THE OFFICIAL® 2002–2003 PRICE GUIDE TO BASEBALL CARDS

DR. JAMES BECKETT

TWENTY-SECOND EDITION

HOUSE OF COLLECTIBLES
The Crown Publishing Group
New York

Important Notice: All of the information, including valuations, in this book has been compiled from the most reliable sources, and every effort has been made to eliminate errors and questionable data. Nevertheless, the possibility of error, in a work of such immense scope, always exists. The publisher will not be held responsible for losses that may occur in the purchase, sale, or other transaction of items because of information contained herein. Readers who feel they have discovered errors are invited to *write* and inform us, so they may be corrected in subsequent editions. Those seeking further information on the topics covered in this book are advised to refer to the complete line of *Official Price Guides* published by the House of Collectibles.

House of Collectibles is a registered trademark and the colophon is a trademark of Random House, Inc.

Published by:
House of Collectibles
The Crown Publishing Group
New York, New York

Distributed by The Crown Publishing Group,
a division of Random House, Inc.,
New York, and simultaneously in Canada by
Random House of Canada Limited, Toronto.

www.randomhouse.com

Manufactured in the United States of America

ISSN: 1062-7138

ISBN: 0-609-80902-4

10 9 8 7 6 5 4 3 2 1

Twenty-second Edition: April 2002

Table of Contents

About the Author 7
How to Use This Book 7
How to Collect 8
Obtaining Cards 8
Preserving Your Cards 9
Collecting vs. Investing 9
Terminology 10
Glossary/Legend 11
Understanding Card Values 15
Determining Value 15
Regional Variation 15
Set Prices 16
Scarce Series 16
Grading Your Cards 17
Centering 17
Corner Wear 17
Creases 17
Alterations 18
Categorization of Defects 18
Condition Guide 18
Grades 18
Selling Your Cards 19
Interesting Notes 20
History of Baseball Cards 22
Increasing Popularity 24
Intensified Competition 26
Sharing the Pie 26
Finding Out More 32
Additional Reading 33
Advertising 33
Prices in This Guide 34
Acknowledgements 694

1948 Bowman 35
1949 Bowman 35
1950 Bowman 36
1951 Bowman 37
1952 Bowman 38
1953 Bowman B/W 39
1953 Bowman Color 40
1954 Bowman 41
1955 Bowman 42
1989 Bowman 43
1990 Bowman 45
1991 Bowman 47
1992 Bowman 50
1993 Bowman 53
1994 Bowman 56
1995 Bowman 59
1996 Bowman 60
1997 Bowman 62
1998 Bowman 64
1999 Bowman 66
2000 Bowman 67
2000 Bowman Draft Picks 69
2001 Bowman 70
2001 Bowman Draft Picks 72
1997 Bowman Chrome 72
1998 Bowman Chrome 73
1999 Bowman Chrome 75
2000 Bowman Chrome 77
2000 Bowman Chrome Draft Picks 79
2001 Bowman Chrome 79
2001 Bowman Heritage 81
1994 Bowman's Best 83
1995 Bowman's Best 84
1996 Bowman's Best 85
1997 Bowman's Best 85
1998 Bowman's Best 86
1999 Bowman's Best 87
2000 Bowman's Best 88
2001 Bowman's Best 89
1981 Donruss 90
1982 Donruss 93
1983 Donruss 96
1984 Donruss 99
1985 Donruss 102
1986 Donruss 104
1986 Donruss Rookies 107
1987 Donruss 108
1987 Donruss Rookies 110
1987 Donruss Opening Day 111
1988 Donruss 112
1988 Donruss Rookies 114
1989 Donruss 115
1989 Donruss Rookies 118
1989 Donruss Baseball's Best 118
1990 Donruss 119
1990 Donruss Rookies 123
1991 Donruss 123
1991 Donruss Rookies 127
1992 Donruss 127
1992 Donruss Rookies 130
1993 Donruss 131
1994 Donruss 134
1995 Donruss 137
1996 Donruss 139
1997 Donruss 141
1998 Donruss 143
2001 Donruss 145
2001 Donruss Classics 146
1997 Donruss Elite 147
1998 Donruss Elite 147
2001 Donruss Elite 148
1997 Donruss Signature 149
1998 Donruss Signature 150
2001 Donruss Signature 150
1995 Emotion 152
1996 Emotion-XL 152
2001 eTopps 154
1997 E-X2000 154
1998 E-X2001 155

1999 E-X Century 155
2000 E-X 156
2001 E-X 156
1993 Finest 157
1994 Finest 158
1995 Finest 159
1996 Finest 161
1997 Finest 162
1998 Finest 164
1999 Finest 165
2000 Finest 166
2001 Finest 168
1993 Flair 168
1994 Flair 170
1995 Flair 171
1996 Flair 173
1997 Flair Showcase Row 2 175
1998 Flair Showcase Row 3 176
1999 Flair Showcase Row 3 176
1963 Fleer 177
1981 Fleer 177
1982 Fleer 181
1983 Fleer 184
1984 Fleer 186
1984 Fleer Update 189
1985 Fleer 190
1985 Fleer Update 193
1986 Fleer 193
1986 Fleer Update 196
1987 Fleer 197
1987 Fleer Update 200
1988 Fleer 200
1988 Fleer Update 203
1989 Fleer 204
1989 Fleer Update 208
1990 Fleer 208
1990 Fleer Update 211
1991 Fleer 212
1991 Fleer Update 215
1992 Fleer 216
1992 Fleer Update 219
1993 Fleer 220
1993 Fleer Final Edition 223
1994 Fleer 224
1994 Fleer Update 227
1995 Fleer 228
1995 Fleer Update 230
1996 Fleer 231
1996 Fleer Update 234
1997 Fleer 235
1998 Fleer 238
1998 Fleer Update 240
1999 Fleer 241
1999 Fleer Update 243
2000 Fleer 244
2000 Fleer Glossy 246
2000 Fleer Update 246
2001 Fleer 247
1999 Fleer Brilliants 249
2000 Fleer Focus 250
2001 Fleer Focus 251
2001 Fleer Futures 252
2001 Fleer Game Time 253
2001 Fleer Genuine 254
2000 Fleer Greats of the Game 255
2001 Fleer Greats of the Game 255
2001 Fleer Legacy 256
2001 Fleer Platinum 256
2001 Fleer Premium 258
2001 Fleer Red Sox 100th 259
2000 Fleer Showcase 259
2001 Fleer Showcase 260
2001 Fleer Triple Crown 261
1949 Leaf 262
1990 Leaf 263
1991 Leaf 265
1992 Leaf 267
1993 Leaf 269
1994 Leaf 271
1995 Leaf 273
1996 Leaf 275
1997 Leaf 276
1998 Leaf 277
2001 Leaf Certified Materials 278
1994 Leaf Limited 279
1994 Leaf Limited Rookies 280
1995 Leaf Limited 280
1996 Leaf Limited 281
1998 Leaf Rookies and Stars 281
2001 Leaf Rookies and Stars 283
1996 Leaf Signature 284
2000 MLB Showdown 1st Edition 285
2000 MLB Showdown Pennant Run 1st Edition 287
2001 MLB Showdown 1st Edition 287
2001 MLB Showdown Pennant Run 289
1994 Pacific 290
1995 Pacific 293
1996 Pacific 294
1997 Pacific 296
1998 Pacific 298
1999 Pacific 300
2000 Pacific 302
2001 Pacific 304
2000 Pacific Private Stock 306
2001 Pacific Private Stock 307
1992 Pinnacle 308
1993 Pinnacle 310
1994 Pinnacle 313
1995 Pinnacle 315
1996 Pinnacle 317
1997 Pinnacle 318

1998 Pinnacle 319
2001 Playoff Absolute Memorabilia 320
1988 Score Rookie/Traded 324
1989 Score 325
1989 Score Rookie/Traded 328
1990 Score 328
1990 Score Rookie/Traded 331
1991 Score 332
1991 Score Rookie/Traded 336
1992 Score 337
1992 Score Rookie/Traded 340
1993 Score 341
1994 Score 343
1994 Score Rookie/Traded 346
1995 Score 347
1996 Score 349
1997 Score 351
1998 Score 354
1998 Score Rookie/Traded 355
1993 SP 356
1994 SP 357
1995 SP 358
1996 SP 359
1997 SP 360
1998 SP Authentic 361
1999 SP Authentic 362
2000 SP Authentic 362
2001 SP Authentic 363
2001 SP Game Bat Edition 364
2001 SP Game Bat Milestone 364
2001 SP Game-Used Edition 365
2001 SP Legendary Cuts 365
1996 SPx 366
1997 SPx 366
1998 SPx Finite 366
1999 SPx 368
2000 SPx 368
2001 SPx 369
1991 Stadium Club 370
1992 Stadium Club Dome 373
1992 Stadium Club 373
1993 Stadium Club Murphy 377
1993 Stadium Club 378
1994 Stadium Club 381
1994 Stadium Club Draft Picks 384
1995 Stadium Club 384
1996 Stadium Club 387
1997 Stadium Club 389
1998 Stadium Club 391
1999 Stadium Club 392
2000 Stadium Club 394
2001 Stadium Club 395
2002 Stadium Club 396
2000 Stadium Club Chrome 396
1991 Studio 397
1992 Studio 398
1993 Studio 400
1994 Studio 401
1995 Studio 401
1996 Studio 402
1997 Studio 403
1998 Studio 404
2001 Studio 405
1952 Topps 406
1953 Topps 408
1954 Topps 409
1955 Topps 410
1956 Topps 411
1957 Topps 413
1958 Topps 415
1959 Topps 417
1960 Topps 420
1961 Topps 422
1962 Topps 425
1963 Topps 429
1964 Topps 432
1965 Topps 436
1966 Topps 439
1967 Topps 442
1968 Topps 445
1969 Topps 448
1970 Topps 452
1971 Topps 456
1972 Topps 459
1973 Topps 463
1974 Topps 467
1974 Topps Traded 471
1975 Topps 471
1976 Topps 474
1976 Topps Traded 478
1977 Topps 478
1978 Topps 481
1979 Topps 485
1980 Topps 488
1981 Topps 492
1981 Topps Traded 495
1982 Topps 496
1982 Topps Traded 500
1983 Topps 500
1983 Topps Traded 504
1984 Topps 504
1984 Topps Traded 508
1985 Topps 509
1985 Topps Traded 512
1986 Topps 513
1986 Topps Traded 516
1987 Topps 516
1987 Topps Traded 520
1988 Topps 521
1988 Topps Traded 524
1989 Topps 525
1989 Topps Traded 528

1990 Topps 529
1990 Topps Traded 532
1991 Topps 533
1991 Topps Traded 537
1992 Topps 537
1992 Topps Traded 541
1993 Topps 541
1993 Topps Traded 545
1994 Topps 546
1994 Topps Traded 549
1995 Topps 550
1995 Topps Traded 553
1996 Topps 554
1997 Topps 556
1998 Topps 558
1999 Topps 560
1999 Topps Traded 563
2000 Topps 563
2000 Topps Limited 566
2001 Topps 567
2001 Topps Limited 570
2001 Topps Traded 570
2002 Topps 571
2001 Topps American Pie 573
2001 Topps Archives 574
2001 Topps Archives Reserve 576
1996 Topps Chrome 577
1997 Topps Chrome 577
1998 Topps Chrome 578
1999 Topps Chrome 580
1999 Topps Chrome Traded 583
2000 Topps Chrome 584
2000 Topps Chrome Traded 586
2001 Topps Chrome 587
2001 Topps Chrome Traded 590
2001 Topps Fusion 591
1996 Topps Gallery 592
1997 Topps Gallery 593
1998 Topps Gallery 594
1999 Topps Gallery 594
2000 Topps Gallery 595
2001 Topps Gallery 596
1998 Topps Gold Label Class 1 597
1999 Topps Gold Label Class 1 597
2000 Topps Gold Label Class 1 598
2001 Topps Gold Label Class 1 598
2000 Topps HD 599
2001 Topps HD 599
2001 Topps Heritage 600
1998 Topps Opening Day 602
1999 Topps Opening Day 602
2000 Topps Opening Day 603
2001 Topps Opening Day 604
2001 Topps Reserve 605
1997 Topps Stars 605
1998 Topps Stars 606
1999 Topps Stars 607
2000 Topps Stars 607
2001 Topps Stars 608
2001 UD Reserve 609
1991 Ultra 610
1991 Ultra Update 612
1992 Ultra 612
1993 Ultra 615
1994 Ultra 618
1995 Ultra 620
1996 Ultra 622
1997 Ultra 624
1998 Ultra 627
1999 Ultra 629
2000 Ultra 630
2001 Ultra 631
2002 Ultra 632
1989 Upper Deck 634
1990 Upper Deck 637
1991 Upper Deck 641
1991 Upper Deck Final Edition 644
1992 Upper Deck 645
1993 Upper Deck 648
1994 Upper Deck 652
1995 Upper Deck 654
1996 Upper Deck 656
1997 Upper Deck 658
1998 Upper Deck 661
1999 Upper Deck 664
2000 Upper Deck 666
2001 Upper Deck 668
2002 Upper Deck 670
2001 Upper Deck Decade 1970s 672
2001 Upper Deck Evolution 673
2001 Upper Deck Gold Glove 673
2001 Upper Deck Hall of Famers 674
2000 Upper Deck Legends 675
2001 Upper Deck Legends 675
1999 Upper Deck MVP 676
2000 Upper Deck MVP 677
2001 Upper Deck MVP 678
1999 Upper Deck Ovation 679
2000 Upper Deck Ovation 679
2001 Upper Deck Ovation 680
2000 Upper Deck Pros and Prospects 680
2001 Upper Deck Pros and Prospects 681
2001 Upper Deck Prospect Premieres 682
1999 Upper Deck Retro 682
2001 Upper Deck Sweet Spot 683
1999 Upper Deck Victory 683
2000 Upper Deck Victory 685
2001 Upper Deck Victory 687
2001 Upper Deck Vintage 690

About the Author

Jim Beckett, the leading authority on sports card values in the United States, maintains a wide range of activities in the world of sports. He possesses one of the finest collections of sports cards and autographs in the world, has made numerous appearances on radio and television, and has been frequently cited in many national publications. He was awarded the first "Special Achievement Award" for Contributions to the Hobby by the National Sports Collectors Convention in 1980, the "Jock-Jaspersen Award" for Hobby Dedication in 1983, and the "Buck Barker, Spirit of the Hobby" Award in 1991.

Dr. Beckett is the author of *Beckett Baseball Card Price Guide, The Official Price Guide to Baseball Cards, Price Guide to Baseball Collectibles, The Sport Americana Baseball Memorabilia* and *Autograph Price Guide, Beckett Almanac of Baseball Cards* and *Collectibles, Beckett Football Card Price Guide, The Official Price Guide to Football Cards, Beckett Hockey Card Price Guide, The Official Price Guide to Hockey Cards, Beckett Basketball Card Price Guide, The Official Price Guide to Basketball Cards, The Beckett Baseball Card Alphabetical Checklist, The Beckett Basketball Card Alphabetical Checklist,* and *The Beckett Football Card Alphabetical Checklist*. In addition, he is the founder, publisher, and editor of *Beckett Baseball Card Monthly, Beckett Basketball Monthly, Beckett Football Card Monthly, Beckett Hockey Collector, Beckett Sports Collectibles,* and *Beckett Racing* and *Motorsports Marketplace.*

Jim Beckett received his Ph.D. in Statistics from Southern Methodist University in 1975. Prior to starting Beckett Publications in 1984, Dr. Beckett served as an Associate Professor of Statistics at Bowling Green State University and as a vice president of a consulting firm in Dallas, Texas.

How to Use This Book

Isn't it great? Every year this book gets better with all the new sets coming out. But even more exciting is that every year there are more options in collecting the cards we love so much. This edition has been enhanced and expanded from the previous edition. The cards you collect — who appears on them, what they look like, where they are from, and (most important to most of you) what their current values are — are enumerated within. Many of the features contained in the other *Beckett Price Guides* have been incorporated into this volume since condition grading, terminology, and many other aspects of collecting are common to the card hobby in general. We hope you find the book both interesting and useful in your collecting pursuits.

The *Beckett Guide* has been successful where other attempts have failed because it is complete, current, and valid. This Price Guide contains not just one, but three prices by condition for all the baseball cards listed. The prices were added to the card lists just prior to printing and reflect not the author's opinions or desires but the going retail prices for each card, based on the marketplace (sports memorabilia conventions and shows, sports card shops, hobby papers, current mail-order catalogs, local club meetings, auction results, and other firsthand reportings of actually realized prices).

What is the best price guide available on the market today? Of course, card sellers prefer the price guide with the highest prices, while card buyers naturally prefer the one with the lowest prices. Accuracy, however, is the true test. Use the price guide trusted by more collectors and dealers than all the others combined. Look for the *Beckett®* name. I won't put my name on anything I won't stake my reputation on. Not the lowest and not the highest — but the most accurate, with integrity.

To facilitate your use of this book, read the complete introductory section on the following pages before going to the pricing pages. Every collectible field has its own terminology; we've tried to capture most of these terms and definitions in our glossary. Please read carefully the section on grading and the condition of your cards, as you cannot determine which price column is appropriate for a given card without first knowing its condition.

Welcome to the world of baseball cards.

How to Collect

Each collection is personal and reflects the individuality of its owner. There are no set rules on how to collect cards. Since card collecting is a hobby or leisure pastime, what you collect, how much you collect, and how much time and money you spend collecting are entirely up to you. The funds you have available for collecting and your own personal taste should determine how you collect. Information and ideas presented here are intended to help you get the most enjoyment from this hobby.

It is impossible to collect every card ever produced. Therefore, beginners as well as intermediate and advanced collectors usually specialize in some way. One of the reasons this hobby is popular is that individual collectors can define and tailor their collecting methods to match their own tastes. To give you some idea of the various approaches to collecting, we will list some of the more popular areas of specialization.

Many collectors select complete sets from particular years. For example, they may concentrate on assembling complete sets from all the years since their birth or since they became avid sports fans. They may try to collect a card for every player during that specified period of time.

Many others wish to acquire only certain players. Usually such players are the superstars of the sport, but occasionally collectors will specialize in all the cards of players who attended a particular college or came from a certain town. Some collectors are interested in only the first cards or Rookie Cards of certain players. A handy guide for collectors interested in pursuing the hobby this way is *The Sport Americana Baseball Card Alphabetical Checklist.*

Another fun way to collect cards is by team. Most fans have a favorite team, and it is natural for that loyalty to be translated into a desire for cards of the players on that favorite team. For most of the recent years, team sets (all the cards from a given team for that year) are readily available at a reasonable price. *The Sport Americana Team Baseball Card Checklist* will open up this field to the collector.

Obtaining Cards

Several avenues are open to card collectors. Cards still can be purchased in the traditional way: by the pack at the local candy, grocery, drug, or major discount stores.

But there are also thousands of card shops across the country that specialize in selling cards individually or by the pack, box, or set. Another alternative is the thousands of card shows held each month around the country, which feature anywhere from eight to 800 tables of sports cards and memorabilia for sale.

For many years, it has been possible to purchase complete sets of baseball cards through mail-order advertisers found in traditional sports media publications, such as *The Sporting News, Baseball Digest, Street & Smith* yearbooks, and others. These sets also are advertised in the card collecting periodicals. Many collectors will begin by subscribing to at least one of the hobby periodicals, all with good up-to-date information. In fact, subscription offers can be found in the advertising section of this book.

Most serious card collectors obtain old (and new) cards from one or more of several main sources: (1) trading or buying from other collectors or dealers; (2) responding to sale or auction ads in the hobby publications; (3) buying at a local hobby store; (4) attending sports collectibles shows or conventions; and/or (5) purchasing cards over the Internet .

We advise that you try all four methods since each has its own distinct advantages: (1) trading is a great way to make new friends; (2) hobby periodicals help you keep up with what's going on in the hobby (including when and where the conventions are happening); (3) stores provide the opportunity to enjoy personalized service and consider a great diversity of material in a relaxed sports-oriented atmosphere; (4) shows allow you to choose from multiple dealers and thousands of cards under one roof in a competitive situation; and (5) the Internet allows one to purchase cards in a convenient manner from almost anywhere in the world.

Preserving Your Cards

Cards are fragile. They must be handled properly in order to retain their value. Careless handling can easily result in creased or bent cards. It is, however, not recommended that tweezers or tongs be used to pick up your cards since such utensils might mar or indent card surfaces and thus reduce those cards' conditions and values.

In general, your cards should be handled directly as little as possible. This is sometimes easier to say than to do.

Although there are still many who use custom boxes, storage trays, or even shoe boxes, plastic sheets are the preferred method of many collectors for storing cards.

A collection stored in plastic pages in a three-ring album allows you to view your collection at any time without the need to touch the card itself. Cards can also be kept in single holders (of various types and thickness) designed for the enjoyment of each card individually.

For a large collection, some collectors may use a combination of the above methods. When purchasing plastic sheets for your cards, be sure that you find the pocket size that fits the cards snugly. Don't put your 1951 Bowman in a sheet designed to fit 1981 Topps.

Most hobby and collectibles shops and virtually all collectors' conventions will have these plastic pages available in quantity for the various sizes offered, or you can purchase them directly from the advertisers in this book.

Also, remember that pocket size isn't the only factor to consider when looking for plastic sheets. Other factors such as safety, economy, appearance, availability, or personal preference also may indicate which types of sheets a collector may want to buy.

Damp, sunny, and/or hot conditions — no, this is not a weather forecast — are three elements to avoid in extremes if you are interested in preserving your collection. Too much (or too little) humidity can cause the gradual deterioration of a card. Direct, bright sun (or fluorescent light) over time will bleach out the color of a card. Extreme heat accelerates the decomposition of the card. On the other hand, many cards have lasted more than 75 years without much scientific intervention. So be cautious, even if the above factors typically present a problem only when present in the extreme. It never hurts to be prudent.

Collecting vs. Investing

Collecting individual players and collecting complete sets are both popular vehicles for investment and speculation.

Most investors and speculators stock up on complete sets or on quantities of players they think have good investment potential.

There is obviously no guarantee in this book, or anywhere else for that matter, that cards will outperform the stock market or other investment alternatives in the future. After all, baseball cards do not pay quarterly dividends and cards cannot be sold at their "current values" as easily as stocks or bonds.

Nevertheless, investors have noticed a favorable long-term trend in the past performance of baseball and other sports collectibles, and certain cards and sets have outperformed just about any other investment in some years.

Many hobbyists maintain that the best investment is and always will be the building of a collection, which traditionally has held up better than outright speculation.

Some of the obvious questions are: Which cards? When to buy? When to sell? The best investment you can make is in your own education.

The more you know about your collection and the hobby, the more informed the decisions you will be able to make. We're not selling investment tips. We're selling information about the current value of baseball cards. It's up to you to use that information to your best advantage.

Terminology

Each hobby has its own language to describe its area of interest. The nomenclature traditionally used for trading cards is derived from the *American Card Catalog*, published in 1960 by Nostalgia Press. That catalog, written by Jefferson Burdick (who is called the "Father of Card Collecting" for his pioneering work), uses letter and number designations for each separate set of cards. The letter used in the ACC designation refers to the generic type of card. While both sport and non-sport issues are classified in the ACC, we shall confine ourselves to the sport issues. The following list defines the letters and their meanings as used by the *American Card Catalog*.

(none) or N - 19th Century U.S. Tobacco
B - Blankets
D - Bakery Inserts Including Bread
E - Early Candy and Gum
F - Food Inserts
H - Advertising
M - Periodicals
PC - Postcards
R - Candy and Gum since 1930

Following the letter prefix and an optional hyphen are one-, two-, or three-digit numbers, R(-)999. These typically represent the company or entity issuing the cards. In several cases, the ACC number is extended by an additional hyphen and another one- or two-digit numerical suffix. For example, the 1957 Topps regular-series baseball card issue carries an ACC designation of R414-11. The "R" indicates a Candy or Gum card produced since 1930. The "414" is the ACC designation for Topps Chewing Gum baseball card issues, and the "11" is the ACC designation for the 1957 regular issue (Topps' eleventh baseball set). Like other traditional methods of identification, this system provides order to the process of cataloging cards; however, most serious collectors learn the ACC designation of the popular sets by repetition and familiarity, rather than by attempting to "figure out" what they might or should be. From 1948 forward, collectors and dealers commonly refer to all sets by their year, maker, type of issue, and any other distinguishing characteristic. For example, such a characteristic could be an unusual issue or one of several regular issues put out by a specific maker in a single year. Regional issues are usually referred to by year, maker, and sometimes by title or theme of the set.

Glossary/Legend

Our glossary defines terms used in the card collecting hobby and in this book. Many of these terms are also common to other types of sports memorabilia collecting. Some terms may have several meanings depending on use and context.

ACETATE - A transparent plastic.

AS - All-Star card. A card portraying an All-Star Player of the previous year that says "All-Star" on its face.

ATG - All-Time Great card.

ATL - All-Time Leaders card.

AU(TO) - Autographed card.

BC - Bonus Card.

BL - Blue letters.

BOX CARD - Card issued on a box (i.e., 1987 Topps Box Bottoms).

BRICK - A group of 50 or more cards having common characteristics that is intended to be bought, sold, or traded as a unit.

CABINETS - Popular and highly valuable photographs on thick card stock produced in the 19th and early 20th century.

CHECKLIST - A list of the cards contained in a particular set. The list is always in numerical order if the cards are numbered. Some unnumbered sets are artificially numbered in alphabetical order, by team and alphabetically within the team, or by uniform number for convenience.

CL - Checklist card. A card that lists in order the cards and players in the set or series. Older checklist cards in Mint condition that have not been marked are very desirable and command premiums.

CO - Coach.

COMM - Commissioner.

COMMON CARD - The typical card of any set; it has no premium value accruing from subject matter, numerical scarcity, popular demand, or anomaly.

CONVENTION - A gathering of dealers and collectors at a single location for the purpose of buying, selling, and trading sports memorabilia items. Conventions are open to the public and sometimes feature autograph guests, door prizes, contests, seminars, etc. They are frequently referred to simply as "shows."

COOP - Cooperstown.

COR - Corrected card.

CY - Cy Young Award.

DEALER - A person who engages in buying, selling, and trading sports collectibles or supplies. A dealer may also be a collector, but as a dealer, his main goal is to earn a profit.

DIE-CUT - A card with part of its stock partially cut, allowing one or more parts to be folded or removed. After removal or appropriate folding, the remaining part of the card can frequently be made to stand up.

DK - Diamond King.

DL - Division Leaders.

DP - Double Print (a card that was printed in double the quantity compared to the other cards in the same series) or a Draft Pick card.

DUFEX - A method of card manufacturing technology patented by Pinnacle Brands, Inc. It involves a refractive quality to a card with a foil coating.

ERA - Earned Run Average.

ERR - Error card. A card with erroneous information, spelling, or depiction on either side of the card. Most errors are not corrected by the producing card company.

FDP - First or First Round Draft Pick.

FOIL - Foil embossed stamp on card.

FOLD - Foldout.
FS - Father/son card.
FUN - Fun Cards.
GL - Green letters.
GLOSS - A card with luster; a shiny finish as in a card with UV coating.
HIGH NUMBER - The cards in the last series of numbers in a year in which such higher-numbered cards were printed or distributed in significantly lesser amounts than the lower-numbered cards. The high-number designation refers to a scarcity of the high-numbered cards. Not all years have high numbers in terms of this definition.
HL - Highlight card.
HOF - Hall of Fame, or a card that portrays a Hall of Famer (HOFer).
HOLOGRAM - A three-dimensional photographic image.
HOR - Horizontal pose on card as opposed to the standard vertical orientation found on most cards.
IA - In Action card.
IF - Infielder.
INSERT - A card of a different type or any other sports collectible (typically a poster or sticker) contained and sold in the same package along with a card or cards of a major set. An insert card is either unnumbered or not numbered in the same sequence as the major set. Sometimes the inserts are randomly distributed and are not found in every pack.
INTERACTIVE - A concept that involves collector participation.
ISSUE - Synonymous with set, but usually used in conjunction with a manufacturer; e.g., a Topps issue.
LHP - Left handed pitcher.
LL - League leaders or large letters on card.
MAJOR SET - A set produced by a national manufacturer of cards containing a large number of cards. Usually 100 or more different cards comprise a major set.
MEM - Memorial card. For example, the 1990 Donruss and Topps Bart Giamatti cards.
METALLIC - A glossy design method that enhances card features.
MG - Manager.
MINI - A small card; for example, a 1975 Topps card of identical design but smaller dimensions than the regular Topps issue of 1975.
ML - Major League.
MULTI-PLAYER CARD - A single card depicting two or more players (but not a team card).
MVP - Most Valuable Player.
NAU - No autograph on card.
NH - No-Hitter.
NNOF - No Name on Front.
NOF - Name on Front.
NOTCHING - The grooving of the card, usually caused by fingernails, rubber bands, or bumping card edges against other objects.
OF - Outfield or Outfielder.
OLY - Olympics Card.
P - Pitcher or Pitching pose.
P1 - First Printing.
P2 - Second Printing.
P3 - Third Printing.
PACKS - A means with which cards are issued in terms of pack type (wax, cello, foil, rack, etc.) and channels of distribution (hobby, retail, etc.).
PARALLEL- A card that is similar in design to its counterpart from a basic set,

but offers a distinguishing quality.

PF - Profiles.

PLASTIC SHEET - A clear, plastic page that is punched for insertion into a binder (with standard three-ring spacing) containing pockets for displaying cards. Many different styles of sheets exist with pockets of varying sizes to hold the many differing card formats. Also called a display sheet or storage sheet.

PLATINUM - A metallic element used in the process of creating a glossy card.

PR - Printed name on back.

PREMIUM - A card, sometimes on photographic stock, that is purchased or obtained in conjunction with, or redemption for, another card or product. The premium is not packaged in the same unit as the primary item.

PRES - President.

PRISMATIC/PRISM - A glossy or bright design that refracts or disperses light.

PUZZLE CARD - A card whose back contains a part of a picture which, when joined correctly with other puzzle cards, forms the completed picture.

PUZZLE PIECE - A die-cut piece designed to interlock with similar pieces (e.g., early 1980's Donruss).

PVC - Polyvinyl chloride, a substance used to make many of the popular card display protective sheets. Non-PVC sheets are considered preferable for long-term storage of cards by many.

RARE - A card or series of cards of very limited availability. Unfortunately, "rare" is a subjective term frequently used indiscriminately to hype value. "Rare" cards are harder to obtain than "scarce" cards.

RB - Record Breaker.

REDEMPTION- A program established by multiple card manufacturers that allows collectors to mail in a special card (usually a random insert) in return for special cards, sets, or other prizes not available through conventional channels.

REFRACTORS - A card that features a design element which enhances (distorts) its color/appearance through deflecting light.

REV NEG - Reversed or flopped photo side of the card. This is a major type of error card, but only some are corrected.

RHP - Right handed pitcher.

ROY - Rookie of the Year.

RP - Relief pitcher.

SA - Super Action card.

SASE - Self-Addressed, Stamped Envelope.

SB - Stolen Bases.

SCARCE - A card or series of cards of limited availability. This subjective term is sometimes used indiscriminately to hype value. "Scarce" cards are not as difficult to obtain as "rare" cards.

SCR - Script name on back.

SD - San Diego Padres.

SEMI-HIGH - A card from the next-to-last series of a sequentially issued set. It has more value than an average card and generally less value than a high number. A card is not called a semi-high unless the next-to-last series in which it exists has an additional premium attached to it.

SERIES - The entire set of cards issued by a particular producer in a particular year; e.g., the 1971 Topps series. Also, within a particular set, series can refer to a group of (consecutively numbered) cards printed at the same time; e.g., the first series of the 1957 Topps issue (#1 through #88).

SET - One each of the entire run of cards of the same type produced by a particular manufacturer during a single year. In other words, if you have a complete set of 1976 Topps then you have every card from #1 up to and

including #660; i.e., all the different cards that were produced.
SF - Starflics.
SHEEN - Brightness or luster emitted by card.
SKIP-NUMBERED - A set that has many unissued card numbers between the lowest number in the set and the highest number in the set; e.g., the 1948 Leaf baseball set contains 98 cards skip-numbered from #1 to #168. A major set in which a few numbers were not printed is not considered to be skip-numbered.
SP - Single or Short Print (a card which was printed in lesser quantity compared to the other cards in the same series; see also DP and TP).
SPECIAL CARD - A card that portrays something other than a single player or team; for example, a card that portrays the previous year's statistical leaders or the results from the previous year's World Series.
SS - Shortstop.
STANDARD SIZE - Most modern sports cards measure 2-1/2 by 3-1/2 inches. Exceptions are noted in card descriptions throughout this book.
STAR CARD - A card that portrays a player of some repute, usually determined by his ability; however, sometimes referring to sheer popularity.
STOCK - The cardboard or paper on which the card is printed.
SUPERIMPOSED - To be affixed on top of something; i.e., a player photo over a solid background.
SUPERSTAR CARD - A card that portrays a superstar; e.g., a Hall of Famer or player with strong Hall of Fame potential.
TC - Team Checklist.
TEAM CARD - A card that depicts an entire team.
THREE-DIMENSIONAL (3D) - A visual image that provides an illusion of depth and perspective.
TOPICAL - a subset or group of cards that have a common theme (e.g., MVP award winners).
TP - Triple Print (a card that was printed in triple the quantity compared to the other cards in the same series).
TRANSPARENT - Clear, see-through.
TR - Trade reference on card.
UDCA - Upper Deck Classic Alumni.
UER - Uncorrected Error.
UMP - Umpire.
USA - Team USA.
UV - Ultraviolet, a glossy coating used in producing cards.
VAR - Variation card. One of two or more cards from the same series with the same number (or player with identical pose if the series is unnumbered) differing from one another by some aspect, the different feature stemming from the printing or stock of the card. This can be caused when the manufacturer of the cards notices an error in one or more of the cards, makes the changes, and then resumes the print run. In this case there will be two versions or variations of the same card. Sometimes one of the variations is relatively scarce.
VERT - Vertical pose on card.
WAS - Washington National League (1974 Topps).
WC - What's the Call?
WL - White letter on front.
WS - World Series card.
YL - Yellow letters on front
YT - Yellow team name on front.
* - to denote multi-sport sets.

Understanding Card Values

Determining Value

Why are some cards more valuable than others? Obviously, the economic laws of supply and demand are applicable to card collecting just as they are to any other field where a commodity is bought, sold, or traded in a free, unregulated market.

Supply (the number of cards available on the market) is less than the total number of cards originally produced since attrition diminishes that original quantity. Each year a percentage of cards is typically thrown away, destroyed,or otherwise lost to collectors. This percentage is much, much smaller today than it was in the past because more and more people have become increasingly aware of the value of their cards.

For those who collect only Mint condition cards, the supply of older cards can be quite small indeed. Until recently, collectors were not so conscious of the need to preserve the condition of their cards. For this reason, it is difficult to know exactly how many 1953 Topps are currently available, Mint or otherwise. It is generally accepted that there are fewer 1953 Topps available than 1963, 1973 or 1983 Topps cards. If demand were equal for each of these sets, the law of supply and demand would increase the price for the least available sets. Demand, however, is never equal for all sets, so price correlations can be complicated. The demand for a card is influenced by many factors. These include: (1) the age of the card; (2) the number of cards printed; (3) the player(s) portrayed on the card; (4) the attractiveness and popularity of the set; and (5) the physical condition of the card.

In general, (1) the older the card, (2) the fewer the number of the cards printed, (3) the more famous, popular, and talented the player, (4) the more attractive and popular the set, and (5) the better the condition of the card, the higher the value of the card will be. There are exceptions to all but one of these factors: the condition of the card. Given two cards similar in all respects except condition, the one in the best condition will always be valued higher.

While those guidelines help to establish the value of a card, the countless exceptions and peculiarities make any simple, direct mathematical formula to determine card values impossible.

Regional Variation

Since the market varies from region to region, card prices of local players may be higher. This is known as a regional premium. How significant the premium is — and if there is any premium at all — depends on the local popularity of the team and the player.

The largest regional premiums usually do not apply to superstars, who often are so well known nationwide that the prices of their key cards are too high for local dealers to realize a premium.

Lesser stars often command the strongest premiums. Their popularity is concentrated in their home region, creating local demand that greatly exceeds overall demand.

Regional premiums can apply to popular retired players and sometimes can be found in the areas where the players grew up or starred in college.

A regional discount is the converse of a regional premium. Regional discounts occur when a player has been so popular in his region for so long that local collectors and dealers have accumulated quantities of his key cards. The abundant supply may make the cards available in that area at the lowest prices anywhere.

Set Prices

A somewhat paradoxical situation exists in the price of a complete set vs. the combined cost of the individual cards in the set. In nearly every case, the sum of the prices for the individual cards is higher than the cost for the complete set. This is prevalent especially in the cards of the last few years. The reasons for this apparent anomaly stem from the habits of collectors and from the carrying costs to dealers. Today, each card in a set normally is produced in the same quantity as all other cards in its set.

Many collectors pick up only stars, superstars, and particular teams. As a result, the dealer is left with a shortage of certain player cards and an abundance of others. He therefore incurs an expense in simply "carrying" these less desirable cards in stock. On the other hand, if he sells a complete set, he gets rid of large numbers of cards at one time. For this reason, he generally is willing to receive less money for a complete set. By doing this, he recovers all of his costs and also makes a profit.

The disparity between the price of the complete set and the sum of the individual cards also has been influenced by the fact that some of the major manufacturers now are pre-collating card sets. Since "pulling" individual cards from the sets involves a specific type of labor (and cost), the singles or star card market is not affected significantly by pre-collation.

Set prices also do not include rare card varieties, unless specifically stated. Of course, the prices for sets do include one example of each type for the given set, but this is the least expensive variety.

Scarce Series

Scarce series occur because cards issued before 1974 were made available to the public each year in several series of finite numbers of cards, rather than all cards of the set being available for purchase at one time. At some point during the year, usually toward the end of the baseball season, interest in current year baseball cards waned. Consequently, the manufacturers produced smaller numbers of these later-series cards.

Nearly all nationwide issues from post–World War II manufacturers (1948 to 1973) exhibit these series variations. In the past, Topps, for example, may have issued series consisting of many different numbers of cards, including 55, 66, 80, 88, and others. Recently, Topps has settled on what is now its standard sheet size of 132 cards, six of which comprise its 792-card set.

While the number of cards within a given series is usually the same as the number of cards on one printed sheet, this is not always the case. For example, Bowman used 36 cards on its standard printed sheets, but in 1948 substituted 12 cards during later print runs of that year's baseball cards. Twelve of the cards from the initial sheet of 36 cards were removed and replaced by 12 different cards, giving, in effect, a first series of 36 cards and a second series of 12 new cards. This replacement produced a scarcity of 24 cards — the 12 cards removed from the original sheet and the 12 new cards added to the sheet. A full sheet of 1948 Bowman cards (second printing) shows that card numbers 37 through 48 have replaced 12 of the cards on the first printing sheet.

The Topps Company also has created scarcities and/or excesses of certain cards in many of its sets. Topps, however, has most frequently gone the other direction by double printing some of the cards. Double printing causes an abundance of cards of the players who are on the same sheet more than one time. During the years from 1978 to 1981, Topps double printed 66 cards out of their large 726-card set. The Topps practice of double printing cards in earlier years is the most logical explanation for the known scarcities of particular cards in some of these Topps sets.

From 1988 through 1990, Donruss short printed and double printed certain cards in its major sets. Ostensibly this was because of its addition of bonus team MVP cards in its regular-issue wax packs.

We are always looking for information or photographs of printing sheets of cards for research. Each year, we try to update the hobby's knowledge of distribution anomalies. Please let us know at the address in this book if you have first-hand knowledge that would be helpful in this pursuit.

Grading Your Cards

Each hobby has its own grading terminology — stamps, coins, comic books, record collecting, etc. Collectors of sports cards are no exception. The one invariable criterion for determining the value of a card is its condition: The better the condition of the card, the more valuable it is. Condition grading, however, is subjective. Individual card dealers and collectors differ in the strictness of their grading, but the stated condition of a card should be determined without regard to whether it is being bought or sold.

No allowance is made for age. A 1952 card is judged by the same standards as a 1992 card. But there are specific sets and cards that are condition-sensitive (marked with "!" in the Price Guide) because of their border color, consistently poor centering, etc. Such cards and sets sometimes command premiums above the listed percentages in Mint condition.

Centering

Current centering terminology uses numbers representing the percentage of border on either side of the main design. Obviously, centering is diminished in importance for borderless cards such as Stadium Club.

Slightly Off-Center (60/40): A slightly off-center card is one that, upon close inspection, is found to have one border bigger than the opposite border. This degree once was offensive only to purists, but now some hobbyists try to avoid cards that are anything other than perfectly centered.

Off-Center (70/30): An off-center card has one border that is noticeably more than twice as wide as the opposite border.

Badly Off-Center (80/20 or worse): A badly off-center card has virtually no border on one side of the card.

Miscut: A miscut card actually shows part of the adjacent card in its larger border and consequently a corresponding amount of its card is cut off.

Corner Wear

Corner wear is the most scrutinized grading criteria in the hobby. These are the major categories of corner wear:

Corner with a slight touch of wear: The corner still is sharp, but there is a slight touch of wear showing. On a dark-bordered card, this shows as a dot of white.

Fuzzy corner: The corner still comes to a point, but the point has just begun to fray. A slightly "dinged" corner is considered the same as a fuzzy corner.

Slightly rounded corner: The fraying of the corner has increased to where there is only a hint of a point. Mild layering may be evident. A "dinged" corner is considered the same as a slightly rounded corner.

Rounded corner: The point is completely gone. Some layering is noticeable.

Badly rounded corner: The corner is completely round and rough. Severe layering is evident.

Creases

A third common defect is the crease. The degree of creasing in a card is difficult to show in a drawing or picture. On giving the specific condition of an expensive card for sale, the seller should note any creases additionally. Creases can be categorized as to severity according to the following scale:

Light Crease: A light crease is a crease that is barely noticeable upon close inspection. In fact, when cards are in plastic sheets or holders, a light crease may not be seen (until the card is taken out of the holder). A light crease on the front is much more serious than a light crease on the card back only.

Medium Crease: A medium crease is noticeable when held and studied at arm's length by the naked eye, but does not overly detract from the appearance of the card. It is an obvious crease, but not one that breaks the picture surface of the card.

Heavy Crease: A heavy crease is one that has torn or broken through the card's picture surface; e.g., puts a tear in the photo surface.

Alterations

Deceptive Trimming: This occurs when someone alters the card in order (1) to shave off edge wear, (2) to improve the sharpness of the corners, or (3) to improve centering — obviously their objective is to falsely increase the perceived value of the card to an unsuspecting buyer. The shrinkage usually is evident only if the trimmed card is compared to an adjacent full-sized card or if the trimmed card is itself measured.

Obvious Trimming: Obvious trimming is noticeable and unfortunate. It is usually performed by non-collectors who give no thought to the present or future value of their cards.

Deceptively Retouched Borders: This occurs when the borders (especially on those cards with dark borders) are touched up on the edges and corners with magic marker or crayons of appropriate color in order to make the card appear Mint.

Categorization of Defects—Miscellaneous Flaws

The following are common minor flaws that, depending on severity, lower a card's condition by one to four grades and often render it no better than Excellent-Mint: bubbles (lumps in surface), gum and wax stains, diamond cutting (slanted borders), notching, off-centered backs, paper wrinkles, scratched-off cartoons or puzzles on back, rubber band marks, scratches, surface impressions, and warping.

The following are common serious flaws that, depending on severity, lower a card's condition at least four grades and often render it no better than Good: chemical or sun fading, erasure marks, mildew, miscutting (severe off-centering), holes, bleached or re-touched borders, tape marks, tears, trimming, water or coffee stains, and writing.

Condition Guide

Grades

Mint (Mt) - A card with no flaws or wear. The card has four perfect corners, 60/40 or better centering from top to bottom and from left to right, original gloss, smooth edges, and original color borders. A Mint card does not have print spots, color or focus imperfections.

Near Mint-Mint (NrMt-Mt) - A card with one minor flaw. Any one of the following would lower a Mint card to Near Mint-Mint: one corner with a slight touch of wear, barely noticeable print spots, color or focus imperfections. The card must have 60/40 or better centering in both directions, original gloss, smooth edges and original color borders.

Near Mint (NrMt) - A card with one minor flaw. Any one of the following would lower a Mint card to Near Mint: one fuzzy corner or two to four corners with slight touches of wear, 70/30 to 60/40 centering, slightly rough edges, minor print spots, color or focus imperfections. The card must have original gloss and original color borders.

Excellent-Mint (ExMt) - A card with two or three fuzzy, but not rounded, corners and centering no worse than 80/20. The card may have no more than two of the following: slightly rough edges, very slightly discolored borders, minor print spots, color or focus imperfections. The card must have original gloss.

Excellent (Ex) - A card with four fuzzy but definitely not rounded corners and centering no worse than 80/20. The card may have a small amount of original gloss lost, rough edges, slightly discolored borders and minor print spots, color or focus imperfections.

Very Good (Vg) - A card that has been handled but not abused: slightly rounded corners with slight layering, slight notching on edges, a significant amount of gloss lost from the surface but no scuffing and moderate discoloration of borders. The card may have a few light creases.

Good (G), Fair (F), Poor (P) - A well-worn, mishandled, or abused card: badly rounded and layered corners, scuffing, most or all original gloss missing, seriously discolored borders, moderate or heavy creases, and one or more serious flaws. The grade of Good, Fair, or Poor depends on the severity of wear and flaws. Good, Fair, and Poor cards generally are used only as fillers.

The most widely used grades are defined above. Obviously, many cards will not perfectly fit one of the definitions.

Therefore, categories between the major grades known as in-between grades are used, such as Good to Very Good (G-Vg), Very Good to Excellent (VgEx), and Excellent-Mint to Near Mint (ExMt-NrMt). Such grades indicate a card with all qualities of the lower category but with at least a few qualities of the higher category.

Beckett Baseball Card Price Guide lists each card and set in two grades, with the middle grade valued at about 40-45% of the top grade.

The value of cards that fall between the listed columns can also be calculated using a percentage of the top grade. For example, a card that falls between the top and middle grades (Ex, ExMt, or NrMt in most cases) will generally be valued at anywhere from 50% to 90% of the top grade.

Similarly, a card that falls between the middle and bottom grades (G-Vg, Vg, or VgEx in most cases) will generally be valued at anywhere from 20% to 40% of the top grade.

There are also cases where cards are in better condition than the top grade or worse than the bottom grade. Cards that grade worse than the lowest grade are generally valued at 5-10% of the top grade.

When a card exceeds the top grade by one — such as NrMt-Mt when the top grade is NrMt, or Mint when the top grade is NrMt-Mt — a premium of up to 50% is possible, with 10-20% the usual norm.

When a card exceeds the top grade by two — such as Mint when the top grade is NrMt, or NrMt-Mt when the top grade is ExMt — a premium of 25-50% is the usual norm. But certain condition-sensitive cards or sets, particularly those from the pre-war era, can bring premiums of up to 100% or even more.

Unopened packs, boxes, and factory-collated sets are considered Mint in their unknown (and presumed perfect) state. Once opened, however, each card can be graded (and valued) in its own right by taking into account any defects that may be present in spite of the fact that the card has never been handled.

Selling Your Cards

Just about every collector sells cards or will sell cards eventually. Someday you may be interested in selling your duplicates or maybe even your whole collection. You may sell to other collectors, friends, or dealers. You may even sell cards you purchased from a certain dealer back to that same dealer. In any event, it helps to know some of the mechanics of the typical transaction between buyer and seller.

Dealers will buy cards in order to resell them to other collectors who are interested in the cards. Dealers will always pay a higher percentage for items that (in their opinion) can be resold quickly, and a much lower percentage for those items that are perceived as having low demand and hence are slow moving. In either case, dealers must buy at a price that allows for the expense of doing business and a margin for profit.

If you have cards for sale, the best advice we can give is that you get several offers for your cards — either from card shops or at a card show — and take the best offer, all things considered. Note, the "best" offer may not be the one for the highest amount. And remember, if a dealer really wants your cards, he won't let you get away without making his best competitive offer. Another alternative is to place your cards in an auction as one or several lots.

Many people think nothing of going into a department store and paying $15 for an item of clothing for which the store paid $5. But if you were selling your $15 card to a dealer and he offered you $5 for it, you might consider his markup unreasonable. To complete the analogy: Most department stores (and card dealers) that consistently pay $10 for $15 items eventually go out of business. An exception is when the dealer has lined up a willing buyer for the item(s) you are attempting to sell, or if the cards are so Hot that it's likely he'll have to hold the cards for just a short period of time.

In those cases, an offer of up to 75% of book value still will allow the dealer to make a reasonable profit considering the short time he will need to hold the merchandise. In general, however, most cards and collections will bring offers in the range of 25 to 50% of retail price. Also consider that most material from the last 5 to 10 years is plentiful. If that's what you're selling, don't be surprised if your best offer is well below that range.

Interesting Notes

The first card numerically of an issue is the single card most likely to obtain excessive wear.

Consequently, you typically will find the price on the #1 card (in NrMt or Mint condition) somewhat higher than might otherwise be the case.

Similarly, but to a lesser extent (because normally the less important, reverse side of the card is the one exposed), the last card numerically in an issue also is prone to abnormal wear. This extra wear and tear occurs because the first and last cards are exposed to the elements (human element included) more than any of the other cards. They are generally end cards in any brick formations, rubber bandings, stackings on wet surfaces and like activities.

Sports cards have no intrinsic value. The value of a card, like the value of other collectibles, can be determined only by you and your enjoyment in viewing

Centering

Well-centered

Slightly Off-centered

Off-centered

Badly Off-centered

Miscut

and possessing these cardboard treasures.

Remember, the buyer ultimately determines the price of each baseball card. You are the determining price factor because you have the ability to say "No" to the price of any card by not exchanging your hard-earned money for a given issue. When the cost of a trading card exceeds the enjoyment you will receive from it, your answer should be "No." We assess and report the prices. You set them!

We are always interested in receiving the price input of collectors and dealers. We happily credit major contributors.

We welcome your opinions, since your contributions assist us in ensuring a better guide each year.

If you would like to join our survey list for the next editions of this book and others authored by Dr. Beckett, please send your name and address to Dr. James Beckett, 15850 Dallas Parkway, Dallas, TX 75248.

History of Baseball Cards

Today's version of the baseball card, with its colorful and ofttimes high-tech fronts and backs, is a far cry from its earliest predecessors. The issue remains cloudy as to which was the very first baseball card ever produced, but the institution of baseball cards dates from the latter half of the 19th century, more than 100 years ago. Early issues, generally printed on heavy cardboard, were of poor quality, with photographs, drawings, and printing far short of today's standards.

Goodwin & Co., of New York, makers of Gypsy Queen, Old Judge, and other cigarette brands, is considered by many to be the first issuer of baseball and other sports cards. Its issues, predominantly sized 1-1/2 by 2-1/2 inches, generally consisted of photographs of baseball players, boxers, wrestlers, and other subjects mounted on stiff cardboard. More than 2,000 different photos of baseball players alone have been identified. These "Old Judges," a collective name commonly used for the Goodwin & Co. cards, were issued from 1886 to 1890 and are treasured parts of many collections today.

Among the other cigarette companies that issued baseball cards still attracting attention today are Allen & Ginter, D. Buchner & Co. (Gold Coin Chewing Tobacco), and P.H. Mayo & Brother. Cards from the first two companies bear colored line drawings, while the Mayos are sepia photographs on black cardboard. In addition to the small-size cards from this era, several tobacco companies issued cabinet-size baseball cards. These "cabinets" were considerably larger than the small cards, usually about 4-1/4 by 6-1/2 inches, and were printed on heavy stock. Goodwin & Co.'s Old Judge cabinets and the National Tobacco Works' "Newsboy" baseball photos are two that remain popular today.

By 1895, the American Tobacco Company began to dominate its competition. They discontinued baseball card inserts in their cigarette packages (actually slide boxes in those days). The lack of competition in the cigarette market had made these inserts unnecessary. This marked the end of the first era of baseball cards. At the dawn of the 20th century, few baseball cards were being issued. But once again, it was the cigarette companies - particularly, the American Tobacco Company - followed to a lesser extent by the candy and gum makers that revived the practice of including baseball cards with their products. The bulk of these cards, identified in the American Card Catalog (designated hereafter as ACC) as T or E cards for 20th century "Tobacco" or "Early Candy and Gum" issues, respectively, were released from 1909 to 1915.

This romantic and popular era of baseball card collecting produced many desirable items. The most outstanding is the fabled T-206 Honus Wagner card. Other perennial favorites among collectors are the T-206 Eddie Plank card, and the T-206 Magee error card. The former was once the second most valuable card and only recently relinquished that position to a more distinctive and aesthetically pleasing Napoleon Lajoie card from the 1933-34 Goudey Gum series. The latter misspells the player's name as "Magie," the most famous and most valuable blooper card.

Corner Wear

The partial cards here have been photographed at 300%. This was done in order to magnify each card's corner wear to such a degree that differences could be shown on a printed page.

The 1962 Topps Mickey Mantle card definitely has a rounded corner. Some may say that this card is badly rounded, but that is a judgment call.

The 1962 Topps Hank Aaron card has a sligh-ly rounded corner. Note that there is definite corner wear evident by the fraying and that the corner no longer sports a sharp point.

The 1962 Topps Gil Hodges card has corner wear; it is slightly better than the Aaron card above. Nevertheless, some collectors might classify this Hodges corner as slightly rounded.

The 1962 Topps Manager's Dream card showing Mantle and Mays has slight corner wear. This is not a fuzzy corner as very slight wear is noticeable on the card's photo surface.

The 1962 Topps Don Mossi card has very slight corner wear such that it might be called a fuzzy corner. A close look at the original card shows the corner is not perfect, but almost. However, note that corner wear is somewhat academic on this card. As you can plainly see, the heavy crease going across his name breaks through the photo surface.

The ingenuity and distinctiveness of this era has yet to be surpassed. Highlights include:

the T-202 Hassan triple-folders, one of the best looking and the most distinctive cards ever issued;

the durable T-201 Mecca double-folders, one of the first sets with players' records on the reverse;

the T-3 Turkey Reds, the hobby's most popular cabinet card;

the E-145 Cracker Jacks, the only major set containing Federal League player cards;

the T-204 Ramlys, with their distinctive black-and-white oval photos and ornate gold borders.

These are but a few of the varieties issued during this period.

Increasing Popularity

While the American Tobacco Company dominated the field, several other tobacco companies, as well as clothing manufacturers, newspapers and periodicals, game makers, and companies whose identities remain anonymous, also issued cards during this period. In fact, the Collins-McCarthy Candy Company, makers of Zeenuts Pacific Coast League baseball cards, issued cards yearly from 1911 to 1938. Its record for continuous annual card production has been exceeded only by the Topps Chewing Gum Company. The era of the tobacco card issues closed with the onset of World War I, with the exception of the Red Man chewing tobacco sets produced from 1952 to 1955.

The next flurry of card issues broke out in the roaring and prosperous 1920s, the era of the E card. The caramel companies (National Caramel, American Caramel, York Caramel) were the leading distributors of these E cards. In addition, the strip card, a continuous strip with several cards divided by dotted lines or other sectioning features, flourished during this time. While the E cards and the strip cards generally are considered less imaginative than the T cards or the recent candy and gum issues, they still are pursued by many advanced collectors.

Another significant event of the 1920s was the introduction of the arcade card. Taking its designation from its issuer, the Exhibit Supply Company of Chicago, it is usually known as the "Exhibit" card. Once a trademark of the penny arcades, amusement parks and county fairs across the country, Exhibit machines dispensed nearly postcard-size photos on thick stock for one penny. These picture cards bore likenesses of a favorite cowboy, actor, actress or baseball player. Exhibit Supply and its associated companies produced baseball cards during a longer time span, although discontinuous, than any other manufacturer. Its first cards appeared in 1921, while its last issue was in 1966. In 1979, the Exhibit Supply Company was bought and somewhat revived by a collector/dealer who has since reprinted Exhibit photos of the past.

If the T card period, from 1909 to 1915, can be designated the "Golden Age" of baseball card collecting, then perhaps the "Silver Age" commenced with the introduction of the Big League Gum series of 239 cards in 1933 (a 240th card was added in 1934). These are the forerunners of today's baseball gum cards, and the Goudey Gum Company of Boston is responsible for their success. This era spanned the period from the Depression days of 1933 to America's formal involvement in World War II in 1941.

Goudey's attractive designs, with full-color line drawings on thick card stock, greatly influenced other cards being issued at that time. As a result, the most attractive and popular vintage cards in history were produced in this "Silver Age." The 1933 Goudey Big League Gum series also owes its popularity to the more than 40 Hall of Fame players in the set. These include four cards of Babe Ruth and two of Lou Gehrig. Goudey's reign continued in 1934, when it issued a 96-card set in color, together with the single remaining card from the 1933 series, #106, the Napoleon Lajoie card.

In addition to Goudey, several other bubblegum manufacturers issued baseball cards during this era. DeLong Gum Company issued an extremely attractive set in 1933. National Chicle Company's 192-card "Batter-Up" series of 1934-1936 became the largest die-cut set in card history. In addition, that company offered the popular "Diamond Stars" series during the same period. Other popular sets included the "Tattoo Orbit" set of 60 color cards issued in 1933 and Gum Products' 75-card "Double Play" set, featuring sepia depictions of two players per card.

In 1939, Gum Inc., which later became Bowman Gum, replaced Goudey Gum as the leading baseball card producer. In 1939 and the following year, it issued two important sets of black-and-white cards. In 1939, its "Play Ball America" set consisted of 162 cards. The larger, 240-card "Play Ball" set of 1940 still is considered by many to be the most attractive black-and-white cards ever produced. That firm introduced its only color set in 1941, consisting of 72 cards titled "Play Ball Sports Hall of Fame." Many of these were colored repeats of poses from the black-and-white 1940 series.

In addition to regular gum cards, many manufacturers distributed premium issues during the 1930s. These premiums were printed on paper or photographic stock, rather than card stock. They were much larger than the regular cards and were sold for a penny across the counter with gum (which was packaged separately from the premium). They often were redeemed at the store or through the mail in exchange for the wrappers of previously purchased gum cards, like proof-of-purchase box-top premiums today. The gum premiums are scarcer than the card issues of the 1930s and in most cases no manufacturer's name is present.

World War II brought an end to this popular era of card collecting when paper and rubber shortages curtailed the production of bubblegum baseball cards. They were resurrected again in 1948 by the Bowman Gum Company (the direct descendent of Gum, Inc.). This marked the beginning of the modern era of card collecting.

In 1948, Bowman Gum issued a 48-card set in black and white consisting of one card and one slab of gum in every 1 cent pack. That same year, the Leaf Gum Company also issued a set of cards. Although rather poor in quality, these cards were issued in color. A squabble over the rights to use players' pictures developed between Bowman and Leaf. Eventually Leaf dropped out of the card market, but not before it had left a lasting heritage to the hobby by issuing some of the rarest cards now in existence. Leaf's baseball card series of 1948-49 contained 98 cards, skip numbered to #168 (not all numbers were printed). Of these 98 cards, 49 are relatively plentiful; the other 49, however, are rare and quite valuable.

Bowman continued its production of cards in 1949 with a color series of 240 cards. Because there are many scarce "high numbers," this series remains the most difficult Bowman regular issue to complete. Although the set was printed in color and commands great interest due to its scarcity, it is considered aesthetically inferior to the Goudey and National Chicle issues of the 1930s. In addition to the regular issue of 1949, Bowman also produced a set of 36 Pacific Coast League players. While this was not a regular issue, it still is prized by collectors. In fact, it has become the most valuable Bowman series.

In 1950 (representing Bowman's one-year monopoly of the baseball card market), the company began a string of top quality cards that continued until its demise in 1955. The 1950 series was itself something of an oddity because the low numbers, rather than the traditional high numbers, were the more difficult cards to obtain.

The year 1951 marked the beginning of the most competitive and perhaps the highest quality period of baseball card production. In that year, Topps Chewing Gum Company of Brooklyn entered the market. Topps' 1951 series consisted of two sets of 52 cards each, one set with red backs and the other with blue backs. In addition, Topps also issued 31 insert cards, three of which remain the rarest Topps cards ("Current All-Stars" Konstanty, Roberts and Stanky). The 1951 Topps cards were unattractive and paled in comparison to the 1951 Bowman issues. They were successful, however, and Topps has continued to produce cards ever since.

Intensified Competition

Topps issued a larger and more attractive card set in 1952. This larger size became standard for the next five years. (Bowman followed with larger-size baseball cards in 1953.) This 1952 Topps set has become, like the 1933 Goudey series and the T-206 white border series, the classic set of its era. The 407-card set is a collector's dream of scarcities, rarities, errors and variations. It also contains the first Topps issues of Mickey Mantle and Willie Mays.

As with Bowman and Leaf in the late 1940s, competition over player rights arose. Ensuing court battles occurred between Topps and Bowman. The market split due to stiff competition, and in January 1956, Topps bought out Bowman. (Topps, using the Bowman name, resurrected Bowman as a later label in 1989.) Topps remained essentially unchallenged as the primary producer of baseball cards through 1980. So, the story of major baseball card sets from 1956 through 1980 is by and large the story of Topps' issues. Notable exceptions include the small sets produced by Fleer Gum in 1959, 1960, 1961 and 1963, and the Kellogg's Cereal and Hostess Cakes baseball cards issued to promote their products.

A court decision in 1980 paved the way for two other large gum companies to enter (or reenter, in Fleer's case) the baseball card arena. Fleer, which had last made photo cards in 1963, and the Donruss Company (then a division of General Mills) secured rights to produce baseball cards of current players, thus breaking Topps' monopoly. Each company issued major card sets in 1981 with bubblegum products.

Then a higher court decision in that year overturned the lower court ruling against Topps. It appeared that Topps had regained its sole position as a producer of baseball cards. Undaunted by the revocation ruling, Fleer and Donruss continued to issue cards in 1982 but without bubblegum or any other edible product. Fleer issued its current player baseball cards with "team logo stickers," while Donruss issued its cards with a piece of a baseball jigsaw puzzle.

Sharing the Pie

Since 1981, these three major baseball card producers all have thrived, sharing relatively equal recognition. Each has steadily increased its involvement in terms of numbers of issues per year. To the delight of collectors, their competition has generated novel, and in some cases exceptional, issues of current Major League Baseball players. Collectors also eagerly accepted the debut efforts of Score (1988) and Upper Deck (1989). These five companies were about to embark on a wild ride through the 1990's.

Upper Deck's successful entry into the market turned out to be very important. The company's card stock, photography, packaging and marketing gave baseball cards a new standard for quality, and began the "premium card" trend that continues today. The second premium baseball card set to be issued was the 1990 Leaf set, named for and issued by the parent company of Donruss. To gauge the significance of the premium card trend, one need only note that two of the most valuable post-1986 regular-issue cards in the hobby are the 1989 Upper Deck Ken Griffey Jr. and 1990 Leaf Frank Thomas Rookie Cards.

The impressive debut of Leaf in 1990 was followed by Studio, Ultra, and Stadium Club in 1991. Of those, Stadium Club with it's dramatic borderless photo, Un-coated card fronts made the biggest impact. In 1992, Bowman, and Pinnacle joined the premium fray. In 1992, Donruss and Fleer abandoned the traditional 50-cent pack market and instead produced premium sets comparable to (and presumably designed to compete against) Upper Deck's set. Those moves, combined with the almost instantaneous spread of premium cards to the other major team sports cards, serve as strong indicators that premium cards were here to stay. Bowman had been a lower-level product from 1989 to '91.

In 1993, Fleer, Topps and Upper Deck produced the first "super premium" cards with Flair, Finest and SP, respectively. The success of all three products was an indication the baseball card market was headed toward even higher price levels, and that turned out to be the case in 1994 with the introduction of Bowman's Best (a Topps hybrid of prospect-oriented Bowman and the superpremium Finest) and Leaf Limited. Other 1994 debuts included Upper Deck's entry-level Collector's Choice and Pinnacle's hobby-only Select.

Overall, inserts continued to dominate the hobby scene. Specifically, the parallel chase cards first introduced in 1992 with Topps Gold became the latest major hobby trend. Topps Gold was followed by 1993 Finest Refractors (at the time the scarcest insert ever produced and still a landmark set), and the one-per-box Stadium Club First Day Issue.

Of course, the biggest on-field news of 1994 was the owner-provoked players strike that halted the season prematurely. While the baseball card hobby suffered noticeably from the strike, there was no catastrophic market crash as some had feared. However, the strike pulled the plug on a market that was both strong and growing, and contributed to a serious hobby contraction that continues to this day.

By 1995, parallel insert sets were commonplace and had taken on a new complexion: the most popular ones were those that had announced (or at least suspected) print runs of 500 or less, such as Finest Refractors and Select Artist's Proofs.

This trend continued in 1996, with several parallel inserts that were printed in quantities of 250 or less such as Finest Gold Refractors, Fleer Circa Rave, Studio Silver Press Proofs and three of the six Select Certified parallels. It could be argued that the high price tags on these extremely limited parallel cards (many exceeded the $1000 plateau) were driving many single-player collectors to frustration, and even completely out of the hobby. At the same time, average pack prices soared while average number of cards per pack dropped, making the baseball card hobby increasingly more expensive.

On the positive side, two trends from 1996 clearly brought in new collectors: Topps' Mickey Mantle retrospective inserts in both series of Topps and Stadium Club; and Leaf's Signature Series, which included one certified autograph per pack. While the Mantle craze following his passing seemed to be a short-term phenomenon, the inclusion of autographs in packs seemed to have more long-term significance.

In 1997 the print runs in selected sets got even lower. Both Fleer/SkyBox and Pinnacle brands issued cards of which only one exists.

The growth in popularity of autographs also continued. Many products had autographed cards in their packs. A very positive trend was a return to basics. Many collectors bought Rookie Cards as they understood that concept and worked on finishing sets.

There was also an increase in international players collecting. Hideo Nomo was incredibly popular in Japan while Chan Ho Park was in demand in Korea. This bodes well for an international growth in the hobby.

Clearly, 1998 was a year of rebirth and growth for the hobby. The big boost came from the home run chase being conducted by Mark McGwire and Sammy Sosa, as well as the continued brilliance of stalwarts like Ken Griffey Jr. and Roger Clemens. The baseball card hobby received a great deal of positive publicity from the renewed interest in the game.

Rookie Cards of the key players of '98 made significant gains in value as the hobby once again turned to Rookie Cards as the collectible of choice. Also, cards professionally graded by companies such as PSA and SGC were becoming more heavily traded in both older and newer material.

In addition, the internet and various services such as eBay, contributed to the strong growth in collecting interest over the last year.

There were down sides in 1998 though. Pinnacle Brands folded, leaving a legacy of innovation and promotions not seen by other companies. In addition, there still was the problem of collectors being frustrated by the extremely short printed cards of their favorite players, making set completion almost impossible.

During 1998, Pacific received a full baseball license and added many innovations to the card market. Their 1998 OnLine set for example is the most comprehensive set issued in the last five years and many veteran collectors applauded Pacific's continuing attempts to get as many different players as possible into their sets.

In the last couple of years, card companies have been printing specific subsets (usually young players or Rookie Cards) in shorter supply than the regular cards. This is not in every set, but in many sets produced since 1998.

In 1999, many of the trends of the last couple of years continued to gain strength. Buying, selling and trading cards over the Internet became a dominant factor in the secondary market. Beckett Publications began its own Marketplace, offering the collectors a chance to search across inventory from many of the finest dealers nationwide in one comprehensive online database. eBay continued to flourish, while many other parties began to reap the benefits of the burgeoning online auction market. The Barry Halper collection was auctioned off bringing many museum quality items to the market and giving the older memorabilia market a significant boost as many treasures were made available to collectors.

Also, the boom in Internet trading created a perfect fit for professionally graded cards as buyers and sellers traded cards sight unseen with the confidence established by a third party grader.

From a field of almost a dozen contenders, three companies emerged in 1999 to dominate the field of professional grading - BGS (Beckett Grading Services), PSA (Professional Sports Authenticator) and SGC (Sportscard Guaranty L.L.C.). In 1999 these companies made dramatic expansions in onsite grading and submissions at card shows throughout the nation. In response to the widespread acceptance of graded cards, the line of monthly Beckett Price Guides each added a separate section within the price guide area for professionally graded cards.

As was similar to 1998, four licensed manufacturers (Fleer/SkyBox, Pacific, Topps and Upper Deck) produced slightly more than fifty different products for 1999.

Perhaps the biggest hit of the 1999 card season was created by Topps. Card #220 within the basic issue first series 1999 Topps brand featured Home Run King Mark McGwire in 70 variations, one for each homer he slugged in 1998 and many collectors went after the whole set. Continuing a legacy as strong as the Yankees, the basic Topps issue was the one of the most popular sets released in 1999.

Closely trailing the Topps McGwire promotion was Upper Deck's dynamic A Piece of History bat card promotion. The card that kicked off the frenzy was the Babe Ruth A Piece of History distributed in 1999 Upper Deck series 1 packs. Upper Deck actually purchased a cracked game-used Babe Ruth bat for $24,000 and proceeded to cut it up into approximately 350-400 chips of wood to create the now famous Ruth bat card. The card instantly created polar opposites of opinion amongst hobbyists. Traditional collectors howled at the sacreligious act of destroying such a historic piece of memorabilia while more open-minded collectors jumped at the opportunity to chase such an important card. The Ruth card was followed up by the cross-brand "500 Club" bat card promotion, whereby UD produced bat cards from every major league ballplayer that hit 500 or more home runs in their career (except for Mark McGwire of whom hit his 500th in the midst of the 1999 season and promptly stated that he did not support Upper Deck's promotion).

More memorabilia cards than ever were offered to collectors in 1999 as Fleer/SkyBox kicked up their efforts to match the standards set by Upper Deck in previous years. Batting Gloves, hats and shoes joined the typical bats and jerseys as pieces of game-used equipment to be featured on trading cards. Sets like E-X Century Authen-Kicks and Fleer Mystique Feel the Game typified the new offerings.

Topps only dabbled with memorabilia cards in 1999, but continued to offer some of the hottest autographed inserts highlighted by the Topps Stars Rookie Reprint Autographs and the Topps Nolan Ryan Autographs.

Pacific made a clear decision to steer free of memorabilia and autograph inserts, instead focusing on offering collectors a wide selection of beautifully designed insert and parallel cards. Those themes worked beautifully with their established presence for making comprehensive sets - providing collectors with the necessary challenge to pursue regional stars and a favorite team in addition to the typical superstars.

An astounding total of 264 different players made their first appearance on a major league licensed trading card in 1999. What may go down as the deepest class of Rookie Cards of all time features a cornucopia of talented youngsters led by Rick Ankiel, Josh Beckett, Pat Burrell, Josh Hamilton, Eric Munson, Corey Patterson and Alfonso Soriano.

As in years past, Topps continued to provide collectors with a fistful of Rookie Cards within their Bowman, Bowman Chrome and Bowman's Best brands. In a trend established in 1998 by Fleer when they released their Fleer Update set (fueled largely by a J.D. Drew Rookie Card), hobbyists enjoyed a bevy of late season sets chock full of RC's. Fleer/SkyBox made an all out effort by stuffing more than 100 Rookie Cards into their 1999 Fleer Update set. Topps produced their first boxed Traded set since 1994. Each 1999 Topps Traded set contained one of 75 different cards autographed by a rookie prospect. Considering how much wider the selection of Rookie Cards became in 1999, it's amazing to see that so few of these RC's were serial numbered. When one looks at the success established with serial numbered Rookie Cards in the basketball and football card markets with brands like SP Authentic and SPx Finite, one can only scratch their head when realizing that Fleer Mystique was the only brand to offer baseball collectors serial numbered RC's. Thus, it's not surprising to see that despite having twenty-five different Rookie Cards issued in 1999, Pat Burrell's Fleer Mystique RC (#'d of 2,999) had been established as his "best" RC by year's end.

Youngsters weren't the only players in the limelight last year as retired stars and Hall of Famers were featured on more cards than any other year in the '90s. Upper Deck's Century Legends brand, featuring the top 50 active and top 50 retired players of the decade as chosen by The Sporting News was a runaway hit.

Perhaps the most popular insert set of the year, outpacing all of the dazzling high dollar memorabilia cards, was Topps Gallery Heritage. Utilizing the design and painting style of artist Gerry Dvorak from the classic 1953 Topps set, these modern masterpieces proved that insert cards can still be a hot commodity in the secondary market - albeit assuming they're well conceived and well made - an unfortunate rarity these days.

The spate of basic issue sets with short-printed subsets continued across many brands in 1999. In reaction to many frustrated dealers and collectors struggling to complete these sets, Fleer/SkyBox created dual versions of each prospect card for the 1999 SkyBox Premium set - an action shot was short-printed and a posed shot was seeded at the same rate as other basic issue cards. The idea was well received by collectors, but enjoyed a surprisingly short-lived period of active trading in the secondary market.

2000 was a year marked by several major developments that would continue shaping the future of our hobby. First off, Pacific decided to forfeit their baseball card license on January 1st, 2001 in an effort to more sharply focus their production expenditures into football and hockey. Though official word was not divulged by Major League Baseball Players Association and Properties at the time we went to press, speculation that another current manufacturer would fill the void was rampant.

In a separate development, Wizards of the Coast (primarily known for their non-sport gaming cards) was granted a license to produce baseball trading cards and debuted their MLB Showdown brand. The cards proved to be quite successful in that they were collected as a set by veteran collectors and played as a game by children (and some adults) both inside and outside of the typical collecting community. By year's end, Fleer fazed out their SkyBox and Flair brand names in an effort to take full advantage of the historic significance and brand recognition of their flagship Fleer sets issued sporadically from the late '50's-70's and consistently from 1981-present.

Almost sixty different brands of MLB-licensed cards, issued by five manufacturers were produced in 2000. In addition, Just Minors and Team Best produced a variety of attractive minor league products. Most shop owners continued to generate their income primarily through the sales of packs and boxes of new product and as in years past, they had to make careful decisions as to what to keep in stock for customers and what to pass up in fear of a low sell through.

Vintage (or retro-themed) sets dominated the market highlighted by Fleer Greats of the Game, Upper Deck Yankees Legends and the run of 3000 hit club and Joe DiMaggio game used cards issued by Fleer and Upper Deck. In 2001, Topps Heritage (mimicking the style of the classic '52 Topps cards), Upper Deck Vintage (in an homage to '63 Topps baseball) and the return of Topps Archives (after a six year hiatus) will add fuel to the fire.

Using the vintage-theme to tap into a base of wealthy consumers, Upper Deck rolled out their line of Master Collection products (of which debuted in basketball a year prior with a Michael Jordan set). Both the Yankees Master Collection and Brooklyn Dodgers Master Collection sets carried initial SRP's of $4,000 or more - making the most expensive "factory set" of all-time. Each of these sets was serial numbered (500 Yankees and 250 Dodgers), came in a stylish wood box and contained an assortion of game-used and autograph cards from legends of days gone by.

Game-used memorabilia cards became more prolific in all products to the point where a few early 2001 releases (2001 Pacific Private Stock and 2001 SP

Game Bat Edition both carrying SRP's in the $15-$20 range) included them at a rate of one per pack. Both products enjoyed a dynamic sell through and proved to be very popular in the secondary market. The result, however, on the secondary market values of game-used memorabilia cards has been dramatic. An Alex Rodriguez or Ken Griffey Jr. game bat or game jersey card that sold for $200+ in 1999 could be had for as little as $25-$50 in early 2001.

Patch cards (aka a swatch of jersey that contains part of a multi-colored patch) really caught on by year's end as the market formalized premium values on these cards. Upper Deck was the first to create separate "super-premium" jersey Patch inserts within 2000 Upper Deck 1 and 2000 Upper Deck Game Jersey Edition (aka series 2). Pacific followed suit with their Game Gear patch subset within the Invincible brand.

By early 2001, Major League Baseball Properties had gotten involved with the trading card autograph and memorabilia programs. From 2001-on, all MLB-licensed trading cards produced by the manufacturers that involved an autograph or game-used memorabilia item had to have the procurement of the item witnessed by a representative of Anderson Consulting - a firm hired by MLB to oversee this historic program. Never before, had consumers been provided such an effort by the league and manufacturers to be offered autographed or game-used memorabilia trading cards of such authentic provenance.

Short-printed subset cards - a trend started in 1999 - continued to be a common element in most basic sets. The trend, however, evolved to the point where these short prints were now being serial numbered, autographed by the player or incorporating an element of game-used material onto the card. The result was higher values on the key singles - but lower odds of actually finding a good RC in a pack. By year's end, a general sentiment of frustration over not being able to pull good Rookie Cards from a box was beginning to be heard more and more often from collectors. As we enter 2001, we may see some manufacturers trim back the number of products of which serial numbered RC's are included.

Rookie Cards incorporating game-used material debuted at year's end in 2000 Black Diamond Rookie Edition. Also, Rookie Cards signed by the player, first introduced within the basketball and football card markets in 1999 (with Upper Deck's SPx brand), made their baseball debut in 2000 SPx. Serial-numbered Rookie Cards grew in total usage, but shrank in print run numbers as production figures reached an all-time low of 999 copies for a basic issue RC within the 2000 Pacific Omega set.

Year-end boxed sets, a trend brought back from a four year hiatus by Fleer in 1998 with their Fleer Update set, continued to expand as Topps issued their Bowman Draft Picks and Bowman Chrome Draft Picks sets to cap the now single-series accompanying standard Bowman and Bowman Chrome products.

Fleer broke new ground by blending a 1980's "old-school" concept with some post-modern angles in their 2000 Fleer Glossy boxed set. Harkening back to the run of Glossy parallel factory sets produced from 1987-1989, the 2000 Fleer Glossy set included a parallel version of the complete 400-card basic 2000 Fleer set. In addition, fifty new cards (card #'s 401-450 - each serial numbered to 1,000 copies) featuring a selection of prospects and rookies were created. Each Glossy factory set contained five of the 50 new cards - making a real challenge to complete the Glossy set.

In a first of it's kind for the baseball market, Upper Deck issued a product in December, 2000 called Rookie Update that incorporated new cards for three separate popular brands (SP Authentic, SPx and UD Pros and Prospects) into each pack of cards.

Upper Deck came to terms with Major League Baseball for a license to produce cards featuring members of past and present Team USA squads (bringing back a run of cards last seen seven years ago in 1993 Topps Traded). That allowed Upper Deck the opportunity to radically expand their production of "true" Rookie Cards in year-end 2000 products, adding a spate of cards featuring heroes from the Olympics in Sydney, Australia like Ben Sheets. Not surprisingly, the number of prospects making their Rookie Card debut in 2000 sets jumped from about 280 players in 1999 to slightly more than 350 players in 2000.

The influence of sportscard dealers and collectors from the Far East (and most noticeably Japan) continued to grow in 2000 as stateside buying approached frenzied levels over scarce Hideo Nomo and Kazuhiro Sasaki cards. A much-traveled starter these days, Nomo's first-ever certified autograph card (issued within the Fleer Mystique Fresh Ink insert set) was the hottest card in the hobby for two months (initially trading for as much as $600-$800).

Not all trends were met with success this year. In particular, low-end products geared towards the youth audience (like 2000 Impact by Fleer) were roundly ignored. The hobby still faces a tough road ahead to keep new waves of collectors involved from generation to generation. Part of the "Catch-22" with creating affordable brands catered to youths is that the same customers are most interested in the high-end, expensive material.

Also, Upper Deck's PowerDeck product faced an indifferent audience for a second year in a row - as collectors and even general sports enthusiasts outside the hobby failed to get excited over the CD Rom cards. More success was met with UD's e-Card insert program, whereby collectors that pulled an e-Card from a pack of UD cards had to go to their website and check the serial number printed on the card to see if it could evolve into an autograph, game jersey or game jersey autograph exchange.

The impact of the Internet continued to have profound ramifications upon shaping the destiny of sportscard collecting. By 2000, nearly every dealer (and hardcore collector) was buying or selling cards to some degree in on-line auctions. Auction sales had become so prolific, that they were now having a strong effect on the secondary market sales levels of trading cards in arenas entirely outside of cyberspace like shops, shows and mail-order.

eBay continued to dominate the online auction action - introducing what appears to be a popular "Buy It Now" option to their already established auction format. The Pit.com opened in mid-year with their concept of buying and selling a portfolio of professionally graded sportscards through their website. The concept is based almost exactly upon the methodology used for buying and selling stocks through a brokerage house - with daily ebbs and flows in posted buy and sell prices on your inventory.

Beckett.com made radical improvements to their Marketplace search engines and expanded their inventory of sports cards to the point where they were providing both a wider and deeper selection of trading cards than any site on the Internet. In addition, a company-wide effort to provide daily news content on their site (coupled with a weekly newsletter sent to over 400,000 collectors) began at year's end and the hobby has reaped the benefits ever since.

As the 2001 season approached, hobbyists were waiting with bated breath for seven-time Japanese batting champ Ichiro Suzuki to make his debut in the Seattle Mariner's outfield. And what a stunning debut it was. Ichiro led the league in hitting, led the Mariners to their best record ever and walked off with the A.L. Rookie of the Year and Most Valuable Player awards. Upper Deck obtained the exclusive rights to produce his autograph cards and they hit a grand slam home run in mid-Summer by releasing his SPx Rookie Card, featuring a game jersey swatch and a cut signature autograph. In a year, studded with notable cards, this one was likely the most memorable.

In the National League, 37-year old San Francisco Giants superstar Barry Bonds captivated the nation by bashing a jaw-dropping 73 home runs, shattering Mark McGwire's 1998 single-season home run record.

Cardinals rookie Albert Pujols emerged out of the low minor leagues to become an instant hobby superstar and walk away with N.L. Rookie of the Year honors.

2001 was a tumultuous year for sports cards. Topps started the year of with a bang by celebrating their 50th Anniversary producing baseball cards. Pacific forfeited it's license to make baseball cards after an eight year run to focus on football and hockey cards. Playoff, a company based out of Grand Prairie, Texas that had earned it's stripes producing football cards in the late 1990s, purchased the rights to the much-hallowed Donruss corporate name and became a formal MLB licensee in the

Spring of 2001. Their entrance into the baseball card market heralded the return of benchmark brands like Donruss, Donruss Signature and Leaf.

Competition was more fierce than ever amongst the four primary licensees (Donruss-Playoff, Fleer, Topps and Upper Deck) as they cranked out almost 80 different products over the course of 2001.

Of all these, likely the most historically impactful product, Upper Deck Prospect Premieres was widely overlooked upon release. In a bold move, Upper Deck created a set of 102 prospects, none of which had played a day in the majors. Each player was pictured, however, in the major league uniforms of their parent ballclubs and signed to individual contracts. Because no active major leaguers were featured, Upper Deck did not have to include licensing rights from the MLB Player's Association though they did get licensing from Major League Properties. The industry had never seen a major release featuring active ballplayers marketed to the mainstream audience that lacked licensing from the MLBPA. Because of it's lack of historical predecessors and a mixed reception from collectors, the cards were tagged by Beckett Baseball Card Monthly as XRC's (or Extended Rookie Cards) – a term that had not been used since 1989.

UD's Prospect Premieres was the first major effort by a manufacturer to level the playing field between Topps and everyone else in that Topps has exclusive rights from the MLBPA to include minor leaguers in their basic brands. Whether Fleer or Donruss-Playoff will follow suit, or even if Prospect Premieres returns for another run around the block in 2002 remains to be seen.

Rookie Cards continued to fascinate collectors, especially in a year with talents like Ichiro and Albert Pujols. The number of players featured on Rookie Cards in 2001 ballooned to an almost absurd figure of 505.

Exchange cards became more prevalent than ever, as manufacturers expanded their use from autograph cards that didn't get returned in time for pack out to slots within basic sets left open in brands released early in the year to fill in with late-season rookie call-ups.

Certified autograph cards remained a huge player in how brands were structured, but the quality of the players suffered greatly as autograph fees continued to spiral out of control. Signatures from superstars like Barry Bonds and Derek Jeter were now being featured on cards with miniscule print runs of 25 or 50 copies while unknown (and often aging and talentless) prospects signed their serial-numbered Rookies Cards by the hundred count.

More serial-numbered Rookie Cards were produced than ever before, but the quantities produced kept sinking lower and lower as companies tried to create secondary market value by simply limiting supply, a dangerous move to say the least. Donruss-Playoff produced the scarcest Rookie Cards of the year, a handful of Game Base cards (including Ichiro) each serial #'d to a scant 100 copies, within their Leaf Limited set.

After a six-month delay, Topps released their much awaited e-Topps program - a product sold entirely on their website whereby trading is conducted in a similar fashion to the buying and selling of stocks – in September.

Several products incorporated non-card memorabilia such as signed caps, bobbing head dolls and signed baseballs with mixed results.

Memorabilia cards continued their slide into mediocrity as the number of cards featuring various bits and pieces of balls, bases, bats, jerseys, pants, shoes, seats and whatever else could be dreamt up continued to be offered to consumers that found the cards less appealing with each passing month. To battle consumer apathy, companies often started to offer combination memorabilia cards featuring notable teammates or several pieces of equipment from a notable star.

Retro-themed cards continued to grow in popularity and some of the innovations seen in these sets were remarkable. Of particular note was Upper Deck's SP Legendary Cuts Autographs set, featuring 84 deceased players. The set required UD to purchase more than 3,300 autograph cuts, of which were then incorporated into a windowpane card design. The result was the first certified autograph cards for legends like Roger Maris, Satchell Paige and Jackie Robinson. Also, Topps Tribute released at year's end and carrying a hefty $40 per pack suggested retail was widely

hailed as one of the most beautiful retro-themed cards ever designed with their crystal-board fronts encasing full-color, razor-sharp photos.
Pack prices continued to escalate, but surprisingly, the public did not balk as long as they delivered value. The most notable high-end product to hit the market in 2001 was Upper Deck Ultimate Collection with a suggested retail of $100 per pack.

September 11th, 2001 is a day that will go down as one of the most devastating in the history of the United States of America. The game of baseball and the hobby of collecting sports cards was rightfully cast aside as the nation mourned the tragic loss of lives in New York, Pennsylvania and Washington DC. America's economy tumbled as airline traveling ground to a near halt and threats of Anthrax crippled the mail system. An economy threatening to slip into recession at the beginning of the year dove headlong into it. The sports card market, along with many other industries felt the hit for several months. Slowly, Americans looked to move past the grief and the sports card industry, steeped in American nostalgia, provided an ideal repast for many.

The Arizona Diamondbacks beat the New York Yankees in one of the finest World Series ever played, a much-needed diversion for a grief-stricken nation and a calling card for the dramatic power and glory of our National Pastime.

As we enter 2002, the nation is still struggling to dig out of recession and the sport of baseball had yet to come to a long-term agreement between players and owners. Commissioner Bud Selig failed in an attempt to contract the league by eliminating the Minnesota Twins and Montreal Expos. The baseball card market, however, has stepped back to the forefront of the card collecting hobby – clearly outpacing football, basketball, hockey, golf or motorsports. As the hobby of collecting baseball cards heads into the 21st century, we face a market that is blessed with bold creativity and superlative quality and also challenged with the need to reach new consumers both in mass retail and in cyberspace to continue it's growth.

Finding Out More

The above has been a thumbnail sketch of card collecting from its inception in the 1880s to the present. It is difficult to tell the whole story in just a few pages - there are several other good sources of information. Serious collectors should subscribe to at least one of the excellent hobby periodicals. We also suggest that collectors visit their local card shop(s) and also attend a sports collectibles show in their area. Card collecting is still a young and informal hobby. You can learn more about it in either place. After all, smart dealers realize that spending a few minutes teaching beginners about the hobby often pays off in the long run.

Additional Reading

Each year Beckett Publications produces comprehensive annual price guides for these sports: Beckett Baseball Card Price Guide, Beckett Basketball Card Price Guide, Beckett Football Card Price Guide, Beckett Hockey Card Price Guide, Beckett Racing Price Guide and a line of Beckett Alphabetical Checklists Books have been released as well. The aim of these annual guides is to provide information and accurate pricing on a wide array of sports cards, ranging from main issues by the major card manufacturers to various regional, promotional, and food issues. Also alphabetical checklist books are published to assist the collector in identifying all the cards of any particular player. The seasoned collector will find these tools valuable sources of information that will enable him to pursue his hobby interests.

In addition, abridged editions of the Beckett Price Guides have been published for each of these major sports as part of the House of Collectibles series: The Official Price Guide to Baseball Cards, The Official Price Guide to Football Cards, The Official Price Guide to Basketball Cards. Published in a convenient mass-market paperback format, these price guides provide information and accurate pricing on all the main issues by the major card manufacturers.

Advertising

Within this Price Guide you will find advertisements for sports memorabilia material, mail order, and retail sports collectibles establishments. All advertisements were accepted in good faith based on the reputation of the advertiser; however, neither the author, the publisher, the distributors, nor the other advertisers in this Price Guide accept any responsibility for any particular advertiser not complying with the terms of his or her ad.

Readers also should be aware that prices in advertisements are subject to change over the annual period before a new edition of this volume is issued each spring. When replying to an advertisement late in the baseball year, the reader should take this into account, and contact the dealer by phone or in writing for up-to-date price information. Should you come into contact with any of the advertisers in this guide as a result of their advertisement herein, please mention this source as your contact.

Prices in this Guide

Prices found in this guide reflect current retail rates just prior to the printing of this book. They do not reflect the FOR SALE prices of the author, the publisher, the distributors, the advertisers, or any card dealers associated with this guide. No one is obligated in any way to buy, sell or trade his or her cards based on these prices. The price listings were compiled by the author from actual buy/sell transactions at sports conventions, sports card shops, buy/sell advertisements in the hobby papers, for sale prices from dealer catalogs and price lists, and discussions with leading hobbyists in the U.S. and Canada. All prices are in U.S. dollars.

Acknowledgments

A great deal of diligence, hard work, and dedicated effort went into this year's volume. However, the high standards to which we hold ourselves could not have been met without the expert input and generous amount of time contributed by many people. Our sincere thanks are extended to each and every one of you.

A complete list of these invaluable contributors appears after the Price Guide section.

Work in Progress

Because we intend the Almanac to be the most comprehensive Price Guide book available, we occasionally include sets with incomplete checklists and/or information. In these cases we have exhausted our resources in an attempt to fill in the missing data but have been unsuccessful. This is where you can help. We always appreciate assistance from our readers to make sure the next edition of this book is even more accurate and more complete. Write to Dr. James Beckett, 15850 Dallas Parkway, Dallas, Texas 75248.

1948 Bowman

	NRMT	VG-E
COMPLETE SET (48)	3400.00	1500.00
COMMON CARD (1-36)	20.00	9.00
COMMON CARD (37-48)	30.00	13.50
WRAPPER (5-CENT)	700.00	325.00
❑ 1 Bob Elliott RC	125.00	19.00
❑ 2 Ewell Blackwell RC	50.00	22.00
❑ 3 Ralph Kiner RC	150.00	70.00
❑ 4 Johnny Mize	100.00	45.00
❑ 5 Bob Feller	250.00	110.00
❑ 6 Yogi Berra RC	450.00	200.00
❑ 7 Pete Reiser SP	120.00	55.00
❑ 8 Phil Rizzuto SP	350.00	160.00
❑ 9 Walker Cooper RC	20.00	9.00
❑ 10 Buddy Rosar	20.00	9.00
❑ 11 Johnny Lindell	25.00	11.00
❑ 12 Johnny Sain RC	50.00	22.00
❑ 13 Willard Marshall SP	40.00	18.00
❑ 14 Allie Reynolds RC	50.00	22.00
❑ 15 Eddie Joost	20.00	9.00
❑ 16 Jack Lohrke SP	40.00	18.00
❑ 17 Enos Slaughter	100.00	45.00
❑ 18 Warren Spahn RC	300.00	135.00
❑ 19 Tommy Henrich	50.00	22.00
❑ 20 Buddy Kerr SP	40.00	18.00
❑ 21 Ferris Fain RC	40.00	18.00
❑ 22 Floyd Bevens SP RC	50.00	22.00
❑ 23 Larry Jansen RC	25.00	11.00
❑ 24 Dutch Leonard SP	40.00	18.00
❑ 25 Barney McCosky	20.00	9.00
❑ 26 Frank Shea SP RC	50.00	22.00
❑ 27 Sid Gordon RC	25.00	11.00
❑ 28 Emil Verban SP	40.00	18.00
❑ 29 Joe Page SP RC	75.00	34.00
❑ 30 W.Lockman SP RC	50.00	22.00
❑ 31 Bill McCahan	20.00	9.00
❑ 32 Bill Rigney RC	20.00	9.00
❑ 33 Bill Johnson	25.00	11.00
❑ 34 Sheldon Jones SP	40.00	18.00
❑ 35 Snuffy Stirnweiss RC	40.00	18.00
❑ 36 Stan Musial RC	800.00	350.00
❑ 37 Clint Hartung RC	30.00	13.50
❑ 38 Red Schoendienst RC	200.00	90.00
❑ 39 Augie Galan	30.00	13.50
❑ 40 Marty Marion RC	80.00	36.00
❑ 41 Rex Barney RC	60.00	27.00
❑ 42 Ray Poat	30.00	13.50
❑ 43 Bruce Edwards	40.00	18.00
❑ 44 Johnny Wyrostek	30.00	13.50
❑ 45 Hank Sauer RC	60.00	27.00
❑ 46 Herman Wehmeier	30.00	13.50
❑ 47 Bobby Thomson RC	100.00	45.00
❑ 48 Dave Koslo RC	80.00	19.50

1949 Bowman

	NRMT	VG-E
COMP. MASTER SET (252)	16000.00	7200.00
COMPLETE SET (240)	13000.00	5800.00
COMMON CARD (1-144)	15.00	6.75
COMMON CARD (145-240)	50.00	22.00
WRAPPER (5-CENT, GR.)	250.00	110.00
WRAPPER (5-CENT, BL.)	200.00	90.00
❑ 1 Vern Bickford RC	125.00	25.00
❑ 2 Whitey Lockman	40.00	18.00
❑ 3 Bob Porterfield	15.00	6.75
❑ 4A Jerry Priddy NNOF	15.00	6.75
❑ 4B Jerry Priddy NOF	50.00	22.00
❑ 5 Hank Sauer	40.00	18.00
❑ 6 Phil Cavarretta	40.00	18.00
❑ 7 Joe Dobson	15.00	6.75
❑ 8 Murry Dickson	15.00	6.75
❑ 9 Ferris Fain	40.00	18.00
❑ 10 Ted Gray	15.00	6.75
❑ 11 Lou Boudreau	75.00	34.00
❑ 12 Cass Michaels	15.00	6.75
❑ 13 Bob Chesnes	15.00	6.75
❑ 14 Curt Simmons RC	40.00	18.00
❑ 15 Ned Garver	15.00	6.75
❑ 16 Al Kozar	15.00	6.75
❑ 17 Earl Torgeson	15.00	6.75
❑ 18 Bobby Thomson	40.00	18.00
❑ 19 Bobby Brown RC	60.00	27.00
❑ 20 Gene Hermanski	15.00	6.75
❑ 21 Frank Baumholtz	25.00	11.00
❑ 22 Peanuts Lowrey	15.00	6.75
❑ 23 Bobby Doerr	75.00	34.00
❑ 24 Stan Musial	500.00	220.00
❑ 25 Carl Scheib	15.00	6.75
❑ 26 George Kell RC	75.00	34.00
❑ 27 Bob Feller	200.00	90.00
❑ 28 Don Kolloway	15.00	6.75
❑ 29 Ralph Kiner	125.00	55.00
❑ 30 Andy Seminick	40.00	18.00
❑ 31 Dick Kokos	15.00	6.75
❑ 32 Eddie Yost RC	60.00	27.00
❑ 33 Warren Spahn	200.00	90.00
❑ 34 Dave Koslo	15.00	6.75
❑ 35 Vic Raschi RC	60.00	27.00
❑ 36 Pee Wee Reese	200.00	90.00
❑ 37 Johnny Wyrostek	15.00	6.75
❑ 38 Emil Verban	15.00	6.75
❑ 39 Billy Goodman	25.00	11.00
❑ 40 Red Munger	15.00	6.75
❑ 41 Lou Brissie	15.00	6.75
❑ 42 Hoot Evers	15.00	6.75
❑ 43 Dale Mitchell RC	40.00	18.00
❑ 44 Dave Philley	15.00	6.75
❑ 45 Wally Westlake	15.00	6.75
❑ 46 Robin Roberts RC	250.00	110.00
❑ 47 Johnny Sain	60.00	27.00
❑ 48 Willard Marshall	15.00	6.75
❑ 49 Frank Shea	25.00	11.00
❑ 50 Jackie Robinson RC	1100.00	500.00
❑ 51 Herman Wehmeier	15.00	6.75
❑ 52 Johnny Schmitz	15.00	6.75
❑ 53 Jack Kramer	15.00	6.75
❑ 54 Marty Marion	60.00	27.00
❑ 55 Eddie Joost	15.00	6.75
❑ 56 Pat Mullin	15.00	6.75
❑ 57 Gene Bearden	40.00	18.00
❑ 58 Bob Elliott	40.00	18.00
❑ 59 Jack Lohrke	15.00	6.75
❑ 60 Yogi Berra	300.00	135.00
❑ 61 Rex Barney	40.00	18.00
❑ 62 Grady Hatton	15.00	6.75
❑ 63 Andy Pafko	40.00	18.00
❑ 64 Dom DiMaggio	60.00	27.00
❑ 65 Enos Slaughter	75.00	34.00
❑ 66 Elmer Valo	15.00	6.75
❑ 67 Alvin Dark	40.00	18.00
❑ 68 Sheldon Jones	15.00	6.75
❑ 69 Tommy Henrich	40.00	18.00
❑ 70 Carl Furillo RC	125.00	55.00
❑ 71 Vern Stephens	15.00	6.75
❑ 72 Tommy Holmes	40.00	18.00
❑ 73 Billy Cox RC	40.00	18.00
❑ 74 Tom McBride	15.00	6.75
❑ 75 Eddie Mayo	15.00	6.75
❑ 76 Bill Nicholson RC	25.00	11.00
❑ 77 Ernie Bonham	15.00	6.75
❑ 78A Sam Zoldak NNOF	15.00	6.75
❑ 78B Sam Zoldak NOF	50.00	22.00
❑ 79 Ron Northey	15.00	6.75
❑ 80 Bill McCahan	15.00	6.75
❑ 81 Virgil Stallcup	15.00	6.75
❑ 82 Joe Page	60.00	27.00
❑ 83A Bob Scheffing NNOF	15.00	6.75
❑ 83B Bob Scheffing NOF	50.00	22.00
❑ 84 Roy Campanella RC !	700.00	325.00
❑ 85A Johnny Mize NNOF	100.00	45.00
❑ 85B Johnny Mize NOF	150.00	70.00
❑ 86 Johnny Pesky	60.00	27.00
❑ 87 Randy Gumpert	15.00	6.75
❑ 88A Bill Salkeld NNOF	15.00	6.75
❑ 88B Bill Salkeld NOF	50.00	22.00
❑ 89 Mizell Platt	15.00	6.75
❑ 90 Gil Coan	15.00	6.75
❑ 91 Dick Wakefield	15.00	6.75
❑ 92 Willie Jones	40.00	18.00
❑ 93 Ed Stevens	15.00	6.75
❑ 94 Mickey Vernon RC	40.00	18.00
❑ 95 Howie Pollet RC	15.00	6.75
❑ 96 Taft Wright	15.00	6.75
❑ 97 Danny Litwhiler	15.00	6.75
❑ 98A Phil Rizzuto NNOF	200.00	90.00
❑ 98B Phil Rizzuto NOF	250.00	110.00
❑ 99 Frank Gustine	15.00	6.75
❑ 100 Gil Hodges RC	250.00	110.00
❑ 101 Sid Gordon	15.00	6.75
❑ 102 Stan Spence	15.00	6.75
❑ 103 Joe Tipton	15.00	6.75
❑ 104 Eddie Stanky RC	40.00	18.00
❑ 105 Bill Kennedy	15.00	6.75
❑ 106 Jake Early	15.00	6.75
❑ 107 Eddie Lake	15.00	6.75
❑ 108 Ken Heintzelman	15.00	6.75
❑ 109A Ed Fitzgerald SCR	15.00	6.75
❑ 109B Ed Fitzgerald PR	60.00	27.00
❑ 110 Early Wynn RC	125.00	55.00
❑ 111 Red Schoendienst	80.00	36.00
❑ 112 Sam Chapman	40.00	18.00
❑ 113 Ray LaManno	15.00	6.75
❑ 114 Allie Reynolds	60.00	27.00
❑ 115 Dutch Leonard	15.00	6.75
❑ 116 Joe Hatton	15.00	6.75
❑ 117 Walker Cooper	15.00	6.75
❑ 118 Sam Mele	15.00	6.75
❑ 119 Floyd Baker	15.00	6.75
❑ 120 Cliff Fannin	15.00	6.75
❑ 121 Mark Christman	15.00	6.75
❑ 122 George Vico	15.00	6.75
❑ 123 Johnny Blatnick	15.00	6.75
❑ 124A D.Murtaugh SCR RC	50.00	22.00
❑ 124B D.Murtaugh PR RC	70.00	32.00
❑ 125 Ken Keltner	25.00	11.00
❑ 126A Al Brazle SCR	15.00	6.75
❑ 126B Al Brazle PR	60.00	27.00
❑ 127A Hank Majeski SCR	15.00	6.75
❑ 127B Hank Majeski PR	60.00	27.00
❑ 128 Johnny VanderMeer	60.00	27.00
❑ 129 Bill Johnson	40.00	18.00
❑ 130 Harry Walker	15.00	6.75
❑ 131 Paul Lehner	15.00	6.75
❑ 132A Al Evans SCR	15.00	6.75
❑ 132B Al Evans PR	60.00	27.00
❑ 133 Aaron Robinson	15.00	6.75
❑ 134 Hank Borowy	15.00	6.75
❑ 135 Stan Rojek	15.00	6.75
❑ 136 Hank Edwards	15.00	6.75
❑ 137 Ted Wilks	15.00	6.75
❑ 138 Buddy Rosar	15.00	6.75
❑ 139 Hank Arft	15.00	6.75
❑ 140 Ray Scarborough	15.00	6.75
❑ 141 Tony Lupien	15.00	6.75
❑ 142 Eddie Waitkus RC	40.00	18.00
❑ 143A B.Dillinger RC SCR	25.00	11.00
❑ 143B Bob Dillinger RC PR	60.00	27.00
❑ 144 Mickey Haefner	15.00	6.75
❑ 145 Sylvester Donnelly	50.00	22.00
❑ 146 Mike McCormick	50.00	22.00
❑ 147 Bert Singleton	50.00	22.00
❑ 148 Bob Swift	50.00	22.00

❑ 149 Roy Partee 50.00 22.00
❑ 150 Allie Clark 50.00 22.00
❑ 151 Mickey Harris 50.00 22.00
❑ 152 Clarence Maddern 50.00 22.00
❑ 153 Phil Masi 50.00 22.00
❑ 154 Clint Hartung 60.00 27.00
❑ 155 Mickey Guerra 50.00 22.00
❑ 156 Al Zarilla 50.00 22.00
❑ 157 Walt Masterson 50.00 22.00
❑ 158 Harry Brecheen 60.00 27.00
❑ 159 Glen Moulder 50.00 22.00
❑ 160 Jim Blackburn 50.00 22.00
❑ 161 Jocko Thompson 50.00 22.00
❑ 162 Preacher Roe RC 125.00 55.00
❑ 163 Clyde McCullough 50.00 22.00
❑ 164 Vic Wertz RC 75.00 34.00
❑ 165 Snuffy Stirnweiss 75.00 34.00
❑ 166 Mike Tresh 50.00 22.00
❑ 167 Babe Martin 50.00 22.00
❑ 168 Doyle Lade 50.00 22.00
❑ 169 Jeff Heath 60.00 27.00
❑ 170 Bill Rigney 60.00 27.00
❑ 171 Dick Fowler 50.00 22.00
❑ 172 Eddie Pellagrini 50.00 22.00
❑ 173 Eddie Stewart 50.00 22.00
❑ 174 Terry Moore RC 75.00 34.00
❑ 175 Luke Appling 125.00 55.00
❑ 176 Ken Raffensberger 50.00 22.00
❑ 177 Stan Lopata 60.00 27.00
❑ 178 Tom Brown 60.00 27.00
❑ 179 Hugh Casey 75.00 34.00
❑ 180 Connie Berry 50.00 22.00
❑ 181 Gus Niarhos 50.00 22.00
❑ 182 Hal Peck 50.00 22.00
❑ 183 Lou Stringer 50.00 22.00
❑ 184 Bob Chipman 50.00 22.00
❑ 185 Pete Reiser 75.00 34.00
❑ 186 Buddy Kerr 50.00 22.00
❑ 187 Phil Marchildon 50.00 22.00
❑ 188 Karl Drews 50.00 22.00
❑ 189 Earl Wooten 50.00 22.00
❑ 190 Jim Hearn 50.00 22.00
❑ 191 Joe Haynes 50.00 22.00
❑ 192 Harry Gumbert 50.00 22.00
❑ 193 Ken Trinkle 50.00 22.00
❑ 194 Ralph Branca RC 100.00 45.00
❑ 195 Eddie Bockman 50.00 22.00
❑ 196 Fred Hutchinson 60.00 27.00
❑ 197 Johnny Lindell 60.00 27.00
❑ 198 Steve Gromek 50.00 22.00
❑ 199 Tex Hughson 50.00 22.00
❑ 200 Jess Dobernic 50.00 22.00
❑ 201 Sibby Sisti 50.00 22.00
❑ 202 Larry Jansen 60.00 27.00
❑ 203 Barney McCosky 50.00 22.00
❑ 204 Bob Savage 50.00 22.00
❑ 205 Dick Sisler 60.00 27.00
❑ 206 Bruce Edwards 50.00 22.00
❑ 207 Johnny Hopp 50.00 22.00
❑ 208 Dizzy Trout 60.00 27.00
❑ 209 Charlie Keller 75.00 34.00
❑ 210 Joe Gordon 75.00 34.00
❑ 211 Boo Ferriss 50.00 22.00
❑ 212 Ralph Hamner 50.00 22.00
❑ 213 Red Barrett 50.00 22.00
❑ 214 Richie Ashburn RC 600.00 275.00
❑ 215 Kirby Higbe 50.00 22.00
❑ 216 Schoolboy Rowe 60.00 27.00
❑ 217 Marino Pieretti 50.00 22.00
❑ 218 Dick Kryhoski 50.00 22.00
❑ 219 Virgil Fire Trucks 60.00 27.00
❑ 220 Johnny McCarthy 50.00 22.00
❑ 221 Bob Muncrief 50.00 22.00
❑ 222 Alex Kellner 50.00 22.00
❑ 223 Bobby Hofman 50.00 22.00
❑ 224 Satchell Paige RC 1200.00 550.00
❑ 225 Jerry Coleman RC 75.00 34.00
❑ 226 Duke Snider RC 900.00 400.00
❑ 227 Fritz Ostermueller 50.00 22.00
❑ 228 Jackie Mayo 50.00 22.00
❑ 229 Ed Lopat RC 125.00 55.00
❑ 230 Augie Galan 60.00 27.00
❑ 231 Earl Johnson 50.00 22.00
❑ 232 George McQuinn 60.00 27.00
❑ 233 Larry Doby RC 200.00 90.00
❑ 234 Rip Sewell 50.00 22.00
❑ 235 Jim Russell 50.00 22.00
❑ 236 Fred Sanford 50.00 22.00
❑ 237 Monte Kennedy 50.00 22.00
❑ 238 Bob Lemon RC 200.00 90.00
❑ 239 Frank McCormick 50.00 22.00
❑ 240 Babe Young UER 100.00 25.00
(Photo actually Bobby Young)

1950 Bowman

	NRMT	VG-E
COMPLETE SET (252)	8500.00	3800.00
COMMON CARD (1-72)	50.00	22.00
COMMON CARD (73-252)	15.00	6.75
WRAPPER (1-CENT)	250.00	110.00
WRAPPER (5-CENT)	250.00	110.00

❑ 1 Mel Parnell RC 150.00 30.00
❑ 2 Vern Stephens 60.00 27.00
❑ 3 Dom DiMaggio 80.00 36.00
❑ 4 Gus Zernial RC 60.00 27.00
❑ 5 Bob Kuzava 50.00 22.00
❑ 6 Bob Feller 300.00 135.00
❑ 7 Jim Hegan 60.00 27.00
❑ 8 George Kell 80.00 36.00
❑ 9 Vic Wertz 60.00 27.00
❑ 10 Tommy Henrich 80.00 36.00
❑ 11 Phil Rizzuto 225.00 100.00
❑ 12 Joe Page 80.00 36.00
❑ 13 Ferris Fain 60.00 27.00
❑ 14 Alex Kellner 50.00 22.00
❑ 15 Al Kozar 50.00 22.00
❑ 16 Roy Sievers RC 80.00 36.00
❑ 17 Sid Hudson 50.00 22.00
❑ 18 Eddie Robinson 50.00 22.00
❑ 19 Warren Spahn 300.00 135.00
❑ 20 Bob Elliott 60.00 27.00
❑ 21 Pee Wee Reese 300.00 135.00
❑ 22 Jackie Robinson 1000.00 450.00
❑ 23 Don Newcombe RC 150.00 70.00
❑ 24 Johnny Schmitz 50.00 22.00
❑ 25 Hank Sauer 60.00 27.00
❑ 26 Grady Hatton 50.00 22.00
❑ 27 Herman Wehmeier 50.00 22.00
❑ 28 Bobby Thomson 80.00 36.00
❑ 29 Eddie Stanky 60.00 27.00
❑ 30 Eddie Waitkus 60.00 27.00
❑ 31 Del Ennis 80.00 36.00
❑ 32 Robin Roberts 150.00 70.00
❑ 33 Ralph Kiner 100.00 45.00
❑ 34 Murry Dickson 50.00 22.00
❑ 35 Enos Slaughter 100.00 45.00
❑ 36 Eddie Kazak 60.00 27.00
❑ 37 Luke Appling 80.00 36.00
❑ 38 Bill Wight 50.00 22.00
❑ 39 Larry Doby 100.00 45.00
❑ 40 Bob Lemon 80.00 36.00
❑ 41 Hoot Evers 50.00 22.00
❑ 42 Art Houtteman 50.00 22.00
❑ 43 Bobby Doerr 80.00 36.00
❑ 44 Joe Dobson 50.00 22.00
❑ 45 Al Zarilla 50.00 22.00
❑ 46 Yogi Berra 375.00 170.00
❑ 47 Jerry Coleman 80.00 36.00
❑ 48 Lou Brissie 50.00 22.00
❑ 49 Elmer Valo 50.00 22.00
❑ 50 Dick Kokos 50.00 22.00
❑ 51 Ned Garver 60.00 27.00
❑ 52 Sam Mele 50.00 22.00
❑ 53 Clyde Vollmer 50.00 22.00
❑ 54 Gil Coan 50.00 22.00
❑ 55 Buddy Kerr 50.00 22.00
❑ 56 Del Crandall RC 60.00 27.00
❑ 57 Vern Bickford 50.00 22.00
❑ 58 Carl Furillo 80.00 36.00
❑ 59 Ralph Branca 80.00 36.00
❑ 60 Andy Pafko 60.00 27.00
❑ 61 Bob Rush 50.00 22.00
❑ 62 Ted Kluszewski 125.00 55.00
❑ 63 Ewell Blackwell 60.00 27.00
❑ 64 Alvin Dark 60.00 27.00
❑ 65 Dave Koslo 50.00 22.00
❑ 66 Larry Jansen 60.00 27.00
❑ 67 Willie Jones 60.00 27.00
❑ 68 Curt Simmons 60.00 27.00
❑ 69 Wally Westlake 50.00 22.00
❑ 70 Bob Chesnes 50.00 22.00
❑ 71 Red Schoendienst 80.00 36.00
❑ 72 Howie Pollet 50.00 22.00
❑ 73 Willard Marshall 15.00 6.75
❑ 74 Johnny Antonelli RC 60.00 27.00
❑ 75 Roy Campanella 275.00 125.00
❑ 76 Rex Barney 40.00 18.00
❑ 77 Duke Snider 275.00 125.00
❑ 78 Mickey Owen 25.00 11.00
❑ 79 Johnny VanderMeer 40.00 18.00
❑ 80 Howard Fox 15.00 6.75
❑ 81 Ron Northey 15.00 6.75
❑ 82 Whitey Lockman 25.00 11.00
❑ 83 Sheldon Jones 15.00 6.75
❑ 84 Richie Ashburn 100.00 45.00
❑ 85 Ken Heintzelman 15.00 6.75
❑ 86 Stan Rojek 15.00 6.75
❑ 87 Bill Werle 15.00 6.75
❑ 88 Marty Marion 40.00 18.00
❑ 89 Red Munger 15.00 6.75
❑ 90 Harry Brecheen 40.00 18.00
❑ 91 Cass Michaels 15.00 6.75
❑ 92 Hank Majeski 15.00 6.75
❑ 93 Gene Bearden 40.00 18.00
❑ 94 Lou Boudreau 60.00 27.00
❑ 95 Aaron Robinson 15.00 6.75
❑ 96 Virgil Trucks 25.00 11.00
❑ 97 Maurice McDermott 15.00 6.75
❑ 98 Ted Williams 1000.00 450.00
❑ 99 Billy Goodman 25.00 11.00
❑ 100 Vic Raschi 60.00 27.00
❑ 101 Bobby Brown 60.00 27.00
❑ 102 Billy Johnson 25.00 11.00
❑ 103 Eddie Joost 15.00 6.75
❑ 104 Sam Chapman 15.00 6.75
❑ 105 Bob Dillinger 15.00 6.75
❑ 106 Cliff Fannin 15.00 6.75
❑ 107 Sam Dente 15.00 6.75
❑ 108 Ray Scarborough 15.00 6.75
❑ 109 Sid Gordon 15.00 6.75
❑ 110 Tommy Holmes 25.00 11.00
❑ 111 Walker Cooper 15.00 6.75
❑ 112 Gil Hodges 100.00 45.00
❑ 113 Gene Hermanski 15.00 6.75
❑ 114 Wayne Terwilliger RC 15.00 6.75
❑ 115 Roy Smalley 15.00 6.75
❑ 116 Virgil Stallcup 15.00 6.75
❑ 117 Bill Rigney 15.00 6.75
❑ 118 Clint Hartung 15.00 6.75
❑ 119 Dick Sisler 25.00 11.00
❑ 120 John Thompson 15.00 6.75
❑ 121 Andy Seminick 25.00 11.00
❑ 122 Johnny Hopp 25.00 11.00
❑ 123 Dino Restelli 15.00 6.75
❑ 124 Clyde McCullough 15.00 6.75
❑ 125 Del Rice 15.00 6.75
❑ 126 Al Brazle 15.00 6.75
❑ 127 Dave Philley 15.00 6.75
❑ 128 Phil Masi 15.00 6.75
❑ 129 Joe Gordon 25.00 11.00
❑ 130 Dale Mitchell 25.00 11.00
❑ 131 Steve Gromek 15.00 6.75
❑ 132 Mickey Vernon 25.00 11.00
❑ 133 Don Kolloway 15.00 6.75
❑ 134 Paul Trout 15.00 6.75
❑ 135 Pat Mullin 15.00 6.75
❑ 136 Warren Rosar 15.00 6.75
❑ 137 Johnny Pesky 25.00 11.00
❑ 138 Allie Reynolds 60.00 27.00
❑ 139 Johnny Mize 80.00 36.00

❑ 140 Pete Suder 15.00 6.75
❑ 141 Joe Coleman 25.00 11.00
❑ 142 Sherman Lollar RC 40.00 18.00
❑ 143 Eddie Stewart 15.00 6.75
❑ 144 Al Evans 15.00 6.75
❑ 145 Jack Graham 15.00 6.75
❑ 146 Floyd Baker 15.00 6.75
❑ 147 Mike Garcia RC 40.00 18.00
❑ 148 Early Wynn 80.00 36.00
❑ 149 Bob Swift 15.00 6.75
❑ 150 George Vico 15.00 6.75
❑ 151 Fred Hutchinson 25.00 11.00
❑ 152 Ellis Kinder RC 15.00 6.75
❑ 153 Walt Masterson 15.00 6.75
❑ 154 Gus Niarhos 15.00 6.75
❑ 155 Frank Shea 25.00 11.00
❑ 156 Fred Sanford 25.00 11.00
❑ 157 Mike Guerra 15.00 6.75
❑ 158 Paul Lehner 15.00 6.75
❑ 159 Joe Tipton 15.00 6.75
❑ 160 Mickey Harris 15.00 6.75
❑ 161 Sherry Robertson 15.00 6.75
❑ 162 Eddie Yost 25.00 11.00
❑ 163 Earl Torgeson 15.00 6.75
❑ 164 Sibby Sisti 15.00 6.75
❑ 165 Bruce Edwards 15.00 6.75
❑ 166 Joe Hatton 15.00 6.75
❑ 167 Preacher Roe 60.00 27.00
❑ 168 Bob Scheffing 15.00 6.75
❑ 169 Hank Edwards 15.00 6.75
❑ 170 Dutch Leonard 15.00 6.75
❑ 171 Harry Gumbert 15.00 6.75
❑ 172 Peanuts Lowrey 15.00 6.75
❑ 173 Lloyd Merriman 15.00 6.75
❑ 174 Hank Thompson RC 40.00 18.00
❑ 175 Monte Kennedy 15.00 6.75
❑ 176 Sylvester Donnelly 15.00 6.75
❑ 177 Hank Borowy 15.00 6.75
❑ 178 Ed Fitzgerald 15.00 6.75
❑ 179 Chuck Diering 15.00 6.75
❑ 180 Harry Walker 25.00 11.00
❑ 181 Marino Pieretti 15.00 6.75
❑ 182 Sam Zoldak 15.00 6.75
❑ 183 Mickey Haefner 15.00 6.75
❑ 184 Randy Gumpert 15.00 6.75
❑ 185 Howie Judson 15.00 6.75
❑ 186 Ken Keltner 25.00 11.00
❑ 187 Lou Stringer 15.00 6.75
❑ 188 Earl Johnson 15.00 6.75
❑ 189 Owen Friend 15.00 6.75
❑ 190 Ken Wood 15.00 6.75
❑ 191 Dick Starr 15.00 6.75
❑ 192 Bob Chipman 15.00 6.75
❑ 193 Pete Reiser 40.00 18.00
❑ 194 Billy Cox 60.00 27.00
❑ 195 Phil Cavarretta 40.00 18.00
❑ 196 Doyle Lade 15.00 6.75
❑ 197 Johnny Wyrostek 15.00 6.75
❑ 198 Danny Litwhiler 15.00 6.75
❑ 199 Jack Kramer 15.00 6.75
❑ 200 Kirby Higbe 25.00 11.00
❑ 201 Pete Castiglione 15.00 6.75
❑ 202 Cliff Chambers 15.00 6.75
❑ 203 Danny Murtaugh 25.00 11.00
❑ 204 Granny Hamner RC 40.00 18.00
❑ 205 Mike Goliat 15.00 6.75
❑ 206 Stan Lopata 25.00 11.00
❑ 207 Max Lanier 15.00 6.75
❑ 208 Jim Hearn 15.00 6.75
❑ 209 Johnny Lindell 15.00 6.75
❑ 210 Ted Gray 15.00 6.75
❑ 211 Charlie Keller 40.00 18.00
❑ 212 Jerry Priddy 15.00 6.75
❑ 213 Carl Scheib 15.00 6.75
❑ 214 Dick Fowler 15.00 6.75
❑ 215 Ed Lopat 60.00 27.00
❑ 216 Bob Porterfield 25.00 11.00
❑ 217 Casey Stengel MG 125.00 55.00
❑ 218 Cliff Mapes RC 25.00 11.00
❑ 219 Hank Bauer RC 100.00 45.00
❑ 220 Leo Durocher MG 60.00 27.00
❑ 221 Don Mueller RC 40.00 18.00
❑ 222 Bobby Morgan 15.00 6.75
❑ 223 Jim Russell 15.00 6.75
❑ 224 Jack Banta 15.00 6.75
❑ 225 Eddie Sawyer MG 25.00 11.00
❑ 226 Jim Konstanty RC 60.00 27.00
❑ 227 Bob Miller 25.00 11.00
❑ 228 Bill Nicholson 25.00 11.00
❑ 229 Frank Frisch MG 60.00 27.00
❑ 230 Bill Serena 15.00 6.75
❑ 231 Preston Ward 15.00 6.75
❑ 232 Al Rosen RC 60.00 27.00
❑ 233 Allie Clark 15.00 6.75
❑ 234 Bobby Shantz RC 60.00 27.00
❑ 235 Harold Gilbert 15.00 6.75
❑ 236 Bob Cain 15.00 6.75
❑ 237 Bill Salkeld 15.00 6.75
❑ 238 Nippy Jones 15.00 6.75
❑ 239 Bill Howerton 15.00 6.75
❑ 240 Eddie Lake 15.00 6.75
❑ 241 Neil Berry 15.00 6.75
❑ 242 Dick Kryhoski 15.00 6.75
❑ 243 Johnny Groth 15.00 6.75
❑ 244 Dale Coogan 15.00 6.75
❑ 245 Al Papai 15.00 6.75
❑ 246 Walt Dropo RC 40.00 18.00
❑ 247 Irv Noren RC 25.00 11.00
❑ 248 Sam Jethroe RC 60.00 27.00
❑ 249 Snuffy Stirnweiss 25.00 11.00
❑ 250 Ray Coleman 15.00 6.75
❑ 251 Les Moss 15.00 6.75
❑ 252 Billy DeMars RC 60.00 16.50

1951 Bowman

	NRMT	VG-E
COMPLETE SET (324)	16000.00	7200.00
COMMON CARD (1-252)	18.00	8.00
COMMON CARD (253-324)	50.00	22.00
WRAPPER (1-CENT)	200.00	90.00
WRAPPER (5-CENT)	250.00	110.00

❑ 1 Whitey Ford RC 1400.00 350.00
❑ 2 Yogi Berra 350.00 160.00
❑ 3 Robin Roberts 75.00 34.00
❑ 4 Del Ennis 25.00 11.00
❑ 5 Dale Mitchell 25.00 11.00
❑ 6 Don Newcombe 60.00 27.00
❑ 7 Gil Hodges 100.00 45.00
❑ 8 Paul Lehner 18.00 8.00
❑ 9 Sam Chapman 18.00 8.00
❑ 10 Red Schoendienst 60.00 27.00
❑ 11 Red Munger 18.00 8.00
❑ 12 Hank Majeski 18.00 8.00
❑ 13 Eddie Stanky 25.00 11.00
❑ 14 Alvin Dark 40.00 18.00
❑ 15 Johnny Pesky 25.00 11.00
❑ 16 Maurice McDermott 18.00 8.00
❑ 17 Pete Castiglione 18.00 8.00
❑ 18 Gil Coan 18.00 8.00
❑ 19 Sid Gordon 18.00 8.00
❑ 20 Del Crandall UER 25.00 11.00
(Misspelled Crandell on card)
❑ 21 Snuffy Stirnweiss 25.00 11.00
❑ 22 Hank Sauer 25.00 11.00
❑ 23 Hoot Evers 18.00 8.00
❑ 24 Ewell Blackwell 40.00 18.00
❑ 25 Vic Raschi 60.00 27.00
❑ 26 Phil Rizzuto 125.00 55.00
❑ 27 Jim Konstanty 25.00 11.00
❑ 28 Eddie Waitkus 18.00 8.00
❑ 29 Allie Clark 18.00 8.00
❑ 30 Bob Feller 125.00 55.00
❑ 31 Roy Campanella 250.00 110.00
❑ 32 Duke Snider 250.00 110.00
❑ 33 Bob Hooper 18.00 8.00
❑ 34 Marty Marion 40.00 18.00
❑ 35 Al Zarilla 18.00 8.00
❑ 36 Joe Dobson 18.00 8.00
❑ 37 Whitey Lockman 40.00 18.00
❑ 38 Al Evans 18.00 8.00
❑ 39 Ray Scarborough 18.00 8.00
❑ 40 Gus Bell RC 60.00 27.00
❑ 41 Eddie Yost 25.00 11.00
❑ 42 Vern Bickford 18.00 8.00
❑ 43 Billy DeMars 18.00 8.00
❑ 44 Roy Smalley 18.00 8.00
❑ 45 Art Houtteman 18.00 8.00
❑ 46 George Kell 1941 UER 60.00 27.00
❑ 47 Grady Hatton 18.00 8.00
❑ 48 Ken Raffensberger 18.00 8.00
❑ 49 Jerry Coleman 25.00 11.00
❑ 50 Johnny Mize 60.00 27.00
❑ 51 Andy Seminick 18.00 8.00
❑ 52 Dick Sisler 40.00 18.00
❑ 53 Bob Lemon 60.00 27.00
❑ 54 Ray Boone RC 40.00 18.00
❑ 55 Gene Hermanski 18.00 8.00
❑ 56 Ralph Branca 60.00 27.00
❑ 57 Alex Kellner 18.00 8.00
❑ 58 Enos Slaughter 60.00 27.00
❑ 59 Randy Gumpert 18.00 8.00
❑ 60 Chico Carrasquel RC 60.00 27.00
❑ 61 Jim Hearn 25.00 11.00
❑ 62 Lou Boudreau 60.00 27.00
❑ 63 Bob Dillinger 18.00 8.00
❑ 64 Bill Werle 18.00 8.00
❑ 65 Mickey Vernon 40.00 18.00
❑ 66 Bob Elliott 25.00 11.00
❑ 67 Roy Sievers 25.00 11.00
❑ 68 Dick Kokos 18.00 8.00
❑ 69 Johnny Schmitz 18.00 8.00
❑ 70 Ron Northey 18.00 8.00
❑ 71 Jerry Priddy 18.00 8.00
❑ 72 Lloyd Merriman 18.00 8.00
❑ 73 Tommy Byrne 18.00 8.00
❑ 74 Billy Johnson 25.00 11.00
❑ 75 Russ Meyer RC 25.00 11.00
❑ 76 Stan Lopata 25.00 11.00
❑ 77 Mike Goliat 18.00 8.00
❑ 78 Early Wynn 60.00 27.00
❑ 79 Jim Hegan 25.00 11.00
❑ 80 Pee Wee Reese 150.00 70.00
❑ 81 Carl Furillo 40.00 18.00
❑ 82 Joe Tipton 18.00 8.00
❑ 83 Carl Scheib 18.00 8.00
❑ 84 Barney McCosky 18.00 8.00
❑ 85 Eddie Kazak 18.00 8.00
❑ 86 Harry Brecheen 25.00 11.00
❑ 87 Floyd Baker 18.00 8.00
❑ 88 Eddie Robinson 18.00 8.00
❑ 89 Hank Thompson 25.00 11.00
❑ 90 Dave Koslo 18.00 8.00
❑ 91 Clyde Vollmer 18.00 8.00
❑ 92 Vern Stephens 25.00 11.00
❑ 93 Danny O'Connell 18.00 8.00
❑ 94 Clyde McCullough 18.00 8.00
❑ 95 Sherry Robertson 18.00 8.00
❑ 96 Sandy Consuegra 18.00 8.00
❑ 97 Bob Kuzava 18.00 8.00
❑ 98 Willard Marshall 18.00 8.00
❑ 99 Earl Torgeson 18.00 8.00
❑ 100 Sherm Lollar 25.00 11.00
❑ 101 Owen Friend 18.00 8.00
❑ 102 Dutch Leonard 18.00 8.00
❑ 103 Andy Pafko 40.00 18.00
❑ 104 Virgil Trucks 25.00 11.00
❑ 105 Don Kolloway 18.00 8.00
❑ 106 Pat Mullin 18.00 8.00
❑ 107 Johnny Wyrostek 18.00 8.00
❑ 108 Virgil Stallcup 18.00 8.00
❑ 109 Allie Reynolds 60.00 27.00
❑ 110 Bobby Brown 40.00 18.00
❑ 111 Curt Simmons 25.00 11.00
❑ 112 Willie Jones 18.00 8.00
❑ 113 Bill Nicholson 18.00 8.00
❑ 114 Sam Zoldak 18.00 8.00
❑ 115 Steve Gromek 18.00 8.00

❑ 116 Bruce Edwards 18.00 8.00
❑ 117 Eddie Miksis 18.00 8.00
❑ 118 Preacher Roe 60.00 27.00
❑ 119 Eddie Joost 18.00 8.00
❑ 120 Joe Coleman 25.00 11.00
❑ 121 Jerry Staley 18.00 8.00
❑ 122 Joe Garagiola RC 80.00 36.00
❑ 123 Howie Judson 18.00 8.00
❑ 124 Gus Niarhos 18.00 8.00
❑ 125 Bill Rigney 25.00 11.00
❑ 126 Bobby Thomson 60.00 27.00
❑ 127 Sal Maglie RC 60.00 27.00
❑ 128 Ellis Kinder 18.00 8.00
❑ 129 Matt Batts 18.00 8.00
❑ 130 Tom Saffell 18.00 8.00
❑ 131 Cliff Chambers 18.00 8.00
❑ 132 Cass Michaels 18.00 8.00
❑ 133 Sam Dente 18.00 8.00
❑ 134 Warren Spahn 125.00 55.00
❑ 135 Walker Cooper 18.00 8.00
❑ 136 Ray Coleman 18.00 8.00
❑ 137 Dick Starr 18.00 8.00
❑ 138 Phil Cavarretta 25.00 11.00
❑ 139 Doyle Lade 18.00 8.00
❑ 140 Eddie Lake 18.00 8.00
❑ 141 Fred Hutchinson 25.00 11.00
❑ 142 Aaron Robinson 18.00 8.00
❑ 143 Ted Kluszewski 60.00 27.00
❑ 144 Herman Wehmeier 18.00 8.00
❑ 145 Fred Sanford 25.00 11.00
❑ 146 Johnny Hopp 25.00 11.00
❑ 147 Ken Heintzelman 18.00 8.00
❑ 148 Granny Hamner 18.00 8.00
❑ 149 Bubba Church 18.00 8.00
❑ 150 Mike Garcia 25.00 11.00
❑ 151 Larry Doby 60.00 27.00
❑ 152 Cal Abrams 18.00 8.00
❑ 153 Rex Barney 25.00 11.00
❑ 154 Pete Suder 18.00 8.00
❑ 155 Lou Brissie 18.00 8.00
❑ 156 Del Rice 18.00 8.00
❑ 157 Al Brazle 18.00 8.00
❑ 158 Chuck Diering 18.00 8.00
❑ 159 Eddie Stewart 18.00 8.00
❑ 160 Phil Masi 18.00 8.00
❑ 161 Wes Westrum RC 18.00 8.00
❑ 162 Larry Jansen 25.00 11.00
❑ 163 Monte Kennedy 18.00 8.00
❑ 164 Bill Wight 18.00 8.00
❑ 165 Ted Williams 750.00 350.00
❑ 166 Stan Rojek 18.00 8.00
❑ 167 Murry Dickson 18.00 8.00
❑ 168 Sam Mele 18.00 8.00
❑ 169 Sid Hudson 18.00 8.00
❑ 170 Sibby Sisti 18.00 8.00
❑ 171 Buddy Kerr 18.00 8.00
❑ 172 Ned Garver 18.00 8.00
❑ 173 Hank Arft 18.00 8.00
❑ 174 Mickey Owen 25.00 11.00
❑ 175 Wayne Terwilliger 18.00 8.00
❑ 176 Vic Wertz 40.00 18.00
❑ 177 Charlie Keller 25.00 11.00
❑ 178 Ted Gray 18.00 8.00
❑ 179 Danny Litwhiler 18.00 8.00
❑ 180 Howie Fox 18.00 8.00
❑ 181 Casey Stengel MG 75.00 34.00
❑ 182 Tom Ferrick 18.00 8.00
❑ 183 Hank Bauer 60.00 27.00
❑ 184 Eddie Sawyer MG 40.00 18.00
❑ 185 Jimmy Bloodworth 18.00 8.00
❑ 186 Richie Ashburn 100.00 45.00
❑ 187 Al Rosen 40.00 18.00
❑ 188 Bobby Avila RC 25.00 11.00
❑ 189 Erv Palica 18.00 8.00
❑ 190 Joe Hatten 18.00 8.00
❑ 191 Billy Hitchcock 18.00 8.00
❑ 192 Hank Wyse 18.00 8.00
❑ 193 Ted Wilks 18.00 8.00
❑ 194 Peanuts Lowrey 18.00 8.00
❑ 195 Paul Richards MG 25.00 11.00
(Caricature)
❑ 196 Billy Pierce RC 60.00 27.00
❑ 197 Bob Cain 18.00 8.00
❑ 198 Monte Irvin RC 100.00 45.00
❑ 199 Sheldon Jones 18.00 8.00
❑ 200 Jack Kramer 18.00 8.00
❑ 201 Steve O'Neill MG 18.00 8.00
❑ 202 Mike Guerra 18.00 8.00
❑ 203 Vernon Law RC 60.00 27.00
❑ 204 Vic Lombardi 18.00 8.00
❑ 205 Mickey Grasso 18.00 8.00
❑ 206 Conrado Marrero 18.00 8.00
❑ 207 Billy Southworth MG 18.00 8.00
❑ 208 Blix Donnelly 18.00 8.00
❑ 209 Ken Wood 18.00 8.00
❑ 210 Les Moss 18.00 8.00
❑ 211 Hal Jeffcoat 18.00 8.00
❑ 212 Bob Rush 18.00 8.00
❑ 213 Neil Berry 18.00 8.00
❑ 214 Bob Swift 18.00 8.00
❑ 215 Ken Peterson 18.00 8.00
❑ 216 Connie Ryan 18.00 8.00
❑ 217 Joe Page 25.00 11.00
❑ 218 Ed Lopat 60.00 27.00
❑ 219 Gene Woodling RC 60.00 27.00
❑ 220 Bob Miller 18.00 8.00
❑ 221 Dick Whitman 18.00 8.00
❑ 222 Thurman Tucker 18.00 8.00
❑ 223 Johnny VanderMeer 40.00 18.00
❑ 224 Billy Cox 25.00 11.00
❑ 225 Dan Bankhead 40.00 18.00
❑ 226 Jimmy Dykes MG 18.00 8.00
❑ 227 Bobby Shantz UER 25.00 11.00
Sic, Schantz
❑ 228 Cloyd Boyer 25.00 11.00
❑ 229 Bill Howerton 18.00 8.00
❑ 230 Max Lanier 18.00 8.00
❑ 231 Luis Aloma 18.00 8.00
❑ 232 Nelson Fox RC 250.00 110.00
❑ 233 Leo Durocher MG 60.00 27.00
❑ 234 Clint Hartung 25.00 11.00
❑ 235 Jack Lohrke 18.00 8.00
❑ 236 Warren Rosar 18.00 8.00
❑ 237 Billy Goodman 25.00 11.00
❑ 238 Pete Reiser 40.00 18.00
❑ 239 Bill MacDonald 18.00 8.00
❑ 240 Joe Haynes 18.00 8.00
❑ 241 Irv Noren 25.00 11.00
❑ 242 Sam Jethroe 25.00 11.00
❑ 243 Johnny Antonelli 25.00 11.00
❑ 244 Cliff Fannin 18.00 8.00
❑ 245 John Berardino RC 60.00 27.00
❑ 246 Bill Serena 18.00 8.00
❑ 247 Bob Ramazzotti 18.00 8.00
❑ 248 Johnny Klippstein 18.00 8.00
❑ 249 Johnny Groth 18.00 8.00
❑ 250 Hank Borowy 18.00 8.00
❑ 251 Willard Ramsdell 18.00 8.00
❑ 252 Dixie Howell 18.00 8.00
❑ 253 Mickey Mantle RC 8500.00 3800.00
❑ 254 Jackie Jensen RC 100.00 45.00
❑ 255 Milo Candini 50.00 22.00
❑ 256 Ken Sylvestri 50.00 22.00
❑ 257 Birdie Tebbetts RC 60.00 27.00
❑ 258 Luke Easter RC 60.00 27.00
❑ 259 Chuck Dressen MG 60.00 27.00
❑ 260 Carl Erskine RC 100.00 45.00
❑ 261 Wally Moses 60.00 27.00
❑ 262 Gus Zernial 60.00 27.00
❑ 263 Howie Pollet 60.00 27.00
❑ 264 Don Richmond 50.00 22.00
❑ 265 Steve Bilko 50.00 22.00
❑ 266 Harry Dorish 50.00 22.00
❑ 267 Ken Holcombe 50.00 22.00
❑ 268 Don Mueller 60.00 27.00
❑ 269 Ray Noble 50.00 22.00
❑ 270 Willard Nixon 50.00 22.00
❑ 271 Tommy Wright 50.00 22.00
❑ 272 Billy Meyer MG 50.00 22.00
❑ 273 Danny Murtaugh 60.00 27.00
❑ 274 George Metkovich 50.00 22.00
❑ 275 Bucky Harris MG 60.00 27.00
❑ 276 Frank Quinn 50.00 22.00
❑ 277 Roy Hartsfield 50.00 22.00
❑ 278 Norman Roy 50.00 22.00
❑ 279 Jim Delsing 50.00 22.00
❑ 280 Frank Overmire 50.00 22.00
❑ 281 Al Widmar 50.00 22.00
❑ 282 Frank Frisch MG 100.00 45.00
❑ 283 Walt Dubiel 50.00 22.00
❑ 284 Gene Bearden 60.00 27.00
❑ 285 Johnny Lipon 50.00 22.00
❑ 286 Bob Usher 50.00 22.00
❑ 287 Jim Blackburn 50.00 22.00
❑ 288 Bobby Adams 50.00 22.00
❑ 289 Cliff Mapes 60.00 27.00
❑ 290 Bill Dickey CO 100.00 45.00
❑ 291 Tommy Henrich CO 80.00 36.00
❑ 292 Eddie Pellegrini 50.00 22.00
❑ 293 Ken Johnson 50.00 22.00
❑ 294 Jocko Thompson 50.00 22.00
❑ 295 Al Lopez MG 125.00 55.00
❑ 296 Bob Kennedy 60.00 27.00
❑ 297 Dave Philley 50.00 22.00
❑ 298 Joe Astroth 50.00 22.00
❑ 299 Clyde King 50.00 22.00
❑ 300 Hal Rice 50.00 22.00
❑ 301 Tommy Glaviano 50.00 22.00
❑ 302 Jim Busby 50.00 22.00
❑ 303 Marv Rotblatt 50.00 22.00
❑ 304 Al Gettell 50.00 22.00
❑ 305 Willie Mays RC 3000.00 1350.00
❑ 306 Jim Piersall RC 125.00 55.00
❑ 307 Walt Masterson 50.00 22.00
❑ 308 Ted Beard 50.00 22.00
❑ 309 Mel Queen 50.00 22.00
❑ 310 Erv Dusak 50.00 22.00
❑ 311 Mickey Harris 50.00 22.00
❑ 312 Gene Mauch RC 60.00 27.00
❑ 313 Ray Mueller 50.00 22.00
❑ 314 Johnny Sain 60.00 27.00
❑ 315 Zack Taylor MG 50.00 22.00
❑ 316 Duane Pillette 50.00 22.00
❑ 317 Smoky Burgess RC 80.00 36.00
❑ 318 Warren Hacker 50.00 22.00
❑ 319 Red Rolfe MG 60.00 27.00
❑ 320 Hal White 50.00 22.00
❑ 321 Earl Johnson 50.00 22.00
❑ 322 Luke Sewell MG 60.00 27.00
❑ 323 Joe Adcock RC 80.00 36.00
❑ 324 Johnny Pramesa RC 100.00 30.00

1952 Bowman

	NRMT	VG-E
COMPLETE SET (252)	7500.00	3400.00
COMMON CARD (1-216)	15.00	6.75
COMMON CARD (217-252)	60.00	27.00
WRAPPER (1-CENT)	200.00	90.00
WRAPPER (5-CENT)	100.00	45.00

❑ 1 Yogi Berra 600.00 190.00
❑ 2 Bobby Thomson 40.00 18.00
❑ 3 Fred Hutchinson 25.00 11.00
❑ 4 Robin Roberts 60.00 27.00
❑ 5 Minnie Minoso RC 125.00 55.00
❑ 6 Virgil Stallcup 15.00 6.75
❑ 7 Mike Garcia 25.00 11.00
❑ 8 Pee Wee Reese 150.00 70.00
❑ 9 Vern Stephens 25.00 11.00
❑ 10 Bob Hooper 15.00 6.75
❑ 11 Ralph Kiner 60.00 27.00
❑ 12 Max Surkont 15.00 6.75
❑ 13 Cliff Mapes 15.00 6.75
❑ 14 Cliff Chambers 15.00 6.75
❑ 15 Sam Mele 15.00 6.75
❑ 16 Turk Lown 15.00 6.75
❑ 17 Ed Lopat 40.00 18.00
❑ 18 Don Mueller 25.00 11.00
❑ 19 Bob Cain 15.00 6.75

❑ 20	Willie Jones	15.00	6.75
❑ 21	Nellie Fox	100.00	45.00
❑ 22	Willard Ramsdell	15.00	6.75
❑ 23	Bob Lemon	60.00	27.00
❑ 24	Carl Furillo	40.00	18.00
❑ 25	Mickey McDermott	15.00	6.75
❑ 26	Eddie Joost	15.00	6.75
❑ 27	Joe Garagiola	40.00	18.00
❑ 28	Roy Hartsfield	15.00	6.75
❑ 29	Ned Garver	15.00	6.75
❑ 30	Red Schoendienst	60.00	27.00
❑ 31	Eddie Yost	25.00	11.00
❑ 32	Eddie Miksis	15.00	6.75
❑ 33	Gil McDougald RC	80.00	36.00
❑ 34	Alvin Dark	25.00	11.00
❑ 35	Granny Hamner	15.00	6.75
❑ 36	Cass Michaels	15.00	6.75
❑ 37	Vic Raschi	25.00	11.00
❑ 38	Whitey Lockman	25.00	11.00
❑ 39	Vic Wertz	25.00	11.00
❑ 40	Bubba Church	15.00	6.75
❑ 41	Chico Carrasquel	25.00	11.00
❑ 42	Johnny Wyrostek	15.00	6.75
❑ 43	Bob Feller	150.00	70.00
❑ 44	Roy Campanella	250.00	110.00
❑ 45	Johnny Pesky	25.00	11.00
❑ 46	Carl Scheib	15.00	6.75
❑ 47	Pete Castiglione	15.00	6.75
❑ 48	Vern Bickford	15.00	6.75
❑ 49	Jim Hearn	15.00	6.75
❑ 50	Jerry Staley	15.00	6.75
❑ 51	Gil Coan	15.00	6.75
❑ 52	Phil Rizzuto	150.00	70.00
❑ 53	Richie Ashburn	100.00	45.00
❑ 54	Billy Pierce	25.00	11.00
❑ 55	Ken Raffensberger	15.00	6.75
❑ 56	Clyde King	25.00	11.00
❑ 57	Clyde Vollmer	15.00	6.75
❑ 58	Hank Majeski	15.00	6.75
❑ 59	Murry Dickson	15.00	6.75
❑ 60	Sid Gordon	15.00	6.75
❑ 61	Tommy Byrne	15.00	6.75
❑ 62	Joe Presko	15.00	6.75
❑ 63	Irv Noren	15.00	6.75
❑ 64	Roy Smalley	15.00	6.75
❑ 65	Hank Bauer	25.00	11.00
❑ 66	Sal Maglie	25.00	11.00
❑ 67	Johnny Groth	15.00	6.75
❑ 68	Jim Busby	15.00	6.75
❑ 69	Joe Adcock	25.00	11.00
❑ 70	Carl Erskine	40.00	18.00
❑ 71	Vernon Law	25.00	11.00
❑ 72	Earl Torgeson	15.00	6.75
❑ 73	Jerry Coleman	25.00	11.00
❑ 74	Wes Westrum	25.00	11.00
❑ 75	George Kell	60.00	27.00
❑ 76	Del Ennis	25.00	11.00
❑ 77	Eddie Robinson	15.00	6.75
❑ 78	Lloyd Merriman	15.00	6.75
❑ 79	Lou Brissie	15.00	6.75
❑ 80	Gil Hodges	90.00	40.00
❑ 81	Billy Goodman	25.00	11.00
❑ 82	Gus Zernial	25.00	11.00
❑ 83	Howie Pollet	15.00	6.75
❑ 84	Sam Jethroe	25.00	11.00
❑ 85	Marty Marion CO	25.00	11.00
❑ 86	Cal Abrams	15.00	6.75
❑ 87	Mickey Vernon	25.00	11.00
❑ 88	Bruce Edwards	15.00	6.75
❑ 89	Billy Hitchcock	15.00	6.75
❑ 90	Larry Jansen	25.00	11.00
❑ 91	Don Kolloway	15.00	6.75
❑ 92	Eddie Waitkus	25.00	11.00
❑ 93	Paul Richards MG	25.00	11.00
❑ 94	Luke Sewell MG	25.00	11.00
❑ 95	Luke Easter	25.00	11.00
❑ 96	Ralph Branca	25.00	11.00
❑ 97	Willard Marshall	15.00	6.75
❑ 98	Jimmy Dykes MG	25.00	11.00
❑ 99	Clyde McCullough	15.00	6.75
❑ 100	Sibby Sisti	15.00	6.75
❑ 101	Mickey Mantle	2500.00	1100.00
❑ 102	Peanuts Lowrey	15.00	6.75
❑ 103	Joe Haynes	15.00	6.75
❑ 104	Hal Jeffcoat	15.00	6.75
❑ 105	Bobby Brown	25.00	11.00
❑ 106	Randy Gumpert	15.00	6.75
❑ 107	Del Rice	15.00	6.75
❑ 108	George Metkovich	15.00	6.75
❑ 109	Tom Morgan	15.00	6.75
❑ 110	Max Lanier	15.00	6.75
❑ 111	Hoot Evers	15.00	6.75
❑ 112	Smoky Burgess	25.00	11.00
❑ 113	Al Zarilla	15.00	6.75
❑ 114	Frank Hiller	15.00	6.75
❑ 115	Larry Doby	60.00	27.00
❑ 116	Duke Snider	200.00	90.00
❑ 117	Bill Wight	15.00	6.75
❑ 118	Ray Murray	15.00	6.75
❑ 119	Bill Howerton	15.00	6.75
❑ 120	Chet Nichols	15.00	6.75
❑ 121	Al Corwin	15.00	6.75
❑ 122	Billy Johnson	15.00	6.75
❑ 123	Sid Hudson	15.00	6.75
❑ 124	Birdie Tebbetts	15.00	6.75
❑ 125	Howie Fox	15.00	6.75
❑ 126	Phil Cavarretta	25.00	11.00
❑ 127	Dick Sisler	15.00	6.75
❑ 128	Don Newcombe	40.00	18.00
❑ 129	Gus Niarhos	15.00	6.75
❑ 130	Allie Clark	15.00	6.75
❑ 131	Bob Swift	15.00	6.75
❑ 132	Dave Cole	15.00	6.75
❑ 133	Dick Kryhoski	15.00	6.75
❑ 134	Al Brazle	15.00	6.75
❑ 135	Mickey Harris	15.00	6.75
❑ 136	Gene Hermanski	15.00	6.75
❑ 137	Stan Rojek	15.00	6.75
❑ 138	Ted Wilks	15.00	6.75
❑ 139	Jerry Priddy	15.00	6.75
❑ 140	Ray Scarborough	15.00	6.75
❑ 141	Hank Edwards	15.00	6.75
❑ 142	Early Wynn	60.00	27.00
❑ 143	Sandy Consuegra	15.00	6.75
❑ 144	Joe Hatton	15.00	6.75
❑ 145	Johnny Mize	60.00	27.00
❑ 146	Leo Durocher MG	60.00	27.00
❑ 147	Marlin Stuart	15.00	6.75
❑ 148	Ken Heintzelman	15.00	6.75
❑ 149	Howie Judson	15.00	6.75
❑ 150	Herman Wehmeier	15.00	6.75
❑ 151	Al Rosen	25.00	11.00
❑ 152	Billy Cox	15.00	6.75
❑ 153	Fred Hatfield	15.00	6.75
❑ 154	Ferris Fain	25.00	11.00
❑ 155	Billy Meyer MG	15.00	6.75
❑ 156	Warren Spahn	125.00	55.00
❑ 157	Jim Delsing	15.00	6.75
❑ 158	Bucky Harris MG	25.00	11.00
❑ 159	Dutch Leonard	15.00	6.75
❑ 160	Eddie Stanky	25.00	11.00
❑ 161	Jackie Jensen	40.00	18.00
❑ 162	Monte Irvin	60.00	27.00
❑ 163	Johnny Lipon	15.00	6.75
❑ 164	Connie Ryan	15.00	6.75
❑ 165	Saul Rogovin	15.00	6.75
❑ 166	Bobby Adams	15.00	6.75
❑ 167	Bobby Avila	25.00	11.00
❑ 168	Preacher Roe	25.00	11.00
❑ 169	Walt Dropo	25.00	11.00
❑ 170	Joe Astroth	15.00	6.75
❑ 171	Mel Queen	15.00	6.75
❑ 172	Ebba St.Claire	15.00	6.75
❑ 173	Gene Bearden	15.00	6.75
❑ 174	Mickey Grasso	15.00	6.75
❑ 175	Randy Jackson	15.00	6.75
❑ 176	Harry Brecheen	25.00	11.00
❑ 177	Gene Woodling	25.00	11.00
❑ 178	Dave Williams RC	25.00	11.00
❑ 179	Pete Suder	15.00	6.75
❑ 180	Ed Fitzgerald	15.00	6.75
❑ 181	Joe Collins RC	25.00	11.00
❑ 182	Dave Koslo	15.00	6.75
❑ 183	Pat Mullin	15.00	6.75
❑ 184	Curt Simmons	25.00	11.00
❑ 185	Eddie Stewart	15.00	6.75
❑ 186	Frank Smith	15.00	6.75
❑ 187	Jim Hegan	25.00	11.00
❑ 188	Chuck Dressen MG	25.00	11.00
❑ 189	Jimmy Piersall	25.00	11.00
❑ 190	Dick Fowler	15.00	6.75
❑ 191	Bob Friend RC	40.00	18.00
❑ 192	John Cusick	15.00	6.75
❑ 193	Bobby Young	15.00	6.75
❑ 194	Bob Porterfield	15.00	6.75
❑ 195	Frank Baumholtz	15.00	6.75
❑ 196	Stan Musial	600.00	275.00
❑ 197	Charlie Silvera RC	15.00	6.75
❑ 198	Chuck Diering	15.00	6.75
❑ 199	Ted Gray	15.00	6.75
❑ 200	Ken Silvestri	15.00	6.75
❑ 201	Ray Coleman	15.00	6.75
❑ 202	Harry Perkowski	15.00	6.75
❑ 203	Steve Gromek	15.00	6.75
❑ 204	Andy Pafko	25.00	11.00
❑ 205	Walt Masterson	15.00	6.75
❑ 206	Elmer Valo	15.00	6.75
❑ 207	George Strickland	15.00	6.75
❑ 208	Walker Cooper	15.00	6.75
❑ 209	Dick Littlefield	15.00	6.75
❑ 210	Archie Wilson	15.00	6.75
❑ 211	Paul Minner	15.00	6.75
❑ 212	Solly Hemus	15.00	6.75
❑ 213	Monte Kennedy	15.00	6.75
❑ 214	Ray Boone	15.00	6.75
❑ 215	Sheldon Jones	15.00	6.75
❑ 216	Matt Batts	15.00	6.75
❑ 217	Casey Stengel MG	150.00	70.00
❑ 218	Willie Mays	1200.00	550.00
❑ 219	Neil Berry	60.00	27.00
❑ 220	Russ Meyer	60.00	27.00
❑ 221	Lou Kretlow	60.00	27.00
❑ 222	Dixie Howell	60.00	27.00
❑ 223	Harry Simpson	60.00	27.00
❑ 224	Johnny Schmitz	60.00	27.00
❑ 225	Del Wilber	60.00	27.00
❑ 226	Alex Kellner	60.00	27.00
❑ 227	Clyde Sukeforth CO	60.00	27.00
❑ 228	Bob Chipman	60.00	27.00
❑ 229	Hank Arft	60.00	27.00
❑ 230	Frank Shea	60.00	27.00
❑ 231	Dee Fondy	60.00	27.00
❑ 232	Enos Slaughter	90.00	40.00
❑ 233	Bob Kuzava	60.00	27.00
❑ 234	Fred Fitzsimmons CO	70.00	32.00
❑ 235	Steve Souchock	60.00	27.00
❑ 236	Tommy Brown	60.00	27.00
❑ 237	Sherm Lollar	70.00	32.00
❑ 238	Roy McMillan RC	70.00	32.00
❑ 239	Dale Mitchell	70.00	32.00
❑ 240	Billy Loes RC	70.00	32.00
❑ 241	Mel Parnell	70.00	32.00
❑ 242	Everett Kell	60.00	27.00
❑ 243	Red Munger	60.00	27.00
❑ 244	Lew Burdette RC	80.00	36.00
❑ 245	George Schmees	60.00	27.00
❑ 246	Jerry Snyder	60.00	27.00
❑ 247	Johnny Pramesa	60.00	27.00
❑ 248	Bill Werle Full name in signature	60.00	27.00
❑ 248A	Bill Werle Signature on front has no W	60.00	27.00
❑ 249	Hank Thompson	70.00	32.00
❑ 250	Ike Delock	60.00	27.00
❑ 251	Jack Lohrke	60.00	27.00
❑ 252	Frank Crosetti CO	110.00	28.00

1953 Bowman B/W

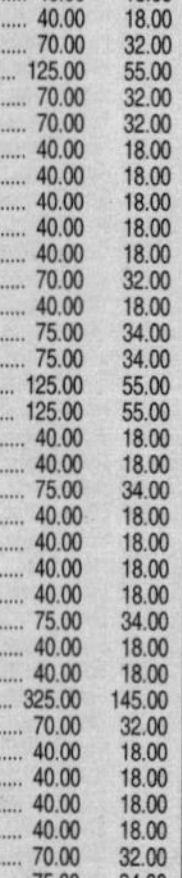

	NRMT	VG-E
COMPLETE SET (64)	2400.00	1100.00
WRAPPER (1-CENT)	350.00	160.00
❑ 1 Gus Bell	125.00	25.00
❑ 2 Willard Nixon	40.00	18.00
❑ 3 Bill Rigney	40.00	18.00
❑ 4 Pat Mullin	40.00	18.00
❑ 5 Dee Fondy	40.00	18.00
❑ 6 Ray Murray	40.00	18.00
❑ 7 Andy Seminick	40.00	18.00
❑ 8 Pete Suder	40.00	18.00
❑ 9 Walt Masterson	40.00	18.00
❑ 10 Dick Sisler	70.00	32.00
❑ 11 Dick Gernert	40.00	18.00
❑ 12 Randy Jackson	40.00	18.00
❑ 13 Joe Tipton	40.00	18.00
❑ 14 Bill Nicholson	70.00	32.00
❑ 15 Johnny Mize	125.00	55.00
❑ 16 Stu Miller RC	70.00	32.00
❑ 17 Virgil Trucks	70.00	32.00
❑ 18 Billy Hoeft	40.00	18.00
❑ 19 Paul LaPalme	40.00	18.00
❑ 20 Eddie Robinson	40.00	18.00
❑ 21 Clarence Podbielan	40.00	18.00
❑ 22 Matt Batts	40.00	18.00
❑ 23 Wilmer Mizell	70.00	32.00
❑ 24 Del Wilber	40.00	18.00
❑ 25 Johnny Sain	75.00	34.00
❑ 26 Preacher Roe	75.00	34.00
❑ 27 Bob Lemon	125.00	55.00
❑ 28 Hoyt Wilhelm	125.00	55.00
❑ 29 Sid Hudson	40.00	18.00
❑ 30 Walker Cooper	40.00	18.00
❑ 31 Gene Woodling	75.00	34.00
❑ 32 Rocky Bridges	40.00	18.00
❑ 33 Bob Kuzava	40.00	18.00
❑ 34 Ebba St.Claire	40.00	18.00
❑ 35 Johnny Wyrostek	40.00	18.00
❑ 36 Jimmy Piersall	75.00	34.00
❑ 37 Hal Jeffcoat	40.00	18.00
❑ 38 Dave Cole	40.00	18.00
❑ 39 Casey Stengel MG	325.00	145.00
❑ 40 Larry Jansen	70.00	32.00
❑ 41 Bob Ramazzotti	40.00	18.00
❑ 42 Howie Judson	40.00	18.00
❑ 43 Hal Bevan	40.00	18.00
❑ 44 Jim Delsing	40.00	18.00
❑ 45 Irv Noren	70.00	32.00
❑ 46 Bucky Harris MG	75.00	34.00
❑ 47 Jack Lohrke	40.00	18.00
❑ 48 Steve Ridzik	40.00	18.00
❑ 49 Floyd Baker	40.00	18.00
❑ 50 Dutch Leonard	40.00	18.00
❑ 51 Lou Burdette	75.00	34.00
❑ 52 Ralph Branca	75.00	34.00
❑ 53 Morrie Martin	40.00	18.00
❑ 54 Bill Miller	40.00	18.00
❑ 55 Don Johnson	40.00	18.00
❑ 56 Roy Smalley	40.00	18.00
❑ 57 Andy Pafko	70.00	32.00
❑ 58 Jim Konstanty	70.00	32.00
❑ 59 Duane Pillette	40.00	18.00
❑ 60 Billy Cox	75.00	34.00
❑ 61 Tom Gorman	40.00	18.00
❑ 62 Keith Thomas	40.00	18.00
❑ 63 Steve Gromek	40.00	18.00
❑ 64 Andy Hansen	75.00	24.00

1953 Bowman Color

	NRMT	VG-E
COMPLETE SET (160)	12000.00	5400.00
COMMON CARD (1-112)	40.00	18.00
COMMON CARD (113-128)	80.00	36.00
COMMON CARD (129-160)	75.00	34.00
WRAPPER (1-CENT)	400.00	180.00
WRAPPER (5-CENT)	300.00	135.00
❑ 1 Dave Williams	175.00	35.00
❑ 2 Vic Wertz	50.00	22.00
❑ 3 Sam Jethroe	50.00	22.00
❑ 4 Art Houtteman	40.00	18.00
❑ 5 Sid Gordon	40.00	18.00
❑ 6 Joe Ginsberg	40.00	18.00
❑ 7 Harry Chiti	40.00	18.00
❑ 8 Al Rosen	50.00	22.00
❑ 9 Phil Rizzuto	225.00	100.00
❑ 10 Richie Ashburn	150.00	70.00
❑ 11 Bobby Shantz	50.00	22.00
❑ 12 Carl Erskine	60.00	27.00
❑ 13 Gus Zernial	50.00	22.00
❑ 14 Billy Loes	50.00	22.00
❑ 15 Jim Busby	40.00	18.00
❑ 16 Bob Friend	50.00	22.00
❑ 17 Gerry Staley	40.00	18.00
❑ 18 Nellie Fox	150.00	70.00
❑ 19 Alvin Dark	50.00	22.00
❑ 20 Don Lenhardt	40.00	18.00
❑ 21 Joe Garagiola	60.00	27.00
❑ 22 Bob Porterfield	40.00	18.00
❑ 23 Herman Wehmeier	40.00	18.00
❑ 24 Jackie Jensen	60.00	27.00
❑ 25 Hoot Evers	40.00	18.00
❑ 26 Roy McMillan	50.00	22.00
❑ 27 Vic Raschi	60.00	27.00
❑ 28 Smoky Burgess	50.00	22.00
❑ 29 Bobby Avila	50.00	22.00
❑ 30 Phil Cavarretta	50.00	22.00
❑ 31 Jimmy Dykes MG	50.00	22.00
❑ 32 Stan Musial	700.00	325.00
❑ 33 Pee Wee Reese	900.00	400.00
❑ 34 Gil Coan	40.00	18.00
❑ 35 Maurice McDermott	40.00	18.00
❑ 36 Minnie Minoso	80.00	36.00
❑ 37 Jim Wilson	40.00	18.00
❑ 38 Harry Byrd	40.00	18.00
❑ 39 Paul Richards MG	50.00	22.00
❑ 40 Larry Doby	80.00	36.00
❑ 41 Sammy White	40.00	18.00
❑ 42 Tommy Brown	40.00	18.00
❑ 43 Mike Garcia	50.00	22.00
❑ 44 Yogi Berra Hank Bauer Mickey Mantle	700.00	325.00
❑ 45 Walt Dropo	50.00	22.00
❑ 46 Roy Campanella	350.00	160.00
❑ 47 Ned Garver	40.00	18.00
❑ 48 Hank Sauer	50.00	22.00
❑ 49 Eddie Stanky MG	50.00	22.00
❑ 50 Lou Kretlow	40.00	18.00
❑ 51 Monte Irvin	80.00	36.00
❑ 52 Marty Marion MG	50.00	22.00
❑ 53 Del Rice	40.00	18.00
❑ 54 Chico Carrasquel	40.00	18.00
❑ 55 Leo Durocher MG	80.00	36.00
❑ 56 Bob Cain	40.00	18.00
❑ 57 Lou Boudreau MG	80.00	36.00
❑ 58 Willard Marshall	40.00	18.00
❑ 59 Mickey Mantle	2500.00	1100.00
❑ 60 Granny Hamner	40.00	18.00
❑ 61 George Kell	80.00	36.00
❑ 62 Ted Kluszewski	100.00	45.00
❑ 63 Gil McDougald	60.00	27.00
❑ 64 Curt Simmons	50.00	22.00
❑ 65 Robin Roberts	110.00	50.00
❑ 66 Mel Parnell	50.00	22.00
❑ 67 Mel Clark	40.00	18.00
❑ 68 Allie Reynolds	60.00	27.00
❑ 69 Charlie Grimm MG	50.00	22.00
❑ 70 Clint Courtney	40.00	18.00
❑ 71 Paul Minner	40.00	18.00
❑ 72 Ted Gray	40.00	18.00
❑ 73 Billy Pierce	50.00	22.00
❑ 74 Don Mueller	50.00	22.00
❑ 75 Saul Rogovin	40.00	18.00
❑ 76 Jim Hearn	40.00	18.00
❑ 77 Mickey Grasso	40.00	18.00
❑ 78 Carl Furillo	60.00	27.00
❑ 79 Ray Boone	50.00	22.00
❑ 80 Ralph Kiner	80.00	36.00
❑ 81 Enos Slaughter	80.00	36.00
❑ 82 Joe Astroth	40.00	18.00
❑ 83 Jack Daniels	40.00	18.00
❑ 84 Hank Bauer	60.00	27.00
❑ 85 Solly Hemus	40.00	18.00
❑ 86 Harry Simpson	40.00	18.00
❑ 87 Harry Perkowski	40.00	18.00
❑ 88 Joe Dobson	40.00	18.00
❑ 89 Sandy Consuegra	40.00	18.00
❑ 90 Joe Nuxhall	50.00	22.00
❑ 91 Steve Souchock	40.00	18.00
❑ 92 Gil Hodges	200.00	90.00
❑ 93 Phil Rizzuto and Billy Martin	275.00	125.00
❑ 94 Bob Addis	40.00	18.00
❑ 95 Wally Moses CO	50.00	22.00
❑ 96 Sal Maglie	50.00	22.00
❑ 97 Eddie Mathews	300.00	135.00
❑ 98 Hector Rodriguez	40.00	18.00
❑ 99 Warren Spahn	350.00	160.00
❑ 100 Bill Wight	40.00	18.00
❑ 101 Red Schoendienst	80.00	36.00
❑ 102 Jim Hegan	50.00	22.00
❑ 103 Del Ennis	50.00	22.00
❑ 104 Luke Easter	50.00	22.00
❑ 105 Eddie Joost	40.00	18.00
❑ 106 Ken Raffensberger	40.00	18.00
❑ 107 Alex Kellner	40.00	18.00
❑ 108 Bobby Adams	40.00	18.00
❑ 109 Ken Wood	40.00	18.00
❑ 110 Bob Rush	40.00	18.00
❑ 111 Jim Dyck	40.00	18.00
❑ 112 Toby Atwell	40.00	18.00
❑ 113 Karl Drews	80.00	36.00
❑ 114 Bob Feller	500.00	220.00
❑ 115 Cloyd Boyer	80.00	36.00
❑ 116 Eddie Yost	100.00	45.00
❑ 117 Duke Snider	600.00	275.00
❑ 118 Billy Martin	400.00	180.00
❑ 119 Dale Mitchell	100.00	45.00
❑ 120 Marlin Stuart	80.00	36.00
❑ 121 Yogi Berra	700.00	325.00
❑ 122 Bill Serena	80.00	36.00
❑ 123 Johnny Lipon	80.00	36.00
❑ 124 Charlie Dressen MG	100.00	45.00
❑ 125 Fred Hatfield	80.00	36.00
❑ 126 Al Corwin	80.00	36.00
❑ 127 Dick Kryhoski	80.00	36.00
❑ 128 Whitey Lockman	100.00	45.00
❑ 129 Russ Meyer	75.00	34.00
❑ 130 Cass Michaels	75.00	34.00
❑ 131 Connie Ryan	75.00	34.00
❑ 132 Fred Hutchinson	90.00	40.00
❑ 133 Willie Jones	75.00	34.00
❑ 134 Johnny Pesky	90.00	40.00
❑ 135 Bobby Morgan	75.00	34.00
❑ 136 Jim Brideweser	75.00	34.00
❑ 137 Sam Dente	75.00	34.00
❑ 138 Bubba Church	75.00	34.00
❑ 139 Pete Runnels	90.00	40.00
❑ 140 Al Brazle	75.00	34.00
❑ 141 Frank Shea	75.00	34.00
❑ 142 Larry Miggins	75.00	34.00
❑ 143 Al Lopez MG	110.00	50.00
❑ 144 Warren Hacker	75.00	34.00
❑ 145 George Shuba	90.00	40.00
❑ 146 Early Wynn	200.00	90.00
❑ 147 Clem Koshorek	75.00	34.00
❑ 148 Billy Goodman	90.00	40.00
❑ 149 Al Corwin	75.00	34.00
❑ 150 Carl Scheib	75.00	34.00
❑ 151 Joe Adcock	90.00	40.00
❑ 152 Clyde Vollmer	75.00	34.00
❑ 153 Whitey Ford	600.00	275.00
❑ 154 Turk Lown	75.00	34.00
❑ 155 Allie Clark	75.00	34.00
❑ 156 Max Surkont	75.00	34.00
❑ 157 Sherm Lollar	90.00	40.00

❑ 158 Howard Fox 75.00 34.00
❑ 159 Mickey Vernon UER .. 90.00 40.00
(Photo actually
Floyd Baker)
❑ 160 Cal Abrams 200.00 70.00

1954 Bowman

	NRMT	VG-E
COMPLETE SET (224)	4000.00	1800.00
WRAP.(1-CENT, DATED)	150.00	70.00
WRAP.(1-CENT, UNDAT)	200.00	90.00
WRAP.(5-CENT, DATED)	150.00	70.00
WRAP.(5-CENT, UNDAT)	60.00	27.00

❑ 1 Phil Rizzuto 160.00 47.50
❑ 2 Jackie Jensen 30.00 13.50
❑ 3 Marion Fricano 12.00 5.50
❑ 4 Bob Hooper 12.00 5.50
❑ 5 Billy Hunter 12.00 5.50
❑ 6 Nellie Fox 75.00 34.00
❑ 7 Walt Dropo 20.00 9.00
❑ 8 Jim Busby 12.00 5.50
❑ 9 Dave Williams 12.00 5.50
❑ 10 Carl Erskine 20.00 9.00
❑ 11 Sid Gordon 12.00 5.50
❑ 12 Roy McMillan 20.00 9.00
❑ 13 Paul Minner 12.00 5.50
❑ 14 Jerry Staley 12.00 5.50
❑ 15 Richie Ashburn 75.00 34.00
❑ 16 Jim Wilson 12.00 5.50
❑ 17 Tom Gorman 12.00 5.50
❑ 18 Hoot Evers 12.00 5.50
❑ 19 Bobby Shantz 20.00 9.00
❑ 20 Art Houtteman 12.00 5.50
❑ 21 Vic Wertz 20.00 9.00
❑ 22 Sam Mele 12.00 5.50
❑ 23 Harvey Kuenn RC 30.00 13.50
❑ 24 Bob Porterfield 12.00 5.50
❑ 25 Wes Westrum 20.00 9.00
❑ 26 Billy Cox 20.00 9.00
❑ 27 Dick Cole 12.00 5.50
❑ 28 Jim Greengrass 12.00 5.50
❑ 29 Johnny Klippstein 12.00 5.50
❑ 30 Del Rice 12.00 5.50
❑ 31 Smoky Burgess 20.00 9.00
❑ 32 Del Crandall 20.00 9.00
❑ 33A Vic Raschi 20.00 9.00
(No mention of
trade on back)
❑ 33B Vic Raschi 30.00 13.50
(Traded to St.Louis)
❑ 34 Sammy White 12.00 5.50
❑ 35 Eddie Joost 12.00 5.50
❑ 36 George Strickland 12.00 5.50
❑ 37 Dick Kokos 12.00 5.50
❑ 38 Minnie Minoso 30.00 13.50
❑ 39 Ned Garver 12.00 5.50
❑ 40 Gil Coan 12.00 5.50
❑ 41 Alvin Dark 20.00 9.00
❑ 42 Billy Loes 20.00 9.00
❑ 43 Bob Friend 20.00 9.00
❑ 44 Harry Perkowski 12.00 5.50
❑ 45 Ralph Kiner 50.00 22.00
❑ 46 Rip Repulski 12.00 5.50
❑ 47 Granny Hamner 12.00 5.50
❑ 48 Jack Dittmer 12.00 5.50
❑ 49 Harry Byrd 12.00 5.50
❑ 50 George Kell 50.00 22.00
❑ 51 Alex Kellner 12.00 5.50
❑ 52 Joe Ginsberg 12.00 5.50
❑ 53 Don Lenhardt 12.00 5.50
❑ 54 Chico Carrasquel 12.00 5.50
❑ 55 Jim Delsing 12.00 5.50
❑ 56 Maurice McDermott 12.00 5.50
❑ 57 Hoyt Wilhelm 50.00 22.00
❑ 58 Pee Wee Reese 75.00 34.00
❑ 59 Bob Schultz 12.00 5.50
❑ 60 Fred Baczewski 12.00 5.50
❑ 61 Eddie Miksis 12.00 5.50
❑ 62 Enos Slaughter 50.00 22.00
❑ 63 Earl Torgeson 12.00 5.50
❑ 64 Eddie Mathews 75.00 34.00
❑ 65 Mickey Mantle 1400.00 650.00
❑ 66A Ted Williams 3500.00 1600.00
❑ 66B Jimmy Piersall 75.00 34.00
❑ 67 Carl Scheib 12.00 5.50
❑ 68 Bobby Avila 20.00 9.00
❑ 69 Clint Courtney 12.00 5.50
❑ 70 Willard Marshall 12.00 5.50
❑ 71 Ted Gray 12.00 5.50
❑ 72 Eddie Yost 20.00 9.00
❑ 73 Don Mueller 20.00 9.00
❑ 74 Jim Gilliam 30.00 13.50
❑ 75 Max Surkont 12.00 5.50
❑ 76 Joe Nuxhall 20.00 9.00
❑ 77 Bob Rush 12.00 5.50
❑ 78 Sal Yvars 12.00 5.50
❑ 79 Curt Simmons 20.00 9.00
❑ 80 Johnny Logan 12.00 5.50
❑ 81 Jerry Coleman 20.00 9.00
❑ 82 Billy Goodman 20.00 9.00
❑ 83 Ray Murray 12.00 5.50
❑ 84 Larry Doby 50.00 22.00
❑ 85 Jim Dyck 12.00 5.50
❑ 86 Harry Dorish 12.00 5.50
❑ 87 Don Lund 12.00 5.50
❑ 88 Tom Umphlett 12.00 5.50
❑ 89 Willie Mays 400.00 180.00
❑ 90 Roy Campanella 150.00 70.00
❑ 91 Cal Abrams 12.00 5.50
❑ 92 Ken Raffensberger 12.00 5.50
❑ 93 Bill Serena 12.00 5.50
❑ 94 Solly Hemus 12.00 5.50
❑ 95 Robin Roberts 50.00 22.00
❑ 96 Joe Adcock 20.00 9.00
❑ 97 Gil McDougald 20.00 9.00
❑ 98 Ellis Kinder 12.00 5.50
❑ 99 Pete Suder 12.00 5.50
❑ 100 Mike Garcia 20.00 9.00
❑ 101 Don Larsen RC 75.00 34.00
❑ 102 Billy Pierce 20.00 9.00
❑ 103 Steve Souchock 12.00 5.50
❑ 104 Frank Shea 12.00 5.50
❑ 105 Sal Maglie 20.00 9.00
❑ 106 Clem Labine 20.00 9.00
❑ 107 Paul LaPalme 12.00 5.50
❑ 108 Bobby Adams 12.00 5.50
❑ 109 Roy Smalley 12.00 5.50
❑ 110 Red Schoendienst 50.00 22.00
❑ 111 Murry Dickson 12.00 5.50
❑ 112 Andy Pafko 20.00 9.00
❑ 113 Allie Reynolds 20.00 9.00
❑ 114 Willard Nixon 12.00 5.50
❑ 115 Don Bollweg 12.00 5.50
❑ 116 Luke Easter 20.00 9.00
❑ 117 Dick Kryhoski 12.00 5.50
❑ 118 Bob Boyd 12.00 5.50
❑ 119 Fred Hatfield 12.00 5.50
❑ 120 Mel Hoderlein 12.00 5.50
❑ 121 Ray Katt 12.00 5.50
❑ 122 Carl Furillo 30.00 13.50
❑ 123 Toby Atwell 12.00 5.50
❑ 124 Gus Bell 20.00 9.00
❑ 125 Warren Hacker 12.00 5.50
❑ 126 Cliff Chambers 12.00 5.50
❑ 127 Del Ennis 20.00 9.00
❑ 128 Ebba St.Claire 12.00 5.50
❑ 129 Hank Bauer 30.00 13.50
❑ 130 Milt Bolling 12.00 5.50
❑ 131 Joe Astroth 12.00 5.50
❑ 132 Bob Feller 75.00 34.00
❑ 133 Duane Pillette 12.00 5.50
❑ 134 Luis Aloma 12.00 5.50
❑ 135 Johnny Pesky 20.00 9.00
❑ 136 Clyde Vollmer 12.00 5.50
❑ 137 Al Corwin 12.00 5.50
❑ 138 Gil Hodges 75.00 34.00
❑ 139 Preston Ward 12.00 5.50
❑ 140 Saul Rogovin 12.00 5.50
❑ 141 Joe Garagiola 30.00 13.50
❑ 142 Al Brazle 12.00 5.50
❑ 143 Willie Jones 12.00 5.50
❑ 144 Ernie Johnson RC 30.00 13.50
❑ 145 Billy Martin 75.00 34.00
❑ 146 Dick Gernert 12.00 5.50
❑ 147 Joe DeMaestri 12.00 5.50
❑ 148 Dale Mitchell 20.00 9.00
❑ 149 Bob Young 12.00 5.50
❑ 150 Cass Michaels 12.00 5.50
❑ 151 Pat Mullin 12.00 5.50
❑ 152 Mickey Vernon 20.00 9.00
❑ 153 Whitey Lockman 20.00 9.00
❑ 154 Don Newcombe 30.00 13.50
❑ 155 Frank Thomas RC 20.00 9.00
❑ 156 Rocky Bridges 12.00 5.50
❑ 157 Turk Lown 12.00 5.50
❑ 158 Stu Miller 20.00 9.00
❑ 159 Johnny Lindell 12.00 5.50
❑ 160 Danny O'Connell 12.00 5.50
❑ 161 Yogi Berra 175.00 80.00
❑ 162 Ted Lepcio 12.00 5.50
❑ 163A Dave Philley 20.00 9.00
(No mention of
trade on back)
❑ 163B Dave Philley 30.00 13.50
(Traded to
Cleveland)
❑ 164 Early Wynn 50.00 22.00
❑ 165 Johnny Groth 12.00 5.50
❑ 166 Sandy Consuegra 12.00 5.50
❑ 167 Billy Hoeft 12.00 5.50
❑ 168 Ed Fitzgerald 12.00 5.50
❑ 169 Larry Jansen 20.00 9.00
❑ 170 Duke Snider 150.00 70.00
❑ 171 Carlos Bernier 12.00 5.50
❑ 172 Andy Seminick 12.00 5.50
❑ 173 Dee Fondy 12.00 5.50
❑ 174 Pete Castiglione 12.00 5.50
❑ 175 Mel Clark 12.00 5.50
❑ 176 Vern Bickford 12.00 5.50
❑ 177 Whitey Ford 100.00 45.00
❑ 178 Del Wilber 12.00 5.50
❑ 179 Morrie Martin 12.00 5.50
❑ 180 Joe Tipton 12.00 5.50
❑ 181 Les Moss 12.00 5.50
❑ 182 Sherm Lollar 20.00 9.00
❑ 183 Matt Batts 12.00 5.50
❑ 184 Mickey Grasso 12.00 5.50
❑ 185 Daryl Spencer 12.00 5.50
❑ 186 Russ Meyer 12.00 5.50
❑ 187 Vern Law 20.00 9.00
❑ 188 Frank Smith 12.00 5.50
❑ 189 Randy Jackson 12.00 5.50
❑ 190 Joe Presko 12.00 5.50
❑ 191 Karl Drews 12.00 5.50
❑ 192 Lou Burdette 20.00 9.00
❑ 193 Eddie Robinson 12.00 5.50
❑ 194 Sid Hudson 12.00 5.50
❑ 195 Bob Cain 12.00 5.50
❑ 196 Bob Lemon 50.00 22.00
❑ 197 Lou Kretlow 12.00 5.50
❑ 198 Virgil Trucks 12.00 5.50
❑ 199 Steve Gromek 12.00 5.50
❑ 200 Conrado Marrero 12.00 5.50
❑ 201 Bobby Thomson 30.00 13.50
❑ 202 George Shuba 20.00 9.00
❑ 203 Vic Janowicz 20.00 9.00
❑ 204 Jack Collum 12.00 5.50
❑ 205 Hal Jeffcoat 12.00 5.50
❑ 206 Steve Bilko 12.00 5.50
❑ 207 Stan Lopata 12.00 5.50
❑ 208 Johnny Antonelli 20.00 9.00
❑ 209 Gene Woodling 12.00 5.50
❑ 210 Jimmy Piersall 30.00 13.50
❑ 211 Al Robertson 12.00 5.50
❑ 212 Owen Friend 12.00 5.50
❑ 213 Dick Littlefield 12.00 5.50
❑ 214 Ferris Fain 20.00 9.00
❑ 215 Johnny Bucha 12.00 5.50

Card	NRMT	VG-E
❑ 216 Jerry Snyder	12.00	5.50
❑ 217 Hank Thompson	20.00	9.00
❑ 218 Preacher Roe	20.00	9.00
❑ 219 Hal Rice	12.00	5.50
❑ 220 Hobie Landrith	12.00	5.50
❑ 221 Frank Baumholtz	12.00	5.50
❑ 222 Memo Luna	12.00	5.50
❑ 223 Steve Ridzik	12.00	5.50
❑ 224 Bill Bruton	50.00	12.50

1955 Bowman

	NRMT	VG-E
COMPLETE SET (320)	4600.00	2100.00
COMMON CARD (1-96)	12.00	5.50
COM. CARD (97-224)	10.00	4.50
COM. CARD (225-320)	15.00	6.75
COM. UMPIRE (225-320)	30.00	13.50
WRAPPER (1-CENT)	60.00	27.00
WRAPPER (5-CENT)	60.00	27.00

Card	NRMT	VG-E
❑ 1 Hoyt Wilhelm	100.00	22.00
❑ 2 Alvin Dark	15.00	6.75
❑ 3 Joe Coleman	15.00	6.75
❑ 4 Eddie Waitkus	15.00	6.75
❑ 5 Jim Robertson	12.00	5.50
❑ 6 Pete Suder	12.00	5.50
❑ 7 Gene Baker	12.00	5.50
❑ 8 Warren Hacker	12.00	5.50
❑ 9 Gil McDougald	20.00	9.00
❑ 10 Phil Rizzuto	100.00	45.00
❑ 11 Bill Bruton	15.00	6.75
❑ 12 Andy Pafko	15.00	6.75
❑ 13 Clyde Vollmer	12.00	5.50
❑ 14 Gus Keriazakos	12.00	5.50
❑ 15 Frank Sullivan	12.00	5.50
❑ 16 Jimmy Piersall	20.00	9.00
❑ 17 Del Ennis	15.00	6.75
❑ 18 Stan Lopata	12.00	5.50
❑ 19 Bobby Avila	15.00	6.75
❑ 20 Al Smith	15.00	6.75
❑ 21 Don Hoak	12.00	5.50
❑ 22 Roy Campanella	125.00	55.00
❑ 23 Al Kaline	150.00	70.00
❑ 24 Al Aber	12.00	5.50
❑ 25 Minnie Minoso	30.00	13.50
❑ 26 Virgil Trucks	15.00	6.75
❑ 27 Preston Ward	12.00	5.50
❑ 28 Dick Cole	12.00	5.50
❑ 29 Red Schoendienst	30.00	13.50
❑ 30 Bill Sarni	12.00	5.50
❑ 31 Johnny Temple RC	15.00	6.75
❑ 32 Wally Post	15.00	6.75
❑ 33 Nellie Fox	50.00	22.00
❑ 34 Clint Courtney	12.00	5.50
❑ 35 Bill Tuttle	12.00	5.50
❑ 36 Wayne Belardi	12.00	5.50
❑ 37 Pee Wee Reese	75.00	34.00
❑ 38 Early Wynn	30.00	13.50
❑ 39 Bob Darnell	15.00	6.75
❑ 40 Vic Wertz	15.00	6.75
❑ 41 Mel Clark	12.00	5.50
❑ 42 Bob Greenwood	12.00	5.50
❑ 43 Bob Buhl	15.00	6.75
❑ 44 Danny O'Connell	12.00	5.50
❑ 45 Tom Umphlett	12.00	5.50
❑ 46 Mickey Vernon	15.00	6.75
❑ 47 Sammy White	12.00	5.50
❑ 48A Milt Bolling ERR (Name on back is Frank Bolling)	20.00	9.00
❑ 48B Milt Bolling COR	20.00	9.00
❑ 49 Jim Greengrass	12.00	5.50
❑ 50 Hobie Landrith	12.00	5.50
❑ 51 Elvin Tappe	12.00	5.50
❑ 52 Hal Rice	12.00	5.50
❑ 53 Alex Kellner	12.00	5.50
❑ 54 Don Bollweg	12.00	5.50
❑ 55 Cal Abrams	12.00	5.50
❑ 56 Billy Cox	15.00	6.75
❑ 57 Bob Friend	15.00	6.75
❑ 58 Frank Thomas	15.00	6.75
❑ 59 Whitey Ford	100.00	45.00
❑ 60 Enos Slaughter	30.00	13.50
❑ 61 Paul LaPalme	12.00	5.50
❑ 62 Royce Lint	12.00	5.50
❑ 63 Irv Noren	15.00	6.75
❑ 64 Curt Simmons	15.00	6.75
❑ 65 Don Zimmer RC	20.00	9.00
❑ 66 George Shuba	20.00	9.00
❑ 67 Don Larsen	20.00	9.00
❑ 68 Elston Howard RC	75.00	34.00
❑ 69 Billy Hunter	12.00	5.50
❑ 70 Lou Burdette	20.00	9.00
❑ 71 Dave Jolly	12.00	5.50
❑ 72 Chet Nichols	12.00	5.50
❑ 73 Eddie Yost	15.00	6.75
❑ 74 Jerry Snyder	12.00	5.50
❑ 75 Brooks Lawrence RC	12.00	5.50
❑ 76 Tom Poholsky	12.00	5.50
❑ 77 Jim McDonald	12.00	5.50
❑ 78 Gil Coan	12.00	5.50
❑ 79 Willie Miranda	12.00	5.50
❑ 80 Lou Limmer	12.00	5.50
❑ 81 Bobby Morgan	12.00	5.50
❑ 82 Lee Walls	12.00	5.50
❑ 83 Max Surkont	12.00	5.50
❑ 84 George Freese	12.00	5.50
❑ 85 Cass Michaels	12.00	5.50
❑ 86 Ted Gray	12.00	5.50
❑ 87 Randy Jackson	12.00	5.50
❑ 88 Steve Bilko	12.00	5.50
❑ 89 Lou Boudreau MG	30.00	13.50
❑ 90 Art Ditmar	12.00	5.50
❑ 91 Dick Marlowe	12.00	5.50
❑ 92 George Zuverink	12.00	5.50
❑ 93 Andy Seminick	12.00	5.50
❑ 94 Hank Thompson	15.00	6.75
❑ 95 Sal Maglie	15.00	6.75
❑ 96 Ray Narleski RC	12.00	5.50
❑ 97 Johnny Podres	30.00	13.50
❑ 98 Jim Gilliam	20.00	9.00
❑ 99 Jerry Coleman	15.00	6.75
❑ 100 Tom Morgan	10.00	4.50
❑ 101A Don Johnson ERR (Photo actually Ernie Johnson)	20.00	9.00
❑ 101B Don Johnson COR	20.00	9.00
❑ 102 Bobby Thomson	15.00	6.75
❑ 103 Eddie Mathews	60.00	27.00
❑ 104 Bob Porterfield	10.00	4.50
❑ 105 Johnny Schmitz	10.00	4.50
❑ 106 Del Rice	10.00	4.50
❑ 107 Solly Hemus	10.00	4.50
❑ 108 Lou Kretlow	10.00	4.50
❑ 109 Vern Stephens	15.00	6.75
❑ 110 Bob Miller	10.00	4.50
❑ 111 Steve Ridzik	10.00	4.50
❑ 112 Granny Hamner	10.00	4.50
❑ 113 Bob Hall	10.00	4.50
❑ 114 Vic Janowicz	15.00	6.75
❑ 115 Roger Bowman	10.00	4.50
❑ 116 Sandy Consuegra	10.00	4.50
❑ 117 Johnny Groth	10.00	4.50
❑ 118 Bobby Adams	10.00	4.50
❑ 119 Joe Astroth	10.00	4.50
❑ 120 Ed Burtschy	10.00	4.50
❑ 121 Rufus Crawford	10.00	4.50
❑ 122 Al Corwin	10.00	4.50
❑ 123 Marv Grissom	10.00	4.50
❑ 124 Johnny Antonelli	15.00	6.75
❑ 125 Paul Giel	15.00	6.75
❑ 126 Billy Goodman	15.00	6.75
❑ 127 Hank Majeski	10.00	4.50
❑ 128 Mike Garcia	15.00	6.75
❑ 129 Hal Naragon	10.00	4.50
❑ 130 Richie Ashburn	50.00	22.00
❑ 131 Willard Marshall	10.00	4.50
❑ 132A Harvey Kueen ERR (Sic, Kuenn)	50.00	22.00
❑ 132B Harvey Kuenn COR	30.00	13.50
❑ 133 Charles King	10.00	4.50
❑ 134 Bob Feller	70.00	32.00
❑ 135 Lloyd Merriman	10.00	4.50
❑ 136 Rocky Bridges	10.00	4.50
❑ 137 Bob Talbot	10.00	4.50
❑ 138 Davey Williams	15.00	6.75
❑ 139 Shantz Brothers (Wilmer Shantz, Bobby Shantz)	15.00	6.75
❑ 140 Bobby Shantz	15.00	6.75
❑ 141 Wes Westrum	15.00	6.75
❑ 142 Rudy Regalado	10.00	4.50
❑ 143 Don Newcombe	30.00	13.50
❑ 144 Art Houtteman	10.00	4.50
❑ 145 Bob Nieman	10.00	4.50
❑ 146 Don Liddle	10.00	4.50
❑ 147 Sam Mele	10.00	4.50
❑ 148 Bob Chakales	10.00	4.50
❑ 149 Cloyd Boyer	10.00	4.50
❑ 150 Billy Klaus	10.00	4.50
❑ 151 Jim Brideweser	10.00	4.50
❑ 152 Johnny Klippstein	10.00	4.50
❑ 153 Eddie Robinson	10.00	4.50
❑ 154 Frank Lary RC	15.00	6.75
❑ 155 Gerry Staley	10.00	4.50
❑ 156 Jim Hughes	15.00	6.75
❑ 157A Ernie Johnson ERR (Photo actually Don Johnson)	20.00	9.00
❑ 157B Ernie Johnson COR	20.00	9.00
❑ 158 Gil Hodges	50.00	22.00
❑ 159 Harry Byrd	10.00	4.50
❑ 160 Bill Skowron	20.00	9.00
❑ 161 Matt Batts	10.00	4.50
❑ 162 Charlie Maxwell	10.00	4.50
❑ 163 Sid Gordon	15.00	6.75
❑ 164 Toby Atwell	10.00	4.50
❑ 165 Maurice McDermott	10.00	4.50
❑ 166 Jim Busby	10.00	4.50
❑ 167 Bob Grim RC	20.00	9.00
❑ 168 Yogi Berra	100.00	45.00
❑ 169 Carl Furillo	30.00	13.50
❑ 170 Carl Erskine	20.00	9.00
❑ 171 Robin Roberts	50.00	22.00
❑ 172 Willie Jones	10.00	4.50
❑ 173 Chico Carrasquel	10.00	4.50
❑ 174 Sherm Lollar	15.00	6.75
❑ 175 Wilmer Shantz	10.00	4.50
❑ 176 Joe DeMaestri	10.00	4.50
❑ 177 Willard Nixon	10.00	4.50
❑ 178 Tom Brewer	10.00	4.50
❑ 179 Hank Aaron	225.00	100.00
❑ 180 Johnny Logan	15.00	6.75
❑ 181 Eddie Miksis	10.00	4.50
❑ 182 Bob Rush	10.00	4.50
❑ 183 Ray Katt	10.00	4.50
❑ 184 Willie Mays	225.00	100.00
❑ 185 Vic Raschi	10.00	4.50
❑ 186 Alex Grammas	10.00	4.50
❑ 187 Fred Hatfield	10.00	4.50
❑ 188 Ned Garver	10.00	4.50
❑ 189 Jack Collum	10.00	4.50
❑ 190 Fred Baczewski	10.00	4.50
❑ 191 Bob Lemon	30.00	13.50
❑ 192 George Strickland	10.00	4.50
❑ 193 Howie Judson	10.00	4.50
❑ 194 Joe Nuxhall	15.00	6.75
❑ 195A Erv Palica (Without trade)	15.00	6.75
❑ 195B Erv Palica (With trade)	40.00	18.00
❑ 196 Russ Meyer	15.00	6.75
❑ 197 Ralph Kiner	30.00	13.50
❑ 198 Dave Pope	10.00	4.50
❑ 199 Vern Law	15.00	6.75
❑ 200 Dick Littlefield	10.00	4.50
❑ 201 Allie Reynolds	20.00	9.00
❑ 202 Mickey Mantle UER (Birthdate listed as 10/30/31)	900.00	400.00

Should be 10/20/31
❑ 203 Steve Gromek 10.00 4.50
❑ 204A Frank Bolling ERR 20.00 9.00
(Name on back is
Milt Bolling)
❑ 204B Frank Bolling COR 20.00 9.00
❑ 205 Rip Repulski 10.00 4.50
❑ 206 Ralph Beard 10.00 4.50
❑ 207 Frank Shea 10.00 4.50
❑ 208 Ed Fitzgerald 10.00 4.50
❑ 209 Smoky Burgess 15.00 6.75
❑ 210 Earl Torgeson 10.00 4.50
❑ 211 Sonny Dixon 10.00 4.50
❑ 212 Jack Dittmer 10.00 4.50
❑ 213 George Kell 30.00 13.50
❑ 214 Billy Pierce 15.00 6.75
❑ 215 Bob Kuzava 10.00 4.50
❑ 216 Preacher Roe 20.00 9.00
❑ 217 Del Crandall 15.00 6.75
❑ 218 Joe Adcock 15.00 6.75
❑ 219 Whitey Lockman 15.00 6.75
❑ 220 Jim Hearn 10.00 4.50
❑ 221 Hector Brown 10.00 4.50
❑ 222 Russ Kemmerer 10.00 4.50
❑ 223 Hal Jeffcoat 10.00 4.50
❑ 224 Dee Fondy 10.00 4.50
❑ 225 Paul Richards MG 15.00 6.75
❑ 226 Bill McKinley UMP 30.00 13.50
❑ 227 Frank Baumholtz 15.00 6.75
❑ 228 John Phillips 15.00 6.75
❑ 229 Jim Brosnan RC 20.00 9.00
❑ 230 Al Brazle 15.00 6.75
❑ 231 Jim Konstanty 20.00 9.00
❑ 232 Birdie Tebbetts MG 20.00 9.00
❑ 233 Bill Serena 15.00 6.75
❑ 234 Dick Bartell CO 20.00 9.00
❑ 235 Joe Paparella UMP 30.00 13.50
❑ 236 Murry Dickson 15.00 6.75
❑ 237 Johnny Wyrostek 15.00 6.75
❑ 238 Eddie Stanky MG 20.00 9.00
❑ 239 Edwin Rommel UMP 40.00 18.00
❑ 240 Billy Loes 20.00 9.00
❑ 241 Johnny Pesky CO 20.00 9.00
❑ 242 Ernie Banks 350.00 160.00
❑ 243 Gus Bell 20.00 9.00
❑ 244 Duane Pillette 15.00 6.75
❑ 245 Bill Miller 15.00 6.75
❑ 246 Hank Bauer 30.00 13.50
❑ 247 Dutch Leonard CO 15.00 6.75
❑ 248 Harry Dorish 15.00 6.75
❑ 249 Billy Gardner 20.00 9.00
❑ 250 Larry Napp UMP 30.00 13.50
❑ 251 Stan Jok 15.00 6.75
❑ 252 Roy Smalley 15.00 6.75
❑ 253 Jim Wilson 15.00 6.75
❑ 254 Bennett Flowers 15.00 6.75
❑ 255 Pete Runnels 20.00 9.00
❑ 256 Owen Friend 15.00 6.75
❑ 257 Tom Alston 15.00 6.75
❑ 258 John Stevens UMP 30.00 13.50
❑ 259 Don Mossi RC 30.00 13.50
❑ 260 Edwin Hurley UMP 30.00 13.50
❑ 261 Walt Moryn 20.00 9.00
❑ 262 Jim Lemon 15.00 6.75
❑ 263 Eddie Joost 15.00 6.75
❑ 264 Bill Henry 15.00 6.75
❑ 265 Albert Barlick UMP 75.00 34.00
❑ 266 Mike Fornieles 15.00 6.75
❑ 267 Jim Honochick UMP 75.00 34.00
❑ 268 Roy Lee Hawes 15.00 6.75
❑ 269 Joe Amalfitano RC 20.00 9.00
❑ 270 Chico Fernandez 20.00 9.00
❑ 271 Bob Hooper 15.00 6.75
❑ 272 John Flaherty UMP 30.00 13.50
❑ 273 Bubba Church 15.00 6.75
❑ 274 Jim Delsing 15.00 6.75
❑ 275 William Grieve UMP 30.00 13.50
❑ 276 Ike Delock 15.00 6.75
❑ 277 Ed Runge UMP 30.00 13.50
❑ 278 Charlie Neal RC 40.00 18.00
❑ 279 Hank Soar UMP 40.00 18.00
❑ 280 Clyde McCullough 15.00 6.75
❑ 281 Charles Berry UMP 40.00 18.00
❑ 282 Phil Cavarretta 20.00 9.00
❑ 283 Nestor Chylak UMP 75.00 34.00
❑ 284 Bill Jackowski UMP 30.00 13.50
❑ 285 Walt Dropo 20.00 9.00
❑ 286 Frank Secory UMP 30.00 13.50
❑ 287 Ron Mrozinski 15.00 6.75
❑ 288 Dick Smith 15.00 6.75
❑ 289 Arthur Gore UMP 30.00 13.50
❑ 290 Hershell Freeman 15.00 6.75
❑ 291 Frank Dascoli UMP 30.00 13.50
❑ 292 Marv Blaylock 15.00 6.75
❑ 293 Thomas Gorman UMP 40.00 18.00
❑ 294 Wally Moses CO 15.00 6.75
❑ 295 Lee Ballanfant UMP 30.00 13.50
❑ 296 Bill Virdon RC 30.00 13.50
❑ 297 Dusty Boggess UMP 30.00 13.50
❑ 298 Charlie Grimm MG 20.00 9.00
❑ 299 Lon Warneke UMP 40.00 18.00
❑ 300 Tommy Byrne 20.00 9.00
❑ 301 William Engeln UMP 30.00 13.50
❑ 302 Frank Malzone RC 30.00 13.50
❑ 303 Jocko Conlan UMP 75.00 34.00
❑ 304 Harry Chiti 15.00 6.75
❑ 305 Frank Umont UMP 30.00 13.50
❑ 306 Bob Cerv 20.00 9.00
❑ 307 Babe Pinelli UMP 40.00 18.00
❑ 308 Al Lopez MG 50.00 22.00
❑ 309 Hal Dixon UMP 30.00 13.50
❑ 310 Ken Lehman 15.00 6.75
❑ 311 Lawrence Goetz UMP 30.00 13.50
❑ 312 Bill Wight 15.00 6.75
❑ 313 Augie Donatelli UMP 50.00 22.00
❑ 314 Dale Mitchell 20.00 9.00
❑ 315 Cal Hubbard UMP 75.00 34.00
❑ 316 Marion Fricano 15.00 6.75
❑ 317 W. Summers UMP 20.00 9.00
❑ 318 Sid Hudson 15.00 6.75
❑ 319 Al Schroll 15.00 6.75
❑ 320 George Susce RC 50.00 10.00

1989 Bowman

	MINT	NRMT
COMPLETE SET (484)	25.00	11.00
COMP.FACT.SET (484)	30.00	13.50

❑ 1 Oswald Peraza .05 .02
❑ 2 Brian Holton .05 .02
❑ 3 Jose Bautista .05 .02
❑ 4 Pete Harnisch RC .25 .11
❑ 5 Dave Schmidt .05 .02
❑ 6 Gregg Olson RC .20 .09
❑ 7 Jeff Ballard .05 .02
❑ 8 Bob Melvin .05 .02
❑ 9 Cal Ripken .75 .35
❑ 10 Randy Milligan .05 .02
❑ 11 Juan Bell RC .05 .02
❑ 12 Billy Ripken .05 .02
❑ 13 Jim Traber .05 .02
❑ 14 Pete Stanicek .05 .02
❑ 15 Steve Finley RC .50 .23
❑ 16 Larry Sheets .05 .02
❑ 17 Phil Bradley .05 .02
❑ 18 Brady Anderson RC .40 .18
❑ 19 Lee Smith .10 .05
❑ 20 Tom Fischer .05 .02
❑ 21 Mike Boddicker .05 .02
❑ 22 Rob Murphy .05 .02
❑ 23 Wes Gardner .05 .02
❑ 24 John Dopson .05 .02
❑ 25 Bob Stanley .05 .02
❑ 26 Roger Clemens .50 .23
❑ 27 Rich Gedman .05 .02
❑ 28 Marty Barrett .05 .02
❑ 29 Luis Rivera .05 .02
❑ 30 Jody Reed .05 .02
❑ 31 Nick Esasky .05 .02
❑ 32 Wade Boggs .20 .09
❑ 33 Jim Rice .10 .05
❑ 34 Mike Greenwell .05 .02
❑ 35 Dwight Evans .10 .05
❑ 36 Ellis Burks .10 .05
❑ 37 Chuck Finley .10 .05
❑ 38 Kirk McCaskill .05 .02
❑ 39 Jim Abbott RC* .20 .09
❑ 40 Bryan Harvey RC* .05 .02
❑ 41 Bert Blyleven .10 .05
❑ 42 Mike Witt .05 .02
❑ 43 Bob McClure .05 .02
❑ 44 Bill Schroeder .05 .02
❑ 45 Lance Parrish .05 .02
❑ 46 Dick Schofield .05 .02
❑ 47 Wally Joyner .10 .05
❑ 48 Jack Howell .05 .02
❑ 49 Johnny Ray .05 .02
❑ 50 Chili Davis .10 .05
❑ 51 Tony Armas .05 .02
❑ 52 Claudell Washington .05 .02
❑ 53 Brian Downing .05 .02
❑ 54 Devon White .10 .05
❑ 55 Bobby Thigpen .05 .02
❑ 56 Bill Long .05 .02
❑ 57 Jerry Reuss .05 .02
❑ 58 Shawn Hillegas .05 .02
❑ 59 Melido Perez .05 .02
❑ 60 Jeff Bittiger .05 .02
❑ 61 Jack McDowell .10 .05
❑ 62 Carlton Fisk .20 .09
❑ 63 Steve Lyons .05 .02
❑ 64 Ozzie Guillen .05 .02
❑ 65 Robin Ventura RC .75 .35
❑ 66 Fred Manrique .05 .02
❑ 67 Dan Pasqua .05 .02
❑ 68 Ivan Calderon .05 .02
❑ 69 Ron Kittle .05 .02
❑ 70 Daryl Boston .05 .02
❑ 71 Dave Gallagher .05 .02
❑ 72 Harold Baines .10 .05
❑ 73 Charles Nagy RC .25 .11
❑ 74 John Farrell .05 .02
❑ 75 Kevin Wickander .05 .02
❑ 76 Greg Swindell .05 .02
❑ 77 Mike Walker .05 .02
❑ 78 Doug Jones .05 .02
❑ 79 Rich Yett .05 .02
❑ 80 Tom Candiotti .05 .02
❑ 81 Jesse Orosco .05 .02
❑ 82 Bud Black .05 .02
❑ 83 Andy Allanson .05 .02
❑ 84 Pete O'Brien .05 .02
❑ 85 Jerry Browne .05 .02
❑ 86 Brook Jacoby .05 .02
❑ 87 Mark Lewis RC .10 .05
❑ 88 Luis Aguayo .05 .02
❑ 89 Cory Snyder .05 .02
❑ 90 Oddibe McDowell .05 .02
❑ 91 Joe Carter .10 .05
❑ 92 Frank Tanana .05 .02
❑ 93 Jack Morris .10 .05
❑ 94 Doyle Alexander .05 .02
❑ 95 Steve Searcy .05 .02
❑ 96 Randy Bockus .05 .02
❑ 97 Jeff M. Robinson .05 .02
❑ 98 Mike Henneman .05 .02
❑ 99 Paul Gibson .05 .02
❑ 100 Frank Williams .05 .02
❑ 101 Matt Nokes .05 .02
❑ 102 Rico Brogna RC UER .25 .11
(Misspelled Ricco
on card back)
❑ 103 Lou Whitaker .10 .05
❑ 104 Al Pedrique .05 .02
❑ 105 Alan Trammell .10 .05
❑ 106 Chris Brown .05 .02
❑ 107 Pat Sheridan .05 .02
❑ 108 Chet Lemon .05 .02
❑ 109 Keith Moreland .05 .02

❑ 110 Mel Stottlemyre Jr. .05 .02
❑ 111 Bret Saberhagen .10 .05
❑ 112 Floyd Bannister .05 .02
❑ 113 Jeff Montgomery .10 .05
❑ 114 Steve Farr .05 .02
❑ 115 Tom Gordon RC UER .20 .09
(Front shows autograph of Don Gordon)
❑ 116 Charlie Leibrandt .05 .02
❑ 117 Mark Gubicza .05 .02
❑ 118 Mike Macfarlane RC .05 .02
❑ 119 Bob Boone .10 .05
❑ 120 Kurt Stillwell .05 .02
❑ 121 George Brett .40 .18
❑ 122 Frank White .10 .05
❑ 123 Kevin Seitzer .05 .02
❑ 124 Willie Wilson .05 .02
❑ 125 Pat Tabler .05 .02
❑ 126 Bo Jackson .10 .05
❑ 127 Hugh Walker RC .05 .02
❑ 128 Danny Tartabull .05 .02
❑ 129 Teddy Higuera .05 .02
❑ 130 Don August .05 .02
❑ 131 Juan Nieves .05 .02
❑ 132 Mike Birkbeck .05 .02
❑ 133 Dan Plesac .05 .02
❑ 134 Chris Bosio .05 .02
❑ 135 Bill Wegman .05 .02
❑ 136 Chuck Crim .05 .02
❑ 137 B.J. Surhoff .10 .05
❑ 138 Joey Meyer .05 .02
❑ 139 Dale Sveum .05 .02
❑ 140 Paul Molitor .20 .09
❑ 141 Jim Gantner .05 .02
❑ 142 Gary Sheffield RC 1.00 .45
❑ 143 Greg Brock .05 .02
❑ 144 Robin Yount .20 .09
❑ 145 Glenn Braggs .05 .02
❑ 146 Rob Deer .05 .02
❑ 147 Fred Toliver .05 .02
❑ 148 Jeff Reardon .10 .05
❑ 149 Allan Anderson .05 .02
❑ 150 Frank Viola .05 .02
❑ 151 Shane Rawley .05 .02
❑ 152 Juan Berenguer .05 .02
❑ 153 Johnny Ard .05 .02
❑ 154 Tim Laudner .05 .02
❑ 155 Brian Harper .05 .02
❑ 156 Al Newman .05 .02
❑ 157 Kent Hrbek .10 .05
❑ 158 Gary Gaetti .10 .05
❑ 159 Wally Backman .05 .02
❑ 160 Gene Larkin .05 .02
❑ 161 Greg Gagne .05 .02
❑ 162 Kirby Puckett .50 .23
❑ 163 Dan Gladden .05 .02
❑ 164 Randy Bush .05 .02
❑ 165 Dave LaPoint .05 .02
❑ 166 Andy Hawkins .05 .02
❑ 167 Dave Righetti .05 .02
❑ 168 Lance McCullers .05 .02
❑ 169 Jimmy Jones .05 .02
❑ 170 Al Leiter .20 .09
❑ 171 John Candelaria .05 .02
❑ 172 Don Slaught .05 .02
❑ 173 Jamie Quirk .05 .02
❑ 174 Rafael Santana .05 .02
❑ 175 Mike Pagliarulo .05 .02
❑ 176 Don Mattingly .50 .23
❑ 177 Ken Phelps .05 .02
❑ 178 Steve Sax .05 .02
❑ 179 Dave Winfield .20 .09
❑ 180 Stan Jefferson .05 .02
❑ 181 Rickey Henderson .40 .18
❑ 182 Bob Brower .05 .02
❑ 183 Roberto Kelly .10 .05
❑ 184 Curt Young .05 .02
❑ 185 Gene Nelson .05 .02
❑ 186 Bob Welch .05 .02
❑ 187 Rick Honeycutt .05 .02
❑ 188 Dave Stewart .10 .05
❑ 189 Mike Moore .05 .02
❑ 190 Dennis Eckersley .10 .05
❑ 191 Eric Plunk .05 .02
❑ 192 Storm Davis .05 .02
❑ 193 Terry Steinbach .10 .05
❑ 194 Ron Hassey .05 .02
❑ 195 Stan Royer RC .05 .02
❑ 196 Walt Weiss .05 .02
❑ 197 Mark McGwire 1.00 .45
❑ 198 Carney Lansford .10 .05
❑ 199 Glenn Hubbard .05 .02
❑ 200 Dave Henderson .05 .02
❑ 201 Jose Canseco .20 .09
❑ 202 Dave Parker .10 .05
❑ 203 Scott Bankhead .05 .02
❑ 204 Tom Niedenfuer .05 .02
❑ 205 Mark Langston .05 .02
❑ 206 Erik Hanson RC .10 .05
❑ 207 Mike Jackson .05 .02
❑ 208 Dave Valle .05 .02
❑ 209 Scott Bradley .05 .02
❑ 210 Harold Reynolds .05 .02
❑ 211 Tino Martinez RC .50 .23
❑ 212 Rich Renteria .05 .02
❑ 213 Rey Quinones .05 .02
❑ 214 Jim Presley .05 .02
❑ 215 Alvin Davis .05 .02
❑ 216 Edgar Martinez .10 .05
❑ 217 Darnell Coles .05 .02
❑ 218 Jeffrey Leonard .05 .02
❑ 219 Jay Buhner .10 .05
❑ 220 Ken Griffey Jr. RC 15.00 6.75
❑ 221 Drew Hall .05 .02
❑ 222 Bobby Witt .05 .02
❑ 223 Jamie Moyer .05 .02
❑ 224 Charlie Hough .10 .05
❑ 225 Nolan Ryan 1.00 .45
❑ 226 Jeff Russell .05 .02
❑ 227 Jim Sundberg .05 .02
❑ 228 Julio Franco .05 .02
❑ 229 Buddy Bell .10 .05
❑ 230 Scott Fletcher .05 .02
❑ 231 Jeff Kunkel .05 .02
❑ 232 Steve Buechele .05 .02
❑ 233 Monty Fariss .05 .02
❑ 234 Rick Leach .05 .02
❑ 235 Ruben Sierra .05 .02
❑ 236 Cecil Espy .05 .02
❑ 237 Rafael Palmeiro .25 .11
❑ 238 Pete Incaviglia .05 .02
❑ 239 Dave Stieb .05 .02
❑ 240 Jeff Musselman .05 .02
❑ 241 Mike Flanagan .05 .02
❑ 242 Todd Stottlemyre .10 .05
❑ 243 Jimmy Key .10 .05
❑ 244 Tony Castillo .05 .02
❑ 245 Alex Sanchez .05 .02
❑ 246 Tom Henke .05 .02
❑ 247 John Cerutti .05 .02
❑ 248 Ernie Whitt .05 .02
❑ 249 Bob Brenly .05 .02
❑ 250 Rance Mulliniks .05 .02
❑ 251 Kelly Gruber .05 .02
❑ 252 Ed Sprague RC .10 .05
❑ 253 Fred McGriff .20 .09
❑ 254 Tony Fernandez .05 .02
❑ 255 Tom Lawless .05 .02
❑ 256 George Bell .05 .02
❑ 257 Jesse Barfield .05 .02
❑ 258 Roberto Alomar .20 .09
Sandy Alomar
❑ 259 Ken Griffey Jr. 2.00 .90
Ken Griffey Sr.
❑ 260 Cal Ripken Jr. .25 .11
Cal Ripken Sr.
❑ 261 Mel Stottlemyre Jr. .05 .02
Mel Stottlemyre Sr.
❑ 262 Zane Smith .05 .02
❑ 263 Charlie Puleo .05 .02
❑ 264 Derek Lilliquist RC .05 .02
❑ 265 Paul Assenmacher .05 .02
❑ 266 John Smoltz RC .40 .18
❑ 267 Tom Glavine .20 .09
❑ 268 Steve Avery RC .20 .09
❑ 269 Pete Smith .05 .02
❑ 270 Jody Davis .05 .02
❑ 271 Bruce Benedict .05 .02
❑ 272 Andres Thomas .05 .02
❑ 273 Gerald Perry .05 .02
❑ 274 Ron Gant .10 .05
❑ 275 Darrell Evans .10 .05
❑ 276 Dale Murphy .20 .09
❑ 277 Dion James .05 .02
❑ 278 Lonnie Smith .05 .02
❑ 279 Geronimo Berroa .05 .02
❑ 280 Steve Wilson .05 .02
❑ 281 Rick Sutcliffe .10 .05
❑ 282 Kevin Coffman .05 .02
❑ 283 Mitch Williams .05 .02
❑ 284 Greg Maddux .60 .25
❑ 285 Paul Kilgus .05 .02
❑ 286 Mike Harkey RC .05 .02
❑ 287 Lloyd McClendon .05 .02
❑ 288 Damon Berryhill .05 .02
❑ 289 Ty Griffin .05 .02
❑ 290 Ryne Sandberg .25 .11
❑ 291 Mark Grace .20 .09
❑ 292 Curt Wilkerson .05 .02
❑ 293 Vance Law .05 .02
❑ 294 Shawon Dunston .05 .02
❑ 295 Jerome Walton .20 .09
❑ 296 Mitch Webster .05 .02
❑ 297 Dwight Smith RC .10 .05
❑ 298 Andre Dawson .10 .05
❑ 299 Jeff Sellers .05 .02
❑ 300 Jose Rijo .05 .02
❑ 301 John Franco .10 .05
❑ 302 Rick Mahler .05 .02
❑ 303 Ron Robinson .05 .02
❑ 304 Danny Jackson .05 .02
❑ 305 Rob Dibble RC* .10 .05
❑ 306 Tom Browning .05 .02
❑ 307 Bo Diaz .05 .02
❑ 308 Manny Trillo .05 .02
❑ 309 Chris Sabo RC* .05 .02
❑ 310 Ron Oester .05 .02
❑ 311 Barry Larkin .20 .09
❑ 312 Todd Benzinger .05 .02
❑ 313 Paul O'Neill .20 .09
❑ 314 Kal Daniels .05 .02
❑ 315 Joel Youngblood .05 .02
❑ 316 Eric Davis .10 .05
❑ 317 Dave Smith .05 .02
❑ 318 Mark Portugal .05 .02
❑ 319 Brian Meyer .05 .02
❑ 320 Jim Deshaies .05 .02
❑ 321 Juan Agosto .05 .02
❑ 322 Mike Scott .05 .02
❑ 323 Rick Rhoden .05 .02
❑ 324 Jim Clancy .05 .02
❑ 325 Larry Andersen .05 .02
❑ 326 Alex Trevino .05 .02
❑ 327 Alan Ashby .05 .02
❑ 328 Craig Reynolds .05 .02
❑ 329 Bill Doran .05 .02
❑ 330 Rafael Ramirez .05 .02
❑ 331 Glenn Davis .05 .02
❑ 332 Willie Ansley RC .05 .02
❑ 333 Gerald Young .05 .02
❑ 334 Cameron Drew .05 .02
❑ 335 Jay Howell .05 .02
❑ 336 Tim Belcher .05 .02
❑ 337 Fernando Valenzuela .10 .05
❑ 338 Ricky Horton .05 .02
❑ 339 Tim Leary .05 .02
❑ 340 Bill Bene .05 .02
❑ 341 Orel Hershiser .10 .05
❑ 342 Mike Scioscia .05 .02
❑ 343 Rick Dempsey .05 .02
❑ 344 Willie Randolph .10 .05
❑ 345 Alfredo Griffin .05 .02
❑ 346 Eddie Murray .20 .09
❑ 347 Mickey Hatcher .05 .02
❑ 348 Mike Sharperson .05 .02
❑ 349 John Shelby .05 .02
❑ 350 Mike Marshall .05 .02
❑ 351 Kirk Gibson .10 .05
❑ 352 Mike Davis .05 .02
❑ 353 Bryn Smith .05 .02
❑ 354 Pascual Perez .05 .02
❑ 355 Kevin Gross .05 .02
❑ 356 Andy McGaffigan .05 .02
❑ 357 Brian Holman RC* .05 .02
❑ 358 Dave Wainhouse RC .05 .02
❑ 359 Dennis Martinez .10 .05
❑ 360 Tim Burke .05 .02
❑ 361 Nelson Santovenia .05 .02

Card	Player	Mint	NRMT
❑ 362	Tim Wallach	.05	.02
❑ 363	Spike Owen	.05	.02
❑ 364	Rex Hudler	.05	.02
❑ 365	Andres Galarraga	.10	.05
❑ 366	Otis Nixon	.05	.02
❑ 367	Hubie Brooks	.05	.02
❑ 368	Mike Aldrete	.05	.02
❑ 369	Tim Raines	.10	.05
❑ 370	Dave Martinez	.05	.02
❑ 371	Bob Ojeda	.05	.02
❑ 372	Ron Darling	.05	.02
❑ 373	Wally Whitehurst RC	.05	.02
❑ 374	Randy Myers	.10	.05
❑ 375	David Cone	.10	.05
❑ 376	Dwight Gooden	.10	.05
❑ 377	Sid Fernandez	.05	.02
❑ 378	Dave Proctor	.05	.02
❑ 379	Gary Carter	.10	.05
❑ 380	Keith Miller	.05	.02
❑ 381	Gregg Jefferies	.10	.05
❑ 382	Tim Teufel	.05	.02
❑ 383	Kevin Elster	.05	.02
❑ 384	Dave Magadan	.05	.02
❑ 385	Keith Hernandez	.10	.05
❑ 386	Mookie Wilson	.10	.05
❑ 387	Darryl Strawberry	.10	.05
❑ 388	Kevin McReynolds	.05	.02
❑ 389	Mark Carreon	.05	.02
❑ 390	Jeff Parrett	.05	.02
❑ 391	Mike Maddux	.05	.02
❑ 392	Don Carman	.05	.02
❑ 393	Bruce Ruffin	.05	.02
❑ 394	Ken Howell	.05	.02
❑ 395	Steve Bedrosian	.05	.02
❑ 396	Floyd Youmans	.05	.02
❑ 397	Larry McWilliams	.05	.02
❑ 398	Pat Combs RC*	.05	.02
❑ 399	Steve Lake	.05	.02
❑ 400	Dickie Thon	.05	.02
❑ 401	Ricky Jordan RC*	.05	.02
❑ 402	Mike Schmidt	.40	.18
❑ 403	Tom Herr	.05	.02
❑ 404	Chris James	.05	.02
❑ 405	Juan Samuel	.05	.02
❑ 406	Von Hayes	.05	.02
❑ 407	Ron Jones	.05	.02
❑ 408	Curt Ford	.05	.02
❑ 409	Bob Walk	.05	.02
❑ 410	Jeff D. Robinson	.05	.02
❑ 411	Jim Gott	.05	.02
❑ 412	Scott Medvin	.05	.02
❑ 413	John Smiley	.05	.02
❑ 414	Bob Kipper	.05	.02
❑ 415	Brian Fisher	.05	.02
❑ 416	Doug Drabek	.05	.02
❑ 417	Mike LaValliere	.05	.02
❑ 418	Ken Oberkfell	.05	.02
❑ 419	Sid Bream	.05	.02
❑ 420	Austin Manahan	.05	.02
❑ 421	Jose Lind	.05	.02
❑ 422	Bobby Bonilla	.10	.05
❑ 423	Glenn Wilson	.05	.02
❑ 424	Andy Van Slyke	.10	.05
❑ 425	Gary Redus	.05	.02
❑ 426	Barry Bonds	.75	.35
❑ 427	Don Heinkel	.05	.02
❑ 428	Ken Dayley	.05	.02
❑ 429	Todd Worrell	.05	.02
❑ 430	Brad DuVall	.05	.02
❑ 431	Jose DeLeon	.05	.02
❑ 432	Joe Magrane	.05	.02
❑ 433	John Ericks	.05	.02
❑ 434	Frank DiPino	.05	.02
❑ 435	Tony Pena	.05	.02
❑ 436	Ozzie Smith	.25	.11
❑ 437	Terry Pendleton	.10	.05
❑ 438	Jose Oquendo	.05	.02
❑ 439	Tim Jones	.05	.02
❑ 440	Pedro Guerrero	.05	.02
❑ 441	Milt Thompson	.05	.02
❑ 442	Willie McGee	.10	.05
❑ 443	Vince Coleman	.05	.02
❑ 444	Tom Brunansky	.05	.02
❑ 445	Walt Terrell	.05	.02
❑ 446	Eric Show	.05	.02
❑ 447	Mark Davis	.05	.02
❑ 448	Andy Benes RC*	.10	.05
❑ 449	Ed Whitson	.05	.02
❑ 450	Dennis Rasmussen	.05	.02
❑ 451	Bruce Hurst	.05	.02
❑ 452	Pat Clements	.05	.02
❑ 453	Benito Santiago	.05	.02
❑ 454	Sandy Alomar Jr. RC	.25	.11
❑ 455	Garry Templeton	.05	.02
❑ 456	Jack Clark	.05	.02
❑ 457	Tim Flannery	.05	.02
❑ 458	Roberto Alomar	.30	.14
❑ 459	Carmelo Martinez	.05	.02
❑ 460	John Kruk	.10	.05
❑ 461	Tony Gwynn	.40	.18
❑ 462	Jerald Clark RC	.05	.02
❑ 463	Don Robinson	.05	.02
❑ 464	Craig Lefferts	.05	.02
❑ 465	Kelly Downs	.05	.02
❑ 466	Rick Reuschel	.05	.02
❑ 467	Scott Garrelts	.05	.02
❑ 468	Wil Tejada	.05	.02
❑ 469	Kirt Manwaring	.05	.02
❑ 470	Terry Kennedy	.05	.02
❑ 471	Jose Uribe	.05	.02
❑ 472	Royce Clayton RC	.25	.11
❑ 473	Robby Thompson	.05	.02
❑ 474	Kevin Mitchell	.10	.05
❑ 475	Ernie Riles	.05	.02
❑ 476	Will Clark	.20	.09
❑ 477	Donell Nixon	.05	.02
❑ 478	Candy Maldonado	.05	.02
❑ 479	Tracy Jones	.05	.02
❑ 480	Brett Butler	.10	.05
❑ 481	Checklist 1-121	.05	.02
❑ 482	Checklist 122-242	.05	.02
❑ 483	Checklist 243-363	.05	.02
❑ 484	Checklist 364-484	.05	.02

1990 Bowman

	MINT	NRMT
COMPLETE SET (528)	30.00	13.50
COMP.FACT.SET (528)	30.00	13.50

Card	Player	Mint	NRMT
❑ 1	Tommy Greene RC	.05	.02
❑ 2	Tom Glavine	.20	.09
❑ 3	Andy Nezelek	.05	.02
❑ 4	Mike Stanton RC	.05	.02
❑ 5	Rick Luecken	.05	.02
❑ 6	Kent Mercker RC	.05	.02
❑ 7	Derek Lilliquist	.05	.02
❑ 8	Charlie Leibrandt	.05	.02
❑ 9	Steve Avery	.05	.02
❑ 10	John Smoltz	.10	.05
❑ 11	Mark Lemke	.05	.02
❑ 12	Lonnie Smith	.05	.02
❑ 13	Oddibe McDowell	.05	.02
❑ 14	Tyler Houston RC	.15	.07
❑ 15	Jeff Blauser	.05	.02
❑ 16	Ernie Whitt	.05	.02
❑ 17	Alexis Infante	.05	.02
❑ 18	Jim Presley	.05	.02
❑ 19	Dale Murphy	.20	.09
❑ 20	Nick Esasky	.05	.02
❑ 21	Rick Sutcliffe	.10	.05
❑ 22	Mike Bielecki	.05	.02
❑ 23	Steve Wilson	.05	.02
❑ 24	Kevin Blankenship	.05	.02
❑ 25	Mitch Williams	.05	.02
❑ 26	Dean Wilkins	.05	.02
❑ 27	Greg Maddux	.50	.23
❑ 28	Mike Harkey	.05	.02
❑ 29	Mark Grace	.20	.09
❑ 30	Ryne Sandberg	.25	.11
❑ 31	Greg Smith	.05	.02
❑ 32	Dwight Smith	.05	.02
❑ 33	Damon Berryhill	.05	.02
❑ 34	E.Cunningham RC UER (Errant * by the word "in")	.05	.02
❑ 35	Jerome Walton	.05	.02
❑ 36	Lloyd McClendon	.05	.02
❑ 37	Ty Griffin	.05	.02
❑ 38	Shawon Dunston	.05	.02
❑ 39	Andre Dawson	.15	.07
❑ 40	Luis Salazar	.05	.02
❑ 41	Tim Layana	.05	.02
❑ 42	Rob Dibble	.05	.02
❑ 43	Tom Browning	.05	.02
❑ 44	Danny Jackson	.05	.02
❑ 45	Jose Rijo	.05	.02
❑ 46	Scott Scudder	.05	.02
❑ 47	Randy Myers UER (Career ERA .274, should be 2.74)	.10	.05
❑ 48	Brian Lane RC	.05	.02
❑ 49	Paul O'Neill	.20	.09
❑ 50	Barry Larkin	.20	.09
❑ 51	Reggie Jefferson RC	.20	.09
❑ 52	Jeff Branson RC**	.05	.02
❑ 53	Chris Sabo	.05	.02
❑ 54	Joe Oliver	.05	.02
❑ 55	Todd Benzinger	.05	.02
❑ 56	Rolando Roomes	.05	.02
❑ 57	Hal Morris	.05	.02
❑ 58	Eric Davis	.10	.05
❑ 59	Scott Bryant	.05	.02
❑ 60	Ken Griffey Sr.	.10	.05
❑ 61	Darryl Kile RC	.75	.35
❑ 62	Dave Smith	.05	.02
❑ 63	Mark Portugal	.05	.02
❑ 64	Jeff Juden RC	.05	.02
❑ 65	Bill Gullickson	.05	.02
❑ 66	Danny Darwin	.05	.02
❑ 67	Larry Andersen	.05	.02
❑ 68	Jose Cano	.05	.02
❑ 69	Dan Schatzeder	.05	.02
❑ 70	Jim Deshaies	.05	.02
❑ 71	Mike Scott	.05	.02
❑ 72	Gerald Young	.05	.02
❑ 73	Ken Caminiti	.10	.05
❑ 74	Ken Oberkfell	.05	.02
❑ 75	Dave Rohde	.05	.02
❑ 76	Bill Doran	.05	.02
❑ 77	Andujar Cedeno RC	.05	.02
❑ 78	Craig Biggio	.15	.07
❑ 79	Karl Rhodes RC	.05	.02
❑ 80	Glenn Davis	.05	.02
❑ 81	Eric Anthony RC	.05	.02
❑ 82	John Wetteland	.20	.09
❑ 83	Jay Howell	.05	.02
❑ 84	Orel Hershiser	.10	.05
❑ 85	Tim Belcher	.05	.02
❑ 86	Kiki Jones	.05	.02
❑ 87	Mike Hartley	.05	.02
❑ 88	Ramon Martinez	.05	.02
❑ 89	Mike Scioscia	.05	.02
❑ 90	Willie Randolph	.10	.05
❑ 91	Juan Samuel	.05	.02
❑ 92	Jose Offerman RC	.10	.05
❑ 93	Dave Hansen RC	.05	.02
❑ 94	Jeff Hamilton	.05	.02
❑ 95	Alfredo Griffin	.05	.02
❑ 96	Tom Goodwin RC	.20	.09
❑ 97	Kirk Gibson	.10	.05
❑ 98	Jose Vizcaino RC	.15	.07
❑ 99	Kal Daniels	.05	.02
❑ 100	Hubie Brooks	.05	.02
❑ 101	Eddie Murray	.20	.09
❑ 102	Dennis Boyd	.05	.02
❑ 103	Tim Burke	.05	.02
❑ 104	Bill Sampen	.05	.02
❑ 105	Brett Gideon	.05	.02
❑ 106	Mark Gardner RC	.05	.02

❑ 107 Howard Farmer .05 .02
❑ 108 Mel Rojas RC .10 .05
❑ 109 Kevin Gross .05 .02
❑ 110 Dave Schmidt .05 .02
❑ 111 Dennis Martinez .10 .05
❑ 112 Jerry Goff .05 .02
❑ 113 Andres Galarraga .15 .07
❑ 114 Tim Wallach .05 .02
❑ 115 Marquis Grissom RC .10 .05
❑ 116 Spike Owen .05 .02
❑ 117 Larry Walker RC 1.25 .55
❑ 118 Tim Raines .10 .05
❑ 119 Delino DeShields RC .20 .09
❑ 120 Tom Foley .05 .02
❑ 121 Dave Martinez .05 .02
❑ 122 Frank Viola UER .05 .02
(Career ERA .384
should be 3.84)
❑ 123 Julio Valera RC .05 .02
❑ 124 Alejandro Pena .05 .02
❑ 125 David Cone .10 .05
❑ 126 Dwight Gooden .10 .05
❑ 127 Kevin D. Brown .05 .02
❑ 128 John Franco .10 .05
❑ 129 Terry Bross .05 .02
❑ 130 Blaine Beatty .05 .02
❑ 131 Sid Fernandez .05 .02
❑ 132 Mike Marshall .05 .02
❑ 133 Howard Johnson .05 .02
❑ 134 Jaime Roseboro .05 .02
❑ 135 Alan Zinter RC .05 .02
❑ 136 Keith Miller .05 .02
❑ 137 Kevin Elster .05 .02
❑ 138 Kevin McReynolds .05 .02
❑ 139 Barry Lyons .05 .02
❑ 140 Gregg Jefferies .10 .05
❑ 141 Darryl Strawberry .10 .05
❑ 142 Todd Hundley RC .20 .09
❑ 143 Scott Service .05 .02
❑ 144 Chuck Malone .05 .02
❑ 145 Steve Ontiveros .05 .02
❑ 146 Roger McDowell .05 .02
❑ 147 Ken Howell .05 .02
❑ 148 Pat Combs .05 .02
❑ 149 Jeff Parrett .05 .02
❑ 150 Chuck McElroy RC .05 .02
❑ 151 Jason Grimsley RC .05 .02
❑ 152 Len Dykstra .10 .05
❑ 153 M.Morandini RC .20 .09
❑ 154 John Kruk .10 .05
❑ 155 Dickie Thon .05 .02
❑ 156 Ricky Jordan .05 .02
❑ 157 Jeff Jackson RC .05 .02
❑ 158 Darren Daulton .10 .05
❑ 159 Tom Herr .05 .02
❑ 160 Von Hayes .05 .02
❑ 161 Dave Hollins RC .20 .09
❑ 162 Carmelo Martinez .05 .02
❑ 163 Bob Walk .05 .02
❑ 164 Doug Drabek .05 .02
❑ 165 Walt Terrell .05 .02
❑ 166 Bill Landrum .05 .02
❑ 167 Scott Ruskin .05 .02
❑ 168 Bob Patterson .05 .02
❑ 169 Bobby Bonilla .10 .05
❑ 170 Jose Lind .05 .02
❑ 171 Andy Van Slyke .10 .05
❑ 172 Mike LaValliere .05 .02
❑ 173 Willie Greene RC .10 .05
❑ 174 Jay Bell .10 .05
❑ 175 Sid Bream .05 .02
❑ 176 Tom Prince .05 .02
❑ 177 Wally Backman .05 .02
❑ 178 Moises Alou RC 1.00 .45
❑ 179 Steve Carter .05 .02
❑ 180 Gary Redus .05 .02
❑ 181 Barry Bonds .50 .23
❑ 182 Don Slaught UER .05 .02
(Card back shows
headings for a pitcher)
❑ 183 Joe Magrane .05 .02
❑ 184 Bryn Smith .05 .02
❑ 185 Todd Worrell .05 .02
❑ 186 Jose DeLeon .05 .02
❑ 187 Frank DiPino .05 .02
❑ 188 John Tudor .05 .02
❑ 189 Howard Hilton .05 .02
❑ 190 John Ericks .05 .02
❑ 191 Ken Dayley .05 .02
❑ 192 Ray Lankford RC .40 .18
❑ 193 Todd Zeile .10 .05
❑ 194 Willie McGee .10 .05
❑ 195 Ozzie Smith .25 .11
❑ 196 Milt Thompson .05 .02
❑ 197 Terry Pendleton .10 .05
❑ 198 Vince Coleman .05 .02
❑ 199 Paul Coleman RC .05 .02
❑ 200 Jose Oquendo .05 .02
❑ 201 Pedro Guerrero .05 .02
❑ 202 Tom Brunansky .05 .02
❑ 203 Roger Smithberg .05 .02
❑ 204 Eddie Whitson .05 .02
❑ 205 Dennis Rasmussen .05 .02
❑ 206 Craig Lefferts .05 .02
❑ 207 Andy Benes .05 .02
❑ 208 Bruce Hurst .05 .02
❑ 209 Eric Show .05 .02
❑ 210 Rafael Valdez .05 .02
❑ 211 Joey Cora .10 .05
❑ 212 Thomas Howard .05 .02
❑ 213 Rob Nelson .05 .02
❑ 214 Jack Clark .10 .05
❑ 215 Garry Templeton .05 .02
❑ 216 Fred Lynn .05 .02
❑ 217 Tony Gwynn .40 .18
❑ 218 Benito Santiago .05 .02
❑ 219 Mike Pagliarulo .05 .02
❑ 220 Joe Carter .10 .05
❑ 221 Roberto Alomar .20 .09
❑ 222 Bip Roberts .05 .02
❑ 223 Rick Reuschel .05 .02
❑ 224 Russ Swan .05 .02
❑ 225 Eric Gunderson .05 .02
❑ 226 Steve Bedrosian .05 .02
❑ 227 Mike Remlinger .05 .02
❑ 228 Scott Garrelts .05 .02
❑ 229 Ernie Camacho .05 .02
❑ 230 Andres Santana RC .05 .02
❑ 231 Will Clark .20 .09
❑ 232 Kevin Mitchell .05 .02
❑ 233 Robby Thompson .05 .02
❑ 234 Bill Bathe .05 .02
❑ 235 Tony Perezchica .05 .02
❑ 236 Gary Carter .15 .07
❑ 237 Brett Butler .10 .05
❑ 238 Matt Williams .15 .07
❑ 239 Earnie Riles .05 .02
❑ 240 Kevin Bass .05 .02
❑ 241 Terry Kennedy .05 .02
❑ 242 Steve Hosey RC .05 .02
❑ 243 Ben McDonald RC .10 .05
❑ 244 Jeff Ballard .05 .02
❑ 245 Joe Price .05 .02
❑ 246 Curt Schilling 1.00 .45
❑ 247 Pete Harnisch .05 .02
❑ 248 Mark Williamson .05 .02
❑ 249 Gregg Olson .10 .05
❑ 250 Chris Myers .05 .02
❑ 251 David Segui RC ERR .40 .18
(Missing vital stats
at top of card back
under name)
❑ 251B David Segui COR RC .20 .09
❑ 252 Joe Orsulak .05 .02
❑ 253 Craig Worthington .05 .02
❑ 254 Mickey Tettleton .05 .02
❑ 255 Cal Ripken .75 .35
❑ 256 Bill Ripken .05 .02
❑ 257 Randy Milligan .05 .02
❑ 258 Brady Anderson .20 .09
❑ 259 Chris Hoiles RC UER .20 .09
Baltimore is spelled Balitmore
❑ 260 Mike Devereaux .05 .02
❑ 261 Phil Bradley .05 .02
❑ 262 Leo Gomez RC .05 .02
❑ 263 Lee Smith .10 .05
❑ 264 Mike Rochford .05 .02
❑ 265 Jeff Reardon .10 .05
❑ 266 Wes Gardner .05 .02
❑ 267 Mike Boddicker .05 .02
❑ 268 Roger Clemens .50 .23
❑ 269 Rob Murphy .05 .02
❑ 270 Mickey Pina .05 .02
❑ 271 Tony Pena .05 .02
❑ 272 Jody Reed .05 .02
❑ 273 Kevin Romine .05 .02
❑ 274 Mike Greenwell .05 .02
❑ 275 Maurice Vaughn RC .75 .35
❑ 276 Danny Heep .05 .02
❑ 277 Scott Cooper RC .05 .02
❑ 278 Greg Blosser RC .05 .02
❑ 279 Dwight Evans UER .10 .05
(* by "1990 Team
Breakdown")
❑ 280 Ellis Burks .15 .07
❑ 281 Wade Boggs .20 .09
❑ 282 Marty Barrett .05 .02
❑ 283 Kirk McCaskill .05 .02
❑ 284 Mark Langston .05 .02
❑ 285 Bert Blyleven .10 .05
❑ 286 Mike Fetters RC .05 .02
❑ 287 Kyle Abbott .05 .02
❑ 288 Jim Abbott .15 .07
❑ 289 Chuck Finley .10 .05
❑ 290 Gary DiSarcina RC .15 .07
❑ 291 Dick Schofield .05 .02
❑ 292 Devon White .05 .02
❑ 293 Bobby Rose .05 .02
❑ 294 Brian Downing .05 .02
❑ 295 Lance Parrish .05 .02
❑ 296 Jack Howell .05 .02
❑ 297 Claudell Washington .05 .02
❑ 298 John Orton RC .05 .02
❑ 299 Wally Joyner .10 .05
❑ 300 Lee Stevens .10 .05
❑ 301 Chili Davis .10 .05
❑ 302 Johnny Ray .05 .02
❑ 303 Greg Hibbard RC .05 .02
❑ 304 Eric King .05 .02
❑ 305 Jack McDowell .05 .02
❑ 306 Bobby Thigpen .05 .02
❑ 307 Adam Peterson .05 .02
❑ 308 Scott Radinsky RC .05 .02
❑ 309 Wayne Edwards .05 .02
❑ 310 Melido Perez .05 .02
❑ 311 Robin Ventura .20 .09
❑ 312 Sammy Sosa RC 6.00 2.70
❑ 313 Dan Pasqua .05 .02
❑ 314 Carlton Fisk .20 .09
❑ 315 Ozzie Guillen .05 .02
❑ 316 Ivan Calderon .05 .02
❑ 317 Daryl Boston .05 .02
❑ 318 Craig Grebeck RC .05 .02
❑ 319 Scott Fletcher .05 .02
❑ 320 Frank Thomas RC 3.00 1.35
❑ 321 Steve Lyons .05 .02
❑ 322 Carlos Martinez .05 .02
❑ 323 Joe Skalski .05 .02
❑ 324 Tom Candiotti .05 .02
❑ 325 Greg Swindell .05 .02
❑ 326 Steve Olin RC .10 .05
❑ 327 Kevin Wickander .05 .02
❑ 328 Doug Jones .05 .02
❑ 329 Jeff Shaw .05 .02
❑ 330 Kevin Bearse .05 .02
❑ 331 Dion James .05 .02
❑ 332 Jerry Browne .05 .02
❑ 333 Joey Belle .20 .09
❑ 334 Felix Fermin .05 .02
❑ 335 Candy Maldonado .05 .02
❑ 336 Cory Snyder .05 .02
❑ 337 Sandy Alomar Jr. .10 .05
❑ 338 Mark Lewis .05 .02
❑ 339 Carlos Baerga RC .10 .05
❑ 340 Chris James .05 .02
❑ 341 Brook Jacoby .05 .02
❑ 342 Keith Hernandez .10 .05
❑ 343 Frank Tanana .05 .02
❑ 344 Scott Aldred .05 .02
❑ 345 Mike Henneman .05 .02
❑ 346 Steve Wapnick .05 .02
❑ 347 Greg Gohr RC .05 .02
❑ 348 Eric Stone .05 .02
❑ 349 Brian DuBois .05 .02
❑ 350 Kevin Ritz .05 .02
❑ 351 Rico Brogna .20 .09
❑ 352 Mike Heath .05 .02
❑ 353 Alan Trammell .15 .07

Card	Player	MINT	NRMT
❑ 354	Chet Lemon	.05	.02
❑ 355	Dave Bergman	.05	.02
❑ 356	Lou Whitaker	.10	.05
❑ 357	Cecil Fielder UER * by 1990 Team Breakdown	.10	.05
❑ 358	Milt Cuyler RC	.05	.02
❑ 359	Tony Phillips	.05	.02
❑ 360	Travis Fryman RC	.40	.18
❑ 361	Ed Romero	.05	.02
❑ 362	Lloyd Moseby	.05	.02
❑ 363	Mark Gubicza	.05	.02
❑ 364	Bret Saberhagen	.10	.05
❑ 365	Tom Gordon	.10	.05
❑ 366	Steve Farr	.05	.02
❑ 367	Kevin Appier	.15	.07
❑ 368	Storm Davis	.05	.02
❑ 369	Mark Davis	.05	.02
❑ 370	Jeff Montgomery	.10	.05
❑ 371	Frank White	.10	.05
❑ 372	Brent Mayne RC	.05	.02
❑ 373	Bob Boone	.10	.05
❑ 374	Jim Eisenreich	.05	.02
❑ 375	Danny Tartabull	.05	.02
❑ 376	Kurt Stillwell	.05	.02
❑ 377	Bill Pecota	.05	.02
❑ 378	Bo Jackson	.10	.05
❑ 379	Bob Hamelin RC	.20	.09
❑ 380	Kevin Seitzer	.05	.02
❑ 381	Rey Palacios	.05	.02
❑ 382	George Brett	.40	.18
❑ 383	Gerald Perry	.05	.02
❑ 384	Teddy Higuera	.05	.02
❑ 385	Tom Filer	.05	.02
❑ 386	Dan Plesac	.05	.02
❑ 387	Cal Eldred RC	.10	.05
❑ 388	Jaime Navarro	.05	.02
❑ 389	Chris Bosio	.05	.02
❑ 390	Randy Veres	.05	.02
❑ 391	Gary Sheffield	.10	.05
❑ 392	George Canale	.05	.02
❑ 393	B.J. Surhoff	.10	.05
❑ 394	Tim McIntosh	.05	.02
❑ 395	Greg Brock	.05	.02
❑ 396	Greg Vaughn	.20	.09
❑ 397	Darryl Hamilton	.05	.02
❑ 398	Dave Parker	.10	.05
❑ 399	Paul Molitor	.20	.09
❑ 400	Jim Gantner	.05	.02
❑ 401	Rob Deer	.05	.02
❑ 402	Billy Spiers	.05	.02
❑ 403	Glenn Braggs	.05	.02
❑ 404	Robin Yount	.20	.09
❑ 405	Rick Aguilera	.10	.05
❑ 406	Johnny Ard	.05	.02
❑ 407	Kevin Tapani RC	.20	.09
❑ 408	Park Pittman	.05	.02
❑ 409	Allan Anderson	.05	.02
❑ 410	Juan Berenguer	.05	.02
❑ 411	Willie Banks RC	.05	.02
❑ 412	Rich Yett	.05	.02
❑ 413	Dave West	.05	.02
❑ 414	Greg Gagne	.05	.02
❑ 415	Chuck Knoblauch RC	.40	.18
❑ 416	Randy Bush	.05	.02
❑ 417	Gary Gaetti	.10	.05
❑ 418	Kent Hrbek	.10	.05
❑ 419	Al Newman	.05	.02
❑ 420	Danny Gladden	.05	.02
❑ 421	Paul Sorrento RC	.15	.07
❑ 422	Derek Parks RC	.05	.02
❑ 423	Scott Leius RC	.05	.02
❑ 424	Kirby Puckett	.50	.23
❑ 425	Willie Smith	.05	.02
❑ 426	Dave Righetti	.05	.02
❑ 427	Jeff D. Robinson	.05	.02
❑ 428	Alan Mills RC	.05	.02
❑ 429	Tim Leary	.05	.02
❑ 430	Pascual Perez	.05	.02
❑ 431	Alvaro Espinoza	.05	.02
❑ 432	Dave Winfield	.20	.09
❑ 433	Jesse Barfield	.05	.02
❑ 434	Randy Velarde	.05	.02
❑ 435	Rick Cerone	.05	.02
❑ 436	Steve Balboni	.05	.02
❑ 437	Mel Hall	.05	.02
❑ 438	Bob Geren	.05	.02

Card	Player	MINT	NRMT
❑ 439	Bernie Williams RC	2.00	.90
❑ 440	Kevin Maas RC	.10	.05
❑ 441	Mike Blowers RC	.10	.05
❑ 442	Steve Sax	.05	.02
❑ 443	Don Mattingly	.50	.23
❑ 444	Roberto Kelly	.05	.02
❑ 445	Mike Moore	.05	.02
❑ 446	Reggie Harris RC	.05	.02
❑ 447	Scott Sanderson	.05	.02
❑ 448	Dave Otto	.05	.02
❑ 449	Dave Stewart	.10	.05
❑ 450	Rick Honeycutt	.05	.02
❑ 451	Dennis Eckersley	.15	.07
❑ 452	Carney Lansford	.10	.05
❑ 453	Scott Hemond RC	.05	.02
❑ 454	Mark McGwire	.75	.35
❑ 455	Felix Jose	.05	.02
❑ 456	Terry Steinbach	.05	.02
❑ 457	Rickey Henderson	.40	.18
❑ 458	Dave Henderson	.05	.02
❑ 459	Mike Gallego	.05	.02
❑ 460	Jose Canseco	.20	.09
❑ 461	Walt Weiss	.05	.02
❑ 462	Ken Phelps	.05	.02
❑ 463	Darren Lewis RC	.05	.02
❑ 464	Ron Hassey	.05	.02
❑ 465	Roger Salkeld RC	.05	.02
❑ 466	Scott Bankhead	.05	.02
❑ 467	Keith Comstock	.05	.02
❑ 468	Randy Johnson	.40	.18
❑ 469	Erik Hanson	.05	.02
❑ 470	Mike Schooler	.05	.02
❑ 471	Gary Eave	.05	.02
❑ 472	Jeffrey Leonard	.05	.02
❑ 473	Dave Valle	.05	.02
❑ 474	Omar Vizquel	.20	.09
❑ 475	Pete O'Brien	.05	.02
❑ 476	Henry Cotto	.05	.02
❑ 477	Jay Buhner	.10	.05
❑ 478	Harold Reynolds	.05	.02
❑ 479	Alvin Davis	.05	.02
❑ 480	Darnell Coles	.05	.02
❑ 481	Ken Griffey Jr.	1.25	.55
❑ 482	Greg Briley	.05	.02
❑ 483	Scott Bradley	.05	.02
❑ 484	Tino Martinez	.20	.09
❑ 485	Jeff Russell	.05	.02
❑ 486	Nolan Ryan	1.00	.45
❑ 487	Robb Nen RC	.75	.35
❑ 488	Kevin Brown	.20	.09
❑ 489	Brian Bohanon RC	.05	.02
❑ 490	Ruben Sierra	.05	.02
❑ 491	Pete Incaviglia	.05	.02
❑ 492	Juan Gonzalez RC	2.50	1.10
❑ 493	Steve Buechele	.05	.02
❑ 494	Scott Coolbaugh	.05	.02
❑ 495	Geno Petralli	.05	.02
❑ 496	Rafael Palmeiro	.20	.09
❑ 497	Julio Franco	.05	.02
❑ 498	Gary Pettis	.05	.02
❑ 499	Donald Harris	.05	.02
❑ 500	Monty Fariss	.05	.02
❑ 501	Harold Baines	.10	.05
❑ 502	Cecil Espy	.05	.02
❑ 503	Jack Daugherty	.05	.02
❑ 504	Willie Blair RC	.05	.02
❑ 505	Dave Stieb	.10	.05
❑ 506	Tom Henke	.05	.02
❑ 507	John Cerutti	.05	.02
❑ 508	Paul Kilgus	.05	.02
❑ 509	Jimmy Key	.10	.05
❑ 510	John Olerud RC	1.00	.45
❑ 511	Ed Sprague	.10	.05
❑ 512	Manuel Lee	.05	.02
❑ 513	Fred McGriff	.20	.09
❑ 514	Glenallen Hill	.05	.02
❑ 515	George Bell	.05	.02
❑ 516	Mookie Wilson	.10	.05
❑ 517	Luis Sojo RC	.05	.02
❑ 518	Nelson Liriano	.05	.02
❑ 519	Kelly Gruber	.05	.02
❑ 520	Greg Myers	.05	.02
❑ 521	Pat Borders	.05	.02
❑ 522	Junior Felix	.05	.02
❑ 523	Eddie Zosky RC	.05	.02
❑ 524	Tony Fernandez	.05	.02
❑ 525	Checklist 1-132 UER (No copyright mark on the back)	.05	.02
❑ 526	Checklist 133-264	.05	.02
❑ 527	Checklist 265-396	.05	.02
❑ 528	Checklist 397-528	.05	.02

1991 Bowman

	MINT	NRMT
COMPLETE SET (704)	40.00	18.00
COMP.FACT.SET (704)	50.00	22.00

Card	Player	MINT	NRMT
❑ 1	Rod Carew I	.20	.09
❑ 2	Rod Carew II	.20	.09
❑ 3	Rod Carew III	.20	.09
❑ 4	Rod Carew IV	.20	.09
❑ 5	Rod Carew V	.20	.09
❑ 6	Willie Fraser	.05	.02
❑ 7	John Olerud	.15	.07
❑ 8	William Suero	.05	.02
❑ 9	Roberto Alomar	.20	.09
❑ 10	Todd Stottlemyre	.05	.02
❑ 11	Joe Carter	.10	.05
❑ 12	Steve Karsay RC	.10	.05
❑ 13	Mark Whiten	.05	.02
❑ 14	Pat Borders	.05	.02
❑ 15	Mike Timlin RC	.10	.05
❑ 16	Tom Henke	.05	.02
❑ 17	Eddie Zosky	.05	.02
❑ 18	Kelly Gruber	.05	.02
❑ 19	Jimmy Key	.10	.05
❑ 20	Jerry Schunk	.05	.02
❑ 21	Manuel Lee	.05	.02
❑ 22	Dave Stieb	.05	.02
❑ 23	Pat Hentgen RC	.10	.05
❑ 24	Glenallen Hill	.05	.02
❑ 25	Rene Gonzales	.05	.02
❑ 26	Ed Sprague	.05	.02
❑ 27	Ken Dayley	.05	.02
❑ 28	Pat Tabler	.05	.02
❑ 29	Denis Boucher RC	.05	.02
❑ 30	Devon White	.05	.02
❑ 31	Dante Bichette	.10	.05
❑ 32	Paul Molitor	.20	.09
❑ 33	Greg Vaughn	.10	.05
❑ 34	Dan Plesac	.05	.02
❑ 35	Chris George RC	.05	.02
❑ 36	Tim McIntosh	.05	.02
❑ 37	Franklin Stubbs	.05	.02
❑ 38	Bo Dodson RC	.05	.02
❑ 39	Ron Robinson	.05	.02
❑ 40	Ed Nunez	.05	.02
❑ 41	Greg Brock	.05	.02
❑ 42	Jaime Navarro	.05	.02
❑ 43	Chris Bosio	.05	.02
❑ 44	B.J. Surhoff	.10	.05
❑ 45	Chris Johnson	.05	.02
❑ 46	Willie Randolph	.10	.05
❑ 47	Narciso Elvira	.05	.02
❑ 48	Jim Gantner	.05	.02
❑ 49	Kevin Brown	.10	.05
❑ 50	Julio Machado	.05	.02
❑ 51	Chuck Crim	.05	.02
❑ 52	Gary Sheffield	.10	.05
❑ 53	Angel Miranda RC	.05	.02
❑ 54	Ted Higuera	.05	.02
❑ 55	Robin Yount	.20	.09

Card	Player	Price 1	Price 2
❑ 56	Cal Eldred	.05	.02
❑ 57	Sandy Alomar Jr.	.10	.05
❑ 58	Greg Swindell	.05	.02
❑ 59	Brook Jacoby	.05	.02
❑ 60	Efrain Valdez	.05	.02
❑ 61	Ever Magallanes	.05	.02
❑ 62	Tom Candiotti	.05	.02
❑ 63	Eric King	.05	.02
❑ 64	Alex Cole	.05	.02
❑ 65	Charles Nagy	.05	.02
❑ 66	Mitch Webster	.05	.02
❑ 67	Chris James	.05	.02
❑ 68	Jim Thome RC	2.50	1.10
❑ 69	Carlos Baerga	.05	.02
❑ 70	Mark Lewis	.05	.02
❑ 71	Jerry Browne	.05	.02
❑ 72	Jesse Orosco	.05	.02
❑ 73	Mike Huff	.05	.02
❑ 74	Jose Escobar	.05	.02
❑ 75	Jeff Manto	.05	.02
❑ 76	Turner Ward RC	.10	.05
❑ 77	Doug Jones	.05	.02
❑ 78	Bruce Egloff	.05	.02
❑ 79	Tim Costo RC	.05	.02
❑ 80	Beau Allred	.05	.02
❑ 81	Albert Belle	.10	.05
❑ 82	John Farrell	.05	.02
❑ 83	Glenn Davis	.05	.02
❑ 84	Joe Orsulak	.05	.02
❑ 85	Mark Williamson	.05	.02
❑ 86	Ben McDonald	.05	.02
❑ 87	Billy Ripken	.05	.02
❑ 88	Leo Gomez UER Baltimore is spelled Balitmore	.05	.02
❑ 89	Bob Melvin	.05	.02
❑ 90	Jeff M. Robinson	.05	.02
❑ 91	Jose Mesa	.05	.02
❑ 92	Gregg Olson	.05	.02
❑ 93	Mike Devereaux	.05	.02
❑ 94	Luis Mercedes RC	.05	.02
❑ 95	Arthur Rhodes RC	.10	.05
❑ 96	Juan Bell	.05	.02
❑ 97	Mike Mussina RC	2.50	1.10
❑ 98	Jeff Ballard	.05	.02
❑ 99	Chris Hoiles	.05	.02
❑ 100	Brady Anderson	.10	.05
❑ 101	Bob Milacki	.05	.02
❑ 102	David Segui	.05	.02
❑ 103	Dwight Evans	.10	.05
❑ 104	Cal Ripken	.75	.35
❑ 105	Mike Linskey	.05	.02
❑ 106	Jeff Tackett RC	.05	.02
❑ 107	Jeff Reardon	.10	.05
❑ 108	Dana Kiecker	.05	.02
❑ 109	Ellis Burks	.10	.05
❑ 110	Dave Owen	.05	.02
❑ 111	Danny Darwin	.05	.02
❑ 112	Mo Vaughn	.10	.05
❑ 113	Jeff McNeely RC	.05	.02
❑ 114	Tom Bolton	.05	.02
❑ 115	Greg Blosser	.05	.02
❑ 116	Mike Greenwell	.05	.02
❑ 117	Phil Plantier RC	.05	.02
❑ 118	Roger Clemens	.50	.23
❑ 119	John Marzano	.05	.02
❑ 120	Jody Reed	.05	.02
❑ 121	Scott Taylor	.05	.02
❑ 122	Jack Clark	.10	.05
❑ 123	Derek Livernois	.05	.02
❑ 124	Tony Pena	.05	.02
❑ 125	Tom Brunansky	.05	.02
❑ 126	Carlos Quintana	.05	.02
❑ 127	Tim Naehring	.05	.02
❑ 128	Matt Young	.05	.02
❑ 129	Wade Boggs	.20	.09
❑ 130	Kevin Morton	.05	.02
❑ 131	Pete Incaviglia	.05	.02
❑ 132	Rob Deer	.05	.02
❑ 133	Bill Gullickson	.05	.02
❑ 134	Rico Brogna	.05	.02
❑ 135	Lloyd Moseby	.05	.02
❑ 136	Cecil Fielder	.10	.05
❑ 137	Tony Phillips	.05	.02
❑ 138	Mark Leiter RC	.05	.02
❑ 139	John Cerutti	.05	.02
❑ 140	Mickey Tettleton	.05	.02
❑ 141	Milt Cuyler	.05	.02
❑ 142	Greg Gohr	.05	.02
❑ 143	Tony Bernazard	.05	.02
❑ 144	Dan Gakeler	.05	.02
❑ 145	Travis Fryman	.10	.05
❑ 146	Dan Petry	.05	.02
❑ 147	Scott Aldred	.05	.02
❑ 148	John DeSilva	.05	.02
❑ 149	Rusty Meacham RC	.05	.02
❑ 150	Lou Whitaker	.10	.05
❑ 151	Dave Haas	.05	.02
❑ 152	Luis de los Santos	.05	.02
❑ 153	Ivan Cruz	.05	.02
❑ 154	Alan Trammell	.15	.07
❑ 155	Pat Kelly RC	.05	.02
❑ 156	Carl Everett RC	1.00	.45
❑ 157	Greg Cadaret	.05	.02
❑ 158	Kevin Maas	.05	.02
❑ 159	Jeff Johnson	.05	.02
❑ 160	Willie Smith	.05	.02
❑ 161	Gerald Williams RC	.20	.09
❑ 162	Mike Humphreys RC	.05	.02
❑ 163	Alvaro Espinoza	.05	.02
❑ 164	Matt Nokes	.05	.02
❑ 165	Wade Taylor	.05	.02
❑ 166	Roberto Kelly	.05	.02
❑ 167	John Habyan	.05	.02
❑ 168	Steve Farr	.05	.02
❑ 169	Jesse Barfield	.05	.02
❑ 170	Steve Sax	.05	.02
❑ 171	Jim Leyritz	.05	.02
❑ 172	Robert Eenhoorn RC	.05	.02
❑ 173	Bernie Williams	.25	.11
❑ 174	Scott Lusader	.05	.02
❑ 175	Torey Lovullo	.05	.02
❑ 176	Chuck Cary	.05	.02
❑ 177	Scott Sanderson	.05	.02
❑ 178	Don Mattingly	.50	.23
❑ 179	Mel Hall	.05	.02
❑ 180	Juan Gonzalez	.25	.11
❑ 181	Hensley Meulens	.05	.02
❑ 182	Jose Offerman	.05	.02
❑ 183	Jeff Bagwell RC	4.00	1.80
❑ 184	Jeff Conine RC	.10	.05
❑ 185	Henry Rodriguez RC	.20	.09
❑ 186	Jimmie Reese CO	.10	.05
❑ 187	Kyle Abbott	.05	.02
❑ 188	Lance Parrish	.10	.05
❑ 189	Rafael Montalvo	.05	.02
❑ 190	Floyd Bannister	.05	.02
❑ 191	Dick Schofield	.05	.02
❑ 192	Scott Lewis	.05	.02
❑ 193	Jeff D. Robinson	.05	.02
❑ 194	Kent Anderson	.05	.02
❑ 195	Wally Joyner	.10	.05
❑ 196	Chuck Finley	.10	.05
❑ 197	Luis Sojo	.05	.02
❑ 198	Jeff Richardson	.05	.02
❑ 199	Dave Parker	.10	.05
❑ 200	Jim Abbott	.10	.05
❑ 201	Junior Felix	.05	.02
❑ 202	Mark Langston	.05	.02
❑ 203	Tim Salmon RC	1.00	.45
❑ 204	Cliff Young	.05	.02
❑ 205	Scott Bailes	.05	.02
❑ 206	Bobby Rose	.05	.02
❑ 207	Gary Gaetti	.10	.05
❑ 208	Ruben Amaro RC	.05	.02
❑ 209	Luis Polonia	.05	.02
❑ 210	Dave Winfield	.20	.09
❑ 211	Bryan Harvey	.05	.02
❑ 212	Mike Moore	.05	.02
❑ 213	Rickey Henderson	.40	.18
❑ 214	Steve Chitren	.05	.02
❑ 215	Bob Welch	.05	.02
❑ 216	Terry Steinbach	.05	.02
❑ 217	Earnest Riles	.05	.02
❑ 218	Todd Van Poppel RC	.05	.02
❑ 219	Mike Gallego	.05	.02
❑ 220	Curt Young	.05	.02
❑ 221	Todd Burns	.05	.02
❑ 222	Vance Law	.05	.02
❑ 223	Eric Show	.05	.02
❑ 224	Don Peters	.05	.02
❑ 225	Dave Stewart	.10	.05
❑ 226	Dave Henderson	.05	.02
❑ 227	Jose Canseco	.20	.09
❑ 228	Walt Weiss	.05	.02
❑ 229	Dann Howitt	.05	.02
❑ 230	Willie Wilson	.05	.02
❑ 231	Harold Baines	.10	.05
❑ 232	Scott Hemond	.05	.02
❑ 233	Joe Slusarski	.05	.02
❑ 234	Mark McGwire	.75	.35
❑ 235	K.Dressendorfer RC	.05	.02
❑ 236	Craig Paquette RC	.10	.05
❑ 237	Dennis Eckersley	.10	.05
❑ 238	Dana Allison	.05	.02
❑ 239	Scott Bradley	.05	.02
❑ 240	Brian Holman	.05	.02
❑ 241	Mike Schooler	.05	.02
❑ 242	Rich DeLucia	.05	.02
❑ 243	Edgar Martinez	.15	.07
❑ 244	Henry Cotto	.05	.02
❑ 245	Omar Vizquel	.10	.05
❑ 246	Ken Griffey Jr. (See also 255)	.75	.35
❑ 247	Jay Buhner	.10	.05
❑ 248	Bill Krueger	.05	.02
❑ 249	Dave Fleming RC	.05	.02
❑ 250	Patrick Lennon	.05	.02
❑ 251	Dave Valle	.05	.02
❑ 252	Harold Reynolds	.05	.02
❑ 253	Randy Johnson	.30	.14
❑ 254	Scott Bankhead	.05	.02
❑ 255	Ken Griffey Sr. UER (Card number is 246)	.05	.02
❑ 256	Greg Briley	.05	.02
❑ 257	Tino Martinez	.10	.05
❑ 258	Alvin Davis	.05	.02
❑ 259	Pete O'Brien	.05	.02
❑ 260	Erik Hanson	.05	.02
❑ 261	Bret Boone RC	6.00	2.70
❑ 262	Roger Salkeld	.05	.02
❑ 263	Dave Burba RC	.10	.05
❑ 264	Kerry Woodson RC	.05	.02
❑ 265	Julio Franco	.10	.05
❑ 266	Dan Peltier RC	.05	.02
❑ 267	Jeff Russell	.05	.02
❑ 268	Steve Buechele	.05	.02
❑ 269	Donald Harris	.05	.02
❑ 270	Robb Nen	.05	.02
❑ 271	Rich Gossage	.10	.05
❑ 272	Ivan Rodriguez RC	3.00	1.35
❑ 273	Jeff Huson	.05	.02
❑ 274	Kevin Brown	.10	.05
❑ 275	Dan Smith RC	.05	.02
❑ 276	Gary Pettis	.05	.02
❑ 277	Jack Daugherty	.05	.02
❑ 278	Mike Jeffcoat	.05	.02
❑ 279	Brad Arnsberg	.05	.02
❑ 280	Nolan Ryan	1.00	.45
❑ 281	Eric McCray	.05	.02
❑ 282	Scott Chiamparino	.05	.02
❑ 283	Ruben Sierra	.05	.02
❑ 284	Geno Petralli	.05	.02
❑ 285	Monty Fariss	.05	.02
❑ 286	Rafael Palmeiro	.20	.09
❑ 287	Bobby Witt	.05	.02
❑ 288	Dean Palmer UER Photo is Dan Peltier	.10	.05
❑ 289	Tony Scruggs	.05	.02
❑ 290	Kenny Rogers	.05	.02
❑ 291	Bret Saberhagen	.10	.05
❑ 292	Brian McRae RC	.10	.05
❑ 293	Storm Davis	.05	.02
❑ 294	Danny Tartabull	.05	.02
❑ 295	David Howard	.05	.02
❑ 296	Mike Boddicker	.05	.02
❑ 297	Joel Johnston RC	.05	.02
❑ 298	Tim Spehr	.05	.02
❑ 299	Hector Wagner	.05	.02
❑ 300	George Brett	.40	.18
❑ 301	Mike Macfarlane	.05	.02
❑ 302	Kirk Gibson	.10	.05
❑ 303	Harvey Pulliam RC	.05	.02
❑ 304	Jim Eisenreich	.05	.02
❑ 305	Kevin Seitzer	.05	.02
❑ 306	Mark Davis	.05	.02
❑ 307	Kurt Stillwell	.05	.02
❑ 308	Jeff Montgomery	.05	.02
❑ 309	Kevin Appier	.10	.05

❑	310	Bob Hamelin	.05	.02
❑	311	Tom Gordon	.05	.02
❑	312	Kerwin Moore RC	.05	.02
❑	313	Hugh Walker	.05	.02
❑	314	Terry Shumpert	.05	.02
❑	315	Warren Cromartie	.05	.02
❑	316	Gary Thurman	.05	.02
❑	317	Steve Bedrosian	.05	.02
❑	318	Danny Gladden	.05	.02
❑	319	Jack Morris	.10	.05
❑	320	Kirby Puckett	.50	.23
❑	321	Kent Hrbek	.10	.05
❑	322	Kevin Tapani	.05	.02
❑	323	Denny Neagle RC	.20	.09
❑	324	Rich Garces RC	.05	.02
❑	325	Larry Casian	.05	.02
❑	326	Shane Mack	.05	.02
❑	327	Allan Anderson	.05	.02
❑	328	Junior Ortiz	.05	.02
❑	329	Paul Abbott RC	.50	.23
❑	330	Chuck Knoblauch	.10	.05
❑	331	Chili Davis	.10	.05
❑	332	Todd Ritchie RC	.10	.05
❑	333	Brian Harper	.05	.02
❑	334	Rick Aguilera	.10	.05
❑	335	Scott Erickson	.05	.02
❑	336	Pedro Munoz RC	.05	.02
❑	337	Scott Leius	.05	.02
❑	338	Greg Gagne	.05	.02
❑	339	Mike Pagliarulo	.05	.02
❑	340	Terry Leach	.05	.02
❑	341	Willie Banks	.05	.02
❑	342	Bobby Thigpen	.05	.02
❑	343	R.Hernandez RC	.10	.05
❑	344	Melido Perez	.05	.02
❑	345	Carlton Fisk	.20	.09
❑	346	Norberto Martin	.05	.02
❑	347	Johnny Ruffin RC	.05	.02
❑	348	Jeff Carter	.05	.02
❑	349	Lance Johnson	.05	.02
❑	350	Sammy Sosa	.50	.23
❑	351	Alex Fernandez	.05	.02
❑	352	Jack McDowell	.05	.02
❑	353	Bob Wickman RC	.05	.02
❑	354	Wilson Alvarez	.05	.02
❑	355	Charlie Hough	.10	.05
❑	356	Ozzie Guillen	.05	.02
❑	357	Cory Snyder	.05	.02
❑	358	Robin Ventura	.10	.05
❑	359	Scott Fletcher	.05	.02
❑	360	Cesar Bernhardt	.05	.02
❑	361	Dan Pasqua	.05	.02
❑	362	Tim Raines	.10	.05
❑	363	Brian Drahman	.05	.02
❑	364	Wayne Edwards	.05	.02
❑	365	Scott Radinsky	.05	.02
❑	366	Frank Thomas	.30	.14
❑	367	Cecil Fielder SLUG	.05	.02
❑	368	Julio Franco SLUG	.05	.02
❑	369	Kelly Gruber SLUG	.05	.02
❑	370	Alan Trammell SLUG	.10	.05
❑	371	R.Henderson SLUG	.20	.09
❑	372	Jose Canseco SLUG	.10	.05
❑	373	Ellis Burks SLUG	.05	.02
❑	374	Lance Parrish SLUG	.05	.02
❑	375	Dave Parker SLUG	.05	.02
❑	376	Eddie Murray SLUG	.10	.05
❑	377	Ryne Sandberg SLUG	.15	.07
❑	378	Matt Williams SLUG	.10	.05
❑	379	Barry Larkin SLUG	.10	.05
❑	380	Barry Bonds SLUG	.25	.11
❑	381	Bobby Bonilla SLUG	.05	.02
❑	382	D.Strawberry SLUG	.05	.02
❑	383	Benny Santiago SLUG	.05	.02
❑	384	Don Robinson SLUG	.05	.02
❑	385	Paul Coleman	.05	.02
❑	386	Milt Thompson	.05	.02
❑	387	Lee Smith	.10	.05
❑	388	Ray Lankford	.10	.05
❑	389	Tom Pagnozzi	.05	.02
❑	390	Ken Hill	.05	.02
❑	391	Jamie Moyer	.05	.02
❑	392	Greg Carmona	.05	.02
❑	393	John Ericks	.05	.02
❑	394	Bob Tewksbury	.05	.02
❑	395	Jose Oquendo	.05	.02
❑	396	Rheal Cormier RC	.05	.02
❑	397	Mike Milchin	.05	.02
❑	398	Ozzie Smith	.25	.11
❑	399	Aaron Holbert RC	.05	.02
❑	400	Jose DeLeon	.05	.02
❑	401	Felix Jose	.05	.02
❑	402	Juan Agosto	.05	.02
❑	403	Pedro Guerrero	.10	.05
❑	404	Todd Zeile	.05	.02
❑	405	Gerald Perry	.05	.02
❑	406	D.Osborne UER RC Card number is 410	.10	.05
❑	407	Bryn Smith	.05	.02
❑	408	Bernard Gilkey	.05	.02
❑	409	Rex Hudler	.05	.02
❑	410	Bobby Thomson Ralph Branca Shot Heard Round the World See also 406	.20	.09
❑	411	Lance Dickson RC	.05	.02
❑	412	Danny Jackson	.05	.02
❑	413	Jerome Walton	.05	.02
❑	414	Sean Cheetham	.05	.02
❑	415	Joe Girardi	.05	.02
❑	416	Ryne Sandberg	.25	.11
❑	417	Mike Harkey	.05	.02
❑	418	George Bell	.05	.02
❑	419	Rick Wilkins RC	.05	.02
❑	420	Earl Cunningham	.05	.02
❑	421	H.Slocumb RC	.10	.05
❑	422	Mike Bielecki	.05	.02
❑	423	Jessie Hollins RC	.05	.02
❑	424	Shawon Dunston	.05	.02
❑	425	Dave Smith	.05	.02
❑	426	Greg Maddux	.50	.23
❑	427	Jose Vizcaino	.05	.02
❑	428	Luis Salazar	.05	.02
❑	429	Andre Dawson	.15	.07
❑	430	Rick Sutcliffe	.10	.05
❑	431	Paul Assenmacher	.05	.02
❑	432	Erik Pappas	.05	.02
❑	433	Mark Grace	.20	.09
❑	434	Dennis Martinez	.10	.05
❑	435	Marquis Grissom	.05	.02
❑	436	Wil Cordero RC	.10	.05
❑	437	Tim Wallach	.05	.02
❑	438	Brian Barnes	.05	.02
❑	439	Barry Jones	.05	.02
❑	440	Ivan Calderon	.05	.02
❑	441	Stan Spencer	.05	.02
❑	442	Larry Walker	.15	.07
❑	443	Chris Haney RC	.05	.02
❑	444	Hector Rivera	.05	.02
❑	445	Delino DeShields	.10	.05
❑	446	Andres Galarraga	.15	.07
❑	447	Gilberto Reyes	.05	.02
❑	448	Willie Greene	.05	.02
❑	449	Greg Colbrunn RC	.10	.05
❑	450	Rondell White RC	.75	.35
❑	451	Steve Frey	.05	.02
❑	452	Shane Andrews RC	.10	.05
❑	453	Mike Fitzgerald	.05	.02
❑	454	Spike Owen	.05	.02
❑	455	Dave Martinez	.05	.02
❑	456	Dennis Boyd	.05	.02
❑	457	Eric Bullock	.05	.02
❑	458	Reid Cornelius RC	.05	.02
❑	459	Chris Nabholz	.05	.02
❑	460	David Cone	.10	.05
❑	461	Hubie Brooks	.05	.02
❑	462	Sid Fernandez	.05	.02
❑	463	Doug Simons	.05	.02
❑	464	Howard Johnson	.05	.02
❑	465	Chris Donnels	.05	.02
❑	466	Anthony Young RC	.05	.02
❑	467	Todd Hundley	.05	.02
❑	468	Rick Cerone	.05	.02
❑	469	Kevin Elster	.05	.02
❑	470	Wally Whitehurst	.05	.02
❑	471	Vince Coleman	.05	.02
❑	472	Dwight Gooden	.10	.05
❑	473	Charlie O'Brien	.05	.02
❑	474	Jeromy Burnitz RC	1.00	.45
❑	475	John Franco	.10	.05
❑	476	Daryl Boston	.05	.02
❑	477	Frank Viola	.10	.05
❑	478	D.J. Dozier	.05	.02
❑	479	Kevin McReynolds	.05	.02
❑	480	Tom Herr	.05	.02
❑	481	Gregg Jefferies	.05	.02
❑	482	Pete Schourek RC	.05	.02
❑	483	Ron Darling	.05	.02
❑	484	Dave Magadan	.05	.02
❑	485	Andy Ashby RC	.20	.09
❑	486	Dale Murphy	.20	.09
❑	487	Von Hayes	.05	.02
❑	488	Kim Batiste RC	.05	.02
❑	489	Tony Longmire RC	.05	.02
❑	490	Wally Backman	.05	.02
❑	491	Jeff Jackson	.05	.02
❑	492	Mickey Morandini	.05	.02
❑	493	Darrel Akerfelds	.05	.02
❑	494	Ricky Jordan	.05	.02
❑	495	Randy Ready	.05	.02
❑	496	Darrin Fletcher	.05	.02
❑	497	Chuck Malone	.05	.02
❑	498	Pat Combs	.05	.02
❑	499	Dickie Thon	.05	.02
❑	500	Roger McDowell	.05	.02
❑	501	Len Dykstra	.10	.05
❑	502	Joe Boever	.05	.02
❑	503	John Kruk	.10	.05
❑	504	Terry Mulholland	.05	.02
❑	505	Wes Chamberlain RC	.05	.02
❑	506	Mike Lieberthal RC	1.00	.45
❑	507	Darren Daulton	.10	.05
❑	508	Charlie Hayes	.05	.02
❑	509	John Smiley	.05	.02
❑	510	Gary Varsho	.05	.02
❑	511	Curt Wilkerson	.05	.02
❑	512	Orlando Merced RC	.05	.02
❑	513	Barry Bonds	.50	.23
❑	514	Mike LaValliere	.05	.02
❑	515	Doug Drabek	.05	.02
❑	516	Gary Redus	.05	.02
❑	517	W.Pennyfeather RC	.05	.02
❑	518	Randy Tomlin RC	.05	.02
❑	519	Mike Zimmerman RC	.05	.02
❑	520	Jeff King	.05	.02
❑	521	Kurt Miller RC	.05	.02
❑	522	Jay Bell	.10	.05
❑	523	Bill Landrum	.05	.02
❑	524	Zane Smith	.05	.02
❑	525	Bobby Bonilla	.10	.05
❑	526	Bob Walk	.05	.02
❑	527	Austin Manahan	.05	.02
❑	528	Joe Ausanio	.05	.02
❑	529	Andy Van Slyke	.10	.05
❑	530	Jose Lind	.05	.02
❑	531	Carlos Garcia RC	.05	.02
❑	532	Don Slaught	.05	.02
❑	533	Gen.Colin Powell	.50	.23
❑	534	Frank Bolick RC	.05	.02
❑	535	Gary Scott	.05	.02
❑	536	Nikco Riesgo	.05	.02
❑	537	Reggie Sanders RC	1.00	.45
❑	538	Tim Howard RC	.05	.02
❑	539	Ryan Bowen RC	.05	.02
❑	540	Eric Anthony	.05	.02
❑	541	Jim Deshaies	.05	.02
❑	542	Tom Nevers RC	.05	.02
❑	543	Ken Caminiti	.10	.05
❑	544	Karl Rhodes	.05	.02
❑	545	Xavier Hernandez	.05	.02
❑	546	Mike Scott	.05	.02
❑	547	Jeff Juden	.05	.02
❑	548	Darryl Kile	.10	.05
❑	549	Willie Ansley	.05	.02
❑	550	Luis Gonzalez RC	4.00	1.80
❑	551	Mike Simms	.05	.02
❑	552	Mark Portugal	.05	.02
❑	553	Jimmy Jones	.05	.02
❑	554	Jim Clancy	.05	.02
❑	555	Pete Harnisch	.05	.02
❑	556	Craig Biggio	.15	.07
❑	557	Eric Yelding	.05	.02
❑	558	Dave Rohde	.05	.02
❑	559	Casey Candaele	.05	.02
❑	560	Curt Schilling	.20	.09
❑	561	Steve Finley	.10	.05
❑	562	Javier Ortiz	.05	.02
❑	563	Andujar Cedeno	.05	.02

	No.	Player	MINT	NRMT
❑	564	Rafael Ramirez	.05	.02
❑	565	Kenny Lofton RC	1.00	.45
❑	566	Steve Avery	.05	.02
❑	567	Lonnie Smith	.05	.02
❑	568	Kent Mercker	.05	.02
❑	569	Chipper Jones RC	5.00	2.20
❑	570	Terry Pendleton	.10	.05
❑	571	Otis Nixon	.05	.02
❑	572	Juan Berenguer	.05	.02
❑	573	Charlie Leibrandt	.05	.02
❑	574	David Justice	.20	.09
❑	575	Keith Mitchell RC	.05	.02
❑	576	Tom Glavine	.20	.09
❑	577	Greg Olson	.05	.02
❑	578	Rafael Belliard	.05	.02
❑	579	Ben Rivera RC	.05	.02
❑	580	John Smoltz	.10	.05
❑	581	Tyler Houston	.05	.02
❑	582	Mark Wohlers RC	.10	.05
❑	583	Ron Gant	.05	.02
❑	584	Ramon Caraballo RC	.05	.02
❑	585	Sid Bream	.05	.02
❑	586	Jeff Treadway	.05	.02
❑	587	Javy Lopez RC	1.00	.45
❑	588	Deion Sanders	.10	.05
❑	589	Mike Heath	.05	.02
❑	590	Ryan Klesko RC	1.50	.70
❑	591	Bob Ojeda	.05	.02
❑	592	Alfredo Griffin	.05	.02
❑	593	Raul Mondesi RC	1.00	.45
❑	594	Greg Smith	.05	.02
❑	595	Orel Hershiser	.10	.05
❑	596	Juan Samuel	.05	.02
❑	597	Brett Butler	.10	.05
❑	598	Gary Carter	.15	.07
❑	599	Stan Javier	.05	.02
❑	600	Kal Daniels	.05	.02
❑	601	Jamie McAndrew RC	.05	.02
❑	602	Mike Sharperson	.05	.02
❑	603	Jay Howell	.05	.02
❑	604	Eric Karros RC	1.00	.45
❑	605	Tim Belcher	.05	.02
❑	606	Dan Opperman	.05	.02
❑	607	Lenny Harris	.05	.02
❑	608	Tom Goodwin	.05	.02
❑	609	Darryl Strawberry	.10	.05
❑	610	Ramon Martinez	.05	.02
❑	611	Kevin Gross	.05	.02
❑	612	Zakary Shinall	.05	.02
❑	613	Mike Scioscia	.05	.02
❑	614	Eddie Murray	.20	.09
❑	615	Ronnie Walden RC	.05	.02
❑	616	Will Clark	.20	.09
❑	617	Adam Hyzdu RC	.05	.02
❑	618	Matt Williams	.15	.07
❑	619	Don Robinson	.05	.02
❑	620	Jeff Brantley	.05	.02
❑	621	Greg Litton	.05	.02
❑	622	Steve Decker	.05	.02
❑	623	Robby Thompson	.05	.02
❑	624	Mark Leonard	.05	.02
❑	625	Kevin Bass	.05	.02
❑	626	Scott Garrelts	.05	.02
❑	627	Jose Uribe	.05	.02
❑	628	Eric Gunderson	.05	.02
❑	629	Steve Hosey	.05	.02
❑	630	Trevor Wilson	.05	.02
❑	631	Terry Kennedy	.05	.02
❑	632	Dave Righetti	.10	.05
❑	633	Kelly Downs	.05	.02
❑	634	Johnny Ard	.05	.02
❑	635	E.Christopherson RC	.05	.02
❑	636	Kevin Mitchell	.05	.02
❑	637	John Burkett	.05	.02
❑	638	Kevin Rogers RC	.05	.02
❑	639	Bud Black	.05	.02
❑	640	Willie McGee	.10	.05
❑	641	Royce Clayton	.05	.02
❑	642	Tony Fernandez	.05	.02
❑	643	Ricky Bones RC	.05	.02
❑	644	Thomas Howard	.05	.02
❑	645	Dave Staton RC	.05	.02
❑	646	Jim Presley	.05	.02
❑	647	Tony Gwynn	.40	.18
❑	648	Marty Barrett	.05	.02
❑	649	Scott Coolbaugh	.05	.02
❑	650	Craig Lefferts	.05	.02
❑	651	Eddie Whitson	.05	.02
❑	652	Oscar Azocar	.05	.02
❑	653	Wes Gardner	.05	.02
❑	654	Bip Roberts	.05	.02
❑	655	Robbie Beckett RC	.05	.02
❑	656	Benito Santiago	.05	.02
❑	657	Greg W.Harris	.05	.02
❑	658	Jerald Clark	.05	.02
❑	659	Fred McGriff	.15	.07
❑	660	Larry Andersen	.05	.02
❑	661	Bruce Hurst	.05	.02
❑	662	Steve Martin UER Card said he pitched at Waterloo He's an outfielder	.05	.02
❑	663	Rafael Valdez	.05	.02
❑	664	Paul Faries	.05	.02
❑	665	Andy Benes	.05	.02
❑	666	Randy Myers	.05	.02
❑	667	Rob Dibble	.05	.02
❑	668	Glenn Sutko	.05	.02
❑	669	Glenn Braggs	.05	.02
❑	670	Billy Hatcher	.05	.02
❑	671	Joe Oliver	.05	.02
❑	672	Freddy Benavides	.05	.02
❑	673	Barry Larkin	.20	.09
❑	674	Chris Sabo	.05	.02
❑	675	Mariano Duncan	.05	.02
❑	676	Chris Jones RC	.05	.02
❑	677	Gino Minutelli	.05	.02
❑	678	Reggie Jefferson	.05	.02
❑	679	Jack Armstrong	.05	.02
❑	680	Chris Hammond	.05	.02
❑	681	Jose Rijo	.05	.02
❑	682	Bill Doran	.05	.02
❑	683	Terry Lee	.05	.02
❑	684	Tom Browning	.05	.02
❑	685	Paul O'Neill	.20	.09
❑	686	Eric Davis	.10	.05
❑	687	Dan Wilson RC	.20	.09
❑	688	Ted Power	.05	.02
❑	689	Tim Layana	.05	.02
❑	690	Norm Charlton	.05	.02
❑	691	Hal Morris	.05	.02
❑	692	Rickey Henderson	.20	.09
❑	693	Sam Militello RC	.05	.02
❑	694	Matt Mieske RC	.05	.02
❑	695	Paul Russo RC	.05	.02
❑	696	Domingo Mota	.05	.02
❑	697	Todd Guggiana RC	.05	.02
❑	698	Marc Newfield RC	.05	.02
❑	699	Checklist 1-122	.05	.02
❑	700	Checklist 123-244	.05	.02
❑	701	Checklist 245-366	.05	.02
❑	702	Checklist 367-471	.05	.02
❑	703	Checklist 472-593	.05	.02
❑	704	Checklist 594-704	.05	.02

1992 Bowman

			MINT	NRMT
		COMPLETE SET (705)	200.00	90.00
❑	1	Ivan Rodriguez	2.50	1.10
❑	2	Kirk McCaskill	.40	.18
❑	3	Scott Livingstone	.40	.18
❑	4	Salomon Torres RC	.40	.18
❑	5	Carlos Hernandez	.40	.18
❑	6	Dave Hollins	.40	.18
❑	7	Scott Fletcher	.40	.18
❑	8	Jorge Fabregas RC	.40	.18
❑	9	Andujar Cedeno	.40	.18
❑	10	Howard Johnson	.40	.18
❑	11	Trevor Hoffman RC	4.00	1.80
❑	12	Roberto Kelly	.40	.18
❑	13	Gregg Jefferies	.40	.18
❑	14	Marquis Grissom	.40	.18
❑	15	Mike Ignasiak	.40	.18
❑	16	Jack Morris	.60	.25
❑	17	William Pennyfeather	.40	.18
❑	18	Todd Stottlemyre	.40	.18
❑	19	Chito Martinez	.40	.18
❑	20	Roberto Alomar	1.50	.70
❑	21	Sam Militello	.40	.18
❑	22	Hector Fajardo RC	.40	.18

	No.	Player	MINT	NRMT
❑	23	Paul Quantrill RC	.40	.18
❑	24	Chuck Knoblauch	.60	.25
❑	25	Reggie Jefferson	.40	.18
❑	26	Jeremy McGarity RC	.40	.18
❑	27	Jerome Walton	.40	.18
❑	28	Chipper Jones	20.00	9.00
❑	29	Brian Barber RC	.40	.18
❑	30	Ron Darling	.40	.18
❑	31	Roberto Petagine RC	.40	.18
❑	32	Chuck Finley	.60	.25
❑	33	Edgar Martinez	1.00	.45
❑	34	Napoleon Robinson	.40	.18
❑	35	Andy Van Slyke	.60	.25
❑	36	Bobby Thigpen	.40	.18
❑	37	Travis Fryman	.60	.25
❑	38	Eric Christopherson	.40	.18
❑	39	Terry Mulholland	.40	.18
❑	40	Darryl Strawberry	.60	.25
❑	41	Manny Alexander RC	.40	.18
❑	42	Tracy Sanders RC	.40	.18
❑	43	Pete Incaviglia	.40	.18
❑	44	Kim Batiste	.40	.18
❑	45	Frank Rodriguez	.40	.18
❑	46	Greg Swindell	.40	.18
❑	47	Delino DeShields	.40	.18
❑	48	John Ericks	.40	.18
❑	49	Franklin Stubbs	.40	.18
❑	50	Tony Gwynn	3.00	1.35
❑	51	Clifton Garrett RC	.40	.18
❑	52	Mike Gardella	.40	.18
❑	53	Scott Erickson	.40	.18
❑	54	Gary Caraballo RC	.40	.18
❑	55	Jose Oliva RC	.40	.18
❑	56	Brook Fordyce	.40	.18
❑	57	Mark Whiten	.40	.18
❑	58	Joe Slusarski	.40	.18
❑	59	J.R. Phillips RC	.60	.25
❑	60	Barry Bonds	4.00	1.80
❑	61	Bob Milacki	.40	.18
❑	62	Keith Mitchell	.40	.18
❑	63	Angel Miranda	.40	.18
❑	64	Raul Mondesi	6.00	2.70
❑	65	Brian Koelling RC	.40	.18
❑	66	Brian McRae	.40	.18
❑	67	John Patterson	.40	.18
❑	68	John Wetteland	.60	.25
❑	69	Wilson Alvarez	.40	.18
❑	70	Wade Boggs	1.50	.70
❑	71	Darryl Ratliff RC	.40	.18
❑	72	Jeff Jackson	.40	.18
❑	73	Jeremy Hernandez RC	.40	.18
❑	74	Darryl Hamilton	.40	.18
❑	75	Rafael Belliard	.40	.18
❑	76	Rick Trlicek RC	.40	.18
❑	77	Felipe Crespo RC	.40	.18
❑	78	Carney Lansford	.60	.25
❑	79	Ryan Long RC	.40	.18
❑	80	Kirby Puckett	4.00	1.80
❑	81	Earl Cunningham	.40	.18
❑	82	Pedro Martinez	25.00	11.00
❑	83	Scott Hatteberg RC	.40	.18
❑	84	Juan Gonzalez UER (65 doubles vs. Tigers)	1.50	.70
❑	85	Robert Nutting RC	.40	.18
❑	86	Pokey Reese RC	2.00	.90
❑	87	Dave Silvestri	.40	.18
❑	88	Scott Ruffcorn RC	.40	.18

89	Rick Aguilera	.60	.25
90	Cecil Fielder	.60	.25
91	Kirk Dressendorfer	.40	.18
92	Jerry DiPoto RC	.40	.18
93	Mike Felder	.40	.18
94	Craig Paquette	.40	.18
95	Elvin Paulino RC	.40	.18
96	Donovan Osborne	.40	.18
97	Hubie Brooks	.40	.18
98	Derek Lowe RC	1.50	.70
99	David Zancanaro	.40	.18
100	Ken Griffey Jr.	5.00	2.20
101	Todd Hundley	.40	.18
102	Mike Trombley RC	.40	.18
103	Ricky Gutierrez RC	.40	.18
104	Braulio Castillo	.40	.18
105	Craig Lefferts	.40	.18
106	Rick Sutcliffe	.60	.25
107	Dean Palmer	.60	.25
108	Henry Rodriguez	.40	.18
109	Mark Clark RC	.60	.25
110	Kenny Lofton	2.00	.90
111	Mark Carreon	.40	.18
112	J.T. Bruett	.40	.18
113	Gerald Williams	.40	.18
114	Frank Thomas	2.00	.90
115	Kevin Reimer	.40	.18
116	Sammy Sosa	3.00	1.35
117	Mickey Tettleton	.40	.18
118	Reggie Sanders	.40	.18
119	Trevor Wilson	.40	.18
120	Cliff Brantley	.40	.18
121	Spike Owen	.40	.18
122	Jeff Montgomery	.40	.18
123	Alex Sutherland	.40	.18
124	Brien Taylor RC	.60	.25
125	Brian Williams RC	.40	.18
126	Kevin Seitzer	.40	.18
127	Carlos Delgado RC	20.00	9.00
128	Gary Scott	.40	.18
129	Scott Cooper	.40	.18
130	Domingo Jean RC	.40	.18
131	Pat Mahomes RC	.40	.18
132	Mike Boddicker	.40	.18
133	Roberto Hernandez	.40	.18
134	Dave Valle	.40	.18
135	Kurt Stillwell	.40	.18
136	Brad Pennington RC	.40	.18
137	Jermaine Swinton RC	.40	.18
138	Ryan Hawblitzel RC	.40	.18
139	Tito Navarro RC	.40	.18
140	Sandy Alomar Jr.	.60	.25
141	Todd Benzinger	.40	.18
142	Danny Jackson	.40	.18
143	Melvin Nieves RC	.40	.18
144	Jim Campanis	.40	.18
145	Luis Gonzalez	1.50	.70
146	D.Doorneweerd RC	.40	.18
147	Charlie Hayes	.40	.18
148	Greg Maddux	4.00	1.80
149	Brian Harper	.40	.18
150	Brent Miller RC	.40	.18
151	Shawn Estes RC	2.00	.90
152	Mike Williams RC	.40	.18
153	Charlie Hough	.60	.25
154	Randy Myers	.40	.18
155	Kevin Young RC	1.50	.70
156	Rick Wilkins	.40	.18
157	Terry Shumpert	.40	.18
158	Steve Karsay	.40	.18
159	Gary DiSarcina	.40	.18
160	Deion Sanders	.60	.25
161	Tom Browning	.40	.18
162	Dickie Thon	.40	.18
163	Luis Mercedes	.40	.18
164	Riccardo Ingram	.40	.18
165	Tavo Alvarez RC	.40	.18
166	Rickey Henderson	3.00	1.35
167	Jaime Navarro	.40	.18
168	Billy Ashley RC	.40	.18
169	Phil Dauphin RC	.40	.18
170	Ivan Cruz	.40	.18
171	Harold Baines	.60	.25
172	Bryan Harvey	.40	.18
173	Alex Cole	.40	.18
174	Curtis Shaw RC	.40	.18
175	Matt Williams	1.00	.45
176	Felix Jose	.40	.18
177	Sam Horn	.40	.18
178	Randy Johnson	2.00	.90
179	Ivan Calderon	.40	.18
180	Steve Avery	.40	.18
181	William Suero	.40	.18
182	Bill Swift	.40	.18
183	Howard Battle RC	.40	.18
184	Ruben Amaro	.40	.18
185	Jim Abbott	.60	.25
186	Mike Fitzgerald	.40	.18
187	Bruce Hurst	.40	.18
188	Jeff Juden	.40	.18
189	Jeromy Burnitz	2.00	.90
190	Dave Burba	.40	.18
191	Kevin Brown	.60	.25
192	Patrick Lennon	.40	.18
193	Jeff McNeely	.40	.18
194	Wil Cordero	.40	.18
195	Chili Davis	.60	.25
196	Milt Cuyler	.40	.18
197	Von Hayes	.40	.18
198	Todd Revenig RC	.40	.18
199	Joel Johnston	.40	.18
200	Jeff Bagwell	3.00	1.35
201	Alex Fernandez	.40	.18
202	Todd Jones RC	.60	.25
203	Charles Nagy	.40	.18
204	Tim Raines	.60	.25
205	Kevin Maas	.40	.18
206	Julio Franco	.60	.25
207	Randy Velarde	.40	.18
208	Lance Johnson	.40	.18
209	Scott Leius	.40	.18
210	Derek Lee	.40	.18
211	Joe Sondrini RC	.40	.18
212	Royce Clayton	.40	.18
213	Chris George	.40	.18
214	Gary Sheffield	.60	.25
215	Mark Gubicza	.40	.18
216	Mike Moore	.40	.18
217	Rick Huisman RC	.40	.18
218	Jeff Russell	.40	.18
219	D.J. Dozier	.40	.18
220	Dave Martinez	.40	.18
221	Alan Newman RC	.40	.18
222	Nolan Ryan	8.00	3.60
223	Teddy Higuera	.40	.18
224	Damon Buford RC	.40	.18
225	Ruben Sierra	.40	.18
226	Tom Nevers	.40	.18
227	Tommy Greene	.40	.18
228	Nigel Wilson RC	.40	.18
229	John DeSilva	.40	.18
230	Bobby Witt	.40	.18
231	Greg Cadaret	.40	.18
232	John Vander Wal RC	.40	.18
233	Jack Clark	.60	.25
234	Bill Doran	.40	.18
235	Bobby Bonilla	.60	.25
236	Steve Olin	.40	.18
237	Derek Bell	.60	.25
238	David Cone	.60	.25
239	Victor Cole	.40	.18
240	Rod Bolton RC	.40	.18
241	Tom Pagnozzi	.40	.18
242	Rob Dibble	.40	.18
243	Michael Carter RC	.40	.18
244	Don Peters	.40	.18
245	Mike LaValliere	.40	.18
246	Joe Perona RC	.40	.18
247	Mitch Williams	.40	.18
248	Jay Buhner	.60	.25
249	Andy Benes	.40	.18
250	Alex Ochoa RC	.60	.25
251	Greg Blosser	.40	.18
252	Jack Armstrong	.40	.18
253	Juan Samuel	.40	.18
254	Terry Pendleton	.60	.25
255	Ramon Martinez	.40	.18
256	Rico Brogna	.40	.18
257	John Smiley	.40	.18
258	Carl Everett	2.00	.90
259	Tim Salmon	2.00	.90
260	Will Clark	1.50	.70
261	Ugueth Urbina RC	.60	.25
262	Jason Wood RC	.40	.18
263	Dave Magadan	.40	.18
264	Dante Bichette	.60	.25
265	Jose DeLeon	.40	.18
266	Mike Neill RC	.60	.25
267	Paul O'Neill	1.50	.70
268	Anthony Young	.40	.18
269	Greg W. Harris	.40	.18
270	Todd Van Poppel	.40	.18
271	Pedro Castellano RC	.40	.18
272	Tony Phillips	.40	.18
273	Mike Gallego	.40	.18
274	Steve Cooke RC	.40	.18
275	Robin Ventura	.60	.25
276	Kevin Mitchell	.40	.18
277	Doug Linton	.40	.18
278	Robert Eenhoorn	.40	.18
279	Gabe White RC	.40	.18
280	Dave Stewart	.60	.25
281	Mo Sanford	.40	.18
282	Greg Perschke	.40	.18
283	Kevin Flora RC	.40	.18
284	Jeff Williams RC	.40	.18
285	Keith Miller	.40	.18
286	Andy Ashby	.40	.18
287	Doug Dascenzo	.40	.18
288	Eric Karros	.60	.25
289	Glenn Murray RC	.40	.18
290	Troy Percival RC	2.00	.90
291	Orlando Merced	.40	.18
292	Peter Hoy	.40	.18
293	Tony Fernandez	.40	.18
294	Juan Guzman	.40	.18
295	Jesse Barfield	.40	.18
296	Sid Fernandez	.40	.18
297	Scott Cepicky	.40	.18
298	Garret Anderson RC	4.00	1.80
299	Cal Eldred	.40	.18
300	Ryne Sandberg	2.00	.90
301	Jim Gantner	.40	.18
302	Mariano Rivera RC	10.00	4.50
303	Ron Lockett RC	.40	.18
304	Jose Offerman	.40	.18
305	Dennis Martinez	.60	.25
306	Luis Ortiz RC	.40	.18
307	David Howard	.40	.18
308	Russ Springer RC	.40	.18
309	Chris Howard	.40	.18
310	Kyle Abbott	.40	.18
311	Aaron Sele RC	5.00	2.20
312	David Justice	.60	.25
313	Pete O'Brien	.40	.18
314	Greg Hansell RC	.40	.18
315	Dave Winfield	1.50	.70
316	Lance Dickson	.40	.18
317	Eric King	.40	.18
318	Vaughn Eshelman RC	.40	.18
319	Tim Belcher	.40	.18
320	Andres Galarraga	1.00	.45
321	Scott Bullett RC	.40	.18
322	Doug Strange	.40	.18
323	Jerald Clark	.40	.18
324	Dave Righetti	.60	.25
325	Greg Hibbard	.40	.18
326	Eric Hillman RC	.40	.18
327	Shane Reynolds RC	.60	.25
328	Chris Hammond	.40	.18
329	Albert Belle	.60	.25
330	Rich Becker RC	.60	.25
331	Eddie Williams RC	.40	.18
332	Donald Harris	.40	.18
333	Dave Smith	.40	.18
334	Steve Fireovid	.40	.18
335	Steve Buechele	.40	.18
336	Mike Schooler	.40	.18
337	Kevin McReynolds	.40	.18
338	Hensley Meulens	.40	.18
339	Benji Gil RC	.40	.18
340	Don Mattingly	4.00	1.80
341	Alvin Davis	.40	.18
342	Alan Mills	.40	.18
343	Kelly Downs	.40	.18
344	Leo Gomez	.40	.18
345	Tarrik Brock RC	.40	.18
346	Ryan Turner RC	.40	.18

❑ 347	John Smoltz	.60	.25
❑ 348	Bill Sampen	.40	.18
❑ 349	Paul Byrd RC	.60	.25
❑ 350	Mike Bordick	.40	.18
❑ 351	Jose Lind	.40	.18
❑ 352	David Wells	.60	.25
❑ 353	Barry Larkin	1.50	.70
❑ 354	Bruce Ruffin	.40	.18
❑ 355	Luis Rivera	.40	.18
❑ 356	Sid Bream	.40	.18
❑ 357	Julian Vasquez RC	.40	.18
❑ 358	Jason Bere RC	1.50	.70
❑ 359	Ben McDonald	.40	.18
❑ 360	Scott Stahoviak RC	.40	.18
❑ 361	Kirt Manwaring	.40	.18
❑ 362	Jeff Johnson	.40	.18
❑ 363	Rob Deer	.40	.18
❑ 364	Tony Pena	.40	.18
❑ 365	Melido Perez	.40	.18
❑ 366	Clay Parker	.40	.18
❑ 367	Dale Sveum	.40	.18
❑ 368	Mike Scioscia	.40	.18
❑ 369	Roger Salkeld	.40	.18
❑ 370	Mike Stanley	.40	.18
❑ 371	Jack McDowell	.40	.18
❑ 372	Tim Wallach	.40	.18
❑ 373	Billy Ripken	.40	.18
❑ 374	Mike Christopher	.40	.18
❑ 375	Paul Molitor	1.50	.70
❑ 376	Dave Stieb	.40	.18
❑ 377	Pedro Guerrero	.60	.25
❑ 378	Russ Swan	.40	.18
❑ 379	Bob Ojeda	.40	.18
❑ 380	Donn Pall	.40	.18
❑ 381	Eddie Zosky	.40	.18
❑ 382	Darnell Coles	.40	.18
❑ 383	Tom Smith RC	.40	.18
❑ 384	Mark McGwire	6.00	2.70
❑ 385	Gary Carter	1.00	.45
❑ 386	Rich Amaral RC	.40	.18
❑ 387	Alan Embree RC	.40	.18
❑ 388	Jonathan Hurst RC	.40	.18
❑ 389	Bobby Jones RC	.60	.25
❑ 390	Rico Rossy	.40	.18
❑ 391	Dan Smith	.40	.18
❑ 392	Terry Steinbach	.40	.18
❑ 393	Jon Farrell RC	.40	.18
❑ 394	Dave Anderson	.40	.18
❑ 395	Benny Santiago	.40	.18
❑ 396	Mark Wohlers	.40	.18
❑ 397	Mo Vaughn	.60	.25
❑ 398	Randy Kramer	.40	.18
❑ 399	John Jaha RC	.60	.25
❑ 400	Cal Ripken	6.00	2.70
❑ 401	Ryan Bowen	.40	.18
❑ 402	Tim McIntosh	.40	.18
❑ 403	Bernard Gilkey	.40	.18
❑ 404	Junior Felix	.40	.18
❑ 405	Cris Colon RC	.40	.18
❑ 406	Marc Newfield	.40	.18
❑ 407	Bernie Williams	1.50	.70
❑ 408	Jay Howell	.40	.18
❑ 409	Zane Smith	.40	.18
❑ 410	Jeff Shaw	.40	.18
❑ 411	Kerry Woodson	.40	.18
❑ 412	Wes Chamberlain	.40	.18
❑ 413	Dave Mlicki RC	.60	.25
❑ 414	Benny Distefano	.40	.18
❑ 415	Kevin Rogers	.40	.18
❑ 416	Tim Naehring	.40	.18
❑ 417	Clemente Nunez RC	.40	.18
❑ 418	Luis Sojo	.40	.18
❑ 419	Kevin Ritz	.40	.18
❑ 420	Omar Olivares	.40	.18
❑ 421	Manuel Lee	.40	.18
❑ 422	Julio Valera	.40	.18
❑ 423	Omar Vizquel	.60	.25
❑ 424	Darren Burton RC	.40	.18
❑ 425	Mel Hall	.40	.18
❑ 426	Dennis Powell	.40	.18
❑ 427	Lee Stevens	.40	.18
❑ 428	Glenn Davis	.40	.18
❑ 429	Willie Greene	.40	.18
❑ 430	Kevin Wickander	.40	.18
❑ 431	Dennis Eckersley	.60	.25
❑ 432	Joe Orsulak	.40	.18
❑ 433	Eddie Murray	1.50	.70
❑ 434	Matt Stairs RC	1.50	.70
❑ 435	Wally Joyner	.60	.25
❑ 436	Rondell White	1.50	.70
❑ 437	Rob Maurer	.40	.18
❑ 438	Joe Redfield	.40	.18
❑ 439	Mark Lewis	.40	.18
❑ 440	Darren Daulton	.60	.25
❑ 441	Mike Henneman	.40	.18
❑ 442	John Cangelosi	.40	.18
❑ 443	Vince Moore RC	.40	.18
❑ 444	John Wehner	.40	.18
❑ 445	Kent Hrbek	.60	.25
❑ 446	Mark McLemore	.40	.18
❑ 447	Bill Wegman	.40	.18
❑ 448	Robby Thompson	.40	.18
❑ 449	Mark Anthony RC	.40	.18
❑ 450	Archi Cianfrocco RC	.40	.18
❑ 451	Johnny Ruffin	.40	.18
❑ 452	Javier Lopez	2.00	.90
❑ 453	Greg Gohr	.40	.18
❑ 454	Tim Scott	.40	.18
❑ 455	Stan Belinda	.40	.18
❑ 456	Darrin Jackson	.40	.18
❑ 457	Chris Gardner	.40	.18
❑ 458	Esteban Beltre	.40	.18
❑ 459	Phil Plantier	.40	.18
❑ 460	Jim Thome	6.00	2.70
❑ 461	Mike Piazza RC	50.00	22.00
❑ 462	Matt Sinatro	.40	.18
❑ 463	Scott Servais	.40	.18
❑ 464	Brian Jordan RC	3.00	1.35
❑ 465	Doug Drabek	.40	.18
❑ 466	Carl Willis	.40	.18
❑ 467	Bret Barberie	.40	.18
❑ 468	Hal Morris	.40	.18
❑ 469	Steve Sax	.40	.18
❑ 470	Jerry Willard	.40	.18
❑ 471	Dan Wilson	.40	.18
❑ 472	Chris Hoiles	.40	.18
❑ 473	Rheal Cormier	.40	.18
❑ 474	John Morris	.40	.18
❑ 475	Jeff Reardon	.60	.25
❑ 476	Mark Leiter	.40	.18
❑ 477	Tom Gordon	.40	.18
❑ 478	Kent Bottenfield RC	.60	.25
❑ 479	Gene Larkin	.40	.18
❑ 480	Dwight Gooden	.60	.25
❑ 481	B.J. Surhoff	.60	.25
❑ 482	Andy Stankiewicz	.40	.18
❑ 483	Tino Martinez	.60	.25
❑ 484	Craig Biggio	1.00	.45
❑ 485	Denny Neagle	.60	.25
❑ 486	Rusty Meacham	.40	.18
❑ 487	Kal Daniels	.40	.18
❑ 488	Dave Henderson	.40	.18
❑ 489	Tim Costo	.40	.18
❑ 490	Doug Davis	.40	.18
❑ 491	Frank Viola	.60	.25
❑ 492	Cory Snyder	.40	.18
❑ 493	Chris Martin	.40	.18
❑ 494	Dion James	.40	.18
❑ 495	Randy Tomlin	.40	.18
❑ 496	Greg Vaughn	.60	.25
❑ 497	Dennis Cook	.40	.18
❑ 498	Rosario Rodriguez	.40	.18
❑ 499	Dave Staton	.40	.18
❑ 500	George Brett	3.00	1.35
❑ 501	Brian Barnes	.40	.18
❑ 502	Butch Henry RC	.40	.18
❑ 503	Harold Reynolds	.40	.18
❑ 504	David Nied RC	.40	.18
❑ 505	Lee Smith	.60	.25
❑ 506	Steve Chitren	.40	.18
❑ 507	Ken Hill	.40	.18
❑ 508	Robbie Beckett	.40	.18
❑ 509	Troy Afenir	.40	.18
❑ 510	Kelly Gruber	.40	.18
❑ 511	Bret Boone	2.00	.90
❑ 512	Jeff Branson	.40	.18
❑ 513	Mike Jackson	.40	.18
❑ 514	Pete Harnisch	.40	.18
❑ 515	Chad Kreuter	.40	.18
❑ 516	Joe Vitko RC	.40	.18
❑ 517	Orel Hershiser	.60	.25
❑ 518	John Doherty RC	.40	.18
❑ 519	Jay Bell	.60	.25
❑ 520	Mark Langston	.40	.18
❑ 521	Dann Howitt	.40	.18
❑ 522	Bobby Reed RC	.40	.18
❑ 523	Bobby Munoz RC	.40	.18
❑ 524	Todd Ritchie	.40	.18
❑ 525	Bip Roberts	.40	.18
❑ 526	Pat Listach RC	.60	.25
❑ 527	Scott Brosius RC	3.00	1.35
❑ 528	John Roper RC	.40	.18
❑ 529	Phil Hiatt RC	.40	.18
❑ 530	Denny Walling	.40	.18
❑ 531	Carlos Baerga	.40	.18
❑ 532	Manny Ramirez RC	40.00	18.00
❑ 533	Pat Clements UER (Mistakenly numbered 553)	.40	.18
❑ 534	Ron Gant	.40	.18
❑ 535	Pat Kelly	.40	.18
❑ 536	Bill Spiers	.40	.18
❑ 537	Darren Reed	.40	.18
❑ 538	Ken Caminiti	.60	.25
❑ 539	Butch Huskey RC	.60	.25
❑ 540	Matt Nokes	.40	.18
❑ 541	John Kruk	.60	.25
❑ 542	John Jaha FOIL	.60	.25
❑ 543	Justin Thompson RC	.60	.25
❑ 544	Steve Hosey	.40	.18
❑ 545	Joe Kmak	.40	.18
❑ 546	John Franco	.60	.25
❑ 547	Devon White	.40	.18
❑ 548	E.Hansen FOIL RC	.40	.18
❑ 549	Ryan Klesko	2.00	.90
❑ 550	Danny Tartabull	.40	.18
❑ 551	Frank Thomas FOIL	2.00	.90
❑ 552	Kevin Tapani	.40	.18
❑ 553	Willie Banks (See also 533)	.40	.18
❑ 554	B.J. Wallace RC FOIL	.40	.18
❑ 555	Orlando Miller RC	.40	.18
❑ 556	Mark Smith RC	.40	.18
❑ 557	Tim Wallach FOIL	.40	.18
❑ 558	Bill Gullickson	.40	.18
❑ 559	Derek Bell FOIL	.60	.25
❑ 560	Joe Randa FOIL RC	1.50	.70
❑ 561	Frank Seminara RC	.40	.18
❑ 562	Mark Gardner	.40	.18
❑ 563	Rick Greene RC FOIL	.40	.18
❑ 564	Gary Gaetti	.60	.25
❑ 565	Ozzie Guillen	.40	.18
❑ 566	Charles Nagy FOIL	.40	.18
❑ 567	Mike Milchin	.40	.18
❑ 568	Ben Shelton RC	.40	.18
❑ 569	Chris Roberts FOIL	.40	.18
❑ 570	Ellis Burks	.60	.25
❑ 571	Scott Scudder	.40	.18
❑ 572	Jim Abbott FOIL	.40	.18
❑ 573	Joe Carter	.60	.25
❑ 574	Steve Finley	.60	.25
❑ 575	Jim Olander FOIL	.40	.18
❑ 576	Carlos Garcia	.40	.18
❑ 577	Gregg Olson	.40	.18
❑ 578	Greg Swindell FOIL	.40	.18
❑ 579	Matt Williams FOIL	1.00	.45
❑ 580	Mark Grace	1.50	.70
❑ 581	H.House RC FOIL	.40	.18
❑ 582	Luis Polonia	.40	.18
❑ 583	Erik Hanson	.40	.18
❑ 584	Salomon Torres FOIL	.40	.18
❑ 585	Carlton Fisk	1.50	.70
❑ 586	Bret Saberhagen	.60	.25
❑ 587	C.McConnell FOIL RC	.40	.18
❑ 588	Jimmy Key	.60	.25
❑ 589	Mike Macfarlane	.40	.18
❑ 590	Barry Bonds FOIL	4.00	1.80
❑ 591	Jamie McAndrew	.40	.18
❑ 592	Shane Mack	.40	.18
❑ 593	Kerwin Moore	.40	.18
❑ 594	Joe Oliver	.40	.18
❑ 595	Chris Sabo	.40	.18
❑ 596	Alex Gonzalez RC	1.50	.70
❑ 597	Brett Butler	.60	.25
❑ 598	Mark Hutton RC	.40	.18
❑ 599	Andy Benes FOIL	.40	.18
❑ 600	Jose Canseco	1.50	.70
❑ 601	Darryl Kile	.60	.25
❑ 602	Matt Stairs FOIL	.60	.25

❑ 603 R.Butler RC FOIL .40 .18
❑ 604 Willie McGee .60 .25
❑ 605 Jack McDowell FOIL .40 .18
❑ 606 Tom Candiotti .40 .18
❑ 607 Ed Martel RC .40 .18
❑ 608 Matt Mieske FOIL .40 .18
❑ 609 Darrin Fletcher .40 .18
❑ 610 Rafael Palmeiro 1.50 .70
❑ 611 Bill Swift FOIL .40 .18
❑ 612 Mike Mussina 1.50 .70
❑ 613 Vince Coleman .40 .18
❑ 614 S.Cepicky FOIL UER .40 .18
Bats: LEFLT
❑ 615 Mike Greenwell .40 .18
❑ 616 Kevin McGehee RC .40 .18
❑ 617 J.Hammonds FOIL .60 .25
❑ 618 Scott Taylor .40 .18
❑ 619 Dave Otto .40 .18
❑ 620 Mark McGwire FOIL 6.00 2.70
❑ 621 Kevin Tatar RC .40 .18
❑ 622 Steve Farr .40 .18
❑ 623 Ryan Klesko FOIL .60 .25
❑ 624 Dave Fleming .40 .18
❑ 625 Andre Dawson 1.00 .45
❑ 626 Tino Martinez FOIL .60 .25
❑ 627 Chad Curtis RC .60 .25
❑ 628 Mickey Morandini .40 .18
❑ 629 Gregg Olson FOIL .40 .18
❑ 630 Lou Whitaker .60 .25
❑ 631 Arthur Rhodes .40 .18
❑ 632 Brandon Wilson RC .40 .18
❑ 633 Lance Jennings RC .40 .18
❑ 634 Allen Watson RC .40 .18
❑ 635 Len Dykstra .60 .25
❑ 636 Joe Girardi .40 .18
❑ 637 K.Hernandez RC FOIL .40 .18
❑ 638 Mike Hampton RC 5.00 2.20
❑ 639 Al Osuna .40 .18
❑ 640 Kevin Appier .60 .25
❑ 641 Rick Helling FOIL .40 .18
❑ 642 Jody Reed .40 .18
❑ 643 Ray Lankford .40 .18
❑ 644 John Olerud .60 .25
❑ 645 Paul Molitor FOIL 1.50 .70
❑ 646 Pat Borders .40 .18
❑ 647 Mike Morgan .40 .18
❑ 648 Larry Walker 1.00 .45
❑ 649 P.Castellano FOIL .40 .18
❑ 650 Fred McGriff 1.00 .45
❑ 651 Walt Weiss .40 .18
❑ 652 C.Murray RC FOIL .40 .18
❑ 653 Dave Nilsson .40 .18
❑ 654 Greg Pirkl RC .40 .18
❑ 655 Robin Ventura FOIL .60 .25
❑ 656 Mark Portugal .40 .18
❑ 657 Roger McDowell .40 .18
❑ 658 R.Hirtensteiner RC .40 .18
FOIL
❑ 659 Glenallen Hill .40 .18
❑ 660 Greg Gagne .40 .18
❑ 661 Charles Johnson FOIL 2.00 .90
❑ 662 Brian Hunter .40 .18
❑ 663 Mark Lemke .40 .18
❑ 664 Tim Belcher FOIL .40 .18
❑ 665 Rich DeLucia .40 .18
❑ 666 Bob Walk .40 .18
❑ 667 Joe Carter FOIL .60 .25
❑ 668 Jose Guzman .40 .18
❑ 669 Otis Nixon .40 .18
❑ 670 Phil Nevin FOIL 2.00 .90
❑ 671 Eric Davis .60 .25
❑ 672 Damion Easley RC .60 .25
❑ 673 Will Clark FOIL 1.50 .70
❑ 674 Mark Kiefer RC .40 .18
❑ 675 Ozzie Smith 2.00 .90
❑ 676 Manny Ramirez FOIL 10.00 4.50
❑ 677 Gregg Olson .40 .18
❑ 678 Cliff Floyd RC 8.00 3.60
❑ 679 Duane Singleton RC .40 .18
❑ 680 Jose Rijo .40 .18
❑ 681 Willie Randolph .60 .25
❑ 682 M.Tucker FOIL RC .60 .25
❑ 683 Darren Lewis .40 .18
❑ 684 Dale Murphy 1.50 .70
❑ 685 Mike Pagliarulo .40 .18
❑ 686 Paul Miller RC .40 .18
❑ 687 Mike Robertson RC .40 .18
❑ 688 Mike Devereaux .40 .18
❑ 689 Pedro Astacio RC 2.00 .90
❑ 690 Alan Trammell 1.00 .45
❑ 691 Roger Clemens 4.00 1.80
❑ 692 Bud Black .40 .18
❑ 693 Turk Wendell RC .60 .25
❑ 694 Barry Larkin FOIL 1.50 .70
❑ 695 Todd Zeile .40 .18
❑ 696 Pat Hentgen .40 .18
❑ 697 Eddie Taubensee RC .60 .25
❑ 698 G.Velasquez RC .40 .18
❑ 699 Tom Glavine 1.50 .70
❑ 700 Robin Yount 1.50 .70
❑ 701 Checklist 1-141 .40 .18
❑ 702 Checklist 142-282 .40 .18
❑ 703 Checklist 283-423 .40 .18
❑ 704 Checklist 424-564 .40 .18
❑ 705 Checklist 565-705 .40 .18

1993 Bowman

	MINT	NRMT
COMPLETE SET (708)	60.00	27.00

❑ 1 Glenn Davis .15 .07
❑ 2 Hector Roa RC .15 .07
❑ 3 Ken Ryan RC .15 .07
❑ 4 Derek Wallace RC .15 .07
❑ 5 Jorge Fabregas .15 .07
❑ 6 Joe Oliver .15 .07
❑ 7 Brandon Wilson .15 .07
❑ 8 Mark Thompson RC .15 .07
❑ 9 Tracy Sanders .15 .07
❑ 10 Rich Renteria .15 .07
❑ 11 Lou Whitaker .25 .11
❑ 12 Brian L. Hunter RC .25 .11
❑ 13 Joe Vitiello .15 .07
❑ 14 Eric Karros .25 .11
❑ 15 Joe Kmak .15 .07
❑ 16 Tavo Alvarez .15 .07
❑ 17 Steve Dunn RC .15 .07
❑ 18 Tony Fernandez .15 .07
❑ 19 Melido Perez .15 .07
❑ 20 Mike Lieberthal .25 .11
❑ 21 Terry Steinbach .15 .07
❑ 22 Stan Belinda .15 .07
❑ 23 Jay Buhner .25 .11
❑ 24 Allen Watson .15 .07
❑ 25 Daryl Henderson RC .15 .07
❑ 26 Ray McDavid RC .15 .07
❑ 27 Shawn Green 2.00 .90
❑ 28 Bud Black .15 .07
❑ 29 Sherman Obando RC .15 .07
❑ 30 Mike Hostetler RC .15 .07
❑ 31 Nate Minchey RC .15 .07
❑ 32 Randy Myers .15 .07
❑ 33 Brian Grebeck .15 .07
❑ 34 John Roper .15 .07
❑ 35 Larry Thomas .15 .07
❑ 36 Alex Cole .15 .07
❑ 37 Tom Kramer RC .15 .07
❑ 38 Matt Whisenant RC .15 .07
❑ 39 Chris Gomez RC .25 .11
❑ 40 Luis Gonzalez .60 .25
❑ 41 Kevin Appier .25 .11
❑ 42 Omar Daal RC 1.00 .45
❑ 43 Duane Singleton .15 .07
❑ 44 Bill Risley .15 .07
❑ 45 Pat Meares RC .25 .11
❑ 46 Butch Huskey .15 .07
❑ 47 Bobby Munoz .15 .07
❑ 48 Juan Bell .15 .07
❑ 49 Scott Lydy RC .15 .07
❑ 50 Dennis Moeller .15 .07
❑ 51 Marc Newfield .15 .07
❑ 52 Tripp Cromer RC .15 .07
❑ 53 Kurt Miller .15 .07
❑ 54 Jim Pena .15 .07
❑ 55 Juan Guzman .15 .07
❑ 56 Matt Williams .40 .18
❑ 57 Harold Reynolds .15 .07
❑ 58 Donnie Elliott RC .15 .07
❑ 59 Jon Shave RC .15 .07
❑ 60 Kevin Roberson RC .15 .07
❑ 61 Hilly Hathaway RC .15 .07
❑ 62 Jose Rijo .15 .07
❑ 63 Kerry Taylor RC .15 .07
❑ 64 Ryan Hawblitzel .15 .07
❑ 65 Glenallen Hill .15 .07
❑ 66 Ramon Martinez RC .15 .07
❑ 67 Travis Fryman .25 .11
❑ 68 Tom Nevers .15 .07
❑ 69 Phil Hiatt .15 .07
❑ 70 Tim Wallach .15 .07
❑ 71 B.J. Surhoff .25 .11
❑ 72 Rondell White .25 .11
❑ 73 Denny Hocking RC .15 .07
❑ 74 Mike Oquist RC .15 .07
❑ 75 Paul O'Neill .60 .25
❑ 76 Willie Banks .15 .07
❑ 77 Bob Welch .15 .07
❑ 78 Jose Sandoval RC .15 .07
❑ 79 Bill Haselman .15 .07
❑ 80 Rheal Cormier .15 .07
❑ 81 Dean Palmer .25 .11
❑ 82 Pat Gomez RC .15 .07
❑ 83 Steve Karsay .15 .07
❑ 84 Carl Hanselman RC .15 .07
❑ 85 T.R. Lewis RC .15 .07
❑ 86 Chipper Jones 1.50 .70
❑ 87 Scott Hatteberg .15 .07
❑ 88 Greg Hibbard .15 .07
❑ 89 Lance Painter RC .15 .07
❑ 90 Chad Mottola RC .15 .07
❑ 91 Jason Bere .15 .07
❑ 92 Dante Bichette .25 .11
❑ 93 Sandy Alomar Jr. .25 .11
❑ 94 Carl Everett .25 .11
❑ 95 Danny Bautista RC .15 .07
❑ 96 Steve Finley .25 .11
❑ 97 David Cone .25 .11
❑ 98 Todd Hollandsworth .15 .07
❑ 99 Matt Mieske .15 .07
❑ 100 Larry Walker .40 .18
❑ 101 Shane Mack .15 .07
❑ 102 Aaron Ledesma RC .15 .07
❑ 103 Andy Pettitte RC 5.00 2.20
❑ 104 Kevin Stocker .15 .07
❑ 105 Mike Mohler RC .15 .07
❑ 106 Tony Menendez .15 .07
❑ 107 Derek Lowe .25 .11
❑ 108 Basil Shabazz .15 .07
❑ 109 Dan Smith .15 .07
❑ 110 Scott Sanders RC .15 .07
❑ 111 Todd Stottlemyre .15 .07
❑ 112 Benji Simonton RC .15 .07
❑ 113 Rick Sutcliffe .25 .11
❑ 114 Lee Heath RC .15 .07
❑ 115 Jeff Russell .15 .07
❑ 116 Dave Stevens RC .15 .07
❑ 117 Mark Holzemer RC .15 .07
❑ 118 Tim Belcher .15 .07
❑ 119 Bobby Thigpen .15 .07
❑ 120 Roger Bailey RC .15 .07
❑ 121 Tony Mitchell RC .15 .07
❑ 122 Junior Felix .15 .07
❑ 123 Rich Robertson RC .15 .07
❑ 124 Andy Cook RC .15 .07
❑ 125 Brian Bevil RC .15 .07
❑ 126 Darryl Strawberry .25 .11
❑ 127 Cal Eldred .15 .07
❑ 128 Cliff Floyd .25 .11
❑ 129 Alan Newman .15 .07

❑	130	Howard Johnson	.15	.07
❑	131	Jim Abbott	.25	.11
❑	132	Chad McConnell	.15	.07
❑	133	Miguel Jimenez RC	.15	.07
❑	134	Brett Backlund RC	.15	.07
❑	135	John Cummings RC	.15	.07
❑	136	Brian Barber	.15	.07
❑	137	Rafael Palmeiro	.60	.25
❑	138	Tim Worrell RC	.15	.07
❑	139	Jose Pett RC	.15	.07
❑	140	Barry Bonds	1.50	.70
❑	141	Damon Buford	.15	.07
❑	142	Jeff Blauser	.15	.07
❑	143	Frankie Rodriguez	.15	.07
❑	144	Mike Morgan	.15	.07
❑	145	Gary DiSarcina	.15	.07
❑	146	Pokey Reese	.15	.07
❑	147	Johnny Ruffin	.15	.07
❑	148	David Nied	.15	.07
❑	149	Charles Nagy	.15	.07
❑	150	Mike Myers RC	.15	.07
❑	151	Kenny Carlyle RC	.15	.07
❑	152	Eric Anthony	.15	.07
❑	153	Jose Lind	.15	.07
❑	154	Pedro Martinez	1.50	.70
❑	155	Mark Kiefer	.15	.07
❑	156	Tim Laker RC	.15	.07
❑	157	Pat Mahomes	.15	.07
❑	158	Bobby Bonilla	.25	.11
❑	159	Domingo Jean	.15	.07
❑	160	Darren Daulton	.25	.11
❑	161	Mark McGwire	2.50	1.10
❑	162	Jason Kendall RC	4.00	1.80
❑	163	Desi Relaford	.15	.07
❑	164	Ozzie Canseco	.15	.07
❑	165	Rick Helling	.15	.07
❑	166	Steve Pegues RC	.15	.07
❑	167	Paul Molitor	.60	.25
❑	168	Larry Carter	.15	.07
❑	169	Arthur Rhodes	.15	.07
❑	170	Damon Hollins RC	.15	.07
❑	171	Frank Viola	.25	.11
❑	172	Steve Trachsel RC	.25	.11
❑	173	J.T. Snow RC	1.50	.70
❑	174	Keith Gordon RC	.15	.07
❑	175	Carlton Fisk	.60	.25
❑	176	Jason Bates RC	.15	.07
❑	177	Mike Crosby RC	.15	.07
❑	178	Benny Santiago	.15	.07
❑	179	Mike Moore	.15	.07
❑	180	Jeff Juden	.15	.07
❑	181	Darren Burton	.15	.07
❑	182	Todd Williams RC	.25	.11
❑	183	John Jaha	.15	.07
❑	184	Mike Lansing RC	.25	.11
❑	185	Pedro Grifol RC	.15	.07
❑	186	Vince Coleman	.15	.07
❑	187	Pat Kelly	.15	.07
❑	188	Clemente Alvarez RC	.15	.07
❑	189	Ron Darling	.15	.07
❑	190	Orlando Merced	.15	.07
❑	191	Chris Bosio	.15	.07
❑	192	Steve Dixon RC	.15	.07
❑	193	Doug Dascenzo	.15	.07
❑	194	Ray Holbert RC	.15	.07
❑	195	Howard Battle	.15	.07
❑	196	Willie McGee	.25	.11
❑	197	John O'Donoghue RC	.15	.07
❑	198	Steve Avery	.15	.07
❑	199	Greg Blosser	.15	.07
❑	200	Ryne Sandberg	.75	.35
❑	201	Joe Grahe	.15	.07
❑	202	Dan Wilson	.25	.11
❑	203	Domingo Martinez RC	.15	.07
❑	204	Andres Galarraga	.40	.18
❑	205	Jamie Taylor RC	.15	.07
❑	206	Darrell Whitmore RC	.15	.07
❑	207	Ben Blomdahl RC	.15	.07
❑	208	Doug Drabek	.15	.07
❑	209	Keith Miller	.15	.07
❑	210	Billy Ashley	.15	.07
❑	211	Mike Farrell RC	.15	.07
❑	212	John Wetteland	.25	.11
❑	213	Randy Tomlin	.15	.07
❑	214	Sid Fernandez	.15	.07
❑	215	Quilvio Veras RC	1.00	.45
❑	216	Dave Hollins	.15	.07
❑	217	Mike Neill	.15	.07
❑	218	Andy Van Slyke	.25	.11
❑	219	Bret Boone	.25	.11
❑	220	Tom Pagnozzi	.15	.07
❑	221	Mike Welch RC	.15	.07
❑	222	Frank Seminara	.15	.07
❑	223	Ron Villone	.15	.07
❑	224	D.J. Thielen RC	.15	.07
❑	225	Cal Ripken	2.50	1.10
❑	226	Pedro Borbon Jr. RC	.15	.07
❑	227	Carlos Quintana	.15	.07
❑	228	Tommy Shields	.15	.07
❑	229	Tim Salmon	.25	.11
❑	230	John Smiley	.15	.07
❑	231	Ellis Burks	.25	.11
❑	232	Pedro Castellano	.15	.07
❑	233	Paul Byrd	.15	.07
❑	234	Bryan Harvey	.15	.07
❑	235	Scott Livingstone	.15	.07
❑	236	James Mouton RC	.15	.07
❑	237	Joe Randa	.25	.11
❑	238	Pedro Astacio	.15	.07
❑	239	Darryl Hamilton	.15	.07
❑	240	Joey Eischen RC	.15	.07
❑	241	Edgar Herrera RC	.15	.07
❑	242	Dwight Gooden	.25	.11
❑	243	Sam Militello	.15	.07
❑	244	Ron Blazier RC	.15	.07
❑	245	Ruben Sierra	.15	.07
❑	246	Al Martin	.15	.07
❑	247	Mike Felder	.15	.07
❑	248	Bob Tewksbury	.15	.07
❑	249	Craig Lefferts	.15	.07
❑	250	Luis Lopez RC	.15	.07
❑	251	Devon White	.15	.07
❑	252	Will Clark	.60	.25
❑	253	Mark Smith	.15	.07
❑	254	Terry Pendleton	.25	.11
❑	255	Aaron Sele	.25	.11
❑	256	Jose Viera RC	.15	.07
❑	257	Damion Easley	.15	.07
❑	258	Rod Lofton RC	.15	.07
❑	259	Chris Snopek RC	.15	.07
❑	260	Q.McCracken RC	.25	.11
❑	261	Mike Matthews RC	.15	.07
❑	262	Hector Carrasco RC	.15	.07
❑	263	Rick Greene	.15	.07
❑	264	Chris Holt RC	.25	.11
❑	265	George Brett	1.25	.55
❑	266	Rick Gorecki RC	.15	.07
❑	267	Francisco Gamez RC	.15	.07
❑	268	Marquis Grissom	.15	.07
❑	269	Kevin Tapani UER (Misspelled Tapan on card front)	.15	.07
❑	270	Ryan Thompson	.15	.07
❑	271	Gerald Williams	.15	.07
❑	272	Paul Fletcher RC	.15	.07
❑	273	Lance Blankenship	.15	.07
❑	274	Marty Neff RC	.15	.07
❑	275	Shawn Estes	.25	.11
❑	276	Rene Arocha RC	.25	.11
❑	277	Scott Eyre RC	.15	.07
❑	278	Phil Plantier	.15	.07
❑	279	Paul Spoljaric RC	.15	.07
❑	280	Chris Gambs	.15	.07
❑	281	Harold Baines	.25	.11
❑	282	Jose Oliva	.15	.07
❑	283	Matt Whiteside RC	.15	.07
❑	284	Brant Brown RC	.25	.11
❑	285	Russ Springer	.15	.07
❑	286	Chris Sabo	.15	.07
❑	287	Ozzie Guillen	.15	.07
❑	288	Marcus Moore RC	.15	.07
❑	289	Chad Ogea	.15	.07
❑	290	Walt Weiss	.15	.07
❑	291	Brian Edmondson	.15	.07
❑	292	Jimmy Gonzalez	.15	.07
❑	293	Danny Miceli RC	.15	.07
❑	294	Jose Offerman	.15	.07
❑	295	Greg Vaughn	.25	.11
❑	296	Frank Bolick	.15	.07
❑	297	Mike Maksudian RC	.15	.07
❑	298	John Franco	.25	.11
❑	299	Danny Tartabull	.15	.07
❑	300	Len Dykstra	.25	.11
❑	301	Bobby Witt	.15	.07
❑	302	Trey Beamon RC	.15	.07
❑	303	Tino Martinez	.25	.11
❑	304	Aaron Holbert	.15	.07
❑	305	Juan Gonzalez	.60	.25
❑	306	Billy Hall RC	.15	.07
❑	307	Duane Ward	.15	.07
❑	308	Rod Beck	.15	.07
❑	309	Jose Mercedes RC	.15	.07
❑	310	Otis Nixon	.15	.07
❑	311	Gettys Glaze RC	.15	.07
❑	312	Candy Maldonado	.15	.07
❑	313	Chad Curtis	.15	.07
❑	314	Tim Costo	.15	.07
❑	315	Mike Robertson	.15	.07
❑	316	Nigel Wilson	.15	.07
❑	317	Greg McMichael RC	.15	.07
❑	318	Scott Pose RC	.15	.07
❑	319	Ivan Cruz	.15	.07
❑	320	Greg Swindell	.15	.07
❑	321	Kevin McReynolds	.15	.07
❑	322	Tom Candiotti	.15	.07
❑	323	Rob Wishnevski RC	.15	.07
❑	324	Ken Hill	.15	.07
❑	325	Kirby Puckett	1.50	.70
❑	326	Tim Bogar RC	.15	.07
❑	327	Mariano Rivera	1.00	.45
❑	328	Mitch Williams	.15	.07
❑	329	Craig Paquette	.15	.07
❑	330	Jay Bell	.25	.11
❑	331	Jose Martinez RC	.15	.07
❑	332	Rob Deer	.15	.07
❑	333	Brook Fordyce	.15	.07
❑	334	Matt Nokes	.15	.07
❑	335	Derek Lee	.15	.07
❑	336	Paul Ellis RC	.15	.07
❑	337	Desi Wilson RC	.15	.07
❑	338	Roberto Alomar	.60	.25
❑	339	Jim Tatum FOIL RC	.15	.07
❑	340	J.T. Snow FOIL	.60	.25
❑	341	Tim Salmon FOIL	.25	.11
❑	342	Russ Davis FOIL RC	.25	.11
❑	343	Javier Lopez FOIL	.25	.11
❑	344	Troy O'Leary FOIL RC	.60	.25
❑	345	M.Cordova FOIL RC	2.00	.90
❑	346	Bubba Smith RC FOIL	.15	.07
❑	347	Chipper Jones FOIL	1.50	.70
❑	348	Jessie Hollins FOIL	.15	.07
❑	349	Willie Greene FOIL	.15	.07
❑	350	Mark Thompson FOIL	.15	.07
❑	351	Nigel Wilson FOIL	.15	.07
❑	352	Todd Jones FOIL	.15	.07
❑	353	Raul Mondesi FOIL	.25	.11
❑	354	Cliff Floyd FOIL	.25	.11
❑	355	Bobby Jones FOIL	.25	.11
❑	356	Kevin Stocker FOIL	.15	.07
❑	357	M.Cummings FOIL	.15	.07
❑	358	Allen Watson FOIL	.15	.07
❑	359	Ray McDavid FOIL	.15	.07
❑	360	Steve Hosey FOIL	.15	.07
❑	361	B.Pennington FOIL	.15	.07
❑	362	F.Rodriguez FOIL	.15	.07
❑	363	Troy Percival FOIL	.25	.11
❑	364	Jason Bere FOIL	.15	.07
❑	365	Manny Ramirez FOIL	1.50	.70
❑	366	J.Thompson FOIL	.15	.07
❑	367	Joe Vitiello FOIL	.15	.07
❑	368	Tyrone Hill FOIL	.15	.07
❑	369	David McCarty FOIL	.15	.07
❑	370	Brien Taylor FOIL	.15	.07
❑	371	T.Van Poppel FOIL	.15	.07
❑	372	Marc Newfield FOIL	.15	.07
❑	373	T.Lowery RC FOIL	.15	.07
❑	374	Alex Gonzalez FOIL	.15	.07
❑	375	Ken Griffey Jr.	2.00	.90
❑	376	Donovan Osborne	.15	.07
❑	377	Ritchie Moody RC	.15	.07
❑	378	Shane Andrews	.15	.07
❑	379	Carlos Delgado	1.25	.55
❑	380	Bill Swift	.15	.07
❑	381	Leo Gomez	.15	.07
❑	382	Ron Gant	.15	.07
❑	383	Scott Fletcher	.15	.07
❑	384	Matt Walbeck RC	.15	.07
❑	385	Chuck Finley	.25	.11

❑ 386 Kevin Mitchell .15 .07
❑ 387 Wilson Alvarez UER .15 .07
(Misspelled Alverez on card front)
❑ 388 John Burke RC .15 .07
❑ 389 Alan Embree .15 .07
❑ 390 Trevor Hoffman .25 .11
❑ 391 Alan Trammell .40 .18
❑ 392 Todd Jones .15 .07
❑ 393 Felix Jose .15 .07
❑ 394 Orel Hershiser .25 .11
❑ 395 Pat Listach .15 .07
❑ 396 Gabe White .15 .07
❑ 397 Dan Serafini RC .15 .07
❑ 398 Todd Hundley .15 .07
❑ 399 Wade Boggs .60 .25
❑ 400 Tyler Green .15 .07
❑ 401 Mike Bordick .15 .07
❑ 402 Scott Bullett .15 .07
❑ 403 LaGrande Russell RC .15 .07
❑ 404 Ray Lankford .15 .07
❑ 405 Nolan Ryan 3.00 1.35
❑ 406 Robbie Beckett .15 .07
❑ 407 Brent Bowers RC .15 .07
❑ 408 Adell Davenport RC .15 .07
❑ 409 Brady Anderson .25 .11
❑ 410 Tom Glavine .60 .25
❑ 411 Doug Hecker RC .15 .07
❑ 412 Jose Guzman .15 .07
❑ 413 Luis Polonia .15 .07
❑ 414 Brian Williams .15 .07
❑ 415 Bo Jackson .25 .11
❑ 416 Eric Young .15 .07
❑ 417 Kenny Lofton .25 .11
❑ 418 Orestes Destrade .15 .07
❑ 419 Tony Phillips .15 .07
❑ 420 Jeff Bagwell .75 .35
❑ 421 Mark Gardner .15 .07
❑ 422 Brett Butler .25 .11
❑ 423 Graeme Lloyd RC .25 .11
❑ 424 Delino DeShields .15 .07
❑ 425 Scott Erickson .15 .07
❑ 426 Jeff Kent .60 .25
❑ 427 Jimmy Key .25 .11
❑ 428 Mickey Morandini .15 .07
❑ 429 Marcos Armas RC .15 .07
❑ 430 Don Slaught .15 .07
❑ 431 Randy Johnson .75 .35
❑ 432 Omar Olivares .15 .07
❑ 433 Charlie Leibrandt .15 .07
❑ 434 Kurt Stillwell .15 .07
❑ 435 Scott Brow RC .15 .07
❑ 436 Robby Thompson .15 .07
❑ 437 Ben McDonald .15 .07
❑ 438 Deion Sanders .25 .11
❑ 439 Tony Pena .15 .07
❑ 440 Mark Grace .60 .25
❑ 441 Eduardo Perez .15 .07
❑ 442 Tim Pugh RC .15 .07
❑ 443 Scott Ruffcorn .15 .07
❑ 444 Jay Gainer RC .15 .07
❑ 445 Albert Belle .25 .11
❑ 446 Bret Barberie .15 .07
❑ 447 Justin Mashore .15 .07
❑ 448 Pete Harnisch .15 .07
❑ 449 Greg Gagne .15 .07
❑ 450 Eric Davis .25 .11
❑ 451 Dave Mlicki .15 .07
❑ 452 Moises Alou .25 .11
❑ 453 Rick Aguilera .15 .07
❑ 454 Eddie Murray .60 .25
❑ 455 Bob Wickman .15 .07
❑ 456 Wes Chamberlain .15 .07
❑ 457 Brent Gates .15 .07
❑ 458 Paul Wagner .15 .07
❑ 459 Mike Hampton .60 .25
❑ 460 Ozzie Smith .75 .35
❑ 461 Tom Henke .15 .07
❑ 462 Ricky Gutierrez .15 .07
❑ 463 Jack Morris .25 .11
❑ 464 Joel Chimelis .15 .07
❑ 465 Gregg Olson .15 .07
❑ 466 Javier Lopez .25 .11
❑ 467 Scott Cooper .15 .07
❑ 468 Willie Wilson .15 .07
❑ 469 Mark Langston .15 .07
❑ 470 Barry Larkin .60 .25
❑ 471 Rod Bolton .15 .07
❑ 472 Freddie Benavides .15 .07
❑ 473 Ken Ramos RC .15 .07
❑ 474 Chuck Carr .15 .07
❑ 475 Cecil Fielder .25 .11
❑ 476 Eddie Taubensee .15 .07
❑ 477 Chris Eddy RC .15 .07
❑ 478 Greg Hansell .15 .07
❑ 479 Kevin Reimer .15 .07
❑ 480 Dennis Martinez .25 .11
❑ 481 Chuck Knoblauch .25 .11
❑ 482 Mike Draper .15 .07
❑ 483 Spike Owen .15 .07
❑ 484 Terry Mulholland .15 .07
❑ 485 Dennis Eckersley .25 .11
❑ 486 Blas Minor .15 .07
❑ 487 Dave Fleming .15 .07
❑ 488 Dan Cholowsky .15 .07
❑ 489 Ivan Rodriguez .60 .25
❑ 490 Gary Sheffield .25 .11
❑ 491 Ed Sprague .15 .07
❑ 492 Steve Hosey .15 .07
❑ 493 Jimmy Haynes RC .25 .11
❑ 494 John Smoltz .25 .11
❑ 495 Andre Dawson .40 .18
❑ 496 Rey Sanchez .15 .07
❑ 497 Ty Van Burkleo .15 .07
❑ 498 Bobby Ayala RC .15 .07
❑ 499 Tim Raines .25 .11
❑ 500 Charlie Hayes .15 .07
❑ 501 Paul Sorrento .15 .07
❑ 502 Richie Lewis RC .15 .07
❑ 503 Jason Pfaff RC .15 .07
❑ 504 Ken Caminiti .25 .11
❑ 505 Mike Macfarlane .15 .07
❑ 506 Jody Reed .15 .07
❑ 507 Bobby Hughes RC .15 .07
❑ 508 Wil Cordero .15 .07
❑ 509 George Tsamis RC .15 .07
❑ 510 Bret Saberhagen .25 .11
❑ 511 Derek Jeter RC 25.00 11.00
❑ 512 Gene Schall .15 .07
❑ 513 Curtis Shaw .15 .07
❑ 514 Steve Cooke .15 .07
❑ 515 Edgar Martinez .40 .18
❑ 516 Mike Milchin .15 .07
❑ 517 Billy Ripken .15 .07
❑ 518 Andy Benes .15 .07
❑ 519 Juan de la Rosa RC .15 .07
❑ 520 John Burkett .15 .07
❑ 521 Alex Ochoa .15 .07
❑ 522 Tony Tarasco RC .15 .07
❑ 523 Luis Ortiz .15 .07
❑ 524 Rick Wilkins .15 .07
❑ 525 Chris Turner RC .15 .07
❑ 526 Rob Dibble .15 .07
❑ 527 Jack McDowell .15 .07
❑ 528 Daryl Boston .15 .07
❑ 529 Bill Wertz RC .15 .07
❑ 530 Charlie Hough .25 .11
❑ 531 Sean Bergman .15 .07
❑ 532 Doug Jones .15 .07
❑ 533 Jeff Montgomery .15 .07
❑ 534 Roger Cedeno RC .25 .11
❑ 535 Robin Yount .60 .25
❑ 536 Mo Vaughn .25 .11
❑ 537 Brian Harper .15 .07
❑ 538 Juan Castillo .15 .07
❑ 539 Steve Farr .15 .07
❑ 540 John Kruk .25 .11
❑ 541 Troy Neel .15 .07
❑ 542 Danny Clyburn RC .15 .07
❑ 543 Jim Converse RC .15 .07
❑ 544 Gregg Jefferies .15 .07
❑ 545 Jose Canseco .60 .25
❑ 546 Julio Bruno RC .15 .07
❑ 547 Rob Butler .15 .07
❑ 548 Royce Clayton .15 .07
❑ 549 Chris Hoiles .15 .07
❑ 550 Greg Maddux 1.50 .70
❑ 551 Joe Ciccarella RC .15 .07
❑ 552 Ozzie Timmons .15 .07
❑ 553 Chili Davis .25 .11
❑ 554 Brian Koelling .15 .07
❑ 555 Frank Thomas .75 .35
❑ 556 Vinny Castilla .25 .11
❑ 557 Reggie Jefferson .15 .07
❑ 558 Rob Natal .15 .07
❑ 559 Mike Henneman .15 .07
❑ 560 Craig Biggio .40 .18
❑ 561 Billy Brewer .15 .07
❑ 562 Dan Melendez .15 .07
❑ 563 Kenny Felder RC .15 .07
❑ 564 Miguel Batista RC .15 .07
❑ 565 Dave Winfield .60 .25
❑ 566 Al Shirley .15 .07
❑ 567 Robert Eenhoorn .15 .07
❑ 568 Mike Williams .15 .07
❑ 569 Tanyon Sturtze RC .15 .07
❑ 570 Tim Wakefield .15 .07
❑ 571 Greg Pirkl .15 .07
❑ 572 Sean Lowe RC .15 .07
❑ 573 Terry Burrows RC .15 .07
❑ 574 Kevin Higgins .15 .07
❑ 575 Joe Carter .25 .11
❑ 576 Kevin Rogers .15 .07
❑ 577 Manny Alexander .15 .07
❑ 578 David Justice .25 .11
❑ 579 Brian Conroy RC .15 .07
❑ 580 Jessie Hollins .15 .07
❑ 581 Ron Watson RC .15 .07
❑ 582 Bip Roberts .15 .07
❑ 583 Tom Urbani RC .15 .07
❑ 584 Jason Hutchins RC .15 .07
❑ 585 Carlos Baerga .15 .07
❑ 586 Jeff Mutis .15 .07
❑ 587 Justin Thompson .15 .07
❑ 588 Orlando Miller .15 .07
❑ 589 Brian McRae .15 .07
❑ 590 Ramon Martinez .15 .07
❑ 591 Dave Nilsson .15 .07
❑ 592 Jose Vidro RC 4.00 1.80
❑ 593 Rich Becker .15 .07
❑ 594 Preston Wilson RC 2.50 1.10
❑ 595 Don Mattingly 1.50 .70
❑ 596 Tony Longmire .15 .07
❑ 597 Kevin Seitzer .15 .07
❑ 598 Midre Cummings RC .15 .07
❑ 599 Omar Vizquel .25 .11
❑ 600 Lee Smith .25 .11
❑ 601 David Hulse RC .15 .07
❑ 602 Darrell Sherman RC .15 .07
❑ 603 Alex Gonzalez .15 .07
❑ 604 Geronimo Pena .15 .07
❑ 605 Mike Devereaux .15 .07
❑ 606 S.Hitchcock RC .25 .11
❑ 607 Mike Greenwell .15 .07
❑ 608 Steve Buechele .15 .07
❑ 609 Troy Percival .25 .11
❑ 610 Roberto Kelly .15 .07
❑ 611 James Baldwin RC 1.00 .45
❑ 612 Jerald Clark .15 .07
❑ 613 Albie Lopez RC .25 .11
❑ 614 Dave Magadan .15 .07
❑ 615 Mickey Tettleton .15 .07
❑ 616 Sean Runyan RC .15 .07
❑ 617 Bob Hamelin .15 .07
❑ 618 Raul Mondesi .25 .11
❑ 619 Tyrone Hill .15 .07
❑ 620 Darrin Fletcher .15 .07
❑ 621 Mike Trombley .15 .07
❑ 622 Jeromy Burnitz .25 .11
❑ 623 Bernie Williams .60 .25
❑ 624 Mike Farmer RC .15 .07
❑ 625 Rickey Henderson 1.25 .55
❑ 626 Carlos Garcia .15 .07
❑ 627 Jeff Darwin RC .15 .07
❑ 628 Todd Zeile .15 .07
❑ 629 Benji Gil .15 .07
❑ 630 Tony Gwynn 1.25 .55
❑ 631 Aaron Small RC .15 .07
❑ 632 Joe Rosselli RC .15 .07
❑ 633 Mike Mussina .60 .25
❑ 634 Ryan Klesko .25 .11
❑ 635 Roger Clemens 1.50 .70
❑ 636 Sammy Sosa 1.25 .55
❑ 637 Orlando Palmeiro RC .15 .07
❑ 638 Willie Greene .15 .07
❑ 639 George Bell .15 .07
❑ 640 Garvin Alston RC .15 .07
❑ 641 Pete Janicki RC .15 .07

- ❑ 642 Chris Sheff RC .15 .07
- ❑ 643 Felipe Lira RC .15 .07
- ❑ 644 Roberto Petagine .15 .07
- ❑ 645 Wally Joyner .25 .11
- ❑ 646 Mike Piazza 3.00 1.35
- ❑ 647 Jaime Navarro .15 .07
- ❑ 648 Jeff Hartsock .15 .07
- ❑ 649 David McCarty .15 .07
- ❑ 650 Bobby Jones .25 .11
- ❑ 651 Mark Hutton .15 .07
- ❑ 652 Kyle Abbott .15 .07
- ❑ 653 Steve Cox RC .25 .11
- ❑ 654 Jeff King .15 .07
- ❑ 655 Norm Charlton .15 .07
- ❑ 656 Mike Gulan RC .15 .07
- ❑ 657 Julio Franco .25 .11
- ❑ 658 C.Cairncross RC .15 .07
- ❑ 659 John Olerud .25 .11
- ❑ 660 Salomon Torres .15 .07
- ❑ 661 Brad Pennington .15 .07
- ❑ 662 Melvin Nieves .15 .07
- ❑ 663 Ivan Calderon .15 .07
- ❑ 664 Turk Wendell .15 .07
- ❑ 665 Chris Pritchett .15 .07
- ❑ 666 Reggie Sanders .15 .07
- ❑ 667 Robin Ventura .25 .11
- ❑ 668 Joe Girardi .15 .07
- ❑ 669 Manny Ramirez 1.50 .70
- ❑ 670 Jeff Conine .15 .07
- ❑ 671 Greg Gohr .15 .07
- ❑ 672 Andujar Cedeno .15 .07
- ❑ 673 Les Norman RC .15 .07
- ❑ 674 Mike James RC .15 .07
- ❑ 675 Marshall Boze RC .15 .07
- ❑ 676 B.J. Wallace .15 .07
- ❑ 677 Kent Hrbek .25 .11
- ❑ 678 Jack Voigt RC .15 .07
- ❑ 679 Brien Taylor .15 .07
- ❑ 680 Curt Schilling .60 .25
- ❑ 681 Todd Van Poppel .15 .07
- ❑ 682 Kevin Young .25 .11
- ❑ 683 Tommy Adams .15 .07
- ❑ 684 Bernard Gilkey .15 .07
- ❑ 685 Kevin Brown .25 .11
- ❑ 686 Fred McGriff .40 .18
- ❑ 687 Pat Borders .15 .07
- ❑ 688 Kirt Manwaring .15 .07
- ❑ 689 Sid Bream .15 .07
- ❑ 690 John Valentin .15 .07
- ❑ 691 Steve Olsen RC .15 .07
- ❑ 692 Roberto Mejia RC .15 .07
- ❑ 693 Carlos Delgado FOIL 1.25 .55
- ❑ 694 S.Gibralter FOIL RC .15 .07
- ❑ 695 Gary Mota RC FOIL .15 .07
- ❑ 696 Jose Malave FOIL RC .15 .07
- ❑ 697 Larry Sutton FOIL RC .15 .07
- ❑ 698 Dan Frye FOIL RC .15 .07
- ❑ 699 Tim Clark RC FOIL .15 .07
- ❑ 700 Brian Rupp RC FOIL .15 .07
- ❑ 701 Felipe Alou FOIL .25 .11
  Moises Alou
- ❑ 702 Barry Bonds FOIL .75 .35
  Bobby Bonds
- ❑ 703 Ken Griffey Sr. FOIL .75 .35
  Ken Griffey Jr.
- ❑ 704 Brian McRae FOIL .15 .07
  Hal McRae
- ❑ 705 Checklist 1 .15 .07
- ❑ 706 Checklist 2 .15 .07
- ❑ 707 Checklist 3 .15 .07
- ❑ 708 Checklist 4 .15 .07

1994 Bowman

	MINT	NRMT
COMPLETE SET (682)	100.00	45.00

- ❑ 1 Joe Carter .30 .14
- ❑ 2 Marcus Moore .20 .09
- ❑ 3 Doug Creek RC .20 .09
- ❑ 4 Pedro Martinez 1.00 .45
- ❑ 5 Ken Griffey Jr. 2.50 1.10
- ❑ 6 Greg Swindell .20 .09
- ❑ 7 J.J. Johnson .20 .09
- ❑ 8 Homer Bush RC .75 .35
- ❑ 9 Arquimedez Pozo RC .20 .09

- ❑ 10 Bryan Harvey .20 .09
- ❑ 11 J.T. Snow .30 .14
- ❑ 12 Alan Benes RC .30 .14
- ❑ 13 Chad Kreuter .20 .09
- ❑ 14 Eric Karros .30 .14
- ❑ 15 Frank Thomas 1.00 .45
- ❑ 16 Bret Saberhagen .30 .14
- ❑ 17 Terrell Lowery .20 .09
- ❑ 18 Rod Bolton .20 .09
- ❑ 19 Harold Baines .30 .14
- ❑ 20 Matt Walbeck .20 .09
- ❑ 21 Tom Glavine .75 .35
- ❑ 22 Todd Jones .20 .09
- ❑ 23 Alberto Castillo RC .20 .09
- ❑ 24 Ruben Sierra .20 .09
- ❑ 25 Don Mattingly 2.00 .90
- ❑ 26 Mike Morgan .20 .09
- ❑ 27 Jim Musselwhite RC .20 .09
- ❑ 28 Matt Brunson RC .20 .09
- ❑ 29 A.Meinershagen RC .20 .09
- ❑ 30 Joe Girardi .20 .09
- ❑ 31 Shane Halter .20 .09
- ❑ 32 Jose Paniagua RC .30 .14
- ❑ 33 Paul Perkins RC .20 .09
- ❑ 34 John Hudek RC .20 .09
- ❑ 35 Frank Viola .30 .14
- ❑ 36 David Lamb RC .20 .09
- ❑ 37 Marshall Boze .20 .09
- ❑ 38 Jorge Posada RC 6.00 2.70
- ❑ 39 Brian Anderson RC .30 .14
- ❑ 40 Mark Whiten .20 .09
- ❑ 41 Sean Bergman .20 .09
- ❑ 42 Jose Parra RC .20 .09
- ❑ 43 Mike Robertson .20 .09
- ❑ 44 Pete Walker RC .20 .09
- ❑ 45 Juan Gonzalez .75 .35
- ❑ 46 Cleveland Ladell RC .20 .09
- ❑ 47 Mark Smith .20 .09
- ❑ 48 Kevin Jarvis UER .20 .09
  (team listed as Yankees on back)
- ❑ 49 Amaury Telemaco RC .20 .09
- ❑ 50 Andy Van Slyke .30 .14
- ❑ 51 Rikkert Faneyte RC .20 .09
- ❑ 52 Curtis Shaw .20 .09
- ❑ 53 Matt Drews RC .20 .09
- ❑ 54 Wilson Alvarez .20 .09
- ❑ 55 Manny Ramirez 1.25 .55
- ❑ 56 Bobby Munoz .20 .09
- ❑ 57 Ed Sprague .20 .09
- ❑ 58 Jamey Wright RC 1.00 .45
- ❑ 59 Jeff Montgomery .20 .09
- ❑ 60 Kirk Rueter .20 .09
- ❑ 61 Edgar Martinez .50 .23
- ❑ 62 Luis Gonzalez .75 .35
- ❑ 63 Tim Vanegmond RC .20 .09
- ❑ 64 Bip Roberts .20 .09
- ❑ 65 John Jaha .20 .09
- ❑ 66 Chuck Carr .20 .09
- ❑ 67 Chuck Finley .30 .14
- ❑ 68 Aaron Holbert .20 .09
- ❑ 69 Cecil Fielder .30 .14
- ❑ 70 Tom Engle RC .20 .09
- ❑ 71 Ron Karkovice .20 .09
- ❑ 72 Joe Orsulak .20 .09
- ❑ 73 Duff Brumley RC .20 .09
- ❑ 74 Craig Clayton RC .20 .09
- ❑ 75 Cal Ripken 3.00 1.35
- ❑ 76 Brad Fulmer RC 4.00 1.80
- ❑ 77 Tony Tarasco .20 .09
- ❑ 78 Terry Farrar RC .20 .09
- ❑ 79 Matt Williams .50 .23
- ❑ 80 Rickey Henderson 1.50 .70
- ❑ 81 Terry Mulholland .20 .09
- ❑ 82 Sammy Sosa 1.50 .70
- ❑ 83 Paul Sorrento .20 .09
- ❑ 84 Pete Incaviglia .20 .09
- ❑ 85 Darren Hall RC .20 .09
- ❑ 86 Scott Klingenbeck .20 .09
- ❑ 87 Dario Perez RC .20 .09
- ❑ 88 Ugueth Urbina .20 .09
- ❑ 89 Dave Vanhof RC .20 .09
- ❑ 90 Domingo Jean .20 .09
- ❑ 91 Otis Nixon .20 .09
- ❑ 92 Andres Berumen .20 .09
- ❑ 93 Jose Valentin .20 .09
- ❑ 94 Edgar Renteria RC 2.00 .90
- ❑ 95 Chris Turner .20 .09
- ❑ 96 Ray Lankford .20 .09
- ❑ 97 Danny Bautista .20 .09
- ❑ 98 Chan Ho Park RC 5.00 2.20
- ❑ 99 Glenn DiSarcina RC .20 .09
- ❑ 100 Butch Huskey .20 .09
- ❑ 101 Ivan Rodriguez .75 .35
- ❑ 102 Johnny Ruffin .20 .09
- ❑ 103 Alex Ochoa .20 .09
- ❑ 104 Torii Hunter RC 3.00 1.35
- ❑ 105 Ryan Klesko .30 .14
- ❑ 106 Jay Bell .30 .14
- ❑ 107 Kurt Peltzer RC .20 .09
- ❑ 108 Miguel Jimenez .20 .09
- ❑ 109 Russ Davis .20 .09
- ❑ 110 Derek Wallace .20 .09
- ❑ 111 Keith Lockhart RC .30 .14
- ❑ 112 Mike Lieberthal .30 .14
- ❑ 113 Dave Stewart .30 .14
- ❑ 114 Tom Schmidt .20 .09
- ❑ 115 Brian McRae .20 .09
- ❑ 116 Moises Alou .30 .14
- ❑ 117 Dave Fleming .20 .09
- ❑ 118 Jeff Bagwell 1.00 .45
- ❑ 119 Luis Ortiz .20 .09
- ❑ 120 Tony Gwynn 1.50 .70
- ❑ 121 Jaime Navarro .20 .09
- ❑ 122 Benito Santiago .20 .09
- ❑ 123 Darrell Whitmore .20 .09
- ❑ 124 John Mabry RC .20 .09
- ❑ 125 Mickey Tettleton .20 .09
- ❑ 126 Tom Candiotti .20 .09
- ❑ 127 Tim Raines .30 .14
- ❑ 128 Bobby Bonilla .30 .14
- ❑ 129 John Dettmer .20 .09
- ❑ 130 Hector Carrasco .20 .09
- ❑ 131 Chris Hoiles .20 .09
- ❑ 132 Rick Aguilera .20 .09
- ❑ 133 David Justice .30 .14
- ❑ 134 Esteban Loaiza RC 1.00 .45
- ❑ 135 Barry Bonds 2.00 .90
- ❑ 136 Bob Welch .20 .09
- ❑ 137 Mike Stanley .20 .09
- ❑ 138 Roberto Hernandez .20 .09
- ❑ 139 Sandy Alomar Jr. .30 .14
- ❑ 140 Darren Daulton .30 .14
- ❑ 141 Angel Martinez RC .20 .09
- ❑ 142 Howard Johnson .20 .09
- ❑ 143 Bob Hamelin UER .20 .09
  (name and card number colors don't match)
- ❑ 144 J.J. Thobe RC .20 .09
- ❑ 145 Roger Salkeld .20 .09
- ❑ 146 Orlando Miller .20 .09
- ❑ 147 Dmitri Young .30 .14
- ❑ 148 Tim Hyers RC .20 .09
- ❑ 149 Mark Loretta RC .30 .14
- ❑ 150 Chris Hammond .20 .09
- ❑ 151 Joel Moore RC .20 .09
- ❑ 152 Todd Zeile .20 .09
- ❑ 153 Wil Cordero .20 .09
- ❑ 154 Chris Smith .20 .09
- ❑ 155 James Baldwin .20 .09
- ❑ 156 Edgardo Alfonzo RC 6.00 2.70
- ❑ 157 Kym Ashworth RC .20 .09
- ❑ 158 Paul Bako RC .20 .09
- ❑ 159 Rick Krivda RC .20 .09

❑	160	Pat Mahomes	.20	.09
❑	161	Damon Hollins	.30	.14
❑	162	Felix Martinez RC	.30	.14
❑	163	Jason Myers RC	.20	.09
❑	164	Izzy Molina RC	.20	.09
❑	165	Brien Taylor	.20	.09
❑	166	Kevin Orie RC	.20	.09
❑	167	Casey Whitten RC	.20	.09
❑	168	Tony Longmire	.20	.09
❑	169	John Olerud	.30	.14
❑	170	Mark Thompson	.20	.09
❑	171	Jorge Fabregas	.20	.09
❑	172	John Wetteland	.30	.14
❑	173	Dan Wilson	.20	.09
❑	174	Doug Drabek	.20	.09
❑	175	Jeff McNeely	.20	.09
❑	176	Melvin Nieves	.20	.09
❑	177	Doug Glanville RC	1.00	.45
❑	178	Javier De La Hoya RC	.20	.09
❑	179	Chad Curtis	.20	.09
❑	180	Brian Barber	.20	.09
❑	181	Mike Henneman	.20	.09
❑	182	Jose Offerman	.20	.09
❑	183	Robert Ellis RC	.20	.09
❑	184	John Franco	.30	.14
❑	185	Benji Gil	.20	.09
❑	186	Hal Morris	.20	.09
❑	187	Chris Sabo	.20	.09
❑	188	Blaise Ilsley RC	.20	.09
❑	189	Steve Avery	.20	.09
❑	190	Rick White RC	.20	.09
❑	191	Rod Beck	.20	.09
❑	192	Mark McGwire UER (No card number on back)	3.00	1.35
❑	193	Jim Abbott	.30	.14
❑	194	Randy Myers	.20	.09
❑	195	Kenny Lofton	.30	.14
❑	196	Mariano Duncan	.20	.09
❑	197	Lee Daniels RC	.20	.09
❑	198	Armando Reynoso	.20	.09
❑	199	Joe Randa	.30	.14
❑	200	Cliff Floyd	.30	.14
❑	201	Tim Harkrider RC	.20	.09
❑	202	Kevin Gallaher RC	.20	.09
❑	203	Scott Cooper	.20	.09
❑	204	Phil Stidham RC	.20	.09
❑	205	Jeff D'Amico RC	1.00	.45
❑	206	Matt Whisenant	.20	.09
❑	207	De Shawn Warren	.20	.09
❑	208	Rene Arocha	.20	.09
❑	209	Tony Clark RC	3.00	1.35
❑	210	Jason Jacome RC	.20	.09
❑	211	Scott Christman RC	.20	.09
❑	212	Bill Pulsipher	.30	.14
❑	213	Dean Palmer	.30	.14
❑	214	Chad Mottola	.20	.09
❑	215	Manny Alexander	.20	.09
❑	216	Rich Becker	.20	.09
❑	217	Andre King RC	.20	.09
❑	218	Carlos Garcia	.20	.09
❑	219	Ron Pezzoni RC	.20	.09
❑	220	Steve Karsay	.20	.09
❑	221	Jose Musset RC	.20	.09
❑	222	Karl Rhodes	.20	.09
❑	223	Frank Cimorelli RC	.20	.09
❑	224	Kevin Jordan RC	.20	.09
❑	225	Duane Ward	.20	.09
❑	226	John Burke	.20	.09
❑	227	Mike Macfarlane	.20	.09
❑	228	Mike Lansing	.20	.09
❑	229	Chuck Knoblauch	.30	.14
❑	230	Ken Caminiti	.30	.14
❑	231	Gar Finnvold RC	.20	.09
❑	232	Derrek Lee RC	2.00	.90
❑	233	Brady Anderson	.30	.14
❑	234	Vic Darensbourg RC	.20	.09
❑	235	Mark Langston	.20	.09
❑	236	T.J. Mathews RC	.30	.14
❑	237	Lou Whitaker	.30	.14
❑	238	Roger Cedeno	.20	.09
❑	239	Alex Fernandez	.20	.09
❑	240	Ryan Thompson	.20	.09
❑	241	Kerry Lacy RC	.20	.09
❑	242	Reggie Sanders	.20	.09
❑	243	Brad Pennington	.20	.09
❑	244	Bryan Eversgerd RC	.20	.09
❑	245	Greg Maddux	2.00	.90
❑	246	Jason Kendall	.30	.14
❑	247	J.R. Phillips	.20	.09
❑	248	Bobby Witt	.20	.09
❑	249	Paul O'Neill	.75	.35
❑	250	Ryne Sandberg	1.00	.45
❑	251	Charles Nagy	.20	.09
❑	252	Kevin Stocker	.20	.09
❑	253	Shawn Green	1.00	.45
❑	254	Charlie Hayes	.20	.09
❑	255	Donnie Elliott	.20	.09
❑	256	Rob Fitzpatrick RC	.20	.09
❑	257	Tim Davis	.20	.09
❑	258	James Mouton	.20	.09
❑	259	Mike Greenwell	.20	.09
❑	260	Ray McDavid	.20	.09
❑	261	Mike Kelly	.20	.09
❑	262	Andy Larkin RC	.20	.09
❑	263	Marquis Riley UER (No card number on back)	.20	.09
❑	264	Bob Tewksbury	.20	.09
❑	265	Brian Edmondson	.20	.09
❑	266	Eduardo Lantigua RC	.20	.09
❑	267	Brandon Wilson	.20	.09
❑	268	Mike Welch	.20	.09
❑	269	Tom Henke	.20	.09
❑	270	Pokey Reese	.20	.09
❑	271	Greg Zaun RC	.20	.09
❑	272	Todd Ritchie	.20	.09
❑	273	Javier Lopez	.30	.14
❑	274	Kevin Young	.20	.09
❑	275	Kirt Manwaring	.20	.09
❑	276	Bill Taylor RC	.30	.14
❑	277	Robert Eenhoorn	.20	.09
❑	278	Jessie Hollins	.20	.09
❑	279	Julian Tavarez RC	.30	.14
❑	280	Gene Schall	.20	.09
❑	281	Paul Molitor	.75	.35
❑	282	Neifi Perez RC	2.00	.90
❑	283	Greg Gagne	.20	.09
❑	284	Marquis Grissom	.20	.09
❑	285	Randy Johnson	1.00	.45
❑	286	Pete Harnisch	.20	.09
❑	287	Joel Bennett RC	.20	.09
❑	288	Derek Bell	.20	.09
❑	289	Darryl Hamilton	.20	.09
❑	290	Gary Sheffield	.30	.14
❑	291	Eduardo Perez	.20	.09
❑	292	Basil Shabazz	.20	.09
❑	293	Eric Davis	.30	.14
❑	294	Pedro Astacio	.20	.09
❑	295	Robin Ventura	.30	.14
❑	296	Jeff Kent	.50	.23
❑	297	Rick Helling	.20	.09
❑	298	Joe Oliver	.20	.09
❑	299	Lee Smith	.30	.14
❑	300	Dave Winfield	.75	.35
❑	301	Deion Sanders	.30	.14
❑	302	R.Manzanillo RC	.20	.09
❑	303	Mark Portugal	.20	.09
❑	304	Brent Gates	.20	.09
❑	305	Wade Boggs	.75	.35
❑	306	Rick Wilkins	.20	.09
❑	307	Carlos Baerga	.20	.09
❑	308	Curt Schilling	.75	.35
❑	309	Shannon Stewart	.75	.35
❑	310	Darren Holmes	.20	.09
❑	311	Robert Toth RC	.20	.09
❑	312	Gabe White	.20	.09
❑	313	Mac Suzuki RC	.30	.14
❑	314	Alvin Morman RC	.20	.09
❑	315	Mo Vaughn	.30	.14
❑	316	Bryce Florie RC	.20	.09
❑	317	Gabby Martinez RC	.20	.09
❑	318	Carl Everett	.30	.14
❑	319	Kerwin Moore	.20	.09
❑	320	Tom Pagnozzi	.20	.09
❑	321	Chris Gomez	.20	.09
❑	322	Todd Williams	.20	.09
❑	323	Pat Hentgen	.20	.09
❑	324	Kirk Presley RC	.20	.09
❑	325	Kevin Brown	.30	.14
❑	326	J.Isringhausen RC	2.00	.90
❑	327	Rick Forney RC	.20	.09
❑	328	Carlos Pulido RC	.20	.09
❑	329	Terrell Wade RC	.20	.09
❑	330	Al Martin	.20	.09
❑	331	Dan Carlson RC	.20	.09
❑	332	Mark Acre RC	.20	.09
❑	333	Sterling Hitchcock	.20	.09
❑	334	Jon Ratliff RC	.20	.09
❑	335	Alex Ramirez RC	.30	.14
❑	336	Phil Geisler RC	.20	.09
❑	337	E.Zambrano FOIL RC	.20	.09
❑	338	Jim Thome FOIL	.75	.35
❑	339	James Mouton FOIL	.20	.09
❑	340	Cliff Floyd FOIL	.30	.14
❑	341	Carlos Delgado FOIL	1.25	.55
❑	342	R.Petagine FOIL	.20	.09
❑	343	Tim Clark FOIL	.20	.09
❑	344	Bubba Smith FOIL	.20	.09
❑	345	Randy Curtis FOIL RC	.20	.09
❑	346	Joe Biasucci FOIL RC	.20	.09
❑	347	D.J. Boston FOIL RC	.20	.09
❑	348	R.Rivera FOIL RC	.30	.14
❑	349	Bryan Link FOIL RC	.20	.09
❑	350	Mike Bell FOIL RC	.20	.09
❑	351	M.Watson FOIL RC	.20	.09
❑	352	Jason Myers FOIL	.20	.09
❑	353	Chipper Jones FOIL	1.50	.70
❑	354	B.Kieschnick FOIL	.20	.09
❑	355	Pokey Reese FOIL	.20	.09
❑	356	John Burke FOIL	.20	.09
❑	357	Kurt Miller FOIL	.20	.09
❑	358	Orlando Miller FOIL	.20	.09
❑	359	T.Hollandsworth FOIL	.20	.09
❑	360	Rondell White FOIL	.30	.14
❑	361	Bill Pulsipher FOIL	.30	.14
❑	362	Tyler Green FOIL	.20	.09
❑	363	M.Cummings FOIL	.20	.09
❑	364	Brian Barber FOIL	.20	.09
❑	365	Melvin Nieves FOIL	.20	.09
❑	366	Salomon Torres FOIL	.20	.09
❑	367	Alex Ochoa FOIL	.20	.09
❑	368	F.Rodriguez FOIL	.20	.09
❑	369	Brian Anderson FOIL	.30	.14
❑	370	James Baldwin FOIL	.20	.09
❑	371	Manny Ramirez FOIL	1.25	.55
❑	372	J.Thompson FOIL	.20	.09
❑	373	Johnny Damon FOIL	.75	.35
❑	374	Jeff D'Amico FOIL	1.00	.45
❑	375	Rich Becker FOIL	.20	.09
❑	376	Derek Jeter FOIL	4.00	1.80
❑	377	Steve Karsay FOIL	.20	.09
❑	378	Mac Suzuki FOIL	.30	.14
❑	379	Benji Gil FOIL	.20	.09
❑	380	Alex Gonzalez FOIL	.20	.09
❑	381	Jason Bere FOIL	.20	.09
❑	382	Brett Butler FOIL	.30	.14
❑	383	Jeff Conine FOIL	.20	.09
❑	384	Darren Daulton FOIL	.30	.14
❑	385	Jeff Kent FOIL	.50	.23
❑	386	Don Mattingly FOIL	2.00	.90
❑	387	Mike Piazza FOIL	2.50	1.10
❑	388	Ryne Sandberg FOIL	1.00	.45
❑	389	Rich Amaral	.20	.09
❑	390	Craig Biggio	.50	.23
❑	391	Jeff Suppan RC	.30	.14
❑	392	Andy Benes	.20	.09
❑	393	Cal Eldred	.20	.09
❑	394	Jeff Conine	.20	.09
❑	395	Tim Salmon	.30	.14
❑	396	Ray Suplee RC	.20	.09
❑	397	Tony Phillips	.20	.09
❑	398	Ramon Martinez	.20	.09
❑	399	Julio Franco	.30	.14
❑	400	Dwight Gooden	.30	.14
❑	401	Kevin Lomon RC	.20	.09
❑	402	Jose Rijo	.20	.09
❑	403	Mike Devereaux	.20	.09
❑	404	Mike Zolecki RC	.20	.09
❑	405	Fred McGriff	.50	.23
❑	406	Danny Clyburn	.20	.09
❑	407	Robby Thompson	.20	.09
❑	408	Terry Steinbach	.20	.09
❑	409	Luis Polonia	.20	.09
❑	410	Mark Grace	.75	.35
❑	411	Albert Belle	.30	.14
❑	412	John Kruk	.30	.14
❑	413	Scott Spiezio RC	.30	.14
❑	414	Ellis Burks UER (Name spelled Elkis on front)	.30	.14

❑ 415 Joe Vitiello .20 .09
❑ 416 Tim Costo .20 .09
❑ 417 Marc Newfield .20 .09
❑ 418 Oscar Henriquez RC .20 .09
❑ 419 Matt Perisho RC .30 .14
❑ 420 Julio Bruno .20 .09
❑ 421 Kenny Felder .20 .09
❑ 422 Tyler Green .20 .09
❑ 423 Jim Edmonds .75 .35
❑ 424 Ozzie Smith 1.00 .45
❑ 425 Rick Greene .20 .09
❑ 426 Todd Hollandsworth .20 .09
❑ 427 Eddie Pearson RC .20 .09
❑ 428 Quilvio Veras .20 .09
❑ 429 Kenny Rogers .20 .09
❑ 430 Willie Greene .20 .09
❑ 431 Vaughn Eshelman .20 .09
❑ 432 Pat Meares .20 .09
❑ 433 Jermaine Dye RC 10.00 4.50
❑ 434 Steve Cooke .20 .09
❑ 435 Bill Swift .20 .09
❑ 436 Fausto Cruz RC .20 .09
❑ 437 Mark Hutton .20 .09
❑ 438 B.Kieschnick RC .20 .09
❑ 439 Yorkis Perez .20 .09
❑ 440 Len Dykstra .30 .14
❑ 441 Pat Borders .20 .09
❑ 442 Doug Walls RC .20 .09
❑ 443 Wally Joyner .30 .14
❑ 444 Ken Hill .20 .09
❑ 445 Eric Anthony .20 .09
❑ 446 Mitch Williams .20 .09
❑ 447 Cory Bailey RC .20 .09
❑ 448 Dave Staton .20 .09
❑ 449 Greg Vaughn .30 .14
❑ 450 Dave Magadan .20 .09
❑ 451 Chili Davis .30 .14
❑ 452 Gerald Santos RC .20 .09
❑ 453 Joe Perona .20 .09
❑ 454 Delino DeShields .20 .09
❑ 455 Jack McDowell .20 .09
❑ 456 Todd Hundley .20 .09
❑ 457 Ritchie Moody .20 .09
❑ 458 Bret Boone .30 .14
❑ 459 Ben McDonald .20 .09
❑ 460 Kirby Puckett 2.00 .90
❑ 461 Gregg Olson .20 .09
❑ 462 Rich Aude RC .20 .09
❑ 463 John Burkett .20 .09
❑ 464 Troy Neel .20 .09
❑ 465 Jimmy Key .30 .14
❑ 466 Ozzie Timmons .20 .09
❑ 467 Eddie Murray .75 .35
❑ 468 Mark Tranberg RC .20 .09
❑ 469 Alex Gonzalez .20 .09
❑ 470 David Nied .20 .09
❑ 471 Barry Larkin .75 .35
❑ 472 Brian Looney RC .20 .09
❑ 473 Shawn Estes .30 .14
❑ 474 A.J. Sager RC .20 .09
❑ 475 Roger Clemens 2.00 .90
❑ 476 Vince Moore .20 .09
❑ 477 Scott Karl RC .30 .14
❑ 478 Kurt Miller .20 .09
❑ 479 Garret Anderson .30 .14
❑ 480 Allen Watson .20 .09
❑ 481 Jose Lima RC 1.00 .45
❑ 482 Rick Gorecki .20 .09
❑ 483 Jimmy Hurst RC .20 .09
❑ 484 Preston Wilson .75 .35
❑ 485 Will Clark .75 .35
❑ 486 Mike Ferry RC .20 .09
❑ 487 Curtis Goodwin RC .30 .14
❑ 488 Mike Myers .20 .09
❑ 489 Chipper Jones 1.50 .70
❑ 490 Jeff King .20 .09
❑ 491 W.VanLandingham RC .20 .09
❑ 492 Carlos Reyes RC .20 .09
❑ 493 Andy Pettitte 1.00 .45
❑ 494 Brant Brown .20 .09
❑ 495 Daron Kirkreit .20 .09
❑ 496 Ricky Bottalico RC .30 .14
❑ 497 Devon White .20 .09
❑ 498 Jason Johnson RC .20 .09
❑ 499 Vince Coleman .20 .09
❑ 500 Larry Walker .50 .23
❑ 501 Bobby Ayala .20 .09
❑ 502 Steve Finley .30 .14
❑ 503 Scott Fletcher .20 .09
❑ 504 Brad Ausmus .20 .09
❑ 505 Scott Talanoa RC .20 .09
❑ 506 Orestes Destrade .20 .09
❑ 507 Gary DiSarcina .20 .09
❑ 508 Willie Smith RC .20 .09
❑ 509 Alan Trammell .50 .23
❑ 510 Mike Piazza 2.50 1.10
❑ 511 Ozzie Guillen .20 .09
❑ 512 Jeromy Burnitz .30 .14
❑ 513 Darren Oliver RC .75 .35
❑ 514 Kevin Mitchell .20 .09
❑ 515 Rafael Palmeiro .75 .35
❑ 516 David McCarty .20 .09
❑ 517 Jeff Blauser .20 .09
❑ 518 Trey Beamon .20 .09
❑ 519 Royce Clayton .20 .09
❑ 520 Dennis Eckersley .30 .14
❑ 521 Bernie Williams .75 .35
❑ 522 Steve Buechele .20 .09
❑ 523 Dennis Martinez .30 .14
❑ 524 Dave Hollins .20 .09
❑ 525 Joey Hamilton .20 .09
❑ 526 Andres Galarraga .50 .23
❑ 527 Jeff Granger .20 .09
❑ 528 Joey Eischen .20 .09
❑ 529 Desi Relaford .20 .09
❑ 530 Roberto Petagine .20 .09
❑ 531 Andre Dawson .50 .23
❑ 532 Ray Holbert .20 .09
❑ 533 Duane Singleton .20 .09
❑ 534 Kurt Abbott RC .30 .14
❑ 535 Bo Jackson .30 .14
❑ 536 Gregg Jefferies .20 .09
❑ 537 David Mysel .20 .09
❑ 538 Raul Mondesi .30 .14
❑ 539 Chris Snopek .20 .09
❑ 540 Brook Fordyce .20 .09
❑ 541 Ron Frazier RC .20 .09
❑ 542 Brian Koelling .20 .09
❑ 543 Jimmy Haynes .20 .09
❑ 544 Marty Cordova .20 .09
❑ 545 Jason Green RC .20 .09
❑ 546 Orlando Merced .20 .09
❑ 547 Lou Pote RC .20 .09
❑ 548 Todd Van Poppel .20 .09
❑ 549 Pat Kelly .20 .09
❑ 550 Turk Wendell .20 .09
❑ 551 Herbert Perry RC .30 .14
❑ 552 Ryan Karp RC .20 .09
❑ 553 Juan Guzman .20 .09
❑ 554 Bryan Rekar RC .20 .09
❑ 555 Kevin Appier .30 .14
❑ 556 Chris Schwab RC .20 .09
❑ 557 Jay Buhner .30 .14
❑ 558 Andujar Cedeno .20 .09
❑ 559 Ryan McGuire RC .30 .14
❑ 560 Ricky Gutierrez .20 .09
❑ 561 Keith Kimsey RC .20 .09
❑ 562 Tim Clark .20 .09
❑ 563 Damion Easley .20 .09
❑ 564 Clint Davis RC .20 .09
❑ 565 Mike Moore .20 .09
❑ 566 Orel Hershiser .30 .14
❑ 567 Jason Bere .20 .09
❑ 568 Kevin McReynolds .20 .09
❑ 569 Leland Macon RC .20 .09
❑ 570 John Courtright RC .20 .09
❑ 571 Sid Fernandez .20 .09
❑ 572 Chad Roper .20 .09
❑ 573 Terry Pendleton .30 .14
❑ 574 Danny Miceli .20 .09
❑ 575 Joe Rosselli .20 .09
❑ 576 Mike Bordick .20 .09
❑ 577 Danny Tartabull .20 .09
❑ 578 Jose Guzman .20 .09
❑ 579 Omar Vizquel .30 .14
❑ 580 Tommy Greene .20 .09
❑ 581 Paul Spoljaric .20 .09
❑ 582 Walt Weiss .20 .09
❑ 583 Oscar Jimenez RC .20 .09
❑ 584 Rod Henderson .20 .09
❑ 585 Derek Lowe .20 .09
❑ 586 Richard Hidalgo RC 10.00 4.50
❑ 587 Shayne Bennett RC .20 .09
❑ 588 Tim Belk RC .20 .09
❑ 589 Matt Mieske .20 .09
❑ 590 Nigel Wilson .20 .09
❑ 591 Jeff Knox RC .20 .09
❑ 592 Bernard Gilkey .20 .09
❑ 593 David Cone .30 .14
❑ 594 Paul LoDuca RC 12.00 5.50
❑ 595 Scott Ruffcorn .20 .09
❑ 596 Chris Roberts .20 .09
❑ 597 Oscar Munoz RC .20 .09
❑ 598 Scott Sullivan RC .20 .09
❑ 599 Matt Jarvis RC .20 .09
❑ 600 Jose Canseco .75 .35
❑ 601 Tony Graffanino RC .30 .14
❑ 602 Don Slaught .20 .09
❑ 603 Brett King RC .20 .09
❑ 604 Jose Herrera RC .20 .09
❑ 605 Melido Perez .20 .09
❑ 606 Mike Hubbard RC .20 .09
❑ 607 Chad Ogea .20 .09
❑ 608 Wayne Gomes RC .20 .09
❑ 609 Roberto Alomar .75 .35
❑ 610 Angel Echevarria RC .20 .09
❑ 611 Jose Lind .20 .09
❑ 612 Darrin Fletcher .20 .09
❑ 613 Chris Bosio .20 .09
❑ 614 Darryl Kile .30 .14
❑ 615 Frankie Rodriguez .20 .09
❑ 616 Phil Plantier .20 .09
❑ 617 Pat Listach .20 .09
❑ 618 Charlie Hough .30 .14
❑ 619 Ryan Hancock RC .20 .09
❑ 620 Darrel Deak RC .20 .09
❑ 621 Travis Fryman .30 .14
❑ 622 Brett Butler .30 .14
❑ 623 Lance Johnson .20 .09
❑ 624 Pete Smith .20 .09
❑ 625 James Hurst RC .20 .09
❑ 626 Roberto Kelly .20 .09
❑ 627 Mike Mussina .75 .35
❑ 628 Kevin Tapani .20 .09
❑ 629 John Smoltz .30 .14
❑ 630 Midre Cummings .20 .09
❑ 631 Salomon Torres .20 .09
❑ 632 Willie Adams .20 .09
❑ 633 Derek Jeter 4.00 1.80
❑ 634 Steve Trachsel .20 .09
❑ 635 Albie Lopez .20 .09
❑ 636 Jason Moler .20 .09
❑ 637 Carlos Delgado 1.25 .55
❑ 638 Roberto Mejia .20 .09
❑ 639 Darren Burton .20 .09
❑ 640 B.J. Wallace .20 .09
❑ 641 Brad Clontz RC .20 .09
❑ 642 Billy Wagner RC 2.00 .90
❑ 643 Aaron Sele .30 .14
❑ 644 Cameron Cairncross .20 .09
❑ 645 Brian Harper .20 .09
❑ 646 Marc Valdes UER .20 .09
(No card number on back)
❑ 647 Mark Ratekin .20 .09
❑ 648 Terry Bradshaw RC .20 .09
❑ 649 Justin Thompson .20 .09
❑ 650 Mike Busch RC .20 .09
❑ 651 Joe Hall RC .20 .09
❑ 652 Bobby Jones .20 .09
❑ 653 Kelly Stinnett RC .30 .14
❑ 654 Rod Steph RC .20 .09
❑ 655 Jay Powell RC .20 .09
❑ 656 K.Garagozzo RC UER .20 .09
No card number on back
❑ 657 Todd Dunn .20 .09
❑ 658 Charles Peterson RC .20 .09
❑ 659 Darren Lewis .20 .09
❑ 660 John Wasdin RC .20 .09
❑ 661 Tate Seefried RC .20 .09
❑ 662 Hector Trinidad RC .20 .09
❑ 663 John Carter RC .20 .09
❑ 664 Larry Mitchell .20 .09
❑ 665 David Catlett RC .20 .09
❑ 666 Dante Bichette .30 .14
❑ 667 Felix Jose .20 .09
❑ 668 Rondell White .30 .14
❑ 669 Tino Martinez .30 .14
❑ 670 Brian L. Hunter .20 .09

Card	MINT	NRMT
❑ 671 Jose Malave	.20	.09
❑ 672 Archi Cianfrocco	.20	.09
❑ 673 Mike Matheny RC	.20	.09
❑ 674 Bret Barberie	.20	.09
❑ 675 Andrew Lorraine RC	.20	.09
❑ 676 Brian Jordan	.30	.14
❑ 677 Tim Belcher	.20	.09
❑ 678 Antonio Osuna RC	.30	.14
❑ 679 Checklist	.20	.09
❑ 680 Checklist	.20	.09
❑ 681 Checklist	.20	.09
❑ 682 Checklist	.20	.09

1995 Bowman

	MINT	NRMT
COMPLETE SET (439)	250.00	110.00
❑ 1 Billy Wagner	.40	.18
❑ 2 Chris Widger	.25	.11
❑ 3 Brent Bowers	.25	.11
❑ 4 Bob Abreu RC	10.00	4.50
❑ 5 Lou Collier RC	.25	.11
❑ 6 Juan Acevedo RC	.25	.11
❑ 7 Jason Kelley RC	.25	.11
❑ 8 Brian Sackinsky	.25	.11
❑ 9 Scott Christman	.25	.11
❑ 10 Damon Hollins	.25	.11
❑ 11 Willis Otanez RC	.25	.11
❑ 12 Jason Ryan RC	.25	.11
❑ 13 Jason Giambi	1.00	.45
❑ 14 Andy Taulbee RC	.25	.11
❑ 15 Mark Thompson	.25	.11
❑ 16 Hugo Pivaral RC	.25	.11
❑ 17 Brien Taylor	.25	.11
❑ 18 Antonio Osuna	.25	.11
❑ 19 Edgardo Alfonzo	1.00	.45
❑ 20 Carl Everett	.40	.18
❑ 21 Matt Drews	.25	.11
❑ 22 Bartolo Colon RC	6.00	2.70
❑ 23 Andruw Jones RC	30.00	13.50
❑ 24 Robert Person RC	2.00	.90
❑ 25 Derrek Lee	.40	.18
❑ 26 John Ambrose RC	.25	.11
❑ 27 Eric Knowles RC	.25	.11
❑ 28 Chris Roberts	.25	.11
❑ 29 Don Wengert	.25	.11
❑ 30 Marcus Jensen RC	.40	.18
❑ 31 Brian Barber	.25	.11
❑ 32 Kevin Brown C	.40	.18
❑ 33 Benji Gil	.25	.11
❑ 34 Mike Hubbard	.25	.11
❑ 35 Bart Evans RC	.25	.11
❑ 36 Enrique Wilson RC	.40	.18
❑ 37 Brian Buchanan RC	.25	.11
❑ 38 Ken Ray RC	.25	.11
❑ 39 Micah Franklin RC	.25	.11
❑ 40 Ricky Otero RC	.25	.11
❑ 41 Jason Kendall	.40	.18
❑ 42 Jimmy Hurst	.25	.11
❑ 43 Jerry Wolak RC	.25	.11
❑ 44 Jayson Peterson RC	.25	.11
❑ 45 Allen Battle RC	.25	.11
❑ 46 Scott Stahoviak	.25	.11
❑ 47 Steve Schrenk RC	.25	.11
❑ 48 Travis Miller RC	.25	.11
❑ 49 Eddie Rios RC	.25	.11
❑ 50 Mike Hampton	.40	.18
❑ 51 Chad Frontera RC	.25	.11
❑ 52 Tom Evans	.25	.11
❑ 53 C.J. Nitkowski	.25	.11
❑ 54 Clay Caruthers RC	.25	.11
❑ 55 Shannon Stewart	.40	.18
❑ 56 Jorge Posada	.40	.18
❑ 57 Aaron Holbert	.25	.11
❑ 58 Harry Berrios RC	.25	.11
❑ 59 Steve Rodriguez	.25	.11
❑ 60 Shane Andrews	.25	.11
❑ 61 Will Cunnane RC	.25	.11
❑ 62 Richard Hidalgo	.60	.25
❑ 63 Bill Selby RC	.25	.11
❑ 64 Jay Cranford RC	.25	.11
❑ 65 Jeff Suppan	.25	.11
❑ 66 Curtis Goodwin	.25	.11
❑ 67 John Thomson RC	.25	.11
❑ 68 Justin Thompson	.25	.11
❑ 69 Troy Percival	.25	.11
❑ 70 Matt Wagner RC	.25	.11
❑ 71 Terry Bradshaw	.25	.11
❑ 72 Greg Hansell	.25	.11
❑ 73 John Burke	.25	.11
❑ 74 Jeff D'Amico	.25	.11
❑ 75 Ernie Young	.25	.11
❑ 76 Jason Bates	.25	.11
❑ 77 Chris Stynes	.25	.11
❑ 78 Cade Gaspar RC	.25	.11
❑ 79 Melvin Nieves	.25	.11
❑ 80 Rick Gorecki	.25	.11
❑ 81 Felix Rodriguez RC	.40	.18
❑ 82 Ryan Hancock	.25	.11
❑ 83 Chris Carpenter RC	2.00	.90
❑ 84 Ray McDavid	.25	.11
❑ 85 Chris Wimmer	.25	.11
❑ 86 Doug Glanville	.25	.11
❑ 87 DeShawn Warren	.25	.11
❑ 88 Damian Moss RC	.40	.18
❑ 89 Rafael Orellano RC	.25	.11
❑ 90 Vladimir Guerrero RC	40.00	18.00
❑ 91 Raul Casanova RC	.25	.11
❑ 92 Karim Garcia RC	.40	.18
❑ 93 Bryce Florie	.25	.11
❑ 94 Kevin Orie	.25	.11
❑ 95 Ryan Nye RC	.25	.11
❑ 96 Matt Sachse RC	.25	.11
❑ 97 Ivan Arteaga RC	.25	.11
❑ 98 Glenn Murray	.25	.11
❑ 99 Stacy Hollins RC	.25	.11
❑ 100 Jim Pittsley	.25	.11
❑ 101 Craig Mattson RC	.25	.11
❑ 102 Neifi Perez	.25	.11
❑ 103 Keith Williams	.25	.11
❑ 104 Roger Cedeno	.25	.11
❑ 105 Tony Terry RC	.25	.11
❑ 106 Jose Malave	.25	.11
❑ 107 Joe Rosselli	.25	.11
❑ 108 Kevin Jordan	.25	.11
❑ 109 Sid Roberson RC	.25	.11
❑ 110 Alan Embree	.25	.11
❑ 111 Terrell Wade	.25	.11
❑ 112 Bob Wolcott	.25	.11
❑ 113 Carlos Perez RC	.40	.18
❑ 114 Mike Bovee RC	.25	.11
❑ 115 Tommy Davis RC	.25	.11
❑ 116 Jeremey Kendall RC	.25	.11
❑ 117 Rich Aude	.25	.11
❑ 118 Rick Huisman	.25	.11
❑ 119 Tim Belk	.25	.11
❑ 120 Edgar Renteria	.25	.11
❑ 121 Calvin Maduro RC	.25	.11
❑ 122 Jerry Martin RC	.25	.11
❑ 123 Ramon Fermin RC	.25	.11
❑ 124 Kimera Bartee RC	.25	.11
❑ 125 Mark Farris	.25	.11
❑ 126 Frank Rodriguez	.25	.11
❑ 127 Bobby Higginson RC	4.00	1.80
❑ 128 Bret Wagner	.25	.11
❑ 129 Edwin Diaz RC	.25	.11
❑ 130 Jimmy Haynes	.25	.11
❑ 131 Chris Weinke RC	6.00	2.70
❑ 132 Damian Jackson RC	1.50	.70
❑ 133 Felix Martinez	.25	.11
❑ 134 Edwin Hurtado RC	.25	.11
❑ 135 Matt Raleigh RC	.25	.11
❑ 136 Paul Wilson	.25	.11
❑ 137 Ron Villone	.25	.11
❑ 138 E.Stuckenschneider RC	.25	.11
❑ 139 Tate Seefried	.25	.11
❑ 140 Rey Ordonez RC	2.00	.90
❑ 141 Eddie Pearson	.25	.11
❑ 142 Kevin Gallaher	.25	.11
❑ 143 Torii Hunter	.40	.18
❑ 144 Daron Kirkreit	.25	.11
❑ 145 Craig Wilson	.25	.11
❑ 146 Ugueth Urbina	.25	.11
❑ 147 Chris Snopek	.25	.11
❑ 148 Kym Ashworth	.25	.11
❑ 149 Wayne Gomes	.25	.11
❑ 150 Mark Loretta	.25	.11
❑ 151 Ramon Morel RC	.25	.11
❑ 152 Trot Nixon	.40	.18
❑ 153 Desi Relaford	.25	.11
❑ 154 Scott Sullivan	.25	.11
❑ 155 Marc Barcelo	.25	.11
❑ 156 Willie Adams	.25	.11
❑ 157 Derrick Gibson RC	.40	.18
❑ 158 Brian Meadows RC	.40	.18
❑ 159 Julian Tavarez	.25	.11
❑ 160 Bryan Rekar	.25	.11
❑ 161 Steve Gibralter	.25	.11
❑ 162 Esteban Loaiza	.25	.11
❑ 163 John Wasdin	.25	.11
❑ 164 Kirk Presley	.25	.11
❑ 165 Mariano Rivera	.40	.18
❑ 166 Andy Larkin	.25	.11
❑ 167 Sean Whiteside RC	.25	.11
❑ 168 Matt Apana RC	.25	.11
❑ 169 Shawn Senior RC	.25	.11
❑ 170 Scott Gentile	.25	.11
❑ 171 Quilvio Veras	.25	.11
❑ 172 Eli Marrero RC	.40	.18
❑ 173 Mendy Lopez RC	.25	.11
❑ 174 Homer Bush	.25	.11
❑ 175 Brian Stephenson RC	.25	.11
❑ 176 Jon Nunnally	.25	.11
❑ 177 Jose Herrera	.25	.11
❑ 178 Corey Avrard RC	.25	.11
❑ 179 David Bell	.25	.11
❑ 180 Jason Isringhausen	.40	.18
❑ 181 Jamey Wright	.25	.11
❑ 182 Lonell Roberts RC	.25	.11
❑ 183 Marty Cordova	.25	.11
❑ 184 Amaury Telemaco	.25	.11
❑ 185 John Mabry	.25	.11
❑ 186 Andrew Vessel RC	.25	.11
❑ 187 Jim Cole RC	.25	.11
❑ 188 Marquis Riley	.25	.11
❑ 189 Todd Dunn	.25	.11
❑ 190 John Carter	.25	.11
❑ 191 Donnie Sadler RC	.40	.18
❑ 192 Mike Bell	.25	.11
❑ 193 Chris Cumberland RC	.25	.11
❑ 194 Jason Schmidt	.25	.11
❑ 195 Matt Brunson	.25	.11
❑ 196 James Baldwin	.25	.11
❑ 197 Bill Simas RC	.25	.11
❑ 198 Gus Gandarillas	.25	.11
❑ 199 Mac Suzuki	.25	.11
❑ 200 Rick Holifield RC	.25	.11
❑ 201 Fernando Lunar RC	.25	.11
❑ 202 Kevin Jarvis	.25	.11
❑ 203 Everett Stull	.25	.11
❑ 204 Steve Wojciechowski	.25	.11
❑ 205 Shawn Estes	.40	.18
❑ 206 Jermaine Dye	1.00	.45
❑ 207 Marc Kroon	.25	.11
❑ 208 Peter Munro RC	.25	.11
❑ 209 Pat Watkins	.25	.11
❑ 210 Matt Smith	.25	.11
❑ 211 Joe Vitiello	.25	.11
❑ 212 Gerald Witasick Jr.	.25	.11
❑ 213 Freddy Adrian Garcia RC	.25	.11
❑ 214 Glenn Dishman RC	.25	.11
❑ 215 Jay Canizaro RC	.25	.11
❑ 216 Angel Martinez	.25	.11
❑ 217 Yamil Benitez RC	.25	.11
❑ 218 Fausto Macey RC	.25	.11
❑ 219 Eric Owens	.25	.11
❑ 220 Checklist	.25	.11
❑ 221 D.Hosey FOIL RC	.25	.11
❑ 222 B.Woodall FOIL RC	.25	.11

❑ 223 Billy Ashley FOIL .25 .11
❑ 224 M.Grudzielanek FOIL RC 2.00 .90
❑ 225 M.Johnson FOIL RC .40 .18
❑ 226 Tim Unroe FOIL RC .25 .11
❑ 227 Todd Greene FOIL .25 .11
❑ 228 Larry Sutton FOIL .25 .11
❑ 229 Derek Jeter FOIL 5.00 2.20
❑ 230 Sal Fasano FOIL RC .40 .18
❑ 231 Ruben Rivera FOIL .25 .11
❑ 232 Chris Truby FOIL RC 1.50 .70
❑ 233 John Donati FOIL .25 .11
❑ 234 D.Conner FOIL RC .25 .11
❑ 235 Sergio Nunez FOIL RC .25 .11
❑ 236 Ray Brown RC FOIL .25 .11
❑ 237 Juan Melo FOIL RC .40 .18
❑ 238 Hideo Nomo FOIL RC 6.00 2.70
❑ 239 Jamie Bluma RC FOIL .25 .11
❑ 240 Jay Payton FOIL RC 2.00 .90
❑ 241 Paul Konerko FOIL 2.00 .90
❑ 242 Scott Elarton FOIL RC 2.00 .90
❑ 243 Jeff Abbott FOIL RC .40 .18
❑ 244 Jim Brower RC FOIL .25 .11
❑ 245 Geoff Blum FOIL RC 1.00 .45
❑ 246 Aaron Boone FOIL RC .40 .18
❑ 247 J.R. Phillips FOIL .25 .11
❑ 248 Alex Ochoa FOIL .25 .11
❑ 249 N.Garciaparra FOIL 10.00 4.50
❑ 250 Garret Anderson FOIL .40 .18
❑ 251 Ray Durham FOIL .40 .18
❑ 252 Paul Shuey FOIL .25 .11
❑ 253 Tony Clark FOIL .40 .18
❑ 254 Johnny Damon FOIL .60 .25
❑ 255 Duane Singleton FOIL .25 .11
❑ 256 LaTroy Hawkins FOIL .25 .11
❑ 257 Andy Pettitte FOIL .40 .18
❑ 258 Ben Grieve FOIL 2.00 .90
❑ 259 Marc Newfield FOIL .25 .11
❑ 260 Terrell Lowery FOIL .25 .11
❑ 261 Shawn Green FOIL 1.00 .45
❑ 262 Chipper Jones FOIL 2.00 .90
❑ 263 B.Kieschnick FOIL .25 .11
❑ 264 Pokey Reese FOIL .25 .11
❑ 265 Doug Million FOIL .25 .11
❑ 266 Marc Valdes FOIL .25 .11
❑ 267 Brian L.Hunter FOIL .25 .11
❑ 268 T.Hollandsworth FOIL .25 .11
❑ 269 Rod Henderson FOIL .25 .11
❑ 270 Bill Pulsipher FOIL .25 .11
❑ 271 Scott Rolen FOIL RC 20.00 9.00
❑ 272 Trey Beamon FOIL .25 .11
❑ 273 Alan Benes FOIL .25 .11
❑ 274 D.Hermanson FOIL .25 .11
❑ 275 Ricky Bottalico .25 .11
❑ 276 Albert Belle .40 .18
❑ 277 Deion Sanders .40 .18
❑ 278 Matt Williams .60 .25
❑ 279 Jeff Bagwell 1.25 .55
❑ 280 Kirby Puckett 2.50 1.10
❑ 281 Dave Hollins .25 .11
❑ 282 Don Mattingly 2.50 1.10
❑ 283 Joey Hamilton .25 .11
❑ 284 Bobby Bonilla .40 .18
❑ 285 Moises Alou .40 .18
❑ 286 Tom Glavine 1.00 .45
❑ 287 Brett Butler .40 .18
❑ 288 Chris Hoiles .25 .11
❑ 289 Kenny Rogers .25 .11
❑ 290 Larry Walker .60 .25
❑ 291 Tim Raines .40 .18
❑ 292 Kevin Appier .40 .18
❑ 293 Roger Clemens 2.50 1.10
❑ 294 Chuck Carr .25 .11
❑ 295 Randy Myers .25 .11
❑ 296 Dave Nilsson .25 .11
❑ 297 Joe Carter .40 .18
❑ 298 Chuck Finley .40 .18
❑ 299 Ray Lankford .25 .11
❑ 300 Roberto Kelly .25 .11
❑ 301 Jon Lieber .25 .11
❑ 302 Travis Fryman .40 .18
❑ 303 Mark McGwire 4.00 1.80
❑ 304 Tony Gwynn 2.00 .90
❑ 305 Kenny Lofton .40 .18
❑ 306 Mark Whiten .25 .11
❑ 307 Doug Drabek .25 .11
❑ 308 Terry Steinbach .25 .11
❑ 309 Ryan Klesko .40 .18
❑ 310 Mike Piazza 2.50 1.10
❑ 311 Ben McDonald .25 .11
❑ 312 Reggie Sanders .25 .11
❑ 313 Alex Fernandez .25 .11
❑ 314 Aaron Sele .40 .18
❑ 315 Gregg Jefferies .25 .11
❑ 316 Rickey Henderson 2.00 .90
❑ 317 Brian Anderson .25 .11
❑ 318 Jose Valentin .25 .11
❑ 319 Rod Beck .25 .11
❑ 320 Marquis Grissom .25 .11
❑ 321 Ken Griffey Jr. 3.00 1.35
❑ 322 Bret Saberhagen .40 .18
❑ 323 Juan Gonzalez 1.00 .45
❑ 324 Paul Molitor 1.00 .45
❑ 325 Gary Sheffield .40 .18
❑ 326 Darren Daulton .40 .18
❑ 327 Bill Swift .25 .11
❑ 328 Brian McRae .25 .11
❑ 329 Robin Ventura .40 .18
❑ 330 Lee Smith .40 .18
❑ 331 Fred McGriff .60 .25
❑ 332 Delino DeShields .25 .11
❑ 333 Edgar Martinez .60 .25
❑ 334 Mike Mussina 1.00 .45
❑ 335 Orlando Merced .25 .11
❑ 336 Carlos Baerga .25 .11
❑ 337 Wil Cordero .25 .11
❑ 338 Tom Pagnozzi .25 .11
❑ 339 Pat Hentgen .25 .11
❑ 340 Chad Curtis .25 .11
❑ 341 Darren Lewis .25 .11
❑ 342 Jeff Kent .60 .25
❑ 343 Bip Roberts .25 .11
❑ 344 Ivan Rodriguez 1.00 .45
❑ 345 Jeff Montgomery .25 .11
❑ 346 Hal Morris .25 .11
❑ 347 Danny Tartabull .25 .11
❑ 348 Raul Mondesi .40 .18
❑ 349 Ken Hill .25 .11
❑ 350 Pedro Martinez 1.25 .55
❑ 351 Frank Thomas 1.25 .55
❑ 352 Manny Ramirez 1.25 .55
❑ 353 Tim Salmon .40 .18
❑ 354 W. VanLandingham .25 .11
❑ 355 Andres Galarraga .60 .25
❑ 356 Paul O'Neill 1.00 .45
❑ 357 Brady Anderson .40 .18
❑ 358 Ramon Martinez .25 .11
❑ 359 John Olerud .40 .18
❑ 360 Ruben Sierra .25 .11
❑ 361 Cal Eldred .25 .11
❑ 362 Jay Buhner .40 .18
❑ 363 Jay Bell .40 .18
❑ 364 Wally Joyner .40 .18
❑ 365 Chuck Knoblauch .40 .18
❑ 366 Len Dykstra .40 .18
❑ 367 John Wetteland .40 .18
❑ 368 Roberto Alomar 1.00 .45
❑ 369 Craig Biggio .60 .25
❑ 370 Ozzie Smith 1.25 .55
❑ 371 Terry Pendleton .40 .18
❑ 372 Sammy Sosa 2.00 .90
❑ 373 Carlos Garcia .25 .11
❑ 374 Jose Rijo .25 .11
❑ 375 Chris Gomez .25 .11
❑ 376 Barry Bonds 2.50 1.10
❑ 377 Steve Avery .25 .11
❑ 378 Rick Wilkins .25 .11
❑ 379 Pete Harnisch .25 .11
❑ 380 Dean Palmer .40 .18
❑ 381 Bob Hamelin .25 .11
❑ 382 Jason Bere .25 .11
❑ 383 Jimmy Key .40 .18
❑ 384 Dante Bichette .40 .18
❑ 385 Rafael Palmeiro 1.00 .45
❑ 386 David Justice .40 .18
❑ 387 Chili Davis .40 .18
❑ 388 Mike Greenwell .25 .11
❑ 389 Todd Zeile .25 .11
❑ 390 Jeff Conine .25 .11
❑ 391 Rick Aguilera .25 .11
❑ 392 Eddie Murray 1.00 .45
❑ 393 Mike Stanley .25 .11
❑ 394 Cliff Floyd UER .40 .18
(numbered 294)
❑ 395 Randy Johnson 1.25 .55
❑ 396 David Nied .25 .11
❑ 397 Devon White .40 .18
❑ 398 Royce Clayton .25 .11
❑ 399 Andy Benes .25 .11
❑ 400 John Hudek .25 .11
❑ 401 Bobby Jones .25 .11
❑ 402 Eric Karros .40 .18
❑ 403 Will Clark 1.00 .45
❑ 404 Mark Langston .25 .11
❑ 405 Kevin Brown .40 .18
❑ 406 Greg Maddux 2.50 1.10
❑ 407 David Cone .40 .18
❑ 408 Wade Boggs 1.00 .45
❑ 409 Steve Trachsel .25 .11
❑ 410 Greg Vaughn .40 .18
❑ 411 Mo Vaughn .40 .18
❑ 412 Wilson Alvarez .25 .11
❑ 413 Cal Ripken 4.00 1.80
❑ 414 Rico Brogna .25 .11
❑ 415 Barry Larkin 1.00 .45
❑ 416 Cecil Fielder .40 .18
❑ 417 Jose Canseco 1.00 .45
❑ 418 Jack McDowell .25 .11
❑ 419 Mike Lieberthal .40 .18
❑ 420 Andrew Lorraine .25 .11
❑ 421 Rich Becker .25 .11
❑ 422 Tony Phillips .25 .11
❑ 423 Scott Ruffcorn .25 .11
❑ 424 Jeff Granger .25 .11
❑ 425 Greg Pirkl .25 .11
❑ 426 Dennis Eckersley .40 .18
❑ 427 Jose Lima .25 .11
❑ 428 Russ Davis .25 .11
❑ 429 Armando Benitez .40 .18
❑ 430 Alex Gonzalez .25 .11
❑ 431 Carlos Delgado 1.00 .45
❑ 432 Chan Ho Park .40 .18
❑ 433 Mickey Tettleton .25 .11
❑ 434 Dave Winfield 1.00 .45
❑ 435 John Burkett .25 .11
❑ 436 Orlando Miller .25 .11
❑ 437 Rondell White .40 .18
❑ 438 Jose Oliva .25 .11
❑ 439 Checklist .25 .11

1996 Bowman

	MINT	NRMT
COMPLETE SET (385)	100.00	45.00

❑ 1 Cal Ripken 2.50 1.10
❑ 2 Ray Durham .25 .11
❑ 3 Ivan Rodriguez .60 .25
❑ 4 Fred McGriff .40 .18
❑ 5 Hideo Nomo .75 .35
❑ 6 Troy Percival .15 .07
❑ 7 Moises Alou .25 .11
❑ 8 Mike Stanley .15 .07
❑ 9 Jay Buhner .25 .11
❑ 10 Shawn Green .60 .25
❑ 11 Ryan Klesko .25 .11
❑ 12 Andres Galarraga .40 .18
❑ 13 Dean Palmer .25 .11
❑ 14 Jeff Conine .15 .07
❑ 15 Brian L.Hunter .15 .07
❑ 16 J.T. Snow .25 .11

❑ 17 Larry Walker .40 .18
❑ 18 Barry Larkin .60 .25
❑ 19 Alex Gonzalez .15 .07
❑ 20 Edgar Martinez .40 .18
❑ 21 Mo Vaughn .25 .11
❑ 22 Mark McGwire 2.50 1.10
❑ 23 Jose Canseco .60 .25
❑ 24 Jack McDowell .15 .07
❑ 25 Dante Bichette .25 .11
❑ 26 Wade Boggs .60 .25
❑ 27 Mike Piazza 1.50 .70
❑ 28 Ray Lankford .15 .07
❑ 29 Craig Biggio .40 .18
❑ 30 Rafael Palmeiro .60 .25
❑ 31 Ron Gant .15 .07
❑ 32 Javy Lopez .25 .11
❑ 33 Brian Jordan .25 .11
❑ 34 Paul O'Neill .60 .25
❑ 35 Mark Grace .60 .25
❑ 36 Matt Williams .40 .18
❑ 37 Pedro Martinez .75 .35
❑ 38 Rickey Henderson 1.25 .55
❑ 39 Bobby Bonilla .25 .11
❑ 40 Todd Hollandsworth .15 .07
❑ 41 Jim Thome .60 .25
❑ 42 Gary Sheffield .60 .25
❑ 43 Tim Salmon .25 .11
❑ 44 Gregg Jefferies .15 .07
❑ 45 Roberto Alomar .60 .25
❑ 46 Carlos Baerga .15 .07
❑ 47 Mark Grudzielanek .15 .07
❑ 48 Randy Johnson .75 .35
❑ 49 Tino Martinez .25 .11
❑ 50 Robin Ventura .25 .11
❑ 51 Ryne Sandberg .75 .35
❑ 52 Jay Bell .25 .11
❑ 53 Jason Schmidt .15 .07
❑ 54 Frank Thomas .75 .35
❑ 55 Kenny Lofton .25 .11
❑ 56 Ariel Prieto .15 .07
❑ 57 David Cone .25 .11
❑ 58 Reggie Sanders .15 .07
❑ 59 Michael Tucker .15 .07
❑ 60 Vinny Castilla .25 .11
❑ 61 Len Dykstra .25 .11
❑ 62 Todd Hundley .15 .07
❑ 63 Brian McRae .15 .07
❑ 64 Dennis Eckersley .25 .11
❑ 65 Rondell White .25 .11
❑ 66 Eric Karros .25 .11
❑ 67 Greg Maddux 1.50 .70
❑ 68 Kevin Appier .25 .11
❑ 69 Eddie Murray .60 .25
❑ 70 John Olerud .25 .11
❑ 71 Tony Gwynn 1.25 .55
❑ 72 David Justice .25 .11
❑ 73 Ken Caminiti .25 .11
❑ 74 Terry Steinbach .15 .07
❑ 75 Alan Benes .15 .07
❑ 76 Chipper Jones 1.25 .55
❑ 77 Jeff Bagwell .75 .35
❑ 78 Barry Bonds 1.50 .70
❑ 79 Ken Griffey Jr. 2.50 1.10
❑ 80 Roger Cedeno .15 .07
❑ 81 Joe Carter .25 .11
❑ 82 Henry Rodriguez .15 .07
❑ 83 Jason Isringhausen .25 .11
❑ 84 Chuck Knoblauch .25 .11
❑ 85 Manny Ramirez .75 .35
❑ 86 Tom Glavine .60 .25
❑ 87 Jeffrey Hammonds .15 .07
❑ 88 Paul Molitor .60 .25
❑ 89 Roger Clemens 1.50 .70
❑ 90 Greg Vaughn .25 .11
❑ 91 Marty Cordova .15 .07
❑ 92 Albert Belle .25 .11
❑ 93 Mike Mussina .60 .25
❑ 94 Garret Anderson .25 .11
❑ 95 Juan Gonzalez .60 .25
❑ 96 John Valentin .15 .07
❑ 97 Jason Giambi .60 .25
❑ 98 Kirby Puckett 1.50 .70
❑ 99 Jim Edmonds .40 .18
❑ 100 Cecil Fielder .25 .11
❑ 101 Mike Aldrete .15 .07
❑ 102 Marquis Grissom .15 .07
❑ 103 Derek Bell .15 .07
❑ 104 Raul Mondesi .25 .11
❑ 105 Sammy Sosa 1.25 .55
❑ 106 Travis Fryman .25 .11
❑ 107 Rico Brogna .15 .07
❑ 108 Will Clark .60 .25
❑ 109 Bernie Williams .60 .25
❑ 110 Brady Anderson .25 .11
❑ 111 Torii Hunter .25 .11
❑ 112 Derek Jeter 2.50 1.10
❑ 113 Mike Kusiewicz RC .25 .11
❑ 114 Scott Rolen 1.25 .55
❑ 115 Ramon Castro .15 .07
❑ 116 Jose Guillen RC .60 .25
❑ 117 Wade Walker RC .15 .07
❑ 118 Shawn Senior .15 .07
❑ 119 Onan Masaoka RC .60 .25
❑ 120 Marlon Anderson RC 1.00 .45
❑ 121 Katsuhiro Maeda RC .15 .07
❑ 122 G.Stephenson RC 1.00 .45
❑ 123 Butch Huskey .15 .07
❑ 124 D'Angelo Jimenez RC 3.00 1.35
❑ 125 Tony Mounce RC .15 .07
❑ 126 Jay Canizaro .15 .07
❑ 127 Juan Melo .15 .07
❑ 128 Steve Gibralter .15 .07
❑ 129 Freddy Garcia .15 .07
❑ 130 Julio Santana UER .15 .07
Card has him born in 1993
❑ 131 Richard Hidalgo .25 .11
❑ 132 Jermaine Dye .25 .11
❑ 133 Willie Adams .15 .07
❑ 134 Everett Stull .15 .07
❑ 135 Ramon Morel .15 .07
❑ 136 Chan Ho Park .25 .11
❑ 137 Jamey Wright .15 .07
❑ 138 Luis Garcia RC .15 .07
❑ 139 Dan Serafini .15 .07
❑ 140 Ryan Dempster RC 5.00 2.20
❑ 141 Tate Seefried .15 .07
❑ 142 Jimmy Hurst .15 .07
❑ 143 Travis Miller .15 .07
❑ 144 Curtis Goodwin .15 .07
❑ 145 Rocky Coppinger RC .15 .07
❑ 146 Enrique Wilson .15 .07
❑ 147 Jaime Bluma .15 .07
❑ 148 Andrew Vessel .15 .07
❑ 149 Damian Moss .15 .07
❑ 150 Shawn Gallagher RC .15 .07
❑ 151 Pat Watkins .15 .07
❑ 152 Jose Paniagua .15 .07
❑ 153 Danny Graves .25 .11
❑ 154 Bryon Gainey RC .15 .07
❑ 155 Steve Soderstrom .15 .07
❑ 156 Cliff Brumbaugh RC .15 .07
❑ 157 Eugene Kingsale RC .25 .11
❑ 158 Lou Collier .15 .07
❑ 159 Todd Walker .25 .11
❑ 160 Kris Detmers RC .15 .07
❑ 161 Josh Booty RC 1.00 .45
❑ 162 Greg Whiteman RC .15 .07
❑ 163 Damian Jackson .15 .07
❑ 164 Tony Clark .25 .11
❑ 165 Jeff D'Amico .15 .07
❑ 166 Johnny Damon .25 .11
❑ 167 Rafael Orellano .15 .07
❑ 168 Ruben Rivera .15 .07
❑ 169 Alex Ochoa .15 .07
❑ 170 Jay Powell .15 .07
❑ 171 Tom Evans .15 .07
❑ 172 Ron Villone .15 .07
❑ 173 Shawn Estes .25 .11
❑ 174 John Wasdin .15 .07
❑ 175 Bill Simas .15 .07
❑ 176 Kevin Brown .25 .11
❑ 177 Shannon Stewart .25 .11
❑ 178 Todd Greene .15 .07
❑ 179 Bob Wolcott .15 .07
❑ 180 Chris Snopek .15 .07
❑ 181 Nomar Garciaparra 2.00 .90
❑ 182 Cameron Smith RC .15 .07
❑ 183 Matt Drews .15 .07
❑ 184 Jimmy Haynes .15 .07
❑ 185 Chris Carpenter .15 .07
❑ 186 Desi Relaford .15 .07
❑ 187 Ben Grieve .25 .11
❑ 188 Mike Bell .15 .07
❑ 189 Luis Castillo RC 2.00 .90
❑ 190 Ugueth Urbina .15 .07
❑ 191 Paul Wilson .15 .07
❑ 192 Andruw Jones 1.50 .70
❑ 193 Wayne Gomes .15 .07
❑ 194 Craig Counsell RC 2.00 .90
❑ 195 Jim Cole .15 .07
❑ 196 Brooks Kieschnick .15 .07
❑ 197 Trey Beamon .15 .07
❑ 198 Marino Santana RC .15 .07
❑ 199 Bob Abreu .60 .25
❑ 200 Pokey Reese .15 .07
❑ 201 Dante Powell .15 .07
❑ 202 George Arias .15 .07
❑ 203 Jorge Velandia RC .15 .07
❑ 204 George Lombard RC .60 .25
❑ 205 Byron Browne RC .15 .07
❑ 206 John Frascatore .15 .07
❑ 207 Terry Adams .15 .07
❑ 208 Wilson Delgado RC .15 .07
❑ 209 Billy McMillon .15 .07
❑ 210 Jeff Abbott .15 .07
❑ 211 Trot Nixon .25 .11
❑ 212 Amaury Telemaco .15 .07
❑ 213 Scott Sullivan .15 .07
❑ 214 Justin Thompson .15 .07
❑ 215 Decomba Conner .15 .07
❑ 216 Ryan McGuire .15 .07
❑ 217 Matt Luke .15 .07
❑ 218 Doug Million .15 .07
❑ 219 Jason Dickson RC .25 .11
❑ 220 Ramon Hernandez RC 2.00 .90
❑ 221 Mark Bellhorn RC .15 .07
❑ 222 Eric Ludwick RC .15 .07
❑ 223 Luke Wilcox RC .15 .07
❑ 224 Marty Malloy RC .15 .07
❑ 225 Gary Coffee RC .15 .07
❑ 226 Wendell Magee RC .25 .11
❑ 227 Brett Tomko RC .25 .11
❑ 228 Derek Lowe .15 .07
❑ 229 Jose Rosado RC .15 .07
❑ 230 Steve Bourgeois RC .15 .07
❑ 231 Neil Weber RC .15 .07
❑ 232 Jeff Ware .15 .07
❑ 233 Edwin Diaz .15 .07
❑ 234 Greg Norton .15 .07
❑ 235 Aaron Boone .15 .07
❑ 236 Jeff Suppan .15 .07
❑ 237 Bret Wagner .15 .07
❑ 238 Elieser Marrero .15 .07
❑ 239 Will Cunnane .15 .07
❑ 240 Brian Barkley RC .15 .07
❑ 241 Jay Payton .15 .07
❑ 242 Marcus Jensen .15 .07
❑ 243 Ryan Nye .15 .07
❑ 244 Chad Mottola .15 .07
❑ 245 Scott McClain RC .15 .07
❑ 246 Jessie Ibarra RC .15 .07
❑ 247 Mike Darr RC 1.50 .70
❑ 248 Bobby Estalella RC 1.00 .45
❑ 249 Michael Barrett .15 .07
❑ 250 Jamie Lopiccolo RC .15 .07
❑ 251 Shane Spencer RC 3.00 1.35
❑ 252 Ben Petrick RC 3.00 1.35
❑ 253 Jason Bell RC .15 .07
❑ 254 Arnold Gooch RC .15 .07
❑ 255 T.J. Mathews .15 .07
❑ 256 Jason Ryan .15 .07
❑ 257 Pat Cline RC .15 .07
❑ 258 Rafael Carmona RC .15 .07
❑ 259 Carl Pavano RC .60 .25
❑ 260 Ben Davis .25 .11
❑ 261 Matt Lawton RC 2.00 .90
❑ 262 Kevin Sefcik RC .15 .07
❑ 263 Chris Fussell RC .15 .07
❑ 264 Mike Cameron RC 4.00 1.80
❑ 265 Marty Janzen RC .15 .07
❑ 266 Livan Hernandez RC 2.00 .90
❑ 267 Raul Ibanez RC .15 .07
❑ 268 Juan Encarnacion .60 .25
❑ 269 David Yocum RC .15 .07
❑ 270 Jonathan Johnson RC .15 .07
❑ 271 Reggie Taylor .15 .07
❑ 272 Danny Buxbaum RC .15 .07
❑ 273 Jacob Cruz .15 .07

❑ 274 Bobby Morris RC .15 .07
❑ 275 Andy Fox RC .15 .07
❑ 276 Greg Keagle .15 .07
❑ 277 Charles Peterson .15 .07
❑ 278 Derrek Lee .25 .11
❑ 279 Bryant Nelson RC .15 .07
❑ 280 Antone Williamson .15 .07
❑ 281 Scott Elarton .15 .07
❑ 282 Shad Williams RC .15 .07
❑ 283 Rich Hunter RC .15 .07
❑ 284 Chris Sheff .15 .07
❑ 285 Derrick Gibson .15 .07
❑ 286 Felix Rodriguez .15 .07
❑ 287 Brian Banks RC .15 .07
❑ 288 Jason McDonald .15 .07
❑ 289 Glendon Rusch RC 1.50 .70
❑ 290 Gary Rath .15 .07
❑ 291 Peter Munro .15 .07
❑ 292 Tom Fordham .15 .07
❑ 293 Jason Kendall .25 .11
❑ 294 Russ Johnson .15 .07
❑ 295 Joe Long .15 .07
❑ 296 Robert Smith RC .25 .11
❑ 297 Jarrod Washburn RC 2.50 1.10
❑ 298 Dave Coggin RC 1.00 .45
❑ 299 Jeff Yoder RC .15 .07
❑ 300 Jed Hansen RC .15 .07
❑ 301 Matt Morris RC 4.00 1.80
❑ 302 Josh Bishop RC .15 .07
❑ 303 Dustin Hermanson .15 .07
❑ 304 Mike Gulan .15 .07
❑ 305 Felipe Crespo .15 .07
❑ 306 Quinton McCracken .15 .07
❑ 307 Jim Bonnici RC .15 .07
❑ 308 Sal Fasano .15 .07
❑ 309 Gabe Alvarez RC .15 .07
❑ 310 Heath Murray RC .25 .11
❑ 311 Jose Valentin RC .15 .07
❑ 312 Bartolo Colon .25 .11
❑ 313 Olmedo Saenz .15 .07
❑ 314 Norm Hutchins RC .15 .07
❑ 315 Chris Holt .15 .07
❑ 316 David Doster RC .15 .07
❑ 317 Robert Person .15 .07
❑ 318 Donne Wall RC .15 .07
❑ 319 Adam Riggs RC .15 .07
❑ 320 Homer Bush .15 .07
❑ 321 Brad Rigby RC .15 .07
❑ 322 Lou Merloni RC 2.00 .90
❑ 323 Neifi Perez .15 .07
❑ 324 Chris Cumberland .15 .07
❑ 325 Alvie Shepherd RC .15 .07
❑ 326 Jarrod Patterson RC .15 .07
❑ 327 Ray Ricken RC .15 .07
❑ 328 Danny Klassen RC .15 .07
❑ 329 David Miller RC .15 .07
❑ 330 Chad Alexander RC .15 .07
❑ 331 Matt Beaumont .15 .07
❑ 332 Damon Hollins .15 .07
❑ 333 Todd Dunn .15 .07
❑ 334 Mike Sweeney RC 6.00 2.70
❑ 335 Richie Sexson .60 .25
❑ 336 Billy Wagner .15 .07
❑ 337 Ron Wright RC .25 .11
❑ 338 Paul Konerko .25 .11
❑ 339 Tommy Phelps RC .15 .07
❑ 340 Karim Garcia .15 .07
❑ 341 Mike Grace RC .15 .07
❑ 342 Russell Branyan RC 6.00 2.70
❑ 343 Randy Winn RC .15 .07
❑ 344 A.J. Pierzynski RC 1.00 .45
❑ 345 Mike Busby RC .15 .07
❑ 346 Matt Beech RC .15 .07
❑ 347 Jose Cepeda RC .15 .07
❑ 348 Brian Stephenson .15 .07
❑ 349 Rey Ordonez .15 .07
❑ 350 Rich Aurilia RC 5.00 2.20
❑ 351 Edgard Velazquez RC .25 .11
❑ 352 Raul Casanova .15 .07
❑ 353 Carlos Guillen RC 2.00 .90
❑ 354 Bruce Aven RC .15 .07
❑ 355 Ryan Jones RC .15 .07
❑ 356 Derek Aucoin RC .15 .07
❑ 357 Brian Rose RC .25 .11
❑ 358 Richard Almanzar RC .15 .07
❑ 359 Fletcher Bates RC .15 .07
❑ 360 Russ Ortiz RC 2.00 .90
❑ 361 Wilton Guerrero RC .25 .11
❑ 362 Geoff Jenkins RC 5.00 2.20
❑ 363 Pete Janicki .15 .07
❑ 364 Yamil Benitez .15 .07
❑ 365 Aaron Holbert .15 .07
❑ 366 Tim Belk .15 .07
❑ 367 Terrell Wade .15 .07
❑ 368 Terrence Long .60 .25
❑ 369 Brad Fullmer .25 .11
❑ 370 Matt Wagner .15 .07
❑ 371 Craig Wilson RC .15 .07
❑ 372 Mark Loretta .15 .07
❑ 373 Eric Owens .15 .07
❑ 374 Vladimir Guerrero 2.00 .90
❑ 375 Tommy Davis .15 .07
❑ 376 Donnie Sadler .15 .07
❑ 377 Edgar Renteria .15 .07
❑ 378 Todd Helton 3.00 1.35
❑ 379 Ralph Milliard RC .15 .07
❑ 380 Darin Blood RC .15 .07
❑ 381 Shayne Bennett .15 .07
❑ 382 Mark Redman .25 .11
❑ 383 Felix Martinez .15 .07
❑ 384 Sean Watkins RC .15 .07
❑ 385 Oscar Henriquez .15 .07
❑ M20 Mickey Mantle 8.00 3.60
1952 Bowman Reprint
❑ NNO Checklists .15 .07

1997 Bowman

	MINT	NRMT
COMPLETE SET (441)	80.00	36.00
COMPLETE SERIES 1 (221)	40.00	18.00
COMPLETE SERIES 2 (220)	40.00	18.00

❑ 1 Derek Jeter 2.50 1.10
❑ 2 Edgar Renteria .15 .07
❑ 3 Chipper Jones 1.25 .55
❑ 4 Hideo Nomo .60 .25
❑ 5 Tim Salmon .25 .11
❑ 6 Jason Giambi .60 .25
❑ 7 Robin Ventura .25 .11
❑ 8 Tony Clark .25 .11
❑ 9 Barry Larkin .60 .25
❑ 10 Paul Molitor .60 .25
❑ 11 Bernard Gilkey .15 .07
❑ 12 Jack McDowell .15 .07
❑ 13 Andy Benes .15 .07
❑ 14 Ryan Klesko .25 .11
❑ 15 Mark McGwire 2.50 1.10
❑ 16 Ken Griffey Jr. 2.00 .90
❑ 17 Robb Nen .15 .07
❑ 18 Cal Ripken 2.50 1.10
❑ 19 John Valentin .15 .07
❑ 20 Ricky Bottalico .15 .07
❑ 21 Mike Lansing .15 .07
❑ 22 Ryne Sandberg .75 .35
❑ 23 Carlos Delgado .60 .25
❑ 24 Craig Biggio .40 .18
❑ 25 Eric Karros .25 .11
❑ 26 Kevin Appier .25 .11
❑ 27 Mariano Rivera .25 .11
❑ 28 Vinny Castilla .25 .11
❑ 29 Juan Gonzalez .60 .25
❑ 30 Al Martin .15 .07
❑ 31 Jeff Cirillo .25 .11
❑ 32 Eddie Murray .60 .25
❑ 33 Ray Lankford .15 .07
❑ 34 Manny Ramirez .75 .35
❑ 35 Roberto Alomar .60 .25
❑ 36 Will Clark .60 .25
❑ 37 Chuck Knoblauch .25 .11
❑ 38 Harold Baines .25 .11
❑ 39 Trevor Hoffman .25 .11
❑ 40 Edgar Martinez .40 .18
❑ 41 Geronimo Berroa .15 .07
❑ 42 Rey Ordonez .15 .07
❑ 43 Mike Stanley .15 .07
❑ 44 Mike Mussina .60 .25
❑ 45 Kevin Brown .25 .11
❑ 46 Dennis Eckersley .25 .11
❑ 47 Henry Rodriguez .15 .07
❑ 48 Tino Martinez .25 .11
❑ 49 Eric Young .15 .07
❑ 50 Bret Boone .25 .11
❑ 51 Raul Mondesi .25 .11
❑ 52 Sammy Sosa 1.25 .55
❑ 53 John Smoltz .25 .11
❑ 54 Billy Wagner .15 .07
❑ 55 Jeff D'Amico .15 .07
❑ 56 Ken Caminiti .25 .11
❑ 57 Jason Kendall .25 .11
❑ 58 Wade Boggs .60 .25
❑ 59 Andres Galarraga .40 .18
❑ 60 Jeff Brantley .15 .07
❑ 61 Mel Rojas .15 .07
❑ 62 Brian L. Hunter .15 .07
❑ 63 Bobby Bonilla .25 .11
❑ 64 Roger Clemens 1.50 .70
❑ 65 Jeff Kent .40 .18
❑ 66 Matt Williams .40 .18
❑ 67 Albert Belle .25 .11
❑ 68 Jeff King .15 .07
❑ 69 John Wetteland .25 .11
❑ 70 Deion Sanders .25 .11
❑ 71 Bubba Trammell RC .75 .35
❑ 72 Felix Heredia RC .15 .07
❑ 73 Billy Koch RC 1.00 .45
❑ 74 Sidney Ponson RC .75 .35
❑ 75 Ricky Ledee RC .50 .23
❑ 76 Brett Tomko .15 .07
❑ 77 Braden Looper RC .15 .07
❑ 78 Damian Jackson .15 .07
❑ 79 Jason Dickson .15 .07
❑ 80 Chad Green RC .15 .07
❑ 81 R.A. Dickey RC .15 .07
❑ 82 Jeff Liefer .15 .07
❑ 83 Matt Wagner .15 .07
❑ 84 Richard Hidalgo .25 .11
❑ 85 Adam Riggs .15 .07
❑ 86 Robert Smith .15 .07
❑ 87 Chad Hermansen RC .50 .23
❑ 88 Felix Martinez .15 .07
❑ 89 J.J. Johnson .15 .07
❑ 90 Todd Dunwoody .15 .07
❑ 91 Katsuhiro Maeda .15 .07
❑ 92 Darin Erstad .60 .25
❑ 93 Elieser Marrero .15 .07
❑ 94 Bartolo Colon .25 .11
❑ 95 Chris Fussell .15 .07
❑ 96 Ugueth Urbina .15 .07
❑ 97 Josh Paul RC .50 .23
❑ 98 Jaime Bluma .15 .07
❑ 99 Seth Greisinger RC .25 .11
❑ 100 Jose Cruz Jr. RC 2.50 1.10
❑ 101 Todd Dunn .15 .07
❑ 102 Joe Young RC .15 .07
❑ 103 Jonathan Johnson .15 .07
❑ 104 Justin Towle RC .15 .07
❑ 105 Brian Rose .15 .07
❑ 106 Jose Guillen .15 .07
❑ 107 Andruw Jones .75 .35
❑ 108 Mark Kotsay RC 1.00 .45
❑ 109 Wilton Guerrero .15 .07
❑ 110 Jacob Cruz .15 .07
❑ 111 Mike Sweeney .25 .11
❑ 112 Julio Mosquera .15 .07
❑ 113 Matt Morris .25 .11
❑ 114 Wendell Magee .15 .07
❑ 115 John Thomson .15 .07
❑ 116 Javier (Jose) Valentin .15 .07
❑ 117 Tom Fordham .15 .07

❑ 118 Ruben Rivera .15 .07
❑ 119 Mike Drumright RC .15 .07
❑ 120 Chris Holt .15 .07
❑ 121 Sean Maloney .15 .07
❑ 122 Michael Barrett .15 .07
❑ 123 Tony Saunders RC .15 .07
❑ 124 Kevin Brown C .15 .07
❑ 125 Richard Almanzar .15 .07
❑ 126 Mark Redman .15 .07
❑ 127 Anthony Sanders RC .15 .07
❑ 128 Jeff Abbott .15 .07
❑ 129 Eugene Kingsale .15 .07
❑ 130 Paul Konerko .25 .11
❑ 131 Randall Simon RC .15 .07
❑ 132 Andy Larkin .15 .07
❑ 133 Rafael Medina .15 .07
❑ 134 Mendy Lopez .15 .07
❑ 135 Freddy Adrian Garcia .15 .07
❑ 136 Karim Garcia .15 .07
❑ 137 Larry Rodriguez RC .15 .07
❑ 138 Carlos Guillen .15 .07
❑ 139 Aaron Boone .15 .07
❑ 140 Donnie Sadler .15 .07
❑ 141 Brooks Kieschnick .15 .07
❑ 142 Scott Spiezio .15 .07
❑ 143 Everett Stull .15 .07
❑ 144 Enrique Wilson .15 .07
❑ 145 Milton Bradley RC 2.00 .90
❑ 146 Kevin Orie .15 .07
❑ 147 Derek Wallace .15 .07
❑ 148 Russ Johnson .15 .07
❑ 149 Joe Lagarde RC .15 .07
❑ 150 Luis Castillo .15 .07
❑ 151 Jay Payton .15 .07
❑ 152 Joe Long .25 .11
❑ 153 Livan Hernandez .15 .07
❑ 154 Vladimir Nunez RC .25 .11
❑ 155 Pokey Reese UER .15 .07
Card actually numbered 156
❑ 156 George Arias .15 .07
❑ 157 Homer Bush .15 .07
❑ 158 Chris Carpenter UER .15 .07
Card numbered 159
❑ 159 Eric Milton RC 2.00 .90
❑ 160 Richie Sexson .25 .11
❑ 161 Carl Pavano .15 .07
❑ 162 Chris Gissell RC .50 .23
❑ 163 Mac Suzuki .15 .07
❑ 164 Pat Cline .15 .07
❑ 165 Ron Wright .15 .07
❑ 166 Dante Powell .15 .07
❑ 167 Mark Bellhorn .15 .07
❑ 168 George Lombard .15 .07
❑ 169 Pee Wee Lopez RC .50 .23
❑ 170 Paul Wilder RC .15 .07
❑ 171 Brad Fullmer .25 .11
❑ 172 Willie Martinez RC .25 .11
❑ 173 Dario Veras RC .15 .07
❑ 174 Dave Coggin .15 .07
❑ 175 Kris Benson RC 1.50 .70
❑ 176 Torii Hunter .25 .11
❑ 177 D.T. Cromer .15 .07
❑ 178 Nelson Figueroa RC .60 .25
❑ 179 Hiram Bocachica RC .50 .23
❑ 180 Shane Monahan .15 .07
❑ 181 Jimmy Anderson RC .15 .07
❑ 182 Juan Melo .15 .07
❑ 183 Pablo Ortega RC .15 .07
❑ 184 Calvin Pickering RC .25 .11
❑ 185 Reggie Taylor .15 .07
❑ 186 Jeff Farnsworth RC .15 .07
❑ 187 Terrence Long .25 .11
❑ 188 Geoff Jenkins .40 .18
❑ 189 Steve Rain RC .15 .07
❑ 190 Nerio Rodriguez RC .15 .07
❑ 191 Derrick Gibson .15 .07
❑ 192 Darin Blood .15 .07
❑ 193 Ben Davis .25 .11
❑ 194 Adrian Beltre RC 4.00 1.80
❑ 195 Damian Sapp RC UER .15 .07
❑ 196 Kerry Wood RC 5.00 2.20
❑ 197 Nate Rolison RC .40 .18
❑ 198 Fernando Tatis RC .75 .35
❑ 199 Brad Penny RC 3.00 1.35
❑ 200 Jake Westbrook RC .50 .23
❑ 201 Edwin Diaz .15 .07
❑ 202 Joe Fontenot RC .25 .11
❑ 203 Matt Halloran RC .15 .07
❑ 204 Blake Stein RC .15 .07
❑ 205 Onan Masaoka .15 .07
❑ 206 Ben Petrick .15 .07
❑ 207 Matt Clement RC 1.00 .45
❑ 208 Todd Greene .15 .07
❑ 209 Ray Ricken .15 .07
❑ 210 Eric Chavez RC 3.00 1.35
❑ 211 Edgard Velazquez .15 .07
❑ 212 Bruce Chen RC .75 .35
❑ 213 Danny Patterson .15 .07
❑ 214 Jeff Yoder .15 .07
❑ 215 Luis Ordaz RC .15 .07
❑ 216 Chris Widger .15 .07
❑ 217 Jason Brester .15 .07
❑ 218 Carlton Loewer .15 .07
❑ 219 Chris Reitsma RC .75 .35
❑ 220 Neifi Perez .15 .07
❑ 221 Hideki Irabu RC .25 .11
❑ 222 Ellis Burks .25 .11
❑ 223 Pedro Martinez .75 .35
❑ 224 Kenny Lofton .25 .11
❑ 225 Randy Johnson .75 .35
❑ 226 Terry Steinbach .15 .07
❑ 227 Bernie Williams .60 .25
❑ 228 Dean Palmer .25 .11
❑ 229 Alan Benes .15 .07
❑ 230 Marquis Grissom .15 .07
❑ 231 Gary Sheffield .25 .11
❑ 232 Curt Schilling .60 .25
❑ 233 Reggie Sanders .15 .07
❑ 234 Bobby Higginson .25 .11
❑ 235 Moises Alou .25 .11
❑ 236 Tom Glavine .60 .25
❑ 237 Mark Grace .60 .25
❑ 238 Ramon Martinez .15 .07
❑ 239 Rafael Palmeiro .60 .25
❑ 240 John Olerud .25 .11
❑ 241 Dante Bichette .25 .11
❑ 242 Greg Vaughn .25 .11
❑ 243 Jeff Bagwell .75 .35
❑ 244 Barry Bonds 1.50 .70
❑ 245 Pat Hentgen .15 .07
❑ 246 Jim Thome .60 .25
❑ 247 J.Allensworth .15 .07
❑ 248 Andy Pettitte .25 .11
❑ 249 Jay Bell .25 .11
❑ 250 John Jaha .15 .07
❑ 251 Jim Edmonds .40 .18
❑ 252 Ron Gant .15 .07
❑ 253 David Cone .25 .11
❑ 254 Jose Canseco .60 .25
❑ 255 Jay Buhner .25 .11
❑ 256 Greg Maddux 1.50 .70
❑ 257 Brian McRae .15 .07
❑ 258 Lance Johnson .15 .07
❑ 259 Travis Fryman .25 .11
❑ 260 Paul O'Neill .60 .25
❑ 261 Ivan Rodriguez .60 .25
❑ 262 Gregg Jefferies .15 .07
❑ 263 Fred McGriff .40 .18
❑ 264 Derek Bell .15 .07
❑ 265 Jeff Conine .15 .07
❑ 266 Mike Piazza 1.50 .70
❑ 267 Mark Grudzielanek .15 .07
❑ 268 Brady Anderson .25 .11
❑ 269 Marty Cordova .15 .07
❑ 270 Ray Durham .25 .11
❑ 271 Joe Carter .25 .11
❑ 272 Brian Jordan .25 .11
❑ 273 David Justice .25 .11
❑ 274 Tony Gwynn 1.25 .55
❑ 275 Larry Walker .40 .18
❑ 276 Cecil Fielder .25 .11
❑ 277 Mo Vaughn .25 .11
❑ 278 Alex Fernandez .15 .07
❑ 279 Michael Tucker .15 .07
❑ 280 Jose Valentin .15 .07
❑ 281 Sandy Alomar Jr. .25 .11
❑ 282 Todd Hollandsworth .15 .07
❑ 283 Rico Brogna .15 .07
❑ 284 Rusty Greer .25 .11
❑ 285 Roberto Hernandez .15 .07
❑ 286 Hal Morris .15 .07
❑ 287 Johnny Damon .25 .11
❑ 288 Todd Hundley .15 .07
❑ 289 Rondell White .25 .11
❑ 290 Frank Thomas .75 .35
❑ 291 Don Denbow RC .15 .07
❑ 292 Derrek Lee .25 .11
❑ 293 Todd Walker .15 .07
❑ 294 Scott Rolen .60 .25
❑ 295 Wes Helms .25 .11
❑ 296 Bob Abreu .25 .11
❑ 297 John Patterson RC .60 .25
❑ 298 Alex Gonzalez RC .50 .23
❑ 299 Grant Roberts RC .50 .23
❑ 300 Jeff Suppan .15 .07
❑ 301 Luke Wilcox .15 .07
❑ 302 Marlon Anderson .15 .07
❑ 303 Ray Brown .15 .07
❑ 304 Mike Caruso RC .15 .07
❑ 305 Sam Marsonek RC .50 .23
❑ 306 Brady Raggio RC .15 .07
❑ 307 Kevin McGlinchy RC .25 .11
❑ 308 Roy Halladay RC .25 .11
❑ 309 Jeremi Gonzalez RC .15 .07
❑ 310 Aramis Ramirez RC 3.00 1.35
❑ 311 Dermal Brown RC 2.00 .90
❑ 312 Justin Thompson .15 .07
❑ 313 Jay Tessmer RC .15 .07
❑ 314 Mike Johnson RC .15 .07
❑ 315 Danny Clyburn .15 .07
❑ 316 Bruce Aven .15 .07
❑ 317 Keith Foulke RC .25 .11
❑ 318 Jimmy Osting RC .25 .11
❑ 319 Val.De Los Santos RC .15 .07
❑ 320 Shannon Stewart .25 .11
❑ 321 Willie Adams .15 .07
❑ 322 Larry Barnes RC .15 .07
❑ 323 Mark Johnson RC .15 .07
❑ 324 Chris Stowers RC .15 .07
❑ 325 Brandon Reed .15 .07
❑ 326 Randy Winn .15 .07
❑ 327 Steve Chavez RC .15 .07
❑ 328 Nomar Garciaparra 1.50 .70
❑ 329 Jacque Jones RC 2.00 .90
❑ 330 Chris Clemons .15 .07
❑ 331 Todd Helton 1.00 .45
❑ 332 Ryan Brannan RC .15 .07
❑ 333 Alex Sanchez RC .25 .11
❑ 334 Arnold Gooch .15 .07
❑ 335 Russell Branyan .25 .11
❑ 336 Daryle Ward 1.00 .45
❑ 337 John LeRoy RC .15 .07
❑ 338 Steve Cox .15 .07
❑ 339 Kevin Witt .15 .07
❑ 340 Norm Hutchins .15 .07
❑ 341 Gabby Martinez .15 .07
❑ 342 Kris Detmers .15 .07
❑ 343 Mike Villano RC .15 .07
❑ 344 Preston Wilson .25 .11
❑ 345 James Manias RC .15 .07
❑ 346 Deivi Cruz RC 1.25 .55
❑ 347 Donzell McDonald RC .15 .07
❑ 348 Rod Myers RC .15 .07
❑ 349 Shawn Chacon RC .75 .35
❑ 350 Elvin Hernandez RC .25 .11
❑ 351 Orlando Cabrera RC .60 .25
❑ 352 Brian Banks .15 .07
❑ 353 Robbie Bell .60 .25
❑ 354 Brad Rigby .15 .07
❑ 355 Scott Elarton .15 .07
❑ 356 Kevin Sweeney RC .15 .07
❑ 357 Steve Soderstrom .15 .07
❑ 358 Ryan Nye .15 .07
❑ 360 Donny Leon RC .25 .11
❑ 361 Garrett Neubart RC .25 .11
❑ 362 Abraham Nunez RC .25 .11
❑ 363 Adam Eaton RC 2.00 .90
❑ 364 Octavio Dotel RC .75 .35
❑ 365 Dean Crow RC .15 .07
❑ 366 Jason Baker RC .15 .07
❑ 367 Sean Casey 3.00 1.35
❑ 368 Joe Lawrence RC .60 .25
❑ 369 Adam Johnson RC .15 .07
❑ 370 S.Schoeneweis RC .75 .35
❑ 371 Gerald Witasick Jr. .15 .07
❑ 372 Ronnie Belliard RC .40 .18
❑ 373 Russ Ortiz .25 .11
❑ 374 Robert Stratton RC .75 .35

❑	375	Bobby Estalella	.15	.07
❑	376	Corey Lee RC	.15	.07
❑	377	Carlos Beltran	.60	.25
❑	378	Mike Cameron	.25	.11
❑	379	Scott Randall RC	.15	.07
❑	380	Corey Erickson RC	.50	.23
❑	381	Jay Canizaro	.15	.07
❑	382	Kerry Robinson RC	.15	.07
❑	383	Todd Noel RC	.60	.25
❑	384	A.J. Zapp RC	.40	.18
❑	385	Jarrod Washburn	.15	.07
❑	386	Ben Grieve	.25	.11
❑	387	Javier Vazquez RC	3.00	1.35
❑	388	Tony Graffanino	.15	.07
❑	389	Travis Lee RC	1.50	.70
❑	390	DaRond Stovall	.15	.07
❑	391	Dennis Reyes RC	.25	.11
❑	392	Danny Buxbaum	.15	.07
❑	393	Marc Lewis RC	.15	.07
❑	394	Kelvim Escobar RC	.50	.23
❑	395	Danny Klassen	.15	.07
❑	396	Ken Cloude RC	.15	.07
❑	397	Gabe Alvarez	.15	.07
❑	398	Jaret Wright RC	.25	.11
❑	399	Raul Casanova	.15	.07
❑	400	Clayton Bruner RC	.15	.07
❑	401	Jason Marquis RC	1.00	.45
❑	402	Marc Kroon	.15	.07
❑	403	Jamey Wright	.15	.07
❑	404	Matt Snyder RC	.15	.07
❑	405	Josh Garrett RC	.50	.23
❑	406	Juan Encarnacion	.25	.11
❑	407	Heath Murray	.15	.07
❑	408	Brett Herbison RC	.25	.11
❑	409	Brent Butler RC	.50	.23
❑	410	Danny Peoples RC	.25	.11
❑	411	Miguel Tejada RC	4.00	1.80
❑	412	Damian Moss	.15	.07
❑	413	Jim Pittsley	.15	.07
❑	414	Dmitri Young	.25	.11
❑	415	Glendon Rusch	.15	.07
❑	416	Vladimir Guerrero	1.00	.45
❑	417	Cole Liniak RC	.25	.11
❑	418	R.Hernandez UER	.15	.07
		Card back says 1st Bowman card is 1997, he had a 1996 Bowman		
❑	419	Cliff Politte RC	.15	.07
❑	420	Mel Rosario RC	.15	.07
❑	421	Jorge Carrion RC	.15	.07
❑	422	John Barnes RC	.25	.11
❑	423	Chris Stowe RC	.15	.07
❑	424	Vernon Wells RC	2.50	1.10
❑	425	Brett Caradonna RC	.50	.23
❑	426	Scott Hodges RC	.50	.23
❑	427	Jon Garland RC	1.00	.45
❑	428	Nathan Haynes RC	.50	.23
❑	429	Geoff Goetz RC	.50	.23
❑	430	Adam Kennedy RC	1.00	.45
❑	431	T.J. Tucker RC	.50	.23
❑	432	Aaron Akin RC	.25	.11
❑	433	Jayson Werth RC	.40	.18
❑	434	Glenn Davis RC	.15	.07
❑	435	Mark Mangum RC	.50	.23
❑	436	Troy Cameron RC	.50	.23
❑	437	J.J. Davis RC	1.00	.45
❑	438	Lance Berkman RC	8.00	3.60
❑	439	Jason Standridge RC	.60	.25
❑	440	Jason Dellaero RC	.25	.11
❑	441	Hideki Irabu	.25	.11

1998 Bowman

	MINT	NRMT
COMPLETE SET (441)	80.00	36.00
COMPLETE SERIES 1 (221)	50.00	22.00
COMPLETE SERIES 2 (220)	30.00	13.50

❑	1	Nomar Garciaparra	1.50	.70
❑	2	Scott Rolen	.60	.25
❑	3	Andy Pettitte	.25	.11
❑	4	Ivan Rodriguez	.60	.25
❑	5	Mark McGwire	2.50	1.10
❑	6	Jason Dickson	.15	.07
❑	7	Jose Cruz Jr.	.25	.11
❑	8	Jeff Kent	.40	.18
❑	9	Mike Mussina	.60	.25

❑	10	Jason Kendall	.25	.11
❑	11	Brett Tomko	.15	.07
❑	12	Jeff King	.15	.07
❑	13	Brad Radke	.25	.11
❑	14	Robin Ventura	.25	.11
❑	15	Jeff Bagwell	.75	.35
❑	16	Greg Maddux	1.50	.70
❑	17	John Jaha	.25	.11
❑	18	Mike Piazza	1.50	.70
❑	19	Edgar Martinez	.40	.18
❑	20	David Justice	.25	.11
❑	21	Todd Hundley	.15	.07
❑	22	Tony Gwynn	1.25	.55
❑	23	Larry Walker	.40	.18
❑	24	Bernie Williams	.60	.25
❑	25	Edgar Renteria	.15	.07
❑	26	Rafael Palmeiro	.60	.25
❑	27	Tim Salmon	.25	.11
❑	28	Matt Morris	.25	.11
❑	29	Shawn Estes	.25	.11
❑	30	Vladimir Guerrero	.75	.35
❑	31	Fernando Tatis	.15	.07
❑	32	Justin Thompson	.15	.07
❑	33	Ken Griffey Jr.	2.00	.90
❑	34	Edgardo Alfonzo	.25	.11
❑	35	Mo Vaughn	.25	.11
❑	36	Marty Cordova	.15	.07
❑	37	Craig Biggio	.40	.18
❑	38	Roger Clemens	1.50	.70
❑	39	Mark Grace	.60	.25
❑	40	Ken Caminiti	.25	.11
❑	41	Tony Womack	.15	.07
❑	42	Albert Belle	.25	.11
❑	43	Tino Martinez	.25	.11
❑	44	Sandy Alomar Jr.	.25	.11
❑	45	Jeff Cirillo	.25	.11
❑	46	Jason Giambi	.60	.25
❑	47	Darin Erstad	.60	.25
❑	48	Livan Hernandez	.15	.07
❑	49	Mark Grudzielanek	.15	.07
❑	50	Sammy Sosa	1.25	.55
❑	51	Curt Schilling	.60	.25
❑	52	Brian Hunter	.15	.07
❑	53	Neifi Perez	.15	.07
❑	54	Todd Walker	.15	.07
❑	55	Jose Guillen	.15	.07
❑	56	Jim Thome	.60	.25
❑	57	Tom Glavine	.60	.25
❑	58	Todd Greene	.15	.07
❑	59	Rondell White	.25	.11
❑	60	Roberto Alomar	.60	.25
❑	61	Tony Clark	.25	.11
❑	62	Vinny Castilla	.25	.11
❑	63	Barry Larkin	.60	.25
❑	64	Hideki Irabu	.15	.07
❑	65	Johnny Damon	.25	.11
❑	66	Juan Gonzalez	.60	.25
❑	67	John Olerud	.25	.11
❑	68	Gary Sheffield	.25	.11
❑	69	Raul Mondesi	.25	.11
❑	70	Chipper Jones	1.25	.55
❑	71	David Ortiz	.25	.11
❑	72	Warren Morris RC	.50	.23
❑	73	Alex Gonzalez	.25	.11
❑	74	Nick Bierbrodt	.60	.25
❑	75	Roy Halladay	.15	.07
❑	76	Danny Buxbaum	.15	.07
❑	77	Adam Kennedy	.15	.07
❑	78	Jared Sandberg	.25	.11
❑	79	Michael Barrett	.15	.07
❑	80	Gil Meche	.75	.35
❑	81	Jayson Werth	.15	.07
❑	82	Abraham Nunez	.15	.07
❑	83	Ben Petrick	.15	.07
❑	84	Brett Caradonna	.15	.07
❑	85	Mike Lowell RC	1.50	.70
❑	86	Clayton Bruner	.25	.11
❑	87	John Curtice RC	.25	.11
❑	88	Bobby Estalella	.15	.07
❑	89	Juan Melo	.15	.07
❑	90	Arnold Gooch	.15	.07
❑	91	Kevin Millwood RC	1.25	.55
❑	92	Richie Sexson	.25	.11
❑	93	Orlando Cabrera	.15	.07
❑	94	Pat Cline	.15	.07
❑	95	Anthony Sanders	.15	.07
❑	96	Russ Johnson	.15	.07
❑	97	Ben Grieve	.25	.11
❑	98	Kevin McGlinchy	.15	.07
❑	99	Paul Wilder	.15	.07
❑	100	Russ Ortiz	.25	.11
❑	101	Ryan Jackson RC	.15	.07
❑	102	Heath Murray	.15	.07
❑	103	Brian Rose	.15	.07
❑	104	R.Radmanovich RC	.15	.07
❑	105	Ricky Ledee	.15	.07
❑	106	Jeff Wallace RC	.25	.11
❑	107	Ryan Minor RC	.25	.11
❑	108	Dennis Reyes	.15	.07
❑	109	James Manias	.15	.07
❑	110	Chris Carpenter	.15	.07
❑	111	Daryle Ward	.15	.07
❑	112	Vernon Wells	.40	.18
❑	113	Chad Green	.15	.07
❑	114	Mike Stoner RC	.15	.07
❑	115	Brad Fullmer	.25	.11
❑	116	Adam Eaton	.25	.11
❑	117	Jeff Liefer	.15	.07
❑	118	Corey Koskie RC	1.50	.70
❑	119	Todd Helton	.75	.35
❑	120	Jaime Jones RC	.25	.11
❑	121	Mel Rosario	.15	.07
❑	122	Geoff Goetz	.15	.07
❑	123	Adrian Beltre	.25	.11
❑	124	Jason Dellaero	.15	.07
❑	125	Gabe Kapler RC	2.00	.90
❑	126	Scott Schoeneweis	.15	.07
❑	127	Ryan Brannan	.15	.07
❑	128	Aaron Akin	.15	.07
❑	129	Ryan Anderson RC	3.00	1.35
❑	130	Brad Penny	.25	.11
❑	131	Bruce Chen	.15	.07
❑	132	Eli Marrero	.15	.07
❑	133	Eric Chavez	.25	.11
❑	134	Troy Glaus RC	6.00	2.70
❑	135	Troy Cameron	.15	.07
❑	136	Brian Sikorski RC	.15	.07
❑	137	Mike Kinkade RC	.25	.11
❑	138	Braden Looper	.15	.07
❑	139	Mark Mangum	.15	.07
❑	140	Danny Peoples	.15	.07
❑	141	J.J. Davis	.25	.11
❑	142	Ben Davis	.25	.11
❑	143	Jacque Jones	.25	.11
❑	144	Derrick Gibson	.15	.07
❑	145	Bronson Arroyo	.25	.11
❑	146	L.De Los Santos RC UER	.25	.11
		has hitting stat line instead of pitching		
❑	147	Jeff Abbott	.15	.07
❑	148	Mike Cuddyer RC	2.00	.90
❑	149	Jason Romano	.15	.07
❑	150	Shane Monahan	.15	.07
❑	151	Ntema Ndungidi RC	.25	.11
❑	152	Alex Sanchez	.15	.07
❑	153	Jack Cust RC	2.50	1.10
❑	154	Brent Butler	.15	.07
❑	155	Ramon Hernandez	.15	.07
❑	156	Norm Hutchins	.15	.07
❑	157	Jason Marquis	.25	.11
❑	158	Jacob Cruz	.15	.07
❑	159	Rob Burger RC	.15	.07
❑	160	Dave Coggin	.15	.07

❑ 161 Preston Wilson .25 .11
❑ 162 Jason Fitzgerald RC .15 .07
❑ 163 Dan Serafini .15 .07
❑ 164 Peter Munro .15 .07
❑ 165 Trot Nixon .25 .11
❑ 166 Homer Bush .15 .07
❑ 167 Dermal Brown .15 .07
❑ 168 Chad Hermansen .15 .07
❑ 169 Julio Moreno RC .50 .23
❑ 170 John Roskos RC .25 .11
❑ 171 Grant Roberts .15 .07
❑ 172 Ken Cloude .15 .07
❑ 173 Jason Brester .15 .07
❑ 174 Jason Conti .15 .07
❑ 175 Jon Garland .15 .07
❑ 176 Robbie Bell .15 .07
❑ 177 Nathan Haynes .15 .07
❑ 178 Ramon Ortiz RC 1.50 .70
❑ 179 Shannon Stewart .25 .11
❑ 180 Pablo Ortega .15 .07
❑ 181 Jimmy Rollins RC 3.00 1.35
❑ 182 Sean Casey .40 .18
❑ 183 Ted Lilly RC 1.00 .45
❑ 184 Chris Enochs RC .25 .11
❑ 185 M.Ordonez RC UER 4.00 1.80
Front photo is Mario Valdez
❑ 186 Mike Drumright .15 .07
❑ 187 Aaron Boone .15 .07
❑ 188 Matt Clement .15 .07
❑ 189 Todd Dunwoody .15 .07
❑ 190 Larry Rodriguez .15 .07
❑ 191 Todd Noel .15 .07
❑ 192 Geoff Jenkins .25 .11
❑ 193 George Lombard .15 .07
❑ 194 Lance Berkman .60 .25
❑ 195 Marcus McCain .25 .11
❑ 196 Ryan McGuire .15 .07
❑ 197 Jhensy Sandoval .15 .07
❑ 198 Corey Lee .15 .07
❑ 199 Mario Valdez .15 .07
❑ 200 Robert Fick RC 1.25 .55
❑ 201 Donnie Sadler .15 .07
❑ 202 Marc Kroon .15 .07
❑ 203 David Miller .15 .07
❑ 204 Jarrod Washburn .15 .07
❑ 205 Miguel Tejada .40 .18
❑ 206 Raul Ibanez .15 .07
❑ 207 John Patterson .15 .07
❑ 208 Calvin Pickering .15 .07
❑ 209 Felix Martinez .15 .07
❑ 210 Mark Redman .15 .07
❑ 211 Scott Elarton .15 .07
❑ 212 Jose Amado RC .15 .07
❑ 213 Kerry Wood .60 .25
❑ 214 Dante Powell .15 .07
❑ 215 Aramis Ramirez .25 .11
❑ 216 A.J. Hinch .15 .07
❑ 217 Dustin Carr RC .50 .23
❑ 218 Mark Kotsay .25 .11
❑ 219 Jason Standridge .15 .07
❑ 220 Luis Ordaz .15 .07
❑ 221 O.Hernandez RC 1.50 .70
❑ 222 Cal Ripken 2.50 1.10
❑ 223 Paul Molitor .60 .25
❑ 224 Derek Jeter 2.50 1.10
❑ 225 Barry Bonds 1.50 .70
❑ 226 Jim Edmonds .40 .18
❑ 227 John Smoltz .25 .11
❑ 228 Eric Karros .25 .11
❑ 229 Ray Lankford .15 .07
❑ 230 Rey Ordonez .15 .07
❑ 231 Kenny Lofton .25 .11
❑ 232 Alex Rodriguez 1.50 .70
❑ 233 Dante Bichette .25 .11
❑ 234 Pedro Martinez .75 .35
❑ 235 Carlos Delgado .60 .25
❑ 236 Rod Beck .15 .07
❑ 237 Matt Williams .40 .18
❑ 238 Charles Johnson .25 .11
❑ 239 Rico Brogna .15 .07
❑ 240 Frank Thomas .75 .35
❑ 241 Paul O'Neill .60 .25
❑ 242 Jaret Wright .15 .07
❑ 243 Brant Brown .15 .07
❑ 244 Ryan Klesko .25 .11
❑ 245 Chuck Finley .25 .11
❑ 246 Derek Bell .15 .07
❑ 247 Delino DeShields .15 .07
❑ 248 Chan Ho Park .25 .11
❑ 249 Wade Boggs .60 .25
❑ 250 Jay Buhner .25 .11
❑ 251 Butch Huskey .15 .07
❑ 252 Steve Finley .25 .11
❑ 253 Will Clark .60 .25
❑ 254 John Valentin .15 .07
❑ 255 Bobby Higginson .25 .11
❑ 256 Darryl Strawberry .25 .11
❑ 257 Randy Johnson .75 .35
❑ 258 Al Martin .15 .07
❑ 259 Travis Fryman .25 .11
❑ 260 Fred McGriff .40 .18
❑ 261 Jose Valentin .15 .07
❑ 262 Andruw Jones .60 .25
❑ 263 Kenny Rogers .15 .07
❑ 264 Moises Alou .25 .11
❑ 265 Denny Neagle .15 .07
❑ 266 Ugueth Urbina .15 .07
❑ 267 Derrek Lee .25 .11
❑ 268 Ellis Burks .25 .11
❑ 269 Mariano Rivera .25 .11
❑ 270 Dean Palmer .25 .11
❑ 271 Eddie Taubensee .15 .07
❑ 272 Brady Anderson .25 .11
❑ 273 Brian Giles .25 .11
❑ 274 Quinton McCracken .15 .07
❑ 275 Henry Rodriguez .15 .07
❑ 276 Andres Galarraga .40 .18
❑ 277 Jose Canseco .60 .25
❑ 278 David Segui .15 .07
❑ 279 Bret Saberhagen .25 .11
❑ 280 Kevin Brown .40 .18
❑ 281 Chuck Knoblauch .25 .11
❑ 282 Jeromy Burnitz .25 .11
❑ 283 Jay Bell .25 .11
❑ 284 Manny Ramirez .75 .35
❑ 285 Rick Helling .15 .07
❑ 286 Francisco Cordova .15 .07
❑ 287 Bob Abreu .25 .11
❑ 288 J.T. Snow .25 .11
❑ 289 Hideo Nomo .60 .25
❑ 290 Brian Jordan .25 .11
❑ 291 Javy Lopez .25 .11
❑ 292 Travis Lee .25 .11
❑ 293 Russell Branyan .25 .11
❑ 294 Paul Konerko .25 .11
❑ 295 Masato Yoshii RC 1.00 .45
❑ 296 Kris Benson .25 .11
❑ 297 Juan Encarnacion .25 .11
❑ 298 Eric Milton .25 .11
❑ 299 Mike Caruso .15 .07
❑ 300 R.Aramboles RC 1.00 .45
❑ 301 Bobby Smith .15 .07
❑ 302 Billy Koch .15 .07
❑ 303 Richard Hidalgo .25 .11
❑ 304 Justin Baughman RC .15 .07
❑ 305 Chris Gissell .15 .07
❑ 306 Donnie Bridges RC .50 .23
❑ 307 Nelson Lara RC .25 .11
❑ 308 Randy Wolf RC 1.00 .45
❑ 309 Jason LaRue RC 1.00 .45
❑ 310 Jason Gooding RC .15 .07
❑ 311 Edgard Clemente .15 .07
❑ 312 Andrew Vessel .15 .07
❑ 313 Chris Reitsma .15 .07
❑ 314 Jesus Sanchez RC .25 .11
❑ 315 Buddy Carlyle RC .50 .23
❑ 316 Randy Winn .15 .07
❑ 317 Luis Rivera RC .50 .23
❑ 318 Marcus Thames RC 1.25 .55
❑ 319 A.J. Pierzynski .15 .07
❑ 320 Scott Randall .15 .07
❑ 321 Damian Sapp .15 .07
❑ 322 Ed Yarnall RC .50 .23
❑ 323 Luke Allen RC .25 .11
❑ 324 J.D. Smart .15 .07
❑ 325 Willie Martinez .25 .11
❑ 326 Alex Ramirez .15 .07
❑ 327 Eric DuBose RC .25 .11
❑ 328 Kevin Witt .15 .07
❑ 329 Dan McKinley RC .25 .11
❑ 330 Cliff Politte .15 .07
❑ 331 Vladimir Nunez .15 .07
❑ 332 John Halama RC 1.00 .45
❑ 333 Nerio Rodriguez .15 .07
❑ 334 Desi Relaford .15 .07
❑ 335 Robinson Checo .15 .07
❑ 336 John Nicholson .40 .18
❑ 337 Tom LaRosa RC .15 .07
❑ 338 Kevin Nicholson RC .25 .11
❑ 339 Javier Vazquez .25 .11
❑ 340 A.J. Zapp .15 .07
❑ 341 Tom Evans .15 .07
❑ 342 Kerry Robinson .15 .07
❑ 343 Gabe Gonzalez RC .15 .07
❑ 344 Ralph Milliard .15 .07
❑ 345 Enrique Wilson .15 .07
❑ 346 Elvin Hernandez .15 .07
❑ 347 Mike Lincoln RC .15 .07
❑ 348 Cesar King RC .25 .11
❑ 349 Cristian Guzman RC 2.50 1.10
❑ 350 Donzell McDonald .15 .07
❑ 351 Jim Parque RC .50 .23
❑ 352 Mike Saipe RC .15 .07
❑ 353 Carlos Febles RC .50 .23
❑ 354 Dernell Stenson RC 1.00 .45
❑ 355 Mark Osborne RC .25 .11
❑ 356 Odalis Perez RC .60 .25
❑ 357 Jason Dewey RC .25 .11
❑ 358 Joe Fontenot .15 .07
❑ 359 Jason Grilli RC .25 .11
❑ 360 Kevin Haverbusch RC .25 .11
❑ 361 Jay Yennaco RC .25 .11
❑ 362 Brian Buchanan .15 .07
❑ 363 John Barnes .15 .07
❑ 364 Chris Fussell .15 .07
❑ 365 Kevin Gibbs RC .15 .07
❑ 366 Joe Lawrence .15 .07
❑ 367 DaRond Stovall .15 .07
❑ 368 Brian Fuentes RC .15 .07
❑ 369 Jimmy Anderson .15 .07
❑ 370 Lariel Gonzalez RC .25 .11
❑ 371 Scott Williamson RC .25 .11
❑ 372 Milton Bradley .15 .07
❑ 373 Jason Halper RC .25 .11
❑ 374 Brent Billingsley RC .15 .07
❑ 375 Joe DePastino RC .15 .07
❑ 376 Jake Westbrook .15 .07
❑ 377 Octavio Dotel .15 .07
❑ 378 Jason Williams RC .15 .07
❑ 379 Julio Ramirez RC .25 .11
❑ 380 Seth Greisinger .15 .07
❑ 381 Mike Judd RC .25 .11
❑ 382 Ben Ford RC .25 .11
❑ 383 Tom Bennett RC .15 .07
❑ 384 Adam Butler RC .15 .07
❑ 385 Wade Miller RC 3.00 1.35
❑ 386 Kyle Peterson RC .25 .11
❑ 387 Tommy Peterman RC .15 .07
❑ 388 Onan Masaoka .15 .07
❑ 389 Jason Rakers RC .15 .07
❑ 390 Rafael Medina .15 .07
❑ 391 Luis Lopez .15 .07
❑ 392 Jeff Yoder .15 .07
❑ 393 Vance Wilson RC .15 .07
❑ 394 F.Seguignol RC .25 .11
❑ 395 Ron Wright .15 .07
❑ 396 Ruben Mateo RC 1.50 .70
❑ 397 Steve Lomasney RC .25 .11
❑ 398 Damian Jackson .15 .07
❑ 399 Mike Jerzembeck RC .25 .11
❑ 400 Luis Rivas RC 1.25 .55
❑ 401 Kevin Burford RC .25 .11
❑ 402 Glenn Davis .15 .07
❑ 403 Robert Luce RC .15 .07
❑ 404 Cole Liniak .15 .07
❑ 405 Matt LeCroy RC .50 .23
❑ 406 Jeremy Giambi RC 1.00 .45
❑ 407 Shawn Chacon .15 .07
❑ 408 Dewayne Wise RC .25 .11
❑ 409 Steve Woodard .15 .07
❑ 410 F.Cordero RC .40 .18
❑ 411 Damon Minor RC .25 .11
❑ 412 Lou Collier .15 .07
❑ 413 Justin Towle .15 .07
❑ 414 Juan LeBron .15 .07
❑ 415 Michael Coleman .15 .07
❑ 416 Felix Rodriguez .15 .07
❑ 417 Paul Ah Yat RC .15 .07

		MINT	NRMT
❑ 418	Kevin Barker RC	.25	.11
❑ 419	Brian Meadows	.15	.07
❑ 420	Darnell McDonald RC	.25	.11
❑ 421	Matt Kinney RC	.50	.23
❑ 422	Mike Vavrek RC	.15	.07
❑ 423	Courtney Duncan RC	.15	.07
❑ 424	Kevin Millar RC	.60	.25
❑ 425	Ruben Rivera	.15	.07
❑ 426	Steve Shoemaker RC	.15	.07
❑ 427	Dan Reichert RC	1.00	.45
❑ 428	Carlos Lee RC	2.00	.90
❑ 429	Rod Barajas	.25	.11
❑ 430	Pablo Ozuna RC	.25	.11
❑ 431	Todd Belitz RC	.50	.23
❑ 432	Sidney Ponson	.15	.07
❑ 433	Steve Carver RC	.15	.07
❑ 434	Esteban Yan RC	.50	.23
❑ 435	Cedrick Bowers	.25	.11
❑ 436	Marlon Anderson	.15	.07
❑ 437	Carl Pavano	.15	.07
❑ 438	Jae Weong Seo RC	1.00	.45
❑ 439	Jose Taveras RC	.25	.11
❑ 440	Matt Anderson RC	.25	.11
❑ 441	Darron Ingram RC	.25	.11
❑ NNO	S.Hasegawa '91 BBM	10.00	4.50
❑ NNO	H.Irabu '91 BBM	10.00	4.50
❑ NNO	H.Nomo '91 BBM	25.00	11.00

1999 Bowman

	MINT	NRMT
COMPLETE SET (440)	120.00	55.00
COMPLETE SERIES 1 (220)	50.00	22.00
COMPLETE SERIES 2 (220)	70.00	32.00

		MINT	NRMT
❑ 1	Ben Grieve	.25	.11
❑ 2	Kerry Wood	.60	.25
❑ 3	Ruben Rivera	.15	.07
❑ 4	Sandy Alomar Jr.	.25	.11
❑ 5	Cal Ripken	2.50	1.10
❑ 6	Mark McGwire	2.50	1.10
❑ 7	Vladimir Guerrero	.75	.35
❑ 8	Moises Alou	.25	.11
❑ 9	Jim Edmonds	.40	.18
❑ 10	Greg Maddux	1.50	.70
❑ 11	Gary Sheffield	.25	.11
❑ 12	John Valentin	.15	.07
❑ 13	Chuck Knoblauch	.25	.11
❑ 14	Tony Clark	.25	.11
❑ 15	Rusty Greer	.25	.11
❑ 16	Al Leiter	.25	.11
❑ 17	Travis Lee	.15	.07
❑ 18	Jose Cruz Jr.	.25	.11
❑ 19	Pedro Martinez	.75	.35
❑ 20	Paul O'Neill	.60	.25
❑ 21	Todd Walker	.15	.07
❑ 22	Vinny Castilla	.25	.11
❑ 23	Barry Larkin	.60	.25
❑ 24	Curt Schilling	.60	.25
❑ 25	Jason Kendall	.25	.11
❑ 26	Scott Erickson	.15	.07
❑ 27	Andres Galarraga	.40	.18
❑ 28	Jeff Shaw	.15	.07
❑ 29	John Olerud	.25	.11
❑ 30	Orlando Hernandez	.25	.11
❑ 31	Larry Walker	.40	.18
❑ 32	Andruw Jones	.60	.25
❑ 33	Jeff Cirillo	.25	.11
❑ 34	Barry Bonds	1.50	.70
❑ 35	Manny Ramirez	.75	.35
❑ 36	Mark Kotsay	.15	.07
❑ 37	Ivan Rodriguez	.60	.25
❑ 38	Jeff King	.15	.07
❑ 39	Brian Hunter	.15	.07
❑ 40	Ray Durham	.25	.11
❑ 41	Bernie Williams	.60	.25
❑ 42	Darin Erstad	.60	.25
❑ 43	Chipper Jones	1.25	.55
❑ 44	Pat Hentgen	.15	.07
❑ 45	Eric Young	.15	.07
❑ 46	Jaret Wright	.15	.07
❑ 47	Juan Guzman	.15	.07
❑ 48	Jorge Posada	.25	.11
❑ 49	Bobby Higginson	.25	.11
❑ 50	Jose Guillen	.15	.07
❑ 51	Trevor Hoffman	.25	.11
❑ 52	Ken Griffey Jr.	2.00	.90
❑ 53	David Justice	.25	.11
❑ 54	Matt Williams	.40	.18
❑ 55	Eric Karros	.25	.11
❑ 56	Derek Bell	.15	.07
❑ 57	Ray Lankford	.15	.07
❑ 58	Mariano Rivera	.25	.11
❑ 59	Brett Tomko	.15	.07
❑ 60	Mike Mussina	.60	.25
❑ 61	Kenny Lofton	.25	.11
❑ 62	Chuck Finley	.25	.11
❑ 63	Alex Gonzalez	.15	.07
❑ 64	Mark Grace	.60	.25
❑ 65	Raul Mondesi	.25	.11
❑ 66	David Cone	.25	.11
❑ 67	Brad Fullmer	.25	.11
❑ 68	Andy Benes	.15	.07
❑ 69	John Smoltz	.25	.11
❑ 70	Shane Reynolds	.15	.07
❑ 71	Bruce Chen	.15	.07
❑ 72	Adam Kennedy	.15	.07
❑ 73	Jack Cust	.25	.11
❑ 74	Matt Clement	.15	.07
❑ 75	Derrick Gibson	.15	.07
❑ 76	Darnell McDonald	.15	.07
❑ 77	Adam Everett RC	.75	.35
❑ 78	Ricardo Aramboles	.15	.07
❑ 79	Mark Quinn RC	1.50	.70
❑ 80	Jason Rakers	.15	.07
❑ 81	Seth Etherton RC	.60	.25
❑ 82	Jeff Urban RC	.25	.11
❑ 83	Manny Aybar	.15	.07
❑ 84	Mike Nannini RC	1.00	.45
❑ 85	Onan Masaoka	.15	.07
❑ 86	Rod Barajas	.15	.07
❑ 87	Mike Frank	.15	.07
❑ 88	Scott Randall	.15	.07
❑ 89	Justin Bowles RC	.15	.07
❑ 90	Chris Haas	.15	.07
❑ 91	Arturo McDowell RC	.50	.23
❑ 92	Matt Belisle RC	1.00	.45
❑ 93	Scott Elarton	.15	.07
❑ 94	Vernon Wells	.25	.11
❑ 95	Pat Cline	.15	.07
❑ 96	Ryan Anderson	.25	.11
❑ 97	Kevin Barker	.15	.07
❑ 98	Ruben Mateo	.25	.11
❑ 99	Robert Fick	.15	.07
❑ 100	Corey Koskie	.25	.11
❑ 101	Ricky Ledee	.15	.07
❑ 102	Rick Elder RC	1.25	.55
❑ 103	Jack Cressend RC	.15	.07
❑ 104	Joe Lawrence	.25	.11
❑ 105	Mike Lincoln	.15	.07
❑ 106	Kit Pellow RC	.60	.25
❑ 107	Matt Burch RC	.25	.11
❑ 108	Cole Liniak	.15	.07
❑ 109	Jason Dewey	.15	.07
❑ 110	Cesar King	.15	.07
❑ 111	Julio Ramirez	.15	.07
❑ 112	Jake Westbrook	.15	.07
❑ 113	Eric Valent RC	1.25	.55
❑ 114	Roosevelt Brown RC	.60	.25
❑ 115	Choo Freeman RC	.75	.35
❑ 116	Juan Melo	.15	.07
❑ 117	Jason Grilli	.15	.07
❑ 118	Jared Sandberg	.15	.07
❑ 119	Glenn Davis	.15	.07
❑ 120	David Riske RC	.50	.23
❑ 121	Jacque Jones	.25	.11
❑ 122	Corey Lee	.15	.07
❑ 123	Michael Barrett	.15	.07
❑ 124	Lariel Gonzalez	.15	.07
❑ 125	Mitch Meluskey	.15	.07
❑ 126	Freddy Adrian Garcia	.15	.07
❑ 127	Tony Torcato RC	1.25	.55
❑ 128	Jeff Liefer	.15	.07
❑ 129	Ntema Ndungidi	.15	.07
❑ 130	Andy Brown RC	.75	.35
❑ 131	Ryan Mills RC	.50	.23
❑ 132	Andy Abad RC	.15	.07
❑ 133	Carlos Febles	.15	.07
❑ 134	Jason Tyner RC	.60	.25
❑ 135	Mark Osborne	.15	.07
❑ 136	Phil Norton RC	.15	.07
❑ 137	Nathan Haynes	.15	.07
❑ 138	Roy Halladay	.15	.07
❑ 139	Juan Encarnacion	.25	.11
❑ 140	Brad Penny	.25	.11
❑ 141	Grant Roberts	.15	.07
❑ 142	Aramis Ramirez	.25	.11
❑ 143	Cristian Guzman	.25	.11
❑ 144	Mamon Tucker RC	.60	.25
❑ 145	Ryan Bradley	.15	.07
❑ 146	Brian Simmons	.15	.07
❑ 147	Dan Reichert	.15	.07
❑ 148	Russ Branyan	.25	.11
❑ 149	Victor Valencia RC	.25	.11
❑ 150	Scott Schoeneweis	.15	.07
❑ 151	Sean Spencer RC	.15	.07
❑ 152	Odalis Perez	.15	.07
❑ 153	Joe Fontenot	.15	.07
❑ 154	Milton Bradley	.15	.07
❑ 155	Josh McKinley RC	.60	.25
❑ 156	Terrence Long	.25	.11
❑ 157	Danny Klassen	.15	.07
❑ 158	Paul Hoover RC	.25	.11
❑ 159	Ron Belliard	.15	.07
❑ 160	Armando Rios	.15	.07
❑ 161	Ramon Hernandez	.15	.07
❑ 162	Jason Conti	.15	.07
❑ 163	Chad Hermansen	.15	.07
❑ 164	Jason Standridge	.15	.07
❑ 165	Jason Dellaero	.15	.07
❑ 166	John Curtice	.15	.07
❑ 167	Clayton Andrews RC	.50	.23
❑ 168	Jeremy Giambi	.15	.07
❑ 169	Alex Ramirez	.15	.07
❑ 170	Gabe Molina RC	.15	.07
❑ 171	M.Encarnacion RC	.60	.25
❑ 172	Mike Zywica RC	.15	.07
❑ 173	Chip Ambres RC	.75	.35
❑ 174	Trot Nixon	.25	.11
❑ 175	Pat Burrell RC	3.00	1.35
❑ 176	Jeff Yoder	.15	.07
❑ 177	Chris Jones RC	.60	.25
❑ 178	Kevin Witt	.15	.07
❑ 179	Keith Luuloa RC	.15	.07
❑ 180	Billy Koch	.15	.07
❑ 181	Damaso Marte RC	.15	.07
❑ 182	Ryan Glynn RC	.60	.25
❑ 183	Calvin Pickering	.15	.07
❑ 184	Michael Cuddyer	.25	.11
❑ 185	Nick Johnson RC	3.00	1.35
❑ 186	D.Mientkiewicz RC	2.50	1.10
❑ 187	Nate Cornejo RC	2.00	.90
❑ 188	Octavio Dotel	.15	.07
❑ 189	Wes Helms	.15	.07
❑ 190	Nelson Lara	.15	.07
❑ 191	Chuck Abbott RC	.15	.07
❑ 192	Tony Armas Jr.	.25	.11
❑ 193	Gil Meche	.15	.07
❑ 194	Ben Petrick	.15	.07
❑ 195	Chris George RC	1.25	.55
❑ 196	Scott Hunter RC	.15	.07
❑ 197	Ryan Brannan	.15	.07
❑ 198	Amaury Garcia RC	.25	.11
❑ 199	Chris Gissell	.15	.07
❑ 200	Austin Kearns RC	4.00	1.80
❑ 201	Alex Gonzalez	.15	.07
❑ 202	Wade Miller	.25	.11
❑ 203	Scott Williamson	.15	.07
❑ 204	Chris Enochs	.15	.07
❑ 205	Fernando Seguignol	.15	.07

		MINT	NRMT
❑ 206	Marlon Anderson	.15	.07
❑ 207	Todd Sears RC	.50	.23
❑ 208	Nate Bump RC	.50	.23
❑ 209	J.M. Gold RC	.60	.25
❑ 210	Matt LeCroy	.15	.07
❑ 211	Alex Hernandez	.15	.07
❑ 212	Luis Rivera	.15	.07
❑ 213	Troy Cameron	.15	.07
❑ 214	Alex Escobar RC	2.50	1.10
❑ 215	Jason LaRue	.15	.07
❑ 216	Kyle Peterson	.15	.07
❑ 217	Brent Butler	.15	.07
❑ 218	Dernell Stenson	.15	.07
❑ 219	Adrian Beltre	.25	.11
❑ 220	Daryle Ward	.15	.07
❑ 221	Jim Thome	.60	.25
❑ 222	Cliff Floyd	.25	.11
❑ 223	Rickey Henderson	1.25	.55
❑ 224	Garret Anderson	.25	.11
❑ 225	Ken Caminiti	.25	.11
❑ 226	Bret Boone	.25	.11
❑ 227	Jeromy Burnitz	.25	.11
❑ 228	Steve Finley	.25	.11
❑ 229	Miguel Tejada	.25	.11
❑ 230	Greg Vaughn	.25	.11
❑ 231	Jose Offerman	.15	.07
❑ 232	Andy Ashby	.15	.07
❑ 233	Albert Belle	.25	.11
❑ 234	Fernando Tatis	.15	.07
❑ 235	Todd Helton	.75	.35
❑ 236	Sean Casey	.40	.18
❑ 237	Brian Giles	.25	.11
❑ 238	Andy Pettitte	.25	.11
❑ 239	Fred McGriff	.40	.18
❑ 240	Roberto Alomar	.60	.25
❑ 241	Edgar Martinez	.40	.18
❑ 242	Lee Stevens	.15	.07
❑ 243	Shawn Green	.60	.25
❑ 244	Ryan Klesko	.25	.11
❑ 245	Sammy Sosa	1.25	.55
❑ 246	Todd Hundley	.15	.07
❑ 247	Shannon Stewart	.25	.11
❑ 248	Randy Johnson	.75	.35
❑ 249	Rondell White	.25	.11
❑ 250	Mike Piazza	1.50	.70
❑ 251	Craig Biggio	.40	.18
❑ 252	David Wells	.25	.11
❑ 253	Brian Jordan	.25	.11
❑ 254	Edgar Renteria	.15	.07
❑ 255	Bartolo Colon	.25	.11
❑ 256	Frank Thomas	.75	.35
❑ 257	Will Clark	.60	.25
❑ 258	Dean Palmer	.25	.11
❑ 259	Dmitri Young	.25	.11
❑ 260	Scott Rolen	.60	.25
❑ 261	Jeff Kent	.40	.18
❑ 262	Dante Bichette	.25	.11
❑ 263	Nomar Garciaparra	1.50	.70
❑ 264	Tony Gwynn	1.25	.55
❑ 265	Alex Rodriguez	1.50	.70
❑ 266	Jose Canseco	.60	.25
❑ 267	Jason Giambi	.60	.25
❑ 268	Jeff Bagwell	.75	.35
❑ 269	Carlos Delgado	.60	.25
❑ 270	Tom Glavine	.60	.25
❑ 271	Eric Davis	.25	.11
❑ 272	Edgardo Alfonzo	.25	.11
❑ 273	Tim Salmon	.25	.11
❑ 274	Johnny Damon	.25	.11
❑ 275	Rafael Palmeiro	.60	.25
❑ 276	Denny Neagle	.15	.07
❑ 277	Neifi Perez	.15	.07
❑ 278	Roger Clemens	1.50	.70
❑ 279	Brant Brown	.15	.07
❑ 280	Kevin Brown	.40	.18
❑ 281	Jay Bell	.25	.11
❑ 282	Jay Buhner	.25	.11
❑ 283	Matt Lawton	.25	.11
❑ 284	Robin Ventura	.25	.11
❑ 285	Juan Gonzalez	.60	.25
❑ 286	Mo Vaughn	.25	.11
❑ 287	Kevin Millwood	.15	.07
❑ 288	Tino Martinez	.25	.11
❑ 289	Justin Thompson	.15	.07
❑ 290	Derek Jeter	2.50	1.10
❑ 291	Ben Davis	.25	.11
❑ 292	Mike Lowell	.25	.11
❑ 293	Calvin Murray	.15	.07
❑ 294	Micah Bowie RC	.15	.07
❑ 295	Lance Berkman	.60	.25
❑ 296	Jason Marquis	.25	.11
❑ 297	Chad Green	.15	.07
❑ 298	Dee Brown	.25	.11
❑ 299	Jerry Hairston Jr.	.25	.11
❑ 300	Gabe Kapler	.25	.11
❑ 301	Brent Stentz RC	.25	.11
❑ 302	Scott Mullen RC	.15	.07
❑ 303	Brandon Reed	.15	.07
❑ 304	Shea Hillenbrand RC	1.50	.70
❑ 305	J.D. Closser RC	1.00	.45
❑ 306	Gary Matthews Jr.	.15	.07
❑ 307	Toby Hall RC	2.50	1.10
❑ 308	Jason Phillips RC	.50	.23
❑ 309	Jose Macias RC	.15	.07
❑ 310	Jung Bong RC	1.00	.45
❑ 311	Ramon Soler RC	.60	.25
❑ 312	Kelly Dransfeldt RC	.15	.07
❑ 313	Carlos E. Hernandez RC	.25	.11
❑ 314	Kevin Haverbusch	.15	.07
❑ 315	Aaron Myette RC	.60	.25
❑ 316	Chad Harville RC	.25	.11
❑ 317	Kyle Farnsworth RC	.75	.35
❑ 318	Travis Dawkins RC	.60	.25
❑ 319	Willie Martinez	.15	.07
❑ 320	Carlos Lee	.25	.11
❑ 321	Carlos Pena RC	3.00	1.35
❑ 322	Peter Bergeron RC	1.00	.45
❑ 323	A.J. Burnett RC	1.50	.70
❑ 324	Bucky Jacobsen RC	.15	.07
❑ 325	Mo Bruce RC	.15	.07
❑ 326	Reggie Taylor	.15	.07
❑ 327	Jackie Rexrode	.15	.07
❑ 328	Alvin Morrow RC	.50	.23
❑ 329	Carlos Beltran	.25	.11
❑ 330	Eric Chavez	.25	.11
❑ 331	John Patterson	.15	.07
❑ 332	Jayson Werth	.15	.07
❑ 333	Richie Sexson	.25	.11
❑ 334	Randy Wolf	.15	.07
❑ 335	Eli Marrero	.15	.07
❑ 336	Paul LoDuca	.25	.11
❑ 337	J.D Smart	.15	.07
❑ 338	Ryan Minor	.15	.07
❑ 339	Kris Benson	.25	.11
❑ 340	George Lombard	.15	.07
❑ 341	Troy Glaus	.60	.25
❑ 342	Eddie Yarnall	.15	.07
❑ 343	Kip Wells RC	1.00	.45
❑ 344	C.C. Sabathia RC	4.00	1.80
❑ 345	Sean Burroughs RC	5.00	2.20
❑ 346	Felipe Lopez RC	2.00	.90
❑ 347	Ryan Rupe RC	.60	.25
❑ 348	Orber Moreno RC	.50	.23
❑ 349	Rafael Roque RC	.15	.07
❑ 350	Alfonso Soriano RC	5.00	2.20
❑ 351	Pablo Ozuna	.15	.07
❑ 352	Corey Patterson RC	3.00	1.35
❑ 353	Braden Looper	.15	.07
❑ 354	Robbie Bell	.15	.07
❑ 355	Mark Mulder RC	4.00	1.80
❑ 356	Angel Pena	.15	.07
❑ 357	Kevin McGlinchy	.15	.07
❑ 358	M.Restovich RC	2.00	.90
❑ 359	Eric DuBose	.15	.07
❑ 360	Geoff Jenkins	.25	.11
❑ 361	Mark Harriger RC	.15	.07
❑ 362	Junior Herndon RC	.60	.25
❑ 363	Tim Raines Jr. RC	1.25	.55
❑ 364	Rafael Furcal RC	3.00	1.35
❑ 365	Marcus Giles RC	2.50	1.10
❑ 366	Ted Lilly	.15	.07
❑ 367	Jorge Toca RC	.50	.23
❑ 368	David Kelton RC	1.50	.70
❑ 369	Adam Dunn RC	12.00	5.50
❑ 370	Guillermo Mota RC	.15	.07
❑ 371	Brett Laxton RC	.15	.07
❑ 372	Travis Harper RC	.25	.11
❑ 373	Tom Davey RC	.15	.07
❑ 374	Darren Blakely RC	.60	.25
❑ 375	Tim Hudson RC	5.00	2.20
❑ 376	Jason Romano	.15	.07
❑ 377	Dan Reichert	.15	.07
❑ 378	Julio Lugo RC	1.00	.45
❑ 379	Jose Garcia RC	.50	.23
❑ 380	Erubiel Durazo RC	1.50	.70
❑ 381	Jose Jimenez	.15	.07
❑ 382	Chris Fussell	.15	.07
❑ 383	Steve Lomasney	.15	.07
❑ 384	Juan Pena RC	.25	.11
❑ 385	Allen Levrault RC	1.00	.45
❑ 386	Juan Rivera RC	2.50	1.10
❑ 387	Steve Colyer RC	.50	.23
❑ 388	Joe Nathan RC	.15	.07
❑ 389	Ron Walker RC	.15	.07
❑ 390	Nick Bierbrodt	.15	.07
❑ 391	Luke Prokopec RC	1.25	.55
❑ 392	Dave Roberts RC	.15	.07
❑ 393	Mike Darr	.15	.07
❑ 394	Abraham Nunez RC	1.50	.70
❑ 395	G.Chiaramonte RC	.60	.25
❑ 396	J.Van Buren RC	.60	.25
❑ 397	Mike Kusiewicz	.15	.07
❑ 398	Matt Wise RC	.15	.07
❑ 399	Joe McEwing RC	.25	.11
❑ 400	Matt Holliday RC	1.00	.45
❑ 401	Willi Mo Pena RC	3.00	1.35
❑ 402	Ruben Quevedo RC	1.00	.45
❑ 403	Rob Ryan RC	.15	.07
❑ 404	Freddy Garcia RC	3.00	1.35
❑ 405	Kevin Eberwein RC	.50	.23
❑ 406	Jesus Colome RC	1.00	.45
❑ 407	Chris Singleton	.15	.07
❑ 408	Bubba Crosby RC	.25	.11
❑ 409	Jesus Cordero RC	.50	.23
❑ 410	Donny Leon	.15	.07
❑ 411	G.Tomlinson RC	.25	.11
❑ 412	Jeff Winchester RC	.60	.25
❑ 413	Adam Piatt RC	1.25	.55
❑ 414	Robert Stratton	.15	.07
❑ 415	T.J. Tucker	.15	.07
❑ 416	Ryan Langerhans RC	.60	.25
❑ 417	A.Shumaker RC	.15	.07
❑ 418	Matt Miller RC	.15	.07
❑ 419	Doug Clark RC	.15	.07
❑ 420	Kory DeHaan RC	.15	.07
❑ 421	David Eckstein RC	1.00	.45
❑ 422	Brian Cooper RC	.50	.23
❑ 423	Brady Clark RC	.15	.07
❑ 424	Chris Magruder RC	.25	.11
❑ 425	Bobby Seay RC	.60	.25
❑ 426	Aubrey Huff RC	1.50	.70
❑ 427	Mike Jerzembeck	.15	.07
❑ 428	Matt Blank RC	.25	.11
❑ 429	Benny Agbayani RC	1.25	.55
❑ 430	Kevin Beirne RC	.15	.07
❑ 431	Josh Hamilton RC	5.00	2.20
❑ 432	Josh Girdley RC	.75	.35
❑ 433	Kyle Snyder RC	.50	.23
❑ 434	Mike Paradis RC	.50	.23
❑ 435	Jason Jennings RC	1.50	.70
❑ 436	David Walling RC	.60	.25
❑ 437	Omar Ortiz RC	.25	.11
❑ 438	Jay Gehrke RC	.25	.11
❑ 439	Casey Burns RC	.25	.11
❑ 440	Carl Crawford RC	2.00	.90

2000 Bowman

	MINT	NRMT
COMPLETE SET (440)	100.00	45.00

❑ 1 Vladimir Guerrero .75 .35
❑ 2 Chipper Jones 1.25 .55
❑ 3 Todd Walker .15 .07
❑ 4 Barry Larkin .60 .25
❑ 5 Bernie Williams .60 .25
❑ 6 Todd Helton .75 .35
❑ 7 Jermaine Dye .25 .11
❑ 8 Brian Giles .25 .11
❑ 9 Freddy Garcia .40 .18
❑ 10 Greg Vaughn .25 .11
❑ 11 Alex Gonzalez .15 .07
❑ 12 Luis Gonzalez .60 .25
❑ 13 Ron Belliard .15 .07
❑ 14 Ben Grieve .25 .11
❑ 15 Carlos Delgado .60 .25
❑ 16 Brian Jordan .25 .11
❑ 17 Fernando Tatis .15 .07
❑ 18 Ryan Rupe .15 .07
❑ 19 Miguel Tejada .25 .11
❑ 20 Mark Grace .60 .25
❑ 21 Kenny Lofton .25 .11
❑ 22 Eric Karros .25 .11
❑ 23 Cliff Floyd .25 .11
❑ 24 John Halama .15 .07
❑ 25 Cristian Guzman .25 .11
❑ 26 Scott Williamson .15 .07
❑ 27 Mike Lieberthal .25 .11
❑ 28 Tim Hudson .60 .25
❑ 29 Warren Morris .15 .07
❑ 30 Pedro Martinez .75 .35
❑ 31 John Smoltz .25 .11
❑ 32 Ray Durham .25 .11
❑ 33 Chad Allen .15 .07
❑ 34 Tony Clark .25 .11
❑ 35 Tino Martinez .25 .11
❑ 36 J.T. Snow .25 .11
❑ 37 Kevin Brown .25 .11
❑ 38 Bartolo Colon .25 .11
❑ 39 Rey Ordonez .15 .07
❑ 40 Jeff Bagwell .75 .35
❑ 41 Ivan Rodriguez .60 .25
❑ 42 Eric Chavez .25 .11
❑ 43 Eric Milton .25 .11
❑ 44 Jose Canseco .60 .25
❑ 45 Shawn Green .60 .25
❑ 46 Rich Aurilia .25 .11
❑ 47 Roberto Alomar .60 .25
❑ 48 Brian Daubach .25 .11
❑ 49 Magglio Ordonez .25 .11
❑ 50 Derek Jeter 2.50 1.10
❑ 51 Kris Benson .25 .11
❑ 52 Albert Belle .25 .11
❑ 53 Rondell White .25 .11
❑ 54 Justin Thompson .15 .07
❑ 55 Nomar Garciaparra 1.50 .70
❑ 56 Chuck Finley .25 .11
❑ 57 Omar Vizquel .25 .11
❑ 58 Luis Castillo .15 .07
❑ 59 Richard Hidalgo .25 .11
❑ 60 Barry Bonds 1.50 .70
❑ 61 Craig Biggio .40 .18
❑ 62 Doug Glanville .15 .07
❑ 63 Gabe Kapler .25 .11
❑ 64 Johnny Damon .25 .11
❑ 65 Pokey Reese .15 .07
❑ 66 Andy Pettitte .25 .11
❑ 67 B.J. Surhoff .25 .11
❑ 68 Richie Sexson .25 .11
❑ 69 Javy Lopez .25 .11
❑ 70 Raul Mondesi .25 .11
❑ 71 Darin Erstad .60 .25
❑ 72 Kevin Millwood .15 .07
❑ 73 Ricky Ledee .15 .07
❑ 74 John Olerud .25 .11
❑ 75 Sean Casey .40 .18
❑ 76 Carlos Febles .15 .07
❑ 77 Paul O'Neill .60 .25
❑ 78 Bob Abreu .25 .11
❑ 79 Neifi Perez .15 .07
❑ 80 Tony Gwynn 1.25 .55
❑ 81 Russ Ortiz .25 .11
❑ 82 Matt Williams .40 .18
❑ 83 Chris Carpenter .15 .07
❑ 84 Roger Cedeno .15 .07
❑ 85 Tim Salmon .25 .11
❑ 86 Billy Koch .15 .07
❑ 87 Jeromy Burnitz .25 .11
❑ 88 Edgardo Alfonzo .25 .11
❑ 89 Jay Bell .25 .11
❑ 90 Manny Ramirez .75 .35
❑ 91 Frank Thomas .75 .35
❑ 92 Mike Mussina .60 .25
❑ 93 J.D. Drew .60 .25
❑ 94 Adrian Beltre .25 .11
❑ 95 Alex Rodriguez 1.50 .70
❑ 96 Larry Walker .40 .18
❑ 97 Juan Encarnacion .25 .11
❑ 98 Mike Sweeney .25 .11
❑ 99 Rusty Greer .25 .11
❑ 100 Randy Johnson .75 .35
❑ 101 Jose Vidro .25 .11
❑ 102 Preston Wilson .25 .11
❑ 103 Greg Maddux 1.50 .70
❑ 104 Jason Giambi .60 .25
❑ 105 Cal Ripken 2.50 1.10
❑ 106 Carlos Beltran .25 .11
❑ 107 Vinny Castilla .25 .11
❑ 108 Mariano Rivera .25 .11
❑ 109 Mo Vaughn .25 .11
❑ 110 Rafael Palmeiro .60 .25
❑ 111 Shannon Stewart .25 .11
❑ 112 Mike Hampton .25 .11
❑ 113 Joe Nathan .15 .07
❑ 114 Ben Davis .25 .11
❑ 115 Andruw Jones .60 .25
❑ 116 Robin Ventura .25 .11
❑ 117 Damion Easley .15 .07
❑ 118 Jeff Cirillo .25 .11
❑ 119 Kerry Wood .60 .25
❑ 120 Scott Rolen .60 .25
❑ 121 Sammy Sosa 1.25 .55
❑ 122 Ken Griffey Jr. 2.00 .90
❑ 123 Shane Reynolds .15 .07
❑ 124 Troy Glaus .60 .25
❑ 125 Tom Glavine .60 .25
❑ 126 Michael Barrett .15 .07
❑ 127 Al Leiter .15 .07
❑ 128 Jason Kendall .25 .11
❑ 129 Roger Clemens 1.50 .70
❑ 130 Juan Gonzalez .60 .25
❑ 131 Corey Koskie .25 .11
❑ 132 Curt Schilling .60 .25
❑ 133 Mike Piazza 1.50 .70
❑ 134 Gary Sheffield .25 .11
❑ 135 Jim Thome .60 .25
❑ 136 Orlando Hernandez .25 .11
❑ 137 Ray Lankford .15 .07
❑ 138 Geoff Jenkins .25 .11
❑ 139 Jose Lima .15 .07
❑ 140 Mark McGwire 2.50 1.10
❑ 141 Adam Piatt .40 .18
❑ 142 Pat Manning RC 1.25 .55
❑ 143 Marcos Castillo RC .50 .23
❑ 144 Leslie Brea RC .50 .23
❑ 145 Humberto Cota RC 1.00 .45
❑ 146 Ben Petrick .15 .07
❑ 147 Kip Wells .25 .11
❑ 148 Wily Pena .60 .25
❑ 149 Chris Wakeland RC .50 .23
❑ 150 Brad Baker RC 1.25 .55
❑ 151 Robbie Morrison RC .50 .23
❑ 152 Reggie Taylor .15 .07
❑ 153 Matt Ginter RC .75 .35
❑ 154 Peter Bergeron .15 .07
❑ 155 Roosevelt Brown .15 .07
❑ 156 Matt Cepicky RC .60 .25
❑ 157 Ramon Castro .15 .07
❑ 158 Brad Baisley RC .75 .35
❑ 159 Jeff Goldbach RC .75 .35
❑ 160 Mitch Meluskey .15 .07
❑ 161 Chad Harville .15 .07
❑ 162 Brian Cooper .15 .07
❑ 163 Marcus Giles .25 .11
❑ 164 Jim Morris .15 .07
❑ 165 Geoff Goetz .15 .07
❑ 166 Bobby Bradley RC 1.25 .55
❑ 167 Rob Bell .15 .07
❑ 168 Joe Crede .25 .11
❑ 169 Michael Restovich .25 .11
❑ 170 Quincy Foster RC .50 .23
❑ 171 Enrique Cruz RC 1.25 .55
❑ 172 Mark Quinn .25 .11
❑ 173 Nick Johnson .60 .25
❑ 174 Jeff Liefer .15 .07
❑ 175 Kevin Mench RC 2.50 1.10
❑ 176 Steve Lomasney .15 .07
❑ 177 Jayson Werth .15 .07
❑ 178 Tim Drew .15 .07
❑ 179 Chip Ambres .25 .11
❑ 180 Ryan Anderson .25 .11
❑ 181 Matt Blank .15 .07
❑ 182 G.Chiaramonte .15 .07
❑ 183 Corey Myers RC .75 .35
❑ 184 Jeff Yoder .15 .07
❑ 185 Craig Dingman RC .50 .23
❑ 186 Jon Hamilton RC .75 .35
❑ 187 Toby Hall .40 .18
❑ 188 Russell Branyan .25 .11
❑ 189 Brian Falkenborg RC .50 .23
❑ 190 Aaron Harang RC .50 .23
❑ 191 Juan Pena .15 .07
❑ 192 Travis Thompson RC .50 .23
❑ 193 Alfonso Soriano .60 .25
❑ 194 Alejandro Diaz RC .60 .25
❑ 195 Carlos Pena .60 .25
❑ 196 Kevin Nicholson .15 .07
❑ 197 Mo Bruce .15 .07
❑ 198 C.C. Sabathia .60 .25
❑ 199 Carl Crawford .25 .11
❑ 200 Rafael Furcal .60 .25
❑ 201 Andrew Beinbrink RC .50 .23
❑ 202 Jimmy Osting .15 .07
❑ 203 Aaron McNeal RC .60 .25
❑ 204 Brett Laxton .15 .07
❑ 205 Chris George .25 .11
❑ 206 Felipe Lopez .25 .11
❑ 207 Ben Sheets RC 3.00 1.35
❑ 208 Mike Meyers RC .60 .25
❑ 209 Jason Conti .15 .07
❑ 210 Milton Bradley .15 .07
❑ 211 Chris Mears RC .60 .25
❑ 212 Carlos Hernandez RC 2.00 .90
❑ 213 Jason Romano .15 .07
❑ 214 Geofrey Tomlinson .15 .07
❑ 215 Jimmy Rollins .25 .11
❑ 216 Pablo Ozuna .15 .07
❑ 217 Steve Cox .15 .07
❑ 218 Terrence Long .25 .11
❑ 219 Jeff DaVanon RC .50 .23
❑ 220 Rick Ankiel .60 .25
❑ 221 Jason Standridge .15 .07
❑ 222 Tony Armas Jr. .25 .11
❑ 223 Jason Tyner .15 .07
❑ 224 Ramon Ortiz .25 .11
❑ 225 Daryle Ward .15 .07
❑ 226 Enger Veras RC .50 .23
❑ 227 Chris Jones .15 .07
❑ 228 Eric Cammack RC .50 .23
❑ 229 Ruben Mateo .25 .11
❑ 230 Ken Harvey RC 2.50 1.10
❑ 231 Jake Westbrook .15 .07
❑ 232 Rob Purvis RC .50 .23
❑ 233 Choo Freeman .25 .11
❑ 234 Aramis Ramirez .25 .11
❑ 235 A.J. Burnett .25 .11
❑ 236 Kevin Barker .15 .07
❑ 237 Chance Caple RC .75 .35
❑ 238 Jarrod Washburn .15 .07
❑ 239 Lance Berkman .60 .25
❑ 240 Michael Wenner RC .60 .25
❑ 241 Alex Sanchez .15 .07
❑ 242 Pat Daneker .15 .07
❑ 243 Grant Roberts .15 .07
❑ 244 Mark Ellis RC 1.00 .45
❑ 245 Donny Leon .15 .07
❑ 246 David Eckstein .15 .07
❑ 247 Dicky Gonzalez RC .75 .35
❑ 248 John Patterson .15 .07
❑ 249 Chad Green .15 .07
❑ 250 Scot Shields RC .50 .23
❑ 251 Troy Cameron .15 .07
❑ 252 Jose Molina .15 .07
❑ 253 Rob Pugmire RC .60 .25
❑ 254 Rick Elder .25 .11
❑ 255 Sean Burroughs .60 .25
❑ 256 Josh Kalinowski RC .50 .23
❑ 257 Matt LeCroy .15 .07
❑ 258 Alex Graman RC 1.00 .45

❑ 259 Tomokazu Ohka RC .... 1.00 .45
❑ 260 Brady Clark .... .15 .07
❑ 261 Rico Washington RC .... .60 .25
❑ 262 Gary Matthews Jr. .... .15 .07
❑ 263 Matt Wise .... .15 .07
❑ 264 Keith Reed RC .... 1.00 .45
❑ 265 Santiago Ramirez RC .... .50 .23
❑ 266 Ben Broussard RC .... 1.50 .70
❑ 267 Ryan Langerhans .... .15 .07
❑ 268 Juan Rivera .... .25 .11
❑ 269 Shawn Gallagher .... .15 .07
❑ 270 Jorge Toca .... .15 .07
❑ 271 Brad Lidge .... .15 .07
❑ 272 Leoncio Estrella RC .... .50 .23
❑ 273 Ruben Quevedo .... .15 .07
❑ 274 Jack Cust .... .25 .11
❑ 275 T.J. Tucker .... .15 .07
❑ 276 Mike Colangelo .... .15 .07
❑ 277 Brian Schneider .... .15 .07
❑ 278 Calvin Murray .... .15 .07
❑ 279 Josh Girdley .... .15 .07
❑ 280 Mike Paradis .... .15 .07
❑ 281 Chad Hermansen .... .15 .07
❑ 282 Ty Howington RC .... 1.50 .70
❑ 283 Aaron Myette .... .25 .11
❑ 284 D'Angelo Jimenez .... .25 .11
❑ 285 Dernell Stenson .... .15 .07
❑ 286 Jerry Hairston Jr. .... .15 .07
❑ 287 Gary Majewski RC .... .60 .25
❑ 288 Derrin Ebert .... .15 .07
❑ 289 Steve Fish RC .... .50 .23
❑ 290 Carlos E. Hernandez .... .15 .07
❑ 291 Allen Levrault .... .15 .07
❑ 292 Sean McNally RC .... .50 .23
❑ 293 Randey Dorame RC .... .60 .25
❑ 294 Wes Anderson RC .... .75 .35
❑ 295 B.J. Ryan .... .15 .07
❑ 296 Alan Webb RC .... .50 .23
❑ 297 Brandon Inge RC .... 1.25 .55
❑ 298 David Walling .... .15 .07
❑ 299 Sun Woo Kim RC .... .75 .35
❑ 300 Pat Burrell .... .60 .25
❑ 301 Rick Guttormson RC .... .50 .23
❑ 302 Gil Meche .... .15 .07
❑ 303 Carlos Zambrano RC .. 1.25 .55
❑ 304 Eric Byrnes UER RC .... .60 .25
Bo Porter pictured
❑ 305 Robb Quinlan RC .... .75 .35
❑ 306 Jackie Rexrode .... .15 .07
❑ 307 Nate Bump .... .15 .07
❑ 308 Sean DePaula RC .... .50 .23
❑ 309 Matt Riley .... .15 .07
❑ 310 Ryan Minor .... .15 .07
❑ 311 J.J. Davis .... .25 .11
❑ 312 Randy Wolf .... .15 .07
❑ 313 Jason Jennings .... .25 .11
❑ 314 Scott Seabol RC .... .50 .23
❑ 315 Doug Davis .... .15 .07
❑ 316 Todd Moser RC .... .50 .23
❑ 317 Rob Ryan .... .15 .07
❑ 318 Bubba Crosby .... .15 .07
❑ 319 Ryan Knox RC .... 1.50 .70
❑ 320 Mario Encarnacion .... .15 .07
❑ 321 F.Rodriguez RC .... .75 .35
❑ 322 Michael Cuddyer .... .25 .11
❑ 323 Ed Yarnall .... .15 .07
❑ 324 Cesar Saba RC .... .75 .35
❑ 325 Travis Dawkins .... .25 .11
❑ 326 Alex Escobar .... .25 .11
❑ 327 Julio Zuleta RC .... .75 .35
❑ 328 Josh Hamilton .... .75 .35
❑ 329 Nick Neugebauer RC .. 6.00 2.70
❑ 330 Matt Belisle .... .25 .11
❑ 331 Kurt Ainsworth RC .... 1.25 .55
❑ 332 Tim Raines Jr. .... .25 .11
❑ 333 Eric Munson .... .25 .11
❑ 334 Donzell McDonald .... .15 .07
❑ 335 Larry Bigbie RC .... 1.00 .45
❑ 336 Matt Watson RC .... .50 .23
❑ 337 Aubrey Huff .... .15 .07
❑ 338 Julio Ramirez .... .15 .07
❑ 339 Jason Grabowski RC .... .75 .35
❑ 340 Jon Garland .... .15 .07
❑ 341 Austin Kearns .... .60 .25
❑ 342 Josh Pressley RC .... .60 .25
❑ 343 Miguel Olivo RC .... .60 .25
❑ 344 Julio Lugo .... .15 .07
❑ 345 Roberto Vaz .... .15 .07
❑ 346 Ramon Soler .... .15 .07
❑ 347 Brandon Phillips RC .... 1.25 .55
❑ 348 Vince Faison RC .... .75 .35
❑ 349 Mike Venafro .... .15 .07
❑ 350 Rick Asadoorian RC .... 1.25 .55
❑ 351 B.J. Garbe RC .... 1.50 .70
❑ 352 Dan Reichert .... .15 .07
❑ 353 Jason Stumm RC .... 1.00 .45
❑ 354 Ruben Salazar RC .... 1.25 .55
❑ 355 Francisco Cordero .... .15 .07
❑ 356 Juan Guzman RC .... .50 .23
❑ 357 Mike Bacsik RC .... .50 .23
❑ 358 Jared Sandberg .... .15 .07
❑ 359 Rod Barajas .... .15 .07
❑ 360 Junior Brignac RC .... .50 .23
❑ 361 J.M. Gold .... .15 .07
❑ 362 Octavio Dotel .... .15 .07
❑ 363 David Kelton .... .25 .11
❑ 364 Scott Morgan .... .15 .07
❑ 365 Wascar Serrano RC .... .75 .35
❑ 366 Wilton Veras .... .15 .07
❑ 367 Eugene Kingsale .... .15 .07
❑ 368 Ted Lilly .... .15 .07
❑ 369 George Lombard .... .15 .07
❑ 370 Chris Haas .... .15 .07
❑ 371 Wilton Pena RC .... .50 .23
❑ 372 Vernon Wells .... .25 .11
❑ 373 Jason Royer RC .... .50 .23
❑ 374 Jeff Heaverlo RC .... 1.25 .55
❑ 375 Calvin Pickering .... .15 .07
❑ 376 Mike Lamb RC .... .60 .25
❑ 377 Kyle Snyder .... .15 .07
❑ 378 Javier Cardona RC .... .50 .23
❑ 379 Aaron Rowand RC .... 1.25 .55
❑ 380 Dee Brown .... .15 .07
❑ 381 Brett Myers RC .... 1.00 .45
❑ 382 Abraham Nunez .... .25 .11
❑ 383 Eric Valent .... .25 .11
❑ 384 Jody Gerut RC .... .60 .25
❑ 385 Adam Dunn .... 1.50 .70
❑ 386 Jay Gehrke .... .15 .07
❑ 387 Omar Ortiz .... .15 .07
❑ 388 Darnell McDonald .... .15 .07
❑ 389 Tony Schrager RC .... .50 .23
❑ 390 J.D. Closser .... .15 .07
❑ 391 Ben Christensen RC .... .60 .25
❑ 392 Adam Kennedy .... .15 .07
❑ 393 Nick Green RC .... .50 .23
❑ 394 Ramon Hernandez .... .15 .07
❑ 395 Roy Oswalt RC 5.00 2.20
❑ 396 Andy Tracy RC .... .50 .23
❑ 397 Eric Gagne .... .15 .07
❑ 398 Michael Tejera RC .... .50 .23
❑ 399 Adam Everett .... .25 .11
❑ 400 Corey Patterson .... .60 .25
❑ 401 Gary Knotts RC .... .50 .23
❑ 402 Ryan Christianson RC .. 1.25 .55
❑ 403 Eric Ireland RC .... .75 .35
❑ 404 Andrew Good RC .... .50 .23
❑ 405 Brad Penny .... .25 .11
❑ 406 Jason LaRue .... .15 .07
❑ 407 Kit Pellow .... .15 .07
❑ 408 Kevin Beirne .... .15 .07
❑ 409 Kelly Dransfeldt .... .15 .07
❑ 410 Jason Grilli .... .15 .07
❑ 411 Scott Downs RC .... .50 .23
❑ 412 Jesus Colome .... .25 .11
❑ 413 John Sneed RC .... .50 .23
❑ 414 Tony McKnight .... .15 .07
❑ 415 Luis Rivera .... .15 .07
❑ 416 Adam Eaton .... .25 .11
❑ 417 Mike MacDougal RC .... .60 .25
❑ 418 Mike Nannini .... .15 .07
❑ 419 Barry Zito RC 4.00 1.80
❑ 420 DeWayne Wise .... .15 .07
❑ 421 Jason Dellaero .... .15 .07
❑ 422 Chad Moeller .... .15 .07
❑ 423 Jason Marquis .... .25 .11
❑ 424 Tim Redding RC .... 2.00 .90
❑ 425 Mark Mulder .... .60 .25
❑ 426 Josh Paul .... .15 .07
❑ 427 Chris Enochs .... .15 .07
❑ 428 W.Rodriguez RC .... 1.00 .45
❑ 429 Kevin Witt .... .15 .07
❑ 430 Scott Sobkowiak RC .... .60 .25
❑ 431 McKay Christensen .... .15 .07
❑ 432 Jung Bong .... .15 .07
❑ 433 Keith Evans RC .... .50 .23
❑ 434 Garry Maddox Jr. RC .... .50 .23
❑ 435 Ramon Santiago RC .... 1.00 .45
❑ 436 Alex Cora .... .15 .07
❑ 437 Carlos Lee .... .25 .11
❑ 438 Jason Repko RC .... .75 .35
❑ 439 Matt Burch .... .15 .07
❑ 440 Shawn Sonnier RC .... .50 .23

2000 Bowman Draft Picks

	MINT	NRMT
COMP.FACT.SET (111)	30.00	13.50
COMPLETE SET (110)	25.00	11.00

❑ 1 Pat Burrell .... .60 .25
❑ 2 Rafael Furcal .... .60 .25
❑ 3 Grant Roberts .... .15 .07
❑ 4 Barry Zito .... 1.25 .55
❑ 5 Julio Zuleta .... .25 .11
❑ 6 Mark Mulder .... .60 .25
❑ 7 Rob Bell .... .15 .07
❑ 8 Adam Piatt .... .40 .18
❑ 9 Mike Lamb .... .40 .18
❑ 10 Pablo Ozuna .... .15 .07
❑ 11 Jason Tyner .... .15 .07
❑ 12 Jason Marquis .... .25 .11
❑ 13 Eric Munson .... .25 .11
❑ 14 Seth Etherton .... .15 .07
❑ 15 Milton Bradley .... .15 .07
❑ 16 Nick Green .... .25 .11
❑ 17 Chin-Feng Chen RC .... 2.00 .90
❑ 18 Matt Boone RC .... .40 .18
❑ 19 Kevin Gregg RC .... .40 .18
❑ 20 Eddy Garabito RC .... .40 .18
❑ 21 Aaron Capista RC .... .40 .18
❑ 22 Esteban German RC .... .60 .25
❑ 23 Derek Thompson RC .... .40 .18
❑ 24 Phil Merrell RC .... .40 .18
❑ 25 Brian O'Connor RC .... .50 .23
❑ 26 Yamid Haad .... .15 .07
❑ 27 Hector Mercado RC .... .40 .18
❑ 28 Jason Woolf RC .... .40 .18
❑ 29 Eddy Furniss RC .... .40 .18
❑ 30 Cha Sueng Baek RC .... .75 .35
❑ 31 Colby Lewis RC .... .50 .23
❑ 32 Pasqual Coco RC .... .40 .18
❑ 33 Jorge Cantu RC .... .40 .18
❑ 34 Erasmo Ramirez RC .... .40 .18
❑ 35 Bobby Kielty RC .... 1.00 .45
❑ 36 Joaquin Benoit RC .... .75 .35
❑ 37 Brian Esposito RC .... .40 .18
❑ 38 Michael Wenner .... .25 .11
❑ 39 Juan Rincon RC .... .40 .18
❑ 40 Yorvit Torrealba RC .... .40 .18
❑ 41 Chad Durham RC .... .40 .18
❑ 42 Jim Mann RC .... .40 .18
❑ 43 Shane Loux RC .... .50 .23
❑ 44 Luis Rivas .... .25 .11
❑ 45 Ken Chenard RC .... .40 .18
❑ 46 Mike Lockwood RC .... .40 .18
❑ 47 Yovanny Lara RC .... .40 .18
❑ 48 Bubba Carpenter RC .... .40 .18
❑ 49 Ryan Dittfurth RC .... .40 .18

❑ 50 John Stephens RC	.60	.25
❑ 51 Pedro Feliz RC	1.00	.45
❑ 52 Kenny Kelly RC	.75	.35
❑ 53 Neil Jenkins RC	.75	.35
❑ 54 Mike Glendenning RC	.40	.18
❑ 55 Bo Porter	.15	.07
❑ 56 Eric Byrnes	.25	.11
❑ 57 Tony Alvarez RC	.75	.35
❑ 58 Kazuhiro Sasaki RC	2.00	.90
❑ 59 Chad Durbin RC	.40	.18
❑ 60 Mike Bynum RC	.75	.35
❑ 61 Travis Wilson RC	.75	.35
❑ 62 Jose Leon RC	.40	.18
❑ 63 Ryan Vogelsong RC	.75	.35
❑ 64 Geraldo Guzman RC	.40	.18
❑ 65 Craig Anderson RC	.60	.25
❑ 66 Carlos Silva RC	.40	.18
❑ 67 Brad Thomas RC	.50	.23
❑ 68 Chin-Hui Tsao RC	1.25	.55
❑ 69 Mark Buehrle RC	3.00	1.35
❑ 70 Juan Salas RC	.50	.23
❑ 71 Denny Abreu RC	.40	.18
❑ 72 Keith McDonald RC	.40	.18
❑ 73 Chris Richard RC	1.00	.45
❑ 74 Tomas De la Rosa RC	.40	.18
❑ 75 Vicente Padilla RC	.40	.18
❑ 76 Justin Brunette RC	.40	.18
❑ 77 Scott Linebrink RC	.40	.18
❑ 78 Jeff Sparks RC	.40	.18
❑ 79 Tike Redman RC	.50	.23
❑ 80 John Lackey RC	.50	.23
❑ 81 Joe Strong RC	.40	.18
❑ 82 Brian Tollberg RC	.40	.18
❑ 83 Steve Sisco RC	.40	.18
❑ 84 Chris Clapinski RC	.40	.18
❑ 85 Augie Ojeda RC	.40	.18
❑ 86 Adrian Gonzalez RC	4.00	1.80
❑ 87 Mike Stodolka RC	.75	.35
❑ 88 Adam Johnson RC	1.00	.45
❑ 89 Matt Wheatland RC	.75	.35
❑ 90 Corey Smith RC	1.25	.55
❑ 91 Rocco Baldelli RC	1.00	.45
❑ 92 Keith Bucktrot RC	.50	.23
❑ 93 Adam Wainwright RC	1.25	.55
❑ 94 Blaine Boyer RC	.50	.23
❑ 95 Aaron Herr RC	.60	.25
❑ 96 Scott Thorman RC	1.00	.45
❑ 97 Bryan Digby RC	.50	.23
❑ 98 Josh Shortslef RC	.75	.35
❑ 99 Sean Smith RC	.50	.23
❑ 100 Alex Cruz RC	.40	.18
❑ 101 Marc Love RC	.50	.23
❑ 102 Kevin Lee RC	.40	.18
❑ 103 Victor Ramos RC	.50	.23
❑ 104 Jason Kaanoi RC	.50	.23
❑ 105 Luis Escobar RC	.50	.23
❑ 106 Tripper Johnson RC	.75	.35
❑ 107 Phil Dumatrait RC	.75	.35
❑ 108 Bryan Edwards RC	.50	.23
❑ 109 Grady Sizemore RC	2.50	1.10
❑ 110 Thomas Mitchell RC	1.00	.45

2001 Bowman

	MINT	NRMT
COMPLETE SET (440)	150.00	70.00
❑ 1 Jason Giambi	.60	.25
❑ 2 Rafael Furcal	.25	.11
❑ 3 Rick Ankiel	.40	.18
❑ 4 Freddy Garcia	.25	.11
❑ 5 Magglio Ordonez	.25	.11
❑ 6 Bernie Williams	.60	.25
❑ 7 Kenny Lofton	.25	.11
❑ 8 Al Leiter	.25	.11
❑ 9 Albert Belle	.25	.11
❑ 10 Craig Biggio	.40	.18
❑ 11 Mark Mulder	.40	.18
❑ 12 Carlos Delgado	.60	.25
❑ 13 Darin Erstad	.60	.25
❑ 14 Richie Sexson	.25	.11
❑ 15 Randy Johnson	.75	.35
❑ 16 Greg Maddux	1.50	.70
❑ 17 Cliff Floyd	.25	.11
❑ 18 Mark Buehrle	.60	.25

❑ 19 Chris Singleton	.15	.07
❑ 20 Orlando Hernandez	.25	.11
❑ 21 Javier Vazquez	.25	.11
❑ 22 Jeff Kent	.40	.18
❑ 23 Jim Thome	.60	.25
❑ 24 John Olerud	.25	.11
❑ 25 Jason Kendall	.25	.11
❑ 26 Scott Rolen	.60	.25
❑ 27 Tony Gwynn	1.25	.55
❑ 28 Edgardo Alfonzo	.25	.11
❑ 29 Pokey Reese	.15	.07
❑ 30 Todd Helton	.75	.35
❑ 31 Mark Quinn	.25	.11
❑ 32 Dan Tosca RC	.75	.35
❑ 33 Dean Palmer	.25	.11
❑ 34 Jacque Jones	.25	.11
❑ 35 Ray Durham	.25	.11
❑ 36 Rafael Palmeiro	.60	.25
❑ 37 Carl Everett	.25	.11
❑ 38 Ryan Dempster	.25	.11
❑ 39 Randy Wolf	.15	.07
❑ 40 Vladimir Guerrero	.75	.35
❑ 41 Livan Hernandez	.25	.11
❑ 42 Mo Vaughn	.25	.11
❑ 43 Shannon Stewart	.25	.11
❑ 44 Preston Wilson	.25	.11
❑ 45 Jose Vidro	.25	.11
❑ 46 Fred McGriff	.40	.18
❑ 47 Kevin Brown	.25	.11
❑ 48 Peter Bergeron	.15	.07
❑ 49 Miguel Tejada	.25	.11
❑ 50 Chipper Jones	1.25	.55
❑ 51 Edgar Martinez	.40	.18
❑ 52 Tony Batista	.25	.11
❑ 53 Jorge Posada	.25	.11
❑ 54 Ricky Ledee	.15	.07
❑ 55 Sammy Sosa	1.25	.55
❑ 56 Steve Cox	.15	.07
❑ 57 Tony Armas Jr.	.25	.11
❑ 58 Gary Sheffield	.25	.11
❑ 59 Bartolo Colon	.25	.11
❑ 60 Pat Burrell	.25	.11
❑ 61 Jay Payton	.15	.07
❑ 62 Sean Casey	.40	.18
❑ 63 Larry Walker	.40	.18
❑ 64 Mike Mussina	.60	.25
❑ 65 Nomar Garciaparra	1.50	.70
❑ 66 Darren Dreifort	.15	.07
❑ 67 Richard Hidalgo	.25	.11
❑ 68 Troy Glaus	.60	.25
❑ 69 Ben Grieve	.25	.11
❑ 70 Jim Edmonds	.40	.18
❑ 71 Raul Mondesi	.25	.11
❑ 72 Andruw Jones	.60	.25
❑ 73 Luis Castillo	.15	.07
❑ 74 Mike Sweeney	.25	.11
❑ 75 Derek Jeter	2.50	1.10
❑ 76 Ruben Mateo	.25	.11
❑ 77 Carlos Lee	.25	.11
❑ 78 Cristian Guzman	.25	.11
❑ 79 Mike Hampton	.25	.11
❑ 80 J.D. Drew	.60	.25
❑ 81 Matt Lawton	.25	.11
❑ 82 Moises Alou	.25	.11
❑ 83 Terrence Long	.25	.11
❑ 84 Geoff Jenkins	.25	.11
❑ 85 Manny Ramirez	.75	.35
❑ 86 Johnny Damon	.25	.11
❑ 87 Barry Larkin	.60	.25
❑ 88 Pedro Martinez	.75	.35
❑ 89 Juan Gonzalez	.60	.25
❑ 90 Roger Clemens	1.50	.70
❑ 91 Carlos Beltran	.25	.11
❑ 92 Brad Radke	.25	.11
❑ 93 Orlando Cabrera	.15	.07
❑ 94 Roberto Alomar	.60	.25
❑ 95 Barry Bonds	1.50	.70
❑ 96 Tim Hudson	.60	.25
❑ 97 Tom Glavine	.60	.25
❑ 98 Jeromy Burnitz	.25	.11
❑ 99 Adrian Beltre	.25	.11
❑ 100 Mike Piazza	1.50	.70
❑ 101 Kerry Wood	.60	.25
❑ 102 Steve Finley	.25	.11
❑ 103 Alex Cora	.15	.07
❑ 104 Bob Abreu	.25	.11
❑ 105 Neifi Perez	.15	.07
❑ 106 Mark Redman	.15	.07
❑ 107 Paul Konerko	.25	.11
❑ 108 Jermaine Dye	.25	.11
❑ 109 Brian Giles	.25	.11
❑ 110 Ivan Rodriguez	.60	.25
❑ 111 Vinny Castilla	.25	.11
❑ 112 Adam Kennedy	.15	.07
❑ 113 Eric Chavez	.25	.11
❑ 114 Billy Koch	.15	.07
❑ 115 Shawn Green	.60	.25
❑ 116 Matt Williams	.40	.18
❑ 117 Greg Vaughn	.25	.11
❑ 118 Gabe Kapler	.25	.11
❑ 119 Jeff Cirillo	.25	.11
❑ 120 Frank Thomas	.75	.35
❑ 121 David Justice	.25	.11
❑ 122 Cal Ripken	2.50	1.10
❑ 123 Rich Aurilia	.25	.11
❑ 124 Curt Schilling	.60	.25
❑ 125 Barry Zito	.60	.25
❑ 126 Brian Jordan	.25	.11
❑ 127 Chan Ho Park	.25	.11
❑ 128 J.T. Snow	.25	.11
❑ 129 Kazuhiro Sasaki	.60	.25
❑ 130 Alex Rodriguez	1.50	.70
❑ 131 Mariano Rivera	.25	.11
❑ 132 Eric Milton	.25	.11
❑ 133 Andy Pettitte	.25	.11
❑ 134 Scott Elarton	.15	.07
❑ 135 Ken Griffey Jr.	2.00	.90
❑ 136 Bengie Molina	.15	.07
❑ 137 Jeff Bagwell	.75	.35
❑ 138 Kevin Millwood	.15	.07
❑ 139 Tino Martinez	.25	.11
❑ 140 Mark McGwire	2.50	1.10
❑ 141 Larry Barnes	.15	.07
❑ 142 John Buck RC	1.00	.45
❑ 143 Freddie Bynum RC	1.25	.55
❑ 144 Abraham Nunez	.25	.11
❑ 145 Felix Diaz RC	.50	.23
❑ 146 Horacio Estrada	.15	.07
❑ 147 Ben Diggins	.25	.11
❑ 148 Tsuyoshi Shinjo RC	2.50	1.10
❑ 149 Rocco Baldelli	.25	.11
❑ 150 Rod Barajas	.15	.07
❑ 151 Luis Terrero	.15	.07
❑ 152 Milton Bradley	.15	.07
❑ 153 Kurt Ainsworth	.25	.11
❑ 154 Russell Branyan	.25	.11
❑ 155 Ryan Anderson	.25	.11
❑ 156 Mitch Jones RC	1.00	.45
❑ 157 Chip Ambres	.25	.11
❑ 158 Steve Bennett RC	.50	.23
❑ 159 Ivanon Coffie	.15	.07
❑ 160 Sean Burroughs	.60	.25
❑ 161 Keith Bucktrot	.15	.07
❑ 162 Tony Alvarez	.15	.07
❑ 163 Joaquin Benoit	.15	.07
❑ 164 Rick Asadoorian	.25	.11
❑ 165 Ben Broussard	.25	.11
❑ 166 Ryan Madson RC	.75	.35
❑ 167 Dee Brown	.15	.07
❑ 168 Sergio Contreras RC	.75	.35
❑ 169 John Barnes	.15	.07
❑ 170 Ben Washburn RC	.75	.35
❑ 171 Erick Almonte RC	1.00	.45

❑ 172 Shawn Fagan RC .50 .23
❑ 173 Gary Johnson RC .75 .35
❑ 174 Brady Clark .15 .07
❑ 175 Grant Roberts .15 .07
❑ 176 Tony Torcato .15 .07
❑ 177 Ramon Castro .15 .07
❑ 178 Esteban German .15 .07
❑ 179 Joe Hamer RC .75 .35
❑ 180 Nick Neugebauer .60 .25
❑ 181 Dernell Stenson .15 .07
❑ 182 Yhency Brazoban RC 1.00 .45
❑ 183 Aaron Myette .15 .07
❑ 184 Juan Sosa .15 .07
❑ 185 Brandon Inge .25 .11
❑ 186 Domingo Guante RC .50 .23
❑ 187 Adrian Brown .15 .07
❑ 188 Deivi Mendez RC 1.25 .55
❑ 189 Luis Matos .15 .07
❑ 190 Pedro Liriano RC 1.25 .55
❑ 191 Donnie Bridges .15 .07
❑ 192 Alex Cintron .15 .07
❑ 193 Jace Brewer .15 .07
❑ 194 Ron Davenport RC 1.00 .45
❑ 195 Jason Belcher RC 2.00 .90
❑ 196 Adrian Hernandez RC 1.00 .45
❑ 197 Bobby Kielty .15 .07
❑ 198 Reggie Griggs RC .75 .35
❑ 199 Reggie Abercrombie RC .75 .35
❑ 200 Troy Farnsworth RC .75 .35
❑ 201 Matt Belisle .15 .07
❑ 202 Miguel Villilo RC .50 .23
❑ 203 Adam Everett .15 .07
❑ 204 John Lackey .15 .07
❑ 205 Pasqual Coco .15 .07
❑ 206 Adam Wainwright .25 .11
❑ 207 Matt White RC 1.00 .45
❑ 208 Chin-Feng Chen .40 .18
❑ 209 Jeff Andra RC .50 .23
❑ 210 Willie Bloomquist .25 .11
❑ 211 Wes Anderson .15 .07
❑ 212 Enrique Cruz .15 .07
❑ 213 Jerry Hairston Jr. .15 .07
❑ 214 Mike Bynum .15 .07
❑ 215 Brian Hitchcox RC .50 .23
❑ 216 Ryan Christianson .15 .07
❑ 217 J.J. Davis .15 .07
❑ 218 Jovanny Cedeno .25 .11
❑ 219 Elvin Nina .15 .07
❑ 220 Alex Graman .15 .07
❑ 221 Arturo McDowell .15 .07
❑ 222 Deivis Santos RC 1.00 .45
❑ 223 Jody Gerut .15 .07
❑ 224 Sun Woo Kim .15 .07
❑ 225 Jimmy Rollins .25 .11
❑ 226 Ntema Ndungidi .15 .07
❑ 227 Ruben Salazar .15 .07
❑ 228 Josh Girdley .15 .07
❑ 229 Carl Crawford .25 .11
❑ 230 Luis Montanez RC 1.50 .70
❑ 231 Ramon Carvajal RC .75 .35
❑ 232 Matt Riley .15 .07
❑ 233 Ben Davis .25 .11
❑ 234 Jason Grabowski .15 .07
❑ 235 Chris George .25 .11
❑ 236 Hank Blalock RC 4.00 1.80
❑ 237 Roy Oswalt .60 .25
❑ 238 Eric Reynolds RC .60 .25
❑ 239 Brian Cole .15 .07
❑ 240 Denny Bautista RC 1.00 .45
❑ 241 Hector Garcia RC .60 .25
❑ 242 Joe Thurston RC .75 .35
❑ 243 Brad Cresse 1.50 .70
❑ 244 Corey Patterson .25 .11
❑ 245 Brett Evert RC 1.00 .45
❑ 246 Elpidio Guzman RC 1.00 .45
❑ 247 Vernon Wells .25 .11
❑ 248 Roberto Miniel RC .75 .35
❑ 249 Brian Bass RC .75 .35
❑ 250 Mark Burnett RC .75 .35
❑ 251 Juan Silvestre .15 .07
❑ 252 Pablo Ozuna .15 .07
❑ 253 Jayson Werth .15 .07
❑ 254 Russ Jacobson .15 .07
❑ 255 Chad Hermansen .15 .07
❑ 256 Travis Hafner RC 1.25 .55
❑ 257 Brad Baker .25 .11
❑ 258 Gookie Dawkins .15 .07
❑ 259 Michael Cuddyer .25 .11
❑ 260 Mark Buehrle .60 .25
❑ 261 Ricardo Aramboles .15 .07
❑ 262 Esix Snead RC .75 .35
❑ 263 Wilson Betemit RC 2.50 1.10
❑ 264 Albert Pujols RC 20.00 9.00
❑ 265 Joe Lawrence .15 .07
❑ 266 Ramon Ortiz .25 .11
❑ 267 Ben Sheets .40 .18
❑ 268 Luke Lockwood RC .60 .25
❑ 269 Toby Hall .25 .11
❑ 270 Jack Cust .25 .11
❑ 271 Pedro Feliz UER .15 .07
No facsimile signature on card
❑ 272 Noel Devarez RC .75 .35
❑ 273 Josh Beckett .60 .25
❑ 274 Alex Escobar .25 .11
❑ 275 Doug Gredvig RC 1.00 .45
❑ 276 Marcus Giles .25 .11
❑ 277 Jon Rauch .25 .11
❑ 278 Brian Schmitt RC .75 .35
❑ 279 Seung Song RC 1.50 .70
❑ 280 Kevin Mench .40 .18
❑ 281 Adam Eaton .25 .11
❑ 282 Shawn Sonnier .15 .07
❑ 283 Andy Van Hekken RC 1.25 .55
❑ 284 Aaron Rowand .25 .11
❑ 285 Tony Blanco RC 2.00 .90
❑ 286 Ryan Kohlmeier .15 .07
❑ 287 C.C. Sabathia .40 .18
❑ 288 Bubba Crosby .15 .07
❑ 289 Josh Hamilton .60 .25
❑ 290 Dee Haynes RC .60 .25
❑ 291 Jason Marquis .25 .11
❑ 292 Julio Zuleta .25 .11
❑ 293 Carlos Hernandez .25 .11
❑ 294 Matt Lecroy .15 .07
❑ 295 Andy Beal RC .60 .25
❑ 296 Carlos Pena .25 .11
❑ 297 Reggie Taylor .15 .07
❑ 298 Bob Keppel RC 1.00 .45
❑ 299 Miguel Cabrera UER .25 .11
Photo is Manuel Esquivia
❑ 300 Ryan Franklin .15 .07
❑ 301 Brandon Phillips .25 .11
❑ 302 Victor Hall RC .75 .35
❑ 303 Tony Pena Jr. .15 .07
❑ 304 Jim Journell RC 1.00 .45
❑ 305 Cristian Guerrero .60 .25
❑ 306 Miguel Olivo .15 .07
❑ 307 Jin Ho Cho .15 .07
❑ 308 Choo Freeman .15 .07
❑ 309 Danny Borrell RC 1.00 .45
❑ 310 Doug Mientkiewicz .25 .11
❑ 311 Aaron Herr .15 .07
❑ 312 Keith Ginter .25 .11
❑ 313 Felipe Lopez .15 .07
❑ 314 Jeff Goldbach .15 .07
❑ 315 Travis Harper .15 .07
❑ 316 Paul LoDuca .25 .11
❑ 317 Joe Torres .25 .11
❑ 318 Eric Byrnes .15 .07
❑ 319 George Lombard .15 .07
❑ 320 David Krynzel .25 .11
❑ 321 Ben Christensen .15 .07
❑ 322 Aubrey Huff .15 .07
❑ 323 Lyle Overbay .25 .11
❑ 324 Sean McGowan .15 .07
❑ 325 Jeff Heaverlo .25 .11
❑ 326 Timo Perez .15 .07
❑ 327 Octavio Martinez RC .75 .35
❑ 328 Vince Faison .15 .07
❑ 329 David Parrish RC 1.00 .45
❑ 330 Bobby Bradley .25 .11
❑ 331 Jason Miller RC .75 .35
❑ 332 Corey Spencer RC .50 .23
❑ 333 Craig House .15 .07
❑ 334 Maxim St. Pierre RC .75 .35
❑ 335 Adam Johnson .25 .11
❑ 336 Joe Crede .25 .11
❑ 337 Greg Nash RC 3.00 1.35
❑ 338 Chad Durbin .15 .07
❑ 339 Pat Magness RC .75 .35
❑ 340 Matt Wheatland .15 .07
❑ 341 Julio Lugo .15 .07
❑ 342 Grady Sizemore .25 .11
❑ 343 Adrian Gonzalez .75 .35
❑ 344 Tim Raines Jr. .15 .07
❑ 345 Ranier Olmedo RC .60 .25
❑ 346 Phil Dumatrait .15 .07
❑ 347 Brandon Mims RC 1.00 .45
❑ 348 Jason Jennings .25 .11
❑ 349 Phil Wilson RC .75 .35
❑ 350 Jason Hart .40 .18
❑ 351 Cesar Izturis .15 .07
❑ 352 Matt Butler RC 1.00 .45
❑ 353 David Kelton .25 .11
❑ 354 Luke Prokopec .25 .11
❑ 355 Corey Smith .25 .11
❑ 356 Joel Pineiro 2.50 1.10
❑ 357 Ken Chenard .15 .07
❑ 358 Keith Reed .25 .11
❑ 359 David Walling .15 .07
❑ 360 Alexis Gomez RC 1.00 .45
❑ 361 Justin Morneau RC 2.00 .90
❑ 362 Josh Fogg RC .75 .35
❑ 363 J.R. House .60 .25
❑ 364 Andy Tracy .15 .07
❑ 365 Kenny Kelly .15 .07
❑ 366 Aaron McNeal .15 .07
❑ 367 Nick Johnson .25 .11
❑ 368 Brian Esposito .15 .07
❑ 369 Charles Frazier RC .75 .35
❑ 370 Scott Heard .25 .11
❑ 371 Pat Strange .25 .11
❑ 372 Mike Meyers .15 .07
❑ 373 Ryan Ludwick RC 1.50 .70
❑ 374 Brad Wilkerson .15 .07
❑ 375 Allen Levrault .15 .07
❑ 376 Seth McClung RC .75 .35
❑ 377 Joe Nathan .15 .07
❑ 378 Rafael Soriano RC 1.00 .45
❑ 379 Chris Richard .25 .11
❑ 380 Jared Sandberg .15 .07
❑ 381 Tike Redman .15 .07
❑ 382 Adam Dunn UER 1.00 .45
Card lists him as a pitcher
❑ 383 Jared Abruzzo RC 1.00 .45
❑ 384 Jason Richardson RC .75 .35
❑ 385 Matt Holliday .15 .07
❑ 386 Darwin Cubillan RC .75 .35
❑ 387 Mike Nannini .15 .07
❑ 388 Blake Williams RC .75 .35
❑ 389 Valentino Pascucci RC .60 .25
❑ 390 Jon Garland .15 .07
❑ 391 Josh Pressley .15 .07
❑ 392 Jose Ortiz .40 .18
❑ 393 Ryan Hannaman RC .75 .35
❑ 394 Steve Smyth RC .75 .35
❑ 395 John Patterson .15 .07
❑ 396 Chad Petty RC 1.00 .45
❑ 397 Jake Peavy RC 1.25 .55
UER last name misspelled Peavey
❑ 398 Onix Mercado RC .75 .35
❑ 399 Jason Romano .15 .07
❑ 400 Luis Torres RC .75 .35
❑ 401 Casey Fossum RC 1.50 .70
❑ 402 Eduardo Figueroa RC .60 .25
❑ 403 Bryan Barnowski RC .75 .35
❑ 404 Tim Redding .25 .11
❑ 405 Jason Standridge .15 .07
❑ 406 Marvin Seale RC .75 .35
❑ 407 Todd Moser .15 .07
❑ 408 Alex Gordon .15 .07
❑ 409 Steve Smitherman RC .75 .35
❑ 410 Ben Petrick .15 .07
❑ 411 Eric Munson .25 .11
❑ 412 Luis Rivas .15 .07
❑ 413 Matt Ginter .15 .07
❑ 414 Alfonso Soriano .60 .25
❑ 415 Rafael Boitel RC .75 .35
❑ 416 Dany Morban RC .75 .35
❑ 417 Justin Woodrow RC .75 .35
❑ 418 Wilfredo Rodriguez .15 .07
❑ 419 Derrick Van Dusen RC .75 .35
❑ 420 Josh Spoerl RC .75 .35
❑ 421 Juan Pierre .25 .11
❑ 422 J.C. Romero .15 .07
❑ 423 Ed Rogers RC 1.25 .55
❑ 424 Tomo Ohka .25 .11
❑ 425 Ben Hendrickson RC .75 .35

❑ 426 Carlos Zambrano .... .15 .07
❑ 427 Brett Myers .... .15 .07
❑ 428 Scott Seabol .... .15 .07
❑ 429 Thomas Mitchell .... .15 .07
❑ 430 Jose Reyes RC .... 1.00 .45
❑ 431 Kip Wells .... .15 .07
❑ 432 Donzell McDonald .... .15 .07
❑ 433 Adam Pettyjohn RC...... 1.00 .45
❑ 434 Austin Kearns .... .40 .18
❑ 435 Rico Washington .... .15 .07
❑ 436 Doug Nickle RC.............. .50 .23
❑ 437 Steve Lomasney .... .15 .07
❑ 438 Jason Jones RC .... .60 .25
❑ 439 Bobby Seay.................... .15 .07
❑ 440 Justin Wayne RC .... 1.25 .55
❑ ROYR Kazuhiro Sasaki 60.00 27.00
Rafael Furcal ROY Jsy
❑ NNO S.Burroughs Ball EXCH/80 80.00 36.00

2001 Bowman Draft Picks

	MINT	NRMT
COMP.FACT.SET (112)..........	45.00	20.00
COMPLETE SET (110)	30.00	13.50

❑ BDP1 Alfredo Amezaga RC .. .50 .23
❑ BDP2 Andrew Good.............. .15 .07
❑ BDP3 Kelly Johnson RC .... 1.50 .70
❑ BDP4 Larry Bigbie .... .15 .07
❑ BDP5 Matt Thompson RC .... .50 .23
❑ BDP6 Wilton Chavez RC ...... .50 .23
❑ BDP7 Joe Borchard RC...... 4.00 1.80
❑ BDP8 David Espinosa .... .25 .11
❑ BDP9 Zach Day RC .... .50 .23
❑ BDP10 Brad Hawpe RC......... .50 .23
❑ BDP11 Nate Cornejo .... .25 .11
❑ BDP12 Matt Cooper RC......... .50 .23
❑ BDP13 Brad Lidge .... .15 .07
❑ BDP14 Angel Berroa RC .... .75 .35
❑ BDP15 Lamont Matthews RC .75 .35
❑ BDP16 Jose Garcia .... .15 .07
❑ BDP17 Grant Balfour RC ...... .50 .23
❑ BDP18 Ron Chiavacci RC .... .50 .23
❑ BDP19 Jae Seo .... .25 .11
❑ BDP20 Juan Rivera .... .25 .11
❑ BDP21 D'Angelo Jimenez .... .25 .11
❑ BDP22 Juan A.Pena RC ...... .50 .23
❑ BDP23 Marlon Byrd RC 2.50 1.10
❑ BDP24 Sean Burnett .... .15 .07
❑ BDP25 Josh Pearce RC........ .50 .23
❑ BDP26 B. Duckworth RC .... 2.00 .90
❑ BDP27 Jack Taschner RC .... .50 .23
❑ BDP28 Marcus Thames......... .25 .11
❑ BDP29 Brent Abernathy......... .15 .07
❑ BDP30 David Elder RC .... .50 .23
❑ BDP31 Scott Cassidy RC...... .50 .23
❑ BDP32 Dennis Tankersley RC 2.00 .90
❑ BDP33 Denny Stark............... .15 .07
❑ BDP34 Dave Williams RC .... .75 .35
❑ BDP35 Boof Bonser RC...... 1.50 .70
❑ BDP36 Kris Foster RC.......... .50 .23
❑ BDP37 Luis Garcia RC .... .75 .35
❑ BDP38 Shawn Chacon .... .15 .07
❑ BDP39 Mike Rivera RC ...... 1.25 .55
❑ BDP40 Will Smith RC......... 1.25 .55
❑ BDP41 Morgan Ensberg RC 1.50 .70
❑ BDP42 Ken Harvey .... .25 .11
❑ BDP43 Ricardo Rodriguez RC 1.25 .55
❑ BDP44 Jose Mieses RC........ .50 .23
❑ BDP45 Luis Maza RC .... .50 .23
❑ BDP46 Julio Perez RC.......... .50 .23
❑ BDP47 Dustan Mohr RC ...... .75 .35
❑ BDP48 Randy Flores RC ...... .50 .23
❑ BDP49 Covelli Crisp RC ...... .75 .35
❑ BDP50 Kevin Reese RC ...... .50 .23
❑ BDP51 Brad Thomas UER.... .15 .07
Card back is BDP71 Alex Herrera
❑ BDP52 Xavier Nady.............. .40 .18
❑ BDP53 Ryan Vogelsong ...... .15 .07
❑ BDP54 Carlos Silva .... .15 .07
❑ BDP55 Dan Wright................ .25 .11
❑ BDP56 Brent Butler .... .15 .07
❑ BDP57 Brandon Knight RC .. .50 .23
❑ BDP58 Brian Reith RC.......... .50 .23
❑ BDP59 Mario Valenzuela RC .50 .23
❑ BDP60 Bobby Hill RC .... 1.25 .55
❑ BDP61 Rich Rundles RC...... .50 .23
❑ BDP62 Rick Elder .... .15 .07
❑ BDP63 J.D. Closser.............. .15 .07
❑ BDP64 Scot Shields.............. .15 .07
❑ BDP65 Miguel Olivo.............. .15 .07
❑ BDP66 Stubby Clapp RC...... .50 .23
❑ BDP67 Jerome Williams RC 1.50 .70

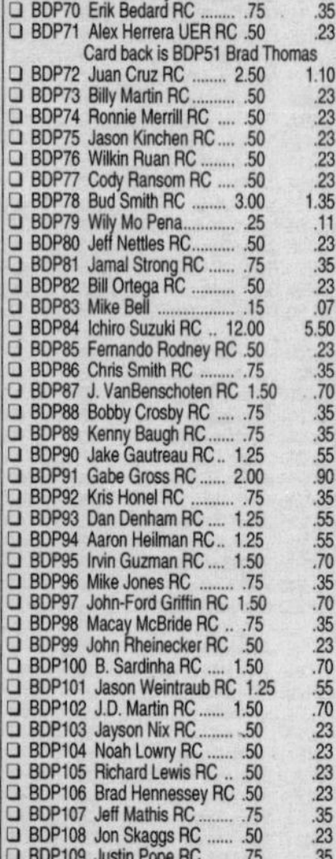

❑ BDP68 Jason Lane RC ...... 2.00 .90
❑ BDP69 Chase Utley RC ...... 1.25 .55
❑ BDP70 Erik Bedard RC .... .75 .35
❑ BDP71 Alex Herrera UER RC .50 .23
Card back is BDP51 Brad Thomas
❑ BDP72 Juan Cruz RC 2.50 1.10
❑ BDP73 Billy Martin RC.......... .50 .23
❑ BDP74 Ronnie Merrill RC .... .50 .23
❑ BDP75 Jason Kinchen RC.... .50 .23
❑ BDP76 Wilkin Ruan RC .... .50 .23
❑ BDP77 Cody Ransom RC .... .50 .23
❑ BDP78 Bud Smith RC 3.00 1.35
❑ BDP79 Wily Mo Pena............ .25 .11
❑ BDP80 Jeff Nettles RC.......... .50 .23
❑ BDP81 Jamal Strong RC ...... .75 .35
❑ BDP82 Bill Ortega RC .... .50 .23
❑ BDP83 Mike Bell .... .15 .07
❑ BDP84 Ichiro Suzuki RC .. 12.00 5.50
❑ BDP85 Fernando Rodney RC .50 .23
❑ BDP86 Chris Smith RC .... .75 .35
❑ BDP87 J. VanBenschoten RC 1.50 .70
❑ BDP88 Bobby Crosby RC .... .75 .35
❑ BDP89 Kenny Baugh RC...... .75 .35
❑ BDP90 Jake Gautreau RC.. 1.25 .55
❑ BDP91 Gabe Gross RC ...... 2.00 .90
❑ BDP92 Kris Honel RC .... .75 .35
❑ BDP93 Dan Denham RC .... 1.25 .55
❑ BDP94 Aaron Heilman RC.. 1.25 .55
❑ BDP95 Irvin Guzman RC .... 1.50 .70
❑ BDP96 Mike Jones RC .... .75 .35
❑ BDP97 John-Ford Griffin RC 1.50 .70
❑ BDP98 Macay McBride RC .. .75 .35
❑ BDP99 John Rheinecker RC .50 .23
❑ BDP100 B. Sardinha RC .... 1.50 .70
❑ BDP101 Jason Weintraub RC 1.25 .55
❑ BDP102 J.D. Martin RC ...... 1.50 .70
❑ BDP103 Jayson Nix RC........ .50 .23
❑ BDP104 Noah Lowry RC ...... .50 .23
❑ BDP105 Richard Lewis RC .. .50 .23
❑ BDP106 Brad Hennessey RC .50 .23
❑ BDP107 Jeff Mathis RC .... .75 .35
❑ BDP108 Jon Skaggs RC ...... .50 .23
❑ BDP109 Justin Pope RC ...... .75 .35
❑ BDP110 Josh Burrus RC ...... .75 .35

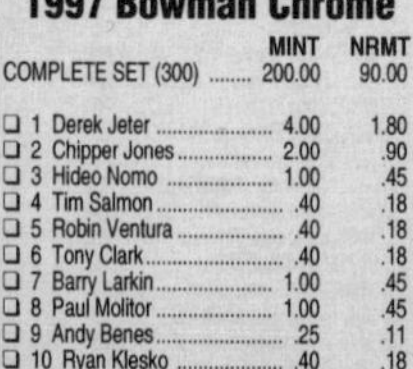

1997 Bowman Chrome

	MINT	NRMT
COMPLETE SET (300)	200.00	90.00

❑ 1 Derek Jeter 4.00 1.80
❑ 2 Chipper Jones................ 2.00 .90
❑ 3 Hideo Nomo .... 1.00 .45
❑ 4 Tim Salmon.................... .40 .18
❑ 5 Robin Ventura................ .40 .18
❑ 6 Tony Clark...................... .40 .18
❑ 7 Barry Larkin.................. 1.00 .45
❑ 8 Paul Molitor.................. 1.00 .45
❑ 9 Andy Benes.................... .25 .11
❑ 10 Ryan Klesko .... .40 .18

❑ 11 Mark McGwire.............. 4.00 1.80
❑ 12 Ken Griffey Jr. 3.00 1.35
❑ 13 Robb Nen .... .25 .11
❑ 14 Cal Ripken.................. 4.00 1.80
❑ 15 John Valentin .... .25 .11
❑ 16 Ricky Bottalico................ .25 .11
❑ 17 Mike Lansing.................. .25 .11
❑ 18 Ryne Sandberg .... 1.25 .55
❑ 19 Carlos Delgado .... 1.00 .45
❑ 20 Craig Biggio.................... .60 .25
❑ 21 Eric Karros .... .40 .18
❑ 22 Kevin Appier .... .40 .18
❑ 23 Mariano Rivera .... .40 .18
❑ 24 Vinny Castilla .... .40 .18
❑ 25 Juan Gonzalez .... 1.00 .45
❑ 26 Al Martin .... .25 .11
❑ 27 Jeff Cirillo .... .40 .18
❑ 28 Ray Lankford.................... .25 .11
❑ 29 Manny Ramirez .... 1.25 .55
❑ 30 Roberto Alomar .... 1.00 .45
❑ 31 Will Clark .... 1.00 .45
❑ 32 Chuck Knoblauch .... .40 .18
❑ 33 Harold Baines .... .40 .18
❑ 34 Edgar Martinez .... .60 .25
❑ 35 Mike Mussina .... 1.00 .45
❑ 36 Kevin Brown .... .40 .18
❑ 37 Dennis Eckersley .... .40 .18
❑ 38 Tino Martinez .... .40 .18
❑ 39 Raul Mondesi .... .40 .18
❑ 40 Sammy Sosa .... 2.00 .90
❑ 41 John Smoltz .... .40 .18
❑ 42 Billy Wagner .... .25 .11
❑ 43 Ken Caminiti .... .40 .18
❑ 44 Wade Boggs .... 1.00 .45
❑ 45 Andres Galarraga .... .60 .25
❑ 46 Roger Clemens 2.50 1.10
❑ 47 Matt Williams.................... .60 .25
❑ 48 Albert Belle .... .40 .18
❑ 49 Jeff King .... .25 .11
❑ 50 John Wetteland .... .40 .18
❑ 51 Deion Sanders .... .40 .18
❑ 52 Ellis Burks .... .40 .18
❑ 53 Pedro Martinez .... 1.25 .55
❑ 54 Kenny Lofton .... .40 .18
❑ 55 Randy Johnson .... 1.25 .55
❑ 56 Bernie Williams .... 1.00 .45
❑ 57 Marquis Grissom .... .25 .11
❑ 58 Gary Sheffield .... .40 .18
❑ 59 Curt Schilling.................. 1.00 .45
❑ 60 Reggie Sanders .... .25 .11
❑ 61 Bobby Higginson .... .40 .18
❑ 62 Moises Alou...................... .40 .18
❑ 63 Tom Glavine .... 1.00 .45
❑ 64 Mark Grace .... 1.00 .45
❑ 65 Rafael Palmeiro.............. 1.00 .45
❑ 66 John Olerud...................... .40 .18
❑ 67 Dante Bichette.................. .40 .18
❑ 68 Jeff Bagwell.................... 1.25 .55
❑ 69 Barry Bonds 2.50 1.10
❑ 70 Pat Hentgen .... .25 .11
❑ 71 Jim Thome .... 1.00 .45
❑ 72 Andy Pettitte .... .40 .18
❑ 73 Jay Bell .... .40 .18
❑ 74 Jim Edmonds .... .60 .25
❑ 75 Ron Gant............................ .25 .11
❑ 76 David Cone .... .40 .18
❑ 77 Jose Canseco .... 1.00 .45

❑ 78 Jay Buhner .40 .18
❑ 79 Greg Maddux 2.50 1.10
❑ 80 Lance Johnson .25 .11
❑ 81 Travis Fryman .40 .18
❑ 82 Paul O'Neill 1.00 .45
❑ 83 Ivan Rodriguez 1.00 .45
❑ 84 Fred McGriff .60 .25
❑ 85 Mike Piazza 2.50 1.10
❑ 86 Brady Anderson .40 .18
❑ 87 Marty Cordova .25 .11
❑ 88 Joe Carter .40 .18
❑ 89 Brian Jordan .40 .18
❑ 90 David Justice .40 .18
❑ 91 Tony Gwynn 2.00 .90
❑ 92 Larry Walker .60 .25
❑ 93 Mo Vaughn .40 .18
❑ 94 Sandy Alomar Jr. .40 .18
❑ 95 Rusty Greer .40 .18
❑ 96 Roberto Hernandez .25 .11
❑ 97 Hal Morris .25 .11
❑ 98 Todd Hundley .25 .11
❑ 99 Rondell White .40 .18
❑ 100 Frank Thomas 1.25 .55
❑ 101 Bubba Trammell RC 3.00 1.35
❑ 102 Sidney Ponson RC 3.00 1.35
❑ 103 Ricky Ledee RC 2.00 .90
❑ 104 Brett Tomko .25 .11
❑ 105 Braden Looper RC .25 .11
❑ 106 Jason Dickson .25 .11
❑ 107 Chad Green RC .25 .11
❑ 108 R.A. Dickey RC .25 .11
❑ 109 Jeff Liefer .25 .11
❑ 110 Richard Hidalgo .40 .18
❑ 111 Chad Hermansen RC 2.00 .90
❑ 112 Felix Martinez .25 .11
❑ 113 J.J. Johnson .25 .11
❑ 114 Todd Dunwoody .25 .11
❑ 115 Katsuhiro Maeda .25 .11
❑ 116 Darin Erstad 1.00 .45
❑ 117 Elieser Marrero .25 .11
❑ 118 Bartolo Colon .40 .18
❑ 119 Ugueth Urbina .25 .11
❑ 120 Jaime Bluma .25 .11
❑ 121 Seth Greisinger RC .40 .18
❑ 122 Jose Cruz Jr. RC 10.00 4.50
❑ 123 Todd Dunn .25 .11
❑ 124 Justin Towle RC .25 .11
❑ 125 Brian Rose .25 .11
❑ 126 Jose Guillen .25 .11
❑ 127 Andruw Jones 1.50 .70
❑ 128 Mark Kotsay RC 4.00 1.80
❑ 129 Wilton Guerrero .25 .11
❑ 130 Jacob Cruz .25 .11
❑ 131 Mike Sweeney .40 .18
❑ 132 Matt Morris .40 .18
❑ 133 John Thomson .25 .11
❑ 134 Javier Valentin .25 .11
❑ 135 Mike Drumright RC .25 .11
❑ 136 Michael Barrett .25 .11
❑ 137 Tony Saunders RC .25 .11
❑ 138 Kevin Brown .40 .18
❑ 139 Anthony Sanders RC 1.50 .70
❑ 140 Jeff Abbott .25 .11
❑ 141 Eugene Kingsale .25 .11
❑ 142 Paul Konerko .40 .18
❑ 143 Randall Simon RC .25 .11
❑ 144 Freddy Adrian Garcia .25 .11
❑ 145 Karim Garcia .25 .11
❑ 146 Carlos Guillen .25 .11
❑ 147 Aaron Boone .25 .11
❑ 148 Donnie Sadler .25 .11
❑ 149 Brooks Kieschnick .25 .11
❑ 150 Scott Spiezio .25 .11
❑ 151 Kevin Orie .25 .11
❑ 152 Russ Johnson .25 .11
❑ 153 Livan Hernandez .25 .11
❑ 154 Vladimir Nunez RC .40 .18
❑ 155 Pokey Reese .25 .11
❑ 156 Chris Carpenter .25 .11
❑ 157 Eric Milton RC 8.00 3.60
❑ 158 Richie Sexson .40 .18
❑ 159 Carl Pavano .25 .11
❑ 160 Pat Cline .25 .11
❑ 161 Ron Wright .25 .11
❑ 162 Dante Powell .25 .11
❑ 163 Mark Bellhorn .25 .11
❑ 164 George Lombard .25 .11
❑ 165 Paul Wilder RC .25 .11
❑ 166 Brad Fullmer .40 .18
❑ 167 Kris Benson RC 6.00 2.70
❑ 168 Torii Hunter .40 .18
❑ 169 D.T. Cromer RC .25 .11
❑ 170 Nelson Figueroa RC 2.50 1.10
❑ 171 Hiram Bocachica RC 1.50 .70
❑ 172 Shane Monahan .25 .11
❑ 173 Juan Melo .25 .11
❑ 174 Calvin Pickering RC .40 .18
❑ 175 Reggie Taylor .25 .11
❑ 176 Geoff Jenkins .60 .25
❑ 177 Steve Rain RC .25 .11
❑ 178 Nerio Rodriguez RC .25 .11
❑ 179 Derrick Gibson .25 .11
❑ 180 Darin Blood .25 .11
❑ 181 Ben Davis .40 .18
❑ 182 Adrian Beltre RC 15.00 6.75
❑ 183 Kerry Wood RC 20.00 9.00
❑ 184 Nate Rolison RC 1.50 .70
❑ 185 Fernando Tatis RC 3.00 1.35
❑ 186 Jake Westbrook RC 2.00 .90
❑ 187 Edwin Diaz .25 .11
❑ 188 Joe Fontenot RC .40 .18
❑ 189 Matt Halloran RC .25 .11
❑ 190 Matt Clement RC 4.00 1.80
❑ 191 Todd Greene .25 .11
❑ 192 Eric Chavez RC 12.00 5.50
❑ 193 Edgard Velazquez .25 .11
❑ 194 Bruce Chen RC 3.00 1.35
❑ 195 Jason Brester .25 .11
❑ 196 Chris Reitsma RC 3.00 1.35
❑ 197 Neifi Perez .25 .11
❑ 198 Hideki Irabu RC 1.00 .45
❑ 199 Don Denbow RC .25 .11
❑ 200 Derrek Lee .40 .18
❑ 201 Todd Walker .25 .11
❑ 202 Scott Rolen 1.00 .45
❑ 203 Wes Helms .40 .18
❑ 204 Bob Abreu .40 .18
❑ 205 John Patterson RC 2.50 1.10
❑ 206 Alex Gonzalez RC 2.00 .90
❑ 207 Grant Roberts RC 2.00 .90
❑ 208 Jeff Suppan .25 .11
❑ 209 Luke Wilcox .25 .11
❑ 210 Marlon Anderson .25 .11
❑ 211 Mike Caruso RC .25 .11
❑ 212 Roy Halladay RC 1.00 .45
❑ 213 Jeremi Gonzalez RC .25 .11
❑ 214 Aramis Ramirez RC 12.00 5.50
❑ 215 Dermal Brown RC 8.00 3.60
❑ 216 Justin Thompson .25 .11
❑ 217 Danny Clyburn .25 .11
❑ 218 Bruce Aven .25 .11
❑ 219 Keith Foulke RC .40 .18
❑ 220 Shannon Stewart .40 .18
❑ 221 Larry Barnes RC .25 .11
❑ 222 Mark Johnson RC .25 .11
❑ 223 Randy Winn .25 .11
❑ 224 Nomar Garciaparra 2.50 1.10
❑ 225 Jacque Jones RC 8.00 3.60
❑ 226 Chris Clemons .25 .11
❑ 227 Todd Helton 2.00 .90
❑ 228 Ryan Brannan RC .25 .11
❑ 229 Alex Sanchez RC .40 .18
❑ 230 Russell Branyan .40 .18
❑ 231 Daryle Ward 3.00 1.35
❑ 232 Kevin Witt .25 .11
❑ 233 Gabby Martinez .25 .11
❑ 234 Preston Wilson .40 .18
❑ 235 Donzell McDonald RC .25 .11
❑ 236 Orlando Cabrera RC 2.50 1.10
❑ 237 Brian Banks .25 .11
❑ 238 Robbie Bell 1.00 .45
❑ 239 Brad Rigby .25 .11
❑ 240 Scott Elarton .25 .11
❑ 241 Donny Leon RC .40 .18
❑ 242 Abraham Nunez RC 1.00 .45
❑ 243 Adam Eaton RC 8.00 3.60
❑ 244 Octavio Dotel RC 3.00 1.35
❑ 245 Sean Casey 10.00 4.50
❑ 246 Joe Lawrence RC 2.50 1.10
❑ 247 Adam Johnson RC .25 .11
❑ 248 Ronnie Belliard RC 1.50 .70
❑ 249 Bobby Estalella .25 .11
❑ 250 Corey Lee RC .25 .11
❑ 251 Mike Cameron .40 .18
❑ 252 Kerry Robinson RC .25 .11
❑ 253 A.J. Zapp RC 1.50 .70
❑ 254 Jarrod Washburn .25 .11
❑ 255 Ben Grieve .40 .18
❑ 256 Javier Vazquez RC 12.00 5.50
❑ 257 Travis Lee RC 6.00 2.70
❑ 258 Dennis Reyes RC 1.00 .45
❑ 259 Danny Buxbaum .25 .11
❑ 260 Kelvim Escobar RC 1.50 .70
❑ 261 Danny Klassen .25 .11
❑ 262 Ken Cloude RC .25 .11
❑ 263 Gabe Alvarez .25 .11
❑ 264 Clayton Bruner RC .25 .11
❑ 265 Jason Marquis RC 4.00 1.80
❑ 266 Jamey Wright .25 .11
❑ 267 Matt Snyder RC .25 .11
❑ 268 Josh Garrett RC 1.50 .70
❑ 269 Juan Encarnacion .40 .18
❑ 270 Heath Murray .25 .11
❑ 271 Brent Butler RC 1.50 .70
❑ 272 Danny Peoples RC 1.00 .45
❑ 273 Miguel Tejada RC 15.00 6.75
❑ 274 Jim Pittsley .25 .11
❑ 275 Dmitri Young .40 .18
❑ 276 Vladimir Guerrero 2.00 .90
❑ 277 Cole Liniak RC .40 .18
❑ 278 Ramon Hernandez .25 .11
❑ 279 Cliff Politte RC .25 .11
❑ 280 Mel Rosario RC .25 .11
❑ 281 Jorge Carrion RC .25 .11
❑ 282 John Barnes RC 1.00 .45
❑ 283 Chris Stowe RC .25 .11
❑ 284 Vernon Wells RC 10.00 4.50
❑ 285 Brett Caradonna RC 1.50 .70
❑ 286 Scott Hodges RC 2.00 .90
❑ 287 Jon Garland RC 4.00 1.80
❑ 288 Nathan Haynes RC 2.00 .90
❑ 289 Geoff Goetz RC 1.50 .70
❑ 290 Adam Kennedy RC 4.00 1.80
❑ 291 T.J. Tucker RC 1.50 .70
❑ 292 Aaron Akin RC 1.00 .45
❑ 293 Jayson Werth RC 1.50 .70
❑ 294 Glenn Davis RC .25 .11
❑ 295 Mark Mangum RC 1.50 .70
❑ 296 Troy Cameron RC 2.00 .90
❑ 297 J.J. Davis RC 4.00 1.80
❑ 298 Lance Berkman RC 25.00 11.00
❑ 299 Jason Standridge RC 2.00 .90
❑ 300 Jason Dellaero RC .40 .18

1998 Bowman Chrome

	MINT	NRMT
COMPLETE SET (441)	200.00	90.00
COMPLETE SERIES 1 (221)	120.00	55.00
COMPLETE SERIES 2 (220)	80.00	36.00

❑ 1 Nomar Garciaparra 2.50 1.10
❑ 2 Scott Rolen 1.00 .45
❑ 3 Andy Pettitte .40 .18
❑ 4 Ivan Rodriguez 1.00 .45
❑ 5 Mark McGwire 4.00 1.80
❑ 6 Jason Dickson .25 .11
❑ 7 Jose Cruz Jr. .40 .18
❑ 8 Jeff Kent .60 .25
❑ 9 Mike Mussina 1.00 .45

❑	10	Jason Kendall	.40	.18
❑	11	Brett Tomko	.25	.11
❑	12	Jeff King	.25	.11
❑	13	Brad Radke	.40	.18
❑	14	Robin Ventura	.40	.18
❑	15	Jeff Bagwell	1.25	.55
❑	16	Greg Maddux	2.50	1.10
❑	17	John Jaha	.40	.18
❑	18	Mike Piazza	2.50	1.10
❑	19	Edgar Martinez	.60	.25
❑	20	David Justice	.40	.18
❑	21	Todd Hundley	.25	.11
❑	22	Tony Gwynn	2.00	.90
❑	23	Larry Walker	.60	.25
❑	24	Bernie Williams	1.00	.45
❑	25	Edgar Renteria	.25	.11
❑	26	Rafael Palmeiro	1.00	.45
❑	27	Tim Salmon	.40	.18
❑	28	Matt Morris	.40	.18
❑	29	Shawn Estes	.40	.18
❑	30	Vladimir Guerrero	1.25	.55
❑	31	Fernando Tatis	.25	.11
❑	32	Justin Thompson	.25	.11
❑	33	Ken Griffey Jr.	3.00	1.35
❑	34	Edgardo Alfonzo	.40	.18
❑	35	Mo Vaughn	.40	.18
❑	36	Marty Cordova	.25	.11
❑	37	Craig Biggio	.60	.25
❑	38	Roger Clemens	2.50	1.10
❑	39	Mark Grace	1.00	.45
❑	40	Ken Caminiti	.40	.18
❑	41	Tony Womack	.25	.11
❑	42	Albert Belle	.40	.18
❑	43	Tino Martinez	.40	.18
❑	44	Sandy Alomar Jr.	.40	.18
❑	45	Jeff Cirillo	.40	.18
❑	46	Jason Giambi	1.00	.45
❑	47	Darin Erstad	1.00	.45
❑	48	Livan Hernandez	.25	.11
❑	49	Mark Grudzielanek	.25	.11
❑	50	Sammy Sosa	2.00	.90
❑	51	Curt Schilling	1.00	.45
❑	52	Brian Hunter	.25	.11
❑	53	Neifi Perez	.25	.11
❑	54	Todd Walker	.25	.11
❑	55	Jose Guillen	.25	.11
❑	56	Jim Thome	1.00	.45
❑	57	Tom Glavine	1.00	.45
❑	58	Todd Greene	.25	.11
❑	59	Rondell White	.40	.18
❑	60	Roberto Alomar	1.00	.45
❑	61	Tony Clark	.40	.18
❑	62	Vinny Castilla	.40	.18
❑	63	Barry Larkin	1.00	.45
❑	64	Hideki Irabu	.25	.11
❑	65	Johnny Damon	.40	.18
❑	66	Juan Gonzalez	1.00	.45
❑	67	John Olerud	.40	.18
❑	68	Gary Sheffield	.40	.18
❑	69	Raul Mondesi	.40	.18
❑	70	Chipper Jones	2.00	.90
❑	71	David Ortiz	2.00	.90
❑	72	Warren Morris RC	2.00	.90
❑	73	Alex Gonzalez	.25	.11
❑	74	Nick Bierbrodt	1.00	.45
❑	75	Roy Halladay	.25	.11
❑	76	Danny Buxbaum	.25	.11
❑	77	Adam Kennedy	.25	.11
❑	78	Jared Sandberg	.40	.18
❑	79	Michael Barrett	.25	.11
❑	80	Gil Meche	2.00	.90
❑	81	Jayson Werth	.25	.11
❑	82	Abraham Nunez	.25	.11
❑	83	Ben Petrick	.25	.11
❑	84	Brett Caradonna	.25	.11
❑	85	Mike Lowell RC	5.00	2.20
❑	86	Clay Bruner	.40	.18
❑	87	John Curtice RC	1.50	.70
❑	88	Bobby Estalella	.25	.11
❑	89	Juan Melo	.25	.11
❑	90	Arnold Gooch	.25	.11
❑	91	Kevin Millwood RC	4.00	1.80
❑	92	Richie Sexson	.40	.18
❑	93	Orlando Cabrera	.25	.11
❑	94	Pat Cline	.25	.11
❑	95	Anthony Sanders	.25	.11
❑	96	Russ Johnson	.25	.11
❑	97	Ben Grieve	.40	.18
❑	98	Kevin McGlinchy	.25	.11
❑	99	Paul Wilder	.25	.11
❑	100	Russ Ortiz	.40	.18
❑	101	Ryan Jackson RC	.25	.11
❑	102	Heath Murray	.25	.11
❑	103	Brian Rose	.25	.11
❑	104	R.Radmanovich RC	.25	.11
❑	105	Ricky Ledee	.25	.11
❑	106	Jeff Wallace RC	.40	.18
❑	107	Ryan Minor RC	1.00	.45
❑	108	Dennis Reyes	.25	.11
❑	109	James Manias	.25	.11
❑	110	Chris Carpenter	.25	.11
❑	111	Daryle Ward	.25	.11
❑	112	Vernon Wells	.60	.25
❑	113	Chad Green	.25	.11
❑	114	Mike Stoner RC	.25	.11
❑	115	Brad Fullmer	.40	.18
❑	116	Adam Eaton	.40	.18
❑	117	Jeff Liefer	.25	.11
❑	118	Corey Koskie RC	5.00	2.20
❑	119	Todd Helton	1.25	.55
❑	120	Jaime Jones RC	.40	.18
❑	121	Mel Rosario	.25	.11
❑	122	Geoff Goetz	.25	.11
❑	123	Adrian Beltre	.40	.18
❑	124	Jason Dellaero	.25	.11
❑	125	Gabe Kapler RC	6.00	2.70
❑	126	Scott Schoeneweis	.25	.11
❑	127	Ryan Brannan	.25	.11
❑	128	Aaron Akin	.25	.11
❑	129	Ryan Anderson RC	10.00	4.50
❑	130	Brad Penny	.40	.18
❑	131	Bruce Chen	.25	.11
❑	132	Eli Marrero	.25	.11
❑	133	Eric Chavez	.40	.18
❑	134	Troy Glaus RC	25.00	11.00
❑	135	Troy Cameron	.25	.11
❑	136	Brian Sikorski RC	.25	.11
❑	137	Mike Kinkade RC	1.50	.70
❑	138	Braden Looper	.25	.11
❑	139	Mark Mangum	.25	.11
❑	140	Danny Peoples	.25	.11
❑	141	J.J. Davis	.40	.18
❑	142	Ben Davis	.40	.18
❑	143	Jacque Jones	.40	.18
❑	144	Derrick Gibson	.25	.11
❑	145	Bronson Arroyo	1.50	.70
❑	146	L.De Los Santos RC	1.00	.45
❑	147	Jeff Abbott	.25	.11
❑	148	Mike Cuddyer RC	6.00	2.70
❑	149	Jason Romano	.25	.11
❑	150	Shane Monahan	.25	.11
❑	151	Ntema Ndungidi RC	1.50	.70
❑	152	Alex Sanchez	.25	.11
❑	153	Jack Cust RC	6.00	2.70
❑	154	Brent Butler	.25	.11
❑	155	Ramon Hernandez	.25	.11
❑	156	Norm Hutchins	.25	.11
❑	157	Jason Marquis	.40	.18
❑	158	Jacob Cruz	.25	.11
❑	159	Rob Burger RC	.25	.11
❑	160	Dave Coggin	.25	.11
❑	161	Preston Wilson	.40	.18
❑	162	Jason Fitzgerald RC	.25	.11
❑	163	Dan Serafini	.25	.11
❑	164	Pete Munro	.25	.11
❑	165	Trot Nixon	.40	.18
❑	166	Homer Bush	.25	.11
❑	167	Dermal Brown	.25	.11
❑	168	Chad Hermansen	.25	.11
❑	169	Julio Moreno RC	1.50	.70
❑	170	John Roskos RC	.40	.18
❑	171	Grant Roberts	.25	.11
❑	172	Ken Cloude	.25	.11
❑	173	Jason Brester	.25	.11
❑	174	Jason Conti	.25	.11
❑	175	Jon Garland	.25	.11
❑	176	Robbie Bell	.25	.11
❑	177	Nathan Haynes	.25	.11
❑	178	Ramon Ortiz RC	8.00	3.60
❑	179	Shannon Stewart	.40	.18
❑	180	Pablo Ortega	.25	.11
❑	181	Jimmy Rollins RC	10.00	4.50
❑	182	Sean Casey	.60	.25
❑	183	Ted Lilly RC	3.00	1.35
❑	184	Chris Enochs RC	.40	.18
❑	185	M.Ordonez RC UER	12.00	5.50
		Front photo is Mario Valdez		
❑	186	Mike Drumright	.25	.11
❑	187	Aaron Boone	.25	.11
❑	188	Matt Clement	.25	.11
❑	189	Todd Dunwoody	.25	.11
❑	190	Larry Rodriguez	.25	.11
❑	191	Todd Noel	.25	.11
❑	192	Geoff Jenkins	.40	.18
❑	193	George Lombard	.25	.11
❑	194	Lance Berkman	1.00	.45
❑	195	Marcus McCain	.40	.18
❑	196	Ryan McGuire	.25	.11
❑	197	Jhensy Sandoval	.25	.11
❑	198	Corey Lee	.25	.11
❑	199	Mario Valdez	.25	.11
❑	200	Robert Fick RC	4.00	1.80
❑	201	Donnie Sadler	.25	.11
❑	202	Marc Kroon	.25	.11
❑	203	David Miller	.25	.11
❑	204	Jarrod Washburn	.25	.11
❑	205	Miguel Tejada	.60	.25
❑	206	Raul Ibanez	.25	.11
❑	207	John Patterson	.25	.11
❑	208	Calvin Pickering	.25	.11
❑	209	Felix Martinez	.25	.11
❑	210	Mark Redman	.25	.11
❑	211	Scott Elarton	.25	.11
❑	212	Jose Amado RC	.25	.11
❑	213	Kerry Wood	1.00	.45
❑	214	Dante Powell	.25	.11
❑	215	Aramis Ramirez	.40	.18
❑	216	A.J. Hinch	.25	.11
❑	217	Dustin Carr RC	1.50	.70
❑	218	Mark Kotsay	.40	.18
❑	219	Jason Standridge	.25	.11
❑	220	Luis Ordaz	.25	.11
❑	221	O.Hernandez RC	5.00	2.20
❑	222	Cal Ripken	4.00	1.80
❑	223	Paul Molitor	1.00	.45
❑	224	Derek Jeter	4.00	1.80
❑	225	Barry Bonds	2.50	1.10
❑	226	Jim Edmonds	.60	.25
❑	227	John Smoltz	.40	.18
❑	228	Eric Karros	.40	.18
❑	229	Ray Lankford	.25	.11
❑	230	Rey Ordonez	.25	.11
❑	231	Kenny Lofton	.40	.18
❑	232	Alex Rodriguez	2.50	1.10
❑	233	Dante Bichette	.40	.18
❑	234	Pedro Martinez	1.25	.55
❑	235	Carlos Delgado	1.00	.45
❑	236	Rod Beck	.25	.11
❑	237	Matt Williams	.60	.25
❑	238	Charles Johnson	.40	.18
❑	239	Rico Brogna	.25	.11
❑	240	Frank Thomas	1.25	.55
❑	241	Paul O'Neill	1.00	.45
❑	242	Jaret Wright	.25	.11
❑	243	Brant Brown	.25	.11
❑	244	Ryan Klesko	.40	.18
❑	245	Chuck Finley	.40	.18
❑	246	Derek Bell	.25	.11
❑	247	Delino DeShields	.25	.11
❑	248	Chan Ho Park	.40	.18
❑	249	Wade Boggs	1.00	.45
❑	250	Jay Buhner	.40	.18
❑	251	Butch Huskey	.25	.11
❑	252	Steve Finley	.40	.18
❑	253	Will Clark	1.00	.45
❑	254	John Valentin	.25	.11
❑	255	Bobby Higginson	.40	.18
❑	256	Darryl Strawberry	.40	.18
❑	257	Randy Johnson	1.25	.55
❑	258	Al Martin	.25	.11
❑	259	Travis Fryman	.40	.18
❑	260	Fred McGriff	.60	.25
❑	261	Jose Valentin	.25	.11
❑	262	Andruw Jones	1.00	.45
❑	263	Kenny Rogers	.25	.11
❑	264	Moises Alou	.40	.18
❑	265	Denny Neagle	.25	.11
❑	266	Ugueth Urbina	.25	.11

		MINT	NRMT
❑	267 Derrek Lee	.40	.18
❑	268 Ellis Burks	.40	.18
❑	269 Mariano Rivera	.40	.18
❑	270 Dean Palmer	.40	.18
❑	271 Eddie Taubensee	.25	.11
❑	272 Brady Anderson	.40	.18
❑	273 Brian Giles	.40	.18
❑	274 Quinton McCracken	.25	.11
❑	275 Henry Rodriguez	.25	.11
❑	276 Andres Galarraga	.60	.25
❑	277 Jose Canseco	1.00	.45
❑	278 David Segui	.25	.11
❑	279 Bret Saberhagen	.40	.18
❑	280 Kevin Brown	.60	.25
❑	281 Chuck Knoblauch	.40	.18
❑	282 Jeromy Burnitz	.40	.18
❑	283 Jay Bell	.40	.18
❑	284 Manny Ramirez	1.25	.55
❑	285 Rick Helling	.25	.11
❑	286 Francisco Cordova	.25	.11
❑	287 Bob Abreu	.40	.18
❑	288 J.T. Snow	.25	.11
❑	289 Hideo Nomo	1.00	.45
❑	290 Brian Jordan	.40	.18
❑	291 Javy Lopez	.40	.18
❑	292 Travis Lee	.40	.18
❑	293 Russell Branyan	.40	.18
❑	294 Paul Konerko	.40	.18
❑	295 Masato Yoshii RC	3.00	1.35
❑	296 Kris Benson	.40	.18
❑	297 Juan Encarnacion	.40	.18
❑	298 Eric Milton	.40	.18
❑	299 Mike Caruso	.25	.11
❑	300 R. Aramboles RC	3.00	1.35
❑	301 Bobby Smith	.25	.11
❑	302 Billy Koch	.25	.11
❑	303 Richard Hidalgo	.40	.18
❑	304 Justin Baughman RC	.25	.11
❑	305 Chris Gissell	.25	.11
❑	306 Donnie Bridges RC	2.00	.90
❑	307 Nelson Lara RC	1.00	.45
❑	308 Randy Wolf RC	3.00	1.35
❑	309 Jason LaRue RC	3.00	1.35
❑	310 Jason Gooding RC	.25	.11
❑	311 Edgard Clemente	.25	.11
❑	312 Andrew Vessel	.25	.11
❑	313 Chris Reitsma	.25	.11
❑	314 Jesus Sanchez RC	.40	.18
❑	315 Buddy Carlyle RC	1.00	.45
❑	316 Randy Winn	.25	.11
❑	317 Luis Rivera RC	1.00	.45
❑	318 Marcus Thames RC	4.00	1.80
❑	319 A.J. Pierzynski	.25	.11
❑	320 Scott Randall	.25	.11
❑	321 Damian Sapp	.25	.11
❑	322 Ed Yarnall RC	1.00	.45
❑	323 Luke Allen RC	1.50	.70
❑	324 J.D. Smart	.25	.11
❑	325 Willie Martinez	.40	.18
❑	326 Alex Ramirez	.25	.11
❑	327 Eric DuBose RC	.40	.18
❑	328 Kevin Witt	.25	.11
❑	329 Dan McKinley RC	.40	.18
❑	330 Cliff Politte	.25	.11
❑	331 Vladimir Nunez	.25	.11
❑	332 John Halama RC	3.00	1.35
❑	333 Nerio Rodriguez	.25	.11
❑	334 Desi Relaford	.25	.11
❑	335 Robinson Checo	.25	.11
❑	336 John Nicholson	.60	.25
❑	337 Tom LaRosa RC	.25	.11
❑	338 Kevin Nicholson RC	.40	.18
❑	339 Javier Vazquez	.40	.18
❑	340 A.J. Zapp	.25	.11
❑	341 Tom Evans	.25	.11
❑	342 Kerry Robinson	.25	.11
❑	343 Gabe Gonzalez RC	.25	.11
❑	344 Ralph Milliard	.25	.11
❑	345 Enrique Wilson	.25	.11
❑	346 Elvin Hernandez	.25	.11
❑	347 Mike Lincoln RC	.25	.11
❑	348 Cesar King RC	.40	.18
❑	349 Cristian Guzman RC	8.00	3.60
❑	350 Donzell McDonald	.25	.11
❑	351 Jim Parque RC	2.00	.90
❑	352 Mike Saipe RC	.25	.11
❑	353 Carlos Febles RC	2.00	.90
❑	354 Dernell Stenson RC	3.00	1.35
❑	355 Mark Osborne RC	1.00	.45
❑	356 Odalis Perez RC	2.00	.90
❑	357 Jason Dewey RC	1.00	.45
❑	358 Joe Fontenot	.25	.11
❑	359 Jason Grilli RC	.40	.18
❑	360 Kevin Haverbusch RC	.40	.18
❑	361 Jay Yennaco RC	.40	.18
❑	362 Brian Buchanan	.25	.11
❑	363 John Barnes	.25	.11
❑	364 Chris Fussell	.25	.11
❑	365 Kevin Gibbs RC	.25	.11
❑	366 Joe Lawrence	.25	.11
❑	367 DaRond Stovall	.25	.11
❑	368 Brian Fuentes RC	.25	.11
❑	369 Jimmy Anderson	.25	.11
❑	370 Lariel Gonzalez RC	.40	.18
❑	371 Scott Williamson RC	1.50	.70
❑	372 Milton Bradley	.25	.11
❑	373 Jason Halper RC	.40	.18
❑	374 Brent Billingsley RC	.25	.11
❑	375 Joe DePastino RC	.25	.11
❑	376 Jake Westbrook	.25	.11
❑	377 Octavio Dotel	.25	.11
❑	378 Jason Williams RC	.25	.11
❑	379 Julio Ramirez RC		
❑	380 Seth Greisinger	.25	.11
❑	381 Mike Judd RC	.40	.18
❑	382 Ben Ford RC	.40	.18
❑	383 Tom Bennett RC	.25	.11
❑	384 Adam Butler RC	.25	.11
❑	385 Wade Miller RC	10.00	4.50
❑	386 Kyle Peterson RC	.40	.18
❑	387 Tommy Peterman RC	.25	.11
❑	388 Onan Masaoka	.25	.11
❑	389 Jason Rakers RC	.25	.11
❑	390 Rafael Medina	.25	.11
❑	391 Luis Lopez	.25	.11
❑	392 Jeff Yoder	.25	.11
❑	393 Vance Wilson RC	.25	.11
❑	394 F. Seguignol RC	.40	.18
❑	395 Ron Wright	.25	.11
❑	396 Ruben Mateo RC	5.00	2.20
❑	397 Steve Lomasney RC	1.50	.70
❑	398 Damian Jackson	.25	.11
❑	399 Mike Jerzembeck RC	.40	.18
❑	400 Luis Rivas RC	5.00	2.20
❑	401 Kevin Burford RC	1.50	.70
❑	402 Glenn Davis	.25	.11
❑	403 Robert Luce RC	.25	.11
❑	404 Cole Liniak	.25	.11
❑	405 Matt LeCroy RC	2.00	.90
❑	406 Jeremy Giambi RC	3.00	1.35
❑	407 Shawn Chacon	.25	.11
❑	408 Dewayne Wise RC	.40	.18
❑	409 Steve Woodard	.25	.11
❑	410 F.Cordero RC	1.25	.55
❑	411 Damon Minor RC	1.50	.70
❑	412 Lou Collier	.25	.11
❑	413 Justin Towle	.25	.11
❑	414 Juan LeBron	.25	.11
❑	415 Michael Coleman	.25	.11
❑	416 Felix Rodriguez	.25	.11
❑	417 Paul Ah Yat RC	.25	.11
❑	418 Kevin Barker RC	1.00	.45
❑	419 Brian Meadows	.25	.11
❑	420 Darnell McDonald RC	1.50	.70
❑	421 Matt Kinney RC	2.00	.90
❑	422 Mike Vavrek RC	.25	.11
❑	423 Courtney Duncan RC	.25	.11
❑	424 Kevin Millar RC	2.00	.90
❑	425 Ruben Rivera	.25	.11
❑	426 Steve Shoemaker RC	.25	.11
❑	427 Dan Reichert RC	3.00	1.35
❑	428 Carlos Lee RC	6.00	2.70
❑	429 Rod Barajas	.40	.18
❑	430 Pablo Ozuna RC	1.50	.70
❑	431 Todd Belitz RC	1.50	.70
❑	432 Sidney Ponson	.25	.11
❑	433 Steve Carver RC	.25	.11
❑	434 Esteban Yan RC	1.50	.70
❑	435 Cedrick Bowers	.40	.18
❑	436 Marlon Anderson	.25	.11
❑	437 Carl Pavano	.25	.11
❑	438 Jae Weong Seo RC	3.00	1.35
❑	439 Jose Taveras RC	.40	.18
❑	440 Matt Anderson RC	1.00	.45
❑	441 Darron Ingram RC	.40	.18

1999 Bowman Chrome

	MINT	NRMT
COMPLETE SET (440)	400.00	180.00
COMPLETE SERIES 1 (220)	150.00	70.00
COMPLETE SERIES 2 (220)	250.00	110.00

		MINT	NRMT
❑	1 Ben Grieve	.40	.18
❑	2 Kerry Wood	1.00	.45
❑	3 Ruben Rivera	.25	.11
❑	4 Sandy Alomar Jr.	.40	.18
❑	5 Cal Ripken	4.00	1.80
❑	6 Mark McGwire	4.00	1.80
❑	7 Vladimir Guerrero	1.25	.55
❑	8 Moises Alou	.40	.18
❑	9 Jim Edmonds	.60	.25
❑	10 Greg Maddux	2.50	1.10
❑	11 Gary Sheffield	.40	.18
❑	12 John Valentin	.25	.11
❑	13 Chuck Knoblauch	.40	.18
❑	14 Tony Clark	.40	.18
❑	15 Rusty Greer	.40	.18
❑	16 Al Leiter	.40	.18
❑	17 Travis Lee	.25	.11
❑	18 Jose Cruz Jr.	.40	.18
❑	19 Pedro Martinez	1.25	.55
❑	20 Paul O'Neill	1.00	.45
❑	21 Todd Walker	.25	.11
❑	22 Vinny Castilla	.40	.18
❑	23 Barry Larkin	1.00	.45
❑	24 Curt Schilling	1.00	.45
❑	25 Jason Kendall	.40	.18
❑	26 Scott Erickson	.25	.11
❑	27 Andres Galarraga	.60	.25
❑	28 Jeff Shaw	.25	.11
❑	29 John Olerud	.40	.18
❑	30 Orlando Hernandez	.40	.18
❑	31 Larry Walker	.60	.25
❑	32 Andruw Jones	1.00	.45
❑	33 Jeff Cirillo	.40	.18
❑	34 Barry Bonds	2.50	1.10
❑	35 Manny Ramirez	1.25	.55
❑	36 Mark Kotsay	.25	.11
❑	37 Ivan Rodriguez	1.00	.45
❑	38 Jeff King	.25	.11
❑	39 Brian Hunter	.25	.11
❑	40 Ray Durham	.40	.18
❑	41 Bernie Williams	1.00	.45
❑	42 Darin Erstad	1.00	.45
❑	43 Chipper Jones	2.00	.90
❑	44 Pat Hentgen	.25	.11
❑	45 Eric Young	.25	.11
❑	46 Jaret Wright	.25	.11
❑	47 Juan Guzman	.25	.11
❑	48 Jorge Posada	.40	.18
❑	49 Bobby Higginson	.40	.18
❑	50 Jose Guillen	.25	.11
❑	51 Trevor Hoffman	.40	.18
❑	52 Ken Griffey Jr.	3.00	1.35
❑	53 David Justice	.40	.18
❑	54 Matt Williams	.60	.25
❑	55 Eric Karros	.40	.18
❑	56 Derek Bell	.25	.11
❑	57 Ray Lankford	.25	.11

❑ 58 Mariano Rivera .40 .18
❑ 59 Brett Tomko .25 .11
❑ 60 Mike Mussina 1.00 .45
❑ 61 Kenny Lofton .40 .18
❑ 62 Chuck Finley .40 .18
❑ 63 Alex Gonzalez .25 .11
❑ 64 Mark Grace 1.00 .45
❑ 65 Raul Mondesi .40 .18
❑ 66 David Cone .40 .18
❑ 67 Brad Fullmer .40 .18
❑ 68 Andy Benes .25 .11
❑ 69 John Smoltz .40 .18
❑ 70 Shane Reynolds .25 .11
❑ 71 Bruce Chen .25 .11
❑ 72 Adam Kennedy .25 .11
❑ 73 Jack Cust .40 .18
❑ 74 Matt Clement .25 .11
❑ 75 Derrick Gibson .25 .11
❑ 76 Darnell McDonald .25 .11
❑ 77 Adam Everett RC 2.50 1.10
❑ 78 Ricardo Aramboles .25 .11
❑ 79 Mark Quinn RC 5.00 2.20
❑ 80 Jason Rakers .25 .11
❑ 81 Seth Etherton RC 2.00 .90
❑ 82 Jeff Urban RC 1.00 .45
❑ 83 Manny Aybar .25 .11
❑ 84 Mike Nannini RC 3.00 1.35
❑ 85 Onan Masaoka .25 .11
❑ 86 Rod Barajas .25 .11
❑ 87 Mike Frank .25 .11
❑ 88 Scott Randall .25 .11
❑ 89 Justin Bowles RC .25 .11
❑ 90 Chris Haas .25 .11
❑ 91 Arturo McDowell RC 1.50 .70
❑ 92 Matt Belisle RC 3.00 1.35
❑ 93 Scott Elarton .25 .11
❑ 94 Vernon Wells .40 .18
❑ 95 Pat Cline .25 .11
❑ 96 Ryan Anderson .40 .18
❑ 97 Kevin Barker .25 .11
❑ 98 Ruben Mateo .40 .18
❑ 99 Robert Fick .25 .11
❑ 100 Corey Koskie .40 .18
❑ 101 Ricky Ledee .25 .11
❑ 102 Rick Elder RC 4.00 1.80
❑ 103 Jack Cressend RC .25 .11
❑ 104 Joe Lawrence .40 .18
❑ 105 Mike Lincoln .25 .11
❑ 106 Kit Pellow RC 1.00 .45
❑ 107 Matt Burch RC 1.00 .45
❑ 108 Cole Liniak .25 .11
❑ 109 Jason Dewey .25 .11
❑ 110 Cesar King .25 .11
❑ 111 Julio Ramirez .25 .11
❑ 112 Jake Westbrook .25 .11
❑ 113 Eric Valent RC 4.00 1.80
❑ 114 Roosevelt Brown RC 2.00 .90
❑ 115 Choo Freeman RC 2.50 1.10
❑ 116 Juan Melo .25 .11
❑ 117 Jason Grilli .25 .11
❑ 118 Jared Sandberg .25 .11
❑ 119 Glenn Davis .25 .11
❑ 120 David Riske RC 1.50 .70
❑ 121 Jacque Jones .40 .18
❑ 122 Corey Lee .25 .11
❑ 123 Michael Barrett .25 .11
❑ 124 Lariel Gonzalez .25 .11
❑ 125 Mitch Meluskey .25 .11
❑ 126 Freddy Adrian Garcia .25 .11
❑ 127 Tony Torcato RC 4.00 1.80
❑ 128 Jeff Liefer .25 .11
❑ 129 Ntema Ndungidi .25 .11
❑ 130 Andy Brown RC 2.50 1.10
❑ 131 Ryan Mills RC 1.50 .70
❑ 132 Andy Abad RC .25 .11
❑ 133 Carlos Febles .25 .11
❑ 134 Jason Tyner RC 2.00 .90
❑ 135 Mark Osborne .25 .11
❑ 136 Phil Norton RC .25 .11
❑ 137 Nathan Haynes .25 .11
❑ 138 Roy Halladay .25 .11
❑ 139 Juan Encarnacion .40 .18
❑ 140 Brad Penny .40 .18
❑ 141 Grant Roberts .25 .11
❑ 142 Aramis Ramirez .40 .18
❑ 143 Cristian Guzman .40 .18
❑ 144 Mamon Tucker RC 2.00 .90
❑ 145 Ryan Bradley .25 .11
❑ 146 Brian Simmons .25 .11
❑ 147 Dan Reichert .25 .11
❑ 148 Russell Branyan .40 .18
❑ 149 Victor Valencia RC 1.00 .45
❑ 150 Scott Schoeneweis .25 .11
❑ 151 Sean Spencer RC .25 .11
❑ 152 Odalis Perez .25 .11
❑ 153 Joe Fontenot .25 .11
❑ 154 Milton Bradley .25 .11
❑ 155 Josh McKinley RC 2.00 .90
❑ 156 Terrence Long .40 .18
❑ 157 Danny Klassen .25 .11
❑ 158 Paul Hoover RC 1.00 .45
❑ 159 Ron Belliard .25 .11
❑ 160 Armando Rios .25 .11
❑ 161 Ramon Hernandez .25 .11
❑ 162 Jason Conti .25 .11
❑ 163 Chad Hermansen .25 .11
❑ 164 Jason Standridge .25 .11
❑ 165 Jason Dellaero .25 .11
❑ 166 John Curtice .25 .11
❑ 167 Clayton Andrews RC 1.50 .70
❑ 168 Jeremy Giambi .25 .11
❑ 169 Alex Ramirez .25 .11
❑ 170 Gabe Molina RC .25 .11
❑ 171 M.Encarnacion RC 2.00 .90
❑ 172 Mike Zywica RC .25 .11
❑ 173 Chip Ambres RC 2.50 1.10
❑ 174 Trot Nixon .40 .18
❑ 175 Pat Burrell RC 10.00 4.50
❑ 176 Jeff Yoder .25 .11
❑ 177 Chris Jones RC 2.00 .90
❑ 178 Kevin Witt .25 .11
❑ 179 Keith Luuloa RC .25 .11
❑ 180 Billy Koch .25 .11
❑ 181 Damaso Marte RC .25 .11
❑ 182 Ryan Glynn RC 2.00 .90
❑ 183 Calvin Pickering .25 .11
❑ 184 Michael Cuddyer .40 .18
❑ 185 Nick Johnson RC 10.00 4.50
❑ 186 D.Mientkiewicz RC 8.00 3.60
❑ 187 Nate Cornejo RC 6.00 2.70
❑ 188 Octavio Dotel .25 .11
❑ 189 Wes Helms .25 .11
❑ 190 Nelson Lara .25 .11
❑ 191 Chuck Abbott RC .25 .11
❑ 192 Tony Armas Jr. .40 .18
❑ 193 Gil Meche .25 .11
❑ 194 Ben Petrick .25 .11
❑ 195 Chris George RC 4.00 1.80
❑ 196 Scott Hunter RC .25 .11
❑ 197 Ryan Brannan .25 .11
❑ 198 Amaury Garcia RC 1.00 .45
❑ 199 Chris Gissell .25 .11
❑ 200 Austin Kearns RC 12.00 5.50
❑ 201 Alex Gonzalez .25 .11
❑ 202 Wade Miller .40 .18
❑ 203 Scott Williamson .25 .11
❑ 204 Chris Enochs .25 .11
❑ 205 Fernando Seguignol .25 .11
❑ 206 Marlon Anderson .25 .11
❑ 207 Todd Sears RC 1.50 .70
❑ 208 Nate Bump RC 1.50 .70
❑ 209 J.M. Gold RC 2.00 .90
❑ 210 Matt LeCroy .25 .11
❑ 211 Alex Hernandez .25 .11
❑ 212 Luis Rivera .25 .11
❑ 213 Troy Cameron .25 .11
❑ 214 Alex Escobar RC 8.00 3.60
❑ 215 Jason LaRue .25 .11
❑ 216 Kyle Peterson .25 .11
❑ 217 Brent Butler .25 .11
❑ 218 Dernell Stenson .25 .11
❑ 219 Adrian Beltre .40 .18
❑ 220 Daryle Ward .25 .11
❑ 221 Jim Thome 1.00 .45
❑ 222 Cliff Floyd .40 .18
❑ 223 Rickey Henderson 2.00 .90
❑ 224 Garret Anderson .40 .18
❑ 225 Ken Caminiti .40 .18
❑ 226 Bret Boone .40 .18
❑ 227 Jeromy Burnitz .40 .18
❑ 228 Steve Finley .40 .18
❑ 229 Miguel Tejada .40 .18
❑ 230 Greg Vaughn .40 .18
❑ 231 Jose Offerman .25 .11
❑ 232 Andy Ashby .25 .11
❑ 233 Albert Belle .40 .18
❑ 234 Fernando Tatis .25 .11
❑ 235 Todd Helton 1.25 .55
❑ 236 Sean Casey .60 .25
❑ 237 Brian Giles .40 .18
❑ 238 Andy Pettitte .40 .18
❑ 239 Fred McGriff .60 .25
❑ 240 Roberto Alomar 1.00 .45
❑ 241 Edgar Martinez .60 .25
❑ 242 Lee Stevens .25 .11
❑ 243 Shawn Green 1.00 .45
❑ 244 Ryan Klesko .40 .18
❑ 245 Sammy Sosa 2.00 .90
❑ 246 Todd Hundley .25 .11
❑ 247 Shannon Stewart .40 .18
❑ 248 Randy Johnson 1.25 .55
❑ 249 Rondell White .40 .18
❑ 250 Mike Piazza 2.50 1.10
❑ 251 Craig Biggio .60 .25
❑ 252 David Wells .40 .18
❑ 253 Brian Jordan .40 .18
❑ 254 Edgar Renteria .25 .11
❑ 255 Bartolo Colon .40 .18
❑ 256 Frank Thomas 1.25 .55
❑ 257 Will Clark 1.00 .45
❑ 258 Dean Palmer .40 .18
❑ 259 Dmitri Young .40 .18
❑ 260 Scott Rolen 1.00 .45
❑ 261 Jeff Kent .60 .25
❑ 262 Dante Bichette .40 .18
❑ 263 Nomar Garciaparra 2.50 1.10
❑ 264 Tony Gwynn 2.00 .90
❑ 265 Alex Rodriguez 2.50 1.10
❑ 266 Jose Canseco 1.00 .45
❑ 267 Jason Giambi 1.00 .45
❑ 268 Jeff Bagwell 1.25 .55
❑ 269 Carlos Delgado 1.00 .45
❑ 270 Tom Glavine 1.00 .45
❑ 271 Eric Davis .40 .18
❑ 272 Edgardo Alfonzo .40 .18
❑ 273 Tim Salmon .40 .18
❑ 274 Johnny Damon .40 .18
❑ 275 Rafael Palmeiro 1.00 .45
❑ 276 Denny Neagle .25 .11
❑ 277 Neifi Perez .25 .11
❑ 278 Roger Clemens 2.50 1.10
❑ 279 Brant Brown .25 .11
❑ 280 Kevin Brown .60 .25
❑ 281 Jay Bell .40 .18
❑ 282 Jay Buhner .40 .18
❑ 283 Matt Lawton .40 .18
❑ 284 Robin Ventura .40 .18
❑ 285 Juan Gonzalez 1.00 .45
❑ 286 Mo Vaughn .40 .18
❑ 287 Kevin Millwood .25 .11
❑ 288 Tino Martinez .40 .18
❑ 289 Justin Thompson .25 .11
❑ 290 Derek Jeter 4.00 1.80
❑ 291 Ben Davis .40 .18
❑ 292 Mike Lowell .40 .18
❑ 293 Calvin Murray .25 .11
❑ 294 Micah Bowie RC .25 .11
❑ 295 Lance Berkman 1.00 .45
❑ 296 Jason Marquis .40 .18
❑ 297 Chad Green .25 .11
❑ 298 Dee Brown .25 .11
❑ 299 Jerry Hairston Jr. .40 .18
❑ 300 Gabe Kapler .40 .18
❑ 301 Brent Stentz RC 1.00 .45
❑ 302 Scott Mullen RC .25 .11
❑ 303 Brandon Reed .25 .11
❑ 304 Shea Hillenbrand RC 5.00 2.20
❑ 305 J.D. Closser RC 3.00 1.35
❑ 306 Gary Matthews Jr. .25 .11
❑ 307 Toby Hall RC 8.00 3.60
❑ 308 Jason Phillips RC 1.50 .70
❑ 309 Jose Macias RC .25 .11
❑ 310 Jung Bong RC 3.00 1.35
❑ 311 Ramon Soler RC 2.00 .90
❑ 312 Kelly Dransfeldt RC .25 .11
❑ 313 Carlos E. Hernandez RC .40 .18
❑ 314 Kevin Haverbusch .25 .11
❑ 315 Aaron Myette RC 2.00 .90

❑ 316 Chad Harville RC 1.00 .45
❑ 317 Kyle Farnsworth RC 2.50 1.10
❑ 318 Travis Dawkins RC 2.00 .90
❑ 319 Willie Martinez .25 .11
❑ 320 Carlos Lee .40 .18
❑ 321 Carlos Pena RC 10.00 4.50
❑ 322 Peter Bergeron RC 3.00 1.35
❑ 323 A.J. Burnett RC 5.00 2.20
❑ 324 Bucky Jacobsen RC .25 .11
❑ 325 Mo Bruce RC .25 .11
❑ 326 Reggie Taylor .25 .11
❑ 327 Jackie Rexrode .25 .11
❑ 328 Alvin Morrow RC 1.50 .70
❑ 329 Carlos Beltran .40 .18
❑ 330 Eric Chavez .40 .18
❑ 331 John Patterson .25 .11
❑ 332 Jayson Werth .25 .11
❑ 333 Richie Sexson .40 .18
❑ 334 Randy Wolf .25 .11
❑ 335 Eli Marrero .25 .11
❑ 336 Paul LoDuca .40 .18
❑ 337 J.D Smart .25 .11
❑ 338 Ryan Minor .25 .11
❑ 339 Kris Benson .40 .18
❑ 340 George Lombard .25 .11
❑ 341 Troy Glaus 1.00 .45
❑ 342 Eddie Yarnall .25 .11
❑ 343 Kip Wells RC 3.00 1.35
❑ 344 C.C. Sabathia RC 12.00 5.50
❑ 345 Sean Burroughs RC 15.00 6.75
❑ 346 Felipe Lopez RC 6.00 2.70
❑ 347 Ryan Rupe RC 1.50 .70
❑ 348 Orber Moreno RC 1.50 .70
❑ 349 Rafael Roque RC .25 .11
❑ 350 Alfonso Soriano RC 15.00 6.75
❑ 351 Pablo Ozuna .25 .11
❑ 352 Corey Patterson RC 10.00 4.50
❑ 353 Braden Looper .25 .11
❑ 354 Robbie Bell .25 .11
❑ 355 Mark Mulder RC 12.00 5.50
❑ 356 Angel Pena .25 .11
❑ 357 Kevin McGlinchy .25 .11
❑ 358 M.Restovich RC 6.00 2.70
❑ 359 Eric DuBose .25 .11
❑ 360 Geoff Jenkins .40 .18
❑ 361 Mark Harriger RC .25 .11
❑ 362 Junior Herndon RC 2.00 .90
❑ 363 Tim Raines Jr. RC 4.00 1.80
❑ 364 Rafael Furcal RC 10.00 4.50
❑ 365 Marcus Giles RC 8.00 3.60
❑ 366 Ted Lilly .25 .11
❑ 367 Jorge Toca RC 1.50 .70
❑ 368 David Kelton RC 5.00 2.20
❑ 369 Adam Dunn RC 40.00 18.00
❑ 370 Guillermo Mota RC .25 .11
❑ 371 Brett Laxton RC .25 .11
❑ 372 Travis Harper RC 1.00 .45
❑ 373 Tom Davey RC .25 .11
❑ 374 Darren Blakely RC 2.00 .90
❑ 375 Tim Hudson RC 15.00 6.75
❑ 376 Jason Romano .25 .11
❑ 377 Dan Reichert .25 .11
❑ 378 Julio Lugo RC 3.00 1.35
❑ 379 Jose Garcia RC 1.50 .70
❑ 380 Erubiel Durazo RC 6.00 2.70
❑ 381 Jose Jimenez .25 .11
❑ 382 Chris Fussell .25 .11
❑ 383 Steve Lomasney .25 .11
❑ 384 Juan Pena RC 1.50 .70
❑ 385 Allen Levrault RC 3.00 1.35
❑ 386 Juan Rivera RC 8.00 3.60
❑ 387 Steve Colyer RC 1.50 .70
❑ 388 Joe Nathan RC .25 .11
❑ 389 Ron Walker RC .25 .11
❑ 390 Nick Bierbrodt .25 .11
❑ 391 Luke Prokopec RC 4.00 1.80
❑ 392 Dave Roberts RC .25 .11
❑ 393 Mike Darr .25 .11
❑ 394 Abraham Nunez RC 5.00 2.20
❑ 395 G.Chiaramonte RC 1.50 .70
❑ 396 J.Van Buren RC 2.00 .90
❑ 397 Mike Kusiewicz .25 .11
❑ 398 Matt Wise RC .25 .11
❑ 399 Joe McEwing RC .40 .18
❑ 400 Matt Holliday RC 3.00 1.35
❑ 401 Willi Mo Pena RC 10.00 4.50
❑ 402 Ruben Quevedo RC 3.00 1.35
❑ 403 Rob Ryan RC .25 .11
❑ 404 Freddy Garcia RC 10.00 4.50
❑ 405 Kevin Eberwein RC 1.50 .70
❑ 406 Jesus Colome RC 3.00 1.35
❑ 407 Chris Singleton .25 .11
❑ 408 Bubba Crosby RC 1.00 .45
❑ 409 Jesus Cordero RC 1.50 .70
❑ 410 Donny Leon .25 .11
❑ 411 G.Tomlinson RC 1.00 .45
❑ 412 Jeff Winchester RC 2.00 .90
❑ 413 Adam Piatt RC 4.00 1.80
❑ 414 Robert Stratton .25 .11
❑ 415 T.J. Tucker .25 .11
❑ 416 Ryan Langerhans RC 2.00 .90
❑ 417 A.Shumaker RC .25 .11
❑ 418 Matt Miller RC .25 .11
❑ 419 Doug Clark RC .25 .11
❑ 420 Kory DeHaan RC .25 .11
❑ 421 David Eckstein RC 3.00 1.35
❑ 422 Brian Cooper RC 1.50 .70
❑ 423 Brady Clark RC .25 .11
❑ 424 Chris Magruder RC 1.00 .45
❑ 425 Bobby Seay RC 2.00 .90
❑ 426 Aubrey Huff RC 5.00 2.20
❑ 427 Mike Jerzembeck .25 .11
❑ 428 Matt Blank RC 1.00 .45
❑ 429 Benny Agbayani RC 4.00 1.80
❑ 430 Kevin Beirne RC .25 .11
❑ 431 Josh Hamilton RC 20.00 9.00
❑ 432 Josh Girdley RC 2.50 1.10
❑ 433 Kyle Snyder RC 1.50 .70
❑ 434 Mike Paradis RC 1.50 .70
❑ 435 Jason Jennings RC 5.00 2.20
❑ 436 David Walling RC 2.00 .90
❑ 437 Omar Ortiz RC 1.00 .45
❑ 438 Jay Gehrke RC 1.00 .45
❑ 439 Casey Burns RC 1.00 .45
❑ 440 Carl Crawford RC 6.00 2.70

2000 Bowman Chrome

	MINT	NRMT
COMPLETE SET (440)	300.00	135.00

❑ 1 Vladimir Guerrero 1.25 .55
❑ 2 Chipper Jones 2.00 .90
❑ 3 Todd Walker .25 .11
❑ 4 Barry Larkin 1.00 .45
❑ 5 Bernie Williams 1.00 .45
❑ 6 Todd Helton 1.25 .55
❑ 7 Jermaine Dye .40 .18
❑ 8 Brian Giles .40 .18
❑ 9 Freddy Garcia .60 .25
❑ 10 Greg Vaughn .40 .18
❑ 11 Alex Gonzalez .25 .11
❑ 12 Luis Gonzalez 1.00 .45
❑ 13 Ron Belliard .25 .11
❑ 14 Ben Grieve .40 .18
❑ 15 Carlos Delgado 1.00 .45
❑ 16 Brian Jordan .40 .18
❑ 17 Fernando Tatis .25 .11
❑ 18 Ryan Rupe .25 .11
❑ 19 Miguel Tejada .40 .18
❑ 20 Mark Grace 1.00 .45
❑ 21 Kenny Lofton .40 .18
❑ 22 Eric Karros .40 .18
❑ 23 Cliff Floyd .40 .18
❑ 24 John Halama .25 .11
❑ 25 Cristian Guzman .40 .18
❑ 26 Scott Williamson .25 .11
❑ 27 Mike Lieberthal .40 .18
❑ 28 Tim Hudson 1.00 .45
❑ 29 Warren Morris .25 .11
❑ 30 Pedro Martinez 1.25 .55
❑ 31 John Smoltz .40 .18
❑ 32 Ray Durham .40 .18
❑ 33 Chad Allen .25 .11
❑ 34 Tony Clark .40 .18
❑ 35 Tino Martinez .40 .18
❑ 36 J.T. Snow .40 .18
❑ 37 Kevin Brown .60 .25
❑ 38 Bartolo Colon .40 .18
❑ 39 Rey Ordonez .25 .11
❑ 40 Jeff Bagwell 1.25 .55
❑ 41 Ivan Rodriguez 1.00 .45
❑ 42 Eric Chavez .40 .18
❑ 43 Eric Milton .40 .18
❑ 44 Jose Canseco 1.00 .45
❑ 45 Shawn Green 1.00 .45
❑ 46 Rich Aurilia .40 .18
❑ 47 Roberto Alomar 1.00 .45
❑ 48 Brian Daubach .40 .18
❑ 49 Maggio Ordonez .40 .18
❑ 50 Derek Jeter 4.00 1.80
❑ 51 Kris Benson .40 .18
❑ 52 Albert Belle .40 .18
❑ 53 Rondell White .40 .18
❑ 54 Justin Thompson .25 .11
❑ 55 Nomar Garciaparra 2.50 1.10
❑ 56 Chuck Finley .40 .18
❑ 57 Omar Vizquel .40 .18
❑ 58 Luis Castillo .25 .11
❑ 59 Richard Hidalgo .40 .18
❑ 60 Barry Bonds 2.50 1.10
❑ 61 Craig Biggio .60 .25
❑ 62 Doug Glanville .25 .11
❑ 63 Gabe Kapler .40 .18
❑ 64 Johnny Damon .40 .18
❑ 65 Pokey Reese .25 .11
❑ 66 Andy Pettitte .40 .18
❑ 67 B.J. Surhoff .40 .18
❑ 68 Richie Sexson .40 .18
❑ 69 Javy Lopez .40 .18
❑ 70 Raul Mondesi .40 .18
❑ 71 Darin Erstad 1.00 .45
❑ 72 Kevin Millwood .25 .11
❑ 73 Ricky Ledee .25 .11
❑ 74 John Olerud .40 .18
❑ 75 Sean Casey .60 .25
❑ 76 Carlos Febles .25 .11
❑ 77 Paul O'Neill 1.00 .45
❑ 78 Bob Abreu .40 .18
❑ 79 Neifi Perez .25 .11
❑ 80 Tony Gwynn 2.00 .90
❑ 81 Russ Ortiz .40 .18
❑ 82 Matt Williams .60 .25
❑ 83 Chris Carpenter .25 .11
❑ 84 Roger Cedeno .25 .11
❑ 85 Tim Salmon .40 .18
❑ 86 Billy Koch .25 .11
❑ 87 Jeromy Burnitz .40 .18
❑ 88 Edgardo Alfonzo .40 .18
❑ 89 Jay Bell .40 .18
❑ 90 Manny Ramirez 1.25 .55
❑ 91 Frank Thomas 1.25 .55
❑ 92 Mike Mussina 1.00 .45
❑ 93 J.D. Drew 1.00 .45
❑ 94 Adrian Beltre .40 .18
❑ 95 Alex Rodriguez 2.50 1.10
❑ 96 Larry Walker .60 .25
❑ 97 Juan Encarnacion .40 .18
❑ 98 Mike Sweeney .40 .18
❑ 99 Rusty Greer .40 .18
❑ 100 Randy Johnson 1.25 .55
❑ 101 Jose Vidro .40 .18
❑ 102 Preston Wilson .40 .18
❑ 103 Greg Maddux 2.50 1.10
❑ 104 Jason Giambi 1.00 .45
❑ 105 Cal Ripken 4.00 1.80
❑ 106 Carlos Beltran .40 .18
❑ 107 Vinny Castilla .40 .18
❑ 108 Mariano Rivera .40 .18
❑ 109 Mo Vaughn .40 .18

❑ 110 Rafael Palmeiro 1.00 .45
❑ 111 Shannon Stewart .40 .18
❑ 112 Mike Hampton .40 .18
❑ 113 Joe Nathan .25 .11
❑ 114 Ben Davis .40 .18
❑ 115 Andruw Jones 1.00 .45
❑ 116 Robin Ventura .40 .18
❑ 117 Damion Easley .25 .11
❑ 118 Jeff Cirillo .40 .18
❑ 119 Kerry Wood 1.00 .45
❑ 120 Scott Rolen 1.00 .45
❑ 121 Sammy Sosa 2.00 .90
❑ 122 Ken Griffey Jr. 3.00 1.35
❑ 123 Shane Reynolds .25 .11
❑ 124 Troy Glaus 1.00 .45
❑ 125 Tom Glavine 1.00 .45
❑ 126 Michael Barrett .25 .11
❑ 127 Al Leiter .25 .11
❑ 128 Jason Kendall .40 .18
❑ 129 Roger Clemens 2.50 1.10
❑ 130 Juan Gonzalez 1.00 .45
❑ 131 Corey Koskie .40 .18
❑ 132 Curt Schilling 1.00 .45
❑ 133 Mike Piazza 2.50 1.10
❑ 134 Gary Sheffield .40 .18
❑ 135 Jim Thome 1.00 .45
❑ 136 Orlando Hernandez .40 .18
❑ 137 Ray Lankford .25 .11
❑ 138 Geoff Jenkins .40 .18
❑ 139 Jose Lima .25 .11
❑ 140 Mark McGwire 4.00 1.80
❑ 141 Adam Piatt .60 .25
❑ 142 Pat Manning RC 4.00 1.80
❑ 143 Marcos Castillo RC 1.50 .70
❑ 144 Leslie Brea RC 1.50 .70
❑ 145 Humberto Cota RC 3.00 1.35
❑ 146 Ben Petrick .25 .11
❑ 147 Kip Wells .40 .18
❑ 148 Wily Pena 1.00 .45
❑ 149 Chris Wakeland RC 1.50 .70
❑ 150 Brad Baker RC 4.00 1.80
❑ 151 Robbie Morrison RC 1.50 .70
❑ 152 Reggie Taylor .25 .11
❑ 153 Matt Ginter RC 2.50 1.10
❑ 154 Peter Bergeron .25 .11
❑ 155 Roosevelt Brown .25 .11
❑ 156 Matt Cepicky RC 2.00 .90
❑ 157 Ramon Castro .25 .11
❑ 158 Brad Baisley RC 2.50 1.10
❑ 159 Jason Hart RC 10.00 4.50
❑ 160 Mitch Meluskey .25 .11
❑ 161 Chad Harville .25 .11
❑ 162 Brian Cooper .25 .11
❑ 163 Marcus Giles .40 .18
❑ 164 Jim Morris .25 .11
❑ 165 Geoff Goetz .25 .11
❑ 166 Bobby Bradley RC 4.00 1.80
❑ 167 Rob Bell .25 .11
❑ 168 Joe Crede .40 .18
❑ 169 Michael Restovich .40 .18
❑ 170 Quincy Foster RC 1.50 .70
❑ 171 Enrique Cruz RC 4.00 1.80
❑ 172 Mark Quinn .40 .18
❑ 173 Nick Johnson 1.00 .45
❑ 174 Jeff Liefer .25 .11
❑ 175 Kevin Mench RC 8.00 3.60
❑ 176 Steve Lomasney .25 .11
❑ 177 Jayson Werth .25 .11
❑ 178 Tim Drew .25 .11
❑ 179 Chip Ambres .40 .18
❑ 180 Ryan Anderson .40 .18
❑ 181 Matt Blank .25 .11
❑ 182 G. Chiaramonte .25 .11
❑ 183 Corey Myers RC 2.50 1.10
❑ 184 Jeff Yoder .25 .11
❑ 185 Craig Dingman RC 1.50 .70
❑ 186 Jon Hamilton RC 2.00 .90
❑ 187 Toby Hall .60 .25
❑ 188 Russell Branyan .40 .18
❑ 189 Brian Falkenborg RC 1.50 .70
❑ 190 Aaron Harang RC 2.00 .90
❑ 191 Juan Pena .25 .11
❑ 192 Chin-Hui Tsao RC 5.00 2.20
❑ 193 Alfonso Soriano 1.00 .45
❑ 194 Alejandro Diaz RC 2.00 .90
❑ 195 Carlos Pena 1.00 .45
❑ 196 Kevin Nicholson .25 .11
❑ 197 Mo Bruce .25 .11
❑ 198 C.C. Sabathia 1.00 .45
❑ 199 Carl Crawford .40 .18
❑ 200 Rafael Furcal 1.00 .45
❑ 201 Andrew Beinbrink RC 1.50 .70
❑ 202 Jimmy Osting .25 .11
❑ 203 Aaron McNeal RC 2.00 .90
❑ 204 Brett Laxton .25 .11
❑ 205 Chris George .40 .18
❑ 206 Felipe Lopez .40 .18
❑ 207 Ben Sheets RC 8.00 3.60
❑ 208 Mike Meyers RC 2.00 .90
❑ 209 Jason Conti .25 .11
❑ 210 Milton Bradley .25 .11
❑ 211 Chris Mears RC 1.50 .70
❑ 212 Carlos Hernandez RC 6.00 2.70
❑ 213 Jason Romano .25 .11
❑ 214 Geofrey Tomlinson .25 .11
❑ 215 Jimmy Rollins .40 .18
❑ 216 Pablo Ozuna .25 .11
❑ 217 Steve Cox .25 .11
❑ 218 Terrence Long .40 .18
❑ 219 Jeff DaVanon RC 1.50 .70
❑ 220 Rick Ankiel 1.00 .45
❑ 221 Jason Standridge .25 .11
❑ 222 Tony Armas Jr. .40 .18
❑ 223 Jason Tyner .25 .11
❑ 224 Ramon Ortiz .40 .18
❑ 225 Daryle Ward .25 .11
❑ 226 Enger Veras RC 1.50 .70
❑ 227 Chris Jones .25 .11
❑ 228 Eric Cammack RC 1.50 .70
❑ 229 Ruben Mateo .40 .18
❑ 230 Ken Harvey RC 8.00 3.60
❑ 231 Jake Westbrook .25 .11
❑ 232 Rob Purvis RC 1.50 .70
❑ 233 Choo Freeman .40 .18
❑ 234 Aramis Ramirez .40 .18
❑ 235 A.J. Burnett .40 .18
❑ 236 Kevin Barker .25 .11
❑ 237 Chance Caple RC 2.50 1.10
❑ 238 Jarrod Washburn .25 .11
❑ 239 Lance Berkman 1.00 .45
❑ 240 Michael Wenner RC 1.50 .70
❑ 241 Alex Sanchez .25 .11
❑ 242 Pat Daneker .25 .11
❑ 243 Grant Roberts .25 .11
❑ 244 Mark Ellis RC 3.00 1.35
❑ 245 Donny Leon .25 .11
❑ 246 David Eckstein .25 .11
❑ 247 Dicky Gonzalez RC 2.00 .90
❑ 248 John Patterson .25 .11
❑ 249 Chad Green .25 .11
❑ 250 Scot Shields RC 1.50 .70
❑ 251 Troy Cameron .25 .11
❑ 252 Jose Molina .25 .11
❑ 253 Rob Pugmire RC 2.00 .90
❑ 254 Rick Elder .40 .18
❑ 255 Sean Burroughs 1.00 .45
❑ 256 Josh Kalinowski RC 1.50 .70
❑ 257 Matt LeCroy .25 .11
❑ 258 Alex Graman RC 3.00 1.35
❑ 259 Juan Silvestre RC 2.50 1.10
❑ 260 Brady Clark .40 .18
❑ 261 Rico Washington RC 2.00 .90
❑ 262 Gary Matthews Jr. .25 .11
❑ 263 Matt Wise .25 .11
❑ 264 Keith Reed RC 3.00 1.35
❑ 265 Santiago Ramirez RC 1.50 .70
❑ 266 Ben Broussard RC 5.00 2.20
❑ 267 Ryan Langerhans .25 .11
❑ 268 Juan Rivera .40 .18
❑ 269 Shawn Gallagher .25 .11
❑ 270 Jorge Toca .25 .11
❑ 271 Brad Lidge .25 .11
❑ 272 Leoncio Estrella RC 1.50 .70
❑ 273 Ruben Quevedo .25 .11
❑ 274 Jack Cust .40 .18
❑ 275 T.J. Tucker .25 .11
❑ 276 Mike Colangelo .25 .11
❑ 277 Brian Schneider .25 .11
❑ 278 Calvin Murray .25 .11
❑ 279 Josh Girdley .25 .11
❑ 280 Mike Paradis .25 .11
❑ 281 Chad Hermansen .25 .11
❑ 282 Ty Howington RC 5.00 2.20
❑ 283 Aaron Myette .40 .18
❑ 284 D'Angelo Jimenez .40 .18
❑ 285 Dernell Stenson .25 .11
❑ 286 Jerry Hairston Jr. .25 .11
❑ 287 Gary Majewski RC 2.00 .90
❑ 288 Derrin Ebert .25 .11
❑ 289 Steve Fish RC 1.50 .70
❑ 290 Carlos E. Hernandez .25 .11
❑ 291 Allen Levrault .25 .11
❑ 292 Sean McNally RC 1.50 .70
❑ 293 Randey Dorame RC 2.00 .90
❑ 294 Wes Anderson RC 2.50 1.10
❑ 295 B.J. Ryan .25 .11
❑ 296 Alan Webb RC 1.50 .70
❑ 297 Brandon Inge RC 4.00 1.80
❑ 298 David Walling .25 .11
❑ 299 Sun Woo Kim RC 2.50 1.10
❑ 300 Pat Burrell 1.00 .45
❑ 301 Rick Guttormson RC 1.50 .70
❑ 302 Gil Meche .25 .11
❑ 303 Carlos Zambrano RC 4.00 1.80
❑ 304 Eric Byrnes UER RC 2.00 .90
Bo Porter pictured
❑ 305 Robb Quinlan RC 2.00 .90
❑ 306 Jackie Rexrode .25 .11
❑ 307 Nate Bump .25 .11
❑ 308 Sean DePaula RC 1.50 .70
❑ 309 Matt Riley .25 .11
❑ 310 Ryan Minor .25 .11
❑ 311 J.J. Davis .40 .18
❑ 312 Randy Wolf .25 .11
❑ 313 Jason Jennings .40 .18
❑ 314 Scott Seabol RC 1.50 .70
❑ 315 Doug Davis .25 .11
❑ 316 Todd Moser RC 1.50 .70
❑ 317 Rob Ryan .25 .11
❑ 318 Bubba Crosby .25 .11
❑ 319 Ryan Knox RC 5.00 2.20
❑ 320 Mario Encarnacion .25 .11
❑ 321 F.Rodriguez RC 2.50 1.10
❑ 322 Michael Cuddyer .40 .18
❑ 323 Ed Yarnall .25 .11
❑ 324 Cesar Saba RC 2.50 1.10
❑ 325 Travis Dawkins .40 .18
❑ 326 Alex Escobar .40 .18
❑ 327 Julio Zuleta RC 2.50 1.10
❑ 328 Josh Hamilton 1.25 .55
❑ 329 Carlos Urquiola RC 4.00 1.80
❑ 330 Matt Belisle .40 .18
❑ 331 Kurt Ainsworth RC 4.00 1.80
❑ 332 Tim Raines Jr. .40 .18
❑ 333 Eric Munson .40 .18
❑ 334 Donzell McDonald .25 .11
❑ 335 Larry Bigbie RC 3.00 1.35
❑ 336 Matt Watson RC 1.50 .70
❑ 337 Aubrey Huff .25 .11
❑ 338 Julio Ramirez .25 .11
❑ 339 Jason Grabowski RC 2.50 1.10
❑ 340 Jon Garland .25 .11
❑ 341 Austin Kearns 1.00 .45
❑ 342 Josh Pressley RC 2.00 .90
❑ 343 Miguel Olivo RC 2.00 .90
❑ 344 Julio Lugo .25 .11
❑ 345 Roberto Vaz .25 .11
❑ 346 Ramon Soler .25 .11
❑ 347 Brandon Phillips RC 4.00 1.80
❑ 348 Vince Faison RC 2.50 1.10
❑ 349 Mike Venafro .25 .11
❑ 350 Rick Asadoorian RC 4.00 1.80
❑ 351 B.J. Garbe RC 5.00 2.20
❑ 352 Dan Reichert .25 .11
❑ 353 Jason Stumm RC 3.00 1.35
❑ 354 Ruben Salazar RC 4.00 1.80
❑ 355 Francisco Cordero .25 .11
❑ 356 Juan Guzman RC 1.50 .70
❑ 357 Mike Bacsik RC 1.50 .70
❑ 358 Jared Sandberg .25 .11
❑ 359 Rod Barajas .25 .11
❑ 360 Junior Brignac RC 1.50 .70
❑ 361 J.M. Gold .25 .11
❑ 362 Octavio Dotel .25 .11
❑ 363 David Kelton .40 .18
❑ 364 Scott Morgan .25 .11
❑ 365 Wascar Serrano RC 2.50 1.10
❑ 366 Wilton Veras .25 .11

Card	MINT	NRMT
❑ 367 Eugene Kingsale	.25	.11
❑ 368 Ted Lilly	.25	.11
❑ 369 George Lombard	.25	.11
❑ 370 Chris Haas	.25	.11
❑ 371 Wilton Pena RC	1.50	.70
❑ 372 Vernon Wells	.40	.18
❑ 373 Keith Ginter RC	6.00	2.70
❑ 374 Jeff Heaverlo RC	4.00	1.80
❑ 375 Calvin Pickering	.25	.11
❑ 376 Mike Lamb RC	2.00	.90
❑ 377 Kyle Snyder	.25	.11
❑ 378 Javier Cardona RC	1.50	.70
❑ 379 Aaron Rowand RC	4.00	1.80
❑ 380 Dee Brown	.25	.11
❑ 381 Brett Myers RC	3.00	1.35
❑ 382 Abraham Nunez	.40	.18
❑ 383 Eric Valent	.40	.18
❑ 384 Jody Gerut RC	1.50	.70
❑ 385 Adam Dunn	2.50	1.10
❑ 386 Jay Gehrke	.25	.11
❑ 387 Omar Ortiz	.25	.11
❑ 388 Darnell McDonald	.25	.11
❑ 389 Tony Schrager RC	1.50	.70
❑ 390 J.D. Closser	.25	.11
❑ 391 Ben Christensen RC	2.00	.90
❑ 392 Adam Kennedy	.25	.11
❑ 393 Nick Green RC	1.25	.55
❑ 394 Ramon Hernandez	.25	.11
❑ 395 Roy Oswalt RC	15.00	6.75
❑ 396 Andy Tracy RC	1.50	.70
❑ 397 Eric Gagne	.25	.11
❑ 398 Michael Tejera RC	1.50	.70
❑ 399 Adam Everett	.40	.18
❑ 400 Corey Patterson	1.00	.45
❑ 401 Gary Knotts RC	1.50	.70
❑ 402 Ryan Christianson RC	4.00	1.80
❑ 403 Eric Ireland RC	2.00	.90
❑ 404 Andrew Good RC	1.50	.70
❑ 405 Brad Penny	.40	.18
❑ 406 Jason LaRue	.25	.11
❑ 407 Kit Pellow	.25	.11
❑ 408 Kevin Beirne	.25	.11
❑ 409 Kelly Dransfeldt	.25	.11
❑ 410 Jason Grilli	.25	.11
❑ 411 Scott Downs RC	1.50	.70
❑ 412 Jesus Colome	.40	.18
❑ 413 John Sneed RC	1.50	.70
❑ 414 Tony McKnight	.25	.11
❑ 415 Luis Rivera	.25	.11
❑ 416 Adam Eaton	.40	.18
❑ 417 Mike MacDougal RC	2.00	.90
❑ 418 Mike Nannini	.25	.11
❑ 419 Barry Zito RC	10.00	4.50
❑ 420 DeWayne Wise	.25	.11
❑ 421 Jason Dellaero	.25	.11
❑ 422 Chad Moeller	.25	.11
❑ 423 Jason Marquis	.40	.18
❑ 424 Tim Redding RC	6.00	2.70
❑ 425 Mark Mulder	1.00	.45
❑ 426 Josh Paul	.25	.11
❑ 427 Chris Enochs	.25	.11
❑ 428 W.Rodriguez RC	3.00	1.35
❑ 429 Kevin Witt	.25	.11
❑ 430 Scott Sobkowiak RC	2.00	.90
❑ 431 McKay Christensen	.25	.11
❑ 432 Jung Bong	.25	.11
❑ 433 Keith Evans RC	1.50	.70
❑ 434 Garry Maddox Jr. RC	1.50	.70
❑ 435 Ramon Santiago RC	3.00	1.35
❑ 436 Alex Cora	.25	.11
❑ 437 Carlos Lee	.40	.18
❑ 438 Jason Repko RC	2.50	1.10
❑ 439 Matt Burch	.25	.11
❑ 440 Shawn Sonnier RC	1.50	.70

2000 Bowman Chrome Draft Picks

	MINT	NRMT
COMP.FACT.SET (110)	70.00	32.00

Card	MINT	NRMT
❑ 1 Pat Burrell	1.00	.45
❑ 2 Rafael Furcal	1.00	.45
❑ 3 Grant Roberts	.25	.11
❑ 4 Barry Zito	4.00	1.80
❑ 5 Julio Zuleta	1.25	.55
❑ 6 Mark Mulder	1.00	.45
❑ 7 Rob Bell	.25	.11
❑ 8 Adam Piatt	.60	.25
❑ 9 Mike Lamb	.60	.25
❑ 10 Pablo Ozuna	.25	.11
❑ 11 Jason Tyner	.25	.11
❑ 12 Jason Marquis	.40	.18
❑ 13 Eric Munson	.40	.18
❑ 14 Seth Etherton	.25	.11
❑ 15 Milton Bradley	.25	.11
❑ 16 Nick Green	.40	.18
❑ 17 Chin-Feng Chen RC	6.00	2.70
❑ 18 Matt Boone RC	1.25	.55
❑ 19 Kevin Gregg RC	1.00	.45
❑ 20 Eddy Garabito RC	1.00	.45
❑ 21 Aaron Capista RC	1.00	.45
❑ 22 Esteban German RC	2.00	.90
❑ 23 Derek Thompson RC	1.00	.45
❑ 24 Phil Merrell RC	1.00	.45
❑ 25 Brian O'Connor RC	1.50	.70
❑ 26 Yamid Haad	.25	.11
❑ 27 Hector Mercado RC	1.00	.45
❑ 28 Jason Woolf RC	1.00	.45
❑ 29 Eddy Furniss RC	1.00	.45
❑ 30 Cha Sueng Baek RC	2.50	1.10
❑ 31 Colby Lewis RC	1.50	.70
❑ 32 Pasqual Coco RC	1.00	.45
❑ 33 Jorge Cantu RC	1.00	.45
❑ 34 Erasmo Ramirez RC	1.00	.45
❑ 35 Bobby Kielty RC	3.00	1.35
❑ 36 Joaquin Benoit RC	2.50	1.10
❑ 37 Brian Esposito RC	1.25	.55
❑ 38 Michael Wenner	.40	.18
❑ 39 Juan Rincon RC	1.00	.45
❑ 40 Yorvit Torrealba RC	1.00	.45
❑ 41 Chad Durham RC	1.00	.45
❑ 42 Jim Mann RC	1.00	.45
❑ 43 Shane Loux RC	1.50	.70
❑ 44 Luis Rivas	.40	.18
❑ 45 Ken Chenard RC	1.00	.45
❑ 46 Mike Lockwood RC	1.00	.45
❑ 47 Yovanny Lara RC	1.00	.45
❑ 48 Bubba Carpenter RC	1.00	.45
❑ 49 Ryan Dittfurth RC	1.00	.45
❑ 50 John Stephens RC	2.00	.90
❑ 51 Pedro Feliz RC	3.00	1.35
❑ 52 Kenny Kelly RC	2.50	1.10
❑ 53 Neil Jenkins RC	2.50	1.10
❑ 54 Mike Glendenning RC	1.00	.45
❑ 55 Bo Porter	.25	.11
❑ 56 Eric Byrnes	.40	.18
❑ 57 Tony Alvarez RC	2.50	1.10
❑ 58 Kazuhiro Sasaki RC	5.00	2.20
❑ 59 Chad Durbin RC	1.00	.45
❑ 60 Mike Bynum RC	2.50	1.10
❑ 61 Travis Wilson RC	2.50	1.10
❑ 62 Jose Leon RC	1.00	.45
❑ 63 Ryan Vogelsong RC	2.50	1.10
❑ 64 Geraldo Guzman RC	1.00	.45
❑ 65 Craig Anderson RC	2.00	.90
❑ 66 Carlos Silva RC	1.00	.45
❑ 67 Brad Thomas RC	1.25	.55
❑ 68 Chin-Hui Tsao	2.00	.90
❑ 69 Mark Buehrle RC	8.00	3.60
❑ 70 Juan Salas RC	1.50	.70
❑ 71 Denny Abreu RC	1.00	.45
❑ 72 Keith McDonald RC	1.00	.45
❑ 73 Chris Richard RC	3.00	1.35
❑ 74 Tomas De la Rosa RC	1.00	.45
❑ 75 Vicente Padilla RC	1.00	.45
❑ 76 Justin Brunette RC	1.00	.45
❑ 77 Scott Linebrink RC	1.00	.45
❑ 78 Jeff Sparks RC	1.00	.45
❑ 79 Tike Redman RC	1.25	.55
❑ 80 John Lackey RC	1.50	.70
❑ 81 Joe Strong RC	1.00	.45
❑ 82 Brian Tollberg RC	1.00	.45
❑ 83 Steve Sisco RC	1.00	.45
❑ 84 Chris Clapinski RC	1.00	.45
❑ 85 Augie Ojeda RC	1.00	.45
❑ 86 Adrian Gonzalez RC	12.00	5.50
❑ 87 Mike Stodolka RC	2.50	1.10
❑ 88 Adam Johnson RC	3.00	1.35
❑ 89 Matt Wheatland RC	2.50	1.10
❑ 90 Corey Smith RC	4.00	1.80
❑ 91 Rocco Baldelli RC	3.00	1.35
❑ 92 Keith Bucktrot RC	1.50	.70
❑ 93 Adam Wainwright RC	4.00	1.80
❑ 94 Blaine Boyer RC	1.50	.70
❑ 95 Aaron Herr RC	2.00	.90
❑ 96 Scott Thorman RC	3.00	1.35
❑ 97 Bryan Digby RC	1.50	.70
❑ 98 Josh Shortslef RC	2.00	.90
❑ 99 Sean Smith RC	1.50	.70
❑ 100 Alex Cruz RC	1.00	.45
❑ 101 Marc Love RC	1.50	.70
❑ 102 Kevin Lee RC	1.00	.45
❑ 103 Timo Perez RC	3.00	1.35
❑ 104 Alex Cabrera RC	2.50	1.10
❑ 105 Shane Heams RC	1.50	.70
❑ 106 Tripper Johnson RC	2.50	1.10
❑ 107 Brent Abernathy RC	3.00	1.35
❑ 108 John Cotton RC	1.00	.45
❑ 109 Brad Wilkerson RC	2.50	1.10
❑ 110 Jon Rauch RC	6.00	2.70

2001 Bowman Chrome

	MINT	NRMT
COMP.SET w/o SP's (220)	50.00	22.00
COMMON (1-110/201-310)	.25	.11
COM.REF (111-200/311-330)	5.00	2.20
COMMON AU REF (331-350)	50.00	22.00

Card	MINT	NRMT
❑ 1 Jason Giambi	1.00	.45
❑ 2 Rafael Furcal	.40	.18
❑ 3 Bernie Williams	1.00	.45
❑ 4 Kenny Lofton	.40	.18
❑ 5 Al Leiter	.40	.18
❑ 6 Albert Belle	.40	.18
❑ 7 Craig Biggio	.60	.25
❑ 8 Mark Mulder	.60	.25
❑ 9 Carlos Delgado	1.00	.45
❑ 10 Darin Erstad	1.00	.45
❑ 11 Richie Sexson	.40	.18
❑ 12 Randy Johnson	1.25	.55
❑ 13 Greg Maddux	2.50	1.10
❑ 14 Orlando Hernandez	.40	.18
❑ 15 Javier Vazquez	.40	.18
❑ 16 Jeff Kent	.60	.25
❑ 17 Jim Thome	1.00	.45
❑ 18 John Olerud	.40	.18
❑ 19 Jason Kendall	.40	.18

❑ 20 Scott Rolen 1.00 .45
❑ 21 Tony Gwynn 2.00 .90
❑ 22 Edgardo Alfonzo .40 .18
❑ 23 Pokey Reese .25 .11
❑ 24 Todd Helton 1.25 .55
❑ 25 Mark Quinn .40 .18
❑ 26 Dean Palmer .40 .18
❑ 27 Ray Durham .40 .18
❑ 28 Rafael Palmeiro 1.00 .45
❑ 29 Carl Everett .40 .18
❑ 30 Vladimir Guerrero 1.25 .55
❑ 31 Livan Hernandez .40 .18
❑ 32 Preston Wilson .40 .18
❑ 33 Jose Vidro .40 .18
❑ 34 Fred McGriff .60 .25
❑ 35 Kevin Brown .40 .18
❑ 36 Miguel Tejada .40 .18
❑ 37 Chipper Jones 2.00 .90
❑ 38 Edgar Martinez .60 .25
❑ 39 Tony Batista .40 .18
❑ 40 Jorge Posada .40 .18
❑ 41 Sammy Sosa 2.00 .90
❑ 42 Gary Sheffield .40 .18
❑ 43 Bartolo Colon .40 .18
❑ 44 Pat Burrell .40 .18
❑ 45 Jay Payton .25 .11
❑ 46 Mike Mussina 1.00 .45
❑ 47 Nomar Garciaparra 2.50 1.10
❑ 48 Darren Dreifort .25 .11
❑ 49 Richard Hidalgo .40 .18
❑ 50 Troy Glaus 1.00 .45
❑ 51 Ben Grieve .40 .18
❑ 52 Jim Edmonds .60 .25
❑ 53 Raul Mondesi .40 .18
❑ 54 Andruw Jones 1.00 .45
❑ 55 Mike Sweeney .40 .18
❑ 56 Derek Jeter 4.00 1.80
❑ 57 Ruben Mateo .40 .18
❑ 58 Cristian Guzman .40 .18
❑ 59 Mike Hampton .40 .18
❑ 60 J.D. Drew 1.00 .45
❑ 61 Matt Lawton .40 .18
❑ 62 Moises Alou .40 .18
❑ 63 Terrence Long .40 .18
❑ 64 Geoff Jenkins .40 .18
❑ 65 Manny Ramirez 1.25 .55
❑ 66 Johnny Damon .40 .18
❑ 67 Pedro Martinez 1.25 .55
❑ 68 Juan Gonzalez 1.00 .45
❑ 69 Roger Clemens 2.50 1.10
❑ 70 Carlos Beltran .40 .18
❑ 71 Roberto Alomar 1.00 .45
❑ 72 Barry Bonds 2.50 1.10
❑ 73 Tim Hudson 1.00 .45
❑ 74 Tom Glavine 1.00 .45
❑ 75 Jeromy Burnitz .40 .18
❑ 76 Adrian Beltre .40 .18
❑ 77 Mike Piazza 2.50 1.10
❑ 78 Kerry Wood 1.00 .45
❑ 79 Steve Finley .40 .18
❑ 80 Bob Abreu .40 .18
❑ 81 Neifi Perez .25 .11
❑ 82 Mark Redman .25 .11
❑ 83 Paul Konerko .40 .18
❑ 84 Jermaine Dye .40 .18
❑ 85 Brian Giles .40 .18
❑ 86 Ivan Rodriguez 1.00 .45
❑ 87 Adam Kennedy .25 .11
❑ 88 Eric Chavez .40 .18
❑ 89 Billy Koch .25 .11
❑ 90 Shawn Green 1.00 .45
❑ 91 Matt Williams .60 .25
❑ 92 Greg Vaughn .40 .18
❑ 93 Jeff Cirillo .40 .18
❑ 94 Frank Thomas 1.25 .55
❑ 95 David Justice .40 .18
❑ 96 Cal Ripken 4.00 1.80
❑ 97 Curt Schilling 1.00 .45
❑ 98 Barry Zito 1.00 .45
❑ 99 Brian Jordan .40 .18
❑ 100 Chan Ho Park .40 .18
❑ 101 J.T. Snow .40 .18
❑ 102 Kazuhiro Sasaki 1.00 .45
❑ 103 Alex Rodriguez 2.50 1.10
❑ 104 Mariano Rivera .40 .18
❑ 105 Eric Milton .40 .18
❑ 106 Andy Pettitte .40 .18
❑ 107 Ken Griffey Jr. 3.00 1.35
❑ 108 Bengie Molina .25 .11
❑ 109 Jeff Bagwell 1.25 .55
❑ 110 Mark McGwire 4.00 1.80
❑ 111 Dan Tosca RC 8.00 3.60
❑ 112 Sergio Contreras RC 8.00 3.60
❑ 113 Mitch Jones RC 8.00 3.60
❑ 114 Ramon Carvajal RC 8.00 3.60
❑ 115 Ryan Madson RC 8.00 3.60
❑ 116 Hank Blalock RC 40.00 18.00
❑ 117 Ben Washburn RC 8.00 3.60
❑ 118 Erick Almonte RC 10.00 4.50
❑ 119 Shawn Fagan RC 8.00 3.60
❑ 120 Gary Johnson RC 8.00 3.60
❑ 121 Brett Evert RC 10.00 4.50
❑ 122 Joe Hamer RC 8.00 3.60
❑ 123 Yhency Brazoban RC 8.00 3.60
❑ 124 Domingo Guante RC 8.00 3.60
❑ 125 Deivi Mendez RC 10.00 4.50
❑ 126 Adrian Hernandez RC 5.00 2.20
❑ 127 Reggie Abercrombie RC 8.00 3.60
❑ 128 Steve Bennett RC 5.00 2.20
❑ 129 Matt White RC 8.00 3.60
❑ 130 Brian Hitchcox RC 5.00 2.20
❑ 131 Deivis Santos RC 10.00 4.50
❑ 132 Luis Montanez RC 12.00 5.50
❑ 133 Eric Reynolds RC 5.00 2.20
❑ 134 Denny Bautista RC 10.00 4.50
❑ 135 Hector Garcia RC 8.00 3.60
❑ 136 Joe Thurston RC 8.00 3.60
❑ 137 Tsuyoshi Shinjo RC 15.00 6.75
❑ 138 Elpidio Guzman RC 8.00 3.60
❑ 139 Brian Bass RC 8.00 3.60
❑ 140 Mark Burnett RC 8.00 3.60
❑ 141 Russ Jacobson UER 5.00 2.20
Last name misspelled Jacobsen on front
❑ 142 Travis Hafner RC 10.00 4.50
❑ 143 Wilson Betemit RC 25.00 11.00
❑ 144 Luke Lockwood RC 8.00 3.60
❑ 145 Noel Devarez RC 8.00 3.60
❑ 146 Doug Gredvig RC 8.00 3.60
❑ 147 Seung Song RC 12.00 5.50
❑ 148 Andy Van Hekken RC 10.00 4.50
❑ 149 Ryan Kohlmeier 5.00 2.20
❑ 150 Dee Haynes RC 8.00 3.60
❑ 151 Jim Journell RC 10.00 4.50
❑ 152 Chad Petty RC 10.00 4.50
❑ 153 Danny Borrell RC 8.00 3.60
❑ 154 David Krynzel 8.00 3.60
❑ 155 Octavio Martinez RC 8.00 3.60
❑ 156 David Parrish RC 10.00 4.50
❑ 157 Jason Miller RC 8.00 3.60
❑ 158 Corey Spencer RC 5.00 2.20
❑ 159 Maxim St. Pierre RC 8.00 3.60
❑ 160 Pat Magness RC 8.00 3.60
❑ 161 Ranier Olmedo RC 8.00 3.60
❑ 162 Brandon Mims RC 8.00 3.60
❑ 163 Phil Wilson RC 8.00 3.60
❑ 164 Jose Reyes RC 10.00 4.50
❑ 165 Matt Butler RC 8.00 3.60
❑ 166 Joel Pineiro 20.00 9.00
❑ 167 Ken Chenard 5.00 2.20
❑ 168 Alexis Gomez RC 8.00 3.60
❑ 169 Justin Morneau RC 15.00 6.75
❑ 170 Josh Fogg RC 5.00 2.20
❑ 171 Charles Frazier RC 8.00 3.60
❑ 172 Ryan Ludwick RC 12.00 5.50
❑ 173 Seth McClung RC 8.00 3.60
❑ 174 Justin Wayne RC 10.00 4.50
❑ 175 Rafael Soriano RC 10.00 4.50
❑ 176 Jared Abruzzo RC 8.00 3.60
❑ 177 Jason Richardson RC 8.00 3.60
❑ 178 Darwin Cubillan RC 5.00 2.20
❑ 179 Blake Williams RC 8.00 3.60
❑ 180 Valentino Pascucci RC 8.00 3.60
❑ 181 Ryan Hannaman RC 8.00 3.60
❑ 182 Steve Smyth RC 8.00 3.60
❑ 183 Jake Peavy RC 10.00 4.50
❑ 184 Onix Mercado RC 8.00 3.60
❑ 185 Luis Torres RC 8.00 3.60
❑ 186 Casey Fossum RC 12.00 5.50
❑ 187 Eduardo Figueroa RC 8.00 3.60
❑ 188 Bryan Barnowski RC 8.00 3.60
❑ 189 Jason Standridge 5.00 2.20
❑ 190 Marvin Seale RC 8.00 3.60
❑ 191 Steve Smitherman RC 8.00 3.60
❑ 192 Rafael Boitel RC 8.00 3.60
❑ 193 Dany Morban RC 8.00 3.60
❑ 194 Justin Woodrow RC 8.00 3.60
❑ 195 Ed Rogers RC 10.00 4.50
❑ 196 Ben Hendrickson RC 8.00 3.60
❑ 197 Thomas Mitchell 5.00 2.20
❑ 198 Adam Pettyjohn RC 8.00 3.60
❑ 199 Doug Nickle RC 5.00 2.20
❑ 200 Jason Jones RC 8.00 3.60
❑ 201 Larry Barnes .25 .11
❑ 202 Ben Diggins .40 .18
❑ 203 Dee Brown .25 .11
❑ 204 Rocco Baldelli .40 .18
❑ 205 Luis Terrero .25 .11
❑ 206 Milton Bradley .25 .11
❑ 207 Kurt Ainsworth .40 .18
❑ 208 Sean Burroughs 1.00 .45
❑ 209 Rick Asadoorian .40 .18
❑ 210 Ramon Castro .25 .11
❑ 211 Nick Neugebauer 1.00 .45
❑ 212 Aaron Myette .25 .11
❑ 213 Luis Matos .25 .11
❑ 214 Donnie Bridges .25 .11
❑ 215 Alex Cintron .25 .11
❑ 216 Bobby Kielty .25 .11
❑ 217 Matt Belisle .25 .11
❑ 218 Adam Everett .25 .11
❑ 219 John Lackey .25 .11
❑ 220 Adam Wainwright .40 .18
❑ 221 Jerry Hairston Jr. .25 .11
❑ 222 Mike Bynum .25 .11
❑ 223 Ryan Christianson .25 .11
❑ 224 J.J. Davis .25 .11
❑ 225 Alex Graman .25 .11
❑ 226 Abraham Nunez .40 .18
❑ 227 Sun Woo Kim .25 .11
❑ 228 Jimmy Rollins .40 .18
❑ 229 Ruben Salazar .25 .11
❑ 230 Josh Girdley .25 .11
❑ 231 Carl Crawford .40 .18
❑ 232 Ben Davis .40 .18
❑ 233 Jason Grabowski .25 .11
❑ 234 Chris George .40 .18
❑ 235 Roy Oswalt 1.00 .45
❑ 236 Brian Cole .25 .11
❑ 237 Corey Patterson .40 .18
❑ 238 Vernon Wells .40 .18
❑ 239 Brad Baker .40 .18
❑ 240 Gookie Dawkins .25 .11
❑ 241 Michael Cuddyer .40 .18
❑ 242 Ricardo Aramboles .25 .11
❑ 243 Ben Sheets .60 .25
❑ 244 Toby Hall .40 .18
❑ 245 Jack Cust .40 .18
❑ 246 Pedro Feliz .25 .11
❑ 247 Josh Beckett 1.00 .45
❑ 248 Alex Escobar .40 .18
❑ 249 Marcus Giles .40 .18
❑ 250 Jon Rauch .40 .18
❑ 251 Kevin Mench .60 .25
❑ 252 Shawn Sonnier .25 .11
❑ 253 Aaron Rowand .40 .18
❑ 254 C.C. Sabathia .60 .25
❑ 255 Bubba Crosby .25 .11
❑ 256 Josh Hamilton 1.00 .45
❑ 257 Carlos Hernandez .40 .18
❑ 258 Carlos Pena .40 .18
❑ 259 Miguel Cabrera .40 .18
❑ 260 Brandon Phillips .40 .18
❑ 261 Tony Pena Jr. .25 .11
❑ 262 Cristian Guerrero 1.00 .45
❑ 263 Jin Ho Cho .25 .11
❑ 264 Aaron Herr .25 .11
❑ 265 Keith Ginter .40 .18
❑ 266 Felipe Lopez .25 .11
❑ 267 Travis Harper .25 .11
❑ 268 Joe Torres .40 .18
❑ 269 Eric Byrnes .25 .11
❑ 270 Ben Christensen .25 .11
❑ 271 Aubrey Huff .25 .11
❑ 272 Lyle Overbay .40 .18
❑ 273 Vince Faison .25 .11
❑ 274 Bobby Bradley .40 .18
❑ 275 Joe Crede .40 .18

❑ 276 Matt Wheatland .25 .11
❑ 277 Grady Sizemore .40 .18
❑ 278 Adrian Gonzalez 1.25 .55
❑ 279 Tim Raines Jr. .25 .11
❑ 280 Phil Dumatrait .25 .11
❑ 281 Jason Hart .60 .25
❑ 282 David Kelton .40 .18
❑ 283 David Walling .25 .11
❑ 284 J.R. House 1.00 .45
❑ 285 Kenny Kelly .25 .11
❑ 286 Aaron McNeal .25 .11
❑ 287 Nick Johnson .40 .18
❑ 288 Scott Heard .40 .18
❑ 289 Brad Wilkerson .25 .11
❑ 290 Allen Levrault .25 .11
❑ 291 Chris Richard .40 .18
❑ 292 Jared Sandberg .25 .11
❑ 293 Tike Redman .25 .11
❑ 294 Adam Dunn 4.00 1.80
❑ 295 Josh Pressley .25 .11
❑ 296 Jose Ortiz .60 .25
❑ 297 Jason Romano .25 .11
❑ 298 Tim Redding .40 .18
❑ 299 Alex Gordon .25 .11
❑ 300 Ben Petrick .25 .11
❑ 301 Eric Munson .40 .18
❑ 302 Luis Rivas .25 .11
❑ 303 Matt Ginter .25 .11
❑ 304 Alfonso Soriano 1.00 .45
❑ 305 Wilfredo Rodriguez .25 .11
❑ 306 Brett Myers .25 .11
❑ 307 Scott Seabol .25 .11
❑ 308 Tony Alvarez .25 .11
❑ 309 Donzell McDonald .25 .11
❑ 310 Austin Kearns .60 .25
❑ 311 Will Ohman RC 8.00 3.60
❑ 312 Ryan Soules RC 5.00 2.20
❑ 313 Cody Ross RC 10.00 4.50
❑ 314 Bill Whitecotton RC 8.00 3.60
❑ 315 Mike Burns RC 5.00 2.20
❑ 316 Manuel Acosta RC 8.00 3.60
❑ 317 Lance Niekro RC 10.00 4.50
❑ 318 Travis Thompson RC 8.00 3.60
❑ 319 Zach Sorensen RC 8.00 3.60
❑ 320 Austin Evans RC 5.00 2.20
❑ 321 Brad Stiles RC 8.00 3.60
❑ 322 Joe Kennedy RC 10.00 4.50
❑ 323 Luke Martin RC 8.00 3.60
❑ 324 Juan Diaz RC 8.00 3.60
❑ 325 Pat Hallmark RC 5.00 2.20
❑ 326 Christian Parker RC 5.00 2.20
❑ 327 Ronny Corona RC 8.00 3.60
❑ 328 Jermaine Clark RC 5.00 2.20
❑ 329 Scott Dunn RC 8.00 3.60
❑ 330 Scott Chiasson RC 8.00 3.60
❑ 331 Greg Nash AU RC 125.00 55.00
❑ 332 Brad Cresse AU 60.00 27.00
❑ 333 John Buck AU RC 60.00 27.00
❑ 334 Freddie Bynum AU RC 50.00 22.00
❑ 335 Felix Diaz AU RC 50.00 22.00
❑ 336 Jason Belcher AU RC 60.00 27.00
❑ 337 Troy Farnsworth AU RC 50.00 22.00
❑ 338 Roberto Miniel AU RC 50.00 22.00
❑ 339 Esix Snead AU RC 60.00 27.00
❑ 340 Albert Pujols AU RC 400.00 180.00
❑ 340 Albert Pujols AU EXCH 400.00 180.00
❑ 341 Jeff Andra AU RC 50.00 22.00
❑ 342 Victor Hall AU RC 50.00 22.00
❑ 343 Pedro Liriano AU RC 60.00 27.00
❑ 344 Andy Beal AU RC 50.00 22.00
❑ 345 Bob Keppel AU RC 50.00 22.00
❑ 346 Brian Schmitt AU RC 50.00 22.00
❑ 347 Ron Davenport AU RC 60.00 27.00
❑ 348 Tony Blanco AU RC 100.00 45.00
❑ 349 Reggie Griggs AU RC 50.00 22.00
❑ 350 D. Van Dusen AU RC 50.00 22.00
❑ 351 Ichiro Suzuki English RC 100.00 45.00
❑ 351 Ichiro Suzuki Japan RC 80.00 36.00
❑ NNO I.Suzuki English EXCH 100.00 45.00
❑ NNO I. Suzuki Japan EXCH 80.00 36.00

2001 Bowman Heritage

	MINT	NRMT
COMP.SET w/o SP's (330)	50.00	22.00
COMMON CARD (1-330)	.20	.09

COMMON RC (1-330)	.50	.23
COMMON CARD (331-440)	2.00	.90

❑ 1 Chipper Jones 1.50 .70
❑ 2 Pete Harnisch .20 .09
❑ 3 Brian Giles .30 .14
❑ 4 J.T. Snow .30 .14
❑ 5 Bartolo Colon .30 .14
❑ 6 Jorge Posada .30 .14
❑ 7 Shawn Green .75 .35
❑ 8 Derek Jeter 3.00 1.35
❑ 9 Benito Santiago .20 .09
❑ 10 Ramon Hernandez .20 .09
❑ 11 Bernie Williams .75 .35
❑ 12 Greg Maddux 2.00 .90
❑ 13 Barry Bonds 2.00 .90
❑ 14 Roger Clemens 2.00 .90
❑ 15 Miguel Tejada .30 .14
❑ 16 Pedro Feliz .20 .09
❑ 17 Jim Edmonds .50 .23
❑ 18 Tom Glavine .75 .35
❑ 19 David Justice .50 .23
❑ 20 Rich Aurilia .30 .14
❑ 21 Jason Giambi .75 .35
❑ 22 Orlando Hernandez .30 .14
❑ 23 Shawn Estes .20 .09
❑ 24 Nelson Figueroa .20 .09
❑ 25 Terrence Long .30 .14
❑ 26 Mike Mussina .75 .35
❑ 27 Eric Davis .30 .14
❑ 28 Jimmy Rollins .30 .14
❑ 29 Andy Pettitte .30 .14
❑ 30 Shawon Dunston .20 .09
❑ 31 Tim Hudson .75 .35
❑ 32 Jeff Kent .50 .23
❑ 33 Scott Brosius .30 .14
❑ 34 Livan Hernandez .20 .09
❑ 35 Alfonso Soriano .75 .35
❑ 36 Mark McGwire 3.00 1.35
❑ 37 Russ Ortiz .30 .14
❑ 38 Fernando Vina .20 .09
❑ 39 Ken Griffey Jr. 2.50 1.10
❑ 40 Edgar Renteria .30 .14
❑ 41 Kevin Brown .30 .14
❑ 42 Robb Nen .30 .14
❑ 43 Paul LoDuca .30 .14
❑ 44 Bobby Abreu .30 .14
❑ 45 Adam Dunn 1.25 .55
❑ 46 Osvaldo Fernandez .20 .09
❑ 47 Marvin Benard .20 .09
❑ 48 Mark Gardner .20 .09
❑ 49 Alex Rodriguez 2.00 .90
❑ 50 Preston Wilson .30 .14
❑ 51 Roberto Alomar .75 .35
❑ 52 Ben Davis .30 .14
❑ 53 Derek Bell .20 .09
❑ 54 Ken Caminiti .30 .14
❑ 55 Barry Zito .75 .35
❑ 56 Scott Rolen .75 .35
❑ 57 Geoff Jenkins .30 .14
❑ 58 Mike Cameron .30 .14
❑ 59 Ben Grieve .30 .14
❑ 60 Chuck Knoblauch .30 .14
❑ 61 Matt Lawton .30 .14
❑ 62 Chan Ho Park .30 .14
❑ 63 Lance Berkman .75 .35
❑ 64 Carlos Beltran .30 .14
❑ 65 Dean Palmer .30 .14
❑ 66 Alex Gonzalez .20 .09
❑ 67 Larry Walker .50 .23
❑ 68 Magglio Ordonez .30 .14
❑ 69 Ellis Burks .30 .14
❑ 70 Mark Mulder .50 .23
❑ 71 Randy Johnson 1.00 .45
❑ 72 John Smoltz .30 .14
❑ 73 Jerry Hairston Jr. .20 .09
❑ 74 Pedro Martinez 1.00 .45
❑ 75 Fred McGriff .50 .23
❑ 76 Sean Casey .50 .23
❑ 77 C.C. Sabathia .50 .23
❑ 78 Todd Helton 1.00 .45
❑ 79 Brad Penny .30 .14
❑ 80 Mike Sweeney .30 .14
❑ 81 Billy Wagner .30 .14
❑ 82 Mark Buehrle .75 .35
❑ 83 Cristian Guzman .30 .14
❑ 84 Jose Vidro .30 .14
❑ 85 Pat Burrell .30 .14
❑ 86 Jermaine Dye .30 .14
❑ 87 Brandon Inge .30 .14
❑ 88 David Wells .30 .14
❑ 89 Mike Piazza 2.00 .90
❑ 90 Jose Cabrera .20 .09
❑ 91 Cliff Floyd .30 .14
❑ 92 Matt Morris .30 .14
❑ 93 Raul Mondesi .30 .14
❑ 94 Joe Kennedy RC 1.50 .70
❑ 95 Jack Wilson RC .60 .25
❑ 96 Andruw Jones .75 .35
❑ 97 Mariano Rivera .30 .14
❑ 98 Mike Hampton .30 .14
❑ 99 Roger Cedeno .20 .09
❑ 100 Jose Cruz .30 .14
❑ 101 Mike Lowell .30 .14
❑ 102 Pedro Astacio .20 .09
❑ 103 Joe Mays .30 .14
❑ 104 John Franco .30 .14
❑ 105 Tim Redding .30 .14
❑ 106 Sandy Alomar Jr. .30 .14
❑ 107 Bret Boone .30 .14
❑ 108 Josh Towers RC 2.00 .90
❑ 109 Matt Stairs .20 .09
❑ 110 Chris Truby .20 .09
❑ 111 Jeff Suppan .20 .09
❑ 112 J.C. Romero .20 .09
❑ 113 Felipe Lopez .30 .14
❑ 114 Ben Sheets .50 .23
❑ 115 Frank Thomas 1.00 .45
❑ 116 A.J. Burnett .30 .14
❑ 117 Tony Clark .30 .14
❑ 118 Mac Suzuki .20 .09
❑ 119 Brad Radke .30 .14
❑ 120 Jeff Shaw .20 .09
❑ 121 Nick Neugebauer .30 .14
❑ 122 Kenny Lofton .30 .14
❑ 123 Jacque Jones .30 .14
❑ 124 Brent Mayne .20 .09
❑ 125 Carlos Hernandez .30 .14
❑ 126 Shane Spencer .30 .14
❑ 127 John Lackey .20 .09
❑ 128 Sterling Hitchcock .20 .09
❑ 129 Darren Dreifort .20 .09
❑ 130 Rusty Greer .30 .14
❑ 131 Michael Cuddyer .30 .14
❑ 132 Tyler Houston .20 .09
❑ 133 Chin-Feng Chen .50 .23
❑ 134 Ken Harvey .50 .23
❑ 135 Marquis Grissom .20 .09
❑ 136 Russell Branyan .30 .14
❑ 137 Eric Karros .30 .14
❑ 138 Josh Beckett .75 .35
❑ 139 Todd Zeile .30 .14
❑ 140 Corey Koskie .30 .14
❑ 141 Steve Sparks .20 .09
❑ 142 Bobby Seay .20 .09
❑ 143 Tim Raines Jr. .30 .14
❑ 144 Julio Zuleta .20 .09
❑ 145 Jose Lima .20 .09
❑ 146 Dante Bichette .30 .14
❑ 147 Randy Keisler .20 .09
❑ 148 Brent Butler .20 .09
❑ 149 Antonio Alfonseca .20 .09
❑ 150 Bryan Rekar .20 .09

❑ 151 Jeffrey Hammonds .20 .09
❑ 152 Larry Bigbie .20 .09
❑ 153 Blake Stein .20 .09
❑ 154 Robin Ventura .30 .14
❑ 155 Rondell White .30 .14
❑ 156 Juan Silvestre .20 .09
❑ 157 Marcus Thames .30 .14
❑ 158 Sidney Ponson .20 .09
❑ 159 Juan A. Pena RC .60 .25
❑ 160 C.J. Nitkowski .20 .09
❑ 161 Adam Everett .20 .09
❑ 162 Eric Munson .30 .14
❑ 163 Jason Isringhausen .30 .14
❑ 164 Brad Fullmer .30 .14
❑ 165 Miguel Olivo .20 .09
❑ 166 Fernando Tatis .20 .09
❑ 167 Freddy Garcia .30 .14
❑ 168 Tom Goodwin .20 .09
❑ 169 Armando Benitez .30 .14
❑ 170 Paul Konerko .30 .14
❑ 171 Jeff Cirillo .30 .14
❑ 172 Shane Reynolds .20 .09
❑ 173 Kevin Tapani .20 .09
❑ 174 Joe Crede .30 .14
❑ 175 Omar Infante RC .60 .25
❑ 176 Jake Peavy RC 1.50 .70
❑ 177 Corey Patterson .30 .14
❑ 178 Mike Penney RC .50 .23
❑ 179 Jeromy Burnitz .30 .14
❑ 180 David Segui .20 .09
❑ 181 Marcus Giles .30 .14
❑ 182 Paul O'Neill .75 .35
❑ 183 John Olerud .30 .14
❑ 184 Andy Benes .20 .09
❑ 185 Brad Cresse .50 .23
❑ 186 Ricky Ledee .20 .09
❑ 187 Allen Levrault UER .20 .09
Last name misspelled Leverault
❑ 188 Royce Clayton .20 .09
❑ 189 Kelly Johnson RC 2.00 .90
❑ 190 Quilvio Veras .20 .09
❑ 191 Mike Williams .20 .09
❑ 192 Jason Lane RC 2.50 1.10
❑ 193 Rick Helling .30 .14
❑ 194 Tim Wakefield .20 .09
❑ 195 James Baldwin .20 .09
❑ 196 Cody Ransom RC .50 .23
❑ 197 Bobby Kielty .20 .09
❑ 198 Bobby Jones .20 .09
❑ 199 Steve Cox .20 .09
❑ 200 Jamal Strong RC 1.00 .45
❑ 201 Steve Lomasney .20 .09
❑ 202 Brian Cardwell RC .60 .25
❑ 203 Mike Matheny .20 .09
❑ 204 Jeff Randazzo RC .60 .25
❑ 205 Aubrey Huff .20 .09
❑ 206 Chuck Finley .30 .14
❑ 207 Denny Bautista RC 1.50 .70
❑ 208 Terry Mulholland .20 .09
❑ 209 Rey Ordonez .20 .09
❑ 210 Keith Surkont RC .60 .25
❑ 211 Orlando Cabrera .20 .09
❑ 212 Juan Encarnacion .30 .14
❑ 213 Dustin Hermanson .20 .09
❑ 214 Luis Rivas .20 .09
❑ 215 Mark Quinn .30 .14
❑ 216 Randy Velarde .20 .09
❑ 217 Billy Koch .20 .09
❑ 218 Ryan Rupe .20 .09
❑ 219 Keith Ginter .30 .14
❑ 220 Woody Williams .20 .09
❑ 221 Ryan Franklin .20 .09
❑ 222 Aaron Myette .20 .09
❑ 223 Joe Borchard RC 5.00 2.20
❑ 224 Nate Cornejo .30 .14
❑ 225 Julian Tavarez .20 .09
❑ 226 Kevin Millwood .20 .09
❑ 227 Travis Hafner RC 1.50 .70
❑ 228 Charles Nagy .20 .09
❑ 229 Mike Lieberthal .30 .14
❑ 230 Jeff Nelson .20 .09
❑ 231 Ryan Dempster .30 .14
❑ 232 Andres Galarraga .50 .23
❑ 233 Chad Durbin .20 .09
❑ 234 Timo Perez .20 .09
❑ 235 Troy O'Leary .20 .09
❑ 236 Kevin Young .20 .09
❑ 237 Gabe Kapler .30 .14
❑ 238 Juan Cruz RC 3.00 1.35
❑ 239 Masato Yoshii .30 .14
❑ 240 Aramis Ramirez .30 .14
❑ 241 Matt Cooper RC .60 .25
❑ 242 Randy Flores RC .60 .25
❑ 243 Rafael Furcal .30 .14
❑ 244 David Eckstein .20 .09
❑ 245 Matt Clement .20 .09
❑ 246 Craig Biggio .50 .23
❑ 247 Rick Reed .20 .09
❑ 248 Jose Macias .20 .09
❑ 249 Alex Escobar .30 .14
❑ 250 Roberto Hernandez .20 .09
❑ 251 Andy Ashby .20 .09
❑ 252 Tony Armas Jr. .30 .14
❑ 253 Jamie Moyer .30 .14
❑ 254 Jason Tyner .20 .09
❑ 255 Charles Kegley RC .60 .25
❑ 256 Jeff Conine .30 .14
❑ 257 Francisco Cordova .20 .09
❑ 258 Ted Lilly .20 .09
❑ 259 Joe Randa .20 .09
❑ 260 Jeff D'Amico .20 .09
❑ 261 Albie Lopez .20 .09
❑ 262 Kevin Appier .30 .14
❑ 263 Richard Hidalgo .30 .14
❑ 264 Omar Daal .20 .09
❑ 265 Ricky Gutierrez .20 .09
❑ 266 John Rocker .30 .14
❑ 267 Ray Lankford .30 .14
❑ 268 Beau Hale RC 1.50 .70
❑ 269 Tony Blanco RC 2.50 1.10
❑ 270 Derrek Lee UER .20 .09
First name misspelled Derrick
❑ 271 Jamey Wright .20 .09
❑ 272 Alex Gordon .20 .09
❑ 273 Jeff Weaver .30 .14
❑ 274 Jaret Wright .20 .09
❑ 275 Jose Hernandez .20 .09
❑ 276 Bruce Chen .20 .09
❑ 277 Todd Hollandsworth .20 .09
❑ 278 Wade Miller .30 .14
❑ 279 Luke Prokopec .20 .09
❑ 280 Rafael Soriano RC 1.50 .70
❑ 281 Damion Easley .20 .09
❑ 282 Darren Oliver .20 .09
❑ 283 Brandon Duckworth RC 2.50 1.10
❑ 284 Aaron Herr .20 .09
❑ 285 Ray Durham .30 .14
❑ 286 Wilmy Caceras RC .60 .25
❑ 287 Ugueth Urbina .20 .09
❑ 288 Scott Seabol .20 .09
❑ 289 Lance Niekro RC 1.50 .70
❑ 290 Trot Nixon .30 .14
❑ 291 Adam Kennedy .20 .09
❑ 292 Brian Schmitt RC .60 .25
❑ 293 Grant Roberts .20 .09
❑ 294 Benny Agbayani .20 .09
❑ 295 Travis Lee .30 .14
❑ 296 Erick Almonte RC 1.50 .70
❑ 297 Jim Thome .75 .35
❑ 298 Eric Young .20 .09
❑ 299 Dan Denham RC 1.50 .70
❑ 300 Boof Bonser RC 2.00 .90
❑ 301 Denny Neagle .20 .09
❑ 302 Kenny Rogers .20 .09
❑ 303 J.D. Closser .20 .09
❑ 304 Chase Utley RC 1.50 .70
❑ 305 Rey Sanchez .20 .09
❑ 306 Sean McGowan .20 .09
❑ 307 Justin Pope RC 1.00 .45
❑ 308 Torii Hunter .30 .14
❑ 309 B.J. Surhoff .30 .14
❑ 310 Aaron Heilman RC 1.50 .70
❑ 311 Gabe Gross RC 2.00 .90
❑ 312 Lee Stevens .20 .09
❑ 313 Todd Hundley .20 .09
❑ 314 Macay McBride RC 1.00 .45
❑ 315 Edgar Martinez .50 .23
❑ 316 Omar Vizquel .30 .14
❑ 317 Reggie Sanders .30 .14
❑ 318 John-Ford Griffin RC 2.00 .90
❑ 319 Tim Salmon .30 .14
❑ 320 Pokey Reese .20 .09
❑ 321 Jay Payton .20 .09
❑ 322 Doug Glanville .20 .09
❑ 323 Greg Vaughn .30 .14
❑ 324 Ruben Sierra .20 .09
❑ 325 Kip Wells .20 .09
❑ 326 Carl Everett .30 .14
❑ 327 Garret Anderson .30 .14
❑ 328 Jay Bell .30 .14
❑ 329 Barry Larkin .75 .35
❑ 330 Jeff Mathis RC 1.00 .45
❑ 331 Adrian Gonzalez SP 5.00 2.20
❑ 332 Juan Rivera SP 2.00 .90
❑ 333 Tony Alvarez SP 2.00 .90
❑ 334 Xavier Nady SP 3.00 1.35
❑ 335 Josh Hamilton SP 5.00 2.20
❑ 336 Will Smith SP RC 5.00 2.20
❑ 337 Israel Alcantara SP 2.00 .90
❑ 338 Chris George SP 2.00 .90
❑ 339 Sean Burroughs SP 5.00 2.20
❑ 340 Jack Cust SP 2.00 .90
❑ 341 Henry Mateo SP RC 2.00 .90
❑ 342 Carlos Pena SP 2.00 .90
❑ 343 J.R. House SP 5.00 2.20
❑ 344 Carlos Silva SP 2.00 .90
❑ 345 Mike Rivera SP RC 5.00 2.20
❑ 346 Adam Johnson SP 2.00 .90
❑ 347 Scott Heard SP 2.00 .90
❑ 348 Alex Cintron SP 2.00 .90
❑ 349 Miguel Cabrera SP 2.00 .90
❑ 350 Nick Johnson SP 2.00 .90
❑ 351 Albert Pujols SP RC 40.00 18.00
❑ 352 Ichiro Suzuki SP RC 60.00 27.00
❑ 353 Carlos Delgado SP 5.00 2.20
❑ 354 Troy Glaus SP 5.00 2.20
❑ 355 Sammy Sosa SP 10.00 4.50
❑ 356 Ivan Rodriguez SP 5.00 2.20
❑ 357 Vladimir Guerrero SP 6.00 2.70
❑ 358 Manny Ramirez SP 6.00 2.70
❑ 359 Luis Gonzalez SP 5.00 2.20
❑ 360 Roy Oswalt SP 5.00 2.20
❑ 361 Moises Alou SP 2.00 .90
❑ 362 Juan Gonzalez SP 5.00 2.20
❑ 363 Tony Gwynn SP 10.00 4.50
❑ 364 Hideo Nomo SP 5.00 2.20
❑ 365 Tsuyoshi Shinjo SP RC 10.00 4.50
❑ 366 Kazuhiro Sasaki SP 5.00 2.20
❑ 367 Cal Ripken SP 20.00 9.00
❑ 368 Rafael Palmeiro SP 5.00 2.20
❑ 369 J.D. Drew SP 5.00 2.20
❑ 370 Doug Mientkiewicz SP 2.00 .90
❑ 371 Jeff Bagwell SP 6.00 2.70
❑ 372 Darin Erstad SP 5.00 2.20
❑ 373 Tom Gordon SP 2.00 .90
❑ 374 Ben Petrick SP 2.00 .90
❑ 375 Eric Milton SP 2.00 .90
❑ 376 Nomar Garciaparra SP 12.00 5.50
❑ 377 Julio Lugo SP 2.00 .90
❑ 378 Tino Martinez SP 2.00 .90
❑ 379 Javier Vazquez SP 2.00 .90
❑ 380 Jeremy Giambi SP 2.00 .90
❑ 381 Marty Cordova SP 2.00 .90
❑ 382 Adrian Beltre SP 2.00 .90
❑ 383 John Burkett SP 2.00 .90
❑ 384 Aaron Boone SP 2.00 .90
❑ 385 Eric Chavez SP 2.00 .90
❑ 386 Curt Schilling SP 5.00 2.20
❑ 387 Cory Lidle UER 2.00 .90
First name misspelled Corey
❑ 388 Jason Schmidt SP 2.00 .90
❑ 389 Johnny Damon SP 2.00 .90
❑ 390 Steve Finley SP 2.00 .90
❑ 391 Edgardo Alfonzo SP 2.00 .90
❑ 392 Jose Valentin SP 2.00 .90
❑ 393 Jose Canseco SP 5.00 2.20
❑ 394 Ryan Klesko SP 2.00 .90
❑ 395 David Cone SP 2.00 .90
❑ 396 Jason Kendall UER 2.00 .90
Last name misspelled Kendell
❑ 397 Placido Polanco SP 2.00 .90
❑ 398 Glendon Rusch SP 2.00 .90
❑ 399 Aaron Sele SP 2.00 .90
❑ 400 D'Angelo Jimenez SP 2.00 .90
❑ 401 Mark Grace SP 5.00 2.20
❑ 402 Al Leiter SP 2.00 .90
❑ 403 Brian Jordan SP 2.00 .90
❑ 404 Phil Nevin SP 2.00 .90

- ❑ 405 Brent Abernathy SP .... 2.00 .90
- ❑ 406 Kerry Wood SP 5.00 2.20
- ❑ 407 Alex Gonzalez SP .... 2.00 .90
- ❑ 408 Robert Fick SP .... 2.00 .90
- ❑ 409 Dmitri Young UER........ 2.00 .90
  First name misspelled Dimitri
- ❑ 410 Wes Helms SP .... 2.00 .90
- ❑ 411 Trevor Hoffman SP ...... 2.00 .90
- ❑ 412 Rickey Henderson SP 10.00 4.50
- ❑ 413 Bobby Higginson SP .... 2.00 .90
- ❑ 414 Gary Sheffield SP .... 2.00 .90
- ❑ 415 Darryl Kile SP .... 2.00 .90
- ❑ 416 Richie Sexson SP .... 2.00 .90
- ❑ 417 Frank Menechino SP RC 2.00 .90
- ❑ 418 Javy Lopez SP .... 2.00 .90
- ❑ 419 Carlos Lee SP .... 2.00 .90
- ❑ 420 Jon Lieber SP .... 2.00 .90
- ❑ 421 Hank Blalock SP RC .. 15.00 6.75
- ❑ 422 Marlon Byrd SP RC 10.00 4.50
- ❑ 423 Jason Kinchen SP RC.. 2.00 .90
- ❑ 424 Morgan Ensberg SP RC 6.00 2.70
- ❑ 425 Greg Nash SP RC...... 10.00 4.50
- ❑ 426 D. Tankersley SP RC .. 8.00 3.60
- ❑ 427 Nate Murphy SP RC .... 2.00 .90
- ❑ 428 Chris Smith SP RC 3.00 1.35
- ❑ 429 Jake Gautreau SP RC.. 5.00 2.20
- ❑ 430 J. VanBenschoten SP RC 6.00 2.70
- ❑ 431 Travis Thompson SP RC 2.00 .90
- ❑ 432 Orlando Hudson SP RC 2.00 .90
- ❑ 433 Jerome Williams SP RC 6.00 2.70
- ❑ 434 Kevin Reese SP RC .... 2.00 .90
- ❑ 435 Ed Rogers SP RC 5.00 2.20
- ❑ 436 Ryan Jamison SP RC .. 2.00 .90
- ❑ 437 Adam Pettyjohn SP RC 2.00 .90
- ❑ 438 Hee Seop Choi SP RC 8.00 3.60
- ❑ 439 Justin Morneau SP RC 8.00 3.60
- ❑ 440 Mitch Jones SP RC 3.00 1.35

1994 Bowman's Best

	MINT	NRMT
COMPLETE SET (200)	60.00	27.00

- ❑ B1 Chipper Jones................ 2.00 .90
- ❑ B2 Derek Jeter 5.00 2.20
- ❑ B3 Bill Pulsipher .... .40 .18
- ❑ B4 James Baldwin .... .25 .11
- ❑ B5 Brooks Kieschnick RC .... .25 .11
- ❑ B6 Justin Thompson .... .25 .11
- ❑ B7 Midre Cummings.............. .25 .11
- ❑ B8 Joey Hamilton.................. .25 .11
- ❑ B9 Pokey Reese .... .25 .11
- ❑ B10 Brian Barber .... .25 .11
- ❑ B11 John Burke .... .25 .11
- ❑ B12 DeShawn Warren .... .25 .11
- ❑ B13 Edgardo Alfonzo RC 8.00 3.60
- ❑ B14 Eddie Pearson RC .... .25 .11
- ❑ B15 Jimmy Haynes .... .25 .11
- ❑ B16 Danny Bautista .... .25 .11
- ❑ B17 Roger Cedeno .... .25 .11
- ❑ B18 Jon Lieber...................... .40 .18
- ❑ B19 Billy Wagner RC 2.50 1.10
- ❑ B20 Tate Seefried RC .... .25 .11
- ❑ B21 Chad Mottola .... .25 .11
- ❑ B22 Jose Malave .... .25 .11
- ❑ B23 Terrell Wade RC............ .25 .11
- ❑ B24 Shane Andrews .... .25 .11
- ❑ B25 Chan Ho Park RC........ 6.00 2.70
- ❑ B26 Kirk Presley RC .... .25 .11
- ❑ B27 Robbie Beckett .... .25 .11
- ❑ B28 Orlando Miller .... .25 .11
- ❑ B29 Jorge Posada RC 10.00 4.50
- ❑ B30 Frankie Rodriguez .... .25 .11
- ❑ B31 Brian L. Hunter .... .25 .11
- ❑ B32 Billy Ashley .... .25 .11
- ❑ B33 Rondell White .... .40 .18
- ❑ B34 John Roper..................... .25 .11
- ❑ B35 Marc Valdes .... .25 .11
- ❑ B36 Scott Ruffcorn .... .25 .11
- ❑ B37 Rod Henderson.............. .25 .11
- ❑ B38 Curtis Goodwin RC........ .40 .18
- ❑ B39 Russ Davis .... .25 .11
- ❑ B40 Rick Gorecki .... .25 .11
- ❑ B41 Johnny Damon .... 1.00 .45
- ❑ B42 Roberto Petagine .... .25 .11
- ❑ B43 Chris Snopek .... .25 .11
- ❑ B44 Mark Acre RC .... .25 .11
- ❑ B45 Todd Hollandsworth ...... .25 .11
- ❑ B46 Shawn Green .... 1.25 .55
- ❑ B47 John Carter RC.............. .25 .11
- ❑ B48 Jim Pittsley RC .... .25 .11
- ❑ B49 John Wasdin RC............ .25 .11
- ❑ B50 D.J. Boston RC .... .25 .11
- ❑ B51 Tim Clark .... .25 .11
- ❑ B52 Alex Ochoa .... .25 .11
- ❑ B53 Chad Roper .... .25 .11
- ❑ B54 Mike Kelly .... .25 .11
- ❑ B55 Brad Fullmer RC 5.00 2.20
- ❑ B56 Carl Everett..................... .40 .18
- ❑ B57 Tim Belk RC .... .25 .11
- ❑ B58 Jimmy Hurst RC .... .25 .11
- ❑ B59 Mac Suzuki RC .... .40 .18
- ❑ B60 Michael Moore .... .25 .11
- ❑ B61 Alan Benes RC .... .40 .18
- ❑ B62 Tony Clark RC 4.00 1.80
- ❑ B63 Edgar Renteria RC 2.50 1.10
- ❑ B64 Trey Beamon .... .25 .11
- ❑ B65 LaTroy Hawkins RC ...... .40 .18
- ❑ B66 Wayne Gomes RC .... .25 .11
- ❑ B67 Ray McDavid .... .25 .11
- ❑ B68 John Dettmer .... .25 .11
- ❑ B69 Willie Greene .... .25 .11
- ❑ B70 Dave Stevens .... .25 .11
- ❑ B71 Kevin Orie RC................ .25 .11
- ❑ B72 Chad Ogea .... .25 .11
- ❑ B73 Ben Van Ryn RC .... .25 .11
- ❑ B74 Kym Ashworth RC .... .25 .11
- ❑ B75 Dmitri Young.................. .40 .18
- ❑ B76 Herbert Perry RC .... .40 .18
- ❑ B77 Joey Eischen .... .25 .11
- ❑ B78 Arquimedez Pozo RC .... .25 .11
- ❑ B79 Ugueth Urbina................ .25 .11
- ❑ B80 Keith Williams RC.......... .25 .11
- ❑ B81 John Frascatore RC ...... .25 .11
- ❑ B82 Garey Ingram RC .... .25 .11
- ❑ B83 Aaron Small .... .25 .11
- ❑ B84 Olmedo Saenz RC .... .40 .18
- ❑ B85 Jesus Tavarez RC .... .25 .11
- ❑ B86 Jose Silva RC .... .40 .18
- ❑ B87 Jay Witasick RC .... .25 .11
- ❑ B88 Jay Maldonado RC .... .25 .11
- ❑ B89 Keith Heberling RC........ .25 .11
- ❑ B90 Rusty Greer RC 3.00 1.35
- ❑ R1 Paul Molitor.................. 1.00 .45
- ❑ R2 Eddie Murray .... 1.00 .45
- ❑ R3 Ozzie Smith .... 1.25 .55
- ❑ R4 Rickey Henderson .... 2.00 .90
- ❑ R5 Lee Smith .... .40 .18
- ❑ R6 Dave Winfield .... 1.00 .45
- ❑ R7 Roberto Alomar .... 1.00 .45
- ❑ R8 Matt Williams .... .60 .25
- ❑ R9 Mark Grace.................. 1.00 .45
- ❑ R10 Lance Johnson .... .25 .11
- ❑ R11 Darren Daulton .... .40 .18
- ❑ R12 Tom Glavine .... 1.00 .45
- ❑ R13 Gary Sheffield .... .40 .18
- ❑ R14 Rod Beck .... .25 .11
- ❑ R15 Fred McGriff .... .60 .25
- ❑ R16 Joe Carter....................... .40 .18
- ❑ R17 Dante Bichette .... .40 .18
- ❑ R18 Danny Tartabull .... .25 .11
- ❑ R19 Juan Gonzalez .... 1.00 .45
- ❑ R20 Steve Avery .... .25 .11
- ❑ R21 John Wetteland.............. .40 .18
- ❑ R22 Ben McDonald .... .25 .11
- ❑ R23 Jack McDowell .... .25 .11
- ❑ R24 Jose Canseco............. 1.00 .45
- ❑ R25 Tim Salmon .... .40 .18
- ❑ R26 Wilson Alvarez .... .25 .11
- ❑ R27 Gregg Jefferies.............. .25 .11
- ❑ R28 John Burkett .... .25 .11
- ❑ R29 Greg Vaughn .... .40 .18
- ❑ R30 Robin Ventura................. .40 .18
- ❑ R31 Paul O'Neill .... 1.00 .45
- ❑ R32 Cecil Fielder .... .40 .18
- ❑ R33 Kevin Mitchell .... .25 .11
- ❑ R34 Jeff Conine .... .25 .11
- ❑ R35 Carlos Baerga................. .25 .11
- ❑ R36 Greg Maddux 2.50 1.10
- ❑ R37 Roger Clemens........... 2.50 1.10
- ❑ R38 Deion Sanders .... .40 .18
- ❑ R39 Delino DeShields .... .25 .11
- ❑ R40 Ken Griffey Jr. 3.00 1.35
- ❑ R41 Albert Belle .... .40 .18
- ❑ R42 Wade Boggs............... 1.00 .45
- ❑ R43 Andres Galarraga .... .60 .25
- ❑ R44 Aaron Sele .... .40 .18
- ❑ R45 Don Mattingly 2.50 1.10
- ❑ R46 David Cone..................... .40 .18
- ❑ R47 Len Dykstra .... .40 .18
- ❑ R48 Brett Butler .... .40 .18
- ❑ R49 Bill Swift .... .25 .11
- ❑ R50 Bobby Bonilla .... .40 .18
- ❑ R51 Rafael Palmeiro .... 1.00 .45
- ❑ R52 Moises Alou .... .40 .18
- ❑ R53 Jeff Bagwell .... 1.25 .55
- ❑ R54 Mike Mussina .... 1.00 .45
- ❑ R55 Frank Thomas .... 1.25 .55
- ❑ R56 Jose Rijo......................... .25 .11
- ❑ R57 Ruben Sierra .... .25 .11
- ❑ R58 Randy Myers .... .25 .11
- ❑ R59 Barry Bonds 2.50 1.10
- ❑ R60 Jimmy Key .... .40 .18
- ❑ R61 Travis Fryman................. .40 .18
- ❑ R62 John Olerud .... .40 .18
- ❑ R63 David Justice .... .40 .18
- ❑ R64 Ray Lankford .... .25 .11
- ❑ R65 Bob Tewksbury............... .25 .11
- ❑ R66 Chuck Carr .... .25 .11
- ❑ R67 Jay Buhner .... .40 .18
- ❑ R68 Kenny Lofton .... .40 .18
- ❑ R69 Marquis Grissom .... .25 .11
- ❑ R70 Sammy Sosa .... 2.00 .90
- ❑ R71 Cal Ripken 4.00 1.80
- ❑ R72 Ellis Burks...................... .40 .18
- ❑ R73 Jeff Montgomery............ .25 .11
- ❑ R74 Julio Franco .... .40 .18
- ❑ R75 Kirby Puckett 2.50 1.10
- ❑ R76 Larry Walker .... .60 .25
- ❑ R77 Andy Van Slyke .... .40 .18
- ❑ R78 Tony Gwynn .... 2.00 .90
- ❑ R79 Will Clark .... 1.00 .45
- ❑ R80 Mo Vaughn .... .40 .18
- ❑ R81 Mike Piazza 3.00 1.35
- ❑ R82 James Mouton .... .25 .11
- ❑ R83 Carlos Delgado........... 1.50 .70
- ❑ R84 Ryan Klesko .... .40 .18
- ❑ R85 Javier Lopez .... .40 .18
- ❑ R86 Raul Mondesi .... .40 .18
- ❑ R87 Cliff Floyd .... .40 .18
- ❑ R88 Manny Ramirez .... 1.50 .70
- ❑ R89 Hector Carrasco .... .25 .11
- ❑ R90 Jeff Granger .... .25 .11
- ❑ X91 Frank Thomas................ .60 .25
  Dmitri Young
- ❑ X92 Fred McGriff .... .40 .18
  Brooks Kieschnick
- ❑ X93 Matt Williams .... .40 .18
  Shane Andrews
- ❑ X94 Cal Ripken .... 2.00 .90
  Kevin Orie
- ❑ X95 Barry Larkin 2.50 1.10
  Derek Jeter
- ❑ X96 Ken Griffey Jr. .... 1.50 .70
  Johnny Damon
- ❑ X97 Barry Bonds .... 1.25 .55
  Rondell White
- ❑ X98 Albert Belle .... .40 .18
  Jimmy Hurst
- ❑ X99 Raul Mondesi .... .40 .18

Card	MINT	NRMT
Ruben Rivera RC		
❑ X100 Roger Clemens	1.25	.55
Scott Ruffcorn		
❑ X101 Greg Maddux	1.25	.55
John Wasdin		
❑ X102 Tim Salmon	.40	.18
Chad Mottola		
❑ X103 Carlos Baerga	.25	.11
Arquimedez Pozo		
❑ X104 Mike Piazza	1.50	.70
Bobby Hughes		
❑ X105 Carlos Delgado	.60	.25
Melvin Nieves		
❑ X106 Javier Lopez	2.50	1.10
Jorge Posada		
❑ X107 Manny Ramirez	1.00	.45
Jose Malave		
❑ X108 Travis Fryman	1.00	.45
Chipper Jones		
❑ X109 Steve Avery	.25	.11
Bill Pulsipher		
❑ X110 John Olerud	1.00	.45
Shawn Green		

1995 Bowman's Best

	MINT	NRMT
COMPLETE SET (195)	350.00	160.00
COMMON CARD (B1-R90)	.25	.11
COMMON MIR.IM.(X1-X15)	.50	.23

Card	MINT	NRMT
❑ B1 Derek Jeter	4.00	1.80
❑ B2 Vladimir Guerrero RC	80.00	36.00
❑ B3 Bob Abreu RC	15.00	6.75
❑ B4 Chan Ho Park	.40	.18
❑ B5 Paul Wilson	.25	.11
❑ B6 Chad Ogea	.25	.11
❑ B7 Andruw Jones RC	50.00	22.00
❑ B8 Brian Barber	.25	.11
❑ B9 Andy Larkin	.25	.11
❑ B10 Richie Sexson RC	15.00	6.75
❑ B11 Everett Stull	.25	.11
❑ B12 Brooks Kieschnick	.25	.11
❑ B13 Matt Murray	.25	.11
❑ B14 John Wasdin	.25	.11
❑ B15 Shannon Stewart	.40	.18
❑ B16 Luis Ortiz	.25	.11
❑ B17 Marc Kroon	.25	.11
❑ B18 Todd Greene	.25	.11
❑ B19 Juan Acevedo RC	.25	.11
❑ B20 Tony Clark	.40	.18
❑ B21 Jermaine Dye	1.00	.45
❑ B22 Derrek Lee	.40	.18
❑ B23 Pat Watkins	.25	.11
❑ B24 Pokey Reese	.25	.11
❑ B25 Ben Grieve	3.00	1.35
❑ B26 Julio Santana	.25	.11
❑ B27 Felix Rodriguez RC	.40	.18
❑ B28 Paul Konerko	3.00	1.35
❑ B29 Nomar Garciaparra	12.00	5.50
❑ B30 Pat Ahearne	.25	.11
❑ B31 Jason Schmidt	.25	.11
❑ B32 Billy Wagner	.40	.18
❑ B33 Rey Ordonez RC	4.00	1.80
❑ B34 Curtis Goodwin	.25	.11
❑ B35 Sergio Nunez RC	.25	.11
❑ B36 Tim Belk	.25	.11
❑ B37 Scott Elarton RC	4.00	1.80
❑ B38 Jason Isringhausen	.40	.18
❑ B39 Trot Nixon	.40	.18
❑ B40 Sid Roberson RC	.25	.11
❑ B41 Ron Villone	.25	.11
❑ B42 Ruben Rivera	.25	.11
❑ B43 Rick Huisman	.25	.11
❑ B44 Todd Hollandsworth	.25	.11
❑ B45 Johnny Damon	.60	.25
❑ B46 Garret Anderson	.40	.18
❑ B47 Jeff D'Amico	.25	.11
❑ B48 Dustin Hermanson	.25	.11
❑ B49 Juan Encarnacion RC	8.00	3.60
❑ B50 Andy Pettitte	.40	.18
❑ B51 Chris Stynes	.25	.11
❑ B52 Troy Percival	.25	.11
❑ B53 LaTroy Hawkins	.25	.11
❑ B54 Roger Cedeno	.25	.11
❑ B55 Alan Benes	.25	.11
❑ B56 Karim Garcia RC	.40	.18
❑ B57 Andrew Lorraine	.25	.11
❑ B58 Gary Rath RC	.25	.11
❑ B59 Bret Wagner	.25	.11
❑ B60 Jeff Suppan	.25	.11
❑ B61 Bill Pulsipher	.25	.11
❑ B62 Jay Payton RC	4.00	1.80
❑ B63 Alex Ochoa	.25	.11
❑ B64 Ugueth Urbina	.25	.11
❑ B65 Armando Benitez	.40	.18
❑ B66 George Arias	.25	.11
❑ B67 Raul Casanova RC	.25	.11
❑ B68 Matt Drews	.25	.11
❑ B69 Jimmy Haynes	.25	.11
❑ B70 Jimmy Hurst	.25	.11
❑ B71 C.J. Nitkowski	.25	.11
❑ B72 Tommy Davis RC	.25	.11
❑ B73 Bartolo Colon RC	10.00	4.50
❑ B74 Chris Carpenter RC	4.00	1.80
❑ B75 Trey Beamon	.25	.11
❑ B76 Bryan Rekar	.25	.11
❑ B77 James Baldwin	.25	.11
❑ B78 Marc Valdes	.25	.11
❑ B79 Tom Fordham RC	.25	.11
❑ B80 Marc Newfield	.25	.11
❑ B81 Angel Martinez	.25	.11
❑ B82 Brian L. Hunter	.25	.11
❑ B83 Jose Herrera	.25	.11
❑ B84 Glenn Dishman RC	.25	.11
❑ B85 Jacob Cruz RC	.40	.18
❑ B86 Paul Shuey	.25	.11
❑ B87 Scott Rolen RC	30.00	13.50
❑ B88 Doug Million	.25	.11
❑ B89 Desi Relaford	.25	.11
❑ B90 Michael Tucker	.25	.11
❑ R1 Randy Johnson	1.25	.55
❑ R2 Joe Carter	.40	.18
❑ R3 Chili Davis	.40	.18
❑ R4 Moises Alou	.40	.18
❑ R5 Gary Sheffield	.40	.18
❑ R6 Kevin Appier	.40	.18
❑ R7 Denny Neagle	.40	.18
❑ R8 Ruben Sierra	.25	.11
❑ R9 Darren Daulton	.40	.18
❑ R10 Cal Ripken	4.00	1.80
❑ R11 Bobby Bonilla	.40	.18
❑ R12 Manny Ramirez	1.25	.55
❑ R13 Barry Bonds	2.50	1.10
❑ R14 Eric Karros	.40	.18
❑ R15 Greg Maddux	2.50	1.10
❑ R16 Jeff Bagwell	1.25	.55
❑ R17 Paul Molitor	1.00	.45
❑ R18 Ray Lankford	.25	.11
❑ R19 Mark Grace	1.00	.45
❑ R20 Kenny Lofton	.40	.18
❑ R21 Tony Gwynn	2.00	.90
❑ R22 Will Clark	1.00	.45
❑ R23 Roger Clemens	2.50	1.10
❑ R24 Dante Bichette	.40	.18
❑ R25 Barry Larkin	1.00	.45
❑ R26 Wade Boggs	1.00	.45
❑ R27 Kirby Puckett	2.50	1.10
❑ R28 Cecil Fielder	.40	.18
❑ R29 Jose Canseco	1.00	.45
❑ R30 Juan Gonzalez	1.00	.45
❑ R31 David Cone	.40	.18
❑ R32 Craig Biggio	.60	.25
❑ R33 Tim Salmon	.40	.18
❑ R34 David Justice	.40	.18
❑ R35 Sammy Sosa	2.00	.90
❑ R36 Mike Piazza	2.50	1.10
❑ R37 Carlos Baerga	.25	.11
❑ R38 Jeff Conine	.25	.11
❑ R39 Rafael Palmeiro	1.00	.45
❑ R40 Bret Saberhagen	.40	.18
❑ R41 Len Dykstra	.40	.18
❑ R42 Mo Vaughn	.40	.18
❑ R43 Wally Joyner	.40	.18
❑ R44 Chuck Knoblauch	.40	.18
❑ R45 Robin Ventura	.40	.18
❑ R46 Don Mattingly	2.50	1.10
❑ R47 Dave Hollins	.25	.11
❑ R48 Andy Benes	.25	.11
❑ R49 Ken Griffey Jr.	3.00	1.35
❑ R50 Albert Belle	.40	.18
❑ R51 Matt Williams	.60	.25
❑ R52 Rondell White	.40	.18
❑ R53 Raul Mondesi	.40	.18
❑ R54 Brian Jordan	.40	.18
❑ R55 Greg Vaughn	.40	.18
❑ R56 Fred McGriff	.60	.25
❑ R57 Roberto Alomar	1.00	.45
❑ R58 Dennis Eckersley	.40	.18
❑ R59 Lee Smith	.40	.18
❑ R60 Eddie Murray	1.00	.45
❑ R61 Kenny Rogers	.25	.11
❑ R62 Ron Gant	.25	.11
❑ R63 Larry Walker	.60	.25
❑ R64 Chad Curtis	.25	.11
❑ R65 Frank Thomas	1.25	.55
❑ R66 Paul O'Neill	1.00	.45
❑ R67 Kevin Seitzer	.25	.11
❑ R68 Marquis Grissom	.25	.11
❑ R69 Mark McGwire	5.00	2.20
❑ R70 Travis Fryman	.40	.18
❑ R71 Andres Galarraga	.60	.25
❑ R72 Carlos Perez RC	1.00	.45
❑ R73 Tyler Green	.25	.11
❑ R74 Marty Cordova	.25	.11
❑ R75 Shawn Green	1.00	.45
❑ R76 Vaughn Eshelman	.25	.11
❑ R77 John Mabry	.25	.11
❑ R78 Jason Bates	.25	.11
❑ R79 Jon Nunnally	.25	.11
❑ R80 Ray Durham	.40	.18
❑ R81 Edgardo Alfonzo	1.00	.45
❑ R82 Esteban Loaiza	.25	.11
❑ R83 Hideo Nomo RC	10.00	4.50
❑ R84 Orlando Miller	.25	.11
❑ R85 Alex Gonzalez	.25	.11
❑ R86 M.Grudzielanek RC	3.00	1.35
❑ R87 Julian Tavarez	.25	.11
❑ R88 Benji Gil	.25	.11
❑ R89 Quilvio Veras	.25	.11
❑ R90 Ricky Bottalico	.25	.11
❑ X1 Ben Davis RC	1.00	.45
Ivan Rodriguez		
❑ X2 Mark Redman RC	2.00	.90
Manny Ramirez		
❑ X3 Reggie Taylor RC	1.00	.45
Deion Sanders		
❑ X4 Ryan Jaroncyk RC	1.00	.45
Shawn Green		
❑ X5 Juan LeBron RC	1.50	.70
Juan Gonzalez UER		
Card pictures Carlos Beltran		
instead of Juan LeBron.		
❑ X6 Tony McKnight RC	1.00	.45
Craig Biggio		
❑ X7 Michael Barrett RC	2.00	.90
Travis Fryman		
❑ X8 Corey Jenkins RC	.40	.18
Mo Vaughn		
❑ X9 Ruben Rivera	.60	.25
Frank Thomas		
❑ X10 Curtis Goodwin	.40	.18
Kenny Lofton		
❑ X11 Brian L. Hunter	1.00	.45
Tony Gwynn		
❑ X12 Todd Greene	1.50	.70
Ken Griffey Jr.		
❑ X13 Karim Garcia	.60	.25
Matt Williams		
❑ X14 Billy Wagner	1.00	.45

Randy Johnson		
❑ X15 Pat Watkins	1.00	.45
Jeff Bagwell		

1996 Bowman's Best

	MINT	NRMT
COMPLETE SET (180)	60.00	27.00
❑ 1 Hideo Nomo	1.00	.45
❑ 2 Edgar Martinez	.50	.23
❑ 3 Cal Ripken	3.00	1.35
❑ 4 Wade Boggs	.75	.35
❑ 5 Cecil Fielder	.30	.14
❑ 6 Albert Belle	.30	.14
❑ 7 Chipper Jones	1.50	.70
❑ 8 Ryne Sandberg	1.00	.45
❑ 9 Tim Salmon	.30	.14
❑ 10 Barry Bonds	2.00	.90
❑ 11 Ken Caminiti	.30	.14
❑ 12 Ron Gant	.20	.09
❑ 13 Frank Thomas	1.00	.45
❑ 14 Dante Bichette	.30	.14
❑ 15 Jason Kendall	.30	.14
❑ 16 Mo Vaughn	.30	.14
❑ 17 Rey Ordonez	.20	.09
❑ 18 Henry Rodriguez	.20	.09
❑ 19 Ryan Klesko	.30	.14
❑ 20 Jeff Bagwell	1.00	.45
❑ 21 Randy Johnson	1.00	.45
❑ 22 Jim Edmonds	.50	.23
❑ 23 Kenny Lofton	.30	.14
❑ 24 Andy Pettitte	.30	.14
❑ 25 Brady Anderson	.30	.14
❑ 26 Mike Piazza	2.00	.90
❑ 27 Greg Vaughn	.30	.14
❑ 28 Joe Carter	.30	.14
❑ 29 Jason Giambi	.75	.35
❑ 30 Ivan Rodriguez	.75	.35
❑ 31 Jeff Conine	.20	.09
❑ 32 Rafael Palmeiro	.75	.35
❑ 33 Roger Clemens	2.00	.90
❑ 34 Chuck Knoblauch	.30	.14
❑ 35 Reggie Sanders	.20	.09
❑ 36 Andres Galarraga	.50	.23
❑ 37 Paul O'Neill	.75	.35
❑ 38 Tony Gwynn	1.50	.70
❑ 39 Paul Wilson	.20	.09
❑ 40 Garret Anderson	.30	.14
❑ 41 David Justice	.30	.14
❑ 42 Eddie Murray	.75	.35
❑ 43 Mike Grace RC	.20	.09
❑ 44 Marty Cordova	.20	.09
❑ 45 Kevin Appier	.30	.14
❑ 46 Raul Mondesi	.30	.14
❑ 47 Jim Thome	.75	.35
❑ 48 Sammy Sosa	1.50	.70
❑ 49 Craig Biggio	.50	.23
❑ 50 Marquis Grissom	.20	.09
❑ 51 Alan Benes	.20	.09
❑ 52 Manny Ramirez	1.00	.45
❑ 53 Gary Sheffield	.30	.14
❑ 54 Mike Mussina	.75	.35
❑ 55 Robin Ventura	.30	.14
❑ 56 Johnny Damon	.30	.14
❑ 57 Jose Canseco	.75	.35
❑ 58 Juan Gonzalez	.75	.35
❑ 59 Tino Martinez	.30	.14
❑ 60 Brian Hunter	.20	.09
❑ 61 Fred McGriff	.50	.23
❑ 62 Jay Buhner	.30	.14
❑ 63 Carlos Delgado	.75	.35
❑ 64 Moises Alou	.30	.14
❑ 65 Roberto Alomar	.75	.35
❑ 66 Barry Larkin	.75	.35
❑ 67 Vinny Castilla	.30	.14
❑ 68 Ray Durham	.30	.14
❑ 69 Travis Fryman	.30	.14
❑ 70 Jason Isringhausen	.30	.14
❑ 71 Ken Griffey Jr.	2.50	1.10
❑ 72 John Smoltz	.30	.14
❑ 73 Matt Williams	.50	.23
❑ 74 Chan Ho Park	.30	.14
❑ 75 Mark McGwire	4.00	1.80
❑ 76 Jeffrey Hammonds	.20	.09
❑ 77 Will Clark	.75	.35
❑ 78 Kirby Puckett	2.00	.90
❑ 79 Derek Jeter	3.00	1.35
❑ 80 Derek Bell	.20	.09
❑ 81 Eric Karros	.30	.14
❑ 82 Len Dykstra	.30	.14
❑ 83 Larry Walker	.50	.23
❑ 84 Mark Grudzielanek	.20	.09
❑ 85 Greg Maddux	2.00	.90
❑ 86 Carlos Baerga	.20	.09
❑ 87 Paul Molitor	.75	.35
❑ 88 John Valentin	.20	.09
❑ 89 Mark Grace	.75	.35
❑ 90 Ray Lankford	.20	.09
❑ 91 Andruw Jones	2.00	.90
❑ 92 Nomar Garciaparra	2.50	1.10
❑ 93 Alex Ochoa	.20	.09
❑ 94 Derrick Gibson	.20	.09
❑ 95 Jeff D'Amico	.20	.09
❑ 96 Ruben Rivera	.20	.09
❑ 97 Vladimir Guerrero	2.50	1.10
❑ 98 Pokey Reese	.20	.09
❑ 99 Richard Hidalgo	.30	.14
❑ 100 Bartolo Colon	.30	.14
❑ 101 Karim Garcia	.20	.09
❑ 102 Ben Davis	.30	.14
❑ 103 Jay Powell	.20	.09
❑ 104 Chris Snopek	.20	.09
❑ 105 Glendon Rusch RC	2.50	1.10
❑ 106 Enrique Wilson	.20	.09
❑ 107 A.Alfonseca RC	1.50	.70
❑ 108 Wilton Guerrero RC	.30	.14
❑ 109 Jose Guillen RC	.75	.35
❑ 110 Miguel Mejia RC	.20	.09
❑ 111 Jay Payton	.20	.09
❑ 112 Scott Elarton	.20	.09
❑ 113 Brooks Kieschnick	.20	.09
❑ 114 Dustin Hermanson	.20	.09
❑ 115 Roger Cedeno	.20	.09
❑ 116 Matt Wagner	.20	.09
❑ 117 Lee Daniels	.20	.09
❑ 118 Ben Grieve	.30	.14
❑ 119 Ugueth Urbina	.20	.09
❑ 120 Danny Graves	.30	.14
❑ 121 Dan Donato RC	.20	.09
❑ 122 Matt Ruebel RC	.20	.09
❑ 123 Mark Sievert RC	.20	.09
❑ 124 Chris Stynes	.20	.09
❑ 125 Jeff Abbott	.20	.09
❑ 126 Rocky Coppinger RC	.20	.09
❑ 127 Jermaine Dye	.30	.14
❑ 128 Todd Greene	.20	.09
❑ 129 Chris Carpenter	.20	.09
❑ 130 Edgar Renteria	.20	.09
❑ 131 Matt Drews	.20	.09
❑ 132 Edgard Velazquez RC	.30	.14
❑ 133 Casey Whitten	.20	.09
❑ 134 Ryan Jones RC	.20	.09
❑ 135 Todd Walker	.30	.14
❑ 136 Geoff Jenkins RC	10.00	4.50
❑ 137 Matt Morris RC	8.00	3.60
❑ 138 Richie Sexson	.75	.35
❑ 139 Todd Dunwoody RC	.20	.09
❑ 140 Gabe Alvarez RC	.20	.09
❑ 141 J.J. Johnson	.20	.09
❑ 142 Shannon Stewart	.30	.14
❑ 143 Brad Fullmer	.30	.14
❑ 144 Julio Santana	.20	.09
❑ 145 Scott Rolen	1.50	.70
❑ 146 Amaury Telemaco	.20	.09
❑ 147 Trey Beamon	.20	.09
❑ 148 Billy Wagner	.20	.09
❑ 149 Todd Hollandsworth	.20	.09
❑ 150 Doug Million	.20	.09
❑ 151 Jose Valentin RC	.20	.09
❑ 152 Wes Helms RC	3.00	1.35
❑ 153 Jeff Suppan	.20	.09
❑ 154 Luis Castillo RC	3.00	1.35
❑ 155 Bob Abreu	.75	.35
❑ 156 Paul Konerko	.30	.14
❑ 157 Jamey Wright	.20	.09
❑ 158 Eddie Pearson	.20	.09
❑ 159 Jimmy Haynes	.20	.09
❑ 160 Derrek Lee	.30	.14
❑ 161 Damian Moss	.20	.09
❑ 162 Carlos Guillen RC	3.00	1.35
❑ 163 Chris Fussell RC	.20	.09
❑ 164 Mike Sweeney RC	12.00	5.50
❑ 165 Donnie Sadler	.20	.09
❑ 166 Desi Relaford	.20	.09
❑ 167 Steve Gibralter	.20	.09
❑ 168 Neifi Perez	.20	.09
❑ 169 Antone Williamson	.20	.09
❑ 170 Marty Janzen RC	.20	.09
❑ 171 Todd Helton	5.00	2.20
❑ 172 Raul Ibanez RC	.20	.09
❑ 173 Bill Selby	.20	.09
❑ 174 Shane Monahan RC	.20	.09
❑ 175 Robin Jennings	.20	.09
❑ 176 Bobby Chouinard	.20	.09
❑ 177 Einar Diaz	.20	.09
❑ 178 Jason Thompson	.20	.09
❑ 179 Rafael Medina RC	.20	.09
❑ 180 Kevin Orie	.20	.09
❑ NNO Mickey Mantle	5.00	2.20
1952 Bowman Chrome		
❑ NNO Mickey Mantle	30.00	13.50
1952 Bowman Atomic Ref.		
❑ NNO Mickey Mantle	15.00	6.75
1952 Bowman Refractor		

1997 Bowman's Best

	MINT	NRMT
COMPLETE SET (200)	50.00	22.00
❑ 1 Ken Griffey Jr.	2.50	1.10
❑ 2 Cecil Fielder	.30	.14
❑ 3 Albert Belle	.30	.14
❑ 4 Todd Hundley	.20	.09
❑ 5 Mike Piazza	2.00	.90
❑ 6 Matt Williams	.50	.23
❑ 7 Mo Vaughn	.30	.14
❑ 8 Ryne Sandberg	1.00	.45
❑ 9 Chipper Jones	1.50	.70
❑ 10 Edgar Martinez	.50	.23
❑ 11 Kenny Lofton	.30	.14
❑ 12 Ron Gant	.20	.09
❑ 13 Moises Alou	.30	.14
❑ 14 Pat Hentgen	.20	.09
❑ 15 Steve Finley	.30	.14
❑ 16 Mark Grace	.75	.35
❑ 17 Jay Buhner	.30	.14
❑ 18 Jeff Conine	.20	.09
❑ 19 Jim Edmonds	.50	.23
❑ 20 Todd Hollandsworth	.20	.09
❑ 21 Andy Pettitte	.30	.14

☐ 22	Jim Thome	.75	.35
☐ 23	Eric Young	.20	.09
☐ 24	Ray Lankford	.20	.09
☐ 25	Marquis Grissom	.20	.09
☐ 26	Tony Clark	.30	.14
☐ 27	Jermaine Allensworth	.20	.09
☐ 28	Ellis Burks	.30	.14
☐ 29	Tony Gwynn	1.50	.70
☐ 30	Barry Larkin	.75	.35
☐ 31	John Olerud	.30	.14
☐ 32	Mariano Rivera	.30	.14
☐ 33	Paul Molitor	.75	.35
☐ 34	Ken Caminiti	.30	.14
☐ 35	Gary Sheffield	.30	.14
☐ 36	Al Martin	.20	.09
☐ 37	John Valentin	.20	.09
☐ 38	Frank Thomas	1.00	.45
☐ 39	John Jaha	.20	.09
☐ 40	Greg Maddux	2.00	.90
☐ 41	Alex Fernandez	.20	.09
☐ 42	Dean Palmer	.30	.14
☐ 43	Bernie Williams	.75	.35
☐ 44	Deion Sanders	.30	.14
☐ 45	Mark McGwire	4.00	1.80
☐ 46	Brian Jordan	.30	.14
☐ 47	Bernard Gilkey	.20	.09
☐ 48	Will Clark	.75	.35
☐ 49	Kevin Appier	.30	.14
☐ 50	Tom Glavine	.75	.35
☐ 51	Chuck Knoblauch	.30	.14
☐ 52	Rondell White	.30	.14
☐ 53	Greg Vaughn	.30	.14
☐ 54	Mike Mussina	.75	.35
☐ 55	Brian McRae	.20	.09
☐ 56	Chili Davis	.30	.14
☐ 57	Wade Boggs	.75	.35
☐ 58	Jeff Bagwell	1.00	.45
☐ 59	Roberto Alomar	.75	.35
☐ 60	Dennis Eckersley	.30	.14
☐ 61	Ryan Klesko	.30	.14
☐ 62	Manny Ramirez	1.00	.45
☐ 63	John Wetteland	.30	.14
☐ 64	Cal Ripken	3.00	1.35
☐ 65	Edgar Renteria	.20	.09
☐ 66	Tino Martinez	.30	.14
☐ 67	Larry Walker	.50	.23
☐ 68	Gregg Jefferies	.20	.09
☐ 69	Lance Johnson	.20	.09
☐ 70	Carlos Delgado	.75	.35
☐ 71	Craig Biggio	.50	.23
☐ 72	Jose Canseco	.75	.35
☐ 73	Barry Bonds	2.00	.90
☐ 74	Juan Gonzalez	.75	.35
☐ 75	Eric Karros	.30	.14
☐ 76	Reggie Sanders	.20	.09
☐ 77	Robin Ventura	.30	.14
☐ 78	Hideo Nomo	.75	.35
☐ 79	David Justice	.30	.14
☐ 80	Vinny Castilla	.30	.14
☐ 81	Travis Fryman	.30	.14
☐ 82	Derek Jeter	3.00	1.35
☐ 83	Sammy Sosa	1.50	.70
☐ 84	Ivan Rodriguez	.75	.35
☐ 85	Rafael Palmeiro	.75	.35
☐ 86	Roger Clemens	2.00	.90
☐ 87	Jason Giambi	.75	.35
☐ 88	Andres Galarraga	.50	.23
☐ 89	Jermaine Dye	.30	.14
☐ 90	Joe Carter	.30	.14
☐ 91	Brady Anderson	.30	.14
☐ 92	Derek Bell	.20	.09
☐ 93	Randy Johnson	1.00	.45
☐ 94	Fred McGriff	.50	.23
☐ 95	John Smoltz	.30	.14
☐ 96	Harold Baines	.30	.14
☐ 97	Raul Mondesi	.30	.14
☐ 98	Tim Salmon	.30	.14
☐ 99	Carlos Baerga	.20	.09
☐ 100	Dante Bichette	.30	.14
☐ 101	Vladimir Guerrero	1.25	.55
☐ 102	Richard Hidalgo	.30	.14
☐ 103	Paul Konerko	.30	.14
☐ 104	Alex Gonzalez RC	.60	.25
☐ 105	Jason Dickson	.20	.09
☐ 106	Jose Rosado	.20	.09
☐ 107	Todd Walker	.20	.09
☐ 108	Seth Greisinger RC	.30	.14
☐ 109	Todd Helton	1.25	.55
☐ 110	Ben Davis	.30	.14
☐ 111	Bartolo Colon	.30	.14
☐ 112	Elieser Marrero	.20	.09
☐ 113	Jeff D'Amico	.20	.09
☐ 114	Miguel Tejada RC	5.00	2.20
☐ 115	Darin Erstad	.75	.35
☐ 116	Kris Benson RC	2.00	.90
☐ 117	Adrian Beltre RC	5.00	2.20
☐ 118	Neifi Perez	.20	.09
☐ 119	Pokey Reese	.20	.09
☐ 120	Carl Pavano	.20	.09
☐ 121	Juan Melo	.20	.09
☐ 122	Kevin McGlinchy RC	.30	.14
☐ 123	Pat Cline	.20	.09
☐ 124	Felix Heredia RC	.20	.09
☐ 125	Aaron Boone	.20	.09
☐ 126	Glendon Rusch	.20	.09
☐ 127	Mike Cameron	.30	.14
☐ 128	Justin Thompson	.20	.09
☐ 129	Chad Hermansen RC	.60	.25
☐ 130	Sidney Ponson RC	1.00	.45
☐ 131	Willie Martinez RC	.30	.14
☐ 132	Paul Wilder RC	.20	.09
☐ 133	Geoff Jenkins	.50	.23
☐ 134	Roy Halladay RC	.30	.14
☐ 135	Carlos Guillen	.20	.09
☐ 136	Tony Batista	.30	.14
☐ 137	Todd Greene	.20	.09
☐ 138	Luis Castillo	.20	.09
☐ 139	Jimmy Anderson RC	.20	.09
☐ 140	Edgard Velazquez	.20	.09
☐ 141	Chris Snopek	.20	.09
☐ 142	Ruben Rivera	.20	.09
☐ 143	Javier Valentin	.20	.09
☐ 144	Brian Rose	.20	.09
☐ 145	Fernando Tatis RC	1.00	.45
☐ 146	Dean Crow RC	.20	.09
☐ 147	Karim Garcia	.20	.09
☐ 148	Dante Powell	.20	.09
☐ 149	Hideki Irabu RC	.30	.14
☐ 150	Matt Morris	.30	.14
☐ 151	Wes Helms	.30	.14
☐ 152	Russ Johnson	.20	.09
☐ 153	Jarrod Washburn	.20	.09
☐ 154	Kerry Wood RC	6.00	2.70
☐ 155	Joe Fontenot RC	.30	.14
☐ 156	Eugene Kingsale	.20	.09
☐ 157	Terrence Long	.30	.14
☐ 158	Calvin Maduro	.20	.09
☐ 159	Jeff Suppan	.20	.09
☐ 160	DaRond Stovall	.20	.09
☐ 161	Mark Redman	.20	.09
☐ 162	Ken Cloude RC	.20	.09
☐ 163	Bobby Estalella	.20	.09
☐ 164	Abraham Nunez RC	.30	.14
☐ 165	Derrick Gibson	.20	.09
☐ 166	Mike Drumright RC	.20	.09
☐ 167	Katsuhiro Maeda	.20	.09
☐ 168	Jeff Liefer	.20	.09
☐ 169	Ben Grieve	.30	.14
☐ 170	Bob Abreu	.30	.14
☐ 171	Shannon Stewart	.30	.14
☐ 172	Braden Looper RC	.20	.09
☐ 173	Brant Brown	.20	.09
☐ 174	Marlon Anderson	.20	.09
☐ 175	Brad Fullmer	.30	.14
☐ 176	Carlos Beltran	.75	.35
☐ 177	Nomar Garciaparra	2.00	.90
☐ 178	Derrek Lee	.30	.14
☐ 179	Val.De Los Santos RC	.20	.09
☐ 180	Dmitri Young	.30	.14
☐ 181	Jamey Wright	.20	.09
☐ 182	Hiram Bocachica RC	.30	.14
☐ 183	Wilton Guerrero	.20	.09
☐ 184	Chris Carpenter	.20	.09
☐ 185	Scott Spiezio	.20	.09
☐ 186	Andruw Jones	1.00	.45
☐ 187	Travis Lee RC	2.00	.90
☐ 188	Jose Cruz Jr. RC	3.00	1.35
☐ 189	Jose Guillen	.20	.09
☐ 190	Jeff Abbott	.20	.09
☐ 191	Ricky Ledee RC	.75	.35
☐ 192	Mike Sweeney	.30	.14
☐ 193	Donnie Sadler	.20	.09
☐ 194	Scott Rolen	.75	.35
☐ 195	Kevin Orie	.20	.09
☐ 196	Jason Conti RC	.30	.14
☐ 197	Mark Kotsay RC	1.25	.55
☐ 198	Eric Milton RC	2.50	1.10
☐ 199	Russell Branyan	.30	.14
☐ 200	Alex Sanchez RC	.30	.14

1998 Bowman's Best

		MINT	NRMT
COMPLETE SET (200)		60.00	27.00
☐ 1	Mark McGwire	3.00	1.35
☐ 2	Jeromy Burnitz	.30	.14
☐ 3	Barry Bonds	2.00	.90
☐ 4	Dante Bichette	.30	.14
☐ 5	Chipper Jones	1.50	.70
☐ 6	Frank Thomas	1.00	.45
☐ 7	Kevin Brown	.50	.23
☐ 8	Juan Gonzalez	.75	.35
☐ 9	Jay Buhner	.30	.14
☐ 10	Chuck Knoblauch	.30	.14
☐ 11	Cal Ripken	3.00	1.35
☐ 12	Matt Williams	.50	.23
☐ 13	Jim Edmonds	.50	.23
☐ 14	Manny Ramirez	1.00	.45
☐ 15	Tony Clark	.30	.14
☐ 16	Mo Vaughn	.30	.14
☐ 17	Bernie Williams	.75	.35
☐ 18	Scott Rolen	.75	.35
☐ 19	Gary Sheffield	.30	.14
☐ 20	Albert Belle	.30	.14
☐ 21	Mike Piazza	2.00	.90
☐ 22	John Olerud	.30	.14
☐ 23	Tony Gwynn	1.50	.70
☐ 24	Jay Bell	.30	.14
☐ 25	Jose Cruz Jr.	.30	.14
☐ 26	Justin Thompson	.20	.09
☐ 27	Ken Griffey Jr.	2.50	1.10
☐ 28	Sandy Alomar Jr.	.30	.14
☐ 29	Mark Grudzielanek	.20	.09
☐ 30	Mark Grace	.75	.35
☐ 31	Ron Gant	.30	.14
☐ 32	Javy Lopez	.30	.14
☐ 33	Jeff Bagwell	1.00	.45
☐ 34	Fred McGriff	.50	.23
☐ 35	Rafael Palmeiro	.75	.35
☐ 36	Vinny Castilla	.30	.14
☐ 37	Andy Benes	.20	.09
☐ 38	Pedro Martinez	1.00	.45
☐ 39	Andy Pettitte	.30	.14
☐ 40	Marty Cordova	.20	.09
☐ 41	Rusty Greer	.30	.14
☐ 42	Kevin Orie	.20	.09
☐ 43	Chan Ho Park	.30	.14
☐ 44	Ryan Klesko	.30	.14
☐ 45	Alex Rodriguez	2.00	.90
☐ 46	Travis Fryman	.30	.14
☐ 47	Jeff King	.20	.09
☐ 48	Roger Clemens	2.00	.90
☐ 49	Darin Erstad	.75	.35
☐ 50	Brady Anderson	.30	.14
☐ 51	Jason Kendall	.30	.14
☐ 52	John Valentin	.20	.09
☐ 53	Ellis Burks	.30	.14
☐ 54	Brian Hunter	.20	.09
☐ 55	Paul O'Neill	.75	.35

Card	MINT	NRMT
❑ 56 Ken Caminiti	.30	.14
❑ 57 David Justice	.30	.14
❑ 58 Eric Karros	.30	.14
❑ 59 Pat Hentgen	.20	.09
❑ 60 Greg Maddux	2.00	.90
❑ 61 Craig Biggio	.50	.23
❑ 62 Edgar Martinez	.50	.23
❑ 63 Mike Mussina	.75	.35
❑ 64 Larry Walker	.50	.23
❑ 65 Tino Martinez	.30	.14
❑ 66 Jim Thome	.75	.35
❑ 67 Tom Glavine	.75	.35
❑ 68 Raul Mondesi	.30	.14
❑ 69 Marquis Grissom	.20	.09
❑ 70 Randy Johnson	1.00	.45
❑ 71 Steve Finley	.30	.14
❑ 72 Jose Guillen	.20	.09
❑ 73 Nomar Garciaparra	2.00	.90
❑ 74 Wade Boggs	.75	.35
❑ 75 Bobby Higginson	.30	.14
❑ 76 Robin Ventura	.30	.14
❑ 77 Derek Jeter	3.00	1.35
❑ 78 Andruw Jones	.75	.35
❑ 79 Ray Lankford	.20	.09
❑ 80 Vladimir Guerrero	1.00	.45
❑ 81 Kenny Lofton	.30	.14
❑ 82 Ivan Rodriguez	.75	.35
❑ 83 Neifi Perez	.20	.09
❑ 84 John Smoltz	.30	.14
❑ 85 Tim Salmon	.30	.14
❑ 86 Carlos Delgado	.75	.35
❑ 87 Sammy Sosa	1.50	.70
❑ 88 Jaret Wright	.20	.09
❑ 89 Roberto Alomar	.75	.35
❑ 90 Paul Molitor	.75	.35
❑ 91 Dean Palmer	.30	.14
❑ 92 Barry Larkin	.75	.35
❑ 93 Jason Giambi	.75	.35
❑ 94 Curt Schilling	.75	.35
❑ 95 Eric Young	.20	.09
❑ 96 Denny Neagle	.20	.09
❑ 97 Moises Alou	.30	.14
❑ 98 Livan Hernandez	.20	.09
❑ 99 Todd Hundley	.20	.09
❑ 100 Andres Galarraga	.50	.23
❑ 101 Travis Lee	.30	.14
❑ 102 Lance Berkman	.75	.35
❑ 103 Orlando Cabrera	.20	.09
❑ 104 Mike Lowell RC	2.00	.90
❑ 105 Ben Grieve	.30	.14
❑ 106 Jae Weong Seo RC	1.25	.55
❑ 107 Richie Sexson	.30	.14
❑ 108 Eli Marrero	.20	.09
❑ 109 Aramis Ramirez	.30	.14
❑ 110 Paul Konerko	.30	.14
❑ 111 Carl Pavano	.20	.09
❑ 112 Brad Fullmer	.30	.14
❑ 113 Matt Clement	.20	.09
❑ 114 Donzell McDonald	.20	.09
❑ 115 Todd Helton	1.00	.45
❑ 116 Mike Caruso	.20	.09
❑ 117 Donnie Sadler	.20	.09
❑ 118 Bruce Chen	.20	.09
❑ 119 Jarrod Washburn	.20	.09
❑ 120 Adrian Beltre	.30	.14
❑ 121 Ryan Jackson RC	.20	.09
❑ 122 Kevin Millar RC	.20	.09
❑ 123 Corey Koskie RC	2.00	.90
❑ 124 Dermal Brown	.20	.09
❑ 125 Kerry Wood	.75	.35
❑ 126 Juan Melo	.20	.09
❑ 127 Ramon Hernandez	.20	.09
❑ 128 Roy Halladay	.20	.09
❑ 129 Ron Wright	.20	.09
❑ 130 Darnell McDonald RC	.30	.14
❑ 131 Odalis Perez RC	.75	.35
❑ 132 Alex Cora RC	1.00	.45
❑ 133 Justin Towle	.20	.09
❑ 134 Juan Encarnacion	.30	.14
❑ 135 Brian Rose	.20	.09
❑ 136 Russell Branyan	.30	.14
❑ 137 Cesar King RC	.30	.14
❑ 138 Ruben Rivera	.20	.09
❑ 139 Ricky Ledee	.20	.09
❑ 140 Vernon Wells	.50	.23
❑ 141 Luis Rivas RC	1.50	.70
❑ 142 Brent Butler	.20	.09
❑ 143 Karim Garcia	.20	.09
❑ 144 George Lombard	.20	.09
❑ 145 Masato Yoshii RC	1.25	.55
❑ 146 Braden Looper	.20	.09
❑ 147 Alex Sanchez	.20	.09
❑ 148 Kris Benson	.30	.14
❑ 149 Mark Kotsay	.30	.14
❑ 150 Richard Hidalgo	.30	.14
❑ 151 Scott Elarton	.20	.09
❑ 152 Ryan Minor RC	.30	.14
❑ 153 Troy Glaus RC	8.00	3.60
❑ 154 Carlos Lee RC	2.50	1.10
❑ 155 Michael Coleman	.20	.09
❑ 156 Jason Grilli RC	.30	.14
❑ 157 Julio Ramirez RC	.30	.14
❑ 158 Randy Wolf RC	1.25	.55
❑ 159 Ryan Brannan	.20	.09
❑ 160 Edgard Clemente	.20	.09
❑ 161 Miguel Tejada	.50	.23
❑ 162 Chad Hermansen	.20	.09
❑ 163 Ryan Anderson RC	4.00	1.80
❑ 164 Ben Petrick	.20	.09
❑ 165 Alex Gonzalez	.20	.09
❑ 166 Ben Davis	.30	.14
❑ 167 John Patterson	.20	.09
❑ 168 Cliff Politte	.20	.09
❑ 169 Randall Simon	.20	.09
❑ 170 Javier Vazquez	.30	.14
❑ 171 Kevin Witt	.20	.09
❑ 172 Geoff Jenkins	.30	.14
❑ 173 David Ortiz	.30	.14
❑ 174 Derrick Gibson	.20	.09
❑ 175 Abraham Nunez	.20	.09
❑ 176 A.J. Hinch	.20	.09
❑ 177 Ruben Mateo RC	2.00	.90
❑ 178 Magglio Ordonez RC	5.00	2.20
❑ 179 Todd Dunwoody	.20	.09
❑ 180 Daryle Ward	.20	.09
❑ 181 Mike Kinkade RC	.30	.14
❑ 182 Willie Martinez	.30	.14
❑ 183 O.Hernandez RC	2.00	.90
❑ 184 Eric Milton	.30	.14
❑ 185 Eric Chavez	.30	.14
❑ 186 Damian Jackson	.20	.09
❑ 187 Jim Parque RC	.75	.35
❑ 188 Dan Reichert RC	1.25	.55
❑ 189 Mike Drumright	.20	.09
❑ 190 Todd Walker	.20	.09
❑ 191 Shane Monahan	.20	.09
❑ 192 Derrek Lee	.30	.14
❑ 193 Jeremy Giambi RC	1.25	.55
❑ 194 Dan McKinley RC	.30	.14
❑ 195 Tony Armas Jr. RC	3.00	1.35
❑ 196 Matt Anderson RC	.30	.14
❑ 197 Jim Chamblee RC	.20	.09
❑ 198 F.Cordero RC	.50	.23
❑ 199 Calvin Pickering	.20	.09
❑ 200 Reggie Taylor	.20	.09

1999 Bowman's Best

	MINT	NRMT
COMPLETE SET (200)	100.00	45.00
COMP.SET w/o SP's (150)	30.00	13.50
COMMON CARD (1-150)	.20	.09
COMMON ROOKIE (151-200)	.60	.25

Card	MINT	NRMT
❑ 1 Chipper Jones	1.50	.70
❑ 2 Brian Jordan	.30	.14
❑ 3 David Justice	.30	.14
❑ 4 Jason Kendall	.30	.14
❑ 5 Mo Vaughn	.30	.14
❑ 6 Jim Edmonds	.50	.23
❑ 7 Wade Boggs	.75	.35
❑ 8 Jeromy Burnitz	.30	.14
❑ 9 Todd Hundley	.20	.09
❑ 10 Rondell White	.30	.14
❑ 11 Cliff Floyd	.30	.14
❑ 12 Sean Casey	.50	.23
❑ 13 Bernie Williams	.75	.35
❑ 14 Dante Bichette	.30	.14
❑ 15 Greg Vaughn	.30	.14
❑ 16 Andres Galarraga	.50	.23
❑ 17 Ray Durham	.30	.14
❑ 18 Jim Thome	.75	.35
❑ 19 Gary Sheffield	.30	.14
❑ 20 Frank Thomas	1.00	.45
❑ 21 Orlando Hernandez	.30	.14
❑ 22 Ivan Rodriguez	.75	.35
❑ 23 Jose Cruz Jr.	.30	.14
❑ 24 Jason Giambi	.75	.35
❑ 25 Craig Biggio	.50	.23
❑ 26 Kerry Wood	.75	.35
❑ 27 Manny Ramirez	1.00	.45
❑ 28 Curt Schilling	.75	.35
❑ 29 Mike Mussina	.75	.35
❑ 30 Tim Salmon	.30	.14
❑ 31 Mike Piazza	2.00	.90
❑ 32 Roberto Alomar	.75	.35
❑ 33 Larry Walker	.50	.23
❑ 34 Barry Larkin	.75	.35
❑ 35 Nomar Garciaparra	2.00	.90
❑ 36 Paul O'Neill	.75	.35
❑ 37 Todd Walker	.20	.09
❑ 38 Eric Karros	.30	.14
❑ 39 Brad Fullmer	.30	.14
❑ 40 John Olerud	.30	.14
❑ 41 Todd Helton	1.00	.45
❑ 42 Raul Mondesi	.30	.14
❑ 43 Jose Canseco	.75	.35
❑ 44 Matt Williams	.50	.23
❑ 45 Ray Lankford	.20	.09
❑ 46 Carlos Delgado	.75	.35
❑ 47 Darin Erstad	.75	.35
❑ 48 Vladimir Guerrero	1.00	.45
❑ 49 Robin Ventura	.30	.14
❑ 50 Alex Rodriguez	2.00	.90
❑ 51 Vinny Castilla	.30	.14
❑ 52 Tony Clark	.30	.14
❑ 53 Pedro Martinez	1.00	.45
❑ 54 Rafael Palmeiro	.75	.35
❑ 55 Scott Rolen	.75	.35
❑ 56 Tino Martinez	.30	.14
❑ 57 Tony Gwynn	1.50	.70
❑ 58 Barry Bonds	2.00	.90
❑ 59 Kenny Lofton	.30	.14
❑ 60 Javy Lopez	.30	.14
❑ 61 Mark Grace	.75	.35
❑ 62 Travis Lee	.20	.09
❑ 63 Kevin Brown	.50	.23
❑ 64 Al Leiter	.30	.14
❑ 65 Albert Belle	.30	.14
❑ 66 Sammy Sosa	1.50	.70
❑ 67 Greg Maddux	2.00	.90
❑ 68 Mark Kotsay	.20	.09
❑ 69 Dmitri Young	.30	.14
❑ 70 Mark McGwire	3.00	1.35
❑ 71 Juan Gonzalez	.75	.35
❑ 72 Andruw Jones	.75	.35
❑ 73 Derek Jeter	3.00	1.35
❑ 74 Randy Johnson	1.00	.45
❑ 75 Cal Ripken	3.00	1.35
❑ 76 Shawn Green	.75	.35
❑ 77 Moises Alou	.30	.14
❑ 78 Tom Glavine	.75	.35
❑ 79 Sandy Alomar Jr.	.30	.14
❑ 80 Ken Griffey Jr.	2.50	1.10
❑ 81 Ryan Klesko	.30	.14
❑ 82 Jeff Bagwell	1.00	.45
❑ 83 Ben Grieve	.30	.14
❑ 84 John Smoltz	.30	.14
❑ 85 Roger Clemens	2.00	.90
❑ 86 Ken Griffey Jr. BP	1.25	.55

❑ 87	Roger Clemens BP	1.00	.45
❑ 88	Derek Jeter BP	1.50	.70
❑ 89	Nomar Garciaparra BP	1.00	.45
❑ 90	Mark McGwire BP	1.50	.70
❑ 91	Sammy Sosa BP	.75	.35
❑ 92	Alex Rodriguez BP	1.00	.45
❑ 93	Greg Maddux BP	1.00	.45
❑ 94	Vladimir Guerrero BP	.50	.23
❑ 95	Chipper Jones BP	.75	.35
❑ 96	Kerry Wood BP	.30	.14
❑ 97	Ben Grieve BP	.30	.14
❑ 98	Tony Gwynn BP	.75	.35
❑ 99	Juan Gonzalez BP	.30	.14
❑ 100	Mike Piazza BP	1.00	.45
❑ 101	Eric Chavez	.30	.14
❑ 102	Billy Koch	.20	.09
❑ 103	Dernell Stenson	.20	.09
❑ 104	Marlon Anderson	.20	.09
❑ 105	Ron Belliard	.20	.09
❑ 106	Bruce Chen	.20	.09
❑ 107	Carlos Beltran	.30	.14
❑ 108	Chad Hermansen	.20	.09
❑ 109	Ryan Anderson	.30	.14
❑ 110	Michael Barrett	.20	.09
❑ 111	Matt Clement	.20	.09
❑ 112	Ben Davis	.30	.14
❑ 113	Calvin Pickering	.20	.09
❑ 114	Brad Penny	.30	.14
❑ 115	Paul Konerko	.30	.14
❑ 116	Alex Gonzalez	.20	.09
❑ 117	George Lombard	.20	.09
❑ 118	John Patterson	.20	.09
❑ 119	Rob Bell	.20	.09
❑ 120	Ruben Mateo	.30	.14
❑ 121	Troy Glaus	.75	.35
❑ 122	Ryan Bradley	.20	.09
❑ 123	Carlos Lee	.30	.14
❑ 124	Gabe Kapler	.30	.14
❑ 125	Ramon Hernandez	.20	.09
❑ 126	Carlos Febles	.20	.09
❑ 127	Mitch Meluskey	.20	.09
❑ 128	Michael Cuddyer	.30	.14
❑ 129	Pablo Ozuna	.20	.09
❑ 130	Jayson Werth	.20	.09
❑ 131	Ricky Ledee	.20	.09
❑ 132	Jeremy Giambi	.20	.09
❑ 133	Danny Klassen	.20	.09
❑ 134	Mark DeRosa	.20	.09
❑ 135	Randy Wolf	.20	.09
❑ 136	Roy Halladay	.20	.09
❑ 137	Derrick Gibson	.20	.09
❑ 138	Ben Petrick	.20	.09
❑ 139	Warren Morris	.20	.09
❑ 140	Lance Berkman	.75	.35
❑ 141	Russell Branyan	.30	.14
❑ 142	Adrian Beltre	.30	.14
❑ 143	Juan Encarnacion	.30	.14
❑ 144	Fernando Seguignol	.20	.09
❑ 145	Corey Koskie	.30	.14
❑ 146	Preston Wilson	.30	.14
❑ 147	Homer Bush	.20	.09
❑ 148	Daryle Ward	.20	.09
❑ 149	Joe McEwing RC	.30	.14
❑ 150	Peter Bergeron RC	1.25	.55
❑ 151	Pat Burrell RC	4.00	1.80
❑ 152	Choo Freeman RC	1.00	.45
❑ 153	Matt Belisle RC	1.25	.55
❑ 154	Carlos Pena RC	4.00	1.80
❑ 155	A.J. Burnett RC	2.00	.90
❑ 156	D.Mientkiewicz RC	3.00	1.35
❑ 157	Sean Burroughs RC	6.00	2.70
❑ 158	Mike Zywica RC	.20	.09
❑ 159	Corey Patterson RC	4.00	1.80
❑ 160	Austin Kearns RC	5.00	2.20
❑ 161	Chip Ambres RC	1.00	.45
❑ 162	Kelly Dransfeldt RC	.20	.09
❑ 163	Mike Nannini RC	1.25	.55
❑ 164	Mark Mulder RC	5.00	2.20
❑ 165	Jason Tyner RC	.75	.35
❑ 166	Bobby Seay RC	.75	.35
❑ 167	Alex Escobar RC	3.00	1.35
❑ 168	Nick Johnson RC	4.00	1.80
❑ 169	Alfonso Soriano RC	6.00	2.70
❑ 170	Clayton Andrews RC	.60	.25
❑ 171	C.C. Sabathia RC	5.00	2.20
❑ 172	Matt Holliday RC	1.25	.55
❑ 173	Brad Lidge RC	.60	.25
❑ 174	Kit Pellow RC	.75	.35
❑ 175	J.M. Gold RC	.75	.35
❑ 176	Roosevelt Brown RC	.75	.35
❑ 177	Eric Valent RC	1.50	.70
❑ 178	Adam Everett RC	1.00	.45
❑ 179	Jorge Toca RC	.60	.25
❑ 180	Matt Roney RC	.75	.35
❑ 181	Andy Brown RC	1.00	.45
❑ 182	Phil Norton RC	.20	.09
❑ 183	Mickey Lopez RC	.20	.09
❑ 184	Chris George RC	1.50	.70
❑ 185	Arturo McDowell RC	.60	.25
❑ 186	Jose Fernandez RC	.20	.09
❑ 187	Seth Etherton RC	.75	.35
❑ 188	Josh McKinley RC	.75	.35
❑ 189	Nate Cornejo RC	2.50	1.10
❑ 190	G.Chiaramonte RC	.75	.35
❑ 191	Mamon Tucker RC	.75	.35
❑ 192	Ryan Mills RC	.60	.25
❑ 193	Chad Moeller RC	.20	.09
❑ 194	Tony Torcato RC	1.50	.70
❑ 195	Jeff Winchester RC	.75	.35
❑ 196	Rick Elder RC	1.50	.70
❑ 197	Matt Burch RC	.30	.14
❑ 198	Jeff Urban RC	.30	.14
❑ 199	Chris Jones RC	.75	.35
❑ 200	Masao Kida RC	.75	.35

2000 Bowman's Best

	MINT	NRMT
COMPLETE SET (200)	500.00	220.00
COMP.SET w/o RC's (150)	60.00	27.00
COMMON CARD (1-150)	.20	.09
COMMON ROOKIE (151-200)	8.00	3.60

❑ 1	Nomar Garciaparra	2.00	.90
❑ 2	Chipper Jones	1.50	.70
❑ 3	Tony Clark	.30	.14
❑ 4	Bernie Williams	.75	.35
❑ 5	Barry Bonds	2.00	.90
❑ 6	Jermaine Dye	.30	.14
❑ 7	John Olerud	.30	.14
❑ 8	Mike Hampton	.30	.14
❑ 9	Cal Ripken	3.00	1.35
❑ 10	Jeff Bagwell	1.00	.45
❑ 11	Troy Glaus	.75	.35
❑ 12	J.D. Drew	.75	.35
❑ 13	Jeromy Burnitz	.30	.14
❑ 14	Carlos Delgado	.75	.35
❑ 15	Shawn Green	.75	.35
❑ 16	Kevin Millwood	.20	.09
❑ 17	Rondell White	.30	.14
❑ 18	Scott Rolen	.75	.35
❑ 19	Jeff Cirillo	.30	.14
❑ 20	Barry Larkin	.75	.35
❑ 21	Brian Giles	.30	.14
❑ 22	Roger Clemens	2.00	.90
❑ 23	Manny Ramirez	1.00	.45
❑ 24	Alex Gonzalez	.20	.09
❑ 25	Mark Grace	.75	.35
❑ 26	Fernando Tatis	.20	.09
❑ 27	Randy Johnson	1.00	.45
❑ 28	Roger Cedeno	.20	.09
❑ 29	Brian Jordan	.30	.14
❑ 30	Kevin Brown	.30	.14
❑ 31	Greg Vaughn	.30	.14
❑ 32	Roberto Alomar	.75	.35
❑ 33	Larry Walker	.50	.23
❑ 34	Rafael Palmeiro	.75	.35
❑ 35	Curt Schilling	.75	.35
❑ 36	Orlando Hernandez	.30	.14
❑ 37	Todd Walker	.20	.09
❑ 38	Juan Gonzalez	.75	.35
❑ 39	Sean Casey	.50	.23
❑ 40	Tony Gwynn	1.50	.70
❑ 41	Albert Belle	.30	.14
❑ 42	Gary Sheffield	.30	.14
❑ 43	Michael Barrett	.20	.09
❑ 44	Preston Wilson	.30	.14
❑ 45	Jim Thome	.75	.35
❑ 46	Shannon Stewart	.30	.14
❑ 47	Mo Vaughn	.30	.14
❑ 48	Ben Grieve	.30	.14
❑ 49	Adrian Beltre	.30	.14
❑ 50	Sammy Sosa	1.50	.70
❑ 51	Bob Abreu	.30	.14
❑ 52	Edgardo Alfonzo	.30	.14
❑ 53	Carlos Febles	.20	.09
❑ 54	Frank Thomas	1.00	.45
❑ 55	Alex Rodriguez	2.00	.90
❑ 56	Cliff Floyd	.30	.14
❑ 57	Jose Canseco	.75	.35
❑ 58	Erubiel Durazo	.30	.14
❑ 59	Tim Hudson	.75	.35
❑ 60	Craig Biggio	.50	.23
❑ 61	Eric Karros	.30	.14
❑ 62	Mike Mussina	.75	.35
❑ 63	Robin Ventura	.30	.14
❑ 64	Carlos Beltran	.30	.14
❑ 65	Pedro Martinez	1.00	.45
❑ 66	Gabe Kapler	.30	.14
❑ 67	Jason Kendall	.30	.14
❑ 68	Derek Jeter	3.00	1.35
❑ 69	Magglio Ordonez	.30	.14
❑ 70	Mike Piazza	2.00	.90
❑ 71	Mike Lieberthal	.30	.14
❑ 72	Andres Galarraga	.50	.23
❑ 73	Raul Mondesi	.30	.14
❑ 74	Eric Chavez	.30	.14
❑ 75	Greg Maddux	2.00	.90
❑ 76	Matt Williams	.50	.23
❑ 77	Kris Benson	.30	.14
❑ 78	Ivan Rodriguez	.75	.35
❑ 79	Pokey Reese	.20	.09
❑ 80	Vladimir Guerrero	1.00	.45
❑ 81	Mark McGwire	3.00	1.35
❑ 82	Vinny Castilla	.30	.14
❑ 83	Todd Helton	1.00	.45
❑ 84	Andruw Jones	.75	.35
❑ 85	Ken Griffey Jr.	2.50	1.10
❑ 86	Mark McGwire BP	1.50	.70
❑ 87	Derek Jeter BP	1.50	.70
❑ 88	Chipper Jones BP	.75	.35
❑ 89	Nomar Garciaparra BP	1.00	.45
❑ 90	Sammy Sosa BP	.75	.35
❑ 91	Cal Ripken BP	1.50	.70
❑ 92	Juan Gonzalez BP	.30	.14
❑ 93	Alex Rodriguez BP	1.00	.45
❑ 94	Barry Bonds BP	1.00	.45
❑ 95	Sean Casey BP	.50	.23
❑ 96	Vladimir Guerrero BP	.50	.23
❑ 97	Mike Piazza BP	1.00	.45
❑ 98	Shawn Green BP	.30	.14
❑ 99	Jeff Bagwell BP	.50	.23
❑ 100	Ken Griffey Jr. BP	1.25	.55
❑ 101	Rick Ankiel	.75	.35
❑ 102	John Patterson	.20	.09
❑ 103	David Walling	.20	.09
❑ 104	Michael Restovich	.30	.14
❑ 105	A.J. Burnett	.30	.14
❑ 106	Pablo Ozuna	.20	.09
❑ 107	Chad Hermansen	.20	.09
❑ 108	Choo Freeman	.30	.14
❑ 109	Mark Quinn	.30	.14
❑ 110	Corey Patterson	.75	.35
❑ 111	Ramon Ortiz	.30	.14
❑ 112	Vernon Wells	.30	.14
❑ 113	Milton Bradley	.20	.09
❑ 114	Travis Dawkins	.30	.14
❑ 115	Sean Burroughs	.75	.35
❑ 116	Wily Mo Pena	.75	.35
❑ 117	Dee Brown	.20	.09

❑ 118 C.C. Sabathia .75 .35
❑ 119 Adam Kennedy .20 .09
❑ 120 Octavio Dotel .20 .09
❑ 121 Kip Wells .30 .14
❑ 122 Ben Petrick .20 .09
❑ 123 Mark Mulder .75 .35
❑ 124 Jason Standridge .20 .09
❑ 125 Adam Piatt .50 .23
❑ 126 Steve Lomasney .20 .09
❑ 127 Jayson Werth .20 .09
❑ 128 Alex Escobar .30 .14
❑ 129 Ryan Anderson .30 .14
❑ 130 Adam Dunn 2.00 .90
❑ 131 Ted Lilly .20 .09
❑ 132 Brad Penny .30 .14
❑ 133 Daryle Ward .20 .09
❑ 134 Eric Munson .30 .14
❑ 135 Nick Johnson .75 .35
❑ 136 Jason Jennings .30 .14
❑ 137 Tim Raines Jr. .30 .14
❑ 138 Ruben Mateo .30 .14
❑ 139 Jack Cust .30 .14
❑ 140 Rafael Furcal .75 .35
❑ 141 Eric Gagne .20 .09
❑ 142 Tony Armas Jr. .30 .14
❑ 143 Mike Paradis .20 .09
❑ 144 Peter Bergeron .20 .09
❑ 145 Alfonso Soriano .75 .35
❑ 146 Josh Hamilton 1.00 .45
❑ 147 Michael Cuddyer .30 .14
❑ 148 Jay Gehrke .20 .09
❑ 149 Josh Girdley .20 .09
❑ 150 Pat Burrell .75 .35
❑ 151 Brett Myers RC 12.00 5.50
❑ 152 Scott Seabol RC 8.00 3.60
❑ 153 Keith Reed RC 12.00 5.50
❑ 154 F.Rodriguez RC 10.00 4.50
❑ 155 Barry Zito RC 40.00 18.00
❑ 156 Pat Manning RC 15.00 6.75
❑ 157 Ben Christensen RC 8.00 3.60
❑ 158 Corey Myers RC 10.00 4.50
❑ 159 Wascar Serrano RC 10.00 4.50
❑ 160 Wes Anderson RC 10.00 4.50
❑ 161 Andy Tracy RC 8.00 3.60
❑ 162 Cesar Saba RC 8.00 3.60
❑ 163 Mike Lamb RC 10.00 4.50
❑ 164 Bobby Bradley RC 15.00 6.75
❑ 165 Vince Faison RC 10.00 4.50
❑ 166 Ty Howington RC 20.00 9.00
❑ 167 Ken Harvey RC 30.00 13.50
❑ 168 Josh Kalinowski RC 8.00 3.60
❑ 169 Ruben Salazar RC 15.00 6.75
❑ 170 Aaron Rowand RC 15.00 6.75
❑ 171 Ramon Santiago RC 12.00 5.50
❑ 172 Scott Sobkowiak RC 8.00 3.60
❑ 173 Lyle Overbay RC 20.00 9.00
❑ 174 Rico Washington RC 8.00 3.60
❑ 175 Rick Asadoorian RC 15.00 6.75
❑ 176 Matt Ginter RC 10.00 4.50
❑ 177 Jason Stumm RC 12.00 5.50
❑ 178 B.J. Garbe RC 20.00 9.00
❑ 179 Mike MacDougal RC 10.00 4.50
❑ 180 Ryan Christianson RC 15.00 6.75
❑ 181 Kurt Ainsworth RC 15.00 6.75
❑ 182 Brad Baisley RC 10.00 4.50
❑ 183 Ben Broussard RC 20.00 9.00
❑ 184 Aaron McNeal RC 8.00 3.60
❑ 185 John Sneed RC 8.00 3.60
❑ 186 Junior Brignac RC 8.00 3.60
❑ 187 Chance Caple RC 10.00 4.50
❑ 188 Scott Downs RC 8.00 3.60
❑ 189 Matt Cepicky RC 10.00 4.50
❑ 190 Chin-Feng Chen RC 30.00 13.50
❑ 191 Johan Santana RC 8.00 3.60
❑ 192 Brad Baker RC 15.00 6.75
❑ 193 Jason Repko RC 10.00 4.50
❑ 194 Craig Dingman RC 8.00 3.60
❑ 195 Chris Wakeland RC 8.00 3.60
❑ 196 Rogelio Arias RC 8.00 3.60
❑ 197 Luis Matos RC 8.00 3.60
❑ 198 Robert Ramsay 8.00 3.60
❑ 199 Willie Bloomquist RC 20.00 9.00
❑ 200 Tony Pena Jr. RC 10.00 4.50

2001 Bowman's Best

	MINT	NRMT
COMP.SET w/o SP's (150)	60.00	27.00
COMMON CARD (1-150)	.20	.09
COMMON CARD (151-200)	8.00	3.60

❑ 1 Vladimir Guerrero 1.00 .45
❑ 2 Miguel Tejada .30 .14
❑ 3 Geoff Jenkins .30 .14
❑ 4 Jeff Bagwell 1.00 .45
❑ 5 Todd Helton 1.00 .45
❑ 6 Ken Griffey Jr. 2.50 1.10
❑ 7 Nomar Garciaparra 2.00 .90
❑ 8 Chipper Jones 1.50 .70
❑ 9 Darin Erstad .75 .35
❑ 10 Frank Thomas 1.00 .45
❑ 11 Jim Thome .75 .35
❑ 12 Preston Wilson .30 .14
❑ 13 Kevin Brown .30 .14
❑ 14 Derek Jeter 3.00 1.35
❑ 15 Scott Rolen .75 .35
❑ 16 Ryan Klesko .30 .14
❑ 17 Jeff Kent .50 .23
❑ 18 Raul Mondesi .30 .14
❑ 19 Greg Vaughn .30 .14
❑ 20 Bernie Williams .75 .35
❑ 21 Mike Piazza 2.00 .90
❑ 22 Richard Hidalgo .30 .14
❑ 23 Dean Palmer .30 .14
❑ 24 Roberto Alomar .75 .35
❑ 25 Sammy Sosa 1.50 .70
❑ 26 Randy Johnson 1.00 .45
❑ 27 Manny Ramirez 1.00 .45
❑ 28 Roger Clemens 2.00 .90
❑ 29 Terrence Long .30 .14
❑ 30 Jason Kendall .30 .14
❑ 31 Richie Sexson .30 .14
❑ 32 David Wells .30 .14
❑ 33 Andruw Jones .75 .35
❑ 34 Pokey Reese .20 .09
❑ 35 Juan Gonzalez .75 .35
❑ 36 Carlos Beltran .30 .14
❑ 37 Shawn Green .75 .35
❑ 38 Mariano Rivera .30 .14
❑ 39 John Olerud .30 .14
❑ 40 Jim Edmonds .50 .23
❑ 41 Andres Galarraga .50 .23
❑ 42 Carlos Delgado .75 .35
❑ 43 Kris Benson .30 .14
❑ 44 Andy Pettitte .30 .14
❑ 45 Jeff Cirillo .30 .14
❑ 46 Magglio Ordonez .30 .14
❑ 47 Tom Glavine .75 .35
❑ 48 Garret Anderson .30 .14
❑ 49 Cal Ripken 3.00 1.35
❑ 50 Pedro Martinez 1.00 .45
❑ 51 Barry Bonds 2.00 .90
❑ 52 Alex Rodriguez 2.00 .90
❑ 53 Ben Grieve .30 .14
❑ 54 Edgar Martinez .50 .23
❑ 55 Jason Giambi .75 .35
❑ 56 Jeromy Burnitz .30 .14
❑ 57 Mike Mussina .75 .35
❑ 58 Moises Alou .30 .14
❑ 59 Sean Casey .50 .23
❑ 60 Greg Maddux 2.00 .90
❑ 61 Tim Hudson .75 .35
❑ 62 Mark McGwire 3.00 1.35
❑ 63 Rafael Palmeiro .75 .35
❑ 64 Tony Batista .30 .14
❑ 65 Kazuhiro Sasaki .75 .35
❑ 66 Jorge Posada .30 .14
❑ 67 Johnny Damon .30 .14
❑ 68 Brian Giles .30 .14
❑ 69 Jose Vidro .30 .14
❑ 70 Jermaine Dye .30 .14
❑ 71 Craig Biggio .50 .23
❑ 72 Larry Walker .50 .23
❑ 73 Eric Chavez .30 .14
❑ 74 David Segui .20 .09
❑ 75 Tim Salmon .30 .14
❑ 76 Javy Lopez .30 .14
❑ 77 Paul Konerko .30 .14
❑ 78 Barry Larkin .75 .35
❑ 79 Mike Hampton .30 .14
❑ 80 Bobby Higginson .30 .14
❑ 81 Mark Mulder .50 .23
❑ 82 Pat Burrell .30 .14
❑ 83 Kerry Wood .75 .35
❑ 84 J.T. Snow .30 .14
❑ 85 Ivan Rodriguez .75 .35
❑ 86 Edgardo Alfonzo .30 .14
❑ 87 Orlando Hernandez .30 .14
❑ 88 Gary Sheffield .30 .14
❑ 89 Mike Sweeney .30 .14
❑ 90 Carlos Lee .30 .14
❑ 91 Rafael Furcal .30 .14
❑ 92 Troy Glaus .75 .35
❑ 93 Bartolo Colon .30 .14
❑ 94 Cliff Floyd .30 .14
❑ 95 Barry Zito .75 .35
❑ 96 J.D. Drew .75 .35
❑ 97 Eric Karros .30 .14
❑ 98 Jose Valentin .20 .09
❑ 99 Ellis Burks .30 .14
❑ 100 David Justice .30 .14
❑ 101 Larry Barnes .20 .09
❑ 102 Rod Barajas .20 .09
❑ 103 Tony Pena Jr. .20 .09
❑ 104 Jerry Hairston Jr. .20 .09
❑ 105 Keith Ginter .30 .14
❑ 106 Corey Patterson .30 .14
❑ 107 Aaron Rowand .30 .14
❑ 108 Miguel Olivo .20 .09
❑ 109 Gookie Dawkins .20 .09
❑ 110 C.C. Sabathia .50 .23
❑ 111 Ben Petrick .20 .09
❑ 112 Eric Munson .30 .14
❑ 113 Ramon Castro .20 .09
❑ 114 Alex Escobar .30 .14
❑ 115 Josh Hamilton .75 .35
❑ 116 Jason Marquis .30 .14
❑ 117 Ben Davis .30 .14
❑ 118 Alex Cintron .20 .09
❑ 119 Julio Zuleta .20 .09
❑ 120 Ben Broussard .30 .14
❑ 121 Adam Everett .20 .09
❑ 122 Ramon Carvajal RC .75 .35
❑ 123 Felipe Lopez .30 .14
❑ 124 Alfonso Soriano .75 .35
❑ 125 Jayson Werth .20 .09
❑ 126 Donzell McDonald .20 .09
❑ 127 Jason Hart .50 .23
❑ 128 Joe Crede .30 .14
❑ 129 Sean Burroughs .75 .35
❑ 130 Jack Cust .30 .14
❑ 131 Corey Smith .30 .14
❑ 132 Adrian Gonzalez 1.00 .45
❑ 133 J.R. House .75 .35
❑ 134 Steve Lomasney .20 .09
❑ 135 Tim Raines Jr. .20 .09
❑ 136 Tony Alvarez .20 .09
❑ 137 Doug Mientkiewicz .30 .14
❑ 138 Rocco Baldelli .30 .14
❑ 139 Jason Romano .20 .09
❑ 140 Vernon Wells .30 .14
❑ 141 Mike Bynum .20 .09
❑ 142 Xavier Nady .50 .23
❑ 143 Brad Wilkerson .20 .09
❑ 144 Ben Diggins .30 .14
❑ 145 Aubrey Huff .20 .09
❑ 146 Eric Byrnes .20 .09
❑ 147 Alex Gordon .20 .09

❑ 148 Roy Oswalt .75 .35
❑ 149 Brian Esposito .20 .09
❑ 150 Scott Seabol .20 .09
❑ 151 Erick Almonte RC 8.00 3.60
❑ 152 Gary Johnson RC 8.00 3.60
❑ 153 Pedro Liriano RC 10.00 4.50
❑ 154 Matt White RC 8.00 3.60
❑ 155 Luis Montanez RC 12.00 5.50
❑ 156 Brad Cresse 12.00 5.50
❑ 157 Wilson Betemit RC 25.00 11.00
❑ 158 Octavio Martinez RC 8.00 3.60
❑ 159 Adam Pettyjohn RC 8.00 3.60
❑ 160 Corey Spencer RC 8.00 3.60
❑ 161 Mark Burnett RC 8.00 3.60
❑ 162 Ichiro Suzuki RC 100.00 45.00
❑ 163 Alexis Gomez RC 8.00 3.60
❑ 164 Greg Nash RC 25.00 11.00
❑ 165 Roberto Miniel RC 8.00 3.60
❑ 166 Justin Morneau RC 15.00 6.75
❑ 167 Ben Washburn RC 10.00 4.50
❑ 168 Bob Keppel RC 8.00 3.60
❑ 169 Deivi Mendez RC 10.00 4.50
❑ 170 Tsuyoshi Shinjo RC 20.00 9.00
❑ 171 Jared Abruzzo RC 8.00 3.60
❑ 172 Derrick Van Dusen RC 8.00 3.60
❑ 173 Hee Seop Choi RC 20.00 9.00
❑ 174 Albert Pujols RC 60.00 27.00
❑ 175 Travis Hafner RC 10.00 4.50
❑ 176 Ron Davenport RC 8.00 3.60
❑ 177 Luis Torres RC 8.00 3.60
❑ 178 Jake Peavy RC 10.00 4.50
❑ 179 Elvis Corporan RC 8.00 3.60
❑ 180 David Krynzel 8.00 3.60
❑ 181 Tony Blanco RC 15.00 6.75
❑ 182 Elpidio Guzman RC 8.00 3.60
❑ 183 Matt Butler RC 8.00 3.60
❑ 184 Joe Thurston RC 8.00 3.60
❑ 185 Andy Beal RC 8.00 3.60
❑ 186 Kevin Nulton RC 8.00 3.60
❑ 187 Sneideer Santos RC 8.00 3.60
❑ 188 Joe Dillon RC 8.00 3.60
❑ 189 Jeremy Blevins RC 8.00 3.60
❑ 190 Chris Amador RC 8.00 3.60
❑ 191 Mark Hendrickson RC 8.00 3.60
❑ 192 Willy Aybar RC 20.00 9.00
❑ 193 Antoine Cameron RC 8.00 3.60
❑ 194 Jonathan Johnson RC 10.00 4.50
❑ 195 Ryan Ketchner RC 8.00 3.60
❑ 196 Bjorn Ivy RC 8.00 3.60
❑ 197 Josh Kroeger RC 8.00 3.60
❑ 198 Ty Wigginton RC 8.00 3.60
❑ 199 Stubby Clapp RC 8.00 3.60
❑ 200 Jerrod Riggan RC 8.00 3.60

1981 Donruss

	NRMT	VG-E
COMPLETE SET (605)	30.00	13.50

❑ 1 Ozzie Smith 3.00 1.35
❑ 2 Rollie Fingers 1.00 .45
❑ 3 Rick Wise .10 .05
❑ 4 Gene Richards .10 .05
❑ 5 Alan Trammell .50 .23
❑ 6 Tom Brookens .10 .05
❑ 7A Duffy Dyer P1 .25 .11
1980 batting average
has decimal point
❑ 7B Duffy Dyer P2 .10 .05
1980 batting average
has no decimal point
❑ 8 Mark Fidrych 1.00 .45
❑ 9 Dave Rozema .10 .05
❑ 10 Ricky Peters .10 .05
❑ 11 Mike Schmidt 2.00 .90
❑ 12 Willie Stargell 1.00 .45
❑ 13 Tim Foli .10 .05
❑ 14 Manny Sanguillen .25 .11
❑ 15 Grant Jackson .10 .05
❑ 16 Eddie Solomon .10 .05
❑ 17 Omar Moreno .10 .05
❑ 18 Joe Morgan 1.00 .45
❑ 19 Rafael Landestoy .10 .05
❑ 20 Bruce Bochy .10 .05
❑ 21 Joe Sambito .10 .05
❑ 22 Manny Trillo .10 .05
❑ 23A Dave Smith RC P1 .25 .11
Line box around stats
is not complete
❑ 23B Dave Smith RC P2 .25 .11
Box totally encloses
stats at top
❑ 24 Terry Puhl .10 .05
❑ 25 Bump Wills .10 .05
❑ 26A John Ellis P1 ERR .50 .23
Danny Walton photo on front
❑ 26B John Ellis P2 COR .25 .11
❑ 27 Jim Kern .10 .05
❑ 28 Richie Zisk .10 .05
❑ 29 John Mayberry .10 .05
❑ 30 Bob Davis .10 .05
❑ 31 Jackson Todd .10 .05
❑ 32 Alvis Woods .10 .05
❑ 33 Steve Carlton 1.00 .45
❑ 34 Lee Mazzilli .10 .05
❑ 35 John Stearns .10 .05
❑ 36 Roy Lee Jackson .10 .05
❑ 37 Mike Scott .25 .11
❑ 38 Lamar Johnson .10 .05
❑ 39 Kevin Bell .10 .05
❑ 40 Ed Farmer .10 .05
❑ 41 Ross Baumgarten .10 .05
❑ 42 Leo Sutherland .10 .05
❑ 43 Dan Meyer .10 .05
❑ 44 Ron Reed .10 .05
❑ 45 Mario Mendoza .10 .05
❑ 46 Rick Honeycutt .10 .05
❑ 47 Glenn Abbott .10 .05
❑ 48 Leon Roberts .10 .05
❑ 49 Rod Carew 1.00 .45
❑ 50 Bert Campaneris .25 .11
❑ 51A T.Donahue P1 ERR .25 .11
Name on front
misspelled Donahue
❑ 51B Tom Donohue .10 .05
P2 COR
❑ 52 Dave Frost .10 .05
❑ 53 Ed Halicki .10 .05
❑ 54 Dan Ford .10 .05
❑ 55 Garry Maddox .10 .05
❑ 56A Steve Garvey P1 1.00 .45
Surpassed 25 HR
❑ 56B Steve Garvey P2 1.00 .45
Surpassed 21 HR
❑ 57 Bill Russell .25 .11
❑ 58 Don Sutton 1.00 .45
❑ 59 Reggie Smith .25 .11
❑ 60 Rick Monday .25 .11
❑ 61 Ray Knight .25 .11
❑ 62 Johnny Bench 1.50 .70
❑ 63 Mario Soto .10 .05
❑ 64 Doug Bair .10 .05
❑ 65 George Foster .25 .11
❑ 66 Jeff Burroughs .10 .05
❑ 67 Keith Hernandez .25 .11
❑ 68 Tom Herr .25 .11
❑ 69 Bob Forsch .10 .05
❑ 70 John Fulgham .10 .05
❑ 71A Bobby Bonds P1 ERR 1.00 .45
986 lifetime HR
❑ 71B Bobby Bonds P2 COR .50 .23
326 lifetime HR
❑ 72A Rennie Stennett P1 .25 .11
Breaking broke leg
❑ 72B Rennie Stennett P2 .10 .05
Word "broke" deleted
❑ 73 Joe Strain .10 .05
❑ 74 Ed Whitson .10 .05
❑ 75 Tom Griffin .10 .05
❑ 76 Billy North .10 .05
❑ 77 Gene Garber .10 .05
❑ 78 Mike Hargrove .25 .11
❑ 79 Dave Rosello .10 .05
❑ 80 Ron Hassey .10 .05
❑ 81 Sid Monge .10 .05
❑ 82A J.Charboneau RC P1 1.00 .45
'78 highlights
For some reason
❑ 82B J.Charboneau RC P2 1.00 .45
Phrase "For some reason" deleted
❑ 83 Cecil Cooper .25 .11
❑ 84 Sal Bando .25 .11
❑ 85 Moose Haas .10 .05
❑ 86 Mike Caldwell .10 .05
❑ 87A Larry Hisle P1 .25 .11
'77 highlights
line ends with "28 RBI"
❑ 87B Larry Hisle P2 .10 .05
Correct line "28 HR"
❑ 88 Luis Gomez .10 .05
❑ 89 Larry Parrish .10 .05
❑ 90 Gary Carter .50 .23
❑ 91 Bill Gullickson RC .50 .23
❑ 92 Fred Norman .10 .05
❑ 93 Tommy Hutton .10 .05
❑ 94 Carl Yastrzemski 1.00 .45
❑ 95 Glenn Hoffman .10 .05
❑ 96 Dennis Eckersley 1.00 .45
❑ 97A Tom Burgmeier P1 .25 .11
ERR Throws: Right
❑ 97B Tom Burgmeier P2 .10 .05
COR Throws: Left
❑ 98 Win Remmerswaal .10 .05
❑ 99 Bob Horner .25 .11
❑ 100 George Brett 2.50 1.10
❑ 101 Dave Chalk .10 .05
❑ 102 Dennis Leonard .10 .05
❑ 103 Renie Martin .10 .05
❑ 104 Amos Otis .25 .11
❑ 105 Graig Nettles .25 .11
❑ 106 Eric Soderholm .10 .05
❑ 107 Tommy John .50 .23
❑ 108 Tom Underwood .10 .05
❑ 109 Lou Piniella .25 .11
❑ 110 Mickey Klutts .10 .05
❑ 111 Bobby Murcer .25 .11
❑ 112 Eddie Murray 2.00 .90
❑ 113 Rick Dempsey .25 .11
❑ 114 Scott McGregor .10 .05
❑ 115 Ken Singleton .25 .11
❑ 116 Gary Roenicke .10 .05
❑ 117 Dave Revering .10 .05
❑ 118 Mike Norris .10 .05
❑ 119 Rickey Henderson 6.00 2.70
❑ 120 Mike Heath .10 .05
❑ 121 Dave Cash .10 .05
❑ 122 Randy Jones .10 .05
❑ 123 Eric Rasmussen .10 .05
❑ 124 Jerry Mumphrey .10 .05
❑ 125 Richie Hebner .10 .05
❑ 126 Mark Wagner .10 .05
❑ 127 Jack Morris 1.00 .45
❑ 128 Dan Petry .10 .05
❑ 129 Bruce Robbins .10 .05
❑ 130 Champ Summers .10 .05
❑ 131 Pete Rose P1 3.00 1.35
Last line ends with
see card 251
❑ 131B Pete Rose P2 2.00 .90
Last line corrected
see card 371
❑ 132 Willie Stargell 1.00 .45
❑ 133 Ed Ott .10 .05
❑ 134 Jim Bibby .10 .05
❑ 135 Bert Blyleven .50 .23
❑ 136 Dave Parker .25 .11
❑ 137 Bill Robinson .25 .11
❑ 138 Enos Cabell .10 .05
❑ 139 Dave Bergman .10 .05
❑ 140 J.R. Richard .25 .11
❑ 141 Ken Forsch .10 .05

❑ 142 Larry Bowa UER .25 .11
Shortshop on front
❑ 143 Frank LaCorte UER .10 .05
Photo actually Randy Niemann
❑ 144 Denny Walling .10 .05
❑ 145 Buddy Bell .25 .11
❑ 146 Ferguson Jenkins 1.00 .45
❑ 147 Danny Darwin .25 .11
❑ 148 John Grubb .10 .05
❑ 149 Alfredo Griffin .10 .05
❑ 150 Jerry Garvin .10 .05
❑ 151 Paul Mirabella .10 .05
❑ 152 Rick Bosetti .10 .05
❑ 153 Dick Ruthven .10 .05
❑ 154 Frank Taveras .10 .05
❑ 155 Craig Swan .10 .05
❑ 156 Jeff Reardon RC 1.00 .45
❑ 157 Steve Henderson .10 .05
❑ 158 Jim Morrison .10 .05
❑ 159 Glenn Borgmann .10 .05
❑ 160 LaMarr Hoyt RC .25 .11
❑ 161 Rich Wortham .10 .05
❑ 162 Thad Bosley .10 .05
❑ 163 Julio Cruz .10 .05
❑ 164A Del Unser P1 .25 .11
No "3B" heading
❑ 164B Del Unser P2 .10 .05
Batting record on back
corrected "3B"
❑ 165 Jim Anderson .10 .05
❑ 166 Jim Beattie .10 .05
❑ 167 Shane Rawley .10 .05
❑ 168 Joe Simpson .10 .05
❑ 169 Rod Carew 1.00 .45
❑ 170 Fred Patek .10 .05
❑ 171 Frank Tanana .25 .11
❑ 172 Alfredo Martinez .10 .05
❑ 173 Chris Knapp .10 .05
❑ 174 Joe Rudi .25 .11
❑ 175 Greg Luzinski .25 .11
❑ 176 Steve Garvey .50 .23
❑ 177 Joe Ferguson .10 .05
❑ 178 Bob Welch .25 .11
❑ 179 Dusty Baker .50 .23
❑ 180 Rudy Law .10 .05
❑ 181 Dave Concepcion .25 .11
❑ 182 Johnny Bench 1.50 .70
❑ 183 Mike LaCoss .10 .05
❑ 184 Ken Griffey .50 .23
❑ 185 Dave Collins .10 .05
❑ 186 Brian Asselstine .10 .05
❑ 187 Garry Templeton .10 .05
❑ 188 Mike Phillips .10 .05
❑ 189 Pete Vuckovich .25 .11
❑ 190 John Urrea .10 .05
❑ 191 Tony Scott .10 .05
❑ 192 Darrell Evans .25 .11
❑ 193 Milt May .10 .05
❑ 194 Bob Knepper .10 .05
❑ 195 Randy Moffitt .10 .05
❑ 196 Larry Herndon .10 .05
❑ 197 Rick Camp .10 .05
❑ 198 Andre Thornton .25 .11
❑ 199 Tom Veryzer .10 .05
❑ 200 Gary Alexander .10 .05
❑ 201 Rick Waits .10 .05
❑ 202 Rick Manning .10 .05
❑ 203 Paul Molitor 2.00 .90
❑ 204 Jim Gantner .25 .11
❑ 205 Paul Mitchell .10 .05
❑ 206 Reggie Cleveland .10 .05
❑ 207 Sixto Lezcano .10 .05
❑ 208 Bruce Benedict .10 .05
❑ 209 Rodney Scott .10 .05
❑ 210 John Tamargo .10 .05
❑ 211 Bill Lee .25 .11
❑ 212 Andre Dawson UER .50 .23
Middle name Fernando
should be Nolan
❑ 213 Rowland Office .10 .05
❑ 214 Carl Yastrzemski 1.00 .45
❑ 215 Jerry Remy .10 .05
❑ 216 Mike Torrez .10 .05
❑ 217 Skip Lockwood .10 .05
❑ 218 Fred Lynn .25 .11

❑ 219 Chris Chambliss .25 .11
❑ 220 Willie Aikens .10 .05
❑ 221 John Wathan .10 .05
❑ 222 Dan Quisenberry .25 .11
❑ 223 Willie Wilson .25 .11
❑ 224 Clint Hurdle .10 .05
❑ 225 Bob Watson .25 .11
❑ 226 Jim Spencer .10 .05
❑ 227 Ron Guidry .25 .11
❑ 228 Reggie Jackson 1.25 .55
❑ 229 Oscar Gamble .10 .05
❑ 230 Jeff Cox .10 .05
❑ 231 Luis Tiant .25 .11
❑ 232 Rich Dauer .10 .05
❑ 233 Dan Graham .10 .05
❑ 234 Mike Flanagan .25 .11
❑ 235 John Lowenstein .10 .05
❑ 236 Benny Ayala .10 .05
❑ 237 Wayne Gross .10 .05
❑ 238 Rick Langford .10 .05
❑ 239 Tony Armas .25 .11
❑ 240A Bob Lacey P1 ERR .50 .23
Name misspelled Lacy
❑ 240B Bob Lacey P2 COR .10 .05
❑ 241 Gene Tenace .25 .11
❑ 242 Bob Shirley .10 .05
❑ 243 Gary Lucas .10 .05
❑ 244 Jerry Turner .10 .05
❑ 245 John Wockenfuss .10 .05
❑ 246 Stan Papi .10 .05
❑ 247 Milt Wilcox .10 .05
❑ 248 Dan Schatzeder .10 .05
❑ 249 Steve Kemp .10 .05
❑ 250 Jim Lentine .10 .05
❑ 251 Pete Rose 3.00 1.35
❑ 252 Bill Madlock .25 .11
❑ 253 Dale Berra .10 .05
❑ 254 Kent Tekulve .25 .11
❑ 255 Enrique Romo .10 .05
❑ 256 Mike Easler .10 .05
❑ 257 Chuck Tanner MG .25 .11
❑ 258 Art Howe .25 .11
❑ 259 Alan Ashby .10 .05
❑ 260 Nolan Ryan 5.00 2.20
❑ 261A Vern Ruhle P1 ERR .50 .23
Ken Forsch photo on front
❑ 261B Vern Ruhle P2 COR .25 .11
❑ 262 Bob Boone .25 .11
❑ 263 Cesar Cedeno .25 .11
❑ 264 Jeff Leonard .25 .11
❑ 265 Pat Putnam .10 .05
❑ 266 Jon Matlack .10 .05
❑ 267 Dave Rajsich .10 .05
❑ 268 Billy Sample .10 .05
❑ 269 Damaso Garcia .10 .05
❑ 270 Tom Buskey .10 .05
❑ 271 Joey McLaughlin .10 .05
❑ 272 Barry Bonnell .10 .05
❑ 273 Tug McGraw .25 .11
❑ 274 Mike Jorgensen .10 .05
❑ 275 Pat Zachry .10 .05
❑ 276 Neil Allen .10 .05
❑ 277 Joel Youngblood .10 .05
❑ 278 Greg Pryor .10 .05
❑ 279 Britt Burns .10 .05
❑ 280 Rich Dotson .10 .05
❑ 281 Chet Lemon .10 .05
❑ 282 Rusty Kuntz .10 .05
❑ 283 Ted Cox .10 .05
❑ 284 Sparky Lyle .25 .11
❑ 285 Larry Cox .10 .05
❑ 286 Floyd Bannister .10 .05
❑ 287 Byron McLaughlin .10 .05
❑ 288 Rodney Craig .10 .05
❑ 289 Bobby Grich .25 .11
❑ 290 Dickie Thon .25 .11
❑ 291 Mark Clear .10 .05
❑ 292 Dave Lemanczyk .10 .05
❑ 293 Jason Thompson .10 .05
❑ 294 Rick Miller .10 .05
❑ 295 Lonnie Smith .25 .11
❑ 296 Ron Cey .25 .11
❑ 297 Steve Yeager .10 .05
❑ 298 Bobby Castillo .10 .05
❑ 299 Manny Mota .25 .11
❑ 300 Jay Johnstone .25 .11

❑ 301 Dan Driessen .10 .05
❑ 302 Joe Nolan .10 .05
❑ 303 Paul Householder .10 .05
❑ 304 Harry Spilman .10 .05
❑ 305 Cesar Geronimo .10 .05
❑ 306A G.Mathews P1 ERR .50 .23
Name misspelled
❑ 306B G.Matthews P2 .25 .11
COR
❑ 307 Ken Reitz .10 .05
❑ 308 Ted Simmons .25 .11
❑ 309 John Littlefield .10 .05
❑ 310 George Frazier .10 .05
❑ 311 Dane Iorg .10 .05
❑ 312 Mike Ivie .10 .05
❑ 313 Dennis Littlejohn .10 .05
❑ 314 Gary Lavelle .10 .05
❑ 315 Jack Clark .25 .11
❑ 316 Jim Wohlford .10 .05
❑ 317 Rick Matula .10 .05
❑ 318 Toby Harrah .25 .11
❑ 319A D.Kuiper P1 ERR .25 .11
Name misspelled
❑ 319B D.Kuiper P2 COR .10 .05
❑ 320 Len Barker .10 .05
❑ 321 Victor Cruz .10 .05
❑ 322 Dell Alston .10 .05
❑ 323 Robin Yount 1.00 .45
❑ 324 Charlie Moore .10 .05
❑ 325 Lary Sorensen .10 .05
❑ 326A Gorman Thomas P1 .50 .23
2nd line on back:
"30 HR mark 4th"
❑ 326B Gorman Thomas P2 .25 .11
30 HR mark 3rd
❑ 327 Bob Rodgers MG .10 .05
❑ 328 Phil Niekro 1.00 .45
❑ 329 Chris Speier .10 .05
❑ 330A Steve Rodgers P1 .25 .11
ERR Name misspelled
❑ 330B S.Rogers P2 COR .10 .05
❑ 331 Woodie Fryman .10 .05
❑ 332 Warren Cromartie .10 .05
❑ 333 Jerry White .10 .05
❑ 334 Tony Perez 1.00 .45
❑ 335 Carlton Fisk 1.00 .45
❑ 336 Dick Drago .10 .05
❑ 337 Steve Renko .10 .05
❑ 338 Jim Rice .25 .11
❑ 339 Jerry Royster .10 .05
❑ 340 Frank White .25 .11
❑ 341 Jamie Quirk .10 .05
❑ 342A P.Spittorff P1 ERR .25 .11
Name misspelled
❑ 342B Paul Splittorff .10 .05
P2 COR
❑ 343 Marty Pattin .10 .05
❑ 344 Pete LaCock .10 .05
❑ 345 Willie Randolph .25 .11
❑ 346 Rick Cerone .10 .05
❑ 347 Rich Gossage .50 .23
❑ 348 Reggie Jackson 1.25 .55
❑ 349 Ruppert Jones .10 .05
❑ 350 Dave McKay .10 .05
❑ 351 Yogi Berra CO .50 .23
❑ 352 Doug DeCinces .25 .11
❑ 353 Jim Palmer 1.00 .45
❑ 354 Tippy Martinez .10 .05
❑ 355 Al Bumbry .25 .11
❑ 356 Earl Weaver MG 1.00 .45
❑ 357A Bob Picciolo P1 ERR .25 .11
Name misspelled
❑ 357B R.Picciolo P2 COR .10 .05
❑ 358 Matt Keough .10 .05
❑ 359 Dwayne Murphy .10 .05
❑ 360 Brian Kingman .10 .05
❑ 361 Bill Fahey .10 .05
❑ 362 Steve Mura .10 .05
❑ 363 Dennis Kinney .10 .05
❑ 364 Dave Winfield 1.00 .45
❑ 365 Lou Whitaker 1.00 .45
❑ 366 Lance Parrish .25 .11
❑ 367 Tim Corcoran .10 .05
❑ 368 Pat Underwood .10 .05
❑ 369 Al Cowens .10 .05
❑ 370 Sparky Anderson MG .25 .11

No.	Card	Mint	Ex
❑ 371	Pete Rose	3.00	1.35
❑ 372	Phil Garner	.25	.11
❑ 373	Steve Nicosia	.10	.05
❑ 374	John Candelaria	.25	.11
❑ 375	Don Robinson	.10	.05
❑ 376	Lee Lacy	.10	.05
❑ 377	John Milner	.10	.05
❑ 378	Craig Reynolds	.10	.05
❑ 379A	Luis Pujols P1 ERR Name misspelled Pujois	.25	.11
❑ 379B	Luis Pujols P2 COR	.10	.05
❑ 380	Joe Niekro	.25	.11
❑ 381	Joaquin Andujar	.25	.11
❑ 382	Keith Moreland	.25	.11
❑ 383	Jose Cruz	.25	.11
❑ 384	Bill Virdon MG	.10	.05
❑ 385	Jim Sundberg	.25	.11
❑ 386	Doc Medich	.10	.05
❑ 387	Al Oliver	.25	.11
❑ 388	Jim Norris	.10	.05
❑ 389	Bob Bailor	.10	.05
❑ 390	Ernie Whitt	.10	.05
❑ 391	Otto Velez	.10	.05
❑ 392	Roy Howell	.10	.05
❑ 393	Bob Walk RC	.25	.11
❑ 394	Doug Flynn	.10	.05
❑ 395	Pete Falcone	.10	.05
❑ 396	Tom Hausman	.10	.05
❑ 397	Elliott Maddox	.10	.05
❑ 398	Mike Squires	.10	.05
❑ 399	Marvis Foley	.10	.05
❑ 400	Steve Trout	.10	.05
❑ 401	Wayne Nordhagen	.10	.05
❑ 402	Tony LaRussa MG	.25	.11
❑ 403	Bruce Bochte	.10	.05
❑ 404	Bake McBride	.10	.05
❑ 405	Jerry Narron	.10	.05
❑ 406	Rob Dressler	.10	.05
❑ 407	Dave Heaverlo	.10	.05
❑ 408	Tom Paciorek	.25	.11
❑ 409	Carney Lansford	.25	.11
❑ 410	Brian Downing	.25	.11
❑ 411	Don Aase	.10	.05
❑ 412	Jim Barr	.10	.05
❑ 413	Don Baylor	.50	.23
❑ 414	Jim Fregosi MG	.10	.05
❑ 415	Dallas Green MG	.10	.05
❑ 416	Dave Lopes	.25	.11
❑ 417	Jerry Reuss	.25	.11
❑ 418	Rick Sutcliffe	.25	.11
❑ 419	Derrel Thomas	.10	.05
❑ 420	Tom Lasorda MG	1.00	.45
❑ 421	Charlie Leibrandt RC	.50	.23
❑ 422	Tom Seaver	1.50	.70
❑ 423	Ron Oester	.10	.05
❑ 424	Junior Kennedy	.10	.05
❑ 425	Tom Seaver	1.50	.70
❑ 426	Bobby Cox MG	.25	.11
❑ 427	Leon Durham	.25	.11
❑ 428	Terry Kennedy	.10	.05
❑ 429	Silvio Martinez	.10	.05
❑ 430	George Hendrick	.10	.05
❑ 431	Red Schoendienst MG	.50	.23
❑ 432	Johnnie LeMaster	.10	.05
❑ 433	Vida Blue	.25	.11
❑ 434	John Montefusco	.10	.05
❑ 435	Terry Whitfield	.10	.05
❑ 436	Dave Bristol MG	.10	.05
❑ 437	Dale Murphy	1.00	.45
❑ 438	Jerry Dybzinski	.10	.05
❑ 439	Jorge Orta	.10	.05
❑ 440	Wayne Garland	.10	.05
❑ 441	Miguel Dilone	.10	.05
❑ 442	Dave Garcia MG	.10	.05
❑ 443	Don Money	.10	.05
❑ 444A	B.Martinez P1 ERR Reverse negative	.25	.11
❑ 444B	Buck Martinez P2 COR	.10	.05
❑ 445	Jerry Augustine	.10	.05
❑ 446	Ben Oglivie	.25	.11
❑ 447	Jim Slaton	.10	.05
❑ 448	Doyle Alexander	.10	.05
❑ 449	Tony Bernazard	.10	.05
❑ 450	Scott Sanderson	.10	.05
❑ 451	David Palmer	.10	.05
❑ 452	Stan Bahnsen	.10	.05
❑ 453	Dick Williams MG	.10	.05
❑ 454	Rick Burleson	.10	.05
❑ 455	Gary Allenson	.10	.05
❑ 456	Bob Stanley	.10	.05
❑ 457A	John Tudor RC P1 ERR Lifetime W-L 9.7	.25	.11
❑ 457B	John Tudor RC P2 COR Lifetime W-L 9-7	.25	.11
❑ 458	Dwight Evans	.50	.23
❑ 459	Glenn Hubbard	.10	.05
❑ 460	U.L. Washington	.10	.05
❑ 461	Larry Gura	.10	.05
❑ 462	Rich Gale	.10	.05
❑ 463	Hal McRae	.25	.11
❑ 464	Jim Frey MG	.10	.05
❑ 465	Bucky Dent	.25	.11
❑ 466	Dennis Werth	.10	.05
❑ 467	Ron Davis	.10	.05
❑ 468	Reggie Jackson UER 32 HR in 1970 should be 23	1.25	.55
❑ 469	Bobby Brown	.10	.05
❑ 470	Mike Davis	.10	.05
❑ 471	Gaylord Perry	1.00	.45
❑ 472	Mark Belanger	.25	.11
❑ 473	Jim Palmer	1.00	.45
❑ 474	Sammy Stewart	.10	.05
❑ 475	Tim Stoddard	.10	.05
❑ 476	Steve Stone	.25	.11
❑ 477	Jeff Newman	.10	.05
❑ 478	Steve McCatty	.10	.05
❑ 479	Billy Martin MG	.50	.23
❑ 480	Mitchell Page	.10	.05
❑ 481	Steve Carlton CY	.50	.23
❑ 482	Bill Buckner	.25	.11
❑ 483A	Ivan DeJesus P1 ERR Lifetime hits 702	.25	.11
❑ 483B	Ivan DeJesus P2 COR Lifetime hits 642	.10	.05
❑ 484	Cliff Johnson	.10	.05
❑ 485	Lenny Randle	.10	.05
❑ 486	Larry Milbourne	.10	.05
❑ 487	Roy Smalley	.10	.05
❑ 488	John Castino	.10	.05
❑ 489	Ron Jackson	.10	.05
❑ 490A	Dave Roberts P1 Career Highlights Showed pop in	.25	.11
❑ 490B	Dave Roberts P2 Declared himself	.10	.05
❑ 491	George Brett MVP	1.25	.55
❑ 492	Mike Cubbage	.10	.05
❑ 493	Rob Wilfong	.10	.05
❑ 494	Danny Goodwin	.10	.05
❑ 495	Jose Morales	.10	.05
❑ 496	Mickey Rivers	.25	.11
❑ 497	Mike Edwards	.10	.05
❑ 498	Mike Sadek	.10	.05
❑ 499	Lenn Sakata	.10	.05
❑ 500	Gene Michael MG	.10	.05
❑ 501	Dave Roberts	.10	.05
❑ 502	Steve Dillard	.10	.05
❑ 503	Jim Essian	.10	.05
❑ 504	Rance Mulliniks	.10	.05
❑ 505	Darrell Porter	.10	.05
❑ 506	Joe Torre MG	.25	.11
❑ 507	Terry Crowley	.10	.05
❑ 508	Bill Travers	.10	.05
❑ 509	Nelson Norman	.10	.05
❑ 510	Bob McClure	.10	.05
❑ 511	Steve Howe	.25	.11
❑ 512	Dave Rader	.10	.05
❑ 513	Mick Kelleher	.10	.05
❑ 514	Kiko Garcia	.10	.05
❑ 515	Larry Biittner	.10	.05
❑ 516A	Willie Norwood P1 Career Highlights Spent most of	.25	.11
❑ 516B	Willie Norwood P2 Traded to Seattle	.10	.05
❑ 517	Bo Diaz	.10	.05
❑ 518	Juan Beniquez	.10	.05
❑ 519	Scot Thompson	.10	.05
❑ 520	Jim Tracy	.10	.05
❑ 521	Carlos Lezcano	.10	.05
❑ 522	Joe Amalfitano MG	.10	.05
❑ 523	Preston Hanna	.10	.05
❑ 524A	Ray Burris P1 Career Highlights Went on ...	.25	.11
❑ 524B	Ray Burris P2 Drafted by ...	.10	.05
❑ 525	Broderick Perkins	.10	.05
❑ 526	Mickey Hatcher	.25	.11
❑ 527	John Goryl MG	.10	.05
❑ 528	Dick Davis	.10	.05
❑ 529	Butch Wynegar	.10	.05
❑ 530	Sal Butera	.10	.05
❑ 531	Jerry Koosman	.25	.11
❑ 532A	Geoff Zahn P1 (Career Highlights Was 2nd in	.25	.11
❑ 532B	Geoff Zahn P2 Signed a 3 year	.10	.05
❑ 533	Dennis Martinez	.50	.23
❑ 534	Gary Thomasson	.10	.05
❑ 535	Steve Macko	.10	.05
❑ 536	Jim Kaat	.25	.11
❑ 537	Best Hitters George Brett Rod Carew	1.50	.70
❑ 538	Tim Raines RC	2.00	.90
❑ 539	Keith Smith	.10	.05
❑ 540	Ken Macha	.10	.05
❑ 541	Burt Hooton	.10	.05
❑ 542	Butch Hobson	.10	.05
❑ 543	Bill Stein	.10	.05
❑ 544	Dave Stapleton	.10	.05
❑ 545	Bob Pate	.10	.05
❑ 546	Doug Corbett	.10	.05
❑ 547	Darrell Jackson	.10	.05
❑ 548	Pete Redfern	.10	.05
❑ 549	Roger Erickson	.10	.05
❑ 550	Al Hrabosky	.10	.05
❑ 551	Dick Tidrow	.10	.05
❑ 552	Dave Ford	.10	.05
❑ 553	Dave Kingman	.50	.23
❑ 554A	Mike Vail P1 Career Highlights After two	.25	.11
❑ 554B	Mike Vail P2 Traded to	.10	.05
❑ 555A	Jerry Martin P1 Career Highlights Overcame a	.25	.11
❑ 555B	Jerry Martin P2 Traded to	.10	.05
❑ 556A	Jesus Figueroa P1 Career Highlights Had an	.25	.11
❑ 556B	Jesus Figueroa P2 Traded to	.10	.05
❑ 557	Don Stanhouse	.10	.05
❑ 558	Barry Foote	.10	.05
❑ 559	Tim Blackwell	.10	.05
❑ 560	Bruce Sutter	.25	.11
❑ 561	Rick Reuschel	.25	.11
❑ 562	Lynn McGlothen	.10	.05
❑ 563A	Bob Owchinko P1 Career Highlights Traded to	.25	.11
❑ 563B	Bob Owchinko P2 Involved in a	.10	.05
❑ 564	John Verhoeven	.10	.05
❑ 565	Ken Landreaux	.10	.05
❑ 566A	Glen Adams P1 ERR Name misspelled	.25	.11
❑ 566B	G. Adams P2 COR	.10	.05
❑ 567	Hosken Powell	.10	.05
❑ 568	Dick Noles	.10	.05
❑ 569	Danny Ainge RC	2.00	.90
❑ 570	Bobby Mattick MG	.10	.05
❑ 571	Joe Lefebvre	.10	.05
❑ 572	Bobby Clark	.10	.05
❑ 573	Dennis Lamp	.10	.05
❑ 574	Randy Lerch	.10	.05
❑ 575	Mookie Wilson RC	.50	.23
❑ 576	Ron LeFlore	.25	.11
❑ 577	Jim Dwyer	.10	.05
❑ 578	Bill Castro	.10	.05

❑ 579 Greg Minton .10 .05
❑ 580 Mark Littell .10 .05
❑ 581 Andy Hassler .10 .05
❑ 582 Dave Stieb .25 .11
❑ 583 Ken Oberkfell .10 .05
❑ 584 Larry Bradford .10 .05
❑ 585 Fred Stanley .10 .05
❑ 586 Bill Caudill .10 .05
❑ 587 Doug Capilla .10 .05
❑ 588 George Riley .10 .05
❑ 589 Willie Hernandez .25 .11
❑ 590 Mike Schmidt MVP 2.00 .90
❑ 591 Steve Stone CY .10 .05
❑ 592 Rick Sofield .10 .05
❑ 593 Bombo Rivera .10 .05
❑ 594 Gary Ward .10 .05
❑ 595A Dave Edwards P1 .25 .11
Career Highlights
Sidelined the
❑ 595B Dave Edwards P2 .10 .05
Traded to
❑ 596 Mike Proly .10 .05
❑ 597 Tommy Boggs .10 .05
❑ 598 Greg Gross .10 .05
❑ 599 Elias Sosa .10 .05
❑ 600 Pat Kelly .10 .05
❑ 601A Checklist 1-120 P1 .25 .11
ERR Unnumbered
51 Donahue
❑ 601B Checklist 1-120 P2 .50 .23
COR Unnumbered
51 Donohue
❑ 602 Checklist 121-240 .25 .11
Unnumbered
❑ 603A CL 241-360 P1 .25 .11
ERR Unnumbered
306 Mathews
❑ 603B CL 241-360 P2 .25 .11
COR Unnumbered
306 Matthews
❑ 604A CL 361-480 P1 .25 .11
ERR Unnumbered
379 Pujois
❑ 604B CL 361-480 P2 .25 .11
COR Unnumbered
379 Pujols
❑ 605A CL 481-600 P1 .25 .11
ERR Unnumbered
566 Glen Adams
❑ 605B CL 481-600 P2 .25 .11
COR Unnumbered
566 Glenn Adams

1982 Donruss

	NRMT	VG-E
COMPLETE SET (660)	60.00	27.00
COMP.FACT.SET (660)	70.00	32.00
COMP.RUTH PUZZLE	10.00	4.50

❑ 1 Pete Rose DK 2.50 1.10
❑ 2 Gary Carter DK .20 .09
❑ 3 Steve Garvey DK .20 .09
❑ 4 Vida Blue DK .10 .05
❑ 5 Alan Trammell DK .10 .05
COR
❑ 5A Alan Trammel DK ERR .40 .18
(Name misspelled)
❑ 6 Len Barker DK .10 .05
❑ 7 Dwight Evans DK .40 .18
❑ 8 Rod Carew DK .75 .35
❑ 9 George Hendrick DK .20 .09
❑ 10 Phil Niekro DK .40 .18
❑ 11 Richie Zisk DK .10 .05
❑ 12 Dave Parker DK .20 .09
❑ 13 Nolan Ryan DK 4.00 1.80
❑ 14 Ivan DeJesus DK .10 .05
❑ 15 George Brett DK .75 .35
❑ 16 Tom Seaver DK 1.25 .55
❑ 17 Dave Kingman DK .20 .09
❑ 18 Dave Winfield DK .20 .09
❑ 19 Mike Norris DK .10 .05
❑ 20 Carlton Fisk DK .40 .18
❑ 21 Ozzie Smith DK 1.50 .70
❑ 22 Roy Smalley DK .20 .09
❑ 23 Buddy Bell DK .20 .09
❑ 24 Ken Singleton DK .10 .05
❑ 25 John Mayberry DK .10 .05
❑ 26 Gorman Thomas DK .20 .09
❑ 27 Earl Weaver MG .40 .18
❑ 28 Rollie Fingers .75 .35
❑ 29 Sparky Anderson MG .20 .09
❑ 30 Dennis Eckersley .75 .35
❑ 31 Dave Winfield .75 .35
❑ 32 Burt Hooton .10 .05
❑ 33 Rick Waits .10 .05
❑ 34 George Brett 1.50 .70
❑ 35 Steve McCatty .10 .05
❑ 36 Steve Rogers .10 .05
❑ 37 Bill Stein .10 .05
❑ 38 Steve Renko .10 .05
❑ 39 Mike Squires .10 .05
❑ 40 George Hendrick .10 .05
❑ 41 Bob Knepper .10 .05
❑ 42 Steve Carlton .75 .35
❑ 43 Larry Biittner .10 .05
❑ 44 Chris Welsh .10 .05
❑ 45 Steve Nicosia .10 .05
❑ 46 Jack Clark .20 .09
❑ 47 Chris Chambliss .20 .09
❑ 48 Ivan DeJesus .10 .05
❑ 49 Lee Mazzilli .10 .05
❑ 50 Julio Cruz .10 .05
❑ 51 Pete Redfern .10 .05
❑ 52 Dave Stieb .20 .09
❑ 53 Doug Corbett .10 .05
❑ 54 Jorge Bell RC .75 .35
❑ 55 Joe Simpson .10 .05
❑ 56 Rusty Staub .20 .09
❑ 57 Hector Cruz .10 .05
❑ 58 Claudell Washington .10 .05
❑ 59 Enrique Romo .10 .05
❑ 60 Gary Lavelle .10 .05
❑ 61 Tim Flannery .10 .05
❑ 62 Joe Nolan .10 .05
❑ 63 Larry Bowa .20 .09
❑ 64 Sixto Lezcano .10 .05
❑ 65 Joe Sambito .10 .05
❑ 66 Bruce Kison .10 .05
❑ 67 Wayne Nordhagen .10 .05
❑ 68 Woodie Fryman .10 .05
❑ 69 Billy Sample .10 .05
❑ 70 Amos Otis .20 .09
❑ 71 Matt Keough .10 .05
❑ 72 Toby Harrah .20 .09
❑ 73 Dave Righetti RC .75 .35
❑ 74 Carl Yastrzemski .75 .35
❑ 75 Bob Welch .20 .09
❑ 76 Alan Trammell COR .40 .18
❑ 76A Alan Trammel ERR .40 .18
(Name misspelled)
❑ 77 Rick Dempsey .20 .09
❑ 78 Paul Molitor 1.00 .45
❑ 79 Dennis Martinez .40 .18
❑ 80 Jim Slaton .10 .05
❑ 81 Champ Summers .10 .05
❑ 82 Carney Lansford .20 .09
❑ 83 Barry Foote .10 .05
❑ 84 Steve Garvey .40 .18
❑ 85 Rick Manning .10 .05
❑ 86 John Wathan .10 .05
❑ 87 Brian Kingman .10 .05
❑ 88 Andre Dawson UER .40 .18
(Middle name Fernando
should be Nolan)
❑ 89 Jim Kern .10 .05
❑ 90 Bobby Grich .20 .09
❑ 91 Bob Forsch .10 .05
❑ 92 Art Howe .20 .09
❑ 93 Marty Bystrom .10 .05
❑ 94 Ozzie Smith 1.50 .70
❑ 95 Dave Parker .20 .09
❑ 96 Doyle Alexander .10 .05
❑ 97 Al Hrabosky .10 .05
❑ 98 Frank Taveras .10 .05
❑ 99 Tim Blackwell .10 .05
❑ 100 Floyd Bannister .10 .05
❑ 101 Alfredo Griffin .10 .05
❑ 102 Dave Engle .10 .05
❑ 103 Mario Soto .10 .05
❑ 104 Ross Baumgarten .10 .05
❑ 105 Ken Singleton .20 .09
❑ 106 Ted Simmons .20 .09
❑ 107 Jack Morris .20 .09
❑ 108 Bob Watson .20 .09
❑ 109 Dwight Evans .40 .18
❑ 110 Tom Lasorda MG .40 .18
❑ 111 Bert Blyleven .40 .18
❑ 112 Dan Quisenberry .20 .09
❑ 113 Rickey Henderson 2.50 1.10
❑ 114 Gary Carter .40 .18
❑ 115 Brian Downing .10 .05
❑ 116 Al Oliver .20 .09
❑ 117 LaMarr Hoyt .10 .05
❑ 118 Cesar Cedeno .20 .09
❑ 119 Keith Moreland .10 .05
❑ 120 Bob Shirley .10 .05
❑ 121 Terry Kennedy .10 .05
❑ 122 Frank Pastore .10 .05
❑ 123 Gene Garber .10 .05
❑ 124 Tony Pena .20 .09
❑ 125 Allen Ripley .10 .05
❑ 126 Randy Martz .10 .05
❑ 127 Richie Zisk .10 .05
❑ 128 Mike Scott .20 .09
❑ 129 Lloyd Moseby .10 .05
❑ 130 Rob Wilfong .10 .05
❑ 131 Tim Stoddard .10 .05
❑ 132 Gorman Thomas .20 .09
❑ 133 Dan Petry .10 .05
❑ 134 Bob Stanley .10 .05
❑ 135 Lou Piniella .20 .09
❑ 136 Pedro Guerrero .20 .09
❑ 137 Len Barker .10 .05
❑ 138 Rich Gale .10 .05
❑ 139 Wayne Gross .10 .05
❑ 140 Tim Wallach RC .40 .18
❑ 141 Gene Mauch MG .10 .05
❑ 142 Doc Medich .10 .05
❑ 143 Tony Bernazard .10 .05
❑ 144 Bill Virdon MG .10 .05
❑ 145 John Littlefield .10 .05
❑ 146 Dave Bergman .10 .05
❑ 147 Dick Davis .10 .05
❑ 148 Tom Seaver 1.25 .55
❑ 149 Matt Sinatro .10 .05
❑ 150 Chuck Tanner MG .10 .05
❑ 151 Leon Durham .10 .05
❑ 152 Gene Tenace .20 .09
❑ 153 Al Bumbry .10 .05
❑ 154 Mark Brouhard .10 .05
❑ 155 Rick Peters .10 .05
❑ 156 Jerry Remy .10 .05
❑ 157 Rick Reuschel .20 .09
❑ 158 Steve Howe .10 .05
❑ 159 Alan Bannister .10 .05
❑ 160 U.L. Washington .10 .05
❑ 161 Rick Langford .10 .05
❑ 162 Bill Gullickson .10 .05
❑ 163 Mark Wagner .10 .05
❑ 164 Geoff Zahn .10 .05
❑ 165 Ron LeFlore .20 .09
❑ 166 Dane Iorg .10 .05
❑ 167 Joe Niekro .20 .09
❑ 168 Pete Rose 2.50 1.10
❑ 169 Dave Collins .10 .05
❑ 170 Rick Wise .10 .05
❑ 171 Jim Bibby .10 .05
❑ 172 Larry Herndon .10 .05
❑ 173 Bob Horner .20 .09
❑ 174 Steve Dillard .10 .05

❑ 175 Mookie Wilson .20 .09
❑ 176 Dan Meyer .10 .05
❑ 177 Fernando Arroyo .10 .05
❑ 178 Jackson Todd .10 .05
❑ 179 Darrell Jackson .10 .05
❑ 180 Alvis Woods .10 .05
❑ 181 Jim Anderson .10 .05
❑ 182 Dave Kingman .20 .09
❑ 183 Steve Henderson .10 .05
❑ 184 Brian Asselstine .10 .05
❑ 185 Rod Scurry .10 .05
❑ 186 Fred Breining .10 .05
❑ 187 Danny Boone .10 .05
❑ 188 Junior Kennedy .10 .05
❑ 189 Sparky Lyle .20 .09
❑ 190 Whitey Herzog MG .20 .09
❑ 191 Dave Smith .10 .05
❑ 192 Ed Ott .10 .05
❑ 193 Greg Luzinski .20 .09
❑ 194 Bill Lee .20 .09
❑ 195 Don Zimmer MG .10 .05
❑ 196 Hal McRae .20 .09
❑ 197 Mike Norris .10 .05
❑ 198 Duane Kuiper .10 .05
❑ 199 Rick Cerone .10 .05
❑ 200 Jim Rice .20 .09
❑ 201 Steve Yeager .10 .05
❑ 202 Tom Brookens .10 .05
❑ 203 Jose Morales .10 .05
❑ 204 Roy Howell .10 .05
❑ 205 Tippy Martinez .10 .05
❑ 206 Moose Haas .10 .05
❑ 207 Al Cowens .10 .05
❑ 208 Dave Stapleton .10 .05
❑ 209 Bucky Dent .20 .09
❑ 210 Ron Cey .20 .09
❑ 211 Jorge Orta .10 .05
❑ 212 Jamie Quirk .10 .05
❑ 213 Jeff Jones .10 .05
❑ 214 Tim Raines .75 .35
❑ 215 Jon Matlack .10 .05
❑ 216 Rod Carew .75 .35
❑ 217 Jim Kaat .20 .09
❑ 218 Joe Pittman .10 .05
❑ 219 Larry Christenson .10 .05
❑ 220 Juan Bonilla .10 .05
❑ 221 Mike Easler .10 .05
❑ 222 Vida Blue .20 .09
❑ 223 Rick Camp .10 .05
❑ 224 Mike Jorgensen .10 .05
❑ 225 Jody Davis .10 .05
❑ 226 Mike Parrott .10 .05
❑ 227 Jim Clancy .10 .05
❑ 228 Hosken Powell .10 .05
❑ 229 Tom Hume .10 .05
❑ 230 Britt Burns .10 .05
❑ 231 Jim Palmer .75 .35
❑ 232 Bob Rodgers MG .10 .05
❑ 233 Milt Wilcox .10 .05
❑ 234 Dave Revering .10 .05
❑ 235 Mike Torrez .10 .05
❑ 236 Robert Castillo .10 .05
❑ 237 Von Hayes .20 .09
❑ 238 Renie Martin .10 .05
❑ 239 Dwayne Murphy .10 .05
❑ 240 Rodney Scott .10 .05
❑ 241 Fred Patek .10 .05
❑ 242 Mickey Rivers .10 .05
❑ 243 Steve Trout .10 .05
❑ 244 Jose Cruz .20 .09
❑ 245 Manny Trillo .10 .05
❑ 246 Lary Sorensen .10 .05
❑ 247 Dave Edwards .10 .05
❑ 248 Dan Driessen .10 .05
❑ 249 Tommy Boggs .10 .05
❑ 250 Dale Berra .10 .05
❑ 251 Ed Whitson .10 .05
❑ 252 Lee Smith RC 2.00 .90
❑ 253 Tom Paciorek .20 .09
❑ 254 Pat Zachry .10 .05
❑ 255 Luis Leal .10 .05
❑ 256 John Castino .10 .05
❑ 257 Rich Dauer .10 .05
❑ 258 Cecil Cooper .20 .09
❑ 259 Dave Rozema .10 .05
❑ 260 John Tudor .10 .05
❑ 261 Jerry Mumphrey .10 .05
❑ 262 Jay Johnstone .20 .09
❑ 263 Bo Diaz .10 .05
❑ 264 Dennis Leonard .10 .05
❑ 265 Jim Spencer .10 .05
❑ 266 John Milner .10 .05
❑ 267 Don Aase .10 .05
❑ 268 Jim Sundberg .10 .05
❑ 269 Lamar Johnson .10 .05
❑ 270 Frank LaCorte .10 .05
❑ 271 Barry Evans .10 .05
❑ 272 Enos Cabell .10 .05
❑ 273 Del Unser .10 .05
❑ 274 George Foster .20 .09
❑ 275 Brett Butler RC 1.00 .45
❑ 276 Lee Lacy .10 .05
❑ 277 Ken Reitz .10 .05
❑ 278 Keith Hernandez .20 .09
❑ 279 Doug DeCinces .20 .09
❑ 280 Charlie Moore .10 .05
❑ 281 Lance Parrish .40 .18
❑ 282 Ralph Houk MG .20 .09
❑ 283 Rich Gossage .40 .18
❑ 284 Jerry Reuss .20 .09
❑ 285 Mike Stanton .10 .05
❑ 286 Frank White .20 .09
❑ 287 Bob Owchinko .10 .05
❑ 288 Scott Sanderson .10 .05
❑ 289 Bump Wills .10 .05
❑ 290 Dave Frost .10 .05
❑ 291 Chet Lemon .10 .05
❑ 292 Tito Landrum .10 .05
❑ 293 Vern Ruhle .10 .05
❑ 294 Mike Schmidt 1.50 .70
❑ 295 Sam Mejias .10 .05
❑ 296 Gary Lucas .10 .05
❑ 297 John Candelaria .10 .05
❑ 298 Jerry Martin .10 .05
❑ 299 Dale Murphy .75 .35
❑ 300 Mike Lum .10 .05
❑ 301 Tom Hausman .10 .05
❑ 302 Glenn Abbott .10 .05
❑ 303 Roger Erickson .10 .05
❑ 304 Otto Velez .10 .05
❑ 305 Danny Goodwin .10 .05
❑ 306 John Mayberry .10 .05
❑ 307 Lenny Randle .10 .05
❑ 308 Bob Bailor .10 .05
❑ 309 Jerry Morales .10 .05
❑ 310 Rufino Linares .10 .05
❑ 311 Kent Tekulve .20 .09
❑ 312 Joe Morgan .75 .35
❑ 313 John Urrea .10 .05
❑ 314 Paul Householder .10 .05
❑ 315 Garry Maddox .10 .05
❑ 316 Mike Ramsey .10 .05
❑ 317 Alan Ashby .10 .05
❑ 318 Bob Clark .10 .05
❑ 319 Tony LaRussa MG .20 .09
❑ 320 Charlie Lea .10 .05
❑ 321 Danny Darwin .10 .05
❑ 322 Cesar Geronimo .10 .05
❑ 323 Tom Underwood .10 .05
❑ 324 Andre Thornton .10 .05
❑ 325 Rudy May .10 .05
❑ 326 Frank Tanana .20 .09
❑ 327 Dave Lopes .20 .09
❑ 328 Richie Hebner .20 .09
❑ 329 Mike Flanagan .20 .09
❑ 330 Mike Caldwell .10 .05
❑ 331 Scott McGregor .10 .05
❑ 332 Jerry Augustine .10 .05
❑ 333 Stan Papi .10 .05
❑ 334 Rick Miller .10 .05
❑ 335 Graig Nettles .20 .09
❑ 336 Dusty Baker .40 .18
❑ 337 Dave Garcia MG .10 .05
❑ 338 Larry Gura .10 .05
❑ 339 Cliff Johnson .10 .05
❑ 340 Warren Cromartie .10 .05
❑ 341 Steve Comer .10 .05
❑ 342 Rick Burleson .10 .05
❑ 343 John Martin .10 .05
❑ 344 Craig Reynolds .10 .05
❑ 345 Mike Proly .10 .05
❑ 346 Ruppert Jones .10 .05
❑ 347 Omar Moreno .10 .05
❑ 348 Greg Minton .10 .05
❑ 349 Rick Mahler .10 .05
❑ 350 Alex Trevino .10 .05
❑ 351 Mike Krukow .10 .05
❑ 352A Shane Rawley ERR .40 .18
(Photo actually
Jim Anderson)
❑ 352B Shane Rawley COR .10 .05
❑ 353 Garth Iorg .10 .05
❑ 354 Pete Mackanin .10 .05
❑ 355 Paul Moskau .10 .05
❑ 356 Richard Dotson .10 .05
❑ 357 Steve Stone .20 .09
❑ 358 Larry Hisle .10 .05
❑ 359 Aurelio Lopez .10 .05
❑ 360 Oscar Gamble .10 .05
❑ 361 Tom Burgmeier .10 .05
❑ 362 Terry Forster .10 .05
❑ 363 Joe Charboneau .20 .09
❑ 364 Ken Brett .10 .05
❑ 365 Tony Armas .10 .05
❑ 366 Chris Speier .10 .05
❑ 367 Fred Lynn .20 .09
❑ 368 Buddy Bell .20 .09
❑ 369 Jim Essian .10 .05
❑ 370 Terry Puhl .10 .05
❑ 371 Greg Gross .10 .05
❑ 372 Bruce Sutter .20 .09
❑ 373 Joe Lefebvre .10 .05
❑ 374 Ray Knight .20 .09
❑ 375 Bruce Benedict .10 .05
❑ 376 Tim Foli .10 .05
❑ 377 Al Holland .10 .05
❑ 378 Ken Kravec .10 .05
❑ 379 Jeff Burroughs .10 .05
❑ 380 Pete Falcone .10 .05
❑ 381 Ernie Whitt .10 .05
❑ 382 Brad Havens .10 .05
❑ 383 Terry Crowley .10 .05
❑ 384 Don Money .10 .05
❑ 385 Dan Schatzeder .10 .05
❑ 386 Gary Allenson .10 .05
❑ 387 Yogi Berra CO .40 .18
❑ 388 Ken Landreaux .10 .05
❑ 389 Mike Hargrove .20 .09
❑ 390 Darryl Motley .10 .05
❑ 391 Dave McKay .10 .05
❑ 392 Stan Bahnsen .10 .05
❑ 393 Ken Forsch .10 .05
❑ 394 Mario Mendoza .10 .05
❑ 395 Jim Morrison .10 .05
❑ 396 Mike Ivie .10 .05
❑ 397 Broderick Perkins .10 .05
❑ 398 Darrell Evans .20 .09
❑ 399 Ron Reed .10 .05
❑ 400 Johnny Bench 1.25 .55
❑ 401 Steve Bedrosian RC .20 .09
❑ 402 Bill Robinson .10 .05
❑ 403 Bill Buckner .20 .09
❑ 404 Ken Oberkfell .10 .05
❑ 405 Cal Ripken RC ! 40.00 18.00
❑ 406 Jim Gantner .20 .09
❑ 407 Kirk Gibson .75 .35
❑ 408 Tony Perez .75 .35
❑ 409 Tommy John UER .40 .18
(Text says 52-56 as
Yankee, should be
52-26)
❑ 410 Dave Stewart RC 1.00 .45
❑ 411 Dan Spillner .10 .05
❑ 412 Willie Aikens .10 .05
❑ 413 Mike Heath .10 .05
❑ 414 Ray Burris .10 .05
❑ 415 Leon Roberts .10 .05
❑ 416 Mike Witt .20 .09
❑ 417 Bob Molinaro .10 .05
❑ 418 Steve Braun .10 .05
❑ 419 Nolan Ryan UER 4.00 1.80
(Nisnumbering of
Nolan's no-hitters
on card back)
❑ 420 Tug McGraw .20 .09
❑ 421 Dave Concepcion .20 .09
❑ 422A Juan Eichelberger .40 .18
ERR (Photo actually

Gary Lucas)
❑ 422B Juan Eichelberger .10 .05
COR
❑ 423 Rick Rhoden .10 .05
❑ 424 Frank Robinson MG .40 .18
❑ 425 Eddie Miller .10 .05
❑ 426 Bill Caudill .10 .05
❑ 427 Doug Flynn .10 .05
❑ 428 Larry Andersen UER .10 .05
(Misspelled Anderson
on card front)
❑ 429 Al Williams .10 .05
❑ 430 Jerry Garvin .10 .05
❑ 431 Glenn Adams .10 .05
❑ 432 Barry Bonnell .10 .05
❑ 433 Jerry Narron .10 .05
❑ 434 John Stearns .10 .05
❑ 435 Mike Tyson .10 .05
❑ 436 Glenn Hubbard .10 .05
❑ 437 Eddie Solomon .10 .05
❑ 438 Jeff Leonard .10 .05
❑ 439 Randy Bass RC .10 .05
❑ 440 Mike LaCoss .10 .05
❑ 441 Gary Matthews .20 .09
❑ 442 Mark Littell .10 .05
❑ 443 Don Sutton .75 .35
❑ 444 John Harris .10 .05
❑ 445 Vada Pinson CO .20 .09
❑ 446 Elias Sosa .10 .05
❑ 447 Charlie Hough .20 .09
❑ 448 Willie Wilson .20 .09
❑ 449 Fred Stanley .10 .05
❑ 450 Tom Veryzer .10 .05
❑ 451 Ron Davis .10 .05
❑ 452 Mark Clear .10 .05
❑ 453 Bill Russell .10 .05
❑ 454 Lou Whitaker .75 .35
❑ 455 Dan Graham .10 .05
❑ 456 Reggie Cleveland .10 .05
❑ 457 Sammy Stewart .10 .05
❑ 458 Pete Vuckovich .10 .05
❑ 459 John Wockenfuss .10 .05
❑ 460 Glenn Hoffman .10 .05
❑ 461 Willie Randolph .20 .09
❑ 462 Fernando Valenzuela .75 .35
❑ 463 Ron Hassey .10 .05
❑ 464 Paul Splittorff .10 .05
❑ 465 Rob Picciolo .10 .05
❑ 466 Larry Parrish .10 .05
❑ 467 Johnny Grubb .10 .05
❑ 468 Dan Ford .10 .05
❑ 469 Silvio Martinez .10 .05
❑ 470 Kiko Garcia .10 .05
❑ 471 Bob Boone .20 .09
❑ 472 Luis Salazar .10 .05
❑ 473 Randy Niemann .10 .05
❑ 474 Tom Griffin .10 .05
❑ 475 Phil Niekro .75 .35
❑ 476 Hubie Brooks .20 .09
❑ 477 Dick Tidrow .10 .05
❑ 478 Jim Beattie .10 .05
❑ 479 Damaso Garcia .10 .05
❑ 480 Mickey Hatcher .10 .05
❑ 481 Joe Price .10 .05
❑ 482 Ed Farmer .10 .05
❑ 483 Eddie Murray 1.00 .45
❑ 484 Ben Oglivie .20 .09
❑ 485 Kevin Saucier .10 .05
❑ 486 Bobby Murcer .20 .09
❑ 487 Bill Campbell .10 .05
❑ 488 Reggie Smith .20 .09
❑ 489 Wayne Garland .10 .05
❑ 490 Jim Wright .10 .05
❑ 491 Billy Martin MG .20 .09
❑ 492 Jim Fanning MG .10 .05
❑ 493 Don Baylor .40 .18
❑ 494 Rick Honeycutt .10 .05
❑ 495 Carlton Fisk .75 .35
❑ 496 Denny Walling .10 .05
❑ 497 Bake McBride .10 .05
❑ 498 Darrell Porter .20 .09
❑ 499 Gene Richards .10 .05
❑ 500 Ron Oester .10 .05
❑ 501 Ken Dayley .10 .05
❑ 502 Jason Thompson .10 .05
❑ 503 Milt May .10 .05
❑ 504 Doug Bird .10 .05
❑ 505 Bruce Bochte .10 .05
❑ 506 Neil Allen .10 .05
❑ 507 Joey McLaughlin .10 .05
❑ 508 Butch Wynegar .10 .05
❑ 509 Gary Roenicke .10 .05
❑ 510 Robin Yount .75 .35
❑ 511 Dave Tobik .10 .05
❑ 512 Rich Gedman .20 .09
❑ 513 Gene Nelson .10 .05
❑ 514 Rick Monday .10 .05
❑ 515 Miguel Dilone .10 .05
❑ 516 Clint Hurdle .10 .05
❑ 517 Jeff Newman .10 .05
❑ 518 Grant Jackson .10 .05
❑ 519 Andy Hassler .10 .05
❑ 520 Pat Putnam .10 .05
❑ 521 Greg Pryor .10 .05
❑ 522 Tony Scott .10 .05
❑ 523 Steve Mura .10 .05
❑ 524 Johnnie LeMaster .10 .05
❑ 525 Dick Ruthven .10 .05
❑ 526 John McNamara MG .10 .05
❑ 527 Larry McWilliams .10 .05
❑ 528 Johnny Ray .20 .09
❑ 529 Pat Tabler .20 .09
❑ 530 Tom Herr .20 .09
❑ 531A SD Chicken RC .75 .35
ERR (Without TM)
❑ 531B San Diego Chicken .75 .35
COR (With TM)
❑ 532 Sal Butera .10 .05
❑ 533 Mike Griffin .10 .05
❑ 534 Kelvin Moore .10 .05
❑ 535 Reggie Jackson 1.00 .45
❑ 536 Ed Romero .10 .05
❑ 537 Derrel Thomas .10 .05
❑ 538 Mike O'Berry .10 .05
❑ 539 Jack O'Connor .10 .05
❑ 540 Bob Ojeda RC .40 .18
❑ 541 Roy Lee Jackson .10 .05
❑ 542 Lynn Jones .10 .05
❑ 543 Gaylord Perry .75 .35
❑ 544A Phil Garner ERR .40 .18
(Reverse negative)
❑ 544B Phil Garner COR .20 .09
❑ 545 Garry Templeton .10 .05
❑ 546 Rafael Ramirez .10 .05
❑ 547 Jeff Reardon .40 .18
❑ 548 Ron Guidry .20 .09
❑ 549 Tim Laudner .10 .05
❑ 550 John Henry Johnson .10 .05
❑ 551 Chris Bando .10 .05
❑ 552 Bobby Brown .10 .05
❑ 553 Larry Bradford .10 .05
❑ 554 Scott Fletcher RC .20 .09
❑ 555 Jerry Royster .10 .05
❑ 556 Shooty Babitt UER .10 .05
(Spelled Babbitt
on front)
❑ 557 Kent Hrbek RC 1.00 .45
❑ 558 Yankee Winners .20 .09
Ron Guidry
Tommy John
❑ 559 Mark Bomback .10 .05
❑ 560 Julio Valdez .10 .05
❑ 561 Buck Martinez .10 .05
❑ 562 Mike A. Marshall .20 .09
❑ 563 Rennie Stennett .10 .05
❑ 564 Steve Crawford .10 .05
❑ 565 Bob Babcock .10 .05
❑ 566 Johnny Podres CO .20 .09
❑ 567 Paul Serna .10 .05
❑ 568 Harold Baines .75 .35
❑ 569 Dave LaRoche .10 .05
❑ 570 Lee May .20 .09
❑ 571 Gary Ward .10 .05
❑ 572 John Denny .10 .05
❑ 573 Roy Smalley .10 .05
❑ 574 Bob Brenly .40 .18
❑ 575 Bronx Bombers .75 .35
Reggie Jackson
Dave Winfield
❑ 576 Luis Pujols .10 .05
❑ 577 Butch Hobson .10 .05
❑ 578 Harvey Kuenn MG .20 .09
❑ 579 Cal Ripken Sr. CO .20 .09
❑ 580 Juan Berenguer .10 .05
❑ 581 Benny Ayala .10 .05
❑ 582 Vance Law .10 .05
❑ 583 Rick Leach .10 .05
❑ 584 George Frazier .10 .05
❑ 585 Phillies Finest 1.00 .45
Pete Rose
Mike Schmidt
❑ 586 Joe Rudi .10 .05
❑ 587 Juan Beniquez .10 .05
❑ 588 Luis DeLeon .10 .05
❑ 589 Craig Swan .10 .05
❑ 590 Dave Chalk .10 .05
❑ 591 Billy Gardner MG .10 .05
❑ 592 Sal Bando .20 .09
❑ 593 Bert Campaneris .20 .09
❑ 594 Steve Kemp .10 .05
❑ 595A Randy Lerch ERR .40 .18
(Braves)
❑ 595B Randy Lerch COR .10 .05
(Brewers)
❑ 596 Bryan Clark .10 .05
❑ 597 Dave Ford .10 .05
❑ 598 Mike Scioscia .20 .09
❑ 599 John Lowenstein .10 .05
❑ 600 Rene Lachemann MG .10 .05
❑ 601 Mick Kelleher .10 .05
❑ 602 Ron Jackson .10 .05
❑ 603 Jerry Koosman .20 .09
❑ 604 Dave Goltz .10 .05
❑ 605 Ellis Valentine .10 .05
❑ 606 Lonnie Smith .20 .09
❑ 607 Joaquin Andujar .20 .09
❑ 608 Garry Hancock .10 .05
❑ 609 Jerry Turner .10 .05
❑ 610 Bob Bonner .10 .05
❑ 611 Jim Dwyer .10 .05
❑ 612 Terry Bulling .10 .05
❑ 613 Joel Youngblood .10 .05
❑ 614 Larry Milbourne .10 .05
❑ 615 Gene Roof UER .10 .05
(Name on front
is Phil Roof)
❑ 616 Keith Drumwright .10 .05
❑ 617 Dave Rosello .10 .05
❑ 618 Rickey Keeton .10 .05
❑ 619 Dennis Lamp .10 .05
❑ 620 Sid Monge .10 .05
❑ 621 Jerry White .10 .05
❑ 622 Luis Aguayo .10 .05
❑ 623 Jamie Easterly .10 .05
❑ 624 Steve Sax RC .75 .35
❑ 625 Dave Roberts .10 .05
❑ 626 Rick Bosetti .10 .05
❑ 627 Terry Francona .40 .18
❑ 628 Pride of Reds 1.00 .45
Tom Seaver
Johnny Bench
❑ 629 Paul Mirabella .10 .05
❑ 630 Rance Mulliniks .10 .05
❑ 631 Kevin Hickey .10 .05
❑ 632 Reid Nichols .10 .05
❑ 633 Dave Geisel .10 .05
❑ 634 Ken Griffey .20 .09
❑ 635 Bob Lemon MG .75 .35
❑ 636 Orlando Sanchez .10 .05
❑ 637 Bill Almon .10 .05
❑ 638 Danny Ainge 1.00 .45
❑ 639 Willie Stargell .75 .35
❑ 640 Bob Sykes .10 .05
❑ 641 Ed Lynch .10 .05
❑ 642 John Ellis .10 .05
❑ 643 Ferguson Jenkins .75 .35
❑ 644 Lenn Sakata .10 .05
❑ 645 Julio Gonzalez .10 .05
❑ 646 Jesse Orosco .10 .05
❑ 647 Jerry Dybzinski .10 .05
❑ 648 Tommy Davis CO .20 .09
❑ 649 Ron Gardenhire .10 .05
❑ 650 Felipe Alou CO .20 .09
❑ 651 Harvey Haddix CO .20 .09
❑ 652 Willie Upshaw .10 .05
❑ 653 Bill Madlock .20 .09
❑ 654A DK Checklist 1-26 .75 .35
ERR (Unnumbered)

No.	Card	NRMT	VG-E
	(With Trammel)		
654B	DK Checklist 1-26 COR (Unnumbered) (With Trammell)	.20	.09
655	Checklist 27-130 (Unnumbered)	.20	.09
656	Checklist 131-234 (Unnumbered)	.20	.09
657	Checklist 235-338 (Unnumbered)	.20	.09
658	Checklist 339-442 (Unnumbered)	.20	.09
659	Checklist 443-544 (Unnumbered)	.20	.09
660	Checklist 545-653 (Unnumbered)	.20	.09

1983 Donruss

	NRMT	VG-E
COMPLETE SET (660)	60.00	27.00
COMP.FACT.SET (660)	80.00	36.00
COMP.COBB PUZZLE	5.00	2.20

No.	Player	NRMT	VG-E
1	Fernando Valenzuela DK	.40	.18
2	Rollie Fingers DK	.40	.18
3	Reggie Jackson DK	1.00	.45
4	Jim Palmer DK	.40	.18
5	Jack Morris DK	.10	.05
6	George Foster DK	.20	.09
7	Jim Sundberg DK	.10	.05
8	Willie Stargell DK	.40	.18
9	Dave Stieb DK	.20	.09
10	Joe Niekro DK	.20	.09
11	Rickey Henderson DK	1.50	.70
12	Dale Murphy DK	.40	.18
13	Toby Harrah DK	.10	.05
14	Bill Buckner DK	.10	.05
15	Willie Wilson DK	.10	.05
16	Steve Carlton DK	.40	.18
17	Ron Guidry DK	.10	.05
18	Steve Rogers DK	.10	.05
19	Kent Hrbek DK	.20	.09
20	Keith Hernandez DK	.20	.09
21	Floyd Bannister DK	.10	.05
22	Johnny Bench DK	1.25	.55
23	Britt Burns DK	.10	.05
24	Joe Morgan DK	.40	.18
25	Carl Yastrzemski DK	.40	.18
26	Terry Kennedy DK	.10	.05
27	Gary Roenicke	.10	.05
28	Dwight Bernard	.10	.05
29	Pat Underwood	.10	.05
30	Gary Allenson	.10	.05
31	Ron Guidry	.20	.09
32	Burt Hooton	.10	.05
33	Chris Bando	.10	.05
34	Vida Blue	.20	.09
35	Rickey Henderson	1.50	.70
36	Ray Burris	.10	.05
37	John Butcher	.10	.05
38	Don Aase	.10	.05
39	Jerry Koosman	.20	.09
40	Bruce Sutter	.20	.09
41	Jose Cruz	.20	.09
42	Pete Rose	2.50	1.10
43	Cesar Cedeno	.20	.09
44	Floyd Chiffer	.10	.05
45	Larry McWilliams	.10	.05
46	Alan Fowlkes	.10	.05
47	Dale Murphy	.75	.35
48	Doug Bird	.10	.05
49	Hubie Brooks	.20	.09
50	Floyd Bannister	.10	.05
51	Jack O'Connor	.10	.05
52	Steve Senteney	.10	.05
53	Gary Gaetti RC	.75	.35
54	Damaso Garcia	.10	.05
55	Gene Nelson	.10	.05
56	Mookie Wilson	.20	.09
57	Allen Ripley	.10	.05
58	Bob Horner	.10	.05
59	Tony Pena	.10	.05
60	Gary Lavelle	.10	.05
61	Tim Lollar	.10	.05
62	Frank Pastore	.10	.05
63	Garry Maddox	.10	.05
64	Bob Forsch	.10	.05
65	Harry Spilman	.10	.05
66	Geoff Zahn	.10	.05
67	Salome Barojas	.10	.05
68	David Palmer	.10	.05
69	Charlie Hough	.20	.09
70	Dan Quisenberry	.20	.09
71	Tony Armas	.10	.05
72	Rick Sutcliffe	.20	.09
73	Steve Balboni	.10	.05
74	Jerry Remy	.10	.05
75	Mike Scioscia	.20	.09
76	John Wockenfuss	.10	.05
77	Jim Palmer	.75	.35
78	Rollie Fingers	.75	.35
79	Joe Nolan	.10	.05
80	Pete Vuckovich	.10	.05
81	Rick Leach	.10	.05
82	Rick Miller	.10	.05
83	Graig Nettles	.20	.09
84	Ron Cey	.20	.09
85	Miguel Dilone	.10	.05
86	John Wathan	.10	.05
87	Kelvin Moore	.10	.05
88A	Byrn Smith ERR (Sic, Bryn)	.20	.09
88B	Bryn Smith COR	.40	.18
89	Dave Hostetler	.10	.05
90	Rod Carew	.75	.35
91	Lonnie Smith	.10	.05
92	Bob Knepper	.10	.05
93	Marty Bystrom	.10	.05
94	Chris Welsh	.10	.05
95	Jason Thompson	.10	.05
96	Tom O'Malley	.10	.05
97	Phil Niekro	.75	.35
98	Neil Allen	.10	.05
99	Bill Buckner	.20	.09
100	Ed VandeBerg	.10	.05
101	Jim Clancy	.10	.05
102	Robert Castillo	.10	.05
103	Bruce Berenyi	.10	.05
104	Carlton Fisk	.75	.35
105	Mike Flanagan	.20	.09
106	Cecil Cooper	.20	.09
107	Jack Morris	.20	.09
108	Mike Morgan	.10	.05
109	Luis Aponte	.10	.05
110	Pedro Guerrero	.20	.09
111	Len Barker	.10	.05
112	Willie Wilson	.20	.09
113	Dave Beard	.10	.05
114	Mike Gates	.10	.05
115	Reggie Jackson	1.00	.45
116	George Wright	.10	.05
117	Vance Law	.10	.05
118	Nolan Ryan	4.00	1.80
119	Mike Krukow	.10	.05
120	Ozzie Smith	1.25	.55
121	Broderick Perkins	.10	.05
122	Tom Seaver	1.25	.55
123	Chris Chambliss	.20	.09
124	Chuck Tanner MG	.10	.05
125	Johnnie LeMaster	.10	.05
126	Mel Hall RC	.20	.09
127	Bruce Bochte	.10	.05
128	Charlie Puleo	.10	.05
129	Luis Leal	.10	.05
130	John Pacella	.10	.05
131	Glenn Gulliver	.10	.05
132	Don Money	.10	.05
133	Dave Rozema	.10	.05
134	Bruce Hurst	.10	.05
135	Rudy May	.10	.05
136	Tom Lasorda MG	.40	.18
137	Dan Spillner UER (Photo actually Ed Whitson)	.10	.05
138	Jerry Martin	.10	.05
139	Mike Norris	.10	.05
140	Al Oliver	.20	.09
141	Daryl Sconiers	.10	.05
142	Lamar Johnson	.10	.05
143	Harold Baines	.75	.35
144	Alan Ashby	.10	.05
145	Garry Templeton	.10	.05
146	Al Holland	.10	.05
147	Bo Diaz	.10	.05
148	Dave Concepcion	.20	.09
149	Rick Camp	.10	.05
150	Jim Morrison	.10	.05
151	Randy Martz	.10	.05
152	Keith Hernandez	.20	.09
153	John Lowenstein	.10	.05
154	Mike Caldwell	.10	.05
155	Milt Wilcox	.10	.05
156	Rich Gedman	.10	.05
157	Rich Gossage	.40	.18
158	Jerry Reuss	.20	.09
159	Ron Hassey	.10	.05
160	Larry Gura	.10	.05
161	Dwayne Murphy	.10	.05
162	Woodie Fryman	.10	.05
163	Steve Comer	.10	.05
164	Ken Forsch	.10	.05
165	Dennis Lamp	.10	.05
166	David Green	.10	.05
167	Terry Puhl	.10	.05
168	Mike Schmidt (Wearing 37 rather than 20)	1.50	.70
169	Eddie Milner	.10	.05
170	John Curtis	.10	.05
171	Don Robinson	.10	.05
172	Rich Gale	.10	.05
173	Steve Bedrosian	.20	.09
174	Willie Hernandez	.20	.09
175	Ron Gardenhire	.10	.05
176	Jim Beattie	.10	.05
177	Tim Laudner	.10	.05
178	Buck Martinez	.10	.05
179	Kent Hrbek	.20	.09
180	Alfredo Griffin	.10	.05
181	Larry Andersen	.10	.05
182	Pete Falcone	.10	.05
183	Jody Davis	.10	.05
184	Glenn Hubbard	.10	.05
185	Dale Berra	.10	.05
186	Greg Minton	.10	.05
187	Gary Lucas	.10	.05
188	Dave Van Gorder	.10	.05
189	Bob Dernier	.10	.05
190	Willie McGee RC	1.50	.70
191	Dickie Thon	.10	.05
192	Bob Boone	.20	.09
193	Britt Burns	.10	.05
194	Jeff Reardon	.20	.09
195	Jon Matlack	.10	.05
196	Don Slaught RC	.40	.18
197	Fred Stanley	.10	.05
198	Rick Manning	.10	.05
199	Dave Righetti	.20	.09
200	Dave Stapleton	.10	.05
201	Steve Yeager	.10	.05
202	Enos Cabell	.10	.05
203	Sammy Stewart	.10	.05
204	Moose Haas	.10	.05
205	Lenn Sakata	.10	.05
206	Charlie Moore	.10	.05
207	Alan Trammell	.40	.18
208	Jim Rice	.20	.09
209	Roy Smalley	.10	.05
210	Bill Russell	.10	.05

❑ 211 Andre Thornton .10 .05
❑ 212 Willie Aikens .10 .05
❑ 213 Dave McKay .10 .05
❑ 214 Tim Blackwell .10 .05
❑ 215 Buddy Bell .20 .09
❑ 216 Doug DeCinces .20 .09
❑ 217 Tom Herr .20 .09
❑ 218 Frank LaCorte .10 .05
❑ 219 Steve Carlton .75 .35
❑ 220 Terry Kennedy .10 .05
❑ 221 Mike Easler .10 .05
❑ 222 Jack Clark .20 .09
❑ 223 Gene Garber .10 .05
❑ 224 Scott Holman .10 .05
❑ 225 Mike Proly .10 .05
❑ 226 Terry Bulling .10 .05
❑ 227 Jerry Garvin .10 .05
❑ 228 Ron Davis .10 .05
❑ 229 Tom Hume .10 .05
❑ 230 Marc Hill .10 .05
❑ 231 Dennis Martinez .20 .09
❑ 232 Jim Gantner .10 .05
❑ 233 Larry Pashnick .10 .05
❑ 234 Dave Collins .10 .05
❑ 235 Tom Burgmeier .10 .05
❑ 236 Ken Landreaux .10 .05
❑ 237 John Denny .10 .05
❑ 238 Hal McRae .20 .09
❑ 239 Matt Keough .10 .05
❑ 240 Doug Flynn .10 .05
❑ 241 Fred Lynn .20 .09
❑ 242 Billy Sample .10 .05
❑ 243 Tom Paciorek .20 .09
❑ 244 Joe Sambito .10 .05
❑ 245 Sid Monge .10 .05
❑ 246 Ken Oberkfell .10 .05
❑ 247 Joe Pittman UER .10 .05
(Photo actually
Juan Eichelberger)
❑ 248 Mario Soto .10 .05
❑ 249 Claudell Washington .10 .05
❑ 250 Rick Rhoden .10 .05
❑ 251 Darrell Evans .20 .09
❑ 252 Steve Henderson .10 .05
❑ 253 Manny Castillo .10 .05
❑ 254 Craig Swan .10 .05
❑ 255 Joey McLaughlin .10 .05
❑ 256 Pete Redfern .10 .05
❑ 257 Ken Singleton .10 .05
❑ 258 Robin Yount .75 .35
❑ 259 Elias Sosa .10 .05
❑ 260 Bob Ojeda .10 .05
❑ 261 Bobby Murcer .20 .09
❑ 262 Candy Maldonado RC .20 .09
❑ 263 Rick Waits .10 .05
❑ 264 Greg Pryor .10 .05
❑ 265 Bob Owchinko .10 .05
❑ 266 Chris Speier .10 .05
❑ 267 Bruce Kison .10 .05
❑ 268 Mark Wagner .10 .05
❑ 269 Steve Kemp .10 .05
❑ 270 Phil Garner .20 .09
❑ 271 Gene Richards .10 .05
❑ 272 Renie Martin .10 .05
❑ 273 Dave Roberts .10 .05
❑ 274 Dan Driessen .10 .05
❑ 275 Rufino Linares .10 .05
❑ 276 Lee Lacy .10 .05
❑ 277 Ryne Sandberg RC 10.00 4.50
❑ 278 Darrell Porter .10 .05
❑ 279 Cal Ripken 8.00 3.60
❑ 280 Jamie Easterly .10 .05
❑ 281 Bill Fahey .10 .05
❑ 282 Glenn Hoffman .10 .05
❑ 283 Willie Randolph .20 .09
❑ 284 Fernando Valenzuela .40 .18
❑ 285 Alan Bannister .10 .05
❑ 286 Paul Splittorff .10 .05
❑ 287 Joe Rudi .10 .05
❑ 288 Bill Gullickson .10 .05
❑ 289 Danny Darwin .10 .05
❑ 290 Andy Hassler .10 .05
❑ 291 Ernesto Escarrega .10 .05
❑ 292 Steve Mura .10 .05
❑ 293 Tony Scott .10 .05
❑ 294 Manny Trillo .10 .05
❑ 295 Greg Harris .10 .05
❑ 296 Luis DeLeon .10 .05
❑ 297 Kent Tekulve .20 .09
❑ 298 Atlee Hammaker .10 .05
❑ 299 Bruce Benedict .10 .05
❑ 300 Fergie Jenkins .75 .35
❑ 301 Dave Kingman .40 .18
❑ 302 Bill Caudill .10 .05
❑ 303 John Castino .10 .05
❑ 304 Ernie Whitt .10 .05
❑ 305 Randy Johnson .10 .05
❑ 306 Garth Iorg .10 .05
❑ 307 Gaylord Perry .75 .35
❑ 308 Ed Lynch .10 .05
❑ 309 Keith Moreland .10 .05
❑ 310 Rafael Ramirez .10 .05
❑ 311 Bill Madlock .20 .09
❑ 312 Milt May .10 .05
❑ 313 John Montefusco .10 .05
❑ 314 Wayne Krenchicki .10 .05
❑ 315 George Vukovich .10 .05
❑ 316 Joaquin Andujar .10 .05
❑ 317 Craig Reynolds .10 .05
❑ 318 Rick Burleson .10 .05
❑ 319 Richard Dotson .10 .05
❑ 320 Steve Rogers .10 .05
❑ 321 Dave Schmidt .10 .05
❑ 322 Bud Black RC .20 .09
❑ 323 Jeff Burroughs .10 .05
❑ 324 Von Hayes .20 .09
❑ 325 Butch Wynegar .10 .05
❑ 326 Carl Yastrzemski .75 .35
❑ 327 Ron Roenicke .10 .05
❑ 328 Howard Johnson RC .75 .35
❑ 329 Rick Dempsey UER .20 .09
(Posing as a left-
handed batter)
❑ 330A Jim Slaton .10 .05
(Bio printed
black on white)
❑ 330B Jim Slaton .20 .09
(Bio printed
black on yellow)
❑ 331 Benny Ayala .10 .05
❑ 332 Ted Simmons .20 .09
❑ 333 Lou Whitaker .40 .18
❑ 334 Chuck Rainey .10 .05
❑ 335 Lou Piniella .20 .09
❑ 336 Steve Sax .20 .09
❑ 337 Toby Harrah .10 .05
❑ 338 George Brett 1.50 .70
❑ 339 Dave Lopes .20 .09
❑ 340 Gary Carter .40 .18
❑ 341 John Grubb .10 .05
❑ 342 Tim Foli .10 .05
❑ 343 Jim Kaat .20 .09
❑ 344 Mike LaCoss .10 .05
❑ 345 Larry Christenson .10 .05
❑ 346 Juan Bonilla .10 .05
❑ 347 Omar Moreno .10 .05
❑ 348 Chili Davis .75 .35
❑ 349 Tommy Boggs .10 .05
❑ 350 Rusty Staub .20 .09
❑ 351 Bump Wills .10 .05
❑ 352 Rick Sweet .10 .05
❑ 353 Jim Gott RC .10 .05
❑ 354 Terry Felton .10 .05
❑ 355 Jim Kern .10 .05
❑ 356 Bill Almon UER .10 .05
(Expos/Mets in 1983,
not Padres/Mets)
❑ 357 Tippy Martinez .10 .05
❑ 358 Roy Howell .10 .05
❑ 359 Dan Petry .10 .05
❑ 360 Jerry Mumphrey .10 .05
❑ 361 Mark Clear .10 .05
❑ 362 Mike Marshall .10 .05
❑ 363 Lary Sorensen .10 .05
❑ 364 Amos Otis .20 .09
❑ 365 Rick Langford .10 .05
❑ 366 Brad Mills .10 .05
❑ 367 Brian Downing .10 .05
❑ 368 Mike Richardt .10 .05
❑ 369 Aurelio Rodriguez .10 .05
❑ 370 Dave Smith .10 .05
❑ 371 Tug McGraw .20 .09
❑ 372 Doug Bair .10 .05
❑ 373 Ruppert Jones .10 .05
❑ 374 Alex Trevino .10 .05
❑ 375 Ken Dayley .10 .05
❑ 376 Rod Scurry .10 .05
❑ 377 Bob Brenly .10 .05
❑ 378 Scot Thompson .10 .05
❑ 379 Julio Cruz .10 .05
❑ 380 John Stearns .10 .05
❑ 381 Dale Murray .10 .05
❑ 382 Frank Viola RC .75 .35
❑ 383 Al Bumbry .10 .05
❑ 384 Ben Oglivie .10 .05
❑ 385 Dave Tobik .10 .05
❑ 386 Bob Stanley .10 .05
❑ 387 Andre Robertson .10 .05
❑ 388 Jorge Orta .10 .05
❑ 389 Ed Whitson .10 .05
❑ 390 Don Hood .10 .05
❑ 391 Tom Underwood .10 .05
❑ 392 Tim Wallach .20 .09
❑ 393 Steve Renko .10 .05
❑ 394 Mickey Rivers .10 .05
❑ 395 Greg Luzinski .20 .09
❑ 396 Art Howe .20 .09
❑ 397 Alan Wiggins .10 .05
❑ 398 Jim Barr .10 .05
❑ 399 Ivan DeJesus .10 .05
❑ 400 Tom Lawless .10 .05
❑ 401 Bob Walk .10 .05
❑ 402 Jimmy Smith .10 .05
❑ 403 Lee Smith .75 .35
❑ 404 George Hendrick .10 .05
❑ 405 Eddie Murray 1.00 .45
❑ 406 Marshall Edwards .10 .05
❑ 407 Lance Parrish .20 .09
❑ 408 Carney Lansford .20 .09
❑ 409 Dave Winfield .75 .35
❑ 410 Bob Welch .20 .09
❑ 411 Larry Milbourne .10 .05
❑ 412 Dennis Leonard .10 .05
❑ 413 Dan Meyer .10 .05
❑ 414 Charlie Lea .10 .05
❑ 415 Rick Honeycutt .10 .05
❑ 416 Mike Witt .10 .05
❑ 417 Steve Trout .10 .05
❑ 418 Glenn Brummer .10 .05
❑ 419 Denny Walling .10 .05
❑ 420 Gary Matthews .20 .09
❑ 421 Charlie Leibrandt UER .10 .05
(Liebrandt on
front of card)
❑ 422 J.Eichelberger UER .10 .05
Photo actually
Joe Pittman
❑ 423 Cecilio Guante UER .10 .05
(Listed as Matt
on card)
❑ 424 Bill Laskey .10 .05
❑ 425 Jerry Royster .10 .05
❑ 426 Dickie Noles .10 .05
❑ 427 George Foster .20 .09
❑ 428 Mike Moore RC .20 .09
❑ 429 Gary Ward .10 .05
❑ 430 Barry Bonnell .10 .05
❑ 431 Ron Washington .10 .05
❑ 432 Rance Mulliniks .10 .05
❑ 433 Mike Stanton .10 .05
❑ 434 Jesse Orosco .10 .05
❑ 435 Larry Bowa .20 .09
❑ 436 Biff Pocoroba .10 .05
❑ 437 Johnny Ray .10 .05
❑ 438 Joe Morgan .75 .35
❑ 439 Eric Show .10 .05
❑ 440 Larry Biittner .10 .05
❑ 441 Greg Gross .10 .05
❑ 442 Gene Tenace .20 .09
❑ 443 Danny Heep .10 .05
❑ 444 Bobby Clark .10 .05
❑ 445 Kevin Hickey .10 .05
❑ 446 Scott Sanderson .10 .05
❑ 447 Frank Tanana .20 .09
❑ 448 Cesar Geronimo .10 .05
❑ 449 Jimmy Sexton .10 .05
❑ 450 Mike Hargrove .20 .09
❑ 451 Doyle Alexander .10 .05

❑ 452 Dwight Evans .20 .09
❑ 453 Terry Forster .10 .05
❑ 454 Tom Brookens .10 .05
❑ 455 Rich Dauer .10 .05
❑ 456 Rob Picciolo .10 .05
❑ 457 Terry Crowley .10 .05
❑ 458 Ned Yost .10 .05
❑ 459 Kirk Gibson .75 .35
❑ 460 Reid Nichols .10 .05
❑ 461 Oscar Gamble .10 .05
❑ 462 Dusty Baker .20 .09
❑ 463 Jack Perconte .10 .05
❑ 464 Frank White .20 .09
❑ 465 Mickey Klutts .10 .05
❑ 466 Warren Cromartie .10 .05
❑ 467 Larry Parrish .10 .05
❑ 468 Bobby Grich .20 .09
❑ 469 Dane Iorg .10 .05
❑ 470 Joe Niekro .20 .09
❑ 471 Ed Farmer .10 .05
❑ 472 Tim Flannery .10 .05
❑ 473 Dave Parker .20 .09
❑ 474 Jeff Leonard .10 .05
❑ 475 Al Hrabosky .10 .05
❑ 476 Ron Hodges .10 .05
❑ 477 Leon Durham .10 .05
❑ 478 Jim Essian .10 .05
❑ 479 Roy Lee Jackson .10 .05
❑ 480 Brad Havens .10 .05
❑ 481 Joe Price .10 .05
❑ 482 Tony Bernazard .10 .05
❑ 483 Scott McGregor .10 .05
❑ 484 Paul Molitor 1.00 .45
❑ 485 Mike Ivie .10 .05
❑ 486 Ken Griffey .20 .09
❑ 487 Dennis Eckersley .75 .35
❑ 488 Steve Garvey .40 .18
❑ 489 Mike Fischlin .10 .05
❑ 490 U.L. Washington .10 .05
❑ 491 Steve McCatty .10 .05
❑ 492 Roy Johnson .10 .05
❑ 493 Don Baylor .40 .18
❑ 494 Bobby Johnson .10 .05
❑ 495 Mike Squires .10 .05
❑ 496 Bert Roberge .10 .05
❑ 497 Dick Ruthven .10 .05
❑ 498 Tito Landrum .10 .05
❑ 499 Sixto Lezcano .10 .05
❑ 500 Johnny Bench 1.25 .55
❑ 501 Larry Whisenton .10 .05
❑ 502 Manny Sarmiento .10 .05
❑ 503 Fred Breining .10 .05
❑ 504 Bill Campbell .10 .05
❑ 505 Todd Cruz .10 .05
❑ 506 Bob Bailor .10 .05
❑ 507 Dave Stieb .20 .09
❑ 508 Al Williams .10 .05
❑ 509 Dan Ford .10 .05
❑ 510 Gorman Thomas .10 .05
❑ 511 Chet Lemon .10 .05
❑ 512 Mike Torrez .10 .05
❑ 513 Shane Rawley .10 .05
❑ 514 Mark Belanger .10 .05
❑ 515 Rodney Craig .10 .05
❑ 516 Onix Concepcion .10 .05
❑ 517 Mike Heath .10 .05
❑ 518 Andre Dawson UER .40 .18
(Middle name Fernando,
should be Nolan)
❑ 519 Luis Sanchez .10 .05
❑ 520 Terry Bogener .10 .05
❑ 521 Rudy Law .10 .05
❑ 522 Ray Knight .20 .09
❑ 523 Joe Lefebvre .10 .05
❑ 524 Jim Wohlford .10 .05
❑ 525 Julio Franco RC 1.00 .45
❑ 526 Ron Oester .10 .05
❑ 527 Rick Mahler .10 .05
❑ 528 Steve Nicosia .10 .05
❑ 529 Junior Kennedy .10 .05
❑ 530A Whitey Herzog MG .20 .09
(Bio printed
black on white)
❑ 530B Whitey Herzog MG .20 .09
(Bio printed
black on yellow)
❑ 531A Don Sutton .75 .35
(Blue border
on photo)
❑ 531B Don Sutton .75 .35
(Green border
on photo)
❑ 532 Mark Brouhard .10 .05
❑ 533A S.Anderson MG .20 .09
Bio printed
black on white
❑ 533B S.Anderson MG .20 .09
Bio printed
black on yellow
❑ 534 Roger LaFrancois .10 .05
❑ 535 George Frazier .10 .05
❑ 536 Tom Niedenfuer .10 .05
❑ 537 Ed Glynn .10 .05
❑ 538 Lee May .20 .09
❑ 539 Bob Kearney .10 .05
❑ 540 Tim Raines .75 .35
❑ 541 Paul Mirabella .10 .05
❑ 542 Luis Tiant .20 .09
❑ 543 Ron LeFlore .10 .05
❑ 544 Dave LaPoint .10 .05
❑ 545 Randy Moffitt .10 .05
❑ 546 Luis Aguayo .10 .05
❑ 547 Brad Lesley .20 .09
❑ 548 Luis Salazar .10 .05
❑ 549 John Candelaria .10 .05
❑ 550 Dave Bergman .10 .05
❑ 551 Bob Watson .20 .09
❑ 552 Pat Tabler .10 .05
❑ 553 Brent Gaff .10 .05
❑ 554 Al Cowens .10 .05
❑ 555 Tom Brunansky .20 .09
❑ 556 Lloyd Moseby .10 .05
❑ 557A Pascual Perez ERR 2.00 .90
(Twins in glove)
❑ 557B Pascual Perez COR .20 .09
(Braves in glove)
❑ 558 Willie Upshaw .10 .05
❑ 559 Richie Zisk .10 .05
❑ 560 Pat Zachry .10 .05
❑ 561 Jay Johnstone .20 .09
❑ 562 Carlos Diaz .10 .05
❑ 563 John Tudor .10 .05
❑ 564 Frank Robinson MG .40 .18
❑ 565 Dave Edwards .10 .05
❑ 566 Paul Householder .10 .05
❑ 567 Ron Reed .10 .05
❑ 568 Mike Ramsey .10 .05
❑ 569 Kiko Garcia .10 .05
❑ 570 Tommy John .40 .18
❑ 571 Tony LaRussa MG .20 .09
❑ 572 Joel Youngblood .10 .05
❑ 573 Wayne Tolleson .10 .05
❑ 574 Keith Creel .10 .05
❑ 575 Billy Martin MG .20 .09
❑ 576 Jerry Dybzinski .10 .05
❑ 577 Rick Cerone .10 .05
❑ 578 Tony Perez .75 .35
❑ 579 Greg Brock .10 .05
❑ 580 Glenn Wilson .10 .05
❑ 581 Tim Stoddard .10 .05
❑ 582 Bob McClure .10 .05
❑ 583 Jim Dwyer .10 .05
❑ 584 Ed Romero .10 .05
❑ 585 Larry Herndon .10 .05
❑ 586 Wade Boggs RC 10.00 4.50
❑ 587 Jay Howell .10 .05
❑ 588 Dave Stewart .20 .09
❑ 589 Bert Blyleven .40 .18
❑ 590 Dick Howser MG .10 .05
❑ 591 Wayne Gross .10 .05
❑ 592 Terry Francona .10 .05
❑ 593 Don Werner .10 .05
❑ 594 Bill Stein .10 .05
❑ 595 Jesse Barfield .20 .09
❑ 596 Bob Molinaro .10 .05
❑ 597 Mike Vail .10 .05
❑ 598 Tony Gwynn RC 20.00 9.00
❑ 599 Gary Rajsich .10 .05
❑ 600 Jerry Ujdur .10 .05
❑ 601 Cliff Johnson .10 .05
❑ 602 Jerry White .10 .05
❑ 603 Bryan Clark .10 .05
❑ 604 Joe Ferguson .10 .05
❑ 605 Guy Sularz .10 .05
❑ 606A Ozzie Virgil .20 .09
(Green border
on photo)
❑ 606B Ozzie Virgil .20 .09
(Orange border
on photo)
❑ 607 Terry Harper .10 .05
❑ 608 Harvey Kuenn MG .10 .05
❑ 609 Jim Sundberg .20 .09
❑ 610 Willie Stargell .75 .35
❑ 611 Reggie Smith .20 .09
❑ 612 Rob Wilfong .10 .05
❑ 613 The Niekro Brothers .40 .18
Joe Niekro
Phil Niekro
❑ 614 Lee Elia MG .10 .05
❑ 615 Mickey Hatcher .10 .05
❑ 616 Jerry Hairston .10 .05
❑ 617 John Martin .10 .05
❑ 618 Wally Backman .10 .05
❑ 619 Storm Davis RC .10 .05
❑ 620 Alan Knicely .10 .05
❑ 621 John Stuper .10 .05
❑ 622 Matt Sinatro .10 .05
❑ 623 Geno Petralli .40 .18
❑ 624 Duane Walker .10 .05
❑ 625 Dick Williams MG .10 .05
❑ 626 Pat Corrales MG .10 .05
❑ 627 Vern Ruhle .10 .05
❑ 628 Joe Torre MG .20 .09
❑ 629 Anthony Johnson .10 .05
❑ 630 Steve Howe .10 .05
❑ 631 Gary Woods .10 .05
❑ 632 LaMarr Hoyt .20 .09
❑ 633 Steve Swisher .10 .05
❑ 634 Terry Leach .10 .05
❑ 635 Jeff Newman .10 .05
❑ 636 Brett Butler .75 .35
❑ 637 Gary Gray .10 .05
❑ 638 Lee Mazzilli .10 .05
❑ 639A Ron Jackson ERR 5.00 2.20
(A's in glove)
❑ 639B Ron Jackson COR .10 .05
(Angels in glove,
red border
on photo)
❑ 639C Ron Jackson COR .75 .35
(Angels in glove,
green border
on photo)
❑ 640 Juan Beniquez .10 .05
❑ 641 Dave Rucker .10 .05
❑ 642 Luis Pujols .10 .05
❑ 643 Rick Monday .10 .05
❑ 644 Hosken Powell .10 .05
❑ 645 The Chicken .75 .35
❑ 646 Dave Engle .10 .05
❑ 647 Dick Davis .10 .05
❑ 648 Frank Robinson .20 .09
Vida Blue
Joe Morgan
❑ 649 Al Chambers .10 .05
❑ 650 Jesus Vega .10 .05
❑ 651 Jeff Jones .10 .05
❑ 652 Marvis Foley .10 .05
❑ 653 Ty Cobb Puzzle Card .75 .35
❑ 654A Dick Perez/Diamond .75 .35
King Checklist 1-26
(Unnumbered) ERR
(Word "checklist"
omitted from back)
❑ 654B Dick Perez/Diamond .75 .35
King Checklist 1-26
(Unnumbered) COR
(Word "checklist"
is on back)
❑ 655 Checklist 27-130 .10 .05
(Unnumbered)
❑ 656 Checklist 131-234 .10 .05
(Unnumbered)
❑ 657 Checklist 235-338 .10 .05
(Unnumbered)
❑ 658 Checklist 339-442 .10 .05
(Unnumbered)

❑ 659 Checklist 443-544 .... .10 .05
(Unnumbered)
❑ 660 Checklist 545-653 .... .10 .05
(Unnumbered)

1984 Donruss

	NRMT	VG-E
COMPLETE SET (660)	80.00	36.00
COMP.FACT.SET (658)	120.00	55.00
COMP.SNIDER PUZZLE	5.00	2.20

❑ 1 Robin Yount DK COR ...... 2.00 .90
❑ 1A Robin Yount DK ERR 3.00 1.35
❑ 2 Dave Concepcion DK ...... 1.50 .70
COR
❑ 2A Dave Concepcion DK ...... .75 .35
ERR (Perez Steel)
❑ 3 Dwayne Murphy DK .... .75 .35
COR
❑ 3A Dwayne Murphy DK .... .25 .11
ERR (Perez Steel)
❑ 4 John Castino DK COR ...... .75 .35
❑ 4A John Castino DK ERR .... .25 .11
(Perez Steel)
❑ 5 Leon Durham DK COR ...... .75 .35
❑ 5A Leon Durham DK ERR .... .25 .11
(Perez Steel)
❑ 6 Rusty Staub DK COR ...... 1.50 .70
❑ 6A Rusty Staub DK ERR ...... .75 .35
(Perez Steel)
❑ 7 Jack Clark DK COR .... .75 .35
❑ 7A Jack Clark DK ERR .... .75 .35
(Perez Steel)
❑ 8 Dave Dravecky DK .... .75 .35
COR
❑ 8A Dave Dravecky DK .... .75 .35
ERR (Perez Steel)
❑ 9 Al Oliver DK COR .... 1.50 .70
❑ 9A Al Oliver DK ERR .... .75 .35
(Perez Steel)
❑ 10 Dave Righetti DK............. .75 .35
COR
❑ 10A Dave Righetti DK .... .75 .35
ERR (Perez Steel)
❑ 11 Hal McRae DK COR ...... 1.50 .70
❑ 11A Hal McRae DK ERR ...... .75 .35
(Perez Steel)
❑ 12 Ray Knight DK COR .... .75 .35
❑ 12A Ray Knight DK ERR ...... .75 .35
(Perez Steel)
❑ 13 Bruce Sutter DK COR .... 1.50 .70
❑ 13A Bruce Sutter DK ERR .... .75 .35
(Perez Steel)
❑ 14 Bob Horner DK COR......... .75 .35
❑ 14A Bob Horner DK ERR...... .75 .35
(Perez Steel)
❑ 15 Lance Parrish DK .... 1.50 .70
COR
❑ 15A Lance Parrish DK .... .75 .35
ERR (Perez Steel)
❑ 16 Matt Young DK COR........ .75 .35
❑ 16A Matt Young DK ERR...... .25 .11
(Perez Steel)
❑ 17 Fred Lynn DK COR.......... .75 .35
❑ 17A Fred Lynn DK ERR .... .25 .11
(Perez Steel)
(A's logo on back
❑ 18 Ron Kittle DK COR .... .75 .35
❑ 18A Ron Kittle DK ERR .... .25 .11
(Perez Steel)
❑ 19 Jim Clancy DK COR .... .75 .35
❑ 19A Jim Clancy DK ERR ...... .25 .11
(Perez Steel)
❑ 20 Bill Madlock DK COR .... 1.50 .70
❑ 20A Bill Madlock DK ERR .... .75 .35
(Perez Steel)
❑ 21 Larry Parrish DK .... .75 .35
COR
❑ 21A Larry Parrish DK .... .25 .11
ERR (Perez Steel)
❑ 22 Eddie Murray DK COR .. 3.00 1.35
❑ 22A Eddie Murray DK ERR 2.50 1.10
❑ 23 Mike Schmidt DK COR .. 4.00 1.80
❑ 23A M.Schmidt DK ERR 4.00 1.80
❑ 24 Pedro Guerrero DK .... .75 .35
COR
❑ 24A Pedro Guerrero DK........ .75 .35
ERR (Perez Steel)
❑ 25 Andre Thornton DK .... .75 .35
COR
❑ 25A Andre Thornton DK........ .75 .35
ERR (Perez Steel)
❑ 26 Wade Boggs DK COR.... 3.00 1.35
❑ 26A Wade Boggs DK ERR.. 2.50 1.10
❑ 27 Joel Skinner RR RC .... .25 .11
❑ 28 Tommy Dunbar RR RC .... .25 .11
❑ 29A M.Stenhouse RC RR ..... .25 .11
ERR No number on back
❑ 29B Mike Stenhouse RR 3.00 1.35
COR Numbered on back
❑ 30A R.Darling RC RR ERR .. .75 .35
No number on back
❑ 30B Ron Darling RR COR .. 3.00 1.35
(Numbered on back)
❑ 31 Dion James RR RC.......... .25 .11
❑ 32 Tony Fernandez RR RC 3.00 1.35
❑ 33 Angel Salazar RR RC ...... .25 .11
❑ 34 Kevin McReynolds RR RC 1.50 .70
❑ 35 Dick Schofield RR RC ...... .75 .35
❑ 36 Brad Komminsk RR RC .. .25 .11
❑ 37 Tim Teufel RR RC............ .25 .11
❑ 38 Doug Frobel RR RC .... .25 .11
❑ 39 Greg Gagne RR RC .... .75 .35
❑ 40 Mike Fuentes RR RC ...... .25 .11
❑ 41 Joe Carter RR RC........ 10.00 4.50
❑ 42 Mike Brown RC RR .... .25 .11
(Angels OF)
❑ 43 Mike Jeffcoat RR RC......... .25 .11
❑ 44 Sid Fernandez RR RC .. 1.50 .70
❑ 45 Brian Dayett RR RC .... .25 .11
❑ 46 Chris Smith RR RC .... .25 .11
❑ 47 Eddie Murray................. 3.00 1.35
❑ 48 Robin Yount 3.00 1.35
❑ 49 Lance Parrish .... 1.50 .70
❑ 50 Jim Rice .... .75 .35
❑ 51 Dave Winfield 3.00 1.35
❑ 52 Fernando Valenzuela ...... .75 .35
❑ 53 George Brett 6.00 2.70
❑ 54 Rickey Henderson.......... 6.00 2.70
❑ 55 Gary Carter .... 1.50 .70
❑ 56 Buddy Bell .... .75 .35
❑ 57 Reggie Jackson............. 4.00 1.80
❑ 58 Harold Baines 3.00 1.35
❑ 59 Ozzie Smith.................... 4.00 1.80
❑ 60 Nolan Ryan UER.......... 15.00 6.75
(Text on back refers to 1972 as
the year he struck out 383;
the year was 1973)
❑ 61 Pete Rose 10.00 4.50
❑ 62 Ron Oester .... .25 .11
❑ 63 Steve Garvey .... 1.50 .70
❑ 64 Jason Thompson.............. .25 .11
❑ 65 Jack Clark .... .75 .35
❑ 66 Dale Murphy 3.00 1.35
❑ 67 Leon Durham .... .25 .11
❑ 68 Darryl Strawberry RC 5.00 2.20
❑ 69 Richie Zisk...................... .25 .11
❑ 70 Kent Hrbek .... .75 .35
❑ 71 Dave Stieb........................ .25 .11
❑ 72 Ken Schrom .... .25 .11
❑ 73 George Bell .... .75 .35
❑ 74 John Moses...................... .25 .11
❑ 75 Ed Lynch .... .25 .11
❑ 76 Chuck Rainey .... .25 .11
❑ 77 Biff Pocoroba.................... .25 .11
❑ 78 Cecilio Guante.................. .25 .11
❑ 79 Jim Barr............................ .25 .11
❑ 80 Kurt Bevacqua.................. .25 .11
❑ 81 Tom Foley .... .25 .11
❑ 82 Joe Lefebvre .... .25 .11
❑ 83 Andy Van Slyke RC........ 3.00 1.35
❑ 84 Bob Lillis MG .... .25 .11
❑ 85 Ricky Adams .... .25 .11
❑ 86 Jerry Hairston .... .25 .11
❑ 87 Bob James .... .25 .11
❑ 88 Joe Altobelli MG .... .25 .11
❑ 89 Ed Romero .... .25 .11
❑ 90 John Grubb .... .25 .11
❑ 91 John Henry Johnson .... .25 .11
❑ 92 Juan Espino .... .25 .11
❑ 93 Candy Maldonado .... .25 .11
❑ 94 Andre Thornton .... .25 .11
❑ 95 Onix Concepcion .... .25 .11
❑ 96 Donnie Hill UER .... .25 .11
(Listed as P,
should be 2B)
❑ 97 Andre Dawson UER ...... 1.50 .70
(Wrong middle name,
should be Nolan)
❑ 98 Frank Tanana .... .75 .35
❑ 99 Curtis Wilkerson .... .25 .11
❑ 100 Larry Gura .... .25 .11
❑ 101 Dwayne Murphy .... .25 .11
❑ 102 Tom Brennan .... .25 .11
❑ 103 Dave Righetti.................. .75 .35
❑ 104 Steve Sax .... .75 .35
❑ 105 Dan Petry .... .75 .35
❑ 106 Cal Ripken................. 20.00 9.00
❑ 107 Paul Molitor UER.......... 3.00 1.35
('83 stats should
say .270 BA, 608 AB,
and 164 hits)
❑ 108 Fred Lynn .... .75 .35
❑ 109 Neil Allen....................... .25 .11
❑ 110 Joe Niekro .... .75 .35
❑ 111 Steve Carlton 3.00 1.35
❑ 112 Terry Kennedy................ .25 .11
❑ 113 Bill Madlock .... .75 .35
❑ 114 Chili Davis .... 1.50 .70
❑ 115 Jim Gantner.................... .25 .11
❑ 116 Tom Seaver.................. 5.00 2.20
❑ 117 Bill Buckner .... .75 .35
❑ 118 Bill Caudill .... .25 .11
❑ 119 Jim Clancy .... .25 .11
❑ 120 John Castino .... .25 .11
❑ 121 Dave Concepcion .... .75 .35
❑ 122 Greg Luzinski .... .75 .35
❑ 123 Mike Boddicker .... .25 .11
❑ 124 Pete Ladd .... .25 .11
❑ 125 Juan Berenguer.............. .25 .11
❑ 126 John Montefusco .... .25 .11
❑ 127 Ed Jurak .... .25 .11
❑ 128 Tom Niedenfuer .... .25 .11
❑ 129 Bert Blyleven .... .75 .35
❑ 130 Bud Black .... .25 .11
❑ 131 Gorman Heimueller .... .25 .11
❑ 132 Dan Schatzeder .... .25 .11
❑ 133 Ron Jackson .... .25 .11
❑ 134 Tom Henke RC .... 1.50 .70
❑ 135 Kevin Hickey .... .25 .11
❑ 136 Mike Scott .... .75 .35
❑ 137 Bo Diaz .... .25 .11
❑ 138 Glenn Brummer.............. .25 .11
❑ 139 Sid Monge .... .25 .11
❑ 140 Rich Gale .... .25 .11
❑ 141 Brett Butler .... 1.50 .70
❑ 142 Brian Harper RC .... .75 .35
❑ 143 John Rabb....................... .25 .11
❑ 144 Gary Woods .... .25 .11
❑ 145 Pat Putnam .... .25 .11
❑ 146 Jim Acker .... .25 .11
❑ 147 Mickey Hatcher .... .25 .11
❑ 148 Todd Cruz .... .25 .11
❑ 149 Tom Tellmann .... .25 .11
❑ 150 John Wockenfuss .... .25 .11
❑ 151 Wade Boggs UER......... 8.00 3.60
1983 runs 10; should be 100
❑ 152 Don Baylor .... 1.50 .70
❑ 153 Bob Welch....................... .25 .11

❑ 154 Alan Bannister .25 .11
❑ 155 Willie Aikens .25 .11
❑ 156 Jeff Burroughs .25 .11
❑ 157 Bryan Little .25 .11
❑ 158 Bob Boone .75 .35
❑ 159 Dave Hostetler .25 .11
❑ 160 Jerry Dybzinski .25 .11
❑ 161 Mike Madden .25 .11
❑ 162 Luis DeLeon .25 .11
❑ 163 Willie Hernandez .75 .35
❑ 164 Frank Pastore .25 .11
❑ 165 Rick Camp .25 .11
❑ 166 Lee Mazzilli .25 .11
❑ 167 Scot Thompson .25 .11
❑ 168 Bob Forsch .25 .11
❑ 169 Mike Flanagan .25 .11
❑ 170 Rick Manning .25 .11
❑ 171 Chet Lemon .25 .11
❑ 172 Jerry Remy .25 .11
❑ 173 Ron Guidry .75 .35
❑ 174 Pedro Guerrero .75 .35
❑ 175 Willie Wilson .25 .11
❑ 176 Carney Lansford .75 .35
❑ 177 Al Oliver .75 .35
❑ 178 Jim Sundberg .75 .35
❑ 179 Bobby Grich .75 .35
❑ 180 Rich Dotson .25 .11
❑ 181 Joaquin Andujar .25 .11
❑ 182 Jose Cruz .75 .35
❑ 183 Mike Schmidt 6.00 2.70
❑ 184 Gary Redus RC* .25 .11
❑ 185 Garry Templeton .25 .11
❑ 186 Tony Pena .25 .11
❑ 187 Greg Minton .25 .11
❑ 188 Phil Niekro 3.00 1.35
❑ 189 Ferguson Jenkins 3.00 1.35
❑ 190 Mookie Wilson .75 .35
❑ 191 Jim Beattie .25 .11
❑ 192 Gary Ward .25 .11
❑ 193 Jesse Barfield .75 .35
❑ 194 Pete Filson .25 .11
❑ 195 Roy Lee Jackson .25 .11
❑ 196 Rick Sweet .25 .11
❑ 197 Jesse Orosco .25 .11
❑ 198 Steve Lake .25 .11
❑ 199 Ken Dayley .25 .11
❑ 200 Manny Sarmiento .25 .11
❑ 201 Mark Davis .25 .11
❑ 202 Tim Flannery .25 .11
❑ 203 Bill Scherrer .25 .11
❑ 204 Al Holland .25 .11
❑ 205 Dave Von Ohlen .25 .11
❑ 206 Mike LaCoss .25 .11
❑ 207 Juan Beniquez .25 .11
❑ 208 Juan Agosto .25 .11
❑ 209 Bobby Ramos .25 .11
❑ 210 Al Bumbry .25 .11
❑ 211 Mark Brouhard .25 .11
❑ 212 Howard Bailey .25 .11
❑ 213 Bruce Hurst .25 .11
❑ 214 Bob Shirley .25 .11
❑ 215 Pat Zachry .25 .11
❑ 216 Julio Franco 1.50 .70
❑ 217 Mike Armstrong .25 .11
❑ 218 Dave Beard .25 .11
❑ 219 Steve Rogers .25 .11
❑ 220 John Butcher .25 .11
❑ 221 Mike Smithson .25 .11
❑ 222 Frank White .75 .35
❑ 223 Mike Heath .25 .11
❑ 224 Chris Bando .25 .11
❑ 225 Roy Smalley .25 .11
❑ 226 Dusty Baker .75 .35
❑ 227 Lou Whitaker 3.00 1.35
❑ 228 John Lowenstein .25 .11
❑ 229 Ben Oglivie .25 .11
❑ 230 Doug DeCinces .25 .11
❑ 231 Lonnie Smith .25 .11
❑ 232 Ray Knight .75 .35
❑ 233 Gary Matthews .75 .35
❑ 234 Juan Bonilla .25 .11
❑ 235 Rod Scurry .25 .11
❑ 236 Atlee Hammaker .25 .11
❑ 237 Mike Caldwell .25 .11
❑ 238 Keith Hernandez .75 .35
❑ 239 Larry Bowa .75 .35
❑ 240 Tony Bernazard .25 .11
❑ 241 Damaso Garcia .25 .11
❑ 242 Tom Brunansky .75 .35
❑ 243 Dan Driessen .25 .11
❑ 244 Ron Kittle .25 .11
❑ 245 Tim Stoddard .25 .11
❑ 246 Bob L. Gibson .25 .11
(Brewers Pitcher)
❑ 247 Marty Castillo .25 .11
❑ 248 D.Mattingly RC UER .. 30.00 13.50
traiing on back
❑ 249 Jeff Newman .25 .11
❑ 250 Alejandro Pena RC* .75 .35
❑ 251 Toby Harrah .75 .35
❑ 252 Cesar Geronimo .25 .11
❑ 253 Tom Underwood .25 .11
❑ 254 Doug Flynn .25 .11
❑ 255 Andy Hassler .25 .11
❑ 256 Odell Jones .25 .11
❑ 257 Rudy Law .25 .11
❑ 258 Harry Spilman .25 .11
❑ 259 Marty Bystrom .25 .11
❑ 260 Dave Rucker .25 .11
❑ 261 Ruppert Jones .25 .11
❑ 262 Jeff R. Jones .25 .11
(Reds OF)
❑ 263 Gerald Perry .75 .35
❑ 264 Gene Tenace .75 .35
❑ 265 Brad Wellman .25 .11
❑ 266 Dickie Noles .25 .11
❑ 267 Jamie Allen .25 .11
❑ 268 Jim Gott .25 .11
❑ 269 Ron Davis .25 .11
❑ 270 Benny Ayala .25 .11
❑ 271 Ned Yost .25 .11
❑ 272 Dave Rozema .25 .11
❑ 273 Dave Stapleton .25 .11
❑ 274 Lou Piniella .75 .35
❑ 275 Jose Morales .25 .11
❑ 276 Broderick Perkins .25 .11
❑ 277 Butch Davis RC .25 .11
❑ 278 Tony Phillips RC 3.00 1.35
❑ 279 Jeff Reardon .75 .35
❑ 280 Ken Forsch .25 .11
❑ 281 Pete O'Brien RC* .75 .35
❑ 282 Tom Paciorek .75 .35
❑ 283 Frank LaCorte .25 .11
❑ 284 Tim Lollar .25 .11
❑ 285 Greg Gross .25 .11
❑ 286 Alex Trevino .25 .11
❑ 287 Gene Garber .25 .11
❑ 288 Dave Parker .75 .35
❑ 289 Lee Smith 3.00 1.35
❑ 290 Dave LaPoint .25 .11
❑ 291 John Shelby .25 .11
❑ 292 Charlie Moore .25 .11
❑ 293 Alan Trammell 1.50 .70
❑ 294 Tony Armas .25 .11
❑ 295 Shane Rawley .25 .11
❑ 296 Greg Brock .25 .11
❑ 297 Hal McRae .75 .35
❑ 298 Mike Davis .25 .11
❑ 299 Tim Raines 1.50 .70
❑ 300 Bucky Dent .75 .35
❑ 301 Tommy John 1.50 .70
❑ 302 Carlton Fisk 3.00 1.35
❑ 303 Darrell Porter .25 .11
❑ 304 Dickie Thon .25 .11
❑ 305 Garry Maddox .25 .11
❑ 306 Cesar Cedeno .75 .35
❑ 307 Gary Lucas .25 .11
❑ 308 Johnny Ray .25 .11
❑ 309 Andy McGaffigan .25 .11
❑ 310 Claudell Washington .25 .11
❑ 311 Ryne Sandberg 10.00 4.50
❑ 312 George Foster .75 .35
❑ 313 Spike Owen RC .75 .35
❑ 314 Gary Gaetti 1.50 .70
❑ 315 Willie Upshaw .25 .11
❑ 316 Al Williams .25 .11
❑ 317 Jorge Orta .25 .11
❑ 318 Orlando Mercado .25 .11
❑ 319 Junior Ortiz .25 .11
❑ 320 Mike Proly .25 .11
❑ 321 Randy Johnson UER .25 .11
('72-'82 stats are
from Twins' Randy John-
son, '83 stats are from
Braves' Randy Johnson)
❑ 322 Jim Morrison .25 .11
❑ 323 Max Venable .25 .11
❑ 324 Tony Gwynn 15.00 6.75
❑ 325 Duane Walker .25 .11
❑ 326 Ozzie Virgil .25 .11
❑ 327 Jeff Lahti .25 .11
❑ 328 Bill Dawley .25 .11
❑ 329 Rob Wilfong .25 .11
❑ 330 Marc Hill .25 .11
❑ 331 Ray Burris .25 .11
❑ 332 Allan Ramirez .25 .11
❑ 333 Chuck Porter .25 .11
❑ 334 Wayne Krenchicki .25 .11
❑ 335 Gary Allenson .25 .11
❑ 336 Bobby Meacham .25 .11
❑ 337 Joe Beckwith .25 .11
❑ 338 Rick Sutcliffe .75 .35
❑ 339 Mark Huismann .25 .11
❑ 340 Tim Conroy .25 .11
❑ 341 Scott Sanderson .25 .11
❑ 342 Larry Biittner .25 .11
❑ 343 Dave Stewart .75 .35
❑ 344 Darryl Motley .25 .11
❑ 345 Chris Codiroli .25 .11
❑ 346 Rich Behenna .25 .11
❑ 347 Andre Robertson .25 .11
❑ 348 Mike Marshall .25 .11
❑ 349 Larry Herndon .75 .35
❑ 350 Rich Dauer .25 .11
❑ 351 Cecil Cooper .75 .35
❑ 352 Rod Carew 3.00 1.35
❑ 353 Willie McGee 1.50 .70
❑ 354 Phil Garner .75 .35
❑ 355 Joe Morgan 3.00 1.35
❑ 356 Luis Salazar .25 .11
❑ 357 John Candelaria .25 .11
❑ 358 Bill Laskey .25 .11
❑ 359 Bob McClure .25 .11
❑ 360 Dave Kingman 1.50 .70
❑ 361 Ron Cey .75 .35
❑ 362 Matt Young .25 .11
❑ 363 Lloyd Moseby .25 .11
❑ 364 Frank Viola 1.50 .70
❑ 365 Eddie Milner .25 .11
❑ 366 Floyd Bannister .25 .11
❑ 367 Dan Ford .25 .11
❑ 368 Moose Haas .25 .11
❑ 369 Doug Bair .25 .11
❑ 370 Ray Fontenot .25 .11
❑ 371 Luis Aponte .25 .11
❑ 372 Jack Fimple .25 .11
❑ 373 Neal Heaton .25 .11
❑ 374 Greg Pryor .25 .11
❑ 375 Wayne Gross .25 .11
❑ 376 Charlie Lea .25 .11
❑ 377 Steve Lubratich .25 .11
❑ 378 Jon Matlack .25 .11
❑ 379 Julio Cruz .25 .11
❑ 380 John Mizerock .25 .11
❑ 381 Kevin Gross RC .25 .11
❑ 382 Mike Ramsey .25 .11
❑ 383 Doug Gwosdz .25 .11
❑ 384 Kelly Paris .25 .11
❑ 385 Pete Falcone .25 .11
❑ 386 Milt May .25 .11
❑ 387 Fred Breining .25 .11
❑ 388 Craig Lefferts RC .25 .11
❑ 389 Steve Henderson .25 .11
❑ 390 Randy Moffitt .25 .11
❑ 391 Ron Washington .25 .11
❑ 392 Gary Roenicke .25 .11
❑ 393 Tom Candiotti RC 3.00 1.35
❑ 394 Larry Pashnick .25 .11
❑ 395 Dwight Evans .75 .35
❑ 396 Rich Gossage 1.50 .70
❑ 397 Derrel Thomas .25 .11
❑ 398 Juan Eichelberger .25 .11
❑ 399 Leon Roberts .25 .11
❑ 400 Dave Lopes .75 .35
❑ 401 Bill Gullickson .25 .11
❑ 402 Geoff Zahn .25 .11
❑ 403 Billy Sample .25 .11
❑ 404 Mike Squires .25 .11

❑ 405 Craig Reynolds .25 .11
❑ 406 Eric Show .25 .11
❑ 407 John Denny .25 .11
❑ 408 Dann Bilardello .25 .11
❑ 409 Bruce Benedict .25 .11
❑ 410 Kent Tekulve .75 .35
❑ 411 Mel Hall .75 .35
❑ 412 John Stuper .25 .11
❑ 413 Rick Dempsey .25 .11
❑ 414 Don Sutton 3.00 1.35
❑ 415 Jack Morris 3.00 1.35
❑ 416 John Tudor .25 .11
❑ 417 Willie Randolph .75 .35
❑ 418 Jerry Reuss .25 .11
❑ 419 Don Slaught .75 .35
❑ 420 Steve McCatty .25 .11
❑ 421 Tim Wallach .75 .35
❑ 422 Larry Parrish .25 .11
❑ 423 Brian Downing .25 .11
❑ 424 Britt Burns .25 .11
❑ 425 David Green .25 .11
❑ 426 Jerry Mumphrey .25 .11
❑ 427 Ivan DeJesus .25 .11
❑ 428 Mario Soto .25 .11
❑ 429 Gene Richards .25 .11
❑ 430 Dale Berra .25 .11
❑ 431 Darrell Evans .75 .35
❑ 432 Glenn Hubbard .25 .11
❑ 433 Jody Davis .25 .11
❑ 434 Danny Heep .25 .11
❑ 435 Ed Nunez RC .25 .11
❑ 436 Bobby Castillo .25 .11
❑ 437 Ernie Whitt .25 .11
❑ 438 Scott Ullger .25 .11
❑ 439 Doyle Alexander .25 .11
❑ 440 Domingo Ramos .25 .11
❑ 441 Craig Swan .25 .11
❑ 442 Warren Brusstar .25 .11
❑ 443 Len Barker .25 .11
❑ 444 Mike Easler .25 .11
❑ 445 Renie Martin .25 .11
❑ 446 D.Rasmussen RC .25 .11
❑ 447 Ted Power .25 .11
❑ 448 Charles Hudson .25 .11
❑ 449 Danny Cox RC .25 .11
❑ 450 Kevin Bass .25 .11
❑ 451 Daryl Sconiers .25 .11
❑ 452 Scott Fletcher .25 .11
❑ 453 Bryn Smith .25 .11
❑ 454 Jim Dwyer .25 .11
❑ 455 Rob Picciolo .25 .11
❑ 456 Enos Cabell .25 .11
❑ 457 Dennis Boyd .75 .35
❑ 458 Butch Wynegar .25 .11
❑ 459 Burt Hooton .25 .11
❑ 460 Ron Hassey .25 .11
❑ 461 Danny Jackson RC 1.50 .70
❑ 462 Bob Kearney .25 .11
❑ 463 Terry Francona .25 .11
❑ 464 Wayne Tolleson .25 .11
❑ 465 Mickey Rivers .25 .11
❑ 466 John Wathan .25 .11
❑ 467 Bill Almon .25 .11
❑ 468 George Vukovich .25 .11
❑ 469 Steve Kemp .25 .11
❑ 470 Ken Landreaux .25 .11
❑ 471 Milt Wilcox .25 .11
❑ 472 Tippy Martinez .25 .11
❑ 473 Ted Simmons .75 .35
❑ 474 Tim Foli .25 .11
❑ 475 George Hendrick .25 .11
❑ 476 Terry Puhl .25 .11
❑ 477 Von Hayes .25 .11
❑ 478 Bobby Brown .25 .11
❑ 479 Lee Lacy .25 .11
❑ 480 Joel Youngblood .25 .11
❑ 481 Jim Slaton .25 .11
❑ 482 Mike Fitzgerald .25 .11
❑ 483 Keith Moreland .25 .11
❑ 484 Ron Roenicke .25 .11
❑ 485 Luis Leal .25 .11
❑ 486 Bryan Oelkers .25 .11
❑ 487 Bruce Berenyi .25 .11
❑ 488 LaMarr Hoyt .25 .11
❑ 489 Joe Nolan .25 .11
❑ 490 Marshall Edwards .25 .11
❑ 491 Mike Laga .75 .35
❑ 492 Rick Cerone .25 .11
❑ 493 Rick Miller UER .25 .11
(Listed as Mike
on card front)
❑ 494 Rick Honeycutt .25 .11
❑ 495 Mike Hargrove .75 .35
❑ 496 Joe Simpson .25 .11
❑ 497 Keith Atherton .25 .11
❑ 498 Chris Welsh .25 .11
❑ 499 Bruce Kison .25 .11
❑ 500 Bobby Johnson .25 .11
❑ 501 Jerry Koosman .75 .35
❑ 502 Frank DiPino .25 .11
❑ 503 Tony Perez 3.00 1.35
❑ 504 Ken Oberkfell .25 .11
❑ 505 Mark Thurmond .25 .11
❑ 506 Joe Price .25 .11
❑ 507 Pascual Perez .25 .11
❑ 508 Marvell Wynne .25 .11
❑ 509 Mike Krukow .25 .11
❑ 510 Dick Ruthven .25 .11
❑ 511 Al Cowens .25 .11
❑ 512 Cliff Johnson .25 .11
❑ 513 Randy Bush .25 .11
❑ 514 Sammy Stewart .25 .11
❑ 515 Bill Schroeder .25 .11
❑ 516 Aurelio Lopez .75 .35
❑ 517 Mike G. Brown .25 .11
❑ 518 Graig Nettles .75 .35
❑ 519 Dave Sax .25 .11
❑ 520 Jerry Willard .25 .11
❑ 521 Paul Splittorff .25 .11
❑ 522 Tom Burgmeier .25 .11
❑ 523 Chris Speier .25 .11
❑ 524 Bobby Clark .25 .11
❑ 525 George Wright .25 .11
❑ 526 Dennis Lamp .25 .11
❑ 527 Tony Scott .25 .11
❑ 528 Ed Whitson .25 .11
❑ 529 Ron Reed .25 .11
❑ 530 Charlie Puleo .25 .11
❑ 531 Jerry Royster .25 .11
❑ 532 Don Robinson .25 .11
❑ 533 Steve Trout .25 .11
❑ 534 Bruce Sutter .75 .35
❑ 535 Bob Horner .25 .11
❑ 536 Pat Tabler .25 .11
❑ 537 Chris Chambliss .75 .35
❑ 538 Bob Ojeda .25 .11
❑ 539 Alan Ashby .25 .11
❑ 540 Jay Johnstone .75 .35
❑ 541 Bob Dernier .25 .11
❑ 542 Brook Jacoby .75 .35
❑ 543 U.L. Washington .25 .11
❑ 544 Danny Darwin .25 .11
❑ 545 Kiko Garcia .25 .11
❑ 546 Vance Law UER .25 .11
(Listed as P
on card front)
❑ 547 Tug McGraw .75 .35
❑ 548 Dave Smith .25 .11
❑ 549 Len Matuszek .25 .11
❑ 550 Tom Hume .25 .11
❑ 551 Dave Dravecky .75 .35
❑ 552 Rick Rhoden .25 .11
❑ 553 Duane Kuiper .25 .11
❑ 554 Rusty Staub .75 .35
❑ 555 Bill Campbell .25 .11
❑ 556 Mike Torrez .25 .11
❑ 557 Dave Henderson .75 .35
❑ 558 Len Whitehouse .25 .11
❑ 559 Barry Bonnell .25 .11
❑ 560 Rick Lysander .25 .11
❑ 561 Garth Iorg .25 .11
❑ 562 Bryan Clark .25 .11
❑ 563 Brian Giles .25 .11
❑ 564 Vern Ruhle .25 .11
❑ 565 Steve Bedrosian .25 .11
❑ 566 Larry McWilliams .25 .11
❑ 567 Jeff Leonard UER .25 .11
(Listed as P
on card front)
❑ 568 Alan Wiggins .25 .11
❑ 569 Jeff Russell RC .75 .35
❑ 570 Salome Barojas .25 .11
❑ 571 Dane Iorg .25 .11
❑ 572 Bob Knepper .25 .11
❑ 573 Gary Lavelle .25 .11
❑ 574 Gorman Thomas .25 .11
❑ 575 Manny Trillo .25 .11
❑ 576 Jim Palmer 3.00 1.35
❑ 577 Dale Murray .25 .11
❑ 578 Tom Brookens .75 .35
❑ 579 Rich Gedman .25 .11
❑ 580 Bill Doran RC* .75 .35
❑ 581 Steve Yeager .25 .11
❑ 582 Dan Spillner .25 .11
❑ 583 Dan Quisenberry .25 .11
❑ 584 Rance Mulliniks .25 .11
❑ 585 Storm Davis .25 .11
❑ 586 Dave Schmidt .25 .11
❑ 587 Bill Russell .25 .11
❑ 588 Pat Sheridan .25 .11
❑ 589 Rafael Ramirez .25 .11
UER (A's on front)
❑ 590 Bud Anderson .25 .11
❑ 591 George Frazier .25 .11
❑ 592 Lee Tunnell .25 .11
❑ 593 Kirk Gibson 3.00 1.35
❑ 594 Scott McGregor .25 .11
❑ 595 Bob Bailor .25 .11
❑ 596 Tom Herr .75 .35
❑ 597 Luis Sanchez .25 .11
❑ 598 Dave Engle .25 .11
❑ 599 Craig McMurtry .25 .11
❑ 600 Carlos Diaz .25 .11
❑ 601 Tom O'Malley .25 .11
❑ 602 Nick Esasky .25 .11
❑ 603 Ron Hodges .25 .11
❑ 604 Ed VandeBerg .25 .11
❑ 605 Alfredo Griffin .25 .11
❑ 606 Glenn Hoffman .25 .11
❑ 607 Hubie Brooks .25 .11
❑ 608 Richard Barnes UER .25 .11
(Photo actually
Neal Heaton)
❑ 609 Greg Walker .75 .35
❑ 610 Ken Singleton .25 .11
❑ 611 Mark Clear .25 .11
❑ 612 Buck Martinez .25 .11
❑ 613 Ken Griffey .75 .35
❑ 614 Reid Nichols .25 .11
❑ 615 Doug Sisk .25 .11
❑ 616 Bob Brenly .25 .11
❑ 617 Joey McLaughlin .25 .11
❑ 618 Glenn Wilson .75 .35
❑ 619 Bob Stoddard .25 .11
❑ 620 Lenn Sakata UER .25 .11
(Listed as Len
on card front)
❑ 621 Mike Young .25 .11
❑ 622 John Stefero .25 .11
❑ 623 Carmelo Martinez .25 .11
❑ 624 Dave Bergman .25 .11
❑ 625 Runnin' Reds UER 3.00 1.35
(Sic, Redbirds)
David Green
Willie McGee
Lonnie Smith
Ozzie Smith
❑ 626 Rudy May .25 .11
❑ 627 Matt Keough .25 .11
❑ 628 Jose DeLeon .25 .11
❑ 629 Jim Essian .25 .11
❑ 630 Darnell Coles RC .25 .11
❑ 631 Mike Warren .25 .11
❑ 632 Del Crandall MG .25 .11
❑ 633 Dennis Martinez .75 .35
❑ 634 Mike Moore .75 .35
❑ 635 Lary Sorensen .25 .11
❑ 636 Ricky Nelson .25 .11
❑ 637 Omar Moreno .25 .11
❑ 638 Charlie Hough .75 .35
❑ 639 Dennis Eckersley 3.00 1.35
❑ 640 Walt Terrell .25 .11
❑ 641 Denny Walling .25 .11
❑ 642 Dave Anderson .25 .11
❑ 643 Jose Oquendo RC .75 .35
❑ 644 Bob Stanley .25 .11
❑ 645 Dave Geisel .25 .11
❑ 646 Scott Garrelts .25 .11

❑ 647 Gary Pettis .25 .11
❑ 648 Duke Snider 1.50 .70
Puzzle Card
❑ 649 Johnnie LeMaster .25 .11
❑ 650 Dave Collins .25 .11
❑ 651 The Chicken 1.50 .70
❑ 652 DK Checklist 1-26 .75 .35
(Unnumbered)
❑ 653 Checklist 27-130 .25 .11
(Unnumbered)
❑ 654 Checklist 131-234 .25 .11
(Unnumbered)
❑ 655 Checklist 235-338 .25 .11
(Unnumbered)
❑ 656 Checklist 339-442 .25 .11
(Unnumbered)
❑ 657 Checklist 443-546 .25 .11
(Unnumbered)
❑ 658 Checklist 547-651 .25 .11
(Unnumbered)
❑ A Living Legends A 2.50 1.10
Gaylord Perry
Rollie Fingers
❑ B Living Legends B 5.00 2.20
Carl Yastrzemski
Johnny Bench

1985 Donruss

	NRMT	VG-E
COMPLETE SET (660)	60.00	27.00
COMP.FACT.SET (660)	100.00	45.00
COMP.GEHRIG PUZZLE	4.00	1.80

❑ 1 Ryne Sandberg DK 2.00 .90
❑ 2 Doug DeCinces DK .15 .07
❑ 3 Richard Dotson DK .15 .07
❑ 4 Bert Blyleven DK .15 .07
❑ 5 Lou Whitaker DK .40 .18
❑ 6 Dan Quisenberry DK .40 .18
❑ 7 Don Mattingly DK 2.00 .90
❑ 8 Carney Lansford DK .15 .07
❑ 9 Frank Tanana DK .15 .07
❑ 10 Willie Upshaw DK .15 .07
❑ 11 C.Washington DK .15 .07
❑ 12 Mike Marshall DK .15 .07
❑ 13 Joaquin Andujar DK .15 .07
❑ 14 Cal Ripken DK 3.00 1.35
❑ 15 Jim Rice DK .15 .07
❑ 16 Don Sutton DK .40 .18
❑ 17 Frank Viola DK .15 .07
❑ 18 Alvin Davis DK .15 .07
❑ 19 Mario Soto DK .15 .07
❑ 20 Jose Cruz DK .15 .07
❑ 21 Charlie Lea DK .15 .07
❑ 22 Jesse Orosco DK .15 .07
❑ 23 Juan Samuel DK .15 .07
❑ 24 Tony Pena DK .15 .07
❑ 25 Tony Gwynn DK 2.00 .90
❑ 26 Bob Brenly DK .15 .07
❑ 27 Danny Tartabull RR RC 1.25 .55
❑ 28 Mike Bielecki RR .15 .07
❑ 29 Steve Lyons RR RC .40 .18
❑ 30 Jeff Reed RR .15 .07
❑ 31 Tony Brewer RR .15 .07
❑ 32 John Morris RR .15 .07
❑ 33 Daryl Boston RR RC .15 .07
❑ 34 Al Pulido RR .15 .07
❑ 35 Steve Kiefer RR .15 .07
❑ 36 Larry Sheets RR .15 .07
❑ 37 Scott Bradley RR .15 .07
❑ 38 Calvin Schiraldi RR .15 .07
❑ 39 S.Dunston RR RC 1.00 .45
❑ 40 Charlie Mitchell RR .15 .07
❑ 41 Billy Hatcher RR RC .75 .35
❑ 42 Russ Stephans RR .15 .07
❑ 43 Alejandro Sanchez RR .15 .07
❑ 44 Steve Jeltz RR .15 .07
❑ 45 Jim Traber RR .15 .07
❑ 46 Doug Loman RR .15 .07
❑ 47 Eddie Murray 1.25 .55
❑ 48 Robin Yount 1.25 .55
❑ 49 Lance Parrish .40 .18
❑ 50 Jim Rice .40 .18
❑ 51 Dave Winfield 1.25 .55
❑ 52 Fernando Valenzuela .40 .18
❑ 53 George Brett 2.50 1.10
❑ 54 Dave Kingman .40 .18
❑ 55 Gary Carter .75 .35
❑ 56 Buddy Bell .40 .18
❑ 57 Reggie Jackson 1.50 .70
❑ 58 Harold Baines .40 .18
❑ 59 Ozzie Smith 1.50 .70
❑ 60 Nolan Ryan UER 6.00 2.70
(Set strikeout record
in 1973, not 1972)
❑ 61 Mike Schmidt 2.50 1.10
❑ 62 Dave Parker .40 .18
❑ 63 Tony Gwynn 4.00 1.80
❑ 64 Tony Pena .15 .07
❑ 65 Jack Clark .40 .18
❑ 66 Dale Murphy 1.25 .55
❑ 67 Ryne Sandberg 2.50 1.10
❑ 68 Keith Hernandez .40 .18
❑ 69 Alvin Davis RC* .40 .18
❑ 70 Kent Hrbek .40 .18
❑ 71 Willie Upshaw .15 .07
❑ 72 Dave Engle .15 .07
❑ 73 Alfredo Griffin .15 .07
❑ 74A Jack Perconte .15 .07
(Career Highlights
takes four lines)
❑ 74B Jack Perconte .15 .07
(Career Highlights
takes three lines)
❑ 75 Jesse Orosco .15 .07
❑ 76 Jody Davis .15 .07
❑ 77 Bob Horner .15 .07
❑ 78 Larry McWilliams .15 .07
❑ 79 Joel Youngblood .15 .07
❑ 80 Alan Wiggins .15 .07
❑ 81 Ron Oester .15 .07
❑ 82 Ozzie Virgil .15 .07
❑ 83 Ricky Horton .15 .07
❑ 84 Bill Doran .15 .07
❑ 85 Rod Carew 1.25 .55
❑ 86 LaMarr Hoyt .15 .07
❑ 87 Tim Wallach .40 .18
❑ 88 Mike Flanagan .15 .07
❑ 89 Jim Sundberg .15 .07
❑ 90 Chet Lemon .15 .07
❑ 91 Bob Stanley .15 .07
❑ 92 Willie Randolph .40 .18
❑ 93 Bill Russell .15 .07
❑ 94 Julio Franco .75 .35
❑ 95 Dan Quisenberry .40 .18
❑ 96 Bill Caudill .15 .07
❑ 97 Bill Gullickson .15 .07
❑ 98 Danny Darwin .15 .07
❑ 99 Curtis Wilkerson .15 .07
❑ 100 Bud Black .15 .07
❑ 101 Tony Phillips .15 .07
❑ 102 Tony Bernazard .15 .07
❑ 103 Jay Howell .15 .07
❑ 104 Burt Hooton .15 .07
❑ 105 Milt Wilcox .15 .07
❑ 106 Rich Dauer .15 .07
❑ 107 Don Sutton 1.25 .55
❑ 108 Mike Witt .15 .07
❑ 109 Bruce Sutter .40 .18
❑ 110 Enos Cabell .15 .07
❑ 111 John Denny .15 .07
❑ 112 Dave Dravecky .40 .18
❑ 113 Marvell Wynne .15 .07
❑ 114 Johnnie LeMaster .15 .07
❑ 115 Chuck Porter .15 .07
❑ 116 John Gibbons .15 .07
❑ 117 Keith Moreland .15 .07
❑ 118 Darnell Coles .15 .07
❑ 119 Dennis Lamp .15 .07
❑ 120 Ron Davis .15 .07
❑ 121 Nick Esasky .15 .07
❑ 122 Vance Law .15 .07
❑ 123 Gary Roenicke .15 .07
❑ 124 Bill Schroeder .15 .07
❑ 125 Dave Rozema .15 .07
❑ 126 Bobby Meacham .15 .07
❑ 127 Marty Barrett .15 .07
❑ 128 R.J. Reynolds .15 .07
❑ 129 Ernie Camacho UER .15 .07
(Photo actually
Rich Thompson)
❑ 130 Jorge Orta .15 .07
❑ 131 Lary Sorensen .15 .07
❑ 132 Terry Francona .15 .07
❑ 133 Fred Lynn .40 .18
❑ 134 Bob Jones .15 .07
❑ 135 Jerry Hairston .15 .07
❑ 136 Kevin Bass .15 .07
❑ 137 Garry Maddox .15 .07
❑ 138 Dave LaPoint .15 .07
❑ 139 Kevin McReynolds .40 .18
❑ 140 Wayne Krenchicki .15 .07
❑ 141 Rafael Ramirez .15 .07
❑ 142 Rod Scurry .15 .07
❑ 143 Greg Minton .15 .07
❑ 144 Tim Stoddard .15 .07
❑ 145 Steve Henderson .15 .07
❑ 146 George Bell .40 .18
❑ 147 Dave Meier .15 .07
❑ 148 Sammy Stewart .15 .07
❑ 149 Mark Brouhard .15 .07
❑ 150 Larry Herndon .15 .07
❑ 151 Oil Can Boyd .15 .07
❑ 152 Brian Dayett .15 .07
❑ 153 Tom Niedenfuer .15 .07
❑ 154 Brook Jacoby .15 .07
❑ 155 Onix Concepcion .15 .07
❑ 156 Tim Conroy .15 .07
❑ 157 Joe Hesketh .15 .07
❑ 158 Brian Downing .15 .07
❑ 159 Tommy Dunbar .15 .07
❑ 160 Marc Hill .15 .07
❑ 161 Phil Garner .40 .18
❑ 162 Jerry Davis .15 .07
❑ 163 Bill Campbell .15 .07
❑ 164 John Franco RC 1.25 .55
❑ 165 Len Barker .15 .07
❑ 166 Benny Distefano .15 .07
❑ 167 George Frazier .15 .07
❑ 168 Tito Landrum .15 .07
❑ 169 Cal Ripken 5.00 2.20
❑ 170 Cecil Cooper .40 .18
❑ 171 Alan Trammell .75 .35
❑ 172 Wade Boggs 1.25 .55
❑ 173 Don Baylor .40 .18
❑ 174 Pedro Guerrero .40 .18
❑ 175 Frank White .40 .18
❑ 176 Rickey Henderson 2.50 1.10
❑ 177 Charlie Lea .15 .07
❑ 178 Pete O'Brien .15 .07
❑ 179 Doug DeCinces .15 .07
❑ 180 Ron Kittle .15 .07
❑ 181 George Hendrick .15 .07
❑ 182 Joe Niekro .15 .07
❑ 183 Juan Samuel .15 .07
❑ 184 Mario Soto .15 .07
❑ 185 Rich Gossage .40 .18
❑ 186 Johnny Ray .15 .07
❑ 187 Bob Brenly .15 .07
❑ 188 Craig McMurtry .15 .07
❑ 189 Leon Durham .15 .07
❑ 190 Dwight Gooden RC 2.00 .90
❑ 191 Barry Bonnell .15 .07
❑ 192 Tim Teufel .15 .07
❑ 193 Dave Stieb .40 .18
❑ 194 Mickey Hatcher .15 .07
❑ 195 Jesse Barfield .15 .07
❑ 196 Al Cowens .15 .07
❑ 197 Hubie Brooks .15 .07

❑	198	Steve Trout	.15	.07
❑	199	Glenn Hubbard	.15	.07
❑	200	Bill Madlock	.40	.18
❑	201	Jeff D. Robinson	.15	.07
❑	202	Eric Show	.15	.07
❑	203	Dave Concepcion	.40	.18
❑	204	Ivan DeJesus	.15	.07
❑	205	Neil Allen	.15	.07
❑	206	Jerry Mumphrey	.15	.07
❑	207	Mike C. Brown	.15	.07
❑	208	Carlton Fisk	1.25	.55
❑	209	Bryn Smith	.15	.07
❑	210	Tippy Martinez	.15	.07
❑	211	Dion James	.15	.07
❑	212	Willie Hernandez	.15	.07
❑	213	Mike Easler	.15	.07
❑	214	Ron Guidry	.40	.18
❑	215	Rick Honeycutt	.15	.07
❑	216	Brett Butler	.40	.18
❑	217	Larry Gura	.15	.07
❑	218	Ray Burris	.15	.07
❑	219	Steve Rogers	.15	.07
❑	220	Frank Tanana UER (Bats Left listed twice on card back)	.15	.07
❑	221	Ned Yost	.15	.07
❑	222	B.Saberhagen RC UER 18 career IP on back	1.00	.45
❑	223	Mike Davis	.15	.07
❑	224	Bert Blyleven	.40	.18
❑	225	Steve Kemp	.15	.07
❑	226	Jerry Reuss	.15	.07
❑	227	Darrell Evans UER (80 homers in 1980)	.40	.18
❑	228	Wayne Gross	.15	.07
❑	229	Jim Gantner	.15	.07
❑	230	Bob Boone	.40	.18
❑	231	Lonnie Smith	.15	.07
❑	232	Frank DiPino	.15	.07
❑	233	Jerry Koosman	.40	.18
❑	234	Graig Nettles	.40	.18
❑	235	John Tudor	.15	.07
❑	236	John Rabb	.15	.07
❑	237	Rick Manning	.15	.07
❑	238	Mike Fitzgerald	.15	.07
❑	239	Gary Matthews	.15	.07
❑	240	Jim Presley	.40	.18
❑	241	Dave Collins	.15	.07
❑	242	Gary Gaetti	.40	.18
❑	243	Dann Bilardello	.15	.07
❑	244	Rudy Law	.15	.07
❑	245	John Lowenstein	.15	.07
❑	246	Tom Tellmann	.15	.07
❑	247	Howard Johnson	.40	.18
❑	248	Ray Fontenot	.15	.07
❑	249	Tony Armas	.15	.07
❑	250	Candy Maldonado	.15	.07
❑	251	Mike Jeffcoat	.15	.07
❑	252	Dane Iorg	.15	.07
❑	253	Bruce Bochte	.15	.07
❑	254	Pete Rose Expos	4.00	1.80
❑	255	Don Aase	.15	.07
❑	256	George Wright	.15	.07
❑	257	Britt Burns	.15	.07
❑	258	Mike Scott	.15	.07
❑	259	Len Matuszek	.15	.07
❑	260	Dave Rucker	.15	.07
❑	261	Craig Lefferts	.15	.07
❑	262	Jay Tibbs	.15	.07
❑	263	Bruce Benedict	.15	.07
❑	264	Don Robinson	.15	.07
❑	265	Gary Lavelle	.15	.07
❑	266	Scott Sanderson	.15	.07
❑	267	Matt Young	.15	.07
❑	268	Ernie Whitt	.15	.07
❑	269	Houston Jimenez	.15	.07
❑	270	Ken Dixon	.15	.07
❑	271	Pete Ladd	.15	.07
❑	272	Juan Berenguer	.15	.07
❑	273	Roger Clemens RC	30.00	13.50
❑	274	Rick Cerone	.15	.07
❑	275	Dave Anderson	.15	.07
❑	276	George Vukovich	.15	.07
❑	277	Greg Pryor	.15	.07
❑	278	Mike Warren	.15	.07
❑	279	Bob James	.15	.07
❑	280	Bobby Grich	.40	.18
❑	281	Mike Mason	.15	.07
❑	282	Ron Reed	.15	.07
❑	283	Alan Ashby	.15	.07
❑	284	Mark Thurmond	.15	.07
❑	285	Joe Lefebvre	.15	.07
❑	286	Ted Power	.15	.07
❑	287	Chris Chambliss	.40	.18
❑	288	Lee Tunnell	.15	.07
❑	289	Rich Bordi	.15	.07
❑	290	Glenn Brummer	.15	.07
❑	291	Mike Boddicker	.15	.07
❑	292	Rollie Fingers	1.25	.55
❑	293	Lou Whitaker	.75	.35
❑	294	Dwight Evans	.40	.18
❑	295	Don Mattingly	4.00	1.80
❑	296	Mike Marshall	.15	.07
❑	297	Willie Wilson	.15	.07
❑	298	Mike Heath	.15	.07
❑	299	Tim Raines	.40	.18
❑	300	Larry Parrish	.15	.07
❑	301	Geoff Zahn	.15	.07
❑	302	Rich Dotson	.15	.07
❑	303	David Green	.15	.07
❑	304	Jose Cruz	.40	.18
❑	305	Steve Carlton	1.25	.55
❑	306	Gary Redus	.15	.07
❑	307	Steve Garvey	.75	.35
❑	308	Jose DeLeon	.15	.07
❑	309	Randy Lerch	.15	.07
❑	310	Claudell Washington	.15	.07
❑	311	Lee Smith	.75	.35
❑	312	Darryl Strawberry	1.25	.55
❑	313	Jim Beattie	.15	.07
❑	314	John Butcher	.15	.07
❑	315	Damaso Garcia	.15	.07
❑	316	Mike Smithson	.15	.07
❑	317	Luis Leal	.15	.07
❑	318	Ken Phelps	.15	.07
❑	319	Wally Backman	.15	.07
❑	320	Ron Cey	.40	.18
❑	321	Brad Komminsk	.15	.07
❑	322	Jason Thompson	.15	.07
❑	323	Frank Williams	.15	.07
❑	324	Tim Lollar	.15	.07
❑	325	Eric Davis RC	2.00	.90
❑	326	Von Hayes	.15	.07
❑	327	Andy Van Slyke	.75	.35
❑	328	Craig Reynolds	.15	.07
❑	329	Dick Schofield	.15	.07
❑	330	Scott Fletcher	.15	.07
❑	331	Jeff Reardon	.40	.18
❑	332	Rick Dempsey	.15	.07
❑	333	Ben Oglivie	.15	.07
❑	334	Dan Petry	.15	.07
❑	335	Jackie Gutierrez	.15	.07
❑	336	Dave Righetti	.40	.18
❑	337	Alejandro Pena	.15	.07
❑	338	Mel Hall	.15	.07
❑	339	Pat Sheridan	.15	.07
❑	340	Keith Atherton	.15	.07
❑	341	David Palmer	.15	.07
❑	342	Gary Ward	.15	.07
❑	343	Dave Stewart	.40	.18
❑	344	Mark Gubicza RC*	.40	.18
❑	345	Carney Lansford	.40	.18
❑	346	Jerry Willard	.15	.07
❑	347	Ken Griffey	.40	.18
❑	348	Franklin Stubbs	.15	.07
❑	349	Aurelio Lopez	.15	.07
❑	350	Al Bumbry	.15	.07
❑	351	Charlie Moore	.15	.07
❑	352	Luis Sanchez	.15	.07
❑	353	Darrell Porter	.15	.07
❑	354	Bill Dawley	.15	.07
❑	355	Charles Hudson	.15	.07
❑	356	Garry Templeton	.15	.07
❑	357	Cecilio Guante	.15	.07
❑	358	Jeff Leonard	.15	.07
❑	359	Paul Molitor	1.25	.55
❑	360	Ron Gardenhire	.15	.07
❑	361	Larry Bowa	.40	.18
❑	362	Bob Kearney	.15	.07
❑	363	Garth Iorg	.15	.07
❑	364	Tom Brunansky	.40	.18
❑	365	Brad Gulden	.15	.07
❑	366	Greg Walker	.15	.07
❑	367	Mike Young	.15	.07
❑	368	Rick Waits	.15	.07
❑	369	Doug Bair	.15	.07
❑	370	Bob Shirley	.15	.07
❑	371	Bob Ojeda	.15	.07
❑	372	Bob Welch	.15	.07
❑	373	Neal Heaton	.15	.07
❑	374	Danny Jackson UER (Photo actually Frank Wills)	.15	.07
❑	375	Donnie Hill	.15	.07
❑	376	Mike Stenhouse	.15	.07
❑	377	Bruce Kison	.15	.07
❑	378	Wayne Tolleson	.15	.07
❑	379	Floyd Bannister	.15	.07
❑	380	Vern Ruhle	.15	.07
❑	381	Tim Corcoran	.15	.07
❑	382	Kurt Kepshire	.15	.07
❑	383	Bobby Brown	.15	.07
❑	384	Dave Van Gorder	.15	.07
❑	385	Rick Mahler	.15	.07
❑	386	Lee Mazzilli	.15	.07
❑	387	Bill Laskey	.15	.07
❑	388	Thad Bosley	.15	.07
❑	389	Al Chambers	.15	.07
❑	390	Tony Fernandez	.40	.18
❑	391	Ron Washington	.15	.07
❑	392	Bill Swaggerty	.15	.07
❑	393	Bob L. Gibson	.15	.07
❑	394	Marty Castillo	.15	.07
❑	395	Steve Crawford	.15	.07
❑	396	Clay Christiansen	.15	.07
❑	397	Bob Bailor	.15	.07
❑	398	Mike Hargrove	.40	.18
❑	399	Charlie Leibrandt	.15	.07
❑	400	Tom Burgmeier	.15	.07
❑	401	Razor Shines	.15	.07
❑	402	Rob Wilfong	.15	.07
❑	403	Tom Henke	.40	.18
❑	404	Al Jones	.15	.07
❑	405	Mike LaCoss	.15	.07
❑	406	Luis DeLeon	.15	.07
❑	407	Greg Gross	.15	.07
❑	408	Tom Hume	.15	.07
❑	409	Rick Camp	.15	.07
❑	410	Milt May	.15	.07
❑	411	Henry Cotto RC	.15	.07
❑	412	David Von Ohlen	.15	.07
❑	413	Scott McGregor	.15	.07
❑	414	Ted Simmons	.40	.18
❑	415	Jack Morris	.40	.18
❑	416	Bill Buckner	.40	.18
❑	417	Butch Wynegar	.15	.07
❑	418	Steve Sax	.15	.07
❑	419	Steve Balboni	.15	.07
❑	420	Dwayne Murphy	.15	.07
❑	421	Andre Dawson	.75	.35
❑	422	Charlie Hough	.40	.18
❑	423	Tommy John	.75	.35
❑	424A	Tom Seaver ERR (Photo actually Floyd Bannister)	2.00	.90
❑	424B	Tom Seaver COR	15.00	6.75
❑	425	Tom Herr	.40	.18
❑	426	Terry Puhl	.15	.07
❑	427	Al Holland	.15	.07
❑	428	Eddie Milner	.15	.07
❑	429	Terry Kennedy	.15	.07
❑	430	John Candelaria	.15	.07
❑	431	Manny Trillo	.15	.07
❑	432	Ken Oberkfell	.15	.07
❑	433	Rick Sutcliffe	.40	.18
❑	434	Ron Darling	.40	.18
❑	435	Spike Owen	.15	.07
❑	436	Frank Viola	.40	.18
❑	437	Lloyd Moseby	.15	.07
❑	438	Kirby Puckett RC	20.00	9.00
❑	439	Jim Clancy	.15	.07
❑	440	Mike Moore	.15	.07
❑	441	Doug Sisk	.15	.07
❑	442	Dennis Eckersley	1.25	.55
❑	443	Gerald Perry	.15	.07
❑	444	Dale Berra	.15	.07
❑	445	Dusty Baker	.40	.18
❑	446	Ed Whitson	.15	.07

❑	447	Cesar Cedeno	.40	.18
❑	448	Rick Schu	.15	.07
❑	449	Joaquin Andujar	.15	.07
❑	450	Mark Bailey	.15	.07
❑	451	Ron Romanick	.15	.07
❑	452	Julio Cruz	.15	.07
❑	453	Miguel Dilone	.15	.07
❑	454	Storm Davis	.15	.07
❑	455	Jaime Cocanower	.15	.07
❑	456	Barbaro Garbey	.15	.07
❑	457	Rich Gedman	.15	.07
❑	458	Phil Niekro	1.25	.55
❑	459	Mike Scioscia	.15	.07
❑	460	Pat Tabler	.15	.07
❑	461	Darryl Motley	.15	.07
❑	462	Chris Codiroli	.15	.07
❑	463	Doug Flynn	.15	.07
❑	464	Billy Sample	.15	.07
❑	465	Mickey Rivers	.15	.07
❑	466	John Wathan	.15	.07
❑	467	Bill Krueger	.15	.07
❑	468	Andre Thornton	.15	.07
❑	469	Rex Hudler	.15	.07
❑	470	Sid Bream RC	.40	.18
❑	471	Kirk Gibson	.40	.18
❑	472	John Shelby	.15	.07
❑	473	Moose Haas	.15	.07
❑	474	Doug Corbett	.15	.07
❑	475	Willie McGee	.40	.18
❑	476	Bob Knepper	.15	.07
❑	477	Kevin Gross	.15	.07
❑	478	Carmelo Martinez	.15	.07
❑	479	Kent Tekulve	.15	.07
❑	480	Chili Davis	.40	.18
❑	481	Bobby Clark	.15	.07
❑	482	Mookie Wilson	.40	.18
❑	483	Dave Owen	.15	.07
❑	484	Ed Nunez	.15	.07
❑	485	Rance Mulliniks	.15	.07
❑	486	Ken Schrom	.15	.07
❑	487	Jeff Russell	.15	.07
❑	488	Tom Paciorek	.40	.18
❑	489	Dan Ford	.15	.07
❑	490	Mike Caldwell	.15	.07
❑	491	Scottie Earl	.15	.07
❑	492	Jose Rijo RC	.75	.35
❑	493	Bruce Hurst	.15	.07
❑	494	Ken Landreaux	.15	.07
❑	495	Mike Fischlin	.15	.07
❑	496	Don Slaught	.15	.07
❑	497	Steve McCatty	.15	.07
❑	498	Gary Lucas	.15	.07
❑	499	Gary Pettis	.15	.07
❑	500	Marvis Foley	.15	.07
❑	501	Mike Squires	.15	.07
❑	502	Jim Pankovits	.15	.07
❑	503	Luis Aguayo	.15	.07
❑	504	Ralph Citarella	.15	.07
❑	505	Bruce Bochy	.15	.07
❑	506	Bob Owchinko	.15	.07
❑	507	Pascual Perez	.15	.07
❑	508	Lee Lacy	.15	.07
❑	509	Atlee Hammaker	.15	.07
❑	510	Bob Dernier	.15	.07
❑	511	Ed VandeBerg	.15	.07
❑	512	Cliff Johnson	.15	.07
❑	513	Len Whitehouse	.15	.07
❑	514	Dennis Martinez	.40	.18
❑	515	Ed Romero	.15	.07
❑	516	Rusty Kuntz	.15	.07
❑	517	Rick Miller	.15	.07
❑	518	Dennis Rasmussen	.15	.07
❑	519	Steve Yeager	.15	.07
❑	520	Chris Bando	.15	.07
❑	521	U.L. Washington	.15	.07
❑	522	Curt Young	.15	.07
❑	523	Angel Salazar	.15	.07
❑	524	Curt Kaufman	.15	.07
❑	525	Odell Jones	.15	.07
❑	526	Juan Agosto	.15	.07
❑	527	Denny Walling	.15	.07
❑	528	Andy Hawkins	.15	.07
❑	529	Sixto Lezcano	.15	.07
❑	530	Skeeter Barnes RC	.15	.07
❑	531	Randy Johnson	.15	.07
❑	532	Jim Morrison	.15	.07
❑	533	Warren Brusstar	.15	.07
❑	534A	J.Pendleton RC ERR	1.25	.55
		Wrong first name		
❑	534B	T.Pendleton RC COR	2.00	.90
❑	535	Vic Rodriguez	.15	.07
❑	536	Bob McClure	.15	.07
❑	537	Dave Bergman	.15	.07
❑	538	Mark Clear	.15	.07
❑	539	Mike Pagliarulo	.15	.07
❑	540	Terry Whitfield	.15	.07
❑	541	Joe Beckwith	.15	.07
❑	542	Jeff Burroughs	.15	.07
❑	543	Dan Schatzeder	.15	.07
❑	544	Donnie Scott	.15	.07
❑	545	Jim Slaton	.15	.07
❑	546	Greg Luzinski	.40	.18
❑	547	Mark Salas	.15	.07
❑	548	Dave Smith	.15	.07
❑	549	John Wockenfuss	.15	.07
❑	550	Frank Pastore	.15	.07
❑	551	Tim Flannery	.15	.07
❑	552	Rick Rhoden	.15	.07
❑	553	Mark Davis	.15	.07
❑	554	Jeff Dedmon	.15	.07
❑	555	Gary Woods	.15	.07
❑	556	Danny Heep	.15	.07
❑	557	Mark Langston RC	.75	.35
❑	558	Darrell Brown	.15	.07
❑	559	Jimmy Key RC	1.25	.55
❑	560	Rick Lysander	.15	.07
❑	561	Doyle Alexander	.15	.07
❑	562	Mike Stanton	.15	.07
❑	563	Sid Fernandez	.40	.18
❑	564	Richie Hebner	.15	.07
❑	565	Alex Trevino	.15	.07
❑	566	Brian Harper	.15	.07
❑	567	Dan Gladden RC	.40	.18
❑	568	Luis Salazar	.15	.07
❑	569	Tom Foley	.15	.07
❑	570	Larry Andersen	.15	.07
❑	571	Danny Cox	.15	.07
❑	572	Joe Sambito	.15	.07
❑	573	Juan Beniquez	.15	.07
❑	574	Joel Skinner	.15	.07
❑	575	Randy St.Claire	.15	.07
❑	576	Floyd Rayford	.15	.07
❑	577	Roy Howell	.15	.07
❑	578	John Grubb	.15	.07
❑	579	Ed Jurak	.15	.07
❑	580	John Montefusco	.15	.07
❑	581	Orel Hershiser RC	2.00	.90
❑	582	Tom Waddell	.15	.07
❑	583	Mark Huismann	.15	.07
❑	584	Joe Morgan	1.25	.55
❑	585	Jim Wohlford	.15	.07
❑	586	Dave Schmidt	.15	.07
❑	587	Jeff Kunkel	.15	.07
❑	588	Hal McRae	.40	.18
❑	589	Bill Almon	.15	.07
❑	590	Carmen Castillo	.15	.07
❑	591	Omar Moreno	.15	.07
❑	592	Ken Howell	.15	.07
❑	593	Tom Brookens	.15	.07
❑	594	Joe Nolan	.15	.07
❑	595	Willie Lozado	.15	.07
❑	596	Tom Nieto	.15	.07
❑	597	Walt Terrell	.15	.07
❑	598	Al Oliver	.40	.18
❑	599	Shane Rawley	.15	.07
❑	600	Denny Gonzalez	.15	.07
❑	601	Mark Grant	.15	.07
❑	602	Mike Armstrong	.15	.07
❑	603	George Foster	.40	.18
❑	604	Dave Lopes	.40	.18
❑	605	Salome Barojas	.15	.07
❑	606	Roy Lee Jackson	.15	.07
❑	607	Pete Filson	.15	.07
❑	608	Duane Walker	.15	.07
❑	609	Glenn Wilson	.15	.07
❑	610	Rafael Santana	.15	.07
❑	611	Roy Smith	.15	.07
❑	612	Ruppert Jones	.15	.07
❑	613	Joe Cowley	.15	.07
❑	614	Al Nipper UER	.15	.07
		(Photo actually Mike Brown)		
❑	615	Gene Nelson	.15	.07
❑	616	Joe Carter	1.25	.55
❑	617	Ray Knight	.15	.07
❑	618	Chuck Rainey	.15	.07
❑	619	Dan Driessen	.15	.07
❑	620	Daryl Sconiers	.15	.07
❑	621	Bill Stein	.15	.07
❑	622	Roy Smalley	.15	.07
❑	623	Ed Lynch	.15	.07
❑	624	Jeff Stone	.15	.07
❑	625	Bruce Berenyi	.15	.07
❑	626	Kelvin Chapman	.15	.07
❑	627	Joe Price	.15	.07
❑	628	Steve Bedrosian	.15	.07
❑	629	Vic Mata	.15	.07
❑	630	Mike Krukow	.15	.07
❑	631	Phil Bradley	.40	.18
❑	632	Jim Gott	.15	.07
❑	633	Randy Bush	.15	.07
❑	634	Tom Browning RC	.40	.18
❑	635	Lou Gehrig Puzzle Card	1.25	.55
❑	636	Reid Nichols	.15	.07
❑	637	Dan Pasqua RC	.40	.18
❑	638	German Rivera	.15	.07
❑	639	Don Schulze	.15	.07
❑	640A	Mike Jones (Career Highlights, takes five lines)	.15	.07
❑	640B	Mike Jones (Career Highlights, takes four lines)	.15	.07
❑	641	Pete Rose	4.00	1.80
❑	642	Wade Rowdon	.15	.07
❑	643	Jerry Narron	.15	.07
❑	644	Darrell Miller	.15	.07
❑	645	Tim Hulett RC	.15	.07
❑	646	Andy McGaffigan	.15	.07
❑	647	Kurt Bevacqua	.15	.07
❑	648	John Russell	.15	.07
❑	649	Ron Robinson	.15	.07
❑	650	Donnie Moore	.15	.07
❑	651A	Two for the Title Dave Winfield Don Mattingly (Yellow letters)	1.50	.70
❑	651B	Two for the Title Dave Winfield Don Mattingly (White letters)	4.00	1.80
❑	652	Tim Laudner	.15	.07
❑	653	Steve Farr RC	.40	.18
❑	654	DK Checklist 1-26 (Unnumbered)	.15	.07
❑	655	Checklist 27-130 (Unnumbered)	.15	.07
❑	656	Checklist 131-234 (Unnumbered)	.15	.07
❑	657	Checklist 235-338 (Unnumbered)	.15	.07
❑	658	Checklist 339-442 (Unnumbered)	.15	.07
❑	659	Checklist 443-546 (Unnumbered)	.15	.07
❑	660	Checklist 547-653 (Unnumbered)	.15	.07

1986 Donruss

	MINT	NRMT
COMPLETE SET (660)	50.00	22.00
COMP.FACT.SET (660)	50.00	22.00
COMP.AARON PUZZLE	2.00	.90
❑ 1 Kirk Gibson DK	.25	.11
❑ 2 Rich Gossage DK	.25	.11
❑ 3 Willie McGee DK	.25	.11
❑ 4 George Bell DK	.15	.07
❑ 5 Tony Armas DK	.15	.07
❑ 6 Chili Davis DK	.50	.23
❑ 7 Cecil Cooper DK	.15	.07
❑ 8 Mike Boddicker DK	.15	.07
❑ 9 Dave Lopes DK	.25	.11
❑ 10 Bill Doran DK	.15	.07
❑ 11 Bret Saberhagen DK	.25	.11
❑ 12 Brett Butler DK	.15	.07
❑ 13 Harold Baines DK	.50	.23
❑ 14 Mike Davis DK	.15	.07
❑ 15 Tony Perez DK	.25	.11
❑ 16 Willie Randolph DK	.15	.07
❑ 17 Bob Boone DK	.15	.07
❑ 18 Orel Hershiser DK	.25	.11
❑ 19 Johnny Ray DK	.15	.07
❑ 20 Gary Ward DK	.15	.07
❑ 21 Rick Mahler DK	.15	.07
❑ 22 Phil Bradley DK	.15	.07
❑ 23 Jerry Koosman DK	.25	.11
❑ 24 Tom Brunansky DK	.15	.07
❑ 25 Andre Dawson DK	.25	.11
❑ 26 Dwight Gooden DK	.75	.35
❑ 27 Kal Daniels RR	.25	.11
❑ 28 Fred McGriff RR RC	8.00	3.60
❑ 29 Cory Snyder RR	.15	.07
❑ 30 Jose Guzman RR RC	.15	.07
❑ 31 Ty Gainey RR	.15	.07
❑ 32 Johnny Abrego RR	.15	.07
❑ 33 A.Galarraga RC RR	6.00	2.70
No accent		
❑ 33B A.Galarraga RC RR	6.00	2.70
Accent over e		
❑ 34 Dave Shipanoff RR	.15	.07
❑ 35 M.McLemore RR RC	.75	.35
❑ 36 Marty Clary RR	.15	.07
❑ 37 Paul O'Neill RR RC	6.00	2.70
❑ 38 Danny Tartabull RR	.25	.11
❑ 39 Jose Canseco RR RC	15.00	6.75
❑ 40 Juan Nieves RR	.15	.07
❑ 41 Lance McCullers RR	.15	.07
❑ 42 Rick Surhoff RR	.15	.07
❑ 43 Todd Worrell RR RC	.75	.35
❑ 44 Bob Kipper RR	.15	.07
❑ 45 John Habyan RR RC	.15	.07
❑ 46 Mike Woodard RR	.15	.07
❑ 47 Mike Boddicker	.15	.07
❑ 48 Robin Yount	.75	.35
❑ 49 Lou Whitaker	.25	.11
❑ 50 Oil Can Boyd	.15	.07
❑ 51 Rickey Henderson	1.50	.70
❑ 52 Mike Marshall	.15	.07
❑ 53 George Brett	1.50	.70
❑ 54 Dave Kingman	.25	.11
❑ 55 Hubie Brooks	.15	.07
❑ 56 Oddibe McDowell	.15	.07
❑ 57 Doug DeCinces	.15	.07
❑ 58 Britt Burns	.15	.07
❑ 59 Ozzie Smith	1.00	.45
❑ 60 Jose Cruz	.25	.11
❑ 61 Mike Schmidt	1.50	.70
❑ 62 Pete Rose	2.50	1.10
❑ 63 Steve Garvey	.50	.23
❑ 64 Tony Pena	.15	.07
❑ 65 Chili Davis	.50	.23
❑ 66 Dale Murphy	.75	.35
❑ 67 Ryne Sandberg	1.00	.45
❑ 68 Gary Carter	.50	.23
❑ 69 Alvin Davis	.15	.07
❑ 70 Kent Hrbek	.25	.11
❑ 71 George Bell	.25	.11
❑ 72 Kirby Puckett	3.00	1.35
❑ 73 Lloyd Moseby	.15	.07
❑ 74 Bob Kearney	.15	.07
❑ 75 Dwight Gooden	.75	.35
❑ 76 Gary Matthews	.15	.07
❑ 77 Rick Mahler	.15	.07
❑ 78 Benny Distefano	.15	.07
❑ 79 Jeff Leonard	.15	.07
❑ 80 Kevin McReynolds	.25	.11
❑ 81 Ron Oester	.15	.07
❑ 82 John Russell	.15	.07
❑ 83 Tommy Herr	.15	.07
❑ 84 Jerry Mumphrey	.15	.07
❑ 85 Ron Romanick	.15	.07
❑ 86 Daryl Boston	.15	.07
❑ 87 Andre Dawson	.50	.23
❑ 88 Eddie Murray	.75	.35
❑ 89 Dion James	.15	.07
❑ 90 Chet Lemon	.15	.07
❑ 91 Bob Stanley	.15	.07
❑ 92 Willie Randolph	.25	.11
❑ 93 Mike Scioscia	.15	.07
❑ 94 Tom Waddell	.15	.07
❑ 95 Danny Jackson	.15	.07
❑ 96 Mike Davis	.15	.07
❑ 97 Mike Fitzgerald	.15	.07
❑ 98 Gary Ward	.15	.07
❑ 99 Pete O'Brien	.15	.07
❑ 100 Bret Saberhagen	.25	.11
❑ 101 Alfredo Griffin	.15	.07
❑ 102 Brett Butler	.25	.11
❑ 103 Ron Guidry	.25	.11
❑ 104 Jerry Reuss	.15	.07
❑ 105 Jack Morris	.25	.11
❑ 106 Rick Dempsey	.15	.07
❑ 107 Ray Burris	.15	.07
❑ 108 Brian Downing	.15	.07
❑ 109 Willie McGee	.25	.11
❑ 110 Bill Doran	.15	.07
❑ 111 Kent Tekulve	.15	.07
❑ 112 Tony Gwynn	1.50	.70
❑ 113 Marvell Wynne	.15	.07
❑ 114 David Green	.15	.07
❑ 115 Jim Gantner	.15	.07
❑ 116 George Foster	.25	.11
❑ 117 Steve Trout	.15	.07
❑ 118 Mark Langston	.15	.07
❑ 119 Tony Fernandez	.15	.07
❑ 120 John Butcher	.15	.07
❑ 121 Ron Robinson	.15	.07
❑ 122 Dan Spillner	.15	.07
❑ 123 Mike Young	.15	.07
❑ 124 Paul Molitor	.75	.35
❑ 125 Kirk Gibson	.25	.11
❑ 126 Ken Griffey	.25	.11
❑ 127 Tony Armas	.15	.07
❑ 128 Mariano Duncan RC*	.75	.35
❑ 129 Pat Tabler	.15	.07
❑ 130 Frank White	.25	.11
❑ 131 Carney Lansford	.25	.11
❑ 132 Vance Law	.15	.07
❑ 133 Dick Schofield	.15	.07
❑ 134 Wayne Tolleson	.15	.07
❑ 135 Greg Walker	.15	.07
❑ 136 Denny Walling	.15	.07
❑ 137 Ozzie Virgil	.15	.07
❑ 138 Ricky Horton	.15	.07
❑ 139 LaMarr Hoyt	.15	.07
❑ 140 Wayne Krenchicki	.15	.07
❑ 141 Glenn Hubbard	.15	.07
❑ 142 Cecilio Guante	.15	.07
❑ 143 Mike Krukow	.15	.07
❑ 144 Lee Smith	.50	.23
❑ 145 Edwin Nunez	.15	.07
❑ 146 Dave Stieb	.15	.07
❑ 147 Mike Smithson	.15	.07
❑ 148 Ken Dixon	.15	.07
❑ 149 Danny Darwin	.15	.07
❑ 150 Chris Pittaro	.15	.07
❑ 151 Bill Buckner	.25	.11
❑ 152 Mike Pagliarulo	.15	.07
❑ 153 Bill Russell	.15	.07
❑ 154 Brook Jacoby	.15	.07
❑ 155 Pat Sheridan	.15	.07
❑ 156 Mike Gallego RC	.25	.11
❑ 157 Jim Wohlford	.15	.07
❑ 158 Gary Pettis	.15	.07
❑ 159 Toby Harrah	.15	.07
❑ 160 Richard Dotson	.15	.07
❑ 161 Bob Knepper	.15	.07
❑ 162 Dave Dravecky	.25	.11
❑ 163 Greg Gross	.15	.07
❑ 164 Eric Davis	.50	.23
❑ 165 Gerald Perry	.15	.07
❑ 166 Rick Rhoden	.15	.07
❑ 167 Keith Moreland	.15	.07
❑ 168 Jack Clark	.25	.11
❑ 169 Storm Davis	.15	.07
❑ 170 Cecil Cooper	.25	.11
❑ 171 Alan Trammell	.50	.23
❑ 172 Roger Clemens	4.00	1.80
❑ 173 Don Mattingly	2.00	.90
❑ 174 Pedro Guerrero	.25	.11
❑ 175 Willie Wilson	.15	.07
❑ 176 Dwayne Murphy	.15	.07
❑ 177 Tim Raines	.25	.11
❑ 178 Larry Parrish	.15	.07
❑ 179 Mike Witt	.15	.07
❑ 180 Harold Baines	.50	.23
❑ 181 V.Coleman RC* UER	.75	.35
BA 2.67 on back		
❑ 182 Jeff Heathcock	.15	.07
❑ 183 Steve Carlton	.75	.35
❑ 184 Mario Soto	.15	.07
❑ 185 Rich Gossage	.25	.11
❑ 186 Johnny Ray	.15	.07
❑ 187 Dan Gladden	.15	.07
❑ 188 Bob Horner	.15	.07
❑ 189 Rick Sutcliffe	.25	.11
❑ 190 Keith Hernandez	.25	.11
❑ 191 Phil Bradley	.15	.07
❑ 192 Tom Brunansky	.15	.07
❑ 193 Jesse Barfield	.15	.07
❑ 194 Frank Viola	.25	.11
❑ 195 Willie Upshaw	.15	.07
❑ 196 Jim Beattie	.15	.07
❑ 197 Darryl Strawberry	.75	.35
❑ 198 Ron Cey	.25	.11
❑ 199 Steve Bedrosian	.15	.07
❑ 200 Steve Kemp	.15	.07
❑ 201 Manny Trillo	.15	.07
❑ 202 Garry Templeton	.15	.07
❑ 203 Dave Parker	.25	.11
❑ 204 John Denny	.15	.07
❑ 205 Terry Pendleton	.25	.11
❑ 206 Terry Puhl	.15	.07
❑ 207 Bobby Grich	.25	.11
❑ 208 Ozzie Guillen RC*	.50	.23
❑ 209 Jeff Reardon	.15	.07
❑ 210 Cal Ripken	3.00	1.35
❑ 211 Bill Schroeder	.15	.07
❑ 212 Dan Petry	.15	.07
❑ 213 Jim Rice	.25	.11
❑ 214 Dave Righetti	.15	.07
❑ 215 Fernando Valenzuela	.25	.11
❑ 216 Julio Franco	.25	.11
❑ 217 Darryl Motley	.15	.07
❑ 218 Dave Collins	.15	.07
❑ 219 Tim Wallach	.15	.07
❑ 220 George Wright	.15	.07
❑ 221 Tommy Dunbar	.15	.07
❑ 222 Steve Balboni	.15	.07
❑ 223 Jay Howell	.15	.07
❑ 224 Joe Carter	.75	.35
❑ 225 Ed Whitson	.15	.07
❑ 226 Orel Hershiser	.50	.23
❑ 227 Willie Hernandez	.15	.07
❑ 228 Lee Lacy	.15	.07
❑ 229 Rollie Fingers	.75	.35
❑ 230 Bob Boone	.25	.11
❑ 231 Joaquin Andujar	.15	.07
❑ 232 Craig Reynolds	.15	.07
❑ 233 Shane Rawley	.15	.07
❑ 234 Eric Show	.15	.07
❑ 235 Jose DeLeon	.15	.07
❑ 236 Jose Uribe	.15	.07
❑ 237 Moose Haas	.15	.07
❑ 238 Wally Backman	.15	.07
❑ 239 Dennis Eckersley	.75	.35
❑ 240 Mike Moore	.15	.07
❑ 241 Damaso Garcia	.15	.07
❑ 242 Tim Teufel	.15	.07
❑ 243 Dave Concepcion	.25	.11
❑ 244 Floyd Bannister	.15	.07
❑ 245 Fred Lynn	.25	.11
❑ 246 Charlie Moore	.15	.07
❑ 247 Walt Terrell	.15	.07
❑ 248 Dave Winfield	.75	.35

❑	249	Dwight Evans	.25	.11
❑	250	Dennis Powell	.15	.07
❑	251	Andre Thornton	.15	.07
❑	252	Onix Concepcion	.15	.07
❑	253	Mike Heath	.15	.07
❑	254A	David Palmer ERR (Position 2B)	.15	.07
❑	254B	David Palmer COR (Position P)	.75	.35
❑	255	Donnie Moore	.15	.07
❑	256	Curtis Wilkerson	.15	.07
❑	257	Julio Cruz	.15	.07
❑	258	Nolan Ryan	4.00	1.80
❑	259	Jeff Stone	.15	.07
❑	260	John Tudor	.15	.07
❑	261	Mark Thurmond	.15	.07
❑	262	Jay Tibbs	.15	.07
❑	263	Rafael Ramirez	.15	.07
❑	264	Larry McWilliams	.15	.07
❑	265	Mark Davis	.15	.07
❑	266	Bob Dernier	.15	.07
❑	267	Matt Young	.15	.07
❑	268	Jim Clancy	.15	.07
❑	269	Mickey Hatcher	.15	.07
❑	270	Sammy Stewart	.15	.07
❑	271	Bob L. Gibson	.15	.07
❑	272	Nelson Simmons	.15	.07
❑	273	Rich Gedman	.15	.07
❑	274	Butch Wynegar	.15	.07
❑	275	Ken Howell	.15	.07
❑	276	Mel Hall	.15	.07
❑	277	Jim Sundberg	.15	.07
❑	278	Chris Codiroli	.15	.07
❑	279	Herm Winningham	.15	.07
❑	280	Rod Carew	.75	.35
❑	281	Don Slaught	.15	.07
❑	282	Scott Fletcher	.15	.07
❑	283	Bill Dawley	.15	.07
❑	284	Andy Hawkins	.15	.07
❑	285	Glenn Wilson	.15	.07
❑	286	Nick Esasky	.15	.07
❑	287	Claudell Washington	.15	.07
❑	288	Lee Mazzilli	.15	.07
❑	289	Jody Davis	.15	.07
❑	290	Darrell Porter	.25	.11
❑	291	Scott McGregor	.15	.07
❑	292	Ted Simmons	.25	.11
❑	293	Aurelio Lopez	.15	.07
❑	294	Marty Barrett	.15	.07
❑	295	Dale Berra	.15	.07
❑	296	Greg Brock	.15	.07
❑	297	Charlie Leibrandt	.15	.07
❑	298	Bill Krueger	.15	.07
❑	299	Bryn Smith	.15	.07
❑	300	Burt Hooton	.15	.07
❑	301	Stu Cliburn	.15	.07
❑	302	Luis Salazar	.15	.07
❑	303	Ken Dayley	.15	.07
❑	304	Frank DiPino	.15	.07
❑	305	Von Hayes	.15	.07
❑	306	Gary Redus	.15	.07
❑	307	Craig Lefferts	.15	.07
❑	308	Sammy Khalifa	.15	.07
❑	309	Scott Garrelts	.15	.07
❑	310	Rick Cerone	.15	.07
❑	311	Shawon Dunston	.25	.11
❑	312	Howard Johnson	.25	.11
❑	313	Jim Presley	.15	.07
❑	314	Gary Gaetti	.25	.11
❑	315	Luis Leal	.15	.07
❑	316	Mark Salas	.15	.07
❑	317	Bill Caudill	.15	.07
❑	318	Dave Henderson	.15	.07
❑	319	Rafael Santana	.15	.07
❑	320	Leon Durham	.15	.07
❑	321	Bruce Sutter	.25	.11
❑	322	Jason Thompson	.15	.07
❑	323	Bob Brenly	.15	.07
❑	324	Carmelo Martinez	.15	.07
❑	325	Eddie Milner	.15	.07
❑	326	Juan Samuel	.15	.07
❑	327	Tom Nieto	.15	.07
❑	328	Dave Smith	.15	.07
❑	329	Urbano Lugo	.15	.07
❑	330	Joel Skinner	.15	.07
❑	331	Bill Gullickson	.15	.07
❑	332	Floyd Rayford	.15	.07
❑	333	Ben Oglivie	.15	.07
❑	334	Lance Parrish	.25	.11
❑	335	Jackie Gutierrez	.15	.07
❑	336	Dennis Rasmussen	.15	.07
❑	337	Terry Whitfield	.15	.07
❑	338	Neal Heaton	.15	.07
❑	339	Jorge Orta	.15	.07
❑	340	Donnie Hill	.15	.07
❑	341	Joe Hesketh	.15	.07
❑	342	Charlie Hough	.25	.11
❑	343	Dave Rozema	.15	.07
❑	344	Greg Pryor	.15	.07
❑	345	Mickey Tettleton RC	.25	.11
❑	346	George Vukovich	.15	.07
❑	347	Don Baylor	.50	.23
❑	348	Carlos Diaz	.15	.07
❑	349	Barbaro Garbey	.15	.07
❑	350	Larry Sheets	.15	.07
❑	351	Ted Higuera RC*	.25	.11
❑	352	Juan Beniquez	.15	.07
❑	353	Bob Forsch	.15	.07
❑	354	Mark Bailey	.15	.07
❑	355	Larry Andersen	.15	.07
❑	356	Terry Kennedy	.15	.07
❑	357	Don Robinson	.15	.07
❑	358	Jim Gott	.15	.07
❑	359	Earnie Riles	.15	.07
❑	360	John Christensen	.15	.07
❑	361	Ray Fontenot	.15	.07
❑	362	Spike Owen	.15	.07
❑	363	Jim Acker	.15	.07
❑	364	Ron Davis	.15	.07
❑	365	Tom Hume	.15	.07
❑	366	Carlton Fisk	.75	.35
❑	367	Nate Snell	.15	.07
❑	368	Rick Manning	.15	.07
❑	369	Darrell Evans	.25	.11
❑	370	Ron Hassey	.15	.07
❑	371	Wade Boggs	.75	.35
❑	372	Rick Honeycutt	.15	.07
❑	373	Chris Bando	.15	.07
❑	374	Bud Black	.15	.07
❑	375	Steve Henderson	.15	.07
❑	376	Charlie Lea	.15	.07
❑	377	Reggie Jackson	1.00	.45
❑	378	Dave Schmidt	.15	.07
❑	379	Bob James	.15	.07
❑	380	Glenn Davis	.25	.11
❑	381	Tim Corcoran	.15	.07
❑	382	Danny Cox	.15	.07
❑	383	Tim Flannery	.15	.07
❑	384	Tom Browning	.15	.07
❑	385	Rick Camp	.15	.07
❑	386	Jim Morrison	.15	.07
❑	387	Dave LaPoint	.15	.07
❑	388	Dave Lopes	.25	.11
❑	389	Al Cowens	.15	.07
❑	390	Doyle Alexander	.15	.07
❑	391	Tim Laudner	.15	.07
❑	392	Don Aase	.15	.07
❑	393	Jaime Cocanower	.15	.07
❑	394	Randy O'Neal	.15	.07
❑	395	Mike Easler	.15	.07
❑	396	Scott Bradley	.15	.07
❑	397	Tom Niedenfuer	.15	.07
❑	398	Jerry Willard	.15	.07
❑	399	Lonnie Smith	.15	.07
❑	400	Bruce Bochte	.15	.07
❑	401	Terry Francona	.15	.07
❑	402	Jim Slaton	.15	.07
❑	403	Bill Stein	.15	.07
❑	404	Tim Hulett	.15	.07
❑	405	Alan Ashby	.15	.07
❑	406	Tim Stoddard	.15	.07
❑	407	Garry Maddox	.15	.07
❑	408	Ted Power	.15	.07
❑	409	Len Barker	.15	.07
❑	410	Denny Gonzalez	.15	.07
❑	411	George Frazier	.15	.07
❑	412	Andy Van Slyke	.25	.11
❑	413	Jim Dwyer	.15	.07
❑	414	Paul Householder	.15	.07
❑	415	Alejandro Sanchez	.15	.07
❑	416	Steve Crawford	.15	.07
❑	417	Dan Pasqua	.15	.07
❑	418	Enos Cabell	.15	.07
❑	419	Mike Jones	.15	.07
❑	420	Steve Kiefer	.15	.07
❑	421	Tim Burke	.15	.07
❑	422	Mike Mason	.15	.07
❑	423	Ruppert Jones	.15	.07
❑	424	Jerry Hairston	.15	.07
❑	425	Tito Landrum	.15	.07
❑	426	Jeff Calhoun	.15	.07
❑	427	Don Carman	.15	.07
❑	428	Tony Perez	.75	.35
❑	429	Jerry Davis	.15	.07
❑	430	Bob Walk	.15	.07
❑	431	Brad Wellman	.15	.07
❑	432	Terry Forster	.15	.07
❑	433	Billy Hatcher	.15	.07
❑	434	Clint Hurdle	.15	.07
❑	435	Ivan Calderon RC*	.25	.11
❑	436	Pete Filson	.15	.07
❑	437	Tom Henke	.25	.11
❑	438	Dave Engle	.15	.07
❑	439	Tom Filer	.15	.07
❑	440	Gorman Thomas	.15	.07
❑	441	Rick Aguilera RC	.75	.35
❑	442	Scott Sanderson	.15	.07
❑	443	Jeff Dedmon	.15	.07
❑	444	Joe Orsulak RC*	.15	.07
❑	445	Atlee Hammaker	.15	.07
❑	446	Jerry Royster	.15	.07
❑	447	Buddy Bell	.25	.11
❑	448	Dave Rucker	.15	.07
❑	449	Ivan DeJesus	.15	.07
❑	450	Jim Pankovits	.15	.07
❑	451	Jerry Narron	.15	.07
❑	452	Bryan Little	.15	.07
❑	453	Gary Lucas	.15	.07
❑	454	Dennis Martinez	.25	.11
❑	455	Ed Romero	.15	.07
❑	456	Bob Melvin	.15	.07
❑	457	Glenn Hoffman	.15	.07
❑	458	Bob Shirley	.15	.07
❑	459	Bob Welch	.15	.07
❑	460	Carmen Castillo	.15	.07
❑	461	Dave Leeper	.15	.07
❑	462	Tim Birtsas	.15	.07
❑	463	Randy St.Claire	.15	.07
❑	464	Chris Welsh	.15	.07
❑	465	Greg Harris	.15	.07
❑	466	Lynn Jones	.15	.07
❑	467	Dusty Baker	.25	.11
❑	468	Roy Smith	.15	.07
❑	469	Andre Robertson	.15	.07
❑	470	Ken Landreaux	.15	.07
❑	471	Dave Bergman	.15	.07
❑	472	Gary Roenicke	.15	.07
❑	473	Pete Vuckovich	.15	.07
❑	474	Kirk McCaskill RC	.25	.11
❑	475	Jeff Lahti	.15	.07
❑	476	Mike Scott	.15	.07
❑	477	Darren Daulton RC	1.50	.70
❑	478	Graig Nettles	.25	.11
❑	479	Bill Almon	.15	.07
❑	480	Greg Minton	.15	.07
❑	481	Randy Ready	.15	.07
❑	482	Len Dykstra RC	1.50	.70
❑	483	Thad Bosley	.15	.07
❑	484	Harold Reynolds RC	.75	.35
❑	485	Al Oliver	.25	.11
❑	486	Roy Smalley	.15	.07
❑	487	John Franco	.75	.35
❑	488	Juan Agosto	.15	.07
❑	489	Al Pardo	.15	.07
❑	490	Bill Wegman RC	.15	.07
❑	491	Frank Tanana	.15	.07
❑	492	Brian Fisher	.15	.07
❑	493	Mark Clear	.15	.07
❑	494	Len Matuszek	.15	.07
❑	495	Ramon Romero	.15	.07
❑	496	John Wathan	.15	.07
❑	497	Rob Picciolo	.15	.07
❑	498	U.L. Washington	.15	.07
❑	499	John Candelaria	.15	.07
❑	500	Duane Walker	.15	.07
❑	501	Gene Nelson	.15	.07
❑	502	John Mizerock	.15	.07
❑	503	Luis Aguayo	.15	.07

❑ 504 Kurt Kepshire .15 .07
❑ 505 Ed Wojna .15 .07
❑ 506 Joe Price .15 .07
❑ 507 Milt Thompson RC .25 .11
❑ 508 Junior Ortiz .15 .07
❑ 509 Vida Blue .25 .11
❑ 510 Steve Engel .15 .07
❑ 511 Karl Best .15 .07
❑ 512 Cecil Fielder RC 1.50 .70
❑ 513 Frank Eufemia .15 .07
❑ 514 Tippy Martinez .15 .07
❑ 515 Billy Joe Robidoux .15 .07
❑ 516 Bill Scherrer .15 .07
❑ 517 Bruce Hurst .15 .07
❑ 518 Rich Bordi .15 .07
❑ 519 Steve Yeager .15 .07
❑ 520 Tony Bernazard .15 .07
❑ 521 Hal McRae .25 .11
❑ 522 Jose Rijo .15 .07
❑ 523 Mitch Webster .15 .07
❑ 524 Jack Howell .15 .07
❑ 525 Alan Bannister .15 .07
❑ 526 Ron Kittle .15 .07
❑ 527 Phil Garner .25 .11
❑ 528 Kurt Bevacqua .15 .07
❑ 529 Kevin Gross .15 .07
❑ 530 Bo Diaz .15 .07
❑ 531 Ken Oberkfell .15 .07
❑ 532 Rick Reuschel .15 .07
❑ 533 Ron Meridith .15 .07
❑ 534 Steve Braun .15 .07
❑ 535 Wayne Gross .15 .07
❑ 536 Ray Searage .15 .07
❑ 537 Tom Brookens .15 .07
❑ 538 Al Nipper .15 .07
❑ 539 Billy Sample .15 .07
❑ 540 Steve Sax .15 .07
❑ 541 Dan Quisenberry .15 .07
❑ 542 Tony Phillips .15 .07
❑ 543 Floyd Youmans .15 .07
❑ 544 Steve Buechele RC .25 .11
❑ 545 Craig Gerber .15 .07
❑ 546 Joe DeSa .15 .07
❑ 547 Brian Harper .15 .07
❑ 548 Kevin Bass .15 .07
❑ 549 Tom Foley .15 .07
❑ 550 Dave Van Gorder .15 .07
❑ 551 Bruce Bochy .15 .07
❑ 552 R.J. Reynolds .15 .07
❑ 553 Chris Brown .15 .07
❑ 554 Bruce Benedict .15 .07
❑ 555 Warren Brusstar .15 .07
❑ 556 Danny Heep .15 .07
❑ 557 Darnell Coles .15 .07
❑ 558 Greg Gagne .15 .07
❑ 559 Ernie Whitt .15 .07
❑ 560 Ron Washington .15 .07
❑ 561 Jimmy Key .75 .35
❑ 562 Billy Swift .15 .07
❑ 563 Ron Darling .15 .07
❑ 564 Dick Ruthven .15 .07
❑ 565 Zane Smith .15 .07
❑ 566 Sid Bream .15 .07
❑ 567A J.Youngblood ERR .15 .07
Position P
❑ 567B J.Youngblood COR .75 .35
Position IF
❑ 568 Mario Ramirez .15 .07
❑ 569 Tom Runnells .15 .07
❑ 570 Rick Schu .15 .07
❑ 571 Bill Campbell .15 .07
❑ 572 Dickie Thon .15 .07
❑ 573 Al Holland .15 .07
❑ 574 Reid Nichols .15 .07
❑ 575 Bert Roberge .15 .07
❑ 576 Mike Flanagan .15 .07
❑ 577 Tim Leary .15 .07
❑ 578 Mike Laga .15 .07
❑ 579 Steve Lyons .15 .07
❑ 580 Phil Niekro .75 .35
❑ 581 Gilberto Reyes .15 .07
❑ 582 Jamie Easterly .15 .07
❑ 583 Mark Gubicza .15 .07
❑ 584 Stan Javier RC .25 .11
❑ 585 Bill Laskey .15 .07
❑ 586 Jeff Russell .15 .07
❑ 587 Dickie Noles .15 .07
❑ 588 Steve Farr .15 .07
❑ 589 Steve Ontiveros RC .25 .11
❑ 590 Mike Hargrove .25 .11
❑ 591 Marty Bystrom .15 .07
❑ 592 Franklin Stubbs .15 .07
❑ 593 Larry Herndon .15 .07
❑ 594 Bill Swaggerty .15 .07
❑ 595 Carlos Ponce .15 .07
❑ 596 Pat Perry .15 .07
❑ 597 Ray Knight .25 .11
❑ 598 Steve Lombardozzi .15 .07
❑ 599 Brad Havens .15 .07
❑ 600 Pat Clements .15 .07
❑ 601 Joe Niekro .15 .07
❑ 602 Hank Aaron .75 .35
Puzzle Card
❑ 603 Dwayne Henry .15 .07
❑ 604 Mookie Wilson .25 .11
❑ 605 Buddy Biancalana .15 .07
❑ 606 Rance Mulliniks .15 .07
❑ 607 Alan Wiggins .15 .07
❑ 608 Joe Cowley .15 .07
❑ 609 Tom Seaver 1.25 .55
(Green borders
on name)
❑ 609B Tom Seaver 2.00 .90
(Yellow borders
on name)
❑ 610 Neil Allen .15 .07
❑ 611 Don Sutton .75 .35
❑ 612 Fred Toliver .15 .07
❑ 613 Jay Baller .15 .07
❑ 614 Marc Sullivan .15 .07
❑ 615 John Grubb .15 .07
❑ 616 Bruce Kison .15 .07
❑ 617 Bill Madlock .15 .07
❑ 618 Chris Chambliss .25 .11
❑ 619 Dave Stewart .25 .11
❑ 620 Tim Lollar .15 .07
❑ 621 Gary Lavelle .15 .07
❑ 622 Charles Hudson .15 .07
❑ 623 Joel Davis .15 .07
❑ 624 Joe Johnson .15 .07
❑ 625 Sid Fernandez .25 .11
❑ 626 Dennis Lamp .15 .07
❑ 627 Terry Harper .15 .07
❑ 628 Jack Lazorko .15 .07
❑ 629 Roger McDowell RC* .25 .11
❑ 630 Mark Funderburk .15 .07
❑ 631 Ed Lynch .15 .07
❑ 632 Rudy Law .15 .07
❑ 633 Roger Mason RC .15 .07
❑ 634 Mike Felder RC .15 .07
❑ 635 Ken Schrom .15 .07
❑ 636 Bob Ojeda .15 .07
❑ 637 Ed VandeBerg .15 .07
❑ 638 Bobby Meacham .15 .07
❑ 639 Cliff Johnson .15 .07
❑ 640 Garth Iorg .15 .07
❑ 641 Dan Driessen .15 .07
❑ 642 Mike Brown OF .15 .07
❑ 643 John Shelby .15 .07
❑ 644 Pete Rose .75 .35
(Ty-Breaking)
❑ 645 The Knuckle Brothers .25 .11
Phil Niekro
Joe Niekro
❑ 646 Jesse Orosco .15 .07
❑ 647 Billy Beane .15 .07
❑ 648 Cesar Cedeno .25 .11
❑ 649 Bert Blyleven .25 .11
❑ 650 Max Venable .15 .07
❑ 651 Fleet Feet .15 .07
Vince Coleman
Willie McGee
❑ 652 Calvin Schiraldi .15 .07
❑ 653 King of Kings .75 .35
(Pete Rose)
❑ 654 Dia. Kings CL 1-26 .15 .07
Unnumbered
❑ 655A CL 1: 27-130 .15 .07
(Unnumbered)
(45 Beane ERR)
❑ 655B CL 1: 27-130 .15 .07
(Unnumbered)
(45 Habyan COR)
❑ 656 CL 2: 131-234 .15 .07
(Unnumbered)
❑ 657 CL 3: 235-338 .15 .07
(Unnumbered)
❑ 658 CL 4: 339-442 .15 .07
(Unnumbered)
❑ 659 CL 5: 443-546 .15 .07
(Unnumbered)
❑ 660 CL 6: 547-653 .15 .07
(Unnumbered)

1986 Donruss Rookies

	MINT	NRMT
COMP.FACT.SET (56)	50.00	22.00

❑ 1 Wally Joyner XRC 1.00 .45
❑ 2 Tracy Jones .10 .05
❑ 3 Allan Anderson .10 .05
❑ 4 Ed Correa .10 .05
❑ 5 Reggie Williams .10 .05
❑ 6 Charlie Kerfeld .10 .05
❑ 7 Andres Galarraga 2.00 .90
❑ 8 Bob Tewksbury XRC .25 .11
❑ 9 Al Newman .25 .11
❑ 10 Andres Thomas .10 .05
❑ 11 Barry Bonds XRC 30.00 13.50
❑ 12 Juan Nieves .10 .05
❑ 13 Mark Eichhorn .10 .05
❑ 14 Dan Plesac XRC .10 .05
❑ 15 Cory Snyder .10 .05
❑ 16 Kelly Gruber XRC** .10 .05
❑ 17 Kevin Mitchell XRC 1.00 .45
❑ 18 Steve Lombardozzi .10 .05
❑ 19 Mitch Williams XRC .25 .11
❑ 20 John Cerutti .10 .05
❑ 21 Todd Worrell 1.00 .45
❑ 22 Jose Canseco 5.00 2.20
❑ 23 Pete Incaviglia XRC 1.00 .45
❑ 24 Jose Guzman .10 .05
❑ 25 Scott Bailes .10 .05
❑ 26 Greg Mathews .10 .05
❑ 27 Eric King .10 .05
❑ 28 Paul Assenmacher .10 .05
❑ 29 Jeff Sellers .10 .05
❑ 30 Bobby Bonilla XRC 1.00 .45
❑ 31 Doug Drabek XRC 1.00 .45
❑ 32 Will Clark UER 3.00 1.35
(Listed as throwing
right, should be left) XRC
❑ 33 Bip Roberts XRC 1.00 .45
❑ 34 Jim Deshaies XRC .10 .05
❑ 35 Mike LaValliere XRC .10 .05
❑ 36 Scott Bankhead .10 .05
❑ 37 Dale Sveum .10 .05
❑ 38 Bo Jackson XRC 2.50 1.10
❑ 39 Robby Thompson XRC .25 .11
❑ 40 Eric Plunk .10 .05
❑ 41 Bill Bathe .10 .05
❑ 42 John Kruk XRC 1.00 .45
❑ 43 Andy Allanson .10 .05
❑ 44 Mark Portugal XRC .50 .23
❑ 45 Danny Tartabull .25 .11
❑ 46 Bob Kipper .10 .05
❑ 47 Gene Walter .10 .05
❑ 48 Rey Quinones UER .10 .05
(Misspelled Quinonez)

❑ 49 Bobby Witt XRC .50 .23
❑ 50 Bill Mooneyham .10 .05
❑ 51 John Cangelosi .10 .05
❑ 52 Ruben Sierra XRC 1.00 .45
❑ 53 Rob Woodward .10 .05
❑ 54 Ed Hearn .10 .05
❑ 55 Joel McKeon .10 .05
❑ 56 Checklist 1-56 .10 .05

1987 Donruss

	MINT	NRMT
COMPLETE SET (660)	50.00	22.00
COMP.FACT.SET (660)	80.00	36.00
COMP.CLEMENTE PUZZLE	1.50	.70

❑ 1 Wally Joyner DK .40 .18
❑ 2 Roger Clemens DK .50 .23
❑ 3 Dale Murphy DK .15 .07
❑ 4 Darryl Strawberry DK .15 .07
❑ 5 Ozzie Smith DK .40 .18
❑ 6 Jose Canseco DK .60 .25
❑ 7 Charlie Hough DK .10 .05
❑ 8 Brook Jacoby DK .10 .05
❑ 9 Fred Lynn DK .15 .07
❑ 10 Rick Rhoden DK .10 .05
❑ 11 Chris Brown DK .10 .05
❑ 12 Von Hayes DK .10 .05
❑ 13 Jack Morris DK .15 .07
❑ 14A Kevin McReynolds DK .40 .18
ERR (Yellow strip missing on back)
❑ 14B Kevin McReynolds DK .10 .05
COR
❑ 15 George Brett DK .40 .18
❑ 16 Ted Higuera DK .10 .05
❑ 17 Hubie Brooks DK .10 .05
❑ 18 Mike Scott DK .10 .05
❑ 19 Kirby Puckett DK .40 .18
❑ 20 Dave Winfield DK .15 .07
❑ 21 Lloyd Moseby DK .10 .05
❑ 22A Eric Davis DK ERR .40 .18
(Yellow strip missing on back)
❑ 22B Eric Davis DK COR .15 .07
❑ 23 Jim Presley DK .10 .05
❑ 24 Keith Moreland DK .10 .05
❑ 25A Greg Walker DK ERR .40 .18
(Yellow strip missing on back)
❑ 25B Greg Walker DK COR .10 .05
❑ 26 Steve Sax DK .10 .05
❑ 27 DK Checklist 1-26 .10 .05
❑ 28 B.J. Surhoff RR RC 1.00 .45
❑ 29 Randy Myers RR RC .40 .18
❑ 30 Ken Gerhart RR .10 .05
❑ 31 Benito Santiago RR .15 .07
❑ 32 Greg Swindell RR RC .40 .18
❑ 33 Mike Birkbeck RR .10 .05
❑ 34 Terry Steinbach RR RC .40 .18
❑ 35 Bo Jackson RR RC 1.00 .45
❑ 36 Greg Maddux UER RC 15.00 6.75
middle name misspelled "Allen"
❑ 37 Jim Lindeman RR .10 .05
❑ 38 Devon White RR RC .50 .23
❑ 39 Eric Bell RR .10 .05
❑ 40 Willie Fraser RR .10 .05
❑ 41 Jerry Browne RR RC .10 .05
❑ 42 Chris James RR RC* .10 .05
❑ 43 Rafael Palmeiro RR RC 8.00 3.60
❑ 44 Pat Dodson RR .10 .05
❑ 45 Duane Ward RR RC* .15 .07
❑ 46 Mark McGwire RR 15.00 6.75
❑ 47 Bruce Fields RR UER .10 .05
(Photo actually Darnell Coles)
❑ 48 Eddie Murray .40 .18
❑ 49 Ted Higuera .10 .05
❑ 50 Kirk Gibson .15 .07
❑ 51 Oil Can Boyd .10 .05
❑ 52 Don Mattingly 1.00 .45
❑ 53 Pedro Guerrero .10 .05
❑ 54 George Brett .75 .35
❑ 55 Jose Rijo .10 .05
❑ 56 Tim Raines .15 .07
❑ 57 Ed Correa .10 .05
❑ 58 Mike Witt .10 .05
❑ 59 Greg Walker .10 .05
❑ 60 Ozzie Smith .50 .23
❑ 61 Glenn Davis .10 .05
❑ 62 Glenn Wilson .10 .05
❑ 63 Tom Browning .10 .05
❑ 64 Tony Gwynn .75 .35
❑ 65 R.J. Reynolds .10 .05
❑ 66 Will Clark RC 1.50 .70
❑ 67 Ozzie Virgil .10 .05
❑ 68 Rick Sutcliffe .15 .07
❑ 69 Gary Carter .25 .11
❑ 70 Mike Moore .10 .05
❑ 71 Bert Blyleven .15 .07
❑ 72 Tony Fernandez .10 .05
❑ 73 Kent Hrbek .15 .07
❑ 74 Lloyd Moseby .10 .05
❑ 75 Alvin Davis .10 .05
❑ 76 Keith Hernandez .15 .07
❑ 77 Ryne Sandberg .50 .23
❑ 78 Dale Murphy .40 .18
❑ 79 Sid Bream .10 .05
❑ 80 Chris Brown .10 .05
❑ 81 Steve Garvey .25 .11
❑ 82 Mario Soto .10 .05
❑ 83 Shane Rawley .10 .05
❑ 84 Willie McGee .15 .07
❑ 85 Jose Cruz .15 .07
❑ 86 Brian Downing .10 .05
❑ 87 Ozzie Guillen .10 .05
❑ 88 Hubie Brooks .10 .05
❑ 89 Cal Ripken 1.50 .70
❑ 90 Juan Nieves .10 .05
❑ 91 Lance Parrish .15 .07
❑ 92 Jim Rice .15 .07
❑ 93 Ron Guidry .15 .07
❑ 94 Fernando Valenzuela .15 .07
❑ 95 Andy Allanson .10 .05
❑ 96 Willie Wilson .15 .07
❑ 97 Jose Canseco 1.25 .55
❑ 98 Jeff Reardon .15 .07
❑ 99 Bobby Witt RC .15 .07
❑ 100 Checklist 28-133 .10 .05
❑ 101 Jose Guzman .10 .05
❑ 102 Steve Balboni .10 .05
❑ 103 Tony Phillips .10 .05
❑ 104 Brook Jacoby .10 .05
❑ 105 Dave Winfield .40 .18
❑ 106 Orel Hershiser .15 .07
❑ 107 Lou Whitaker .15 .07
❑ 108 Fred Lynn .15 .07
❑ 109 Bill Wegman .10 .05
❑ 110 Donnie Moore .10 .05
❑ 111 Jack Clark .15 .07
❑ 112 Bob Knepper .10 .05
❑ 113 Von Hayes .10 .05
❑ 114 Bip Roberts RC* .40 .18
❑ 115 Tony Pena .10 .05
❑ 116 Scott Garrelts .10 .05
❑ 117 Paul Molitor .40 .18
❑ 118 Darryl Strawberry .25 .11
❑ 119 Shawon Dunston .10 .05
❑ 120 Jim Presley .10 .05
❑ 121 Jesse Barfield .10 .05
❑ 122 Gary Gaetti .15 .07
❑ 123 Kurt Stillwell .10 .05
❑ 124 Joel Davis .10 .05
❑ 125 Mike Boddicker .10 .05
❑ 126 Robin Yount .40 .18
❑ 127 Alan Trammell .25 .11
❑ 128 Dave Righetti .10 .05
❑ 129 Dwight Evans .15 .07
❑ 130 Mike Scioscia .10 .05
❑ 131 Julio Franco .10 .05
❑ 132 Bret Saberhagen .15 .07
❑ 133 Mike Davis .10 .05
❑ 134 Joe Hesketh .10 .05
❑ 135 Wally Joyner RC .40 .18
❑ 136 Don Slaught .10 .05
❑ 137 Daryl Boston .10 .05
❑ 138 Nolan Ryan 2.00 .90
❑ 139 Mike Schmidt .75 .35
❑ 140 Tommy Herr .10 .05
❑ 141 Garry Templeton .10 .05
❑ 142 Kal Daniels .10 .05
❑ 143 Billy Sample .10 .05
❑ 144 Johnny Ray .10 .05
❑ 145 Rob Thompson RC* .15 .07
❑ 146 Bob Dernier .10 .05
❑ 147 Danny Tartabull .10 .05
❑ 148 Ernie Whitt .10 .05
❑ 149 Kirby Puckett 1.00 .45
❑ 150 Mike Young .10 .05
❑ 151 Ernest Riles .10 .05
❑ 152 Frank Tanana .10 .05
❑ 153 Rich Gedman .10 .05
❑ 154 Willie Randolph .15 .07
❑ 155 Bill Madlock .15 .07
❑ 156 Joe Carter .40 .18
❑ 157 Danny Jackson .10 .05
❑ 158 Carney Lansford .15 .07
❑ 159 Bryn Smith .10 .05
❑ 160 Gary Pettis .10 .05
❑ 161 Oddibe McDowell .10 .05
❑ 162 John Cangelosi .10 .05
❑ 163 Mike Scott .10 .05
❑ 164 Eric Show .10 .05
❑ 165 Juan Samuel .10 .05
❑ 166 Nick Esasky .10 .05
❑ 167 Zane Smith .10 .05
❑ 168 Mike C. Brown OF .10 .05
❑ 169 Keith Moreland .10 .05
❑ 170 John Tudor .10 .05
❑ 171 Ken Dixon .10 .05
❑ 172 Jim Gantner .10 .05
❑ 173 Jack Morris .15 .07
❑ 174 Bruce Hurst .10 .05
❑ 175 Dennis Rasmussen .10 .05
❑ 176 Mike Marshall .10 .05
❑ 177 Dan Quisenberry .10 .05
❑ 178 Eric Plunk .10 .05
❑ 179 Tim Wallach .10 .05
❑ 180 Steve Buechele .10 .05
❑ 181 Don Sutton .40 .18
❑ 182 Dave Schmidt .10 .05
❑ 183 Terry Pendleton .15 .07
❑ 184 Jim Deshaies RC* .10 .05
❑ 185 Steve Bedrosian .10 .05
❑ 186 Pete Rose 1.25 .55
❑ 187 Dave Dravecky .15 .07
❑ 188 Rick Reuschel .10 .05
❑ 189 Dan Gladden .10 .05
❑ 190 Rick Mahler .10 .05
❑ 191 Thad Bosley .10 .05
❑ 192 Ron Darling .10 .05
❑ 193 Matt Young .10 .05
❑ 194 Tom Brunansky .10 .05
❑ 195 Dave Stieb .10 .05
❑ 196 Frank Viola .10 .05
❑ 197 Tom Henke .10 .05
❑ 198 Karl Best .10 .05
❑ 199 Dwight Gooden .25 .11
❑ 200 Checklist 134-239 .10 .05
❑ 201 Steve Trout .10 .05
❑ 202 Rafael Ramirez .10 .05
❑ 203 Bob Walk .10 .05
❑ 204 Roger Mason .10 .05
❑ 205 Terry Kennedy .10 .05
❑ 206 Ron Oester .10 .05
❑ 207 John Russell .10 .05
❑ 208 Greg Mathews .10 .05
❑ 209 Charlie Kerfeld .10 .05
❑ 210 Reggie Jackson .50 .23
❑ 211 Floyd Bannister .10 .05

❑ 212 Vance Law .10 .05
❑ 213 Rich Bordi .10 .05
❑ 214 Dan Plesac .10 .05
❑ 215 Dave Collins .10 .05
❑ 216 Bob Stanley .10 .05
❑ 217 Joe Niekro .10 .05
❑ 218 Tom Niedenfuer .10 .05
❑ 219 Brett Butler .15 .07
❑ 220 Charlie Leibrandt .10 .05
❑ 221 Steve Ontiveros .10 .05
❑ 222 Tim Burke .10 .05
❑ 223 Curtis Wilkerson .10 .05
❑ 224 Pete Incaviglia RC* .15 .07
❑ 225 Lonnie Smith .10 .05
❑ 226 Chris Codiroli .10 .05
❑ 227 Scott Bailes .10 .05
❑ 228 Rickey Henderson .75 .35
❑ 229 Ken Howell .10 .05
❑ 230 Darnell Coles .10 .05
❑ 231 Don Aase .10 .05
❑ 232 Tim Leary .10 .05
❑ 233 Bob Boone .15 .07
❑ 234 Ricky Horton .10 .05
❑ 235 Mark Bailey .10 .05
❑ 236 Kevin Gross .10 .05
❑ 237 Lance McCullers .10 .05
❑ 238 Cecilio Guante .10 .05
❑ 239 Bob Melvin .10 .05
❑ 240 Billy Joe Robidoux .10 .05
❑ 241 Roger McDowell .10 .05
❑ 242 Leon Durham .10 .05
❑ 243 Ed Nunez .10 .05
❑ 244 Jimmy Key .15 .07
❑ 245 Mike Smithson .10 .05
❑ 246 Bo Diaz .10 .05
❑ 247 Carlton Fisk .40 .18
❑ 248 Larry Sheets .10 .05
❑ 249 Juan Castillo .10 .05
❑ 250 Eric King .10 .05
❑ 251 Doug Drabek RC .40 .18
❑ 252 Wade Boggs .40 .18
❑ 253 Mariano Duncan .10 .05
❑ 254 Pat Tabler .10 .05
❑ 255 Frank White .15 .07
❑ 256 Alfredo Griffin .10 .05
❑ 257 Floyd Youmans .10 .05
❑ 258 Rob Wilfong .10 .05
❑ 259 Pete O'Brien .10 .05
❑ 260 Tim Hulett .10 .05
❑ 261 Dickie Thon .10 .05
❑ 262 Darren Daulton .25 .11
❑ 263 Vince Coleman .10 .05
❑ 264 Andy Hawkins .10 .05
❑ 265 Eric Davis .25 .11
❑ 266 Andres Thomas .10 .05
❑ 267 Mike Diaz .10 .05
❑ 268 Chili Davis .25 .11
❑ 269 Jody Davis .10 .05
❑ 270 Phil Bradley .10 .05
❑ 271 George Bell .10 .05
❑ 272 Keith Atherton .10 .05
❑ 273 Storm Davis .10 .05
❑ 274 Rob Deer .10 .05
❑ 275 Walt Terrell .10 .05
❑ 276 Roger Clemens 1.00 .45
❑ 277 Mike Easler .10 .05
❑ 278 Steve Sax .10 .05
❑ 279 Andre Thornton .10 .05
❑ 280 Jim Sundberg .10 .05
❑ 281 Bill Bathe .10 .05
❑ 282 Jay Tibbs .10 .05
❑ 283 Dick Schofield .10 .05
❑ 284 Mike Mason .10 .05
❑ 285 Jerry Hairston .10 .05
❑ 286 Bill Doran .10 .05
❑ 287 Tim Flannery .10 .05
❑ 288 Gary Redus .10 .05
❑ 289 John Franco .15 .07
❑ 290 Paul Assenmacher .25 .11
❑ 291 Joe Orsulak .10 .05
❑ 292 Lee Smith .25 .11
❑ 293 Mike Laga .10 .05
❑ 294 Rick Dempsey .15 .07
❑ 295 Mike Felder .10 .05
❑ 296 Tom Brookens .10 .05
❑ 297 Al Nipper .10 .05
❑ 298 Mike Pagliarulo .10 .05
❑ 299 Franklin Stubbs .10 .05
❑ 300 Checklist 240-345 .10 .05
❑ 301 Steve Farr .10 .05
❑ 302 Bill Mooneyham .10 .05
❑ 303 Andres Galarraga .40 .18
❑ 304 Scott Fletcher .10 .05
❑ 305 Jack Howell .10 .05
❑ 306 Russ Morman .10 .05
❑ 307 Todd Worrell .15 .07
❑ 308 Dave Smith .10 .05
❑ 309 Jeff Stone .10 .05
❑ 310 Ron Robinson .10 .05
❑ 311 Bruce Bochy .10 .05
❑ 312 Jim Winn .10 .05
❑ 313 Mark Davis .10 .05
❑ 314 Jeff Dedmon .10 .05
❑ 315 Jamie Moyer RC .75 .35
❑ 316 Wally Backman .10 .05
❑ 317 Ken Phelps .10 .05
❑ 318 Steve Lombardozzi .10 .05
❑ 319 Rance Mulliniks .10 .05
❑ 320 Tim Laudner .10 .05
❑ 321 Mark Eichhorn .10 .05
❑ 322 Lee Guetterman .10 .05
❑ 323 Sid Fernandez .10 .05
❑ 324 Jerry Mumphrey .10 .05
❑ 325 David Palmer .10 .05
❑ 326 Bill Almon .10 .05
❑ 327 Candy Maldonado .10 .05
❑ 328 John Kruk RC .40 .18
❑ 329 John Denny .10 .05
❑ 330 Milt Thompson .10 .05
❑ 331 Mike LaValliere RC* .10 .05
❑ 332 Alan Ashby .10 .05
❑ 333 Doug Corbett .10 .05
❑ 334 Ron Karkovice RC .15 .07
❑ 335 Mitch Webster .10 .05
❑ 336 Lee Lacy .10 .05
❑ 337 Glenn Braggs RC .10 .05
❑ 338 Dwight Lowry .10 .05
❑ 339 Don Baylor .15 .07
❑ 340 Brian Fisher .10 .05
❑ 341 Reggie Williams .10 .05
❑ 342 Tom Candiotti .10 .05
❑ 343 Rudy Law .10 .05
❑ 344 Curt Young .10 .05
❑ 345 Mike Fitzgerald .10 .05
❑ 346 Ruben Sierra RC .50 .23
❑ 347 Mitch Williams RC* .15 .07
❑ 348 Jorge Orta .10 .05
❑ 349 Mickey Tettleton .10 .05
❑ 350 Ernie Camacho .10 .05
❑ 351 Ron Kittle .10 .05
❑ 352 Ken Landreaux .10 .05
❑ 353 Chet Lemon .10 .05
❑ 354 John Shelby .10 .05
❑ 355 Mark Clear .10 .05
❑ 356 Doug DeCinces .10 .05
❑ 357 Ken Dayley .10 .05
❑ 358 Phil Garner .10 .05
❑ 359 Steve Jeltz .10 .05
❑ 360 Ed Whitson .10 .05
❑ 361 Barry Bonds RC 15.00 6.75
❑ 362 Vida Blue .15 .07
❑ 363 Cecil Cooper .15 .07
❑ 364 Bob Ojeda .10 .05
❑ 365 Dennis Eckersley .40 .18
❑ 366 Mike Morgan .10 .05
❑ 367 Willie Upshaw .10 .05
❑ 368 Allan Anderson .10 .05
❑ 369 Bill Gullickson .10 .05
❑ 370 Bobby Thigpen RC .15 .07
❑ 371 Juan Beniquez .10 .05
❑ 372 Charlie Moore .10 .05
❑ 373 Dan Petry .10 .05
❑ 374 Rod Scurry .10 .05
❑ 375 Tom Seaver .40 .18
❑ 376 Ed VandeBerg .10 .05
❑ 377 Tony Bernazard .10 .05
❑ 378 Greg Pryor .10 .05
❑ 379 Dwayne Murphy .10 .05
❑ 380 Andy McGaffigan .10 .05
❑ 381 Kirk McCaskill .10 .05
❑ 382 Greg Harris .10 .05
❑ 383 Rich Dotson .10 .05
❑ 384 Craig Reynolds .10 .05
❑ 385 Greg Gross .10 .05
❑ 386 Tito Landrum .10 .05
❑ 387 Craig Lefferts .10 .05
❑ 388 Dave Parker .15 .07
❑ 389 Bob Horner .10 .05
❑ 390 Pat Clements .10 .05
❑ 391 Jeff Leonard .10 .05
❑ 392 Chris Speier .10 .05
❑ 393 John Moses .10 .05
❑ 394 Garth Iorg .10 .05
❑ 395 Greg Gagne .10 .05
❑ 396 Nate Snell .10 .05
❑ 397 Bryan Clutterbuck .10 .05
❑ 398 Darrell Evans .15 .07
❑ 399 Steve Crawford .10 .05
❑ 400 Checklist 346-451 .10 .05
❑ 401 Phil Lombardi .10 .05
❑ 402 Rick Honeycutt .10 .05
❑ 403 Ken Schrom .10 .05
❑ 404 Bud Black .10 .05
❑ 405 Donnie Hill .10 .05
❑ 406 Wayne Krenchicki .10 .05
❑ 407 Chuck Finley RC .75 .35
❑ 408 Toby Harrah .10 .05
❑ 409 Steve Lyons .10 .05
❑ 410 Kevin Bass .10 .05
❑ 411 Marvell Wynne .10 .05
❑ 412 Ron Roenicke .10 .05
❑ 413 Tracy Jones .10 .05
❑ 414 Gene Garber .10 .05
❑ 415 Mike Bielecki .10 .05
❑ 416 Frank DiPino .10 .05
❑ 417 Andy Van Slyke .15 .07
❑ 418 Jim Dwyer .10 .05
❑ 419 Ben Oglivie .10 .05
❑ 420 Dave Bergman .10 .05
❑ 421 Joe Sambito .10 .05
❑ 422 Bob Tewksbury RC* .15 .07
❑ 423 Len Matuszek .10 .05
❑ 424 Mike Kingery RC .10 .05
❑ 425 Dave Kingman .15 .07
❑ 426 Al Newman .10 .05
❑ 427 Gary Ward .10 .05
❑ 428 Ruppert Jones .10 .05
❑ 429 Harold Baines .15 .07
❑ 430 Pat Perry .10 .05
❑ 431 Terry Puhl .10 .05
❑ 432 Don Carman .10 .05
❑ 433 Eddie Milner .10 .05
❑ 434 LaMarr Hoyt .10 .05
❑ 435 Rick Rhoden .10 .05
❑ 436 Jose Uribe .10 .05
❑ 437 Ken Oberkfell .10 .05
❑ 438 Ron Davis .10 .05
❑ 439 Jesse Orosco .10 .05
❑ 440 Scott Bradley .10 .05
❑ 441 Randy Bush .10 .05
❑ 442 John Cerutti .10 .05
❑ 443 Roy Smalley .10 .05
❑ 444 Kelly Gruber .10 .05
❑ 445 Bob Kearney .10 .05
❑ 446 Ed Hearn .10 .05
❑ 447 Scott Sanderson .10 .05
❑ 448 Bruce Benedict .10 .05
❑ 449 Junior Ortiz .10 .05
❑ 450 Mike Aldrete .10 .05
❑ 451 Kevin McReynolds .10 .05
❑ 452 Rob Murphy .10 .05
❑ 453 Kent Tekulve .10 .05
❑ 454 Curt Ford .10 .05
❑ 455 Dave Lopes .15 .07
❑ 456 Bob Grich .15 .07
❑ 457 Jose DeLeon .10 .05
❑ 458 Andre Dawson .25 .11
❑ 459 Mike Flanagan .10 .05
❑ 460 Joey Meyer .10 .05
❑ 461 Chuck Cary .10 .05
❑ 462 Bill Buckner .15 .07
❑ 463 Bob Shirley .10 .05
❑ 464 Jeff Hamilton .10 .05
❑ 465 Phil Niekro .40 .18
❑ 466 Mark Gubicza .10 .05
❑ 467 Jerry Willard .10 .05
❑ 468 Bob Sebra .10 .05
❑ 469 Larry Parrish .10 .05

❑ 470 Charlie Hough .15 .07
❑ 471 Hal McRae .15 .07
❑ 472 Dave Leiper .10 .05
❑ 473 Mel Hall .10 .05
❑ 474 Dan Pasqua .10 .05
❑ 475 Bob Welch .10 .05
❑ 476 Johnny Grubb .10 .05
❑ 477 Jim Traber .10 .05
❑ 478 Chris Bosio RC .15 .07
❑ 479 Mark McLemore .15 .07
❑ 480 John Morris .10 .05
❑ 481 Billy Hatcher .10 .05
❑ 482 Dan Schatzeder .10 .05
❑ 483 Rich Gossage .15 .07
❑ 484 Jim Morrison .10 .05
❑ 485 Bob Brenly .10 .05
❑ 486 Bill Schroeder .10 .05
❑ 487 Mookie Wilson .15 .07
❑ 488 Dave Martinez RC .15 .07
❑ 489 Harold Reynolds .15 .07
❑ 490 Jeff Hearron .10 .05
❑ 491 Mickey Hatcher .10 .05
❑ 492 Barry Larkin RC 2.00 .90
❑ 493 Bob James .10 .05
❑ 494 John Habyan .10 .05
❑ 495 Jim Adduci .10 .05
❑ 496 Mike Heath .10 .05
❑ 497 Tim Stoddard .10 .05
❑ 498 Tony Armas .10 .05
❑ 499 Dennis Powell .10 .05
❑ 500 Checklist 452-557 .10 .05
❑ 501 Chris Bando .10 .05
❑ 502 David Cone RC 2.00 .90
❑ 503 Jay Howell .10 .05
❑ 504 Tom Foley .10 .05
❑ 505 Ray Chadwick .10 .05
❑ 506 Mike Loynd .10 .05
❑ 507 Neil Allen .10 .05
❑ 508 Danny Darwin .10 .05
❑ 509 Rick Schu .10 .05
❑ 510 Jose Oquendo .10 .05
❑ 511 Gene Walter .10 .05
❑ 512 Terry McGriff .10 .05
❑ 513 Ken Griffey .15 .07
❑ 514 Benny Distefano .10 .05
❑ 515 Terry Mulholland RC .15 .07
❑ 516 Ed Lynch .10 .05
❑ 517 Bill Swift .10 .05
❑ 518 Manny Lee .10 .05
❑ 519 Andre David .10 .05
❑ 520 Scott McGregor .10 .05
❑ 521 Rick Manning .10 .05
❑ 522 Willie Hernandez .10 .05
❑ 523 Marty Barrett .10 .05
❑ 524 Wayne Tolleson .10 .05
❑ 525 Jose Gonzalez .10 .05
❑ 526 Cory Snyder .10 .05
❑ 527 Buddy Biancalana .10 .05
❑ 528 Moose Haas .10 .05
❑ 529 Wilfredo Tejada .10 .05
❑ 530 Stu Cliburn .10 .05
❑ 531 Dale Mohorcic .10 .05
❑ 532 Ron Hassey .10 .05
❑ 533 Ty Gainey .10 .05
❑ 534 Jerry Royster .10 .05
❑ 535 Mike Maddux .10 .05
❑ 536 Ted Power .10 .05
❑ 537 Ted Simmons .15 .07
❑ 538 Rafael Belliard RC .10 .05
❑ 539 Chico Walker .10 .05
❑ 540 Bob Forsch .10 .05
❑ 541 John Stefero .10 .05
❑ 542 Dale Sveum .10 .05
❑ 543 Mark Thurmond .10 .05
❑ 544 Jeff Sellers .10 .05
❑ 545 Joel Skinner .10 .05
❑ 546 Alex Trevino .10 .05
❑ 547 Randy Kutcher .10 .05
❑ 548 Joaquin Andujar .10 .05
❑ 549 Casey Candaele .10 .05
❑ 550 Jeff Russell .10 .05
❑ 551 John Candelaria .10 .05
❑ 552 Joe Cowley .10 .05
❑ 553 Danny Cox .10 .05
❑ 554 Denny Walling .10 .05
❑ 555 Bruce Ruffin RC .10 .05
❑ 556 Buddy Bell .15 .07
❑ 557 Jimmy Jones RC .10 .05
❑ 558 Bobby Bonilla RC .50 .23
❑ 559 Jeff D. Robinson .10 .05
❑ 560 Ed Olwine .10 .05
❑ 561 Glenallen Hill RC .40 .18
❑ 562 Lee Mazzilli .10 .05
❑ 563 Mike G. Brown P .10 .05
❑ 564 George Frazier .10 .05
❑ 565 Mike Sharperson RC .10 .05
❑ 566 Mark Portugal RC* .15 .07
❑ 567 Rick Leach .10 .05
❑ 568 Mark Langston .10 .05
❑ 569 Rafael Santana .10 .05
❑ 570 Manny Trillo .10 .05
❑ 571 Cliff Speck .10 .05
❑ 572 Bob Kipper .10 .05
❑ 573 Kelly Downs RC .10 .05
❑ 574 Randy Asadoor .10 .05
❑ 575 Dave Magadan RC .15 .07
❑ 576 Marvin Freeman RC .10 .05
❑ 577 Jeff Lahti .10 .05
❑ 578 Jeff Calhoun .10 .05
❑ 579 Gus Polidor .10 .05
❑ 580 Gene Nelson .10 .05
❑ 581 Tim Teufel .10 .05
❑ 582 Odell Jones .10 .05
❑ 583 Mark Ryal .10 .05
❑ 584 Randy O'Neal .10 .05
❑ 585 Mike Greenwell RC .40 .18
❑ 586 Ray Knight .10 .05
❑ 587 Ralph Bryant .10 .05
❑ 588 Carmen Castillo .10 .05
❑ 589 Ed Wojna .10 .05
❑ 590 Stan Javier .10 .05
❑ 591 Jeff Musselman .10 .05
❑ 592 Mike Stanley RC .40 .18
❑ 593 Darrell Porter .10 .05
❑ 594 Drew Hall .10 .05
❑ 595 Rob Nelson .10 .05
❑ 596 Bryan Oelkers .10 .05
❑ 597 Scott Nielsen .10 .05
❑ 598 Brian Holton .10 .05
❑ 599 Kevin Mitchell RC* .25 .11
❑ 600 Checklist 558-660 .10 .05
❑ 601 Jackie Gutierrez .10 .05
❑ 602 Barry Jones .10 .05
❑ 603 Jerry Narron .10 .05
❑ 604 Steve Lake .10 .05
❑ 605 Jim Pankovits .10 .05
❑ 606 Ed Romero .10 .05
❑ 607 Dave LaPoint .10 .05
❑ 608 Don Robinson .10 .05
❑ 609 Mike Krukow .10 .05
❑ 610 Dave Valle RC** .10 .05
❑ 611 Len Dykstra .25 .11
❑ 612 R.Clemente PUZ .50 .23
❑ 613 Mike Trujillo .10 .05
❑ 614 Damaso Garcia .10 .05
❑ 615 Neal Heaton .10 .05
❑ 616 Juan Berenguer .10 .05
❑ 617 Steve Carlton .40 .18
❑ 618 Gary Lucas .10 .05
❑ 619 Geno Petralli .10 .05
❑ 620 Rick Aguilera .15 .07
❑ 621 Fred McGriff .50 .23
❑ 622 Dave Henderson .10 .05
❑ 623 Dave Clark RC .15 .07
❑ 624 Angel Salazar .10 .05
❑ 625 Randy Hunt .10 .05
❑ 626 John Gibbons .10 .05
❑ 627 Kevin Brown RC 2.00 .90
❑ 628 Bill Dawley .10 .05
❑ 629 Aurelio Lopez .10 .05
❑ 630 Charles Hudson .10 .05
❑ 631 Ray Soff .10 .05
❑ 632 Ray Hayward .10 .05
❑ 633 Spike Owen .10 .05
❑ 634 Glenn Hubbard .10 .05
❑ 635 Kevin Elster RC .15 .07
❑ 636 Mike LaCoss .10 .05
❑ 637 Dwayne Henry .10 .05
❑ 638 Rey Quinones .10 .05
❑ 639 Jim Clancy .10 .05
❑ 640 Larry Andersen .10 .05
❑ 641 Calvin Schiraldi .10 .05
❑ 642 Stan Jefferson .10 .05
❑ 643 Marc Sullivan .10 .05
❑ 644 Mark Grant .10 .05
❑ 645 Cliff Johnson .10 .05
❑ 646 Howard Johnson .10 .05
❑ 647 Dave Sax .10 .05
❑ 648 Dave Stewart .15 .07
❑ 649 Danny Heep .10 .05
❑ 650 Joe Johnson .10 .05
❑ 651 Bob Brower .10 .05
❑ 652 Rob Woodward .10 .05
❑ 653 John Mizerock .10 .05
❑ 654 Tim Pyznarski .10 .05
❑ 655 Luis Aquino .10 .05
❑ 656 Mickey Brantley .10 .05
❑ 657 Doyle Alexander .10 .05
❑ 658 Sammy Stewart .10 .05
❑ 659 Jim Acker .10 .05
❑ 660 Pete Ladd .10 .05

1987 Donruss Rookies

	MINT	NRMT
COMP.FACT.SET (56)	40.00	18.00
❑ 1 Mark McGwire	25.00	11.00
❑ 2 Eric Bell	.10	.05
❑ 3 Mark Williamson	.10	.05
❑ 4 Mike Greenwell	.75	.35
❑ 5 Ellis Burks XRC	1.50	.70
❑ 6 DeWayne Buice	.10	.05
❑ 7 Mark McLemore	.25	.11
❑ 8 Devon White	.75	.35
❑ 9 Willie Fraser	.10	.05
❑ 10 Les Lancaster	.10	.05
❑ 11 Ken Williams XRC	.10	.05
❑ 12 Matt Nokes XRC	.25	.11
❑ 13 Jeff M. Robinson	.10	.05
❑ 14 Bo Jackson	.75	.35
❑ 15 Kevin Seitzer XRC	.75	.35
❑ 16 Billy Ripken XRC	.10	.05
❑ 17 B.J. Surhoff	.75	.35
❑ 18 Chuck Crim	.10	.05
❑ 19 Mike Birkbeck	.10	.05
❑ 20 Chris Bosio	.25	.11
❑ 21 Les Straker	.10	.05
❑ 22 Mark Davidson	.10	.05
❑ 23 Gene Larkin XRC	.10	.05
❑ 24 Ken Gerhart	.10	.05
❑ 25 Luis Polonia XRC	.25	.11
❑ 26 Terry Steinbach	.75	.35
❑ 27 Mickey Brantley	.10	.05
❑ 28 Mike Stanley	.75	.35
❑ 29 Jerry Browne	.10	.05
❑ 30 Todd Benzinger XRC	.10	.05
❑ 31 Fred McGriff	1.00	.45
❑ 32 Mike Henneman XRC	.50	.23
❑ 33 Casey Candaele	.10	.05
❑ 34 Dave Magadan	.25	.11
❑ 35 David Cone	1.50	.70
❑ 36 Mike Jackson XRC	.25	.11
❑ 37 John Mitchell	.10	.05
❑ 38 Mike Dunne	.10	.05
❑ 39 John Smiley XRC	.10	.05
❑ 40 Joe Magrane XRC	.10	.05
❑ 41 Jim Lindeman	.10	.05
❑ 42 Shane Mack XRC**	.25	.11
❑ 43 Stan Jefferson	.10	.05

❑ 44 Benito Santiago	.25	.11
❑ 45 Matt Williams XRC	3.00	1.35
❑ 46 Dave Meads	.10	.05
❑ 47 Rafael Palmeiro	5.00	2.20
❑ 48 Bill Long	.10	.05
❑ 49 Bob Brower	.10	.05
❑ 50 James Steels	.10	.05
❑ 51 Paul Noce	.10	.05
❑ 52 Greg Maddux	10.00	4.50
❑ 53 Jeff Musselman	.10	.05
❑ 54 Brian Holton	.10	.05
❑ 55 Chuck Jackson	.10	.05
❑ 56 Checklist 1-56	.10	.05

1987 Donruss Opening Day

	MINT	NRMT
COMP.FACT.SET (272)	50.00	22.00
❑ 1 Doug DeCinces	.10	.05
❑ 2 Mike Witt	.10	.05
❑ 3 George Hendrick	.10	.05
❑ 4 Dick Schofield	.10	.05
❑ 5 Devon White	.15	.07
❑ 6 Butch Wynegar	.10	.05
❑ 7 Wally Joyner	.40	.18
❑ 8 Mark McLemore	.15	.07
❑ 9 Brian Downing	.10	.05
❑ 10 Gary Pettis	.10	.05
❑ 11 Bill Doran	.10	.05
❑ 12 Phil Garner	.15	.07
❑ 13 Jose Cruz	.15	.07
❑ 14 Kevin Bass	.10	.05
❑ 15 Mike Scott	.10	.05
❑ 16 Glenn Davis	.10	.05
❑ 17 Alan Ashby	.10	.05
❑ 18 Billy Hatcher	.10	.05
❑ 19 Craig Reynolds	.10	.05
❑ 20 Carney Lansford	.15	.07
❑ 21 Mike Davis	.10	.05
❑ 22 Reggie Jackson	.50	.23
❑ 23 Mickey Tettleton	.10	.05
❑ 24 Jose Canseco	1.25	.55
❑ 25 Rob Nelson	.10	.05
❑ 26 Tony Phillips	.10	.05
❑ 27 Dwayne Murphy	.10	.05
❑ 28 Alfredo Griffin	.10	.05
❑ 29 Curt Young	.10	.05
❑ 30 Willie Upshaw	.10	.05
❑ 31 Mike Sharperson	.10	.05
❑ 32 Rance Mulliniks	.10	.05
❑ 33 Ernie Whitt	.10	.05
❑ 34 Jesse Barfield	.10	.05
❑ 35 Tony Fernandez	.10	.05
❑ 36 Lloyd Moseby	.10	.05
❑ 37 Jimmy Key	.15	.07
❑ 38 Fred McGriff	.50	.23
❑ 39 George Bell	.10	.05
❑ 40 Dale Murphy	.40	.18
❑ 41 Rick Mahler	.10	.05
❑ 42 Ken Griffey	.15	.07
❑ 43 Andres Thomas	.10	.05
❑ 44 Dion James	.10	.05
❑ 45 Ozzie Virgil	.10	.05
❑ 46 Ken Oberkfell	.10	.05
❑ 47 Gary Roenicke	.10	.05
❑ 48 Glenn Hubbard	.10	.05
❑ 49 Bill Schroeder	.10	.05
❑ 50 Greg Brock	.10	.05
❑ 51 Billy Joe Robidoux	.10	.05
❑ 52 Glenn Braggs	.10	.05
❑ 53 Jim Gantner	.10	.05
❑ 54 Paul Molitor	.40	.18
❑ 55 Dale Sveum	.10	.05
❑ 56 Ted Higuera	.10	.05
❑ 57 Rob Deer	.10	.05
❑ 58 Robin Yount	.40	.18
❑ 59 Jim Lindeman	.10	.05
❑ 60 Vince Coleman	.10	.05
❑ 61 Tommy Herr	.10	.05
❑ 62 Terry Pendleton	.15	.07
❑ 63 John Tudor	.10	.05
❑ 64 Tony Pena	.10	.05
❑ 65 Ozzie Smith	.50	.23
❑ 66 Tito Landrum	.10	.05
❑ 67 Jack Clark	.15	.07
❑ 68 Bob Dernier	.10	.05
❑ 69 Rick Sutcliffe	.15	.07
❑ 70 Andre Dawson	.25	.11
❑ 71 Keith Moreland	.10	.05
❑ 72 Jody Davis	.10	.05
❑ 73 Brian Dayett	.10	.05
❑ 74 Leon Durham	.10	.05
❑ 75 Ryne Sandberg	.50	.23
❑ 76 Shawon Dunston	.10	.05
❑ 77 Mike Marshall	.10	.05
❑ 78 Bill Madlock	.15	.07
❑ 79 Orel Hershiser	.15	.07
❑ 80 Mike Ramsey	.10	.05
❑ 81 Ken Landreaux	.10	.05
❑ 82 Mike Scioscia	.10	.05
❑ 83 Franklin Stubbs	.10	.05
❑ 84 Mariano Duncan	.10	.05
❑ 85 Steve Sax	.10	.05
❑ 86 Mitch Webster	.10	.05
❑ 87 Reid Nichols	.10	.05
❑ 88 Tim Wallach	.10	.05
❑ 89 Floyd Youmans	.10	.05
❑ 90 Andres Galarraga	.40	.18
❑ 91 Hubie Brooks	.10	.05
❑ 92 Jeff Reed	.10	.05
❑ 93 Alonzo Powell	.10	.05
❑ 94 Vance Law	.10	.05
❑ 95 Bob Brenly	.10	.05
❑ 96 Will Clark	1.00	.45
❑ 97 Chili Davis	.25	.11
❑ 98 Mike Krukow	.10	.05
❑ 99 Jose Uribe	.10	.05
❑ 100 Chris Brown	.10	.05
❑ 101 Robby Thompson	.15	.07
❑ 102 Candy Maldonado	.10	.05
❑ 103 Jeff Leonard	.10	.05
❑ 104 Tom Candiotti	.10	.05
❑ 105 Chris Bando	.10	.05
❑ 106 Cory Snyder	.10	.05
❑ 107 Pat Tabler	.10	.05
❑ 108 Andre Thornton	.10	.05
❑ 109 Joe Carter	.40	.18
❑ 110 Tony Bernazard	.10	.05
❑ 111 Julio Franco	.15	.07
❑ 112 Brook Jacoby	.10	.05
❑ 113 Brett Butler	.15	.07
❑ 114 Donell Nixon	.10	.05
❑ 115 Alvin Davis	.10	.05
❑ 116 Mark Langston	.10	.05
❑ 117 Harold Reynolds	.15	.07
❑ 118 Ken Phelps	.10	.05
❑ 119 Mike Kingery	.10	.05
❑ 120 Dave Valle	.10	.05
❑ 121 Rey Quinones	.10	.05
❑ 122 Phil Bradley	.10	.05
❑ 123 Jim Presley	.10	.05
❑ 124 Keith Hernandez	.15	.07
❑ 125 Kevin McReynolds	.10	.05
❑ 126 Rafael Santana	.10	.05
❑ 127 Bob Ojeda	.10	.05
❑ 128 Darryl Strawberry	.25	.11
❑ 129 Mookie Wilson	.15	.07
❑ 130 Gary Carter	.25	.11
❑ 131 Tim Teufel	.10	.05
❑ 132 Howard Johnson	.10	.05
❑ 133 Cal Ripken	1.50	.70
❑ 134 Rick Burleson	.10	.05
❑ 135 Fred Lynn	.15	.07
❑ 136 Eddie Murray	.40	.18
❑ 137 Ray Knight	.10	.05
❑ 138 Alan Wiggins	.10	.05
❑ 139 John Shelby	.10	.05
❑ 140 Mike Boddicker	.10	.05
❑ 141 Ken Gerhart	.10	.05
❑ 142 Terry Kennedy	.10	.05
❑ 143 Steve Garvey	.25	.11
❑ 144 Marvell Wynne	.10	.05
❑ 145 Kevin Mitchell	.25	.11
❑ 146 Tony Gwynn	.75	.35
❑ 147 Joey Cora	.25	.11
❑ 148 Benito Santiago	.15	.07
❑ 149 Eric Show	.10	.05
❑ 150 Garry Templeton	.10	.05
❑ 151 Carmelo Martinez	.10	.05
❑ 152 Von Hayes	.10	.05
❑ 153 Lance Parrish	.15	.07
❑ 154 Milt Thompson	.10	.05
❑ 155 Mike Easler	.10	.05
❑ 156 Juan Samuel	.10	.05
❑ 157 Steve Jeltz	.10	.05
❑ 158 Glenn Wilson	.10	.05
❑ 159 Shane Rawley	.10	.05
❑ 160 Mike Schmidt	.75	.35
❑ 161 Andy Van Slyke	.15	.07
❑ 162 Johnny Ray	.10	.05
❑ 163A Barry Bonds ERR (Photo actually Johnny Ray wearing a black shirt)	250.00	110.00
❑ 163B Barry Bonds COR	15.00	6.75
❑ 164 Junior Ortiz	.10	.05
❑ 165 Rafael Belliard	.10	.05
❑ 166 Bob Patterson	.10	.05
❑ 167 Bobby Bonilla	.40	.18
❑ 168 Sid Bream	.10	.05
❑ 169 Jim Morrison	.10	.05
❑ 170 Jerry Browne	.10	.05
❑ 171 Scott Fletcher	.10	.05
❑ 172 Ruben Sierra	.50	.23
❑ 173 Larry Parrish	.10	.05
❑ 174 Pete O'Brien	.10	.05
❑ 175 Pete Incaviglia	.15	.07
❑ 176 Don Slaught	.10	.05
❑ 177 Oddibe McDowell	.10	.05
❑ 178 Charlie Hough	.15	.07
❑ 179 Steve Buechele	.10	.05
❑ 180 Bob Stanley	.10	.05
❑ 181 Wade Boggs	.40	.18
❑ 182 Jim Rice	.15	.07
❑ 183 Bill Buckner	.15	.07
❑ 184 Dwight Evans	.15	.07
❑ 185 Spike Owen	.10	.05
❑ 186 Don Baylor	.15	.07
❑ 187 Marc Sullivan	.10	.05
❑ 188 Marty Barrett	.10	.05
❑ 189 Dave Henderson	.10	.05
❑ 190 Bo Diaz	.10	.05
❑ 191 Barry Larkin	2.00	.90
❑ 192 Kal Daniels	.10	.05
❑ 193 Terry Francona	.15	.07
❑ 194 Tom Browning	.10	.05
❑ 195 Ron Oester	.10	.05
❑ 196 Buddy Bell	.15	.07
❑ 197 Eric Davis	.25	.11
❑ 198 Dave Parker	.15	.07
❑ 199 Steve Balboni	.10	.05
❑ 200 Danny Tartabull	.10	.05
❑ 201 Ed Hearn	.10	.05
❑ 202 Buddy Biancalana	.10	.05
❑ 203 Danny Jackson	.10	.05
❑ 204 Frank White	.15	.07
❑ 205 Bo Jackson	.40	.18
❑ 206 George Brett	.75	.35
❑ 207 Kevin Seitzer	.40	.18
❑ 208 Willie Wilson	.15	.07
❑ 209 Orlando Mercado	.10	.05
❑ 210 Darrell Evans	.15	.07
❑ 211 Larry Herndon	.10	.05
❑ 212 Jack Morris	.15	.07
❑ 213 Chet Lemon	.10	.05
❑ 214 Mike Heath	.10	.05
❑ 215 Darnell Coles	.10	.05
❑ 216 Alan Trammell	.25	.11

❑ 217 Terry Harper	.10	.05
❑ 218 Lou Whitaker	.15	.07
❑ 219 Gary Gaetti	.15	.07
❑ 220 Tom Nieto	.10	.05
❑ 221 Kirby Puckett	1.00	.45
❑ 222 Tom Brunansky	.10	.05
❑ 223 Greg Gagne	.10	.05
❑ 224 Dan Gladden	.10	.05
❑ 225 Mark Davidson	.10	.05
❑ 226 Bert Blyleven	.15	.07
❑ 227 Steve Lombardozzi	.10	.05
❑ 228 Kent Hrbek	.15	.07
❑ 229 Gary Redus	.10	.05
❑ 230 Ivan Calderon	.10	.05
❑ 231 Tim Hulett	.10	.05
❑ 232 Carlton Fisk	.40	.18
❑ 233 Greg Walker	.10	.05
❑ 234 Ron Karkovice	.10	.05
❑ 235 Ozzie Guillen	.10	.05
❑ 236 Harold Baines	.25	.11
❑ 237 Donnie Hill	.10	.05
❑ 238 Rich Dotson	.10	.05
❑ 239 Mike Pagliarulo	.10	.05
❑ 240 Joel Skinner	.10	.05
❑ 241 Don Mattingly	1.00	.45
❑ 242 Gary Ward	.10	.05
❑ 243 Dave Winfield	.40	.18
❑ 244 Dan Pasqua	.10	.05
❑ 245 Wayne Tolleson	.10	.05
❑ 246 Willie Randolph	.15	.07
❑ 247 Dennis Rasmussen	.10	.05
❑ 248 Rickey Henderson	.75	.35
❑ 249 Angels Logo	.05	.02
❑ 250 Astros Logo	.05	.02
❑ 251 A's Logo	.05	.02
❑ 252 Blue Jays Logo	.05	.02
❑ 253 Braves Logo	.05	.02
❑ 254 Brewers Logo	.05	.02
❑ 255 Cardinals Logo	.05	.02
❑ 256 Dodgers Logo	.05	.02
❑ 257 Expos Logo	.05	.02
❑ 258 Giants Logo	.05	.02
❑ 259 Indians Logo	.05	.02
❑ 260 Mariners Logo	.05	.02
❑ 261 Orioles Logo	.05	.02
❑ 262 Padres Logo	.05	.02
❑ 263 Phillies Logo	.05	.02
❑ 264 Pirates Logo	.05	.02
❑ 265 Rangers Logo	.05	.02
❑ 266 Red Sox Logo	.05	.02
❑ 267 Reds Logo	.05	.02
❑ 268 Royals Logo	.05	.02
❑ 269 Tigers Logo	.05	.02
❑ 270 Twins Logo	.05	.02
❑ 271 Chicago Logos	.05	.02
❑ 272 New York Logos	.05	.02

1988 Donruss

	MINT	NRMT
COMPLETE SET (660)	12.00	5.50
COMP.FACT.SET (660)	15.00	6.75
COMMON CARD (1-660)	.05	.02
COMMON SP (648-660)	.07	.03
COMP.MUSIAL PUZZLE	1.00	.45

❑ 1 Mark McGwire DK	1.00	.45
❑ 2 Tim Raines DK	.10	.05
❑ 3 Benito Santiago DK	.05	.02
❑ 4 Alan Trammell DK	.05	.02
❑ 5 Danny Tartabull DK	.05	.02
❑ 6 Ron Darling DK	.05	.02
❑ 7 Paul Molitor DK	.20	.09
❑ 8 Devon White DK	.05	.02
❑ 9 Andre Dawson DK	.10	.05
❑ 10 Julio Franco DK	.05	.02
❑ 11 Scott Fletcher DK	.05	.02
❑ 12 Tony Fernandez DK	.05	.02
❑ 13 Shane Rawley DK	.05	.02
❑ 14 Kal Daniels DK	.05	.02
❑ 15 Jack Clark DK	.10	.05
❑ 16 Dwight Evans DK	.05	.02
❑ 17 Tommy John DK	.05	.02
❑ 18 Andy Van Slyke DK	.05	.02
❑ 19 Gary Gaetti DK	.05	.02
❑ 20 Mark Langston DK	.05	.02
❑ 21 Will Clark DK	.20	.09
❑ 22 Glenn Hubbard DK	.05	.02
❑ 23 Billy Hatcher DK	.05	.02
❑ 24 Bob Welch DK	.05	.02
❑ 25 Ivan Calderon DK	.05	.02
❑ 26 Cal Ripken DK	.40	.18
❑ 27 DK Checklist 1-26	.05	.02
❑ 28 Mackey Sasser RR RC	.05	.02
❑ 29 Jeff Treadway RR RC	.05	.02
❑ 30 Mike Campbell RR	.05	.02
❑ 31 Lance Johnson RR RC	.20	.09
❑ 32 Nelson Liriano RR	.05	.02
❑ 33 Shawn Abner RR	.05	.02
❑ 34 Roberto Alomar RR RC	1.50	.70
❑ 35 Shawn Hillegas RR	.05	.02
❑ 36 Joey Meyer RR	.05	.02
❑ 37 Kevin Elster RR	.05	.02
❑ 38 Jose Lind RR RC	.05	.02
❑ 39 Kirt Manwaring RR RC	.05	.02
❑ 40 Mark Grace RR RC	1.00	.45
❑ 41 Jody Reed RR RC	.10	.05
❑ 42 John Farrell RR	.05	.02
❑ 43 Al Leiter RR RC	.40	.18
❑ 44 Gary Thurman RR	.05	.02
❑ 45 Vicente Palacios RR	.05	.02
❑ 46 Eddie Williams RR RC	.05	.02
❑ 47 Jack McDowell RR RC	.20	.09
❑ 48 Ken Dixon	.05	.02
❑ 49 Mike Birkbeck	.05	.02
❑ 50 Eric King	.05	.02
❑ 51 Roger Clemens	.50	.23
❑ 52 Pat Clements	.05	.02
❑ 53 Fernando Valenzuela	.10	.05
❑ 54 Mark Gubicza	.05	.02
❑ 55 Jay Howell	.05	.02
❑ 56 Floyd Youmans	.05	.02
❑ 57 Ed Correa	.05	.02
❑ 58 DeWayne Buice	.05	.02
❑ 59 Jose DeLeon	.05	.02
❑ 60 Danny Cox	.05	.02
❑ 61 Nolan Ryan	1.00	.45
❑ 62 Steve Bedrosian	.05	.02
❑ 63 Tom Browning	.05	.02
❑ 64 Mark Davis	.05	.02
❑ 65 R.J. Reynolds	.05	.02
❑ 66 Kevin Mitchell	.10	.05
❑ 67 Ken Oberkfell	.05	.02
❑ 68 Rick Sutcliffe	.10	.05
❑ 69 Dwight Gooden	.10	.05
❑ 70 Scott Bankhead	.05	.02
❑ 71 Bert Blyleven	.10	.05
❑ 72 Jimmy Key	.10	.05
❑ 73 Les Straker	.05	.02
❑ 74 Jim Clancy	.05	.02
❑ 75 Mike Moore	.05	.02
❑ 76 Ron Darling	.05	.02
❑ 77 Ed Lynch	.05	.02
❑ 78 Dale Murphy	.20	.09
❑ 79 Doug Drabek	.05	.02
❑ 80 Scott Garrelts	.05	.02
❑ 81 Ed Whitson	.05	.02
❑ 82 Rob Murphy	.05	.02
❑ 83 Shane Rawley	.05	.02
❑ 84 Greg Mathews	.05	.02
❑ 85 Jim Deshaies	.05	.02
❑ 86 Mike Witt	.05	.02
❑ 87 Donnie Hill	.05	.02
❑ 88 Jeff Reed	.05	.02
❑ 89 Mike Boddicker	.05	.02
❑ 90 Ted Higuera	.05	.02
❑ 91 Walt Terrell	.05	.02
❑ 92 Bob Stanley	.05	.02
❑ 93 Dave Righetti	.05	.02
❑ 94 Orel Hershiser	.10	.05
❑ 95 Chris Bando	.05	.02
❑ 96 Bret Saberhagen	.10	.05
❑ 97 Curt Young	.05	.02
❑ 98 Tim Burke	.05	.02
❑ 99 Charlie Hough	.10	.05
❑ 100A Checklist 28-137	.05	.02
❑ 100B Checklist 28-133	.05	.02
❑ 101 Bobby Witt	.05	.02
❑ 102 George Brett	.40	.18
❑ 103 Mickey Tettleton	.05	.02
❑ 104 Scott Bailes	.05	.02
❑ 105 Mike Pagliarulo	.05	.02
❑ 106 Mike Scioscia	.05	.02
❑ 107 Tom Brookens	.05	.02
❑ 108 Ray Knight	.05	.02
❑ 109 Dan Plesac	.05	.02
❑ 110 Wally Joyner	.15	.07
❑ 111 Bob Forsch	.05	.02
❑ 112 Mike Scott	.05	.02
❑ 113 Kevin Gross	.05	.02
❑ 114 Benito Santiago	.05	.02
❑ 115 Bob Kipper	.05	.02
❑ 116 Mike Krukow	.05	.02
❑ 117 Chris Bosio	.05	.02
❑ 118 Sid Fernandez	.05	.02
❑ 119 Jody Davis	.05	.02
❑ 120 Mike Morgan	.05	.02
❑ 121 Mark Eichhorn	.05	.02
❑ 122 Jeff Reardon	.10	.05
❑ 123 John Franco	.10	.05
❑ 124 Richard Dotson	.05	.02
❑ 125 Eric Bell	.05	.02
❑ 126 Juan Nieves	.05	.02
❑ 127 Jack Morris	.10	.05
❑ 128 Rick Rhoden	.05	.02
❑ 129 Rich Gedman	.05	.02
❑ 130 Ken Howell	.05	.02
❑ 131 Brook Jacoby	.05	.02
❑ 132 Danny Jackson	.05	.02
❑ 133 Gene Nelson	.05	.02
❑ 134 Neal Heaton	.05	.02
❑ 135 Willie Fraser	.05	.02
❑ 136 Jose Guzman	.05	.02
❑ 137 Ozzie Guillen	.05	.02
❑ 138 Bob Knepper	.05	.02
❑ 139 Mike Jackson RC*	.10	.05
❑ 140 Joe Magrane RC*	.05	.02
❑ 141 Jimmy Jones	.05	.02
❑ 142 Ted Power	.05	.02
❑ 143 Ozzie Virgil	.05	.02
❑ 144 Felix Fermin	.05	.02
❑ 145 Kelly Downs	.05	.02
❑ 146 Shawon Dunston	.05	.02
❑ 147 Scott Bradley	.05	.02
❑ 148 Dave Stieb	.05	.02
❑ 149 Frank Viola	.05	.02
❑ 150 Terry Kennedy	.05	.02
❑ 151 Bill Wegman	.05	.02
❑ 152 Matt Nokes RC*	.05	.02
❑ 153 Wade Boggs	.20	.09
❑ 154 Wayne Tolleson	.05	.02
❑ 155 Mariano Duncan	.05	.02
❑ 156 Julio Franco	.05	.02
❑ 157 Charlie Leibrandt	.05	.02
❑ 158 Terry Steinbach	.10	.05
❑ 159 Mike Fitzgerald	.05	.02
❑ 160 Jack Lazorko	.05	.02
❑ 161 Mitch Williams	.05	.02
❑ 162 Greg Walker	.05	.02
❑ 163 Alan Ashby	.05	.02
❑ 164 Tony Gwynn	.40	.18
❑ 165 Bruce Ruffin	.05	.02
❑ 166 Ron Robinson	.05	.02
❑ 167 Zane Smith	.05	.02
❑ 168 Junior Ortiz	.05	.02
❑ 169 Jamie Moyer	.10	.05
❑ 170 Tony Pena	.05	.02
❑ 171 Cal Ripken	.75	.35
❑ 172 B.J. Surhoff	.10	.05
❑ 173 Lou Whitaker	.10	.05

❑ 174	Ellis Burks RC	.40	.18
❑ 175	Ron Guidry	.05	.02
❑ 176	Steve Sax	.05	.02
❑ 177	Danny Tartabull	.05	.02
❑ 178	Carney Lansford	.10	.05
❑ 179	Casey Candaele	.05	.02
❑ 180	Scott Fletcher	.05	.02
❑ 181	Mark McLemore	.05	.02
❑ 182	Ivan Calderon	.05	.02
❑ 183	Jack Clark	.10	.05
❑ 184	Glenn Davis	.05	.02
❑ 185	Luis Aguayo	.05	.02
❑ 186	Bo Diaz	.05	.02
❑ 187	Stan Jefferson	.05	.02
❑ 188	Sid Bream	.05	.02
❑ 189	Bob Brenly	.05	.02
❑ 190	Dion James	.05	.02
❑ 191	Leon Durham	.05	.02
❑ 192	Jesse Orosco	.05	.02
❑ 193	Alvin Davis	.05	.02
❑ 194	Gary Gaetti	.10	.05
❑ 195	Fred McGriff	.20	.09
❑ 196	Steve Lombardozzi	.05	.02
❑ 197	Rance Mulliniks	.05	.02
❑ 198	Rey Quinones	.05	.02
❑ 199	Gary Carter	.15	.07
❑ 200A	Checklist 138-247	.05	.02
❑ 200B	Checklist 134-239	.05	.02
❑ 201	Keith Moreland	.05	.02
❑ 202	Ken Griffey	.10	.05
❑ 203	Tommy Gregg	.05	.02
❑ 204	Will Clark	.25	.11
❑ 205	John Kruk	.10	.05
❑ 206	Buddy Bell	.10	.05
❑ 207	Von Hayes	.05	.02
❑ 208	Tommy Herr	.05	.02
❑ 209	Craig Reynolds	.05	.02
❑ 210	Gary Pettis	.05	.02
❑ 211	Harold Baines	.10	.05
❑ 212	Vance Law	.05	.02
❑ 213	Ken Gerhart	.05	.02
❑ 214	Jim Gantner	.05	.02
❑ 215	Chet Lemon	.05	.02
❑ 216	Dwight Evans	.10	.05
❑ 217	Don Mattingly	.50	.23
❑ 218	Franklin Stubbs	.05	.02
❑ 219	Pat Tabler	.05	.02
❑ 220	Bo Jackson	.20	.09
❑ 221	Tony Phillips	.05	.02
❑ 222	Tim Wallach	.05	.02
❑ 223	Ruben Sierra	.05	.02
❑ 224	Steve Buechele	.05	.02
❑ 225	Frank White	.10	.05
❑ 226	Alfredo Griffin	.05	.02
❑ 227	Greg Swindell	.05	.02
❑ 228	Willie Randolph	.10	.05
❑ 229	Mike Marshall	.05	.02
❑ 230	Alan Trammell	.15	.07
❑ 231	Eddie Murray	.20	.09
❑ 232	Dale Sveum	.05	.02
❑ 233	Dick Schofield	.05	.02
❑ 234	Jose Oquendo	.05	.02
❑ 235	Bill Doran	.05	.02
❑ 236	Milt Thompson	.05	.02
❑ 237	Marvell Wynne	.05	.02
❑ 238	Bobby Bonilla	.10	.05
❑ 239	Chris Speier	.05	.02
❑ 240	Glenn Braggs	.05	.02
❑ 241	Wally Backman	.05	.02
❑ 242	Ryne Sandberg	.25	.11
❑ 243	Phil Bradley	.05	.02
❑ 244	Kelly Gruber	.05	.02
❑ 245	Tom Brunansky	.05	.02
❑ 246	Ron Oester	.05	.02
❑ 247	Bobby Thigpen	.05	.02
❑ 248	Fred Lynn	.05	.02
❑ 249	Paul Molitor	.20	.09
❑ 250	Darrell Evans	.10	.05
❑ 251	Gary Ward	.05	.02
❑ 252	Bruce Hurst	.05	.02
❑ 253	Bob Welch	.05	.02
❑ 254	Joe Carter	.20	.09
❑ 255	Willie Wilson	.05	.02
❑ 256	Mark McGwire	2.00	.90
❑ 257	Mitch Webster	.05	.02
❑ 258	Brian Downing	.05	.02
❑ 259	Mike Stanley	.10	.05
❑ 260	Carlton Fisk	.20	.09
❑ 261	Billy Hatcher	.05	.02
❑ 262	Glenn Wilson	.05	.02
❑ 263	Ozzie Smith	.25	.11
❑ 264	Randy Ready	.05	.02
❑ 265	Kurt Stillwell	.05	.02
❑ 266	David Palmer	.05	.02
❑ 267	Mike Diaz	.05	.02
❑ 268	Robby Thompson	.05	.02
❑ 269	Andre Dawson	.15	.07
❑ 270	Lee Guetterman	.05	.02
❑ 271	Willie Upshaw	.05	.02
❑ 272	Randy Bush	.05	.02
❑ 273	Larry Sheets	.05	.02
❑ 274	Rob Deer	.05	.02
❑ 275	Kirk Gibson	.10	.05
❑ 276	Marty Barrett	.05	.02
❑ 277	Rickey Henderson	.40	.18
❑ 278	Pedro Guerrero	.05	.02
❑ 279	Brett Butler	.10	.05
❑ 280	Kevin Seitzer	.10	.05
❑ 281	Mike Davis	.05	.02
❑ 282	Andres Galarraga	.15	.07
❑ 283	Devon White	.10	.05
❑ 284	Pete O'Brien	.05	.02
❑ 285	Jerry Hairston	.05	.02
❑ 286	Kevin Bass	.05	.02
❑ 287	Carmelo Martinez	.05	.02
❑ 288	Juan Samuel	.05	.02
❑ 289	Kal Daniels	.05	.02
❑ 290	Albert Hall	.05	.02
❑ 291	Andy Van Slyke	.10	.05
❑ 292	Lee Smith	.10	.05
❑ 293	Vince Coleman	.05	.02
❑ 294	Tom Niedenfuer	.05	.02
❑ 295	Robin Yount	.20	.09
❑ 296	Jeff M. Robinson	.05	.02
❑ 297	Todd Benzinger RC*	.05	.02
❑ 298	Dave Winfield	.20	.09
❑ 299	Mickey Hatcher	.05	.02
❑ 300A	Checklist 248-357	.05	.02
❑ 300B	Checklist 240-345	.05	.02
❑ 301	Bud Black	.05	.02
❑ 302	Jose Canseco	.30	.14
❑ 303	Tom Foley	.05	.02
❑ 304	Pete Incaviglia	.05	.02
❑ 305	Bob Boone	.10	.05
❑ 306	Bill Long	.05	.02
❑ 307	Willie McGee	.10	.05
❑ 308	Ken Caminiti RC	.50	.23
❑ 309	Darren Daulton	.10	.05
❑ 310	Tracy Jones	.05	.02
❑ 311	Greg Booker	.05	.02
❑ 312	Mike LaValliere	.05	.02
❑ 313	Chili Davis	.15	.07
❑ 314	Glenn Hubbard	.05	.02
❑ 315	Paul Noce	.05	.02
❑ 316	Keith Hernandez	.10	.05
❑ 317	Mark Langston	.05	.02
❑ 318	Keith Atherton	.05	.02
❑ 319	Tony Fernandez	.05	.02
❑ 320	Kent Hrbek	.10	.05
❑ 321	John Cerutti	.05	.02
❑ 322	Mike Kingery	.05	.02
❑ 323	Dave Magadan	.05	.02
❑ 324	Rafael Palmeiro	.40	.18
❑ 325	Jeff Dedmon	.05	.02
❑ 326	Barry Bonds	1.50	.70
❑ 327	Jeffrey Leonard	.05	.02
❑ 328	Tim Flannery	.05	.02
❑ 329	Dave Concepcion	.10	.05
❑ 330	Mike Schmidt	.40	.18
❑ 331	Bill Dawley	.05	.02
❑ 332	Larry Andersen	.05	.02
❑ 333	Jack Howell	.05	.02
❑ 334	Ken Williams RC	.05	.02
❑ 335	Bryn Smith	.05	.02
❑ 336	Bill Ripken RC*	.05	.02
❑ 337	Greg Brock	.05	.02
❑ 338	Mike Heath	.05	.02
❑ 339	Mike Greenwell	.05	.02
❑ 340	Claudell Washington	.05	.02
❑ 341	Jose Gonzalez	.05	.02
❑ 342	Mel Hall	.05	.02
❑ 343	Jim Eisenreich	.20	.09
❑ 344	Tony Bernazard	.05	.02
❑ 345	Tim Raines	.10	.05
❑ 346	Bob Brower	.05	.02
❑ 347	Larry Parrish	.05	.02
❑ 348	Thad Bosley	.05	.02
❑ 349	Dennis Eckersley	.10	.05
❑ 350	Cory Snyder	.05	.02
❑ 351	Rick Cerone	.05	.02
❑ 352	John Shelby	.05	.02
❑ 353	Larry Herndon	.05	.02
❑ 354	John Habyan	.05	.02
❑ 355	Chuck Crim	.05	.02
❑ 356	Gus Polidor	.05	.02
❑ 357	Ken Dayley	.05	.02
❑ 358	Danny Darwin	.05	.02
❑ 359	Lance Parrish	.05	.02
❑ 360	James Steels	.05	.02
❑ 361	Al Pedrique	.05	.02
❑ 362	Mike Aldrete	.05	.02
❑ 363	Juan Castillo	.05	.02
❑ 364	Len Dykstra	.10	.05
❑ 365	Luis Quinones	.05	.02
❑ 366	Jim Presley	.05	.02
❑ 367	Lloyd Moseby	.05	.02
❑ 368	Kirby Puckett	.50	.23
❑ 369	Eric Davis	.10	.05
❑ 370	Gary Redus	.05	.02
❑ 371	Dave Schmidt	.05	.02
❑ 372	Mark Clear	.05	.02
❑ 373	Dave Bergman	.05	.02
❑ 374	Charles Hudson	.05	.02
❑ 375	Calvin Schiraldi	.05	.02
❑ 376	Alex Trevino	.05	.02
❑ 377	Tom Candiotti	.05	.02
❑ 378	Steve Farr	.05	.02
❑ 379	Mike Gallego	.05	.02
❑ 380	Andy McGaffigan	.05	.02
❑ 381	Kirk McCaskill	.05	.02
❑ 382	Oddibe McDowell	.05	.02
❑ 383	Floyd Bannister	.05	.02
❑ 384	Denny Walling	.05	.02
❑ 385	Don Carman	.05	.02
❑ 386	Todd Worrell	.10	.05
❑ 387	Eric Show	.05	.02
❑ 388	Dave Parker	.10	.05
❑ 389	Rick Mahler	.05	.02
❑ 390	Mike Dunne	.05	.02
❑ 391	Candy Maldonado	.05	.02
❑ 392	Bob Dernier	.05	.02
❑ 393	Dave Valle	.05	.02
❑ 394	Ernie Whitt	.05	.02
❑ 395	Juan Berenguer	.05	.02
❑ 396	Mike Young	.05	.02
❑ 397	Mike Felder	.05	.02
❑ 398	Willie Hernandez	.05	.02
❑ 399	Jim Rice	.10	.05
❑ 400A	Checklist 358-467	.05	.02
❑ 400B	Checklist 346-451	.05	.02
❑ 401	Tommy John	.10	.05
❑ 402	Brian Holton	.05	.02
❑ 403	Carmen Castillo	.05	.02
❑ 404	Jamie Quirk	.05	.02
❑ 405	Dwayne Murphy	.05	.02
❑ 406	Jeff Parrett	.05	.02
❑ 407	Don Sutton	.20	.09
❑ 408	Jerry Browne	.05	.02
❑ 409	Jim Winn	.05	.02
❑ 410	Dave Smith	.05	.02
❑ 411	Shane Mack	.05	.02
❑ 412	Greg Gross	.05	.02
❑ 413	Nick Esasky	.05	.02
❑ 414	Damaso Garcia	.05	.02
❑ 415	Brian Fisher	.05	.02
❑ 416	Brian Dayett	.05	.02
❑ 417	Curt Ford	.05	.02
❑ 418	Mark Williamson	.05	.02
❑ 419	Bill Schroeder	.05	.02
❑ 420	Mike Henneman RC*	.10	.05
❑ 421	John Marzano	.05	.02
❑ 422	Ron Kittle	.05	.02
❑ 423	Matt Young	.05	.02
❑ 424	Steve Balboni	.05	.02
❑ 425	Luis Polonia RC*	.05	.02
❑ 426	Randy St.Claire	.05	.02
❑ 427	Greg Harris	.05	.02
❑ 428	Johnny Ray	.05	.02

❑ 429 Ray Searage	.05	.02
❑ 430 Ricky Horton	.05	.02
❑ 431 Gerald Young	.05	.02
❑ 432 Rick Schu	.05	.02
❑ 433 Paul O'Neill	.20	.09
❑ 434 Rich Gossage	.10	.05
❑ 435 John Cangelosi	.05	.02
❑ 436 Mike LaCoss	.05	.02
❑ 437 Gerald Perry	.05	.02
❑ 438 Dave Martinez	.05	.02
❑ 439 Darryl Strawberry	.10	.05
❑ 440 John Moses	.05	.02
❑ 441 Greg Gagne	.05	.02
❑ 442 Jesse Barfield	.05	.02
❑ 443 George Frazier	.05	.02
❑ 444 Garth Iorg	.05	.02
❑ 445 Ed Nunez	.05	.02
❑ 446 Rick Aguilera	.10	.05
❑ 447 Jerry Mumphrey	.05	.02
❑ 448 Rafael Ramirez	.05	.02
❑ 449 John Smiley RC*	.10	.05
❑ 450 Atlee Hammaker	.05	.02
❑ 451 Lance McCullers	.05	.02
❑ 452 Guy Hoffman	.05	.02
❑ 453 Chris James	.05	.02
❑ 454 Terry Pendleton	.10	.05
❑ 455 Dave Meads	.05	.02
❑ 456 Bill Buckner	.10	.05
❑ 457 John Pawlowski	.05	.02
❑ 458 Bob Sebra	.05	.02
❑ 459 Jim Dwyer	.05	.02
❑ 460 Jay Aldrich	.05	.02
❑ 461 Frank Tanana	.05	.02
❑ 462 Oil Can Boyd	.05	.02
❑ 463 Dan Pasqua	.05	.02
❑ 464 Tim Crews RC	.05	.02
❑ 465 Andy Allanson	.05	.02
❑ 466 Bill Pecota RC*	.05	.02
❑ 467 Steve Ontiveros	.05	.02
❑ 468 Hubie Brooks	.05	.02
❑ 469 Paul Kilgus	.05	.02
❑ 470 Dale Mohorcic	.05	.02
❑ 471 Dan Quisenberry	.05	.02
❑ 472 Dave Stewart	.10	.05
❑ 473 Dave Clark	.05	.02
❑ 474 Joel Skinner	.05	.02
❑ 475 Dave Anderson	.05	.02
❑ 476 Dan Petry	.05	.02
❑ 477 Carl Nichols	.05	.02
❑ 478 Ernest Riles	.05	.02
❑ 479 George Hendrick	.05	.02
❑ 480 John Morris	.05	.02
❑ 481 Manny Hernandez	.05	.02
❑ 482 Jeff Stone	.05	.02
❑ 483 Chris Brown	.05	.02
❑ 484 Mike Bielecki	.05	.02
❑ 485 Dave Dravecky	.10	.05
❑ 486 Rick Manning	.05	.02
❑ 487 Bill Almon	.05	.02
❑ 488 Jim Sundberg	.05	.02
❑ 489 Ken Phelps	.05	.02
❑ 490 Tom Henke	.05	.02
❑ 491 Dan Gladden	.05	.02
❑ 492 Barry Larkin	.20	.09
❑ 493 Fred Manrique	.05	.02
❑ 494 Mike Griffin	.05	.02
❑ 495 Mark Knudson	.05	.02
❑ 496 Bill Madlock	.10	.05
❑ 497 Tim Stoddard	.05	.02
❑ 498 Sam Horn RC	.05	.02
❑ 499 Tracy Woodson RC	.05	.02
❑ 500A Checklist 468-577	.05	.02
❑ 500B Checklist 452-557	.05	.02
❑ 501 Ken Schrom	.05	.02
❑ 502 Angel Salazar	.05	.02
❑ 503 Eric Plunk	.05	.02
❑ 504 Joe Hesketh	.05	.02
❑ 505 Greg Minton	.05	.02
❑ 506 Geno Petralli	.05	.02
❑ 507 Bob James	.05	.02
❑ 508 Robbie Wine	.05	.02
❑ 509 Jeff Calhoun	.05	.02
❑ 510 Steve Lake	.05	.02
❑ 511 Mark Grant	.05	.02
❑ 512 Frank Williams	.05	.02
❑ 513 Jeff Blauser RC	.20	.09
❑ 514 Bob Walk	.05	.02
❑ 515 Craig Lefferts	.05	.02
❑ 516 Manny Trillo	.05	.02
❑ 517 Jerry Reed	.05	.02
❑ 518 Rick Leach	.05	.02
❑ 519 Mark Davidson	.05	.02
❑ 520 Jeff Ballard	.05	.02
❑ 521 Dave Stapleton	.05	.02
❑ 522 Pat Sheridan	.05	.02
❑ 523 Al Nipper	.05	.02
❑ 524 Steve Trout	.05	.02
❑ 525 Jeff Hamilton	.05	.02
❑ 526 Tommy Hinzo	.05	.02
❑ 527 Lonnie Smith	.05	.02
❑ 528 Greg Cadaret	.05	.02
❑ 529 Bob McClure UER (Rob on front)	.05	.02
❑ 530 Chuck Finley	.15	.07
❑ 531 Jeff Russell	.05	.02
❑ 532 Steve Lyons	.05	.02
❑ 533 Terry Puhl	.05	.02
❑ 534 Eric Nolte	.05	.02
❑ 535 Kent Tekulve	.05	.02
❑ 536 Pat Pacillo	.05	.02
❑ 537 Charlie Puleo	.05	.02
❑ 538 Tom Prince	.05	.02
❑ 539 Greg Maddux	1.00	.45
❑ 540 Jim Lindeman	.05	.02
❑ 541 Pete Stanicek	.05	.02
❑ 542 Steve Kiefer	.05	.02
❑ 543A Jim Morrison ERR (No decimal before lifetime average)	.20	.09
❑ 543B Jim Morrison COR	.05	.02
❑ 544 Spike Owen	.05	.02
❑ 545 Jay Buhner RC	.40	.18
❑ 546 Mike Devereaux RC	.10	.05
❑ 547 Jerry Don Gleaton	.05	.02
❑ 548 Jose Rijo	.05	.02
❑ 549 Dennis Martinez	.10	.05
❑ 550 Mike Loynd	.05	.02
❑ 551 Darrell Miller	.05	.02
❑ 552 Dave LaPoint	.05	.02
❑ 553 John Tudor	.05	.02
❑ 554 Rocky Childress	.05	.02
❑ 555 Wally Ritchie	.05	.02
❑ 556 Terry McGriff	.05	.02
❑ 557 Dave Leiper	.05	.02
❑ 558 Jeff D. Robinson	.05	.02
❑ 559 Jose Uribe	.05	.02
❑ 560 Ted Simmons	.10	.05
❑ 561 Les Lancaster	.05	.02
❑ 562 Keith A. Miller RC	.05	.02
❑ 563 Harold Reynolds	.10	.05
❑ 564 Gene Larkin RC*	.05	.02
❑ 565 Cecil Fielder	.15	.07
❑ 566 Roy Smalley	.05	.02
❑ 567 Duane Ward	.05	.02
❑ 568 Bill Wilkinson	.05	.02
❑ 569 Howard Johnson	.05	.02
❑ 570 Frank DiPino	.05	.02
❑ 571 Pete Smith RC	.05	.02
❑ 572 Darnell Coles	.05	.02
❑ 573 Don Robinson	.05	.02
❑ 574 Rob Nelson UER (Career 0 RBI, but 1 RBI in '87)	.05	.02
❑ 575 Dennis Rasmussen	.05	.02
❑ 576 Steve Jeltz UER (Photo actually Juan Samuel; Samuel noted for one batting glove and black bat)	.05	.02
❑ 577 Tom Pagnozzi RC	.05	.02
❑ 578 Ty Gainey	.05	.02
❑ 579 Gary Lucas	.05	.02
❑ 580 Ron Hassey	.05	.02
❑ 581 Herm Winningham	.05	.02
❑ 582 Rene Gonzales RC	.05	.02
❑ 583 Brad Komminsk	.05	.02
❑ 584 Doyle Alexander	.05	.02
❑ 585 Jeff Sellers	.05	.02
❑ 586 Bill Gullickson	.05	.02
❑ 587 Tim Belcher	.10	.05
❑ 588 Doug Jones RC	.20	.09
❑ 589 Melido Perez RC	.05	.02
❑ 590 Rick Honeycutt	.05	.02
❑ 591 Pascual Perez	.05	.02
❑ 592 Curt Wilkerson	.05	.02
❑ 593 Steve Howe	.05	.02
❑ 594 John Davis	.05	.02
❑ 595 Storm Davis	.05	.02
❑ 596 Sammy Stewart	.05	.02
❑ 597 Neil Allen	.05	.02
❑ 598 Alejandro Pena	.05	.02
❑ 599 Mark Thurmond	.05	.02
❑ 600A Checklist 578-660 BC1-BC26	.05	.02
❑ 600B Checklist 558-660	.05	.02
❑ 601 Jose Mesa RC	.15	.07
❑ 602 Don August	.05	.02
❑ 603 Terry Leach SP	.07	.03
❑ 604 Tom Newell	.05	.02
❑ 605 Randall Byers SP	.07	.03
❑ 606 Jim Gott	.05	.02
❑ 607 Harry Spilman	.05	.02
❑ 608 John Candelaria	.05	.02
❑ 609 Mike Brumley	.05	.02
❑ 610 Mickey Brantley	.05	.02
❑ 611 Jose Nunez SP	.07	.03
❑ 612 Tom Nieto	.05	.02
❑ 613 Rick Reuschel	.05	.02
❑ 614 Lee Mazzilli SP	.07	.03
❑ 615 Scott Lusader	.05	.02
❑ 616 Bobby Meacham	.05	.02
❑ 617 Kevin McReynolds SP	.07	.03
❑ 618 Gene Garber	.05	.02
❑ 619 Barry Lyons SP	.07	.03
❑ 620 Randy Myers	.15	.07
❑ 621 Donnie Moore	.05	.02
❑ 622 Domingo Ramos	.05	.02
❑ 623 Ed Romero	.05	.02
❑ 624 Greg Myers RC	.05	.02
❑ 625 Ripken Family: Cal Ripken Sr., Cal Ripken Jr., Billy Ripken	.40	.18
❑ 626 Pat Perry	.05	.02
❑ 627 Andres Thomas SP	.07	.03
❑ 628 Matt Williams SP RC	.75	.35
❑ 629 Dave Hengel	.05	.02
❑ 630 Jeff Musselman SP	.07	.03
❑ 631 Tim Laudner	.05	.02
❑ 632 Bob Ojeda SP	.07	.03
❑ 633 Rafael Santana	.05	.02
❑ 634 Wes Gardner	.05	.02
❑ 635 Roberto Kelly RC SP	.20	.09
❑ 636 Mike Flanagan SP	.07	.03
❑ 637 Jay Bell RC	.40	.18
❑ 638 Bob Melvin	.05	.02
❑ 639 D.Berryhill RC UER (Bats: Swithch)	.05	.02
❑ 640 David Wells SP RC	1.00	.45
❑ 641 Stan Musial PUZ	.20	.09
❑ 642 Doug Sisk	.05	.02
❑ 643 Keith Hughes	.05	.02
❑ 644 Tom Glavine RC	1.25	.55
❑ 645 Al Newman	.05	.02
❑ 646 Scott Sanderson	.05	.02
❑ 647 Scott Terry	.05	.02
❑ 648 Tim Teufel SP	.07	.03
❑ 649 Garry Templeton SP	.07	.03
❑ 650 Manny Lee SP	.07	.03
❑ 651 Roger McDowell SP	.07	.03
❑ 652 Mookie Wilson SP	.20	.09
❑ 653 David Cone SP	.10	.05
❑ 654 Ron Gant SP RC	.25	.11
❑ 655 Joe Price SP	.07	.03
❑ 656 George Bell SP	.10	.05
❑ 657 Gregg Jefferies SP RC	.20	.09
❑ 658 T.Stottlemyre SP RC	.20	.09
❑ 659 G.Berroa SP RC	.25	.11
❑ 660 Jerry Royster SP	.07	.03
❑ XX Kirby Puckett Blister Pack	2.00	.90

1988 Donruss Rookies

	MINT	NRMT
COMP.FACT.SET (56)	12.00	5.50
❑ 1 Mark Grace	2.50	1.10

	Card	MINT	NRMT
❑	2 Mike Campbell	.15	.07
❑	3 Todd Frohwirth	.15	.07
❑	4 Dave Stapleton	.15	.07
❑	5 Shawn Abner	.15	.07
❑	6 Jose Cecena	.15	.07
❑	7 Dave Gallagher	.15	.07
❑	8 Mark Parent	.15	.07
❑	9 Cecil Espy	.15	.07
❑	10 Pete Smith	.15	.07
❑	11 Jay Buhner	1.00	.45
❑	12 Pat Borders XRC	.30	.14
❑	13 Doug Jennings	.15	.07
❑	14 Brady Anderson XRC	1.50	.70
❑	15 Pete Stanicek	.15	.07
❑	16 Roberto Kelly	.30	.14
❑	17 Jeff Treadway	.15	.07
❑	18 Walt Weiss XRC*	1.00	.45
❑	19 Paul Gibson	.15	.07
❑	20 Tim Crews	.15	.07
❑	21 Melido Perez	.15	.07
❑	22 Steve Peters	.15	.07
❑	23 Craig Worthington	.15	.07
❑	24 John Trautwein	.15	.07
❑	25 DeWayne Vaughn	.15	.07
❑	26 David Wells	3.00	1.35
❑	27 Al Leiter	1.50	.70
❑	28 Tim Belcher	.30	.14
❑	29 Johnny Paredes	.15	.07
❑	30 Chris Sabo XRC	.30	.14
❑	31 Damon Berryhill	.15	.07
❑	32 Randy Milligan XRC*	.15	.07
❑	33 Gary Thurman	.15	.07
❑	34 Kevin Elster	.15	.07
❑	35 Roberto Alomar	5.00	2.20
❑	36 E.Martinez UER XRC	3.00	1.35
	Photo actually Edwin Nunez		
❑	37 Todd Stottlemyre	.30	.14
❑	38 Joey Meyer	.15	.07
❑	39 Carl Nichols	.15	.07
❑	40 Jack McDowell	.60	.25
❑	41 Jose Bautista	.15	.07
❑	42 Sil Campusano	.15	.07
❑	43 John Dopson	.15	.07
❑	44 Jody Reed	.30	.14
❑	45 Darrin Jackson XRC*	.15	.07
❑	46 Mike Capel	.15	.07
❑	47 Ron Gant	.30	.14
❑	48 John Davis	.15	.07
❑	49 Kevin Coffman	.15	.07
❑	50 Cris Carpenter XRC	.15	.07
❑	51 Mackey Sasser	.15	.07
❑	52 Luis Alicea XRC	.15	.07
❑	53 Bryan Harvey XRC	.30	.14
❑	54 Steve Ellsworth	.15	.07
❑	55 Mike Macfarlane XRC	.15	.07
❑	56 Checklist 1-56	.15	.07

1989 Donruss

	MINT	NRMT
COMPLETE SET (660)	25.00	11.00
COMP.FACT.SET (672)	30.00	13.50
COMP.SPAHN PUZZLE	1.00	.45

	Card	MINT	NRMT
❑	1 Mike Greenwell DK	.05	.02
❑	2 Bobby Bonilla DK DP	.10	.05
❑	3 Pete Incaviglia DK	.05	.02
❑	4 Chris Sabo DK DP	.05	.02
❑	5 Robin Yount DK	.10	.05
❑	6 Tony Gwynn DK DP	.20	.09
❑	7 Carlton Fisk DK UER	.10	.05
	(OF on back)		
❑	8 Cory Snyder DK	.05	.02
❑	9 David Cone DK UER	.05	.02
	("hurdlers")		
❑	10 Kevin Seitzer DK	.05	.02
❑	11 Rick Reuschel DK	.05	.02
❑	12 Johnny Ray DK	.05	.02
❑	13 Dave Schmidt DK	.05	.02
❑	14 Andres Galarraga DK	.05	.02
❑	15 Kirk Gibson DK	.05	.02
❑	16 Fred McGriff DK	.10	.05
❑	17 Mark Grace DK	.10	.05
❑	18 Jeff M. Robinson DK	.05	.02
❑	19 Vince Coleman DK DP	.05	.02
❑	20 Dave Henderson DK	.05	.02
❑	21 Harold Reynolds DK	.05	.02
❑	22 Gerald Perry DK	.05	.02
❑	23 Frank Viola DK	.05	.02
❑	24 Steve Bedrosian DK	.05	.02
❑	25 Glenn Davis DK	.05	.02
❑	26 Don Mattingly DK UER	.15	.07
	(Doesn't mention Don's previous DK in 1985)		
❑	27 DK Checklist 1-26 DP	.05	.02
❑	28 S.Alomar Jr. RR RC	.25	.11
❑	29 Steve Searcy RR	.05	.02
❑	30 Cameron Drew RR	.05	.02
❑	31 Gary Sheffield RR RC	1.25	.55
❑	32 Erik Hanson RR RC	.10	.05
❑	33 Ken Griffey Jr. RR RC	15.00	6.75
❑	34 Greg W. Harris RR RC	.05	.02
❑	35 Gregg Jefferies RR	.10	.05
❑	36 Luis Medina RR	.05	.02
❑	37 Carlos Quintana RR RC	.05	.02
❑	38 Felix Jose RR RC	.05	.02
❑	39 Cris Carpenter RR RC*	.05	.02
❑	40 Ron Jones RR	.05	.02
❑	41 Dave West RR RC	.05	.02
❑	42 R.Johnson RC RR UER	3.00	1.35
	Card says born in 1964 he was born in 1963		
❑	43 Mike Harkey RR RC	.05	.02
❑	44 P.Harnisch RR DP RC	.25	.11
❑	45 Tom Gordon RR DP RC	.20	.09
❑	46 Gregg Olson RC RR DP	.20	.09
❑	47 Alex Sanchez RR DP	.05	.02
❑	48 Ruben Sierra	.05	.02
❑	49 Rafael Palmeiro	.25	.11
❑	50 Ron Gant	.10	.05
❑	51 Cal Ripken	.75	.35
❑	52 Wally Joyner	.10	.05
❑	53 Gary Carter	.15	.07
❑	54 Andy Van Slyke	.10	.05
❑	55 Robin Yount	.20	.09
❑	56 Pete Incaviglia	.05	.02
❑	57 Greg Brock	.05	.02
❑	58 Melido Perez	.05	.02
❑	59 Craig Lefferts	.05	.02
❑	60 Gary Pettis	.05	.02
❑	61 Danny Tartabull	.05	.02
❑	62 Guillermo Hernandez	.05	.02
❑	63 Ozzie Smith	.25	.11
❑	64 Gary Gaetti	.10	.05
❑	65 Mark Davis	.05	.02
❑	66 Lee Smith	.10	.05
❑	67 Dennis Eckersley	.15	.07
❑	68 Wade Boggs	.20	.09
❑	69 Mike Scott	.05	.02
❑	70 Fred McGriff	.20	.09
❑	71 Tom Browning	.05	.02
❑	72 Claudell Washington	.05	.02
❑	73 Mel Hall	.05	.02
❑	74 Don Mattingly	.50	.23
❑	75 Steve Bedrosian	.05	.02
❑	76 Juan Samuel	.05	.02
❑	77 Mike Scioscia	.05	.02
❑	78 Dave Righetti	.05	.02
❑	79 Alfredo Griffin	.05	.02
❑	80 Eric Davis UER	.10	.05
	(165 games in 1988, should be 135)		
❑	81 Juan Berenguer	.05	.02
❑	82 Todd Worrell	.05	.02
❑	83 Joe Carter	.15	.07
❑	84 Steve Sax	.05	.02
❑	85 Frank White	.10	.05
❑	86 John Kruk	.10	.05
❑	87 Rance Mulliniks	.05	.02
❑	88 Alan Ashby	.05	.02
❑	89 Charlie Leibrandt	.05	.02
❑	90 Frank Tanana	.05	.02
❑	91 Jose Canseco	.20	.09
❑	92 Barry Bonds	.75	.35
❑	93 Harold Reynolds	.05	.02
❑	94 Mark McLemore	.05	.02
❑	95 Mark McGwire	1.00	.45
❑	96 Eddie Murray	.20	.09
❑	97 Tim Raines	.10	.05
❑	98 Robby Thompson	.05	.02
❑	99 Kevin McReynolds	.05	.02
❑	100 Checklist 28-137	.05	.02
❑	101 Carlton Fisk	.20	.09
❑	102 Dave Martinez	.05	.02
❑	103 Glenn Braggs	.05	.02
❑	104 Dale Murphy	.20	.09
❑	105 Ryne Sandberg	.25	.11
❑	106 Dennis Martinez	.10	.05
❑	107 Pete O'Brien	.05	.02
❑	108 Dick Schofield	.05	.02
❑	109 Henry Cotto	.05	.02
❑	110 Mike Marshall	.05	.02
❑	111 Keith Moreland	.05	.02
❑	112 Tom Brunansky	.05	.02
❑	113 Kelly Gruber UER	.05	.02
	(Wrong birthdate)		
❑	114 Brook Jacoby	.05	.02
❑	115 Keith Brown	.05	.02
❑	116 Matt Nokes	.05	.02
❑	117 Keith Hernandez	.10	.05
❑	118 Bob Forsch	.05	.02
❑	119 Bert Blyleven UER	.10	.05
	(... 3000 strikeouts in 1987, should be 1986)		
❑	120 Willie Wilson	.05	.02
❑	121 Tommy Gregg	.05	.02
❑	122 Jim Rice	.10	.05
❑	123 Bob Knepper	.05	.02
❑	124 Danny Jackson	.05	.02
❑	125 Eric Plunk	.05	.02
❑	126 Brian Fisher	.05	.02
❑	127 Mike Pagliarulo	.05	.02
❑	128 Tony Gwynn	.40	.18
❑	129 Lance McCullers	.05	.02
❑	130 Andres Galarraga	.15	.07
❑	131 Jose Uribe	.05	.02
❑	132 Kirk Gibson UER	.10	.05
	(Wrong birthdate)		
❑	133 David Palmer	.05	.02
❑	134 R.J. Reynolds	.05	.02
❑	135 Greg Walker	.05	.02
❑	136 Kirk McCaskill UER	.05	.02
	(Wrong birthdate)		
❑	137 Shawon Dunston	.05	.02
❑	138 Andy Allanson	.05	.02
❑	139 Rob Murphy	.05	.02
❑	140 Mike Aldrete	.05	.02
❑	141 Terry Kennedy	.05	.02
❑	142 Scott Fletcher	.05	.02

❑ 143 Steve Balboni .05 .02
❑ 144 Bret Saberhagen .10 .05
❑ 145 Ozzie Virgil .05 .02
❑ 146 Dale Sveum .05 .02
❑ 147 Darryl Strawberry .10 .05
❑ 148 Harold Baines .10 .05
❑ 149 George Bell .05 .02
❑ 150 Dave Parker .10 .05
❑ 151 Bobby Bonilla .10 .05
❑ 152 Mookie Wilson .10 .05
❑ 153 Ted Power .05 .02
❑ 154 Nolan Ryan 1.00 .45
❑ 155 Jeff Reardon .10 .05
❑ 156 Tim Wallach .05 .02
❑ 157 Jamie Moyer .05 .02
❑ 158 Rich Gossage .10 .05
❑ 159 Dave Winfield .20 .09
❑ 160 Von Hayes .05 .02
❑ 161 Willie McGee .10 .05
❑ 162 Rich Gedman .05 .02
❑ 163 Tony Pena .05 .02
❑ 164 Mike Morgan .05 .02
❑ 165 Charlie Hough .10 .05
❑ 166 Mike Stanley .05 .02
❑ 167 Andre Dawson .15 .07
❑ 168 Joe Boever .05 .02
❑ 169 Pete Stanicek .05 .02
❑ 170 Bob Boone .10 .05
❑ 171 Ron Darling .05 .02
❑ 172 Bob Walk .05 .02
❑ 173 Rob Deer .05 .02
❑ 174 Steve Buechele .05 .02
❑ 175 Ted Higuera .05 .02
❑ 176 Ozzie Guillen .05 .02
❑ 177 Candy Maldonado .05 .02
❑ 178 Doyle Alexander .05 .02
❑ 179 Mark Gubicza .05 .02
❑ 180 Alan Trammell .15 .07
❑ 181 Vince Coleman .05 .02
❑ 182 Kirby Puckett .50 .23
❑ 183 Chris Brown .05 .02
❑ 184 Marty Barrett .05 .02
❑ 185 Stan Javier .05 .02
❑ 186 Mike Greenwell .05 .02
❑ 187 Billy Hatcher .05 .02
❑ 188 Jimmy Key .10 .05
❑ 189 Nick Esasky .05 .02
❑ 190 Don Slaught .05 .02
❑ 191 Cory Snyder .05 .02
❑ 192 John Candelaria .05 .02
❑ 193 Mike Schmidt .40 .18
❑ 194 Kevin Gross .05 .02
❑ 195 John Tudor .05 .02
❑ 196 Neil Allen .05 .02
❑ 197 Orel Hershiser .10 .05
❑ 198 Kal Daniels .05 .02
❑ 199 Kent Hrbek .10 .05
❑ 200 Checklist 138-247 .05 .02
❑ 201 Joe Magrane .05 .02
❑ 202 Scott Bailes .05 .02
❑ 203 Tim Belcher .05 .02
❑ 204 George Brett .40 .18
❑ 205 Benito Santiago .05 .02
❑ 206 Tony Fernandez .05 .02
❑ 207 Gerald Young .05 .02
❑ 208 Bo Jackson .15 .07
❑ 209 Chet Lemon .05 .02
❑ 210 Storm Davis .05 .02
❑ 211 Doug Drabek .05 .02
❑ 212 Mickey Brantley UER .05 .02
(Photo actually Nelson Simmons)
❑ 213 Devon White .10 .05
❑ 214 Dave Stewart .10 .05
❑ 215 Dave Schmidt .05 .02
❑ 216 Bryn Smith .05 .02
❑ 217 Brett Butler .10 .05
❑ 218 Bob Ojeda .05 .02
❑ 219 Steve Rosenberg .05 .02
❑ 220 Hubie Brooks .05 .02
❑ 221 B.J. Surhoff .10 .05
❑ 222 Rick Mahler .05 .02
❑ 223 Rick Sutcliffe .10 .05
❑ 224 Neal Heaton .05 .02
❑ 225 Mitch Williams .05 .02
❑ 226 Chuck Finley .10 .05
❑ 227 Mark Langston .05 .02
❑ 228 Jesse Orosco .05 .02
❑ 229 Ed Whitson .05 .02
❑ 230 Terry Pendleton .10 .05
❑ 231 Lloyd Moseby .05 .02
❑ 232 Greg Swindell .05 .02
❑ 233 John Franco .10 .05
❑ 234 Jack Morris .10 .05
❑ 235 Howard Johnson .05 .02
❑ 236 Glenn Davis .05 .02
❑ 237 Frank Viola .05 .02
❑ 238 Kevin Seitzer .05 .02
❑ 239 Gerald Perry .05 .02
❑ 240 Dwight Evans .10 .05
❑ 241 Jim Deshaies .05 .02
❑ 242 Bo Diaz .05 .02
❑ 243 Carney Lansford .10 .05
❑ 244 Mike LaValliere .05 .02
❑ 245 Rickey Henderson .40 .18
❑ 246 Roberto Alomar .30 .14
❑ 247 Jimmy Jones .05 .02
❑ 248 Pascual Perez .05 .02
❑ 249 Will Clark .20 .09
❑ 250 Fernando Valenzuela .10 .05
❑ 251 Shane Rawley .05 .02
❑ 252 Sid Bream .05 .02
❑ 253 Steve Lyons .05 .02
❑ 254 Brian Downing .05 .02
❑ 255 Mark Grace .20 .09
❑ 256 Tom Candiotti .05 .02
❑ 257 Barry Larkin .20 .09
❑ 258 Mike Krukow .05 .02
❑ 259 Billy Ripken .05 .02
❑ 260 Cecilio Guante .05 .02
❑ 261 Scott Bradley .05 .02
❑ 262 Floyd Bannister .05 .02
❑ 263 Pete Smith .05 .02
❑ 264 Jim Gantner UER .05 .02
(Wrong birthdate)
❑ 265 Roger McDowell .05 .02
❑ 266 Bobby Thigpen .05 .02
❑ 267 Jim Clancy .05 .02
❑ 268 Terry Steinbach .10 .05
❑ 269 Mike Dunne .05 .02
❑ 270 Dwight Gooden .10 .05
❑ 271 Mike Heath .05 .02
❑ 272 Dave Smith .05 .02
❑ 273 Keith Atherton .05 .02
❑ 274 Tim Burke .05 .02
❑ 275 Damon Berryhill .05 .02
❑ 276 Vance Law .05 .02
❑ 277 Rich Dotson .05 .02
❑ 278 Lance Parrish .05 .02
❑ 279 Denny Walling .05 .02
❑ 280 Roger Clemens .50 .23
❑ 281 Greg Mathews .05 .02
❑ 282 Tom Niedenfuer .05 .02
❑ 283 Paul Kilgus .05 .02
❑ 284 Jose Guzman .05 .02
❑ 285 Calvin Schiraldi .05 .02
❑ 286 Charlie Puleo UER .05 .02
(Career ERA 4.24, should be 4.23)
❑ 287 Joe Orsulak .05 .02
❑ 288 Jack Howell .05 .02
❑ 289 Kevin Elster .05 .02
❑ 290 Jose Lind .05 .02
❑ 291 Paul Molitor .20 .09
❑ 292 Cecil Espy .05 .02
❑ 293 Bill Wegman .05 .02
❑ 294 Dan Pasqua .05 .02
❑ 295 Scott Garrelts UER .05 .02
(Wrong birthdate)
❑ 296 Walt Terrell .05 .02
❑ 297 Ed Hearn .05 .02
❑ 298 Lou Whitaker .10 .05
❑ 299 Ken Dayley .05 .02
❑ 300 Checklist 248-357 .05 .02
❑ 301 Tommy Herr .05 .02
❑ 302 Mike Brumley .05 .02
❑ 303 Ellis Burks .15 .07
❑ 304 Curt Young UER .05 .02
(Wrong birthdate)
❑ 305 Jody Reed .05 .02
❑ 306 Bill Doran .05 .02
❑ 307 David Wells .05 .02
❑ 308 Ron Robinson .05 .02
❑ 309 Rafael Santana .05 .02
❑ 310 Julio Franco .05 .02
❑ 311 Jack Clark .05 .02
❑ 312 Chris James .05 .02
❑ 313 Milt Thompson .05 .02
❑ 314 John Shelby .05 .02
❑ 315 Al Leiter .20 .09
❑ 316 Mike Davis .05 .02
❑ 317 Chris Sabo RC* .05 .02
❑ 318 Greg Gagne .05 .02
❑ 319 Jose Oquendo .05 .02
❑ 320 John Farrell .05 .02
❑ 321 Franklin Stubbs .05 .02
❑ 322 Kurt Stillwell .05 .02
❑ 323 Shawn Abner .05 .02
❑ 324 Mike Flanagan .05 .02
❑ 325 Kevin Bass .05 .02
❑ 326 Pat Tabler .05 .02
❑ 327 Mike Henneman .05 .02
❑ 328 Rick Honeycutt .05 .02
❑ 329 John Smiley .05 .02
❑ 330 Rey Quinones .05 .02
❑ 331 Johnny Ray .05 .02
❑ 332 Bob Welch .05 .02
❑ 333 Larry Sheets .05 .02
❑ 334 Jeff Parrett .05 .02
❑ 335 Rick Reuschel UER .05 .02
(For Don Robinson, should be Jeff)
❑ 336 Randy Myers .10 .05
❑ 337 Ken Williams .05 .02
❑ 338 Andy McGaffigan .05 .02
❑ 339 Joey Meyer .05 .02
❑ 340 Dion James .05 .02
❑ 341 Les Lancaster .05 .02
❑ 342 Tom Foley .05 .02
❑ 343 Geno Petralli .05 .02
❑ 344 Dan Petry .05 .02
❑ 345 Alvin Davis .05 .02
❑ 346 Mickey Hatcher .05 .02
❑ 347 Marvell Wynne .05 .02
❑ 348 Danny Cox .05 .02
❑ 349 Dave Stieb .05 .02
❑ 350 Jay Bell .15 .07
❑ 351 Jeff Treadway .05 .02
❑ 352 Luis Salazar .05 .02
❑ 353 Len Dykstra .10 .05
❑ 354 Juan Agosto .05 .02
❑ 355 Gene Larkin .05 .02
❑ 356 Steve Farr .05 .02
❑ 357 Paul Assenmacher .05 .02
❑ 358 Todd Benzinger .05 .02
❑ 359 Larry Andersen .05 .02
❑ 360 Paul O'Neill .20 .09
❑ 361 Ron Hassey .05 .02
❑ 362 Jim Gott .05 .02
❑ 363 Ken Phelps .05 .02
❑ 364 Tim Flannery .05 .02
❑ 365 Randy Ready .05 .02
❑ 366 Nelson Santovenia .05 .02
❑ 367 Kelly Downs .05 .02
❑ 368 Danny Heep .05 .02
❑ 369 Phil Bradley .05 .02
❑ 370 Jeff D. Robinson .05 .02
❑ 371 Ivan Calderon .05 .02
❑ 372 Mike Witt .05 .02
❑ 373 Greg Maddux .60 .25
❑ 374 Carmen Castillo .05 .02
❑ 375 Jose Rijo .05 .02
❑ 376 Joe Price .05 .02
❑ 377 Rene Gonzales .05 .02
❑ 378 Oddibe McDowell .05 .02
❑ 379 Jim Presley .05 .02
❑ 380 Brad Wellman .05 .02
❑ 381 Tom Glavine .20 .09
❑ 382 Dan Plesac .05 .02
❑ 383 Wally Backman .05 .02
❑ 384 Dave Gallagher .05 .02
❑ 385 Tom Henke .05 .02
❑ 386 Luis Polonia .05 .02
❑ 387 Junior Ortiz .05 .02
❑ 388 David Cone .10 .05
❑ 389 Dave Bergman .05 .02
❑ 390 Danny Darwin .05 .02
❑ 391 Dan Gladden .05 .02

❑ 392 John Dopson .05 .02
❑ 393 Frank DiPino .05 .02
❑ 394 Al Nipper .05 .02
❑ 395 Willie Randolph .10 .05
❑ 396 Don Carman .05 .02
❑ 397 Scott Terry .05 .02
❑ 398 Rick Cerone .05 .02
❑ 399 Tom Pagnozzi .05 .02
❑ 400 Checklist 358-467 .05 .02
❑ 401 Mickey Tettleton .05 .02
❑ 402 Curtis Wilkerson .05 .02
❑ 403 Jeff Russell .05 .02
❑ 404 Pat Perry .05 .02
❑ 405 Jose Alvarez .05 .02
❑ 406 Rick Schu .05 .02
❑ 407 Sherman Corbett .05 .02
❑ 408 Dave Magadan .05 .02
❑ 409 Bob Kipper .05 .02
❑ 410 Don August .05 .02
❑ 411 Bob Brower .05 .02
❑ 412 Chris Bosio .05 .02
❑ 413 Jerry Reuss .05 .02
❑ 414 Atlee Hammaker .05 .02
❑ 415 Jim Walewander .05 .02
❑ 416 Mike Macfarlane RC* .05 .02
❑ 417 Pat Sheridan .05 .02
❑ 418 Pedro Guerrero .05 .02
❑ 419 Allan Anderson .05 .02
❑ 420 Mark Parent .05 .02
❑ 421 Bob Stanley .05 .02
❑ 422 Mike Gallego .05 .02
❑ 423 Bruce Hurst .05 .02
❑ 424 Dave Meads .05 .02
❑ 425 Jesse Barfield .05 .02
❑ 426 Rob Dibble RC* .10 .05
❑ 427 Joel Skinner .05 .02
❑ 428 Ron Kittle .05 .02
❑ 429 Rick Rhoden .05 .02
❑ 430 Bob Dernier .05 .02
❑ 431 Steve Jeltz .05 .02
❑ 432 Rick Dempsey .05 .02
❑ 433 Roberto Kelly .10 .05
❑ 434 Dave Anderson .05 .02
❑ 435 Herm Winningham .05 .02
❑ 436 Al Newman .05 .02
❑ 437 Jose DeLeon .05 .02
❑ 438 Doug Jones .05 .02
❑ 439 Brian Holton .05 .02
❑ 440 Jeff Montgomery .10 .05
❑ 441 Dickie Thon .05 .02
❑ 442 Cecil Fielder .10 .05
❑ 443 John Fishel .05 .02
❑ 444 Jerry Don Gleaton .05 .02
❑ 445 Paul Gibson .05 .02
❑ 446 Walt Weiss .05 .02
❑ 447 Glenn Wilson .05 .02
❑ 448 Mike Moore .05 .02
❑ 449 Chili Davis .10 .05
❑ 450 Dave Henderson .05 .02
❑ 451 Jose Bautista .05 .02
❑ 452 Rex Hudler .05 .02
❑ 453 Bob Brenly .05 .02
❑ 454 Mackey Sasser .05 .02
❑ 455 Daryl Boston .05 .02
❑ 456 Mike R. Fitzgerald .05 .02
❑ 457 Jeffrey Leonard .05 .02
❑ 458 Bruce Sutter .05 .02
❑ 459 Mitch Webster .05 .02
❑ 460 Joe Hesketh .05 .02
❑ 461 Bobby Witt .05 .02
❑ 462 Stew Cliburn .05 .02
❑ 463 Scott Bankhead .05 .02
❑ 464 Ramon Martinez RC .25 .11
❑ 465 Dave Leiper .05 .02
❑ 466 Luis Alicea RC* .05 .02
❑ 467 John Cerutti .05 .02
❑ 468 Ron Washington .05 .02
❑ 469 Jeff Reed .05 .02
❑ 470 Jeff M. Robinson .05 .02
❑ 471 Sid Fernandez .05 .02
❑ 472 Terry Puhl .05 .02
❑ 473 Charlie Lea .05 .02
❑ 474 Israel Sanchez .05 .02
❑ 475 Bruce Benedict .05 .02
❑ 476 Oil Can Boyd .05 .02
❑ 477 Craig Reynolds .05 .02
❑ 478 Frank Williams .05 .02
❑ 479 Greg Cadaret .05 .02
❑ 480 Randy Kramer .05 .02
❑ 481 Dave Eiland .05 .02
❑ 482 Eric Show .05 .02
❑ 483 Garry Templeton .05 .02
❑ 484 Wallace Johnson .05 .02
❑ 485 Kevin Mitchell .10 .05
❑ 486 Tim Crews .05 .02
❑ 487 Mike Maddux .05 .02
❑ 488 Dave LaPoint .05 .02
❑ 489 Fred Manrique .05 .02
❑ 490 Greg Minton .05 .02
❑ 491 Doug Dascenzo UER .05 .02
(Photo actually
Damon Berryhill)
❑ 492 Willie Upshaw .05 .02
❑ 493 Jack Armstrong RC* .05 .02
❑ 494 Kirt Manwaring .05 .02
❑ 495 Jeff Ballard .05 .02
❑ 496 Jeff Kunkel .05 .02
❑ 497 Mike Campbell .05 .02
❑ 498 Gary Thurman .05 .02
❑ 499 Zane Smith .05 .02
❑ 500 Checklist 468-577 DP .05 .02
❑ 501 Mike Birkbeck .05 .02
❑ 502 Terry Leach .05 .02
❑ 503 Shawn Hillegas .05 .02
❑ 504 Manny Lee .05 .02
❑ 505 Doug Jennings .05 .02
❑ 506 Ken Oberkfell .05 .02
❑ 507 Tim Teufel .05 .02
❑ 508 Tom Brookens .05 .02
❑ 509 Rafael Ramirez .05 .02
❑ 510 Fred Toliver .05 .02
❑ 511 Brian Holman RC* .05 .02
❑ 512 Mike Bielecki .05 .02
❑ 513 Jeff Pico .05 .02
❑ 514 Charles Hudson .05 .02
❑ 515 Bruce Ruffin .05 .02
❑ 516 L.McWilliams UER .05 .02
New Richland, should
be North Richland
❑ 517 Jeff Sellers .05 .02
❑ 518 John Costello .05 .02
❑ 519 Brady Anderson RC .40 .18
❑ 520 Craig McMurtry .05 .02
❑ 521 Ray Hayward DP .05 .02
❑ 522 Drew Hall DP .05 .02
❑ 523 Mark Lemke DP RC .15 .07
❑ 524 Oswald Peraza DP .05 .02
❑ 525 Bryan Harvey DP RC* .05 .02
❑ 526 Rick Aguilera DP .10 .05
❑ 527 Tom Prince DP .05 .02
❑ 528 Mark Clear DP .05 .02
❑ 529 Jerry Browne DP .05 .02
❑ 530 Juan Castillo DP .05 .02
❑ 531 Jack McDowell DP .10 .05
❑ 532 Chris Speier DP .05 .02
❑ 533 Darrell Evans DP .10 .05
❑ 534 Luis Aquino DP .05 .02
❑ 535 Eric King DP .05 .02
❑ 536 Ken Hill DP RC .20 .09
❑ 537 Randy Bush DP .05 .02
❑ 538 Shane Mack DP .05 .02
❑ 539 Tom Bolton DP .05 .02
❑ 540 Gene Nelson DP .05 .02
❑ 541 Wes Gardner DP .05 .02
❑ 542 Ken Caminiti DP .10 .05
❑ 543 Duane Ward DP .05 .02
❑ 544 Norm Charlton DP RC .10 .05
❑ 545 Hal Morris DP RC .20 .09
❑ 546 Rich Yett DP .05 .02
❑ 547 H.Meulens DP RC .05 .02
❑ 548 Greg A. Harris DP .05 .02
❑ 549 Darren Daulton DP .10 .05
(Posing as right-
handed hitter)
❑ 550 Jeff Hamilton DP .05 .02
❑ 551 Luis Aguayo DP .05 .02
❑ 552 Tim Leary DP .05 .02
(Resembles M.Marshall)
❑ 553 Ron Oester DP .05 .02
❑ 554 S.Lombardozzi DP .05 .02
❑ 555 Tim Jones DP .05 .02
❑ 556 Bud Black DP .05 .02
❑ 557 Alejandro Pena DP .05 .02
❑ 558 Jose DeJesus DP .05 .02
❑ 559 D.Rasmussen DP .05 .02
❑ 560 Pat Borders DP RC* .10 .05
❑ 561 Craig Biggio DP RC .75 .35
❑ 562 Luis DeLosSantos DP .05 .02
❑ 563 Fred Lynn DP .05 .02
❑ 564 Todd Burns DP .05 .02
❑ 565 Felix Fermin DP .05 .02
❑ 566 Darnell Coles DP .05 .02
❑ 567 Willie Fraser DP .05 .02
❑ 568 Glenn Hubbard DP .05 .02
❑ 569 Craig Worthington DP .05 .02
❑ 570 Johnny Paredes DP .05 .02
❑ 571 Don Robinson DP .05 .02
❑ 572 Barry Lyons DP .05 .02
❑ 573 Bill Long DP .05 .02
❑ 574 Tracy Jones DP .05 .02
❑ 575 Juan Nieves DP .05 .02
❑ 576 Andres Thomas DP .05 .02
❑ 577 Rolando Roomes DP .05 .02
❑ 578 Luis Rivera UER DP .05 .02
(Wrong birthdate)
❑ 579 Chad Kreuter DP RC .05 .02
❑ 580 Tony Armas DP .05 .02
❑ 581 Jay Buhner .10 .05
❑ 582 Ricky Horton DP .05 .02
❑ 583 Andy Hawkins DP .05 .02
❑ 584 Sil Campusano .05 .02
❑ 585 Dave Clark .05 .02
❑ 586 Van Snider DP .05 .02
❑ 587 Todd Frohwirth DP .05 .02
❑ 588 W.Spahn DP PUZ .20 .09
❑ 589 William Brennan .05 .02
❑ 590 German Gonzalez .05 .02
❑ 591 Ernie Whitt DP .05 .02
❑ 592 Jeff Blauser .10 .05
❑ 593 Spike Owen DP .05 .02
❑ 594 Matt Williams .15 .07
❑ 595 Lloyd McClendon DP .05 .02
❑ 596 Steve Ontiveros .05 .02
❑ 597 Scott Medvin .05 .02
❑ 598 Hipolito Pena DP .05 .02
❑ 599 Jerald Clark DP RC .05 .02
❑ 600A CL 578-660 DP .05 .02
635 KurtSchilling
❑ 600B CL 578-660 DP .05 .02
635 CurtSchilling;
MVP's not listed
on checklist card
❑ 600C CL 578-660 DP .05 .02
635 CurtSchilling;
MVP's listed
following 660
❑ 601 Carmelo Martinez DP .05 .02
❑ 602 Mike LaCoss .05 .02
❑ 603 Mike Devereaux .05 .02
❑ 604 Alex Madrid DP .05 .02
❑ 605 Gary Redus DP .05 .02
❑ 606 Lance Johnson .10 .05
❑ 607 Terry Clark DP .05 .02
❑ 608 Manny Trillo DP .05 .02
❑ 609 Scott Jordan RC .10 .05
❑ 610 Jay Howell DP .05 .02
❑ 611 Francisco Melendez .05 .02
❑ 612 Mike Boddicker .05 .02
❑ 613 Kevin Brown DP .40 .18
❑ 614 Dave Valle .05 .02
❑ 615 Tim Laudner DP .05 .02
❑ 616 Andy Nezelek UER .05 .02
(Wrong birthdate)
❑ 617 Chuck Crim .05 .02
❑ 618 Jack Savage DP .05 .02
❑ 619 Adam Peterson .05 .02
❑ 620 Todd Stottlemyre .15 .07
❑ 621 Lance Blankenship RC .05 .02
❑ 622 Miguel Garcia DP .05 .02
❑ 623 Keith A. Miller DP .05 .02
❑ 624 Ricky Jordan DP RC* .10 .05
❑ 625 Ernest Riles DP .05 .02
❑ 626 John Moses DP .05 .02
❑ 627 Nelson Liriano DP .05 .02
❑ 628 Mike Smithson DP .05 .02
❑ 629 Scott Sanderson .05 .02
❑ 630 Dale Mohorcic .05 .02
❑ 631 Marvin Freeman DP .05 .02

Card	MINT	NRMT
❑ 632 Mike Young DP	.05	.02
❑ 633 Dennis Lamp	.05	.02
❑ 634 Dante Bichette DP RC	.40	.18
❑ 635 Curt Schilling DP RC	4.00	1.80
❑ 636 Scott May DP	.05	.02
❑ 637 Mike Schooler	.05	.02
❑ 638 Rick Leach	.05	.02
❑ 639 Tom Lampkin UER (Throws Left, should be Throws Right)	.05	.02
❑ 640 Brian Meyer	.05	.02
❑ 641 Brian Harper	.05	.02
❑ 642 John Smoltz RC	.40	.18
❑ 643 Jose Canseco (40/40 Club)	.10	.05
❑ 644 Bill Schroeder	.05	.02
❑ 645 Edgar Martinez	.15	.07
❑ 646 Dennis Cook RC	.05	.02
❑ 647 Barry Jones	.05	.02
❑ 648 Orel Hershiser (59 and Counting)	.10	.05
❑ 649 Rod Nichols	.05	.02
❑ 650 Jody Davis	.05	.02
❑ 651 Bob Milacki	.05	.02
❑ 652 Mike Jackson	.05	.02
❑ 653 Derek Lilliquist RC	.05	.02
❑ 654 Paul Mirabella	.05	.02
❑ 655 Mike Diaz	.05	.02
❑ 656 Jeff Musselman	.05	.02
❑ 657 Jerry Reed	.05	.02
❑ 658 Kevin Blankenship	.05	.02
❑ 659 Wayne Tolleson	.05	.02
❑ 660 Eric Hetzel	.05	.02

1989 Donruss Rookies

	MINT	NRMT
COMP.FACT.SET (56)	20.00	9.00
❑ 1 Gary Sheffield	1.25	.55
❑ 2 Gregg Jefferies	.10	.05
❑ 3 Ken Griffey Jr.	15.00	6.75
❑ 4 Tom Gordon	.20	.09
❑ 5 Billy Spiers RC	.05	.02
❑ 6 Deion Sanders RC	.40	.18
❑ 7 Donn Pall	.05	.02
❑ 8 Steve Carter	.05	.02
❑ 9 Francisco Oliveras	.05	.02
❑ 10 Steve Wilson	.05	.02
❑ 11 Bob Geren	.05	.02
❑ 12 Tony Castillo	.05	.02
❑ 13 Kenny Rogers RC	.20	.09
❑ 14 Carlos Martinez RC	.05	.02
❑ 15 Edgar Martinez	.15	.07
❑ 16 Jim Abbott RC*	.20	.09
❑ 17 Torey Lovullo RC	.05	.02
❑ 18 Mark Carreon	.05	.02
❑ 19 Geronimo Berroa	.05	.02
❑ 20 Luis Medina	.05	.02
❑ 21 Sandy Alomar Jr.	.25	.11
❑ 22 Bob Milacki	.05	.02
❑ 23 Joe Girardi RC	.20	.09
❑ 24 German Gonzalez	.05	.02
❑ 25 Craig Worthington	.05	.02
❑ 26 Jerome Walton	.20	.09
❑ 27 Gary Wayne	.05	.02
❑ 28 Tim Jones	.05	.02
❑ 29 Dante Bichette	.40	.18
❑ 30 Alexis Infante	.05	.02
❑ 31 Ken Hill	.20	.09
❑ 32 Dwight Smith RC	.10	.05
❑ 33 Luis de los Santos	.05	.02
❑ 34 Eric Yelding	.05	.02
❑ 35 Gregg Olson	.20	.09
❑ 36 Phil Stephenson	.05	.02
❑ 37 Ken Patterson	.05	.02
❑ 38 Rick Wrona	.05	.02
❑ 39 Mike Brumley	.05	.02
❑ 40 Cris Carpenter	.05	.02
❑ 41 Jeff Brantley RC	.15	.07
❑ 42 Ron Jones	.05	.02
❑ 43 Randy Johnson	3.00	1.35
❑ 44 Kevin Brown	.40	.18
❑ 45 Ramon Martinez	.10	.05
❑ 46 Greg W.Harris	.05	.02
❑ 47 Steve Finley RC	.50	.23
❑ 48 Randy Kramer	.05	.02
❑ 49 Erik Hanson	.10	.05
❑ 50 Matt Merullo	.05	.02
❑ 51 Mike Devereaux	.05	.02
❑ 52 Clay Parker	.05	.02
❑ 53 Omar Vizquel RC	.50	.23
❑ 54 Derek Lilliquist	.05	.02
❑ 55 Junior Felix RC	.05	.02
❑ 56 Checklist 1-56	.05	.02

1989 Donruss Baseball's Best

	MINT	NRMT
COMP.FACT.SET (336)	100.00	45.00
❑ 1 Don Mattingly	1.25	.55
❑ 2 Tom Glavine	.50	.23
❑ 3 Bert Blyleven	.25	.11
❑ 4 Andre Dawson	.40	.18
❑ 5 Pete O'Brien	.15	.07
❑ 6 Eric Davis	.25	.11
❑ 7 George Brett	1.00	.45
❑ 8 Glenn Davis	.15	.07
❑ 9 Ellis Burks	.40	.18
❑ 10 Kirk Gibson	.25	.11
❑ 11 Carlton Fisk	.50	.23
❑ 12 Andres Galarraga	.40	.18
❑ 13 Alan Trammell	.40	.18
❑ 14 Dwight Gooden	.25	.11
❑ 15 Paul Molitor	.50	.23
❑ 16 Roger McDowell	.15	.07
❑ 17 Doug Drabek	.15	.07
❑ 18 Kent Hrbek	.25	.11
❑ 19 Vince Coleman	.15	.07
❑ 20 Steve Sax	.15	.07
❑ 21 Roberto Alomar	.75	.35
❑ 22 Carney Lansford	.25	.11
❑ 23 Will Clark	.50	.23
❑ 24 Alvin Davis	.15	.07
❑ 25 Bobby Thigpen	.15	.07
❑ 26 Ryne Sandberg	.60	.25
❑ 27 Devon White	.25	.11
❑ 28 Mike Greenwell	.15	.07
❑ 29 Dale Murphy	.50	.23
❑ 30 Jeff Ballard	.15	.07
❑ 31 Kelly Gruber	.15	.07
❑ 32 Julio Franco	.15	.07
❑ 33 Bobby Bonilla	.25	.11
❑ 34 Tim Wallach	.15	.07
❑ 35 Lou Whitaker	.25	.11
❑ 36 Jay Howell	.15	.07
❑ 37 Greg Maddux	1.50	.70
❑ 38 Bill Doran	.15	.07
❑ 39 Danny Tartabull	.15	.07
❑ 40 Darryl Strawberry	.25	.11
❑ 41 Ron Darling	.15	.07
❑ 42 Tony Gwynn	1.00	.45
❑ 43 Mark McGwire	2.50	1.10
❑ 44 Ozzie Smith	.60	.25
❑ 45 Andy Van Slyke	.25	.11
❑ 46 Juan Berenguer	.15	.07
❑ 47 Von Hayes	.15	.07
❑ 48 Tony Fernandez	.15	.07
❑ 49 Eric Plunk	.15	.07
❑ 50 Ernest Riles	.15	.07
❑ 51 Harold Reynolds	.15	.07
❑ 52 Andy Hawkins	.15	.07
❑ 53 Robin Yount	.50	.23
❑ 54 Danny Jackson	.15	.07
❑ 55 Nolan Ryan	2.50	1.10
❑ 56 Joe Carter	.40	.18
❑ 57 Jose Canseco	.50	.23
❑ 58 Jody Davis	.15	.07
❑ 59 Lance Parrish	.15	.07
❑ 60 Mitch Williams	.15	.07
❑ 61 Brook Jacoby	.15	.07
❑ 62 Tom Browning	.15	.07
❑ 63 Kurt Stillwell	.15	.07
❑ 64 Rafael Ramirez	.15	.07
❑ 65 Roger Clemens	1.25	.55
❑ 66 Mike Scioscia	.15	.07
❑ 67 Dave Gallagher	.15	.07
❑ 68 Mark Langston	.15	.07
❑ 69 Chet Lemon	.15	.07
❑ 70 Kevin McReynolds	.15	.07
❑ 71 Rob Deer	.15	.07
❑ 72 Tommy Herr	.15	.07
❑ 73 Barry Bonds	2.00	.90
❑ 74 Frank Viola	.15	.07
❑ 75 Pedro Guerrero	.15	.07
❑ 76 Dave Righetti UER (ML total of 7 wins incorrect)	.15	.07
❑ 77 Bruce Hurst	.15	.07
❑ 78 Rickey Henderson	1.00	.45
❑ 79 Robby Thompson	.15	.07
❑ 80 Randy Johnson	6.00	2.70
❑ 81 Harold Baines	.25	.11
❑ 82 Calvin Schiraldi	.15	.07
❑ 83 Kirk McCaskill	.15	.07
❑ 84 Lee Smith	.25	.11
❑ 85 John Smoltz	.75	.35
❑ 86 Mickey Tettleton	.15	.07
❑ 87 Jimmy Key	.25	.11
❑ 88 Rafael Palmeiro	.60	.25
❑ 89 Sid Bream	.15	.07
❑ 90 Dennis Martinez	.25	.11
❑ 91 Frank Tanana	.15	.07
❑ 92 Eddie Murray	.50	.23
❑ 93 Shawon Dunston	.15	.07
❑ 94 Mike Scott	.15	.07
❑ 95 Bret Saberhagen	.25	.11
❑ 96 David Cone	.25	.11
❑ 97 Kevin Elster	.15	.07
❑ 98 Jack Clark	.15	.07
❑ 99 Dave Stewart	.25	.11
❑ 100 Jose Oquendo	.15	.07
❑ 101 Jose Lind	.15	.07
❑ 102 Gary Gaetti	.25	.11
❑ 103 Ricky Jordan	.15	.07
❑ 104 Fred McGriff	.50	.23
❑ 105 Don Slaught	.15	.07
❑ 106 Jose Uribe	.15	.07
❑ 107 Jeffrey Leonard	.15	.07
❑ 108 Lee Guetterman	.15	.07
❑ 109 Chris Bosio	.15	.07
❑ 110 Barry Larkin	.50	.23
❑ 111 Ruben Sierra	.15	.07
❑ 112 Greg Swindell	.15	.07
❑ 113 Gary Sheffield	2.50	1.10
❑ 114 Lonnie Smith	.15	.07
❑ 115 Chili Davis	.25	.11
❑ 116 Damon Berryhill	.15	.07
❑ 117 Tom Candiotti	.15	.07
❑ 118 Kal Daniels	.15	.07

❑ 119 Mark Gubicza	.15	.07
❑ 120 Jim Deshaies	.15	.07
❑ 121 Dwight Evans	.25	.11
❑ 122 Mike Morgan	.15	.07
❑ 123 Dan Pasqua	.15	.07
❑ 124 Bryn Smith	.15	.07
❑ 125 Doyle Alexander	.15	.07
❑ 126 Howard Johnson	.15	.07
❑ 127 Chuck Crim	.15	.07
❑ 128 Darren Daulton	.25	.11
❑ 129 Jeff Robinson	.15	.07
❑ 130 Kirby Puckett	1.25	.55
❑ 131 Joe Magrane	.15	.07
❑ 132 Jesse Barfield	.15	.07
❑ 133 Mark Davis UER (Photo actually Dave Leiper)	.15	.07
❑ 134 Dennis Eckersley	.40	.18
❑ 135 Mike Krukow	.15	.07
❑ 136 Jay Buhner	.25	.11
❑ 137 Ozzie Guillen	.15	.07
❑ 138 Rick Sutcliffe	.25	.11
❑ 139 Wally Joyner	.25	.11
❑ 140 Wade Boggs	.50	.23
❑ 141 Jeff Treadway	.15	.07
❑ 142 Cal Ripken	2.00	.90
❑ 143 Dave Stieb	.15	.07
❑ 144 Pete Incaviglia	.15	.07
❑ 145 Bob Walk	.15	.07
❑ 146 Nelson Santovenia	.15	.07
❑ 147 Mike Heath	.15	.07
❑ 148 Willie Randolph	.25	.11
❑ 149 Paul Kilgus	.15	.07
❑ 150 Billy Hatcher	.15	.07
❑ 151 Steve Farr	.15	.07
❑ 152 Gregg Jefferies	.25	.11
❑ 153 Randy Myers	.25	.11
❑ 154 Garry Templeton	.15	.07
❑ 155 Walt Weiss	.15	.07
❑ 156 Terry Pendleton	.25	.11
❑ 157 John Smiley	.15	.07
❑ 158 Greg Gagne	.15	.07
❑ 159 Len Dykstra	.25	.11
❑ 160 Nelson Liriano	.15	.07
❑ 161 Alvaro Espinoza	.15	.07
❑ 162 Rick Reuschel	.15	.07
❑ 163 Omar Vizquel UER Photo actually Darnell Coles	.40	.18
❑ 164 Clay Parker	.15	.07
❑ 165 Dan Plesac	.15	.07
❑ 166 John Franco	.25	.11
❑ 167 Scott Fletcher	.15	.07
❑ 168 Cory Snyder	.15	.07
❑ 169 Bo Jackson	.40	.18
❑ 170 Tommy Gregg	.15	.07
❑ 171 Jim Abbott	.25	.11
❑ 172 Jerome Walton	.50	.23
❑ 173 Doug Jones	.15	.07
❑ 174 Todd Benzinger	.15	.07
❑ 175 Frank White	.25	.11
❑ 176 Craig Biggio	2.00	.90
❑ 177 John Dopson	.15	.07
❑ 178 Alfredo Griffin	.15	.07
❑ 179 Melido Perez	.15	.07
❑ 180 Tim Burke	.15	.07
❑ 181 Matt Nokes	.15	.07
❑ 182 Gary Carter	.40	.18
❑ 183 Ted Higuera	.15	.07
❑ 184 Ken Howell	.15	.07
❑ 185 Rey Quinones	.15	.07
❑ 186 Wally Backman	.15	.07
❑ 187 Tom Brunansky	.15	.07
❑ 188 Steve Balboni	.15	.07
❑ 189 Marvell Wynne	.15	.07
❑ 190 Dave Henderson	.15	.07
❑ 191 Don Robinson	.15	.07
❑ 192 Ken Griffey Jr.	25.00	11.00
❑ 193 Ivan Calderon	.15	.07
❑ 194 Mike Bielecki	.15	.07
❑ 195 Johnny Ray	.15	.07
❑ 196 Rob Murphy	.15	.07
❑ 197 Andres Thomas	.15	.07
❑ 198 Phil Bradley	.15	.07
❑ 199 Junior Felix	.15	.07
❑ 200 Jeff Russell	.15	.07
❑ 201 Mike LaValliere	.15	.07
❑ 202 Kevin Gross	.15	.07
❑ 203 Keith Moreland	.15	.07
❑ 204 Mike Marshall	.15	.07
❑ 205 Dwight Smith	.25	.11
❑ 206 Jim Clancy	.15	.07
❑ 207 Kevin Seitzer	.15	.07
❑ 208 Keith Hernandez	.25	.11
❑ 209 Bob Ojeda	.15	.07
❑ 210 Ed Whitson	.15	.07
❑ 211 Tony Phillips	.15	.07
❑ 212 Milt Thompson	.15	.07
❑ 213 Randy Kramer	.15	.07
❑ 214 Randy Bush	.15	.07
❑ 215 Randy Ready	.15	.07
❑ 216 Duane Ward	.15	.07
❑ 217 Jimmy Jones	.15	.07
❑ 218 Scott Garrelts	.15	.07
❑ 219 Scott Bankhead	.15	.07
❑ 220 Lance McCullers	.15	.07
❑ 221 B.J. Surhoff	.25	.11
❑ 222 Chris Sabo	.15	.07
❑ 223 Steve Buechele	.15	.07
❑ 224 Joel Skinner	.15	.07
❑ 225 Orel Hershiser	.25	.11
❑ 226 Derek Lilliquist	.15	.07
❑ 227 Claudell Washington	.15	.07
❑ 228 Lloyd McClendon	.15	.07
❑ 229 Felix Fermin	.15	.07
❑ 230 Paul O'Neill	.50	.23
❑ 231 Charlie Leibrandt	.15	.07
❑ 232 Dave Smith	.15	.07
❑ 233 Bob Stanley	.15	.07
❑ 234 Tim Belcher	.15	.07
❑ 235 Eric King	.15	.07
❑ 236 Spike Owen	.15	.07
❑ 237 Mike Henneman	.15	.07
❑ 238 Juan Samuel	.15	.07
❑ 239 Greg Brock	.15	.07
❑ 240 John Kruk	.25	.11
❑ 241 Glenn Wilson	.15	.07
❑ 242 Jeff Reardon	.25	.11
❑ 243 Todd Worrell	.15	.07
❑ 244 Dave LaPoint	.15	.07
❑ 245 Walt Terrell	.15	.07
❑ 246 Mike Moore	.15	.07
❑ 247 Kelly Downs	.15	.07
❑ 248 Dave Valle	.15	.07
❑ 249 Ron Kittle	.15	.07
❑ 250 Steve Wilson	.15	.07
❑ 251 Dick Schofield	.15	.07
❑ 252 Marty Barrett	.15	.07
❑ 253 Dion James	.15	.07
❑ 254 Bob Milacki	.15	.07
❑ 255 Ernie Whitt	.15	.07
❑ 256 Kevin Brown	.60	.25
❑ 257 R.J. Reynolds	.15	.07
❑ 258 Tim Raines	.25	.11
❑ 259 Frank Williams	.15	.07
❑ 260 Jose Gonzalez	.15	.07
❑ 261 Mitch Webster	.15	.07
❑ 262 Ken Caminiti	.25	.11
❑ 263 Bob Boone	.25	.11
❑ 264 Dave Magadan	.15	.07
❑ 265 Rick Aguilera	.25	.11
❑ 266 Chris James	.15	.07
❑ 267 Bob Welch	.15	.07
❑ 268 Ken Dayley	.15	.07
❑ 269 Junior Ortiz	.15	.07
❑ 270 Allan Anderson	.15	.07
❑ 271 Steve Jeltz	.15	.07
❑ 272 George Bell	.15	.07
❑ 273 Roberto Kelly	.25	.11
❑ 274 Brett Butler	.25	.11
❑ 275 Mike Schooler	.15	.07
❑ 276 Ken Phelps	.15	.07
❑ 277 Glenn Braggs	.15	.07
❑ 278 Jose Rijo	.15	.07
❑ 279 Bobby Witt	.15	.07
❑ 280 Jerry Browne	.15	.07
❑ 281 Kevin Mitchell	.25	.11
❑ 282 Craig Worthington	.15	.07
❑ 283 Greg Minton	.15	.07
❑ 284 Nick Esasky	.15	.07
❑ 285 John Farrell	.15	.07
❑ 286 Rick Mahler	.15	.07
❑ 287 Tom Gordon	.50	.23
❑ 288 Gerald Young	.15	.07
❑ 289 Jody Reed	.15	.07
❑ 290 Jeff Hamilton	.15	.07
❑ 291 Gerald Perry	.15	.07
❑ 292 Hubie Brooks	.15	.07
❑ 293 Bo Diaz	.15	.07
❑ 294 Terry Puhl	.15	.07
❑ 295 Jim Gantner	.15	.07
❑ 296 Jeff Parrett	.15	.07
❑ 297 Mike Boddicker	.15	.07
❑ 298 Dan Gladden	.15	.07
❑ 299 Tony Pena	.15	.07
❑ 300 Checklist Card	.15	.07
❑ 301 Tom Henke	.15	.07
❑ 302 Pascual Perez	.15	.07
❑ 303 Steve Bedrosian	.15	.07
❑ 304 Ken Hill	.25	.11
❑ 305 Jerry Reuss	.15	.07
❑ 306 Jim Eisenreich	.15	.07
❑ 307 Jack Howell	.15	.07
❑ 308 Rick Cerone	.15	.07
❑ 309 Tim Leary	.15	.07
❑ 310 Joe Orsulak	.15	.07
❑ 311 Jim Dwyer	.15	.07
❑ 312 Geno Petralli	.15	.07
❑ 313 Rick Honeycutt	.15	.07
❑ 314 Tom Foley	.15	.07
❑ 315 Kenny Rogers	.50	.23
❑ 316 Mike Flanagan	.15	.07
❑ 317 Bryan Harvey	.15	.07
❑ 318 Billy Ripken	.15	.07
❑ 319 Jeff Montgomery	.25	.11
❑ 320 Erik Hanson	.25	.11
❑ 321 Brian Downing	.15	.07
❑ 322 Gregg Olson	.50	.23
❑ 323 Terry Steinbach	.25	.11
❑ 324 Sammy Sosa	25.00	11.00
❑ 325 Gene Harris	.15	.07
❑ 326 Mike Devereaux	.15	.07
❑ 327 Dennis Cook	.15	.07
❑ 328 David Wells	.15	.07
❑ 329 Checklist Card	.15	.07
❑ 330 Kirt Manwaring	.15	.07
❑ 331 Jim Presley	.15	.07
❑ 332 Checklist Card	.15	.07
❑ 333 Chuck Finley	.25	.11
❑ 334 Rob Dibble	.25	.11
❑ 335 Cecil Espy	.15	.07
❑ 336 Dave Parker	.25	.11

1990 Donruss

	MINT	NRMT
COMPLETE SET (716)	15.00	6.75
COMP.FACT.SET (728)	20.00	9.00
COMP.YAZ PUZZLE	1.00	.45
❑ 1 Bo Jackson DK	.10	.05
❑ 2 Steve Sax DK	.05	.02
❑ 3A Ruben Sierra DK ERR (No small line on top border on card back)	.05	.02
❑ 3B Ruben Sierra DK COR	.05	.02
❑ 4 Ken Griffey Jr. DK	.60	.25
❑ 5 Mickey Tettleton DK	.05	.02
❑ 6 Dave Stewart DK	.05	.02
❑ 7 Jim Deshaies DK DP	.05	.02

❑ 8	John Smoltz DK	.10	.05
❑ 9	Mike Bielecki DK	.05	.02
❑ 10A	Brian Downing DK ERR (Reverse negative on card front)	.20	.09
❑ 10B	Brian Downing DK COR	.05	.02
❑ 11	Kevin Mitchell DK	.05	.02
❑ 12	Kelly Gruber DK	.05	.02
❑ 13	Joe Magrané DK	.05	.02
❑ 14	John Franco DK	.05	.02
❑ 15	Ozzie Guillen DK	.05	.02
❑ 16	Lou Whitaker DK	.05	.02
❑ 17	John Smiley DK	.05	.02
❑ 18	Howard Johnson DK	.05	.02
❑ 19	Willie Randolph DK	.10	.05
❑ 20	Chris Bosio DK	.05	.02
❑ 21	Tommy Herr DK DP	.05	.02
❑ 22	Dan Gladden DK	.05	.02
❑ 23	Ellis Burks DK	.10	.05
❑ 24	Pete O'Brien DK	.05	.02
❑ 25	Bryn Smith DK	.05	.02
❑ 26	Ed Whitson DK DP	.05	.02
❑ 27	DK Checklist 1-27 DP (Comments on Perez-Steele on back)	.05	.02
❑ 28	Robin Ventura RR	.20	.09
❑ 29	Todd Zeile RR	.10	.05
❑ 30	Sandy Alomar Jr. RR	.10	.05
❑ 31	Kent Mercker RR RC	.05	.02
❑ 32	B.McDonald RC UER Middle name Benard not Benjamin	.10	.05
❑ 33A	J.Gonzalez RC ERR Reverse negative	5.00	2.20
❑ 33B	J.Gonzalez COR RC	2.00	.90
❑ 34	Eric Anthony RR RC	.05	.02
❑ 35	Mike Fetters RR RC	.05	.02
❑ 36	Marquis Grissom RC	.10	.05
❑ 37	Greg Vaughn RR	.20	.09
❑ 38	Brian DuBois RR	.05	.02
❑ 39	Steve Avery RR UER (Born in MI, not NJ)	.05	.02
❑ 40	Mark Gardner RR RC	.05	.02
❑ 41	Andy Benes RR	.05	.02
❑ 42	D.DeShields RR RC	.20	.09
❑ 43	Scott Coolbaugh RR	.05	.02
❑ 44	Pat Combs RR DP	.05	.02
❑ 45	Alex Sanchez RR DP	.05	.02
❑ 46	Kelly Mann RR DP	.05	.02
❑ 47	Julio Machado RR DP	.05	.02
❑ 48	Pete Incaviglia	.05	.02
❑ 49	Shawon Dunston	.05	.02
❑ 50	Jeff Treadway	.05	.02
❑ 51	Jeff Ballard	.05	.02
❑ 52	Claudell Washington	.05	.02
❑ 53	Juan Samuel	.05	.02
❑ 54	John Smiley	.05	.02
❑ 55	Rob Deer	.05	.02
❑ 56	Geno Petralli	.05	.02
❑ 57	Chris Bosio	.05	.02
❑ 58	Carlton Fisk	.20	.09
❑ 59	Kirt Manwaring	.05	.02
❑ 60	Chet Lemon	.05	.02
❑ 61	Bo Jackson	.10	.05
❑ 62	Doyle Alexander	.05	.02
❑ 63	Pedro Guerrero	.05	.02
❑ 64	Allan Anderson	.05	.02
❑ 65	Greg W. Harris	.05	.02
❑ 66	Mike Greenwell	.05	.02
❑ 67	Walt Weiss	.05	.02
❑ 68	Wade Boggs	.20	.09
❑ 69	Jim Clancy	.05	.02
❑ 70	Junior Felix	.05	.02
❑ 71	Barry Larkin	.20	.09
❑ 72	Dave LaPoint	.05	.02
❑ 73	Joel Skinner	.05	.02
❑ 74	Jesse Barfield	.05	.02
❑ 75	Tommy Herr	.05	.02
❑ 76	Ricky Jordan	.05	.02
❑ 77	Eddie Murray	.20	.09
❑ 78	Steve Sax	.05	.02
❑ 79	Tim Belcher	.05	.02
❑ 80	Danny Jackson	.05	.02
❑ 81	Kent Hrbek	.10	.05
❑ 82	Milt Thompson	.05	.02
❑ 83	Brook Jacoby	.05	.02
❑ 84	Mike Marshall	.05	.02
❑ 85	Kevin Seitzer	.05	.02
❑ 86	Tony Gwynn	.40	.18
❑ 87	Dave Stieb	.10	.05
❑ 88	Dave Smith	.05	.02
❑ 89	Bret Saberhagen	.10	.05
❑ 90	Alan Trammell	.15	.07
❑ 91	Tony Phillips	.05	.02
❑ 92	Doug Drabek	.05	.02
❑ 93	Jeffrey Leonard	.05	.02
❑ 94	Wally Joyner	.10	.05
❑ 95	Carney Lansford	.10	.05
❑ 96	Cal Ripken	.75	.35
❑ 97	Andres Galarraga	.15	.07
❑ 98	Kevin Mitchell	.05	.02
❑ 99	Howard Johnson	.05	.02
❑ 100A	Checklist 28-129	.05	.02
❑ 100B	Checklist 28-125	.05	.02
❑ 101	Melido Perez	.05	.02
❑ 102	Spike Owen	.05	.02
❑ 103	Paul Molitor	.20	.09
❑ 104	Geronimo Berroa	.05	.02
❑ 105	Ryne Sandberg	.25	.11
❑ 106	Bryn Smith	.05	.02
❑ 107	Steve Buechele	.05	.02
❑ 108	Jim Abbott	.15	.07
❑ 109	Alvin Davis	.05	.02
❑ 110	Lee Smith	.10	.05
❑ 111	Roberto Alomar	.20	.09
❑ 112	Rick Reuschel	.05	.02
❑ 113A	Kelly Gruber ERR (Born 2/22)	.05	.02
❑ 113B	Kelly Gruber COR (Born 2/26; corrected in factory sets)	.05	.02
❑ 114	Joe Carter	.10	.05
❑ 115	Jose Rijo	.05	.02
❑ 116	Greg Minton	.05	.02
❑ 117	Bob Ojeda	.05	.02
❑ 118	Glenn Davis	.05	.02
❑ 119	Jeff Reardon	.10	.05
❑ 120	Kurt Stillwell	.05	.02
❑ 121	John Smoltz	.10	.05
❑ 122	Dwight Evans	.10	.05
❑ 123	Eric Yelding	.05	.02
❑ 124	John Franco	.10	.05
❑ 125	Jose Canseco	.20	.09
❑ 126	Barry Bonds	.50	.23
❑ 127	Lee Guetterman	.05	.02
❑ 128	Jack Clark	.10	.05
❑ 129	Dave Valle	.05	.02
❑ 130	Hubie Brooks	.05	.02
❑ 131	Ernest Riles	.05	.02
❑ 132	Mike Morgan	.05	.02
❑ 133	Steve Jeltz	.05	.02
❑ 134	Jeff D. Robinson	.05	.02
❑ 135	Ozzie Guillen	.05	.02
❑ 136	Chili Davis	.10	.05
❑ 137	Mitch Webster	.05	.02
❑ 138	Jerry Browne	.05	.02
❑ 139	Bo Diaz	.05	.02
❑ 140	Robby Thompson	.05	.02
❑ 141	Craig Worthington	.05	.02
❑ 142	Julio Franco	.05	.02
❑ 143	Brian Holman	.05	.02
❑ 144	George Brett	.40	.18
❑ 145	Tom Glavine	.20	.09
❑ 146	Robin Yount	.20	.09
❑ 147	Gary Carter	.15	.07
❑ 148	Ron Kittle	.05	.02
❑ 149	Tony Fernandez	.05	.02
❑ 150	Dave Stewart	.10	.05
❑ 151	Gary Gaetti	.10	.05
❑ 152	Kevin Elster	.05	.02
❑ 153	Gerald Perry	.05	.02
❑ 154	Jesse Orosco	.05	.02
❑ 155	Wally Backman	.05	.02
❑ 156	Dennis Martinez	.10	.05
❑ 157	Rick Sutcliffe	.10	.05
❑ 158	Greg Maddux	.50	.23
❑ 159	Andy Hawkins	.05	.02
❑ 160	John Kruk	.10	.05
❑ 161	Jose Oquendo	.05	.02
❑ 162	John Dopson	.05	.02
❑ 163	Joe Magrane	.05	.02
❑ 164	Bill Ripken	.05	.02
❑ 165	Fred Manrique	.05	.02
❑ 166	Nolan Ryan UER (Did not lead NL in K's in '89 as he was in AL in '89)	1.00	.45
❑ 167	Damon Berryhill	.05	.02
❑ 168	Dale Murphy	.20	.09
❑ 169	Mickey Tettleton	.05	.02
❑ 170A	Kirk McCaskill ERR (Born 4/19)	.05	.02
❑ 170B	Kirk McCaskill COR (Born 4/9; corrected in factory sets)	.05	.02
❑ 171	Dwight Gooden	.10	.05
❑ 172	Jose Lind	.05	.02
❑ 173	B.J. Surhoff	.10	.05
❑ 174	Ruben Sierra	.05	.02
❑ 175	Dan Plesac	.05	.02
❑ 176	Dan Pasqua	.05	.02
❑ 177	Kelly Downs	.05	.02
❑ 178	Matt Nokes	.05	.02
❑ 179	Luis Aquino	.05	.02
❑ 180	Frank Tanana	.05	.02
❑ 181	Tony Pena	.05	.02
❑ 182	Dan Gladden	.05	.02
❑ 183	Bruce Hurst	.05	.02
❑ 184	Roger Clemens	.50	.23
❑ 185	Mark McGwire	.75	.35
❑ 186	Rob Murphy	.05	.02
❑ 187	Jim Deshaies	.05	.02
❑ 188	Fred McGriff	.20	.09
❑ 189	Rob Dibble	.05	.02
❑ 190	Don Mattingly	.50	.23
❑ 191	Felix Fermin	.05	.02
❑ 192	Roberto Kelly	.05	.02
❑ 193	Dennis Cook	.05	.02
❑ 194	Darren Daulton	.10	.05
❑ 195	Alfredo Griffin	.05	.02
❑ 196	Eric Plunk	.05	.02
❑ 197	Orel Hershiser	.10	.05
❑ 198	Paul O'Neill	.20	.09
❑ 199	Randy Bush	.05	.02
❑ 200A	Checklist 130-231	.05	.02
❑ 200B	Checklist 126-223	.05	.02
❑ 201	Ozzie Smith	.25	.11
❑ 202	Pete O'Brien	.05	.02
❑ 203	Jay Howell	.05	.02
❑ 204	Mark Gubicza	.05	.02
❑ 205	Ed Whitson	.05	.02
❑ 206	George Bell	.05	.02
❑ 207	Mike Scott	.05	.02
❑ 208	Charlie Leibrandt	.05	.02
❑ 209	Mike Heath	.05	.02
❑ 210	Dennis Eckersley	.15	.07
❑ 211	Mike LaValliere	.05	.02
❑ 212	Darnell Coles	.05	.02
❑ 213	Lance Parrish	.05	.02
❑ 214	Mike Moore	.05	.02
❑ 215	Steve Finley	.10	.05
❑ 216	Tim Raines	.10	.05
❑ 217A	Scott Garrelts ERR (Born 10/20)	.05	.02
❑ 217B	Scott Garrelts COR (Born 10/30; corrected in factory sets)	.05	.02
❑ 218	Kevin McReynolds	.05	.02
❑ 219	Dave Gallagher	.05	.02
❑ 220	Tim Wallach	.05	.02
❑ 221	Chuck Crim	.05	.02
❑ 222	Lonnie Smith	.05	.02
❑ 223	Andre Dawson	.15	.07
❑ 224	Nelson Santovenia	.05	.02
❑ 225	Rafael Palmeiro	.20	.09
❑ 226	Devon White	.05	.02
❑ 227	Harold Reynolds	.05	.02
❑ 228	Ellis Burks	.15	.07
❑ 229	Mark Parent	.05	.02
❑ 230	Will Clark	.20	.09
❑ 231	Jimmy Key	.10	.05
❑ 232	John Farrell	.05	.02
❑ 233	Eric Davis	.10	.05
❑ 234	Johnny Ray	.05	.02
❑ 235	Darryl Strawberry	.10	.05
❑ 236	Bill Doran	.05	.02
❑ 237	Greg Gagne	.05	.02

❑ 238 Jim Eisenreich .05 .02
❑ 239 Tommy Gregg .05 .02
❑ 240 Marty Barrett .05 .02
❑ 241 Rafael Ramirez .05 .02
❑ 242 Chris Sabo .05 .02
❑ 243 Dave Henderson .05 .02
❑ 244 Andy Van Slyke .10 .05
❑ 245 Alvaro Espinoza .05 .02
❑ 246 Garry Templeton .05 .02
❑ 247 Gene Harris .05 .02
❑ 248 Kevin Gross .05 .02
❑ 249 Brett Butler .10 .05
❑ 250 Willie Randolph .10 .05
❑ 251 Roger McDowell .05 .02
❑ 252 Rafael Belliard .05 .02
❑ 253 Steve Rosenberg .05 .02
❑ 254 Jack Howell .05 .02
❑ 255 Marvell Wynne .05 .02
❑ 256 Tom Candiotti .05 .02
❑ 257 Todd Benzinger .05 .02
❑ 258 Don Robinson .05 .02
❑ 259 Phil Bradley .05 .02
❑ 260 Cecil Espy .05 .02
❑ 261 Scott Bankhead .05 .02
❑ 262 Frank White .10 .05
❑ 263 Andres Thomas .05 .02
❑ 264 Glenn Braggs .05 .02
❑ 265 David Cone .10 .05
❑ 266 Bobby Thigpen .05 .02
❑ 267 Nelson Liriano .05 .02
❑ 268 Terry Steinbach .05 .02
❑ 269 Kirby Puckett UER .50 .23
(Back doesn't consider
Joe Torre's .363 in '71)
❑ 270 Gregg Jefferies .10 .05
❑ 271 Jeff Blauser .05 .02
❑ 272 Cory Snyder .05 .02
❑ 273 Roy Smith .05 .02
❑ 274 Tom Foley .05 .02
❑ 275 Mitch Williams .05 .02
❑ 276 Paul Kilgus .05 .02
❑ 277 Don Slaught .05 .02
❑ 278 Von Hayes .05 .02
❑ 279 Vince Coleman .05 .02
❑ 280 Mike Boddicker .05 .02
❑ 281 Ken Dayley .05 .02
❑ 282 Mike Devereaux .05 .02
❑ 283 Kenny Rogers .10 .05
❑ 284 Jeff Russell .05 .02
❑ 285 Jerome Walton .05 .02
❑ 286 Derek Lilliquist .05 .02
❑ 287 Joe Orsulak .05 .02
❑ 288 Dick Schofield .05 .02
❑ 289 Ron Darling .05 .02
❑ 290 Bobby Bonilla .10 .05
❑ 291 Jim Gantner .05 .02
❑ 292 Bobby Witt .05 .02
❑ 293 Greg Brock .05 .02
❑ 294 Ivan Calderon .05 .02
❑ 295 Steve Bedrosian .05 .02
❑ 296 Mike Henneman .05 .02
❑ 297 Tom Gordon .10 .05
❑ 298 Lou Whitaker .10 .05
❑ 299 Terry Pendleton .10 .05
❑ 300A Checklist 232-333 .05 .02
❑ 300B Checklist 224-321 .05 .02
❑ 301 Juan Berenguer .05 .02
❑ 302 Mark Davis .05 .02
❑ 303 Nick Esasky .05 .02
❑ 304 Rickey Henderson .40 .18
❑ 305 Rick Cerone .05 .02
❑ 306 Craig Biggio .15 .07
❑ 307 Duane Ward .05 .02
❑ 308 Tom Browning .05 .02
❑ 309 Walt Terrell .05 .02
❑ 310 Greg Swindell .05 .02
❑ 311 Dave Righetti .05 .02
❑ 312 Mike Maddux .05 .02
❑ 313 Len Dykstra .10 .05
❑ 314 Jose Gonzalez .05 .02
❑ 315 Steve Balboni .05 .02
❑ 316 Mike Scioscia .05 .02
❑ 317 Ron Oester .05 .02
❑ 318 Gary Wayne .05 .02
❑ 319 Todd Worrell .05 .02
❑ 320 Doug Jones .05 .02
❑ 321 Jeff Hamilton .05 .02
❑ 322 Danny Tartabull .05 .02
❑ 323 Chris James .05 .02
❑ 324 Mike Flanagan .05 .02
❑ 325 Gerald Young .05 .02
❑ 326 Bob Boone .10 .05
❑ 327 Frank Williams .05 .02
❑ 328 Dave Parker .10 .05
❑ 329 Sid Bream .05 .02
❑ 330 Mike Schooler .05 .02
❑ 331 Bert Blyleven .10 .05
❑ 332 Bob Welch .05 .02
❑ 333 Bob Milacki .05 .02
❑ 334 Tim Burke .05 .02
❑ 335 Jose Uribe .05 .02
❑ 336 Randy Myers .10 .05
❑ 337 Eric King .05 .02
❑ 338 Mark Langston .05 .02
❑ 339 Teddy Higuera .05 .02
❑ 340 Oddibe McDowell .05 .02
❑ 341 Lloyd McClendon .05 .02
❑ 342 Pascual Perez .05 .02
❑ 343 Kevin Brown UER .20 .09
(Signed is misspelled
as signeed on back)
❑ 344 Chuck Finley .10 .05
❑ 345 Erik Hanson .05 .02
❑ 346 Rich Gedman .05 .02
❑ 347 Bip Roberts .05 .02
❑ 348 Matt Williams .15 .07
❑ 349 Tom Henke .05 .02
❑ 350 Brad Komminsk .05 .02
❑ 351 Jeff Reed .05 .02
❑ 352 Brian Downing .05 .02
❑ 353 Frank Viola .05 .02
❑ 354 Terry Puhl .05 .02
❑ 355 Brian Harper .05 .02
❑ 356 Steve Farr .05 .02
❑ 357 Joe Boever .05 .02
❑ 358 Danny Heep .05 .02
❑ 359 Larry Andersen .05 .02
❑ 360 Rolando Roomes .05 .02
❑ 361 Mike Gallego .05 .02
❑ 362 Bob Kipper .05 .02
❑ 363 Clay Parker .05 .02
❑ 364 Mike Pagliarulo .05 .02
❑ 365 Ken Griffey Jr. UER 1.25 .55
(Signed through 1990,
should be 1991)
❑ 366 Rex Hudler .05 .02
❑ 367 Pat Sheridan .05 .02
❑ 368 Kirk Gibson .10 .05
❑ 369 Jeff Parrett .05 .02
❑ 370 Bob Walk .05 .02
❑ 371 Ken Patterson .05 .02
❑ 372 Bryan Harvey .05 .02
❑ 373 Mike Bielecki .05 .02
❑ 374 Tom Magrann .05 .02
❑ 375 Rick Mahler .05 .02
❑ 376 Craig Lefferts .05 .02
❑ 377 Gregg Olson .10 .05
❑ 378 Jamie Moyer .05 .02
❑ 379 Randy Johnson .40 .18
❑ 380 Jeff Montgomery .10 .05
❑ 381 Marty Clary .05 .02
❑ 382 Bill Spiers .05 .02
❑ 383 Dave Magadan .05 .02
❑ 384 Greg Hibbard RC .05 .02
❑ 385 Ernie Whitt .05 .02
❑ 386 Rick Honeycutt .05 .02
❑ 387 Dave West .05 .02
❑ 388 Keith Hernandez .10 .05
❑ 389 Jose Alvarez .05 .02
❑ 390 Joey Belle .20 .09
❑ 391 Rick Aguilera .10 .05
❑ 392 Mike Fitzgerald .05 .02
❑ 393 Dwight Smith .05 .02
❑ 394 Steve Wilson .05 .02
❑ 395 Bob Geren .05 .02
❑ 396 Randy Ready .05 .02
❑ 397 Ken Hill .10 .05
❑ 398 Jody Reed .05 .02
❑ 399 Tom Brunansky .05 .02
❑ 400A Checklist 334-435 .05 .02
❑ 400B Checklist 322-419 .05 .02
❑ 401 Rene Gonzales .05 .02
❑ 402 Harold Baines .10 .05
❑ 403 Cecilio Guante .05 .02
❑ 404 Joe Girardi .15 .07
❑ 405A Sergio Valdez ERR .05 .02
(Card front shows
black line crossing
S in Sergio)
❑ 405B Sergio Valdez COR .05 .02
❑ 406 Mark Williamson .05 .02
❑ 407 Glenn Hoffman .05 .02
❑ 408 Jeff Innis .05 .02
❑ 409 Randy Kramer .05 .02
❑ 410 Charlie O'Brien .05 .02
❑ 411 Charlie Hough .10 .05
❑ 412 Gus Polidor .05 .02
❑ 413 Ron Karkovice .05 .02
❑ 414 Trevor Wilson .05 .02
❑ 415 Kevin Ritz .05 .02
❑ 416 Gary Thurman .05 .02
❑ 417 Jeff M. Robinson .05 .02
❑ 418 Scott Terry .05 .02
❑ 419 Tim Laudner .05 .02
❑ 420 Dennis Rasmussen .05 .02
❑ 421 Luis Rivera .05 .02
❑ 422 Jim Corsi .05 .02
❑ 423 Dennis Lamp .05 .02
❑ 424 Ken Caminiti .10 .05
❑ 425 David Wells .10 .05
❑ 426 Norm Charlton .05 .02
❑ 427 Deion Sanders .20 .09
❑ 428 Dion James .05 .02
❑ 429 Chuck Cary .05 .02
❑ 430 Ken Howell .05 .02
❑ 431 Steve Lake .05 .02
❑ 432 Kal Daniels .05 .02
❑ 433 Lance McCullers .05 .02
❑ 434 Lenny Harris .05 .02
❑ 435 Scott Scudder .05 .02
❑ 436 Gene Larkin .05 .02
❑ 437 Dan Quisenberry .05 .02
❑ 438 Steve Olin RC .10 .05
❑ 439 Mickey Hatcher .05 .02
❑ 440 Willie Wilson .05 .02
❑ 441 Mark Grant .05 .02
❑ 442 Mookie Wilson .10 .05
❑ 443 Alex Trevino .05 .02
❑ 444 Pat Tabler .05 .02
❑ 445 Dave Bergman .05 .02
❑ 446 Todd Burns .05 .02
❑ 447 R.J. Reynolds .05 .02
❑ 448 Jay Buhner .10 .05
❑ 449 Lee Stevens .10 .05
❑ 450 Ron Hassey .05 .02
❑ 451 Bob Melvin .05 .02
❑ 452 Dave Martinez .05 .02
❑ 453 Greg Litton .05 .02
❑ 454 Mark Carreon .05 .02
❑ 455 Scott Fletcher .05 .02
❑ 456 Otis Nixon .05 .02
❑ 457 Tony Fossas .05 .02
❑ 458 John Russell .05 .02
❑ 459 Paul Assenmacher .05 .02
❑ 460 Zane Smith .05 .02
❑ 461 Jack Daugherty .05 .02
❑ 462 Rich Monteleone .05 .02
❑ 463 Greg Briley .05 .02
❑ 464 Mike Smithson .05 .02
❑ 465 Benito Santiago .05 .02
❑ 466 Jeff Brantley .05 .02
❑ 467 Jose Nunez .05 .02
❑ 468 Scott Bailes .05 .02
❑ 469 Ken Griffey Sr. .10 .05
❑ 470 Bob McClure .05 .02
❑ 471 Mackey Sasser .05 .02
❑ 472 Glenn Wilson .05 .02
❑ 473 Kevin Tapani RC .20 .09
❑ 474 Bill Buckner .05 .02
❑ 475 Ron Gant .10 .05
❑ 476 Kevin Romine .05 .02
❑ 477 Juan Agosto .05 .02
❑ 478 Herm Winningham .05 .02
❑ 479 Storm Davis .05 .02
❑ 480 Jeff King .05 .02
❑ 481 Kevin Mmahat .05 .02
❑ 482 Carmelo Martinez .05 .02
❑ 483 Omar Vizquel .20 .09

- ❑ 484 Jim Dwyer .05 .02
- ❑ 485 Bob Knepper .05 .02
- ❑ 486 Dave Anderson .05 .02
- ❑ 487 Ron Jones .05 .02
- ❑ 488 Jay Bell .10 .05
- ❑ 489 Sammy Sosa RC 5.00 2.20
- ❑ 490 Kent Anderson .05 .02
- ❑ 491 Domingo Ramos .05 .02
- ❑ 492 Dave Clark .05 .02
- ❑ 493 Tim Birtsas .05 .02
- ❑ 494 Ken Oberkfell .05 .02
- ❑ 495 Larry Sheets .05 .02
- ❑ 496 Jeff Kunkel .05 .02
- ❑ 497 Jim Presley .05 .02
- ❑ 498 Mike Macfarlane .05 .02
- ❑ 499 Pete Smith .05 .02
- ❑ 500A Checklist 436-537 DP .05 .02
- ❑ 500B Checklist 420-517 .05 .02
- ❑ 501 Gary Sheffield .10 .05
- ❑ 502 Terry Bross .05 .02
- ❑ 503 Jerry Kutzler .05 .02
- ❑ 504 Lloyd Moseby .05 .02
- ❑ 505 Curt Young .05 .02
- ❑ 506 Al Newman .05 .02
- ❑ 507 Keith Miller .05 .02
- ❑ 508 Mike Stanton RC .05 .02
- ❑ 509 Rich Yett .05 .02
- ❑ 510 Tim Drummond .05 .02
- ❑ 511 Joe Hesketh .05 .02
- ❑ 512 Rick Wrona .05 .02
- ❑ 513 Luis Salazar .05 .02
- ❑ 514 Hal Morris .05 .02
- ❑ 515 Terry Mulholland .05 .02
- ❑ 516 John Morris .05 .02
- ❑ 517 Carlos Quintana .05 .02
- ❑ 518 Frank DiPino .05 .02
- ❑ 519 Randy Milligan .05 .02
- ❑ 520 Chad Kreuter .05 .02
- ❑ 521 Mike Jeffcoat .05 .02
- ❑ 522 Mike Harkey .05 .02
- ❑ 523A Andy Nezelek ERR .05 .02 (Wrong birth year)
- ❑ 523B Andy Nezelek COR .20 .09 (Finally corrected in factory sets)
- ❑ 524 Dave Schmidt .05 .02
- ❑ 525 Tony Armas .05 .02
- ❑ 526 Barry Lyons .05 .02
- ❑ 527 Rick Reed RC .25 .11
- ❑ 528 Jerry Reuss .05 .02
- ❑ 529 Dean Palmer RC .40 .18
- ❑ 530 Jeff Peterek .05 .02
- ❑ 531 Carlos Martinez .05 .02
- ❑ 532 Atlee Hammaker .05 .02
- ❑ 533 Mike Brumley .05 .02
- ❑ 534 Terry Leach .05 .02
- ❑ 535 Doug Strange .05 .02
- ❑ 536 Jose DeLeon .05 .02
- ❑ 537 Shane Rawley .05 .02
- ❑ 538 Joey Cora .10 .05
- ❑ 539 Eric Hetzel .05 .02
- ❑ 540 Gene Nelson .05 .02
- ❑ 541 Wes Gardner .05 .02
- ❑ 542 Mark Portugal .05 .02
- ❑ 543 Al Leiter .20 .09
- ❑ 544 Jack Armstrong .05 .02
- ❑ 545 Greg Cadaret .05 .02
- ❑ 546 Rod Nichols .05 .02
- ❑ 547 Luis Polonia .05 .02
- ❑ 548 Charlie Hayes .05 .02
- ❑ 549 Dickie Thon .05 .02
- ❑ 550 Tim Crews .05 .02
- ❑ 551 Dave Winfield .20 .09
- ❑ 552 Mike Davis .05 .02
- ❑ 553 Ron Robinson .05 .02
- ❑ 554 Carmen Castillo .05 .02
- ❑ 555 John Costello .05 .02
- ❑ 556 Bud Black .05 .02
- ❑ 557 Rick Dempsey .05 .02
- ❑ 558 Jim Acker .05 .02
- ❑ 559 Eric Show .05 .02
- ❑ 560 Pat Borders .05 .02
- ❑ 561 Danny Darwin .05 .02
- ❑ 562 Rick Luecken .05 .02
- ❑ 563 Edwin Nunez .05 .02
- ❑ 564 Felix Jose .05 .02
- ❑ 565 John Cangelosi .05 .02
- ❑ 566 Bill Swift .05 .02
- ❑ 567 Bill Schroeder .05 .02
- ❑ 568 Stan Javier .05 .02
- ❑ 569 Jim Traber .05 .02
- ❑ 570 Wallace Johnson .05 .02
- ❑ 571 Donell Nixon .05 .02
- ❑ 572 Sid Fernandez .05 .02
- ❑ 573 Lance Johnson .05 .02
- ❑ 574 Andy McGaffigan .05 .02
- ❑ 575 Mark Knudson .05 .02
- ❑ 576 Tommy Greene RC .05 .02
- ❑ 577 Mark Grace .20 .09
- ❑ 578 Larry Walker RC .60 .25
- ❑ 579 Mike Stanley .05 .02
- ❑ 580 Mike Witt DP .05 .02
- ❑ 581 Scott Bradley .05 .02
- ❑ 582 Greg A. Harris .05 .02
- ❑ 583A Kevin Hickey ERR .20 .09
- ❑ 583B Kevin Hickey COR .05 .02
- ❑ 584 Lee Mazzilli .05 .02
- ❑ 585 Jeff Pico .05 .02
- ❑ 586 Joe Oliver .05 .02
- ❑ 587 Willie Fraser DP .05 .02
- ❑ 588 Carl Yastrzemski .20 .09 Puzzle Card DP
- ❑ 589 Kevin Bass DP .05 .02
- ❑ 590 John Moses DP .05 .02
- ❑ 591 Tom Pagnozzi DP .05 .02
- ❑ 592 Tony Castillo DP .05 .02
- ❑ 593 Jerald Clark DP .05 .02
- ❑ 594 Dan Schatzeder .05 .02
- ❑ 595 Luis Quinones DP .05 .02
- ❑ 596 Pete Harnisch DP .05 .02
- ❑ 597 Gary Redus .05 .02
- ❑ 598 Mel Hall .05 .02
- ❑ 599 Rick Schu .05 .02
- ❑ 600A Checklist 538-639 .05 .02
- ❑ 600B Checklist 518-617 .05 .02
- ❑ 601 Mike Kingery DP .05 .02
- ❑ 602 Terry Kennedy DP .05 .02
- ❑ 603 Mike Sharperson DP .05 .02
- ❑ 604 Don Carman DP .05 .02
- ❑ 605 Jim Gott .05 .02
- ❑ 606 Donn Pall DP .05 .02
- ❑ 607 Rance Mulliniks .05 .02
- ❑ 608 Curt Wilkerson DP .05 .02
- ❑ 609 Mike Felder DP .05 .02
- ❑ 610 G.Hernandez DP .05 .02
- ❑ 611 Candy Maldonado DP .05 .02
- ❑ 612 Mark Thurmond DP .05 .02
- ❑ 613 Rick Leach DP .05 .02
- ❑ 614 Jerry Reed DP .05 .02
- ❑ 615 Franklin Stubbs .05 .02
- ❑ 616 Billy Hatcher DP .05 .02
- ❑ 617 Don August DP .05 .02
- ❑ 618 Tim Teufel .05 .02
- ❑ 619 Shawn Hillegas DP .05 .02
- ❑ 620 Manny Lee .05 .02
- ❑ 621 Gary Ward DP .05 .02
- ❑ 622 Mark Guthrie DP .05 .02
- ❑ 623 Jeff Musselman DP .05 .02
- ❑ 624 Mark Lemke DP .05 .02
- ❑ 625 Fernando Valenzuela .10 .05
- ❑ 626 Paul Sorrento DP RC .15 .07
- ❑ 627 Glenallen Hill DP .05 .02
- ❑ 628 Les Lancaster DP .05 .02
- ❑ 629 Vance Law DP .05 .02
- ❑ 630 Randy Velarde DP .05 .02
- ❑ 631 Todd Frohwirth DP .05 .02
- ❑ 632 Willie McGee .10 .05
- ❑ 633 Dennis Boyd DP .05 .02
- ❑ 634 Cris Carpenter DP .05 .02
- ❑ 635 Brian Holton .05 .02
- ❑ 636 Tracy Jones DP .05 .02
- ❑ 637A Terry Steinbach AS .05 .02 (Recent Major League Performance)
- ❑ 637B Terry Steinbach AS .05 .02 (All-Star Game Performance)
- ❑ 638 Brady Anderson .20 .09
- ❑ 639A Jack Morris ERR .10 .05 (Card front shows black line crossing J in Jack)
- ❑ 639B Jack Morris COR .10 .05
- ❑ 640 Jaime Navarro .05 .02
- ❑ 641 Darrin Jackson .05 .02
- ❑ 642 Mike Dyer .05 .02
- ❑ 643 Mike Schmidt .40 .18
- ❑ 644 Henry Cotto .05 .02
- ❑ 645 John Cerutti .05 .02
- ❑ 646 Francisco Cabrera .05 .02
- ❑ 647 Scott Sanderson .05 .02
- ❑ 648 Brian Meyer .05 .02
- ❑ 649 Ray Searage .05 .02
- ❑ 650A Bo Jackson AS .10 .05 (Recent Major League Performance)
- ❑ 650B Bo Jackson AS .10 .05 (All-Star Game Performance)
- ❑ 651 Steve Lyons .05 .02
- ❑ 652 Mike LaCoss .05 .02
- ❑ 653 Ted Power .05 .02
- ❑ 654A Howard Johnson AS .05 .02 (Recent Major League Performance)
- ❑ 654B Howard Johnson AS .05 .02 (All-Star Game Performance)
- ❑ 655 Mauro Gozzo .05 .02
- ❑ 656 Mike Blowers RC .10 .05
- ❑ 657 Paul Gibson .05 .02
- ❑ 658 Neal Heaton .05 .02
- ❑ 659 Nolan Ryan 5000K .40 .18 COR (Still an error as Ryan did not lead AL in K's in '75)
- ❑ 659A Nolan Ryan 5000K 1.50 .70 (665 King of Kings back) ERR
- ❑ 660A Harold Baines AS .75 .35 (Black line through star on front; Recent Major League Performance)
- ❑ 660B Harold Baines AS 1.00 .45 (Black line through star on front; All-Star Game Performance)
- ❑ 660C Harold Baines AS .20 .09 (Black line behind star on front; Recent Major League Performance)
- ❑ 660D Harold Baines AS .05 .02 (Black line behind star on front; All-Star Game Performance)
- ❑ 661 Gary Pettis .05 .02
- ❑ 662 Clint Zavaras .05 .02
- ❑ 663A Rick Reuschel AS .05 .02 (Recent Major League Performance)
- ❑ 663B Rick Reuschel AS .05 .02 (All-Star Game Performance)
- ❑ 664 Alejandro Pena .05 .02
- ❑ 665 N.Ryan KING COR .40 .18
- ❑ 665A Nolan Ryan KING 1.50 .70 (659 5000 K back) ERR
- ❑ 665C N.Ryan KING ERR .75 .35 No number on back in factory sets
- ❑ 666 Ricky Horton .05 .02
- ❑ 667 Curt Schilling 1.00 .45
- ❑ 668 Bill Landrum .05 .02
- ❑ 669 Todd Stottlemyre .10 .05
- ❑ 670 Tim Leary .05 .02
- ❑ 671 John Wetteland .20 .09
- ❑ 672 Calvin Schiraldi .05 .02
- ❑ 673A Ruben Sierra AS .05 .02 (Recent Major League Performance)
- ❑ 673B Ruben Sierra AS .05 .02 (All-Star Game Performance)

❑ 674A Pedro Guerrero AS ...... .05 .02
(Recent Major
League Performance)
❑ 674B Pedro Guerrero AS ...... .05 .02
(All-Star Game
Performance)
❑ 675 Ken Phelps .... .05 .02
❑ 676A Cal Ripken AS .... .40 .18
(All-Star Game
Performance)
❑ 676B Cal Ripken AS .... .75 .35
(Recent Major
League Performance)
❑ 677 Denny Walling .... .05 .02
❑ 678 Goose Gossage .... .10 .05
❑ 679 Gary Mielke .... .05 .02
❑ 680 Bill Bathe .... .05 .02
❑ 681 Tom Lawless .... .05 .02
❑ 682 Xavier Hernandez RC .... .05 .02
❑ 683A Kirby Puckett AS .... .25 .11
(Recent Major
League Performance)
❑ 683B Kirby Puckett AS .... .25 .11
(All-Star Game
Performance)
❑ 684 Mariano Duncan .... .05 .02
❑ 685 Ramon Martinez .... .05 .02
❑ 686 Tim Jones .... .05 .02
❑ 687 Tom Filer .... .05 .02
❑ 688 Steve Lombardozzi .... .05 .02
❑ 689 Bernie Williams RC ...... 1.00 .45
❑ 690 Chip Hale .... .05 .02
❑ 691 Beau Allred .... .05 .02
❑ 692A Ryne Sandberg AS ...... .20 .09
(Recent Major
League Performance)
❑ 692B Ryne Sandberg AS ...... .20 .09
(All-Star Game
Performance)
❑ 693 Jeff Huson RC .... .05 .02
❑ 694 Curt Ford .... .05 .02
❑ 695A Eric Davis AS .... .05 .02
(Recent Major
League Performance)
❑ 695B Eric Davis AS .... .05 .02
(All-Star Game
Performance)
❑ 696 Scott Lusader .... .05 .02
❑ 697A Mark McGwire AS .... .20 .09
(Recent Major
League Performance)
❑ 697B Mark McGwire AS .... .20 .09
(All-Star Game
Performance)
❑ 698 Steve Cummings .... .05 .02
❑ 699 George Canale .... .05 .02
❑ 700A Checklist 640-715 .... .20 .09
and BC1-BC26
❑ 700B Checklist 640-716 .... .10 .05
and BC1-BC26
❑ 700C Checklist 618-716 .... .05 .02
❑ 701A Julio Franco AS .... .05 .02
(Recent Major
League Performance)
❑ 701B Julio Franco AS .... .05 .02
(All-Star Game
Performance)
❑ 702 Dave Johnson (P) .... .05 .02
❑ 703A Dave Stewart AS .... .05 .02
(Recent Major
League Performance)
❑ 703B Dave Stewart AS .... .05 .02
(All-Star Game
Performance)
❑ 704 Dave Justice RC .... .60 .25
❑ 705 Tony Gwynn AS .... .20 .09
(All-Star Game
Performance)
❑ 705A Tony Gwynn AS .... .20 .09
(Recent Major
League Performance)
❑ 706 Greg Myers .... .05 .02
❑ 707A Will Clark AS .... .20 .09
(Recent Major
League Performance)
❑ 707B Will Clark AS .... .20 .09
(All-Star Game
Performance)
❑ 708A Benito Santiago AS ...... .05 .02
(Recent Major
League Performance)
❑ 708B Benito Santiago AS ...... .05 .02
(All-Star Game
Performance)
❑ 709 Larry McWilliams .... .05 .02
❑ 710A Ozzie Smith AS .... .20 .09
(Recent Major
League Performance)
❑ 710B Ozzie Smith AS .... .10 .05
(All-Star Game
Performance)
❑ 711 John Olerud RC .... .50 .23
❑ 712A Wade Boggs AS .... .10 .05
(Recent Major
League Performance)
❑ 712B Wade Boggs AS .... .10 .05
(All-Star Game
Performance)
❑ 713 Gary Eave .... .05 .02
❑ 714 Bob Tewksbury .... .05 .02
❑ 715A Kevin Mitchell AS .... .05 .02
(Recent Major
League Performance)
❑ 715B Kevin Mitchell AS .... .05 .02
(All-Star Game
Performance)
❑ 716 B.Giamatti RC COMM .... .20 .09
In Memoriam

1990 Donruss Rookies

	MINT	NRMT
COMP.FACT.SET (56)	2.00	.90

❑ 1 Sandy Alomar Jr. UER ...... .10 .05
(No stitches on base-
ball on Donruss logo
on card front)
❑ 2 John Olerud .... .20 .09
❑ 3 Pat Combs .... .05 .02
❑ 4 Brian DuBois .... .05 .02
❑ 5 Felix Jose .... .05 .02
❑ 6 Delino DeShields .... .20 .09
❑ 7 Mike Stanton .... .05 .02
❑ 8 Mike Munoz .... .05 .02
❑ 9 Craig Grebeck RC .... .05 .02
❑ 10 Joe Kraemer .... .05 .02
❑ 11 Jeff Huson .... .05 .02
❑ 12 Bill Sampen .... .05 .02
❑ 13 Brian Bohanon RC .... .05 .02
❑ 14 Dave Justice .... .60 .25
❑ 15 Robin Ventura .... .20 .09
❑ 16 Greg Vaughn .... .20 .09
❑ 17 Wayne Edwards .... .05 .02
❑ 18 Shawn Boskie RC .... .05 .02
❑ 19 Carlos Baerga RC .... .10 .05
❑ 20 Mark Gardner .... .05 .02
❑ 21 Kevin Appier .... .15 .07
❑ 22 Mike Harkey .... .05 .02
❑ 23 Tim Layana .... .05 .02
❑ 24 Glenallen Hill .... .05 .02
❑ 25 Jerry Kutzler .... .05 .02
❑ 26 Mike Blowers .... .10 .05
❑ 27 Scott Ruskin .... .05 .02
❑ 28 Dana Kiecker .... .05 .02
❑ 29 Willie Blair RC .... .05 .02
❑ 30 Ben McDonald .... .05 .02
❑ 31 Todd Zeile .... .10 .05
❑ 32 Scott Coolbaugh .... .05 .02
❑ 33 Xavier Hernandez .... .05 .02
❑ 34 Mike Hartley .... .05 .02
❑ 35 Kevin Tapani .... .20 .09
❑ 36 Kevin Wickander .... .05 .02
❑ 37 Carlos Hernandez RC .... .20 .09
❑ 38 Brian Traxler RC .... .05 .02
❑ 39 Marty Brown .... .05 .02
❑ 40 Scott Radinsky RC .... .05 .02
❑ 41 Julio Machado .... .05 .02
❑ 42 Steve Avery .... .05 .02
❑ 43 Mark Lemke .... .05 .02
❑ 44 Alan Mills RC .... .05 .02
❑ 45 Marquis Grissom .... .10 .05
❑ 46 Greg Olson RC .... .05 .02
❑ 47 Dave Hollins RC .... .20 .09
❑ 48 Jerald Clark .... .05 .02
❑ 49 Eric Anthony .... .05 .02
❑ 50 Tim Drummond .... .05 .02
❑ 51 John Burkett .... .05 .02
❑ 52 Brent Knackert RC .... .05 .02
❑ 53 Jeff Shaw .... .05 .02
❑ 54 John Orton RC .... .05 .02
❑ 55 Terry Shumpert .... .05 .02
❑ 56 Checklist 1-56 .... .05 .02

1991 Donruss

	MINT	NRMT
COMPLETE SET (770)	8.00	3.60
COMP.FACT.w/LEAF PREV	10.00	4.50
COMP.FACT.w/STUDIO PREV	10.00	4.50
COMP.STARGELL PUZZLE	1.00	.45

❑ 1 Dave Stieb DK .... .05 .02
❑ 2 Craig Biggio DK .... .10 .05
❑ 3 Cecil Fielder DK .... .05 .02
❑ 4 Barry Bonds DK .... .25 .11
❑ 5 Barry Larkin DK .... .10 .05
❑ 6 Dave Parker DK .... .05 .02
❑ 7 Len Dykstra DK .... .05 .02
❑ 8 Bobby Thigpen DK .... .05 .02
❑ 9 Roger Clemens DK .... .25 .11
❑ 10 Ron Gant DK UER .... .05 .02
(No trademark on
team logo on back)
❑ 11 Delino DeShields DK .... .05 .02
❑ 12 R.Alomar DK UER .... .10 .05
No trademark on
team logo on back
❑ 13 Sandy Alomar Jr. DK .... .05 .02
❑ 14 R.Sandberg DK UER .... .15 .07
Was DK in '85, not
'83 as shown
❑ 15 Ramon Martinez DK .... .05 .02
❑ 16 Edgar Martinez DK .... .10 .05
❑ 17 Dave Magadan DK .... .05 .02
❑ 18 Matt Williams DK .... .10 .05
❑ 19 Rafael Palmeiro DK .... .10 .05
UER (No trademark on
team logo on back)
❑ 20 Bob Welch DK .... .05 .02
❑ 21 Dave Righetti DK .... .05 .02
❑ 22 Brian Harper DK .... .05 .02

❑ 23 Gregg Olson DK .05 .02
❑ 24 Kurt Stillwell DK .05 .02
❑ 25 P.Guerrero DK UER .05 .02
No trademark on
team logo on back
❑ 26 Chuck Finley DK UER .05 .02
(No trademark on
team logo on back)
❑ 27 DK Checklist 1-27 .05 .02
❑ 28 Tino Martinez RR .10 .05
❑ 29 Mark Lewis RR .05 .02
❑ 30 Bernard Gilkey RR .05 .02
❑ 31 Hensley Meulens RR .05 .02
❑ 32 Derek Bell RR .10 .05
❑ 33 Jose Offerman RR .05 .02
❑ 34 Terry Bross RR .05 .02
❑ 35 Leo Gomez RR .05 .02
❑ 36 Derrick May RR .05 .02
❑ 37 Kevin Morton RR .05 .02
❑ 38 Moises Alou RR .10 .05
❑ 39 Julio Valera RR .05 .02
❑ 40 Milt Cuyler RR .05 .02
❑ 41 Phil Plantier RR RC .05 .02
❑ 42 Scott Chiamparino RR .05 .02
❑ 43 Ray Lankford RR .10 .05
❑ 44 Mickey Morandini RR .05 .02
❑ 45 Dave Hansen RR .05 .02
❑ 46 Kevin Belcher RR .05 .02
❑ 47 Darrin Fletcher RR .05 .02
❑ 48 Steve Sax AS .05 .02
❑ 49 Ken Griffey Jr. AS .40 .18
❑ 50A J.Canseco AS ERR .10 .05
Team in stat box
should be AL, not A's
❑ 50B J.Canseco AS COR .20 .09
❑ 51 Sandy Alomar Jr. AS .05 .02
❑ 52 Cal Ripken AS .40 .18
❑ 53 Rickey Henderson AS .20 .09
❑ 54 Bob Welch AS .05 .02
❑ 55 Wade Boggs AS .10 .05
❑ 56 Mark McGwire AS .40 .18
❑ 57A Jack McDowell ERR .20 .09
(Career stats do
not include 1990)
❑ 57B Jack McDowell COR .50 .23
(Career stats do
not include 1990)
❑ 58 Jose Lind .05 .02
❑ 59 Alex Fernandez .05 .02
❑ 60 Pat Combs .05 .02
❑ 61 Mike Walker .05 .02
❑ 62 Juan Samuel .05 .02
❑ 63 Mike Blowers UER .05 .02
(Last line has
aseball, not baseball)
❑ 64 Mark Guthrie .05 .02
❑ 65 Mark Salas .05 .02
❑ 66 Tim Jones .05 .02
❑ 67 Tim Leary .05 .02
❑ 68 Andres Galarraga .15 .07
❑ 69 Bob Milacki .05 .02
❑ 70 Tim Belcher .05 .02
❑ 71 Todd Zeile .05 .02
❑ 72 Jerome Walton .05 .02
❑ 73 Kevin Seitzer .05 .02
❑ 74 Jerald Clark .05 .02
❑ 75 John Smoltz UER .10 .05
(Born in Detroit,
not Warren)
❑ 76 Mike Henneman .05 .02
❑ 77 Ken Griffey Jr. .75 .35
❑ 78 Jim Abbott .10 .05
❑ 79 Gregg Jefferies .05 .02
❑ 80 Kevin Reimer .05 .02
❑ 81 Roger Clemens .50 .23
❑ 82 Mike Fitzgerald .05 .02
❑ 83 Bruce Hurst UER .05 .02
(Middle name is
Lee, not Vee)
❑ 84 Eric Davis .10 .05
❑ 85 Paul Molitor .20 .09
❑ 86 Will Clark .20 .09
❑ 87 Mike Bielecki .05 .02
❑ 88 Bret Saberhagen .10 .05
❑ 89 Nolan Ryan 1.00 .45
❑ 90 Bobby Thigpen .05 .02
❑ 91 Dickie Thon .05 .02
❑ 92 Duane Ward .05 .02
❑ 93 Luis Polonia .05 .02
❑ 94 Terry Kennedy .05 .02
❑ 95 Kent Hrbek .10 .05
❑ 96 Danny Jackson .05 .02
❑ 97 Sid Fernandez .05 .02
❑ 98 Jimmy Key .10 .05
❑ 99 Franklin Stubbs .05 .02
❑ 100 Checklist 28-103 .05 .02
❑ 101 R.J. Reynolds .05 .02
❑ 102 Dave Stewart .10 .05
❑ 103 Dan Pasqua .05 .02
❑ 104 Dan Plesac .05 .02
❑ 105 Mark McGwire .75 .35
❑ 106 John Farrell .05 .02
❑ 107 Don Mattingly .50 .23
❑ 108 Carlton Fisk .20 .09
❑ 109 Ken Oberkfell .05 .02
❑ 110 Darrel Akerfelds .05 .02
❑ 111 Gregg Olson .05 .02
❑ 112 Mike Scioscia .05 .02
❑ 113 Bryn Smith .05 .02
❑ 114 Bob Geren .05 .02
❑ 115 Tom Candiotti .05 .02
❑ 116 Kevin Tapani .05 .02
❑ 117 Jeff Treadway .05 .02
❑ 118 Alan Trammell .15 .07
❑ 119 Pete O'Brien .05 .02
(Blue shading goes
through stats)
❑ 120 Joel Skinner .05 .02
❑ 121 Mike LaValliere .05 .02
❑ 122 Dwight Evans .10 .05
❑ 123 Jody Reed .05 .02
❑ 124 Lee Guetterman .05 .02
❑ 125 Tim Burke .05 .02
❑ 126 Dave Johnson .05 .02
❑ 127 Fernando Valenzuela .10 .05
(Lower large stripe
in yellow instead
of blue) UER
❑ 128 Jose DeLeon .05 .02
❑ 129 Andre Dawson .15 .07
❑ 130 Gerald Perry .05 .02
❑ 131 Greg W. Harris .05 .02
❑ 132 Tom Glavine .20 .09
❑ 133 Lance McCullers .05 .02
❑ 134 Randy Johnson .25 .11
❑ 135 Lance Parrish UER .10 .05
(Born in McKeesport,
not Clairton)
❑ 136 Mackey Sasser .05 .02
❑ 137 Geno Petralli .05 .02
❑ 138 Dennis Lamp .05 .02
❑ 139 Dennis Martinez .10 .05
❑ 140 Mike Pagliarulo .05 .02
❑ 141 Hal Morris .05 .02
❑ 142 Dave Parker .10 .05
❑ 143 Brett Butler .10 .05
❑ 144 Paul Assenmacher .05 .02
❑ 145 Mark Gubicza .05 .02
❑ 146 Charlie Hough .10 .05
❑ 147 Sammy Sosa .50 .23
❑ 148 Randy Ready .05 .02
❑ 149 Kelly Gruber .05 .02
❑ 150 Devon White .05 .02
❑ 151 Gary Carter .15 .07
❑ 152 Gene Larkin .05 .02
❑ 153 Chris Sabo .05 .02
❑ 154 David Cone .10 .05
❑ 155 Todd Stottlemyre .05 .02
❑ 156 Glenn Wilson .05 .02
❑ 157 Bob Walk .05 .02
❑ 158 Mike Gallego .05 .02
❑ 159 Greg Hibbard .05 .02
❑ 160 Chris Bosio .05 .02
❑ 161 Mike Moore .05 .02
❑ 162 Jerry Browne UER .05 .02
(Born Christiansted,
should be St. Croix)
❑ 163 Steve Sax UER .05 .02
(No asterisk next to
his 1989 At Bats)
❑ 164 Melido Perez .05 .02
❑ 165 Danny Darwin .05 .02
❑ 166 Roger McDowell .05 .02
❑ 167 Bill Ripken .05 .02
❑ 168 Mike Sharperson .05 .02
❑ 169 Lee Smith .10 .05
❑ 170 Matt Nokes .05 .02
❑ 171 Jesse Orosco .05 .02
❑ 172 Rick Aguilera .10 .05
❑ 173 Jim Presley .05 .02
❑ 174 Lou Whitaker .10 .05
❑ 175 Harold Reynolds .05 .02
❑ 176 Brook Jacoby .05 .02
❑ 177 Wally Backman .05 .02
❑ 178 Wade Boggs .20 .09
❑ 179 Chuck Cary .05 .02
(Comma after DOB,
not on other cards)
❑ 180 Tom Foley .05 .02
❑ 181 Pete Harnisch .05 .02
❑ 182 Mike Morgan .05 .02
❑ 183 Bob Tewksbury .05 .02
❑ 184 Joe Girardi .05 .02
❑ 185 Storm Davis .05 .02
❑ 186 Ed Whitson .05 .02
❑ 187 Steve Avery UER .05 .02
(Born in New Jersey,
should be Michigan)
❑ 188 Lloyd Moseby .05 .02
❑ 189 Scott Bankhead .05 .02
❑ 190 Mark Langston .05 .02
❑ 191 Kevin McReynolds .05 .02
❑ 192 Julio Franco .10 .05
❑ 193 John Dopson .05 .02
❑ 194 Dennis Boyd .05 .02
❑ 195 Bip Roberts .05 .02
❑ 196 Billy Hatcher .05 .02
❑ 197 Edgar Diaz .05 .02
❑ 198 Greg Litton .05 .02
❑ 199 Mark Grace .20 .09
❑ 200 Checklist 104-179 .05 .02
❑ 201 George Brett .40 .18
❑ 202 Jeff Russell .05 .02
❑ 203 Ivan Calderon .05 .02
❑ 204 Ken Howell .05 .02
❑ 205 Tom Henke .05 .02
❑ 206 Bryan Harvey .05 .02
❑ 207 Steve Bedrosian .05 .02
❑ 208 Al Newman .05 .02
❑ 209 Randy Myers .05 .02
❑ 210 Daryl Boston .05 .02
❑ 211 Manny Lee .05 .02
❑ 212 Dave Smith .05 .02
❑ 213 Don Slaught .05 .02
❑ 214 Walt Weiss .05 .02
❑ 215 Donn Pall .05 .02
❑ 216 Jaime Navarro .05 .02
❑ 217 Willie Randolph .10 .05
❑ 218 Rudy Seanez .05 .02
❑ 219 Jim Leyritz .05 .02
❑ 220 Ron Karkovice .05 .02
❑ 221 Ken Caminiti .10 .05
❑ 222 Von Hayes .05 .02
❑ 223 Cal Ripken .75 .35
❑ 224 Lenny Harris .05 .02
❑ 225 Milt Thompson .05 .02
❑ 226 Alvaro Espinoza .05 .02
❑ 227 Chris James .05 .02
❑ 228 Dan Gladden .05 .02
❑ 229 Jeff Blauser .05 .02
❑ 230 Mike Heath .05 .02
❑ 231 Omar Vizquel .10 .05
❑ 232 Doug Jones .05 .02
❑ 233 Jeff King .05 .02
❑ 234 Luis Rivera .05 .02
❑ 235 Ellis Burks .10 .05
❑ 236 Greg Cadaret .05 .02
❑ 237 Dave Martinez .05 .02
❑ 238 Mark Williamson .05 .02
❑ 239 Stan Javier .05 .02
❑ 240 Ozzie Smith .25 .11
❑ 241 Shawn Boskie .05 .02
❑ 242 Tom Gordon .05 .02
❑ 243 Tony Gwynn .40 .18
❑ 244 Tommy Gregg .05 .02
❑ 245 Jeff M. Robinson .05 .02
❑ 246 Keith Comstock .05 .02
❑ 247 Jack Howell .05 .02

❑ 248 Keith Miller .05 .02
❑ 249 Bobby Witt .05 .02
❑ 250 Rob Murphy UER .05 .02
(Shown as on Reds
in '89 in stats,
should be Red Sox)
❑ 251 Spike Owen .05 .02
❑ 252 Garry Templeton .05 .02
❑ 253 Glenn Braggs .05 .02
❑ 254 Ron Robinson .05 .02
❑ 255 Kevin Mitchell .05 .02
❑ 256 Les Lancaster .05 .02
❑ 257 Mel Stottlemyre Jr. .05 .02
❑ 258 Kenny Rogers UER .05 .02
(IP listed as 171,
should be 172)
❑ 259 Lance Johnson .05 .02
❑ 260 John Kruk .10 .05
❑ 261 Fred McGriff .15 .07
❑ 262 Dick Schofield .05 .02
❑ 263 Trevor Wilson .05 .02
❑ 264 David West .05 .02
❑ 265 Scott Scudder .05 .02
❑ 266 Dwight Gooden .10 .05
❑ 267 Willie Blair .05 .02
❑ 268 Mark Portugal .05 .02
❑ 269 Doug Drabek .05 .02
❑ 270 Dennis Eckersley .10 .05
❑ 271 Eric King .05 .02
❑ 272 Robin Yount .20 .09
❑ 273 Carney Lansford .10 .05
❑ 274 Carlos Baerga .05 .02
❑ 275 Dave Righetti .10 .05
❑ 276 Scott Fletcher .05 .02
❑ 277 Eric Yelding .05 .02
❑ 278 Charlie Hayes .05 .02
❑ 279 Jeff Ballard .05 .02
❑ 280 Orel Hershiser .10 .05
❑ 281 Jose Oquendo .05 .02
❑ 282 Mike Witt .05 .02
❑ 283 Mitch Webster .05 .02
❑ 284 Greg Gagne .05 .02
❑ 285 Greg Olson .05 .02
❑ 286 Tony Phillips UER .05 .02
(Born 4/15
should be 4/25)
❑ 287 Scott Bradley .05 .02
❑ 288 Cory Snyder UER .05 .02
(In text, led is re-
peated and Inglewood is
misspelled as Englewood)
❑ 289 Jay Bell UER .10 .05
(Born in Pensacola,
not Eglin AFB)
❑ 290 Kevin Romine .05 .02
❑ 291 Jeff D. Robinson .05 .02
❑ 292 Steve Frey UER .05 .02
(Bats left,
should be right)
❑ 293 Craig Worthington .05 .02
❑ 294 Tim Crews .05 .02
❑ 295 Joe Magrane .05 .02
❑ 296 Hector Villanueva .05 .02
❑ 297 Terry Shumpert .05 .02
❑ 298 Joe Carter .10 .05
❑ 299 Kent Mercker UER .05 .02
(IP listed as 53,
should be 52)
❑ 300 Checklist 180-255 .05 .02
❑ 301 Chet Lemon .05 .02
❑ 302 Mike Schooler .05 .02
❑ 303 Dante Bichette .10 .05
❑ 304 Kevin Elster .05 .02
❑ 305 Jeff Huson .05 .02
❑ 306 Greg A. Harris .05 .02
❑ 307 Marquis Grissom UER .05 .02
(Middle name Deon,
should be Dean)
❑ 308 Calvin Schiraldi .05 .02
❑ 309 Mariano Duncan .05 .02
❑ 310 Bill Spiers .05 .02
❑ 311 Scott Garrelts .05 .02
❑ 312 Mitch Williams .05 .02
❑ 313 Mike Macfarlane .05 .02
❑ 314 Kevin Brown .10 .05
❑ 315 Robin Ventura .10 .05
❑ 316 Darren Daulton .10 .05
❑ 317 Pat Borders .05 .02
❑ 318 Mark Eichhorn .05 .02
❑ 319 Jeff Brantley .05 .02
❑ 320 Shane Mack .05 .02
❑ 321 Rob Dibble .05 .02
❑ 322 John Franco .10 .05
❑ 323 Junior Felix .05 .02
❑ 324 Casey Candaele .05 .02
❑ 325 Bobby Bonilla .10 .05
❑ 326 Dave Henderson .05 .02
❑ 327 Wayne Edwards .05 .02
❑ 328 Mark Knudson .05 .02
❑ 329 Terry Steinbach .05 .02
❑ 330 Colby Ward UER .05 .02
(No comma between
city and state)
❑ 331 Oscar Azocar .05 .02
❑ 332 Scott Radinsky .05 .02
❑ 333 Eric Anthony .05 .02
❑ 334 Steve Lake .05 .02
❑ 335 Bob Melvin .05 .02
❑ 336 Kal Daniels .05 .02
❑ 337 Tom Pagnozzi .05 .02
❑ 338 Alan Mills .05 .02
❑ 339 Steve Olin .05 .02
❑ 340 Juan Berenguer .05 .02
❑ 341 Francisco Cabrera .05 .02
❑ 342 Dave Bergman .05 .02
❑ 343 Henry Cotto .05 .02
❑ 344 Sergio Valdez .05 .02
❑ 345 Bob Patterson .05 .02
❑ 346 John Marzano .05 .02
❑ 347 Dana Kiecker .05 .02
❑ 348 Dion James .05 .02
❑ 349 Hubie Brooks .05 .02
❑ 350 Bill Landrum .05 .02
❑ 351 Bill Sampen .05 .02
❑ 352 Greg Briley .05 .02
❑ 353 Paul Gibson .05 .02
❑ 354 Dave Eiland .05 .02
❑ 355 Steve Finley .10 .05
❑ 356 Bob Boone .10 .05
❑ 357 Steve Buechele .05 .02
❑ 358 Chris Hoiles .05 .02
❑ 359 Larry Walker .15 .07
❑ 360 Frank DiPino .05 .02
❑ 361 Mark Grant .05 .02
❑ 362 Dave Magadan .05 .02
❑ 363 Robby Thompson .05 .02
❑ 364 Lonnie Smith .05 .02
❑ 365 Steve Farr .05 .02
❑ 366 Dave Valle .05 .02
❑ 367 Tim Naehring .05 .02
❑ 368 Jim Acker .05 .02
❑ 369 Jeff Reardon UER .10 .05
(Born in Pittsfield,
not Dalton)
❑ 370 Tim Teufel .05 .02
❑ 371 Juan Gonzalez .25 .11
❑ 372 Luis Salazar .05 .02
❑ 373 Rick Honeycutt .05 .02
❑ 374 Greg Maddux .50 .23
❑ 375 Jose Uribe UER .05 .02
(Middle name Elta,
should be Altá)
❑ 376 Donnie Hill .05 .02
❑ 377 Don Carman .05 .02
❑ 378 Craig Grebeck .05 .02
❑ 379 Willie Fraser .05 .02
❑ 380 Glenallen Hill .05 .02
❑ 381 Joe Oliver .05 .02
❑ 382 Randy Bush .05 .02
❑ 383 Alex Cole .05 .02
❑ 384 Norm Charlton .05 .02
❑ 385 Gene Nelson .05 .02
❑ 386 Checklist 256-331 .05 .02
❑ 387 Rickey Henderson MVP .20 .09
❑ 388 Lance Parrish MVP .05 .02
❑ 389 Fred McGriff MVP .10 .05
❑ 390 Dave Parker MVP .05 .02
❑ 391 Candy Maldonado MVP .05 .02
❑ 392 Ken Griffey Jr. MVP .40 .18
❑ 393 Gregg Olson MVP .05 .02
❑ 394 Rafael Palmeiro MVP .10 .05
❑ 395 Roger Clemens MVP .25 .11
❑ 396 George Brett MVP .20 .09
❑ 397 Cecil Fielder MVP .05 .02
❑ 398 Brian Harper MVP .05 .02
UER (Major League
Performance, should
be Career)
❑ 399 Bobby Thigpen MVP .05 .02
❑ 400 Roberto Kelly MVP .05 .02
UER (Second Base on
front and OF on back)
❑ 401 Danny Darwin MVP .05 .02
❑ 402 Dave Justice MVP .10 .05
❑ 403 Lee Smith MVP .05 .02
❑ 404 Ryne Sandberg MVP .15 .07
❑ 405 Eddie Murray MVP .10 .05
❑ 406 Tim Wallach MVP .05 .02
❑ 407 Kevin Mitchell MVP .05 .02
❑ 408 Darryl Strawberry MVP .05 .02
❑ 409 Joe Carter MVP .05 .02
❑ 410 Len Dykstra MVP .05 .02
❑ 411 Doug Drabek MVP .05 .02
❑ 412 Chris Sabo MVP .05 .02
❑ 413 Paul Marak RR .05 .02
❑ 414 Tim McIntosh RR .05 .02
❑ 415 Brian Barnes RR .05 .02
❑ 416 Eric Gunderson RR .05 .02
❑ 417 Mike Gardiner RR .05 .02
❑ 418 Steve Carter RR .05 .02
❑ 419 Gerald Alexander RR .05 .02
❑ 420 Rich Garces RR RC .05 .02
❑ 421 Chuck Knoblauch RR .10 .05
❑ 422 Scott Aldred RR .05 .02
❑ 423 W.Chamberlain RR RC .05 .02
❑ 424 Lance Dickson RR RC .05 .02
❑ 425 Greg Colbrunn RR RC .10 .05
❑ 426 Rich DeLucia RR UER .05 .02
(Misspelled Delucia
on card)
❑ 427 Jeff Conine RR RC .10 .05
❑ 428 Steve Decker RR .05 .02
❑ 429 Turner Ward RR RC .10 .05
❑ 430 Mo Vaughn RR .10 .05
❑ 431 Steve Chitren RR .05 .02
❑ 432 Mike Benjamin RR .05 .02
❑ 433 Ryne Sandberg AS .15 .07
❑ 434 Len Dykstra AS .05 .02
❑ 435 Andre Dawson AS .10 .05
❑ 436A Mike Scioscia AS .05 .02
(White star by name)
❑ 436B Mike Scioscia AS .05 .02
(Yellow star by name)
❑ 437 Ozzie Smith AS .15 .07
❑ 438 Kevin Mitchell AS .05 .02
❑ 439 Jack Armstrong AS .05 .02
❑ 440 Chris Sabo AS .05 .02
❑ 441 Will Clark AS .10 .05
❑ 442 Mel Hall .05 .02
❑ 443 Mark Gardner .05 .02
❑ 444 Mike Devereaux .05 .02
❑ 445 Kirk Gibson .10 .05
❑ 446 Terry Pendleton .10 .05
❑ 447 Mike Harkey .05 .02
❑ 448 Jim Eisenreich .05 .02
❑ 449 Benito Santiago .05 .02
❑ 450 Oddibe McDowell .05 .02
❑ 451 Cecil Fielder .10 .05
❑ 452 Ken Griffey Sr. .10 .05
❑ 453 Bert Blyleven .10 .05
❑ 454 Howard Johnson .05 .02
❑ 455 Monty Fariss UER .05 .02
(Misspelled Farris
on card)
❑ 456 Tony Pena .05 .02
❑ 457 Tim Raines .10 .05
❑ 458 Dennis Rasmussen .05 .02
❑ 459 Luis Quinones .05 .02
❑ 460 B.J. Surhoff .10 .05
❑ 461 Ernest Riles .05 .02
❑ 462 Rick Sutcliffe .10 .05
❑ 463 Danny Tartabull .05 .02
❑ 464 Pete Incaviglia .05 .02
❑ 465 Carlos Martinez .05 .02
❑ 466 Ricky Jordan .05 .02
❑ 467 John Cerutti .05 .02
❑ 468 Dave Winfield .20 .09
❑ 469 Francisco Oliveras .05 .02

☐ 470	Roy Smith	.05	.02
☐ 471	Barry Larkin	.20	.09
☐ 472	Ron Darling	.05	.02
☐ 473	David Wells	.10	.05
☐ 474	Glenn Davis	.05	.02
☐ 475	Neal Heaton	.05	.02
☐ 476	Ron Hassey	.05	.02
☐ 477	Frank Thomas	.30	.14
☐ 478	Greg Vaughn	.10	.05
☐ 479	Todd Burns	.05	.02
☐ 480	Candy Maldonado	.05	.02
☐ 481	Dave LaPoint	.05	.02
☐ 482	Alvin Davis	.05	.02
☐ 483	Mike Scott	.05	.02
☐ 484	Dale Murphy	.20	.09
☐ 485	Ben McDonald	.05	.02
☐ 486	Jay Howell	.05	.02
☐ 487	Vince Coleman	.05	.02
☐ 488	Alfredo Griffin	.05	.02
☐ 489	Sandy Alomar Jr.	.10	.05
☐ 490	Kirby Puckett	.50	.23
☐ 491	Andres Thomas	.05	.02
☐ 492	Jack Morris	.10	.05
☐ 493	Matt Young	.05	.02
☐ 494	Greg Myers	.05	.02
☐ 495	Barry Bonds	.50	.23
☐ 496	Scott Cooper UER (No BA for 1990 and career)	.05	.02
☐ 497	Dan Schatzeder	.05	.02
☐ 498	Jesse Barfield	.05	.02
☐ 499	Jerry Goff	.05	.02
☐ 500	Checklist 332-408	.05	.02
☐ 501	Anthony Telford	.05	.02
☐ 502	Eddie Murray	.20	.09
☐ 503	Omar Olivares RC	.10	.05
☐ 504	Ryne Sandberg	.25	.11
☐ 505	Jeff Montgomery	.05	.02
☐ 506	Mark Parent	.05	.02
☐ 507	Ron Gant	.05	.02
☐ 508	Frank Tanana	.05	.02
☐ 509	Jay Buhner	.10	.05
☐ 510	Max Venable	.05	.02
☐ 511	Wally Whitehurst	.05	.02
☐ 512	Gary Pettis	.05	.02
☐ 513	Tom Brunansky	.05	.02
☐ 514	Tim Wallach	.05	.02
☐ 515	Craig Lefferts	.05	.02
☐ 516	Tim Layana	.05	.02
☐ 517	Darryl Hamilton	.05	.02
☐ 518	Rick Reuschel	.05	.02
☐ 519	Steve Wilson	.05	.02
☐ 520	Kurt Stillwell	.05	.02
☐ 521	Rafael Palmeiro	.20	.09
☐ 522	Ken Patterson	.05	.02
☐ 523	Len Dykstra	.10	.05
☐ 524	Tony Fernandez	.05	.02
☐ 525	Kent Anderson	.05	.02
☐ 526	Mark Leonard	.05	.02
☐ 527	Allan Anderson	.05	.02
☐ 528	Tom Browning	.05	.02
☐ 529	Frank Viola	.10	.05
☐ 530	John Olerud	.15	.07
☐ 531	Juan Agosto	.05	.02
☐ 532	Zane Smith	.05	.02
☐ 533	Scott Sanderson	.05	.02
☐ 534	Barry Jones	.05	.02
☐ 535	Mike Felder	.05	.02
☐ 536	Jose Canseco	.20	.09
☐ 537	Felix Fermin	.05	.02
☐ 538	Roberto Kelly	.05	.02
☐ 539	Brian Holman	.05	.02
☐ 540	Mark Davidson	.05	.02
☐ 541	Terry Mulholland	.05	.02
☐ 542	Randy Milligan	.05	.02
☐ 543	Jose Gonzalez	.05	.02
☐ 544	Craig Wilson	.05	.02
☐ 545	Mike Hartley	.05	.02
☐ 546	Greg Swindell	.05	.02
☐ 547	Gary Gaetti	.10	.05
☐ 548	Dave Justice	.20	.09
☐ 549	Steve Searcy	.05	.02
☐ 550	Erik Hanson	.05	.02
☐ 551	Dave Stieb	.05	.02
☐ 552	Andy Van Slyke	.10	.05
☐ 553	Mike Greenwell	.05	.02
☐ 554	Kevin Maas	.05	.02
☐ 555	Delino DeShields	.10	.05
☐ 556	Curt Schilling	.20	.09
☐ 557	Ramon Martinez	.05	.02
☐ 558	Pedro Guerrero	.10	.05
☐ 559	Dwight Smith	.05	.02
☐ 560	Mark Davis	.05	.02
☐ 561	Shawn Abner	.05	.02
☐ 562	Charlie Leibrandt	.05	.02
☐ 563	John Shelby	.05	.02
☐ 564	Bill Swift	.05	.02
☐ 565	Mike Fetters	.05	.02
☐ 566	Alejandro Pena	.05	.02
☐ 567	Ruben Sierra	.05	.02
☐ 568	Carlos Quintana	.05	.02
☐ 569	Kevin Gross	.05	.02
☐ 570	Derek Lilliquist	.05	.02
☐ 571	Jack Armstrong	.05	.02
☐ 572	Greg Brock	.05	.02
☐ 573	Mike Kingery	.05	.02
☐ 574	Greg Smith	.05	.02
☐ 575	Brian McRae RC	.10	.05
☐ 576	Jack Daugherty	.05	.02
☐ 577	Ozzie Guillen	.05	.02
☐ 578	Joe Boever	.05	.02
☐ 579	Luis Sojo	.05	.02
☐ 580	Chili Davis	.10	.05
☐ 581	Don Robinson	.05	.02
☐ 582	Brian Harper	.05	.02
☐ 583	Paul O'Neill	.20	.09
☐ 584	Bob Ojeda	.05	.02
☐ 585	Mookie Wilson	.10	.05
☐ 586	Rafael Ramirez	.05	.02
☐ 587	Gary Redus	.05	.02
☐ 588	Jamie Quirk	.05	.02
☐ 589	Shawn Hillegas	.05	.02
☐ 590	Tom Edens	.05	.02
☐ 591	Joe Klink	.05	.02
☐ 592	Charles Nagy	.05	.02
☐ 593	Eric Plunk	.05	.02
☐ 594	Tracy Jones	.05	.02
☐ 595	Craig Biggio	.15	.07
☐ 596	Jose DeJesus	.05	.02
☐ 597	Mickey Tettleton	.05	.02
☐ 598	Chris Gwynn	.05	.02
☐ 599	Rex Hudler	.05	.02
☐ 600	Checklist 409-506	.05	.02
☐ 601	Jim Gott	.05	.02
☐ 602	Jeff Manto	.05	.02
☐ 603	Nelson Liriano	.05	.02
☐ 604	Mark Lemke	.05	.02
☐ 605	Clay Parker	.05	.02
☐ 606	Edgar Martinez	.15	.07
☐ 607	Mark Whiten	.05	.02
☐ 608	Ted Power	.05	.02
☐ 609	Tom Bolton	.05	.02
☐ 610	Tom Herr	.05	.02
☐ 611	Andy Hawkins UER (Pitched No-Hitter on 7/1, not 7/2)	.05	.02
☐ 612	Scott Ruskin	.05	.02
☐ 613	Ron Kittle	.05	.02
☐ 614	John Wetteland	.10	.05
☐ 615	Mike Perez RC	.05	.02
☐ 616	Dave Clark	.05	.02
☐ 617	Brent Mayne	.05	.02
☐ 618	Jack Clark	.10	.05
☐ 619	Marvin Freeman	.05	.02
☐ 620	Edwin Nunez	.05	.02
☐ 621	Russ Swan	.05	.02
☐ 622	Johnny Ray	.05	.02
☐ 623	Charlie O'Brien	.05	.02
☐ 624	Joe Bitker	.05	.02
☐ 625	Mike Marshall	.05	.02
☐ 626	Otis Nixon	.05	.02
☐ 627	Andy Benes	.05	.02
☐ 628	Ron Oester	.05	.02
☐ 629	Ted Higuera	.05	.02
☐ 630	Kevin Bass	.05	.02
☐ 631	Damon Berryhill	.05	.02
☐ 632	Bo Jackson	.10	.05
☐ 633	Brad Arnsberg	.05	.02
☐ 634	Jerry Willard	.05	.02
☐ 635	Tommy Greene	.05	.02
☐ 636	Bob MacDonald	.05	.02
☐ 637	Kirk McCaskill	.05	.02
☐ 638	John Burkett	.05	.02
☐ 639	Paul Abbott RC	.10	.05
☐ 640	Todd Benzinger	.05	.02
☐ 641	Todd Hundley	.05	.02
☐ 642	George Bell	.05	.02
☐ 643	Javier Ortiz	.05	.02
☐ 644	Sid Bream	.05	.02
☐ 645	Bob Welch	.05	.02
☐ 646	Phil Bradley	.05	.02
☐ 647	Bill Krueger	.05	.02
☐ 648	Rickey Henderson	.40	.18
☐ 649	Kevin Wickander	.05	.02
☐ 650	Steve Balboni	.05	.02
☐ 651	Gene Harris	.05	.02
☐ 652	Jim Deshaies	.05	.02
☐ 653	Jason Grimsley	.05	.02
☐ 654	Joe Orsulak	.05	.02
☐ 655	Jim Poole	.05	.02
☐ 656	Felix Jose	.05	.02
☐ 657	Denis Cook	.05	.02
☐ 658	Tom Brookens	.05	.02
☐ 659	Junior Ortiz	.05	.02
☐ 660	Jeff Parrett	.05	.02
☐ 661	Jerry Don Gleaton	.05	.02
☐ 662	Brent Knackert	.05	.02
☐ 663	Rance Mulliniks	.05	.02
☐ 664	John Smiley	.05	.02
☐ 665	Larry Andersen	.05	.02
☐ 666	Willie McGee	.10	.05
☐ 667	Chris Nabholz	.05	.02
☐ 668	Brady Anderson	.10	.05
☐ 669	D.Holmes UER RC 19 CG's, should be 0	.10	.05
☐ 670	Ken Hill	.05	.02
☐ 671	Gary Varsho	.05	.02
☐ 672	Bill Pecota	.05	.02
☐ 673	Fred Lynn	.05	.02
☐ 674	Kevin D. Brown	.05	.02
☐ 675	Dan Petry	.05	.02
☐ 676	Mike Jackson	.05	.02
☐ 677	Wally Joyner	.10	.05
☐ 678	Danny Jackson	.05	.02
☐ 679	Bill Haselman	.05	.02
☐ 680	Mike Boddicker	.05	.02
☐ 681	Mel Rojas	.05	.02
☐ 682	Roberto Alomar	.20	.09
☐ 683	Dave Justice ROY	.10	.05
☐ 684	Chuck Crim	.05	.02
☐ 685	Matt Williams	.15	.07
☐ 686	Shawon Dunston	.05	.02
☐ 687	Jeff Schulz	.05	.02
☐ 688	John Barfield	.05	.02
☐ 689	Gerald Young	.05	.02
☐ 690	Luis Gonzalez RC	2.00	.90
☐ 691	Frank Wills	.05	.02
☐ 692	Chuck Finley	.10	.05
☐ 693	S.Alomar Jr. ROY	.05	.02
☐ 694	Tim Drummond	.05	.02
☐ 695	Herm Winningham	.05	.02
☐ 696	Darryl Strawberry	.10	.05
☐ 697	Al Leiter	.10	.05
☐ 698	Karl Rhodes	.05	.02
☐ 699	Stan Belinda	.05	.02
☐ 700	Checklist 507-604	.05	.02
☐ 701	Lance Blankenship	.05	.02
☐ 702	Willie Stargell PUZ	.20	.09
☐ 703	Jim Gantner	.05	.02
☐ 704	Reggie Harris	.05	.02
☐ 705	Rob Ducey	.05	.02
☐ 706	Tim Hulett	.05	.02
☐ 707	Atlee Hammaker	.05	.02
☐ 708	Xavier Hernandez	.05	.02
☐ 709	Chuck McElroy	.05	.02
☐ 710	John Mitchell	.05	.02
☐ 711	Carlos Hernandez	.05	.02
☐ 712	Geronimo Pena	.05	.02
☐ 713	Jim Neidlinger	.05	.02
☐ 714	John Orton	.05	.02
☐ 715	Terry Leach	.05	.02
☐ 716	Mike Stanton	.05	.02
☐ 717	Walt Terrell	.05	.02
☐ 718	Luis Aquino	.05	.02
☐ 719	Bud Black (Blue Jays uniform, but Giants logo)	.05	.02
☐ 720	Bob Kipper	.05	.02

Card	Mint	Nrmt
❑ 721 Jeff Gray	.05	.02
❑ 722 Jose Rijo	.05	.02
❑ 723 Curt Young	.05	.02
❑ 724 Jose Vizcaino	.05	.02
❑ 725 Randy Tomlin RC	.05	.02
❑ 726 Junior Noboa	.05	.02
❑ 727 Bob Welch CY	.05	.02
❑ 728 Gary Ward	.05	.02
❑ 729 Rob Deer (Brewers uniform, but Tigers logo)	.05	.02
❑ 730 David Segui	.05	.02
❑ 731 Mark Carreon	.05	.02
❑ 732 Vicente Palacios	.05	.02
❑ 733 Sam Horn	.05	.02
❑ 734 Howard Farmer	.05	.02
❑ 735 Ken Dayley (Cardinals uniform, but Blue Jays logo)	.05	.02
❑ 736 Kelly Mann	.05	.02
❑ 737 Joe Grahe RC	.05	.02
❑ 738 Kelly Downs	.05	.02
❑ 739 Jimmy Kremers	.05	.02
❑ 740 Kevin Appier	.10	.05
❑ 741 Jeff Reed	.05	.02
❑ 742 Jose Rijo WS	.05	.02
❑ 743 Dave Rohde	.05	.02
❑ 744 Dr.Dirt/Mr.Clean Len Dykstra Dale Murphy UER (No '91 Donruss logo on card front)	.10	.05
❑ 745 Paul Sorrento	.05	.02
❑ 746 Thomas Howard	.05	.02
❑ 747 Matt Stark	.05	.02
❑ 748 Harold Baines	.10	.05
❑ 749 Doug Dascenzo	.05	.02
❑ 750 Doug Drabek CY	.05	.02
❑ 751 Gary Sheffield	.10	.05
❑ 752 Terry Lee	.05	.02
❑ 753 Jim Vatcher	.05	.02
❑ 754 Lee Stevens	.05	.02
❑ 755 Randy Veres	.05	.02
❑ 756 Bill Doran	.05	.02
❑ 757 Gary Wayne	.05	.02
❑ 758 Pedro Munoz RC	.05	.02
❑ 759 Chris Hammond	.05	.02
❑ 760 Checklist 605-702	.05	.02
❑ 761 R.Henderson MVP	.20	.09
❑ 762 Barry Bonds MVP	.25	.11
❑ 763 Billy Hatcher WS UER (Line 13, on should be one)	.05	.02
❑ 764 Julio Machado	.05	.02
❑ 765 Jose Mesa	.05	.02
❑ 766 Willie Randolph WS	.05	.02
❑ 767 Scott Erickson	.05	.02
❑ 768 Travis Fryman	.10	.05
❑ 769 Rich Rodriguez	.05	.02
❑ 770 Checklist 703-770 and BC1-BC22	.05	.02

1991 Donruss Rookies

	MINT	NRMT
COMP.FACT.SET (56)	6.00	2.70

Card	Mint	Nrmt
❑ 1 Pat Kelly RC	.05	.02
❑ 2 Rich DeLucia	.05	.02
❑ 3 Wes Chamberlain	.05	.02
❑ 4 Scott Leius	.05	.02
❑ 5 Darryl Kile	.10	.05
❑ 6 Milt Cuyler	.05	.02
❑ 7 Todd Van Poppel RC	.05	.02
❑ 8 Ray Lankford	.10	.05
❑ 9 Brian R. Hunter RC	.10	.05
❑ 10 Tony Perezchica	.05	.02
❑ 11 Ced Landrum	.05	.02
❑ 12 Dave Burba RC	.10	.05
❑ 13 Ramon Garcia	.05	.02
❑ 14 Ed Sprague	.05	.02
❑ 15 Warren Newson	.05	.02
❑ 16 Paul Faries	.05	.02
❑ 17 Luis Gonzalez	2.00	.90
❑ 18 Charles Nagy	.05	.02
❑ 19 Chris Hammond	.05	.02

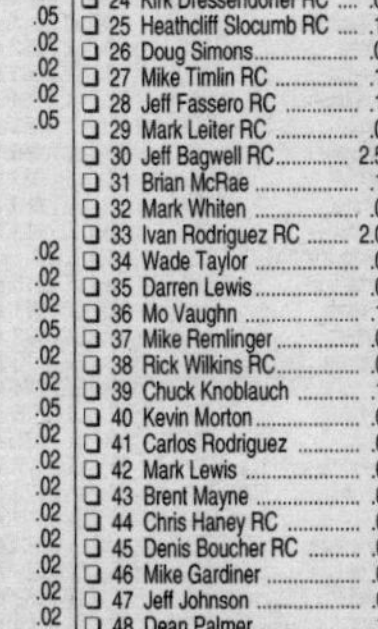

Card	Mint	Nrmt
❑ 20 Frank Castillo RC	.10	.05
❑ 21 Pedro Munoz	.05	.02
❑ 22 Orlando Merced RC	.05	.02
❑ 23 Jose Melendez	.05	.02
❑ 24 Kirk Dressendorfer RC	.05	.02
❑ 25 Heathcliff Slocumb RC	.10	.05
❑ 26 Doug Simons	.05	.02
❑ 27 Mike Timlin RC	.10	.05
❑ 28 Jeff Fassero RC	.10	.05
❑ 29 Mark Leiter RC	.05	.02
❑ 30 Jeff Bagwell RC	2.50	1.10
❑ 31 Brian McRae	.10	.05
❑ 32 Mark Whiten	.05	.02
❑ 33 Ivan Rodriguez RC	2.00	.90
❑ 34 Wade Taylor	.05	.02
❑ 35 Darren Lewis	.05	.02
❑ 36 Mo Vaughn	.10	.05
❑ 37 Mike Remlinger	.05	.02
❑ 38 Rick Wilkins RC	.05	.02
❑ 39 Chuck Knoblauch	.10	.05
❑ 40 Kevin Morton	.05	.02
❑ 41 Carlos Rodriguez	.05	.02
❑ 42 Mark Lewis	.05	.02
❑ 43 Brent Mayne	.05	.02
❑ 44 Chris Haney RC	.05	.02
❑ 45 Denis Boucher RC	.05	.02
❑ 46 Mike Gardiner	.05	.02
❑ 47 Jeff Johnson	.05	.02
❑ 48 Dean Palmer	.10	.05
❑ 49 Chuck McElroy	.05	.02
❑ 50 Chris Jones RC	.05	.02
❑ 51 Scott Kamieniecki RC	.05	.02
❑ 52 Al Osuna RC	.05	.02
❑ 53 Rusty Meacham RC	.05	.02
❑ 54 Chito Martinez	.05	.02
❑ 55 Reggie Jefferson	.05	.02
❑ 56 Checklist 1-56	.05	.02

1992 Donruss

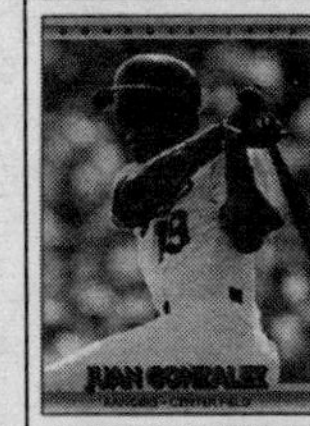

	MINT	NRMT
COMPLETE SET (784)	10.00	4.50
COMP.HOBBY SET (788)	15.00	6.75
COMP.RETAIL SET (788)	10.00	4.50
COMPLETE SERIES 1 (396)	5.00	2.20
COMPLETE SERIES 2 (388)	5.00	2.20
COMP.CAREW PUZZLE	1.00	.45

Card	Mint	Nrmt
❑ 1 Mark Wohlers RR	.05	.02
❑ 2 Wil Cordero RR	.05	.02
❑ 3 Kyle Abbott RR	.05	.02
❑ 4 Dave Nilsson RR	.05	.02
❑ 5 Kenny Lofton RR	.20	.09
❑ 6 Luis Mercedes RR	.05	.02
❑ 7 Roger Salkeld RR	.05	.02
❑ 8 Eddie Zosky RR	.05	.02
❑ 9 Todd Van Poppel RR	.05	.02
❑ 10 Frank Seminara RR RC	.05	.02
❑ 11 Andy Ashby RR	.05	.02
❑ 12 Reggie Jefferson RR	.05	.02
❑ 13 Ryan Klesko RR	.10	.05
❑ 14 Carlos Garcia RR	.05	.02
❑ 15 John Ramos RR	.05	.02
❑ 16 Eric Karros RR	.10	.05
❑ 17 Patrick Lennon RR	.05	.02
❑ 18 E.Taubensee RR RC	.10	.05
❑ 19 Roberto Hernandez RR	.05	.02
❑ 20 D.J. Dozier RR	.05	.02
❑ 21 Dave Henderson AS	.05	.02
❑ 22 Cal Ripken AS	.40	.18
❑ 23 Wade Boggs AS	.10	.05
❑ 24 Ken Griffey Jr. AS	.50	.23
❑ 25 Jack Morris AS	.05	.02
❑ 26 Danny Tartabull AS	.05	.02
❑ 27 Cecil Fielder AS	.05	.02
❑ 28 Roberto Alomar AS	.10	.05
❑ 29 Sandy Alomar Jr. AS	.10	.05
❑ 30 Rickey Henderson AS	.20	.09
❑ 31 Ken Hill	.05	.02
❑ 32 John Habyan	.05	.02
❑ 33 Otis Nixon HL	.05	.02
❑ 34 Tim Wallach	.05	.02
❑ 35 Cal Ripken	.75	.35
❑ 36 Gary Carter	.15	.07
❑ 37 Juan Agosto	.05	.02
❑ 38 Doug Dascenzo	.05	.02
❑ 39 Kirk Gibson	.10	.05
❑ 40 Benito Santiago	.05	.02
❑ 41 Otis Nixon	.05	.02
❑ 42 Andy Allanson	.05	.02
❑ 43 Brian Holman	.05	.02
❑ 44 Dick Schofield	.05	.02
❑ 45 Dave Magadan	.05	.02
❑ 46 Rafael Palmeiro	.20	.09
❑ 47 Jody Reed	.05	.02
❑ 48 Ivan Calderon	.05	.02
❑ 49 Greg W. Harris	.05	.02
❑ 50 Chris Sabo	.05	.02
❑ 51 Paul Molitor	.20	.09
❑ 52 Robby Thompson	.05	.02
❑ 53 Dave Smith	.05	.02
❑ 54 Mark Davis	.05	.02
❑ 55 Kevin Brown	.10	.05
❑ 56 Donn Pall	.05	.02
❑ 57 Len Dykstra	.10	.05
❑ 58 Roberto Alomar	.20	.09
❑ 59 Jeff D. Robinson	.05	.02
❑ 60 Willie McGee	.10	.05
❑ 61 Jay Buhner	.10	.05
❑ 62 Mike Pagliarulo	.05	.02
❑ 63 Paul O'Neill	.20	.09
❑ 64 Hubie Brooks	.05	.02
❑ 65 Kelly Gruber	.05	.02
❑ 66 Ken Caminiti	.10	.05
❑ 67 Gary Redus	.05	.02
❑ 68 Harold Baines	.10	.05
❑ 69 Charlie Hough	.10	.05
❑ 70 B.J. Surhoff	.10	.05
❑ 71 Walt Weiss	.05	.02
❑ 72 Shawn Hillegas	.05	.02
❑ 73 Roberto Kelly	.05	.02
❑ 74 Jeff Ballard	.05	.02
❑ 75 Craig Biggio	.15	.07
❑ 76 Pat Combs	.05	.02
❑ 77 Jeff M. Robinson	.05	.02
❑ 78 Tim Belcher	.05	.02
❑ 79 Cris Carpenter	.05	.02
❑ 80 Checklist 1-79	.05	.02
❑ 81 Steve Avery	.05	.02
❑ 82 Chris James	.05	.02
❑ 83 Brian Harper	.05	.02
❑ 84 Charlie Leibrandt	.05	.02
❑ 85 Mickey Tettleton	.05	.02
❑ 86 Pete O'Brien	.05	.02
❑ 87 Danny Darwin	.05	.02
❑ 88 Bob Walk	.05	.02

❑	89	Jeff Reardon	.10	.05
❑	90	Bobby Rose	.05	.02
❑	91	Danny Jackson	.05	.02
❑	92	John Morris	.05	.02
❑	93	Bud Black	.05	.02
❑	94	Tommy Greene HL	.05	.02
❑	95	Rick Aguilera	.10	.05
❑	96	Gary Gaetti	.10	.05
❑	97	David Cone	.10	.05
❑	98	John Olerud	.10	.05
❑	99	Joel Skinner	.05	.02
❑	100	Jay Bell	.10	.05
❑	101	Bob Milacki	.05	.02
❑	102	Norm Charlton	.05	.02
❑	103	Chuck Crim	.05	.02
❑	104	Terry Steinbach	.05	.02
❑	105	Juan Samuel	.05	.02
❑	106	Steve Howe	.05	.02
❑	107	Rafael Belliard	.05	.02
❑	108	Joey Cora	.05	.02
❑	109	Tommy Greene	.05	.02
❑	110	Gregg Olson	.05	.02
❑	111	Frank Tanana	.05	.02
❑	112	Lee Smith	.10	.05
❑	113	Greg A. Harris	.05	.02
❑	114	Dwayne Henry	.05	.02
❑	115	Chili Davis	.10	.05
❑	116	Kent Mercker	.05	.02
❑	117	Brian Barnes	.05	.02
❑	118	Rich DeLucia	.05	.02
❑	119	Andre Dawson	.15	.07
❑	120	Carlos Baerga	.05	.02
❑	121	Mike LaValliere	.05	.02
❑	122	Jeff Gray	.05	.02
❑	123	Bruce Hurst	.05	.02
❑	124	Alvin Davis	.05	.02
❑	125	John Candelaria	.05	.02
❑	126	Matt Nokes	.05	.02
❑	127	George Bell	.05	.02
❑	128	Bret Saberhagen	.10	.05
❑	129	Jeff Russell	.05	.02
❑	130	Jim Abbott	.10	.05
❑	131	Bill Gullickson	.05	.02
❑	132	Todd Zeile	.05	.02
❑	133	Dave Winfield	.20	.09
❑	134	Wally Whitehurst	.05	.02
❑	135	Matt Williams	.15	.07
❑	136	Tom Browning	.05	.02
❑	137	Marquis Grissom	.05	.02
❑	138	Erik Hanson	.05	.02
❑	139	Rob Dibble	.05	.02
❑	140	Don August	.05	.02
❑	141	Tom Henke	.05	.02
❑	142	Dan Pasqua	.05	.02
❑	143	George Brett	.40	.18
❑	144	Jerald Clark	.05	.02
❑	145	Robin Ventura	.10	.05
❑	146	Dale Murphy	.20	.09
❑	147	Dennis Eckersley	.10	.05
❑	148	Eric Yelding	.05	.02
❑	149	Mario Diaz	.05	.02
❑	150	Casey Candaele	.05	.02
❑	151	Steve Olin	.05	.02
❑	152	Luis Salazar	.05	.02
❑	153	Kevin Maas	.05	.02
❑	154	Nolan Ryan HL	.50	.23
❑	155	Barry Jones	.05	.02
❑	156	Chris Hoiles	.05	.02
❑	157	Bob Ojeda	.05	.02
❑	158	Pedro Guerrero	.10	.05
❑	159	Paul Assenmacher	.05	.02
❑	160	Checklist 80-157	.05	.02
❑	161	Mike Macfarlane	.05	.02
❑	162	Craig Lefferts	.05	.02
❑	163	Brian Hunter	.05	.02
❑	164	Alan Trammell	.15	.07
❑	165	Ken Griffey Jr.	.60	.25
❑	166	Lance Parrish	.10	.05
❑	167	Brian Downing	.05	.02
❑	168	John Barfield	.05	.02
❑	169	Jack Clark	.10	.05
❑	170	Chris Nabholz	.05	.02
❑	171	Tim Teufel	.05	.02
❑	172	Chris Hammond	.05	.02
❑	173	Robin Yount	.20	.09
❑	174	Dave Righetti	.10	.05
❑	175	Joe Girardi	.05	.02
❑	176	Mike Boddicker	.05	.02
❑	177	Dean Palmer	.10	.05
❑	178	Greg Hibbard	.05	.02
❑	179	Randy Ready	.05	.02
❑	180	Devon White	.05	.02
❑	181	Mark Eichhorn	.05	.02
❑	182	Mike Felder	.05	.02
❑	183	Joe Klink	.05	.02
❑	184	Steve Bedrosian	.05	.02
❑	185	Barry Larkin	.20	.09
❑	186	John Franco	.10	.05
❑	187	Ed Sprague	.05	.02
❑	188	Mark Portugal	.05	.02
❑	189	Jose Lind	.05	.02
❑	190	Bob Welch	.05	.02
❑	191	Alex Fernandez	.05	.02
❑	192	Gary Sheffield	.10	.05
❑	193	Rickey Henderson	.40	.18
❑	194	Rod Nichols	.05	.02
❑	195	Scott Kamieniecki	.05	.02
❑	196	Mike Flanagan	.05	.02
❑	197	Steve Finley	.10	.05
❑	198	Darren Daulton	.10	.05
❑	199	Leo Gomez	.05	.02
❑	200	Mike Morgan	.05	.02
❑	201	Bob Tewksbury	.05	.02
❑	202	Sid Bream	.05	.02
❑	203	Sandy Alomar Jr.	.10	.05
❑	204	Greg Gagne	.05	.02
❑	205	Juan Berenguer	.05	.02
❑	206	Cecil Fielder	.10	.05
❑	207	Randy Johnson	.25	.11
❑	208	Tony Pena	.05	.02
❑	209	Doug Drabek	.05	.02
❑	210	Wade Boggs	.20	.09
❑	211	Bryan Harvey	.05	.02
❑	212	Jose Vizcaino	.05	.02
❑	213	Alonzo Powell	.05	.02
❑	214	Will Clark	.20	.09
❑	215	Rickey Henderson HL	.20	.09
❑	216	Jack Morris	.10	.05
❑	217	Junior Felix	.05	.02
❑	218	Vince Coleman	.05	.02
❑	219	Jimmy Key	.10	.05
❑	220	Alex Cole	.05	.02
❑	221	Bill Landrum	.05	.02
❑	222	Randy Milligan	.05	.02
❑	223	Jose Rijo	.05	.02
❑	224	Greg Vaughn	.10	.05
❑	225	Dave Stewart	.10	.05
❑	226	Lenny Harris	.05	.02
❑	227	Scott Sanderson	.05	.02
❑	228	Jeff Blauser	.05	.02
❑	229	Ozzie Guillen	.05	.02
❑	230	John Kruk	.10	.05
❑	231	Bob Melvin	.05	.02
❑	232	Milt Cuyler	.05	.02
❑	233	Felix Jose	.05	.02
❑	234	Ellis Burks	.10	.05
❑	235	Pete Harnisch	.05	.02
❑	236	Kevin Tapani	.05	.02
❑	237	Terry Pendleton	.10	.05
❑	238	Mark Gardner	.05	.02
❑	239	Harold Reynolds	.05	.02
❑	240	Checklist 158-237	.05	.02
❑	241	Mike Harkey	.05	.02
❑	242	Felix Fermin	.05	.02
❑	243	Barry Bonds	.50	.23
❑	244	Roger Clemens	.50	.23
❑	245	Dennis Rasmussen	.05	.02
❑	246	Jose DeLeon	.05	.02
❑	247	Orel Hershiser	.10	.05
❑	248	Mel Hall	.05	.02
❑	249	Rick Wilkins	.05	.02
❑	250	Tom Gordon	.05	.02
❑	251	Kevin Reimer	.05	.02
❑	252	Luis Polonia	.05	.02
❑	253	Mike Henneman	.05	.02
❑	254	Tom Pagnozzi	.05	.02
❑	255	Chuck Finley	.10	.05
❑	256	Mackey Sasser	.05	.02
❑	257	John Burkett	.05	.02
❑	258	Hal Morris	.05	.02
❑	259	Larry Walker	.15	.07
❑	260	Bill Swift	.05	.02
❑	261	Joe Oliver	.05	.02
❑	262	Julio Machado	.05	.02
❑	263	Todd Stottlemyre	.05	.02
❑	264	Matt Merullo	.05	.02
❑	265	Brent Mayne	.05	.02
❑	266	Thomas Howard	.05	.02
❑	267	Lance Johnson	.05	.02
❑	268	Terry Mulholland	.05	.02
❑	269	Rick Honeycutt	.05	.02
❑	270	Luis Gonzalez	.20	.09
❑	271	Jose Guzman	.05	.02
❑	272	Jimmy Jones	.05	.02
❑	273	Mark Lewis	.05	.02
❑	274	Rene Gonzales	.05	.02
❑	275	Jeff Johnson	.05	.02
❑	276	Dennis Martinez HL	.05	.02
❑	277	Delino DeShields	.05	.02
❑	278	Sam Horn	.05	.02
❑	279	Kevin Gross	.05	.02
❑	280	Jose Oquendo	.05	.02
❑	281	Mark Grace	.20	.09
❑	282	Mark Gubicza	.05	.02
❑	283	Fred McGriff	.15	.07
❑	284	Ron Gant	.05	.02
❑	285	Lou Whitaker	.10	.05
❑	286	Edgar Martinez	.15	.07
❑	287	Ron Tingley	.05	.02
❑	288	Kevin McReynolds	.05	.02
❑	289	Ivan Rodriguez	.25	.11
❑	290	Mike Gardiner	.05	.02
❑	291	Chris Haney	.05	.02
❑	292	Darrin Jackson	.05	.02
❑	293	Bill Doran	.05	.02
❑	294	Ted Higuera	.05	.02
❑	295	Jeff Brantley	.05	.02
❑	296	Les Lancaster	.05	.02
❑	297	Jim Eisenreich	.05	.02
❑	298	Ruben Sierra	.05	.02
❑	299	Scott Radinsky	.05	.02
❑	300	Jose DeJesus	.05	.02
❑	301	Mike Timlin	.05	.02
❑	302	Luis Sojo	.05	.02
❑	303	Kelly Downs	.05	.02
❑	304	Scott Bankhead	.05	.02
❑	305	Pedro Munoz	.05	.02
❑	306	Scott Scudder	.05	.02
❑	307	Kevin Elster	.05	.02
❑	308	Duane Ward	.05	.02
❑	309	Darryl Kile	.10	.05
❑	310	Orlando Merced	.05	.02
❑	311	Dave Henderson	.05	.02
❑	312	Tim Raines	.10	.05
❑	313	Mark Lee	.05	.02
❑	314	Mike Gallego	.05	.02
❑	315	Charles Nagy	.05	.02
❑	316	Jesse Barfield	.05	.02
❑	317	Todd Frohwirth	.05	.02
❑	318	Al Osuna	.05	.02
❑	319	Darrin Fletcher	.05	.02
❑	320	Checklist 238-316	.05	.02
❑	321	David Segui	.05	.02
❑	322	Stan Javier	.05	.02
❑	323	Bryn Smith	.05	.02
❑	324	Jeff Treadway	.05	.02
❑	325	Mark Whiten	.05	.02
❑	326	Kent Hrbek	.10	.05
❑	327	Dave Justice	.10	.05
❑	328	Tony Phillips	.05	.02
❑	329	Rob Murphy	.05	.02
❑	330	Kevin Morton	.05	.02
❑	331	John Smiley	.05	.02
❑	332	Luis Rivera	.05	.02
❑	333	Wally Joyner	.10	.05
❑	334	Heathcliff Slocumb	.05	.02
❑	335	Rick Cerone	.05	.02
❑	336	Mike Remlinger	.05	.02
❑	337	Mike Moore	.05	.02
❑	338	Lloyd McClendon	.05	.02
❑	339	Al Newman	.05	.02
❑	340	Kirk McCaskill	.05	.02
❑	341	Howard Johnson	.05	.02
❑	342	Greg Myers	.05	.02
❑	343	Kal Daniels	.05	.02
❑	344	Bernie Williams	.20	.09
❑	345	Shane Mack	.05	.02
❑	346	Gary Thurman	.05	.02

❑ 347 Dante Bichette .10 .05
❑ 348 Mark McGwire .75 .35
❑ 349 Travis Fryman .10 .05
❑ 350 Ray Lankford .05 .02
❑ 351 Mike Jeffcoat .05 .02
❑ 352 Jack McDowell .05 .02
❑ 353 Mitch Williams .05 .02
❑ 354 Mike Devereaux .05 .02
❑ 355 Andres Galarraga .15 .07
❑ 356 Henry Cotto .05 .02
❑ 357 Scott Bailes .05 .02
❑ 358 Jeff Bagwell .40 .18
❑ 359 Scott Leius .05 .02
❑ 360 Zane Smith .05 .02
❑ 361 Bill Pecota .05 .02
❑ 362 Tony Fernandez .05 .02
❑ 363 Glenn Braggs .05 .02
❑ 364 Bill Spiers .05 .02
❑ 365 Vicente Palacios .05 .02
❑ 366 Tim Burke .05 .02
❑ 367 Randy Tomlin .05 .02
❑ 368 Kenny Rogers .05 .02
❑ 369 Brett Butler .10 .05
❑ 370 Pat Kelly .05 .02
❑ 371 Bip Roberts .05 .02
❑ 372 Gregg Jefferies .05 .02
❑ 373 Kevin Bass .05 .02
❑ 374 Ron Karkovice .05 .02
❑ 375 Paul Gibson .05 .02
❑ 376 Bernard Gilkey .05 .02
❑ 377 Dave Gallagher .05 .02
❑ 378 Bill Wegman .05 .02
❑ 379 Pat Borders .05 .02
❑ 380 Ed Whitson .05 .02
❑ 381 Gilberto Reyes .05 .02
❑ 382 Russ Swan .05 .02
❑ 383 Andy Van Slyke .10 .05
❑ 384 Wes Chamberlain .05 .02
❑ 385 Steve Chitren .05 .02
❑ 386 Greg Olson .05 .02
❑ 387 Brian McRae .05 .02
❑ 388 Rich Rodriguez .05 .02
❑ 389 Steve Decker .05 .02
❑ 390 Chuck Knoblauch .10 .05
❑ 391 Bobby Witt .05 .02
❑ 392 Eddie Murray .20 .09
❑ 393 Juan Gonzalez .20 .09
❑ 394 Scott Ruskin .05 .02
❑ 395 Jay Howell .05 .02
❑ 396 Checklist 317-396 .05 .02
❑ 397 Royce Clayton RR .05 .02
❑ 398 John Jaha RR RC .10 .05
❑ 399 Dan Wilson RR .05 .02
❑ 400 Archie Corbin RR .05 .02
❑ 401 Barry Manuel RR .05 .02
❑ 402 Kim Batiste RR .05 .02
❑ 403 Pat Mahomes RR RC .05 .02
❑ 404 Dave Fleming RR .05 .02
❑ 405 Jeff Juden RR .05 .02
❑ 406 Jim Thome RR .20 .09
❑ 407 Sam Militello RR .05 .02
❑ 408 Jeff Nelson RR RC .10 .05
❑ 409 Anthony Young RR .05 .02
❑ 410 Tino Martinez RR .10 .05
❑ 411 Jeff Mutis RR .05 .02
❑ 412 Rey Sanchez RR RC .10 .05
❑ 413 Chris Gardner RR .05 .02
❑ 414 John Vander Wal RR .05 .02
❑ 415 Reggie Sanders RR .05 .02
❑ 416 Brian Williams RR RC .05 .02
❑ 417 Mo Sanford RR .05 .02
❑ 418 D.Weathers RR RC .05 .02
❑ 419 Hector Fajardo RR RC .05 .02
❑ 420 Steve Foster RR .05 .02
❑ 421 Lance Dickson RR .05 .02
❑ 422 Andre Dawson AS .10 .05
❑ 423 Ozzie Smith AS .15 .07
❑ 424 Chris Sabo AS .05 .02
❑ 425 Tony Gwynn AS .20 .09
❑ 426 Tom Glavine AS .10 .05
❑ 427 Bobby Bonilla AS .05 .02
❑ 428 Will Clark AS .10 .05
❑ 429 Ryne Sandberg AS .15 .07
❑ 430 Benito Santiago AS .05 .02
❑ 431 Ivan Calderon AS .05 .02
❑ 432 Ozzie Smith .25 .11
❑ 433 Tim Leary .05 .02
❑ 434 Bret Saberhagen HL .05 .02
❑ 435 Mel Rojas .05 .02
❑ 436 Ben McDonald .05 .02
❑ 437 Tim Crews .05 .02
❑ 438 Rex Hudler .05 .02
❑ 439 Chico Walker .05 .02
❑ 440 Kurt Stillwell .05 .02
❑ 441 Tony Gwynn .40 .18
❑ 442 John Smoltz .10 .05
❑ 443 Lloyd Moseby .05 .02
❑ 444 Mike Schooler .05 .02
❑ 445 Joe Grahe .05 .02
❑ 446 Dwight Gooden .10 .05
❑ 447 Oil Can Boyd .05 .02
❑ 448 John Marzano .05 .02
❑ 449 Bret Barberie .05 .02
❑ 450 Mike Maddux .05 .02
❑ 451 Jeff Reed .05 .02
❑ 452 Dale Sveum .05 .02
❑ 453 Jose Uribe .05 .02
❑ 454 Bob Scanlan .05 .02
❑ 455 Kevin Appier .10 .05
❑ 456 Jeff Huson .05 .02
❑ 457 Ken Patterson .05 .02
❑ 458 Ricky Jordan .05 .02
❑ 459 Tom Candiotti .05 .02
❑ 460 Lee Stevens .05 .02
❑ 461 Rod Beck RC .20 .09
❑ 462 Dave Valle .05 .02
❑ 463 Scott Erickson .05 .02
❑ 464 Chris Jones .05 .02
❑ 465 Mark Carreon .05 .02
❑ 466 Rob Ducey .05 .02
❑ 467 Jim Corsi .05 .02
❑ 468 Jeff King .05 .02
❑ 469 Curt Young .05 .02
❑ 470 Bo Jackson .10 .05
❑ 471 Chris Bosio .05 .02
❑ 472 Jamie Quirk .05 .02
❑ 473 Jesse Orosco .05 .02
❑ 474 Alvaro Espinoza .05 .02
❑ 475 Joe Orsulak .05 .02
❑ 476 Checklist 397-477 .05 .02
❑ 477 Gerald Young .05 .02
❑ 478 Wally Backman .05 .02
❑ 479 Juan Bell .05 .02
❑ 480 Mike Scioscia .05 .02
❑ 481 Omar Olivares .05 .02
❑ 482 Francisco Cabrera .05 .02
❑ 483 Greg Swindell UER .05 .02
(Shown on Indians,
but listed on Reds)
❑ 484 Terry Leach .05 .02
❑ 485 Tommy Gregg .05 .02
❑ 486 Scott Aldred .05 .02
❑ 487 Greg Briley .05 .02
❑ 488 Phil Plantier .05 .02
❑ 489 Curtis Wilkerson .05 .02
❑ 490 Tom Brunansky .05 .02
❑ 491 Mike Fetters .05 .02
❑ 492 Frank Castillo .05 .02
❑ 493 Joe Boever .05 .02
❑ 494 Kirt Manwaring .05 .02
❑ 495 Wilson Alvarez HL .05 .02
❑ 496 Gene Larkin .05 .02
❑ 497 Gary DiSarcina .05 .02
❑ 498 Frank Viola .10 .05
❑ 499 Manuel Lee .05 .02
❑ 500 Albert Belle .10 .05
❑ 501 Stan Belinda .05 .02
❑ 502 Dwight Evans .10 .05
❑ 503 Eric Davis .10 .05
❑ 504 Darren Holmes .05 .02
❑ 505 Mike Bordick .05 .02
❑ 506 Dave Hansen .05 .02
❑ 507 Lee Guetterman .05 .02
❑ 508 Keith Mitchell .05 .02
❑ 509 Melido Perez .05 .02
❑ 510 Dickie Thon .05 .02
❑ 511 Mark Williamson .05 .02
❑ 512 Mark Salas .05 .02
❑ 513 Milt Thompson .05 .02
❑ 514 Mo Vaughn .10 .05
❑ 515 Jim Deshaies .05 .02
❑ 516 Rich Garces .05 .02
❑ 517 Lonnie Smith .05 .02
❑ 518 Spike Owen .05 .02
❑ 519 Tracy Jones .05 .02
❑ 520 Greg Maddux .50 .23
❑ 521 Carlos Martinez .05 .02
❑ 522 Neal Heaton .05 .02
❑ 523 Mike Greenwell .05 .02
❑ 524 Andy Benes .05 .02
❑ 525 Jeff Schaefer UER .05 .02
(Photo actually
Tino Martinez)
❑ 526 Mike Sharperson .05 .02
❑ 527 Wade Taylor .05 .02
❑ 528 Jerome Walton .05 .02
❑ 529 Storm Davis .05 .02
❑ 530 Jose Hernandez RC .05 .02
❑ 531 Mark Langston .05 .02
❑ 532 Rob Deer .05 .02
❑ 533 Geronimo Pena .05 .02
❑ 534 Juan Guzman .05 .02
❑ 535 Pete Schourek .05 .02
❑ 536 Todd Benzinger .05 .02
❑ 537 Billy Hatcher .05 .02
❑ 538 Tom Foley .05 .02
❑ 539 Dave Cochrane .05 .02
❑ 540 Mariano Duncan .05 .02
❑ 541 Edwin Nunez .05 .02
❑ 542 Rance Mulliniks .05 .02
❑ 543 Carlton Fisk .20 .09
❑ 544 Luis Aquino .05 .02
❑ 545 Ricky Bones .05 .02
❑ 546 Craig Grebeck .05 .02
❑ 547 Charlie Hayes .05 .02
❑ 548 Jose Canseco .20 .09
❑ 549 Andujar Cedeno .05 .02
❑ 550 Geno Petralli .05 .02
❑ 551 Javier Ortiz .05 .02
❑ 552 Rudy Seanez .05 .02
❑ 553 Rich Gedman .05 .02
❑ 554 Eric Plunk .05 .02
❑ 555 Nolan Ryan HL .40 .18
(With Rich Gossage)
❑ 556 Checklist 478-555 .05 .02
❑ 557 Greg Colbrunn .05 .02
❑ 558 Chito Martinez .05 .02
❑ 559 Darryl Strawberry .10 .05
❑ 560 Luis Alicea .05 .02
❑ 561 Dwight Smith .05 .02
❑ 562 Terry Shumpert .05 .02
❑ 563 Jim Vatcher .05 .02
❑ 564 Deion Sanders .10 .05
❑ 565 Walt Terrell .05 .02
❑ 566 Dave Burba .05 .02
❑ 567 Dave Howard .05 .02
❑ 568 Todd Hundley .05 .02
❑ 569 Jack Daugherty .05 .02
❑ 570 Scott Cooper .05 .02
❑ 571 Bill Sampen .05 .02
❑ 572 Jose Melendez .05 .02
❑ 573 Freddie Benavides .05 .02
❑ 574 Jim Gantner .05 .02
❑ 575 Trevor Wilson .05 .02
❑ 576 Ryne Sandberg .25 .11
❑ 577 Kevin Seitzer .05 .02
❑ 578 Gerald Alexander .05 .02
❑ 579 Mike Huff .05 .02
❑ 580 Von Hayes .05 .02
❑ 581 Derek Bell .10 .05
❑ 582 Mike Stanley .05 .02
❑ 583 Kevin Mitchell .05 .02
❑ 584 Mike Jackson .05 .02
❑ 585 Dan Gladden .05 .02
❑ 586 Ted Power UER .05 .02
(Wrong year given for
signing with Reds)
❑ 587 Jeff Innis .05 .02
❑ 588 Bob MacDonald .05 .02
❑ 589 Jose Tolentino .05 .02
❑ 590 Bob Patterson .05 .02
❑ 591 Scott Brosius RC .50 .23
❑ 592 Frank Thomas .25 .11
❑ 593 Darryl Hamilton .05 .02
❑ 594 Kirk Dressendorfer .05 .02
❑ 595 Jeff Shaw .05 .02
❑ 596 Don Mattingly .50 .23
❑ 597 Glenn Davis .05 .02

❑ 598 Andy Mota .05 .02
❑ 599 Jason Grimsley .05 .02
❑ 600 Jim Poole .05 .02
❑ 601 Jim Gott .05 .02
❑ 602 Stan Royer .05 .02
❑ 603 Marvin Freeman .05 .02
❑ 604 Denis Boucher .05 .02
❑ 605 Denny Neagle .10 .05
❑ 606 Mark Lemke .05 .02
❑ 607 Jerry Don Gleaton .05 .02
❑ 608 Brent Knackert .05 .02
❑ 609 Carlos Quintana .05 .02
❑ 610 Bobby Bonilla .10 .05
❑ 611 Joe Hesketh .05 .02
❑ 612 Daryl Boston .05 .02
❑ 613 Shawon Dunston .05 .02
❑ 614 Danny Cox .05 .02
❑ 615 Darren Lewis .05 .02
❑ 616 Braves No-Hitter UER .05 .02
Kent Mercker
(Misspelled Merker
on card front)
Alejandro Pena
Mark Wohlers
❑ 617 Kirby Puckett .50 .23
❑ 618 Franklin Stubbs .05 .02
❑ 619 Chris Donnels .05 .02
❑ 620 David Wells UER .10 .05
(Career Highlights
in black not red)
❑ 621 Mike Aldrete .05 .02
❑ 622 Bob Kipper .05 .02
❑ 623 Anthony Telford .05 .02
❑ 624 Randy Myers .05 .02
❑ 625 Willie Randolph .10 .05
❑ 626 Joe Slusarski .05 .02
❑ 627 John Wetteland .10 .05
❑ 628 Greg Cadaret .05 .02
❑ 629 Tom Glavine .20 .09
❑ 630 Wilson Alvarez .05 .02
❑ 631 Wally Ritchie .05 .02
❑ 632 Mike Mussina .30 .14
❑ 633 Mark Leiter .05 .02
❑ 634 Gerald Perry .05 .02
❑ 635 Matt Young .05 .02
❑ 636 Checklist 556-635 .05 .02
❑ 637 Scott Hemond .05 .02
❑ 638 David West .05 .02
❑ 639 Jim Clancy .05 .02
❑ 640 Doug Piatt UER .05 .02
(Not born in 1955 as
on card; incorrect info
on How Acquired)
❑ 641 Omar Vizquel .10 .05
❑ 642 Rick Sutcliffe .10 .05
❑ 643 Glenallen Hill .05 .02
❑ 644 Gary Varsho .05 .02
❑ 645 Tony Fossas .05 .02
❑ 646 Jack Howell .05 .02
❑ 647 Jim Campanis .05 .02
❑ 648 Chris Gwynn .05 .02
❑ 649 Jim Leyritz .05 .02
❑ 650 Chuck McElroy .05 .02
❑ 651 Sean Berry .05 .02
❑ 652 Donald Harris .05 .02
❑ 653 Don Slaught .05 .02
❑ 654 Rusty Meacham .05 .02
❑ 655 Scott Terry .05 .02
❑ 656 Ramon Martinez .05 .02
❑ 657 Keith Miller .05 .02
❑ 658 Ramon Garcia .05 .02
❑ 659 Milt Hill .05 .02
❑ 660 Steve Frey .05 .02
❑ 661 Bob McClure .05 .02
❑ 662 Ced Landrum .05 .02
❑ 663 Doug Henry RC .05 .02
❑ 664 Candy Maldonado .05 .02
❑ 665 Carl Willis .05 .02
❑ 666 Jeff Montgomery .05 .02
❑ 667 Craig Shipley .05 .02
❑ 668 Warren Newson .05 .02
❑ 669 Mickey Morandini .05 .02
❑ 670 Brook Jacoby .05 .02
❑ 671 Ryan Bowen .05 .02
❑ 672 Bill Krueger .05 .02
❑ 673 Rob Mallicoat .05 .02
❑ 674 Doug Jones .05 .02
❑ 675 Scott Livingstone .05 .02
❑ 676 Danny Tartabull .05 .02
❑ 677 Joe Carter HL .05 .02
❑ 678 Cecil Espy .05 .02
❑ 679 Randy Velarde .05 .02
❑ 680 Bruce Ruffin .05 .02
❑ 681 Ted Wood .05 .02
❑ 682 Dan Plesac .05 .02
❑ 683 Eric Bullock .05 .02
❑ 684 Junior Ortiz .05 .02
❑ 685 Dave Hollins .05 .02
❑ 686 Dennis Martinez .10 .05
❑ 687 Larry Andersen .05 .02
❑ 688 Doug Simons .05 .02
❑ 689 Tim Spehr .05 .02
❑ 690 Calvin Jones .05 .02
❑ 691 Mark Guthrie .05 .02
❑ 692 Alfredo Griffin .05 .02
❑ 693 Joe Carter .10 .05
❑ 694 Terry Mathews .05 .02
❑ 695 Pascual Perez .05 .02
❑ 696 Gene Nelson .05 .02
❑ 697 Gerald Williams .05 .02
❑ 698 Chris Cron .05 .02
❑ 699 Steve Buechele .05 .02
❑ 700 Paul McClellan .05 .02
❑ 701 Jim Lindeman .05 .02
❑ 702 Francisco Oliveras .05 .02
❑ 703 Rob Maurer .05 .02
❑ 704 Pat Hentgen .05 .02
❑ 705 Jaime Navarro .05 .02
❑ 706 Mike Magnante RC .05 .02
❑ 707 Nolan Ryan 1.00 .45
❑ 708 Bobby Thigpen .05 .02
❑ 709 John Cerutti .05 .02
❑ 710 Steve Wilson .05 .02
❑ 711 Hensley Meulens .05 .02
❑ 712 Rheal Cormier .05 .02
❑ 713 Scott Bradley .05 .02
❑ 714 Mitch Webster .05 .02
❑ 715 Roger Mason .05 .02
❑ 716 Checklist 636-716 .05 .02
❑ 717 Jeff Fassero .05 .02
❑ 718 Cal Eldred .05 .02
❑ 719 Sid Fernandez .05 .02
❑ 720 Bob Zupcic RC .05 .02
❑ 721 Jose Offerman .05 .02
❑ 722 Cliff Brantley .05 .02
❑ 723 Ron Darling .05 .02
❑ 724 Dave Stieb .05 .02
❑ 725 Hector Villanueva .05 .02
❑ 726 Mike Hartley .05 .02
❑ 727 Arthur Rhodes .05 .02
❑ 728 Randy Bush .05 .02
❑ 729 Steve Sax .05 .02
❑ 730 Dave Otto .05 .02
❑ 731 John Wehner .05 .02
❑ 732 Dave Martinez .05 .02
❑ 733 Ruben Amaro .05 .02
❑ 734 Billy Ripken .05 .02
❑ 735 Steve Farr .05 .02
❑ 736 Shawn Abner .05 .02
❑ 737 Gil Heredia RC .10 .05
❑ 738 Ron Jones .05 .02
❑ 739 Tony Castillo .05 .02
❑ 740 Sammy Sosa .40 .18
❑ 741 Julio Franco .10 .05
❑ 742 Tim Naehring .05 .02
❑ 743 Steve Wapnick .05 .02
❑ 744 Craig Wilson .05 .02
❑ 745 Darrin Chapin .05 .02
❑ 746 Chris George .05 .02
❑ 747 Mike Simms .05 .02
❑ 748 Rosario Rodriguez .05 .02
❑ 749 Skeeter Barnes .05 .02
❑ 750 Roger McDowell .05 .02
❑ 751 Dann Howitt .05 .02
❑ 752 Paul Sorrento .05 .02
❑ 753 Braulio Castillo .05 .02
❑ 754 Yorkis Perez .05 .02
❑ 755 Willie Fraser .05 .02
❑ 756 Jeremy Hernandez RC .05 .02
❑ 757 Curt Schilling .20 .09
❑ 758 Steve Lyons .05 .02
❑ 759 Dave Anderson .05 .02
❑ 760 Willie Banks .05 .02
❑ 761 Mark Leonard .05 .02
❑ 762 Jack Armstrong .05 .02
(Listed on Indians,
but shown on Reds)
❑ 763 Scott Servais .05 .02
❑ 764 Ray Stephens .05 .02
❑ 765 Junior Noboa .05 .02
❑ 766 Jim Olander .05 .02
❑ 767 Joe Magrane .05 .02
❑ 768 Lance Blankenship .05 .02
❑ 769 Mike Humphreys .05 .02
❑ 770 Jarvis Brown .05 .02
❑ 771 Damon Berryhill .05 .02
❑ 772 Alejandro Pena .05 .02
❑ 773 Jose Mesa .05 .02
❑ 774 Gary Cooper .05 .02
❑ 775 Carney Lansford .10 .05
❑ 776 Mike Bielecki .05 .02
(Shown on Cubs,
but listed on Braves)
❑ 777 Charlie O'Brien .05 .02
❑ 778 Carlos Hernandez .05 .02
❑ 779 Howard Farmer .05 .02
❑ 780 Mike Stanton .05 .02
❑ 781 Reggie Harris .05 .02
❑ 782 Xavier Hernandez .05 .02
❑ 783 Bryan Hickerson RC .05 .02
❑ 784 Checklist 717-784 .05 .02
and BC1-BC8

1992 Donruss Rookies

	MINT	NRMT
COMPLETE SET (132)	10.00	4.50

❑ 1 Kyle Abbott .05 .02
❑ 2 Troy Afenir .05 .02
❑ 3 Rich Amaral RC .05 .02
❑ 4 Ruben Amaro .05 .02
❑ 5 Billy Ashley RC .05 .02
❑ 6 Pedro Astacio RC .10 .05
❑ 7 Jim Austin .05 .02
❑ 8 Robert Ayrault .05 .02
❑ 9 Kevin Baez .05 .02
❑ 10 Esteban Beltre .05 .02
❑ 11 Brian Bohanon .05 .02
❑ 12 Kent Bottenfield RC .10 .05
❑ 13 Jeff Branson .05 .02
❑ 14 Brad Brink .05 .02
❑ 15 John Briscoe .05 .02
❑ 16 Doug Brocail RC .05 .02
❑ 17 Rico Brogna .05 .02
❑ 18 J.T. Bruett .05 .02
❑ 19 Jacob Brumfield .05 .02
❑ 20 Jim Bullinger .05 .02
❑ 21 Kevin Campbell .05 .02
❑ 22 Pedro Castellano RC .05 .02
❑ 23 Mike Christopher .05 .02
❑ 24 Archi Cianfrocco RC .05 .02
❑ 25 Mark Clark RC .10 .05
❑ 26 Craig Colbert .05 .02
❑ 27 Victor Cole .05 .02
❑ 28 Steve Cooke RC .05 .02
❑ 29 Tim Costo .05 .02
❑ 30 Chad Curtis RC .10 .05
❑ 31 Doug Davis .05 .02
❑ 32 Gary DiSarcina .05 .02

	MINT	NRMT
❑ 33 John Doherty RC	.05	.02
❑ 34 Mike Draper	.05	.02
❑ 35 Monty Fariss	.05	.02
❑ 36 Bien Figueroa	.05	.02
❑ 37 John Flaherty	.05	.02
❑ 38 Tim Fortugno	.05	.02
❑ 39 Eric Fox RC	.05	.02
❑ 40 Jeff Frye RC	.10	.05
❑ 41 Ramon Garcia	.05	.02
❑ 42 Brent Gates RC	.05	.02
❑ 43 Tom Goodwin	.05	.02
❑ 44 Buddy Groom	.05	.02
❑ 45 Jeff Grotewold	.05	.02
❑ 46 Juan Guerrero	.05	.02
❑ 47 Johnny Guzman RC	.05	.02
❑ 48 Shawn Hare RC	.05	.02
❑ 49 Ryan Hawblitzel RC	.05	.02
❑ 50 Bert Hefferman	.05	.02
❑ 51 Butch Henry	.05	.02
❑ 52 Cesar Hernandez RC	.05	.02
❑ 53 Vince Horsman	.05	.02
❑ 54 Steve Hosey	.05	.02
❑ 55 Pat Howell	.05	.02
❑ 56 Peter Hoy	.05	.02
❑ 57 Jonathan Hurst RC	.05	.02
❑ 58 Mark Hutton RC	.05	.02
❑ 59 Shawn Jeter RC	.05	.02
❑ 60 Joel Johnston	.05	.02
❑ 61 Jeff Kent RC	2.00	.90
❑ 62 Kurt Knudsen RC	.05	.02
❑ 63 Kevin Koslofski	.05	.02
❑ 64 Danny Leon	.05	.02
❑ 65 Jesse Levis	.05	.02
❑ 66 Tom Marsh	.05	.02
❑ 67 Ed Martel	.05	.02
❑ 68 Al Martin RC	.10	.05
❑ 69 Pedro Martinez	3.00	1.35
❑ 70 Derrick May	.05	.02
❑ 71 Matt Maysey	.05	.02
❑ 72 Russ McGinnis	.05	.02
❑ 73 Tim McIntosh	.05	.02
❑ 74 Jim McNamara	.05	.02
❑ 75 Jeff McNeely	.05	.02
❑ 76 Rusty Meacham	.05	.02
❑ 77 Tony Menendez	.05	.02
❑ 78 Henry Mercedes	.05	.02
❑ 79 Paul Miller	.05	.02
❑ 80 Joe Millette	.05	.02
❑ 81 Blas Minor	.05	.02
❑ 82 Dennis Moeller	.05	.02
❑ 83 Raul Mondesi	.20	.09
❑ 84 Rob Natal	.05	.02
❑ 85 Troy Neel RC	.05	.02
❑ 86 David Nied RC	.05	.02
❑ 87 Jerry Nielson	.05	.02
❑ 88 Donovan Osborne	.05	.02
❑ 89 John Patterson	.05	.02
❑ 90 Roger Pavlik RC	.05	.02
❑ 91 Dan Peltier	.05	.02
❑ 92 Jim Pena	.05	.02
❑ 93 William Pennyfeather	.05	.02
❑ 94 Mike Perez	.05	.02
❑ 95 Hipolito Pichardo RC	.05	.02
❑ 96 Greg Pirkl RC	.05	.02
❑ 97 Harvey Pulliam	.05	.02
❑ 98 Manny Ramirez RC	5.00	2.20
❑ 99 Pat Rapp RC	.10	.05
❑ 100 Jeff Reboulet	.05	.02
❑ 101 Darren Reed	.05	.02
❑ 102 Shane Reynolds RC	.10	.05
❑ 103 Bill Risley	.05	.02
❑ 104 Ben Rivera	.05	.02
❑ 105 Henry Rodriguez	.05	.02
❑ 106 Rico Rossy	.05	.02
❑ 107 Johnny Ruffin	.05	.02
❑ 108 Steve Scarsone	.05	.02
❑ 109 Tim Scott	.05	.02
❑ 110 Steve Shifflett	.05	.02
❑ 111 Dave Silvestri	.05	.02
❑ 112 Matt Stairs RC	.10	.05
❑ 113 William Suero	.05	.02
❑ 114 Jeff Tackett	.05	.02
❑ 115 Eddie Taubensee	.10	.05
❑ 116 Rick Trlicek RC	.05	.02
❑ 117 Scooter Tucker	.05	.02
❑ 118 Shane Turner	.05	.02
❑ 119 Julio Valera	.05	.02
❑ 120 Paul Wagner RC	.05	.02
❑ 121 Tim Wakefield RC	.10	.05
❑ 122 Mike Walker	.05	.02
❑ 123 Bruce Walton	.05	.02
❑ 124 Lenny Webster	.05	.02
❑ 125 Bob Wickman	.05	.02
❑ 126 Mike Williams RC	.05	.02
❑ 127 Kerry Woodson	.05	.02
❑ 128 Eric Young RC	.10	.05
❑ 129 Kevin Young RC	.20	.09
❑ 130 Pete Young	.05	.02
❑ 131 Checklist 1-66	.05	.02
❑ 132 Checklist 67-132	.05	.02

1993 Donruss

	MINT	NRMT
COMPLETE SET (792)	30.00	13.50
COMPLETE SERIES 1 (396)	15.00	6.75
COMPLETE SERIES 2 (396)	15.00	6.75

	MINT	NRMT
❑ 1 Craig Lefferts	.10	.05
❑ 2 Kent Mercker	.10	.05
❑ 3 Phil Plantier	.10	.05
❑ 4 Alex Arias	.10	.05
❑ 5 Julio Valera	.10	.05
❑ 6 Dan Wilson	.15	.07
❑ 7 Frank Thomas	.50	.23
❑ 8 Eric Anthony	.10	.05
❑ 9 Derek Lilliquist	.10	.05
❑ 10 Rafael Bournigal	.10	.05
❑ 11 Manny Alexander RR	.10	.05
❑ 12 Bret Barberie	.10	.05
❑ 13 Mickey Tettleton	.10	.05
❑ 14 Anthony Young	.10	.05
❑ 15 Tim Spehr	.10	.05
❑ 16 Bob Ayrault	.10	.05
❑ 17 Bill Wegman	.10	.05
❑ 18 Jay Bell	.15	.07
❑ 19 Rick Aguilera	.10	.05
❑ 20 Todd Zeile	.10	.05
❑ 21 Steve Farr	.10	.05
❑ 22 Andy Benes	.10	.05
❑ 23 Lance Blankenship	.10	.05
❑ 24 Ted Wood	.10	.05
❑ 25 Omar Vizquel	.15	.07
❑ 26 Steve Avery	.10	.05
❑ 27 Brian Bohanon	.10	.05
❑ 28 Rick Wilkins	.10	.05
❑ 29 Devon White	.10	.05
❑ 30 Bobby Ayala RC	.10	.05
❑ 31 Leo Gomez	.10	.05
❑ 32 Mike Simms	.10	.05
❑ 33 Ellis Burks	.15	.07
❑ 34 Steve Wilson	.10	.05
❑ 35 Jim Abbott	.15	.07
❑ 36 Tim Wallach	.10	.05
❑ 37 Wilson Alvarez	.10	.05
❑ 38 Daryl Boston	.10	.05
❑ 39 Sandy Alomar Jr.	.15	.07
❑ 40 Mitch Williams	.10	.05
❑ 41 Rico Brogna	.10	.05
❑ 42 Gary Varsho	.10	.05
❑ 43 Kevin Appier	.15	.07
❑ 44 Eric Wedge RR RC	.10	.05
❑ 45 Dante Bichette	.15	.07
❑ 46 Jose Oquendo	.10	.05
❑ 47 Mike Trombley	.10	.05
❑ 48 Dan Walters	.10	.05
❑ 49 Gerald Williams	.10	.05
❑ 50 Bud Black	.10	.05
❑ 51 Bobby Witt	.10	.05
❑ 52 Mark Davis	.10	.05
❑ 53 Shawn Barton RC	.10	.05
❑ 54 Paul Assenmacher	.10	.05
❑ 55 Kevin Reimer	.10	.05
❑ 56 Billy Ashley RR	.10	.05
❑ 57 Eddie Zosky	.10	.05
❑ 58 Chris Sabo	.10	.05
❑ 59 Billy Ripken	.10	.05
❑ 60 Scooter Tucker	.10	.05
❑ 61 Tim Wakefield RR	.10	.05
❑ 62 Mitch Webster	.10	.05
❑ 63 Jack Clark	.15	.07
❑ 64 Mark Gardner	.10	.05
❑ 65 Lee Stevens	.10	.05
❑ 66 Todd Hundley	.10	.05
❑ 67 Bobby Thigpen	.10	.05
❑ 68 Dave Hollins	.10	.05
❑ 69 Jack Armstrong	.10	.05
❑ 70 Alex Cole	.10	.05
❑ 71 Mark Carreon	.10	.05
❑ 72 Todd Worrell	.10	.05
❑ 73 Steve Shifflett	.10	.05
❑ 74 Jerald Clark	.10	.05
❑ 75 Paul Molitor	.40	.18
❑ 76 Larry Carter	.10	.05
❑ 77 Rich Rowland RR	.10	.05
❑ 78 Damon Berryhill	.10	.05
❑ 79 Willie Banks	.10	.05
❑ 80 Hector Villanueva	.10	.05
❑ 81 Mike Gallego	.10	.05
❑ 82 Tim Belcher	.10	.05
❑ 83 Mike Bordick	.10	.05
❑ 84 Craig Biggio	.25	.11
❑ 85 Lance Parrish	.15	.07
❑ 86 Brett Butler	.15	.07
❑ 87 Mike Timlin	.10	.05
❑ 88 Brian Barnes	.10	.05
❑ 89 Brady Anderson	.15	.07
❑ 90 D.J. Dozier	.10	.05
❑ 91 Frank Viola	.15	.07
❑ 92 Darren Daulton	.15	.07
❑ 93 Chad Curtis	.10	.05
❑ 94 Zane Smith	.10	.05
❑ 95 George Bell	.10	.05
❑ 96 Rex Hudler	.10	.05
❑ 97 Mark Whiten	.10	.05
❑ 98 Tim Teufel	.10	.05
❑ 99 Kevin Ritz	.10	.05
❑ 100 Jeff Brantley	.10	.05
❑ 101 Jeff Conine	.10	.05
❑ 102 Vinny Castilla	.15	.07
❑ 103 Greg Vaughn	.15	.07
❑ 104 Steve Buechele	.10	.05
❑ 105 Darren Reed	.10	.05
❑ 106 Bip Roberts	.10	.05
❑ 107 John Habyan	.10	.05
❑ 108 Scott Servais	.10	.05
❑ 109 Walt Weiss	.10	.05
❑ 110 J.T. Snow RR RC	.50	.23
❑ 111 Jay Buhner	.15	.07
❑ 112 Darryl Strawberry	.15	.07
❑ 113 Roger Pavlik	.10	.05
❑ 114 Chris Nabholz	.10	.05
❑ 115 Pat Borders	.10	.05
❑ 116 Pat Howell	.10	.05
❑ 117 Gregg Olson	.10	.05
❑ 118 Curt Schilling	.40	.18
❑ 119 Roger Clemens	1.00	.45
❑ 120 Victor Cole	.10	.05
❑ 121 Gary DiSarcina	.10	.05
❑ 122 Checklist 1-80 Gary Carter and Kirt Manwaring	.15	.07
❑ 123 Steve Sax	.10	.05
❑ 124 Chuck Carr	.10	.05
❑ 125 Mark Lewis	.10	.05
❑ 126 Tony Gwynn	.75	.35
❑ 127 Travis Fryman	.15	.07
❑ 128 Dave Burba	.10	.05
❑ 129 Wally Joyner	.15	.07
❑ 130 John Smoltz	.15	.07

❑ 131 Cal Eldred .10 .05
❑ 132 Checklist 81-159 .15 .07
Roberto Alomar and
Devon White
❑ 133 Arthur Rhodes .10 .05
❑ 134 Jeff Blauser .10 .05
❑ 135 Scott Cooper .10 .05
❑ 136 Doug Strange .10 .05
❑ 137 Luis Sojo .10 .05
❑ 138 Jeff Branson .10 .05
❑ 139 Alex Fernandez .10 .05
❑ 140 Ken Caminiti .15 .07
❑ 141 Charles Nagy .10 .05
❑ 142 Tom Candiotti .10 .05
❑ 143 Willie Greene RR .10 .05
❑ 144 John Vander Wal .10 .05
❑ 145 Kurt Knudsen .10 .05
❑ 146 John Franco .15 .07
❑ 147 Eddie Pierce RC .10 .05
❑ 148 Kim Batiste .10 .05
❑ 149 Darren Holmes .10 .05
❑ 150 Steve Cooke .10 .05
❑ 151 Terry Jorgensen .10 .05
❑ 152 Mark Clark .10 .05
❑ 153 Randy Velarde .10 .05
❑ 154 Greg W. Harris .10 .05
❑ 155 Kevin Campbell .10 .05
❑ 156 John Burkett .10 .05
❑ 157 Kevin Mitchell .10 .05
❑ 158 Deion Sanders .15 .07
❑ 159 Jose Canseco .40 .18
❑ 160 Jeff Hartsock .10 .05
❑ 161 Tom Quinlan RC .10 .05
❑ 162 Tim Pugh RC .10 .05
❑ 163 Glenn Davis .10 .05
❑ 164 Shane Reynolds .10 .05
❑ 165 Jody Reed .10 .05
❑ 166 Mike Sharperson .10 .05
❑ 167 Scott Lewis .10 .05
❑ 168 Dennis Martinez .15 .07
❑ 169 Scott Radinsky .10 .05
❑ 170 Dave Gallagher .10 .05
❑ 171 Jim Thome .40 .18
❑ 172 Terry Mulholland .10 .05
❑ 173 Milt Cuyler .10 .05
❑ 174 Bob Patterson .10 .05
❑ 175 Jeff Montgomery .10 .05
❑ 176 Tim Salmon RR .15 .07
❑ 177 Franklin Stubbs .10 .05
❑ 178 Donovan Osborne .10 .05
❑ 179 Jeff Reboulet .10 .05
❑ 180 Jeremy Hernandez .10 .05
❑ 181 Charlie Hayes .10 .05
❑ 182 Matt Williams .25 .11
❑ 183 Mike Raczka .10 .05
❑ 184 Francisco Cabrera .10 .05
❑ 185 Rich DeLucia .10 .05
❑ 186 Sammy Sosa .75 .35
❑ 187 Ivan Rodriguez .40 .18
❑ 188 Bret Boone RR .15 .07
❑ 189 Juan Guzman .10 .05
❑ 190 Tom Browning .10 .05
❑ 191 Randy Milligan .10 .05
❑ 192 Steve Finley .15 .07
❑ 193 John Patterson RR .10 .05
❑ 194 Kip Gross .10 .05
❑ 195 Tony Fossas .10 .05
❑ 196 Ivan Calderon .10 .05
❑ 197 Junior Felix .10 .05
❑ 198 Pete Schourek .10 .05
❑ 199 Craig Grebeck .10 .05
❑ 200 Juan Bell .10 .05
❑ 201 Glenallen Hill .10 .05
❑ 202 Danny Jackson .10 .05
❑ 203 John Kiely .10 .05
❑ 204 Bob Tewksbury .10 .05
❑ 205 Kevin Koslofski .10 .05
❑ 206 Craig Shipley .10 .05
❑ 207 John Jaha .10 .05
❑ 208 Royce Clayton .10 .05
❑ 209 Mike Piazza RR 2.00 .90
❑ 210 Ron Gant .10 .05
❑ 211 Scott Erickson .10 .05
❑ 212 Doug Dascenzo .10 .05
❑ 213 Andy Stankiewicz .10 .05
❑ 214 Geronimo Berroa .10 .05
❑ 215 Dennis Eckersley .15 .07
❑ 216 Al Osuna .10 .05
❑ 217 Tino Martinez .15 .07
❑ 218 Henry Rodriguez .10 .05
❑ 219 Ed Sprague .10 .05
❑ 220 Ken Hill .10 .05
❑ 221 Chito Martinez .10 .05
❑ 222 Bret Saberhagen .15 .07
❑ 223 Mike Greenwell .10 .05
❑ 224 Mickey Morandini .10 .05
❑ 225 Chuck Finley .15 .07
❑ 226 Denny Neagle .15 .07
❑ 227 Kirk McCaskill .10 .05
❑ 228 Rheal Cormier .10 .05
❑ 229 Paul Sorrento .10 .05
❑ 230 Darrin Jackson .10 .05
❑ 231 Rob Deer .10 .05
❑ 232 Bill Swift .10 .05
❑ 233 Kevin McReynolds .10 .05
❑ 234 Terry Pendleton .15 .07
❑ 235 Dave Nilsson .10 .05
❑ 236 Chuck McElroy .10 .05
❑ 237 Derek Parks .10 .05
❑ 238 Norm Charlton .10 .05
❑ 239 Matt Nokes .10 .05
❑ 240 Juan Guerrero .10 .05
❑ 241 Jeff Parrett .10 .05
❑ 242 Ryan Thompson RR .10 .05
❑ 243 Dave Fleming .10 .05
❑ 244 Dave Hansen .10 .05
❑ 245 Monty Fariss .10 .05
❑ 246 Archi Cianfrocco .10 .05
❑ 247 Pat Hentgen .10 .05
❑ 248 Bill Pecota .10 .05
❑ 249 Ben McDonald .10 .05
❑ 250 Cliff Brantley .10 .05
❑ 251 John Valentin .10 .05
❑ 252 Jeff King .10 .05
❑ 253 Reggie Williams .10 .05
❑ 254 Checklist 160-238 .10 .05
(Damon Berryhill
and Alex Arias)
❑ 255 Ozzie Guillen .10 .05
❑ 256 Mike Perez .10 .05
❑ 257 Thomas Howard .10 .05
❑ 258 Kurt Stillwell .10 .05
❑ 259 Mike Henneman .10 .05
❑ 260 Steve Decker .10 .05
❑ 261 Brent Mayne .10 .05
❑ 262 Otis Nixon .10 .05
❑ 263 Mark Kiefer .10 .05
❑ 264 Checklist 239-317 .25 .11
(Don Mattingly
and Mike Bordick)
❑ 265 Richie Lewis RC .10 .05
❑ 266 Pat Gomez RC .10 .05
❑ 267 Scott Taylor .10 .05
❑ 268 Shawon Dunston .10 .05
❑ 269 Greg Myers .10 .05
❑ 270 Tim Costo .10 .05
❑ 271 Greg Hibbard .10 .05
❑ 272 Pete Harnisch .10 .05
❑ 273 Dave Mlicki .10 .05
❑ 274 Orel Hershiser .15 .07
❑ 275 Sean Berry RR .10 .05
❑ 276 Doug Simons .10 .05
❑ 277 John Doherty .10 .05
❑ 278 Eddie Murray .40 .18
❑ 279 Chris Haney .10 .05
❑ 280 Stan Javier .10 .05
❑ 281 Jaime Navarro .10 .05
❑ 282 Orlando Merced .10 .05
❑ 283 Kent Hrbek .15 .07
❑ 284 Bernard Gilkey .10 .05
❑ 285 Russ Springer .10 .05
❑ 286 Mike Maddux .10 .05
❑ 287 Eric Fox .10 .05
❑ 288 Mark Leonard .10 .05
❑ 289 Tim Leary .10 .05
❑ 290 Brian Hunter .10 .05
❑ 291 Donald Harris .10 .05
❑ 292 Bob Scanlan .10 .05
❑ 293 Turner Ward .10 .05
❑ 294 Hal Morris .10 .05
❑ 295 Jimmy Poole .10 .05
❑ 296 Doug Jones .10 .05
❑ 297 Tony Pena .10 .05
❑ 298 Ramon Martinez .10 .05
❑ 299 Tim Fortugno .10 .05
❑ 300 Marquis Grissom .10 .05
❑ 301 Lance Johnson .10 .05
❑ 302 Jeff Kent .40 .18
❑ 303 Reggie Jefferson .10 .05
❑ 304 Wes Chamberlain .10 .05
❑ 305 Shawn Hare .10 .05
❑ 306 Mike LaValliere .10 .05
❑ 307 Gregg Jefferies .10 .05
❑ 308 Troy Neel RR .10 .05
❑ 309 Pat Listach .10 .05
❑ 310 Geronimo Pena .10 .05
❑ 311 Pedro Munoz .10 .05
❑ 312 Guillermo Velasquez .10 .05
❑ 313 Roberto Kelly .10 .05
❑ 314 Mike Jackson .10 .05
❑ 315 Rickey Henderson .75 .35
❑ 316 Mark Lemke .10 .05
❑ 317 Erik Hanson .10 .05
❑ 318 Derrick May .10 .05
❑ 319 Geno Petralli .10 .05
❑ 320 Melvin Nieves RR .10 .05
❑ 321 Doug Linton .10 .05
❑ 322 Rob Dibble .10 .05
❑ 323 Chris Hoiles .10 .05
❑ 324 Jimmy Jones .10 .05
❑ 325 Dave Staton RR .10 .05
❑ 326 Pedro Martinez 1.00 .45
❑ 327 Paul Quantrill .10 .05
❑ 328 Greg Colbrunn .10 .05
❑ 329 Hilly Hathaway RC .10 .05
❑ 330 Jeff Innis .10 .05
❑ 331 Ron Karkovice .10 .05
❑ 332 Keith Shepherd RC .10 .05
❑ 333 Alan Embree .10 .05
❑ 334 Paul Wagner .10 .05
❑ 335 Dave Haas .10 .05
❑ 336 Ozzie Canseco .10 .05
❑ 337 Bill Sampen .10 .05
❑ 338 Rich Rodriguez .10 .05
❑ 339 Dean Palmer .15 .07
❑ 340 Greg Litton .10 .05
❑ 341 Jim Tatum RR RC .10 .05
❑ 342 Todd Haney RC .10 .05
❑ 343 Larry Casian .10 .05
❑ 344 Ryne Sandberg .50 .23
❑ 345 Sterling Hitchcock RC .15 .07
❑ 346 Chris Hammond .10 .05
❑ 347 Vince Horsman .10 .05
❑ 348 Butch Henry .10 .05
❑ 349 Dann Howitt .10 .05
❑ 350 Roger McDowell .10 .05
❑ 351 Jack Morris .15 .07
❑ 352 Bill Krueger .10 .05
❑ 353 Cris Colon .10 .05
❑ 354 Joe Vitko .10 .05
❑ 355 Willie McGee .15 .07
❑ 356 Jay Baller .10 .05
❑ 357 Pat Mahomes .10 .05
❑ 358 Roger Mason .10 .05
❑ 359 Jerry Nielsen .10 .05
❑ 360 Tom Pagnozzi .10 .05
❑ 361 Kevin Baez .10 .05
❑ 362 Tim Scott .10 .05
❑ 363 Domingo Martinez RC .10 .05
❑ 364 Kirt Manwaring .10 .05
❑ 365 Rafael Palmeiro .40 .18
❑ 366 Ray Lankford .10 .05
❑ 367 Tim McIntosh .10 .05
❑ 368 Jessie Hollins .10 .05
❑ 369 Scott Leius .10 .05
❑ 370 Bill Doran .10 .05
❑ 371 Sam Militello .10 .05
❑ 372 Ryan Bowen .10 .05
❑ 373 Dave Henderson .10 .05
❑ 374 Dan Smith RR .10 .05
❑ 375 Steve Reed RR RC .10 .05
❑ 376 Jose Offerman .10 .05
❑ 377 Kevin Brown .15 .07
❑ 378 Darrin Fletcher .10 .05
❑ 379 Duane Ward .10 .05
❑ 380 Wayne Kirby RR .10 .05
❑ 381 Steve Scarsone .10 .05
❑ 382 Mariano Duncan .10 .05

383	Ken Ryan RC	.10	.05
384	Lloyd McClendon	.10	.05
385	Brian Holman	.10	.05
386	Braulio Castillo	.10	.05
387	Danny Leon	.10	.05
388	Omar Olivares	.10	.05
389	Kevin Wickander	.10	.05
390	Fred McGriff	.25	.11
391	Phil Clark	.10	.05
392	Darren Lewis	.10	.05
393	Phil Hiatt	.10	.05
394	Mike Morgan	.10	.05
395	Shane Mack	.10	.05
396	Checklist 318-396 (Dennis Eckersley and Art Kusnyer CO)	.15	.07
397	David Segui	.10	.05
398	Rafael Belliard	.10	.05
399	Tim Naehring	.10	.05
400	Frank Castillo	.10	.05
401	Joe Grahe	.10	.05
402	Reggie Sanders	.10	.05
403	Roberto Hernandez	.10	.05
404	Luis Gonzalez	.40	.18
405	Carlos Baerga	.10	.05
406	Carlos Hernandez	.10	.05
407	Pedro Astacio RR	.10	.05
408	Mel Rojas	.10	.05
409	Scott Livingstone	.10	.05
410	Chico Walker	.10	.05
411	Brian McRae	.10	.05
412	Ben Rivera	.10	.05
413	Ricky Bones	.10	.05
414	Andy Van Slyke	.15	.07
415	Chuck Knoblauch	.15	.07
416	Luis Alicea	.10	.05
417	Bob Wickman	.10	.05
418	Doug Brocail	.10	.05
419	Scott Brosius	.15	.07
420	Rod Beck	.10	.05
421	Edgar Martinez	.25	.11
422	Ryan Klesko	.15	.07
423	Nolan Ryan	2.00	.90
424	Rey Sanchez	.10	.05
425	Roberto Alomar	.40	.18
426	Barry Larkin	.40	.18
427	Mike Mussina	.40	.18
428	Jeff Bagwell	.50	.23
429	Mo Vaughn	.15	.07
430	Eric Karros	.15	.07
431	John Orton	.10	.05
432	Wil Cordero	.10	.05
433	Jack McDowell	.10	.05
434	Howard Johnson	.10	.05
435	Albert Belle	.15	.07
436	John Kruk	.15	.07
437	Skeeter Barnes	.10	.05
438	Don Slaught	.10	.05
439	Rusty Meacham	.10	.05
440	Tim Laker RR RC	.10	.05
441	Robin Yount	.40	.18
442	Brian Jordan	.15	.07
443	Kevin Tapani	.10	.05
444	Gary Sheffield	.15	.07
445	Rich Monteleone	.10	.05
446	Will Clark	.40	.18
447	Jerry Browne	.10	.05
448	Jeff Treadway	.10	.05
449	Mike Schooler	.10	.05
450	Mike Harkey	.10	.05
451	Julio Franco	.15	.07
452	Kevin Young RR	.15	.07
453	Kelly Gruber	.10	.05
454	Jose Rijo	.10	.05
455	Mike Devereaux	.10	.05
456	Andujar Cedeno	.10	.05
457	Damion Easley RR	.10	.05
458	Kevin Gross	.10	.05
459	Matt Young	.10	.05
460	Matt Stairs	.10	.05
461	Luis Polonia	.10	.05
462	Dwight Gooden	.15	.07
463	Warren Newson	.10	.05
464	Jose DeLeon	.10	.05
465	Jose Mesa	.10	.05
466	Danny Cox	.10	.05
467	Dan Gladden	.10	.05
468	Gerald Perry	.10	.05
469	Mike Boddicker	.10	.05
470	Jeff Gardner	.10	.05
471	Doug Henry	.10	.05
472	Mike Benjamin	.10	.05
473	Dan Peltier RR	.10	.05
474	Mike Stanton	.10	.05
475	John Smiley	.10	.05
476	Dwight Smith	.10	.05
477	Jim Leyritz	.10	.05
478	Dwayne Henry	.10	.05
479	Mark McGwire	1.50	.70
480	Pete Incaviglia	.10	.05
481	Dave Cochrane	.10	.05
482	Eric Davis	.15	.07
483	John Olerud	.15	.07
484	Kent Bottenfield	.10	.05
485	Mark McLemore	.10	.05
486	Dave Magadan	.10	.05
487	John Marzano	.10	.05
488	Ruben Amaro	.10	.05
489	Rob Ducey	.10	.05
490	Stan Belinda	.10	.05
491	Dan Pasqua	.10	.05
492	Joe Magrane	.10	.05
493	Brook Jacoby	.10	.05
494	Gene Harris	.10	.05
495	Mark Leiter	.10	.05
496	Bryan Hickerson	.10	.05
497	Tom Gordon	.10	.05
498	Pete Smith	.10	.05
499	Chris Bosio	.10	.05
500	Shawn Boskie	.10	.05
501	Dave West	.10	.05
502	Milt Hill	.10	.05
503	Pat Kelly	.10	.05
504	Joe Boever	.10	.05
505	Terry Steinbach	.10	.05
506	Butch Huskey RR	.10	.05
507	David Valle	.10	.05
508	Mike Scioscia	.10	.05
509	Kenny Rogers	.10	.05
510	Moises Alou	.15	.07
511	David Wells	.15	.07
512	Mackey Sasser	.10	.05
513	Todd Frohwirth	.10	.05
514	Ricky Jordan	.10	.05
515	Mike Gardiner	.10	.05
516	Gary Redus	.10	.05
517	Gary Gaetti	.15	.07
518	Checklist	.10	.05
519	Carlton Fisk	.40	.18
520	Ozzie Smith	.50	.23
521	Rod Nichols	.10	.05
522	Benito Santiago	.10	.05
523	Bill Gullickson	.10	.05
524	Robby Thompson	.10	.05
525	Mike Macfarlane	.10	.05
526	Sid Bream	.10	.05
527	Darryl Hamilton	.10	.05
528	Checklist	.10	.05
529	Jeff Tackett	.10	.05
530	Greg Olson	.10	.05
531	Bob Zupcic	.10	.05
532	Mark Grace	.40	.18
533	Steve Frey	.10	.05
534	Dave Martinez	.10	.05
535	Robin Ventura	.15	.07
536	Casey Candaele	.10	.05
537	Kenny Lofton	.15	.07
538	Jay Howell	.10	.05
539	Fern.Ramsey RR RC	.10	.05
540	Larry Walker	.25	.11
541	Cecil Fielder	.15	.07
542	Lee Guetterman	.10	.05
543	Keith Miller	.10	.05
544	Len Dykstra	.15	.07
545	B.J. Surhoff	.15	.07
546	Bob Walk	.10	.05
547	Brian Harper	.10	.05
548	Lee Smith	.15	.07
549	Danny Tartabull	.10	.05
550	Frank Seminara	.10	.05
551	Henry Mercedes	.10	.05
552	Dave Righetti	.15	.07
553	Ken Griffey Jr.	1.25	.55
554	Tom Glavine	.40	.18
555	Juan Gonzalez	.40	.18
556	Jim Bullinger	.10	.05
557	Derek Bell	.10	.05
558	Cesar Hernandez	.10	.05
559	Cal Ripken	1.50	.70
560	Eddie Taubensee	.10	.05
561	John Flaherty	.10	.05
562	Todd Benzinger	.10	.05
563	Hubie Brooks	.10	.05
564	Delino DeShields	.10	.05
565	Tim Raines	.15	.07
566	Sid Fernandez	.10	.05
567	Steve Olin	.10	.05
568	Tommy Greene	.10	.05
569	Buddy Groom	.10	.05
570	Randy Tomlin	.10	.05
571	Hipolito Pichardo	.10	.05
572	Rene Arocha RR RC	.15	.07
573	Mike Fetters	.10	.05
574	Felix Jose	.10	.05
575	Gene Larkin	.10	.05
576	Bruce Hurst	.10	.05
577	Bernie Williams	.40	.18
578	Trevor Wilson	.10	.05
579	Bob Welch	.10	.05
580	David Justice	.15	.07
581	Randy Johnson	.50	.23
582	Jose Vizcaino	.10	.05
583	Jeff Huson	.10	.05
584	Rob Maurer RR	.10	.05
585	Todd Stottlemyre	.10	.05
586	Joe Oliver	.10	.05
587	Bob Milacki	.10	.05
588	Rob Murphy	.10	.05
589	Greg Pirkl RR	.10	.05
590	Lenny Harris	.10	.05
591	Luis Rivera	.10	.05
592	John Wetteland	.15	.07
593	Mark Langston	.10	.05
594	Bobby Bonilla	.15	.07
595	Esteban Beltre	.10	.05
596	Mike Hartley	.10	.05
597	Felix Fermin	.10	.05
598	Carlos Garcia	.10	.05
599	Frank Tanana	.10	.05
600	Pedro Guerrero	.15	.07
601	Terry Shumpert	.10	.05
602	Wally Whitehurst	.10	.05
603	Kevin Seitzer	.10	.05
604	Chris James	.10	.05
605	Greg Gohr RR	.10	.05
606	Mark Wohlers	.10	.05
607	Kirby Puckett	1.00	.45
608	Greg Maddux	1.00	.45
609	Don Mattingly	1.00	.45
610	Greg Cadaret	.10	.05
611	Dave Stewart	.15	.07
612	Mark Portugal	.10	.05
613	Pete O'Brien	.10	.05
614	Bob Ojeda	.10	.05
615	Joe Carter	.15	.07
616	Pete Young	.10	.05
617	Sam Horn	.10	.05
618	Vince Coleman	.10	.05
619	Wade Boggs	.40	.18
620	Todd Pratt RC	.15	.07
621	Ron Tingley	.10	.05
622	Doug Drabek	.10	.05
623	Scott Hemond	.10	.05
624	Tim Jones	.10	.05
625	Dennis Cook	.10	.05
626	Jose Melendez	.10	.05
627	Mike Munoz	.10	.05
628	Jim Pena	.10	.05
629	Gary Thurman	.10	.05
630	Charlie Leibrandt	.10	.05
631	Scott Fletcher	.10	.05
632	Andre Dawson	.25	.11
633	Greg Gagne	.10	.05
634	Greg Swindell	.10	.05
635	Kevin Maas	.10	.05
636	Xavier Hernandez	.10	.05
637	Ruben Sierra	.10	.05
638	Dmitri Young RR	.15	.07

	Mint	NrMt
❑ 639 Harold Reynolds	.10	.05
❑ 640 Tom Goodwin	.10	.05
❑ 641 Todd Burns	.10	.05
❑ 642 Jeff Fassero	.10	.05
❑ 643 Dave Winfield	.40	.18
❑ 644 Willie Randolph	.15	.07
❑ 645 Luis Mercedes	.10	.05
❑ 646 Dale Murphy	.25	.11
❑ 647 Danny Darwin	.10	.05
❑ 648 Dennis Moeller	.10	.05
❑ 649 Chuck Crim	.10	.05
❑ 650 Checklist	.10	.05
❑ 651 Shawn Abner	.10	.05
❑ 652 Tracy Woodson	.10	.05
❑ 653 Scott Scudder	.10	.05
❑ 654 Tom Lampkin	.10	.05
❑ 655 Alan Trammell	.25	.11
❑ 656 Cory Snyder	.10	.05
❑ 657 Chris Gwynn	.10	.05
❑ 658 Lonnie Smith	.10	.05
❑ 659 Jim Austin	.10	.05
❑ 660 Checklist	.10	.05
❑ 661 Tim Hulett	.10	.05
❑ 662 Marvin Freeman	.10	.05
❑ 663 Greg A. Harris	.10	.05
❑ 664 Heathcliff Slocumb	.10	.05
❑ 665 Mike Butcher	.10	.05
❑ 666 Steve Foster	.10	.05
❑ 667 Donn Pall	.10	.05
❑ 668 Darryl Kile	.15	.07
❑ 669 Jesse Levis	.10	.05
❑ 670 Jim Gott	.10	.05
❑ 671 Mark Hutton RR	.10	.05
❑ 672 Brian Drahman	.10	.05
❑ 673 Chad Kreuter	.10	.05
❑ 674 Tony Fernandez	.10	.05
❑ 675 Jose Lind	.10	.05
❑ 676 Kyle Abbott	.10	.05
❑ 677 Dan Plesac	.10	.05
❑ 678 Barry Bonds	1.00	.45
❑ 679 Chili Davis	.15	.07
❑ 680 Stan Royer	.10	.05
❑ 681 Scott Kamieniecki	.10	.05
❑ 682 Carlos Martinez	.10	.05
❑ 683 Mike Moore	.10	.05
❑ 684 Candy Maldonado	.10	.05
❑ 685 Jeff Nelson	.10	.05
❑ 686 Lou Whitaker	.15	.07
❑ 687 Jose Guzman	.10	.05
❑ 688 Manuel Lee	.10	.05
❑ 689 Bob MacDonald	.10	.05
❑ 690 Scott Bankhead	.10	.05
❑ 691 Alan Mills	.10	.05
❑ 692 Brian Williams	.10	.05
❑ 693 Tom Brunansky	.10	.05
❑ 694 Lenny Webster	.10	.05
❑ 695 Greg Briley	.10	.05
❑ 696 Paul O'Neill	.40	.18
❑ 697 Joey Cora	.10	.05
❑ 698 Charlie O'Brien	.10	.05
❑ 699 Junior Ortiz	.10	.05
❑ 700 Ron Darling	.10	.05
❑ 701 Tony Phillips	.10	.05
❑ 702 William Pennyfeather	.10	.05
❑ 703 Mark Gubicza	.10	.05
❑ 704 Steve Hosey RR	.10	.05
❑ 705 Henry Cotto	.10	.05
❑ 706 David Hulse RC	.10	.05
❑ 707 Mike Pagliarulo	.10	.05
❑ 708 Dave Stieb	.10	.05
❑ 709 Melido Perez	.10	.05
❑ 710 Jimmy Key	.15	.07
❑ 711 Jeff Russell	.10	.05
❑ 712 David Cone	.15	.07
❑ 713 Russ Swan	.10	.05
❑ 714 Mark Guthrie	.10	.05
❑ 715 Checklist	.10	.05
❑ 716 Al Martin RR	.10	.05
❑ 717 Randy Knorr	.10	.05
❑ 718 Mike Stanley	.10	.05
❑ 719 Rick Sutcliffe	.15	.07
❑ 720 Terry Leach	.10	.05
❑ 721 Chipper Jones RR	1.00	.45
❑ 722 Jim Eisenreich	.10	.05
❑ 723 Tom Henke	.10	.05
❑ 724 Jeff Frye	.10	.05
❑ 725 Harold Baines	.15	.07
❑ 726 Scott Sanderson	.10	.05
❑ 727 Tom Foley	.10	.05
❑ 728 Bryan Harvey	.10	.05
❑ 729 Tom Edens	.10	.05
❑ 730 Eric Young	.10	.05
❑ 731 Dave Weathers	.10	.05
❑ 732 Spike Owen	.10	.05
❑ 733 Scott Aldred	.10	.05
❑ 734 Cris Carpenter	.10	.05
❑ 735 Dion James	.10	.05
❑ 736 Joe Girardi	.10	.05
❑ 737 Nigel Wilson RR	.10	.05
❑ 738 Scott Chiamparino	.10	.05
❑ 739 Jeff Reardon	.15	.07
❑ 740 Willie Blair	.10	.05
❑ 741 Jim Corsi	.10	.05
❑ 742 Ken Patterson	.10	.05
❑ 743 Andy Ashby	.10	.05
❑ 744 Rob Natal	.10	.05
❑ 745 Kevin Bass	.10	.05
❑ 746 Freddie Benavides	.10	.05
❑ 747 Chris Donnels	.10	.05
❑ 748 Kerry Woodson	.10	.05
❑ 749 Calvin Jones	.10	.05
❑ 750 Gary Scott	.10	.05
❑ 751 Joe Orsulak	.10	.05
❑ 752 Armando Reynoso	.10	.05
❑ 753 Monty Fariss	.10	.05
❑ 754 Billy Hatcher	.10	.05
❑ 755 Denis Boucher	.10	.05
❑ 756 Walt Weiss	.10	.05
❑ 757 Mike Fitzgerald	.10	.05
❑ 758 Rudy Seanez	.10	.05
❑ 759 Bret Barberie	.10	.05
❑ 760 Mo Sanford	.10	.05
❑ 761 Pedro Castellano	.10	.05
❑ 762 Chuck Carr	.10	.05
❑ 763 Steve Howe	.10	.05
❑ 764 Andres Galarraga	.25	.11
❑ 765 Jeff Conine	.10	.05
❑ 766 Ted Power	.10	.05
❑ 767 Butch Henry	.10	.05
❑ 768 Steve Decker	.10	.05
❑ 769 Storm Davis	.10	.05
❑ 770 Vinny Castilla	.15	.07
❑ 771 Junior Felix	.10	.05
❑ 772 Walt Terrell	.10	.05
❑ 773 Brad Ausmus	.10	.05
❑ 774 Jamie McAndrew	.10	.05
❑ 775 Milt Thompson	.10	.05
❑ 776 Charlie Hayes	.10	.05
❑ 777 Jack Armstrong	.10	.05
❑ 778 Dennis Rasmussen	.10	.05
❑ 779 Darren Holmes	.10	.05
❑ 780 Alex Arias	.10	.05
❑ 781 Randy Bush	.10	.05
❑ 782 Javier Lopez RR	.15	.07
❑ 783 Dante Bichette	.15	.07
❑ 784 John Johnstone RC	.10	.05
❑ 785 Rene Gonzales	.10	.05
❑ 786 Alex Cole	.10	.05
❑ 787 Jeromy Burnitz RR	.15	.07
❑ 788 Michael Huff	.10	.05
❑ 789 Anthony Telford	.10	.05
❑ 790 Jerald Clark	.10	.05
❑ 791 Joel Johnston	.10	.05
❑ 792 David Nied RR	.10	.05

1994 Donruss

	MINT	NRMT
COMPLETE SET (660)	30.00	13.50
COMPLETE SERIES 1 (330)	15.00	6.75
COMPLETE SERIES 2 (330)	15.00	6.75
❑ 1 Nolan Ryan	4.00	1.80
❑ 2 Mike Piazza	2.00	.90
❑ 3 Moises Alou	.25	.11
❑ 4 Ken Griffey Jr.	2.00	.90
❑ 5 Gary Sheffield	.25	.11
❑ 6 Roberto Alomar	.60	.25
❑ 7 John Kruk	.25	.11
❑ 8 Gregg Olson	.15	.07
❑ 9 Gregg Jefferies	.15	.07
❑ 10 Tony Gwynn	1.25	.55

	MINT	NRMT
❑ 11 Chad Curtis	.15	.07
❑ 12 Craig Biggio	.40	.18
❑ 13 John Burkett	.15	.07
❑ 14 Carlos Baerga	.15	.07
❑ 15 Robin Yount	.60	.25
❑ 16 Dennis Eckersley	.25	.11
❑ 17 Dwight Gooden	.25	.11
❑ 18 Ryne Sandberg	.75	.35
❑ 19 Rickey Henderson	1.25	.55
❑ 20 Jack McDowell	.15	.07
❑ 21 Jay Bell	.25	.11
❑ 22 Kevin Brown	.25	.11
❑ 23 Robin Ventura	.25	.11
❑ 24 Paul Molitor	.60	.25
❑ 25 David Justice	.25	.11
❑ 26 Rafael Palmeiro	.60	.25
❑ 27 Cecil Fielder	.25	.11
❑ 28 Chuck Knoblauch	.25	.11
❑ 29 Dave Hollins	.15	.07
❑ 30 Jimmy Key	.25	.11
❑ 31 Mark Langston	.15	.07
❑ 32 Darryl Kile	.25	.11
❑ 33 Ruben Sierra	.15	.07
❑ 34 Ron Gant	.15	.07
❑ 35 Ozzie Smith	.75	.35
❑ 36 Wade Boggs	.60	.25
❑ 37 Marquis Grissom	.15	.07
❑ 38 Will Clark	.60	.25
❑ 39 Kenny Lofton	.25	.11
❑ 40 Cal Ripken	2.50	1.10
❑ 41 Steve Avery	.15	.07
❑ 42 Mo Vaughn	.25	.11
❑ 43 Brian McRae	.15	.07
❑ 44 Mickey Tettleton	.15	.07
❑ 45 Barry Larkin	.60	.25
❑ 46 Charlie Hayes	.15	.07
❑ 47 Kevin Appier	.25	.11
❑ 48 Robby Thompson	.15	.07
❑ 49 Juan Gonzalez	.60	.25
❑ 50 Paul O'Neill	.60	.25
❑ 51 Marcos Armas	.15	.07
❑ 52 Mike Butcher	.15	.07
❑ 53 Ken Caminiti	.25	.11
❑ 54 Pat Borders	.15	.07
❑ 55 Pedro Munoz	.15	.07
❑ 56 Tim Belcher	.15	.07
❑ 57 Paul Assenmacher	.15	.07
❑ 58 Damon Berryhill	.15	.07
❑ 59 Ricky Bones	.15	.07
❑ 60 Rene Arocha	.15	.07
❑ 61 Shawn Boskie	.15	.07
❑ 62 Pedro Astacio	.15	.07
❑ 63 Frank Bolick	.15	.07
❑ 64 Bud Black	.15	.07
❑ 65 Sandy Alomar Jr.	.25	.11
❑ 66 Rich Amaral	.15	.07
❑ 67 Luis Aquino	.15	.07
❑ 68 Kevin Baez	.15	.07
❑ 69 Mike Devereaux	.15	.07
❑ 70 Andy Ashby	.15	.07
❑ 71 Larry Andersen	.15	.07
❑ 72 Steve Cooke	.15	.07
❑ 73 Mario Diaz	.15	.07
❑ 74 Rob Deer	.15	.07
❑ 75 Bobby Ayala	.15	.07
❑ 76 Freddie Benavides	.15	.07
❑ 77 Stan Belinda	.15	.07

❑ 78 John Doherty .15 .07
❑ 79 Willie Banks .15 .07
❑ 80 Spike Owen .15 .07
❑ 81 Mike Bordick .15 .07
❑ 82 Chili Davis .25 .11
❑ 83 Luis Gonzalez .60 .25
❑ 84 Ed Sprague .15 .07
❑ 85 Jeff Reboulet .15 .07
❑ 86 Jason Bere .15 .07
❑ 87 Mark Hutton .15 .07
❑ 88 Jeff Blauser .15 .07
❑ 89 Cal Eldred .15 .07
❑ 90 Bernard Gilkey .15 .07
❑ 91 Frank Castillo .15 .07
❑ 92 Jim Gott .15 .07
❑ 93 Greg Colbrunn .15 .07
❑ 94 Jeff Brantley .15 .07
❑ 95 Jeremy Hernandez .15 .07
❑ 96 Norm Charlton .15 .07
❑ 97 Alex Arias .15 .07
❑ 98 John Franco .25 .11
❑ 99 Chris Hoiles .15 .07
❑ 100 Brad Ausmus .15 .07
❑ 101 Wes Chamberlain .15 .07
❑ 102 Mark Dewey .15 .07
❑ 103 Benji Gil .15 .07
❑ 104 John Dopson .15 .07
❑ 105 John Smiley .15 .07
❑ 106 David Nied .15 .07
❑ 107 George Brett 1.25 .55
❑ 108 Kirk Gibson .25 .11
❑ 109 Larry Casian .15 .07
❑ 110 Ryne Sandberg CL .40 .18
❑ 111 Brent Gates .15 .07
❑ 112 Damion Easley .15 .07
❑ 113 Pete Harnisch .15 .07
❑ 114 Danny Cox .15 .07
❑ 115 Kevin Tapani .15 .07
❑ 116 Roberto Hernandez .15 .07
❑ 117 Domingo Jean .15 .07
❑ 118 Sid Bream .15 .07
❑ 119 Doug Henry .15 .07
❑ 120 Omar Olivares .15 .07
❑ 121 Mike Harkey .15 .07
❑ 122 Carlos Hernandez .15 .07
❑ 123 Jeff Fassero .15 .07
❑ 124 Dave Burba .15 .07
❑ 125 Wayne Kirby .15 .07
❑ 126 John Cummings .15 .07
❑ 127 Bret Barberie .15 .07
❑ 128 Todd Hundley .15 .07
❑ 129 Tim Hulett .15 .07
❑ 130 Phil Clark .15 .07
❑ 131 Danny Jackson .15 .07
❑ 132 Tom Foley .15 .07
❑ 133 Donald Harris .15 .07
❑ 134 Scott Fletcher .15 .07
❑ 135 Johnny Ruffin .15 .07
❑ 136 Jerald Clark .15 .07
❑ 137 Billy Brewer .15 .07
❑ 138 Dan Gladden .15 .07
❑ 139 Eddie Guardado .15 .07
❑ 140 Cal Ripken CL .60 .25
❑ 141 Scott Hemond .15 .07
❑ 142 Steve Frey .15 .07
❑ 143 Xavier Hernandez .15 .07
❑ 144 Mark Eichhorn .15 .07
❑ 145 Ellis Burks .25 .11
❑ 146 Jim Leyritz .15 .07
❑ 147 Mark Lemke .15 .07
❑ 148 Pat Listach .15 .07
❑ 149 Donovan Osborne .15 .07
❑ 150 Glenallen Hill .15 .07
❑ 151 Orel Hershiser .25 .11
❑ 152 Darrin Fletcher .15 .07
❑ 153 Royce Clayton .15 .07
❑ 154 Derek Lilliquist .15 .07
❑ 155 Mike Felder .15 .07
❑ 156 Jeff Conine .15 .07
❑ 157 Ryan Thompson .15 .07
❑ 158 Ben McDonald .15 .07
❑ 159 Ricky Gutierrez .15 .07
❑ 160 Terry Mulholland .15 .07
❑ 161 Carlos Garcia .15 .07
❑ 162 Tom Henke .15 .07
❑ 163 Mike Greenwell .15 .07
❑ 164 Thomas Howard .15 .07
❑ 165 Joe Girardi .15 .07
❑ 166 Hubie Brooks .15 .07
❑ 167 Greg Gohr .15 .07
❑ 168 Chip Hale .15 .07
❑ 169 Rick Honeycutt .15 .07
❑ 170 Hilly Hathaway .15 .07
❑ 171 Todd Jones .15 .07
❑ 172 Tony Fernandez .15 .07
❑ 173 Bo Jackson .25 .11
❑ 174 Bobby Munoz .15 .07
❑ 175 Greg McMichael .15 .07
❑ 176 Graeme Lloyd .15 .07
❑ 177 Tom Pagnozzi .15 .07
❑ 178 Derrick May .15 .07
❑ 179 Pedro Martinez 1.00 .45
❑ 180 Ken Hill .15 .07
❑ 181 Bryan Hickerson .15 .07
❑ 182 Jose Mesa .15 .07
❑ 183 Dave Fleming .15 .07
❑ 184 Henry Cotto .15 .07
❑ 185 Jeff Kent .40 .18
❑ 186 Mark McLemore .15 .07
❑ 187 Trevor Hoffman .25 .11
❑ 188 Todd Pratt .15 .07
❑ 189 Blas Minor .15 .07
❑ 190 Charlie Leibrandt .15 .07
❑ 191 Tony Pena .15 .07
❑ 192 Larry Luebbers RC .15 .07
❑ 193 Greg W. Harris .15 .07
❑ 194 David Cone .25 .11
❑ 195 Bill Gullickson .15 .07
❑ 196 Brian Harper .15 .07
❑ 197 Steve Karsay .15 .07
❑ 198 Greg Myers .15 .07
❑ 199 Mark Portugal .15 .07
❑ 200 Pat Hentgen .15 .07
❑ 201 Mike LaValliere .15 .07
❑ 202 Mike Stanley .15 .07
❑ 203 Kent Mercker .15 .07
❑ 204 Dave Nilsson .15 .07
❑ 205 Erik Pappas .15 .07
❑ 206 Mike Morgan .15 .07
❑ 207 Roger McDowell .15 .07
❑ 208 Mike Lansing .15 .07
❑ 209 Kirt Manwaring .15 .07
❑ 210 Randy Milligan .15 .07
❑ 211 Erik Hanson .15 .07
❑ 212 Orestes Destrade .15 .07
❑ 213 Mike Maddux .15 .07
❑ 214 Alan Mills .15 .07
❑ 215 Tim Mauser .15 .07
❑ 216 Ben Rivera .15 .07
❑ 217 Don Slaught .15 .07
❑ 218 Bob Patterson .15 .07
❑ 219 Carlos Quintana .15 .07
❑ 220 Tim Raines CL .15 .07
❑ 221 Hal Morris .15 .07
❑ 222 Darren Holmes .15 .07
❑ 223 Chris Gwynn .15 .07
❑ 224 Chad Kreuter .15 .07
❑ 225 Mike Hartley .15 .07
❑ 226 Scott Lydy .15 .07
❑ 227 Eduardo Perez .15 .07
❑ 228 Greg Swindell .15 .07
❑ 229 Al Leiter .25 .11
❑ 230 Scott Radinsky .15 .07
❑ 231 Bob Wickman .15 .07
❑ 232 Otis Nixon .15 .07
❑ 233 Kevin Reimer .15 .07
❑ 234 Geronimo Pena .15 .07
❑ 235 Kevin Roberson .15 .07
❑ 236 Jody Reed .15 .07
❑ 237 Kirk Rueter .15 .07
❑ 238 Willie McGee .25 .11
❑ 239 Charles Nagy .15 .07
❑ 240 Tim Leary .15 .07
❑ 241 Carl Everett .25 .11
❑ 242 Charlie O'Brien .15 .07
❑ 243 Mike Pagliarulo .15 .07
❑ 244 Kerry Taylor .15 .07
❑ 245 Kevin Stocker .15 .07
❑ 246 Joel Johnston .15 .07
❑ 247 Geno Petralli .15 .07
❑ 248 Jeff Russell .15 .07
❑ 249 Joe Oliver .15 .07
❑ 250 Roberto Mejia .15 .07
❑ 251 Chris Haney .15 .07
❑ 252 Bill Krueger .15 .07
❑ 253 Shane Mack .15 .07
❑ 254 Terry Steinbach .15 .07
❑ 255 Luis Polonia .15 .07
❑ 256 Eddie Taubensee .15 .07
❑ 257 Dave Stewart .25 .11
❑ 258 Tim Raines .25 .11
❑ 259 Bernie Williams .60 .25
❑ 260 John Smoltz .25 .11
❑ 261 Kevin Seitzer .15 .07
❑ 262 Bob Tewksbury .15 .07
❑ 263 Bob Scanlan .15 .07
❑ 264 Henry Rodriguez .15 .07
❑ 265 Tim Scott .15 .07
❑ 266 Scott Sanderson .15 .07
❑ 267 Eric Plunk .15 .07
❑ 268 Edgar Martinez .40 .18
❑ 269 Charlie Hough .25 .11
❑ 270 Joe Orsulak .15 .07
❑ 271 Harold Reynolds .15 .07
❑ 272 Tim Teufel .15 .07
❑ 273 Bobby Thigpen .15 .07
❑ 274 Randy Tomlin .15 .07
❑ 275 Gary Redus .15 .07
❑ 276 Ken Ryan .15 .07
❑ 277 Tim Pugh .15 .07
❑ 278 J. Owens .15 .07
❑ 279 Phil Hiatt .15 .07
❑ 280 Alan Trammell .40 .18
❑ 281 Dave McCarty .15 .07
❑ 282 Bob Welch .15 .07
❑ 283 J.T. Snow .25 .11
❑ 284 Brian Williams .15 .07
❑ 285 Devon White .15 .07
❑ 286 Steve Sax .15 .07
❑ 287 Tony Tarasco .15 .07
❑ 288 Bill Spiers .15 .07
❑ 289 Allen Watson .15 .07
❑ 290 Rickey Henderson CL .60 .25
❑ 291 Jose Vizcaino .15 .07
❑ 292 Darryl Strawberry .25 .11
❑ 293 John Wetteland .25 .11
❑ 294 Bill Swift .15 .07
❑ 295 Jeff Treadway .15 .07
❑ 296 Tino Martinez .25 .11
❑ 297 Richie Lewis .15 .07
❑ 298 Bret Saberhagen .25 .11
❑ 299 Arthur Rhodes .15 .07
❑ 300 Guillermo Velasquez .15 .07
❑ 301 Milt Thompson .15 .07
❑ 302 Doug Strange .15 .07
❑ 303 Aaron Sele .25 .11
❑ 304 Bip Roberts .15 .07
❑ 305 Bruce Ruffin .15 .07
❑ 306 Jose Lind .15 .07
❑ 307 David Wells .25 .11
❑ 308 Bobby Witt .15 .07
❑ 309 Mark Wohlers .15 .07
❑ 310 B.J. Surhoff .25 .11
❑ 311 Mark Whiten .15 .07
❑ 312 Turk Wendell .15 .07
❑ 313 Raul Mondesi .25 .11
❑ 314 Brian Turang RC .15 .07
❑ 315 Chris Hammond .15 .07
❑ 316 Tim Bogar .15 .07
❑ 317 Brad Pennington .15 .07
❑ 318 Tim Worrell .15 .07
❑ 319 Mitch Williams .15 .07
❑ 320 Rondell White .25 .11
❑ 321 Frank Viola .25 .11
❑ 322 Manny Ramirez 1.00 .45
❑ 323 Gary Wayne .15 .07
❑ 324 Mike Macfarlane .15 .07
❑ 325 Russ Springer .15 .07
❑ 326 Tim Wallach .15 .07
❑ 327 Salomon Torres .15 .07
❑ 328 Omar Vizquel .25 .11
❑ 329 Andy Tomberlin RC .15 .07
❑ 330 Chris Sabo .15 .07
❑ 331 Mike Mussina .60 .25
❑ 332 Andy Benes .15 .07
❑ 333 Darren Daulton .25 .11
❑ 334 Orlando Merced .15 .07
❑ 335 Mark McGwire 2.50 1.10

❑ 336 Dave Winfield .60 .25
❑ 337 Sammy Sosa 1.25 .55
❑ 338 Eric Karros .25 .11
❑ 339 Greg Vaughn .25 .11
❑ 340 Don Mattingly 1.50 .70
❑ 341 Frank Thomas .75 .35
❑ 342 Fred McGriff .40 .18
❑ 343 Kirby Puckett 1.50 .70
❑ 344 Roberto Kelly .15 .07
❑ 345 Wally Joyner .25 .11
❑ 346 Andres Galarraga .40 .18
❑ 347 Bobby Bonilla .25 .11
❑ 348 Benito Santiago .15 .07
❑ 349 Barry Bonds 1.50 .70
❑ 350 Delino DeShields .15 .07
❑ 351 Albert Belle .25 .11
❑ 352 Randy Johnson .75 .35
❑ 353 Tim Salmon .25 .11
❑ 354 John Olerud .25 .11
❑ 355 Dean Palmer .25 .11
❑ 356 Roger Clemens 1.50 .70
❑ 357 Jim Abbott .25 .11
❑ 358 Mark Grace .60 .25
❑ 359 Ozzie Guillen .15 .07
❑ 360 Lou Whitaker .25 .11
❑ 361 Jose Rijo .15 .07
❑ 362 Jeff Montgomery .15 .07
❑ 363 Chuck Finley .25 .11
❑ 364 Tom Glavine .60 .25
❑ 365 Jeff Bagwell .75 .35
❑ 366 Joe Carter .25 .11
❑ 367 Ray Lankford .15 .07
❑ 368 Ramon Martinez .15 .07
❑ 369 Jay Buhner .25 .11
❑ 370 Matt Williams .40 .18
❑ 371 Larry Walker .40 .18
❑ 372 Jose Canseco .60 .25
❑ 373 Lenny Dykstra .25 .11
❑ 374 Bryan Harvey .15 .07
❑ 375 Andy Van Slyke .25 .11
❑ 376 Ivan Rodriguez .60 .25
❑ 377 Kevin Mitchell .15 .07
❑ 378 Travis Fryman .25 .11
❑ 379 Duane Ward .15 .07
❑ 380 Greg Maddux 1.50 .70
❑ 381 Scott Servais .15 .07
❑ 382 Greg Olson .15 .07
❑ 383 Rey Sanchez .15 .07
❑ 384 Tom Kramer .15 .07
❑ 385 David Valle .15 .07
❑ 386 Eddie Murray .60 .25
❑ 387 Kevin Higgins .15 .07
❑ 388 Dan Wilson .15 .07
❑ 389 Todd Frohwirth .15 .07
❑ 390 Gerald Williams .15 .07
❑ 391 Hipolito Pichardo .15 .07
❑ 392 Pat Meares .15 .07
❑ 393 Luis Lopez .15 .07
❑ 394 Ricky Jordan .15 .07
❑ 395 Bob Walk .15 .07
❑ 396 Sid Fernandez .15 .07
❑ 397 Todd Worrell .15 .07
❑ 398 Darryl Hamilton .15 .07
❑ 399 Randy Myers .15 .07
❑ 400 Rod Brewer .15 .07
❑ 401 Lance Blankenship .15 .07
❑ 402 Steve Finley .25 .11
❑ 403 Phil Leftwich RC .15 .07
❑ 404 Juan Guzman .15 .07
❑ 405 Anthony Young .15 .07
❑ 406 Jeff Gardner .15 .07
❑ 407 Ryan Bowen .15 .07
❑ 408 Fernando Valenzuela .25 .11
❑ 409 David West .15 .07
❑ 410 Kenny Rogers .15 .07
❑ 411 Bob Zupcic .15 .07
❑ 412 Eric Young .15 .07
❑ 413 Bret Boone .25 .11
❑ 414 Danny Tartabull .15 .07
❑ 415 Bob MacDonald .15 .07
❑ 416 Ron Karkovice .15 .07
❑ 417 Scott Cooper .15 .07
❑ 418 Dante Bichette .25 .11
❑ 419 Tripp Cromer .15 .07
❑ 420 Billy Ashley .15 .07
❑ 421 Roger Smithberg .15 .07
❑ 422 Dennis Martinez .25 .11
❑ 423 Mike Blowers .15 .07
❑ 424 Darren Lewis .15 .07
❑ 425 Junior Ortiz .15 .07
❑ 426 Butch Huskey .15 .07
❑ 427 Jimmy Poole .15 .07
❑ 428 Walt Weiss .15 .07
❑ 429 Scott Bankhead .15 .07
❑ 430 Deion Sanders .25 .11
❑ 431 Scott Bullett .15 .07
❑ 432 Jeff Huson .15 .07
❑ 433 Tyler Green .15 .07
❑ 434 Billy Hatcher .15 .07
❑ 435 Bob Hamelin .15 .07
❑ 436 Reggie Sanders .15 .07
❑ 437 Scott Erickson .15 .07
❑ 438 Steve Reed .15 .07
❑ 439 Randy Velarde .15 .07
❑ 440 Tony Gwynn CL .60 .25
❑ 441 Terry Leach .15 .07
❑ 442 Danny Bautista .15 .07
❑ 443 Kent Hrbek .25 .11
❑ 444 Rick Wilkins .15 .07
❑ 445 Tony Phillips .15 .07
❑ 446 Dion James .15 .07
❑ 447 Joey Cora .15 .07
❑ 448 Andre Dawson .40 .18
❑ 449 Pedro Castellano .15 .07
❑ 450 Tom Gordon .15 .07
❑ 451 Rob Dibble .15 .07
❑ 452 Ron Darling .15 .07
❑ 453 Chipper Jones 1.25 .55
❑ 454 Joe Grahe .15 .07
❑ 455 Domingo Cedeno .15 .07
❑ 456 Tom Edens .15 .07
❑ 457 Mitch Webster .15 .07
❑ 458 Jose Bautista .15 .07
❑ 459 Troy O'Leary .15 .07
❑ 460 Todd Zeile .15 .07
❑ 461 Sean Berry .15 .07
❑ 462 Brad Holman RC .15 .07
❑ 463 Dave Martinez .15 .07
❑ 464 Mark Lewis .15 .07
❑ 465 Paul Carey .15 .07
❑ 466 Jack Armstrong .15 .07
❑ 467 David Telgheder .15 .07
❑ 468 Gene Harris .15 .07
❑ 469 Danny Darwin .15 .07
❑ 470 Kim Batiste .15 .07
❑ 471 Tim Wakefield .15 .07
❑ 472 Craig Lefferts .15 .07
❑ 473 Jacob Brumfield .15 .07
❑ 474 Lance Painter .15 .07
❑ 475 Milt Cuyler .15 .07
❑ 476 Melido Perez .15 .07
❑ 477 Derek Parks .15 .07
❑ 478 Gary DiSarcina .15 .07
❑ 479 Steve Bedrosian .15 .07
❑ 480 Eric Anthony .15 .07
❑ 481 Julio Franco .25 .11
❑ 482 Tommy Greene .15 .07
❑ 483 Pat Kelly .15 .07
❑ 484 Nate Minchey .15 .07
❑ 485 William Pennyfeather .15 .07
❑ 486 Harold Baines .25 .11
❑ 487 Howard Johnson .15 .07
❑ 488 Angel Miranda .15 .07
❑ 489 Scott Sanders .15 .07
❑ 490 Shawon Dunston .15 .07
❑ 491 Mel Rojas .15 .07
❑ 492 Jeff Nelson .15 .07
❑ 493 Archi Cianfrocco .15 .07
❑ 494 Al Martin .15 .07
❑ 495 Mike Gallego .15 .07
❑ 496 Mike Henneman .15 .07
❑ 497 Armando Reynoso .15 .07
❑ 498 Mickey Morandini .15 .07
❑ 499 Rick Renteria .15 .07
❑ 500 Rick Sutcliffe .25 .11
❑ 501 Bobby Jones .15 .07
❑ 502 Gary Gaetti .25 .11
❑ 503 Rick Aguilera .15 .07
❑ 504 Todd Stottlemyre .15 .07
❑ 505 Mike Mohler .15 .07
❑ 506 Mike Stanton .15 .07
❑ 507 Jose Guzman .15 .07
❑ 508 Kevin Rogers .15 .07
❑ 509 Chuck Carr .15 .07
❑ 510 Chris Jones .15 .07
❑ 511 Brent Mayne .15 .07
❑ 512 Greg Harris .15 .07
❑ 513 Dave Henderson .15 .07
❑ 514 Eric Hillman .15 .07
❑ 515 Dan Peltier .15 .07
❑ 516 Craig Shipley .15 .07
❑ 517 John Valentin .15 .07
❑ 518 Wilson Alvarez .15 .07
❑ 519 Andujar Cedeno .15 .07
❑ 520 Troy Neel .15 .07
❑ 521 Tom Candiotti .15 .07
❑ 522 Matt Mieske .15 .07
❑ 523 Jim Thome .60 .25
❑ 524 Lou Frazier .15 .07
❑ 525 Mike Jackson .15 .07
❑ 526 Pedro Martinez RC .15 .07
❑ 527 Roger Pavlik .15 .07
❑ 528 Kent Bottenfield .15 .07
❑ 529 Felix Jose .15 .07
❑ 530 Mark Guthrie .15 .07
❑ 531 Steve Farr .15 .07
❑ 532 Craig Paquette .15 .07
❑ 533 Doug Jones .15 .07
❑ 534 Luis Alicea .15 .07
❑ 535 Cory Snyder .15 .07
❑ 536 Paul Sorrento .15 .07
❑ 537 Nigel Wilson .15 .07
❑ 538 Jeff King .15 .07
❑ 539 Willie Greene .15 .07
❑ 540 Kirk McCaskill .15 .07
❑ 541 Al Osuna .15 .07
❑ 542 Greg Hibbard .15 .07
❑ 543 Brett Butler .25 .11
❑ 544 Jose Valentin .15 .07
❑ 545 Wil Cordero .15 .07
❑ 546 Chris Bosio .15 .07
❑ 547 Jamie Moyer .15 .07
❑ 548 Jim Eisenreich .15 .07
❑ 549 Vinny Castilla .25 .11
❑ 550 Dave Winfield CL .25 .11
❑ 551 John Roper .15 .07
❑ 552 Lance Johnson .15 .07
❑ 553 Scott Kamieniecki .15 .07
❑ 554 Mike Moore .15 .07
❑ 555 Steve Buechele .15 .07
❑ 556 Terry Pendleton .25 .11
❑ 557 Todd Van Poppel .15 .07
❑ 558 Rob Butler .15 .07
❑ 559 Zane Smith .15 .07
❑ 560 David Hulse .15 .07
❑ 561 Tim Costo .15 .07
❑ 562 John Habyan .15 .07
❑ 563 Terry Jorgensen .15 .07
❑ 564 Matt Nokes .15 .07
❑ 565 Kevin McReynolds .15 .07
❑ 566 Phil Plantier .15 .07
❑ 567 Chris Turner .15 .07
❑ 568 Carlos Delgado 1.00 .45
❑ 569 John Jaha .15 .07
❑ 570 Dwight Smith .15 .07
❑ 571 John Vander Wal .15 .07
❑ 572 Trevor Wilson .15 .07
❑ 573 Felix Fermin .15 .07
❑ 574 Marc Newfield .15 .07
❑ 575 Jeromy Burnitz .25 .11
❑ 576 Leo Gomez .15 .07
❑ 577 Curt Schilling .60 .25
❑ 578 Kevin Young .15 .07
❑ 579 Jerry Spradlin RC .15 .07
❑ 580 Curt Leskanic .15 .07
❑ 581 Carl Willis .15 .07
❑ 582 Alex Fernandez .15 .07
❑ 583 Mark Holzemer .15 .07
❑ 584 Domingo Martinez .15 .07
❑ 585 Pete Smith .15 .07
❑ 586 Brian Jordan .25 .11
❑ 587 Kevin Gross .15 .07
❑ 588 J.R. Phillips .15 .07
❑ 589 Chris Nabholz .15 .07
❑ 590 Bill Wertz .15 .07
❑ 591 Derek Bell .15 .07
❑ 592 Brady Anderson .25 .11
❑ 593 Matt Turner .15 .07

❑ 594 Pete Incaviglia .15 .07
❑ 595 Greg Gagne .15 .07
❑ 596 John Flaherty .15 .07
❑ 597 Scott Livingstone .15 .07
❑ 598 Rod Bolton .15 .07
❑ 599 Mike Perez .15 .07
❑ 600 Roger Clemens CL .75 .35
❑ 601 Tony Castillo .15 .07
❑ 602 Henry Mercedes .15 .07
❑ 603 Mike Fetters .15 .07
❑ 604 Rod Beck .15 .07
❑ 605 Damon Buford .15 .07
❑ 606 Matt Whiteside .15 .07
❑ 607 Shawn Green .75 .35
❑ 608 Midre Cummings .15 .07
❑ 609 Jeff McNeely .15 .07
❑ 610 Danny Sheaffer .15 .07
❑ 611 Paul Wagner .15 .07
❑ 612 Torey Lovullo .15 .07
❑ 613 Javier Lopez .25 .11
❑ 614 Mariano Duncan .15 .07
❑ 615 Doug Brocail .15 .07
❑ 616 Dave Hansen .15 .07
❑ 617 Ryan Klesko .25 .11
❑ 618 Eric Davis .25 .11
❑ 619 Scott Ruffcorn .15 .07
❑ 620 Mike Trombley .15 .07
❑ 621 Jaime Navarro .15 .07
❑ 622 Rheal Cormier .15 .07
❑ 623 Jose Offerman .15 .07
❑ 624 David Segui .15 .07
❑ 625 Robb Nen .15 .07
❑ 626 Dave Gallagher .15 .07
❑ 627 Julian Tavarez RC .25 .11
❑ 628 Chris Gomez .15 .07
❑ 629 Jeffrey Hammonds .25 .11
❑ 630 Scott Brosius .25 .11
❑ 631 Willie Blair .15 .07
❑ 632 Doug Drabek .15 .07
❑ 633 Bill Wegman .15 .07
❑ 634 Jeff McKnight .15 .07
❑ 635 Rich Rodriguez .15 .07
❑ 636 Steve Trachsel .15 .07
❑ 637 Buddy Groom .15 .07
❑ 638 Sterling Hitchcock .15 .07
❑ 639 Chuck McElroy .15 .07
❑ 640 Rene Gonzales .15 .07
❑ 641 Dan Plesac .15 .07
❑ 642 Jeff Branson .15 .07
❑ 643 Darrell Whitmore .15 .07
❑ 644 Paul Quantrill .15 .07
❑ 645 Rich Rowland .15 .07
❑ 646 Curtis Pride RC .25 .11
❑ 647 Erik Plantenberg RC .15 .07
❑ 648 Albie Lopez .15 .07
❑ 649 Rich Batchelor RC .15 .07
❑ 650 Lee Smith .25 .11
❑ 651 Cliff Floyd .25 .11
❑ 652 Pete Schourek .15 .07
❑ 653 Reggie Jefferson .15 .07
❑ 654 Bill Haselman .15 .07
❑ 655 Steve Hosey .15 .07
❑ 656 Mark Clark .15 .07
❑ 657 Mark Davis .15 .07
❑ 658 Dave Magadan .15 .07
❑ 659 Candy Maldonado .15 .07
❑ 660 Mark Langston CL .15 .07

1995 Donruss

	MINT	NRMT
COMPLETE SET (550)	30.00	13.50
COMPLETE SERIES 1 (330)	20.00	9.00
COMPLETE SERIES 2 (220)	10.00	4.50

❑ 1 David Justice .25 .11
❑ 2 Rene Arocha .15 .07
❑ 3 Sandy Alomar Jr. .25 .11
❑ 4 Luis Lopez .15 .07
❑ 5 Mike Piazza 1.50 .70
❑ 6 Bobby Jones .15 .07
❑ 7 Damion Easley .15 .07
❑ 8 Barry Bonds 1.50 .70
❑ 9 Mike Mussina .60 .25
❑ 10 Kevin Seitzer .15 .07
❑ 11 John Smiley .15 .07

❑ 12 Wm.VanLandingham .15 .07
❑ 13 Ron Darling .15 .07
❑ 14 Walt Weiss .15 .07
❑ 15 Mike Lansing .15 .07
❑ 16 Allen Watson .15 .07
❑ 17 Aaron Sele .25 .11
❑ 18 Randy Johnson .75 .35
❑ 19 Dean Palmer .25 .11
❑ 20 Jeff Bagwell .75 .35
❑ 21 Curt Schilling .60 .25
❑ 22 Darrell Whitmore .15 .07
❑ 23 Steve Trachsel .15 .07
❑ 24 Dan Wilson .15 .07
❑ 25 Steve Finley .25 .11
❑ 26 Bret Boone .25 .11
❑ 27 Charles Johnson .25 .11
❑ 28 Mike Stanton .15 .07
❑ 29 Ismael Valdes .15 .07
❑ 30 Salomon Torres .15 .07
❑ 31 Eric Anthony .15 .07
❑ 32 Spike Owen .15 .07
❑ 33 Joey Cora .15 .07
❑ 34 Robert Eenhoorn .15 .07
❑ 35 Rick White .15 .07
❑ 36 Omar Vizquel .25 .11
❑ 37 Carlos Delgado .60 .25
❑ 38 Eddie Williams .15 .07
❑ 39 Shawon Dunston .15 .07
❑ 40 Darrin Fletcher .15 .07
❑ 41 Leo Gomez .15 .07
❑ 42 Juan Gonzalez .60 .25
❑ 43 Luis Alicea .15 .07
❑ 44 Ken Ryan .15 .07
❑ 45 Lou Whitaker .25 .11
❑ 46 Mike Blowers .15 .07
❑ 47 Willie Blair .15 .07
❑ 48 Todd Van Poppel .15 .07
❑ 49 Roberto Alomar .60 .25
❑ 50 Ozzie Smith .75 .35
❑ 51 Sterling Hitchcock .15 .07
❑ 52 Mo Vaughn .25 .11
❑ 53 Rick Aguilera .15 .07
❑ 54 Kent Mercker .15 .07
❑ 55 Don Mattingly 1.50 .70
❑ 56 Bob Scanlan .15 .07
❑ 57 Wilson Alvarez .15 .07
❑ 58 Jose Mesa .15 .07
❑ 59 Scott Kamieniecki .15 .07
❑ 60 Todd Jones .15 .07
❑ 61 John Kruk .25 .11
❑ 62 Mike Stanley .15 .07
❑ 63 Tino Martinez .25 .11
❑ 64 Eddie Zambrano .15 .07
❑ 65 Todd Hundley .15 .07
❑ 66 Jamie Moyer .15 .07
❑ 67 Rich Amaral .15 .07
❑ 68 Jose Valentin .15 .07
❑ 69 Alex Gonzalez .15 .07
❑ 70 Kurt Abbott .15 .07
❑ 71 Delino DeShields .15 .07
❑ 72 Brian Anderson .15 .07
❑ 73 John Vander Wal .15 .07
❑ 74 Turner Ward .15 .07
❑ 75 Tim Raines .25 .11
❑ 76 Mark Acre .15 .07
❑ 77 Jose Offerman .15 .07
❑ 78 Jimmy Key .25 .11

❑ 79 Mark Whiten .15 .07
❑ 80 Mark Gubicza .15 .07
❑ 81 Darren Hall .15 .07
❑ 82 Travis Fryman .25 .11
❑ 83 Cal Ripken 2.50 1.10
❑ 84 Geronimo Berroa .15 .07
❑ 85 Bret Barberie .15 .07
❑ 86 Andy Ashby .15 .07
❑ 87 Steve Avery .15 .07
❑ 88 Rich Becker .15 .07
❑ 89 John Valentin .15 .07
❑ 90 Glenallen Hill .15 .07
❑ 91 Carlos Garcia .15 .07
❑ 92 Dennis Martinez .25 .11
❑ 93 Pat Kelly .15 .07
❑ 94 Orlando Miller .15 .07
❑ 95 Felix Jose .15 .07
❑ 96 Mike Kingery .15 .07
❑ 97 Jeff Kent .40 .18
❑ 98 Pete Incaviglia .15 .07
❑ 99 Chad Curtis .15 .07
❑ 100 Thomas Howard .15 .07
❑ 101 Hector Carrasco .15 .07
❑ 102 Tom Pagnozzi .15 .07
❑ 103 Danny Tartabull .15 .07
❑ 104 Donnie Elliott .15 .07
❑ 105 Danny Jackson .15 .07
❑ 106 Steve Dunn .15 .07
❑ 107 Roger Salkeld .15 .07
❑ 108 Jeff King .15 .07
❑ 109 Cecil Fielder .25 .11
❑ 110 Paul Molitor CL .25 .11
❑ 111 Denny Neagle .25 .11
❑ 112 Troy Neel .15 .07
❑ 113 Rod Beck .15 .07
❑ 114 Alex Rodriguez 2.00 .90
❑ 115 Joey Eischen .15 .07
❑ 116 Tom Candiotti .15 .07
❑ 117 Ray McDavid .15 .07
❑ 118 Vince Coleman .15 .07
❑ 119 Pete Harnisch .15 .07
❑ 120 David Nied .15 .07
❑ 121 Pat Rapp .15 .07
❑ 122 Sammy Sosa 1.25 .55
❑ 123 Steve Reed .15 .07
❑ 124 Jose Oliva .15 .07
❑ 125 Ricky Bottalico .15 .07
❑ 126 Jose DeLeon .15 .07
❑ 127 Pat Hentgen .15 .07
❑ 128 Will Clark .60 .25
❑ 129 Mark Dewey .15 .07
❑ 130 Greg Vaughn .25 .11
❑ 131 Darren Dreifort .15 .07
❑ 132 Ed Sprague .15 .07
❑ 133 Lee Smith .25 .11
❑ 134 Charles Nagy .15 .07
❑ 135 Phil Plantier .15 .07
❑ 136 Jason Jacome .15 .07
❑ 137 Jose Lima .15 .07
❑ 138 J.R. Phillips .15 .07
❑ 139 J.T. Snow .25 .11
❑ 140 Michael Huff .15 .07
❑ 141 Billy Brewer .15 .07
❑ 142 Jeromy Burnitz .25 .11
❑ 143 Ricky Bones .15 .07
❑ 144 Carlos Rodriguez .15 .07
❑ 145 Luis Gonzalez .60 .25
❑ 146 Mark Lemke .15 .07
❑ 147 Al Martin .15 .07
❑ 148 Mike Bordick .15 .07
❑ 149 Robb Nen .15 .07
❑ 150 Wil Cordero .15 .07
❑ 151 Edgar Martinez .40 .18
❑ 152 Gerald Williams .15 .07
❑ 153 Esteban Beltre .15 .07
❑ 154 Mike Moore .15 .07
❑ 155 Mark Langston .15 .07
❑ 156 Mark Clark .15 .07
❑ 157 Bobby Ayala .15 .07
❑ 158 Rick Wilkins .15 .07
❑ 159 Bobby Munoz .15 .07
❑ 160 Brett Butler CL .15 .07
❑ 161 Scott Erickson .15 .07
❑ 162 Paul Molitor .60 .25
❑ 163 Jon Lieber .15 .07
❑ 164 Jason Grimsley .15 .07

❑ 165 Norberto Martin .15 .07
❑ 166 Javier Lopez .25 .11
❑ 167 Brian McRae .15 .07
❑ 168 Gary Sheffield .25 .11
❑ 169 Marcus Moore .15 .07
❑ 170 John Hudek .15 .07
❑ 171 Kelly Stinnett .15 .07
❑ 172 Chris Gomez .15 .07
❑ 173 Rey Sanchez .15 .07
❑ 174 Juan Guzman .15 .07
❑ 175 Chan Ho Park .25 .11
❑ 176 Terry Shumpert .15 .07
❑ 177 Steve Ontiveros .15 .07
❑ 178 Brad Ausmus .15 .07
❑ 179 Tim Davis .15 .07
❑ 180 Billy Ashley .15 .07
❑ 181 Vinny Castilla .25 .11
❑ 182 Bill Spiers .15 .07
❑ 183 Randy Knorr .15 .07
❑ 184 Brian Hunter .15 .07
❑ 185 Pat Meares .15 .07
❑ 186 Steve Buechele .15 .07
❑ 187 Kirt Manwaring .15 .07
❑ 188 Tim Naehring .15 .07
❑ 189 Matt Mieske .15 .07
❑ 190 Josias Manzanillo .15 .07
❑ 191 Greg McMichael .15 .07
❑ 192 Chuck Carr .15 .07
❑ 193 Midre Cummings .15 .07
❑ 194 Darryl Strawberry .25 .11
❑ 195 Greg Gagne .15 .07
❑ 196 Steve Cooke .15 .07
❑ 197 Woody Williams .15 .07
❑ 198 Ron Karkovice .15 .07
❑ 199 Phil Leftwich .15 .07
❑ 200 Jim Thome .60 .25
❑ 201 Brady Anderson .25 .11
❑ 202 Pedro A.Martinez .15 .07
❑ 203 Steve Karsay .15 .07
❑ 204 Reggie Sanders .15 .07
❑ 205 Bill Risley .15 .07
❑ 206 Jay Bell .25 .11
❑ 207 Kevin Brown .25 .11
❑ 208 Tim Scott .15 .07
❑ 209 Lenny Dykstra .25 .11
❑ 210 Willie Greene .15 .07
❑ 211 Jim Eisenreich .15 .07
❑ 212 Cliff Floyd .25 .11
❑ 213 Otis Nixon .15 .07
❑ 214 Eduardo Perez .15 .07
❑ 215 Manuel Lee .15 .07
❑ 216 Armando Benitez .25 .11
❑ 217 Dave McCarty .15 .07
❑ 218 Scott Livingstone .15 .07
❑ 219 Chad Kreuter .15 .07
❑ 220 Don Mattingly CL .75 .35
❑ 221 Brian Jordan .25 .11
❑ 222 Matt Whiteside .15 .07
❑ 223 Jim Edmonds .40 .18
❑ 224 Tony Gwynn 1.25 .55
❑ 225 Jose Lind .15 .07
❑ 226 Marvin Freeman .15 .07
❑ 227 Ken Hill .15 .07
❑ 228 David Hulse .15 .07
❑ 229 Joe Hesketh .15 .07
❑ 230 Roberto Petagine .15 .07
❑ 231 Jeffrey Hammonds .15 .07
❑ 232 John Jaha .15 .07
❑ 233 John Burkett .15 .07
❑ 234 Hal Morris .15 .07
❑ 235 Tony Castillo .15 .07
❑ 236 Ryan Bowen .15 .07
❑ 237 Wayne Kirby .15 .07
❑ 238 Brent Mayne .15 .07
❑ 239 Jim Bullinger .15 .07
❑ 240 Mike Lieberthal .25 .11
❑ 241 Barry Larkin .60 .25
❑ 242 David Segui .15 .07
❑ 243 Jose Bautista .15 .07
❑ 244 Hector Fajardo .15 .07
❑ 245 Orel Hershiser .25 .11
❑ 246 James Mouton .15 .07
❑ 247 Scott Leius .15 .07
❑ 248 Tom Glavine .60 .25
❑ 249 Danny Bautista .15 .07
❑ 250 Jose Mercedes .15 .07
❑ 251 Marquis Grissom .15 .07
❑ 252 Charlie Hayes .15 .07
❑ 253 Ryan Klesko .25 .11
❑ 254 Vicente Palacios .15 .07
❑ 255 Matias Carrillo .15 .07
❑ 256 Gary DiSarcina .15 .07
❑ 257 Kirk Gibson .25 .11
❑ 258 Garey Ingram .15 .07
❑ 259 Alex Fernandez .15 .07
❑ 260 John Mabry .15 .07
❑ 261 Chris Howard .15 .07
❑ 262 Miguel Jimenez .15 .07
❑ 263 Heathcliff Slocumb .15 .07
❑ 264 Albert Belle .25 .11
❑ 265 Dave Clark .15 .07
❑ 266 Joe Orsulak .15 .07
❑ 267 Joey Hamilton .15 .07
❑ 268 Mark Portugal .15 .07
❑ 269 Kevin Tapani .15 .07
❑ 270 Sid Fernandez .15 .07
❑ 271 Steve Dreyer .15 .07
❑ 272 Denny Hocking .15 .07
❑ 273 Troy O'Leary .15 .07
❑ 274 Milt Cuyler .15 .07
❑ 275 Frank Thomas .75 .35
❑ 276 Jorge Fabregas .15 .07
❑ 277 Mike Gallego .15 .07
❑ 278 Mickey Morandini .15 .07
❑ 279 Roberto Hernandez .15 .07
❑ 280 Henry Rodriguez .15 .07
❑ 281 Garret Anderson .25 .11
❑ 282 Bob Wickman .15 .07
❑ 283 Gar Finnvold .15 .07
❑ 284 Paul O'Neill .60 .25
❑ 285 Royce Clayton .15 .07
❑ 286 Chuck Knoblauch .25 .11
❑ 287 Johnny Ruffin .15 .07
❑ 288 Dave Nilsson .15 .07
❑ 289 David Cone .25 .11
❑ 290 Chuck McElroy .15 .07
❑ 291 Kevin Stocker .15 .07
❑ 292 Jose Rijo .15 .07
❑ 293 Sean Berry .15 .07
❑ 294 Ozzie Guillen .15 .07
❑ 295 Chris Hoiles .15 .07
❑ 296 Kevin Foster .15 .07
❑ 297 Jeff Frye .15 .07
❑ 298 Lance Johnson .15 .07
❑ 299 Mike Kelly .15 .07
❑ 300 Ellis Burks .25 .11
❑ 301 Roberto Kelly .15 .07
❑ 302 Dante Bichette .25 .11
❑ 303 Alvaro Ezpinoza .15 .07
❑ 304 Alex Cole .15 .07
❑ 305 Rickey Henderson 1.25 .55
❑ 306 Dave Weathers .15 .07
❑ 307 Shane Reynolds .15 .07
❑ 308 Bobby Bonilla .25 .11
❑ 309 Junior Felix .15 .07
❑ 310 Jeff Fassero .15 .07
❑ 311 Darren Lewis .15 .07
❑ 312 John Doherty .15 .07
❑ 313 Scott Servais .15 .07
❑ 314 Rick Helling .15 .07
❑ 315 Pedro Martinez .75 .35
❑ 316 Wes Chamberlain .15 .07
❑ 317 Bryan Eversgerd .15 .07
❑ 318 Trevor Hoffman .25 .11
❑ 319 John Patterson .15 .07
❑ 320 Matt Walbeck .15 .07
❑ 321 Jeff Montgomery .15 .07
❑ 322 Mel Rojas .15 .07
❑ 323 Eddie Taubensee .15 .07
❑ 324 Ray Lankford .15 .07
❑ 325 Jose Vizcaino .15 .07
❑ 326 Carlos Baerga .15 .07
❑ 327 Jack Voigt .15 .07
❑ 328 Julio Franco .25 .11
❑ 329 Brent Gates .15 .07
❑ 330 Kirby Puckett CL .75 .35
❑ 331 Greg Maddux 1.50 .70
❑ 332 Jason Bere .15 .07
❑ 333 Bill Wegman .15 .07
❑ 334 Tuffy Rhodes .15 .07
❑ 335 Kevin Young .15 .07
❑ 336 Andy Benes .15 .07
❑ 337 Pedro Astacio .15 .07
❑ 338 Reggie Jefferson .15 .07
❑ 339 Tim Belcher .15 .07
❑ 340 Ken Griffey Jr. 2.00 .90
❑ 341 Mariano Duncan .15 .07
❑ 342 Andres Galarraga .40 .18
❑ 343 Rondell White .25 .11
❑ 344 Cory Bailey .15 .07
❑ 345 Bryan Harvey .15 .07
❑ 346 John Franco .25 .11
❑ 347 Greg Swindell .15 .07
❑ 348 David West .15 .07
❑ 349 Fred McGriff .40 .18
❑ 350 Jose Canseco .60 .25
❑ 351 Orlando Merced .15 .07
❑ 352 Rheal Cormier .15 .07
❑ 353 Carlos Pulido .15 .07
❑ 354 Terry Steinbach .15 .07
❑ 355 Wade Boggs .60 .25
❑ 356 B.J. Surhoff .25 .11
❑ 357 Rafael Palmeiro .60 .25
❑ 358 Anthony Young .15 .07
❑ 359 Tom Brunansky .15 .07
❑ 360 Todd Stottlemyre .15 .07
❑ 361 Chris Turner .15 .07
❑ 362 Joe Boever .15 .07
❑ 363 Jeff Blauser .15 .07
❑ 364 Derek Bell .15 .07
❑ 365 Matt Williams .40 .18
❑ 366 Jeremy Hernandez .15 .07
❑ 367 Joe Girardi .15 .07
❑ 368 Mike Devereaux .15 .07
❑ 369 Jim Abbott .25 .11
❑ 370 Manny Ramirez .75 .35
❑ 371 Kenny Lofton .25 .11
❑ 372 Mark Smith .15 .07
❑ 373 Dave Fleming .15 .07
❑ 374 Dave Stewart .25 .11
❑ 375 Roger Pavlik .15 .07
❑ 376 Hipolito Pichardo .15 .07
❑ 377 Bill Taylor .15 .07
❑ 378 Robin Ventura .25 .11
❑ 379 Bernard Gilkey .15 .07
❑ 380 Kirby Puckett 1.50 .70
❑ 381 Steve Howe .15 .07
❑ 382 Devon White .25 .11
❑ 383 Roberto Mejia .15 .07
❑ 384 Darrin Jackson .15 .07
❑ 385 Mike Morgan .15 .07
❑ 386 Rusty Meacham .15 .07
❑ 387 Bill Swift .15 .07
❑ 388 Lou Frazier .15 .07
❑ 389 Andy Van Slyke .25 .11
❑ 390 Brett Butler .25 .11
❑ 391 Bobby Witt .15 .07
❑ 392 Jeff Conine .15 .07
❑ 393 Tim Hyers .15 .07
❑ 394 Terry Pendleton .25 .11
❑ 395 Ricky Jordan .15 .07
❑ 396 Eric Plunk .15 .07
❑ 397 Melido Perez .15 .07
❑ 398 Darryl Kile .25 .11
❑ 399 Mark McLemore .15 .07
❑ 400 Greg W.Harris .15 .07
❑ 401 Jim Leyritz .15 .07
❑ 402 Doug Strange .15 .07
❑ 403 Tim Salmon .25 .11
❑ 404 Terry Mulholland .15 .07
❑ 405 Robby Thompson .15 .07
❑ 406 Ruben Sierra .15 .07
❑ 407 Tony Phillips .15 .07
❑ 408 Moises Alou .25 .11
❑ 409 Felix Fermin .15 .07
❑ 410 Pat Listach .15 .07
❑ 411 Kevin Bass .15 .07
❑ 412 Ben McDonald .15 .07
❑ 413 Scott Cooper .15 .07
❑ 414 Jody Reed .15 .07
❑ 415 Deion Sanders .25 .11
❑ 416 Ricky Gutierrez .15 .07
❑ 417 Gregg Jefferies .15 .07
❑ 418 Jack McDowell .15 .07
❑ 419 Al Leiter .25 .11
❑ 420 Tony Longmire .15 .07
❑ 421 Paul Wagner .15 .07
❑ 422 Geronimo Pena .15 .07

❑ 423 Ivan Rodriguez .60 .25
❑ 424 Kevin Gross .15 .07
❑ 425 Kirk McCaskill .15 .07
❑ 426 Greg Myers .15 .07
❑ 427 Roger Clemens 1.50 .70
❑ 428 Chris Hammond .15 .07
❑ 429 Randy Myers .15 .07
❑ 430 Roger Mason .15 .07
❑ 431 Bret Saberhagen .25 .11
❑ 432 Jeff Reboulet .15 .07
❑ 433 John Olerud .25 .11
❑ 434 Bill Gullickson .15 .07
❑ 435 Eddie Murray .60 .25
❑ 436 Pedro Munoz .15 .07
❑ 437 Charlie O'Brien .15 .07
❑ 438 Jeff Nelson .15 .07
❑ 439 Mike Macfarlane .15 .07
❑ 440 Don Mattingly CL .75 .35
❑ 441 Derrick May .15 .07
❑ 442 John Roper .15 .07
❑ 443 Darryl Hamilton .15 .07
❑ 444 Dan Miceli .15 .07
❑ 445 Tony Eusebio .15 .07
❑ 446 Jerry Browne .15 .07
❑ 447 Wally Joyner .25 .11
❑ 448 Brian Harper .15 .07
❑ 449 Scott Fletcher .15 .07
❑ 450 Bip Roberts .15 .07
❑ 451 Pete Smith .15 .07
❑ 452 Chili Davis .25 .11
❑ 453 Dave Hollins .15 .07
❑ 454 Tony Pena .15 .07
❑ 455 Butch Henry .15 .07
❑ 456 Craig Biggio .40 .18
❑ 457 Zane Smith .15 .07
❑ 458 Ryan Thompson .15 .07
❑ 459 Mike Jackson .15 .07
❑ 460 Mark McGwire 2.50 1.10
❑ 461 John Smoltz .25 .11
❑ 462 Steve Scarsone .15 .07
❑ 463 Greg Colbrunn .15 .07
❑ 464 Shawn Green .60 .25
❑ 465 David Wells .25 .11
❑ 466 Jose Hernandez .15 .07
❑ 467 Chip Hale .15 .07
❑ 468 Tony Tarasco .15 .07
❑ 469 Kevin Mitchell .15 .07
❑ 470 Billy Hatcher .15 .07
❑ 471 Jay Buhner .25 .11
❑ 472 Ken Caminiti .25 .11
❑ 473 Tom Henke .15 .07
❑ 474 Todd Worrell .15 .07
❑ 475 Mark Eichhorn .15 .07
❑ 476 Bruce Ruffin .15 .07
❑ 477 Chuck Finley .25 .11
❑ 478 Marc Newfield .15 .07
❑ 479 Paul Shuey .15 .07
❑ 480 Bob Tewksbury .15 .07
❑ 481 Ramon J.Martinez .15 .07
❑ 482 Melvin Nieves .15 .07
❑ 483 Todd Zeile .15 .07
❑ 484 Benito Santiago .15 .07
❑ 485 Stan Javier .15 .07
❑ 486 Kirk Rueter .15 .07
❑ 487 Andre Dawson .40 .18
❑ 488 Eric Karros .25 .11
❑ 489 Dave Magadan .15 .07
❑ 490 Joe Carter CL .15 .07
❑ 491 Randy Velarde .15 .07
❑ 492 Larry Walker .40 .18
❑ 493 Cris Carpenter .15 .07
❑ 494 Tom Gordon .15 .07
❑ 495 Dave Burba .15 .07
❑ 496 Darren Bragg .15 .07
❑ 497 Darren Daulton .25 .11
❑ 498 Don Slaught .15 .07
❑ 499 Pat Borders .15 .07
❑ 500 Lenny Harris .15 .07
❑ 501 Joe Ausanio .15 .07
❑ 502 Alan Trammell .40 .18
❑ 503 Mike Fetters .15 .07
❑ 504 Scott Ruffcorn .15 .07
❑ 505 Rich Rowland .15 .07
❑ 506 Juan Samuel .15 .07
❑ 507 Bo Jackson .25 .11
❑ 508 Jeff Branson .15 .07
❑ 509 Bernie Williams .60 .25
❑ 510 Paul Sorrento .15 .07
❑ 511 Dennis Eckersley .25 .11
❑ 512 Pat Mahomes .15 .07
❑ 513 Rusty Greer .25 .11
❑ 514 Luis Polonia .15 .07
❑ 515 Willie Banks .15 .07
❑ 516 John Wetteland .25 .11
❑ 517 Mike LaValliere .15 .07
❑ 518 Tommy Greene .15 .07
❑ 519 Mark Grace .60 .25
❑ 520 Bob Hamelin .15 .07
❑ 521 Scott Sanderson .15 .07
❑ 522 Joe Carter .25 .11
❑ 523 Jeff Brantley .15 .07
❑ 524 Andrew Lorraine .15 .07
❑ 525 Rico Brogna .15 .07
❑ 526 Shane Mack .15 .07
❑ 527 Mark Wohlers .15 .07
❑ 528 Scott Sanders .15 .07
❑ 529 Chris Bosio .15 .07
❑ 530 Andujar Cedeno .15 .07
❑ 531 Kenny Rogers .15 .07
❑ 532 Doug Drabek .15 .07
❑ 533 Curt Leskanic .15 .07
❑ 534 Craig Shipley .15 .07
❑ 535 Craig Grebeck .15 .07
❑ 536 Cal Eldred .15 .07
❑ 537 Mickey Tettleton .15 .07
❑ 538 Harold Baines .25 .11
❑ 539 Tim Wallach .15 .07
❑ 540 Damon Buford .15 .07
❑ 541 Lenny Webster .15 .07
❑ 542 Kevin Appier .25 .11
❑ 543 Raul Mondesi .25 .11
❑ 544 Eric Young .15 .07
❑ 545 Russ Davis .15 .07
❑ 546 Mike Benjamin .15 .07
❑ 547 Mike Greenwell .15 .07
❑ 548 Scott Brosius .25 .11
❑ 549 Brian Dorsett .15 .07
❑ 550 Chili Davis CL .15 .07

1996 Donruss

	MINT	NRMT
COMPLETE SET (550)	40.00	18.00
COMPLETE SERIES 1 (330)	25.00	11.00
COMPLETE SERIES 2 (220)	15.00	6.75

❑ 1 Frank Thomas .75 .35
❑ 2 Jason Bates .15 .07
❑ 3 Steve Sparks .15 .07
❑ 4 Scott Servais .15 .07
❑ 5 Angelo Encarnacion RC .15 .07
❑ 6 Scott Sanders .15 .07
❑ 7 Billy Ashley .15 .07
❑ 8 Alex Rodriguez 1.50 .70
❑ 9 Sean Bergman .15 .07
❑ 10 Brad Radke .25 .11
❑ 11 Andy Van Slyke .25 .11
❑ 12 Joe Girardi .15 .07
❑ 13 Mark Grudzielanek .15 .07
❑ 14 Rick Aguilera .15 .07
❑ 15 Randy Veres .15 .07
❑ 16 Tim Bogar .15 .07
❑ 17 Dave Veres .15 .07
❑ 18 Kevin Stocker .15 .07
❑ 19 Marquis Grissom .15 .07
❑ 20 Will Clark .60 .25
❑ 21 Jay Bell .25 .11
❑ 22 Allen Battle .15 .07
❑ 23 Frank Rodriguez .15 .07
❑ 24 Terry Steinbach .15 .07
❑ 25 Gerald Williams .15 .07
❑ 26 Sid Roberson .15 .07
❑ 27 Greg Zaun .15 .07
❑ 28 Ozzie Timmons .15 .07
❑ 29 Vaughn Eshelman .15 .07
❑ 30 Ed Sprague .15 .07
❑ 31 Gary DiSarcina .15 .07
❑ 32 Joe Boever .15 .07
❑ 33 Steve Avery .15 .07
❑ 34 Brad Ausmus .15 .07
❑ 35 Kirt Manwaring .15 .07
❑ 36 Gary Sheffield .25 .11
❑ 37 Jason Bere .15 .07
❑ 38 Jeff Manto .15 .07
❑ 39 David Cone .25 .11
❑ 40 Manny Ramirez .75 .35
❑ 41 Sandy Alomar Jr. .25 .11
❑ 42 Curtis Goodwin .15 .07
❑ 43 Tino Martinez .25 .11
❑ 44 Woody Williams .15 .07
❑ 45 Dean Palmer .25 .11
❑ 46 Hipolito Pichardo .15 .07
❑ 47 Jason Giambi .60 .25
❑ 48 Lance Johnson .15 .07
❑ 49 Bernard Gilkey .15 .07
❑ 50 Kirby Puckett 1.50 .70
❑ 51 Tony Fernandez .15 .07
❑ 52 Alex Gonzalez .15 .07
❑ 53 Bret Saberhagen .25 .11
❑ 54 Lyle Mouton .15 .07
❑ 55 Brian McRae .15 .07
❑ 56 Mark Gubicza .15 .07
❑ 57 Sergio Valdez .15 .07
❑ 58 Darrin Fletcher .15 .07
❑ 59 Steve Parris .15 .07
❑ 60 Johnny Damon .25 .11
❑ 61 Rickey Henderson 1.25 .55
❑ 62 Darrell Whitmore .15 .07
❑ 63 Roberto Petagine .15 .07
❑ 64 Trenidad Hubbard .15 .07
❑ 65 Heathcliff Slocumb .15 .07
❑ 66 Steve Finley .25 .11
❑ 67 Mariano Rivera .25 .11
❑ 68 Brian L.Hunter .15 .07
❑ 69 Jamie Moyer .15 .07
❑ 70 Ellis Burks .25 .11
❑ 71 Pat Kelly .15 .07
❑ 72 Mickey Tettleton .15 .07
❑ 73 Garret Anderson .25 .11
❑ 74 Andy Pettitte .25 .11
❑ 75 Glenallen Hill .15 .07
❑ 76 Brent Gates .15 .07
❑ 77 Lou Whitaker .25 .11
❑ 78 David Segui .15 .07
❑ 79 Dan Wilson .15 .07
❑ 80 Pat Listach .15 .07
❑ 81 Jeff Bagwell .75 .35
❑ 82 Ben McDonald .15 .07
❑ 83 John Valentin .15 .07
❑ 84 John Jaha .15 .07
❑ 85 Pete Schourek .15 .07
❑ 86 Bryce Florie .15 .07
❑ 87 Brian Jordan .25 .11
❑ 88 Ron Karkovice .15 .07
❑ 89 Al Leiter .25 .11
❑ 90 Tony Longmire .15 .07
❑ 91 Nelson Liriano .15 .07
❑ 92 David Bell .15 .07
❑ 93 Kevin Gross .15 .07
❑ 94 Tom Candiotti .15 .07
❑ 95 Dave Martinez .15 .07
❑ 96 Greg Myers .15 .07
❑ 97 Rheal Cormier .15 .07
❑ 98 Chris Hammond .15 .07
❑ 99 Randy Myers .15 .07
❑ 100 Bill Pulsipher .15 .07
❑ 101 Jason Isringhausen .25 .11
❑ 102 Dave Stevens .15 .07
❑ 103 Roberto Alomar .60 .25
❑ 104 Bob Higginson .25 .11

❑ 105 Eddie Murray .60 .25
❑ 106 Matt Walbeck .15 .07
❑ 107 Mark Wohlers .15 .07
❑ 108 Jeff Nelson .15 .07
❑ 109 Tom Goodwin .15 .07
❑ 110 Cal Ripken CL 1.25 .55
❑ 111 Rey Sanchez .15 .07
❑ 112 Hector Carrasco .15 .07
❑ 113 B.J. Surhoff .25 .11
❑ 114 Dan Miceli .15 .07
❑ 115 Dean Hartgraves .15 .07
❑ 116 John Burkett .15 .07
❑ 117 Gary Gaetti .25 .11
❑ 118 Ricky Bones .15 .07
❑ 119 Mike Macfarlane .15 .07
❑ 120 Bip Roberts .15 .07
❑ 121 Dave Mlicki .15 .07
❑ 122 Chili Davis .25 .11
❑ 123 Mark Whiten .15 .07
❑ 124 Herbert Perry .15 .07
❑ 125 Butch Henry .15 .07
❑ 126 Derek Bell .15 .07
❑ 127 Al Martin .15 .07
❑ 128 John Franco .25 .11
❑ 129 W. VanLandingham .15 .07
❑ 130 Mike Bordick .15 .07
❑ 131 Mike Mordecai .15 .07
❑ 132 Robby Thompson .15 .07
❑ 133 Greg Colbrunn .15 .07
❑ 134 Domingo Cedeno .15 .07
❑ 135 Chad Curtis .15 .07
❑ 136 Jose Hernandez .15 .07
❑ 137 Scott Klingenbeck .15 .07
❑ 138 Ryan Klesko .25 .11
❑ 139 John Smiley .15 .07
❑ 140 Charlie Hayes .15 .07
❑ 141 Jay Buhner .25 .11
❑ 142 Doug Drabek .15 .07
❑ 143 Roger Pavlik .15 .07
❑ 144 Todd Worrell .15 .07
❑ 145 Cal Ripken 2.50 1.10
❑ 146 Steve Reed .15 .07
❑ 147 Chuck Finley .25 .11
❑ 148 Mike Blowers .15 .07
❑ 149 Orel Hershiser .25 .11
❑ 150 Allen Watson .15 .07
❑ 151 Ramon Martinez .15 .07
❑ 152 Melvin Nieves .15 .07
❑ 153 Tripp Cromer .15 .07
❑ 154 Yorkis Perez .15 .07
❑ 155 Stan Javier .15 .07
❑ 156 Mel Rojas .15 .07
❑ 157 Aaron Sele .25 .11
❑ 158 Eric Karros .25 .11
❑ 159 Robb Nen .15 .07
❑ 160 Raul Mondesi .25 .11
❑ 161 John Wetteland .25 .11
❑ 162 Tim Scott .15 .07
❑ 163 Kenny Rogers .15 .07
❑ 164 Melvin Bunch .15 .07
❑ 165 Rod Beck .15 .07
❑ 166 Andy Benes .15 .07
❑ 167 Lenny Dykstra .25 .11
❑ 168 Orlando Merced .15 .07
❑ 169 Tomas Perez .15 .07
❑ 170 Xavier Hernandez .15 .07
❑ 171 Ruben Sierra .15 .07
❑ 172 Alan Trammell .40 .18
❑ 173 Mike Fetters .15 .07
❑ 174 Wilson Alvarez .15 .07
❑ 175 Erik Hanson .15 .07
❑ 176 Travis Fryman .25 .11
❑ 177 Jim Abbott .25 .11
❑ 178 Bret Boone .25 .11
❑ 179 Sterling Hitchcock .15 .07
❑ 180 Pat Mahomes .15 .07
❑ 181 Mark Acre .15 .07
❑ 182 Charles Nagy .15 .07
❑ 183 Rusty Greer .25 .11
❑ 184 Mike Stanley .15 .07
❑ 185 Jim Bullinger .15 .07
❑ 186 Shane Andrews .15 .07
❑ 187 Brian Keyser .15 .07
❑ 188 Tyler Green .15 .07
❑ 189 Mark Grace .60 .25
❑ 190 Bob Hamelin .15 .07
❑ 191 Luis Ortiz .15 .07
❑ 192 Joe Carter .25 .11
❑ 193 Eddie Taubensee .15 .07
❑ 194 Brian Anderson .15 .07
❑ 195 Edgardo Alfonzo .25 .11
❑ 196 Pedro Munoz .15 .07
❑ 197 David Justice .25 .11
❑ 198 Trevor Hoffman .25 .11
❑ 199 Bobby Ayala .15 .07
❑ 200 Tony Eusebio .15 .07
❑ 201 Jeff Russell .15 .07
❑ 202 Mike Hampton .25 .11
❑ 203 Walt Weiss .15 .07
❑ 204 Joey Hamilton .15 .07
❑ 205 Roberto Hernandez .15 .07
❑ 206 Greg Vaughn .25 .11
❑ 207 Felipe Lira .15 .07
❑ 208 Harold Baines .25 .11
❑ 209 Tim Wallach .15 .07
❑ 210 Manny Alexander .15 .07
❑ 211 Tim Laker .15 .07
❑ 212 Chris Haney .15 .07
❑ 213 Brian Maxcy .15 .07
❑ 214 Eric Young .15 .07
❑ 215 Darryl Strawberry .25 .11
❑ 216 Barry Bonds 1.50 .70
❑ 217 Tim Naehring .15 .07
❑ 218 Scott Brosius .25 .11
❑ 219 Reggie Sanders .15 .07
❑ 220 Eddie Murray CL .25 .11
❑ 221 Luis Alicea .15 .07
❑ 222 Albert Belle .25 .11
❑ 223 Benji Gil .15 .07
❑ 224 Dante Bichette .25 .11
❑ 225 Bobby Bonilla .25 .11
❑ 226 Todd Stottlemyre .15 .07
❑ 227 Jim Edmonds .40 .18
❑ 228 Todd Jones .15 .07
❑ 229 Shawn Green .60 .25
❑ 230 Javier Lopez .25 .11
❑ 231 Ariel Prieto .15 .07
❑ 232 Tony Phillips .15 .07
❑ 233 James Mouton .15 .07
❑ 234 Jose Oquendo .15 .07
❑ 235 Royce Clayton .15 .07
❑ 236 Chuck Carr .15 .07
❑ 237 Doug Jones .15 .07
❑ 238 Mark McLemore .15 .07
❑ 239 Bill Swift .15 .07
❑ 240 Scott Leius .15 .07
❑ 241 Russ Davis .15 .07
❑ 242 Ray Durham .25 .11
❑ 243 Matt Mieske .15 .07
❑ 244 Brent Mayne .15 .07
❑ 245 Thomas Howard .15 .07
❑ 246 Troy O'Leary .15 .07
❑ 247 Jacob Brumfield .15 .07
❑ 248 Mickey Morandini .15 .07
❑ 249 Todd Hundley .15 .07
❑ 250 Chris Bosio .15 .07
❑ 251 Omar Vizquel .25 .11
❑ 252 Mike Lansing .15 .07
❑ 253 John Mabry .15 .07
❑ 254 Mike Perez .15 .07
❑ 255 Delino DeShields .15 .07
❑ 256 Wil Cordero .15 .07
❑ 257 Mike James .15 .07
❑ 258 Todd Van Poppel .15 .07
❑ 259 Joey Cora .15 .07
❑ 260 Andre Dawson .40 .18
❑ 261 Jerry DiPoto .15 .07
❑ 262 Rick Krivda .15 .07
❑ 263 Glenn Dishman .15 .07
❑ 264 Mike Mimbs .15 .07
❑ 265 John Ericks .15 .07
❑ 266 Jose Canseco .60 .25
❑ 267 Jeff Branson .15 .07
❑ 268 Curt Leskanic .15 .07
❑ 269 Jon Nunnally .15 .07
❑ 270 Scott Stahoviak .15 .07
❑ 271 Jeff Montgomery .15 .07
❑ 272 Hal Morris .15 .07
❑ 273 Esteban Loaiza .15 .07
❑ 274 Rico Brogna .15 .07
❑ 275 Dave Winfield .60 .25
❑ 276 J.R. Phillips .15 .07
❑ 277 Todd Zeile .15 .07
❑ 278 Tom Pagnozzi .15 .07
❑ 279 Mark Lemke .15 .07
❑ 280 Dave Magadan .15 .07
❑ 281 Greg McMichael .15 .07
❑ 282 Mike Morgan .15 .07
❑ 283 Moises Alou .25 .11
❑ 284 Dennis Martinez .25 .11
❑ 285 Jeff Kent .40 .18
❑ 286 Mark Johnson .15 .07
❑ 287 Darren Lewis .15 .07
❑ 288 Brad Clontz .15 .07
❑ 289 Chad Fonville .15 .07
❑ 290 Paul Sorrento .15 .07
❑ 291 Lee Smith .25 .11
❑ 292 Tom Glavine .60 .25
❑ 293 Antonio Osuna .15 .07
❑ 294 Kevin Foster .15 .07
❑ 295 Sandy Martinez .15 .07
❑ 296 Mark Leiter .15 .07
❑ 297 Julian Tavarez .15 .07
❑ 298 Mike Kelly .15 .07
❑ 299 Joe Oliver .15 .07
❑ 300 John Flaherty .15 .07
❑ 301 Don Mattingly 1.50 .70
❑ 302 Pat Meares .15 .07
❑ 303 John Doherty .15 .07
❑ 304 Joe Vitiello .15 .07
❑ 305 Vinny Castilla .25 .11
❑ 306 Jeff Brantley .15 .07
❑ 307 Mike Greenwell .15 .07
❑ 308 Midre Cummings .15 .07
❑ 309 Curt Schilling .60 .25
❑ 310 Ken Caminiti .25 .11
❑ 311 Scott Erickson .15 .07
❑ 312 Carl Everett .25 .11
❑ 313 Charles Johnson .25 .11
❑ 314 Alex Diaz .15 .07
❑ 315 Jose Mesa .15 .07
❑ 316 Mark Carreon .15 .07
❑ 317 Carlos Perez .15 .07
❑ 318 Ismael Valdes .15 .07
❑ 319 Frank Castillo .15 .07
❑ 320 Tom Henke .15 .07
❑ 321 Spike Owen .15 .07
❑ 322 Joe Orsulak .15 .07
❑ 323 Paul Menhart .15 .07
❑ 324 Pedro Borbon .15 .07
❑ 325 Paul Molitor CL .25 .11
❑ 326 Jeff Cirillo .25 .11
❑ 327 Edwin Hurtado .15 .07
❑ 328 Orlando Miller .15 .07
❑ 329 Steve Ontiveros .15 .07
❑ 330 Kirby Puckett CL .75 .35
❑ 331 Scott Bullett .15 .07
❑ 332 Andres Galarraga .40 .18
❑ 333 Cal Eldred .15 .07
❑ 334 Sammy Sosa 1.25 .55
❑ 335 Don Slaught .15 .07
❑ 336 Jody Reed .15 .07
❑ 337 Roger Cedeno .15 .07
❑ 338 Ken Griffey Jr. 2.00 .90
❑ 339 Todd Hollandsworth .15 .07
❑ 340 Mike Trombley .15 .07
❑ 341 Gregg Jefferies .15 .07
❑ 342 Larry Walker .40 .18
❑ 343 Pedro Martinez .75 .35
❑ 344 Dwayne Hosey .15 .07
❑ 345 Terry Pendleton .25 .11
❑ 346 Pete Harnisch .15 .07
❑ 347 Tony Castillo .15 .07
❑ 348 Paul Quantrill .15 .07
❑ 349 Fred McGriff .40 .18
❑ 350 Ivan Rodriguez .60 .25
❑ 351 Butch Huskey .15 .07
❑ 352 Ozzie Smith .75 .35
❑ 353 Marty Cordova .15 .07
❑ 354 John Wasdin .15 .07
❑ 355 Wade Boggs .60 .25
❑ 356 Dave Nilsson .15 .07
❑ 357 Rafael Palmeiro .60 .25
❑ 358 Luis Gonzalez .60 .25
❑ 359 Reggie Jefferson .15 .07
❑ 360 Carlos Delgado .60 .25
❑ 361 Orlando Palmeiro .15 .07
❑ 362 Chris Gomez .15 .07

❑ 363 John Smoltz .25 .11
❑ 364 Marc Newfield .15 .07
❑ 365 Matt Williams .40 .18
❑ 366 Jesus Tavarez .15 .07
❑ 367 Bruce Ruffin .15 .07
❑ 368 Sean Berry .15 .07
❑ 369 Randy Velarde .15 .07
❑ 370 Tony Pena .15 .07
❑ 371 Jim Thome .60 .25
❑ 372 Jeffrey Hammonds .15 .07
❑ 373 Bob Wolcott .15 .07
❑ 374 Juan Guzman .15 .07
❑ 375 Juan Gonzalez .60 .25
❑ 376 Michael Tucker .15 .07
❑ 377 Doug Johns .15 .07
❑ 378 Mike Cameron RC 1.50 .70
❑ 379 Ray Lankford .15 .07
❑ 380 Jose Parra .15 .07
❑ 381 Jimmy Key .25 .11
❑ 382 John Olerud .25 .11
❑ 383 Kevin Ritz .15 .07
❑ 384 Tim Raines .25 .11
❑ 385 Rich Amaral .15 .07
❑ 386 Keith Lockhart .15 .07
❑ 387 Steve Scarsone .15 .07
❑ 388 Cliff Floyd .25 .11
❑ 389 Rich Aude .15 .07
❑ 390 Hideo Nomo .75 .35
❑ 391 Geronimo Berroa .15 .07
❑ 392 Pat Rapp .15 .07
❑ 393 Dustin Hermanson .15 .07
❑ 394 Greg Maddux 1.50 .70
❑ 395 Darren Daulton .25 .11
❑ 396 Kenny Lofton .25 .11
❑ 397 Ruben Rivera .15 .07
❑ 398 Billy Wagner .15 .07
❑ 399 Kevin Brown .25 .11
❑ 400 Mike Kingery .15 .07
❑ 401 Bernie Williams .60 .25
❑ 402 Otis Nixon .15 .07
❑ 403 Damion Easley .15 .07
❑ 404 Paul O'Neill .60 .25
❑ 405 Deion Sanders .25 .11
❑ 406 Dennis Eckersley .25 .11
❑ 407 Tony Clark .25 .11
❑ 408 Rondell White .25 .11
❑ 409 Luis Sojo .15 .07
❑ 410 David Hulse .15 .07
❑ 411 Shane Reynolds .15 .07
❑ 412 Chris Hoiles .15 .07
❑ 413 Lee Tinsley .15 .07
❑ 414 Scott Karl .15 .07
❑ 415 Ron Gant .15 .07
❑ 416 Brian Johnson .15 .07
❑ 417 Jose Oliva .15 .07
❑ 418 Jack McDowell .15 .07
❑ 419 Paul Molitor .60 .25
❑ 420 Ricky Bottalico .15 .07
❑ 421 Paul Wagner .15 .07
❑ 422 Terry Bradshaw .15 .07
❑ 423 Bob Tewksbury .15 .07
❑ 424 Mike Piazza 1.50 .70
❑ 425 Luis Andujar .15 .07
❑ 426 Mark Langston .15 .07
❑ 427 Stan Belinda .15 .07
❑ 428 Kurt Abbott .15 .07
❑ 429 Shawon Dunston .15 .07
❑ 430 Bobby Jones .15 .07
❑ 431 Jose Vizcaino .15 .07
❑ 432 Matt Lawton RC .75 .35
❑ 433 Pat Hentgen .15 .07
❑ 434 Cecil Fielder .25 .11
❑ 435 Carlos Baerga .15 .07
❑ 436 Rich Becker .15 .07
❑ 437 Chipper Jones 1.25 .55
❑ 438 Bill Risley .15 .07
❑ 439 Kevin Appier .25 .11
❑ 440 Wade Boggs CL .25 .11
❑ 441 Jaime Navarro .15 .07
❑ 442 Barry Larkin .60 .25
❑ 443 Jose Valentin .15 .07
❑ 444 Bryan Rekar .15 .07
❑ 445 Rick Wilkins .15 .07
❑ 446 Quilvio Veras .15 .07
❑ 447 Greg Gagne .15 .07
❑ 448 Mark Kiefer .15 .07
❑ 449 Bobby Witt .15 .07
❑ 450 Andy Ashby .15 .07
❑ 451 Alex Ochoa .15 .07
❑ 452 Jorge Fabregas .15 .07
❑ 453 Gene Schall .15 .07
❑ 454 Ken Hill .15 .07
❑ 455 Tony Tarasco .15 .07
❑ 456 Donnie Wall .15 .07
❑ 457 Carlos Garcia .15 .07
❑ 458 Ryan Thompson .15 .07
❑ 459 Marvin Benard RC .25 .11
❑ 460 Jose Herrera .15 .07
❑ 461 Jeff Blauser .15 .07
❑ 462 Chris Hook .15 .07
❑ 463 Jeff Conine .15 .07
❑ 464 Devon White .25 .11
❑ 465 Danny Bautista .15 .07
❑ 466 Steve Trachsel .15 .07
❑ 467 C.J. Nitkowski .15 .07
❑ 468 Mike Devereaux .15 .07
❑ 469 David Wells .25 .11
❑ 470 Jim Eisenreich .15 .07
❑ 471 Edgar Martinez .40 .18
❑ 472 Craig Biggio .40 .18
❑ 473 Jeff Frye .15 .07
❑ 474 Karim Garcia .15 .07
❑ 475 Jimmy Haynes .15 .07
❑ 476 Darren Holmes .15 .07
❑ 477 Tim Salmon .25 .11
❑ 478 Randy Johnson .75 .35
❑ 479 Eric Plunk .15 .07
❑ 480 Scott Cooper .15 .07
❑ 481 Chan Ho Park .25 .11
❑ 482 Ray McDavid .15 .07
❑ 483 Mark Petkovsek .15 .07
❑ 484 Greg Swindell .15 .07
❑ 485 George Williams .15 .07
❑ 486 Yamil Benitez .15 .07
❑ 487 Tim Wakefield .15 .07
❑ 488 Kevin Tapani .15 .07
❑ 489 Derrick May .15 .07
❑ 490 Ken Griffey Jr. CL 1.00 .45
❑ 491 Derek Jeter 2.50 1.10
❑ 492 Jeff Fassero .15 .07
❑ 493 Benito Santiago .15 .07
❑ 494 Tom Gordon .15 .07
❑ 495 Jamie Brewington RC .15 .07
❑ 496 Vince Coleman .15 .07
❑ 497 Kevin Jordan .15 .07
❑ 498 Jeff King .15 .07
❑ 499 Mike Simms .15 .07
❑ 500 Jose Rijo .15 .07
❑ 501 Denny Neagle .25 .11
❑ 502 Jose Lima .15 .07
❑ 503 Kevin Seitzer .15 .07
❑ 504 Alex Fernandez .15 .07
❑ 505 Mo Vaughn .25 .11
❑ 506 Phil Nevin .25 .11
❑ 507 J.T. Snow .25 .11
❑ 508 Andujar Cedeno .15 .07
❑ 509 Ozzie Guillen .15 .07
❑ 510 Mark Clark .15 .07
❑ 511 Mark McGwire 2.50 1.10
❑ 512 Jeff Reboulet .15 .07
❑ 513 Armando Benitez .15 .07
❑ 514 LaTroy Hawkins .15 .07
❑ 515 Brett Butler .25 .11
❑ 516 Tavo Alvarez .15 .07
❑ 517 Chris Snopek .15 .07
❑ 518 Mike Mussina .60 .25
❑ 519 Darryl Kile .25 .11
❑ 520 Wally Joyner .25 .11
❑ 521 Willie McGee .25 .11
❑ 522 Kent Mercker .15 .07
❑ 523 Mike Jackson .15 .07
❑ 524 Troy Percival .15 .07
❑ 525 Tony Gwynn 1.25 .55
❑ 526 Ron Coomer .15 .07
❑ 527 Darryl Hamilton .15 .07
❑ 528 Phil Plantier .15 .07
❑ 529 Norm Charlton .15 .07
❑ 530 Craig Paquette .15 .07
❑ 531 Dave Burba .15 .07
❑ 532 Mike Henneman .15 .07
❑ 533 Terrell Wade .15 .07
❑ 534 Eddie Williams .15 .07
❑ 535 Robin Ventura .25 .11
❑ 536 Chuck Knoblauch .25 .11
❑ 537 Les Norman .15 .07
❑ 538 Brady Anderson .25 .11
❑ 539 Roger Clemens 1.50 .70
❑ 540 Mark Portugal .15 .07
❑ 541 Mike Matheny .15 .07
❑ 542 Jeff Parrett .15 .07
❑ 543 Roberto Kelly .15 .07
❑ 544 Damon Buford .15 .07
❑ 545 Chad Ogea .15 .07
❑ 546 Jose Offerman .15 .07
❑ 547 Brian Barber .15 .07
❑ 548 Danny Tartabull .15 .07
❑ 549 Duane Singleton .15 .07
❑ 550 Tony Gwynn CL .60 .25

1997 Donruss

	MINT	NRMT
COMPLETE SET (450)	40.00	18.00
COMPLETE SERIES 1 (270)	20.00	9.00
COMPLETE UPDATE (180)	20.00	9.00

❑ 1 Juan Gonzalez .60 .25
❑ 2 Jim Edmonds .40 .18
❑ 3 Tony Gwynn 1.25 .55
❑ 4 Andres Galarraga .40 .18
❑ 5 Joe Carter .25 .11
❑ 6 Raul Mondesi .25 .11
❑ 7 Greg Maddux 1.50 .70
❑ 8 Travis Fryman .25 .11
❑ 9 Brian Jordan .25 .11
❑ 10 Henry Rodriguez .15 .07
❑ 11 Manny Ramirez .75 .35
❑ 12 Mark McGwire 2.50 1.10
❑ 13 Marc Newfield .15 .07
❑ 14 Craig Biggio .40 .18
❑ 15 Sammy Sosa 1.25 .55
❑ 16 Brady Anderson .25 .11
❑ 17 Wade Boggs .60 .25
❑ 18 Charles Johnson .25 .11
❑ 19 Matt Williams .40 .18
❑ 20 Denny Neagle .25 .11
❑ 21 Ken Griffey Jr. 2.00 .90
❑ 22 Robin Ventura .25 .11
❑ 23 Barry Larkin .60 .25
❑ 24 Todd Zeile .15 .07
❑ 25 Chuck Knoblauch .25 .11
❑ 26 Todd Hundley .15 .07
❑ 27 Roger Clemens 1.50 .70
❑ 28 Michael Tucker .15 .07
❑ 29 Rondell White .25 .11
❑ 30 Osvaldo Fernandez .15 .07
❑ 31 Ivan Rodriguez .60 .25
❑ 32 Alex Fernandez .15 .07
❑ 33 Jason Isringhausen .15 .07
❑ 34 Chipper Jones 1.25 .55
❑ 35 Paul O'Neill .60 .25
❑ 36 Hideo Nomo .60 .25
❑ 37 Roberto Alomar .60 .25
❑ 38 Derek Bell .15 .07
❑ 39 Paul Molitor .60 .25
❑ 40 Andy Benes .15 .07
❑ 41 Steve Trachsel .15 .07
❑ 42 J.T. Snow .25 .11
❑ 43 Jason Kendall .25 .11
❑ 44 Alex Rodriguez 1.50 .70

❑	45	Joey Hamilton	.15	.07
❑	46	Carlos Delgado	.60	.25
❑	47	Jason Giambi	.60	.25
❑	48	Larry Walker	.40	.18
❑	49	Derek Jeter	2.50	1.10
❑	50	Kenny Lofton	.25	.11
❑	51	Devon White	.25	.11
❑	52	Matt Mieske	.15	.07
❑	53	Melvin Nieves	.15	.07
❑	54	Jose Canseco	.60	.25
❑	55	Tino Martinez	.25	.11
❑	56	Rafael Palmeiro	.60	.25
❑	57	Edgardo Alfonzo	.25	.11
❑	58	Jay Buhner	.25	.11
❑	59	Shane Reynolds	.15	.07
❑	60	Steve Finley	.25	.11
❑	61	Bobby Higginson	.25	.11
❑	62	Dean Palmer	.25	.11
❑	63	Terry Pendleton	.25	.11
❑	64	Marquis Grissom	.15	.07
❑	65	Mike Stanley	.15	.07
❑	66	Moises Alou	.25	.11
❑	67	Ray Lankford	.15	.07
❑	68	Marty Cordova	.15	.07
❑	69	John Olerud	.25	.11
❑	70	David Cone	.25	.11
❑	71	Benito Santiago	.15	.07
❑	72	Ryne Sandberg	.75	.35
❑	73	Rickey Henderson	1.25	.55
❑	74	Roger Cedeno	.15	.07
❑	75	Wilson Alvarez	.15	.07
❑	76	Tim Salmon	.25	.11
❑	77	Orlando Merced	.15	.07
❑	78	Vinny Castilla	.25	.11
❑	79	Ismael Valdes	.15	.07
❑	80	Dante Bichette	.25	.11
❑	81	Kevin Brown	.25	.11
❑	82	Andy Pettitte	.25	.11
❑	83	Scott Stahoviak	.15	.07
❑	84	Mickey Tettleton	.15	.07
❑	85	Jack McDowell	.15	.07
❑	86	Tom Glavine	.60	.25
❑	87	Gregg Jefferies	.15	.07
❑	88	Chili Davis	.25	.11
❑	89	Randy Johnson	.75	.35
❑	90	John Mabry	.15	.07
❑	91	Billy Wagner	.15	.07
❑	92	Jeff Cirillo	.25	.11
❑	93	Trevor Hoffman	.25	.11
❑	94	Juan Guzman	.15	.07
❑	95	Geronimo Berroa	.15	.07
❑	96	Bernard Gilkey	.15	.07
❑	97	Danny Tartabull	.15	.07
❑	98	Johnny Damon	.25	.11
❑	99	Charlie Hayes	.15	.07
❑	100	Reggie Sanders	.15	.07
❑	101	Robby Thompson	.15	.07
❑	102	Bobby Bonilla	.25	.11
❑	103	Reggie Jefferson	.15	.07
❑	104	John Smoltz	.25	.11
❑	105	Jim Thome	.60	.25
❑	106	Ruben Rivera	.15	.07
❑	107	Darren Oliver	.15	.07
❑	108	Mo Vaughn	.25	.11
❑	109	Roger Pavlik	.15	.07
❑	110	Terry Steinbach	.15	.07
❑	111	Jermaine Dye	.25	.11
❑	112	Mark Grudzielanek	.15	.07
❑	113	Rick Aguilera	.15	.07
❑	114	Jamey Wright	.15	.07
❑	115	Eddie Murray	.60	.25
❑	116	Brian L. Hunter	.15	.07
❑	117	Hal Morris	.15	.07
❑	118	Tom Pagnozzi	.15	.07
❑	119	Mike Mussina	.60	.25
❑	120	Mark Grace	.60	.25
❑	121	Cal Ripken	2.50	1.10
❑	122	Tom Goodwin	.15	.07
❑	123	Paul Sorrento	.15	.07
❑	124	Jay Bell	.25	.11
❑	125	Todd Hollandsworth	.15	.07
❑	126	Edgar Martinez	.40	.18
❑	127	George Arias	.15	.07
❑	128	Greg Vaughn	.25	.11
❑	129	Roberto Hernandez	.15	.07
❑	130	Delino DeShields	.15	.07
❑	131	Bill Pulsipher	.15	.07
❑	132	Joey Cora	.15	.07
❑	133	Mariano Rivera	.25	.11
❑	134	Mike Piazza	1.50	.70
❑	135	Carlos Baerga	.15	.07
❑	136	Jose Mesa	.15	.07
❑	137	Will Clark	.60	.25
❑	138	Frank Thomas	.75	.35
❑	139	John Wetteland	.25	.11
❑	140	Shawn Estes	.25	.11
❑	141	Garret Anderson	.25	.11
❑	142	Andre Dawson	.40	.18
❑	143	Eddie Taubensee	.15	.07
❑	144	Ryan Klesko	.25	.11
❑	145	Rocky Coppinger	.15	.07
❑	146	Jeff Bagwell	.75	.35
❑	147	Donovan Osborne	.15	.07
❑	148	Greg Myers	.15	.07
❑	149	Brant Brown	.15	.07
❑	150	Kevin Elster	.15	.07
❑	151	Bob Wells	.15	.07
❑	152	Wally Joyner	.25	.11
❑	153	Rico Brogna	.15	.07
❑	154	Dwight Gooden	.25	.11
❑	155	Jermaine Allensworth	.15	.07
❑	156	Ray Durham	.25	.11
❑	157	Cecil Fielder	.25	.11
❑	158	John Burkett	.15	.07
❑	159	Gary Sheffield	.25	.11
❑	160	Albert Belle	.25	.11
❑	161	Tomas Perez	.15	.07
❑	162	David Doster	.15	.07
❑	163	John Valentin	.15	.07
❑	164	Danny Graves	.15	.07
❑	165	Jose Paniagua	.15	.07
❑	166	Brian Giles RC	2.50	1.10
❑	167	Barry Bonds	1.50	.70
❑	168	Sterling Hitchcock	.15	.07
❑	169	Bernie Williams	.60	.25
❑	170	Fred McGriff	.40	.18
❑	171	George Williams	.15	.07
❑	172	Amaury Telemaco	.15	.07
❑	173	Ken Caminiti	.25	.11
❑	174	Ron Gant	.15	.07
❑	175	Dave Justice	.25	.11
❑	176	James Baldwin	.15	.07
❑	177	Pat Hentgen	.15	.07
❑	178	Ben McDonald	.15	.07
❑	179	Tim Naehring	.15	.07
❑	180	Jim Eisenreich	.15	.07
❑	181	Ken Hill	.15	.07
❑	182	Paul Wilson	.15	.07
❑	183	Marvin Benard	.15	.07
❑	184	Alan Benes	.15	.07
❑	185	Ellis Burks	.25	.11
❑	186	Scott Servais	.15	.07
❑	187	David Segui	.15	.07
❑	188	Scott Brosius	.25	.11
❑	189	Jose Offerman	.15	.07
❑	190	Eric Davis	.25	.11
❑	191	Brett Butler	.25	.11
❑	192	Curtis Pride	.15	.07
❑	193	Yamil Benitez	.15	.07
❑	194	Chan Ho Park	.25	.11
❑	195	Bret Boone	.25	.11
❑	196	Omar Vizquel	.25	.11
❑	197	Orlando Miller	.15	.07
❑	198	Ramon Martinez	.15	.07
❑	199	Harold Baines	.25	.11
❑	200	Eric Young	.15	.07
❑	201	Fernando Vina	.15	.07
❑	202	Alex Gonzalez	.15	.07
❑	203	Fernando Valenzuela	.25	.11
❑	204	Steve Avery	.15	.07
❑	205	Ernie Young	.15	.07
❑	206	Kevin Appier	.25	.11
❑	207	Randy Myers	.15	.07
❑	208	Jeff Suppan	.15	.07
❑	209	James Mouton	.15	.07
❑	210	Russ Davis	.15	.07
❑	211	Al Martin	.15	.07
❑	212	Troy Percival	.15	.07
❑	213	Al Leiter	.25	.11
❑	214	Dennis Eckersley	.25	.11
❑	215	Mark Johnson	.15	.07
❑	216	Eric Karros	.25	.11
❑	217	Royce Clayton	.15	.07
❑	218	Tony Phillips	.15	.07
❑	219	Tim Wakefield	.15	.07
❑	220	Alan Trammell	.40	.18
❑	221	Eduardo Perez	.15	.07
❑	222	Butch Huskey	.15	.07
❑	223	Tim Belcher	.15	.07
❑	224	Jamie Moyer	.15	.07
❑	225	F.P. Santangelo	.15	.07
❑	226	Rusty Greer	.25	.11
❑	227	Jeff Brantley	.15	.07
❑	228	Mark Langston	.15	.07
❑	229	Ray Montgomery	.15	.07
❑	230	Rich Becker	.15	.07
❑	231	Ozzie Smith	.75	.35
❑	232	Rey Ordonez	.15	.07
❑	233	Ricky Otero	.15	.07
❑	234	Mike Cameron	.25	.11
❑	235	Mike Sweeney	.25	.11
❑	236	Mark Lewis	.15	.07
❑	237	Luis Gonzalez	.60	.25
❑	238	Marcus Jensen	.15	.07
❑	239	Ed Sprague	.15	.07
❑	240	Jose Valentin	.15	.07
❑	241	Jeff Frye	.15	.07
❑	242	Charles Nagy	.15	.07
❑	243	Carlos Garcia	.15	.07
❑	244	Mike Hampton	.25	.11
❑	245	B.J. Surhoff	.25	.11
❑	246	Wilton Guerrero	.15	.07
❑	247	Frank Rodriguez	.15	.07
❑	248	Gary Gaetti	.25	.11
❑	249	Lance Johnson	.15	.07
❑	250	Darren Bragg	.15	.07
❑	251	Darryl Hamilton	.15	.07
❑	252	John Jaha	.15	.07
❑	253	Craig Paquette	.15	.07
❑	254	Jaime Navarro	.15	.07
❑	255	Shawon Dunston	.15	.07
❑	256	Mark Loretta	.15	.07
❑	257	Tim Belk	.15	.07
❑	258	Jeff Darwin	.15	.07
❑	259	Ruben Sierra	.15	.07
❑	260	Chuck Finley	.25	.11
❑	261	Darryl Strawberry	.25	.11
❑	262	Shannon Stewart	.25	.11
❑	263	Pedro Martinez	.75	.35
❑	264	Neifi Perez	.15	.07
❑	265	Jeff Conine	.15	.07
❑	266	Orel Hershiser	.25	.11
❑	267	Eddie Murray CL	.25	.11
❑	268	Paul Molitor CL	.25	.11
❑	269	Barry Bonds CL	.75	.35
❑	270	Mark McGwire CL	1.25	.55
❑	271	Matt Williams	.40	.18
❑	272	Todd Zeile	.15	.07
❑	273	Roger Clemens	1.50	.70
❑	274	Michael Tucker	.15	.07
❑	275	J.T. Snow	.25	.11
❑	276	Kenny Lofton	.25	.11
❑	277	Jose Canseco	.60	.25
❑	278	Marquis Grissom	.15	.07
❑	279	Moises Alou	.25	.11
❑	280	Benito Santiago	.15	.07
❑	281	Willie McGee	.25	.11
❑	282	Chili Davis	.25	.11
❑	283	Ron Coomer	.15	.07
❑	284	Orlando Merced	.15	.07
❑	285	Delino DeShields	.15	.07
❑	286	John Wetteland	.25	.11
❑	287	Darren Daulton	.25	.11
❑	288	Lee Stevens	.15	.07
❑	289	Albert Belle	.25	.11
❑	290	Sterling Hitchcock	.15	.07
❑	291	David Justice	.25	.11
❑	292	Eric Davis	.25	.11
❑	293	Brian Hunter	.15	.07
❑	294	Darryl Hamilton	.15	.07
❑	295	Steve Avery	.15	.07
❑	296	Joe Vitiello	.15	.07
❑	297	Jaime Navarro	.15	.07
❑	298	Eddie Murray	.60	.25
❑	299	Randy Myers	.15	.07
❑	300	Francisco Cordova	.15	.07
❑	301	Javier Lopez	.25	.11
❑	302	Geronimo Berroa	.15	.07

❑ 303 Jeffrey Hammonds .15 .07
❑ 304 Deion Sanders .25 .11
❑ 305 Jeff Fassero .15 .07
❑ 306 Curt Schilling .60 .25
❑ 307 Robb Nen .15 .07
❑ 308 Mark McLemore .15 .07
❑ 309 Jimmy Key .25 .11
❑ 310 Quilvio Veras .15 .07
❑ 311 Bip Roberts .15 .07
❑ 312 Esteban Loaiza .15 .07
❑ 313 Andy Ashby .15 .07
❑ 314 Sandy Alomar Jr. .25 .11
❑ 315 Shawn Green .60 .25
❑ 316 Luis Castillo .15 .07
❑ 317 Benji Gil .15 .07
❑ 318 Otis Nixon .15 .07
❑ 319 Aaron Sele .25 .11
❑ 320 Brad Ausmus .15 .07
❑ 321 Troy O'Leary .15 .07
❑ 322 Terrell Wade .15 .07
❑ 323 Jeff King .15 .07
❑ 324 Kevin Seitzer .15 .07
❑ 325 Mark Wohlers .15 .07
❑ 326 Edgar Renteria .15 .07
❑ 327 Dan Wilson .15 .07
❑ 328 Brian McRae .15 .07
❑ 329 Rod Beck .15 .07
❑ 330 Julio Franco .25 .11
❑ 331 Dave Nilsson .15 .07
❑ 332 Glenallen Hill .15 .07
❑ 333 Kevin Elster .15 .07
❑ 334 Joe Girardi .15 .07
❑ 335 David Wells .25 .11
❑ 336 Jeff Blauser .15 .07
❑ 337 Darryl Kile .25 .11
❑ 338 Jeff Kent .40 .18
❑ 339 Jim Leyritz .15 .07
❑ 340 Todd Stottlemyre .15 .07
❑ 341 Tony Clark .25 .11
❑ 342 Chris Hoiles .15 .07
❑ 343 Mike Lieberthal .25 .11
❑ 344 Matt Lawton .25 .11
❑ 345 Alex Ochoa .15 .07
❑ 346 Chris Snopek .15 .07
❑ 347 Rudy Pemberton .15 .07
❑ 348 Eric Owens .15 .07
❑ 349 Joe Randa .15 .07
❑ 350 John Olerud .25 .11
❑ 351 Steve Karsay .15 .07
❑ 352 Mark Whiten .15 .07
❑ 353 Bob Abreu .25 .11
❑ 354 Bartolo Colon .25 .11
❑ 355 Vladimir Guerrero 1.00 .45
❑ 356 Darin Erstad .60 .25
❑ 357 Scott Rolen .60 .25
❑ 358 Andruw Jones .75 .35
❑ 359 Scott Spiezio .15 .07
❑ 360 Karim Garcia .15 .07
❑ 361 Hideki Irabu RC .25 .11
❑ 362 Nomar Garciaparra 1.50 .70
❑ 363 Dmitri Young .25 .11
❑ 364 Bubba Trammell RC .25 .11
❑ 365 Kevin Orie .15 .07
❑ 366 Jose Rosado .15 .07
❑ 367 Jose Guillen .15 .07
❑ 368 Brooks Kieschnick .15 .07
❑ 369 Pokey Reese .15 .07
❑ 370 Glendon Rusch .15 .07
❑ 371 Jason Dickson .15 .07
❑ 372 Todd Walker .15 .07
❑ 373 Justin Thompson .15 .07
❑ 374 Todd Greene .15 .07
❑ 375 Jeff Suppan .15 .07
❑ 376 Trey Beamon .15 .07
❑ 377 Damon Mashore .15 .07
❑ 378 Wendell Magee .15 .07
❑ 379 S. Hasegawa RC .40 .18
❑ 380 Bill Mueller RC .40 .18
❑ 381 Chris Widger .15 .07
❑ 382 Tony Graffanino .15 .07
❑ 383 Derrek Lee .25 .11
❑ 384 Brian Moehler .15 .07
❑ 385 Quinton McCracken .15 .07
❑ 386 Matt Morris .25 .11
❑ 387 Marvin Benard .15 .07
❑ 388 Deivi Cruz RC .75 .35
❑ 389 Javier Valentin .15 .07
❑ 390 Todd Dunwoody .15 .07
❑ 391 Derrick Gibson .15 .07
❑ 392 Raul Casanova .15 .07
❑ 393 George Arias .15 .07
❑ 394 Tony Womack RC .50 .23
❑ 395 Antone Williamson .15 .07
❑ 396 Jose Cruz Jr. RC 1.50 .70
❑ 397 Desi Relaford .15 .07
❑ 398 Frank Thomas HIT .60 .25
❑ 399 Ken Griffey Jr. HIT 1.00 .45
❑ 400 Cal Ripken HIT 1.25 .55
❑ 401 Chipper Jones HIT .60 .25
❑ 402 Mike Piazza HIT .75 .35
❑ 403 Gary Sheffield HIT .15 .07
❑ 404 Alex Rodriguez HIT .75 .35
❑ 405 Wade Boggs HIT .25 .11
❑ 406 Juan Gonzalez HIT .25 .11
❑ 407 Tony Gwynn HIT .60 .25
❑ 408 Edgar Martinez HIT .25 .11
❑ 409 Jeff Bagwell HIT .40 .18
❑ 410 Larry Walker HIT .15 .07
❑ 411 Kenny Lofton HIT .15 .07
❑ 412 Manny Ramirez HIT .40 .18
❑ 413 Mark McGwire HIT 1.25 .55
❑ 414 Roberto Alomar HIT .25 .11
❑ 415 Derek Jeter HIT 1.25 .55
❑ 416 Brady Anderson HIT .15 .07
❑ 417 Paul Molitor HIT .25 .11
❑ 418 Dante Bichette HIT .15 .07
❑ 419 Jim Edmonds HIT .25 .11
❑ 420 Mo Vaughn HIT .15 .07
❑ 421 Barry Bonds HIT .75 .35
❑ 422 Rusty Greer HIT .15 .07
❑ 423 Greg Maddux KING .75 .35
❑ 424 Andy Pettitte KING .15 .07
❑ 425 John Smoltz KING .15 .07
❑ 426 Randy Johnson KING .40 .18
❑ 427 Hideo Nomo KING .25 .11
❑ 428 Roger Clemens KING .75 .35
❑ 429 Tom Glavine KING .25 .11
❑ 430 Pat Hentgen KING .15 .07
❑ 431 Kevin Brown KING .15 .07
❑ 432 Mike Mussina KING .25 .11
❑ 433 Alex Fernandez KING .15 .07
❑ 434 Kevin Appier KING .15 .07
❑ 435 David Cone KING .15 .07
❑ 436 Jeff Fassero KING .15 .07
❑ 437 John Wetteland KING .15 .07
❑ 438 Barry Bonds IS .75 .35
Ivan Rodriguez
❑ 439 Ken Griffey Jr. IS .75 .35
Andres Galarraga
❑ 440 Fred McGriff IS .25 .11
Rafael Palmeiro
❑ 441 Barry Larkin IS .25 .11
Jim Thome
❑ 442 Sammy Sosa IS .60 .25
Albert Belle
❑ 443 Bernie Williams IS .25 .11
Todd Hundley
❑ 444 Chuck Knoblauch IS .15 .07
Brian Jordan
❑ 445 Mo Vaughn IS .15 .07
Jeff Conine
❑ 446 Ken Caminiti IS .25 .11
Jason Giambi
❑ 447 Raul Mondesi IS .15 .07
Tim Salmon
❑ 448 Cal Ripken CL 1.25 .55
❑ 449 Greg Maddux CL .75 .35
❑ 450 Ken Griffey Jr. CL 1.00 .45

1998 Donruss

	MINT	NRMT
COMPLETE SET (420)	50.00	22.00
COMPLETE SERIES 1 (170)	20.00	9.00
COMPLETE UPDATE (250)	30.00	13.50

❑ 1 Paul Molitor .50 .23
❑ 2 Juan Gonzalez .50 .23
❑ 3 Darryl Kile .20 .09
❑ 4 Randy Johnson .60 .25
❑ 5 Tom Glavine .50 .23
❑ 6 Pat Hentgen .10 .05

❑ 7 David Justice .20 .09
❑ 8 Kevin Brown .30 .14
❑ 9 Mike Mussina .50 .23
❑ 10 Ken Caminiti .20 .09
❑ 11 Todd Hundley .10 .05
❑ 12 Frank Thomas .60 .25
❑ 13 Ray Lankford .10 .05
❑ 14 Justin Thompson .10 .05
❑ 15 Jason Dickson .10 .05
❑ 16 Kenny Lofton .20 .09
❑ 17 Ivan Rodriguez .50 .23
❑ 18 Pedro Martinez .60 .25
❑ 19 Brady Anderson .20 .09
❑ 20 Barry Larkin .50 .23
❑ 21 Chipper Jones 1.00 .45
❑ 22 Tony Gwynn 1.00 .45
❑ 23 Roger Clemens 1.25 .55
❑ 24 Sandy Alomar Jr. .20 .09
❑ 25 Tino Martinez .20 .09
❑ 26 Jeff Bagwell .60 .25
❑ 27 Shawn Estes .20 .09
❑ 28 Ken Griffey Jr. 1.50 .70
❑ 29 Javier Lopez .20 .09
❑ 30 Denny Neagle .10 .05
❑ 31 Mike Piazza 1.25 .55
❑ 32 Andres Galarraga .30 .14
❑ 33 Larry Walker .30 .14
❑ 34 Alex Rodriguez 1.25 .55
❑ 35 Greg Maddux 1.25 .55
❑ 36 Albert Belle .20 .09
❑ 37 Barry Bonds 1.25 .55
❑ 38 Mo Vaughn .20 .09
❑ 39 Kevin Appier .20 .09
❑ 40 Wade Boggs .50 .23
❑ 41 Garret Anderson .20 .09
❑ 42 Jeffrey Hammonds .10 .05
❑ 43 Marquis Grissom .10 .05
❑ 44 Jim Edmonds .30 .14
❑ 45 Brian Jordan .20 .09
❑ 46 Raul Mondesi .20 .09
❑ 47 John Valentin .10 .05
❑ 48 Brad Radke .20 .09
❑ 49 Ismael Valdes .10 .05
❑ 50 Matt Stairs .10 .05
❑ 51 Matt Williams .30 .14
❑ 52 Reggie Jefferson .10 .05
❑ 53 Alan Benes .10 .05
❑ 54 Charles Johnson .20 .09
❑ 55 Chuck Knoblauch .20 .09
❑ 56 Edgar Martinez .30 .14
❑ 57 Nomar Garciaparra 1.25 .55
❑ 58 Craig Biggio .30 .14
❑ 59 Bernie Williams .50 .23
❑ 60 David Cone .20 .09
❑ 61 Cal Ripken 2.00 .90
❑ 62 Mark McGwire 2.00 .90
❑ 63 Roberto Alomar .50 .23
❑ 64 Fred McGriff .30 .14
❑ 65 Eric Karros .20 .09
❑ 66 Robin Ventura .20 .09
❑ 67 Darin Erstad .50 .23
❑ 68 Michael Tucker .10 .05
❑ 69 Jim Thome .50 .23
❑ 70 Mark Grace .50 .23
❑ 71 Lou Collier .10 .05
❑ 72 Karim Garcia .10 .05
❑ 73 Alex Fernandez .10 .05

❑ 74 J.T. Snow .20 .09
❑ 75 Reggie Sanders .10 .05
❑ 76 John Smoltz .20 .09
❑ 77 Tim Salmon .20 .09
❑ 78 Paul O'Neill .50 .23
❑ 79 Vinny Castilla .20 .09
❑ 80 Rafael Palmeiro .50 .23
❑ 81 Jaret Wright .10 .05
❑ 82 Jay Buhner .20 .09
❑ 83 Brett Butler .20 .09
❑ 84 Todd Greene .10 .05
❑ 85 Scott Rolen .50 .23
❑ 86 Sammy Sosa 1.00 .45
❑ 87 Jason Giambi .50 .23
❑ 88 Carlos Delgado .50 .23
❑ 89 Deion Sanders .20 .09
❑ 90 Wilton Guerrero .10 .05
❑ 91 Andy Pettitte .20 .09
❑ 92 Brian Giles .20 .09
❑ 93 Dmitri Young .20 .09
❑ 94 Ron Coomer .10 .05
❑ 95 Mike Cameron .20 .09
❑ 96 Edgardo Alfonzo .20 .09
❑ 97 Jimmy Key .20 .09
❑ 98 Ryan Klesko .20 .09
❑ 99 Andy Benes .10 .05
❑ 100 Derek Jeter 2.00 .90
❑ 101 Jeff Fassero .10 .05
❑ 102 Neifi Perez .10 .05
❑ 103 Hideo Nomo .50 .23
❑ 104 Andruw Jones .50 .23
❑ 105 Todd Helton .60 .25
❑ 106 Livan Hernandez .10 .05
❑ 107 Brett Tomko .10 .05
❑ 108 Shannon Stewart .20 .09
❑ 109 Bartolo Colon .20 .09
❑ 110 Matt Morris .20 .09
❑ 111 Miguel Tejada .30 .14
❑ 112 Pokey Reese .10 .05
❑ 113 Fernando Tatis .10 .05
❑ 114 Todd Dunwoody .10 .05
❑ 115 Jose Cruz Jr. .20 .09
❑ 116 Chan Ho Park .20 .09
❑ 117 Kevin Young .20 .09
❑ 118 Rickey Henderson 1.00 .45
❑ 119 Hideki Irabu .10 .05
❑ 120 Francisco Cordova .10 .05
❑ 121 Al Martin .10 .05
❑ 122 Tony Clark .20 .09
❑ 123 Curt Schilling .50 .23
❑ 124 Rusty Greer .20 .09
❑ 125 Jose Canseco .50 .23
❑ 126 Edgar Renteria .10 .05
❑ 127 Todd Walker .10 .05
❑ 128 Wally Joyner .20 .09
❑ 129 Bill Mueller .10 .05
❑ 130 Jose Guillen .10 .05
❑ 131 Manny Ramirez .60 .25
❑ 132 Bobby Higginson .20 .09
❑ 133 Kevin Orie .10 .05
❑ 134 Will Clark .50 .23
❑ 135 Dave Nilsson .10 .05
❑ 136 Jason Kendall .20 .09
❑ 137 Ivan Cruz .10 .05
❑ 138 Gary Sheffield .20 .09
❑ 139 Bubba Trammell .10 .05
❑ 140 Vladimir Guerrero .60 .25
❑ 141 Dennis Reyes .10 .05
❑ 142 Bobby Bonilla .20 .09
❑ 143 Ruben Rivera .10 .05
❑ 144 Ben Grieve .20 .09
❑ 145 Moises Alou .20 .09
❑ 146 Tony Womack .10 .05
❑ 147 Eric Young .10 .05
❑ 148 Paul Konerko .20 .09
❑ 149 Dante Bichette .20 .09
❑ 150 Joe Carter .20 .09
❑ 151 Rondell White .20 .09
❑ 152 Chris Holt .10 .05
❑ 153 Shawn Green .50 .23
❑ 154 Mark Grudzielanek .10 .05
UER back rudzielanek
❑ 155 Jermaine Dye .20 .09
❑ 156 Ken Griffey Jr. FC .75 .35
❑ 157 Frank Thomas FC .30 .14
❑ 158 Chipper Jones FC .50 .23
❑ 159 Mike Piazza FC .60 .25
❑ 160 Cal Ripken FC 1.00 .45
❑ 161 Greg Maddux FC .60 .25
❑ 162 Juan Gonzalez FC .20 .09
❑ 163 Alex Rodriguez FC .60 .25
❑ 164 Mark McGwire FC 1.00 .45
❑ 165 Derek Jeter FC 1.00 .45
❑ 166 Larry Walker CL .30 .14
❑ 167 Tony Gwynn CL .50 .23
❑ 168 Tino Martinez CL .10 .05
❑ 169 Scott Rolen CL .50 .23
❑ 170 Nomar Garciaparra CL .60 .25
❑ 171 Mike Sweeney .20 .09
❑ 172 Dustin Hermanson .10 .05
❑ 173 Darren Dreifort .10 .05
❑ 174 Ron Gant .20 .09
❑ 175 Todd Hollandsworth .10 .05
❑ 176 John Jaha .20 .09
❑ 177 Kerry Wood .50 .23
❑ 178 Chris Stynes .10 .05
❑ 179 Kevin Elster .10 .05
❑ 180 Derek Bell .10 .05
❑ 181 Darryl Strawberry .20 .09
❑ 182 Damion Easley .10 .05
❑ 183 Jeff Cirillo .20 .09
❑ 184 John Thomson .10 .05
❑ 185 Dan Wilson .10 .05
❑ 186 Jay Bell .20 .09
❑ 187 Bernard Gilkey .10 .05
❑ 188 Marc Valdes .10 .05
❑ 189 Ramon Martinez .10 .05
❑ 190 Charles Nagy .10 .05
❑ 191 Derek Lowe .10 .05
❑ 192 Andy Benes .10 .05
❑ 193 Delino DeShields .10 .05
❑ 194 Ryan Jackson RC .10 .05
❑ 195 Kenny Lofton .20 .09
❑ 196 Chuck Knoblauch .20 .09
❑ 197 Andres Galarraga .30 .14
❑ 198 Jose Canseco .50 .23
❑ 199 John Olerud .20 .09
❑ 200 Lance Johnson .10 .05
❑ 201 Darryl Kile .20 .09
❑ 202 Luis Castillo .10 .05
❑ 203 Joe Carter .20 .09
❑ 204 Dennis Eckersley .20 .09
❑ 205 Steve Finley .20 .09
❑ 206 Esteban Loaiza .10 .05
❑ 207 R.Christenson RC UER .20 .09
birthdate says 1988
❑ 208 Deivi Cruz .10 .05
❑ 209 Mariano Rivera .20 .09
❑ 210 Mike Judd RC .20 .09
❑ 211 Billy Wagner .10 .05
❑ 212 Scott Spiezio .10 .05
❑ 213 Russ Davis .10 .05
❑ 214 Jeff Suppan .10 .05
❑ 215 Doug Glanville .10 .05
❑ 216 Dmitri Young .20 .09
❑ 217 Rey Ordonez .10 .05
❑ 218 Cecil Fielder .20 .09
❑ 219 Masato Yoshii RC .40 .18
❑ 220 Raul Casanova .10 .05
❑ 221 Rolando Arrojo RC .40 .18
❑ 222 Ellis Burks .20 .09
❑ 223 Butch Huskey .10 .05
❑ 224 Brian Hunter .10 .05
❑ 225 Marquis Grissom .10 .05
❑ 226 Kevin Brown .30 .14
❑ 227 Joe Randa .10 .05
❑ 228 Henry Rodriguez .10 .05
❑ 229 Omar Vizquel .20 .09
❑ 230 Fred McGriff .30 .14
❑ 231 Matt Williams .30 .14
❑ 232 Moises Alou .20 .09
❑ 233 Travis Fryman .20 .09
❑ 234 Wade Boggs .50 .23
❑ 235 Pedro Martinez .60 .25
❑ 236 Rickey Henderson 1.00 .45
❑ 237 Bubba Trammell .10 .05
❑ 238 Mike Caruso .10 .05
❑ 239 Wilson Alvarez .10 .05
❑ 240 Geronimo Berroa .10 .05
❑ 241 Eric Milton .20 .09
❑ 242 Scott Erickson .10 .05
❑ 243 Todd Erdos RC .20 .09
❑ 244 Bobby Hughes .10 .05
❑ 245 Dave Hollins .10 .05
❑ 246 Dean Palmer .20 .09
❑ 247 Carlos Baerga .10 .05
❑ 248 Jose Silva .10 .05
❑ 249 Jose Cabrera RC .10 .05
❑ 250 Tom Evans .10 .05
❑ 251 Marty Cordova .10 .05
❑ 252 Hanley Frias RC .10 .05
❑ 253 Javier Valentin .10 .05
❑ 254 Mario Valdez .10 .05
❑ 255 Joey Cora .10 .05
❑ 256 Mike Lansing .10 .05
❑ 257 Jeff Kent .30 .14
❑ 258 Dave Dellucci RC .10 .05
❑ 259 Curtis King RC .10 .05
❑ 260 David Segui .10 .05
❑ 261 Royce Clayton .10 .05
❑ 262 Jeff Blauser .10 .05
❑ 263 Manny Aybar RC .20 .09
❑ 264 Mike Cather RC .10 .05
❑ 265 Todd Zeile .20 .09
❑ 266 Richard Hidalgo .20 .09
❑ 267 Dante Powell .10 .05
❑ 268 Mike DeJean RC .10 .05
❑ 269 Ken Cloude .10 .05
❑ 270 Danny Klassen .10 .05
❑ 271 Sean Casey .30 .14
❑ 272 A.J. Hinch .10 .05
❑ 273 Rich Butler RC .10 .05
❑ 274 Ben Ford RC .20 .09
❑ 275 Billy McMillon .10 .05
❑ 276 Wilson Delgado .10 .05
❑ 277 Orlando Cabrera .10 .05
❑ 278 Geoff Jenkins .20 .09
❑ 279 Enrique Wilson .10 .05
❑ 280 Derrek Lee .20 .09
❑ 281 Marc Pisciotta RC .10 .05
❑ 282 Abraham Nunez .10 .05
❑ 283 Aaron Boone .10 .05
❑ 284 Brad Fullmer .20 .09
❑ 285 Rob Stanifer RC .10 .05
❑ 286 Preston Wilson .20 .09
❑ 287 Greg Norton .10 .05
❑ 288 Bobby Smith .10 .05
❑ 289 Josh Booty .10 .05
❑ 290 Russell Branyan .20 .09
❑ 291 Jeremi Gonzalez .10 .05
❑ 292 Michael Coleman .10 .05
❑ 293 Cliff Politte .10 .05
❑ 294 Eric Ludwick .10 .05
❑ 295 Rafael Medina .10 .05
❑ 296 Jason Varitek .20 .09
❑ 297 Ron Wright .10 .05
❑ 298 Mark Kotsay .20 .09
❑ 299 David Ortiz .20 .09
❑ 300 Frank Catalanotto RC .50 .23
❑ 301 Robinson Checo .10 .05
❑ 302 Kevin Millwood RC .50 .23
❑ 303 Jacob Cruz .10 .05
❑ 304 Javier Vazquez .20 .09
❑ 305 Magglio Ordonez RC 1.50 .70
❑ 306 Kevin Witt .10 .05
❑ 307 Derrick Gibson .10 .05
❑ 308 Shane Monahan .10 .05
❑ 309 Brian Rose .10 .05
❑ 310 Bobby Estalella .10 .05
❑ 311 Felix Heredia .10 .05
❑ 312 Desi Relaford .10 .05
❑ 313 Esteban Yan RC .30 .14
❑ 314 Ricky Ledee .10 .05
❑ 315 Steve Woodard .10 .05
❑ 316 Pat Watkins .10 .05
❑ 317 Damian Moss .10 .05
❑ 318 Bob Abreu .20 .09
❑ 319 Jeff Abbott .10 .05
❑ 320 Miguel Cairo .10 .05
❑ 321 Rigo Beltran RC .10 .05
❑ 322 Tony Saunders .10 .05
❑ 323 Randall Simon .10 .05
❑ 324 Hiram Bocachica .10 .05
❑ 325 Richie Sexson .20 .09
❑ 326 Karim Garcia .10 .05
❑ 327 Mike Lowell RC .60 .25
❑ 328 Pat Cline .10 .05
❑ 329 Matt Clement .20 .09

❑	330 Scott Elarton	.10	.05
❑	331 Manuel Barrios RC	.10	.05
❑	332 Bruce Chen	.10	.05
❑	333 Juan Encarnacion	.20	.09
❑	334 Travis Lee	.20	.09
❑	335 Wes Helms	.10	.05
❑	336 Chad Fox RC	.10	.05
❑	337 Donnie Sadler	.10	.05
❑	338 Carlos Mendoza RC	.20	.09
❑	339 Damian Jackson	.10	.05
❑	340 Julio Ramirez RC	.20	.09
❑	341 John Halama RC	.40	.18
❑	342 Edwin Diaz	.10	.05
❑	343 Felix Martinez	.10	.05
❑	344 Eli Marrero	.10	.05
❑	345 Carl Pavano	.10	.05
❑	346 Vladimir Guerrero HL	.30	.14
❑	347 Barry Bonds HL	.60	.25
❑	348 Darin Erstad HL	.20	.09
❑	349 Albert Belle HL	.10	.05
❑	350 Kenny Lofton HL	.10	.05
❑	351 Mo Vaughn HL	.20	.09
❑	352 Jose Cruz Jr. HL	.10	.05
❑	353 Tony Clark HL	.10	.05
❑	354 Roberto Alomar HL	.20	.09
❑	355 Manny Ramirez HL	.30	.14
❑	356 Paul Molitor HL	.20	.09
❑	357 Jim Thome HL	.20	.09
❑	358 Tino Martinez HL	.10	.05
❑	359 Tim Salmon HL	.10	.05
❑	360 David Justice HL	.10	.05
❑	361 Raul Mondesi HL	.10	.05
❑	362 Mark Grace HL	.20	.09
❑	363 Craig Biggio HL	.30	.14
❑	364 Larry Walker HL	.30	.14
❑	365 Mark McGwire HL	1.00	.45
❑	366 Juan Gonzalez HL	.20	.09
❑	367 Derek Jeter HL	1.00	.45
❑	368 Chipper Jones HL	.50	.23
❑	369 Frank Thomas HL	.30	.14
❑	370 Alex Rodriguez HL	.60	.25
❑	371 Mike Piazza HL	.60	.25
❑	372 Tony Gwynn HL	.50	.23
❑	373 Jeff Bagwell HL	.30	.14
❑	374 N.Garciaparra HL	.60	.25
❑	375 Ken Griffey Jr. HL	.75	.35
❑	376 Livan Hernandez UN	.10	.05
❑	377 Chan Ho Park UN	.10	.05
❑	378 Mike Mussina UN	.20	.09
❑	379 Andy Pettitte UN	.10	.05
❑	380 Greg Maddux UN	.60	.25
❑	381 Hideo Nomo UN	.20	.09
❑	382 Roger Clemens UN	.60	.25
❑	383 Randy Johnson UN	.20	.09
❑	384 Pedro Martinez UN	.30	.14
❑	385 Jaret Wright UN	.10	.05
❑	386 Ken Griffey Jr. SG	.75	.35
❑	387 Todd Helton SG	.50	.23
❑	388 Paul Konerko SG	.10	.05
❑	389 Cal Ripken SG	1.00	.45
❑	390 Larry Walker SG	.30	.14
❑	391 Ken Caminiti SG	.10	.05
❑	392 Jose Guillen SG	.10	.05
❑	393 Jim Edmonds SG	.20	.09
❑	394 Barry Larkin SG	.20	.09
❑	395 Bernie Williams SG	.20	.09
❑	396 Tony Clark SG	.10	.05
❑	397 Jose Cruz Jr. SG	.10	.05
❑	398 Ivan Rodriguez SG	.20	.09
❑	399 Darin Erstad SG	.20	.09
❑	400 Scott Rolen SG	.50	.23
❑	401 Mark McGwire SG	1.00	.45
❑	402 Andruw Jones SG	.20	.09
❑	403 Juan Gonzalez SG	.20	.09
❑	404 Derek Jeter SG	1.00	.45
❑	405 Chipper Jones SG	.50	.23
❑	406 Greg Maddux SG	.60	.25
❑	407 Frank Thomas SG	.30	.14
❑	408 Alex Rodriguez SG	.60	.25
❑	409 Mike Piazza SG	.60	.25
❑	410 Tony Gwynn SG	.50	.23
❑	411 Jeff Bagwell SG	.30	.14
❑	412 N.Garciaparra SG	.60	.25
❑	413 Hideo Nomo SG	.20	.09
❑	414 Barry Bonds SG	.60	.25
❑	415 Ben Grieve SG	.20	.09
❑	416 Barry Bonds CL	.60	.25
❑	417 Mark McGwire CL	1.00	.45
❑	418 Roger Clemens CL	.60	.25
❑	419 Livan Hernandez CL	.10	.05
❑	420 Ken Griffey Jr. CL	.75	.35

2001 Donruss

	MINT	NRMT
COMP.SET w/o SP's (150)	25.00	11.00
COMMON CARD (1-150)	.15	.07
COMMON CARD (151-200)	8.00	3.60
COMMON CARD (201-220)	3.00	1.35

	Card	MINT	NRMT
❑	1 Alex Rodriguez	1.50	.70
❑	2 Barry Bonds	1.50	.70
❑	3 Cal Ripken	2.50	1.10
❑	4 Chipper Jones	1.25	.55
❑	5 Derek Jeter	2.50	1.10
❑	6 Troy Glaus	.60	.25
❑	7 Frank Thomas	.75	.35
❑	8 Greg Maddux	1.50	.70
❑	9 Ivan Rodriguez	.60	.25
❑	10 Jeff Bagwell	.75	.35
❑	11 Jose Canseco	.60	.25
❑	12 Todd Helton	.75	.35
❑	13 Ken Griffey Jr.	2.00	.90
❑	14 Manny Ramirez	.75	.35
❑	15 Mark McGwire	2.50	1.10
❑	16 Mike Piazza	1.50	.70
❑	17 Nomar Garciaparra	1.50	.70
❑	18 Pedro Martinez	.75	.35
❑	19 Randy Johnson	.75	.35
❑	20 Rick Ankiel	.40	.18
❑	21 Rickey Henderson	1.25	.55
❑	22 Roger Clemens	1.50	.70
❑	23 Sammy Sosa	1.25	.55
❑	24 Tony Gwynn	1.25	.55
❑	25 Vladimir Guerrero	.75	.35
❑	26 Eric Davis	.25	.11
❑	27 Roberto Alomar	.25	.11
❑	28 Mark Mulder	.40	.18
❑	29 Pat Burrell	.25	.11
❑	30 Harold Baines	.25	.11
❑	31 Carlos Delgado	.60	.25
❑	32 J.D. Drew	.60	.25
❑	33 Jim Edmonds	.40	.18
❑	34 Darin Erstad	.60	.25
❑	35 Jason Giambi	.60	.25
❑	36 Tom Glavine	.60	.25
❑	37 Juan Gonzalez	.60	.25
❑	38 Mark Grace	.60	.25
❑	39 Shawn Green	.60	.25
❑	40 Tim Hudson	.60	.25
❑	41 Andruw Jones	.60	.25
❑	42 David Justice	.25	.11
❑	43 Jeff Kent	.40	.18
❑	44 Barry Larkin	.60	.25
❑	45 Pokey Reese	.15	.07
❑	46 Mike Mussina	.60	.25
❑	47 Hideo Nomo	.60	.25
❑	48 Rafael Palmeiro	.60	.25
❑	49 Adam Piatt	.25	.11
❑	50 Scott Rolen	.60	.25
❑	51 Gary Sheffield	.25	.11
❑	52 Bernie Williams	.60	.25
❑	53 Bob Abreu	.25	.11
❑	54 Edgardo Alfonzo	.25	.11
❑	55 Jermaine Clark RC	.40	.18
❑	56 Albert Belle	.25	.11
❑	57 Craig Biggio	.40	.18
❑	58 Andres Galarraga	.40	.18
❑	59 Edgar Martinez	.40	.18
❑	60 Fred McGriff	.40	.18
❑	61 Magglio Ordonez	.25	.11
❑	62 Jim Thome	.60	.25
❑	63 Matt Williams	.40	.18
❑	64 Kerry Wood	.60	.25
❑	65 Moises Alou	.25	.11
❑	66 Brady Anderson	.25	.11
❑	67 Garret Anderson	.25	.11
❑	68 Tony Armas Jr.	.15	.07
❑	69 Tony Batista	.25	.11
❑	70 Jose Cruz Jr.	.25	.11
❑	71 Carlos Beltran	.25	.11
❑	72 Adrian Beltre	.25	.11
❑	73 Kris Benson	.25	.11
❑	74 Lance Berkman	.60	.25
❑	75 Kevin Brown	.25	.11
❑	76 Jay Buhner	.25	.11
❑	77 Jeromy Burnitz	.25	.11
❑	78 Ken Caminiti	.25	.11
❑	79 Sean Casey	.40	.18
❑	80 Luis Castillo	.15	.07
❑	81 Eric Chavez	.25	.11
❑	82 Jeff Cirillo	.25	.11
❑	83 Bartolo Colon	.25	.11
❑	84 David Cone	.25	.11
❑	85 Freddy Garcia	.25	.11
❑	86 Johnny Damon	.25	.11
❑	87 Ray Durham	.25	.11
❑	88 Jermaine Dye	.25	.11
❑	89 Juan Encarnacion	.25	.11
❑	90 Terrence Long	.25	.11
❑	91 Carl Everett	.25	.11
❑	92 Steve Finley	.25	.11
❑	93 Cliff Floyd	.25	.11
❑	94 Brad Fullmer	.25	.11
❑	95 Brian Giles	.25	.11
❑	96 Luis Gonzalez	.60	.25
❑	97 Rusty Greer	.25	.11
❑	98 Jeffrey Hammonds	.15	.07
❑	99 Mike Hampton	.25	.11
❑	100 Orlando Hernandez	.25	.11
❑	101 Richard Hidalgo	.25	.11
❑	102 Geoff Jenkins	.25	.11
❑	103 Jacque Jones	.25	.11
❑	104 Brian Jordan	.25	.11
❑	105 Gabe Kapler	.25	.11
❑	106 Eric Karros	.25	.11
❑	107 Jason Kendall	.25	.11
❑	108 Adam Kennedy	.15	.07
❑	109 Byung-Hyun Kim	.25	.11
❑	110 Ryan Klesko	.25	.11
❑	111 Chuck Knoblauch	.25	.11
❑	112 Paul Konerko	.25	.11
❑	113 Carlos Lee	.25	.11
❑	114 Kenny Lofton	.25	.11
❑	115 Javy Lopez	.25	.11
❑	116 Tino Martinez	.25	.11
❑	117 Ruben Mateo	.25	.11
❑	118 Kevin Millwood	.15	.07
❑	119 Ben Molina	.15	.07
❑	120 Raul Mondesi	.25	.11
❑	121 Trot Nixon	.25	.11
❑	122 John Olerud	.25	.11
❑	123 Paul O'Neill	.60	.25
❑	124 Chan Ho Park	.25	.11
❑	125 Andy Pettitte	.25	.11
❑	126 Jorge Posada	.25	.11
❑	127 Mark Quinn	.25	.11
❑	128 Aramis Ramirez	.25	.11
❑	129 Mariano Rivera	.25	.11
❑	130 Tim Salmon	.25	.11
❑	131 Curt Schilling	.60	.25
❑	132 Richie Sexson	.25	.11
❑	133 John Smoltz	.25	.11
❑	134 J.T. Snow	.25	.11
❑	135 Jay Payton	.15	.07
❑	136 Shannon Stewart	.25	.11
❑	137 B.J. Surhoff	.25	.11
❑	138 Mike Sweeney	.25	.11
❑	139 Fernando Tatis	.15	.07

❑ 140 Miguel Tejada .... .25 .11
❑ 141 Jason Varitek .... .25 .11
❑ 142 Greg Vaughn .... .25 .11
❑ 143 Mo Vaughn .... .25 .11
❑ 144 Robin Ventura UER .... .25 .11
Listed as playing for
Yankees last 2 years
Also Bat and Throw
information is wrong
❑ 145 Jose Vidro .... .25 .11
❑ 146 Omar Vizquel .... .25 .11
❑ 147 Larry Walker .... .40 .18
❑ 148 David Wells .... .25 .11
❑ 149 Rondell White .... .25 .11
❑ 150 Preston Wilson .... .25 .11
❑ 151 Brent Abernathy RR 8.00 3.60
❑ 152 Cory Aldridge RR RC .. 8.00 3.60
❑ 153 Gene Altman RR RC 8.00 3.60
❑ 154 Josh Beckett RR 10.00 4.50
❑ 155 Wilson Betemit RR RC 20.00 9.00
❑ 156 A. Pujols RR/500 EXCH 150.00 70.00
❑ 157 Joe Crede RR 8.00 3.60
❑ 158 Jack Cust RR 8.00 3.60
❑ 159 B. Sheets RR/500 EXCH 40.00 18.00
❑ 160 Alex Escobar RR.......... 8.00 3.60
❑ 161 Adrian Hernandez RR RC 8.00 3.60
❑ 162 Pedro Feliz RR 8.00 3.60
❑ 163 Nate Frese RR RC 8.00 3.60
❑ 164 Carlos Garcia RR RC .. 8.00 3.60
❑ 165 Marcus Giles RR.......... 8.00 3.60
❑ 166 Alexis Gomez RR RC .. 8.00 3.60
❑ 167 Jason Hart RR.............. 8.00 3.60
❑ 168 Eric Hinske RR RC 10.00 4.50
❑ 169 Cesar Izturis RR 8.00 3.60
❑ 170 Nick Johnson RR 8.00 3.60
❑ 171 Mike Young RR............ 8.00 3.60
❑ 172 Brian Lawrence RR RC 8.00 3.60
❑ 173 Steve Lomasney RR 8.00 3.60
❑ 174 Nick Maness RR 8.00 3.60
❑ 175 Jose Mieses RR RC 8.00 3.60
❑ 176 Greg Miller RR RC 8.00 3.60
❑ 177 Eric Munson RR 8.00 3.60
❑ 178 Xavier Nady RR 8.00 3.60
❑ 179 Blaine Neal RR RC 8.00 3.60
❑ 180 Abraham Nunez RR 8.00 3.60
❑ 181 Jose Ortiz RR 8.00 3.60
❑ 182 Jeremy Owens RR RC 8.00 3.60
❑ 183 Pablo Ozuna RR 8.00 3.60
❑ 184 Corey Patterson RR 8.00 3.60
❑ 185 Carlos Pena RR 8.00 3.60
❑ 186 Wily Mo Pena RR 8.00 3.60
❑ 187 Timo Perez RR 8.00 3.60
❑ 188 Adam Pettyjohn RR RC 8.00 3.60
❑ 189 Luis Rivas RR 8.00 3.60
❑ 190 Jackson Melian RR RC 8.00 3.60
❑ 191 Wilken Ruan RR RC 8.00 3.60
❑ 192 Duaner Sanchez RR RC 8.00 3.60
❑ 193 Alfonso Soriano RR.... 10.00 4.50
❑ 194 Rafael Soriano RR RC 10.00 4.50
❑ 195 Ichiro Suzuki RR RC 100.00 45.00
❑ 196 Billy Sylvester RR RC .. 8.00 3.60
❑ 197 Juan Uribe RR RC 12.00 5.50
❑ 198 Eric Valent RR.............. 8.00 3.60
❑ 199 C. Valderrama RR RC.. 8.00 3.60
❑ 200 Matt White RR RC........ 8.00 3.60
❑ 201 Alex Rodriguez FC 8.00 3.60
❑ 202 Barry Bonds FC............ 8.00 3.60
❑ 203 Cal Ripken FC........... 12.00 5.50
❑ 204 Chipper Jones FC 6.00 2.70
❑ 205 Derek Jeter FC 12.00 5.50
❑ 206 Troy Glaus FC.............. 3.00 1.35
❑ 207 Frank Thomas FC 4.00 1.80
❑ 208 Greg Maddux FC.......... 8.00 3.60
❑ 209 Ivan Rodriguez FC 3.00 1.35
❑ 210 Jeff Bagwell FC 4.00 1.80
❑ 211 Todd Helton FC............ 4.00 1.80
❑ 212 Ken Griffey Jr. FC 10.00 4.50
❑ 213 Manny Ramirez FC 4.00 1.80
❑ 214 Mark McGwire FC 12.00 5.50
❑ 215 Mike Piazza FC 8.00 3.60
❑ 216 Pedro Martinez FC 4.00 1.80
❑ 217 Sammy Sosa FC 6.00 2.70
❑ 218 Tony Gwynn FC 6.00 2.70
❑ 219 Vladimir Guerrero FC .. 4.00 1.80
❑ 220 Nomar Garciaparra FC 8.00 3.60

❑ NNO Baseball's Best Coupon 150.00 70.00
❑ NNO The Rookies Coupon 25.00 11.00

2001 Donruss Classics

	MINT	NRMT
COMP.SET w/o SP's (100).....	40.00	18.00
COMMON CARD (1-100)............	.75	.35
COMMON CARD (101-150)....	10.00	4.50
COMMON CARD (151-200)......	5.00	2.20

❑ 1 Alex Rodriguez 5.00 2.20
❑ 2 Barry Bonds 5.00 2.20
❑ 3 Cal Ripken....................... 8.00 3.60
❑ 4 Chipper Jones.................. 4.00 1.80
❑ 5 Derek Jeter 8.00 3.60
❑ 6 Troy Glaus....................... 2.00 .90
❑ 7 Frank Thomas.................. 2.50 1.10
❑ 8 Greg Maddux 5.00 2.20
❑ 9 Ivan Rodriguez .... 2.00 .90
❑ 10 Jeff Bagwell.................... 2.50 1.10
❑ 11 Cliff Floyd .... .75 .35
❑ 12 Todd Helton.................... 2.50 1.10
❑ 13 Ken Griffey Jr. 6.00 2.70
❑ 14 Manny Ramirez 2.50 1.10
❑ 15 Mark McGwire 8.00 3.60
❑ 16 Mike Piazza.................... 5.00 2.20
❑ 17 Nomar Garciaparra 5.00 2.20
❑ 18 Pedro Martinez 2.50 1.10
❑ 19 Randy Johnson 2.50 1.10
❑ 20 Rick Ankiel .... 1.25 .55
❑ 21 Rickey Henderson.......... 4.00 1.80
❑ 22 Roger Clemens 5.00 2.20
❑ 23 Sammy Sosa.................. 4.00 1.80
❑ 24 Tony Gwynn 4.00 1.80
❑ 25 Vladimir Guerrero 2.50 1.10
❑ 26 Kazuhiro Sasaki .... 2.00 .90
❑ 27 Roberto Alomar.............. 2.00 .90
❑ 28 Barry Zito........................ 2.00 .90
❑ 29 Pat Burrell .... .75 .35
❑ 30 Harold Baines .... .75 .35
❑ 31 Carlos Delgado .... 2.00 .90
❑ 32 J.D. Drew .... 2.00 .90
❑ 33 Jim Edmonds .... 1.25 .55
❑ 34 Darin Erstad .... 2.00 .90
❑ 35 Jason Giambi .... 2.00 .90
❑ 36 Tom Glavine .... 2.00 .90
❑ 37 Juan Gonzalez .... 2.00 .90
❑ 38 Mark Grace .... 2.00 .90
❑ 39 Shawn Green .... 2.00 .90
❑ 40 Tim Hudson.................... 2.00 .90
❑ 41 Andruw Jones .... 2.00 .90
❑ 42 Jeff Kent .... 1.25 .55
❑ 43 Barry Larkin.................... 2.00 .90
❑ 44 Rafael Furcal................... .75 .35
❑ 45 Mike Mussina .... 2.00 .90
❑ 46 Hideo Nomo .... 2.00 .90
❑ 47 Rafael Palmeiro.............. 2.00 .90
❑ 48 Scott Rolen .... 2.00 .90
❑ 49 Gary Sheffield .... .75 .35
❑ 50 Bernie Williams .... 2.00 .90
❑ 51 Bob Abreu .... .75 .35
❑ 52 Edgardo Alfonzo .... .75 .35
❑ 53 Edgar Martinez .... 1.25 .55
❑ 54 Magglio Ordonez............. .75 .35
❑ 55 Kerry Wood .... 2.00 .90
❑ 56 Adrian Beltre .... .75 .35
❑ 57 Lance Berkman.............. 2.00 .90
❑ 58 Kevin Brown .... .75 .35
❑ 59 Sean Casey.................... 1.25 .55
❑ 60 Eric Chavez...................... .75 .35
❑ 61 Bartolo Colon .... .75 .35
❑ 62 Johnny Damon .... .75 .35
❑ 63 Jermaine Dye .... .75 .35
❑ 64 Juan Encarnacion .... .75 .35
❑ 65 Carl Everett .... .75 .35
❑ 66 Brian Giles....................... .75 .35
❑ 67 Mike Hampton.................. .75 .35
❑ 68 Richard Hidalgo............... .75 .35
❑ 69 Geoff Jenkins .... .75 .35
❑ 70 Jacque Jones .... .75 .35
❑ 71 Jason Kendall .... .75 .35
❑ 72 Ryan Klesko .... .75 .35
❑ 73 Chan Ho Park .... .75 .35
❑ 74 Richie Sexson.................. .75 .35
❑ 75 Mike Sweeney.................. .75 .35
❑ 76 Fernando Tatis .... .75 .35
❑ 77 Miguel Tejada .... .75 .35
❑ 78 Jose Vidro .... .75 .35
❑ 79 Larry Walker .... 1.25 .55
❑ 80 Preston Wilson .... .75 .35
❑ 81 Craig Biggio.................... 1.25 .55
❑ 82 Fred McGriff .... 1.25 .55
❑ 83 Jim Thome .... 2.00 .90
❑ 84 Garret Anderson .... .75 .35
❑ 85 Russell Branyan .... .75 .35
❑ 86 Tony Batista .... .75 .35
❑ 87 Terrence Long.................. .75 .35
❑ 88 Brad Fullmer .... .75 .35
❑ 89 Rusty Greer...................... .75 .35
❑ 90 Orlando Hernandez .... .75 .35
❑ 91 Gabe Kapler .... .75 .35
❑ 92 Paul Konerko.................... .75 .35
❑ 93 Carlos Lee........................ .75 .35
❑ 94 Kenny Lofton.................... .75 .35
❑ 95 Raul Mondesi .... .75 .35
❑ 96 Jorge Posada .... .75 .35
❑ 97 Tim Salmon...................... .75 .35
❑ 98 Greg Vaughn.................... .75 .35
❑ 99 Mo Vaughn .... .75 .35
❑ 100 Omar Vizquel .... .75 .35
❑ 101 Aubrey Huff SP 10.00 4.50
❑ 102 Jimmy Rollins SP 10.00 4.50
❑ 103 Cory Aldridge SP RC 10.00 4.50
❑ 104 Wilmy Caceres SP RC 10.00 4.50
❑ 105 Josh Beckett SP 20.00 9.00
❑ 106 Wilson Betemit SP RC 30.00 13.50
❑ 107 Timo Perez SP 10.00 4.50
❑ 108 Albert Pujols SP RC 100.00 45.00
❑ 109 Bud Smith SP RC 40.00 18.00
❑ 110 Jack Wilson SP RC.... 10.00 4.50
❑ 111 Alex Escobar SP 10.00 4.50
❑ 112 Johnny Estrada SP RC 20.00 9.00
❑ 113 Pedro Feliz SP 10.00 4.50
❑ 114 Nate Frese SP RC 10.00 4.50
❑ 115 Carlos Garcia SP RC 10.00 4.50
❑ 116 Brandon Larson SP RC 10.00 4.50
❑ 117 Alexis Gomez SP RC 10.00 4.50
❑ 118 Jason Hart SP 15.00 6.75
❑ 119 Adam Dunn SP 30.00 13.50
❑ 120 Marcus Giles SP 10.00 4.50
❑ 121 Christian Parker SP RC 10.00 4.50
❑ 122 Jackson Melian SP RC 10.00 4.50
❑ 123 Endy Chavez SP RC.. 10.00 4.50
❑ 124 Adrian Hernandez SP RC 10.00 4.50
❑ 125 Joe Kennedy SP RC .. 15.00 6.75
❑ 126 Jose Mieses SP RC .. 10.00 4.50
❑ 127 C.C. Sabathia SP 15.00 6.75
❑ 128 Eric Munson SP 10.00 4.50
❑ 129 Xavier Nady SP......... 15.00 6.75
❑ 130 Horacio Ramirez SP RC 10.00 4.50
❑ 131 Abraham Nunez SP .. 10.00 4.50
❑ 132 Jose Ortiz SP 15.00 6.75
❑ 133 Jeremy Owens SP RC 10.00 4.50
❑ 134 Claudio Vargas SP RC 10.00 4.50
❑ 135 Corey Patterson SP .. 10.00 4.50
❑ 136 Andres Torres SP RC 10.00 4.50
❑ 137 Ben Sheets SP 15.00 6.75
❑ 138 Joe Crede SP 10.00 4.50
❑ 139 Adam Pettyjohn SP RC 10.00 4.50
❑ 140 Elpidio Guzman SP RC 10.00 4.50
❑ 141 Jay Gibbons SP RC .. 15.00 6.75
❑ 142 Wilkin Ruan SP RC.... 10.00 4.50
❑ 143 Tsuyoshi Shinjo SP RC 30.00 13.50

		MINT	NRMT
❑ 144	Alfonso Soriano SP	20.00	9.00
❑ 145	Nick Johnson SP	10.00	4.50
❑ 146	Ichiro Suzuki SP RC	180.00	80.00
❑ 147	Juan Uribe SP RC	20.00	9.00
❑ 148	Jack Cust SP	10.00	4.50
❑ 149	C. Valderrama SP RC	10.00	4.50
❑ 150	Matt White SP RC	10.00	4.50
❑ 151	Hank Aaron LGD	15.00	6.75
❑ 152	Ernie Banks LGD	8.00	3.60
❑ 153	Johnny Bench LGD	10.00	4.50
❑ 154	George Brett LGD	12.00	5.50
❑ 155	Lou Brock LGD	8.00	3.60
❑ 156	Rod Carew LGD	8.00	3.60
❑ 157	Steve Carlton LGD	8.00	3.60
❑ 158	Bob Feller LGD	5.00	2.20
❑ 159	Bob Gibson LGD	8.00	3.60
❑ 160	Reggie Jackson LGD	10.00	4.50
❑ 161	Al Kaline LGD	8.00	3.60
❑ 162	Sandy Koufax LGD		
❑ 163	Don Mattingly LGD	20.00	9.00
❑ 164	Willie Mays LGD	15.00	6.75
❑ 165	Willie McCovey LGD	8.00	3.60
❑ 166	Joe Morgan LGD	8.00	3.60
❑ 167	Stan Musial LGD	12.00	5.50
❑ 168	Jim Palmer LGD	8.00	3.60
❑ 169	Brooks Robinson LGD	8.00	3.60
❑ 170	Frank Robinson LGD	8.00	3.60
❑ 171	Nolan Ryan LGD	25.00	11.00
❑ 172	Mike Schmidt LGD	12.00	5.50
❑ 173	Tom Seaver LGD	10.00	4.50
❑ 174	Warren Spahn LGD	8.00	3.60
❑ 175	Robin Yount LGD	8.00	3.60
❑ 176	Wade Boggs LGD	8.00	3.60
❑ 177	Ty Cobb LGD	10.00	4.50
❑ 178	Lou Gehrig LGD	12.00	5.50
❑ 179	Luis Aparicio LGD	5.00	2.20
❑ 180	Babe Ruth LGD	20.00	9.00
❑ 181	Ryne Sandberg LGD	15.00	6.75
❑ 182	Yogi Berra LGD	8.00	3.60
❑ 183	Roberto Clemente LGD	15.00	6.75
❑ 184	Eddie Murray LGD	8.00	3.60
❑ 185	Robin Roberts LGD	80.00	36.00
❑ 186	Duke Snider LGD	8.00	3.60
❑ 187	Orlando Cepeda LGD	5.00	2.20
❑ 188	Billy Williams LGD	5.00	2.20
❑ 189	Juan Marichal LGD	5.00	2.20
❑ 190	Harmon Killebrew LGD	8.00	3.60
❑ 191	Kirby Puckett LGD	15.00	6.75
❑ 192	Carlton Fisk LGD	8.00	3.60
❑ 193	Dave Winfield LGD	8.00	3.60
❑ 194	Whitey Ford LGD	8.00	3.60
❑ 195	Paul Molitor LGD	8.00	3.60
❑ 196	Tony Perez LGD	5.00	2.20
❑ 197	Ozzie Smith LGD	8.00	3.60
❑ 198	Ralph Kiner LGD	5.00	2.20
❑ 199	Fergie Jenkins LGD	5.00	2.20
❑ 200	Phil Rizzuto LGD	8.00	3.60

1997 Donruss Elite

		MINT	NRMT
	COMPLETE SET (150)	40.00	18.00
❑ 1	Juan Gonzalez	.75	.35
❑ 2	Alex Rodriguez	2.00	.90
❑ 3	Frank Thomas	1.00	.45
❑ 4	Greg Maddux	2.00	.90
❑ 5	Ken Griffey Jr.	2.50	1.10
❑ 6	Cal Ripken	3.00	1.35
❑ 7	Mike Piazza	2.00	.90
❑ 8	Chipper Jones	1.50	.70
❑ 9	Albert Belle	.30	.14
❑ 10	Andruw Jones	1.00	.45
❑ 11	Vladimir Guerrero	1.25	.55
❑ 12	Mo Vaughn UER front Gonzales	.30	.14
❑ 13	Ivan Rodriguez	.75	.35
❑ 14	Andy Pettitte	.30	.14
❑ 15	Tony Gwynn	1.50	.70
❑ 16	Barry Bonds	2.00	.90
❑ 17	Jeff Bagwell	1.00	.45
❑ 18	Manny Ramirez	1.00	.45
❑ 19	Kenny Lofton	.30	.14
❑ 20	Roberto Alomar	.75	.35
❑ 21	Mark McGwire	3.00	1.35
❑ 22	Ryan Klesko	.30	.14
❑ 23	Tim Salmon	.30	.14
❑ 24	Derek Jeter	3.00	1.35
❑ 25	Eddie Murray	.75	.35
❑ 26	Jermaine Dye	.30	.14
❑ 27	Ruben Rivera	.20	.09
❑ 28	Jim Edmonds	.50	.23
❑ 29	Mike Mussina	.75	.35
❑ 30	Randy Johnson	1.00	.45
❑ 31	Sammy Sosa	1.50	.70
❑ 32	Hideo Nomo	.75	.35
❑ 33	Chuck Knoblauch	.30	.14
❑ 34	Paul Molitor	.75	.35
❑ 35	Rafael Palmeiro	.75	.35
❑ 36	Brady Anderson	.30	.14
❑ 37	Will Clark	.75	.35
❑ 38	Craig Biggio	.50	.23
❑ 39	Jason Giambi	.75	.35
❑ 40	Roger Clemens	2.00	.90
❑ 41	Jay Buhner	.30	.14
❑ 42	Edgar Martinez	.50	.23
❑ 43	Gary Sheffield	.30	.14
❑ 44	Fred McGriff	.50	.23
❑ 45	Bobby Bonilla	.30	.14
❑ 46	Tom Glavine	.75	.35
❑ 47	Wade Boggs	.75	.35
❑ 48	Jeff Conine	.20	.09
❑ 49	John Smoltz	.30	.14
❑ 50	Jim Thome	.75	.35
❑ 51	Billy Wagner	.20	.09
❑ 52	Jose Canseco	.75	.35
❑ 53	Javy Lopez	.30	.14
❑ 54	Cecil Fielder	.30	.14
❑ 55	Garret Anderson	.30	.14
❑ 56	Alex Ochoa	.20	.09
❑ 57	Scott Rolen	.75	.35
❑ 58	Darin Erstad	.75	.35
❑ 59	Rey Ordonez	.20	.09
❑ 60	Dante Bichette	.30	.14
❑ 61	Joe Carter	.30	.14
❑ 62	Moises Alou	.30	.14
❑ 63	Jason Isringhausen	.20	.09
❑ 64	Karim Garcia	.20	.09
❑ 65	Brian Jordan	.30	.14
❑ 66	Ruben Sierra	.20	.09
❑ 67	Todd Hollandsworth	.20	.09
❑ 68	Paul Wilson	.20	.09
❑ 69	Ernie Young	.20	.09
❑ 70	Ryne Sandberg	1.00	.45
❑ 71	Raul Mondesi	.30	.14
❑ 72	George Arias	.20	.09
❑ 73	Ray Durham	.30	.14
❑ 74	Dean Palmer	.30	.14
❑ 75	Shawn Green	.75	.35
❑ 76	Eric Young	.20	.09
❑ 77	Jason Kendall	.30	.14
❑ 78	Greg Vaughn	.30	.14
❑ 79	Terrell Wade	.20	.09
❑ 80	Bill Pulsipher	.20	.09
❑ 81	Bobby Higginson	.30	.14
❑ 82	Mark Grudzielanek	.20	.09
❑ 83	Ken Caminiti	.30	.14
❑ 84	Todd Greene	.20	.09
❑ 85	Carlos Delgado	.75	.35
❑ 86	Mark Grace	.75	.35
❑ 87	Rondell White	.30	.14
❑ 88	Barry Larkin	.75	.35
❑ 89	J.T. Snow	.30	.14
❑ 90	Alex Gonzalez	.20	.09
❑ 91	Raul Casanova	.20	.09
❑ 92	Marc Newfield	.20	.09
❑ 93	Jermaine Allensworth	.20	.09
❑ 94	John Mabry	.20	.09
❑ 95	Kirby Puckett	2.00	.90
❑ 96	Travis Fryman	.30	.14
❑ 97	Kevin Brown	.30	.14
❑ 98	Andres Galarraga	.50	.23
❑ 99	Marty Cordova	.20	.09
❑ 100	Henry Rodriguez	.20	.09
❑ 101	Sterling Hitchcock	.20	.09
❑ 102	Trey Beamon	.20	.09
❑ 103	Brett Butler	.30	.14
❑ 104	Rickey Henderson	1.50	.70
❑ 105	Tino Martinez	.30	.14
❑ 106	Kevin Appier	.30	.14
❑ 107	Brian Hunter	.20	.09
❑ 108	Eric Karros	.30	.14
❑ 109	Andre Dawson	.50	.23
❑ 110	Darryl Strawberry	.30	.14
❑ 111	James Baldwin	.20	.09
❑ 112	Chad Mottola	.20	.09
❑ 113	Dave Nilsson	.20	.09
❑ 114	Carlos Baerga	.20	.09
❑ 115	Chan Ho Park	.30	.14
❑ 116	John Jaha	.20	.09
❑ 117	Alan Benes	.20	.09
❑ 118	Mariano Rivera	.30	.14
❑ 119	Ellis Burks	.30	.14
❑ 120	Tony Clark	.30	.14
❑ 121	Todd Walker	.20	.09
❑ 122	Dwight Gooden	.30	.14
❑ 123	Ugueth Urbina	.20	.09
❑ 124	David Cone	.30	.14
❑ 125	Ozzie Smith	1.00	.45
❑ 126	Kimera Bartee	.20	.09
❑ 127	Rusty Greer	.30	.14
❑ 128	Pat Hentgen	.20	.09
❑ 129	Charles Johnson	.30	.14
❑ 130	Quinton McCracken	.20	.09
❑ 131	Troy Percival	.20	.09
❑ 132	Shane Reynolds	.20	.09
❑ 133	Charles Nagy	.20	.09
❑ 134	Tom Goodwin	.20	.09
❑ 135	Ron Gant	.20	.09
❑ 136	Dan Wilson	.20	.09
❑ 137	Matt Williams	.50	.23
❑ 138	LaTroy Hawkins	.20	.09
❑ 139	Kevin Seitzer	.20	.09
❑ 140	Michael Tucker	.20	.09
❑ 141	Todd Hundley	.20	.09
❑ 142	Alex Fernandez	.20	.09
❑ 143	Marquis Grissom	.20	.09
❑ 144	Steve Finley	.30	.14
❑ 145	Curtis Pride	.20	.09
❑ 146	Derek Bell	.20	.09
❑ 147	Butch Huskey	.20	.09
❑ 148	Dwight Gooden CL	.30	.14
❑ 149	Al Leiter CL	.20	.09
❑ 150	Hideo Nomo CL	.30	.14

1998 Donruss Elite

		MINT	NRMT
	COMPLETE SET (150)	30.00	13.50
❑ 1	Ken Griffey Jr.	2.00	.90
❑ 2	Frank Thomas	.75	.35
❑ 3	Alex Rodriguez	1.50	.70
❑ 4	Mike Piazza	1.50	.70

❑ 5 Greg Maddux	1.50	.70
❑ 6 Cal Ripken	2.50	1.10
❑ 7 Chipper Jones	1.25	.55
❑ 8 Derek Jeter	2.50	1.10
❑ 9 Tony Gwynn	1.25	.55
❑ 10 Andruw Jones	.60	.25
❑ 11 Juan Gonzalez	.60	.25
❑ 12 Jeff Bagwell	.75	.35
❑ 13 Mark McGwire	2.50	1.10
❑ 14 Roger Clemens	1.50	.70
❑ 15 Albert Belle	.25	.11
❑ 16 Barry Bonds	1.50	.70
❑ 17 Kenny Lofton	.25	.11
❑ 18 Ivan Rodriguez	.60	.25
❑ 19 Manny Ramirez	.75	.35
❑ 20 Jim Thome	.60	.25
❑ 21 Chuck Knoblauch	.25	.11
❑ 22 Paul Molitor	.60	.25
❑ 23 Barry Larkin	.60	.25
❑ 24 Andy Pettitte	.25	.11
❑ 25 John Smoltz	.25	.11
❑ 26 Randy Johnson	.75	.35
❑ 27 Bernie Williams	.60	.25
❑ 28 Larry Walker	.40	.18
❑ 29 Mo Vaughn	.25	.11
❑ 30 Bobby Higginson	.25	.11
❑ 31 Edgardo Alfonzo	.25	.11
❑ 32 Justin Thompson	.15	.07
❑ 33 Jeff Suppan	.15	.07
❑ 34 Roberto Alomar	.60	.25
❑ 35 Hideo Nomo	.60	.25
❑ 36 Rusty Greer	.25	.11
❑ 37 Tim Salmon	.25	.11
❑ 38 Jim Edmonds	.40	.18
❑ 39 Gary Sheffield	.25	.11
❑ 40 Ken Caminiti	.25	.11
❑ 41 Sammy Sosa	1.25	.55
❑ 42 Tony Womack	.15	.07
❑ 43 Matt Williams	.40	.18
❑ 44 Andres Galarraga	.40	.18
❑ 45 Garret Anderson	.25	.11
❑ 46 Rafael Palmeiro	.60	.25
❑ 47 Mike Mussina	.60	.25
❑ 48 Craig Biggio	.40	.18
❑ 49 Wade Boggs	.60	.25
❑ 50 Tom Glavine	.60	.25
❑ 51 Jason Giambi	.60	.25
❑ 52 Will Clark	.60	.25
❑ 53 David Justice	.25	.11
❑ 54 Sandy Alomar Jr.	.25	.11
❑ 55 Edgar Martinez	.40	.18
❑ 56 Brady Anderson	.25	.11
❑ 57 Eric Young	.15	.07
❑ 58 Ray Lankford	.15	.07
❑ 59 Kevin Brown	.40	.18
❑ 60 Raul Mondesi	.25	.11
❑ 61 Bobby Bonilla	.25	.11
❑ 62 Javier Lopez	.25	.11
❑ 63 Fred McGriff	.40	.18
❑ 64 Rondell White	.25	.11
❑ 65 Todd Hundley	.15	.07
❑ 66 Mark Grace	.60	.25
❑ 67 Alan Benes	.15	.07
❑ 68 Jeff Abbott	.15	.07
❑ 69 Bob Abreu	.25	.11
❑ 70 Deion Sanders	.25	.11
❑ 71 Tino Martinez	.25	.11
❑ 72 Shannon Stewart	.25	.11
❑ 73 Homer Bush	.15	.07
❑ 74 Carlos Delgado	.60	.25
❑ 75 Raul Ibanez	.15	.07
❑ 76 Hideki Irabu	.15	.07
❑ 77 Jose Cruz Jr.	.25	.11
❑ 78 Tony Clark	.25	.11
❑ 79 Wilton Guerrero	.15	.07
❑ 80 Vladimir Guerrero	.75	.35
❑ 81 Scott Rolen	.60	.25
❑ 82 Nomar Garciaparra	1.50	.70
❑ 83 Darin Erstad	.60	.25
❑ 84 Chan Ho Park	.25	.11
❑ 85 Mike Cameron	.25	.11
❑ 86 Todd Walker	.15	.07
❑ 87 Todd Dunwoody	.15	.07
❑ 88 Neifi Perez	.15	.07
❑ 89 Brett Tomko	.15	.07
❑ 90 Jose Guillen	.15	.07
❑ 91 Matt Morris	.25	.11
❑ 92 Bartolo Colon	.25	.11
❑ 93 Jaret Wright	.15	.07
❑ 94 Shawn Estes	.25	.11
❑ 95 Livan Hernandez	.15	.07
❑ 96 Bobby Estalella	.15	.07
❑ 97 Ben Grieve	.25	.11
❑ 98 Paul Konerko	.25	.11
❑ 99 David Ortiz	.25	.11
❑ 100 Todd Helton	.75	.35
❑ 101 Juan Encarnacion	.25	.11
❑ 102 Bubba Trammell	.15	.07
❑ 103 Miguel Tejada	.40	.18
❑ 104 Jacob Cruz	.15	.07
❑ 105 Todd Greene	.15	.07
❑ 106 Kevin Orie	.15	.07
❑ 107 Mark Kotsay	.25	.11
❑ 108 Fernando Tatis	.15	.07
❑ 109 Jay Payton	.15	.07
❑ 110 Pokey Reese	.15	.07
❑ 111 Derrek Lee	.25	.11
❑ 112 Richard Hidalgo	.25	.11
❑ 113 Ricky Ledee UER front Rickey	.15	.07
❑ 114 Lou Collier	.15	.07
❑ 115 Ruben Rivera	.15	.07
❑ 116 Shawn Green	.60	.25
❑ 117 Moises Alou	.25	.11
❑ 118 Ken Griffey Jr. GEN	1.00	.45
❑ 119 Frank Thomas GEN	.40	.18
❑ 120 Alex Rodriguez GEN	.75	.35
❑ 121 Mike Piazza GEN	.75	.35
❑ 122 Greg Maddux GEN	.75	.35
❑ 123 Cal Ripken GEN	1.25	.55
❑ 124 Chipper Jones GEN	.60	.25
❑ 125 Derek Jeter GEN	1.25	.55
❑ 126 Tony Gwynn GEN	.60	.25
❑ 127 Andruw Jones GEN	.25	.11
❑ 128 Juan Gonzalez GEN	.25	.11
❑ 129 Jeff Bagwell GEN	.40	.18
❑ 130 Mark McGwire GEN	1.25	.55
❑ 131 Roger Clemens GEN	.75	.35
❑ 132 Albert Belle GEN	.15	.07
❑ 133 Barry Bonds GEN	.75	.35
❑ 134 Kenny Lofton GEN	.15	.07
❑ 135 Ivan Rodriguez GEN	.25	.11
❑ 136 Manny Ramirez GEN	.40	.18
❑ 137 Jim Thome GEN	.25	.11
❑ 138 C.Knoblauch GEN	.15	.07
❑ 139 Paul Molitor GEN	.25	.11
❑ 140 Barry Larkin GEN	.25	.11
❑ 141 Mo Vaughn GEN	.25	.11
❑ 142 Hideki Irabu GEN	.15	.07
❑ 143 Jose Cruz Jr. GEN	.15	.07
❑ 144 Tony Clark GEN	.25	.11
❑ 145 V.Guerrero GEN	.40	.18
❑ 146 Scott Rolen GEN	.60	.25
❑ 147 N.Garciaparra GEN	.75	.35
❑ 148 Nomar Garciaparra CL	.75	.35
❑ 149 Larry Walker CL	.40	.18
❑ 150 Tino Martinez CL	.15	.07
❑ AU2 F.Thomas AUTO/100	150.00	70.00

2001 Donruss Elite

	MINT	NRMT
COMPLETE SET (250)		
COMP.SET w/o SP's (150)	40.00	18.00
COMMON CARD (1-150)	.40	.18
COMMON CARD (151-200)	10.00	4.50
COMMON COUPON (201-250)	5.00	2.20

Card	MINT	NRMT
❑ 1 Alex Rodriguez	2.50	1.10
❑ 2 Barry Bonds	2.50	1.10
❑ 3 Cal Ripken	4.00	1.80
❑ 4 Chipper Jones	2.00	.90
❑ 5 Derek Jeter	4.00	1.80
❑ 6 Troy Glaus	1.00	.45
❑ 7 Frank Thomas	1.25	.55
❑ 8 Greg Maddux	2.50	1.10
❑ 9 Ivan Rodriguez	1.00	.45
❑ 10 Jeff Bagwell	1.25	.55
❑ 11 Jose Canseco	1.00	.45
❑ 12 Todd Helton	1.25	.55
❑ 13 Ken Griffey Jr.	3.00	1.35
❑ 14 Manny Ramirez	1.25	.55

Card	MINT	NRMT
❑ 15 Mark McGwire	4.00	1.80
❑ 16 Mike Piazza	2.50	1.10
❑ 17 Nomar Garciaparra	2.50	1.10
❑ 18 Pedro Martinez	1.25	.55
❑ 19 Randy Johnson	1.25	.55
❑ 20 Rick Ankiel	.60	.25
❑ 21 Rickey Henderson	2.00	.90
❑ 22 Roger Clemens	2.50	1.10
❑ 23 Sammy Sosa	2.00	.90
❑ 24 Tony Gwynn	2.00	.90
❑ 25 Vladimir Guerrero	1.25	.55
❑ 26 Eric Davis	.40	.18
❑ 27 Roberto Alomar	1.00	.45
❑ 28 Mark Mulder	.60	.25
❑ 29 Pat Burrell	.40	.18
❑ 30 Harold Baines	.40	.18
❑ 31 Carlos Delgado	1.00	.45
❑ 32 J.D. Drew	1.00	.45
❑ 33 Jim Edmonds	.60	.25
❑ 34 Darin Erstad	1.00	.45
❑ 35 Jason Giambi	1.00	.45
❑ 36 Tom Glavine	1.00	.45
❑ 37 Juan Gonzalez	1.00	.45
❑ 38 Mark Grace	1.00	.45
❑ 39 Shawn Green	1.00	.45
❑ 40 Tim Hudson	1.00	.45
❑ 41 Andruw Jones	1.00	.45
❑ 42 David Justice	.40	.18
❑ 43 Jeff Kent	.60	.25
❑ 44 Barry Larkin	1.00	.45
❑ 45 Pokey Reese	.40	.18
❑ 46 Mike Mussina	1.00	.45
❑ 47 Hideo Nomo	1.00	.45
❑ 48 Rafael Palmeiro	1.00	.45
❑ 49 Adam Piatt	.40	.18
❑ 50 Scott Rolen	1.00	.45
❑ 51 Gary Sheffield	.40	.18
❑ 52 Bernie Williams	1.00	.45
❑ 53 Bob Abreu	.40	.18
❑ 54 Edgardo Alfonzo	.40	.18
❑ 55 Jermaine Clark RC	.60	.25
❑ 56 Albert Belle	.40	.18
❑ 57 Craig Biggio	.60	.25
❑ 58 Andres Galarraga	.60	.25
❑ 59 Edgar Martinez	.60	.25
❑ 60 Fred McGriff	.60	.25
❑ 61 Magglio Ordonez	.40	.18
❑ 62 Jim Thome	1.00	.45
❑ 63 Matt Williams	.60	.25
❑ 64 Kerry Wood	1.00	.45
❑ 65 Moises Alou	.40	.18
❑ 66 Brady Anderson	.40	.18
❑ 67 Garret Anderson	.40	.18
❑ 68 Tony Armas Jr.	.40	.18
❑ 69 Tony Batista	.40	.18
❑ 70 Jose Cruz Jr.	.40	.18
❑ 71 Carlos Beltran	.40	.18
❑ 72 Adrian Beltre	.40	.18
❑ 73 Kris Benson	.40	.18
❑ 74 Lance Berkman	1.00	.45
❑ 75 Kevin Brown	.40	.18
❑ 76 Jay Buhner	.40	.18
❑ 77 Jeromy Burnitz	.40	.18
❑ 78 Ken Caminiti	.40	.18
❑ 79 Sean Casey	.60	.25
❑ 80 Luis Castillo	.40	.18
❑ 81 Eric Chavez	.40	.18

- 82 Jeff Cirillo .40 .18
- 83 Bartolo Colon .40 .18
- 84 David Cone .40 .18
- 85 Freddy Garcia .40 .18
- 86 Johnny Damon .40 .18
- 87 Ray Durham .40 .18
- 88 Jermaine Dye .40 .18
- 89 Juan Encarnacion .40 .18
- 90 Terrence Long .40 .18
- 91 Carl Everett .40 .18
- 92 Steve Finley .40 .18
- 93 Cliff Floyd .40 .18
- 94 Brad Fullmer .40 .18
- 95 Brian Giles .40 .18
- 96 Luis Gonzalez 1.00 .45
- 97 Rusty Greer .40 .18
- 98 Jeffrey Hammonds .40 .18
- 99 Mike Hampton .40 .18
- 100 Orlando Hernandez .40 .18
- 101 Richard Hidalgo .40 .18
- 102 Geoff Jenkins .40 .18
- 103 Jacque Jones .40 .18
- 104 Brian Jordan .40 .18
- 105 Gabe Kapler .40 .18
- 106 Eric Karros .40 .18
- 107 Jason Kendall .40 .18
- 108 Adam Kennedy .40 .18
- 109 Byung-Hyun Kim .40 .18
- 110 Ryan Klesko .40 .18
- 111 Chuck Knoblauch .40 .18
- 112 Paul Konerko .40 .18
- 113 Carlos Lee .40 .18
- 114 Kenny Lofton .40 .18
- 115 Javy Lopez .40 .18
- 116 Tino Martinez .40 .18
- 117 Ruben Mateo .40 .18
- 118 Kevin Millwood .40 .18
- 119 Ben Molina .40 .18
- 120 Raul Mondesi .40 .18
- 121 Trot Nixon .40 .18
- 122 John Olerud .40 .18
- 123 Paul O'Neill 1.00 .45
- 124 Chan Ho Park .40 .18
- 125 Andy Pettitte .40 .18
- 126 Jorge Posada .40 .18
- 127 Mark Quinn .40 .18
- 128 Aramis Ramirez .40 .18
- 129 Mariano Rivera .40 .18
- 130 Tim Salmon .40 .18
- 131 Curt Schilling 1.00 .45
- 132 Richie Sexson .40 .18
- 133 John Smoltz .40 .18
- 134 J.T. Snow .40 .18
- 135 Jay Payton .40 .18
- 136 Shannon Stewart .40 .18
- 137 B.J. Surhoff .40 .18
- 138 Mike Sweeney .40 .18
- 139 Fernando Tatis .40 .18
- 140 Miguel Tejada .40 .18
- 141 Jason Varitek .40 .18
- 142 Greg Vaughn .40 .18
- 143 Mo Vaughn .40 .18
- 144 Robin Ventura UER .40 .18
  Listed as playing for Yankees last 2 years, Also Bat and Throw information is wrong
- 145 Jose Vidro .40 .18
- 146 Omar Vizquel .40 .18
- 147 Larry Walker .60 .25
- 148 David Wells .40 .18
- 149 Rondell White .40 .18
- 150 Preston Wilson .40 .18
- 151 Brent Abernathy SP 10.00 4.50
- 152 Cory Aldridge SP RC 10.00 4.50
- 153 Gene Altman SP RC 10.00 4.50
- 154 Josh Beckett SP 15.00 6.75
- 155 Wilson Betemit SP RC 25.00 11.00
- 156 Albert Pujols SP RC 100.00 45.00
- 157 Joe Crede SP 10.00 4.50
- 158 Jack Cust SP 10.00 4.50
- 159 Ben Sheets SP 10.00 4.50
- 160 Alex Escobar SP 10.00 4.50
- 161 Adrian Hernandez SP RC 10.00 4.50
- 162 Pedro Feliz SP 10.00 4.50
- 163 Nate Frese SP RC 10.00 4.50
- 164 Carlos Garcia SP RC 10.00 4.50
- 165 Marcus Giles SP 10.00 4.50
- 166 Alexis Gomez SP RC 10.00 4.50
- 167 Jason Hart SP 10.00 4.50
- 168 Aubrey Huff SP 10.00 4.50
- 169 Cesar Izturis SP 10.00 4.50
- 170 Nick Johnson SP 10.00 4.50
- 171 Jack Wilson SP RC 10.00 4.50
- 172 Brian Lawrence SP RC 10.00 4.50
- 173 Christian Parker SP RC 10.00 4.50
- 174 Nick Maness SP RC 10.00 4.50
- 175 Jose Mieses SP RC 10.00 4.50
- 176 Greg Miller SP RC 10.00 4.50
- 177 Eric Munson SP 10.00 4.50
- 178 Xavier Nady SP 10.00 4.50
- 179 Blaine Neal SP RC 10.00 4.50
- 180 Abraham Nunez SP 10.00 4.50
- 181 Jose Ortiz SP 10.00 4.50
- 182 Jeremy Owens SP RC 10.00 4.50
- 183 Jay Gibbons SP RC 12.00 5.50
- 184 Corey Patterson SP 10.00 4.50
- 185 Carlos Pena SP 10.00 4.50
- 186 C.C. Sabathia SP 10.00 4.50
- 187 Timo Perez SP 10.00 4.50
- 188 Adam Pettyjohn SP RC 10.00 4.50
- 189 Donaldo Mendez SP RC 10.00 4.50
- 190 Jackson Melian SP RC 10.00 4.50
- 191 Wilkin Ruan SP RC 10.00 4.50
- 192 Duaner Sanchez SP RC 10.00 4.50
- 193 Alfonso Soriano SP 15.00 6.75
- 194 Rafael Soriano SP RC 10.00 4.50
- 195 Ichiro Suzuki SP RC 200.00 90.00
- 196 Billy Sylvester SP RC 10.00 4.50
- 197 Juan Uribe SP RC 15.00 6.75
- 198 Tsuyoshi Shinjo SP RC 25.00 11.00
- 199 C. Valderrama SP RC 10.00 4.50
- 200 Matt White SP RC 10.00 4.50
- 201 Adam Dunn EXCH 20.00 9.00
- 202 Joe Kennedy EXCH 8.00 3.60
- 203 Mike Rivera EXCH 5.00 2.20
- 204 Erick Almonte EXCH 5.00 2.20
- 205 B. Duckworth EXCH 15.00 6.75
- 206 Victor Martinez EXCH 5.00 2.20
- 207 Rick Bauer EXCH 5.00 2.20
- 208 Jeff Deardorff EXCH 5.00 2.20
- 209 Antonio Perez EXCH 8.00 3.60
- 210 Bill Hall EXCH 5.00 2.20
- 211 Dennis Tankersley EXCH 10.00 4.50
- 212 Jeremy Affeldt EXCH 5.00 2.20
- 213 Junior Spivey EXCH 5.00 2.20
- 214 Casey Fossum EXCH 5.00 2.20
- 215 Brandon Lyon EXCH 5.00 2.20
- 216 Angel Santos EXCH 5.00 2.20
- 217 Cody Ransom EXCH 5.00 2.20
- 218 Jason Lane EXCH 10.00 4.50
- 219 David Williams EXCH 5.00 2.20
- 220 Alex Herrera EXCH 5.00 2.20
- 221 Ryan Drese EXCH 5.00 2.20
- 222 Travis Hafner EXCH 5.00 2.20
- 223 Bud Smith EXCH 30.00 13.50
- 224 Johnny Estrada EXCH 10.00 4.50
- 225 Ricardo Rodriguez EXCH 8.00 3.60
- 226 Brandon Berger EXCH 5.00 2.20
- 227 Claudio Vargas EXCH 5.00 2.20
- 228 Luis Garcia EXCH 5.00 2.20
- 229 Marlon Byrd EXCH 12.00 5.50
- 230 Hee Seop Choi EXCH 15.00 6.75
- 231 Corky Miller EXCH 5.00 2.20
- 232 J. Duchscherer EXCH 5.00 2.20
- 233 T. Spooneybarger EXCH 8.00 3.60
- 234 Roy Oswalt EXCH 10.00 4.50
- 235 Willie Harris EXCH 5.00 2.20
- 236 Josh Towers EXCH 15.00 6.75
- 237 Juan A.Pena EXCH 5.00 2.20
- 238 Alfredo Amezaga EXCH 5.00 2.20
- 239 Geronimo Gil EXCH 5.00 2.20
- 240 Juan Cruz EXCH 25.00 11.00
- 241 Ed Rogers EXCH 8.00 3.60
- 242 Joe Thurston EXCH 5.00 2.20
- 243 Orlando Hudson EXCH 5.00 2.20
- 244 John Buck EXCH 5.00 2.20
- 245 Martin Vargas EXCH 5.00 2.20
- 246 David Brous EXCH 5.00 2.20
- 247 Dewon Brazelton EXCH 15.00 6.75
- 248 Mark Prior EXCH 50.00 22.00
- 249 Angel Berroa EXCH 5.00 2.20
- 250 Mark Teixeira EXCH 60.00 27.00

1997 Donruss Signature

	MINT	NRMT
COMPLETE SET (100)	50.00	22.00

- 1 Mark McGwire 4.00 1.80
- 2 Kenny Lofton .40 .18
- 3 Tony Gwynn 2.00 .90
- 4 Tony Clark .40 .18
- 5 Tim Salmon .40 .18
- 6 Ken Griffey Jr. 3.00 1.35
- 7 Mike Piazza 2.50 1.10
- 8 Greg Maddux 2.50 1.10
- 9 Roberto Alomar 1.00 .45
- 10 Andres Galarraga .60 .25
- 11 Roger Clemens 2.50 1.10
- 12 Bernie Williams 1.00 .45
- 13 Rondell White .40 .18
- 14 Kevin Appier .40 .18
- 15 Ray Lankford .25 .11
- 16 Frank Thomas 1.25 .55
- 17 Will Clark 1.00 .45
- 18 Chipper Jones 2.00 .90
- 19 Jeff Bagwell 1.25 .55
- 20 Manny Ramirez 1.25 .55
- 21 Ryne Sandberg 1.25 .55
- 22 Paul Molitor 1.00 .45
- 23 Gary Sheffield .40 .18
- 24 Jim Edmonds .60 .25
- 25 Barry Larkin 1.00 .45
- 26 Rafael Palmeiro 1.00 .45
- 27 Alan Benes .25 .11
- 28 Dave Justice .40 .18
- 29 Randy Johnson 1.25 .55
- 30 Barry Bonds 2.50 1.10
- 31 Mo Vaughn .40 .18
- 32 Michael Tucker .25 .11
- 33 Larry Walker .60 .25
- 34 Tino Martinez .40 .18
- 35 Jose Guillen .25 .11
- 36 Carlos Delgado 1.00 .45
- 37 Jason Dickson .25 .11
- 38 Tom Glavine 1.00 .45
- 39 Raul Mondesi .40 .18
- 40 Jose Cruz Jr. RC 2.50 1.10
- 41 Johnny Damon .40 .18
- 42 Mark Grace 1.00 .45
- 43 Juan Gonzalez 1.00 .45
- 44 Vladimir Guerrero 1.50 .70
- 45 Kevin Brown .40 .18
- 46 Justin Thompson .25 .11
- 47 Eric Young .25 .11
- 48 Ron Coomer .25 .11
- 49 Mark Kotsay RC .75 .35
- 50 Scott Rolen 1.00 .45
- 51 Derek Jeter 4.00 1.80
- 52 Jim Thome 1.00 .45
- 53 Fred McGriff .60 .25
- 54 Albert Belle .40 .18
- 55 Garret Anderson .40 .18
- 56 Wilton Guerrero .25 .11
- 57 Jose Canseco 1.00 .45
- 58 Cal Ripken 4.00 1.80
- 59 Sammy Sosa 2.00 .90
- 60 Dmitri Young .40 .18

		MINT	NRMT
❑ 61	Alex Rodriguez	2.50	1.10
❑ 62	Javier Lopez	.40	.18
❑ 63	Sandy Alomar Jr.	.40	.18
❑ 64	Joe Carter	.40	.18
❑ 65	Dante Bichette	.40	.18
❑ 66	Al Martin	.25	.11
❑ 67	Darin Erstad	1.00	.45
❑ 68	Pokey Reese	.25	.11
❑ 69	Brady Anderson	.40	.18
❑ 70	Andruw Jones	1.25	.55
❑ 71	Ivan Rodriguez	1.00	.45
❑ 72	Nomar Garciaparra	2.50	1.10
❑ 73	Moises Alou	.40	.18
❑ 74	Andy Pettitte	.40	.18
❑ 75	Jay Buhner	.40	.18
❑ 76	Craig Biggio	.60	.25
❑ 77	Wade Boggs	1.00	.45
❑ 78	Shawn Estes	.40	.18
❑ 79	Neifi Perez	.25	.11
❑ 80	Rusty Greer	.40	.18
❑ 81	Pedro Martinez	1.25	.55
❑ 82	Mike Mussina	1.00	.45
❑ 83	Jason Giambi	1.00	.45
❑ 84	Hideo Nomo	1.00	.45
❑ 85	Todd Hundley	.25	.11
❑ 86	Deion Sanders	.40	.18
❑ 87	Mike Cameron	.40	.18
❑ 88	Bobby Bonilla	.40	.18
❑ 89	Todd Greene	.25	.11
❑ 90	Kevin Orie	.25	.11
❑ 91	Ken Caminiti	.40	.18
❑ 92	Chuck Knoblauch	.40	.18
❑ 93	Matt Morris	.40	.18
❑ 94	Matt Williams	.60	.25
❑ 95	Pat Hentgen	.25	.11
❑ 96	John Smoltz	.40	.18
❑ 97	Edgar Martinez	.60	.25
❑ 98	Jason Kendall	.40	.18
❑ 99	Ken Griffey Jr. CL	1.50	.70
❑ 100	Frank Thomas CL	.60	.25

1998 Donruss Signature

	MINT	NRMT
COMPLETE SET (140)	120.00	55.00

		MINT	NRMT
❑ 1	David Justice	.40	.18
❑ 2	Derek Jeter	4.00	1.80
❑ 3	Nomar Garciaparra	2.50	1.10
❑ 4	Ryan Klesko	.40	.18
❑ 5	Jeff Bagwell	1.25	.55
❑ 6	Dante Bichette	.40	.18
❑ 7	Ivan Rodriguez	1.00	.45
❑ 8	Albert Belle	.40	.18
❑ 9	Cal Ripken	4.00	1.80
❑ 10	Craig Biggio	.60	.25
❑ 11	Barry Larkin	1.00	.45
❑ 12	Jose Guillen	.25	.11
❑ 13	Will Clark	1.00	.45
❑ 14	J.T. Snow	.40	.18
❑ 15	Chuck Knoblauch	.40	.18
❑ 16	Todd Walker	.25	.11
❑ 17	Scott Rolen	1.00	.45
❑ 18	Rickey Henderson	2.00	.90
❑ 19	Juan Gonzalez	1.00	.45
❑ 20	Justin Thompson	.25	.11
❑ 21	Roger Clemens	2.50	1.10
❑ 22	Ray Lankford	.25	.11
❑ 23	Jose Cruz Jr.	.40	.18
❑ 24	Ken Griffey Jr.	3.00	1.35
❑ 25	Andruw Jones	1.00	.45
❑ 26	Darin Erstad	1.00	.45
❑ 27	Jim Thome	1.00	.45
❑ 28	Wade Boggs	1.00	.45
❑ 29	Ken Caminiti	.40	.18
❑ 30	Todd Hundley	.25	.11
❑ 31	Mike Piazza	2.50	1.10
❑ 32	Sammy Sosa	2.00	.90
❑ 33	Larry Walker	.60	.25
❑ 34	Matt Williams	.60	.25
❑ 35	Frank Thomas	1.25	.55
❑ 36	Gary Sheffield	.40	.18
❑ 37	Alex Rodriguez	2.50	1.10
❑ 38	Hideo Nomo	1.00	.45
❑ 39	Kenny Lofton	.40	.18
❑ 40	John Smoltz	.40	.18
❑ 41	Mo Vaughn	.40	.18
❑ 42	Edgar Martinez	.60	.25
❑ 43	Paul Molitor	1.00	.45
❑ 44	Rafael Palmeiro	1.00	.45
❑ 45	Barry Bonds	2.50	1.10
❑ 46	Vladimir Guerrero	1.25	.55
❑ 47	Carlos Delgado	1.00	.45
❑ 48	Bobby Higginson	.40	.18
❑ 49	Greg Maddux	2.50	1.10
❑ 50	Jim Edmonds	.60	.25
❑ 51	Randy Johnson	1.25	.55
❑ 52	Mark McGwire	4.00	1.80
❑ 53	Rondell White	.40	.18
❑ 54	Raul Mondesi	.40	.18
❑ 55	Manny Ramirez	1.25	.55
❑ 56	Pedro Martinez	1.25	.55
❑ 57	Tim Salmon	.40	.18
❑ 58	Moises Alou	.40	.18
❑ 59	Fred McGriff	.60	.25
❑ 60	Garret Anderson	.40	.18
❑ 61	Sandy Alomar Jr.	.40	.18
❑ 62	Chan Ho Park	.40	.18
❑ 63	Mark Kotsay	.40	.18
❑ 64	Mike Mussina	1.00	.45
❑ 65	Tom Glavine	1.00	.45
❑ 66	Tony Clark	.40	.18
❑ 67	Mark Grace	1.00	.45
❑ 68	Tony Gwynn	2.00	.90
❑ 69	Tino Martinez	.40	.18
❑ 70	Kevin Brown	.60	.25
❑ 71	Todd Greene	.25	.11
❑ 72	Andy Pettitte	.40	.18
❑ 73	Livan Hernandez	.25	.11
❑ 74	Curt Schilling	1.00	.45
❑ 75	Andres Galarraga	.60	.25
❑ 76	Rusty Greer	.40	.18
❑ 77	Jay Buhner	.40	.18
❑ 78	Bobby Bonilla	.40	.18
❑ 79	Chipper Jones	2.00	.90
❑ 80	Eric Young	.25	.11
❑ 81	Jason Giambi	1.00	.45
❑ 82	Javy Lopez	.40	.18
❑ 83	Roberto Alomar	1.00	.45
❑ 84	Bernie Williams	1.00	.45
❑ 85	A.J. Hinch	.25	.11
❑ 86	Kerry Wood	1.00	.45
❑ 87	Juan Encarnacion	.40	.18
❑ 88	Brad Fullmer	.40	.18
❑ 89	Ben Grieve	.40	.18
❑ 90	Magglio Ordonez RC	8.00	3.60
❑ 91	Todd Helton	1.25	.55
❑ 92	Richard Hidalgo	.40	.18
❑ 93	Paul Konerko	.40	.18
❑ 94	Aramis Ramirez	.40	.18
❑ 95	Ricky Ledee	.25	.11
❑ 96	Derrek Lee	.40	.18
❑ 97	Travis Lee	.40	.18
❑ 98	Matt Anderson RC	.40	.18
❑ 99	Jaret Wright	.25	.11
❑ 100	David Ortiz	.40	.18
❑ 101	Carl Pavano	.25	.11
❑ 102	O.Hernandez RC	2.50	1.10
❑ 103	Fernando Tatis	.25	.11
❑ 104	Miguel Tejada	.60	.25
❑ 105	Rolando Arrojo RC	1.50	.70
❑ 106	Kevin Millwood RC	2.00	.90
❑ 107	Ken Griffey Jr. CL	1.50	.70
❑ 108	Frank Thomas CL	.60	.25
❑ 109	Cal Ripken CL	2.00	.90
❑ 110	Greg Maddux CL	1.25	.55
❑ 111	John Olerud	.40	.18
❑ 112	David Cone	.40	.18
❑ 113	Vinny Castilla	.40	.18
❑ 114	Jason Kendall	.40	.18
❑ 115	Brian Jordan	.40	.18
❑ 116	Hideki Irabu	.25	.11
❑ 117	Bartolo Colon	.40	.18
❑ 118	Greg Vaughn	.40	.18
❑ 119	David Segui	.25	.11
❑ 120	Bruce Chen	.25	.11
❑ 121	Julio Ramirez RC	.40	.18
❑ 122	Troy Glaus RC	15.00	6.75
❑ 123	Jeremy Giambi RC	1.50	.70
❑ 124	Ryan Minor RC	.40	.18
❑ 125	Richie Sexson	.40	.18
❑ 126	Dermal Brown	.25	.11
❑ 127	Adrian Beltre	.40	.18
❑ 128	Eric Chavez	.40	.18
❑ 129	J.D. Drew RC	15.00	6.75
❑ 130	Gabe Kapler RC	3.00	1.35
❑ 131	Masato Yoshii RC	1.50	.70
❑ 132	Mike Lowell RC	2.50	1.10
❑ 133	Jim Parque RC	1.00	.45
❑ 134	Roy Halladay	.25	.11
❑ 135	Carlos Lee RC	3.00	1.35
❑ 136	Jin Ho Cho RC	.40	.18
❑ 137	Michael Barrett	.25	.11
❑ 138	F.Seguignol RC	.40	.18
❑ 139	Odalis Perez RC UER.. Back pictures John Rocker	1.00	.45
❑ 140	Mark McGwire CL	2.00	.90

2001 Donruss Signature

	MINT	NRMT
COMP.SET w/o SP'S (110)	50.00	22.00
COMMON CARD (1-110)	.75	.35
COMMON CARD (111-165)	15.00	6.75
COMMON CARD (166-311)	8.00	3.60

		MINT	NRMT
❑ 1	Alex Rodriguez	5.00	2.20
❑ 2	Barry Bonds	5.00	2.20
❑ 3	Cal Ripken	8.00	3.60
❑ 4	Chipper Jones	4.00	1.80
❑ 5	Derek Jeter	8.00	3.60
❑ 6	Troy Glaus	2.00	.90
❑ 7	Frank Thomas	2.50	1.10
❑ 8	Greg Maddux	5.00	2.20
❑ 9	Ivan Rodriguez	2.00	.90
❑ 10	Jeff Bagwell	2.50	1.10
❑ 11	John Olerud	.75	.35
❑ 12	Todd Helton	2.50	1.10
❑ 13	Ken Griffey Jr.	6.00	2.70
❑ 14	Manny Ramirez	2.50	1.10
❑ 15	Mark McGwire	8.00	3.60
❑ 16	Mike Piazza	5.00	2.20
❑ 17	Nomar Garciaparra	5.00	2.20
❑ 18	Moises Alou	.75	.35
❑ 19	Aramis Ramirez	.75	.35
❑ 20	Curt Schilling	2.00	.90
❑ 21	Pat Burrell	.75	.35
❑ 22	Doug Mientkiewicz	.75	.35
❑ 23	Carlos Delgado	2.00	.90
❑ 24	J.D. Drew	2.00	.90
❑ 25	Cliff Floyd	.75	.35
❑ 26	Freddy Garcia	.75	.35

❑	27	Roberto Alomar	2.00	.90
❑	28	Barry Zito	2.00	.90
❑	29	Juan Encarnacion	.75	.35
❑	30	Paul Konerko	.75	.35
❑	31	Mark Mulder	1.25	.55
❑	32	Andy Pettitte	.75	.35
❑	33	Jim Edmonds	1.25	.55
❑	34	Darin Erstad	2.00	.90
❑	35	Jason Giambi	2.00	.90
❑	36	Tom Glavine	2.00	.90
❑	37	Juan Gonzalez	2.00	.90
❑	38	Fred McGriff	1.25	.55
❑	39	Shawn Green	2.00	.90
❑	40	Tim Hudson	2.00	.90
❑	41	Andruw Jones	2.00	.90
❑	42	Jeff Kent	1.25	.55
❑	43	Barry Larkin	2.00	.90
❑	44	Brad Radke	.75	.35
❑	45	Mike Mussina	2.00	.90
❑	46	Hideo Nomo	2.00	.90
❑	47	Rafael Palmeiro	2.00	.90
❑	48	Scott Rolen	2.00	.90
❑	49	Gary Sheffield	.75	.35
❑	50	Bernie Williams	2.00	.90
❑	51	Bob Abreu	.75	.35
❑	52	Edgardo Alfonzo	.75	.35
❑	53	Edgar Martinez	1.25	.55
❑	54	Magglio Ordonez	.75	.35
❑	55	Kerry Wood	2.00	.90
❑	56	Adrian Beltre	.75	.35
❑	57	Lance Berkman	2.00	.90
❑	58	Kevin Brown	2.00	.90
❑	59	Sean Casey	1.25	.55
❑	60	Eric Chavez	.75	.35
❑	61	Bartolo Colon	.75	.35
❑	62	Sammy Sosa	4.00	1.80
❑	63	Jermaine Dye	.75	.35
❑	64	Tony Gwynn	4.00	1.80
❑	65	Carl Everett	.75	.35
❑	66	Brian Giles	.75	.35
❑	67	Mike Hampton	.75	.35
❑	68	Richard Hidalgo	.75	.35
❑	69	Geoff Jenkins	.75	.35
❑	70	Tony Clark	.75	.35
❑	71	Roger Clemens	5.00	2.20
❑	72	Ryan Klesko	.75	.35
❑	73	Chan Ho Park	.75	.35
❑	74	Richie Sexson	.75	.35
❑	75	Mike Sweeney	.75	.35
❑	76	Kazuhiro Sasaki	2.00	.90
❑	77	Miguel Tejada	.75	.35
❑	78	Jose Vidro	.75	.35
❑	79	Larry Walker	.75	.35
❑	80	Preston Wilson	.75	.35
❑	81	Craig Biggio	1.25	.55
❑	82	Andres Galarraga	1.25	.55
❑	83	Jim Thome	2.00	.90
❑	84	Vladimir Guerrero	2.50	1.10
❑	85	Rafael Furcal	.75	.35
❑	86	Cristian Guzman	.75	.35
❑	87	Terrence Long	.75	.35
❑	88	Bret Boone	.75	.35
❑	89	Wade Miller	.75	.35
❑	90	Eric Milton	.75	.35
❑	91	Gabe Kapler	.75	.35
❑	92	Johnny Damon	.75	.35
❑	93	Carlos Lee	.75	.35
❑	94	Kenny Lofton	.75	.35
❑	95	Raul Mondesi	.75	.35
❑	96	Jorge Posada	.75	.35
❑	97	Mark Grace	2.00	.90
❑	98	Robert Fick	.75	.35
❑	99	Joe Mays	.75	.35
❑	100	Aaron Sele	.75	.35
❑	101	Ben Grieve	.75	.35
❑	102	Luis Gonzalez	2.00	.90
❑	103	Ray Durham	.75	.35
❑	104	Mark Quinn	.75	.35
❑	105	Jose Canseco	2.00	.90
❑	106	David Justice	1.25	.55
❑	107	Pedro Martinez	2.50	1.10
❑	108	Randy Johnson	2.50	1.10
❑	109	Phil Nevin	.75	.35
❑	110	Rickey Henderson	4.00	1.80
❑	111	Alex Escobar AU	15.00	6.75
❑	112	Johnny Estrada AU RC	30.00	13.50
❑	113	Pedro Feliz AU	15.00	6.75
❑	114	Nate Frese AU RC	15.00	6.75
❑	115	R. Rodriguez AU RC	25.00	11.00
❑	116	Brandon Larson AU RC	15.00	6.75
❑	117	Alexis Gomez AU RC	15.00	6.75
❑	118	Jason Hart AU	20.00	9.00
❑	119	C.C. Sabathia AU	30.00	13.50
❑	120	Endy Chavez AU RC	15.00	6.75
❑	121	Christian Parker AU RC	15.00	6.75
❑	122	Jackson Melian RC	10.00	4.50
❑	123	Joe Kennedy AU RC	25.00	11.00
❑	124	Adrian Hernandez AU RC	15.00	6.75
❑	125	Cesar Izturis AU	15.00	6.75
❑	126	Jose Mieses AU RC	15.00	6.75
❑	127	Roy Oswalt AU	40.00	18.00
❑	128	Eric Munson AU	20.00	9.00
❑	129	Xavier Nady AU	20.00	9.00
❑	130	Horacio Ramirez AU RC	15.00	6.75
❑	131	Abraham Nunez AU	15.00	6.75
❑	132	Jose Ortiz AU	20.00	9.00
❑	133	Jeremy Owens AU RC	15.00	6.75
❑	134	Claudio Vargas AU RC	15.00	6.75
❑	135	Corey Patterson AU	25.00	11.00
❑	136	Carlos Pena	10.00	4.50
❑	137	Bud Smith AU RC	60.00	27.00
❑	138	Adam Dunn AU	50.00	22.00
❑	139	Adam Pettyjohn AU RC	15.00	6.75
❑	140	Elpidio Guzman AU RC	15.00	6.75
❑	141	Jay Gibbons AU RC	25.00	11.00
❑	142	Wilkin Ruan AU RC	15.00	6.75
❑	143	Tsuyoshi Shinjo RC	50.00	22.00
❑	144	Alfonso Soriano AU	40.00	18.00
❑	145	Marcus Giles AU	25.00	11.00
❑	146	Ichiro Suzuki RC	200.00	90.00
❑	147	Juan Uribe AU RC	30.00	13.50
❑	148	David Williams AU RC	25.00	11.00
❑	149	C. Valderrama AU RC	15.00	6.75
❑	150	Matt White AU RC	15.00	6.75
❑	151	Albert Pujols AU RC	200.00	90.00
❑	152	Donaldo Mendez AU RC	15.00	6.75
❑	153	Cory Aldridge AU RC	15.00	6.75
❑	154	B. Duckworth AU RC	40.00	18.00
❑	155	Josh Beckett AU	40.00	18.00
❑	156	Wilson Betemit AU RC	50.00	22.00
❑	157	Ben Sheets AU	20.00	9.00
❑	158	Andres Torres AU RC	15.00	6.75
❑	159	Aubrey Huff AU	15.00	6.75
❑	160	Jack Wilson AU RC	15.00	6.75
❑	161	Rafael Soriano AU RC	25.00	11.00
❑	162	Nick Johnson AU	25.00	11.00
❑	163	Carlos Garcia AU RC	15.00	6.75
❑	164	Josh Towers AU RC	30.00	13.50
❑	165	Jason Michaels AU RC	15.00	6.75
❑	166	Ryan Drese RC	8.00	3.60
❑	167	Dewon Brazelton RC	15.00	6.75
❑	168	Kevin Olsen RC	8.00	3.60
❑	169	Benito Baez RC	8.00	3.60
❑	170	Mark Prior RC	40.00	18.00
❑	171	Wilmy Caceres RC	8.00	3.60
❑	172	Mark Teixeira RC	50.00	22.00
❑	173	Willie Harris RC	8.00	3.60
❑	174	Mike Koplove RC	8.00	3.60
❑	175	Brandon Knight RC	8.00	3.60
❑	176	John Grabow RC	8.00	3.60
❑	177	Jeremy Affeldt RC	8.00	3.60
❑	178	Brandon Inge	8.00	3.60
❑	179	Casey Fossum RC	12.00	5.50
❑	180	Scott Stewart RC	8.00	3.60
❑	181	Luke Hudson RC	8.00	3.60
❑	182	Ken Vining RC	8.00	3.60
❑	183	Toby Hall	8.00	3.60
❑	184	Eric Knott RC	8.00	3.60
❑	185	Kris Foster RC	8.00	3.60
❑	186	David Brous RC	8.00	3.60
❑	187	Roy Smith RC	8.00	3.60
❑	188	Grant Balfour RC	8.00	3.60
❑	189	Jeremy Fikac RC	8.00	3.60
❑	190	Morgan Ensberg RC	12.00	5.50
❑	191	Ryan Freel RC	8.00	3.60
❑	192	Ryan Jensen RC	8.00	3.60
❑	193	Lance Davis RC	8.00	3.60
❑	194	Delvin James RC	8.00	3.60
❑	195	Timo Perez	8.00	3.60
❑	196	Michael Cuddyer	8.00	3.60
❑	197	Bob File RC	8.00	3.60
❑	198	Martin Vargas RC	8.00	3.60
❑	199	Kris Keller RC	8.00	3.60
❑	200	Tim Spooneybarger RC	8.00	3.60
❑	201	Adam Everett	8.00	3.60
❑	202	Josh Fogg RC	8.00	3.60
❑	203	Kip Wells	8.00	3.60
❑	204	Rick Bauer RC	8.00	3.60
❑	205	Brent Abernathy	8.00	3.60
❑	206	Erick Almonte RC	10.00	4.50
❑	207	Pedro Santana RC	8.00	3.60
❑	208	Ken Harvey	8.00	3.60
❑	209	Jerrod Riggan RC	8.00	3.60
❑	210	Nick Punto RC	8.00	3.60
❑	211	Steve Green RC	8.00	3.60
❑	212	Nick Neugebauer	15.00	6.75
❑	213	Chris George	8.00	3.60
❑	214	Mike Penney RC	8.00	3.60
❑	215	Bret Prinz RC	8.00	3.60
❑	216	Tim Christman RC	8.00	3.60
❑	217	Sean Douglass RC	8.00	3.60
❑	218	Brett Jodie RC	8.00	3.60
❑	219	Juan Diaz RC	8.00	3.60
❑	220	Carlos Hernandez	8.00	3.60
❑	221	Alex Cintron	8.00	3.60
❑	222	Juan Cruz RC	20.00	9.00
❑	223	Larry Bigbie	8.00	3.60
❑	224	Junior Spivey RC	8.00	3.60
❑	225	Luis Rivas	8.00	3.60
❑	226	Brandon Lyon RC	10.00	4.50
❑	227	Tony Cogan RC	8.00	3.60
❑	228	Justin Duchscherer RC	8.00	3.60
❑	229	Tike Redman	8.00	3.60
❑	230	Jimmy Rollins	8.00	3.60
❑	231	Scott Podsednik RC	8.00	3.60
❑	232	Jose Acevedo RC	8.00	3.60
❑	233	Luis Pineda RC	8.00	3.60
❑	234	Josh Phelps	8.00	3.60
❑	235	Paul Phillips RC	8.00	3.60
❑	236	Brian Roberts RC	8.00	3.60
❑	237	Orlando Woodards RC	8.00	3.60
❑	238	Bart Miadich RC	8.00	3.60
❑	239	Les Walrond RC	8.00	3.60
❑	240	Brad Voyles RC	8.00	3.60
❑	241	Joe Crede	8.00	3.60
❑	242	Juan Moreno RC	8.00	3.60
❑	243	Matt Ginter	8.00	3.60
❑	244	Brian Rogers RC	8.00	3.60
❑	245	Pablo Ozuna	8.00	3.60
❑	246	Geronimo Gil RC	8.00	3.60
❑	247	Mike Maroth RC	8.00	3.60
❑	248	Josue Perez RC	8.00	3.60
❑	249	Dee Brown	8.00	3.60
❑	250	Victor Zambrano RC	8.00	3.60
❑	251	Nick Maness RC	8.00	3.60
❑	252	Kyle Lohse RC	12.00	5.50
❑	253	Greg Miller RC	8.00	3.60
❑	254	Henry Mateo RC	8.00	3.60
❑	255	Duaner Sanchez RC	8.00	3.60
❑	256	Rob MacKowiak RC	8.00	3.60
❑	257	Steve Lomasney	8.00	3.60
❑	258	Angel Santos RC	8.00	3.60
❑	259	Winston Abreu RC	8.00	3.60
❑	260	Brandon Berger RC	8.00	3.60
❑	261	Tomas De La Rosa	8.00	3.60
❑	262	Ramon Vazquez RC	10.00	4.50
❑	263	Mickey Callaway RC	8.00	3.60
❑	264	Corky Miller RC	8.00	3.60
❑	265	Keith Ginter	8.00	3.60
❑	266	Cody Ransom RC	8.00	3.60
❑	267	Doug Nickle RC	8.00	3.60
❑	268	Derrick Lewis RC	8.00	3.60
❑	269	Eric Hinske RC	10.00	4.50
❑	270	Travis Phelps RC	8.00	3.60
❑	271	Eric Valent	8.00	3.60
❑	272	Michael Rivera RC	8.00	3.60
❑	273	Esix Snead RC	8.00	3.60
❑	274	Troy Mattes RC	8.00	3.60
❑	275	Jermaine Clark RC	8.00	3.60
❑	276	Nate Cornejo	8.00	3.60
❑	277	George Perez RC	8.00	3.60
❑	278	Juan Rivera	8.00	3.60
❑	279	Justin Atchley RC	8.00	3.60
❑	280	Adam Johnson	8.00	3.60
❑	281	Gene Altman RC	8.00	3.60
❑	282	Jason Jennings	8.00	3.60
❑	283	Scott MacRae RC	8.00	3.60
❑	284	Craig Monroe RC	10.00	4.50

❏ 285 Bert Snow RC	8.00	3.60
❏ 286 Stubby Clapp RC	8.00	3.60
❏ 287 Jack Cust	8.00	3.60
❏ 288 Will Ohman RC	8.00	3.60
❏ 289 Wily Mo Pena	8.00	3.60
❏ 290 Joe Beimel RC	8.00	3.60
❏ 291 Jason Karnuth RC	8.00	3.60
❏ 292 Bill Ortega RC	8.00	3.60
❏ 293 Nate Teut RC	8.00	3.60
❏ 294 Erik Hiljus RC	8.00	3.60
❏ 295 Jason Smith RC	8.00	3.60
❏ 296 Juan A.Pena RC	8.00	3.60
❏ 297 David Espinosa	8.00	3.60
❏ 298 Tim Redding	15.00	6.75
❏ 299 Brian Lawrence RC	8.00	3.60
❏ 300 Brian Reith RC	8.00	3.60
❏ 301 Chad Durbin	8.00	3.60
❏ 302 Kurt Ainsworth	8.00	3.60
❏ 303 Blaine Neal RC	8.00	3.60
❏ 304 Jorge Julio RC	8.00	3.60
❏ 305 Adam Bernero	8.00	3.60
❏ 306 Travis Hafner RC	10.00	4.50
❏ 307 Dustan Mohr RC	8.00	3.60
❏ 308 Cesar Crespo RC	8.00	3.60
❏ 309 Billy Sylvester RC	8.00	3.60
❏ 310 Zach Day RC	8.00	3.60
❏ 311 Angel Berroa RC	8.00	3.60

1995 Emotion

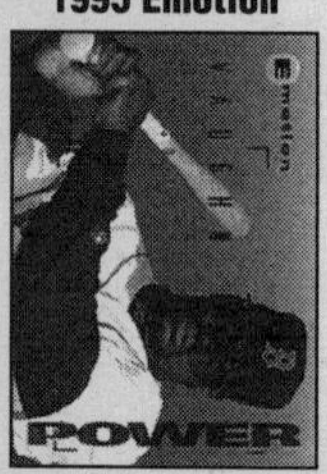

	MINT	NRMT
COMPLETE SET (200)	40.00	18.00
❏ 1 Brady Anderson	.30	.14
❏ 2 Kevin Brown	.30	.14
❏ 3 Curtis Goodwin	.20	.09
❏ 4 Jeffrey Hammonds	.20	.09
❏ 5 Ben McDonald	.20	.09
❏ 6 Mike Mussina	.75	.35
❏ 7 Rafael Palmeiro	.75	.35
❏ 8 Cal Ripken Jr.	3.00	1.35
❏ 9 Jose Canseco	.75	.35
❏ 10 Roger Clemens	2.00	.90
❏ 11 Vaughn Eshelman	.20	.09
❏ 12 Mike Greenwell	.20	.09
❏ 13 Erik Hanson	.20	.09
❏ 14 Tim Naehring	.20	.09
❏ 15 Aaron Sele	.30	.14
❏ 16 John Valentin	.20	.09
❏ 17 Mo Vaughn	.30	.14
❏ 18 Chili Davis	.30	.14
❏ 19 Gary DiSarcina	.20	.09
❏ 20 Chuck Finley	.30	.14
❏ 21 Tim Salmon	.30	.14
❏ 22 Lee Smith	.30	.14
❏ 23 J.T. Snow	.30	.14
❏ 24 Jim Abbott	.30	.14
❏ 25 Jason Bere	.20	.09
❏ 26 Ray Durham	.30	.14
❏ 27 Ozzie Guillen	.20	.09
❏ 28 Tim Raines	.30	.14
❏ 29 Frank Thomas	1.00	.45
❏ 30 Robin Ventura	.30	.14
❏ 31 Carlos Baerga	.20	.09
❏ 32 Albert Belle	.30	.14
❏ 33 Orel Hershiser	.30	.14
❏ 34 Kenny Lofton	.30	.14
❏ 35 Dennis Martinez	.30	.14
❏ 36 Eddie Murray	.75	.35
❏ 37 Manny Ramirez	1.00	.45
❏ 38 Julian Tavarez	.20	.09
❏ 39 Jim Thome	.75	.35
❏ 40 Dave Winfield	.75	.35
❏ 41 Chad Curtis	.20	.09
❏ 42 Cecil Fielder	.30	.14
❏ 43 Travis Fryman	.30	.14
❏ 44 Kirk Gibson	.30	.14
❏ 45 Bobby Higginson RC	1.25	.55
❏ 46 Alan Trammell	.50	.23
❏ 47 Lou Whitaker	.30	.14
❏ 48 Kevin Appier	.30	.14
❏ 49 Gary Gaetti	.30	.14
❏ 50 Jeff Montgomery	.20	.09
❏ 51 Jon Nunnally	.20	.09
❏ 52 Ricky Bones	.20	.09
❏ 53 Cal Eldred	.20	.09
❏ 54 Joe Oliver	.20	.09
❏ 55 Kevin Seitzer	.20	.09
❏ 56 Marty Cordova	.20	.09
❏ 57 Chuck Knoblauch	.30	.14
❏ 58 Kirby Puckett	2.00	.90
❏ 59 Wade Boggs	.75	.35
❏ 60 Derek Jeter	3.00	1.35
❏ 61 Jimmy Key	.30	.14
❏ 62 Don Mattingly	2.00	.90
❏ 63 Jack McDowell	.20	.09
❏ 64 Paul O'Neill	.75	.35
❏ 65 Andy Pettitte	.30	.14
❏ 66 Ruben Rivera	.20	.09
❏ 67 Mike Stanley	.20	.09
❏ 68 John Wetteland	.30	.14
❏ 69 Geronimo Berroa	.20	.09
❏ 70 Dennis Eckersley	.30	.14
❏ 71 Rickey Henderson	1.50	.70
❏ 72 Mark McGwire	3.00	1.35
❏ 73 Steve Ontiveros	.20	.09
❏ 74 Ruben Sierra	.20	.09
❏ 75 Terry Steinbach	.20	.09
❏ 76 Jay Buhner	.30	.14
❏ 77 Ken Griffey Jr.	2.50	1.10
❏ 78 Randy Johnson	1.00	.45
❏ 79 Edgar Martinez	.50	.23
❏ 80 Tino Martinez	.30	.14
❏ 81 Marc Newfield	.20	.09
❏ 82 Alex Rodriguez	2.50	1.10
❏ 83 Will Clark	.75	.35
❏ 84 Benji Gil	.20	.09
❏ 85 Juan Gonzalez	.75	.35
❏ 86 Rusty Greer	.30	.14
❏ 87 Dean Palmer	.30	.14
❏ 88 Ivan Rodriguez	.75	.35
❏ 89 Kenny Rogers	.20	.09
❏ 90 Roberto Alomar	.75	.35
❏ 91 Joe Carter	.30	.14
❏ 92 David Cone	.30	.14
❏ 93 Alex Gonzalez	.20	.09
❏ 94 Shawn Green	.75	.35
❏ 95 Pat Hentgen	.20	.09
❏ 96 Paul Molitor	.75	.35
❏ 97 John Olerud	.30	.14
❏ 98 Devon White	.30	.14
❏ 99 Steve Avery	.20	.09
❏ 100 Tom Glavine	.75	.35
❏ 101 Marquis Grissom	.20	.09
❏ 102 Chipper Jones	1.50	.70
❏ 103 David Justice	.30	.14
❏ 104 Ryan Klesko	.30	.14
❏ 105 Javier Lopez	.30	.14
❏ 106 Greg Maddux	2.00	.90
❏ 107 Fred McGriff	.50	.23
❏ 108 John Smoltz	.30	.14
❏ 109 Shawon Dunston	.20	.09
❏ 110 Mark Grace	.75	.35
❏ 111 Brian McRae	.20	.09
❏ 112 Randy Myers	.20	.09
❏ 113 Sammy Sosa	1.50	.70
❏ 114 Steve Trachsel	.20	.09
❏ 115 Bret Boone	.30	.14
❏ 116 Ron Gant	.20	.09
❏ 117 Barry Larkin	.75	.35
❏ 118 Deion Sanders	.30	.14
❏ 119 Reggie Sanders	.20	.09
❏ 120 Pete Schourek	.20	.09
❏ 121 John Smiley	.20	.09
❏ 122 Jason Bates	.20	.09
❏ 123 Dante Bichette	.30	.14
❏ 124 Vinny Castilla	.30	.14
❏ 125 Andres Galarraga	.50	.23
❏ 126 Larry Walker	.50	.23
❏ 127 Greg Colbrunn	.20	.09
❏ 128 Jeff Conine	.20	.09
❏ 129 Andre Dawson	.50	.23
❏ 130 Chris Hammond	.20	.09
❏ 131 Charles Johnson	.30	.14
❏ 132 Gary Sheffield	.30	.14
❏ 133 Quilvio Veras	.20	.09
❏ 134 Jeff Bagwell	1.00	.45
❏ 135 Derek Bell	.20	.09
❏ 136 Craig Biggio	.50	.23
❏ 137 Jim Dougherty RC	.20	.09
❏ 138 John Hudek	.20	.09
❏ 139 Orlando Miller	.20	.09
❏ 140 Phil Plantier	.20	.09
❏ 141 Eric Karros	.30	.14
❏ 142 Ramon Martinez	.20	.09
❏ 143 Raul Mondesi	.30	.14
❏ 144 Hideo Nomo RC	2.00	.90
❏ 145 Mike Piazza	2.00	.90
❏ 146 Ismael Valdes	.20	.09
❏ 147 Todd Worrell	.20	.09
❏ 148 Moises Alou	.30	.14
❏ 149 Yamil Benitez RC	.20	.09
❏ 150 Wil Cordero	.20	.09
❏ 151 Jeff Fassero	.20	.09
❏ 152 Cliff Floyd	.30	.14
❏ 153 Pedro Martinez	1.00	.45
❏ 154 Carlos Perez RC	.30	.14
❏ 155 Tony Tarasco	.20	.09
❏ 156 Rondell White	.30	.14
❏ 157 Edgardo Alfonzo	.75	.35
❏ 158 Bobby Bonilla	.30	.14
❏ 159 Rico Brogna	.20	.09
❏ 160 Bobby Jones	.20	.09
❏ 161 Bill Pulsipher	.20	.09
❏ 162 Bret Saberhagen	.30	.14
❏ 163 Ricky Bottalico	.20	.09
❏ 164 Darren Daulton	.30	.14
❏ 165 Lenny Dykstra	.30	.14
❏ 166 Charlie Hayes	.20	.09
❏ 167 Dave Hollins	.20	.09
❏ 168 Gregg Jefferies	.20	.09
❏ 169 Michael Mimbs RC	.20	.09
❏ 170 Curt Schilling	.75	.35
❏ 171 Heathcliff Slocumb	.20	.09
❏ 172 Jay Bell	.30	.14
❏ 173 Micah Franklin RC	.20	.09
❏ 174 Mark Johnson RC	.30	.14
❏ 175 Jeff King	.20	.09
❏ 176 Al Martin	.20	.09
❏ 177 Dan Miceli	.20	.09
❏ 178 Denny Neagle	.30	.14
❏ 179 Bernard Gilkey	.20	.09
❏ 180 Ken Hill	.20	.09
❏ 181 Brian Jordan	.30	.14
❏ 182 Ray Lankford	.20	.09
❏ 183 Ozzie Smith	1.00	.45
❏ 184 Andy Benes	.20	.09
❏ 185 Ken Caminiti	.30	.14
❏ 186 Steve Finley	.30	.14
❏ 187 Tony Gwynn	1.50	.70
❏ 188 Joey Hamilton	.20	.09
❏ 189 Melvin Nieves	.20	.09
❏ 190 Scott Sanders	.20	.09
❏ 191 Rod Beck	.20	.09
❏ 192 Barry Bonds	2.00	.90
❏ 193 Royce Clayton	.20	.09
❏ 194 Glenallen Hill	.20	.09
❏ 195 Darren Lewis	.20	.09
❏ 196 Mark Portugal	.20	.09
❏ 197 Matt Williams	.50	.23
❏ 198 Checklist 1-82	.20	.09
❏ 199 Checklist 83-162	.20	.09
❏ 200 CL 163-200/Inserts	.20	.09
❏ P8 Cal Ripken Promo	2.00	.90

1996 Emotion-XL

	MINT	NRMT
COMPLETE SET (300)	80.00	36.00

❑	1	Roberto Alomar	1.50	.70
❑	2	Brady Anderson	.60	.25
❑	3	Bobby Bonilla	.60	.25
❑	4	Jeffrey Hammonds	.40	.18
❑	5	Chris Hoiles	.40	.18
❑	6	Mike Mussina	1.50	.70
❑	7	Randy Myers	.40	.18
❑	8	Rafael Palmeiro	1.50	.70
❑	9	Cal Ripken	6.00	2.70
❑	10	B.J. Surhoff	.60	.25
❑	11	Jose Canseco	1.50	.70
❑	12	Roger Clemens	4.00	1.80
❑	13	Wil Cordero	.40	.18
❑	14	Mike Greenwell	.40	.18
❑	15	Dwayne Hosey	.40	.18
❑	16	Tim Naehring	.40	.18
❑	17	Troy O'Leary	.40	.18
❑	18	Mike Stanley	.40	.18
❑	19	John Valentin	.40	.18
❑	20	Mo Vaughn	.60	.25
❑	21	Jim Abbott	.60	.25
❑	22	Garret Anderson	.60	.25
❑	23	George Arias	.40	.18
❑	24	Chili Davis	.60	.25
❑	25	Jim Edmonds	1.00	.45
❑	26	Chuck Finley	.60	.25
❑	27	Todd Greene	.40	.18
❑	28	Mark Langston	.40	.18
❑	29	Troy Percival	.40	.18
❑	30	Tim Salmon	.60	.25
❑	31	Lee Smith	.60	.25
❑	32	J.T. Snow	.60	.25
❑	33	Harold Baines	.60	.25
❑	34	Jason Bere	.40	.18
❑	35	Ray Durham	.60	.25
❑	36	Alex Fernandez	.40	.18
❑	37	Ozzie Guillen	.40	.18
❑	38	Darren Lewis	.40	.18
❑	39	Lyle Mouton	.40	.18
❑	40	Tony Phillips	.40	.18
❑	41	Danny Tartabull	.40	.18
❑	42	Frank Thomas	2.00	.90
❑	43	Robin Ventura	.60	.25
❑	44	Sandy Alomar Jr.	.60	.25
❑	45	Carlos Baerga	.40	.18
❑	46	Albert Belle	.60	.25
❑	47	Julio Franco	.60	.25
❑	48	Orel Hershiser	.60	.25
❑	49	Kenny Lofton	.60	.25
❑	50	Dennis Martinez	.60	.25
❑	51	Jack McDowell	.40	.18
❑	52	Jose Mesa	.40	.18
❑	53	Eddie Murray	1.50	.70
❑	54	Charles Nagy	.40	.18
❑	55	Manny Ramirez	2.00	.90
❑	56	Jim Thome	1.50	.70
❑	57	Omar Vizquel	.60	.25
❑	58	Chad Curtis	.40	.18
❑	59	Cecil Fielder	.60	.25
❑	60	Travis Fryman	.60	.25
❑	61	Chris Gomez	.40	.18
❑	62	Felipe Lira	.40	.18
❑	63	Alan Trammell	1.00	.45
❑	64	Kevin Appier	.60	.25
❑	65	Johnny Damon	.60	.25
❑	66	Tom Goodwin	.40	.18
❑	67	Mark Gubicza	.40	.18
❑	68	Jeff Montgomery	.40	.18
❑	69	Jon Nunnally	.40	.18
❑	70	Bip Roberts	.40	.18
❑	71	Ricky Bones	.40	.18
❑	72	Chuck Carr	.40	.18
❑	73	John Jaha	.40	.18
❑	74	Ben McDonald	.40	.18
❑	75	Matt Mieske	.40	.18
❑	76	Dave Nilsson	.40	.18
❑	77	Kevin Seitzer	.40	.18
❑	78	Greg Vaughn	.60	.25
❑	79	Rick Aguilera	.40	.18
❑	80	Marty Cordova	.40	.18
❑	81	Roberto Kelly	.40	.18
❑	82	Chuck Knoblauch	.60	.25
❑	83	Pat Meares	.40	.18
❑	84	Paul Molitor	1.50	.70
❑	85	Kirby Puckett	4.00	1.80
❑	86	Brad Radke	.60	.25
❑	87	Wade Boggs	1.50	.70
❑	88	David Cone	.60	.25
❑	89	Dwight Gooden	.60	.25
❑	90	Derek Jeter	6.00	2.70
❑	91	Tino Martinez	.60	.25
❑	92	Paul O'Neill	1.50	.70
❑	93	Andy Pettitte	.60	.25
❑	94	Tim Raines	.60	.25
❑	95	Ruben Rivera	.40	.18
❑	96	Kenny Rogers	.40	.18
❑	97	Ruben Sierra	.40	.18
❑	98	John Wetteland	.60	.25
❑	99	Bernie Williams	1.50	.70
❑	100	Allen Battle	.40	.18
❑	101	Geronimo Berroa	.40	.18
❑	102	Brent Gates	.40	.18
❑	103	Doug Johns	.40	.18
❑	104	Mark McGwire	6.00	2.70
❑	105	Pedro Munoz	.40	.18
❑	106	Ariel Prieto	.40	.18
❑	107	Terry Steinbach	.40	.18
❑	108	Todd Van Poppel	.40	.18
❑	109	Chris Bosio	.40	.18
❑	110	Jay Buhner	.60	.25
❑	111	Joey Cora	.40	.18
❑	112	Russ Davis	.40	.18
❑	113	Ken Griffey Jr.	5.00	2.20
❑	114	Sterling Hitchcock	.40	.18
❑	115	Randy Johnson	2.00	.90
❑	116	Edgar Martinez	1.00	.45
❑	117	Alex Rodriguez	4.00	1.80
❑	118	Paul Sorrento	.40	.18
❑	119	Dan Wilson	.40	.18
❑	120	Will Clark	1.50	.70
❑	121	Juan Gonzalez	1.50	.70
❑	122	Rusty Greer	.60	.25
❑	123	Kevin Gross	.40	.18
❑	124	Ken Hill	.40	.18
❑	125	Dean Palmer	.60	.25
❑	126	Roger Pavlik	.40	.18
❑	127	Ivan Rodriguez	1.50	.70
❑	128	Mickey Tettleton	.40	.18
❑	129	Joe Carter	.60	.25
❑	130	Carlos Delgado	1.50	.70
❑	131	Alex Gonzalez	.40	.18
❑	132	Shawn Green	1.50	.70
❑	133	Erik Hanson	.40	.18
❑	134	Pat Hentgen	.40	.18
❑	135	Otis Nixon	.40	.18
❑	136	John Olerud	.60	.25
❑	137	Ed Sprague	.40	.18
❑	138	Steve Avery	.40	.18
❑	139	Jermaine Dye	.60	.25
❑	140	Tom Glavine	1.50	.70
❑	141	Marquis Grissom	.40	.18
❑	142	Chipper Jones	3.00	1.35
❑	143	David Justice	.60	.25
❑	144	Ryan Klesko	.60	.25
❑	145	Javier Lopez	.60	.25
❑	146	Greg Maddux	4.00	1.80
❑	147	Fred McGriff	1.00	.45
❑	148	Jason Schmidt	.40	.18
❑	149	John Smoltz	.60	.25
❑	150	Mark Wohlers	.40	.18
❑	151	Jim Bullinger	.40	.18
❑	152	Frank Castillo	.40	.18
❑	153	Kevin Foster	.40	.18
❑	154	Luis Gonzalez	1.50	.70
❑	155	Mark Grace	1.50	.70
❑	156	Brian McRae	.40	.18
❑	157	Jaime Navarro	.40	.18
❑	158	Rey Sanchez	.40	.18
❑	159	Ryne Sandberg	2.00	.90
❑	160	Sammy Sosa	3.00	1.35
❑	161	Bret Boone	.60	.25
❑	162	Jeff Brantley	.40	.18
❑	163	Vince Coleman	.40	.18
❑	164	Steve Gibralter	.40	.18
❑	165	Barry Larkin	1.50	.70
❑	166	Hal Morris	.40	.18
❑	167	Mark Portugal	.40	.18
❑	168	Reggie Sanders	.40	.18
❑	169	Pete Schourek	.40	.18
❑	170	John Smiley	.40	.18
❑	171	Jason Bates	.40	.18
❑	172	Dante Bichette	.60	.25
❑	173	Ellis Burks	.60	.25
❑	174	Vinny Castilla	.60	.25
❑	175	Andres Galarraga	1.00	.45
❑	176	Kevin Ritz	.40	.18
❑	177	Bill Swift	.40	.18
❑	178	Larry Walker	1.00	.45
❑	179	Walt Weiss	.40	.18
❑	180	Eric Young	.40	.18
❑	181	Kurt Abbott	.40	.18
❑	182	Kevin Brown	.60	.25
❑	183	John Burkett	.40	.18
❑	184	Greg Colbrunn	.40	.18
❑	185	Jeff Conine	.40	.18
❑	186	Chris Hammond	.40	.18
❑	187	Charles Johnson	.60	.25
❑	188	Terry Pendleton	.60	.25
❑	189	Pat Rapp	.40	.18
❑	190	Gary Sheffield	.60	.25
❑	191	Quilvio Veras	.40	.18
❑	192	Devon White	.60	.25
❑	193	Jeff Bagwell	2.00	.90
❑	194	Derek Bell	.40	.18
❑	195	Sean Berry	.40	.18
❑	196	Craig Biggio	1.00	.45
❑	197	Doug Drabek	.40	.18
❑	198	Tony Eusebio	.40	.18
❑	199	Mike Hampton	.60	.25
❑	200	Brian L.Hunter	.40	.18
❑	201	Derrick May	.40	.18
❑	202	Orlando Miller	.40	.18
❑	203	Shane Reynolds	.40	.18
❑	204	Mike Blowers	.40	.18
❑	205	Tom Candiotti	.40	.18
❑	206	Delino DeShields	.40	.18
❑	207	Greg Gagne	.40	.18
❑	208	Karim Garcia	.40	.18
❑	209	Todd Hollandsworth	.40	.18
❑	210	Eric Karros	.60	.25
❑	211	Ramon Martinez	.40	.18
❑	212	Raul Mondesi	.60	.25
❑	213	Hideo Nomo	2.00	.90
❑	214	Chan Ho Park	.60	.25
❑	215	Mike Piazza	4.00	1.80
❑	216	Ismael Valdes	.40	.18
❑	217	Todd Worrell	.40	.18
❑	218	Moises Alou	.60	.25
❑	219	Yamil Benitez	.40	.18
❑	220	Jeff Fassero	.40	.18
❑	221	Darrin Fletcher	.40	.18
❑	222	Cliff Floyd	.60	.25
❑	223	Pedro Martinez	2.00	.90
❑	224	Carlos Perez	.40	.18
❑	225	Mel Rojas	.40	.18
❑	226	David Segui	.40	.18
❑	227	Rondell White	.60	.25
❑	228	Rico Brogna	.40	.18
❑	229	Carl Everett	.60	.25
❑	230	John Franco	.60	.25
❑	231	Bernard Gilkey	.40	.18
❑	232	Todd Hundley	.40	.18
❑	233	Jason Isringhausen	.60	.25
❑	234	Lance Johnson	.40	.18
❑	235	Bobby Jones	.40	.18
❑	236	Jeff Kent	1.00	.45
❑	237	Rey Ordonez	.40	.18
❑	238	Bill Pulsipher	.40	.18
❑	239	Jose Vizcaino	.40	.18

❑ 240 Paul Wilson	.40	.18
❑ 241 Ricky Bottalico	.40	.18
❑ 242 Darren Daulton	.60	.25
❑ 243 Lenny Dykstra	.60	.25
❑ 244 Jim Eisenreich	.40	.18
❑ 245 Sid Fernandez	.40	.18
❑ 246 Gregg Jefferies	.40	.18
❑ 247 Mickey Morandini	.40	.18
❑ 248 Benito Santiago	.40	.18
❑ 249 Curt Schilling	1.50	.70
❑ 250 Mark Whiten	.40	.18
❑ 251 Todd Zeile	.40	.18
❑ 252 Jay Bell	.60	.25
❑ 253 Carlos Garcia	.40	.18
❑ 254 Charlie Hayes	.40	.18
❑ 255 Jason Kendall	.60	.25
❑ 256 Jeff King	.40	.18
❑ 257 Al Martin	.40	.18
❑ 258 Orlando Merced	.40	.18
❑ 259 Dan Miceli	.40	.18
❑ 260 Denny Neagle	.60	.25
❑ 261 Alan Benes	.40	.18
❑ 262 Andy Benes	.40	.18
❑ 263 Royce Clayton	.40	.18
❑ 264 Dennis Eckersley	.60	.25
❑ 265 Gary Gaetti	.60	.25
❑ 266 Ron Gant	.40	.18
❑ 267 Brian Jordan	.60	.25
❑ 268 Ray Lankford	.40	.18
❑ 269 John Mabry	.40	.18
❑ 270 Tom Pagnozzi	.40	.18
❑ 271 Ozzie Smith	2.00	.90
❑ 272 Todd Stottlemyre	.40	.18
❑ 273 Andy Ashby	.40	.18
❑ 274 Brad Ausmus	.40	.18
❑ 275 Ken Caminiti	.60	.25
❑ 276 Steve Finley	.60	.25
❑ 277 Tony Gwynn	3.00	1.35
❑ 278 Joey Hamilton	.40	.18
❑ 279 Rickey Henderson	3.00	1.35
❑ 280 Trevor Hoffman	.60	.25
❑ 281 Wally Joyner	.60	.25
❑ 282 Jody Reed	.40	.18
❑ 283 Bob Tewksbury	.40	.18
❑ 284 Fernando Valenzuela	.60	.25
❑ 285 Rod Beck	.40	.18
❑ 286 Barry Bonds	4.00	1.80
❑ 287 Mark Carreon	.40	.18
❑ 288 Shawon Dunston	.40	.18
❑ 289 O.Fernandez RC	.40	.18
❑ 290 Glenallen Hill	.40	.18
❑ 291 Stan Javier	.40	.18
❑ 292 Mark Leiter	.40	.18
❑ 293 Kirt Manwaring	.40	.18
❑ 294 Robby Thompson	.40	.18
❑ 295 W.VanLandingham	.40	.18
❑ 296 Allen Watson	.40	.18
❑ 297 Matt Williams	1.00	.45
❑ 298 Checklist	.40	.18
❑ 299 Checklist	.40	.18
❑ 300 Checklist	.40	.18
❑ P55 Manny Ramirez Promo	1.00	.45

2001 eTopps

	MINT	NRMT
❑ 1 Nomar Garciaparra/1315	25.00	11.00
❑ 2 Chipper Jones/674	20.00	9.00
❑ 3 Jeff Bagwell/485	50.00	22.00
❑ 4 Randy Johnson/1499	12.00	5.50
❑ 7 Adam Dunn/4197	10.00	4.50
❑ 8 J.D. Drew/767	12.00	5.50
❑ 9 Larry Walker/420	30.00	13.50
❑ 10 Edgardo Alfonzo/338	25.00	11.00
❑ 11 Lance Berkman/595	12.00	5.50
❑ 12 Tony Gwynn/828	20.00	9.00
❑ 13 Andruw Jones/908	10.00	4.50
❑ 15 Troy Glaus/862	10.00	4.50
❑ 17 Sammy Sosa/2487	12.00	5.50
❑ 21 Darin Erstad/664	8.00	3.60
❑ 22 Barry Bonds/1567	40.00	18.00
❑ 27 Derek Jeter/1041	25.00	11.00
❑ 29 Curt Schilling/2125	12.00	5.50
❑ 30 Roberto Alomar/448	30.00	13.50

❑ 31 Luis Gonzalez/1104	12.00	5.50
❑ 32 Jimmy Rollins/1307	8.00	3.60
❑ 34 Joe Crede/1050	6.00	2.70
❑ 39 Sean Casey/537	10.00	4.50
❑ 46 Alex Rodriguez/2212	20.00	9.00
❑ 47 Tom Glavine/437	20.00	9.00
❑ 50 Jose Ortiz/738	6.00	2.70
❑ 51 Cal Ripken/2201	20.00	9.00
❑ 52 Bob Abreu/677	8.00	3.60
❑ 55 Alex Escobar/931	8.00	3.60
❑ 56 Ivan Rodriguez/698	15.00	6.75
❑ 59 Jeff Kent/452	12.00	5.50
❑ 62 Rick Ankiel/752	10.00	4.50
❑ 65 Craig Biggio/410	25.00	11.00
❑ 66 Carlos Delgado/398	20.00	9.00
❑ 68 Greg Maddux/1031	15.00	6.75
❑ 69 Kerry Wood/1056	8.00	3.60
❑ 71 Todd Helton/978	10.00	4.50
❑ 72 Mariano Rivera/824	10.00	4.50
❑ 73 Jason Kendall/672	8.00	3.60
❑ 75 Scott Rolen/498	10.00	4.50
❑ 76 Kazuhiro Sasaki/5000	12.00	5.50
❑ 77 Roy Oswalt/915	10.00	4.50
❑ 78 C.C. Sabathia/1974	12.00	5.50
❑ 83 Brian Giles/400	15.00	6.75
❑ 87 Rafael Furcal/646	8.00	3.60
❑ 88 Mike Mussina/793	12.00	5.50
❑ 89 Gary Sheffield/359	15.00	6.75
❑ 92 Mark McGwire/2908	15.00	6.75
❑ 94 Tsuyoshi Shinjo/3000	8.00	3.60
❑ 99 Jose Vidro /443	10.00	4.50
❑ 100 Ichiro Suzuki/10000	30.00	13.50
❑ 105 Manny Ramirez/1074	10.00	4.50
❑ 109 Juan Gonzalez/558	12.00	5.50
❑ 112 Ken Griffey Jr./2398	15.00	6.75
❑ 114 Tim Hudson/663	10.00	4.50
❑ 115 Nick Johnson/1217	10.00	4.50
❑ 118 Jason Giambi/897	15.00	6.75
❑ 122 Rafael Palmeiro/464	25.00	11.00
❑ 124 Vladimir Guerrero/854	15.00	6.75
❑ 125 Vernon Wells/349	15.00	6.75
❑ 127 Roger Clemens/1462	15.00	6.75
❑ 128 Frank Thomas/834	12.00	5.50
❑ 129 Carlos Beltran/489	8.00	3.60
❑ 130 Pat Burrell/1253	6.00	2.70
❑ 131 Pedro Martinez/1038	12.00	5.50
❑ 132 Mike Piazza/1379	12.00	5.50
❑ 135 Luis Montanez/5000	8.00	3.60
❑ 140 Sean Burroughs/5000	8.00	3.60
❑ 141 Barry Zito/843	6.00	8.70
❑ 142 Bobby Bradley/5000	5.00	2.20
❑ 143 Albert Pujols/5000	15.00	6.75
❑ 144 Ben Sheets/1713	6.00	2.70
❑ 145 Alfonso Soriano/1699	10.00	4.50
❑ 146 Josh Hamilton/5000	8.00	3.60
❑ 147 Eric Munson/5000	5.00	2.20
❑ 150 Mark Mulder/4335	5.00	2.20

1997 E-X2000

	MINT	NRMT
COMPLETE SET (100)	80.00	36.00
❑ 1 Jim Edmonds	1.00	.45
❑ 2 Darin Erstad	1.50	.70
❑ 3 Eddie Murray	1.50	.70
❑ 4 Roberto Alomar	1.50	.70
❑ 5 Brady Anderson	.60	.25

❑ 6 Mike Mussina	1.50	.70
❑ 7 Rafael Palmeiro	1.50	.70
❑ 8 Cal Ripken	6.00	2.70
❑ 9 Steve Avery	.40	.18
❑ 10 Nomar Garciaparra	4.00	1.80
❑ 11 Mo Vaughn	.60	.25
❑ 12 Albert Belle	.60	.25
❑ 13 Mike Cameron	.60	.25
❑ 14 Ray Durham	.60	.25
❑ 15 Frank Thomas	2.00	.90
❑ 16 Robin Ventura	.60	.25
❑ 17 Manny Ramirez	2.00	.90
❑ 18 Jim Thome	1.50	.70
❑ 19 Matt Williams	1.00	.45
❑ 20 Tony Clark	.60	.25
❑ 21 Travis Fryman	.60	.25
❑ 22 Bob Higginson	.60	.25
❑ 23 Kevin Appier	.60	.25
❑ 24 Johnny Damon	.60	.25
❑ 25 Jermaine Dye	.60	.25
❑ 26 Jeff Cirillo	.60	.25
❑ 27 Ben McDonald	.40	.18
❑ 28 Chuck Knoblauch	.60	.25
❑ 29 Paul Molitor	1.50	.70
❑ 30 Todd Walker	.40	.18
❑ 31 Wade Boggs	1.50	.70
❑ 32 Cecil Fielder	.60	.25
❑ 33 Derek Jeter	6.00	2.70
❑ 34 Andy Pettitte	.60	.25
❑ 35 Ruben Rivera	.40	.18
❑ 36 Bernie Williams	1.50	.70
❑ 37 Jose Canseco	1.50	.70
❑ 38 Mark McGwire	6.00	2.70
❑ 39 Jay Buhner	.60	.25
❑ 40 Ken Griffey Jr.	5.00	2.20
❑ 41 Randy Johnson	2.00	.90
❑ 42 Edgar Martinez	1.00	.45
❑ 43 Alex Rodriguez	4.00	1.80
❑ 44 Dan Wilson	.40	.18
❑ 45 Will Clark	1.50	.70
❑ 46 Juan Gonzalez	1.50	.70
❑ 47 Ivan Rodriguez	1.50	.70
❑ 48 Joe Carter	.60	.25
❑ 49 Roger Clemens	4.00	1.80
❑ 50 Juan Guzman	.40	.18
❑ 51 Pat Hentgen	.40	.18
❑ 52 Tom Glavine	1.50	.70
❑ 53 Andruw Jones	2.00	.90
❑ 54 Chipper Jones	3.00	1.35
❑ 55 Ryan Klesko	.60	.25
❑ 56 Kenny Lofton	.60	.25
❑ 57 Greg Maddux	4.00	1.80
❑ 58 Fred McGriff	1.00	.45
❑ 59 John Smoltz	.60	.25
❑ 60 Mark Wohlers	.40	.18
❑ 61 Mark Grace	1.50	.70
❑ 62 Ryne Sandberg	2.00	.90
❑ 63 Sammy Sosa	3.00	1.35
❑ 64 Barry Larkin	1.50	.70
❑ 65 Deion Sanders	.60	.25
❑ 66 Reggie Sanders	.40	.18
❑ 67 Dante Bichette	.60	.25
❑ 68 Ellis Burks	.60	.25
❑ 69 Andres Galarraga	1.00	.45
❑ 70 Moises Alou	.60	.25
❑ 71 Kevin Brown	.60	.25
❑ 72 Cliff Floyd	.60	.25

Card	MINT	NRMT
❑ 73 Edgar Renteria	.40	.18
❑ 74 Gary Sheffield	.60	.25
❑ 75 Bob Abreu	.60	.25
❑ 76 Jeff Bagwell	2.00	.90
❑ 77 Craig Biggio	1.00	.45
❑ 78 Todd Hollandsworth	.40	.18
❑ 79 Eric Karros	.60	.25
❑ 80 Raul Mondesi	.60	.25
❑ 81 Hideo Nomo	1.50	.70
❑ 82 Mike Piazza	4.00	1.80
❑ 83 Vladimir Guerrero	2.50	1.10
❑ 84 Henry Rodriguez	.40	.18
❑ 85 Todd Hundley	.40	.18
❑ 86 Alex Ochoa	.60	.25
❑ 87 Rey Ordonez	.40	.18
❑ 88 Gregg Jefferies	.40	.18
❑ 89 Scott Rolen	1.50	.70
❑ 90 Jermaine Allensworth	.40	.18
❑ 91 Jason Kendall	.60	.25
❑ 92 Ken Caminiti	.60	.25
❑ 93 Tony Gwynn	3.00	1.35
❑ 94 Rickey Henderson	3.00	1.35
❑ 95 Barry Bonds	4.00	1.80
❑ 96 J.T. Snow	.60	.25
❑ 97 Dennis Eckersley	.60	.25
❑ 98 Ron Gant	.40	.18
❑ 99 Brian Jordan	.60	.25
❑ 100 Ray Lankford	.40	.18
❑ 101 Checklist	.40	.18
❑ 102 Checklist	.40	.18
❑ P43 Alex Rodriguez Three card promo strip	1.50	.70
❑ S43 Alex Rodriguez Mailed to Dealers who ordered Cases Card is numbered out of 3,000	15.00	6.75
❑ NNO Alex Rodriguez Ball Exch 100 produced	80.00	36.00

1998 E-X2001

	MINT	NRMT
COMPLETE SET (100)	100.00	45.00

Card	MINT	NRMT
❑ 1 Alex Rodriguez	4.00	1.80
❑ 2 Barry Bonds	4.00	1.80
❑ 3 Greg Maddux	4.00	1.80
❑ 4 Roger Clemens	4.00	1.80
❑ 5 Juan Gonzalez	1.50	.70
❑ 6 Chipper Jones	3.00	1.35
❑ 7 Derek Jeter	6.00	2.70
❑ 8 Frank Thomas	2.00	.90
❑ 9 Cal Ripken	6.00	2.70
❑ 10 Ken Griffey Jr.	5.00	2.20
❑ 11 Mark McGwire	6.00	2.70
❑ 12 Hideo Nomo	1.50	.70
❑ 13 Tony Gwynn	3.00	1.35
❑ 14 Ivan Rodriguez	1.50	.70
❑ 15 Mike Piazza	4.00	1.80
❑ 16 Roberto Alomar	1.50	.70
❑ 17 Jeff Bagwell	2.00	.90
❑ 18 Andruw Jones	1.50	.70
❑ 19 Albert Belle	.60	.25
❑ 20 Mo Vaughn	.60	.25
❑ 21 Kenny Lofton	.60	.25
❑ 22 Gary Sheffield	.60	.25
❑ 23 Tony Clark	.60	.25
❑ 24 Mike Mussina	1.50	.70
❑ 25 Barry Larkin	1.50	.70
❑ 26 Moises Alou	.60	.25
❑ 27 Brady Anderson	.60	.25
❑ 28 Andy Pettitte	.60	.25
❑ 29 Sammy Sosa	3.00	1.35
❑ 30 Raul Mondesi	.60	.25
❑ 31 Andres Galarraga	1.00	.45
❑ 32 Chuck Knoblauch	.60	.25
❑ 33 Jim Thome	1.50	.70
❑ 34 Craig Biggio	1.00	.45
❑ 35 Jay Buhner	.60	.25
❑ 36 Rafael Palmeiro	1.50	.70
❑ 37 Curt Schilling	1.50	.70
❑ 38 Tino Martinez	.60	.25
❑ 39 Pedro Martinez	2.00	.90
❑ 40 Jose Canseco	1.50	.70
❑ 41 Jeff Cirillo	.60	.25
❑ 42 Dean Palmer	.60	.25
❑ 43 Tim Salmon	.60	.25
❑ 44 Jason Giambi	1.50	.70
❑ 45 Bobby Higginson	.60	.25
❑ 46 Jim Edmonds	1.00	.45
❑ 47 David Justice	.60	.25
❑ 48 John Olerud	.60	.25
❑ 49 Ray Lankford	.40	.18
❑ 50 Al Martin	.40	.18
❑ 51 Mike Lieberthal	.60	.25
❑ 52 Henry Rodriguez	.40	.18
❑ 53 Edgar Renteria	.40	.18
❑ 54 Eric Karros	.60	.25
❑ 55 Marquis Grissom	.40	.18
❑ 56 Wilson Alvarez	.40	.18
❑ 57 Darryl Kile	.60	.25
❑ 58 Jeff King	.40	.18
❑ 59 Shawn Estes	.60	.25
❑ 60 Tony Womack	.40	.18
❑ 61 Willie Greene	.40	.18
❑ 62 Ken Caminiti	.60	.25
❑ 63 Vinny Castilla	.60	.25
❑ 64 Mark Grace	1.50	.70
❑ 65 Ryan Klesko	.60	.25
❑ 66 Robin Ventura	.60	.25
❑ 67 Todd Hundley	.40	.18
❑ 68 Travis Fryman	.60	.25
❑ 69 Edgar Martinez	1.00	.45
❑ 70 Matt Williams	1.00	.45
❑ 71 Paul Molitor	1.50	.70
❑ 72 Kevin Brown	1.00	.45
❑ 73 Randy Johnson	2.00	.90
❑ 74 Bernie Williams	1.50	.70
❑ 75 Manny Ramirez	2.00	.90
❑ 76 Fred McGriff	1.00	.45
❑ 77 Tom Glavine	1.50	.70
❑ 78 Carlos Delgado	1.50	.70
❑ 79 Larry Walker	1.00	.45
❑ 80 Hideki Irabu	.40	.18
❑ 81 Ryan McGuire	.40	.18
❑ 82 Justin Thompson	.40	.18
❑ 83 Kevin Orie	.40	.18
❑ 84 Jon Nunnally	.40	.18
❑ 85 Mark Kotsay	.60	.25
❑ 86 Todd Walker	.40	.18
❑ 87 Jason Dickson	.40	.18
❑ 88 Fernando Tatis	.40	.18
❑ 89 Karim Garcia	.40	.18
❑ 90 Ricky Ledee	.40	.18
❑ 91 Paul Konerko	.60	.25
❑ 92 Jaret Wright	.40	.18
❑ 93 Darin Erstad	1.50	.70
❑ 94 Livan Hernandez	.40	.18
❑ 95 Nomar Garciaparra	4.00	1.80
❑ 96 Jose Cruz Jr.	.60	.25
❑ 97 Scott Rolen	1.50	.70
❑ 98 Ben Grieve	.60	.25
❑ 99 Vladimir Guerrero	2.00	.90
❑ 100 Travis Lee	.60	.25
❑ 101 K.Wood Redemption	4.00	1.80
❑ NNO Kerry Wood EXCH	2.00	.90
❑ NNO A.Rodriguez Sample	2.00	.90

1999 E-X Century

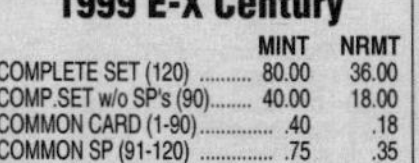

	MINT	NRMT
COMPLETE SET (120)	80.00	36.00
COMP.SET w/o SP's (90)	40.00	18.00
COMMON CARD (1-90)	.40	.18
COMMON SP (91-120)	.75	.35

Card	MINT	NRMT
❑ 1 Scott Rolen	1.50	.70
❑ 2 Nomar Garciaparra	4.00	1.80
❑ 3 Mike Piazza	4.00	1.80
❑ 4 Tony Gwynn	3.00	1.35
❑ 5 Sammy Sosa	3.00	1.35
❑ 6 Alex Rodriguez	4.00	1.80
❑ 7 Vladimir Guerrero	2.00	.90
❑ 8 Chipper Jones	3.00	1.35
❑ 9 Derek Jeter	6.00	2.70
❑ 10 Kerry Wood	1.50	.70
❑ 11 Juan Gonzalez	1.50	.70
❑ 12 Frank Thomas	2.00	.90
❑ 13 Mo Vaughn	.60	.25
❑ 14 Greg Maddux	4.00	1.80
❑ 15 Jeff Bagwell	2.00	.90
❑ 16 Mark McGwire	6.00	2.70
❑ 17 Ken Griffey Jr.	5.00	2.20
❑ 18 Roger Clemens	4.00	1.80
❑ 19 Cal Ripken	6.00	2.70
❑ 20 Travis Lee	.40	.18
❑ 21 Todd Helton	2.00	.90
❑ 22 Darin Erstad	1.50	.70
❑ 23 Pedro Martinez	2.00	.90
❑ 24 Barry Bonds	4.00	1.80
❑ 25 Andruw Jones	1.50	.70
❑ 26 Larry Walker	1.00	.45
❑ 27 Albert Belle	.60	.25
❑ 28 Ivan Rodriguez	1.50	.70
❑ 29 Magglio Ordonez	1.00	.45
❑ 30 Andres Galarraga	1.00	.45
❑ 31 Mike Mussina	1.50	.70
❑ 32 Randy Johnson	2.00	.90
❑ 33 Tom Glavine	1.50	.70
❑ 34 Barry Larkin	1.50	.70
❑ 35 Jim Thome	1.50	.70
❑ 36 Gary Sheffield	.60	.25
❑ 37 Bernie Williams	1.50	.70
❑ 38 Carlos Delgado	1.50	.70
❑ 39 Rafael Palmeiro	1.50	.70
❑ 40 Edgar Renteria	.40	.18
❑ 41 Brad Fullmer	.60	.25
❑ 42 David Wells	.60	.25
❑ 43 Dante Bichette	.60	.25
❑ 44 Jaret Wright	.40	.18
❑ 45 Ricky Ledee	.40	.18
❑ 46 Ray Lankford	.40	.18
❑ 47 Mark Grace	1.50	.70
❑ 48 Jeff Cirillo	.60	.25
❑ 49 Rondell White	.60	.25
❑ 50 Jeromy Burnitz	.60	.25
❑ 51 Sean Casey	1.00	.45
❑ 52 Rolando Arrojo	.40	.18
❑ 53 Jason Giambi	1.50	.70
❑ 54 John Olerud	.60	.25
❑ 55 Will Clark	1.50	.70
❑ 56 Raul Mondesi	.60	.25
❑ 57 Scott Brosius	.60	.25
❑ 58 Bartolo Colon	.60	.25
❑ 59 Steve Finley	.60	.25
❑ 60 Javy Lopez	.60	.25
❑ 61 Tim Salmon	.60	.25
❑ 62 Roberto Alomar	1.50	.70
❑ 63 Vinny Castilla	.60	.25
❑ 64 Craig Biggio	1.00	.45
❑ 65 Jose Guillen	.40	.18
❑ 66 Greg Vaughn	.60	.25
❑ 67 Jose Canseco	1.50	.70

Card	MINT	NRMT
❑ 68 Shawn Green	1.50	.70
❑ 69 Curt Schilling	1.50	.70
❑ 70 Orlando Hernandez	.60	.25
❑ 71 Jose Cruz Jr.	.60	.25
❑ 72 Alex Gonzalez	.40	.18
❑ 73 Tino Martinez	.60	.25
❑ 74 Todd Hundley	.40	.18
❑ 75 Brian Giles	.60	.25
❑ 76 Cliff Floyd	.60	.25
❑ 77 Paul O'Neill	1.50	.70
❑ 78 Ken Caminiti	.60	.25
❑ 79 Ron Gant	.60	.25
❑ 80 Juan Encarnacion	.60	.25
❑ 81 Ben Grieve	.60	.25
❑ 82 Brian Jordan	.60	.25
❑ 83 Rickey Henderson	3.00	1.35
❑ 84 Tony Clark	.60	.25
❑ 85 Shannon Stewart	.60	.25
❑ 86 Robin Ventura	.60	.25
❑ 87 Todd Walker	.40	.18
❑ 88 Kevin Brown	1.00	.45
❑ 89 Moises Alou	.60	.25
❑ 90 Manny Ramirez	2.00	.90
❑ 91 Gabe Alvarez SP	.75	.35
❑ 92 Jeremy Giambi SP	.75	.35
❑ 93 Adrian Beltre SP	1.25	.55
❑ 94 George Lombard SP	.75	.35
❑ 95 Ryan Minor SP	.75	.35
❑ 96 Kevin Witt SP	.75	.35
❑ 97 Scott Hunter SP RC	.40	.18
❑ 98 Carlos Guillen SP	.75	.35
❑ 99 Derrick Gibson SP	.75	.35
❑ 100 Trot Nixon SP	1.25	.55
❑ 101 Troy Glaus SP	1.50	.70
❑ 102 Armando Rios SP	.75	.35
❑ 103 Preston Wilson SP	1.25	.55
❑ 104 Pat Burrell SP RC	5.00	2.20
❑ 105 J.D. Drew SP	3.00	1.35
❑ 106 Bruce Chen SP	.75	.35
❑ 107 Matt Clement SP	.75	.35
❑ 108 Carlos Beltran SP	1.25	.55
❑ 109 Carlos Febles SP	.75	.35
❑ 110 Rob Fick SP	.75	.35
❑ 111 Russell Branyan SP	1.25	.55
❑ 112 R.Brown SP RC	1.00	.45
❑ 113 Corey Koskie SP	1.25	.55
❑ 114 M.Encarnacion SP RC	1.00	.45
❑ 115 Peter Tucci SP	.75	.35
❑ 116 Eric Chavez SP	1.25	.55
❑ 117 Gabe Kapler SP	1.25	.55
❑ 118 Marlon Anderson SP	.75	.35
❑ 119 A.J. Burnett SP RC	2.50	1.10
❑ 120 Ryan Bradley SP	.75	.35
❑ P81 Ben Grieve Sample	1.00	.45

2000 E-X

	MINT	NRMT
COMPLETE SET (90)	100.00	45.00
COMP.SET w/o SP's (60)	20.00	9.00
COMMON CARD (1-60)	.20	.09
COMMON PROS (61-90)	4.00	1.80

Card	MINT	NRMT
❑ 1 Alex Rodriguez	2.00	.90
❑ 2 Jeff Bagwell	1.00	.45
❑ 3 Mike Piazza	2.00	.90
❑ 4 Tony Gwynn	1.50	.70
❑ 5 Ken Griffey Jr.	2.50	1.10
❑ 6 Juan Gonzalez	.75	.35
❑ 7 Vladimir Guerrero	1.00	.45
❑ 8 Cal Ripken	3.00	1.35
❑ 9 Mo Vaughn	.20	.09
❑ 10 Chipper Jones	1.50	.70
❑ 11 Derek Jeter	3.00	1.35
❑ 12 Nomar Garciaparra	2.00	.90
❑ 13 Mark McGwire	3.00	1.35
❑ 14 Sammy Sosa	1.50	.70
❑ 15 Pedro Martinez	1.00	.45
❑ 16 Greg Maddux	2.00	.90
❑ 17 Frank Thomas	1.00	.45
❑ 18 Shawn Green	.75	.35
❑ 19 Carlos Beltran	.25	.11
❑ 20 Roger Clemens	2.00	.90
❑ 21 Randy Johnson	1.00	.45
❑ 22 Bernie Williams	.75	.35
❑ 23 Carlos Delgado	.75	.35
❑ 24 Manny Ramirez	1.00	.45
❑ 25 Freddy Garcia	.50	.23
❑ 26 Barry Bonds	2.00	.90
❑ 27 Tim Hudson	.75	.35
❑ 28 Larry Walker	.50	.23
❑ 29 Raul Mondesi	.20	.09
❑ 30 Ivan Rodriguez	.75	.35
❑ 31 Magglio Ordonez	.20	.09
❑ 32 Scott Rolen	.75	.35
❑ 33 Mike Mussina	.75	.35
❑ 34 J.D. Drew	.75	.35
❑ 35 Tom Glavine	.75	.35
❑ 36 Barry Larkin	.75	.35
❑ 37 Jim Thome	.25	.11
❑ 38 Erubiel Durazo	.25	.11
❑ 39 Curt Schilling	.25	.11
❑ 40 Orlando Hernandez	.25	.11
❑ 41 Rafael Palmeiro	.75	.35
❑ 42 Gabe Kapler	.25	.11
❑ 43 Mark Grace	.75	.35
❑ 44 Jeff Cirillo	.25	.11
❑ 45 Jeromy Burnitz	.20	.09
❑ 46 Sean Casey	.50	.23
❑ 47 Kevin Millwood	.20	.09
❑ 48 Vinny Castilla	.25	.11
❑ 49 Jose Canseco	.75	.35
❑ 50 Roberto Alomar	.75	.35
❑ 51 Craig Biggio	.50	.23
❑ 52 Preston Wilson	.20	.09
❑ 53 Jeff Weaver	.25	.11
❑ 54 Robin Ventura	.20	.09
❑ 55 Ben Grieve	.25	.11
❑ 56 Troy Glaus	.75	.35
❑ 57 Jacque Jones	.20	.09
❑ 58 Brian Giles	.20	.09
❑ 59 Kevin Brown	.20	.09
❑ 60 Todd Helton	1.00	.45
❑ 61 Ben Petrick PROS	4.00	1.80
❑ 62 C.Hermansen PROS	4.00	1.80
❑ 63 Kevin Barker PROS	4.00	1.80
❑ 64 Matt LeCroy PROS	4.00	1.80
❑ 65 Brad Penny PROS	5.00	2.20
❑ 66 D.T. Cromer PROS	4.00	1.80
❑ 67 Steve Lomasney PROS	4.00	1.80
❑ 68 Cole Liniak PROS	4.00	1.80
❑ 69 B.J. Ryan PROS	4.00	1.80
❑ 70 Wilton Veras PROS	4.00	1.80
❑ 71 A.McNeal PROS RC	4.00	1.80
❑ 72 Nick Johnson PROS	6.00	2.70
❑ 73 Adam Piatt PROS	5.00	2.20
❑ 74 Adam Kennedy PROS	4.00	1.80
❑ 75 Cesar King PROS	4.00	1.80
❑ 76 Peter Bergeron PROS	4.00	1.80
❑ 77 Rob Bell PROS	4.00	1.80
❑ 78 Wily Pena PROS	6.00	2.70
❑ 79 Ruben Mateo PROS	5.00	2.20
❑ 80 Kip Wells PROS	5.00	2.20
❑ 81 Alex Escobar PROS	5.00	2.20
❑ 82 Danys Baez PROS RC	5.00	2.20
❑ 83 Travis Dawkins PROS	5.00	2.20
❑ 84 Mark Quinn PROS	5.00	2.20
❑ 85 Jimmy Anderson PROS	4.00	1.80
❑ 86 Rick Ankiel PROS	6.00	2.70
❑ 87 Alfonso Soriano PROS	6.00	2.70
❑ 88 Pat Burrell PROS	6.00	2.70
❑ 89 Eric Munson PROS	5.00	2.20
❑ 90 Josh Beckett PROS	8.00	3.60

2001 E-X

	MINT	NRMT
COMP.SET w/o SP's (100)	25.00	11.00
COMMON CARD (1-100)	.40	.18
COMMON CARD (101-130)	8.00	3.60

Card	MINT	NRMT
❑ 1 Jason Kendall	.40	.18
❑ 2 Derek Jeter	4.00	1.80
❑ 3 Greg Vaughn	.40	.18
❑ 4 Eric Chavez	.40	.18
❑ 5 Nomar Garciaparra	2.50	1.10
❑ 6 Roberto Alomar	1.00	.45
❑ 7 Barry Larkin	1.00	.45
❑ 8 Matt Lawton	.40	.18
❑ 9 Larry Walker	.60	.25
❑ 10 Chipper Jones	2.00	.90
❑ 11 Scott Rolen	1.00	.45
❑ 12 Carlos Lee	.40	.18
❑ 13 Adrian Beltre	.40	.18
❑ 14 Ben Grieve	.40	.18
❑ 15 Mike Sweeney	.40	.18
❑ 16 John Olerud	.40	.18
❑ 17 Gabe Kapler	.40	.18
❑ 18 Brian Giles	.40	.18
❑ 19 Luis Gonzalez	1.00	.45
❑ 20 Sammy Sosa	2.00	.90
❑ 21 Roger Clemens	2.50	1.10
❑ 22 Vladimir Guerrero	1.25	.55
❑ 23 Ken Griffey Jr.	3.00	1.35
❑ 24 Mark McGwire	4.00	1.80
❑ 25 Orlando Hernandez	.40	.18
❑ 26 Shannon Stewart	.40	.18
❑ 27 Fred McGriff	.60	.25
❑ 28 Lance Berkman	1.00	.45
❑ 29 Carlos Delgado	1.00	.45
❑ 30 Mike Piazza	2.50	1.10
❑ 31 Juan Encarnacion	.40	.18
❑ 32 David Justice	.40	.18
❑ 33 Greg Maddux	2.50	1.10
❑ 34 Frank Thomas	1.25	.55
❑ 35 Jason Giambi	1.00	.45
❑ 36 Ruben Mateo	.40	.18
❑ 37 Todd Helton	1.25	.55
❑ 38 Jim Edmonds	.60	.25
❑ 39 Steve Finley	.40	.18
❑ 40 Tom Glavine	1.00	.45
❑ 41 Mo Vaughn	.40	.18
❑ 42 Phil Nevin	.40	.18
❑ 43 Richie Sexson	.40	.18
❑ 44 Craig Biggio	.60	.25
❑ 45 Kerry Wood	1.00	.45
❑ 46 Pat Burrell	.40	.18
❑ 47 Edgar Martinez	.60	.25
❑ 48 Jim Thome	1.00	.45
❑ 49 Jeff Bagwell	1.25	.55
❑ 50 Bernie Williams	1.00	.45
❑ 51 Andruw Jones	1.00	.45
❑ 52 Gary Sheffield	.40	.18
❑ 53 Johnny Damon	.40	.18
❑ 54 Rondell White	.40	.18
❑ 55 J.D. Drew	1.00	.45
❑ 56 Tony Batista	.40	.18
❑ 57 Paul Konerko	.40	.18
❑ 58 Rafael Palmeiro	1.00	.45
❑ 59 Cal Ripken	4.00	1.80
❑ 60 Darin Erstad	1.00	.45
❑ 61 Ivan Rodriguez	1.00	.45

❑ 62 Barry Bonds 2.50 1.10
❑ 63 Edgardo Alfonzo .40 .18
❑ 64 Ellis Burks .40 .18
❑ 65 Mike Lieberthal .40 .18
❑ 66 Robin Ventura .40 .18
❑ 67 Richard Hidalgo .40 .18
❑ 68 Magglio Ordonez .40 .18
❑ 69 Kazuhiro Sasaki 1.00 .45
❑ 70 Miguel Tejada .40 .18
❑ 71 David Wells .40 .18
❑ 72 Troy Glaus 1.00 .45
❑ 73 Jose Vidro .40 .18
❑ 74 Shawn Green 1.00 .45
❑ 75 Barry Zito 1.00 .45
❑ 76 Jermaine Dye .40 .18
❑ 77 Geoff Jenkins .40 .18
❑ 78 Jeff Kent .60 .25
❑ 79 Al Leiter .40 .18
❑ 80 Deivi Cruz .40 .18
❑ 81 Eric Karros .40 .18
❑ 82 Albert Belle .40 .18
❑ 83 Pedro Martinez 1.25 .55
❑ 84 Raul Mondesi .40 .18
❑ 85 Preston Wilson .40 .18
❑ 86 Rafael Furcal .40 .18
❑ 87 Rick Ankiel .60 .25
❑ 88 Randy Johnson 1.25 .55
❑ 89 Kevin Brown .40 .18
❑ 90 Sean Casey .60 .25
❑ 91 Mike Mussina 1.00 .45
❑ 92 Alex Rodriguez 2.50 1.10
❑ 93 Andres Galarraga .60 .25
❑ 94 Juan Gonzalez 1.00 .45
❑ 95 Manny Ramirez 1.25 .55
❑ 96 Mark Grace 1.00 .45
❑ 97 Carl Everett .40 .18
❑ 98 Tony Gwynn 2.00 .90
❑ 99 Mike Hampton .40 .18
❑ 100 Ken Caminiti .40 .18
❑ 101 Jason Hart/1749 10.00 4.50
❑ 102 Corey Patterson/1199 8.00 3.60
❑ 103 Timo Perez/1999 8.00 3.60
❑ 104 Marcus Giles/1999 8.00 3.60
❑ 105 Ichiro Suzuki/1999 RC 120.00 55.00
❑ 106 Aubrey Huff/1499 8.00 3.60
❑ 107 Joe Crede/1999 8.00 3.60
❑ 108 Larry Barnes/1499 8.00 3.60
❑ 109 Esix Snead/1999 RC 8.00 3.60
❑ 110 Kenny Kelly/2249 8.00 3.60
❑ 111 Justin Miller/2249 8.00 3.60
❑ 112 Jack Cust/1999 8.00 3.60
❑ 113 Xavier Nady/999 10.00 4.50
❑ 114 Eric Munson/1499 8.00 3.60
❑ 115 Elpidio Guzman/1749 RC 8.00 3.60
❑ 116 Juan Pierre/2189 8.00 3.60
❑ 117 Winston Abreu/1749 RC 8.00 3.60
❑ 118 Keith Ginter/1999 8.00 3.60
❑ 119 Jace Brewer/2699 8.00 3.60
❑ 120 Paxton Crawford/2249 8.00 3.60
❑ 121 Jason Tyner/2249 8.00 3.60
❑ 122 Tike Redman/1999 8.00 3.60
❑ 123 John Riedling/2499 8.00 3.60
❑ 124 Jose Ortiz/1499 10.00 4.50
❑ 125 Oswaldo Mairena/2499 8.00 3.60
❑ 126 Eric Byrnes/2249 8.00 3.60
❑ 127 Brian Cole/999 8.00 3.60
❑ 128 Adam Piatt/2249 8.00 3.60
❑ 129 Nate Rolison/2499 8.00 3.60
❑ 130 Keith McDonald/2249 8.00 3.60
❑ NNO Derek Jeter 200.00 90.00
Base Inks AU/500
❑ MM2 Derek Jeter 15.00 6.75
Monumental Moments
❑ NNO Derek Jeter 200.00 90.00
Monumental Moments AU/96

1993 Finest

	MINT	NRMT
COMPLETE SET (199)	150.00	70.00

❑ 1 David Justice 2.00 .90
❑ 2 Lou Whitaker 2.00 .90
❑ 3 Bryan Harvey 1.00 .45
❑ 4 Carlos Garcia 1.00 .45
❑ 5 Sid Fernandez 1.00 .45

❑ 6 Brett Butler 2.00 .90
❑ 7 Scott Cooper 1.00 .45
❑ 8 B.J. Surhoff 2.00 .90
❑ 9 Steve Finley 2.00 .90
❑ 10 Curt Schilling 5.00 2.20
❑ 11 Jeff Bagwell 6.00 2.70
❑ 12 Alex Cole 1.00 .45
❑ 13 John Olerud 2.00 .90
❑ 14 John Smiley 1.00 .45
❑ 15 Bip Roberts 1.00 .45
❑ 16 Albert Belle 2.00 .90
❑ 17 Duane Ward 1.00 .45
❑ 18 Alan Trammell 3.00 1.35
❑ 19 Andy Benes 1.00 .45
❑ 20 Reggie Sanders 1.00 .45
❑ 21 Todd Zeile 1.00 .45
❑ 22 Rick Aguilera 1.00 .45
❑ 23 Dave Hollins 1.00 .45
❑ 24 Jose Rijo 1.00 .45
❑ 25 Matt Williams 3.00 1.35
❑ 26 Sandy Alomar Jr. 2.00 .90
❑ 27 Alex Fernandez 1.00 .45
❑ 28 Ozzie Smith 6.00 2.70
❑ 29 Ramon Martinez 1.00 .45
❑ 30 Bernie Williams 5.00 2.20
❑ 31 Gary Sheffield 2.00 .90
❑ 32 Eric Karros 2.00 .90
❑ 33 Frank Viola 2.00 .90
❑ 34 Kevin Young 2.00 .90
❑ 35 Ken Hill 1.00 .45
❑ 36 Tony Fernandez 1.00 .45
❑ 37 Tim Wakefield 1.00 .45
❑ 38 John Kruk 2.00 .90
❑ 39 Chris Sabo 1.00 .45
❑ 40 Marquis Grissom 1.00 .45
❑ 41 Glenn Davis 1.00 .45
❑ 42 Jeff Montgomery 1.00 .45
❑ 43 Kenny Lofton 2.00 .90
❑ 44 John Burkett 1.00 .45
❑ 45 Darryl Hamilton 1.00 .45
❑ 46 Jim Abbott 2.00 .90
❑ 47 Ivan Rodriguez 5.00 2.20
❑ 48 Eric Young 1.00 .45
❑ 49 Mitch Williams 1.00 .45
❑ 50 Harold Reynolds 1.00 .45
❑ 51 Brian Harper 1.00 .45
❑ 52 Rafael Palmeiro 5.00 2.20
❑ 53 Bret Saberhagen 2.00 .90
❑ 54 Jeff Conine 1.00 .45
❑ 55 Ivan Calderon 1.00 .45
❑ 56 Juan Guzman 1.00 .45
❑ 57 Carlos Baerga 1.00 .45
❑ 58 Charles Nagy 1.00 .45
❑ 59 Wally Joyner 2.00 .90
❑ 60 Charlie Hayes 1.00 .45
❑ 61 Shane Mack 1.00 .45
❑ 62 Pete Harnisch 1.00 .45
❑ 63 George Brett 10.00 4.50
❑ 64 Lance Johnson 1.00 .45
❑ 65 Ben McDonald 1.00 .45
❑ 66 Bobby Bonilla 2.00 .90
❑ 67 Terry Steinbach 1.00 .45
❑ 68 Ron Gant 1.00 .45
❑ 69 Doug Jones 1.00 .45
❑ 70 Paul Molitor 5.00 2.20
❑ 71 Brady Anderson 2.00 .90
❑ 72 Chuck Finley 2.00 .90
❑ 73 Mark Grace 5.00 2.20
❑ 74 Mike Devereaux 1.00 .45
❑ 75 Tony Phillips 1.00 .45
❑ 76 Chuck Knoblauch 2.00 .90
❑ 77 Tony Gwynn 10.00 4.50
❑ 78 Kevin Appier 2.00 .90
❑ 79 Sammy Sosa 10.00 4.50
❑ 80 Mickey Tettleton 1.00 .45
❑ 81 Felix Jose 1.00 .45
❑ 82 Mark Langston 1.00 .45
❑ 83 Gregg Jefferies 1.00 .45
❑ 84 Andre Dawson AS 3.00 1.35
❑ 85 Greg Maddux AS 12.00 5.50
❑ 86 Rickey Henderson AS 10.00 4.50
❑ 87 Tom Glavine AS 5.00 2.20
❑ 88 Roberto Alomar AS 5.00 2.20
❑ 89 Darryl Strawberry AS 2.00 .90
❑ 90 Wade Boggs AS 5.00 2.20
❑ 91 Bo Jackson AS 2.00 .90
❑ 92 Mark McGwire AS 20.00 9.00
❑ 93 Robin Ventura AS 2.00 .90
❑ 94 Joe Carter AS 2.00 .90
❑ 95 Lee Smith AS 2.00 .90
❑ 96 Cal Ripken AS 20.00 9.00
❑ 97 Larry Walker AS 3.00 1.35
❑ 98 Don Mattingly AS 12.00 5.50
❑ 99 Jose Canseco AS 5.00 2.20
❑ 100 Dennis Eckersley AS 1.00 .45
❑ 101 Terry Pendleton AS 2.00 .90
❑ 102 Frank Thomas AS 6.00 2.70
❑ 103 Barry Bonds AS 12.00 5.50
❑ 104 Roger Clemens AS 12.00 5.50
❑ 105 Ryne Sandberg AS 6.00 2.70
❑ 106 Fred McGriff AS 3.00 1.35
❑ 107 Nolan Ryan AS 25.00 11.00
❑ 108 Will Clark AS 5.00 2.20
❑ 109 Pat Listach AS 1.00 .45
❑ 110 Ken Griffey Jr. AS 15.00 6.75
❑ 111 Cecil Fielder AS 2.00 .90
❑ 112 Kirby Puckett AS 12.00 5.50
❑ 113 Dwight Gooden AS 2.00 .90
❑ 114 Barry Larkin AS 5.00 2.20
❑ 115 David Cone AS 2.00 .90
❑ 116 Juan Gonzalez AS 5.00 2.20
❑ 117 Kent Hrbek 2.00 .90
❑ 118 Tim Wallach 1.00 .45
❑ 119 Craig Biggio 3.00 1.35
❑ 120 Roberto Kelly 1.00 .45
❑ 121 Gregg Olson 1.00 .45
❑ 122 Eddie Murray UER 5.00 2.20
122 career strikeouts
should be 1224
❑ 123 Wil Cordero 1.00 .45
❑ 124 Jay Buhner 2.00 .90
❑ 125 Carlton Fisk 5.00 2.20
❑ 126 Eric Davis 2.00 .90
❑ 127 Doug Drabek 1.00 .45
❑ 128 Ozzie Guillen 1.00 .45
❑ 129 John Wetteland 2.00 .90
❑ 130 Andres Galarraga 3.00 1.35
❑ 131 Ken Caminiti 2.00 .90
❑ 132 Tom Candiotti 1.00 .45
❑ 133 Pat Borders 1.00 .45
❑ 134 Kevin Brown 2.00 .90
❑ 135 Travis Fryman 2.00 .90
❑ 136 Kevin Mitchell 1.00 .45
❑ 137 Greg Swindell 1.00 .45
❑ 138 Benito Santiago 1.00 .45
❑ 139 Reggie Jefferson 1.00 .45
❑ 140 Chris Bosio 1.00 .45
❑ 141 Deion Sanders 2.00 .90
❑ 142 Scott Erickson 1.00 .45
❑ 143 Howard Johnson 1.00 .45
❑ 144 Orestes Destrade 1.00 .45
❑ 145 Jose Guzman 1.00 .45
❑ 146 Chad Curtis 1.00 .45
❑ 147 Cal Eldred 1.00 .45
❑ 148 Willie Greene 1.00 .45
❑ 149 Tommy Greene 1.00 .45
❑ 150 Erik Hanson 1.00 .45
❑ 151 Bob Welch 1.00 .45
❑ 152 John Jaha 1.00 .45
❑ 153 Harold Baines 2.00 .90
❑ 154 Randy Johnson 6.00 2.70
❑ 155 Al Martin 1.00 .45
❑ 156 J.T. Snow RC 6.00 2.70

❑ 157 Mike Mussina 5.00 2.20
❑ 158 Ruben Sierra .... 1.00 .45
❑ 159 Dean Palmer .... 2.00 .90
❑ 160 Steve Avery .... 1.00 .45
❑ 161 Julio Franco .... 2.00 .90
❑ 162 Dave Winfield 5.00 2.20
❑ 163 Tim Salmon .... 2.00 .90
❑ 164 Tom Henke .... 1.00 .45
❑ 165 Mo Vaughn .... 2.00 .90
❑ 166 John Smoltz .... 2.00 .90
❑ 167 Danny Tartabull .... 1.00 .45
❑ 168 Delino DeShields .... 1.00 .45
❑ 169 Charlie Hough .... 2.00 .90
❑ 170 Paul O'Neill 5.00 2.20
❑ 171 Darren Daulton .... 2.00 .90
❑ 172 Jack McDowell .... 1.00 .45
❑ 173 Junior Felix .... 1.00 .45
❑ 174 Jimmy Key .... 2.00 .90
❑ 175 George Bell .... 1.00 .45
❑ 176 Mike Stanton .... 1.00 .45
❑ 177 Len Dykstra .... 2.00 .90
❑ 178 Norm Charlton .... 1.00 .45
❑ 179 Eric Anthony .... 1.00 .45
❑ 180 Rob Dibble .... 1.00 .45
❑ 181 Otis Nixon .... 1.00 .45
❑ 182 Randy Myers .... 1.00 .45
❑ 183 Tim Raines .... 2.00 .90
❑ 184 Orel Hershiser .... 2.00 .90
❑ 185 Andy Van Slyke .... 2.00 .90
❑ 186 Mike Lansing RC .... 2.00 .90
❑ 187 Ray Lankford .... 1.00 .45
❑ 188 Mike Morgan .... 1.00 .45
❑ 189 Moises Alou .... 2.00 .90
❑ 190 Edgar Martinez 3.00 1.35
❑ 191 John Franco .... 2.00 .90
❑ 192 Robin Yount 5.00 2.20
❑ 193 Bob Tewksbury .... 1.00 .45
❑ 194 Jay Bell .... 2.00 .90
❑ 195 Luis Gonzalez 5.00 2.20
❑ 196 Dave Fleming .... 1.00 .45
❑ 197 Mike Greenwell .... 1.00 .45
❑ 198 David Nied .... 1.00 .45
❑ 199 Mike Piazza 25.00 11.00

1994 Finest

	MINT	NRMT
COMPLETE SET (440)	120.00	55.00
COMPLETE SERIES 1 (220) ..	60.00	27.00
COMPLETE SERIES 2 (220) ..	60.00	27.00

❑ 1 Mike Piazza FIN 8.00 3.60
❑ 2 Kevin Stocker FIN .... .50 .23
❑ 3 Greg McMichael FIN .... .50 .23
❑ 4 Jeff Conine FIN .... .50 .23
❑ 5 Rene Arocha FIN .... .50 .23
❑ 6 Aaron Sele FIN .... 1.00 .45
❑ 7 Brent Gates FIN .... .50 .23
❑ 8 Chuck Carr FIN .... .50 .23
❑ 9 Kirk Rueter FIN .... .50 .23
❑ 10 Mike Lansing FIN .... .50 .23
❑ 11 Al Martin FIN .... .50 .23
❑ 12 Jason Bere FIN .... .50 .23
❑ 13 Troy Neel FIN .... .50 .23
❑ 14 Armando Reynoso FIN ..... .50 .23
❑ 15 Jeromy Burnitz FIN .... 1.00 .45
❑ 16 Rich Amaral FIN .... .50 .23
❑ 17 David McCarty FIN .... .50 .23
❑ 18 Tim Salmon FIN .... 1.00 .45
❑ 19 Steve Cooke FIN .... .50 .23
❑ 20 Wil Cordero FIN .... .50 .23
❑ 21 Kevin Tapani .... .50 .23
❑ 22 Deion Sanders .... 1.00 .45
❑ 23 Jose Offerman .... .50 .23
❑ 24 Mark Langston .... .50 .23
❑ 25 Ken Hill .... .50 .23
❑ 26 Alex Fernandez .... .50 .23
❑ 27 Jeff Blauser .... .50 .23
❑ 28 Royce Clayton .... .50 .23
❑ 29 Brad Ausmus .... .50 .23
❑ 30 Ryan Bowen .... .50 .23
❑ 31 Steve Finley .... 1.00 .45
❑ 32 Charlie Hayes .... .50 .23
❑ 33 Jeff Kent .... 1.50 .70
❑ 34 Mike Henneman .... .50 .23
❑ 35 Andres Galarraga .... 1.50 .70
❑ 36 Wayne Kirby .... .50 .23
❑ 37 Joe Oliver .... .50 .23
❑ 38 Terry Steinbach .... .50 .23
❑ 39 Ryan Thompson .... .50 .23
❑ 40 Luis Alicea .... .50 .23
❑ 41 Randy Velarde .... .50 .23
❑ 42 Bob Tewksbury .... .50 .23
❑ 43 Reggie Sanders .... .50 .23
❑ 44 Brian Williams .... .50 .23
❑ 45 Joe Orsulak .... .50 .23
❑ 46 Jose Lind .... .50 .23
❑ 47 Dave Hollins .... .50 .23
❑ 48 Graeme Lloyd .... .50 .23
❑ 49 Jim Gott .... .50 .23
❑ 50 Andre Dawson .... 1.50 .70
❑ 51 Steve Buechele .... .50 .23
❑ 52 David Cone .... 1.00 .45
❑ 53 Ricky Gutierrez .... .50 .23
❑ 54 Lance Johnson .... .50 .23
❑ 55 Tino Martinez .... 1.00 .45
❑ 56 Phil Hiatt .... .50 .23
❑ 57 Carlos Garcia .... .50 .23
❑ 58 Danny Darwin .... .50 .23
❑ 59 Dante Bichette .... 1.00 .45
❑ 60 Scott Kamieniecki .... .50 .23
❑ 61 Orlando Merced .... .50 .23
❑ 62 Brian McRae .... .50 .23
❑ 63 Pat Kelly .... .50 .23
❑ 64 Tom Henke .... .50 .23
❑ 65 Jeff King .... .50 .23
❑ 66 Mike Mussina 2.50 1.10
❑ 67 Tim Pugh .... .50 .23
❑ 68 Robby Thompson .... .50 .23
❑ 69 Paul O'Neill 2.50 1.10
❑ 70 Hal Morris .... .50 .23
❑ 71 Ron Karkovice .... .50 .23
❑ 72 Joe Girardi .... .50 .23
❑ 73 Eduardo Perez .... .50 .23
❑ 74 Raul Mondesi .... 1.00 .45
❑ 75 Mike Gallego .... .50 .23
❑ 76 Mike Stanley .... .50 .23
❑ 77 Kevin Roberson .... .50 .23
❑ 78 Mark McGwire 10.00 4.50
❑ 79 Pat Listach .... .50 .23
❑ 80 Eric Davis .... 1.00 .45
❑ 81 Mike Bordick .... .50 .23
❑ 82 Dwight Gooden .... 1.00 .45
❑ 83 Mike Moore .... .50 .23
❑ 84 Phil Plantier .... .50 .23
❑ 85 Darren Lewis .... .50 .23
❑ 86 Rick Wilkins .... .50 .23
❑ 87 Darryl Strawberry .... 1.00 .45
❑ 88 Rob Dibble .... .50 .23
❑ 89 Greg Vaughn .... 1.00 .45
❑ 90 Jeff Russell .... .50 .23
❑ 91 Mark Lewis .... .50 .23
❑ 92 Gregg Jefferies .... .50 .23
❑ 93 Jose Guzman .... .50 .23
❑ 94 Kenny Rogers .... .50 .23
❑ 95 Mark Lemke .... .50 .23
❑ 96 Mike Morgan .... .50 .23
❑ 97 Andujar Cedeno .... .50 .23
❑ 98 Orel Hershiser .... 1.00 .45
❑ 99 Greg Swindell .... .50 .23
❑ 100 John Smoltz .... 1.00 .45
❑ 101 Pedro A.Martinez RC ...... .50 .23
❑ 102 Jim Thome 2.50 1.10
❑ 103 David Segui .... .50 .23
❑ 104 Charles Nagy .... .50 .23
❑ 105 Shane Mack .... .50 .23
❑ 106 John Jaha .... .50 .23
❑ 107 Tom Candiotti .... .50 .23
❑ 108 David Wells .... 1.00 .45
❑ 109 Bobby Jones .... .50 .23
❑ 110 Bob Hamelin .... .50 .23
❑ 111 Bernard Gilkey .... .50 .23
❑ 112 Chili Davis .... 1.00 .45
❑ 113 Todd Stottlemyre .... .50 .23
❑ 114 Derek Bell .... .50 .23
❑ 115 Mark McLemore .... .50 .23
❑ 116 Mark Whiten .... .50 .23
❑ 117 Mike Devereaux .... .50 .23
❑ 118 Terry Pendleton .... 1.00 .45
❑ 119 Pat Meares .... .50 .23
❑ 120 Pete Harnisch .... .50 .23
❑ 121 Moises Alou .... 1.00 .45
❑ 122 Jay Buhner .... 1.00 .45
❑ 123 Wes Chamberlain .... .50 .23
❑ 124 Mike Perez .... .50 .23
❑ 125 Devon White .... .50 .23
❑ 126 Ivan Rodriguez 2.50 1.10
❑ 127 Don Slaught .... .50 .23
❑ 128 John Valentin .... .50 .23
❑ 129 Jaime Navarro .... .50 .23
❑ 130 Dave Magadan .... .50 .23
❑ 131 Brady Anderson .... 1.00 .45
❑ 132 Juan Guzman .... .50 .23
❑ 133 John Wetteland .... 1.00 .45
❑ 134 Dave Stewart .... 1.00 .45
❑ 135 Scott Servais .... .50 .23
❑ 136 Ozzie Smith 3.00 1.35
❑ 137 Darrin Fletcher .... .50 .23
❑ 138 Jose Mesa .... .50 .23
❑ 139 Wilson Alvarez .... .50 .23
❑ 140 Pete Incaviglia .... .50 .23
❑ 141 Chris Hoiles .... .50 .23
❑ 142 Darryl Hamilton .... .50 .23
❑ 143 Chuck Finley .... 1.00 .45
❑ 144 Archi Cianfrocco .... .50 .23
❑ 145 Bill Wegman .... .50 .23
❑ 146 Joey Cora .... .50 .23
❑ 147 Darrell Whitmore .... .50 .23
❑ 148 David Hulse .... .50 .23
❑ 149 Jim Abbott .... 1.00 .45
❑ 150 Curt Schilling 2.50 1.10
❑ 151 Bill Swift .... .50 .23
❑ 152 Tommy Greene .... .50 .23
❑ 153 Roberto Mejia .... .50 .23
❑ 154 Edgar Martinez .... 1.50 .70
❑ 155 Roger Pavlik .... .50 .23
❑ 156 Randy Tomlin .... .50 .23
❑ 157 J.T. Snow .... 1.00 .45
❑ 158 Bob Welch .... .50 .23
❑ 159 Alan Trammell .... 1.50 .70
❑ 160 Ed Sprague .... .50 .23
❑ 161 Ben McDonald .... .50 .23
❑ 162 Derrick May .... .50 .23
❑ 163 Roberto Kelly .... .50 .23
❑ 164 Bryan Harvey .... .50 .23
❑ 165 Ron Gant .... .50 .23
❑ 166 Scott Erickson .... .50 .23
❑ 167 Anthony Young .... .50 .23
❑ 168 Scott Cooper .... .50 .23
❑ 169 Rod Beck .... .50 .23
❑ 170 John Franco .... 1.00 .45
❑ 171 Gary DiSarcina .... .50 .23
❑ 172 Dave Fleming .... .50 .23
❑ 173 Wade Boggs 2.50 1.10
❑ 174 Kevin Appier .... 1.00 .45
❑ 175 Jose Bautista .... .50 .23
❑ 176 Wally Joyner .... 1.00 .45
❑ 177 Dean Palmer .... 1.00 .45
❑ 178 Tony Phillips .... .50 .23
❑ 179 John Smiley .... .50 .23
❑ 180 Charlie Hough .... 1.00 .45
❑ 181 Scott Fletcher .... .50 .23
❑ 182 Todd Van Poppel .... .50 .23
❑ 183 Mike Blowers .... .50 .23
❑ 184 Willie McGee .... 1.00 .45
❑ 185 Paul Sorrento .... .50 .23
❑ 186 Eric Young .... .50 .23
❑ 187 Bret Barberie .... .50 .23
❑ 188 Manuel Lee .... .50 .23
❑ 189 Jeff Branson .... .50 .23

- ❑ 190 Jim Deshaies .50 .23
- ❑ 191 Ken Caminiti 1.00 .45
- ❑ 192 Tim Raines 1.00 .45
- ❑ 193 Joe Grahe .50 .23
- ❑ 194 Hipolito Pichardo .50 .23
- ❑ 195 Denny Neagle 1.00 .45
- ❑ 196 Jeff Gardner .50 .23
- ❑ 197 Mike Benjamin .50 .23
- ❑ 198 Milt Thompson .50 .23
- ❑ 199 Bruce Ruffin .50 .23
- ❑ 200 Chris Hammond UER .50 .23
  (Back of card has Mariners; should be Marlins)
- ❑ 201 Tony Gwynn FIN 5.00 2.20
- ❑ 202 Robin Ventura FIN 1.00 .45
- ❑ 203 Frank Thomas FIN 3.00 1.35
- ❑ 204 Kirby Puckett FIN 6.00 2.70
- ❑ 205 Roberto Alomar FIN 2.50 1.10
- ❑ 206 Dennis Eckersley FIN 1.00 .45
- ❑ 207 Joe Carter FIN 1.00 .45
- ❑ 208 Albert Belle FIN 1.00 .45
- ❑ 209 Greg Maddux FIN 6.00 2.70
- ❑ 210 Ryne Sandberg FIN 3.00 1.35
- ❑ 211 Juan Gonzalez FIN 2.50 1.10
- ❑ 212 Jeff Bagwell FIN 3.00 1.35
- ❑ 213 Randy Johnson FIN 3.00 1.35
- ❑ 214 Matt Williams FIN 1.50 .70
- ❑ 215 Dave Winfield FIN 2.50 1.10
- ❑ 216 Larry Walker FIN 1.50 .70
- ❑ 217 Roger Clemens FIN 6.00 2.70
- ❑ 218 Kenny Lofton FIN 1.00 .45
- ❑ 219 Cecil Fielder FIN 1.00 .45
- ❑ 220 Darren Daulton FIN 1.00 .45
- ❑ 221 John Olerud FIN 1.00 .45
- ❑ 222 Jose Canseco FIN 2.50 1.10
- ❑ 223 Rickey Henderson FIN 5.00 2.20
- ❑ 224 Fred McGriff FIN 1.50 .70
- ❑ 225 Gary Sheffield FIN 1.00 .45
- ❑ 226 Jack McDowell FIN .50 .23
- ❑ 227 Rafael Palmeiro FIN 2.50 1.10
- ❑ 228 Travis Fryman FIN 1.00 .45
- ❑ 229 Marquis Grissom FIN .50 .23
- ❑ 230 Barry Bonds FIN 6.00 2.70
- ❑ 231 Carlos Baerga FIN .50 .23
- ❑ 232 Ken Griffey Jr. FIN 8.00 3.60
- ❑ 233 David Justice FIN 1.00 .45
- ❑ 234 Bobby Bonilla FIN 1.00 .45
- ❑ 235 Cal Ripken FIN 10.00 4.50
- ❑ 236 Sammy Sosa FIN 5.00 2.20
- ❑ 237 Len Dykstra FIN 1.00 .45
- ❑ 238 Will Clark FIN 2.50 1.10
- ❑ 239 Paul Molitor FIN 2.50 1.10
- ❑ 240 Barry Larkin FIN 2.50 1.10
- ❑ 241 Bo Jackson 1.00 .45
- ❑ 242 Mitch Williams .50 .23
- ❑ 243 Ron Darling .50 .23
- ❑ 244 Darryl Kile 1.00 .45
- ❑ 245 Geronimo Berroa .50 .23
- ❑ 246 Gregg Olson .50 .23
- ❑ 247 Brian Harper .50 .23
- ❑ 248 Rheal Cormier .50 .23
- ❑ 249 Rey Sanchez .50 .23
- ❑ 250 Jeff Fassero .50 .23
- ❑ 251 Sandy Alomar Jr. 1.00 .45
- ❑ 252 Chris Bosio .50 .23
- ❑ 253 Andy Stankiewicz .50 .23
- ❑ 254 Harold Baines 1.00 .45
- ❑ 255 Andy Ashby .50 .23
- ❑ 256 Tyler Green .50 .23
- ❑ 257 Kevin Brown 1.00 .45
- ❑ 258 Mo Vaughn 1.00 .45
- ❑ 259 Mike Harkey .50 .23
- ❑ 260 Dave Henderson .50 .23
- ❑ 261 Kent Hrbek 1.00 .45
- ❑ 262 Darrin Jackson .50 .23
- ❑ 263 Bob Wickman .50 .23
- ❑ 264 Spike Owen .50 .23
- ❑ 265 Todd Jones .50 .23
- ❑ 266 Pat Borders .50 .23
- ❑ 267 Tom Glavine 2.50 1.10
- ❑ 268 Dave Nilsson .50 .23
- ❑ 269 Rich Batchelor .50 .23
- ❑ 270 Delino DeShields .50 .23
- ❑ 271 Felix Fermin .50 .23
- ❑ 272 Orestes Destrade .50 .23
- ❑ 273 Mickey Morandini .50 .23
- ❑ 274 Otis Nixon .50 .23
- ❑ 275 Ellis Burks 1.00 .45
- ❑ 276 Greg Gagne .50 .23
- ❑ 277 John Doherty .50 .23
- ❑ 278 Julio Franco 1.00 .45
- ❑ 279 Bernie Williams 2.50 1.10
- ❑ 280 Rick Aguilera .50 .23
- ❑ 281 Mickey Tettleton .50 .23
- ❑ 282 David Nied .50 .23
- ❑ 283 Johnny Ruffin .50 .23
- ❑ 284 Dan Wilson .50 .23
- ❑ 285 Omar Vizquel 1.00 .45
- ❑ 286 Willie Banks .50 .23
- ❑ 287 Erik Pappas .50 .23
- ❑ 288 Cal Eldred .50 .23
- ❑ 289 Bobby Witt .50 .23
- ❑ 290 Luis Gonzalez 2.50 1.10
- ❑ 291 Greg Pirkl .50 .23
- ❑ 292 Alex Cole .50 .23
- ❑ 293 Ricky Bones .50 .23
- ❑ 294 Denis Boucher .50 .23
- ❑ 295 John Burkett .50 .23
- ❑ 296 Steve Trachsel .50 .23
- ❑ 297 Ricky Jordan .50 .23
- ❑ 298 Mark Dewey .50 .23
- ❑ 299 Jimmy Key 1.00 .45
- ❑ 300 Mike Macfarlane .50 .23
- ❑ 301 Tim Belcher .50 .23
- ❑ 302 Carlos Reyes .50 .23
- ❑ 303 Greg A. Harris .50 .23
- ❑ 304 Brian Anderson RC 1.00 .45
- ❑ 305 Terry Mulholland .50 .23
- ❑ 306 Felix Jose .50 .23
- ❑ 307 Darren Holmes .50 .23
- ❑ 308 Jose Rijo .50 .23
- ❑ 309 Paul Wagner .50 .23
- ❑ 310 Bob Scanlan .50 .23
- ❑ 311 Mike Jackson .50 .23
- ❑ 312 Jose Vizcaino .50 .23
- ❑ 313 Rob Butler .50 .23
- ❑ 314 Kevin Seitzer .50 .23
- ❑ 315 Geronimo Pena .50 .23
- ❑ 316 Hector Carrasco .50 .23
- ❑ 317 Eddie Murray 2.50 1.10
- ❑ 318 Roger Salkeld .50 .23
- ❑ 319 Todd Hundley .50 .23
- ❑ 320 Danny Jackson .50 .23
- ❑ 321 Kevin Young .50 .23
- ❑ 322 Mike Greenwell .50 .23
- ❑ 323 Kevin Mitchell .50 .23
- ❑ 324 Chuck Knoblauch 1.00 .45
- ❑ 325 Danny Tartabull .50 .23
- ❑ 326 Vince Coleman .50 .23
- ❑ 327 Marvin Freeman .50 .23
- ❑ 328 Andy Benes .50 .23
- ❑ 329 Mike Kelly .50 .23
- ❑ 330 Karl Rhodes .50 .23
- ❑ 331 Allen Watson .50 .23
- ❑ 332 Damion Easley .50 .23
- ❑ 333 Reggie Jefferson .50 .23
- ❑ 334 Kevin McReynolds .50 .23
- ❑ 335 Arthur Rhodes .50 .23
- ❑ 336 Brian R. Hunter .50 .23
- ❑ 337 Tom Browning .50 .23
- ❑ 338 Pedro Munoz .50 .23
- ❑ 339 Billy Ripken .50 .23
- ❑ 340 Gene Harris .50 .23
- ❑ 341 Fernando Vina .50 .23
- ❑ 342 Sean Berry .50 .23
- ❑ 343 Pedro Astacio .50 .23
- ❑ 344 B.J. Surhoff 1.00 .45
- ❑ 345 Doug Drabek .50 .23
- ❑ 346 Jody Reed .50 .23
- ❑ 347 Ray Lankford .50 .23
- ❑ 348 Steve Farr .50 .23
- ❑ 349 Eric Anthony .50 .23
- ❑ 350 Pete Smith .50 .23
- ❑ 351 Lee Smith 1.00 .45
- ❑ 352 Mariano Duncan .50 .23
- ❑ 353 Doug Strange .50 .23
- ❑ 354 Tim Bogar .50 .23
- ❑ 355 Dave Weathers .50 .23
- ❑ 356 Eric Karros 1.00 .45
- ❑ 357 Randy Myers .50 .23
- ❑ 358 Chad Curtis .50 .23
- ❑ 359 Steve Avery .50 .23
- ❑ 360 Brian Jordan 1.00 .45
- ❑ 361 Tim Wallach .50 .23
- ❑ 362 Pedro Martinez 4.00 1.80
- ❑ 363 Bip Roberts .50 .23
- ❑ 364 Lou Whitaker 1.00 .45
- ❑ 365 Luis Polonia .50 .23
- ❑ 366 Benito Santiago .50 .23
- ❑ 367 Brett Butler 1.00 .45
- ❑ 368 Shawon Dunston .50 .23
- ❑ 369 Kelly Stinnett RC 1.00 .45
- ❑ 370 Chris Turner .50 .23
- ❑ 371 Ruben Sierra .50 .23
- ❑ 372 Greg A. Harris .50 .23
- ❑ 373 Xavier Hernandez .50 .23
- ❑ 374 Howard Johnson .50 .23
- ❑ 375 Duane Ward .50 .23
- ❑ 376 Roberto Hernandez .50 .23
- ❑ 377 Scott Leius .50 .23
- ❑ 378 Dave Valle .50 .23
- ❑ 379 Sid Fernandez .50 .23
- ❑ 380 Doug Jones .50 .23
- ❑ 381 Zane Smith .50 .23
- ❑ 382 Craig Biggio 1.50 .70
- ❑ 383 Rick White RC .50 .23
- ❑ 384 Tom Pagnozzi .50 .23
- ❑ 385 Chris James .50 .23
- ❑ 386 Bret Boone 1.00 .45
- ❑ 387 Jeff Montgomery .50 .23
- ❑ 388 Chad Kreuter .50 .23
- ❑ 389 Greg Hibbard .50 .23
- ❑ 390 Mark Grace 2.50 1.10
- ❑ 391 Phil Leftwich RC .50 .23
- ❑ 392 Don Mattingly 6.00 2.70
- ❑ 393 Ozzie Guillen .50 .23
- ❑ 394 Gary Gaetti 1.00 .45
- ❑ 395 Erik Hanson .50 .23
- ❑ 396 Scott Brosius 1.00 .45
- ❑ 397 Tom Gordon .50 .23
- ❑ 398 Bill Gullickson .50 .23
- ❑ 399 Matt Mieske .50 .23
- ❑ 400 Pat Hentgen .50 .23
- ❑ 401 Walt Weiss .50 .23
- ❑ 402 Greg Blosser .50 .23
- ❑ 403 Stan Javier .50 .23
- ❑ 404 Doug Henry .50 .23
- ❑ 405 Ramon Martinez .50 .23
- ❑ 406 Frank Viola 1.00 .45
- ❑ 407 Mike Hampton 1.00 .45
- ❑ 408 Andy Van Slyke 1.00 .45
- ❑ 409 Bobby Ayala .50 .23
- ❑ 410 Todd Zeile .50 .23
- ❑ 411 Jay Bell 1.00 .45
- ❑ 412 Dennis Martinez 1.00 .45
- ❑ 413 Mark Portugal .50 .23
- ❑ 414 Bobby Munoz .50 .23
- ❑ 415 Kirt Manwaring .50 .23
- ❑ 416 John Kruk 1.00 .45
- ❑ 417 Trevor Hoffman 1.00 .45
- ❑ 418 Chris Sabo .50 .23
- ❑ 419 Bret Saberhagen 1.00 .45
- ❑ 420 Chris Nabholz .50 .23
- ❑ 421 James Mouton FIN .50 .23
- ❑ 422 Tony Tarasco FIN .50 .23
- ❑ 423 Carlos Delgado FIN 4.00 1.80
- ❑ 424 Rondell White FIN 1.00 .45
- ❑ 425 Javier Lopez FIN 1.00 .45
- ❑ 426 Chan Ho Park FIN RC 8.00 3.60
- ❑ 427 Cliff Floyd FIN 1.00 .45
- ❑ 428 Dave Staton FIN .50 .23
- ❑ 429 J.R. Phillips FIN .50 .23
- ❑ 430 Manny Ramirez FIN 4.00 1.80
- ❑ 431 Kurt Abbott FIN RC 1.00 .45
- ❑ 432 Melvin Nieves FIN .50 .23
- ❑ 433 Alex Gonzalez FIN .50 .23
- ❑ 434 Rick Helling FIN .50 .23
- ❑ 435 Danny Bautista FIN .50 .23
- ❑ 436 Matt Walbeck FIN .50 .23
- ❑ 437 Ryan Klesko FIN 1.00 .45
- ❑ 438 Steve Karsay FIN .50 .23
- ❑ 439 Salomon Torres FIN .50 .23
- ❑ 440 Scott Ruffcorn FIN .50 .23

1995 Finest

	MINT	NRMT
COMPLETE SET (330)	80.00	36.00

COMPLETE SERIES 1 (220) .. 60.00 27.00
COMPLETE SERIES 2 (110) .. 20.00 9.00

❑ 1 Raul Mondesi .75 .35
❑ 2 Kurt Abbott .50 .23
❑ 3 Chris Gomez .50 .23
❑ 4 Manny Ramirez 2.50 1.10
❑ 5 Rondell White .75 .35
❑ 6 William VanLandingham .50 .23
❑ 7 Jon Lieber .50 .23
❑ 8 Ryan Klesko .75 .35
❑ 9 John Hudek .50 .23
❑ 10 Joey Hamilton .50 .23
❑ 11 Bob Hamelin .50 .23
❑ 12 Brian Anderson .50 .23
❑ 13 Mike Lieberthal .75 .35
❑ 14 Rico Brogna .50 .23
❑ 15 Rusty Greer .75 .35
❑ 16 Carlos Delgado 2.00 .90
❑ 17 Jim Edmonds 1.25 .55
❑ 18 Steve Trachsel .50 .23
❑ 19 Matt Walbeck .50 .23
❑ 20 Armando Benitez .75 .35
❑ 21 Steve Karsay .50 .23
❑ 22 Jose Oliva .50 .23
❑ 23 Cliff Floyd .75 .35
❑ 24 Kevin Foster .50 .23
❑ 25 Javier Lopez .75 .35
❑ 26 Jose Valentin .50 .23
❑ 27 James Mouton .50 .23
❑ 28 Hector Carrasco .50 .23
❑ 29 Orlando Miller .50 .23
❑ 30 Garret Anderson .75 .35
❑ 31 Marvin Freeman .50 .23
❑ 32 Brett Butler .75 .35
❑ 33 Roberto Kelly .50 .23
❑ 34 Rod Beck .50 .23
❑ 35 Jose Rijo .50 .23
❑ 36 Edgar Martinez 1.25 .55
❑ 37 Jim Thome 2.00 .90
❑ 38 Rick Wilkins .50 .23
❑ 39 Wally Joyner .75 .35
❑ 40 Wil Cordero .50 .23
❑ 41 Tommy Greene .50 .23
❑ 42 Travis Fryman .75 .35
❑ 43 Don Slaught .50 .23
❑ 44 Brady Anderson .75 .35
❑ 45 Matt Williams 1.25 .55
❑ 46 Rene Arocha .50 .23
❑ 47 Rickey Henderson 4.00 1.80
❑ 48 Mike Mussina 2.00 .90
❑ 49 Greg McMichael .50 .23
❑ 50 Jody Reed .50 .23
❑ 51 Tino Martinez .75 .35
❑ 52 Dave Clark .50 .23
❑ 53 John Valentin .50 .23
❑ 54 Bret Boone .75 .35
❑ 55 Walt Weiss .50 .23
❑ 56 Kenny Lofton .75 .35
❑ 57 Scott Leius .50 .23
❑ 58 Eric Karros .75 .35
❑ 59 John Olerud .75 .35
❑ 60 Chris Hoiles .50 .23
❑ 61 Sandy Alomar Jr. .75 .35
❑ 62 Tim Wallach .50 .23
❑ 63 Cal Eldred .50 .23
❑ 64 Tom Glavine 2.00 .90
❑ 65 Mark Grace 2.00 .90
❑ 66 Rey Sanchez .50 .23
❑ 67 Bobby Ayala .50 .23
❑ 68 Dante Bichette .75 .35
❑ 69 Andres Galarraga 1.25 .55
❑ 70 Chuck Carr .50 .23
❑ 71 Bobby Witt .50 .23
❑ 72 Steve Avery .50 .23
❑ 73 Bobby Jones .50 .23
❑ 74 Delino DeShields .50 .23
❑ 75 Kevin Tapani .50 .23
❑ 76 Randy Johnson 2.50 1.10
❑ 77 David Nied .50 .23
❑ 78 Pat Hentgen .50 .23
❑ 79 Tim Salmon .75 .35
❑ 80 Todd Zeile .50 .23
❑ 81 John Wetteland .75 .35
❑ 82 Albert Belle .75 .35
❑ 83 Ben McDonald .50 .23
❑ 84 Bobby Munoz .50 .23
❑ 85 Bip Roberts .50 .23
❑ 86 Mo Vaughn .75 .35
❑ 87 Chuck Finley .75 .35
❑ 88 Chuck Knoblauch .75 .35
❑ 89 Frank Thomas 2.50 1.10
❑ 90 Danny Tartabull .50 .23
❑ 91 Dean Palmer .75 .35
❑ 92 Len Dykstra .75 .35
❑ 93 J.R. Phillips .50 .23
❑ 94 Tom Candiotti .50 .23
❑ 95 Marquis Grissom .50 .23
❑ 96 Barry Larkin 2.00 .90
❑ 97 Bryan Harvey .50 .23
❑ 98 David Justice .75 .35
❑ 99 David Cone .75 .35
❑ 100 Wade Boggs 2.00 .90
❑ 101 Jason Bere .50 .23
❑ 102 Hal Morris .50 .23
❑ 103 Fred McGriff 1.25 .55
❑ 104 Bobby Bonilla .75 .35
❑ 105 Jay Buhner .75 .35
❑ 106 Allen Watson .50 .23
❑ 107 Mickey Tettleton .50 .23
❑ 108 Kevin Appier .75 .35
❑ 109 Ivan Rodriguez 2.00 .90
❑ 110 Carlos Garcia .50 .23
❑ 111 Andy Benes .50 .23
❑ 112 Eddie Murray 2.00 .90
❑ 113 Mike Piazza 5.00 2.20
❑ 114 Greg Vaughn .75 .35
❑ 115 Paul Molitor 2.00 .90
❑ 116 Terry Steinbach .50 .23
❑ 117 Jeff Bagwell 2.50 1.10
❑ 118 Ken Griffey Jr. 6.00 2.70
❑ 119 Gary Sheffield .75 .35
❑ 120 Cal Ripken 8.00 3.60
❑ 121 Jeff Kent 1.25 .55
❑ 122 Jay Bell .75 .35
❑ 123 Will Clark 2.00 .90
❑ 124 Cecil Fielder .75 .35
❑ 125 Alex Fernandez .50 .23
❑ 126 Don Mattingly 5.00 2.20
❑ 127 Reggie Sanders .50 .23
❑ 128 Moises Alou .75 .35
❑ 129 Craig Biggio 1.25 .55
❑ 130 Eddie Williams .50 .23
❑ 131 John Franco .75 .35
❑ 132 John Kruk .75 .35
❑ 133 Jeff King .50 .23
❑ 134 Royce Clayton .50 .23
❑ 135 Doug Drabek .50 .23
❑ 136 Ray Lankford .50 .23
❑ 137 Roberto Alomar 2.00 .90
❑ 138 Todd Hundley .50 .23
❑ 139 Alex Cole .50 .23
❑ 140 Shawon Dunston .50 .23
❑ 141 John Roper .50 .23
❑ 142 Mark Langston .50 .23
❑ 143 Tom Pagnozzi .50 .23
❑ 144 Wilson Alvarez .50 .23
❑ 145 Scott Cooper .50 .23
❑ 146 Kevin Mitchell .50 .23
❑ 147 Mark Whiten .50 .23
❑ 148 Jeff Conine .50 .23
❑ 149 Chili Davis .75 .35
❑ 150 Luis Gonzalez 2.00 .90
❑ 151 Juan Guzman .50 .23
❑ 152 Mike Greenwell .50 .23
❑ 153 Mike Henneman .50 .23
❑ 154 Rick Aguilera .50 .23
❑ 155 Dennis Eckersley .75 .35
❑ 156 Darrin Fletcher .50 .23
❑ 157 Darren Lewis .50 .23
❑ 158 Juan Gonzalez 2.00 .90
❑ 159 Dave Hollins .50 .23
❑ 160 Jimmy Key .75 .35
❑ 161 Roberto Hernandez .50 .23
❑ 162 Randy Myers .50 .23
❑ 163 Joe Carter .75 .35
❑ 164 Darren Daulton .75 .35
❑ 165 Mike Macfarlane .50 .23
❑ 166 Bret Saberhagen .75 .35
❑ 167 Kirby Puckett 5.00 2.20
❑ 168 Lance Johnson .50 .23
❑ 169 Mark McGwire 8.00 3.60
❑ 170 Jose Canseco 2.00 .90
❑ 171 Mike Stanley .50 .23
❑ 172 Lee Smith .75 .35
❑ 173 Robin Ventura .75 .35
❑ 174 Greg Gagne .50 .23
❑ 175 Brian McRae .50 .23
❑ 176 Mike Bordick .50 .23
❑ 177 Rafael Palmeiro 2.00 .90
❑ 178 Kenny Rogers .50 .23
❑ 179 Chad Curtis .50 .23
❑ 180 Devon White .75 .35
❑ 181 Paul O'Neill 2.00 .90
❑ 182 Ken Caminiti .75 .35
❑ 183 Dave Nilsson .50 .23
❑ 184 Tim Naehring .50 .23
❑ 185 Roger Clemens 5.00 2.20
❑ 186 Otis Nixon .50 .23
❑ 187 Tim Raines .75 .35
❑ 188 Denny Martinez .75 .35
❑ 189 Pedro Martinez 2.50 1.10
❑ 190 Jim Abbott .75 .35
❑ 191 Ryan Thompson .50 .23
❑ 192 Barry Bonds 5.00 2.20
❑ 193 Joe Girardi .50 .23
❑ 194 Steve Finley .75 .35
❑ 195 John Jaha .50 .23
❑ 196 Tony Gwynn 4.00 1.80
❑ 197 Sammy Sosa 4.00 1.80
❑ 198 John Burkett .50 .23
❑ 199 Carlos Baerga .50 .23
❑ 200 Ramon Martinez .50 .23
❑ 201 Aaron Sele .75 .35
❑ 202 Eduardo Perez .50 .23
❑ 203 Alan Trammell 1.25 .55
❑ 204 Orlando Merced .50 .23
❑ 205 Deion Sanders .75 .35
❑ 206 Robb Nen .50 .23
❑ 207 Jack McDowell .50 .23
❑ 208 Ruben Sierra .50 .23
❑ 209 Bernie Williams 2.00 .90
❑ 210 Kevin Seitzer .50 .23
❑ 211 Charles Nagy .50 .23
❑ 212 Tony Phillips .50 .23
❑ 213 Greg Maddux 5.00 2.20
❑ 214 Jeff Montgomery .50 .23
❑ 215 Larry Walker 1.25 .55
❑ 216 Andy Van Slyke .75 .35
❑ 217 Ozzie Smith 2.50 1.10
❑ 218 Geronimo Pena .50 .23
❑ 219 Gregg Jefferies .50 .23
❑ 220 Lou Whitaker .75 .35
❑ 221 Chipper Jones 4.00 1.80
❑ 222 Benji Gil .50 .23
❑ 223 Tony Phillips .50 .23
❑ 224 Trevor Wilson .50 .23
❑ 225 Tony Tarasco .50 .23
❑ 226 Roberto Petagine .50 .23
❑ 227 Mike Macfarlane .50 .23
❑ 228 Hideo Nomo RCUER .. 8.00 3.60
(In 3rd line agianst)
❑ 229 Mark McLemore .50 .23
❑ 230 Ron Gant .50 .23
❑ 231 Andujar Cedeno .50 .23
❑ 232 Mike Mimbs RC .50 .23
❑ 233 Jim Abbott .75 .35
❑ 234 Ricky Bones .50 .23
❑ 235 Marty Cordova .50 .23

❑ 236 Mark Johnson RC .75 .35
❑ 237 Marquis Grissom .50 .23
❑ 238 Tom Henke .50 .23
❑ 239 Terry Pendleton .75 .35
❑ 240 John Wetteland .75 .35
❑ 241 Lee Smith .75 .35
❑ 242 Jaime Navarro .50 .23
❑ 243 Luis Alicea .50 .23
❑ 244 Scott Cooper .50 .23
❑ 245 Gary Gaetti .75 .35
❑ 246 Edgardo Alfonzo UER .. 2.00 .90
(Incomplete career BA)
❑ 247 Brad Clontz .50 .23
❑ 248 Dave Mlicki .50 .23
❑ 249 Dave Winfield 2.00 .90
❑ 250 Mark Grudzielanek RC 2.50 1.10
❑ 251 Alex Gonzalez .50 .23
❑ 252 Kevin Brown .75 .35
❑ 253 Esteban Loaiza .50 .23
❑ 254 Vaughn Eshelman .50 .23
❑ 255 Bill Swift .50 .23
❑ 256 Brian McRae .50 .23
❑ 257 Bobby Higginson RC 5.00 2.20
❑ 258 Jack McDowell .50 .23
❑ 259 Scott Stahoviak .50 .23
❑ 260 Jon Nunnally .50 .23
❑ 261 Charlie Hayes .50 .23
❑ 262 Jacob Brumfield .50 .23
❑ 263 Chad Curtis .50 .23
❑ 264 Heathcliff Slocumb .50 .23
❑ 265 Mark Whiten .50 .23
❑ 266 Mickey Tettleton .50 .23
❑ 267 Jose Mesa .50 .23
❑ 268 Doug Jones .50 .23
❑ 269 Trevor Hoffman .75 .35
❑ 270 Paul Sorrento .50 .23
❑ 271 Shane Andrews .50 .23
❑ 272 Brett Butler .75 .35
❑ 273 Curtis Goodwin .50 .23
❑ 274 Larry Walker 1.25 .55
❑ 275 Phil Plantier .50 .23
❑ 276 Ken Hill .50 .23
❑ 277 Vinny Castilla UER .75 .35
Rockies spelled Rockie
❑ 278 Billy Ashley .50 .23
❑ 279 Derek Jeter 8.00 3.60
❑ 280 Bob Tewksbury .50 .23
❑ 281 Jose Offerman .50 .23
❑ 282 Glenallen Hill .50 .23
❑ 283 Tony Fernandez .50 .23
❑ 284 Mike Devereaux .50 .23
❑ 285 John Burkett .50 .23
❑ 286 Geronimo Berroa .50 .23
❑ 287 Quilvio Veras .50 .23
❑ 288 Jason Bates .50 .23
❑ 289 Lee Tinsley .50 .23
❑ 290 Derek Bell .50 .23
❑ 291 Jeff Fassero .50 .23
❑ 292 Ray Durham .75 .35
❑ 293 Chad Ogea .50 .23
❑ 294 Bill Pulsipher .50 .23
❑ 295 Phil Nevin .75 .35
❑ 296 Carlos Perez RC .75 .35
❑ 297 Roberto Kelly .50 .23
❑ 298 Tim Wakefield .50 .23
❑ 299 Jeff Manto .50 .23
❑ 300 Brian Hunter .50 .23
❑ 301 C.J. Nitkowski .50 .23
❑ 302 Dustin Hermanson .50 .23
❑ 303 John Mabry .50 .23
❑ 304 Orel Hershiser .75 .35
❑ 305 Ron Villone .50 .23
❑ 306 Sean Bergman .50 .23
❑ 307 Tom Goodwin .50 .23
❑ 308 Al Reyes .50 .23
❑ 309 Todd Stottlemyre .50 .23
❑ 310 Rich Becker .50 .23
❑ 311 Joey Cora .50 .23
❑ 312 Ed Sprague .50 .23
❑ 313 John Smoltz UER .75 .35
(3rd line; from spelled as form)
❑ 314 Frank Castillo .50 .23
❑ 315 Chris Hammond .50 .23
❑ 316 Ismael Valdes .50 .23
❑ 317 Pete Harnisch .50 .23
❑ 318 Bernard Gilkey .50 .23
❑ 319 John Kruk .75 .35
❑ 320 Marc Newfield .50 .23
❑ 321 Brian Johnson .50 .23
❑ 322 Mark Portugal .50 .23
❑ 323 David Hulse .50 .23
❑ 324 Luis Ortiz UER .50 .23
(Below spelled beloe)
❑ 325 Mike Benjamin .50 .23
❑ 326 Brian Jordan .75 .35
❑ 327 Shawn Green 2.00 .90
❑ 328 Joe Oliver .50 .23
❑ 329 Felipe Lira .50 .23
❑ 330 Andre Dawson 1.25 .55

1996 Finest

	MINT	NRMT
COMP.BRONZE SER.1 (110)	25.00	11.00
COMP.BRONZE SER.2 (110)	30.00	13.50
COMMON BRONZE	.25	.11
COMP.GOLD SER.1 (26)	500.00	220.00
COMP.GOLD SER.2 (22)	250.00	110.00
COMMON GOLD	4.00	1.80
COMP.SILVER SER.1 (55)	150.00	70.00
COMP.SILVER SER.2 (36)	80.00	36.00
COMMON SILVER	1.50	.70

❑ B5 Roberto Hernandez B .25 .11
❑ B8 Terry Pendleton B .40 .18
❑ B12 Ken Caminiti B .40 .18
❑ B15 Dan Miceli B .25 .11
❑ B16 Chipper Jones B 2.00 .90
❑ B17 John Wetteland B .40 .18
❑ B19 Tim Naehring B .25 .11
❑ B21 Eddie Murray B 1.00 .45
❑ B23 Kevin Appier B .40 .18
❑ B24 Ken Griffey Jr. B 3.00 1.35
❑ B26 Brian McRae B .25 .11
❑ B27 Pedro Martinez B 1.25 .55
❑ B28 Brian Jordan B .40 .18
❑ B29 Mike Fetters B .25 .11
❑ B30 Carlos Delgado B 1.00 .45
❑ B31 Shane Reynolds B .25 .11
❑ B32 Terry Steinbach B .25 .11
❑ B34 Mark Leiter B .25 .11
❑ B36 David Segui B .25 .11
❑ B40 Fred McGriff B .60 .25
❑ B44 Glenallen Hill B .25 .11
❑ B45 Brady Anderson B .40 .18
❑ B47 Jim Thome B 1.00 .45
❑ B48 Frank Thomas B 1.25 .55
❑ B49 Chuck Knoblauch B .40 .18
❑ B50 Len Dykstra B .40 .18
❑ B53 Tom Pagnozzi B .25 .11
❑ B55 Ricky Bones B .25 .11
❑ B56 David Justice B .40 .18
❑ B57 Steve Avery B .25 .11
❑ B58 Robby Thompson B .25 .11
❑ B61 Tony Gwynn B 2.00 .90
❑ B63 Denny Neagle B .40 .18
❑ B67 Robin Ventura B .40 .18
❑ B70 Kevin Seitzer B .25 .11
❑ B71 Ramon Martinez B .25 .11
❑ B75 Brian L.Hunter B .25 .11
❑ B76 Alan Benes B .25 .11
❑ B80 Ozzie Guillen B .25 .11
❑ B82 Benji Gil B .25 .11
❑ B85 Todd Hundley B .25 .11
❑ B87 Pat Hentgen B .25 .11
❑ B89 Chuck Finley B .40 .18
❑ B92 Derek Jeter B 4.00 1.80
❑ B93 Paul O'Neill B 1.00 .45
❑ B94 Darrin Fletcher B .25 .11
❑ B96 Delino DeShields B .25 .11
❑ B97 Tim Salmon B .40 .18
❑ B98 John Olerud B .40 .18
❑ B101 Tim Wakefield B .25 .11
❑ B103 Dave Stevens B .25 .11
❑ B104 Orlando Merced B .25 .11
❑ B106 Jay Bell B .40 .18
❑ B107 John Burkett B .25 .11
❑ B108 Chris Hoiles B .25 .11
❑ B110 Dave Nilsson B .25 .11
❑ B111 Rod Beck B .25 .11
❑ B113 Mike Piazza B 2.50 1.10
❑ B114 Mark Langston B .25 .11
❑ B116 Rico Brogna B .25 .11
❑ B118 Tom Goodwin B .25 .11
❑ B119 Bryan Rekar B .25 .11
❑ B120 David Cone B .40 .18
❑ B122 Andy Pettitte B .40 .18
❑ B123 Chili Davis B .40 .18
❑ B124 John Smoltz B .40 .18
❑ B125 H.Slocumb B .25 .11
❑ B126 Dante Bichette B .40 .18
❑ B128 Alex Gonzalez B .25 .11
❑ B129 Jeff Montgomery B .25 .11
❑ B131 Denny Martinez B .40 .18
❑ B132 Mel Rojas B .25 .11
❑ B133 Derek Bell B .25 .11
❑ B134 Trevor Hoffman B .40 .18
❑ B136 Darren Daulton B .40 .18
❑ B137 Pete Schourek B .25 .11
❑ B138 Phil Nevin B .40 .18
❑ B139 Andres Galarraga B .60 .25
❑ B140 Chad Fonville B .25 .11
❑ B144 J.T. Snow B .40 .18
❑ B146 Barry Bonds B 2.50 1.10
❑ B147 Orel Hershiser B .40 .18
❑ B148 Quilvio Veras B .25 .11
❑ B149 Will Clark B 1.00 .45
❑ B150 Jose Rijo B .25 .11
❑ B152 Travis Fryman B .40 .18
❑ B154 Alex Fernandez B .25 .11
❑ B155 Wade Boggs B 1.00 .45
❑ B156 Troy Percival B .25 .11
❑ B157 Moises Alou B .40 .18
❑ B158 Javy Lopez B .40 .18
❑ B159 Jason Giambi B 1.00 .45
❑ B162 Mark McGwire B 4.00 1.80
❑ B163 Eric Karros B .40 .18
❑ B166 Mickey Tettleton B .25 .11
❑ B167 Barry Larkin B 1.00 .45
❑ B169 Ruben Sierra B .25 .11
❑ B170 Bill Swift B .25 .11
❑ B172 Chad Curtis B .25 .11
❑ B173 Dean Palmer B .40 .18
❑ B175 Bobby Bonilla B .40 .18
❑ B176 Greg Colbrunn B .25 .11
❑ B177 Jose Mesa B .25 .11
❑ B178 Mike Greenwell B .25 .11
❑ B181 Doug Drabek B .25 .11
❑ B183 Wilson Alvarez B .25 .11
❑ B184 Marty Cordova B .25 .11
❑ B185 Hal Morris B .25 .11
❑ B187 Carlos Garcia B .25 .11
❑ B190 Marquis Grissom B .25 .11
❑ B193 Will Clark B 1.00 .45
❑ B194 Paul Molitor B 1.00 .45
❑ B195 Kenny Rogers B .25 .11
❑ B196 Reggie Sanders B .25 .11
❑ B199 Raul Mondesi B .40 .18
❑ B200 Lance Johnson B .25 .11
❑ B201 Alvin Morman B .25 .11
❑ B203 Jack McDowell B .25 .11
❑ B204 Randy Myers B .25 .11
❑ B205 Harold Baines B .40 .18
❑ B206 Marty Cordova B .25 .11
❑ B207 Rich Hunter B RC .25 .11
❑ B208 Al Leiter B .40 .18
❑ B209 Greg Gagne B .25 .11
❑ B210 Ben McDonald B .25 .11
❑ B212 Terry Adams B .25 .11
❑ B213 Paul Sorrento B .25 .11

Card	Player	Mint	NRMT
❑ B214	Albert Belle B	.40	.18
❑ B215	Mike Blowers B	.25	.11
❑ B216	Jim Edmonds B	.60	.25
❑ B217	Felipe Crespo B	.25	.11
❑ B219	Shawon Dunston B	.25	.11
❑ B220	Jimmy Haynes B	.25	.11
❑ B221	Jose Canseco B	1.00	.45
❑ B222	Eric Davis B	.40	.18
❑ B224	Tim Raines B	.40	.18
❑ B225	Tony Phillips B	.25	.11
❑ B226	Charlie Hayes B	.25	.11
❑ B227	Eric Owens B	.25	.11
❑ B228	Roberto Alomar B	1.00	.45
❑ B233	Kenny Lofton B	.40	.18
❑ B236	Mark McGwire B	4.00	1.80
❑ B237	Jay Buhner B	.40	.18
❑ B238	Craig Biggio B	.60	.25
❑ B240	Barry Bonds B	2.50	1.10
❑ B244	Ron Gant B	.25	.11
❑ B245	Paul Wilson B	.25	.11
❑ B246	T.Hollandsworth B	.25	.11
❑ B247	Todd Zeile B	.25	.11
❑ B248	David Justice B	.40	.18
❑ B250	Moises Alou B	.40	.18
❑ B251	Bob Wolcott B	.25	.11
❑ B252	David Wells B	.40	.18
❑ B253	Juan Gonzalez B	1.00	.45
❑ B254	Andres Galarraga B	.60	.25
❑ B255	Dave Hollins B	.25	.11
❑ B257	Sammy Sosa B	2.00	.90
❑ B258	Ivan Rodriguez B	1.00	.45
❑ B259	Bip Roberts B	.25	.11
❑ B260	Tino Martinez B	.40	.18
❑ B262	Mike Stanley B	.25	.11
❑ B264	Butch Huskey B	.25	.11
❑ B265	Jeff Conine B	.25	.11
❑ B267	Mark Grace B	1.00	.45
❑ B268	Jason Schmidt B	.25	.11
❑ B269	Otis Nixon B	.25	.11
❑ B271	Kirby Puckett B	2.50	1.10
❑ B273	Andy Benes B	.25	.11
❑ B275	Mike Piazza B	2.50	1.10
❑ B276	Rey Ordonez B	.25	.11
❑ B278	Gary Gaetti B	.40	.18
❑ B280	Robin Ventura B	.40	.18
❑ B281	Cal Ripken B	4.00	1.80
❑ B282	Carlos Baerga B	.25	.11
❑ B283	Roger Cedeno B	.25	.11
❑ B285	Terrell Wade B	.25	.11
❑ B286	Kevin Brown B	.40	.18
❑ B287	Rafael Palmeiro B	1.00	.45
❑ B288	Mo Vaughn B	.40	.18
❑ B292	Bob Tewksbury B	.25	.11
❑ B297	T.J. Mathews B	.25	.11
❑ B298	Manny Ramirez B	1.25	.55
❑ B299	Jeff Bagwell B	1.25	.55
❑ B301	Wade Boggs B	1.00	.45
❑ B303	Steve Gibralter B	.25	.11
❑ B304	B.J. Surhoff B	.40	.18
❑ B306	Royce Clayton B	.25	.11
❑ B307	Sal Fasano B	.25	.11
❑ B309	Gary Sheffield B	.40	.18
❑ B310	Ken Hill B	.25	.11
❑ B311	Joe Girardi B	.25	.11
❑ B312	Matt Lawton B RC	1.50	.70
❑ B314	Julio Franco B	.40	.18
❑ B315	Joe Carter B	.40	.18
❑ B316	Brooks Kieschnick B	.25	.11
❑ B318	H.Slocumb B	.25	.11
❑ B319	Barry Larkin B	1.00	.45
❑ B320	Tony Gwynn B	2.00	.90
❑ B322	Frank Thomas B	1.25	.55
❑ B323	Edgar Martinez B	.60	.25
❑ B325	Henry Rodriguez B	.25	.11
❑ B326	Marvin Benard B RC	.40	.18
❑ B329	Ugueth Urbina B	.25	.11
❑ B331	Roger Salkeld B	.25	.11
❑ B332	Edgar Renteria B	.25	.11
❑ B333	Ryan Klesko B	.40	.18
❑ B334	Ray Lankford B	.25	.11
❑ B336	Justin Thompson B	.25	.11
❑ B339	Mark Clark B	.25	.11
❑ B340	Ruben Rivera B	.25	.11
❑ B342	Matt Williams B	.60	.25
❑ B343	F.Cordova B RC	.25	.11
❑ B344	Cecil Fielder B	.40	.18
❑ B348	Mark Grudzielanek B	.25	.11
❑ B349	Ron Coomer B	.25	.11
❑ B351	Rich Aurilia B RC	3.00	1.35
❑ B352	Jose Herrera B	.25	.11
❑ B356	Tony Clark B	.40	.18
❑ B358	Dan Naulty B	.25	.11
❑ B359	Checklist B	.25	.11
❑ G4	Marty Cordova G	4.00	1.80
❑ G6	Tony Gwynn G	20.00	9.00
❑ G9	Albert Belle G	4.00	1.80
❑ G18	Kirby Puckett G	25.00	11.00
❑ G20	Karim Garcia G	4.00	1.80
❑ G25	Cal Ripken G	40.00	18.00
❑ G33	Hideo Nomo G	12.00	5.50
❑ G39	Ryne Sandberg G	12.00	5.50
❑ G42	Jeff Bagwell G	12.00	5.50
❑ G51	Jason Isringhausen G	4.00	1.80
❑ G64	Mo Vaughn G	4.00	1.80
❑ G66	Dante Bichette G	4.00	1.80
❑ G74	Mark McGwire G	40.00	18.00
❑ G81	Kenny Lofton G	4.00	1.80
❑ G83	Jim Edmonds G	6.00	2.70
❑ G90	Mike Mussina G	10.00	4.50
❑ G100	Jeff Conine G	4.00	1.80
❑ G102	Johnny Damon G	4.00	1.80
❑ G105	Barry Bonds G	25.00	11.00
❑ G117	Jose Canseco G	1.00	.45
❑ G135	Ken Griffey Jr. G	30.00	13.50
❑ G141	Chipper Jones G	20.00	9.00
❑ G145	Greg Maddux G	25.00	11.00
❑ G164	Jay Buhner G	4.00	1.80
❑ G186	Frank Thomas G	12.00	5.50
❑ G191	Checklist G	4.00	1.80
❑ G192	Chipper Jones G	20.00	9.00
❑ G197	Roberto Alomar G	10.00	4.50
❑ G198	Dennis Eckersley G	4.00	1.80
❑ G202	George Arias G	4.00	1.80
❑ G232	Hideo Nomo G	12.00	5.50
❑ G243	Chris Snopek G	4.00	1.80
❑ G249	Tim Salmon G	4.00	1.80
❑ G266	Matt Williams G	6.00	2.70
❑ G270	Randy Johnson G	12.00	5.50
❑ G279	Paul Molitor G	10.00	4.50
❑ G290	Cecil Fielder G	4.00	1.80
❑ G294	L.Hernandez G RC	8.00	3.60
❑ G300	Marty Janzen G RC	4.00	1.80
❑ G308	Ron Gant G	4.00	1.80
❑ G321	Ryan Klesko G	4.00	1.80
❑ G324	Jermaine Dye G	4.00	1.80
❑ G330	Jason Giambi G	10.00	4.50
❑ G335	Edgar Martinez G	6.00	2.70
❑ G338	Rey Ordonez G	4.00	1.80
❑ G347	Sammy Sosa G	20.00	9.00
❑ G354	Juan Gonzalez G	10.00	4.50
❑ G355	Craig Biggio G	6.00	2.70
❑ S1	Greg Maddux S UER 95 stats listed as Mariners	12.00	5.50
❑ S2	Bernie Williams S	5.00	2.20
❑ S3	Ivan Rodriguez S	1.00	.45
❑ S7	Barry Larkin S	5.00	2.20
❑ S10	Ray Lankford S	1.50	.70
❑ S11	Mike Piazza S	12.00	5.50
❑ S13	Larry Walker S	3.00	1.35
❑ S14	Matt Williams S	3.00	1.35
❑ S22	Tim Salmon S	2.50	1.10
❑ S35	Edgar Martinez S	3.00	1.35
❑ S37	Gregg Jefferies S	1.50	.70
❑ S38	Bill Pulsipher S	1.50	.70
❑ S41	Shawn Green S	5.00	2.20
❑ S43	Jim Abbott S	2.50	1.10
❑ S46	Roger Clemens S	12.00	5.50
❑ S52	Rondell White S	2.50	1.10
❑ S54	Dennis Eckersley S	2.50	1.10
❑ S59	Hideo Nomo S	6.00	2.70
❑ S60	Gary Sheffield S	2.50	1.10
❑ S62	Will Clark S	5.00	2.20
❑ S65	Bret Boone S	2.50	1.10
❑ S68	Rafael Palmeiro S	5.00	2.20
❑ S69	Carlos Baerga S	1.50	.70
❑ S72	Tom Glavine S	5.00	2.20
❑ S73	Garret Anderson S	2.50	1.10
❑ S77	Randy Johnson S	6.00	2.70
❑ S78	Jeff King S	1.50	.70
❑ S79	Kirby Puckett S	12.00	5.50
❑ S84	Cecil Fielder S	2.50	1.10
❑ S86	Reggie Sanders S	1.50	.70
❑ S88	Ryan Klesko S	2.50	1.10
❑ S91	John Valentin S	1.50	.70
❑ S95	Manny Ramirez S	6.00	2.70
❑ S99	Vinny Castilla S	2.50	1.10
❑ S109	Carlos Perez S	1.50	.70
❑ S112	Craig Biggio S	3.00	1.35
❑ S115	Juan Gonzalez S	5.00	2.20
❑ S121	Ray Durham S	2.50	1.10
❑ S127	C.J. Nitkowski S	1.50	.70
❑ S130	Raul Mondesi S	2.50	1.10
❑ S142	Lee Smith S	2.50	1.10
❑ S143	Joe Carter S	2.50	1.10
❑ S151	Mo Vaughn S	2.50	1.10
❑ S153	Frank Rodriguez S	1.50	.70
❑ S160	Steve Finley S	2.50	1.10
❑ S161	Jeff Bagwell S	6.00	2.70
❑ S165	Cal Ripken S	20.00	9.00
❑ S168	Lyle Mouton S	1.50	.70
❑ S171	Sammy Sosa S	10.00	4.50
❑ S174	John Franco S	2.50	1.10
❑ S179	Greg Vaughn S	2.50	1.10
❑ S180	Mark Wohlers S	1.50	.70
❑ S182	Paul O'Neill S	5.00	2.20
❑ S188	Albert Belle S	2.50	1.10
❑ S189	Mark Grace S	5.00	2.20
❑ S211	Ernie Young S	1.50	.70
❑ S218	Fred McGriff S	3.00	1.35
❑ S223	Kimera Bartee S	1.50	.70
❑ S229	Rickey Henderson S	10.00	4.50
❑ S230	Sterling Hitchcock S	1.50	.70
❑ S231	Bernard Gilkey S	1.50	.70
❑ S234	Ryne Sandberg S	6.00	2.70
❑ S235	Greg Maddux S	12.00	5.50
❑ S239	Todd Stottlemyre S	1.50	.70
❑ S241	Jason Kendall S	2.50	1.10
❑ S242	Paul O'Neill S	5.00	2.20
❑ S256	Devon White S	2.50	1.10
❑ S261	Chuck Knoblauch S	2.50	1.10
❑ S263	Wally Joyner S	2.50	1.10
❑ S272	Andy Fox S	1.50	.70
❑ S274	Sean Berry S	1.50	.70
❑ S277	Benito Santiago S	1.50	.70
❑ S284	Chad Mottola S	1.50	.70
❑ S289	Dante Bichette S	2.50	1.10
❑ S291	Dwight Gooden S	2.50	1.10
❑ S293	Kevin Mitchell S	1.50	.70
❑ S295	Russ Davis S	1.50	.70
❑ S296	Chan Ho Park S	2.50	1.10
❑ S302	Larry Walker S	3.00	1.35
❑ S305	Ken Griffey Jr. S	15.00	6.75
❑ S313	Billy Wagner S	1.50	.70
❑ S317	Mike Grace S RC	1.50	.70
❑ S327	Kenny Lofton S	2.50	1.10
❑ S328	Derek Bell S	1.50	.70
❑ S337	Gary Sheffield S	2.50	1.10
❑ S341	Mark Grace S	5.00	2.20
❑ S345	Andres Galarraga S	3.00	1.35
❑ S346	Brady Anderson S	2.50	1.10
❑ S350	Derek Jeter S	15.00	6.75
❑ S353	Jay Buhner S	2.50	1.10
❑ S357	Tino Martinez S	2.50	1.10

1997 Finest

	MINT	NRMT
COMP.BRONZE SER.1 (100)	30.00	13.50
COMP.BRONZE SER.2 (100)	30.00	13.50
COM.BRON.(1-100/176-275)	.25	.11

COMP.SILVER SER.1 (50)	120.00	55.00
COMP.SILVER SER.2 (50)	150.00	70.00
COM.SILV.(101-150/276-325)	2.00	.90
COMP.GOLD SER.1 (25)	300.00	135.00
COMP.GOLD SER.2 (25)	250.00	110.00
COM.GOLD (151-175/326-350)	5.00	2.20
❑ 1 Barry Bonds B	2.50	1.10
❑ 2 Ryne Sandberg B	1.25	.55
❑ 3 Brian Jordan B	.40	.18
❑ 4 Rocky Coppinger B	.25	.11
❑ 5 Dante Bichette B UER	.40	.18
Card is erroneously numbered 155		
❑ 6 Al Martin B	.25	.11
❑ 7 Charles Nagy B	.25	.11
❑ 8 Otis Nixon B	.25	.11
❑ 9 Mark Johnson B	.25	.11
❑ 10 Jeff Bagwell B	1.25	.55
❑ 11 Ken Hill B	.25	.11
❑ 12 Willie Adams B	.25	.11
❑ 13 Raul Mondesi B	.40	.18
❑ 14 Reggie Sanders B	.25	.11
❑ 15 Derek Jeter B	4.00	1.80
❑ 16 Jermaine Dye B	.40	.18
❑ 17 Edgar Renteria B	.25	.11
❑ 18 Travis Fryman B	.40	.18
❑ 19 Roberto Hernandez B	.25	.11
❑ 20 Sammy Sosa B	2.00	.90
❑ 21 Garret Anderson B	.40	.18
❑ 22 Rey Ordonez B	.25	.11
❑ 23 Glenallen Hill B	.25	.11
❑ 24 Dave Nilsson B	.25	.11
❑ 25 Kevin Brown B	.40	.18
❑ 26 Brian McRae B	.25	.11
❑ 27 Joey Hamilton B	.25	.11
❑ 28 Jamey Wright B	.25	.11
❑ 29 Frank Thomas B	1.25	.55
❑ 30 Mark McGwire B	4.00	1.80
❑ 31 Ramon Martinez B	.25	.11
❑ 32 Jaime Bluma B	.25	.11
❑ 33 Frank Rodriguez B	.25	.11
❑ 34 Andy Benes B	.25	.11
❑ 35 Jay Buhner B	.40	.18
❑ 36 Justin Thompson B	.25	.11
❑ 37 Darin Erstad B	1.00	.45
❑ 38 Gregg Jefferies B	.25	.11
❑ 39 Jeff D'Amico B	.25	.11
❑ 40 Pedro Martinez B	1.25	.55
❑ 41 Nomar Garciaparra B	2.50	1.10
❑ 42 Jose Valentin B	.25	.11
❑ 43 Pat Hentgen B	.25	.11
❑ 44 Will Clark B	1.00	.45
❑ 45 Bernie Williams B	1.00	.45
❑ 46 Luis Castillo B	.25	.11
❑ 47 B.J. Surhoff B	.40	.18
❑ 48 Greg Gagne B	.25	.11
❑ 49 Pete Schourek B	.25	.11
❑ 50 Mike Piazza B	2.50	1.10
❑ 51 Dwight Gooden B	.40	.18
❑ 52 Javy Lopez B	.40	.18
❑ 53 Chuck Finley B	.40	.18
❑ 54 James Baldwin B	.25	.11
❑ 55 Jack McDowell B	.25	.11
❑ 56 Royce Clayton B	.25	.11
❑ 57 Carlos Delgado B	1.00	.45
❑ 58 Neifi Perez B	.25	.11
❑ 59 Eddie Taubensee B	.25	.11
❑ 60 Rafael Palmeiro B	1.00	.45
❑ 61 Marty Cordova B	.25	.11
❑ 62 Wade Boggs B	1.00	.45
❑ 63 Rickey Henderson B	2.00	.90
❑ 64 Mike Hampton B	.40	.18
❑ 65 Troy Percival B	.25	.11
❑ 66 Barry Larkin B	1.00	.45
❑ 67 J.Allensworth B	.25	.11
❑ 68 Mark Clark B	.25	.11
❑ 69 Mike Lansing B	.25	.11
❑ 70 Mark Grudzielanek B	.25	.11
❑ 71 Todd Stottlemyre B	.25	.11
❑ 72 Juan Guzman B	.25	.11
❑ 73 John Burkett B	.25	.11
❑ 74 Wilson Alvarez B	.25	.11
❑ 75 Ellis Burks B	.40	.18
❑ 76 Bobby Higginson B	.40	.18
❑ 77 Ricky Bottalico B	.25	.11
❑ 78 Omar Vizquel B	.40	.18
❑ 79 Paul Sorrento B	.25	.11
❑ 80 Denny Neagle B	.40	.18
❑ 81 Roger Pavlik B	.25	.11
❑ 82 Mike Lieberthal B	.40	.18
❑ 83 Devon White B	.40	.18
❑ 84 John Olerud B	.40	.18
❑ 85 Kevin Appier B	.40	.18
❑ 86 Joe Girardi B	.25	.11
❑ 87 Paul O'Neill B	1.00	.45
❑ 88 Mike Sweeney B	.40	.18
❑ 89 John Smiley B	.25	.11
❑ 90 Ivan Rodriguez B	1.00	.45
❑ 91 Randy Myers B	.25	.11
❑ 92 Bip Roberts B	.25	.11
❑ 93 Jose Mesa B	.25	.11
❑ 94 Paul Wilson B	.25	.11
❑ 95 Mike Mussina B	1.00	.45
❑ 96 Ben McDonald B	.25	.11
❑ 97 John Mabry B	.25	.11
❑ 98 Tom Goodwin B	.25	.11
❑ 99 Edgar Martinez B	.60	.25
❑ 100 Andruw Jones B	1.25	.55
❑ 101 Jose Canseco S	4.00	1.80
❑ 102 Billy Wagner S	2.00	.90
❑ 103 Dante Bichette S	2.50	1.10
❑ 104 Curt Schilling S	4.00	1.80
❑ 105 Dean Palmer S	2.50	1.10
❑ 106 Larry Walker S	3.00	1.35
❑ 107 Bernie Williams S	4.00	1.80
❑ 108 Chipper Jones S	8.00	3.60
❑ 109 Gary Sheffield S	2.50	1.10
❑ 110 Randy Johnson S	5.00	2.20
❑ 111 Roberto Alomar S	4.00	1.80
❑ 112 Todd Walker S	2.00	.90
❑ 113 Sandy Alomar Jr. S	2.50	1.10
❑ 114 John Jaha S	2.00	.90
❑ 115 Ken Caminiti S UER	2.50	1.10
Card is numbered 135		
❑ 116 Ryan Klesko S	2.50	1.10
❑ 117 Mariano Rivera S	2.50	1.10
❑ 118 Jason Giambi S	4.00	1.80
❑ 119 Lance Johnson S	2.00	.90
❑ 120 Robin Ventura S	2.50	1.10
❑ 121 Todd Hollandsworth S	2.00	.90
❑ 122 Johnny Damon S	2.50	1.10
❑ 123 W. VanLandingham S	2.00	.90
❑ 124 Jason Kendall S	2.50	1.10
❑ 125 Vinny Castilla S	2.50	1.10
❑ 126 Harold Baines S	2.50	1.10
❑ 127 Joe Carter S	2.50	1.10
❑ 128 Craig Biggio S	3.00	1.35
❑ 129 Tony Clark S	2.50	1.10
❑ 130 Ron Gant S	2.00	.90
❑ 131 David Segui S	2.00	.90
❑ 132 Steve Trachsel S	2.00	.90
❑ 133 Scott Rolen S	4.00	1.80
❑ 134 Mike Stanley S	2.00	.90
❑ 135 Cal Ripken S	15.00	6.75
❑ 136 John Smoltz S	2.50	1.10
❑ 137 Bobby Jones S	2.00	.90
❑ 138 Manny Ramirez S	5.00	2.20
❑ 139 Ken Griffey Jr. S	12.00	5.50
❑ 140 Chuck Knoblauch S	2.50	1.10
❑ 141 Mark Grace S	4.00	1.80
❑ 142 Chris Snopek S	2.00	.90
❑ 143 Hideo Nomo S	4.00	1.80
❑ 144 Tim Salmon S	2.50	1.10
❑ 145 David Cone S	2.50	1.10
❑ 146 Eric Young S	2.00	.90
❑ 147 Jeff Brantley S	2.00	.90
❑ 148 Jim Thome S	4.00	1.80
❑ 149 Trevor Hoffman S	2.50	1.10
❑ 150 Juan Gonzalez S	4.00	1.80
❑ 151 Mike Piazza G	25.00	11.00
❑ 152 Ivan Rodriguez G	1.00	.45
❑ 153 Mo Vaughn G	6.00	2.70
❑ 154 Brady Anderson G	6.00	2.70
❑ 155 Mark McGwire G	40.00	18.00
❑ 156 Rafael Palmeiro G	10.00	4.50
❑ 157 Barry Larkin G	10.00	4.50
❑ 158 Greg Maddux G	25.00	11.00
❑ 159 Jeff Bagwell G	12.00	5.50
❑ 160 Frank Thomas G	12.00	5.50
❑ 161 Ken Caminiti G	6.00	2.70
❑ 162 Andruw Jones G	12.00	5.50
❑ 163 Dennis Eckersley G	6.00	2.70
❑ 164 Jeff Conine G	5.00	2.20
❑ 165 Jim Edmonds G	8.00	3.60
❑ 166 Derek Jeter G	40.00	18.00
❑ 167 Vladimir Guerrero G	15.00	6.75
❑ 168 Sammy Sosa G	20.00	9.00
❑ 169 Tony Gwynn G	20.00	9.00
❑ 170 Andres Galarraga G	8.00	3.60
❑ 171 Todd Hundley G	5.00	2.20
❑ 172 Jay Buhner G UER	6.00	2.70
Card is numbered 164		
❑ 173 Paul Molitor G	10.00	4.50
❑ 174 Kenny Lofton G	6.00	2.70
❑ 175 Barry Bonds G	25.00	11.00
❑ 176 Gary Sheffield B	.40	.18
❑ 177 Dmitri Young B	.40	.18
❑ 178 Jay Bell B	.40	.18
❑ 179 David Wells B	.40	.18
❑ 180 Walt Weiss B	.25	.11
❑ 181 Paul Molitor B	1.00	.45
❑ 182 Jose Guillen B	.25	.11
❑ 183 Al Leiter B	.40	.18
❑ 184 Mike Fetters B	.25	.11
❑ 185 Mark Langston B	.25	.11
❑ 186 Fred McGriff B	.60	.25
❑ 187 Darrin Fletcher B	.25	.11
❑ 188 Brant Brown B	.25	.11
❑ 189 Geronimo Berroa B	.25	.11
❑ 190 Jim Thome B	1.00	.45
❑ 191 Jose Vizcaino B	.25	.11
❑ 192 Andy Ashby B	.25	.11
❑ 193 Rusty Greer B	.40	.18
❑ 194 Brian Hunter B	.25	.11
❑ 195 Chris Hoiles B	.25	.11
❑ 196 Orlando Merced B	.25	.11
❑ 197 Brett Butler B	.40	.18
❑ 198 Derek Bell B	.25	.11
❑ 199 Bobby Bonilla B	.40	.18
❑ 200 Alex Ochoa B	.25	.11
❑ 201 Wally Joyner B	.40	.18
❑ 202 Mo Vaughn B	.40	.18
❑ 203 Doug Drabek B	.25	.11
❑ 204 Tino Martinez B	.40	.18
❑ 205 Roberto Alomar B	1.00	.45
❑ 206 Brian Giles B RC	5.00	2.20
❑ 207 Todd Worrell B	.25	.11
❑ 208 Alan Benes B	.25	.11
❑ 209 Jim Leyritz B	.25	.11
❑ 210 Darryl Hamilton B	.25	.11
❑ 211 Jimmy Key B	.40	.18
❑ 212 Juan Gonzalez B	1.00	.45
❑ 213 Vinny Castilla B	.40	.18
❑ 214 Chuck Knoblauch B	.40	.18
❑ 215 Tony Phillips B	.25	.11
❑ 216 Jeff Cirillo B	.40	.18
❑ 217 Carlos Garcia B	.25	.11
❑ 218 Brooks Kieschnick B	.25	.11
❑ 219 Marquis Grissom B	.25	.11
❑ 220 Dan Wilson B	.25	.11
❑ 221 Greg Vaughn B	.40	.18
❑ 222 John Wetteland B	.40	.18
❑ 223 Andres Galarraga B	.60	.25
❑ 224 Ozzie Guillen B	.25	.11
❑ 225 Kevin Elster B	.25	.11
❑ 226 Bernard Gilkey B	.25	.11
❑ 227 Mike Macfarlane B	.25	.11
❑ 228 Heathcliff Slocumb B	.25	.11
❑ 229 Wendell Magee Jr. B	.25	.11
❑ 230 Carlos Baerga B	.25	.11
❑ 231 Kevin Seitzer B	.25	.11
❑ 232 Henry Rodriguez B	.25	.11
❑ 233 Roger Clemens B	2.50	1.10
❑ 234 Mark Wohlers B	.25	.11
❑ 235 Eddie Murray B	1.00	.45
❑ 236 Todd Zeile B	.25	.11
❑ 237 J.T. Snow B	.40	.18
❑ 238 Ken Griffey Jr. B	3.00	1.35
❑ 239 Sterling Hitchcock B	.25	.11
❑ 240 Albert Belle B	.40	.18
❑ 241 Terry Steinbach B	.25	.11
❑ 242 Robb Nen B	.25	.11
❑ 243 Mark McLemore B	.25	.11
❑ 244 Jeff King B	.25	.11
❑ 245 Tony Clark B	.40	.18
❑ 246 Tim Salmon B	.40	.18
❑ 247 Benito Santiago B	.25	.11
❑ 248 Robin Ventura B	.40	.18

No.	Player	Mint	Nrmt
249	Bubba Trammell B RC	.40	.18
250	Chili Davis B	.40	.18
251	John Valentin B	.25	.11
252	Cal Ripken B	4.00	1.80
253	Matt Williams B	.60	.25
254	Jeff Kent B	.60	.25
255	Eric Karros B	.40	.18
256	Ray Lankford B	.25	.11
257	Ed Sprague B	.25	.11
258	Shane Reynolds B	.25	.11
259	Jaime Navarro B	.25	.11
260	Eric Davis B	.40	.18
261	Orel Hershiser B	.40	.18
262	Mark Grace B	1.00	.45
263	Rod Beck B	.25	.11
264	Ismael Valdes B	.25	.11
265	Manny Ramirez B	1.25	.55
266	Ken Caminiti B	.40	.18
267	Tim Naehring B	.25	.11
268	Jose Rosado B	.25	.11
269	Greg Colbrunn B	.25	.11
270	Dean Palmer B	.40	.18
271	David Justice B	.40	.18
272	Scott Spiezio B	.25	.11
273	Chipper Jones B	2.00	.90
274	Mel Rojas B	.25	.11
275	Bartolo Colon B	.40	.18
276	Darin Erstad S	1.00	.45
277	Sammy Sosa S	6.00	2.70
278	Rafael Palmeiro S	4.00	1.80
279	Frank Thomas S	6.00	2.70
280	Ruben Rivera S	2.00	.90
281	Hal Morris S	2.00	.90
282	Jay Buhner S	2.50	1.10
283	Kenny Lofton S	2.50	1.10
284	Jose Canseco S	4.00	1.80
285	Alex Fernandez S	2.00	.90
286	Todd Helton S	6.00	2.70
287	Andy Pettitte S	2.50	1.10
288	John Franco S	2.50	1.10
289	Ivan Rodriguez S	1.00	.45
290	Ellis Burks S	2.50	1.10
291	Julio Franco S	2.50	1.10
292	Mike Piazza S	10.00	4.50
293	Brian Jordan S	2.50	1.10
294	Greg Maddux S	10.00	4.50
295	Bob Abreu S	2.50	1.10
296	Rondell White S	2.50	1.10
297	Moises Alou S	2.50	1.10
298	Tony Gwynn S	8.00	3.60
299	Deion Sanders S	2.50	1.10
300	Jeff Montgomery S	2.00	.90
301	Ray Durham S	2.50	1.10
302	John Wasdin S	2.00	.90
303	Ryne Sandberg S	5.00	2.20
304	Delino DeShields S	2.00	.90
305	Mark McGwire S	15.00	6.75
306	Andruw Jones S	5.00	2.20
307	Kevin Orie S	2.00	.90
308	Matt Williams S	3.00	1.35
309	Karim Garcia S	2.00	.90
310	Derek Jeter S	15.00	6.75
311	Mo Vaughn S	2.50	1.10
312	Brady Anderson S	2.50	1.10
313	Barry Bonds S	10.00	4.50
314	Steve Finley S	2.50	1.10
315	Vladimir Guerrero S	6.00	2.70
316	Matt Morris S	2.50	1.10
317	Tom Glavine S	4.00	1.80
318	Jeff Bagwell S	5.00	2.20
319	Albert Belle S	2.50	1.10
320	Hideki Irabu S RC	2.50	1.10
321	Andres Galarraga S	3.00	1.35
322	Cecil Fielder S	2.50	1.10
323	Barry Larkin S	4.00	1.80
324	Todd Hundley S	2.00	.90
325	Fred McGriff S	3.00	1.35
326	Gary Sheffield G	6.00	2.70
327	Craig Biggio G	8.00	3.60
328	Raul Mondesi G	6.00	2.70
329	Edgar Martinez G	8.00	3.60
330	Chipper Jones G	20.00	9.00
331	Bernie Williams G	10.00	4.50
332	Juan Gonzalez G	10.00	4.50
333	Ron Gant G	5.00	2.20
334	Cal Ripken G	40.00	18.00
335	Larry Walker G	8.00	3.60
336	Matt Williams G	8.00	3.60
337	Jose Cruz Jr. G RC	20.00	9.00
338	Joe Carter G	6.00	2.70
339	Wilton Guerrero G	5.00	2.20
340	Cecil Fielder G	6.00	2.70
341	Todd Walker G	5.00	2.20
342	Ken Griffey Jr. G	30.00	13.50
343	Ryan Klesko G	6.00	2.70
344	Roger Clemens G	25.00	11.00
345	Hideo Nomo G	10.00	4.50
346	Dante Bichette G	6.00	2.70
347	Albert Belle G	6.00	2.70
348	Randy Johnson G	12.00	5.50
349	Manny Ramirez G	12.00	5.50
350	John Smoltz G	6.00	2.70

1998 Finest

	MINT	NRMT
COMPLETE SET (275)	70.00	32.00
COMPLETE SERIES 1 (150)	40.00	18.00
COMPLETE SERIES 2 (125)	30.00	13.50

No.	Player	Mint	Nrmt
1	Larry Walker	.60	.25
2	Andruw Jones	1.00	.45
3	Ramon Martinez	.25	.11
4	Geronimo Berroa	.25	.11
5	David Justice	.40	.18
6	Rusty Greer	.40	.18
7	Chad Ogea	.25	.11
8	Tom Goodwin	.25	.11
9	Tino Martinez	.40	.18
10	Jose Guillen	.25	.11
11	Jeffrey Hammonds	.25	.11
12	Brian McRae	.25	.11
13	Jeremi Gonzalez	.25	.11
14	Craig Counsell	.25	.11
15	Mike Piazza	2.50	1.10
16	Greg Maddux	2.50	1.10
17	Todd Greene	.25	.11
18	Rondell White	.40	.18
19	Kirk Rueter	.25	.11
20	Tony Clark	.40	.18
21	Brad Radke	.40	.18
22	Jaret Wright	.25	.11
23	Carlos Delgado	1.00	.45
24	Dustin Hermanson	.25	.11
25	Gary Sheffield	.40	.18
26	Jose Canseco	1.00	.45
27	Kevin Young	.40	.18
28	David Wells	.40	.18
29	Mariano Rivera	.40	.18
30	Reggie Sanders	.25	.11
31	Mike Cameron	.40	.18
32	Bobby Witt	.25	.11
33	Kevin Orie	.25	.11
34	Royce Clayton	.25	.11
35	Edgar Martinez	.60	.25
36	Neifi Perez	.25	.11
37	Kevin Appier	.40	.18
38	Darryl Hamilton	.25	.11
39	Michael Tucker	.25	.11
40	Roger Clemens	2.50	1.10
41	Carl Everett	.40	.18
42	Mike Sweeney	.40	.18
43	Pat Meares	.25	.11
44	Brian Giles	.40	.18
45	Matt Morris	.40	.18
46	Jason Dickson	.25	.11
47	Rich Loiselle RC	.40	.18
48	Joe Girardi	.25	.11
49	Steve Trachsel	.25	.11
50	Ben Grieve	.40	.18
51	Brian Johnson	.25	.11
52	Hideki Irabu	.25	.11
53	J.T. Snow	.40	.18
54	Mike Hampton	.40	.18
55	Dave Nilsson	.25	.11
56	Alex Fernandez	.25	.11
57	Brett Tomko	.25	.11
58	Wally Joyner	.40	.18
59	Kelvim Escobar	.25	.11
60	Roberto Alomar	1.00	.45
61	Todd Jones	.25	.11
62	Paul O'Neill	1.00	.45
63	Jamie Moyer	.25	.11
64	Mark Wohlers	.25	.11
65	Jose Cruz Jr.	.40	.18
66	Troy Percival	.25	.11
67	Rick Reed	.25	.11
68	Will Clark	1.00	.45
69	Jamey Wright	.25	.11
70	Mike Mussina	1.00	.45
71	David Cone	.40	.18
72	Ryan Klesko	.40	.18
73	Scott Hatteberg	.25	.11
74	James Baldwin	.25	.11
75	Tony Womack	.25	.11
76	Carlos Perez	.25	.11
77	Charles Nagy	.25	.11
78	Jeromy Burnitz	.40	.18
79	Shane Reynolds	.25	.11
80	Cliff Floyd	.40	.18
81	Jason Kendall	.40	.18
82	Chad Curtis	.25	.11
83	Matt Karchner	.25	.11
84	Ricky Bottalico	.25	.11
85	Sammy Sosa	2.00	.90
86	Javy Lopez	.40	.18
87	Jeff Kent	.60	.25
88	Shawn Green	1.00	.45
89	Joey Cora	.25	.11
90	Tony Gwynn	2.00	.90
91	Bob Tewksbury	.25	.11
92	Derek Jeter	4.00	1.80
93	Eric Davis	.40	.18
94	Jeff Fassero	.25	.11
95	Denny Neagle	.25	.11
96	Ismael Valdes	.25	.11
97	Tim Salmon	.40	.18
98	Mark Grudzielanek	.25	.11
99	Curt Schilling	1.00	.45
100	Ken Griffey Jr.	3.00	1.35
101	Edgardo Alfonzo	.40	.18
102	Vinny Castilla	.40	.18
103	Jose Rosado	.25	.11
104	Scott Erickson	.25	.11
105	Alan Benes	.25	.11
106	Shannon Stewart	.40	.18
107	Delino DeShields	.25	.11
108	Mark Loretta	.25	.11
109	Todd Hundley	.25	.11
110	Chuck Knoblauch	.40	.18
111	Todd Helton	1.25	.55
112	F.P. Santangelo	.25	.11
113	Jeff Cirillo	.40	.18
114	Omar Vizquel	.40	.18
115	John Valentin	.25	.11
116	Damion Easley	.25	.11
117	Matt Lawton	.25	.11
118	Jim Thome	1.00	.45
119	Sandy Alomar Jr.	.40	.18
120	Albert Belle	.40	.18
121	Chris Stynes	.25	.11
122	Butch Huskey	.25	.11
123	Shawn Estes	.40	.18
124	Terry Adams	.25	.11
125	Ivan Rodriguez	1.00	.45
126	Ron Gant	.40	.18
127	John Mabry	.25	.11
128	Jeff Shaw	.25	.11
129	Jeff Montgomery	.25	.11
130	Justin Thompson	.25	.11

Card	Mint	NrMt
❑ 131 Livan Hernandez	.25	.11
❑ 132 Ugueth Urbina	.25	.11
❑ 133 Scott Servais	.25	.11
❑ 134 Troy O'Leary	.25	.11
❑ 135 Cal Ripken	4.00	1.80
❑ 136 Quilvio Veras	.25	.11
❑ 137 Pedro Astacio	.25	.11
❑ 138 Willie Greene	.25	.11
❑ 139 Lance Johnson	.25	.11
❑ 140 Nomar Garciaparra	2.50	1.10
❑ 141 Jose Offerman	.25	.11
❑ 142 Scott Rolen	1.00	.45
❑ 143 Derek Bell	.25	.11
❑ 144 Johnny Damon	.40	.18
❑ 145 Mark McGwire	4.00	1.80
❑ 146 Chan Ho Park	.40	.18
❑ 147 Edgar Renteria	.25	.11
❑ 148 Eric Young	.25	.11
❑ 149 Craig Biggio	.60	.25
❑ 150 Checklist (1-150)	.25	.11
❑ 151 Frank Thomas	1.25	.55
❑ 152 John Wetteland	.40	.18
❑ 153 Mike Lansing	.25	.11
❑ 154 Pedro Martinez	1.25	.55
❑ 155 Rico Brogna	.25	.11
❑ 156 Kevin Brown	.60	.25
❑ 157 Alex Rodriguez	2.50	1.10
❑ 158 Wade Boggs	1.00	.45
❑ 159 Richard Hidalgo	.40	.18
❑ 160 Mark Grace	1.00	.45
❑ 161 Jose Mesa	.25	.11
❑ 162 John Olerud	.40	.18
❑ 163 Tim Belcher	.25	.11
❑ 164 Chuck Finley	.40	.18
❑ 165 Brian Hunter	.25	.11
❑ 166 Joe Carter	.40	.18
❑ 167 Stan Javier	.25	.11
❑ 168 Jay Bell	.40	.18
❑ 169 Ray Lankford	.25	.11
❑ 170 John Smoltz	.40	.18
❑ 171 Ed Sprague	.25	.11
❑ 172 Jason Giambi	1.00	.45
❑ 173 Todd Walker	.25	.11
❑ 174 Paul Konerko	.40	.18
❑ 175 Rey Ordonez	.25	.11
❑ 176 Dante Bichette	.40	.18
❑ 177 Bernie Williams	1.00	.45
❑ 178 Jon Nunnally	.25	.11
❑ 179 Rafael Palmeiro	1.00	.45
❑ 180 Jay Buhner	.40	.18
❑ 181 Devon White	.25	.11
❑ 182 Jeff D'Amico	.25	.11
❑ 183 Walt Weiss	.40	.18
❑ 184 Scott Spiezio	.25	.11
❑ 185 Moises Alou	.40	.18
❑ 186 Carlos Baerga	.25	.11
❑ 187 Todd Zeile	.40	.18
❑ 188 Gregg Jefferies	.25	.11
❑ 189 Mo Vaughn	.40	.18
❑ 190 Terry Steinbach	.25	.11
❑ 191 Ray Durham	.40	.18
❑ 192 Robin Ventura	.40	.18
❑ 193 Jeff Reed	.25	.11
❑ 194 Ken Caminiti	.40	.18
❑ 195 Eric Karros	.40	.18
❑ 196 Wilson Alvarez	.25	.11
❑ 197 Gary Gaetti	.40	.18
❑ 198 Andres Galarraga	.60	.25
❑ 199 Alex Gonzalez	.25	.11
❑ 200 Garret Anderson	.40	.18
❑ 201 Andy Benes	.25	.11
❑ 202 Harold Baines	.40	.18
❑ 203 Ron Coomer	.25	.11
❑ 204 Dean Palmer	.40	.18
❑ 205 Reggie Jefferson	.25	.11
❑ 206 John Burkett	.25	.11
❑ 207 Jermaine Allensworth	.25	.11
❑ 208 Bernard Gilkey	.25	.11
❑ 209 Jeff Bagwell	1.25	.55
❑ 210 Kenny Lofton	.40	.18
❑ 211 Bobby Jones	.25	.11
❑ 212 Bartolo Colon	.40	.18
❑ 213 Jim Edmonds	.60	.25
❑ 214 Pat Hentgen	.25	.11
❑ 215 Matt Williams	.60	.25
❑ 216 Bob Abreu	.40	.18
❑ 217 Jorge Posada	.40	.18
❑ 218 Marty Cordova	.25	.11
❑ 219 Ken Hill	.25	.11
❑ 220 Steve Finley	.40	.18
❑ 221 Jeff King	.25	.11
❑ 222 Quinton McCracken	.25	.11
❑ 223 Matt Stairs	.25	.11
❑ 224 Darin Erstad	1.00	.45
❑ 225 Fred McGriff	.60	.25
❑ 226 Marquis Grissom	.25	.11
❑ 227 Doug Glanville	.25	.11
❑ 228 Tom Glavine	1.00	.45
❑ 229 John Franco	.40	.18
❑ 230 Darren Bragg	.25	.11
❑ 231 Barry Larkin	1.00	.45
❑ 232 Trevor Hoffman	.40	.18
❑ 233 Brady Anderson	.40	.18
❑ 234 Al Martin	.25	.11
❑ 235 B.J. Surhoff	.40	.18
❑ 236 Ellis Burks	.40	.18
❑ 237 Randy Johnson	1.25	.55
❑ 238 Mark Clark	.25	.11
❑ 239 Tony Saunders	.25	.11
❑ 240 Hideo Nomo	1.00	.45
❑ 241 Brad Fullmer	.40	.18
❑ 242 Chipper Jones	2.00	.90
❑ 243 Jose Valentin	.25	.11
❑ 244 Manny Ramirez	1.25	.55
❑ 245 Derrek Lee	.40	.18
❑ 246 Jimmy Key	.40	.18
❑ 247 Tim Naehring	.25	.11
❑ 248 Bobby Higginson	.40	.18
❑ 249 Charles Johnson	.40	.18
❑ 250 Chili Davis	.40	.18
❑ 251 Tom Gordon	.40	.18
❑ 252 Mike Lieberthal	.40	.18
❑ 253 Billy Wagner	.25	.11
❑ 254 Juan Guzman	.25	.11
❑ 255 Todd Stottlemyre	.25	.11
❑ 256 Brian Jordan	.40	.18
❑ 257 Barry Bonds	2.50	1.10
❑ 258 Dan Wilson	.25	.11
❑ 259 Paul Molitor	1.00	.45
❑ 260 Juan Gonzalez	1.00	.45
❑ 261 Francisco Cordova	.25	.11
❑ 262 Cecil Fielder	.40	.18
❑ 263 Travis Lee	.40	.18
❑ 264 Kevin Tapani	.25	.11
❑ 265 Raul Mondesi	.40	.18
❑ 266 Travis Fryman	.40	.18
❑ 267 Armando Benitez	.25	.11
❑ 268 Pokey Reese	.25	.11
❑ 269 Rick Aguilera	.25	.11
❑ 270 Andy Pettitte	.40	.18
❑ 271 Jose Vizcaino	.25	.11
❑ 272 Kerry Wood	1.00	.45
❑ 273 Vladimir Guerrero	1.25	.55
❑ 274 John Smiley	.25	.11
❑ 275 Checklist (151-275)	.25	.11

1999 Finest

	MINT	NRMT
COMPLETE SET (300)	150.00	70.00
COMPLETE SERIES 1 (150)	80.00	36.00
COMPLETE SERIES 2 (150)	75.00	34.00
COMP.SER.1 w/o SP's (100)	30.00	13.50
COMP.SER.2 w/o SP's (100)	30.00	13.50
COMMON (1-100/151-250)	.20	.09
COMMON (101-150/251-300)	.50	.23

Card	Mint	NrMt
❑ 1 Darin Erstad	.75	.35
❑ 2 Javy Lopez	.30	.14
❑ 3 Vinny Castilla	.30	.14
❑ 4 Jim Thome	.75	.35
❑ 5 Tino Martinez	.30	.14
❑ 6 Mark Grace	.75	.35
❑ 7 Shawn Green	.75	.35
❑ 8 Dustin Hermanson	.20	.09
❑ 9 Kevin Young	.30	.14
❑ 10 Tony Clark	.30	.14
❑ 11 Scott Brosius	.30	.14
❑ 12 Craig Biggio	.50	.23
❑ 13 Brian McRae	.20	.09
❑ 14 Chan Ho Park	.30	.14
❑ 15 Manny Ramirez	1.00	.45
❑ 16 Chipper Jones	1.50	.70
❑ 17 Rico Brogna	.20	.09
❑ 18 Quinton McCracken	.20	.09
❑ 19 J.T. Snow	.30	.14
❑ 20 Tony Gwynn	1.50	.70
❑ 21 Juan Guzman	.20	.09
❑ 22 John Valentin	.20	.09
❑ 23 Rick Helling	.20	.09
❑ 24 Sandy Alomar Jr.	.30	.14
❑ 25 Frank Thomas	1.00	.45
❑ 26 Jorge Posada	.30	.14
❑ 27 Dmitri Young	.30	.14
❑ 28 Rick Reed	.20	.09
❑ 29 Kevin Tapani	.20	.09
❑ 30 Troy Glaus	.75	.35
❑ 31 Kenny Rogers	.20	.09
❑ 32 Jeromy Burnitz	.30	.14
❑ 33 Mark Grudzielanek	.20	.09
❑ 34 Mike Mussina	.75	.35
❑ 35 Scott Rolen	.75	.35
❑ 36 Neifi Perez	.20	.09
❑ 37 Brad Radke	.30	.14
❑ 38 Darryl Strawberry	.30	.14
❑ 39 Robb Nen	.20	.09
❑ 40 Moises Alou	.30	.14
❑ 41 Eric Young	.20	.09
❑ 42 Livan Hernandez	.20	.09
❑ 43 John Wetteland	.30	.14
❑ 44 Matt Lawton	.30	.14
❑ 45 Ben Grieve	.30	.14
❑ 46 Fernando Tatis	.20	.09
❑ 47 Travis Fryman	.30	.14
❑ 48 David Segui	.20	.09
❑ 49 Bob Abreu	.30	.14
❑ 50 Nomar Garciaparra	2.00	.90
❑ 51 Paul O'Neill	.75	.35
❑ 52 Jeff King	.20	.09
❑ 53 Francisco Cordova	.20	.09
❑ 54 John Olerud	.30	.14
❑ 55 Vladimir Guerrero	1.00	.45
❑ 56 Fernando Vina	.20	.09
❑ 57 Shane Reynolds	.20	.09
❑ 58 Chuck Finley	.30	.14
❑ 59 Rondell White	.30	.14
❑ 60 Greg Vaughn	.30	.14
❑ 61 Ryan Minor	.20	.09
❑ 62 Tom Gordon	.20	.09
❑ 63 Damion Easley	.20	.09
❑ 64 Ray Durham	.30	.14
❑ 65 Orlando Hernandez	.30	.14
❑ 66 Bartolo Colon	.30	.14
❑ 67 Jaret Wright	.20	.09
❑ 68 Royce Clayton	.20	.09
❑ 69 Tim Salmon	.30	.14
❑ 70 Mark McGwire	3.00	1.35
❑ 71 Alex Gonzalez	.20	.09
❑ 72 Tom Glavine	.75	.35
❑ 73 David Justice	.30	.14
❑ 74 Omar Vizquel	.30	.14
❑ 75 Juan Gonzalez	.75	.35
❑ 76 Bobby Higginson	.30	.14
❑ 77 Todd Walker	.20	.09
❑ 78 Dante Bichette	.30	.14
❑ 79 Kevin Millwood	.20	.09
❑ 80 Roger Clemens	2.00	.90
❑ 81 Kerry Wood	.75	.35
❑ 82 Cal Ripken	3.00	1.35
❑ 83 Jay Bell	.30	.14

No.	Player	MINT	NRMT
❑ 84	Barry Bonds	2.00	.90
❑ 85	Alex Rodriguez	2.00	.90
❑ 86	Doug Glanville	.20	.09
❑ 87	Jason Kendall	.30	.14
❑ 88	Sean Casey	.50	.23
❑ 89	Aaron Sele	.30	.14
❑ 90	Derek Jeter	3.00	1.35
❑ 91	Andy Ashby	.20	.09
❑ 92	Rusty Greer	.30	.14
❑ 93	Rod Beck	.20	.09
❑ 94	Matt Williams	.50	.23
❑ 95	Mike Piazza	2.00	.90
❑ 96	Wally Joyner	.30	.14
❑ 97	Barry Larkin	.75	.35
❑ 98	Eric Milton	.30	.14
❑ 99	Gary Sheffield	.30	.14
❑ 100	Greg Maddux	2.00	.90
❑ 101	Ken Griffey Jr. GEM	4.00	1.80
❑ 102	Frank Thomas GEM	1.50	.70
❑ 103	N.Garciaparra GEM	3.00	1.35
❑ 104	Mark McGwire GEM	5.00	2.20
❑ 105	Alex Rodriguez GEM	3.00	1.35
❑ 106	Tony Gwynn GEM	2.50	1.10
❑ 107	Juan Gonzalez GEM	.75	.35
❑ 108	Jeff Bagwell GEM	1.50	.70
❑ 109	Sammy Sosa GEM	2.50	1.10
❑ 110	V.Guerrero GEM	1.50	.70
❑ 111	Roger Clemens GEM	3.00	1.35
❑ 112	Barry Bonds GEM	3.00	1.35
❑ 113	Darin Erstad GEM	1.25	.55
❑ 114	Mike Piazza GEM	3.00	1.35
❑ 115	Derek Jeter GEM	5.00	2.20
❑ 116	Chipper Jones GEM	2.50	1.10
❑ 117	Larry Walker GEM	.75	.35
❑ 118	Scott Rolen GEM	1.25	.55
❑ 119	Cal Ripken GEM	5.00	2.20
❑ 120	Greg Maddux GEM	3.00	1.35
❑ 121	Troy Glaus SENS	.75	.35
❑ 122	Ben Grieve SENS	.50	.23
❑ 123	Ryan Minor SENS	.50	.23
❑ 124	Kerry Wood SENS	1.25	.55
❑ 125	Travis Lee SENS	.50	.23
❑ 126	Adrian Beltre SENS	.50	.23
❑ 127	Brad Fullmer SENS	.50	.23
❑ 128	Aramis Ramirez SENS	.50	.23
❑ 129	Eric Chavez SENS	.50	.23
❑ 130	Todd Helton SENS	1.50	.70
❑ 131	Pat Burrell RC	5.00	2.20
❑ 132	Ryan Mills RC	.75	.35
❑ 133	Austin Kearns RC	6.00	2.70
❑ 134	Josh McKinley RC	1.00	.45
❑ 135	Adam Everett RC	1.25	.55
❑ 136	Marlon Anderson	.50	.23
❑ 137	Bruce Chen	.20	.09
❑ 138	Matt Clement	.50	.23
❑ 139	Alex Gonzalez	.50	.23
❑ 140	Roy Halladay	.50	.23
❑ 141	Calvin Pickering	.50	.23
❑ 142	Randy Wolf	.50	.23
❑ 143	Ryan Anderson	.50	.23
❑ 144	Ruben Mateo	.50	.23
❑ 145	Alex Escobar RC	4.00	1.80
❑ 146	Jeremy Giambi	.50	.23
❑ 147	Lance Berkman	1.25	.55
❑ 148	Michael Barrett	.50	.23
❑ 149	Preston Wilson	.50	.23
❑ 150	Gabe Kapler	.50	.23
❑ 151	Roger Clemens	2.00	.90
❑ 152	Jay Buhner	.30	.14
❑ 153	Brad Fullmer	.30	.14
❑ 154	Ray Lankford	.20	.09
❑ 155	Jim Edmonds	.50	.23
❑ 156	Jason Giambi	.75	.35
❑ 157	Bret Boone	.30	.14
❑ 158	Jeff Cirillo	.30	.14
❑ 159	Rickey Henderson	1.50	.70
❑ 160	Edgar Martinez	.50	.23
❑ 161	Ron Gant	.30	.14
❑ 162	Mark Kotsay	.20	.09
❑ 163	Trevor Hoffman	.30	.14
❑ 164	Jason Schmidt	.20	.09
❑ 165	Brett Tomko	.20	.09
❑ 166	David Ortiz	.30	.14
❑ 167	Dean Palmer	.30	.14
❑ 168	Hideki Irabu	.20	.09
❑ 169	Mike Cameron	.30	.14
❑ 170	Pedro Martinez	1.00	.45
❑ 171	Tom Goodwin	.20	.09
❑ 172	Brian Hunter	.20	.09
❑ 173	Al Leiter	.30	.14
❑ 174	Charles Johnson	.30	.14
❑ 175	Curt Schilling	.75	.35
❑ 176	Robin Ventura	.30	.14
❑ 177	Travis Lee	.20	.09
❑ 178	Jeff Shaw	.20	.09
❑ 179	Ugueth Urbina	.20	.09
❑ 180	Roberto Alomar	.75	.35
❑ 181	Cliff Floyd	.30	.14
❑ 182	Adrian Beltre	.30	.14
❑ 183	Tony Womack	.20	.09
❑ 184	Brian Jordan	.30	.14
❑ 185	Randy Johnson	1.00	.45
❑ 186	Mickey Morandini	.20	.09
❑ 187	Todd Hundley	.20	.09
❑ 188	Jose Valentin	.20	.09
❑ 189	Eric Davis	.30	.14
❑ 190	Ken Caminiti	.30	.14
❑ 191	David Wells	.30	.14
❑ 192	Ryan Klesko	.30	.14
❑ 193	Garret Anderson	.30	.14
❑ 194	Eric Karros	.30	.14
❑ 195	Ivan Rodriguez	.75	.35
❑ 196	Aramis Ramirez	.30	.14
❑ 197	Mike Lieberthal	.30	.14
❑ 198	Will Clark	.75	.35
❑ 199	Rey Ordonez	.20	.09
❑ 200	Ken Griffey Jr.	2.50	1.10
❑ 201	Jose Guillen	.20	.09
❑ 202	Scott Erickson	.20	.09
❑ 203	Paul Konerko	.30	.14
❑ 204	Johnny Damon	.30	.14
❑ 205	Larry Walker	.50	.23
❑ 206	Denny Neagle	.20	.09
❑ 207	Jose Offerman	.20	.09
❑ 208	Andy Pettitte	.30	.14
❑ 209	Bobby Jones	.20	.09
❑ 210	Kevin Brown	.50	.23
❑ 211	John Smoltz	.30	.14
❑ 212	Henry Rodriguez	.20	.09
❑ 213	Tim Belcher	.20	.09
❑ 214	Carlos Delgado	.75	.35
❑ 215	Andruw Jones	.75	.35
❑ 216	Andy Benes	.20	.09
❑ 217	Fred McGriff	.50	.23
❑ 218	Edgar Renteria	.20	.09
❑ 219	Miguel Tejada	.30	.14
❑ 220	Bernie Williams	.75	.35
❑ 221	Justin Thompson	.20	.09
❑ 222	Marty Cordova	.20	.09
❑ 223	Delino DeShields	.20	.09
❑ 224	Ellis Burks	.30	.14
❑ 225	Kenny Lofton	.30	.14
❑ 226	Steve Finley	.30	.14
❑ 227	Eric Chavez	.30	.14
❑ 228	Jose Cruz Jr.	.30	.14
❑ 229	Marquis Grissom	.20	.09
❑ 230	Jeff Bagwell	1.00	.45
❑ 231	Jose Canseco	.75	.35
❑ 232	Edgardo Alfonzo	.30	.14
❑ 233	Richie Sexson	.30	.14
❑ 234	Jeff Kent	.50	.23
❑ 235	Rafael Palmeiro	.75	.35
❑ 236	David Cone	.30	.14
❑ 237	Gregg Jefferies	.20	.09
❑ 238	Mike Lansing	.20	.09
❑ 239	Mariano Rivera	.30	.14
❑ 240	Albert Belle	.30	.14
❑ 241	Chuck Knoblauch	.30	.14
❑ 242	Derek Bell	.20	.09
❑ 243	Pat Hentgen	.20	.09
❑ 244	Andres Galarraga	.50	.23
❑ 245	Mo Vaughn	.30	.14
❑ 246	Wade Boggs	.75	.35
❑ 247	Devon White	.20	.09
❑ 248	Todd Helton	1.00	.45
❑ 249	Raul Mondesi	.30	.14
❑ 250	Sammy Sosa	1.50	.70
❑ 251	Nomar Garciaparra ST	3.00	1.35
❑ 252	Mark McGwire ST	5.00	2.20
❑ 253	Alex Rodriguez ST	3.00	1.35
❑ 254	Juan Gonzalez ST	.75	.35
❑ 255	Vladimir Guerrero ST	1.50	.70
❑ 256	Ken Griffey Jr. ST	4.00	1.80
❑ 257	Mike Piazza ST	3.00	1.35
❑ 258	Derek Jeter ST	5.00	2.20
❑ 259	Albert Belle ST	.50	.23
❑ 260	Greg Vaughn ST	.50	.23
❑ 261	Sammy Sosa ST	2.50	1.10
❑ 262	Greg Maddux ST	3.00	1.35
❑ 263	Frank Thomas ST	1.50	.70
❑ 264	Mark Grace ST	1.25	.55
❑ 265	Ivan Rodriguez ST	.75	.35
❑ 266	Roger Clemens GM	3.00	1.35
❑ 267	Mo Vaughn GM	.50	.23
❑ 268	Jim Thome GM	1.25	.55
❑ 269	Darin Erstad GM	1.25	.55
❑ 270	Chipper Jones GM	2.50	1.10
❑ 271	Larry Walker GM	.75	.35
❑ 272	Cal Ripken GM	5.00	2.20
❑ 273	Scott Rolen GM	1.25	.55
❑ 274	Randy Johnson GM	1.50	.70
❑ 275	Tony Gwynn GM	2.50	1.10
❑ 276	Barry Bonds GM	3.00	1.35
❑ 277	Sean Burroughs RC	8.00	3.60
❑ 278	J.M. Gold RC	1.00	.45
❑ 279	Carlos Lee	.50	.23
❑ 280	George Lombard	.50	.23
❑ 281	Carlos Beltran	.50	.23
❑ 282	Fernando Seguignol	.50	.23
❑ 283	Eric Chavez	.50	.23
❑ 284	Carlos Pena RC	5.00	2.20
❑ 285	Corey Patterson RC	5.00	2.20
❑ 286	Alfonso Soriano RC	8.00	3.60
❑ 287	Nick Johnson RC	5.00	2.20
❑ 288	Jorge Toca RC	.75	.35
❑ 289	A.J. Burnett RC	2.50	1.10
❑ 290	Andy Brown RC	1.25	.55
❑ 291	D.Mientkiewicz RC	4.00	1.80
❑ 292	Bobby Seay RC	1.00	.45
❑ 293	Chip Ambres RC	1.25	.55
❑ 294	C.C. Sabathia RC	6.00	2.70
❑ 295	Choo Freeman RC	1.25	.55
❑ 296	Eric Valent RC	2.00	.90
❑ 297	Matt Belisle RC	1.25	.55
❑ 298	Jason Tyner RC	1.00	.45
❑ 299	Masao Kida RC	.50	.23
❑ 300	Hank Aaron Mark McGwire	4.00	1.80

2000 Finest

	MINT	NRMT
COMPLETE SET (287)	700.00	325.00
COMPLETE SERIES 1 (147)	500.00	220.00
COMPLETE SERIES 2 (140)	300.00	135.00
COMP.SERIES 1 w/o SP's (100)	25.00	11.00
COMP.SERIES 2 w/o SP's (100)	25.00	11.00
COMMON (1-100/147-246)	.20	.09
COMMON ROOKIE (101-120)	8.00	3.60
COMMON FEATURES (121-135)	1.50	.70
COMM.GEM (136-145/277-286)	2.50	1.10
COMMON ROOKIE (247-266)	6.00	2.70
COMMON COUNTER (267-276)	1.00	.45

No.	Player	MINT	NRMT
❑ 1	Nomar Garciaparra	2.00	.90
❑ 2	Chipper Jones	1.50	.70
❑ 3	Erubiel Durazo	.30	.14
❑ 4	Robin Ventura	.50	.23
❑ 5	Garret Anderson	.30	.14
❑ 6	Dean Palmer	.30	.14

❑ 7 Mariano Rivera .30 .14
❑ 8 Rusty Greer .30 .14
❑ 9 Jim Thome .75 .35
❑ 10 Jeff Bagwell 1.00 .45
❑ 11 Jason Giambi .75 .35
❑ 12 Jeromy Burnitz .30 .14
❑ 13 Mark Grace .75 .35
❑ 14 Russ Ortiz .30 .14
❑ 15 Kevin Brown .50 .23
❑ 16 Kevin Millwood .20 .09
❑ 17 Scott Williamson .20 .09
❑ 18 Orlando Hernandez .30 .14
❑ 19 Todd Walker .20 .09
❑ 20 Carlos Beltran .30 .14
❑ 21 Ruben Rivera .20 .09
❑ 22 Curt Schilling .75 .35
❑ 23 Brian Giles .30 .14
❑ 24 Eric Karros .30 .14
❑ 25 Preston Wilson .30 .14
❑ 26 Al Leiter .20 .09
❑ 27 Juan Encarnacion .30 .14
❑ 28 Tim Salmon .30 .14
❑ 29 B.J. Surhoff .30 .14
❑ 30 Bernie Williams .75 .35
❑ 31 Lee Stevens .20 .09
❑ 32 Pokey Reese .20 .09
❑ 33 Mike Sweeney .30 .14
❑ 34 Corey Koskie .30 .14
❑ 35 Roberto Alomar .75 .35
❑ 36 Tim Hudson .75 .35
❑ 37 Tom Glavine .75 .35
❑ 38 Jeff Kent .50 .23
❑ 39 Mike Lieberthal .30 .14
❑ 40 Barry Larkin .75 .35
❑ 41 Paul O'Neill .75 .35
❑ 42 Rico Brogna .20 .09
❑ 43 Brian Daubach .30 .14
❑ 44 Rich Aurilia .30 .14
❑ 45 Vladimir Guerrero 1.00 .45
❑ 46 Luis Castillo .20 .09
❑ 47 Bartolo Colon .30 .14
❑ 48 Kevin Appier .20 .09
❑ 49 Mo Vaughn .30 .14
❑ 50 Alex Rodriguez 2.00 .90
❑ 51 Randy Johnson 1.00 .45
❑ 52 Kris Benson .30 .14
❑ 53 Tony Clark .30 .14
❑ 54 Chad Allen .20 .09
❑ 55 Larry Walker .50 .23
❑ 56 Freddy Garcia .50 .23
❑ 57 Paul Konerko .30 .14
❑ 58 Edgardo Alfonzo .30 .14
❑ 59 Brady Anderson .30 .14
❑ 60 Derek Jeter 3.00 1.35
❑ 61 John Smoltz .30 .14
❑ 62 Doug Glanville .20 .09
❑ 63 Shannon Stewart .30 .14
❑ 64 Greg Maddux 2.00 .90
❑ 65 Mark McGwire 3.00 1.35
❑ 66 Gary Sheffield .30 .14
❑ 67 Kevin Young .20 .09
❑ 68 Tony Gwynn 1.50 .70
❑ 69 Rey Ordonez .20 .09
❑ 70 Cal Ripken 3.00 1.35
❑ 71 Todd Helton 1.00 .45
❑ 72 Brian Jordan .30 .14
❑ 73 Jose Canseco .75 .35
❑ 74 Luis Gonzalez .75 .35
❑ 75 Barry Bonds 2.00 .90
❑ 76 Jermaine Dye .30 .14
❑ 77 Jose Offerman .20 .09
❑ 78 Magglio Ordonez .30 .14
❑ 79 Fred McGriff .50 .23
❑ 80 Ivan Rodriguez .75 .35
❑ 81 Josh Hamilton 1.00 .45
❑ 82 Vernon Wells .30 .14
❑ 83 Mark Mulder .75 .35
❑ 84 John Patterson .20 .09
❑ 85 Nick Johnson .75 .35
❑ 86 Pablo Ozuna .20 .09
❑ 87 A.J. Burnett .30 .14
❑ 88 Jack Cust .30 .14
❑ 89 Adam Piatt .50 .23
❑ 90 Rob Ryan .20 .09
❑ 91 Sean Burroughs .75 .35
❑ 92 D'Angelo Jimenez .30 .14
❑ 93 Chad Hermansen .20 .09
❑ 94 Robert Fick .20 .09
❑ 95 Ruben Mateo .30 .14
❑ 96 Alex Escobar .30 .14
❑ 97 Wily Pena .75 .35
❑ 98 Corey Patterson .75 .35
❑ 99 Eric Munson .30 .14
❑ 100 Pat Burrell .75 .35
❑ 101 Michael Tejera RC 8.00 3.60
❑ 102 Bobby Bradley RC 15.00 6.75
❑ 103 Larry Bigbie RC 12.00 5.50
❑ 104 B.J. Garbe RC 20.00 9.00
❑ 105 Josh Kalinowski RC 8.00 3.60
❑ 106 Brett Myers RC 12.00 5.50
❑ 107 Chris Mears RC 8.00 3.60
❑ 108 Aaron Rowand RC 15.00 6.75
❑ 109 Corey Myers RC 10.00 4.50
❑ 110 John Sneed RC 8.00 3.60
❑ 111 Ryan Christianson RC 15.00 6.75
❑ 112 Kyle Snyder 8.00 3.60
❑ 113 Mike Paradis 8.00 3.60
❑ 114 Chance Caple RC 10.00 4.50
❑ 115 Ben Christensen RC 8.00 3.60
❑ 116 Brad Baker RC 15.00 6.75
❑ 117 Rob Purvis RC 8.00 3.60
❑ 118 Rick Asadoorian RC 15.00 6.75
❑ 119 Ruben Salazar RC 15.00 6.75
❑ 120 Julio Zuleta RC 10.00 4.50
❑ 121 Alex Rodriguez 6.00 2.70
Ken Griffey Jr.
❑ 122 Nomar Garciaparra 8.00 3.60
Derek Jeter
❑ 123 Mark Mcgwire 8.00 3.60
Sammy Sosa
❑ 124 Randy Johnson 2.50 1.10
Pedro Martinez
❑ 125 Ivan Rodriguez 5.00 2.20
Mike Piazza
❑ 126 Manny Ramirez 2.50 1.10
Roberto Alomar
❑ 127 Chipper Jones 4.00 1.80
Andruw Jones
❑ 128 Cal Ripken 8.00 3.60
Tony Gwynn
❑ 129 Jeff Bagwell 2.50 1.10
Craig Biggio
❑ 130 Barry Bonds 5.00 2.20
Vladimir Guerrero
❑ 131 Nick Johnson 2.00 .90
Alfonso Soriano
❑ 132 Josh Hamilton 2.50 1.10
Pat Burrell
❑ 133 Corey Patterson 3.00 1.35
Ruben Mateo
❑ 134 Larry Walker 2.50 1.10
Todd Helton
❑ 135 Rey Ordonez 1.50 .70
Edgardo Alfonzo
❑ 136 Derek Jeter GEM 15.00 6.75
❑ 137 Alex Rodriguez GEM 10.00 4.50
❑ 138 Chipper Jones GEM 8.00 3.60
❑ 139 Mike Piazza GEM 10.00 4.50
❑ 140 Mark McGwire GEM 15.00 6.75
❑ 141 Ivan Rodriguez GEM 4.00 1.80
❑ 142 Cal Ripken GEM 15.00 6.75
❑ 143 V.Guerrero GEM 5.00 2.20
❑ 144 Randy Johnson GEM 5.00 2.20
❑ 145 Jeff Bagwell GEM 5.00 2.20
❑ 146 K.Griffey Jr. ACTION 2.50 1.10
❑ 146A Ken Griffey Jr. PORT 2.50 1.10
❑ 147 Andruw Jones .75 .35
❑ 148 Kerry Wood .75 .35
❑ 149 Jim Edmonds .50 .23
❑ 150 Pedro Martinez 1.00 .45
❑ 151 Warren Morris .20 .09
❑ 152 Trevor Hoffman .30 .14
❑ 153 Ryan Klesko .30 .14
❑ 154 Andy Pettitte .30 .14
❑ 155 Frank Thomas 1.00 .45
❑ 156 Damion Easley .20 .09
❑ 157 Cliff Floyd .30 .14
❑ 158 Ben Davis .30 .14
❑ 159 John Valentin .20 .09
❑ 160 Rafael Palmeiro .75 .35
❑ 161 Andy Ashby .20 .09
❑ 162 J.D. Drew .75 .35
❑ 163 Jay Bell .30 .14
❑ 164 Adam Kennedy .20 .09
❑ 165 Manny Ramirez 1.00 .45
❑ 166 John Halama .20 .09
❑ 167 Octavio Dotel .20 .09
❑ 168 Darin Erstad .75 .35
❑ 169 Jose Lima .20 .09
❑ 170 Andres Galarraga .50 .23
❑ 171 Scott Rolen .75 .35
❑ 172 Delino DeShields .20 .09
❑ 173 J.T. Snow .30 .14
❑ 174 Tony Womack .20 .09
❑ 175 John Olerud .30 .14
❑ 176 Jason Kendall .30 .14
❑ 177 Carlos Lee .30 .14
❑ 178 Eric Milton .30 .14
❑ 179 Jeff Cirillo .30 .14
❑ 180 Gabe Kapler .30 .14
❑ 181 Greg Vaughn .30 .14
❑ 182 Denny Neagle .20 .09
❑ 183 Tino Martinez .30 .14
❑ 184 Doug Mientkiewicz .50 .23
❑ 185 Juan Gonzalez .75 .35
❑ 186 Ellis Burks .30 .14
❑ 187 Mike Hampton .30 .14
❑ 188 Royce Clayton .20 .09
❑ 189 Mike Mussina .75 .35
❑ 190 Carlos Delgado .75 .35
❑ 191 Ben Grieve .30 .14
❑ 192 Fernando Tatis .20 .09
❑ 193 Matt Williams .50 .23
❑ 194 Rondell White .30 .14
❑ 195 Shawn Green .75 .35
❑ 196 Hideki Irabu .20 .09
❑ 197 Troy Glaus .75 .35
❑ 198 Roger Cedeno .20 .09
❑ 199 Ray Lankford .20 .09
❑ 200 Sammy Sosa 1.50 .70
❑ 201 Kenny Lofton .30 .14
❑ 202 Edgar Martinez .50 .23
❑ 203 Mark Kotsay .20 .09
❑ 204 David Wells .30 .14
❑ 205 Craig Biggio .50 .23
❑ 206 Ray Durham .30 .14
❑ 207 Troy O'Leary .20 .09
❑ 208 Rickey Henderson 1.50 .70
❑ 209 Bob Abreu .30 .14
❑ 210 Neifi Perez .20 .09
❑ 211 Carlos Febles .20 .09
❑ 212 Chuck Knoblauch .30 .14
❑ 213 Moises Alou .30 .14
❑ 214 Omar Vizquel .30 .14
❑ 215 Vinny Castilla .30 .14
❑ 216 Javy Lopez .30 .14
❑ 217 Johnny Damon .30 .14
❑ 218 Roger Clemens 2.00 .90
❑ 219 Miguel Tejada .30 .14
❑ 220 Carl Everett .30 .14
❑ 221 Matt Lawton .30 .14
❑ 222 Albert Belle .30 .14
❑ 223 Adrian Beltre .30 .14
❑ 224 Dante Bichette .30 .14
❑ 225 Raul Mondesi .30 .14
❑ 226 Mike Piazza 2.00 .90
❑ 227 Brad Penny .30 .14
❑ 228 Kip Wells .30 .14
❑ 229 Adam Everett .20 .09
❑ 230 Eddie Yarnall .20 .09
❑ 231 Matt LeCroy .20 .09
❑ 232 Jason Tyner .20 .09
❑ 233 Rick Ankiel .75 .35
❑ 234 Lance Berkman .75 .35
❑ 235 Rafael Furcal .75 .35
❑ 236 Dee Brown .20 .09
❑ 237 Gookie Dawkins .30 .14
❑ 238 Eric Valent .30 .14
❑ 239 Peter Bergeron .20 .09
❑ 240 Alfonso Soriano .75 .35
❑ 241 Adam Dunn 2.00 .90
❑ 242 Jorge Toca .20 .09
❑ 243 Ryan Anderson .30 .14
❑ 244 Jason Dellaero .20 .09
❑ 245 Jason Grilli .20 .09
❑ 246 Milton Bradley .20 .09
❑ 247 Scott Downs RC 6.00 2.70
❑ 248 Keith Reed RC 10.00 4.50

Card	MINT	NRMT
❑ 249 Edgar Cruz RC	6.00	2.70
❑ 250 Wes Anderson RC	8.00	3.60
❑ 251 Lyle Overbay RC	15.00	6.75
❑ 252 Mike Lamb RC	8.00	3.60
❑ 253 Vince Faison RC	8.00	3.60
❑ 254 Chad Alexander	6.00	2.70
❑ 255 Chris Wakeland RC	8.00	3.60
❑ 256 Aaron McNeal RC	8.00	3.60
❑ 257 Tomokazu Ohka RC	10.00	4.50
❑ 258 Ty Howington RC	15.00	6.75
❑ 259 Javier Colina RC	6.00	2.70
❑ 260 Jason Jennings	6.00	2.70
❑ 261 Ramon Santiago RC	8.00	3.60
❑ 262 Johan Santana RC	6.00	2.70
❑ 263 Quincy Foster RC	6.00	2.70
❑ 264 Junior Brignac RC	6.00	2.70
❑ 265 Rico Washington RC	8.00	3.60
❑ 266 Scott Sobkowiak RC	8.00	3.60
❑ 267 Pedro Martinez Rick Ankiel	3.00	1.35
❑ 268 Manny Ramirez Vladimir Guerrero	2.50	1.10
❑ 269 A.J.Burnett Mark Mulder	2.00	.90
❑ 270 Mike Piazza Eric Munson	5.00	2.20
❑ 271 Josh Hamilton Corey Patterson	2.50	1.10
❑ 272 Ken Griffey Jr. Sammy Sosa	5.00	2.20
❑ 273 Derek Jeter Alfonso Soriano	8.00	3.60
❑ 274 Mark McGwire Pat Burrell	8.00	3.60
❑ 275 Chipper Jones Cal Ripken	6.00	2.70
❑ 276 Nomar Garciaparra Alex Rodriguez	6.00	2.70
❑ 277 Pedro Martinez GEM	5.00	2.20
❑ 278 Tony Gwynn GEM	8.00	3.60
❑ 279 Barry Bonds GEM	10.00	4.50
❑ 280 Juan Gonzalez GEM	4.00	1.80
❑ 281 Larry Walker GEM	2.50	1.10
❑ 282 N.Garciaparra GEM	10.00	4.50
❑ 283 Ken Griffey Jr. GEM	12.00	5.50
❑ 284 Manny Ramirez GEM	5.00	2.20
❑ 285 Shawn Green GEM	.75	.35
❑ 286 Sammy Sosa GEM	8.00	3.60
❑ NNO Graded Gems Ser.1 EXCH/10		
❑ NNO Graded Gems Ser.2 EXCH/10		

2001 Finest

	MINT	NRMT
COMP.SET w/o SP's (100)	30.00	13.50
COMMON CARD (1-110)	.30	.14
COMMON SP	10.00	4.50
COMMON PROSPECT (111-140)	10.00	4.50
❑ 1 Mike Piazza SP	20.00	9.00
❑ 2 Andruw Jones	.75	.35
❑ 3 Jason Giambi	.75	.35
❑ 4 Fred McGriff	.50	.23
❑ 5 Vladimir Guerrero SP	10.00	4.50
❑ 6 Adrian Gonzalez	1.00	.45
❑ 7 Pedro Martinez	1.00	.45
❑ 8 Mike Lieberthal	.30	.14
❑ 9 Warren Morris	.30	.14
❑ 10 Juan Gonzalez	.75	.35
❑ 11 Jose Canseco	.75	.35
❑ 12 Jose Valentin	.30	.14
❑ 13 Jeff Cirillo	.30	.14
❑ 14 Pokey Reese	.30	.14
❑ 15 Scott Rolen	.75	.35
❑ 16 Greg Maddux	2.00	.90
❑ 17 Carlos Delgado	.75	.35
❑ 18 Rick Ankiel	.50	.23
❑ 19 Steve Finley	.30	.14
❑ 20 Shawn Green	.75	.35
❑ 21 Orlando Cabrera	.30	.14
❑ 22 Roberto Alomar	.75	.35
❑ 23 John Olerud	.30	.14
❑ 24 Albert Belle	.30	.14
❑ 25 Edgardo Alfonzo	.30	.14
❑ 26 Rafael Palmeiro	.75	.35
❑ 27 Mike Sweeney	.30	.14
❑ 28 Bernie Williams	.75	.35
❑ 29 Larry Walker	.50	.23
❑ 30 Barry Bonds SP	20.00	9.00
❑ 31 Orlando Hernandez	.30	.14
❑ 32 Randy Johnson	1.00	.45
❑ 33 Shannon Stewart	.30	.14
❑ 34 Mark Grace	.75	.35
❑ 35 Alex Rodriguez SP	25.00	11.00
❑ 36 Tino Martinez	.30	.14
❑ 37 Carlos Febles	.30	.14
❑ 38 Al Leiter	.30	.14
❑ 39 Omar Vizquel	.30	.14
❑ 40 Chuck Knoblauch	.30	.14
❑ 41 Tim Salmon	.30	.14
❑ 42 Brian Jordan	.30	.14
❑ 43 Edgar Renteria	.30	.14
❑ 44 Preston Wilson	.30	.14
❑ 45 Mariano Rivera	.30	.14
❑ 46 Gabe Kapler	.30	.14
❑ 47 Jason Kendall	.30	.14
❑ 48 Rickey Henderson	1.25	.55
❑ 49 Luis Gonzalez	.75	.35
❑ 50 Tom Glavine	.75	.35
❑ 51 Jeromy Burnitz	.30	.14
❑ 52 Garret Anderson	.30	.14
❑ 53 Craig Biggio	.50	.23
❑ 54 Vinny Castilla	.30	.14
❑ 55 Jeff Kent	.50	.23
❑ 56 Gary Sheffield	.30	.14
❑ 57 Jorge Posada	.30	.14
❑ 58 Sean Casey	.50	.23
❑ 59 Johnny Damon	.30	.14
❑ 60 Dean Palmer	.30	.14
❑ 61 Todd Helton	1.00	.45
❑ 62 Barry Larkin	.75	.35
❑ 63 Robin Ventura	.30	.14
❑ 64 Kenny Lofton	.30	.14
❑ 65 Sammy Sosa SP	15.00	6.75
❑ 66 Rafael Furcal	.30	.14
❑ 67 Jay Bell	.30	.14
❑ 68 J.T. Snow	.30	.14
❑ 69 Jose Vidro	.30	.14
❑ 70 Ivan Rodriguez	.75	.35
❑ 71 Jermaine Dye	.30	.14
❑ 72 Chipper Jones SP	15.00	6.75
❑ 73 Fernando Vina	.30	.14
❑ 74 Ben Grieve	.30	.14
❑ 75 Mark McGwire SP	30.00	13.50
❑ 76 Matt Williams	.50	.23
❑ 77 Mark Grudzielanek	.30	.14
❑ 78 Mike Hampton	.30	.14
❑ 79 Brian Giles	.30	.14
❑ 80 Tony Gwynn	1.50	.70
❑ 81 Carlos Beltran	.30	.14
❑ 82 Ray Durham	.30	.14
❑ 83 Brad Radke	.30	.14
❑ 84 David Justice	.30	.14
❑ 85 Frank Thomas	1.00	.45
❑ 86 Todd Zeile	.30	.14
❑ 87 Pat Burrell	.30	.14
❑ 88 Jim Thome	.75	.35
❑ 89 Greg Vaughn	.30	.14
❑ 90 Ken Griffey Jr. SP	25.00	11.00
❑ 91 Mike Mussina	.75	.35
❑ 92 Magglio Ordonez	.30	.14
❑ 93 Bob Abreu	.30	.14
❑ 94 Alex Gonzalez	.30	.14
❑ 95 Kevin Brown	.30	.14
❑ 96 Jay Buhner	.30	.14
❑ 97 Roger Clemens	2.00	.90
❑ 98 Nomar Garciaparra SP	25.00	11.00
❑ 99 Derrek Lee	.30	.14
❑ 100 Derek Jeter SP	30.00	13.50
❑ 101 Adrian Beltre	.30	.14
❑ 102 Geoff Jenkins	.30	.14
❑ 103 Javy Lopez	.30	.14
❑ 104 Raul Mondesi	.30	.14
❑ 105 Troy Glaus	.75	.35
❑ 106 Jeff Bagwell	1.00	.45
❑ 107 Eric Karros	.30	.14
❑ 108 Mo Vaughn	.30	.14
❑ 109 Cal Ripken	3.00	1.35
❑ 110 Manny Ramirez	1.00	.45
❑ 111 Scott Heard PROS	10.00	4.50
❑ 112 Luis Montanez PROS RC	30.00	13.50
❑ 113 Ben Diggins PROS	10.00	4.50
❑ 114 Shaun Boyd PROS RC	15.00	6.75
❑ 115 Sean Burnett PROS	10.00	4.50
❑ 116 Carmen Cali PROS RC	15.00	6.75
❑ 117 Derek Thompson PROS	10.00	4.50
❑ 118 David Parrish PROS RC	15.00	6.75
❑ 119 Dominic Rich PROS RC	15.00	6.75
❑ 120 Chad Petty PROS RC	15.00	6.75
❑ 121 Steve Smyth PROS RC	15.00	6.75
❑ 122 John Lackey PROS	10.00	4.50
❑ 123 Matt Galante PROS RC	15.00	6.75
❑ 124 Danny Borrell PROS RC	15.00	6.75
❑ 125 Bob Keppel PROS RC	15.00	6.75
❑ 126 Justin Wayne PROS RC	20.00	9.00
❑ 127 J.R. House PROS	20.00	9.00
❑ 128 Brian Sellier PROS RC	15.00	6.75
❑ 129 Dan Moylan PROS RC	15.00	6.75
❑ 130 Scott Pratt PROS RC	15.00	6.75
❑ 131 Victor Hall PROS RC	15.00	6.75
❑ 132 Joel Pineiro PROS	15.00	6.75
❑ 133 Josh Axelson PROS RC	15.00	6.75
❑ 134 Jose Reyes PROS RC	20.00	9.00
❑ 135 Greg Runser PROS RC	15.00	6.75
❑ 136 Bryan Hebson PROS RC	15.00	6.75
❑ 137 S. Serrano PROS RC	15.00	6.75
❑ 138 Kevin Joseph PROS RC	15.00	6.75
❑ 139 J. Richardson PROS RC	10.00	4.50
❑ 140 Mark Fischer PROS RC	15.00	6.75

1993 Flair

	MINT	NRMT
COMPLETE SET (300)	50.00	22.00
❑ 1 Steve Avery	.25	.11
❑ 2 Jeff Blauser	.25	.11
❑ 3 Ron Gant	.25	.11
❑ 4 Tom Glavine	1.00	.45
❑ 5 David Justice	.40	.18
❑ 6 Mark Lemke	.25	.11
❑ 7 Greg Maddux	2.50	1.10
❑ 8 Fred McGriff	.60	.25
❑ 9 Terry Pendleton	.40	.18
❑ 10 Deion Sanders	.40	.18
❑ 11 John Smoltz	.40	.18
❑ 12 Mike Stanton	.25	.11
❑ 13 Steve Buechele	.25	.11
❑ 14 Mark Grace	1.00	.45
❑ 15 Greg Hibbard	.25	.11
❑ 16 Derrick May	.25	.11
❑ 17 Chuck McElroy	.25	.11
❑ 18 Mike Morgan	.25	.11

❑ 19	Randy Myers	.25	.11
❑ 20	Ryne Sandberg	1.25	.55
❑ 21	Dwight Smith	.25	.11
❑ 22	Sammy Sosa	2.00	.90
❑ 23	Jose Vizcaino	.25	.11
❑ 24	Tim Belcher	.25	.11
❑ 25	Rob Dibble	.25	.11
❑ 26	Roberto Kelly	.25	.11
❑ 27	Barry Larkin	1.00	.45
❑ 28	Kevin Mitchell	.25	.11
❑ 29	Hal Morris	.25	.11
❑ 30	Joe Oliver	.25	.11
❑ 31	Jose Rijo	.25	.11
❑ 32	Bip Roberts	.25	.11
❑ 33	Chris Sabo	.25	.11
❑ 34	Reggie Sanders	.25	.11
❑ 35	Dante Bichette	.40	.18
❑ 36	Willie Blair	.25	.11
❑ 37	Jerald Clark	.25	.11
❑ 38	Alex Cole	.25	.11
❑ 39	Andres Galarraga	.60	.25
❑ 40	Joe Girardi	.25	.11
❑ 41	Charlie Hayes	.25	.11
❑ 42	Chris Jones	.25	.11
❑ 43	David Nied	.25	.11
❑ 44	Eric Young	.25	.11
❑ 45	Alex Arias	.25	.11
❑ 46	Jack Armstrong	.25	.11
❑ 47	Bret Barberie	.25	.11
❑ 48	Chuck Carr	.25	.11
❑ 49	Jeff Conine	.25	.11
❑ 50	Orestes Destrade	.25	.11
❑ 51	Chris Hammond	.25	.11
❑ 52	Bryan Harvey	.25	.11
❑ 53	Benito Santiago	.25	.11
❑ 54	Gary Sheffield	.40	.18
❑ 55	Walt Weiss	.25	.11
❑ 56	Eric Anthony	.25	.11
❑ 57	Jeff Bagwell	1.25	.55
❑ 58	Craig Biggio	.60	.25
❑ 59	Ken Caminiti	.40	.18
❑ 60	Andujar Cedeno	.25	.11
❑ 61	Doug Drabek	.25	.11
❑ 62	Steve Finley	.40	.18
❑ 63	Luis Gonzalez	1.00	.45
❑ 64	Pete Harnisch	.25	.11
❑ 65	Doug Jones	.25	.11
❑ 66	Darryl Kile	.40	.18
❑ 67	Greg Swindell	.25	.11
❑ 68	Brett Butler	.40	.18
❑ 69	Jim Gott	.25	.11
❑ 70	Orel Hershiser	.40	.18
❑ 71	Eric Karros	.40	.18
❑ 72	Pedro Martinez	2.50	1.10
❑ 73	Ramon Martinez	.25	.11
❑ 74	Roger McDowell	.25	.11
❑ 75	Mike Piazza	5.00	2.20
❑ 76	Jody Reed	.25	.11
❑ 77	Tim Wallach	.25	.11
❑ 78	Moises Alou	.40	.18
❑ 79	Greg Colbrunn	.25	.11
❑ 80	Wil Cordero	.25	.11
❑ 81	Delino DeShields	.25	.11
❑ 82	Jeff Fassero	.25	.11
❑ 83	Marquis Grissom	.25	.11
❑ 84	Ken Hill	.25	.11
❑ 85	Mike Lansing RC	.40	.18
❑ 86	Dennis Martinez	.40	.18
❑ 87	Larry Walker	.60	.25
❑ 88	John Wetteland	.40	.18
❑ 89	Bobby Bonilla	.40	.18
❑ 90	Vince Coleman	.25	.11
❑ 91	Dwight Gooden	.40	.18
❑ 92	Todd Hundley	.25	.11
❑ 93	Howard Johnson	.25	.11
❑ 94	Eddie Murray	1.00	.45
❑ 95	Joe Orsulak	.25	.11
❑ 96	Bret Saberhagen	.40	.18
❑ 97	Darren Daulton	.40	.18
❑ 98	Mariano Duncan	.25	.11
❑ 99	Len Dykstra	.40	.18
❑ 100	Jim Eisenreich	.25	.11
❑ 101	Tommy Greene	.25	.11
❑ 102	Dave Hollins	.25	.11
❑ 103	Pete Incaviglia	.25	.11
❑ 104	Danny Jackson	.25	.11
❑ 105	John Kruk	.40	.18
❑ 106	Terry Mulholland	.25	.11
❑ 107	Curt Schilling	1.00	.45
❑ 108	Mitch Williams	.25	.11
❑ 109	Stan Belinda	.25	.11
❑ 110	Jay Bell	.40	.18
❑ 111	Steve Cooke	.25	.11
❑ 112	Carlos Garcia	.25	.11
❑ 113	Jeff King	.25	.11
❑ 114	Al Martin	.25	.11
❑ 115	Orlando Merced	.25	.11
❑ 116	Don Slaught	.25	.11
❑ 117	Andy Van Slyke	.40	.18
❑ 118	Tim Wakefield	.25	.11
❑ 119	Rene Arocha RC	.40	.18
❑ 120	Bernard Gilkey	.25	.11
❑ 121	Gregg Jefferies	.25	.11
❑ 122	Ray Lankford	.25	.11
❑ 123	Donovan Osborne	.25	.11
❑ 124	Tom Pagnozzi	.25	.11
❑ 125	Erik Pappas	.25	.11
❑ 126	Geronimo Pena	.25	.11
❑ 127	Lee Smith	.40	.18
❑ 128	Ozzie Smith	1.25	.55
❑ 129	Bob Tewksbury	.25	.11
❑ 130	Mark Whiten	.25	.11
❑ 131	Derek Bell	.25	.11
❑ 132	Andy Benes	.25	.11
❑ 133	Tony Gwynn	2.00	.90
❑ 134	Gene Harris	.25	.11
❑ 135	Trevor Hoffman	.40	.18
❑ 136	Phil Plantier	.25	.11
❑ 137	Rod Beck	.25	.11
❑ 138	Barry Bonds	2.50	1.10
❑ 139	John Burkett	.25	.11
❑ 140	Will Clark	1.00	.45
❑ 141	Royce Clayton	.25	.11
❑ 142	Mike Jackson	.25	.11
❑ 143	Darren Lewis	.25	.11
❑ 144	Kirt Manwaring	.25	.11
❑ 145	Willie McGee	.40	.18
❑ 146	Bill Swift	.25	.11
❑ 147	Robby Thompson	.25	.11
❑ 148	Matt Williams	.60	.25
❑ 149	Brady Anderson	.40	.18
❑ 150	Mike Devereaux	.25	.11
❑ 151	Chris Hoiles	.25	.11
❑ 152	Ben McDonald	.25	.11
❑ 153	Mark McLemore	.25	.11
❑ 154	Mike Mussina	1.00	.45
❑ 155	Gregg Olson	.25	.11
❑ 156	Harold Reynolds	.25	.11
❑ 157	Cal Ripken UER (Back refers to his games streak going into 1992; should be 1993) Also streak is spelled steak	4.00	1.80
❑ 158	Rick Sutcliffe	.40	.18
❑ 159	Fernando Valenzuela	.40	.18
❑ 160	Roger Clemens	2.50	1.10
❑ 161	Scott Cooper	.25	.11
❑ 162	Andre Dawson	.60	.25
❑ 163	Scott Fletcher	.25	.11
❑ 164	Mike Greenwell	.25	.11
❑ 165	Greg A. Harris	.25	.11
❑ 166	Billy Hatcher	.25	.11
❑ 167	Jeff Russell	.25	.11
❑ 168	Mo Vaughn	.40	.18
❑ 169	Frank Viola	.40	.18
❑ 170	Chad Curtis	.25	.11
❑ 171	Chili Davis	.40	.18
❑ 172	Gary DiSarcina	.25	.11
❑ 173	Damion Easley	.25	.11
❑ 174	Chuck Finley	.40	.18
❑ 175	Mark Langston	.25	.11
❑ 176	Luis Polonia	.25	.11
❑ 177	Tim Salmon	.40	.18
❑ 178	Scott Sanderson	.25	.11
❑ 179	J.T.Snow RC	1.25	.55
❑ 180	Wilson Alvarez	.25	.11
❑ 181	Ellis Burks	.40	.18
❑ 182	Joey Cora	.25	.11
❑ 183	Alex Fernandez	.25	.11
❑ 184	Ozzie Guillen	.25	.11
❑ 185	Roberto Hernandez	.25	.11
❑ 186	Bo Jackson	.40	.18
❑ 187	Lance Johnson	.25	.11
❑ 188	Jack McDowell	.25	.11
❑ 189	Frank Thomas	1.25	.55
❑ 190	Robin Ventura	.40	.18
❑ 191	Carlos Baerga	.25	.11
❑ 192	Albert Belle	.40	.18
❑ 193	Wayne Kirby	.25	.11
❑ 194	Derek Lilliquist	.25	.11
❑ 195	Kenny Lofton	.40	.18
❑ 196	Carlos Martinez	.25	.11
❑ 197	Jose Mesa	.25	.11
❑ 198	Eric Plunk	.25	.11
❑ 199	Paul Sorrento	.25	.11
❑ 200	John Doherty	.25	.11
❑ 201	Cecil Fielder	.40	.18
❑ 202	Travis Fryman	.40	.18
❑ 203	Kirk Gibson	.40	.18
❑ 204	Mike Henneman	.25	.11
❑ 205	Chad Kreuter	.25	.11
❑ 206	Scott Livingstone	.25	.11
❑ 207	Tony Phillips	.25	.11
❑ 208	Mickey Tettleton	.25	.11
❑ 209	Alan Trammell	.60	.25
❑ 210	David Wells	.40	.18
❑ 211	Lou Whitaker	.40	.18
❑ 212	Kevin Appier	.40	.18
❑ 213	George Brett	2.00	.90
❑ 214	David Cone	.40	.18
❑ 215	Tom Gordon	.25	.11
❑ 216	Phil Hiatt	.25	.11
❑ 217	Felix Jose	.25	.11
❑ 218	Wally Joyner	.40	.18
❑ 219	Jose Lind	.25	.11
❑ 220	Mike Macfarlane	.25	.11
❑ 221	Brian McRae	.25	.11
❑ 222	Jeff Montgomery	.25	.11
❑ 223	Cal Eldred	.25	.11
❑ 224	Darryl Hamilton	.25	.11
❑ 225	John Jaha	.25	.11
❑ 226	Pat Listach	.25	.11
❑ 227	Graeme Lloyd RC	.40	.18
❑ 228	Kevin Reimer	.25	.11
❑ 229	Bill Spiers	.25	.11
❑ 230	B.J. Surhoff	.40	.18
❑ 231	Greg Vaughn	.40	.18
❑ 232	Robin Yount	1.00	.45
❑ 233	Rick Aguilera	.25	.11
❑ 234	Jim Deshaies	.25	.11
❑ 235	Brian Harper	.25	.11
❑ 236	Kent Hrbek	.40	.18
❑ 237	Chuck Knoblauch	.40	.18
❑ 238	Shane Mack	.25	.11
❑ 239	David McCarty	.25	.11
❑ 240	Pedro Munoz	.25	.11
❑ 241	Mike Pagliarulo	.25	.11
❑ 242	Kirby Puckett	2.50	1.10
❑ 243	Dave Winfield	1.00	.45
❑ 244	Jim Abbott	.40	.18
❑ 245	Wade Boggs	1.00	.45
❑ 246	Pat Kelly	.25	.11
❑ 247	Jimmy Key	.40	.18
❑ 248	Jim Leyritz	.25	.11
❑ 249	Don Mattingly	2.50	1.10
❑ 250	Matt Nokes	.25	.11
❑ 251	Paul O'Neill	1.00	.45
❑ 252	Mike Stanley	.25	.11
❑ 253	Danny Tartabull	.25	.11
❑ 254	Bob Wickman	.25	.11
❑ 255	Bernie Williams	1.00	.45
❑ 256	Mike Bordick	.25	.11
❑ 257	Dennis Eckersley	.40	.18
❑ 258	Brent Gates	.25	.11
❑ 259	Rich Gossage	.40	.18
❑ 260	Rickey Henderson	2.00	.90
❑ 261	Mark McGwire	4.00	1.80
❑ 262	Ruben Sierra	.25	.11
❑ 263	Terry Steinbach	.25	.11
❑ 264	Bob Welch	.25	.11
❑ 265	Bobby Witt	.25	.11
❑ 266	Rich Amaral	.25	.11
❑ 267	Chris Bosio	.25	.11
❑ 268	Jay Buhner	.40	.18
❑ 269	Norm Charlton	.25	.11
❑ 270	Ken Griffey Jr.	3.00	1.35
❑ 271	Erik Hanson	.25	.11
❑ 272	Randy Johnson	1.25	.55
❑ 273	Edgar Martinez	.60	.25

❑ 274	Tino Martinez	.40	.18
❑ 275	Dave Valle	.25	.11
❑ 276	Omar Vizquel	.40	.18
❑ 277	Kevin Brown	.40	.18
❑ 278	Jose Canseco	1.00	.45
❑ 279	Julio Franco	.40	.18
❑ 280	Juan Gonzalez	1.00	.45
❑ 281	Tom Henke	.25	.11
❑ 282	David Hulse RC	.25	.11
❑ 283	Rafael Palmeiro	1.00	.45
❑ 284	Dean Palmer	.40	.18
❑ 285	Ivan Rodriguez	1.00	.45
❑ 286	Nolan Ryan	5.00	2.20
❑ 287	Roberto Alomar	1.00	.45
❑ 288	Pat Borders	.25	.11
❑ 289	Joe Carter	.40	.18
❑ 290	Juan Guzman	.25	.11
❑ 291	Pat Hentgen	.25	.11
❑ 292	Paul Molitor	1.00	.45
❑ 293	John Olerud	.40	.18
❑ 294	Ed Sprague	.25	.11
❑ 295	Dave Stewart	.40	.18
❑ 296	Duane Ward	.25	.11
❑ 297	Devon White	.25	.11
❑ 298	Checklist 1-100	.25	.11
❑ 299	Checklist 101-200	.25	.11
❑ 300	Checklist 201-300	.25	.11

1994 Flair

	MINT	NRMT
COMPLETE SET (450)	100.00	45.00
COMPLETE SERIES 1 (250)	25.00	11.00
COMPLETE SERIES 2 (200)	75.00	34.00

❑ 1	Harold Baines	.40	.18
❑ 2	Jeffrey Hammonds	.40	.18
❑ 3	Chris Hoiles	.25	.11
❑ 4	Ben McDonald	.25	.11
❑ 5	Mark McLemore	.25	.11
❑ 6	Jamie Moyer	.25	.11
❑ 7	Jim Poole	.25	.11
❑ 8	Cal Ripken Jr.	4.00	1.80
❑ 9	Chris Sabo	.25	.11
❑ 10	Scott Bankhead	.25	.11
❑ 11	Scott Cooper	.25	.11
❑ 12	Danny Darwin	.25	.11
❑ 13	Andre Dawson	.60	.25
❑ 14	Billy Hatcher	.25	.11
❑ 15	Aaron Sele	.40	.18
❑ 16	John Valentin	.25	.11
❑ 17	Dave Valle	.25	.11
❑ 18	Mo Vaughn	.40	.18
❑ 19	Brian Anderson RC	.40	.18
❑ 20	Gary DiSarcina	.25	.11
❑ 21	Jim Edmonds	1.00	.45
❑ 22	Chuck Finley	.40	.18
❑ 23	Bo Jackson	.40	.18
❑ 24	Mark Leiter	.25	.11
❑ 25	Greg Myers	.25	.11
❑ 26	Eduardo Perez	.25	.11
❑ 27	Tim Salmon	.40	.18
❑ 28	Wilson Alvarez	.25	.11
❑ 29	Jason Bere	.25	.11
❑ 30	Alex Fernandez	.25	.11
❑ 31	Ozzie Guillen	.25	.11
❑ 32	Joe Hall RC	.25	.11
❑ 33	Darrin Jackson	.25	.11
❑ 34	Kirk McCaskill	.25	.11
❑ 35	Tim Raines	.40	.18
❑ 36	Frank Thomas	1.25	.55
❑ 37	Carlos Baerga	.25	.11
❑ 38	Albert Belle	.40	.18
❑ 39	Mark Clark	.25	.11
❑ 40	Wayne Kirby	.25	.11
❑ 41	Dennis Martinez	.40	.18
❑ 42	Charles Nagy	.25	.11
❑ 43	Manny Ramirez	1.50	.70
❑ 44	Paul Sorrento	.25	.11
❑ 45	Jim Thome	1.00	.45
❑ 46	Eric Davis	.40	.18
❑ 47	John Doherty	.25	.11
❑ 48	Junior Felix	.25	.11
❑ 49	Cecil Fielder	.40	.18
❑ 50	Kirk Gibson	.40	.18
❑ 51	Mike Moore	.25	.11
❑ 52	Tony Phillips	.25	.11
❑ 53	Alan Trammell	.60	.25
❑ 54	Kevin Appier	.40	.18
❑ 55	Stan Belinda	.25	.11
❑ 56	Vince Coleman	.25	.11
❑ 57	Greg Gagne	.25	.11
❑ 58	Bob Hamelin	.25	.11
❑ 59	Dave Henderson	.25	.11
❑ 60	Wally Joyner	.40	.18
❑ 61	Mike Macfarlane	.25	.11
❑ 62	Jeff Montgomery	.25	.11
❑ 63	Ricky Bones	.25	.11
❑ 64	Jeff Bronkey	.25	.11
❑ 65	Alex Diaz RC	.25	.11
❑ 66	Cal Eldred	.25	.11
❑ 67	Darryl Hamilton	.25	.11
❑ 68	John Jaha	.25	.11
❑ 69	Mark Kiefer	.25	.11
❑ 70	Kevin Seitzer	.25	.11
❑ 71	Turner Ward	.25	.11
❑ 72	Rich Becker	.25	.11
❑ 73	Scott Erickson	.25	.11
❑ 74	Keith Garagozzo RC	.25	.11
❑ 75	Kent Hrbek	.40	.18
❑ 76	Scott Leius	.25	.11
❑ 77	Kirby Puckett	2.50	1.10
❑ 78	Matt Walbeck	.25	.11
❑ 79	Dave Winfield	1.00	.45
❑ 80	Mike Gallego	.25	.11
❑ 81	Xavier Hernandez	.25	.11
❑ 82	Jimmy Key	.40	.18
❑ 83	Jim Leyritz	.25	.11
❑ 84	Don Mattingly	2.50	1.10
❑ 85	Matt Nokes	.25	.11
❑ 86	Paul O'Neill	1.00	.45
❑ 87	Melido Perez	.25	.11
❑ 88	Danny Tartabull	.25	.11
❑ 89	Mike Bordick	.25	.11
❑ 90	Ron Darling	.25	.11
❑ 91	Dennis Eckersley	.40	.18
❑ 92	Stan Javier	.25	.11
❑ 93	Steve Karsay	.25	.11
❑ 94	Mark McGwire	4.00	1.80
❑ 95	Troy Neel	.25	.11
❑ 96	Terry Steinbach	.25	.11
❑ 97	Bill Taylor RC	.40	.18
❑ 98	Eric Anthony	.25	.11
❑ 99	Chris Bosio	.25	.11
❑ 100	Tim Davis	.25	.11
❑ 101	Felix Fermin	.25	.11
❑ 102	Dave Fleming	.25	.11
❑ 103	Ken Griffey Jr.	3.00	1.35
❑ 104	Greg Hibbard	.25	.11
❑ 105	Reggie Jefferson	.25	.11
❑ 106	Tino Martinez	.40	.18
❑ 107	Jack Armstrong	.25	.11
❑ 108	Will Clark	1.00	.45
❑ 109	Juan Gonzalez	1.00	.45
❑ 110	Rick Helling	.25	.11
❑ 111	Tom Henke	.25	.11
❑ 112	David Hulse	.25	.11
❑ 113	Manuel Lee	.25	.11
❑ 114	Doug Strange	.25	.11
❑ 115	Roberto Alomar	1.00	.45
❑ 116	Joe Carter	.40	.18
❑ 117	Carlos Delgado	1.50	.70
❑ 118	Pat Hentgen	.25	.11
❑ 119	Paul Molitor	1.00	.45
❑ 120	John Olerud	.40	.18
❑ 121	Dave Stewart	.40	.18
❑ 122	Todd Stottlemyre	.25	.11
❑ 123	Mike Timlin	.25	.11
❑ 124	Jeff Blauser	.25	.11
❑ 125	Tom Glavine	1.00	.45
❑ 126	David Justice	.40	.18
❑ 127	Mike Kelly	.25	.11
❑ 128	Ryan Klesko	.40	.18
❑ 129	Javier Lopez	.40	.18
❑ 130	Greg Maddux	2.50	1.10
❑ 131	Fred McGriff	.60	.25
❑ 132	Kent Mercker	.25	.11
❑ 133	Mark Wohlers	.25	.11
❑ 134	Willie Banks	.25	.11
❑ 135	Steve Buechele	.25	.11
❑ 136	Shawon Dunston	.25	.11
❑ 137	Jose Guzman	.25	.11
❑ 138	Glenallen Hill	.25	.11
❑ 139	Randy Myers	.25	.11
❑ 140	Karl Rhodes	.25	.11
❑ 141	Ryne Sandberg	1.25	.55
❑ 142	Steve Trachsel	.25	.11
❑ 143	Bret Boone	.40	.18
❑ 144	Tom Browning	.25	.11
❑ 145	Hector Carrasco	.25	.11
❑ 146	Barry Larkin	1.00	.45
❑ 147	Hal Morris	.25	.11
❑ 148	Jose Rijo	.25	.11
❑ 149	Reggie Sanders	.25	.11
❑ 150	John Smiley	.25	.11
❑ 151	Dante Bichette	.40	.18
❑ 152	Ellis Burks	.40	.18
❑ 153	Joe Girardi	.25	.11
❑ 154	Mike Harkey	.25	.11
❑ 155	Roberto Mejia	.25	.11
❑ 156	Marcus Moore	.25	.11
❑ 157	Armando Reynoso	.25	.11
❑ 158	Bruce Ruffin	.25	.11
❑ 159	Eric Young	.25	.11
❑ 160	Kurt Abbott RC	.40	.18
❑ 161	Jeff Conine	.25	.11
❑ 162	Orestes Destrade	.25	.11
❑ 163	Chris Hammond	.25	.11
❑ 164	Bryan Harvey	.25	.11
❑ 165	Dave Magadan	.25	.11
❑ 166	Gary Sheffield	.40	.18
❑ 167	David Weathers	.25	.11
❑ 168	Andujar Cedeno	.25	.11
❑ 169	Tom Edens	.25	.11
❑ 170	Luis Gonzalez	1.00	.45
❑ 171	Pete Harnisch	.25	.11
❑ 172	Todd Jones	.25	.11
❑ 173	Darryl Kile	.40	.18
❑ 174	James Mouton	.25	.11
❑ 175	Scott Servais	.25	.11
❑ 176	Mitch Williams	.25	.11
❑ 177	Pedro Astacio	.25	.11
❑ 178	Orel Hershiser	.40	.18
❑ 179	Raul Mondesi	.40	.18
❑ 180	Jose Offerman	.25	.11
❑ 181	Chan Ho Park RC	3.00	1.35
❑ 182	Mike Piazza	3.00	1.35
❑ 183	Cory Snyder	.25	.11
❑ 184	Tim Wallach	.25	.11
❑ 185	Todd Worrell	.25	.11
❑ 186	Sean Berry	.25	.11
❑ 187	Wil Cordero	.25	.11
❑ 188	Darrin Fletcher	.25	.11
❑ 189	Cliff Floyd	.40	.18
❑ 190	Marquis Grissom	.25	.11
❑ 191	Rod Henderson	.25	.11
❑ 192	Ken Hill	.25	.11
❑ 193	Pedro Martinez	1.50	.70
❑ 194	Kirk Rueter	.25	.11
❑ 195	Jeromy Burnitz	.40	.18
❑ 196	John Franco	.40	.18
❑ 197	Dwight Gooden	.40	.18
❑ 198	Todd Hundley	.25	.11
❑ 199	Bobby Jones	.25	.11
❑ 200	Jeff Kent	.60	.25
❑ 201	Mike Maddux	.25	.11
❑ 202	Ryan Thompson	.25	.11
❑ 203	Jose Vizcaino	.25	.11
❑ 204	Darren Daulton	.40	.18
❑ 205	Lenny Dykstra	.40	.18

No.	Player	MINT	NRMT
❑ 206	Jim Eisenreich	.25	.11
❑ 207	Dave Hollins	.25	.11
❑ 208	Danny Jackson	.25	.11
❑ 209	Doug Jones	.25	.11
❑ 210	Jeff Juden	.25	.11
❑ 211	Ben Rivera	.25	.11
❑ 212	Kevin Stocker	.25	.11
❑ 213	Milt Thompson	.25	.11
❑ 214	Jay Bell	.40	.18
❑ 215	Steve Cooke	.25	.11
❑ 216	Mark Dewey	.25	.11
❑ 217	Al Martin	.25	.11
❑ 218	Orlando Merced	.25	.11
❑ 219	Don Slaught	.25	.11
❑ 220	Zane Smith	.25	.11
❑ 221	Rick White RC	.25	.11
❑ 222	Kevin Young	.25	.11
❑ 223	Rene Arocha	.25	.11
❑ 224	Rheal Cormier	.25	.11
❑ 225	Brian Jordan	.40	.18
❑ 226	Ray Lankford	.25	.11
❑ 227	Mike Perez	.25	.11
❑ 228	Ozzie Smith	1.25	.55
❑ 229	Mark Whiten	.25	.11
❑ 230	Todd Zeile	.25	.11
❑ 231	Derek Bell	.25	.11
❑ 232	Archi Cianfrocco	.25	.11
❑ 233	Ricky Gutierrez	.25	.11
❑ 234	Trevor Hoffman	.40	.18
❑ 235	Phil Plantier	.25	.11
❑ 236	Dave Staton	.25	.11
❑ 237	Wally Whitehurst	.25	.11
❑ 238	Todd Benzinger	.25	.11
❑ 239	Barry Bonds	2.50	1.10
❑ 240	John Burkett	.25	.11
❑ 241	Royce Clayton	.25	.11
❑ 242	Bryan Hickerson	.25	.11
❑ 243	Mike Jackson	.25	.11
❑ 244	Darren Lewis	.25	.11
❑ 245	Kirt Manwaring	.25	.11
❑ 246	Mark Portugal	.25	.11
❑ 247	Salomon Torres	.25	.11
❑ 248	Checklist	.25	.11
❑ 249	Checklist	.25	.11
❑ 250	Checklist	.25	.11
❑ 251	Brady Anderson	.40	.18
❑ 252	Mike Devereaux	.25	.11
❑ 253	Sid Fernandez	.25	.11
❑ 254	Leo Gomez	.25	.11
❑ 255	Mike Mussina	1.00	.45
❑ 256	Mike Oquist	.25	.11
❑ 257	Rafael Palmeiro	1.00	.45
❑ 258	Lee Smith	.40	.18
❑ 259	Damon Berryhill	.25	.11
❑ 260	Wes Chamberlain	.25	.11
❑ 261	Roger Clemens	2.50	1.10
❑ 262	Gar Finnvold RC	.25	.11
❑ 263	Mike Greenwell	.25	.11
❑ 264	Tim Naehring	.25	.11
❑ 265	Otis Nixon	.25	.11
❑ 266	Ken Ryan	.25	.11
❑ 267	Chad Curtis	.25	.11
❑ 268	Chili Davis	.40	.18
❑ 269	Damion Easley	.25	.11
❑ 270	Jorge Fabregas	.25	.11
❑ 271	Mark Langston	.25	.11
❑ 272	Phil Leftwich RC	.25	.11
❑ 273	Harold Reynolds	.25	.11
❑ 274	J.T. Snow	.40	.18
❑ 275	Joey Cora	.25	.11
❑ 276	Julio Franco	.40	.18
❑ 277	Roberto Hernandez	.25	.11
❑ 278	Lance Johnson	.25	.11
❑ 279	Ron Karkovice	.25	.11
❑ 280	Jack McDowell	.25	.11
❑ 281	Robin Ventura	.40	.18
❑ 282	Sandy Alomar Jr.	.40	.18
❑ 283	Kenny Lofton	.40	.18
❑ 284	Jose Mesa	.25	.11
❑ 285	Jack Morris	.40	.18
❑ 286	Eddie Murray	1.00	.45
❑ 287	Chad Ogea	.25	.11
❑ 288	Eric Plunk	.25	.11
❑ 289	Paul Shuey	.25	.11
❑ 290	Omar Vizquel	.40	.18
❑ 291	Danny Bautista	.25	.11
❑ 292	Travis Fryman	.40	.18
❑ 293	Greg Gohr	.25	.11
❑ 294	Chris Gomez	.25	.11
❑ 295	Mickey Tettleton	.25	.11
❑ 296	Lou Whitaker	.40	.18
❑ 297	David Cone	.40	.18
❑ 298	Gary Gaetti	.40	.18
❑ 299	Tom Gordon	.25	.11
❑ 300	Felix Jose	.25	.11
❑ 301	Jose Lind	.25	.11
❑ 302	Brian McRae	.25	.11
❑ 303	Mike Fetters	.25	.11
❑ 304	Brian Harper	.25	.11
❑ 305	Pat Listach	.25	.11
❑ 306	Matt Mieske	.25	.11
❑ 307	Dave Nilsson	.25	.11
❑ 308	Jody Reed	.25	.11
❑ 309	Greg Vaughn	.40	.18
❑ 310	Bill Wegman	.25	.11
❑ 311	Rick Aguilera	.25	.11
❑ 312	Alex Cole	.25	.11
❑ 313	Denny Hocking	.25	.11
❑ 314	Chuck Knoblauch	.40	.18
❑ 315	Shane Mack	.25	.11
❑ 316	Pat Meares	.25	.11
❑ 317	Kevin Tapani	.25	.11
❑ 318	Jim Abbott	.40	.18
❑ 319	Wade Boggs	1.00	.45
❑ 320	Sterling Hitchcock	.25	.11
❑ 321	Pat Kelly	.25	.11
❑ 322	Terry Mulholland	.25	.11
❑ 323	Luis Polonia	.25	.11
❑ 324	Mike Stanley	.25	.11
❑ 325	Bob Wickman	.25	.11
❑ 326	Bernie Williams	1.00	.45
❑ 327	Mark Acre RC	.25	.11
❑ 328	Geronimo Berroa	.25	.11
❑ 329	Scott Brosius	.40	.18
❑ 330	Brent Gates	.25	.11
❑ 331	Rickey Henderson	2.00	.90
❑ 332	Carlos Reyes RC	.25	.11
❑ 333	Ruben Sierra	.25	.11
❑ 334	Bobby Witt	.25	.11
❑ 335	Bobby Ayala	.25	.11
❑ 336	Jay Buhner	.40	.18
❑ 337	Randy Johnson	1.25	.55
❑ 338	Edgar Martinez	.60	.25
❑ 339	Bill Risley	.25	.11
❑ 340	Alex Rodriguez RC	50.00	22.00
❑ 341	Roger Salkeld	.25	.11
❑ 342	Dan Wilson	.25	.11
❑ 343	Kevin Brown	.40	.18
❑ 344	Jose Canseco	1.00	.45
❑ 345	Dean Palmer	.40	.18
❑ 346	Ivan Rodriguez	1.00	.45
❑ 347	Kenny Rogers	.25	.11
❑ 348	Pat Borders	.25	.11
❑ 349	Juan Guzman	.25	.11
❑ 350	Ed Sprague	.25	.11
❑ 351	Devon White	.25	.11
❑ 352	Steve Avery	.25	.11
❑ 353	Roberto Kelly	.25	.11
❑ 354	Mark Lemke	.25	.11
❑ 355	Greg McMichael	.25	.11
❑ 356	Terry Pendleton	.40	.18
❑ 357	John Smoltz	.40	.18
❑ 358	Mike Stanton	.25	.11
❑ 359	Tony Tarasco	.25	.11
❑ 360	Mark Grace	1.00	.45
❑ 361	Derrick May	.25	.11
❑ 362	Rey Sanchez	.25	.11
❑ 363	Sammy Sosa	2.00	.90
❑ 364	Rick Wilkins	.25	.11
❑ 365	Jeff Brantley	.25	.11
❑ 366	Tony Fernandez	.25	.11
❑ 367	Chuck McElroy	.25	.11
❑ 368	Kevin Mitchell	.25	.11
❑ 369	John Roper	.25	.11
❑ 370	Johnny Ruffin	.25	.11
❑ 371	Deion Sanders	.40	.18
❑ 372	Marvin Freeman	.25	.11
❑ 373	Andres Galarraga	.60	.25
❑ 374	Charlie Hayes	.25	.11
❑ 375	Nelson Liriano	.25	.11
❑ 376	David Nied	.25	.11
❑ 377	Walt Weiss	.25	.11
❑ 378	Bret Barberie	.25	.11
❑ 379	Jerry Browne	.25	.11
❑ 380	Chuck Carr	.25	.11
❑ 381	Greg Colbrunn	.25	.11
❑ 382	Charlie Hough	.40	.18
❑ 383	Kurt Miller	.25	.11
❑ 384	Benito Santiago	.25	.11
❑ 385	Jeff Bagwell	1.25	.55
❑ 386	Craig Biggio	.60	.25
❑ 387	Ken Caminiti	.40	.18
❑ 388	Doug Drabek	.25	.11
❑ 389	Steve Finley	.40	.18
❑ 390	John Hudek RC	.25	.11
❑ 391	Orlando Miller	.25	.11
❑ 392	Shane Reynolds	.25	.11
❑ 393	Brett Butler	.40	.18
❑ 394	Tom Candiotti	.25	.11
❑ 395	Delino DeShields	.25	.11
❑ 396	Kevin Gross	.25	.11
❑ 397	Eric Karros	.40	.18
❑ 398	Ramon Martinez	.25	.11
❑ 399	Henry Rodriguez	.25	.11
❑ 400	Moises Alou	.40	.18
❑ 401	Jeff Fassero	.25	.11
❑ 402	Mike Lansing	.25	.11
❑ 403	Mel Rojas	.25	.11
❑ 404	Larry Walker	.60	.25
❑ 405	John Wetteland	.40	.18
❑ 406	Gabe White	.25	.11
❑ 407	Bobby Bonilla	.40	.18
❑ 408	Josias Manzanillo	.25	.11
❑ 409	Bret Saberhagen	.40	.18
❑ 410	David Segui	.25	.11
❑ 411	Mariano Duncan	.25	.11
❑ 412	Tommy Greene	.25	.11
❑ 413	Billy Hatcher	.25	.11
❑ 414	Ricky Jordan	.25	.11
❑ 415	John Kruk	.40	.18
❑ 416	Bobby Munoz	.25	.11
❑ 417	Curt Schilling	1.00	.45
❑ 418	Fernando Valenzuela	.40	.18
❑ 419	David West	.25	.11
❑ 420	Carlos Garcia	.25	.11
❑ 421	Brian Hunter	.25	.11
❑ 422	Jeff King	.25	.11
❑ 423	Jon Lieber	.40	.18
❑ 424	Ravelo Manzanillo	.25	.11
❑ 425	Denny Neagle	.40	.18
❑ 426	Andy Van Slyke	.40	.18
❑ 427	Bryan Eversgerd RC	.25	.11
❑ 428	Bernard Gilkey	.25	.11
❑ 429	Gregg Jefferies	.25	.11
❑ 430	Tom Pagnozzi	.25	.11
❑ 431	Bob Tewksbury	.25	.11
❑ 432	Allen Watson	.25	.11
❑ 433	Andy Ashby	.25	.11
❑ 434	Andy Benes	.25	.11
❑ 435	Donnie Elliott	.25	.11
❑ 436	Tony Gwynn	2.00	.90
❑ 437	Joey Hamilton	.25	.11
❑ 438	Tim Hyers RC	.25	.11
❑ 439	Luis Lopez	.25	.11
❑ 440	Bip Roberts	.25	.11
❑ 441	Scott Sanders	.25	.11
❑ 442	Rod Beck	.25	.11
❑ 443	Dave Burba	.25	.11
❑ 444	Darryl Strawberry	.40	.18
❑ 445	Bill Swift	.25	.11
❑ 446	Robby Thompson	.25	.11
❑ 447	B.VanLandingham RC	.25	.11
❑ 448	Matt Williams	.60	.25
❑ 449	Checklist	.25	.11
❑ 450	Checklist	.25	.11
❑ P15	Aaron Sele Promo	1.00	.45

1995 Flair

	MINT	NRMT
COMPLETE SET (432)	60.00	27.00
COMPLETE SERIES 1 (216)	35.00	16.00
COMPLETE SERIES 2 (216)	25.00	11.00

No.	Player	MINT	NRMT
❑ 1	Brady Anderson	.40	.18
❑ 2	Harold Baines	.40	.18
❑ 3	Leo Gomez	.25	.11
❑ 4	Alan Mills	.25	.11

❑	5	Jamie Moyer	.25	.11
❑	6	Mike Mussina	1.00	.45
❑	7	Mike Oquist	.25	.11
❑	8	Arthur Rhodes	.25	.11
❑	9	Cal Ripken Jr.	4.00	1.80
❑	10	Roger Clemens	2.50	1.10
❑	11	Scott Cooper	.25	.11
❑	12	Mike Greenwell	.25	.11
❑	13	Aaron Sele	.40	.18
❑	14	John Valentin	.25	.11
❑	15	Mo Vaughn	.40	.18
❑	16	Chad Curtis	.25	.11
❑	17	Gary DiSarcina	.25	.11
❑	18	Chuck Finley	.40	.18
❑	19	Andrew Lorraine	.25	.11
❑	20	Spike Owen	.25	.11
❑	21	Tim Salmon	.40	.18
❑	22	J.T. Snow	.40	.18
❑	23	Wilson Alvarez	.25	.11
❑	24	Jason Bere	.25	.11
❑	25	Ozzie Guillen	.25	.11
❑	26	Mike LaValliere	.25	.11
❑	27	Frank Thomas	1.25	.55
❑	28	Robin Ventura	.40	.18
❑	29	Carlos Baerga	.25	.11
❑	30	Albert Belle	.40	.18
❑	31	Jason Grimsley	.25	.11
❑	32	Dennis Martinez	.40	.18
❑	33	Eddie Murray	1.00	.45
❑	34	Charles Nagy	.25	.11
❑	35	Manny Ramirez	1.25	.55
❑	36	Paul Sorrento	.25	.11
❑	37	John Doherty	.25	.11
❑	38	Cecil Fielder	.40	.18
❑	39	Travis Fryman	.40	.18
❑	40	Chris Gomez	.25	.11
❑	41	Tony Phillips	.25	.11
❑	42	Lou Whitaker	.40	.18
❑	43	David Cone	.40	.18
❑	44	Gary Gaetti	.40	.18
❑	45	Mark Gubicza	.25	.11
❑	46	Bob Hamelin	.25	.11
❑	47	Wally Joyner	.40	.18
❑	48	Rusty Meacham	.25	.11
❑	49	Jeff Montgomery	.25	.11
❑	50	Ricky Bones	.25	.11
❑	51	Cal Eldred	.25	.11
❑	52	Pat Listach	.25	.11
❑	53	Matt Mieske	.25	.11
❑	54	Dave Nilsson	.25	.11
❑	55	Greg Vaughn	.40	.18
❑	56	Bill Wegman	.25	.11
❑	57	Chuck Knoblauch	.40	.18
❑	58	Scott Leius	.25	.11
❑	59	Pat Mahomes	.25	.11
❑	60	Pat Meares	.25	.11
❑	61	Pedro Munoz	.25	.11
❑	62	Kirby Puckett	2.50	1.10
❑	63	Wade Boggs	1.00	.45
❑	64	Jimmy Key	.40	.18
❑	65	Jim Leyritz	.25	.11
❑	66	Don Mattingly	2.50	1.10
❑	67	Paul O'Neill	1.00	.45
❑	68	Melido Perez	.25	.11
❑	69	Danny Tartabull	.25	.11
❑	70	John Briscoe	.25	.11
❑	71	Scott Brosius	.40	.18
❑	72	Ron Darling	.25	.11
❑	73	Brent Gates	.25	.11
❑	74	Rickey Henderson	2.00	.90
❑	75	Stan Javier	.25	.11
❑	76	Mark McGwire	4.00	1.80
❑	77	Todd Van Poppel	.25	.11
❑	78	Bobby Ayala	.25	.11
❑	79	Mike Blowers	.25	.11
❑	80	Jay Buhner	.40	.18
❑	81	Ken Griffey Jr.	3.00	1.35
❑	82	Randy Johnson	1.25	.55
❑	83	Tino Martinez	.40	.18
❑	84	Jeff Nelson	.25	.11
❑	85	Alex Rodriguez	3.00	1.35
❑	86	Will Clark	1.00	.45
❑	87	Jeff Frye	.25	.11
❑	88	Juan Gonzalez	1.00	.45
❑	89	Rusty Greer	.40	.18
❑	90	Darren Oliver	.25	.11
❑	91	Dean Palmer	.40	.18
❑	92	Ivan Rodriguez	1.00	.45
❑	93	Matt Whiteside	.25	.11
❑	94	Roberto Alomar	1.00	.45
❑	95	Joe Carter	.40	.18
❑	96	Tony Castillo	.25	.11
❑	97	Juan Guzman	.25	.11
❑	98	Pat Hentgen	.25	.11
❑	99	Mike Huff	.25	.11
❑	100	John Olerud	.40	.18
❑	101	Woody Williams	.25	.11
❑	102	Roberto Kelly	.25	.11
❑	103	Ryan Klesko	.40	.18
❑	104	Javier Lopez	.40	.18
❑	105	Greg Maddux	2.50	1.10
❑	106	Fred McGriff	.60	.25
❑	107	Jose Oliva	.25	.11
❑	108	John Smoltz	.40	.18
❑	109	Tony Tarasco	.25	.11
❑	110	Mark Wohlers	.25	.11
❑	111	Jim Bullinger	.25	.11
❑	112	Shawon Dunston	.25	.11
❑	113	Derrick May	.25	.11
❑	114	Randy Myers	.25	.11
❑	115	Karl Rhodes	.25	.11
❑	116	Rey Sanchez	.25	.11
❑	117	Steve Trachsel	.25	.11
❑	118	Eddie Zambrano	.25	.11
❑	119	Bret Boone	.40	.18
❑	120	Brian Dorsett	.25	.11
❑	121	Hal Morris	.25	.11
❑	122	Jose Rijo	.25	.11
❑	123	John Roper	.25	.11
❑	124	Reggie Sanders	.25	.11
❑	125	Pete Schourek	.25	.11
❑	126	John Smiley	.25	.11
❑	127	Ellis Burks	.40	.18
❑	128	Vinny Castilla	.40	.18
❑	129	Marvin Freeman	.25	.11
❑	130	Andres Galarraga	.60	.25
❑	131	Mike Munoz	.25	.11
❑	132	David Nied	.25	.11
❑	133	Bruce Ruffin	.25	.11
❑	134	Walt Weiss	.25	.11
❑	135	Eric Young	.25	.11
❑	136	Greg Colbrunn	.25	.11
❑	137	Jeff Conine	.25	.11
❑	138	Jeremy Hernandez	.25	.11
❑	139	Charles Johnson	.40	.18
❑	140	Robb Nen	.25	.11
❑	141	Gary Sheffield	.40	.18
❑	142	Dave Weathers	.25	.11
❑	143	Jeff Bagwell	1.25	.55
❑	144	Craig Biggio	.60	.25
❑	145	Tony Eusebio	.25	.11
❑	146	Luis Gonzalez	1.00	.45
❑	147	John Hudek	.25	.11
❑	148	Darryl Kile	.40	.18
❑	149	Dave Veres	.25	.11
❑	150	Billy Ashley	.25	.11
❑	151	Pedro Astacio	.25	.11
❑	152	Rafael Bournigal	.25	.11
❑	153	Delino DeShields	.25	.11
❑	154	Raul Mondesi	.40	.18
❑	155	Mike Piazza	2.50	1.10
❑	156	Rudy Seanez	.25	.11
❑	157	Ismael Valdes	.25	.11
❑	158	Tim Wallach	.25	.11
❑	159	Todd Worrell	.25	.11
❑	160	Moises Alou	.40	.18
❑	161	Cliff Floyd	.40	.18
❑	162	Gil Heredia	.25	.11
❑	163	Mike Lansing	.25	.11
❑	164	Pedro Martinez	1.25	.55
❑	165	Kirk Rueter	.25	.11
❑	166	Tim Scott	.25	.11
❑	167	Jeff Shaw	.25	.11
❑	168	Rondell White	.40	.18
❑	169	Bobby Bonilla	.40	.18
❑	170	Rico Brogna	.25	.11
❑	171	Todd Hundley	.25	.11
❑	172	Jeff Kent	.60	.25
❑	173	Jim Lindeman	.25	.11
❑	174	Joe Orsulak	.25	.11
❑	175	Bret Saberhagen	.40	.18
❑	176	Toby Borland	.25	.11
❑	177	Darren Daulton	.40	.18
❑	178	Lenny Dykstra	.40	.18
❑	179	Jim Eisenreich	.25	.11
❑	180	Tommy Greene	.25	.11
❑	181	Tony Longmire	.25	.11
❑	182	Bobby Munoz	.25	.11
❑	183	Kevin Stocker	.25	.11
❑	184	Jay Bell	.40	.18
❑	185	Steve Cooke	.25	.11
❑	186	Ravelo Manzanillo	.25	.11
❑	187	Al Martin	.25	.11
❑	188	Denny Neagle	.40	.18
❑	189	Don Slaught	.25	.11
❑	190	Paul Wagner	.25	.11
❑	191	Rene Arocha	.25	.11
❑	192	Bernard Gilkey	.25	.11
❑	193	Jose Oquendo	.25	.11
❑	194	Tom Pagnozzi	.25	.11
❑	195	Ozzie Smith	1.25	.55
❑	196	Allen Watson	.25	.11
❑	197	Mark Whiten	.25	.11
❑	198	Andy Ashby	.25	.11
❑	199	Donnie Elliott	.25	.11
❑	200	Bryce Florie	.25	.11
❑	201	Tony Gwynn	2.00	.90
❑	202	Trevor Hoffman	.40	.18
❑	203	Brian Johnson	.25	.11
❑	204	Tim Mauser	.25	.11
❑	205	Bip Roberts	.25	.11
❑	206	Rod Beck	.25	.11
❑	207	Barry Bonds	2.50	1.10
❑	208	Royce Clayton	.25	.11
❑	209	Darren Lewis	.25	.11
❑	210	Mark Portugal	.25	.11
❑	211	Kevin Rogers	.25	.11
❑	212	W.VanLandingham	.25	.11
❑	213	Matt Williams	.60	.25
❑	214	Checklist	.25	.11
❑	215	Checklist	.25	.11
❑	216	Checklist	.25	.11
❑	217	Bret Barberie	.25	.11
❑	218	Armando Benitez	.40	.18
❑	219	Kevin Brown	.40	.18
❑	220	Sid Fernandez	.25	.11
❑	221	Chris Hoiles	.25	.11
❑	222	Doug Jones	.25	.11
❑	223	Ben McDonald	.25	.11
❑	224	Rafael Palmeiro	1.00	.45
❑	225	Andy Van Slyke	.40	.18
❑	226	Jose Canseco	1.00	.45
❑	227	Vaughn Eshelman	.25	.11
❑	228	Mike Macfarlane	.25	.11
❑	229	Tim Naehring	.25	.11
❑	230	Frank Rodriguez	.25	.11
❑	231	Lee Tinsley	.25	.11
❑	232	Mark Whiten	.25	.11
❑	233	Garret Anderson	.40	.18
❑	234	Chili Davis	.40	.18
❑	235	Jim Edmonds	.60	.25
❑	236	Mark Langston	.25	.11
❑	237	Troy Percival	.25	.11
❑	238	Tony Phillips	.25	.11
❑	239	Lee Smith	.40	.18
❑	240	Jim Abbott	.40	.18
❑	241	James Baldwin	.25	.11
❑	242	Mike Devereaux	.25	.11
❑	243	Ray Durham	.40	.18

	No.	Player	Mint	Nrmt
❑	244	Alex Fernandez	.25	.11
❑	245	Roberto Hernandez	.25	.11
❑	246	Lance Johnson	.25	.11
❑	247	Ron Karkovice	.25	.11
❑	248	Tim Raines	.40	.18
❑	249	Sandy Alomar Jr.	.40	.18
❑	250	Orel Hershiser	.40	.18
❑	251	Julian Tavarez	.25	.11
❑	252	Jim Thome	1.00	.45
❑	253	Omar Vizquel	.40	.18
❑	254	Dave Winfield	1.00	.45
❑	255	Chad Curtis	.25	.11
❑	256	Kirk Gibson	.40	.18
❑	257	Mike Henneman	.25	.11
❑	258	Bob Higginson RC	1.50	.70
❑	259	Felipe Lira	.25	.11
❑	260	Rudy Pemberton	.25	.11
❑	261	Alan Trammell	.60	.25
❑	262	Kevin Appier	.40	.18
❑	263	Pat Borders	.25	.11
❑	264	Tom Gordon	.25	.11
❑	265	Jose Lind	.25	.11
❑	266	Jon Nunnally	.25	.11
❑	267	Dilson Torres RC	.25	.11
❑	268	Michael Tucker	.25	.11
❑	269	Jeff Cirillo	.40	.18
❑	270	Darryl Hamilton	.25	.11
❑	271	David Hulse	.25	.11
❑	272	Mark Kiefer	.25	.11
❑	273	Graeme Lloyd	.25	.11
❑	274	Joe Oliver	.25	.11
❑	275	Al Reyes RC	.25	.11
❑	276	Kevin Seitzer	.25	.11
❑	277	Rick Aguilera	.25	.11
❑	278	Marty Cordova	.25	.11
❑	279	Scott Erickson	.25	.11
❑	280	LaTroy Hawkins	.25	.11
❑	281	Brad Radke RC	4.00	1.80
❑	282	Kevin Tapani	.25	.11
❑	283	Tony Fernandez	.25	.11
❑	284	Sterling Hitchcock	.25	.11
❑	285	Pat Kelly	.25	.11
❑	286	Jack McDowell	.25	.11
❑	287	Andy Pettitte	.40	.18
❑	288	Mike Stanley	.25	.11
❑	289	John Wetteland	.40	.18
❑	290	Bernie Williams	1.00	.45
❑	291	Mark Acre	.25	.11
❑	292	Geronimo Berroa	.25	.11
❑	293	Dennis Eckersley	.40	.18
❑	294	Steve Ontiveros	.25	.11
❑	295	Ruben Sierra	.25	.11
❑	296	Terry Steinbach	.25	.11
❑	297	Dave Stewart	.40	.18
❑	298	Todd Stottlemyre	.25	.11
❑	299	Darren Bragg	.25	.11
❑	300	Joey Cora	.25	.11
❑	301	Edgar Martinez	.60	.25
❑	302	Bill Risley	.25	.11
❑	303	Ron Villone	.25	.11
❑	304	Dan Wilson	.25	.11
❑	305	Benji Gil	.25	.11
❑	306	Wilson Heredia	.25	.11
❑	307	Mark McLemore	.25	.11
❑	308	Otis Nixon	.25	.11
❑	309	Kenny Rogers	.25	.11
❑	310	Jeff Russell	.25	.11
❑	311	Mickey Tettleton	.25	.11
❑	312	Bob Tewksbury	.25	.11
❑	313	David Cone	.40	.18
❑	314	Carlos Delgado	1.00	.45
❑	315	Alex Gonzalez	.25	.11
❑	316	Shawn Green	1.00	.45
❑	317	Paul Molitor	1.00	.45
❑	318	Ed Sprague	.25	.11
❑	319	Devon White	.40	.18
❑	320	Steve Avery	.25	.11
❑	321	Jeff Blauser	.25	.11
❑	322	Brad Clontz	.25	.11
❑	323	Tom Glavine	1.00	.45
❑	324	Marquis Grissom	.25	.11
❑	325	Chipper Jones	2.00	.90
❑	326	David Justice	.40	.18
❑	327	Mark Lemke	.25	.11
❑	328	Kent Mercker	.25	.11
❑	329	Jason Schmidt	.25	.11
❑	330	Steve Buechele	.25	.11
❑	331	Kevin Foster	.25	.11
❑	332	Mark Grace	1.00	.45
❑	333	Brian McRae	.25	.11
❑	334	Sammy Sosa	2.00	.90
❑	335	Ozzie Timmons	.25	.11
❑	336	Rick Wilkins	.25	.11
❑	337	Hector Carrasco	.25	.11
❑	338	Ron Gant	.25	.11
❑	339	Barry Larkin	1.00	.45
❑	340	Deion Sanders	.40	.18
❑	341	Benito Santiago	.25	.11
❑	342	Roger Bailey	.25	.11
❑	343	Jason Bates	.25	.11
❑	344	Dante Bichette	.40	.18
❑	345	Joe Girardi	.25	.11
❑	346	Bill Swift	.25	.11
❑	347	Mark Thompson	.25	.11
❑	348	Larry Walker	.60	.25
❑	349	Kurt Abbott	.25	.11
❑	350	John Burkett	.25	.11
❑	351	Chuck Carr	.25	.11
❑	352	Andre Dawson	.60	.25
❑	353	Chris Hammond	.25	.11
❑	354	Charles Johnson	.40	.18
❑	355	Terry Pendleton	.40	.18
❑	356	Quilvio Veras	.25	.11
❑	357	Derek Bell	.25	.11
❑	358	Jim Dougherty RC	.25	.11
❑	359	Doug Drabek	.25	.11
❑	360	Todd Jones	.25	.11
❑	361	Orlando Miller	.25	.11
❑	362	James Mouton	.25	.11
❑	363	Phil Plantier	.25	.11
❑	364	Shane Reynolds	.25	.11
❑	365	Todd Hollandsworth	.25	.11
❑	366	Eric Karros	.40	.18
❑	367	Ramon Martinez	.25	.11
❑	368	Hideo Nomo RC	3.00	1.35
❑	369	Jose Offerman	.25	.11
❑	370	Antonio Osuna	.25	.11
❑	371	Todd Williams	.25	.11
❑	372	Shane Andrews	.25	.11
❑	373	Wil Cordero	.25	.11
❑	374	Jeff Fassero	.25	.11
❑	375	Darrin Fletcher	.25	.11
❑	376	Mark Grudzielanek RC	.40	.18
❑	377	Carlos Perez RC	.40	.18
❑	378	Mel Rojas	.25	.11
❑	379	Tony Tarasco	.25	.11
❑	380	Edgardo Alfonzo	1.00	.45
❑	381	Brett Butler	.40	.18
❑	382	Carl Everett	.40	.18
❑	383	John Franco	.40	.18
❑	384	Pete Harnisch	.25	.11
❑	385	Bobby Jones	.25	.11
❑	386	Dave Mlicki	.25	.11
❑	387	Jose Vizcaino	.25	.11
❑	388	Ricky Bottalico	.25	.11
❑	389	Tyler Green	.25	.11
❑	390	Charlie Hayes	.25	.11
❑	391	Dave Hollins	.25	.11
❑	392	Gregg Jefferies	.25	.11
❑	393	Michael Mimbs RC	.25	.11
❑	394	Mickey Morandini	.25	.11
❑	395	Curt Schilling	1.00	.45
❑	396	Heathcliff Slocumb	.25	.11
❑	397	J.Christiansen RC	.25	.11
❑	398	Midre Cummings	.25	.11
❑	399	Carlos Garcia	.25	.11
❑	400	Mark Johnson RC	.40	.18
❑	401	Jeff King	.25	.11
❑	402	Jon Lieber	.25	.11
❑	403	Esteban Loaiza	.25	.11
❑	404	Orlando Merced	.25	.11
❑	405	Gary Wilson RC	.25	.11
❑	406	Scott Cooper	.25	.11
❑	407	Tom Henke	.25	.11
❑	408	Ken Hill	.25	.11
❑	409	Danny Jackson	.25	.11
❑	410	Brian Jordan	.40	.18
❑	411	Ray Lankford	.25	.11
❑	412	John Mabry	.25	.11
❑	413	Todd Zeile	.25	.11
❑	414	Andy Benes	.25	.11
❑	415	Andres Berumen	.25	.11
❑	416	Ken Caminiti	.40	.18
❑	417	Andujar Cedeno	.25	.11
❑	418	Steve Finley	.40	.18
❑	419	Joey Hamilton	.25	.11
❑	420	Dustin Hermanson	.25	.11
❑	421	Melvin Nieves	.25	.11
❑	422	Roberto Petagine	.25	.11
❑	423	Eddie Williams	.25	.11
❑	424	Glenallen Hill	.25	.11
❑	425	Kirt Manwaring	.25	.11
❑	426	Terry Mulholland	.25	.11
❑	427	J.R. Phillips	.25	.11
❑	428	Joe Rosselli	.25	.11
❑	429	Robby Thompson	.25	.11
❑	430	Checklist	.25	.11
❑	431	Checklist	.25	.11
❑	432	Checklist	.25	.11

1996 Flair

		MINT	NRMT
COMPLETE SET (400)		100.00	45.00

	No.	Player	Mint	Nrmt
❑	1	Roberto Alomar	2.00	.90
❑	2	Brady Anderson	.75	.35
❑	3	Bobby Bonilla	.75	.35
❑	4	Scott Erickson	.50	.23
❑	5	Jeffrey Hammonds	.50	.23
❑	6	Jimmy Haynes	.50	.23
❑	7	Chris Hoiles	.50	.23
❑	8	Kent Mercker	.50	.23
❑	9	Mike Mussina	2.00	.90
❑	10	Randy Myers	.50	.23
❑	11	Rafael Palmeiro	2.00	.90
❑	12	Cal Ripken	8.00	3.60
❑	13	B.J. Surhoff	.75	.35
❑	14	David Wells	.75	.35
❑	15	Jose Canseco	2.00	.90
❑	16	Roger Clemens	5.00	2.20
❑	17	Wil Cordero	.50	.23
❑	18	Tom Gordon	.50	.23
❑	19	Mike Greenwell	.50	.23
❑	20	Dwayne Hosey	.50	.23
❑	21	Jose Malave	.50	.23
❑	22	Tim Naehring	.50	.23
❑	23	Troy O'Leary	.50	.23
❑	24	Aaron Sele	.75	.35
❑	25	Heathcliff Slocumb	.50	.23
❑	26	Mike Stanley	.50	.23
❑	27	Jeff Suppan	.50	.23
❑	28	John Valentin	.50	.23
❑	29	Mo Vaughn	.75	.35
❑	30	Tim Wakefield	.50	.23
❑	31	Jim Abbott	.75	.35
❑	32	Garret Anderson	.75	.35
❑	33	George Arias	.50	.23
❑	34	Chili Davis	.75	.35
❑	35	Gary DiSarcina	.50	.23
❑	36	Jim Edmonds	1.25	.55
❑	37	Chuck Finley	.75	.35
❑	38	Todd Greene	.50	.23
❑	39	Mark Langston	.50	.23
❑	40	Troy Percival	.50	.23
❑	41	Tim Salmon	.75	.35
❑	42	Lee Smith	.75	.35
❑	43	J.T. Snow	.75	.35
❑	44	Randy Velarde	.50	.23
❑	45	Tim Wallach	.50	.23

❑ 46 Wilson Alvarez .50 .23
❑ 47 Harold Baines .75 .35
❑ 48 Jason Bere .50 .23
❑ 49 Ray Durham .75 .35
❑ 50 Alex Fernandez .50 .23
❑ 51 Ozzie Guillen .50 .23
❑ 52 Roberto Hernandez .50 .23
❑ 53 Ron Karkovice .50 .23
❑ 54 Darren Lewis .50 .23
❑ 55 Lyle Mouton .50 .23
❑ 56 Tony Phillips .50 .23
❑ 57 Chris Snopek .50 .23
❑ 58 Kevin Tapani .50 .23
❑ 59 Danny Tartabull .50 .23
❑ 60 Frank Thomas 2.50 1.10
❑ 61 Robin Ventura .75 .35
❑ 62 Sandy Alomar Jr. .75 .35
❑ 63 Carlos Baerga .50 .23
❑ 64 Albert Belle .75 .35
❑ 65 Julio Franco .75 .35
❑ 66 Orel Hershiser .75 .35
❑ 67 Kenny Lofton .75 .35
❑ 68 Dennis Martinez .75 .35
❑ 69 Jack McDowell .50 .23
❑ 70 Jose Mesa .50 .23
❑ 71 Eddie Murray 2.00 .90
❑ 72 Charles Nagy .50 .23
❑ 73 Tony Pena .50 .23
❑ 74 Manny Ramirez 2.50 1.10
❑ 75 Julian Tavarez .50 .23
❑ 76 Jim Thome 2.00 .90
❑ 77 Omar Vizquel .75 .35
❑ 78 Chad Curtis .50 .23
❑ 79 Cecil Fielder .75 .35
❑ 80 Travis Fryman .75 .35
❑ 81 Chris Gomez .50 .23
❑ 82 Bob Higginson .75 .35
❑ 83 Mark Lewis .50 .23
❑ 84 Felipe Lira .50 .23
❑ 85 Alan Trammell 1.25 .55
❑ 86 Kevin Appier .75 .35
❑ 87 Johnny Damon .75 .35
❑ 88 Tom Goodwin .50 .23
❑ 89 Mark Gubicza .50 .23
❑ 90 Bob Hamelin .50 .23
❑ 91 Keith Lockhart .50 .23
❑ 92 Jeff Montgomery .50 .23
❑ 93 Jon Nunnally .50 .23
❑ 94 Bip Roberts .50 .23
❑ 95 Michael Tucker .50 .23
❑ 96 Joe Vitiello .50 .23
❑ 97 Ricky Bones .50 .23
❑ 98 Chuck Carr .50 .23
❑ 99 Jeff Cirillo .75 .35
❑ 100 Mike Fetters .50 .23
❑ 101 John Jaha .50 .23
❑ 102 Mike Matheny .50 .23
❑ 103 Ben McDonald .50 .23
❑ 104 Matt Mieske .50 .23
❑ 105 Dave Nilsson .50 .23
❑ 106 Kevin Seitzer .50 .23
❑ 107 Steve Sparks .50 .23
❑ 108 Jose Valentin .50 .23
❑ 109 Greg Vaughn .75 .35
❑ 110 Rick Aguilera .50 .23
❑ 111 Rich Becker .50 .23
❑ 112 Marty Cordova .50 .23
❑ 113 LaTroy Hawkins .50 .23
❑ 114 Dave Hollins .50 .23
❑ 115 Roberto Kelly .50 .23
❑ 116 Chuck Knoblauch .75 .35
❑ 117 Matt Lawton RC 2.50 1.10
❑ 118 Pat Meares .50 .23
❑ 119 Paul Molitor 2.00 .90
❑ 120 Kirby Puckett 5.00 2.20
❑ 121 Brad Radke .75 .35
❑ 122 Frank Rodriguez .50 .23
❑ 123 Scott Stahoviak .50 .23
❑ 124 Matt Walbeck .50 .23
❑ 125 Wade Boggs 2.00 .90
❑ 126 David Cone .75 .35
❑ 127 Joe Girardi .50 .23
❑ 128 Dwight Gooden .75 .35
❑ 129 Derek Jeter 8.00 3.60
❑ 130 Jimmy Key .75 .35
❑ 131 Jim Leyritz .50 .23
❑ 132 Tino Martinez .75 .35
❑ 133 Paul O'Neill 2.00 .90
❑ 134 Andy Pettitte .75 .35
❑ 135 Tim Raines .75 .35
❑ 136 Ruben Rivera .50 .23
❑ 137 Kenny Rogers .50 .23
❑ 138 Ruben Sierra .50 .23
❑ 139 John Wetteland .75 .35
❑ 140 Bernie Williams 2.00 .90
❑ 141 Tony Batista RC 6.00 2.70
❑ 142 Allen Battle .50 .23
❑ 143 Geronimo Berroa .50 .23
❑ 144 Mike Bordick .50 .23
❑ 145 Scott Brosius .75 .35
❑ 146 Steve Cox .50 .23
❑ 147 Brent Gates .50 .23
❑ 148 Jason Giambi 2.00 .90
❑ 149 Doug Johns .50 .23
❑ 150 Mark McGwire 8.00 3.60
❑ 151 Pedro Munoz .50 .23
❑ 152 Ariel Prieto .50 .23
❑ 153 Terry Steinbach .50 .23
❑ 154 Todd Van Poppel .50 .23
❑ 155 Bobby Ayala .50 .23
❑ 156 Chris Bosio .50 .23
❑ 157 Jay Buhner .75 .35
❑ 158 Joey Cora .50 .23
❑ 159 Russ Davis .50 .23
❑ 160 Ken Griffey Jr. 6.00 2.70
❑ 161 Sterling Hitchcock .50 .23
❑ 162 Randy Johnson 2.50 1.10
❑ 163 Edgar Martinez 1.25 .55
❑ 164 Alex Rodriguez 5.00 2.20
❑ 165 Paul Sorrento .50 .23
❑ 166 Dan Wilson .50 .23
❑ 167 Will Clark 2.00 .90
❑ 168 Benji Gil .50 .23
❑ 169 Juan Gonzalez 2.00 .90
❑ 170 Rusty Greer .75 .35
❑ 171 Kevin Gross .50 .23
❑ 172 Darryl Hamilton .50 .23
❑ 173 Mike Henneman .50 .23
❑ 174 Ken Hill .50 .23
❑ 175 Mark McLemore .50 .23
❑ 176 Dean Palmer .75 .35
❑ 177 Roger Pavlik .50 .23
❑ 178 Ivan Rodriguez 2.00 .90
❑ 179 Mickey Tettleton .50 .23
❑ 180 Bobby Witt .50 .23
❑ 181 Joe Carter .75 .35
❑ 182 Felipe Crespo .50 .23
❑ 183 Alex Gonzalez .50 .23
❑ 184 Shawn Green 2.00 .90
❑ 185 Juan Guzman .50 .23
❑ 186 Erik Hanson .50 .23
❑ 187 Pat Hentgen .50 .23
❑ 188 Sandy Martinez .50 .23
❑ 189 Otis Nixon .50 .23
❑ 190 John Olerud .75 .35
❑ 191 Paul Quantrill .50 .23
❑ 192 Bill Risley .50 .23
❑ 193 Ed Sprague .50 .23
❑ 194 Steve Avery .50 .23
❑ 195 Jeff Blauser .50 .23
❑ 196 Brad Clontz .50 .23
❑ 197 Jermaine Dye .75 .35
❑ 198 Tom Glavine 2.00 .90
❑ 199 Marquis Grissom .50 .23
❑ 200 Chipper Jones 4.00 1.80
❑ 201 David Justice .75 .35
❑ 202 Ryan Klesko .75 .35
❑ 203 Mark Lemke .50 .23
❑ 204 Javier Lopez .75 .35
❑ 205 Greg Maddux 5.00 2.20
❑ 206 Fred McGriff 1.25 .55
❑ 207 Greg McMichael .50 .23
❑ 208 Wonderful Monds RC .50 .23
❑ 209 Jason Schmidt .50 .23
❑ 210 John Smoltz .75 .35
❑ 211 Mark Wohlers .50 .23
❑ 212 Jim Bullinger .50 .23
❑ 213 Frank Castillo .50 .23
❑ 214 Kevin Foster .50 .23
❑ 215 Luis Gonzalez 2.00 .90
❑ 216 Mark Grace 2.00 .90
❑ 217 Robin Jennings .50 .23
❑ 218 Doug Jones .50 .23
❑ 219 Dave Magadan .50 .23
❑ 220 Brian McRae .50 .23
❑ 221 Jaime Navarro .50 .23
❑ 222 Rey Sanchez .50 .23
❑ 223 Ryne Sandberg 2.50 1.10
❑ 224 Scott Servais .50 .23
❑ 225 Sammy Sosa 4.00 1.80
❑ 226 Ozzie Timmons .50 .23
❑ 227 Bret Boone .75 .35
❑ 228 Jeff Branson .50 .23
❑ 229 Jeff Brantley .50 .23
❑ 230 Dave Burba .50 .23
❑ 231 Vince Coleman .50 .23
❑ 232 Steve Gibralter .50 .23
❑ 233 Mike Kelly .50 .23
❑ 234 Barry Larkin 2.00 .90
❑ 235 Hal Morris .50 .23
❑ 236 Mark Portugal .50 .23
❑ 237 Jose Rijo .50 .23
❑ 238 Reggie Sanders .50 .23
❑ 239 Pete Schourek .50 .23
❑ 240 John Smiley .50 .23
❑ 241 Eddie Taubensee .50 .23
❑ 242 Jason Bates .50 .23
❑ 243 Dante Bichette .75 .35
❑ 244 Ellis Burks .75 .35
❑ 245 Vinny Castilla .75 .35
❑ 246 Andres Galarraga 1.25 .55
❑ 247 Darren Holmes .50 .23
❑ 248 Curt Leskanic .50 .23
❑ 249 Steve Reed .50 .23
❑ 250 Kevin Ritz .50 .23
❑ 251 Bret Saberhagen .75 .35
❑ 252 Bill Swift .50 .23
❑ 253 Larry Walker 1.25 .55
❑ 254 Walt Weiss .50 .23
❑ 255 Eric Young .50 .23
❑ 256 Kurt Abbott .50 .23
❑ 257 Kevin Brown .75 .35
❑ 258 John Burkett .50 .23
❑ 259 Greg Colbrunn .50 .23
❑ 260 Jeff Conine .50 .23
❑ 261 Andre Dawson 1.25 .55
❑ 262 Chris Hammond .50 .23
❑ 263 Charles Johnson .75 .35
❑ 264 Al Leiter .75 .35
❑ 265 Robb Nen .50 .23
❑ 266 Terry Pendleton .75 .35
❑ 267 Pat Rapp .50 .23
❑ 268 Gary Sheffield .75 .35
❑ 269 Quilvio Veras .50 .23
❑ 270 Devon White .75 .35
❑ 271 Bob Abreu 2.00 .90
❑ 272 Jeff Bagwell 2.50 1.10
❑ 273 Derek Bell .50 .23
❑ 274 Sean Berry .50 .23
❑ 275 Craig Biggio 1.25 .55
❑ 276 Doug Drabek .50 .23
❑ 277 Tony Eusebio .50 .23
❑ 278 Richard Hidalgo .75 .35
❑ 279 Brian L.Hunter .50 .23
❑ 280 Todd Jones .50 .23
❑ 281 Derrick May .50 .23
❑ 282 Orlando Miller .50 .23
❑ 283 James Mouton .50 .23
❑ 284 Shane Reynolds .50 .23
❑ 285 Greg Swindell .50 .23
❑ 286 Mike Blowers .50 .23
❑ 287 Brett Butler .75 .35
❑ 288 Tom Candiotti .50 .23
❑ 289 Roger Cedeno .50 .23
❑ 290 Delino DeShields .50 .23
❑ 291 Greg Gagne .50 .23
❑ 292 Karim Garcia .50 .23
❑ 293 Todd Hollandsworth .50 .23
❑ 294 Eric Karros .75 .35
❑ 295 Ramon Martinez .50 .23
❑ 296 Raul Mondesi .75 .35
❑ 297 Hideo Nomo 2.50 1.10
❑ 298 Mike Piazza 5.00 2.20
❑ 299 Ismael Valdes .50 .23
❑ 300 Todd Worrell .50 .23
❑ 301 Moises Alou .75 .35
❑ 302 Shane Andrews .50 .23
❑ 303 Yamil Benitez .50 .23

Card	Mint	NrMt
❑ 304 Jeff Fassero	.50	.23
❑ 305 Darrin Fletcher	.50	.23
❑ 306 Cliff Floyd	.75	.35
❑ 307 Mark Grudzielanek	.50	.23
❑ 308 Mike Lansing	.50	.23
❑ 309 Pedro Martinez	2.50	1.10
❑ 310 Ryan McGuire	.50	.23
❑ 311 Carlos Perez	.50	.23
❑ 312 Mel Rojas	.50	.23
❑ 313 David Segui	.50	.23
❑ 314 Rondell White	.75	.35
❑ 315 Edgardo Alfonzo	.75	.35
❑ 316 Rico Brogna	.50	.23
❑ 317 Carl Everett	.75	.35
❑ 318 John Franco	.75	.35
❑ 319 Bernard Gilkey	.50	.23
❑ 320 Todd Hundley	.50	.23
❑ 321 Jason Isringhausen	.75	.35
❑ 322 Lance Johnson	.50	.23
❑ 323 Bobby Jones	.50	.23
❑ 324 Jeff Kent	1.25	.55
❑ 325 Rey Ordonez	.50	.23
❑ 326 Bill Pulsipher	.50	.23
❑ 327 Jose Vizcaino	.50	.23
❑ 328 Paul Wilson	.50	.23
❑ 329 Ricky Bottalico	.50	.23
❑ 330 Darren Daulton	.75	.35
❑ 331 David Doster	.50	.23
❑ 332 Lenny Dykstra	.75	.35
❑ 333 Jim Eisenreich	.50	.23
❑ 334 Sid Fernandez	.50	.23
❑ 335 Gregg Jefferies	.50	.23
❑ 336 Mickey Morandini	.50	.23
❑ 337 Benito Santiago	.50	.23
❑ 338 Curt Schilling	2.00	.90
❑ 339 Kevin Stocker	.50	.23
❑ 340 David West	.50	.23
❑ 341 Mark Whiten	.50	.23
❑ 342 Todd Zeile	.50	.23
❑ 343 Jay Bell	.75	.35
❑ 344 John Ericks	.50	.23
❑ 345 Carlos Garcia	.50	.23
❑ 346 Charlie Hayes	.50	.23
❑ 347 Jason Kendall	.75	.35
❑ 348 Jeff King	.50	.23
❑ 349 Mike Kingery	.50	.23
❑ 350 Al Martin	.50	.23
❑ 351 Orlando Merced	.50	.23
❑ 352 Dan Miceli	.50	.23
❑ 353 Denny Neagle	.75	.35
❑ 354 Alan Benes	.50	.23
❑ 355 Andy Benes	.50	.23
❑ 356 Royce Clayton	.50	.23
❑ 357 Dennis Eckersley	.75	.35
❑ 358 Gary Gaetti	.75	.35
❑ 359 Ron Gant	.50	.23
❑ 360 Brian Jordan	.75	.35
❑ 361 Ray Lankford	.50	.23
❑ 362 John Mabry	.50	.23
❑ 363 T.J. Mathews	.50	.23
❑ 364 Mike Morgan	.50	.23
❑ 365 Donovan Osborne	.50	.23
❑ 366 Tom Pagnozzi	.50	.23
❑ 367 Ozzie Smith	2.50	1.10
❑ 368 Todd Stottlemyre	.50	.23
❑ 369 Andy Ashby	.50	.23
❑ 370 Brad Ausmus	.50	.23
❑ 371 Ken Caminiti	.75	.35
❑ 372 Andujar Cedeno	.50	.23
❑ 373 Steve Finley	.75	.35
❑ 374 Tony Gwynn	4.00	1.80
❑ 375 Joey Hamilton	.50	.23
❑ 376 Rickey Henderson	4.00	1.80
❑ 377 Trevor Hoffman	.75	.35
❑ 378 Wally Joyner	.75	.35
❑ 379 Marc Newfield	.50	.23
❑ 380 Jody Reed	.50	.23
❑ 381 Bob Tewksbury	.50	.23
❑ 382 Fernando Valenzuela	.75	.35
❑ 383 Rod Beck	.50	.23
❑ 384 Barry Bonds	5.00	2.20
❑ 385 Mark Carreon	.50	.23
❑ 386 Shawon Dunston	.50	.23
❑ 387 O.Fernandez RC	.50	.23
❑ 388 Glenallen Hill	.50	.23
❑ 389 Stan Javier	.50	.23
❑ 390 Mark Leiter	.50	.23
❑ 391 Kirt Manwaring	.50	.23
❑ 392 Robby Thompson	.50	.23
❑ 393 W.VanLandingham	.50	.23
❑ 394 Allen Watson	.50	.23
❑ 395 Matt Williams	1.25	.55
❑ 396 Checklist 1-92	.50	.23
❑ 397 Checklist 93-180	.50	.23
❑ 398 Checklist 181-272	.50	.23
❑ 399 Checklist 273-365	.50	.23
❑ 400 CL 366-400/Inserts	.50	.23

1997 Flair Showcase Row 2

	MINT	NRMT
COMPLETE SET (180)	80.00	36.00
COMMON CARD (1-60)	.25	.11
COMMON CARD (61-120)	.40	.18
COMMON CARD (121-180)	.30	.14

Card	Mint	NrMt
❑ 1 Andruw Jones	1.25	.55
❑ 2 Derek Jeter	4.00	1.80
❑ 3 Alex Rodriguez	2.50	1.10
❑ 4 Paul Molitor	1.00	.45
❑ 5 Jeff Bagwell	1.25	.55
❑ 6 Scott Rolen	1.00	.45
❑ 7 Kenny Lofton	.40	.18
❑ 8 Cal Ripken	4.00	1.80
❑ 9 Brady Anderson	.40	.18
❑ 10 Chipper Jones	2.00	.90
❑ 11 Todd Greene	.25	.11
❑ 12 Todd Walker	.25	.11
❑ 13 Billy Wagner	.25	.11
❑ 14 Craig Biggio	.60	.25
❑ 15 Kevin Orie	.25	.11
❑ 16 Hideo Nomo	1.00	.45
❑ 17 Kevin Appier	.40	.18
❑ 18 B.Trammell RC	.40	.18
❑ 19 Juan Gonzalez	1.00	.45
❑ 20 Randy Johnson	1.25	.55
❑ 21 Roger Clemens	2.50	1.10
❑ 22 Johnny Damon	.40	.18
❑ 23 Ryne Sandberg	1.25	.55
❑ 24 Ken Griffey Jr.	3.00	1.35
❑ 25 Barry Bonds	2.50	1.10
❑ 26 Nomar Garciaparra	2.50	1.10
❑ 27 Vladimir Guerrero	1.50	.70
❑ 28 Ron Gant	.25	.11
❑ 29 Joe Carter	.40	.18
❑ 30 Tim Salmon	.40	.18
❑ 31 Mike Piazza	2.50	1.10
❑ 32 Barry Larkin	1.00	.45
❑ 33 Manny Ramirez	1.25	.55
❑ 34 Sammy Sosa	2.00	.90
❑ 35 Frank Thomas	1.25	.55
❑ 36 Melvin Nieves	.25	.11
❑ 37 Tony Gwynn	2.00	.90
❑ 38 Gary Sheffield	.40	.18
❑ 39 Darin Erstad	1.00	.45
❑ 40 Ken Caminiti	.40	.18
❑ 41 Jermaine Dye	.40	.18
❑ 42 Mo Vaughn	.40	.18
❑ 43 Raul Mondesi	.40	.18
❑ 44 Greg Maddux	2.50	1.10
❑ 45 Chuck Knoblauch	.40	.18
❑ 46 Andy Pettitte	.40	.18
❑ 47 Deion Sanders	.40	.18
❑ 48 Albert Belle	.40	.18
❑ 49 Jamey Wright	.25	.11
❑ 50 Rey Ordonez	.25	.11
❑ 51 Bernie Williams	1.00	.45
❑ 52 Mark McGwire	4.00	1.80
❑ 53 Mike Mussina	1.00	.45
❑ 54 Bob Abreu	.40	.18
❑ 55 Reggie Sanders	.25	.11
❑ 56 Brian Jordan	.40	.18
❑ 57 Ivan Rodriguez	1.00	.45
❑ 58 Roberto Alomar	1.00	.45
❑ 59 Tim Naehring	.25	.11
❑ 60 Edgar Renteria	.25	.11
❑ 61 Dean Palmer	.60	.25
❑ 62 Benito Santiago	.40	.18
❑ 63 David Cone	.60	.25
❑ 64 Carlos Delgado	1.50	.70
❑ 65 Brian Giles RC	3.00	1.35
❑ 66 Alex Ochoa	.40	.18
❑ 67 Rondell White	.60	.25
❑ 68 Robin Ventura	.60	.25
❑ 69 Eric Karros	.60	.25
❑ 70 Jose Valentin	.40	.18
❑ 71 Rafael Palmeiro	1.50	.70
❑ 72 Chris Snopek	.40	.18
❑ 73 David Justice	.60	.25
❑ 74 Tom Glavine	1.50	.70
❑ 75 Rudy Pemberton	.40	.18
❑ 76 Larry Walker	.60	.25
❑ 77 Jim Thome	1.50	.70
❑ 78 Charles Johnson	.60	.25
❑ 79 Dante Powell	.40	.18
❑ 80 Derrek Lee	.60	.25
❑ 81 Jason Kendall	.60	.25
❑ 82 Todd Hollandsworth	.40	.18
❑ 83 Bernard Gilkey	.40	.18
❑ 84 Mel Rojas	.40	.18
❑ 85 Dmitri Young	.60	.25
❑ 86 Bret Boone	.60	.25
❑ 87 Pat Hentgen	.40	.18
❑ 88 Bobby Bonilla	.60	.25
❑ 89 John Wetteland	.60	.25
❑ 90 Todd Hundley	.40	.18
❑ 91 Wilton Guerrero	.40	.18
❑ 92 Geronimo Berroa	.40	.18
❑ 93 Al Martin	.40	.18
❑ 94 Danny Tartabull	.40	.18
❑ 95 Brian McRae	.40	.18
❑ 96 Steve Finley	.60	.25
❑ 97 Todd Stottlemyre	.40	.18
❑ 98 John Smoltz	.60	.25
❑ 99 Matt Williams	1.00	.45
❑ 100 Eddie Murray	1.50	.70
❑ 101 Henry Rodriguez	.40	.18
❑ 102 Marty Cordova	.40	.18
❑ 103 Juan Guzman	.40	.18
❑ 104 Chili Davis	.60	.25
❑ 105 Eric Young	.40	.18
❑ 106 Jeff Abbott	.40	.18
❑ 107 Shannon Stewart	.60	.25
❑ 108 Rocky Coppinger	.40	.18
❑ 109 Jose Canseco	1.00	.45
❑ 110 Dante Bichette	.60	.25
❑ 111 Dwight Gooden	.60	.25
❑ 112 Scott Brosius	.60	.25
❑ 113 Steve Avery	.40	.18
❑ 114 Andres Galarraga	1.00	.45
❑ 115 Sandy Alomar Jr.	.60	.25
❑ 116 Ray Lankford	.40	.18
❑ 117 Jorge Posada	.60	.25
❑ 118 Ryan Klesko	.60	.25
❑ 119 Jay Buhner	.60	.25
❑ 120 Jose Guillen	.40	.18
❑ 121 Paul O'Neill	1.25	.55
❑ 122 Jimmy Key	.50	.23
❑ 123 Hal Morris	.30	.14
❑ 124 Travis Fryman	.50	.23
❑ 125 Jim Edmonds	.75	.35
❑ 126 Jeff Cirillo	.50	.23
❑ 127 Fred McGriff	.75	.35
❑ 128 Alan Benes	.30	.14
❑ 129 Derek Bell	.30	.14
❑ 130 Tony Graffanino	.30	.14
❑ 131 Shawn Green	1.25	.55
❑ 132 Denny Neagle	.50	.23
❑ 133 Alex Fernandez	.30	.14

❑ 134 Mickey Morandini .30 .14
❑ 135 Royce Clayton .30 .14
❑ 136 Jose Mesa .30 .14
❑ 137 Edgar Martinez .75 .35
❑ 138 Curt Schilling 1.25 .55
❑ 139 Lance Johnson .30 .14
❑ 140 Andy Benes .30 .14
❑ 141 Charles Nagy .30 .14
❑ 142 Mariano Rivera .50 .23
❑ 143 Mark Wohlers .30 .14
❑ 144 Ken Hill .30 .14
❑ 145 Jay Bell .50 .23
❑ 146 Bob Higginson .50 .23
❑ 147 Mark Grudzielanek .30 .14
❑ 148 Ray Durham .50 .23
❑ 149 John Olerud .50 .23
❑ 150 Joey Hamilton .30 .14
❑ 151 Trevor Hoffman .50 .23
❑ 152 Dan Wilson .30 .14
❑ 153 J.T. Snow .50 .23
❑ 154 Marquis Grissom .30 .14
❑ 155 Yamil Benitez .30 .14
❑ 156 Rusty Greer .50 .23
❑ 157 Darryl Kile .50 .23
❑ 158 Ismael Valdes .30 .14
❑ 159 Jeff Conine .30 .14
❑ 160 Darren Daulton .50 .23
❑ 161 Chan Ho Park .50 .23
❑ 162 Troy Percival .30 .14
❑ 163 Wade Boggs 1.00 .45
❑ 164 Dave Nilsson .30 .14
❑ 165 Vinny Castilla .50 .23
❑ 166 Kevin Brown .50 .23
❑ 167 Dennis Eckersley .50 .23
❑ 168 Wendell Magee Jr. .30 .14
❑ 169 John Jaha .30 .14
❑ 170 Garret Anderson .50 .23
❑ 171 Jason Giambi 1.25 .55
❑ 172 Mark Grace 1.25 .55
❑ 173 Tony Clark .50 .23
❑ 174 Moises Alou .50 .23
❑ 175 Brett Butler .50 .23
❑ 176 Cecil Fielder .50 .23
❑ 177 Chris Widger .30 .14
❑ 178 Doug Drabek .30 .14
❑ 179 Ellis Burks .50 .23
❑ 180 S. Hasegawa RC 1.00 .45
❑ NNO A. Rod. Glove EXCH/25 150.00 70.00

1998 Flair Showcase Row 3

	MINT	NRMT
COMPLETE SET (120)	60.00	27.00
COMMON CARD (1-30)	.40	.18
COMMON CARD (31-60)	.40	.18
COMMON CARD (61-90)	.50	.23
COMMON CARD (91-120)	.60	.25

❑ 1 Ken Griffey Jr. 3.00 1.35
❑ 2 Travis Lee .40 .18
❑ 3 Frank Thomas 1.25 .55
❑ 4 Ben Grieve .40 .18
❑ 5 Nomar Garciaparra 2.50 1.10
❑ 6 Jose Cruz Jr. .40 .18
❑ 7 Alex Rodriguez 2.50 1.10
❑ 8 Cal Ripken 4.00 1.80
❑ 9 Mark McGwire 4.00 1.80
❑ 10 Chipper Jones 2.00 .90
❑ 11 Paul Konerko .40 .18
❑ 12 Todd Helton 1.25 .55
❑ 13 Greg Maddux 2.50 1.10
❑ 14 Derek Jeter 4.00 1.80
❑ 15 Jaret Wright .40 .18
❑ 16 Livan Hernandez .40 .18
❑ 17 Mike Piazza 2.50 1.10
❑ 18 Juan Encarnacion .40 .18
❑ 19 Tony Gwynn 2.00 .90
❑ 20 Scott Rolen 1.00 .45
❑ 21 Roger Clemens 2.50 1.10
❑ 22 Tony Clark .40 .18
❑ 23 Albert Belle .40 .18
❑ 24 Mo Vaughn .40 .18
❑ 25 Andruw Jones 1.00 .45
❑ 26 Jason Dickson .40 .18
❑ 27 Fernando Tatis .40 .18
❑ 28 Ivan Rodriguez 1.00 .45
❑ 29 Ricky Ledee .40 .18
❑ 30 Darin Erstad 1.00 .45
❑ 31 Brian Rose .40 .18
❑ 32 Magglio Ordonez RC 3.00 1.35
❑ 33 Larry Walker .60 .25
❑ 34 Bobby Higginson .40 .18
❑ 35 Chili Davis .40 .18
❑ 36 Barry Bonds 2.50 1.10
❑ 37 Vladimir Guerrero 1.25 .55
❑ 38 Jeff Bagwell 1.25 .55
❑ 39 Kenny Lofton .40 .18
❑ 40 Ryan Klesko .40 .18
❑ 41 Mike Cameron .40 .18
❑ 42 Charles Johnson .40 .18
❑ 43 Andy Pettitte .40 .18
❑ 44 Juan Gonzalez 1.00 .45
❑ 45 Tim Salmon .40 .18
❑ 46 Hideki Irabu .40 .18
❑ 47 Paul Molitor 1.00 .45
❑ 48 Edgar Renteria .40 .18
❑ 49 Manny Ramirez 1.25 .55
❑ 50 Jim Edmonds .60 .25
❑ 51 Bernie Williams 1.00 .45
❑ 52 Roberto Alomar 1.00 .45
❑ 53 David Justice .40 .18
❑ 54 Rey Ordonez .40 .18
❑ 55 Ken Caminiti .40 .18
❑ 56 Jose Guillen .40 .18
❑ 57 Randy Johnson 1.25 .55
❑ 58 Brady Anderson .40 .18
❑ 59 Hideo Nomo 1.00 .45
❑ 60 Tino Martinez .40 .18
❑ 61 John Smoltz .50 .23
❑ 62 Joe Carter .50 .23
❑ 63 Matt Williams .75 .35
❑ 64 Robin Ventura .50 .23
❑ 65 Barry Larkin 1.25 .55
❑ 66 Dante Bichette .50 .23
❑ 67 Travis Fryman .50 .23
❑ 68 Gary Sheffield .50 .23
❑ 69 Eric Karros .50 .23
❑ 70 Matt Stairs .50 .23
❑ 71 Al Martin .50 .23
❑ 72 Jay Buhner .50 .23
❑ 73 Ray Lankford .50 .23
❑ 74 Carlos Delgado 1.25 .55
❑ 75 Edgardo Alfonzo .50 .23
❑ 76 Rondell White .50 .23
❑ 77 Chuck Knoblauch .50 .23
❑ 78 Raul Mondesi .50 .23
❑ 79 Johnny Damon .50 .23
❑ 80 Matt Morris .50 .23
❑ 81 Tom Glavine 1.25 .55
❑ 82 Kevin Brown .75 .35
❑ 83 Garret Anderson .50 .23
❑ 84 Mike Mussina 1.25 .55
❑ 85 Pedro Martinez 1.25 .55
❑ 86 Craig Biggio .75 .35
❑ 87 Darryl Kile .50 .23
❑ 88 Rafael Palmeiro 1.25 .55
❑ 89 Jim Thome 1.25 .55
❑ 90 Andres Galarraga .75 .35
❑ 91 Sammy Sosa 3.00 1.35
❑ 92 Willie Greene .60 .25
❑ 93 Vinny Castilla .60 .25
❑ 94 Justin Thompson .60 .25
❑ 95 Jeff King .60 .25
❑ 96 Jeff Cirillo .60 .25
❑ 97 Mark Grudzielanek .60 .25
❑ 98 Brad Radke .60 .25
❑ 99 John Olerud .60 .25
❑ 100 Curt Schilling 1.50 .70
❑ 101 Steve Finley .60 .25
❑ 102 J.T. Snow .60 .25
❑ 103 Edgar Martinez 1.00 .45
❑ 104 Wilson Alvarez .60 .25
❑ 105 Rusty Greer .60 .25
❑ 106 Pat Hentgen .60 .25
❑ 107 David Cone .60 .25
❑ 108 Fred McGriff 1.00 .45
❑ 109 Jason Giambi 1.50 .70
❑ 110 Tony Womack .60 .25
❑ 111 Bernard Gilkey .60 .25
❑ 112 Alan Benes .60 .25
❑ 113 Mark Grace 1.50 .70
❑ 114 Reggie Sanders .60 .25
❑ 115 Moises Alou .60 .25
❑ 116 John Jaha .60 .25
❑ 117 Henry Rodriguez .60 .25
❑ 118 Dean Palmer .60 .25
❑ 119 Mike Lieberthal .60 .25
❑ 120 Shawn Estes .60 .25

1999 Flair Showcase Row 3

	MINT	NRMT
COMPLETE SET (144)	60.00	27.00
COMMON CARD (1-48)	.25	.11
COMMON CARD (49-96)	.25	.11
COMMON CARD (97-144)	.30	.14

❑ 1 Mark McGwire 4.00 1.80
❑ 2 Sammy Sosa 2.00 .90
❑ 3 Ken Griffey Jr. 3.00 1.35
❑ 4 Chipper Jones 2.00 .90
❑ 5 Ben Grieve .40 .18
❑ 6 J.D. Drew 1.00 .45
❑ 7 Jeff Bagwell 1.25 .55
❑ 8 Cal Ripken 4.00 1.80
❑ 9 Tony Gwynn 2.00 .90
❑ 10 Nomar Garciaparra 2.50 1.10
❑ 11 Travis Lee .25 .11
❑ 12 Troy Glaus UER 1.00 .45
Spelled Tony on back
❑ 13 Mike Piazza 2.50 1.10
❑ 14 Alex Rodriguez 2.50 1.10
❑ 15 Kevin Brown .60 .25
❑ 16 Darin Erstad 1.00 .45
❑ 17 Scott Rolen 1.00 .45
❑ 18 Micah Bowie RC .25 .11
❑ 19 Juan Gonzalez 1.00 .45
❑ 20 Kerry Wood 1.00 .45
❑ 21 Roger Clemens 2.50 1.10
❑ 22 Derek Jeter 4.00 1.80
❑ 23 Pat Burrell RC 3.00 1.35
❑ 24 Tim Salmon .40 .18
❑ 25 Barry Bonds 2.50 1.10
❑ 26 Roosevelt Brown RC .50 .23
❑ 27 Vladimir Guerrero 1.25 .55
❑ 28 Randy Johnson 1.25 .55
❑ 29 Mo Vaughn .40 .18
❑ 30 Fernando Seguignol .25 .11
❑ 31 Greg Maddux 2.50 1.10
❑ 32 Tony Clark .40 .18
❑ 33 Eric Chavez .40 .18

❑ 34 Kris Benson .40 .18
❑ 35 Frank Thomas 1.25 .55
❑ 36 Mario Encarnacion RC .50 .23
❑ 37 Gabe Kapler .40 .18
❑ 38 Jeremy Giambi .25 .11
❑ 39 Peter Tucci .25 .11
❑ 40 Manny Ramirez 1.25 .55
❑ 41 Albert Belle .40 .18
❑ 42 Warren Morris .25 .11
❑ 43 Michael Barrett .25 .11
❑ 44 Andruw Jones 1.00 .45
❑ 45 Carlos Delgado 1.00 .45
❑ 46 Jaret Wright .25 .11
❑ 47 Juan Encarnacion .40 .18
❑ 48 Scott Hunter RC .25 .11
❑ 49 Tino Martinez .40 .18
❑ 50 Craig Biggio .60 .25
❑ 51 Jim Thome 1.00 .45
❑ 52 Vinny Castilla .40 .18
❑ 53 Tom Glavine 1.00 .45
❑ 54 Bob Higginson .40 .18
❑ 55 Moises Alou .40 .18
❑ 56 Robin Ventura .40 .18
❑ 57 Bernie Williams 1.00 .45
❑ 58 Pedro Martinez 1.25 .55
❑ 59 Greg Vaughn .40 .18
❑ 60 Ray Lankford .25 .11
❑ 61 Jose Canseco 1.00 .45
❑ 62 Ivan Rodriguez 1.00 .45
❑ 63 Shawn Green 1.00 .45
❑ 64 Rafael Palmeiro 1.00 .45
❑ 65 Ellis Burks .40 .18
❑ 66 Jason Kendall .40 .18
❑ 67 David Wells .40 .18
❑ 68 Rondell White .40 .18
❑ 69 Gary Sheffield .40 .18
❑ 70 Ken Caminiti .40 .18
❑ 71 Cliff Floyd .40 .18
❑ 72 Larry Walker .60 .25
❑ 73 Bartolo Colon .40 .18
❑ 74 Barry Larkin 1.00 .45
❑ 75 Calvin Pickering .25 .11
❑ 76 Jim Edmonds .60 .25
❑ 77 Henry Rodriguez .25 .11
❑ 78 Roberto Alomar 1.00 .45
❑ 79 Andres Galarraga .60 .25
❑ 80 Richie Sexson .40 .18
❑ 81 Todd Helton 1.25 .55
❑ 82 Damion Easley .25 .11
❑ 83 Livan Hernandez .25 .11
❑ 84 Carlos Beltran .40 .18
❑ 85 Todd Hundley .25 .11
❑ 86 Todd Walker .25 .11
❑ 87 Scott Brosius .40 .18
❑ 88 Bob Abreu .40 .18
❑ 89 Corey Koskie .40 .18
❑ 90 Ruben Rivera .25 .11
❑ 91 Edgar Renteria .25 .11
❑ 92 Quinton McCracken .25 .11
❑ 93 Bernard Gilkey .25 .11
❑ 94 Shannon Stewart .40 .18
❑ 95 Dustin Hermanson .25 .11
❑ 96 Mike Caruso .25 .11
❑ 97 Alex Gonzalez .30 .14
❑ 98 Raul Mondesi .50 .23
❑ 99 David Cone .50 .23
❑ 100 Curt Schilling 1.25 .55
❑ 101 Brian Giles .50 .23
❑ 102 Edgar Martinez .75 .35
❑ 103 Rolando Arrojo .30 .14
❑ 104 Derek Bell .30 .14
❑ 105 Denny Neagle .30 .14
❑ 106 Marquis Grissom .30 .14
❑ 107 Bret Boone .50 .23
❑ 108 Mike Mussina 1.25 .55
❑ 109 John Smoltz .50 .23
❑ 110 Brett Tomko .30 .14
❑ 111 David Justice .50 .23
❑ 112 Andy Pettitte .50 .23
❑ 113 Eric Karros .50 .23
❑ 114 Dante Bichette .50 .23
❑ 115 Jeromy Burnitz .50 .23
❑ 116 Paul Konerko .50 .23
❑ 117 Steve Finley .50 .23
❑ 118 Ricky Ledee .30 .14
❑ 119 Edgardo Alfonzo .50 .23
❑ 120 Dean Palmer .50 .23
❑ 121 Rusty Greer .50 .23
❑ 122 Luis Gonzalez 1.25 .55
❑ 123 Randy Winn .30 .14
❑ 124 Jeff Kent .75 .35
❑ 125 Doug Glanville .30 .14
❑ 126 Justin Thompson .30 .14
❑ 127 Bret Saberhagen .50 .23
❑ 128 Wade Boggs 1.00 .45
❑ 129 Al Leiter .50 .23
❑ 130 Paul O'Neill 1.25 .55
❑ 131 Chan Ho Park .50 .23
❑ 132 Johnny Damon .50 .23
❑ 133 Darryl Kile .50 .23
❑ 134 Reggie Sanders .30 .14
❑ 135 Kevin Millwood .30 .14
❑ 136 Charles Johnson .50 .23
❑ 137 Ray Durham .50 .23
❑ 138 Rico Brogna .30 .14
❑ 139 Matt Williams .50 .23
❑ 140 Sandy Alomar Jr. .50 .23
❑ 141 Jeff Cirillo .50 .23
❑ 142 Devon White .30 .14
❑ 143 Andy Benes .30 .14
❑ 144 Mike Stanley .30 .14

1963 Fleer

	NRMT	VG-E
COMPLETE SET (67)	2000.00	900.00
WRAPPER (5-CENT)	100.00	45.00

❑ 1 Steve Barber 25.00 7.50
❑ 2 Ron Hansen 15.00 6.75
❑ 3 Milt Pappas 20.00 9.00
❑ 4 Brooks Robinson 100.00 45.00
❑ 5 Willie Mays 200.00 90.00
❑ 6 Lou Clinton 15.00 6.75
❑ 7 Bill Monbouquette 15.00 6.75
❑ 8 Carl Yastrzemski 100.00 45.00
❑ 9 Ray Herbert 15.00 6.75
❑ 10 Jim Landis 15.00 6.75
❑ 11 Dick Donovan 15.00 6.75
❑ 12 Tito Francona 15.00 6.75
❑ 13 Jerry Kindall 15.00 6.75
❑ 14 Frank Lary 20.00 9.00
❑ 15 Dick Howser 20.00 9.00
❑ 16 Jerry Lumpe 15.00 6.75
❑ 17 Norm Siebern 15.00 6.75
❑ 18 Don Lee 15.00 6.75
❑ 19 Albie Pearson 20.00 9.00
❑ 20 Bob Rodgers 20.00 9.00
❑ 21 Leon Wagner 15.00 6.75
❑ 22 Jim Kaat 25.00 11.00
❑ 23 Vic Power 20.00 9.00
❑ 24 Rich Rollins 20.00 9.00
❑ 25 Bobby Richardson 25.00 11.00
❑ 26 Ralph Terry 20.00 9.00
❑ 27 Tom Cheney 15.00 6.75
❑ 28 Chuck Cottier 15.00 6.75
❑ 29 Jimmy Piersall 20.00 9.00
❑ 30 Dave Stenhouse 15.00 6.75
❑ 31 Glen Hobbie 15.00 6.75
❑ 32 Ron Santo 25.00 11.00
❑ 33 Gene Freese 15.00 6.75
❑ 34 Vada Pinson 25.00 11.00
❑ 35 Bob Purkey 15.00 6.75
❑ 36 Joe Amalfitano 15.00 6.75
❑ 37 Bob Aspromonte 15.00 6.75
❑ 38 Dick Farrell 15.00 6.75
❑ 39 Al Spangler 15.00 6.75
❑ 40 Tommy Davis 20.00 9.00
❑ 41 Don Drysdale 75.00 34.00
❑ 42 Sandy Koufax 200.00 90.00
❑ 43 Maury Wills RC 100.00 45.00
❑ 44 Frank Bolling 15.00 6.75
❑ 45 Warren Spahn 75.00 34.00
❑ 46 Joe Adcock SP 150.00 70.00
❑ 47 Roger Craig 20.00 9.00
❑ 48 Al Jackson 20.00 9.00
❑ 49 Rod Kanehl 20.00 9.00
❑ 50 Ruben Amaro 15.00 6.75
❑ 51 Johnny Callison 20.00 9.00
❑ 52 Clay Dalrymple 15.00 6.75
❑ 53 Don Demeter 15.00 6.75
❑ 54 Art Mahaffey 15.00 6.75
❑ 55 Smoky Burgess 20.00 9.00
❑ 56 Roberto Clemente 200.00 90.00
❑ 57 Roy Face 20.00 9.00
❑ 58 Vern Law 20.00 9.00
❑ 59 Bill Mazeroski 30.00 13.50
❑ 60 Ken Boyer 25.00 11.00
❑ 61 Bob Gibson 75.00 34.00
❑ 62 Gene Oliver 15.00 6.75
❑ 63 Bill White 20.00 9.00
❑ 64 Orlando Cepeda 30.00 13.50
❑ 65 Jim Davenport 15.00 6.75
❑ 66 Billy O'Dell 25.00 7.50
❑ NNO Checklist card 500.00 160.00

1981 Fleer

	NRMT	VG-E
COMPLETE SET (660)	30.00	13.50

❑ 1 Pete Rose UER 3.00 1.35
270 hits in 63
should be 170
❑ 2 Larry Bowa .25 .11
❑ 3 Manny Trillo .10 .05
❑ 4 Bob Boone .25 .11
❑ 5 Mike Schmidt 2.00 .90
See also 640A
❑ 6 Steve Carlton P1 1.00 .45
Golden Arm
Back 1066 Cardinals
Number on back 6
❑ 6B Steve Carlton P2 1.50 .70
Pitcher of Year
Back 1066 Cardinals
❑ 6C Steve Carlton P3 2.00 .90
1966 Cardinals
❑ 7 Tug McGraw .25 .11
See 657A
❑ 8 Larry Christenson .10 .05
❑ 9 Bake McBride .10 .05
❑ 10 Greg Luzinski .25 .11
❑ 11 Ron Reed .10 .05
❑ 12 Dickie Noles .10 .05
❑ 13 Keith Moreland .25 .11
❑ 14 Bob Walk RC .25 .11
❑ 15 Lonnie Smith .25 .11
❑ 16 Dick Ruthven .10 .05
❑ 17 Sparky Lyle .25 .11
❑ 18 Greg Gross .10 .05
❑ 19 Garry Maddox .10 .05

	No.	Player		
☐	20	Nino Espinosa	.10	.05
☐	21	George Vukovich	.10	.05
☐	22	John Vukovich	.10	.05
☐	23	Ramon Aviles	.10	.05
☐	24A	Kevin Saucier P1 Name on back Ken	.10	.05
☐	24B	Kevin Saucier P2 Name on back Ken	.10	.05
☐	24C	Kevin Saucier P3 Name on back Kevin	1.00	.45
☐	25	Randy Lerch	.10	.05
☐	26	Del Unser	.10	.05
☐	27	Tim McCarver	.50	.23
☐	28	George Brett See also 655A	2.50	1.10
☐	29	Willie Wilson See also 653A	.25	.11
☐	30	Paul Splittorff	.10	.05
☐	31	Dan Quisenberry	.25	.11
☐	32A	Amos Otis P1 (Batting Pose Outfield 32 on back	.25	.11
☐	32B	Amos Otis P2 Series Starter 483 on back	.25	.11
☐	33	Steve Busby	.10	.05
☐	34	U.L. Washington	.10	.05
☐	35	Dave Chalk	.10	.05
☐	36	Darrell Porter	.10	.05
☐	37	Marty Pattin	.10	.05
☐	38	Larry Gura	.10	.05
☐	39	Renie Martin	.10	.05
☐	40	Rich Gale	.10	.05
☐	41A	Hal McRae P1 (Royals on front in black letters	.50	.23
☐	41B	Hal McRae P2 (Royals on front in blue letters	.25	.11
☐	42	Dennis Leonard	.10	.05
☐	43	Willie Aikens	.10	.05
☐	44	Frank White	.25	.11
☐	45	Clint Hurdle	.10	.05
☐	46	John Wathan	.10	.05
☐	47	Pete LaCock	.10	.05
☐	48	Rance Mulliniks	.10	.05
☐	49	Jeff Twitty	.10	.05
☐	50	Jamie Quirk	.10	.05
☐	51	Art Howe	.25	.11
☐	52	Ken Forsch	.10	.05
☐	53	Vern Ruhle	.10	.05
☐	54	Joe Niekro	.25	.11
☐	55	Frank LaCorte	.10	.05
☐	56	J.R. Richard	.25	.11
☐	57	Nolan Ryan	5.00	2.20
☐	58	Enos Cabell	.10	.05
☐	59	Cesar Cedeno	.25	.11
☐	60	Jose Cruz	.25	.11
☐	61	Bill Virdon MG	.10	.05
☐	62	Terry Puhl	.10	.05
☐	63	Joaquin Andujar	.25	.11
☐	64	Alan Ashby	.10	.05
☐	65	Joe Sambito	.10	.05
☐	66	Denny Walling	.10	.05
☐	67	Jeff Leonard	.25	.11
☐	68	Luis Pujols	.10	.05
☐	69	Bruce Bochy	.10	.05
☐	70	Rafael Landestoy	.10	.05
☐	71	Dave Smith RC	.25	.11
☐	72	Danny Heep	.10	.05
☐	73	Julio Gonzalez	.10	.05
☐	74	Craig Reynolds	.10	.05
☐	75	Gary Woods	.10	.05
☐	76	Dave Bergman	.10	.05
☐	77	Randy Niemann	.10	.05
☐	78	Joe Morgan	1.00	.45
☐	79	Reggie Jackson See also 650A	1.25	.55
☐	80	Bucky Dent	.25	.11
☐	81	Tommy John	.50	.23
☐	82	Luis Tiant	.25	.11
☐	83	Rick Cerone	.10	.05
☐	84	Dick Howser MG	.25	.11
☐	85	Lou Piniella	.25	.11
☐	86	Ron Davis	.10	.05
☐	87A	Graig Nettles ERR Name on back spelled Craig	5.00	2.20
☐	87B	Graig Nettles COR Graig	.25	.11
☐	88	Ron Guidry	.25	.11
☐	89	Rich Gossage	.50	.23
☐	90	Rudy May	.10	.05
☐	91	Gaylord Perry	1.00	.45
☐	92	Eric Soderholm	.10	.05
☐	93	Bob Watson	.25	.11
☐	94	Bobby Murcer	.25	.11
☐	95	Bobby Brown	.10	.05
☐	96	Jim Spencer	.10	.05
☐	97	Tom Underwood	.10	.05
☐	98	Oscar Gamble	.10	.05
☐	99	Johnny Oates	.25	.11
☐	100	Fred Stanley	.10	.05
☐	101	Ruppert Jones	.10	.05
☐	102	Dennis Werth	.10	.05
☐	103	Joe Lefebvre	.10	.05
☐	104	Brian Doyle	.10	.05
☐	105	Aurelio Rodriguez	.10	.05
☐	106	Doug Bird	.10	.05
☐	107	Mike Griffin RC	.10	.05
☐	108	Tim Lollar	.10	.05
☐	109	Willie Randolph	.25	.11
☐	110	Steve Garvey	.50	.23
☐	111	Reggie Smith	.25	.11
☐	112	Don Sutton	1.00	.45
☐	113	Burt Hooton	.10	.05
☐	114A	Dave Lopes P1 Small hand on back	.50	.23
☐	114B	Dave Lopes P2 No hand	.25	.11
☐	115	Dusty Baker	.50	.23
☐	116	Tom Lasorda MG	.25	.11
☐	117	Bill Russell	.25	.11
☐	118	Jerry Reuss UER Home omitted	.25	.11
☐	119	Terry Forster	.10	.05
☐	120A	Bob Welch P1 (Name on back is Bob	.25	.11
☐	120B	Bob Welch P2 Name on back is Robert	.50	.23
☐	121	Don Stanhouse	.10	.05
☐	122	Rick Monday	.25	.11
☐	123	Derrel Thomas	.10	.05
☐	124	Joe Ferguson	.10	.05
☐	125	Rick Sutcliffe	.25	.11
☐	126A	Ron Cey P1 Small hand on back	.50	.23
☐	126B	Ron Cey P2 No hand	.25	.11
☐	127	Dave Goltz	.10	.05
☐	128	Jay Johnstone	.25	.11
☐	129	Steve Yeager	.10	.05
☐	130	Gary Weiss	.10	.05
☐	131	Mike Scioscia RC	1.00	.45
☐	132	Vic Davalillo	.10	.05
☐	133	Doug Rau	.10	.05
☐	134	Pepe Frias	.10	.05
☐	135	Mickey Hatcher	.25	.11
☐	136	Steve Howe	.25	.11
☐	137	Robert Castillo	.10	.05
☐	138	Gary Thomasson	.10	.05
☐	139	Rudy Law	.10	.05
☐	140	F.Valenzuela RC UER Misspelled Fernand on card	2.00	.90
☐	141	Manny Mota	.25	.11
☐	142	Gary Carter	.50	.23
☐	143	Steve Rogers	.10	.05
☐	144	Warren Cromartie	.10	.05
☐	145	Andre Dawson	.50	.23
☐	146	Larry Parrish	.10	.05
☐	147	Rowland Office	.10	.05
☐	148	Ellis Valentine	.10	.05
☐	149	Dick Williams MG	.10	.05
☐	150	Bill Gullickson RC	.50	.23
☐	151	Elias Sosa	.10	.05
☐	152	John Tamargo	.10	.05
☐	153	Chris Speier	.10	.05
☐	154	Ron LeFlore	.25	.11
☐	155	Rodney Scott	.10	.05
☐	156	Stan Bahnsen	.10	.05
☐	157	Bill Lee	.25	.11
☐	158	Fred Norman	.10	.05
☐	159	Woodie Fryman	.10	.05
☐	160	David Palmer	.10	.05
☐	161	Jerry White	.10	.05
☐	162	Roberto Ramos	.10	.05
☐	163	John D'Acquisto	.10	.05
☐	164	Tommy Hutton	.10	.05
☐	165	Charlie Lea	.10	.05
☐	166	Scott Sanderson	.10	.05
☐	167	Ken Macha	.10	.05
☐	168	Tony Bernazard	.10	.05
☐	169	Jim Palmer	1.00	.45
☐	170	Steve Stone	.25	.11
☐	171	Mike Flanagan	.25	.11
☐	172	Al Bumbry	.25	.11
☐	173	Doug DeCinces	.25	.11
☐	174	Scott McGregor	.10	.05
☐	175	Mark Belanger	.25	.11
☐	176	Tim Stoddard	.10	.05
☐	177A	Rick Dempsey P1 Small hand on front	.50	.23
☐	177B	Rick Dempsey P2 No hand	.25	.11
☐	178	Earl Weaver MG	1.00	.45
☐	179	Tippy Martinez	.10	.05
☐	180	Dennis Martinez	.50	.23
☐	181	Sammy Stewart	.10	.05
☐	182	Rich Dauer	.10	.05
☐	183	Lee May	.25	.11
☐	184	Eddie Murray	2.00	.90
☐	185	Benny Ayala	.10	.05
☐	186	John Lowenstein	.10	.05
☐	187	Gary Roenicke	.10	.05
☐	188	Ken Singleton	.25	.11
☐	189	Dan Graham	.10	.05
☐	190	Terry Crowley	.10	.05
☐	191	Kiko Garcia	.10	.05
☐	192	Dave Ford	.10	.05
☐	193	Mark Corey	.10	.05
☐	194	Lenn Sakata	.10	.05
☐	195	Doug DeCinces	.25	.11
☐	196	Johnny Bench	1.50	.70
☐	197	Dave Concepcion	.25	.11
☐	198	Ray Knight	.25	.11
☐	199	Ken Griffey	.50	.23
☐	200	Tom Seaver	1.50	.70
☐	201	Dave Collins	.10	.05
☐	202A	George Foster P1 Slugger Number on back 216	.50	.23
☐	202B	George Foster P2 Slugger Number on back 202	.50	.23
☐	203	Junior Kennedy	.10	.05
☐	204	Frank Pastore	.10	.05
☐	205	Dan Driessen	.10	.05
☐	206	Hector Cruz	.10	.05
☐	207	Paul Moskau	.10	.05
☐	208	Charlie Leibrandt RC	.50	.23
☐	209	Harry Spilman	.10	.05
☐	210	Joe Price	.10	.05
☐	211	Tom Hume	.10	.05
☐	212	Joe Nolan	.10	.05
☐	213	Doug Bair	.10	.05
☐	214	Mario Soto	.10	.05
☐	215A	Bill Bonham P1 (Small hand on back)	.50	.23
☐	215B	Bill Bonham P2 (No hand)	.10	.05
☐	216	George Foster (See 202)	.25	.11
☐	217	Paul Householder	.10	.05
☐	218	Ron Oester	.10	.05
☐	219	Sam Mejias	.10	.05
☐	220	Sheldon Burnside	.10	.05
☐	221	Carl Yastrzemski	1.00	.45
☐	222	Jim Rice	.25	.11
☐	223	Fred Lynn	.25	.11
☐	224	Carlton Fisk	1.00	.45
☐	225	Rick Burleson	.10	.05
☐	226	Dennis Eckersley	1.00	.45
☐	227	Butch Hobson	.10	.05
☐	228	Tom Burgmeier	.10	.05
☐	229	Garry Hancock	.10	.05
☐	230	Don Zimmer MG	.25	.11
☐	231	Steve Renko	.10	.05
☐	232	Dwight Evans	.50	.23

- ❑ 233 Mike Torrez .10 .05
- ❑ 234 Bob Stanley .10 .05
- ❑ 235 Jim Dwyer .10 .05
- ❑ 236 Dave Stapleton .10 .05
- ❑ 237 Glenn Hoffman .10 .05
- ❑ 238 Jerry Remy .10 .05
- ❑ 239 Dick Drago .10 .05
- ❑ 240 Bill Campbell .10 .05
- ❑ 241 Tony Perez 1.00 .45
- ❑ 242 Phil Niekro 1.00 .45
- ❑ 243 Dale Murphy 1.00 .45
- ❑ 244 Bob Horner .25 .11
- ❑ 245 Jeff Burroughs .10 .05
- ❑ 246 Rick Camp .10 .05
- ❑ 247 Bobby Cox MG .25 .11
- ❑ 248 Bruce Benedict .10 .05
- ❑ 249 Gene Garber .10 .05
- ❑ 250 Jerry Royster .10 .05
- ❑ 251A Gary Matthews P1 .50 .23
  Small hand on back
- ❑ 251B Gary Matthews P2 .25 .11
  No hand
- ❑ 252 Chris Chambliss .25 .11
- ❑ 253 Luis Gomez .10 .05
- ❑ 254 Bill Nahorodny .10 .05
- ❑ 255 Doyle Alexander .10 .05
- ❑ 256 Brian Asselstine .10 .05
- ❑ 257 Biff Pocoroba .10 .05
- ❑ 258 Mike Lum .10 .05
- ❑ 259 Charlie Spikes .10 .05
- ❑ 260 Glenn Hubbard .10 .05
- ❑ 261 Tommy Boggs .10 .05
- ❑ 262 Al Hrabosky UER .10 .05
  Card lists him as 5' 1"
- ❑ 263 Rick Matula .10 .05
- ❑ 264 Preston Hanna .10 .05
- ❑ 265 Larry Bradford .10 .05
- ❑ 266 Rafael Ramirez .10 .05
- ❑ 267 Larry McWilliams .10 .05
- ❑ 268 Rod Carew 1.00 .45
- ❑ 269 Bobby Grich .25 .11
- ❑ 270 Carney Lansford .25 .11
- ❑ 271 Don Baylor .50 .23
- ❑ 272 Joe Rudi .25 .11
- ❑ 273 Dan Ford .10 .05
- ❑ 274 Jim Fregosi MG .10 .05
- ❑ 275 Dave Frost .10 .05
- ❑ 276 Frank Tanana .25 .11
- ❑ 277 Dickie Thon .25 .11
- ❑ 278 Jason Thompson .10 .05
- ❑ 279 Rick Miller .10 .05
- ❑ 280 Bert Campaneris .25 .11
- ❑ 281 Tom Donohue .10 .05
- ❑ 282 Brian Downing .25 .11
- ❑ 283 Fred Patek .10 .05
- ❑ 284 Bruce Kison .10 .05
- ❑ 285 Dave LaRoche .10 .05
- ❑ 286 Don Aase .10 .05
- ❑ 287 Jim Barr .10 .05
- ❑ 288 Alfredo Martinez .10 .05
- ❑ 289 Larry Harlow .10 .05
- ❑ 290 Andy Hassler .10 .05
- ❑ 291 Dave Kingman .50 .23
- ❑ 292 Bill Buckner .25 .11
- ❑ 293 Rick Reuschel .25 .11
- ❑ 294 Bruce Sutter .25 .11
- ❑ 295 Jerry Martin .10 .05
- ❑ 296 Scot Thompson .10 .05
- ❑ 297 Ivan DeJesus .10 .05
- ❑ 298 Steve Dillard .10 .05
- ❑ 299 Dick Tidrow .10 .05
- ❑ 300 Randy Martz .10 .05
- ❑ 301 Lenny Randle .10 .05
- ❑ 302 Lynn McGlothen .10 .05
- ❑ 303 Cliff Johnson .10 .05
- ❑ 304 Tim Blackwell .10 .05
- ❑ 305 Dennis Lamp .10 .05
- ❑ 306 Bill Caudill .10 .05
- ❑ 307 Carlos Lezcano .10 .05
- ❑ 308 Jim Tracy .10 .05
- ❑ 309 Doug Capilla UER .10 .05
  Cubs on front but
  Braves on back
- ❑ 310 Willie Hernandez .25 .11
- ❑ 311 Mike Vail .10 .05
- ❑ 312 Mike Krukow .10 .05
- ❑ 313 Barry Foote .10 .05
- ❑ 314 Larry Biittner .10 .05
- ❑ 315 Mike Tyson .10 .05
- ❑ 316 Lee Mazzilli .10 .05
- ❑ 317 John Stearns .10 .05
- ❑ 318 Alex Trevino .10 .05
- ❑ 319 Craig Swan .10 .05
- ❑ 320 Frank Taveras .10 .05
- ❑ 321 Steve Henderson .10 .05
- ❑ 322 Neil Allen .10 .05
- ❑ 323 Mark Bomback .10 .05
- ❑ 324 Mike Jorgensen .10 .05
- ❑ 325 Joe Torre MG .25 .11
- ❑ 326 Elliott Maddox .10 .05
- ❑ 327 Pete Falcone .10 .05
- ❑ 328 Ray Burris .10 .05
- ❑ 329 Claudell Washington .10 .05
- ❑ 330 Doug Flynn .10 .05
- ❑ 331 Joel Youngblood .10 .05
- ❑ 332 Bill Almon .10 .05
- ❑ 333 Tom Hausman .10 .05
- ❑ 334 Pat Zachry .10 .05
- ❑ 335 Jeff Reardon RC 1.00 .45
- ❑ 336 Wally Backman .25 .11
- ❑ 337 Dan Norman .10 .05
- ❑ 338 Jerry Morales .10 .05
- ❑ 339 Ed Farmer .10 .05
- ❑ 340 Bob Molinaro .10 .05
- ❑ 341 Todd Cruz .10 .05
- ❑ 342A Britt Burns P1 .50 .23
  Small hand on front
- ❑ 342B Britt Burns P2 .25 .11
  No hand
- ❑ 343 Kevin Bell .10 .05
- ❑ 344 Tony LaRussa MG .25 .11
- ❑ 345 Steve Trout .10 .05
- ❑ 346 Harold Baines RC 5.00 2.20
- ❑ 347 Richard Wortham .10 .05
- ❑ 348 Wayne Nordhagen .10 .05
- ❑ 349 Mike Squires .10 .05
- ❑ 350 Lamar Johnson .10 .05
- ❑ 351 Rickey Henderson 3.00 1.35
  Most Stolen Bases AL
- ❑ 352 Francisco Barrios .10 .05
- ❑ 353 Thad Bosley .10 .05
- ❑ 354 Chet Lemon .10 .05
- ❑ 355 Bruce Kimm .10 .05
- ❑ 356 Richard Dotson .10 .05
- ❑ 357 Jim Morrison .10 .05
- ❑ 358 Mike Proly .10 .05
- ❑ 359 Greg Pryor .10 .05
- ❑ 360 Dave Parker .25 .11
- ❑ 361 Omar Moreno .10 .05
- ❑ 362A Kent Tekulve P1 .25 .11
  Back 1071 Waterbury
  and 1078 Pirates
- ❑ 362B Kent Tekulve P2 .25 .11
  1971 Waterbury and
  1978 Pirates
- ❑ 363 Willie Stargell 1.00 .45
- ❑ 364 Phil Garner .25 .11
- ❑ 365 Ed Ott .10 .05
- ❑ 366 Don Robinson .10 .05
- ❑ 367 Chuck Tanner MG .25 .11
- ❑ 368 Jim Rooker .10 .05
- ❑ 369 Dale Berra .10 .05
- ❑ 370 Jim Bibby .10 .05
- ❑ 371 Steve Nicosia .10 .05
- ❑ 372 Mike Easler .10 .05
- ❑ 373 Bill Robinson .25 .11
- ❑ 374 Lee Lacy .10 .05
- ❑ 375 John Candelaria .25 .11
- ❑ 376 Manny Sanguillen .25 .11
- ❑ 377 Rick Rhoden .10 .05
- ❑ 378 Grant Jackson .10 .05
- ❑ 379 Tim Foli .10 .05
- ❑ 380 Rod Scurry .10 .05
- ❑ 381 Bill Madlock .25 .11
- ❑ 382A Kurt Bevacqua .25 .11
  P1 ERR
  P on cap backwards
- ❑ 382B Kurt Bevacqua P2 .10 .05
  COR
- ❑ 383 Bert Blyleven .50 .23
- ❑ 384 Eddie Solomon .10 .05
- ❑ 385 Enrique Romo .10 .05
- ❑ 386 John Milner .10 .05
- ❑ 387 Mike Hargrove .25 .11
- ❑ 388 Jorge Orta .10 .05
- ❑ 389 Toby Harrah .25 .11
- ❑ 390 Tom Veryzer .10 .05
- ❑ 391 Miguel Dilone .10 .05
- ❑ 392 Dan Spillner .10 .05
- ❑ 393 Jack Brohamer .10 .05
- ❑ 394 Wayne Garland .10 .05
- ❑ 395 Sid Monge .10 .05
- ❑ 396 Rick Waits .10 .05
- ❑ 397 Joe Charboneau RC 1.00 .45
- ❑ 398 Gary Alexander .10 .05
- ❑ 399 Jerry Dybzinski .10 .05
- ❑ 400 Mike Stanton .10 .05
- ❑ 401 Mike Paxton .10 .05
- ❑ 402 Gary Gray .10 .05
- ❑ 403 Rick Manning .10 .05
- ❑ 404 Bo Diaz .10 .05
- ❑ 405 Ron Hassey .10 .05
- ❑ 406 Ross Grimsley .10 .05
- ❑ 407 Victor Cruz .10 .05
- ❑ 408 Len Barker .10 .05
- ❑ 409 Bob Bailor .10 .05
- ❑ 410 Otto Velez .10 .05
- ❑ 411 Ernie Whitt .10 .05
- ❑ 412 Jim Clancy .10 .05
- ❑ 413 Barry Bonnell .10 .05
- ❑ 414 Dave Stieb .25 .11
- ❑ 415 Damaso Garcia .10 .05
- ❑ 416 John Mayberry .10 .05
- ❑ 417 Roy Howell .10 .05
- ❑ 418 Danny Ainge RC 2.00 .90
- ❑ 419A Jesse Jefferson P1 .10 .05
  Back says Pirates
- ❑ 419B Jesse Jefferson P2 .10 .05
  Back says Pirates
- ❑ 419C Jesse Jefferson P3 1.00 .45
  Back says Blue Jays
- ❑ 420 Joey McLaughlin .10 .05
- ❑ 421 Lloyd Moseby .25 .11
- ❑ 422 Alvis Woods .10 .05
- ❑ 423 Garth Iorg .10 .05
- ❑ 424 Doug Ault .10 .05
- ❑ 425 Ken Schrom .10 .05
- ❑ 426 Mike Willis .10 .05
- ❑ 427 Steve Braun .10 .05
- ❑ 428 Bob Davis .10 .05
- ❑ 429 Jerry Garvin .10 .05
- ❑ 430 Alfredo Griffin .10 .05
- ❑ 431 Bob Mattick MG .10 .05
- ❑ 432 Vida Blue .25 .11
- ❑ 433 Jack Clark .25 .11
- ❑ 434 Willie McCovey 1.00 .45
- ❑ 435 Mike Ivie .10 .05
- ❑ 436A Darrel Evans P1 ERR .50 .23
  (Name on front Darrel
- ❑ 436B Darrell Evans P2 COR .50 .23
  Name on front Darrell
- ❑ 437 Terry Whitfield .10 .05
- ❑ 438 Rennie Stennett .10 .05
- ❑ 439 John Montefusco .10 .05
- ❑ 440 Jim Wohlford .10 .05
- ❑ 441 Bill North .10 .05
- ❑ 442 Milt May .10 .05
- ❑ 443 Max Venable .10 .05
- ❑ 444 Ed Whitson .10 .05
- ❑ 445 Al Holland .10 .05
- ❑ 446 Randy Moffitt .10 .05
- ❑ 447 Bob Knepper .10 .05
- ❑ 448 Gary Lavelle .10 .05
- ❑ 449 Greg Minton .10 .05
- ❑ 450 Johnnie LeMaster .10 .05
- ❑ 451 Larry Herndon .10 .05
- ❑ 452 Rich Murray .10 .05
- ❑ 453 Joe Pettini .10 .05
- ❑ 454 Allen Ripley .10 .05
- ❑ 455 Dennis Littlejohn .10 .05
- ❑ 456 Tom Griffin .10 .05
- ❑ 457 Alan Hargesheimer .10 .05
- ❑ 458 Joe Strain .10 .05
- ❑ 459 Steve Kemp .10 .05
- ❑ 460 Sparky Anderson MG .25 .11
- ❑ 461 Alan Trammell .50 .23
- ❑ 462 Mark Fidrych 1.00 .45
- ❑ 463 Lou Whitaker 1.00 .45

❑ 464 Dave Rozema .10 .05
❑ 465 Milt Wilcox .10 .05
❑ 466 Champ Summers .10 .05
❑ 467 Lance Parrish .25 .11
❑ 468 Dan Petry .10 .05
❑ 469 Pat Underwood .10 .05
❑ 470 Rick Peters .10 .05
❑ 471 Al Cowens .10 .05
❑ 472 John Wockenfuss .10 .05
❑ 473 Tom Brookens .10 .05
❑ 474 Richie Hebner .10 .05
❑ 475 Jack Morris 1.00 .45
❑ 476 Jim Lentine .10 .05
❑ 477 Bruce Robbins .10 .05
❑ 478 Mark Wagner .10 .05
❑ 479 Tim Corcoran .10 .05
❑ 480A Stan Papi P1 .25 .11
Front as Pitcher
❑ 480B Stan Papi P2 .10 .05
Front as Shortstop
❑ 481 Kirk Gibson RC 2.00 .90
❑ 482 Dan Schatzeder .10 .05
❑ 483A Amos Otis P1 .25 .11
See card 32
❑ 483B Amos Otis P2 .25 .11
See card 32
❑ 484 Dave Winfield 1.00 .45
❑ 485 Rollie Fingers 1.00 .45
❑ 486 Gene Richards .10 .05
❑ 487 Randy Jones .10 .05
❑ 488 Ozzie Smith 3.00 1.35
❑ 489 Gene Tenace .25 .11
❑ 490 Bill Fahey .10 .05
❑ 491 John Curtis .10 .05
❑ 492 Dave Cash .10 .05
❑ 493A Tim Flannery P1 .25 .11
Batting right
❑ 493B Tim Flannery P2 .10 .05
Batting left
❑ 494 Jerry Mumphrey .10 .05
❑ 495 Bob Shirley .10 .05
❑ 496 Steve Mura .10 .05
❑ 497 Eric Rasmussen .10 .05
❑ 498 Broderick Perkins .10 .05
❑ 499 Barry Evans .10 .05
❑ 500 Chuck Baker .10 .05
❑ 501 Luis Salazar RC .10 .05
❑ 502 Gary Lucas .10 .05
❑ 503 Mike Armstrong .10 .05
❑ 504 Jerry Turner .10 .05
❑ 505 Dennis Kinney .10 .05
❑ 506 Willie Montanez UER .10 .05
Spelled Willy on card front
❑ 507 Gorman Thomas .25 .11
❑ 508 Ben Oglivie .25 .11
❑ 509 Larry Hisle .10 .05
❑ 510 Sal Bando .25 .11
❑ 511 Robin Yount 1.00 .45
❑ 512 Mike Caldwell .10 .05
❑ 513 Sixto Lezcano .10 .05
❑ 514A Bill Travers P1 ERR .25 .11
Jerry Augustine
with Augustine back
❑ 514B Bill Travers P2 COR .10 .05
❑ 515 Paul Molitor 2.00 .90
❑ 516 Moose Haas .10 .05
❑ 517 Bill Castro .10 .05
❑ 518 Jim Slaton .10 .05
❑ 519 Lary Sorensen .10 .05
❑ 520 Bob McClure .10 .05
❑ 521 Charlie Moore .10 .05
❑ 522 Jim Gantner .25 .11
❑ 523 Reggie Cleveland .10 .05
❑ 524 Don Money .10 .05
❑ 525 Bill Travers .10 .05
❑ 526 Buck Martinez .10 .05
❑ 527 Dick Davis .10 .05
❑ 528 Ted Simmons .25 .11
❑ 529 Garry Templeton .10 .05
❑ 530 Ken Reitz .10 .05
❑ 531 Tony Scott .10 .05
❑ 532 Ken Oberkfell .10 .05
❑ 533 Bob Sykes .10 .05
❑ 534 Keith Smith .10 .05
❑ 535 John Littlefield .10 .05
❑ 536 Jim Kaat .25 .11
❑ 537 Bob Forsch .10 .05
❑ 538 Mike Phillips .10 .05
❑ 539 Terry Landrum .10 .05
❑ 540 Leon Durham .25 .11
❑ 541 Terry Kennedy .10 .05
❑ 542 George Hendrick .10 .05
❑ 543 Dane Iorg .10 .05
❑ 544 Mark Littell .10 .05
❑ 545 Keith Hernandez .25 .11
❑ 546 Silvio Martinez .10 .05
❑ 547A Don Hood P1 ERR .25 .11
Pete Vuckovich
with Vuckovich back
❑ 547B Don Hood P2 COR .10 .05
❑ 548 Bobby Bonds .25 .11
❑ 549 Mike Ramsey .10 .05
❑ 550 Tom Herr .25 .11
❑ 551 Roy Smalley .10 .05
❑ 552 Jerry Koosman .25 .11
❑ 553 Ken Landreaux .10 .05
❑ 554 John Castino .10 .05
❑ 555 Doug Corbett .10 .05
❑ 556 Bombo Rivera .10 .05
❑ 557 Ron Jackson .10 .05
❑ 558 Butch Wynegar .10 .05
❑ 559 Hosken Powell .10 .05
❑ 560 Pete Redfern .10 .05
❑ 561 Roger Erickson .10 .05
❑ 562 Glenn Adams .10 .05
❑ 563 Rick Sofield .10 .05
❑ 564 Geoff Zahn .10 .05
❑ 565 Pete Mackanin .10 .05
❑ 566 Mike Cubbage .10 .05
❑ 567 Darrell Jackson .10 .05
❑ 568 Dave Edwards .10 .05
❑ 569 Rob Wilfong .10 .05
❑ 570 Sal Butera .10 .05
❑ 571 Jose Morales .10 .05
❑ 572 Rick Langford .10 .05
❑ 573 Mike Norris .10 .05
❑ 574 Rickey Henderson 6.00 2.70
❑ 575 Tony Armas .25 .11
❑ 576 Dave Revering .10 .05
❑ 577 Jeff Newman .10 .05
❑ 578 Bob Lacey .10 .05
❑ 579 Brian Kingman .10 .05
❑ 580 Mitchell Page .10 .05
❑ 581 Billy Martin MG .50 .23
❑ 582 Rob Picciolo .10 .05
❑ 583 Mike Heath .10 .05
❑ 584 Mickey Klutts .10 .05
❑ 585 Orlando Gonzalez .10 .05
❑ 586 Mike Davis .10 .05
❑ 587 Wayne Gross .10 .05
❑ 588 Matt Keough .10 .05
❑ 589 Steve McCatty .10 .05
❑ 590 Dwayne Murphy .10 .05
❑ 591 Mario Guerrero .10 .05
❑ 592 Dave McKay .10 .05
❑ 593 Jim Essian .10 .05
❑ 594 Dave Heaverlo .10 .05
❑ 595 Maury Wills MG .25 .11
❑ 596 Juan Beniquez .10 .05
❑ 597 Rodney Craig .10 .05
❑ 598 Jim Anderson .10 .05
❑ 599 Floyd Bannister .10 .05
❑ 600 Bruce Bochte .10 .05
❑ 601 Julio Cruz .10 .05
❑ 602 Ted Cox .10 .05
❑ 603 Dan Meyer .10 .05
❑ 604 Larry Cox .10 .05
❑ 605 Bill Stein .10 .05
❑ 606 Steve Garvey .50 .23
Most Hits NL
❑ 607 Dave Roberts .10 .05
❑ 608 Leon Roberts .10 .05
❑ 609 Reggie Walton .10 .05
❑ 610 Dave Edler .10 .05
❑ 611 Larry Milbourne .10 .05
❑ 612 Kim Allen .10 .05
❑ 613 Mario Mendoza .10 .05
❑ 614 Tom Paciorek .25 .11
❑ 615 Glenn Abbott .10 .05
❑ 616 Joe Simpson .10 .05
❑ 617 Mickey Rivers .25 .11
❑ 618 Jim Kern .10 .05
❑ 619 Jim Sundberg .25 .11
❑ 620 Richie Zisk .10 .05
❑ 621 Jon Matlack .10 .05
❑ 622 Ferguson Jenkins 1.00 .45
❑ 623 Pat Corrales MG .10 .05
❑ 624 Ed Figueroa .10 .05
❑ 625 Buddy Bell .25 .11
❑ 626 Al Oliver .25 .11
❑ 627 Doc Medich .10 .05
❑ 628 Bump Wills .10 .05
❑ 629 Rusty Staub .25 .11
❑ 630 Pat Putnam .10 .05
❑ 631 John Grubb .10 .05
❑ 632 Danny Darwin .10 .05
❑ 633 Ken Clay .10 .05
❑ 634 Jim Norris .10 .05
❑ 635 John Butcher .10 .05
❑ 636 Dave Roberts .10 .05
❑ 637 Billy Sample .10 .05
❑ 638 Carl Yastrzemski 1.00 .45
❑ 639 Cecil Cooper .25 .11
❑ 640 Mike Schmidt P1 2.00 .90
Portrait
Third Base
number on back 5
❑ 640B Mike Schmidt P2 2.00 .90
1980 Home Run King
640 on back
❑ 641A CL: Phils/Royals P1 .25 .11
41 is Hal McRae
❑ 641B CL: Phils/Royals P2 .25 .11
41 is Hal McRae
Double Threat
❑ 642 CL: Astros/Yankees .10 .05
❑ 643 CL: Expos/Dodgers .10 .05
❑ 644A CL: Reds/Orioles P1 .25 .11
202 is George Foster
Joe Nolan pitcher
should be catcher
❑ 644B CL: Reds/Orioles P2 .25 .11
202 is Foster Slugger
Joe Nolan pitcher
should be catcher
❑ 645 Pete Rose 1.25 .55
Larry Bowa
Mike Schmidt
Triple Threat P1
No number on back
❑ 645B Pete Rose 2.00 .90
Larry Bowa
Mike Schmidt
Triple Threat P2
Back numbered 645
❑ 646 CL: Braves/Red Sox .10 .05
❑ 647 CL: Cubs/Angels .10 .05
❑ 648 CL: Mets/White Sox .10 .05
❑ 649 CL: Indians/Pirates .10 .05
❑ 650 Reggie Jackson 1.25 .55
Mr. Baseball P1
Number on back 79
❑ 650B Reggie Jackson 1.00 .45
Mr. Baseball P2
Number on back 650
❑ 651 CL: Giants/Blue Jays .10 .05
❑ 652A CL:Tigers/Padres P1 .25 .11
483 is listed
❑ 652B CL:Tigers/Padres P2 .25 .11
483 is deleted
❑ 653A Willie Wilson P1 .25 .11
Most Hits Most Runs
Number on back 29
❑ 653B Willie Wilson P2 .25 .11
Most Hits Most Runs
Number on back 653
❑ 654A Checklist Brewers .25 .11
Cards P1
514 Jerry Augustine
547 Pete Vuckovich
❑ 654B Checklist Brewers .25 .11
Cards P2
514 Billy Travers
547 Don Hood
❑ 655 George Brett P1 2.50 1.10
.390 Average
Number on back 28
❑ 655B George Brett P2 4.00 1.80

.390 Average
Number on back 655
❑ 656 CL:Twins/Oakland A's .... .25 .11
❑ 657A Tug McGraw P1 .... .25 .11
Game Saver
Number on back 7
❑ 657B Tug McGraw P2 .... .25 .11
Game Saver
Number on back 657
❑ 658 CL: Rangers/Mariners .... .10 .05
❑ 659A Checklist P1 .... .10 .05
of Special Cards
Last lines on front
Wilson Most Hits
❑ 659B Checklist P2 .... .10 .05
of Special Cards
Last lines on front
Otis Series Starter
❑ 660 Steve Carlton P1 .... 1.00 .45
Golden Arm
(Number on back 660
Back 1066 Cardinals
❑ 660B Steve Carlton P2........ 2.00 .90
Golden Arm
1966 Cardinals

1982 Fleer

	NRMT	VG-E
COMPLETE SET (660)	60.00	27.00

❑ 1 Dusty Baker .40 .18
❑ 2 Robert Castillo .10 .05
❑ 3 Ron Cey .20 .09
❑ 4 Terry Forster .10 .05
❑ 5 Steve Garvey .40 .18
❑ 6 Dave Goltz .10 .05
❑ 7 Pedro Guerrero .20 .09
❑ 8 Burt Hooton .10 .05
❑ 9 Steve Howe .10 .05
❑ 10 Jay Johnstone .20 .09
❑ 11 Ken Landreaux .10 .05
❑ 12 Dave Lopes .20 .09
❑ 13 Mike A. Marshall .20 .09
❑ 14 Bobby Mitchell .10 .05
❑ 15 Rick Monday .10 .05
❑ 16 Tom Niedenfuer .10 .05
❑ 17 Ted Power RC .10 .05
❑ 18 Jerry Reuss UER .20 .09
("Home:" omitted)
❑ 19 Ron Roenicke .10 .05
❑ 20 Bill Russell .10 .05
❑ 21 Steve Sax RC .75 .35
❑ 22 Mike Scioscia .20 .09
❑ 23 Reggie Smith .20 .09
❑ 24 Dave Stewart RC 1.00 .45
❑ 25 Rick Sutcliffe .20 .09
❑ 26 Derrel Thomas .10 .05
❑ 27 Fernando Valenzuela .75 .35
❑ 28 Bob Welch .20 .09
❑ 29 Steve Yeager .10 .05
❑ 30 Bobby Brown .10 .05
❑ 31 Rick Cerone .10 .05
❑ 32 Ron Davis .10 .05
❑ 33 Bucky Dent .20 .09
❑ 34 Barry Foote .10 .05
❑ 35 George Frazier .10 .05
❑ 36 Oscar Gamble .10 .05
❑ 37 Rich Gossage .40 .18
❑ 38 Ron Guidry .20 .09
❑ 39 Reggie Jackson 1.00 .45
❑ 40 Tommy John .40 .18
❑ 41 Rudy May .10 .05
❑ 42 Larry Milbourne .10 .05
❑ 43 Jerry Mumphrey .10 .05
❑ 44 Bobby Murcer .20 .09
❑ 45 Gene Nelson .10 .05
❑ 46 Graig Nettles .20 .09
❑ 47 Johnny Oates .20 .09
❑ 48 Lou Piniella .20 .09
❑ 49 Willie Randolph .20 .09
❑ 50 Rick Reuschel .20 .09
❑ 51 Dave Revering .10 .05
❑ 52 Dave Righetti RC .75 .35
❑ 53 Aurelio Rodriguez .10 .05
❑ 54 Bob Watson .20 .09
❑ 55 Dennis Werth .10 .05
❑ 56 Dave Winfield .75 .35
❑ 57 Johnny Bench 1.25 .55
❑ 58 Bruce Berenyi .10 .05
❑ 59 Larry Biittner .10 .05
❑ 60 Scott Brown .10 .05
❑ 61 Dave Collins .10 .05
❑ 62 Geoff Combe .10 .05
❑ 63 Dave Concepcion .20 .09
❑ 64 Dan Driessen .10 .05
❑ 65 Joe Edelen .10 .05
❑ 66 George Foster .20 .09
❑ 67 Ken Griffey .20 .09
❑ 68 Paul Householder .10 .05
❑ 69 Tom Hume .10 .05
❑ 70 Junior Kennedy .10 .05
❑ 71 Ray Knight .20 .09
❑ 72 Mike LaCoss .10 .05
❑ 73 Rafael Landestoy .10 .05
❑ 74 Charlie Leibrandt .10 .05
❑ 75 Sam Mejias .10 .05
❑ 76 Paul Moskau .10 .05
❑ 77 Joe Nolan .10 .05
❑ 78 Mike O'Berry .10 .05
❑ 79 Ron Oester .10 .05
❑ 80 Frank Pastore .10 .05
❑ 81 Joe Price .10 .05
❑ 82 Tom Seaver 1.25 .55
❑ 83 Mario Soto .10 .05
❑ 84 Mike Vail .10 .05
❑ 85 Tony Armas .10 .05
❑ 86 Shooty Babitt .10 .05
❑ 87 Dave Beard .10 .05
❑ 88 Rick Bosetti .10 .05
❑ 89 Keith Drumwright .10 .05
❑ 90 Wayne Gross .10 .05
❑ 91 Mike Heath .10 .05
❑ 92 Rickey Henderson 2.50 1.10
❑ 93 Cliff Johnson .10 .05
❑ 94 Jeff Jones .10 .05
❑ 95 Matt Keough .10 .05
❑ 96 Brian Kingman .10 .05
❑ 97 Mickey Klutts .10 .05
❑ 98 Rick Langford .10 .05
❑ 99 Steve McCatty .10 .05
❑ 100 Dave McKay .10 .05
❑ 101 Dwayne Murphy .10 .05
❑ 102 Jeff Newman .10 .05
❑ 103 Mike Norris .10 .05
❑ 104 Bob Owchinko .10 .05
❑ 105 Mitchell Page .10 .05
❑ 106 Rob Picciolo .10 .05
❑ 107 Jim Spencer .10 .05
❑ 108 Fred Stanley .10 .05
❑ 109 Tom Underwood .10 .05
❑ 110 Joaquin Andujar .20 .09
❑ 111 Steve Braun .10 .05
❑ 112 Bob Forsch .10 .05
❑ 113 George Hendrick .10 .05
❑ 114 Keith Hernandez .20 .09
❑ 115 Tom Herr .20 .09
❑ 116 Dane Iorg .10 .05
❑ 117 Jim Kaat .20 .09
❑ 118 Tito Landrum .10 .05
❑ 119 Sixto Lezcano .10 .05
❑ 120 Mark Littell .10 .05
❑ 121 John Martin .10 .05
❑ 122 Silvio Martinez .10 .05
❑ 123 Ken Oberkfell .10 .05
❑ 124 Darrell Porter .20 .09
❑ 125 Mike Ramsey .10 .05
❑ 126 Orlando Sanchez .10 .05
❑ 127 Bob Shirley .10 .05
❑ 128 Lary Sorensen .10 .05
❑ 129 Bruce Sutter .20 .09
❑ 130 Bob Sykes .10 .05
❑ 131 Garry Templeton .10 .05
❑ 132 Gene Tenace .20 .09
❑ 133 Jerry Augustine .10 .05
❑ 134 Sal Bando .20 .09
❑ 135 Mark Brouhard .10 .05
❑ 136 Mike Caldwell .10 .05
❑ 137 Reggie Cleveland .10 .05
❑ 138 Cecil Cooper .20 .09
❑ 139 Jamie Easterly .10 .05
❑ 140 Marshall Edwards .10 .05
❑ 141 Rollie Fingers .75 .35
❑ 142 Jim Gantner .20 .09
❑ 143 Moose Haas .10 .05
❑ 144 Larry Hisle .10 .05
❑ 145 Roy Howell .10 .05
❑ 146 Rickey Keeton .10 .05
❑ 147 Randy Lerch .10 .05
❑ 148 Paul Molitor 1.00 .45
❑ 149 Don Money .10 .05
❑ 150 Charlie Moore .10 .05
❑ 151 Ben Oglivie .20 .09
❑ 152 Ted Simmons .20 .09
❑ 153 Jim Slaton .10 .05
❑ 154 Gorman Thomas .20 .09
❑ 155 Robin Yount .75 .35
❑ 156 Pete Vuckovich .10 .05
(Should precede Yount
in the team order)
❑ 157 Benny Ayala .10 .05
❑ 158 Mark Belanger .10 .05
❑ 159 Al Bumbry .10 .05
❑ 160 Terry Crowley .10 .05
❑ 161 Rich Dauer .10 .05
❑ 162 Doug DeCinces .20 .09
❑ 163 Rick Dempsey .20 .09
❑ 164 Jim Dwyer .10 .05
❑ 165 Mike Flanagan .20 .09
❑ 166 Dave Ford .10 .05
❑ 167 Dan Graham .10 .05
❑ 168 Wayne Krenchicki .10 .05
❑ 169 John Lowenstein .10 .05
❑ 170 Dennis Martinez .40 .18
❑ 171 Tippy Martinez .10 .05
❑ 172 Scott McGregor .10 .05
❑ 173 Jose Morales .10 .05
❑ 174 Eddie Murray 1.00 .45
❑ 175 Jim Palmer .75 .35
❑ 176 Cal Ripken RC 40.00 18.00
Fleer Ripken cards from 1982
through 1993 erroneously have 22
games played in 1981;not 23.
❑ 177 Gary Roenicke .10 .05
❑ 178 Lenn Sakata .10 .05
❑ 179 Ken Singleton .20 .09
❑ 180 Sammy Stewart .10 .05
❑ 181 Tim Stoddard .10 .05
❑ 182 Steve Stone .20 .09
❑ 183 Stan Bahnsen .10 .05
❑ 184 Ray Burris .10 .05
❑ 185 Gary Carter .40 .18
❑ 186 Warren Cromartie .10 .05
❑ 187 Andre Dawson .40 .18
❑ 188 Terry Francona .40 .18
❑ 189 Woodie Fryman .10 .05
❑ 190 Bill Gullickson .10 .05
❑ 191 Grant Jackson .10 .05
❑ 192 Wallace Johnson .10 .05
❑ 193 Charlie Lea .10 .05
❑ 194 Bill Lee .20 .09
❑ 195 Jerry Manuel .10 .05
❑ 196 Brad Mills .10 .05
❑ 197 John Milner .10 .05
❑ 198 Rowland Office .10 .05
❑ 199 David Palmer .10 .05
❑ 200 Larry Parrish .10 .05
❑ 201 Mike Phillips .10 .05
❑ 202 Tim Raines .75 .35
❑ 203 Bobby Ramos .10 .05

❑ 204 Jeff Reardon .40 .18
❑ 205 Steve Rogers .10 .05
❑ 206 Scott Sanderson .10 .05
❑ 207 Rodney Scott UER .40 .18
(Photo actually
Tim Raines)
❑ 208 Elias Sosa .10 .05
❑ 209 Chris Speier .10 .05
❑ 210 Tim Wallach RC .40 .18
❑ 211 Jerry White .10 .05
❑ 212 Alan Ashby .10 .05
❑ 213 Cesar Cedeno .20 .09
❑ 214 Jose Cruz .20 .09
❑ 215 Kiko Garcia .10 .05
❑ 216 Phil Garner .20 .09
❑ 217 Danny Heep .10 .05
❑ 218 Art Howe .20 .09
❑ 219 Bob Knepper .10 .05
❑ 220 Frank LaCorte .10 .05
❑ 221 Joe Niekro .20 .09
❑ 222 Joe Pittman .10 .05
❑ 223 Terry Puhl .10 .05
❑ 224 Luis Pujols .10 .05
❑ 225 Craig Reynolds .10 .05
❑ 226 J.R. Richard .20 .09
❑ 227 Dave Roberts .10 .05
❑ 228 Vern Ruhle .10 .05
❑ 229 Nolan Ryan 4.00 1.80
❑ 230 Joe Sambito .10 .05
❑ 231 Tony Scott .10 .05
❑ 232 Dave Smith .10 .05
❑ 233 Harry Spilman .10 .05
❑ 234 Don Sutton .75 .35
❑ 235 Dickie Thon .10 .05
❑ 236 Denny Walling .10 .05
❑ 237 Gary Woods .10 .05
❑ 238 Luis Aguayo .10 .05
❑ 239 Ramon Aviles .10 .05
❑ 240 Bob Boone .20 .09
❑ 241 Larry Bowa .20 .09
❑ 242 Warren Brusstar .10 .05
❑ 243 Steve Carlton .75 .35
❑ 244 Larry Christenson .10 .05
❑ 245 Dick Davis .10 .05
❑ 246 Greg Gross .10 .05
❑ 247 Sparky Lyle .20 .09
❑ 248 Garry Maddox .10 .05
❑ 249 Gary Matthews .20 .09
❑ 250 Bake McBride .10 .05
❑ 251 Tug McGraw .20 .09
❑ 252 Keith Moreland .10 .05
❑ 253 Dickie Noles .10 .05
❑ 254 Mike Proly .10 .05
❑ 255 Ron Reed .10 .05
❑ 256 Pete Rose 2.50 1.10
❑ 257 Dick Ruthven .10 .05
❑ 258 Mike Schmidt 1.50 .70
❑ 259 Lonnie Smith .20 .09
❑ 260 Manny Trillo .10 .05
❑ 261 Del Unser .10 .05
❑ 262 George Vukovich .10 .05
❑ 263 Tom Brookens .10 .05
❑ 264 George Cappuzzello .10 .05
❑ 265 Marty Castillo .10 .05
❑ 266 Al Cowens .10 .05
❑ 267 Kirk Gibson .75 .35
❑ 268 Richie Hebner .20 .09
❑ 269 Ron Jackson .10 .05
❑ 270 Lynn Jones .10 .05
❑ 271 Steve Kemp .10 .05
❑ 272 Rick Leach .10 .05
❑ 273 Aurelio Lopez .10 .05
❑ 274 Jack Morris .20 .09
❑ 275 Kevin Saucier .10 .05
❑ 276 Lance Parrish .40 .18
❑ 277 Rick Peters .10 .05
❑ 278 Dan Petry .10 .05
❑ 279 Dave Rozema .10 .05
❑ 280 Stan Papi .10 .05
❑ 281 Dan Schatzeder .10 .05
❑ 282 Champ Summers .10 .05
❑ 283 Alan Trammell .40 .18
❑ 284 Lou Whitaker .75 .35
❑ 285 Milt Wilcox .10 .05
❑ 286 John Wockenfuss .10 .05
❑ 287 Gary Allenson .10 .05
❑ 288 Tom Burgmeier .10 .05
❑ 289 Bill Campbell .10 .05
❑ 290 Mark Clear .10 .05
❑ 291 Steve Crawford .10 .05
❑ 292 Dennis Eckersley .75 .35
❑ 293 Dwight Evans .40 .18
❑ 294 Rich Gedman .20 .09
❑ 295 Garry Hancock .10 .05
❑ 296 Glenn Hoffman .10 .05
❑ 297 Bruce Hurst .10 .05
❑ 298 Carney Lansford .20 .09
❑ 299 Rick Miller .10 .05
❑ 300 Reid Nichols .10 .05
❑ 301 Bob Ojeda RC .40 .18
❑ 302 Tony Perez .75 .35
❑ 303 Chuck Rainey .10 .05
❑ 304 Jerry Remy .10 .05
❑ 305 Jim Rice .20 .09
❑ 306 Joe Rudi .10 .05
❑ 307 Bob Stanley .10 .05
❑ 308 Dave Stapleton .10 .05
❑ 309 Frank Tanana .20 .09
❑ 310 Mike Torrez .10 .05
❑ 311 John Tudor .10 .05
❑ 312 Carl Yastrzemski .75 .35
❑ 313 Buddy Bell .20 .09
❑ 314 Steve Comer .10 .05
❑ 315 Danny Darwin .10 .05
❑ 316 John Ellis .10 .05
❑ 317 John Grubb .10 .05
❑ 318 Rick Honeycutt .10 .05
❑ 319 Charlie Hough .20 .09
❑ 320 Ferguson Jenkins .75 .35
❑ 321 John Henry Johnson .10 .05
❑ 322 Jim Kern .10 .05
❑ 323 Jon Matlack .10 .05
❑ 324 Doc Medich .10 .05
❑ 325 Mario Mendoza .10 .05
❑ 326 Al Oliver .20 .09
❑ 327 Pat Putnam .10 .05
❑ 328 Mickey Rivers .10 .05
❑ 329 Leon Roberts .10 .05
❑ 330 Billy Sample .10 .05
❑ 331 Bill Stein .10 .05
❑ 332 Jim Sundberg .10 .05
❑ 333 Mark Wagner .10 .05
❑ 334 Bump Wills .10 .05
❑ 335 Bill Almon .10 .05
❑ 336 Harold Baines .75 .35
❑ 337 Ross Baumgarten .10 .05
❑ 338 Tony Bernazard .10 .05
❑ 339 Britt Burns .10 .05
❑ 340 Richard Dotson .10 .05
❑ 341 Jim Essian .10 .05
❑ 342 Ed Farmer .10 .05
❑ 343 Carlton Fisk .75 .35
❑ 344 Kevin Hickey .10 .05
❑ 345 LaMarr Hoyt .10 .05
❑ 346 Lamar Johnson .10 .05
❑ 347 Jerry Koosman .20 .09
❑ 348 Rusty Kuntz .10 .05
❑ 349 Dennis Lamp .10 .05
❑ 350 Ron LeFlore .20 .09
❑ 351 Chet Lemon .10 .05
❑ 352 Greg Luzinski .20 .09
❑ 353 Bob Molinaro .10 .05
❑ 354 Jim Morrison .10 .05
❑ 355 Wayne Nordhagen .10 .05
❑ 356 Greg Pryor .10 .05
❑ 357 Mike Squires .10 .05
❑ 358 Steve Trout .10 .05
❑ 359 Alan Bannister .10 .05
❑ 360 Len Barker .10 .05
❑ 361 Bert Blyleven .40 .18
❑ 362 Joe Charboneau .20 .09
❑ 363 John Denny .10 .05
❑ 364 Bo Diaz .10 .05
❑ 365 Miguel Dilone .10 .05
❑ 366 Jerry Dybzinski .10 .05
❑ 367 Wayne Garland .10 .05
❑ 368 Mike Hargrove .20 .09
❑ 369 Toby Harrah .20 .09
❑ 370 Ron Hassey .10 .05
❑ 371 Von Hayes .20 .09
❑ 372 Pat Kelly .10 .05
❑ 373 Duane Kuiper .10 .05
❑ 374 Rick Manning .10 .05
❑ 375 Sid Monge .10 .05
❑ 376 Jorge Orta .10 .05
❑ 377 Dave Rosello .10 .05
❑ 378 Dan Spillner .10 .05
❑ 379 Mike Stanton .10 .05
❑ 380 Andre Thornton .10 .05
❑ 381 Tom Veryzer .10 .05
❑ 382 Rick Waits .10 .05
❑ 383 Doyle Alexander .10 .05
❑ 384 Vida Blue .20 .09
❑ 385 Fred Breining .10 .05
❑ 386 Enos Cabell .10 .05
❑ 387 Jack Clark .20 .09
❑ 388 Darrell Evans .20 .09
❑ 389 Tom Griffin .10 .05
❑ 390 Larry Herndon .10 .05
❑ 391 Al Holland .10 .05
❑ 392 Gary Lavelle .10 .05
❑ 393 Johnnie LeMaster .10 .05
❑ 394 Jerry Martin .10 .05
❑ 395 Milt May .10 .05
❑ 396 Greg Minton .10 .05
❑ 397 Joe Morgan .75 .35
❑ 398 Joe Pettini .10 .05
❑ 399 Allen Ripley .10 .05
❑ 400 Billy Smith .10 .05
❑ 401 Rennie Stennett .10 .05
❑ 402 Ed Whitson .10 .05
❑ 403 Jim Wohlford .10 .05
❑ 404 Willie Aikens .10 .05
❑ 405 George Brett 1.50 .70
❑ 406 Ken Brett .10 .05
❑ 407 Dave Chalk .10 .05
❑ 408 Rich Gale .10 .05
❑ 409 Cesar Geronimo .10 .05
❑ 410 Larry Gura .10 .05
❑ 411 Clint Hurdle .10 .05
❑ 412 Mike Jones .10 .05
❑ 413 Dennis Leonard .10 .05
❑ 414 Renie Martin .10 .05
❑ 415 Lee May .20 .09
❑ 416 Hal McRae .20 .09
❑ 417 Darryl Motley .10 .05
❑ 418 Rance Mulliniks .10 .05
❑ 419 Amos Otis .20 .09
❑ 420 Ken Phelps .10 .05
❑ 421 Jamie Quirk .10 .05
❑ 422 Dan Quisenberry .20 .09
❑ 423 Paul Splittorff .10 .05
❑ 424 U.L. Washington .10 .05
❑ 425 John Wathan .10 .05
❑ 426 Frank White .20 .09
❑ 427 Willie Wilson .20 .09
❑ 428 Brian Asselstine .10 .05
❑ 429 Bruce Benedict .10 .05
❑ 430 Tommy Boggs .10 .05
❑ 431 Larry Bradford .10 .05
❑ 432 Rick Camp .10 .05
❑ 433 Chris Chambliss .20 .09
❑ 434 Gene Garber .10 .05
❑ 435 Preston Hanna .10 .05
❑ 436 Bob Horner .20 .09
❑ 437 Glenn Hubbard .10 .05
❑ 438A Al Hrabosky ERR 8.00 3.60
(Height 5'1"
All on reverse)
❑ 438B Al Hrabosky ERR .40 .18
(Height 5'1")
❑ 438C Al Hrabosky .20 .09
(Height 5'10")
❑ 439 Rufino Linares .10 .05
❑ 440 Rick Mahler .10 .05
❑ 441 Ed Miller .10 .05
❑ 442 John Montefusco .10 .05
❑ 443 Dale Murphy .75 .35
❑ 444 Phil Niekro .75 .35
❑ 445 Gaylord Perry .75 .35
❑ 446 Biff Pocoroba .10 .05
❑ 447 Rafael Ramirez .10 .05
❑ 448 Jerry Royster .10 .05
❑ 449 Claudell Washington .10 .05
❑ 450 Don Aase .10 .05
❑ 451 Don Baylor .40 .18
❑ 452 Juan Beniquez .10 .05
❑ 453 Rick Burleson .10 .05

	No.	Player		
❑	454	Bert Campaneris	.20	.09
❑	455	Rod Carew	.75	.35
❑	456	Bob Clark	.10	.05
❑	457	Brian Downing	.10	.05
❑	458	Dan Ford	.10	.05
❑	459	Ken Forsch	.10	.05
❑	460A	Dave Frost (5 mm space before ERA)	.10	.05
❑	460B	Dave Frost (1 mm space)	.10	.05
❑	461	Bobby Grich	.20	.09
❑	462	Larry Harlow	.10	.05
❑	463	John Harris	.10	.05
❑	464	Andy Hassler	.10	.05
❑	465	Butch Hobson	.10	.05
❑	466	Jesse Jefferson	.10	.05
❑	467	Bruce Kison	.10	.05
❑	468	Fred Lynn	.20	.09
❑	469	Angel Moreno	.10	.05
❑	470	Ed Ott	.10	.05
❑	471	Fred Patek	.10	.05
❑	472	Steve Renko	.10	.05
❑	473	Mike Witt	.20	.09
❑	474	Geoff Zahn	.10	.05
❑	475	Gary Alexander	.10	.05
❑	476	Dale Berra	.10	.05
❑	477	Kurt Bevacqua	.10	.05
❑	478	Jim Bibby	.10	.05
❑	479	John Candelaria	.10	.05
❑	480	Victor Cruz	.10	.05
❑	481	Mike Easler	.10	.05
❑	482	Tim Foli	.10	.05
❑	483	Lee Lacy	.10	.05
❑	484	Vance Law	.10	.05
❑	485	Bill Madlock	.20	.09
❑	486	Willie Montanez	.10	.05
❑	487	Omar Moreno	.10	.05
❑	488	Steve Nicosia	.10	.05
❑	489	Dave Parker	.20	.09
❑	490	Tony Pena	.20	.09
❑	491	Pascual Perez	.10	.05
❑	492	Johnny Ray	.20	.09
❑	493	Rick Rhoden	.10	.05
❑	494	Bill Robinson	.10	.05
❑	495	Don Robinson	.10	.05
❑	496	Enrique Romo	.10	.05
❑	497	Rod Scurry	.10	.05
❑	498	Eddie Solomon	.10	.05
❑	499	Willie Stargell	.75	.35
❑	500	Kent Tekulve	.20	.09
❑	501	Jason Thompson	.10	.05
❑	502	Glenn Abbott	.10	.05
❑	503	Jim Anderson	.10	.05
❑	504	Floyd Bannister	.10	.05
❑	505	Bruce Bochte	.10	.05
❑	506	Jeff Burroughs	.10	.05
❑	507	Bryan Clark	.10	.05
❑	508	Ken Clay	.10	.05
❑	509	Julio Cruz	.10	.05
❑	510	Dick Drago	.10	.05
❑	511	Gary Gray	.10	.05
❑	512	Dan Meyer	.10	.05
❑	513	Jerry Narron	.10	.05
❑	514	Tom Paciorek	.20	.09
❑	515	Casey Parsons	.10	.05
❑	516	Lenny Randle	.10	.05
❑	517	Shane Rawley	.10	.05
❑	518	Joe Simpson	.10	.05
❑	519	Richie Zisk	.10	.05
❑	520	Neil Allen	.10	.05
❑	521	Bob Bailor	.10	.05
❑	522	Hubie Brooks	.20	.09
❑	523	Mike Cubbage	.10	.05
❑	524	Pete Falcone	.10	.05
❑	525	Doug Flynn	.10	.05
❑	526	Tom Hausman	.10	.05
❑	527	Ron Hodges	.10	.05
❑	528	Randy Jones	.10	.05
❑	529	Mike Jorgensen	.10	.05
❑	530	Dave Kingman	.20	.09
❑	531	Ed Lynch	.10	.05
❑	532	Mike G. Marshall	.10	.05
❑	533	Lee Mazzilli	.10	.05
❑	534	Dyar Miller	.10	.05
❑	535	Mike Scott	.20	.09
❑	536	Rusty Staub	.20	.09
❑	537	John Stearns	.10	.05
❑	538	Craig Swan	.10	.05
❑	539	Frank Taveras	.10	.05
❑	540	Alex Trevino	.10	.05
❑	541	Ellis Valentine	.10	.05
❑	542	Mookie Wilson	.20	.09
❑	543	Joel Youngblood	.10	.05
❑	544	Pat Zachry	.10	.05
❑	545	Glenn Adams	.10	.05
❑	546	Fernando Arroyo	.10	.05
❑	547	John Verhoeven	.10	.05
❑	548	Sal Butera	.10	.05
❑	549	John Castino	.10	.05
❑	550	Don Cooper	.10	.05
❑	551	Doug Corbett	.10	.05
❑	552	Dave Engle	.10	.05
❑	553	Roger Erickson	.10	.05
❑	554	Danny Goodwin	.10	.05
❑	555A	Darrell Jackson (Black cap)	.40	.18
❑	555B	Darrell Jackson (Red cap with T)	.20	.09
❑	555C	Darrell Jackson (Red cap, no emblem)	3.00	1.35
❑	556	Pete Mackanin	.10	.05
❑	557	Jack O'Connor	.10	.05
❑	558	Hosken Powell	.10	.05
❑	559	Pete Redfern	.10	.05
❑	560	Roy Smalley	.10	.05
❑	561	Chuck Baker UER (Shortshop on front)	.10	.05
❑	562	Gary Ward	.10	.05
❑	563	Rob Wilfong	.10	.05
❑	564	Al Williams	.10	.05
❑	565	Butch Wynegar	.10	.05
❑	566	Randy Bass RC	.10	.05
❑	567	Juan Bonilla	.10	.05
❑	568	Danny Boone	.10	.05
❑	569	John Curtis	.10	.05
❑	570	Juan Eichelberger	.10	.05
❑	571	Barry Evans	.10	.05
❑	572	Tim Flannery	.10	.05
❑	573	Ruppert Jones	.10	.05
❑	574	Terry Kennedy	.10	.05
❑	575	Joe Lefebvre	.10	.05
❑	576A	John Littlefield ERR (Left handed; reverse negative)	80.00	36.00
❑	576B	John Littlefield COR (Right handed)	.20	.09
❑	577	Gary Lucas	.10	.05
❑	578	Steve Mura	.10	.05
❑	579	Broderick Perkins	.10	.05
❑	580	Gene Richards	.10	.05
❑	581	Luis Salazar	.10	.05
❑	582	Ozzie Smith	1.50	.70
❑	583	John Urrea	.10	.05
❑	584	Chris Welsh	.10	.05
❑	585	Rick Wise	.10	.05
❑	586	Doug Bird	.10	.05
❑	587	Tim Blackwell	.10	.05
❑	588	Bobby Bonds	.20	.09
❑	589	Bill Buckner	.20	.09
❑	590	Bill Caudill	.10	.05
❑	591	Hector Cruz	.10	.05
❑	592	Jody Davis	.10	.05
❑	593	Ivan DeJesus	.10	.05
❑	594	Steve Dillard	.10	.05
❑	595	Leon Durham	.10	.05
❑	596	Rawly Eastwick	.10	.05
❑	597	Steve Henderson	.10	.05
❑	598	Mike Krukow	.10	.05
❑	599	Mike Lum	.10	.05
❑	600	Randy Martz	.10	.05
❑	601	Jerry Morales	.10	.05
❑	602	Ken Reitz	.10	.05
❑	603	Lee Smith RC ERR (Cubs logo reversed)	2.00	.90
❑	603B	Lee Smith RC COR	6.00	2.70
❑	604	Dick Tidrow	.10	.05
❑	605	Jim Tracy	.10	.05
❑	606	Mike Tyson	.10	.05
❑	607	Ty Waller	.10	.05
❑	608	Danny Ainge	1.00	.45
❑	609	Jorge Bell RC	.75	.35
❑	610	Mark Bomback	.10	.05
❑	611	Barry Bonnell	.10	.05
❑	612	Jim Clancy	.10	.05
❑	613	Damaso Garcia	.10	.05
❑	614	Jerry Garvin	.10	.05
❑	615	Alfredo Griffin	.10	.05
❑	616	Garth Iorg	.10	.05
❑	617	Luis Leal	.10	.05
❑	618	Ken Macha	.10	.05
❑	619	John Mayberry	.10	.05
❑	620	Joey McLaughlin	.10	.05
❑	621	Lloyd Moseby	.10	.05
❑	622	Dave Stieb	.20	.09
❑	623	Jackson Todd	.10	.05
❑	624	Willie Upshaw	.10	.05
❑	625	Otto Velez	.10	.05
❑	626	Ernie Whitt	.10	.05
❑	627	Alvis Woods	.10	.05
❑	628	All Star Game Cleveland, Ohio	.20	.09
❑	629	All Star Infielders Frank White Bucky Dent	.20	.09
❑	630	Big Red Machine Dan Driessen Dave Concepcion George Foster	.20	.09
❑	631	Bruce Sutter Top NL Relief Pitcher	.10	.05
❑	632	Steve and Carlton Steve Carlton Carlton Fisk	.40	.18
❑	633	Carl Yastrzemski 3000th Game	.75	.35
❑	634	Dynamic Duo Johnny Bench Tom Seaver	1.00	.45
❑	635	West Meets East Fernando Valenzuela Gary Carter	.20	.09
❑	636A	F.Valenzuela: NL SO King "he" NL	.75	.35
❑	636B	F.Valenzuela: NL SO King "the" NL	.75	.35
❑	637	Mike Schmidt Home Run King	.40	.18
❑	638	NL All Stars Gary Carter Dave Parker	.20	.09
❑	639	Perfect Game UER Len Barker Bo Diaz (Catcher actually Ron Hassey)	.20	.09
❑	640	Pete and Re-Pete Pete Rose Pete Rose Jr.	.75	.35
❑	641	Phillies Finest Lonnie Smith Mike Schmidt Steve Carlton	.75	.35
❑	642	Red Sox Reunion Fred Lynn Dwight Evans	.20	.09
❑	643	Rickey Henderson Most Hits and Runs	1.25	.55
❑	644	Rollie Fingers Most Saves AL	.20	.09
❑	645	Tom Seaver Most 1981 Wins	.40	.18
❑	646	Yankee Powerhouse Reggie Jackson Dave Winfield (Comma on back after outfielder)	.75	.35
❑	646B	Yankee Powerhouse Reggie Jackson Dave Winfield (No comma)	2.00	.90
❑	647	CL: Yankees/Dodgers	.10	.05
❑	648	CL: A's/Reds	.10	.05
❑	649	CL: Cards/Brewers	.10	.05
❑	650	CL: Expos/Orioles	.10	.05
❑	651	CL: Astros/Phillies	.10	.05
❑	652	CL: Tigers/Red Sox	.10	.05
❑	653	CL: Rangers/White Sox	.10	.05
❑	654	CL: Giants/Indians	.10	.05

Card		
❑ 655 CL: Royals/Braves	.10	.05
❑ 656 CL: Angels/Pirates	.10	.05
❑ 657 CL: Mariners/Mets	.10	.05
❑ 658 CL: Padres/Twins	.10	.05
❑ 659 CL: Blue Jays/Cubs	.10	.05
❑ 660 Specials Checklist	.10	.05

1983 Fleer

	NRMT	VG-E
COMPLETE SET (660)	60.00	27.00
❑ 1 Joaquin Andujar	.10	.05
❑ 2 Doug Bair	.10	.05
❑ 3 Steve Braun	.10	.05
❑ 4 Glenn Brummer	.10	.05
❑ 5 Bob Forsch	.10	.05
❑ 6 David Green	.10	.05
❑ 7 George Hendrick	.10	.05
❑ 8 Keith Hernandez	.20	.09
❑ 9 Tom Herr	.20	.09
❑ 10 Dane Iorg	.10	.05
❑ 11 Jim Kaat	.20	.09
❑ 12 Jeff Lahti	.10	.05
❑ 13 Tito Landrum	.10	.05
❑ 14 Dave LaPoint	.10	.05
❑ 15 Willie McGee RC	1.50	.70
❑ 16 Steve Mura	.10	.05
❑ 17 Ken Oberkfell	.10	.05
❑ 18 Darrell Porter	.10	.05
❑ 19 Mike Ramsey	.10	.05
❑ 20 Gene Roof	.10	.05
❑ 21 Lonnie Smith	.10	.05
❑ 22 Ozzie Smith	1.25	.55
❑ 23 John Stuper	.10	.05
❑ 24 Bruce Sutter	.20	.09
❑ 25 Gene Tenace	.20	.09
❑ 26 Jerry Augustine	.10	.05
❑ 27 Dwight Bernard	.10	.05
❑ 28 Mark Brouhard	.10	.05
❑ 29 Mike Caldwell	.10	.05
❑ 30 Cecil Cooper	.20	.09
❑ 31 Jamie Easterly	.10	.05
❑ 32 Marshall Edwards	.10	.05
❑ 33 Rollie Fingers	.75	.35
❑ 34 Jim Gantner	.10	.05
❑ 35 Moose Haas	.10	.05
❑ 36 Roy Howell	.10	.05
❑ 37 Pete Ladd	.10	.05
❑ 38 Bob McClure	.10	.05
❑ 39 Doc Medich	.10	.05
❑ 40 Paul Molitor	1.00	.45
❑ 41 Don Money	.10	.05
❑ 42 Charlie Moore	.10	.05
❑ 43 Ben Oglivie	.10	.05
❑ 44 Ed Romero	.10	.05
❑ 45 Ted Simmons	.20	.09
❑ 46 Jim Slaton	.10	.05
❑ 47 Don Sutton	.75	.35
❑ 48 Gorman Thomas	.10	.05
❑ 49 Pete Vuckovich	.10	.05
❑ 50 Ned Yost	.10	.05
❑ 51 Robin Yount	.75	.35
❑ 52 Benny Ayala	.10	.05
❑ 53 Bob Bonner	.10	.05
❑ 54 Al Bumbry	.10	.05
❑ 55 Terry Crowley	.10	.05
❑ 56 Storm Davis RC	.10	.05
❑ 57 Rich Dauer	.10	.05
❑ 58 Rick Dempsey UER (Posing batting lefty)	.20	.09
❑ 59 Jim Dwyer	.10	.05
❑ 60 Mike Flanagan	.20	.09
❑ 61 Dan Ford	.10	.05
❑ 62 Glenn Gulliver	.10	.05
❑ 63 John Lowenstein	.10	.05
❑ 64 Dennis Martinez	.20	.09
❑ 65 Tippy Martinez	.10	.05
❑ 66 Scott McGregor	.10	.05
❑ 67 Eddie Murray	1.00	.45
❑ 68 Joe Nolan	.10	.05
❑ 69 Jim Palmer	.75	.35
❑ 70 Cal Ripken	8.00	3.60
❑ 71 Gary Roenicke	.10	.05
❑ 72 Lenn Sakata	.10	.05
❑ 73 Ken Singleton	.10	.05
❑ 74 Sammy Stewart	.10	.05
❑ 75 Tim Stoddard	.10	.05
❑ 76 Don Aase	.10	.05
❑ 77 Don Baylor	.40	.18
❑ 78 Juan Beniquez	.10	.05
❑ 79 Bob Boone	.20	.09
❑ 80 Rick Burleson	.10	.05
❑ 81 Rod Carew	.75	.35
❑ 82 Bobby Clark	.10	.05
❑ 83 Doug Corbett	.10	.05
❑ 84 John Curtis	.10	.05
❑ 85 Doug DeCinces	.20	.09
❑ 86 Brian Downing	.10	.05
❑ 87 Joe Ferguson	.10	.05
❑ 88 Tim Foli	.10	.05
❑ 89 Ken Forsch	.10	.05
❑ 90 Dave Goltz	.10	.05
❑ 91 Bobby Grich	.20	.09
❑ 92 Andy Hassler	.10	.05
❑ 93 Reggie Jackson	1.00	.45
❑ 94 Ron Jackson	.10	.05
❑ 95 Tommy John	.40	.18
❑ 96 Bruce Kison	.10	.05
❑ 97 Fred Lynn	.20	.09
❑ 98 Ed Ott	.10	.05
❑ 99 Steve Renko	.10	.05
❑ 100 Luis Sanchez	.10	.05
❑ 101 Rob Wilfong	.10	.05
❑ 102 Mike Witt	.10	.05
❑ 103 Geoff Zahn	.10	.05
❑ 104 Willie Aikens	.10	.05
❑ 105 Mike Armstrong	.10	.05
❑ 106 Vida Blue	.20	.09
❑ 107 Bud Black RC	.20	.09
❑ 108 George Brett	1.50	.70
❑ 109 Bill Castro	.10	.05
❑ 110 Onix Concepcion	.10	.05
❑ 111 Dave Frost	.10	.05
❑ 112 Cesar Geronimo	.10	.05
❑ 113 Larry Gura	.10	.05
❑ 114 Steve Hammond	.10	.05
❑ 115 Don Hood	.10	.05
❑ 116 Dennis Leonard	.10	.05
❑ 117 Jerry Martin	.10	.05
❑ 118 Lee May	.20	.09
❑ 119 Hal McRae	.20	.09
❑ 120 Amos Otis	.20	.09
❑ 121 Greg Pryor	.10	.05
❑ 122 Dan Quisenberry	.20	.09
❑ 123 Don Slaught RC	.40	.18
❑ 124 Paul Splittorff	.10	.05
❑ 125 U.L. Washington	.10	.05
❑ 126 John Wathan	.10	.05
❑ 127 Frank White	.20	.09
❑ 128 Willie Wilson	.20	.09
❑ 129 Steve Bedrosian UER (Height 6'33")	.20	.09
❑ 130 Bruce Benedict	.10	.05
❑ 131 Tommy Boggs	.10	.05
❑ 132 Brett Butler	.75	.35
❑ 133 Rick Camp	.10	.05
❑ 134 Chris Chambliss	.20	.09
❑ 135 Ken Dayley	.10	.05
❑ 136 Gene Garber	.10	.05
❑ 137 Terry Harper	.10	.05
❑ 138 Bob Horner	.10	.05
❑ 139 Glenn Hubbard	.10	.05
❑ 140 Rufino Linares	.10	.05
❑ 141 Rick Mahler	.10	.05
❑ 142 Dale Murphy	.75	.35
❑ 143 Phil Niekro	.75	.35
❑ 144 Pascual Perez	.10	.05
❑ 145 Biff Pocoroba	.10	.05
❑ 146 Rafael Ramirez	.10	.05
❑ 147 Jerry Royster	.10	.05
❑ 148 Ken Smith	.10	.05
❑ 149 Bob Walk	.10	.05
❑ 150 Claudell Washington	.10	.05
❑ 151 Bob Watson	.20	.09
❑ 152 Larry Whisenton	.10	.05
❑ 153 Porfirio Altamirano	.10	.05
❑ 154 Marty Bystrom	.10	.05
❑ 155 Steve Carlton	.75	.35
❑ 156 Larry Christenson	.10	.05
❑ 157 Ivan DeJesus	.10	.05
❑ 158 John Denny	.10	.05
❑ 159 Bob Dernier	.10	.05
❑ 160 Bo Diaz	.10	.05
❑ 161 Ed Farmer	.10	.05
❑ 162 Greg Gross	.10	.05
❑ 163 Mike Krukow	.10	.05
❑ 164 Garry Maddox	.10	.05
❑ 165 Gary Matthews	.20	.09
❑ 166 Tug McGraw	.20	.09
❑ 167 Bob Molinaro	.10	.05
❑ 168 Sid Monge	.10	.05
❑ 169 Ron Reed	.10	.05
❑ 170 Bill Robinson	.10	.05
❑ 171 Pete Rose	2.50	1.10
❑ 172 Dick Ruthven	.10	.05
❑ 173 Mike Schmidt	1.50	.70
❑ 174 Manny Trillo	.10	.05
❑ 175 Ozzie Virgil	.10	.05
❑ 176 George Vukovich	.10	.05
❑ 177 Gary Allenson	.10	.05
❑ 178 Luis Aponte	.10	.05
❑ 179 Wade Boggs RC	10.00	4.50
❑ 180 Tom Burgmeier	.10	.05
❑ 181 Mark Clear	.10	.05
❑ 182 Dennis Eckersley	.75	.35
❑ 183 Dwight Evans	.20	.09
❑ 184 Rich Gedman	.10	.05
❑ 185 Glenn Hoffman	.10	.05
❑ 186 Bruce Hurst	.10	.05
❑ 187 Carney Lansford	.20	.09
❑ 188 Rick Miller	.10	.05
❑ 189 Reid Nichols	.10	.05
❑ 190 Bob Ojeda	.10	.05
❑ 191 Tony Perez	.75	.35
❑ 192 Chuck Rainey	.10	.05
❑ 193 Jerry Remy	.10	.05
❑ 194 Jim Rice	.20	.09
❑ 195 Bob Stanley	.10	.05
❑ 196 Dave Stapleton	.10	.05
❑ 197 Mike Torrez	.10	.05
❑ 198 John Tudor	.10	.05
❑ 199 Julio Valdez	.10	.05
❑ 200 Carl Yastrzemski	.75	.35
❑ 201 Dusty Baker	.20	.09
❑ 202 Joe Beckwith	.10	.05
❑ 203 Greg Brock	.10	.05
❑ 204 Ron Cey	.20	.09
❑ 205 Terry Forster	.10	.05
❑ 206 Steve Garvey	.40	.18
❑ 207 Pedro Guerrero	.20	.09
❑ 208 Burt Hooton	.10	.05
❑ 209 Steve Howe	.10	.05
❑ 210 Ken Landreaux	.10	.05
❑ 211 Mike Marshall	.10	.05
❑ 212 Candy Maldonado RC	.20	.09
❑ 213 Rick Monday	.10	.05
❑ 214 Tom Niedenfuer	.10	.05
❑ 215 Jorge Orta	.10	.05
❑ 216 Jerry Reuss UER ("Home:" omitted)	.20	.09
❑ 217 Ron Roenicke	.10	.05
❑ 218 Vicente Romo	.10	.05
❑ 219 Bill Russell	.10	.05
❑ 220 Steve Sax	.20	.09
❑ 221 Mike Scioscia	.20	.09
❑ 222 Dave Stewart	.20	.09
❑ 223 Derrel Thomas	.10	.05
❑ 224 Fernando Valenzuela	.40	.18
❑ 225 Bob Welch	.20	.09

❑ 226 Ricky Wright .10 .05
❑ 227 Steve Yeager .10 .05
❑ 228 Bill Almon .10 .05
❑ 229 Harold Baines .75 .35
❑ 230 Salome Barojas .10 .05
❑ 231 Tony Bernazard .10 .05
❑ 232 Britt Burns .10 .05
❑ 233 Richard Dotson .10 .05
❑ 234 Ernesto Escarrega .10 .05
❑ 235 Carlton Fisk .75 .35
❑ 236 Jerry Hairston .10 .05
❑ 237 Kevin Hickey .10 .05
❑ 238 LaMarr Hoyt .20 .09
❑ 239 Steve Kemp .10 .05
❑ 240 Jim Kern .10 .05
❑ 241 Ron Kittle RC .40 .18
❑ 242 Jerry Koosman .20 .09
❑ 243 Dennis Lamp .10 .05
❑ 244 Rudy Law .10 .05
❑ 245 Vance Law .10 .05
❑ 246 Ron LeFlore .10 .05
❑ 247 Greg Luzinski .20 .09
❑ 248 Tom Paciorek .20 .09
❑ 249 Aurelio Rodriguez .10 .05
❑ 250 Mike Squires .10 .05
❑ 251 Steve Trout .10 .05
❑ 252 Jim Barr .10 .05
❑ 253 Dave Bergman .10 .05
❑ 254 Fred Breining .10 .05
❑ 255 Bob Brenly .10 .05
❑ 256 Jack Clark .20 .09
❑ 257 Chili Davis .75 .35
❑ 258 Darrell Evans .20 .09
❑ 259 Alan Fowlkes .10 .05
❑ 260 Rich Gale .10 .05
❑ 261 Atlee Hammaker .10 .05
❑ 262 Al Holland .10 .05
❑ 263 Duane Kuiper .10 .05
❑ 264 Bill Laskey .10 .05
❑ 265 Gary Lavelle .10 .05
❑ 266 Johnnie LeMaster .10 .05
❑ 267 Renie Martin .10 .05
❑ 268 Milt May .10 .05
❑ 269 Greg Minton .10 .05
❑ 270 Joe Morgan .75 .35
❑ 271 Tom O'Malley .10 .05
❑ 272 Reggie Smith .20 .09
❑ 273 Guy Sularz .10 .05
❑ 274 Champ Summers .10 .05
❑ 275 Max Venable .10 .05
❑ 276 Jim Wohlford .10 .05
❑ 277 Ray Burris .10 .05
❑ 278 Gary Carter .40 .18
❑ 279 Warren Cromartie .10 .05
❑ 280 Andre Dawson .40 .18
❑ 281 Terry Francona .10 .05
❑ 282 Doug Flynn .10 .05
❑ 283 Woodie Fryman .10 .05
❑ 284 Bill Gullickson .10 .05
❑ 285 Wallace Johnson .10 .05
❑ 286 Charlie Lea .10 .05
❑ 287 Randy Lerch .10 .05
❑ 288 Brad Mills .10 .05
❑ 289 Dan Norman .10 .05
❑ 290 Al Oliver .20 .09
❑ 291 David Palmer .10 .05
❑ 292 Tim Raines .75 .35
❑ 293 Jeff Reardon .20 .09
❑ 294 Steve Rogers .10 .05
❑ 295 Scott Sanderson .10 .05
❑ 296 Dan Schatzeder .10 .05
❑ 297 Bryn Smith .10 .05
❑ 298 Chris Speier .10 .05
❑ 299 Tim Wallach .20 .09
❑ 300 Jerry White .10 .05
❑ 301 Joel Youngblood .10 .05
❑ 302 Ross Baumgarten .10 .05
❑ 303 Dale Berra .10 .05
❑ 304 John Candelaria .10 .05
❑ 305 Dick Davis .10 .05
❑ 306 Mike Easler .10 .05
❑ 307 Richie Hebner .20 .09
❑ 308 Lee Lacy .10 .05
❑ 309 Bill Madlock .20 .09
❑ 310 Larry McWilliams .10 .05
❑ 311 John Milner .10 .05
❑ 312 Omar Moreno .10 .05
❑ 313 Jim Morrison .10 .05
❑ 314 Steve Nicosia .10 .05
❑ 315 Dave Parker .20 .09
❑ 316 Tony Pena .10 .05
❑ 317 Johnny Ray .10 .05
❑ 318 Rick Rhoden .10 .05
❑ 319 Don Robinson .10 .05
❑ 320 Enrique Romo .10 .05
❑ 321 Manny Sarmiento .10 .05
❑ 322 Rod Scurry .10 .05
❑ 323 Jimmy Smith .10 .05
❑ 324 Willie Stargell .75 .35
❑ 325 Jason Thompson .10 .05
❑ 326 Kent Tekulve .20 .09
❑ 327A Tom Brookens .10 .05
(Short .375" brown box shaded in on card back)
❑ 327B Tom Brookens .10 .05
(Longer 1.25" brown box shaded in on card back)
❑ 328 Enos Cabell .10 .05
❑ 329 Kirk Gibson .75 .35
❑ 330 Larry Herndon .10 .05
❑ 331 Mike Ivie .10 .05
❑ 332 Howard Johnson RC .75 .35
❑ 333 Lynn Jones .10 .05
❑ 334 Rick Leach .10 .05
❑ 335 Chet Lemon .10 .05
❑ 336 Jack Morris .20 .09
❑ 337 Lance Parrish .20 .09
❑ 338 Larry Pashnick .10 .05
❑ 339 Dan Petry .10 .05
❑ 340 Dave Rozema .10 .05
❑ 341 Dave Rucker .10 .05
❑ 342 Elias Sosa .10 .05
❑ 343 Dave Tobik .10 .05
❑ 344 Alan Trammell .40 .18
❑ 345 Jerry Turner .10 .05
❑ 346 Jerry Ujdur .10 .05
❑ 347 Pat Underwood .10 .05
❑ 348 Lou Whitaker .40 .18
❑ 349 Milt Wilcox .10 .05
❑ 350 Glenn Wilson .20 .09
❑ 351 John Wockenfuss .10 .05
❑ 352 Kurt Bevacqua .10 .05
❑ 353 Juan Bonilla .10 .05
❑ 354 Floyd Chiffer .10 .05
❑ 355 Luis DeLeon .10 .05
❑ 356 Dave Dravecky RC .75 .35
❑ 357 Dave Edwards .10 .05
❑ 358 Juan Eichelberger .10 .05
❑ 359 Tim Flannery .10 .05
❑ 360 Tony Gwynn RC 20.00 9.00
❑ 361 Ruppert Jones .10 .05
❑ 362 Terry Kennedy .10 .05
❑ 363 Joe Lefebvre .10 .05
❑ 364 Sixto Lezcano .10 .05
❑ 365 Tim Lollar .10 .05
❑ 366 Gary Lucas .10 .05
❑ 367 John Montefusco .10 .05
❑ 368 Broderick Perkins .10 .05
❑ 369 Joe Pittman .10 .05
❑ 370 Gene Richards .10 .05
❑ 371 Luis Salazar .10 .05
❑ 372 Eric Show .10 .05
❑ 373 Garry Templeton .10 .05
❑ 374 Chris Welsh .10 .05
❑ 375 Alan Wiggins .10 .05
❑ 376 Rick Cerone .10 .05
❑ 377 Dave Collins .10 .05
❑ 378 Roger Erickson .10 .05
❑ 379 George Frazier .10 .05
❑ 380 Oscar Gamble .10 .05
❑ 381 Rich Gossage .40 .18
❑ 382 Ken Griffey .20 .09
❑ 383 Ron Guidry .20 .09
❑ 384 Dave LaRoche .10 .05
❑ 385 Rudy May .10 .05
❑ 386 John Mayberry .10 .05
❑ 387 Lee Mazzilli .10 .05
❑ 388 Mike Morgan .10 .05
❑ 389 Jerry Mumphrey .10 .05
❑ 390 Bobby Murcer .20 .09
❑ 391 Graig Nettles .20 .09
❑ 392 Lou Piniella .20 .09
❑ 393 Willie Randolph .20 .09
❑ 394 Shane Rawley .10 .05
❑ 395 Dave Righetti .20 .09
❑ 396 Andre Robertson .10 .05
❑ 397 Roy Smalley .10 .05
❑ 398 Dave Winfield .75 .35
❑ 399 Butch Wynegar .10 .05
❑ 400 Chris Bando .10 .05
❑ 401 Alan Bannister .10 .05
❑ 402 Len Barker .10 .05
❑ 403 Tom Brennan .10 .05
❑ 404 Carmelo Castillo .10 .05
❑ 405 Miguel Dilone .10 .05
❑ 406 Jerry Dybzinski .10 .05
❑ 407 Mike Fischlin .10 .05
❑ 408 Ed Glynn UER .10 .05
(Photo actually Bud Anderson)
❑ 409 Mike Hargrove .20 .09
❑ 410 Toby Harrah .10 .05
❑ 411 Ron Hassey .10 .05
❑ 412 Von Hayes .20 .09
❑ 413 Rick Manning .10 .05
❑ 414 Bake McBride .10 .05
❑ 415 Larry Milbourne .10 .05
❑ 416 Bill Nahorodny .10 .05
❑ 417 Jack Perconte .10 .05
❑ 418 Lary Sorensen .10 .05
❑ 419 Dan Spillner .10 .05
❑ 420 Rick Sutcliffe .20 .09
❑ 421 Andre Thornton .10 .05
❑ 422 Rick Waits .10 .05
❑ 423 Eddie Whitson .10 .05
❑ 424 Jesse Barfield .20 .09
❑ 425 Barry Bonnell .10 .05
❑ 426 Jim Clancy .10 .05
❑ 427 Damaso Garcia .10 .05
❑ 428 Jerry Garvin .10 .05
❑ 429 Alfredo Griffin .10 .05
❑ 430 Garth Iorg .10 .05
❑ 431 Roy Lee Jackson .10 .05
❑ 432 Luis Leal .10 .05
❑ 433 Buck Martinez .10 .05
❑ 434 Joey McLaughlin .10 .05
❑ 435 Lloyd Moseby .10 .05
❑ 436 Rance Mulliniks .10 .05
❑ 437 Dale Murray .10 .05
❑ 438 Wayne Nordhagen .10 .05
❑ 439 Geno Petralli .20 .09
❑ 440 Hosken Powell .10 .05
❑ 441 Dave Stieb .20 .09
❑ 442 Willie Upshaw .10 .05
❑ 443 Ernie Whitt .10 .05
❑ 444 Alvis Woods .10 .05
❑ 445 Alan Ashby .10 .05
❑ 446 Jose Cruz .20 .09
❑ 447 Kiko Garcia .10 .05
❑ 448 Phil Garner .20 .09
❑ 449 Danny Heep .10 .05
❑ 450 Art Howe .20 .09
❑ 451 Bob Knepper .10 .05
❑ 452 Alan Knicely .10 .05
❑ 453 Ray Knight .20 .09
❑ 454 Frank LaCorte .10 .05
❑ 455 Mike LaCoss .10 .05
❑ 456 Randy Moffitt .10 .05
❑ 457 Joe Niekro .20 .09
❑ 458 Terry Puhl .10 .05
❑ 459 Luis Pujols .10 .05
❑ 460 Craig Reynolds .10 .05
❑ 461 Bert Roberge .10 .05
❑ 462 Vern Ruhle .10 .05
❑ 463 Nolan Ryan 4.00 1.80
❑ 464 Joe Sambito .10 .05
❑ 465 Tony Scott .10 .05
❑ 466 Dave Smith .10 .05
❑ 467 Harry Spilman .10 .05
❑ 468 Dickie Thon .10 .05
❑ 469 Denny Walling .10 .05
❑ 470 Larry Andersen .10 .05
❑ 471 Floyd Bannister .10 .05
❑ 472 Jim Beattie .10 .05
❑ 473 Bruce Bochte .10 .05
❑ 474 Manny Castillo .10 .05
❑ 475 Bill Caudill .10 .05
❑ 476 Bryan Clark .10 .05

❑ 477 Al Cowens .10 .05
❑ 478 Julio Cruz .10 .05
❑ 479 Todd Cruz .10 .05
❑ 480 Gary Gray .10 .05
❑ 481 Dave Henderson .10 .05
❑ 482 Mike Moore RC .20 .09
❑ 483 Gaylord Perry .75 .35
❑ 484 Dave Revering .10 .05
❑ 485 Joe Simpson .10 .05
❑ 486 Mike Stanton .10 .05
❑ 487 Rick Sweet .10 .05
❑ 488 Ed VandeBerg .10 .05
❑ 489 Richie Zisk .10 .05
❑ 490 Doug Bird .10 .05
❑ 491 Larry Bowa .20 .09
❑ 492 Bill Buckner .20 .09
❑ 493 Bill Campbell .10 .05
❑ 494 Jody Davis .10 .05
❑ 495 Leon Durham .10 .05
❑ 496 Steve Henderson .10 .05
❑ 497 Willie Hernandez .20 .09
❑ 498 Ferguson Jenkins .75 .35
❑ 499 Jay Johnstone .20 .09
❑ 500 Junior Kennedy .10 .05
❑ 501 Randy Martz .10 .05
❑ 502 Jerry Morales .10 .05
❑ 503 Keith Moreland .10 .05
❑ 504 Dickie Noles .10 .05
❑ 505 Mike Proly .10 .05
❑ 506 Allen Ripley .10 .05
❑ 507 R.Sandberg RC UER 10.00 4.50
Should say High School
in Spokane, Washington
❑ 508 Lee Smith .75 .35
❑ 509 Pat Tabler .10 .05
❑ 510 Dick Tidrow .10 .05
❑ 511 Bump Wills .10 .05
❑ 512 Gary Woods .10 .05
❑ 513 Tony Armas .10 .05
❑ 514 Dave Beard .10 .05
❑ 515 Jeff Burroughs .10 .05
❑ 516 John D'Acquisto .10 .05
❑ 517 Wayne Gross .10 .05
❑ 518 Mike Heath .10 .05
❑ 519 R.Henderson UER 1.50 .70
Brock record listed
as 120 steals
❑ 520 Cliff Johnson .10 .05
❑ 521 Matt Keough .10 .05
❑ 522 Brian Kingman .10 .05
❑ 523 Rick Langford .10 .05
❑ 524 Dave Lopes .20 .09
❑ 525 Steve McCatty .10 .05
❑ 526 Dave McKay .10 .05
❑ 527 Dan Meyer .10 .05
❑ 528 Dwayne Murphy .10 .05
❑ 529 Jeff Newman .10 .05
❑ 530 Mike Norris .10 .05
❑ 531 Bob Owchinko .10 .05
❑ 532 Joe Rudi .10 .05
❑ 533 Jimmy Sexton .10 .05
❑ 534 Fred Stanley .10 .05
❑ 535 Tom Underwood .10 .05
❑ 536 Neil Allen .10 .05
❑ 537 Wally Backman .10 .05
❑ 538 Bob Bailor .10 .05
❑ 539 Hubie Brooks .20 .09
❑ 540 Carlos Diaz .10 .05
❑ 541 Pete Falcone .10 .05
❑ 542 George Foster .20 .09
❑ 543 Ron Gardenhire .10 .05
❑ 544 Brian Giles .10 .05
❑ 545 Ron Hodges .10 .05
❑ 546 Randy Jones .10 .05
❑ 547 Mike Jorgensen .10 .05
❑ 548 Dave Kingman .40 .18
❑ 549 Ed Lynch .10 .05
❑ 550 Jesse Orosco .10 .05
❑ 551 Rick Ownbey .10 .05
❑ 552 Charlie Puleo .10 .05
❑ 553 Gary Rajsich .10 .05
❑ 554 Mike Scott .20 .09
❑ 555 Rusty Staub .20 .09
❑ 556 John Stearns .10 .05
❑ 557 Craig Swan .10 .05
❑ 558 Ellis Valentine .10 .05
❑ 559 Tom Veryzer .10 .05
❑ 560 Mookie Wilson .20 .09
❑ 561 Pat Zachry .10 .05
❑ 562 Buddy Bell .20 .09
❑ 563 John Butcher .10 .05
❑ 564 Steve Comer .10 .05
❑ 565 Danny Darwin .10 .05
❑ 566 Bucky Dent .20 .09
❑ 567 John Grubb .10 .05
❑ 568 Rick Honeycutt .10 .05
❑ 569 Dave Hostetler .10 .05
❑ 570 Charlie Hough .20 .09
❑ 571 Lamar Johnson .10 .05
❑ 572 Jon Matlack .10 .05
❑ 573 Paul Mirabella .10 .05
❑ 574 Larry Parrish .10 .05
❑ 575 Mike Richardt .10 .05
❑ 576 Mickey Rivers .10 .05
❑ 577 Billy Sample .10 .05
❑ 578 Dave Schmidt .10 .05
❑ 579 Bill Stein .10 .05
❑ 580 Jim Sundberg .20 .09
❑ 581 Frank Tanana .20 .09
❑ 582 Mark Wagner .10 .05
❑ 583 George Wright .10 .05
❑ 584 Johnny Bench 1.25 .55
❑ 585 Bruce Berenyi .10 .05
❑ 586 Larry Biittner .10 .05
❑ 587 Cesar Cedeno .20 .09
❑ 588 Dave Concepcion .20 .09
❑ 589 Dan Driessen .10 .05
❑ 590 Greg Harris .10 .05
❑ 591 Ben Hayes .10 .05
❑ 592 Paul Householder .10 .05
❑ 593 Tom Hume .10 .05
❑ 594 Wayne Krenchicki .10 .05
❑ 595 Rafael Landestoy .10 .05
❑ 596 Charlie Leibrandt .10 .05
❑ 597 Eddie Milner .10 .05
❑ 598 Ron Oester .10 .05
❑ 599 Frank Pastore .10 .05
❑ 600 Joe Price .10 .05
❑ 601 Tom Seaver 1.25 .55
❑ 602 Bob Shirley .10 .05
❑ 603 Mario Soto .10 .05
❑ 604 Alex Trevino .10 .05
❑ 605 Mike Vail .10 .05
❑ 606 Duane Walker .10 .05
❑ 607 Tom Brunansky .20 .09
❑ 608 Bobby Castillo .10 .05
❑ 609 John Castino .10 .05
❑ 610 Ron Davis .10 .05
❑ 611 Lenny Faedo .10 .05
❑ 612 Terry Felton .10 .05
❑ 613 Gary Gaetti RC .75 .35
❑ 614 Mickey Hatcher .10 .05
❑ 615 Brad Havens .10 .05
❑ 616 Kent Hrbek .20 .09
❑ 617 Randy Johnson .10 .05
❑ 618 Tim Laudner .10 .05
❑ 619 Jeff Little .10 .05
❑ 620 Bobby Mitchell .10 .05
❑ 621 Jack O'Connor .10 .05
❑ 622 John Pacella .10 .05
❑ 623 Pete Redfern .10 .05
❑ 624 Jesus Vega .10 .05
❑ 625 Frank Viola RC .75 .35
❑ 626 Ron Washington .10 .05
❑ 627 Gary Ward .10 .05
❑ 628 Al Williams .10 .05
❑ 629 Red Sox All-Stars .75 .35
Carl Yastrzemski
Dennis Eckersley
Mark Clear
❑ 630 300 Career Wins .20 .09
Gaylord Perry
Terry Bulling 5/6/82
❑ 631 Pride of Venezuela .20 .09
Dave Concepcion and
Manny Trillo
❑ 632 All-Star Infielders .75 .35
Robin Yount and
Buddy Bell
❑ 633 Mr.Vet and Mr.Rookie .20 .09
Dave Winfield and
Kent Hrbek
❑ 634 Fountain of Youth .75 .35
Willie Stargell and
Pete Rose
❑ 635 Big Chiefs .20 .09
Toby Harrah and
Andre Thornton
❑ 636 Smith Brothers .75 .35
Ozzie Smith
Lonnie Smith
❑ 637 Base Stealers' Threat .20 .09
Bo Diaz and
Gary Carter
❑ 638 All-Star Catchers .40 .18
Carlton Fisk and
Gary Carter
❑ 639 The Silver Shoe .75 .35
Rickey Henderson
❑ 640 Home Run Threats .75 .35
Ben Oglivie and
Reggie Jackson
❑ 641 Two Teams Same Day .10 .05
Joel Youngblood
August 4, 1982
❑ 642 Last Perfect Game .20 .09
Ron Hassey and
Len Barker
❑ 643 Black and Blue .20 .09
Vida Blue
❑ 644 Black and Blue .10 .05
Bud Black
❑ 645 Speed and Power .40 .18
Reggie Jackson
❑ 646 Speed and Power .75 .35
Rickey Henderson
❑ 647 CL: Cards/Brewers .10 .05
❑ 648 CL: Orioles/Angels .10 .05
❑ 649 CL: Royals/Braves .10 .05
❑ 650 CL: Phillies/Red Sox .10 .05
❑ 651 CL: Dodgers/White Sox .10 .05
❑ 652 CL: Giants/Expos .10 .05
❑ 653 CL: Pirates/Tigers .10 .05
❑ 654 CL: Padres/Yankees .10 .05
❑ 655 CL: Indians/Blue Jays .10 .05
❑ 656 CL: Astros/Mariners .10 .05
❑ 657 CL: Cubs/A's .10 .05
❑ 658 CL: Mets/Rangers .10 .05
❑ 659 CL: Reds/Twins .10 .05
❑ 660 CL: Specials/Teams .10 .05

1984 Fleer

	NRMT	VG-E
COMPLETE SET (660)	50.00	22.00

❑ 1 Mike Boddicker .15 .07
❑ 2 Al Bumbry .15 .07
❑ 3 Todd Cruz .15 .07
❑ 4 Rich Dauer .15 .07
❑ 5 Storm Davis .15 .07
❑ 6 Rick Dempsey .15 .07
❑ 7 Jim Dwyer .15 .07
❑ 8 Mike Flanagan .15 .07
❑ 9 Dan Ford .15 .07
❑ 10 John Lowenstein .15 .07
❑ 11 Dennis Martinez .40 .18
❑ 12 Tippy Martinez .15 .07
❑ 13 Scott McGregor .15 .07
❑ 14 Eddie Murray 1.50 .70

	#	Player		
❑	15	Joe Nolan	.15	.07
❑	16	Jim Palmer	1.50	.70
❑	17	Cal Ripken	10.00	4.50
❑	18	Gary Roenicke	.15	.07
❑	19	Lenn Sakata	.15	.07
❑	20	John Shelby	.15	.07
❑	21	Ken Singleton	.15	.07
❑	22	Sammy Stewart	.15	.07
❑	23	Tim Stoddard	.15	.07
❑	24	Marty Bystrom	.15	.07
❑	25	Steve Carlton	1.50	.70
❑	26	Ivan DeJesus	.15	.07
❑	27	John Denny	.15	.07
❑	28	Bob Dernier	.15	.07
❑	29	Bo Diaz	.15	.07
❑	30	Kiko Garcia	.15	.07
❑	31	Greg Gross	.15	.07
❑	32	Kevin Gross RC	.15	.07
❑	33	Von Hayes	.15	.07
❑	34	Willie Hernandez	.40	.18
❑	35	Al Holland	.15	.07
❑	36	Charles Hudson	.15	.07
❑	37	Joe Lefebvre	.15	.07
❑	38	Sixto Lezcano	.15	.07
❑	39	Garry Maddox	.15	.07
❑	40	Gary Matthews	.40	.18
❑	41	Len Matuszek	.15	.07
❑	42	Tug McGraw	.40	.18
❑	43	Joe Morgan	1.50	.70
❑	44	Tony Perez	1.50	.70
❑	45	Ron Reed	.15	.07
❑	46	Pete Rose	5.00	2.20
❑	47	Juan Samuel RC	.75	.35
❑	48	Mike Schmidt	3.00	1.35
❑	49	Ozzie Virgil	.15	.07
❑	50	Juan Agosto	.15	.07
❑	51	Harold Baines	1.50	.70
❑	52	Floyd Bannister	.15	.07
❑	53	Salome Barojas	.15	.07
❑	54	Britt Burns	.15	.07
❑	55	Julio Cruz	.15	.07
❑	56	Richard Dotson	.15	.07
❑	57	Jerry Dybzinski	.15	.07
❑	58	Carlton Fisk	1.50	.70
❑	59	Scott Fletcher	.15	.07
❑	60	Jerry Hairston	.15	.07
❑	61	Kevin Hickey	.15	.07
❑	62	Marc Hill	.15	.07
❑	63	LaMarr Hoyt	.15	.07
❑	64	Ron Kittle	.15	.07
❑	65	Jerry Koosman	.40	.18
❑	66	Dennis Lamp	.15	.07
❑	67	Rudy Law	.15	.07
❑	68	Vance Law	.15	.07
❑	69	Greg Luzinski	.40	.18
❑	70	Tom Paciorek	.40	.18
❑	71	Mike Squires	.15	.07
❑	72	Dick Tidrow	.15	.07
❑	73	Greg Walker	.40	.18
❑	74	Glenn Abbott	.15	.07
❑	75	Howard Bailey	.15	.07
❑	76	Doug Bair	.15	.07
❑	77	Juan Berenguer	.15	.07
❑	78	Tom Brookens	.40	.18
❑	79	Enos Cabell	.15	.07
❑	80	Kirk Gibson	1.50	.70
❑	81	John Grubb	.15	.07
❑	82	Larry Herndon	.40	.18
❑	83	Wayne Krenchicki	.15	.07
❑	84	Rick Leach	.15	.07
❑	85	Chet Lemon	.15	.07
❑	86	Aurelio Lopez	.40	.18
❑	87	Jack Morris	1.50	.70
❑	88	Lance Parrish	.75	.35
❑	89	Dan Petry	.40	.18
❑	90	Dave Rozema	.15	.07
❑	91	Alan Trammell	.75	.35
❑	92	Lou Whitaker	1.50	.70
❑	93	Milt Wilcox	.15	.07
❑	94	Glenn Wilson	.40	.18
❑	95	John Wockenfuss	.15	.07
❑	96	Dusty Baker	.40	.18
❑	97	Joe Beckwith	.15	.07
❑	98	Greg Brock	.15	.07
❑	99	Jack Fimple	.15	.07
❑	100	Pedro Guerrero	.40	.18
❑	101	Rick Honeycutt	.15	.07
❑	102	Burt Hooton	.15	.07
❑	103	Steve Howe	.15	.07
❑	104	Ken Landreaux	.15	.07
❑	105	Mike Marshall	.15	.07
❑	106	Rick Monday	.15	.07
❑	107	Jose Morales	.15	.07
❑	108	Tom Niedenfuer	.15	.07
❑	109	Alejandro Pena RC*	.40	.18
❑	110	Jerry Reuss UER ("Home:" omitted)	.15	.07
❑	111	Bill Russell	.15	.07
❑	112	Steve Sax	.40	.18
❑	113	Mike Scioscia	.15	.07
❑	114	Derrel Thomas	.15	.07
❑	115	Fernando Valenzuela	.40	.18
❑	116	Bob Welch	.15	.07
❑	117	Steve Yeager	.15	.07
❑	118	Pat Zachry	.15	.07
❑	119	Don Baylor	.75	.35
❑	120	Bert Campaneris	.40	.18
❑	121	Rick Cerone	.15	.07
❑	122	Ray Fontenot	.15	.07
❑	123	George Frazier	.15	.07
❑	124	Oscar Gamble	.15	.07
❑	125	Rich Gossage	.75	.35
❑	126	Ken Griffey	.40	.18
❑	127	Ron Guidry	.40	.18
❑	128	Jay Howell	.15	.07
❑	129	Steve Kemp	.15	.07
❑	130	Matt Keough	.15	.07
❑	131	Don Mattingly RC	20.00	9.00
❑	132	John Montefusco	.15	.07
❑	133	Omar Moreno	.15	.07
❑	134	Dale Murray	.15	.07
❑	135	Graig Nettles	.40	.18
❑	136	Lou Piniella	.40	.18
❑	137	Willie Randolph	.40	.18
❑	138	Shane Rawley	.15	.07
❑	139	Dave Righetti	.40	.18
❑	140	Andre Robertson	.15	.07
❑	141	Bob Shirley	.15	.07
❑	142	Roy Smalley	.15	.07
❑	143	Dave Winfield	1.50	.70
❑	144	Butch Wynegar	.15	.07
❑	145	Jim Acker	.15	.07
❑	146	Doyle Alexander	.15	.07
❑	147	Jesse Barfield	.40	.18
❑	148	Jorge Bell	.40	.18
❑	149	Barry Bonnell	.15	.07
❑	150	Jim Clancy	.15	.07
❑	151	Dave Collins	.15	.07
❑	152	Tony Fernandez RC	2.00	.90
❑	153	Damaso Garcia	.15	.07
❑	154	Dave Geisel	.15	.07
❑	155	Jim Gott	.15	.07
❑	156	Alfredo Griffin	.15	.07
❑	157	Garth Iorg	.15	.07
❑	158	Roy Lee Jackson	.15	.07
❑	159	Cliff Johnson	.15	.07
❑	160	Luis Leal	.15	.07
❑	161	Buck Martinez	.15	.07
❑	162	Joey McLaughlin	.15	.07
❑	163	Randy Moffitt	.15	.07
❑	164	Lloyd Moseby	.15	.07
❑	165	Rance Mulliniks	.15	.07
❑	166	Jorge Orta	.15	.07
❑	167	Dave Stieb	.15	.07
❑	168	Willie Upshaw	.15	.07
❑	169	Ernie Whitt	.15	.07
❑	170	Len Barker	.15	.07
❑	171	Steve Bedrosian	.15	.07
❑	172	Bruce Benedict	.15	.07
❑	173	Brett Butler	.75	.35
❑	174	Rick Camp	.15	.07
❑	175	Chris Chambliss	.40	.18
❑	176	Ken Dayley	.15	.07
❑	177	Pete Falcone	.15	.07
❑	178	Terry Forster	.15	.07
❑	179	Gene Garber	.15	.07
❑	180	Terry Harper	.15	.07
❑	181	Bob Horner	.15	.07
❑	182	Glenn Hubbard	.15	.07
❑	183	Randy Johnson	.15	.07
❑	184	Craig McMurtry	.15	.07
❑	185	Donnie Moore	.15	.07
❑	186	Dale Murphy	1.50	.70
❑	187	Phil Niekro	1.50	.70
❑	188	Pascual Perez	.15	.07
❑	189	Biff Pocoroba	.15	.07
❑	190	Rafael Ramirez	.15	.07
❑	191	Jerry Royster	.15	.07
❑	192	Claudell Washington	.15	.07
❑	193	Bob Watson	.40	.18
❑	194	Jerry Augustine	.15	.07
❑	195	Mark Brouhard	.15	.07
❑	196	Mike Caldwell	.15	.07
❑	197	Tom Candiotti RC	1.50	.70
❑	198	Cecil Cooper	.40	.18
❑	199	Rollie Fingers	1.50	.70
❑	200	Jim Gantner	.15	.07
❑	201	Bob L. Gibson	.15	.07
❑	202	Moose Haas	.15	.07
❑	203	Roy Howell	.15	.07
❑	204	Pete Ladd	.15	.07
❑	205	Rick Manning	.15	.07
❑	206	Bob McClure	.15	.07
❑	207	Paul Molitor UER ('83 stats should say .270 BA and 608 AB)	1.50	.70
❑	208	Don Money	.15	.07
❑	209	Charlie Moore	.15	.07
❑	210	Ben Oglivie	.15	.07
❑	211	Chuck Porter	.15	.07
❑	212	Ed Romero	.15	.07
❑	213	Ted Simmons	.40	.18
❑	214	Jim Slaton	.15	.07
❑	215	Don Sutton	1.50	.70
❑	216	Tom Tellmann	.15	.07
❑	217	Pete Vuckovich	.15	.07
❑	218	Ned Yost	.15	.07
❑	219	Robin Yount	1.50	.70
❑	220	Alan Ashby	.15	.07
❑	221	Kevin Bass	.15	.07
❑	222	Jose Cruz	.40	.18
❑	223	Bill Dawley	.15	.07
❑	224	Frank DiPino	.15	.07
❑	225	Bill Doran RC*	.40	.18
❑	226	Phil Garner	.40	.18
❑	227	Art Howe	.40	.18
❑	228	Bob Knepper	.15	.07
❑	229	Ray Knight	.40	.18
❑	230	Frank LaCorte	.15	.07
❑	231	Mike LaCoss	.15	.07
❑	232	Mike Madden	.15	.07
❑	233	Jerry Mumphrey	.15	.07
❑	234	Joe Niekro	.40	.18
❑	235	Terry Puhl	.15	.07
❑	236	Luis Pujols	.15	.07
❑	237	Craig Reynolds	.15	.07
❑	238	Vern Ruhle	.15	.07
❑	239	Nolan Ryan	8.00	3.60
❑	240	Mike Scott	.40	.18
❑	241	Tony Scott	.15	.07
❑	242	Dave Smith	.15	.07
❑	243	Dickie Thon	.15	.07
❑	244	Denny Walling	.15	.07
❑	245	Dale Berra	.15	.07
❑	246	Jim Bibby	.15	.07
❑	247	John Candelaria	.15	.07
❑	248	Jose DeLeon	.15	.07
❑	249	Mike Easler	.15	.07
❑	250	Cecilio Guante	.15	.07
❑	251	Richie Hebner	.15	.07
❑	252	Lee Lacy	.15	.07
❑	253	Bill Madlock	.40	.18
❑	254	Milt May	.15	.07
❑	255	Lee Mazzilli	.15	.07
❑	256	Larry McWilliams	.15	.07
❑	257	Jim Morrison	.15	.07
❑	258	Dave Parker	.40	.18
❑	259	Tony Pena	.15	.07
❑	260	Johnny Ray	.15	.07
❑	261	Rick Rhoden	.15	.07
❑	262	Don Robinson	.15	.07
❑	263	Manny Sarmiento	.15	.07
❑	264	Rod Scurry	.15	.07
❑	265	Kent Tekulve	.40	.18
❑	266	Gene Tenace	.40	.18
❑	267	Jason Thompson	.15	.07
❑	268	Lee Tunnell	.15	.07
❑	269	Marvell Wynne	.15	.07

	No.	Player		
❑	270	Ray Burris	.15	.07
❑	271	Gary Carter	.75	.35
❑	272	Warren Cromartie	.15	.07
❑	273	Andre Dawson	.75	.35
❑	274	Doug Flynn	.15	.07
❑	275	Terry Francona	.15	.07
❑	276	Bill Gullickson	.15	.07
❑	277	Bob James	.15	.07
❑	278	Charlie Lea	.15	.07
❑	279	Bryan Little	.15	.07
❑	280	Al Oliver	.40	.18
❑	281	Tim Raines	.75	.35
❑	282	Bobby Ramos	.15	.07
❑	283	Jeff Reardon	.40	.18
❑	284	Steve Rogers	.15	.07
❑	285	Scott Sanderson	.15	.07
❑	286	Dan Schatzeder	.15	.07
❑	287	Bryn Smith	.15	.07
❑	288	Chris Speier	.15	.07
❑	289	Manny Trillo	.15	.07
❑	290	Mike Vail	.15	.07
❑	291	Tim Wallach	.40	.18
❑	292	Chris Welsh	.15	.07
❑	293	Jim Wohlford	.15	.07
❑	294	Kurt Bevacqua	.15	.07
❑	295	Juan Bonilla	.15	.07
❑	296	Bobby Brown	.15	.07
❑	297	Luis DeLeon	.15	.07
❑	298	Dave Dravecky	.40	.18
❑	299	Tim Flannery	.15	.07
❑	300	Steve Garvey	.75	.35
❑	301	Tony Gwynn	8.00	3.60
❑	302	Andy Hawkins	.15	.07
❑	303	Ruppert Jones	.15	.07
❑	304	Terry Kennedy	.15	.07
❑	305	Tim Lollar	.15	.07
❑	306	Gary Lucas	.15	.07
❑	307	Kevin McReynolds RC	.75	.35
❑	308	Sid Monge	.15	.07
❑	309	Mario Ramirez	.15	.07
❑	310	Gene Richards	.15	.07
❑	311	Luis Salazar	.15	.07
❑	312	Eric Show	.15	.07
❑	313	Elias Sosa	.15	.07
❑	314	Garry Templeton	.15	.07
❑	315	Mark Thurmond	.15	.07
❑	316	Ed Whitson	.15	.07
❑	317	Alan Wiggins	.15	.07
❑	318	Neil Allen	.15	.07
❑	319	Joaquin Andujar	.15	.07
❑	320	Steve Braun	.15	.07
❑	321	Glenn Brummer	.15	.07
❑	322	Bob Forsch	.15	.07
❑	323	David Green	.15	.07
❑	324	George Hendrick	.15	.07
❑	325	Tom Herr	.40	.18
❑	326	Dane Iorg	.15	.07
❑	327	Jeff Lahti	.15	.07
❑	328	Dave LaPoint	.15	.07
❑	329	Willie McGee	.75	.35
❑	330	Ken Oberkfell	.15	.07
❑	331	Darrell Porter	.15	.07
❑	332	Jamie Quirk	.15	.07
❑	333	Mike Ramsey	.15	.07
❑	334	Floyd Rayford	.15	.07
❑	335	Lonnie Smith	.15	.07
❑	336	Ozzie Smith	2.00	.90
❑	337	John Stuper	.15	.07
❑	338	Bruce Sutter	.40	.18
❑	339	A.Van Slyke RC UER Batting and throwing both wrong on card back	1.50	.70
❑	340	Dave Von Ohlen	.15	.07
❑	341	Willie Aikens	.15	.07
❑	342	Mike Armstrong	.15	.07
❑	343	Bud Black	.15	.07
❑	344	George Brett	3.00	1.35
❑	345	Onix Concepcion	.15	.07
❑	346	Keith Creel	.15	.07
❑	347	Larry Gura	.15	.07
❑	348	Don Hood	.15	.07
❑	349	Dennis Leonard	.15	.07
❑	350	Hal McRae	.40	.18
❑	351	Amos Otis	.40	.18
❑	352	Gaylord Perry	1.50	.70
❑	353	Greg Pryor	.15	.07
❑	354	Dan Quisenberry	.15	.07
❑	355	Steve Renko	.15	.07
❑	356	Leon Roberts	.15	.07
❑	357	Pat Sheridan	.15	.07
❑	358	Joe Simpson	.15	.07
❑	359	Don Slaught	.40	.18
❑	360	Paul Splittorff	.15	.07
❑	361	U.L. Washington	.15	.07
❑	362	John Wathan	.15	.07
❑	363	Frank White	.40	.18
❑	364	Willie Wilson	.15	.07
❑	365	Jim Barr	.15	.07
❑	366	Dave Bergman	.15	.07
❑	367	Fred Breining	.15	.07
❑	368	Bob Brenly	.15	.07
❑	369	Jack Clark	.40	.18
❑	370	Chili Davis	.75	.35
❑	371	Mark Davis	.15	.07
❑	372	Darrell Evans	.40	.18
❑	373	Atlee Hammaker	.15	.07
❑	374	Mike Krukow	.15	.07
❑	375	Duane Kuiper	.15	.07
❑	376	Bill Laskey	.15	.07
❑	377	Gary Lavelle	.15	.07
❑	378	Johnnie LeMaster	.15	.07
❑	379	Jeff Leonard	.15	.07
❑	380	Randy Lerch	.15	.07
❑	381	Renie Martin	.15	.07
❑	382	Andy McGaffigan	.15	.07
❑	383	Greg Minton	.15	.07
❑	384	Tom O'Malley	.15	.07
❑	385	Max Venable	.15	.07
❑	386	Brad Wellman	.15	.07
❑	387	Joel Youngblood	.15	.07
❑	388	Gary Allenson	.15	.07
❑	389	Luis Aponte	.15	.07
❑	390	Tony Armas	.15	.07
❑	391	Doug Bird	.15	.07
❑	392	Wade Boggs	4.00	1.80
❑	393	Dennis Boyd	.40	.18
❑	394	Mike Brown UER P (shown with record of 31-104)	.15	.07
❑	395	Mark Clear	.15	.07
❑	396	Dennis Eckersley	1.50	.70
❑	397	Dwight Evans	.40	.18
❑	398	Rich Gedman	.15	.07
❑	399	Glenn Hoffman	.15	.07
❑	400	Bruce Hurst	.15	.07
❑	401	John Henry Johnson	.15	.07
❑	402	Ed Jurak	.15	.07
❑	403	Rick Miller	.15	.07
❑	404	Jeff Newman	.15	.07
❑	405	Reid Nichols	.15	.07
❑	406	Bob Ojeda	.15	.07
❑	407	Jerry Remy	.15	.07
❑	408	Jim Rice	.40	.18
❑	409	Bob Stanley	.15	.07
❑	410	Dave Stapleton	.15	.07
❑	411	John Tudor	.15	.07
❑	412	Carl Yastrzemski	1.50	.70
❑	413	Buddy Bell	.40	.18
❑	414	Larry Biittner	.15	.07
❑	415	John Butcher	.15	.07
❑	416	Danny Darwin	.15	.07
❑	417	Bucky Dent	.40	.18
❑	418	Dave Hostetler	.15	.07
❑	419	Charlie Hough	.40	.18
❑	420	Bobby Johnson	.15	.07
❑	421	Odell Jones	.15	.07
❑	422	Jon Matlack	.15	.07
❑	423	Pete O'Brien RC*	.40	.18
❑	424	Larry Parrish	.15	.07
❑	425	Mickey Rivers	.15	.07
❑	426	Billy Sample	.15	.07
❑	427	Dave Schmidt	.15	.07
❑	428	Mike Smithson	.15	.07
❑	429	Bill Stein	.15	.07
❑	430	Dave Stewart	.40	.18
❑	431	Jim Sundberg	.40	.18
❑	432	Frank Tanana	.40	.18
❑	433	Dave Tobik	.15	.07
❑	434	Wayne Tolleson	.15	.07
❑	435	George Wright	.15	.07
❑	436	Bill Almon	.15	.07
❑	437	Keith Atherton	.15	.07
❑	438	Dave Beard	.15	.07
❑	439	Tom Burgmeier	.15	.07
❑	440	Jeff Burroughs	.15	.07
❑	441	Chris Codiroli	.15	.07
❑	442	Tim Conroy	.15	.07
❑	443	Mike Davis	.15	.07
❑	444	Wayne Gross	.15	.07
❑	445	Garry Hancock	.15	.07
❑	446	Mike Heath	.15	.07
❑	447	Rickey Henderson	3.00	1.35
❑	448	Donnie Hill	.15	.07
❑	449	Bob Kearney	.15	.07
❑	450	Bill Krueger RC	.15	.07
❑	451	Rick Langford	.15	.07
❑	452	Carney Lansford	.40	.18
❑	453	Dave Lopes	.40	.18
❑	454	Steve McCatty	.15	.07
❑	455	Dan Meyer	.15	.07
❑	456	Dwayne Murphy	.15	.07
❑	457	Mike Norris	.15	.07
❑	458	Ricky Peters	.15	.07
❑	459	Tony Phillips RC	1.50	.70
❑	460	Tom Underwood	.15	.07
❑	461	Mike Warren	.15	.07
❑	462	Johnny Bench	2.50	1.10
❑	463	Bruce Berenyi	.15	.07
❑	464	Dann Bilardello	.15	.07
❑	465	Cesar Cedeno	.40	.18
❑	466	Dave Concepcion	.40	.18
❑	467	Dan Driessen	.15	.07
❑	468	Nick Esasky	.15	.07
❑	469	Rich Gale	.15	.07
❑	470	Ben Hayes	.15	.07
❑	471	Paul Householder	.15	.07
❑	472	Tom Hume	.15	.07
❑	473	Alan Knicely	.15	.07
❑	474	Eddie Milner	.15	.07
❑	475	Ron Oester	.15	.07
❑	476	Kelly Paris	.15	.07
❑	477	Frank Pastore	.15	.07
❑	478	Ted Power	.15	.07
❑	479	Joe Price	.15	.07
❑	480	Charlie Puleo	.15	.07
❑	481	Gary Redus RC*	.15	.07
❑	482	Bill Scherrer	.15	.07
❑	483	Mario Soto	.15	.07
❑	484	Alex Trevino	.15	.07
❑	485	Duane Walker	.15	.07
❑	486	Larry Bowa	.40	.18
❑	487	Warren Brusstar	.15	.07
❑	488	Bill Buckner	.40	.18
❑	489	Bill Campbell	.15	.07
❑	490	Ron Cey	.40	.18
❑	491	Jody Davis	.15	.07
❑	492	Leon Durham	.15	.07
❑	493	Mel Hall	.40	.18
❑	494	Ferguson Jenkins	1.50	.70
❑	495	Jay Johnstone	.40	.18
❑	496	Craig Lefferts RC	.15	.07
❑	497	Carmelo Martinez	.15	.07
❑	498	Jerry Morales	.15	.07
❑	499	Keith Moreland	.15	.07
❑	500	Dickie Noles	.15	.07
❑	501	Mike Proly	.15	.07
❑	502	Chuck Rainey	.15	.07
❑	503	Dick Ruthven	.15	.07
❑	504	Ryne Sandberg	5.00	2.20
❑	505	Lee Smith	1.50	.70
❑	506	Steve Trout	.15	.07
❑	507	Gary Woods	.15	.07
❑	508	Juan Beniquez	.15	.07
❑	509	Bob Boone	.40	.18
❑	510	Rick Burleson	.15	.07
❑	511	Rod Carew	1.50	.70
❑	512	Bobby Clark	.15	.07
❑	513	John Curtis	.15	.07
❑	514	Doug DeCinces	.15	.07
❑	515	Brian Downing	.15	.07
❑	516	Tim Foli	.15	.07
❑	517	Ken Forsch	.15	.07
❑	518	Bobby Grich	.40	.18
❑	519	Andy Hassler	.15	.07
❑	520	Reggie Jackson	2.00	.90
❑	521	Ron Jackson	.15	.07
❑	522	Tommy John	.75	.35
❑	523	Bruce Kison	.15	.07

❑ 524 Steve Lubratich .... .15 .07
❑ 525 Fred Lynn .... .40 .18
❑ 526 Gary Pettis .... .15 .07
❑ 527 Luis Sanchez................. .15 .07
❑ 528 Daryl Sconiers............... .15 .07
❑ 529 Ellis Valentine .... .15 .07
❑ 530 Rob Wilfong.................. .15 .07
❑ 531 Mike Witt .... .15 .07
❑ 532 Geoff Zahn .... .15 .07
❑ 533 Bud Anderson .... .15 .07
❑ 534 Chris Bando .... .15 .07
❑ 535 Alan Bannister................ .15 .07
❑ 536 Bert Blyleven .... .40 .18
❑ 537 Tom Brennan .... .15 .07
❑ 538 Jamie Easterly................ .15 .07
❑ 539 Juan Eichelberger .... .15 .07
❑ 540 Jim Essian...................... .15 .07
❑ 541 Mike Fischlin .... .15 .07
❑ 542 Julio Franco................... .75 .35
❑ 543 Mike Hargrove................ .40 .18
❑ 544 Toby Harrah .... .40 .18
❑ 545 Ron Hassey.................... .15 .07
❑ 546 Neal Heaton .... .15 .07
❑ 547 Bake McBride .... .15 .07
❑ 548 Broderick Perkins .... .15 .07
❑ 549 Lary Sorensen................ .15 .07
❑ 550 Dan Spillner................... .15 .07
❑ 551 Rick Sutcliffe .... .40 .18
❑ 552 Pat Tabler .... .15 .07
❑ 553 Gorman Thomas .... .15 .07
❑ 554 Andre Thornton .... .15 .07
❑ 555 George Vukovich............ .15 .07
❑ 556 Darrell Brown .... .15 .07
❑ 557 Tom Brunansky.............. .40 .18
❑ 558 Randy Bush.................... .15 .07
❑ 559 Bobby Castillo .... .15 .07
❑ 560 John Castino .... .15 .07
❑ 561 Ron Davis .... .15 .07
❑ 562 Dave Engle .... .15 .07
❑ 563 Lenny Faedo .... .15 .07
❑ 564 Pete Filson .... .15 .07
❑ 565 Gary Gaetti .... .75 .35
❑ 566 Mickey Hatcher .... .15 .07
❑ 567 Kent Hrbek .... .40 .18
❑ 568 Rusty Kuntz.................... .15 .07
❑ 569 Tim Laudner .... .15 .07
❑ 570 Rick Lysander .... .15 .07
❑ 571 Bobby Mitchell................ .15 .07
❑ 572 Ken Schrom .... .15 .07
❑ 573 Ray Smith .... .15 .07
❑ 574 Tim Teufel RC .... .15 .07
❑ 575 Frank Viola .... .75 .35
❑ 576 Gary Ward...................... .15 .07
❑ 577 Ron Washington .... .15 .07
❑ 578 Len Whitehouse .... .15 .07
❑ 579 Al Williams..................... .15 .07
❑ 580 Bob Bailor .... .15 .07
❑ 581 Mark Bradley.................. .15 .07
❑ 582 Hubie Brooks.................. .15 .07
❑ 583 Carlos Diaz .... .15 .07
❑ 584 George Foster................ .40 .18
❑ 585 Brian Giles..................... .15 .07
❑ 586 Danny Heep .... .15 .07
❑ 587 Keith Hernandez .... .40 .18
❑ 588 Ron Hodges .... .15 .07
❑ 589 Scott Holman.................. .15 .07
❑ 590 Dave Kingman................ .75 .35
❑ 591 Ed Lynch .... .15 .07
❑ 592 Jose Oquendo RC.......... .40 .18
❑ 593 Jesse Orosco .... .15 .07
❑ 594 Junior Ortiz .... .15 .07
❑ 595 Tom Seaver.................. 2.50 1.10
❑ 596 Doug Sisk .... .15 .07
❑ 597 Rusty Staub.................... .40 .18
❑ 598 John Stearns.................. .15 .07
❑ 599 Darryl Strawberry RC .. 3.00 1.35
❑ 600 Craig Swan .... .15 .07
❑ 601 Walt Terrell .... .15 .07
❑ 602 Mike Torrez.................... .15 .07
❑ 603 Mookie Wilson................ .40 .18
❑ 604 Jamie Allen .... .15 .07
❑ 605 Jim Beattie .... .15 .07
❑ 606 Tony Bernazard.............. .15 .07
❑ 607 Manny Castillo............... .15 .07
❑ 608 Bill Caudill .... .15 .07
❑ 609 Bryan Clark .... .15 .07
❑ 610 Al Cowens .... .15 .07
❑ 611 Dave Henderson .... .40 .18
❑ 612 Steve Henderson .... .15 .07
❑ 613 Orlando Mercado .... .15 .07
❑ 614 Mike Moore .... .15 .07
❑ 615 Ricky Nelson UER.......... .15 .07
(Jamie Nelson's
stats on back)
❑ 616 Spike Owen RC.............. .40 .18
❑ 617 Pat Putnam .... .15 .07
❑ 618 Ron Roenicke .... .15 .07
❑ 619 Mike Stanton .... .15 .07
❑ 620 Bob Stoddard .... .15 .07
❑ 621 Rick Sweet .... .15 .07
❑ 622 Roy Thomas .... .15 .07
❑ 623 Ed VandeBerg................ .15 .07
❑ 624 Matt Young .... .15 .07
❑ 625 Richie Zisk..................... .15 .07
❑ 626 Fred Lynn .... .40 .18
1982 AS Game RB
❑ 627 Manny Trillo................... .15 .07
1983 AS Game RB
❑ 628 Steve Garvey .... .40 .18
NL Iron Man
❑ 629 Rod Carew .... .75 .35
AL Batting Runner-Up
❑ 630 Wade Boggs .... 1.50 .70
AL Batting Champion
❑ 631 Tim Raines: Letting .... .40 .18
Go of the Raines
❑ 632 Al Oliver........................ .40 .18
Double Trouble
❑ 633 Steve Sax .... .15 .07
AS Second Base
❑ 634 Dickie Thon .... .15 .07
AS Shortstop
❑ 635 Ace Firemen .... .15 .07
Dan Quisenberry
and Tippy Martinez
❑ 636 Reds Reunited .... 1.50 .70
Joe Morgan
Pete Rose
Tony Perez
❑ 637 Backstop Stars .... .75 .35
Lance Parrish
Bob Boone
❑ 638 George Brett and.......... 2.00 .90
Gaylord Perry
Pine Tar 7/24/83
❑ 639 1983 No Hitters.............. .75 .35
Dave Righetti
Mike Warren
Bob Forsch
❑ 640 Johnny Bench and ...... 2.00 .90
Carl Yastrzemski
Retiring Superstars
❑ 641 Gaylord Perry .... 1.50 .70
Going Out In Style
❑ 642 Steve Carlton .... .75 .35
300 Club and
Strikeout Record
❑ 643 Joe Altobelli and .... .15 .07
Paul Owens
World Series Managers
❑ 644 Rick Dempsey .... .40 .18
World Series MVP
❑ 645 Mike Boddicker .... .15 .07
WS Rookie Winner
❑ 646 Scott McGregor.............. .15 .07
WS Clincher
❑ 647 CL: Orioles/Royals .... .15 .07
Joe Altobelli MG
❑ 648 CL: Phillies/Giants.......... .15 .07
Paul Owens MG
❑ 649 CL: White Sox/Red Sox .75 .35
Tony LaRussa MG
❑ 650 CL: Tigers/Rangers........ .75 .35
Sparky Anderson MG
❑ 651 CL: Dodgers/A's .... .75 .35
Tommy Lasorda MG
❑ 652 CL: Yankees/Reds .... .75 .35
Billy Martin MG
❑ 653 CL: Blue Jays/Cubs........ .40 .18
Bobby Cox MG
❑ 654 CL: Braves/Angels .... .75 .35
Joe Torre MG
❑ 655 CL: Brewers/Indians ...... .15 .07
Rene Lachemann MG
❑ 656 CL: Astros/Twins .... .15 .07
Bob Lillis MG
❑ 657 CL: Pirates/Mets .... .15 .07
Chuck Tanner MG
❑ 658 CL: Expos/Mariners........ .15 .07
Bill Virdon MG
❑ 659 CL: Padres/Specials ...... .40 .18
Dick Williams MG
❑ 660 CL: Cardinals/Teams .... .75 .35
Whitey Herzog MG

1984 Fleer Update

	NRMT	VG-E
COMP.FACT.SET (132)........	400.00	180.00

❑ 1 Willie Aikens .... 1.00 .45
❑ 2 Luis Aponte .... 1.00 .45
❑ 3 Mark Bailey .... 1.00 .45
❑ 4 Bob Bailor .... 1.00 .45
❑ 5 Dusty Baker...................... 1.50 .70
❑ 6 Steve Balboni .... 1.00 .45
❑ 7 Alan Bannister.................. 1.00 .45
❑ 8 Marty Barrett .... 1.50 .70
❑ 9 Dave Beard .... 1.00 .45
❑ 10 Joe Beckwith .... 1.00 .45
❑ 11 Dave Bergman .... 1.00 .45
❑ 12 Tony Bernazard.............. 1.00 .45
❑ 13 Bruce Bochte.................. 1.00 .45
❑ 14 Barry Bonnell.................. 1.00 .45
❑ 15 Phil Bradley.................... 1.50 .70
❑ 16 Fred Breining.................. 1.00 .45
❑ 17 Mike C. Brown .... 1.00 .45
❑ 18 Bill Buckner .... 1.50 .70
❑ 19 Ray Burris .... 1.00 .45
❑ 20 John Butcher.................. 1.00 .45
❑ 21 Brett Butler 2.50 1.10
❑ 22 Enos Cabell.................... 1.00 .45
❑ 23 Bill Campbell .... 1.00 .45
❑ 24 Bill Caudill .... 1.00 .45
❑ 25 Bobby Clark.................... 1.00 .45
❑ 26 Bryan Clark .... 1.00 .45
❑ 27 Roger Clemens XRC.. 200.00 90.00
❑ 28 Jaime Cocanower .... 1.00 .45
❑ 29 Ron Darling XRC* 2.50 1.10
❑ 30 Alvin Davis XRC .... 1.50 .70
❑ 31 Bob Dernier.................... 1.00 .45
❑ 32 Carlos Diaz .... 1.00 .45
❑ 33 Mike Easler .... 1.00 .45
❑ 34 Dennis Eckersley 4.00 1.80
❑ 35 Jim Essian...................... 1.00 .45
❑ 36 Darrell Evans.................. 1.50 .70
❑ 37 Mike Fitzgerald .... 1.00 .45
❑ 38 Tim Foli .... 1.00 .45
❑ 39 John Franco XRC 8.00 3.60
❑ 40 George Frazier .... 1.00 .45
❑ 41 Rich Gale .... 1.00 .45
❑ 42 Barbaro Garbey.............. 1.00 .45
❑ 43 Dwight Gooden XRC.... 15.00 6.75
❑ 44 Rich Gossage 2.50 1.10
❑ 45 Wayne Gross .... 1.00 .45
❑ 46 Mark Gubicza XRC .... 1.50 .70
❑ 47 Jackie Gutierrez .... 1.00 .45
❑ 48 Toby Harrah .... 1.50 .70
❑ 49 Ron Hassey.................... 1.00 .45
❑ 50 Richie Hebner .... 1.00 .45

❑ 51 Willie Hernandez	1.50	.70
❑ 52 Ed Hodge	1.00	.45
❑ 53 Ricky Horton	1.00	.45
❑ 54 Art Howe	1.50	.70
❑ 55 Dane Iorg	1.00	.45
❑ 56 Brook Jacoby	1.50	.70
❑ 57 Dion James XRC*	1.00	.45
❑ 58 Mike Jeffcoat	1.00	.45
❑ 59 Ruppert Jones	1.00	.45
❑ 60 Bob Kearney	1.00	.45
❑ 61 Jimmy Key XRC	2.50	1.10
❑ 62 Dave Kingman	2.50	1.10
❑ 63 Brad Komminsk	1.00	.45
❑ 64 Jerry Koosman	1.50	.70
❑ 65 Wayne Krenchicki	1.00	.45
❑ 66 Rusty Kuntz	1.00	.45
❑ 67 Frank LaCorte	1.00	.45
❑ 68 Dennis Lamp	1.00	.45
❑ 69 Tito Landrum	1.00	.45
❑ 70 Mark Langston XRC	4.00	1.80
❑ 71 Rick Leach	1.00	.45
❑ 72 Craig Lefferts	1.50	.70
❑ 73 Gary Lucas	1.00	.45
❑ 74 Jerry Martin	1.00	.45
❑ 75 Carmelo Martinez	1.00	.45
❑ 76 Mike Mason	1.00	.45
❑ 77 Gary Matthews	1.50	.70
❑ 78 Andy McGaffigan	1.00	.45
❑ 79 Joey McLaughlin	1.00	.45
❑ 80 Joe Morgan	4.00	1.80
❑ 81 Darryl Motley	1.00	.45
❑ 82 Graig Nettles	1.50	.70
❑ 83 Phil Niekro	4.00	1.80
❑ 84 Ken Oberkfell	1.00	.45
❑ 85 Al Oliver	1.50	.70
❑ 86 Jorge Orta	1.00	.45
❑ 87 Amos Otis	1.50	.70
❑ 88 Bob Owchinko	1.00	.45
❑ 89 Dave Parker	1.50	.70
❑ 90 Jack Perconte	1.00	.45
❑ 91 Tony Perez	4.00	1.80
❑ 92 Gerald Perry	1.50	.70
❑ 93 Kirby Puckett XRC	100.00	45.00
❑ 94 Shane Rawley	1.00	.45
❑ 95 Floyd Rayford	1.00	.45
❑ 96 Ron Reed	1.00	.45
❑ 97 R.J. Reynolds	1.00	.45
❑ 98 Gene Richards	1.00	.45
❑ 99 Jose Rijo XRC	4.00	1.80
❑ 100 Jeff D. Robinson	1.00	.45
❑ 101 Ron Romanick	1.00	.45
❑ 102 Pete Rose	12.00	5.50
❑ 103 Bret Saberhagen XRC	10.00	4.50
❑ 104 Scott Sanderson	1.00	.45
❑ 105 Dick Schofield XRC*	1.50	.70
❑ 106 Tom Seaver	6.00	2.70
❑ 107 Jim Slaton	1.00	.45
❑ 108 Mike Smithson	1.00	.45
❑ 109 Lary Sorensen	1.00	.45
❑ 110 Tim Stoddard	1.00	.45
❑ 111 Jeff Stone	1.00	.45
❑ 112 Champ Summers	1.00	.45
❑ 113 Jim Sundberg	1.50	.70
❑ 114 Rick Sutcliffe	1.50	.70
❑ 115 Craig Swan	1.00	.45
❑ 116 Derrel Thomas	1.00	.45
❑ 117 Gorman Thomas	1.00	.45
❑ 118 Alex Trevino	1.00	.45
❑ 119 Manny Trillo	1.00	.45
❑ 120 John Tudor	1.00	.45
❑ 121 Tom Underwood	1.00	.45
❑ 122 Mike Vail	1.00	.45
❑ 123 Tom Waddell	1.00	.45
❑ 124 Gary Ward	1.00	.45
❑ 125 Terry Whitfield	1.00	.45
❑ 126 Curtis Wilkerson	1.00	.45
❑ 127 Frank Williams	1.00	.45
❑ 128 Glenn Wilson	1.00	.45
❑ 129 John Wockenfuss	1.00	.45
❑ 130 Ned Yost	1.00	.45
❑ 131 Mike Young	1.00	.45
❑ 132 Checklist 1-132	1.00	.45

1985 Fleer

	NRMT	VG-E
COMPLETE SET (660)	80.00	36.00
❑ 1 Doug Bair	.15	.07
❑ 2 Juan Berenguer	.15	.07
❑ 3 Dave Bergman	.15	.07
❑ 4 Tom Brookens	.15	.07
❑ 5 Marty Castillo	.15	.07
❑ 6 Darrell Evans	.40	.18
❑ 7 Barbaro Garbey	.15	.07
❑ 8 Kirk Gibson	.40	.18
❑ 9 John Grubb	.15	.07
❑ 10 Willie Hernandez	.15	.07
❑ 11 Larry Herndon	.15	.07
❑ 12 Howard Johnson	.40	.18
❑ 13 Ruppert Jones	.15	.07
❑ 14 Rusty Kuntz	.15	.07
❑ 15 Chet Lemon	.15	.07
❑ 16 Aurelio Lopez	.15	.07
❑ 17 Sid Monge	.15	.07
❑ 18 Jack Morris	.40	.18
❑ 19 Lance Parrish	.40	.18
❑ 20 Dan Petry	.15	.07
❑ 21 Dave Rozema	.15	.07
❑ 22 Bill Scherrer	.15	.07
❑ 23 Alan Trammell	.75	.35
❑ 24 Lou Whitaker	.75	.35
❑ 25 Milt Wilcox	.15	.07
❑ 26 Kurt Bevacqua	.15	.07
❑ 27 Greg Booker	.15	.07
❑ 28 Bobby Brown	.15	.07
❑ 29 Luis DeLeon	.15	.07
❑ 30 Dave Dravecky	.40	.18
❑ 31 Tim Flannery	.15	.07
❑ 32 Steve Garvey	.75	.35
❑ 33 Rich Gossage	.40	.18
❑ 34 Tony Gwynn	4.00	1.80
❑ 35 Greg Harris	.15	.07
❑ 36 Andy Hawkins	.15	.07
❑ 37 Terry Kennedy	.15	.07
❑ 38 Craig Lefferts	.15	.07
❑ 39 Tim Lollar	.15	.07
❑ 40 Carmelo Martinez	.15	.07
❑ 41 Kevin McReynolds	.40	.18
❑ 42 Graig Nettles	.40	.18
❑ 43 Luis Salazar	.15	.07
❑ 44 Eric Show	.15	.07
❑ 45 Garry Templeton	.15	.07
❑ 46 Mark Thurmond	.15	.07
❑ 47 Ed Whitson	.15	.07
❑ 48 Alan Wiggins	.15	.07
❑ 49 Rich Bordi	.15	.07
❑ 50 Larry Bowa	.40	.18
❑ 51 Warren Brusstar	.15	.07
❑ 52 Ron Cey	.40	.18
❑ 53 Henry Cotto RC	.15	.07
❑ 54 Jody Davis	.15	.07
❑ 55 Bob Dernier	.15	.07
❑ 56 Leon Durham	.15	.07
❑ 57 Dennis Eckersley	1.25	.55
❑ 58 George Frazier	.15	.07
❑ 59 Richie Hebner	.15	.07
❑ 60 Dave Lopes	.40	.18
❑ 61 Gary Matthews	.15	.07
❑ 62 Keith Moreland	.15	.07
❑ 63 Rick Reuschel	.15	.07
❑ 64 Dick Ruthven	.15	.07
❑ 65 Ryne Sandberg	2.50	1.10
❑ 66 Scott Sanderson	.15	.07
❑ 67 Lee Smith	.75	.35
❑ 68 Tim Stoddard	.15	.07
❑ 69 Rick Sutcliffe	.40	.18
❑ 70 Steve Trout	.15	.07
❑ 71 Gary Woods	.15	.07
❑ 72 Wally Backman	.15	.07
❑ 73 Bruce Berenyi	.15	.07
❑ 74 Hubie Brooks UER (Kelvin Chapman's stats on card back)	.15	.07
❑ 75 Kelvin Chapman	.15	.07
❑ 76 Ron Darling	.40	.18
❑ 77 Sid Fernandez	.40	.18
❑ 78 Mike Fitzgerald	.15	.07
❑ 79 George Foster	.40	.18
❑ 80 Brent Gaff	.15	.07
❑ 81 Ron Gardenhire	.15	.07
❑ 82 Dwight Gooden RC	2.00	.90
❑ 83 Tom Gorman	.15	.07
❑ 84 Danny Heep	.15	.07
❑ 85 Keith Hernandez	.40	.18
❑ 86 Ray Knight	.15	.07
❑ 87 Ed Lynch	.15	.07
❑ 88 Jose Oquendo	.15	.07
❑ 89 Jesse Orosco	.15	.07
❑ 90 Rafael Santana	.15	.07
❑ 91 Doug Sisk	.15	.07
❑ 92 Rusty Staub	.40	.18
❑ 93 Darryl Strawberry	1.25	.55
❑ 94 Walt Terrell	.15	.07
❑ 95 Mookie Wilson	.40	.18
❑ 96 Jim Acker	.15	.07
❑ 97 Willie Aikens	.15	.07
❑ 98 Doyle Alexander	.15	.07
❑ 99 Jesse Barfield	.15	.07
❑ 100 George Bell	.40	.18
❑ 101 Jim Clancy	.15	.07
❑ 102 Dave Collins	.15	.07
❑ 103 Tony Fernandez	.40	.18
❑ 104 Damaso Garcia	.15	.07
❑ 105 Jim Gott	.15	.07
❑ 106 Alfredo Griffin	.15	.07
❑ 107 Garth Iorg	.15	.07
❑ 108 Roy Lee Jackson	.15	.07
❑ 109 Cliff Johnson	.15	.07
❑ 110 Jimmy Key RC	1.25	.55
❑ 111 Dennis Lamp	.15	.07
❑ 112 Rick Leach	.15	.07
❑ 113 Luis Leal	.15	.07
❑ 114 Buck Martinez	.15	.07
❑ 115 Lloyd Moseby	.15	.07
❑ 116 Rance Mulliniks	.15	.07
❑ 117 Dave Stieb	.40	.18
❑ 118 Willie Upshaw	.15	.07
❑ 119 Ernie Whitt	.15	.07
❑ 120 Mike Armstrong	.15	.07
❑ 121 Don Baylor	.40	.18
❑ 122 Marty Bystrom	.15	.07
❑ 123 Rick Cerone	.15	.07
❑ 124 Joe Cowley	.15	.07
❑ 125 Brian Dayett	.15	.07
❑ 126 Tim Foli	.15	.07
❑ 127 Ray Fontenot	.15	.07
❑ 128 Ken Griffey	.40	.18
❑ 129 Ron Guidry	.40	.18
❑ 130 Toby Harrah	.15	.07
❑ 131 Jay Howell	.15	.07
❑ 132 Steve Kemp	.15	.07
❑ 133 Don Mattingly	4.00	1.80
❑ 134 Bobby Meacham	.15	.07
❑ 135 John Montefusco	.15	.07
❑ 136 Omar Moreno	.15	.07
❑ 137 Dale Murray	.15	.07
❑ 138 Phil Niekro	1.25	.55
❑ 139 Mike Pagliarulo	.15	.07
❑ 140 Willie Randolph	.40	.18
❑ 141 Dennis Rasmussen	.15	.07
❑ 142 Dave Righetti	.40	.18
❑ 143 Jose Rijo RC	.75	.35
❑ 144 Andre Robertson	.15	.07
❑ 145 Bob Shirley	.15	.07
❑ 146 Dave Winfield	1.25	.55
❑ 147 Butch Wynegar	.15	.07

❑ 148 Gary Allenson .15 .07
❑ 149 Tony Armas .15 .07
❑ 150 Marty Barrett .15 .07
❑ 151 Wade Boggs 1.25 .55
❑ 152 Dennis Boyd .15 .07
❑ 153 Bill Buckner .40 .18
❑ 154 Mark Clear .15 .07
❑ 155 Roger Clemens RC 30.00 13.50
❑ 156 Steve Crawford .15 .07
❑ 157 Mike Easler .15 .07
❑ 158 Dwight Evans .40 .18
❑ 159 Rich Gedman .15 .07
❑ 160 Jackie Gutierrez .40 .18
(Wade Boggs
shown on deck)
❑ 161 Bruce Hurst .15 .07
❑ 162 John Henry Johnson .15 .07
❑ 163 Rick Miller .15 .07
❑ 164 Reid Nichols .15 .07
❑ 165 Al Nipper .15 .07
❑ 166 Bob Ojeda .15 .07
❑ 167 Jerry Remy .15 .07
❑ 168 Jim Rice .40 .18
❑ 169 Bob Stanley .15 .07
❑ 170 Mike Boddicker .15 .07
❑ 171 Al Bumbry .15 .07
❑ 172 Todd Cruz .15 .07
❑ 173 Rich Dauer .15 .07
❑ 174 Storm Davis .15 .07
❑ 175 Rick Dempsey .15 .07
❑ 176 Jim Dwyer .15 .07
❑ 177 Mike Flanagan .15 .07
❑ 178 Dan Ford .15 .07
❑ 179 Wayne Gross .15 .07
❑ 180 John Lowenstein .15 .07
❑ 181 Dennis Martinez .40 .18
❑ 182 Tippy Martinez .15 .07
❑ 183 Scott McGregor .15 .07
❑ 184 Eddie Murray 1.25 .55
❑ 185 Joe Nolan .15 .07
❑ 186 Floyd Rayford .15 .07
❑ 187 Cal Ripken 5.00 2.20
❑ 188 Gary Roenicke .15 .07
❑ 189 Lenn Sakata .15 .07
❑ 190 John Shelby .15 .07
❑ 191 Ken Singleton .15 .07
❑ 192 Sammy Stewart .15 .07
❑ 193 Bill Swaggerty .15 .07
❑ 194 Tom Underwood .15 .07
❑ 195 Mike Young .15 .07
❑ 196 Steve Balboni .15 .07
❑ 197 Joe Beckwith .15 .07
❑ 198 Bud Black .15 .07
❑ 199 George Brett 2.50 1.10
❑ 200 Onix Concepcion .15 .07
❑ 201 Mark Gubicza RC* .40 .18
❑ 202 Larry Gura .15 .07
❑ 203 Mark Huismann .15 .07
❑ 204 Dane Iorg .15 .07
❑ 205 Danny Jackson .15 .07
❑ 206 Charlie Leibrandt .15 .07
❑ 207 Hal McRae .40 .18
❑ 208 Darryl Motley .15 .07
❑ 209 Jorge Orta .15 .07
❑ 210 Greg Pryor .15 .07
❑ 211 Dan Quisenberry .40 .18
❑ 212 Bret Saberhagen RC 1.00 .45
❑ 213 Pat Sheridan .15 .07
❑ 214 Don Slaught .15 .07
❑ 215 U.L. Washington .15 .07
❑ 216 John Wathan .15 .07
❑ 217 Frank White .40 .18
❑ 218 Willie Wilson .15 .07
❑ 219 Neil Allen .15 .07
❑ 220 Joaquin Andujar .15 .07
❑ 221 Steve Braun .15 .07
❑ 222 Danny Cox .15 .07
❑ 223 Bob Forsch .15 .07
❑ 224 David Green .15 .07
❑ 225 George Hendrick .15 .07
❑ 226 Tom Herr .15 .07
❑ 227 Ricky Horton .15 .07
❑ 228 Art Howe .15 .07
❑ 229 Mike Jorgensen .15 .07
❑ 230 Kurt Kepshire .15 .07
❑ 231 Jeff Lahti .15 .07
❑ 232 Tito Landrum .15 .07
❑ 233 Dave LaPoint .15 .07
❑ 234 Willie McGee .40 .18
❑ 235 Tom Nieto .15 .07
❑ 236 Terry Pendleton RC 1.25 .55
❑ 237 Darrell Porter .15 .07
❑ 238 Dave Rucker .15 .07
❑ 239 Lonnie Smith .15 .07
❑ 240 Ozzie Smith 1.50 .70
❑ 241 Bruce Sutter .40 .18
❑ 242 Andy Van Slyke UER .40 .18
(Bats Right,
Throws Left)
❑ 243 Dave Von Ohlen .15 .07
❑ 244 Larry Andersen .15 .07
❑ 245 Bill Campbell .15 .07
❑ 246 Steve Carlton 1.25 .55
❑ 247 Tim Corcoran .15 .07
❑ 248 Ivan DeJesus .15 .07
❑ 249 John Denny .15 .07
❑ 250 Bo Diaz .15 .07
❑ 251 Greg Gross .15 .07
❑ 252 Kevin Gross .15 .07
❑ 253 Von Hayes .15 .07
❑ 254 Al Holland .15 .07
❑ 255 Charles Hudson .15 .07
❑ 256 Jerry Koosman .40 .18
❑ 257 Joe Lefebvre .15 .07
❑ 258 Sixto Lezcano .15 .07
❑ 259 Garry Maddox .15 .07
❑ 260 Len Matuszek .15 .07
❑ 261 Tug McGraw .40 .18
❑ 262 Al Oliver .40 .18
❑ 263 Shane Rawley .15 .07
❑ 264 Juan Samuel .15 .07
❑ 265 Mike Schmidt 2.50 1.10
❑ 266 Jeff Stone .15 .07
❑ 267 Ozzie Virgil .15 .07
❑ 268 Glenn Wilson .15 .07
❑ 269 John Wockenfuss .15 .07
❑ 270 Darrell Brown .15 .07
❑ 271 Tom Brunansky .40 .18
❑ 272 Randy Bush .15 .07
❑ 273 John Butcher .15 .07
❑ 274 Bobby Castillo .15 .07
❑ 275 Ron Davis .15 .07
❑ 276 Dave Engle .15 .07
❑ 277 Pete Filson .15 .07
❑ 278 Gary Gaetti .40 .18
❑ 279 Mickey Hatcher .15 .07
❑ 280 Ed Hodge .15 .07
❑ 281 Kent Hrbek .40 .18
❑ 282 Houston Jimenez .15 .07
❑ 283 Tim Laudner .15 .07
❑ 284 Rick Lysander .15 .07
❑ 285 Dave Meier .15 .07
❑ 286 Kirby Puckett RC 20.00 9.00
❑ 287 Pat Putnam .15 .07
❑ 288 Ken Schrom .15 .07
❑ 289 Mike Smithson .15 .07
❑ 290 Tim Teufel .15 .07
❑ 291 Frank Viola .40 .18
❑ 292 Ron Washington .15 .07
❑ 293 Don Aase .15 .07
❑ 294 Juan Beniquez .15 .07
❑ 295 Bob Boone .40 .18
❑ 296 Mike C. Brown .15 .07
❑ 297 Rod Carew 1.25 .55
❑ 298 Doug Corbett .15 .07
❑ 299 Doug DeCinces .15 .07
❑ 300 Brian Downing .15 .07
❑ 301 Ken Forsch .15 .07
❑ 302 Bobby Grich .40 .18
❑ 303 Reggie Jackson 1.50 .70
❑ 304 Tommy John .75 .35
❑ 305 Curt Kaufman .15 .07
❑ 306 Bruce Kison .15 .07
❑ 307 Fred Lynn .40 .18
❑ 308 Gary Pettis .15 .07
❑ 309 Ron Romanick .15 .07
❑ 310 Luis Sanchez .15 .07
❑ 311 Dick Schofield .15 .07
❑ 312 Daryl Sconiers .15 .07
❑ 313 Jim Slaton .15 .07
❑ 314 Derrel Thomas .15 .07
❑ 315 Rob Wilfong .15 .07
❑ 316 Mike Witt .15 .07
❑ 317 Geoff Zahn .15 .07
❑ 318 Len Barker .15 .07
❑ 319 Steve Bedrosian .15 .07
❑ 320 Bruce Benedict .15 .07
❑ 321 Rick Camp .15 .07
❑ 322 Chris Chambliss .40 .18
❑ 323 Jeff Dedmon .15 .07
❑ 324 Terry Forster .15 .07
❑ 325 Gene Garber .15 .07
❑ 326 Albert Hall .15 .07
❑ 327 Terry Harper .15 .07
❑ 328 Bob Horner .15 .07
❑ 329 Glenn Hubbard .15 .07
❑ 330 Randy Johnson .15 .07
❑ 331 Brad Komminsk .15 .07
❑ 332 Rick Mahler .15 .07
❑ 333 Craig McMurtry .15 .07
❑ 334 Donnie Moore .15 .07
❑ 335 Dale Murphy 1.25 .55
❑ 336 Ken Oberkfell .15 .07
❑ 337 Pascual Perez .15 .07
❑ 338 Gerald Perry .15 .07
❑ 339 Rafael Ramirez .15 .07
❑ 340 Jerry Royster .15 .07
❑ 341 Alex Trevino .15 .07
❑ 342 Claudell Washington .15 .07
❑ 343 Alan Ashby .15 .07
❑ 344 Mark Bailey .15 .07
❑ 345 Kevin Bass .15 .07
❑ 346 Enos Cabell .15 .07
❑ 347 Jose Cruz .40 .18
❑ 348 Bill Dawley .15 .07
❑ 349 Frank DiPino .15 .07
❑ 350 Bill Doran .15 .07
❑ 351 Phil Garner .40 .18
❑ 352 Bob Knepper .15 .07
❑ 353 Mike LaCoss .15 .07
❑ 354 Jerry Mumphrey .15 .07
❑ 355 Joe Niekro .15 .07
❑ 356 Terry Puhl .15 .07
❑ 357 Craig Reynolds .15 .07
❑ 358 Vern Ruhle .15 .07
❑ 359 Nolan Ryan 6.00 2.70
❑ 360 Joe Sambito .15 .07
❑ 361 Mike Scott .15 .07
❑ 362 Dave Smith .15 .07
❑ 363 Julio Solano .15 .07
❑ 364 Dickie Thon .15 .07
❑ 365 Denny Walling .15 .07
❑ 366 Dave Anderson .15 .07
❑ 367 Bob Bailor .15 .07
❑ 368 Greg Brock .15 .07
❑ 369 Carlos Diaz .15 .07
❑ 370 Pedro Guerrero .40 .18
❑ 371 Orel Hershiser RC 2.00 .90
❑ 372 Rick Honeycutt .15 .07
❑ 373 Burt Hooton .15 .07
❑ 374 Ken Howell .15 .07
❑ 375 Ken Landreaux .15 .07
❑ 376 Candy Maldonado .15 .07
❑ 377 Mike Marshall .15 .07
❑ 378 Tom Niedenfuer .15 .07
❑ 379 Alejandro Pena .15 .07
❑ 380 Jerry Reuss UER .15 .07
("Home:" omitted)
❑ 381 R.J. Reynolds .15 .07
❑ 382 German Rivera .15 .07
❑ 383 Bill Russell .15 .07
❑ 384 Steve Sax .15 .07
❑ 385 Mike Scioscia .15 .07
❑ 386 Franklin Stubbs .15 .07
❑ 387 Fernando Valenzuela .40 .18
❑ 388 Bob Welch .15 .07
❑ 389 Terry Whitfield .15 .07
❑ 390 Steve Yeager .15 .07
❑ 391 Pat Zachry .15 .07
❑ 392 Fred Breining .15 .07
❑ 393 Gary Carter .75 .35
❑ 394 Andre Dawson .75 .35
❑ 395 Miguel Dilone .15 .07
❑ 396 Dan Driessen .15 .07
❑ 397 Doug Flynn .15 .07
❑ 398 Terry Francona .15 .07
❑ 399 Bill Gullickson .15 .07
❑ 400 Bob James .15 .07

❑ 401 Charlie Lea .15 .07
❑ 402 Bryan Little .15 .07
❑ 403 Gary Lucas .15 .07
❑ 404 David Palmer .15 .07
❑ 405 Tim Raines .40 .18
❑ 406 Mike Ramsey .15 .07
❑ 407 Jeff Reardon .40 .18
❑ 408 Steve Rogers .15 .07
❑ 409 Dan Schatzeder .15 .07
❑ 410 Bryn Smith .15 .07
❑ 411 Mike Stenhouse .15 .07
❑ 412 Tim Wallach .40 .18
❑ 413 Jim Wohlford .15 .07
❑ 414 Bill Almon .15 .07
❑ 415 Keith Atherton .15 .07
❑ 416 Bruce Bochte .15 .07
❑ 417 Tom Burgmeier .15 .07
❑ 418 Ray Burris .15 .07
❑ 419 Bill Caudill .15 .07
❑ 420 Chris Codiroli .15 .07
❑ 421 Tim Conroy .15 .07
❑ 422 Mike Davis .15 .07
❑ 423 Jim Essian .15 .07
❑ 424 Mike Heath .15 .07
❑ 425 Rickey Henderson 2.50 1.10
❑ 426 Donnie Hill .15 .07
❑ 427 Dave Kingman .40 .18
❑ 428 Bill Krueger .15 .07
❑ 429 Carney Lansford .40 .18
❑ 430 Steve McCatty .15 .07
❑ 431 Joe Morgan 1.25 .55
❑ 432 Dwayne Murphy .15 .07
❑ 433 Tony Phillips .15 .07
❑ 434 Lary Sorensen .15 .07
❑ 435 Mike Warren .15 .07
❑ 436 Curt Young .15 .07
❑ 437 Luis Aponte .15 .07
❑ 438 Chris Bando .15 .07
❑ 439 Tony Bernazard .15 .07
❑ 440 Bert Blyleven .40 .18
❑ 441 Brett Butler .40 .18
❑ 442 Ernie Camacho .15 .07
❑ 443 Joe Carter 1.25 .55
❑ 444 Carmelo Castillo .15 .07
❑ 445 Jamie Easterly .15 .07
❑ 446 Steve Farr RC .40 .18
❑ 447 Mike Fischlin .15 .07
❑ 448 Julio Franco .75 .35
❑ 449 Mel Hall .15 .07
❑ 450 Mike Hargrove .40 .18
❑ 451 Neal Heaton .15 .07
❑ 452 Brook Jacoby .15 .07
❑ 453 Mike Jeffcoat .15 .07
❑ 454 Don Schulze .15 .07
❑ 455 Roy Smith .15 .07
❑ 456 Pat Tabler .15 .07
❑ 457 Andre Thornton .15 .07
❑ 458 George Vukovich .15 .07
❑ 459 Tom Waddell .15 .07
❑ 460 Jerry Willard .15 .07
❑ 461 Dale Berra .15 .07
❑ 462 John Candelaria .15 .07
❑ 463 Jose DeLeon .15 .07
❑ 464 Doug Frobel .15 .07
❑ 465 Cecilio Guante .15 .07
❑ 466 Brian Harper .15 .07
❑ 467 Lee Lacy .15 .07
❑ 468 Bill Madlock .40 .18
❑ 469 Lee Mazzilli .15 .07
❑ 470 Larry McWilliams .15 .07
❑ 471 Jim Morrison .15 .07
❑ 472 Tony Pena .15 .07
❑ 473 Johnny Ray .15 .07
❑ 474 Rick Rhoden .15 .07
❑ 475 Don Robinson .15 .07
❑ 476 Rod Scurry .15 .07
❑ 477 Kent Tekulve .15 .07
❑ 478 Jason Thompson .15 .07
❑ 479 John Tudor .15 .07
❑ 480 Lee Tunnell .15 .07
❑ 481 Marvell Wynne .15 .07
❑ 482 Salome Barojas .15 .07
❑ 483 Dave Beard .15 .07
❑ 484 Jim Beattie .15 .07
❑ 485 Barry Bonnell .15 .07
❑ 486 Phil Bradley .40 .18
❑ 487 Al Cowens .15 .07
❑ 488 Alvin Davis RC* .40 .18
❑ 489 Dave Henderson .15 .07
❑ 490 Steve Henderson .15 .07
❑ 491 Bob Kearney .15 .07
❑ 492 Mark Langston RC .75 .35
❑ 493 Larry Milbourne .15 .07
❑ 494 Paul Mirabella .15 .07
❑ 495 Mike Moore .15 .07
❑ 496 Edwin Nunez .15 .07
❑ 497 Spike Owen .15 .07
❑ 498 Jack Perconte .15 .07
❑ 499 Ken Phelps .15 .07
❑ 500 Jim Presley .40 .18
❑ 501 Mike Stanton .15 .07
❑ 502 Bob Stoddard .15 .07
❑ 503 Gorman Thomas .15 .07
❑ 504 Ed VandeBerg .15 .07
❑ 505 Matt Young .15 .07
❑ 506 Juan Agosto .15 .07
❑ 507 Harold Baines .40 .18
❑ 508 Floyd Bannister .15 .07
❑ 509 Britt Burns .15 .07
❑ 510 Julio Cruz .15 .07
❑ 511 Richard Dotson .15 .07
❑ 512 Jerry Dybzinski .15 .07
❑ 513 Carlton Fisk 1.25 .55
❑ 514 Scott Fletcher .15 .07
❑ 515 Jerry Hairston .15 .07
❑ 516 Marc Hill .15 .07
❑ 517 LaMarr Hoyt .15 .07
❑ 518 Ron Kittle .15 .07
❑ 519 Rudy Law .15 .07
❑ 520 Vance Law .15 .07
❑ 521 Greg Luzinski .40 .18
❑ 522 Gene Nelson .15 .07
❑ 523 Tom Paciorek .40 .18
❑ 524 Ron Reed .15 .07
❑ 525 Bert Roberge .15 .07
❑ 526 Tom Seaver 2.00 .90
❑ 527 Roy Smalley .15 .07
❑ 528 Dan Spillner .15 .07
❑ 529 Mike Squires .15 .07
❑ 530 Greg Walker .15 .07
❑ 531 Cesar Cedeno .40 .18
❑ 532 Dave Concepcion .40 .18
❑ 533 Eric Davis RC 2.00 .90
❑ 534 Nick Esasky .15 .07
❑ 535 Tom Foley .15 .07
❑ 536 John Franco RC UER 1.25 .55
(Koufax misspelled as Kofax on back)
❑ 537 Brad Gulden .15 .07
❑ 538 Tom Hume .15 .07
❑ 539 Wayne Krenchicki .15 .07
❑ 540 Andy McGaffigan .15 .07
❑ 541 Eddie Milner .15 .07
❑ 542 Ron Oester .15 .07
❑ 543 Bob Owchinko .15 .07
❑ 544 Dave Parker .40 .18
❑ 545 Frank Pastore .15 .07
❑ 546 Tony Perez 1.25 .55
❑ 547 Ted Power .15 .07
❑ 548 Joe Price .15 .07
❑ 549 Gary Redus .15 .07
❑ 550 Pete Rose 4.00 1.80
❑ 551 Jeff Russell .15 .07
❑ 552 Mario Soto .15 .07
❑ 553 Jay Tibbs .15 .07
❑ 554 Duane Walker .15 .07
❑ 555 Alan Bannister .15 .07
❑ 556 Buddy Bell .40 .18
❑ 557 Danny Darwin .15 .07
❑ 558 Charlie Hough .40 .18
❑ 559 Bobby Jones .15 .07
❑ 560 Odell Jones .15 .07
❑ 561 Jeff Kunkel .15 .07
❑ 562 Mike Mason .15 .07
❑ 563 Pete O'Brien .15 .07
❑ 564 Larry Parrish .15 .07
❑ 565 Mickey Rivers .15 .07
❑ 566 Billy Sample .15 .07
❑ 567 Dave Schmidt .15 .07
❑ 568 Donnie Scott .15 .07
❑ 569 Dave Stewart .40 .18
❑ 570 Frank Tanana .15 .07
❑ 571 Wayne Tolleson .15 .07
❑ 572 Gary Ward .15 .07
❑ 573 Curtis Wilkerson .15 .07
❑ 574 George Wright .15 .07
❑ 575 Ned Yost .15 .07
❑ 576 Mark Brouhard .15 .07
❑ 577 Mike Caldwell .15 .07
❑ 578 Bobby Clark .15 .07
❑ 579 Jaime Cocanower .15 .07
❑ 580 Cecil Cooper .40 .18
❑ 581 Rollie Fingers 1.25 .55
❑ 582 Jim Gantner .15 .07
❑ 583 Moose Haas .15 .07
❑ 584 Dion James .15 .07
❑ 585 Pete Ladd .15 .07
❑ 586 Rick Manning .15 .07
❑ 587 Bob McClure .15 .07
❑ 588 Paul Molitor 1.25 .55
❑ 589 Charlie Moore .15 .07
❑ 590 Ben Oglivie .15 .07
❑ 591 Chuck Porter .15 .07
❑ 592 Randy Ready RC* .15 .07
❑ 593 Ed Romero .15 .07
❑ 594 Bill Schroeder .15 .07
❑ 595 Ray Searage .15 .07
❑ 596 Ted Simmons .40 .18
❑ 597 Jim Sundberg .15 .07
❑ 598 Don Sutton 1.25 .55
❑ 599 Tom Tellmann .15 .07
❑ 600 Rick Waits .15 .07
❑ 601 Robin Yount 1.25 .55
❑ 602 Dusty Baker .40 .18
❑ 603 Bob Brenly .15 .07
❑ 604 Jack Clark .40 .18
❑ 605 Chili Davis .40 .18
❑ 606 Mark Davis .15 .07
❑ 607 Dan Gladden RC .40 .18
❑ 608 Atlee Hammaker .15 .07
❑ 609 Mike Krukow .15 .07
❑ 610 Duane Kuiper .15 .07
❑ 611 Bob Lacey .15 .07
❑ 612 Bill Laskey .15 .07
❑ 613 Gary Lavelle .15 .07
❑ 614 Johnnie LeMaster .15 .07
❑ 615 Jeff Leonard .15 .07
❑ 616 Randy Lerch .15 .07
❑ 617 Greg Minton .15 .07
❑ 618 Steve Nicosia .15 .07
❑ 619 Gene Richards .15 .07
❑ 620 Jeff D. Robinson .15 .07
❑ 621 Scot Thompson .15 .07
❑ 622 Manny Trillo .15 .07
❑ 623 Brad Wellman .15 .07
❑ 624 Frank Williams .15 .07
❑ 625 Joel Youngblood .15 .07
❑ 626 Cal Ripken IA 3.00 1.35
❑ 627 Mike Schmidt IA .75 .35
❑ 628 Giving The Signs .40 .18
Sparky Anderson
❑ 629 AL Pitcher's Nightmare 1.25 .55
Dave Winfield
Rickey Henderson
❑ 630 NL Pitcher's Nightmare 2.00 .90
Mike Schmidt
Ryne Sandberg
❑ 631 NL All-Stars 1.25 .55
Darryl Strawberry
Gary Carter
Steve Garvey
Ozzie Smith
❑ 632 A-S Winning Battery .40 .18
Gary Carter
Charlie Lea
❑ 633 NL Pennant Clinchers .75 .35
Steve Garvey
Rich Gossage
❑ 634 NL Rookie Phenoms 1.25 .55
Dwight Gooden
Juan Samuel
❑ 635 Toronto's Big Guns .15 .07
Willie Upshaw
❑ 636 Toronto's Big Guns .15 .07
Lloyd Moseby
❑ 637 HOLLAND: Al Holland .15 .07
❑ 638 TUNNELL .15 .07
Lee Tunnell

❑ 639 Reggie Jackson .... 1.25 .55
500th Homer
❑ 640 4000th Hit .... 1.25 .55
Pete Rose
❑ 641 Father and Son 3.00 1.35
Cal Ripken Jr.
Cal Ripken Sr.
❑ 642 Cubs: Division Champs.. .40 .18
❑ 643 Two Perfect Games ...... .40 .18
and One No-Hitter:
Mike Witt
David Palmer
Jack Morris
❑ 644 Willie Lozado and .... .15 .07
Vic Mata
❑ 645 Kelly Gruber RC and...... .40 .18
Randy O'Neal
❑ 646 Jose Roman and............ .15 .07
Joel Skinner
❑ 647 Steve Kiefer RC and .... 1.25 .55
Danny Tartabull
❑ 648 Rob Dee RC and........... .40 .18
Alejandro Sanchez
❑ 649 Billy Hatcher RC and.... 1.00 .45
Shawon Dunston
❑ 650 Ron Robinson and .... .15 .07
Mike Bielecki
❑ 651 Zane Smith RC and........ .40 .18
Paul Zuvella
❑ 652 Joe Hesketh RC and...... .40 .18
Glenn Davis
❑ 653 John Russell and............ .15 .07
Steve Jeltz
❑ 654 CL: Tigers/Padres .... .15 .07
and Cubs/Mets
❑ 655 CL: Blue Jays/Yankees .. .15 .07
and Red Sox/Orioles
❑ 656 CL: Royals/Cardinals .... .15 .07
and Phillies/Twins
❑ 657 CL: Angels/Braves .... .15 .07
and Astros/Dodgers
❑ 658 CL: Expos/A's .... .15 .07
and Indians/Pirates
❑ 659 CL: Mariners/White Sox .15 .07
and Reds/Rangers
❑ 660 CL: Brewers/Giants........ .15 .07
and Special Cards

1985 Fleer Update

	NRMT	VG-E
COMP.FACT.SET (132)	6.00	2.70

❑ 1 Don Aase .... .15 .07
❑ 2 Bill Almon .... .15 .07
❑ 3 Dusty Baker........................ .40 .18
❑ 4 Dale Berra........................ .15 .07
❑ 5 Karl Best .... .15 .07
❑ 6 Tim Birtsas .... .15 .07
❑ 7 Vida Blue........................ .40 .18
❑ 8 Rich Bordi .... .15. .07
❑ 9 Daryl Boston XRC* .... .15 .07
❑ 10 Hubie Brooks.................. .15 .07
❑ 11 Chris Brown.................... .15 .07
❑ 12 Tom Browning XRC* .... .40 .18
❑ 13 Al Bumbry .... .15 .07
❑ 14 Tim Burke .... .15 .07
❑ 15 Ray Burris .... .15 .07
❑ 16 Jeff Burroughs.................. .15 .07
❑ 17 Ivan Calderon XRC .... .15 .07
❑ 18 Jeff Calhoun .... .15 .07
❑ 19 Bill Campbell .... .15 .07
❑ 20 Don Carman .... .15 .07
❑ 21 Gary Carter .... .75 .35
❑ 22 Bobby Castillo .... .15 .07
❑ 23 Bill Caudill .... .15 .07
❑ 24 Rick Cerone .... .15 .07
❑ 25 Jack Clark .... .40 .18
❑ 26 Pat Clements.................... .15 .07
❑ 27 Stewart Cliburn .... .15 .07
❑ 28 Vince Coleman XRC ...... 1.00 .45
❑ 29 Dave Collins .... .15 .07
❑ 30 Fritz Connally .... .15 .07
❑ 31 Henry Cotto...................... .15 .07
❑ 32 Danny Darwin .... .15 .07
❑ 33 Darren Daulton XRC ...... 2.00 .90
❑ 34 Jerry Davis .... .15 .07
❑ 35 Brian Dayett .... .15 .07
❑ 36 Ken Dixon .... .15 .07
❑ 37 Tommy Dunbar .... .15 .07
❑ 38 Mariano Duncan XRC .... 1.00 .45
❑ 39 Bob Fallon........................ .15 .07
❑ 40 Brian Fisher...................... .15 .07
❑ 41 Mike Fitzgerald .... .15 .07
❑ 42 Ray Fontenot.................... .15 .07
❑ 43 Greg Gagne XRC* .... .40 .18
❑ 44 Oscar Gamble .... .15 .07
❑ 45 Jim Gott............................ .15 .07
❑ 46 David Green .... .15 .07
❑ 47 Alfredo Griffin .... .15 .07
❑ 48 Ozzie Guillen XRC .... 1.00 .45
❑ 49 Toby Harrah .... .15 .07
❑ 50 Ron Hassey...................... .15 .07
❑ 51 Rickey Henderson.......... 3.00 1.35
❑ 52 Steve Henderson .... .15 .07
❑ 53 George Hendrick.............. .15 .07
❑ 54 Teddy Higuera XRC .... .40 .18
❑ 55 Al Holland .... .15 .07
❑ 56 Burt Hooton...................... .15 .07
❑ 57 Jay Howell........................ .15 .07
❑ 58 LaMarr Hoyt .... .15 .07
❑ 59 Tim Hulett XRC* .... .15 .07
❑ 60 Bob James .... .15 .07
❑ 61 Cliff Johnson .... .15 .07
❑ 62 Howard Johnson .... .40 .18
❑ 63 Ruppert Jones.................. .15 .07
❑ 64 Steve Kemp...................... .15 .07
❑ 65 Bruce Kison...................... .15 .07
❑ 66 Mike LaCoss .... .15 .07
❑ 67 Lee Lacy .... .15 .07
❑ 68 Dave LaPoint.................... .15 .07
❑ 69 Gary Lavelle .... .15 .07
❑ 70 Vance Law .... .15 .07
❑ 71 Manny Lee XRC .... .15 .07
❑ 72 Sixto Lezcano .... .15 .07
❑ 73 Tim Lollar .... .15 .07
❑ 74 Urbano Lugo .... .15 .07
❑ 75 Fred Lynn .... .40 .18
❑ 76 Steve Lyons .... .40 .18
❑ 77 Mickey Mahler.................. .15 .07
❑ 78 Ron Mathis .... .15 .07
❑ 79 Len Matuszek .... .15 .07
❑ 80 O.McDowell XRC UER .... .40 .18
Part of bio
actually Roger's
❑ 81 R.McDowell XRC UER .... .40 .18
Part of bio
actually Oddibe's
❑ 82 Donnie Moore .... .15 .07
❑ 83 Ron Musselman .... .15 .07
❑ 84 Al Oliver............................ .40 .18
❑ 85 Joe Orsulak XRC .... .40 .18
❑ 86 Dan Pasqua XRC* .... .40 .18
❑ 87 Chris Pittaro .... .15 .07
❑ 88 Rick Reuschel .... .15 .07
❑ 89 Earnie Riles...................... .15 .07
❑ 90 Jerry Royster.................... .15 .07
❑ 91 Dave Rozema .... .15 .07
❑ 92 Dave Rucker .... .15 .07
❑ 93 Vern Ruhle .... .15 .07
❑ 94 Mark Salas .... .15 .07
❑ 95 Luis Salazar .... .15 .07
❑ 96 Joe Sambito .... .15 .07
❑ 97 Billy Sample .... .15 .07
❑ 98 Alejandro Sanchez .... .15 .07
❑ 99 Calvin Schiraldi .... .15 .07
❑ 100 Rick Schu .... .15 .07
❑ 101 Larry Sheets .... .15 .07
❑ 102 Ron Shephard................ .15 .07
❑ 103 Nelson Simmons............ .15 .07
❑ 104 Don Slaught .... .15 .07
❑ 105 Roy Smalley .... .15 .07
❑ 106 Lonnie Smith .... .15 .07
❑ 107 Nate Snell .... .15 .07
❑ 108 Lary Sorensen................ .15 .07
❑ 109 Chris Speier .... .15 .07
❑ 110 Mike Stenhouse .... .15 .07
❑ 111 Tim Stoddard.................. .15 .07
❑ 112 John Stuper.................... .15 .07
❑ 113 Jim Sundberg .... .15 .07
❑ 114 Bruce Sutter .... .40 .18
❑ 115 Don Sutton .... 1.00 .45
❑ 116 Bruce Tanner .... .15 .07
❑ 117 Kent Tekulve .... .15 .07
❑ 118 Walt Terrell .... .15 .07
❑ 119 Mickey Tettleton XRC .. 1.00 .45
❑ 120 Rich Thompson.............. .15 .07
❑ 121 Louis Thornton .... .15 .07
❑ 122 Alex Trevino .... .15 .07
❑ 123 John Tudor .... .15 .07
❑ 124 Jose Uribe...................... .15 .07
❑ 125 Dave Valle XRC .... .15 .07
❑ 126 Dave Von Ohlen .... .15 .07
❑ 127 Curt Wardle.................... .15 .07
❑ 128 U.L. Washington .... .15 .07
❑ 129 Ed Whitson .... .15 .07
❑ 130 Herm Winningham .... .15 .07
❑ 131 Rich Yett .... .15 .07
❑ 132 Checklist U1-U132 .... .15 .07

1986 Fleer

	MINT	NRMT
COMPLETE SET (660)	40.00	18.00
COMP.FACT.SET (660).........	40.00	18.00

❑ 1 Steve Balboni .... .15 .07
❑ 2 Joe Beckwith.................... .15 .07
❑ 3 Buddy Biancalana.............. .15 .07
❑ 4 Bud Black .... .15 .07
❑ 5 George Brett .... 1.50 .70
❑ 6 Onix Concepcion.............. .15 .07
❑ 7 Steve Farr .... .15 .07
❑ 8 Mark Gubicza .... .15 .07
❑ 9 Dane Iorg .... .15 .07
❑ 10 Danny Jackson .... .15 .07
❑ 11 Lynn Jones .... .15 .07
❑ 12 Mike Jones .... .15 .07
❑ 13 Charlie Leibrandt............ .15 .07
❑ 14 Hal McRae .... .25 .11
❑ 15 Omar Moreno .... .15 .07
❑ 16 Darryl Motley .... .15 .07
❑ 17 Jorge Orta .... .15 .07
❑ 18 Dan Quisenberry .... .15 .07
❑ 19 Bret Saberhagen............ .25 .11
❑ 20 Pat Sheridan .... .15 .07
❑ 21 Lonnie Smith .... .15 .07
❑ 22 Jim Sundberg .... .15 .07
❑ 23 John Wathan .... .15 .07
❑ 24 Frank White.................... .25 .11
❑ 25 Willie Wilson .... .15 .07
❑ 26 Joaquin Andujar .... .15 .07

❑ 27 Steve Braun .15 .07
❑ 28 Bill Campbell .15 .07
❑ 29 Cesar Cedeno .25 .11
❑ 30 Jack Clark .25 .11
❑ 31 Vince Coleman RC* .75 .35
❑ 32 Danny Cox .15 .07
❑ 33 Ken Dayley .15 .07
❑ 34 Ivan DeJesus .15 .07
❑ 35 Bob Forsch .15 .07
❑ 36 Brian Harper .15 .07
❑ 37 Tom Herr .15 .07
❑ 38 Ricky Horton .15 .07
❑ 39 Kurt Kepshire .15 .07
❑ 40 Jeff Lahti .15 .07
❑ 41 Tito Landrum .15 .07
❑ 42 Willie McGee .25 .11
❑ 43 Tom Nieto .15 .07
❑ 44 Terry Pendleton .25 .11
❑ 45 Darrell Porter .25 .11
❑ 46 Ozzie Smith 1.00 .45
❑ 47 John Tudor .15 .07
❑ 48 Andy Van Slyke .25 .11
❑ 49 Todd Worrell RC .75 .35
❑ 50 Jim Acker .15 .07
❑ 51 Doyle Alexander .15 .07
❑ 52 Jesse Barfield .15 .07
❑ 53 George Bell .25 .11
❑ 54 Jeff Burroughs .15 .07
❑ 55 Bill Caudill .15 .07
❑ 56 Jim Clancy .15 .07
❑ 57 Tony Fernandez .15 .07
❑ 58 Tom Filer .15 .07
❑ 59 Damaso Garcia .15 .07
❑ 60 Tom Henke .25 .11
❑ 61 Garth Iorg .15 .07
❑ 62 Cliff Johnson .15 .07
❑ 63 Jimmy Key .75 .35
❑ 64 Dennis Lamp .15 .07
❑ 65 Gary Lavelle .15 .07
❑ 66 Buck Martinez .15 .07
❑ 67 Lloyd Moseby .15 .07
❑ 68 Rance Mulliniks .15 .07
❑ 69 Al Oliver .25 .11
❑ 70 Dave Stieb .15 .07
❑ 71 Louis Thornton .15 .07
❑ 72 Willie Upshaw .15 .07
❑ 73 Ernie Whitt .15 .07
❑ 74 Rick Aguilera RC .75 .35
❑ 75 Wally Backman .15 .07
❑ 76 Gary Carter .50 .23
❑ 77 Ron Darling .15 .07
❑ 78 Len Dykstra RC 1.50 .70
❑ 79 Sid Fernandez .25 .11
❑ 80 George Foster .25 .11
❑ 81 Dwight Gooden .75 .35
❑ 82 Tom Gorman .15 .07
❑ 83 Danny Heep .15 .07
❑ 84 Keith Hernandez .25 .11
❑ 85 Howard Johnson .25 .11
❑ 86 Ray Knight .25 .11
❑ 87 Terry Leach .15 .07
❑ 88 Ed Lynch .15 .07
❑ 89 Roger McDowell RC* .25 .11
❑ 90 Jesse Orosco .15 .07
❑ 91 Tom Paciorek .25 .11
❑ 92 Ronn Reynolds .15 .07
❑ 93 Rafael Santana .15 .07
❑ 94 Doug Sisk .15 .07
❑ 95 Rusty Staub .25 .11
❑ 96 Darryl Strawberry .75 .35
❑ 97 Mookie Wilson .25 .11
❑ 98 Neil Allen .15 .07
❑ 99 Don Baylor .50 .23
❑ 100 Dale Berra .15 .07
❑ 101 Rich Bordi .15 .07
❑ 102 Marty Bystrom .15 .07
❑ 103 Joe Cowley .15 .07
❑ 104 Brian Fisher .15 .07
❑ 105 Ken Griffey .25 .11
❑ 106 Ron Guidry .25 .11
❑ 107 Ron Hassey .15 .07
❑ 108 R.Henderson UER 1.50 .70
SB Record of 120, sic
❑ 109 Don Mattingly 2.00 .90
❑ 110 Bobby Meacham .15 .07
❑ 111 John Montefusco .15 .07
❑ 112 Phil Niekro .75 .35
❑ 113 Mike Pagliarulo .15 .07
❑ 114 Dan Pasqua .15 .07
❑ 115 Willie Randolph .25 .11
❑ 116 Dave Righetti .15 .07
❑ 117 Andre Robertson .15 .07
❑ 118 Billy Sample .15 .07
❑ 119 Bob Shirley .15 .07
❑ 120 Ed Whitson .15 .07
❑ 121 Dave Winfield .75 .35
❑ 122 Butch Wynegar .15 .07
❑ 123 Dave Anderson .15 .07
❑ 124 Bob Bailor .15 .07
❑ 125 Greg Brock .15 .07
❑ 126 Enos Cabell .15 .07
❑ 127 Bobby Castillo .15 .07
❑ 128 Carlos Diaz .15 .07
❑ 129 Mariano Duncan RC* .75 .35
❑ 130 Pedro Guerrero .25 .11
❑ 131 Orel Hershiser .50 .23
❑ 132 Rick Honeycutt .15 .07
❑ 133 Ken Howell .15 .07
❑ 134 Ken Landreaux .15 .07
❑ 135 Bill Madlock .15 .07
❑ 136 Candy Maldonado .15 .07
❑ 137 Mike Marshall .15 .07
❑ 138 Len Matuszek .15 .07
❑ 139 Tom Niedenfuer .15 .07
❑ 140 Alejandro Pena .15 .07
❑ 141 Jerry Reuss .15 .07
❑ 142 Bill Russell .15 .07
❑ 143 Steve Sax .15 .07
❑ 144 Mike Scioscia .15 .07
❑ 145 Fernando Valenzuela .25 .11
❑ 146 Bob Welch .15 .07
❑ 147 Terry Whitfield .15 .07
❑ 148 Juan Beniquez .15 .07
❑ 149 Bob Boone .25 .11
❑ 150 John Candelaria .15 .07
❑ 151 Rod Carew .75 .35
❑ 152 Stewart Cliburn .15 .07
❑ 153 Doug DeCinces .15 .07
❑ 154 Brian Downing .15 .07
❑ 155 Ken Forsch .15 .07
❑ 156 Craig Gerber .15 .07
❑ 157 Bobby Grich .25 .11
❑ 158 George Hendrick .15 .07
❑ 159 Al Holland .15 .07
❑ 160 Reggie Jackson 1.00 .45
❑ 161 Ruppert Jones .15 .07
❑ 162 Urbano Lugo .15 .07
❑ 163 Kirk McCaskill RC .25 .11
❑ 164 Donnie Moore .15 .07
❑ 165 Gary Pettis .15 .07
❑ 166 Ron Romanick .15 .07
❑ 167 Dick Schofield .15 .07
❑ 168 Daryl Sconiers .15 .07
❑ 169 Jim Slaton .15 .07
❑ 170 Don Sutton .75 .35
❑ 171 Mike Witt .15 .07
❑ 172 Buddy Bell .25 .11
❑ 173 Tom Browning .15 .07
❑ 174 Dave Concepcion .25 .11
❑ 175 Eric Davis .50 .23
❑ 176 Bo Diaz .15 .07
❑ 177 Nick Esasky .15 .07
❑ 178 John Franco .75 .35
❑ 179 Tom Hume .15 .07
❑ 180 Wayne Krenchicki .15 .07
❑ 181 Andy McGaffigan .15 .07
❑ 182 Eddie Milner .15 .07
❑ 183 Ron Oester .15 .07
❑ 184 Dave Parker .25 .11
❑ 185 Frank Pastore .15 .07
❑ 186 Tony Perez .75 .35
❑ 187 Ted Power .15 .07
❑ 188 Joe Price .15 .07
❑ 189 Gary Redus .15 .07
❑ 190 Ron Robinson .15 .07
❑ 191 Pete Rose 2.50 1.10
❑ 192 Mario Soto .15 .07
❑ 193 John Stuper .15 .07
❑ 194 Jay Tibbs .15 .07
❑ 195 Dave Van Gorder .15 .07
❑ 196 Max Venable .15 .07
❑ 197 Juan Agosto .15 .07
❑ 198 Harold Baines .50 .23
❑ 199 Floyd Bannister .15 .07
❑ 200 Britt Burns .15 .07
❑ 201 Julio Cruz .15 .07
❑ 202 Joel Davis .15 .07
❑ 203 Richard Dotson .15 .07
❑ 204 Carlton Fisk .75 .35
❑ 205 Scott Fletcher .15 .07
❑ 206 Ozzie Guillen RC* .50 .23
❑ 207 Jerry Hairston .15 .07
❑ 208 Tim Hulett .15 .07
❑ 209 Bob James .15 .07
❑ 210 Ron Kittle .15 .07
❑ 211 Rudy Law .15 .07
❑ 212 Bryan Little .15 .07
❑ 213 Gene Nelson .15 .07
❑ 214 Reid Nichols .15 .07
❑ 215 Luis Salazar .15 .07
❑ 216 Tom Seaver 1.25 .55
❑ 217 Dan Spillner .15 .07
❑ 218 Bruce Tanner .15 .07
❑ 219 Greg Walker .15 .07
❑ 220 Dave Wehrmeister .15 .07
❑ 221 Juan Berenguer .15 .07
❑ 222 Dave Bergman .15 .07
❑ 223 Tom Brookens .15 .07
❑ 224 Darrell Evans .25 .11
❑ 225 Barbaro Garbey .15 .07
❑ 226 Kirk Gibson .25 .11
❑ 227 John Grubb .15 .07
❑ 228 Willie Hernandez .15 .07
❑ 229 Larry Herndon .15 .07
❑ 230 Chet Lemon .15 .07
❑ 231 Aurelio Lopez .15 .07
❑ 232 Jack Morris .25 .11
❑ 233 Randy O'Neal .15 .07
❑ 234 Lance Parrish .25 .11
❑ 235 Dan Petry .15 .07
❑ 236 Alejandro Sanchez .15 .07
❑ 237 Bill Scherrer .15 .07
❑ 238 Nelson Simmons .15 .07
❑ 239 Frank Tanana .15 .07
❑ 240 Walt Terrell .15 .07
❑ 241 Alan Trammell .50 .23
❑ 242 Lou Whitaker .25 .11
❑ 243 Milt Wilcox .15 .07
❑ 244 Hubie Brooks .15 .07
❑ 245 Tim Burke .15 .07
❑ 246 Andre Dawson .50 .23
❑ 247 Mike Fitzgerald .15 .07
❑ 248 Terry Francona .15 .07
❑ 249 Bill Gullickson .15 .07
❑ 250 Joe Hesketh .15 .07
❑ 251 Bill Laskey .15 .07
❑ 252 Vance Law .15 .07
❑ 253 Charlie Lea .15 .07
❑ 254 Gary Lucas .15 .07
❑ 255 David Palmer .15 .07
❑ 256 Tim Raines .25 .11
❑ 257 Jeff Reardon .15 .07
❑ 258 Bert Roberge .15 .07
❑ 259 Dan Schatzeder .15 .07
❑ 260 Bryn Smith .15 .07
❑ 261 Randy St.Claire .15 .07
❑ 262 Scot Thompson .15 .07
❑ 263 Tim Wallach .15 .07
❑ 264 U.L. Washington .15 .07
❑ 265 Mitch Webster .15 .07
❑ 266 Herm Winningham .15 .07
❑ 267 Floyd Youmans .15 .07
❑ 268 Don Aase .15 .07
❑ 269 Mike Boddicker .15 .07
❑ 270 Rich Dauer .15 .07
❑ 271 Storm Davis .15 .07
❑ 272 Rick Dempsey .15 .07
❑ 273 Ken Dixon .15 .07
❑ 274 Jim Dwyer .15 .07
❑ 275 Mike Flanagan .15 .07
❑ 276 Wayne Gross .15 .07
❑ 277 Lee Lacy .15 .07
❑ 278 Fred Lynn .25 .11
❑ 279 Tippy Martinez .15 .07
❑ 280 Dennis Martinez .25 .11
❑ 281 Scott McGregor .15 .07
❑ 282 Eddie Murray .75 .35
❑ 283 Floyd Rayford .15 .07

❑ 284 Cal Ripken 3.00 1.35
❑ 285 Gary Roenicke .... .15 .07
❑ 286 Larry Sheets .... .15 .07
❑ 287 John Shelby .... .15 .07
❑ 288 Nate Snell .... .15 .07
❑ 289 Sammy Stewart .... .15 .07
❑ 290 Alan Wiggins .... .15 .07
❑ 291 Mike Young .... .15 .07
❑ 292 Alan Ashby .... .15 .07
❑ 293 Mark Bailey .... .15 .07
❑ 294 Kevin Bass .... .15 .07
❑ 295 Jeff Calhoun .... .15 .07
❑ 296 Jose Cruz .... .25 .11
❑ 297 Glenn Davis .... .25 .11
❑ 298 Bill Dawley .... .15 .07
❑ 299 Frank DiPino .... .15 .07
❑ 300 Bill Doran .... .15 .07
❑ 301 Phil Garner .... .25 .11
❑ 302 Jeff Heathcock .... .15 .07
❑ 303 Charlie Kerfeld .... .15 .07
❑ 304 Bob Knepper .... .15 .07
❑ 305 Ron Mathis .... .15 .07
❑ 306 Jerry Mumphrey .... .15 .07
❑ 307 Jim Pankovits .... .15 .07
❑ 308 Terry Puhl .... .15 .07
❑ 309 Craig Reynolds .... .15 .07
❑ 310 Nolan Ryan 4.00 1.80
❑ 311 Mike Scott .... .15 .07
❑ 312 Dave Smith .... .15 .07
❑ 313 Dickie Thon .... .15 .07
❑ 314 Denny Walling .... .15 .07
❑ 315 Kurt Bevacqua .... .15 .07
❑ 316 Al Bumbry .... .15 .07
❑ 317 Jerry Davis .... .15 .07
❑ 318 Luis DeLeon .... .15 .07
❑ 319 Dave Dravecky .... .25 .11
❑ 320 Tim Flannery .... .15 .07
❑ 321 Steve Garvey .... .50 .23
❑ 322 Rich Gossage .... .25 .11
❑ 323 Tony Gwynn .... 1.50 .70
❑ 324 Andy Hawkins .... .15 .07
❑ 325 LaMarr Hoyt .... .15 .07
❑ 326 Roy Lee Jackson .... .15 .07
❑ 327 Terry Kennedy .... .15 .07
❑ 328 Craig Lefferts .... .15 .07
❑ 329 Carmelo Martinez .... .15 .07
❑ 330 Lance McCullers .... .15 .07
❑ 331 Kevin McReynolds .... .15 .07
❑ 332 Graig Nettles .... .25 .11
❑ 333 Jerry Royster .... .15 .07
❑ 334 Eric Show .... .15 .07
❑ 335 Tim Stoddard .... .15 .07
❑ 336 Garry Templeton .... .15 .07
❑ 337 Mark Thurmond .... .15 .07
❑ 338 Ed Wojna .... .15 .07
❑ 339 Tony Armas .... .15 .07
❑ 340 Marty Barrett .... .15 .07
❑ 341 Wade Boggs .... .75 .35
❑ 342 Dennis Boyd .... .15 .07
❑ 343 Bill Buckner .... .25 .11
❑ 344 Mark Clear .... .15 .07
❑ 345 Roger Clemens 4.00 1.80
❑ 346 Steve Crawford .... .15 .07
❑ 347 Mike Easler .... .15 .07
❑ 348 Dwight Evans .... .25 .11
❑ 349 Rich Gedman .... .15 .07
❑ 350 Jackie Gutierrez .... .15 .07
❑ 351 Glenn Hoffman .... .15 .07
❑ 352 Bruce Hurst .... .15 .07
❑ 353 Bruce Kison .... .15 .07
❑ 354 Tim Lollar .... .15 .07
❑ 355 Steve Lyons .... .15 .07
❑ 356 Al Nipper .... .15 .07
❑ 357 Bob Ojeda .... .15 .07
❑ 358 Jim Rice .... .25 .11
❑ 359 Bob Stanley .... .15 .07
❑ 360 Mike Trujillo .... .15 .07
❑ 361 Thad Bosley .... .15 .07
❑ 362 Warren Brusstar .... .15 .07
❑ 363 Ron Cey .... .25 .11
❑ 364 Jody Davis .... .15 .07
❑ 365 Bob Dernier .... .15 .07
❑ 366 Shawon Dunston .... .25 .11
❑ 367 Leon Durham .... .15 .07
❑ 368 Dennis Eckersley .... .75 .35
❑ 369 Ray Fontenot .... .15 .07
❑ 370 George Frazier .... .15 .07
❑ 371 Billy Hatcher .... .15 .07
❑ 372 Dave Lopes .... .25 .11
❑ 373 Gary Matthews .... .15 .07
❑ 374 Ron Meridith .... .15 .07
❑ 375 Keith Moreland .... .15 .07
❑ 376 Reggie Patterson .... .15 .07
❑ 377 Dick Ruthven .... .15 .07
❑ 378 Ryne Sandberg .... 1.00 .45
❑ 379 Scott Sanderson .... .15 .07
❑ 380 Lee Smith .... .50 .23
❑ 381 Lary Sorensen .... .15 .07
❑ 382 Chris Speier .... .15 .07
❑ 383 Rick Sutcliffe .... .25 .11
❑ 384 Steve Trout .... .15 .07
❑ 385 Gary Woods .... .15 .07
❑ 386 Bert Blyleven .... .25 .11
❑ 387 Tom Brunansky .... .15 .07
❑ 388 Randy Bush .... .15 .07
❑ 389 John Butcher .... .15 .07
❑ 390 Ron Davis .... .15 .07
❑ 391 Dave Engle .... .15 .07
❑ 392 Frank Eufemia .... .15 .07
❑ 393 Pete Filson .... .15 .07
❑ 394 Gary Gaetti .... .25 .11
❑ 395 Greg Gagne .... .15 .07
❑ 396 Mickey Hatcher .... .15 .07
❑ 397 Kent Hrbek .... .25 .11
❑ 398 Tim Laudner .... .15 .07
❑ 399 Rick Lysander .... .15 .07
❑ 400 Dave Meier .... .15 .07
❑ 401 Kirby Puckett UER 3.00 1.35
(Card has him in NL, should be AL)
❑ 402 Mark Salas .... .15 .07
❑ 403 Ken Schrom .... .15 .07
❑ 404 Roy Smalley .... .15 .07
❑ 405 Mike Smithson .... .15 .07
❑ 406 Mike Stenhouse .... .15 .07
❑ 407 Tim Teufel .... .15 .07
❑ 408 Frank Viola .... .25 .11
❑ 409 Ron Washington .... .15 .07
❑ 410 Keith Atherton .... .15 .07
❑ 411 Dusty Baker .... .25 .11
❑ 412 Tim Birtsas .... .15 .07
❑ 413 Bruce Bochte .... .15 .07
❑ 414 Chris Codiroli .... .15 .07
❑ 415 Dave Collins .... .15 .07
❑ 416 Mike Davis .... .15 .07
❑ 417 Alfredo Griffin .... .15 .07
❑ 418 Mike Heath .... .15 .07
❑ 419 Steve Henderson .... .15 .07
❑ 420 Donnie Hill .... .15 .07
❑ 421 Jay Howell .... .15 .07
❑ 422 Tommy John .... .75 .35
❑ 423 Dave Kingman .... .25 .11
❑ 424 Bill Krueger .... .15 .07
❑ 425 Rick Langford .... .15 .07
❑ 426 Carney Lansford .... .25 .11
❑ 427 Steve McCatty .... .15 .07
❑ 428 Dwayne Murphy .... .15 .07
❑ 429 Steve Ontiveros RC .... .25 .11
❑ 430 Tony Phillips .... .15 .07
❑ 431 Jose Rijo .... .15 .07
❑ 432 Mickey Tettleton RC .... .25 .11
❑ 433 Luis Aguayo .... .15 .07
❑ 434 Larry Andersen .... .15 .07
❑ 435 Steve Carlton .... .75 .35
❑ 436 Don Carman .... .15 .07
❑ 437 Tim Corcoran .... .15 .07
❑ 438 Darren Daulton RC .... 1.50 .70
❑ 439 John Denny .... .15 .07
❑ 440 Tom Foley .... .15 .07
❑ 441 Greg Gross .... .15 .07
❑ 442 Kevin Gross .... .15 .07
❑ 443 Von Hayes .... .15 .07
❑ 444 Charles Hudson .... .15 .07
❑ 445 Garry Maddox .... .15 .07
❑ 446 Shane Rawley .... .15 .07
❑ 447 Dave Rucker .... .15 .07
❑ 448 John Russell .... .15 .07
❑ 449 Juan Samuel .... .15 .07
❑ 450 Mike Schmidt .... 1.50 .70
❑ 451 Rick Schu .... .15 .07
❑ 452 Dave Shipanoff .... .15 .07
❑ 453 Dave Stewart .... .25 .11
❑ 454 Jeff Stone .... .15 .07
❑ 455 Kent Tekulve .... .15 .07
❑ 456 Ozzie Virgil .... .15 .07
❑ 457 Glenn Wilson .... .15 .07
❑ 458 Jim Beattie .... .15 .07
❑ 459 Karl Best .... .15 .07
❑ 460 Barry Bonnell .... .15 .07
❑ 461 Phil Bradley .... .15 .07
❑ 462 Ivan Calderon RC* .... .25 .11
❑ 463 Al Cowens .... .15 .07
❑ 464 Alvin Davis .... .15 .07
❑ 465 Dave Henderson .... .15 .07
❑ 466 Bob Kearney .... .15 .07
❑ 467 Mark Langston .... .15 .07
❑ 468 Bob Long .... .15 .07
❑ 469 Mike Moore .... .15 .07
❑ 470 Edwin Nunez .... .15 .07
❑ 471 Spike Owen .... .15 .07
❑ 472 Jack Perconte .... .15 .07
❑ 473 Jim Presley .... .15 .07
❑ 474 Donnie Scott .... .15 .07
❑ 475 Bill Swift .... .15 .07
❑ 476 Danny Tartabull .... .25 .11
❑ 477 Gorman Thomas .... .15 .07
❑ 478 Roy Thomas .... .15 .07
❑ 479 Ed VandeBerg .... .15 .07
❑ 480 Frank Wills .... .15 .07
❑ 481 Matt Young .... .15 .07
❑ 482 Ray Burris .... .15 .07
❑ 483 Jaime Cocanower .... .15 .07
❑ 484 Cecil Cooper .... .25 .11
❑ 485 Danny Darwin .... .15 .07
❑ 486 Rollie Fingers .... .75 .35
❑ 487 Jim Gantner .... .15 .07
❑ 488 Bob L. Gibson .... .15 .07
❑ 489 Moose Haas .... .15 .07
❑ 490 Teddy Higuera RC* .... .25 .11
❑ 491 Paul Householder .... .15 .07
❑ 492 Pete Ladd .... .15 .07
❑ 493 Rick Manning .... .15 .07
❑ 494 Bob McClure .... .15 .07
❑ 495 Paul Molitor .... .75 .35
❑ 496 Charlie Moore .... .15 .07
❑ 497 Ben Oglivie .... .15 .07
❑ 498 Randy Ready .... .15 .07
❑ 499 Earnie Riles .... .15 .07
❑ 500 Ed Romero .... .15 .07
❑ 501 Bill Schroeder .... .15 .07
❑ 502 Ray Searage .... .15 .07
❑ 503 Ted Simmons .... .25 .11
❑ 504 Pete Vuckovich .... .15 .07
❑ 505 Rick Waits .... .15 .07
❑ 506 Robin Yount .... .75 .35
❑ 507 Len Barker .... .15 .07
❑ 508 Steve Bedrosian .... .15 .07
❑ 509 Bruce Benedict .... .15 .07
❑ 510 Rick Camp .... .15 .07
❑ 511 Rick Cerone .... .15 .07
❑ 512 Chris Chambliss .... .25 .11
❑ 513 Jeff Dedmon .... .15 .07
❑ 514 Terry Forster .... .15 .07
❑ 515 Gene Garber .... .15 .07
❑ 516 Terry Harper .... .15 .07
❑ 517 Bob Horner .... .15 .07
❑ 518 Glenn Hubbard .... .15 .07
❑ 519 Joe Johnson .... .15 .07
❑ 520 Brad Komminsk .... .15 .07
❑ 521 Rick Mahler .... .15 .07
❑ 522 Dale Murphy .... .75 .35
❑ 523 Ken Oberkfell .... .15 .07
❑ 524 Pascual Perez .... .15 .07
❑ 525 Gerald Perry .... .15 .07
❑ 526 Rafael Ramirez .... .15 .07
❑ 527 Steve Shields .... .15 .07
❑ 528 Zane Smith .... .15 .07
❑ 529 Bruce Sutter .... .25 .11
❑ 530 Milt Thompson RC .... .25 .11
❑ 531 Claudell Washington .... .15 .07
❑ 532 Paul Zuvella .... .15 .07
❑ 533 Vida Blue .... .25 .11
❑ 534 Bob Brenly .... .15 .07
❑ 535 Chris Brown .... .15 .07
❑ 536 Chili Davis .... .50 .23
❑ 537 Mark Davis .... .15 .07
❑ 538 Rob Deer .... .15 .07
❑ 539 Dan Driessen .... .15 .07

❑ 540 Scott Garrelts .15 .07
❑ 541 Dan Gladden .15 .07
❑ 542 Jim Gott .15 .07
❑ 543 David Green .15 .07
❑ 544 Atlee Hammaker .15 .07
❑ 545 Mike Jeffcoat .15 .07
❑ 546 Mike Krukow .15 .07
❑ 547 Dave LaPoint .15 .07
❑ 548 Jeff Leonard .15 .07
❑ 549 Greg Minton .15 .07
❑ 550 Alex Trevino .15 .07
❑ 551 Manny Trillo .15 .07
❑ 552 Jose Uribe .15 .07
❑ 553 Brad Wellman .15 .07
❑ 554 Frank Williams .15 .07
❑ 555 Joel Youngblood .15 .07
❑ 556 Alan Bannister .15 .07
❑ 557 Glenn Brummer .15 .07
❑ 558 Steve Buechele RC .25 .11
❑ 559 Jose Guzman RC .15 .07
❑ 560 Toby Harrah .15 .07
❑ 561 Greg Harris .15 .07
❑ 562 Dwayne Henry .15 .07
❑ 563 Burt Hooton .15 .07
❑ 564 Charlie Hough .25 .11
❑ 565 Mike Mason .15 .07
❑ 566 Oddibe McDowell .15 .07
❑ 567 Dickie Noles .15 .07
❑ 568 Pete O'Brien .15 .07
❑ 569 Larry Parrish .15 .07
❑ 570 Dave Rozema .15 .07
❑ 571 Dave Schmidt .15 .07
❑ 572 Don Slaught .15 .07
❑ 573 Wayne Tolleson .15 .07
❑ 574 Duane Walker .15 .07
❑ 575 Gary Ward .15 .07
❑ 576 Chris Welsh .15 .07
❑ 577 Curtis Wilkerson .15 .07
❑ 578 George Wright .15 .07
❑ 579 Chris Bando .15 .07
❑ 580 Tony Bernazard .15 .07
❑ 581 Brett Butler .25 .11
❑ 582 Ernie Camacho .15 .07
❑ 583 Joe Carter .75 .35
❑ 584 Carmen Castillo .15 .07
❑ 585 Jamie Easterly .15 .07
❑ 586 Julio Franco .25 .11
❑ 587 Mel Hall .15 .07
❑ 588 Mike Hargrove .25 .11
❑ 589 Neal Heaton .15 .07
❑ 590 Brook Jacoby .15 .07
❑ 591 Otis Nixon RC .25 .11
❑ 592 Jerry Reed .15 .07
❑ 593 Vern Ruhle .15 .07
❑ 594 Pat Tabler .15 .07
❑ 595 Rich Thompson .15 .07
❑ 596 Andre Thornton .15 .07
❑ 597 Dave Von Ohlen .15 .07
❑ 598 George Vukovich .15 .07
❑ 599 Tom Waddell .15 .07
❑ 600 Curt Wardle .15 .07
❑ 601 Jerry Willard .15 .07
❑ 602 Bill Almon .15 .07
❑ 603 Mike Bielecki .15 .07
❑ 604 Sid Bream .15 .07
❑ 605 Mike C. Brown .15 .07
❑ 606 Pat Clements .15 .07
❑ 607 Jose DeLeon .15 .07
❑ 608 Denny Gonzalez .15 .07
❑ 609 Cecilio Guante .15 .07
❑ 610 Steve Kemp .15 .07
❑ 611 Sammy Khalifa .15 .07
❑ 612 Lee Mazzilli .15 .07
❑ 613 Larry McWilliams .15 .07
❑ 614 Jim Morrison .15 .07
❑ 615 Joe Orsulak RC* .15 .07
❑ 616 Tony Pena .15 .07
❑ 617 Johnny Ray .15 .07
❑ 618 Rick Reuschel .15 .07
❑ 619 R.J. Reynolds .15 .07
❑ 620 Rick Rhoden .15 .07
❑ 621 Don Robinson .15 .07
❑ 622 Jason Thompson .15 .07
❑ 623 Lee Tunnell .15 .07
❑ 624 Jim Winn .15 .07
❑ 625 Marvell Wynne .15 .07

❑ 626 Dwight Gooden IA .25 .11
❑ 627 Don Mattingly IA .75 .35
❑ 628 4192 (Pete Rose) .50 .23
❑ 629 3000 Career Hits .75 .35
Rod Carew
❑ 630 300 Career Wins .75 .35
Tom Seaver
Phil Niekro
❑ 631 Ouch (Don Baylor) .25 .11
❑ 632 Instant Offense .50 .23
Darryl Strawberry
Tim Raines
❑ 633 Shortstops Supreme 1.50 .70
Cal Ripken
Alan Trammell
❑ 634 Boggs and "Hero" 1.00 .45
Wade Boggs
George Brett
❑ 635 Braves Dynamic Duo .25 .11
Bob Horner
Dale Murphy
❑ 636 Cardinal Ignitors .25 .11
Willie McGee
Vince Coleman
❑ 637 Terror on Basepaths .25 .11
Vince Coleman
❑ 638 Charlie Hustle / Dr.K .75 .35
Pete Rose
Dwight Gooden
❑ 639 1984 and 1985 AL 1.00 .45
Batting Champs
Wade Boggs
Don Mattingly
❑ 640 NL West Sluggers .25 .11
Dale Murphy
Steve Garvey
Dave Parker
❑ 641 Staff Aces .25 .11
Fernando Valenzuela
Dwight Gooden
❑ 642 Blue Jay Stoppers .25 .11
Jimmy Key
Dave Stieb
❑ 643 AL All-Star Backstops .25 .11
Carlton Fisk
Rich Gedman
❑ 644 Gene Walter RC and .75 .35
Benito Santiago
❑ 645 Mike Woodard and .15 .07
Colin Ward
❑ 646 Kal Daniels RC and 5.00 2.20
Paul O'Neill
❑ 647 Andres Galarraga RC 5.00 2.20
Fred Toliver
❑ 648 Bob Kipper and .15 .07
Curt Ford
❑ 649 Jose Canseco RC and 10.00 4.50
Eric Plunk
❑ 650 Mark McLemore RC .75 .35
Gus Polidor
❑ 651 Rob Woodward and .15 .07
Mickey Brantley
❑ 652 Billy Joe Robidoux .15 .07
Mark Funderburk
❑ 653 Cecil Fielder RC and 1.50 .70
Cory Snyder
❑ 654 CL: Royals/Cardinals .15 .07
Blue Jays/Mets
❑ 655 CL: Yankees/Dodgers .15 .07
Angels/Reds UER
(168 Darly Sconiers)
❑ 656 CL: White Sox/Tigers .15 .07
Expos/Orioles
(279 Dennis,
280 Tippy)
❑ 657 CL: Astros/Padres .15 .07
Red Sox/Cubs
❑ 658 CL: Twins/A's .15 .07
Phillies/Mariners
❑ 659 CL: Brewers/Braves .15 .07
Giants/Rangers
❑ 660 CL: Indians/Pirates .15 .07
Special Cards

1986 Fleer Update

	MINT	NRMT
COMP.FACT.SET (132)	50.00	22.00
❑ 1 Mike Aldrete	.10	.05
❑ 2 Andy Allanson	.10	.05
❑ 3 Neil Allen	.10	.05
❑ 4 Joaquin Andujar	.10	.05
❑ 5 Paul Assenmacher	.10	.05
❑ 6 Scott Bailes	.10	.05
❑ 7 Jay Baller	.10	.05
❑ 8 Scott Bankhead	.10	.05
❑ 9 Bill Bathe	.10	.05
❑ 10 Don Baylor	.40	.18
❑ 11 Billy Beane	.10	.05
❑ 12 Steve Bedrosian	.10	.05
❑ 13 Juan Beniquez	.10	.05
❑ 14 Barry Bonds XRC !	30.00	13.50
❑ 15 Bobby Bonilla UER (Wrong birthday) XRC	.75	.35
❑ 16 Rich Bordi	.10	.05
❑ 17 Bill Campbell	.10	.05
❑ 18 Tom Candiotti	.10	.05
❑ 19 John Cangelosi	.10	.05
❑ 20 Jose Canseco UER (Headings on back for a pitcher)	3.00	1.35
❑ 21 Chuck Cary	.10	.05
❑ 22 Juan Castillo	.10	.05
❑ 23 Rick Cerone	.10	.05
❑ 24 John Cerutti	.10	.05
❑ 25 Will Clark XRC	2.00	.90
❑ 26 Mark Clear	.10	.05
❑ 27 Darnell Coles	.10	.05
❑ 28 Dave Collins	.10	.05
❑ 29 Tim Conroy	.10	.05
❑ 30 Ed Correa	.10	.05
❑ 31 Joe Cowley	.10	.05
❑ 32 Bill Dawley	.10	.05
❑ 33 Rob Deer	.20	.09
❑ 34 John Denny	.10	.05
❑ 35 Jim Deshaies XRC	.10	.05
❑ 36 Doug Drabek XRC	.75	.35
❑ 37 Mike Easler	.10	.05
❑ 38 Mark Eichhorn	.10	.05
❑ 39 Dave Engle	.10	.05
❑ 40 Mike Fischlin	.10	.05
❑ 41 Scott Fletcher	.10	.05
❑ 42 Terry Forster	.10	.05
❑ 43 Terry Francona	.10	.05
❑ 44 Andres Galarraga	1.50	.70
❑ 45 Lee Guetterman	.10	.05
❑ 46 Bill Gullickson	.10	.05
❑ 47 Jackie Gutierrez	.10	.05
❑ 48 Moose Haas	.10	.05
❑ 49 Billy Hatcher	.10	.05
❑ 50 Mike Heath	.10	.05
❑ 51 Guy Hoffman	.10	.05
❑ 52 Tom Hume	.10	.05
❑ 53 Pete Incaviglia XRC	.75	.35
❑ 54 Dane Iorg	.10	.05
❑ 55 Chris James XRC	.10	.05
❑ 56 Stan Javier XRC*	.20	.09
❑ 57 Tommy John	.75	.35
❑ 58 Tracy Jones	.10	.05
❑ 59 Wally Joyner XRC	.75	.35
❑ 60 Wayne Krenchicki	.10	.05

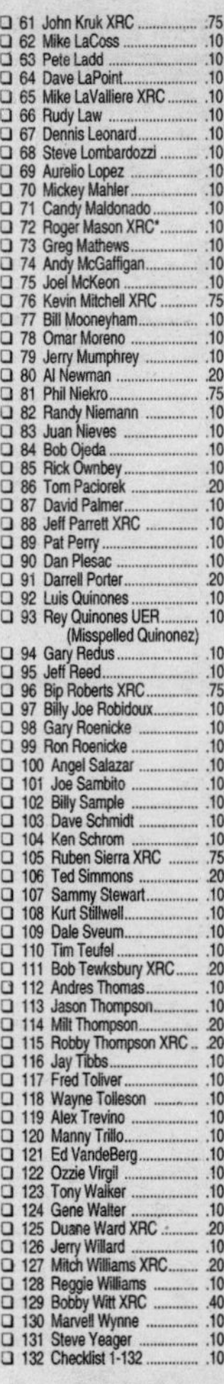

❑	61	John Kruk XRC	.75	.35
❑	62	Mike LaCoss	.10	.05
❑	63	Pete Ladd	.10	.05
❑	64	Dave LaPoint	.10	.05
❑	65	Mike LaValliere XRC	.10	.05
❑	66	Rudy Law	.10	.05
❑	67	Dennis Leonard	.10	.05
❑	68	Steve Lombardozzi	.10	.05
❑	69	Aurelio Lopez	.10	.05
❑	70	Mickey Mahler	.10	.05
❑	71	Candy Maldonado	.10	.05
❑	72	Roger Mason XRC*	.10	.05
❑	73	Greg Mathews	.10	.05
❑	74	Andy McGaffigan	.10	.05
❑	75	Joel McKeon	.10	.05
❑	76	Kevin Mitchell XRC	.75	.35
❑	77	Bill Mooneyham	.10	.05
❑	78	Omar Moreno	.10	.05
❑	79	Jerry Mumphrey	.10	.05
❑	80	Al Newman	.20	.09
❑	81	Phil Niekro	.75	.35
❑	82	Randy Niemann	.10	.05
❑	83	Juan Nieves	.10	.05
❑	84	Bob Ojeda	.10	.05
❑	85	Rick Ownbey	.10	.05
❑	86	Tom Paciorek	.20	.09
❑	87	David Palmer	.10	.05
❑	88	Jeff Parrett XRC	.10	.05
❑	89	Pat Perry	.10	.05
❑	90	Dan Plesac	.10	.05
❑	91	Darrell Porter	.20	.09
❑	92	Luis Quinones	.10	.05
❑	93	Rey Quinones UER (Misspelled Quinonez)	.10	.05
❑	94	Gary Redus	.10	.05
❑	95	Jeff Reed	.10	.05
❑	96	Bip Roberts XRC	.75	.35
❑	97	Billy Joe Robidoux	.10	.05
❑	98	Gary Roenicke	.10	.05
❑	99	Ron Roenicke	.10	.05
❑	100	Angel Salazar	.10	.05
❑	101	Joe Sambito	.10	.05
❑	102	Billy Sample	.10	.05
❑	103	Dave Schmidt	.10	.05
❑	104	Ken Schrom	.10	.05
❑	105	Ruben Sierra XRC	.75	.35
❑	106	Ted Simmons	.20	.09
❑	107	Sammy Stewart	.10	.05
❑	108	Kurt Stillwell	.10	.05
❑	109	Dale Sveum	.10	.05
❑	110	Tim Teufel	.10	.05
❑	111	Bob Tewksbury XRC	.20	.09
❑	112	Andres Thomas	.10	.05
❑	113	Jason Thompson	.10	.05
❑	114	Milt Thompson	.20	.09
❑	115	Robby Thompson XRC	.20	.09
❑	116	Jay Tibbs	.10	.05
❑	117	Fred Toliver	.10	.05
❑	118	Wayne Tolleson	.10	.05
❑	119	Alex Trevino	.10	.05
❑	120	Manny Trillo	.10	.05
❑	121	Ed VandeBerg	.10	.05
❑	122	Ozzie Virgil	.10	.05
❑	123	Tony Walker	.10	.05
❑	124	Gene Walter	.10	.05
❑	125	Duane Ward XRC	.20	.09
❑	126	Jerry Willard	.10	.05
❑	127	Mitch Williams XRC	.20	.09
❑	128	Reggie Williams	.10	.05
❑	129	Bobby Witt XRC	.40	.18
❑	130	Marvell Wynne	.10	.05
❑	131	Steve Yeager	.10	.05
❑	132	Checklist 1-132	.10	.05

1987 Fleer

	MINT	NRMT
COMPLETE SET (660)	60.00	27.00
COMP.FACT.SET (672)	80.00	36.00

	No.	Player	MINT	NRMT
❑	1	Rick Aguilera	.25	.11
❑	2	Richard Anderson	.15	.07
❑	3	Wally Backman	.15	.07
❑	4	Gary Carter	.40	.18
❑	5	Ron Darling	.15	.07
❑	6	Len Dykstra	.40	.18

	No.	Player	MINT	NRMT
❑	7	Kevin Elster RC	.25	.11
❑	8	Sid Fernandez	.15	.07
❑	9	Dwight Gooden	.40	.18
❑	10	Ed Hearn	.15	.07
❑	11	Danny Heep	.15	.07
❑	12	Keith Hernandez	.25	.11
❑	13	Howard Johnson	.15	.07
❑	14	Ray Knight	.15	.07
❑	15	Lee Mazzilli	.15	.07
❑	16	Roger McDowell	.15	.07
❑	17	Kevin Mitchell RC*	.40	.18
❑	18	Randy Niemann	.15	.07
❑	19	Bob Ojeda	.15	.07
❑	20	Jesse Orosco	.15	.07
❑	21	Rafael Santana	.15	.07
❑	22	Doug Sisk	.15	.07
❑	23	Darryl Strawberry	.40	.18
❑	24	Tim Teufel	.15	.07
❑	25	Mookie Wilson	.25	.11
❑	26	Tony Armas	.15	.07
❑	27	Marty Barrett	.15	.07
❑	28	Don Baylor	.25	.11
❑	29	Wade Boggs	.60	.25
❑	30	Oil Can Boyd	.15	.07
❑	31	Bill Buckner	.25	.11
❑	32	Roger Clemens	1.50	.70
❑	33	Steve Crawford	.15	.07
❑	34	Dwight Evans	.25	.11
❑	35	Rich Gedman	.15	.07
❑	36	Dave Henderson	.15	.07
❑	37	Bruce Hurst	.15	.07
❑	38	Tim Lollar	.15	.07
❑	39	Al Nipper	.15	.07
❑	40	Spike Owen	.15	.07
❑	41	Jim Rice	.25	.11
❑	42	Ed Romero	.15	.07
❑	43	Joe Sambito	.15	.07
❑	44	Calvin Schiraldi	.15	.07
❑	45	Tom Seaver UER (Lifetime saves total 0, should be 1)	.60	.25
❑	46	Jeff Sellers	.15	.07
❑	47	Bob Stanley	.15	.07
❑	48	Sammy Stewart	.15	.07
❑	49	Larry Andersen	.15	.07
❑	50	Alan Ashby	.15	.07
❑	51	Kevin Bass	.15	.07
❑	52	Jeff Calhoun	.15	.07
❑	53	Jose Cruz	.25	.11
❑	54	Danny Darwin	.15	.07
❑	55	Glenn Davis	.15	.07
❑	56	Jim Deshaies RC*	.15	.07
❑	57	Bill Doran	.15	.07
❑	58	Phil Garner	.15	.07
❑	59	Billy Hatcher	.15	.07
❑	60	Charlie Kerfeld	.15	.07
❑	61	Bob Knepper	.15	.07
❑	62	Dave Lopes	.25	.11
❑	63	Aurelio Lopez	.15	.07
❑	64	Jim Pankovits	.15	.07
❑	65	Terry Puhl	.15	.07
❑	66	Craig Reynolds	.15	.07
❑	67	Nolan Ryan	3.00	1.35
❑	68	Mike Scott	.15	.07
❑	69	Dave Smith	.15	.07
❑	70	Dickie Thon	.15	.07
❑	71	Tony Walker	.15	.07
❑	72	Denny Walling	.15	.07
❑	73	Bob Boone	.25	.11
❑	74	Rick Burleson	.15	.07
❑	75	John Candelaria	.15	.07
❑	76	Doug Corbett	.15	.07
❑	77	Doug DeCinces	.15	.07
❑	78	Brian Downing	.15	.07
❑	79	Chuck Finley RC	2.00	.90
❑	80	Terry Forster	.15	.07
❑	81	Bob Grich	.25	.11
❑	82	George Hendrick	.15	.07
❑	83	Jack Howell	.15	.07
❑	84	Reggie Jackson	.75	.35
❑	85	Ruppert Jones	.15	.07
❑	86	Wally Joyner RC	1.00	.45
❑	87	Gary Lucas	.15	.07
❑	88	Kirk McCaskill	.15	.07
❑	89	Donnie Moore	.15	.07
❑	90	Gary Pettis	.15	.07
❑	91	Vern Ruhle	.15	.07
❑	92	Dick Schofield	.15	.07
❑	93	Don Sutton	.60	.25
❑	94	Rob Wilfong	.15	.07
❑	95	Mike Witt	.15	.07
❑	96	Doug Drabek RC	.60	.25
❑	97	Mike Easler	.15	.07
❑	98	Mike Fischlin	.15	.07
❑	99	Brian Fisher	.15	.07
❑	100	Ron Guidry	.25	.11
❑	101	Rickey Henderson	1.25	.55
❑	102	Tommy John	.25	.11
❑	103	Ron Kittle	.15	.07
❑	104	Don Mattingly	1.50	.70
❑	105	Bobby Meacham	.15	.07
❑	106	Joe Niekro	.15	.07
❑	107	Mike Pagliarulo	.15	.07
❑	108	Dan Pasqua	.15	.07
❑	109	Willie Randolph	.25	.11
❑	110	Dennis Rasmussen	.15	.07
❑	111	Dave Righetti	.15	.07
❑	112	Gary Roenicke	.15	.07
❑	113	Rod Scurry	.15	.07
❑	114	Bob Shirley	.15	.07
❑	115	Joel Skinner	.15	.07
❑	116	Tim Stoddard	.15	.07
❑	117	Bob Tewksbury RC*	.25	.11
❑	118	Wayne Tolleson	.15	.07
❑	119	Claudell Washington	.15	.07
❑	120	Dave Winfield	.60	.25
❑	121	Steve Buechele	.15	.07
❑	122	Ed Correa	.15	.07
❑	123	Scott Fletcher	.15	.07
❑	124	Jose Guzman	.15	.07
❑	125	Toby Harrah	.15	.07
❑	126	Greg Harris	.15	.07
❑	127	Charlie Hough	.25	.11
❑	128	Pete Incaviglia RC*	.25	.11
❑	129	Mike Mason	.15	.07
❑	130	Oddibe McDowell	.15	.07
❑	131	Dale Mohorcic	.15	.07
❑	132	Pete O'Brien	.15	.07
❑	133	Tom Paciorek	.25	.11
❑	134	Larry Parrish	.15	.07
❑	135	Geno Petralli	.15	.07
❑	136	Darrell Porter	.15	.07
❑	137	Jeff Russell	.15	.07
❑	138	Ruben Sierra RC	1.00	.45
❑	139	Don Slaught	.15	.07
❑	140	Gary Ward	.15	.07
❑	141	Curtis Wilkerson	.15	.07
❑	142	Mitch Williams RC*	.25	.11
❑	143	Bobby Witt RC UER (Tulsa misspelled as Tusla; ERA should be 6.43, not .643)	.25	.11
❑	144	Dave Bergman	.15	.07
❑	145	Tom Brookens	.15	.07
❑	146	Bill Campbell	.15	.07
❑	147	Chuck Cary	.15	.07
❑	148	Darnell Coles	.15	.07
❑	149	Dave Collins	.15	.07
❑	150	Darrell Evans	.25	.11
❑	151	Kirk Gibson	.25	.11
❑	152	John Grubb	.15	.07
❑	153	Willie Hernandez	.15	.07
❑	154	Larry Herndon	.15	.07
❑	155	Eric King	.15	.07

❑ 156	Chet Lemon	.15	.07
❑ 157	Dwight Lowry	.15	.07
❑ 158	Jack Morris	.25	.11
❑ 159	Randy O'Neal	.15	.07
❑ 160	Lance Parrish	.25	.11
❑ 161	Dan Petry	.15	.07
❑ 162	Pat Sheridan	.15	.07
❑ 163	Jim Slaton	.15	.07
❑ 164	Frank Tanana	.15	.07
❑ 165	Walt Terrell	.15	.07
❑ 166	Mark Thurmond	.15	.07
❑ 167	Alan Trammell	.40	.18
❑ 168	Lou Whitaker	.25	.11
❑ 169	Luis Aguayo	.15	.07
❑ 170	Steve Bedrosian	.15	.07
❑ 171	Don Carman	.15	.07
❑ 172	Darren Daulton	.40	.18
❑ 173	Greg Gross	.15	.07
❑ 174	Kevin Gross	.15	.07
❑ 175	Von Hayes	.15	.07
❑ 176	Charles Hudson	.15	.07
❑ 177	Tom Hume	.15	.07
❑ 178	Steve Jeltz	.15	.07
❑ 179	Mike Maddux	.15	.07
❑ 180	Shane Rawley	.15	.07
❑ 181	Gary Redus	.15	.07
❑ 182	Ron Roenicke	.15	.07
❑ 183	Bruce Ruffin RC	.15	.07
❑ 184	John Russell	.15	.07
❑ 185	Juan Samuel	.15	.07
❑ 186	Dan Schatzeder	.15	.07
❑ 187	Mike Schmidt	1.25	.55
❑ 188	Rick Schu	.15	.07
❑ 189	Jeff Stone	.15	.07
❑ 190	Kent Tekulve	.15	.07
❑ 191	Milt Thompson	.15	.07
❑ 192	Glenn Wilson	.15	.07
❑ 193	Buddy Bell	.25	.11
❑ 194	Tom Browning	.15	.07
❑ 195	Sal Butera	.15	.07
❑ 196	Dave Concepcion	.25	.11
❑ 197	Kal Daniels	.15	.07
❑ 198	Eric Davis	.40	.18
❑ 199	John Denny	.15	.07
❑ 200	Bo Diaz	.15	.07
❑ 201	Nick Esasky	.15	.07
❑ 202	John Franco	.25	.11
❑ 203	Bill Gullickson	.15	.07
❑ 204	Barry Larkin RC	5.00	2.20
❑ 205	Eddie Milner	.15	.07
❑ 206	Rob Murphy	.15	.07
❑ 207	Ron Oester	.15	.07
❑ 208	Dave Parker	.25	.11
❑ 209	Tony Perez	.60	.25
❑ 210	Ted Power	.15	.07
❑ 211	Joe Price	.15	.07
❑ 212	Ron Robinson	.15	.07
❑ 213	Pete Rose	2.00	.90
❑ 214	Mario Soto	.15	.07
❑ 215	Kurt Stillwell	.15	.07
❑ 216	Max Venable	.15	.07
❑ 217	Chris Welsh	.15	.07
❑ 218	Carl Willis RC	.15	.07
❑ 219	Jesse Barfield	.15	.07
❑ 220	George Bell	.15	.07
❑ 221	Bill Caudill	.15	.07
❑ 222	John Cerutti	.15	.07
❑ 223	Jim Clancy	.15	.07
❑ 224	Mark Eichhorn	.15	.07
❑ 225	Tony Fernandez	.15	.07
❑ 226	Damaso Garcia	.15	.07
❑ 227	Kelly Gruber ERR (Wrong birth year)	.15	.07
❑ 228	Tom Henke	.15	.07
❑ 229	Garth Iorg	.15	.07
❑ 230	Joe Johnson	.15	.07
❑ 231	Cliff Johnson	.15	.07
❑ 232	Jimmy Key	.25	.11
❑ 233	Dennis Lamp	.15	.07
❑ 234	Rick Leach	.15	.07
❑ 235	Buck Martinez	.15	.07
❑ 236	Lloyd Moseby	.15	.07
❑ 237	Rance Mulliniks	.15	.07
❑ 238	Dave Stieb	.15	.07
❑ 239	Willie Upshaw	.15	.07
❑ 240	Ernie Whitt	.15	.07
❑ 241	Andy Allanson	.15	.07
❑ 242	Scott Bailes	.15	.07
❑ 243	Chris Bando	.15	.07
❑ 244	Tony Bernazard	.15	.07
❑ 245	John Butcher	.15	.07
❑ 246	Brett Butler	.25	.11
❑ 247	Ernie Camacho	.15	.07
❑ 248	Tom Candiotti	.15	.07
❑ 249	Joe Carter	.60	.25
❑ 250	Carmen Castillo	.15	.07
❑ 251	Julio Franco	.25	.11
❑ 252	Mel Hall	.15	.07
❑ 253	Brook Jacoby	.15	.07
❑ 254	Phil Niekro	.60	.25
❑ 255	Otis Nixon	.15	.07
❑ 256	Dickie Noles	.15	.07
❑ 257	Bryan Oelkers	.15	.07
❑ 258	Ken Schrom	.15	.07
❑ 259	Don Schulze	.15	.07
❑ 260	Cory Snyder	.15	.07
❑ 261	Pat Tabler	.15	.07
❑ 262	Andre Thornton	.15	.07
❑ 263	Rich Yett	.15	.07
❑ 264	Mike Aldrete	.15	.07
❑ 265	Juan Berenguer	.15	.07
❑ 266	Vida Blue	.25	.11
❑ 267	Bob Brenly	.15	.07
❑ 268	Chris Brown	.15	.07
❑ 269	Will Clark RC	4.00	1.80
❑ 270	Chili Davis	.40	.18
❑ 271	Mark Davis	.15	.07
❑ 272	Kelly Downs RC	.15	.07
❑ 273	Scott Garrelts	.15	.07
❑ 274	Dan Gladden	.15	.07
❑ 275	Mike Krukow	.15	.07
❑ 276	Randy Kutcher	.15	.07
❑ 277	Mike LaCoss	.15	.07
❑ 278	Jeff Leonard	.15	.07
❑ 279	Candy Maldonado	.15	.07
❑ 280	Roger Mason	.15	.07
❑ 281	Bob Melvin	.15	.07
❑ 282	Greg Minton	.15	.07
❑ 283	Jeff D. Robinson	.15	.07
❑ 284	Harry Spilman	.15	.07
❑ 285	R.Thompson RC*	.25	.11
❑ 286	Jose Uribe	.15	.07
❑ 287	Frank Williams	.15	.07
❑ 288	Joel Youngblood	.15	.07
❑ 289	Jack Clark	.25	.11
❑ 290	Vince Coleman	.15	.07
❑ 291	Tim Conroy	.15	.07
❑ 292	Danny Cox	.15	.07
❑ 293	Ken Dayley	.15	.07
❑ 294	Curt Ford	.15	.07
❑ 295	Bob Forsch	.15	.07
❑ 296	Tom Herr	.15	.07
❑ 297	Ricky Horton	.15	.07
❑ 298	Clint Hurdle	.15	.07
❑ 299	Jeff Lahti	.15	.07
❑ 300	Steve Lake	.15	.07
❑ 301	Tito Landrum	.15	.07
❑ 302	Mike LaValliere RC*	.15	.07
❑ 303	Greg Mathews	.15	.07
❑ 304	Willie McGee	.25	.11
❑ 305	Jose Oquendo	.15	.07
❑ 306	Terry Pendleton	.25	.11
❑ 307	Pat Perry	.15	.07
❑ 308	Ozzie Smith	.75	.35
❑ 309	Ray Soff	.15	.07
❑ 310	John Tudor	.15	.07
❑ 311	Andy Van Slyke UER (Bats R, Throws L)	.25	.11
❑ 312	Todd Worrell	.25	.11
❑ 313	Dann Bilardello	.15	.07
❑ 314	Hubie Brooks	.15	.07
❑ 315	Tim Burke	.15	.07
❑ 316	Andre Dawson	.40	.18
❑ 317	Mike Fitzgerald	.15	.07
❑ 318	Tom Foley	.15	.07
❑ 319	Andres Galarraga	.60	.25
❑ 320	Joe Hesketh	.15	.07
❑ 321	Wallace Johnson	.15	.07
❑ 322	Wayne Krenchicki	.15	.07
❑ 323	Vance Law	.15	.07
❑ 324	Dennis Martinez	.25	.11
❑ 325	Bob McClure	.15	.07
❑ 326	Andy McGaffigan	.15	.07
❑ 327	Al Newman	.15	.07
❑ 328	Tim Raines	.25	.11
❑ 329	Jeff Reardon	.25	.11
❑ 330	Luis Rivera	.15	.07
❑ 331	Bob Sebra	.15	.07
❑ 332	Bryn Smith	.15	.07
❑ 333	Jay Tibbs	.15	.07
❑ 334	Tim Wallach	.15	.07
❑ 335	Mitch Webster	.15	.07
❑ 336	Jim Wohlford	.15	.07
❑ 337	Floyd Youmans	.15	.07
❑ 338	Chris Bosio RC	.25	.11
❑ 339	Glenn Braggs RC	.15	.07
❑ 340	Rick Cerone	.15	.07
❑ 341	Mark Clear	.15	.07
❑ 342	Bryan Clutterbuck	.15	.07
❑ 343	Cecil Cooper	.25	.11
❑ 344	Rob Deer	.15	.07
❑ 345	Jim Gantner	.15	.07
❑ 346	Ted Higuera	.15	.07
❑ 347	John Henry Johnson	.15	.07
❑ 348	Tim Leary	.15	.07
❑ 349	Rick Manning	.15	.07
❑ 350	Paul Molitor	.60	.25
❑ 351	Charlie Moore	.15	.07
❑ 352	Juan Nieves	.15	.07
❑ 353	Ben Oglivie	.15	.07
❑ 354	Dan Plesac	.15	.07
❑ 355	Ernest Riles	.15	.07
❑ 356	Billy Joe Robidoux	.15	.07
❑ 357	Bill Schroeder	.15	.07
❑ 358	Dale Sveum	.15	.07
❑ 359	Gorman Thomas	.15	.07
❑ 360	Bill Wegman	.15	.07
❑ 361	Robin Yount	.60	.25
❑ 362	Steve Balboni	.15	.07
❑ 363	Scott Bankhead	.15	.07
❑ 364	Buddy Biancalana	.15	.07
❑ 365	Bud Black	.15	.07
❑ 366	George Brett	1.25	.55
❑ 367	Steve Farr	.15	.07
❑ 368	Mark Gubicza	.15	.07
❑ 369	Bo Jackson RC	3.00	1.35
❑ 370	Danny Jackson	.15	.07
❑ 371	Mike Kingery RC	.15	.07
❑ 372	Rudy Law	.15	.07
❑ 373	Charlie Leibrandt	.15	.07
❑ 374	Dennis Leonard	.15	.07
❑ 375	Hal McRae	.25	.11
❑ 376	Jorge Orta	.15	.07
❑ 377	Jamie Quirk	.15	.07
❑ 378	Dan Quisenberry	.15	.07
❑ 379	Bret Saberhagen	.25	.11
❑ 380	Angel Salazar	.15	.07
❑ 381	Lonnie Smith	.15	.07
❑ 382	Jim Sundberg	.15	.07
❑ 383	Frank White	.25	.11
❑ 384	Willie Wilson	.25	.11
❑ 385	Joaquin Andujar	.15	.07
❑ 386	Doug Bair	.15	.07
❑ 387	Dusty Baker	.25	.11
❑ 388	Bruce Bochte	.15	.07
❑ 389	Jose Canseco	1.50	.70
❑ 390	Chris Codiroli	.15	.07
❑ 391	Mike Davis	.15	.07
❑ 392	Alfredo Griffin	.15	.07
❑ 393	Moose Haas	.15	.07
❑ 394	Donnie Hill	.15	.07
❑ 395	Jay Howell	.15	.07
❑ 396	Dave Kingman	.25	.11
❑ 397	Carney Lansford	.25	.11
❑ 398	Dave Leiper	.15	.07
❑ 399	Bill Mooneyham	.15	.07
❑ 400	Dwayne Murphy	.15	.07
❑ 401	Steve Ontiveros	.15	.07
❑ 402	Tony Phillips	.15	.07
❑ 403	Eric Plunk	.15	.07
❑ 404	Jose Rijo	.15	.07
❑ 405	Terry Steinbach RC	1.00	.45
❑ 406	Dave Stewart	.25	.11
❑ 407	Mickey Tettleton	.15	.07
❑ 408	Dave Von Ohlen	.15	.07
❑ 409	Jerry Willard	.15	.07
❑ 410	Curt Young	.15	.07
❑ 411	Bruce Bochy	.15	.07

❑ 412 Dave Dravecky .25 .11
❑ 413 Tim Flannery .15 .07
❑ 414 Steve Garvey .40 .18
❑ 415 Rich Gossage .25 .11
❑ 416 Tony Gwynn 1.25 .55
❑ 417 Andy Hawkins .15 .07
❑ 418 LaMarr Hoyt .15 .07
❑ 419 Terry Kennedy .15 .07
❑ 420 John Kruk RC 1.00 .45
❑ 421 Dave LaPoint .15 .07
❑ 422 Craig Lefferts .15 .07
❑ 423 Carmelo Martinez .15 .07
❑ 424 Lance McCullers .15 .07
❑ 425 Kevin McReynolds .15 .07
❑ 426 Graig Nettles .25 .11
❑ 427 Bip Roberts RC .60 .25
❑ 428 Jerry Royster .15 .07
❑ 429 Benito Santiago .25 .11
❑ 430 Eric Show .15 .07
❑ 431 Bob Stoddard .15 .07
❑ 432 Garry Templeton .15 .07
❑ 433 Gene Walter .15 .07
❑ 434 Ed Whitson .15 .07
❑ 435 Marvell Wynne .15 .07
❑ 436 Dave Anderson .15 .07
❑ 437 Greg Brock .15 .07
❑ 438 Enos Cabell .15 .07
❑ 439 Mariano Duncan .15 .07
❑ 440 Pedro Guerrero .15 .07
❑ 441 Orel Hershiser .25 .11
❑ 442 Rick Honeycutt .15 .07
❑ 443 Ken Howell .15 .07
❑ 444 Ken Landreaux .15 .07
❑ 445 Bill Madlock .25 .11
❑ 446 Mike Marshall .15 .07
❑ 447 Len Matuszek .15 .07
❑ 448 Tom Niedenfuer .15 .07
❑ 449 Alejandro Pena .15 .07
❑ 450 Dennis Powell .15 .07
❑ 451 Jerry Reuss .15 .07
❑ 452 Bill Russell .15 .07
❑ 453 Steve Sax .15 .07
❑ 454 Mike Scioscia .15 .07
❑ 455 Franklin Stubbs .15 .07
❑ 456 Alex Trevino .15 .07
❑ 457 Fernando Valenzuela .25 .11
❑ 458 Ed VandeBerg .15 .07
❑ 459 Bob Welch .15 .07
❑ 460 Reggie Williams .15 .07
❑ 461 Don Aase .15 .07
❑ 462 Juan Beniquez .15 .07
❑ 463 Mike Boddicker .15 .07
❑ 464 Juan Bonilla .15 .07
❑ 465 Rich Bordi .15 .07
❑ 466 Storm Davis .15 .07
❑ 467 Rick Dempsey .25 .11
❑ 468 Ken Dixon .15 .07
❑ 469 Jim Dwyer .15 .07
❑ 470 Mike Flanagan .15 .07
❑ 471 Jackie Gutierrez .15 .07
❑ 472 Brad Havens .15 .07
❑ 473 Lee Lacy .15 .07
❑ 474 Fred Lynn .25 .11
❑ 475 Scott McGregor .15 .07
❑ 476 Eddie Murray .60 .25
❑ 477 Tom O'Malley .15 .07
❑ 478 Cal Ripken Jr. 2.50 1.10
❑ 479 Larry Sheets .15 .07
❑ 480 John Shelby .15 .07
❑ 481 Nate Snell .15 .07
❑ 482 Jim Traber .15 .07
❑ 483 Mike Young .15 .07
❑ 484 Neil Allen .15 .07
❑ 485 Harold Baines .25 .11
❑ 486 Floyd Bannister .15 .07
❑ 487 Daryl Boston .15 .07
❑ 488 Ivan Calderon .15 .07
❑ 489 John Cangelosi .15 .07
❑ 490 Steve Carlton .60 .25
❑ 491 Joe Cowley .15 .07
❑ 492 Julio Cruz .15 .07
❑ 493 Bill Dawley .15 .07
❑ 494 Jose DeLeon .15 .07
❑ 495 Richard Dotson .15 .07
❑ 496 Carlton Fisk .60 .25
❑ 497 Ozzie Guillen .15 .07
❑ 498 Jerry Hairston .15 .07
❑ 499 Ron Hassey .15 .07
❑ 500 Tim Hulett .15 .07
❑ 501 Bob James .15 .07
❑ 502 Steve Lyons .15 .07
❑ 503 Joel McKeon .15 .07
❑ 504 Gene Nelson .15 .07
❑ 505 Dave Schmidt .15 .07
❑ 506 Ray Searage .15 .07
❑ 507 Bobby Thigpen RC .25 .11
❑ 508 Greg Walker .15 .07
❑ 509 Jim Acker .15 .07
❑ 510 Doyle Alexander .15 .07
❑ 511 Paul Assenmacher .40 .18
❑ 512 Bruce Benedict .15 .07
❑ 513 Chris Chambliss .25 .11
❑ 514 Jeff Dedmon .15 .07
❑ 515 Gene Garber .15 .07
❑ 516 Ken Griffey .25 .11
❑ 517 Terry Harper .15 .07
❑ 518 Bob Horner .15 .07
❑ 519 Glenn Hubbard .15 .07
❑ 520 Rick Mahler .15 .07
❑ 521 Omar Moreno .15 .07
❑ 522 Dale Murphy .60 .25
❑ 523 Ken Oberkfell .15 .07
❑ 524 Ed Olwine .15 .07
❑ 525 David Palmer .15 .07
❑ 526 Rafael Ramirez .15 .07
❑ 527 Billy Sample .15 .07
❑ 528 Ted Simmons .25 .11
❑ 529 Zane Smith .15 .07
❑ 530 Bruce Sutter .15 .07
❑ 531 Andres Thomas .15 .07
❑ 532 Ozzie Virgil .15 .07
❑ 533 Allan Anderson .15 .07
❑ 534 Keith Atherton .15 .07
❑ 535 Billy Beane .15 .07
❑ 536 Bert Blyleven .25 .11
❑ 537 Tom Brunansky .15 .07
❑ 538 Randy Bush .15 .07
❑ 539 George Frazier .15 .07
❑ 540 Gary Gaetti .25 .11
❑ 541 Greg Gagne .15 .07
❑ 542 Mickey Hatcher .15 .07
❑ 543 Neal Heaton .15 .07
❑ 544 Kent Hrbek .25 .11
❑ 545 Roy Lee Jackson .15 .07
❑ 546 Tim Laudner .15 .07
❑ 547 Steve Lombardozzi .15 .07
❑ 548 Mark Portugal RC* .25 .11
❑ 549 Kirby Puckett 1.50 .70
❑ 550 Jeff Reed .15 .07
❑ 551 Mark Salas .15 .07
❑ 552 Roy Smalley .15 .07
❑ 553 Mike Smithson .15 .07
❑ 554 Frank Viola .15 .07
❑ 555 Thad Bosley .15 .07
❑ 556 Ron Cey .25 .11
❑ 557 Jody Davis .15 .07
❑ 558 Ron Davis .15 .07
❑ 559 Bob Dernier .15 .07
❑ 560 Frank DiPino .15 .07
❑ 561 Shawon Dunston UER .15 .07
(Wrong birth year
listed on card back)
❑ 562 Leon Durham .15 .07
❑ 563 Dennis Eckersley .60 .25
❑ 564 Terry Francona .25 .11
❑ 565 Dave Gumpert .15 .07
❑ 566 Guy Hoffman .15 .07
❑ 567 Ed Lynch .15 .07
❑ 568 Gary Matthews .15 .07
❑ 569 Keith Moreland .15 .07
❑ 570 Jamie Moyer RC 2.00 .90
❑ 571 Jerry Mumphrey .15 .07
❑ 572 Ryne Sandberg .75 .35
❑ 573 Scott Sanderson .15 .07
❑ 574 Lee Smith .40 .18
❑ 575 Chris Speier .15 .07
❑ 576 Rick Sutcliffe .25 .11
❑ 577 Manny Trillo .15 .07
❑ 578 Steve Trout .15 .07
❑ 579 Karl Best .15 .07
❑ 580 Scott Bradley .15 .07
❑ 581 Phil Bradley .15 .07
❑ 582 Mickey Brantley .15 .07
❑ 583 Mike G. Brown P .15 .07
❑ 584 Alvin Davis .15 .07
❑ 585 Lee Guetterman .15 .07
❑ 586 Mark Huismann .15 .07
❑ 587 Bob Kearney .15 .07
❑ 588 Pete Ladd .15 .07
❑ 589 Mark Langston .15 .07
❑ 590 Mike Moore .15 .07
❑ 591 Mike Morgan .15 .07
❑ 592 John Moses .15 .07
❑ 593 Ken Phelps .15 .07
❑ 594 Jim Presley .15 .07
❑ 595 Rey Quinones UER .15 .07
(Quinonez on front)
❑ 596 Harold Reynolds .25 .11
❑ 597 Billy Swift .15 .07
❑ 598 Danny Tartabull .15 .07
❑ 599 Steve Yeager .15 .07
❑ 600 Matt Young .15 .07
❑ 601 Bill Almon .15 .07
❑ 602 Rafael Belliard RC .15 .07
❑ 603 Mike Bielecki .15 .07
❑ 604 Barry Bonds RC 50.00 22.00
❑ 605 Bobby Bonilla RC 1.00 .45
❑ 606 Sid Bream .15 .07
❑ 607 Mike C. Brown .15 .07
❑ 608 Pat Clements .15 .07
❑ 609 Mike Diaz .15 .07
❑ 610 Cecilio Guante .15 .07
❑ 611 Barry Jones .15 .07
❑ 612 Bob Kipper .15 .07
❑ 613 Larry McWilliams .15 .07
❑ 614 Jim Morrison .15 .07
❑ 615 Joe Orsulak .15 .07
❑ 616 Junior Ortiz .15 .07
❑ 617 Tony Pena .15 .07
❑ 618 Johnny Ray .15 .07
❑ 619 Rick Reuschel .15 .07
❑ 620 R.J. Reynolds .15 .07
❑ 621 Rick Rhoden .15 .07
❑ 622 Don Robinson .15 .07
❑ 623 Bob Walk .15 .07
❑ 624 Jim Winn .15 .07
❑ 625 Youthful Power .60 .25
Pete Incaviglia
Jose Canseco
❑ 626 300 Game Winners .40 .18
Don Sutton
Phil Niekro
❑ 627 AL Firemen .15 .07
Dave Righetti
Don Aase
❑ 628 Rookie All-Stars .60 .25
Wally Joyner
Jose Canseco
❑ 629 Magic Mets .40 .18
Gary Carter
Sid Fernandez
Dwight Gooden
Keith Hernandez
Darryl Strawberry
❑ 630 NL Best Righties .15 .07
Mike Scott
Mike Krukow
❑ 631 Sensational Southpaws .15 .07
Fernando Valenzuela
John Franco
❑ 632 Count'Em .15 .07
Bob Horner
❑ 633 AL Pitcher's Nightmare .60 .25
Jose Canseco
Jim Rice
Kirby Puckett
❑ 634 All-Star Battery .75 .35
Gary Carter
Roger Clemens
❑ 635 4000 Strikeouts .25 .11
Steve Carlton
❑ 636 Big Bats at First .60 .25
Glenn Davis
Eddie Murray
❑ 637 On Base .25 .11
Wade Boggs
Keith Hernandez
❑ 638 Sluggers Left Side .60 .25

Don Mattingly
Darryl Strawberry
❑ 639 Former MVP's .25 .11
Dave Parker
Ryne Sandberg
❑ 640 Dr. K and Super K .75 .35
Dwight Gooden
Roger Clemens
❑ 641 AL West Stoppers .15 .07
Mike Witt
Charlie Hough
❑ 642 Doubles and Triples .25 .11
Juan Samuel
Tim Raines
❑ 643 Outfielders with Punch .25 .11
Harold Baines
Jesse Barfield
❑ 644 Dave Clark RC and .60 .25
Greg Swindell
❑ 645 Ron Karkovice RC .25 .11
Russ Morman
❑ 646 Devon White RC and 1.00 .45
Willie Fraser
❑ 647 Mike Stanley RC and .60 .25
Jerry Browne
❑ 648 Dave Magadan RC and .25 .11
Phil Lombardi
❑ 649 Jose Gonzalez and .15 .07
Ralph Bryant
❑ 650 Jimmy Jones RC and .15 .07
Randy Asadoor
❑ 651 Tracy Jones RC and .15 .07
Marvin Freeman
❑ 652 John Stefero and .60 .25
Kevin Seitzer RC
❑ 653 Rob Nelson and .15 .07
Steve Fireovid
❑ 654 CL: Mets/Red Sox .15 .07
Astros/Angels
❑ 655 CL: Yankees/Rangers .15 .07
Tigers/Phillies
❑ 656 CL: Reds/Blue Jays .15 .07
Indians/Giants
ERR (230/231 wrong)
❑ 657 CL: Cardinals/Expos .15 .07
Brewers/Royals
❑ 658 CL: A's/Padres .15 .07
Dodgers/Orioles
❑ 659 CL: White Sox/Braves .15 .07
Twins/Cubs
❑ 660 CL: Mariners/Pirates .15 .07
Special Cards
ER (580/581 wrong)

1987 Fleer Update

	MINT	NRMT
COMP.FACT.SET (132)	20.00	9.00

❑ 1 Scott Bankhead .10 .05
❑ 2 Eric Bell .10 .05
❑ 3 Juan Beniquez .10 .05
❑ 4 Juan Berenguer .10 .05
❑ 5 Mike Birkbeck .10 .05
❑ 6 Randy Bockus .10 .05
❑ 7 Rod Booker .10 .05
❑ 8 Thad Bosley .10 .05
❑ 9 Greg Brock .10 .05
❑ 10 Bob Brower .10 .05
❑ 11 Chris Brown .10 .05
❑ 12 Jerry Browne .10 .05
❑ 13 Ralph Bryant .10 .05
❑ 14 DeWayne Buice .10 .05
❑ 15 Ellis Burks XRC 1.00 .45
❑ 16 Casey Candaele .10 .05
❑ 17 Steve Carlton .40 .18
❑ 18 Juan Castillo .10 .05
❑ 19 Chuck Crim .10 .05
❑ 20 Mark Davidson .10 .05
❑ 21 Mark Davis .10 .05
❑ 22 Storm Davis .10 .05
❑ 23 Bill Dawley .10 .05
❑ 24 Andre Dawson .25 .11
❑ 25 Brian Dayett .10 .05
❑ 26 Rick Dempsey .15 .07
❑ 27 Ken Dowell .10 .05
❑ 28 Dave Dravecky .15 .07
❑ 29 Mike Dunne .10 .05
❑ 30 Dennis Eckersley .40 .18
❑ 31 Cecil Fielder .25 .11
❑ 32 Brian Fisher .10 .05
❑ 33 Willie Fraser .10 .05
❑ 34 Ken Gerhart .10 .05
❑ 35 Jim Gott .10 .05
❑ 36 Dan Gladden .10 .05
❑ 37 Mike Greenwell XRC* .40 .18
❑ 38 Cecilio Guante .10 .05
❑ 39 Albert Hall .10 .05
❑ 40 Atlee Hammaker .10 .05
❑ 41 Mickey Hatcher .10 .05
❑ 42 Mike Heath .10 .05
❑ 43 Neal Heaton .10 .05
❑ 44 Mike Henneman XRC .25 .11
❑ 45 Guy Hoffman .10 .05
❑ 46 Charles Hudson .10 .05
❑ 47 Chuck Jackson .10 .05
❑ 48 Mike Jackson XRC .15 .07
❑ 49 Reggie Jackson .50 .23
❑ 50 Chris James .10 .05
❑ 51 Dion James .10 .05
❑ 52 Stan Javier .10 .05
❑ 53 Stan Jefferson .10 .05
❑ 54 Jimmy Jones .10 .05
❑ 55 Tracy Jones .10 .05
❑ 56 Terry Kennedy .10 .05
❑ 57 Mike Kingery .10 .05
❑ 58 Ray Knight .10 .05
❑ 59 Gene Larkin XRC .10 .05
❑ 60 Mike LaValliere .10 .05
❑ 61 Jack Lazorko .10 .05
❑ 62 Terry Leach .10 .05
❑ 63 Rick Leach .10 .05
❑ 64 Craig Lefferts .10 .05
❑ 65 Jim Lindeman .10 .05
❑ 66 Bill Long .10 .05
❑ 67 Mike Loynd .10 .05
❑ 68 Greg Maddux XRC 8.00 3.60
❑ 69 Bill Madlock .15 .07
❑ 70 Dave Magadan .15 .07
❑ 71 Joe Magrane XRC .10 .05
❑ 72 Fred Manrique .10 .05
❑ 73 Mike Mason .10 .05
❑ 74 Lloyd McClendon XRC .10 .05
❑ 75 Fred McGriff .60 .25
❑ 76 Mark McGwire 8.00 3.60
❑ 77 Mark McLemore .15 .07
❑ 78 Kevin McReynolds .10 .05
❑ 79 Dave Meads .10 .05
❑ 80 Greg Minton .10 .05
❑ 81 John Mitchell .10 .05
❑ 82 Kevin Mitchell .25 .11
❑ 83 John Morris .10 .05
❑ 84 Jeff Musselman .10 .05
❑ 85 Randy Myers XRC .40 .18
❑ 86 Gene Nelson .10 .05
❑ 87 Joe Niekro .10 .05
❑ 88 Tom Nieto .10 .05
❑ 89 Reid Nichols .10 .05
❑ 90 Matt Nokes XRC .15 .07
❑ 91 Dickie Noles .10 .05
❑ 92 Edwin Nunez .10 .05
❑ 93 Jose Nunez .10 .05
❑ 94 Paul O'Neill .40 .18
❑ 95 Jim Paciorek .10 .05
❑ 96 Lance Parrish .15 .07
❑ 97 Bill Pecota XRC .10 .05
❑ 98 Tony Pena .10 .05
❑ 99 Luis Polonia XRC .15 .07
❑ 100 Randy Ready .10 .05
❑ 101 Jeff Reardon .15 .07
❑ 102 Gary Redus .10 .05
❑ 103 Rick Rhoden .10 .05
❑ 104 Wally Ritchie .10 .05
❑ 105 Jeff M. Robinson UER .10 .05
(Wrong Jeff's
stats on back)
❑ 106 Mark Salas .10 .05
❑ 107 Dave Schmidt .10 .05
❑ 108 Kevin Seitzer UER .15 .07
(Wrong birth year)
❑ 109 John Shelby .10 .05
❑ 110 John Smiley XRC .10 .05
❑ 111 Lary Sorensen .10 .05
❑ 112 Chris Speier .10 .05
❑ 113 Randy St.Claire .10 .05
❑ 114 Jim Sundberg .10 .05
❑ 115 B.J. Surhoff XRC .75 .35
❑ 116 Greg Swindell .40 .18
❑ 117 Danny Tartabull .10 .05
❑ 118 Dorn Taylor .10 .05
❑ 119 Lee Tunnell .10 .05
❑ 120 Ed VandeBerg .10 .05
❑ 121 Andy Van Slyke .15 .07
❑ 122 Gary Ward .10 .05
❑ 123 Devon White .40 .18
❑ 124 Alan Wiggins .10 .05
❑ 125 Bill Wilkinson .10 .05
❑ 126 Jim Winn .10 .05
❑ 127 Frank Williams .10 .05
❑ 128 Ken Williams XRC .10 .05
❑ 129 Matt Williams XRC 2.00 .90
❑ 130 Herm Willingham .10 .05
❑ 131 Matt Young .10 .05
❑ 132 Checklist 1-132 .10 .05

1988 Fleer

	MINT	NRMT
COMPLETE SET (660)	15.00	6.75
COMP.RETAIL SET (660)	15.00	6.75
COMP.HOBBY SET (672)	15.00	6.75

❑ 1 Keith Atherton .10 .05
❑ 2 Don Baylor .15 .07
❑ 3 Juan Berenguer .10 .05
❑ 4 Bert Blyleven .15 .07
❑ 5 Tom Brunansky .10 .05
❑ 6 Randy Bush .10 .05
❑ 7 Steve Carlton .30 .14
❑ 8 Mark Davidson .10 .05
❑ 9 George Frazier .10 .05
❑ 10 Gary Gaetti .15 .07
❑ 11 Greg Gagne .10 .05
❑ 12 Dan Gladden .10 .05
❑ 13 Kent Hrbek .15 .07
❑ 14 Gene Larkin RC* .10 .05
❑ 15 Tim Laudner .10 .05
❑ 16 Steve Lombardozzi .10 .05
❑ 17 Al Newman .10 .05
❑ 18 Joe Niekro .10 .05
❑ 19 Kirby Puckett .75 .35
❑ 20 Jeff Reardon .15 .07

Card		
❑ 21A Dan Schatzeder ERR (Misspelled Schatzader on card front)	.15	.07
❑ 21B Dan Schatzeder COR	.10	.05
❑ 22 Roy Smalley	.10	.05
❑ 23 Mike Smithson	.10	.05
❑ 24 Les Straker	.10	.05
❑ 25 Frank Viola	.10	.05
❑ 26 Jack Clark	.15	.07
❑ 27 Vince Coleman	.10	.05
❑ 28 Danny Cox	.10	.05
❑ 29 Bill Dawley	.10	.05
❑ 30 Ken Dayley	.10	.05
❑ 31 Doug DeCinces	.10	.05
❑ 32 Curt Ford	.10	.05
❑ 33 Bob Forsch	.10	.05
❑ 34 David Green	.10	.05
❑ 35 Tom Herr	.10	.05
❑ 36 Ricky Horton	.10	.05
❑ 37 Lance Johnson RC	.30	.14
❑ 38 Steve Lake	.10	.05
❑ 39 Jim Lindeman	.10	.05
❑ 40 Joe Magrane RC*	.10	.05
❑ 41 Greg Mathews	.10	.05
❑ 42 Willie McGee	.15	.07
❑ 43 John Morris	.10	.05
❑ 44 Jose Oquendo	.10	.05
❑ 45 Tony Pena	.10	.05
❑ 46 Terry Pendleton	.15	.07
❑ 47 Ozzie Smith	.40	.18
❑ 48 John Tudor	.10	.05
❑ 49 Lee Tunnell	.10	.05
❑ 50 Todd Worrell	.15	.07
❑ 51 Doyle Alexander	.10	.05
❑ 52 Dave Bergman	.10	.05
❑ 53 Tom Brookens	.10	.05
❑ 54 Darrell Evans	.15	.07
❑ 55 Kirk Gibson	.15	.07
❑ 56 Mike Heath	.10	.05
❑ 57 Mike Henneman RC*	.15	.07
❑ 58 Willie Hernandez	.10	.05
❑ 59 Larry Herndon	.10	.05
❑ 60 Eric King	.10	.05
❑ 61 Chet Lemon	.10	.05
❑ 62 Scott Lusader	.10	.05
❑ 63 Bill Madlock	.15	.07
❑ 64 Jack Morris	.15	.07
❑ 65 Jim Morrison	.10	.05
❑ 66 Matt Nokes RC*	.10	.05
❑ 67 Dan Petry	.10	.05
❑ 68A Jeff M. Robinson ERR, Stats for Jeff D. Robinson on card back Born 12-13-60	.30	.14
❑ 68B Jeff M. Robinson COR, Born 12-14-61	.10	.05
❑ 69 Pat Sheridan	.10	.05
❑ 70 Nate Snell	.10	.05
❑ 71 Frank Tanana	.10	.05
❑ 72 Walt Terrell	.10	.05
❑ 73 Mark Thurmond	.10	.05
❑ 74 Alan Trammell	.20	.09
❑ 75 Lou Whitaker	.15	.07
❑ 76 Mike Aldrete	.10	.05
❑ 77 Bob Brenly	.10	.05
❑ 78 Will Clark	.40	.18
❑ 79 Chili Davis	.20	.09
❑ 80 Kelly Downs	.10	.05
❑ 81 Dave Dravecky	.15	.07
❑ 82 Scott Garrelts	.10	.05
❑ 83 Atlee Hammaker	.10	.05
❑ 84 Dave Henderson	.10	.05
❑ 85 Mike Krukow	.10	.05
❑ 86 Mike LaCoss	.10	.05
❑ 87 Craig Lefferts	.10	.05
❑ 88 Jeff Leonard	.10	.05
❑ 89 Candy Maldonado	.10	.05
❑ 90 Eddie Milner	.10	.05
❑ 91 Bob Melvin	.10	.05
❑ 92 Kevin Mitchell	.15	.07
❑ 93 Jon Perlman	.10	.05
❑ 94 Rick Reuschel	.10	.05
❑ 95 Don Robinson	.10	.05
❑ 96 Chris Speier	.10	.05
❑ 97 Harry Spilman	.10	.05
❑ 98 Robby Thompson	.10	.05
❑ 99 Jose Uribe	.10	.05
❑ 100 Mark Wasinger	.10	.05
❑ 101 Matt Williams RC	1.50	.70
❑ 102 Jesse Barfield	.10	.05
❑ 103 George Bell	.10	.05
❑ 104 Juan Beniquez	.10	.05
❑ 105 John Cerutti	.10	.05
❑ 106 Jim Clancy	.10	.05
❑ 107 Rob Ducey	.10	.05
❑ 108 Mark Eichhorn	.10	.05
❑ 109 Tony Fernandez	.10	.05
❑ 110 Cecil Fielder	.20	.09
❑ 111 Kelly Gruber	.10	.05
❑ 112 Tom Henke	.10	.05
❑ 113A Garth Iorg ERR (Misspelled Iorq on card front)	.30	.14
❑ 113B Garth Iorg COR	.10	.05
❑ 114 Jimmy Key	.15	.07
❑ 115 Rick Leach	.10	.05
❑ 116 Manny Lee	.10	.05
❑ 117 Nelson Liriano	.10	.05
❑ 118 Fred McGriff	.30	.14
❑ 119 Lloyd Moseby	.10	.05
❑ 120 Rance Mulliniks	.10	.05
❑ 121 Jeff Musselman	.10	.05
❑ 122 Jose Nunez	.10	.05
❑ 123 Dave Stieb	.10	.05
❑ 124 Willie Upshaw	.10	.05
❑ 125 Duane Ward	.10	.05
❑ 126 Ernie Whitt	.10	.05
❑ 127 Rick Aguilera	.15	.07
❑ 128 Wally Backman	.10	.05
❑ 129 Mark Carreon RC	.15	.07
❑ 130 Gary Carter	.20	.09
❑ 131 David Cone	.15	.07
❑ 132 Ron Darling	.10	.05
❑ 133 Len Dykstra	.15	.07
❑ 134 Sid Fernandez	.10	.05
❑ 135 Dwight Gooden	.15	.07
❑ 136 Keith Hernandez	.15	.07
❑ 137 Gregg Jefferies RC	.30	.14
❑ 138 Howard Johnson	.10	.05
❑ 139 Terry Leach	.10	.05
❑ 140 Barry Lyons	.10	.05
❑ 141 Dave Magadan	.10	.05
❑ 142 Roger McDowell	.10	.05
❑ 143 Kevin McReynolds	.10	.05
❑ 144 Keith A. Miller RC	.10	.05
❑ 145 John Mitchell	.10	.05
❑ 146 Randy Myers	.20	.09
❑ 147 Bob Ojeda	.10	.05
❑ 148 Jesse Orosco	.10	.05
❑ 149 Rafael Santana	.10	.05
❑ 150 Doug Sisk	.10	.05
❑ 151 Darryl Strawberry	.15	.07
❑ 152 Tim Teufel	.10	.05
❑ 153 Gene Walter	.10	.05
❑ 154 Mookie Wilson	.15	.07
❑ 155 Jay Aldrich	.10	.05
❑ 156 Chris Bosio	.10	.05
❑ 157 Glenn Braggs	.10	.05
❑ 158 Greg Brock	.10	.05
❑ 159 Juan Castillo	.10	.05
❑ 160 Mark Clear	.10	.05
❑ 161 Cecil Cooper	.15	.07
❑ 162 Chuck Crim	.10	.05
❑ 163 Rob Deer	.10	.05
❑ 164 Mike Felder	.10	.05
❑ 165 Jim Gantner	.10	.05
❑ 166 Ted Higuera	.10	.05
❑ 167 Steve Kiefer	.10	.05
❑ 168 Rick Manning	.10	.05
❑ 169 Paul Molitor	.30	.14
❑ 170 Juan Nieves	.10	.05
❑ 171 Dan Plesac	.10	.05
❑ 172 Earnest Riles	.10	.05
❑ 173 Bill Schroeder	.10	.05
❑ 174 Steve Stanicek	.10	.05
❑ 175 B.J. Surhoff	.15	.07
❑ 176 Dale Sveum	.10	.05
❑ 177 Bill Wegman	.10	.05
❑ 178 Robin Yount	.30	.14
❑ 179 Hubie Brooks	.10	.05
❑ 180 Tim Burke	.10	.05
❑ 181 Casey Candaele	.10	.05
❑ 182 Mike Fitzgerald	.10	.05
❑ 183 Tom Foley	.10	.05
❑ 184 Andres Galarraga	.20	.09
❑ 185 Neal Heaton	.10	.05
❑ 186 Wallace Johnson	.10	.05
❑ 187 Vance Law	.10	.05
❑ 188 Dennis Martinez	.15	.07
❑ 189 Bob McClure	.10	.05
❑ 190 Andy McGaffigan	.10	.05
❑ 191 Reid Nichols	.10	.05
❑ 192 Pascual Perez	.10	.05
❑ 193 Tim Raines	.15	.07
❑ 194 Jeff Reed	.10	.05
❑ 195 Bob Sebra	.10	.05
❑ 196 Bryn Smith	.10	.05
❑ 197 Randy St.Claire	.10	.05
❑ 198 Tim Wallach	.10	.05
❑ 199 Mitch Webster	.10	.05
❑ 200 Herm Winningham	.10	.05
❑ 201 Floyd Youmans	.10	.05
❑ 202 Brad Arnsberg	.10	.05
❑ 203 Rick Cerone	.10	.05
❑ 204 Pat Clements	.10	.05
❑ 205 Henry Cotto	.10	.05
❑ 206 Mike Easler	.10	.05
❑ 207 Ron Guidry	.10	.05
❑ 208 Bill Gullickson	.10	.05
❑ 209 Rickey Henderson	.60	.25
❑ 210 Charles Hudson	.10	.05
❑ 211 Tommy John	.15	.07
❑ 212 Roberto Kelly RC	.30	.14
❑ 213 Ron Kittle	.10	.05
❑ 214 Don Mattingly	.75	.35
❑ 215 Bobby Meacham	.10	.05
❑ 216 Mike Pagliarulo	.10	.05
❑ 217 Dan Pasqua	.10	.05
❑ 218 Willie Randolph	.15	.07
❑ 219 Rick Rhoden	.10	.05
❑ 220 Dave Righetti	.10	.05
❑ 221 Jerry Royster	.10	.05
❑ 222 Tim Stoddard	.10	.05
❑ 223 Wayne Tolleson	.10	.05
❑ 224 Gary Ward	.10	.05
❑ 225 Claudell Washington	.10	.05
❑ 226 Dave Winfield	.30	.14
❑ 227 Buddy Bell	.15	.07
❑ 228 Tom Browning	.10	.05
❑ 229 Dave Concepcion	.15	.07
❑ 230 Kal Daniels	.10	.05
❑ 231 Eric Davis	.15	.07
❑ 232 Bo Diaz	.10	.05
❑ 233 Nick Esasky (Has a dollar sign before '87 SB totals)	.10	.05
❑ 234 John Franco	.15	.07
❑ 235 Guy Hoffman	.10	.05
❑ 236 Tom Hume	.10	.05
❑ 237 Tracy Jones	.10	.05
❑ 238 Bill Landrum	.10	.05
❑ 239 Barry Larkin	.30	.14
❑ 240 Terry McGriff	.10	.05
❑ 241 Rob Murphy	.10	.05
❑ 242 Ron Oester	.10	.05
❑ 243 Dave Parker	.15	.07
❑ 244 Pat Perry	.10	.05
❑ 245 Ted Power	.10	.05
❑ 246 Dennis Rasmussen	.10	.05
❑ 247 Ron Robinson	.10	.05
❑ 248 Kurt Stillwell	.10	.05
❑ 249 Jeff Treadway RC	.10	.05
❑ 250 Frank Williams	.10	.05
❑ 251 Steve Balboni	.10	.05
❑ 252 Bud Black	.10	.05
❑ 253 Thad Bosley	.10	.05
❑ 254 George Brett	.60	.25
❑ 255 John Davis	.10	.05
❑ 256 Steve Farr	.10	.05
❑ 257 Gene Garber	.10	.05
❑ 258 Jerry Don Gleaton	.10	.05
❑ 259 Mark Gubicza	.10	.05
❑ 260 Bo Jackson	.30	.14
❑ 261 Danny Jackson	.10	.05
❑ 262 Ross Jones	.10	.05
❑ 263 Charlie Leibrandt	.10	.05
❑ 264 Bill Pecota RC*	.10	.05
❑ 265 Melido Perez RC	.10	.05

Card		
❑ 266 Jamie Quirk	.10	.05
❑ 267 Dan Quisenberry	.10	.05
❑ 268 Bret Saberhagen	.15	.07
❑ 269 Angel Salazar	.10	.05
❑ 270 Kevin Seitzer UER (Wrong birth year)	.15	.07
❑ 271 Danny Tartabull	.10	.05
❑ 272 Gary Thurman	.10	.05
❑ 273 Frank White	.15	.07
❑ 274 Willie Wilson	.10	.05
❑ 275 Tony Bernazard	.10	.05
❑ 276 Jose Canseco	.50	.23
❑ 277 Mike Davis	.10	.05
❑ 278 Storm Davis	.10	.05
❑ 279 Dennis Eckersley	.15	.07
❑ 280 Alfredo Griffin	.10	.05
❑ 281 Rick Honeycutt	.10	.05
❑ 282 Jay Howell	.10	.05
❑ 283 Reggie Jackson	.40	.18
❑ 284 Dennis Lamp	.10	.05
❑ 285 Carney Lansford	.15	.07
❑ 286 Mark McGwire	3.00	1.35
❑ 287 Dwayne Murphy	.10	.05
❑ 288 Gene Nelson	.10	.05
❑ 289 Steve Ontiveros	.10	.05
❑ 290 Tony Phillips	.10	.05
❑ 291 Eric Plunk	.10	.05
❑ 292 Luis Polonia RC*	.10	.05
❑ 293 Rick Rodriguez	.10	.05
❑ 294 Terry Steinbach	.15	.07
❑ 295 Dave Stewart	.15	.07
❑ 296 Curt Young	.10	.05
❑ 297 Luis Aguayo	.10	.05
❑ 298 Steve Bedrosian	.10	.05
❑ 299 Jeff Calhoun	.10	.05
❑ 300 Don Carman	.10	.05
❑ 301 Todd Frohwirth	.10	.05
❑ 302 Greg Gross	.10	.05
❑ 303 Kevin Gross	.10	.05
❑ 304 Von Hayes	.10	.05
❑ 305 Keith Hughes	.10	.05
❑ 306 Mike Jackson RC*	.15	.07
❑ 307 Chris James	.10	.05
❑ 308 Steve Jeltz	.10	.05
❑ 309 Mike Maddux	.10	.05
❑ 310 Lance Parrish	.10	.05
❑ 311 Shane Rawley	.10	.05
❑ 312 Wally Ritchie	.10	.05
❑ 313 Bruce Ruffin	.10	.05
❑ 314 Juan Samuel	.10	.05
❑ 315 Mike Schmidt	.60	.25
❑ 316 Rick Schu	.10	.05
❑ 317 Jeff Stone	.10	.05
❑ 318 Kent Tekulve	.10	.05
❑ 319 Milt Thompson	.10	.05
❑ 320 Glenn Wilson	.10	.05
❑ 321 Rafael Belliard	.10	.05
❑ 322 Barry Bonds	2.50	1.10
❑ 323 Bobby Bonilla UER (Wrong birth year)	.15	.07
❑ 324 Sid Bream	.10	.05
❑ 325 John Cangelosi	.10	.05
❑ 326 Mike Diaz	.10	.05
❑ 327 Doug Drabek	.10	.05
❑ 328 Mike Dunne	.10	.05
❑ 329 Brian Fisher	.10	.05
❑ 330 Brett Gideon	.10	.05
❑ 331 Terry Harper	.10	.05
❑ 332 Bob Kipper	.10	.05
❑ 333 Mike LaValliere	.10	.05
❑ 334 Jose Lind RC	.10	.05
❑ 335 Junior Ortiz	.10	.05
❑ 336 Vicente Palacios	.10	.05
❑ 337 Bob Patterson	.10	.05
❑ 338 Al Pedrique	.10	.05
❑ 339 R.J. Reynolds	.10	.05
❑ 340 John Smiley RC*	.15	.07
❑ 341 Andy Van Slyke UER (Wrong batting and throwing listed)	.15	.07
❑ 342 Bob Walk	.10	.05
❑ 343 Marty Barrett	.10	.05
❑ 344 Todd Benzinger RC*	.10	.05
❑ 345 Wade Boggs	.30	.14
❑ 346 Tom Bolton	.10	.05
❑ 347 Oil Can Boyd	.10	.05
❑ 348 Ellis Burks RC	.75	.35
❑ 349 Roger Clemens	.75	.35
❑ 350 Steve Crawford	.10	.05
❑ 351 Dwight Evans	.15	.07
❑ 352 Wes Gardner	.10	.05
❑ 353 Rich Gedman	.10	.05
❑ 354 Mike Greenwell	.10	.05
❑ 355 Sam Horn RC	.10	.05
❑ 356 Bruce Hurst	.10	.05
❑ 357 John Marzano	.10	.05
❑ 358 Al Nipper	.10	.05
❑ 359 Spike Owen	.10	.05
❑ 360 Jody Reed RC	.15	.07
❑ 361 Jim Rice	.15	.07
❑ 362 Ed Romero	.10	.05
❑ 363 Kevin Romine	.10	.05
❑ 364 Joe Sambito	.10	.05
❑ 365 Calvin Schiraldi	.10	.05
❑ 366 Jeff Sellers	.10	.05
❑ 367 Bob Stanley	.10	.05
❑ 368 Scott Bankhead	.10	.05
❑ 369 Phil Bradley	.10	.05
❑ 370 Scott Bradley	.10	.05
❑ 371 Mickey Brantley	.10	.05
❑ 372 Mike Campbell	.10	.05
❑ 373 Alvin Davis	.10	.05
❑ 374 Lee Guetterman	.10	.05
❑ 375 Dave Hengel	.10	.05
❑ 376 Mike Kingery	.10	.05
❑ 377 Mark Langston	.10	.05
❑ 378 Edgar Martinez RC	3.00	1.35
❑ 379 Mike Moore	.10	.05
❑ 380 Mike Morgan	.10	.05
❑ 381 John Moses	.10	.05
❑ 382 Donell Nixon	.10	.05
❑ 383 Edwin Nunez	.10	.05
❑ 384 Ken Phelps	.10	.05
❑ 385 Jim Presley	.10	.05
❑ 386 Rey Quinones	.10	.05
❑ 387 Jerry Reed	.10	.05
❑ 388 Harold Reynolds	.15	.07
❑ 389 Dave Valle	.10	.05
❑ 390 Bill Wilkinson	.10	.05
❑ 391 Harold Baines	.15	.07
❑ 392 Floyd Bannister	.10	.05
❑ 393 Daryl Boston	.10	.05
❑ 394 Ivan Calderon	.10	.05
❑ 395 Jose DeLeon	.10	.05
❑ 396 Richard Dotson	.10	.05
❑ 397 Carlton Fisk	.30	.14
❑ 398 Ozzie Guillen	.10	.05
❑ 399 Ron Hassey	.10	.05
❑ 400 Donnie Hill	.10	.05
❑ 401 Bob James	.10	.05
❑ 402 Dave LaPoint	.10	.05
❑ 403 Bill Lindsey	.10	.05
❑ 404 Bill Long	.10	.05
❑ 405 Steve Lyons	.10	.05
❑ 406 Fred Manrique	.10	.05
❑ 407 Jack McDowell RC	.30	.14
❑ 408 Gary Redus	.10	.05
❑ 409 Ray Searage	.10	.05
❑ 410 Bobby Thigpen	.10	.05
❑ 411 Greg Walker	.10	.05
❑ 412 Ken Williams RC	.10	.05
❑ 413 Jim Winn	.10	.05
❑ 414 Jody Davis	.10	.05
❑ 415 Andre Dawson	.20	.09
❑ 416 Brian Dayett	.10	.05
❑ 417 Bob Dernier	.10	.05
❑ 418 Frank DiPino	.10	.05
❑ 419 Shawon Dunston	.10	.05
❑ 420 Leon Durham	.10	.05
❑ 421 Les Lancaster	.10	.05
❑ 422 Ed Lynch	.10	.05
❑ 423 Greg Maddux	1.50	.70
❑ 424 Dave Martinez	.10	.05
❑ 425A Keith Moreland ERR (Photo actually Jody Davis)	1.50	.70
❑ 425B Keith Moreland COR (Bat on shoulder)	.15	.07
❑ 426 Jamie Moyer	.15	.07
❑ 427 Jerry Mumphrey	.10	.05
❑ 428 Paul Noce	.10	.05
❑ 429 Rafael Palmeiro	.60	.25
❑ 430 Wade Rowdon	.10	.05
❑ 431 Ryne Sandberg	.40	.18
❑ 432 Scott Sanderson	.10	.05
❑ 433 Lee Smith	.15	.07
❑ 434 Jim Sundberg	.10	.05
❑ 435 Rick Sutcliffe	.15	.07
❑ 436 Manny Trillo	.10	.05
❑ 437 Juan Agosto	.10	.05
❑ 438 Larry Andersen	.10	.05
❑ 439 Alan Ashby	.10	.05
❑ 440 Kevin Bass	.10	.05
❑ 441 Ken Caminiti RC	1.00	.45
❑ 442 Rocky Childress	.10	.05
❑ 443 Jose Cruz	.10	.05
❑ 444 Danny Darwin	.10	.05
❑ 445 Glenn Davis	.10	.05
❑ 446 Jim Deshaies	.10	.05
❑ 447 Bill Doran	.10	.05
❑ 448 Ty Gainey	.10	.05
❑ 449 Billy Hatcher	.10	.05
❑ 450 Jeff Heathcock	.10	.05
❑ 451 Bob Knepper	.10	.05
❑ 452 Rob Mallicoat	.10	.05
❑ 453 Dave Meads	.10	.05
❑ 454 Craig Reynolds	.10	.05
❑ 455 Nolan Ryan	1.50	.70
❑ 456 Mike Scott	.10	.05
❑ 457 Dave Smith	.10	.05
❑ 458 Denny Walling	.10	.05
❑ 459 Robbie Wine	.10	.05
❑ 460 Gerald Young	.10	.05
❑ 461 Bob Brower	.10	.05
❑ 462A Jerry Browne ERR (Photo actually Bob Brower, white player)	1.50	.70
❑ 462B Jerry Browne COR (Black player)	.15	.07
❑ 463 Steve Buechele	.10	.05
❑ 464 Edwin Correa	.10	.05
❑ 465 Cecil Espy	.10	.05
❑ 466 Scott Fletcher	.10	.05
❑ 467 Jose Guzman	.10	.05
❑ 468 Greg Harris	.10	.05
❑ 469 Charlie Hough	.15	.07
❑ 470 Pete Incaviglia	.10	.05
❑ 471 Paul Kilgus	.10	.05
❑ 472 Mike Loynd	.10	.05
❑ 473 Oddibe McDowell	.10	.05
❑ 474 Dale Mohorcic	.10	.05
❑ 475 Pete O'Brien	.10	.05
❑ 476 Larry Parrish	.10	.05
❑ 477 Geno Petralli	.10	.05
❑ 478 Jeff Russell	.10	.05
❑ 479 Ruben Sierra	.10	.05
❑ 480 Mike Stanley	.15	.07
❑ 481 Curtis Wilkerson	.10	.05
❑ 482 Mitch Williams	.10	.05
❑ 483 Bobby Witt	.10	.05
❑ 484 Tony Armas	.10	.05
❑ 485 Bob Boone	.15	.07
❑ 486 Bill Buckner	.15	.07
❑ 487 DeWayne Buice	.10	.05
❑ 488 Brian Downing	.10	.05
❑ 489 Chuck Finley	.20	.09
❑ 490 Willie Fraser UER (Wrong bio stats, for George Hendrick)	.10	.05
❑ 491 Jack Howell	.10	.05
❑ 492 Ruppert Jones	.10	.05
❑ 493 Wally Joyner	.20	.09
❑ 494 Jack Lazorko	.10	.05
❑ 495 Gary Lucas	.10	.05
❑ 496 Kirk McCaskill	.10	.05
❑ 497 Mark McLemore	.10	.05
❑ 498 Darrell Miller	.10	.05
❑ 499 Greg Minton	.10	.05
❑ 500 Donnie Moore	.10	.05
❑ 501 Gus Polidor	.10	.05
❑ 502 Johnny Ray	.10	.05
❑ 503 Mark Ryal	.10	.05
❑ 504 Dick Schofield	.10	.05
❑ 505 Don Sutton	.30	.14
❑ 506 Devon White	.15	.07
❑ 507 Mike Witt	.10	.05
❑ 508 Dave Anderson	.10	.05

No.	Player	Mint	NrMt
❑ 509	Tim Belcher	.15	.07
❑ 510	Ralph Bryant	.10	.05
❑ 511	Tim Crews RC	.10	.05
❑ 512	Mike Devereaux RC	.15	.07
❑ 513	Mariano Duncan	.10	.05
❑ 514	Pedro Guerrero	.10	.05
❑ 515	Jeff Hamilton	.10	.05
❑ 516	Mickey Hatcher	.10	.05
❑ 517	Brad Havens	.10	.05
❑ 518	Orel Hershiser	.15	.07
❑ 519	Shawn Hillegas	.10	.05
❑ 520	Ken Howell	.10	.05
❑ 521	Tim Leary	.10	.05
❑ 522	Mike Marshall	.10	.05
❑ 523	Steve Sax	.10	.05
❑ 524	Mike Scioscia	.10	.05
❑ 525	Mike Sharperson	.10	.05
❑ 526	John Shelby	.10	.05
❑ 527	Franklin Stubbs	.10	.05
❑ 528	Fernando Valenzuela	.15	.07
❑ 529	Bob Welch	.10	.05
❑ 530	Matt Young	.10	.05
❑ 531	Jim Acker	.10	.05
❑ 532	Paul Assenmacher	.10	.05
❑ 533	Jeff Blauser RC	.30	.14
❑ 534	Joe Boever	.10	.05
❑ 535	Martin Clary	.10	.05
❑ 536	Kevin Coffman	.10	.05
❑ 537	Jeff Dedmon	.10	.05
❑ 538	Ron Gant RC	.40	.18
❑ 539	Tom Glavine RC	2.50	1.10
❑ 540	Ken Griffey	.15	.07
❑ 541	Albert Hall	.10	.05
❑ 542	Glenn Hubbard	.10	.05
❑ 543	Dion James	.10	.05
❑ 544	Dale Murphy	.30	.14
❑ 545	Ken Oberkfell	.10	.05
❑ 546	David Palmer	.10	.05
❑ 547	Gerald Perry	.10	.05
❑ 548	Charlie Puleo	.10	.05
❑ 549	Ted Simmons	.15	.07
❑ 550	Zane Smith	.10	.05
❑ 551	Andres Thomas	.10	.05
❑ 552	Ozzie Virgil	.10	.05
❑ 553	Don Aase	.10	.05
❑ 554	Jeff Ballard	.10	.05
❑ 555	Eric Bell	.10	.05
❑ 556	Mike Boddicker	.10	.05
❑ 557	Ken Dixon	.10	.05
❑ 558	Jim Dwyer	.10	.05
❑ 559	Ken Gerhart	.10	.05
❑ 560	Rene Gonzales RC	.10	.05
❑ 561	Mike Griffin	.10	.05
❑ 562	John Habyan UER	.10	.05
	(Misspelled Hayban on		
	both sides of card)		
❑ 563	Terry Kennedy	.10	.05
❑ 564	Ray Knight	.10	.05
❑ 565	Lee Lacy	.10	.05
❑ 566	Fred Lynn	.10	.05
❑ 567	Eddie Murray	.30	.14
❑ 568	Tom Niedenfuer	.10	.05
❑ 569	Bill Ripken RC*	.10	.05
❑ 570	Cal Ripken	1.25	.55
❑ 571	Dave Schmidt	.10	.05
❑ 572	Larry Sheets	.10	.05
❑ 573	Pete Stanicek	.10	.05
❑ 574	Mark Williamson	.10	.05
❑ 575	Mike Young	.10	.05
❑ 576	Shawn Abner	.10	.05
❑ 577	Greg Booker	.10	.05
❑ 578	Chris Brown	.10	.05
❑ 579	Keith Comstock	.10	.05
❑ 580	Joey Cora RC	.30	.14
❑ 581	Mark Davis	.10	.05
❑ 582	Tim Flannery	.30	.14
	(With surfboard)		
❑ 583	Goose Gossage	.20	.09
❑ 584	Mark Grant	.10	.05
❑ 585	Tony Gwynn	.60	.25
❑ 586	Andy Hawkins	.10	.05
❑ 587	Stan Jefferson	.10	.05
❑ 588	Jimmy Jones	.10	.05
❑ 589	John Kruk	.15	.07
❑ 590	Shane Mack	.10	.05
❑ 591	Carmelo Martinez	.10	.05
❑ 592	Lance McCullers UER	.10	.05
	(6'11" tall)		
❑ 593	Eric Nolte	.10	.05
❑ 594	Randy Ready	.10	.05
❑ 595	Luis Salazar	.10	.05
❑ 596	Benito Santiago	.10	.05
❑ 597	Eric Show	.10	.05
❑ 598	Garry Templeton	.10	.05
❑ 599	Ed Whitson	.10	.05
❑ 600	Scott Bailes	.10	.05
❑ 601	Chris Bando	.10	.05
❑ 602	Jay Bell RC	.75	.35
❑ 603	Brett Butler	.15	.07
❑ 604	Tom Candiotti	.10	.05
❑ 605	Joe Carter	.30	.14
❑ 606	Carmen Castillo	.10	.05
❑ 607	Brian Dorsett	.10	.05
❑ 608	John Farrell	.10	.05
❑ 609	Julio Franco	.10	.05
❑ 610	Mel Hall	.10	.05
❑ 611	Tommy Hinzo	.10	.05
❑ 612	Brook Jacoby	.10	.05
❑ 613	Doug Jones RC	.30	.14
❑ 614	Ken Schrom	.10	.05
❑ 615	Cory Snyder	.10	.05
❑ 616	Sammy Stewart	.10	.05
❑ 617	Greg Swindell	.10	.05
❑ 618	Pat Tabler	.10	.05
❑ 619	Ed VandeBerg	.10	.05
❑ 620	Eddie Williams RC	.15	.07
❑ 621	Rich Yett	.10	.05
❑ 622	Slug.Sophomores	.15	.07
	Wally Joyner		
	Cory Snyder		
❑ 623	Dominican Dynamite	.10	.05
	George Bell		
	Pedro Guerrero		
❑ 624	Oakland's Power Team	1.25	.55
	Mark McGwire		
	Jose Canseco		
❑ 625	Classic Relief	.10	.05
	Dave Righetti		
	Dan Plesac		
❑ 626	All Star Righties	.15	.07
	Bret Saberhagen		
	Mike Witt		
	Jack Morris		
❑ 627	Game Closers	.10	.05
	John Franco		
	Steve Bedrosian		
❑ 628	Masters/Double Play	.40	.18
	Ozzie Smith		
	Ryne Sandberg		
❑ 629	Rookie Record Setter	1.50	.70
	Mark McGwire		
❑ 630	Changing the Guard	.30	.14
	Mike Greenwell		
	Ellis Burks		
	Todd Benzinger		
❑ 631	NL Batting Champs	.30	.14
	Tony Gwynn		
	Tim Raines		
❑ 632	Pitching Magic	.15	.07
	Mike Scott		
	Orel Hershiser		
❑ 633	Big Bats at First	1.50	.70
	Pat Tabler		
	Mark McGwire		
❑ 634	Hitting King/Thief	.30	.14
	Tony Gwynn		
	Vince Coleman		
❑ 635	Slugging Shortstops	.40	.18
	Tony Fernandez		
	Cal Ripken		
	Alan Trammell		
❑ 636	Tried/True Sluggers	.20	.09
	Mike Schmidt		
	Gary Carter		
❑ 637	Crunch Time	.15	.07
	Darryl Strawberry		
	Eric Davis		
❑ 638	AL All-Stars	.20	.09
	Matt Nokes		
	Kirby Puckett		
❑ 639	NL All-Stars	.15	.07
	Keith Hernandez		
	Dale Murphy		
❑ 640	The O's Brothers	.60	.25
	Billy Ripken		
	Cal Ripken		
❑ 641	Mark Grace RC and	2.00	.90
	Darrin Jackson		
❑ 642	Damon Berryhill RC	.30	.14
	Jeff Montgomery RC		
❑ 643	Felix Fermin and	.10	.05
	Jesse Reid		
❑ 644	Greg Myers RC and	.10	.05
	Greg Tabor		
❑ 645	Joey Meyer and	.10	.05
	Jim Eppard		
❑ 646	Adam Peterson	.50	.23
	Randy Velarde RC		
❑ 647	Pete Smith and	.15	.07
	Chris Gwynn RC		
❑ 648	Tom Newell and	.10	.05
	Greg Jelks		
❑ 649	Mario Diaz and	.10	.05
	Clay Parker		
❑ 650	Jack Savage and	.10	.05
	Todd Simmons		
❑ 651	John Burkett RC and	.30	.14
	Kirt Manwaring		
❑ 652	Dave Otto RC and	.40	.18
	Walt Weiss		
❑ 653	Jeff King RC and	.15	.07
	Randell Byers		
❑ 654	CL: Twins/Cards	.10	.05
	Tigers/Giants UER		
	(90 Bob Melvin,		
	91 Eddie Milner)		
❑ 655	CL: Blue Jays/Mets	.10	.05
	Brewers/Expos UER		
	(Mets listed before		
	Blue Jays on card)		
❑ 656	CL: Yankees/Reds	.10	.05
	Royals/A's		
❑ 657	CL: Phillies/Pirates	.10	.05
	Red Sox/Mariners		
❑ 658	CL: White Sox/Cubs	.10	.05
	Astros/Rangers		
❑ 659	CL: Angels/Dodgers	.10	.05
	Braves/Orioles		
❑ 660	CL: Padres/Indians	.10	.05
	Rookies/Specials		

1988 Fleer Update

		MINT	NRMT
	COMP.FACT.SET (132)	8.00	3.60
❑ 1	Jose Bautista	.10	.05
❑ 2	Joe Orsulak	.10	.05
❑ 3	Doug Sisk	.10	.05
❑ 4	Craig Worthington	.10	.05
❑ 5	Mike Boddicker	.10	.05
❑ 6	Rick Cerone	.10	.05
❑ 7	Larry Parrish	.10	.05
❑ 8	Lee Smith	.20	.09
❑ 9	Mike Smithson	.10	.05
❑ 10	John Trautwein	.10	.05
❑ 11	Sherman Corbett	.10	.05
❑ 12	Chili Davis	.30	.14
❑ 13	Jim Eppard	.10	.05
❑ 14	Bryan Harvey XRC	.20	.09

❑ 15 John Davis .10 .05
❑ 16 Dave Gallagher .10 .05
❑ 17 Ricky Horton .10 .05
❑ 18 Dan Pasqua .10 .05
❑ 19 Melido Perez .10 .05
❑ 20 Jose Segura .10 .05
❑ 21 Andy Allanson .10 .05
❑ 22 Jon Perlman .10 .05
❑ 23 Domingo Ramos .10 .05
❑ 24 Rick Rodriguez .10 .05
❑ 25 Willie Upshaw .10 .05
❑ 26 Paul Gibson .10 .05
❑ 27 Don Heinkel .10 .05
❑ 28 Ray Knight .10 .05
❑ 29 Gary Pettis .10 .05
❑ 30 Luis Salazar .10 .05
❑ 31 Mike Macfarlane XRC .10 .05
❑ 32 Jeff Montgomery .50 .23
❑ 33 Ted Power .10 .05
❑ 34 Israel Sanchez .10 .05
❑ 35 Kurt Stillwell .10 .05
❑ 36 Pat Tabler .10 .05
❑ 37 Don August .10 .05
❑ 38 Darryl Hamilton XRC .20 .09
❑ 39 Jeff Leonard .10 .05
❑ 40 Joey Meyer .10 .05
❑ 41 Allan Anderson .10 .05
❑ 42 Brian Harper .10 .05
❑ 43 Tom Herr .10 .05
❑ 44 Charlie Lea .10 .05
❑ 45 John Moses .10 .05
(Listed as Hohn on checklist card)
❑ 46 John Candelaria .10 .05
❑ 47 Jack Clark .20 .09
❑ 48 Richard Dotson .10 .05
❑ 49 Al Leiter XRC* 1.00 .45
❑ 50 Rafael Santana .10 .05
❑ 51 Don Slaught .10 .05
❑ 52 Todd Burns .10 .05
❑ 53 Dave Henderson .10 .05
❑ 54 Doug Jennings .10 .05
❑ 55 Dave Parker .20 .09
❑ 56 Walt Weiss .30 .14
❑ 57 Bob Welch .10 .05
❑ 58 Henry Cotto .10 .05
❑ 59 Mario Diaz UER .10 .05
(Listed as Marion on card front)
❑ 60 Mike Jackson .20 .09
❑ 61 Bill Swift .10 .05
❑ 62 Jose Cecena .10 .05
❑ 63 Ray Hayward .10 .05
❑ 64 Jim Steels UER .10 .05
(Listed as Jim Steele on card back)
❑ 65 Pat Borders XRC .20 .09
❑ 66 Sil Campusano .10 .05
❑ 67 Mike Flanagan .10 .05
❑ 68 Todd Stottlemyre XRC .50 .23
❑ 69 David Wells XRC 1.50 .70
❑ 70 Jose Alvarez .10 .05
❑ 71 Paul Runge .10 .05
❑ 72 Cesar Jimenez .10 .05
(Card was intended for German Jiminez, it's his photo)
❑ 73 Pete Smith .10 .05
❑ 74 John Smoltz XRC 1.00 .45
❑ 75 Damon Berryhill .10 .05
❑ 76 Goose Gossage .30 .14
❑ 77 Mark Grace 2.00 .90
❑ 78 Darrin Jackson .10 .05
❑ 79 Vance Law .10 .05
❑ 80 Jeff Pico .10 .05
❑ 81 Gary Varsho .10 .05
❑ 82 Tim Birtsas .10 .05
❑ 83 Rob Dibble XRC .20 .09
❑ 84 Danny Jackson .10 .05
❑ 85 Paul O'Neill .50 .23
❑ 86 Jose Rijo .10 .05
❑ 87 Chris Sabo XRC .20 .09
❑ 88 John Fishel .10 .05
❑ 89 Craig Biggio XRC 2.00 .90
❑ 90 Terry Puhl .10 .05
❑ 91 Rafael Ramirez .10 .05
❑ 92 Louie Meadows .10 .05
❑ 93 Kirk Gibson .50 .23
❑ 94 Alfredo Griffin .10 .05
❑ 95 Jay Howell .10 .05
❑ 96 Jesse Orosco .10 .05
❑ 97 Alejandro Pena .10 .05
❑ 98 Tracy Woodson XRC* .10 .05
❑ 99 John Dopson .10 .05
❑ 100 Brian Holman XRC .10 .05
❑ 101 Rex Hudler .10 .05
❑ 102 Jeff Parrett .10 .05
❑ 103 Nelson Santovenia .10 .05
❑ 104 Kevin Elster .10 .05
❑ 105 Jeff Innis .10 .05
❑ 106 Mackey Sasser XRC* .10 .05
❑ 107 Phil Bradley .10 .05
❑ 108 Danny Clay .10 .05
❑ 109 Greg A.Harris .10 .05
❑ 110 Ricky Jordan XRC .20 .09
❑ 111 David Palmer .10 .05
❑ 112 Jim Gott .10 .05
❑ 113 Tommy Gregg UER .10 .05
(Photo actually Randy Milligan)
❑ 114 Barry Jones .10 .05
❑ 115 Randy Milligan XRC* .10 .05
❑ 116 Luis Alicea XRC .20 .09
❑ 117 Tom Brunansky .10 .05
❑ 118 John Costello .10 .05
❑ 119 Jose DeLeon .10 .05
❑ 120 Bob Horner .10 .05
❑ 121 Scott Terry .10 .05
❑ 122 Roberto Alomar XRC 3.00 1.35
❑ 123 Dave Leiper .10 .05
❑ 124 Keith Moreland .10 .05
❑ 125 Mark Parent .10 .05
❑ 126 Dennis Rasmussen .10 .05
❑ 127 Randy Bockus .10 .05
❑ 128 Brett Butler .20 .09
❑ 129 Donell Nixon .10 .05
❑ 130 Earnest Riles .10 .05
❑ 131 Roger Samuels .10 .05
❑ 132 Checklist U1-U132 .10 .05

1989 Fleer

	MINT	NRMT
COMPLETE SET (660)	25.00	11.00
COMP.FACT.SET (672)	25.00	11.00

❑ 1 Don Baylor .10 .05
❑ 2 Lance Blankenship RC .05 .02
❑ 3 Todd Burns UER .05 .02
(Wrong birthdate; before/after All-Star stats missing)
❑ 4 Greg Cadaret UER .05 .02
(All-Star Break stats show 3 losses, should be 2)
❑ 5 Jose Canseco .20 .09
❑ 6 Storm Davis .05 .02
❑ 7 Dennis Eckersley .15 .07
❑ 8 Mike Gallego .05 .02
❑ 9 Ron Hassey .05 .02
❑ 10 Dave Henderson .05 .02
❑ 11 Rick Honeycutt .05 .02
❑ 12 Glenn Hubbard .05 .02
❑ 13 Stan Javier .05 .02
❑ 14 Doug Jennings .05 .02
❑ 15 Felix Jose RC .05 .02
❑ 16 Carney Lansford .10 .05
❑ 17 Mark McGwire 1.00 .45
❑ 18 Gene Nelson .05 .02
❑ 19 Dave Parker .10 .05
❑ 20 Eric Plunk .05 .02
❑ 21 Luis Polonia .05 .02
❑ 22 Terry Steinbach .10 .05
❑ 23 Dave Stewart .10 .05
❑ 24 Walt Weiss .05 .02
❑ 25 Bob Welch .05 .02
❑ 26 Curt Young .05 .02
❑ 27 Rick Aguilera .10 .05
❑ 28 Wally Backman .05 .02
❑ 29 Mark Carreon UER .05 .02
(After All-Star Break batting 7.14)
❑ 30 Gary Carter .15 .07
❑ 31 David Cone .10 .05
❑ 32 Ron Darling .05 .02
❑ 33 Len Dykstra .10 .05
❑ 34 Kevin Elster .05 .02
❑ 35 Sid Fernandez .05 .02
❑ 36 Dwight Gooden .10 .05
❑ 37 Keith Hernandez .10 .05
❑ 38 Gregg Jefferies .10 .05
❑ 39 Howard Johnson .05 .02
❑ 40 Terry Leach .05 .02
❑ 41 Dave Magadan UER .05 .02
(Bio says 15 doubles, should be 13)
❑ 42 Bob McClure .05 .02
❑ 43 Roger McDowell UER .05 .02
(Led Mets with 58, should be 62)
❑ 44 Kevin McReynolds .05 .02
❑ 45 Keith A. Miller .05 .02
❑ 46 Randy Myers .10 .05
❑ 47 Bob Ojeda .05 .02
❑ 48 Mackey Sasser .05 .02
❑ 49 Darryl Strawberry .10 .05
❑ 50 Tim Teufel .05 .02
❑ 51 Dave West RC .05 .02
❑ 52 Mookie Wilson .10 .05
❑ 53 Dave Anderson .05 .02
❑ 54 Tim Belcher .05 .02
❑ 55 Mike Davis .05 .02
❑ 56 Mike Devereaux .05 .02
❑ 57 Kirk Gibson .10 .05
❑ 58 Alfredo Griffin .05 .02
❑ 59 Chris Gwynn .05 .02
❑ 60 Jeff Hamilton .05 .02
❑ 61A Danny Heep ERR .20 .09
Lake Hills
❑ 61B Danny Heep COR .05 .02
San Antonio
❑ 62 Orel Hershiser .10 .05
❑ 63 Brian Holton .05 .02
❑ 64 Jay Howell .05 .02
❑ 65 Tim Leary .05 .02
❑ 66 Mike Marshall .05 .02
❑ 67 Ramon Martinez RC .25 .11
❑ 68 Jesse Orosco .05 .02
❑ 69 Alejandro Pena .05 .02
❑ 70 Steve Sax .05 .02
❑ 71 Mike Scioscia .05 .02
❑ 72 Mike Sharperson .05 .02
❑ 73 John Shelby .05 .02
❑ 74 Franklin Stubbs .05 .02
❑ 75 John Tudor .05 .02
❑ 76 Fernando Valenzuela .10 .05
❑ 77 Tracy Woodson .05 .02
❑ 78 Marty Barrett .05 .02
❑ 79 Todd Benzinger .05 .02
❑ 80 Mike Boddicker UER .05 .02
(Rochester in '76, should be '78)
❑ 81 Wade Boggs .20 .09
❑ 82 Oil Can Boyd .05 .02
❑ 83 Ellis Burks .15 .07
❑ 84 Rick Cerone .05 .02
❑ 85 Roger Clemens .50 .23
❑ 86 Steve Curry .05 .02
❑ 87 Dwight Evans .10 .05

❑ 88 Wes Gardner .05 .02
❑ 89 Rich Gedman .05 .02
❑ 90 Mike Greenwell .05 .02
❑ 91 Bruce Hurst .05 .02
❑ 92 Dennis Lamp .05 .02
❑ 93 Spike Owen .05 .02
❑ 94 Larry Parrish UER .05 .02
(Before All-Star Break
batting 1.90)
❑ 95 Carlos Quintana RC .05 .02
❑ 96 Jody Reed .05 .02
❑ 97 Jim Rice .10 .05
❑ 98A Kevin Romine ERR .20 .09
(Photo actually
Randy Kutcher batting)
❑ 98B Kevin Romine COR .05 .02
(Arms folded)
❑ 99 Lee Smith .10 .05
❑ 100 Mike Smithson .05 .02
❑ 101 Bob Stanley .05 .02
❑ 102 Allan Anderson .05 .02
❑ 103 Keith Atherton .05 .02
❑ 104 Juan Berenguer .05 .02
❑ 105 Bert Blyleven .10 .05
❑ 106 Eric Bullock UER .05 .02
(Bats/Throws Right,
should be Left)
❑ 107 Randy Bush .05 .02
❑ 108 John Christensen .05 .02
❑ 109 Mark Davidson .05 .02
❑ 110 Gary Gaetti .10 .05
❑ 111 Greg Gagne .05 .02
❑ 112 Dan Gladden .05 .02
❑ 113 German Gonzalez .05 .02
❑ 114 Brian Harper .05 .02
❑ 115 Tom Herr .05 .02
❑ 116 Kent Hrbek .10 .05
❑ 117 Gene Larkin .05 .02
❑ 118 Tim Laudner .05 .02
❑ 119 Charlie Lea .05 .02
❑ 120 Steve Lombardozzi .05 .02
❑ 121A John Moses ERR .20 .09
Tempe
❑ 121B John Moses COR .05 .02
Phoenix
❑ 122 Al Newman .05 .02
❑ 123 Mark Portugal .05 .02
❑ 124 Kirby Puckett .50 .23
❑ 125 Jeff Reardon .10 .05
❑ 126 Fred Toliver .05 .02
❑ 127 Frank Viola .05 .02
❑ 128 Doyle Alexander .05 .02
❑ 129 Dave Bergman .05 .02
❑ 130A Tom Brookens ERR .75 .35
(Mike Heath back)
❑ 130B Tom Brookens COR .05 .02
❑ 131 Paul Gibson .05 .02
❑ 132A Mike Heath ERR .75 .35
(Tom Brookens back)
❑ 132B Mike Heath COR .05 .02
❑ 133 Don Heinkel .05 .02
❑ 134 Mike Henneman .05 .02
❑ 135 Guillermo Hernandez .05 .02
❑ 136 Eric King .05 .02
❑ 137 Chet Lemon .05 .02
❑ 138 Fred Lynn UER .05 .02
('74, '75 stats
missing)
❑ 139 Jack Morris .10 .05
❑ 140 Matt Nokes .05 .02
❑ 141 Gary Pettis .05 .02
❑ 142 Ted Power .05 .02
❑ 143 Jeff M. Robinson .05 .02
❑ 144 Luis Salazar .05 .02
❑ 145 Steve Searcy .05 .02
❑ 146 Pat Sheridan .05 .02
❑ 147 Frank Tanana .05 .02
❑ 148 Alan Trammell .15 .07
❑ 149 Walt Terrell .05 .02
❑ 150 Jim Walewander .05 .02
❑ 151 Lou Whitaker .10 .05
❑ 152 Tim Birtsas .05 .02
❑ 153 Tom Browning .05 .02
❑ 154 Keith Brown .05 .02
❑ 155 Norm Charlton RC .10 .05
❑ 156 Dave Concepcion .10 .05
❑ 157 Kal Daniels .05 .02
❑ 158 Eric Davis .10 .05
❑ 159 Bo Diaz .05 .02
❑ 160 Rob Dibble RC .10 .05
❑ 161 Nick Esasky .05 .02
❑ 162 John Franco .10 .05
❑ 163 Danny Jackson .05 .02
❑ 164 Barry Larkin .20 .09
❑ 165 Rob Murphy .05 .02
❑ 166 Paul O'Neill .20 .09
❑ 167 Jeff Reed .05 .02
❑ 168 Jose Rijo .05 .02
❑ 169 Ron Robinson .05 .02
❑ 170 Chris Sabo RC .05 .02
❑ 171 Candy Sierra .05 .02
❑ 172 Van Snider .05 .02
❑ 173A Jeff Treadway 5.00 2.20
(Target registration
mark above head
on front in
light blue)
❑ 173B Jeff Treadway .05 .02
(No target on front)
❑ 174 Frank Williams UER .05 .02
(After All-Star Break
stats are jumbled)
❑ 175 Herm Winningham .05 .02
❑ 176 Jim Adduci .05 .02
❑ 177 Don August .05 .02
❑ 178 Mike Birkbeck .05 .02
❑ 179 Chris Bosio .05 .02
❑ 180 Glenn Braggs .05 .02
❑ 181 Greg Brock .05 .02
❑ 182 Mark Clear .05 .02
❑ 183 Chuck Crim .05 .02
❑ 184 Rob Deer .05 .02
❑ 185 Tom Filer .05 .02
❑ 186 Jim Gantner .05 .02
❑ 187 Darryl Hamilton RC .05 .02
❑ 188 Ted Higuera .05 .02
❑ 189 Odell Jones .05 .02
❑ 190 Jeffrey Leonard .05 .02
❑ 191 Joey Meyer .05 .02
❑ 192 Paul Mirabella .05 .02
❑ 193 Paul Molitor .20 .09
❑ 194 Charlie O'Brien .05 .02
❑ 195 Dan Plesac .05 .02
❑ 196 Gary Sheffield RC 1.00 .45
❑ 197 B.J. Surhoff .10 .05
❑ 198 Dale Sveum .05 .02
❑ 199 Bill Wegman .05 .02
❑ 200 Robin Yount .20 .09
❑ 201 Rafael Belliard .05 .02
❑ 202 Barry Bonds .75 .35
❑ 203 Bobby Bonilla .10 .05
❑ 204 Sid Bream .05 .02
❑ 205 Benny Distefano .05 .02
❑ 206 Doug Drabek .05 .02
❑ 207 Mike Dunne .05 .02
❑ 208 Felix Fermin .05 .02
❑ 209 Brian Fisher .05 .02
❑ 210 Jim Gott .05 .02
❑ 211 Bob Kipper .05 .02
❑ 212 Dave LaPoint .05 .02
❑ 213 Mike LaValliere .05 .02
❑ 214 Jose Lind .05 .02
❑ 215 Junior Ortiz .05 .02
❑ 216 Vicente Palacios .05 .02
❑ 217 Tom Prince .05 .02
❑ 218 Gary Redus .05 .02
❑ 219 R.J. Reynolds .05 .02
❑ 220 Jeff D. Robinson .05 .02
❑ 221 John Smiley .05 .02
❑ 222 Andy Van Slyke .10 .05
❑ 223 Bob Walk .05 .02
❑ 224 Glenn Wilson .05 .02
❑ 225 Jesse Barfield .05 .02
❑ 226 George Bell .05 .02
❑ 227 Pat Borders RC .10 .05
❑ 228 John Cerutti .05 .02
❑ 229 Jim Clancy .05 .02
❑ 230 Mark Eichhorn .05 .02
❑ 231 Tony Fernandez .05 .02
❑ 232 Cecil Fielder .10 .05
❑ 233 Mike Flanagan .05 .02
❑ 234 Kelly Gruber .05 .02
❑ 235 Tom Henke .05 .02
❑ 236 Jimmy Key .10 .05
❑ 237 Rick Leach .05 .02
❑ 238 Manny Lee UER .05 .02
(Bio says regular
shortstop, sic,
Tony Fernandez)
❑ 239 Nelson Liriano .05 .02
❑ 240 Fred McGriff .20 .09
❑ 241 Lloyd Moseby .05 .02
❑ 242 Rance Mulliniks .05 .02
❑ 243 Jeff Musselman .05 .02
❑ 244 Dave Stieb .05 .02
❑ 245 Todd Stottlemyre .15 .07
❑ 246 Duane Ward .05 .02
❑ 247 David Wells .10 .05
❑ 248 Ernie Whitt UER .05 .02
(HR total 21,
should be 121)
❑ 249 Luis Aguayo .05 .02
❑ 250A Neil Allen ERR .75 .35
Sarasota, FL
❑ 250B Neil Allen COR .05 .02
Syosset, NY
❑ 251 John Candelaria .05 .02
❑ 252 Jack Clark .05 .02
❑ 253 Richard Dotson .05 .02
❑ 254 Rickey Henderson .40 .18
❑ 255 Tommy John .10 .05
❑ 256 Roberto Kelly .10 .05
❑ 257 Al Leiter .20 .09
❑ 258 Don Mattingly .50 .23
❑ 259 Dale Mohorcic .05 .02
❑ 260 Hal Morris RC .20 .09
❑ 261 Scott Nielsen .05 .02
❑ 262 Mike Pagliarulo UER .05 .02
(Wrong birthdate)
❑ 263 Hipolito Pena .05 .02
❑ 264 Ken Phelps .05 .02
❑ 265 Willie Randolph .10 .05
❑ 266 Rick Rhoden .05 .02
❑ 267 Dave Righetti .05 .02
❑ 268 Rafael Santana .05 .02
❑ 269 Steve Shields .05 .02
❑ 270 Joel Skinner .05 .02
❑ 271 Don Slaught .05 .02
❑ 272 Claudell Washington .05 .02
❑ 273 Gary Ward .05 .02
❑ 274 Dave Winfield .20 .09
❑ 275 Luis Aquino .05 .02
❑ 276 Floyd Bannister .05 .02
❑ 277 George Brett .40 .18
❑ 278 Bill Buckner .10 .05
❑ 279 Nick Capra .05 .02
❑ 280 Jose DeJesus .05 .02
❑ 281 Steve Farr .05 .02
❑ 282 Jerry Don Gleaton .05 .02
❑ 283 Mark Gubicza .05 .02
❑ 284 Tom Gordon RC UER .20 .09
(16.2 innings in '88,
should be 15.2)
❑ 285 Bo Jackson .15 .07
❑ 286 Charlie Leibrandt .05 .02
❑ 287 Mike Macfarlane RC .05 .02
❑ 288 Jeff Montgomery .10 .05
❑ 289 Bill Pecota UER .05 .02
(Photo actually
Brad Wellman)
❑ 290 Jamie Quirk .05 .02
❑ 291 Bret Saberhagen .10 .05
❑ 292 Kevin Seitzer .05 .02
❑ 293 Kurt Stillwell .05 .02
❑ 294 Pat Tabler .05 .02
❑ 295 Danny Tartabull .05 .02
❑ 296 Gary Thurman .05 .02
❑ 297 Frank White .10 .05
❑ 298 Willie Wilson .05 .02
❑ 299 Roberto Alomar .30 .14
❑ 300 S.Alomar Jr. RC UER .25 .11
Wrong birthdate, says
6/16/66, should say
6/18/66
❑ 301 Chris Brown .05 .02
❑ 302 Mike Brumley UER .05 .02
(133 hits in '88,
should be 134)

❑ 303 Mark Davis .05 .02
❑ 304 Mark Grant .05 .02
❑ 305 Tony Gwynn .40 .18
❑ 306 Greg W. Harris RC .05 .02
❑ 307 Andy Hawkins .05 .02
❑ 308 Jimmy Jones .05 .02
❑ 309 John Kruk .10 .05
❑ 310 Dave Leiper .05 .02
❑ 311 Carmelo Martinez .05 .02
❑ 312 Lance McCullers .05 .02
❑ 313 Keith Moreland .05 .02
❑ 314 Dennis Rasmussen .05 .02
❑ 315 Randy Ready UER .05 .02
(1214 games in '88, should be 114)
❑ 316 Benito Santiago .05 .02
❑ 317 Eric Show .05 .02
❑ 318 Todd Simmons .05 .02
❑ 319 Garry Templeton .05 .02
❑ 320 Dickie Thon .05 .02
❑ 321 Ed Whitson .05 .02
❑ 322 Marvell Wynne .05 .02
❑ 323 Mike Aldrete .05 .02
❑ 324 Brett Butler .10 .05
❑ 325 Will Clark UER .20 .09
(Three consecutive 100 RBI seasons)
❑ 326 Kelly Downs UER .05 .02
('88 stats missing)
❑ 327 Dave Dravecky .10 .05
❑ 328 Scott Garrelts .05 .02
❑ 329 Atlee Hammaker .05 .02
❑ 330 Charlie Hayes RC .20 .09
❑ 331 Mike Krukow .05 .02
❑ 332 Craig Lefferts .05 .02
❑ 333 Candy Maldonado .05 .02
❑ 334 Kirt Manwaring UER .05 .02
(Bats Rights)
❑ 335 Bob Melvin .05 .02
❑ 336 Kevin Mitchell .10 .05
❑ 337 Donell Nixon .05 .02
❑ 338 Tony Perezchica .05 .02
❑ 339 Joe Price .05 .02
❑ 340 Rick Reuschel .05 .02
❑ 341 Earnest Riles .05 .02
❑ 342 Don Robinson .05 .02
❑ 343 Chris Speier .05 .02
❑ 344 Robby Thompson UER .05 .02
(West Plam Beach)
❑ 345 Jose Uribe .05 .02
❑ 346 Matt Williams .15 .07
❑ 347 Trevor Wilson RC .05 .02
❑ 348 Juan Agosto .05 .02
❑ 349 Larry Andersen .05 .02
❑ 350A Alan Ashby ERR 2.00 .90
(Throws Rig)
❑ 350B Alan Ashby COR .05 .02
❑ 351 Kevin Bass .05 .02
❑ 352 Buddy Bell .10 .05
❑ 353 Craig Biggio RC .75 .35
❑ 354 Danny Darwin .05 .02
❑ 355 Glenn Davis .05 .02
❑ 356 Jim Deshaies .05 .02
❑ 357 Bill Doran .05 .02
❑ 358 John Fishel .05 .02
❑ 359 Billy Hatcher .05 .02
❑ 360 Bob Knepper .05 .02
❑ 361 L.Meadows UER .05 .02
Bio says 10 EBH's and 6 SB's in '88, should be 3 and 4
❑ 362 Dave Meads .05 .02
❑ 363 Jim Pankovits .05 .02
❑ 364 Terry Puhl .05 .02
❑ 365 Rafael Ramirez .05 .02
❑ 366 Craig Reynolds .05 .02
❑ 367 Mike Scott .05 .02
(Card number listed as 368 on Astros CL)
❑ 368 Nolan Ryan 1.00 .45
(Card number listed as 367 on Astros CL)
❑ 369 Dave Smith .05 .02
❑ 370 Gerald Young .05 .02
❑ 371 Hubie Brooks .05 .02
❑ 372 Tim Burke .05 .02
❑ 373 John Dopson .05 .02
❑ 374 Mike R. Fitzgerald .05 .02
❑ 375 Tom Foley .05 .02
❑ 376 Andres Galarraga UER .15 .07
(Home: Caracus)
❑ 377 Neal Heaton .05 .02
❑ 378 Joe Hesketh .05 .02
❑ 379 Brian Holman RC .05 .02
❑ 380 Rex Hudler .05 .02
❑ 381 R.Johnson RC UER 2.50 1.10
Innings for '85 and '86 shown as 27 and 120, should be 27.1 and 119.2
❑ 382 Wallace Johnson .05 .02
❑ 383 Tracy Jones .05 .02
❑ 384 Dave Martinez .05 .02
❑ 385 Dennis Martinez .10 .05
❑ 386 Andy McGaffigan .05 .02
❑ 387 Otis Nixon .05 .02
❑ 388 Johnny Paredes .05 .02
❑ 389 Jeff Parrett .05 .02
❑ 390 Pascual Perez .05 .02
❑ 391 Tim Raines .10 .05
❑ 392 Luis Rivera .05 .02
❑ 393 Nelson Santovenia .05 .02
❑ 394 Bryn Smith .05 .02
❑ 395 Tim Wallach .05 .02
❑ 396 Andy Allanson UER .05 .02
(1214 hits in '88, should be 114)
❑ 397 Rod Allen .05 .02
❑ 398 Scott Bailes .05 .02
❑ 399 Tom Candiotti .05 .02
❑ 400 Joe Carter .15 .07
❑ 401 Carmen Castillo UER .05 .02
(After All-Star Break batting 2.50)
❑ 402 Dave Clark UER .05 .02
(Card front shows position as Rookie; after All-Star Break batting 3.14)
❑ 403 John Farrell UER .05 .02
(Typo in runs allowed in '88)
❑ 404 Julio Franco .05 .02
❑ 405 Don Gordon .05 .02
❑ 406 Mel Hall .05 .02
❑ 407 Brad Havens .05 .02
❑ 408 Brook Jacoby .05 .02
❑ 409 Doug Jones .05 .02
❑ 410 Jeff Kaiser .05 .02
❑ 411 Luis Medina .05 .02
❑ 412 Cory Snyder .05 .02
❑ 413 Greg Swindell .05 .02
❑ 414 Ron Tingley UER .05 .02
(Hit HR in first ML at-bat, should be first AL at-bat)
❑ 415 Willie Upshaw .05 .02
❑ 416 Ron Washington .05 .02
❑ 417 Rich Yett .05 .02
❑ 418 Damon Berryhill .05 .02
❑ 419 Mike Bielecki .05 .02
❑ 420 Doug Dascenzo .05 .02
❑ 421 Jody Davis UER .05 .02
(Braves stats for '88 missing)
❑ 422 Andre Dawson .15 .07
❑ 423 Frank DiPino .05 .02
❑ 424 Shawon Dunston .05 .02
❑ 425 Rich Gossage .10 .05
❑ 426 Mark Grace UER .20 .09
(Minor League stats for '88 missing)
❑ 427 Mike Harkey RC .05 .02
❑ 428 Darrin Jackson .05 .02
❑ 429 Les Lancaster .05 .02
❑ 430 Vance Law .05 .02
❑ 431 Greg Maddux .60 .25
❑ 432 Jamie Moyer .05 .02
❑ 433 Al Nipper .05 .02
❑ 434 Rafael Palmeiro UER .25 .11
(170 hits in '88, should be 178)
❑ 435 Pat Perry .05 .02
❑ 436 Jeff Pico .05 .02
❑ 437 Ryne Sandberg .25 .11
❑ 438 Calvin Schiraldi .05 .02
❑ 439 Rick Sutcliffe .10 .05
❑ 440A Manny Trillo ERR 2.00 .90
(Throws Rig)
❑ 440B Manny Trillo COR .05 .02
❑ 441 Gary Varsho UER .05 .02
(Wrong birthdate; .303 should be .302; 11/28 should be 9/19)
❑ 442 Mitch Webster .05 .02
❑ 443 Luis Alicea RC .05 .02
❑ 444 Tom Brunansky .05 .02
❑ 445 Vince Coleman UER .05 .02
(Third straight with 83, should be fourth straight with 81)
❑ 446 John Costello UER .05 .02
(Home California, should be New York)
❑ 447 Danny Cox .05 .02
❑ 448 Ken Dayley .05 .02
❑ 449 Jose DeLeon .05 .02
❑ 450 Curt Ford .05 .02
❑ 451 Pedro Guerrero .05 .02
❑ 452 Bob Horner .05 .02
❑ 453 Tim Jones .05 .02
❑ 454 Steve Lake .05 .02
❑ 455 Joe Magrane UER .05 .02
(Des Moines, IO)
❑ 456 Greg Mathews .05 .02
❑ 457 Willie McGee .10 .05
❑ 458 Larry McWilliams .05 .02
❑ 459 Jose Oquendo .05 .02
❑ 460 Tony Pena .05 .02
❑ 461 Terry Pendleton .10 .05
❑ 462 Steve Peters UER .05 .02
(Lives in Harrah, not Harah)
❑ 463 Ozzie Smith .25 .11
❑ 464 Scott Terry .05 .02
❑ 465 Denny Walling .05 .02
❑ 466 Todd Worrell .05 .02
❑ 467 Tony Armas UER .05 .02
(Before All-Star Break batting 2.39)
❑ 468 Dante Bichette RC .40 .18
❑ 469 Bob Boone .10 .05
❑ 470 Terry Clark .05 .02
❑ 471 Stew Cliburn .05 .02
❑ 472 Mike Cook UER .05 .02
(TM near Angels logo missing from front)
❑ 473 Sherman Corbett .05 .02
❑ 474 Chili Davis .10 .05
❑ 475 Brian Downing .05 .02
❑ 476 Jim Eppard .05 .02
❑ 477 Chuck Finley .10 .05
❑ 478 Willie Fraser .05 .02
❑ 479 Bryan Harvey UER RC .05 .02
(ML record shows 0-0, should be 7-5)
❑ 480 Jack Howell .05 .02
❑ 481 Wally Joyner UER .10 .05
(Yorba Linda, GA)
❑ 482 Jack Lazorko .05 .02
❑ 483 Kirk McCaskill .05 .02
❑ 484 Mark McLemore .05 .02
❑ 485 Greg Minton .05 .02
❑ 486 Dan Petry .05 .02
❑ 487 Johnny Ray .05 .02
❑ 488 Dick Schofield .05 .02
❑ 489 Devon White .10 .05
❑ 490 Mike Witt .05 .02
❑ 491 Harold Baines .10 .05
❑ 492 Daryl Boston .05 .02
❑ 493 Ivan Calderon UER .05 .02
('80 stats shifted)
❑ 494 Mike Diaz .05 .02
❑ 495 Carlton Fisk .20 .09
❑ 496 Dave Gallagher .05 .02
❑ 497 Ozzie Guillen .05 .02
❑ 498 Shawn Hillegas .05 .02
❑ 499 Lance Johnson .10 .05

❑ 500 Barry Jones .05 .02
❑ 501 Bill Long .05 .02
❑ 502 Steve Lyons .05 .02
❑ 503 Fred Manrique .05 .02
❑ 504 Jack McDowell .10 .05
❑ 505 Donn Pall .05 .02
❑ 506 Kelly Paris .05 .02
❑ 507 Dan Pasqua .05 .02
❑ 508 Ken Patterson .05 .02
❑ 509 Melido Perez .05 .02
❑ 510 Jerry Reuss .05 .02
❑ 511 Mark Salas .05 .02
❑ 512 Bobby Thigpen UER .05 .02
('86 ERA 4.69,
should be 4.68)
❑ 513 Mike Woodard .05 .02
❑ 514 Bob Brower .05 .02
❑ 515 Steve Buechele .05 .02
❑ 516 Jose Cecena .05 .02
❑ 517 Cecil Espy .05 .02
❑ 518 Scott Fletcher .05 .02
❑ 519 Cecilio Guante .05 .02
('87 Yankee stats
are off-centered)
❑ 520 Jose Guzman .05 .02
❑ 521 Ray Hayward .05 .02
❑ 522 Charlie Hough .10 .05
❑ 523 Pete Incaviglia .05 .02
❑ 524 Mike Jeffcoat .05 .02
❑ 525 Paul Kilgus .05 .02
❑ 526 Chad Kreuter RC .05 .02
❑ 527 Jeff Kunkel .05 .02
❑ 528 Oddibe McDowell .05 .02
❑ 529 Pete O'Brien .05 .02
❑ 530 Geno Petralli .05 .02
❑ 531 Jeff Russell .05 .02
❑ 532 Ruben Sierra .05 .02
❑ 533 Mike Stanley .05 .02
❑ 534A Ed VandeBerg ERR .. 2.00 .90
(Throws Lef)
❑ 534B Ed VandeBerg COR .05 .02
❑ 535 Curtis Wilkerson ERR .05 .02
(Pitcher headings
at bottom)
❑ 536 Mitch Williams .05 .02
❑ 537 Bobby Witt UER .05 .02
('85 ERA .643,
should be 6.43)
❑ 538 Steve Balboni .05 .02
❑ 539 Scott Bankhead .05 .02
❑ 540 Scott Bradley .05 .02
❑ 541 Mickey Brantley .05 .02
❑ 542 Jay Buhner .10 .05
❑ 543 Mike Campbell .05 .02
❑ 544 Darnell Coles .05 .02
❑ 545 Henry Cotto .05 .02
❑ 546 Alvin Davis .05 .02
❑ 547 Mario Diaz .05 .02
❑ 548 Ken Griffey Jr. RC 15.00 6.75
❑ 549 Erik Hanson RC .10 .05
❑ 550 Mike Jackson UER .05 .02
(Lifetime ERA 3.345,
should be 3.45)
❑ 551 Mark Langston .05 .02
❑ 552 Edgar Martinez .15 .07
❑ 553 Bill McGuire .05 .02
❑ 554 Mike Moore .05 .02
❑ 555 Jim Presley .05 .02
❑ 556 Rey Quinones .05 .02
❑ 557 Jerry Reed .05 .02
❑ 558 Harold Reynolds .05 .02
❑ 559 Mike Schooler .05 .02
❑ 560 Bill Swift .05 .02
❑ 561 Dave Valle .05 .02
❑ 562 Steve Bedrosian .05 .02
❑ 563 Phil Bradley .05 .02
❑ 564 Don Carman .05 .02
❑ 565 Bob Dernier .05 .02
❑ 566 Marvin Freeman .05 .02
❑ 567 Todd Frohwirth .05 .02
❑ 568 Greg Gross .05 .02
❑ 569 Kevin Gross .05 .02
❑ 570 Greg A. Harris .05 .02
❑ 571 Von Hayes .05 .02
❑ 572 Chris James .05 .02
❑ 573 Steve Jeltz .05 .02
❑ 574 Ron Jones UER .05 .02
(Led IL in '88 with
85, should be 75)
❑ 575 Ricky Jordan RC .10 .05
❑ 576 Mike Maddux .05 .02
❑ 577 David Palmer .05 .02
❑ 578 Lance Parrish .05 .02
❑ 579 Shane Rawley .05 .02
❑ 580 Bruce Ruffin .05 .02
❑ 581 Juan Samuel .05 .02
❑ 582 Mike Schmidt .40 .18
❑ 583 Kent Tekulve .05 .02
❑ 584 Milt Thompson UER .05 .02
(19 hits in '88,
should be 109)
❑ 585 Jose Alvarez .05 .02
❑ 586 Paul Assenmacher .05 .02
❑ 587 Bruce Benedict .05 .02
❑ 588 Jeff Blauser .10 .05
❑ 589 Terry Blocker .05 .02
❑ 590 Ron Gant .10 .05
❑ 591 Tom Glavine .20 .09
❑ 592 Tommy Gregg .05 .02
❑ 593 Albert Hall .05 .02
❑ 594 Dion James .05 .02
❑ 595 Rick Mahler .05 .02
❑ 596 Dale Murphy .20 .09
❑ 597 Gerald Perry .05 .02
❑ 598 Charlie Puleo .05 .02
❑ 599 Ted Simmons .10 .05
❑ 600 Pete Smith .05 .02
❑ 601 Zane Smith .05 .02
❑ 602 John Smoltz RC .40 .18
❑ 603 Bruce Sutter .05 .02
❑ 604 Andres Thomas .05 .02
❑ 605 Ozzie Virgil .05 .02
❑ 606 Brady Anderson RC .40 .18
❑ 607 Jeff Ballard .05 .02
❑ 608 Jose Bautista .05 .02
❑ 609 Ken Gerhart .05 .02
❑ 610 Terry Kennedy .05 .02
❑ 611 Eddie Murray .20 .09
❑ 612 Carl Nichols UER .05 .02
(Before All-Star Break
batting 1.88)
❑ 613 Tom Niedenfuer .05 .02
❑ 614 Joe Orsulak .05 .02
❑ 615 Oswald Peraza UER .05 .02
(Shown as Oswaldo)
❑ 616A Bill Ripken ERR 15.00 6.75
(Rick Face written
on knob of bat)
❑ 616B Bill Ripken 50.00 22.00
(Bat knob
whited out)
❑ 616C Bill Ripken 6.00 2.70
(Words on bat knob
scribbled out in White)
❑ 616D Bill Ripken 20.00 9.00
Words on Bat
scribbled out in Black
❑ 616E Bill Ripken DP .10 .05
(Black box covering
bat knob)
❑ 617 Cal Ripken .75 .35
❑ 618 Dave Schmidt .05 .02
❑ 619 Rick Schu .05 .02
❑ 620 Larry Sheets .05 .02
❑ 621 Doug Sisk .05 .02
❑ 622 Pete Stanicek .05 .02
❑ 623 Mickey Tettleton .05 .02
❑ 624 Jay Tibbs .05 .02
❑ 625 Jim Traber .05 .02
❑ 626 Mark Williamson .05 .02
❑ 627 Craig Worthington .05 .02
❑ 628 Speed/Power .10 .05
Jose Canseco
❑ 629 Pitcher Perfect .05 .02
Tom Browning
❑ 630 Like Father/Like Sons .20 .09
Roberto Alomar
Sandy Alomar Jr.
(Names on card listed
in wrong order) UER
❑ 631 NL All Stars UER .20 .09
Will Clark
Rafael Palmeiro
(Gallaraga, sic;
Clark 3 consecutive
100 RBI seasons;
third with 102 RBI's)
❑ 632 Homeruns - Coast .10 .05
to Coast UER
Darryl Strawberry
Will Clark (Homeruns
should be two words)
❑ 633 Hot Corners - Hot .10 .05
Hitters UER
Wade Boggs
Carney Lansford
(Boggs hit .366 in
'86, should be '88)
❑ 634 Triple A's .50 .23
Jose Canseco
Terry Steinbach
Mark McGwire
❑ 635 Dual Heat .10 .05
Mark Davis
Dwight Gooden
❑ 636 NL Pitch. Power UER .05 .02
Danny Jackson
David Cone
Hersheiser, sic
❑ 637 Cannon Arms UER .10 .05
Chris Sabo
Bobby Bonilla
(Bobby Bonds, sic)
❑ 638 Double Trouble UER .05 .02
Andres Galarraga
(Misspelled Gallaraga
on card back)
Gerald Perry
❑ 639 Power Center .15 .07
Kirby Puckett
Eric Davis
❑ 640 Steve Wilson and .05 .02
Cameron Drew
❑ 641 Kevin Brown and .40 .18
Kevin Reimer
❑ 642 Brad Pounders RC .05 .02
Jerald Clark
❑ 643 Mike Capel and .05 .02
Drew Hall
❑ 644 Joe Girardi RC and .20 .09
Rolando Roomes
❑ 645 Lenny Harris RC and .10 .05
Marty Brown
❑ 646 Luis DeLosSantos .05 .02
and Jim Campbell
❑ 647 Randy Kramer and .05 .02
Miguel Garcia
❑ 648 Torey Lovullo RC and .05 .02
Robert Palacios
❑ 649 Jim Corsi and .05 .02
Bob Milacki
❑ 650 Grady Hall and .05 .02
Mike Rochford
❑ 651 Terry Taylor and .05 .02
Vance Lovelace
❑ 652 Ken Hill RC and .20 .09
Dennis Cook
❑ 653 Scott Service and .05 .02
Shane Turner
❑ 654 CL: Oakland/Mets .05 .02
Dodgers/Red Sox
(10 Henderson;
68 Jess Orosco)
❑ 655A CL: Twins/Tigers ERR .05 .02
Reds/Brewers
(179 Boslo and
Twins/Tigers positions
listed)
❑ 655B CL: Twins/Tigers COR .05 .02
Reds/Brewers
(179 Boslo but
Twins/Tigers positions
not listed)
❑ 656 CL: Pirates/Blue Jays .05 .02
Yankees/Royals
(225 Jess Barfield)
❑ 657 CL: Padres/Giants .05 .02
Astros/Expos

(367/368 wrong)
❑ 658 CL: Indians/Cubs .... .05 .02
Cardinals/Angels
(449 Deleon)
❑ 659 CL: White Sox/Rangers.. .05 .02
Mariners/Phillies
❑ 660 CL: Braves/Orioles .... .05 .02
Specials/Checklists
(632 hyphenated differently and 650 Hali;
595 Rich Mahler;
619 Rich Schu)

1989 Fleer Update

	MINT	NRMT
COMP.FACT.SET (132)	5.00	2.20

❑ 1 Phil Bradley .... .05 .02
❑ 2 Mike Devereaux .... .05 .02
❑ 3 Steve Finley RC .... .50 .23
❑ 4 Kevin Hickey .... .05 .02
❑ 5 Brian Holton .... .05 .02
❑ 6 Bob Milacki .... .05 .02
❑ 7 Randy Milligan .... .05 .02
❑ 8 John Dopson .... .05 .02
❑ 9 Nick Esasky .... .05 .02
❑ 10 Rob Murphy .... .05 .02
❑ 11 Jim Abbott RC* .... .20 .09
❑ 12 Bert Blyleven .... .10 .05
❑ 13 Jeff Manto RC .... .05 .02
❑ 14 Bob McClure .... .05 .02
❑ 15 Lance Parrish .... .05 .02
❑ 16 Lee Stevens RC .... .25 .11
❑ 17 Claudell Washington .... .05 .02
❑ 18 Mark Davis .... .05 .02
❑ 19 Eric King .... .05 .02
❑ 20 Ron Kittle .... .05 .02
❑ 21 Matt Merullo .... .05 .02
❑ 22 Steve Rosenberg .... .05 .02
❑ 23 Robin Ventura RC .... .75 .35
❑ 24 Keith Atherton .... .05 .02
❑ 25 Joey Belle RC .... 2.00 .90
❑ 26 Jerry Browne .... .05 .02
❑ 27 Felix Fermin .... .05 .02
❑ 28 Brad Komminsk .... .05 .02
❑ 29 Pete O'Brien .... .05 .02
❑ 30 Mike Brumley .... .05 .02
❑ 31 Tracy Jones .... .05 .02
❑ 32 Mike Schwabe .... .05 .02
❑ 33 Gary Ward .... .05 .02
❑ 34 Frank Williams .... .05 .02
❑ 35 Kevin Appier RC .... .25 .11
❑ 36 Bob Boone .... .10 .05
❑ 37 Luis DeLosSantos .... .05 .02
❑ 38 Jim Eisenreich .... .05 .02
❑ 39 Jaime Navarro RC .... .05 .02
❑ 40 Bill Spiers RC .... .05 .02
❑ 41 Greg Vaughn RC .... 1.00 .45
❑ 42 Randy Veres .... .05 .02
❑ 43 Wally Backman .... .05 .02
❑ 44 Shane Rawley .... .05 .02
❑ 45 Steve Balboni .... .05 .02
❑ 46 Jesse Barfield .... .05 .02
❑ 47 Alvaro Espinoza .... .05 .02
❑ 48 Bob Geren .... .05 .02
❑ 49 Mel Hall .... .05 .02
❑ 50 Andy Hawkins .... .05 .02
❑ 51 Hensley Meulens RC .... .05 .02
❑ 52 Steve Sax .... .05 .02
❑ 53 Deion Sanders RC .... .40 .18
❑ 54 Rickey Henderson .... .40 .18
❑ 55 Mike Moore .... .05 .02
❑ 56 Tony Phillips .... .05 .02
❑ 57 Greg Briley .... .05 .02
❑ 58 Gene Harris RC .... .05 .02
❑ 59 Randy Johnson 2.50 1.10
❑ 60 Jeffrey Leonard .... .05 .02
❑ 61 Dennis Powell .... .05 .02
❑ 62 Omar Vizquel RC .... .50 .23
❑ 63 Kevin Brown .... .40 .18
❑ 64 Julio Franco .... .05 .02
❑ 65 Jamie Moyer .... .05 .02
❑ 66 Rafael Palmeiro .... .25 .11
❑ 67 Nolan Ryan .... 2.00 .90
❑ 68 Francisco Cabrera RC .... .10 .05
❑ 69 Junior Felix RC .... .05 .02
❑ 70 Al Leiter .... .20 .09
❑ 71 Alex Sanchez .... .05 .02
❑ 72 Geronimo Berroa .... .05 .02
❑ 73 Derek Lilliquist RC .... .05 .02
❑ 74 Lonnie Smith .... .05 .02
❑ 75 Jeff Treadway .... .05 .02
❑ 76 Paul Kilgus .... .05 .02
❑ 77 Lloyd McClendon .... .05 .02
❑ 78 Scott Sanderson .... .05 .02
❑ 79 Dwight Smith RC .... .10 .05
❑ 80 Jerome Walton .... .20 .09
❑ 81 Mitch Williams .... .05 .02
❑ 82 Steve Wilson .... .05 .02
❑ 83 Todd Benzinger .... .05 .02
❑ 84 Ken Griffey Sr. .... .10 .05
❑ 85 Rick Mahler .... .05 .02
❑ 86 Rolando Roomes .... .05 .02
❑ 87 Scott Scudder RC .... .05 .02
❑ 88 Jim Clancy .... .05 .02
❑ 89 Rick Rhoden .... .05 .02
❑ 90 Dan Schatzeder .... .05 .02
❑ 91 Mike Morgan .... .05 .02
❑ 92 Eddie Murray .... .20 .09
❑ 93 Willie Randolph .... .10 .05
❑ 94 Ray Searage .... .05 .02
❑ 95 Mike Aldrete .... .05 .02
❑ 96 Kevin Gross .... .05 .02
❑ 97 Mark Langston .... .05 .02
❑ 98 Spike Owen .... .05 .02
❑ 99 Zane Smith .... .05 .02
❑ 100 Don Aase .... .05 .02
❑ 101 Barry Lyons .... .05 .02
❑ 102 Juan Samuel .... .05 .02
❑ 103 Wally Whitehurst RC .... .05 .02
❑ 104 Dennis Cook .... .05 .02
❑ 105 Len Dykstra .... .10 .05
❑ 106 Charlie Hayes .... .20 .09
❑ 107 Tommy Herr .... .05 .02
❑ 108 Ken Howell .... .05 .02
❑ 109 John Kruk .... .10 .05
❑ 110 Roger McDowell .... .05 .02
❑ 111 Terry Mulholland .... .05 .02
❑ 112 Jeff Parrett .... .05 .02
❑ 113 Neal Heaton .... .05 .02
❑ 114 Jeff King .... .05 .02
❑ 115 Randy Kramer .... .05 .02
❑ 116 Bill Landrum .... .05 .02
❑ 117 Cris Carpenter RC* .... .05 .02
❑ 118 Frank DiPino .... .05 .02
❑ 119 Ken Hill .... .20 .09
❑ 120 Dan Quisenberry .... .05 .02
❑ 121 Milt Thompson .... .05 .02
❑ 122 Todd Zeile RC .... .25 .11
❑ 123 Jack Clark .... .05 .02
❑ 124 Bruce Hurst .... .05 .02
❑ 125 Mark Parent .... .05 .02
❑ 126 Bip Roberts .... .10 .05
❑ 127 Jeff Brantley RC UER .... .15 .07
(Photo actually
Joe Kmak)
❑ 128 Terry Kennedy .... .05 .02
❑ 129 Mike LaCoss .... .05 .02
❑ 130 Greg Litton .... .05 .02
❑ 131 Mike Schmidt .... .60 .25
❑ 132 Checklist 1-132 .... .05 .02

1990 Fleer

	MINT	NRMT
COMPLETE SET (660)	12.00	5.50
COMP.RETAIL SET (660)	8.00	3.60
COMP.HOBBY SET (672)	15.00	6.75

❑ 1 Lance Blankenship .... .05 .02
❑ 2 Todd Burns .... .05 .02
❑ 3 Jose Canseco .... .20 .09
❑ 4 Jim Corsi .... .05 .02
❑ 5 Storm Davis .... .05 .02
❑ 6 Dennis Eckersley .... .15 .07
❑ 7 Mike Gallego .... .05 .02
❑ 8 Ron Hassey .... .05 .02
❑ 9 Dave Henderson .... .05 .02
❑ 10 Rickey Henderson .... .40 .18
❑ 11 Rick Honeycutt .... .05 .02
❑ 12 Stan Javier .... .05 .02
❑ 13 Felix Jose .... .05 .02
❑ 14 Carney Lansford .... .10 .05
❑ 15 Mark McGwire UER .... .75 .35
(1989 runs listed as
4, should be 74)
❑ 16 Mike Moore .... .05 .02
❑ 17 Gene Nelson .... .05 .02
❑ 18 Dave Parker .... .10 .05
❑ 19 Tony Phillips .... .05 .02
❑ 20 Terry Steinbach .... .05 .02
❑ 21 Dave Stewart .... .10 .05
❑ 22 Walt Weiss .... .05 .02
❑ 23 Bob Welch .... .05 .02
❑ 24 Curt Young .... .05 .02
❑ 25 Paul Assenmacher .... .05 .02
❑ 26 Damon Berryhill .... .05 .02
❑ 27 Mike Bielecki .... .05 .02
❑ 28 Kevin Blankenship .... .05 .02
❑ 29 Andre Dawson .... .15 .07
❑ 30 Shawon Dunston .... .05 .02
❑ 31 Joe Girardi .... .15 .07
❑ 32 Mark Grace .... .20 .09
❑ 33 Mike Harkey .... .05 .02
❑ 34 Paul Kilgus .... .05 .02
❑ 35 Les Lancaster .... .05 .02
❑ 36 Vance Law .... .05 .02
❑ 37 Greg Maddux .... .50 .23
❑ 38 Lloyd McClendon .... .05 .02
❑ 39 Jeff Pico .... .05 .02
❑ 40 Ryne Sandberg .... .25 .11
❑ 41 Scott Sanderson .... .05 .02
❑ 42 Dwight Smith .... .05 .02
❑ 43 Rick Sutcliffe .... .10 .05
❑ 44 Jerome Walton .... .05 .02
❑ 45 Mitch Webster .... .05 .02
❑ 46 Curt Wilkerson .... .05 .02
❑ 47 Dean Wilkins .... .05 .02
❑ 48 Mitch Williams .... .05 .02
❑ 49 Steve Wilson .... .05 .02
❑ 50 Steve Bedrosian .... .05 .02
❑ 51 Mike Benjamin RC .... .05 .02
❑ 52 Jeff Brantley .... .05 .02
❑ 53 Brett Butler .... .10 .05
❑ 54 Will Clark UER .... .10 .05
(Did You Know says
first in runs, should
say tied for first)
❑ 55 Kelly Downs .... .05 .02
❑ 56 Scott Garrelts .... .05 .02

❑ 57 Atlee Hammaker .05 .02
❑ 58 Terry Kennedy .05 .02
❑ 59 Mike LaCoss .05 .02
❑ 60 Craig Lefferts .05 .02
❑ 61 Greg Litton .05 .02
❑ 62 Candy Maldonado .05 .02
❑ 63 Kirt Manwaring UER .05 .02
(No '88 Phoenix stats as noted in box)
❑ 64 Randy McCament .05 .02
❑ 65 Kevin Mitchell .05 .02
❑ 66 Donell Nixon .05 .02
❑ 67 Ken Oberkfell .05 .02
❑ 68 Rick Reuschel .05 .02
❑ 69 Ernest Riles .05 .02
❑ 70 Don Robinson .05 .02
❑ 71 Pat Sheridan .05 .02
❑ 72 Chris Speier .05 .02
❑ 73 Robby Thompson .05 .02
❑ 74 Jose Uribe .05 .02
❑ 75 Matt Williams .15 .07
❑ 76 George Bell .05 .02
❑ 77 Pat Borders .05 .02
❑ 78 John Cerutti .05 .02
❑ 79 Junior Felix .05 .02
❑ 80 Tony Fernandez .05 .02
❑ 81 Mike Flanagan .05 .02
❑ 82 Mauro Gozzo .05 .02
❑ 83 Kelly Gruber .05 .02
❑ 84 Tom Henke .05 .02
❑ 85 Jimmy Key .10 .05
❑ 86 Manny Lee .05 .02
❑ 87 Nelson Liriano UER .05 .02
(Should say "led the IL" instead of "led the TL")
❑ 88 Lee Mazzilli .05 .02
❑ 89 Fred McGriff .20 .09
❑ 90 Lloyd Moseby .05 .02
❑ 91 Rance Mulliniks .05 .02
❑ 92 Alex Sanchez .05 .02
❑ 93 Dave Stieb .10 .05
❑ 94 Todd Stottlemyre .10 .05
❑ 95 Duane Ward UER .05 .02
(Double line of '87 Syracuse stats)
❑ 96 David Wells .10 .05
❑ 97 Ernie Whitt .05 .02
❑ 98 Frank Wills .05 .02
❑ 99 Mookie Wilson .10 .05
❑ 100 Kevin Appier .15 .07
❑ 101 Luis Aquino .05 .02
❑ 102 Bob Boone .10 .05
❑ 103 George Brett .40 .18
❑ 104 Jose DeJesus .05 .02
❑ 105 Luis De Los Santos .05 .02
❑ 106 Jim Eisenreich .05 .02
❑ 107 Steve Farr .05 .02
❑ 108 Tom Gordon .10 .05
❑ 109 Mark Gubicza .05 .02
❑ 110 Bo Jackson .10 .05
❑ 111 Terry Leach .05 .02
❑ 112 Charlie Leibrandt .05 .02
❑ 113 Rick Luecken .05 .02
❑ 114 Mike Macfarlane .05 .02
❑ 115 Jeff Montgomery .10 .05
❑ 116 Bret Saberhagen .10 .05
❑ 117 Kevin Seitzer .05 .02
❑ 118 Kurt Stillwell .05 .02
❑ 119 Pat Tabler .05 .02
❑ 120 Danny Tartabull .05 .02
❑ 121 Gary Thurman .05 .02
❑ 122 Frank White .10 .05
❑ 123 Willie Wilson .05 .02
❑ 124 Matt Winters .05 .02
❑ 125 Jim Abbott .15 .07
❑ 126 Tony Armas .05 .02
❑ 127 Dante Bichette .20 .09
❑ 128 Bert Blyleven .10 .05
❑ 129 Chili Davis .10 .05
❑ 130 Brian Downing .05 .02
❑ 131 Mike Fetters RC .05 .02
❑ 132 Chuck Finley .10 .05
❑ 133 Willie Fraser .05 .02
❑ 134 Bryan Harvey .05 .02
❑ 135 Jack Howell .05 .02
❑ 136 Wally Joyner .10 .05
❑ 137 Jeff Manto .05 .02
❑ 138 Kirk McCaskill .05 .02
❑ 139 Bob McClure .05 .02
❑ 140 Greg Minton .05 .02
❑ 141 Lance Parrish .05 .02
❑ 142 Dan Petry .05 .02
❑ 143 Johnny Ray .05 .02
❑ 144 Dick Schofield .05 .02
❑ 145 Lee Stevens .10 .05
❑ 146 Claudell Washington .05 .02
❑ 147 Devon White .05 .02
❑ 148 Mike Witt .05 .02
❑ 149 Roberto Alomar .20 .09
❑ 150 Sandy Alomar Jr. .10 .05
❑ 151 Andy Benes .05 .02
❑ 152 Jack Clark .10 .05
❑ 153 Pat Clements .05 .02
❑ 154 Joey Cora .10 .05
❑ 155 Mark Davis .05 .02
❑ 156 Mark Grant .05 .02
❑ 157 Tony Gwynn .40 .18
❑ 158 Greg W. Harris .05 .02
❑ 159 Bruce Hurst .05 .02
❑ 160 Darrin Jackson .05 .02
❑ 161 Chris James .05 .02
❑ 162 Carmelo Martinez .05 .02
❑ 163 Mike Pagliarulo .05 .02
❑ 164 Mark Parent .05 .02
❑ 165 Dennis Rasmussen .05 .02
❑ 166 Bip Roberts .05 .02
❑ 167 Benito Santiago .05 .02
❑ 168 Calvin Schiraldi .05 .02
❑ 169 Eric Show .05 .02
❑ 170 Garry Templeton .05 .02
❑ 171 Ed Whitson .05 .02
❑ 172 Brady Anderson .20 .09
❑ 173 Jeff Ballard .05 .02
❑ 174 Phil Bradley .05 .02
❑ 175 Mike Devereaux .05 .02
❑ 176 Steve Finley .10 .05
❑ 177 Pete Harnisch .05 .02
❑ 178 Kevin Hickey .05 .02
❑ 179 Brian Holton .05 .02
❑ 180 Ben McDonald RC .10 .05
❑ 181 Bob Melvin .05 .02
❑ 182 Bob Milacki .05 .02
❑ 183 Randy Milligan UER .05 .02
(Double line of '87 stats)
❑ 184 Gregg Olson .10 .05
❑ 185 Joe Orsulak .05 .02
❑ 186 Bill Ripken .05 .02
❑ 187 Cal Ripken .75 .35
❑ 188 Dave Schmidt .05 .02
❑ 189 Larry Sheets .05 .02
❑ 190 Mickey Tettleton .05 .02
❑ 191 Mark Thurmond .05 .02
❑ 192 Jay Tibbs .05 .02
❑ 193 Jim Traber .05 .02
❑ 194 Mark Williamson .05 .02
❑ 195 Craig Worthington .05 .02
❑ 196 Don Aase .05 .02
❑ 197 Blaine Beatty .05 .02
❑ 198 Mark Carreon .05 .02
❑ 199 Gary Carter .15 .07
❑ 200 David Cone .10 .05
❑ 201 Ron Darling .05 .02
❑ 202 Kevin Elster .05 .02
❑ 203 Sid Fernandez .05 .02
❑ 204 Dwight Gooden .10 .05
❑ 205 Keith Hernandez .10 .05
❑ 206 Jeff Innis .05 .02
❑ 207 Gregg Jefferies .10 .05
❑ 208 Howard Johnson .05 .02
❑ 209 Barry Lyons UER .05 .02
(Double line of '87 stats)
❑ 210 Dave Magadan .05 .02
❑ 211 Kevin McReynolds .05 .02
❑ 212 Jeff Musselman .05 .02
❑ 213 Randy Myers .10 .05
❑ 214 Bob Ojeda .05 .02
❑ 215 Juan Samuel .05 .02
❑ 216 Mackey Sasser .05 .02
❑ 217 Darryl Strawberry .10 .05
❑ 218 Tim Teufel .05 .02
❑ 219 Frank Viola .05 .02
❑ 220 Juan Agosto .05 .02
❑ 221 Larry Andersen .05 .02
❑ 222 Eric Anthony RC .05 .02
❑ 223 Kevin Bass .05 .02
❑ 224 Craig Biggio .15 .07
❑ 225 Ken Caminiti .10 .05
❑ 226 Jim Clancy .05 .02
❑ 227 Danny Darwin .05 .02
❑ 228 Glenn Davis .05 .02
❑ 229 Jim Deshaies .05 .02
❑ 230 Bill Doran .05 .02
❑ 231 Bob Forsch .05 .02
❑ 232 Brian Meyer .05 .02
❑ 233 Terry Puhl .05 .02
❑ 234 Rafael Ramirez .05 .02
❑ 235 Rick Rhoden .05 .02
❑ 236 Dan Schatzeder .05 .02
❑ 237 Mike Scott .05 .02
❑ 238 Dave Smith .05 .02
❑ 239 Alex Trevino .05 .02
❑ 240 Glenn Wilson .05 .02
❑ 241 Gerald Young .05 .02
❑ 242 Tom Brunansky .05 .02
❑ 243 Cris Carpenter .05 .02
❑ 244 Alex Cole RC .05 .02
❑ 245 Vince Coleman .05 .02
❑ 246 John Costello .05 .02
❑ 247 Ken Dayley .05 .02
❑ 248 Jose DeLeon .05 .02
❑ 249 Frank DiPino .05 .02
❑ 250 Pedro Guerrero .05 .02
❑ 251 Ken Hill .10 .05
❑ 252 Joe Magrane .05 .02
❑ 253 Willie McGee UER .10 .05
(No decimal point before 353)
❑ 254 John Morris .05 .02
❑ 255 Jose Oquendo .05 .02
❑ 256 Tony Pena .05 .02
❑ 257 Terry Pendleton .10 .05
❑ 258 Ted Power .05 .02
❑ 259 Dan Quisenberry .05 .02
❑ 260 Ozzie Smith .25 .11
❑ 261 Scott Terry .05 .02
❑ 262 Milt Thompson .05 .02
❑ 263 Denny Walling .05 .02
❑ 264 Todd Worrell .05 .02
❑ 265 Todd Zeile .10 .05
❑ 266 Marty Barrett .05 .02
❑ 267 Mike Boddicker .05 .02
❑ 268 Wade Boggs .20 .09
❑ 269 Ellis Burks .15 .07
❑ 270 Rick Cerone .05 .02
❑ 271 Roger Clemens .50 .23
❑ 272 John Dopson .05 .02
❑ 273 Nick Esasky .05 .02
❑ 274 Dwight Evans .10 .05
❑ 275 Wes Gardner .05 .02
❑ 276 Rich Gedman .05 .02
❑ 277 Mike Greenwell .05 .02
❑ 278 Danny Heep .05 .02
❑ 279 Eric Hetzel .05 .02
❑ 280 Dennis Lamp .05 .02
❑ 281 Rob Murphy UER .05 .02
('89 stats say Reds, should say Red Sox)
❑ 282 Joe Price .05 .02
❑ 283 Carlos Quintana .05 .02
❑ 284 Jody Reed .05 .02
❑ 285 Luis Rivera .05 .02
❑ 286 Kevin Romine .05 .02
❑ 287 Lee Smith .10 .05
❑ 288 Mike Smithson .05 .02
❑ 289 Bob Stanley .05 .02
❑ 290 Harold Baines .10 .05
❑ 291 Kevin Brown .20 .09
❑ 292 Steve Buechele .05 .02
❑ 293 Scott Coolbaugh .05 .02
❑ 294 Jack Daugherty .05 .02
❑ 295 Cecil Espy .05 .02
❑ 296 Julio Franco .05 .02
❑ 297 Juan Gonzalez RC 2.00 .90
❑ 298 Cecilio Guante .05 .02
❑ 299 Drew Hall .05 .02

No.	Player		
❑ 300	Charlie Hough	.10	.05
❑ 301	Pete Incaviglia	.05	.02
❑ 302	Mike Jeffcoat	.05	.02
❑ 303	Chad Kreuter	.05	.02
❑ 304	Jeff Kunkel	.05	.02
❑ 305	Rick Leach	.05	.02
❑ 306	Fred Manrique	.05	.02
❑ 307	Jamie Moyer	.05	.02
❑ 308	Rafael Palmeiro	.20	.09
❑ 309	Geno Petralli	.05	.02
❑ 310	Kevin Reimer	.05	.02
❑ 311	Kenny Rogers	.10	.05
❑ 312	Jeff Russell	.05	.02
❑ 313	Nolan Ryan	1.00	.45
❑ 314	Ruben Sierra	.05	.02
❑ 315	Bobby Witt	.05	.02
❑ 316	Chris Bosio	.05	.02
❑ 317	Glenn Braggs UER (Stats say 111 K's, but bio says 117 K's)	.05	.02
❑ 318	Greg Brock	.05	.02
❑ 319	Chuck Crim	.05	.02
❑ 320	Rob Deer	.05	.02
❑ 321	Mike Felder	.05	.02
❑ 322	Tom Filer	.05	.02
❑ 323	Tony Fossas	.05	.02
❑ 324	Jim Gantner	.05	.02
❑ 325	Darryl Hamilton	.05	.02
❑ 326	Teddy Higuera	.05	.02
❑ 327	Mark Knudson	.05	.02
❑ 328	Bill Krueger UER ('86 stats missing)	.05	.02
❑ 329	Tim McIntosh RC	.05	.02
❑ 330	Paul Molitor	.20	.09
❑ 331	Jaime Navarro	.05	.02
❑ 332	Charlie O'Brien	.05	.02
❑ 333	Jeff Peterek	.05	.02
❑ 334	Dan Plesac	.05	.02
❑ 335	Jerry Reuss	.05	.02
❑ 336	Gary Sheffield UER (Bio says played for 3 teams in '87, but stats say in '88)	.10	.05
❑ 337	Bill Spiers	.05	.02
❑ 338	B.J. Surhoff	.10	.05
❑ 339	Greg Vaughn	.20	.09
❑ 340	Robin Yount	.20	.09
❑ 341	Hubie Brooks	.05	.02
❑ 342	Tim Burke	.05	.02
❑ 343	Mike Fitzgerald	.05	.02
❑ 344	Tom Foley	.05	.02
❑ 345	Andres Galarraga	.15	.07
❑ 346	Damaso Garcia	.05	.02
❑ 347	Marquis Grissom RC	.10	.05
❑ 348	Kevin Gross	.05	.02
❑ 349	Joe Hesketh	.05	.02
❑ 350	Jeff Huson RC	.05	.02
❑ 351	Wallace Johnson	.05	.02
❑ 352	Mark Langston	.05	.02
❑ 353A	Dave Martinez (Yellow on front)	2.00	.90
❑ 353B	Dave Martinez (Red on front)	.05	.02
❑ 354	Dennis Martinez UER ('87 ERA is 616, should be 6.16)	.10	.05
❑ 355	Andy McGaffigan	.05	.02
❑ 356	Otis Nixon	.05	.02
❑ 357	Spike Owen	.05	.02
❑ 358	Pascual Perez	.05	.02
❑ 359	Tim Raines	.10	.05
❑ 360	Nelson Santovenia	.05	.02
❑ 361	Bryn Smith	.05	.02
❑ 362	Zane Smith	.05	.02
❑ 363	Larry Walker RC	.60	.25
❑ 364	Tim Wallach	.05	.02
❑ 365	Rick Aguilera	.10	.05
❑ 366	Allan Anderson	.05	.02
❑ 367	Wally Backman	.05	.02
❑ 368	Doug Baker	.05	.02
❑ 369	Juan Berenguer	.05	.02
❑ 370	Randy Bush	.05	.02
❑ 371	Carmen Castillo	.05	.02
❑ 372	Mike Dyer	.05	.02
❑ 373	Gary Gaetti	.10	.05
❑ 374	Greg Gagne	.05	.02
❑ 375	Dan Gladden	.05	.02
❑ 376	G.Gonzalez UER (Bio says 31 saves in '88, but stats say 30)	.05	.02
❑ 377	Brian Harper	.05	.02
❑ 378	Kent Hrbek	.10	.05
❑ 379	Gene Larkin	.05	.02
❑ 380	Tim Laudner UER (No decimal point before '85 BA of 238)	.05	.02
❑ 381	John Moses	.05	.02
❑ 382	Al Newman	.05	.02
❑ 383	Kirby Puckett	.50	.23
❑ 384	Shane Rawley	.05	.02
❑ 385	Jeff Reardon	.10	.05
❑ 386	Roy Smith	.05	.02
❑ 387	Gary Wayne	.05	.02
❑ 388	Dave West	.05	.02
❑ 389	Tim Belcher	.05	.02
❑ 390	Tim Crews UER (Stats say 163 IP for '83, but bio says 136)	.05	.02
❑ 391	Mike Davis	.05	.02
❑ 392	Rick Dempsey	.05	.02
❑ 393	Kirk Gibson	.10	.05
❑ 394	Jose Gonzalez	.05	.02
❑ 395	Alfredo Griffin	.05	.02
❑ 396	Jeff Hamilton	.05	.02
❑ 397	Lenny Harris	.05	.02
❑ 398	Mickey Hatcher	.05	.02
❑ 399	Orel Hershiser	.10	.05
❑ 400	Jay Howell	.05	.02
❑ 401	Mike Marshall	.05	.02
❑ 402	Ramon Martinez	.05	.02
❑ 403	Mike Morgan	.05	.02
❑ 404	Eddie Murray	.20	.09
❑ 405	Alejandro Pena	.05	.02
❑ 406	Willie Randolph	.10	.05
❑ 407	Mike Scioscia	.05	.02
❑ 408	Ray Searage	.05	.02
❑ 409	Fernando Valenzuela	.10	.05
❑ 410	Jose Vizcaino RC	.15	.07
❑ 411	John Wetteland	.20	.09
❑ 412	Jack Armstrong	.05	.02
❑ 413	Todd Benzinger UER (Bio says .323 at Pawtucket, but stats say .321)	.05	.02
❑ 414	Tim Birtsas	.05	.02
❑ 415	Tom Browning	.05	.02
❑ 416	Norm Charlton	.05	.02
❑ 417	Eric Davis	.10	.05
❑ 418	Rob Dibble	.05	.02
❑ 419	John Franco	.10	.05
❑ 420	Ken Griffey Sr.	.10	.05
❑ 421	Chris Hammond RC (No 1989 used for "Did Not Play" stat, actually did play for Nashville in 1989)	.05	.02
❑ 422	Danny Jackson	.05	.02
❑ 423	Barry Larkin	.20	.09
❑ 424	Tim Leary	.05	.02
❑ 425	Rick Mahler	.05	.02
❑ 426	Joe Oliver	.05	.02
❑ 427	Paul O'Neill	.20	.09
❑ 428	Luis Quinones UER ('86-'88 stats are omitted from card but included in totals)	.05	.02
❑ 429	Jeff Reed	.05	.02
❑ 430	Jose Rijo	.05	.02
❑ 431	Ron Robinson	.05	.02
❑ 432	Rolando Roomes	.05	.02
❑ 433	Chris Sabo	.05	.02
❑ 434	Scott Scudder	.05	.02
❑ 435	Herm Winningham	.05	.02
❑ 436	Steve Balboni	.05	.02
❑ 437	Jesse Barfield	.05	.02
❑ 438	Mike Blowers RC	.10	.05
❑ 439	Tom Brookens	.05	.02
❑ 440	Greg Cadaret	.05	.02
❑ 441	Alvaro Espinoza UER (Career games say 218, should be 219)	.05	.02
❑ 442	Bob Geren	.05	.02
❑ 443	Lee Guetterman	.05	.02
❑ 444	Mel Hall	.05	.02
❑ 445	Andy Hawkins	.05	.02
❑ 446	Roberto Kelly	.05	.02
❑ 447	Don Mattingly	.50	.23
❑ 448	Lance McCullers	.05	.02
❑ 449	Hensley Meulens	.05	.02
❑ 450	Dale Mohorcic	.05	.02
❑ 451	Clay Parker	.05	.02
❑ 452	Eric Plunk	.05	.02
❑ 453	Dave Righetti	.05	.02
❑ 454	Deion Sanders	.20	.09
❑ 455	Steve Sax	.05	.02
❑ 456	Don Slaught	.05	.02
❑ 457	Walt Terrell	.05	.02
❑ 458	Dave Winfield	.20	.09
❑ 459	Jay Bell	.10	.05
❑ 460	Rafael Belliard	.05	.02
❑ 461	Barry Bonds	.50	.23
❑ 462	Bobby Bonilla	.10	.05
❑ 463	Sid Bream	.05	.02
❑ 464	Benny Distefano	.05	.02
❑ 465	Doug Drabek	.05	.02
❑ 466	Jim Gott	.05	.02
❑ 467	Billy Hatcher UER (.1 hits for Cubs in 1984)	.05	.02
❑ 468	Neal Heaton	.05	.02
❑ 469	Jeff King	.05	.02
❑ 470	Bob Kipper	.05	.02
❑ 471	Randy Kramer	.05	.02
❑ 472	Bill Landrum	.05	.02
❑ 473	Mike LaValliere	.05	.02
❑ 474	Jose Lind	.05	.02
❑ 475	Junior Ortiz	.05	.02
❑ 476	Gary Redus	.05	.02
❑ 477	Rick Reed RC	.25	.11
❑ 478	R.J. Reynolds	.05	.02
❑ 479	Jeff D. Robinson	.05	.02
❑ 480	John Smiley	.05	.02
❑ 481	Andy Van Slyke	.10	.05
❑ 482	Bob Walk	.05	.02
❑ 483	Andy Allanson	.05	.02
❑ 484	Scott Bailes	.05	.02
❑ 485	Joey Belle UER (Has Jay Bell "Did You Know")	.20	.09
❑ 486	Bud Black	.05	.02
❑ 487	Jerry Browne	.05	.02
❑ 488	Tom Candiotti	.05	.02
❑ 489	Joe Carter	.10	.05
❑ 490	Dave Clark (No '84 stats)	.05	.02
❑ 491	John Farrell	.05	.02
❑ 492	Felix Fermin	.05	.02
❑ 493	Brook Jacoby	.05	.02
❑ 494	Dion James	.05	.02
❑ 495	Doug Jones	.05	.02
❑ 496	Brad Komminsk	.05	.02
❑ 497	Rod Nichols	.05	.02
❑ 498	Pete O'Brien	.05	.02
❑ 499	Steve Olin RC	.10	.05
❑ 500	Jesse Orosco	.05	.02
❑ 501	Joel Skinner	.05	.02
❑ 502	Cory Snyder	.05	.02
❑ 503	Greg Swindell	.05	.02
❑ 504	Rich Yett	.05	.02
❑ 505	Scott Bankhead	.05	.02
❑ 506	Scott Bradley	.05	.02
❑ 507	Greg Briley UER (28 SB's in bio, but 27 in stats)	.05	.02
❑ 508	Jay Buhner	.10	.05
❑ 509	Darnell Coles	.05	.02
❑ 510	Keith Comstock	.05	.02
❑ 511	Henry Cotto	.05	.02
❑ 512	Alvin Davis	.05	.02
❑ 513	Ken Griffey Jr.	1.25	.55
❑ 514	Erik Hanson	.05	.02
❑ 515	Gene Harris	.05	.02
❑ 516	Brian Holman	.05	.02
❑ 517	Mike Jackson	.05	.02
❑ 518	Randy Johnson	.40	.18
❑ 519	Jeffrey Leonard	.05	.02
❑ 520	Edgar Martinez	.15	.07
❑ 521	Dennis Powell	.05	.02

❑ 522 Jim Presley .05 .02
❑ 523 Jerry Reed .05 .02
❑ 524 Harold Reynolds .05 .02
❑ 525 Mike Schooler .05 .02
❑ 526 Bill Swift .05 .02
❑ 527 Dave Valle .05 .02
❑ 528 Omar Vizquel .20 .09
❑ 529 Ivan Calderon .05 .02
❑ 530 Carlton Fisk UER .20 .09
(Bellow Falls, should
be Bellows Falls)
❑ 531 Scott Fletcher .05 .02
❑ 532 Dave Gallagher .05 .02
❑ 533 Ozzie Guillen .05 .02
❑ 534 Greg Hibbard RC .05 .02
❑ 535 Shawn Hillegas .05 .02
❑ 536 Lance Johnson .05 .02
❑ 537 Eric King .05 .02
❑ 538 Ron Kittle .05 .02
❑ 539 Steve Lyons .05 .02
❑ 540 Carlos Martinez .05 .02
❑ 541 Tom McCarthy .05 .02
❑ 542 Matt Merullo .05 .02
(Had 5 ML runs scored
entering '90, not 6)
❑ 543 Donn Pall UER .05 .02
(Stats say pro career
began in '85,
bio says '88)
❑ 544 Dan Pasqua .05 .02
❑ 545 Ken Patterson .05 .02
❑ 546 Melido Perez .05 .02
❑ 547 Steve Rosenberg .05 .02
❑ 548 Sammy Sosa RC 5.00 2.20
❑ 549 Bobby Thigpen .05 .02
❑ 550 Robin Ventura .20 .09
❑ 551 Greg Walker .05 .02
❑ 552 Don Carman .05 .02
❑ 553 Pat Combs .05 .02
(6 walks for Phillies
in '89 in stats,
brief bio says 4)
❑ 554 Dennis Cook .05 .02
❑ 555 Darren Daulton .10 .05
❑ 556 Len Dykstra .10 .05
❑ 557 Curt Ford .05 .02
❑ 558 Charlie Hayes .05 .02
❑ 559 Von Hayes .05 .02
❑ 560 Tommy Herr .05 .02
❑ 561 Ken Howell .05 .02
❑ 562 Steve Jeltz .05 .02
❑ 563 Ron Jones .05 .02
❑ 564 Ricky Jordan UER .05 .02
(Duplicate line of
statistics on back)
❑ 565 John Kruk .10 .05
❑ 566 Steve Lake .05 .02
❑ 567 Roger McDowell .05 .02
❑ 568 Terry Mulholland UER .05 .02
(Did You Know refers
to Dave Magadan)
❑ 569 Dwayne Murphy .05 .02
❑ 570 Jeff Parrett .05 .02
❑ 571 Randy Ready .05 .02
❑ 572 Bruce Ruffin .05 .02
❑ 573 Dickie Thon .05 .02
❑ 574 Jose Alvarez UER .05 .02
('78 and '79 stats
are reversed)
❑ 575 Geronimo Berroa .05 .02
❑ 576 Jeff Blauser .05 .02
❑ 577 Joe Boever .05 .02
❑ 578 Marty Clary UER .05 .02
(No comma between
city and state)
❑ 579 Jody Davis .05 .02
❑ 580 Mark Eichhorn .05 .02
❑ 581 Darrell Evans .10 .05
❑ 582 Ron Gant .10 .05
❑ 583 Tom Glavine .20 .09
❑ 584 Tommy Greene RC .05 .02
❑ 585 Tommy Gregg .05 .02
❑ 586 Dave Justice RC UER .60 .25
(Actually had 16 2B
in Sumter in '86)
❑ 587 Mark Lemke .05 .02
❑ 588 Derek Lilliquist .05 .02
❑ 589 Oddibe McDowell .05 .02
❑ 590 Kent Mercker RC ERA .05 .02
(Bio says 2.75 ERA,
stats say 2.68 ERA)
❑ 591 Dale Murphy .20 .09
❑ 592 Gerald Perry .05 .02
❑ 593 Lonnie Smith .05 .02
❑ 594 Pete Smith .05 .02
❑ 595 John Smoltz .10 .05
❑ 596 Mike Stanton RC UER .05 .02
(No comma between
city and state)
❑ 597 Andres Thomas .05 .02
❑ 598 Jeff Treadway .05 .02
❑ 599 Doyle Alexander .05 .02
❑ 600 Dave Bergman .05 .02
❑ 601 Brian DuBois .05 .02
❑ 602 Paul Gibson .05 .02
❑ 603 Mike Heath .05 .02
❑ 604 Mike Henneman .05 .02
❑ 605 Guillermo Hernandez .05 .02
❑ 606 Shawn Holman .05 .02
❑ 607 Tracy Jones .05 .02
❑ 608 Chet Lemon .05 .02
❑ 609 Fred Lynn .05 .02
❑ 610 Jack Morris .10 .05
❑ 611 Matt Nokes .05 .02
❑ 612 Gary Pettis .05 .02
❑ 613 Kevin Ritz .05 .02
❑ 614 Jeff M. Robinson .05 .02
('88 stats are
not in line)
❑ 615 Steve Searcy .05 .02
❑ 616 Frank Tanana .05 .02
❑ 617 Alan Trammell .15 .07
❑ 618 Gary Ward .05 .02
❑ 619 Lou Whitaker .10 .05
❑ 620 Frank Williams .05 .02
❑ 621A George Brett '80 1.50 .70
ERR (Had 10 .390
hitting seasons)
❑ 621B George Brett '80 .20 .09
COR
❑ 622 Fern.Valenzuela '81 .05 .02
❑ 623 Dale Murphy '82 .10 .05
❑ 624A Cal Ripken '83 ERR 5.00 2.20
(Misspelled Ripkin
on card back)
❑ 624B Cal Ripken '83 COR .40 .18
❑ 625 Ryne Sandberg '84 .20 .09
❑ 626 Don Mattingly '85 .20 .09
❑ 627 Roger Clemens '86 .25 .11
❑ 628 George Bell '87 .05 .02
❑ 629 J.Canseco '88 UER .10 .05
Reggie won MVP in
'83, should say '73
❑ 630A Will Clark '89 ERR 1.00 .45
(32 total bases
on card back)
❑ 630B Will Clark '89 COR .20 .09
(321 total bases;
technically still
an error, listing
only 24 runs)
❑ 631 Game Savers .05 .02
Mark Davis
Mitch Williams
❑ 632 Boston Igniters .10 .05
Wade Boggs
Mike Greenwell
❑ 633 Starter and Stopper .05 .02
Mark Gubicza
Jeff Russell
❑ 634 League's Best .25 .11
Shortstops
Tony Fernandez
Cal Ripken
❑ 635 Human Dynamos .20 .09
Kirby Puckett
Bo Jackson
❑ 636 300 Strikeout Club .40 .18
Nolan Ryan
Mike Scott
❑ 637 The Dynamic Duo .10 .05
Will Clark
Kevin Mitchell
❑ 638 AL All-Stars .40 .18
Don Mattingly
Mark McGwire
❑ 639 NL East Rivals .20 .09
Howard Johnson
Ryne Sandberg
❑ 640 Rudy Seanez RC .05 .02
Colin Charland
❑ 641 George Canale RC .10 .05
Kevin Maas UER
(Canale listed as INF
on front, 1B on back)
❑ 642 Kelly Mann .05 .02
and Dave Hansen RC
❑ 643 Greg Smith .05 .02
and Stu Tate
❑ 644 Tom Drees .05 .02
and Dann Howitt
❑ 645 Mike Roesler RC .20 .09
and Derrick May
❑ 646 Scott Hemond .05 .02
and Mark Gardner RC
❑ 647 John Orton .05 .02
and Scott Leius RC
❑ 648 Rich Monteleone .05 .02
and Dana Williams
❑ 649 Mike Huff .05 .02
and Steve Frey
❑ 650 Chuck McElroy .50 .23
and Moises Alou RC
❑ 651 Bobby Rose .05 .02
and Mike Hartley
❑ 652 Matt Kinzer .05 .02
and Wayne Edwards
❑ 653 Delino DeShields RC .20 .09
and Jason Grimsley
❑ 654 CL: A's/Cubs .05 .02
Giants/Blue Jays
❑ 655 CL: Royals/Angels .05 .02
Padres/Orioles
❑ 656 CL: Mets/Astros .05 .02
Cards/Red Sox
❑ 657 CL: Rangers/Brewers .05 .02
Expos/Twins
❑ 658 CL: Dodgers/Reds .05 .02
Yankees/Pirates
❑ 659 CL: Indians/Mariners .05 .02
White Sox/Phillies
❑ 660A CL: Braves/Tigers .05 .02
Specials/Checklists
(Checklist-660 in small-
er print on card front)
❑ 660B CL: Braves/Tigers .05 .02
Specials/Checklists
(Checklist-660 in nor-
mal print on card front)

1990 Fleer Update

	MINT	NRMT
COMP.FACT.SET (132)	5.00	2.20
❑ 1 Steve Avery	.05	.02
❑ 2 Francisco Cabrera	.05	.02
❑ 3 Nick Esasky	.05	.02
❑ 4 Jim Kremers	.05	.02
❑ 5 Greg Olson RC	.05	.02

❑ 6 Jim Presley .05 .02
❑ 7 Shawn Boskie RC .05 .02
❑ 8 Joe Kraemer .05 .02
❑ 9 Luis Salazar .05 .02
❑ 10 Hector Villanueva .05 .02
❑ 11 Glenn Braggs .05 .02
❑ 12 Mariano Duncan .05 .02
❑ 13 Billy Hatcher .05 .02
❑ 14 Tim Layana .05 .02
❑ 15 Hal Morris .05 .02
❑ 16 Javier Ortiz .05 .02
❑ 17 Dave Rohde .05 .02
❑ 18 Eric Yelding .05 .02
❑ 19 Hubie Brooks .05 .02
❑ 20 Kal Daniels .05 .02
❑ 21 Dave Hansen .05 .02
❑ 22 Mike Hartley .05 .02
❑ 23 Stan Javier .05 .02
❑ 24 Jose Offerman RC .10 .05
❑ 25 Juan Samuel .05 .02
❑ 26 Dennis Boyd .05 .02
❑ 27 Delino DeShields .20 .09
❑ 28 Steve Frey .05 .02
❑ 29 Mark Gardner .05 .02
❑ 30 Chris Nabholz RC .05 .02
❑ 31 Bill Sampen .05 .02
❑ 32 Dave Schmidt .05 .02
❑ 33 Daryl Boston .05 .02
❑ 34 Chuck Carr RC .20 .09
❑ 35 John Franco .10 .05
❑ 36 Todd Hundley RC .20 .09
❑ 37 Julio Machado .05 .02
❑ 38 Alejandro Pena .05 .02
❑ 39 Darren Reed .05 .02
❑ 40 Kelvin Torve .05 .02
❑ 41 Darrel Akerfelds .05 .02
❑ 42 Jose DeJesus .05 .02
❑ 43 Dave Hollins RC UER .20 .09
(Misspelled Dane on card back)
❑ 44 Carmelo Martinez .05 .02
❑ 45 Brad Moore .05 .02
❑ 46 Dale Murphy .20 .09
❑ 47 Wally Backman .05 .02
❑ 48 Stan Belinda RC .05 .02
❑ 49 Bob Patterson .05 .02
❑ 50 Ted Power .05 .02
❑ 51 Don Slaught .05 .02
❑ 52 Geronimo Pena RC .05 .02
❑ 53 Lee Smith .10 .05
❑ 54 John Tudor .05 .02
❑ 55 Joe Carter .10 .05
❑ 56 Thomas Howard .05 .02
❑ 57 Craig Lefferts .05 .02
❑ 58 Rafael Valdez .05 .02
❑ 59 Dave Anderson .05 .02
❑ 60 Kevin Bass .05 .02
❑ 61 John Burkett .05 .02
❑ 62 Gary Carter .15 .07
❑ 63 Rick Parker .05 .02
❑ 64 Trevor Wilson .05 .02
❑ 65 Chris Hoiles RC .20 .09
❑ 66 Tim Hulett .05 .02
❑ 67 Dave Johnson .05 .02
❑ 68 Curt Schilling 1.00 .45
❑ 69 David Segui RC .25 .11
❑ 70 Tom Brunansky .05 .02
❑ 71 Greg A. Harris .05 .02
❑ 72 Dana Kiecker .05 .02
❑ 73 Tim Naehring RC .10 .05
❑ 74 Tony Pena .05 .02
❑ 75 Jeff Reardon .10 .05
❑ 76 Jerry Reed .05 .02
❑ 77 Mark Eichhorn .05 .02
❑ 78 Mark Langston .05 .02
❑ 79 John Orton .05 .02
❑ 80 Luis Polonia .05 .02
❑ 81 Dave Winfield .20 .09
❑ 82 Cliff Young .05 .02
❑ 83 Wayne Edwards .05 .02
❑ 84 Alex Fernandez RC .10 .05
❑ 85 Craig Grebeck RC .05 .02
❑ 86 Scott Radinsky RC .05 .02
❑ 87 Frank Thomas RC 2.00 .90
❑ 88 Beau Allred .05 .02
❑ 89 Sandy Alomar Jr. .10 .05
❑ 90 Carlos Baerga RC .10 .05
❑ 91 Kevin Bearse .05 .02
❑ 92 Chris James .05 .02
❑ 93 Candy Maldonado .05 .02
❑ 94 Jeff Manto .05 .02
❑ 95 Cecil Fielder .10 .05
❑ 96 Travis Fryman RC .25 .11
❑ 97 Lloyd Moseby .05 .02
❑ 98 Edwin Nunez .05 .02
❑ 99 Tony Phillips .05 .02
❑ 100 Larry Sheets .05 .02
❑ 101 Mark Davis .05 .02
❑ 102 Storm Davis .05 .02
❑ 103 Gerald Perry .05 .02
❑ 104 Terry Shumpert .05 .02
❑ 105 Edgar Diaz .05 .02
❑ 106 Dave Parker .10 .05
❑ 107 Tim Drummond .05 .02
❑ 108 Junior Ortiz .05 .02
❑ 109 Park Pittman .05 .02
❑ 110 Kevin Tapani RC .20 .09
❑ 111 Oscar Azocar .05 .02
❑ 112 Jim Leyritz RC .10 .05
❑ 113 Kevin Maas .10 .05
❑ 114 Alan Mills RC .05 .02
❑ 115 Matt Nokes .05 .02
❑ 116 Pascual Perez .05 .02
❑ 117 Ozzie Canseco .05 .02
❑ 118 Scott Sanderson .05 .02
❑ 119 Tino Martinez .20 .09
❑ 120 Jeff Schaefer .05 .02
❑ 121 Matt Young .05 .02
❑ 122 Brian Bohanon RC .05 .02
❑ 123 Jeff Huson .05 .02
❑ 124 Ramon Manon .05 .02
❑ 125 Gary Mielke UER .05 .02
(Shown as Blue Jay on front)
❑ 126 Willie Blair RC .05 .02
❑ 127 Glenallen Hill .05 .02
❑ 128 John Olerud RC UER .50 .23
(Listed as throwing right, should be left)
❑ 129 Luis Sojo .05 .02
❑ 130 Mark Whiten RC .05 .02
❑ 131 Nolan Ryan 1.00 .45
❑ 132 Checklist U1-U132 .05 .02

1991 Fleer

	MINT	NRMT
COMPLETE SET (720)	8.00	3.60
COMP.RETAIL SET (732)	10.00	4.50
COMP.HOBBY SET (732)	10.00	4.50

❑ 1 Troy Afenir .05 .02
❑ 2 Harold Baines .10 .05
❑ 3 Lance Blankenship .05 .02
❑ 4 Todd Burns .05 .02
❑ 5 Jose Canseco .20 .09
❑ 6 Dennis Eckersley .10 .05
❑ 7 Mike Gallego .05 .02
❑ 8 Ron Hassey .05 .02
❑ 9 Dave Henderson .05 .02
❑ 10 Rickey Henderson .40 .18
❑ 11 Rick Honeycutt .05 .02
❑ 12 Doug Jennings .05 .02
❑ 13 Joe Klink .05 .02
❑ 14 Carney Lansford .10 .05
❑ 15 Darren Lewis .05 .02
❑ 16 Willie McGee UER .10 .05
(Height 6'11")
❑ 17 Mark McGwire UER .75 .35
(183 extra base hits in 1987)
❑ 18 Mike Moore .05 .02
❑ 19 Gene Nelson .05 .02
❑ 20 Dave Otto .05 .02
❑ 21 Jamie Quirk .05 .02
❑ 22 Willie Randolph .10 .05
❑ 23 Scott Sanderson .05 .02
❑ 24 Terry Steinbach .05 .02
❑ 25 Dave Stewart .10 .05
❑ 26 Walt Weiss .05 .02
❑ 27 Bob Welch .05 .02
❑ 28 Curt Young .05 .02
❑ 29 Wally Backman .05 .02
❑ 30 Stan Belinda UER .05 .02
(Born in Huntington, should be State College)
❑ 31 Jay Bell .10 .05
❑ 32 Rafael Belliard .05 .02
❑ 33 Barry Bonds .50 .23
❑ 34 Bobby Bonilla .10 .05
❑ 35 Sid Bream .05 .02
❑ 36 Doug Drabek .05 .02
❑ 37 Carlos Garcia RC .05 .02
❑ 38 Neal Heaton .05 .02
❑ 39 Jeff King .05 .02
❑ 40 Bob Kipper .05 .02
❑ 41 Bill Landrum .05 .02
❑ 42 Mike LaValliere .05 .02
❑ 43 Jose Lind .05 .02
❑ 44 Carmelo Martinez .05 .02
❑ 45 Bob Patterson .05 .02
❑ 46 Ted Power .05 .02
❑ 47 Gary Redus .05 .02
❑ 48 R.J. Reynolds .05 .02
❑ 49 Don Slaught .05 .02
❑ 50 John Smiley .05 .02
❑ 51 Zane Smith .05 .02
❑ 52 Randy Tomlin RC .05 .02
❑ 53 Andy Van Slyke .10 .05
❑ 54 Bob Walk .05 .02
❑ 55 Jack Armstrong .05 .02
❑ 56 Todd Benzinger .05 .02
❑ 57 Glenn Braggs .05 .02
❑ 58 Keith Brown .05 .02
❑ 59 Tom Browning .05 .02
❑ 60 Norm Charlton .05 .02
❑ 61 Eric Davis .10 .05
❑ 62 Rob Dibble .05 .02
❑ 63 Bill Doran .05 .02
❑ 64 Mariano Duncan .05 .02
❑ 65 Chris Hammond .05 .02
❑ 66 Billy Hatcher .05 .02
❑ 67 Danny Jackson .05 .02
❑ 68 Barry Larkin .20 .09
❑ 69 Tim Layana .05 .02
(Black line over made in first text line)
❑ 70 Terry Lee .05 .02
❑ 71 Rick Mahler .05 .02
❑ 72 Hal Morris .05 .02
❑ 73 Randy Myers .05 .02
❑ 74 Ron Oester .05 .02
❑ 75 Joe Oliver .05 .02
❑ 76 Paul O'Neill .20 .09
❑ 77 Luis Quinones .05 .02
❑ 78 Jeff Reed .05 .02
❑ 79 Jose Rijo .05 .02
❑ 80 Chris Sabo .05 .02
❑ 81 Scott Scudder .05 .02
❑ 82 Herm Winningham .05 .02
❑ 83 Larry Andersen .05 .02
❑ 84 Marty Barrett .05 .02
❑ 85 Mike Boddicker .05 .02
❑ 86 Wade Boggs .20 .09
❑ 87 Tom Bolton .05 .02
❑ 88 Tom Brunansky .05 .02
❑ 89 Ellis Burks .10 .05
❑ 90 Roger Clemens .50 .23
❑ 91 Scott Cooper .05 .02
❑ 92 John Dopson .05 .02

❑ 93 Dwight Evans .10 .05
❑ 94 Wes Gardner .05 .02
❑ 95 Jeff Gray .05 .02
❑ 96 Mike Greenwell .05 .02
❑ 97 Greg A. Harris .05 .02
❑ 98 Daryl Irvine .05 .02
❑ 99 Dana Kiecker .05 .02
❑ 100 Randy Kutcher .05 .02
❑ 101 Dennis Lamp .05 .02
❑ 102 Mike Marshall .05 .02
❑ 103 John Marzano .05 .02
❑ 104 Rob Murphy .05 .02
❑ 105 Tim Naehring .05 .02
❑ 106 Tony Pena .05 .02
❑ 107 Phil Plantier RC .05 .02
❑ 108 Carlos Quintana .05 .02
❑ 109 Jeff Reardon .10 .05
❑ 110 Jerry Reed .05 .02
❑ 111 Jody Reed .05 .02
❑ 112 Luis Rivera UER .05 .02
(Born 1/3/84)
❑ 113 Kevin Romine .05 .02
❑ 114 Phil Bradley .05 .02
❑ 115 Ivan Calderon .05 .02
❑ 116 Wayne Edwards .05 .02
❑ 117 Alex Fernandez .05 .02
❑ 118 Carlton Fisk .20 .09
❑ 119 Scott Fletcher .05 .02
❑ 120 Craig Grebeck .05 .02
❑ 121 Ozzie Guillen .05 .02
❑ 122 Greg Hibbard .05 .02
❑ 123 Lance Johnson UER .05 .02
(Born Cincinnati, should be Lincoln Heights)
❑ 124 Barry Jones .05 .02
❑ 125 Ron Karkovice .05 .02
❑ 126 Eric King .05 .02
❑ 127 Steve Lyons .05 .02
❑ 128 Carlos Martinez .05 .02
❑ 129 Jack McDowell UER .05 .02
(Stanford misspelled as Standford on back)
❑ 130 Donn Pall .05 .02
(No dots over any i's in text)
❑ 131 Dan Pasqua .05 .02
❑ 132 Ken Patterson .05 .02
❑ 133 Melido Perez .05 .02
❑ 134 Adam Peterson .05 .02
❑ 135 Scott Radinsky .05 .02
❑ 136 Sammy Sosa .50 .23
❑ 137 Bobby Thigpen .05 .02
❑ 138 Frank Thomas .30 .14
❑ 139 Robin Ventura .10 .05
❑ 140 Daryl Boston .05 .02
❑ 141 Chuck Carr .05 .02
❑ 142 Mark Carreon .05 .02
❑ 143 David Cone .10 .05
❑ 144 Ron Darling .05 .02
❑ 145 Kevin Elster .05 .02
❑ 146 Sid Fernandez .05 .02
❑ 147 John Franco .10 .05
❑ 148 Dwight Gooden .10 .05
❑ 149 Tom Herr .05 .02
❑ 150 Todd Hundley .05 .02
❑ 151 Gregg Jefferies .05 .02
❑ 152 Howard Johnson .05 .02
❑ 153 Dave Magadan .05 .02
❑ 154 Kevin McReynolds .05 .02
❑ 155 Keith Miller UER .05 .02
(Text says Rochester in '87, stats say Tidewater, mixed up with other Keith Miller)
❑ 156 Bob Ojeda .05 .02
❑ 157 Tom O'Malley .05 .02
❑ 158 Alejandro Pena .05 .02
❑ 159 Darren Reed .05 .02
❑ 160 Mackey Sasser .05 .02
❑ 161 Darryl Strawberry .10 .05
❑ 162 Tim Teufel .05 .02
❑ 163 Kelvin Torve .05 .02
❑ 164 Julio Valera .05 .02
❑ 165 Frank Viola .10 .05
❑ 166 Wally Whitehurst .05 .02
❑ 167 Jim Acker .05 .02
❑ 168 Derek Bell .10 .05
❑ 169 George Bell .05 .02
❑ 170 Willie Blair .05 .02
❑ 171 Pat Borders .05 .02
❑ 172 John Cerutti .05 .02
❑ 173 Junior Felix .05 .02
❑ 174 Tony Fernandez .05 .02
❑ 175 Kelly Gruber UER .05 .02
(Born in Houston, should be Bellaire)
❑ 176 Tom Henke .05 .02
❑ 177 Glenallen Hill .05 .02
❑ 178 Jimmy Key .10 .05
❑ 179 Manny Lee .05 .02
❑ 180 Fred McGriff .15 .07
❑ 181 Rance Mulliniks .05 .02
❑ 182 Greg Myers .05 .02
❑ 183 John Olerud UER .15 .07
(Listed as throwing right, should be left)
❑ 184 Luis Sojo .05 .02
❑ 185 Dave Stieb .05 .02
❑ 186 Todd Stottlemyre .05 .02
❑ 187 Duane Ward .05 .02
❑ 188 David Wells .10 .05
❑ 189 Mark Whiten .05 .02
❑ 190 Ken Williams .05 .02
❑ 191 Frank Wills .05 .02
❑ 192 Mookie Wilson .10 .05
❑ 193 Don Aase .05 .02
❑ 194 Tim Belcher UER .05 .02
(Born Sparta, Ohio, should say Mt. Gilead)
❑ 195 Hubie Brooks .05 .02
❑ 196 Dennis Cook .05 .02
❑ 197 Tim Crews .05 .02
❑ 198 Kal Daniels .05 .02
❑ 199 Kirk Gibson .10 .05
❑ 200 Jim Gott .05 .02
❑ 201 Alfredo Griffin .05 .02
❑ 202 Chris Gwynn .05 .02
❑ 203 Dave Hansen .05 .02
❑ 204 Lenny Harris .05 .02
❑ 205 Mike Hartley .05 .02
❑ 206 Mickey Hatcher .05 .02
❑ 207 Carlos Hernandez .05 .02
❑ 208 Orel Hershiser .10 .05
❑ 209 Jay Howell UER .05 .02
(No 1982 Yankee stats)
❑ 210 Mike Huff .05 .02
❑ 211 Stan Javier .05 .02
❑ 212 Ramon Martinez .05 .02
❑ 213 Mike Morgan .05 .02
❑ 214 Eddie Murray .20 .09
❑ 215 Jim Neidlinger .05 .02
❑ 216 Jose Offerman .05 .02
❑ 217 Jim Poole .05 .02
❑ 218 Juan Samuel .05 .02
❑ 219 Mike Scioscia .05 .02
❑ 220 Ray Searage .05 .02
❑ 221 Mike Sharperson .05 .02
❑ 222 Fernando Valenzuela .10 .05
❑ 223 Jose Vizcaino .05 .02
❑ 224 Mike Aldrete .05 .02
❑ 225 Scott Anderson .05 .02
❑ 226 Dennis Boyd .05 .02
❑ 227 Tim Burke .05 .02
❑ 228 Delino DeShields .10 .05
❑ 229 Mike Fitzgerald .05 .02
❑ 230 Tom Foley .05 .02
❑ 231 Steve Frey .05 .02
❑ 232 Andres Galarraga .15 .07
❑ 233 Mark Gardner .05 .02
❑ 234 Marquis Grissom .05 .02
❑ 235 Kevin Gross .05 .02
(No date given for first Expos win)
❑ 236 Drew Hall .05 .02
❑ 237 Dave Martinez .05 .02
❑ 238 Dennis Martinez .10 .05
❑ 239 Dale Mohorcic .05 .02
❑ 240 Chris Nabholz .05 .02
❑ 241 Otis Nixon .05 .02
❑ 242 Junior Noboa .05 .02
❑ 243 Spike Owen .05 .02
❑ 244 Tim Raines .10 .05
❑ 245 Mel Rojas UER .05 .02
(Stats show 3.60 ERA, bio says 3.19 ERA)
❑ 246 Scott Ruskin .05 .02
❑ 247 Bill Sampen .05 .02
❑ 248 Nelson Santovenia .05 .02
❑ 249 Dave Schmidt .05 .02
❑ 250 Larry Walker .15 .07
❑ 251 Tim Wallach .05 .02
❑ 252 Dave Anderson .05 .02
❑ 253 Kevin Bass .05 .02
❑ 254 Steve Bedrosian .05 .02
❑ 255 Jeff Brantley .05 .02
❑ 256 John Burkett .05 .02
❑ 257 Brett Butler .10 .05
❑ 258 Gary Carter .15 .07
❑ 259 Will Clark .20 .09
❑ 260 Steve Decker RC .05 .02
❑ 261 Kelly Downs .05 .02
❑ 262 Scott Garrelts .05 .02
❑ 263 Terry Kennedy .05 .02
❑ 264 Mike LaCoss .05 .02
❑ 265 Mark Leonard .05 .02
❑ 266 Greg Litton .05 .02
❑ 267 Kevin Mitchell .05 .02
❑ 268 Randy O'Neal .05 .02
❑ 269 Rick Parker .05 .02
❑ 270 Rick Reuschel .05 .02
❑ 271 Ernest Riles .05 .02
❑ 272 Don Robinson .05 .02
❑ 273 Robby Thompson .05 .02
❑ 274 Mark Thurmond .05 .02
❑ 275 Jose Uribe .05 .02
❑ 276 Matt Williams .15 .07
❑ 277 Trevor Wilson .05 .02
❑ 278 Gerald Alexander .05 .02
❑ 279 Brad Arnsberg .05 .02
❑ 280 Kevin Belcher .05 .02
❑ 281 Joe Bitker .05 .02
❑ 282 Kevin Brown .10 .05
❑ 283 Steve Buechele .05 .02
❑ 284 Jack Daugherty .05 .02
❑ 285 Julio Franco .10 .05
❑ 286 Juan Gonzalez .25 .11
❑ 287 Bill Haselman .05 .02
❑ 288 Charlie Hough .10 .05
❑ 289 Jeff Huson .05 .02
❑ 290 Pete Incaviglia .05 .02
❑ 291 Mike Jeffcoat .05 .02
❑ 292 Jeff Kunkel .05 .02
❑ 293 Gary Mielke .05 .02
❑ 294 Jamie Moyer .05 .02
❑ 295 Rafael Palmeiro .20 .09
❑ 296 Geno Petralli .05 .02
❑ 297 Gary Pettis .05 .02
❑ 298 Kevin Reimer .05 .02
❑ 299 Kenny Rogers .05 .02
❑ 300 Jeff Russell .05 .02
❑ 301 John Russell .05 .02
❑ 302 Nolan Ryan 1.00 .45
❑ 303 Ruben Sierra .05 .02
❑ 304 Bobby Witt .05 .02
❑ 305 Jim Abbott UER .10 .05
(Text on back states he won Sullivan Award (outstanding amateur athlete) in 1989;should be '88)
❑ 306 Kent Anderson .05 .02
❑ 307 Dante Bichette .10 .05
❑ 308 Bert Blyleven .10 .05
❑ 309 Chili Davis .10 .05
❑ 310 Brian Downing .05 .02
❑ 311 Mark Eichhorn .05 .02
❑ 312 Mike Fetters .05 .02
❑ 313 Chuck Finley .10 .05
❑ 314 Willie Fraser .05 .02
❑ 315 Bryan Harvey .05 .02
❑ 316 Donnie Hill .05 .02
❑ 317 Wally Joyner .10 .05
❑ 318 Mark Langston .05 .02
❑ 319 Kirk McCaskill .05 .02
❑ 320 John Orton .05 .02
❑ 321 Lance Parrish .10 .05
❑ 322 Luis Polonia UER .05 .02
(1984 Madfison, should be Madison)
❑ 323 Johnny Ray .05 .02

	No.	Player		
❑	324	Bobby Rose	.05	.02
❑	325	Dick Schofield	.05	.02
❑	326	Rick Schu	.05	.02
❑	327	Lee Stevens	.05	.02
❑	328	Devon White	.05	.02
❑	329	Dave Winfield	.20	.09
❑	330	Cliff Young	.05	.02
❑	331	Dave Bergman	.05	.02
❑	332	Phil Clark RC	.05	.02
❑	333	Darnell Coles	.05	.02
❑	334	Milt Cuyler	.05	.02
❑	335	Cecil Fielder	.10	.05
❑	336	Travis Fryman	.10	.05
❑	337	Paul Gibson	.05	.02
❑	338	Jerry Don Gleaton	.05	.02
❑	339	Mike Heath	.05	.02
❑	340	Mike Henneman	.05	.02
❑	341	Chet Lemon	.05	.02
❑	342	Lance McCullers	.05	.02
❑	343	Jack Morris	.10	.05
❑	344	Lloyd Moseby	.05	.02
❑	345	Edwin Nunez	.05	.02
❑	346	Clay Parker	.05	.02
❑	347	Dan Petry	.05	.02
❑	348	Tony Phillips	.05	.02
❑	349	Jeff M. Robinson	.05	.02
❑	350	Mark Salas	.05	.02
❑	351	Mike Schwabe	.05	.02
❑	352	Larry Sheets	.05	.02
❑	353	John Shelby	.05	.02
❑	354	Frank Tanana	.05	.02
❑	355	Alan Trammell	.15	.07
❑	356	Gary Ward	.05	.02
❑	357	Lou Whitaker	.10	.05
❑	358	Beau Allred	.05	.02
❑	359	Sandy Alomar Jr.	.10	.05
❑	360	Carlos Baerga	.05	.02
❑	361	Kevin Bearse	.05	.02
❑	362	Tom Brookens	.05	.02
❑	363	Jerry Browne UER (No dot over i in first text line)	.05	.02
❑	364	Tom Candiotti	.05	.02
❑	365	Alex Cole	.05	.02
❑	366	John Farrell UER (Born in Neptune, should be Monmouth)	.05	.02
❑	367	Felix Fermin	.05	.02
❑	368	Keith Hernandez	.10	.05
❑	369	Brook Jacoby	.05	.02
❑	370	Chris James	.05	.02
❑	371	Dion James	.05	.02
❑	372	Doug Jones	.05	.02
❑	373	Candy Maldonado	.05	.02
❑	374	Steve Olin	.05	.02
❑	375	Jesse Orosco	.05	.02
❑	376	Rudy Seanez	.05	.02
❑	377	Joel Skinner	.05	.02
❑	378	Cory Snyder	.05	.02
❑	379	Greg Swindell	.05	.02
❑	380	Sergio Valdez	.05	.02
❑	381	Mike Walker	.05	.02
❑	382	Colby Ward	.05	.02
❑	383	Turner Ward RC	.10	.05
❑	384	Mitch Webster	.05	.02
❑	385	Kevin Wickander	.05	.02
❑	386	Darrel Akerfelds	.05	.02
❑	387	Joe Boever	.05	.02
❑	388	Rod Booker	.05	.02
❑	389	Sil Campusano	.05	.02
❑	390	Don Carman	.05	.02
❑	391	Wes Chamberlain RC	.05	.02
❑	392	Pat Combs	.05	.02
❑	393	Darren Daulton	.10	.05
❑	394	Jose DeJesus	.05	.02
❑	395A	Len Dykstra (Name spelled Lenny on back)	.10	.05
❑	395B	Len Dykstra (Name spelled Len on back)	.10	.05
❑	396	Jason Grimsley	.05	.02
❑	397	Charlie Hayes	.05	.02
❑	398	Von Hayes	.05	.02
❑	399	David Hollins UER (Atl-bats, should say at-bats)	.05	.02
❑	400	Ken Howell	.05	.02
❑	401	Ricky Jordan	.05	.02
❑	402	John Kruk	.10	.05
❑	403	Steve Lake	.05	.02
❑	404	Chuck Malone	.05	.02
❑	405	Roger McDowell UER (Says Phillies is saves, should say in)	.05	.02
❑	406	Chuck McElroy	.05	.02
❑	407	Mickey Morandini	.05	.02
❑	408	Terry Mulholland	.05	.02
❑	409	Dale Murphy	.20	.09
❑	410A	Randy Ready ERR (No Brewers stats listed for 1983)	.05	.02
❑	410B	Randy Ready COR	.05	.02
❑	411	Bruce Ruffin	.05	.02
❑	412	Dickie Thon	.05	.02
❑	413	Paul Assenmacher	.05	.02
❑	414	Damon Berryhill	.05	.02
❑	415	Mike Bielecki	.05	.02
❑	416	Shawn Boskie	.05	.02
❑	417	Dave Clark	.05	.02
❑	418	Doug Dascenzo	.05	.02
❑	419A	Andre Dawson ERR (No stats for 1976)	.15	.07
❑	419B	Andre Dawson COR	.15	.07
❑	420	Shawon Dunston	.05	.02
❑	421	Joe Girardi	.05	.02
❑	422	Mark Grace	.20	.09
❑	423	Mike Harkey	.05	.02
❑	424	Les Lancaster	.05	.02
❑	425	Bill Long	.05	.02
❑	426	Greg Maddux	.50	.23
❑	427	Derrick May	.05	.02
❑	428	Jeff Pico	.05	.02
❑	429	Domingo Ramos	.05	.02
❑	430	Luis Salazar	.05	.02
❑	431	Ryne Sandberg	.25	.11
❑	432	Dwight Smith	.05	.02
❑	433	Greg Smith	.05	.02
❑	434	Rick Sutcliffe	.10	.05
❑	435	Gary Varsho	.05	.02
❑	436	Hector Villanueva	.05	.02
❑	437	Jerome Walton	.05	.02
❑	438	Curtis Wilkerson	.05	.02
❑	439	Mitch Williams	.05	.02
❑	440	Steve Wilson	.05	.02
❑	441	Marvell Wynne	.05	.02
❑	442	Scott Bankhead	.05	.02
❑	443	Scott Bradley	.05	.02
❑	444	Greg Briley	.05	.02
❑	445	Mike Brumley UER (Text 40 SB's in 1988, stats say 41)	.05	.02
❑	446	Jay Buhner	.10	.05
❑	447	Dave Burba RC	.10	.05
❑	448	Henry Cotto	.05	.02
❑	449	Alvin Davis	.05	.02
❑	450	Ken Griffey Jr. (Bat around .300)	.75	.35
❑	450A	Ken Griffey Jr. (Bat .300)	.75	.35
❑	451	Erik Hanson	.05	.02
❑	452	Gene Harris UER (63 career runs, should be 73)	.05	.02
❑	453	Brian Holman	.05	.02
❑	454	Mike Jackson	.05	.02
❑	455	Randy Johnson	.30	.14
❑	456	Jeffrey Leonard	.05	.02
❑	457	Edgar Martinez	.15	.07
❑	458	Tino Martinez	.10	.05
❑	459	Pete O'Brien UER (1987 BA .266, should be .286)	.05	.02
❑	460	Harold Reynolds	.05	.02
❑	461	Mike Schooler	.05	.02
❑	462	Bill Swift	.05	.02
❑	463	David Valle	.05	.02
❑	464	Omar Vizquel	.10	.05
❑	465	Matt Young	.05	.02
❑	466	Brady Anderson	.10	.05
❑	467	Jeff Ballard UER (Missing top of right parenthesis after Saberhagen in last text line)	.05	.02
❑	468	Juan Bell	.05	.02
❑	469A	Mike Devereaux (First line of text ends with six)	.10	.05
❑	469B	Mike Devereaux (First line of text ends with runs)	.10	.05
❑	470	Steve Finley	.10	.05
❑	471	Dave Gallagher	.05	.02
❑	472	Leo Gomez	.05	.02
❑	473	Rene Gonzales	.05	.02
❑	474	Pete Harnisch	.05	.02
❑	475	Kevin Hickey	.05	.02
❑	476	Chris Hoiles	.05	.02
❑	477	Sam Horn	.05	.02
❑	478	Tim Hulett (Photo shows National Leaguer sliding into second base)	.05	.02
❑	479	Dave Johnson	.05	.02
❑	480	Ron Kittle UER (Edmonton misspelled as Edmundton)	.05	.02
❑	481	Ben McDonald	.05	.02
❑	482	Bob Melvin	.05	.02
❑	483	Bob Milacki	.05	.02
❑	484	Randy Milligan	.05	.02
❑	485	John Mitchell	.05	.02
❑	486	Gregg Olson	.05	.02
❑	487	Joe Orsulak	.05	.02
❑	488	Joe Price	.05	.02
❑	489	Bill Ripken	.05	.02
❑	490	Cal Ripken	.75	.35
❑	491	Curt Schilling	.20	.09
❑	492	David Segui	.05	.02
❑	493	Anthony Telford	.05	.02
❑	494	Mickey Tettleton	.05	.02
❑	495	Mark Williamson	.05	.02
❑	496	Craig Worthington	.05	.02
❑	497	Juan Agosto	.05	.02
❑	498	Eric Anthony	.05	.02
❑	499	Craig Biggio	.15	.07
❑	500	Ken Caminiti UER (Born 4/4, should be 4/21)	.10	.05
❑	501	Casey Candaele	.05	.02
❑	502	Andujar Cedeno	.05	.02
❑	503	Danny Darwin	.05	.02
❑	504	Mark Davidson	.05	.02
❑	505	Glenn Davis	.05	.02
❑	506	Jim Deshaies	.05	.02
❑	507	Luis Gonzalez RC	2.00	.90
❑	508	Bill Gullickson	.05	.02
❑	509	Xavier Hernandez	.05	.02
❑	510	Brian Meyer	.05	.02
❑	511	Ken Oberkfell	.05	.02
❑	512	Mark Portugal	.05	.02
❑	513	Rafael Ramirez	.05	.02
❑	514	Karl Rhodes	.05	.02
❑	515	Mike Scott	.05	.02
❑	516	Mike Simms	.05	.02
❑	517	Dave Smith	.05	.02
❑	518	Franklin Stubbs	.05	.02
❑	519	Glenn Wilson	.05	.02
❑	520	Eric Yelding UER (Text has 63 steals, stats have 64, which is correct)	.05	.02
❑	521	Gerald Young	.05	.02
❑	522	Shawn Abner	.05	.02
❑	523	Roberto Alomar	.20	.09
❑	524	Andy Benes	.05	.02
❑	525	Joe Carter	.10	.05
❑	526	Jack Clark	.10	.05
❑	527	Joey Cora	.05	.02
❑	528	Paul Faries	.05	.02
❑	529	Tony Gwynn	.40	.18
❑	530	Atlee Hammaker	.05	.02
❑	531	Greg W. Harris	.05	.02
❑	532	Thomas Howard	.05	.02
❑	533	Bruce Hurst	.05	.02
❑	534	Craig Lefferts	.05	.02
❑	535	Derek Lilliquist	.05	.02
❑	536	Fred Lynn	.05	.02
❑	537	Mike Pagliarulo	.05	.02

	Player	MINT	NRMT
❑ 538	Mark Parent	.05	.02
❑ 539	Dennis Rasmussen	.05	.02
❑ 540	Bip Roberts	.05	.02
❑ 541	Richard Rodriguez	.05	.02
❑ 542	Benito Santiago	.05	.02
❑ 543	Calvin Schiraldi	.05	.02
❑ 544	Eric Show	.05	.02
❑ 545	Phil Stephenson	.05	.02
❑ 546	Garry Templeton UER (Born 3/24/57, should be 3/24/56)	.05	.02
❑ 547	Ed Whitson	.05	.02
❑ 548	Eddie Williams	.05	.02
❑ 549	Kevin Appier	.10	.05
❑ 550	Luis Aquino	.05	.02
❑ 551	Bob Boone	.10	.05
❑ 552	George Brett	.40	.18
❑ 553	Jeff Conine RC	.10	.05
❑ 554	Steve Crawford	.05	.02
❑ 555	Mark Davis	.05	.02
❑ 556	Storm Davis	.05	.02
❑ 557	Jim Eisenreich	.05	.02
❑ 558	Steve Farr	.05	.02
❑ 559	Tom Gordon	.05	.02
❑ 560	Mark Gubicza	.05	.02
❑ 561	Bo Jackson	.10	.05
❑ 562	Mike Macfarlane	.05	.02
❑ 563	Brian McRae RC	.10	.05
❑ 564	Jeff Montgomery	.05	.02
❑ 565	Bill Pecota	.05	.02
❑ 566	Gerald Perry	.05	.02
❑ 567	Bret Saberhagen	.10	.05
❑ 568	Jeff Schulz	.05	.02
❑ 569	Kevin Seitzer	.05	.02
❑ 570	Terry Shumpert	.05	.02
❑ 571	Kurt Stillwell	.05	.02
❑ 572	Danny Tartabull	.05	.02
❑ 573	Gary Thurman	.05	.02
❑ 574	Frank White	.10	.05
❑ 575	Willie Wilson	.05	.02
❑ 576	Chris Bosio	.05	.02
❑ 577	Greg Brock	.05	.02
❑ 578	George Canale	.05	.02
❑ 579	Chuck Crim	.05	.02
❑ 580	Rob Deer	.05	.02
❑ 581	Edgar Diaz	.05	.02
❑ 582	Tom Edens	.05	.02
❑ 583	Mike Felder	.05	.02
❑ 584	Jim Gantner	.05	.02
❑ 585	Darryl Hamilton	.05	.02
❑ 586	Ted Higuera	.05	.02
❑ 587	Mark Knudson	.05	.02
❑ 588	Bill Krueger	.05	.02
❑ 589	Tim McIntosh	.05	.02
❑ 590	Paul Mirabella	.05	.02
❑ 591	Paul Molitor	.20	.09
❑ 592	Jaime Navarro	.05	.02
❑ 593	Dave Parker	.10	.05
❑ 594	Dan Plesac	.05	.02
❑ 595	Ron Robinson	.05	.02
❑ 596	Gary Sheffield	.10	.05
❑ 597	Bill Spiers	.05	.02
❑ 598	B.J. Surhoff	.10	.05
❑ 599	Greg Vaughn	.10	.05
❑ 600	Randy Veres	.05	.02
❑ 601	Robin Yount	.20	.09
❑ 602	Rick Aguilera	.10	.05
❑ 603	Allan Anderson	.05	.02
❑ 604	Juan Berenguer	.05	.02
❑ 605	Randy Bush	.05	.02
❑ 606	Carmen Castillo	.05	.02
❑ 607	Tim Drummond	.05	.02
❑ 608	Scott Erickson	.05	.02
❑ 609	Gary Gaetti	.10	.05
❑ 610	Greg Gagne	.05	.02
❑ 611	Dan Gladden	.05	.02
❑ 612	Mark Guthrie	.05	.02
❑ 613	Brian Harper	.05	.02
❑ 614	Kent Hrbek	.10	.05
❑ 615	Gene Larkin	.05	.02
❑ 616	Terry Leach	.05	.02
❑ 617	Nelson Liriano	.05	.02
❑ 618	Shane Mack	.05	.02
❑ 619	John Moses	.05	.02
❑ 620	Pedro Munoz RC	.05	.02
❑ 621	Al Newman	.05	.02
❑ 622	Junior Ortiz	.05	.02
❑ 623	Kirby Puckett	.50	.23
❑ 624	Roy Smith	.05	.02
❑ 625	Kevin Tapani	.05	.02
❑ 626	Gary Wayne	.05	.02
❑ 627	David West	.05	.02
❑ 628	Cris Carpenter	.05	.02
❑ 629	Vince Coleman	.05	.02
❑ 630	Ken Dayley	.05	.02
❑ 631A	Jose DeLeon ERR (missing '79 Bradenton stats)	.05	.02
❑ 631B	Jose DeLeon COR (with '79 Bradenton stats)	.05	.02
❑ 632	Frank DiPino	.05	.02
❑ 633	Bernard Gilkey	.05	.02
❑ 634A	P.Guerrero ERR career SB shown as "$91"	.10	.05
❑ 634B	Pedro Guerrero COR	.10	.05
❑ 635	Ken Hill	.05	.02
❑ 636	Felix Jose	.05	.02
❑ 637	Ray Lankford	.10	.05
❑ 638	Joe Magrane	.05	.02
❑ 639	Tom Niedenfuer	.05	.02
❑ 640	Jose Oquendo	.05	.02
❑ 641	Tom Pagnozzi	.05	.02
❑ 642	Terry Pendleton	.10	.05
❑ 643	Mike Perez RC	.05	.02
❑ 644	Bryn Smith	.05	.02
❑ 645	Lee Smith	.10	.05
❑ 646	Ozzie Smith	.25	.11
❑ 647	Scott Terry	.05	.02
❑ 648	Bob Tewksbury	.05	.02
❑ 649	Milt Thompson	.05	.02
❑ 650	John Tudor	.05	.02
❑ 651	Denny Walling	.05	.02
❑ 652	Craig Wilson	.05	.02
❑ 653	Todd Worrell	.05	.02
❑ 654	Todd Zeile	.05	.02
❑ 655	Oscar Azocar	.05	.02
❑ 656	Steve Balboni UER (Born 1/5/57, should be 1/16)	.05	.02
❑ 657	Jesse Barfield	.05	.02
❑ 658	Greg Cadaret	.05	.02
❑ 659	Chuck Cary	.05	.02
❑ 660	Rick Cerone	.05	.02
❑ 661	Dave Eiland	.05	.02
❑ 662	Alvaro Espinoza	.05	.02
❑ 663	Bob Geren	.05	.02
❑ 664	Lee Guetterman	.05	.02
❑ 665	Mel Hall	.05	.02
❑ 666	Andy Hawkins	.05	.02
❑ 667	Jimmy Jones	.05	.02
❑ 668	Roberto Kelly	.05	.02
❑ 669	Dave LaPoint UER (No '81 Brewers stats, totals also are wrong)	.05	.02
❑ 670	Tim Leary	.05	.02
❑ 671	Jim Leyritz	.05	.02
❑ 672	Kevin Maas	.05	.02
❑ 673	Don Mattingly	.50	.23
❑ 674	Matt Nokes	.05	.02
❑ 675	Pascual Perez	.05	.02
❑ 676	Eric Plunk	.05	.02
❑ 677	Dave Righetti	.10	.05
❑ 678	Jeff D. Robinson	.05	.02
❑ 679	Steve Sax	.05	.02
❑ 680	Mike Witt	.05	.02
❑ 681	Steve Avery UER (Born in New Jersey, should say Michigan)	.05	.02
❑ 682	Mike Bell	.05	.02
❑ 683	Jeff Blauser	.05	.02
❑ 684	F.Cabrera UER Born 10/16, should say 10/10	.05	.02
❑ 685	Tony Castillo	.05	.02
❑ 686	Marty Clary UER (Shown pitching righty, but bio has left)	.05	.02
❑ 687	Nick Esasky	.05	.02
❑ 688	Ron Gant	.05	.02
❑ 689	Tom Glavine	.20	.09
❑ 690	Mark Grant	.05	.02
❑ 691	Tommy Gregg	.05	.02
❑ 692	Dwayne Henry	.05	.02
❑ 693	Dave Justice	.20	.09
❑ 694	Jimmy Kremers	.05	.02
❑ 695	Charlie Leibrandt	.05	.02
❑ 696	Mark Lemke	.05	.02
❑ 697	Oddibe McDowell	.05	.02
❑ 698	Greg Olson	.05	.02
❑ 699	Jeff Parrett	.05	.02
❑ 700	Jim Presley	.05	.02
❑ 701	Victor Rosario	.05	.02
❑ 702	Lonnie Smith	.05	.02
❑ 703	Pete Smith	.05	.02
❑ 704	John Smoltz	.10	.05
❑ 705	Mike Stanton	.05	.02
❑ 706	Andres Thomas	.05	.02
❑ 707	Jeff Treadway	.05	.02
❑ 708	Jim Vatcher	.05	.02
❑ 709	Ryne Sandberg Cecil Fielder Home Run Kings	.20	.09
❑ 710	Barry Bonds Ken Griffey Jr. 2nd Generation Stars	.60	.25
❑ 711	Bobby Bonilla Barry Larkin NLCS Team Leaders	.10	.05
❑ 712	Bobby Thigpen John Franco Top Game Savers	.05	.02
❑ 713	Chicago's 100 Club Andre Dawson Ryne Sandberg UER (Ryno misspelled Rhino)	.10	.05
❑ 714	CL:A's/Pirates Reds/Red Sox	.05	.02
❑ 715	CL:White Sox/Mets Blue Jays/Dodgers	.05	.02
❑ 716	CL:Expos/Giants Rangers/Angels	.05	.02
❑ 717	CL:Tigers/Indians Phillies/Cubs	.05	.02
❑ 718	CL:Mariners/Orioles Astros/Padres	.05	.02
❑ 719	CL:Royals/Brewers Twins/Cardinals	.05	.02
❑ 720	CL:Yankees/Braves Superstars/Specials	.05	.02

1991 Fleer Update

		MINT	NRMT
COMP.FACT.SET (132)		5.00	2.20
❑ 1	Glenn Davis	.05	.02
❑ 2	Dwight Evans	.10	.05
❑ 3	Jose Mesa	.05	.02
❑ 4	Jack Clark	.10	.05
❑ 5	Danny Darwin	.05	.02
❑ 6	Steve Lyons	.05	.02
❑ 7	Mo Vaughn	.10	.05
❑ 8	Floyd Bannister	.05	.02
❑ 9	Gary Gaetti	.10	.05
❑ 10	Dave Parker	.10	.05
❑ 11	Joey Cora	.05	.02
❑ 12	Charlie Hough	.10	.05
❑ 13	Matt Merullo	.05	.02
❑ 14	Warren Newson	.05	.02
❑ 15	Tim Raines	.10	.05
❑ 16	Albert Belle	.10	.05

❑ 17 Glenallen Hill .05 .02
❑ 18 Shawn Hillegas .05 .02
❑ 19 Mark Lewis .05 .02
❑ 20 Charles Nagy .05 .02
❑ 21 Mark Whiten .05 .02
❑ 22 John Cerutti .05 .02
❑ 23 Rob Deer .05 .02
❑ 24 Mickey Tettleton .05 .02
❑ 25 Warren Cromartie .05 .02
❑ 26 Kirk Gibson .10 .05
❑ 27 David Howard .05 .02
❑ 28 Brent Mayne .05 .02
❑ 29 Dante Bichette .10 .05
❑ 30 Mark Lee .05 .02
❑ 31 Julio Machado .05 .02
❑ 32 Edwin Nunez .05 .02
❑ 33 Willie Randolph .10 .05
❑ 34 Franklin Stubbs .05 .02
❑ 35 Bill Wegman .05 .02
❑ 36 Chili Davis .10 .05
❑ 37 Chuck Knoblauch .10 .05
❑ 38 Scott Leius .05 .02
❑ 39 Jack Morris .10 .05
❑ 40 Mike Pagliarulo .05 .02
❑ 41 Lenny Webster .05 .02
❑ 42 John Habyan .05 .02
❑ 43 Steve Howe .05 .02
❑ 44 Jeff Johnson .05 .02
❑ 45 Scott Kamieniecki RC .05 .02
❑ 46 Pat Kelly RC .05 .02
❑ 47 Hensley Meulens .05 .02
❑ 48 Wade Taylor .05 .02
❑ 49 Bernie Williams .25 .11
❑ 50 Kirk Dressendorfer RC .05 .02
❑ 51 Ernest Riles .05 .02
❑ 52 Rich DeLucia .05 .02
❑ 53 Tracy Jones .05 .02
❑ 54 Bill Krueger .05 .02
❑ 55 Alonzo Powell .05 .02
❑ 56 Jeff Schaefer .05 .02
❑ 57 Russ Swan .05 .02
❑ 58 John Barfield .05 .02
❑ 59 Rich Gossage .10 .05
❑ 60 Jose Guzman .05 .02
❑ 61 Dean Palmer .10 .05
❑ 62 Ivan Rodriguez RC 2.00 .90
❑ 63 Roberto Alomar .20 .09
❑ 64 Tom Candiotti .05 .02
❑ 65 Joe Carter .10 .05
❑ 66 Ed Sprague .05 .02
❑ 67 Pat Tabler .05 .02
❑ 68 Mike Timlin RC .10 .05
❑ 69 Devon White .05 .02
❑ 70 Rafael Belliard .05 .02
❑ 71 Juan Berenguer .05 .02
❑ 72 Sid Bream .05 .02
❑ 73 Marvin Freeman .05 .02
❑ 74 Kent Mercker .05 .02
❑ 75 Otis Nixon .05 .02
❑ 76 Terry Pendleton .10 .05
❑ 77 George Bell .05 .02
❑ 78 Danny Jackson .05 .02
❑ 79 Chuck McElroy .05 .02
❑ 80 Gary Scott .05 .02
❑ 81 Heathcliff Slocumb RC .10 .05
❑ 82 Dave Smith .05 .02
❑ 83 Rick Wilkins RC .05 .02
❑ 84 Freddie Benavides .05 .02
❑ 85 Ted Power .05 .02
❑ 86 Mo Sanford .05 .02
❑ 87 Jeff Bagwell RC 2.50 1.10
❑ 88 Steve Finley .10 .05
❑ 89 Pete Harnisch .05 .02
❑ 90 Darryl Kile .10 .05
❑ 91 Brett Butler .10 .05
❑ 92 John Candelaria .05 .02
❑ 93 Gary Carter .15 .07
❑ 94 Kevin Gross .05 .02
❑ 95 Bob Ojeda .05 .02
❑ 96 Darryl Strawberry .10 .05
❑ 97 Ivan Calderon .05 .02
❑ 98 Ron Hassey .05 .02
❑ 99 Gilberto Reyes .05 .02
❑ 100 Hubie Brooks .05 .02
❑ 101 Rick Cerone .05 .02
❑ 102 Vince Coleman .05 .02
❑ 103 Jeff Innis .05 .02
❑ 104 Pete Schourek RC .05 .02
❑ 105 Andy Ashby RC .20 .09
❑ 106 Wally Backman .05 .02
❑ 107 Darrin Fletcher .05 .02
❑ 108 Tommy Greene .05 .02
❑ 109 John Morris .05 .02
❑ 110 Mitch Williams .05 .02
❑ 111 Lloyd McClendon .05 .02
❑ 112 Orlando Merced RC .05 .02
❑ 113 Vicente Palacios .05 .02
❑ 114 Gary Varsho .05 .02
❑ 115 John Wehner .05 .02
❑ 116 Rex Hudler .05 .02
❑ 117 Tim Jones .05 .02
❑ 118 Geronimo Pena .05 .02
❑ 119 Gerald Perry .05 .02
❑ 120 Larry Andersen .05 .02
❑ 121 Jerald Clark .05 .02
❑ 122 Scott Coolbaugh .05 .02
❑ 123 Tony Fernandez .05 .02
❑ 124 Darrin Jackson .05 .02
❑ 125 Fred McGriff .15 .07
❑ 126 Jose Mota .05 .02
❑ 127 Tim Teufel .05 .02
❑ 128 Bud Black .05 .02
❑ 129 Mike Felder .05 .02
❑ 130 Willie McGee .10 .05
❑ 131 Dave Righetti .10 .05
❑ 132 Checklist U1-U132 .05 .02

1992 Fleer

	MINT	NRMT
COMPLETE SET (720)	10.00	4.50
COMP.HOBBY SET (732)	20.00	9.00
COMP.RETAIL SET (732)	20.00	9.00

❑ 1 Brady Anderson .10 .05
❑ 2 Jose Bautista .05 .02
❑ 3 Juan Bell .05 .02
❑ 4 Glenn Davis .05 .02
❑ 5 Mike Devereaux .05 .02
❑ 6 Dwight Evans .10 .05
❑ 7 Mike Flanagan .05 .02
❑ 8 Leo Gomez .05 .02
❑ 9 Chris Hoiles .05 .02
❑ 10 Sam Horn .05 .02
❑ 11 Tim Hulett .05 .02
❑ 12 Dave Johnson .05 .02
❑ 13 Chito Martinez .05 .02
❑ 14 Ben McDonald .05 .02
❑ 15 Bob Melvin .05 .02
❑ 16 Luis Mercedes .05 .02
❑ 17 Jose Mesa .05 .02
❑ 18 Bob Milacki .05 .02
❑ 19 Randy Milligan .05 .02
❑ 20 Mike Mussina UER .30 .14
(Card back refers to him as Jeff)
❑ 21 Gregg Olson .05 .02
❑ 22 Joe Orsulak .05 .02
❑ 23 Jim Poole .05 .02
❑ 24 Arthur Rhodes .05 .02
❑ 25 Billy Ripken .05 .02
❑ 26 Cal Ripken .75 .35
❑ 27 David Segui .05 .02
❑ 28 Roy Smith .05 .02
❑ 29 Anthony Telford .05 .02
❑ 30 Mark Williamson .05 .02
❑ 31 Craig Worthington .05 .02
❑ 32 Wade Boggs .20 .09
❑ 33 Tom Bolton .05 .02
❑ 34 Tom Brunansky .05 .02
❑ 35 Ellis Burks .10 .05
❑ 36 Jack Clark .10 .05
❑ 37 Roger Clemens .50 .23
❑ 38 Danny Darwin .05 .02
❑ 39 Mike Greenwell .05 .02
❑ 40 Joe Hesketh .05 .02
❑ 41 Daryl Irvine .05 .02
❑ 42 Dennis Lamp .05 .02
❑ 43 Tony Pena .05 .02
❑ 44 Phil Plantier .05 .02
❑ 45 Carlos Quintana .05 .02
❑ 46 Jeff Reardon .10 .05
❑ 47 Jody Reed .05 .02
❑ 48 Luis Rivera .05 .02
❑ 49 Mo Vaughn .10 .05
❑ 50 Jim Abbott .10 .05
❑ 51 Kyle Abbott .05 .02
❑ 52 Ruben Amaro .05 .02
❑ 53 Scott Bailes .05 .02
❑ 54 Chris Beasley .05 .02
❑ 55 Mark Eichhorn .05 .02
❑ 56 Mike Fetters .05 .02
❑ 57 Chuck Finley .10 .05
❑ 58 Gary Gaetti .10 .05
❑ 59 Dave Gallagher .05 .02
❑ 60 Donnie Hill .05 .02
❑ 61 Bryan Harvey UER .05 .02
(Lee Smith led the Majors with 47 saves)
❑ 62 Wally Joyner .10 .05
❑ 63 Mark Langston .05 .02
❑ 64 Kirk McCaskill .05 .02
❑ 65 John Orton .05 .02
❑ 66 Lance Parrish .10 .05
❑ 67 Luis Polonia .05 .02
❑ 68 Bobby Rose .05 .02
❑ 69 Dick Schofield .05 .02
❑ 70 Luis Sojo .05 .02
❑ 71 Lee Stevens .05 .02
❑ 72 Dave Winfield .20 .09
❑ 73 Cliff Young .05 .02
❑ 74 Wilson Alvarez .05 .02
❑ 75 Esteban Beltre .05 .02
❑ 76 Joey Cora .05 .02
❑ 77 Brian Drahman .05 .02
❑ 78 Alex Fernandez .05 .02
❑ 79 Carlton Fisk .20 .09
❑ 80 Scott Fletcher .05 .02
❑ 81 Craig Grebeck .05 .02
❑ 82 Ozzie Guillen .05 .02
❑ 83 Greg Hibbard .05 .02
❑ 84 Charlie Hough .10 .05
❑ 85 Mike Huff .05 .02
❑ 86 Bo Jackson .10 .05
❑ 87 Lance Johnson .05 .02
❑ 88 Ron Karkovice .05 .02
❑ 89 Jack McDowell .05 .02
❑ 90 Matt Merullo .05 .02
❑ 91 Warren Newson .05 .02
❑ 92 Donn Pall UER .05 .02
(Called Dunn on card back)
❑ 93 Dan Pasqua .05 .02
❑ 94 Ken Patterson .05 .02
❑ 95 Melido Perez .05 .02
❑ 96 Scott Radinsky .05 .02
❑ 97 Tim Raines .10 .05
❑ 98 Sammy Sosa .40 .18
❑ 99 Bobby Thigpen .05 .02
❑ 100 Frank Thomas .25 .11
❑ 101 Robin Ventura .10 .05
❑ 102 Mike Aldrete .05 .02
❑ 103 Sandy Alomar Jr. .10 .05
❑ 104 Carlos Baerga .05 .02
❑ 105 Albert Belle .10 .05
❑ 106 Willie Blair .05 .02
❑ 107 Jerry Browne .05 .02
❑ 108 Alex Cole .05 .02
❑ 109 Felix Fermin .05 .02
❑ 110 Glenallen Hill .05 .02

❑ 111 Shawn Hillegas .05 .02
❑ 112 Chris James .05 .02
❑ 113 Reggie Jefferson .05 .02
❑ 114 Doug Jones .05 .02
❑ 115 Eric King .05 .02
❑ 116 Mark Lewis .05 .02
❑ 117 Carlos Martinez .05 .02
❑ 118 Charles Nagy UER .05 .02
(Throws right, but
card says left)
❑ 119 Rod Nichols .05 .02
❑ 120 Steve Olin .05 .02
❑ 121 Jesse Orosco .05 .02
❑ 122 Rudy Seanez .05 .02
❑ 123 Joel Skinner .05 .02
❑ 124 Greg Swindell .05 .02
❑ 125 Jim Thome .20 .09
❑ 126 Mark Whiten .05 .02
❑ 127 Scott Aldred .05 .02
❑ 128 Andy Allanson .05 .02
❑ 129 John Cerutti .05 .02
❑ 130 Milt Cuyler .05 .02
❑ 131 Mike Dalton .05 .02
❑ 132 Rob Deer .05 .02
❑ 133 Cecil Fielder .10 .05
❑ 134 Travis Fryman .10 .05
❑ 135 Dan Gakeler .05 .02
❑ 136 Paul Gibson .05 .02
❑ 137 Bill Gullickson .05 .02
❑ 138 Mike Henneman .05 .02
❑ 139 Pete Incaviglia .05 .02
❑ 140 Mark Leiter .05 .02
❑ 141 Scott Livingstone .05 .02
❑ 142 Lloyd Moseby .05 .02
❑ 143 Tony Phillips .05 .02
❑ 144 Mark Salas .05 .02
❑ 145 Frank Tanana .05 .02
❑ 146 Walt Terrell .05 .02
❑ 147 Mickey Tettleton .05 .02
❑ 148 Alan Trammell .15 .07
❑ 149 Lou Whitaker .10 .05
❑ 150 Kevin Appier .10 .05
❑ 151 Luis Aquino .05 .02
❑ 152 Todd Benzinger .05 .02
❑ 153 Mike Boddicker .05 .02
❑ 154 George Brett .40 .18
❑ 155 Storm Davis .05 .02
❑ 156 Jim Eisenreich .05 .02
❑ 157 Kirk Gibson .10 .05
❑ 158 Tom Gordon .05 .02
❑ 159 Mark Gubicza .05 .02
❑ 160 David Howard .05 .02
❑ 161 Mike Macfarlane .05 .02
❑ 162 Brent Mayne .05 .02
❑ 163 Brian McRae .05 .02
❑ 164 Jeff Montgomery .05 .02
❑ 165 Bill Pecota .05 .02
❑ 166 Harvey Pulliam .05 .02
❑ 167 Bret Saberhagen .10 .05
❑ 168 Kevin Seitzer .05 .02
❑ 169 Terry Shumpert .05 .02
❑ 170 Kurt Stillwell .05 .02
❑ 171 Danny Tartabull .05 .02
❑ 172 Gary Thurman .05 .02
❑ 173 Dante Bichette .10 .05
❑ 174 Kevin D. Brown .05 .02
❑ 175 Chuck Crim .05 .02
❑ 176 Jim Gantner .05 .02
❑ 177 Darryl Hamilton .05 .02
❑ 178 Ted Higuera .05 .02
❑ 179 Darren Holmes .05 .02
❑ 180 Mark Lee .05 .02
❑ 181 Julio Machado .05 .02
❑ 182 Paul Molitor .20 .09
❑ 183 Jaime Navarro .05 .02
❑ 184 Edwin Nunez .05 .02
❑ 185 Dan Plesac .05 .02
❑ 186 Willie Randolph .10 .05
❑ 187 Ron Robinson .05 .02
❑ 188 Gary Sheffield .10 .05
❑ 189 Bill Spiers .05 .02
❑ 190 B.J. Surhoff .10 .05
❑ 191 Dale Sveum .05 .02
❑ 192 Greg Vaughn .10 .05
❑ 193 Bill Wegman .05 .02
❑ 194 Robin Yount .20 .09
❑ 195 Rick Aguilera .10 .05
❑ 196 Allan Anderson .05 .02
❑ 197 Steve Bedrosian .05 .02
❑ 198 Randy Bush .05 .02
❑ 199 Larry Casian .05 .02
❑ 200 Chili Davis .10 .05
❑ 201 Scott Erickson .05 .02
❑ 202 Greg Gagne .05 .02
❑ 203 Dan Gladden .05 .02
❑ 204 Brian Harper .05 .02
❑ 205 Kent Hrbek .10 .05
❑ 206 C.Knoblauch UER .10 .05
Career hit total
of 59 is wrong
❑ 207 Gene Larkin .05 .02
❑ 208 Terry Leach .05 .02
❑ 209 Scott Leius .05 .02
❑ 210 Shane Mack .05 .02
❑ 211 Jack Morris .10 .05
❑ 212 Pedro Munoz .05 .02
❑ 213 Denny Neagle .10 .05
❑ 214 Al Newman .05 .02
❑ 215 Junior Ortiz .05 .02
❑ 216 Mike Pagliarulo .05 .02
❑ 217 Kirby Puckett .50 .23
❑ 218 Paul Sorrento .05 .02
❑ 219 Kevin Tapani .05 .02
❑ 220 Lenny Webster .05 .02
❑ 221 Jesse Barfield .05 .02
❑ 222 Greg Cadaret .05 .02
❑ 223 Dave Eiland .05 .02
❑ 224 Alvaro Espinoza .05 .02
❑ 225 Steve Farr .05 .02
❑ 226 Bob Geren .05 .02
❑ 227 Lee Guetterman .05 .02
❑ 228 John Habyan .05 .02
❑ 229 Mel Hall .05 .02
❑ 230 Steve Howe .05 .02
❑ 231 Mike Humphreys .05 .02
❑ 232 Scott Kamieniecki .05 .02
❑ 233 Pat Kelly .05 .02
❑ 234 Roberto Kelly .05 .02
❑ 235 Tim Leary .05 .02
❑ 236 Kevin Maas .05 .02
❑ 237 Don Mattingly .50 .23
❑ 238 Hensley Meulens .05 .02
❑ 239 Matt Nokes .05 .02
❑ 240 Pascual Perez .05 .02
❑ 241 Eric Plunk .05 .02
❑ 242 John Ramos .05 .02
❑ 243 Scott Sanderson .05 .02
❑ 244 Steve Sax .05 .02
❑ 245 Wade Taylor .05 .02
❑ 246 Randy Velarde .05 .02
❑ 247 Bernie Williams .20 .09
❑ 248 Troy Afenir .05 .02
❑ 249 Harold Baines .10 .05
❑ 250 Lance Blankenship .05 .02
❑ 251 Mike Bordick .05 .02
❑ 252 Jose Canseco .20 .09
❑ 253 Steve Chitren .05 .02
❑ 254 Ron Darling .05 .02
❑ 255 Dennis Eckersley .10 .05
❑ 256 Mike Gallego .05 .02
❑ 257 Dave Henderson .05 .02
❑ 258 R.Henderson UER .40 .18
Wearing 24 on front
and 22 on back
❑ 259 Rick Honeycutt .05 .02
❑ 260 Brook Jacoby .05 .02
❑ 261 Carney Lansford .10 .05
❑ 262 Mark McGwire .75 .35
❑ 263 Mike Moore .05 .02
❑ 264 Gene Nelson .05 .02
❑ 265 Jamie Quirk .05 .02
❑ 266 Joe Slusarski .05 .02
❑ 267 Terry Steinbach .05 .02
❑ 268 Dave Stewart .10 .05
❑ 269 Todd Van Poppel .05 .02
❑ 270 Walt Weiss .05 .02
❑ 271 Bob Welch .05 .02
❑ 272 Curt Young .05 .02
❑ 273 Scott Bradley .05 .02
❑ 274 Greg Briley .05 .02
❑ 275 Jay Buhner .10 .05
❑ 276 Henry Cotto .05 .02
❑ 277 Alvin Davis .05 .02
❑ 278 Rich DeLucia .05 .02
❑ 279 Ken Griffey Jr. .60 .25
❑ 280 Erik Hanson .05 .02
❑ 281 Brian Holman .05 .02
❑ 282 Mike Jackson .05 .02
❑ 283 Randy Johnson .25 .11
❑ 284 Tracy Jones .05 .02
❑ 285 Bill Krueger .05 .02
❑ 286 Edgar Martinez .15 .07
❑ 287 Tino Martinez .10 .05
❑ 288 Rob Murphy .05 .02
❑ 289 Pete O'Brien .05 .02
❑ 290 Alonzo Powell .05 .02
❑ 291 Harold Reynolds .05 .02
❑ 292 Mike Schooler .05 .02
❑ 293 Russ Swan .05 .02
❑ 294 Bill Swift .05 .02
❑ 295 Dave Valle .05 .02
❑ 296 Omar Vizquel .10 .05
❑ 297 Gerald Alexander .05 .02
❑ 298 Brad Arnsberg .05 .02
❑ 299 Kevin Brown .10 .05
❑ 300 Jack Daugherty .05 .02
❑ 301 Mario Diaz .05 .02
❑ 302 Brian Downing .05 .02
❑ 303 Julio Franco .10 .05
❑ 304 Juan Gonzalez .20 .09
❑ 305 Rich Gossage .10 .05
❑ 306 Jose Guzman .05 .02
❑ 307 Jose Hernandez RC .05 .02
❑ 308 Jeff Huson .05 .02
❑ 309 Mike Jeffcoat .05 .02
❑ 310 Terry Mathews .05 .02
❑ 311 Rafael Palmeiro .20 .09
❑ 312 Dean Palmer .10 .05
❑ 313 Geno Petralli .05 .02
❑ 314 Gary Pettis .05 .02
❑ 315 Kevin Reimer .05 .02
❑ 316 Ivan Rodriguez .25 .11
❑ 317 Kenny Rogers .05 .02
❑ 318 Wayne Rosenthal .05 .02
❑ 319 Jeff Russell .05 .02
❑ 320 Nolan Ryan 1.00 .45
❑ 321 Ruben Sierra .05 .02
❑ 322 Jim Acker .05 .02
❑ 323 Roberto Alomar .20 .09
❑ 324 Derek Bell .10 .05
❑ 325 Pat Borders .05 .02
❑ 326 Tom Candiotti .05 .02
❑ 327 Joe Carter .10 .05
❑ 328 Rob Ducey .05 .02
❑ 329 Kelly Gruber .05 .02
❑ 330 Juan Guzman .05 .02
❑ 331 Tom Henke .05 .02
❑ 332 Jimmy Key .10 .05
❑ 333 Manny Lee .05 .02
❑ 334 Al Leiter .10 .05
❑ 335 Bob MacDonald .05 .02
❑ 336 Candy Maldonado .05 .02
❑ 337 Rance Mulliniks .05 .02
❑ 338 Greg Myers .05 .02
❑ 339 John Olerud UER .10 .05
(1991 BA has .256,
but text says .258)
❑ 340 Ed Sprague .05 .02
❑ 341 Dave Stieb .05 .02
❑ 342 Todd Stottlemyre .05 .02
❑ 343 Mike Timlin .05 .02
❑ 344 Duane Ward .05 .02
❑ 345 David Wells .10 .05
❑ 346 Devon White .05 .02
❑ 347 Mookie Wilson .10 .05
❑ 348 Eddie Zosky .05 .02
❑ 349 Steve Avery .05 .02
❑ 350 Mike Bell .05 .02
❑ 351 Rafael Belliard .05 .02
❑ 352 Juan Berenguer .05 .02
❑ 353 Jeff Blauser .05 .02
❑ 354 Sid Bream .05 .02
❑ 355 Francisco Cabrera .05 .02
❑ 356 Marvin Freeman .05 .02
❑ 357 Ron Gant .05 .02
❑ 358 Tom Glavine .20 .09
❑ 359 Brian Hunter .05 .02
❑ 360 Dave Justice .10 .05

❑ 361 Charlie Leibrandt .05 .02
❑ 362 Mark Lemke .05 .02
❑ 363 Kent Mercker .05 .02
❑ 364 Keith Mitchell .05 .02
❑ 365 Greg Olson .05 .02
❑ 366 Terry Pendleton .10 .05
❑ 367 Armando Reynoso RC .10 .05
❑ 368 Deion Sanders .10 .05
❑ 369 Lonnie Smith .05 .02
❑ 370 Pete Smith .05 .02
❑ 371 John Smoltz .10 .05
❑ 372 Mike Stanton .05 .02
❑ 373 Jeff Treadway .05 .02
❑ 374 Mark Wohlers .05 .02
❑ 375 Paul Assenmacher .05 .02
❑ 376 George Bell .05 .02
❑ 377 Shawn Boskie .05 .02
❑ 378 Frank Castillo .05 .02
❑ 379 Andre Dawson .15 .07
❑ 380 Shawon Dunston .05 .02
❑ 381 Mark Grace .20 .09
❑ 382 Mike Harkey .05 .02
❑ 383 Danny Jackson .05 .02
❑ 384 Les Lancaster .05 .02
❑ 385 Ced Landrum .05 .02
❑ 386 Greg Maddux .50 .23
❑ 387 Derrick May .05 .02
❑ 388 Chuck McElroy .05 .02
❑ 389 Ryne Sandberg .25 .11
❑ 390 Heathcliff Slocumb .05 .02
❑ 391 Dave Smith .05 .02
❑ 392 Dwight Smith .05 .02
❑ 393 Rick Sutcliffe .10 .05
❑ 394 Hector Villanueva .05 .02
❑ 395 Chico Walker .05 .02
❑ 396 Jerome Walton .05 .02
❑ 397 Rick Wilkins .05 .02
❑ 398 Jack Armstrong .05 .02
❑ 399 Freddie Benavides .05 .02
❑ 400 Glenn Braggs .05 .02
❑ 401 Tom Browning .05 .02
❑ 402 Norm Charlton .05 .02
❑ 403 Eric Davis .10 .05
❑ 404 Rob Dibble .05 .02
❑ 405 Bill Doran .05 .02
❑ 406 Mariano Duncan .05 .02
❑ 407 Kip Gross .05 .02
❑ 408 Chris Hammond .05 .02
❑ 409 Billy Hatcher .05 .02
❑ 410 Chris Jones .05 .02
❑ 411 Barry Larkin .20 .09
❑ 412 Hal Morris .05 .02
❑ 413 Randy Myers .05 .02
❑ 414 Joe Oliver .05 .02
❑ 415 Paul O'Neill .20 .09
❑ 416 Ted Power .05 .02
❑ 417 Luis Quinones .05 .02
❑ 418 Jeff Reed .05 .02
❑ 419 Jose Rijo .05 .02
❑ 420 Chris Sabo .05 .02
❑ 421 Reggie Sanders .05 .02
❑ 422 Scott Scudder .05 .02
❑ 423 Glenn Sutko .05 .02
❑ 424 Eric Anthony .05 .02
❑ 425 Jeff Bagwell .40 .18
❑ 426 Craig Biggio .15 .07
❑ 427 Ken Caminiti .10 .05
❑ 428 Casey Candaele .05 .02
❑ 429 Mike Capel .05 .02
❑ 430 Andujar Cedeno .05 .02
❑ 431 Jim Corsi .05 .02
❑ 432 Mark Davidson .05 .02
❑ 433 Steve Finley .10 .05
❑ 434 Luis Gonzalez .20 .09
❑ 435 Pete Harnisch .05 .02
❑ 436 Dwayne Henry .05 .02
❑ 437 Xavier Hernandez .05 .02
❑ 438 Jimmy Jones .05 .02
❑ 439 Darryl Kile .10 .05
❑ 440 Rob Mallicoat .05 .02
❑ 441 Andy Mota .05 .02
❑ 442 Al Osuna .05 .02
❑ 443 Mark Portugal .05 .02
❑ 444 Scott Servais .05 .02
❑ 445 Mike Simms .05 .02
❑ 446 Gerald Young .05 .02
❑ 447 Tim Belcher .05 .02
❑ 448 Brett Butler .10 .05
❑ 449 John Candelaria .05 .02
❑ 450 Gary Carter .15 .07
❑ 451 Dennis Cook .05 .02
❑ 452 Tim Crews .05 .02
❑ 453 Kal Daniels .05 .02
❑ 454 Jim Gott .05 .02
❑ 455 Alfredo Griffin .05 .02
❑ 456 Kevin Gross .05 .02
❑ 457 Chris Gwynn .05 .02
❑ 458 Lenny Harris .05 .02
❑ 459 Orel Hershiser .10 .05
❑ 460 Jay Howell .05 .02
❑ 461 Stan Javier .05 .02
❑ 462 Eric Karros .10 .05
❑ 463 Ramon Martinez UER .05 .02
(Card says bats right, should be left)
❑ 464 Roger McDowell UER .05 .02
(Wins add up to 54, totals have 51)
❑ 465 Mike Morgan .05 .02
❑ 466 Eddie Murray .20 .09
❑ 467 Jose Offerman .05 .02
❑ 468 Bob Ojeda .05 .02
❑ 469 Juan Samuel .05 .02
❑ 470 Mike Scioscia .05 .02
❑ 471 Darryl Strawberry .10 .05
❑ 472 Bret Barberie .05 .02
❑ 473 Brian Barnes .05 .02
❑ 474 Eric Bullock .05 .02
❑ 475 Ivan Calderon .05 .02
❑ 476 Delino DeShields .05 .02
❑ 477 Jeff Fassero .05 .02
❑ 478 Mike Fitzgerald .05 .02
❑ 479 Steve Frey .05 .02
❑ 480 Andres Galarraga .15 .07
❑ 481 Mark Gardner .05 .02
❑ 482 Marquis Grissom .05 .02
❑ 483 Chris Haney .05 .02
❑ 484 Barry Jones .05 .02
❑ 485 Dave Martinez .05 .02
❑ 486 Dennis Martinez .10 .05
❑ 487 Chris Nabholz .05 .02
❑ 488 Spike Owen .05 .02
❑ 489 Gilberto Reyes .05 .02
❑ 490 Mel Rojas .05 .02
❑ 491 Scott Ruskin .05 .02
❑ 492 Bill Sampen .05 .02
❑ 493 Larry Walker .15 .07
❑ 494 Tim Wallach .05 .02
❑ 495 Daryl Boston .05 .02
❑ 496 Hubie Brooks .05 .02
❑ 497 Tim Burke .05 .02
❑ 498 Mark Carreon .05 .02
❑ 499 Tony Castillo .05 .02
❑ 500 Vince Coleman .05 .02
❑ 501 David Cone .10 .05
❑ 502 Kevin Elster .05 .02
❑ 503 Sid Fernandez .05 .02
❑ 504 John Franco .10 .05
❑ 505 Dwight Gooden .10 .05
❑ 506 Todd Hundley .05 .02
❑ 507 Jeff Innis .05 .02
❑ 508 Gregg Jefferies .05 .02
❑ 509 Howard Johnson .05 .02
❑ 510 Dave Magadan .05 .02
❑ 511 Terry McDaniel .05 .02
❑ 512 Kevin McReynolds .05 .02
❑ 513 Keith Miller .05 .02
❑ 514 Charlie O'Brien .05 .02
❑ 515 Mackey Sasser .05 .02
❑ 516 Pete Schourek .05 .02
❑ 517 Julio Valera .05 .02
❑ 518 Frank Viola .10 .05
❑ 519 Wally Whitehurst .05 .02
❑ 520 Anthony Young .05 .02
❑ 521 Andy Ashby .05 .02
❑ 522 Kim Batiste .05 .02
❑ 523 Joe Boever .05 .02
❑ 524 Wes Chamberlain .05 .02
❑ 525 Pat Combs .05 .02
❑ 526 Danny Cox .05 .02
❑ 527 Darren Daulton .10 .05
❑ 528 Jose DeJesus .05 .02
❑ 529 Len Dykstra .10 .05
❑ 530 Darrin Fletcher .05 .02
❑ 531 Tommy Greene .05 .02
❑ 532 Jason Grimsley .05 .02
❑ 533 Charlie Hayes .05 .02
❑ 534 Von Hayes .05 .02
❑ 535 Dave Hollins .05 .02
❑ 536 Ricky Jordan .05 .02
❑ 537 John Kruk .10 .05
❑ 538 Jim Lindeman .05 .02
❑ 539 Mickey Morandini .05 .02
❑ 540 Terry Mulholland .05 .02
❑ 541 Dale Murphy .20 .09
❑ 542 Randy Ready .05 .02
❑ 543 Wally Ritchie UER .05 .02
(Letters in data are cut off on card)
❑ 544 Bruce Ruffin .05 .02
❑ 545 Steve Searcy .05 .02
❑ 546 Dickie Thon .05 .02
❑ 547 Mitch Williams .05 .02
❑ 548 Stan Belinda .05 .02
❑ 549 Jay Bell .10 .05
❑ 550 Barry Bonds .50 .23
❑ 551 Bobby Bonilla .10 .05
❑ 552 Steve Buechele .05 .02
❑ 553 Doug Drabek .05 .02
❑ 554 Neal Heaton .05 .02
❑ 555 Jeff King .05 .02
❑ 556 Bob Kipper .05 .02
❑ 557 Bill Landrum .05 .02
❑ 558 Mike LaValliere .05 .02
❑ 559 Jose Lind .05 .02
❑ 560 Lloyd McClendon .05 .02
❑ 561 Orlando Merced .05 .02
❑ 562 Bob Patterson .05 .02
❑ 563 Joe Redfield .05 .02
❑ 564 Gary Redus .05 .02
❑ 565 Rosario Rodriguez .05 .02
❑ 566 Don Slaught .05 .02
❑ 567 John Smiley .05 .02
❑ 568 Zane Smith .05 .02
❑ 569 Randy Tomlin .05 .02
❑ 570 Andy Van Slyke .10 .05
❑ 571 Gary Varsho .05 .02
❑ 572 Bob Walk .05 .02
❑ 573 John Wehner UER .05 .02
(Actually played for Carolina in 1991, not Cards)
❑ 574 Juan Agosto .05 .02
❑ 575 Cris Carpenter .05 .02
❑ 576 Jose DeLeon .05 .02
❑ 577 Rich Gedman .05 .02
❑ 578 Bernard Gilkey .05 .02
❑ 579 Pedro Guerrero .10 .05
❑ 580 Ken Hill .05 .02
❑ 581 Rex Hudler .05 .02
❑ 582 Felix Jose .05 .02
❑ 583 Ray Lankford .05 .02
❑ 584 Omar Olivares .05 .02
❑ 585 Jose Oquendo .05 .02
❑ 586 Tom Pagnozzi .05 .02
❑ 587 Geronimo Pena .05 .02
❑ 588 Mike Perez .05 .02
❑ 589 Gerald Perry .05 .02
❑ 590 Bryn Smith .05 .02
❑ 591 Lee Smith .10 .05
❑ 592 Ozzie Smith .25 .11
❑ 593 Scott Terry .05 .02
❑ 594 Bob Tewksbury .05 .02
❑ 595 Milt Thompson .05 .02
❑ 596 Todd Zeile .05 .02
❑ 597 Larry Andersen .05 .02
❑ 598 Oscar Azocar .05 .02
❑ 599 Andy Benes .05 .02
❑ 600 Ricky Bones .05 .02
❑ 601 Jerald Clark .05 .02
❑ 602 Pat Clements .05 .02
❑ 603 Paul Faries .05 .02
❑ 604 Tony Fernandez .05 .02
❑ 605 Tony Gwynn .40 .18
❑ 606 Greg W. Harris .05 .02
❑ 607 Thomas Howard .05 .02
❑ 608 Bruce Hurst .05 .02
❑ 609 Darrin Jackson .05 .02

❑ 610 Tom Lampkin .05 .02
❑ 611 Craig Lefferts .05 .02
❑ 612 Jim Lewis .05 .02
❑ 613 Mike Maddux .05 .02
❑ 614 Fred McGriff .15 .07
❑ 615 Jose Melendez .05 .02
❑ 616 Jose Mota .05 .02
❑ 617 Dennis Rasmussen .05 .02
❑ 618 Bip Roberts .05 .02
❑ 619 Rich Rodriguez .05 .02
❑ 620 Benito Santiago .05 .02
❑ 621 Craig Shipley .05 .02
❑ 622 Tim Teufel .05 .02
❑ 623 Kevin Ward .05 .02
❑ 624 Ed Whitson .05 .02
❑ 625 Dave Anderson .05 .02
❑ 626 Kevin Bass .05 .02
❑ 627 Rod Beck RC .20 .09
❑ 628 Bud Black .05 .02
❑ 629 Jeff Brantley .05 .02
❑ 630 John Burkett .05 .02
❑ 631 Will Clark .20 .09
❑ 632 Royce Clayton .05 .02
❑ 633 Steve Decker .05 .02
❑ 634 Kelly Downs .05 .02
❑ 635 Mike Felder .05 .02
❑ 636 Scott Garrelts .05 .02
❑ 637 Eric Gunderson .05 .02
❑ 638 Bryan Hickerson RC .05 .02
❑ 639 Darren Lewis .05 .02
❑ 640 Greg Litton .05 .02
❑ 641 Kirt Manwaring .05 .02
❑ 642 Paul McClellan .05 .02
❑ 643 Willie McGee .10 .05
❑ 644 Kevin Mitchell .05 .02
❑ 645 Francisco Oliveras .05 .02
❑ 646 Mike Remlinger .05 .02
❑ 647 Dave Righetti .10 .05
❑ 648 Robby Thompson .05 .02
❑ 649 Jose Uribe .05 .02
❑ 650 Matt Williams .15 .07
❑ 651 Trevor Wilson .05 .02
❑ 652 T.Goodwin MLP UER .05 .02
Timed in 3.5,
should be be timed
❑ 653 Terry Bross MLP .05 .02
❑ 654 M.Christopher MLP .05 .02
❑ 655 Kenny Lofton MLP .20 .09
❑ 656 Chris Cron MLP .05 .02
❑ 657 Willie Banks MLP .05 .02
❑ 658 Pat Rice MLP .05 .02
❑ 659A R.Maurer MLP ERR .75 .35
Name misspelled as
Mauer on card front
❑ 659B R.Maurer MLP COR .05 .02
❑ 660 Don Harris MLP .05 .02
❑ 661 Henry Rodriguez MLP .05 .02
❑ 662 Cliff Brantley MLP .05 .02
❑ 663 M.Lihskey MLP UER .05 .02
220 pounds in data,
200 in text
❑ 664 Gary DiSarcina MLP .05 .02
❑ 665 Gil Heredia RC .10 .05
❑ 666 V.Castilla MLP RC .50 .23
❑ 667 Paul Abbott MLP .05 .02
❑ 668 M.Fariss MLP UER .05 .02
Called Paul on back
❑ 669 Jarvis Brown MLP .05 .02
❑ 670 Wayne Kirby MLP RC .05 .02
❑ 671 S.Brosius MLP RC .50 .23
❑ 672 Bob Hamelin MLP .05 .02
❑ 673 Joel Johnston MLP .05 .02
❑ 674 Tim Spehr MLP .05 .02
❑ 675A J.Gardner MLP ERR .75 .35
P on front,
should be SS
❑ 675B Jeff Gardner MLP COR .10 .05
❑ 676 Rico Rossy MLP .05 .02
❑ 677 R.Hernandez MLP RC .05 .02
❑ 678 Ted Wood MLP .05 .02
❑ 679 Cal Eldred MLP .05 .02
❑ 680 Sean Berry MLP .05 .02
❑ 681 Rickey Henderson RS .20 .09
❑ 682 Nolan Ryan RS .50 .23
❑ 683 Dennis Martinez RS .05 .02
❑ 684 Wilson Alvarez RS .05 .02
❑ 685 Joe Carter RS .05 .02
❑ 686 Dave Winfield RS .10 .05
❑ 687 David Cone RS .05 .02
❑ 688 Jose Canseco LL UER .10 .05
(Text on back has 42 stolen
bases in '88; should be 40)
❑ 689 Howard Johnson LL .05 .02
❑ 690 Julio Franco LL .05 .02
❑ 691 Terry Pendleton LL .05 .02
❑ 692 Cecil Fielder LL .05 .02
❑ 693 Scott Erickson LL .05 .02
❑ 694 Tom Glavine LL .10 .05
❑ 695 Dennis Martinez LL .05 .02
❑ 696 Bryan Harvey LL .05 .02
❑ 697 Lee Smith LL .05 .02
❑ 698 Super Siblings .10 .05
Roberto Alomar
Sandy Alomar Jr.
❑ 699 The Indispensables .10 .05
Bobby Bonilla
Will Clark
❑ 700 Teamwork .05 .02
Mark Wohlers
Kent Mercker
Alejandro Pena
❑ 701 Tiger Tandems .15 .07
Stacy Jones
Bo Jackson
Gregg Olson
Frank Thomas
❑ 702 The Ignitors .20 .09
Paul Molitor
Brett Butler
❑ 703 Indispensables II .40 .18
Cal Ripken
Joe Carter
❑ 704 Power Packs .20 .09
Barry Larkin
Kirby Puckett
❑ 705 Today and Tomorrow .10 .05
Mo Vaughn
Cecil Fielder
❑ 706 Teenage Sensations .05 .02
Ramon Martinez
Ozzie Guillen
❑ 707 Designated Hitters .10 .05
Harold Baines
Wade Boggs
❑ 708 Robin Yount PV .10 .05
❑ 709 K.Griffey Jr. PV UER .50 .23
Missing quotations on
back; BA has .322, but
was actually .327
❑ 710 Nolan Ryan PV .50 .23
❑ 711 Cal Ripken PV .40 .18
❑ 712 Frank Thomas PV .15 .07
❑ 713 Dave Justice PV .10 .05
❑ 714 Checklist 1-101 .05 .02
❑ 715 Checklist 102-194 .05 .02
❑ 716 Checklist 195-296 .05 .02
❑ 717 Checklist 297-397 .05 .02
❑ 718 Checklist 398-494 .05 .02
❑ 719 Checklist 495-596 .05 .02
❑ 720A CL 597-720 ERR .05 .02
659 Rob Mauer
❑ 720B CL 597-720 COR .05 .02
659 Rob Maurer

1992 Fleer Update

	MINT	NRMT
COMP.FACT.SET (136)	150.00	70.00
COMPLETE SET (132)	140.00	65.00

❑ 1 Todd Frohwirth .50 .23
❑ 2 Alan Mills .50 .23
❑ 3 Rick Sutcliffe .75 .35
❑ 4 John Valentin RC 2.00 .90
❑ 5 Frank Viola .75 .35
❑ 6 Bob Zupcic RC .50 .23
❑ 7 Mike Butcher .50 .23
❑ 8 Chad Curtis RC .75 .35
❑ 9 Damion Easley RC .75 .35
❑ 10 Tim Salmon 4.00 1.80
❑ 11 Julio Valera .50 .23
❑ 12 George Bell .50 .23

❑ 13 Roberto Hernandez .50 .23
❑ 14 Shawn Jeter RC .50 .23
❑ 15 Thomas Howard .50 .23
❑ 16 Jesse Levis .50 .23
❑ 17 Kenny Lofton 4.00 1.80
❑ 18 Paul Sorrento .50 .23
❑ 19 Rico Brogna .50 .23
❑ 20 John Doherty RC .50 .23
❑ 21 Dan Gladden .50 .23
❑ 22 Buddy Groom .50 .23
❑ 23 Shawn Hare RC .50 .23
❑ 24 John Kiely .50 .23
❑ 25 Kurt Knudsen .50 .23
❑ 26 Gregg Jefferies .50 .23
❑ 27 Wally Joyner .75 .35
❑ 28 Kevin Koslofski .50 .23
❑ 29 Kevin McReynolds .50 .23
❑ 30 Rusty Meacham .50 .23
❑ 31 Keith Miller .50 .23
❑ 32 Hipolito Pichardo RC .50 .23
❑ 33 James Austin .50 .23
❑ 34 Scott Fletcher .50 .23
❑ 35 John Jaha RC .75 .35
❑ 36 Pat Listach RC .75 .35
❑ 37 Dave Nilsson .50 .23
❑ 38 Kevin Seitzer .50 .23
❑ 39 Tom Edens .50 .23
❑ 40 Pat Mahomes RC .50 .23
❑ 41 John Smiley .50 .23
❑ 42 Charlie Hayes .50 .23
❑ 43 Sam Militello .50 .23
❑ 44 Andy Stankiewicz .50 .23
❑ 45 Danny Tartabull .50 .23
❑ 46 Bob Wickman .50 .23
❑ 47 Jerry Browne .50 .23
❑ 48 Kevin Campbell .50 .23
❑ 49 Vince Horsman .50 .23
❑ 50 Troy Neel RC .50 .23
❑ 51 Ruben Sierra .50 .23
❑ 52 Bruce Walton .50 .23
❑ 53 Willie Wilson .50 .23
❑ 54 Bret Boone 4.00 1.80
❑ 55 Dave Fleming .50 .23
❑ 56 Kevin Mitchell .50 .23
❑ 57 Jeff Nelson RC .75 .35
❑ 58 Shane Turner .50 .23
❑ 59 Jose Canseco 2.00 .90
❑ 60 Jeff Frye RC .75 .35
❑ 61 Danny Leon .50 .23
❑ 62 Roger Pavlik RC .50 .23
❑ 63 David Cone .75 .35
❑ 64 Pat Hentgen .50 .23
❑ 65 Randy Knorr .50 .23
❑ 66 Jack Morris .75 .35
❑ 67 Dave Winfield 2.00 .90
❑ 68 David Nied RC .50 .23
❑ 69 Otis Nixon .50 .23
❑ 70 Alejandro Pena .50 .23
❑ 71 Jeff Reardon .75 .35
❑ 72 Alex Arias RC .50 .23
❑ 73 Jim Bullinger .50 .23
❑ 74 Mike Morgan .50 .23
❑ 75 Rey Sanchez RC .75 .35
❑ 76 Bob Scanlan .50 .23
❑ 77 Sammy Sosa 4.00 1.80
❑ 78 Scott Bankhead .50 .23
❑ 79 Tim Belcher .50 .23

		MINT	NRMT
❑ 80	Steve Foster	.50	.23
❑ 81	Willie Greene	.50	.23
❑ 82	Bip Roberts	.50	.23
❑ 83	Scott Ruskin	.50	.23
❑ 84	Greg Swindell	.50	.23
❑ 85	Juan Guerrero	.50	.23
❑ 86	Butch Henry	.50	.23
❑ 87	Doug Jones	.50	.23
❑ 88	Brian Williams RC	.50	.23
❑ 89	Tom Candiotti	.50	.23
❑ 90	Eric Davis	.75	.35
❑ 91	Carlos Hernandez	.50	.23
❑ 92	Mike Piazza RC	100.00	45.00
❑ 93	Mike Sharperson	.50	.23
❑ 94	Eric Young RC	2.00	.90
❑ 95	Moises Alou	2.00	.90
❑ 96	Greg Colbrunn	.50	.23
❑ 97	Wil Cordero	.50	.23
❑ 98	Ken Hill	.50	.23
❑ 99	John Vander Wal RC	.50	.23
❑ 100	John Wetteland	.75	.35
❑ 101	Bobby Bonilla	.75	.35
❑ 102	Eric Hillman RC	.50	.23
❑ 103	Pat Howell	.50	.23
❑ 104	Jeff Kent RC	20.00	9.00
❑ 105	Dick Schofield	.50	.23
❑ 106	Ryan Thompson RC	.50	.23
❑ 107	Chico Walker	.50	.23
❑ 108	Juan Bell	.50	.23
❑ 109	Mariano Duncan	.50	.23
❑ 110	Jeff Grotewold	.50	.23
❑ 111	Ben Rivera	.50	.23
❑ 112	Curt Schilling	2.00	.90
❑ 113	Victor Cole	.50	.23
❑ 114	Al Martin RC	.75	.35
❑ 115	Roger Mason	.50	.23
❑ 116	Blas Minor	.50	.23
❑ 117	Tim Wakefield RC	.75	.35
❑ 118	Mark Clark RC	.75	.35
❑ 119	Rheal Cormier	.50	.23
❑ 120	Donovan Osborne	.50	.23
❑ 121	Todd Worrell	.50	.23
❑ 122	Jeremy Hernandez RC	.50	.23
❑ 123	Randy Myers	.50	.23
❑ 124	Frank Seminara RC	.50	.23
❑ 125	Gary Sheffield	.75	.35
❑ 126	Dan Walters	.50	.23
❑ 127	Steve Hosey	.50	.23
❑ 128	Mike Jackson	.50	.23
❑ 129	Jim Pena	.50	.23
❑ 130	Cory Snyder	.50	.23
❑ 131	Bill Swift	.50	.23
❑ 132	Checklist U1-U132	.50	.23

1993 Fleer

	MINT	NRMT
COMPLETE SET (720)	40.00	18.00
COMPLETE SERIES 1 (360)	20.00	9.00
COMPLETE SERIES 2 (360)	20.00	9.00

		MINT	NRMT
❑ 1	Steve Avery	.10	.05
❑ 2	Sid Bream	.10	.05
❑ 3	Ron Gant	.10	.05
❑ 4	Tom Glavine	.40	.18
❑ 5	Brian Hunter	.10	.05
❑ 6	Ryan Klesko	.15	.07
❑ 7	Charlie Leibrandt	.10	.05
❑ 8	Kent Mercker	.10	.05
❑ 9	David Nied	.10	.05
❑ 10	Otis Nixon	.10	.05
❑ 11	Greg Olson	.10	.05
❑ 12	Terry Pendleton	.15	.07
❑ 13	Deion Sanders	.15	.07
❑ 14	John Smoltz	.15	.07
❑ 15	Mike Stanton	.10	.05
❑ 16	Mark Wohlers	.10	.05
❑ 17	Paul Assenmacher	.10	.05
❑ 18	Steve Buechele	.10	.05
❑ 19	Shawon Dunston	.10	.05
❑ 20	Mark Grace	.40	.18
❑ 21	Derrick May	.10	.05
❑ 22	Chuck McElroy	.10	.05
❑ 23	Mike Morgan	.10	.05
❑ 24	Rey Sanchez	.10	.05
❑ 25	Ryne Sandberg	.50	.23
❑ 26	Bob Scanlan	.10	.05
❑ 27	Sammy Sosa	.75	.35
❑ 28	Rick Wilkins	.10	.05
❑ 29	Bobby Ayala RC	.10	.05
❑ 30	Tim Belcher	.10	.05
❑ 31	Jeff Branson	.10	.05
❑ 32	Norm Charlton	.10	.05
❑ 33	Steve Foster	.10	.05
❑ 34	Willie Greene	.10	.05
❑ 35	Chris Hammond	.10	.05
❑ 36	Milt Hill	.10	.05
❑ 37	Hal Morris	.10	.05
❑ 38	Joe Oliver	.10	.05
❑ 39	Paul O'Neill	.40	.18
❑ 40	Tim Pugh RC	.10	.05
❑ 41	Jose Rijo	.10	.05
❑ 42	Bip Roberts	.10	.05
❑ 43	Chris Sabo	.10	.05
❑ 44	Reggie Sanders	.10	.05
❑ 45	Eric Anthony	.10	.05
❑ 46	Jeff Bagwell	.50	.23
❑ 47	Craig Biggio	.25	.11
❑ 48	Joe Boever	.10	.05
❑ 49	Casey Candaele	.10	.05
❑ 50	Steve Finley	.15	.07
❑ 51	Luis Gonzalez	.40	.18
❑ 52	Pete Harnisch	.10	.05
❑ 53	Xavier Hernandez	.10	.05
❑ 54	Doug Jones	.10	.05
❑ 55	Eddie Taubensee	.10	.05
❑ 56	Brian Williams	.10	.05
❑ 57	Pedro Astacio	.10	.05
❑ 58	Todd Benzinger	.10	.05
❑ 59	Brett Butler	.15	.07
❑ 60	Tom Candiotti	.10	.05
❑ 61	Lenny Harris	.10	.05
❑ 62	Carlos Hernandez	.10	.05
❑ 63	Orel Hershiser	.15	.07
❑ 64	Eric Karros	.15	.07
❑ 65	Ramon Martinez	.10	.05
❑ 66	Jose Offerman	.10	.05
❑ 67	Mike Scioscia	.10	.05
❑ 68	Mike Sharperson	.10	.05
❑ 69	Eric Young	.10	.05
❑ 70	Moises Alou	.15	.07
❑ 71	Ivan Calderon	.10	.05
❑ 72	Archi Cianfrocco	.10	.05
❑ 73	Wil Cordero	.10	.05
❑ 74	Delino DeShields	.10	.05
❑ 75	Mark Gardner	.10	.05
❑ 76	Ken Hill	.10	.05
❑ 77	Tim Laker RC	.10	.05
❑ 78	Chris Nabholz	.10	.05
❑ 79	Mel Rojas	.10	.05
❑ 80	John Vander Wal UER (Misspelled Vander Wall in letters on back)	.10	.05
❑ 81	Larry Walker	.25	.11
❑ 82	Tim Wallach	.10	.05
❑ 83	John Wetteland	.15	.07
❑ 84	Bobby Bonilla	.15	.07
❑ 85	Daryl Boston	.10	.05
❑ 86	Sid Fernandez	.10	.05
❑ 87	Eric Hillman	.10	.05
❑ 88	Todd Hundley	.10	.05
❑ 89	Howard Johnson	.10	.05
❑ 90	Jeff Kent	.40	.18
❑ 91	Eddie Murray	.40	.18
❑ 92	Bill Pecota	.10	.05
❑ 93	Bret Saberhagen	.15	.07
❑ 94	Dick Schofield	.10	.05
❑ 95	Pete Schourek	.10	.05
❑ 96	Anthony Young	.10	.05
❑ 97	Ruben Amaro	.10	.05
❑ 98	Juan Bell	.10	.05
❑ 99	Wes Chamberlain	.10	.05
❑ 100	Darren Daulton	.15	.07
❑ 101	Mariano Duncan	.10	.05
❑ 102	Mike Hartley	.10	.05
❑ 103	Ricky Jordan	.10	.05
❑ 104	John Kruk	.15	.07
❑ 105	Mickey Morandini	.10	.05
❑ 106	Terry Mulholland	.10	.05
❑ 107	Ben Rivera	.10	.05
❑ 108	Curt Schilling	.40	.18
❑ 109	Keith Shepherd RC	.10	.05
❑ 110	Stan Belinda	.10	.05
❑ 111	Jay Bell	.15	.07
❑ 112	Barry Bonds	1.00	.45
❑ 113	Jeff King	.10	.05
❑ 114	Mike LaValliere	.10	.05
❑ 115	Jose Lind	.10	.05
❑ 116	Roger Mason	.10	.05
❑ 117	Orlando Merced	.10	.05
❑ 118	Bob Patterson	.10	.05
❑ 119	Don Slaught	.10	.05
❑ 120	Zane Smith	.10	.05
❑ 121	Randy Tomlin	.10	.05
❑ 122	Andy Van Slyke	.15	.07
❑ 123	Tim Wakefield	.10	.05
❑ 124	Rheal Cormier	.10	.05
❑ 125	Bernard Gilkey	.10	.05
❑ 126	Felix Jose	.10	.05
❑ 127	Ray Lankford	.10	.05
❑ 128	Bob McClure	.10	.05
❑ 129	Donovan Osborne	.10	.05
❑ 130	Tom Pagnozzi	.10	.05
❑ 131	Geronimo Pena	.10	.05
❑ 132	Mike Perez	.10	.05
❑ 133	Lee Smith	.15	.07
❑ 134	Bob Tewksbury	.10	.05
❑ 135	Todd Worrell	.10	.05
❑ 136	Todd Zeile	.10	.05
❑ 137	Jerald Clark	.10	.05
❑ 138	Tony Gwynn	.75	.35
❑ 139	Greg W. Harris	.10	.05
❑ 140	Jeremy Hernandez	.10	.05
❑ 141	Darrin Jackson	.10	.05
❑ 142	Mike Maddux	.10	.05
❑ 143	Fred McGriff	.25	.11
❑ 144	Jose Melendez	.10	.05
❑ 145	Rich Rodriguez	.10	.05
❑ 146	Frank Seminara	.10	.05
❑ 147	Gary Sheffield	.15	.07
❑ 148	Kurt Stillwell	.10	.05
❑ 149	Dan Walters	.10	.05
❑ 150	Rod Beck	.10	.05
❑ 151	Bud Black	.10	.05
❑ 152	Jeff Brantley	.10	.05
❑ 153	John Burkett	.10	.05
❑ 154	Will Clark	.40	.18
❑ 155	Royce Clayton	.10	.05
❑ 156	Mike Jackson	.10	.05
❑ 157	Darren Lewis	.10	.05
❑ 158	Kirt Manwaring	.10	.05
❑ 159	Willie McGee	.15	.07
❑ 160	Cory Snyder	.10	.05
❑ 161	Bill Swift	.10	.05
❑ 162	Trevor Wilson	.10	.05
❑ 163	Brady Anderson	.15	.07
❑ 164	Glenn Davis	.10	.05
❑ 165	Mike Devereaux	.10	.05
❑ 166	Todd Frohwirth	.10	.05
❑ 167	Leo Gomez	.10	.05
❑ 168	Chris Hoiles	.10	.05
❑ 169	Ben McDonald	.10	.05
❑ 170	Randy Milligan	.10	.05
❑ 171	Alan Mills	.10	.05
❑ 172	Mike Mussina	.40	.18
❑ 173	Gregg Olson	.10	.05
❑ 174	Arthur Rhodes	.10	.05
❑ 175	David Segui	.10	.05
❑ 176	Ellis Burks	.15	.07
❑ 177	Roger Clemens	1.00	.45

❑ 178 Scott Cooper .10 .05
❑ 179 Danny Darwin .10 .05
❑ 180 Tony Fossas .10 .05
❑ 181 Paul Quantrill .10 .05
❑ 182 Jody Reed .10 .05
❑ 183 John Valentin .10 .05
❑ 184 Mo Vaughn .15 .07
❑ 185 Frank Viola .15 .07
❑ 186 Bob Zupcic .10 .05
❑ 187 Jim Abbott .15 .07
❑ 188 Gary DiSarcina .10 .05
❑ 189 Damion Easley .10 .05
❑ 190 Junior Felix .10 .05
❑ 191 Chuck Finley .15 .07
❑ 192 Joe Grahe .10 .05
❑ 193 Bryan Harvey .10 .05
❑ 194 Mark Langston .10 .05
❑ 195 John Orton .10 .05
❑ 196 Luis Polonia .10 .05
❑ 197 Tim Salmon .15 .07
❑ 198 Luis Sojo .10 .05
❑ 199 Wilson Alvarez .10 .05
❑ 200 George Bell .10 .05
❑ 201 Alex Fernandez .10 .05
❑ 202 Craig Grebeck .10 .05
❑ 203 Ozzie Guillen .10 .05
❑ 204 Lance Johnson .10 .05
❑ 205 Ron Karkovice .10 .05
❑ 206 Kirk McCaskill .10 .05
❑ 207 Jack McDowell .10 .05
❑ 208 Scott Radinsky .10 .05
❑ 209 Tim Raines .15 .07
❑ 210 Frank Thomas .50 .23
❑ 211 Robin Ventura .15 .07
❑ 212 Sandy Alomar Jr. .15 .07
❑ 213 Carlos Baerga .10 .05
❑ 214 Dennis Cook .10 .05
❑ 215 Thomas Howard .10 .05
❑ 216 Mark Lewis .10 .05
❑ 217 Derek Lilliquist .10 .05
❑ 218 Kenny Lofton .15 .07
❑ 219 Charles Nagy .10 .05
❑ 220 Steve Olin .10 .05
❑ 221 Paul Sorrento .10 .05
❑ 222 Jim Thome .40 .18
❑ 223 Mark Whiten .10 .05
❑ 224 Milt Cuyler .10 .05
❑ 225 Rob Deer .10 .05
❑ 226 John Doherty .10 .05
❑ 227 Cecil Fielder .15 .07
❑ 228 Travis Fryman .15 .07
❑ 229 Mike Henneman .10 .05
❑ 230 John Kiely UER .10 .05
(Card has batting stats of Pat Kelly)
❑ 231 Kurt Knudsen .10 .05
❑ 232 Scott Livingstone .10 .05
❑ 233 Tony Phillips .10 .05
❑ 234 Mickey Tettleton .10 .05
❑ 235 Kevin Appier .15 .07
❑ 236 George Brett .75 .35
❑ 237 Tom Gordon .10 .05
❑ 238 Gregg Jefferies .10 .05
❑ 239 Wally Joyner .15 .07
❑ 240 Kevin Koslofski .10 .05
❑ 241 Mike Macfarlane .10 .05
❑ 242 Brian McRae .10 .05
❑ 243 Rusty Meacham .10 .05
❑ 244 Keith Miller .10 .05
❑ 245 Jeff Montgomery .10 .05
❑ 246 Hipolito Pichardo .10 .05
❑ 247 Ricky Bones .10 .05
❑ 248 Cal Eldred .10 .05
❑ 249 Mike Fetters .10 .05
❑ 250 Darryl Hamilton .10 .05
❑ 251 Doug Henry .10 .05
❑ 252 John Jaha .10 .05
❑ 253 Pat Listach .10 .05
❑ 254 Paul Molitor .40 .18
❑ 255 Jaime Navarro .10 .05
❑ 256 Kevin Seitzer .10 .05
❑ 257 B.J. Surhoff .15 .07
❑ 258 Greg Vaughn .15 .07
❑ 259 Bill Wegman .10 .05
❑ 260 Robin Yount .40 .18
❑ 261 Rick Aguilera .10 .05
❑ 262 Chili Davis .15 .07
❑ 263 Scott Erickson .10 .05
❑ 264 Greg Gagne .10 .05
❑ 265 Mark Guthrie .10 .05
❑ 266 Brian Harper .10 .05
❑ 267 Kent Hrbek .15 .07
❑ 268 Terry Jorgensen .10 .05
❑ 269 Gene Larkin .10 .05
❑ 270 Scott Leius .10 .05
❑ 271 Pat Mahomes .10 .05
❑ 272 Pedro Munoz .10 .05
❑ 273 Kirby Puckett 1.00 .45
❑ 274 Kevin Tapani .10 .05
❑ 275 Carl Willis .10 .05
❑ 276 Steve Farr .10 .05
❑ 277 John Habyan .10 .05
❑ 278 Mel Hall .10 .05
❑ 279 Charlie Hayes .10 .05
❑ 280 Pat Kelly .10 .05
❑ 281 Don Mattingly 1.00 .45
❑ 282 Sam Militello .10 .05
❑ 283 Matt Nokes .10 .05
❑ 284 Melido Perez .10 .05
❑ 285 Andy Stankiewicz .10 .05
❑ 286 Danny Tartabull .10 .05
❑ 287 Randy Velarde .10 .05
❑ 288 Bob Wickman .10 .05
❑ 289 Bernie Williams .40 .18
❑ 290 Lance Blankenship .10 .05
❑ 291 Mike Bordick .10 .05
❑ 292 Jerry Browne .10 .05
❑ 293 Dennis Eckersley .15 .07
❑ 294 Rickey Henderson .75 .35
❑ 295 Vince Horsman .10 .05
❑ 296 Mark McGwire 1.50 .70
❑ 297 Jeff Parrett .10 .05
❑ 298 Ruben Sierra .10 .05
❑ 299 Terry Steinbach .10 .05
❑ 300 Walt Weiss .10 .05
❑ 301 Bob Welch .10 .05
❑ 302 Willie Wilson .10 .05
❑ 303 Bobby Witt .10 .05
❑ 304 Bret Boone .15 .07
❑ 305 Jay Buhner .15 .07
❑ 306 Dave Fleming .10 .05
❑ 307 Ken Griffey Jr. 1.25 .55
❑ 308 Erik Hanson .10 .05
❑ 309 Edgar Martinez .25 .11
❑ 310 Tino Martinez .15 .07
❑ 311 Jeff Nelson .10 .05
❑ 312 Dennis Powell .10 .05
❑ 313 Mike Schooler .10 .05
❑ 314 Russ Swan .10 .05
❑ 315 Dave Valle .10 .05
❑ 316 Omar Vizquel .15 .07
❑ 317 Kevin Brown .15 .07
❑ 318 Todd Burns .10 .05
❑ 319 Jose Canseco .40 .18
❑ 320 Julio Franco .15 .07
❑ 321 Jeff Frye .10 .05
❑ 322 Juan Gonzalez .40 .18
❑ 323 Jose Guzman .10 .05
❑ 324 Jeff Huson .10 .05
❑ 325 Dean Palmer .15 .07
❑ 326 Kevin Reimer .10 .05
❑ 327 Ivan Rodriguez .40 .18
❑ 328 Kenny Rogers .10 .05
❑ 329 Dan Smith .10 .05
❑ 330 Roberto Alomar .40 .18
❑ 331 Derek Bell .10 .05
❑ 332 Pat Borders .10 .05
❑ 333 Joe Carter .15 .07
❑ 334 Kelly Gruber .10 .05
❑ 335 Tom Henke .10 .05
❑ 336 Jimmy Key .15 .07
❑ 337 Manuel Lee .10 .05
❑ 338 Candy Maldonado .10 .05
❑ 339 John Olerud .15 .07
❑ 340 Todd Stottlemyre .10 .05
❑ 341 Duane Ward .10 .05
❑ 342 Devon White .10 .05
❑ 343 Dave Winfield .40 .18
❑ 344 Edgar Martinez LL .15 .07
❑ 345 Cecil Fielder LL .10 .05
❑ 346 Kenny Lofton LL .10 .05
❑ 347 Jack Morris LL .10 .05
❑ 348 Roger Clemens LL .50 .23
❑ 349 Fred McGriff RT .15 .07
❑ 350 Barry Bonds RT .50 .23
❑ 351 Gary Sheffield RT .10 .05
❑ 352 Darren Daulton RT .10 .05
❑ 353 Dave Hollins RT .10 .05
❑ 354 Brothers in Blue .50 .23
Pedro Martinez
Ramon Martinez
❑ 355 Power Packs .25 .11
Ivan Rodriguez
Kirby Puckett
❑ 356 Triple Threats .15 .07
Ryne Sandberg
Gary Sheffield
❑ 357 Infield Trifecta .15 .07
Roberto Alomar
Chuck Knoblauch
Carlos Baerga
❑ 358 Checklist 1-120 .10 .05
❑ 359 Checklist 121-240 .10 .05
❑ 360 Checklist 241-360 .10 .05
❑ 361 Rafael Belliard .10 .05
❑ 362 Damon Berryhill .10 .05
❑ 363 Mike Bielecki .10 .05
❑ 364 Jeff Blauser .10 .05
❑ 365 Francisco Cabrera .10 .05
❑ 366 Marvin Freeman .10 .05
❑ 367 David Justice .15 .07
❑ 368 Mark Lemke .10 .05
❑ 369 Alejandro Pena .10 .05
❑ 370 Jeff Reardon .15 .07
❑ 371 Lonnie Smith .10 .05
❑ 372 Pete Smith .10 .05
❑ 373 Shawn Boskie .10 .05
❑ 374 Jim Bullinger .10 .05
❑ 375 Frank Castillo .10 .05
❑ 376 Doug Dascenzo .10 .05
❑ 377 Andre Dawson .25 .11
❑ 378 Mike Harkey .10 .05
❑ 379 Greg Hibbard .10 .05
❑ 380 Greg Maddux 1.00 .45
❑ 381 Ken Patterson .10 .05
❑ 382 Jeff D. Robinson .10 .05
❑ 383 Luis Salazar .10 .05
❑ 384 Dwight Smith .10 .05
❑ 385 Jose Vizcaino .10 .05
❑ 386 Scott Bankhead .10 .05
❑ 387 Tom Browning .10 .05
❑ 388 Darnell Coles .10 .05
❑ 389 Rob Dibble .10 .05
❑ 390 Bill Doran .10 .05
❑ 391 Dwayne Henry .10 .05
❑ 392 Cesar Hernandez .10 .05
❑ 393 Roberto Kelly .10 .05
❑ 394 Barry Larkin .40 .18
❑ 395 Dave Martinez .10 .05
❑ 396 Kevin Mitchell .10 .05
❑ 397 Jeff Reed .10 .05
❑ 398 Scott Ruskin .10 .05
❑ 399 Greg Swindell .10 .05
❑ 400 Dan Wilson .15 .07
❑ 401 Andy Ashby .10 .05
❑ 402 Freddie Benavides .10 .05
❑ 403 Dante Bichette .15 .07
❑ 404 Willie Blair .10 .05
❑ 405 Denis Boucher .10 .05
❑ 406 Vinny Castilla .15 .07
❑ 407 Braulio Castillo .10 .05
❑ 408 Alex Cole .10 .05
❑ 409 Andres Galarraga .25 .11
❑ 410 Joe Girardi .10 .05
❑ 411 Butch Henry .10 .05
❑ 412 Darren Holmes .10 .05
❑ 413 Calvin Jones .10 .05
❑ 414 Steve Reed RC .10 .05
❑ 415 Kevin Ritz .10 .05
❑ 416 Jim Tatum RC .10 .05
❑ 417 Jack Armstrong .10 .05
❑ 418 Bret Barberie .10 .05
❑ 419 Ryan Bowen .10 .05
❑ 420 Cris Carpenter .10 .05
❑ 421 Chuck Carr .10 .05
❑ 422 Scott Chiamparino .10 .05
❑ 423 Jeff Conine .10 .05
❑ 424 Jim Corsi .10 .05

❑ 425	Steve Decker	.10	.05
❑ 426	Chris Donnels	.10	.05
❑ 427	Monty Fariss	.10	.05
❑ 428	Bob Natal	.10	.05
❑ 429	Pat Rapp	.10	.05
❑ 430	Dave Weathers	.10	.05
❑ 431	Nigel Wilson	.10	.05
❑ 432	Ken Caminiti	.15	.07
❑ 433	Andujar Cedeno	.10	.05
❑ 434	Tom Edens	.10	.05
❑ 435	Juan Guerrero	.10	.05
❑ 436	Pete Incaviglia	.10	.05
❑ 437	Jimmy Jones	.10	.05
❑ 438	Darryl Kile	.15	.07
❑ 439	Rob Murphy	.10	.05
❑ 440	Al Osuna	.10	.05
❑ 441	Mark Portugal	.10	.05
❑ 442	Scott Servais	.10	.05
❑ 443	John Candelaria	.10	.05
❑ 444	Tim Crews	.10	.05
❑ 445	Eric Davis	.15	.07
❑ 446	Tom Goodwin	.10	.05
❑ 447	Jim Gott	.10	.05
❑ 448	Kevin Gross	.10	.05
❑ 449	Dave Hansen	.10	.05
❑ 450	Jay Howell	.10	.05
❑ 451	Roger McDowell	.10	.05
❑ 452	Bob Ojeda	.10	.05
❑ 453	Henry Rodriguez	.10	.05
❑ 454	Darryl Strawberry	.15	.07
❑ 455	Mitch Webster	.10	.05
❑ 456	Steve Wilson	.10	.05
❑ 457	Brian Barnes	.10	.05
❑ 458	Sean Berry	.10	.05
❑ 459	Jeff Fassero	.10	.05
❑ 460	Darrin Fletcher	.10	.05
❑ 461	Marquis Grissom	.10	.05
❑ 462	Dennis Martinez	.15	.07
❑ 463	Spike Owen	.10	.05
❑ 464	Matt Stairs	.10	.05
❑ 465	Sergio Valdez	.10	.05
❑ 466	Kevin Bass	.10	.05
❑ 467	Vince Coleman	.10	.05
❑ 468	Mark Dewey	.10	.05
❑ 469	Kevin Elster	.10	.05
❑ 470	Tony Fernandez	.10	.05
❑ 471	John Franco	.15	.07
❑ 472	Dave Gallagher	.10	.05
❑ 473	Paul Gibson	.10	.05
❑ 474	Dwight Gooden	.15	.07
❑ 475	Lee Guetterman	.10	.05
❑ 476	Jeff Innis	.10	.05
❑ 477	Dave Magadan	.10	.05
❑ 478	Charlie O'Brien	.10	.05
❑ 479	Willie Randolph	.15	.07
❑ 480	Mackey Sasser	.10	.05
❑ 481	Ryan Thompson	.10	.05
❑ 482	Chico Walker	.10	.05
❑ 483	Kyle Abbott	.10	.05
❑ 484	Bob Ayrault	.10	.05
❑ 485	Kim Batiste	.10	.05
❑ 486	Cliff Brantley	.10	.05
❑ 487	Jose DeLeon	.10	.05
❑ 488	Len Dykstra	.15	.07
❑ 489	Tommy Greene	.10	.05
❑ 490	Jeff Grotewold	.10	.05
❑ 491	Dave Hollins	.10	.05
❑ 492	Danny Jackson	.10	.05
❑ 493	Stan Javier	.10	.05
❑ 494	Tom Marsh	.10	.05
❑ 495	Greg Mathews	.10	.05
❑ 496	Dale Murphy	.25	.11
❑ 497	Todd Pratt RC	.15	.07
❑ 498	Mitch Williams	.10	.05
❑ 499	Danny Cox	.10	.05
❑ 500	Doug Drabek	.10	.05
❑ 501	Carlos Garcia	.10	.05
❑ 502	Lloyd McClendon	.10	.05
❑ 503	Denny Neagle	.15	.07
❑ 504	Gary Redus	.10	.05
❑ 505	Bob Walk	.10	.05
❑ 506	John Wehner	.10	.05
❑ 507	Luis Alicea	.10	.05
❑ 508	Mark Clark	.10	.05
❑ 509	Pedro Guerrero	.15	.07
❑ 510	Rex Hudler	.10	.05
❑ 511	Brian Jordan	.15	.07
❑ 512	Omar Olivares	.10	.05
❑ 513	Jose Oquendo	.10	.05
❑ 514	Gerald Perry	.10	.05
❑ 515	Bryn Smith	.10	.05
❑ 516	Craig Wilson	.10	.05
❑ 517	Tracy Woodson	.10	.05
❑ 518	Larry Andersen	.10	.05
❑ 519	Andy Benes	.10	.05
❑ 520	Jim Deshaies	.10	.05
❑ 521	Bruce Hurst	.10	.05
❑ 522	Randy Myers	.10	.05
❑ 523	Benito Santiago	.10	.05
❑ 524	Tim Scott	.10	.05
❑ 525	Tim Teufel	.10	.05
❑ 526	Mike Benjamin	.10	.05
❑ 527	Dave Burba	.10	.05
❑ 528	Craig Colbert	.10	.05
❑ 529	Mike Felder	.10	.05
❑ 530	Bryan Hickerson	.10	.05
❑ 531	Chris James	.10	.05
❑ 532	Mark Leonard	.10	.05
❑ 533	Greg Litton	.10	.05
❑ 534	Francisco Oliveras	.10	.05
❑ 535	John Patterson	.10	.05
❑ 536	Jim Pena	.10	.05
❑ 537	Dave Righetti	.15	.07
❑ 538	Robby Thompson	.10	.05
❑ 539	Jose Uribe	.10	.05
❑ 540	Matt Williams	.25	.11
❑ 541	Storm Davis	.10	.05
❑ 542	Sam Horn	.10	.05
❑ 543	Tim Hulett	.10	.05
❑ 544	Craig Lefferts	.10	.05
❑ 545	Chito Martinez	.10	.05
❑ 546	Mark McLemore	.10	.05
❑ 547	Luis Mercedes	.10	.05
❑ 548	Bob Milacki	.10	.05
❑ 549	Joe Orsulak	.10	.05
❑ 550	Billy Ripken	.10	.05
❑ 551	Cal Ripken Jr.	1.50	.70
❑ 552	Rick Sutcliffe	.15	.07
❑ 553	Jeff Tackett	.10	.05
❑ 554	Wade Boggs	.40	.18
❑ 555	Tom Brunansky	.10	.05
❑ 556	Jack Clark	.15	.07
❑ 557	John Dopson	.10	.05
❑ 558	Mike Gardiner	.10	.05
❑ 559	Mike Greenwell	.10	.05
❑ 560	Greg A. Harris	.10	.05
❑ 561	Billy Hatcher	.10	.05
❑ 562	Joe Hesketh	.10	.05
❑ 563	Tony Pena	.10	.05
❑ 564	Phil Plantier	.10	.05
❑ 565	Luis Rivera	.10	.05
❑ 566	Herm Winningham	.10	.05
❑ 567	Matt Young	.10	.05
❑ 568	Bert Blyleven	.15	.07
❑ 569	Mike Butcher	.10	.05
❑ 570	Chuck Crim	.10	.05
❑ 571	Chad Curtis	.10	.05
❑ 572	Tim Fortugno	.10	.05
❑ 573	Steve Frey	.10	.05
❑ 574	Gary Gaetti	.15	.07
❑ 575	Scott Lewis	.10	.05
❑ 576	Lee Stevens	.10	.05
❑ 577	Ron Tingley	.10	.05
❑ 578	Julio Valera	.10	.05
❑ 579	Shawn Abner	.10	.05
❑ 580	Joey Cora	.10	.05
❑ 581	Chris Cron	.10	.05
❑ 582	Carlton Fisk	.40	.18
❑ 583	Roberto Hernandez	.10	.05
❑ 584	Charlie Hough	.15	.07
❑ 585	Terry Leach	.10	.05
❑ 586	Donn Pall	.10	.05
❑ 587	Dan Pasqua	.10	.05
❑ 588	Steve Sax	.10	.05
❑ 589	Bobby Thigpen	.10	.05
❑ 590	Albert Belle	.15	.07
❑ 591	Felix Fermin	.10	.05
❑ 592	Glenallen Hill	.10	.05
❑ 593	Brook Jacoby	.10	.05
❑ 594	Reggie Jefferson	.10	.05
❑ 595	Carlos Martinez	.10	.05
❑ 596	Jose Mesa	.10	.05
❑ 597	Rod Nichols	.10	.05
❑ 598	Junior Ortiz	.10	.05
❑ 599	Eric Plunk	.10	.05
❑ 600	Ted Power	.10	.05
❑ 601	Scott Scudder	.10	.05
❑ 602	Kevin Wickander	.10	.05
❑ 603	Skeeter Barnes	.10	.05
❑ 604	Mark Carreon	.10	.05
❑ 605	Dan Gladden	.10	.05
❑ 606	Bill Gullickson	.10	.05
❑ 607	Chad Kreuter	.10	.05
❑ 608	Mark Leiter	.10	.05
❑ 609	Mike Munoz	.10	.05
❑ 610	Rich Rowland	.10	.05
❑ 611	Frank Tanana	.10	.05
❑ 612	Walt Terrell	.10	.05
❑ 613	Alan Trammell	.25	.11
❑ 614	Lou Whitaker	.15	.07
❑ 615	Luis Aquino	.10	.05
❑ 616	Mike Boddicker	.10	.05
❑ 617	Jim Eisenreich	.10	.05
❑ 618	Mark Gubicza	.10	.05
❑ 619	David Howard	.10	.05
❑ 620	Mike Magnante	.10	.05
❑ 621	Brent Mayne	.10	.05
❑ 622	Kevin McReynolds	.10	.05
❑ 623	Ed Pierce RC	.10	.05
❑ 624	Bill Sampen	.10	.05
❑ 625	Steve Shifflett	.10	.05
❑ 626	Gary Thurman	.10	.05
❑ 627	Curt Wilkerson	.10	.05
❑ 628	Chris Bosio	.10	.05
❑ 629	Scott Fletcher	.10	.05
❑ 630	Jim Gantner	.10	.05
❑ 631	Dave Nilsson	.10	.05
❑ 632	Jesse Orosco	.10	.05
❑ 633	Dan Plesac	.10	.05
❑ 634	Ron Robinson	.10	.05
❑ 635	Bill Spiers	.10	.05
❑ 636	Franklin Stubbs	.10	.05
❑ 637	Willie Banks	.10	.05
❑ 638	Randy Bush	.10	.05
❑ 639	Chuck Knoblauch	.15	.07
❑ 640	Shane Mack	.10	.05
❑ 641	Mike Pagliarulo	.10	.05
❑ 642	Jeff Reboulet	.10	.05
❑ 643	John Smiley	.10	.05
❑ 644	Mike Trombley	.10	.05
❑ 645	Gary Wayne	.10	.05
❑ 646	Lenny Webster	.10	.05
❑ 647	Tim Burke	.10	.05
❑ 648	Mike Gallego	.10	.05
❑ 649	Dion James	.10	.05
❑ 650	Jeff Johnson	.10	.05
❑ 651	Scott Kamieniecki	.10	.05
❑ 652	Kevin Maas	.10	.05
❑ 653	Rich Monteleone	.10	.05
❑ 654	Jerry Nielsen	.10	.05
❑ 655	Scott Sanderson	.10	.05
❑ 656	Mike Stanley	.10	.05
❑ 657	Gerald Williams	.10	.05
❑ 658	Curt Young	.10	.05
❑ 659	Harold Baines	.15	.07
❑ 660	Kevin Campbell	.10	.05
❑ 661	Ron Darling	.10	.05
❑ 662	Kelly Downs	.10	.05
❑ 663	Eric Fox	.10	.05
❑ 664	Dave Henderson	.10	.05
❑ 665	Rick Honeycutt	.10	.05
❑ 666	Mike Moore	.10	.05
❑ 667	Jamie Quirk	.10	.05
❑ 668	Jeff Russell	.10	.05
❑ 669	Dave Stewart	.15	.07
❑ 670	Greg Briley	.10	.05
❑ 671	Dave Cochrane	.10	.05
❑ 672	Henry Cotto	.10	.05
❑ 673	Rich DeLucia	.10	.05
❑ 674	Brian Fisher	.10	.05
❑ 675	Mark Grant	.10	.05
❑ 676	Randy Johnson	.50	.23
❑ 677	Tim Leary	.10	.05
❑ 678	Pete O'Brien	.10	.05
❑ 679	Lance Parrish	.15	.07
❑ 680	Harold Reynolds	.10	.05
❑ 681	Shane Turner	.10	.05
❑ 682	Jack Daugherty	.10	.05

❑ 683 David Hulse RC	.10	.05
❑ 684 Terry Mathews	.10	.05
❑ 685 Al Newman	.10	.05
❑ 686 Edwin Nunez	.10	.05
❑ 687 Rafael Palmeiro	.40	.18
❑ 688 Roger Pavlik	.10	.05
❑ 689 Geno Petralli	.10	.05
❑ 690 Nolan Ryan	2.00	.90
❑ 691 David Cone	.15	.07
❑ 692 Alfredo Griffin	.10	.05
❑ 693 Juan Guzman	.10	.05
❑ 694 Pat Hentgen	.10	.05
❑ 695 Randy Knorr	.10	.05
❑ 696 Bob MacDonald	.10	.05
❑ 697 Jack Morris	.15	.07
❑ 698 Ed Sprague	.10	.05
❑ 699 Dave Stieb	.10	.05
❑ 700 Pat Tabler	.10	.05
❑ 701 Mike Timlin	.10	.05
❑ 702 David Wells	.15	.07
❑ 703 Eddie Zosky	.10	.05
❑ 704 Gary Sheffield LL	.10	.05
❑ 705 Darren Daulton LL	.10	.05
❑ 706 Marquis Grissom LL	.10	.05
❑ 707 Greg Maddux LL	.50	.23
❑ 708 Bill Swift LL	.10	.05
❑ 709 Juan Gonzalez RT	.15	.07
❑ 710 Mark McGwire RT	.75	.35
❑ 711 Cecil Fielder RT	.10	.05
❑ 712 Albert Belle RT	.15	.07
❑ 713 Joe Carter RT	.10	.05
❑ 714 Cecil Fielder SS Frank Thomas Power Brokers	.25	.11
❑ 715 Larry Walker SS Darren Daulton Unsung Heroes	.25	.11
❑ 716 Edgar Martinez SS Robin Ventura Hot Corner Hammers	.15	.07
❑ 717 Roger Clemens SS Dennis Eckersley Start to Finish	.40	.18
❑ 718 Checklist 361-480	.10	.05
❑ 719 Checklist 481-600	.10	.05
❑ 720 Checklist 601-720	.10	.05

1993 Fleer Final Edition

	MINT	NRMT
COMP.FACT.SET (310)	12.00	5.50
COMPLETE SET (300)	8.00	3.60

❑ 1 Steve Bedrosian	.10	.05
❑ 2 Jay Howell	.10	.05
❑ 3 Greg Maddux	1.00	.45
❑ 4 Greg McMichael RC	.10	.05
❑ 5 Tony Tarasco RC	.10	.05
❑ 6 Jose Bautista	.10	.05
❑ 7 Jose Guzman	.10	.05
❑ 8 Greg Hibbard	.10	.05
❑ 9 Candy Maldonado	.10	.05
❑ 10 Randy Myers	.10	.05
❑ 11 Matt Walbeck RC	.10	.05
❑ 12 Turk Wendell	.10	.05
❑ 13 Willie Wilson	.10	.05
❑ 14 Greg Cadaret	.10	.05
❑ 15 Roberto Kelly	.10	.05
❑ 16 Randy Milligan	.10	.05
❑ 17 Kevin Mitchell	.10	.05
❑ 18 Jeff Reardon	.15	.07
❑ 19 John Roper	.10	.05
❑ 20 John Smiley	.10	.05
❑ 21 Andy Ashby	.10	.05
❑ 22 Dante Bichette	.15	.07
❑ 23 Willie Blair	.10	.05
❑ 24 Pedro Castellano	.10	.05
❑ 25 Vinny Castilla	.15	.07
❑ 26 Jerald Clark	.10	.05
❑ 27 Alex Cole	.10	.05
❑ 28 Scott Fredrickson RC	.10	.05
❑ 29 Jay Gainer RC	.10	.05
❑ 30 Andres Galarraga	.25	.11
❑ 31 Joe Girardi	.10	.05
❑ 32 Ryan Hawblitzel	.10	.05
❑ 33 Charlie Hayes	.10	.05
❑ 34 Darren Holmes	.10	.05
❑ 35 Chris Jones	.10	.05
❑ 36 David Nied	.10	.05
❑ 37 J.Owens RC	.10	.05
❑ 38 Lance Painter RC	.10	.05
❑ 39 Jeff Parrett	.10	.05
❑ 40 Steve Reed	.10	.05
❑ 41 Armando Reynoso	.10	.05
❑ 42 Bruce Ruffin	.10	.05
❑ 43 Danny Sheaffer RC	.10	.05
❑ 44 Keith Shepherd	.10	.05
❑ 45 Jim Tatum	.10	.05
❑ 46 Gary Wayne	.10	.05
❑ 47 Eric Young	.10	.05
❑ 48 Luis Aquino	.10	.05
❑ 49 Alex Arias	.10	.05
❑ 50 Jack Armstrong	.10	.05
❑ 51 Bret Barberie	.10	.05
❑ 52 Geronimo Berroa	.10	.05
❑ 53 Ryan Bowen	.10	.05
❑ 54 Greg Briley	.10	.05
❑ 55 Cris Carpenter	.10	.05
❑ 56 Chuck Carr	.10	.05
❑ 57 Jeff Conine	.10	.05
❑ 58 Jim Corsi	.10	.05
❑ 59 Orestes Destrade	.10	.05
❑ 60 Junior Felix	.10	.05
❑ 61 Chris Hammond	.10	.05
❑ 62 Bryan Harvey	.10	.05
❑ 63 Charlie Hough	.15	.07
❑ 64 Joe Klink	.10	.05
❑ 65 Richie Lewis RC UER (Refers to place of birth and residence as Illinois instead of Indiana)	.10	.05
❑ 66 Mitch Lyden RC	.10	.05
❑ 67 Bob Natal	.10	.05
❑ 68 Scott Pose RC	.10	.05
❑ 69 Rich Renteria	.10	.05
❑ 70 Benito Santiago	.10	.05
❑ 71 Gary Sheffield	.15	.07
❑ 72 Matt Turner RC	.10	.05
❑ 73 Walt Weiss	.10	.05
❑ 74 Darrell Whitmore RC	.10	.05
❑ 75 Nigel Wilson	.10	.05
❑ 76 Kevin Bass	.10	.05
❑ 77 Doug Drabek	.10	.05
❑ 78 Tom Edens	.10	.05
❑ 79 Chris James	.10	.05
❑ 80 Greg Swindell	.10	.05
❑ 81 Omar Daal RC	.50	.23
❑ 82 Raul Mondesi	.15	.07
❑ 83 Jody Reed	.10	.05
❑ 84 Cory Snyder	.10	.05
❑ 85 Rick Trlicek	.10	.05
❑ 86 Tim Wallach	.10	.05
❑ 87 Todd Worrell	.10	.05
❑ 88 Tavo Alvarez	.10	.05
❑ 89 Frank Bolick	.10	.05
❑ 90 Kent Bottenfield	.10	.05
❑ 91 Greg Colbrunn	.10	.05
❑ 92 Cliff Floyd	.15	.07
❑ 93 Lou Frazier RC	.10	.05
❑ 94 Mike Gardiner	.10	.05
❑ 95 Mike Lansing RC	.15	.07
❑ 96 Bill Risley	.10	.05
❑ 97 Jeff Shaw	.10	.05
❑ 98 Kevin Baez	.10	.05
❑ 99 Tim Bogar RC	.10	.05
❑ 100 Jeromy Burnitz	.15	.07
❑ 101 Mike Draper	.10	.05
❑ 102 Darrin Jackson	.10	.05
❑ 103 Mike Maddux	.10	.05
❑ 104 Joe Orsulak	.10	.05
❑ 105 Doug Saunders RC	.10	.05
❑ 106 Frank Tanana	.10	.05
❑ 107 Dave Telgheder RC	.10	.05
❑ 108 Larry Andersen	.10	.05
❑ 109 Jim Eisenreich	.10	.05
❑ 110 Pete Incaviglia	.10	.05
❑ 111 Danny Jackson	.10	.05
❑ 112 David West	.10	.05
❑ 113 Al Martin	.10	.05
❑ 114 Blas Minor	.10	.05
❑ 115 Dennis Moeller	.10	.05
❑ 116 William Pennyfeather	.10	.05
❑ 117 Rich Robertson RC	.10	.05
❑ 118 Ben Shelton	.10	.05
❑ 119 Lonnie Smith	.10	.05
❑ 120 Freddie Toliver	.10	.05
❑ 121 Paul Wagner	.10	.05
❑ 122 Kevin Young	.15	.07
❑ 123 Rene Arocha RC	.15	.07
❑ 124 Gregg Jefferies	.10	.05
❑ 125 Paul Kilgus	.10	.05
❑ 126 Les Lancaster	.10	.05
❑ 127 Joe Magrane	.10	.05
❑ 128 Rob Murphy	.10	.05
❑ 129 Erik Pappas	.10	.05
❑ 130 Stan Royer	.10	.05
❑ 131 Ozzie Smith	.50	.23
❑ 132 Tom Urbani RC	.10	.05
❑ 133 Mark Whiten	.10	.05
❑ 134 Derek Bell	.10	.05
❑ 135 Doug Brocail	.10	.05
❑ 136 Phil Clark	.10	.05
❑ 137 Mark Ettles RC	.10	.05
❑ 138 Jeff Gardner	.10	.05
❑ 139 Pat Gomez RC	.10	.05
❑ 140 Ricky Gutierrez	.10	.05
❑ 141 Gene Harris	.10	.05
❑ 142 Kevin Higgins	.10	.05
❑ 143 Trevor Hoffman	.15	.07
❑ 144 Phil Plantier	.10	.05
❑ 145 Kerry Taylor RC	.10	.05
❑ 146 Guillermo Velasquez	.10	.05
❑ 147 Wally Whitehurst	.10	.05
❑ 148 Tim Worrell RC	.10	.05
❑ 149 Todd Benzinger	.10	.05
❑ 150 Barry Bonds	1.00	.45
❑ 151 Greg Brummett RC	.10	.05
❑ 152 Mark Carreon	.10	.05
❑ 153 Dave Martinez	.10	.05
❑ 154 Jeff Reed	.10	.05
❑ 155 Kevin Rogers	.10	.05
❑ 156 Harold Baines	.15	.07
❑ 157 Damon Buford	.10	.05
❑ 158 Paul Carey RC	.10	.05
❑ 159 Jeffrey Hammonds	.15	.07
❑ 160 Jamie Moyer	.10	.05
❑ 161 Sherman Obando RC	.10	.05
❑ 162 John O'Donoghue RC	.10	.05
❑ 163 Brad Pennington	.10	.05
❑ 164 Jim Poole	.10	.05
❑ 165 Harold Reynolds	.10	.05
❑ 166 Fernando Valenzuela	.15	.07
❑ 167 Jack Voigt RC	.10	.05
❑ 168 Mark Williamson	.10	.05
❑ 169 Scott Bankhead	.10	.05
❑ 170 Greg Blosser	.10	.05
❑ 171 Jim Byrd RC	.10	.05
❑ 172 Ivan Calderon	.10	.05
❑ 173 Andre Dawson	.25	.11
❑ 174 Scott Fletcher	.10	.05
❑ 175 Jose Melendez	.10	.05
❑ 176 Carlos Quintana	.10	.05
❑ 177 Jeff Russell	.10	.05
❑ 178 Aaron Sele	.15	.07
❑ 179 Rod Correia RC	.10	.05
❑ 180 Chili Davis	.15	.07
❑ 181 Jim Edmonds RC	4.00	1.80
❑ 182 Rene Gonzales	.10	.05
❑ 183 Hilly Hathaway RC	.10	.05
❑ 184 Torey Lovullo	.10	.05

❑ 185 Greg Myers	.10	.05
❑ 186 Gene Nelson	.10	.05
❑ 187 Troy Percival	.15	.07
❑ 188 Scott Sanderson	.10	.05
❑ 189 Darryl Scott RC	.10	.05
❑ 190 J.T. Snow RC	.75	.35
❑ 191 Russ Springer	.10	.05
❑ 192 Jason Bere	.10	.05
❑ 193 Rodney Bolton	.10	.05
❑ 194 Ellis Burks	.15	.07
❑ 195 Bo Jackson	.15	.07
❑ 196 Mike LaValliere	.10	.05
❑ 197 Scott Ruffcorn	.10	.05
❑ 198 Jeff Schwartz	.10	.05
❑ 199 Jerry DiPoto	.10	.05
❑ 200 Alvaro Espinoza	.10	.05
❑ 201 Wayne Kirby	.10	.05
❑ 202 Tom Kramer RC	.10	.05
❑ 203 Jesse Levis	.10	.05
❑ 204 Manny Ramirez	.75	.35
❑ 205 Jeff Treadway	.10	.05
❑ 206 Bill Wertz RC	.10	.05
❑ 207 Cliff Young	.10	.05
❑ 208 Matt Young	.10	.05
❑ 209 Kirk Gibson	.15	.07
❑ 210 Greg Gohr	.10	.05
❑ 211 Bill Krueger	.10	.05
❑ 212 Bob MacDonald	.10	.05
❑ 213 Mike Moore	.10	.05
❑ 214 David Wells	.15	.07
❑ 215 Billy Brewer	.10	.05
❑ 216 David Cone	.15	.07
❑ 217 Greg Gagne	.10	.05
❑ 218 Mark Gardner	.10	.05
❑ 219 Chris Haney	.10	.05
❑ 220 Phil Hiatt	.10	.05
❑ 221 Jose Lind	.10	.05
❑ 222 Juan Bell	.10	.05
❑ 223 Tom Brunansky	.10	.05
❑ 224 Mike Ignasiak	.10	.05
❑ 225 Joe Kmak	.10	.05
❑ 226 Tom Lampkin	.10	.05
❑ 227 Graeme Lloyd RC	.15	.07
❑ 228 Carlos Maldonado	.10	.05
❑ 229 Matt Mieske	.10	.05
❑ 230 Angel Miranda	.10	.05
❑ 231 Troy O'Leary RC	.40	.18
❑ 232 Kevin Reimer	.10	.05
❑ 233 Larry Casian	.10	.05
❑ 234 Jim Deshaies	.10	.05
❑ 235 Eddie Guardado RC	.10	.05
❑ 236 Chip Hale	.10	.05
❑ 237 Mike Maksudian RC	.10	.05
❑ 238 David McCarty	.10	.05
❑ 239 Pat Meares RC	.15	.07
❑ 240 George Tsamis RC	.10	.05
❑ 241 Dave Winfield	.40	.18
❑ 242 Jim Abbott	.15	.07
❑ 243 Wade Boggs	.40	.18
❑ 244 Andy Cook RC	.10	.05
❑ 245 Russ Davis RC	.15	.07
❑ 246 Mike Humphreys	.10	.05
❑ 247 Jimmy Key	.15	.07
❑ 248 Jim Leyritz	.10	.05
❑ 249 Bobby Munoz	.10	.05
❑ 250 Paul O'Neill	.40	.18
❑ 251 Spike Owen	.10	.05
❑ 252 Dave Silvestri	.10	.05
❑ 253 Marcos Armas RC	.10	.05
❑ 254 Brent Gates	.10	.05
❑ 255 Rich Gossage	.15	.07
❑ 256 Scott Lydy RC	.10	.05
❑ 257 Henry Mercedes	.10	.05
❑ 258 Mike Mohler RC	.10	.05
❑ 259 Troy Neel	.10	.05
❑ 260 Edwin Nunez	.10	.05
❑ 261 Craig Paquette	.10	.05
❑ 262 Kevin Seitzer	.10	.05
❑ 263 Rich Amaral	.10	.05
❑ 264 Mike Blowers	.10	.05
❑ 265 Chris Bosio	.10	.05
❑ 266 Norm Charlton	.10	.05
❑ 267 Jim Converse RC	.10	.05
❑ 268 John Cummings RC	.10	.05
❑ 269 Mike Felder	.10	.05
❑ 270 Mike Hampton	.40	.18
❑ 271 Bill Haselman	.10	.05
❑ 272 Dwayne Henry	.10	.05
❑ 273 Greg Litton	.10	.05
❑ 274 Mackey Sasser	.10	.05
❑ 275 Lee Tinsley	.10	.05
❑ 276 David Wainhouse	.10	.05
❑ 277 Jeff Bronkey	.10	.05
❑ 278 Benji Gil	.10	.05
❑ 279 Tom Henke	.10	.05
❑ 280 Charlie Leibrandt	.10	.05
❑ 281 Robb Nen	.10	.05
❑ 282 Bill Ripken	.10	.05
❑ 283 Jon Shave RC	.10	.05
❑ 284 Doug Strange	.10	.05
❑ 285 Matt Whiteside RC	.10	.05
❑ 286 Scott Brow RC	.10	.05
❑ 287 Willie Canate RC	.10	.05
❑ 288 Tony Castillo	.10	.05
❑ 289 Domingo Cedeno RC	.10	.05
❑ 290 Darnell Coles	.10	.05
❑ 291 Danny Cox	.10	.05
❑ 292 Mark Eichhorn	.10	.05
❑ 293 Tony Fernandez	.10	.05
❑ 294 Al Leiter	.15	.07
❑ 295 Paul Molitor	.40	.18
❑ 296 Dave Stewart	.15	.07
❑ 297 Woody Williams RC	.15	.07
❑ 298 Checklist F1-F100	.10	.05
❑ 299 Checklist F101-F200	.10	.05
❑ 300 Checklist F201-F300	.10	.05

1994 Fleer

	MINT	NRMT
COMPLETE SET (720)	40.00	18.00
❑ 1 Brady Anderson	.25	.11
❑ 2 Harold Baines	.25	.11
❑ 3 Mike Devereaux	.15	.07
❑ 4 Todd Frohwirth	.15	.07
❑ 5 Jeffrey Hammonds	.25	.11
❑ 6 Chris Hoiles	.15	.07
❑ 7 Tim Hulett	.15	.07
❑ 8 Ben McDonald	.15	.07
❑ 9 Mark McLemore	.15	.07
❑ 10 Alan Mills	.15	.07
❑ 11 Jamie Moyer	.15	.07
❑ 12 Mike Mussina	.60	.25
❑ 13 Gregg Olson	.15	.07
❑ 14 Mike Pagliarulo	.15	.07
❑ 15 Brad Pennington	.15	.07
❑ 16 Jim Poole	.15	.07
❑ 17 Harold Reynolds	.15	.07
❑ 18 Arthur Rhodes	.15	.07
❑ 19 Cal Ripken Jr.	2.50	1.10
❑ 20 David Segui	.15	.07
❑ 21 Rick Sutcliffe	.25	.11
❑ 22 Fernando Valenzuela	.25	.11
❑ 23 Jack Voigt	.15	.07
❑ 24 Mark Williamson	.15	.07
❑ 25 Scott Bankhead	.15	.07
❑ 26 Roger Clemens	1.50	.70
❑ 27 Scott Cooper	.15	.07
❑ 28 Danny Darwin	.15	.07
❑ 29 Andre Dawson	.40	.18
❑ 30 Rob Deer	.15	.07
❑ 31 John Dopson	.15	.07
❑ 32 Scott Fletcher	.15	.07
❑ 33 Mike Greenwell	.15	.07
❑ 34 Greg A. Harris	.15	.07
❑ 35 Billy Hatcher	.15	.07
❑ 36 Bob Melvin	.15	.07
❑ 37 Tony Pena	.15	.07
❑ 38 Paul Quantrill	.15	.07
❑ 39 Carlos Quintana	.15	.07
❑ 40 Ernest Riles	.15	.07
❑ 41 Jeff Russell	.15	.07
❑ 42 Ken Ryan	.15	.07
❑ 43 Aaron Sele	.25	.11
❑ 44 John Valentin	.15	.07
❑ 45 Mo Vaughn	.25	.11
❑ 46 Frank Viola	.25	.11
❑ 47 Bob Zupcic	.15	.07
❑ 48 Mike Butcher	.15	.07
❑ 49 Rod Correia	.15	.07
❑ 50 Chad Curtis	.15	.07
❑ 51 Chili Davis	.25	.11
❑ 52 Gary DiSarcina	.15	.07
❑ 53 Damion Easley	.15	.07
❑ 54 Jim Edmonds	.60	.25
❑ 55 Chuck Finley	.25	.11
❑ 56 Steve Frey	.15	.07
❑ 57 Rene Gonzales	.15	.07
❑ 58 Joe Grahe	.15	.07
❑ 59 Hilly Hathaway	.15	.07
❑ 60 Stan Javier	.15	.07
❑ 61 Mark Langston	.15	.07
❑ 62 Phil Leftwich RC	.15	.07
❑ 63 Torey Lovullo	.15	.07
❑ 64 Joe Magrane	.15	.07
❑ 65 Greg Myers	.15	.07
❑ 66 Ken Patterson	.15	.07
❑ 67 Eduardo Perez	.15	.07
❑ 68 Luis Polonia	.15	.07
❑ 69 Tim Salmon	.25	.11
❑ 70 J.T. Snow	.25	.11
❑ 71 Ron Tingley	.15	.07
❑ 72 Julio Valera	.15	.07
❑ 73 Wilson Alvarez	.15	.07
❑ 74 Tim Belcher	.15	.07
❑ 75 George Bell	.15	.07
❑ 76 Jason Bere	.15	.07
❑ 77 Rod Bolton	.15	.07
❑ 78 Ellis Burks	.25	.11
❑ 79 Joey Cora	.15	.07
❑ 80 Alex Fernandez	.15	.07
❑ 81 Craig Grebeck	.15	.07
❑ 82 Ozzie Guillen	.15	.07
❑ 83 Roberto Hernandez	.15	.07
❑ 84 Bo Jackson	.25	.11
❑ 85 Lance Johnson	.15	.07
❑ 86 Ron Karkovice	.15	.07
❑ 87 Mike LaValliere	.15	.07
❑ 88 Kirk McCaskill	.15	.07
❑ 89 Jack McDowell	.15	.07
❑ 90 Warren Newson	.15	.07
❑ 91 Dan Pasqua	.15	.07
❑ 92 Scott Radinsky	.15	.07
❑ 93 Tim Raines	.25	.11
❑ 94 Steve Sax	.15	.07
❑ 95 Jeff Schwarz	.15	.07
❑ 96 Frank Thomas	.75	.35
❑ 97 Robin Ventura	.25	.11
❑ 98 Sandy Alomar Jr.	.25	.11
❑ 99 Carlos Baerga	.15	.07
❑ 100 Albert Belle	.25	.11
❑ 101 Mark Clark	.15	.07
❑ 102 Jerry DiPoto	.15	.07
❑ 103 Alvaro Espinoza	.15	.07
❑ 104 Felix Fermin	.15	.07
❑ 105 Jeremy Hernandez	.15	.07
❑ 106 Reggie Jefferson	.15	.07
❑ 107 Wayne Kirby	.15	.07
❑ 108 Tom Kramer	.15	.07
❑ 109 Mark Lewis	.15	.07
❑ 110 Derek Lilliquist	.15	.07
❑ 111 Kenny Lofton	.25	.11
❑ 112 Candy Maldonado	.15	.07
❑ 113 Jose Mesa	.15	.07
❑ 114 Jeff Mutis	.15	.07
❑ 115 Charles Nagy	.15	.07
❑ 116 Bob Ojeda	.15	.07
❑ 117 Junior Ortiz	.15	.07
❑ 118 Eric Plunk	.15	.07

❑ 119 Manny Ramirez 1.00 .45
❑ 120 Paul Sorrento .15 .07
❑ 121 Jim Thome .60 .25
❑ 122 Jeff Treadway .15 .07
❑ 123 Bill Wertz .15 .07
❑ 124 Skeeter Barnes .15 .07
❑ 125 Milt Cuyler .15 .07
❑ 126 Eric Davis .25 .11
❑ 127 John Doherty .15 .07
❑ 128 Cecil Fielder .25 .11
❑ 129 Travis Fryman .25 .11
❑ 130 Kirk Gibson .25 .11
❑ 131 Dan Gladden .15 .07
❑ 132 Greg Gohr .15 .07
❑ 133 Chris Gomez .15 .07
❑ 134 Bill Gullickson .15 .07
❑ 135 Mike Henneman .15 .07
❑ 136 Kurt Knudsen .15 .07
❑ 137 Chad Kreuter .15 .07
❑ 138 Bill Krueger .15 .07
❑ 139 Scott Livingstone .15 .07
❑ 140 Bob MacDonald .15 .07
❑ 141 Mike Moore .15 .07
❑ 142 Tony Phillips .15 .07
❑ 143 Mickey Tettleton .15 .07
❑ 144 Alan Trammell .40 .18
❑ 145 David Wells .25 .11
❑ 146 Lou Whitaker .25 .11
❑ 147 Kevin Appier .25 .11
❑ 148 Stan Belinda .15 .07
❑ 149 George Brett 1.25 .55
❑ 150 Billy Brewer .15 .07
❑ 151 Hubie Brooks .15 .07
❑ 152 David Cone .25 .11
❑ 153 Gary Gaetti .25 .11
❑ 154 Greg Gagne .15 .07
❑ 155 Tom Gordon .15 .07
❑ 156 Mark Gubicza .15 .07
❑ 157 Chris Gwynn .15 .07
❑ 158 John Habyan .15 .07
❑ 159 Chris Haney .15 .07
❑ 160 Phil Hiatt .15 .07
❑ 161 Felix Jose .15 .07
❑ 162 Wally Joyner .25 .11
❑ 163 Jose Lind .15 .07
❑ 164 Mike Macfarlane .15 .07
❑ 165 Mike Magnante .15 .07
❑ 166 Brent Mayne .15 .07
❑ 167 Brian McRae .15 .07
❑ 168 Kevin McReynolds .15 .07
❑ 169 Keith Miller .15 .07
❑ 170 Jeff Montgomery .15 .07
❑ 171 Hipolito Pichardo .15 .07
❑ 172 Rico Rossy .15 .07
❑ 173 Juan Bell .15 .07
❑ 174 Ricky Bones .15 .07
❑ 175 Cal Eldred .15 .07
❑ 176 Mike Fetters .15 .07
❑ 177 Darryl Hamilton .15 .07
❑ 178 Doug Henry .15 .07
❑ 179 Mike Ignasiak .15 .07
❑ 180 John Jaha .15 .07
❑ 181 Pat Listach .15 .07
❑ 182 Graeme Lloyd .15 .07
❑ 183 Matt Mieske .15 .07
❑ 184 Angel Miranda .15 .07
❑ 185 Jaime Navarro .15 .07
❑ 186 Dave Nilsson .15 .07
❑ 187 Troy O'Leary .15 .07
❑ 188 Jesse Orosco .15 .07
❑ 189 Kevin Reimer .15 .07
❑ 190 Kevin Seitzer .15 .07
❑ 191 Bill Spiers .15 .07
❑ 192 B.J. Surhoff .25 .11
❑ 193 Dickie Thon .15 .07
❑ 194 Jose Valentin .15 .07
❑ 195 Greg Vaughn .25 .11
❑ 196 Bill Wegman .15 .07
❑ 197 Robin Yount .60 .25
❑ 198 Rick Aguilera .15 .07
❑ 199 Willie Banks .15 .07
❑ 200 Bernardo Brito .15 .07
❑ 201 Larry Casian .15 .07
❑ 202 Scott Erickson .15 .07
❑ 203 Eddie Guardado .15 .07
❑ 204 Mark Guthrie .15 .07
❑ 205 Chip Hale .15 .07
❑ 206 Brian Harper .15 .07
❑ 207 Mike Hartley .15 .07
❑ 208 Kent Hrbek .25 .11
❑ 209 Terry Jorgensen .15 .07
❑ 210 Chuck Knoblauch .25 .11
❑ 211 Gene Larkin .15 .07
❑ 212 Shane Mack .15 .07
❑ 213 David McCarty .15 .07
❑ 214 Pat Meares .15 .07
❑ 215 Pedro Munoz .15 .07
❑ 216 Derek Parks .15 .07
❑ 217 Kirby Puckett 1.50 .70
❑ 218 Jeff Reboulet .15 .07
❑ 219 Kevin Tapani .15 .07
❑ 220 Mike Trombley .15 .07
❑ 221 George Tsamis .15 .07
❑ 222 Carl Willis .15 .07
❑ 223 Dave Winfield .60 .25
❑ 224 Jim Abbott .25 .11
❑ 225 Paul Assenmacher .15 .07
❑ 226 Wade Boggs .60 .25
❑ 227 Russ Davis .15 .07
❑ 228 Steve Farr .15 .07
❑ 229 Mike Gallego .15 .07
❑ 230 Paul Gibson .15 .07
❑ 231 Steve Howe .15 .07
❑ 232 Dion James .15 .07
❑ 233 Domingo Jean .15 .07
❑ 234 Scott Kamieniecki .15 .07
❑ 235 Pat Kelly .15 .07
❑ 236 Jimmy Key .25 .11
❑ 237 Jim Leyritz .15 .07
❑ 238 Kevin Maas .15 .07
❑ 239 Don Mattingly 1.50 .70
❑ 240 Rich Monteleone .15 .07
❑ 241 Bobby Munoz .15 .07
❑ 242 Matt Nokes .15 .07
❑ 243 Paul O'Neill .60 .25
❑ 244 Spike Owen .15 .07
❑ 245 Melido Perez .15 .07
❑ 246 Lee Smith .25 .11
❑ 247 Mike Stanley .15 .07
❑ 248 Danny Tartabull .15 .07
❑ 249 Randy Velarde .15 .07
❑ 250 Bob Wickman .15 .07
❑ 251 Bernie Williams .60 .25
❑ 252 Mike Aldrete .15 .07
❑ 253 Marcos Armas .15 .07
❑ 254 Lance Blankenship .15 .07
❑ 255 Mike Bordick .15 .07
❑ 256 Scott Brosius .25 .11
❑ 257 Jerry Browne .15 .07
❑ 258 Ron Darling .15 .07
❑ 259 Kelly Downs .15 .07
❑ 260 Dennis Eckersley .25 .11
❑ 261 Brent Gates .15 .07
❑ 262 Rich Gossage .25 .11
❑ 263 Scott Hemond .15 .07
❑ 264 Dave Henderson .15 .07
❑ 265 Rick Honeycutt .15 .07
❑ 266 Vince Horsman .15 .07
❑ 267 Scott Lydy .15 .07
❑ 268 Mark McGwire 2.50 1.10
❑ 269 Mike Mohler .15 .07
❑ 270 Troy Neel .15 .07
❑ 271 Edwin Nunez .15 .07
❑ 272 Craig Paquette .15 .07
❑ 273 Ruben Sierra .15 .07
❑ 274 Terry Steinbach .15 .07
❑ 275 Todd Van Poppel .15 .07
❑ 276 Bob Welch .15 .07
❑ 277 Bobby Witt .15 .07
❑ 278 Rich Amaral .15 .07
❑ 279 Mike Blowers .15 .07
❑ 280 Bret Boone UER .25 .11
(Name spelled Brett on front)
❑ 281 Chris Bosio .15 .07
❑ 282 Jay Buhner .25 .11
❑ 283 Norm Charlton .15 .07
❑ 284 Mike Felder .15 .07
❑ 285 Dave Fleming .15 .07
❑ 286 Ken Griffey Jr. 2.00 .90
❑ 287 Erik Hanson .15 .07
❑ 288 Bill Haselman .15 .07
❑ 289 Brad Holman RC .15 .07
❑ 290 Randy Johnson .75 .35
❑ 291 Tim Leary .15 .07
❑ 292 Greg Litton .15 .07
❑ 293 Dave Magadan .15 .07
❑ 294 Edgar Martinez .40 .18
❑ 295 Tino Martinez .25 .11
❑ 296 Jeff Nelson .15 .07
❑ 297 Erik Plantenberg RC .15 .07
❑ 298 Mackey Sasser .15 .07
❑ 299 Brian Turang RC .15 .07
❑ 300 Dave Valle .15 .07
❑ 301 Omar Vizquel .25 .11
❑ 302 Brian Bohanon .15 .07
❑ 303 Kevin Brown .25 .11
❑ 304 Jose Canseco UER .60 .25
(Back mentions 1991 as his 40/40 MVP season; should be '88)
❑ 305 Mario Diaz .15 .07
❑ 306 Julio Franco .25 .11
❑ 307 Juan Gonzalez .60 .25
❑ 308 Tom Henke .15 .07
❑ 309 David Hulse .15 .07
❑ 310 Manuel Lee .15 .07
❑ 311 Craig Lefferts .15 .07
❑ 312 Charlie Leibrandt .15 .07
❑ 313 Rafael Palmeiro .60 .25
❑ 314 Dean Palmer .25 .11
❑ 315 Roger Pavlik .15 .07
❑ 316 Dan Peltier .15 .07
❑ 317 Gene Petralli .15 .07
❑ 318 Gary Redus .15 .07
❑ 319 Ivan Rodriguez .60 .25
❑ 320 Kenny Rogers .15 .07
❑ 321 Nolan Ryan 3.00 1.35
❑ 322 Doug Strange .15 .07
❑ 323 Matt Whiteside .15 .07
❑ 324 Roberto Alomar .60 .25
❑ 325 Pat Borders .15 .07
❑ 326 Joe Carter .25 .11
❑ 327 Tony Castillo .15 .07
❑ 328 Darnell Coles .15 .07
❑ 329 Danny Cox .15 .07
❑ 330 Mark Eichhorn .15 .07
❑ 331 Tony Fernandez .15 .07
❑ 332 Alfredo Griffin .15 .07
❑ 333 Juan Guzman .15 .07
❑ 334 Rickey Henderson 1.25 .55
❑ 335 Pat Hentgen .15 .07
❑ 336 Randy Knorr .15 .07
❑ 337 Al Leiter .25 .11
❑ 338 Paul Molitor .60 .25
❑ 339 Jack Morris .25 .11
❑ 340 John Olerud .25 .11
❑ 341 Dick Schofield .15 .07
❑ 342 Ed Sprague .15 .07
❑ 343 Dave Stewart .25 .11
❑ 344 Todd Stottlemyre .15 .07
❑ 345 Mike Timlin .15 .07
❑ 346 Duane Ward .15 .07
❑ 347 Turner Ward .15 .07
❑ 348 Devon White .15 .07
❑ 349 Woody Williams .15 .07
❑ 350 Steve Avery .15 .07
❑ 351 Steve Bedrosian .15 .07
❑ 352 Rafael Belliard .15 .07
❑ 353 Damon Berryhill .15 .07
❑ 354 Jeff Blauser .15 .07
❑ 355 Sid Bream .15 .07
❑ 356 Francisco Cabrera .15 .07
❑ 357 Marvin Freeman .15 .07
❑ 358 Ron Gant .15 .07
❑ 359 Tom Glavine .60 .25
❑ 360 Jay Howell .15 .07
❑ 361 David Justice .25 .11
❑ 362 Ryan Klesko .25 .11
❑ 363 Mark Lemke .15 .07
❑ 364 Javier Lopez .25 .11
❑ 365 Greg Maddux 1.50 .70
❑ 366 Fred McGriff .40 .18
❑ 367 Greg McMichael .15 .07
❑ 368 Kent Mercker .15 .07
❑ 369 Otis Nixon .15 .07
❑ 370 Greg Olson .15 .07
❑ 371 Bill Pecota .15 .07
❑ 372 Terry Pendleton .25 .11
❑ 373 Deion Sanders .25 .11

❑ 374 Pete Smith .15 .07
❑ 375 John Smoltz .25 .11
❑ 376 Mike Stanton .15 .07
❑ 377 Tony Tarasco .15 .07
❑ 378 Mark Wohlers .15 .07
❑ 379 Jose Bautista .15 .07
❑ 380 Shawn Boskie .15 .07
❑ 381 Steve Buechele .15 .07
❑ 382 Frank Castillo .15 .07
❑ 383 Mark Grace .60 .25
❑ 384 Jose Guzman .15 .07
❑ 385 Mike Harkey .15 .07
❑ 386 Greg Hibbard .15 .07
❑ 387 Glenallen Hill .15 .07
❑ 388 Steve Lake .15 .07
❑ 389 Derrick May .15 .07
❑ 390 Chuck McElroy .15 .07
❑ 391 Mike Morgan .15 .07
❑ 392 Randy Myers .15 .07
❑ 393 Dan Plesac .15 .07
❑ 394 Kevin Roberson .15 .07
❑ 395 Rey Sanchez .15 .07
❑ 396 Ryne Sandberg .75 .35
❑ 397 Bob Scanlan .15 .07
❑ 398 Dwight Smith .15 .07
❑ 399 Sammy Sosa 1.25 .55
❑ 400 Jose Vizcaino .15 .07
❑ 401 Rick Wilkins .15 .07
❑ 402 Willie Wilson .15 .07
❑ 403 Eric Yelding .15 .07
❑ 404 Bobby Ayala .15 .07
❑ 405 Jeff Branson .15 .07
❑ 406 Tom Browning .15 .07
❑ 407 Jacob Brumfield .15 .07
❑ 408 Tim Costo .15 .07
❑ 409 Rob Dibble .15 .07
❑ 410 Willie Greene .15 .07
❑ 411 Thomas Howard .15 .07
❑ 412 Roberto Kelly .15 .07
❑ 413 Bill Landrum .15 .07
❑ 414 Barry Larkin .60 .25
❑ 415 Larry Luebbers RC .15 .07
❑ 416 Kevin Mitchell .15 .07
❑ 417 Hal Morris .15 .07
❑ 418 Joe Oliver .15 .07
❑ 419 Tim Pugh .15 .07
❑ 420 Jeff Reardon .25 .11
❑ 421 Jose Rijo .15 .07
❑ 422 Bip Roberts .15 .07
❑ 423 John Roper .15 .07
❑ 424 Johnny Ruffin .15 .07
❑ 425 Chris Sabo .15 .07
❑ 426 Juan Samuel .15 .07
❑ 427 Reggie Sanders .15 .07
❑ 428 Scott Service .15 .07
❑ 429 John Smiley .15 .07
❑ 430 Jerry Spradlin RC .15 .07
❑ 431 Kevin Wickander .15 .07
❑ 432 Freddie Benavides .15 .07
❑ 433 Dante Bichette .25 .11
❑ 434 Willie Blair .15 .07
❑ 435 Daryl Boston .15 .07
❑ 436 Kent Bottenfield .15 .07
❑ 437 Vinny Castilla .25 .11
❑ 438 Jerald Clark .15 .07
❑ 439 Alex Cole .15 .07
❑ 440 Andres Galarraga .40 .18
❑ 441 Joe Girardi .15 .07
❑ 442 Greg W. Harris .15 .07
❑ 443 Charlie Hayes .15 .07
❑ 444 Darren Holmes .15 .07
❑ 445 Chris Jones .15 .07
❑ 446 Roberto Mejia .15 .07
❑ 447 David Nied .15 .07
❑ 448 J. Owens .15 .07
❑ 449 Jeff Parrett .15 .07
❑ 450 Steve Reed .15 .07
❑ 451 Armando Reynoso .15 .07
❑ 452 Bruce Ruffin .15 .07
❑ 453 Mo Sanford .15 .07
❑ 454 Danny Sheaffer .15 .07
❑ 455 Jim Tatum .15 .07
❑ 456 Gary Wayne .15 .07
❑ 457 Eric Young .15 .07
❑ 458 Luis Aquino .15 .07
❑ 459 Alex Arias .15 .07
❑ 460 Jack Armstrong .15 .07
❑ 461 Bret Barberie .15 .07
❑ 462 Ryan Bowen .15 .07
❑ 463 Chuck Carr .15 .07
❑ 464 Jeff Conine .15 .07
❑ 465 Henry Cotto .15 .07
❑ 466 Orestes Destrade .15 .07
❑ 467 Chris Hammond .15 .07
❑ 468 Bryan Harvey .15 .07
❑ 469 Charlie Hough .25 .11
❑ 470 Joe Klink .15 .07
❑ 471 Richie Lewis .15 .07
❑ 472 Bob Natal .15 .07
❑ 473 Pat Rapp .15 .07
❑ 474 Rich Renteria .15 .07
❑ 475 Rich Rodriguez .15 .07
❑ 476 Benito Santiago .15 .07
❑ 477 Gary Sheffield .25 .11
❑ 478 Matt Turner .15 .07
❑ 479 David Weathers .15 .07
❑ 480 Walt Weiss .15 .07
❑ 481 Darrell Whitmore .15 .07
❑ 482 Eric Anthony .15 .07
❑ 483 Jeff Bagwell .75 .35
❑ 484 Kevin Bass .15 .07
❑ 485 Craig Biggio .40 .18
❑ 486 Ken Caminiti .25 .11
❑ 487 Andujar Cedeno .15 .07
❑ 488 Chris Donnels .15 .07
❑ 489 Doug Drabek .15 .07
❑ 490 Steve Finley .25 .11
❑ 491 Luis Gonzalez .60 .25
❑ 492 Pete Harnisch .15 .07
❑ 493 Xavier Hernandez .15 .07
❑ 494 Doug Jones .15 .07
❑ 495 Todd Jones .15 .07
❑ 496 Darryl Kile .25 .11
❑ 497 Al Osuna .15 .07
❑ 498 Mark Portugal .15 .07
❑ 499 Scott Servais .15 .07
❑ 500 Greg Swindell .15 .07
❑ 501 Eddie Taubensee .15 .07
❑ 502 Jose Uribe .15 .07
❑ 503 Brian Williams .15 .07
❑ 504 Billy Ashley .15 .07
❑ 505 Pedro Astacio .15 .07
❑ 506 Brett Butler .25 .11
❑ 507 Tom Candiotti .15 .07
❑ 508 Omar Daal .15 .07
❑ 509 Jim Gott .15 .07
❑ 510 Kevin Gross .15 .07
❑ 511 Dave Hansen .15 .07
❑ 512 Carlos Hernandez .15 .07
❑ 513 Orel Hershiser .25 .11
❑ 514 Eric Karros .25 .11
❑ 515 Pedro Martinez 1.00 .45
❑ 516 Ramon Martinez .15 .07
❑ 517 Roger McDowell .15 .07
❑ 518 Raul Mondesi .25 .11
❑ 519 Jose Offerman .15 .07
❑ 520 Mike Piazza 2.00 .90
❑ 521 Jody Reed .15 .07
❑ 522 Henry Rodriguez .15 .07
❑ 523 Mike Sharperson .15 .07
❑ 524 Cory Snyder .15 .07
❑ 525 Darryl Strawberry .25 .11
❑ 526 Rick Trlicek .15 .07
❑ 527 Tim Wallach .15 .07
❑ 528 Mitch Webster .15 .07
❑ 529 Steve Wilson .15 .07
❑ 530 Todd Worrell .15 .07
❑ 531 Moises Alou .25 .11
❑ 532 Brian Barnes .15 .07
❑ 533 Sean Berry .15 .07
❑ 534 Greg Colbrunn .15 .07
❑ 535 Delino DeShields .15 .07
❑ 536 Jeff Fassero .15 .07
❑ 537 Darrin Fletcher .15 .07
❑ 538 Cliff Floyd .25 .11
❑ 539 Lou Frazier .15 .07
❑ 540 Marquis Grissom .15 .07
❑ 541 Butch Henry .15 .07
❑ 542 Ken Hill .15 .07
❑ 543 Mike Lansing .15 .07
❑ 544 Brian Looney RC .15 .07
❑ 545 Dennis Martinez .25 .11
❑ 546 Chris Nabholz .15 .07
❑ 547 Randy Ready .15 .07
❑ 548 Mel Rojas .15 .07
❑ 549 Kirk Rueter .15 .07
❑ 550 Tim Scott .15 .07
❑ 551 Jeff Shaw .15 .07
❑ 552 Tim Spehr .15 .07
❑ 553 John VanderWal .15 .07
❑ 554 Larry Walker .40 .18
❑ 555 John Wetteland .25 .11
❑ 556 Rondell White .25 .11
❑ 557 Tim Bogar .15 .07
❑ 558 Bobby Bonilla .25 .11
❑ 559 Jeromy Burnitz .25 .11
❑ 560 Sid Fernandez .15 .07
❑ 561 John Franco .25 .11
❑ 562 Dave Gallagher .15 .07
❑ 563 Dwight Gooden .25 .11
❑ 564 Eric Hillman .15 .07
❑ 565 Todd Hundley .15 .07
❑ 566 Jeff Innis .15 .07
❑ 567 Darrin Jackson .15 .07
❑ 568 Howard Johnson .15 .07
❑ 569 Bobby Jones .15 .07
❑ 570 Jeff Kent .40 .18
❑ 571 Mike Maddux .15 .07
❑ 572 Jeff McKnight .15 .07
❑ 573 Eddie Murray .60 .25
❑ 574 Charlie O'Brien .15 .07
❑ 575 Joe Orsulak .15 .07
❑ 576 Bret Saberhagen .25 .11
❑ 577 Pete Schourek .15 .07
❑ 578 Dave Telgheder .15 .07
❑ 579 Ryan Thompson .15 .07
❑ 580 Anthony Young .15 .07
❑ 581 Ruben Amaro .15 .07
❑ 582 Larry Andersen .15 .07
❑ 583 Kim Batiste .15 .07
❑ 584 Wes Chamberlain .15 .07
❑ 585 Darren Daulton .25 .11
❑ 586 Mariano Duncan .15 .07
❑ 587 Lenny Dykstra .25 .11
❑ 588 Jim Eisenreich .15 .07
❑ 589 Tommy Greene .15 .07
❑ 590 Dave Hollins .15 .07
❑ 591 Pete Incaviglia .15 .07
❑ 592 Danny Jackson .15 .07
❑ 593 Ricky Jordan .15 .07
❑ 594 John Kruk .25 .11
❑ 595 Roger Mason .15 .07
❑ 596 Mickey Morandini .15 .07
❑ 597 Terry Mulholland .15 .07
❑ 598 Todd Pratt .15 .07
❑ 599 Ben Rivera .15 .07
❑ 600 Curt Schilling .60 .25
❑ 601 Kevin Stocker .15 .07
❑ 602 Milt Thompson .15 .07
❑ 603 David West .15 .07
❑ 604 Mitch Williams .15 .07
❑ 605 Jay Bell .25 .11
❑ 606 Dave Clark .15 .07
❑ 607 Steve Cooke .15 .07
❑ 608 Tom Foley .15 .07
❑ 609 Carlos Garcia .15 .07
❑ 610 Joel Johnston .15 .07
❑ 611 Jeff King .15 .07
❑ 612 Al Martin .15 .07
❑ 613 Lloyd McClendon .15 .07
❑ 614 Orlando Merced .15 .07
❑ 615 Blas Minor .15 .07
❑ 616 Denny Neagle .25 .11
❑ 617 Mark Petkovsek RC .15 .07
❑ 618 Tom Prince .15 .07
❑ 619 Don Slaught .15 .07
❑ 620 Zane Smith .15 .07
❑ 621 Randy Tomlin .15 .07
❑ 622 Andy Van Slyke .25 .11
❑ 623 Paul Wagner .15 .07
❑ 624 Tim Wakefield .15 .07
❑ 625 Bob Walk .15 .07
❑ 626 Kevin Young .15 .07
❑ 627 Luis Alicea .15 .07
❑ 628 Rene Arocha .15 .07
❑ 629 Rod Brewer .15 .07
❑ 630 Rheal Cormier .15 .07
❑ 631 Bernard Gilkey .15 .07

❑ 632 Lee Guetterman	.15	.07
❑ 633 Gregg Jefferies	.15	.07
❑ 634 Brian Jordan	.25	.11
❑ 635 Les Lancaster	.15	.07
❑ 636 Ray Lankford	.15	.07
❑ 637 Rob Murphy	.15	.07
❑ 638 Omar Olivares	.15	.07
❑ 639 Jose Oquendo	.15	.07
❑ 640 Donovan Osborne	.15	.07
❑ 641 Tom Pagnozzi	.15	.07
❑ 642 Erik Pappas	.15	.07
❑ 643 Geronimo Pena	.15	.07
❑ 644 Mike Perez	.15	.07
❑ 645 Gerald Perry	.15	.07
❑ 646 Ozzie Smith	.75	.35
❑ 647 Bob Tewksbury	.15	.07
❑ 648 Allen Watson	.15	.07
❑ 649 Mark Whiten	.15	.07
❑ 650 Tracy Woodson	.15	.07
❑ 651 Todd Zeile	.15	.07
❑ 652 Andy Ashby	.15	.07
❑ 653 Brad Ausmus	.15	.07
❑ 654 Billy Bean	.15	.07
❑ 655 Derek Bell	.15	.07
❑ 656 Andy Benes	.15	.07
❑ 657 Doug Brocail	.15	.07
❑ 658 Jarvis Brown	.15	.07
❑ 659 Archi Cianfrocco	.15	.07
❑ 660 Phil Clark	.15	.07
❑ 661 Mark Davis	.15	.07
❑ 662 Jeff Gardner	.15	.07
❑ 663 Pat Gomez	.15	.07
❑ 664 Ricky Gutierrez	.15	.07
❑ 665 Tony Gwynn	1.25	.55
❑ 666 Gene Harris	.15	.07
❑ 667 Kevin Higgins	.15	.07
❑ 668 Trevor Hoffman	.25	.11
❑ 669 Pedro Martinez RC	.15	.07
❑ 670 Tim Mauser	.15	.07
❑ 671 Melvin Nieves	.15	.07
❑ 672 Phil Plantier	.15	.07
❑ 673 Frank Seminara	.15	.07
❑ 674 Craig Shipley	.15	.07
❑ 675 Kerry Taylor	.15	.07
❑ 676 Tim Teufel	.15	.07
❑ 677 Guillermo Velasquez	.15	.07
❑ 678 Wally Whitehurst	.15	.07
❑ 679 Tim Worrell	.15	.07
❑ 680 Rod Beck	.15	.07
❑ 681 Mike Benjamin	.15	.07
❑ 682 Todd Benzinger	.15	.07
❑ 683 Bud Black	.15	.07
❑ 684 Barry Bonds	1.50	.70
❑ 685 Jeff Brantley	.15	.07
❑ 686 Dave Burba	.15	.07
❑ 687 John Burkett	.15	.07
❑ 688 Mark Carreon	.15	.07
❑ 689 Will Clark	.60	.25
❑ 690 Royce Clayton	.15	.07
❑ 691 Bryan Hickerson	.15	.07
❑ 692 Mike Jackson	.15	.07
❑ 693 Darren Lewis	.15	.07
❑ 694 Kirt Manwaring	.15	.07
❑ 695 Dave Martinez	.15	.07
❑ 696 Willie McGee	.25	.11
❑ 697 John Patterson	.15	.07
❑ 698 Jeff Reed	.15	.07
❑ 699 Kevin Rogers	.15	.07
❑ 700 Scott Sanderson	.15	.07
❑ 701 Steve Scarsone	.15	.07
❑ 702 Billy Swift	.15	.07
❑ 703 Robby Thompson	.15	.07
❑ 704 Matt Williams	.40	.18
❑ 705 Trevor Wilson	.15	.07
❑ 706 Brave New World	.15	.07
Fred McGriff		
Ron Gant		
David Justice		
❑ 707 1-2 Punch	.25	.11
John Olerud		
Paul Molitor		
❑ 708 American Heat	.25	.11
Mike Mussina		
Jack McDowell		
❑ 709 Together Again	.25	.11
Lou Whitaker		
Alan Trammell		
❑ 710 Lone Star Lumber	.25	.11
Rafael Palmeiro		
Juan Gonzalez		
❑ 711 Batmen	.60	.25
Brett Butler		
Tony Gwynn		
❑ 712 Twin Peaks	.40	.18
Kirby Puckett		
Chuck Knoblauch		
❑ 713 Back to Back	.75	.35
Mike Piazza		
Eric Karros		
❑ 714 Checklist 1	.15	.07
❑ 715 Checklist 2	.15	.07
❑ 716 Checklist 3	.15	.07
❑ 717 Checklist 4	.15	.07
❑ 718 Checklist 5	.15	.07
❑ 719 Checklist 6	.15	.07
❑ 720 Checklist 7	.15	.07
❑ P69 Tim Salmon Promo	1.00	.45

1994 Fleer Update

	MINT	NRMT
COMP.FACT.SET (210)	60.00	27.00
COMPLETE SET (200)	75.00	34.00

❑ 1 Mark Eichhorn	.25	.11
❑ 2 Sid Fernandez	.25	.11
❑ 3 Leo Gomez	.25	.11
❑ 4 Mike Oquist	.25	.11
❑ 5 Rafael Palmeiro	1.00	.45
❑ 6 Chris Sabo	.25	.11
❑ 7 Dwight Smith	.25	.11
❑ 8 Lee Smith	.40	.18
❑ 9 Damon Berryhill	.25	.11
❑ 10 Wes Chamberlain	.25	.11
❑ 11 Gar Finnvold	.25	.11
❑ 12 Chris Howard	.25	.11
❑ 13 Tim Naehring	.25	.11
❑ 14 Otis Nixon	.25	.11
❑ 15 Brian Anderson RC	.40	.18
❑ 16 Jorge Fabregas	.25	.11
❑ 17 Rex Hudler	.25	.11
❑ 18 Bo Jackson	.40	.18
❑ 19 Mark Leiter	.25	.11
❑ 20 Spike Owen	.25	.11
❑ 21 Harold Reynolds	.25	.11
❑ 22 Chris Turner	.25	.11
❑ 23 Dennis Cook	.25	.11
❑ 24 Jose DeLeon	.25	.11
❑ 25 Julio Franco	.40	.18
❑ 26 Joe Hall	.25	.11
❑ 27 Darrin Jackson	.25	.11
❑ 28 Dane Johnson	.25	.11
❑ 29 Norberto Martin	.25	.11
❑ 30 Scott Sanderson	.25	.11
❑ 31 Jason Grimsley	.25	.11
❑ 32 Dennis Martinez	.40	.18
❑ 33 Jack Morris	.40	.18
❑ 34 Eddie Murray	1.00	.45
❑ 35 Chad Ogea	.25	.11
❑ 36 Tony Pena	.25	.11
❑ 37 Paul Shuey	.25	.11
❑ 38 Omar Vizquel	.40	.18
❑ 39 Danny Bautista	.25	.11
❑ 40 Tim Belcher	.25	.11
❑ 41 Joe Boever	.25	.11
❑ 42 Storm Davis	.25	.11
❑ 43 Junior Felix	.25	.11
❑ 44 Mike Gardiner	.25	.11
❑ 45 Buddy Groom	.25	.11
❑ 46 Juan Samuel	.25	.11
❑ 47 Vince Coleman	.25	.11
❑ 48 Bob Hamelin	.25	.11
❑ 49 Dave Henderson	.25	.11
❑ 50 Rusty Meacham	.25	.11
❑ 51 Terry Shumpert	.25	.11
❑ 52 Jeff Bronkey	.25	.11
❑ 53 Alex Diaz	.25	.11
❑ 54 Brian Harper	.25	.11
❑ 55 Jose Mercedes	.25	.11
❑ 56 Jody Reed	.25	.11
❑ 57 Bob Scanlan	.25	.11
❑ 58 Turner Ward	.25	.11
❑ 59 Rich Becker	.25	.11
❑ 60 Alex Cole	.25	.11
❑ 61 Denny Hocking	.25	.11
❑ 62 Scott Leius	.25	.11
❑ 63 Pat Mahomes	.25	.11
❑ 64 Carlos Pulido	.25	.11
❑ 65 Dave Stevens	.25	.11
❑ 66 Matt Walbeck	.25	.11
❑ 67 Xavier Hernandez	.25	.11
❑ 68 Sterling Hitchcock	.25	.11
❑ 69 Terry Mulholland	.25	.11
❑ 70 Luis Polonia	.25	.11
❑ 71 Gerald Williams	.25	.11
❑ 72 Mark Acre RC	.25	.11
❑ 73 Geronimo Berroa	.25	.11
❑ 74 Rickey Henderson	2.00	.90
❑ 75 Stan Javier	.25	.11
❑ 76 Steve Karsay	.25	.11
❑ 77 Carlos Reyes	.25	.11
❑ 78 Bill Taylor RC	.40	.18
❑ 79 Eric Anthony	.25	.11
❑ 80 Bobby Ayala	.25	.11
❑ 81 Tim Davis	.25	.11
❑ 82 Felix Fermin	.25	.11
❑ 83 Reggie Jefferson	.25	.11
❑ 84 Keith Mitchell	.25	.11
❑ 85 Bill Risley	.25	.11
❑ 86 Alex Rodriguez RC	40.00	18.00
❑ 87 Roger Salkeld	.25	.11
❑ 88 Dan Wilson	.25	.11
❑ 89 Cris Carpenter	.25	.11
❑ 90 Will Clark	1.00	.45
❑ 91 Jeff Frye	.25	.11
❑ 92 Rick Helling	.25	.11
❑ 93 Chris James	.25	.11
❑ 94 Oddibe McDowell	.25	.11
❑ 95 Billy Ripken	.25	.11
❑ 96 Carlos Delgado	1.50	.70
❑ 97 Alex Gonzalez	.25	.11
❑ 98 Shawn Green	1.25	.55
❑ 99 Darren Hall	.25	.11
❑ 100 Mike Huff	.25	.11
❑ 101 Mike Kelly	.25	.11
❑ 102 Roberto Kelly	.25	.11
❑ 103 Charlie O'Brien	.25	.11
❑ 104 Jose Oliva	.25	.11
❑ 105 Gregg Olson	.25	.11
❑ 106 Willie Banks	.25	.11
❑ 107 Jim Bullinger	.25	.11
❑ 108 Chuck Crim	.25	.11
❑ 109 Shawon Dunston	.25	.11
❑ 110 Karl Rhodes	.25	.11
❑ 111 Steve Trachsel	.25	.11
❑ 112 Anthony Young	.25	.11
❑ 113 Eddie Zambrano	.25	.11
❑ 114 Bret Boone	.40	.18
❑ 115 Jeff Brantley	.25	.11
❑ 116 Hector Carrasco	.25	.11
❑ 117 Tony Fernandez	.25	.11
❑ 118 Tim Fortugno	.25	.11
❑ 119 Erik Hanson	.25	.11
❑ 120 Chuck McElroy	.25	.11
❑ 121 Deion Sanders	.40	.18
❑ 122 Ellis Burks	.40	.18
❑ 123 Marvin Freeman	.25	.11
❑ 124 Mike Harkey	.25	.11
❑ 125 Howard Johnson	.25	.11
❑ 126 Mike Kingery	.25	.11

❑ 127 Nelson Liriano .25 .11
❑ 128 Marcus Moore .25 .11
❑ 129 Mike Munoz .25 .11
❑ 130 Kevin Ritz .25 .11
❑ 131 Walt Weiss .25 .11
❑ 132 Kurt Abbott RC .40 .18
❑ 133 Jerry Browne .25 .11
❑ 134 Greg Colbrunn .25 .11
❑ 135 Jeremy Hernandez .25 .11
❑ 136 Dave Magadan .25 .11
❑ 137 Kurt Miller .25 .11
❑ 138 Robb Nen .25 .11
❑ 139 Jesus Tavarez RC .25 .11
❑ 140 Sid Bream .25 .11
❑ 141 Tom Edens .25 .11
❑ 142 Tony Eusebio .25 .11
❑ 143 John Hudek RC .25 .11
❑ 144 Brian L. Hunter .25 .11
❑ 145 Orlando Miller .25 .11
❑ 146 James Mouton .25 .11
❑ 147 Shane Reynolds .25 .11
❑ 148 Rafael Bournigal .25 .11
❑ 149 Delino DeShields .25 .11
❑ 150 Garey Ingram RC .25 .11
❑ 151 Chan Ho Park RC 2.00 .90
❑ 152 Wil Cordero .25 .11
❑ 153 Pedro Martinez 1.50 .70
❑ 154 Randy Milligan .25 .11
❑ 155 Lenny Webster .25 .11
❑ 156 Rico Brogna .25 .11
❑ 157 Josias Manzanillo .25 .11
❑ 158 Kevin McReynolds .25 .11
❑ 159 Mike Remlinger .25 .11
❑ 160 David Segui .25 .11
❑ 161 Pete Smith .25 .11
❑ 162 Kelly Stinnett RC .40 .18
❑ 163 Jose Vizcaino .25 .11
❑ 164 Billy Hatcher .25 .11
❑ 165 Doug Jones .25 .11
❑ 166 Mike Lieberthal .40 .18
❑ 167 Tony Longmire .25 .11
❑ 168 Bobby Munoz .25 .11
❑ 169 Paul Quantrill .25 .11
❑ 170 Heathcliff Slocumb .25 .11
❑ 171 Fernando Valenzuela .40 .18
❑ 172 Mark Dewey .25 .11
❑ 173 Brian R. Hunter .25 .11
❑ 174 Jon Lieber .40 .18
❑ 175 Ravelo Manzanillo .25 .11
❑ 176 Dan Miceli .25 .11
❑ 177 Rick White .25 .11
❑ 178 Bryan Eversgerd .25 .11
❑ 179 John Habyan .25 .11
❑ 180 Terry McGriff .25 .11
❑ 181 Vicente Palacios .25 .11
❑ 182 Rich Rodriguez .25 .11
❑ 183 Rick Sutcliffe .40 .18
❑ 184 Donnie Elliott .25 .11
❑ 185 Joey Hamilton .25 .11
❑ 186 Tim Hyers RC .25 .11
❑ 187 Luis Lopez .25 .11
❑ 188 Ray McDavid .25 .11
❑ 189 Bip Roberts .25 .11
❑ 190 Scott Sanders .25 .11
❑ 191 Eddie Williams .25 .11
❑ 192 Steve Frey .25 .11
❑ 193 Pat Gomez .25 .11
❑ 194 Rich Monteleone .25 .11
❑ 195 Mark Portugal .25 .11
❑ 196 Darryl Strawberry .40 .18
❑ 197 Salomon Torres .25 .11
❑ 198 W.VanLandingham RC .25 .11
❑ 199 Checklist .25 .11
❑ 200 Checklist .25 .11

1995 Fleer

	MINT	NRMT
COMPLETE SET (600)	50.00	22.00

❑ 1 Brady Anderson .25 .11
❑ 2 Harold Baines .25 .11
❑ 3 Damon Buford .15 .07
❑ 4 Mike Devereaux .15 .07
❑ 5 Mark Eichhorn .15 .07
❑ 6 Sid Fernandez .15 .07

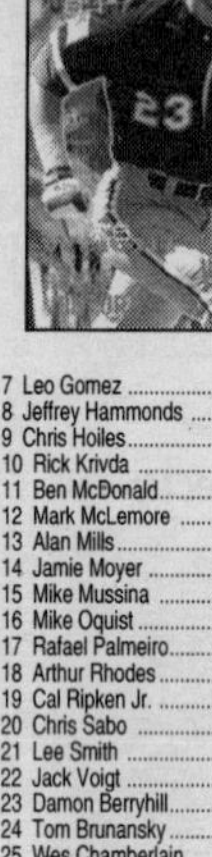

❑ 7 Leo Gomez .15 .07
❑ 8 Jeffrey Hammonds .15 .07
❑ 9 Chris Hoiles .15 .07
❑ 10 Rick Krivda .15 .07
❑ 11 Ben McDonald .15 .07
❑ 12 Mark McLemore .15 .07
❑ 13 Alan Mills .15 .07
❑ 14 Jamie Moyer .15 .07
❑ 15 Mike Mussina .60 .25
❑ 16 Mike Oquist .15 .07
❑ 17 Rafael Palmeiro .60 .25
❑ 18 Arthur Rhodes .15 .07
❑ 19 Cal Ripken Jr. 2.50 1.10
❑ 20 Chris Sabo .15 .07
❑ 21 Lee Smith .25 .11
❑ 22 Jack Voigt .15 .07
❑ 23 Damon Berryhill .15 .07
❑ 24 Tom Brunansky .15 .07
❑ 25 Wes Chamberlain .15 .07
❑ 26 Roger Clemens 1.50 .70
❑ 27 Scott Cooper .15 .07
❑ 28 Andre Dawson .40 .18
❑ 29 Gar Finnvold .15 .07
❑ 30 Tony Fossas .15 .07
❑ 31 Mike Greenwell .15 .07
❑ 32 Joe Hesketh .15 .07
❑ 33 Chris Howard .15 .07
❑ 34 Chris Nabholz .15 .07
❑ 35 Tim Naehring .15 .07
❑ 36 Otis Nixon .15 .07
❑ 37 Carlos Rodriguez .15 .07
❑ 38 Rich Rowland .15 .07
❑ 39 Ken Ryan .15 .07
❑ 40 Aaron Sele .25 .11
❑ 41 John Valentin .15 .07
❑ 42 Mo Vaughn .25 .11
❑ 43 Frank Viola .25 .11
❑ 44 Danny Bautista .15 .07
❑ 45 Joe Boever .15 .07
❑ 46 Milt Cuyler .15 .07
❑ 47 Storm Davis .15 .07
❑ 48 John Doherty .15 .07
❑ 49 Junior Felix .15 .07
❑ 50 Cecil Fielder .25 .11
❑ 51 Travis Fryman .25 .11
❑ 52 Mike Gardiner .15 .07
❑ 53 Kirk Gibson .25 .11
❑ 54 Chris Gomez .15 .07
❑ 55 Buddy Groom .15 .07
❑ 56 Mike Henneman .15 .07
❑ 57 Chad Kreuter .15 .07
❑ 58 Mike Moore .15 .07
❑ 59 Tony Phillips .15 .07
❑ 60 Juan Samuel .15 .07
❑ 61 Mickey Tettleton .15 .07
❑ 62 Alan Trammell .40 .18
❑ 63 David Wells .25 .11
❑ 64 Lou Whitaker .25 .11
❑ 65 Jim Abbott .25 .11
❑ 66 Joe Ausanio .15 .07
❑ 67 Wade Boggs .60 .25
❑ 68 Mike Gallego .15 .07
❑ 69 Xavier Hernandez .15 .07
❑ 70 Sterling Hitchcock .15 .07
❑ 71 Steve Howe .15 .07
❑ 72 Scott Kamieniecki .15 .07
❑ 73 Pat Kelly .15 .07
❑ 74 Jimmy Key .25 .11
❑ 75 Jim Leyritz .15 .07
❑ 76 Don Mattingly UER 1.50 .70
Photo is a reversed negative
❑ 77 Terry Mulholland .15 .07
❑ 78 Paul O'Neill .60 .25
❑ 79 Melido Perez .15 .07
❑ 80 Luis Polonia .15 .07
❑ 81 Mike Stanley .15 .07
❑ 82 Danny Tartabull .15 .07
❑ 83 Randy Velarde .15 .07
❑ 84 Bob Wickman .15 .07
❑ 85 Bernie Williams .60 .25
❑ 86 Gerald Williams .15 .07
❑ 87 Roberto Alomar .60 .25
❑ 88 Pat Borders .15 .07
❑ 89 Joe Carter .25 .11
❑ 90 Tony Castillo .15 .07
❑ 91 Brad Cornett RC .15 .07
❑ 92 Carlos Delgado .60 .25
❑ 93 Alex Gonzalez .15 .07
❑ 94 Shawn Green .60 .25
❑ 95 Juan Guzman .15 .07
❑ 96 Darren Hall .15 .07
❑ 97 Pat Hentgen .15 .07
❑ 98 Mike Huff .15 .07
❑ 99 Randy Knorr .15 .07
❑ 100 Al Leiter .25 .11
❑ 101 Paul Molitor .60 .25
❑ 102 John Olerud .25 .11
❑ 103 Dick Schofield .15 .07
❑ 104 Ed Sprague .15 .07
❑ 105 Dave Stewart .25 .11
❑ 106 Todd Stottlemyre .15 .07
❑ 107 Devon White .25 .11
❑ 108 Woody Williams .15 .07
❑ 109 Wilson Alvarez .15 .07
❑ 110 Paul Assenmacher .15 .07
❑ 111 Jason Bere .15 .07
❑ 112 Dennis Cook .15 .07
❑ 113 Joey Cora .15 .07
❑ 114 Jose DeLeon .15 .07
❑ 115 Alex Fernandez .15 .07
❑ 116 Julio Franco .25 .11
❑ 117 Craig Grebeck .15 .07
❑ 118 Ozzie Guillen .15 .07
❑ 119 Roberto Hernandez .15 .07
❑ 120 Darrin Jackson .15 .07
❑ 121 Lance Johnson .15 .07
❑ 122 Ron Karkovice .15 .07
❑ 123 Mike LaValliere .15 .07
❑ 124 Norberto Martin .15 .07
❑ 125 Kirk McCaskill .15 .07
❑ 126 Jack McDowell .15 .07
❑ 127 Tim Raines .25 .11
❑ 128 Frank Thomas .75 .35
❑ 129 Robin Ventura .25 .11
❑ 130 Sandy Alomar Jr. .25 .11
❑ 131 Carlos Baerga .15 .07
❑ 132 Albert Belle .25 .11
❑ 133 Mark Clark .15 .07
❑ 134 Alvaro Espinoza .15 .07
❑ 135 Jason Grimsley .15 .07
❑ 136 Wayne Kirby .15 .07
❑ 137 Kenny Lofton .25 .11
❑ 138 Albie Lopez .15 .07
❑ 139 Dennis Martinez .25 .11
❑ 140 Jose Mesa .15 .07
❑ 141 Eddie Murray .60 .25
❑ 142 Charles Nagy .15 .07
❑ 143 Tony Pena .15 .07
❑ 144 Eric Plunk .15 .07
❑ 145 Manny Ramirez .75 .35
❑ 146 Jeff Russell .15 .07
❑ 147 Paul Shuey .15 .07
❑ 148 Paul Sorrento .15 .07
❑ 149 Jim Thome .60 .25
❑ 150 Omar Vizquel .25 .11
❑ 151 Dave Winfield .60 .25
❑ 152 Kevin Appier .25 .11
❑ 153 Billy Brewer .15 .07
❑ 154 Vince Coleman .15 .07
❑ 155 David Cone .25 .11
❑ 156 Gary Gaetti .25 .11
❑ 157 Greg Gagne .15 .07
❑ 158 Tom Gordon .15 .07

❑ 159 Mark Gubicza .15 .07
❑ 160 Bob Hamelin .15 .07
❑ 161 Dave Henderson .15 .07
❑ 162 Felix Jose .15 .07
❑ 163 Wally Joyner .25 .11
❑ 164 Jose Lind .15 .07
❑ 165 Mike Macfarlane .15 .07
❑ 166 Mike Magnante .15 .07
❑ 167 Brent Mayne .15 .07
❑ 168 Brian McRae .15 .07
❑ 169 Rusty Meacham .15 .07
❑ 170 Jeff Montgomery .15 .07
❑ 171 Hipolito Pichardo .15 .07
❑ 172 Terry Shumpert .15 .07
❑ 173 Michael Tucker .15 .07
❑ 174 Ricky Bones .15 .07
❑ 175 Jeff Cirillo .25 .11
❑ 176 Alex Diaz .15 .07
❑ 177 Cal Eldred .15 .07
❑ 178 Mike Fetters .15 .07
❑ 179 Darryl Hamilton .15 .07
❑ 180 Brian Harper .15 .07
❑ 181 John Jaha .15 .07
❑ 182 Pat Listach .15 .07
❑ 183 Graeme Lloyd .15 .07
❑ 184 Jose Mercedes .15 .07
❑ 185 Matt Mieske .15 .07
❑ 186 Dave Nilsson .15 .07
❑ 187 Jody Reed .15 .07
❑ 188 Bob Scanlan .15 .07
❑ 189 Kevin Seitzer .15 .07
❑ 190 Bill Spiers .15 .07
❑ 191 B.J. Surhoff .25 .11
❑ 192 Jose Valentin .15 .07
❑ 193 Greg Vaughn .25 .11
❑ 194 Turner Ward .15 .07
❑ 195 Bill Wegman .15 .07
❑ 196 Rick Aguilera .15 .07
❑ 197 Rich Becker .15 .07
❑ 198 Alex Cole .15 .07
❑ 199 Marty Cordova .15 .07
❑ 200 Steve Dunn .15 .07
❑ 201 Scott Erickson .15 .07
❑ 202 Mark Guthrie .15 .07
❑ 203 Chip Hale .15 .07
❑ 204 LaTroy Hawkins .15 .07
❑ 205 Denny Hocking .15 .07
❑ 206 Chuck Knoblauch .25 .11
❑ 207 Scott Leius .15 .07
❑ 208 Shane Mack .15 .07
❑ 209 Pat Mahomes .15 .07
❑ 210 Pat Meares .15 .07
❑ 211 Pedro Munoz .15 .07
❑ 212 Kirby Puckett 1.50 .70
❑ 213 Jeff Reboulet .15 .07
❑ 214 Dave Stevens .15 .07
❑ 215 Kevin Tapani .15 .07
❑ 216 Matt Walbeck .15 .07
❑ 217 Carl Willis .15 .07
❑ 218 Brian Anderson .15 .07
❑ 219 Chad Curtis .15 .07
❑ 220 Chili Davis .25 .11
❑ 221 Gary DiSarcina .15 .07
❑ 222 Damion Easley .15 .07
❑ 223 Jim Edmonds .40 .18
❑ 224 Chuck Finley .25 .11
❑ 225 Joe Grahe .15 .07
❑ 226 Rex Hudler .15 .07
❑ 227 Bo Jackson .25 .11
❑ 228 Mark Langston .15 .07
❑ 229 Phil Leftwich .15 .07
❑ 230 Mark Leiter .15 .07
❑ 231 Spike Owen .15 .07
❑ 232 Bob Patterson .15 .07
❑ 233 Troy Percival .15 .07
❑ 234 Eduardo Perez .15 .07
❑ 235 Tim Salmon .25 .11
❑ 236 J.T. Snow .25 .11
❑ 237 Chris Turner .15 .07
❑ 238 Mark Acre .15 .07
❑ 239 Geronimo Berroa .15 .07
❑ 240 Mike Bordick .15 .07
❑ 241 John Briscoe .15 .07
❑ 242 Scott Brosius .25 .11
❑ 243 Ron Darling .15 .07
❑ 244 Dennis Eckersley .25 .11
❑ 245 Brent Gates .15 .07
❑ 246 Rickey Henderson 1.25 .55
❑ 247 Stan Javier .15 .07
❑ 248 Steve Karsay .15 .07
❑ 249 Mark McGwire 2.50 1.10
❑ 250 Troy Neel .15 .07
❑ 251 Steve Ontiveros .15 .07
❑ 252 Carlos Reyes .15 .07
❑ 253 Ruben Sierra .15 .07
❑ 254 Terry Steinbach .15 .07
❑ 255 Bill Taylor .15 .07
❑ 256 Todd Van Poppel .15 .07
❑ 257 Bobby Witt .15 .07
❑ 258 Rich Amaral .15 .07
❑ 259 Eric Anthony .15 .07
❑ 260 Bobby Ayala .15 .07
❑ 261 Mike Blowers .15 .07
❑ 262 Chris Bosio .15 .07
❑ 263 Jay Buhner .25 .11
❑ 264 John Cummings .15 .07
❑ 265 Tim Davis .15 .07
❑ 266 Felix Fermin .15 .07
❑ 267 Dave Fleming .15 .07
❑ 268 Goose Gossage .25 .11
❑ 269 Ken Griffey Jr. 2.00 .90
❑ 270 Reggie Jefferson .15 .07
❑ 271 Randy Johnson .75 .35
❑ 272 Edgar Martinez .40 .18
❑ 273 Tino Martinez .25 .11
❑ 274 Greg Pirkl .15 .07
❑ 275 Bill Risley .15 .07
❑ 276 Roger Salkeld .15 .07
❑ 277 Luis Sojo .15 .07
❑ 278 Mac Suzuki .15 .07
❑ 279 Dan Wilson .15 .07
❑ 280 Kevin Brown .25 .11
❑ 281 Jose Canseco .60 .25
❑ 282 Cris Carpenter .15 .07
❑ 283 Will Clark .60 .25
❑ 284 Jeff Frye .15 .07
❑ 285 Juan Gonzalez .60 .25
❑ 286 Rick Helling .15 .07
❑ 287 Tom Henke .15 .07
❑ 288 David Hulse .15 .07
❑ 289 Chris James .15 .07
❑ 290 Manuel Lee .15 .07
❑ 291 Oddibe McDowell .15 .07
❑ 292 Dean Palmer .25 .11
❑ 293 Roger Pavlik .15 .07
❑ 294 Bill Ripken .15 .07
❑ 295 Ivan Rodriguez .60 .25
❑ 296 Kenny Rogers .15 .07
❑ 297 Doug Strange .15 .07
❑ 298 Matt Whiteside .15 .07
❑ 299 Steve Avery .15 .07
❑ 300 Steve Bedrosian .15 .07
❑ 301 Rafael Belliard .15 .07
❑ 302 Jeff Blauser .15 .07
❑ 303 Dave Gallagher .15 .07
❑ 304 Tom Glavine .60 .25
❑ 305 David Justice .25 .11
❑ 306 Mike Kelly .15 .07
❑ 307 Roberto Kelly .15 .07
❑ 308 Ryan Klesko .25 .11
❑ 309 Mark Lemke .15 .07
❑ 310 Javier Lopez .25 .11
❑ 311 Greg Maddux 1.50 .70
❑ 312 Fred McGriff .40 .18
❑ 313 Greg McMichael .15 .07
❑ 314 Kent Mercker .15 .07
❑ 315 Charlie O'Brien .15 .07
❑ 316 Jose Oliva .15 .07
❑ 317 Terry Pendleton .25 .11
❑ 318 John Smoltz .25 .11
❑ 319 Mike Stanton .15 .07
❑ 320 Tony Tarasco .15 .07
❑ 321 Terrell Wade .15 .07
❑ 322 Mark Wohlers .15 .07
❑ 323 Kurt Abbott .15 .07
❑ 324 Luis Aquino .15 .07
❑ 325 Bret Barberie .15 .07
❑ 326 Ryan Bowen .15 .07
❑ 327 Jerry Browne .15 .07
❑ 328 Chuck Carr .15 .07
❑ 329 Matias Carrillo .15 .07
❑ 330 Greg Colbrunn .15 .07
❑ 331 Jeff Conine .15 .07
❑ 332 Mark Gardner .15 .07
❑ 333 Chris Hammond .15 .07
❑ 334 Bryan Harvey .15 .07
❑ 335 Richie Lewis .15 .07
❑ 336 Dave Magadan .15 .07
❑ 337 Terry Mathews .15 .07
❑ 338 Robb Nen .15 .07
❑ 339 Yorkis Perez .15 .07
❑ 340 Pat Rapp .15 .07
❑ 341 Benito Santiago .15 .07
❑ 342 Gary Sheffield .25 .11
❑ 343 Dave Weathers .15 .07
❑ 344 Moises Alou .25 .11
❑ 345 Sean Berry .15 .07
❑ 346 Wil Cordero .15 .07
❑ 347 Joey Eischen .15 .07
❑ 348 Jeff Fassero .15 .07
❑ 349 Darrin Fletcher .15 .07
❑ 350 Cliff Floyd .25 .11
❑ 351 Marquis Grissom .15 .07
❑ 352 Butch Henry .15 .07
❑ 353 Gil Heredia .15 .07
❑ 354 Ken Hill .15 .07
❑ 355 Mike Lansing .15 .07
❑ 356 Pedro Martinez .75 .35
❑ 357 Mel Rojas .15 .07
❑ 358 Kirk Rueter .15 .07
❑ 359 Tim Scott .15 .07
❑ 360 Jeff Shaw .15 .07
❑ 361 Larry Walker .40 .18
❑ 362 Lenny Webster .15 .07
❑ 363 John Wetteland .25 .11
❑ 364 Rondell White .25 .11
❑ 365 Bobby Bonilla .25 .11
❑ 366 Rico Brogna .15 .07
❑ 367 Jeromy Burnitz .25 .11
❑ 368 John Franco .25 .11
❑ 369 Dwight Gooden .25 .11
❑ 370 Todd Hundley .15 .07
❑ 371 Jason Jacome .15 .07
❑ 372 Bobby Jones .15 .07
❑ 373 Jeff Kent .40 .18
❑ 374 Jim Lindeman .15 .07
❑ 375 Josias Manzanillo .15 .07
❑ 376 Roger Mason .15 .07
❑ 377 Kevin McReynolds .15 .07
❑ 378 Joe Orsulak .15 .07
❑ 379 Bill Pulsipher .15 .07
❑ 380 Bret Saberhagen .25 .11
❑ 381 David Segui .15 .07
❑ 382 Pete Smith .15 .07
❑ 383 Kelly Stinnett .15 .07
❑ 384 Ryan Thompson .15 .07
❑ 385 Jose Vizcaino .15 .07
❑ 386 Toby Borland .15 .07
❑ 387 Ricky Bottalico .15 .07
❑ 388 Darren Daulton .25 .11
❑ 389 Mariano Duncan .15 .07
❑ 390 Lenny Dykstra .25 .11
❑ 391 Jim Eisenreich .15 .07
❑ 392 Tommy Greene .15 .07
❑ 393 Dave Hollins .15 .07
❑ 394 Pete Incaviglia .15 .07
❑ 395 Danny Jackson .15 .07
❑ 396 Doug Jones .15 .07
❑ 397 Ricky Jordan .15 .07
❑ 398 John Kruk .25 .11
❑ 399 Mike Lieberthal .25 .11
❑ 400 Tony Longmire .15 .07
❑ 401 Mickey Morandini .15 .07
❑ 402 Bobby Munoz .15 .07
❑ 403 Curt Schilling .60 .25
❑ 404 Heathcliff Slocumb .15 .07
❑ 405 Kevin Stocker .15 .07
❑ 406 Fernando Valenzuela .25 .11
❑ 407 David West .15 .07
❑ 408 Willie Banks .15 .07
❑ 409 Jose Bautista .15 .07
❑ 410 Steve Buechele .15 .07
❑ 411 Jim Bullinger .15 .07
❑ 412 Chuck Crim .15 .07
❑ 413 Shawon Dunston .15 .07
❑ 414 Kevin Foster .15 .07
❑ 415 Mark Grace .60 .25
❑ 416 Jose Hernandez .15 .07

❑	Player	MINT	NRMT
❑ 417	Glenallen Hill	.15	.07
❑ 418	Brooks Kieschnick	.15	.07
❑ 419	Derrick May	.15	.07
❑ 420	Randy Myers	.15	.07
❑ 421	Dan Plesac	.15	.07
❑ 422	Karl Rhodes	.15	.07
❑ 423	Rey Sanchez	.15	.07
❑ 424	Sammy Sosa	1.25	.55
❑ 425	Steve Trachsel	.15	.07
❑ 426	Rick Wilkins	.15	.07
❑ 427	Anthony Young	.15	.07
❑ 428	Eddie Zambrano	.15	.07
❑ 429	Bret Boone	.25	.11
❑ 430	Jeff Branson	.15	.07
❑ 431	Jeff Brantley	.15	.07
❑ 432	Hector Carrasco	.15	.07
❑ 433	Brian Dorsett	.15	.07
❑ 434	Tony Fernandez	.15	.07
❑ 435	Tim Fortugno	.15	.07
❑ 436	Erik Hanson	.15	.07
❑ 437	Thomas Howard	.15	.07
❑ 438	Kevin Jarvis	.15	.07
❑ 439	Barry Larkin	.60	.25
❑ 440	Chuck McElroy	.15	.07
❑ 441	Kevin Mitchell	.15	.07
❑ 442	Hal Morris	.15	.07
❑ 443	Jose Rijo	.15	.07
❑ 444	John Roper	.15	.07
❑ 445	Johnny Ruffin	.15	.07
❑ 446	Deion Sanders	.25	.11
❑ 447	Reggie Sanders	.15	.07
❑ 448	Pete Schourek	.15	.07
❑ 449	John Smiley	.15	.07
❑ 450	Eddie Taubensee	.15	.07
❑ 451	Jeff Bagwell	.75	.35
❑ 452	Kevin Bass	.15	.07
❑ 453	Craig Biggio	.40	.18
❑ 454	Ken Caminiti	.25	.11
❑ 455	Andujar Cedeno	.15	.07
❑ 456	Doug Drabek	.15	.07
❑ 457	Tony Eusebio	.15	.07
❑ 458	Mike Felder	.15	.07
❑ 459	Steve Finley	.25	.11
❑ 460	Luis Gonzalez	.60	.25
❑ 461	Mike Hampton	.25	.11
❑ 462	Pete Harnisch	.15	.07
❑ 463	John Hudek	.15	.07
❑ 464	Todd Jones	.15	.07
❑ 465	Darryl Kile	.25	.11
❑ 466	James Mouton	.15	.07
❑ 467	Shane Reynolds	.15	.07
❑ 468	Scott Servais	.15	.07
❑ 469	Greg Swindell	.15	.07
❑ 470	Dave Veres RC	.15	.07
❑ 471	Brian Williams	.15	.07
❑ 472	Jay Bell	.25	.11
❑ 473	Jacob Brumfield	.15	.07
❑ 474	Dave Clark	.15	.07
❑ 475	Steve Cooke	.15	.07
❑ 476	Midre Cummings	.15	.07
❑ 477	Mark Dewey	.15	.07
❑ 478	Tom Foley	.15	.07
❑ 479	Carlos Garcia	.15	.07
❑ 480	Jeff King	.15	.07
❑ 481	Jon Lieber	.15	.07
❑ 482	Ravelo Manzanillo	.15	.07
❑ 483	Al Martin	.15	.07
❑ 484	Orlando Merced	.15	.07
❑ 485	Danny Miceli	.15	.07
❑ 486	Denny Neagle	.25	.11
❑ 487	Lance Parrish	.25	.11
❑ 488	Don Slaught	.15	.07
❑ 489	Zane Smith	.15	.07
❑ 490	Andy Van Slyke	.25	.11
❑ 491	Paul Wagner	.15	.07
❑ 492	Rick White	.15	.07
❑ 493	Luis Alicea	.15	.07
❑ 494	Rene Arocha	.15	.07
❑ 495	Rheal Cormier	.15	.07
❑ 496	Bryan Eversgerd	.15	.07
❑ 497	Bernard Gilkey	.15	.07
❑ 498	John Habyan	.15	.07
❑ 499	Gregg Jefferies	.15	.07
❑ 500	Brian Jordan	.25	.11
❑ 501	Ray Lankford	.15	.07
❑ 502	John Mabry	.15	.07
❑ 503	Terry McGriff	.15	.07
❑ 504	Tom Pagnozzi	.15	.07
❑ 505	Vicente Palacios	.15	.07
❑ 506	Geronimo Pena	.15	.07
❑ 507	Gerald Perry	.15	.07
❑ 508	Rich Rodriguez	.15	.07
❑ 509	Ozzie Smith	.75	.35
❑ 510	Bob Tewksbury	.15	.07
❑ 511	Allen Watson	.15	.07
❑ 512	Mark Whiten	.15	.07
❑ 513	Todd Zeile	.15	.07
❑ 514	Dante Bichette	.25	.11
❑ 515	Willie Blair	.15	.07
❑ 516	Ellis Burks	.25	.11
❑ 517	Marvin Freeman	.15	.07
❑ 518	Andres Galarraga	.40	.18
❑ 519	Joe Girardi	.15	.07
❑ 520	Greg W. Harris	.15	.07
❑ 521	Charlie Hayes	.15	.07
❑ 522	Mike Kingery	.15	.07
❑ 523	Nelson Liriano	.15	.07
❑ 524	Mike Munoz	.15	.07
❑ 525	David Nied	.15	.07
❑ 526	Steve Reed	.15	.07
❑ 527	Kevin Ritz	.15	.07
❑ 528	Bruce Ruffin	.15	.07
❑ 529	John Vander Wal	.15	.07
❑ 530	Walt Weiss	.15	.07
❑ 531	Eric Young	.15	.07
❑ 532	Billy Ashley	.15	.07
❑ 533	Pedro Astacio	.15	.07
❑ 534	Rafael Bournigal	.15	.07
❑ 535	Brett Butler	.25	.11
❑ 536	Tom Candiotti	.15	.07
❑ 537	Omar Daal	.15	.07
❑ 538	Delino DeShields	.15	.07
❑ 539	Darren Dreifort	.15	.07
❑ 540	Kevin Gross	.15	.07
❑ 541	Orel Hershiser	.25	.11
❑ 542	Garey Ingram	.15	.07
❑ 543	Eric Karros	.25	.11
❑ 544	Ramon Martinez	.15	.07
❑ 545	Raul Mondesi	.25	.11
❑ 546	Chan Ho Park	.25	.11
❑ 547	Mike Piazza	1.50	.70
❑ 548	Henry Rodriguez	.15	.07
❑ 549	Rudy Seanez	.15	.07
❑ 550	Ismael Valdes	.15	.07
❑ 551	Tim Wallach	.15	.07
❑ 552	Todd Worrell	.15	.07
❑ 553	Andy Ashby	.15	.07
❑ 554	Brad Ausmus	.15	.07
❑ 555	Derek Bell	.15	.07
❑ 556	Andy Benes	.15	.07
❑ 557	Phil Clark	.15	.07
❑ 558	Donnie Elliott	.15	.07
❑ 559	Ricky Gutierrez	.15	.07
❑ 560	Tony Gwynn	1.25	.55
❑ 561	Joey Hamilton	.15	.07
❑ 562	Trevor Hoffman	.25	.11
❑ 563	Luis Lopez	.15	.07
❑ 564	Pedro A. Martinez	.15	.07
❑ 565	Tim Mauser	.15	.07
❑ 566	Phil Plantier	.15	.07
❑ 567	Bip Roberts	.15	.07
❑ 568	Scott Sanders	.15	.07
❑ 569	Craig Shipley	.15	.07
❑ 570	Jeff Tabaka	.15	.07
❑ 571	Eddie Williams	.15	.07
❑ 572	Rod Beck	.15	.07
❑ 573	Mike Benjamin	.15	.07
❑ 574	Barry Bonds	1.50	.70
❑ 575	Dave Burba	.15	.07
❑ 576	John Burkett	.15	.07
❑ 577	Mark Carreon	.15	.07
❑ 578	Royce Clayton	.15	.07
❑ 579	Steve Frey	.15	.07
❑ 580	Bryan Hickerson	.15	.07
❑ 581	Mike Jackson	.15	.07
❑ 582	Darren Lewis	.15	.07
❑ 583	Kirt Manwaring	.15	.07
❑ 584	Rich Monteleone	.15	.07
❑ 585	John Patterson	.15	.07
❑ 586	J.R. Phillips	.15	.07
❑ 587	Mark Portugal	.15	.07
❑ 588	Joe Rosselli	.15	.07
❑ 589	Darryl Strawberry	.25	.11
❑ 590	Bill Swift	.15	.07
❑ 591	Robby Thompson	.15	.07
❑ 592	W.VanLandingham	.15	.07
❑ 593	Matt Williams	.40	.18
❑ 594	Checklist	.15	.07
❑ 595	Checklist	.15	.07
❑ 596	Checklist	.15	.07
❑ 597	Checklist	.15	.07
❑ 598	Checklist	.15	.07
❑ 599	Checklist	.15	.07
❑ 600	Checklist	.15	.07

1995 Fleer Update

		MINT	NRMT
COMPLETE SET (200)		15.00	6.75
❑ 1	Manny Alexander	.10	.05
❑ 2	Bret Barberie	.10	.05
❑ 3	Armando Benitez	.15	.07
❑ 4	Kevin Brown	.15	.07
❑ 5	Doug Jones	.10	.05
❑ 6	Sherman Obando	.10	.05
❑ 7	Andy Van Slyke	.15	.07
❑ 8	Stan Belinda	.10	.05
❑ 9	Jose Canseco	.40	.18
❑ 10	Vaughn Eshelman	.10	.05
❑ 11	Mike Macfarlane	.10	.05
❑ 12	Troy O'Leary	.10	.05
❑ 13	Steve Rodriguez	.10	.05
❑ 14	Lee Tinsley	.10	.05
❑ 15	Tim Vanegmond	.10	.05
❑ 16	Mark Whiten	.10	.05
❑ 17	Sean Bergman	.10	.05
❑ 18	Chad Curtis	.10	.05
❑ 19	John Flaherty	.10	.05
❑ 20	Bob Higginson RC	.75	.35
❑ 21	Felipe Lira	.10	.05
❑ 22	Shannon Penn	.10	.05
❑ 23	Todd Steverson	.10	.05
❑ 24	Sean Whiteside	.10	.05
❑ 25	Tony Fernandez	.10	.05
❑ 26	Jack McDowell	.10	.05
❑ 27	Andy Pettitte	.15	.07
❑ 28	John Wetteland	.15	.07
❑ 29	David Cone	.15	.07
❑ 30	Mike Timlin	.10	.05
❑ 31	Duane Ward	.10	.05
❑ 32	Jim Abbott	.15	.07
❑ 33	James Baldwin	.10	.05
❑ 34	Mike Devereaux	.10	.05
❑ 35	Ray Durham	.15	.07
❑ 36	Tim Fortugno	.10	.05
❑ 37	Scott Ruffcorn	.10	.05
❑ 38	Chris Sabo	.10	.05
❑ 39	Paul Assenmacher	.10	.05
❑ 40	Bud Black	.10	.05
❑ 41	Orel Hershiser	.15	.07
❑ 42	Julian Tavarez	.10	.05
❑ 43	Dave Winfield	.40	.18
❑ 44	Pat Borders	.10	.05
❑ 45	Melvin Bunch RC	.10	.05
❑ 46	Tom Goodwin	.10	.05
❑ 47	Jon Nunnally	.10	.05
❑ 48	Joe Randa	.10	.05
❑ 49	Dilson Torres RC	.10	.05
❑ 50	Joe Vitiello	.10	.05

❑ 51 David Hulse	.10	.05
❑ 52 Scott Karl	.10	.05
❑ 53 Mark Kiefer	.10	.05
❑ 54 Derrick May	.10	.05
❑ 55 Joe Oliver	.10	.05
❑ 56 Al Reyes RC	.10	.05
❑ 57 Steve Sparks RC	.10	.05
❑ 58 Jerald Clark	.10	.05
❑ 59 Eddie Guardado	.10	.05
❑ 60 Kevin Maas	.10	.05
❑ 61 David McCarty	.10	.05
❑ 62 Brad Radke RC	2.00	.90
❑ 63 Scott Stahoviak	.10	.05
❑ 64 Garret Anderson	.15	.07
❑ 65 Shawn Boskie	.10	.05
❑ 66 Mike James	.10	.05
❑ 67 Tony Phillips	.10	.05
❑ 68 Lee Smith	.15	.07
❑ 69 Mitch Williams	.10	.05
❑ 70 Jim Corsi	.10	.05
❑ 71 Mark Harkey	.10	.05
❑ 72 Dave Stewart	.15	.07
❑ 73 Todd Stottlemyre	.10	.05
❑ 74 Joey Cora	.10	.05
❑ 75 Chad Kreuter	.10	.05
❑ 76 Jeff Nelson	.10	.05
❑ 77 Alex Rodriguez	1.25	.55
❑ 78 Ron Villone	.10	.05
❑ 79 Bob Wells RC	.10	.05
❑ 80 Jose Alberro RC	.10	.05
❑ 81 Terry Burrows	.10	.05
❑ 82 Kevin Gross	.10	.05
❑ 83 Wilson Heredia	.10	.05
❑ 84 Mark McLemore	.10	.05
❑ 85 Otis Nixon	.10	.05
❑ 86 Jeff Russell	.10	.05
❑ 87 Mickey Tettleton	.10	.05
❑ 88 Bob Tewksbury	.10	.05
❑ 89 Pedro Borbon	.10	.05
❑ 90 Marquis Grissom	.10	.05
❑ 91 Chipper Jones	.75	.35
❑ 92 Mike Mordecai	.10	.05
❑ 93 Jason Schmidt	.10	.05
❑ 94 John Burkett	.10	.05
❑ 95 Andre Dawson	.25	.11
❑ 96 Matt Dunbar RC	.10	.05
❑ 97 Charles Johnson	.15	.07
❑ 98 Terry Pendleton	.15	.07
❑ 99 Rich Scheid	.10	.05
❑ 100 Quilvio Veras	.10	.05
❑ 101 Bobby Witt	.10	.05
❑ 102 Eddie Zosky	.10	.05
❑ 103 Shane Andrews	.10	.05
❑ 104 Reid Cornelius	.10	.05
❑ 105 Chad Fonville RC	.10	.05
❑ 106 Mark Grudzielanek RC	.15	.07
❑ 107 Roberto Kelly	.10	.05
❑ 108 Carlos Perez RC	.15	.07
❑ 109 Tony Tarasco	.10	.05
❑ 110 Brett Butler	.15	.07
❑ 111 Carl Everett	.15	.07
❑ 112 Pete Harnisch	.10	.05
❑ 113 Doug Henry	.10	.05
❑ 114 Kevin Lomon RC	.10	.05
❑ 115 Blas Minor	.10	.05
❑ 116 Dave Mlicki	.10	.05
❑ 117 Ricky Otero RC	.10	.05
❑ 118 Norm Charlton	.10	.05
❑ 119 Tyler Green	.10	.05
❑ 120 Gene Harris	.10	.05
❑ 121 Charlie Hayes	.10	.05
❑ 122 Gregg Jefferies	.10	.05
❑ 123 Michael Mimbs RC	.10	.05
❑ 124 Paul Quantrill	.10	.05
❑ 125 Frank Castillo	.10	.05
❑ 126 Brian McRae	.10	.05
❑ 127 Jaime Navarro	.10	.05
❑ 128 Mike Perez	.10	.05
❑ 129 Tanyon Sturtze	.10	.05
❑ 130 Ozzie Timmons	.10	.05
❑ 131 John Courtright	.10	.05
❑ 132 Ron Gant	.10	.05
❑ 133 Xavier Hernandez	.10	.05
❑ 134 Brian Hunter	.10	.05
❑ 135 Benito Santiago	.10	.05
❑ 136 Pete Smith	.10	.05
❑ 137 Scott Sullivan	.10	.05
❑ 138 Derek Bell	.10	.05
❑ 139 Doug Brocail	.10	.05
❑ 140 Ricky Gutierrez	.10	.05
❑ 141 Pedro A.Martinez	.10	.05
❑ 142 Orlando Miller	.10	.05
❑ 143 Phil Plantier	.10	.05
❑ 144 Craig Shipley	.10	.05
❑ 145 Rich Aude	.10	.05
❑ 146 J.Christiansen RC	.10	.05
❑ 147 Freddy Adrian Garcia RC	.10	.05
❑ 148 Jim Gott	.10	.05
❑ 149 Mark Johnson RC	.15	.07
❑ 150 Esteban Loaiza	.10	.05
❑ 151 Dan Plesac	.10	.05
❑ 152 Gary Wilson RC	.10	.05
❑ 153 Allen Battle	.10	.05
❑ 154 Terry Bradshaw	.10	.05
❑ 155 Scott Cooper	.10	.05
❑ 156 Tripp Cromer	.10	.05
❑ 157 John Frascatore RC	.10	.05
❑ 158 John Habyan	.10	.05
❑ 159 Tom Henke	.10	.05
❑ 160 Ken Hill	.10	.05
❑ 161 Danny Jackson	.10	.05
❑ 162 Donovan Osborne	.10	.05
❑ 163 Tom Urbani	.10	.05
❑ 164 Roger Bailey	.10	.05
❑ 165 Jorge Brito RC	.10	.05
❑ 166 Vinny Castilla	.15	.07
❑ 167 Darren Holmes	.10	.05
❑ 168 Roberto Mejia	.10	.05
❑ 169 Bill Swift	.10	.05
❑ 170 Mark Thompson	.10	.05
❑ 171 Larry Walker	.25	.11
❑ 172 Greg Hansell	.10	.05
❑ 173 Dave Hansen	.10	.05
❑ 174 Carlos Hernandez	.10	.05
❑ 175 Hideo Nomo RC	1.50	.70
❑ 176 Jose Offerman	.10	.05
❑ 177 Antonio Osuna	.10	.05
❑ 178 Reggie Williams	.10	.05
❑ 179 Todd Williams	.10	.05
❑ 180 Andres Berumen	.10	.05
❑ 181 Ken Caminiti	.15	.07
❑ 182 Andujar Cedeno	.10	.05
❑ 183 Steve Finley	.15	.07
❑ 184 Bryce Florie	.10	.05
❑ 185 Dustin Hermanson	.10	.05
❑ 186 Ray Holbert	.10	.05
❑ 187 Melvin Nieves	.10	.05
❑ 188 Roberto Petagine	.10	.05
❑ 189 Jody Reed	.10	.05
❑ 190 Fernando Valenzuela	.15	.07
❑ 191 Brian Williams	.10	.05
❑ 192 Mark Dewey	.10	.05
❑ 193 Glenallen Hill	.10	.05
❑ 194 Chris Hook RC	.10	.05
❑ 195 Terry Mulholland	.10	.05
❑ 196 Steve Scarsone	.10	.05
❑ 197 Trevor Wilson	.10	.05
❑ 198 Checklist	.10	.05
❑ 199 Checklist	.10	.05
❑ 200 Checklist	.10	.05

1996 Fleer

	MINT	NRMT
COMPLETE SET (600)	80.00	36.00
❑ 1 Manny Alexander	.15	.07
❑ 2 Brady Anderson	.25	.11
❑ 3 Harold Baines	.25	.11
❑ 4 Armando Benitez	.15	.07
❑ 5 Bobby Bonilla	.25	.11
❑ 6 Kevin Brown	.25	.11
❑ 7 Scott Erickson	.15	.07
❑ 8 Curtis Goodwin	.15	.07
❑ 9 Jeffrey Hammonds	.15	.07
❑ 10 Jimmy Haynes	.15	.07
❑ 11 Chris Hoiles	.15	.07
❑ 12 Doug Jones	.15	.07
❑ 13 Rick Krivda	.15	.07
❑ 14 Jeff Manto	.15	.07
❑ 15 Ben McDonald	.15	.07
❑ 16 Jamie Moyer	.15	.07
❑ 17 Mike Mussina	.60	.25
❑ 18 Jesse Orosco	.15	.07
❑ 19 Rafael Palmeiro	.60	.25
❑ 20 Cal Ripken	2.50	1.10
❑ 21 Rick Aguilera	.15	.07
❑ 22 Luis Alicea	.15	.07
❑ 23 Stan Belinda	.15	.07
❑ 24 Jose Canseco	.60	.25
❑ 25 Roger Clemens	1.50	.70
❑ 26 Vaughn Eshelman	.15	.07
❑ 27 Mike Greenwell	.15	.07
❑ 28 Erik Hanson	.15	.07
❑ 29 Dwayne Hosey	.15	.07
❑ 30 Mike Macfarlane UER	.15	.07
❑ 31 Tim Naehring	.15	.07
❑ 32 Troy O'Leary	.15	.07
❑ 33 Aaron Sele	.25	.11
❑ 34 Zane Smith	.15	.07
❑ 35 Jeff Suppan	.15	.07
❑ 36 Lee Tinsley	.15	.07
❑ 37 John Valentin	.15	.07
❑ 38 Mo Vaughn	.25	.11
❑ 39 Tim Wakefield	.15	.07
❑ 40 Jim Abbott	.25	.11
❑ 41 Brian Anderson	.15	.07
❑ 42 Garret Anderson	.25	.11
❑ 43 Chili Davis	.25	.11
❑ 44 Gary DiSarcina	.15	.07
❑ 45 Damion Easley	.15	.07
❑ 46 Jim Edmonds	.40	.18
❑ 47 Chuck Finley	.25	.11
❑ 48 Todd Greene	.15	.07
❑ 49 Mike Harkey	.15	.07
❑ 50 Mike James	.15	.07
❑ 51 Mark Langston	.15	.07
❑ 52 Greg Myers	.15	.07
❑ 53 Orlando Palmeiro	.15	.07
❑ 54 Bob Patterson	.15	.07
❑ 55 Troy Percival	.15	.07
❑ 56 Tony Phillips	.15	.07
❑ 57 Tim Salmon	.25	.11
❑ 58 Lee Smith	.25	.11
❑ 59 J.T. Snow	.25	.11
❑ 60 Randy Velarde	.15	.07
❑ 61 Wilson Alvarez	.15	.07
❑ 62 Luis Andujar	.15	.07
❑ 63 Jason Bere	.15	.07
❑ 64 Ray Durham	.25	.11
❑ 65 Alex Fernandez	.15	.07
❑ 66 Ozzie Guillen	.15	.07
❑ 67 Roberto Hernandez	.15	.07
❑ 68 Lance Johnson	.15	.07
❑ 69 Matt Karchner	.15	.07
❑ 70 Ron Karkovice	.15	.07
❑ 71 Norberto Martin	.15	.07
❑ 72 Dave Martinez	.15	.07
❑ 73 Kirk McCaskill	.15	.07
❑ 74 Lyle Mouton	.15	.07
❑ 75 Tim Raines	.25	.11
❑ 76 Mike Sirotka RC	.50	.23
❑ 77 Frank Thomas	.75	.35
❑ 78 Larry Thomas	.15	.07
❑ 79 Robin Ventura	.25	.11
❑ 80 Sandy Alomar Jr.	.25	.11
❑ 81 Paul Assenmacher	.15	.07
❑ 82 Carlos Baerga	.15	.07
❑ 83 Albert Belle	.25	.11
❑ 84 Mark Clark	.15	.07
❑ 85 Alan Embree	.15	.07
❑ 86 Alvaro Espinoza	.15	.07

❑ 87	Orel Hershiser	.25	.11
❑ 88	Ken Hill	.15	.07
❑ 89	Kenny Lofton	.25	.11
❑ 90	Dennis Martinez	.25	.11
❑ 91	Jose Mesa	.15	.07
❑ 92	Eddie Murray	.60	.25
❑ 93	Charles Nagy	.15	.07
❑ 94	Chad Ogea	.15	.07
❑ 95	Tony Pena	.15	.07
❑ 96	Herb Perry	.15	.07
❑ 97	Eric Plunk	.15	.07
❑ 98	Jim Poole	.15	.07
❑ 99	Manny Ramirez	.75	.35
❑ 100	Paul Sorrento	.15	.07
❑ 101	Julian Tavarez	.15	.07
❑ 102	Jim Thome	.60	.25
❑ 103	Omar Vizquel	.25	.11
❑ 104	Dave Winfield	.60	.25
❑ 105	Danny Bautista	.15	.07
❑ 106	Joe Boever	.15	.07
❑ 107	Chad Curtis	.15	.07
❑ 108	John Doherty	.15	.07
❑ 109	Cecil Fielder	.25	.11
❑ 110	John Flaherty	.15	.07
❑ 111	Travis Fryman	.25	.11
❑ 112	Chris Gomez	.15	.07
❑ 113	Bob Higginson	.25	.11
❑ 114	Mark Lewis	.15	.07
❑ 115	Jose Lima	.15	.07
❑ 116	Felipe Lira	.15	.07
❑ 117	Brian Maxcy	.15	.07
❑ 118	C.J. Nitkowski	.15	.07
❑ 119	Phil Plantier	.15	.07
❑ 120	Clint Sodowsky	.15	.07
❑ 121	Alan Trammell	.40	.18
❑ 122	Lou Whitaker	.25	.11
❑ 123	Kevin Appier	.25	.11
❑ 124	Johnny Damon	.25	.11
❑ 125	Gary Gaetti	.25	.11
❑ 126	Tom Goodwin	.15	.07
❑ 127	Tom Gordon	.15	.07
❑ 128	Mark Gubicza	.15	.07
❑ 129	Bob Hamelin	.15	.07
❑ 130	David Howard	.15	.07
❑ 131	Jason Jacome	.15	.07
❑ 132	Wally Joyner	.25	.11
❑ 133	Keith Lockhart	.15	.07
❑ 134	Brent Mayne	.15	.07
❑ 135	Jeff Montgomery	.15	.07
❑ 136	Jon Nunnally	.15	.07
❑ 137	Juan Samuel	.15	.07
❑ 138	Mike Sweeney RC	2.50	1.10
❑ 139	Michael Tucker	.15	.07
❑ 140	Joe Vitiello	.15	.07
❑ 141	Ricky Bones	.15	.07
❑ 142	Chuck Carr	.15	.07
❑ 143	Jeff Cirillo	.25	.11
❑ 144	Mike Fetters	.15	.07
❑ 145	Darryl Hamilton	.15	.07
❑ 146	David Hulse	.15	.07
❑ 147	John Jaha	.15	.07
❑ 148	Scott Karl	.15	.07
❑ 149	Mark Kiefer	.15	.07
❑ 150	Pat Listach	.15	.07
❑ 151	Mark Loretta	.15	.07
❑ 152	Mike Matheny	.15	.07
❑ 153	Matt Mieske	.15	.07
❑ 154	Dave Nilsson	.15	.07
❑ 155	Joe Oliver	.15	.07
❑ 156	Al Reyes	.15	.07
❑ 157	Kevin Seitzer	.15	.07
❑ 158	Steve Sparks	.15	.07
❑ 159	B.J. Surhoff	.25	.11
❑ 160	Jose Valentin	.15	.07
❑ 161	Greg Vaughn	.25	.11
❑ 162	Fernando Vina	.15	.07
❑ 163	Rich Becker	.15	.07
❑ 164	Ron Coomer	.15	.07
❑ 165	Marty Cordova	.15	.07
❑ 166	Chuck Knoblauch	.25	.11
❑ 167	Matt Lawton RC	.75	.35
❑ 168	Pat Meares	.15	.07
❑ 169	Paul Molitor	.60	.25
❑ 170	Pedro Munoz	.15	.07
❑ 171	Jose Parra	.15	.07
❑ 172	Kirby Puckett	1.50	.70
❑ 173	Brad Radke	.25	.11
❑ 174	Jeff Reboulet	.15	.07
❑ 175	Rich Robertson	.15	.07
❑ 176	Frank Rodriguez	.15	.07
❑ 177	Scott Stahoviak	.15	.07
❑ 178	Dave Stevens	.15	.07
❑ 179	Matt Walbeck	.15	.07
❑ 180	Wade Boggs	.60	.25
❑ 181	David Cone	.25	.11
❑ 182	Tony Fernandez	.15	.07
❑ 183	Joe Girardi	.15	.07
❑ 184	Derek Jeter	2.50	1.10
❑ 185	Scott Kamieniecki	.15	.07
❑ 186	Pat Kelly	.15	.07
❑ 187	Jim Leyritz	.15	.07
❑ 188	Tino Martinez	.25	.11
❑ 189	Don Mattingly	1.50	.70
❑ 190	Jack McDowell	.15	.07
❑ 191	Jeff Nelson	.15	.07
❑ 192	Paul O'Neill	.60	.25
❑ 193	Melido Perez	.15	.07
❑ 194	Andy Pettitte	.25	.11
❑ 195	Mariano Rivera	.25	.11
❑ 196	Ruben Sierra	.15	.07
❑ 197	Mike Stanley	.15	.07
❑ 198	Darryl Strawberry	.25	.11
❑ 199	John Wetteland	.25	.11
❑ 200	Bob Wickman	.15	.07
❑ 201	Bernie Williams	.60	.25
❑ 202	Mark Acre	.15	.07
❑ 203	Geronimo Berroa	.15	.07
❑ 204	Mike Bordick	.15	.07
❑ 205	Scott Brosius	.25	.11
❑ 206	Dennis Eckersley	.25	.11
❑ 207	Brent Gates	.15	.07
❑ 208	Jason Giambi	.60	.25
❑ 209	Rickey Henderson	1.25	.55
❑ 210	Jose Herrera	.15	.07
❑ 211	Stan Javier	.15	.07
❑ 212	Doug Johns	.15	.07
❑ 213	Mark McGwire	2.50	1.10
❑ 214	Steve Ontiveros	.15	.07
❑ 215	Craig Paquette	.15	.07
❑ 216	Ariel Prieto	.15	.07
❑ 217	Carlos Reyes	.15	.07
❑ 218	Terry Steinbach	.15	.07
❑ 219	Todd Stottlemyre	.15	.07
❑ 220	Danny Tartabull	.15	.07
❑ 221	Todd Van Poppel	.15	.07
❑ 222	John Wasdin	.15	.07
❑ 223	George Williams	.15	.07
❑ 224	Steve Wojciechowski	.15	.07
❑ 225	Rich Amaral	.15	.07
❑ 226	Bobby Ayala	.15	.07
❑ 227	Tim Belcher	.15	.07
❑ 228	Andy Benes	.15	.07
❑ 229	Chris Bosio	.15	.07
❑ 230	Darren Bragg	.15	.07
❑ 231	Jay Buhner	.25	.11
❑ 232	Norm Charlton	.15	.07
❑ 233	Vince Coleman	.15	.07
❑ 234	Joey Cora	.15	.07
❑ 235	Russ Davis	.15	.07
❑ 236	Alex Diaz	.15	.07
❑ 237	Felix Fermin	.15	.07
❑ 238	Ken Griffey Jr.	2.00	.90
❑ 239	Sterling Hitchcock	.15	.07
❑ 240	Randy Johnson	.75	.35
❑ 241	Edgar Martinez	.40	.18
❑ 242	Bill Risley	.15	.07
❑ 243	Alex Rodriguez	1.50	.70
❑ 244	Luis Sojo	.15	.07
❑ 245	Dan Wilson	.15	.07
❑ 246	Bob Wolcott	.15	.07
❑ 247	Will Clark	.60	.25
❑ 248	Jeff Frye	.15	.07
❑ 249	Benji Gil	.15	.07
❑ 250	Juan Gonzalez	.60	.25
❑ 251	Rusty Greer	.25	.11
❑ 252	Kevin Gross	.15	.07
❑ 253	Roger McDowell	.15	.07
❑ 254	Mark McLemore	.15	.07
❑ 255	Otis Nixon	.15	.07
❑ 256	Luis Ortiz	.15	.07
❑ 257	Mike Pagliarulo	.15	.07
❑ 258	Dean Palmer	.25	.11
❑ 259	Roger Pavlik	.15	.07
❑ 260	Ivan Rodriguez	.60	.25
❑ 261	Kenny Rogers	.15	.07
❑ 262	Jeff Russell	.15	.07
❑ 263	Mickey Tettleton	.15	.07
❑ 264	Bob Tewksbury	.15	.07
❑ 265	Dave Valle	.15	.07
❑ 266	Matt Whiteside	.15	.07
❑ 267	Roberto Alomar	.60	.25
❑ 268	Joe Carter	.25	.11
❑ 269	Tony Castillo	.15	.07
❑ 270	Domingo Cedeno	.15	.07
❑ 271	Tim Crabtree UER	.15	.07
❑ 272	Carlos Delgado	.60	.25
❑ 273	Alex Gonzalez	.15	.07
❑ 274	Shawn Green	.60	.25
❑ 275	Juan Guzman	.15	.07
❑ 276	Pat Hentgen	.15	.07
❑ 277	Al Leiter	.25	.11
❑ 278	Sandy Martinez	.15	.07
❑ 279	Paul Menhart	.15	.07
❑ 280	John Olerud	.25	.11
❑ 281	Paul Quantrill	.15	.07
❑ 282	Ken Robinson	.15	.07
❑ 283	Ed Sprague	.15	.07
❑ 284	Mike Timlin	.15	.07
❑ 285	Steve Avery	.15	.07
❑ 286	Rafael Belliard	.15	.07
❑ 287	Jeff Blauser	.15	.07
❑ 288	Pedro Borbon	.15	.07
❑ 289	Brad Clontz	.15	.07
❑ 290	Mike Devereaux	.15	.07
❑ 291	Tom Glavine	.60	.25
❑ 292	Marquis Grissom	.15	.07
❑ 293	Chipper Jones	1.25	.55
❑ 294	David Justice	.25	.11
❑ 295	Mike Kelly	.15	.07
❑ 296	Ryan Klesko	.25	.11
❑ 297	Mark Lemke	.15	.07
❑ 298	Javier Lopez	.25	.11
❑ 299	Greg Maddux	1.50	.70
❑ 300	Fred McGriff	.40	.18
❑ 301	Greg McMichael	.15	.07
❑ 302	Kent Mercker	.15	.07
❑ 303	Mike Mordecai	.15	.07
❑ 304	Charlie O'Brien	.15	.07
❑ 305	Eduardo Perez	.15	.07
❑ 306	Luis Polonia	.15	.07
❑ 307	Jason Schmidt	.15	.07
❑ 308	John Smoltz	.25	.11
❑ 309	Terrell Wade	.15	.07
❑ 310	Mark Wohlers	.15	.07
❑ 311	Scott Bullett	.15	.07
❑ 312	Jim Bullinger	.15	.07
❑ 313	Larry Casian	.15	.07
❑ 314	Frank Castillo	.15	.07
❑ 315	Shawon Dunston	.15	.07
❑ 316	Kevin Foster	.15	.07
❑ 317	Matt Franco	.15	.07
❑ 318	Luis Gonzalez	.60	.25
❑ 319	Mark Grace	.60	.25
❑ 320	Jose Hernandez	.15	.07
❑ 321	Mike Hubbard	.15	.07
❑ 322	Brian McRae	.15	.07
❑ 323	Randy Myers	.15	.07
❑ 324	Jaime Navarro	.15	.07
❑ 325	Mark Parent	.15	.07
❑ 326	Mike Perez	.15	.07
❑ 327	Rey Sanchez	.15	.07
❑ 328	Ryne Sandberg	.75	.35
❑ 329	Scott Servais	.15	.07
❑ 330	Sammy Sosa	1.25	.55
❑ 331	Ozzie Timmons	.15	.07
❑ 332	Steve Trachsel	.15	.07
❑ 333	Todd Zeile	.15	.07
❑ 334	Bret Boone	.25	.11
❑ 335	Jeff Branson	.15	.07
❑ 336	Jeff Brantley	.15	.07
❑ 337	Dave Burba	.15	.07
❑ 338	Hector Carrasco	.15	.07
❑ 339	Mariano Duncan	.15	.07
❑ 340	Ron Gant	.15	.07
❑ 341	Lenny Harris	.15	.07
❑ 342	Xavier Hernandez	.15	.07
❑ 343	Thomas Howard	.15	.07
❑ 344	Mike Jackson	.15	.07

❑ 345 Barry Larkin .60 .25
❑ 346 Darren Lewis .15 .07
❑ 347 Hal Morris .15 .07
❑ 348 Eric Owens .15 .07
❑ 349 Mark Portugal .15 .07
❑ 350 Jose Rijo .15 .07
❑ 351 Reggie Sanders .15 .07
❑ 352 Benito Santiago .15 .07
❑ 353 Pete Schourek .15 .07
❑ 354 John Smiley .15 .07
❑ 355 Eddie Taubensee .15 .07
❑ 356 Jerome Walton .15 .07
❑ 357 David Wells .25 .11
❑ 358 Roger Bailey .15 .07
❑ 359 Jason Bates .15 .07
❑ 360 Dante Bichette .25 .11
❑ 361 Ellis Burks .25 .11
❑ 362 Vinny Castilla .25 .11
❑ 363 Andres Galarraga .40 .18
❑ 364 Darren Holmes .15 .07
❑ 365 Mike Kingery .15 .07
❑ 366 Curt Leskanic .15 .07
❑ 367 Quinton McCracken .15 .07
❑ 368 Mike Munoz .15 .07
❑ 369 David Nied .15 .07
❑ 370 Steve Reed .15 .07
❑ 371 Bryan Rekar .15 .07
❑ 372 Kevin Ritz .15 .07
❑ 373 Bruce Ruffin .15 .07
❑ 374 Bret Saberhagen .25 .11
❑ 375 Bill Swift .15 .07
❑ 376 John Vander Wal .15 .07
❑ 377 Larry Walker .40 .18
❑ 378 Walt Weiss .15 .07
❑ 379 Eric Young .15 .07
❑ 380 Kurt Abbott .15 .07
❑ 381 Alex Arias .15 .07
❑ 382 Jerry Browne .15 .07
❑ 383 John Burkett .15 .07
❑ 384 Greg Colbrunn .15 .07
❑ 385 Jeff Conine .15 .07
❑ 386 Andre Dawson .40 .18
❑ 387 Chris Hammond .15 .07
❑ 388 Charles Johnson .25 .11
❑ 389 Terry Mathews .15 .07
❑ 390 Robb Nen .15 .07
❑ 391 Joe Orsulak .15 .07
❑ 392 Terry Pendleton .25 .11
❑ 393 Pat Rapp .15 .07
❑ 394 Gary Sheffield .25 .11
❑ 395 Jesus Tavarez .15 .07
❑ 396 Marc Valdes .15 .07
❑ 397 Quilvio Veras .15 .07
❑ 398 Randy Veres .15 .07
❑ 399 Devon White .25 .11
❑ 400 Jeff Bagwell .75 .35
❑ 401 Derek Bell .15 .07
❑ 402 Craig Biggio .40 .18
❑ 403 John Cangelosi .15 .07
❑ 404 Jim Dougherty .15 .07
❑ 405 Doug Drabek .15 .07
❑ 406 Tony Eusebio .15 .07
❑ 407 Ricky Gutierrez .15 .07
❑ 408 Mike Hampton .25 .11
❑ 409 Dean Hartgraves .15 .07
❑ 410 John Hudek .15 .07
❑ 411 Brian L. Hunter .15 .07
❑ 412 Todd Jones .15 .07
❑ 413 Darryl Kile .25 .11
❑ 414 Dave Magadan .15 .07
❑ 415 Derrick May .15 .07
❑ 416 Orlando Miller .15 .07
❑ 417 James Mouton .15 .07
❑ 418 Shane Reynolds .15 .07
❑ 419 Greg Swindell .15 .07
❑ 420 Jeff Tabaka .15 .07
❑ 421 Dave Veres .15 .07
❑ 422 Billy Wagner .15 .07
❑ 423 Donne Wall .15 .07
❑ 424 Rick Wilkins .15 .07
❑ 425 Billy Ashley .15 .07
❑ 426 Mike Blowers .15 .07
❑ 427 Brett Butler .25 .11
❑ 428 Tom Candiotti .15 .07
❑ 429 Juan Castro .15 .07
❑ 430 John Cummings .15 .07
❑ 431 Delino DeShields .15 .07
❑ 432 Joey Eischen .15 .07
❑ 433 Chad Fonville .15 .07
❑ 434 Greg Gagne .15 .07
❑ 435 Dave Hansen .15 .07
❑ 436 Carlos Hernandez .15 .07
❑ 437 Todd Hollandsworth .15 .07
❑ 438 Eric Karros .25 .11
❑ 439 Roberto Kelly .15 .07
❑ 440 Ramon Martinez .15 .07
❑ 441 Raul Mondesi .25 .11
❑ 442 Hideo Nomo .75 .35
❑ 443 Antonio Osuna .15 .07
❑ 444 Chan Ho Park .25 .11
❑ 445 Mike Piazza 1.50 .70
❑ 446 Felix Rodriguez .15 .07
❑ 447 Kevin Tapani .15 .07
❑ 448 Ismael Valdes .15 .07
❑ 449 Todd Worrell .15 .07
❑ 450 Moises Alou .25 .11
❑ 451 Shane Andrews .15 .07
❑ 452 Yamil Benitez .15 .07
❑ 453 Sean Berry .15 .07
❑ 454 Wil Cordero .15 .07
❑ 455 Jeff Fassero .15 .07
❑ 456 Darrin Fletcher .15 .07
❑ 457 Cliff Floyd .25 .11
❑ 458 Mark Grudzielanek .15 .07
❑ 459 Gil Heredia .15 .07
❑ 460 Tim Laker .15 .07
❑ 461 Mike Lansing .15 .07
❑ 462 Pedro J.Martinez .75 .35
❑ 463 Carlos Perez .15 .07
❑ 464 Curtis Pride .15 .07
❑ 465 Mel Rojas .15 .07
❑ 466 Kirk Rueter .15 .07
❑ 467 F.P. Santangelo .15 .07
❑ 468 Tim Scott .15 .07
❑ 469 David Segui .15 .07
❑ 470 Tony Tarasco .15 .07
❑ 471 Rondell White .25 .11
❑ 472 Edgardo Alfonzo .25 .11
❑ 473 Tim Bogar .15 .07
❑ 474 Rico Brogna .15 .07
❑ 475 Damon Buford .15 .07
❑ 476 Paul Byrd .15 .07
❑ 477 Carl Everett .25 .11
❑ 478 John Franco .25 .11
❑ 479 Todd Hundley .15 .07
❑ 480 Butch Huskey .15 .07
❑ 481 Jason Isringhausen .25 .11
❑ 482 Bobby Jones .15 .07
❑ 483 Chris Jones .15 .07
❑ 484 Jeff Kent .40 .18
❑ 485 Dave Mlicki .15 .07
❑ 486 Robert Person .15 .07
❑ 487 Bill Pulsipher .15 .07
❑ 488 Kelly Stinnett .15 .07
❑ 489 Ryan Thompson .15 .07
❑ 490 Jose Vizcaino .15 .07
❑ 491 Howard Battle .15 .07
❑ 492 Toby Borland .15 .07
❑ 493 Ricky Bottalico .15 .07
❑ 494 Darren Daulton .25 .11
❑ 495 Lenny Dykstra .25 .11
❑ 496 Jim Eisenreich .15 .07
❑ 497 Sid Fernandez .15 .07
❑ 498 Tyler Green .15 .07
❑ 499 Charlie Hayes .15 .07
❑ 500 Gregg Jefferies .15 .07
❑ 501 Kevin Jordan .15 .07
❑ 502 Tony Longmire .15 .07
❑ 503 Tom Marsh .15 .07
❑ 504 Michael Mimbs .15 .07
❑ 505 Mickey Morandini .15 .07
❑ 506 Gene Schall .15 .07
❑ 507 Curt Schilling .60 .25
❑ 508 Heathcliff Slocumb .15 .07
❑ 509 Kevin Stocker .15 .07
❑ 510 Andy Van Slyke .25 .11
❑ 511 Lenny Webster .15 .07
❑ 512 Mark Whiten .15 .07
❑ 513 Mike Williams .15 .07
❑ 514 Jay Bell .25 .11
❑ 515 Jacob Brumfield .15 .07
❑ 516 Jason Christiansen .15 .07
❑ 517 Dave Clark .15 .07
❑ 518 Midre Cummings .15 .07
❑ 519 Angelo Encarnacion .15 .07
❑ 520 John Ericks .15 .07
❑ 521 Carlos Garcia .15 .07
❑ 522 Mark Johnson .15 .07
❑ 523 Jeff King .15 .07
❑ 524 Nelson Liriano .15 .07
❑ 525 Esteban Loaiza .15 .07
❑ 526 Al Martin .15 .07
❑ 527 Orlando Merced .15 .07
❑ 528 Dan Miceli .15 .07
❑ 529 Ramon Morel .15 .07
❑ 530 Denny Neagle .25 .11
❑ 531 Steve Parris .15 .07
❑ 532 Dan Plesac .15 .07
❑ 533 Don Slaught .15 .07
❑ 534 Paul Wagner .15 .07
❑ 535 John Wehner .15 .07
❑ 536 Kevin Young .15 .07
❑ 537 Allen Battle .15 .07
❑ 538 David Bell .15 .07
❑ 539 Alan Benes .15 .07
❑ 540 Scott Cooper .15 .07
❑ 541 Tripp Cromer .15 .07
❑ 542 Tony Fossas .15 .07
❑ 543 Bernard Gilkey .15 .07
❑ 544 Tom Henke .15 .07
❑ 545 Brian Jordan .25 .11
❑ 546 Ray Lankford .15 .07
❑ 547 John Mabry .15 .07
❑ 548 T.J. Mathews .15 .07
❑ 549 Mike Morgan .15 .07
❑ 550 Jose Oliva .15 .07
❑ 551 Jose Oquendo .15 .07
❑ 552 Donovan Osborne .15 .07
❑ 553 Tom Pagnozzi .15 .07
❑ 554 Mark Petkovsek .15 .07
❑ 555 Danny Sheaffer .15 .07
❑ 556 Ozzie Smith .75 .35
❑ 557 Mark Sweeney .15 .07
❑ 558 Allen Watson .15 .07
❑ 559 Andy Ashby .15 .07
❑ 560 Brad Ausmus .15 .07
❑ 561 Willie Blair .15 .07
❑ 562 Ken Caminiti .25 .11
❑ 563 Andujar Cedeno .15 .07
❑ 564 Glenn Dishman .15 .07
❑ 565 Steve Finley .25 .11
❑ 566 Bryce Florie .15 .07
❑ 567 Tony Gwynn 1.25 .55
❑ 568 Joey Hamilton .15 .07
❑ 569 Dustin Hermanson .15 .07
❑ 570 Trevor Hoffman .25 .11
❑ 571 Brian Johnson .15 .07
❑ 572 Marc Kroon .15 .07
❑ 573 Scott Livingstone .15 .07
❑ 574 Marc Newfield .15 .07
❑ 575 Melvin Nieves .15 .07
❑ 576 Jody Reed .15 .07
❑ 577 Bip Roberts .15 .07
❑ 578 Scott Sanders .15 .07
❑ 579 Fernando Valenzuela .25 .11
❑ 580 Eddie Williams .15 .07
❑ 581 Rod Beck .15 .07
❑ 582 Marvin Benard RC .25 .11
❑ 583 Barry Bonds 1.50 .70
❑ 584 Jamie Brewington RC .15 .07
❑ 585 Mark Carreon .15 .07
❑ 586 Royce Clayton .15 .07
❑ 587 Shawn Estes .25 .11
❑ 588 Glenallen Hill .15 .07
❑ 589 Mark Leiter .15 .07
❑ 590 Kirt Manwaring .15 .07
❑ 591 David McCarty .15 .07
❑ 592 Terry Mulholland .15 .07
❑ 593 John Patterson .15 .07
❑ 594 J.R. Phillips .15 .07
❑ 595 Deion Sanders .25 .11
❑ 596 Steve Scarsone .15 .07
❑ 597 Robby Thompson .15 .07
❑ 598 Sergio Valdez .15 .07
❑ 599 W.Van Landingham .15 .07
❑ 600 Matt Williams .40 .18
❑ P20 Cal Ripken Promo 3.00 1.35

1996 Fleer Update

	MINT	NRMT
COMPLETE SET (250)	30.00	13.50
❑ U1 Roberto Alomar	.60	.25
❑ U2 Mike Devereaux	.15	.07
❑ U3 Scott McClain RC	.15	.07
❑ U4 Roger McDowell	.15	.07
❑ U5 Kent Mercker	.15	.07
❑ U6 Jimmy Myers RC	.15	.07
❑ U7 Randy Myers	.15	.07
❑ U8 B.J. Surhoff	.25	.11
❑ U9 Tony Tarasco	.15	.07
❑ U10 David Wells	.25	.11
❑ U11 Wil Cordero	.15	.07
❑ U12 Tom Gordon	.15	.07
❑ U13 Reggie Jefferson	.15	.07
❑ U14 Jose Malave	.15	.07
❑ U15 Kevin Mitchell	.15	.07
❑ U16 Jamie Moyer	.15	.07
❑ U17 Heathcliff Slocumb	.15	.07
❑ U18 Mike Stanley	.15	.07
❑ U19 George Arias	.15	.07
❑ U20 Jorge Fabregas	.15	.07
❑ U21 Don Slaught	.15	.07
❑ U22 Randy Velarde	.15	.07
❑ U23 Harold Baines	.25	.11
❑ U24 Mike Cameron RC	2.50	1.10
❑ U25 Darren Lewis	.15	.07
❑ U26 Tony Phillips	.15	.07
❑ U27 Bill Simas	.15	.07
❑ U28 Chris Snopek	.15	.07
❑ U29 Kevin Tapani	.15	.07
❑ U30 Danny Tartabull	.15	.07
❑ U31 Julio Franco	.25	.11
❑ U32 Jack McDowell	.15	.07
❑ U33 Kimera Bartee	.15	.07
❑ U34 Mark Lewis	.15	.07
❑ U35 Melvin Nieves	.15	.07
❑ U36 Mark Parent	.15	.07
❑ U37 Eddie Williams	.15	.07
❑ U38 Tim Belcher	.15	.07
❑ U39 Sal Fasano	.15	.07
❑ U40 Chris Haney	.15	.07
❑ U41 Mike Macfarlane	.15	.07
❑ U42 Jose Offerman	.15	.07
❑ U43 Joe Randa	.15	.07
❑ U44 Bip Roberts	.15	.07
❑ U45 Chuck Carr	.15	.07
❑ U46 Bobby Hughes	.15	.07
❑ U47 Graeme Lloyd	.15	.07
❑ U48 Ben McDonald	.15	.07
❑ U49 Kevin Wickander	.15	.07
❑ U50 Rick Aguilera	.15	.07
❑ U51 Mike Durant	.15	.07
❑ U52 Chip Hale	.15	.07
❑ U53 LaTroy Hawkins	.15	.07
❑ U54 Dave Hollins	.15	.07
❑ U55 Roberto Kelly	.15	.07
❑ U56 Paul Molitor	.60	.25
❑ U57 Dan Naulty	.15	.07
❑ U58 Mariano Duncan	.15	.07
❑ U59 Andy Fox	.15	.07
❑ U60 Joe Girardi	.15	.07
❑ U61 Dwight Gooden	.25	.11
❑ U62 Jimmy Key	.25	.11
❑ U63 Matt Luke	.15	.07
❑ U64 Tino Martinez	.25	.11
❑ U65 Jeff Nelson	.15	.07
❑ U66 Tim Raines	.25	.11
❑ U67 Ruben Rivera	.15	.07
❑ U68 Kenny Rogers	.15	.07
❑ U69 Gerald Williams	.15	.07
❑ U70 Tony Batista RC	2.00	.90
❑ U71 Allen Battle	.15	.07
❑ U72 Jim Corsi	.15	.07
❑ U73 Steve Cox	.15	.07
❑ U74 Pedro Munoz	.15	.07
❑ U75 Phil Plantier	.15	.07
❑ U76 Scott Spiezio	.15	.07
❑ U77 Ernie Young	.15	.07
❑ U78 Russ Davis	.15	.07
❑ U79 Sterling Hitchcock	.15	.07
❑ U80 Edwin Hurtado	.15	.07
❑ U81 Raul Ibanez RC	.15	.07
❑ U82 Mike Jackson	.15	.07
❑ U83 Ricky Jordan	.15	.07
❑ U84 Paul Sorrento	.15	.07
❑ U85 Doug Strange	.15	.07
❑ U86 M.Brandenburg RC	.15	.07
❑ U87 Damon Buford	.15	.07
❑ U88 Kevin Elster	.15	.07
❑ U89 Darryl Hamilton	.15	.07
❑ U90 Ken Hill	.15	.07
❑ U91 Ed Vosberg	.15	.07
❑ U92 Craig Worthington	.15	.07
❑ U93 Tilson Brito RC	.15	.07
❑ U94 Giovanni Carrara RC	.15	.07
❑ U95 Felipe Crespo	.15	.07
❑ U96 Erik Hanson	.15	.07
❑ U97 Marty Janzen RC	.15	.07
❑ U98 Otis Nixon	.15	.07
❑ U99 Charlie O'Brien	.15	.07
❑ U100 Robert Perez	.15	.07
❑ U101 Paul Quantrill	.15	.07
❑ U102 Bill Risley	.15	.07
❑ U103 Juan Samuel	.15	.07
❑ U104 Jermaine Dye	.25	.11
❑ U105 W.Monds RC	.15	.07
❑ U106 Dwight Smith	.15	.07
❑ U107 Jerome Walton	.15	.07
❑ U108 Terry Adams	.15	.07
❑ U109 Leo Gomez	.15	.07
❑ U110 Robin Jennings	.15	.07
❑ U111 Doug Jones	.15	.07
❑ U112 Brooks Kieschnick	.15	.07
❑ U113 Dave Magadan	.15	.07
❑ U114 Jason Maxwell RC	.15	.07
❑ U115 Rodney Myers RC	.15	.07
❑ U116 Eric Anthony	.15	.07
❑ U117 Vince Coleman	.15	.07
❑ U118 Eric Davis	.25	.11
❑ U119 Steve Gibralter	.15	.07
❑ U120 Curtis Goodwin	.15	.07
❑ U121 Willie Greene	.15	.07
❑ U122 Mike Kelly	.15	.07
❑ U123 Marcus Moore	.15	.07
❑ U124 Chad Mottola	.15	.07
❑ U125 Chris Sabo	.15	.07
❑ U126 Roger Salkeld	.15	.07
❑ U127 Pedro Castellano	.15	.07
❑ U128 Trenidad Hubbard	.15	.07
❑ U129 Jayhawk Owens	.15	.07
❑ U130 Jeff Reed	.15	.07
❑ U131 Kevin Brown	.25	.11
❑ U132 Al Leiter	.25	.11
❑ U133 Matt Mantei RC	1.00	.45
❑ U134 Dave Weathers	.15	.07
❑ U135 Devon White	.25	.11
❑ U136 Bob Abreu	.60	.25
❑ U137 Sean Berry	.15	.07
❑ U138 Doug Brocail	.15	.07
❑ U139 Richard Hidalgo	.25	.11
❑ U140 Alvin Morman	.15	.07
❑ U141 Mike Blowers	.15	.07
❑ U142 Roger Cedeno	.15	.07
❑ U143 Greg Gagne	.15	.07
❑ U144 Karim Garcia	.15	.07
❑ U145 Wilton Guerrero RC	.25	.11
❑ U146 Israel Alcantara RC	.15	.07
❑ U147 Omar Daal	.15	.07
❑ U148 Ryan McGuire	.15	.07
❑ U149 Sherman Obando	.15	.07
❑ U150 Jose Paniagua	.15	.07
❑ U151 Henry Rodriguez	.15	.07
❑ U152 Andy Stankiewicz	.15	.07
❑ U153 Dave Veres	.15	.07
❑ U154 Juan Acevedo	.15	.07
❑ U155 Mark Clark	.15	.07
❑ U156 Bernard Gilkey	.15	.07
❑ U157 Pete Harnisch	.15	.07
❑ U158 Lance Johnson	.15	.07
❑ U159 Brent Mayne	.15	.07
❑ U160 Rey Ordonez	.15	.07
❑ U161 Kevin Roberson	.15	.07
❑ U162 Paul Wilson	.15	.07
❑ U163 David Doster RC	.15	.07
❑ U164 Mike Grace RC	.15	.07
❑ U165 Rich Hunter RC	.15	.07
❑ U166 Pete Incaviglia	.15	.07
❑ U167 Mike Lieberthal	.25	.11
❑ U168 Terry Mulholland	.15	.07
❑ U169 Ken Ryan	.15	.07
❑ U170 Benito Santiago	.15	.07
❑ U171 Kevin Sefcik RC	.15	.07
❑ U172 Lee Tinsley	.15	.07
❑ U173 Todd Zeile	.15	.07
❑ U174 F.Cordova RC	.15	.07
❑ U175 Danny Darwin	.15	.07
❑ U176 Charlie Hayes	.15	.07
❑ U177 Jason Kendall	.25	.11
❑ U178 Mike Kingery	.15	.07
❑ U179 Jon Lieber	.15	.07
❑ U180 Zane Smith	.15	.07
❑ U181 Luis Alicea	.15	.07
❑ U182 Cory Bailey	.15	.07
❑ U183 Andy Benes	.15	.07
❑ U184 Pat Borders	.15	.07
❑ U185 Mike Busby RC	.15	.07
❑ U186 Royce Clayton	.15	.07
❑ U187 Dennis Eckersley	.25	.11
❑ U188 Gary Gaetti	.25	.11
❑ U189 Ron Gant	.15	.07
❑ U190 Aaron Holbert	.15	.07
❑ U191 Willie McGee	.25	.11
❑ U192 Miguel Mejia RC	.15	.07
❑ U193 Jeff Parrett	.15	.07
❑ U194 Todd Stottlemyre	.15	.07
❑ U195 Sean Bergman	.15	.07
❑ U196 Archi Cianfrocco	.15	.07
❑ U197 Rickey Henderson	1.25	.55
❑ U198 Wally Joyner	.25	.11
❑ U199 Craig Shipley	.15	.07
❑ U200 Bob Tewksbury	.15	.07
❑ U201 Tim Worrell	.15	.07
❑ U202 Rich Aurilia RC	3.00	1.35
❑ U203 Doug Creek	.15	.07
❑ U204 Shawon Dunston	.15	.07
❑ U205 O.Fernandez RC	.15	.07
❑ U206 Mark Gardner	.15	.07
❑ U207 Stan Javier	.15	.07
❑ U208 Marcus Jensen	.15	.07
❑ U209 Chris Singleton RC	1.00	.45
❑ U210 Allen Watson	.15	.07
❑ U211 Jeff Bagwell ENC	.75	.35
❑ U212 Derek Bell ENC	.15	.07
❑ U213 Albert Belle ENC	.25	.11
❑ U214 Wade Boggs ENC	.60	.25
❑ U215 Barry Bonds ENC	1.50	.70
❑ U216 Jose Canseco ENC	.60	.25
❑ U217 Marty Cordova ENC	.15	.07
❑ U218 Jim Edmonds ENC	.40	.18
❑ U219 Cecil Fielder ENC	.25	.11
❑ U220 A.Galarraga ENC	.40	.18
❑ U221 Juan Gonzalez ENC	.60	.25
❑ U222 Mark Grace ENC	.60	.25
❑ U223 Ken Griffey Jr. ENC	2.00	.90
❑ U224 Tony Gwynn ENC	1.25	.55
❑ U225 J. Isringhausen ENC	.15	.07
❑ U226 Derek Jeter ENC	2.50	1.10
❑ U227 Randy Johnson ENC	.75	.35
❑ U228 Chipper Jones ENC	1.25	.55
❑ U229 Ryan Klesko ENC	.25	.11
❑ U230 Barry Larkin ENC	.60	.25
❑ U231 Kenny Lofton ENC	.25	.11
❑ U232 Greg Maddux ENC	1.50	.70
❑ U233 Raul Mondesi ENC	.25	.11
❑ U234 Hideo Nomo ENC	.40	.18
❑ U235 Mike Piazza ENC	1.50	.70

❑ U236 Manny Ramirez ENC .75 .35
❑ U237 Cal Ripken ENC 1.50 .70
❑ U238 Tim Salmon ENC .25 .11
❑ U239 Ryne Sandberg ENC .75 .35
❑ U240 Reggie Sanders ENC .15 .07
❑ U241 Gary Sheffield ENC .25 .11
❑ U242 Sammy Sosa ENC 1.25 .55
❑ U243 Frank Thomas ENC .75 .35
❑ U244 Mo Vaughn ENC .25 .11
❑ U245 Matt Williams ENC .40 .18
❑ U246 Barry Bonds CL .75 .35
❑ U247 Ken Griffey Jr. CL 1.00 .45
❑ U248 Rey Ordonez CL .15 .07
❑ U249 Ryne Sandberg CL .40 .18
❑ U250 Frank Thomas CL .40 .18

1997 Fleer

	MINT	NRMT
COMPLETE SET (761)	90.00	40.00
COMPLETE SERIES 1 (500)	50.00	22.00
COMPLETE SERIES 2 (261)	40.00	18.00
COMMON CARD (1-750)	.15	.07
COMMON CARD (751-761)	.25	.11

❑ 1 Roberto Alomar .60 .25
❑ 2 Brady Anderson .30 .14
❑ 3 Bobby Bonilla .30 .14
❑ 4 Rocky Coppinger .15 .07
❑ 5 Cesar Devarez .15 .07
❑ 6 Scott Erickson .15 .07
❑ 7 Jeffrey Hammonds .15 .07
❑ 8 Chris Hoiles .15 .07
❑ 9 Eddie Murray .60 .25
❑ 10 Mike Mussina .60 .25
❑ 11 Randy Myers .15 .07
❑ 12 Rafael Palmeiro .60 .25
❑ 13 Cal Ripken 2.50 1.10
❑ 14 B.J. Surhoff .30 .14
❑ 15 David Wells .30 .14
❑ 16 Todd Zeile .15 .07
❑ 17 Darren Bragg .15 .07
❑ 18 Jose Canseco .60 .25
❑ 19 Roger Clemens 1.50 .70
❑ 20 Wil Cordero .15 .07
❑ 21 Jeff Frye .15 .07
❑ 22 Nomar Garciaparra 1.50 .70
❑ 23 Tom Gordon .15 .07
❑ 24 Mike Greenwell .15 .07
❑ 25 Reggie Jefferson .15 .07
❑ 26 Jose Malave .15 .07
❑ 27 Tim Naehring .15 .07
❑ 28 Troy O'Leary .15 .07
❑ 29 Heathcliff Slocumb .15 .07
❑ 30 Mike Stanley .15 .07
❑ 31 John Valentin .15 .07
❑ 32 Mo Vaughn .30 .14
❑ 33 Tim Wakefield .15 .07
❑ 34 Garret Anderson .30 .14
❑ 35 George Arias .15 .07
❑ 36 Shawn Boskie .15 .07
❑ 37 Chili Davis .30 .14
❑ 38 Jason Dickson .15 .07
❑ 39 Gary DiSarcina .15 .07
❑ 40 Jim Edmonds .40 .18
❑ 41 Darin Erstad .60 .25
❑ 42 Jorge Fabregas .15 .07
❑ 43 Chuck Finley .30 .14
❑ 44 Todd Greene .15 .07
❑ 45 Mike Holtz .15 .07
❑ 46 Rex Hudler .15 .07
❑ 47 Mike James .15 .07
❑ 48 Mark Langston .15 .07
❑ 49 Troy Percival .15 .07
❑ 50 Tim Salmon .30 .14
❑ 51 Jeff Schmidt .15 .07
❑ 52 J.T. Snow .30 .14
❑ 53 Randy Velarde .15 .07
❑ 54 Wilson Alvarez .15 .07
❑ 55 Harold Baines .30 .14
❑ 56 James Baldwin .15 .07
❑ 57 Jason Bere .15 .07
❑ 58 Mike Cameron .30 .14
❑ 59 Ray Durham .30 .14
❑ 60 Alex Fernandez .15 .07
❑ 61 Ozzie Guillen .15 .07
❑ 62 Roberto Hernandez .15 .07
❑ 63 Ron Karkovice .15 .07
❑ 64 Darren Lewis .15 .07
❑ 65 Dave Martinez .15 .07
❑ 66 Lyle Mouton .15 .07
❑ 67 Greg Norton .15 .07
❑ 68 Tony Phillips .15 .07
❑ 69 Chris Snopek .15 .07
❑ 70 Kevin Tapani .15 .07
❑ 71 Danny Tartabull .15 .07
❑ 72 Frank Thomas .75 .35
❑ 73 Robin Ventura .30 .14
❑ 74 Sandy Alomar Jr. .30 .14
❑ 75 Albert Belle .30 .14
❑ 76 Mark Carreon .15 .07
❑ 77 Julio Franco .30 .14
❑ 78 Brian Giles RC 2.50 1.10
❑ 79 Orel Hershiser .30 .14
❑ 80 Kenny Lofton .30 .14
❑ 81 Dennis Martinez .30 .14
❑ 82 Jack McDowell .15 .07
❑ 83 Jose Mesa .15 .07
❑ 84 Charles Nagy .15 .07
❑ 85 Chad Ogea .15 .07
❑ 86 Eric Plunk .15 .07
❑ 87 Manny Ramirez .75 .35
❑ 88 Kevin Seitzer .15 .07
❑ 89 Julian Tavarez .15 .07
❑ 90 Jim Thome .60 .25
❑ 91 Jose Vizcaino .15 .07
❑ 92 Omar Vizquel .30 .14
❑ 93 Brad Ausmus .15 .07
❑ 94 Kimera Bartee .15 .07
❑ 95 Raul Casanova .15 .07
❑ 96 Tony Clark .30 .14
❑ 97 John Cummings .15 .07
❑ 98 Travis Fryman .30 .14
❑ 99 Bob Higginson .30 .14
❑ 100 Mark Lewis .15 .07
❑ 101 Felipe Lira .15 .07
❑ 102 Phil Nevin .30 .14
❑ 103 Melvin Nieves .15 .07
❑ 104 Curtis Pride .15 .07
❑ 105 A.J. Sager .15 .07
❑ 106 Ruben Sierra .15 .07
❑ 107 Justin Thompson .15 .07
❑ 108 Alan Trammell .40 .18
❑ 109 Kevin Appier .30 .14
❑ 110 Tim Belcher .15 .07
❑ 111 Jaime Bluma .15 .07
❑ 112 Johnny Damon .30 .14
❑ 113 Tom Goodwin .15 .07
❑ 114 Chris Haney .15 .07
❑ 115 Keith Lockhart .15 .07
❑ 116 Mike Macfarlane .15 .07
❑ 117 Jeff Montgomery .15 .07
❑ 118 Jose Offerman .15 .07
❑ 119 Craig Paquette .15 .07
❑ 120 Joe Randa .15 .07
❑ 121 Bip Roberts .15 .07
❑ 122 Jose Rosado .15 .07
❑ 123 Mike Sweeney .30 .14
❑ 124 Michael Tucker .15 .07
❑ 125 Jeromy Burnitz .30 .14
❑ 126 Jeff Cirillo .30 .14
❑ 127 Jeff D'Amico .15 .07
❑ 128 Mike Fetters .15 .07
❑ 129 John Jaha .15 .07
❑ 130 Scott Karl .15 .07
❑ 131 Jesse Levis .15 .07
❑ 132 Mark Loretta .15 .07
❑ 133 Mike Matheny .15 .07
❑ 134 Ben McDonald .15 .07
❑ 135 Matt Mieske .15 .07
❑ 136 Marc Newfield .15 .07
❑ 137 Dave Nilsson .15 .07
❑ 138 Jose Valentin .15 .07
❑ 139 Fernando Vina .15 .07
❑ 140 Bob Wickman .15 .07
❑ 141 Gerald Williams .15 .07
❑ 142 Rick Aguilera .15 .07
❑ 143 Rich Becker .15 .07
❑ 144 Ron Coomer .15 .07
❑ 145 Marty Cordova .15 .07
❑ 146 Roberto Kelly .15 .07
❑ 147 Chuck Knoblauch .30 .14
❑ 148 Matt Lawton .30 .14
❑ 149 Pat Meares .15 .07
❑ 150 Travis Miller .15 .07
❑ 151 Paul Molitor .60 .25
❑ 152 Greg Myers .15 .07
❑ 153 Dan Naulty .15 .07
❑ 154 Kirby Puckett 1.50 .70
❑ 155 Brad Radke .30 .14
❑ 156 Frank Rodriguez .15 .07
❑ 157 Scott Stahoviak .15 .07
❑ 158 Dave Stevens .15 .07
❑ 159 Matt Walbeck .15 .07
❑ 160 Todd Walker .15 .07
❑ 161 Wade Boggs .60 .25
❑ 162 David Cone .30 .14
❑ 163 Mariano Duncan .15 .07
❑ 164 Cecil Fielder .30 .14
❑ 165 Joe Girardi .15 .07
❑ 166 Dwight Gooden .30 .14
❑ 167 Charlie Hayes .15 .07
❑ 168 Derek Jeter 2.50 1.10
❑ 169 Jimmy Key .30 .14
❑ 170 Jim Leyritz .15 .07
❑ 171 Tino Martinez .30 .14
❑ 172 Ramiro Mendoza RC .50 .23
❑ 173 Jeff Nelson .15 .07
❑ 174 Paul O'Neill .60 .25
❑ 175 Andy Pettitte .30 .14
❑ 176 Mariano Rivera .30 .14
❑ 177 Ruben Rivera .15 .07
❑ 178 Kenny Rogers .15 .07
❑ 179 Darryl Strawberry .30 .14
❑ 180 John Wetteland .30 .14
❑ 181 Bernie Williams .60 .25
❑ 182 Willie Adams .15 .07
❑ 183 Tony Batista .30 .14
❑ 184 Geronimo Berroa .15 .07
❑ 185 Mike Bordick .15 .07
❑ 186 Scott Brosius .30 .14
❑ 187 Bobby Chouinard .15 .07
❑ 188 Jim Corsi .15 .07
❑ 189 Brent Gates .15 .07
❑ 190 Jason Giambi .60 .25
❑ 191 Jose Herrera .15 .07
❑ 192 Damon Mashore .15 .07
❑ 193 Mark McGwire 2.50 1.10
❑ 194 Mike Mohler .15 .07
❑ 195 Scott Spiezio .15 .07
❑ 196 Terry Steinbach .15 .07
❑ 197 Bill Taylor .15 .07
❑ 198 John Wasdin .15 .07
❑ 199 Steve Wojciechowski .15 .07
❑ 200 Ernie Young .15 .07
❑ 201 Rich Amaral .15 .07
❑ 202 Jay Buhner .30 .14
❑ 203 Norm Charlton .15 .07
❑ 204 Joey Cora .15 .07
❑ 205 Russ Davis .15 .07
❑ 206 Ken Griffey Jr. 2.00 .90
❑ 207 Sterling Hitchcock .15 .07
❑ 208 Brian Hunter .15 .07
❑ 209 Raul Ibanez .15 .07
❑ 210 Randy Johnson .75 .35
❑ 211 Edgar Martinez .40 .18
❑ 212 Jamie Moyer .15 .07
❑ 213 Alex Rodriguez 1.50 .70
❑ 214 Paul Sorrento .15 .07
❑ 215 Matt Wagner .15 .07

- ❑ 216 Bob Wells .15 .07
- ❑ 217 Dan Wilson .15 .07
- ❑ 218 Damon Buford .15 .07
- ❑ 219 Will Clark .60 .25
- ❑ 220 Kevin Elster .15 .07
- ❑ 221 Juan Gonzalez .60 .25
- ❑ 222 Rusty Greer .30 .14
- ❑ 223 Kevin Gross .15 .07
- ❑ 224 Darryl Hamilton .15 .07
- ❑ 225 Mike Henneman .15 .07
- ❑ 226 Ken Hill .15 .07
- ❑ 227 Mark McLemore .15 .07
- ❑ 228 Darren Oliver .15 .07
- ❑ 229 Dean Palmer .30 .14
- ❑ 230 Roger Pavlik .15 .07
- ❑ 231 Ivan Rodriguez .60 .25
- ❑ 232 Mickey Tettleton .15 .07
- ❑ 233 Bobby Witt .15 .07
- ❑ 234 Jacob Brumfield .15 .07
- ❑ 235 Joe Carter .30 .14
- ❑ 236 Tim Crabtree .15 .07
- ❑ 237 Carlos Delgado .60 .25
- ❑ 238 Huck Flener .15 .07
- ❑ 239 Alex Gonzalez .15 .07
- ❑ 240 Shawn Green .60 .25
- ❑ 241 Juan Guzman .15 .07
- ❑ 242 Pat Hentgen .15 .07
- ❑ 243 Marty Janzen .15 .07
- ❑ 244 Sandy Martinez .15 .07
- ❑ 245 Otis Nixon .15 .07
- ❑ 246 Charlie O'Brien .15 .07
- ❑ 247 John Olerud .30 .14
- ❑ 248 Robert Perez .15 .07
- ❑ 249 Ed Sprague .15 .07
- ❑ 250 Mike Timlin .15 .07
- ❑ 251 Steve Avery .15 .07
- ❑ 252 Jeff Blauser .15 .07
- ❑ 253 Brad Clontz .15 .07
- ❑ 254 Jermaine Dye .30 .14
- ❑ 255 Tom Glavine .60 .25
- ❑ 256 Marquis Grissom .15 .07
- ❑ 257 Andruw Jones .75 .35
- ❑ 258 Chipper Jones 1.25 .55
- ❑ 259 David Justice .30 .14
- ❑ 260 Ryan Klesko .30 .14
- ❑ 261 Mark Lemke .15 .07
- ❑ 262 Javier Lopez .30 .14
- ❑ 263 Greg Maddux 1.50 .70
- ❑ 264 Fred McGriff .40 .18
- ❑ 265 Greg McMichael .15 .07
- ❑ 266 Denny Neagle .30 .14
- ❑ 267 Terry Pendleton .30 .14
- ❑ 268 Eddie Perez .15 .07
- ❑ 269 John Smoltz .30 .14
- ❑ 270 Terrell Wade .15 .07
- ❑ 271 Mark Wohlers .15 .07
- ❑ 272 Terry Adams .15 .07
- ❑ 273 Brant Brown .15 .07
- ❑ 274 Leo Gomez .15 .07
- ❑ 275 Luis Gonzalez .60 .25
- ❑ 276 Mark Grace .60 .25
- ❑ 277 Tyler Houston .15 .07
- ❑ 278 Robin Jennings .15 .07
- ❑ 279 Brooks Kieschnick .15 .07
- ❑ 280 Brian McRae .15 .07
- ❑ 281 Jaime Navarro .15 .07
- ❑ 282 Ryne Sandberg .75 .35
- ❑ 283 Scott Servais .15 .07
- ❑ 284 Sammy Sosa 1.25 .55
- ❑ 285 Dave Swartzbaugh .15 .07
- ❑ 286 Amaury Telemaco .15 .07
- ❑ 287 Steve Trachsel .15 .07
- ❑ 288 Pedro Valdes .15 .07
- ❑ 289 Turk Wendell .15 .07
- ❑ 290 Bret Boone .30 .14
- ❑ 291 Jeff Branson .15 .07
- ❑ 292 Jeff Brantley .15 .07
- ❑ 293 Eric Davis .30 .14
- ❑ 294 Willie Greene .15 .07
- ❑ 295 Thomas Howard .15 .07
- ❑ 296 Barry Larkin .60 .25
- ❑ 297 Kevin Mitchell .15 .07
- ❑ 298 Hal Morris .15 .07
- ❑ 299 Chad Mottola .15 .07
- ❑ 300 Joe Oliver .15 .07
- ❑ 301 Mark Portugal .15 .07
- ❑ 302 Roger Salkeld .15 .07
- ❑ 303 Reggie Sanders .15 .07
- ❑ 304 Pete Schourek .15 .07
- ❑ 305 John Smiley .15 .07
- ❑ 306 Eddie Taubensee .15 .07
- ❑ 307 Dante Bichette .30 .14
- ❑ 308 Ellis Burks .30 .14
- ❑ 309 Vinny Castilla .30 .14
- ❑ 310 Andres Galarraga .40 .18
- ❑ 311 Curt Leskanic .15 .07
- ❑ 312 Quinton McCracken .15 .07
- ❑ 313 Neifi Perez .15 .07
- ❑ 314 Jeff Reed .15 .07
- ❑ 315 Steve Reed .15 .07
- ❑ 316 Armando Reynoso .15 .07
- ❑ 317 Kevin Ritz .15 .07
- ❑ 318 Bruce Ruffin .15 .07
- ❑ 319 Larry Walker .40 .18
- ❑ 320 Walt Weiss .15 .07
- ❑ 321 Jamey Wright .15 .07
- ❑ 322 Eric Young .15 .07
- ❑ 323 Kurt Abbott .15 .07
- ❑ 324 Alex Arias .15 .07
- ❑ 325 Kevin Brown .30 .14
- ❑ 326 Luis Castillo .15 .07
- ❑ 327 Greg Colbrunn .15 .07
- ❑ 328 Jeff Conine .15 .07
- ❑ 329 Andre Dawson .40 .18
- ❑ 330 Charles Johnson .30 .14
- ❑ 331 Al Leiter .30 .14
- ❑ 332 Ralph Milliard .15 .07
- ❑ 333 Robb Nen .15 .07
- ❑ 334 Pat Rapp .15 .07
- ❑ 335 Edgar Renteria .15 .07
- ❑ 336 Gary Sheffield .30 .14
- ❑ 337 Devon White .30 .14
- ❑ 338 Bob Abreu .30 .14
- ❑ 339 Jeff Bagwell .75 .35
- ❑ 340 Derek Bell .15 .07
- ❑ 341 Sean Berry .15 .07
- ❑ 342 Craig Biggio .40 .18
- ❑ 343 Doug Drabek .15 .07
- ❑ 344 Tony Eusebio .15 .07
- ❑ 345 Ricky Gutierrez .15 .07
- ❑ 346 Mike Hampton .30 .14
- ❑ 347 Brian Hunter .15 .07
- ❑ 348 Todd Jones .15 .07
- ❑ 349 Darryl Kile .30 .14
- ❑ 350 Derrick May .15 .07
- ❑ 351 Orlando Miller .15 .07
- ❑ 352 James Mouton .15 .07
- ❑ 353 Shane Reynolds .15 .07
- ❑ 354 Billy Wagner .15 .07
- ❑ 355 Donne Wall .15 .07
- ❑ 356 Mike Blowers .15 .07
- ❑ 357 Brett Butler .30 .14
- ❑ 358 Roger Cedeno .15 .07
- ❑ 359 Chad Curtis .15 .07
- ❑ 360 Delino DeShields .15 .07
- ❑ 361 Greg Gagne .15 .07
- ❑ 362 Karim Garcia .15 .07
- ❑ 363 Wilton Guerrero .15 .07
- ❑ 364 Todd Hollandsworth .15 .07
- ❑ 365 Eric Karros .30 .14
- ❑ 366 Ramon Martinez .15 .07
- ❑ 367 Raul Mondesi .30 .14
- ❑ 368 Hideo Nomo .60 .25
- ❑ 369 Antonio Osuna .15 .07
- ❑ 370 Chan Ho Park .30 .14
- ❑ 371 Mike Piazza 1.50 .70
- ❑ 372 Ismael Valdes .15 .07
- ❑ 373 Todd Worrell .15 .07
- ❑ 374 Moises Alou .30 .14
- ❑ 375 Shane Andrews .15 .07
- ❑ 376 Yamil Benitez .15 .07
- ❑ 377 Jeff Fassero .15 .07
- ❑ 378 Darrin Fletcher .15 .07
- ❑ 379 Cliff Floyd .30 .14
- ❑ 380 Mark Grudzielanek .15 .07
- ❑ 381 Mike Lansing .15 .07
- ❑ 382 Barry Manuel .15 .07
- ❑ 383 Pedro Martinez .75 .35
- ❑ 384 Henry Rodriguez .15 .07
- ❑ 385 Mel Rojas .15 .07
- ❑ 386 F.P. Santangelo .15 .07
- ❑ 387 David Segui .15 .07
- ❑ 388 Ugueth Urbina .15 .07
- ❑ 389 Rondell White .30 .14
- ❑ 390 Edgardo Alfonzo .30 .14
- ❑ 391 Carlos Baerga .15 .07
- ❑ 392 Mark Clark .15 .07
- ❑ 393 Alvaro Espinoza .15 .07
- ❑ 394 John Franco .30 .14
- ❑ 395 Bernard Gilkey .15 .07
- ❑ 396 Pete Harnisch .15 .07
- ❑ 397 Todd Hundley .15 .07
- ❑ 398 Butch Huskey .15 .07
- ❑ 399 Jason Isringhausen .15 .07
- ❑ 400 Lance Johnson .15 .07
- ❑ 401 Bobby Jones .15 .07
- ❑ 402 Alex Ochoa .15 .07
- ❑ 403 Rey Ordonez .15 .07
- ❑ 404 Robert Person .15 .07
- ❑ 405 Paul Wilson .15 .07
- ❑ 406 Matt Beech .15 .07
- ❑ 407 Ron Blazier .15 .07
- ❑ 408 Ricky Bottalico .15 .07
- ❑ 409 Lenny Dykstra .30 .14
- ❑ 410 Jim Eisenreich .15 .07
- ❑ 411 Bobby Estalella .15 .07
- ❑ 412 Mike Grace .15 .07
- ❑ 413 Gregg Jefferies .15 .07
- ❑ 414 Mike Lieberthal .30 .14
- ❑ 415 Wendell Magee .15 .07
- ❑ 416 Mickey Morandini .15 .07
- ❑ 417 Ricky Otero .15 .07
- ❑ 418 Scott Rolen .60 .25
- ❑ 419 Ken Ryan .15 .07
- ❑ 420 Benito Santiago .15 .07
- ❑ 421 Curt Schilling .60 .25
- ❑ 422 Kevin Sefcik .15 .07
- ❑ 423 Jermaine Allensworth .15 .07
- ❑ 424 Trey Beamon .15 .07
- ❑ 425 Jay Bell .30 .14
- ❑ 426 Francisco Cordova .15 .07
- ❑ 427 Carlos Garcia .15 .07
- ❑ 428 Mark Johnson .15 .07
- ❑ 429 Jason Kendall .30 .14
- ❑ 430 Jeff King .15 .07
- ❑ 431 Jon Lieber .15 .07
- ❑ 432 Al Martin .15 .07
- ❑ 433 Orlando Merced .15 .07
- ❑ 434 Ramon Morel .15 .07
- ❑ 435 Matt Ruebel .15 .07
- ❑ 436 Jason Schmidt .15 .07
- ❑ 437 Marc Wilkins .15 .07
- ❑ 438 Alan Benes .15 .07
- ❑ 439 Andy Benes .15 .07
- ❑ 440 Royce Clayton .15 .07
- ❑ 441 Dennis Eckersley .30 .14
- ❑ 442 Gary Gaetti .30 .14
- ❑ 443 Ron Gant .15 .07
- ❑ 444 Aaron Holbert .15 .07
- ❑ 445 Brian Jordan .30 .14
- ❑ 446 Ray Lankford .15 .07
- ❑ 447 John Mabry .15 .07
- ❑ 448 T.J. Mathews .15 .07
- ❑ 449 Willie McGee .30 .14
- ❑ 450 Donovan Osborne .15 .07
- ❑ 451 Tom Pagnozzi .15 .07
- ❑ 452 Ozzie Smith .75 .35
- ❑ 453 Todd Stottlemyre .15 .07
- ❑ 454 Mark Sweeney .15 .07
- ❑ 455 Dmitri Young .30 .14
- ❑ 456 Andy Ashby .15 .07
- ❑ 457 Ken Caminiti .30 .14
- ❑ 458 Archi Cianfrocco .15 .07
- ❑ 459 Steve Finley .30 .14
- ❑ 460 John Flaherty .15 .07
- ❑ 461 Chris Gomez .15 .07
- ❑ 462 Tony Gwynn 1.25 .55
- ❑ 463 Joey Hamilton .15 .07
- ❑ 464 Rickey Henderson 1.25 .55
- ❑ 465 Trevor Hoffman .30 .14
- ❑ 466 Brian Johnson .15 .07
- ❑ 467 Wally Joyner .30 .14
- ❑ 468 Jody Reed .15 .07
- ❑ 469 Scott Sanders .15 .07
- ❑ 470 Bob Tewksbury .15 .07
- ❑ 471 Fernando Valenzuela .30 .14
- ❑ 472 Greg Vaughn .30 .14
- ❑ 473 Tim Worrell .15 .07

❑ 474 Rich Aurilia .30 .14
❑ 475 Rod Beck .15 .07
❑ 476 Marvin Benard .15 .07
❑ 477 Barry Bonds 1.50 .70
❑ 478 Jay Canizaro .15 .07
❑ 479 Shawon Dunston .15 .07
❑ 480 Shawn Estes .30 .14
❑ 481 Mark Gardner .15 .07
❑ 482 Glenallen Hill .15 .07
❑ 483 Stan Javier .15 .07
❑ 484 Marcus Jensen .15 .07
❑ 485 Bill Mueller RC .40 .18
❑ 486 Wm. VanLandingham .15 .07
❑ 487 Allen Watson .15 .07
❑ 488 Rick Wilkins .15 .07
❑ 489 Matt Williams .40 .18
❑ 490 Desi Wilson .15 .07
❑ 491 Albert Belle CL .30 .14
❑ 492 Ken Griffey Jr. CL 1.00 .45
❑ 493 Andruw Jones CL .40 .18
❑ 494 Chipper Jones CL .60 .25
❑ 495 Mark McGwire CL 1.25 .55
❑ 496 Paul Molitor CL .30 .14
❑ 497 Mike Piazza CL .75 .35
❑ 498 Cal Ripken CL 1.25 .55
❑ 499 Alex Rodriguez CL .75 .35
❑ 500 Frank Thomas CL .60 .25
❑ 501 Kenny Lofton .30 .14
❑ 502 Carlos Perez .15 .07
❑ 503 Tim Raines .30 .14
❑ 504 Danny Patterson .15 .07
❑ 505 Derrick May .15 .07
❑ 506 Dave Hollins .15 .07
❑ 507 Felipe Crespo .15 .07
❑ 508 Brian Banks .15 .07
❑ 509 Jeff Kent .40 .18
❑ 510 Bubba Trammell RC .30 .14
❑ 511 Robert Person .15 .07
❑ 512 David Arias-Ortiz RC 1.25 .55
❑ 513 Ryan Jones .15 .07
❑ 514 David Justice .30 .14
❑ 515 Will Cunnane .15 .07
❑ 516 Russ Johnson .15 .07
❑ 517 John Burkett .15 .07
❑ 518 Robinson Checo RC .15 .07
❑ 519 Ricardo Rincon RC .15 .07
❑ 520 Woody Williams .15 .07
❑ 521 Rick Helling .15 .07
❑ 522 Jorge Posada .30 .14
❑ 523 Kevin Orie .15 .07
❑ 524 Fernando Tatis RC .60 .25
❑ 525 Jermaine Dye .30 .14
❑ 526 Brian Hunter .15 .07
❑ 527 Greg McMichael .15 .07
❑ 528 Matt Wagner .15 .07
❑ 529 Richie Sexson .30 .14
❑ 530 Scott Ruffcorn .15 .07
❑ 531 Luis Gonzalez .60 .25
❑ 532 Mike Johnson RC .15 .07
❑ 533 Mark Petkovsek .15 .07
❑ 534 Doug Drabek .15 .07
❑ 535 Jose Canseco .60 .25
❑ 536 Bobby Bonilla .30 .14
❑ 537 J.T. Snow .30 .14
❑ 538 Shawon Dunston .15 .07
❑ 539 John Ericks .15 .07
❑ 540 Terry Steinbach .15 .07
❑ 541 Jay Bell .30 .14
❑ 542 Joe Borowski RC .15 .07
❑ 543 David Wells .30 .14
❑ 544 Justin Towle RC .15 .07
❑ 545 Mike Blowers .15 .07
❑ 546 Shannon Stewart .30 .14
❑ 547 Rudy Pemberton .15 .07
❑ 548 Bill Swift .15 .07
❑ 549 Osvaldo Fernandez .15 .07
❑ 550 Eddie Murray .60 .25
❑ 551 Don Wengert .15 .07
❑ 552 Brad Ausmus .15 .07
❑ 553 Carlos Garcia .15 .07
❑ 554 Jose Guillen .15 .07
❑ 555 Rheal Cormier .15 .07
❑ 556 Doug Brocail .15 .07
❑ 557 Rex Hudler .15 .07
❑ 558 Armando Benitez .15 .07
❑ 559 Eli Marrero .15 .07
❑ 560 Ricky Ledee RC .60 .25
❑ 561 Bartolo Colon .30 .14
❑ 562 Quilvio Veras .15 .07
❑ 563 Alex Fernandez .15 .07
❑ 564 Darren Dreifort .15 .07
❑ 565 Benji Gil .15 .07
❑ 566 Kent Mercker .15 .07
❑ 567 Glendon Rusch .15 .07
❑ 568 Ramon Tatis RC .15 .07
❑ 569 Roger Clemens 1.50 .70
❑ 570 Mark Lewis .15 .07
❑ 571 Emil Brown RC .15 .07
❑ 572 Jaime Navarro .15 .07
❑ 573 Sherman Obando .15 .07
❑ 574 John Wasdin .15 .07
❑ 575 Calvin Maduro .15 .07
❑ 576 Todd Jones .15 .07
❑ 577 Orlando Merced .15 .07
❑ 578 Cal Eldred .15 .07
❑ 579 Mark Gubicza .15 .07
❑ 580 Michael Tucker .15 .07
❑ 581 Tony Saunders RC .15 .07
❑ 582 Garvin Alston .15 .07
❑ 583 Joe Roa .15 .07
❑ 584 Brady Raggio RC .15 .07
❑ 585 Jimmy Key .30 .14
❑ 586 Marc Sagmoen RC .15 .07
❑ 587 Jim Bullinger .15 .07
❑ 588 Yorkis Perez .15 .07
❑ 589 Jose Cruz Jr. RC 1.50 .70
❑ 590 Mike Stanton .15 .07
❑ 591 Deivi Cruz RC .75 .35
❑ 592 Steve Karsay .15 .07
❑ 593 Mike Trombley .15 .07
❑ 594 Doug Glanville .15 .07
❑ 595 Scott Sanders .15 .07
❑ 596 Thomas Howard .15 .07
❑ 597 T.J. Staton RC .15 .07
❑ 598 Garrett Stephenson .15 .07
❑ 599 Rico Brogna .15 .07
❑ 600 Albert Belle .30 .14
❑ 601 Jose Vizcaino .15 .07
❑ 602 Chili Davis .30 .14
❑ 603 Shane Mack .15 .07
❑ 604 Jim Eisenreich .15 .07
❑ 605 Todd Zeile .15 .07
❑ 606 Brian Boehringer RC .15 .07
❑ 607 Paul Shuey .15 .07
❑ 608 Kevin Tapani .15 .07
❑ 609 John Wetteland .30 .14
❑ 610 Jim Leyritz .15 .07
❑ 611 Ray Montgomery RC .15 .07
❑ 612 Doug Bochtler .15 .07
❑ 613 Wady Almonte RC .15 .07
❑ 614 Danny Tartabull .15 .07
❑ 615 Orlando Miller .15 .07
❑ 616 Bobby Ayala .15 .07
❑ 617 Tony Graffanino .15 .07
❑ 618 Marc Valdes .15 .07
❑ 619 Ron Villone .15 .07
❑ 620 Derrek Lee .30 .14
❑ 621 Greg Colbrunn .15 .07
❑ 622 Felix Heredia RC .15 .07
❑ 623 Carl Everett .30 .14
❑ 624 Mark Thompson .15 .07
❑ 625 Jeff Granger .15 .07
❑ 626 Damian Jackson .15 .07
❑ 627 Mark Leiter .15 .07
❑ 628 Chris Holt .15 .07
❑ 629 Dario Veras RC .15 .07
❑ 630 Dave Burba .15 .07
❑ 631 Darryl Hamilton .15 .07
❑ 632 Mark Acre .15 .07
❑ 633 F.Hernandez RC .15 .07
❑ 634 Terry Mulholland .15 .07
❑ 635 Dustin Hermanson .15 .07
❑ 636 Delino DeShields .15 .07
❑ 637 Steve Avery .15 .07
❑ 638 Tony Womack RC .50 .23
❑ 639 Mark Whiten .15 .07
❑ 640 Marquis Grissom .15 .07
❑ 641 Xavier Hernandez .15 .07
❑ 642 Eric Davis .30 .14
❑ 643 Bob Tewksbury .15 .07
❑ 644 Dante Powell .15 .07
❑ 645 Carlos Castillo RC .15 .07
❑ 646 Chris Widger .15 .07
❑ 647 Moises Alou .30 .14
❑ 648 Pat Listach .15 .07
❑ 649 Edgar Ramos RC .15 .07
❑ 650 Deion Sanders .30 .14
❑ 651 John Olerud .30 .14
❑ 652 Todd Dunwoody .15 .07
❑ 653 Randall Simon RC .15 .07
❑ 654 Dan Carlson .15 .07
❑ 655 Matt Williams .40 .18
❑ 656 Jeff King .15 .07
❑ 657 Luis Alicea .15 .07
❑ 658 Brian Moehler RC .15 .07
❑ 659 Ariel Prieto .15 .07
❑ 660 Kevin Elster .15 .07
❑ 661 Mark Hutton .15 .07
❑ 662 Aaron Sele .30 .14
❑ 663 Graeme Lloyd .15 .07
❑ 664 John Burke .15 .07
❑ 665 Mel Rojas .15 .07
❑ 666 Sid Fernandez .15 .07
❑ 667 Pedro Astacio .15 .07
❑ 668 Jeff Abbott .15 .07
❑ 669 Darren Daulton .30 .14
❑ 670 Mike Bordick .15 .07
❑ 671 Sterling Hitchcock .15 .07
❑ 672 Damion Easley .15 .07
❑ 673 Armando Reynoso .15 .07
❑ 674 Pat Cline .15 .07
❑ 675 Orlando Cabrera RC .40 .18
❑ 676 Alan Embree .15 .07
❑ 677 Brian Bevil .15 .07
❑ 678 David Weathers .15 .07
❑ 679 Cliff Floyd .30 .14
❑ 680 Joe Randa .15 .07
❑ 681 Bill Haselman .15 .07
❑ 682 Jeff Fassero .15 .07
❑ 683 Matt Morris .30 .14
❑ 684 Mark Portugal .15 .07
❑ 685 Lee Smith .30 .14
❑ 686 Pokey Reese .15 .07
❑ 687 Benito Santiago .15 .07
❑ 688 Brian Johnson .15 .07
❑ 689 Brent Brede RC .15 .07
❑ 690 S.Hasegawa RC .40 .18
❑ 691 Julio Santana .15 .07
❑ 692 Steve Kline .15 .07
❑ 693 Julian Tavarez .15 .07
❑ 694 John Hudek .15 .07
❑ 695 Manny Alexander .15 .07
❑ 696 Roberto Alomar ENC .30 .14
❑ 697 Jeff Bagwell ENC .40 .18
❑ 698 Barry Bonds ENC .75 .35
❑ 699 Ken Caminiti ENC .15 .07
❑ 700 Juan Gonzalez ENC .30 .14
❑ 701 Ken Griffey Jr. ENC 1.00 .45
❑ 702 Tony Gwynn ENC .60 .25
❑ 703 Derek Jeter ENC 1.25 .55
❑ 704 Andruw Jones ENC .40 .18
❑ 705 Chipper Jones ENC .60 .25
❑ 706 Barry Larkin ENC .30 .14
❑ 707 Greg Maddux ENC .75 .35
❑ 708 Mark McGwire ENC 1.25 .55
❑ 709 Paul Molitor ENC .30 .14
❑ 710 Hideo Nomo ENC .30 .14
❑ 711 Andy Pettitte ENC .15 .07
❑ 712 Mike Piazza ENC .75 .35
❑ 713 Manny Ramirez ENC .40 .18
❑ 714 Cal Ripken ENC 1.25 .55
❑ 715 Alex Rodriguez ENC .75 .35
❑ 716 Ryne Sandberg ENC .40 .18
❑ 717 John Smoltz ENC .15 .07
❑ 718 Frank Thomas ENC .60 .25
❑ 719 Mo Vaughn ENC .15 .07
❑ 720 Bernie Williams ENC .30 .14
❑ 721 Tim Salmon CL .15 .07
❑ 722 Greg Maddux CL .75 .35
❑ 723 Cal Ripken CL 1.25 .55
❑ 724 Mo Vaughn CL .15 .07
❑ 725 Ryne Sandberg CL .40 .18
❑ 726 Frank Thomas CL .60 .25
❑ 727 Barry Larkin CL .30 .14
❑ 728 Manny Ramirez CL .40 .18
❑ 729 Andres Galarraga CL .30 .14
❑ 730 Tony Clark CL .30 .14
❑ 731 Gary Sheffield CL .15 .07

❑ 732	Jeff Bagwell CL	.40	.18
❑ 733	Kevin Appier CL	.15	.07
❑ 734	Mike Piazza CL	.75	.35
❑ 735	Jeff Cirillo CL	.15	.07
❑ 736	Paul Molitor CL	.30	.14
❑ 737	Henry Rodriguez CL	.15	.07
❑ 738	Todd Hundley CL	.15	.07
❑ 739	Derek Jeter CL	1.25	.55
❑ 740	Mark McGwire CL	1.25	.55
❑ 741	Curt Schilling CL	.60	.25
❑ 742	Jason Kendall CL	.15	.07
❑ 743	Tony Gwynn CL	.60	.25
❑ 744	Barry Bonds CL	.75	.35
❑ 745	Ken Griffey Jr. CL	1.00	.45
❑ 746	Brian Jordan CL	.15	.07
❑ 747	Juan Gonzalez CL	.30	.14
❑ 748	Joe Carter CL	.15	.07
❑ 749	Ariz. Diamondbacks CL Inserts	.30	.14
❑ 750	Tampa Bay Devil Rays CL Inserts	.30	.14
❑ 751	Hideki Irabu RC	.30	.14
❑ 752	Jeremi Gonzalez RC	.25	.11
❑ 753	Mario Valdez RC	.25	.11
❑ 754	Aaron Boone	.25	.11
❑ 755	Brett Tomko	.25	.11
❑ 756	Jaret Wright RC	.30	.14
❑ 757	Ryan McGuire	.25	.11
❑ 758	Jason McDonald	.25	.11
❑ 759	Adrian Brown RC	.25	.11
❑ 760	Keith Foulke RC	.25	.11
❑ 761	Bonus Checklist	.25	.11
❑ P489	M.Williams Promo	1.00	.45
❑ NNO	Andruw Jones Circa AU/200	60.00	27.00

1998 Fleer

	MINT	NRMT
COMPLETE SET (600)	150.00	70.00
COMPLETE SERIES 1 (350)	90.00	40.00
COMPLETE SERIES 2 (250)	60.00	27.00
COMMON CARD (1-600)	.15	.07
COMMON GM (311-320)	.40	.18
COMMON TT (321-340)	.50	.23
COMMON UM (576-600)	.60	.25

❑ 1	Ken Griffey Jr.	2.00	.90
❑ 2	Derek Jeter	2.50	1.10
❑ 3	Gerald Williams	.15	.07
❑ 4	Carlos Delgado	.60	.25
❑ 5	Nomar Garciaparra	1.50	.70
❑ 6	Gary Sheffield	.25	.11
❑ 7	Jeff King	.15	.07
❑ 8	Cal Ripken	2.50	1.10
❑ 9	Matt Williams	.40	.18
❑ 10	Chipper Jones	1.25	.55
❑ 11	Chuck Knoblauch	.25	.11
❑ 12	Mark Grudzielanek	.15	.07
❑ 13	Edgardo Alfonzo	.25	.11
❑ 14	Andres Galarraga	.40	.18
❑ 15	Tim Salmon	.25	.11
❑ 16	Reggie Sanders	.15	.07
❑ 17	Tony Clark	.25	.11
❑ 18	Jason Kendall	.25	.11
❑ 19	Juan Gonzalez	.60	.25
❑ 20	Ben Grieve	.25	.11
❑ 21	Roger Clemens	1.50	.70
❑ 22	Raul Mondesi	.25	.11
❑ 23	Robin Ventura	.25	.11
❑ 24	Derrek Lee	.25	.11
❑ 25	Mark McGwire	2.50	1.10
❑ 26	Luis Gonzalez	.60	.25
❑ 27	Kevin Brown	.40	.18
❑ 28	Kirk Rueter	.15	.07
❑ 29	Bobby Estalella	.15	.07
❑ 30	Shawn Green	.60	.25
❑ 31	Greg Maddux	1.50	.70
❑ 32	Jorge Velandia	.15	.07
❑ 33	Larry Walker	.40	.18
❑ 34	Joey Cora	.15	.07
❑ 35	Frank Thomas	.75	.35
❑ 36	Curtis King RC	.15	.07
❑ 37	Aaron Boone	.15	.07
❑ 38	Curt Schilling	.60	.25
❑ 39	Bruce Aven	.15	.07
❑ 40	Ben McDonald	.15	.07
❑ 41	Andy Ashby	.15	.07
❑ 42	Jason McDonald	.15	.07
❑ 43	Eric Davis	.25	.11
❑ 44	Mark Grace	.60	.25
❑ 45	Pedro Martinez	.75	.35
❑ 46	Lou Collier	.15	.07
❑ 47	Chan Ho Park	.25	.11
❑ 48	Shane Halter	.15	.07
❑ 49	Brian Hunter	.15	.07
❑ 50	Jeff Bagwell	.75	.35
❑ 51	Bernie Williams	.60	.25
❑ 52	J.T. Snow	.25	.11
❑ 53	Todd Greene	.15	.07
❑ 54	Shannon Stewart	.25	.11
❑ 55	Darren Bragg	.15	.07
❑ 56	Fernando Tatis	.15	.07
❑ 57	Darryl Kile	.25	.11
❑ 58	Chris Stynes	.15	.07
❑ 59	Javier Valentin	.15	.07
❑ 60	Brian McRae	.15	.07
❑ 61	Tom Evans	.15	.07
❑ 62	Randall Simon	.15	.07
❑ 63	Darrin Fletcher	.15	.07
❑ 64	Jaret Wright	.15	.07
❑ 65	Luis Ordaz	.15	.07
❑ 66	Jose Canseco	.60	.25
❑ 67	Edgar Renteria	.15	.07
❑ 68	Jay Buhner	.25	.11
❑ 69	Paul Konerko	.25	.11
❑ 70	Adrian Brown	.15	.07
❑ 71	Chris Carpenter	.15	.07
❑ 72	Mike Lieberthal	.25	.11
❑ 73	Dean Palmer	.25	.11
❑ 74	Jorge Fabregas	.15	.07
❑ 75	Stan Javier	.15	.07
❑ 76	Damion Easley	.15	.07
❑ 77	David Cone	.25	.11
❑ 78	Aaron Sele	.25	.11
❑ 79	Antonio Alfonseca	.15	.07
❑ 80	Bobby Jones	.15	.07
❑ 81	David Justice	.25	.11
❑ 82	Jeffrey Hammonds	.15	.07
❑ 83	Doug Glanville	.15	.07
❑ 84	Jason Dickson	.15	.07
❑ 85	Brad Radke	.25	.11
❑ 86	David Segui	.15	.07
❑ 87	Greg Vaughn	.25	.11
❑ 88	Mike Cather RC	.15	.07
❑ 89	Alex Fernandez	.15	.07
❑ 90	Billy Taylor	.15	.07
❑ 91	Jason Schmidt	.15	.07
❑ 92	Mike DeJean RC	.15	.07
❑ 93	Domingo Cedeno	.15	.07
❑ 94	Jeff Cirillo	.25	.11
❑ 95	Manny Aybar RC	.25	.11
❑ 96	Jaime Navarro	.15	.07
❑ 97	Dennis Reyes	.15	.07
❑ 98	Barry Larkin	.60	.25
❑ 99	Troy O'Leary	.15	.07
❑ 100	Alex Rodriguez	1.50	.70
❑ 101	Pat Hentgen	.15	.07
❑ 102	Bubba Trammell	.15	.07
❑ 103	Glendon Rusch	.15	.07
❑ 104	Kenny Lofton	.25	.11
❑ 105	Craig Biggio	.40	.18
❑ 106	Kelvim Escobar	.15	.07
❑ 107	Mark Kotsay	.25	.11
❑ 108	Rondell White	.25	.11
❑ 109	Darren Oliver	.15	.07
❑ 110	Jim Thome	.60	.25
❑ 111	Rich Becker	.15	.07
❑ 112	Chad Curtis	.15	.07
❑ 113	Dave Hollins	.15	.07
❑ 114	Bill Mueller	.15	.07
❑ 115	Antone Williamson	.15	.07
❑ 116	Tony Womack	.15	.07
❑ 117	Randy Myers	.25	.11
❑ 118	Rico Brogna	.15	.07
❑ 119	Pat Watkins	.15	.07
❑ 120	Eli Marrero	.15	.07
❑ 121	Jay Bell	.25	.11
❑ 122	Kevin Tapani	.15	.07
❑ 123	Todd Erdos RC	.25	.11
❑ 124	Neifi Perez	.15	.07
❑ 125	Todd Hundley	.15	.07
❑ 126	Jeff Abbott	.15	.07
❑ 127	Todd Zeile	.25	.11
❑ 128	Travis Fryman	.25	.11
❑ 129	Sandy Alomar Jr.	.25	.11
❑ 130	Fred McGriff	.40	.18
❑ 131	Richard Hidalgo	.25	.11
❑ 132	Scott Spiezio	.15	.07
❑ 133	John Valentin	.15	.07
❑ 134	Quilvio Veras	.15	.07
❑ 135	Mike Lansing	.15	.07
❑ 136	Paul Molitor	.60	.25
❑ 137	Randy Johnson	.75	.35
❑ 138	Harold Baines	.25	.11
❑ 139	Doug Jones	.15	.07
❑ 140	Abraham Nunez	.15	.07
❑ 141	Alan Benes	.15	.07
❑ 142	Matt Perisho	.15	.07
❑ 143	Chris Clemons	.15	.07
❑ 144	Andy Pettitte	.25	.11
❑ 145	Jason Giambi	.60	.25
❑ 146	Moises Alou	.25	.11
❑ 147	Chad Fox RC	.15	.07
❑ 148	Felix Martinez	.15	.07
❑ 149	Carlos Mendoza RC	.25	.11
❑ 150	Scott Rolen	.60	.25
❑ 151	Jose Cabrera RC	.15	.07
❑ 152	Justin Thompson	.15	.07
❑ 153	Ellis Burks	.25	.11
❑ 154	Pokey Reese	.15	.07
❑ 155	Bartolo Colon	.25	.11
❑ 156	Ray Durham	.25	.11
❑ 157	Ugueth Urbina	.15	.07
❑ 158	Tom Goodwin	.15	.07
❑ 159	Dave Dellucci RC	.15	.07
❑ 160	Rod Beck	.15	.07
❑ 161	Ramon Martinez	.15	.07
❑ 162	Joe Carter	.25	.11
❑ 163	Kevin Orie	.15	.07
❑ 164	Trevor Hoffman	.25	.11
❑ 165	Emil Brown	.15	.07
❑ 166	Robb Nen	.15	.07
❑ 167	Paul O'Neill	.60	.25
❑ 168	Ryan Long	.15	.07
❑ 169	Ray Lankford	.15	.07
❑ 170	Ivan Rodriguez	.60	.25
❑ 171	Rick Aguilera	.15	.07
❑ 172	Deivi Cruz	.15	.07
❑ 173	Ricky Bottalico	.15	.07
❑ 174	Garret Anderson	.25	.11
❑ 175	Jose Vizcaino	.15	.07
❑ 176	Omar Vizquel	.25	.11
❑ 177	Jeff Blauser	.15	.07
❑ 178	Orlando Cabrera	.15	.07
❑ 179	Russ Johnson	.15	.07
❑ 180	Matt Stairs	.15	.07
❑ 181	Will Cunnane	.15	.07
❑ 182	Adam Riggs	.15	.07
❑ 183	Matt Morris	.25	.11
❑ 184	Mario Valdez	.15	.07
❑ 185	Larry Sutton	.15	.07
❑ 186	Marc Pisciotta RC	.15	.07
❑ 187	Dan Wilson	.15	.07
❑ 188	John Franco	.25	.11
❑ 189	Darren Daulton	.25	.11
❑ 190	Todd Helton	.75	.35
❑ 191	Brady Anderson	.25	.11
❑ 192	Ricardo Rincon	.15	.07
❑ 193	Kevin Stocker	.15	.07

❑ 194	Jose Valentin	.15	.07
❑ 195	Ed Sprague	.15	.07
❑ 196	Ryan McGuire	.15	.07
❑ 197	Scott Eyre	.15	.07
❑ 198	Steve Finley	.25	.11
❑ 199	T.J. Mathews	.15	.07
❑ 200	Mike Piazza	1.50	.70
❑ 201	Mark Wohlers	.15	.07
❑ 202	Brian Giles	.25	.11
❑ 203	Eduardo Perez	.15	.07
❑ 204	Shigetoshi Hasegawa	.25	.11
❑ 205	Mariano Rivera	.25	.11
❑ 206	Jose Rosado	.15	.07
❑ 207	Michael Coleman	.15	.07
❑ 208	James Baldwin	.15	.07
❑ 209	Russ Davis	.15	.07
❑ 210	Billy Wagner	.15	.07
❑ 211	Sammy Sosa	1.25	.55
❑ 212	Frank Catalanotto RC	.60	.25
❑ 213	Delino DeShields	.15	.07
❑ 214	John Olerud	.25	.11
❑ 215	Heath Murray	.15	.07
❑ 216	Jose Vidro	.25	.11
❑ 217	Jim Edmonds	.40	.18
❑ 218	Shawon Dunston	.15	.07
❑ 219	Homer Bush	.15	.07
❑ 220	Midre Cummings	.15	.07
❑ 221	Tony Saunders	.15	.07
❑ 222	Jeromy Burnitz	.25	.11
❑ 223	Enrique Wilson	.15	.07
❑ 224	Chili Davis	.25	.11
❑ 225	Jerry DiPoto	.15	.07
❑ 226	Dante Powell	.15	.07
❑ 227	Javier Lopez	.25	.11
❑ 228	Kevin Polcovich	.15	.07
❑ 229	Deion Sanders	.25	.11
❑ 230	Jimmy Key	.25	.11
❑ 231	Rusty Greer	.25	.11
❑ 232	Reggie Jefferson	.15	.07
❑ 233	Ron Coomer	.15	.07
❑ 234	Bobby Higginson	.25	.11
❑ 235	Magglio Ordonez RC	2.00	.90
❑ 236	Miguel Tejada	.40	.18
❑ 237	Rick Gorecki	.15	.07
❑ 238	Charles Johnson	.25	.11
❑ 239	Lance Johnson	.15	.07
❑ 240	Derek Bell	.15	.07
❑ 241	Will Clark	.60	.25
❑ 242	Brady Raggio	.15	.07
❑ 243	Orel Hershiser	.25	.11
❑ 244	Vladimir Guerrero	.75	.35
❑ 245	John LeRoy	.15	.07
❑ 246	Shawn Estes	.25	.11
❑ 247	Brett Tomko	.15	.07
❑ 248	Dave Nilsson	.15	.07
❑ 249	Edgar Martinez	.40	.18
❑ 250	Tony Gwynn	1.25	.55
❑ 251	Mark Bellhorn	.15	.07
❑ 252	Jed Hansen	.15	.07
❑ 253	Butch Huskey	.15	.07
❑ 254	Eric Young	.15	.07
❑ 255	Vinny Castilla	.25	.11
❑ 256	Hideki Irabu	.15	.07
❑ 257	Mike Cameron	.25	.11
❑ 258	Juan Encarnacion	.25	.11
❑ 259	Brian Rose	.15	.07
❑ 260	Brad Ausmus	.15	.07
❑ 261	Dan Serafini	.15	.07
❑ 262	Willie Greene	.15	.07
❑ 263	Troy Percival	.15	.07
❑ 264	Jeff Wallace	.25	.11
❑ 265	Richie Sexson	.25	.11
❑ 266	Rafael Palmeiro	.60	.25
❑ 267	Brad Fullmer	.25	.11
❑ 268	Jeremi Gonzalez	.15	.07
❑ 269	Rob Stanifer RC	.15	.07
❑ 270	Mickey Morandini	.15	.07
❑ 271	Andruw Jones	.60	.25
❑ 272	Royce Clayton	.15	.07
❑ 273	T.Kashiwada RC	.15	.07
❑ 274	Steve Woodard	.15	.07
❑ 275	Jose Cruz Jr.	.25	.11
❑ 276	Keith Foulke	.15	.07
❑ 277	Brad Rigby	.15	.07
❑ 278	Tino Martinez	.25	.11
❑ 279	Todd Jones	.15	.07
❑ 280	John Wetteland	.25	.11
❑ 281	Alex Gonzalez	.15	.07
❑ 282	Ken Cloude	.15	.07
❑ 283	Jose Guillen	.15	.07
❑ 284	Danny Clyburn	.15	.07
❑ 285	David Ortiz	.25	.11
❑ 286	John Thomson	.15	.07
❑ 287	Kevin Appier	.25	.11
❑ 288	Ismael Valdes	.15	.07
❑ 289	Gary DiSarcina	.15	.07
❑ 290	Todd Dunwoody	.15	.07
❑ 291	Wally Joyner	.25	.11
❑ 292	Charles Nagy	.15	.07
❑ 293	Jeff Shaw	.15	.07
❑ 294	Kevin Millwood RC	.60	.25
❑ 295	Rigo Beltran RC	.15	.07
❑ 296	Jeff Frye	.15	.07
❑ 297	Oscar Henriquez	.15	.07
❑ 298	Mike Thurman	.15	.07
❑ 299	Garrett Stephenson	.15	.07
❑ 300	Barry Bonds	1.50	.70
❑ 301	Roger Clemens SH	.75	.35
❑ 302	David Cone SH	.15	.07
❑ 303	Hideki Irabu SH	.15	.07
❑ 304	Randy Johnson SH	.25	.11
❑ 305	Greg Maddux SH	.75	.35
❑ 306	Pedro Martinez SH	.40	.18
❑ 307	Mike Mussina SH	.25	.11
❑ 308	Andy Pettitte SH	.15	.07
❑ 309	Curt Schilling SH	.25	.11
❑ 310	John Smoltz SH	.15	.07
❑ 311	Roger Clemens GM	2.50	1.10
❑ 312	Jose Cruz JR. GM	.50	.23
❑ 313	N.Garciaparra GM	2.50	1.10
❑ 314	Ken Griffey Jr. GM	3.00	1.35
❑ 315	Tony Gwynn GM	2.00	.90
❑ 316	Hideki Irabu GM	.40	.18
❑ 317	Randy Johnson GM	1.25	.55
❑ 318	Mark McGwire GM	4.00	1.80
❑ 319	Curt Schilling GM	1.00	.45
❑ 320	Larry Walker GM	.60	.25
❑ 321	Jeff Bagwell TT	1.50	.70
❑ 322	Albert Belle TT	.60	.25
❑ 323	Barry Bonds TT	3.00	1.35
❑ 324	Jay Buhner TT	.60	.25
❑ 325	Tony Clark TT	.60	.25
❑ 326	Jose Cruz Jr. TT	.60	.25
❑ 327	Andres Galarraga TT	.75	.35
❑ 328	Juan Gonzalez TT	1.25	.55
❑ 329	Ken Griffey Jr. TT	4.00	1.80
❑ 330	Andruw Jones TT	1.25	.55
❑ 331	Tino Martinez TT	.60	.25
❑ 332	Mark McGwire TT	5.00	2.20
❑ 333	Rafael Palmeiro TT	1.25	.55
❑ 334	Mike Piazza TT	3.00	1.35
❑ 335	Manny Ramirez TT	1.50	.70
❑ 336	Alex Rodriguez TT	3.00	1.35
❑ 337	Frank Thomas TT	1.50	.70
❑ 338	Jim Thome TT	1.25	.55
❑ 339	Mo Vaughn TT	.60	.25
❑ 340	Larry Walker TT	.75	.35
❑ 341	Jose Cruz Jr. CL	.15	.07
❑ 342	Ken Griffey Jr. CL	1.00	.45
❑ 343	Derek Jeter CL	1.25	.55
❑ 344	Andruw Jones CL	.25	.11
❑ 345	Chipper Jones CL	.60	.25
❑ 346	Greg Maddux CL	.75	.35
❑ 347	Mike Piazza CL	.75	.35
❑ 348	Cal Ripken CL	1.25	.55
❑ 349	Alex Rodriguez CL	.75	.35
❑ 350	Frank Thomas CL	.40	.18
❑ 351	Mo Vaughn	.25	.11
❑ 352	Andres Galarraga	.40	.18
❑ 353	Roberto Alomar	.60	.25
❑ 354	Darin Erstad	.60	.25
❑ 355	Albert Belle	.25	.11
❑ 356	Matt Williams	.40	.18
❑ 357	Darryl Kile	.25	.11
❑ 358	Kenny Lofton	.25	.11
❑ 359	Orel Hershiser	.25	.11
❑ 360	Bob Abreu	.25	.11
❑ 361	Chris Widger	.15	.07
❑ 362	Glenallen Hill	.15	.07
❑ 363	Chili Davis	.25	.11
❑ 364	Kevin Brown	.40	.18
❑ 365	Marquis Grissom	.15	.07
❑ 366	Livan Hernandez	.15	.07
❑ 367	Moises Alou	.25	.11
❑ 368	Matt Lawton	.15	.07
❑ 369	Rey Ordonez	.15	.07
❑ 370	Kenny Rogers	.15	.07
❑ 371	Lee Stevens	.15	.07
❑ 372	Wade Boggs	.60	.25
❑ 373	Luis Gonzalez	.60	.25
❑ 374	Jeff Conine	.15	.07
❑ 375	Esteban Loaiza	.15	.07
❑ 376	Jose Canseco	.60	.25
❑ 377	Henry Rodriguez	.15	.07
❑ 378	Dave Burba	.15	.07
❑ 379	Todd Hollandsworth	.15	.07
❑ 380	Ron Gant	.25	.11
❑ 381	Pedro Martinez	.75	.35
❑ 382	Ryan Klesko	.25	.11
❑ 383	Derrek Lee	.25	.11
❑ 384	Doug Glanville	.15	.07
❑ 385	David Wells	.25	.11
❑ 386	Ken Caminiti	.25	.11
❑ 387	Damon Hollins	.15	.07
❑ 388	Manny Ramirez	.75	.35
❑ 389	Mike Mussina	.60	.25
❑ 390	Jay Bell	.25	.11
❑ 391	Mike Piazza	1.50	.70
❑ 392	Mike Lansing	.15	.07
❑ 393	Mike Hampton	.25	.11
❑ 394	Geoff Jenkins	.25	.11
❑ 395	Jimmy Haynes	.15	.07
❑ 396	Scott Servais	.15	.07
❑ 397	Kent Mercker	.15	.07
❑ 398	Jeff Kent	.40	.18
❑ 399	Kevin Elster	.15	.07
❑ 400	Masato Yoshii RC	.50	.23
❑ 401	Jose Vizcaino	.15	.07
❑ 402	Javier Martinez RC	.25	.11
❑ 403	David Segui	.15	.07
❑ 404	Tony Saunders	.15	.07
❑ 405	Karim Garcia	.15	.07
❑ 406	Armando Benitez	.15	.07
❑ 407	Joe Randa	.15	.07
❑ 408	Vic Darensbourg	.15	.07
❑ 409	Sean Casey	.40	.18
❑ 410	Eric Milton	.25	.11
❑ 411	Trey Moore	.15	.07
❑ 412	Mike Stanley	.15	.07
❑ 413	Tom Gordon	.25	.11
❑ 414	Hal Morris	.15	.07
❑ 415	Braden Looper	.15	.07
❑ 416	Mike Kelly	.15	.07
❑ 417	John Smoltz	.25	.11
❑ 418	Roger Cedeno	.15	.07
❑ 419	Al Leiter	.25	.11
❑ 420	Chuck Knoblauch	.25	.11
❑ 421	Felix Rodriguez	.15	.07
❑ 422	Bip Roberts	.15	.07
❑ 423	Ken Hill	.15	.07
❑ 424	Jermaine Allensworth	.15	.07
❑ 425	Esteban Yan RC	.40	.18
❑ 426	Scott Karl	.15	.07
❑ 427	Sean Berry	.15	.07
❑ 428	Rafael Medina	.15	.07
❑ 429	Javier Vazquez	.25	.11
❑ 430	Rickey Henderson	1.25	.55
❑ 431	Adam Butler	.25	.11
❑ 432	Todd Stottlemyre	.15	.07
❑ 433	Yamil Benitez	.15	.07
❑ 434	Sterling Hitchcock	.15	.07
❑ 435	Paul Sorrento	.15	.07
❑ 436	Bobby Ayala	.15	.07
❑ 437	Tim Raines	.25	.11
❑ 438	Chris Hoiles	.15	.07
❑ 439	Rod Beck	.15	.07
❑ 440	Donnie Sadler	.15	.07
❑ 441	Charles Johnson	.25	.11
❑ 442	Russ Ortiz	.25	.11
❑ 443	Pedro Astacio	.15	.07
❑ 444	Wilson Alvarez	.15	.07
❑ 445	Mike Blowers	.15	.07
❑ 446	Todd Zeile	.25	.11
❑ 447	Mel Rojas	.15	.07
❑ 448	F.P. Santangelo	.15	.07
❑ 449	Dmitri Young	.25	.11
❑ 450	Brian Anderson	.15	.07
❑ 451	Cecil Fielder	.25	.11

❑ 452 Roberto Hernandez .15 .07
❑ 453 Todd Walker .15 .07
❑ 454 Tyler Green .15 .07
❑ 455 Jorge Posada .25 .11
❑ 456 Geronimo Berroa .15 .07
❑ 457 Jose Silva .15 .07
❑ 458 Bobby Bonilla .25 .11
❑ 459 Walt Weiss .25 .11
❑ 460 Darren Dreifort .15 .07
❑ 461 B.J. Surhoff .25 .11
❑ 462 Quinton McCracken .15 .07
❑ 463 Derek Lowe .15 .07
❑ 464 Jorge Fabregas .15 .07
❑ 465 Joey Hamilton .15 .07
❑ 466 Brian Jordan .25 .11
❑ 467 Allen Watson .15 .07
❑ 468 John Jaha .25 .11
❑ 469 Heathcliff Slocumb .15 .07
❑ 470 Gregg Jefferies .15 .07
❑ 471 Scott Brosius .25 .11
❑ 472 Chad Ogea .15 .07
❑ 473 A.J. Hinch .15 .07
❑ 474 Bobby Smith .15 .07
❑ 475 Brian Moehler .15 .07
❑ 476 DaRond Stovall .15 .07
❑ 477 Kevin Young .25 .11
❑ 478 Jeff Suppan .15 .07
❑ 479 Marty Cordova .15 .07
❑ 480 John Halama RC .50 .23
❑ 481 Bubba Trammell .15 .07
❑ 482 Mike Caruso .15 .07
❑ 483 Eric Karros .25 .11
❑ 484 Jamey Wright .15 .07
❑ 485 Mike Sweeney .25 .11
❑ 486 Aaron Sele .25 .11
❑ 487 Cliff Floyd .25 .11
❑ 488 Jeff Brantley .15 .07
❑ 489 Jim Leyritz .15 .07
❑ 490 Denny Neagle .15 .07
❑ 491 Travis Fryman .25 .11
❑ 492 Carlos Baerga .15 .07
❑ 493 Eddie Taubensee .15 .07
❑ 494 Darryl Strawberry .25 .11
❑ 495 Brian Johnson .15 .07
❑ 496 Randy Myers .25 .11
❑ 497 Jeff Blauser .15 .07
❑ 498 Jason Wood .15 .07
❑ 499 Rolando Arrojo RC .50 .23
❑ 500 Johnny Damon .25 .11
❑ 501 Jose Mercedes .15 .07
❑ 502 Tony Batista .25 .11
❑ 503 Mike Piazza Mets 1.50 .70
❑ 504 Hideo Nomo .60 .25
❑ 505 Chris Gomez .15 .07
❑ 506 Jesus Sanchez RC .25 .11
❑ 507 Al Martin .15 .07
❑ 508 Brian Edmondson .15 .07
❑ 509 Joe Girardi .15 .07
❑ 510 Shayne Bennett .15 .07
❑ 511 Joe Carter .25 .11
❑ 512 Dave Mlicki .15 .07
❑ 513 Rich Butler RC .15 .07
❑ 514 Dennis Eckersley .25 .11
❑ 515 Travis Lee .25 .11
❑ 516 John Mabry .15 .07
❑ 517 Jose Mesa .15 .07
❑ 518 Phil Nevin .25 .11
❑ 519 Raul Casanova .15 .07
❑ 520 Mike Fetters .15 .07
❑ 521 Gary Sheffield .25 .11
❑ 522 Terry Steinbach .15 .07
❑ 523 Steve Trachsel .15 .07
❑ 524 Josh Booty .15 .07
❑ 525 Darryl Hamilton .15 .07
❑ 526 Mark McLemore .15 .07
❑ 527 Kevin Stocker .15 .07
❑ 528 Bret Boone .25 .11
❑ 529 Shane Andrews .15 .07
❑ 530 Robb Nen .15 .07
❑ 531 Carl Everett .25 .11
❑ 532 LaTroy Hawkins .15 .07
❑ 533 Fernando Vina .15 .07
❑ 534 Michael Tucker .15 .07
❑ 535 Mark Langston .15 .07
❑ 536 Mickey Mantle 5.00 2.20
❑ 537 Bernard Gilkey .15 .07
❑ 538 Francisco Cordova .15 .07
❑ 539 Mike Bordick .15 .07
❑ 540 Fred McGriff .40 .18
❑ 541 Cliff Politte .15 .07
❑ 542 Jason Varitek .25 .11
❑ 543 Shawon Dunston .15 .07
❑ 544 Brian Meadows .15 .07
❑ 545 Pat Meares .15 .07
❑ 546 Carlos Perez .15 .07
❑ 547 Desi Relaford .15 .07
❑ 548 Antonio Osuna .15 .07
❑ 549 Devon White .15 .07
❑ 550 Sean Runyan .15 .07
❑ 551 Mickey Morandini .15 .07
❑ 552 Dave Martinez .15 .07
❑ 553 Jeff Fassero .15 .07
❑ 554 Ryan Jackson RC .15 .07
❑ 555 Stan Javier .15 .07
❑ 556 Jaime Navarro .15 .07
❑ 557 Jose Offerman .15 .07
❑ 558 Mike Lowell RC .75 .35
❑ 559 Darrin Fletcher .15 .07
❑ 560 Mark Lewis .15 .07
❑ 561 Dante Bichette .25 .11
❑ 562 Chuck Finley .25 .11
❑ 563 Kerry Wood .60 .25
❑ 564 Andy Benes .15 .07
❑ 565 Freddy Garcia .15 .07
❑ 566 Tom Glavine .60 .25
❑ 567 Jon Nunnally .15 .07
❑ 568 Miguel Cairo .15 .07
❑ 569 Shane Reynolds .15 .07
❑ 570 Roberto Kelly .15 .07
❑ 571 Jose Cruz Jr. CL .15 .07
❑ 572 Ken Griffey Jr. CL 1.00 .45
❑ 573 Mark McGwire CL 1.25 .55
❑ 574 Cal Ripken CL 1.25 .55
❑ 575 Frank Thomas CL .40 .18
❑ 576 Jeff Bagwell UM 2.00 .90
❑ 577 Barry Bonds UM 4.00 1.80
❑ 578 Tony Clark UM .75 .35
❑ 579 Roger Clemens UM 4.00 1.80
❑ 580 Jose Cruz Jr. UM .75 .35
❑ 581 N.Garciaparra UM 4.00 1.80
❑ 582 Juan Gonzalez UM 1.50 .70
❑ 583 Ben Grieve UM .75 .35
❑ 584 Ken Griffey Jr. UM 5.00 2.20
❑ 585 Tony Gwynn UM 3.00 1.35
❑ 586 Derek Jeter UM 6.00 2.70
❑ 587 Randy Johnson UM 2.00 .90
❑ 588 Chipper Jones UM .60 .25
❑ 589 Greg Maddux UM 4.00 1.80
❑ 590 Mark McGwire UM 6.00 2.70
❑ 591 Paul Molitor UM 1.50 .70
❑ 592 Andy Pettitte UM .75 .35
❑ 593 Cal Ripken UM 6.00 2.70
❑ 594 Alex Rodriguez UM 4.00 1.80
❑ 595 Scott Rolen UM 1.50 .70
❑ 596 Curt Schilling UM 1.50 .70
❑ 597 Frank Thomas UM 2.00 .90
❑ 598 Jim Thome UM 1.50 .70
❑ 599 Larry Walker UM 1.00 .45
❑ 600 Bernie Williams UM 1.50 .70
❑ P100 A.Rodriguez Promo 2.50 1.10

1998 Fleer Update

	MINT	NRMT
COMP.FACT.SET (100)	30.00	13.50

❑ U1 Mark McGwire HL 1.50 .70
❑ U2 Sammy Sosa HL .75 .35
❑ U3 Roger Clemens HL 1.00 .45
❑ U4 Barry Bonds HL 1.00 .45
❑ U5 Kerry Wood HL .40 .18
❑ U6 Paul Molitor HL .15 .07
❑ U7 Ken Griffey Jr. HL 1.25 .55
❑ U8 Cal Ripken HL 1.50 .70
❑ U9 David Wells HL .15 .07
❑ U10 Alex Rodriguez HL 1.00 .45
❑ U11 Angel Pena RC .15 .07
❑ U12 Bruce Chen .10 .05
❑ U13 Craig Wilson .10 .05
❑ U14 O.Hernandez RC 1.25 .55
❑ U15 Aramis Ramirez .15 .07
❑ U16 Aaron Boone .10 .05

❑ U17 Bob Henley .10 .05
❑ U18 Juan Guzman .10 .05
❑ U19 Darryl Hamilton .10 .05
❑ U20 Jay Payton .10 .05
❑ U21 Jeremy Powell .10 .05
❑ U22 Ben Davis .15 .07
❑ U23 Preston Wilson .15 .07
❑ U24 Jim Parque RC .50 .23
❑ U25 Odalis Perez RC .50 .23
❑ U26 Ronnie Belliard .10 .05
❑ U27 Royce Clayton .10 .05
❑ U28 George Lombard .10 .05
❑ U29 Tony Phillips .10 .05
❑ U30 F.Seguignol RC .15 .07
❑ U31 Armando Rios RC .75 .35
❑ U32 Jerry Hairston Jr. RC 1.00 .45
❑ U33 Justin Baughman RC .10 .05
❑ U34 Seth Greisinger .10 .05
❑ U35 Alex Gonzalez .10 .05
❑ U36 Michael Barrett .10 .05
❑ U37 Carlos Beltran .15 .07
❑ U38 Ellis Burks .15 .07
❑ U39 Jose Jimenez RC .10 .05
❑ U40 Carlos Guillen .10 .05
❑ U41 Marlon Anderson .10 .05
❑ U42 Scott Elarton .10 .05
❑ U43 Glenallen Hill .10 .05
❑ U44 Shane Monahan .10 .05
❑ U45 Dennis Martinez .15 .07
❑ U46 Carlos Febles RC .40 .18
❑ U47 Carlos Perez .10 .05
❑ U48 Wilton Guerrero .10 .05
❑ U49 Randy Johnson .50 .23
❑ U50 Brian Simmons RC .10 .05
❑ U51 Carlton Loewer .10 .05
❑ U52 Mark DeRosa RC .10 .05
❑ U53 Tim Young RC .15 .07
❑ U54 Gary Gaetti .15 .07
❑ U55 Eric Chavez .15 .07
❑ U56 Carl Pavano .10 .05
❑ U57 Mike Stanley .10 .05
❑ U58 Todd Stottlemyre .10 .05
❑ U59 Gabe Kapler RC 1.50 .70
❑ U60 Mike Jerzembeck RC .15 .07
❑ U61 Mitch Meluskey RC .15 .07
❑ U62 Bill Pulsipher .10 .05
❑ U63 Derrick Gibson .10 .05
❑ U64 John Rocker RC 2.00 .90
❑ U65 Calvin Pickering .10 .05
❑ U66 Blake Stein .10 .05
❑ U67 Fernando Tatis .10 .05
❑ U68 Gabe Alvarez .10 .05
❑ U69 Jeffrey Hammonds .10 .05
❑ U70 Adrian Beltre .15 .07
❑ U71 Ryan Bradley RC .10 .05
❑ U72 Edgard Clemente .10 .05
❑ U73 Rick Croushore RC .10 .05
❑ U74 Matt Clement .15 .07
❑ U75 Dermal Brown .10 .05
❑ U76 Paul Bako .10 .05
❑ U77 Placido Polanco RC 1.00 .45
❑ U78 Jay Tessmer .10 .05
❑ U79 Jarrod Washburn .10 .05
❑ U80 Kevin Witt .10 .05
❑ U81 Mike Metcalfe .10 .05
❑ U82 Daryle Ward .10 .05
❑ U83 Benj Sampson RC .10 .05

❑	U84 Mike Kinkade RC	.15	.07
❑	U85 Randy Winn	.10	.05
❑	U86 Jeff Shaw	.10	.05
❑	U87 Troy Glaus RC	6.00	2.70
❑	U88 Hideo Nomo	.40	.18
❑	U89 Mark Grudzielanek	.10	.05
❑	U90 Mike Frank RC	.10	.05
❑	U91 Bobby Howry RC	.40	.18
❑	U92 Ryan Minor RC	.15	.07
❑	U93 Corey Koskie RC	1.25	.55
❑	U94 Matt Anderson RC	.15	.07
❑	U95 Joe Carter	.15	.07
❑	U96 Paul Konerko	.15	.07
❑	U97 Sidney Ponson	.10	.05
❑	U98 Jeremy Giambi RC	.75	.35
❑	U99 Jeff Kubenka RC	.10	.05
❑	U100 J.D. Drew RC	10.00	4.50

1999 Fleer

		MINT	NRMT
	COMPLETE SET (600)	60.00	27.00
❑	1 Mark McGwire	2.50	1.10
❑	2 Sammy Sosa	1.25	.55
❑	3 Ken Griffey Jr.	2.00	.90
❑	4 Kerry Wood	.60	.25
❑	5 Derek Jeter	2.50	1.10
❑	6 Stan Musial	2.00	.90
❑	7 J.D. Drew	.60	.25
❑	8 Cal Ripken	2.50	1.10
❑	9 Alex Rodriguez	1.50	.70
❑	10 Travis Lee	.15	.07
❑	11 Andres Galarraga	.40	.18
❑	12 Nomar Garciaparra	1.50	.70
❑	13 Albert Belle	.25	.11
❑	14 Barry Larkin	.60	.25
❑	15 Dante Bichette	.25	.11
❑	16 Tony Clark	.25	.11
❑	17 Moises Alou	.25	.11
❑	18 Rafael Palmeiro	.60	.25
❑	19 Raul Mondesi	.25	.11
❑	20 Vladimir Guerrero	.75	.35
❑	21 John Olerud	.25	.11
❑	22 Bernie Williams	.60	.25
❑	23 Ben Grieve	.25	.11
❑	24 Scott Rolen	.60	.25
❑	25 Jeromy Burnitz	.25	.11
❑	26 Ken Caminiti	.25	.11
❑	27 Barry Bonds	1.50	.70
❑	28 Todd Helton	.75	.35
❑	29 Juan Gonzalez	.60	.25
❑	30 Roger Clemens	1.50	.70
❑	31 Andruw Jones	.60	.25
❑	32 Mo Vaughn	.25	.11
❑	33 Larry Walker	.40	.18
❑	34 Frank Thomas	.75	.35
❑	35 Manny Ramirez	.75	.35
❑	36 Randy Johnson	.75	.35
❑	37 Vinny Castilla	.25	.11
❑	38 Juan Encarnacion	.25	.11
❑	39 Jeff Bagwell	.75	.35
❑	40 Gary Sheffield	.25	.11
❑	41 Mike Piazza	1.50	.70
❑	42 Richie Sexson	.25	.11
❑	43 Tony Gwynn	1.25	.55
❑	44 Chipper Jones	1.25	.55
❑	45 Jim Thome	.60	.25
❑	46 Craig Biggio	.40	.18
❑	47 Carlos Delgado	.60	.25
❑	48 Greg Vaughn	.25	.11
❑	49 Greg Maddux	1.50	.70
❑	50 Troy Glaus	.60	.25
❑	51 Roberto Alomar	.60	.25
❑	52 Dennis Eckersley	.25	.11
❑	53 Mike Caruso	.15	.07
❑	54 Bruce Chen	.15	.07
❑	55 Aaron Boone	.15	.07
❑	56 Bartolo Colon	.25	.11
❑	57 Derrick Gibson	.15	.07
❑	58 Brian Anderson	.15	.07
❑	59 Gabe Alvarez	.15	.07
❑	60 Todd Dunwoody	.15	.07
❑	61 Rod Beck	.15	.07
❑	62 Derek Bell	.15	.07
❑	63 Francisco Cordova	.15	.07
❑	64 Johnny Damon	.25	.11
❑	65 Adrian Beltre	.25	.11
❑	66 Garret Anderson	.25	.11
❑	67 Armando Benitez	.15	.07
❑	68 Edgardo Alfonzo	.25	.11
❑	69 Ryan Bradley	.15	.07
❑	70 Eric Chavez	.25	.11
❑	71 Bobby Abreu	.25	.11
❑	72 Andy Ashby	.15	.07
❑	73 Ellis Burks	.25	.11
❑	74 Jeff Cirillo	.25	.11
❑	75 Jay Buhner	.25	.11
❑	76 Ron Gant	.25	.11
❑	77 Rolando Arrojo	.15	.07
❑	78 Will Clark	.60	.25
❑	79 Chris Carpenter	.15	.07
❑	80 Jim Edmonds	.40	.18
❑	81 Tony Batista	.25	.11
❑	82 Shane Andrews	.15	.07
❑	83 Mark DeRosa	.15	.07
❑	84 Brady Anderson	.25	.11
❑	85 Tom Gordon	.15	.07
❑	86 Brant Brown	.15	.07
❑	87 Ray Durham	.25	.11
❑	88 Ron Coomer	.15	.07
❑	89 Bret Boone	.25	.11
❑	90 Travis Fryman	.25	.11
❑	91 Darryl Kile	.25	.11
❑	92 Paul Bako	.15	.07
❑	93 Cliff Floyd	.25	.11
❑	94 Scott Elarton	.15	.07
❑	95 Jeremy Giambi	.15	.07
❑	96 Darren Dreifort	.15	.07
❑	97 Marquis Grissom	.15	.07
❑	98 Marty Cordova	.15	.07
❑	99 Fernando Seguignol	.15	.07
❑	100 Orlando Hernandez	.25	.11
❑	101 Jose Cruz Jr.	.25	.11
❑	102 Jason Giambi	.60	.25
❑	103 Damion Easley	.15	.07
❑	104 Freddy Garcia	.15	.07
❑	105 Marlon Anderson	.15	.07
❑	106 Kevin Brown	.40	.18
❑	107 Joe Carter	.25	.11
❑	108 Russ Davis	.15	.07
❑	109 Brian Jordan	.25	.11
❑	110 Wade Boggs	.60	.25
❑	111 Tom Goodwin	.15	.07
❑	112 Scott Brosius	.25	.11
❑	113 Darin Erstad	.60	.25
❑	114 Jay Bell	.25	.11
❑	115 Tom Glavine	.60	.25
❑	116 Pedro Martinez	.75	.35
❑	117 Mark Grace	.60	.25
❑	118 Russ Ortiz	.15	.07
❑	119 Magglio Ordonez	.40	.18
❑	120 Sean Casey	.40	.18
❑	121 Rafael Roque RC	.25	.11
❑	122 Brian Giles	.25	.11
❑	123 Mike Lansing	.15	.07
❑	124 David Cone	.25	.11
❑	125 Alex Gonzalez	.15	.07
❑	126 Carl Everett	.25	.11
❑	127 Jeff King	.15	.07
❑	128 Charles Johnson	.25	.11
❑	129 Geoff Jenkins	.25	.11
❑	130 Corey Koskie	.25	.11
❑	131 Brad Fullmer	.25	.11
❑	132 Al Leiter	.25	.11
❑	133 Rickey Henderson	1.25	.55
❑	134 Rico Brogna	.15	.07
❑	135 Jose Guillen	.15	.07
❑	136 Matt Clement	.15	.07
❑	137 Carlos Guillen	.15	.07
❑	138 Orel Hershiser	.25	.11
❑	139 Ray Lankford	.15	.07
❑	140 Miguel Cairo	.15	.07
❑	141 Chuck Finley	.25	.11
❑	142 Rusty Greer	.25	.11
❑	143 Kelvim Escobar	.15	.07
❑	144 Ryan Klesko	.25	.11
❑	145 Andy Benes	.15	.07
❑	146 Eric Davis	.25	.11
❑	147 David Wells	.25	.11
❑	148 Trot Nixon	.25	.11
❑	149 Jose Hernandez	.15	.07
❑	150 Mark Johnson	.15	.07
❑	151 Mike Frank	.15	.07
❑	152 Joey Hamilton	.15	.07
❑	153 David Justice	.25	.11
❑	154 Mike Mussina	.60	.25
❑	155 Neifi Perez	.15	.07
❑	156 Luis Gonzalez	.60	.25
❑	157 Livan Hernandez	.15	.07
❑	158 Dermal Brown	.15	.07
❑	159 Jose Lima	.15	.07
❑	160 Eric Karros	.25	.11
❑	161 Ronnie Belliard	.15	.07
❑	162 Matt Lawton	.25	.11
❑	163 Dustin Hermanson	.15	.07
❑	164 Brian McRae	.15	.07
❑	165 Mike Kinkade	.15	.07
❑	166 A.J. Hinch	.15	.07
❑	167 Doug Glanville	.15	.07
❑	168 Hideo Nomo	.60	.25
❑	169 Jason Kendall	.25	.11
❑	170 Steve Finley	.25	.11
❑	171 Jeff Kent	.40	.18
❑	172 Ben Davis	.25	.11
❑	173 Edgar Martinez	.40	.18
❑	174 Eli Marrero	.15	.07
❑	175 Quinton McCracken	.15	.07
❑	176 Rick Helling	.15	.07
❑	177 Tom Evans	.15	.07
❑	178 Carl Pavano	.15	.07
❑	179 Todd Greene	.15	.07
❑	180 Omar Daal	.15	.07
❑	181 George Lombard	.15	.07
❑	182 Ryan Minor	.15	.07
❑	183 Troy O'Leary	.15	.07
❑	184 Robb Nen	.15	.07
❑	185 Mickey Morandini	.15	.07
❑	186 Robin Ventura	.25	.11
❑	187 Pete Harnisch	.15	.07
❑	188 Kenny Lofton	.25	.11
❑	189 Eric Milton	.25	.11
❑	190 Bobby Higginson	.25	.11
❑	191 Jamie Moyer	.15	.07
❑	192 Mark Kotsay	.15	.07
❑	193 Shane Reynolds	.15	.07
❑	194 Carlos Febles	.15	.07
❑	195 Jeff Kubenka	.15	.07
❑	196 Chuck Knoblauch	.25	.11
❑	197 Kenny Rogers	.15	.07
❑	198 Bill Mueller	.15	.07
❑	199 Shane Monahan	.15	.07
❑	200 Matt Morris	.25	.11
❑	201 Fred McGriff	.40	.18
❑	202 Ivan Rodriguez	.60	.25
❑	203 Kevin Witt	.15	.07
❑	204 Troy Percival	.15	.07
❑	205 David Dellucci	.15	.07
❑	206 Kevin Millwood	.15	.07
❑	207 Jerry Hairston Jr.	.25	.11
❑	208 Mike Stanley	.15	.07
❑	209 Henry Rodriguez	.15	.07
❑	210 Trevor Hoffman	.25	.11
❑	211 Craig Wilson	.15	.07
❑	212 Reggie Sanders	.15	.07
❑	213 Carlton Loewer	.15	.07
❑	214 Omar Vizquel	.25	.11
❑	215 Gabe Kapler	.25	.11
❑	216 Derrek Lee	.25	.11
❑	217 Billy Wagner	.15	.07

❑ 218	Dean Palmer	.25	.11
❑ 219	Chan Ho Park	.25	.11
❑ 220	Fernando Vina	.15	.07
❑ 221	Roy Halladay	.15	.07
❑ 222	Paul Molitor	.60	.25
❑ 223	Ugueth Urbina	.15	.07
❑ 224	Rey Ordonez	.15	.07
❑ 225	Ricky Ledee	.15	.07
❑ 226	Scott Spiezio	.15	.07
❑ 227	Wendell Magee	.15	.07
❑ 228	Aramis Ramirez	.25	.11
❑ 229	Brian Simmons	.15	.07
❑ 230	Fernando Tatis	.15	.07
❑ 231	Bobby Smith	.15	.07
❑ 232	Aaron Sele	.25	.11
❑ 233	Shawn Green	.60	.25
❑ 234	Mariano Rivera	.25	.11
❑ 235	Tim Salmon	.25	.11
❑ 236	Andy Fox	.15	.07
❑ 237	Denny Neagle	.15	.07
❑ 238	John Valentin	.15	.07
❑ 239	Kevin Tapani	.15	.07
❑ 240	Paul Konerko	.25	.11
❑ 241	Robert Fick	.15	.07
❑ 242	Edgar Renteria	.15	.07
❑ 243	Brett Tomko	.15	.07
❑ 244	Daryle Ward	.15	.07
❑ 245	Carlos Beltran	.25	.11
❑ 246	Angel Pena	.15	.07
❑ 247	Steve Woodard	.15	.07
❑ 248	David Ortiz	.25	.11
❑ 249	Justin Thompson	.15	.07
❑ 250	Rondell White	.25	.11
❑ 251	Jaret Wright	.15	.07
❑ 252	Ed Sprague	.15	.07
❑ 253	Jay Payton	.15	.07
❑ 254	Mike Lowell	.25	.11
❑ 255	Orlando Cabrera	.15	.07
❑ 256	Jason Schmidt	.15	.07
❑ 257	David Segui	.15	.07
❑ 258	Paul Sorrento	.15	.07
❑ 259	John Wetteland	.25	.11
❑ 260	Devon White	.15	.07
❑ 261	Odalis Perez	.15	.07
❑ 262	Calvin Pickering	.15	.07
❑ 263	Tyler Green	.15	.07
❑ 264	Preston Wilson	.25	.11
❑ 265	Brad Radke	.25	.11
❑ 266	Walt Weiss	.15	.07
❑ 267	Tim Young	.15	.07
❑ 268	Tino Martinez	.25	.11
❑ 269	Matt Stairs	.15	.07
❑ 270	Curt Schilling	.60	.25
❑ 271	Tony Womack	.15	.07
❑ 272	Ismael Valdes	.15	.07
❑ 273	Wally Joyner	.25	.11
❑ 274	Armando Rios	.15	.07
❑ 275	Andy Pettitte	.25	.11
❑ 276	Bubba Trammell	.15	.07
❑ 277	Todd Zeile	.25	.11
❑ 278	Shannon Stewart	.25	.11
❑ 279	Matt Williams	.40	.18
❑ 280	John Rocker	.25	.11
❑ 281	B.J. Surhoff	.25	.11
❑ 282	Eric Young	.15	.07
❑ 283	Dmitri Young	.25	.11
❑ 284	John Smoltz	.25	.11
❑ 285	Todd Walker	.15	.07
❑ 286	Paul O'Neill	.60	.25
❑ 287	Blake Stein	.15	.07
❑ 288	Kevin Young	.25	.11
❑ 289	Quilvio Veras	.15	.07
❑ 290	Kirk Rueter	.15	.07
❑ 291	Randy Winn	.15	.07
❑ 292	Miguel Tejada	.25	.11
❑ 293	J.T. Snow	.25	.11
❑ 294	Michael Tucker	.15	.07
❑ 295	Jay Tessmer	.15	.07
❑ 296	Scott Erickson	.15	.07
❑ 297	Tim Wakefield	.15	.07
❑ 298	Jeff Abbott	.15	.07
❑ 299	Eddie Taubensee	.15	.07
❑ 300	Darryl Hamilton	.15	.07
❑ 301	Kevin Orie	.15	.07
❑ 302	Jose Offerman	.15	.07
❑ 303	Scott Karl	.15	.07
❑ 304	Chris Widger	.15	.07
❑ 305	Todd Hundley	.15	.07
❑ 306	Desi Relaford	.15	.07
❑ 307	Sterling Hitchcock	.15	.07
❑ 308	Delino DeShields	.15	.07
❑ 309	Alex Gonzalez	.15	.07
❑ 310	Justin Baughman	.15	.07
❑ 311	Jamey Wright	.15	.07
❑ 312	Wes Helms	.15	.07
❑ 313	Dante Powell	.15	.07
❑ 314	Jim Abbott	.25	.11
❑ 315	Manny Alexander	.15	.07
❑ 316	Harold Baines	.25	.11
❑ 317	Danny Graves	.15	.07
❑ 318	Sandy Alomar Jr.	.25	.11
❑ 319	Pedro Astacio	.15	.07
❑ 320	Jermaine Allensworth	.15	.07
❑ 321	Matt Anderson	.15	.07
❑ 322	Chad Curtis	.15	.07
❑ 323	Antonio Osuna	.15	.07
❑ 324	Brad Ausmus	.15	.07
❑ 325	Steve Trachsel	.15	.07
❑ 326	Mike Blowers	.15	.07
❑ 327	Brian Bohanon	.15	.07
❑ 328	Chris Gomez	.15	.07
❑ 329	Valerio De Los Santos	.15	.07
❑ 330	Rich Aurilia	.25	.11
❑ 331	Michael Barrett	.15	.07
❑ 332	Rick Aguilera	.15	.07
❑ 333	Adrian Brown	.15	.07
❑ 334	Bill Spiers	.15	.07
❑ 335	Matt Beech	.15	.07
❑ 336	David Bell	.15	.07
❑ 337	Juan Acevedo	.15	.07
❑ 338	Jose Canseco	.60	.25
❑ 339	Wilson Alvarez	.15	.07
❑ 340	Luis Alicea	.15	.07
❑ 341	Jason Dickson	.15	.07
❑ 342	Mike Bordick	.15	.07
❑ 343	Ben Ford	.15	.07
❑ 344	Javy Lopez	.25	.11
❑ 345	Jason Christiansen	.15	.07
❑ 346	Darren Bragg	.15	.07
❑ 347	Doug Brocail	.15	.07
❑ 348	Jeff Blauser	.15	.07
❑ 349	James Baldwin	.15	.07
❑ 350	Jeffrey Hammonds	.15	.07
❑ 351	Ricky Bottalico	.15	.07
❑ 352	Russ Branyan	.25	.11
❑ 353	Mark Brownson RC	.15	.07
❑ 354	Dave Berg	.15	.07
❑ 355	Sean Bergman	.15	.07
❑ 356	Jeff Conine	.15	.07
❑ 357	Shayne Bennett	.15	.07
❑ 358	Bobby Bonilla	.25	.11
❑ 359	Bob Wickman	.15	.07
❑ 360	Carlos Baerga	.15	.07
❑ 361	Chris Fussell	.15	.07
❑ 362	Chili Davis	.25	.11
❑ 363	Jerry Spradlin	.15	.07
❑ 364	Carlos Hernandez	.15	.07
❑ 365	Roberto Hernandez	.15	.07
❑ 366	Marvin Benard	.15	.07
❑ 367	Ken Cloude	.15	.07
❑ 368	Tony Fernandez	.15	.07
❑ 369	John Burkett	.15	.07
❑ 370	Gary DiSarcina	.15	.07
❑ 371	Alan Benes	.15	.07
❑ 372	Karim Garcia	.15	.07
❑ 373	Carlos Perez	.15	.07
❑ 374	Damon Buford	.15	.07
❑ 375	Mark Clark	.15	.07
❑ 376	Edgard Clemente	.15	.07
❑ 377	Chad Bradford RC	.15	.07
❑ 378	Frank Catalanotto	.15	.07
❑ 379	Vic Darensbourg	.15	.07
❑ 380	Sean Berry	.15	.07
❑ 381	Dave Burba	.15	.07
❑ 382	Sal Fasano	.15	.07
❑ 383	Steve Parris	.15	.07
❑ 384	Roger Cedeno	.15	.07
❑ 385	Chad Fox	.15	.07
❑ 386	Wilton Guerrero	.15	.07
❑ 387	Dennis Cook	.15	.07
❑ 388	Joe Girardi	.15	.07
❑ 389	LaTroy Hawkins	.15	.07
❑ 390	Ryan Christenson	.15	.07
❑ 391	Paul Byrd	.15	.07
❑ 392	Lou Collier	.15	.07
❑ 393	Jeff Fassero	.15	.07
❑ 394	Jim Leyritz	.15	.07
❑ 395	Shawn Estes	.25	.11
❑ 396	Mike Kelly	.15	.07
❑ 397	Rich Croushore	.15	.07
❑ 398	Royce Clayton	.15	.07
❑ 399	Rudy Seanez	.15	.07
❑ 400	Darrin Fletcher	.15	.07
❑ 401	Shigetoshi Hasegawa	.15	.07
❑ 402	Bernard Gilkey	.15	.07
❑ 403	Juan Guzman	.15	.07
❑ 404	Jeff Frye	.15	.07
❑ 405	Donovan Osborne	.15	.07
❑ 406	Alex Fernandez	.15	.07
❑ 407	Gary Gaetti	.15	.07
❑ 408	Dan Miceli	.15	.07
❑ 409	Mike Cameron	.25	.11
❑ 410	Mike Remlinger	.15	.07
❑ 411	Joey Cora	.15	.07
❑ 412	Mark Gardner	.15	.07
❑ 413	Aaron Ledesma	.15	.07
❑ 414	Jerry Dipoto	.15	.07
❑ 415	Ricky Gutierrez	.15	.07
❑ 416	John Franco	.25	.11
❑ 417	Mendy Lopez	.15	.07
❑ 418	Hideki Irabu	.15	.07
❑ 419	Mark Grudzielanek	.15	.07
❑ 420	Bobby Hughes	.15	.07
❑ 421	Pat Meares	.15	.07
❑ 422	Jimmy Haynes	.15	.07
❑ 423	Bob Henley	.15	.07
❑ 424	Bobby Estalella	.15	.07
❑ 425	Jon Lieber	.15	.07
❑ 426	Giomar Guevara RC	.15	.07
❑ 427	Jose Jimenez	.15	.07
❑ 428	Deivi Cruz	.15	.07
❑ 429	Jonathan Johnson	.15	.07
❑ 430	Ken Hill	.15	.07
❑ 431	Craig Grebeck	.15	.07
❑ 432	Jose Rosado	.15	.07
❑ 433	Danny Klassen	.15	.07
❑ 434	Bobby Howry	.15	.07
❑ 435	Gerald Williams	.15	.07
❑ 436	Omar Olivares	.15	.07
❑ 437	Chris Hoiles	.15	.07
❑ 438	Seth Greisinger	.15	.07
❑ 439	Scott Hatteberg	.15	.07
❑ 440	Jeremi Gonzalez	.15	.07
❑ 441	Wil Cordero	.15	.07
❑ 442	Jeff Montgomery	.15	.07
❑ 443	Chris Stynes	.15	.07
❑ 444	Tony Saunders	.15	.07
❑ 445	Einar Diaz	.15	.07
❑ 446	Lariel Gonzalez	.15	.07
❑ 447	Ryan Jackson	.15	.07
❑ 448	Mike Hampton	.25	.11
❑ 449	Todd Hollandsworth	.15	.07
❑ 450	Gabe White	.15	.07
❑ 451	John Jaha	.15	.07
❑ 452	Bret Saberhagen	.25	.11
❑ 453	Otis Nixon	.15	.07
❑ 454	Steve Kline	.15	.07
❑ 455	Butch Huskey	.15	.07
❑ 456	Mike Jerzembeck	.15	.07
❑ 457	Wayne Gomes	.15	.07
❑ 458	Mike Macfarlane	.15	.07
❑ 459	Jesus Sanchez	.15	.07
❑ 460	Al Martin	.15	.07
❑ 461	Dwight Gooden	.25	.11
❑ 462	Ruben Rivera	.15	.07
❑ 463	Pat Hentgen	.15	.07
❑ 464	Jose Valentin	.15	.07
❑ 465	Vladimir Nunez	.15	.07
❑ 466	Charlie Hayes	.15	.07
❑ 467	Jay Powell	.15	.07
❑ 468	Raul Ibanez	.15	.07
❑ 469	Kent Mercker	.15	.07
❑ 470	John Mabry	.15	.07
❑ 471	Woody Williams	.15	.07
❑ 472	Roberto Kelly	.15	.07
❑ 473	Jim Mecir	.15	.07
❑ 474	Dave Hollins	.15	.07
❑ 475	Rafael Medina	.15	.07

		MINT	NRMT
❑ 476	Darren Lewis	.15	.07
❑ 477	Felix Heredia	.15	.07
❑ 478	Brian Hunter	.15	.07
❑ 479	Matt Mantei	.15	.07
❑ 480	Richard Hidalgo	.25	.11
❑ 481	Bobby Jones	.15	.07
❑ 482	Hal Morris	.15	.07
❑ 483	Ramiro Mendoza	.15	.07
❑ 484	Matt Luke	.15	.07
❑ 485	Esteban Loaiza	.15	.07
❑ 486	Mark Loretta	.15	.07
❑ 487	A.J. Pierzynski	.15	.07
❑ 488	Charles Nagy	.15	.07
❑ 489	Kevin Sefcik	.15	.07
❑ 490	Jason McDonald	.15	.07
❑ 491	Jeremy Powell	.15	.07
❑ 492	Scott Servais	.15	.07
❑ 493	Abraham Nunez	.15	.07
❑ 494	Stan Spencer	.15	.07
❑ 495	Stan Javier	.15	.07
❑ 496	Jose Paniagua	.15	.07
❑ 497	Gregg Jefferies	.15	.07
❑ 498	Gregg Olson	.15	.07
❑ 499	Derek Lowe	.15	.07
❑ 500	Willis Otanez	.15	.07
❑ 501	Brian Moehler	.15	.07
❑ 502	Glenallen Hill	.15	.07
❑ 503	Bobby M. Jones	.15	.07
❑ 504	Greg Norton	.15	.07
❑ 505	Mike Jackson	.15	.07
❑ 506	Kirt Manwaring	.15	.07
❑ 507	Eric Weaver RC	.15	.07
❑ 508	Mitch Meluskey	.15	.07
❑ 509	Todd Jones	.15	.07
❑ 510	Mike Matheny	.15	.07
❑ 511	Benj Sampson	.15	.07
❑ 512	Tony Phillips	.15	.07
❑ 513	Mike Thurman	.15	.07
❑ 514	Jorge Posada	.25	.11
❑ 515	Bill Taylor	.15	.07
❑ 516	Mike Sweeney	.25	.11
❑ 517	Jose Silva	.15	.07
❑ 518	Mark Lewis	.15	.07
❑ 519	Chris Peters	.15	.07
❑ 520	Brian Johnson	.15	.07
❑ 521	Mike Timlin	.15	.07
❑ 522	Mark McLemore	.15	.07
❑ 523	Dan Plesac	.15	.07
❑ 524	Kelly Stinnett	.15	.07
❑ 525	Sidney Ponson	.15	.07
❑ 526	Jim Parque	.15	.07
❑ 527	Tyler Houston	.15	.07
❑ 528	John Thomson	.15	.07
❑ 529	Reggie Jefferson	.15	.07
❑ 530	Robert Person	.15	.07
❑ 531	Marc Newfield	.15	.07
❑ 532	Javier Vazquez	.25	.11
❑ 533	Terry Steinbach	.15	.07
❑ 534	Turk Wendell	.15	.07
❑ 535	Tim Raines	.25	.11
❑ 536	Brian Meadows	.15	.07
❑ 537	Mike Lieberthal	.25	.11
❑ 538	Ricardo Rincon	.15	.07
❑ 539	Dan Wilson	.15	.07
❑ 540	John Johnstone	.15	.07
❑ 541	Todd Stottlemyre	.15	.07
❑ 542	Kevin Stocker	.15	.07
❑ 543	Ramon Martinez	.15	.07
❑ 544	Mike Simms	.15	.07
❑ 545	Paul Quantrill	.15	.07
❑ 546	Matt Walbeck	.15	.07
❑ 547	Turner Ward	.15	.07
❑ 548	Bill Pulsipher	.15	.07
❑ 549	Donnie Sadler	.15	.07
❑ 550	Lance Johnson	.15	.07
❑ 551	Bill Simas	.15	.07
❑ 552	Jeff Reed	.15	.07
❑ 553	Jeff Shaw	.15	.07
❑ 554	Joe Randa	.15	.07
❑ 555	Paul Shuey	.15	.07
❑ 556	Mike Redmond RC	.15	.07
❑ 557	Sean Runyan	.15	.07
❑ 558	Enrique Wilson	.15	.07
❑ 559	Scott Radinsky	.15	.07
❑ 560	Larry Sutton	.15	.07
❑ 561	Masato Yoshii	.25	.11
❑ 562	David Nilsson	.15	.07
❑ 563	Mike Trombley	.15	.07
❑ 564	Darryl Strawberry	.25	.11
❑ 565	Dave Mlicki	.15	.07
❑ 566	Placido Polanco	.15	.07
❑ 567	Yorkis Perez	.15	.07
❑ 568	Esteban Yan	.15	.07
❑ 569	Lee Stevens	.15	.07
❑ 570	Steve Sinclair	.15	.07
❑ 571	Jarrod Washburn	.15	.07
❑ 572	Lenny Webster	.15	.07
❑ 573	Mike Sirotka	.15	.07
❑ 574	Jason Varitek	.25	.11
❑ 575	Terry Mulholland	.15	.07
❑ 576	Adrian Beltre FF	.25	.11
❑ 577	Eric Chavez FF	.15	.07
❑ 578	J.D. Drew FF	.60	.25
❑ 579	Juan Encarnacion FF	.15	.07
❑ 580	Nomar Garciaparra FF	.75	.35
❑ 581	Troy Glaus FF	.25	.11
❑ 582	Ben Grieve FF	.25	.11
❑ 583	Vladimir Guerrero FF	.40	.18
❑ 584	Todd Helton FF	.60	.25
❑ 585	Derek Jeter FF	1.25	.55
❑ 586	Travis Lee FF	.15	.07
❑ 587	Alex Rodriguez FF	.75	.35
❑ 588	Scott Rolen FF	.60	.25
❑ 589	Richie Sexson FF	.25	.11
❑ 590	Kerry Wood FF	.25	.11
❑ 591	Ken Griffey Jr. CL	1.00	.45
❑ 592	Chipper Jones CL	.60	.25
❑ 593	Alex Rodriguez CL	.75	.35
❑ 594	Sammy Sosa CL	.60	.25
❑ 595	Mark McGwire CL	1.25	.55
❑ 596	Cal Ripken CL	1.25	.55
❑ 597	Nomar Garciaparra CL	.75	.35
❑ 598	Derek Jeter CL	1.25	.55
❑ 599	Kerry Wood CL	.25	.11
❑ 600	J.D. Drew CL	.60	.25
❑ P7	J.D. Drew Promo	1.50	.70

1999 Fleer Update

		MINT	NRMT
COMP.FACT.SET (150)		30.00	13.50
❑ U1	Rick Ankiel RC	6.00	2.70
❑ U2	Peter Bergeron RC	.60	.25
❑ U3	Pat Burrell RC	2.00	.90
❑ U4	Eric Munson RC	1.50	.70
❑ U5	Alfonso Soriano RC	3.00	1.35
❑ U6	Tim Hudson RC	3.00	1.35
❑ U7	Erubiel Durazo RC	1.00	.45
❑ U8	Chad Hermansen	.10	.05
❑ U9	Jeff Zimmerman RC	.10	.05
❑ U10	Jesus Pena RC	.10	.05
❑ U11	Ramon Hernandez	.10	.05
❑ U12	Trent Durrington RC	.10	.05
❑ U13	Tony Armas Jr.	.15	.07
❑ U14	Mike Fyhrie RC	.10	.05
❑ U15	Danny Kolb RC	.10	.05
❑ U16	Mike Porzio RC	.10	.05
❑ U17	Will Brunson RC	.10	.05
❑ U18	Mike Duvall RC	.10	.05
❑ U19	D.Mientkiewicz RC	1.50	.70
❑ U20	Gabe Molina RC	.10	.05
❑ U21	Luis Vizcaino RC	.15	.07
❑ U22	Robinson Cancel RC	.10	.05
❑ U23	Brett Laxton RC	.10	.05
❑ U24	Joe McEwing RC	.15	.07
❑ U25	Justin Speier RC	.10	.05
❑ U26	Kip Wells RC	.60	.25
❑ U27	Armando Almanza RC	.10	.05
❑ U28	Joe Davenport RC	.10	.05
❑ U29	Yamid Haad RC	.10	.05
❑ U30	John Halama	.10	.05
❑ U31	Adam Kennedy	.10	.05
❑ U32	Micah Bowie RC	.10	.05
❑ U33	Travis Dawkins RC	.40	.18
❑ U34	Ryan Rupe RC	.40	.18
❑ U35	B.J. Ryan RC	.10	.05
❑ U36	Chance Sanford RC	.10	.05
❑ U37	A.Shumaker RC	.10	.05
❑ U38	Ryan Glynn RC	.40	.18
❑ U39	Roosevelt Brown RC	.40	.18
❑ U40	Ben Molina RC	.40	.18
❑ U41	Scott Williamson	.10	.05
❑ U42	Eric Gagne RC	.50	.23
❑ U43	John McDonald RC	.10	.05
❑ U44	Scott Sauerbeck RC	.10	.05
❑ U45	Mike Venafro RC	.10	.05
❑ U46	Edwards Guzman RC	.10	.05
❑ U47	Richard Barker RC	.10	.05
❑ U48	Braden Looper	.10	.05
❑ U49	Chad Meyers RC	.10	.05
❑ U50	Scott Strickland RC	.15	.07
❑ U51	Billy Koch	.10	.05
❑ U52	David Newhan RC	.10	.05
❑ U53	David Riske RC	.25	.11
❑ U54	Jose Santiago RC	.10	.05
❑ U55	Miguel Del Toro RC	.10	.05
❑ U56	Orber Moreno RC	.25	.11
❑ U57	Dave Roberts RC	.10	.05
❑ U58	Tim Byrdak RC	.10	.05
❑ U59	David Lee RC	.10	.05
❑ U60	Guillermo Mota RC	.10	.05
❑ U61	Wilton Veras RC	.25	.11
❑ U62	Joe Mays RC	1.00	.45
❑ U63	Jose Fernandez RC	.10	.05
❑ U64	Ray King RC	.10	.05
❑ U65	Chris Petersen RC	.10	.05
❑ U66	Vernon Wells	.15	.07
❑ U67	Ruben Mateo	.15	.07
❑ U68	Ben Petrick	.10	.05
❑ U69	Chris Tremie RC	.10	.05
❑ U70	Lance Berkman	.40	.18
❑ U71	Dan Smith RC	.25	.11
❑ U72	Carlos E. Hernandez RC	.15	.07
❑ U73	Chad Harville RC	.15	.07
❑ U74	Damaso Marte RC	.10	.05
❑ U75	Aaron Myette RC	.40	.18
❑ U76	Willis Roberts RC	.40	.18
❑ U77	Erik Sabel RC	.10	.05
❑ U78	Hector Almonte RC	.10	.05
❑ U79	Kris Benson	.15	.07
❑ U80	Pat Daneker RC	.10	.05
❑ U81	Freddy Garcia RC	2.00	.90
❑ U82	Byung-Hyun Kim RC	.75	.35
❑ U83	Wily Pena RC	2.00	.90
❑ U84	Dan Wheeler RC	.40	.18
❑ U85	Tim Harikkala RC	.10	.05
❑ U86	Derrin Ebert RC	.15	.07
❑ U87	Horacio Estrada RC	.10	.05
❑ U88	Liu Rodriguez RC	.15	.07
❑ U89	J.Zimmerman RC	.10	.05
❑ U90	A.J. Burnett RC	1.00	.45
❑ U91	Doug Davis RC	.60	.25
❑ U92	Robert Ramsay RC	.10	.05
❑ U93	Clay Bellinger RC	.10	.05
❑ U94	Charlie Greene RC	.10	.05
❑ U95	Bo Porter RC	.10	.05
❑ U96	Jorge Toca RC	.40	.18
❑ U97	Casey Blake RC	.10	.05
❑ U98	Amaury Garcia RC	.15	.07
❑ U99	Jose Molina RC	.10	.05
❑ U100	Melvin Mora RC	.40	.18
❑ U101	Joe Nathan RC	.10	.05
❑ U102	Juan Pena RC	.15	.07
❑ U103	Dave Borkowski RC	.25	.11
❑ U104	Eddie Gaillard RC	.10	.05
❑ U105	Glen Barker RC	.10	.05
❑ U106	Brett Hinchliffe RC	.10	.05
❑ U107	Carlos Lee	.15	.07
❑ U108	Rob Ryan RC	.10	.05

		MINT	NRMT
❑ U109	Jeff Weaver RC	1.00	.45
❑ U110	Ed Yarnall	.10	.05
❑ U111	Nelson Cruz RC	.10	.05
❑ U112	C.Davidson RC	.10	.05
❑ U113	Tim Kubinski RC	.10	.05
❑ U114	Sean Spencer RC	.10	.05
❑ U115	Joe Winkelsas RC	.10	.05
❑ U116	Mike Colangelo RC	.10	.05
❑ U117	Tom Davey RC	.10	.05
❑ U118	Warren Morris	.10	.05
❑ U119	Dan Murray RC	.10	.05
❑ U120	Jose Nieves RC	.10	.05
❑ U121	Mark Quinn RC	1.00	.45
❑ U122	Josh Beckett RC	8.00	3.60
❑ U123	Chad Allen RC	.10	.05
❑ U124	Mike Figga	.10	.05
❑ U125	Beiker Graterol RC	.10	.05
❑ U126	Aaron Scheffer RC	.10	.05
❑ U127	Wiki Gonzalez RC	.15	.07
❑ U128	Ramon E.Martinez RC	.10	.05
❑ U129	Matt Riley RC	.40	.18
❑ U130	Chris Woodward RC	.15	.07
❑ U131	Albert Belle	.15	.07
❑ U132	Roger Cedeno	.10	.05
❑ U133	Roger Clemens	1.00	.45
❑ U134	Brian Giles	.15	.07
❑ U135	Rickey Henderson	.75	.35
❑ U136	Randy Johnson	.50	.23
❑ U137	Brian Jordan	.15	.07
❑ U138	Paul Konerko	.15	.07
❑ U139	Hideo Nomo	.40	.18
❑ U140	Kenny Rogers	.10	.05
❑ U141	Wade Boggs HL	.40	.18
❑ U142	Jose Canseco HL	.15	.07
❑ U143	Roger Clemens HL	1.00	.45
❑ U144	David Cone HL	.10	.05
❑ U145	Tony Gwynn HL	.75	.35
❑ U146	Mark McGwire HL	1.50	.70
❑ U147	Cal Ripken HL	1.50	.70
❑ U148	Alex Rodriguez HL	1.00	.45
❑ U149	Fernando Tatis HL	.10	.05
❑ U150	Robin Ventura HL	.15	.07

2000 Fleer

	MINT	NRMT
COMPLETE SET (450)	80.00	36.00

		MINT	NRMT
❑ 1	AL Home Run LL	1.25	.55
	Ken Griffey Jr		
	Rafael Palmeiro		
	Carlos Delgado		
❑ 2	NL Home Run LL	1.25	.55
	Mark McGwire		
	Sammy Sosa		
	Chipper Jones		
❑ 3	AL RBI LL	.60	.25
	Manny Ramirez		
	Rafael Palmeiro		
	Ken Griffey Jr.		
❑ 4	NL RBI LL	.75	.35
	Mark McGwire		
	Matt Williams		
	Sammy Sosa		
❑ 5	AL Avg LL	.75	.35
	Nomar Garciaparra		
	Derek Jeter		
	Bernie Williams		
❑ 6	NL Avg LL	.40	.18
	Larry Walker		
	Luis Gonzalez		
	Bob Abreu		
❑ 7	AL Wins LL	.25	.11
	Pedro Martinez		
	Bartolo Colon		
	Mike Mussina		
❑ 8	NL Wins LL	.15	.07
	Mike Hampton		
	Jose Lima		
	Greg Maddux		
❑ 9	AL ERA LL	.25	.11
	Pedro Martinez		
	David Cone		
	Mike Mussina		
❑ 10	NL ERA LL	.25	.11
	Randy Johnson		
	Kevin Millwood		
	Mike Hampton		
❑ 11	Matt Mantei	.15	.07
❑ 12	John Rocker	.25	.11
❑ 13	Kyle Farnsworth	.15	.07
❑ 14	Juan Guzman	.15	.07
❑ 15	Manny Ramirez	.75	.35
❑ 16	Matt Riley	.15	.07
	Calvin Pickering		
❑ 17	Tony Clark	.25	.11
❑ 18	Brian Meadows	.15	.07
❑ 19	Orber Moreno	.15	.07
❑ 20	Eric Karros	.25	.11
❑ 21	Steve Woodard	.15	.07
❑ 22	Scott Brosius	.25	.11
❑ 23	Gary Bennett	.15	.07
❑ 24	Jason Wood	.15	.07
	Dave Borkowski		
❑ 25	Joe McEwing	.15	.07
❑ 26	Juan Gonzalez	.60	.25
❑ 27	Roy Halladay	.15	.07
❑ 28	Trevor Hoffman	.25	.11
❑ 29	Arizona Diamondbacks	.25	.11
❑ 30	Domingo Guzman RC	.40	.18
	Wiki Gonzalez		
❑ 31	Bret Boone	.25	.11
❑ 32	Nomar Garciaparra	1.50	.70
❑ 33	Bo Porter	.15	.07
❑ 34	Eddie Taubensee	.15	.07
❑ 35	Pedro Astacio	.15	.07
❑ 36	Derek Bell	.15	.07
❑ 37	Jacque Jones	.25	.11
❑ 38	Ricky Ledee	.15	.07
❑ 39	Jeff Kent	.40	.18
❑ 40	Matt Williams	.40	.18
❑ 41	Alfonso Soriano	.60	.25
	D'Angelo Jimenez		
❑ 42	B.J. Surhoff	.25	.11
❑ 43	Denny Neagle	.15	.07
❑ 44	Omar Vizquel	.25	.11
❑ 45	Jeff Bagwell	.75	.35
❑ 46	Mark Grudzielanek	.15	.07
❑ 47	LaTroy Hawkins	.15	.07
❑ 48	Orlando Hernandez	.25	.11
❑ 49	Ken Griffey Jr. CL	.60	.25
❑ 50	Fernando Tatis	.15	.07
❑ 51	Quilvio Veras	.15	.07
❑ 52	Wayne Gomes	.15	.07
❑ 53	Rick Helling	.15	.07
❑ 54	Shannon Stewart	.25	.11
❑ 55	Dermal Brown	.25	.11
	Mark Quinn		
❑ 56	Randy Johnson	.75	.35
❑ 57	Greg Maddux	1.50	.70
❑ 58	Mike Cameron	.25	.11
❑ 59	Matt Anderson	.15	.07
❑ 60	Milwaukee Brewers	.25	.11
❑ 61	Derrek Lee	.25	.11
❑ 62	Mike Sweeney	.25	.11
❑ 63	Fernando Vina	.15	.07
❑ 64	Orlando Cabrera	.15	.07
❑ 65	Doug Glanville	.15	.07
❑ 66	Stan Spencer	.15	.07
❑ 67	Ray Lankford	.15	.07
❑ 68	Kelly Dransfeldt	.15	.07
❑ 69	Alex Gonzalez	.15	.07
❑ 70	Russ Branyan	.15	.07
	Danny Peoples		
❑ 71	Jim Edmonds	.40	.18
❑ 72	Brady Anderson	.25	.11
❑ 73	Mike Stanley	.15	.07
❑ 74	Travis Fryman	.25	.11
❑ 75	Carlos Febles	.15	.07
❑ 76	Bobby Higginson	.15	.07
❑ 77	Carlos Perez	.15	.07
❑ 78	Steve Cox	.15	.07
	Alex Sanchez		
❑ 79	Dustin Hermanson	.15	.07
❑ 80	Kenny Rogers	.15	.07
❑ 81	Miguel Tejada	.25	.11
❑ 82	Ben Davis	.25	.11
❑ 83	Reggie Sanders	.15	.07
❑ 84	Eric Davis	.25	.11
❑ 85	J.D. Drew	.60	.25
❑ 86	Ryan Rupe	.15	.07
❑ 87	Bobby Smith	.15	.07
❑ 88	Jose Cruz Jr.	.25	.11
❑ 89	Carlos Delgado	.60	.25
❑ 90	Toronto Blue Jays	.25	.11
❑ 91	Denny Stark RC	.15	.07
	Gil Meche		
❑ 92	Randy Velarde	.15	.07
❑ 93	Aaron Boone	.15	.07
❑ 94	Javy Lopez	.25	.11
❑ 95	Johnny Damon	.25	.11
❑ 96	Jon Lieber	.15	.07
❑ 97	Montreal Expos	.25	.11
❑ 98	Mark Kotsay	.15	.07
❑ 99	Luis Gonzalez	.60	.25
❑ 100	Larry Walker	.40	.18
❑ 101	Adrian Beltre	.25	.11
❑ 102	Alex Ochoa	.15	.07
❑ 103	Michael Barrett	.15	.07
❑ 104	Tampa Bay Devil Rays	.25	.11
❑ 105	Rey Ordonez	.15	.07
❑ 106	Derek Jeter	2.00	.90
❑ 107	Mike Lieberthal	.25	.11
❑ 108	Ellis Burks	.25	.11
❑ 109	Steve Finley	.25	.11
❑ 110	Ryan Klesko	.25	.11
❑ 111	Steve Avery	.15	.07
❑ 112	Dave Veres	.15	.07
❑ 113	Cliff Floyd	.25	.11
❑ 114	Shane Reynolds	.15	.07
❑ 115	Kevin Brown	.40	.18
❑ 116	Dave Nilsson	.15	.07
❑ 117	Mike Trombley	.15	.07
❑ 118	Todd Walker	.15	.07
❑ 119	John Olerud	.25	.11
❑ 120	Chuck Knoblauch	.25	.11
❑ 121	Nomar Garciaparra CL	.60	.25
❑ 122	Trot Nixon	.25	.11
❑ 123	Erubiel Durazo	.25	.11
❑ 124	Edwards Guzman	.15	.07
❑ 125	Curt Schilling	.60	.25
❑ 126	Brian Jordan	.25	.11
❑ 127	Cleveland Indians	.25	.11
❑ 128	Benito Santiago	.15	.07
❑ 129	Frank Thomas	.75	.35
❑ 130	Neifi Perez	.15	.07
❑ 131	Alex Fernandez	.15	.07
❑ 132	Jose Lima	.15	.07
❑ 133	Jorge Toca	.15	.07
	Melvin Mora		
❑ 134	Scott Karl	.15	.07
❑ 135	Brad Radke	.25	.11
❑ 136	Paul O'Neill	.60	.25
❑ 137	Kris Benson	.25	.11
❑ 138	Colorado Rockies	.25	.11
❑ 139	Jason Phillips	.15	.07
❑ 140	Robb Nen	.15	.07
❑ 141	Ken Hill	.15	.07
❑ 142	Charles Johnson	.25	.11
❑ 143	Paul Konerko	.25	.11
❑ 144	Dmitri Young	.25	.11
❑ 145	Justin Thompson	.15	.07
❑ 146	Mark Loretta	.15	.07
❑ 147	Edgardo Alfonzo	.25	.11
❑ 148	Armando Benitez	.25	.11
❑ 149	Octavio Dotel	.15	.07
❑ 150	Wade Boggs	.60	.25
❑ 151	Ramon Hernandez	.15	.07
❑ 152	Freddy Garcia	.40	.18
❑ 153	Edgar Martinez	.40	.18

- ❑ 154 Ivan Rodriguez .60 .25
- ❑ 155 Kansas City Royals .25 .11
- ❑ 156 Cleatus Davidson .25 .11
- Cristian Guzman
- ❑ 157 Andy Benes .15 .07
- ❑ 158 Todd Dunwoody .15 .07
- ❑ 159 Pedro Martinez .75 .35
- ❑ 160 Mike Caruso .15 .07
- ❑ 161 Mike Sirotka .15 .07
- ❑ 162 Houston Astros .25 .11
- ❑ 163 Darryl Kile .25 .11
- ❑ 164 Chipper Jones 1.25 .55
- ❑ 165 Carl Everett .25 .11
- ❑ 166 Geoff Jenkins .25 .11
- ❑ 167 Dan Perkins .15 .07
- ❑ 168 Andy Pettitte .25 .11
- ❑ 169 Francisco Cordova .15 .07
- ❑ 170 Jay Buhner .25 .11
- ❑ 171 Jay Bell .25 .11
- ❑ 172 Andruw Jones .60 .25
- ❑ 173 Bobby Howry .15 .07
- ❑ 174 Chris Singleton .15 .07
- ❑ 175 Todd Helton .75 .35
- ❑ 176 A.J. Burnett .25 .11
- ❑ 177 Marquis Grissom .15 .07
- ❑ 178 Eric Milton .25 .11
- ❑ 179 Los Angeles Dodgers .25 .11
- ❑ 180 Kevin Appier .15 .07
- ❑ 181 Brian Giles .25 .11
- ❑ 182 Tom Davey .15 .07
- ❑ 183 Mo Vaughn .25 .11
- ❑ 184 Jose Hernandez .15 .07
- ❑ 185 Jim Parque .15 .07
- ❑ 186 Derrick Gibson .15 .07
- ❑ 187 Bruce Aven .15 .07
- ❑ 188 Jeff Cirillo .25 .11
- ❑ 189 Doug Mientkiewicz .40 .18
- ❑ 190 Eric Chavez .25 .11
- ❑ 191 Al Martin .15 .07
- ❑ 192 Tom Glavine .60 .25
- ❑ 193 Butch Huskey .15 .07
- ❑ 194 Ray Durham .25 .11
- ❑ 195 Greg Vaughn .25 .11
- ❑ 196 Vinny Castilla .25 .11
- ❑ 197 Ken Caminiti .25 .11
- ❑ 198 Joe Mays .25 .11
- ❑ 199 Chicago White Sox .25 .11
- ❑ 200 Mariano Rivera .25 .11
- ❑ 201 Mark McGwire CL .60 .25
- ❑ 202 Pat Meares .15 .07
- ❑ 203 Andres Galarraga .40 .18
- ❑ 204 Tom Gordon .15 .07
- ❑ 205 Henry Rodriguez .15 .07
- ❑ 206 Brett Tomko .15 .07
- ❑ 207 Dante Bichette .25 .11
- ❑ 208 Craig Biggio .40 .18
- ❑ 209 Matt Lawton .15 .07
- ❑ 210 Tino Martinez .25 .11
- ❑ 211 Aaron Myette .25 .11
- Josh Paul
- ❑ 212 Warren Morris .15 .07
- ❑ 213 San Diego Padres .25 .11
- ❑ 214 Ramon E. Martinez .15 .07
- ❑ 215 Troy Percival .15 .07
- ❑ 216 Jason Johnson .15 .07
- ❑ 217 Carlos Lee .25 .11
- ❑ 218 Scott Williamson .15 .07
- ❑ 219 Jeff Weaver .25 .11
- ❑ 220 Ronnie Belliard .15 .07
- ❑ 221 Jason Giambi .60 .25
- ❑ 222 Ken Griffey Jr. 2.00 .90
- ❑ 223 John Halama .15 .07
- ❑ 224 Brett Hinchliffe .15 .07
- ❑ 225 Wilson Alvarez .15 .07
- ❑ 226 Rolando Arrojo .15 .07
- ❑ 227 Ruben Mateo .25 .11
- ❑ 228 Rafael Palmeiro .60 .25
- ❑ 229 David Wells .25 .11
- ❑ 230 Eric Gagne .40 .18
- Jeff Williams RC
- ❑ 231 Tim Salmon .25 .11
- ❑ 232 Mike Mussina .60 .25
- ❑ 233 Magglio Ordonez .25 .11
- ❑ 234 Ron Villone .15 .07
- ❑ 235 Antonio Alfonseca .15 .07
- ❑ 236 Jeromy Burnitz .25 .11
- ❑ 237 Ben Grieve .25 .11
- ❑ 238 Giomar Guevara .15 .07
- ❑ 239 Garret Anderson .25 .11
- ❑ 240 John Smoltz .25 .11
- ❑ 241 Mark Grace .60 .25
- ❑ 242 Cole Liniak .15 .07
- Jose Molina
- ❑ 243 Damion Easley .15 .07
- ❑ 244 Jeff Montgomery .15 .07
- ❑ 245 Kenny Lofton .25 .11
- ❑ 246 Masato Yoshii .15 .07
- ❑ 247 Philadelphia Phillies .25 .11
- ❑ 248 Raul Mondesi .25 .11
- ❑ 249 Marlon Anderson .15 .07
- ❑ 250 Shawn Green .60 .25
- ❑ 251 Sterling Hitchcock .15 .07
- ❑ 252 Randy Wolf .15 .07
- Anthony Shumaker
- ❑ 253 Jeff Fassero .15 .07
- ❑ 254 Eli Marrero .15 .07
- ❑ 255 Cincinnati Reds .25 .11
- ❑ 256 Rick Ankiel .60 .25
- Adam Kennedy
- ❑ 257 Darin Erstad .60 .25
- ❑ 258 Albert Belle .25 .11
- ❑ 259 Bartolo Colon .25 .11
- ❑ 260 Bret Saberhagen .25 .11
- ❑ 261 Carlos Beltran .25 .11
- ❑ 262 Glenallen Hill .15 .07
- ❑ 263 Gregg Jefferies .15 .07
- ❑ 264 Matt Clement .15 .07
- ❑ 265 Miguel Del Toro .15 .07
- ❑ 266 Robinson Cancel .15 .07
- Kevin Barker
- ❑ 267 San Francisco Giants .25 .11
- ❑ 268 Kent Bottenfield .15 .07
- ❑ 269 Fred McGriff .40 .18
- ❑ 270 Chris Carpenter .15 .07
- ❑ 271 Atlanta Braves .25 .11
- ❑ 272 Wilton Veras .50 .23
- Tomokazu Ohka RC
- ❑ 273 Will Clark .60 .25
- ❑ 274 Troy O'Leary .15 .07
- ❑ 275 Sammy Sosa CL .60 .25
- ❑ 276 Travis Lee .15 .07
- ❑ 277 Sean Casey .40 .18
- ❑ 278 Ron Gant .25 .11
- ❑ 279 Roger Clemens 1.50 .70
- ❑ 280 Phil Nevin .25 .11
- ❑ 281 Mike Piazza 1.50 .70
- ❑ 282 Mike Lowell .15 .07
- ❑ 283 Kevin Millwood .15 .07
- ❑ 284 Joe Randa .15 .07
- ❑ 285 Jeff Shaw .15 .07
- ❑ 286 Jason Varitek .25 .11
- ❑ 287 Harold Baines .25 .11
- ❑ 288 Gabe Kapler .25 .11
- ❑ 289 Chuck Finley .25 .11
- ❑ 290 Carl Pavano .15 .07
- ❑ 291 Brad Ausmus .15 .07
- ❑ 292 Brad Fullmer .25 .11
- ❑ 293 Boston Red Sox .25 .11
- ❑ 294 Bob Wickman .15 .07
- ❑ 295 Billy Wagner .15 .07
- ❑ 296 Shawn Estes .25 .11
- ❑ 297 Gary Sheffield .25 .11
- ❑ 298 Fernando Seguignol .15 .07
- ❑ 299 Omar Olivares .15 .07
- ❑ 300 Baltimore Orioles .25 .11
- ❑ 301 Matt Stairs .15 .07
- ❑ 302 Andy Ashby .15 .07
- ❑ 303 Todd Greene .15 .07
- ❑ 304 Jesse Garcia .15 .07
- ❑ 305 Kerry Wood .60 .25
- ❑ 306 Roberto Alomar .60 .25
- ❑ 307 New York Mets .25 .11
- ❑ 308 Dean Palmer .25 .11
- ❑ 309 Mike Hampton .25 .11
- ❑ 310 Devon White .15 .07
- ❑ 311 Chad Hermansen .40 .18
- Mike Garcia RC
- ❑ 312 Tim Hudson .60 .25
- ❑ 313 John Franco .25 .11
- ❑ 314 Jason Schmidt .15 .07
- ❑ 315 J.T. Snow .25 .11
- ❑ 316 Ed Sprague .15 .07
- ❑ 317 Chris Widger .15 .07
- ❑ 318 Ben Petrick .40 .18
- Luther Hackman RC
- ❑ 319 Jose Mesa .15 .07
- ❑ 320 Jose Canseco .60 .25
- ❑ 321 John Wetteland .25 .11
- ❑ 322 Minnesota Twins .25 .11
- ❑ 323 Jeff DaVanon RC .25 .11
- Brian Cooper
- ❑ 324 Tony Womack .15 .07
- ❑ 325 Rod Beck .15 .07
- ❑ 326 Mickey Morandini .15 .07
- ❑ 327 Pokey Reese .15 .07
- ❑ 328 Jaret Wright .15 .07
- ❑ 329 Glen Barker .15 .07
- ❑ 330 Darren Dreifort .15 .07
- ❑ 331 Torii Hunter .25 .11
- ❑ 332 Tony Armas .25 .11
- Peter Bergeron
- ❑ 333 Hideki Irabu .15 .07
- ❑ 334 Desi Relaford .15 .07
- ❑ 335 Barry Bonds 1.50 .70
- ❑ 336 Gary DiSarcina .15 .07
- ❑ 337 Gerald Williams .15 .07
- ❑ 338 John Valentin .15 .07
- ❑ 339 David Justice .25 .11
- ❑ 340 Juan Encarnacion .25 .11
- ❑ 341 Jeremy Giambi .15 .07
- ❑ 342 Chan Ho Park .25 .11
- ❑ 343 Vladimir Guerrero .75 .35
- ❑ 344 Robin Ventura .40 .18
- ❑ 345 Bob Abreu .25 .11
- ❑ 346 Tony Gwynn 1.25 .55
- ❑ 347 Jose Jimenez .15 .07
- ❑ 348 Royce Clayton .15 .07
- ❑ 349 Kelvim Escobar .15 .07
- ❑ 350 Chicago Cubs .25 .11
- ❑ 351 Travis Dawkins .15 .07
- Jason LaRue
- ❑ 352 Barry Larkin .60 .25
- ❑ 353 Cal Ripken 2.50 1.10
- ❑ 354 Alex Rodriguez CL .60 .25
- ❑ 355 Todd Stottlemyre .15 .07
- ❑ 356 Terry Adams .15 .07
- ❑ 357 Pittsburgh Pirates .25 .11
- ❑ 358 Jim Thome .60 .25
- ❑ 359 Corey Lee .15 .07
- Doug Davis
- ❑ 360 Moises Alou .25 .11
- ❑ 361 Todd Hollandsworth .15 .07
- ❑ 362 Marty Cordova .15 .07
- ❑ 363 David Cone .25 .11
- ❑ 364 Joe Nathan .15 .07
- Wilson Delgado
- ❑ 365 Paul Byrd .15 .07
- ❑ 366 Edgar Renteria .15 .07
- ❑ 367 Rusty Greer .25 .11
- ❑ 368 David Segui .15 .07
- ❑ 369 New York Yankees .40 .18
- ❑ 370 Daryle Ward .15 .07
- Carlos Hernandez
- ❑ 371 Troy Glaus .60 .25
- ❑ 372 Delino DeShields .15 .07
- ❑ 373 Jose Offerman .15 .07
- ❑ 374 Sammy Sosa 1.25 .55
- ❑ 375 Sandy Alomar Jr. .15 .07
- ❑ 376 Masao Kida .15 .07
- ❑ 377 Richard Hidalgo .25 .11
- ❑ 378 Ismael Valdes .15 .07
- ❑ 379 Ugueth Urbina .15 .07
- ❑ 380 Darryl Hamilton .15 .07
- ❑ 381 John Jaha .15 .07
- ❑ 382 St. Louis Cardinals .25 .11
- ❑ 383 Scott Sauerbeck .15 .07
- ❑ 384 Russ Ortiz .25 .11
- ❑ 385 Jamie Moyer .15 .07
- ❑ 386 Dave Martinez .15 .07
- ❑ 387 Todd Zeile .25 .11
- ❑ 388 Anaheim Angels .25 .11
- ❑ 389 Rob Ryan .15 .07
- Nick Bierbrodt
- ❑ 390 Rickey Henderson 1.25 .55
- ❑ 391 Alex Rodriguez 1.50 .70
- ❑ 392 Texas Rangers .25 .11
- ❑ 393 Roberto Hernandez .15 .07
- ❑ 394 Tony Batista .25 .11

	#	Player	MINT	NRMT
❑	395	Oakland Athletics	.25	.11
❑	396	Randall Simon	.40	.18
		Dave Cortes RC		
❑	397	Gregg Olson	.15	.07
❑	398	Sidney Ponson	.15	.07
❑	399	Micah Bowie	.15	.07
❑	400	Mark McGwire	2.50	1.10
❑	401	Florida Marlins	.25	.11
❑	402	Chad Allen	.15	.07
❑	403	Casey Blake	.25	.11
		Vernon Wells		
❑	404	Pete Harnisch	.15	.07
❑	405	Preston Wilson	.25	.11
❑	406	Richie Sexson	.25	.11
❑	407	Rico Brogna	.15	.07
❑	408	Todd Hundley	.15	.07
❑	409	Wally Joyner	.25	.11
❑	410	Tom Goodwin	.15	.07
❑	411	Joey Hamilton	.15	.07
❑	412	Detroit Tigers	.25	.11
❑	413	Michael Tejera RC	.40	.18
		Ramon Castro		
❑	414	Alex Gonzalez	.15	.07
❑	415	Jermaine Dye	.25	.11
❑	416	Jose Rosado	.15	.07
❑	417	Wilton Guerrero	.15	.07
❑	418	Rondell White	.25	.11
❑	419	Al Leiter	.15	.07
❑	420	Bernie Williams	.60	.25
❑	421	A.J. Hinch	.15	.07
❑	422	Pat Burrell	.60	.25
❑	423	Scott Rolen	.60	.25
❑	424	Jason Kendall	.25	.11
❑	425	Kevin Young	.15	.07
❑	426	Eric Owens	.15	.07
❑	427	Derek Jeter CL	.60	.25
❑	428	Livan Hernandez	.15	.07
❑	429	Russ Davis	.15	.07
❑	430	Dan Wilson	.15	.07
❑	431	Quinton McCracken	.15	.07
❑	432	Homer Bush	.15	.07
❑	433	Seattle Mariners	.25	.11
❑	434	Chad Harville	.15	.07
		Luis Vizcaino		
❑	435	Carlos Beltran AW	.25	.11
❑	436	Scott Williamson AW	.15	.07
❑	437	Pedro Martinez AW	.40	.18
❑	438	Randy Johnson AW	.40	.18
❑	439	Ivan Rodriguez AW	.25	.11
❑	440	Chipper Jones AW	.60	.25
❑	441	Bernie Williams DIV	.25	.11
❑	442	Pedro Martinez DIV	.40	.18
❑	443	Derek Jeter DIV	1.25	.55
❑	444	Brian Jordan DIV	.15	.07
❑	445	Todd Pratt DIV	.15	.07
❑	446	Kevin Millwood DIV	.15	.07
❑	447	Orl.Hernandez WS	.15	.07
❑	448	Derek Jeter WS	1.25	.55
❑	449	Chad Curtis WS	.15	.07
❑	450	Roger Clemens WS	.75	.35
❑	P353	Cal Ripken Promo	3.00	1.35

2000 Fleer Glossy

	MINT	NRMT
COMPLETE SET (500)	900.00	400.00
COMP.FACT.SET (455)	80.00	36.00
COMMON CARD (1-450)	.30	.14
*STARS 1-450: .75X TO 2X BASIC		
*YNG.STARS 1-450: .75X TO 2X BASIC		
*ROOKIES 1-450: .75X TO 2X BASIC		
COMMON CARD (451-500)	10.00	4.50

	#	Player	MINT	NRMT
❑	451	Carlos Casimiro RC	15.00	6.75
❑	452	Adam Melhuse RC	10.00	4.50
❑	453	Adam Bernero RC	10.00	4.50
❑	454	Dusty Allen RC	10.00	4.50
❑	455	Chan Perry RC	10.00	4.50
❑	456	Damian Rolls RC	10.00	4.50
❑	457	Josh Phelps RC	25.00	11.00
❑	458	Barry Zito	40.00	18.00
❑	459	Hector Ortiz RC	10.00	4.50
❑	460	Juan Pierre RC	25.00	11.00
❑	461	Jose Ortiz RC	60.00	27.00
❑	462	Chad Zerbe RC	25.00	11.00
❑	463	Julio Zuleta RC	15.00	6.75

	#	Player	MINT	NRMT
❑	464	Eric Byrnes	10.00	4.50
❑	465	Wilf. Rodriguez RC	15.00	6.75
❑	466	Wascar Serrano RC	12.00	5.50
❑	467	Aaron McNeal RC	12.00	5.50
❑	468	Paul Rigdon RC	15.00	6.75
❑	469	John Snyder RC	10.00	4.50
❑	470	J.C. Romero RC	10.00	4.50
❑	471	Talmadge Nunnari RC	10.00	4.50
❑	472	Mike Lamb	10.00	4.50
❑	473	Ryan Kohlmeier RC	10.00	4.50
❑	474	Rodney Lindsey RC	10.00	4.50
❑	475	Elvis Pena RC	10.00	4.50
❑	476	Alex Cabrera	12.00	5.50
❑	477	Chris Richard	25.00	11.00
❑	478	Pedro Feliz RC	20.00	9.00
❑	479	Ross Gload RC	10.00	4.50
❑	480	Timo Perez RC	20.00	9.00
❑	481	Jason Woolf RC	10.00	4.50
❑	482	Kenny Kelly RC	15.00	6.75
❑	483	Sang-Hoon Lee	10.00	4.50
❑	484	John Riedling RC	10.00	4.50
❑	485	Chris Wakeland RC	10.00	4.50
❑	486	Britt Reames RC	15.00	6.75
❑	487	Greg LaRocca RC	10.00	4.50
❑	488	Randy Keisler RC	15.00	6.75
❑	489	Xavier Nady RC	40.00	18.00
❑	490	Keith Ginter RC	30.00	13.50
❑	491	Joey Nation RC	10.00	4.50
❑	492	Kazuhiro Sasaki	30.00	13.50
❑	493	Lesli Brea RC	10.00	4.50
❑	494	Jace Brewer	10.00	4.50
❑	495	Yohanny Valera RC	10.00	4.50
❑	496	Adam Piatt	10.00	4.50
❑	497	Nate Rolison	10.00	4.50
❑	498	Aubrey Huff	10.00	4.50
❑	499	Jason Tyner	10.00	4.50
❑	500	Corey Patterson	20.00	9.00

2000 Fleer Update

	MINT	NRMT
COMP.FACT.SET (149)	15.00	6.75

	#	Player	MINT	NRMT
❑	1	Ken Griffey Jr. SH	.75	.35
❑	2	Cal Ripken SH	1.00	.45
❑	3	Randy Velarde SH	.15	.07
❑	4	Fred McGriff SH	.25	.11
❑	5	Derek Jeter SH	1.00	.45
❑	6	Tom Glavine SH	.25	.11
❑	7	Brent Mayne SH	.15	.07
❑	8	Alex Ochoa SH	.15	.07
❑	9	Scott Sheldon SH	.15	.07
❑	10	Randy Johnson SH	.40	.18
❑	11	Daniel Garibay RC	.25	.11
❑	12	Brad Fullmer	.25	.11
❑	13	Kazuhiro Sasaki RC	2.00	.90
❑	14	Andy Tracy RC	.25	.11
❑	15	Bret Boone	.25	.11
❑	16	Chad Durbin RC	.40	.18
❑	17	Mark Buehrle RC	2.50	1.10
❑	18	Julio Zuleta RC	.40	.18
❑	19	Jeremy Giambi	.15	.07
❑	20	Gene Stechschulte RC	.25	.11
❑	21	Lou Pote	.15	.07
		Bengie Molina		
❑	22	Darrell Einertson RC	.25	.11
❑	23	Ken Griffey Jr.	2.00	.90
❑	24	Jeff Sparks RC	.25	.11
		Dan Wheeler		
❑	25	Aaron Fultz RC	.25	.11
❑	26	Derek Bell	.15	.07
❑	27	Rob Bell	.15	.07
		D.T. Cromer		
❑	28	Robert Fick	.15	.07
❑	29	Darryl Kile	.25	.11
❑	30	Clayton Andrews	.25	.11
		John Bale RC		
❑	31	Dave Veres	.15	.07
❑	32	Hector Mercado RC	.25	.11
❑	33	Willie Morales RC	.25	.11
❑	34	Kelly Wunsch	.25	.11
		Kip Wells		
❑	35	Hideki Irabu	.15	.07
❑	36	Sean DePaula RC	.25	.11
❑	37	DeWayne Wise	.15	.07
		Chris Woodward		
❑	38	Curt Schilling	.60	.25
❑	39	Mark Johnson	.15	.07
❑	40	Mike Cameron	.25	.11
❑	41	Scott Sheldon	.15	.07
		Tom Evans		
❑	42	Brett Tomko	.15	.07
❑	43	Johan Santana RC	.40	.18
❑	44	Andy Benes	.15	.07
❑	45	Matt LeCroy	.15	.07
		Mark Redman		
❑	46	Ryan Klesko	.25	.11
❑	47	Andy Ashby	.15	.07
❑	48	Octavio Dotel	.15	.07
❑	49	Eric Byrnes RC	.25	.11
❑	50	Does Not Exist		
❑	51	Kenny Rogers	.15	.07
❑	52	Ben Weber RC	.25	.11
❑	53	Matt Blank	.15	.07
		Scott Strickland		
❑	54	Tom Goodwin	.15	.07
❑	55	Jim Edmonds Cardinals	.40	.18
❑	56	Derrick Turnbow RC	.40	.18
❑	57	Mark Mulder	.60	.25
❑	58	Tarrick Brock	.15	.07
		Ruben Quevedo		
❑	59	Danny Young RC	.25	.11
❑	60	Fernando Vina	.15	.07
❑	61	Justin Brunette RC	.25	.11
❑	62	Jimmy Anderson	.15	.07
❑	63	Reggie Sanders	.15	.07
❑	64	Adam Kennedy	.15	.07
❑	65	Jesse Garcia	.15	.07
		B.J. Ryan		
❑	66	Al Martin	.15	.07
❑	67	Kevin Walker RC	.40	.18
❑	68	Brad Penny	.25	.11
❑	69	B.J. Surhoff	.25	.11
❑	70	Geoff Blum	.25	.11
		Trace Coquillette RC		
❑	71	Jose Jimenez	.15	.07
❑	72	Chuck Finley	.25	.11
❑	73	Valerio De Los Santos	.15	.07
		Everett Stull		
❑	74	Terry Adams	.15	.07
❑	75	Rafael Furcal	.60	.25
❑	76	John Rocker	.15	.07
		Mike Darr		
❑	77	Quilvio Veras	.15	.07
❑	78	Armando Almanza	.15	.07
		Nate Rolison		

❑ 79 Greg Vaughn .25 .11
❑ 80 Keith McDonald RC .25 .11
❑ 81 Eric Cammack RC .25 .11
❑ 82 Horacio Estrada .15 .07
Ray King
❑ 83 Kory DeHaan .15 .07
❑ 84 Kevin Hodges RC .25 .11
❑ 85 Mike Lamb RC .40 .18
❑ 86 Shawn Green .60 .25
❑ 87 Dan Reichert .15 .07
Jason Rakers
❑ 88 Adam Piatt .40 .18
❑ 89 Mike Garcia .15 .07
❑ 90 Rodrigo Lopez RC .40 .18
❑ 91 John Olerud .25 .11
❑ 92 Barry Zito RC 2.00 .90
Terrence Long
❑ 93 Jimmy Rollins .25 .11
❑ 94 Denny Neagle .25 .11
❑ 95 Rickey Henderson 1.25 .55
❑ 96 Adam Eaton .25 .11
Buddy Carlyle
❑ 97 Brian O'Connor RC .25 .11
❑ 98 Andy Thompson RC .40 .18
❑ 99 Jason Boyd RC .25 .11
❑ 100 Joel Pineiro RC 5.00 2.20
Carlos Guillen
❑ 101 Raul Gonzalez RC .25 .11
❑ 102 Brandon Kolb RC .25 .11
❑ 103 Jason Maxwell .15 .07
Mike Lincoln
❑ 104 Luis Matos RC .25 .11
❑ 105 Morgan Burkhart RC .40 .18
❑ 106 Ismael Villegas RC .25 .11
Steve Sisco RC
❑ 107 David Justice Yankees .25 .11
❑ 108 Pablo Ozuna .15 .07
❑ 109 Jose Canseco .60 .25
❑ 110 Alex Cora .15 .07
Shawn Gilbert
❑ 111 Will Clark Cardinals .60 .25
❑ 112 Keith Luuloa .15 .07
Eric Weaver
❑ 113 Bruce Chen .15 .07
❑ 114 Adam Hyzdu .15 .07
❑ 115 Scott Forster RC .25 .11
Yovanny Lara RC
❑ 116 Allen McDill RC .25 .11
Jose Macias
❑ 117 Kevin Nicholson .15 .07
❑ 118 Israel Alcantara .15 .07
Tim Young
❑ 119 Juan Alvarez RC .25 .11
❑ 120 Julio Lugo .15 .07
Mitch Meluskey
❑ 121 B.J. Waszgis RC .25 .11
❑ 122 Jeff M. D'Amico RC .25 .11
Brett Laxton
❑ 123 Ricky Ledee .15 .07
❑ 124 Mark DeRosa .25 .11
Jason Marquis
❑ 125 Alex Cabrera RC 1.00 .45
❑ 126 Augie Ojeda RC .25 .11
Gary Matthews Jr.
❑ 127 Richie Sexson .25 .11
❑ 128 Santiago Perez RC .40 .18
Hector Ramirez RC
❑ 129 Rondell White .25 .11
❑ 130 Craig House RC .25 .11
❑ 131 Kevin Beirne .15 .07
Jon Garland
❑ 132 Wayne Franklin RC .25 .11
❑ 133 Henry Rodriguez .15 .07
❑ 134 Jay Payton .15 .07
Jim Mann
❑ 135 Ron Gant .15 .07
❑ 136 Paxton Crawford RC .40 .18
Sang-Hoon Lee RC
❑ 137 Kent Bottenfield .15 .07
❑ 138 Rocky Biddle RC .40 .18
❑ 139 Travis Lee .15 .07
❑ 140 Ryan Vogelsong RC .60 .25
❑ 141 Jason Conti .25 .11
Geraldo Guzman RC
❑ 142 Tim Drew .25 .11
Mark Watson RC
❑ 143 John Parrish RC .50 .23
Chris Richard RC
❑ 144 Javier Cardona RC .40 .18
Brandon Villafuerte RC
❑ 145 Tike Redman RC .50 .23
Steve Sparks RC
❑ 146 Brian Schneider .25 .11
Matt Skrmetta RC
❑ 147 Pasqual Coco RC .40 .18
❑ 148 Lorenzo Barcelo RC .40 .18
Joe Crede
❑ 149 Jace Brewer RC .25 .11
❑ 150 Milton Bradley .25 .11
Tomas De La Rosa RC
❑ MP1 Mickey Mantle 200.00 90.00

2001 Fleer

	MINT	NRMT
COMP.FACT.SET (485)	60.00	27.00
COMPLETE SET (450)	40.00	18.00
COMMON CARD (1-450)	.15	.07
COMMON CARD (451-485)	.50	.23

❑ 1 Andres Galarraga .40 .18
❑ 2 Armando Rios .15 .07
❑ 3 Julio Lugo .15 .07
❑ 4 Darryl Hamilton .15 .07
❑ 5 Dave Veres .15 .07
❑ 6 Edgardo Alfonzo .25 .11
❑ 7 Brook Fordyce .15 .07
❑ 8 Eric Karros .25 .11
❑ 9 Neifi Perez .15 .07
❑ 10 Jim Edmonds .40 .18
❑ 11 Barry Larkin .60 .25
❑ 12 Trot Nixon .25 .11
❑ 13 Andy Pettitte .25 .11
❑ 14 Jose Guillen .15 .07
❑ 15 David Wells .25 .11
❑ 16 Magglio Ordonez .25 .11
❑ 17 David Segui .15 .07
❑ 17A David Segui ERR .15 .07
Card has no number on the back
❑ 18 Juan Encarnacion .25 .11
❑ 19 Robert Person .15 .07
❑ 20 Quilvio Veras .15 .07
❑ 21 Mo Vaughn .25 .11
❑ 22 B.J. Surhoff .25 .11
❑ 23 Ken Caminiti .25 .11
❑ 24 Frank Catalanotto .15 .07
❑ 25 Luis Gonzalez .60 .25
❑ 26 Pete Harnisch .15 .07
❑ 27 Alex Gonzalez .15 .07
❑ 28 Mark Quinn .25 .11
❑ 29 Luis Castillo .15 .07
❑ 30 Rick Helling .15 .07
❑ 31 Barry Bonds 1.50 .70
❑ 32 Warren Morris .15 .07
❑ 33 Aaron Boone .15 .07
❑ 34 Ricky Gutierrez .15 .07
❑ 35 Preston Wilson .25 .11
❑ 36 Erubiel Durazo .15 .07
❑ 37 Jermaine Dye .25 .11
❑ 38 John Rocker .25 .11
❑ 39 Mark Grudzielanek .15 .07
❑ 40 Pedro Martinez .75 .35
❑ 41 Phil Nevin .25 .11
❑ 42 Luis Matos .15 .07
❑ 43 Orlando Hernandez .25 .11
❑ 44 Steve Cox .15 .07
❑ 45 James Baldwin .15 .07
❑ 46 Rafael Furcal .25 .11
❑ 47 Todd Zeile .25 .11
❑ 48 Elmer Dessens .15 .07
❑ 49 Russell Branyan .25 .11
❑ 50 Juan Gonzalez .60 .25
❑ 51 Mac Suzuki .15 .07
❑ 52 Adam Kennedy .15 .07
❑ 53 Randy Velarde .15 .07
❑ 54 David Bell .15 .07
❑ 55 Royce Clayton .15 .07
❑ 56 Greg Colbrunn .15 .07
❑ 57 Rey Ordonez .15 .07
❑ 58 Kevin Millwood .15 .07
❑ 59 Fernando Vina .15 .07
❑ 60 Eddie Taubensee .15 .07
❑ 61 Enrique Wilson .15 .07
❑ 62 Jay Bell .25 .11
❑ 63 Brian Moehler .15 .07
❑ 64 Brad Fullmer .25 .11
❑ 65 Ben Petrick .15 .07
❑ 66 Orlando Cabrera .15 .07
❑ 67 Shane Reynolds .15 .07
❑ 68 Mitch Meluskey .15 .07
❑ 69 Jeff Shaw .15 .07
❑ 70 Chipper Jones 1.25 .55
❑ 71 Tomo Ohka .25 .11
❑ 72 Ruben Rivera .15 .07
❑ 73 Mike Sirotka .15 .07
❑ 74 Scott Rolen .60 .25
❑ 75 Glendon Rusch .15 .07
❑ 76 Miguel Tejada .25 .11
❑ 77 Brady Anderson .25 .11
❑ 78 Bartolo Colon .25 .11
❑ 79 Ron Coomer .15 .07
❑ 80 Gary DiSarcina .15 .07
❑ 81 Geoff Jenkins .25 .11
❑ 82 Billy Koch .15 .07
❑ 83 Mike Lamb .15 .07
❑ 84 Alex Rodriguez 1.50 .70
❑ 85 Denny Neagle .15 .07
❑ 86 Michael Tucker .15 .07
❑ 87 Edgar Renteria .15 .07
❑ 88 Brian Anderson .15 .07
❑ 89 Glenallen Hill .15 .07
❑ 90 Aramis Ramirez .25 .11
❑ 91 Rondell White .25 .11
❑ 92 Tony Womack .15 .07
❑ 93 Jeffrey Hammonds .15 .07
❑ 94 Freddy Garcia .25 .11
❑ 95 Bill Mueller .15 .07
❑ 96 Mike Lieberthal .25 .11
❑ 97 Michael Barrett .15 .07
❑ 98 Derrek Lee .25 .11
❑ 99 Bill Spiers .15 .07
❑ 100 Derek Lowe .15 .07
❑ 101 Javy Lopez .25 .11
❑ 102 Adrian Beltre .25 .11
❑ 103 Jim Parque .15 .07
❑ 104 Marquis Grissom .15 .07
❑ 105 Eric Chavez .25 .11
❑ 106 Todd Jones .15 .07
❑ 107 Eric Owens .15 .07
❑ 108 Roger Clemens 1.50 .70
❑ 109 Denny Hocking .15 .07
❑ 110 Roberto Hernandez .15 .07
❑ 111 Albert Belle .25 .11
❑ 112 Troy Glaus .60 .25
❑ 113 Ivan Rodriguez .60 .25
❑ 114 Carlos Guillen .15 .07
❑ 115 Chuck Finley .25 .11
❑ 116 Dmitri Young .25 .11
❑ 117 Paul Konerko .25 .11
❑ 118 Damon Buford .15 .07
❑ 119 Fernando Tatis .15 .07
❑ 120 Larry Walker .40 .18
❑ 121 Jason Kendall .25 .11
❑ 122 Matt Williams .40 .18
❑ 123 Henry Rodriguez .15 .07
❑ 124 Placido Polanco .15 .07
❑ 125 Bobby Estalella .15 .07
❑ 126 Pat Burrell .25 .11
❑ 127 Mark Loretta .15 .07
❑ 128 Moises Alou .25 .11

❑ 129 Tino Martinez .25 .11
❑ 130 Milton Bradley .15 .07
❑ 131 Todd Hundley .15 .07
❑ 132 Keith Foulke .15 .07
❑ 133 Robert Fick .15 .07
❑ 134 Cristian Guzman .25 .11
❑ 135 Rusty Greer .25 .11
❑ 136 John Olerud .25 .11
❑ 137 Mariano Rivera .25 .11
❑ 138 Jeromy Burnitz .25 .11
❑ 139 Dave Burba .15 .07
❑ 140 Ken Griffey Jr. 2.00 .90
❑ 141 Tony Gwynn 1.25 .55
❑ 142 Carlos Delgado .60 .25
❑ 143 Edgar Martinez .40 .18
❑ 144 Ramon Hernandez .15 .07
❑ 145 Pedro Astacio .15 .07
❑ 146 Ray Lankford .15 .07
❑ 147 Mike Mussina .60 .25
❑ 148 Ray Durham .25 .11
❑ 149 Lee Stevens .15 .07
❑ 150 Jay Canizaro .15 .07
❑ 151 Adrian Brown .15 .07
❑ 152 Mike Piazza 1.50 .70
❑ 153 Cliff Floyd .25 .11
❑ 154 Jose Vidro .25 .11
❑ 155 Jason Giambi .60 .25
❑ 156 Andruw Jones .60 .25
❑ 157 Robin Ventura .25 .11
❑ 158 Gary Sheffield .25 .11
❑ 159 Jeff D'Amico .15 .07
❑ 160 Chuck Knoblauch .25 .11
❑ 161 Roger Cedeno .15 .07
❑ 162 Jim Thome .60 .25
❑ 163 Peter Bergeron .15 .07
❑ 164 Kerry Wood .60 .25
❑ 165 Gabe Kapler .25 .11
❑ 166 Corey Koskie .25 .11
❑ 167 Doug Glanville .15 .07
❑ 168 Brent Mayne .15 .07
❑ 169 Scott Spiezio .15 .07
❑ 170 Steve Karsay .15 .07
❑ 171 Al Martin .15 .07
❑ 172 Fred McGriff .40 .18
❑ 173 Gabe White .15 .07
❑ 174 Alex Gonzalez .15 .07
❑ 175 Mike Darr .15 .07
❑ 176 Bengie Molina .15 .07
❑ 177 Ben Grieve .25 .11
❑ 178 Marlon Anderson .15 .07
❑ 179 Brian Giles .25 .11
❑ 180 Jose Valentin .15 .07
❑ 181 Brian Jordan .25 .11
❑ 182 Randy Johnson .75 .35
❑ 183 Ricky Ledee .15 .07
❑ 184 Russ Ortiz .25 .11
❑ 185 Mike Lowell .25 .11
❑ 186 Curtis Leskanic .15 .07
❑ 187 Bob Abreu .25 .11
❑ 188 Derek Jeter 2.50 1.10
❑ 189 Lance Berkman .60 .25
❑ 190 Roberto Alomar .60 .25
❑ 191 Darin Erstad .60 .25
❑ 192 Richie Sexson .25 .11
❑ 193 Alex Ochoa .15 .07
❑ 194 Carlos Febles .15 .07
❑ 195 David Ortiz .25 .11
❑ 196 Shawn Green .60 .25
❑ 197 Mike Sweeney .25 .11
❑ 198 Vladimir Guerrero .75 .35
❑ 199 Jose Jimenez .15 .07
❑ 200 Travis Lee .25 .11
❑ 201 Rickey Henderson 1.25 .55
❑ 202 Bob Wickman .15 .07
❑ 203 Miguel Cairo .15 .07
❑ 204 Steve Finley .25 .11
❑ 205 Tony Batista .25 .11
❑ 206 Jamey Wright .15 .07
❑ 207 Terrence Long .25 .11
❑ 208 Trevor Hoffman .25 .11
❑ 209 John VanderWal .15 .07
❑ 210 Greg Maddux 1.50 .70
❑ 211 Tim Salmon .25 .11
❑ 212 Herbert Perry .15 .07
❑ 213 Marvin Benard .15 .07
❑ 214 Jose Offerman .15 .07
❑ 215 Jay Payton .15 .07
❑ 216 Jon Lieber .15 .07
❑ 217 Mark Kotsay .15 .07
❑ 218 Scott Brosius .25 .11
❑ 219 Scott Williamson .15 .07
❑ 220 Omar Vizquel .25 .11
❑ 221 Mike Hampton .25 .11
❑ 222 Richard Hidalgo .25 .11
❑ 223 Rey Sanchez .15 .07
❑ 224 Matt Lawton .25 .11
❑ 225 Bruce Chen .15 .07
❑ 226 Ryan Klesko .25 .11
❑ 227 Garret Anderson .25 .11
❑ 228 Kevin Brown .25 .11
❑ 229 Mike Cameron .25 .11
❑ 230 Tony Clark .25 .11
❑ 231 Curt Schilling .60 .25
❑ 232 Vinny Castilla .25 .11
❑ 233 Carl Pavano .15 .07
❑ 234 Eric Davis .25 .11
❑ 235 Darrin Fletcher .15 .07
❑ 236 Matt Stairs .15 .07
❑ 237 Octavio Dotel .15 .07
❑ 238 Mark Grace .60 .25
❑ 239 John Smoltz .25 .11
❑ 240 Matt Clement .15 .07
❑ 241 Ellis Burks .25 .11
❑ 242 Charles Johnson .25 .11
❑ 243 Jeff Bagwell .75 .35
❑ 244 Derek Bell .15 .07
❑ 245 Nomar Garciaparra 1.50 .70
❑ 246 Jorge Posada .25 .11
❑ 247 Ryan Dempster .25 .11
❑ 248 J.T. Snow .25 .11
❑ 249 Eric Young .15 .07
❑ 250 Daryle Ward .15 .07
❑ 251 Joe Randa .15 .07
❑ 252 Travis Fryman .25 .11
❑ 253 Mike Williams .15 .07
❑ 254 Jacque Jones .25 .11
❑ 255 Scott Elarton .15 .07
❑ 256 Mark McGwire 2.50 1.10
❑ 257 Jay Buhner .25 .11
❑ 258 Randy Wolf .15 .07
❑ 259 Sammy Sosa 1.25 .55
❑ 260 Chan Ho Park .25 .11
❑ 261 Damion Easley .15 .07
❑ 262 Rick Ankiel .40 .18
❑ 263 Frank Thomas .75 .35
❑ 264 Kris Benson .25 .11
❑ 265 Luis Alicea .15 .07
❑ 266 Jeromy Burnitz .25 .11
❑ 267 Geoff Blum .15 .07
❑ 268 Joe Girardi .15 .07
❑ 269 Livan Hernandez .25 .11
❑ 270 Jeff Conine .15 .07
❑ 271 Danny Graves .15 .07
❑ 272 Craig Biggio .40 .18
❑ 273 Jose Canseco .60 .25
❑ 274 Tom Glavine .60 .25
❑ 275 Ruben Mateo .25 .11
❑ 276 Jeff Kent .40 .18
❑ 277 Kevin Young .15 .07
❑ 278 A.J. Burnett .25 .11
❑ 279 Dante Bichette .25 .11
❑ 280 Sandy Alomar Jr. .25 .11
❑ 281 John Wetteland .25 .11
❑ 282 Torii Hunter .25 .11
❑ 283 Jarrod Washburn .15 .07
❑ 284 Rich Aurilia .25 .11
❑ 285 Jeff Cirillo .25 .11
❑ 286 Fernando Seguignol .15 .07
❑ 287 Darren Dreifort .15 .07
❑ 288 Deivi Cruz .15 .07
❑ 289 Pokey Reese .15 .07
❑ 290 Garrett Stephenson .15 .07
❑ 291 Bret Boone .25 .11
❑ 292 Tim Hudson .60 .25
❑ 293 John Flaherty .15 .07
❑ 294 Shannon Stewart .25 .11
❑ 295 Shawn Estes .25 .11
❑ 296 Wilton Guerrero .15 .07
❑ 297 Delino DeShields .15 .07
❑ 298 David Justice .25 .11
❑ 299 Harold Baines .25 .11
❑ 300 Al Leiter .25 .11
❑ 301 Wil Cordero .15 .07
❑ 302 Antonio Alfonseca .15 .07
❑ 303 Sean Casey .40 .18
❑ 304 Carlos Beltran .25 .11
❑ 305 Brad Radke .25 .11
❑ 306 Jason Varitek .25 .11
❑ 307 Shigetoshi Hasegawa .25 .11
❑ 308 Todd Stottlemyre .15 .07
❑ 309 Raul Mondesi .25 .11
❑ 310 Mike Bordick .25 .11
❑ 311 Darryl Kile .25 .11
❑ 312 Dean Palmer .25 .11
❑ 313 Johnny Damon .25 .11
❑ 314 Todd Helton .75 .35
❑ 315 Chad Hermansen .15 .07
❑ 316 Kevin Appier .25 .11
❑ 317 Greg Vaughn .25 .11
❑ 318 Robb Nen .25 .11
❑ 319 Jose Cruz Jr. .25 .11
❑ 320 Ron Belliard .15 .07
❑ 321 Bernie Williams .60 .25
❑ 322 Melvin Mora .15 .07
❑ 323 Kenny Lofton .25 .11
❑ 324 Armando Benitez .25 .11
❑ 325 Carlos Lee .25 .11
❑ 326 Damian Jackson .15 .07
❑ 327 Eric Milton .25 .11
❑ 328 J.D. Drew .60 .25
❑ 329 Byung-Hyun Kim .25 .11
❑ 330 Chris Stynes .15 .07
❑ 331 Kazuhiro Sasaki .75 .35
❑ 332 Troy O'Leary .15 .07
❑ 333 Pat Hentgen .15 .07
❑ 334 Brad Ausmus .15 .07
❑ 335 Todd Walker .15 .07
❑ 336 Jason Isringhausen .25 .11
❑ 337 Gerald Williams .15 .07
❑ 338 Aaron Sele .25 .11
❑ 339 Paul O'Neill .60 .25
❑ 340 Cal Ripken 2.50 1.10
❑ 341 Manny Ramirez .75 .35
❑ 342 Will Clark .60 .25
❑ 343 Mark Redman .15 .07
❑ 344 Bubba Trammell .15 .07
❑ 345 Troy Percival .15 .07
❑ 346 Chris Singleton .15 .07
❑ 347 Rafael Palmeiro .60 .25
❑ 348 Carl Everett .25 .11
❑ 349 Andy Benes .15 .07
❑ 350 Bobby Higginson .25 .11
❑ 351 Alex Cabrera .15 .07
❑ 352 Barry Zito .60 .25
❑ 353 Jace Brewer .15 .07
❑ 354 Paxton Crawford .15 .07
❑ 355 Oswaldo Mairena .15 .07
❑ 356 Joe Crede .25 .11
❑ 357 A.J. Pierzynski .15 .07
❑ 358 Daniel Garibay .15 .07
❑ 359 Jason Tyner .15 .07
❑ 360 Nate Rolison .15 .07
❑ 361 Scott Downs .15 .07
❑ 362 Keith Ginter .25 .11
❑ 363 Juan Pierre .25 .11
❑ 364 Adam Bernero .15 .07
❑ 365 Chris Richard .25 .11
❑ 366 Joey Nation .15 .07
❑ 367 Aubrey Huff .15 .07
❑ 368 Adam Eaton .25 .11
❑ 369 Jose Ortiz 1.00 .45
❑ 370 Eric Munson .25 .11
❑ 371 Matt Kinney .15 .07
❑ 372 Eric Byrnes .15 .07
❑ 373 Keith McDonald .15 .07
❑ 374 Matt Wise .15 .07
❑ 375 Timo Perez .15 .07
❑ 376 Julio Zuleta .15 .07
❑ 377 Jimmy Rollins .25 .11
❑ 378 Xavier Nady .40 .18
❑ 379 Ryan Kohlmeier .15 .07
❑ 380 Corey Patterson .25 .11
❑ 381 Todd Helton LL .40 .18
❑ 382 Moises Alou LL .15 .07
❑ 383 Vladimir Guerrero LL .40 .18
❑ 384 Luis Castillo LL .15 .07
❑ 385 Jeffrey Hammonds LL .15 .07
❑ 386 Nomar Garciaparra LL .75 .35

❑ 387 Carlos Delgado LL .... .25 .11
❑ 388 Darin Erstad LL .... .25 .11
❑ 389 Manny Ramirez LL .... .40 .18
❑ 390 Mike Sweeney LL .... .15 .07
❑ 391 Sammy Sosa LL .... .60 .25
❑ 392 Barry Bonds LL .... .75 .35
❑ 393 Jeff Bagwell LL .... .40 .18
❑ 394 Richard Hidalgo LL .... .15 .07
❑ 395 Vladimir Guerrero LL ...... .40 .18
❑ 396 Troy Glaus LL .... .60 .25
❑ 397 Frank Thomas LL .... .40 .18
❑ 398 Carlos Delgado LL .... .25 .11
❑ 399 David Justice LL .... .25 .11
❑ 400 Jason Giambi LL .... .25 .11
❑ 401 Randy Johnson LL .... .40 .18
❑ 402 Kevin Brown LL .... .15 .07
❑ 403 Greg Maddux LL .... .75 .35
❑ 404 Al Leiter LL .... .15 .07
❑ 405 Mike Hampton LL .... .15 .07
❑ 406 Pedro Martinez LL .... .40 .18
❑ 407 Roger Clemens LL .... .75 .35
❑ 408 Mike Sirotka LL .... .15 .07
❑ 409 Mike Mussina LL .... .25 .11
❑ 410 Bartolo Colon LL .... .15 .07
❑ 411 Subway Series WS .... .40 .18
❑ 412 Jose Vizcaino WS .... .40 .18
Longest Game
❑ 413 Jose Vizcaino WS .... .40 .18
Jose Who?
❑ 414 Roger Clemens WS ...... .60 .25
Retro Rocket
❑ 415 Armando Benitez .... .25 .11
Edgardo Alfonzo
Timo Perez WS
Streak Snappers
❑ 416 Al Leiter WS .... .40 .18
The Warrior
❑ 417 Luis Sojo WS .... .40 .18
Unsung Hero
❑ 418 Yankees 3-Peat WS ...... .60 .25
❑ 419 Derek Jeter WS .... 1.25 .55
Series MVP
❑ 420 Toast of the Town WS .... .40 .18
❑ 421 Atlanta Braves .... .25 .11
Rafael Furcal
Chipper Jones
Greg Maddux
John Rocker
Tom Glavine CL
❑ 422 New York Mets .... .60 .25
Armando Benitez
Mike Piazza
Mike Hampton
Al Leiter CL
❑ 423 Florida Marlins .... .40 .18
Ryan Dempster
Luis Castillo
Antonio Alfonseca
Preston Wilson CL
❑ 424 Philadelphia Phillies ...... .40 .18
Robert Person
Scott Rolen
Randy Wolf
Bob Abreu
Doug Glanville CL
❑ 425 Montreal Expos .... .40 .18
Vladimir Guerrero
Peter Bergeron CL
❑ 426 St. Louis Cardinals .... .40 .18
Fernando Vina
Dave Veres
Jim Edmonds
Rick Ankiel
Edgar Renteria
Darryl Kile CL
❑ 427 Cincinnati Reds .... .40 .18
Danny Graves
Ken Griffey Jr.
Sean Casey
Pokey Reese CL
❑ 428 Chicago Cubs .... .40 .18
Jon Lieber
Sammy Sosa
Eric Young CL
❑ 429 Milwaukee Brewers .... .40 .18
Curtis Leskanic
Geoff Jenkins
Jeff D'Amico
Jeromy Burnitz
Marquis Grissom CL
❑ 430 Houston Astros .... .40 .18
Scott Elarton
Jeff Bagwell
Octavio Dotel
Moises Alou
Roger Cedeno CL
❑ 431 Pittsburgh Pirates .... .40 .18
Mike Williams
Jason Kendall
Kris Benson
Brian Giles CL
❑ 432 San Francisco Giants .... .75 .35
Livan Hernandez
Jeff Kent
Robb Nen
Barry Bonds
Marvin Benard CL
❑ 433 Arizona Diamondbacks .. .25 .11
Luis Gonzalez
Steve Finley
Tony Womack
Randy Johnson CL
❑ 434 Los Angeles Dodgers .... .25 .11
Jeff Shaw
Gary Sheffield
Kevin Brown
Shawn Green
Chan Ho Park
B.Shaw should be J.Shaw CL VER
❑ 435 Colorado Rockies .... .40 .18
Jose Jimenez
Todd Helton
Brian Bohanon
Tom Goodwin
C.Goodwin should be T.Goodwin CL VER
❑ 436 San Diego Padres .... .40 .18
Trevor Hoffman
Phil Nevin
Matt Clement
Eric Owens CL
❑ 437 New York Yankees ...... 1.00 .45
Mariano Rivera
Derek Jeter
Roger Clemens
Bernie Williams
Andy Pettitte CL
❑ 438 Boston Red Sox .... .40 .18
Pedro Martinez
Nomar Garciaparra
Derek Lowe
Carl Everett CL
❑ 439 Baltimore Orioles .... .25 .11
Ryan Kohlmeier
Delino DeShields
Mike Mussina
Albert Belle CL
❑ 440 Toronto Blue Jays .... .40 .18
David Wells
Carlos Delgado
Billy Kch
Raul Mondesi CL
❑ 441 Tampa Bay Devil Rays .. .40 .18
Ramon Hernandez
Fred McGriff
Miguel Cairo
Greg Vaughn CL
❑ 442 Chicago White Sox .... .40 .18
Mike Sirotka
Frank Thomas
Keith Foulke
Ray Durham CL
❑ 443 Cleveland Indians .... .40 .18
Steve Karsay
Manny Ramirez
Bartolo Colon
Roberto Alomar CL
❑ 444 Detoit Tigers .... .40 .18
Brian Moehler
Deivi Cruz
Juan Encarnacion
Todd Jones
Bobby Higginson CL
❑ 445 Kansas City Royals .... .40 .18
Mac Suzuki
Mike Sweeney
Johnny Damon
Jermaine Dye CL
❑ 446 Minnesota Twins .... .40 .18
Brad Radke
Matt Lawton
Eric Milton
Jacque Jones
Cristian Guzman CL
❑ 447 Seattle Mariners .... .60 .25
Kazuhiro Sasaki
Edgar Martinez
Aaron Sele
Rickey Henderson CL
❑ 448 Oakland Athletics .... .60 .25
Jason Isringhausen
Jason Giambi
Tim Hudson
Randy Velarde CL
❑ 449 Anaheim Angels .... .60 .25
Shigetoshi Hasegawa
Darin Erstad
Troy Percival
Troy Glaus CL
❑ 450 Texas Rangers .... .15 .07
Rick Helling
Rafael Palmeiro
John Wetteland
Luis Alicea CL
❑ 451 Albert Pujols RC 10.00 4.50
❑ 452 Ichiro Suzuki RC 15.00 6.75
❑ 453 Tsuyoshi Shinjo RC...... 2.50 1.10
❑ 454 Johnny Estrada RC ...... 1.50 .70
❑ 455 Elpidio Guzman RC........ .50 .23
❑ 456 Adrian Hernandez RC .... .50 .23
❑ 457 Rafael Soriano RC ...... 1.25 .55
❑ 458 Drew Henson RC 5.00 2.20
❑ 459 Juan Uribe RC.............. 1.25 .55
❑ 460 Matt White RC.................. .50 .23
❑ 461 Endy Chavez RC............ .50 .23
❑ 462 Bud Smith RC 3.00 1.35
❑ 463 Morgan Ensberg RC .... 1.50 .70
❑ 464 Jay Gibbons RC .... 1.25 .55
❑ 465 Jackson Melian RC .... .50 .23
❑ 466 Junior Spivey RC .... .50 .23
❑ 467 Juan Cruz RC 2.50 1.10
❑ 468 Wilson Betemit RC 2.50 1.10
❑ 469 Alexis Gomez RC .... .50 .23
❑ 470 Mark Teixeira RC 15.00 6.75
❑ 471 Erick Almonte RC .... 1.25 .55
❑ 472 Travis Hafner RC .... 1.25 .55
❑ 473 Carlos Valderrama RC .. .50 .23
❑ 474 Brandon Duckworth RC 2.00 .90
❑ 475 Ryan Freel RC .... .50 .23
❑ 476 Wilkin Ruan RC................ .50 .23
❑ 477 Andres Torres RC .... .50 .23
❑ 478 Josh Towers RC .... 1.50 .70
❑ 479 Kyle Lohse RC .... 1.50 .70
❑ 480 Jason Michaels RC .... .50 .23
❑ 481 Alfonso Soriano.............. 1.00 .45
❑ 482 C.C. Sabathia .... .75 .35
❑ 483 Roy Oswalt .... 1.00 .45
❑ 484 Ben Sheets .... .75 .35
❑ 485 Adam Dunn 4.00 1.80
❑ NNO Uncut Sheet EXCH/100 30.00 13.50

1999 Fleer Brilliants

	MINT	NRMT
COMPLETE SET (175)	120.00	55.00
COMP.SET w/o SP's (125)......	50.00	22.00
COMMON CARD (1-125)	.25	.11
COMMON CARD (126-175)......	1.00	.45

❑ 1 Mark McGwire 4.00 1.80
❑ 2 Derek Jeter 4.00 1.80
❑ 3 Nomar Garciaparra 2.50 1.10
❑ 4 Travis Lee .... .25 .11
❑ 5 Jeff Bagwell...................... 1.25 .55
❑ 6 Andres Galarraga .... .60 .25
❑ 7 Pedro Martinez .... 1.25 .55
❑ 8 Cal Ripken........................ 4.00 1.80
❑ 9 Vladimir Guerrero .... 1.25 .55
❑ 10 Chipper Jones .... 2.00 .90

❑ 11 Rusty Greer	.40	.18
❑ 12 Omar Vizquel	.40	.18
❑ 13 Quinton McCracken	.25	.11
❑ 14 Jaret Wright	.25	.11
❑ 15 Mike Mussina	1.00	.45
❑ 16 Jason Giambi	1.00	.45
❑ 17 Tony Clark	.40	.18
❑ 18 Troy O'Leary	.25	.11
❑ 19 Troy Percival	.25	.11
❑ 20 Kerry Wood	1.00	.45
❑ 21 Vinny Castilla	.40	.18
❑ 22 Chris Carpenter	.25	.11
❑ 23 Richie Sexson	.40	.18
❑ 24 Ken Griffey Jr.	3.00	1.35
❑ 25 Barry Bonds	2.50	1.10
❑ 26 Carlos Delgado	1.00	.45
❑ 27 Frank Thomas	1.25	.55
❑ 28 Manny Ramirez	1.25	.55
❑ 29 Shawn Green	1.00	.45
❑ 30 Mike Piazza	2.50	1.10
❑ 31 Tino Martinez	.40	.18
❑ 32 Dante Bichette	.40	.18
❑ 33 Scott Rolen	1.00	.45
❑ 34 Gabe Alvarez	.25	.11
❑ 35 Raul Mondesi	.40	.18
❑ 36 Damion Easley	.25	.11
❑ 37 Jeff Kent	.60	.25
❑ 38 Al Leiter	.40	.18
❑ 39 Alex Rodriguez	2.50	1.10
❑ 40 Jeff King	.25	.11
❑ 41 Mark Grace	1.00	.45
❑ 42 Larry Walker	.60	.25
❑ 43 Moises Alou	.40	.18
❑ 44 Juan Gonzalez	1.00	.45
❑ 45 Rolando Arrojo	.25	.11
❑ 46 Tom Glavine	1.00	.45
❑ 47 Johnny Damon	.40	.18
❑ 48 Livan Hernandez	.25	.11
❑ 49 Craig Biggio	.60	.25
❑ 50 Dmitri Young	.40	.18
❑ 51 Chan Ho Park	.40	.18
❑ 52 Todd Walker	.25	.11
❑ 53 Derrek Lee	.40	.18
❑ 54 Todd Helton	1.25	.55
❑ 55 Ray Lankford	.25	.11
❑ 56 Jim Thome	1.00	.45
❑ 57 Matt Lawton	.40	.18
❑ 58 Matt Anderson	.25	.11
❑ 59 Jose Offerman	.25	.11
❑ 60 Eric Karros	.40	.18
❑ 61 Orlando Hernandez	.40	.18
❑ 62 Ben Grieve	.40	.18
❑ 63 Bobby Abreu	.40	.18
❑ 64 Kevin Young	.40	.18
❑ 65 John Olerud	.40	.18
❑ 66 Sammy Sosa	2.00	.90
❑ 67 Andy Ashby	.25	.11
❑ 68 Juan Encarnacion	.40	.18
❑ 69 Shane Reynolds	.25	.11
❑ 70 Bernie Williams	1.00	.45
❑ 71 Mike Cameron	.40	.18
❑ 72 Troy Glaus	1.00	.45
❑ 73 Gary Sheffield	.40	.18
❑ 74 Jeromy Burnitz	.40	.18
❑ 75 Mike Caruso	.25	.11
❑ 76 Chuck Knoblauch	.40	.18
❑ 77 Kenny Rogers	.25	.11
❑ 78 David Cone	.40	.18
❑ 79 Tony Gwynn	2.00	.90
❑ 80 Jay Buhner	.40	.18
❑ 81 Paul O'Neill	1.00	.45
❑ 82 Charles Nagy	.25	.11
❑ 83 Javy Lopez	.40	.18
❑ 84 Scott Erickson	.25	.11
❑ 85 Trevor Hoffman	.40	.18
❑ 86 Andruw Jones	1.00	.45
❑ 87 Ray Durham	.40	.18
❑ 88 Jorge Posada	.40	.18
❑ 89 Edgar Martinez	.60	.25
❑ 90 Tim Salmon	.40	.18
❑ 91 Bobby Higginson	.40	.18
❑ 92 Adrian Beltre	.40	.18
❑ 93 Jason Kendall	.40	.18
❑ 94 Henry Rodriguez	.25	.11
❑ 95 Greg Maddux	2.50	1.10
❑ 96 David Justice	.40	.18
❑ 97 Ivan Rodriguez	1.00	.45
❑ 98 Curt Schilling	1.00	.45
❑ 99 Matt Williams	.60	.25
❑ 100 Darin Erstad	1.00	.45
❑ 101 Rafael Palmeiro	1.00	.45
❑ 102 David Wells	.40	.18
❑ 103 Barry Larkin	1.00	.45
❑ 104 Robin Ventura	.40	.18
❑ 105 Edgar Renteria	.25	.11
❑ 106 Andy Pettitte	.40	.18
❑ 107 Albert Belle	.40	.18
❑ 108 Steve Finley	.40	.18
❑ 109 Fernando Vina	.25	.11
❑ 110 Rondell White	.40	.18
❑ 111 Kevin Brown	.60	.25
❑ 112 Jose Canseco	1.00	.45
❑ 113 Roger Clemens	2.50	1.10
❑ 114 Todd Hundley	.25	.11
❑ 115 Will Clark	1.00	.45
❑ 116 Jim Edmonds	.60	.25
❑ 117 Randy Johnson	1.25	.55
❑ 118 Denny Neagle	.25	.11
❑ 119 Brian Jordan	.40	.18
❑ 120 Dean Palmer	.40	.18
❑ 121 Roberto Alomar	1.00	.45
❑ 122 Ken Caminiti	.40	.18
❑ 123 Brian Giles	.40	.18
❑ 124 Todd Stottlemyre	.25	.11
❑ 125 Mo Vaughn	.40	.18
❑ 126 J.D. Drew	3.00	1.35
❑ 127 Ryan Minor	1.00	.45
❑ 128 Gabe Kapler	1.25	.55
❑ 129 Jeremy Giambi	1.00	.45
❑ 130 Eric Chavez	1.25	.55
❑ 131 Ben Davis	1.25	.55
❑ 132 Rob Fick	1.00	.45
❑ 133 George Lombard	1.00	.45
❑ 134 Calvin Pickering	1.00	.45
❑ 135 Preston Wilson	1.25	.55
❑ 136 Corey Koskie	1.25	.55
❑ 137 Russell Branyan	1.25	.55
❑ 138 Bruce Chen	1.00	.45
❑ 139 Matt Clement	1.00	.45
❑ 140 Pat Burrell RC	4.00	1.80
❑ 141 Freddy Garcia RC	4.00	1.80
❑ 142 Brian Simmons	1.00	.45
❑ 143 Carlos Febles	1.00	.45
❑ 144 Carlos Guillen	1.00	.45
❑ 145 Fernando Seguignol	1.00	.45
❑ 146 Carlos Beltran	1.25	.55
❑ 147 Edgard Clemente	1.00	.45
❑ 148 Mitch Meluskey	1.00	.45
❑ 149 Ryan Bradley	1.00	.45
❑ 150 Marlon Anderson	1.00	.45
❑ 151 A.J. Burnett RC	2.00	.90
❑ 152 Scott Hunter RC	.25	.11
❑ 153 Mark Johnson	1.00	.45
❑ 154 Angel Pena	1.00	.45
❑ 155 Roy Halladay	1.00	.45
❑ 156 Chad Allen RC	.25	.11
❑ 157 Trot Nixon	1.25	.55
❑ 158 Ricky Ledee	1.00	.45
❑ 159 Gary Bennett RC	1.00	.45
❑ 160 Micah Bowie RC	1.00	.45
❑ 161 D.Mientkiewicz RC	3.00	1.35
❑ 162 Danny Klassen	1.00	.45
❑ 163 Willis Otanez	1.00	.45
❑ 164 Jin Ho Cho	1.00	.45
❑ 165 Mike Lowell	1.25	.55
❑ 166 Armando Rios	1.00	.45
❑ 167 Warren Morris	1.00	.45
❑ 168 Michael Barrett	1.00	.45
❑ 169 Alex Gonzalez	1.00	.45
❑ 170 Masao Kida RC	1.25	.55
❑ 171 Peter Tucci	1.00	.45
❑ 172 Luis Saturria RC	.40	.18
❑ 173 Kris Benson	1.25	.55
❑ 174 Mario Encarnacion RC	1.00	.45
❑ 175 Roosevelt Brown RC	1.00	.45
❑ NNO J.D. Drew Sample	1.00	.45

2000 Fleer Focus

	MINT	NRMT
COMP.MASTER SET (275)	500.00	220.00
COMPLETE SET w/2999's (250)	150.00	70.00
COMP.SET w/o SP's (225)	25.00	11.00
COMMON CARD (1-225)	.15	.07
COMMON ROOKIE (226-250)	5.00	2.20
COMMON PORT (226P-250P)	12.00	5.50

❑ 1 Nomar Garciaparra	1.50	.70
❑ 2 Adrian Beltre	.25	.11
❑ 3 Miguel Tejada	.25	.11
❑ 4 Joe Randa	.15	.07
❑ 5 Larry Walker	.40	.18
❑ 6 Jeff Weaver	.25	.11
❑ 7 Jay Bell	.25	.11
❑ 8 Ivan Rodriguez	.60	.25
❑ 9 Edgar Martinez	.40	.18
❑ 10 Desi Relaford	.15	.07
❑ 11 Derek Jeter	2.50	1.10
❑ 12 Delino DeShields	.15	.07
❑ 13 Craig Biggio	.40	.18
❑ 14 Chuck Knoblauch	.25	.11
❑ 15 Chuck Finley	.25	.11
❑ 16 Brett Tomko	.15	.07
❑ 17 Bobby Higginson	.15	.07
❑ 18 Pedro Martinez	.75	.35
❑ 19 Troy O'Leary	.15	.07
❑ 20 Rickey Henderson	1.25	.55
❑ 21 Robb Nen	.15	.07
❑ 22 Rolando Arrojo	.15	.07
❑ 23 Rondell White	.25	.11
❑ 24 Royce Clayton	.15	.07
❑ 25 Rusty Greer	.25	.11
❑ 26 Stan Spencer	.15	.07
❑ 27 Steve Finley	.25	.11
❑ 28 Tom Goodwin	.15	.07
❑ 29 Troy Percival	.15	.07
❑ 30 Wilton Guerrero	.15	.07
❑ 31 Roberto Alomar	.60	.25
❑ 32 Mike Hampton	.25	.11
❑ 33 Michael Barrett	.15	.07
❑ 34 Curt Schilling	.60	.25
❑ 35 Bill Mueller	.15	.07
❑ 36 Bernie Williams	.60	.25
❑ 37 John Smoltz	.25	.11
❑ 38 B.J. Surhoff	.25	.11
❑ 39 Pete Harnisch	.15	.07
❑ 40 Juan Encarnacion	.25	.11
❑ 41 Derrek Lee	.25	.11
❑ 42 Jeff Shaw	.15	.07
❑ 43 David Cone	.25	.11
❑ 44 Jason Christiansen	.15	.07

	Card	Mint	NrMt
❑	45 Jeff Kent	.40	.18
❑	46 Randy Johnson	.75	.35
❑	47 Todd Walker	.15	.07
❑	48 Jose Lima	.15	.07
❑	49 Jason Giambi	.60	.25
❑	50 Ken Griffey Jr. Reds	2.00	.90
❑	51 Bartolo Colon	.25	.11
❑	52 Mike Lieberthal	.25	.11
❑	53 Shane Reynolds	.15	.07
❑	54 Travis Lee	.15	.07
❑	55 Travis Fryman	.25	.11
❑	56 John Valentin	.15	.07
❑	57 Joey Hamilton	.15	.07
❑	58 Jay Buhner	.25	.11
❑	59 Brad Radke	.25	.11
❑	60 A.J. Burnett	.25	.11
❑	61 Roy Halladay	.15	.07
❑	62 Raul Mondesi	.25	.11
❑	63 Matt Mantei	.15	.07
❑	64 Mark Grace	.60	.25
❑	65 David Justice	.25	.11
❑	66 Billy Wagner	.15	.07
❑	67 Eric Milton	.25	.11
❑	68 Eric Chavez	.25	.11
❑	69 Doug Glanville	.15	.07
❑	70 Ray Durham	.25	.11
❑	71 Mike Sirotka	.15	.07
❑	72 Greg Vaughn	.25	.11
❑	73 Brian Jordan	.25	.11
❑	74 Alex Gonzalez	.15	.07
❑	75 Alex Rodriguez	1.50	.70
❑	76 David Nilsson	.15	.07
❑	77 Robin Ventura	.40	.18
❑	78 Kevin Young	.15	.07
❑	79 Wilson Alvarez	.15	.07
❑	80 Matt Williams	.40	.18
❑	81 Ismael Valdes	.15	.07
❑	82 Kenny Lofton	.25	.11
❑	83 Carlos Beltran	.25	.11
❑	84 Doug Mientkiewicz	.40	.18
❑	85 Wally Joyner	.25	.11
❑	86 J.D. Drew	.60	.25
❑	87 Carlos Delgado	.60	.25
❑	88 Tony Womack	.15	.07
❑	89 Eric Young	.15	.07
❑	90 Manny Ramirez	.75	.35
❑	91 Johnny Damon	.25	.11
❑	92 Torii Hunter	.25	.11
❑	93 Kenny Rogers	.15	.07
❑	94 Trevor Hoffman	.25	.11
❑	95 John Wetteland	.25	.11
❑	96 Ray Lankford	.15	.07
❑	97 Tom Glavine	.60	.25
❑	98 Carlos Lee	.25	.11
❑	99 Richie Sexson	.25	.11
❑	100 Carlos Febles	.15	.07
❑	101 Chad Allen	.15	.07
❑	102 Sterling Hitchcock	.15	.07
❑	103 Joe McEwing	.15	.07
❑	104 Justin Thompson	.15	.07
❑	105 Jim Edmonds	.40	.18
❑	106 Kerry Wood	.60	.25
❑	107 Jim Thome	.60	.25
❑	108 Jeremy Giambi	.15	.07
❑	109 Mike Piazza	1.50	.70
❑	110 Darryl Kile	.25	.11
❑	111 Darin Erstad	.60	.25
❑	112 Kyle Farnsworth	.15	.07
❑	113 Omar Vizquel	.25	.11
❑	114 Orber Moreno	.15	.07
❑	115 Al Leiter	.15	.07
❑	116 John Olerud	.25	.11
❑	117 Aaron Sele	.25	.11
❑	118 Chipper Jones	1.25	.55
❑	119 Paul Konerko	.25	.11
❑	120 Chris Singleton	.15	.07
❑	121 Fernando Vina	.15	.07
❑	122 Andy Ashby	.15	.07
❑	123 Eli Marrero	.15	.07
❑	124 Edgar Renteria	.15	.07
❑	125 Roberto Hernandez	.15	.07
❑	126 Andruw Jones	.60	.25
❑	127 Magglio Ordonez	.25	.11
❑	128 Bob Wickman	.15	.07
❑	129 Tony Gwynn	1.25	.55
❑	130 Mark McGwire	2.50	1.10
❑	131 Albert Belle	.25	.11
❑	132 Pokey Reese	.15	.07
❑	133 Tony Clark	.25	.11
❑	134 Jeff Bagwell	.75	.35
❑	135 Mark Grudzielanek	.15	.07
❑	136 Dustin Hermanson	.15	.07
❑	137 Reggie Sanders	.15	.07
❑	138 Ryan Rupe	.15	.07
❑	139 Kevin Millwood	.15	.07
❑	140 Bret Saberhagen	.25	.11
❑	141 Juan Guzman	.15	.07
❑	142 Alex Gonzalez	.15	.07
❑	143 Gary Sheffield	.25	.11
❑	144 Roger Clemens	1.50	.70
❑	145 Ben Grieve	.25	.11
❑	146 Bobby Abreu	.25	.11
❑	147 Brian Giles	.25	.11
❑	148 Quinton McCracken	.15	.07
❑	149 Freddy Garcia	.40	.18
❑	150 Erubiel Durazo	.25	.11
❑	151 Sidney Ponson	.15	.07
❑	152 Scott Williamson	.15	.07
❑	153 Ken Caminiti	.25	.11
❑	154 Vladimir Guerrero	.75	.35
❑	155 Andy Pettitte	.25	.11
❑	156 Edwards Guzman	.15	.07
❑	157 Shannon Stewart	.25	.11
❑	158 Greg Maddux	1.50	.70
❑	159 Mike Stanley	.15	.07
❑	160 Sean Casey	.40	.18
❑	161 Cliff Floyd	.25	.11
❑	162 Devon White	.15	.07
❑	163 Scott Brosius	.25	.11
❑	164 Marlon Anderson	.15	.07
❑	165 Jason Kendall	.25	.11
❑	166 Ryan Klesko	.25	.11
❑	167 Sammy Sosa	1.25	.55
❑	168 Frank Thomas	.75	.35
❑	169 Geoff Jenkins	.25	.11
❑	170 Jason Schmidt	.15	.07
❑	171 Dan Wilson	.15	.07
❑	172 Jose Canseco	.60	.25
❑	173 Troy Glaus	.60	.25
❑	174 Mariano Rivera	.25	.11
❑	175 Scott Rolen	.60	.25
❑	176 J.T. Snow	.25	.11
❑	177 Rafael Palmeiro	.60	.25
❑	178 A.J. Hinch	.15	.07
❑	179 Jose Offerman	.15	.07
❑	180 Jeff Cirillo	.25	.11
❑	181 Dean Palmer	.25	.11
❑	182 Jose Rosado	.15	.07
❑	183 Armando Benitez	.25	.11
❑	184 Brady Anderson	.25	.11
❑	185 Cal Ripken	2.50	1.10
❑	186 Barry Larkin	.60	.25
❑	187 Damion Easley	.15	.07
❑	188 Moises Alou	.25	.11
❑	189 Todd Hundley	.15	.07
❑	190 Tim Hudson	.60	.25
❑	191 Livan Hernandez	.15	.07
❑	192 Fred McGriff	.40	.18
❑	193 Orlando Hernandez	.25	.11
❑	194 Tim Salmon	.25	.11
❑	195 Mike Mussina	.60	.25
❑	196 Todd Helton	.75	.35
❑	197 Juan Gonzalez	.60	.25
❑	198 Kevin Brown	.40	.18
❑	199 Ugueth Urbina	.15	.07
❑	200 Matt Stairs	.15	.07
❑	201 Shawn Estes	.25	.11
❑	202 Gabe Kapler	.25	.11
❑	203 Javy Lopez	.25	.11
❑	204 Henry Rodriguez	.15	.07
❑	205 Dante Bichette	.25	.11
❑	206 Jeromy Burnitz	.25	.11
❑	207 Todd Zeile	.25	.11
❑	208 Rico Brogna	.15	.07
❑	209 Warren Morris	.15	.07
❑	210 David Segui	.15	.07
❑	211 Vinny Castilla	.25	.11
❑	212 Mo Vaughn	.25	.11
❑	213 Charles Johnson	.25	.11
❑	214 Neifi Perez	.15	.07
❑	215 Shawn Green	.60	.25
❑	216 Carl Pavano	.15	.07
❑	217 Tino Martinez	.25	.11
❑	218 Barry Bonds	1.50	.70
❑	219 David Wells	.25	.11
❑	220 Paul O'Neill	.60	.25
❑	221 Masato Yoshii	.15	.07
❑	222 Kris Benson	.25	.11
❑	223 Fernando Tatis	.15	.07
❑	224 Lee Stevens	.15	.07
❑	225 Jose Cruz Jr.	.25	.11
❑	226 Rick Ankiel	10.00	4.50
❑	226P Rick Ankiel PORT	20.00	9.00
❑	227 Matt Riley	5.00	2.20
❑	227P Matt Riley PORT	12.00	5.50
❑	228 Norm Hutchins	5.00	2.20
❑	228P N.Hutchins PORT	12.00	5.50
❑	229 Ruben Mateo	5.00	2.20
❑	229P Ruben Mateo PORT	12.00	5.50
❑	230 Ben Petrick	5.00	2.20
❑	230P Ben Petrick PORT	12.00	5.50
❑	231 Mario Encarnacion	5.00	2.20
❑	231P M.Encarnacion PORT	12.00	5.50
❑	232 Nick Johnson	10.00	4.50
❑	232P Nick Johnson PORT	20.00	9.00
❑	233 Adam Piatt	6.00	2.70
❑	233P Adam Piatt PORT	12.00	5.50
❑	234 Mike Darr	5.00	2.20
❑	234P Mike Darr PORT	12.00	5.50
❑	235 Chad Hermansen	5.00	2.20
❑	235P C.Hermansen PORT	12.00	5.50
❑	236 Wily Pena	10.00	4.50
❑	236P Wily Pena PORT	20.00	9.00
❑	237 Octavio Dotel	5.00	2.20
❑	237P Octavio Dotel PORT	12.00	5.50
❑	238 Vernon Wells	5.00	2.20
❑	238P Vernon Wells PORT	12.00	5.50
❑	239 Daryle Ward	5.00	2.20
❑	239P Daryle Ward PORT	12.00	5.50
❑	240 Adam Kennedy	5.00	2.20
❑	240P A.Kennedy PORT	12.00	5.50
❑	241 Angel Pena	5.00	2.20
❑	241P Angel Pena PORT	12.00	5.50
❑	242 Lance Berkman	10.00	4.50
❑	242P L.Berkman PORT	20.00	9.00
❑	243 Gabe Molina	5.00	2.20
❑	243P Gabe Molina PORT	12.00	5.50
❑	244 Steve Lomasney	5.00	2.20
❑	244P S.Lomasney PORT	12.00	5.50
❑	245 Jacob Cruz	5.00	2.20
❑	245P Jacob Cruz PORT	12.00	5.50
❑	246 Mark Quinn	5.00	2.20
❑	246P Mark Quinn PORT	12.00	5.50
❑	247 Eric Munson	5.00	2.20
❑	247P Eric Munson PORT	12.00	5.50
❑	248 Alfonso Soriano	10.00	4.50
❑	248P A.Soriano PORT	20.00	9.00
❑	249 Kip Wells	5.00	2.20
❑	249P Kip Wells PORT	12.00	5.50
❑	250 Josh Beckett	12.00	5.50
❑	250P Josh Beckett PORT	25.00	11.00

2001 Fleer Focus

		MINT	NRMT
	COMP.SET w/o SP's (200)	25.00	11.00
❑	1 Derek Jeter	2.50	1.10
❑	2 Manny Ramirez	.75	.35
❑	3 Ken Griffey Jr.	2.00	.90

	No.	Player	Mint	NrMt
❑	4	Ken Caminiti	.25	.11
❑	5	Joe Randa	.15	.07
❑	6	Jason Kendall	.25	.11
❑	7	Ron Coomer	.15	.07
❑	8	Rondell White	.25	.11
❑	9	Tino Martinez	.25	.11
❑	10	Nomar Garciaparra	1.50	.70
❑	11	Tony Batista	.25	.11
❑	12	Todd Stottlemyre	.15	.07
❑	13	Ryan Klesko	.25	.11
❑	14	Darin Erstad	.60	.25
❑	15	Todd Walker	.15	.07
❑	16	Al Leiter	.25	.11
❑	17	Carl Everett	.25	.11
❑	18	Bobby Abreu	.25	.11
❑	19	Raul Mondesi	.25	.11
❑	20	Vladimir Guerrero	1.00	.45
❑	21	Mike Bordick	.25	.11
❑	22	Aaron Sele	.25	.11
❑	23	Ray Lankford	.15	.07
❑	24	Roger Clemens	1.50	.70
❑	25	Kevin Young	.15	.07
❑	26	Brad Radke	.25	.11
❑	27	Todd Hundley	.15	.07
❑	28	Ellis Burks	.25	.11
❑	29	Lee Stevens	.15	.07
❑	30	Eric Karros	.25	.11
❑	31	Darren Dreifort	.15	.07
❑	32	Ivan Rodriguez	.60	.25
❑	33	Pedro Martinez	.75	.35
❑	34	Travis Fryman	.25	.11
❑	35	Garret Anderson	.25	.11
❑	36	Rafael Palmeiro	.60	.25
❑	37	Jason Giambi	.60	.25
❑	38	Jeromy Burnitz	.25	.11
❑	39	Robin Ventura	.25	.11
❑	40	Derek Bell	.15	.07
❑	41	Carlos Guillen	.15	.07
❑	42	Albert Belle	.25	.11
❑	43	Henry Rodriguez	.15	.07
❑	44	Brian Jordan	.25	.11
❑	45	Mike Sweeney	.25	.11
❑	46	Ruben Rivera	.15	.07
❑	47	Greg Maddux	1.50	.70
❑	48	Corey Koskie	.25	.11
❑	49	Sandy Alomar Jr.	.25	.11
❑	50	Mike Mussina	.60	.25
❑	51	Tom Glavine	.60	.25
❑	52	Aaron Boone	.15	.07
❑	53	Frank Thomas	.75	.35
❑	54	Kenny Lofton	.25	.11
❑	55	Danny Graves	.15	.07
❑	56	Jose Valentin	.15	.07
❑	57	Travis Lee	.15	.07
❑	58	Jim Edmonds	.40	.18
❑	59	Jim Thome	.60	.25
❑	60	Steve Finley	.25	.11
❑	61	Shawn Green	.60	.25
❑	62	Lance Berkman	.60	.25
❑	63	Mark Quinn	.25	.11
❑	64	Randy Johnson	.75	.35
❑	65	Dmitri Young	.25	.11
❑	66	Andy Pettitte	.25	.11
❑	67	Paul O'Neill	.60	.25
❑	68	Gil Heredia	.15	.07
❑	69	Russell Branyan	.25	.11
❑	70	Alex Rodriguez	1.50	.70
❑	71	Geoff Jenkins	.25	.11
❑	72	Eric Chavez	.25	.11
❑	73	Cal Ripken	2.50	1.10
❑	74	Mark Kotsay	.25	.11
❑	75	Jeff D'Amico	.15	.07
❑	76	Tony Womack	.15	.07
❑	77	Eric Milton	.25	.11
❑	78	Joe Girardi	.15	.07
❑	79	Peter Bergeron	.15	.07
❑	80	Miguel Tejada	.25	.11
❑	81	Luis Gonzalez	.60	.25
❑	82	Doug Glanville	.15	.07
❑	83	Gerald Williams	.15	.07
❑	84	Troy O'Leary	.15	.07
❑	85	Brian Giles	.25	.11
❑	86	Miguel Cairo	.15	.07
❑	87	Magglio Ordonez	.25	.11
❑	88	Rick Helling	.15	.07
❑	89	Bruce Chen	.15	.07
❑	90	Jason Varitek	.25	.11
❑	91	Mike Lieberthal	.25	.11
❑	92	Shawn Estes	.25	.11
❑	93	Rick Ankiel	.40	.18
❑	94	Tim Salmon	.25	.11
❑	95	Jacque Jones	.25	.11
❑	96	Johnny Damon	.25	.11
❑	97	Larry Walker	.40	.18
❑	98	Ruben Mateo	.25	.11
❑	99	Brad Fullmer	.25	.11
❑	100	Edgardo Alfonzo	.25	.11
❑	101	Mark Mulder	.40	.18
❑	102	Tony Gwynn	1.25	.55
❑	103	Mike Cameron	.25	.11
❑	104	Richie Sexson	.25	.11
❑	105	Barry Larkin	.60	.25
❑	106	Mike Piazza	1.50	.70
❑	107	Eric Young	.15	.07
❑	108	Edgar Renteria	.15	.07
❑	109	Todd Zeile	.25	.11
❑	110	Luis Castillo	.15	.07
❑	111	Sammy Sosa	1.25	.55
❑	112	David Justice	.25	.11
❑	113	Delino DeShields	.15	.07
❑	114	Mariano Rivera	.25	.11
❑	115	Edgar Martinez	.25	.11
❑	116	Ray Durham	.25	.11
❑	117	Brady Anderson	.25	.11
❑	118	Eric Owens	.15	.07
❑	119	Alex Gonzalez	.15	.07
❑	120	Jay Buhner	.25	.11
❑	121	Greg Vaughn	.25	.11
❑	122	Mike Lowell	.25	.11
❑	123	Marquis Grissom	.15	.07
❑	124	Matt Williams	.40	.18
❑	125	Dean Palmer	.25	.11
❑	126	Troy Glaus	.75	.35
❑	127	Bret Boone	.25	.11
❑	128	David Ortiz	.25	.11
❑	129	Glenallen Hill	.15	.07
❑	130	Chipper Jones	1.25	.55
❑	131	Tony Clark	.25	.11
❑	132	Terrence Long	.25	.11
❑	133	Chuck Finley	.25	.11
❑	134	Jeff Bagwell	.75	.35
❑	135	J.T. Snow	.25	.11
❑	136	Andruw Jones	.60	.25
❑	137	Carlos Delgado	.60	.25
❑	138	Mo Vaughn	.25	.11
❑	139	Derrek Lee	.15	.07
❑	140	Bobby Estalella	.15	.07
❑	141	Kerry Wood	.60	.25
❑	142	Jose Vidro	.25	.11
❑	143	Ben Grieve	.25	.11
❑	144	Barry Bonds	1.50	.70
❑	145	Javy Lopez	.25	.11
❑	146	Adam Kennedy	.15	.07
❑	147	Jeff Cirillo	.25	.11
❑	148	Cliff Floyd	.25	.11
❑	149	Carl Pavano	.15	.07
❑	150	Bobby Higginson	.25	.11
❑	151	Kevin Brown	.25	.11
❑	152	Fernando Tatis	.15	.07
❑	153	Matt Lawton	.25	.11
❑	154	Damion Easley	.15	.07
❑	155	Curt Schilling	.60	.25
❑	156	Mark McGwire	2.50	1.10
❑	157	Mark Grace	.60	.25
❑	158	Adrian Beltre	.25	.11
❑	159	Jorge Posada	.25	.11
❑	160	Richard Hidalgo	.25	.11
❑	161	Vinny Castilla	.25	.11
❑	162	Bernie Williams	.60	.25
❑	163	John Olerud	.25	.11
❑	164	Todd Helton	.75	.35
❑	165	Craig Biggio	.40	.18
❑	166	David Wells	.25	.11
❑	167	Phil Nevin	.25	.11
❑	168	Andres Galarraga	.40	.18
❑	169	Moises Alou	.25	.11
❑	170	Denny Neagle	.15	.07
❑	171	Jeffrey Hammonds	.15	.07
❑	172	Sean Casey	.40	.18
❑	173	Gary Sheffield	.25	.11
❑	174	Carlos Lee	.25	.11
❑	175	Juan Encarnacion	.25	.11
❑	176	Roberto Alomar	.60	.25
❑	177	Kenny Rogers	.15	.07
❑	178	Charles Johnson	.25	.11
❑	179	Shannon Stewart	.25	.11
❑	180	B.J. Surhoff	.25	.11
❑	181	Paul Konerko	.25	.11
❑	182	Jermaine Dye	.25	.11
❑	183	Scott Rolen	.60	.25
❑	184	Fred McGriff	.40	.18
❑	185	Juan Gonzalez	.60	.25
❑	186	Carlos Beltran	.25	.11
❑	187	Jay Payton	.15	.07
❑	188	Chad Hermansen	.15	.07
❑	189	Pat Burrell	.25	.11
❑	190	Omar Vizquel	.25	.11
❑	191	Trot Nixon	.25	.11
❑	192	Mike Hampton	.25	.11
❑	193	Kris Benson	.25	.11
❑	194	Gabe Kapler	.25	.11
❑	195	Rickey Henderson	1.25	.55
❑	196	J.D. Drew	.60	.25
❑	197	Pokey Reese	.15	.07
❑	198	Jeff Kent	.40	.18
❑	199	Jose Cruz Jr.	.25	.11
❑	200	Preston Wilson	.25	.11
❑	201	Eric Munson/2499	5.00	2.20
❑	202	Alex Cabrera/2499	5.00	2.20
❑	203	Nate Rolison/2499	5.00	2.20
❑	204	Julio Zuleta/2499	5.00	2.20
❑	205	Chris Richard/2499	5.00	2.20
❑	206	Dernell Stenson/2499	5.00	2.20
❑	207	Aaron McNeal/2499	5.00	2.20
❑	208	Aubrey Huff/2999	5.00	2.20
❑	209	Mike Lamb/2999	5.00	2.20
❑	210	Xavier Nady/2999	5.00	2.20
❑	211	Joe Crede/2999	5.00	2.20
❑	212	Ben Petrick/3499	5.00	2.20
❑	213	Morgan Burkhart/1999	5.00	2.20
❑	214	Jason Tyner/1999	5.00	2.20
❑	215	Juan Pierre/1999	5.00	2.20
❑	216	Adam Dunn/1999	12.00	5.50
❑	217	Adam Piatt/1999	5.00	2.20
❑	218	Eric Byrnes/1999	5.00	2.20
❑	219	Corey Patterson/1999	5.00	2.20
❑	220	Kenny Kelly/1999	5.00	2.20
❑	221	Tike Redman/1999	5.00	2.20
❑	222	Luis Matos/1999	5.00	2.20
❑	223	Timo Perez/1999	5.00	2.20
❑	224	Vernon Wells/1999	5.00	2.20
❑	225	Barry Zito/4999	8.00	3.60
❑	226	Adam Bernero/4999	5.00	2.20
❑	227	Kazuhiro Sasaki/4999	10.00	4.50
❑	228	Oswaldo Mairena/4999	5.00	2.20
❑	229	Mark Buehrle/4999	8.00	3.60
❑	230	Ryan Dempster/4999	5.00	2.20
❑	231	Tim Hudson/4999	8.00	3.60
❑	232	Scott Downs/4999	5.00	2.20
❑	233	A.J. Burnett/4999	5.00	2.20
❑	234	Adam Eaton/4999	5.00	2.20
❑	235	Paxton Crawford/4999	5.00	2.20
❑	236	Jace Brewer/3999	5.00	2.20
❑	237	Jose Ortiz/3999	5.00	2.20
❑	238	Rafael Furcal/3999	5.00	2.20
❑	239	Julio Lugo/3999	5.00	2.20
❑	240	Tomas De la Rosa/3999	5.00	2.20

2001 Fleer Futures

	No.	Player	MINT	NRMT
		COMPLETE SET (220)	30.00	13.50
❑	1	Darin Erstad	.60	.25
❑	2	Manny Ramirez	.75	.35
❑	3	Darryl Kile	.25	.11
❑	4	Troy O'Leary	.15	.07
❑	5	Mark Quinn	.25	.11
❑	6	Brian Giles	.25	.11
❑	7	Randy Johnson	.75	.35
❑	8	Todd Walker	.15	.07
❑	9	Mike Piazza	1.50	.70
❑	10	Fred McGriff	.40	.18
❑	11	Sammy Sosa	1.25	.55
❑	12	Chan Ho Park	.25	.11
❑	13	John Rocker	.25	.11
❑	14	Luis Castillo	.15	.07
❑	15	Eric Chavez	.25	.11

❑ 16 Carlos Delgado .60 .25
❑ 17 Sean Casey .40 .18
❑ 18 Corey Koskie .25 .11
❑ 19 John Olerud .25 .11
❑ 20 Nomar Garciaparra 1.50 .70
❑ 21 Craig Biggio .40 .18
❑ 22 Pat Burrell .25 .11
❑ 23 Ben Molina .15 .07
❑ 24 Jim Thome .60 .25
❑ 25 Rey Ordonez .15 .07
❑ 26 Fernando Tatis .15 .07
❑ 27 Eric Young .15 .07
❑ 28 Eric Karros .25 .11
❑ 29 Adam Eaton .25 .11
❑ 30 Brian Jordan .25 .11
❑ 31 Jorge Posada .25 .11
❑ 32 Gabe Kapler .25 .11
❑ 33 Keith Foulke .15 .07
❑ 34 Ron Coomer .15 .07
❑ 35 Chipper Jones 1.25 .55
❑ 36 Miguel Tejada .25 .11
❑ 37 David Wells .25 .11
❑ 38 Carlos Lee .25 .11
❑ 39 Barry Bonds 1.50 .70
❑ 40 Derrek Lee .25 .11
❑ 41 Tim Hudson .60 .25
❑ 42 Billy Koch .15 .07
❑ 43 Dmitri Young .25 .11
❑ 44 Vladimir Guerrero .75 .35
❑ 45 Rickey Henderson 1.25 .55
❑ 46 Jeff Bagwell .75 .35
❑ 47 Robert Person .15 .07
❑ 48 Brady Anderson .25 .11
❑ 49 Lance Berkman .60 .25
❑ 50 Mike Lieberthal .25 .11
❑ 51 Adam Kennedy .15 .07
❑ 52 Russell Branyan .25 .11
❑ 53 Robin Ventura .25 .11
❑ 54 Mark McGwire 2.50 1.10
❑ 55 Tony Gwynn 1.25 .55
❑ 56 Matt Williams .40 .18
❑ 57 Jeff Cirillo .25 .11
❑ 58 Roger Clemens 1.50 .70
❑ 59 Ivan Rodriguez .60 .25
❑ 60 Brad Radke .25 .11
❑ 61 Kazuhiro Sasaki .75 .35
❑ 62 Cal Ripken 2.50 1.10
❑ 63 Ken Caminiti .25 .11
❑ 64 Bob Abreu .25 .11
❑ 65 Troy Glaus .75 .35
❑ 66 Sandy Alomar Jr. .25 .11
❑ 67 Jose Vidro .25 .11
❑ 68 Pedro Martinez .75 .35
❑ 69 Kevin Young .15 .07
❑ 70 Jay Bell .25 .11
❑ 71 Larry Walker .40 .18
❑ 72 Derek Jeter 2.50 1.10
❑ 73 Miguel Cairo .15 .07
❑ 74 Magglio Ordonez .25 .11
❑ 75 Jeromy Burnitz .25 .11
❑ 76 J.T. Snow .25 .11
❑ 77 Andres Galarraga .40 .18
❑ 78 Ryan Dempster .25 .11
❑ 79 Ken Griffey Jr. 2.00 .90
❑ 80 Aaron Sele .25 .11
❑ 81 Tom Glavine .60 .25
❑ 82 Hideo Nomo .60 .25
❑ 83 Orlando Hernandez .25 .11
❑ 84 Tony Batista .25 .11
❑ 85 Aaron Boone .15 .07
❑ 86 Jacque Jones .25 .11
❑ 87 Delino DeShields .15 .07
❑ 88 Garret Anderson .25 .11
❑ 89 Fernando Seguignol .15 .07
❑ 90 Jim Edmonds .40 .18
❑ 91 Frank Thomas .75 .35
❑ 92 Adrian Beltre .25 .11
❑ 93 Ellis Burks .25 .11
❑ 94 Andruw Jones .60 .25
❑ 95 Tony Clark .25 .11
❑ 96 Danny Graves .15 .07
❑ 97 Alex Rodriguez 1.50 .70
❑ 98 Mike Mussina .60 .25
❑ 99 Scott Elarton .15 .07
❑ 100 Jason Giambi .60 .25
❑ 101 Jay Payton .15 .07
❑ 102 Gerald Williams .15 .07
❑ 103 Kerry Wood .60 .25
❑ 104 Shawn Green .60 .25
❑ 105 Greg Maddux 1.50 .70
❑ 106 Juan Encarnacion .25 .11
❑ 107 Bernie Williams .60 .25
❑ 108 Mike Lamb .15 .07
❑ 109 Charles Johnson .15 .07
❑ 110 Richie Sexson .25 .11
❑ 111 Jeff Kent .40 .18
❑ 112 Albert Belle .25 .11
❑ 113 Cliff Floyd .25 .11
❑ 114 Ben Grieve .25 .11
❑ 115 Tim Salmon .25 .11
❑ 116 Carl Pavano .15 .07
❑ 117 Rick Ankiel .40 .18
❑ 118 Dante Bichette .25 .11
❑ 119 Johnny Damon .25 .11
❑ 120 Brian Anderson .15 .07
❑ 121 Roberto Alomar .60 .25
❑ 122 Mike Hampton .25 .11
❑ 123 Greg Vaughn .25 .11
❑ 124 Carl Everett .25 .11
❑ 125 Moises Alou .25 .11
❑ 126 Jason Kendall .25 .11
❑ 127 Omar Vizquel .25 .11
❑ 128 Mark Grace .60 .25
❑ 129 Kevin Brown .25 .11
❑ 130 Phil Nevin .25 .11
❑ 131 Kevin Millwood .15 .07
❑ 132 Bobby Higginson .25 .11
❑ 133 Ruben Mateo .25 .11
❑ 134 Luis Gonzalez .60 .25
❑ 135 Dean Palmer .25 .11
❑ 136 Mariano Rivera .25 .11
❑ 137 Rick Helling .15 .07
❑ 138 Paul Konerko .25 .11
❑ 139 Marquis Grissom .15 .07
❑ 140 Robb Nen .15 .07
❑ 141 Javy Lopez .25 .11
❑ 142 Preston Wilson .25 .11
❑ 143 Terrence Long .25 .11
❑ 144 Shannon Stewart .25 .11
❑ 145 Barry Larkin .60 .25
❑ 146 Cristian Guzman .25 .11
❑ 147 Jay Buhner .25 .11
❑ 148 Jermaine Dye .25 .11
❑ 149 Kris Benson .25 .11
❑ 150 Curt Schilling .60 .25
❑ 151 Todd Helton .75 .35
❑ 152 Paul O'Neill .60 .25
❑ 153 Rafael Palmeiro .60 .25
❑ 154 Ray Durham .25 .11
❑ 155 Geoff Jenkins .25 .11
❑ 156 Livan Hernandez .15 .07
❑ 157 Rafael Furcal .25 .11
❑ 158 Juan Gonzalez .60 .25
❑ 159 Tino Martinez .25 .11
❑ 160 Raul Mondesi .25 .11
❑ 161 Matt Lawton .25 .11
❑ 162 Edgar Martinez .40 .18
❑ 163 Richard Hidalgo .25 .11
❑ 164 Scott Rolen .60 .25
❑ 165 Chuck Finley .25 .11
❑ 166 Edgardo Alfonzo .25 .11
❑ 167 J.D. Drew .60 .25
❑ 168 Trot Nixon .25 .11
❑ 169 Carlos Beltran .25 .11
❑ 170 Ryan Klesko .25 .11
❑ 171 Mo Vaughn .25 .11
❑ 172 Kenny Lofton .25 .11
❑ 173 Al Leiter .25 .11
❑ 174 Rondell White .25 .11
❑ 175 Mike Sweeney .25 .11
❑ 176 Trevor Hoffman .25 .11
❑ 177 Steve Finley .25 .11
❑ 178 Jeffrey Hammonds .15 .07
❑ 179 David Justice .25 .11
❑ 180 Gary Sheffield .25 .11
❑ 181 Eric Munson BF .25 .11
❑ 182 Luis Matos BF .15 .07
❑ 183 Alex Cabrera BF .15 .07
❑ 184 Randy Keisler BF .15 .07
❑ 185 Nate Rolison BF .15 .07
❑ 186 Jason Hart BF .40 .18
❑ 187 Timo Perez BF .15 .07
❑ 188 Adam Bernero BF .15 .07
❑ 189 Barry Zito BF .60 .25
❑ 190 Ryan Kohlmeier BF .15 .07
❑ 191 Joey Nation BF .15 .07
❑ 192 Oswaldo Mairena BF .15 .07
❑ 193 Aubrey Huff BF .15 .07
❑ 194 Mark Buehrle BF .60 .25
❑ 195 Jace Brewer BF .15 .07
❑ 196 Julio Zuleta BF .15 .07
❑ 197 Xavier Nady BF .40 .18
❑ 198 Vernon Wells BF .25 .11
❑ 199 Joe Crede BF .25 .11
❑ 200 Scott Downs BF .15 .07
❑ 201 Ben Petrick BF .15 .07
❑ 202 A.J. Burnett BF .25 .11
❑ 203 Esix Snead BF RC .50 .23
❑ 204 Dernell Stenson BF .15 .07
❑ 205 Jose Ortiz BF .40 .18
❑ 206 Paxton Crawford BF .15 .07
❑ 207 Jason Tyner BF .15 .07
❑ 208 Jimmy Rollins BF .25 .11
❑ 209 Juan Pierre BF .25 .11
❑ 210 Keith Ginter BF .25 .11
❑ 211 Adam Dunn BF 1.00 .45
❑ 212 Larry Barnes BF .15 .07
❑ 213 Adam Piatt BF .25 .11
❑ 214 Rodney Lindsey BF .15 .07
❑ 215 Eric Byrnes BF .15 .07
❑ 216 Julio Lugo BF .15 .07
❑ 217 Corey Patterson BF .25 .11
❑ 218 Reggie Taylor BF .15 .07
❑ 219 Kenny Kelly BF .15 .07
❑ 220 Tike Redman BF .15 .07

2001 Fleer Game Time

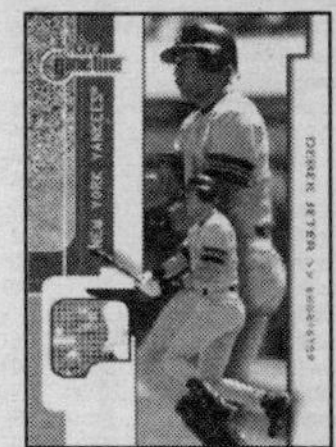

	MINT	NRMT
COMP.SET w/o SP's (90)	25.00	11.00
COMMON CARD (1-90)	.30	.14
COMMON NG (91-121)	5.00	2.20

❑ 1 Derek Jeter 3.00 1.35
❑ 2 Nomar Garciaparra 2.00 .90
❑ 3 Alex Rodriguez 2.00 .90
❑ 4 Jason Kendall .30 .14
❑ 5 Barry Bonds 2.00 .90
❑ 6 David Wells .30 .14
❑ 7 Craig Biggio .50 .23
❑ 8 Adrian Beltre .30 .14

❑ 9 Pat Burrell .30 .14
❑ 10 Rafael Palmeiro .75 .35
❑ 11 Jim Thome .75 .35
❑ 12 Mike Lowell .30 .14
❑ 13 Trevor Hoffman .30 .14
❑ 14 Pokey Reese .30 .14
❑ 15 Juan Encarnacion .30 .14
❑ 16 Shawn Green .75 .35
❑ 17 Kerry Wood .75 .35
❑ 18 Richard Hidalgo .30 .14
❑ 19 Scott Rolen .75 .35
❑ 20 Jeff Kent .50 .23
❑ 21 Alex Gonzalez .30 .14
❑ 22 Matt Williams .50 .23
❑ 23 Mike Sweeney .30 .14
❑ 24 Edgar Martinez .50 .23
❑ 25 Sammy Sosa 1.50 .70
❑ 26 Bobby Higginson .30 .14
❑ 27 Kevin Brown .30 .14
❑ 28 Mike Lieberthal .30 .14
❑ 29 Pedro Martinez 1.00 .45
❑ 30 Jeff Weaver .30 .14
❑ 31 Greg Maddux 2.00 .90
❑ 32 Mike Hampton .30 .14
❑ 33 Vladimir Guerrero 1.00 .45
❑ 34 Greg Vaughn .30 .14
❑ 35 Manny Ramirez 1.00 .45
❑ 36 Carlos Beltran .30 .14
❑ 37 Eric Chavez .30 .14
❑ 38 Troy Glaus .75 .35
❑ 39 Todd Helton 1.00 .45
❑ 40 Gary Sheffield .30 .14
❑ 41 Brady Anderson .30 .14
❑ 42 Juan Gonzalez .75 .35
❑ 43 Tim Hudson .75 .35
❑ 44 Kenny Lofton .30 .14
❑ 45 Al Leiter .30 .14
❑ 46 Eric Owens .30 .14
❑ 47 Roberto Alomar .75 .35
❑ 48 Preston Wilson .30 .14
❑ 49 Tony Gwynn 1.50 .70
❑ 50 Cal Ripken 3.00 1.35
❑ 51 Ben Petrick .30 .14
❑ 52 Jason Giambi .75 .35
❑ 53 Ben Grieve .30 .14
❑ 54 Albert Belle .30 .14
❑ 55 Jose Vidro .30 .14
❑ 56 Barry Zito .75 .35
❑ 57 Ivan Rodriguez 1.00 .45
❑ 58 Jeff Bagwell 1.00 .45
❑ 59 Geoff Jenkins .30 .14
❑ 60 Roger Clemens 2.00 .90
❑ 61 John Olerud .30 .14
❑ 62 Randy Johnson 1.00 .45
❑ 63 Matt Lawton .30 .14
❑ 64 Mark McGwire 3.00 1.35
❑ 65 Brad Radke .30 .14
❑ 66 Frank Thomas 1.00 .45
❑ 67 Edgardo Alfonzo .30 .14
❑ 68 Brian Giles .30 .14
❑ 69 J.T. Snow .30 .14
❑ 70 Carlos Delgado .75 .35
❑ 71 Chipper Jones 1.50 .70
❑ 72 Mark Quinn .30 .14
❑ 73 Mike Mussina .75 .35
❑ 74 Rick Ankiel .50 .23
❑ 75 Rafael Furcal .30 .14
❑ 76 Jim Edmonds .50 .23
❑ 77 Vinny Castilla .30 .14
❑ 78 Sean Casey .50 .23
❑ 79 Derrek Lee .30 .14
❑ 80 Mike Piazza 2.00 .90
❑ 81 Warren Morris .30 .14
❑ 82 Tim Salmon .30 .14
❑ 83 Jeromy Burnitz .30 .14
❑ 84 Freddy Garcia .30 .14
❑ 85 Ken Griffey Jr. 2.50 1.10
❑ 86 Andruw Jones .75 .35
❑ 87 Darryl Kile .30 .14
❑ 88 Magglio Ordonez .30 .14
❑ 89 Bernie Williams .75 .35
❑ 90 Timo Perez .30 .14
❑ 91 Ichiro Suzuki NG RC 80.00 36.00
❑ 92 Larry Barnes 5.00 2.20
Darin Erstad
❑ 93 Jaisen Randolph NG RC 5.00 2.20
❑ 94 Paul Phillips NG RC 5.00 2.20
❑ 95 Esix Snead NG RC 5.00 2.20
❑ 96 Matt White NG RC 5.00 2.20
❑ 97 Ryan Freel NG RC 5.00 2.20
❑ 98 Winston Abreu NG RC 5.00 2.20
❑ 99 Junior Spivey NG RC 5.00 2.20
❑ 100 Randy Keisler 8.00 3.60
Roger Clemens
❑ 101 Mike Piazza 8.00 3.60
Brian Cole
❑ 102 Aubrey Huff 6.00 2.70
Chipper Jones
❑ 103 Corey Patterson 6.00 2.70
Sammy Sosa
❑ 104 Sun Woo Kim 5.00 2.20
Pedro Martinez
❑ 105 Drew Henson NG RC 25.00 11.00
❑ 106 Claudio Vargas NG RC 5.00 2.20
❑ 107 Rafael Furcal 5.00 2.20
Cesar Izturis
❑ 108 Paxton Crawford 5.00 2.20
Pedro Martinez
❑ 109 Adrian Hernandez NG RC 5.00 2.20
❑ 110 Jace Brewer 12.00 5.50
Derek Jeter
❑ 111 Andy Morales NG RC 5.00 2.20
❑ 112 Wilson Betemit NG RC 15.00 6.75
❑ 113 Juan Diaz NG RC 5.00 2.20
❑ 114 Erick Almonte NG RC 5.00 2.20
❑ 115 Nick Punto NG RC 5.00 2.20
❑ 116 Tsuyoshi Shinjo NG RC 12.00 5.50
❑ 117 Jay Gibbons NG RC 8.00 3.60
❑ 118 Andres Torres NG RC 5.00 2.20
❑ 119 Alexis Gomez NG RC 5.00 2.20
❑ 120 Wilkin Ruan NG RC 5.00 2.20
❑ 121 Albert Pujols NG RC 50.00 22.00
❑ MM2 Derek Jeter/1996 15.00 6.75
❑ MM2 Derek Jeter AU/96 200.00 90.00

2001 Fleer Genuine

	MINT	NRMT
COMPLETE SET (130)	550.00	250.00
COMP.SET w/o SP's	25.00	11.00
COMMON CARD (1-100)	.40	.18
COMMON CARD (101-130)	8.00	3.60

❑ 1 Derek Jeter 4.00 1.80
❑ 2 Nomar Garciaparra 2.50 1.10
❑ 3 Alex Rodriguez 2.50 1.10
❑ 4 Frank Thomas 1.25 .55
❑ 5 Travis Fryman .40 .18
❑ 6 Gary Sheffield .40 .18
❑ 7 Jason Giambi 1.00 .45
❑ 8 Trevor Hoffman .40 .18
❑ 9 Todd Helton 1.25 .55
❑ 10 Ivan Rodriguez 1.25 .55
❑ 11 Roberto Alomar 1.00 .45
❑ 12 Barry Zito 1.00 .45
❑ 13 Kevin Brown .40 .18
❑ 14 Shawn Green 1.00 .45
❑ 15 Kenny Lofton .40 .18
❑ 16 Jeff Weaver .40 .18
❑ 17 Geoff Jenkins .40 .18
❑ 18 Carlos Delgado 1.00 .45
❑ 19 Mark Grace 1.00 .45
❑ 20 Ken Griffey Jr. 3.00 1.35
❑ 21 David Justice .40 .18
❑ 22 Brian Giles .40 .18
❑ 23 Scott Williamson .40 .18
❑ 24 Richie Sexson .40 .18
❑ 25 John Olerud .40 .18
❑ 26 Sammy Sosa 2.00 .90
❑ 27 Bobby Higginson .40 .18
❑ 28 Matt Lawton .40 .18
❑ 29 Vinny Castilla .40 .18
❑ 30 Alex Gonzalez .40 .18
❑ 31 Manny Ramirez 1.25 .55
❑ 32 Brad Radke .40 .18
❑ 33 Cal Ripken 4.00 1.80
❑ 34 Richard Hidalgo .40 .18
❑ 35 Al Leiter .40 .18
❑ 36 Freddy Garcia .40 .18
❑ 37 Juan Encarnacion .40 .18
❑ 38 Corey Koskie .40 .18
❑ 39 Greg Vaughn .40 .18
❑ 40 Rafael Palmeiro 1.00 .45
❑ 41 Vladimir Guerrero 1.25 .55
❑ 42 Troy Glaus 1.00 .45
❑ 43 Mike Hampton .40 .18
❑ 44 Jose Vidro .40 .18
❑ 45 Ryan Rupe .40 .18
❑ 46 Troy O'Leary .40 .18
❑ 47 Ben Petrick .40 .18
❑ 48 Mike Lieberthal .40 .18
❑ 49 Mike Sweeney .40 .18
❑ 50 Scott Rolen 1.00 .45
❑ 51 Albert Belle .60 .25
❑ 52 Mark Quinn .40 .18
❑ 53 Mike Piazza 2.50 1.10
❑ 54 Mark McGwire 4.00 1.80
❑ 55 Brady Anderson .40 .18
❑ 56 Carlos Beltran .40 .18
❑ 57 Michael Barrett .40 .18
❑ 58 Jason Kendall .40 .18
❑ 59 Jim Edmonds .60 .25
❑ 60 Matt Williams .60 .25
❑ 61 Pokey Reese .40 .18
❑ 62 Bernie Williams 1.00 .45
❑ 63 Barry Bonds 2.50 1.10
❑ 64 David Wells .40 .18
❑ 65 Chipper Jones 2.00 .90
❑ 66 Jim Parque .40 .18
❑ 67 Derrek Lee .40 .18
❑ 68 Darin Erstad 1.00 .45
❑ 69 Edgar Martinez .60 .25
❑ 70 Kerry Wood 1.00 .45
❑ 71 Omar Vizquel .40 .18
❑ 72 Jeromy Burnitz .40 .18
❑ 73 Warren Morris .40 .18
❑ 74 Rick Ankiel .60 .25
❑ 75 Andruw Jones 1.00 .45
❑ 76 Paul Konerko .40 .18
❑ 77 Mike Lowell .40 .18
❑ 78 Roger Clemens 2.50 1.10
❑ 79 Tim Hudson 1.00 .45
❑ 80 Rafael Furcal .40 .18
❑ 81 Craig Biggio .60 .25
❑ 82 Edgardo Alfonzo .40 .18
❑ 83 Pat Burrell .40 .18
❑ 84 Adrian Beltre .40 .18
❑ 85 Tony Gwynn 2.00 .90
❑ 86 J.T. Snow .40 .18
❑ 87 Randy Johnson 1.25 .55
❑ 88 Sean Casey .60 .25
❑ 89 Preston Wilson .40 .18
❑ 90 Mike Mussina 1.00 .45
❑ 91 Eric Chavez .40 .18
❑ 92 Tim Salmon .40 .18
❑ 93 Pedro Martinez 1.25 .55
❑ 94 Darryl Kile .40 .18
❑ 95 Greg Maddux 2.50 1.10
❑ 96 Magglio Ordonez .40 .18
❑ 97 Jeff Bagwell 1.25 .55
❑ 98 Timo Perez .40 .18
❑ 99 Jeff Kent .60 .25
❑ 100 Eric Owens .40 .18
❑ 101 Ichiro Suzuki GU RC 120.00 55.00
❑ 102 Elpidio Guzman GU RC 8.00 3.60
❑ 103 Tsuyoshi Shinjo GU RC 25.00 11.00
❑ 104 Travis Hafner GU RC 10.00 4.50
❑ 105 Larry Barnes GU 8.00 3.60
❑ 106 Jaisen Randolph GU RC 8.00 3.60
❑ 107 Paul Phillips GU RC 8.00 3.60

Card	MINT	NRMT
❑ 108 Erick Almonte GU RC	10.00	4.50
❑ 109 Nick Punto GU RC	8.00	3.60
❑ 110 Jack Wilson GU RC	8.00	3.60
❑ 111 Jeremy Owens GU RC	8.00	3.60
❑ 112 Esix Snead GU RC	8.00	3.60
❑ 113 Jay Gibbons GU RC	10.00	4.50
❑ 114 Adrian Hernandez GU RC	8.00	3.60
❑ 115 Matt White GU RC	8.00	3.60
❑ 116 Ryan Freel GU RC	8.00	3.60
❑ 117 Martin Vargas GU RC	8.00	3.60
❑ 118 Winston Abreu GU RC	8.00	3.60
❑ 119 Junior Spivey GU RC	8.00	3.60
❑ 120 Paxton Crawford GU	8.00	3.60
❑ 121 Randy Keisler GU	8.00	3.60
❑ 122 Juan Diaz GU RC	8.00	3.60
❑ 123 Aaron Rowand GU	8.00	3.60
❑ 124 Toby Hall GU	8.00	3.60
❑ 125 Brian Cole GU	8.00	3.60
❑ 126 Aubrey Huff GU	8.00	3.60
❑ 127 Corey Patterson GU	8.00	3.60
❑ 128 Sun Woo Kim GU	8.00	3.60
❑ 129 Jace Brewer GU	8.00	3.60
❑ 130 Cesar Izturis GU	8.00	3.60
❑ NNO Derek Jeter AU/500 EXCH	150.00	70.00

2000 Fleer Greats of the Game

	MINT	NRMT
COMPLETE SET (107)	50.00	22.00
❑ 1 Mickey Mantle	15.00	6.75
❑ 2 Gil Hodges	2.00	.90
❑ 3 Monte Irvin	1.25	.55
❑ 4 Satchel Paige	2.50	1.10
❑ 5 Roy Campanella	2.50	1.10
❑ 6 Richie Ashburn	2.00	.90
❑ 7 Roger Maris	2.50	1.10
❑ 8 Ozzie Smith	2.50	1.10
❑ 9 Reggie Jackson	2.50	1.10
❑ 10 Eddie Mathews	2.00	.90
❑ 11 Dave Righetti	.50	.23
❑ 12 Dave Winfield	2.00	.90
❑ 13 Lou Whitaker	.75	.35
❑ 14 Phil Garner	.50	.23
❑ 15 Ron Cey	.75	.35
❑ 16 Brooks Robinson	2.00	.90
❑ 17 Bruce Sutter	.75	.35
❑ 18 Dave Parker	.75	.35
❑ 19 Johnny Bench	3.00	1.35
❑ 20 Fernando Valenzuela	.75	.35
❑ 21 George Brett	4.00	1.80
❑ 22 Paul Molitor	2.00	.90
❑ 23 Hoyt Wilhelm	.75	.35
❑ 24 Luis Aparicio	1.25	.55
❑ 25 Frank White	.50	.23
❑ 26 Herb Score	.75	.35
❑ 27 Kirk Gibson	.75	.35
❑ 28 Mike Schmidt	3.00	1.35
❑ 29 Don Baylor	.75	.35
❑ 30 Joe Pepitone	.50	.23
❑ 31 Hal McRae	.50	.23
❑ 32 Lee Smith	.50	.23
❑ 33 Nolan Ryan	10.00	4.50
❑ 34 Bill Mazeroski	1.25	.55
❑ 35 Bobby Doerr	1.25	.55
❑ 36 Duke Snider	2.50	1.10
❑ 37 Dick Groat	.75	.35
❑ 38 Larry Doby	.75	.35
❑ 39 Kirby Puckett	5.00	2.20
❑ 40 Steve Carlton	2.00	.90
❑ 41 Dennis Eckersley	.75	.35
❑ 42 Jim Bunning	1.25	.55
❑ 43 Ron Guidry	.75	.35
❑ 44 Alan Trammell	1.25	.55
❑ 45 Bob Feller	2.00	.90
❑ 46 Dave Concepcion	.75	.35
❑ 47 Dwight Evans	.75	.35
❑ 48 Enos Slaughter	1.25	.55
❑ 49 Tom Seaver	2.50	1.10
❑ 50 Tony Oliva	.75	.35
❑ 51 Mel Stottlemyre	.50	.23
❑ 52 Tommy John	.75	.35
❑ 53 Willie McCovey	2.00	.90
❑ 54 Red Schoendienst	.75	.35
❑ 55 Gorman Thomas	.50	.23
❑ 56 Ralph Kiner	.75	.35
❑ 57 Robin Yount	2.00	.90
❑ 58 Andre Dawson	1.25	.55
❑ 59 Al Kaline	2.00	.90
❑ 60 Dom DiMaggio	1.25	.55
❑ 61 Juan Marichal	1.25	.55
❑ 62 Jack Morris	.75	.35
❑ 63 Warren Spahn	2.00	.90
❑ 64 Preacher Roe	.75	.35
❑ 65 Darrell Evans	.50	.23
❑ 66 Jim Bouton	.75	.35
❑ 67 Rocky Colavito	1.25	.55
❑ 68 Bob Gibson	2.00	.90
❑ 69 Whitey Ford	2.00	.90
❑ 70 Moose Skowron	.75	.35
❑ 71 Boog Powell	.75	.35
❑ 72 Al Lopez	1.25	.55
❑ 73 Lou Brock	2.00	.90
❑ 74 Mickey Lolich	.50	.23
❑ 75 Rod Carew	2.00	.90
❑ 76 Bob Lemon	1.25	.55
❑ 77 Frank Howard	.75	.35
❑ 78 Phil Rizzuto	2.00	.90
❑ 79 Carl Yastrzemski	2.50	1.10
❑ 80 Rico Carty	.50	.23
❑ 81 Jim Kaat	.75	.35
❑ 82 Bert Blyleven	.75	.35
❑ 83 George Kell	1.25	.55
❑ 84 Jim Palmer	2.00	.90
❑ 85 Maury Wills	.75	.35
❑ 86 Jim Rice	.75	.35
❑ 87 Joe Carter	.75	.35
❑ 88 Clete Boyer	.75	.35
❑ 89 Yogi Berra	2.50	1.10
❑ 90 Cecil Cooper	.50	.23
❑ 91 Davey Johnson	.75	.35
❑ 92 Lou Boudreau	1.25	.55
❑ 93 Orlando Cepeda	1.25	.55
❑ 94 Tommy Henrich	.75	.35
❑ 95 Hank Bauer	.75	.35
❑ 96 Don Larsen	.75	.35
❑ 97 Vida Blue	.50	.23
❑ 98 Ben Oglivie	.50	.23
❑ 99 Don Mattingly	5.00	2.20
❑ 100 Dale Murphy	2.00	.90
❑ 101 Ferguson Jenkins	2.00	.90
❑ 102 Bobby Bonds	.75	.35
❑ 103 Dick Allen	.75	.35
❑ 104 Stan Musial	2.50	1.10
❑ 105 Gaylord Perry	.75	.35
❑ 106 Willie Randolph	.75	.35
❑ 107 Willie Stargell	1.25	.55
❑ P33 Nolan Ryan Promo	4.00	1.80

2001 Fleer Greats of the Game

	MINT	NRMT
COMPLETE SET (137)	50.00	22.00
❑ 1 Roberto Clemente	5.00	2.20
❑ 2 George Anderson	.75	.35
❑ 3 Babe Ruth	8.00	3.60
❑ 4 Paul Molitor	2.00	.90
❑ 5 Don Larsen	.75	.35
❑ 6 Cy Young	2.00	.90
❑ 7 Billy Martin	1.25	.55
❑ 8 Lou Brock	2.00	.90
❑ 9 Fred Lynn	.75	.35
❑ 10 Johnny VanderMeer	.75	.35
❑ 11 Harmon Killebrew	2.00	.90
❑ 12 Dave Winfield	2.00	.90
❑ 13 Orlando Cepeda	1.25	.55
❑ 14 Johnny Mize	1.25	.55
❑ 15 Walter Johnson	2.00	.90
❑ 16 Roy Campanella	2.50	1.10
❑ 17 Monte Irvin	1.25	.55
❑ 18 Mookie Wilson	.50	.23
❑ 19 Elston Howard	.75	.35
❑ 20 Walter Alston	.75	.35
❑ 21 Rollie Fingers	.75	.35
❑ 22 Brooks Robinson	2.00	.90
❑ 23 Hank Greenberg	2.00	.90
❑ 24 Maury Wills	.75	.35
❑ 25 Rich Gossage	.75	.35
❑ 26 Leon Day	.75	.35
❑ 27 Jimmie Foxx	2.00	.90
❑ 28 Alan Trammell	1.25	.55
❑ 29 Dennis Martinez	.75	.35
❑ 30 Don Drysdale	2.00	.90
❑ 31 Bob Feller	2.00	.90
❑ 32 Jackie Robinson	4.00	1.80
❑ 33 Whitey Ford	2.00	.90
❑ 34 Enos Slaughter	.75	.35
❑ 35 Rod Carew	2.00	.90
❑ 36 Eddie Mathews	2.00	.90
❑ 37 Ron Cey	.75	.35
❑ 38 Thurman Munson	3.00	1.35
❑ 39 Henry Kimbro	.50	.23
❑ 40 Ty Cobb	4.00	1.80
❑ 41 Rocky Colavito	1.25	.55
❑ 42 Satchel Paige	2.50	1.10
❑ 43 Andre Dawson	1.25	.55
❑ 44 Phil Rizzuto	2.00	.90
❑ 45 Roger Maris	3.00	1.35
❑ 46 Bobby Bonds	.75	.35
❑ 47 Joe Carter	.75	.35
❑ 48 Christy Mathewson	2.00	.90
❑ 49 Tony Lazzeri	.75	.35
❑ 50 Gil Hodges	2.00	.90
❑ 51 Ray Dandridge	.75	.35
❑ 52 Gaylord Perry	.75	.35
❑ 53 Ernie Banks	2.50	1.10
❑ 54 Lou Gehrig	5.00	2.20
❑ 55 George Kell	1.25	.55
❑ 56 Wes Parker	.50	.23
❑ 57 Sam Jethroe	.75	.35
❑ 58 Joe Morgan	2.00	.90
❑ 59 Steve Garvey	1.25	.55
❑ 60 Joe Torre	.75	.35
❑ 61 Roger Craig	.50	.23
❑ 62 Warren Spahn	2.00	.90
❑ 63 Willie McCovey	2.00	.90
❑ 64 Cool Papa Bell	.75	.35
❑ 65 Frank Robinson	2.00	.90
❑ 66 Richie Allen	.75	.35
❑ 67 Bucky Dent	.75	.35
❑ 68 George Foster	.75	.35
❑ 69 Hoyt Wilhelm	.75	.35
❑ 70 Phil Niekro	1.25	.55
❑ 71 Buck Leonard	.75	.35
❑ 72 Preacher Roe	.75	.35
❑ 73 Yogi Berra	2.50	1.10
❑ 74 Joe Black	.75	.35

Card	MINT	NRMT
❑ 75 Nolan Ryan	8.00	3.60
❑ 76 Pop Lloyd	.75	.35
❑ 77 Lester Lockett	.50	.23
❑ 78 Paul Blair	.50	.23
❑ 79 Ryne Sandberg	2.50	1.10
❑ 80 Bill Perkins	.50	.23
❑ 81 Frank Howard	.75	.35
❑ 82 Hack Wilson	1.25	.55
❑ 83 Robin Yount	2.00	.90
❑ 84 Harry Heilmann	.75	.35
❑ 85 Mike Schmidt	4.00	1.80
❑ 86 Vida Blue	.50	.23
❑ 87 George Brett	4.00	1.80
❑ 88 Juan Marichal	1.25	.55
❑ 89 Tom Seaver	3.00	1.35
❑ 90 Bill Skowron	.75	.35
❑ 91 Don Mattingly	5.00	2.20
❑ 92 Jim Bunning	1.25	.55
❑ 93 Eddie Murray	2.00	.90
❑ 94 Tommy Lasorda	.75	.35
❑ 95 Pee Wee Reese	2.00	.90
❑ 96 Bill Dickey	1.25	.55
❑ 97 Ozzie Smith	2.50	1.10
❑ 98 Dale Murphy	1.25	.55
❑ 99 Artie Wilson	.50	.23
❑ 100 Bill Terry	.50	.23
❑ 101 Jim Hunter	1.25	.55
❑ 102 Don Sutton	.75	.35
❑ 103 Luis Aparicio	1.25	.55
❑ 104 Reggie Jackson	3.00	1.35
❑ 105 Ted Radcliffe	.75	.35
❑ 106 Carl Erskine	.75	.35
❑ 107 Johnny Bench	3.00	1.35
❑ 108 Carl Furillo	.75	.35
❑ 109 Stan Musial	4.00	1.80
❑ 110 Carlton Fisk	2.00	.90
❑ 111 Rube Foster	.75	.35
❑ 112 Tony Oliva	.75	.35
❑ 113 Hank Bauer	.75	.35
❑ 114 Jim Rice	.75	.35
❑ 115 Willie Mays	5.00	2.20
❑ 116 Ralph Kiner	.75	.35
❑ 117 Al Kaline	2.00	.90
❑ 118 Billy Williams	1.25	.55
❑ 119 Buck O'Neil	.75	.35
❑ 120 Tony Perez	1.25	.55
❑ 121 Dave Parker	.75	.35
❑ 122 Kirk Gibson	.75	.35
❑ 123 Lou Piniella	.50	.23
❑ 124 Ted Williams	6.00	2.70
❑ 125 Steve Carlton	2.00	.90
❑ 126 Dizzy Dean	2.00	.90
❑ 127 Willie Stargell	1.25	.55
❑ 128 Joe Niekro	.50	.23
❑ 129 Lloyd Waner	1.25	.55
❑ 130 Wade Boggs	2.00	.90
❑ 131 Wilmer Fields	.50	.23
❑ 132 Bill Mazeroski	1.25	.55
❑ 133 Duke Snider	2.50	1.10
❑ 134 Joe Williams	.50	.23
❑ 135 Bob Gibson	2.00	.90
❑ 136 Jim Palmer	2.00	.90
❑ 137 Oscar Charleston	.75	.35

2001 Fleer Legacy

	MINT	NRMT
COMP.SET w/o SP's (90)	40.00	18.00
COMMON CARD (1-90)	.75	.35
COMMON CARD (91-105)	15.00	6.75

Card	MINT	NRMT
❑ 1 Pedro Martinez	2.50	1.10
❑ 2 Andruw Jones	2.00	.90
❑ 3 Mike Hampton	.75	.35
❑ 4 Gary Sheffield	.75	.35
❑ 5 Barry Zito	2.00	.90
❑ 6 J.D. Drew	2.00	.90
❑ 7 Charles Johnson	.75	.35
❑ 8 David Wells	.75	.35
❑ 9 Kazuhiro Sasaki	2.00	.90
❑ 10 Vladimir Guerrero	2.50	1.10
❑ 11 Pat Burrell	.75	.35
❑ 12 Ruben Mateo	.75	.35
❑ 13 Greg Maddux	5.00	2.20
❑ 14 Sean Casey	1.25	.55
❑ 15 Craig Biggio	1.25	.55
❑ 16 Bernie Williams	2.00	.90
❑ 17 Jeff Kent	1.25	.55
❑ 18 Nomar Garciaparra	5.00	2.20
❑ 19 Cal Ripken	8.00	3.60
❑ 20 Larry Walker	1.25	.55
❑ 21 Adrian Beltre	.75	.35
❑ 22 Johnny Damon	.75	.35
❑ 23 Rick Ankiel	1.25	.55
❑ 24 Matt Williams	1.25	.55
❑ 25 Magglio Ordonez	.75	.35
❑ 26 Richard Hidalgo	.75	.35
❑ 27 Robin Ventura	.75	.35
❑ 28 Jason Kendall	.75	.35
❑ 29 Tony Batista	.75	.35
❑ 30 Chipper Jones	4.00	1.80
❑ 31 Jim Thome	2.00	.90
❑ 32 Kevin Brown	.75	.35
❑ 33 Mike Mussina	2.00	.90
❑ 34 Mark McGwire	8.00	3.60
❑ 35 Darin Erstad	2.00	.90
❑ 36 Manny Ramirez	2.50	1.10
❑ 37 Bobby Higginson	.75	.35
❑ 38 Richie Sexson	.75	.35
❑ 39 Jason Giambi	2.00	.90
❑ 40 Alex Rodriguez	5.00	2.20
❑ 41 Mark Grace	2.00	.90
❑ 42 Ken Griffey Jr.	6.00	2.70
❑ 43 Moises Alou	.75	.35
❑ 44 Edgardo Alfonzo	.75	.35
❑ 45 Phil Nevin	.75	.35
❑ 46 Rafael Palmeiro	2.00	.90
❑ 47 Javy Lopez	.75	.35
❑ 48 Juan Gonzalez	2.00	.90
❑ 49 Jermaine Dye	.75	.35
❑ 50 Roger Clemens	5.00	2.20
❑ 51 Barry Bonds	5.00	2.20
❑ 52 Carl Everett	.75	.35
❑ 53 Ben Sheets	1.25	.55
❑ 54 Juan Encarnacion	.75	.35
❑ 55 Jeromy Burnitz	.75	.35
❑ 56 Miguel Tejada	.75	.35
❑ 57 Ben Grieve	.75	.35
❑ 58 Randy Johnson	2.50	1.10
❑ 59 Frank Thomas	2.50	1.10
❑ 60 Preston Wilson	.75	.35
❑ 61 Mike Piazza	5.00	2.20
❑ 62 Brian Giles	.75	.35
❑ 63 Carlos Delgado	2.00	.90
❑ 64 Tom Glavine	2.00	.90
❑ 65 Roberto Alomar	2.00	.90
❑ 66 Mike Sweeney	.75	.35
❑ 67 Orlando Hernandez	.75	.35
❑ 68 Edgar Martinez	1.25	.55
❑ 69 Tim Salmon	.75	.35
❑ 70 Kerry Wood	2.00	.90
❑ 71 Jack Wilson RC	1.00	.45
❑ 72 Matt Lawton	.75	.35
❑ 73 Scott Rolen	2.00	.90
❑ 74 Ivan Rodriguez	2.00	.90
❑ 75 Steve Finley	.75	.35
❑ 76 Barry Larkin	2.00	.90
❑ 77 Jeff Bagwell	2.50	1.10
❑ 78 Derek Jeter	8.00	3.60
❑ 79 Tony Gwynn	4.00	1.80
❑ 80 Raul Mondesi	.75	.35
❑ 81 Rafael Furcal	.75	.35
❑ 82 Todd Helton	2.50	1.10
❑ 83 Shawn Green	2.00	.90
❑ 84 Tim Hudson	2.00	.90
❑ 85 Jim Edmonds	1.25	.55
❑ 86 Troy Glaus	2.00	.90
❑ 87 Sammy Sosa	4.00	1.80
❑ 88 Cliff Floyd	.75	.35
❑ 89 Jose Vidro	.75	.35
❑ 90 Bob Abreu	.75	.35
❑ 91 Drew Henson AU RC	120.00	55.00
❑ 92 Andy Morales AU RC	20.00	9.00
❑ 93 Wilson Betemit AU RC	40.00	18.00
❑ 94 Elpidio Guzman AU RC	20.00	9.00
❑ 95 Esix Snead AU RC	20.00	9.00
❑ 96 Winston Abreu AU RC	20.00	9.00
❑ 97 Jeremy Owens AU RC	20.00	9.00
❑ 98 Does Not Exist		
❑ 99 Junior Spivey AU RC	20.00	9.00
❑ 100 Jaisen Randolph AU RC	20.00	9.00
❑ 101 Ichiro Suzuki RC	150.00	70.00
❑ 102 Albert Pujols RC/499	100.00	45.00
❑ 102 Albert Pujols AU/300 EX	200.00	90.00
❑ 103 Tsuyoshi Shinjo RC	30.00	13.50
❑ 104 Jay Gibbons RC	15.00	6.75
❑ 105 Juan Uribe RC	20.00	9.00

2001 Fleer Platinum

	MINT	NRMT
COMPLETE SERIES 1 (301)	300.00	135.00
COMP.SER.1 w/o SP's (250)	40.00	18.00
COMMON CARD (1-250)	.20	.09
COMMON PROSPECT (251-280)	4.00	1.80
COMMON AS (281-300)	4.00	1.80

Card	MINT	NRMT
❑ 1 Bobby Abreu	.30	.14
❑ 2 Brad Radke	.30	.14
❑ 3 Bill Mueller	.20	.09
❑ 4 Adam Eaton	.30	.14
❑ 5 Antonio Alfonseca	.20	.09
❑ 6 Manny Ramirez	1.00	.45
❑ 7 Adam Kennedy	.20	.09
❑ 8 Jose Valentin	.20	.09
❑ 9 Jaret Wright	.20	.09
❑ 10 Aramis Ramirez	.30	.14
❑ 11 Jeff Kent	.50	.23
❑ 12 Juan Encarnacion	.30	.14
❑ 13 Sandy Alomar Jr.	.30	.14
❑ 14 Joe Randa	.20	.09
❑ 15 Darryl Kile	.20	.09
❑ 16 Darren Dreifort	.20	.09
❑ 17 Matt Kinney	.20	.09
❑ 18 Pokey Reese	.20	.09
❑ 19 Ryan Klesko	.30	.14
❑ 20 Shawn Estes	.30	.14
❑ 21 Moises Alou	.30	.14
❑ 22 Edgar Renteria	.20	.09
❑ 23 Chuck Knoblauch	.30	.14
❑ 24 Carl Everett	.30	.14
❑ 25 Garret Anderson	.30	.14
❑ 26 Shane Reynolds	.20	.09
❑ 27 Billy Koch	.20	.09
❑ 28 Carlos Febles	.20	.09
❑ 29 Brian Anderson	.20	.09
❑ 30 Armando Rios	.20	.09
❑ 31 Ryan Kohlmeier	.20	.09
❑ 32 Steve Finley	.30	.14
❑ 33 Brady Anderson	.30	.14
❑ 34 Cal Ripken	3.00	1.35

❑	35	Paul Konerko	.30	.14
❑	36	Chuck Finley	.30	.14
❑	37	Rick Ankiel	.50	.23
❑	38	Mariano Rivera	.30	.14
❑	39	Corey Koskie	.30	.14
❑	40	Cliff Floyd	.30	.14
❑	41	Kevin Appier	.30	.14
❑	42	Henry Rodriguez	.20	.09
❑	43	Mark Kotsay	.30	.14
❑	44	Brook Fordyce	.20	.09
❑	45	Brad Ausmus	.20	.09
❑	46	Alfonso Soriano	.75	.35
❑	47	Ray Lankford	.20	.09
❑	48	Keith Foulke	.20	.09
❑	49	Rich Aurilia	.30	.14
❑	50	Alex Rodriguez	2.00	.90
❑	51	Eric Byrnes	.20	.09
❑	52	Travis Fryman	.30	.14
❑	53	Jeff Bagwell	1.00	.45
❑	54	Scott Rolen	.75	.35
❑	55	Matt Lawton	.30	.14
❑	56	Brad Fullmer	.30	.14
❑	57	Tony Batista	.30	.14
❑	58	Nate Rolison	.20	.09
❑	59	Carlos Lee	.30	.14
❑	60	Rafael Furcal	.30	.14
❑	61	Jay Bell	.30	.14
❑	62	Jimmy Rollins	.30	.14
❑	63	Derrek Lee	.20	.09
❑	64	Andres Galarraga	.50	.23
❑	65	Derek Bell	.20	.09
❑	66	Tim Salmon	.30	.14
❑	67	Travis Lee	.30	.14
❑	68	Kevin Millwood	.20	.09
❑	69	Albert Belle	.30	.14
❑	70	Kazuhiro Sasaki	.75	.35
❑	71	Al Leiter	.30	.14
❑	72	Britt Reames	.20	.09
❑	73	Carlos Beltran	.30	.14
❑	74	Curt Schilling	.75	.35
❑	75	Curtis Leskanic	.20	.09
❑	76	Jeremy Giambi	.20	.09
❑	77	Adrian Beltre	.30	.14
❑	78	David Segui	.20	.09
❑	79	Mike Lieberthal	.30	.14
❑	80	Brian Giles	.30	.14
❑	81	Marvin Benard	.20	.09
❑	82	Aaron Sele	.30	.14
❑	83	Kenny Lofton	.30	.14
❑	84	Doug Glanville	.20	.09
❑	85	Kris Benson	.30	.14
❑	86	Richie Sexson	.30	.14
❑	87	Javy Lopez	.30	.14
❑	88	Doug Mientkiewicz	.30	.14
❑	89	Peter Bergeron	.20	.09
❑	90	Gary Sheffield	.30	.14
❑	91	Derek Lowe	.20	.09
❑	92	Tom Glavine	.75	.35
❑	93	Lance Berkman	.75	.35
❑	94	Chris Singleton	.20	.09
❑	95	Mike Lowell	.30	.14
❑	96	Luis Gonzalez	.75	.35
❑	97	Dante Bichette	.30	.14
❑	98	Mike Sirotka	.20	.09
❑	99	Julio Lugo	.20	.09
❑	100	Juan Gonzalez	.75	.35
❑	101	Craig Biggio	.50	.23
❑	102	Armando Benitez	.30	.14
❑	103	Greg Maddux	2.00	.90
❑	104	Mark Grace	.75	.35
❑	105	John Smoltz	.30	.14
❑	106	J.T. Snow	.30	.14
❑	107	Al Martin	.20	.09
❑	108	Danny Graves	.20	.09
❑	109	Barry Bonds	2.00	.90
❑	110	Lee Stevens	.20	.09
❑	111	Pedro Martinez	1.00	.45
❑	112	Shawn Green	.75	.35
❑	113	Bret Boone	.30	.14
❑	114	Matt Stairs	.20	.09
❑	115	Tino Martinez	.30	.14
❑	116	Rusty Greer	.30	.14
❑	117	Mike Bordick	.20	.09
❑	118	Garrett Stephenson	.20	.09
❑	119	Edgar Martinez	.50	.23
❑	120	Ben Grieve	.30	.14
❑	121	Milton Bradley	.20	.09
❑	122	Aaron Boone	.20	.09
❑	123	Ruben Mateo	.30	.14
❑	124	Ken Griffey Jr.	2.50	1.10
❑	125	Russell Branyan	.30	.14
❑	126	Shannon Stewart	.30	.14
❑	127	Fred McGriff	.50	.23
❑	128	Ben Petrick	.20	.09
❑	129	Kevin Brown	.30	.14
❑	130	B.J. Surhoff	.30	.14
❑	131	Mark McGwire	3.00	1.35
❑	132	Carlos Guillen	.20	.09
❑	133	Adrian Brown	.20	.09
❑	134	Mike Sweeney	.30	.14
❑	135	Eric Milton	.30	.14
❑	136	Cristian Guzman	.30	.14
❑	137	Ellis Burks	.30	.14
❑	138	Fernando Tatis	.20	.09
❑	139	Bengie Molina	.20	.09
❑	140	Tony Gwynn	1.50	.70
❑	141	Jeromy Burnitz	.30	.14
❑	142	Miguel Tejada	.30	.14
❑	143	Raul Mondesi	.30	.14
❑	144	Jeffrey Hammonds	.20	.09
❑	145	Pat Burrell	.30	.14
❑	146	Frank Thomas	1.00	.45
❑	147	Eric Munson	.30	.14
❑	148	Mike Hampton	.30	.14
❑	149	Mike Cameron	.30	.14
❑	150	Jim Thome	.75	.35
❑	151	Mike Mussina	.75	.35
❑	152	Rick Helling	.20	.09
❑	153	Ken Caminiti	.30	.14
❑	154	John VanderWal	.20	.09
❑	155	Denny Neagle	.20	.09
❑	156	Robb Nen	.30	.14
❑	157	Jose Canseco	.75	.35
❑	158	Mo Vaughn	.30	.14
❑	159	Phil Nevin	.30	.14
❑	160	Pat Hentgen	.20	.09
❑	161	Sean Casey	.50	.23
❑	162	Greg Vaughn	.30	.14
❑	163	Trot Nixon	.30	.14
❑	164	Roberto Hernandez	.20	.09
❑	165	Vinny Castilla	.30	.14
❑	166	Robin Ventura	.30	.14
❑	167	Alex Ochoa	.20	.09
❑	168	Orlando Hernandez	.30	.14
❑	169	Luis Castillo	.20	.09
❑	170	Quilvio Veras	.20	.09
❑	171	Troy O'Leary	.20	.09
❑	172	Livan Hernandez	.30	.14
❑	173	Roger Cedeno	.20	.09
❑	174	Jose Vidro	.30	.14
❑	175	John Olerud	.30	.14
❑	176	Richard Hidalgo	.30	.14
❑	177	Eric Chavez	.30	.14
❑	178	Fernando Vina	.20	.09
❑	179	Chris Stynes	.20	.09
❑	180	Bobby Higginson	.30	.14
❑	181	Bruce Chen	.20	.09
❑	182	Omar Vizquel	.30	.14
❑	183	Rey Ordonez	.20	.09
❑	184	Trevor Hoffman	.30	.14
❑	185	Jeff Cirillo	.30	.14
❑	186	Billy Wagner	.30	.14
❑	187	David Ortiz	.30	.14
❑	188	Tim Hudson	.75	.35
❑	189	Tony Clark	.30	.14
❑	190	Larry Walker	.50	.23
❑	191	Eric Owens	.20	.09
❑	192	Aubrey Huff	.20	.09
❑	193	Royce Clayton	.20	.09
❑	194	Todd Walker	.20	.09
❑	195	Rafael Palmeiro	.75	.35
❑	196	Todd Hundley	.20	.09
❑	197	Roger Clemens	2.00	.90
❑	198	Jeff Weaver	.30	.14
❑	199	Dean Palmer	.30	.14
❑	200	Geoff Jenkins	.30	.14
❑	201	Matt Clement	.20	.09
❑	202	David Wells	.30	.14
❑	203	Chan Ho Park	.30	.14
❑	204	Hideo Nomo	.75	.35
❑	205	Bartolo Colon	.30	.14
❑	206	John Wetteland	.30	.14
❑	207	Corey Patterson	.30	.14
❑	208	Freddy Garcia	.30	.14
❑	209	David Cone	.30	.14
❑	210	Rondell White	.30	.14
❑	211	Carl Pavano	.20	.09
❑	212	Charles Johnson	.30	.14
❑	213	Ron Coomer	.20	.09
❑	214	Matt Williams	.50	.23
❑	215	Jay Payton	.20	.09
❑	216	Nick Johnson	.30	.14
❑	217	Deivi Cruz	.20	.09
❑	218	Scott Elarton	.20	.09
❑	219	Neifi Perez	.20	.09
❑	220	Jason Isringhausen	.20	.09
❑	221	Jose Cruz Jr.	.30	.14
❑	222	Gerald Williams	.20	.09
❑	223	Timo Perez	.20	.09
❑	224	Damion Easley	.20	.09
❑	225	Jeff D'Amico	.20	.09
❑	226	Preston Wilson	.30	.14
❑	227	Robert Person	.20	.09
❑	228	Jacque Jones	.30	.14
❑	229	Johnny Damon	.30	.14
❑	230	Tony Womack	.20	.09
❑	231	Adam Piatt	.30	.14
❑	232	Brian Jordan	.30	.14
❑	233	Ben Davis	.30	.14
❑	234	Kerry Wood	.75	.35
❑	235	Mike Piazza	2.00	.90
❑	236	David Justice	.30	.14
❑	237	Dave Veres	.20	.09
❑	238	Eric Young	.20	.09
❑	239	Juan Pierre	.30	.14
❑	240	Gabe Kapler	.30	.14
❑	241	Ryan Dempster	.30	.14
❑	242	Dmitri Young	.30	.14
❑	243	Jorge Posada	.30	.14
❑	244	Eric Karros	.30	.14
❑	245	J.D. Drew	.75	.35
❑	246	Todd Zeile	.30	.14
❑	247	Mark Quinn	.30	.14
❑	248	Kenny Kelly UER	.20	.09
		Listed as a Mariner on the front		
❑	249	Jermaine Dye	.30	.14
❑	250	Barry Zito	.75	.35
❑	251	Jason Hart	4.00	1.80
		Larry Barnes		
❑	252	Ichiro Suzuki RC	40.00	18.00
		Elpidio Guzman RC		
❑	253	Tsuyoshi Shinjo RC	8.00	3.60
		Brian Cole		
❑	254	John Barnes	4.00	1.80
		Adrian Hernandez RC		
❑	255	Jason Tyner	4.00	1.80
		Jace Brewer		
❑	256	Brian Buchanan	4.00	1.80
		Luis Rivas		
❑	257	Brent Abernathy	4.00	1.80
		Jose Ortiz		
❑	258	Marcus Giles	4.00	1.80
		Keith Ginter		
❑	259	Tike Redman	4.00	1.80
		Jaisen Randolph RC		
❑	260	Dane Sardinha	4.00	1.80
		David Espinosa		
❑	261	Josh Beckett	5.00	2.20
		Craig House		
❑	262	Jack Cust	4.00	1.80
		Hiram Bocachica		
❑	263	Alex Escobar	4.00	1.80
		Esix Snead RC		
❑	264	Chris Richard	4.00	1.80
		Vernon Wells		
❑	265	Pedro Feliz	4.00	1.80
		Xavier Nady		
❑	266	Brandon Inge	4.00	1.80
		Joe Crede		
❑	267	Ben Sheets	5.00	2.20
		Roy Oswalt		
❑	268	Drew Henson RC	12.00	5.50
		Andy Morales RC		
❑	269	C.C. Sabathia	4.00	1.80
		Justin Miller		
❑	270	David Eckstein	4.00	1.80
		Jason Grabowski		
❑	271	Dee Brown	4.00	1.80

Card	MINT	NRMT
Chris Wakeland		
❑ 272 Junior Spivey RC	4.00	1.80
Alex Cintron		
❑ 273 Elvis Pena	5.00	2.20
Juan Uribe RC		
❑ 274 Carlos Pena	4.00	1.80
Jason Romano		
❑ 275 Winston Abreu	10.00	4.50
Wilson Betemit		
❑ 276 Jose Mieses RC	4.00	1.80
Nick Neugebauer		
❑ 277 Shea Hillenbrand	4.00	1.80
Dernell Stenson		
❑ 278 Jared Sandberg	4.00	1.80
Toby Hall		
❑ 279 Jay Gibbons RC	4.00	1.80
Ivanon Coffie		
❑ 280 Pablo Ozuna	4.00	1.80
Santiago Perez		
❑ 281 Nomar Garciaparra AS	10.00	4.50
❑ 282 Derek Jeter AS	15.00	6.75
❑ 283 Jason Giambi AS	4.00	1.80
❑ 284 Magglio Ordonez AS	4.00	1.80
❑ 285 Ivan Rodriguez AS	.75	.35
❑ 286 Troy Glaus AS	.75	.35
❑ 287 Carlos Delgado AS	4.00	1.80
❑ 288 Darin Erstad AS	4.00	1.80
❑ 289 Bernie Williams AS	4.00	1.80
❑ 290 Roberto Alomar AS	4.00	1.80
❑ 291 Barry Larkin AS	4.00	1.80
❑ 292 Chipper Jones AS	8.00	3.60
❑ 293 Vladimir Guerrero AS	5.00	2.20
❑ 294 Sammy Sosa AS	8.00	3.60
❑ 295 Todd Helton AS	5.00	2.20
❑ 296 Randy Johnson AS	5.00	2.20
❑ 297 Jason Kendall AS	4.00	1.80
❑ 298 Jim Edmonds AS	4.00	1.80
❑ 299 Andruw Jones AS	4.00	1.80
❑ 300 Edgardo Alfonzo AS	4.00	1.80
❑ 301 Albert Pujols RC	80.00	36.00
Donaldo Mendez RC/1500		

2001 Fleer Premium

	MINT	NRMT
COMP.SET w/o SP's (200)	30.00	13.50
COMMON CARD (1-200)	.20	.09
COMMON CARD (201-230)	8.00	3.60
COMMON EXCH. (231-235)	20.00	9.00

Card	MINT	NRMT
❑ 1 Cal Ripken	3.00	1.35
❑ 2 Derek Jeter	3.00	1.35
❑ 3 Edgardo Alfonzo	.30	.14
❑ 4 Luis Castillo	.20	.09
❑ 5 Mike Lieberthal	.30	.14
❑ 6 Kazuhiro Sasaki	1.00	.45
❑ 7 Jeff Kent	.50	.23
❑ 8 Eric Karros	.30	.14
❑ 9 Tom Glavine	.75	.35
❑ 10 Jeromy Burnitz	.30	.14
❑ 11 Travis Fryman	.30	.14
❑ 12 Ron Coomer	.20	.09
❑ 13 Jeff D'Amico	.20	.09
❑ 14 Carlos Febles	.20	.09
❑ 15 Kevin Brown	.30	.14
❑ 16 Deivi Cruz	.20	.09
❑ 17 Tino Martinez	.30	.14
❑ 18 Bobby Abreu	.30	.14
❑ 19 Roger Clemens	2.00	.90
❑ 20 Jeffrey Hammonds	.20	.09
❑ 21 Peter Bergeron	.20	.09
❑ 22 Ray Lankford	.20	.09
❑ 23 Scott Rolen	.75	.35
❑ 24 Jermaine Dye	.30	.14
❑ 25 Rusty Greer	.30	.14
❑ 26 Frank Thomas	1.00	.45
❑ 27 Jeff Bagwell	1.00	.45
❑ 28 Cliff Floyd	.30	.14
❑ 29 Chris Singleton	.20	.09
❑ 30 Steve Finley	.30	.14
❑ 31 Orlando Hernandez	.30	.14
❑ 32 Tom Goodwin	.20	.09
❑ 33 Larry Walker	.50	.23
❑ 34 Mike Sweeney	.30	.14
❑ 35 Tim Hudson	.75	.35
❑ 36 Kerry Wood	.75	.35
❑ 37 Mike Lowell	.30	.14
❑ 38 Andruw Jones	.75	.35
❑ 39 Alex Gonzalez	.20	.09
❑ 40 Juan Gonzalez	.75	.35
❑ 41 J.D. Drew	.75	.35
❑ 42 Mark McLemore	.20	.09
❑ 43 Royce Clayton	.20	.09
❑ 44 Paul O'Neill	.75	.35
❑ 45 Carlos Beltran	.30	.14
❑ 46 Phil Nevin	.30	.14
❑ 47 Rondell White	.30	.14
❑ 48 Gerald Williams	.20	.09
❑ 49 Geoff Jenkins	.30	.14
❑ 50 Marvin Benard	.20	.09
❑ 51 Alex Rodriguez	2.00	.90
❑ 52 Moises Alou	.30	.14
❑ 53 Mike Lansing	.20	.09
❑ 54 Omar Vizquel	.30	.14
❑ 55 Eric Chavez	.30	.14
❑ 56 Mark Quinn	.30	.14
❑ 57 Mike Lamb	.20	.09
❑ 58 Rick Ankiel	.50	.23
❑ 59 Lance Berkman	.75	.35
❑ 60 Jeff Conine	.20	.09
❑ 61 B.J. Surhoff	.30	.14
❑ 62 Todd Helton	1.00	.45
❑ 63 J.T. Snow	.30	.14
❑ 64 John VanderWal	.20	.09
❑ 65 Johnny Damon	.30	.14
❑ 66 Bobby Higginson	.30	.14
❑ 67 Carlos Delgado	.75	.35
❑ 68 Shawn Green	.75	.35
❑ 69 Mike Redmond	.20	.09
❑ 70 Mike Piazza	2.00	.90
❑ 71 Adrian Beltre	.30	.14
❑ 72 Juan Encarnacion	.30	.14
❑ 73 Chipper Jones	1.50	.70
❑ 74 Garret Anderson	.30	.14
❑ 75 Paul Konerko	.30	.14
❑ 76 Barry Larkin	.75	.35
❑ 77 Tony Gwynn	1.50	.70
❑ 78 Rafael Palmeiro	.75	.35
❑ 79 Randy Johnson	1.00	.45
❑ 80 Mark Grace	.75	.35
❑ 81 Javy Lopez	.30	.14
❑ 82 Gabe Kapler	.30	.14
❑ 83 Henry Rodriguez	.20	.09
❑ 84 Raul Mondesi	.30	.14
❑ 85 Adam Piatt	.30	.14
❑ 86 Marquis Grissom	.20	.09
❑ 87 Charles Johnson	.30	.14
❑ 88 Sean Casey	.50	.23
❑ 89 Manny Ramirez	1.00	.45
❑ 90 Curt Schilling	.75	.35
❑ 91 Fernando Tatis	.20	.09
❑ 92 Derek Bell	.20	.09
❑ 93 Tony Clark	.30	.14
❑ 94 Homer Bush	.20	.09
❑ 95 Nomar Garciaparra	2.00	.90
❑ 96 Vinny Castilla	.30	.14
❑ 97 Ben Davis	.30	.14
❑ 98 Carl Everett	.30	.14
❑ 99 Damion Easley	.20	.09
❑ 100 Craig Biggio	.50	.23
❑ 101 Todd Hollandsworth	.20	.09
❑ 102 Jay Payton	.20	.09
❑ 103 Gary Sheffield	.30	.14
❑ 104 Sandy Alomar Jr.	.30	.14
❑ 105 Doug Glanville	.20	.09
❑ 106 Barry Bonds	2.00	.90
❑ 107 Tim Salmon	.30	.14
❑ 108 Terrence Long	.30	.14
❑ 109 Jorge Posada	.30	.14
❑ 110 Jose Offerman	.20	.09
❑ 111 Edgar Martinez	.50	.23
❑ 112 Jeremy Giambi	.20	.09
❑ 113 Dean Palmer	.30	.14
❑ 114 Roberto Alomar	.75	.35
❑ 115 Aaron Boone	.20	.09
❑ 116 Adam Kennedy	.20	.09
❑ 117 Joe Randa	.20	.09
❑ 118 Jose Vidro	.30	.14
❑ 119 Tony Batista	.30	.14
❑ 120 Kevin Young	.20	.09
❑ 121 Preston Wilson	30	.14
❑ 122 Jason Kendall	.30	.14
❑ 123 Mark Kotsay	.30	.14
❑ 124 Timo Perez	.20	.09
❑ 125 Eric Young	.20	.09
❑ 126 Greg Maddux	2.00	.90
❑ 127 Richard Hidalgo	.30	.14
❑ 128 Brian Giles	.30	.14
❑ 129 Fred McGriff	.50	.23
❑ 130 Troy Glaus	.75	.35
❑ 131 Todd Walker	.20	.09
❑ 132 Brady Anderson	.30	.14
❑ 133 Jim Edmonds	.50	.23
❑ 134 Ben Grieve	.30	.14
❑ 135 Greg Vaughn	.30	.14
❑ 136 Robin Ventura	.30	.14
❑ 137 Sammy Sosa	1.50	.70
❑ 138 Rich Aurilia	.30	.14
❑ 139 Jose Valentin	.20	.09
❑ 140 Trot Nixon	.30	.14
❑ 141 Troy Percival	.20	.09
❑ 142 Bernie Williams	.75	.35
❑ 143 Warren Morris	.20	.09
❑ 144 Jacque Jones	.30	.14
❑ 145 Danny Bautista	.20	.09
❑ 146 A.J. Pierzynski	.20	.09
❑ 147 Mark McGwire	3.00	1.35
❑ 148 Rafael Furcal	.30	.14
❑ 149 Ray Durham	.30	.14
❑ 150 Mike Mussina	.75	.35
❑ 151 Jay Bell	.30	.14
❑ 152 David Wells	.30	.14
❑ 153 Ken Caminiti	.30	.14
❑ 154 Jim Thome	.75	.35
❑ 155 Ivan Rodriguez	.75	.35
❑ 156 Milton Bradley	.20	.09
❑ 157 Ken Griffey Jr.	2.50	1.10
❑ 158 Al Leiter	.30	.14
❑ 159 Corey Koskie	.30	.14
❑ 160 Shannon Stewart	.30	.14
❑ 161 Mo Vaughn	.30	.14
❑ 162 Pedro Martinez	1.00	.45
❑ 163 Todd Hundley	.20	.09
❑ 164 Darin Erstad	.75	.35
❑ 165 Ruben Rivera	.20	.09
❑ 166 Richie Sexson	.30	.14
❑ 167 Andres Galarraga	.50	.23
❑ 168 Darryl Kile	.20	.09
❑ 169 Jose Cruz Jr.	.30	.14
❑ 170 David Justice	.30	.14
❑ 171 Vladimir Guerrero	1.00	.45
❑ 172 Jeff Cirillo	.30	.14
❑ 173 John Olerud	.30	.14
❑ 174 Devon White	.20	.09
❑ 175 Ron Belliard	.20	.09
❑ 176 Pokey Reese	.20	.09
❑ 177 Mike Hampton	.30	.14
❑ 178 David Ortiz	.30	.14
❑ 179 Magglio Ordonez	.30	.14
❑ 180 Ruben Mateo	.30	.14
❑ 181 Carlos Lee	.30	.14
❑ 182 Matt Williams	.50	.23
❑ 183 Miguel Tejada	.30	.14
❑ 184 Scott Elarton	.20	.09
❑ 185 Bret Boone	.30	.14
❑ 186 Pat Burrell	.30	.14
❑ 187 Brad Radke	.30	.14
❑ 188 Brian Jordan	.30	.14
❑ 189 Matt Lawton	.30	.14
❑ 190 Al Martin	.20	.09

#	Card	MINT	NRMT
❑ 191	Albert Belle	.30	.14
❑ 192	Tony Womack	.20	.09
❑ 193	Roger Cedeno	.20	.09
❑ 194	Travis Lee	.30	.14
❑ 195	Dmitri Young	.30	.14
❑ 196	Jay Buhner	.30	.14
❑ 197	Jason Giambi	.75	.35
❑ 198	Jason Tyner	.20	.09
❑ 199	Ben Petrick	.20	.09
❑ 200	Jose Canseco	.75	.35
❑ 201	Nick Johnson	8.00	3.60
❑ 202	Jace Brewer	8.00	3.60
❑ 203	Ryan Freel RC	8.00	3.60
❑ 204	Jaisen Randolph RC	8.00	3.60
❑ 205	Marcus Giles	8.00	3.60
❑ 206	Claudio Vargas RC	8.00	3.60
❑ 207	Brian Cole	8.00	3.60
❑ 208	Scott Hodges	8.00	3.60
❑ 209	Winston Abreu RC	8.00	3.60
❑ 210	Shea Hillenbrand	8.00	3.60
❑ 211	Larry Barnes	8.00	3.60
❑ 212	Paul Phillips RC	8.00	3.60
❑ 213	Pedro Santana RC	8.00	3.60
❑ 214	Ivanon Coffie	8.00	3.60
❑ 215	Junior Spivey RC	8.00	3.60
❑ 216	Donzell McDonald	8.00	3.60
❑ 217	Vernon Wells	8.00	3.60
❑ 218	Corey Patterson	8.00	3.60
❑ 219	Sang-Hoon Lee	8.00	3.60
❑ 220	Jack Cust	8.00	3.60
❑ 221	Jason Romano	8.00	3.60
❑ 222	Jack Wilson RC	8.00	3.60
❑ 223	Adam Everett	8.00	3.60
❑ 224	Esix Snead RC	8.00	3.60
❑ 225	Jason Hart	10.00	4.50
❑ 226	Joe Lawrence	8.00	3.60
❑ 227	Brandon Inge	8.00	3.60
❑ 228	Alex Escobar	8.00	3.60
❑ 229	Abraham Nunez	8.00	3.60
❑ 230	Jared Sandberg	8.00	3.60
❑ 231	Ichiro Suzuki RC	100.00	45.00
❑ 232	Tsuyoshi Shinjo RC	25.00	11.00
❑ 233	Albert Pujols RC	60.00	27.00
❑ 234	Wilson Betemit RC	20.00	9.00
❑ 235	Drew Henson RC	40.00	18.00
❑ MM1	Derek Jeter MM/1995	15.00	6.75
❑ NNO	D. Jeter MM AU/95 EXCH	200.00	90.00

2001 Fleer Red Sox 100th

	MINT	NRMT
COMPLETE SET (100)	40.00	18.00

#	Card	MINT	NRMT
❑ 1	Carl Yastrzemski	3.00	1.35
❑ 2	Mel Parnell	.25	.11
❑ 3	Birdie Tebbetts	.25	.11
❑ 4	Tex Hughson	.25	.11
❑ 5	Nomar Garciaparra	4.00	1.80
❑ 6	Fred Lynn	.50	.23
❑ 7	John Valentin	.25	.11
❑ 8	Rico Petrocelli	.25	.11
❑ 9	Ted Williams	5.00	2.20
❑ 10	Roger Clemens	4.00	1.80
❑ 11	Luis Aparicio	1.00	.45
❑ 12	Cy Young	2.00	.90
❑ 13	Carlton Fisk	1.50	.70
❑ 14	Pedro Martinez	2.00	.90
❑ 15	Joe Dobson	.25	.11
❑ 16	Babe Ruth	6.00	2.70
❑ 17	Doc Cramer	.25	.11
❑ 18	Pete Runnels	.25	.11
❑ 19	Tony Conigliaro	1.00	.45
❑ 20	Bill Monbouquette	.25	.11
❑ 21	Boo Ferriss	.25	.11
❑ 22	Harry Hooper	1.00	.45
❑ 23	Tony Armas	.25	.11
❑ 24	Joe Cronin	1.50	.70
❑ 25	Rick Ferrell	.50	.23
❑ 26	Wade Boggs	1.50	.70
❑ 27	Don Baylor	.50	.23
❑ 28	Jeff Reardon	.50	.23
❑ 29	Joe Wood	1.00	.45
❑ 30	Mo Vaughn	.50	.23
❑ 31	Walt Dropo	.25	.11
❑ 32	Vern Stephens	.25	.11
❑ 33	Bernie Carbo	.25	.11
❑ 34	George Scott	.25	.11
❑ 35	Lefty Grove	1.50	.70
❑ 36	Dom DiMaggio	1.50	.70
❑ 37	Dennis Eckersley	.50	.23
❑ 38	Johnny Pesky	.25	.11
❑ 39	Jim Lonborg	.25	.11
❑ 40	Jimmy Piersall	.50	.23
❑ 41	Tris Speaker	1.50	.70
❑ 42	Frank Malzone	.25	.11
❑ 43	Bobby Doerr	1.00	.45
❑ 44	Jimmie Foxx	2.00	.90
❑ 45	Tony Pena	.25	.11
❑ 46	Billy Goodman	.25	.11
❑ 47	Jim Rice	.50	.23
❑ 48	Reggie Smith	.50	.23
❑ 49	Bill Buckner	.50	.23
❑ 50	Earl Wilson	.25	.11
❑ 51	Rick Burleson	.25	.11
❑ 52	George Kell	1.00	.45
❑ 53	Dick Radatz	.25	.11
❑ 54	Dwight Evans	.50	.23
❑ 55	Luis Tiant	.50	.23
❑ 56	Elijah Green	.25	.11
❑ 57	Gene Conley	.25	.11
❑ 58	Jackie Jensen	.50	.23
❑ 59	Mike Fornieles	.25	.11
❑ 60	Dutch Leonard	.25	.11
❑ 61	Jake Stahl	.25	.11
❑ 62	Don Schwall	.25	.11
❑ 63	Jimmy Collins	.50	.23
❑ 64	Herb Pennock	1.00	.45
❑ 65	Red Ruffing	1.00	.45
❑ 66	Carney Lansford	.50	.23
❑ 67	Dick Stuart	.25	.11
❑ 68	Dave Morehead	.25	.11
❑ 69	Harry Agganis	.50	.23
❑ 70	Lou Boudreau MGR	.50	.23
❑ 71	Joe Morgan MGR	.25	.11
❑ 72	Don Zimmer MGR	.50	.23
❑ 73	Tom Yawkey OWN	.50	.23
❑ 74	Jean Yawkey OWN	.25	.11
❑ 75	Boston Red Sox	.50	.23
	Origin of the Red Sox		
❑ 76	Boston Red Sox	.50	.23
	The First Season - 1901		
❑ 77	Boston Red Sox	.50	.23
	World Series Triumphs		
❑ 78	Carl Yastrzemski BB	1.50	.70
❑ 79	Carlton Fisk BB	.50	.23
❑ 80	Dom DiMaggio BB	.50	.23
❑ 81	Wade Boggs BB	.50	.23
❑ 82	Nomar Garciaparra BB	2.00	.90
❑ 83	Pedro Martinez BB	1.00	.45
❑ 84	Ted Williams BB	2.50	1.10
❑ 85	Jim Rice BB	.25	.11
❑ 86	Fred Lynn BB	.25	.11
❑ 87	Mo Vaughn BB	.25	.11
❑ 88	Bobby Doerr BB UER	.50	.23
	Card Pictures Lou Boudreau		
❑ 89	Bernie Carbo BB	.25	.11
❑ 90	Dennis Eckersley BB	.25	.11
❑ 91	Jimmy Piersall BB	.25	.11
❑ 92	Luis Tiant BB	.25	.11
❑ 93	Fenway Park	.25	.11
	Jimmy Fund signage		
❑ 94	Fenway Park	.25	.11
	Green Monster w/Ads		
❑ 95	Fenway Park	.25	.11
	Green Monster w/All-Star logo		
❑ 96	Fenway Park	.25	.11
	Ladder shot on Green Monster		
❑ 97	Fenway Park	.25	.11
	Manual scoreboard		
❑ 98	Fenway Park	.25	.11
	Panoramic of Fenway Park		
❑ 99	Fenway Park	.25	.11
	Lansdowne Street		
❑ 100	Fenway Park	.25	.11
	1999 All-Star Game		
❑ NNO	Field the Game/7150 EXCH	50.00	22.00

2000 Fleer Showcase

	MINT	NRMT
COMPLETE SET (140)	600.00	275.00
COMP.SET w/o SP's (100)	30.00	13.50
COMMON CARD (1-100)	.25	.11
COMMON CARD (101-115)	15.00	6.75
COMMON CARD (116-140)	10.00	4.50

#	Card	MINT	NRMT
❑ 1	Alex Rodriguez	2.50	1.10
❑ 2	Derek Jeter	4.00	1.80
❑ 3	Jeromy Burnitz	.40	.18
❑ 4	John Olerud	.40	.18
❑ 5	Paul Konerko	.40	.18
❑ 6	Johnny Damon	.40	.18
❑ 7	Curt Schilling	1.00	.45
❑ 8	Barry Larkin	1.00	.45
❑ 9	Adrian Beltre	.40	.18
❑ 10	Scott Rolen	.60	.25
❑ 11	Carlos Delgado	1.00	.45
❑ 12	Pedro Martinez	1.25	.55
❑ 13	Todd Helton	1.25	.55
❑ 14	Jacque Jones	.40	.18
❑ 15	Jeff Kent	.60	.25
❑ 16	Darin Erstad	1.00	.45
❑ 17	Juan Encarnacion	.40	.18
❑ 18	Roger Clemens	2.50	1.10
❑ 19	Tony Gwynn	2.00	.90
❑ 20	Nomar Garciaparra	2.50	1.10
❑ 21	Roberto Alomar	1.00	.45
❑ 22	Matt Lawton	.40	.18
❑ 23	Rich Aurilia	.40	.18
❑ 24	Charles Johnson	.40	.18
❑ 25	Jim Thome	1.00	.45
❑ 26	Eric Milton	.40	.18
❑ 27	Barry Bonds	2.50	1.10
❑ 28	Albert Belle	.40	.18
❑ 29	Travis Fryman	.40	.18
❑ 30	Ken Griffey Jr.	3.00	1.35
❑ 31	Phil Nevin	.40	.18
❑ 32	Chipper Jones	2.00	.90
❑ 33	Craig Biggio	.60	.25
❑ 34	Mike Hampton	.40	.18
❑ 35	Fred McGriff	.60	.25
❑ 36	Cal Ripken	4.00	1.80
❑ 37	Manny Ramirez	1.25	.55
❑ 38	Jose Vidro	.40	.18
❑ 39	Trevor Hoffman	.40	.18
❑ 40	Tom Glavine	1.00	.45
❑ 41	Frank Thomas	1.25	.55
❑ 42	Chris Widger	.25	.11
❑ 43	J.D. Drew	1.00	.45
❑ 44	Andres Galarraga	.60	.25
❑ 45	Pokey Reese	.25	.11

❑ 46 Mike Piazza	2.50	1.10
❑ 47 Kevin Young	.25	.11
❑ 48 Sean Casey	.60	.25
❑ 49 Carlos Beltran	.40	.18
❑ 50 Jason Kendall	.40	.18
❑ 51 Vladimir Guerrero	1.25	.55
❑ 52 Jermaine Dye	.40	.18
❑ 53 Brian Giles	.40	.18
❑ 54 Andruw Jones	1.00	.45
❑ 55 Richard Hidalgo	.40	.18
❑ 56 Robin Ventura	.40	.18
❑ 57 Ivan Rodriguez	1.00	.45
❑ 58 Greg Maddux	2.50	1.10
❑ 59 Billy Wagner	.25	.11
❑ 60 Ruben Mateo	.40	.18
❑ 61 Troy Glaus	1.00	.45
❑ 62 Dean Palmer	.40	.18
❑ 63 Eric Chavez	.40	.18
❑ 64 Edgar Martinez	.40	.18
❑ 65 Randy Johnson	1.25	.55
❑ 66 Preston Wilson	.40	.18
❑ 67 Orlando Hernandez	.40	.18
❑ 68 Jim Edmonds	.60	.25
❑ 69 Carl Everett	.40	.18
❑ 70 Larry Walker	.60	.25
❑ 71 Ron Belliard	.25	.11
❑ 72 Sammy Sosa	2.00	.90
❑ 73 Matt Williams	.40	.18
❑ 74 Cliff Floyd	.40	.18
❑ 75 Bernie Williams	1.00	.45
❑ 76 Fernando Tatis	.25	.11
❑ 77 Steve Finley	.40	.18
❑ 78 Jeff Bagwell	1.25	.55
❑ 79 Edgardo Alfonzo	.40	.18
❑ 80 Jose Canseco	1.00	.45
❑ 81 Magglio Ordonez	.40	.18
❑ 82 Shawn Green	1.00	.45
❑ 83 Bobby Abreu	.40	.18
❑ 84 Tony Batista	.40	.18
❑ 85 Mo Vaughn	.40	.18
❑ 86 Juan Gonzalez	1.00	.45
❑ 87 Paul O'Neill	1.00	.45
❑ 88 Mark McGwire	4.00	1.80
❑ 89 Mark Grace	1.00	.45
❑ 90 Kevin Brown	.40	.18
❑ 91 Ben Grieve	.40	.18
❑ 92 Shannon Stewart	.40	.18
❑ 93 Erubiel Durazo	.40	.18
❑ 94 Antonio Alfonseca	.25	.11
❑ 95 Jeff Cirillo	.40	.18
❑ 96 Greg Vaughn	.40	.18
❑ 97 Kerry Wood	1.00	.45
❑ 98 Geoff Jenkins	.40	.18
❑ 99 Jason Giambi	1.00	.45
❑ 100 Rafael Palmeiro	1.00	.45
❑ 101 Rafael Furcal PROS	20.00	9.00
❑ 102 Pablo Ozuna PROS	15.00	6.75
❑ 103 Brad Penny PROS	15.00	6.75
❑ 104 Mark Mulder PROS	20.00	9.00
❑ 105 Adam Piatt PROS	15.00	6.75
❑ 106 Mike Lamb PROS RC	15.00	6.75
❑ 107 K.Sasaki PROS RC	30.00	13.50
❑ 108 A.McNeal PROS RC	15.00	6.75
❑ 109 Pat Burrell PROS	20.00	9.00
❑ 110 Rick Ankiel PROS	20.00	9.00
❑ 111 Eric Munson PROS	15.00	6.75
❑ 112 Josh Beckett PROS	25.00	11.00
❑ 113 Adam Kennedy PROS	15.00	6.75
❑ 114 Alex Escobar PROS	15.00	6.75
❑ 115 C.Hermansen PROS	15.00	6.75
❑ 116 Kip Wells PROS	10.00	4.50
❑ 117 Matt LeCroy PROS	10.00	4.50
❑ 118 Julio Ramirez PROS	10.00	4.50
❑ 119 Ben Petrick PROS	10.00	4.50
❑ 120 Nick Johnson PROS	15.00	6.75
❑ 121 G.Dawkins PROS	10.00	4.50
❑ 122 Julio Zuleta PROS RC	10.00	4.50
❑ 123 A.Soriano PROS	15.00	6.75
❑ 124 K.McDonald RC	10.00	4.50
❑ 125 Kory DeHaan PROS	10.00	4.50
❑ 126 Vernon Wells PROS	10.00	4.50
❑ 127 D.Stenson PROS	10.00	4.50
❑ 128 David Eckstein PROS	10.00	4.50
❑ 129 Robert Fick PROS	10.00	4.50
❑ 130 Cole Liniak PROS	10.00	4.50
❑ 131 Mark Quinn PROS	10.00	4.50
❑ 132 Eric Gagne PROS	10.00	4.50
❑ 133 Wily Mo Pena PROS	15.00	6.75
❑ 134 A.Thompson RC	10.00	4.50
❑ 135 Steve Sisco PROS RC	10.00	4.50
❑ 136 P.Rigdon PROS RC	10.00	4.50
❑ 137 Rob Bell PROS	10.00	4.50
❑ 138 Carlos Guillen PROS	10.00	4.50
❑ 139 Jimmy Rollins PROS	10.00	4.50
❑ 140 Jason Conti PROS	10.00	4.50

2001 Fleer Showcase

	MINT	NRMT
COMP.SET w/o SP's (100)	30.00	13.50
COMMON CARD (1-100)	.40	.18
COMMON CARD (101-115)	6.00	2.70
COMMON CARD (116-125)	20.00	9.00
COMMON CARD (126 -160)	8.00	3.60

❑ 1 Tony Gwynn	2.00	.90
❑ 2 Barry Larkin	1.00	.45
❑ 3 Chan Ho Park	.40	.18
❑ 4 Darin Erstad	1.00	.45
❑ 5 Rafael Furcal	.40	.18
❑ 6 Roger Cedeno	.40	.18
❑ 7 Timo Perez	.40	.18
❑ 8 Rick Ankiel	.60	.25
❑ 9 Pokey Reese	.40	.18
❑ 10 Jeromy Burnitz	.40	.18
❑ 11 Phil Nevin	.40	.18
❑ 12 Matt Williams	.60	.25
❑ 13 Mike Hampton	.40	.18
❑ 14 Fernando Tatis	.40	.18
❑ 15 Kazuhiro Sasaki	1.00	.45
❑ 16 Jim Thome	1.00	.45
❑ 17 Geoff Jenkins	.40	.18
❑ 18 Jeff Kent	.60	.25
❑ 19 Tom Glavine	1.00	.45
❑ 20 Dean Palmer	.40	.18
❑ 21 Todd Zeile	.40	.18
❑ 22 Edgar Renteria	.40	.18
❑ 23 Andruw Jones	1.00	.45
❑ 24 Juan Encarnacion	.40	.18
❑ 25 Robin Ventura	.40	.18
❑ 26 J.D. Drew	1.00	.45
❑ 27 Ray Durham	.40	.18
❑ 28 Richard Hidalgo	.40	.18
❑ 29 Eric Chavez	.40	.18
❑ 30 Rafael Palmeiro	1.00	.45
❑ 31 Steve Finley	.40	.18
❑ 32 Jeff Weaver	.40	.18
❑ 33 Al Leiter	.40	.18
❑ 34 Jim Edmonds	.60	.25
❑ 35 Garret Anderson	.40	.18
❑ 36 Larry Walker	.60	.25
❑ 37 Jose Vidro	.40	.18
❑ 38 Mike Cameron	.40	.18
❑ 39 Brady Anderson	.40	.18
❑ 40 Mike Lowell	.40	.18
❑ 41 Bernie Williams	1.00	.45
❑ 42 Gary Sheffield	.40	.18
❑ 43 John Smoltz	.40	.18
❑ 44 Mike Mussina	1.00	.45
❑ 45 Greg Vaughn	.40	.18
❑ 46 Juan Gonzalez	1.00	.45
❑ 47 Matt Lawton	.40	.18
❑ 48 Robb Nen	.40	.18
❑ 49 Brad Radke	.40	.18
❑ 50 Edgar Martinez	.60	.25
❑ 51 Mike Bordick	.40	.18
❑ 52 Shawn Green	1.00	.45
❑ 53 Carl Everett	.40	.18
❑ 54 Adrian Beltre	.40	.18
❑ 55 Kerry Wood	1.00	.45
❑ 56 Kevin Brown	.40	.18
❑ 57 Brian Giles	.40	.18
❑ 58 Greg Maddux	2.50	1.10
❑ 59 Preston Wilson	.40	.18
❑ 60 Orlando Hernandez	.40	.18
❑ 61 Ben Grieve	.40	.18
❑ 62 Jermaine Dye	.40	.18
❑ 63 Travis Lee	.40	.18
❑ 64 Jose Cruz Jr.	.40	.18
❑ 65 Rondell White	.40	.18
❑ 66 Carlos Beltran	.40	.18
❑ 67 Scott Rolen	1.00	.45
❑ 68 Brad Fullmer	.40	.18
❑ 69 David Wells	.40	.18
❑ 70 Mike Sweeney	.40	.18
❑ 71 Barry Zito	1.00	.45
❑ 72 Tony Batista	.40	.18
❑ 73 Curt Schilling	1.00	.45
❑ 74 Jeff Cirillo	.40	.18
❑ 75 Edgardo Alfonzo	.40	.18
❑ 76 John Olerud	.40	.18
❑ 77 Carlos Lee	.40	.18
❑ 78 Moises Alou	.40	.18
❑ 79 Tim Hudson	1.00	.45
❑ 80 Andres Galarraga	.60	.25
❑ 81 Roberto Alomar	1.00	.45
❑ 82 Richie Sexson	.40	.18
❑ 83 Trevor Hoffman	.40	.18
❑ 84 Omar Vizquel	.40	.18
❑ 85 Jacque Jones	.40	.18
❑ 86 J.T. Snow	.40	.18
❑ 87 Sean Casey	.60	.25
❑ 88 Craig Biggio	.60	.25
❑ 89 Mariano Rivera	.40	.18
❑ 90 Rusty Greer	.40	.18
❑ 91 Barry Bonds	2.50	1.10
❑ 92 Pedro Martinez	1.25	.55
❑ 93 Cal Ripken	4.00	1.80
❑ 94 Pat Burrell	.40	.18
❑ 95 Chipper Jones	2.00	.90
❑ 96 Magglio Ordonez	.40	.18
❑ 97 Jeff Bagwell	1.25	.55
❑ 98 Randy Johnson	1.25	.55
❑ 99 Frank Thomas	1.25	.55
❑ 100 Jason Kendall	.40	.18
❑ 101 Nomar Garciaparra AC	15.00	6.75
❑ 102 Mark McGwire AC	25.00	11.00
❑ 103 Troy Glaus AC	6.00	2.70
❑ 104 Ivan Rodriguez AC	1.00	.45
❑ 105 Manny Ramirez AC	8.00	3.60
❑ 106 Derek Jeter AC	25.00	11.00
❑ 107 Alex Rodriguez AC	15.00	6.75
❑ 108 Ken Griffey Jr. AC	20.00	9.00
❑ 109 Todd Helton AC	8.00	3.60
❑ 110 Sammy Sosa AC	12.00	5.50
❑ 111 Vladimir Guerrero AC	8.00	3.60
❑ 112 Mike Piazza AC	15.00	6.75
❑ 113 Roger Clemens AC	15.00	6.75
❑ 114 Jason Giambi AC	6.00	2.70
❑ 115 Carlos Delgado AC	6.00	2.70
❑ 116 Ichiro Suzuki AC RC	250.00	110.00
❑ 117 Morgan Ensberg AC RC	25.00	11.00
❑ 118 C. Valderrama AC RC	6.00	2.70
❑ 119 Erick Almonte AC RC	25.00	11.00
❑ 120 Tsuyoshi Shinjo AC RC	50.00	22.00
❑ 121 Albert Pujols AC RC	120.00	55.00
❑ 122 Wilson Betemit AC RC	40.00	18.00
❑ 123 Adrian Hernandez AC RC	6.00	2.70
❑ 124 Jackson Melian AC RC	20.00	9.00
❑ 125 Drew Henson AC RC	60.00	27.00
❑ 126 Paul Phillips RS RC	10.00	4.50
❑ 127 Esix Snead RS RC	10.00	4.50
❑ 128 Ryan Freel RS RC	10.00	4.50
❑ 129 Junior Spivey RS RC	10.00	4.50
❑ 130 Elpidio Guzman RS RC	8.00	3.60
❑ 131 Juan Diaz RS RC	10.00	4.50
❑ 132 Andres Torres RS RC	10.00	4.50
❑ 133 Jay Gibbons RS RC	12.00	5.50
❑ 134 Bill Ortega RS RC	10.00	4.50
❑ 135 Alexis Gomez RS RC	10.00	4.50

	Card	Mint	NrMt
❑	136 Wilkin Ruan RS RC	10.00	4.50
❑	137 Henry Mateo RS RC	10.00	4.50
❑	138 Juan Uribe RS RC	15.00	6.75
❑	139 Johnny Estrada RS RC	15.00	6.75
❑	140 Jaisen Randolph RS RC	10.00	4.50
❑	141 Eric Hinske RS RC	10.00	4.50
❑	142 Jack Wilson RS RC	10.00	4.50
❑	143 Cody Ransom RS RC	10.00	4.50
❑	144 Nate Frese RS RC	10.00	4.50
❑	145 John Grabow RS RC	10.00	4.50
❑	146 Christian Parker RS RC	8.00	3.60
❑	147 Brian Lawrence RS RC	8.00	3.60
❑	148 B. Duckworth RS RC	15.00	6.75
❑	149 Winston Abreu RS RC	8.00	3.60
❑	150 Horacio Ramirez RS RC	8.00	3.60
❑	151 Nick Maness RS RC	8.00	3.60
❑	152 Blaine Neal RS RC	8.00	3.60
❑	153 Billy Sylvester RS RC	8.00	3.60
❑	154 David Elder RS RC	8.00	3.60
❑	155 Bert Snow RS RC	8.00	3.60
❑	156 Claudio Vargas RS RC	8.00	3.60
❑	157 Martin Vargas RS RC	8.00	3.60
❑	158 Grant Balfour RS RC	8.00	3.60
❑	159 Randy Keisler RS	8.00	3.60
❑	160 Zach Day RS RC	8.00	3.60
❑	P1 Tony Gwynn Promo	2.00	.90
❑	MM3 Derek Jeter MM/2000	15.00	6.75
❑	NNO Derek Jeter MM AU/100	200.00	90.00

2001 Fleer Triple Crown

		MINT	NRMT
	COMPLETE SET (300)	30.00	13.50
❑	1 Derek Jeter	2.50	1.10
❑	2 Vladimir Guerrero	.75	.35
❑	3 Henry Rodriguez	.15	.07
❑	4 Jason Giambi	.60	.25
❑	5 Nomar Garciaparra	1.50	.70
❑	6 Jeff Kent	.40	.18
❑	7 Garret Anderson	.25	.11
❑	8 Todd Helton	.75	.35
❑	9 Barry Bonds	1.50	.70
❑	10 Preston Wilson	.25	.11
❑	11 Troy Glaus	.60	.25
❑	12 Geoff Jenkins	.25	.11
❑	13 Jim Edmonds	.40	.18
❑	14 Bobby Higginson	.25	.11
❑	15 Mark Quinn	.25	.11
❑	16 Barry Larkin	.60	.25
❑	17 Richie Sexson	.25	.11
❑	18 Fernando Tatis	.15	.07
❑	19 John VanderWal	.15	.07
❑	20 Darin Erstad	.60	.25
❑	21 Shawn Green	.60	.25
❑	22 Scott Rolen	.60	.25
❑	23 Tony Batista	.25	.11
❑	24 Phil Nevin	.25	.11
❑	25 Tim Salmon	.25	.11
❑	26 Gary Sheffield	.25	.11
❑	27 Ben Grieve	.25	.11
❑	28 Jermaine Dye	.25	.11
❑	29 Andres Galarraga	.40	.18
❑	30 Adrian Beltre	.25	.11
❑	31 Rafael Palmeiro	.60	.25
❑	32 J.T. Snow	.25	.11
❑	33 Edgardo Alfonzo	.25	.11
❑	34 Paul Konerko	.25	.11
❑	35 Jim Thome	.60	.25
❑	36 Andruw Jones	.60	.25
❑	37 Mike Sweeney	.25	.11
❑	38 Jose Cruz Jr.	.25	.11
❑	39 David Ortiz	.25	.11
❑	40 Pat Burrell	.25	.11
❑	41 Chipper Jones	1.25	.55
❑	42 Jeff Bagwell	.75	.35
❑	43 Raul Mondesi	.25	.11
❑	44 Rondell White	.25	.11
❑	45 Edgar Martinez	.40	.18
❑	46 Cal Ripken	2.50	1.10
❑	47 Moises Alou	.25	.11
❑	48 Shannon Stewart	.25	.11
❑	49 Tino Martinez	.25	.11
❑	50 Jason Kendall	.25	.11
❑	51 Richard Hidalgo	.25	.11
❑	52 Albert Belle	.25	.11
❑	53 Jay Payton	.15	.07
❑	54 Cliff Floyd	.25	.11
❑	55 Rusty Greer	.25	.11
❑	56 Matt Williams	.40	.18
❑	57 Sammy Sosa	1.25	.55
❑	58 Carl Everett	.25	.11
❑	59 Carlos Delgado	.60	.25
❑	60 Jeremy Giambi	.15	.07
❑	61 Jose Canseco	.60	.25
❑	62 David Segui	.15	.07
❑	63 Jose Vidro	.25	.11
❑	64 Matt Stairs	.15	.07
❑	65 Travis Fryman	.25	.11
❑	66 Ken Griffey Jr.	2.00	.90
❑	67 Mike Piazza	1.50	.70
❑	68 Mark McGwire	2.50	1.10
❑	69 Craig Biggio	.40	.18
❑	70 Eric Chavez	.25	.11
❑	71 Mo Vaughn	.25	.11
❑	72 Matt Lawton	.25	.11
❑	73 Miguel Tejada	.25	.11
❑	74 Brian Giles	.25	.11
❑	75 Sean Casey	.40	.18
❑	76 Robin Ventura	.25	.11
❑	77 Ivan Rodriguez	.60	.25
❑	78 Dean Palmer	.25	.11
❑	79 Frank Thomas	.75	.35
❑	80 Bernie Williams	.60	.25
❑	81 Juan Encarnacion	.25	.11
❑	82 John Olerud	.25	.11
❑	83 Rich Aurilia	.25	.11
❑	84 Juan Gonzalez	.60	.25
❑	85 Ray Durham	.25	.11
❑	86 Steve Finley	.25	.11
❑	87 Ken Caminiti	.25	.11
❑	88 Roberto Alomar	.60	.25
❑	89 Jeromy Burnitz	.25	.11
❑	90 J.D. Drew	.60	.25
❑	91 Lance Berkman	.60	.25
❑	92 Gabe Kapler	.25	.11
❑	93 Larry Walker	.40	.18
❑	94 Alex Rodriguez	1.50	.70
❑	95 Jeffrey Hammonds	.15	.07
❑	96 Magglio Ordonez	.25	.11
❑	97 David Justice	.25	.11
❑	98 Eric Karros	.25	.11
❑	99 Manny Ramirez	.75	.35
❑	100 Paul O'Neill	.60	.25
❑	101 Ron Gant	.15	.07
❑	102 Erubiel Durazo	.15	.07
❑	103 Jason Varitek	.25	.11
❑	104 Chan Ho Park	.25	.11
❑	105 Corey Koskie	.25	.11
❑	106 Jeff Conine	.15	.07
❑	107 Kevin Tapani	.15	.07
❑	108 Mike Lowell	.25	.11
❑	109 Tim Hudson	.60	.25
❑	110 Bobby Abreu	.25	.11
❑	111 Bret Boone	.25	.11
❑	112 David Wells	.25	.11
❑	113 Brian Jordan	.25	.11
❑	114 Mitch Meluskey	.15	.07
❑	115 Terrence Long	.25	.11
❑	116 Matt Clement	.15	.07
❑	117 Fernando Vina	.15	.07
❑	118 Luis Alicea	.15	.07
❑	119 Jay Bell	.25	.11
❑	120 Mark Grace	.60	.25
❑	121 Carlos Febles	.15	.07
❑	122 Mark Redman	.15	.07
❑	123 Kevin Jordan	.15	.07
❑	124 Pat Meares	.15	.07
❑	125 Mark McLemore	.15	.07
❑	126 Chris Singleton	.15	.07
❑	127 Trot Nixon	.25	.11
❑	128 Carlos Beltran	.25	.11
❑	129 Lee Stevens	.15	.07
❑	130 Kris Benson	.25	.11
❑	131 Jay Buhner	.25	.11
❑	132 Greg Vaughn	.25	.11
❑	133 Eric Young	.15	.07
❑	134 Tony Womack	.15	.07
❑	135 Roger Cedeno	.15	.07
❑	136 Travis Lee	.15	.07
❑	137 Marvin Benard	.15	.07
❑	138 Aaron Sele	.25	.11
❑	139 Rick Ankiel	.40	.18
❑	140 Ruben Mateo	.25	.11
❑	141 Randy Johnson	.75	.35
❑	142 Jason Tyner	.15	.07
❑	143 Mike Redmond	.15	.07
❑	144 Ron Coomer	.15	.07
❑	145 Scott Elarton	.15	.07
❑	146 Javy Lopez	.25	.11
❑	147 Carlos Lee	.25	.11
❑	148 Tony Clark	.25	.11
❑	149 Roger Clemens	1.50	.70
❑	150 Mike Lieberthal	.25	.11
❑	151 Shawn Estes	.25	.11
❑	152 Vinny Castilla	.25	.11
❑	153 Alex Gonzalez	.15	.07
❑	154 Troy Percival	.15	.07
❑	155 Pokey Reese	.15	.07
❑	156 Todd Hollandsworth	.15	.07
❑	157 Marquis Grissom	.15	.07
❑	158 Greg Maddux	1.50	.70
❑	159 Dante Bichette	.25	.11
❑	160 Hideo Nomo	.60	.25
❑	161 Jacque Jones	.25	.11
❑	162 Kevin Young	.15	.07
❑	163 B.J. Surhoff	.25	.11
❑	164 Eddie Taubensee	.15	.07
❑	165 Neifi Perez	.15	.07
❑	166 Orlando Hernandez	.25	.11
❑	167 Francisco Cordova	.15	.07
❑	168 Miguel Cairo	.15	.07
❑	169 Rafael Furcal	.25	.11
❑	170 Sandy Alomar Jr.	.25	.11
❑	171 Jeff Cirillo	.25	.11
❑	172 A.J. Pierzynski	.15	.07
❑	173 Fred McGriff	.40	.18
❑	174 Mike Mussina	.60	.25
❑	175 Aaron Boone	.15	.07
❑	176 Nick Johnson	.25	.11
❑	177 Kent Bottenfield	.15	.07
❑	178 Felipe Crespo	.15	.07
❑	179 Ryan Minor	.15	.07
❑	180 Charles Johnson	.25	.11
❑	181 Damion Easley	.15	.07
❑	182 Michael Barrett	.15	.07
❑	183 Doug Glanville	.15	.07
❑	184 Ben Davis	.25	.11
❑	185 Rickey Henderson	1.25	.55
❑	186 Edgard Clemente	.15	.07
❑	187 Dmitri Young	.25	.11
❑	188 Tom Goodwin	.15	.07
❑	189 Mike Hampton	.25	.11
❑	190 Gerald Williams	.15	.07
❑	191 Omar Vizquel	.25	.11
❑	192 Ben Petrick	.15	.07
❑	193 Brad Radke	.25	.11
❑	194 Russ Davis	.15	.07
❑	195 Milton Bradley	.15	.07
❑	196 John Parrish	.15	.07
❑	197 Todd Hundley	.15	.07
❑	198 Carl Pavano	.15	.07
❑	199 Bruce Chen	.15	.07
❑	200 Royce Clayton	.15	.07
❑	201 Homer Bush	.15	.07
❑	202 Mark Grudzielanek	.15	.07
❑	203 Mike Lansing	.15	.07
❑	204 Daryle Ward	.15	.07
❑	205 Jeff D'Amico	.15	.07
❑	206 Ray Lankford	.15	.07

❑ 207 Curt Schilling	.60	.25
❑ 208 Pedro Martinez	.75	.35
❑ 209 Johnny Damon	.25	.11
❑ 210 Al Leiter	.25	.11
❑ 211 Ruben Rivera	.15	.07
❑ 212 Kazuhiro Sasaki	.60	.25
❑ 213 Will Clark	.60	.25
❑ 214 Rick Helling	.15	.07
❑ 215 Adam Piatt	.25	.11
❑ 216 Joe Girardi	.15	.07
❑ 217 A.J. Burnett	.25	.11
❑ 218 Mike Bordick	.25	.11
❑ 219 Mike Cameron	.25	.11
❑ 220 Tony Gwynn	1.25	.55
❑ 221 Deivi Cruz	.15	.07
❑ 222 Bubba Trammell	.15	.07
❑ 223 Scott Erickson	.15	.07
❑ 224 Kerry Wood	.60	.25
❑ 225 Derrek Lee	.25	.11
❑ 226 Peter Bergeron	.15	.07
❑ 227 Chris Gomez	.15	.07
❑ 228 Al Martin	.15	.07
❑ 229 Brady Anderson	.25	.11
❑ 230 Ramon Martinez	.15	.07
❑ 231 Darryl Kile	.25	.11
❑ 232 Devon White	.15	.07
❑ 233 Charlie Hayes	.15	.07
❑ 234 Aramis Ramirez	.25	.11
❑ 235 Mike Lamb	.15	.07
❑ 236 Tom Glavine	.60	.25
❑ 237 Troy O'Leary	.15	.07
❑ 238 Joe Randa	.15	.07
❑ 239 Dustin Hermanson	.15	.07
❑ 240 Adam Kennedy	.15	.07
❑ 241 Jose Valentin	.15	.07
❑ 242 Derek Bell	.15	.07
❑ 243 Mark Kotsay	.15	.07
❑ 244 Ron Belliard	.15	.07
❑ 245 Warren Morris	.15	.07
❑ 246 Ozzie Guillen	.15	.07
❑ 247 Andy Ashby	.15	.07
❑ 248 Jose Offerman	.15	.07
❑ 249 Kevin Brown	.25	.11
❑ 250 Jorge Posada	.25	.11
❑ 251 Alex Cabrera	.15	.07
❑ 252 Chan Perry	.15	.07
❑ 253 Augie Ojeda	.15	.07
❑ 254 Santiago Perez	.15	.07
❑ 255 Grant Roberts	.15	.07
❑ 256 Dusty Allen	.15	.07
❑ 257 Elvis Pena	.15	.07
❑ 258 Matt Kinney	.15	.07
❑ 259 Timo Perez	.15	.07
❑ 260 Adam Eaton	.25	.11
❑ 261 Geraldo Guzman	.15	.07
❑ 262 Damian Rolls	.15	.07
❑ 263 Alfonso Soriano	.60	.25
❑ 264 Corey Patterson	.25	.11
❑ 265 Juan Alvarez	.15	.07
❑ 266 Shawn Gilbert	.15	.07
❑ 267 Adam Bernero	.15	.07
❑ 268 Ben Weber	.15	.07
❑ 269 Tike Redman	.15	.07
❑ 270 Willie Morales	.15	.07
❑ 271 Tomas De la Rosa	.15	.07
❑ 272 Rodney Lindsey	.15	.07
❑ 273 Carlos Casimiro	.15	.07
❑ 274 Jim Mann	.15	.07
❑ 275 Pasqual Coco	.15	.07
❑ 276 Julio Zuleta	.15	
.07❑ 277 Damon Minor	.15	.07
❑ 278 Jose Ortiz	.40	.18
❑ 279 Eric Munson	.25	.11
❑ 280 Andy Thompson	.15	.07
❑ 281 Aubrey Huff	.15	.07
❑ 282 Chris Richard	.25	.11
❑ 283 Ross Gload	.15	.07
❑ 284 Travis Dawkins	.15	.07
❑ 285 Tim Drew	.15	.07
❑ 286 Barry Zito	.60	.25
❑ 287 Andy Tracy	.15	.07
❑ 288 Julio Lugo	.15	.07
❑ 289 Greg LaRocca	.15	.07
❑ 290 Keith McDonald	.15	.07
❑ 291 J.C. Romero	.15	.07
❑ 292 Adam Melhuse	.15	.07
❑ 293 Ryan Kohlmeier	.15	.07
❑ 294 John Bale	.15	.07
❑ 295 Eric Cammack	.15	.07
❑ 296 Morgan Burkhart	.15	.07
❑ 297 Kory DeHaan	.15	.07
❑ 298 Mike Mahoney	.15	.07
❑ 299 Hector Ortiz	.15	.07
❑ 300 Talmadge Nunnari	.15	.07

1949 Leaf

	NRMT	VG-E
COMPLETE SET (98)	25000.00	11200.00
COMMON CARD (1-168)	25.00	11.00
COMMON SP's	300.00	135.00
WRAPPER (1-CENT)	160.00	70.00

Card	NRMT	VG-E
❑ 1 Joe DiMaggio	3000.00	1200.00
❑ 3 Babe Ruth	2500.00	1100.00
❑ 4 Stan Musial	850.00	375.00
❑ 5 Virgil Trucks SP RC	400.00	180.00
❑ 8 Satchel Paige SP RC	6000.00	1800.00
❑ 10 Dizzy Trout	40.00	18.00
❑ 11 Phil Rizzuto	300.00	135.00
❑ 13 Cass Michaels SP	300.00	135.00
❑ 14 Billy Johnson	40.00	18.00
❑ 17 Frank Overmire	25.00	11.00
❑ 19 Johnny Wyrostek SP	300.00	135.00
❑ 20 Hank Sauer SP	400.00	180.00
❑ 22 Al Evans	25.00	11.00
❑ 26 Sam Chapman	40.00	18.00
❑ 27 Mickey Harris	25.00	11.00
❑ 28 Jim Hegan RC	40.00	18.00
❑ 29 Elmer Valo RC	40.00	18.00
❑ 30 Billy Goodman SP RC	400.00	180.00
❑ 31 Lou Brissie	25.00	11.00
❑ 32 Warren Spahn	300.00	125.00
❑ 33 Peanuts Lowrey SP	300.00	135.00
❑ 36 Al Zarilla SP	300.00	135.00
❑ 38 Ted Kluszewski RC	200.00	90.00
❑ 39 Ewell Blackwell	60.00	27.00
❑ 42 Kent Peterson	25.00	11.00
❑ 43 Ed Stevens SP	300.00	135.00
❑ 45 Ken Keltner SP	300.00	135.00
❑ 46 Johnny Mize	100.00	45.00
❑ 47 George Vico	25.00	11.00
❑ 48 Johnny Schmitz SP	300.00	135.00
❑ 49 Del Ennis RC	60.00	27.00
❑ 50 Dick Wakefield	25.00	11.00
❑ 51 Al Dark SP RC	500.00	220.00
❑ 53 Johnny VanderMeer	100.00	45.00
❑ 54 Bobby Adams SP	300.00	135.00
❑ 55 Tommy Henrich SP	500.00	220.00
❑ 56 Larry Jansen RC UER (Misspelled Jensen)	40.00	18.00
❑ 57 Bob McCall	25.00	11.00
❑ 59 Luke Appling	100.00	45.00
❑ 61 Jake Early	25.00	11.00
❑ 62 Eddie Joost SP	300.00	135.00
❑ 63 Barney McCosky SP	300.00	135.00
❑ 65 Robert Elliott RC UER (Misspelled Elliot on card front)	100.00	45.00
❑ 66 Orval Grove SP	300.00	135.00
❑ 68 Eddie Miller SP	300.00	135.00
❑ 70 Honus Wagner CO	300.00	135.00
❑ 72 Hank Edwards	25.00	11.00
❑ 73 Pat Seerey	25.00	11.00
❑ 75 Dom DiMaggio SP	550.00	250.00
❑ 76 Ted Williams	1200.00	550.00
❑ 77 Roy Smalley RC	25.00	11.00
❑ 78 Hoot Evers SP	300.00	135.00
❑ 79 Jackie Robinson RC	1500.00	700.00
❑ 81 Whitey Kurowski SP	300.00	135.00
❑ 82 Johnny Lindell	40.00	18.00
❑ 83 Bobby Doerr	100.00	45.00
❑ 84 Sid Hudson	25.00	11.00
❑ 85 Dave Philley SP RC	400.00	180.00
❑ 86 Ralph Weigel	25.00	11.00
❑ 88 Frank Gustine SP	300.00	135.00
❑ 91 Ralph Kiner	200.00	90.00
❑ 93 Bob Feller SP	1800.00	800.00
❑ 95 George Stirnweiss RC	40.00	18.00
❑ 97 Marty Marion	60.00	27.00
❑ 98 Hal Newhouser SP RC	600.00	275.00
❑ 102A Gene Hermansk ERR	250.00	110.00
❑ 102B G.Hermanski COR	40.00	18.00
❑ 104 Eddie Stewart SP	300.00	135.00
❑ 106 Lou Boudreau	100.00	45.00
❑ 108 Matt Batts SP	300.00	135.00
❑ 111 Jerry Priddy	25.00	11.00
❑ 113 Dutch Leonard SP	300.00	135.00
❑ 117 Joe Gordon	40.00	18.00
❑ 120 George Kell SP RC	600.00	275.00
❑ 121 Johnny Pesky SP RC	400.00	180.00
❑ 123 Cliff Fannin SP	300.00	135.00
❑ 125 Andy Pafko RC	25.00	11.00
❑ 127 Enos Slaughter SP	800.00	350.00
❑ 128 Buddy Rosar	25.00	11.00
❑ 129 Kirby Higbe SP	300.00	135.00
❑ 131 Sid Gordon SP	300.00	135.00
❑ 133 Tommy Holmes SP	500.00	220.00
❑ 136A Cliff Aberson (Full sleeve)	25.00	11.00
❑ 136B Cliff Aberson (Short sleeve)	250.00	110.00
❑ 137 Harry Walker SP	400.00	180.00
❑ 138 Larry Doby SP RC	650.00	300.00
❑ 139 Johnny Hopp RC	25.00	11.00
❑ 142 D.Murtaugh SP RC	400.00	180.00
❑ 143 Dick Sisler SP	300.00	135.00
❑ 144 Bob Dillinger SP	300.00	135.00
❑ 146 Pete Reiser SP	500.00	220.00
❑ 149 Hank Majeski SP	300.00	135.00
❑ 153 Floyd Baker SP	300.00	135.00
❑ 158 Harry Brecheen SP RC	400.00	180.00
❑ 159 Mizell Platt	25.00	11.00
❑ 160 Bob Scheffing SP	300.00	135.00
❑ 161 Vern Stephens SP RC	400.00	180.00
❑ 163 F.Hutchinson SP RC	400.00	180.00
❑ 165 Dale Mitchell SP RC	400.00	180.00
❑ 168 P.Cavarretta SP UER Name spelled Cavaretta	500.00	200.00

1990 Leaf

	MINT	NRMT
COMPLETE SET (528)	150.00	70.00
COMPLETE SERIES 1 (264)	90.00	40.00
COMPLETE SERIES 2 (264)	60.00	27.00
COMP. BERRA PUZZLE	1.00	.45

Card	MINT	NRMT
❑ 1 Introductory Card	.25	.11
❑ 2 Mike Henneman	.25	.11
❑ 3 Steve Bedrosian	.25	.11
❑ 4 Mike Scott	.25	.11
❑ 5 Allan Anderson	.25	.11
❑ 6 Rick Sutcliffe	.50	.23

❑ 7	Gregg Olson	.50	.23
❑ 8	Kevin Elster	.25	.11
❑ 9	Pete O'Brien	.25	.11
❑ 10	Carlton Fisk	1.50	.70
❑ 11	Joe Magrane	.25	.11
❑ 12	Roger Clemens	4.00	1.80
❑ 13	Tom Glavine	1.50	.70
❑ 14	Tom Gordon	.50	.23
❑ 15	Todd Benzinger	.25	.11
❑ 16	Hubie Brooks	.25	.11
❑ 17	Roberto Kelly	.25	.11
❑ 18	Barry Larkin	1.50	.70
❑ 19	Mike Boddicker	.25	.11
❑ 20	Roger McDowell	.25	.11
❑ 21	Nolan Ryan	8.00	3.60
❑ 22	John Farrell	.25	.11
❑ 23	Bruce Hurst	.25	.11
❑ 24	Wally Joyner	.50	.23
❑ 25	Greg Maddux	8.00	3.60
❑ 26	Chris Bosio	.25	.11
❑ 27	John Cerutti	.25	.11
❑ 28	Tim Burke	.25	.11
❑ 29	Dennis Eckersley	1.00	.45
❑ 30	Glenn Davis	.25	.11
❑ 31	Jim Abbott	1.00	.45
❑ 32	Mike LaValliere	.25	.11
❑ 33	Andres Thomas	.25	.11
❑ 34	Lou Whitaker	.50	.23
❑ 35	Alvin Davis	.25	.11
❑ 36	Melido Perez	.25	.11
❑ 37	Craig Biggio	1.00	.45
❑ 38	Rick Aguilera	.50	.23
❑ 39	Pete Harnisch	.25	.11
❑ 40	David Cone	.50	.23
❑ 41	Scott Garrelts	.25	.11
❑ 42	Jay Howell	.25	.11
❑ 43	Eric King	.25	.11
❑ 44	Pedro Guerrero	.25	.11
❑ 45	Mike Bielecki	.25	.11
❑ 46	Bob Boone	.50	.23
❑ 47	Kevin Brown	.50	.23
❑ 48	Jerry Browne	.25	.11
❑ 49	Mike Scioscia	.25	.11
❑ 50	Chuck Cary	.25	.11
❑ 51	Wade Boggs	1.50	.70
❑ 52	Von Hayes	.25	.11
❑ 53	Tony Fernandez	.25	.11
❑ 54	Dennis Martinez	.50	.23
❑ 55	Tom Candiotti	.25	.11
❑ 56	Andy Benes	.25	.11
❑ 57	Rob Dibble	.25	.11
❑ 58	Chuck Crim	.25	.11
❑ 59	John Smoltz	.50	.23
❑ 60	Mike Heath	.25	.11
❑ 61	Kevin Gross	.25	.11
❑ 62	Mark McGwire	6.00	2.70
❑ 63	Bert Blyleven	.50	.23
❑ 64	Bob Walk	.25	.11
❑ 65	Mickey Tettleton	.25	.11
❑ 66	Sid Fernandez	.25	.11
❑ 67	Terry Kennedy	.25	.11
❑ 68	Fernando Valenzuela	.50	.23
❑ 69	Don Mattingly	4.00	1.80
❑ 70	Paul O'Neill	1.50	.70
❑ 71	Robin Yount	1.50	.70
❑ 72	Bret Saberhagen	.50	.23
❑ 73	Geno Petralli	.25	.11
❑ 74	Brook Jacoby	.25	.11
❑ 75	Roberto Alomar	1.50	.70
❑ 76	Devon White	.25	.11
❑ 77	Jose Lind	.25	.11
❑ 78	Pat Combs	.25	.11
❑ 79	Dave Stieb	.50	.23
❑ 80	Tim Wallach	.25	.11
❑ 81	Dave Stewart	.50	.23
❑ 82	Eric Anthony RC	.25	.11
❑ 83	Randy Bush	.25	.11
❑ 84	Rickey Henderson CL	1.50	.70
❑ 85	Jaime Navarro	.25	.11
❑ 86	Tommy Gregg	.25	.11
❑ 87	Frank Tanana	.25	.11
❑ 88	Omar Vizquel	1.50	.70
❑ 89	Ivan Calderon	.25	.11
❑ 90	Vince Coleman	.25	.11
❑ 91	Barry Bonds	4.00	1.80
❑ 92	Randy Milligan	.25	.11
❑ 93	Frank Viola	.25	.11
❑ 94	Matt Williams	1.00	.45
❑ 95	Alfredo Griffin	.25	.11
❑ 96	Steve Sax	.25	.11
❑ 97	Gary Gaetti	.50	.23
❑ 98	Ryne Sandberg	2.00	.90
❑ 99	Danny Tartabull	.25	.11
❑ 100	Rafael Palmeiro	1.50	.70
❑ 101	Jesse Orosco	.25	.11
❑ 102	Garry Templeton	.25	.11
❑ 103	Frank DiPino	.25	.11
❑ 104	Tony Pena	.25	.11
❑ 105	Dickie Thon	.25	.11
❑ 106	Kelly Gruber	.25	.11
❑ 107	Marquis Grissom RC	.50	.23
❑ 108	Jose Canseco	1.50	.70
❑ 109	Mike Blowers RC	.50	.23
❑ 110	Tom Browning	.25	.11
❑ 111	Greg Vaughn	1.50	.70
❑ 112	Oddibe McDowell	.25	.11
❑ 113	Gary Ward	.25	.11
❑ 114	Jay Buhner	.50	.23
❑ 115	Eric Show	.25	.11
❑ 116	Bryan Harvey	.25	.11
❑ 117	Andy Van Slyke	.50	.23
❑ 118	Jeff Ballard	.25	.11
❑ 119	Barry Lyons	.25	.11
❑ 120	Kevin Mitchell	.25	.11
❑ 121	Mike Gallego	.25	.11
❑ 122	Dave Smith	.25	.11
❑ 123	Kirby Puckett	4.00	1.80
❑ 124	Jerome Walton	.25	.11
❑ 125	Bo Jackson	.50	.23
❑ 126	Harold Baines	.50	.23
❑ 127	Scott Bankhead	.25	.11
❑ 128	Ozzie Guillen	.25	.11
❑ 129	Jose Oquendo UER (League misspelled as Legue)	.25	.11
❑ 130	John Dopson	.25	.11
❑ 131	Charlie Hayes	.25	.11
❑ 132	Fred McGriff	1.50	.70
❑ 133	Chet Lemon	.25	.11
❑ 134	Gary Carter	1.00	.45
❑ 135	Rafael Ramirez	.25	.11
❑ 136	Shane Mack	.25	.11
❑ 137	Mark Grace UER (Card back has OB:L, should be B:L)	1.50	.70
❑ 138	Phil Bradley	.25	.11
❑ 139	Dwight Gooden	.50	.23
❑ 140	Harold Reynolds	.25	.11
❑ 141	Scott Fletcher	.25	.11
❑ 142	Ozzie Smith	2.00	.90
❑ 143	Mike Greenwell	.25	.11
❑ 144	Pete Smith	.25	.11
❑ 145	Mark Gubicza	.25	.11
❑ 146	Chris Sabo	.25	.11
❑ 147	Ramon Martinez	.25	.11
❑ 148	Tim Leary	.25	.11
❑ 149	Randy Myers	.50	.23
❑ 150	Jody Reed	.25	.11
❑ 151	Bruce Ruffin	.25	.11
❑ 152	Jeff Russell	.25	.11
❑ 153	Doug Jones	.25	.11
❑ 154	Tony Gwynn	3.00	1.35
❑ 155	Mark Langston	.25	.11
❑ 156	Mitch Williams	.25	.11
❑ 157	Gary Sheffield	2.00	.90
❑ 158	Tom Henke	.25	.11
❑ 159	Oil Can Boyd	.25	.11
❑ 160	Rickey Henderson	3.00	1.35
❑ 161	Bill Doran	.25	.11
❑ 162	Chuck Finley	.50	.23
❑ 163	Jeff King	.25	.11
❑ 164	Nick Esasky	.25	.11
❑ 165	Cecil Fielder	.50	.23
❑ 166	Dave Valle	.25	.11
❑ 167	Robin Ventura	1.50	.70
❑ 168	Jim Deshaies	.25	.11
❑ 169	Juan Berenguer	.25	.11
❑ 170	Craig Worthington	.25	.11
❑ 171	Gregg Jefferies	.50	.23
❑ 172	Will Clark	1.50	.70
❑ 173	Kirk Gibson	.50	.23
❑ 174	Carlton Fisk CL	1.00	.45
❑ 175	Bobby Thigpen	.25	.11
❑ 176	John Tudor	.25	.11
❑ 177	Andre Dawson	1.00	.45
❑ 178	George Brett	3.00	1.35
❑ 179	Steve Buechele	.25	.11
❑ 180	Joey Belle	4.00	1.80
❑ 181	Eddie Murray	1.50	.70
❑ 182	Bob Geren	.25	.11
❑ 183	Rob Murphy	.25	.11
❑ 184	Tom Herr	.25	.11
❑ 185	George Bell	.25	.11
❑ 186	Spike Owen	.25	.11
❑ 187	Cory Snyder	.25	.11
❑ 188	Fred Lynn	.25	.11
❑ 189	Eric Davis	.50	.23
❑ 190	Dave Parker	.50	.23
❑ 191	Jeff Blauser	.25	.11
❑ 192	Matt Nokes	.25	.11
❑ 193	Delino DeShields RC	1.50	.70
❑ 194	Scott Sanderson	.25	.11
❑ 195	Lance Parrish	.25	.11
❑ 196	Bobby Bonilla	.50	.23
❑ 197	Cal Ripken UER (Reistertown, should be Reisterstown)	6.00	2.70
❑ 198	Kevin McReynolds	.25	.11
❑ 199	Robby Thompson	.25	.11
❑ 200	Tim Belcher	.25	.11
❑ 201	Jesse Barfield	.25	.11
❑ 202	Mariano Duncan	.25	.11
❑ 203	Bill Spiers	.25	.11
❑ 204	Frank White	.50	.23
❑ 205	Julio Franco	.25	.11
❑ 206	Greg Swindell	.25	.11
❑ 207	Benito Santiago	.25	.11
❑ 208	Johnny Ray	.25	.11
❑ 209	Gary Redus	.25	.11
❑ 210	Jeff Parrett	.25	.11
❑ 211	Jimmy Key	.50	.23
❑ 212	Tim Raines	.50	.23
❑ 213	Carney Lansford	.50	.23
❑ 214	Gerald Young	.25	.11
❑ 215	Gene Larkin	.25	.11
❑ 216	Dan Plesac	.25	.11
❑ 217	Lonnie Smith	.25	.11
❑ 218	Alan Trammell	1.00	.45
❑ 219	Jeffrey Leonard	.25	.11
❑ 220	Sammy Sosa RC	50.00	22.00
❑ 221	Todd Zeile	.50	.23
❑ 222	Bill Landrum	.25	.11
❑ 223	Mike Devereaux	.25	.11
❑ 224	Mike Marshall	.25	.11
❑ 225	Jose Uribe	.25	.11
❑ 226	Juan Samuel	.25	.11
❑ 227	Mel Hall	.25	.11
❑ 228	Kent Hrbek	.50	.23
❑ 229	Shawon Dunston	.25	.11
❑ 230	Kevin Seitzer	.25	.11
❑ 231	Pete Incaviglia	.25	.11
❑ 232	Sandy Alomar Jr.	.50	.23
❑ 233	Bip Roberts	.25	.11
❑ 234	Scott Terry	.25	.11
❑ 235	Dwight Evans	.50	.23
❑ 236	Ricky Jordan	.25	.11
❑ 237	John Olerud RC	5.00	2.20
❑ 238	Zane Smith	.25	.11
❑ 239	Walt Weiss	.25	.11
❑ 240	Alvaro Espinoza	.25	.11
❑ 241	Billy Hatcher	.25	.11
❑ 242	Paul Molitor	1.50	.70
❑ 243	Dale Murphy	1.50	.70
❑ 244	Dave Bergman	.25	.11
❑ 245	Ken Griffey Jr.	20.00	9.00
❑ 246	Ed Whitson	.25	.11
❑ 247	Kirk McCaskill	.25	.11
❑ 248	Jay Bell	.50	.23
❑ 249	Ben McDonald RC	.50	.23
❑ 250	Darryl Strawberry	.50	.23
❑ 251	Brett Butler	.50	.23
❑ 252	Terry Steinbach	.25	.11
❑ 253	Ken Caminiti	1.50	.70
❑ 254	Dan Gladden	.25	.11
❑ 255	Dwight Smith	.25	.11
❑ 256	Kurt Stillwell	.25	.11
❑ 257	Ruben Sierra	.25	.11
❑ 258	Mike Schooler	.25	.11

❑	259	Lance Johnson	.25	.11
❑	260	Terry Pendleton	.50	.23
❑	261	Ellis Burks	1.00	.45
❑	262	Len Dykstra	.50	.23
❑	263	Mookie Wilson	.50	.23
❑	264	Nolan Ryan CL UER No TM after Ranger logo	1.50	.70
❑	265	Nolan Ryan No Hit King	4.00	1.80
❑	266	Brian DuBois	.25	.11
❑	267	Don Robinson	.25	.11
❑	268	Glenn Wilson	.25	.11
❑	269	Kevin Tapani RC	2.00	.90
❑	270	Marvell Wynne	.25	.11
❑	271	Bill Ripken	.25	.11
❑	272	Howard Johnson	.25	.11
❑	273	Brian Holman	.25	.11
❑	274	Dan Pasqua	.25	.11
❑	275	Ken Dayley	.25	.11
❑	276	Jeff Reardon	.50	.23
❑	277	Jim Presley	.25	.11
❑	278	Jim Eisenreich	.25	.11
❑	279	Danny Jackson	.25	.11
❑	280	Orel Hershiser	.50	.23
❑	281	Andy Hawkins	.25	.11
❑	282	Jose Rijo	.25	.11
❑	283	Luis Rivera	.25	.11
❑	284	John Kruk	.50	.23
❑	285	Jeff Huson RC	.25	.11
❑	286	Joel Skinner	.25	.11
❑	287	Jack Clark	.50	.23
❑	288	Chili Davis	.50	.23
❑	289	Joe Girardi	1.00	.45
❑	290	B.J. Surhoff	.50	.23
❑	291	Luis Sojo	.25	.11
❑	292	Tom Foley	.25	.11
❑	293	Mike Moore	.25	.11
❑	294	Ken Oberkfell	.25	.11
❑	295	Luis Polonia	.25	.11
❑	296	Doug Drabek	.25	.11
❑	297	Dave Justice RC	6.00	2.70
❑	298	Paul Gibson	.25	.11
❑	299	Edgar Martinez	1.00	.45
❑	300	F.Thomas RC UER No B in front of birthdate	25.00	11.00
❑	301	Eric Yelding	.25	.11
❑	302	Greg Gagne	.25	.11
❑	303	Brad Komminsk	.25	.11
❑	304	Ron Darling	.25	.11
❑	305	Kevin Bass	.25	.11
❑	306	Jeff Hamilton	.25	.11
❑	307	Ron Karkovice	.25	.11
❑	308	Milt Thompson UER (Ray Lankford pictured on card back)	.50	.23
❑	309	Mike Harkey	.25	.11
❑	310	Mel Stottlemyre Jr.	.25	.11
❑	311	Kenny Rogers	.50	.23
❑	312	Mitch Webster	.25	.11
❑	313	Kal Daniels	.25	.11
❑	314	Matt Nokes	.25	.11
❑	315	Dennis Lamp	.25	.11
❑	316	Ken Howell	.25	.11
❑	317	Glenallen Hill	.25	.11
❑	318	Dave Martinez	.25	.11
❑	319	Chris James	.25	.11
❑	320	Mike Pagliarulo	.25	.11
❑	321	Hal Morris	.25	.11
❑	322	Rob Deer	.25	.11
❑	323	Greg Olson	.25	.11
❑	324	Tony Phillips	.25	.11
❑	325	Larry Walker RC	10.00	4.50
❑	326	Ron Hassey	.25	.11
❑	327	Jack Howell	.25	.11
❑	328	John Smiley	.25	.11
❑	329	Steve Finley	.50	.23
❑	330	Dave Magadan	.25	.11
❑	331	Greg Litton	.25	.11
❑	332	Mickey Hatcher	.25	.11
❑	333	Lee Guetterman	.25	.11
❑	334	Norm Charlton	.25	11
❑	335	Edgar Diaz	.25	.11
❑	336	Willie Wilson	.25	.11
❑	337	Bobby Witt	.25	.11
❑	338	Candy Maldonado	.25	.11
❑	339	Craig Lefferts	.25	.11
❑	340	Dante Bichette	1.50	.70
❑	341	Wally Backman	.25	.11
❑	342	Dennis Cook	.25	.11
❑	343	Pat Borders	.25	.11
❑	344	Wallace Johnson	.25	.11
❑	345	Willie Randolph	.50	.23
❑	346	Danny Darwin	.25	.11
❑	347	Al Newman	.25	.11
❑	348	Mark Knudson	.25	.11
❑	349	Joe Boever	.25	.11
❑	350	Larry Sheets	.25	.11
❑	351	Mike Jackson	.25	.11
❑	352	Wayne Edwards	.25	.11
❑	353	Bernard Gilkey RC	.50	.23
❑	354	Don Slaught	.25	.11
❑	355	Joe Orsulak	.25	.11
❑	356	John Franco	.50	.23
❑	357	Jeff Brantley	.25	.11
❑	358	Mike Morgan	.25	.11
❑	359	Deion Sanders	2.00	.90
❑	360	Terry Leach	.25	.11
❑	361	Les Lancaster	.25	.11
❑	362	Storm Davis	.25	.11
❑	363	Scott Coolbaugh	.25	.11
❑	364	Ozzie Smith CL	1.00	.45
❑	365	Cecilio Guante	.25	.11
❑	366	Joey Cora	.50	.23
❑	367	Willie McGee	.50	.23
❑	368	Jerry Reed	.25	.11
❑	369	Darren Daulton	.50	.23
❑	370	Manny Lee	.25	.11
❑	371	Mark Gardner	.25	.11
❑	372	Rick Honeycutt	.25	.11
❑	373	Steve Balboni	.25	.11
❑	374	Jack Armstrong	.25	.11
❑	375	Charlie O'Brien	.25	.11
❑	376	Ron Gant	.50	.23
❑	377	Lloyd Moseby	.25	.11
❑	378	Gene Harris	.25	.11
❑	379	Joe Carter	.50	.23
❑	380	Scott Bailes	.25	.11
❑	381	R.J. Reynolds	.25	.11
❑	382	Bob Melvin	.25	.11
❑	383	Tim Teufel	.25	.11
❑	384	John Burkett	.25	.11
❑	385	Felix Jose	.25	.11
❑	386	Larry Andersen	.25	.11
❑	387	David West	.25	.11
❑	388	Luis Salazar	.25	.11
❑	389	Mike Macfarlane	.25	.11
❑	390	Charlie Hough	.50	.23
❑	391	Greg Briley	.25	.11
❑	392	Donn Pall	.25	.11
❑	393	Bryn Smith	.25	.11
❑	394	Carlos Quintana	.25	.11
❑	395	Steve Lake	.25	.11
❑	396	Mark Whiten RC	.25	.11
❑	397	Edwin Nunez	.25	.11
❑	398	Rick Parker	.25	.11
❑	399	Mark Portugal	.25	.11
❑	400	Roy Smith	.25	.11
❑	401	Hector Villanueva	.25	.11
❑	402	Bob Milacki	.25	.11
❑	403	Alejandro Pena	.25	.11
❑	404	Scott Bradley	.25	.11
❑	405	Ron Kittle	.25	.11
❑	406	Bob Tewksbury	.25	.11
❑	407	Wes Gardner	.25	.11
❑	408	Ernie Whitt	.25	.11
❑	409	Terry Shumpert	.25	.11
❑	410	Tim Layana	.25	.11
❑	411	Chris Gwynn	.25	.11
❑	412	Jeff D. Robinson	.25	.11
❑	413	Scott Scudder	.25	.11
❑	414	Kevin Romine	.25	.11
❑	415	Jose DeJesus	.25	.11
❑	416	Mike Jeffcoat	.25	.11
❑	417	Rudy Seanez	.25	.11
❑	418	Mike Dunne	.25	.11
❑	419	Dick Schofield	.25	.11
❑	420	Steve Wilson	.25	.11
❑	421	Bill Krueger	.25	.11
❑	422	Junior Felix	.25	.11
❑	423	Drew Hall	.25	.11
❑	424	Curt Young	.25	.11
❑	425	Franklin Stubbs	.25	.11
❑	426	Dave Winfield	1.50	.70
❑	427	Rick Reed RC	2.00	.90
❑	428	Charlie Leibrandt	.25	.11
❑	429	Jeff M. Robinson	.25	.11
❑	430	Erik Hanson	.25	.11
❑	431	Barry Jones	.25	.11
❑	432	Alex Trevino	.25	.11
❑	433	John Moses	.25	.11
❑	434	Dave Johnson	.25	.11
❑	435	Mackey Sasser	.25	.11
❑	436	Rick Leach	.25	.11
❑	437	Lenny Harris	.25	.11
❑	438	Carlos Martinez	.25	.11
❑	439	Rex Hudler	.25	.11
❑	440	Domingo Ramos	.25	.11
❑	441	Gerald Perry	.25	.11
❑	442	Jeff Russell	.25	.11
❑	443	Carlos Baerga RC	.50	.23
❑	444	Will Clark CL	.50	.23
❑	445	Stan Javier	.25	.11
❑	446	Kevin Maas RC	.50	.23
❑	447	Tom Brunansky	.25	.11
❑	448	Carmelo Martinez	.25	.11
❑	449	Willie Blair RC	.50	.23
❑	450	Andres Galarraga	1.00	.45
❑	451	Bud Black	.25	.11
❑	452	Greg W. Harris	.25	.11
❑	453	Joe Oliver	.25	.11
❑	454	Greg Brock	.25	.11
❑	455	Jeff Treadway	.25	.11
❑	456	Lance McCullers	.25	.11
❑	457	Dave Schmidt	.25	.11
❑	458	Todd Burns	.25	.11
❑	459	Max Venable	.25	.11
❑	460	Neal Heaton	.25	.11
❑	461	Mark Williamson	.25	.11
❑	462	Keith Miller	.25	.11
❑	463	Mike LaCoss	.25	.11
❑	464	Jose Offerman RC	.50	.23
❑	465	Jim Leyritz RC	.50	.23
❑	466	Glenn Braggs	.25	.11
❑	467	Ron Robinson	.25	.11
❑	468	Mark Davis	.25	.11
❑	469	Gary Pettis	.25	.11
❑	470	Keith Hernandez	.50	.23
❑	471	Dennis Rasmussen	.25	.11
❑	472	Mark Eichhorn	.25	.11
❑	473	Ted Power	.25	.11
❑	474	Terry Mulholland	.25	.11
❑	475	Todd Stottlemyre	.50	.23
❑	476	Jerry Goff	.25	.11
❑	477	Gene Nelson	.25	.11
❑	478	Rich Gedman	.25	.11
❑	479	Brian Harper	.25	.11
❑	480	Mike Felder	.25	.11
❑	481	Steve Avery	1.50	.70
❑	482	Jack Morris	.50	.23
❑	483	Randy Johnson	5.00	2.20
❑	484	Scott Radinsky RC	.25	.11
❑	485	Jose DeLeon	.25	.11
❑	486	Stan Belinda RC	.25	.11
❑	487	Brian Holton	.25	.11
❑	488	Mark Carreon	.25	.11
❑	489	Trevor Wilson	.25	.11
❑	490	Mike Sharperson	.25	.11
❑	491	Alan Mills RC	.25	.11
❑	492	John Candelaria	.25	.11
❑	493	Paul Assenmacher	.25	.11
❑	494	Steve Crawford	.25	.11
❑	495	Brad Arnsberg	.25	.11
❑	496	Sergio Valdez	.25	.11
❑	497	Mark Parent	.25	.11
❑	498	Tom Pagnozzi	.25	.11
❑	499	Greg A. Harris	.25	.11
❑	500	Randy Ready	.25	.11
❑	501	Duane Ward	.25	.11
❑	502	Nelson Santovenia	.25	.11
❑	503	Joe Klink	.25	.11
❑	504	Eric Plunk	.25	.11
❑	505	Jeff Reed	.25	.11
❑	506	Ted Higuera	.25	.11
❑	507	Joe Hesketh	.25	.11
❑	508	Dan Petry	.25	.11
❑	509	Matt Young	.25	.11
❑	510	Jerald Clark	.25	.11

#	Player	MINT	NRMT
❑ 511	John Orton	.25	.11
❑ 512	Scott Ruskin	.25	.11
❑ 513	Chris Hoiles RC	.50	.23
❑ 514	Daryl Boston	.25	.11
❑ 515	Francisco Oliveras	.25	.11
❑ 516	Ozzie Canseco	.25	.11
❑ 517	Xavier Hernandez RC	.25	.11
❑ 518	Fred Manrique	.25	.11
❑ 519	Shawn Boskie RC	.25	.11
❑ 520	Jeff Montgomery	.50	.23
❑ 521	Jack Daugherty	.25	.11
❑ 522	Keith Comstock	.25	.11
❑ 523	Greg Hibbard RC	.25	.11
❑ 524	Lee Smith	.50	.23
❑ 525	Dana Kiecker	.25	.11
❑ 526	Darrel Akerfelds	.25	.11
❑ 527	Greg Myers	.25	.11
❑ 528	Ryne Sandberg CL	1.50	.70

1991 Leaf

	MINT	NRMT
COMPLETE SET (528)	15.00	6.75
COMPLETE SERIES 1 (264)	5.00	2.20
COMPLETE SERIES 2 (264)	10.00	4.50
COMP. KILLEBREW PUZZLE	1.00	.45

#	Player	MINT	NRMT
❑ 1	The Leaf Card	.10	.05
❑ 2	Kurt Stillwell	.10	.05
❑ 3	Bobby Witt	.10	.05
❑ 4	Tony Phillips	.10	.05
❑ 5	Scott Garrelts	.10	.05
❑ 6	Greg Swindell	.10	.05
❑ 7	Billy Ripken	.10	.05
❑ 8	Dave Martinez	.10	.05
❑ 9	Kelly Gruber	.10	.05
❑ 10	Juan Samuel	.10	.05
❑ 11	Brian Holman	.10	.05
❑ 12	Craig Biggio	.30	.14
❑ 13	Lonnie Smith	.10	.05
❑ 14	Ron Robinson	.10	.05
❑ 15	Mike LaValliere	.10	.05
❑ 16	Mark Davis	.10	.05
❑ 17	Jack Daugherty	.10	.05
❑ 18	Mike Henneman	.10	.05
❑ 19	Mike Greenwell	.10	.05
❑ 20	Dave Magadan	.10	.05
❑ 21	Mark Williamson	.10	.05
❑ 22	Marquis Grissom	.10	.05
❑ 23	Pat Borders	.10	.05
❑ 24	Mike Scioscia	.10	.05
❑ 25	Shawon Dunston	.10	.05
❑ 26	Randy Bush	.10	.05
❑ 27	John Smoltz	.20	.09
❑ 28	Chuck Crim	.10	.05
❑ 29	Don Slaught	.10	.05
❑ 30	Mike Macfarlane	.10	.05
❑ 31	Wally Joyner	.20	.09
❑ 32	Pat Combs	.10	.05
❑ 33	Tony Pena	.10	.05
❑ 34	Howard Johnson	.10	.05
❑ 35	Leo Gomez	.10	.05
❑ 36	Spike Owen	.10	.05
❑ 37	Eric Davis	.20	.09
❑ 38	Roberto Kelly	.10	.05
❑ 39	Jerome Walton	.10	.05
❑ 40	Shane Mack	.10	.05
❑ 41	Kent Mercker	.10	.05
❑ 42	B.J. Surhoff	.20	.09
❑ 43	Jerry Browne	.10	.05
❑ 44	Lee Smith	.20	.09
❑ 45	Chuck Finley	.20	.09
❑ 46	Terry Mulholland	.10	.05
❑ 47	Tom Bolton	.10	.05
❑ 48	Tom Herr	.10	.05
❑ 49	Jim Deshaies	.10	.05
❑ 50	Walt Weiss	.10	.05
❑ 51	Hal Morris	.10	.05
❑ 52	Lee Guetterman	.10	.05
❑ 53	Paul Assenmacher	.10	.05
❑ 54	Brian Harper	.10	.05
❑ 55	Paul Gibson	.10	.05
❑ 56	John Burkett	.10	.05
❑ 57	Doug Jones	.10	.05
❑ 58	Jose Oquendo	.10	.05
❑ 59	Dick Schofield	.10	.05
❑ 60	Dickie Thon	.10	.05
❑ 61	Ramon Martinez	.10	.05
❑ 62	Jay Buhner	.20	.09
❑ 63	Mark Portugal	.10	.05
❑ 64	Bob Welch	.10	.05
❑ 65	Chris Sabo	.10	.05
❑ 66	Chuck Cary	.10	.05
❑ 67	Mark Langston	.10	.05
❑ 68	Joe Boever	.10	.05
❑ 69	Jody Reed	.10	.05
❑ 70	Alejandro Pena	.10	.05
❑ 71	Jeff King	.10	.05
❑ 72	Tom Pagnozzi	.10	.05
❑ 73	Joe Oliver	.10	.05
❑ 74	Mike Witt	.10	.05
❑ 75	Hector Villanueva	.10	.05
❑ 76	Dan Gladden	.10	.05
❑ 77	Dave Justice	.40	.18
❑ 78	Mike Gallego	.10	.05
❑ 79	Tom Candiotti	.10	.05
❑ 80	Ozzie Smith	.50	.23
❑ 81	Luis Polonia	.10	.05
❑ 82	Randy Ready	.10	.05
❑ 83	Greg A. Harris	.10	.05
❑ 84	David Justice CL	.20	.09
❑ 85	Kevin Mitchell	.10	.05
❑ 86	Mark McLemore	.10	.05
❑ 87	Terry Steinbach	.10	.05
❑ 88	Tom Browning	.10	.05
❑ 89	Matt Nokes	.10	.05
❑ 90	Mike Harkey	.10	.05
❑ 91	Omar Vizquel	.20	.09
❑ 92	Dave Bergman	.10	.05
❑ 93	Matt Williams	.30	.14
❑ 94	Steve Olin	.10	.05
❑ 95	Craig Wilson	.10	.05
❑ 96	Dave Stieb	.10	.05
❑ 97	Ruben Sierra	.10	.05
❑ 98	Jay Howell	.10	.05
❑ 99	Scott Bradley	.10	.05
❑ 100	Eric Yelding	.10	.05
❑ 101	Rickey Henderson	.75	.35
❑ 102	Jeff Reed	.10	.05
❑ 103	Jimmy Key	.20	.09
❑ 104	Terry Shumpert	.10	.05
❑ 105	Kenny Rogers	.10	.05
❑ 106	Cecil Fielder	.20	.09
❑ 107	Robby Thompson	.10	.05
❑ 108	Alex Cole	.10	.05
❑ 109	Randy Milligan	.10	.05
❑ 110	Andres Galarraga	.30	.14
❑ 111	Bill Spiers	.10	.05
❑ 112	Kal Daniels	.10	.05
❑ 113	Henry Cotto	.10	.05
❑ 114	Casey Candaele	.10	.05
❑ 115	Jeff Blauser	.10	.05
❑ 116	Robin Yount	.40	.18
❑ 117	Ben McDonald	.10	.05
❑ 118	Bret Saberhagen	.20	.09
❑ 119	Juan Gonzalez	.50	.23
❑ 120	Lou Whitaker	.20	.09
❑ 121	Ellis Burks	.20	.09
❑ 122	Charlie O'Brien	.10	.05
❑ 123	John Smiley	.10	.05
❑ 124	Tim Burke	.10	.05
❑ 125	John Olerud	.30	.14
❑ 126	Eddie Murray	.40	.18
❑ 127	Greg Maddux	1.00	.45
❑ 128	Kevin Tapani	.10	.05
❑ 129	Ron Gant	.10	.05
❑ 130	Jay Bell	.20	.09
❑ 131	Chris Hoiles	.10	.05
❑ 132	Tom Gordon	.10	.05
❑ 133	Kevin Seitzer	.10	.05
❑ 134	Jeff Huson	.10	.05
❑ 135	Jerry Don Gleaton	.10	.05
❑ 136	Jeff Brantley UER (Photo actually Rick Leach on back)	.10	.05
❑ 137	Felix Fermin	.10	.05
❑ 138	Mike Devereaux	.10	.05
❑ 139	Delino DeShields	.20	.09
❑ 140	David Wells	.20	.09
❑ 141	Tim Crews	.10	.05
❑ 142	Erik Hanson	.10	.05
❑ 143	Mark Davidson	.10	.05
❑ 144	Tommy Gregg	.10	.05
❑ 145	Jim Gantner	.10	.05
❑ 146	Jose Lind	.10	.05
❑ 147	Danny Tartabull	.10	.05
❑ 148	Geno Petralli	.10	.05
❑ 149	Travis Fryman	.20	.09
❑ 150	Tim Naehring	.10	.05
❑ 151	Kevin McReynolds	.10	.05
❑ 152	Joe Orsulak	.10	.05
❑ 153	Steve Frey	.10	.05
❑ 154	Duane Ward	.10	.05
❑ 155	Stan Javier	.10	.05
❑ 156	Damon Berryhill	.10	.05
❑ 157	Gene Larkin	.10	.05
❑ 158	Greg Olson	.10	.05
❑ 159	Mark Knudson	.10	.05
❑ 160	Carmelo Martinez	.10	.05
❑ 161	Storm Davis	.10	.05
❑ 162	Jim Abbott	.20	.09
❑ 163	Len Dykstra	.20	.09
❑ 164	Tom Brunansky	.10	.05
❑ 165	Dwight Gooden	.20	.09
❑ 166	Jose Mesa	.10	.05
❑ 167	Oil Can Boyd	.10	.05
❑ 168	Barry Larkin	.40	.18
❑ 169	Scott Sanderson	.10	.05
❑ 170	Mark Grace	.40	.18
❑ 171	Mark Guthrie	.10	.05
❑ 172	Tom Glavine	.40	.18
❑ 173	Gary Sheffield	.20	.09
❑ 174	Roger Clemens CL	.50	.23
❑ 175	Chris James	.10	.05
❑ 176	Milt Thompson	.10	.05
❑ 177	Donnie Hill	.10	.05
❑ 178	Wes Chamberlain RC	.10	.05
❑ 179	John Marzano	.10	.05
❑ 180	Frank Viola	.20	.09
❑ 181	Eric Anthony	.10	.05
❑ 182	Jose Canseco	.40	.18
❑ 183	Scott Scudder	.10	.05
❑ 184	Dave Eiland	.10	.05
❑ 185	Luis Salazar	.10	.05
❑ 186	Pedro Munoz RC	.10	.05
❑ 187	Steve Searcy	.10	.05
❑ 188	Don Robinson	.10	.05
❑ 189	Sandy Alomar Jr.	.20	.09
❑ 190	Jose DeLeon	.10	.05
❑ 191	John Orton	.10	.05
❑ 192	Darren Daulton	.20	.09
❑ 193	Mike Morgan	.10	.05
❑ 194	Greg Briley	.10	.05
❑ 195	Karl Rhodes	.10	.05
❑ 196	Harold Baines	.20	.09
❑ 197	Bill Doran	.10	.05
❑ 198	Alvaro Espinoza	.10	.05
❑ 199	Kirk McCaskill	.10	.05
❑ 200	Jose DeJesus	.10	.05
❑ 201	Jack Clark	.20	.09
❑ 202	Daryl Boston	.10	.05
❑ 203	Randy Tomlin RC	.10	.05
❑ 204	Pedro Guerrero	.20	.09
❑ 205	Billy Hatcher	.10	.05
❑ 206	Tim Leary	.10	.05
❑ 207	Ryne Sandberg	.50	.23
❑ 208	Kirby Puckett	1.00	.45
❑ 209	Charlie Leibrandt	.10	.05
❑ 210	Rick Honeycutt	.10	.05
❑ 211	Joel Skinner	.10	.05

❑ 212 Rex Hudler .10 .05
❑ 213 Bryan Harvey .10 .05
❑ 214 Charlie Hayes .10 .05
❑ 215 Matt Young .10 .05
❑ 216 Terry Kennedy .10 .05
❑ 217 Carl Nichols .10 .05
❑ 218 Mike Moore .10 .05
❑ 219 Paul O'Neill .40 .18
❑ 220 Steve Sax .10 .05
❑ 221 Shawn Boskie .10 .05
❑ 222 Rich DeLucia .10 .05
❑ 223 Lloyd Moseby .10 .05
❑ 224 Mike Kingery .10 .05
❑ 225 Carlos Baerga .10 .05
❑ 226 Bryn Smith .10 .05
❑ 227 Todd Stottlemyre .10 .05
❑ 228 Julio Franco .20 .09
❑ 229 Jim Gott .10 .05
❑ 230 Mike Schooler .10 .05
❑ 231 Steve Finley .20 .09
❑ 232 Dave Henderson .10 .05
❑ 233 Luis Quinones .10 .05
❑ 234 Mark Whiten .10 .05
❑ 235 Brian McRae RC .20 .09
❑ 236 Rich Gossage .20 .09
❑ 237 Rob Deer .10 .05
❑ 238 Will Clark .40 .18
❑ 239 Albert Belle .20 .09
❑ 240 Bob Melvin .10 .05
❑ 241 Larry Walker .30 .14
❑ 242 Dante Bichette .20 .09
❑ 243 Orel Hershiser .20 .09
❑ 244 Pete O'Brien .10 .05
❑ 245 Pete Harnisch .10 .05
❑ 246 Jeff Treadway .10 .05
❑ 247 Julio Machado .10 .05
❑ 248 Dave Johnson .10 .05
❑ 249 Kirk Gibson .20 .09
❑ 250 Kevin Brown .20 .09
❑ 251 Milt Cuyler .10 .05
❑ 252 Jeff Reardon .20 .09
❑ 253 David Cone .20 .09
❑ 254 Gary Redus .10 .05
❑ 255 Junior Noboa .10 .05
❑ 256 Greg Myers .10 .05
❑ 257 Dennis Cook .10 .05
❑ 258 Joe Girardi .10 .05
❑ 259 Allan Anderson .10 .05
❑ 260 Paul Marak .10 .05
❑ 261 Barry Bonds 1.00 .45
❑ 262 Juan Bell .10 .05
❑ 263 Russ Morman .10 .05
❑ 264 George Brett CL .40 .18
❑ 265 Jerald Clark .10 .05
❑ 266 Dwight Evans .20 .09
❑ 267 Roberto Alomar .40 .18
❑ 268 Danny Jackson .10 .05
❑ 269 Brian Downing .10 .05
❑ 270 John Cerutti .10 .05
❑ 271 Robin Ventura .20 .09
❑ 272 Gerald Perry .10 .05
❑ 273 Wade Boggs .40 .18
❑ 274 Dennis Martinez .20 .09
❑ 275 Andy Benes .10 .05
❑ 276 Tony Fossas .10 .05
❑ 277 Franklin Stubbs .10 .05
❑ 278 John Kruk .20 .09
❑ 279 Kevin Gross .10 .05
❑ 280 Von Hayes .10 .05
❑ 281 Frank Thomas .60 .25
❑ 282 Rob Dibble .10 .05
❑ 283 Mel Hall .10 .05
❑ 284 Rick Mahler .10 .05
❑ 285 Dennis Eckersley .20 .09
❑ 286 Bernard Gilkey .10 .05
❑ 287 Dan Plesac .10 .05
❑ 288 Jason Grimsley .10 .05
❑ 289 Mark Lewis .10 .05
❑ 290 Tony Gwynn .75 .35
❑ 291 Jeff Russell .10 .05
❑ 292 Curt Schilling .40 .18
❑ 293 Pascual Perez .10 .05
❑ 294 Jack Morris .20 .09
❑ 295 Hubie Brooks .10 .05
❑ 296 Alex Fernandez .10 .05
❑ 297 Harold Reynolds .10 .05
❑ 298 Craig Worthington .10 .05
❑ 299 Willie Wilson .10 .05
❑ 300 Mike Maddux .10 .05
❑ 301 Dave Righetti .20 .09
❑ 302 Paul Molitor .40 .18
❑ 303 Gary Gaetti .20 .09
❑ 304 Terry Pendleton .20 .09
❑ 305 Kevin Elster .10 .05
❑ 306 Scott Fletcher .10 .05
❑ 307 Jeff Robinson .10 .05
❑ 308 Jesse Barfield .10 .05
❑ 309 Mike LaCoss .10 .05
❑ 310 Andy Van Slyke .20 .09
❑ 311 Glenallen Hill .10 .05
❑ 312 Bud Black .10 .05
❑ 313 Kent Hrbek .20 .09
❑ 314 Tim Teufel .10 .05
❑ 315 Tony Fernandez .10 .05
❑ 316 Beau Allred .10 .05
❑ 317 Curtis Wilkerson .10 .05
❑ 318 Bill Sampen .10 .05
❑ 319 Randy Johnson .60 .25
❑ 320 Mike Heath .10 .05
❑ 321 Sammy Sosa 1.00 .45
❑ 322 Mickey Tettleton .10 .05
❑ 323 Jose Vizcaino .10 .05
❑ 324 John Candelaria .10 .05
❑ 325 Dave Howard .10 .05
❑ 326 Jose Rijo .10 .05
❑ 327 Todd Zeile .10 .05
❑ 328 Gene Nelson .10 .05
❑ 329 Dwayne Henry .10 .05
❑ 330 Mike Boddicker .10 .05
❑ 331 Ozzie Guillen .10 .05
❑ 332 Sam Horn .10 .05
❑ 333 Wally Whitehurst .10 .05
❑ 334 Dave Parker .20 .09
❑ 335 George Brett .75 .35
❑ 336 Bobby Thigpen .10 .05
❑ 337 Ed Whitson .10 .05
❑ 338 Ivan Calderon .10 .05
❑ 339 Mike Pagliarulo .10 .05
❑ 340 Jack McDowell .10 .05
❑ 341 Dana Kiecker .10 .05
❑ 342 Fred McGriff .30 .14
❑ 343 Mark Lee .10 .05
❑ 344 Alfredo Griffin .10 .05
❑ 345 Scott Bankhead .10 .05
❑ 346 Darrin Jackson .10 .05
❑ 347 Rafael Palmeiro .40 .18
❑ 348 Steve Farr .10 .05
❑ 349 Hensley Meulens .10 .05
❑ 350 Danny Cox .10 .05
❑ 351 Alan Trammell .30 .14
❑ 352 Edwin Nunez .10 .05
❑ 353 Joe Carter .20 .09
❑ 354 Eric Show .10 .05
❑ 355 Vance Law .10 .05
❑ 356 Jeff Gray .10 .05
❑ 357 Bobby Bonilla .20 .09
❑ 358 Ernest Riles .10 .05
❑ 359 Ron Hassey .10 .05
❑ 360 Willie McGee .20 .09
❑ 361 Mackey Sasser .10 .05
❑ 362 Glenn Braggs .10 .05
❑ 363 Mario Diaz .10 .05
❑ 364 Barry Bonds CL .50 .23
❑ 365 Kevin Bass .10 .05
❑ 366 Pete Incaviglia .10 .05
❑ 367 Luis Sojo UER .10 .05
(1989 stats interspersed with 1990's)
❑ 368 Lance Parrish .20 .09
❑ 369 Mark Leonard .10 .05
❑ 370 Heath Slocumb RC .20 .09
❑ 371 Jimmy Jones .10 .05
❑ 372 Ken Griffey Jr. 1.50 .70
❑ 373 Chris Hammond .10 .05
❑ 374 Chili Davis .20 .09
❑ 375 Joey Cora .10 .05
❑ 376 Ken Hill .10 .05
❑ 377 Darryl Strawberry .20 .09
❑ 378 Ron Darling .10 .05
❑ 379 Sid Bream .10 .05
❑ 380 Bill Swift .10 .05
❑ 381 Shawn Abner .10 .05
❑ 382 Eric King .10 .05
❑ 383 Mickey Morandini .10 .05
❑ 384 Carlton Fisk .40 .18
❑ 385 Steve Lake .10 .05
❑ 386 Mike Jeffcoat .10 .05
❑ 387 Darren Holmes RC .20 .09
❑ 388 Tim Wallach .10 .05
❑ 389 George Bell .10 .05
❑ 390 Craig Lefferts .10 .05
❑ 391 Ernie Whitt .10 .05
❑ 392 Felix Jose .10 .05
❑ 393 Kevin Maas .10 .05
❑ 394 Devon White .10 .05
❑ 395 Otis Nixon .10 .05
❑ 396 Chuck Knoblauch .20 .09
❑ 397 Scott Coolbaugh .10 .05
❑ 398 Glenn Davis .10 .05
❑ 399 Manny Lee .10 .05
❑ 400 Andre Dawson .30 .14
❑ 401 Scott Chiamparino .10 .05
❑ 402 Bill Gullickson .10 .05
❑ 403 Lance Johnson .10 .05
❑ 404 Juan Agosto .10 .05
❑ 405 Danny Darwin .10 .05
❑ 406 Barry Jones .10 .05
❑ 407 Larry Andersen .10 .05
❑ 408 Luis Rivera .10 .05
❑ 409 Jaime Navarro .10 .05
❑ 410 Roger McDowell .10 .05
❑ 411 Brett Butler .20 .09
❑ 412 Dale Murphy .40 .18
❑ 413 Tim Raines UER .20 .09
(Listed as hitting .500 in 1980, should be .050)
❑ 414 Norm Charlton .10 .05
❑ 415 Greg Cadaret .10 .05
❑ 416 Chris Nabholz .10 .05
❑ 417 Dave Stewart .20 .09
❑ 418 Rich Gedman .10 .05
❑ 419 Willie Randolph .20 .09
❑ 420 Mitch Williams .10 .05
❑ 421 Brook Jacoby .10 .05
❑ 422 Greg W. Harris .10 .05
❑ 423 Nolan Ryan 2.00 .90
❑ 424 Dave Rohde .10 .05
❑ 425 Don Mattingly 1.00 .45
❑ 426 Greg Gagne .10 .05
❑ 427 Vince Coleman .10 .05
❑ 428 Dan Pasqua .10 .05
❑ 429 Alvin Davis .10 .05
❑ 430 Cal Ripken 1.50 .70
❑ 431 Jamie Quirk .10 .05
❑ 432 Benito Santiago .10 .05
❑ 433 Jose Uribe .10 .05
❑ 434 Candy Maldonado .10 .05
❑ 435 Junior Felix .10 .05
❑ 436 Deion Sanders .20 .09
❑ 437 John Franco .20 .09
❑ 438 Greg Hibbard .10 .05
❑ 439 Floyd Bannister .10 .05
❑ 440 Steve Howe .10 .05
❑ 441 Steve Decker .10 .05
❑ 442 Vicente Palacios .10 .05
❑ 443 Pat Tabler .10 .05
❑ 444 Darryl Strawberry CL .20 .09
❑ 445 Mike Felder .10 .05
❑ 446 Al Newman .10 .05
❑ 447 Chris Donnels .10 .05
❑ 448 Rich Rodriguez .10 .05
❑ 449 Turner Ward RC .20 .09
❑ 450 Bob Walk .10 .05
❑ 451 Gilberto Reyes .10 .05
❑ 452 Mike Jackson .10 .05
❑ 453 Rafael Belliard .10 .05
❑ 454 Wayne Edwards .10 .05
❑ 455 Andy Allanson .10 .05
❑ 456 Dave Smith .10 .05
❑ 457 Gary Carter .30 .14
❑ 458 Warren Cromartie .10 .05
❑ 459 Jack Armstrong .10 .05
❑ 460 Bob Tewksbury .10 .05
❑ 461 Joe Klink .10 .05
❑ 462 Xavier Hernandez .10 .05
❑ 463 Scott Radinsky .10 .05
❑ 464 Jeff Robinson .10 .05
❑ 465 Gregg Jefferies .10 .05

	Card	Mint	Nrmt
❑	466 Denny Neagle RC	.40	.18
❑	467 Carmelo Martinez	.10	.05
❑	468 Donn Pall	.10	.05
❑	469 Bruce Hurst	.10	.05
❑	470 Eric Bullock	.10	.05
❑	471 Rick Aguilera	.20	.09
❑	472 Charlie Hough	.20	.09
❑	473 Carlos Quintana	.10	.05
❑	474 Marty Barrett	.10	.05
❑	475 Kevin D. Brown	.10	.05
❑	476 Bobby Ojeda	.10	.05
❑	477 Edgar Martinez	.30	.14
❑	478 Bip Roberts	.10	.05
❑	479 Mike Flanagan	.10	.05
❑	480 John Habyan	.10	.05
❑	481 Larry Casian	.10	.05
❑	482 Wally Backman	.10	.05
❑	483 Doug Dascenzo	.10	.05
❑	484 Rick Dempsey	.10	.05
❑	485 Ed Sprague	.10	.05
❑	486 Steve Chitren	.10	.05
❑	487 Mark McGwire	1.50	.70
❑	488 Roger Clemens	1.00	.45
❑	489 Orlando Merced RC	.10	.05
❑	490 Rene Gonzales	.10	.05
❑	491 Mike Stanton	.10	.05
❑	492 Al Osuna RC	.10	.05
❑	493 Rick Cerone	.10	.05
❑	494 Mariano Duncan	.10	.05
❑	495 Zane Smith	.10	.05
❑	496 John Morris	.10	.05
❑	497 Frank Tanana	.10	.05
❑	498 Junior Ortiz	.10	.05
❑	499 Dave Winfield	.40	.18
❑	500 Gary Varsho	.10	.05
❑	501 Chico Walker	.10	.05
❑	502 Ken Caminiti	.20	.09
❑	503 Ken Griffey Sr.	.20	.09
❑	504 Randy Myers	.10	.05
❑	505 Steve Bedrosian	.10	.05
❑	506 Cory Snyder	.10	.05
❑	507 Cris Carpenter	.10	.05
❑	508 Tim Belcher	.10	.05
❑	509 Jeff Hamilton	.10	.05
❑	510 Steve Avery	.10	.05
❑	511 Dave Valle	.10	.05
❑	512 Tom Lampkin	.10	.05
❑	513 Shawn Hillegas	.10	.05
❑	514 Reggie Jefferson	.10	.05
❑	515 Ron Karkovice	.10	.05
❑	516 Doug Drabek	.10	.05
❑	517 Tom Henke	.10	.05
❑	518 Chris Bosio	.10	.05
❑	519 Gregg Olson	.10	.05
❑	520 Bob Scanlan	.10	.05
❑	521 Alonzo Powell	.10	.05
❑	522 Jeff Ballard	.10	.05
❑	523 Ray Lankford	.20	.09
❑	524 Tommy Greene	.10	.05
❑	525 Mike Timlin RC	.20	.09
❑	526 Juan Berenguer	.10	.05
❑	527 Scott Erickson	.10	.05
❑	528 Sandy Alomar Jr. CL	.10	.05

1992 Leaf

	MINT	NRMT
COMPLETE SET (528)	15.00	6.75
COMPLETE SERIES 1 (264)	5.00	2.20
COMPLETE SERIES 2 (264)	10.00	4.50

	Card	Mint	Nrmt
❑	1 Jim Abbott	.15	.07
❑	2 Cal Eldred	.05	.02
❑	3 Bud Black	.05	.02
❑	4 Dave Howard	.05	.02
❑	5 Luis Sojo	.05	.02
❑	6 Gary Scott	.05	.02
❑	7 Joe Oliver	.05	.02
❑	8 Chris Gardner	.05	.02
❑	9 Sandy Alomar Jr.	.15	.07
❑	10 Greg W. Harris	.05	.02
❑	11 Doug Drabek	.05	.02
❑	12 Darryl Hamilton	.05	.02
❑	13 Mike Mussina	.50	.23
❑	14 Kevin Tapani	.05	.02
❑	15 Ron Gant	.05	.02
❑	16 Mark McGwire	1.25	.55
❑	17 Robin Ventura	.15	.07
❑	18 Pedro Guerrero	.15	.07
❑	19 Roger Clemens	.75	.35
❑	20 Steve Farr	.05	.02
❑	21 Frank Tanana	.05	.02
❑	22 Joe Hesketh	.05	.02
❑	23 Erik Hanson	.05	.02
❑	24 Greg Cadaret	.05	.02
❑	25 Rex Hudler	.05	.02
❑	26 Mark Grace	.30	.14
❑	27 Kelly Gruber	.05	.02
❑	28 Jeff Bagwell	.60	.25
❑	29 Darryl Strawberry	.15	.07
❑	30 Dave Smith	.05	.02
❑	31 Kevin Appier	.15	.07
❑	32 Steve Chitren	.05	.02
❑	33 Kevin Gross	.05	.02
❑	34 Rick Aguilera	.15	.07
❑	35 Juan Guzman	.05	.02
❑	36 Joe Orsulak	.05	.02
❑	37 Tim Raines	.15	.07
❑	38 Harold Reynolds	.05	.02
❑	39 Charlie Hough	.15	.07
❑	40 Tony Phillips	.05	.02
❑	41 Nolan Ryan	1.50	.70
❑	42 Vince Coleman	.05	.02
❑	43 Andy Van Slyke	.15	.07
❑	44 Tim Burke	.05	.02
❑	45 Luis Polonia	.05	.02
❑	46 Tom Browning	.05	.02
❑	47 Willie McGee	.15	.07
❑	48 Gary DiSarcina	.05	.02
❑	49 Mark Lewis	.05	.02
❑	50 Phil Plantier	.05	.02
❑	51 Doug Dascenzo	.05	.02
❑	52 Cal Ripken	1.25	.55
❑	53 Pedro Munoz	.05	.02
❑	54 Carlos Hernandez	.05	.02
❑	55 Jerald Clark	.05	.02
❑	56 Jeff Brantley	.05	.02
❑	57 Don Mattingly	.75	.35
❑	58 Roger McDowell	.05	.02
❑	59 Steve Avery	.05	.02
❑	60 John Olerud	.15	.07
❑	61 Bill Gullickson	.05	.02
❑	62 Juan Gonzalez	.30	.14
❑	63 Felix Jose	.05	.02
❑	64 Robin Yount	.30	.14
❑	65 Greg Briley	.05	.02
❑	66 Steve Finley	.15	.07
❑	67 Frank Thomas CL	.20	.09
❑	68 Tom Gordon	.05	.02
❑	69 Rob Dibble	.05	.02
❑	70 Glenallen Hill	.05	.02
❑	71 Calvin Jones	.05	.02
❑	72 Joe Girardi	.05	.02
❑	73 Barry Larkin	.30	.14
❑	74 Andy Benes	.05	.02
❑	75 Milt Cuyler	.05	.02
❑	76 Kevin Bass	.05	.02
❑	77 Pete Harnisch	.05	.02
❑	78 Wilson Alvarez	.05	.02
❑	79 Mike Devereaux	.05	.02
❑	80 Doug Henry RC	.05	.02
❑	81 Orel Hershiser	.15	.07
❑	82 Shane Mack	.05	.02
❑	83 Mike Macfarlane	.05	.02
❑	84 Thomas Howard	.05	.02
❑	85 Alex Fernandez	.05	.02
❑	86 Reggie Jefferson	.05	.02
❑	87 Leo Gomez	.05	.02
❑	88 Mel Hall	.05	.02
❑	89 Mike Greenwell	.05	.02
❑	90 Jeff Russell	.05	.02
❑	91 Steve Buechele	.05	.02
❑	92 David Cone	.15	.07
❑	93 Kevin Reimer	.05	.02
❑	94 Mark Lemke	.05	.02
❑	95 Bob Tewksbury	.05	.02
❑	96 Zane Smith	.05	.02
❑	97 Mark Eichhorn	.05	.02
❑	98 Kirby Puckett	.75	.35
❑	99 Paul O'Neill	.30	.14
❑	100 Dennis Eckersley	.15	.07
❑	101 Duane Ward	.05	.02
❑	102 Matt Nokes	.05	.02
❑	103 Mo Vaughn	.15	.07
❑	104 Pat Kelly	.05	.02
❑	105 Ron Karkovice	.05	.02
❑	106 Bill Spiers	.05	.02
❑	107 Gary Gaetti	.15	.07
❑	108 Mackey Sasser	.05	.02
❑	109 Robby Thompson	.05	.02
❑	110 Marvin Freeman	.05	.02
❑	111 Jimmy Key	.15	.07
❑	112 Dwight Gooden	.15	.07
❑	113 Charlie Leibrandt	.05	.02
❑	114 Devon White	.05	.02
❑	115 Charles Nagy	.05	.02
❑	116 Rickey Henderson	.60	.25
❑	117 Paul Assenmacher	.05	.02
❑	118 Junior Felix	.05	.02
❑	119 Julio Franco	.15	.07
❑	120 Norm Charlton	.05	.02
❑	121 Scott Servais	.05	.02
❑	122 Gerald Perry	.05	.02
❑	123 Brian McRae	.05	.02
❑	124 Don Slaught	.05	.02
❑	125 Juan Samuel	.05	.02
❑	126 Harold Baines	.15	.07
❑	127 Scott Livingstone	.05	.02
❑	128 Jay Buhner	.15	.07
❑	129 Darrin Jackson	.05	.02
❑	130 Luis Mercedes	.05	.02
❑	131 Brian Harper	.05	.02
❑	132 Howard Johnson	.05	.02
❑	133 Nolan Ryan CL	.30	.14
❑	134 Dante Bichette	.15	.07
❑	135 Dave Righetti	.15	.07
❑	136 Jeff Montgomery	.05	.02
❑	137 Joe Grahe	.05	.02
❑	138 Delino DeShields	.05	.02
❑	139 Jose Rijo	.05	.02
❑	140 Ken Caminiti	.15	.07
❑	141 Steve Olin	.05	.02
❑	142 Kurt Stillwell	.05	.02
❑	143 Jay Bell	.15	.07
❑	144 Jaime Navarro	.05	.02
❑	145 Ben McDonald	.05	.02
❑	146 Greg Gagne	.05	.02
❑	147 Jeff Blauser	.05	.02
❑	148 Carney Lansford	.15	.07
❑	149 Ozzie Guillen	.05	.02
❑	150 Milt Thompson	.05	.02
❑	151 Jeff Reardon	.15	.07
❑	152 Scott Sanderson	.05	.02
❑	153 Cecil Fielder	.15	.07
❑	154 Greg A. Harris	.05	.02
❑	155 Rich DeLucia	.05	.02
❑	156 Roberto Kelly	.05	.02
❑	157 Bryn Smith	.05	.02
❑	158 Chuck McElroy	.05	.02
❑	159 Tom Henke	.05	.02
❑	160 Luis Gonzalez	.30	.14
❑	161 Steve Wilson	.05	.02
❑	162 Shawn Boskie	.05	.02
❑	163 Mark Davis	.05	.02
❑	164 Mike Moore	.05	.02
❑	165 Mike Scioscia	.05	.02
❑	166 Scott Erickson	.05	.02
❑	167 Todd Stottlemyre	.05	.02
❑	168 Alvin Davis	.05	.02
❑	169 Greg Hibbard	.05	.02

❑ 170 David Valle .05 .02
❑ 171 Dave Winfield .30 .14
❑ 172 Alan Trammell .20 .09
❑ 173 Kenny Rogers .05 .02
❑ 174 John Franco .15 .07
❑ 175 Jose Lind .05 .02
❑ 176 Pete Schourek .05 .02
❑ 177 Von Hayes .05 .02
❑ 178 Chris Hammond .05 .02
❑ 179 John Burkett .05 .02
❑ 180 Dickie Thon .05 .02
❑ 181 Joel Skinner .05 .02
❑ 182 Scott Cooper .05 .02
❑ 183 Andre Dawson .20 .09
❑ 184 Billy Ripken .05 .02
❑ 185 Kevin Mitchell .05 .02
❑ 186 Brett Butler .15 .07
❑ 187 Tony Fernandez .05 .02
❑ 188 Cory Snyder .05 .02
❑ 189 John Habyan .05 .02
❑ 190 Dennis Martinez .15 .07
❑ 191 John Smoltz .15 .07
❑ 192 Greg Myers .05 .02
❑ 193 Rob Deer .05 .02
❑ 194 Ivan Rodriguez .50 .23
❑ 195 Ray Lankford .05 .02
❑ 196 Bill Wegman .05 .02
❑ 197 Edgar Martinez .20 .09
❑ 198 Darryl Kile .15 .07
❑ 199 Cal Ripken CL .30 .14
❑ 200 Brent Mayne .05 .02
❑ 201 Larry Walker .20 .09
❑ 202 Carlos Baerga .05 .02
❑ 203 Russ Swan .05 .02
❑ 204 Mike Morgan .05 .02
❑ 205 Hal Morris .05 .02
❑ 206 Tony Gwynn .60 .25
❑ 207 Mark Leiter .05 .02
❑ 208 Kirt Manwaring .05 .02
❑ 209 Al Osuna .05 .02
❑ 210 Bobby Thigpen .05 .02
❑ 211 Chris Hoiles .05 .02
❑ 212 B.J. Surhoff .15 .07
❑ 213 Lenny Harris .05 .02
❑ 214 Scott Leius .05 .02
❑ 215 Gregg Jefferies .05 .02
❑ 216 Bruce Hurst .05 .02
❑ 217 Steve Sax .05 .02
❑ 218 Dave Otto .05 .02
❑ 219 Sam Horn .05 .02
❑ 220 Charlie Hayes .05 .02
❑ 221 Frank Viola .15 .07
❑ 222 Jose Guzman .05 .02
❑ 223 Gary Redus .05 .02
❑ 224 Dave Gallagher .05 .02
❑ 225 Dean Palmer .15 .07
❑ 226 Greg Olson .05 .02
❑ 227 Jose DeLeon .05 .02
❑ 228 Mike LaValliere .05 .02
❑ 229 Mark Langston .05 .02
❑ 230 Chuck Knoblauch .15 .07
❑ 231 Bill Doran .05 .02
❑ 232 Dave Henderson .05 .02
❑ 233 Roberto Alomar .30 .14
❑ 234 Scott Fletcher .05 .02
❑ 235 Tim Naehring .05 .02
❑ 236 Mike Gallego .05 .02
❑ 237 Lance Johnson .05 .02
❑ 238 Paul Molitor .30 .14
❑ 239 Dan Gladden .05 .02
❑ 240 Willie Randolph .15 .07
❑ 241 Will Clark .30 .14
❑ 242 Sid Bream .05 .02
❑ 243 Derek Bell .15 .07
❑ 244 Bill Pecota .05 .02
❑ 245 Terry Pendleton .15 .07
❑ 246 Randy Ready .05 .02
❑ 247 Jack Armstrong .05 .02
❑ 248 Todd Van Poppel .05 .02
❑ 249 Shawon Dunston .05 .02
❑ 250 Bobby Rose .05 .02
❑ 251 Jeff Huson .05 .02
❑ 252 Bip Roberts .05 .02
❑ 253 Doug Jones .05 .02
❑ 254 Lee Smith .15 .07
❑ 255 George Brett .60 .25
❑ 256 Randy Tomlin .05 .02
❑ 257 Todd Benzinger .05 .02
❑ 258 Dave Stewart .15 .07
❑ 259 Mark Carreon .05 .02
❑ 260 Pete O'Brien .05 .02
❑ 261 Tim Teufel .05 .02
❑ 262 Bob Milacki .05 .02
❑ 263 Mark Guthrie .05 .02
❑ 264 Darrin Fletcher .05 .02
❑ 265 Omar Vizquel .15 .07
❑ 266 Chris Bosio .05 .02
❑ 267 Jose Canseco .30 .14
❑ 268 Mike Boddicker .05 .02
❑ 269 Lance Parrish .15 .07
❑ 270 Jose Vizcaino .05 .02
❑ 271 Chris Sabo .05 .02
❑ 272 Royce Clayton .05 .02
❑ 273 Marquis Grissom .05 .02
❑ 274 Fred McGriff .20 .09
❑ 275 Barry Bonds .75 .35
❑ 276 Greg Vaughn .15 .07
❑ 277 Gregg Olson .05 .02
❑ 278 Dave Hollins .05 .02
❑ 279 Tom Glavine .30 .14
❑ 280 Bryan Hickerson UER .05 .02
Name spelled Brian on front
❑ 281 Scott Radinsky .05 .02
❑ 282 Omar Olivares .05 .02
❑ 283 Ivan Calderon .05 .02
❑ 284 Kevin Maas .05 .02
❑ 285 Mickey Tettleton .05 .02
❑ 286 Wade Boggs .30 .14
❑ 287 Stan Belinda .05 .02
❑ 288 Bret Barberie .05 .02
❑ 289 Jose Oquendo .05 .02
❑ 290 Frank Castillo .05 .02
❑ 291 Dave Stieb .05 .02
❑ 292 Tommy Greene .05 .02
❑ 293 Eric Karros .15 .07
❑ 294 Greg Maddux .75 .35
❑ 295 Jim Eisenreich .05 .02
❑ 296 Rafael Palmeiro .30 .14
❑ 297 Ramon Martinez .05 .02
❑ 298 Tim Wallach .05 .02
❑ 299 Jim Thome .30 .14
❑ 300 Chito Martinez .05 .02
❑ 301 Mitch Williams .05 .02
❑ 302 Randy Johnson .40 .18
❑ 303 Carlton Fisk .30 .14
❑ 304 Travis Fryman .15 .07
❑ 305 Bobby Witt .05 .02
❑ 306 Dave Magadan .05 .02
❑ 307 Alex Cole .05 .02
❑ 308 Bobby Bonilla .15 .07
❑ 309 Bryan Harvey .05 .02
❑ 310 Rafael Belliard .05 .02
❑ 311 Mariano Duncan .05 .02
❑ 312 Chuck Crim .05 .02
❑ 313 John Kruk .15 .07
❑ 314 Ellis Burks .15 .07
❑ 315 Craig Biggio .20 .09
❑ 316 Glenn Davis .05 .02
❑ 317 Ryne Sandberg .40 .18
❑ 318 Mike Sharperson .05 .02
❑ 319 Rich Rodriguez .05 .02
❑ 320 Lee Guetterman .05 .02
❑ 321 Benito Santiago .05 .02
❑ 322 Jose Offerman .05 .02
❑ 323 Tony Pena .05 .02
❑ 324 Pat Borders .05 .02
❑ 325 Mike Henneman .05 .02
❑ 326 Kevin Brown .15 .07
❑ 327 Chris Nabholz .05 .02
❑ 328 Franklin Stubbs .05 .02
❑ 329 Tino Martinez .15 .07
❑ 330 Mickey Morandini .05 .02
❑ 331 Ryne Sandberg CL .20 .09
❑ 332 Mark Gubicza .05 .02
❑ 333 Bill Landrum .05 .02
❑ 334 Mark Whiten .05 .02
❑ 335 Darren Daulton .15 .07
❑ 336 Rick Wilkins .05 .02
❑ 337 Brian Jordan RC .75 .35
❑ 338 Kevin Ward .05 .02
❑ 339 Ruben Amaro .05 .02
❑ 340 Trevor Wilson .05 .02
❑ 341 Andujar Cedeno .05 .02
❑ 342 Michael Huff .05 .02
❑ 343 Brady Anderson .15 .07
❑ 344 Craig Grebeck .05 .02
❑ 345 Bob Ojeda .05 .02
❑ 346 Mike Pagliarulo .05 .02
❑ 347 Terry Shumpert .05 .02
❑ 348 Dann Bilardello .05 .02
❑ 349 Frank Thomas .40 .18
❑ 350 Albert Belle .15 .07
❑ 351 Jose Mesa .05 .02
❑ 352 Rich Monteleone .05 .02
❑ 353 Bob Walk .05 .02
❑ 354 Monty Fariss .05 .02
❑ 355 Luis Rivera .05 .02
❑ 356 Anthony Young .05 .02
❑ 357 Geno Petralli .05 .02
❑ 358 Otis Nixon .05 .02
❑ 359 Tom Pagnozzi .05 .02
❑ 360 Reggie Sanders .05 .02
❑ 361 Lee Stevens .05 .02
❑ 362 Kent Hrbek .15 .07
❑ 363 Orlando Merced .05 .02
❑ 364 Mike Bordick .05 .02
❑ 365 Dion James UER .05 .02
(Blue Jays logo on card back)
❑ 366 Jack Clark .15 .07
❑ 367 Mike Stanley .05 .02
❑ 368 Randy Velarde .05 .02
❑ 369 Dan Pasqua .05 .02
❑ 370 Pat Listach RC .15 .07
❑ 371 Mike Fitzgerald .05 .02
❑ 372 Tom Foley .05 .02
❑ 373 Matt Williams .20 .09
❑ 374 Brian Hunter .05 .02
❑ 375 Joe Carter .15 .07
❑ 376 Bret Saberhagen .15 .07
❑ 377 Mike Stanton .05 .02
❑ 378 Hubie Brooks .05 .02
❑ 379 Eric Bell .05 .02
❑ 380 Walt Weiss .05 .02
❑ 381 Danny Jackson .05 .02
❑ 382 Manuel Lee .05 .02
❑ 383 Ruben Sierra .05 .02
❑ 384 Greg Swindell .05 .02
❑ 385 Ryan Bowen .05 .02
❑ 386 Kevin Ritz .05 .02
❑ 387 Curtis Wilkerson .05 .02
❑ 388 Gary Varsho .05 .02
❑ 389 Dave Hansen .05 .02
❑ 390 Bob Welch .05 .02
❑ 391 Lou Whitaker .15 .07
❑ 392 Ken Griffey Jr. 1.00 .45
❑ 393 Mike Maddux .05 .02
❑ 394 Arthur Rhodes .05 .02
❑ 395 Chili Davis .15 .07
❑ 396 Eddie Murray .30 .14
❑ 397 Robin Yount CL .15 .07
❑ 398 Dave Cochrane .05 .02
❑ 399 Kevin Seitzer .05 .02
❑ 400 Ozzie Smith .40 .18
❑ 401 Paul Sorrento .05 .02
❑ 402 Les Lancaster .05 .02
❑ 403 Junior Noboa .05 .02
❑ 404 David Justice .15 .07
❑ 405 Andy Ashby .05 .02
❑ 406 Danny Tartabull .05 .02
❑ 407 Bill Swift .05 .02
❑ 408 Craig Lefferts .05 .02
❑ 409 Tom Candiotti .05 .02
❑ 410 Lance Blankenship .05 .02
❑ 411 Jeff Tackett .05 .02
❑ 412 Sammy Sosa .60 .25
❑ 413 Jody Reed .05 .02
❑ 414 Bruce Ruffin .05 .02
❑ 415 Gene Larkin .05 .02
❑ 416 John Vander Wal RC .05 .02
❑ 417 Tim Belcher .05 .02
❑ 418 Steve Frey .05 .02
❑ 419 Dick Schofield .05 .02
❑ 420 Jeff King .05 .02
❑ 421 Kim Batiste .05 .02
❑ 422 Jack McDowell .05 .02
❑ 423 Damon Berryhill .05 .02
❑ 424 Gary Wayne .05 .02

	No.	Player	Mint	NrMt
❑	425	Jack Morris	.15	.07
❑	426	Moises Alou	.15	.07
❑	427	Mark McLemore	.05	.02
❑	428	Juan Guerrero	.05	.02
❑	429	Scott Scudder	.05	.02
❑	430	Eric Davis	.15	.07
❑	431	Joe Slusarski	.05	.02
❑	432	Todd Zeile	.05	.02
❑	433	Dwayne Henry	.05	.02
❑	434	Cliff Brantley	.05	.02
❑	435	Butch Henry RC	.05	.02
❑	436	Todd Worrell	.05	.02
❑	437	Bob Scanlan	.05	.02
❑	438	Wally Joyner	.15	.07
❑	439	John Flaherty	.05	.02
❑	440	Brian Downing	.05	.02
❑	441	Darren Lewis	.05	.02
❑	442	Gary Carter	.20	.09
❑	443	Wally Ritchie	.05	.02
❑	444	Chris Jones	.05	.02
❑	445	Jeff Kent RC	2.00	.90
❑	446	Gary Sheffield	.15	.07
❑	447	Ron Darling	.05	.02
❑	448	Deion Sanders	.15	.07
❑	449	Andres Galarraga	.20	.09
❑	450	Chuck Finley	.15	.07
❑	451	Derek Lilliquist	.05	.02
❑	452	Carl Willis	.05	.02
❑	453	Wes Chamberlain	.05	.02
❑	454	Roger Mason	.05	.02
❑	455	Spike Owen	.05	.02
❑	456	Thomas Howard	.05	.02
❑	457	Dave Martinez	.05	.02
❑	458	Pete Incaviglia	.05	.02
❑	459	Keith A. Miller	.05	.02
❑	460	Mike Fetters	.05	.02
❑	461	Paul Gibson	.05	.02
❑	462	George Bell	.05	.02
❑	463	Bobby Bonilla CL	.05	.02
❑	464	Terry Mulholland	.05	.02
❑	465	Storm Davis	.05	.02
❑	466	Gary Pettis	.05	.02
❑	467	Randy Bush	.05	.02
❑	468	Ken Hill	.05	.02
❑	469	Rheal Cormier	.05	.02
❑	470	Andy Stankiewicz	.05	.02
❑	471	Dave Burba	.05	.02
❑	472	Henry Cotto	.05	.02
❑	473	Dale Sveum	.05	.02
❑	474	Rich Gossage	.15	.07
❑	475	William Suero	.05	.02
❑	476	Doug Strange	.05	.02
❑	477	Bill Krueger	.05	.02
❑	478	John Wetteland	.15	.07
❑	479	Melido Perez	.05	.02
❑	480	Lonnie Smith	.05	.02
❑	481	Mike Jackson	.05	.02
❑	482	Mike Gardiner	.05	.02
❑	483	David Wells	.15	.07
❑	484	Barry Jones	.05	.02
❑	485	Scott Bankhead	.05	.02
❑	486	Terry Leach	.05	.02
❑	487	Vince Horsman	.05	.02
❑	488	Dave Eiland	.05	.02
❑	489	Alejandro Pena	.05	.02
❑	490	Julio Valera	.05	.02
❑	491	Joe Boever	.05	.02
❑	492	Paul Miller RC	.05	.02
❑	493	Archi Cianfrocco RC	.05	.02
❑	494	Dave Fleming	.05	.02
❑	495	Kyle Abbott	.05	.02
❑	496	Chad Kreuter	.05	.02
❑	497	Chris James	.05	.02
❑	498	Donnie Hill	.05	.02
❑	499	Jacob Brumfield	.05	.02
❑	500	Ricky Bones	.05	.02
❑	501	Terry Steinbach	.05	.02
❑	502	Bernard Gilkey	.05	.02
❑	503	Dennis Cook	.05	.02
❑	504	Len Dykstra	.15	.07
❑	505	Mike Bielecki	.05	.02
❑	506	Bob Kipper	.05	.02
❑	507	Jose Melendez	.05	.02
❑	508	Rick Sutcliffe	.15	.07
❑	509	Ken Patterson	.05	.02
❑	510	Andy Allanson	.05	.02
❑	511	Al Newman	.05	.02
❑	512	Mark Gardner	.05	.02
❑	513	Jeff Schaefer	.05	.02
❑	514	Jim McNamara	.05	.02
❑	515	Peter Hoy	.05	.02
❑	516	Curt Schilling	.30	.14
❑	517	Kirk McCaskill	.05	.02
❑	518	Chris Gwynn	.05	.02
❑	519	Sid Fernandez	.05	.02
❑	520	Jeff Parrett	.05	.02
❑	521	Scott Ruskin	.05	.02
❑	522	Kevin McReynolds	.05	.02
❑	523	Rick Cerone	.05	.02
❑	524	Jesse Orosco	.05	.02
❑	525	Troy Afenir	.05	.02
❑	526	John Smiley	.05	.02
❑	527	Dale Murphy	.30	.14
❑	528	Leaf Set Card	.05	.02

1993 Leaf

	MINT	NRMT
COMPLETE SET (550)	35.00	16.00
COMPLETE SERIES 1 (220)	15.00	6.75
COMPLETE SERIES 2 (220)	15.00	6.75
COMPLETE UPDATE (110)	5.00	2.20

	No.	Player	Mint	NrMt
❑	1	Ben McDonald	.15	.07
❑	2	Sid Fernandez	.15	.07
❑	3	Juan Guzman	.15	.07
❑	4	Curt Schilling	.60	.25
❑	5	Ivan Rodriguez	.60	.25
❑	6	Don Slaught	.15	.07
❑	7	Terry Steinbach	.15	.07
❑	8	Todd Zeile	.15	.07
❑	9	Andy Stankiewicz	.15	.07
❑	10	Tim Teufel	.15	.07
❑	11	Marvin Freeman	.15	.07
❑	12	Jim Austin	.15	.07
❑	13	Bob Scanlan	.15	.07
❑	14	Rusty Meacham	.15	.07
❑	15	Casey Candaele	.15	.07
❑	16	Travis Fryman	.25	.11
❑	17	Jose Offerman	.15	.07
❑	18	Albert Belle	.25	.11
❑	19	John Vander Wal	.15	.07
❑	20	Dan Pasqua	.15	.07
❑	21	Frank Viola	.25	.11
❑	22	Terry Mulholland	.15	.07
❑	23	Gregg Olson	.15	.07
❑	24	Randy Tomlin	.15	.07
❑	25	Todd Stottlemyre	.15	.07
❑	26	Jose Oquendo	.15	.07
❑	27	Julio Franco	.25	.11
❑	28	Tony Gwynn	1.25	.55
❑	29	Ruben Sierra	.15	.07
❑	30	Robby Thompson	.15	.07
❑	31	Jim Bullinger	.15	.07
❑	32	Rick Aguilera	.15	.07
❑	33	Scott Servais	.15	.07
❑	34	Cal Eldred	.15	.07
❑	35	Mike Piazza	3.00	1.35
❑	36	Brent Mayne	.15	.07
❑	37	Wil Cordero	.15	.07
❑	38	Milt Cuyler	.15	.07
❑	39	Howard Johnson	.15	.07
❑	40	Kenny Lofton	.25	.11
❑	41	Alex Fernandez	.15	.07

	No.	Player	Mint	NrMt
❑	42	Denny Neagle	.25	.11
❑	43	Tony Pena	.15	.07
❑	44	Bob Tewksbury	.15	.07
❑	45	Glenn Davis	.15	.07
❑	46	Fred McGriff	.40	.18
❑	47	John Olerud	.25	.11
❑	48	Steve Hosey	.15	.07
❑	49	Rafael Palmeiro	.60	.25
❑	50	David Justice	.25	.11
❑	51	Pete Harnisch	.15	.07
❑	52	Sam Militello	.15	.07
❑	53	Orel Hershiser	.25	.11
❑	54	Pat Mahomes	.15	.07
❑	55	Greg Colbrunn	.15	.07
❑	56	Greg Vaughn	.25	.11
❑	57	Vince Coleman	.15	.07
❑	58	Brian McRae	.15	.07
❑	59	Len Dykstra	.25	.11
❑	60	Dan Gladden	.15	.07
❑	61	Ted Power	.15	.07
❑	62	Donovan Osborne	.15	.07
❑	63	Ron Karkovice	.15	.07
❑	64	Frank Seminara	.15	.07
❑	65	Bob Zupcic	.15	.07
❑	66	Kirt Manwaring	.15	.07
❑	67	Mike Devereaux	.15	.07
❑	68	Mark Lemke	.15	.07
❑	69	Devon White	.15	.07
❑	70	Sammy Sosa	1.25	.55
❑	71	Pedro Astacio	.15	.07
❑	72	Dennis Eckersley	.25	.11
❑	73	Chris Nabholz	.15	.07
❑	74	Melido Perez	.15	.07
❑	75	Todd Hundley	.15	.07
❑	76	Kent Hrbek	.25	.11
❑	77	Mickey Morandini	.15	.07
❑	78	Tim McIntosh	.15	.07
❑	79	Andy Van Slyke	.25	.11
❑	80	Kevin McReynolds	.15	.07
❑	81	Mike Henneman	.15	.07
❑	82	Greg W. Harris	.15	.07
❑	83	Sandy Alomar Jr.	.25	.11
❑	84	Mike Jackson	.15	.07
❑	85	Ozzie Guillen	.15	.07
❑	86	Jeff Blauser	.15	.07
❑	87	John Valentin	.15	.07
❑	88	Rey Sanchez	.15	.07
❑	89	Rick Sutcliffe	.25	.11
❑	90	Luis Gonzalez	.60	.25
❑	91	Jeff Fassero	.15	.07
❑	92	Kenny Rogers	.15	.07
❑	93	Bret Saberhagen	.25	.11
❑	94	Bob Welch	.15	.07
❑	95	Darren Daulton	.25	.11
❑	96	Mike Gallego	.15	.07
❑	97	Orlando Merced	.15	.07
❑	98	Chuck Knoblauch	.25	.11
❑	99	Bernard Gilkey	.15	.07
❑	100	Billy Ashley	.15	.07
❑	101	Kevin Appier	.25	.11
❑	102	Jeff Brantley	.15	.07
❑	103	Bill Gullickson	.15	.07
❑	104	John Smoltz	.25	.11
❑	105	Paul Sorrento	.15	.07
❑	106	Steve Buechele	.15	.07
❑	107	Steve Sax	.15	.07
❑	108	Andujar Cedeno	.15	.07
❑	109	Billy Hatcher	.15	.07
❑	110	Checklist	.15	.07
❑	111	Alan Mills	.15	.07
❑	112	John Franco	.25	.11
❑	113	Jack Morris	.25	.11
❑	114	Mitch Williams	.15	.07
❑	115	Nolan Ryan	3.00	1.35
❑	116	Jay Bell	.25	.11
❑	117	Mike Bordick	.15	.07
❑	118	Geronimo Pena	.15	.07
❑	119	Danny Tartabull	.15	.07
❑	120	Checklist	.15	.07
❑	121	Steve Avery	.15	.07
❑	122	Ricky Bones	.15	.07
❑	123	Mike Morgan	.15	.07
❑	124	Jeff Montgomery	.15	.07
❑	125	Jeff Bagwell	.75	.35
❑	126	Tony Phillips	.15	.07
❑	127	Lenny Harris	.15	.07

- ❑ 128 Glenallen Hill .15 .07
- ❑ 129 Marquis Grissom .15 .07
- ❑ 130 Gerald Williams UER .15 .07
  (Bernie Williams picture and stats)
- ❑ 131 Greg A. Harris .15 .07
- ❑ 132 Tommy Greene .15 .07
- ❑ 133 Chris Hoiles .15 .07
- ❑ 134 Bob Walk .15 .07
- ❑ 135 Duane Ward .15 .07
- ❑ 136 Tom Pagnozzi .15 .07
- ❑ 137 Jeff Huson .15 .07
- ❑ 138 Kurt Stillwell .15 .07
- ❑ 139 Dave Henderson .15 .07
- ❑ 140 Darrin Jackson .15 .07
- ❑ 141 Frank Castillo .15 .07
- ❑ 142 Scott Erickson .15 .07
- ❑ 143 Darryl Kile .25 .11
- ❑ 144 Bill Wegman .15 .07
- ❑ 145 Steve Wilson .15 .07
- ❑ 146 George Brett 1.25 .55
- ❑ 147 Moises Alou .25 .11
- ❑ 148 Lou Whitaker .25 .11
- ❑ 149 Chico Walker .15 .07
- ❑ 150 Jerry Browne .15 .07
- ❑ 151 Kirk McCaskill .15 .07
- ❑ 152 Zane Smith .15 .07
- ❑ 153 Matt Young .15 .07
- ❑ 154 Lee Smith .25 .11
- ❑ 155 Leo Gomez .15 .07
- ❑ 156 Dan Walters .15 .07
- ❑ 157 Pat Borders .15 .07
- ❑ 158 Matt Williams .40 .18
- ❑ 159 Dean Palmer .25 .11
- ❑ 160 John Patterson .15 .07
- ❑ 161 Doug Jones .15 .07
- ❑ 162 John Habyan .15 .07
- ❑ 163 Pedro Martinez 1.50 .70
- ❑ 164 Carl Willis .15 .07
- ❑ 165 Darrin Fletcher .15 .07
- ❑ 166 B.J. Surhoff .25 .11
- ❑ 167 Eddie Murray .60 .25
- ❑ 168 Keith Miller .15 .07
- ❑ 169 Ricky Jordan .15 .07
- ❑ 170 Juan Gonzalez .60 .25
- ❑ 171 Charles Nagy .15 .07
- ❑ 172 Mark Clark .15 .07
- ❑ 173 Bobby Thigpen .15 .07
- ❑ 174 Tim Scott .15 .07
- ❑ 175 Scott Cooper .15 .07
- ❑ 176 Royce Clayton .15 .07
- ❑ 177 Brady Anderson .25 .11
- ❑ 178 Sid Bream .15 .07
- ❑ 179 Derek Bell .15 .07
- ❑ 180 Otis Nixon .15 .07
- ❑ 181 Kevin Gross .15 .07
- ❑ 182 Ron Darling .15 .07
- ❑ 183 John Wetteland .25 .11
- ❑ 184 Mike Stanley .15 .07
- ❑ 185 Jeff Kent .60 .25
- ❑ 186 Brian Harper .15 .07
- ❑ 187 Mariano Duncan .15 .07
- ❑ 188 Robin Yount .60 .25
- ❑ 189 Al Martin .15 .07
- ❑ 190 Eddie Zosky .15 .07
- ❑ 191 Mike Munoz .15 .07
- ❑ 192 Andy Benes .15 .07
- ❑ 193 Dennis Cook .15 .07
- ❑ 194 Bill Swift .15 .07
- ❑ 195 Frank Thomas .75 .35
- ❑ 195A Frank Thomas 1.25 .55
  Franklin visible on batting glove
- ❑ 196 Damon Berryhill .15 .07
- ❑ 197 Mike Greenwell .15 .07
- ❑ 198 Mark Grace .60 .25
- ❑ 199 Darryl Hamilton .15 .07
- ❑ 200 Derrick May .15 .07
- ❑ 201 Ken Hill .15 .07
- ❑ 202 Kevin Brown .25 .11
- ❑ 203 Dwight Gooden .25 .11
- ❑ 204 Bobby Witt .15 .07
- ❑ 205 Juan Bell .15 .07
- ❑ 206 Kevin Maas .15 .07
- ❑ 207 Jeff King .15 .07
- ❑ 208 Scott Leius .15 .07
- ❑ 209 Rheal Cormier .15 .07
- ❑ 210 Darryl Strawberry .25 .11
- ❑ 211 Tom Gordon .15 .07
- ❑ 212 Bud Black .15 .07
- ❑ 213 Mickey Tettleton .15 .07
- ❑ 214 Pete Smith .15 .07
- ❑ 215 Felix Fermin .15 .07
- ❑ 216 Rick Wilkins .15 .07
- ❑ 217 George Bell .15 .07
- ❑ 218 Eric Anthony .15 .07
- ❑ 219 Pedro Munoz .15 .07
- ❑ 220 Checklist .15 .07
- ❑ 221 Lance Blankenship .15 .07
- ❑ 222 Deion Sanders .25 .11
- ❑ 223 Craig Biggio .40 .18
- ❑ 224 Ryne Sandberg .75 .35
- ❑ 225 Ron Gant .15 .07
- ❑ 226 Tom Brunansky .15 .07
- ❑ 227 Chad Curtis .15 .07
- ❑ 228 Joe Carter .25 .11
- ❑ 229 Brian Jordan .25 .11
- ❑ 230 Brett Butler .25 .11
- ❑ 231 Frank Bolick .15 .07
- ❑ 232 Rod Beck .15 .07
- ❑ 233 Carlos Baerga .15 .07
- ❑ 234 Eric Karros .25 .11
- ❑ 235 Jack Armstrong .15 .07
- ❑ 236 Bobby Bonilla .25 .11
- ❑ 237 Don Mattingly 1.50 .70
- ❑ 238 Jeff Gardner .15 .07
- ❑ 239 Dave Hollins .15 .07
- ❑ 240 Steve Cooke .15 .07
- ❑ 241 Jose Canseco .60 .25
- ❑ 242 Ivan Calderon .15 .07
- ❑ 243 Tim Belcher .15 .07
- ❑ 244 Freddie Benavides .15 .07
- ❑ 245 Roberto Alomar .60 .25
- ❑ 246 Rob Deer .15 .07
- ❑ 247 Will Clark .60 .25
- ❑ 248 Mike Felder .15 .07
- ❑ 249 Harold Baines .25 .11
- ❑ 250 David Cone .25 .11
- ❑ 251 Mark Guthrie .15 .07
- ❑ 252 Ellis Burks .25 .11
- ❑ 253 Jim Abbott .25 .11
- ❑ 254 Chili Davis .25 .11
- ❑ 255 Chris Bosio .15 .07
- ❑ 256 Bret Barberie .15 .07
- ❑ 257 Hal Morris .15 .07
- ❑ 258 Dante Bichette .25 .11
- ❑ 259 Storm Davis .15 .07
- ❑ 260 Gary DiSarcina .15 .07
- ❑ 261 Ken Caminiti .25 .11
- ❑ 262 Paul Molitor .60 .25
- ❑ 263 Joe Oliver .15 .07
- ❑ 264 Pat Listach .15 .07
- ❑ 265 Gregg Jefferies .15 .07
- ❑ 266 Jose Guzman .15 .07
- ❑ 267 Eric Davis .25 .11
- ❑ 268 Delino DeShields .15 .07
- ❑ 269 Barry Bonds 1.50 .70
- ❑ 270 Mike Bielecki .15 .07
- ❑ 271 Jay Buhner .25 .11
- ❑ 272 Scott Pose RC .15 .07
- ❑ 273 Tony Fernandez .15 .07
- ❑ 274 Chito Martinez .15 .07
- ❑ 275 Phil Plantier .15 .07
- ❑ 276 Pete Incaviglia .15 .07
- ❑ 277 Carlos Garcia .15 .07
- ❑ 278 Tom Henke .15 .07
- ❑ 279 Roger Clemens 1.50 .70
- ❑ 280 Rob Dibble .15 .07
- ❑ 281 Daryl Boston .15 .07
- ❑ 282 Greg Gagne .15 .07
- ❑ 283 Cecil Fielder .25 .11
- ❑ 284 Carlton Fisk .60 .25
- ❑ 285 Wade Boggs .60 .25
- ❑ 286 Damion Easley .15 .07
- ❑ 287 Norm Charlton .15 .07
- ❑ 288 Jeff Conine .15 .07
- ❑ 289 Roberto Kelly .15 .07
- ❑ 290 Jerald Clark .15 .07
- ❑ 291 Rickey Henderson 1.25 .55
- ❑ 292 Chuck Finley .25 .11
- ❑ 293 Doug Drabek .15 .07
- ❑ 294 Dave Stewart .25 .11
- ❑ 295 Tom Glavine .60 .25
- ❑ 296 Jaime Navarro .15 .07
- ❑ 297 Ray Lankford .15 .07
- ❑ 298 Greg Hibbard .15 .07
- ❑ 299 Jody Reed .15 .07
- ❑ 300 Dennis Martinez .25 .11
- ❑ 301 Dave Martinez .15 .07
- ❑ 302 Reggie Jefferson .15 .07
- ❑ 303 John Cummings RC .15 .07
- ❑ 304 Orestes Destrade .15 .07
- ❑ 305 Mike Maddux .15 .07
- ❑ 306 David Segui .15 .07
- ❑ 307 Gary Sheffield .25 .11
- ❑ 308 Danny Jackson .15 .07
- ❑ 309 Craig Lefferts .15 .07
- ❑ 310 Andre Dawson .40 .18
- ❑ 311 Barry Larkin .60 .25
- ❑ 312 Alex Cole .15 .07
- ❑ 313 Mark Gardner .15 .07
- ❑ 314 Kirk Gibson .25 .11
- ❑ 315 Shane Mack .15 .07
- ❑ 316 Bo Jackson .25 .11
- ❑ 317 Jimmy Key .25 .11
- ❑ 318 Greg Myers .15 .07
- ❑ 319 Ken Griffey Jr. 2.00 .90
- ❑ 320 Monty Fariss .15 .07
- ❑ 321 Kevin Mitchell .15 .07
- ❑ 322 Andres Galarraga .40 .18
- ❑ 323 Mark McGwire 2.50 1.10
- ❑ 324 Mark Langston .15 .07
- ❑ 325 Steve Finley .25 .11
- ❑ 326 Greg Maddux 1.50 .70
- ❑ 327 Dave Nilsson .15 .07
- ❑ 328 Ozzie Smith .75 .35
- ❑ 329 Candy Maldonado .15 .07
- ❑ 330 Checklist .15 .07
- ❑ 331 Tim Pugh RC .15 .07
- ❑ 332 Joe Girardi .15 .07
- ❑ 333 Junior Felix .15 .07
- ❑ 334 Greg Swindell .15 .07
- ❑ 335 Ramon Martinez .15 .07
- ❑ 336 Sean Berry .15 .07
- ❑ 337 Joe Orsulak .15 .07
- ❑ 338 Wes Chamberlain .15 .07
- ❑ 339 Stan Belinda .15 .07
- ❑ 340 Checklist UER .15 .07
  (306 Luis Mercedes)
- ❑ 341 Bruce Hurst .15 .07
- ❑ 342 John Burkett .15 .07
- ❑ 343 Mike Mussina .60 .25
- ❑ 344 Scott Fletcher .15 .07
- ❑ 345 Rene Gonzales .15 .07
- ❑ 346 Roberto Hernandez .15 .07
- ❑ 347 Carlos Martinez .15 .07
- ❑ 348 Bill Krueger .15 .07
- ❑ 349 Felix Jose .15 .07
- ❑ 350 John Jaha .15 .07
- ❑ 351 Willie Banks .15 .07
- ❑ 352 Matt Nokes .15 .07
- ❑ 353 Kevin Seitzer .15 .07
- ❑ 354 Erik Hanson .15 .07
- ❑ 355 David Hulse RC .15 .07
- ❑ 356 Domingo Martinez RC .15 .07
- ❑ 357 Greg Olson .15 .07
- ❑ 358 Randy Myers .15 .07
- ❑ 359 Tom Browning .15 .07
- ❑ 360 Charlie Hayes .15 .07
- ❑ 361 Bryan Harvey .15 .07
- ❑ 362 Eddie Taubensee .15 .07
- ❑ 363 Tim Wallach .15 .07
- ❑ 364 Mel Rojas .15 .07
- ❑ 365 Frank Tanana .15 .07
- ❑ 366 John Kruk .25 .11
- ❑ 367 Tim Laker RC .15 .07
- ❑ 368 Rich Rodriguez .15 .07
- ❑ 369 Darren Lewis .15 .07
- ❑ 370 Harold Reynolds .15 .07
- ❑ 371 Jose Melendez .15 .07
- ❑ 372 Joe Grahe .15 .07
- ❑ 373 Lance Johnson .15 .07
- ❑ 374 Jose Mesa .15 .07
- ❑ 375 Scott Livingstone .15 .07
- ❑ 376 Wally Joyner .25 .11
- ❑ 377 Kevin Reimer .15 .07
- ❑ 378 Kirby Puckett 1.50 .70
- ❑ 379 Paul O'Neill .60 .25
- ❑ 380 Randy Johnson .75 .35

No.	Player	Mint	NrMt
381	Manuel Lee	.15	.07
382	Dick Schofield	.15	.07
383	Darren Holmes	.15	.07
384	Charlie Hough	.25	.11
385	John Orton	.15	.07
386	Edgar Martinez	.40	.18
387	Terry Pendleton	.25	.11
388	Dan Plesac	.15	.07
389	Jeff Reardon	.25	.11
390	David Nied	.15	.07
391	Dave Magadan	.15	.07
392	Larry Walker	.40	.18
393	Ben Rivera	.15	.07
394	Lonnie Smith	.15	.07
395	Craig Shipley	.15	.07
396	Willie McGee	.25	.11
397	Arthur Rhodes	.15	.07
398	Mike Stanton	.15	.07
399	Luis Polonia	.15	.07
400	Jack McDowell	.15	.07
401	Mike Moore	.15	.07
402	Jose Lind	.15	.07
403	Bill Spiers	.15	.07
404	Kevin Tapani	.15	.07
405	Spike Owen	.15	.07
406	Tino Martinez	.25	.11
407	Charlie Leibrandt	.15	.07
408	Ed Sprague	.15	.07
409	Bryn Smith	.15	.07
410	Benito Santiago	.15	.07
411	Jose Rijo	.15	.07
412	Pete O'Brien	.15	.07
413	Willie Wilson	.15	.07
414	Bip Roberts	.15	.07
415	Eric Young	.15	.07
416	Walt Weiss	.15	.07
417	Milt Thompson	.15	.07
418	Chris Sabo	.15	.07
419	Scott Sanderson	.15	.07
420	Tim Raines	.25	.11
421	Alan Trammell	.40	.18
422	Mike Macfarlane	.15	.07
423	Dave Winfield	.60	.25
424	Bob Wickman	.15	.07
425	David Valle	.15	.07
426	Gary Redus	.15	.07
427	Turner Ward	.15	.07
428	Reggie Sanders	.15	.07
429	Todd Worrell	.15	.07
430	Julio Valera	.15	.07
431	Cal Ripken Jr.	2.50	1.10
432	Mo Vaughn	.25	.11
433	John Smiley	.15	.07
434	Omar Vizquel	.25	.11
435	Billy Ripken	.15	.07
436	Cory Snyder	.15	.07
437	Carlos Quintana	.15	.07
438	Omar Olivares	.15	.07
439	Robin Ventura	.25	.11
440	Checklist	.15	.07
441	Kevin Higgins	.15	.07
442	Carlos Hernandez	.15	.07
443	Dan Peltier	.15	.07
444	Derek Lilliquist	.15	.07
445	Tim Salmon	.25	.11
446	Sherman Obando RC	.15	.07
447	Pat Kelly	.15	.07
448	Todd Van Poppel	.15	.07
449	Mark Whiten	.15	.07
450	Checklist	.15	.07
451	Pat Meares RC	.25	.11
452	Tony Tarasco RC	.15	.07
453	Chris Gwynn	.15	.07
454	Armando Reynoso	.15	.07
455	Danny Darwin	.15	.07
456	Willie Greene	.15	.07
457	Mike Blowers	.15	.07
458	Kevin Roberson RC	.15	.07
459	Graeme Lloyd RC	.25	.11
460	David West	.15	.07
461	Joey Cora	.15	.07
462	Alex Arias	.15	.07
463	Chad Kreuter	.15	.07
464	Mike Lansing RC	.25	.11
465	Mike Timlin	.15	.07
466	Paul Wagner	.15	.07

No.	Player	Mint	NrMt
467	Mark Portugal	.15	.07
468	Jim Leyritz	.15	.07
469	Ryan Klesko	.25	.11
470	Mario Diaz	.15	.07
471	Guillermo Velasquez	.15	.07
472	Fernando Valenzuela	.25	.11
473	Raul Mondesi	.25	.11
474	Mike Pagliarulo	.15	.07
475	Chris Hammond	.15	.07
476	Torey Lovullo	.15	.07
477	Trevor Wilson	.15	.07
478	Marcos Armas RC	.15	.07
479	Dave Gallagher	.15	.07
480	Jeff Treadway	.15	.07
481	Jeff Branson	.15	.07
482	Dickie Thon	.15	.07
483	Eduardo Perez	.15	.07
484	David Wells	.25	.11
485	Brian Williams	.15	.07
486	Domingo Cedeno RC	.15	.07
487	Tom Candiotti	.15	.07
488	Steve Frey	.15	.07
489	Greg McMichael RC	.15	.07
490	Marc Newfield	.15	.07
491	Larry Andersen	.15	.07
492	Damon Buford	.15	.07
493	Ricky Gutierrez	.15	.07
494	Jeff Russell	.15	.07
495	Vinny Castilla	.25	.11
496	Wilson Alvarez	.15	.07
497	Scott Bullett	.15	.07
498	Larry Casian	.15	.07
499	Jose Vizcaino	.15	.07
500	J.T. Snow RC	.75	.35
501	Bryan Hickerson	.15	.07
502	Jeremy Hernandez	.15	.07
503	Jeromy Burnitz	.25	.11
504	Steve Farr	.15	.07
505	J. Owens RC	.15	.07
506	Craig Paquette	.15	.07
507	Jim Eisenreich	.15	.07
508	Matt Whiteside RC	.15	.07
509	Luis Aquino	.15	.07
510	Mike LaValliere	.15	.07
511	Jim Gott	.15	.07
512	Mark McLemore	.15	.07
513	Randy Milligan	.15	.07
514	Gary Gaetti	.25	.11
515	Lou Frazier RC	.15	.07
516	Rich Amaral	.15	.07
517	Gene Harris	.15	.07
518	Aaron Sele	.25	.11
519	Mark Wohlers	.15	.07
520	Scott Kamieniecki	.15	.07
521	Kent Mercker	.15	.07
522	Jim Deshaies	.15	.07
523	Kevin Stocker	.15	.07
524	Jason Bere	.15	.07
525	Tim Bogar RC	.15	.07
526	Brad Pennington	.15	.07
527	Curt Leskanic RC	.15	.07
528	Wayne Kirby	.15	.07
529	Tim Costo	.15	.07
530	Doug Henry	.15	.07
531	Trevor Hoffman	.25	.11
532	Kelly Gruber	.15	.07
533	Mike Harkey	.15	.07
534	John Doherty	.15	.07
535	Erik Pappas	.15	.07
536	Brent Gates	.15	.07
537	Roger McDowell	.15	.07
538	Chris Haney	.15	.07
539	Blas Minor	.15	.07
540	Pat Hentgen	.15	.07
541	Chuck Carr	.15	.07
542	Doug Strange	.15	.07
543	Xavier Hernandez	.15	.07
544	Paul Quantrill	.15	.07
545	Anthony Young	.15	.07
546	Bret Boone	.25	.11
547	Dwight Smith	.15	.07
548	Bobby Munoz	.15	.07
549	Russ Springer	.15	.07
550	Roger Pavlik	.15	.07
DW	Dave Winfield 3000 Hits	1.00	.45

No.	Player	Mint	NrMt
FT	Frank Thomas AU/3500 (Certified autograph)	60.00	27.00

1994 Leaf

	MINT	NRMT
COMPLETE SET (440)	24.00	11.00
COMPLETE SERIES 1 (220)	12.00	5.50
COMPLETE SERIES 2 (220)	12.00	5.50

No.	Player	Mint	NrMt
1	Cal Ripken Jr.	2.50	1.10
2	Tony Tarasco	.15	.07
3	Joe Girardi	.15	.07
4	Bernie Williams	.60	.25
5	Chad Kreuter	.15	.07
6	Troy Neel	.15	.07
7	Tom Pagnozzi	.15	.07
8	Kirk Rueter	.15	.07
9	Chris Bosio	.15	.07
10	Dwight Gooden	.25	.11
11	Mariano Duncan	.15	.07
12	Jay Bell	.25	.11
13	Lance Johnson	.15	.07
14	Richie Lewis	.15	.07
15	Dave Martinez	.15	.07
16	Orel Hershiser	.25	.11
17	Rob Butler	.15	.07
18	Glenallen Hill	.15	.07
19	Chad Curtis	.15	.07
20	Mike Stanton	.15	.07
21	Tim Wallach	.15	.07
22	Milt Thompson	.15	.07
23	Kevin Young	.15	.07
24	John Smiley	.15	.07
25	Jeff Montgomery	.15	.07
26	Robin Ventura	.25	.11
27	Scott Lydy	.15	.07
28	Todd Stottlemyre	.15	.07
29	Mark Whiten	.15	.07
30	Robby Thompson	.15	.07
31	Bobby Bonilla	.25	.11
32	Andy Ashby	.15	.07
33	Greg Myers	.15	.07
34	Billy Hatcher	.15	.07
35	Brad Holman	.15	.07
36	Mark McLemore	.15	.07
37	Scott Sanders	.15	.07
38	Jim Abbott	.25	.11
39	David Wells	.25	.11
40	Roberto Kelly	.15	.07
41	Jeff Conine	.15	.07
42	Sean Berry	.15	.07
43	Mark Grace	.60	.25
44	Eric Young	.15	.07
45	Rick Aguilera	.15	.07
46	Chipper Jones	1.25	.55
47	Mel Rojas	.15	.07
48	Ryan Thompson	.15	.07
49	Al Martin	.15	.07
50	Cecil Fielder	.25	.11
51	Pat Kelly	.15	.07
52	Kevin Tapani	.15	.07
53	Tim Costo	.15	.07
54	Dave Hollins	.15	.07
55	Kirt Manwaring	.15	.07
56	Gregg Jefferies	.15	.07
57	Ron Darling	.15	.07
58	Bill Haselman	.15	.07

❑ 59	Phil Plantier	.15	.07
❑ 60	Frank Viola	.25	.11
❑ 61	Todd Zeile	.15	.07
❑ 62	Bret Barberie	.15	.07
❑ 63	Roberto Mejia	.15	.07
❑ 64	Chuck Knoblauch	.25	.11
❑ 65	Jose Lind	.15	.07
❑ 66	Brady Anderson	.25	.11
❑ 67	Ruben Sierra	.15	.07
❑ 68	Jose Vizcaino	.15	.07
❑ 69	Joe Grahe	.15	.07
❑ 70	Kevin Appier	.25	.11
❑ 71	Wilson Alvarez	.15	.07
❑ 72	Tom Candiotti	.15	.07
❑ 73	John Burkett	.15	.07
❑ 74	Anthony Young	.15	.07
❑ 75	Scott Cooper	.15	.07
❑ 76	Nigel Wilson	.15	.07
❑ 77	John Valentin	.15	.07
❑ 78	David McCarty	.15	.07
❑ 79	Archi Cianfrocco	.15	.07
❑ 80	Lou Whitaker	.25	.11
❑ 81	Dante Bichette	.25	.11
❑ 82	Mark Dewey	.15	.07
❑ 83	Danny Jackson	.15	.07
❑ 84	Harold Baines	.25	.11
❑ 85	Todd Benzinger	.15	.07
❑ 86	Damion Easley	.15	.07
❑ 87	Danny Cox	.15	.07
❑ 88	Jose Bautista	.15	.07
❑ 89	Mike Lansing	.15	.07
❑ 90	Phil Hiatt	.15	.07
❑ 91	Tim Pugh	.15	.07
❑ 92	Tino Martinez	.25	.11
❑ 93	Raul Mondesi	.25	.11
❑ 94	Greg Maddux	1.50	.70
❑ 95	Al Leiter	.25	.11
❑ 96	Benito Santiago	.15	.07
❑ 97	Lenny Dykstra	.25	.11
❑ 98	Sammy Sosa	1.50	.70
❑ 99	Tim Bogar	.15	.07
❑ 100	Checklist	.15	.07
❑ 101	Deion Sanders	.25	.11
❑ 102	Bobby Witt	.15	.07
❑ 103	Wil Cordero	.15	.07
❑ 104	Rich Amaral	.15	.07
❑ 105	Mike Mussina	.60	.25
❑ 106	Reggie Sanders	.15	.07
❑ 107	Ozzie Guillen	.15	.07
❑ 108	Paul O'Neill	.60	.25
❑ 109	Tim Salmon	.25	.11
❑ 110	Rheal Cormier	.15	.07
❑ 111	Billy Ashley	.15	.07
❑ 112	Jeff Kent	.40	.18
❑ 113	Derek Bell	.15	.07
❑ 114	Danny Darwin	.15	.07
❑ 115	Chip Hale	.15	.07
❑ 116	Tim Raines	.25	.11
❑ 117	Ed Sprague	.15	.07
❑ 118	Darrin Fletcher	.15	.07
❑ 119	Darren Holmes	.15	.07
❑ 120	Alan Trammell	.40	.18
❑ 121	Don Mattingly	1.50	.70
❑ 122	Greg Gagne	.15	.07
❑ 123	Jose Offerman	.15	.07
❑ 124	Joe Orsulak	.15	.07
❑ 125	Jack McDowell	.15	.07
❑ 126	Barry Larkin	.60	.25
❑ 127	Ben McDonald	.15	.07
❑ 128	Mike Bordick	.15	.07
❑ 129	Devon White	.15	.07
❑ 130	Mike Perez	.15	.07
❑ 131	Jay Buhner	.25	.11
❑ 132	Phil Leftwich RC	.15	.07
❑ 133	Tommy Greene	.15	.07
❑ 134	Charlie Hayes	.15	.07
❑ 135	Don Slaught	.15	.07
❑ 136	Mike Gallego	.15	.07
❑ 137	Dave Winfield	.60	.25
❑ 138	Steve Avery	.15	.07
❑ 139	Derrick May	.15	.07
❑ 140	Bryan Harvey	.15	.07
❑ 141	Wally Joyner	.25	.11
❑ 142	Andre Dawson	.40	.18
❑ 143	Andy Benes	.15	.07
❑ 144	John Franco	.25	.11
❑ 145	Jeff King	.15	.07
❑ 146	Joe Oliver	.15	.07
❑ 147	Bill Gullickson	.15	.07
❑ 148	Armando Reynoso	.15	.07
❑ 149	Dave Fleming	.15	.07
❑ 150	Checklist	.15	.07
❑ 151	Todd Van Poppel	.15	.07
❑ 152	Bernard Gilkey	.15	.07
❑ 153	Kevin Gross	.15	.07
❑ 154	Mike Devereaux	.15	.07
❑ 155	Tim Wakefield	.15	.07
❑ 156	Andres Galarraga	.40	.18
❑ 157	Pat Meares	.15	.07
❑ 158	Jim Leyritz	.15	.07
❑ 159	Mike Macfarlane	.15	.07
❑ 160	Tony Phillips	.15	.07
❑ 161	Brent Gates	.15	.07
❑ 162	Mark Langston	.15	.07
❑ 163	Allen Watson	.15	.07
❑ 164	Randy Johnson	.75	.35
❑ 165	Doug Brocail	.15	.07
❑ 166	Rob Dibble	.15	.07
❑ 167	Roberto Hernandez	.15	.07
❑ 168	Felix Jose	.15	.07
❑ 169	Steve Cooke	.15	.07
❑ 170	Darren Daulton	.25	.11
❑ 171	Eric Karros	.25	.11
❑ 172	Geronimo Pena	.15	.07
❑ 173	Gary DiSarcina	.15	.07
❑ 174	Marquis Grissom	.15	.07
❑ 175	Joey Cora	.15	.07
❑ 176	Jim Eisenreich	.15	.07
❑ 177	Brad Pennington	.15	.07
❑ 178	Terry Steinbach	.15	.07
❑ 179	Pat Borders	.15	.07
❑ 180	Steve Buechele	.15	.07
❑ 181	Jeff Fassero	.15	.07
❑ 182	Mike Greenwell	.15	.07
❑ 183	Mike Henneman	.15	.07
❑ 184	Ron Karkovice	.15	.07
❑ 185	Pat Hentgen	.15	.07
❑ 186	Jose Guzman	.15	.07
❑ 187	Brett Butler	.25	.11
❑ 188	Charlie Hough	.25	.11
❑ 189	Terry Pendleton	.25	.11
❑ 190	Melido Perez	.15	.07
❑ 191	Orestes Destrade	.15	.07
❑ 192	Mike Morgan	.15	.07
❑ 193	Joe Carter	.25	.11
❑ 194	Jeff Blauser	.15	.07
❑ 195	Chris Hoiles	.15	.07
❑ 196	Ricky Gutierrez	.15	.07
❑ 197	Mike Moore	.15	.07
❑ 198	Carl Willis	.15	.07
❑ 199	Aaron Sele	.25	.11
❑ 200	Checklist	.15	.07
❑ 201	Tim Naehring	.15	.07
❑ 202	Scott Livingstone	.15	.07
❑ 203	Luis Alicea	.15	.07
❑ 204	Torey Lovullo	.15	.07
❑ 205	Jim Gott	.15	.07
❑ 206	Bob Wickman	.15	.07
❑ 207	Greg McMichael	.15	.07
❑ 208	Scott Brosius	.25	.11
❑ 209	Chris Gwynn	.15	.07
❑ 210	Steve Sax	.15	.07
❑ 211	Dick Schofield	.15	.07
❑ 212	Robb Nen	.15	.07
❑ 213	Ben Rivera	.15	.07
❑ 214	Vinny Castilla	.25	.11
❑ 215	Jamie Moyer	.15	.07
❑ 216	Wally Whitehurst	.15	.07
❑ 217	Frank Castillo	.15	.07
❑ 218	Mike Blowers	.15	.07
❑ 219	Tim Scott	.15	.07
❑ 220	Paul Wagner	.15	.07
❑ 221	Jeff Bagwell	.75	.35
❑ 222	Ricky Bones	.15	.07
❑ 223	Sandy Alomar Jr.	.25	.11
❑ 224	Rod Beck	.15	.07
❑ 225	Roberto Alomar	.60	.25
❑ 226	Jack Armstrong	.15	.07
❑ 227	Scott Erickson	.15	.07
❑ 228	Rene Arocha	.15	.07
❑ 229	Eric Anthony	.15	.07
❑ 230	Jeromy Burnitz	.25	.11
❑ 231	Kevin Brown	.25	.11
❑ 232	Tim Belcher	.15	.07
❑ 233	Bret Boone	.25	.11
❑ 234	Dennis Eckersley	.25	.11
❑ 235	Tom Glavine	.60	.25
❑ 236	Craig Biggio	.40	.18
❑ 237	Pedro Astacio	.15	.07
❑ 238	Ryan Bowen	.15	.07
❑ 239	Brad Ausmus	.15	.07
❑ 240	Vince Coleman	.15	.07
❑ 241	Jason Bere	.15	.07
❑ 242	Ellis Burks	.25	.11
❑ 243	Wes Chamberlain	.15	.07
❑ 244	Ken Caminiti	.25	.11
❑ 245	Willie Banks	.15	.07
❑ 246	Sid Fernandez	.15	.07
❑ 247	Carlos Baerga	.15	.07
❑ 248	Carlos Garcia	.15	.07
❑ 249	Jose Canseco	.60	.25
❑ 250	Alex Diaz	.15	.07
❑ 251	Albert Belle	.25	.11
❑ 252	Moises Alou	.25	.11
❑ 253	Bobby Ayala	.15	.07
❑ 254	Tony Gwynn	1.25	.55
❑ 255	Roger Clemens	1.50	.70
❑ 256	Eric Davis	.25	.11
❑ 257	Wade Boggs	.60	.25
❑ 258	Chili Davis	.25	.11
❑ 259	Rickey Henderson	1.25	.55
❑ 260	Andujar Cedeno	.15	.07
❑ 261	Cris Carpenter	.15	.07
❑ 262	Juan Guzman	.15	.07
❑ 263	David Justice	.25	.11
❑ 264	Barry Bonds	1.50	.70
❑ 265	Pete Incaviglia	.15	.07
❑ 266	Tony Fernandez	.15	.07
❑ 267	Cal Eldred	.15	.07
❑ 268	Alex Fernandez	.15	.07
❑ 269	Kent Hrbek	.25	.11
❑ 270	Steve Farr	.15	.07
❑ 271	Doug Drabek	.15	.07
❑ 272	Brian Jordan	.25	.11
❑ 273	Xavier Hernandez	.15	.07
❑ 274	David Cone	.25	.11
❑ 275	Brian Hunter	.15	.07
❑ 276	Mike Harkey	.15	.07
❑ 277	Delino DeShields	.15	.07
❑ 278	David Hulse	.15	.07
❑ 279	Mickey Tettleton	.15	.07
❑ 280	Kevin McReynolds	.15	.07
❑ 281	Darryl Hamilton	.15	.07
❑ 282	Ken Hill	.15	.07
❑ 283	Wayne Kirby	.15	.07
❑ 284	Chris Hammond	.15	.07
❑ 285	Mo Vaughn	.25	.11
❑ 286	Ryan Klesko	.25	.11
❑ 287	Rick Wilkins	.15	.07
❑ 288	Bill Swift	.15	.07
❑ 289	Rafael Palmeiro	.60	.25
❑ 290	Brian Harper	.15	.07
❑ 291	Chris Turner	.15	.07
❑ 292	Luis Gonzalez	.60	.25
❑ 293	Kenny Rogers	.15	.07
❑ 294	Kirby Puckett	1.50	.70
❑ 295	Mike Stanley	.15	.07
❑ 296	Carlos Reyes RC	.15	.07
❑ 297	Charles Nagy	.15	.07
❑ 298	Reggie Jefferson	.15	.07
❑ 299	Bip Roberts	.15	.07
❑ 300	Darrin Jackson	.15	.07
❑ 301	Mike Jackson	.15	.07
❑ 302	Dave Nilsson	.15	.07
❑ 303	Ramon Martinez	.15	.07
❑ 304	Bobby Jones	.15	.07
❑ 305	Johnny Ruffin	.15	.07
❑ 306	Brian McRae	.15	.07
❑ 307	Bo Jackson	.25	.11
❑ 308	Dave Stewart	.25	.11
❑ 309	John Smoltz	.25	.11
❑ 310	Dennis Martinez	.25	.11
❑ 311	Dean Palmer	.25	.11
❑ 312	David Nied	.15	.07
❑ 313	Eddie Murray	.60	.25
❑ 314	Darryl Kile	.25	.11
❑ 315	Rick Sutcliffe	.25	.11
❑ 316	Shawon Dunston	.15	.07

❑ 317	John Jaha	.15	.07
❑ 318	Salomon Torres	.15	.07
❑ 319	Gary Sheffield	.25	.11
❑ 320	Curt Schilling	.60	.25
❑ 321	Greg Vaughn	.25	.11
❑ 322	Jay Howell	.15	.07
❑ 323	Todd Hundley	.15	.07
❑ 324	Chris Sabo	.15	.07
❑ 325	Stan Javier	.15	.07
❑ 326	Willie Greene	.15	.07
❑ 327	Hipolito Pichardo	.15	.07
❑ 328	Doug Strange	.15	.07
❑ 329	Dan Wilson	.15	.07
❑ 330	Checklist	.15	.07
❑ 331	Omar Vizquel	.25	.11
❑ 332	Scott Servais	.15	.07
❑ 333	Bob Tewksbury	.15	.07
❑ 334	Matt Williams	.40	.18
❑ 335	Tom Foley	.15	.07
❑ 336	Jeff Russell	.15	.07
❑ 337	Scott Leius	.15	.07
❑ 338	Ivan Rodriguez	.60	.25
❑ 339	Kevin Seitzer	.15	.07
❑ 340	Jose Rijo	.15	.07
❑ 341	Eduardo Perez	.15	.07
❑ 342	Kirk Gibson	.25	.11
❑ 343	Randy Milligan	.15	.07
❑ 344	Edgar Martinez	.40	.18
❑ 345	Fred McGriff	.40	.18
❑ 346	Kurt Abbott RC	.25	.11
❑ 347	John Kruk	.25	.11
❑ 348	Mike Felder	.15	.07
❑ 349	Dave Staton	.15	.07
❑ 350	Kenny Lofton	.25	.11
❑ 351	Graeme Lloyd	.15	.07
❑ 352	David Segui	.15	.07
❑ 353	Danny Tartabull	.15	.07
❑ 354	Bob Welch	.15	.07
❑ 355	Duane Ward	.15	.07
❑ 356	Karl Rhodes	.15	.07
❑ 357	Lee Smith	.25	.11
❑ 358	Chris James	.15	.07
❑ 359	Walt Weiss	.15	.07
❑ 360	Pedro Munoz	.15	.07
❑ 361	Paul Sorrento	.15	.07
❑ 362	Todd Worrell	.15	.07
❑ 363	Bob Hamelin	.15	.07
❑ 364	Julio Franco	.25	.11
❑ 365	Roberto Petagine	.15	.07
❑ 366	Willie McGee	.25	.11
❑ 367	Pedro Martinez	1.00	.45
❑ 368	Ken Griffey Jr.	2.00	.90
❑ 369	B.J. Surhoff	.25	.11
❑ 370	Kevin Mitchell	.15	.07
❑ 371	John Doherty	.15	.07
❑ 372	Manuel Lee	.15	.07
❑ 373	Terry Mulholland	.15	.07
❑ 374	Zane Smith	.15	.07
❑ 375	Otis Nixon	.15	.07
❑ 376	Jody Reed	.15	.07
❑ 377	Doug Jones	.15	.07
❑ 378	John Olerud	.25	.11
❑ 379	Greg Swindell	.15	.07
❑ 380	Checklist	.15	.07
❑ 381	Royce Clayton	.15	.07
❑ 382	Jim Thome	.60	.25
❑ 383	Steve Finley	.25	.11
❑ 384	Ray Lankford	.15	.07
❑ 385	Henry Rodriguez	.15	.07
❑ 386	Dave Magadan	.15	.07
❑ 387	Gary Redus	.15	.07
❑ 388	Orlando Merced	.15	.07
❑ 389	Tom Gordon	.15	.07
❑ 390	Luis Polonia	.15	.07
❑ 391	Mark McGwire	2.50	1.10
❑ 392	Mark Lemke	.15	.07
❑ 393	Doug Henry	.15	.07
❑ 394	Chuck Finley	.25	.11
❑ 395	Paul Molitor	.60	.25
❑ 396	Randy Myers	.15	.07
❑ 397	Larry Walker	.40	.18
❑ 398	Pete Harnisch	.15	.07
❑ 399	Darren Lewis	.15	.07
❑ 400	Frank Thomas	.75	.35
❑ 401	Jack Morris	.25	.11
❑ 402	Greg Hibbard	.15	.07
❑ 403	Jeffrey Hammonds	.25	.11
❑ 404	Will Clark	.60	.25
❑ 405	Travis Fryman	.25	.11
❑ 406	Scott Sanderson	.15	.07
❑ 407	Gene Harris	.15	.07
❑ 408	Chuck Carr	.15	.07
❑ 409	Ozzie Smith	.75	.35
❑ 410	Kent Mercker	.15	.07
❑ 411	Andy Van Slyke	.25	.11
❑ 412	Jimmy Key	.25	.11
❑ 413	Pat Mahomes	.15	.07
❑ 414	John Wetteland	.25	.11
❑ 415	Todd Jones	.15	.07
❑ 416	Greg Harris	.15	.07
❑ 417	Kevin Stocker	.15	.07
❑ 418	Juan Gonzalez	.60	.25
❑ 419	Pete Smith	.15	.07
❑ 420	Pat Listach	.15	.07
❑ 421	Trevor Hoffman	.25	.11
❑ 422	Scott Fletcher	.15	.07
❑ 423	Mark Lewis	.15	.07
❑ 424	Mickey Morandini	.15	.07
❑ 425	Ryne Sandberg	.75	.35
❑ 426	Erik Hanson	.15	.07
❑ 427	Gary Gaetti	.25	.11
❑ 428	Harold Reynolds	.15	.07
❑ 429	Mark Portugal	.15	.07
❑ 430	David Valle	.15	.07
❑ 431	Mitch Williams	.15	.07
❑ 432	Howard Johnson	.15	.07
❑ 433	Hal Morris	.15	.07
❑ 434	Tom Henke	.15	.07
❑ 435	Shane Mack	.15	.07
❑ 436	Mike Piazza	2.00	.90
❑ 437	Bret Saberhagen	.25	.11
❑ 438	Jose Mesa	.15	.07
❑ 439	Jaime Navarro	.15	.07
❑ 440	Checklist	.15	.07
❑ A300	Frank Thomas Leaf 5th Anniversary	1.25	.55

1995 Leaf

	MINT	NRMT
COMPLETE SET (400)	40.00	18.00
COMPLETE SERIES 1 (200)	15.00	6.75
COMPLETE SERIES 2 (200)	25.00	11.00

❑ 1	Frank Thomas	.75	.35
❑ 2	Carlos Garcia	.15	.07
❑ 3	Todd Hundley	.15	.07
❑ 4	Damion Easley	.15	.07
❑ 5	Roberto Mejia	.15	.07
❑ 6	John Mabry	.15	.07
❑ 7	Aaron Sele	.25	.11
❑ 8	Kenny Lofton	.25	.11
❑ 9	John Doherty	.15	.07
❑ 10	Joe Carter	.25	.11
❑ 11	Mike Lansing	.15	.07
❑ 12	John Valentin	.15	.07
❑ 13	Ismael Valdes	.15	.07
❑ 14	Dave McCarty	.15	.07
❑ 15	Melvin Nieves	.15	.07
❑ 16	Bobby Jones	.15	.07
❑ 17	Trevor Hoffman	.25	.11
❑ 18	John Smoltz	.25	.11
❑ 19	Leo Gomez	.15	.07
❑ 20	Roger Pavlik	.15	.07
❑ 21	Dean Palmer	.25	.11
❑ 22	Rickey Henderson	1.25	.55
❑ 23	Eddie Taubensee	.15	.07
❑ 24	Damon Buford	.15	.07
❑ 25	Mark Wohlers	.15	.07
❑ 26	Jim Edmonds	.40	.18
❑ 27	Wilson Alvarez	.15	.07
❑ 28	Matt Williams	.40	.18
❑ 29	Jeff Montgomery	.15	.07
❑ 30	Shawon Dunston	.15	.07
❑ 31	Tom Pagnozzi	.15	.07
❑ 32	Jose Lind	.15	.07
❑ 33	Royce Clayton	.15	.07
❑ 34	Cal Eldred	.15	.07
❑ 35	Chris Gomez	.15	.07
❑ 36	Henry Rodriguez	.15	.07
❑ 37	Dave Fleming	.15	.07
❑ 38	Jon Lieber	.15	.07
❑ 39	Scott Servais	.15	.07
❑ 40	Wade Boggs	.60	.25
❑ 41	John Olerud	.25	.11
❑ 42	Eddie Williams	.15	.07
❑ 43	Paul Sorrento	.15	.07
❑ 44	Ron Karkovice	.15	.07
❑ 45	Kevin Foster	.15	.07
❑ 46	Miguel Jimenez	.15	.07
❑ 47	Reggie Sanders	.15	.07
❑ 48	Rondell White	.25	.11
❑ 49	Scott Leius	.15	.07
❑ 50	Jose Valentin	.15	.07
❑ 51	Wm. VanLandingham	.15	.07
❑ 52	Denny Hocking	.15	.07
❑ 53	Jeff Fassero	.15	.07
❑ 54	Chris Hoiles	.15	.07
❑ 55	Walt Weiss	.15	.07
❑ 56	Geronimo Berroa	.15	.07
❑ 57	Rich Rowland	.15	.07
❑ 58	Dave Weathers	.15	.07
❑ 59	Sterling Hitchcock	.15	.07
❑ 60	Raul Mondesi	.25	.11
❑ 61	Rusty Greer	.25	.11
❑ 62	David Justice	.25	.11
❑ 63	Cecil Fielder	.25	.11
❑ 64	Brian Jordan	.25	.11
❑ 65	Mike Lieberthal	.25	.11
❑ 66	Rick Aguilera	.15	.07
❑ 67	Chuck Finley	.25	.11
❑ 68	Andy Ashby	.15	.07
❑ 69	Alex Fernandez	.15	.07
❑ 70	Ed Sprague	.15	.07
❑ 71	Steve Buechele	.15	.07
❑ 72	Willie Greene	.15	.07
❑ 73	Dave Nilsson	.15	.07
❑ 74	Bret Saberhagen	.25	.11
❑ 75	Jimmy Key	.25	.11
❑ 76	Darren Lewis	.15	.07
❑ 77	Steve Cooke	.15	.07
❑ 78	Kirk Gibson	.25	.11
❑ 79	Ray Lankford	.15	.07
❑ 80	Paul O'Neill	.60	.25
❑ 81	Mike Bordick	.15	.07
❑ 82	Wes Chamberlain	.15	.07
❑ 83	Rico Brogna	.15	.07
❑ 84	Kevin Appier	.25	.11
❑ 85	Juan Guzman	.15	.07
❑ 86	Kevin Seitzer	.15	.07
❑ 87	Mickey Morandini	.15	.07
❑ 88	Pedro Martinez	.75	.35
❑ 89	Matt Mieske	.15	.07
❑ 90	Tino Martinez	.25	.11
❑ 91	Paul Shuey	.15	.07
❑ 92	Bip Roberts	.15	.07
❑ 93	Chili Davis	.25	.11
❑ 94	Deion Sanders	.25	.11
❑ 95	Darrell Whitmore	.15	.07
❑ 96	Joe Orsulak	.15	.07
❑ 97	Bret Boone	.25	.11
❑ 98	Kent Mercker	.15	.07
❑ 99	Scott Livingstone	.15	.07
❑ 100	Brady Anderson	.25	.11
❑ 101	James Mouton	.15	.07
❑ 102	Jose Rijo	.15	.07
❑ 103	Bobby Munoz	.15	.07
❑ 104	Ramon Martinez	.15	.07
❑ 105	Bernie Williams	.60	.25
❑ 106	Troy Neel	.15	.07

❑	107 Ivan Rodriguez	.60	.25
❑	108 Salomon Torres	.15	.07
❑	109 Johnny Ruffin	.15	.07
❑	110 Darryl Kile	.25	.11
❑	111 Bobby Ayala	.15	.07
❑	112 Ron Darling	.15	.07
❑	113 Jose Lima	.15	.07
❑	114 Joey Hamilton	.15	.07
❑	115 Greg Maddux	1.50	.70
❑	116 Greg Colbrunn	.15	.07
❑	117 Ozzie Guillen	.15	.07
❑	118 Brian Anderson	.15	.07
❑	119 Jeff Bagwell	.75	.35
❑	120 Pat Listach	.15	.07
❑	121 Sandy Alomar Jr.	.25	.11
❑	122 Jose Vizcaino	.15	.07
❑	123 Rick Helling	.15	.07
❑	124 Allen Watson	.15	.07
❑	125 Pedro Munoz	.15	.07
❑	126 Craig Biggio	.40	.18
❑	127 Kevin Stocker	.15	.07
❑	128 Wil Cordero	.15	.07
❑	129 Rafael Palmeiro	.60	.25
❑	130 Gar Finnvold	.15	.07
❑	131 Darren Hall	.15	.07
❑	132 Heathcliff Slocumb	.15	.07
❑	133 Darrin Fletcher	.15	.07
❑	134 Cal Ripken	2.50	1.10
❑	135 Dante Bichette	.25	.11
❑	136 Don Slaught	.15	.07
❑	137 Pedro Astacio	.15	.07
❑	138 Ryan Thompson	.15	.07
❑	139 Greg Gohr	.15	.07
❑	140 Javier Lopez	.25	.11
❑	141 Lenny Dykstra	.25	.11
❑	142 Pat Rapp	.15	.07
❑	143 Mark Kiefer	.15	.07
❑	144 Greg Gagne	.15	.07
❑	145 Eduardo Perez	.15	.07
❑	146 Felix Fermin	.15	.07
❑	147 Jeff Frye	.15	.07
❑	148 Terry Steinbach	.15	.07
❑	149 Jim Eisenreich	.15	.07
❑	150 Brad Ausmus	.15	.07
❑	151 Randy Myers	.15	.07
❑	152 Rick White	.15	.07
❑	153 Mark Portugal	.15	.07
❑	154 Delino DeShields	.15	.07
❑	155 Scott Cooper	.15	.07
❑	156 Pat Hentgen	.15	.07
❑	157 Mark Gubicza	.15	.07
❑	158 Carlos Baerga	.15	.07
❑	159 Joe Girardi	.15	.07
❑	160 Rey Sanchez	.15	.07
❑	161 Todd Jones	.15	.07
❑	162 Luis Polonia	.15	.07
❑	163 Steve Trachsel	.15	.07
❑	164 Roberto Hernandez	.15	.07
❑	165 John Patterson	.15	.07
❑	166 Rene Arocha	.15	.07
❑	167 Will Clark	.60	.25
❑	168 Jim Leyritz	.15	.07
❑	169 Todd Van Poppel	.15	.07
❑	170 Robb Nen	.15	.07
❑	171 Midre Cummings	.15	.07
❑	172 Jay Buhner	.25	.11
❑	173 Kevin Tapani	.15	.07
❑	174 Mark Lemke	.15	.07
❑	175 Marcus Moore	.15	.07
❑	176 Wayne Kirby	.15	.07
❑	177 Rich Amaral	.15	.07
❑	178 Lou Whitaker	.25	.11
❑	179 Jay Bell	.25	.11
❑	180 Rick Wilkins	.15	.07
❑	181 Paul Molitor	.60	.25
❑	182 Gary Sheffield	.25	.11
❑	183 Kirby Puckett	1.50	.70
❑	184 Cliff Floyd	.25	.11
❑	185 Darren Oliver	.15	.07
❑	186 Tim Naehring	.15	.07
❑	187 John Hudek	.15	.07
❑	188 Eric Young	.15	.07
❑	189 Roger Salkeld	.15	.07
❑	190 Kirt Manwaring	.15	.07
❑	191 Kurt Abbott	.15	.07
❑	192 David Nied	.15	.07
❑	193 Todd Zeile	.15	.07
❑	194 Wally Joyner	.25	.11
❑	195 Dennis Martinez	.25	.11
❑	196 Billy Ashley	.15	.07
❑	197 Ben McDonald	.15	.07
❑	198 Bob Hamelin	.15	.07
❑	199 Chris Turner	.15	.07
❑	200 Lance Johnson	.15	.07
❑	201 Willie Banks	.15	.07
❑	202 Juan Gonzalez	.60	.25
❑	203 Scott Sanders	.15	.07
❑	204 Scott Brosius	.25	.11
❑	205 Curt Schilling	.60	.25
❑	206 Alex Gonzalez	.15	.07
❑	207 Travis Fryman	.25	.11
❑	208 Tim Raines	.25	.11
❑	209 Steve Avery	.15	.07
❑	210 Hal Morris	.15	.07
❑	211 Ken Griffey Jr.	2.00	.90
❑	212 Ozzie Smith	.75	.35
❑	213 Chuck Carr	.15	.07
❑	214 Ryan Klesko	.25	.11
❑	215 Robin Ventura	.25	.11
❑	216 Luis Gonzalez	.60	.25
❑	217 Ken Ryan	.15	.07
❑	218 Mike Piazza	1.50	.70
❑	219 Matt Walbeck	.15	.07
❑	220 Jeff Kent	.40	.18
❑	221 Orlando Miller	.15	.07
❑	222 Kenny Rogers	.15	.07
❑	223 J.T. Snow	.25	.11
❑	224 Alan Trammell	.40	.18
❑	225 John Franco	.25	.11
❑	226 Gerald Williams	.15	.07
❑	227 Andy Benes	.15	.07
❑	228 Dan Wilson	.15	.07
❑	229 Dave Hollins	.15	.07
❑	230 Vinny Castilla	.25	.11
❑	231 Devon White	.25	.11
❑	232 Fred McGriff	.40	.18
❑	233 Quilvio Veras	.15	.07
❑	234 Tom Candiotti	.15	.07
❑	235 Jason Bere	.15	.07
❑	236 Mark Langston	.15	.07
❑	237 Mel Rojas	.15	.07
❑	238 Chuck Knoblauch	.25	.11
❑	239 Bernard Gilkey	.15	.07
❑	240 Mark McGwire	2.50	1.10
❑	241 Kirk Rueter	.15	.07
❑	242 Pat Kelly	.15	.07
❑	243 Ruben Sierra	.15	.07
❑	244 Randy Johnson	.75	.35
❑	245 Shane Reynolds	.15	.07
❑	246 Danny Tartabull	.15	.07
❑	247 Darryl Hamilton	.15	.07
❑	248 Danny Bautista	.15	.07
❑	249 Tom Gordon	.15	.07
❑	250 Tom Glavine	.60	.25
❑	251 Orlando Merced	.15	.07
❑	252 Eric Karros	.25	.11
❑	253 Benji Gil	.15	.07
❑	254 Sean Bergman	.15	.07
❑	255 Roger Clemens	1.50	.70
❑	256 Roberto Alomar	.60	.25
❑	257 Benito Santiago	.15	.07
❑	258 Robby Thompson	.15	.07
❑	259 Marvin Freeman	.15	.07
❑	260 Jose Offerman	.15	.07
❑	261 Greg Vaughn	.25	.11
❑	262 David Segui	.15	.07
❑	263 Geronimo Pena	.15	.07
❑	264 Tim Salmon	.25	.11
❑	265 Eddie Murray	.60	.25
❑	266 Mariano Duncan	.15	.07
❑	267 Hideo Nomo RC	1.50	.70
❑	268 Derek Bell	.15	.07
❑	269 Mo Vaughn	.25	.11
❑	270 Jeff King	.15	.07
❑	271 Edgar Martinez	.40	.18
❑	272 Sammy Sosa	1.25	.55
❑	273 Scott Ruffcorn	.15	.07
❑	274 Darren Daulton	.25	.11
❑	275 John Jaha	.15	.07
❑	276 Andres Galarraga	.40	.18
❑	277 Mark Grace	.60	.25
❑	278 Mike Moore	.15	.07
❑	279 Barry Bonds	1.50	.70
❑	280 Manny Ramirez	.75	.35
❑	281 Ellis Burks	.25	.11
❑	282 Greg Swindell	.15	.07
❑	283 Barry Larkin	.60	.25
❑	284 Albert Belle	.25	.11
❑	285 Shawn Green	.60	.25
❑	286 John Roper	.15	.07
❑	287 Scott Erickson	.15	.07
❑	288 Moises Alou	.25	.11
❑	289 Mike Blowers	.15	.07
❑	290 Brent Gates	.15	.07
❑	291 Sean Berry	.15	.07
❑	292 Mike Stanley	.15	.07
❑	293 Jeff Conine	.15	.07
❑	294 Tim Wallach	.15	.07
❑	295 Bobby Bonilla	.25	.11
❑	296 Bruce Ruffin	.15	.07
❑	297 Chad Curtis	.15	.07
❑	298 Mike Greenwell	.15	.07
❑	299 Tony Gwynn	1.25	.55
❑	300 Russ Davis	.15	.07
❑	301 Danny Jackson	.15	.07
❑	302 Pete Harnisch	.15	.07
❑	303 Don Mattingly	1.50	.70
❑	304 Rheal Cormier	.15	.07
❑	305 Larry Walker	.40	.18
❑	306 Hector Carrasco	.15	.07
❑	307 Jason Jacome	.15	.07
❑	308 Phil Plantier	.15	.07
❑	309 Harold Baines	.25	.11
❑	310 Mitch Williams	.15	.07
❑	311 Charles Nagy	.15	.07
❑	312 Ken Caminiti	.25	.11
❑	313 Alex Rodriguez	2.00	.90
❑	314 Chris Sabo	.15	.07
❑	315 Gary Gaetti	.25	.11
❑	316 Andre Dawson	.40	.18
❑	317 Mark Clark	.15	.07
❑	318 Vince Coleman	.15	.07
❑	319 Brad Clontz	.15	.07
❑	320 Steve Finley	.25	.11
❑	321 Doug Drabek	.15	.07
❑	322 Mark McLemore	.15	.07
❑	323 Stan Javier	.15	.07
❑	324 Ron Gant	.15	.07
❑	325 Charlie Hayes	.15	.07
❑	326 Carlos Delgado	.60	.25
❑	327 Ricky Bottalico	.15	.07
❑	328 Rod Beck	.15	.07
❑	329 Mark Acre	.15	.07
❑	330 Chris Bosio	.15	.07
❑	331 Tony Phillips	.15	.07
❑	332 Garret Anderson	.25	.11
❑	333 Pat Meares	.15	.07
❑	334 Todd Worrell	.15	.07
❑	335 Marquis Grissom	.15	.07
❑	336 Brent Mayne	.15	.07
❑	337 Lee Tinsley	.15	.07
❑	338 Terry Pendleton	.25	.11
❑	339 David Cone	.25	.11
❑	340 Tony Fernandez	.15	.07
❑	341 Jim Bullinger	.15	.07
❑	342 Armando Benitez	.25	.11
❑	343 John Smiley	.15	.07
❑	344 Dan Miceli	.15	.07
❑	345 Charles Johnson	.25	.11
❑	346 Lee Smith	.25	.11
❑	347 Brian McRae	.15	.07
❑	348 Jim Thome	.60	.25
❑	349 Jose Oliva	.15	.07
❑	350 Terry Mulholland	.15	.07
❑	351 Tom Henke	.15	.07
❑	352 Dennis Eckersley	.25	.11
❑	353 Sid Fernandez	.15	.07
❑	354 Paul Wagner	.15	.07
❑	355 John Dettmer	.15	.07
❑	356 John Wetteland	.25	.11
❑	357 John Burkett	.15	.07
❑	358 Marty Cordova	.15	.07
❑	359 Norm Charlton	.15	.07
❑	360 Mike Devereaux	.15	.07
❑	361 Alex Cole	.15	.07
❑	362 Brett Butler	.25	.11
❑	363 Mickey Tettleton	.15	.07
❑	364 Al Martin	.15	.07

		MINT	NRMT
❑ 365	Tony Tarasco	.15	.07
❑ 366	Pat Mahomes	.15	.07
❑ 367	Gary DiSarcina	.15	.07
❑ 368	Bill Swift	.15	.07
❑ 369	Chipper Jones	1.25	.55
❑ 370	Orel Hershiser	.25	.11
❑ 371	Kevin Gross	.15	.07
❑ 372	Dave Winfield	.60	.25
❑ 373	Andujar Cedeno	.15	.07
❑ 374	Jim Abbott	.25	.11
❑ 375	Glenallen Hill	.15	.07
❑ 376	Otis Nixon	.15	.07
❑ 377	Roberto Kelly	.15	.07
❑ 378	Chris Hammond	.15	.07
❑ 379	Mike Macfarlane	.15	.07
❑ 380	J.R. Phillips	.15	.07
❑ 381	Luis Alicea	.15	.07
❑ 382	Bret Barberie	.15	.07
❑ 383	Tom Goodwin	.15	.07
❑ 384	Mark Whiten	.15	.07
❑ 385	Jeffrey Hammonds	.15	.07
❑ 386	Omar Vizquel	.25	.11
❑ 387	Mike Mussina	.60	.25
❑ 388	Ricky Bones	.15	.07
❑ 389	Steve Ontiveros	.15	.07
❑ 390	Jeff Blauser	.15	.07
❑ 391	Jose Canseco	.60	.25
❑ 392	Bob Tewksbury	.15	.07
❑ 393	Jacob Brumfield	.15	.07
❑ 394	Doug Jones	.15	.07
❑ 395	Ken Hill	.15	.07
❑ 396	Pat Borders	.15	.07
❑ 397	Carl Everett	.25	.11
❑ 398	Gregg Jefferies	.15	.07
❑ 399	Jack McDowell	.15	.07
❑ 400	Denny Neagle	.25	.11

1996 Leaf

		MINT	NRMT
COMPLETE SET (220)		20.00	9.00
❑ 1	John Smoltz	.25	.11
❑ 2	Dennis Eckersley	.25	.11
❑ 3	Delino DeShields	.15	.07
❑ 4	Cliff Floyd	.25	.11
❑ 5	Chuck Finley	.25	.11
❑ 6	Cecil Fielder	.25	.11
❑ 7	Tim Naehring	.15	.07
❑ 8	Carlos Perez	.15	.07
❑ 9	Brad Ausmus	.15	.07
❑ 10	Matt Lawton RC	.75	.35
❑ 11	Alan Trammell	.40	.18
❑ 12	Steve Finley	.25	.11
❑ 13	Paul O'Neill	.60	.25
❑ 14	Gary Sheffield	.25	.11
❑ 15	Mark McGwire	2.50	1.10
❑ 16	Bernie Williams	.60	.25
❑ 17	Jeff Montgomery	.15	.07
❑ 18	Chan Ho Park	.25	.11
❑ 19	Greg Vaughn	.25	.11
❑ 20	Jeff Kent	.40	.18
❑ 21	Cal Ripken	2.50	1.10
❑ 22	Charles Johnson	.25	.11
❑ 23	Eric Karros	.25	.11
❑ 24	Alex Rodriguez	1.50	.70
❑ 25	Chris Snopek	.15	.07
❑ 26	Jason Isringhausen	.25	.11
❑ 27	Chili Davis	.25	.11
❑ 28	Chipper Jones	1.25	.55
❑ 29	Bret Saberhagen	.25	.11
❑ 30	Tony Clark	.25	.11
❑ 31	Marty Cordova	.15	.07
❑ 32	Dwayne Hosey	.15	.07
❑ 33	Fred McGriff	.40	.18
❑ 34	Deion Sanders	.25	.11
❑ 35	Orlando Merced	.15	.07
❑ 36	Brady Anderson	.25	.11
❑ 37	Ray Lankford	.15	.07
❑ 38	Manny Ramirez	.75	.35
❑ 39	Alex Fernandez	.15	.07
❑ 40	Greg Colbrunn	.15	.07
❑ 41	Ken Griffey, Jr.	2.00	.90
❑ 42	Mickey Morandini	.15	.07
❑ 43	Chuck Knoblauch	.25	.11
❑ 44	Quinton McCracken	.15	.07
❑ 45	Tim Salmon	.25	.11
❑ 46	Jose Mesa	.15	.07
❑ 47	Marquis Grissom	.15	.07
❑ 48	Checklist	.15	.07
❑ 49	Raul Mondesi	.25	.11
❑ 50	Mark Grudzielanek	.15	.07
❑ 51	Ray Durham	.25	.11
❑ 52	Matt Williams	.40	.18
❑ 53	Bob Hamelin	.15	.07
❑ 54	Lenny Dykstra	.25	.11
❑ 55	Jeff King	.15	.07
❑ 56	LaTroy Hawkins	.15	.07
❑ 57	Terry Pendleton	.25	.11
❑ 58	Kevin Stocker	.15	.07
❑ 59	Ozzie Timmons	.15	.07
❑ 60	David Justice	.25	.11
❑ 61	Ricky Bottalico	.15	.07
❑ 62	Andy Ashby	.15	.07
❑ 63	Larry Walker	.40	.18
❑ 64	Jose Canseco	.60	.25
❑ 65	Bret Boone	.25	.11
❑ 66	Shawn Green	.60	.25
❑ 67	Chad Curtis	.15	.07
❑ 68	Travis Fryman	.25	.11
❑ 69	Roger Clemens	1.50	.70
❑ 70	David Bell	.15	.07
❑ 71	Rusty Greer	.25	.11
❑ 72	Bob Higginson	.25	.11
❑ 73	Joey Hamilton	.15	.07
❑ 74	Kevin Seitzer	.15	.07
❑ 75	Julian Tavarez	.15	.07
❑ 76	Troy Percival	.15	.07
❑ 77	Kirby Puckett	1.50	.70
❑ 78	Barry Bonds	1.50	.70
❑ 79	Michael Tucker	.15	.07
❑ 80	Paul Molitor	.60	.25
❑ 81	Carlos Garcia	.15	.07
❑ 82	Johnny Damon	.25	.11
❑ 83	Mike Hampton	.25	.11
❑ 84	Ariel Prieto	.15	.07
❑ 85	Tony Tarasco	.15	.07
❑ 86	Pete Schourek	.15	.07
❑ 87	Tom Glavine	.60	.25
❑ 88	Rondell White	.25	.11
❑ 89	Jim Edmonds	.40	.18
❑ 90	Robby Thompson	.15	.07
❑ 91	Wade Boggs	.60	.25
❑ 92	Pedro Martinez	.75	.35
❑ 93	Gregg Jefferies	.15	.07
❑ 94	Albert Belle	.25	.11
❑ 95	Benji Gil	.15	.07
❑ 96	Denny Neagle	.25	.11
❑ 97	Mark Langston	.15	.07
❑ 98	Sandy Alomar Jr.	.25	.11
❑ 99	Tony Gwynn	1.25	.55
❑ 100	Todd Hundley	.15	.07
❑ 101	Dante Bichette	.25	.11
❑ 102	Eddie Murray	.60	.25
❑ 103	Lyle Mouton	.15	.07
❑ 104	John Jaha	.15	.07
❑ 105	Checklist	.15	.07
❑ 106	Jon Nunnally	.15	.07
❑ 107	Juan Gonzalez	.60	.25
❑ 108	Kevin Appier	.25	.11
❑ 109	Brian McRae	.15	.07
❑ 110	Lee Smith	.25	.11
❑ 111	Tim Wakefield	.15	.07
❑ 112	Sammy Sosa	1.25	.55
❑ 113	Jay Buhner	.25	.11
❑ 114	Garret Anderson	.25	.11
❑ 115	Edgar Martinez	.40	.18
❑ 116	Edgardo Alfonzo	.25	.11
❑ 117	Billy Ashley	.15	.07
❑ 118	Joe Carter	.25	.11
❑ 119	Javy Lopez	.25	.11
❑ 120	Bobby Bonilla	.25	.11
❑ 121	Ken Caminiti	.25	.11
❑ 122	Barry Larkin	.60	.25
❑ 123	Shannon Stewart	.25	.11
❑ 124	Orel Hershiser	.25	.11
❑ 125	Jeff Conine	.15	.07
❑ 126	Mark Grace	.60	.25
❑ 127	Kenny Lofton	.25	.11
❑ 128	Luis Gonzalez	.60	.25
❑ 129	Rico Brogna	.15	.07
❑ 130	Mo Vaughn	.25	.11
❑ 131	Brad Radke	.25	.11
❑ 132	Jose Herrera	.15	.07
❑ 133	Rick Aguilera	.15	.07
❑ 134	Gary DiSarcina	.15	.07
❑ 135	Andres Galarraga	.40	.18
❑ 136	Carl Everett	.25	.11
❑ 137	Steve Avery	.15	.07
❑ 138	Vinny Castilla	.25	.11
❑ 139	Dennis Martinez	.25	.11
❑ 140	John Wetteland	.25	.11
❑ 141	Alex Gonzalez	.15	.07
❑ 142	Brian Jordan	.25	.11
❑ 143	Todd Hollandsworth	.15	.07
❑ 144	Terrell Wade	.15	.07
❑ 145	Wilson Alvarez	.15	.07
❑ 146	Reggie Sanders	.15	.07
❑ 147	Will Clark	.60	.25
❑ 148	Hideo Nomo	.75	.35
❑ 149	J.T.Snow	.25	.11
❑ 150	Frank Thomas	.75	.35
❑ 151	Ivan Rodriguez	.60	.25
❑ 152	Jay Bell	.25	.11
❑ 153	Checklist	.15	.07
❑ 154	David Cone	.25	.11
❑ 155	Roberto Alomar	.60	.25
❑ 156	Carlos Delgado	.60	.25
❑ 157	Carlos Baerga	.15	.07
❑ 158	Geronimo Berroa	.15	.07
❑ 159	Joe Vitiello	.15	.07
❑ 160	Terry Steinbach	.15	.07
❑ 161	Doug Drabek	.15	.07
❑ 162	David Segui	.15	.07
❑ 163	Ozzie Smith	.75	.35
❑ 164	Kurt Abbott	.15	.07
❑ 165	Randy Johnson	.75	.35
❑ 166	John Valentin	.15	.07
❑ 167	Mickey Tettleton	.15	.07
❑ 168	Ruben Sierra	.15	.07
❑ 169	Jim Thome	.60	.25
❑ 170	Mike Greenwell	.15	.07
❑ 171	Quilvio Veras	.15	.07
❑ 172	Robin Ventura	.25	.11
❑ 173	Bill Pulsipher	.15	.07
❑ 174	Rafael Palmeiro	.60	.25
❑ 175	Hal Morris	.15	.07
❑ 176	Ryan Klesko	.25	.11
❑ 177	Eric Young	.15	.07
❑ 178	Shane Andrews	.15	.07
❑ 179	Brian L.Hunter	.15	.07
❑ 180	Brett Butler	.25	.11
❑ 181	John Olerud	.25	.11
❑ 182	Moises Alou	.25	.11
❑ 183	Glenallen Hill	.15	.07
❑ 184	Ismael Valdes	.15	.07
❑ 185	Andy Pettitte	.25	.11
❑ 186	Yamil Benitez	.15	.07
❑ 187	Jason Bere	.15	.07
❑ 188	Dean Palmer	.25	.11
❑ 189	Jimmy Haynes	.15	.07
❑ 190	Trevor Hoffman	.25	.11
❑ 191	Mike Mussina	.60	.25
❑ 192	Greg Maddux	1.50	.70
❑ 193	Ozzie Guillen	.15	.07
❑ 194	Pat Listach	.15	.07
❑ 195	Derek Bell	.15	.07
❑ 196	Darren Daulton	.25	.11
❑ 197	John Mabry	.15	.07
❑ 198	Ramon Martinez	.15	.07

Card	Player	MINT	NRMT
❑ 199	Jeff Bagwell	.75	.35
❑ 200	Mike Piazza	1.50	.70
❑ 201	Al Martin	.15	.07
❑ 202	Aaron Sele	.25	.11
❑ 203	Ed Sprague	.15	.07
❑ 204	Rod Beck	.15	.07
❑ 205	Checklist	.15	.07
❑ 206	Mike Lansing	.15	.07
❑ 207	Craig Biggio	.40	.18
❑ 208	Jeffrey Hammonds	.15	.07
❑ 209	Dave Nilsson	.15	.07
❑ 210	Checklist	.15	.07
❑ 211	Derek Jeter	2.50	1.10
❑ 212	Alan Benes	.15	.07
❑ 213	Jason Schmidt	.15	.07
❑ 214	Alex Ochoa	.15	.07
❑ 215	Ruben Rivera	.15	.07
❑ 216	Roger Cedeno	.15	.07
❑ 217	Jeff Suppan	.15	.07
❑ 218	Billy Wagner	.15	.07
❑ 219	Mark Loretta	.15	.07
❑ 220	Karim Garcia	.15	.07

1997 Leaf

	MINT	NRMT
COMPLETE SET (400)	40.00	18.00
COMPLETE SERIES 1 (200)	20.00	9.00
COMPLETE SERIES 2 (200)	20.00	9.00

Card	Player	MINT	NRMT
❑ 1	Wade Boggs	.60	.25
❑ 2	Brian McRae	.15	.07
❑ 3	Jeff D'Amico	.15	.07
❑ 4	George Arias	.15	.07
❑ 5	Billy Wagner	.15	.07
❑ 6	Ray Lankford	.15	.07
❑ 7	Will Clark	.60	.25
❑ 8	Edgar Renteria	.15	.07
❑ 9	Alex Ochoa	.15	.07
❑ 10	Roberto Hernandez	.15	.07
❑ 11	Joe Carter	.25	.11
❑ 12	Gregg Jefferies	.15	.07
❑ 13	Mark Grace	.60	.25
❑ 14	Roberto Alomar	.60	.25
❑ 15	Joe Randa	.15	.07
❑ 16	Alex Rodriguez	.75	.35
❑ 17	Tony Gwynn	1.25	.55
❑ 18	Steve Gibralter	.15	.07
❑ 19	Scott Stahoviak	.15	.07
❑ 20	Matt Williams	.40	.18
❑ 21	Quinton McCracken	.15	.07
❑ 22	Ugueth Urbina	.15	.07
❑ 23	Jermaine Allensworth	.15	.07
❑ 24	Paul Molitor	.60	.25
❑ 25	Carlos Delgado	.60	.25
❑ 26	Bob Abreu	.25	.11
❑ 27	John Jaha	.15	.07
❑ 28	Rusty Greer	.25	.11
❑ 29	Kimera Bartee	.15	.07
❑ 30	Ruben Rivera	.15	.07
❑ 31	Jason Kendall	.25	.11
❑ 32	Lance Johnson	.15	.07
❑ 33	Robin Ventura	.25	.11
❑ 34	Kevin Appier	.25	.11
❑ 35	John Mabry	.15	.07
❑ 36	Ricky Otero	.15	.07
❑ 37	Mike Lansing	.15	.07
❑ 38	Mark McGwire	2.50	1.10
❑ 39	Tim Naehring	.15	.07
❑ 40	Tom Glavine	.60	.25
❑ 41	Rey Ordonez	.15	.07
❑ 42	Tony Clark	.25	.11
❑ 43	Rafael Palmeiro	.60	.25
❑ 44	Pedro Martinez	.75	.35
❑ 45	Keith Lockhart	.15	.07
❑ 46	Dan Wilson	.15	.07
❑ 47	John Wetteland	.25	.11
❑ 48	Chan Ho Park	.25	.11
❑ 49	Gary Sheffield	.25	.11
❑ 50	Shawn Estes	.25	.11
❑ 51	Royce Clayton	.15	.07
❑ 52	Jaime Navarro	.15	.07
❑ 53	Raul Casanova	.15	.07
❑ 54	Jeff Bagwell	.75	.35
❑ 55	Barry Larkin	.60	.25
❑ 56	Charles Nagy	.15	.07
❑ 57	Ken Caminiti	.25	.11
❑ 58	Todd Hollandsworth	.15	.07
❑ 59	Pat Hentgen	.15	.07
❑ 60	Jose Valentin	.15	.07
❑ 61	Frank Rodriguez	.15	.07
❑ 62	Mickey Tettleton	.15	.07
❑ 63	Marty Cordova	.15	.07
❑ 64	Cecil Fielder	.25	.11
❑ 65	Barry Bonds	1.50	.70
❑ 66	Scott Servais	.15	.07
❑ 67	Ernie Young	.15	.07
❑ 68	Wilson Alvarez	.15	.07
❑ 69	Mike Grace	.15	.07
❑ 70	Shane Reynolds	.15	.07
❑ 71	Henry Rodriguez	.15	.07
❑ 72	Eric Karros	.25	.11
❑ 73	Mark Langston	.15	.07
❑ 74	Scott Karl	.15	.07
❑ 75	Trevor Hoffman	.25	.11
❑ 76	Orel Hershiser	.25	.11
❑ 77	John Smoltz	.25	.11
❑ 78	Raul Mondesi	.25	.11
❑ 79	Jeff Brantley	.15	.07
❑ 80	Donne Wall	.15	.07
❑ 81	Joey Cora	.15	.07
❑ 82	Mel Rojas	.15	.07
❑ 83	Chad Mottola	.15	.07
❑ 84	Omar Vizquel	.25	.11
❑ 85	Greg Maddux	1.50	.70
❑ 86	Jamey Wright	.15	.07
❑ 87	Chuck Finley	.25	.11
❑ 88	Brady Anderson	.25	.11
❑ 89	Alex Gonzalez	.15	.07
❑ 90	Andy Benes	.15	.07
❑ 91	Reggie Jefferson	.15	.07
❑ 92	Paul O'Neill	.60	.25
❑ 93	Javier Lopez	.25	.11
❑ 94	Mark Grudzielanek	.15	.07
❑ 95	Marc Newfield	.15	.07
❑ 96	Kevin Ritz	.15	.07
❑ 97	Fred McGriff	.40	.18
❑ 98	Dwight Gooden	.25	.11
❑ 99	Hideo Nomo	.60	.25
❑ 100	Steve Finley	.25	.11
❑ 101	Juan Gonzalez	.60	.25
❑ 102	Jay Buhner	.25	.11
❑ 103	Paul Wilson	.15	.07
❑ 104	Alan Benes	.15	.07
❑ 105	Manny Ramirez	.75	.35
❑ 106	Kevin Elster	.15	.07
❑ 107	Frank Thomas	.75	.35
❑ 108	Orlando Miller	.15	.07
❑ 109	Ramon Martinez	.15	.07
❑ 110	Kenny Lofton	.25	.11
❑ 111	Bernie Williams	.60	.25
❑ 112	Robby Thompson	.15	.07
❑ 113	Bernard Gilkey	.15	.07
❑ 114	Ray Durham	.25	.11
❑ 115	Jeff Cirillo	.25	.11
❑ 116	Brian Jordan	.25	.11
❑ 117	Rich Becker	.15	.07
❑ 118	Al Leiter	.25	.11
❑ 119	Mark Johnson	.15	.07
❑ 120	Ellis Burks	.25	.11
❑ 121	Sammy Sosa	1.25	.55
❑ 122	Willie Greene	.15	.07
❑ 123	Michael Tucker	.15	.07
❑ 124	Eddie Murray	.60	.25
❑ 125	Joey Hamilton	.15	.07
❑ 126	Antonio Osuna	.15	.07
❑ 127	Bobby Higginson	.25	.11
❑ 128	Tomas Perez	.15	.07
❑ 129	Tim Salmon	.25	.11
❑ 130	Mark Wohlers	.15	.07
❑ 131	Charles Johnson	.25	.11
❑ 132	Randy Johnson	.75	.35
❑ 133	Brooks Kieschnick	.15	.07
❑ 134	Al Martin	.15	.07
❑ 135	Dante Bichette	.25	.11
❑ 136	Andy Pettitte	.25	.11
❑ 137	Jason Giambi	.60	.25
❑ 138	James Baldwin	.15	.07
❑ 139	Ben McDonald	.15	.07
❑ 140	Shawn Green	.60	.25
❑ 141	Geronimo Berroa	.15	.07
❑ 142	Jose Offerman	.15	.07
❑ 143	Curtis Pride	.15	.07
❑ 144	Terrell Wade	.15	.07
❑ 145	Ismael Valdes	.15	.07
❑ 146	Mike Mussina	.60	.25
❑ 147	Mariano Rivera	.25	.11
❑ 148	Ken Hill	.15	.07
❑ 149	Darin Erstad	.60	.25
❑ 150	Jay Bell	.25	.11
❑ 151	Mo Vaughn	.25	.11
❑ 152	Ozzie Smith	.75	.35
❑ 153	Jose Mesa	.15	.07
❑ 154	Osvaldo Fernandez	.15	.07
❑ 155	Vinny Castilla	.25	.11
❑ 156	Jason Isringhausen	.15	.07
❑ 157	B.J. Surhoff	.25	.11
❑ 158	Robert Perez	.15	.07
❑ 159	Ron Coomer	.15	.07
❑ 160	Darren Oliver	.15	.07
❑ 161	Mike Mohler	.15	.07
❑ 162	Russ Davis	.15	.07
❑ 163	Bret Boone	.25	.11
❑ 164	Ricky Bottalico	.15	.07
❑ 165	Derek Jeter	2.50	1.10
❑ 166	Orlando Merced	.15	.07
❑ 167	John Valentin	.15	.07
❑ 168	Andruw Jones	.75	.35
❑ 169	Angel Echevarria	.15	.07
❑ 170	Todd Walker	.15	.07
❑ 171	Desi Relaford	.15	.07
❑ 172	Trey Beamon	.15	.07
❑ 173	Brian Giles RC	2.50	1.10
❑ 174	Scott Rolen	.60	.25
❑ 175	Shannon Stewart	.25	.11
❑ 176	Dmitri Young	.25	.11
❑ 177	Justin Thompson	.15	.07
❑ 178	Trot Nixon	.25	.11
❑ 179	Josh Booty	.15	.07
❑ 180	Robin Jennings	.15	.07
❑ 181	Marvin Benard	.15	.07
❑ 182	Luis Castillo	.15	.07
❑ 183	Wendell Magee	.15	.07
❑ 184	Vladimir Guerrero	1.00	.45
❑ 185	Nomar Garciaparra	1.50	.70
❑ 186	Ryan Hancock	.15	.07
❑ 187	Mike Cameron	.25	.11
❑ 188	Cal Ripken LG	1.25	.55
❑ 189	Chipper Jones LG	.60	.25
❑ 190	Albert Belle LG	.25	.11
❑ 191	Mike Piazza LG	.75	.35
❑ 192	Chuck Knoblauch LG	.15	.07
❑ 193	Ken Griffey Jr. LG	1.00	.45
❑ 194	Ivan Rodriguez LG	.25	.11
❑ 195	Jose Canseco LG	.25	.11
❑ 196	Ryne Sandberg LG	.40	.18
❑ 197	Jim Thome LG	.25	.11
❑ 198	Andy Pettitte CL	.15	.07
❑ 199	Andruw Jones CL	.40	.18
❑ 200	Derek Jeter CL	1.25	.55
❑ 201	Chipper Jones	1.25	.55
❑ 202	Albert Belle	.25	.11
❑ 203	Mike Piazza	1.50	.70
❑ 204	Ken Griffey Jr.	2.00	.90
❑ 205	Ryne Sandberg	.75	.35
❑ 206	Jose Canseco	.60	.25
❑ 207	Chili Davis	.25	.11
❑ 208	Roger Clemens	1.50	.70
❑ 209	Deion Sanders	.25	.11
❑ 210	Darryl Hamilton	.15	.07

❑ 211 Jermaine Dye .25 .11
❑ 212 Matt Williams .40 .18
❑ 213 Kevin Elster .15 .07
❑ 214 John Wetteland .25 .11
❑ 215 Garret Anderson .25 .11
❑ 216 Kevin Brown .25 .11
❑ 217 Matt Lawton .25 .11
❑ 218 Cal Ripken 2.50 1.10
❑ 219 Moises Alou .25 .11
❑ 220 Chuck Knoblauch .25 .11
❑ 221 Ivan Rodriguez .60 .25
❑ 222 Travis Fryman .25 .11
❑ 223 Jim Thome .60 .25
❑ 224 Eddie Murray .60 .25
❑ 225 Eric Young .15 .07
❑ 226 Ron Gant .15 .07
❑ 227 Tony Phillips .15 .07
❑ 228 Reggie Sanders .15 .07
❑ 229 Johnny Damon .25 .11
❑ 230 Bill Pulsipher .15 .07
❑ 231 Jim Edmonds .40 .18
❑ 232 Melvin Nieves .15 .07
❑ 233 Ryan Klesko .25 .11
❑ 234 David Cone .25 .11
❑ 235 Derek Bell .15 .07
❑ 236 Julio Franco .25 .11
❑ 237 Juan Guzman .15 .07
❑ 238 Larry Walker .40 .18
❑ 239 Delino DeShields .15 .07
❑ 240 Troy Percival .15 .07
❑ 241 Andres Galarraga .40 .18
❑ 242 Rondell White .25 .11
❑ 243 John Burkett .15 .07
❑ 244 J.T. Snow .25 .11
❑ 245 Alex Fernandez .15 .07
❑ 246 Edgar Martinez .40 .18
❑ 247 Craig Biggio .40 .18
❑ 248 Todd Hundley .15 .07
❑ 249 Jimmy Key .25 .11
❑ 250 Cliff Floyd .25 .11
❑ 251 Jeff Conine .15 .07
❑ 252 Curt Schilling .60 .25
❑ 253 Jeff King .15 .07
❑ 254 Tino Martinez .25 .11
❑ 255 Carlos Baerga .15 .07
❑ 256 Jeff Fassero .15 .07
❑ 257 Dean Palmer .25 .11
❑ 258 Robb Nen .15 .07
❑ 259 Sandy Alomar Jr. .25 .11
❑ 260 Carlos Perez .15 .07
❑ 261 Rickey Henderson 1.25 .55
❑ 262 Bobby Bonilla .25 .11
❑ 263 Darren Daulton .25 .11
❑ 264 Jim Leyritz .15 .07
❑ 265 Dennis Martinez .25 .11
❑ 266 Butch Huskey .15 .07
❑ 267 Joe Vitiello .15 .07
❑ 268 Steve Trachsel .15 .07
❑ 269 Glenallen Hill .15 .07
❑ 270 Terry Steinbach .15 .07
❑ 271 Mark McLemore .15 .07
❑ 272 Devon White .25 .11
❑ 273 Jeff Kent .40 .18
❑ 274 Tim Raines .25 .11
❑ 275 Carlos Garcia .15 .07
❑ 276 Hal Morris .15 .07
❑ 277 Gary Gaetti .25 .11
❑ 278 John Olerud .25 .11
❑ 279 Wally Joyner .25 .11
❑ 280 Brian Hunter .15 .07
❑ 281 Steve Karsay .15 .07
❑ 282 Denny Neagle .25 .11
❑ 283 Jose Herrera .15 .07
❑ 284 Todd Stottlemyre .15 .07
❑ 285 Bip Roberts .15 .07
❑ 286 Kevin Seitzer .15 .07
❑ 287 Benji Gil .15 .07
❑ 288 Dennis Eckersley .25 .11
❑ 289 Brad Ausmus .15 .07
❑ 290 Otis Nixon .15 .07
❑ 291 Darryl Strawberry .25 .11
❑ 292 Marquis Grissom .15 .07
❑ 293 Darryl Kile .25 .11
❑ 294 Quilvio Veras .15 .07
❑ 295 Tom Goodwin .15 .07
❑ 296 Benito Santiago .15 .07
❑ 297 Mike Bordick .15 .07
❑ 298 Roberto Kelly .15 .07
❑ 299 David Justice .25 .11
❑ 300 Carl Everett .25 .11
❑ 301 Mark Whiten .15 .07
❑ 302 Aaron Sele .25 .11
❑ 303 Darren Dreifort .15 .07
❑ 304 Bobby Jones .15 .07
❑ 305 Fernando Vina .15 .07
❑ 306 Ed Sprague .15 .07
❑ 307 Andy Ashby .15 .07
❑ 308 Tony Fernandez .15 .07
❑ 309 Roger Pavlik .15 .07
❑ 310 Mark Clark .15 .07
❑ 311 Mariano Duncan .15 .07
❑ 312 Tyler Houston .15 .07
❑ 313 Eric Davis .25 .11
❑ 314 Greg Vaughn .25 .11
❑ 315 David Segui .15 .07
❑ 316 Dave Nilsson .15 .07
❑ 317 F.P. Santangelo .15 .07
❑ 318 Wilton Guerrero .15 .07
❑ 319 Jose Guillen .15 .07
❑ 320 Kevin Orie .15 .07
❑ 321 Derrek Lee .25 .11
❑ 322 Bubba Trammell RC .25 .11
❑ 323 Pokey Reese .15 .07
❑ 324 Hideki Irabu RC .25 .11
❑ 325 Scott Spiezio .15 .07
❑ 326 Bartolo Colon .25 .11
❑ 327 Damon Mashore .15 .07
❑ 329 Chris Carpenter .15 .07
❑ 330 Jose Cruz Jr. RC 1.50 .70
❑ 331 Todd Greene .15 .07
❑ 332 Brian Moehler .15 .07
❑ 333 Mike Sweeney .25 .11
❑ 334 Neifi Perez .15 .07
❑ 335 Matt Morris .25 .11
❑ 336 Marvin Benard .15 .07
❑ 337 Karim Garcia .15 .07
❑ 338 Jason Dickson .15 .07
❑ 339 Brant Brown .15 .07
❑ 340 Jeff Suppan .15 .07
❑ 341 Deivi Cruz RC .75 .35
❑ 342 Antone Williamson .15 .07
❑ 343 Curtis Goodwin .15 .07
❑ 344 Brooks Kieschnick .15 .07
❑ 345 Tony Womack RC .50 .23
❑ 346 Rudy Pemberton .15 .07
❑ 347 Todd Dunwoody .15 .07
❑ 348 Frank Thomas LG .40 .18
❑ 349 Andruw Jones LG .40 .18
❑ 350 Alex Rodriguez LG .75 .35
❑ 351 Greg Maddux LG .75 .35
❑ 352 Jeff Bagwell LG .40 .18
❑ 353 Juan Gonzalez LG .25 .11
❑ 354 Barry Bonds LG .75 .35
❑ 355 Mark McGwire LG 1.25 .55
❑ 356 Tony Gwynn LG .60 .25
❑ 357 Gary Sheffield LG .15 .07
❑ 358 Derek Jeter LG 1.25 .55
❑ 359 Manny Ramirez LG .40 .18
❑ 360 Hideo Nomo LG .25 .11
❑ 361 Sammy Sosa LG .60 .25
❑ 362 Paul Molitor LG .25 .11
❑ 363 Kenny Lofton LG .15 .07
❑ 364 Eddie Murray LG .25 .11
❑ 365 Barry Larkin LG .25 .11
❑ 366 Roger Clemens LG .75 .35
❑ 367 John Smoltz LG .15 .07
❑ 368 Alex Rodriguez GM .75 .35
❑ 369 Frank Thomas GM .40 .18
❑ 370 Cal Ripken GM 1.25 .55
❑ 371 Ken Griffey Jr. GM 1.00 .45
❑ 372 Greg Maddux GM .75 .35
❑ 373 Mike Piazza GM .75 .35
❑ 374 Chipper Jones GM .60 .25
❑ 375 Albert Belle GM .25 .11
❑ 376 Chuck Knoblauch GM .15 .07
❑ 377 Brady Anderson GM .15 .07
❑ 378 David Justice GM .15 .07
❑ 379 Randy Johnson GM .40 .18
❑ 380 Wade Boggs GM .25 .11
❑ 381 Kevin Brown GM .15 .07
❑ 382 Tom Glavine GM .25 .11
❑ 383 Raul Mondesi GM .15 .07
❑ 384 Ivan Rodriguez GM .25 .11
❑ 385 Larry Walker GM .15 .07
❑ 386 Bernie Williams GM .25 .11
❑ 387 Rusty Greer GM .15 .07
❑ 388 Rafael Palmeiro GM .25 .11
❑ 389 Matt Williams GM .25 .11
❑ 390 Eric Young GM .15 .07
❑ 391 Fred McGriff GM .25 .11
❑ 392 Ken Caminiti GM .15 .07
❑ 393 Roberto Alomar GM .25 .11
❑ 394 Brian Jordan GM .15 .07
❑ 395 Mark Grace GM .25 .11
❑ 396 Jim Edmonds GM .25 .11
❑ 397 Deion Sanders GM .15 .07
❑ 398 Vladimir Guerrero CL .60 .25
❑ 399 Darin Erstad CL .25 .11
❑ 400 N. Garciaparra CL .75 .35
❑ NNO J.Robinson Reprint 25.00 11.00

1998 Leaf

	MINT	NRMT
COMPLETE SET (200)	150.00	70.00
COMP.SET w/o SP's (147)	15.00	6.75
COMMON CARD (1-201)	.15	.07
COMMON SP (148-197)	1.00	.45

❑ 1 Rusty Greer .25 .11
❑ 2 Tino Martinez .25 .11
❑ 3 Bobby Bonilla .25 .11
❑ 4 Jason Giambi .60 .25
❑ 5 Matt Morris .25 .11
❑ 6 Craig Counsell .15 .07
❑ 7 Reggie Jefferson .15 .07
❑ 8 Brian Rose .15 .07
❑ 9 Ruben Rivera .15 .07
❑ 10 Shawn Estes .25 .11
❑ 11 Tony Gwynn 1.25 .55
❑ 12 Jeff Abbott .15 .07
❑ 13 Jose Cruz Jr. .25 .11
❑ 14 Francisco Cordova .15 .07
❑ 15 Ryan Klesko .25 .11
❑ 16 Tim Salmon .25 .11
❑ 17 Brett Tomko .15 .07
❑ 18 Matt Williams .40 .18
❑ 19 Joe Carter .25 .11
❑ 20 Harold Baines .25 .11
❑ 21 Gary Sheffield .25 .11
❑ 22 Charles Johnson .25 .11
❑ 23 Aaron Boone .15 .07
❑ 24 Eddie Murray .60 .25
❑ 25 Matt Stairs .15 .07
❑ 26 David Cone .25 .11
❑ 27 Jon Nunnally .15 .07
❑ 28 Chris Stynes .15 .07
❑ 29 Enrique Wilson .15 .07
❑ 30 Randy Johnson .75 .35
❑ 31 Garret Anderson .25 .11
❑ 32 Manny Ramirez .75 .35
❑ 33 Jeff Suppan .15 .07
❑ 34 Rickey Henderson 1.25 .55
❑ 35 Scott Spiezio .15 .07
❑ 36 Rondell White .25 .11
❑ 37 Todd Greene .15 .07
❑ 38 Delino DeShields .15 .07
❑ 39 Kevin Brown .40 .18
❑ 40 Chili Davis .25 .11
❑ 41 Jimmy Key .25 .11

❑ 43 Mike Mussina .60 .25
❑ 44 Joe Randa .15 .07
❑ 45 Chan Ho Park .25 .11
❑ 46 Brad Radke .25 .11
❑ 47 Geronimo Berroa .15 .07
❑ 48 Wade Boggs .60 .25
❑ 49 Kevin Appier .25 .11
❑ 50 Moises Alou .25 .11
❑ 51 David Justice .25 .11
❑ 52 Ivan Rodriguez .60 .25
❑ 53 J.T. Snow .25 .11
❑ 54 Brian Giles .25 .11
❑ 55 Will Clark .60 .25
❑ 56 Justin Thompson .15 .07
❑ 57 Javier Lopez .25 .11
❑ 58 Hideki Irabu .15 .07
❑ 59 Mark Grudzielanek .15 .07
❑ 60 Abraham Nunez .15 .07
❑ 61 Todd Hollandsworth .15 .07
❑ 62 Jay Bell .25 .11
❑ 63 Nomar Garciaparra 1.50 .70
❑ 64 Vinny Castilla .25 .11
❑ 65 Lou Collier .15 .07
❑ 66 Kevin Orie .15 .07
❑ 67 John Valentin .15 .07
❑ 68 Robin Ventura .25 .11
❑ 69 Denny Neagle .15 .07
❑ 70 Tony Womack .15 .07
❑ 71 Dennis Reyes .15 .07
❑ 72 Wally Joyner .25 .11
❑ 73 Kevin Brown .40 .18
❑ 74 Ray Durham .25 .11
❑ 75 Mike Cameron .25 .11
❑ 76 Dante Bichette .25 .11
❑ 77 Jose Guillen .15 .07
❑ 78 Carlos Delgado .60 .25
❑ 79 Paul Molitor .60 .25
❑ 80 Jason Kendall .25 .11
❑ 81 Mark Bellhorn .15 .07
❑ 82 Damian Jackson .15 .07
❑ 83 Bill Mueller .15 .07
❑ 84 Kevin Young .25 .11
❑ 85 Curt Schilling .60 .25
❑ 86 Jeffrey Hammonds .15 .07
❑ 87 Sandy Alomar Jr. .25 .11
❑ 88 Bartolo Colon .25 .11
❑ 89 Wilton Guerrero .15 .07
❑ 90 Bernie Williams .60 .25
❑ 91 Deion Sanders .25 .11
❑ 92 Mike Piazza 1.50 .70
❑ 93 Butch Huskey .15 .07
❑ 94 Edgardo Alfonzo .25 .11
❑ 95 Alan Benes .15 .07
❑ 96 Craig Biggio .40 .18
❑ 97 Mark Grace .60 .25
❑ 98 Shawn Green .60 .25
❑ 99 Derrek Lee .25 .11
❑ 100 Ken Griffey Jr. 2.00 .90
❑ 101 Tim Raines .25 .11
❑ 102 Pokey Reese .15 .07
❑ 103 Lee Stevens .15 .07
❑ 104 Shannon Stewart .25 .11
❑ 105 John Smoltz .25 .11
❑ 106 Frank Thomas .75 .35
❑ 107 Jeff Fassero .15 .07
❑ 108 Jay Buhner .25 .11
❑ 109 Jose Canseco .60 .25
❑ 110 Omar Vizquel .25 .11
❑ 111 Travis Fryman .25 .11
❑ 112 Dave Nilsson .15 .07
❑ 113 John Olerud .25 .11
❑ 114 Larry Walker .40 .18
❑ 115 Jim Edmonds .40 .18
❑ 116 Bobby Higginson .25 .11
❑ 117 Todd Hundley .15 .07
❑ 118 Paul O'Neill .60 .25
❑ 119 Bip Roberts .15 .07
❑ 120 Ismael Valdes .15 .07
❑ 121 Pedro Martinez .75 .35
❑ 122 Jeff Cirillo .25 .11
❑ 123 Andy Benes .15 .07
❑ 124 Bobby Jones .15 .07
❑ 125 Brian Hunter .15 .07
❑ 126 Darryl Kile .25 .11
❑ 127 Pat Hentgen .15 .07
❑ 128 Marquis Grissom .15 .07
❑ 129 Eric Davis .25 .11
❑ 130 Chipper Jones 1.25 .55
❑ 131 Edgar Martinez .40 .18
❑ 132 Andy Pettitte .25 .11
❑ 133 Cal Ripken 2.50 1.10
❑ 134 Scott Rolen .60 .25
❑ 135 Ron Coomer .15 .07
❑ 136 Luis Castillo .15 .07
❑ 137 Fred McGriff .40 .18
❑ 138 Neifi Perez .15 .07
❑ 139 Eric Karros .25 .11
❑ 140 Alex Fernandez .15 .07
❑ 141 Jason Dickson .15 .07
❑ 142 Lance Johnson .15 .07
❑ 143 Ray Lankford .15 .07
❑ 144 Sammy Sosa 1.25 .55
❑ 145 Eric Young .15 .07
❑ 146 Bubba Trammell .15 .07
❑ 147 Todd Walker .15 .07
❑ 148 Mo Vaughn CC 1.50 .70
❑ 149 Jeff Bagwell CC 4.00 1.80
❑ 150 Kenny Lofton CC 1.50 .70
❑ 151 Raul Mondesi CC 1.50 .70
❑ 152 Mike Piazza CC 8.00 3.60
❑ 153 Chipper Jones CC 6.00 2.70
❑ 154 Larry Walker CC 2.00 .90
❑ 155 Greg Maddux CC 8.00 3.60
❑ 156 Ken Griffey Jr. CC 10.00 4.50
❑ 157 Frank Thomas CC 4.00 1.80
❑ 158 Darin Erstad GLS 3.00 1.35
❑ 159 Roberto Alomar GLS 3.00 1.35
❑ 160 Albert Belle GLS 1.50 .70
❑ 161 Jim Thome GLS 3.00 1.35
❑ 162 Tony Clark GLS 1.50 .70
❑ 163 Chuck Knoblauch GLS 1.50 .70
❑ 164 Derek Jeter GLS 12.00 5.50
❑ 165 Alex Rodriguez GLS 8.00 3.60
❑ 166 Tony Gwynn GLS 6.00 2.70
❑ 167 Roger Clemens GLS 8.00 3.60
❑ 168 Barry Larkin GLS 3.00 1.35
❑ 169 Andres Galarraga GLS 2.00 .90
❑ 170 Vlad. Guerrero GLS 4.00 1.80
❑ 171 Mark McGwire GLS 12.00 5.50
❑ 172 Barry Bonds GLS 8.00 3.60
❑ 173 Juan Gonzalez GLS 3.00 1.35
❑ 174 Andruw Jones GLS 3.00 1.35
❑ 175 Paul Molitor GLS 3.00 1.35
❑ 176 Hideo Nomo GLS 3.00 1.35
❑ 177 Cal Ripken GLS 12.00 5.50
❑ 178 Brad Fullmer GLR 1.50 .70
❑ 179 Jaret Wright GLR 1.00 .45
❑ 180 Bobby Estalella GLR 1.00 .45
❑ 181 Ben Grieve GLR 1.50 .70
❑ 182 Paul Konerko GLR 1.50 .70
❑ 183 David Ortiz GLR 1.50 .70
❑ 184 Todd Helton GLR 4.00 1.80
❑ 185 J.Encarnacion GLR 1.50 .70
❑ 186 Miguel Tejada GLR .40 .18
❑ 187 Jacob Cruz GLR 1.00 .45
❑ 188 Mark Kotsay GLR 1.50 .70
❑ 189 Fernando Tatis GLR 1.00 .45
❑ 190 Ricky Ledee GLR 1.00 .45
❑ 191 Richard Hidalgo GLR 1.50 .70
❑ 192 Richie Sexson GLR 1.50 .70
❑ 193 Luis Ordaz GLR 1.00 .45
❑ 194 Eli Marrero GLR 1.00 .45
❑ 195 Livan Hernandez GLR 1.00 .45
❑ 196 Homer Bush GLR 1.00 .45
❑ 197 Raul Ibanez GLR 1.00 .45
❑ 198 Nomar Garciaparra CL .75 .35
❑ 199 Scott Rolen CL .60 .25
❑ 200 Jose Cruz Jr. CL .15 .07
❑ 201 Al Martin .15 .07

2001 Leaf Certified Materials

	MINT	NRMT
COMP.SET w/o SP's (110)	40.00	18.00
COMMON CARD (1-110)	.75	.35
COMMON FABRIC (111-160)	20.00	9.00

❑ 1 Alex Rodriguez 5.00 2.20
❑ 2 Barry Bonds 5.00 2.20
❑ 3 Cal Ripken 8.00 3.60

❑ 4 Chipper Jones 4.00 1.80
❑ 5 Derek Jeter 8.00 3.60
❑ 6 Troy Glaus 2.00 .90
❑ 7 Frank Thomas 2.50 1.10
❑ 8 Greg Maddux 5.00 2.20
❑ 9 Ivan Rodriguez 2.00 .90
❑ 10 Jeff Bagwell 2.50 1.10
❑ 11 Eric Karros .75 .35
❑ 12 Todd Helton 2.50 1.10
❑ 13 Ken Griffey Jr. 6.00 2.70
❑ 14 Manny Ramirez 2.50 1.10
❑ 15 Mark McGwire 8.00 3.60
❑ 16 Mike Piazza 5.00 2.20
❑ 17 Nomar Garciaparra 6.00 2.70
❑ 18 Pedro Martinez 2.50 1.10
❑ 19 Randy Johnson 2.50 1.10
❑ 20 Rick Ankiel 1.25 .55
❑ 21 Rickey Henderson 4.00 1.80
❑ 22 Roger Clemens 5.00 2.20
❑ 23 Sammy Sosa 4.00 1.80
❑ 24 Tony Gwynn 4.00 1.80
❑ 25 Vladimir Guerrero 2.50 1.10
❑ 26 Kazuhiro Sasaki 2.00 .90
❑ 27 Roberto Alomar 2.00 .90
❑ 28 Barry Zito 2.00 .90
❑ 29 Pat Burrell .75 .35
❑ 30 Harold Baines .75 .35
❑ 31 Carlos Delgado 2.00 .90
❑ 32 J.D. Drew 2.00 .90
❑ 33 Jim Edmonds 1.25 .55
❑ 34 Darin Erstad 2.00 .90
❑ 35 Jason Giambi 2.00 .90
❑ 36 Tom Glavine 2.00 .90
❑ 37 Juan Gonzalez 2.00 .90
❑ 38 Mark Grace 2.00 .90
❑ 39 Shawn Green 2.00 .90
❑ 40 Tim Hudson 2.00 .90
❑ 41 Andruw Jones 2.00 .90
❑ 42 Jeff Kent 1.25 .55
❑ 43 Barry Larkin 2.00 .90
❑ 44 Rafael Furcal .75 .35
❑ 45 Mike Mussina 2.00 .90
❑ 46 Hideo Nomo 2.00 .90
❑ 47 Rafael Palmeiro 2.00 .90
❑ 48 Scott Rolen 2.00 .90
❑ 49 Gary Sheffield .75 .35
❑ 50 Bernie Williams 2.00 .90
❑ 51 Bob Abreu .75 .35
❑ 52 Edgardo Alfonzo .75 .35
❑ 53 Edgar Martinez 1.25 .55
❑ 54 Magglio Ordonez .75 .35
❑ 55 Kerry Wood 2.00 .90
❑ 56 Adrian Beltre .75 .35
❑ 57 Lance Berkman 2.00 .90
❑ 58 Kevin Brown .75 .35
❑ 59 Sean Casey 1.25 .55
❑ 60 Eric Chavez .75 .35
❑ 61 Bartolo Colon .75 .35
❑ 62 Johnny Damon .75 .35
❑ 63 Jermaine Dye .75 .35
❑ 64 Juan Encarnacion .75 .35
❑ 65 Carl Everett .75 .35
❑ 66 Brian Giles .75 .35
❑ 67 Mike Hampton .75 .35
❑ 68 Richard Hidalgo .75 .35
❑ 69 Geoff Jenkins .75 .35
❑ 70 Jacque Jones .75 .35

❑ 71 Jason Kendall .75 .35
❑ 72 Ryan Klesko .75 .35
❑ 73 Chan Ho Park .75 .35
❑ 74 Richie Sexson .75 .35
❑ 75 Mike Sweeney .75 .35
❑ 76 Fernando Tatis .75 .35
❑ 77 Miguel Tejada .75 .35
❑ 78 Jose Vidro .75 .35
❑ 79 Larry Walker 1.25 .55
❑ 80 Preston Wilson .75 .35
❑ 81 Craig Biggio 1.25 .55
❑ 82 Fred McGriff 1.25 .55
❑ 83 Jim Thome 2.00 .90
❑ 84 Garret Anderson .75 .35
❑ 85 Russell Branyan .75 .35
❑ 86 Tony Batista .75 .35
❑ 87 Terrence Long .75 .35
❑ 88 Deion Sanders .75 .35
❑ 89 Rusty Greer .75 .35
❑ 90 Orlando Hernandez .75 .35
❑ 91 Gabe Kapler .75 .35
❑ 92 Paul Konerko .75 .35
❑ 93 Carlos Lee .75 .35
❑ 94 Kenny Lofton .75 .35
❑ 95 Raul Mondesi .75 .35
❑ 96 Jorge Posada .75 .35
❑ 97 Tim Salmon .75 .35
❑ 98 Greg Vaughn .75 .35
❑ 99 Mo Vaughn .75 .35
❑ 100 Omar Vizquel .75 .35
❑ 101 Ray Durham .75 .35
❑ 102 Jeff Cirillo .75 .35
❑ 103 Dean Palmer .75 .35
❑ 104 Ryan Dempster .75 .35
❑ 105 Carlos Beltran .75 .35
❑ 106 Timo Perez .75 .35
❑ 107 Robin Ventura .75 .35
❑ 108 Andy Pettitte .75 .35
❑ 109 Aramis Ramirez .75 .35
❑ 110 Phil Nevin .75 .35
❑ 111 Alex Escobar FF 20.00 9.00
❑ 112 Johnny Estrada FF RC 30.00 13.50
❑ 113 Pedro Feliz FF 20.00 9.00
❑ 114 Nate Frese FF RC 20.00 9.00
❑ 115 Joe Kennedy FF RC 25.00 11.00
❑ 116 Brandon Larson FF RC 20.00 9.00
❑ 117 Alexis Gomez FF RC 20.00 9.00
❑ 118 Jason Hart FF 25.00 11.00
❑ 119 Jason Michaels FF RC 20.00 9.00
❑ 120 Marcus Giles FF 20.00 9.00
❑ 121 Christian Parker FF RC 20.00 9.00
❑ 122 Jackson Melian FF RC 20.00 9.00
❑ 123 Donaldo Mendez FF RC 20.00 9.00
❑ 124 Adrian Hernandez FF RC 20.00 9.00
❑ 125 Bud Smith FF RC 60.00 27.00
❑ 126 Jose Mieses FF RC 20.00 9.00
❑ 127 Roy Oswalt FF 40.00 18.00
❑ 128 Eric Munson FF 20.00 9.00
❑ 129 Xavier Nady FF 25.00 11.00
❑ 130 Horacio Ramirez FF RC 20.00 9.00
❑ 131 Abraham Nunez FF 20.00 9.00
❑ 132 Jose Ortiz FF 25.00 11.00
❑ 133 Jeremy Owens FF RC 20.00 9.00
❑ 134 Claudio Vargas FF RC 20.00 9.00
❑ 135 Ricardo Rodriguez FF RC 25.00 11.00
❑ 136 Aubrey Huff FF 20.00 9.00
❑ 137 Ben Sheets FF 25.00 11.00
❑ 138 Adam Dunn FF 50.00 22.00
❑ 139 Andres Torres FF RC 20.00 9.00
❑ 140 Elpidio Guzman FF RC 20.00 9.00
❑ 141 Jay Gibbons FF RC 25.00 11.00
❑ 142 Wilkin Ruan FF RC 20.00 9.00
❑ 143 Tsuyoshi Shinjo FF RC 80.00 36.00
❑ 144 Alfonso Soriano FF 40.00 18.00
❑ 145 Josh Towers FF RC 30.00 13.50
❑ 146 Ichiro Suzuki FF RC 300.00 135.00
❑ 147 Juan Uribe FF RC 30.00 13.50
❑ 148 Joe Crede FF 20.00 9.00
❑ 149 Carlos Valderrama FF RC 20.00 9.00
❑ 150 Matt White FF RC 20.00 9.00
❑ 151 Dee Brown FF 20.00 9.00
❑ 152 Juan Cruz FF RC 50.00 22.00
❑ 153 Cory Aldridge FF RC 20.00 9.00
❑ 154 Wilmy Caceres FF RC 20.00 9.00
❑ 155 Josh Beckett FF 40.00 18.00
❑ 156 Wilson Betemit FF RC 50.00 22.00
❑ 157 Corey Patterson FF 20.00 9.00
❑ 158 Albert Pujols FF RC 150.00 70.00
❑ 159 Rafael Soriano FF RC 25.00 11.00
❑ 160 Jack Wilson FF RC 20.00 9.00

1994 Leaf Limited

	MINT	NRMT
COMPLETE SET (160)	80.00	36.00

❑ 1 Jeffrey Hammonds .75 .35
❑ 2 Ben McDonald .50 .23
❑ 3 Mike Mussina 2.00 .90
❑ 4 Rafael Palmeiro 2.00 .90
❑ 5 Cal Ripken Jr. 8.00 3.60
❑ 6 Lee Smith .75 .35
❑ 7 Roger Clemens 5.00 2.20
❑ 8 Scott Cooper .50 .23
❑ 9 Andre Dawson 1.25 .55
❑ 10 Mike Greenwell .50 .23
❑ 11 Aaron Sele .75 .35
❑ 12 Mo Vaughn .75 .35
❑ 13 Brian Anderson RC .75 .35
❑ 14 Chad Curtis .50 .23
❑ 15 Chili Davis .75 .35
❑ 16 Gary DiSarcina .50 .23
❑ 17 Mark Langston .50 .23
❑ 18 Tim Salmon .75 .35
❑ 19 Wilson Alvarez .50 .23
❑ 20 Jason Bere .50 .23
❑ 21 Julio Franco .75 .35
❑ 22 Jack McDowell .50 .23
❑ 23 Tim Raines .75 .35
❑ 24 Frank Thomas 2.50 1.10
❑ 25 Robin Ventura .75 .35
❑ 26 Carlos Baerga .50 .23
❑ 27 Albert Belle .75 .35
❑ 28 Kenny Lofton .75 .35
❑ 29 Eddie Murray 2.00 .90
❑ 30 Manny Ramirez 3.00 1.35
❑ 31 Cecil Fielder .75 .35
❑ 32 Travis Fryman .75 .35
❑ 33 Mickey Tettleton .50 .23
❑ 34 Alan Trammell 1.25 .55
❑ 35 Lou Whitaker .75 .35
❑ 36 David Cone .75 .35
❑ 37 Gary Gaetti .75 .35
❑ 38 Greg Gagne .50 .23
❑ 39 Bob Hamelin .50 .23
❑ 40 Wally Joyner .75 .35
❑ 41 Brian McRae .50 .23
❑ 42 Ricky Bones .50 .23
❑ 43 Brian Harper .50 .23
❑ 44 John Jaha .50 .23
❑ 45 Pat Listach .50 .23
❑ 46 Dave Nilsson .50 .23
❑ 47 Greg Vaughn .75 .35
❑ 48 Kent Hrbek .75 .35
❑ 49 Chuck Knoblauch .75 .35
❑ 50 Shane Mack .50 .23
❑ 51 Kirby Puckett 5.00 2.20
❑ 52 Dave Winfield 2.00 .90
❑ 53 Jim Abbott .75 .35
❑ 54 Wade Boggs 2.00 .90
❑ 55 Jimmy Key .75 .35
❑ 56 Don Mattingly 5.00 2.20
❑ 57 Paul O'Neill 2.00 .90
❑ 58 Danny Tartabull .50 .23
❑ 59 Dennis Eckersley .75 .35
❑ 60 Rickey Henderson 4.00 1.80
❑ 61 Mark McGwire 8.00 3.60
❑ 62 Troy Neel .50 .23
❑ 63 Ruben Sierra .50 .23
❑ 64 Eric Anthony .50 .23
❑ 65 Jay Buhner .75 .35
❑ 66 Ken Griffey Jr. 6.00 2.70
❑ 67 Randy Johnson 2.50 1.10
❑ 68 Edgar Martinez 1.25 .55
❑ 69 Tino Martinez .75 .35
❑ 70 Jose Canseco 2.00 .90
❑ 71 Will Clark 2.00 .90
❑ 72 Juan Gonzalez 2.00 .90
❑ 73 Dean Palmer .75 .35
❑ 74 Ivan Rodriguez 2.00 .90
❑ 75 Roberto Alomar 2.00 .90
❑ 76 Joe Carter .75 .35
❑ 77 Carlos Delgado 3.00 1.35
❑ 78 Paul Molitor 2.00 .90
❑ 79 John Olerud .75 .35
❑ 80 Devon White .50 .23
❑ 81 Steve Avery .50 .23
❑ 82 Tom Glavine 2.00 .90
❑ 83 David Justice .75 .35
❑ 84 Roberto Kelly .50 .23
❑ 85 Ryan Klesko .75 .35
❑ 86 Javier Lopez .75 .35
❑ 87 Greg Maddux 5.00 2.20
❑ 88 Fred McGriff 1.25 .55
❑ 89 Shawon Dunston .50 .23
❑ 90 Mark Grace 2.00 .90
❑ 91 Derrick May .50 .23
❑ 92 Sammy Sosa 4.00 1.80
❑ 93 Rick Wilkins .50 .23
❑ 94 Bret Boone .75 .35
❑ 95 Barry Larkin 2.00 .90
❑ 96 Kevin Mitchell .50 .23
❑ 97 Hal Morris .50 .23
❑ 98 Deion Sanders .75 .35
❑ 99 Reggie Sanders .50 .23
❑ 100 Dante Bichette .75 .35
❑ 101 Ellis Burks .75 .35
❑ 102 Andres Galarraga 1.25 .55
❑ 103 Joe Girardi .50 .23
❑ 104 Charlie Hayes .50 .23
❑ 105 Chuck Carr .50 .23
❑ 106 Jeff Conine .50 .23
❑ 107 Bryan Harvey .50 .23
❑ 108 Benito Santiago .50 .23
❑ 109 Gary Sheffield .75 .35
❑ 110 Jeff Bagwell 2.50 1.10
❑ 111 Craig Biggio 1.25 .55
❑ 112 Ken Caminiti .75 .35
❑ 113 Andujar Cedeno .50 .23
❑ 114 Doug Drabek .50 .23
❑ 115 Luis Gonzalez 2.00 .90
❑ 116 Brett Butler .75 .35
❑ 117 Delino DeShields .50 .23
❑ 118 Eric Karros .75 .35
❑ 119 Raul Mondesi .75 .35
❑ 120 Mike Piazza 6.00 2.70
❑ 121 Henry Rodriguez .50 .23
❑ 122 Tim Wallach .50 .23
❑ 123 Moises Alou .75 .35
❑ 124 Cliff Floyd .75 .35
❑ 125 Marquis Grissom .50 .23
❑ 126 Ken Hill .50 .23
❑ 127 Larry Walker 1.25 .55
❑ 128 John Wetteland .75 .35
❑ 129 Bobby Bonilla .75 .35
❑ 130 John Franco .75 .35
❑ 131 Jeff Kent 1.25 .55
❑ 132 Bret Saberhagen .75 .35
❑ 133 Ryan Thompson .50 .23
❑ 134 Darren Daulton .75 .35
❑ 135 Mariano Duncan .50 .23
❑ 136 Lenny Dykstra .75 .35
❑ 137 Danny Jackson .50 .23
❑ 138 John Kruk .75 .35
❑ 139 Jay Bell .75 .35
❑ 140 Jeff King .50 .23
❑ 141 Al Martin .50 .23
❑ 142 Orlando Merced .50 .23
❑ 143 Andy Van Slyke .75 .35
❑ 144 Bernard Gilkey .50 .23

	MINT	NRMT
❑ 145 Gregg Jefferies	.50	.23
❑ 146 Ray Lankford	.50	.23
❑ 147 Ozzie Smith	2.50	1.10
❑ 148 Mark Whiten	.50	.23
❑ 149 Todd Zeile	.50	.23
❑ 150 Derek Bell	.50	.23
❑ 151 Andy Benes	.50	.23
❑ 152 Tony Gwynn	4.00	1.80
❑ 153 Phil Plantier	.50	.23
❑ 154 Bip Roberts	.50	.23
❑ 155 Rod Beck	.50	.23
❑ 156 Barry Bonds	5.00	2.20
❑ 157 John Burkett	.50	.23
❑ 158 Royce Clayton	.50	.23
❑ 159 Bill Swift	.50	.23
❑ 160 Matt Williams	1.25	.55

1994 Leaf Limited Rookies

	MINT	NRMT
COMPLETE SET (80)	25.00	11.00
❑ 1 Charles Johnson	.60	.25
❑ 2 Rico Brogna	.40	.18
❑ 3 Melvin Nieves	.40	.18
❑ 4 Rich Becker	.40	.18
❑ 5 Russ Davis	.40	.18
❑ 6 Matt Mieske	.40	.18
❑ 7 Paul Shuey	.40	.18
❑ 8 Hector Carrasco	.40	.18
❑ 9 J.R. Phillips	.40	.18
❑ 10 Scott Ruffcorn	.40	.18
❑ 11 Kurt Abbott RC	.60	.25
❑ 12 Danny Bautista	.40	.18
❑ 13 Rick White	.40	.18
❑ 14 Steve Dunn	.40	.18
❑ 15 Joe Ausanio	.40	.18
❑ 16 Salomon Torres	.40	.18
❑ 17 Ricky Bottalico RC	.60	.25
❑ 18 Johnny Ruffin	.40	.18
❑ 19 Kevin Foster RC	.40	.18
❑ 20 W.VanLandingham RC	.40	.18
❑ 21 Troy O'Leary	.40	.18
❑ 22 Mark Acre RC	.40	.18
❑ 23 Norberto Martin	.40	.18
❑ 24 Jason Jacome RC	.40	.18
❑ 25 Steve Trachsel	.40	.18
❑ 26 Denny Hocking	.40	.18
❑ 27 Mike Lieberthal	.60	.25
❑ 28 Gerald Williams	.40	.18
❑ 29 John Mabry RC	.40	.18
❑ 30 Greg Blosser	.40	.18
❑ 31 Carl Everett	.60	.25
❑ 32 Steve Karsay	.40	.18
❑ 33 Jose Valentin	.40	.18
❑ 34 Jon Lieber	.60	.25
❑ 35 Chris Gomez	.40	.18
❑ 36 Jesus Tavarez RC	.40	.18
❑ 37 Tony Longmire	.40	.18
❑ 38 Luis Lopez	.40	.18
❑ 39 Matt Walbeck	.40	.18
❑ 40 Rikkert Faneyte RC	.40	.18
❑ 41 Shane Reynolds	.40	.18
❑ 42 Joey Hamilton	.40	.18
❑ 43 Ismael Valdes RC	.60	.25
❑ 44 Danny Miceli	.40	.18
❑ 45 Darren Bragg RC	.60	.25
❑ 46 Alex Gonzalez	.40	.18
❑ 47 Rick Helling	.40	.18
❑ 48 Jose Oliva	.40	.18
❑ 49 Jim Edmonds	1.50	.70
❑ 50 Miguel Jimenez	.40	.18
❑ 51 Tony Eusebio	.40	.18
❑ 52 Shawn Green	2.50	1.10
❑ 53 Billy Ashley	.40	.18
❑ 54 Rondell White	.60	.25
❑ 55 Cory Bailey RC	.40	.18
❑ 56 Tim Davis	.40	.18
❑ 57 John Hudek RC	.40	.18
❑ 58 Darren Hall	.40	.18
❑ 59 Darren Dreifort	.40	.18
❑ 60 Mike Kelly	.40	.18
❑ 61 Marcus Moore	.40	.18
❑ 62 Garret Anderson	.60	.25
❑ 63 Brian L. Hunter	.40	.18
❑ 64 Mark Smith	.40	.18
❑ 65 Garey Ingram RC	.40	.18
❑ 66 Rusty Greer RC	3.00	1.35
❑ 67 Marc Newfield	.40	.18
❑ 68 Gar Finnvold	.40	.18
❑ 69 Paul Spoljaric	.40	.18
❑ 70 Ray McDavid	.40	.18
❑ 71 Orlando Miller	.40	.18
❑ 72 Jorge Fabregas	.40	.18
❑ 73 Ray Holbert	.40	.18
❑ 74 Armando Benitez RC	2.00	.90
❑ 75 Ernie Young RC	.60	.25
❑ 76 James Mouton	.40	.18
❑ 77 Robert Perez RC	.40	.18
❑ 78 Chan Ho Park RC	5.00	2.20
❑ 79 Roger Salkeld	.40	.18
❑ 80 Tony Tarasco	.40	.18

1995 Leaf Limited

	MINT	NRMT
COMPLETE SET (192)	50.00	22.00
COMPLETE SERIES 1 (96)	25.00	11.00
COMPLETE SERIES 2 (96)	25.00	11.00
❑ 1 Frank Thomas	1.50	.70
❑ 2 Geronimo Berroa	.30	.14
❑ 3 Tony Phillips	.30	.14
❑ 4 Roberto Alomar	1.25	.55
❑ 5 Steve Avery	.30	.14
❑ 6 Darryl Hamilton	.30	.14
❑ 7 Scott Cooper	.30	.14
❑ 8 Mark Grace	1.25	.55
❑ 9 Billy Ashley	.30	.14
❑ 10 Wil Cordero	.30	.14
❑ 11 Barry Bonds	3.00	1.35
❑ 12 Kenny Lofton	.50	.23
❑ 13 Jay Buhner	.50	.23
❑ 14 Alex Rodriguez	4.00	1.80
❑ 15 Bobby Bonilla	.50	.23
❑ 16 Brady Anderson	.50	.23
❑ 17 Ken Caminiti	.50	.23
❑ 18 Charlie Hayes	.30	.14
❑ 19 Jay Bell	.50	.23
❑ 20 Will Clark	1.25	.55
❑ 21 Jose Canseco	1.25	.55
❑ 22 Bret Boone	.50	.23
❑ 23 Dante Bichette	.50	.23
❑ 24 Kevin Appier	.50	.23
❑ 25 Chad Curtis	.30	.14
❑ 26 Marty Cordova	.30	.14
❑ 27 Jason Bere	.30	.14
❑ 28 Jimmy Key	.50	.23
❑ 29 Rickey Henderson	2.50	1.10
❑ 30 Tim Salmon	.50	.23
❑ 31 Joe Carter	.50	.23
❑ 32 Tom Glavine	1.25	.55
❑ 33 Pat Listach	.30	.14
❑ 34 Brian Jordan	.50	.23
❑ 35 Brian McRae	.30	.14
❑ 36 Eric Karros	.50	.23
❑ 37 Pedro Martinez	1.50	.70
❑ 38 Royce Clayton	.30	.14
❑ 39 Eddie Murray	1.25	.55
❑ 40 Randy Johnson	1.50	.70
❑ 41 Jeff Conine	.30	.14
❑ 42 Brett Butler	.50	.23
❑ 43 Jeffrey Hammonds	.30	.14
❑ 44 Andujar Cedeno	.30	.14
❑ 45 Dave Hollins	.30	.14
❑ 46 Jeff King	.30	.14
❑ 47 Benji Gil	.30	.14
❑ 48 Roger Clemens	3.00	1.35
❑ 49 Barry Larkin	1.25	.55
❑ 50 Joe Girardi	.30	.14
❑ 51 Bob Hamelin	.30	.14
❑ 52 Travis Fryman	.50	.23
❑ 53 Chuck Knoblauch	.50	.23
❑ 54 Ray Durham	.50	.23
❑ 55 Don Mattingly	3.00	1.35
❑ 56 Ruben Sierra	.30	.14
❑ 57 J.T. Snow	.50	.23
❑ 58 Derek Bell	.30	.14
❑ 59 David Cone	.50	.23
❑ 60 Marquis Grissom	.30	.14
❑ 61 Kevin Seitzer	.30	.14
❑ 62 Ozzie Smith	1.50	.70
❑ 63 Rick Wilkins	.30	.14
❑ 64 Hideo Nomo RC	3.00	1.35
❑ 65 Tony Tarasco	.30	.14
❑ 66 Manny Ramirez	1.50	.70
❑ 67 Charles Johnson	.50	.23
❑ 68 Craig Biggio	.75	.35
❑ 69 Bobby Jones	.30	.14
❑ 70 Mike Mussina	1.25	.55
❑ 71 Alex Gonzalez	.30	.14
❑ 72 Gregg Jefferies	.30	.14
❑ 73 Rusty Greer	.50	.23
❑ 74 Mike Greenwell	.30	.14
❑ 75 Hal Morris	.30	.14
❑ 76 Paul O'Neill	1.25	.55
❑ 77 Luis Gonzalez	1.25	.55
❑ 78 Chipper Jones	2.50	1.10
❑ 79 Mike Piazza	3.00	1.35
❑ 80 Rondell White	.50	.23
❑ 81 Glenallen Hill	.30	.14
❑ 82 Shawn Green	1.25	.55
❑ 83 Bernie Williams	1.25	.55
❑ 84 Jim Thome	1.25	.55
❑ 85 Terry Pendleton	.50	.23
❑ 86 Rafael Palmeiro	1.25	.55
❑ 87 Tony Gwynn	2.50	1.10
❑ 88 Mickey Tettleton	.30	.14
❑ 89 John Valentin	.30	.14
❑ 90 Deion Sanders	.50	.23
❑ 91 Larry Walker	.75	.35
❑ 92 Michael Tucker	.30	.14
❑ 93 Alan Trammell	.75	.35
❑ 94 Tim Raines	.50	.23
❑ 95 David Justice	.50	.23
❑ 96 Tino Martinez	.50	.23
❑ 97 Cal Ripken Jr.	5.00	2.20
❑ 98 Deion Sanders	.50	.23
❑ 99 Darren Daulton	.50	.23
❑ 100 Paul Molitor	1.25	.55
❑ 101 Randy Myers	.30	.14
❑ 102 Wally Joyner	.50	.23
❑ 103 Carlos Perez RC	.50	.23
❑ 104 Brian Hunter	.30	.14
❑ 105 Wade Boggs	1.25	.55
❑ 106 Bob Higginson RC	2.00	.90
❑ 107 Jeff Kent	.75	.35
❑ 108 Jose Offerman	.30	.14
❑ 109 Dennis Eckersley	.50	.23
❑ 110 Dave Nilsson	.30	.14
❑ 111 Chuck Finley	.50	.23

		MINT	NRMT
❑ 112	Devon White	.50	.23
❑ 113	Bip Roberts	.30	.14
❑ 114	Ramon Martinez	.30	.14
❑ 115	Greg Maddux	3.00	1.35
❑ 116	Curtis Goodwin	.30	.14
❑ 117	John Jaha	.30	.14
❑ 118	Ken Griffey Jr.	4.00	1.80
❑ 119	Geronimo Pena	.30	.14
❑ 120	Shawon Dunston	.30	.14
❑ 121	Ariel Prieto RC	.30	.14
❑ 122	Kirby Puckett	3.00	1.35
❑ 123	Carlos Baerga	.30	.14
❑ 124	Todd Hundley	.30	.14
❑ 125	Tim Naehring	.30	.14
❑ 126	Gary Sheffield	.50	.23
❑ 127	Dean Palmer	.50	.23
❑ 128	Rondell White	.50	.23
❑ 129	Greg Gagne	.30	.14
❑ 130	Jose Rijo	.30	.14
❑ 131	Ivan Rodriguez	1.25	.55
❑ 132	Jeff Bagwell	1.50	.70
❑ 133	Greg Vaughn	.50	.23
❑ 134	Chili Davis	.50	.23
❑ 135	Al Martin	.30	.14
❑ 136	Kenny Rogers	.30	.14
❑ 137	Aaron Sele	.50	.23
❑ 138	Raul Mondesi	.50	.23
❑ 139	Cecil Fielder	.50	.23
❑ 140	Tim Wallach	.30	.14
❑ 141	Andres Galarraga	.75	.35
❑ 142	Lou Whitaker	.50	.23
❑ 143	Jack McDowell	.30	.14
❑ 144	Matt Williams	.75	.35
❑ 145	Ryan Klesko	.50	.23
❑ 146	Carlos Garcia	.30	.14
❑ 147	Albert Belle	.50	.23
❑ 148	Ryan Thompson	.30	.14
❑ 149	Roberto Kelly	.30	.14
❑ 150	Edgar Martinez	.75	.35
❑ 151	Robby Thompson	.30	.14
❑ 152	Mo Vaughn	.50	.23
❑ 153	Todd Zeile	.30	.14
❑ 154	Harold Baines	.50	.23
❑ 155	Phil Plantier	.30	.14
❑ 156	Mike Stanley	.30	.14
❑ 157	Ed Sprague	.30	.14
❑ 158	Moises Alou	.50	.23
❑ 159	Quilvio Veras	.30	.14
❑ 160	Reggie Sanders	.30	.14
❑ 161	Delino DeShields	.30	.14
❑ 162	Rico Brogna	.30	.14
❑ 163	Greg Colbrunn	.30	.14
❑ 164	Steve Finley	.50	.23
❑ 165	Orlando Merced	.30	.14
❑ 166	Mark McGwire	5.00	2.20
❑ 167	Garret Anderson	.50	.23
❑ 168	Paul Sorrento	.30	.14
❑ 169	Mark Langston	.30	.14
❑ 170	Danny Tartabull	.30	.14
❑ 171	Vinny Castilla	.50	.23
❑ 172	Javier Lopez	.50	.23
❑ 173	Bret Saberhagen	.50	.23
❑ 174	Eddie Williams	.30	.14
❑ 175	Scott Leius	.30	.14
❑ 176	Juan Gonzalez	1.25	.55
❑ 177	Gary Gaetti	.50	.23
❑ 178	Jim Edmonds	.75	.35
❑ 179	John Olerud	.50	.23
❑ 180	Lenny Dykstra	.50	.23
❑ 181	Ray Lankford	.30	.14
❑ 182	Ron Gant	.30	.14
❑ 183	Doug Drabek	.30	.14
❑ 184	Fred McGriff	.75	.35
❑ 185	Andy Benes	.30	.14
❑ 186	Kurt Abbott	.30	.14
❑ 187	Bernard Gilkey	.30	.14
❑ 188	Sammy Sosa	2.50	1.10
❑ 189	Lee Smith	.50	.23
❑ 190	Dennis Martinez	.50	.23
❑ 191	Ozzie Guillen	.30	.14
❑ 192	Robin Ventura	.50	.23

1996 Leaf Limited

	MINT	NRMT
COMPLETE SET (90)	50.00	22.00

		MINT	NRMT
❑ 1	Ivan Rodriguez	1.25	.55
❑ 2	Roger Clemens	3.00	1.35
❑ 3	Gary Sheffield	.50	.23
❑ 4	Tino Martinez	.50	.23
❑ 5	Sammy Sosa	2.50	1.10
❑ 6	Reggie Sanders	.30	.14
❑ 7	Ray Lankford	.30	.14
❑ 8	Manny Ramirez	1.50	.70
❑ 9	Jeff Bagwell	1.50	.70
❑ 10	Greg Maddux	3.00	1.35
❑ 11	Ken Griffey Jr.	4.00	1.80
❑ 12	Rondell White	.50	.23
❑ 13	Mike Piazza	3.00	1.35
❑ 14	Marc Newfield	.30	.14
❑ 15	Cal Ripken	5.00	2.20
❑ 16	Carlos Delgado	1.25	.55
❑ 17	Tim Salmon	.50	.23
❑ 18	Andres Galarraga	.75	.35
❑ 19	Chuck Knoblauch	.50	.23
❑ 20	Matt Williams	.75	.35
❑ 21	Mark McGwire	5.00	2.20
❑ 22	Ben McDonald	.30	.14
❑ 23	Frank Thomas	1.50	.70
❑ 24	Johnny Damon	.50	.23
❑ 25	Gregg Jefferies	.30	.14
❑ 26	Travis Fryman	.50	.23
❑ 27	Chipper Jones	2.50	1.10
❑ 28	David Cone	.50	.23
❑ 29	Kenny Lofton	.50	.23
❑ 30	Mike Mussina	1.25	.55
❑ 31	Alex Rodriguez	3.00	1.35
❑ 32	Carlos Baerga	.30	.14
❑ 33	Brian Hunter	.30	.14
❑ 34	Juan Gonzalez	1.25	.55
❑ 35	Bernie Williams	1.25	.55
❑ 36	Wally Joyner	.50	.23
❑ 37	Fred McGriff	.75	.35
❑ 38	Randy Johnson	1.50	.70
❑ 39	Marty Cordova	.30	.14
❑ 40	Garret Anderson	.50	.23
❑ 41	Albert Belle	.50	.23
❑ 42	Edgar Martinez	.75	.35
❑ 43	Barry Larkin	1.25	.55
❑ 44	Paul O'Neill	1.25	.55
❑ 45	Cecil Fielder	.50	.23
❑ 46	Rusty Greer	.50	.23
❑ 47	Mo Vaughn	.50	.23
❑ 48	Dante Bichette	.50	.23
❑ 49	Ryan Klesko	.50	.23
❑ 50	Roberto Alomar	1.25	.55
❑ 51	Raul Mondesi	.50	.23
❑ 52	Robin Ventura	.50	.23
❑ 53	Tony Gwynn	2.50	1.10
❑ 54	Mark Grace	1.25	.55
❑ 55	Jim Thome	1.25	.55
❑ 56	Jason Giambi	1.25	.55
❑ 57	Tom Glavine	1.25	.55
❑ 58	Jim Edmonds	.75	.35
❑ 59	Pedro Martinez	1.50	.70
❑ 60	Charles Johnson	.50	.23
❑ 61	Wade Boggs	1.25	.55
❑ 62	Orlando Merced	.30	.14
❑ 63	Craig Biggio	.75	.35
❑ 64	Brady Anderson	.50	.23
❑ 65	Hideo Nomo	1.50	.70
❑ 66	Ozzie Smith	1.50	.70
❑ 67	Eddie Murray	1.25	.55
❑ 68	Will Clark	1.25	.55
❑ 69	Jay Buhner	.50	.23
❑ 70	Kirby Puckett	3.00	1.35
❑ 71	Barry Bonds	3.00	1.35
❑ 72	Ray Durham	.50	.23
❑ 73	Sterling Hitchcock	.30	.14
❑ 74	John Smoltz	.50	.23
❑ 75	Andre Dawson	.75	.35
❑ 76	Joe Carter	.50	.23
❑ 77	Ryne Sandberg	1.50	.70
❑ 78	Rickey Henderson	2.50	1.10
❑ 79	Brian Jordan	.50	.23
❑ 80	Greg Vaughn	.50	.23
❑ 81	Andy Pettitte	.50	.23
❑ 82	Dean Palmer	.50	.23
❑ 83	Paul Molitor	1.25	.55
❑ 84	Rafael Palmeiro	1.25	.55
❑ 85	Henry Rodriguez	.30	.14
❑ 86	Larry Walker	.75	.35
❑ 87	Ismael Valdes	.30	.14
❑ 88	Derek Bell	.30	.14
❑ 89	J.T. Snow	.50	.23
❑ 90	Jack McDowell	.30	.14

1998 Leaf Rookies and Stars

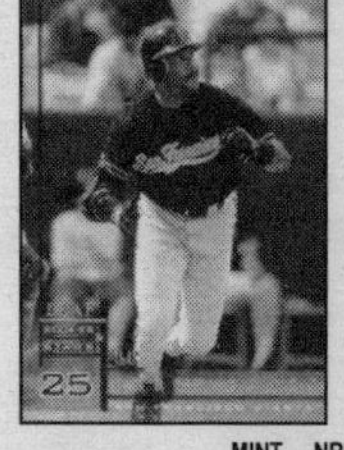

	MINT	NRMT
COMPLETE SET (339)	500.00	220.00
COMP.SET w/o SP's (200)	30.00	13.50
COMMON (1-130/231-300)	.15	.07
COMMON CARD (131-190)	.50	.23
COMMON CARD (191-230)	1.00	.45
COMMON RC (191-230)	2.50	1.10
COMMON CARD (301-339)	1.25	.55
COMMON RC (301-339)	3.00	1.35

		MINT	NRMT
❑ 2	Roberto Alomar	.60	.25
❑ 3	Randy Johnson	.75	.35
❑ 4	Manny Ramirez	.75	.35
❑ 5	Paul Molitor	.60	.25
❑ 6	Mike Mussina	.60	.25
❑ 7	Jim Thome	.60	.25
❑ 8	Tino Martinez	.25	.11
❑ 9	Gary Sheffield	.25	.11
❑ 10	Chuck Knoblauch	.25	.11
❑ 11	Bernie Williams	.60	.25
❑ 12	Tim Salmon	.25	.11
❑ 13	Sammy Sosa	1.25	.55
❑ 14	Wade Boggs	.60	.25
❑ 15	Andres Galarraga	.40	.18
❑ 16	Pedro Martinez	.75	.35
❑ 17	David Justice	.25	.11
❑ 18	Chan Ho Park	.25	.11
❑ 19	Jay Buhner	.25	.11
❑ 20	Ryan Klesko	.25	.11
❑ 21	Barry Larkin	.60	.25
❑ 22	Will Clark	.60	.25
❑ 23	Raul Mondesi	.25	.11
❑ 24	Rickey Henderson	1.25	.55
❑ 25	Jim Edmonds	.40	.18
❑ 26	Ken Griffey Jr.	2.00	.90
❑ 27	Frank Thomas	.75	.35
❑ 28	Cal Ripken	2.50	1.10
❑ 29	Alex Rodriguez	1.50	.70
❑ 30	Mike Piazza	1.50	.70
❑ 31	Greg Maddux	1.50	.70
❑ 32	Chipper Jones	1.25	.55
❑ 33	Tony Gwynn	1.25	.55

❑ 34 Derek Jeter 2.50 1.10
❑ 35 Jeff Bagwell .75 .35
❑ 36 Juan Gonzalez .60 .25
❑ 37 Nomar Garciaparra 1.50 .70
❑ 38 Andruw Jones .60 .25
❑ 39 Hideo Nomo .60 .25
❑ 40 Roger Clemens 1.50 .70
❑ 41 Mark McGwire 2.50 1.10
❑ 42 Scott Rolen .60 .25
❑ 43 Vladimir Guerrero .75 .35
❑ 44 Barry Bonds 1.50 .70
❑ 45 Darin Erstad .60 .25
❑ 46 Albert Belle .25 .11
❑ 47 Kenny Lofton .25 .11
❑ 48 Mo Vaughn .25 .11
❑ 49 Ivan Rodriguez .60 .25
❑ 50 Jose Cruz Jr. .25 .11
❑ 51 Tony Clark .25 .11
❑ 52 Larry Walker .40 .18
❑ 53 Mark Grace .60 .25
❑ 54 Edgar Martinez .40 .18
❑ 55 Fred McGriff .40 .18
❑ 56 Rafael Palmeiro .60 .25
❑ 57 Matt Williams .40 .18
❑ 58 Craig Biggio .40 .18
❑ 59 Ken Caminiti .25 .11
❑ 60 Jose Canseco .60 .25
❑ 61 Brady Anderson .25 .11
❑ 62 Moises Alou .25 .11
❑ 63 Justin Thompson .15 .07
❑ 64 John Smoltz .25 .11
❑ 65 Carlos Delgado .60 .25
❑ 66 J.T. Snow .25 .11
❑ 67 Jason Giambi .60 .25
❑ 68 Garret Anderson .25 .11
❑ 69 Rondell White .25 .11
❑ 70 Eric Karros .25 .11
❑ 71 Javier Lopez .25 .11
❑ 72 Pat Hentgen .15 .07
❑ 73 Dante Bichette .25 .11
❑ 74 Charles Johnson .25 .11
❑ 75 Tom Glavine .60 .25
❑ 76 Rusty Greer .25 .11
❑ 77 Travis Fryman .25 .11
❑ 78 Todd Hundley .15 .07
❑ 79 Ray Lankford .15 .07
❑ 80 Denny Neagle .15 .07
❑ 81 Henry Rodriguez .15 .07
❑ 82 Sandy Alomar Jr. .25 .11
❑ 83 Robin Ventura .25 .11
❑ 84 John Olerud .25 .11
❑ 85 Omar Vizquel .25 .11
❑ 86 Darren Dreifort .15 .07
❑ 87 Kevin Brown .25 .11
❑ 88 Curt Schilling .60 .25
❑ 89 Francisco Cordova .15 .07
❑ 90 Brad Radke .25 .11
❑ 91 David Cone .25 .11
❑ 92 Paul O'Neill .60 .25
❑ 93 Vinny Castilla .25 .11
❑ 94 Marquis Grissom .15 .07
❑ 95 Brian L.Hunter .15 .07
❑ 96 Kevin Appier .25 .11
❑ 97 Bobby Bonilla .25 .11
❑ 98 Eric Young .15 .07
❑ 99 Jason Kendall .25 .11
❑ 100 Shawn Green .60 .25
❑ 101 Edgardo Alfonzo .25 .11
❑ 102 Alan Benes .15 .07
❑ 103 Bobby Higginson .25 .11
❑ 104 Todd Greene .15 .07
❑ 105 Jose Guillen .15 .07
❑ 106 Neifi Perez .15 .07
❑ 107 Edgar Renteria .15 .07
❑ 108 Chris Stynes .15 .07
❑ 109 Todd Walker .15 .07
❑ 110 Brian Jordan .25 .11
❑ 111 Joe Carter .25 .11
❑ 112 Ellis Burks .25 .11
❑ 113 Brett Tomko .15 .07
❑ 114 Mike Cameron .25 .11
❑ 115 Shannon Stewart .25 .11
❑ 116 Kevin Orie .15 .07
❑ 117 Brian Giles .25 .11
❑ 118 Hideki Irabu .15 .07
❑ 119 Delino DeShields .15 .07
❑ 120 David Segui .15 .07
❑ 121 Dustin Hermanson .15 .07
❑ 122 Kevin Young .15 .07
❑ 123 Jay Bell .25 .11
❑ 124 Doug Glanville .15 .07
❑ 125 John Roskos RC .25 .11
❑ 126 Damon Hollins .15 .07
❑ 127 Matt Stairs .15 .07
❑ 128 Cliff Floyd .25 .11
❑ 129 Derek Bell .15 .07
❑ 130 Darryl Strawberry .25 .11
❑ 131 Ken Griffey Jr. PT SP 6.00 2.70
❑ 132 Tim Salmon PT SP .75 .35
❑ 133 M.Ramirez PT SP 2.50 1.10
❑ 134 Paul Konerko PT SP .75 .35
❑ 135 Frank Thomas PT SP 2.50 1.10
❑ 136 Todd Helton PT SP 2.50 1.10
❑ 137 Larry Walker PT SP 1.25 .55
❑ 138 Mo Vaughn PT SP .75 .35
❑ 139 Travis Lee PT SP .75 .35
❑ 140 Ivan Rodriguez PT SP .60 .25
❑ 141 Ben Grieve PT SP .75 .35
❑ 142 Brad Fullmer PT SP .75 .35
❑ 143 Alex Rodriguez PT SP 5.00 2.20
❑ 144 Mike Piazza PT SP 5.00 2.20
❑ 145 Greg Maddux PT SP 5.00 2.20
❑ 146 Chipper Jones PT SP 4.00 1.80
❑ 147 Kenny Lofton PT SP .75 .35
❑ 148 Albert Belle PT SP .75 .35
❑ 149 Barry Bonds PT SP 5.00 2.20
❑ 150 V.Guerrero PT SP 2.50 1.10
❑ 151 Tony Gwynn PT SP 4.00 1.80
❑ 152 Derek Jeter PT SP 8.00 3.60
❑ 153 Jeff Bagwell PT SP 2.50 1.10
❑ 154 Juan Gonzalez PT SP 2.00 .90
❑ 155 N.Garciaparra PT SP 5.00 2.20
❑ 156 Andruw Jones PT SP 2.00 .90
❑ 157 Hideo Nomo PT SP 2.00 .90
❑ 158 Roger Clemens PT SP 5.00 2.20
❑ 159 Mark McGwire PT SP 8.00 3.60
❑ 160 Scott Rolen PT SP 2.00 .90
❑ 161 Travis Lee TLU SP .75 .35
❑ 162 Ben Grieve TLU SP .75 .35
❑ 163 Jose Guillen TLU SP .50 .23
❑ 164 Mike Piazza TLU SP 5.00 2.20
❑ 165 Kevin Appier TLU SP .75 .35
❑ 166 M.Grissom TLU SP .50 .23
❑ 167 Rusty Greer TLU SP .75 .35
❑ 168 Ken Caminiti TLU SP .75 .35
❑ 169 Craig Biggio TLU SP 1.25 .55
❑ 170 K.Griffey Jr. TLU SP 6.00 2.70
❑ 171 Larry Walker TLU SP 1.25 .55
❑ 172 Barry Larkin TLU SP 2.00 .90
❑ 173 A.Galarraga TLU SP 1.25 .55
❑ 174 Wade Boggs TLU SP 2.00 .90
❑ 175 Sammy Sosa TLU SP 4.00 1.80
❑ 176 T.Dunwoody TLU SP .50 .23
❑ 177 Jim Thome TLU SP 2.00 .90
❑ 178 Paul Molitor TLU SP 2.00 .90
❑ 179 Tony Clark TLU SP .75 .35
❑ 180 Jose Cruz Jr. TLU SP .75 .35
❑ 181 Darin Erstad TLU SP 2.00 .90
❑ 182 Barry Bonds TLU SP 5.00 2.20
❑ 183 Vlad.Guerrero TLU SP 2.50 1.10
❑ 184 Scott Rolen TLU SP 2.00 .90
❑ 185 M.McGwire TLU SP 8.00 3.60
❑ 186 N.Garciaparra TLU SP 5.00 2.20
❑ 187 Gary Sheffield TLU SP .75 .35
❑ 188 Cal Ripken TLU SP 8.00 3.60
❑ 189 F.Thomas TLU SP 2.50 1.10
❑ 190 Andy Pettitte TLU SP .75 .35
❑ 191 Paul Konerko SP 1.50 .70
❑ 192 Todd Helton SP 5.00 2.20
❑ 193 Mark Kotsay SP 1.50 .70
❑ 194 Brad Fullmer SP 1.50 .70
❑ 195 K.Millwood SP RC 10.00 4.50
❑ 196 David Ortiz SP 1.50 .70
❑ 197 Kerry Wood SP 4.00 1.80
❑ 198 Miguel Tejada SP 2.50 1.10
❑ 199 Fernando Tatis SP 1.00 .45
❑ 200 Jaret Wright SP 1.00 .45
❑ 201 Ben Grieve SP 1.50 .70
❑ 202 Travis Lee SP 1.50 .70
❑ 203 Wes Helms SP 1.00 .45
❑ 204 Geoff Jenkins SP 1.50 .70
❑ 205 Russell Branyan SP 1.50 .70
❑ 206 Esteban Yan SP RC 4.00 1.80
❑ 207 Ben Ford SP RC 2.50 1.10
❑ 208 Rich Butler SP RC 2.50 1.10
❑ 209 Ryan Jackson SP RC 2.50 1.10
❑ 210 A.J. Hinch SP 1.00 .45
❑ 211 M.Ordonez SP RC 40.00 18.00
❑ 212 Dave Dellucci SP RC 2.50 1.10
❑ 213 Billy McMillon SP 1.00 .45
❑ 214 Mike Lowell SP RC 12.00 5.50
❑ 215 Todd Erdos SP RC 2.50 1.10
❑ 216 C.Mendoza SP RC 2.50 1.10
❑ 217 F.Catalanotto SP RC 15.00 6.75
❑ 218 Julio Ramirez SP RC 4.00 1.80
❑ 219 John Halama SP RC 6.00 2.70
❑ 220 Wilson Delgado SP 1.00 .45
❑ 221 Mike Judd SP RC 4.00 1.80
❑ 222 Rolando Arrojo SP RC 8.00 3.60
❑ 223 Jason LaRue SP RC 12.00 5.50
❑ 224 Manny Aybar SP RC 4.00 1.80
❑ 225 Jorge Velandia SP 1.00 .45
❑ 226 Mike Kinkade SP RC 4.00 1.80
❑ 227 Carlos Lee SP RC 25.00 11.00
❑ 228 Bobby Hughes SP 1.00 .45
❑ 229 R.Christenson SP RC 2.50 1.10
❑ 230 Masato Yoshii SP RC 8.00 3.60
❑ 231 Richard Hidalgo .25 .11
❑ 232 Rafael Medina .15 .07
❑ 233 Damian Jackson .15 .07
❑ 234 Derek Lowe .15 .07
❑ 235 Mario Valdez .15 .07
❑ 236 Eli Marrero .15 .07
❑ 237 Juan Encarnacion .25 .11
❑ 238 Livan Hernandez .15 .07
❑ 239 Bruce Chen .15 .07
❑ 240 Eric Milton .25 .11
❑ 241 Jason Varitek .25 .11
❑ 242 Scott Elarton .15 .07
❑ 243 Manuel Barrios RC .15 .07
❑ 244 Mike Caruso .15 .07
❑ 245 Tom Evans .15 .07
❑ 246 Pat Cline .15 .07
❑ 247 Matt Clement .25 .11
❑ 248 Karim Garcia .15 .07
❑ 249 Richie Sexson .25 .11
❑ 250 Sidney Ponson .15 .07
❑ 251 Randall Simon .15 .07
❑ 252 Tony Saunders .15 .07
❑ 253 Javier Valentin .15 .07
❑ 254 Danny Clyburn .15 .07
❑ 255 Michael Coleman .15 .07
❑ 256 Hanley Frias RC .15 .07
❑ 257 Miguel Cairo .15 .07
❑ 258 Rob Stanifer RC .15 .07
❑ 259 Lou Collier .15 .07
❑ 260 Abraham Nunez .15 .07
❑ 261 Ricky Ledee .15 .07
❑ 262 Carl Pavano .15 .07
❑ 263 Derrek Lee .25 .11
❑ 264 Jeff Abbott .15 .07
❑ 265 Bob Abreu .25 .11
❑ 266 Bartolo Colon .25 .11
❑ 267 Mike Drumright .15 .07
❑ 268 Daryle Ward .15 .07
❑ 269 Gabe Alvarez .15 .07
❑ 270 Josh Booty .15 .07
❑ 271 Damian Moss .15 .07
❑ 272 Brian Rose .15 .07
❑ 273 Jarrod Washburn .15 .07
❑ 274 Bobby Estalella .15 .07
❑ 275 Enrique Wilson .15 .07
❑ 276 Derrick Gibson .15 .07
❑ 277 Ken Cloude .15 .07
❑ 278 Kevin Witt .15 .07
❑ 279 Donnie Sadler .15 .07
❑ 280 Sean Casey .40 .18
❑ 281 Jacob Cruz .15 .07
❑ 282 Ron Wright .15 .07
❑ 283 Jeremi Gonzalez .15 .07
❑ 284 Desi Relaford .15 .07
❑ 285 Bobby Smith .15 .07
❑ 286 Javier Vazquez .25 .11
❑ 287 Steve Woodard .15 .07
❑ 288 Greg Norton .15 .07
❑ 289 Cliff Politte .15 .07
❑ 290 Felix Heredia .15 .07
❑ 291 Braden Looper .15 .07

❑ 292 Felix Martinez	.15	.07
❑ 293 Brian Meadows	.15	.07
❑ 294 Edwin Diaz	.15	.07
❑ 295 Pat Watkins	.15	.07
❑ 296 Marc Pisciotta RC	.15	.07
❑ 297 Rick Gorecki	.15	.07
❑ 298 DaRond Stovall	.15	.07
❑ 299 Andy Larkin	.15	.07
❑ 300 Felix Rodriguez	.15	.07
❑ 301 Blake Stein SP	1.25	.55
❑ 302 John Rocker SP RC	10.00	4.50
❑ 303 J.Baughman SP RC	3.00	1.35
❑ 304 Jesus Sanchez SP RC	5.00	2.20
❑ 305 Randy Winn SP	1.25	.55
❑ 306 Lou Merloni SP	1.25	.55
❑ 307 Jim Parque SP RC	6.00	2.70
❑ 308 Dennis Reyes SP	1.25	.55
❑ 309 O.Hernandez SP RC	15.00	6.75
❑ 310 Jason Johnson SP	1.25	.55
❑ 311 Torii Hunter SP	2.00	.90
❑ 312 M.Piazza Marlins SP	12.00	5.50
❑ 313 Mike Frank SP RC	3.00	1.35
❑ 314 Troy Glaus SP RC	200.00	90.00
❑ 315 Jin Ho Cho SP RC	5.00	2.20
❑ 316 Ruben Mateo SP RC	20.00	9.00
❑ 317 Ryan Minor SP RC	20.00	9.00
❑ 318 Aramis Ramirez SP	2.00	.90
❑ 319 Adrian Beltre SP	2.00	.90
❑ 320 Matt Anderson SP RC	5.00	2.20
❑ 321 Gabe Kapler SP RC	25.00	11.00
❑ 322 Jeremy Giambi SP RC	12.00	5.50
❑ 323 Carlos Beltran SP	2.00	.90
❑ 324 Dermal Brown SP	1.25	.55
❑ 325 Ben Davis SP	2.00	.90
❑ 326 Eric Chavez SP	2.00	.90
❑ 327 Bobby Howry SP RC	5.00	2.20
❑ 328 Roy Halladay SP	1.25	.55
❑ 329 George Lombard SP	1.25	.55
❑ 330 Michael Barrett SP	1.25	.55
❑ 331 F. Seguignol SP RC	5.00	2.20
❑ 332 J.D. Drew SP RC	80.00	36.00
❑ 333 Odalis Perez SP RC	5.00	2.20
❑ 334 Alex Cora SP RC	5.00	2.20
❑ 335 P.Polanco SP RC	15.00	6.75
❑ 336 Armando Rios SP RC	8.00	3.60
❑ 337 Sammy Sosa HR SP	10.00	4.50
❑ 338 Mark McGwire HR SP	20.00	9.00
❑ 339 Sammy Sosa / Mark McGwire CL SP	15.00	6.75

2001 Leaf Rookies and Stars

	MINT	NRMT
COMP.SET w/o SP'S (100)	20.00	9.00
COMMON CARD (1-100)	.25	.11
COMMON CARD (101-200)	3.00	1.35
COMMON CARD (201-300)	10.00	4.50

Card	MINT	NRMT
❑ 1 Alex Rodriguez	1.50	.70
❑ 2 Derek Jeter	2.50	1.10
❑ 3 Aramis Ramirez	.25	.11
❑ 4 Cliff Floyd	.25	.11
❑ 5 Nomar Garciaparra	1.50	.70
❑ 6 Craig Biggio	.40	.18
❑ 7 Ivan Rodriguez	.60	.25
❑ 8 Cal Ripken	2.50	1.10
❑ 9 Fred McGriff	.40	.18
❑ 10 Chipper Jones	1.25	.55
❑ 11 Roberto Alomar	.60	.25
❑ 12 Moises Alou	.25	.11
❑ 13 Freddy Garcia	.25	.11
❑ 14 Bobby Abreu	.25	.11
❑ 15 Shawn Green	.60	.25
❑ 16 Jason Giambi	.60	.25
❑ 17 Todd Helton	.75	.35
❑ 18 Robert Fick	.25	.11
❑ 19 Tony Gwynn	1.25	.55
❑ 20 Luis Gonzalez	.60	.25
❑ 21 Sean Casey	.40	.18
❑ 22 Roger Clemens	1.50	.70
❑ 23 Brian Giles	.25	.11
❑ 24 Manny Ramirez	.75	.35
❑ 25 Barry Bonds	1.50	.70
❑ 26 Richard Hidalgo	.25	.11
❑ 27 Vladimir Guerrero	.75	.35
❑ 28 Kevin Brown	.25	.11
❑ 29 Mike Sweeney	.25	.11
❑ 30 Ken Griffey Jr.	2.00	.90
❑ 31 Mike Piazza	1.50	.70
❑ 32 Richie Sexson	.25	.11
❑ 33 Matt Morris	.25	.11
❑ 34 Jorge Posada	.25	.11
❑ 35 Eric Chavez	.25	.11
❑ 36 Mark Buehrle	.60	.25
❑ 37 Jeff Bagwell	.75	.35
❑ 38 Curt Schilling	.60	.25
❑ 39 Bartolo Colon	.25	.11
❑ 40 Mark Quinn	.25	.11
❑ 41 Tony Clark	.25	.11
❑ 42 Brad Radke	.25	.11
❑ 43 Gary Sheffield	.25	.11
❑ 44 Doug Mientkiewicz	.25	.11
❑ 45 Pedro Martinez	.75	.35
❑ 46 Carlos Lee	.25	.11
❑ 47 Troy Glaus	.60	.25
❑ 48 Preston Wilson	.25	.11
❑ 49 Phil Nevin	.25	.11
❑ 50 Chan Ho Park	.25	.11
❑ 51 Randy Johnson	.75	.35
❑ 52 Jermaine Dye	.25	.11
❑ 53 Terrence Long	.25	.11
❑ 54 Joe Mays	.25	.11
❑ 55 Scott Rolen	.60	.25
❑ 56 Miguel Tejada	.25	.11
❑ 57 Jim Thome	.60	.25
❑ 58 Jose Vidro	.25	.11
❑ 59 Gabe Kapler	.25	.11
❑ 60 Darin Erstad	.60	.25
❑ 61 Jim Edmonds	.40	.18
❑ 62 Jarrod Washburn	.25	.11
❑ 63 Tom Glavine	.60	.25
❑ 64 Adrian Beltre	.25	.11
❑ 65 Sammy Sosa	1.25	.55
❑ 66 Juan Gonzalez	.60	.25
❑ 67 Rafael Furcal	.25	.11
❑ 68 Mike Mussina	.60	.25
❑ 69 Mark McGwire	2.50	1.10
❑ 70 Ryan Klesko	.25	.11
❑ 71 Raul Mondesi	.25	.11
❑ 72 Trot Nixon	.25	.11
❑ 73 Barry Larkin	.60	.25
❑ 74 Rafael Palmeiro	.60	.25
❑ 75 Mark Mulder	.40	.18
❑ 76 Carlos Delgado	.60	.25
❑ 77 Mike Hampton	.25	.11
❑ 78 Carl Everett	.25	.11
❑ 79 Paul Konerko	.25	.11
❑ 80 Larry Walker	.25	.11
❑ 81 Kerry Wood	.60	.25
❑ 82 Frank Thomas	.75	.35
❑ 83 Andruw Jones	.60	.25
❑ 84 Eric Milton	.25	.11
❑ 85 Ben Grieve	.25	.11
❑ 86 Carlos Beltran	.25	.11
❑ 87 Tim Hudson	.60	.25
❑ 88 Hideo Nomo	.60	.25
❑ 89 Greg Maddux	1.50	.70
❑ 90 Edgar Martinez	.40	.18
❑ 91 Lance Berkman	.60	.25
❑ 92 Pat Burrell	.25	.11
❑ 93 Jeff Kent	.40	.18
❑ 94 Magglio Ordonez	.25	.11
❑ 95 Cristian Guzman	.25	.11
❑ 96 Jose Canseco	.60	.25
❑ 97 J.D. Drew	.60	.25
❑ 98 Bernie Williams	.60	.25
❑ 99 Kazuhiro Sasaki	.60	.25
❑ 100 Rickey Henderson	1.25	.55
❑ 101 Wilson Guzman RC	3.00	1.35
❑ 102 Nick Neugebauer	5.00	2.20
❑ 103 Lance Davis RC	3.00	1.35
❑ 104 Felipe Lopez	3.00	1.35
❑ 105 Toby Hall	3.00	1.35
❑ 106 Jack Cust	3.00	1.35
❑ 107 Jason Karnuth RC	3.00	1.35
❑ 108 Bart Miadich RC	3.00	1.35
❑ 109 Brian Roberts RC	3.00	1.35
❑ 110 Brandon Larson RC	3.00	1.35
❑ 111 Sean Douglass RC	3.00	1.35
❑ 112 Joe Crede	3.00	1.35
❑ 113 Tim Redding	3.00	1.35
❑ 114 Adam Johnson	3.00	1.35
❑ 115 Marcus Giles	3.00	1.35
❑ 116 Jose Ortiz	3.00	1.35
❑ 117 Jose Mieses RC	3.00	1.35
❑ 118 Nick Maness RC	3.00	1.35
❑ 119 Les Walrond RC	3.00	1.35
❑ 120 Travis Phelps RC	3.00	1.35
❑ 121 Troy Mattes RC	3.00	1.35
❑ 122 Carlos Garcia RC	3.00	1.35
❑ 123 Bill Ortega RC	3.00	1.35
❑ 124 Gene Altman RC	3.00	1.35
❑ 125 Nate Frese RC	3.00	1.35
❑ 126 Alfonso Soriano	5.00	2.20
❑ 127 Jose Nunez RC	3.00	1.35
❑ 128 Bob File RC	3.00	1.35
❑ 129 Dan Wright	3.00	1.35
❑ 130 Nick Johnson	3.00	1.35
❑ 131 Brent Abernathy	3.00	1.35
❑ 132 Steve Green RC	3.00	1.35
❑ 133 Billy Sylvester RC	3.00	1.35
❑ 134 Scott MacRae RC	3.00	1.35
❑ 135 Kris Keller RC	3.00	1.35
❑ 136 Scott Stewart RC	3.00	1.35
❑ 137 Henry Mateo RC	3.00	1.35
❑ 138 Timo Perez	3.00	1.35
❑ 139 Nate Teut RC	3.00	1.35
❑ 140 Jason Michaels RC	3.00	1.35
❑ 141 Junior Spivey RC	3.00	1.35
❑ 142 Carlos Pena	3.00	1.35
❑ 143 Wilmy Caceres RC	3.00	1.35
❑ 144 David Lundquist	3.00	1.35
❑ 145 Jack Wilson RC	3.00	1.35
❑ 146 Jeremy Fikac RC	3.00	1.35
❑ 147 Alex Escobar	3.00	1.35
❑ 148 Abraham Nunez	3.00	1.35
❑ 149 Xavier Nady	3.00	1.35
❑ 150 Michael Cuddyer	3.00	1.35
❑ 151 Greg Miller RC	3.00	1.35
❑ 152 Eric Munson	3.00	1.35
❑ 153 Aubrey Huff	3.00	1.35
❑ 154 Tim Christman RC	3.00	1.35
❑ 155 Erick Almonte RC	5.00	2.20
❑ 156 Mike Penney RC	3.00	1.35
❑ 157 Delvin James RC	3.00	1.35
❑ 158 Ben Sheets	3.00	1.35
❑ 159 Jason Hart	3.00	1.35
❑ 160 Jose Acevedo RC	3.00	1.35
❑ 161 Will Ohman RC	3.00	1.35
❑ 162 Erik Hiljus RC	3.00	1.35
❑ 163 Juan Moreno RC	3.00	1.35
❑ 164 Mike Koplove RC	3.00	1.35
❑ 165 Pedro Santana RC	3.00	1.35
❑ 166 Jimmy Rollins	3.00	1.35
❑ 167 Matt White RC	3.00	1.35
❑ 168 Cesar Crespo RC	3.00	1.35
❑ 169 Carlos Hernandez	3.00	1.35
❑ 170 Chris George	3.00	1.35
❑ 171 Brad Voyles RC	3.00	1.35
❑ 172 Luis Pineda RC	3.00	1.35
❑ 173 Carlos Zambrano RC	3.00	1.35
❑ 174 Nate Cornejo	3.00	1.35
❑ 175 Jason Smith RC	3.00	1.35
❑ 176 Craig Monroe RC	5.00	2.20
❑ 177 Cody Ransom RC	3.00	1.35
❑ 178 John Grabow RC	3.00	1.35
❑ 179 Pedro Feliz	3.00	1.35
❑ 180 Jeremy Owens RC	3.00	1.35
❑ 181 Kurt Ainsworth	3.00	1.35

Card	MINT	NRMT
❑ 182 Luis Lopez RC	3.00	1.35
❑ 183 Stubby Clapp RC	3.00	1.35
❑ 184 Ryan Freel RC	3.00	1.35
❑ 185 Duaner Sanchez RC	3.00	1.35
❑ 186 Jason Jennings	3.00	1.35
❑ 187 Kyle Lohse RC	6.00	2.70
❑ 188 Jerrod Riggan RC	3.00	1.35
❑ 189 Joe Beimel RC	3.00	1.35
❑ 190 Nick Punto RC	3.00	1.35
❑ 191 Willie Harris RC	3.00	1.35
❑ 192 Ryan Jensen RC	3.00	1.35
❑ 193 Adam Pettyjohn RC	3.00	1.35
❑ 194 Donaldo Mendez RC	3.00	1.35
❑ 195 Bret Prinz RC	3.00	1.35
❑ 196 Paul Phillips RC	3.00	1.35
❑ 197 Brian Lawrence RC	3.00	1.35
❑ 198 Cesar Izturis	3.00	1.35
❑ 199 Blaine Neal RC	3.00	1.35
❑ 200 Josh Fogg RC	3.00	1.35
❑ 201 Josh Towers RC	15.00	6.75
❑ 202 Tim Spooneybarger RC	10.00	4.50
❑ 203 Michael Rivera RC	12.00	5.50
❑ 204 Juan Cruz RC	25.00	11.00
❑ 205 Albert Pujols RC	100.00	45.00
❑ 206 Josh Beckett	12.00	5.50
❑ 207 Roy Oswalt	12.00	5.50
❑ 208 Elpidio Guzman RC	10.00	4.50
❑ 209 Horacio Ramirez RC	10.00	4.50
❑ 210 Corey Patterson	10.00	4.50
❑ 211 Geronimo Gil RC	10.00	4.50
❑ 212 Jay Gibbons RC	12.00	5.50
❑ 213 Orlando Woodards RC	10.00	4.50
❑ 214 David Espinosa	10.00	4.50
❑ 215 Angel Berroa RC	10.00	4.50
❑ 216 Brandon Duckworth RC	20.00	9.00
❑ 217 Brian Reith RC	10.00	4.50
❑ 218 David Brous RC	10.00	4.50
❑ 219 Bud Smith RC	30.00	13.50
❑ 220 Ramon Vazquez RC	12.00	5.50
❑ 221 Mark Teixeira RC	80.00	36.00
❑ 222 Justin Atchley RC	10.00	4.50
❑ 223 Tony Cogan RC	10.00	4.50
❑ 224 Grant Balfour RC	10.00	4.50
❑ 225 Ricardo Rodriguez RC	12.00	5.50
❑ 226 Brian Rogers RC	10.00	4.50
❑ 227 Adam Dunn	20.00	9.00
❑ 228 Wilson Betemit RC	30.00	13.50
❑ 229 Juan Diaz RC	10.00	4.50
❑ 230 Jackson Melian RC	10.00	4.50
❑ 231 Claudio Vargas RC	10.00	4.50
❑ 232 Wilkin Ruan RC	10.00	4.50
❑ 233 Justin Duchscherer RC	10.00	4.50
❑ 234 Kevin Olsen RC	10.00	4.50
❑ 235 Tony Fiore RC	10.00	4.50
❑ 236 Jeremy Affeldt RC	10.00	4.50
❑ 237 Mike Maroth RC	10.00	4.50
❑ 238 C.C. Sabathia	10.00	4.50
❑ 239 Cory Aldridge RC	10.00	4.50
❑ 240 Zach Day RC	10.00	4.50
❑ 241 Brett Jodie RC	10.00	4.50
❑ 242 Winston Abreu RC	10.00	4.50
❑ 243 Travis Hafner RC	12.00	5.50
❑ 244 Joe Kennedy RC	12.00	5.50
❑ 245 Rick Bauer RC	10.00	4.50
❑ 246 Mike Young	10.00	4.50
❑ 247 Ken Vining RC	10.00	4.50
❑ 248 Doug Nickle RC	10.00	4.50
❑ 249 Pablo Ozuna	10.00	4.50
❑ 250 Dustan Mohr RC	10.00	4.50
❑ 251 Ichiro Suzuki RC	120.00	55.00
❑ 252 Ryan Drese RC	10.00	4.50
❑ 253 Morgan Ensberg RC	15.00	6.75
❑ 254 George Perez RC	10.00	4.50
❑ 255 Roy Smith RC	10.00	4.50
❑ 256 Juan Uribe RC	15.00	6.75
❑ 257 Dewon Brazelton RC	25.00	11.00
❑ 258 Endy Chavez RC	10.00	4.50
❑ 259 Kris Foster	10.00	4.50
❑ 260 Eric Knott RC	10.00	4.50
❑ 261 Corky Miller RC	10.00	4.50
❑ 262 Larry Bigbie	10.00	4.50
❑ 263 Andres Torres RC	10.00	4.50
❑ 264 Adrian Hernandez RC	10.00	4.50
❑ 265 Johnny Estrada RC	15.00	6.75
❑ 266 David Williams RC	12.00	5.50
❑ 267 Steve Lomasney	10.00	4.50
❑ 268 Victor Zambrano RC	10.00	4.50
❑ 269 Keith Ginter	10.00	4.50
❑ 270 Casey Fossum RC	15.00	6.75
❑ 271 Josue Perez RC	10.00	4.50
❑ 272 Josh Phelps	10.00	4.50
❑ 273 Mark Prior RC	60.00	27.00
❑ 274 Brandon Berger RC	10.00	4.50
❑ 275 Scott Podsednik RC	10.00	4.50
❑ 276 Jorge Julio RC	10.00	4.50
❑ 277 Esix Snead RC	10.00	4.50
❑ 278 Brandon Knight RC	10.00	4.50
❑ 279 Saul Rivera RC	10.00	4.50
❑ 280 Benito Baez RC	10.00	4.50
❑ 281 Rob MacKowiak RC	10.00	4.50
❑ 282 Eric Hinske RC	12.00	5.50
❑ 283 Juan Rivera	10.00	4.50
❑ 284 Kevin Joseph RC	10.00	4.50
❑ 285 Juan A. Pena RC	10.00	4.50
❑ 286 Brandon Lyon RC	12.00	5.50
❑ 287 Adam Everett	10.00	4.50
❑ 288 Eric Valent	10.00	4.50
❑ 289 Ken Harvey	10.00	4.50
❑ 290 Bert Snow RC	10.00	4.50
❑ 291 Wily Mo Pena	10.00	4.50
❑ 292 Rafael Soriano RC	12.00	5.50
❑ 293 Carlos Valderrama RC	10.00	4.50
❑ 294 Christian Parker RC	10.00	4.50
❑ 295 Tsuyoshi Shinjo RC	25.00	11.00
❑ 296 Martin Vargas RC	10.00	4.50
❑ 297 Luke Hudson RC	10.00	4.50
❑ 298 Dee Brown	10.00	4.50
❑ 299 Alexis Gomez RC	10.00	4.50
❑ 300 Angel Santos RC	10.00	4.50

1996 Leaf Signature

	MINT	NRMT
COMPLETE SET (150)	100.00	45.00
COMPLETE SERIES 1 (100)	60.00	27.00
COMPLETE SERIES 2 (50)	40.00	18.00
COMMON CARD (1-100)	.25	.11
COMMON CARD (101-150)	.30	.14

Card	MINT	NRMT
❑ 1 Mike Piazza	2.50	1.10
❑ 2 Juan Gonzalez	1.00	.45
❑ 3 Greg Maddux	2.50	1.10
❑ 4 Marc Newfield	.25	.11
❑ 5 Wade Boggs	1.00	.45
❑ 6 Ray Lankford	.25	.11
❑ 7 Frank Thomas	1.25	.55
❑ 8 Rico Brogna	.25	.11
❑ 9 Tim Salmon	.40	.18
❑ 10 Ken Griffey Jr.	3.00	1.35
❑ 11 Manny Ramirez	1.25	.55
❑ 12 Cecil Fielder	.40	.18
❑ 13 Gregg Jefferies	.25	.11
❑ 14 Rondell White	.40	.18
❑ 15 Cal Ripken	4.00	1.80
❑ 16 Alex Rodriguez	2.50	1.10
❑ 17 Bernie Williams	1.00	.45
❑ 18 Andres Galarraga	.60	.25
❑ 19 Mike Mussina	1.00	.45
❑ 20 Chuck Knoblauch	.40	.18
❑ 21 Joe Carter	.40	.18
❑ 22 Jeff Bagwell	1.25	.55
❑ 23 Mark McGwire	4.00	1.80
❑ 24 Sammy Sosa	2.00	.90
❑ 25 Reggie Sanders	.25	.11
❑ 26 Chipper Jones	2.00	.90
❑ 27 Jeff Cirillo	.40	.18
❑ 28 Roger Clemens	2.50	1.10
❑ 29 Craig Biggio	.60	.25
❑ 30 Gary Sheffield	.40	.18
❑ 31 Paul O'Neill	1.00	.45
❑ 32 Johnny Damon	.40	.18
❑ 33 Jason Isringhausen	.40	.18
❑ 34 Jay Bell	.40	.18
❑ 35 Henry Rodriguez	.25	.11
❑ 36 Matt Williams	.60	.25
❑ 37 Randy Johnson	1.25	.55
❑ 38 Fred McGriff	.60	.25
❑ 39 Jason Giambi	1.00	.45
❑ 40 Ivan Rodriguez	1.00	.45
❑ 41 Raul Mondesi	.40	.18
❑ 42 Barry Larkin	1.00	.45
❑ 43 Ryan Klesko	.40	.18
❑ 44 Joey Hamilton	.25	.11
❑ 45 Todd Hundley	.25	.11
❑ 46 Jim Edmonds	.60	.25
❑ 47 Dante Bichette	.40	.18
❑ 48 Roberto Alomar	1.00	.45
❑ 49 Mark Grace	1.00	.45
❑ 50 Brady Anderson	.40	.18
❑ 51 Hideo Nomo	1.25	.55
❑ 52 Ozzie Smith	1.25	.55
❑ 53 Robin Ventura	.40	.18
❑ 54 Andy Pettitte	.40	.18
❑ 55 Kenny Lofton	.40	.18
❑ 56 John Mabry	.25	.11
❑ 57 Paul Molitor	1.00	.45
❑ 58 Rey Ordonez	.25	.11
❑ 59 Albert Belle	.40	.18
❑ 60 Charles Johnson	.40	.18
❑ 61 Edgar Martinez	.60	.25
❑ 62 Derek Bell	.25	.11
❑ 63 Carlos Delgado	1.00	.45
❑ 64 Raul Casanova	.25	.11
❑ 65 Ismael Valdes	.25	.11
❑ 66 J.T. Snow	.40	.18
❑ 67 Derek Jeter	4.00	1.80
❑ 68 Jason Kendall	.40	.18
❑ 69 John Smoltz	.40	.18
❑ 70 Chad Mottola	.25	.11
❑ 71 Jim Thome	1.00	.45
❑ 72 Will Clark	1.00	.45
❑ 73 Mo Vaughn	.40	.18
❑ 74 John Wasdin	.25	.11
❑ 75 Rafael Palmeiro	1.00	.45
❑ 76 Mark Grudzielanek	.25	.11
❑ 77 Larry Walker	.60	.25
❑ 78 Alan Benes	.25	.11
❑ 79 Michael Tucker	.25	.11
❑ 80 Billy Wagner	.25	.11
❑ 81 Paul Wilson	.25	.11
❑ 82 Greg Vaughn	.40	.18
❑ 83 Dean Palmer	.40	.18
❑ 84 Ryne Sandberg	1.25	.55
❑ 85 Eric Young	.25	.11
❑ 86 Jay Buhner	.40	.18
❑ 87 Tony Clark	.40	.18
❑ 88 Jermaine Dye	.40	.18
❑ 89 Barry Bonds	2.50	1.10
❑ 90 Ugueth Urbina	.25	.11
❑ 91 Charles Nagy	.25	.11
❑ 92 Ruben Rivera	.25	.11
❑ 93 Todd Hollandsworth	.25	.11
❑ 94 Darin Erstad RC	8.00	3.60
❑ 95 Brooks Kieschnick	.25	.11
❑ 96 Edgar Renteria	.25	.11
❑ 97 Lenny Dykstra	.40	.18
❑ 98 Tony Gwynn	2.00	.90
❑ 99 Kirby Puckett	2.50	1.10
❑ 100 Checklist	.25	.11
❑ 101 Andruw Jones	3.00	1.35
❑ 102 Alex Ochoa	.30	.14
❑ 103 David Cone	.50	.23
❑ 104 Rusty Greer	.50	.23
❑ 105 Jose Canseco	1.00	.45
❑ 106 Ken Caminiti	.50	.23
❑ 107 Mariano Rivera	.50	.23
❑ 108 Ron Gant	.30	.14
❑ 109 Darryl Strawberry	.50	.23
❑ 110 Vladimir Guerrero	4.00	1.80
❑ 111 George Arias	.30	.14

		MINT	NRMT
❑ 112	Jeff Conine	.30	.14
❑ 113	Bobby Higginson	.50	.23
❑ 114	Eric Karros	.50	.23
❑ 115	Brian Hunter	.30	.14
❑ 116	Eddie Murray	1.25	.55
❑ 117	Todd Walker	.50	.23
❑ 118	Chan Ho Park	.50	.23
❑ 119	John Jaha	.30	.14
❑ 120	Dave Justice	.50	.23
❑ 121	Makoto Suzuki	.30	.14
❑ 122	Scott Rolen	2.50	1.10
❑ 123	Tino Martinez	.50	.23
❑ 124	Kimera Bartee	.30	.14
❑ 125	Garret Anderson	.50	.23
❑ 126	Brian Jordan	.50	.23
❑ 127	Andre Dawson	.75	.35
❑ 128	Javier Lopez	.50	.23
❑ 129	Bill Pulsipher	.30	.14
❑ 130	Dwight Gooden	.50	.23
❑ 131	Al Martin	.30	.14
❑ 132	Terrell Wade	.30	.14
❑ 133	Steve Gibralter	.30	.14
❑ 134	Tom Glavine	1.25	.55
❑ 135	Kevin Appier	.50	.23
❑ 136	Tim Raines	.50	.23
❑ 137	Curtis Pride	.30	.14
❑ 138	Todd Greene	.30	.14
❑ 139	Bobby Bonilla	.50	.23
❑ 140	Trey Beamon	.30	.14
❑ 141	Marty Cordova	.30	.14
❑ 142	Rickey Henderson	2.50	1.10
❑ 143	Ellis Burks	.50	.23
❑ 144	Dennis Eckersley	.50	.23
❑ 145	Kevin Brown	.50	.23
❑ 146	Carlos Baerga	.30	.14
❑ 147	Brett Butler	.50	.23
❑ 148	Marquis Grissom	.30	.14
❑ 149	Karim Garcia	.30	.14
❑ 150	Frank Thomas CL	.75	.35

2000 MLB Showdown 1st Edition

	MINT	NRMT
COMPLETE SET (462)	300.00	135.00
COMP.SET w/o FOIL (400)	100.00	45.00
COMMON CARD (1-462)	.25	.11
COMMON FOIL	5.00	2.20

		MINT	NRMT
❑ 1	Garret Anderson	.75	.35
❑ 2	Tim Belcher	.25	.11
❑ 3	Gary DiSarcina UER Tim Salmon incorrectly pictured	.25	.11
❑ 4	Darin Erstad	2.00	.90
❑ 5	Chuck Finley FOIL	8.00	3.60
❑ 6	Troy Glaus	2.00	.90
❑ 7	Todd Greene	.25	.11
❑ 8	Jeff Huson	.25	.11
❑ 9	Orlando Palmeiro	.25	.11
❑ 10	Troy Percival	.25	.11
❑ 11	Mark Petkovsek	.25	.11
❑ 12	Tim Salmon	.75	.35
❑ 13	Steve Sparks	.25	.11
❑ 14	Mo Vaughn	.75	.35
❑ 15	Matt Walbeck	.25	.11
❑ 16	Jay Bell FOIL	8.00	3.60
❑ 17	Andy Benes	.25	.11
❑ 18	Omar Daal	.25	.11
❑ 19	Steve Finley	.75	.35
❑ 20	Andy Fox	.25	.11
❑ 21	Hanley Frias	.25	.11
❑ 22	Bernard Gilkey	.25	.11
❑ 23	Luis Gonzalez FOIL	5.00	2.20
❑ 24	Randy Johnson FOIL	15.00	6.75
❑ 25	Travis Lee	.25	.11
❑ 26	Matt Mantei	.25	.11
❑ 27	Dan Plesac	.25	.11
❑ 28	Kelly Stinnett	.25	.11
❑ 29	Greg Swindell	.25	.11
❑ 30	Matt Williams FOIL	5.00	2.20
❑ 31	Tony Womack	.25	.11
❑ 32	Bret Boone	.75	.35
❑ 33	Tom Glavine	2.00	.90
❑ 34	Jose Hernandez	.25	.11
❑ 35	Brian Hunter	.25	.11
❑ 36	Andruw Jones	2.00	.90
❑ 37	Chipper Jones FOIL	10.00	4.50
❑ 38	Brian Jordan	.25	.11
❑ 39	Ryan Klesko	.75	.35
❑ 40	Keith Lockhart	.25	.11
❑ 41	Greg Maddux FOIL *	4.00	1.80
❑ 42	Kevin Millwood FOIL	5.00	2.20
❑ 43	Eddie Perez	.25	.11
❑ 44	Mike Remlinger	.25	.11
❑ 45	John Rocker	.75	.35
❑ 46	John Smoltz	.75	.35
❑ 47	Walt Weiss	.25	.11
❑ 48	Gerald Williams	.25	.11
❑ 49	Rich Amaral	.25	.11
❑ 50	Brady Anderson	.75	.35
❑ 51	Albert Belle	.75	.35
❑ 52	Mike Bordick	.25	.11
❑ 53	Jeff Conine	.25	.11
❑ 54	Delino DeShields	.75	.35
❑ 55	Scott Erickson	.25	.11
❑ 56	Charles Johnson	.75	.35
❑ 57	Mike Mussina	2.00	.90
❑ 58	Jesse Orosco	.25	.11
❑ 59	Sidney Ponson	.25	.11
❑ 60	Jeff Reboulet	.25	.11
❑ 61	Cal Ripken FOIL	20.00	9.00
❑ 62	B.J. Surhoff	.75	.35
❑ 63	Mike Timlin	.25	.11
❑ 64	Rod Beck	.25	.11
❑ 65	Damon Buford	.25	.11
❑ 66	Rheal Cormier	.25	.11
❑ 67	N.Garciaparra FOIL	12.00	5.50
❑ 68	Butch Huskey	.25	.11
❑ 69	Darren Lewis	.25	.11
❑ 70	Derek Lowe	.25	.11
❑ 71	Pedro Martinez FOIL	20.00	9.00
❑ 72	Trot Nixon	.75	.35
❑ 73	Jose Offerman	.25	.11
❑ 74	Troy O'Leary	.25	.11
❑ 75	Mark Portugal	.25	.11
❑ 76	Pat Rapp	.25	.11
❑ 77	Mike Stanley	.25	.11
❑ 78	John Valentin	.25	.11
❑ 79	Jason Varitek	.25	.11
❑ 80	Tim Wakefield	.25	.11
❑ 81	Rick Aguilera	.75	.35
❑ 82	Jeff Blauser	.25	.11
❑ 83	Kyle Farnsworth	.25	.11
❑ 84	Gary Gaetti	.75	.35
❑ 85	Mark Grace	2.00	.90
❑ 86	Lance Johnson	.25	.11
❑ 87	Jon Lieber	.25	.11
❑ 88	Mickey Morandini	.25	.11
❑ 89	Jose Nieves	.25	.11
❑ 90	Jeff Reed	.25	.11
❑ 91	Henry Rodriguez	.25	.11
❑ 92	Scott Sanders	.25	.11
❑ 93	Benito Santiago	.25	.11
❑ 94	Sammy Sosa FOIL	20.00	9.00
❑ 95	Steve Trachsel	.25	.11
❑ 96	James Baldwin	.25	.11
❑ 97	Mike Caruso	.25	.11
❑ 98	Ray Durham	.75	.35
❑ 99	Brook Fordyce	.25	.11
❑ 100	Bob Howry	.25	.11
❑ 101	Paul Konerko	.75	.35
❑ 102	Carlos Lee	.75	.35
❑ 103	Greg Norton	.25	.11
❑ 104	Magglio Ordonez	.75	.35
❑ 105	Jim Parque	.25	.11
❑ 106	Bill Simas	.25	.11
❑ 107	Chris Singleton	.25	.11
❑ 108	Mike Sirotka	.25	.11
❑ 109	Frank Thomas FOIL	6.00	2.70
❑ 110	Craig Wilson	.25	.11
❑ 111	Aaron Boone	.25	.11
❑ 112	Mike Cameron	.75	.35
❑ 113	Sean Casey FOIL	5.00	2.20
❑ 114	Danny Graves	.25	.11
❑ 115	Pete Harnisch	.25	.11
❑ 116	Barry Larkin FOIL	5.00	2.20
❑ 117	Pokey Reese	.25	.11
❑ 118	Scott Sullivan	.25	.11
❑ 119	Eddie Taubensee	.25	.11
❑ 120	Brett Tomko	.25	.11
❑ 121	Michael Tucker	.25	.11
❑ 122	Greg Vaughn	.75	.35
❑ 123	Ron Villone	.25	.11
❑ 124	Scott Williamson FOIL	5.00	2.20
❑ 125	Dmitri Young	.75	.35
❑ 126	Roberto Alomar FOIL	5.00	2.20
❑ 127	Harold Baines	.75	.35
❑ 128	Dave Burba	.25	.11
❑ 129	Bartolo Colon	.25	.11
❑ 130	Einar Diaz	.25	.11
❑ 131	Travis Fryman	.75	.35
❑ 132	Mike Jackson	.25	.11
❑ 133	David Justice	.75	.35
❑ 134	Kenny Lofton FOIL	8.00	3.60
❑ 135	Charles Nagy	.25	.11
❑ 136	Manny Ramirez FOIL	10.00	4.50
❑ 137	Richie Sexson	.75	.35
❑ 138	Paul Shuey	.25	.11
❑ 139	Jim Thome FOIL	5.00	2.20
❑ 140	Omar Vizquel	.75	.35
❑ 141	Enrique Wilson	.25	.11
❑ 142	Kurt Abbott	.25	.11
❑ 143	Pedro Astacio	.25	.11
❑ 144	Jeff Barry	.25	.11
❑ 145	Dante Bichette	.75	.35
❑ 146	Henry Blanco	.25	.11
❑ 147	Brian Bohanon	.25	.11
❑ 148	Vinny Castilla	.75	.35
❑ 149	Jerry Dipoto	.25	.11
❑ 150	Todd Helton	2.50	1.10
❑ 151	Darryl Kile	.75	.35
❑ 152	Curtis Leskanic	.25	.11
❑ 153	Neifi Perez	.25	.11
❑ 154	Terry Shumpert	.25	.11
❑ 155	Dave Veres	.25	.11
❑ 156	Larry Walker FOIL	5.00	2.20
❑ 157	Brad Ausmus	.25	.11
❑ 158	Frank Catalanotto	.25	.11
❑ 159	Tony Clark	.75	.35
❑ 160	Deivi Cruz	.25	.11
❑ 161	Damion Easley	.25	.11
❑ 162	Juan Encarnacion	.75	.35
❑ 163	Karim Garcia	.25	.11
❑ 164	Bobby Higginson	.25	.11
❑ 165	Todd Jones	.25	.11
❑ 166	Gabe Kapler	.75	.35
❑ 167	Dave Mlicki	.25	.11
❑ 168	Brian Moehler	.25	.11
❑ 169	C.J. Nitkowski	.25	.11
❑ 170	Dean Palmer FOIL	8.00	3.60
❑ 171	Jeff Weaver	.75	.35
❑ 172	Antonio Alfonseca	.25	.11
❑ 173	Bruce Aven	.25	.11
❑ 174	Dave Berg	.25	.11
❑ 175	Luis Castillo FOIL	5.00	2.20
❑ 176	Ryan Dempster	.75	.35
❑ 177	Brian Edmondson	.25	.11
❑ 178	Alex Gonzalez	.25	.11
❑ 179	Mark Kotsay	.25	.11
❑ 180	Derrek Lee	.75	.35
❑ 181	Braden Looper	.25	.11
❑ 182	Mike Lowell	.25	.11
❑ 183	Brian Meadows	.25	.11
❑ 184	Mike Redmond	.25	.11
❑ 185	Dennis Springer	.25	.11
❑ 186	Preston Wilson	.75	.35
❑ 187	Jeff Bagwell FOIL	10.00	4.50
❑ 188	Derek Bell	.25	.11
❑ 189	Craig Biggio	1.25	.55
❑ 190	Tim Bogar	.25	.11

❑ 191 Ken Caminiti .75 .35
❑ 192 Scott Elarton .25 .11
❑ 193 Tony Eusebio .25 .11
❑ 194 Carl Everett FOIL 8.00 3.60
❑ 195 Mike Hampton FOIL 8.00 3.60
❑ 196 Richard Hidalgo .75 .35
❑ 197 Stan Javier .25 .11
❑ 198 Jose Lima .25 .11
❑ 199 Jay Powell .25 .11
❑ 200 Shane Reynolds .25 .11
❑ 201 Bill Spiers .25 .11
❑ 202 Billy Wagner FOIL 5.00 2.20
❑ 203 Carlos Beltran FOIL 8.00 3.60
❑ 204 Johnny Damon .75 .35
❑ 205 Jermaine Dye .25 .11
❑ 206 Carlos Febles .25 .11
❑ 207 Jeremy Giambi .25 .11
❑ 208 Chad Kreuter .25 .11
❑ 209 Jeff Montgomery .25 .11
❑ 210 Joe Randa .75 .35
❑ 211 Jose Rosado .25 .11
❑ 212 Rey Sanchez .25 .11
❑ 213 Scott Service .25 .11
❑ 214 Tim Spehr .25 .11
❑ 215 Jeff Suppan .25 .11
❑ 216 Mike Sweeney .75 .35
❑ 217 Jay Witasick .25 .11
❑ 218 Adrian Beltre .25 .11
❑ 219 Pedro Borbon .25 .11
❑ 220 Kevin Brown FOIL 5.00 2.20
❑ 221 Mark Grudzielanek .25 .11
❑ 222 Dave Hansen .25 .11
❑ 223 Todd Hundley .25 .11
❑ 224 Eric Karros .75 .35
❑ 225 Raul Mondesi .75 .35
❑ 226 Chan Ho Park .75 .35
❑ 227 Jeff Shaw .25 .11
❑ 228 Gary Sheffield FOIL 8.00 3.60
❑ 229 Ismael Valdes .25 .11
❑ 230 Jose Vizcaino .25 .11
❑ 231 Devon White .25 .11
❑ 232 Eric Young .25 .11
❑ 233 Ron Belliard .25 .11
❑ 234 Sean Berry .25 .11
❑ 235 Jeromy Burnitz FOIL 8.00 3.60
❑ 236 Jeff Cirillo .75 .35
❑ 237 Marquis Grissom .25 .11
❑ 238 Geoff Jenkins .75 .35
❑ 239 Scott Karl .25 .11
❑ 240 Mark Loretta .25 .11
❑ 241 Mike Myers .25 .11
❑ 242 David Nilsson FOIL 5.00 2.20
❑ 243 Hideo Nomo 2.00 .90
❑ 244 Alex Ochoa .25 .11
❑ 245 Jose Valentin .25 .11
❑ 246 Bob Wickman .25 .11
❑ 247 Steve Woodard .25 .11
❑ 248 Chad Allen .25 .11
❑ 249 Ron Coomer .25 .11
❑ 250 Cristian Guzman .75 .35
❑ 251 Denny Hocking .25 .11
❑ 252 Torii Hunter .75 .35
❑ 253 Corey Koskie .75 .35
❑ 254 Matt Lawton .75 .35
❑ 255 Joe Mays .75 .35
❑ 256 Doug Mientkiewicz 1.25 .55
❑ 257 Eric Milton .75 .35
❑ 258 Brad Radke FOIL 8.00 3.60
❑ 259 Terry Steinbach .25 .11
❑ 260 Mike Trombley .25 .11
❑ 261 Todd Walker .25 .11
❑ 262 Bob Wells .25 .11
❑ 263 Shane Andrews .25 .11
❑ 264 Michael Barrett .25 .11
❑ 265 Orlando Cabrera .25 .11
❑ 266 Brad Fullmer .75 .35
❑ 267 Vlad. Guerrero FOIL 8.00 3.60
❑ 268 Wilton Guerrero .25 .11
❑ 269 Dustin Hermanson .25 .11
❑ 270 Steve Kline .25 .11
❑ 271 Manny Martinez .25 .11
❑ 272 Mike Thurman .25 .11
❑ 273 Ugueth Urbina .25 .11
❑ 274 Javier Vazquez .75 .35
❑ 275 Jose Vidro .75 .35
❑ 276 Rondell White .75 .35
❑ 277 Chris Widger .25 .11
❑ 278 Edgardo Alfonzo FOIL 8.00 3.60
❑ 279 Armando Benitez .75 .35
❑ 280 Roger Cedeno .25 .11
❑ 281 Dennis Cook UER .25 .11
Mistakenly printed as a RHP
❑ 282 Shawon Dunston .25 .11
❑ 283 Matt Franco .25 .11
❑ 284 Darryl Hamilton .25 .11
❑ 285 R. Henderson FOIL 15.00 6.75
❑ 286 Orel Hershiser .75 .35
❑ 287 Al Leiter UER .75 .35
Mistakenly printed as a RHP
❑ 288 John Olerud .75 .35
❑ 289 Rey Ordonez .25 .11
❑ 290 Mike Piazza FOIL 12.00 5.50
❑ 291 Kenny Rogers UER .25 .11
Mistakenly printed as a RHP
❑ 292 Robin Ventura 1.25 .55
❑ 293 Turk Wendell .25 .11
❑ 294 Masato Yoshii .25 .11
❑ 295 Scott Brosius .25 .11
❑ 296 Roger Clemens FOIL 12.00 5.50
❑ 297 David Cone FOIL * 2.50 1.10
❑ 298 Chad Curtis .25 .11
❑ 299 Chili Davis .75 .35
❑ 300 Orlando Hernandez .75 .35
❑ 301 Derek Jeter FOIL 15.00 6.75
❑ 302 Chuck Knoblauch .75 .35
❑ 303 Ricky Ledee .25 .11
❑ 304 Tino Martinez .75 .35
❑ 305 Ramiro Mendoza .25 .11
❑ 306 Paul O'Neill 2.00 .90
❑ 307 Andy Pettitte .75 .35
❑ 308 Jorge Posada .75 .35
❑ 309 Mariano Rivera FOIL 8.00 3.60
❑ 310 Mike Stanton .25 .11
❑ 311 Bernie Williams FOIL 5.00 2.20
❑ 312 Kevin Appier .25 .11
❑ 313 Eric Chavez .75 .35
❑ 314 Ryan Christenson .25 .11
❑ 315 Jason Giambi FOIL 5.00 2.20
❑ 316 Ben Grieve .75 .35
❑ 317 Buddy Groom .25 .11
❑ 318 Gil Heredia .25 .11
❑ 319 A.J. Hinch .25 .11
❑ 320 John Jaha .25 .11
❑ 321 Doug Jones .25 .11
❑ 322 Omar Olivares .25 .11
❑ 323 Tony Phillips .25 .11
❑ 324 Matt Stairs .25 .11
❑ 325 Miguel Tejada .75 .35
❑ 326 Randy Velarde FOIL 5.00 2.20
❑ 327 Bobby Abreu FOIL 8.00 3.60
❑ 328 Marlon Anderson .25 .11
❑ 329 Alex Arias .25 .11
❑ 330 Rico Brogna .25 .11
❑ 331 Paul Byrd .25 .11
❑ 332 Ron Gant .25 .11
❑ 333 Doug Glanville .25 .11
❑ 334 Wayne Gomes .25 .11
❑ 335 Kevin Jordan .25 .11
❑ 336 Mike Lieberthal .75 .35
❑ 337 Steve Montgomery .25 .11
❑ 338 Chad Ogea .25 .11
❑ 339 Scott Rolen 2.00 .90
❑ 340 Curt Schilling FOIL 5.00 2.20
❑ 341 Kevin Sefcik .25 .11
❑ 342 Mike Benjamin .25 .11
❑ 343 Kris Benson .75 .35
❑ 344 Adrian Brown .25 .11
❑ 345 Tom Goodwin .25 .11
❑ 345 Brant Brown .25 .11
❑ 346 Brad Clontz .25 .11
❑ 347 Brian Giles FOIL 8.00 3.60
❑ 348 Jason Kendall FOIL 8.00 3.60
❑ 349 Al Martin .25 .11
❑ 350 Warren Morris .25 .11
❑ 351 Todd Ritchie .25 .11
❑ 352 Scott Sauerbeck .25 .11
❑ 353 Jason Schmidt .25 .11
❑ 354 Ed Sprague .25 .11
❑ 355 Mike Williams .25 .11
❑ 356 Kevin Young .25 .11
❑ 357 Andy Ashby .25 .11
❑ 358 Ben Davis .75 .35
❑ 359 Tony Gwynn FOIL 10.00 4.50
❑ 360 Sterling Hitchcock .25 .11
❑ 361 Trevor Hoffman FOIL 8.00 3.60
❑ 362 Damian Jackson .25 .11
❑ 363 Wally Joyner .75 .35
❑ 364 Phil Nevin .75 .35
❑ 365 Eric Owens .25 .11
❑ 366 Ruben Rivera .25 .11
❑ 367 Reggie Sanders .25 .11
❑ 368 John VanderWal .25 .11
❑ 369 Quilvio Veras .25 .11
❑ 370 Matt Whisenant .25 .11
❑ 371 Woody Williams .25 .11
❑ 372 Rich Aurilia .75 .35
❑ 373 Marvin Benard .25 .11
❑ 374 Barry Bonds FOIL 15.00 6.75
❑ 375 Ellis Burks .25 .11
❑ 376 Alan Embree .25 .11
❑ 377 Shawn Estes .75 .35
❑ 378 John Johnstone .25 .11
❑ 379 Jeff Kent .25 .11
❑ 380 Brent Mayne .25 .11
❑ 381 Bill Mueller .25 .11
❑ 382 Robb Nen .25 .11
❑ 383 Russ Ortiz .25 .11
❑ 384 Kirk Rueter .25 .11
❑ 385 F.P. Santangelo .25 .11
❑ 386 J.T. Snow .75 .35
❑ 387 David Bell .25 .11
❑ 388 Jay Buhner .75 .35
❑ 389 Russ Davis .25 .11
❑ 390 Freddy Garcia 1.25 .55
❑ 391 Ken Griffey Jr. FOIL 20.00 9.00
❑ 392 John Halama .25 .11
❑ 393 Brian Hunter .25 .11
❑ 394 Raul Ibanez .25 .11
❑ 395 Tom Lampkin .25 .11
❑ 396 Edgar Martinez FOIL 5.00 2.20
❑ 397 Jose Mesa .25 .11
❑ 398 Jamie Moyer .25 .11
❑ 399 Jose Paniagua .25 .11
❑ 400 Alex Rodriguez FOIL 12.00 5.50
❑ 401 Dan Wilson .25 .11
❑ 402 Manny Aybar .25 .11
❑ 403 Ricky Bottalico .25 .11
❑ 404 Kent Bottenfield .25 .11
❑ 405 Darren Bragg .25 .11
❑ 406 Alberto Castillo .25 .11
❑ 407 J.D. Drew 2.00 .90
❑ 408 Jose Jimenez .25 .11
❑ 409 Ray Lankford .25 .11
❑ 410 Joe McEwing .25 .11
❑ 411 Willie McGee .75 .35
❑ 412 Mark McGwire FOIL 30.00 13.50
❑ 413 Darren Oliver .25 .11
❑ 414 Lance Painter .25 .11
❑ 415 Edgar Renteria .25 .11
❑ 416 Fernando Tatis FOIL 5.00 2.20
❑ 417 Wilson Alvarez .25 .11
❑ 418 Rolando Arrojo .25 .11
❑ 419 Wade Boggs 2.00 .90
❑ 420 Miguel Cairo .25 .11
❑ 421 Jose Canseco FOIL 5.00 2.20
❑ 422 John Flaherty .25 .11
❑ 423 Roberto Hernandez .25 .11
❑ 424 Dave Martinez .25 .11
❑ 425 Fred McGriff 1.25 .55
❑ 426 Paul Sorrento .25 .11
❑ 427 Kevin Stocker .25 .11
❑ 428 Bubba Trammell .25 .11
❑ 429 Rick White .25 .11
❑ 430 Randy Winn .25 .11
❑ 431 Bobby Witt .25 .11
❑ 432 Royce Clayton .25 .11
❑ 433 Tim Crabtree .25 .11
❑ 434 Juan Gonzalez 2.00 .90
❑ 436 Rusty Greer .25 .11
❑ 437 Rick Helling .25 .11
❑ 438 Mark McLemore .25 .11
❑ 439 Mike Morgan .25 .11
❑ 440 Rafael Palmeiro FOIL 5.00 2.20
❑ 441 Ivan Rodriguez FOIL 8.00 3.60
❑ 442 Aaron Sele .75 .35
❑ 443 Lee Stevens .25 .11
❑ 444 Mike Venafro .25 .11
❑ 445 John Wetteland .25 .11

❑ 446 Todd Zeile .75 .35
❑ 447 Jeff Zimmerman FOIL 5.00 2.20
❑ 448 Tony Batista .75 .35
❑ 449 Homer Bush .25 .11
❑ 450 Jose Cruz Jr. .25 .11
❑ 451 Carlos Delgado 2.00 .90
❑ 452 Kelvim Escobar .25 .11
❑ 453 Tony Fernandez FOIL 5.00 2.20
❑ 454 Darrin Fletcher .25 .11
❑ 455 Shawn Green FOIL 5.00 2.20
❑ 456 Pat Hentgen .25 .11
❑ 457 Billy Koch .25 .11
❑ 458 Graeme Lloyd .25 .11
❑ 459 Brian McRae .25 .11
❑ 460 David Segui .25 .11
❑ 461 Shannon Stewart .75 .35
❑ 462 David Wells .25 .11

2000 MLB Showdown Pennant Run 1st Edition

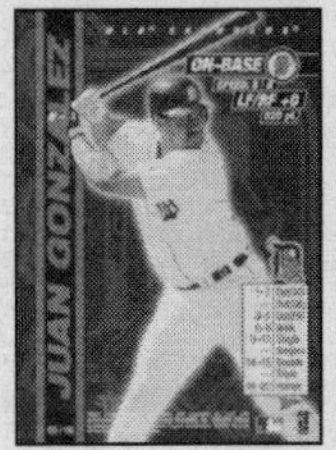

	MINT	NRMT
COMPLETE SET (150)	150.00	70.00
COMP.SET w/o FOIL (130)	30.00	13.50
COMMON CARD (1-150)	.25	.11
COMMON FOIL	4.00	1.80

❑ 1 Kent Bottenfield .25 .11
❑ 2 Ken Hill .25 .11
❑ 3 Adam Kennedy .25 .11
❑ 4 Ben Molina .25 .11
❑ 5 Scott Spiezio .25 .11
❑ 6 Brian Anderson .25 .11
❑ 7 Erubiel Durazo FOIL 4.00 1.80
❑ 8 Armando Reynoso .25 .11
❑ 9 Russ Springer .25 .11
❑ 10 Todd Stottlemyre .25 .11
❑ 11 Tony Womack .25 .11
❑ 12 Andres Galarraga FOIL 6.00 2.70
❑ 13 Javy Lopez FOIL 4.00 1.80
❑ 14 Kevin McGlinchy .25 .11
❑ 15 Terry Mulholland .25 .11
❑ 16 Reggie Sanders .25 .11
❑ 17 Harold Baines .75 .35
❑ 18 Will Clark 2.00 .90
❑ 19 Mike Trombley .25 .11
❑ 20 Manny Alexander .25 .11
❑ 21 Carl Everett FOIL 4.00 1.80
❑ 22 Ramon Martinez FOIL 4.00 1.80
❑ 23 Bret Saberhagen .75 .35
❑ 24 John Wasdin .25 .11
❑ 25 Joe Girardi .25 .11
❑ 26 Ricky Gutierrez .25 .11
❑ 27 Glenallen Hill .25 .11
❑ 28 Kevin Tapani .25 .11
❑ 29 Kerry Wood FOIL 8.00 3.60
❑ 30 Eric Young .25 .11
❑ 31 Keith Foulke FOIL 4.00 1.80
❑ 32 Mark Johnson .25 .11
❑ 33 Sean Lowe .25 .11
❑ 34 Jose Valentin .25 .11
❑ 35 Dante Bichette .75 .35
❑ 36 Ken Griffey Jr. FOIL 20.00 9.00
❑ 37 Denny Neagle .25 .11
❑ 38 Steve Parris .25 .11
❑ 39 Dennys Reyes .25 .11
❑ 40 Sandy Alomar Jr. .25 .11
❑ 41 Chuck Finley FOIL 4.00 1.80
❑ 42 Steve Karsay .25 .11
❑ 43 Steve Reed .25 .11
❑ 44 Jaret Wright .25 .11
❑ 45 Jeff Cirillo .75 .35
❑ 46 Tom Goodwin .25 .11
❑ 47 Jeffrey Hammonds .25 .11
❑ 48 Mike Lansing .25 .11
❑ 49 Aaron Ledesma .25 .11
❑ 50 Brent Mayne .25 .11
❑ 51 Doug Brocail .25 .11
❑ 52 Robert Fick .25 .11
❑ 53 Juan Gonzalez 2.00 .90
❑ 54 Hideo Nomo 2.00 .90
❑ 55 Luis Polonia .25 .11
❑ 56 Brant Brown .25 .11
❑ 57 Alex Fernandez .25 .11
❑ 58 Cliff Floyd .75 .35
❑ 59 Dan Miceli .25 .11
❑ 60 Vladimir Nunez .25 .11
❑ 61 Moises Alou FOIL 4.00 1.80
❑ 62 Roger Cedeno FOIL 4.00 1.80
❑ 63 Octavio Dotel .25 .11
❑ 64 Mitch Meluskey .25 .11
❑ 65 Daryle Ward .25 .11
❑ 66 Mark Quinn FOIL 4.00 1.80
❑ 67 Brad Rigby .25 .11
❑ 68 Blake Stein .25 .11
❑ 69 Mac Suzuki .25 .11
❑ 70 Terry Adams .25 .11
❑ 71 Darren Dreifort .25 .11
❑ 72 Kevin Elster .25 .11
❑ 73 Shawn Green FOIL 8.00 3.60
❑ 74 Todd Hollandsworth .25 .11
❑ 75 Gregg Olson .25 .11
❑ 76 Kevin Barker .25 .11
❑ 77 Jose Hernandez .25 .11
❑ 78 Dave Weathers .25 .11
❑ 79 Hector Carrasco .25 .11
❑ 80 Eddie Guardado .25 .11
❑ 81 Jacque Jones .75 .35
❑ 82 David Ortiz .75 .35
❑ 83 Peter Bergeron .25 .11
❑ 84 Hideki Irabu .25 .11
❑ 85 Lee Stevens .25 .11
❑ 86 Anthony Telford .25 .11
❑ 87 Derek Bell .25 .11
❑ 88 John Franco .75 .35
❑ 89 Mike Hampton FOIL 4.00 1.80
❑ 90 Bobby Jones .25 .11
❑ 91 Todd Pratt .25 .11
❑ 92 Todd Zeile .75 .35
❑ 93 Jason Grimsley .25 .11
❑ 94 Roberto Kelly .25 .11
❑ 95 Jim Leyritz .25 .11
❑ 96 Ramiro Mendoza .25 .11
❑ 97 Rich Becker .25 .11
❑ 98 Ramon Hernandez .25 .11
❑ 99 Tim Hudson FOIL 8.00 3.60
❑ 100 Jason Isringhausen .25 .11
❑ 101 Mike Magnante .25 .11
❑ 102 Olmedo Saenz .25 .11
❑ 103 Mickey Morandini .25 .11
❑ 104 Robert Person .25 .11
❑ 105 Desi Relaford .25 .11
❑ 106 Jason Christiansen .25 .11
❑ 107 Wil Cordero .25 .11
❑ 108 Francisco Cordova .25 .11
❑ 109 Chad Hermansen .25 .11
❑ 110 Pat Meares .25 .11
❑ 111 Aramis Ramirez .75 .35
❑ 112 Bret Boone .75 .35
❑ 113 Matt Clement .25 .11
❑ 114 Carlos Hernandez .25 .11
❑ 115 Ryan Klesko .75 .35
❑ 116 Dave Magadan .25 .11
❑ 117 Al Martin .25 .11
❑ 118 Bobby Estalella .25 .11
❑ 119 Livan Hernandez .25 .11
❑ 120 Doug Mirabelli .25 .11
❑ 121 Joe Nathan .25 .11
❑ 122 Mike Cameron .75 .35
❑ 123 Mark McLemore .25 .11
❑ 124 Gil Meche .25 .11
❑ 125 John Olerud .75 .35
❑ 126 Arthur Rhodes .25 .11
❑ 127 Aaron Sele FOIL 4.00 1.80
❑ 128 Jim Edmonds FOIL 6.00 2.70
❑ 129 Pat Hentgen .25 .11
❑ 130 Darryl Kile .75 .35
❑ 131 Eli Marrero .25 .11
❑ 132 Dave Veres .25 .11
❑ 133 Fernando Vina .25 .11
❑ 134 Vinny Castilla .75 .35
❑ 135 Juan Guzman .25 .11
❑ 136 Ryan Rupe .25 .11
❑ 137 Greg Vaughn FOIL 4.00 1.80
❑ 138 Gerald Williams .25 .11
❑ 139 Esteban Yan .25 .11
❑ 140 Tom Evans .25 .11
❑ 141 Gabe Kapler .75 .35
❑ 142 Ruben Mateo FOIL 4.00 1.80
❑ 143 Kenny Rogers .25 .11
❑ 144 David Segui .25 .11
❑ 145 Tony Batista .75 .35
❑ 146 Chris Carpenter .25 .11
❑ 147 Brad Fullmer .75 .35
❑ 148 Alex Gonzalez .25 .11
❑ 149 Roy Halladay .25 .11
❑ 150 Raul Mondesi FOIL 4.00 1.80

2001 MLB Showdown 1st Edition

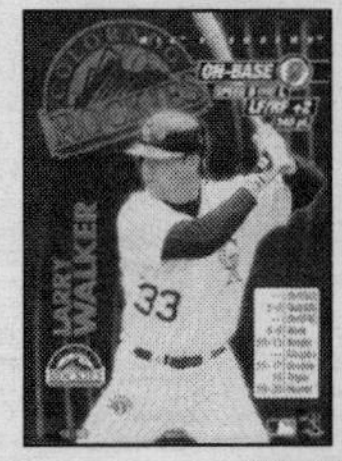

	MINT	NRMT
COMPLETE SET (462)	400.00	180.00
COMP.SET w/o FOIL (400)	100.00	45.00

ERSTAD/VLADDIE IN EVERY STARTER DECK

❑ 1 Garret Anderson .75 .35
❑ 2 Darin Erstad FOIL * 5.00 2.20
❑ 3 Ron Gant .75 .35
❑ 4 Troy Glaus FOIL 8.00 3.60
❑ 5 Shigetoshi Hasegawa .75 .35
❑ 6 Adam Kennedy .25 .11
❑ 7 Al Levine RC .25 .11
❑ 8 Ben Molina .25 .11
❑ 9 Troy Percival .25 .11
❑ 10 Mark Petkovsek .25 .11
❑ 11 Tim Salmon .75 .35
❑ 12 Scott Schoeneweis .25 .11
❑ 13 Scott Spiezio .25 .11
❑ 14 Mo Vaughn .75 .35
❑ 15 Jarrod Washburn .25 .11
❑ 16 Brian Anderson .25 .11
❑ 17 Danny Bautista .25 .11
❑ 18 Jay Bell .75 .35
❑ 19 Greg Colbrunn .25 .11
❑ 20 Steve Finley .75 .35
❑ 21 Luis Gonzalez 8.00 3.60
❑ 22 Randy Johnson FOIL 15.00 6.75
❑ 23 Byung-Hyun Kim .75 .35
❑ 24 Matt Mantei .25 .11
❑ 25 Mike Morgan .25 .11
❑ 26 Curt Schilling 2.00 .90
❑ 27 Kelly Stinnett .25 .11
❑ 28 Greg Swindell .25 .11
❑ 29 Matt Williams 1.25 .55
❑ 30 Tony Womack .25 .11
❑ 31 Andy Ashby .25 .11
❑ 32 Bobby Bonilla .75 .35
❑ 33 Rafael Furcal FOIL 5.00 2.20
❑ 34 Andres Galarraga 1.25 .55
❑ 35 Tom Glavine FOIL 8.00 3.60
❑ 36 Andruw Jones 2.00 .90

❑ 37 Chipper Jones FOIL 10.00 4.50
❑ 38 Brian Jordan .75 .35
❑ 39 Wally Joyner .75 .35
❑ 40 Keith Lockhart .25 .11
❑ 41 Javy Lopez .75 .35
❑ 42 Greg Maddux FOIL 12.00 5.50
❑ 43 Kevin Millwood .25 .11
❑ 44 Mike Remlinger .25 .11
❑ 45 John Rocker .75 .35
❑ 46 B.J. Surhoff .75 .35
❑ 47 Quilvio Veras .25 .11
❑ 48 Brady Anderson .75 .35
❑ 49 Albert Belle .75 .35
❑ 50 Jeff Conine .25 .11
❑ 51 Delino DeShields .25 .11
❑ 52 Buddy Groom .25 .11
❑ 53 Trenidad Hubbard .25 .11
❑ 54 Luis Matos .25 .11
❑ 55 Jose Mercedes .25 .11
❑ 56 Melvin Mora .25 .11
❑ 57 Mike Mussina FOIL 8.00 3.60
❑ 58 Sidney Ponson .25 .11
❑ 59 Pat Rapp .25 .11
❑ 60 Chris Richard .75 .35
❑ 61 Cal Ripken FOIL 15.00 6.75
❑ 62 Mike Trombley .25 .11
❑ 63 Rolando Arrojo .25 .11
❑ 64 Dante Bichette .75 .35
❑ 65 Rheal Cormier .25 .11
❑ 66 Carl Everett .75 .35
❑ 67 Rich Garces .25 .11
❑ 68 Nomar Garciaparra FOIL 12.00 5.50
❑ 69 Mike Lansing .25 .11
❑ 70 Darren Lewis .25 .11
❑ 71 Derek Lowe .25 .11
❑ 72 Pedro Martinez FOIL 20.00 9.00
❑ 73 Ramon Martinez .25 .11
❑ 74 Trot Nixon .75 .35
❑ 75 Jose Offerman .25 .11
❑ 76 Troy O'Leary .25 .11
❑ 77 Jason Varitek .75 .35
❑ 78 Rick Aguilera .25 .11
❑ 79 Damon Buford .25 .11
❑ 80 Joe Girardi .25 .11
❑ 81 Mark Grace 2.00 .90
❑ 82 Willie Greene .25 .11
❑ 83 Ricky Gutierrez .25 .11
❑ 84 Felix Heredia .25 .11
❑ 85 Jon Lieber .25 .11
❑ 86 Jeff Reed .25 .11
❑ 87 Sammy Sosa FOIL 15.00 6.75
❑ 88 Kevin Tapani .25 .11
❑ 89 Todd Van Poppel .25 .11
❑ 90 Rondell White .75 .35
❑ 91 Kerry Wood 2.00 .90
❑ 92 Eric Young .25 .11
❑ 93 James Baldwin .25 .11
❑ 94 Ray Durham .75 .35
❑ 95 Keith Foulke FOIL 5.00 2.20
❑ 96 Bob Howry .25 .11
❑ 97 Charles Johnson FOIL 5.00 2.20
❑ 98 Mark Johnson .25 .11
❑ 99 Paul Konerko .75 .35
❑ 100 Carlos Lee .75 .35
❑ 101 Magglio Ordonez .75 .35
❑ 102 Jim Parque .25 .11
❑ 103 Herbert Perry .25 .11
❑ 104 Bill Simas .25 .11
❑ 105 Chris Singleton .25 .11
❑ 106 Mike Sirotka .25 .11
❑ 107 Frank Thomas FOIL 10.00 4.50
❑ 108 Jose Valentin .25 .11
❑ 109 Kelly Wunsch .25 .11
❑ 110 Aaron Boone .25 .11
❑ 111 Sean Casey 1.25 .55
❑ 112 Danny Graves .25 .11
❑ 113 Ken Griffey Jr. FOIL 20.00 9.00
❑ 114 Pete Harnisch .25 .11
❑ 115 Barry Larkin FOIL 8.00 3.60
❑ 116 Alex Ochoa .25 .11
❑ 117 Steve Parris .25 .11
❑ 118 Pokey Reese .25 .11
❑ 119 Chris Stynes .25 .11
❑ 120 Scott Sullivan .25 .11
❑ 121 Eddie Taubensee .25 .11
❑ 122 Michael Tucker .25 .11
❑ 123 Ron Villone .25 .11
❑ 124 Dmitri Young .75 .35
❑ 125 Roberto Alomar FOIL 8.00 3.60
❑ 126 Sandy Alomar Jr. .75 .35
❑ 127 Jason Bere .25 .11
❑ 128 Dave Burba .25 .11
❑ 129 Bartolo Colon .75 .35
❑ 130 Wil Cordero .25 .11
❑ 131 Chuck Finley .75 .35
❑ 132 Travis Fryman .75 .35
❑ 133 Steve Karsay .25 .11
❑ 134 Kenny Lofton .75 .35
❑ 135 Manny Ramirez FOIL 10.00 4.50
❑ 136 David Segui .25 .11
❑ 137 Jim Thome 2.00 .90
❑ 138 Omar Vizquel .75 .35
❑ 139 Bob Wickman .25 .11
❑ 140 Pedro Astacio .25 .11
❑ 141 Brian Bohanon .25 .11
❑ 142 Jeff Cirillo .75 .35
❑ 143 Jeff Frye .25 .11
❑ 144 Jeffrey Hammonds .25 .11
❑ 145 Todd Helton FOIL 15.00 6.75
❑ 146 Todd Hollandsworth .25 .11
❑ 147 Butch Huskey .25 .11
❑ 148 Jose Jimenez .25 .11
❑ 149 Brent Mayne .25 .11
❑ 150 Neifi Perez .25 .11
❑ 151 Terry Shumpert .25 .11
❑ 152 Larry Walker 1.25 .55
❑ 153 Gabe White FOIL 5.00 2.20
❑ 154 Masato Yoshii .75 .35
❑ 155 Matt Anderson .25 .11
❑ 156 Brad Ausmus .25 .11
❑ 157 Rich Becker .25 .11
❑ 158 Tony Clark .75 .35
❑ 159 Deivi Cruz .25 .11
❑ 160 Damion Easley .25 .11
❑ 161 Juan Encarnacion .75 .35
❑ 162 Juan Gonzalez 2.00 .90
❑ 163 Shane Halter .25 .11
❑ 164 Bobby Higginson .75 .35
❑ 165 Todd Jones FOIL 5.00 2.20
❑ 166 Brian Moehler .25 .11
❑ 167 Hideo Nomo 2.00 .90
❑ 168 Dean Palmer .75 .35
❑ 169 Jeff Weaver .75 .35
❑ 170 Antonio Alfonseca .25 .11
❑ 171 Luis Castillo FOIL 5.00 2.20
❑ 172 Ryan Dempster FOIL 5.00 2.20
❑ 173 Cliff Floyd .75 .35
❑ 174 Alex Gonzalez .25 .11
❑ 175 Mark Kotsay .75 .35
❑ 176 Derrek Lee .75 .35
❑ 177 Braden Looper .25 .11
❑ 178 Mike Lowell .75 .35
❑ 179 Brad Penny .25 .11
❑ 180 Mike Redmond .25 .11
❑ 181 Henry Rodriguez .25 .11
❑ 182 Jesus Sanchez .25 .11
❑ 183 Mark Smith .25 .11
❑ 184 Preston Wilson .75 .35
❑ 185 Moises Alou .75 .35
❑ 186 Jeff Bagwell FOIL 15.00 6.75
❑ 187 Lance Berkman 2.00 .90
❑ 188 Craig Biggio 1.25 .55
❑ 189 Tim Bogar .25 .11
❑ 190 Jose Cabrera .25 .11
❑ 191 Octavio Dotel .75 .35
❑ 192 Scott Elarton FOIL 5.00 2.20
❑ 193 Richard Hidalgo .75 .35
❑ 194 Chris Holt .25 .11
❑ 195 Jose Lima .25 .11
❑ 196 Julio Lugo .25 .11
❑ 197 Mitch Meluskey .25 .11
❑ 198 Bill Spiers .25 .11
❑ 199 Daryle Ward .25 .11
❑ 200 Carlos Beltran .75 .35
❑ 201 Ricky Bottalico .25 .11
❑ 202 Johnny Damon FOIL 5.00 2.20
❑ 203 Jermaine Dye .75 .35
❑ 204 Carlos Febles .25 .11
❑ 205 Dave McCarty .25 .11
❑ 206 Mark Quinn .75 .35
❑ 207 Joe Randa .25 .11
❑ 208 Dan Reichert .25 .11
❑ 209 Rey Sanchez .25 .11
❑ 210 Jose Santiago .25 .11
❑ 211 Jeff Suppan .25 .11
❑ 212 Mac Suzuki .75 .35
❑ 213 Mike Sweeney .75 .35
❑ 214 Gregg Zaun .25 .11
❑ 215 Terry Adams .25 .11
❑ 216 Adrian Beltre .75 .35
❑ 217 Kevin Brown FOIL 5.00 2.20
❑ 218 Alex Cora .25 .11
❑ 219 Darren Dreifort .25 .11
❑ 220 Tom Goodwin .25 .11
❑ 221 Shawn Green 2.00 .90
❑ 222 Mark Grudzielanek .25 .11
❑ 223 Dave Hansen .25 .11
❑ 224 Todd Hundley .25 .11
❑ 225 Eric Karros .75 .35
❑ 226 Chad Kreuter .25 .11
❑ 227 Chan Ho Park .75 .35
❑ 228 Jeff Shaw .25 .11
❑ 229 Gary Sheffield FOIL 5.00 2.20
❑ 230 Juan Acevedo .25 .11
❑ 231 Ron Belliard .25 .11
❑ 232 Henry Blanco .25 .11
❑ 233 Jeromy Burnitz .75 .35
❑ 234 Jeff D'Amico FOIL 5.00 2.20
❑ 235 Valerio De Los Santos .25 .11
❑ 236 Marquis Grissom .25 .11
❑ 237 Charlie Hayes .25 .11
❑ 238 Jimmy Haynes .25 .11
❑ 239 Jose Hernandez .25 .11
❑ 240 Geoff Jenkins .75 .35
❑ 241 Curtis Leskanic .25 .11
❑ 242 Mark Loretta .25 .11
❑ 243 Richie Sexson .75 .35
❑ 244 Dave Weathers .25 .11
❑ 245 Jay Canizaro .25 .11
❑ 246 Ron Coomer .25 .11
❑ 247 Cristian Guzman .75 .35
❑ 248 LaTroy Hawkins .25 .11
❑ 249 Denny Hocking .25 .11
❑ 250 Torii Hunter .75 .35
❑ 251 Jacque Jones .75 .35
❑ 252 Corey Koskie .75 .35
❑ 253 Matt Lawton .75 .35
❑ 254 Matt LeCroy .25 .11
❑ 255 Eric Milton .75 .35
❑ 256 David Ortiz .75 .35
❑ 257 Brad Radke FOIL 5.00 2.20
❑ 258 Mark Redman .25 .11
❑ 259 Bob Wells .25 .11
❑ 260 Michael Barrett .25 .11
❑ 261 Peter Bergeron .25 .11
❑ 262 Milton Bradley .25 .11
❑ 263 Orlando Cabrera .25 .11
❑ 264 Vladimir Guerrero FOIL * 5.00 2.20
❑ 265 Wilton Guerrero .25 .11
❑ 266 Dustin Hermanson .25 .11
❑ 267 Terry Jones .25 .11
❑ 268 Steve Kline .25 .11
❑ 269 Felipe Lira .25 .11
❑ 270 Mike Mordecai .25 .11
❑ 271 Lee Stevens .25 .11
❑ 272 Anthony Telford .25 .11
❑ 273 Javier Vazquez .75 .35
❑ 274 Jose Vidro FOIL 5.00 2.20
❑ 275 Edgardo Alfonzo FOIL 5.00 2.20
❑ 276 Derek Bell .25 .11
❑ 277 Armando Benitez .75 .35
❑ 278 Mike Bordick .25 .11
❑ 279 Mike Hampton FOIL 5.00 2.20
❑ 280 Lenny Harris .25 .11
❑ 281 Al Leiter .75 .35
❑ 282 Jay Payton .25 .11
❑ 283 Mike Piazza FOIL 12.00 5.50
❑ 284 Todd Pratt .25 .11
❑ 285 Glendon Rusch .25 .11
❑ 286 Bubba Trammell .25 .11
❑ 287 Robin Ventura .75 .35
❑ 288 Turk Wendell .25 .11
❑ 289 Rick White .25 .11
❑ 290 Todd Zeile .75 .35
❑ 291 Scott Brosius .75 .35
❑ 292 Roger Clemens FOIL 12.00 5.50
❑ 293 Jason Grimsley .25 .11
❑ 294 Orlando Hernandez .75 .35

	No.	Player	Mint	NrMt
❑	295	Derek Jeter FOIL	15.00	6.75
❑	296	Dave Justice	.75	.35
❑	297	Chuck Knoblauch	.75	.35
❑	298	Tino Martinez	.75	.35
❑	299	Denny Neagle	.25	.11
❑	300	Jeff Nelson	.25	.11
❑	301	Paul O'Neill	2.00	.90
❑	302	Andy Pettitte	.75	.35
❑	303	Jorge Posada	.75	.35
❑	304	Mariano Rivera FOIL	5.00	2.20
❑	305	Jose Vizcaino	.25	.11
❑	306	Bernie Williams FOIL	8.00	3.60
❑	307	Kevin Appier	.75	.35
❑	308	Eric Chavez	.75	.35
❑	309	Ryan Christenson	.25	.11
❑	310	Jason Giambi FOIL	20.00	9.00
❑	311	Jeremy Giambi	.25	.11
❑	312	Ben Grieve	.75	.35
❑	313	Gil Heredia	.25	.11
❑	314	Ramon Hernandez	.25	.11
❑	315	Tim Hudson FOIL	8.00	3.60
❑	316	Jason Isringhausen	.25	.11
❑	317	Terrence Long FOIL	5.00	2.20
❑	318	Jim Mecir	.25	.11
❑	319	Mark Mulder	1.25	.55
❑	320	Matt Stairs	.25	.11
❑	321	Miguel Tejada	.75	.35
❑	322	Randy Velarde	.25	.11
❑	323	Bobby Abreu	.75	.35
❑	324	Jeff Brantley	.25	.11
❑	325	Pat Burrell	.75	.35
❑	326	Omar Daal	.25	.11
❑	327	Rob Ducey	.25	.11
❑	328	Doug Glanville	.25	.11
❑	329	Wayne Gomes	.25	.11
❑	330	Kevin Jordan	.25	.11
❑	331	Travis Lee	.75	.35
❑	332	Mike Lieberthal	.75	.35
❑	333	Vicente Padilla	.25	.11
❑	334	Robert Person	.25	.11
❑	335	Scott Rolen FOIL	8.00	3.60
❑	336	Kevin Sefcik	.25	.11
❑	337	Randy Wolf	.25	.11
❑	338	Jimmy Anderson	.25	.11
❑	339	Mike Benjamin	.25	.11
❑	340	Kris Benson	.75	.35
❑	341	Adrian Brown	.25	.11
❑	342	Brian Giles FOIL	5.00	2.20
❑	343	Jason Kendall FOIL	5.00	2.20
❑	344	Pat Meares	.25	.11
❑	345	Warren Morris	.25	.11
❑	346	Aramis Ramirez	.75	.35
❑	347	Todd Ritchie	.25	.11
❑	348	Scott Sauerbeck	.25	.11
❑	349	Jose Silva	.25	.11
❑	350	John VanderWal	.25	.11
❑	351	Mike Williams	.25	.11
❑	352	Kevin Young	.25	.11
❑	353	Carlos Almanzar	.25	.11
❑	354	Bret Boone	.75	.35
❑	355	Matt Clement	.25	.11
❑	356	Adam Eaton	.75	.35
❑	357	Wiki Gonzalez	.25	.11
❑	358	Trevor Hoffman FOIL	5.00	2.20
❑	359	Damian Jackson	.25	.11
❑	360	Ryan Klesko	.75	.35
❑	361	Phil Nevin FOIL	5.00	2.20
❑	362	Eric Owens	.25	.11
❑	363	Desi Relaford	.25	.11
❑	364	Ruben Rivera	.25	.11
❑	365	Kevin Walker	.25	.11
❑	366	Woody Williams	.25	.11
❑	367	Jay Witasick	.25	.11
❑	368	Rich Aurilia	.75	.35
❑	369	Marvin Benard	.25	.11
❑	370	Barry Bonds FOIL	20.00	9.00
❑	371	Ellis Burks	.75	.35
❑	372	Bobby Estalella	.25	.11
❑	373	Doug Henry	.25	.11
❑	374	Livan Hernandez	.75	.35
❑	375	Jeff Kent FOIL	5.00	2.20
❑	376	Doug Mirabelli	.25	.11
❑	377	Bill Mueller	.25	.11
❑	378	Calvin Murray	.25	.11
❑	379	Robb Nen FOIL	5.00	2.20
❑	380	Russ Ortiz	.25	.11
❑	381	Armando Rios	.25	.11
❑	382	Felix Rodriguez	.25	.11
❑	383	Kirk Rueter	.25	.11
❑	384	J.T. Snow	.75	.35
❑	385	Paul Abbott	.25	.11
❑	386	David Bell	.25	.11
❑	387	Jay Buhner	.75	.35
❑	388	Mike Cameron	.75	.35
❑	389	John Halama	.25	.11
❑	390	Rickey Henderson	4.00	1.80
❑	391	Al Martin	.25	.11
❑	392	Edgar Martinez FOIL	5.00	2.20
❑	393	Mark McLemore	.25	.11
❑	394	John Olerud	.75	.35
❑	395	Jose Paniagua	.25	.11
❑	396	Arthur Rhodes	.25	.11
❑	397	Alex Rodriguez FOIL	12.00	5.50
❑	398	Kazuhiro Sasaki FOIL	10.00	4.50
❑	399	Aaron Sele	.75	.35
❑	400	Dan Wilson	.25	.11
❑	401	Rick Ankiel FOIL	5.00	2.20
❑	402	Will Clark	2.00	.90
❑	403	J.D. Drew	2.00	.90
❑	404	Jim Edmonds FOIL	5.00	2.20
❑	405	Pat Hentgen	.25	.11
❑	406	Darryl Kile	.25	.11
❑	407	Ray Lankford	.25	.11
❑	408	Mike Matheny	.25	.11
❑	409	Mark McGwire FOIL	25.00	11.00
❑	410	Craig Paquette	.25	.11
❑	411	Placido Polanco	.25	.11
❑	412	Edgar Renteria	.25	.11
❑	413	Garrett Stephenson	.25	.11
❑	414	Fernando Tatis	.25	.11
❑	415	Mike Timlin	.25	.11
❑	416	Dave Veres	.25	.11
❑	417	Fernando Vina	.25	.11
❑	418	Miguel Cairo	.25	.11
❑	419	Vinny Castilla	.75	.35
❑	420	Steve Cox	.25	.11
❑	421	Doug Creek	.25	.11
❑	422	John Flaherty	.25	.11
❑	423	Jose Guillen	.25	.11
❑	424	Roberto Hernandez FOIL	5.00	2.20
❑	425	Russ Johnson	.25	.11
❑	426	Albie Lopez	.25	.11
❑	427	Felix Martinez	.25	.11
❑	428	Fred McGriff	1.25	.55
❑	429	Bryan Rekar	.25	.11
❑	430	Greg Vaughn	.75	.35
❑	431	Gerald Williams	.25	.11
❑	432	Esteban Yan	.25	.11
❑	433	Luis Alicea	.25	.11
❑	434	Frank Catalanotto	.25	.11
❑	435	Royce Clayton	.25	.11
❑	436	Tim Crabtree	.25	.11
❑	437	Chad Curtis	.25	.11
❑	438	Rusty Greer	.75	.35
❑	439	Rick Helling	.25	.11
❑	440	Gabe Kapler	.75	.35
❑	441	Mike Lamb	.25	.11
❑	442	Ricky Ledee	.25	.11
❑	443	Rafael Palmeiro	2.00	.90
❑	444	Ivan Rodriguez FOIL	8.00	3.60
❑	445	Kenny Rogers	.25	.11
❑	446	Mike Venafro	.25	.11
❑	447	John Wetteland	.75	.35
❑	448	Tony Batista FOIL	5.00	2.20
❑	449	Jose Cruz Jr.	.75	.35
❑	450	Carlos Delgado FOIL	15.00	6.75
❑	451	Kelvim Escobar	.25	.11
❑	452	Darrin Fletcher	.25	.11
❑	453	Brad Fullmer	.75	.35
❑	454	Alex Gonzalez	.25	.11
❑	455	Mark Guthrie	.25	.11
❑	456	Billy Koch	.25	.11
❑	457	Esteban Loaiza	.25	.11
❑	458	Raul Mondesi	.75	.35
❑	459	Mickey Morandini	.25	.11
❑	460	Paul Quantrill	.25	.11
❑	461	Shannon Stewart	.75	.35
❑	462	David Wells FOIL	5.00	2.20

2001 MLB Showdown Pennant Run

	MINT	NRMT
COMPLETE SET (175)	200.00	90.00
COMP.SET w/o FOIL (150)	40.00	18.00
COMMON CARD (1-175)	.25	.11
COMMON FOIL	5.00	2.20

	No.	Player	Mint	NrMt
❑	1	Randy Velarde	.25	.11
❑	2	Dustin Hermanson	.25	.11
❑	3	Jamie Moyer	.25	.11
❑	4	Aaron Fultz	.25	.11
❑	5	Barry Zito FOIL	10.00	4.50
❑	6	Adam Piatt	.75	.35
❑	7	Ben Grieve	.75	.35
❑	8	C.C. Sabathia FOIL	8.00	3.60
❑	9	Eddie Guardado	.25	.11
❑	10	Matt Kinney	.25	.11
❑	11	Blake Stein	.25	.11
❑	12	Billy Wagner FOIL	8.00	3.60
❑	13	Chris Holt	.25	.11
❑	14	Homer Bush	.25	.11
❑	15	Vladimir Nunez	.25	.11
❑	16	C.J. Nitkowski	.25	.11
❑	17	Juan Pierre	.75	.35
❑	18	Jose Valentin	.25	.11
❑	19	Juan Gonzalez	2.00	.90
❑	20	Derek Bell	.25	.11
❑	21	Wade Miller	.75	.35
❑	22	Shawn Estes	.75	.35
❑	23	Enrique Wilson	.25	.11
❑	24	Dave Magadan	.25	.11
❑	25	Jason Christiansen	.25	.11
❑	26	Paul Shuey	.25	.11
❑	27	Mark Wohlers	.25	.11
❑	28	John Riedling	.25	.11
❑	29	Francisco Cordova	.25	.11
❑	30	Craig House	.25	.11
❑	31	Scott Strickland	.25	.11
❑	32	Octavio Dotel	.25	.11
❑	33	Jimmy Rollins FOIL	8.00	3.60
❑	34	Carl Pavano	.25	.11
❑	35	Sandy Alomar Jr.	.75	.35
❑	36	Hideki Irabu	.25	.11
❑	37	Tom Gordon	.25	.11
❑	38	Roosevelt Brown	.25	.11
❑	39	Alex Rodriguez FOIL	20.00	9.00
❑	40	Andres Galarraga	1.25	.55
❑	41	Rob Bell	.25	.11
❑	42	Jason Schmidt	.25	.11
❑	43	Rod Beck	.25	.11
❑	44	Paul Rigdon	.25	.11
❑	45	Dan Miceli	.25	.11
❑	46	Ricky Bones	.25	.11
❑	47	Mike Hampton FOIL	8.00	3.60
❑	48	Cliff Politte	.25	.11
❑	49	Chris Stynes	.25	.11
❑	50	Ramiro Mendoza	.25	.11
❑	51	Todd Walker	.25	.11
❑	52	Fernando Seguignol	.25	.11
❑	53	Mark Guthrie	.25	.11
❑	54	Tony Armas Jr.	.75	.35
❑	55	Billy McMillon	.25	.11
❑	56	Gary Bennett	.25	.11
❑	57	Corey Patterson FOIL	5.00	2.20
❑	58	Juan Guzman	.25	.11
❑	59	Joe Crede	.75	.35

❑ 60	A.J. Pierzynski	.25	.11
❑ 61	Ben Davis	.75	.35
❑ 62	Alan Embree	.25	.11
❑ 63	Jon Garland FOIL	8.00	3.60
❑ 64	Ryan Kohlmeier	.25	.11
❑ 65	Andy Benes	.25	.11
❑ 66	Ron Gant	.75	.35
❑ 67	Jerry Hairston Jr.	.25	.11
❑ 68	Odalis Perez	.25	.11
❑ 69	Lance Painter	.25	.11
❑ 70	David Segui	.25	.11
❑ 71	Russ Davis	.25	.11
❑ 72	Jeff Zimmerman	.25	.11
❑ 73	Dennys Reyes	.25	.11
❑ 74	Jamey Wright	.25	.11
❑ 75	Rico Brogna	.25	.11
❑ 76	Geraldo Guzman	.25	.11
❑ 77	Eric Gagne	.25	.11
❑ 78	Bruce Chen	.25	.11
❑ 79	Justin Speier	.25	.11
❑ 80	Randy Keisler	.25	.11
❑ 81	Ellis Burks FOIL	8.00	3.60
❑ 82	Alfonso Soriano	2.00	.90
❑ 83	Jeff Nelson	.25	.11
❑ 84	Wes Helms	.25	.11
❑ 85	Freddy Garcia FOIL	8.00	3.60
❑ 86	Erubiel Durazo	.25	.11
❑ 87	Ben Sheets FOIL	8.00	3.60
❑ 88	Jose Ortiz FOIL	8.00	3.60
❑ 89	Paul Wilson	.25	.11
❑ 90	Onan Masaoka	.25	.11
❑ 91	Jose Rosado	.25	.11
❑ 92	A.J. Burnett	.75	.35
❑ 93	Bubba Trammell	.25	.11
❑ 94	Mike Fetters	.25	.11
❑ 95	Jacob Cruz	.25	.11
❑ 96	John Franco	.75	.35
❑ 97	Armando Reynoso	.75	.35
❑ 98	Lou Pote	.25	.11
❑ 99	D'Angelo Jimenez FOIL	5.00	2.20
❑ 100	Julio Zuleta	.25	.11
❑ 101	Charles Johnson FOIL	8.00	3.60
❑ 102	Tsuyoshi Shinjo RC	4.00	1.80
❑ 103	Brett Tomko	.25	.11
❑ 104	Marcus Giles	.75	.35
❑ 105	Craig Counsell	.25	.11
❑ 106	Ruben Mateo	.75	.35
❑ 107	Andy Ashby	.25	.11
❑ 108	Marlon Anderson	.25	.11
❑ 109	Mark Grace	2.00	.90
❑ 110	Russ Branyan	.75	.35
❑ 111	Julian Tavarez	.25	.11
❑ 112	Joey Hamilton	.25	.11
❑ 113	Jason LaRue	.25	.11
❑ 114	Benji Gil	.25	.11
❑ 115	Bill Mueller	.25	.11
❑ 116	Mike Stanton	.25	.11
❑ 117	Ray King	.25	.11
❑ 118	Timo Perez	.25	.11
❑ 119	Johnny Damon FOIL	5.00	2.20
❑ 120	Matt Morris	.75	.35
❑ 121	Kevin Appier	.75	.35
❑ 122	Frank Castillo	.25	.11
❑ 123	Mike Darr	.25	.11
❑ 124	Felipe Crespo	.25	.11
❑ 125	John Smoltz FOIL	8.00	3.60
❑ 126	Ben Weber	.25	.11
❑ 127	Luis Rivas	.25	.11
❑ 128	Travis Harper	.25	.11
❑ 129	Aubrey Huff	.25	.11
❑ 130	Paul LoDuca	.75	.35
❑ 131	Eric Davis	.75	.35
❑ 132	Fernando Tatis	.25	.11
❑ 133	Ugueth Urbina	.25	.11
❑ 134	Steve Kline	.25	.11
❑ 135	Tanyon Sturtze	.25	.11
❑ 136	Scott Hatteberg	.25	.11
❑ 137	Tomokazu Ohka FOIL	8.00	3.60
❑ 138	Melvin Mora	.25	.11
❑ 139	Kip Wells	.25	.11
❑ 140	Ken Caminiti	.75	.35
❑ 141	Dave Martinez	.25	.11
❑ 142	Robert Fick	.25	.11
❑ 143	Mike Bordick	.75	.35
❑ 144	Doug Mientkiewicz	.75	.35
❑ 145	Darryl Hamilton	.25	.11
❑ 146	Shane Reynolds	.25	.11
❑ 147	Vernon Wells FOIL	5.00	2.20
❑ 148	Rey Ordonez	.25	.11
❑ 149	Brad Ausmus	.25	.11
❑ 150	Jay Powell	.25	.11
❑ 151	Todd Hundley	.25	.11
❑ 152	Travis Miller	.25	.11
❑ 153	Tyler Houston	.25	.11
❑ 154	Nelson Cruz	.25	.11
❑ 155	Manny Ramirez FOIL	12.00	5.50
❑ 156	Luis Lopez	.25	.11
❑ 157	Luis Sojo	.25	.11
❑ 158	Tony Gwynn FOIL	10.00	4.50
❑ 159	Roger Cedeno	.25	.11
❑ 160	Royce Clayton	.25	.11
❑ 161	Olmedo Saenz	.25	.11
❑ 162	Brook Fordyce	.25	.11
❑ 163	Dee Brown	.25	.11
❑ 164	David Wells FOIL	5.00	2.20
❑ 165	Jack Wilson RC	.75	.35
❑ 166	Pedro Feliz	.25	.11
❑ 167	Hideo Nomo	2.00	.90
❑ 168	Albert Pujols FOIL RC	20.00	9.00
❑ 169	Ichiro Suzuki FOIL RC	40.00	18.00
❑ 170	Ramon Ortiz	.75	.35
❑ 171	Mike Holtz	.25	.11
❑ 172	Chris Woodward	.25	.11
❑ 173	Mike Mussina FOIL	10.00	4.50
❑ 174	Carlos Guillen	.25	.11
❑ 175	Ben Petrick FOIL	5.00	2.20

1994 Pacific

	MINT	NRMT
COMPLETE SET (660)	40.00	18.00

❑ 1	Steve Avery	.10	.05
❑ 2	Steve Bedrosian	.10	.05
❑ 3	Damon Berryhill	.10	.05
❑ 4	Jeff Blauser	.10	.05
❑ 5	Sid Bream	.10	.05
❑ 6	Francisco Cabrera	.10	.05
❑ 7	Ramon Caraballo	.10	.05
❑ 8	Ron Gant	.10	.05
❑ 9	Tom Glavine	.40	.18
❑ 10	Chipper Jones	.75	.35
❑ 11	Dave Justice	.15	.07
❑ 12	Ryan Klesko	.15	.07
❑ 13	Mark Lemke	.10	.05
❑ 14	Javier Lopez	.15	.07
❑ 15	Greg Maddux	1.00	.45
❑ 16	Fred McGriff	.25	.11
❑ 17	Greg McMichael	.10	.05
❑ 18	Kent Mercker	.10	.05
❑ 19	Otis Nixon	.10	.05
❑ 20	Terry Pendleton	.15	.07
❑ 21	Deion Sanders	.15	.07
❑ 22	John Smoltz	.15	.07
❑ 23	Tony Tarasco	.10	.05
❑ 24	Manny Alexander	.10	.05
❑ 25	Brady Anderson	.15	.07
❑ 26	Harold Baines	.15	.07
❑ 27	Damon Buford	.10	.05
❑ 28	Paul Carey	.10	.05
❑ 29	Mike Devereaux	.10	.05
❑ 30	Todd Frohwirth	.10	.05
❑ 31	Leo Gomez	.10	.05
❑ 32	Jeffrey Hammonds	.15	.07
❑ 33	Chris Hoiles	.10	.05
❑ 34	Tim Hulett	.10	.05
❑ 35	Ben McDonald	.10	.05
❑ 36	Mark McLemore	.10	.05
❑ 37	Alan Mills	.10	.05
❑ 38	Mike Mussina	.40	.18
❑ 39	Sherman Obando	.10	.05
❑ 40	Gregg Olson	.10	.05
❑ 41	Mike Pagliarulo	.10	.05
❑ 42	Jim Poole	.10	.05
❑ 43	Harold Reynolds	.10	.05
❑ 44	Cal Ripken	1.50	.70
❑ 45	David Segui	.10	.05
❑ 46	Fernando Valenzuela	.15	.07
❑ 47	Jack Voigt	.10	.05
❑ 48	Scott Bankhead	.10	.05
❑ 49	Roger Clemens	1.00	.45
❑ 50	Scott Cooper	.10	.05
❑ 51	Danny Darwin	.10	.05
❑ 52	Andre Dawson	.25	.11
❑ 53	John Dopson	.10	.05
❑ 54	Scott Fletcher	.10	.05
❑ 55	Tony Fossas	.10	.05
❑ 56	Mike Greenwell	.10	.05
❑ 57	Billy Hatcher	.10	.05
❑ 58	Jeff McNeely	.10	.05
❑ 59	Jose Melendez	.10	.05
❑ 60	Tim Naehring	.10	.05
❑ 61	Tony Pena	.10	.05
❑ 62	Paul Quantrill	.10	.05
❑ 63	Carlos Quintana	.10	.05
❑ 64	Luis Rivera	.10	.05
❑ 65	Jeff Russell	.10	.05
❑ 66	Aaron Sele	.15	.07
❑ 67	John Valentin	.10	.05
❑ 68	Mo Vaughn	.15	.07
❑ 69	Frank Viola	.15	.07
❑ 70	Bob Zupcic	.10	.05
❑ 71	Mike Butcher	.10	.05
❑ 72	Rod Correia	.10	.05
❑ 73	Chad Curtis	.10	.05
❑ 74	Chili Davis	.15	.07
❑ 75	Gary DiSarcina	.10	.05
❑ 76	Damion Easley	.10	.05
❑ 77	John Farrell	.10	.05
❑ 78	Chuck Finley	.15	.07
❑ 79	Joe Grahe	.10	.05
❑ 80	Stan Javier	.10	.05
❑ 81	Mark Langston	.10	.05
❑ 82	Phil Leftwich RC	.10	.05
❑ 83	Torey Lovullo	.10	.05
❑ 84	Joe Magrane	.10	.05
❑ 85	Greg Myers	.10	.05
❑ 86	Eduardo Perez	.10	.05
❑ 87	Luis Polonia	.10	.05
❑ 88	Tim Salmon	.15	.07
❑ 89	J.T. Snow	.15	.07
❑ 90	Kurt Stillwell	.10	.05
❑ 91	Ron Tingley	.10	.05
❑ 92	Chris Turner	.10	.05
❑ 93	Julio Valera	.10	.05
❑ 94	Jose Bautista	.10	.05
❑ 95	Shawn Boskie	.10	.05
❑ 96	Steve Buechele	.10	.05
❑ 97	Frank Castillo	.10	.05
❑ 98	Mark Grace UER (stats have 98 home runs in 1993; should be 14)	.40	.18
❑ 99	Jose Guzman	.10	.05
❑ 100	Mike Harkey	.10	.05
❑ 101	Greg Hibbard	.10	.05
❑ 102	Doug Jennings	.10	.05
❑ 103	Derrick May	.10	.05
❑ 104	Mike Morgan	.10	.05
❑ 105	Randy Myers	.10	.05
❑ 106	Karl Rhodes	.10	.05
❑ 107	Kevin Roberson	.10	.05
❑ 108	Rey Sanchez	.10	.05
❑ 109	Ryne Sandberg	.50	.23
❑ 110	Tommy Shields	.10	.05
❑ 111	Dwight Smith	.10	.05
❑ 112	Sammy Sosa	.75	.35
❑ 113	Jose Vizcaino	.10	.05
❑ 114	Turk Wendell	.10	.05
❑ 115	Rick Wilkins	.10	.05
❑ 116	Willie Wilson	.10	.05

❑ 117 Ed. Zambrano RC .10 .05
❑ 118 Wilson Alvarez .10 .05
❑ 119 Tim Belcher .10 .05
❑ 120 Jason Bere .10 .05
❑ 121 Rodney Bolton .10 .05
❑ 122 Ellis Burks .15 .07
❑ 123 Joey Cora .10 .05
❑ 124 Alex Fernandez .10 .05
❑ 125 Ozzie Guillen .10 .05
❑ 126 Craig Grebeck .10 .05
❑ 127 Roberto Hernandez .10 .05
❑ 128 Bo Jackson .15 .07
❑ 129 Lance Johnson .10 .05
❑ 130 Ron Karkovice .10 .05
❑ 131 Mike LaValliere .10 .05
❑ 132 Norberto Martin .10 .05
❑ 133 Kirk McCaskill .10 .05
❑ 134 Jack McDowell .10 .05
❑ 135 Scott Radinsky .10 .05
❑ 136 Tim Raines .15 .07
❑ 137 Steve Sax .10 .05
❑ 138 Frank Thomas .50 .23
❑ 139 Dan Pasqua .10 .05
❑ 140 Robin Ventura .15 .07
❑ 141 Jeff Branson .10 .05
❑ 142 Tom Browning .10 .05
❑ 143 Jacob Brumfield .10 .05
❑ 144 Tim Costo .10 .05
❑ 145 Rob Dibble .10 .05
❑ 146 Brian Dorsett .10 .05
❑ 147 Steve Foster .10 .05
❑ 148 Cesar Hernandez .10 .05
❑ 149 Roberto Kelly .10 .05
❑ 150 Barry Larkin .40 .18
❑ 151 Larry Luebbers .10 .05
❑ 152 Kevin Mitchell .10 .05
❑ 153 Joe Oliver .10 .05
❑ 154 Tim Pugh .10 .05
❑ 155 Jeff Reardon .15 .07
❑ 156 Jose Rijo .10 .05
❑ 157 Bip Roberts .10 .05
❑ 158 Chris Sabo .10 .05
❑ 159 Juan Samuel .10 .05
❑ 160 Reggie Sanders .10 .05
❑ 161 John Smiley .10 .05
❑ 162 Jerry Spradlin .10 .05
❑ 163 Gary Varsho .10 .05
❑ 164 Sandy Alomar Jr. .15 .07
❑ 165 Albert Belle .15 .07
❑ 166 Carlos Baerga .10 .05
❑ 167 Mark Clark .10 .05
❑ 168 Alvaro Espinoza .10 .05
❑ 169 Felix Fermin .10 .05
❑ 170 Reggie Jefferson .10 .05
❑ 171 Wayne Kirby .10 .05
❑ 172 Tom Kramer .10 .05
❑ 173 Kenny Lofton .15 .07
❑ 174 Jesse Levis .10 .05
❑ 175 Candy Maldonado .10 .05
❑ 176 Carlos Martinez .10 .05
❑ 177 Jose Mesa .10 .05
❑ 178 Jeff Mutis .10 .05
❑ 179 Charles Nagy .10 .05
❑ 180 Bob Ojeda .10 .05
❑ 181 Junior Ortiz .10 .05
❑ 182 Eric Plunk .10 .05
❑ 183 Manny Ramirez .60 .25
❑ 184 Paul Sorrento .10 .05
❑ 185 Jeff Treadway .10 .05
❑ 186 Bill Wertz .10 .05
❑ 187 Freddie Benavides .10 .05
❑ 188 Dante Bichette .15 .07
❑ 189 Willie Blair .10 .05
❑ 190 Daryl Boston .10 .05
❑ 191 Pedro Castellano .10 .05
❑ 192 Vinny Castilla .15 .07
❑ 193 Jerald Clark .10 .05
❑ 194 Alex Cole .10 .05
❑ 195 Andres Galarraga .25 .11
❑ 196 Joe Girardi .10 .05
❑ 197 Charlie Hayes .10 .05
❑ 198 Darren Holmes .10 .05
❑ 199 Chris Jones .10 .05
❑ 200 Curt Leskanic .10 .05
❑ 201 Roberto Mejia .10 .05
❑ 202 David Nied .10 .05
❑ 203 J. Owens .10 .05
❑ 204 Steve Reed .10 .05
❑ 205 Armando Reynoso .10 .05
❑ 206 Bruce Ruffin .10 .05
❑ 207 Keith Shepherd .10 .05
❑ 208 Jim Tatum .10 .05
❑ 209 Eric Young .10 .05
❑ 210 Skeeter Barnes .10 .05
❑ 211 Danny Bautista .10 .05
❑ 212 Tom Bolton .10 .05
❑ 213 Eric Davis .15 .07
❑ 214 Storm Davis .10 .05
❑ 215 Cecil Fielder .15 .07
❑ 216 Travis Fryman .15 .07
❑ 217 Kirk Gibson .15 .07
❑ 218 Dan Gladden .10 .05
❑ 219 John Doherty .10 .05
❑ 220 Chris Gomez .10 .05
❑ 221 David Haas .10 .05
❑ 222 Bill Krueger .10 .05
❑ 223 Chad Kreuter .10 .05
❑ 224 Mark Leiter .10 .05
❑ 225 Bob MacDonald .10 .05
❑ 226 Mike Moore .10 .05
❑ 227 Tony Phillips .10 .05
❑ 228 Rich Rowland .10 .05
❑ 229 Mickey Tettleton .10 .05
❑ 230 Alan Trammell .25 .11
❑ 231 Lou Whitaker .15 .07
❑ 232 David Wells .15 .07
❑ 233 Luis Aquino .10 .05
❑ 234 Alex Arias .10 .05
❑ 235 Jack Armstrong .10 .05
❑ 236 Ryan Bowen .10 .05
❑ 237 Chuck Carr .10 .05
❑ 238 Matias Carrillo .10 .05
❑ 239 Jeff Conine .10 .05
❑ 240 Henry Cotto .10 .05
❑ 241 Orestes Destrade .10 .05
❑ 242 Chris Hammond .10 .05
❑ 243 Bryan Harvey .10 .05
❑ 244 Charlie Hough .15 .07
❑ 245 Richie Lewis .10 .05
❑ 246 Mitch Lyden .10 .05
❑ 247 Dave Magadan .10 .05
❑ 248 Bob Natal .10 .05
❑ 249 Benito Santiago .10 .05
❑ 250 Gary Sheffield .15 .07
❑ 251 Matt Turner .10 .05
❑ 252 David Weathers .10 .05
❑ 253 Walt Weiss .10 .05
❑ 254 Darrell Whitmore .10 .05
❑ 255 Nigel Wilson .10 .05
❑ 256 Eric Anthony .10 .05
❑ 257 Jeff Bagwell .50 .23
❑ 258 Kevin Bass .10 .05
❑ 259 Craig Biggio .25 .11
❑ 260 Ken Caminiti .15 .07
❑ 261 Andujar Cedeno .10 .05
❑ 262 Chris Donnels .10 .05
❑ 263 Doug Drabek .10 .05
❑ 264 Tom Edens .10 .05
❑ 265 Steve Finley .15 .07
❑ 266 Luis Gonzalez .40 .18
❑ 267 Pete Harnisch .10 .05
❑ 268 Xavier Hernandez .10 .05
❑ 269 Todd Jones .10 .05
❑ 270 Darryl Kile .15 .07
❑ 271 Al Osuna .10 .05
❑ 272 Rick Parker .10 .05
❑ 273 Mark Portugal .10 .05
❑ 274 Scott Servais .10 .05
❑ 275 Greg Swindell .10 .05
❑ 276 Eddie Taubensee .10 .05
❑ 277 Jose Uribe .10 .05
❑ 278 Brian Williams .10 .05
❑ 279 Kevin Appier .15 .07
❑ 280 Billy Brewer .10 .05
❑ 281 David Cone .15 .07
❑ 282 Greg Gagne .10 .05
❑ 283 Tom Gordon .10 .05
❑ 284 Chris Gwynn .10 .05
❑ 285 John Habyan .10 .05
❑ 286 Chris Haney .10 .05
❑ 287 Phil Hiatt .10 .05
❑ 288 David Howard .10 .05
❑ 289 Felix Jose .10 .05
❑ 290 Wally Joyner .15 .07
❑ 291 Kevin Koslofski .10 .05
❑ 292 Jose Lind .10 .05
❑ 293 Brent Mayne .10 .05
❑ 294 Mike Macfarlane .10 .05
❑ 295 Brian McRae .10 .05
❑ 296 Kevin McReynolds .10 .05
❑ 297 Keith Miller .10 .05
❑ 298 Jeff Montgomery .10 .05
❑ 299 Hipolito Pichardo .10 .05
❑ 300 Rico Rossy .10 .05
❑ 301 Curtis Wilkerson .10 .05
❑ 302 Pedro Astacio .10 .05
❑ 303 Rafael Bournigal .10 .05
❑ 304 Brett Butler .15 .07
❑ 305 Tom Candiotti .10 .05
❑ 306 Omar Daal .10 .05
❑ 307 Jim Gott .10 .05
❑ 308 Kevin Gross .10 .05
❑ 309 Dave Hansen .10 .05
❑ 310 Carlos Hernandez .10 .05
❑ 311 Orel Hershiser .15 .07
❑ 312 Eric Karros .15 .07
❑ 313 Pedro Martinez .60 .25
❑ 314 Ramon Martinez .10 .05
❑ 315 Roger McDowell .10 .05
❑ 316 Raul Mondesi .15 .07
❑ 317 Jose Offerman .10 .05
❑ 318 Mike Piazza 1.25 .55
❑ 319 Jody Reed .10 .05
❑ 320 Henry Rodriguez .10 .05
❑ 321 Cory Snyder .10 .05
❑ 322 Darryl Strawberry .15 .07
❑ 323 Tim Wallach .10 .05
❑ 324 Steve Wilson .10 .05
❑ 325 Juan Bell .10 .05
❑ 326 Ricky Bones .10 .05
❑ 327 Alex Diaz RC .10 .05
❑ 328 Cal Eldred .10 .05
❑ 329 Darryl Hamilton .10 .05
❑ 330 Doug Henry .10 .05
❑ 331 John Jaha .10 .05
❑ 332 Pat Listach .10 .05
❑ 333 Graeme Lloyd .10 .05
❑ 334 Carlos Maldonado .10 .05
❑ 335 Angel Miranda .10 .05
❑ 336 Jaime Navarro .10 .05
❑ 337 Dave Nilsson .10 .05
❑ 338 Rafael Novoa .10 .05
❑ 339 Troy O'Leary .10 .05
❑ 340 Jesse Orosco .10 .05
❑ 341 Kevin Seitzer .10 .05
❑ 342 Bill Spiers .10 .05
❑ 343 William Suero .10 .05
❑ 344 B.J. Surhoff .15 .07
❑ 345 Dickie Thon .10 .05
❑ 346 Jose Valentin .10 .05
❑ 347 Greg Vaughn .15 .07
❑ 348 Robin Yount .40 .18
❑ 349 Willie Banks .10 .05
❑ 350 Bernardo Brito .10 .05
❑ 351 Scott Erickson .10 .05
❑ 352 Mark Guthrie .10 .05
❑ 353 Chip Hale .10 .05
❑ 354 Brian Harper .10 .05
❑ 355 Kent Hrbek .15 .07
❑ 356 Terry Jorgensen .10 .05
❑ 357 Chuck Knoblauch .15 .07
❑ 358 Gene Larkin .10 .05
❑ 359 Scott Leius .10 .05
❑ 360 Shane Mack .10 .05
❑ 361 David McCarty .10 .05
❑ 362 Pat Meares .10 .05
❑ 363 Pedro Munoz .10 .05
❑ 364 Derek Parks .10 .05
❑ 365 Kirby Puckett 1.00 .45
❑ 366 Jeff Reboulet .10 .05
❑ 367 Kevin Tapani .10 .05
❑ 368 Mike Trombley .10 .05
❑ 369 George Tsamis .10 .05
❑ 370 Carl Willis .10 .05
❑ 371 Dave Winfield .40 .18
❑ 372 Moises Alou .15 .07
❑ 373 Brian Barnes .10 .05
❑ 374 Sean Berry .10 .05

❑ 375 Frank Bolick .10 .05
❑ 376 Wil Cordero .10 .05
❑ 377 Delino DeShields .10 .05
❑ 378 Jeff Fassero .10 .05
❑ 379 Darrin Fletcher .10 .05
❑ 380 Cliff Floyd .15 .07
❑ 381 Lou Frazier .10 .05
❑ 382 Marquis Grissom .10 .05
❑ 383 Gil Heredia .10 .05
❑ 384 Mike Lansing .10 .05
❑ 385 Oreste Marrero RC .10 .05
❑ 386 Dennis Martinez .15 .07
❑ 387 Curtis Pride RC .15 .07
❑ 388 Mel Rojas .10 .05
❑ 389 Kirk Rueter .10 .05
❑ 390 Joe Siddall .10 .05
❑ 391 John Vander Wal .10 .05
❑ 392 Larry Walker .25 .11
❑ 393 John Wetteland .15 .07
❑ 394 Rondell White .15 .07
❑ 395 Tim Bogar .10 .05
❑ 396 Bobby Bonilla .15 .07
❑ 397 Jeromy Burnitz .15 .07
❑ 398 Mike Draper .10 .05
❑ 399 Sid Fernandez .10 .05
❑ 400 John Franco .15 .07
❑ 401 Dave Gallagher .10 .05
❑ 402 Dwight Gooden .15 .07
❑ 403 Eric Hillman .10 .05
❑ 404 Todd Hundley .10 .05
❑ 405 Butch Huskey .10 .05
❑ 406 Jeff Innis .10 .05
❑ 407 Howard Johnson .10 .05
❑ 408 Jeff Kent .25 .11
❑ 409 Ced Landrum .10 .05
❑ 410 Mike Maddux .10 .05
❑ 411 Josias Manzanillo .10 .05
❑ 412 Jeff McKnight .10 .05
❑ 413 Eddie Murray .40 .18
❑ 414 Tito Navarro .10 .05
❑ 415 Joe Orsulak .10 .05
❑ 416 Bret Saberhagen .15 .07
❑ 417 Dave Telgheder .10 .05
❑ 418 Ryan Thompson .10 .05
❑ 419 Chico Walker .10 .05
❑ 420 Jim Abbott .15 .07
❑ 421 Wade Boggs .40 .18
❑ 422 Mike Gallego .10 .05
❑ 423 Mark Hutton .10 .05
❑ 424 Dion James .10 .05
❑ 425 Domingo Jean .10 .05
❑ 426 Pat Kelly .10 .05
❑ 427 Jimmy Key .15 .07
❑ 428 Jim Leyritz .10 .05
❑ 429 Kevin Maas .10 .05
❑ 430 Don Mattingly 1.00 .45
❑ 431 Bobby Munoz .10 .05
❑ 432 Matt Nokes .10 .05
❑ 433 Paul O'Neill .40 .18
❑ 434 Spike Owen .10 .05
❑ 435 Melido Perez .10 .05
❑ 436 Lee Smith .15 .07
❑ 437 Andy Stankiewicz .10 .05
❑ 438 Mike Stanley .10 .05
❑ 439 Danny Tartabull .10 .05
❑ 440 Randy Velarde .10 .05
❑ 441 Bernie Williams .40 .18
❑ 442 Gerald Williams .10 .05
❑ 443 Mike Witt .10 .05
❑ 444 Marcos Armas .10 .05
❑ 445 Lance Blankenship .10 .05
❑ 446 Mike Bordick .10 .05
❑ 447 Ron Darling UER .10 .05
Reversed negative on front
❑ 448 Dennis Eckersley .15 .07
❑ 449 Brent Gates .10 .05
❑ 450 Rich Gossage .15 .07
❑ 451 Scott Hemond .10 .05
❑ 452 Dave Henderson .10 .05
❑ 453 Shawn Hillegas .10 .05
❑ 454 Rick Honeycutt .10 .05
❑ 455 Scott Lydy .10 .05
❑ 456 Mark McGwire 1.50 .70
❑ 457 Henry Mercedes .10 .05
❑ 458 Mike Mohler .10 .05
❑ 459 Troy Neel .10 .05
❑ 460 Edwin Nunez .10 .05
❑ 461 Craig Paquette .10 .05
❑ 462 Ruben Sierra .10 .05
❑ 463 Terry Steinbach .10 .05
❑ 464 Todd Van Poppel .10 .05
❑ 465 Bob Welch .10 .05
❑ 466 Bobby Witt .10 .05
❑ 467 Ruben Amaro .10 .05
❑ 468 Larry Andersen .10 .05
❑ 469 Kim Batiste .10 .05
❑ 470 Wes Chamberlain .10 .05
❑ 471 Darren Daulton .15 .07
❑ 472 Mariano Duncan .10 .05
❑ 473 Len Dykstra .15 .07
❑ 474 Jim Eisenreich .10 .05
❑ 475 Tommy Greene .10 .05
❑ 476 Dave Hollins .10 .05
❑ 477 Pete Incaviglia .10 .05
❑ 478 Danny Jackson .10 .05
❑ 479 John Kruk .15 .07
❑ 480 Tony Longmire .10 .05
❑ 481 Jeff Manto .10 .05
❑ 482 Mickey Morandini .10 .05
❑ 483 Terry Mulholland .10 .05
❑ 484 Todd Pratt .10 .05
❑ 485 Ben Rivera .10 .05
❑ 486 Curt Schilling .40 .18
❑ 487 Kevin Stocker .10 .05
❑ 488 Milt Thompson .10 .05
❑ 489 David West .10 .05
❑ 490 Mitch Williams .10 .05
❑ 491 Jeff Ballard .10 .05
❑ 492 Jay Bell .15 .07
❑ 493 Scott Bullett .10 .05
❑ 494 Dave Clark .10 .05
❑ 495 Steve Cooke .10 .05
❑ 496 Midre Cummings .10 .05
❑ 497 Mark Dewey .10 .05
❑ 498 Carlos Garcia .10 .05
❑ 499 Jeff King .10 .05
❑ 500 Al Martin .10 .05
❑ 501 Lloyd McClendon .10 .05
❑ 502 Orlando Merced .10 .05
❑ 503 Blas Minor .10 .05
❑ 504 Denny Neagle .15 .07
❑ 505 Tom Prince .10 .05
❑ 506 Don Slaught .10 .05
❑ 507 Zane Smith .10 .05
❑ 508 Randy Tomlin .10 .05
❑ 509 Andy Van Slyke .15 .07
❑ 510 Paul Wagner .10 .05
❑ 511 Tim Wakefield .10 .05
❑ 512 Bob Walk .10 .05
❑ 513 John Wehner .10 .05
❑ 514 Kevin Young .10 .05
❑ 515 Billy Bean .10 .05
❑ 516 Andy Benes .10 .05
❑ 517 Derek Bell .10 .05
❑ 518 Doug Brocail .10 .05
❑ 519 Jarvis Brown .10 .05
❑ 520 Phil Clark .10 .05
❑ 521 Mark Davis .10 .05
❑ 522 Jeff Gardner .10 .05
❑ 523 Pat Gomez .10 .05
❑ 524 Ricky Gutierrez .10 .05
❑ 525 Tony Gwynn .75 .35
❑ 526 Gene Harris .10 .05
❑ 527 Kevin Higgins .10 .05
❑ 528 Trevor Hoffman .15 .07
❑ 529 Luis Lopez .10 .05
❑ 530 Pedro A.Martinez RC .10 .05
❑ 531 Melvin Nieves .10 .05
❑ 532 Phil Plantier .10 .05
❑ 533 Frank Seminara .10 .05
❑ 534 Craig Shipley .10 .05
❑ 535 Tim Teufel .10 .05
❑ 536 Guillermo Velasquez .10 .05
❑ 537 Wally Whitehurst .10 .05
❑ 538 Rod Beck .10 .05
❑ 539 Todd Benzinger .10 .05
❑ 540 Barry Bonds 1.00 .45
❑ 541 Jeff Brantley .10 .05
❑ 542 Dave Burba .10 .05
❑ 543 John Burkett .10 .05
❑ 544 Will Clark .40 .18
❑ 545 Royce Clayton .10 .05
❑ 546 Bryan Hickerson .10 .05
❑ 547 Mike Jackson .10 .05
❑ 548 Darren Lewis .10 .05
❑ 549 Kirt Manwaring .10 .05
❑ 550 Dave Martinez .10 .05
❑ 551 Willie McGee .15 .07
❑ 552 Jeff Reed .10 .05
❑ 553 Dave Righetti .15 .07
❑ 554 Kevin Rogers .10 .05
❑ 555 Steve Scarsone .10 .05
❑ 556 Bill Swift .10 .05
❑ 557 Robby Thompson .10 .05
❑ 558 Salomon Torres .10 .05
❑ 559 Matt Williams .25 .11
❑ 560 Trevor Wilson .10 .05
❑ 561 Rich Amaral .10 .05
❑ 562 Mike Blowers .10 .05
❑ 563 Chris Bosio .10 .05
❑ 564 Jay Buhner .15 .07
❑ 565 Norm Charlton .10 .05
❑ 566 Jim Converse .10 .05
❑ 567 Rich DeLucia .10 .05
❑ 568 Mike Felder .10 .05
❑ 569 Dave Fleming .10 .05
❑ 570 Ken Griffey Jr. 1.25 .55
❑ 571 Bill Haselman .10 .05
❑ 572 Dwayne Henry .10 .05
❑ 573 Brad Holman .10 .05
❑ 574 Randy Johnson .50 .23
❑ 575 Greg Litton .10 .05
❑ 576 Edgar Martinez .25 .11
❑ 577 Tino Martinez .15 .07
❑ 578 Jeff Nelson .10 .05
❑ 579 Marc Newfield .10 .05
❑ 580 Roger Salkeld .10 .05
❑ 581 Mackey Sasser .10 .05
❑ 582 Brian Turang RC .10 .05
❑ 583 Omar Vizquel .15 .07
❑ 584 Dave Valle .10 .05
❑ 585 Luis Alicea .10 .05
❑ 586 Rene Arocha .10 .05
❑ 587 Rheal Cormier .10 .05
❑ 588 Tripp Cromer .10 .05
❑ 589 Bernard Gilkey .10 .05
❑ 590 Lee Guetterman .10 .05
❑ 591 Gregg Jefferies .10 .05
❑ 592 Tim Jones .10 .05
❑ 593 Paul Kilgus .10 .05
❑ 594 Les Lancaster .10 .05
❑ 595 Omar Olivares .10 .05
❑ 596 Jose Oquendo .10 .05
❑ 597 Donovan Osborne .10 .05
❑ 598 Tom Pagnozzi .10 .05
❑ 599 Erik Pappas .10 .05
❑ 600 Geronimo Pena .10 .05
❑ 601 Mike Perez .10 .05
❑ 602 Gerald Perry .10 .05
❑ 603 Stan Royer .10 .05
❑ 604 Ozzie Smith .50 .23
❑ 605 Bob Tewksbury .10 .05
❑ 606 Allen Watson .10 .05
❑ 607 Mark Whiten .10 .05
❑ 608 Todd Zeile .10 .05
❑ 609 Jeff Bronkey .10 .05
❑ 610 Kevin Brown .15 .07
❑ 611 Jose Canseco .40 .18
❑ 612 Doug Dascenzo .10 .05
❑ 613 Butch Davis .10 .05
❑ 614 Mario Diaz .10 .05
❑ 615 Julio Franco .15 .07
❑ 616 Benji Gil .10 .05
❑ 617 Juan Gonzalez .40 .18
❑ 618 Tom Henke .10 .05
❑ 619 Jeff Huson .10 .05
❑ 620 David Hulse .10 .05
❑ 621 Craig Lefferts .10 .05
❑ 622 Rafael Palmeiro .40 .18
❑ 623 Dean Palmer .15 .07
❑ 624 Bob Patterson .10 .05
❑ 625 Roger Pavlik .10 .05
❑ 626 Gary Redus .10 .05
❑ 627 Ivan Rodriguez .40 .18
❑ 628 Kenny Rogers .10 .05
❑ 629 Jon Shave .10 .05
❑ 630 Doug Strange .10 .05
❑ 631 Matt Whiteside .10 .05

No.	Player	Mint	NrMt
632	Roberto Alomar	.40	.18
633	Pat Borders	.10	.05
634	Scott Brow	.10	.05
635	Rob Butler	.10	.05
636	Joe Carter	.15	.07
637	Tony Castillo	.10	.05
638	Mark Eichhorn	.10	.05
639	Tony Fernandez	.10	.05
640	Huck Flener RC	.10	.05
641	Alfredo Griffin	.10	.05
642	Juan Guzman	.10	.05
643	Rickey Henderson	.75	.35
644	Pat Hentgen	.10	.05
645	Randy Knorr	.10	.05
646	Al Leiter	.15	.07
647	Domingo Martinez	.10	.05
648	Paul Molitor	.40	.18
649	Jack Morris	.15	.07
650	John Olerud	.15	.07
651	Ed Sprague	.10	.05
652	Dave Stewart	.15	.07
653	Devon White	.10	.05
654	Woody Williams	.10	.05
655	Barry Bonds MVP	.50	.23
656	Greg Maddux CY	.50	.23
657	Jack McDowell CY	.10	.05
658	Mike Piazza ROY	.60	.25
659	Tim Salmon ROY	.10	.05
660	Frank Thomas MVP	.25	.11

1995 Pacific

	MINT	NRMT
COMPLETE SET (450)	40.00	18.00

No.	Player	Mint	NrMt
1	Steve Avery	.10	.05
2	Rafael Belliard	.10	.05
3	Jeff Blauser	.10	.05
4	Tom Glavine	.40	.18
5	David Justice	.15	.07
6	Mike Kelly	.10	.05
7	Roberto Kelly	.10	.05
8	Ryan Klesko	.15	.07
9	Mark Lemke	.10	.05
10	Javier Lopez	.15	.07
11	Greg Maddux	1.00	.45
12	Fred McGriff	.25	.11
13	Greg McMichael	.10	.05
14	Jose Oliva	.10	.05
15	John Smoltz	.15	.07
16	Tony Tarasco	.10	.05
17	Brady Anderson	.15	.07
18	Harold Baines	.15	.07
19	Armando Benitez	.15	.07
20	Mike Devereaux	.10	.05
21	Leo Gomez	.10	.05
22	Jeffrey Hammonds	.10	.05
23	Chris Hoiles	.10	.05
24	Ben McDonald	.10	.05
25	Mark McLemore	.10	.05
26	Jamie Moyer	.10	.05
27	Mike Mussina	.40	.18
28	Rafael Palmeiro	.40	.18
29	Jim Poole	.10	.05
30	Cal Ripken Jr.	1.50	.70
31	Lee Smith	.15	.07
32	Mark Smith	.10	.05
33	Jose Canseco	.40	.18
34	Roger Clemens	1.00	.45
35	Scott Cooper	.10	.05
36	Andre Dawson	.25	.11
37	Tony Fossas	.10	.05
38	Mike Greenwell	.10	.05
39	Chris Howard	.10	.05
40	Jose Melendez	.10	.05
41	Nate Minchey	.10	.05
42	Tim Naehring	.10	.05
43	Otis Nixon	.10	.05
44	Carlos Rodriguez	.10	.05
45	Aaron Sele	.15	.07
46	Lee Tinsley	.10	.05
47	Sergio Valdez	.10	.05
48	John Valentin	.10	.05
49	Mo Vaughn	.15	.07
50	Brian Anderson	.10	.05
51	Garret Anderson	.15	.07
52	Rod Correia	.10	.05
53	Chad Curtis	.10	.05
54	Mark Dalesandro	.10	.05
55	Chili Davis	.15	.07
56	Gary DiSarcina	.10	.05
57	Damion Easley	.10	.05
58	Jim Edmonds	.25	.11
59	Jorge Fabregas	.10	.05
60	Chuck Finley	.15	.07
61	Bo Jackson	.15	.07
62	Mark Langston	.10	.05
63	Eduardo Perez	.10	.05
64	Tim Salmon	.15	.07
65	J.T. Snow	.15	.07
66	Willie Banks	.10	.05
67	Jose Bautista	.10	.05
68	Shawon Dunston	.10	.05
69	Kevin Foster	.10	.05
70	Mark Grace	.40	.18
71	Jose Guzman	.10	.05
72	Jose Hernandez	.10	.05
73	Blaise Ilsley	.10	.05
74	Derrick May	.10	.05
75	Randy Myers	.10	.05
76	Karl Rhodes	.10	.05
77	Kevin Roberson	.10	.05
78	Rey Sanchez	.10	.05
79	Sammy Sosa	.75	.35
80	Steve Trachsel	.10	.05
81	Eddie Zambrano	.10	.05
82	Wilson Alvarez	.10	.05
83	Jason Bere	.10	.05
84	Joey Cora	.10	.05
85	Jose DeLeon	.10	.05
86	Alex Fernandez	.10	.05
87	Julio Franco	.15	.07
88	Ozzie Guillen	.10	.05
89	Joe Hall	.10	.05
90	Roberto Hernandez	.10	.05
91	Darrin Jackson	.10	.05
92	Lance Johnson	.10	.05
93	Norberto Martin	.10	.05
94	Jack McDowell	.10	.05
95	Tim Raines	.15	.07
96	Olmedo Saenz	.10	.05
97	Frank Thomas	.50	.23
98	Robin Ventura	.15	.07
99	Bret Boone	.15	.07
100	Jeff Brantley	.10	.05
101	Jacob Brumfield	.10	.05
102	Hector Carrasco	.10	.05
103	Brian Dorsett	.10	.05
104	Tony Fernandez	.10	.05
105	Willie Greene	.10	.05
106	Erik Hanson	.10	.05
107	Kevin Jarvis	.10	.05
108	Barry Larkin	.40	.18
109	Kevin Mitchell	.10	.05
110	Hal Morris	.10	.05
111	Jose Rijo	.10	.05
112	Johnny Ruffin	.10	.05
113	Deion Sanders	.15	.07
114	Reggie Sanders	.10	.05
115	Sandy Alomar Jr.	.15	.07
116	Ruben Amaro	.10	.05
117	Carlos Baerga	.10	.05
118	Albert Belle	.15	.07
119	Alvaro Espinoza	.10	.05
120	Rene Gonzales	.10	.05
121	Wayne Kirby	.10	.05
122	Kenny Lofton	.15	.07
123	Candy Maldonado	.10	.05
124	Dennis Martinez	.15	.07
125	Eddie Murray	.40	.18
126	Charles Nagy	.10	.05
127	Tony Pena	.10	.05
128	Manny Ramirez	.50	.23
129	Paul Sorrento	.10	.05
130	Jim Thome	.40	.18
131	Omar Vizquel	.15	.07
132	Dante Bichette	.15	.07
133	Ellis Burks	.15	.07
134	Vinny Castilla	.15	.07
135	Marvin Freeman	.10	.05
136	Andres Galarraga	.25	.11
137	Joe Girardi	.10	.05
138	Charlie Hayes	.10	.05
139	Mike Kingery	.10	.05
140	Nelson Liriano	.10	.05
141	Roberto Mejia	.10	.05
142	David Nied	.10	.05
143	Steve Reed	.10	.05
144	Armando Reynoso	.10	.05
145	Bruce Ruffin	.10	.05
146	John Vander Wal	.10	.05
147	Walt Weiss	.10	.05
148	Skeeter Barnes	.10	.05
149	Tim Belcher	.10	.05
150	Junior Felix	.10	.05
151	Cecil Fielder	.15	.07
152	Travis Fryman	.15	.07
153	Kirk Gibson	.15	.07
154	Chris Gomez	.10	.05
155	Buddy Groom	.10	.05
156	Chad Kreuter	.10	.05
157	Mike Moore	.10	.05
158	Tony Phillips	.10	.05
159	Juan Samuel	.10	.05
160	Mickey Tettleton	.10	.05
161	Alan Trammell	.25	.11
162	David Wells	.15	.07
163	Lou Whitaker	.15	.07
164	Kurt Abbott	.10	.05
165	Luis Aquino	.10	.05
166	Alex Arias	.10	.05
167	Bret Barberie	.10	.05
168	Jerry Browne	.10	.05
169	Chuck Carr	.10	.05
170	Matias Carrillo	.10	.05
171	Greg Colbrunn	.10	.05
172	Jeff Conine	.10	.05
173	Carl Everett	.15	.07
174	Robb Nen	.10	.05
175	Yorkis Perez	.10	.05
176	Pat Rapp	.10	.05
177	Benito Santiago	.10	.05
178	Gary Sheffield	.15	.07
179	Darrell Whitmore	.10	.05
180	Jeff Bagwell	.50	.23
181	Kevin Bass	.10	.05
182	Craig Biggio	.25	.11
183	Andujar Cedeno	.10	.05
184	Doug Drabek	.10	.05
185	Tony Eusebio	.10	.05
186	Steve Finley	.15	.07
187	Luis Gonzalez	.40	.18
188	Pete Harnisch	.10	.05
189	John Hudek	.10	.05
190	Orlando Miller	.10	.05
191	James Mouton	.10	.05
192	Roberto Petagine	.10	.05
193	Shane Reynolds	.10	.05
194	Greg Swindell	.10	.05
195	Dave Veres	.10	.05
196	Kevin Appier	.15	.07
197	Stan Belinda	.10	.05
198	Vince Coleman	.10	.05
199	David Cone	.15	.07
200	Gary Gaetti	.15	.07
201	Greg Gagne	.10	.05
202	Mark Gubicza	.10	.05
203	Bob Hamelin	.10	.05
204	Dave Henderson	.10	.05
205	Felix Jose	.10	.05

	No.	Player	Mint	NrMt
❑	206	Wally Joyner	.15	.07
❑	207	Jose Lind	.10	.05
❑	208	Mike Macfarlane	.10	.05
❑	209	Brian McRae	.10	.05
❑	210	Jeff Montgomery	.10	.05
❑	211	Hipolito Pichardo	.10	.05
❑	212	Pedro Astacio	.10	.05
❑	213	Brett Butler	.15	.07
❑	214	Omar Daal	.10	.05
❑	215	Delino DeShields	.10	.05
❑	216	Darren Dreifort	.10	.05
❑	217	Carlos Hernandez	.10	.05
❑	218	Orel Hershiser	.15	.07
❑	219	Garey Ingram	.10	.05
❑	220	Eric Karros	.15	.07
❑	221	Ramon Martinez	.10	.05
❑	222	Raul Mondesi	.15	.07
❑	223	Jose Offerman	.10	.05
❑	224	Mike Piazza	1.00	.45
❑	225	Henry Rodriguez	.10	.05
❑	226	Ismael Valdes	.10	.05
❑	227	Tim Wallach	.10	.05
❑	228	Jeff Cirillo	.15	.07
❑	229	Alex Diaz	.10	.05
❑	230	Cal Eldred	.10	.05
❑	231	Mike Fetters	.10	.05
❑	232	Brian Harper	.10	.05
❑	233	Ted Higuera	.10	.05
❑	234	John Jaha	.10	.05
❑	235	Graeme Lloyd	.10	.05
❑	236	Jose Mercedes	.10	.05
❑	237	Jaime Navarro	.10	.05
❑	238	Dave Nilsson	.10	.05
❑	239	Jesse Orosco	.10	.05
❑	240	Jody Reed	.10	.05
❑	241	Jose Valentin	.10	.05
❑	242	Greg Vaughn	.15	.07
❑	243	Turner Ward	.10	.05
❑	244	Rick Aguilera	.10	.05
❑	245	Rich Becker	.10	.05
❑	246	Jim Deshaies	.10	.05
❑	247	Steve Dunn	.10	.05
❑	248	Scott Erickson	.10	.05
❑	249	Kent Hrbek	.15	.07
❑	250	Chuck Knoblauch	.15	.07
❑	251	Scott Leius	.10	.05
❑	252	David McCarty	.10	.05
❑	253	Pat Meares	.10	.05
❑	254	Pedro Munoz	.10	.05
❑	255	Kirby Puckett	1.00	.45
❑	256	Carlos Pulido	.10	.05
❑	257	Kevin Tapani	.10	.05
❑	258	Matt Walbeck	.10	.05
❑	259	Dave Winfield	.40	.18
❑	260	Moises Alou	.15	.07
❑	261	Juan Bell	.10	.05
❑	262	Freddie Benavides	.10	.05
❑	263	Sean Berry	.10	.05
❑	264	Wil Cordero	.10	.05
❑	265	Jeff Fassero	.10	.05
❑	266	Darrin Fletcher	.10	.05
❑	267	Cliff Floyd	.15	.07
❑	268	Marquis Grissom	.10	.05
❑	269	Gil Heredia	.10	.05
❑	270	Ken Hill	.10	.05
❑	271	Pedro Martinez	.50	.23
❑	272	Mel Rojas	.10	.05
❑	273	Larry Walker	.25	.11
❑	274	John Wetteland	.15	.07
❑	275	Rondell White	.15	.07
❑	276	Tim Bogar	.10	.05
❑	277	Bobby Bonilla	.15	.07
❑	278	Rico Brogna	.10	.05
❑	279	Jeromy Burnitz	.15	.07
❑	280	John Franco	.15	.07
❑	281	Eric Hillman	.10	.05
❑	282	Todd Hundley	.10	.05
❑	283	Jeff Kent	.25	.11
❑	284	Mike Maddux	.10	.05
❑	285	Joe Orsulak	.10	.05
❑	286	Luis Rivera	.10	.05
❑	287	Bret Saberhagen	.15	.07
❑	288	David Segui	.10	.05
❑	289	Ryan Thompson	.10	.05
❑	290	Fernando Vina	.10	.05
❑	291	Jose Vizcaino	.10	.05
❑	292	Jim Abbott	.15	.07
❑	293	Wade Boggs	.40	.18
❑	294	Russ Davis	.10	.05
❑	295	Mike Gallego	.10	.05
❑	296	Xavier Hernandez	.10	.05
❑	297	Steve Howe	.10	.05
❑	298	Jimmy Key	.15	.07
❑	299	Don Mattingly	1.00	.45
❑	300	Terry Mulholland	.10	.05
❑	301	Paul O'Neill	.40	.18
❑	302	Luis Polonia	.10	.05
❑	303	Mike Stanley	.10	.05
❑	304	Danny Tartabull	.10	.05
❑	305	Randy Velarde	.10	.05
❑	306	Bob Wickman	.10	.05
❑	307	Bernie Williams	.40	.18
❑	308	Mark Acre	.10	.05
❑	309	Geronimo Berroa	.10	.05
❑	310	Mike Bordick	.10	.05
❑	311	Dennis Eckersley	.15	.07
❑	312	Rickey Henderson	.75	.35
❑	313	Stan Javier	.10	.05
❑	314	Miguel Jimenez	.10	.05
❑	315	Francisco Matos RC	.10	.05
❑	316	Mark McGwire	1.50	.70
❑	317	Troy Neel	.10	.05
❑	318	Steve Ontiveros	.10	.05
❑	319	Carlos Reyes	.10	.05
❑	320	Ruben Sierra	.10	.05
❑	321	Terry Steinbach	.10	.05
❑	322	Bob Welch	.10	.05
❑	323	Bobby Witt	.10	.05
❑	324	Larry Andersen	.10	.05
❑	325	Kim Batiste	.10	.05
❑	326	Darren Daulton	.15	.07
❑	327	Mariano Duncan	.10	.05
❑	328	Lenny Dykstra	.15	.07
❑	329	Jim Eisenreich	.10	.05
❑	330	Danny Jackson	.10	.05
❑	331	John Kruk	.15	.07
❑	332	Tony Longmire	.10	.05
❑	333	Tom Marsh	.10	.05
❑	334	Mickey Morandini	.10	.05
❑	335	Bobby Munoz	.10	.05
❑	336	Todd Pratt	.10	.05
❑	337	Tom Quinlan	.10	.05
❑	338	Kevin Stocker	.10	.05
❑	339	Fernando Valenzuela	.15	.07
❑	340	Jay Bell	.15	.07
❑	341	Dave Clark	.10	.05
❑	342	Steve Cooke	.10	.05
❑	343	Carlos Garcia	.10	.05
❑	344	Jeff King	.10	.05
❑	345	Jon Lieber	.10	.05
❑	346	Ravelo Manzanillo	.10	.05
❑	347	Al Martin	.10	.05
❑	348	Orlando Merced	.10	.05
❑	349	Denny Neagle	.15	.07
❑	350	Alejandro Pena	.10	.05
❑	351	Don Slaught	.10	.05
❑	352	Zane Smith	.10	.05
❑	353	Andy Van Slyke	.15	.07
❑	354	Rick White	.10	.05
❑	355	Kevin Young	.10	.05
❑	356	Andy Ashby	.10	.05
❑	357	Derek Bell	.10	.05
❑	358	Andy Benes	.10	.05
❑	359	Phil Clark	.10	.05
❑	360	Donnie Elliott	.10	.05
❑	361	Ricky Gutierrez	.10	.05
❑	362	Tony Gwynn	.75	.35
❑	363	Trevor Hoffman	.15	.07
❑	364	Tim Hyers	.10	.05
❑	365	Luis Lopez	.10	.05
❑	366	Jose Martinez	.10	.05
❑	367	Pedro A. Martinez	.10	.05
❑	368	Phil Plantier	.10	.05
❑	369	Bip Roberts	.10	.05
❑	370	A.J. Sager	.10	.05
❑	371	Jeff Tabaka	.10	.05
❑	372	Todd Benzinger	.10	.05
❑	373	Barry Bonds	.60	.25
❑	374	John Burkett	.10	.05
❑	375	Mark Carreon	.10	.05
❑	376	Royce Clayton	.10	.05
❑	377	Pat Gomez	.10	.05
❑	378	Erik Johnson	.10	.05
❑	379	Darren Lewis	.10	.05
❑	380	Kirt Manwaring	.10	.05
❑	381	Dave Martinez	.10	.05
❑	382	John Patterson	.10	.05
❑	383	Mark Portugal	.10	.05
❑	384	Darryl Strawberry	.15	.07
❑	385	Salomon Torres	.10	.05
❑	386	W. VanLandingham	.10	.05
❑	387	Matt Williams	.25	.11
❑	388	Rich Amaral	.10	.05
❑	389	Bobby Ayala	.10	.05
❑	390	Mike Blowers	.10	.05
❑	391	Chris Bosio	.10	.05
❑	392	Jay Buhner	.15	.07
❑	393	Jim Converse	.10	.05
❑	394	Tim Davis	.10	.05
❑	395	Felix Fermin	.10	.05
❑	396	Dave Fleming	.10	.05
❑	397	Goose Gossage	.15	.07
❑	398	Ken Griffey Jr.	1.25	.55
❑	399	Randy Johnson	.50	.23
❑	400	Edgar Martinez	.25	.11
❑	401	Tino Martinez	.15	.07
❑	402	Alex Rodriguez	1.25	.55
❑	403	Dan Wilson	.10	.05
❑	404	Luis Alicea	.10	.05
❑	405	Rene Arocha	.10	.05
❑	406	Bernard Gilkey	.10	.05
❑	407	Gregg Jefferies	.10	.05
❑	408	Ray Lankford	.10	.05
❑	409	Terry McGriff	.10	.05
❑	410	Omar Olivares	.10	.05
❑	411	Jose Oquendo	.10	.05
❑	412	Vicente Palacios	.10	.05
❑	413	Geronimo Pena	.10	.05
❑	414	Mike Perez	.10	.05
❑	415	Gerald Perry	.10	.05
❑	416	Ozzie Smith	.50	.23
❑	417	Bob Tewksbury	.10	.05
❑	418	Mark Whiten	.10	.05
❑	419	Todd Zeile	.10	.05
❑	420	Esteban Beltre	.10	.05
❑	421	Kevin Brown	.15	.07
❑	422	Cris Carpenter	.10	.05
❑	423	Will Clark	.40	.18
❑	424	Hector Fajardo	.10	.05
❑	425	Jeff Frye	.10	.05
❑	426	Juan Gonzalez	.40	.18
❑	427	Rusty Greer	.15	.07
❑	428	Rick Honeycutt	.10	.05
❑	429	David Hulse	.10	.05
❑	430	Manny Lee	.10	.05
❑	431	Junior Ortiz	.10	.05
❑	432	Dean Palmer	.15	.07
❑	433	Ivan Rodriguez	.40	.18
❑	434	Dan Smith	.10	.05
❑	435	Roberto Alomar	.40	.18
❑	436	Pat Borders	.10	.05
❑	437	Scott Brow	.10	.05
❑	438	Rob Butler	.10	.05
❑	439	Joe Carter	.15	.07
❑	440	Tony Castillo	.10	.05
❑	441	Domingo Cedeno	.10	.05
❑	442	Brad Cornett	.10	.05
❑	443	Carlos Delgado	.40	.18
❑	444	Alex Gonzalez	.10	.05
❑	445	Juan Guzman	.10	.05
❑	446	Darren Hall	.10	.05
❑	447	Paul Molitor	.40	.18
❑	448	John Olerud	.15	.07
❑	449	Robert Perez	.10	.05
❑	450	Devon White	.15	.07

1996 Pacific

	MINT	NRMT
COMPLETE SET (450)	40.00	18.00

	No.	Player	Mint	NrMt
❑	1	Steve Avery	.10	.05
❑	2	Ryan Klesko	.15	.07
❑	3	Pedro Borbon	.10	.05
❑	4	Chipper Jones	.75	.35
❑	5	Kent Mercker	.10	.05
❑	6	Greg Maddux	1.00	.45
❑	7	Greg McMichael	.10	.05

❑	8	Mark Wohlers	.10	.05
❑	9	Fred McGriff	.25	.11
❑	10	John Smoltz	.15	.07
❑	11	Rafael Belliard	.10	.05
❑	12	Mark Lemke	.10	.05
❑	13	Tom Glavine	.40	.18
❑	14	Javier Lopez	.15	.07
❑	15	Jeff Blauser	.10	.05
❑	16	David Justice	.15	.07
❑	17	Marquis Grissom	.10	.05
❑	18	Greg Maddux CY	.50	.23
❑	19	Randy Myers	.10	.05
❑	20	Scott Servais	.10	.05
❑	21	Sammy Sosa	.75	.35
❑	22	Kevin Foster	.10	.05
❑	23	Jose Hernandez	.10	.05
❑	24	Jim Bullinger	.10	.05
❑	25	Mike Perez	.10	.05
❑	26	Shawon Dunston	.10	.05
❑	27	Rey Sanchez	.10	.05
❑	28	Frank Castillo	.10	.05
❑	29	Jaime Navarro	.10	.05
❑	30	Brian McRae	.10	.05
❑	31	Mark Grace	.40	.18
❑	32	Roberto Rivera	.10	.05
❑	33	Luis Gonzalez	.40	.18
❑	34	Hector Carrasco	.10	.05
❑	35	Bret Boone	.15	.07
❑	36	Thomas Howard	.10	.05
❑	37	Hal Morris	.10	.05
❑	38	John Smiley	.10	.05
❑	39	Jeff Brantley	.10	.05
❑	40	Barry Larkin	.40	.18
❑	41	Mariano Duncan	.10	.05
❑	42	Xavier Hernandez	.10	.05
❑	43	Pete Schourek	.10	.05
❑	44	Reggie Sanders	.10	.05
❑	45	Dave Burba	.10	.05
❑	46	Jeff Branson	.10	.05
❑	47	Mark Portugal	.10	.05
❑	48	Ron Gant	.10	.05
❑	49	Benito Santiago	.10	.05
❑	50	Barry Larkin MVP	.15	.07
❑	51	Steve Reed	.10	.05
❑	52	Kevin Ritz	.10	.05
❑	53	Dante Bichette	.15	.07
❑	54	Darren Holmes	.10	.05
❑	55	Ellis Burks	.15	.07
❑	56	Walt Weiss	.10	.05
❑	57	Armando Reynoso	.10	.05
❑	58	Vinny Castilla	.15	.07
❑	59	Jason Bates	.10	.05
❑	60	Mike Kingery	.10	.05
❑	61	Bryan Rekar	.10	.05
❑	62	Curtis Leskanic	.10	.05
❑	63	Bret Saberhagen	.15	.07
❑	64	Andres Galarraga	.25	.11
❑	65	Larry Walker	.25	.11
❑	66	Joe Girardi	.10	.05
❑	67	Quilvio Veras	.10	.05
❑	68	Robb Nen	.10	.05
❑	69	Mario Diaz	.10	.05
❑	70	Chuck Carr	.10	.05
❑	71	Alex Arias	.10	.05
❑	72	Pat Rapp	.10	.05
❑	73	Rich Garces	.10	.05
❑	74	Kurt Abbott	.10	.05
❑	75	Andre Dawson	.25	.11
❑	76	Greg Colbrunn	.10	.05
❑	77	John Burkett	.10	.05
❑	78	Terry Pendleton	.15	.07
❑	79	Jesus Tavarez	.10	.05
❑	80	Charles Johnson	.15	.07
❑	81	Yorkis Perez	.10	.05
❑	82	Jeff Conine	.10	.05
❑	83	Gary Sheffield	.15	.07
❑	84	Brian L. Hunter	.10	.05
❑	85	Derrick May	.10	.05
❑	86	Greg Swindell	.10	.05
❑	87	Derek Bell	.10	.05
❑	88	Dave Veres	.10	.05
❑	89	Jeff Bagwell	.50	.23
❑	90	Todd Jones	.10	.05
❑	91	Orlando Miller	.10	.05
❑	92	Pedro A. Martinez	.10	.05
❑	93	Tony Eusebio	.10	.05
❑	94	Craig Biggio	.25	.11
❑	95	Shane Reynolds	.10	.05
❑	96	James Mouton	.10	.05
❑	97	Doug Drabek	.10	.05
❑	98	Dave Magadan	.10	.05
❑	99	Ricky Gutierrez	.10	.05
❑	100	Hideo Nomo	.50	.23
❑	101	Delino DeShields	.10	.05
❑	102	Tom Candiotti	.10	.05
❑	103	Mike Piazza	1.00	.45
❑	104	Ramon Martinez	.10	.05
❑	105	Pedro Astacio	.10	.05
❑	106	Chad Fonville	.10	.05
❑	107	Raul Mondesi	.15	.07
❑	108	Ismael Valdes	.10	.05
❑	109	Jose Offerman	.10	.05
❑	110	Todd Worrell	.10	.05
❑	111	Eric Karros	.15	.07
❑	112	Brett Butler	.15	.07
❑	113	Juan Castro	.10	.05
❑	114	Roberto Kelly	.10	.05
❑	115	Omar Daal	.10	.05
❑	116	Antonio Osuna	.10	.05
❑	117	Hideo Nomo ROY	.15	.07
❑	118	Mike Lansing	.10	.05
❑	119	Mel Rojas	.10	.05
❑	120	Sean Berry	.10	.05
❑	121	David Segui	.10	.05
❑	122	Tavo Alvarez	.10	.05
❑	123	Pedro J.Martinez	.50	.23
❑	124	F.P. Santangelo	.10	.05
❑	125	Rondell White	.15	.07
❑	126	Cliff Floyd	.15	.07
❑	127	Henry Rodriguez	.10	.05
❑	128	Tony Tarasco	.10	.05
❑	129	Yamil Benitez	.10	.05
❑	130	Carlos Perez	.10	.05
❑	131	Wil Cordero	.10	.05
❑	132	Jeff Fassero	.10	.05
❑	133	Moises Alou	.15	.07
❑	134	John Franco	.15	.07
❑	135	Rico Brogna	.10	.05
❑	136	Dave Mlicki	.10	.05
❑	137	Bill Pulsipher	.10	.05
❑	138	Jose Vizcaino	.10	.05
❑	139	Carl Everett	.15	.07
❑	140	Edgardo Alfonzo	.15	.07
❑	141	Bobby Jones	.10	.05
❑	142	Alberto Castillo	.10	.05
❑	143	Joe Orsulak	.10	.05
❑	144	Jeff Kent	.25	.11
❑	145	Ryan Thompson	.10	.05
❑	146	Jason Isringhausen	.15	.07
❑	147	Todd Hundley	.10	.05
❑	148	Alex Ochoa	.10	.05
❑	149	Charlie Hayes	.10	.05
❑	150	Michael Mimbs	.10	.05
❑	151	Darren Daulton	.15	.07
❑	152	Toby Borland	.10	.05
❑	153	Andy Van Slyke	.15	.07
❑	154	Mickey Morandini	.10	.05
❑	155	Sid Fernandez	.10	.05
❑	156	Tom Marsh	.10	.05
❑	157	Kevin Stocker	.10	.05
❑	158	Paul Quantrill	.10	.05
❑	159	Gregg Jefferies	.10	.05
❑	160	Ricky Bottalico	.10	.05
❑	161	Lenny Dykstra	.15	.07
❑	162	Mark Whiten	.10	.05
❑	163	Tyler Green	.10	.05
❑	164	Jim Eisenreich	.10	.05
❑	165	Heathcliff Slocumb	.10	.05
❑	166	Esteban Loaiza	.10	.05
❑	167	Rich Aude	.10	.05
❑	168	Jason Christiansen	.10	.05
❑	169	Ramon Morel	.10	.05
❑	170	Orlando Merced	.10	.05
❑	171	Paul Wagner	.10	.05
❑	172	Jeff King	.10	.05
❑	173	Jay Bell	.15	.07
❑	174	Jacob Brumfield	.10	.05
❑	175	Nelson Liriano	.10	.05
❑	176	Dan Miceli	.10	.05
❑	177	Carlos Garcia	.10	.05
❑	178	Denny Neagle	.15	.07
❑	179	Angelo Encarnacion	.10	.05
❑	180	Al Martin	.10	.05
❑	181	Midre Cummings	.10	.05
❑	182	Eddie Williams	.10	.05
❑	183	Roberto Petagine	.10	.05
❑	184	Tony Gwynn	.75	.35
❑	185	Andy Ashby	.10	.05
❑	186	Melvin Nieves	.10	.05
❑	187	Phil Clark	.10	.05
❑	188	Brad Ausmus	.10	.05
❑	189	Bip Roberts	.10	.05
❑	190	Fernando Valenzuela	.15	.07
❑	191	Marc Newfield	.10	.05
❑	192	Steve Finley	.15	.07
❑	193	Trevor Hoffman	.15	.07
❑	194	Andujar Cedeno	.10	.05
❑	195	Jody Reed	.10	.05
❑	196	Ken Caminiti	.15	.07
❑	197	Joey Hamilton	.10	.05
❑	198	Tony Gwynn BAC	.40	.18
❑	199	Shawn Barton	.10	.05
❑	200	Deion Sanders	.15	.07
❑	201	Rikkert Faneyte	.10	.05
❑	202	Barry Bonds	1.00	.45
❑	203	Matt Williams	.25	.11
❑	204	Jose Bautista	.10	.05
❑	205	Mark Leiter	.10	.05
❑	206	Mark Carreon	.10	.05
❑	207	Robby Thompson	.10	.05
❑	208	Terry Mulholland	.10	.05
❑	209	Rod Beck	.10	.05
❑	210	Royce Clayton	.10	.05
❑	211	J.R. Phillips	.10	.05
❑	212	Kirt Manwaring	.10	.05
❑	213	Glenallen Hill	.10	.05
❑	214	W.VanLandingham	.10	.05
❑	215	Scott Cooper	.10	.05
❑	216	Bernard Gilkey	.10	.05
❑	217	Allen Watson	.10	.05
❑	218	Donovan Osborne	.10	.05
❑	219	Ray Lankford	.10	.05
❑	220	Tony Fossas	.10	.05
❑	221	Tom Pagnozzi	.10	.05
❑	222	John Mabry	.10	.05
❑	223	Tripp Cromer	.10	.05
❑	224	Mark Petkovsek	.10	.05
❑	225	Mike Morgan	.10	.05
❑	226	Ozzie Smith	.50	.23
❑	227	Tom Henke	.10	.05
❑	228	Jose Oquendo	.10	.05
❑	229	Brian Jordan	.15	.07
❑	230	Cal Ripken	1.50	.70
❑	231	Scott Erickson	.10	.05
❑	232	Harold Baines	.15	.07
❑	233	Jeff Manto	.10	.05
❑	234	Jesse Orosco	.10	.05
❑	235	Jeffrey Hammonds	.10	.05
❑	236	Brady Anderson	.15	.07
❑	237	Manny Alexander	.10	.05
❑	238	Chris Hoiles	.10	.05
❑	239	Rafael Palmeiro	.40	.18
❑	240	Ben McDonald	.10	.05
❑	241	Curtis Goodwin	.10	.05
❑	242	Bobby Bonilla	.15	.07
❑	243	Mike Mussina	.40	.18
❑	244	Kevin Brown	.15	.07
❑	245	Armando Benitez	.10	.05
❑	246	Jose Canseco	.40	.18

❑ 247 Erik Hanson .10 .05
❑ 248 Mo Vaughn .15 .07
❑ 249 Tim Naehring .10 .05
❑ 250 Vaughn Eshelman .10 .05
❑ 251 Mike Greenwell .10 .05
❑ 252 Troy O'Leary .10 .05
❑ 253 Tim Wakefield .10 .05
❑ 254 Dwayne Hosey .10 .05
❑ 255 John Valentin .10 .05
❑ 256 Rick Aguilera .10 .05
❑ 257 Mike Macfarlane .10 .05
❑ 258 Roger Clemens 1.00 .45
❑ 259 Luis Alicea .10 .05
❑ 260 Mo Vaughn MVP .10 .05
❑ 261 Mark Langston .10 .05
❑ 262 Jim Edmonds .25 .11
❑ 263 Rod Correia .10 .05
❑ 264 Tim Salmon .15 .07
❑ 265 J.T. Snow .15 .07
❑ 266 Orlando Palmeiro .10 .05
❑ 267 Jorge Fabregas .10 .05
❑ 268 Jim Abbott .15 .07
❑ 269 Eduardo Perez .10 .05
❑ 270 Lee Smith .15 .07
❑ 271 Gary DiSarcina .10 .05
❑ 272 Damion Easley .10 .05
❑ 273 Tony Phillips .10 .05
❑ 274 Garret Anderson .15 .07
❑ 275 Chuck Finley .15 .07
❑ 276 Chili Davis .15 .07
❑ 277 Lance Johnson .10 .05
❑ 278 Alex Fernandez .10 .05
❑ 279 Robin Ventura .15 .07
❑ 280 Chris Snopek .10 .05
❑ 281 Brian Keyser .10 .05
❑ 282 Lyle Mouton .10 .05
❑ 283 Luis Andujar .10 .05
❑ 284 Tim Raines .15 .07
❑ 285 Larry Thomas .10 .05
❑ 286 Ozzie Guillen .10 .05
❑ 287 Frank Thomas .50 .23
❑ 288 Roberto Hernandez .10 .05
❑ 289 Dave Martinez .10 .05
❑ 290 Ray Durham .15 .07
❑ 291 Ron Karkovice .10 .05
❑ 292 Wilson Alvarez .10 .05
❑ 293 Omar Vizquel .15 .07
❑ 294 Eddie Murray .40 .18
❑ 295 Sandy Alomar Jr. .15 .07
❑ 296 Orel Hershiser .15 .07
❑ 297 Jose Mesa .10 .05
❑ 298 Julian Tavarez .10 .05
❑ 299 Dennis Martinez .15 .07
❑ 300 Carlos Baerga .10 .05
❑ 301 Manny Ramirez .50 .23
❑ 302 Jim Thome .40 .18
❑ 303 Kenny Lofton .15 .07
❑ 304 Tony Pena .10 .05
❑ 305 Alvaro Espinoza .10 .05
❑ 306 Paul Sorrento .10 .05
❑ 307 Albert Belle .15 .07
❑ 308 Danny Bautista .10 .05
❑ 309 Chris Gomez .10 .05
❑ 310 Jose Lima .10 .05
❑ 311 Phil Nevin .15 .07
❑ 312 Alan Trammell .25 .11
❑ 313 Chad Curtis .10 .05
❑ 314 John Flaherty .10 .05
❑ 315 Travis Fryman .15 .07
❑ 316 Todd Steverson .10 .05
❑ 317 Brian Bohanon .10 .05
❑ 318 Lou Whitaker .15 .07
❑ 319 Bobby Higginson .15 .07
❑ 320 Steve Rodriguez .10 .05
❑ 321 Cecil Fielder .15 .07
❑ 322 Felipe Lira .10 .05
❑ 323 Juan Samuel .10 .05
❑ 324 Bob Hamelin .10 .05
❑ 325 Tom Goodwin .10 .05
❑ 326 Johnny Damon .15 .07
❑ 327 Hipolito Pichardo .10 .05
❑ 328 Dilson Torres .10 .05
❑ 329 Kevin Appier .15 .07
❑ 330 Mark Gubicza .10 .05
❑ 331 Jon Nunnally .10 .05
❑ 332 Gary Gaetti .15 .07
❑ 333 Brent Mayne .10 .05
❑ 334 Brent Cookson .10 .05
❑ 335 Tom Gordon .10 .05
❑ 336 Wally Joyner .15 .07
❑ 337 Greg Gagne .10 .05
❑ 338 Fernando Vina .10 .05
❑ 339 Joe Oliver .10 .05
❑ 340 John Jaha .10 .05
❑ 341 Jeff Cirillo .15 .07
❑ 342 Pat Listach .10 .05
❑ 343 Dave Nilsson .10 .05
❑ 344 Steve Sparks .10 .05
❑ 345 Ricky Bones .10 .05
❑ 346 David Hulse .10 .05
❑ 347 Scott Karl .10 .05
❑ 348 Darryl Hamilton .10 .05
❑ 349 B.J. Surhoff .15 .07
❑ 350 Angel Miranda .10 .05
❑ 351 Sid Roberson .10 .05
❑ 352 Matt Mieske .10 .05
❑ 353 Jose Valentin .10 .05
❑ 354 Matt Lawton RC .50 .23
❑ 355 Eddie Guardado .10 .05
❑ 356 Brad Radke .15 .07
❑ 357 Pedro Munoz .10 .05
❑ 358 Scott Stahoviak .10 .05
❑ 359 Erik Schullstrom .10 .05
❑ 360 Pat Meares .10 .05
❑ 361 Marty Cordova .10 .05
❑ 362 Scott Leius .10 .05
❑ 363 Matt Walbeck .10 .05
❑ 364 Rich Becker .10 .05
❑ 365 Kirby Puckett 1.00 .45
❑ 366 Oscar Munoz .10 .05
❑ 367 Chuck Knoblauch .15 .07
❑ 368 Marty Cordova ROY .10 .05
❑ 369 Bernie Williams .40 .18
❑ 370 Mike Stanley .10 .05
❑ 371 Andy Pettitte .15 .07
❑ 372 Jack McDowell .10 .05
❑ 373 Sterling Hitchcock .10 .05
❑ 374 David Cone .15 .07
❑ 375 Randy Velarde .10 .05
❑ 376 Don Mattingly 1.00 .45
❑ 377 Melido Perez .10 .05
❑ 378 Wade Boggs .40 .18
❑ 379 Ruben Sierra .10 .05
❑ 380 Tony Fernandez .10 .05
❑ 381 John Wetteland .15 .07
❑ 382 Mariano Rivera .15 .07
❑ 383 Derek Jeter 1.50 .70
❑ 384 Paul O'Neill .40 .18
❑ 385 Mark McGwire 1.50 .70
❑ 386 Scott Brosius .15 .07
❑ 387 Don Wengert .10 .05
❑ 388 Terry Steinbach .10 .05
❑ 389 Brent Gates .10 .05
❑ 390 Craig Paquette .10 .05
❑ 391 Mike Bordick .10 .05
❑ 392 Ariel Prieto .10 .05
❑ 393 Dennis Eckersley .15 .07
❑ 394 Carlos Reyes .10 .05
❑ 395 Todd Stottlemyre .10 .05
❑ 396 Rickey Henderson .75 .35
❑ 397 Geronimo Berroa .10 .05
❑ 398 Steve Ontiveros .10 .05
❑ 399 Mike Gallego .10 .05
❑ 400 Stan Javier .10 .05
❑ 401 Randy Johnson .50 .23
❑ 402 Norm Charlton .10 .05
❑ 403 Mike Blowers .10 .05
❑ 404 Tino Martinez .15 .07
❑ 405 Dan Wilson .10 .05
❑ 406 Andy Benes .10 .05
❑ 407 Alex Diaz .10 .05
❑ 408 Edgar Martinez .25 .11
❑ 409 Chris Bosio .10 .05
❑ 410 Ken Griffey Jr. 1.25 .55
❑ 411 Luis Sojo .10 .05
❑ 412 Bob Wolcott .10 .05
❑ 413 Vince Coleman .10 .05
❑ 414 Rich Amaral .10 .05
❑ 415 Jay Buhner .15 .07
❑ 416 Alex Rodriguez 1.00 .45
❑ 417 Joey Cora .10 .05
❑ 418 Randy Johnson CY .25 .11
❑ 419 Edgar Martinez BAC .15 .07
❑ 420 Ivan Rodriguez .40 .18
❑ 421 Mark McLemore .10 .05
❑ 422 Mickey Tettleton .10 .05
❑ 423 Juan Gonzalez .40 .18
❑ 424 Will Clark .40 .18
❑ 425 Kevin Gross .10 .05
❑ 426 Dean Palmer .15 .07
❑ 427 Kenny Rogers .10 .05
❑ 428 Bob Tewksbury .10 .05
❑ 429 Benji Gil .10 .05
❑ 430 Jeff Russell .10 .05
❑ 431 Rusty Greer .15 .07
❑ 432 Roger Pavlik .10 .05
❑ 433 Esteban Beltre .10 .05
❑ 434 Otis Nixon .10 .05
❑ 435 Paul Molitor .40 .18
❑ 436 Carlos Delgado .40 .18
❑ 437 Ed Sprague .10 .05
❑ 438 Juan Guzman .10 .05
❑ 439 Domingo Cedeno .10 .05
❑ 440 Pat Hentgen .10 .05
❑ 441 Tomas Perez .10 .05
❑ 442 John Olerud .15 .07
❑ 443 Shawn Green .40 .18
❑ 444 Al Leiter .15 .07
❑ 445 Joe Carter .15 .07
❑ 446 Robert Perez .10 .05
❑ 447 Devon White .15 .07
❑ 448 Tony Castillo .10 .05
❑ 449 Alex Gonzalez .10 .05
❑ 450 Roberto Alomar .40 .18

1997 Pacific

	MINT	NRMT
COMPLETE SET (450)	40.00	18.00

❑ 1 Garret Anderson .25 .11
❑ 2 George Arias .15 .07
❑ 3 Chili Davis .25 .11
❑ 4 Gary DiSarcina .15 .07
❑ 5 Jim Edmonds .40 .18
❑ 6 Darin Erstad .60 .25
❑ 7 Jorge Fabregas .15 .07
❑ 8 Chuck Finley .25 .11
❑ 9 Rex Hudler .15 .07
❑ 10 Mark Langston .15 .07
❑ 11 Orlando Palmeiro .15 .07
❑ 12 Troy Percival .15 .07
❑ 13 Tim Salmon .25 .11
❑ 14 J.T. Snow .25 .11
❑ 15 Randy Velarde .15 .07
❑ 16 Manny Alexander .15 .07
❑ 17 Roberto Alomar .60 .25
❑ 18 Brady Anderson .25 .11
❑ 19 Armando Benitez .15 .07
❑ 20 Bobby Bonilla .25 .11
❑ 21 Rocky Coppinger .15 .07
❑ 22 Scott Erickson .15 .07
❑ 23 Jeffrey Hammonds .15 .07
❑ 24 Chris Hoiles .15 .07
❑ 25 Eddie Murray .60 .25
❑ 26 Mike Mussina .60 .25
❑ 27 Randy Myers .15 .07
❑ 28 Rafael Palmeiro .60 .25
❑ 29 Cal Ripken 2.50 1.10
❑ 30 B.J. Surhoff .25 .11

No.	Player	Price 1	Price 2
❑ 31	Tony Tarasco	.15	.07
❑ 32	Esteban Beltre	.15	.07
❑ 33	Darren Bragg	.15	.07
❑ 34	Jose Canseco	.60	.25
❑ 35	Roger Clemens	1.50	.70
❑ 36	Wil Cordero	.15	.07
❑ 37	Alex Delgado	.15	.07
❑ 38	Jeff Frye	.15	.07
❑ 39	Nomar Garciaparra	1.50	.70
❑ 40	Tom Gordon	.15	.07
❑ 41	Mike Greenwell	.15	.07
❑ 42	Reggie Jefferson	.15	.07
❑ 43	Tim Naehring	.15	.07
❑ 44	Troy O'Leary	.15	.07
❑ 45	Heathcliff Slocumb	.15	.07
❑ 46	Lee Tinsley	.15	.07
❑ 47	John Valentin	.15	.07
❑ 48	Mo Vaughn	.25	.11
❑ 49	Wilson Alvarez	.15	.07
❑ 50	Harold Baines	.25	.11
❑ 51	Ray Durham	.25	.11
❑ 52	Alex Fernandez	.15	.07
❑ 53	Ozzie Guillen	.15	.07
❑ 54	Roberto Hernandez	.15	.07
❑ 55	Ron Karkovice	.15	.07
❑ 56	Darren Lewis	.15	.07
❑ 57	Norberto Martin	.15	.07
❑ 58	Dave Martinez	.15	.07
❑ 59	Lyle Mouton	.15	.07
❑ 60	Jose Munoz	.15	.07
❑ 61	Tony Phillips	.15	.07
❑ 62	Kevin Tapani	.15	.07
❑ 63	Danny Tartabull	.15	.07
❑ 64	Frank Thomas	.75	.35
❑ 65	Robin Ventura	.25	.11
❑ 66	Sandy Alomar Jr.	.25	.11
❑ 67	Albert Belle	.25	.11
❑ 68	Julio Franco	.25	.11
❑ 69	Brian Giles RC	2.50	1.10
❑ 70	Danny Graves	.15	.07
❑ 71	Orel Hershiser	.25	.11
❑ 72	Jeff Kent	.40	.18
❑ 73	Kenny Lofton	.25	.11
❑ 74	Dennis Martinez	.25	.11
❑ 75	Jack McDowell	.15	.07
❑ 76	Jose Mesa	.15	.07
❑ 77	Charles Nagy	.15	.07
❑ 78	Manny Ramirez	.75	.35
❑ 79	Julian Tavarez	.15	.07
❑ 80	Jim Thome	.60	.25
❑ 81	Jose Vizcaino	.15	.07
❑ 82	Omar Vizquel	.25	.11
❑ 83	Brad Ausmus	.15	.07
❑ 84	Kimera Bartee	.15	.07
❑ 85	Raul Casanova	.15	.07
❑ 86	Tony Clark	.25	.11
❑ 87	Travis Fryman	.25	.11
❑ 88	Bobby Higginson	.25	.11
❑ 89	Mark Lewis	.15	.07
❑ 90	Jose Lima	.15	.07
❑ 91	Felipe Lira	.15	.07
❑ 92	Phil Nevin	.25	.11
❑ 93	Melvin Nieves	.15	.07
❑ 94	Curtis Pride	.15	.07
❑ 95	Ruben Sierra	.15	.07
❑ 96	Alan Trammell	.40	.18
❑ 97	Kevin Appier	.25	.11
❑ 98	Tim Belcher	.15	.07
❑ 99	Johnny Damon	.25	.11
❑ 100	Tom Goodwin	.15	.07
❑ 101	Bob Hamelin	.15	.07
❑ 102	David Howard	.15	.07
❑ 103	Jason Jacome	.15	.07
❑ 104	Keith Lockhart	.15	.07
❑ 105	Mike Macfarlane	.15	.07
❑ 106	Jeff Montgomery	.15	.07
❑ 107	Jose Offerman	.15	.07
❑ 108	Hipolito Pichardo	.15	.07
❑ 109	Joe Randa	.15	.07
❑ 110	Bip Roberts	.15	.07
❑ 111	Chris Stynes	.15	.07
❑ 112	Mike Sweeney	.25	.11
❑ 113	Joe Vitiello	.15	.07
❑ 114	Jeromy Burnitz	.25	.11
❑ 115	Chuck Carr	.15	.07
❑ 116	Jeff Cirillo	.25	.11
❑ 117	Mike Fetters	.15	.07
❑ 118	David Hulse	.15	.07
❑ 119	John Jaha	.15	.07
❑ 120	Scott Karl	.15	.07
❑ 121	Jesse Levis	.15	.07
❑ 122	Mark Loretta	.15	.07
❑ 123	Mike Matheny	.15	.07
❑ 124	Ben McDonald	.15	.07
❑ 125	Matt Mieske	.15	.07
❑ 126	Angel Miranda	.15	.07
❑ 127	Dave Nilsson	.15	.07
❑ 128	Jose Valentin	.15	.07
❑ 129	Fernando Vina	.15	.07
❑ 130	Ron Villone	.15	.07
❑ 131	Gerald Williams	.15	.07
❑ 132	Rick Aguilera	.15	.07
❑ 133	Rich Becker	.15	.07
❑ 134	Ron Coomer	.15	.07
❑ 135	Marty Cordova	.15	.07
❑ 136	Eddie Guardado	.15	.07
❑ 137	Denny Hocking	.15	.07
❑ 138	Roberto Kelly	.15	.07
❑ 139	Chuck Knoblauch	.25	.11
❑ 140	Matt Lawton	.25	.11
❑ 141	Pat Meares	.15	.07
❑ 142	Paul Molitor	.60	.25
❑ 143	Greg Myers	.15	.07
❑ 144	Jeff Reboulet	.15	.07
❑ 145	Scott Stahoviak	.15	.07
❑ 146	Todd Walker	.15	.07
❑ 147	Wade Boggs	.60	.25
❑ 148	David Cone	.25	.11
❑ 149	Mariano Duncan	.15	.07
❑ 150	Cecil Fielder	.25	.11
❑ 151	Dwight Gooden	.25	.11
❑ 152	Derek Jeter	2.50	1.10
❑ 153	Jim Leyritz	.15	.07
❑ 154	Tino Martinez	.25	.11
❑ 155	Paul O'Neill	.60	.25
❑ 156	Andy Pettitte	.25	.11
❑ 157	Tim Raines	.25	.11
❑ 158	Mariano Rivera	.25	.11
❑ 159	Ruben Rivera	.15	.07
❑ 160	Kenny Rogers	.15	.07
❑ 161	Darryl Strawberry	.25	.11
❑ 162	John Wetteland	.25	.11
❑ 163	Bernie Williams	.60	.25
❑ 164	Tony Batista	.25	.11
❑ 165	Geronimo Berroa	.15	.07
❑ 166	Mike Bordick	.15	.07
❑ 167	Scott Brosius	.25	.11
❑ 168	Brent Gates	.15	.07
❑ 169	Jason Giambi	.60	.25
❑ 170	Jose Herrera	.15	.07
❑ 171	Brian Lesher RC	.15	.07
❑ 172	Damon Mashore	.15	.07
❑ 173	Mark McGwire	2.50	1.10
❑ 174	Ariel Prieto	.15	.07
❑ 175	Carlos Reyes	.15	.07
❑ 176	Matt Stairs	.15	.07
❑ 177	Terry Steinbach	.15	.07
❑ 178	John Wasdin	.15	.07
❑ 179	Ernie Young	.15	.07
❑ 180	Rich Amaral	.15	.07
❑ 181	Bobby Ayala	.15	.07
❑ 182	Jay Buhner	.25	.11
❑ 183	Rafael Carmona	.15	.07
❑ 184	Norm Charlton	.15	.07
❑ 185	Joey Cora	.15	.07
❑ 186	Ken Griffey Jr.	2.00	.90
❑ 187	Sterling Hitchcock	.15	.07
❑ 188	Dave Hollins	.15	.07
❑ 189	Randy Johnson	.75	.35
❑ 190	Edgar Martinez	.40	.18
❑ 191	Jamie Moyer	.15	.07
❑ 192	Alex Rodriguez	1.50	.70
❑ 193	Paul Sorrento	.15	.07
❑ 194	Salomon Torres	.15	.07
❑ 195	Bob Wells	.15	.07
❑ 196	Dan Wilson	.15	.07
❑ 197	Will Clark	.60	.25
❑ 198	Kevin Elster	.15	.07
❑ 199	Rene Gonzales	.15	.07
❑ 200	Juan Gonzalez	.60	.25
❑ 201	Rusty Greer	.25	.11
❑ 202	Darryl Hamilton	.15	.07
❑ 203	Mike Henneman	.15	.07
❑ 204	Ken Hill	.15	.07
❑ 205	Mark McLemore	.15	.07
❑ 206	Darren Oliver	.15	.07
❑ 207	Dean Palmer	.25	.11
❑ 208	Roger Pavlik	.15	.07
❑ 209	Ivan Rodriguez	.60	.25
❑ 210	Kurt Stillwell	.15	.07
❑ 211	Mickey Tettleton	.15	.07
❑ 212	Bobby Witt	.15	.07
❑ 213	Tilson Brito	.15	.07
❑ 214	Jacob Brumfield	.15	.07
❑ 215	Miguel Cairo	.15	.07
❑ 216	Joe Carter	.25	.11
❑ 217	Felipe Crespo	.15	.07
❑ 218	Carlos Delgado	.60	.25
❑ 219	Alex Gonzalez	.15	.07
❑ 220	Shawn Green	.60	.25
❑ 221	Juan Guzman	.15	.07
❑ 222	Pat Hentgen	.15	.07
❑ 223	Charlie O'Brien	.15	.07
❑ 224	John Olerud	.25	.11
❑ 225	Robert Perez	.15	.07
❑ 226	Tomas Perez	.15	.07
❑ 227	Juan Samuel	.15	.07
❑ 228	Ed Sprague	.15	.07
❑ 229	Mike Timlin	.15	.07
❑ 230	Rafael Belliard	.15	.07
❑ 231	Jermaine Dye	.25	.11
❑ 232	Tom Glavine	.60	.25
❑ 233	Marquis Grissom	.15	.07
❑ 234	Andruw Jones	.75	.35
❑ 235	Chipper Jones	1.25	.55
❑ 236	David Justice	.25	.11
❑ 237	Ryan Klesko	.25	.11
❑ 238	Mark Lemke	.15	.07
❑ 239	Javier Lopez	.25	.11
❑ 240	Greg Maddux	1.50	.70
❑ 241	Fred McGriff	.40	.18
❑ 242	Denny Neagle	.25	.11
❑ 243	Eddie Perez	.15	.07
❑ 244	John Smoltz	.25	.11
❑ 245	Mark Wohlers	.15	.07
❑ 246	Brant Brown	.15	.07
❑ 247	Scott Bullett	.15	.07
❑ 248	Leo Gomez	.15	.07
❑ 249	Luis Gonzalez	.60	.25
❑ 250	Mark Grace	.60	.25
❑ 251	Jose Hernandez	.15	.07
❑ 252	Brooks Kieschnick	.15	.07
❑ 253	Brian McRae	.15	.07
❑ 254	Jaime Navarro	.15	.07
❑ 255	Mike Perez	.15	.07
❑ 256	Rey Sanchez	.15	.07
❑ 257	Ryne Sandberg	.75	.35
❑ 258	Scott Servais	.15	.07
❑ 259	Sammy Sosa	1.25	.55
❑ 260	Pedro Valdes	.15	.07
❑ 261	Turk Wendell	.15	.07
❑ 262	Bret Boone	.25	.11
❑ 263	Jeff Branson	.15	.07
❑ 264	Jeff Brantley	.15	.07
❑ 265	Dave Burba	.15	.07
❑ 266	Hector Carrasco	.15	.07
❑ 267	Eric Davis	.25	.11
❑ 268	Willie Greene	.15	.07
❑ 269	Lenny Harris	.15	.07
❑ 270	Thomas Howard	.15	.07
❑ 271	Barry Larkin	.60	.25
❑ 272	Hal Morris	.15	.07
❑ 273	Joe Oliver	.15	.07
❑ 274	Eric Owens	.15	.07
❑ 275	Jose Rijo	.15	.07
❑ 276	Reggie Sanders	.15	.07
❑ 277	Eddie Taubensee	.15	.07
❑ 278	Jason Bates	.15	.07
❑ 279	Dante Bichette	.25	.11
❑ 280	Ellis Burks	.25	.11
❑ 281	Vinny Castilla	.25	.11
❑ 282	Andres Galarraga	.40	.18
❑ 283	Quinton McCracken	.15	.07
❑ 284	Jayhawk Owens	.15	.07
❑ 285	Jeff Reed	.15	.07
❑ 286	Bryan Rekar	.15	.07
❑ 287	Armando Reynoso	.15	.07
❑ 288	Kevin Ritz	.15	.07

	Card	Player	Mint	NrMt
❑	289	Bruce Ruffin	.15	.07
❑	290	John Vander Wal	.15	.07
❑	291	Larry Walker	.40	.18
❑	292	Walt Weiss	.15	.07
❑	293	Eric Young	.15	.07
❑	294	Kurt Abbott	.15	.07
❑	295	Alex Arias	.15	.07
❑	296	Miguel Batista	.15	.07
❑	297	Kevin Brown	.25	.11
❑	298	Luis Castillo	.15	.07
❑	299	Greg Colbrunn	.15	.07
❑	300	Jeff Conine	.15	.07
❑	301	Charles Johnson	.25	.11
❑	302	Al Leiter	.25	.11
❑	303	Robb Nen	.15	.07
❑	304	Joe Orsulak	.15	.07
❑	305	Yorkis Perez	.15	.07
❑	306	Edgar Renteria	.15	.07
❑	307	Gary Sheffield	.25	.11
❑	308	Jesus Tavarez	.15	.07
❑	309	Quilvio Veras	.15	.07
❑	310	Devon White	.25	.11
❑	311	Jeff Bagwell	.75	.35
❑	312	Derek Bell	.15	.07
❑	313	Sean Berry	.15	.07
❑	314	Craig Biggio	.40	.18
❑	315	Doug Drabek	.15	.07
❑	316	Tony Eusebio	.15	.07
❑	317	Ricky Gutierrez	.15	.07
❑	318	Xavier Hernandez	.15	.07
❑	319	Brian L. Hunter	.15	.07
❑	320	Darryl Kile	.25	.11
❑	321	Derrick May	.15	.07
❑	322	Orlando Miller	.15	.07
❑	323	James Mouton	.15	.07
❑	324	Bill Spiers	.15	.07
❑	325	Pedro Astacio	.15	.07
❑	326	Brett Butler	.25	.11
❑	327	Juan Castro	.15	.07
❑	328	Roger Cedeno	.15	.07
❑	329	Delino DeShields	.15	.07
❑	330	Karim Garcia	.15	.07
❑	331	Todd Hollandsworth	.15	.07
❑	332	Eric Karros	.25	.11
❑	333	Oreste Marrero	.15	.07
❑	334	Ramon Martinez	.15	.07
❑	335	Raul Mondesi	.25	.11
❑	336	Hideo Nomo	.60	.25
❑	337	Antonio Osuna	.15	.07
❑	338	Chan Ho Park	.25	.11
❑	339	Mike Piazza	1.50	.70
❑	340	Ismael Valdes	.15	.07
❑	341	Moises Alou	.25	.11
❑	342	Omar Daal	.15	.07
❑	343	Jeff Fassero	.15	.07
❑	344	Cliff Floyd	.25	.11
❑	345	Mark Grudzielanek	.15	.07
❑	346	Mike Lansing	.15	.07
❑	347	Pedro Martinez	.75	.35
❑	348	Sherman Obando	.15	.07
❑	349	Jose Paniagua	.15	.07
❑	350	Henry Rodriguez	.15	.07
❑	351	Mel Rojas	.15	.07
❑	352	F.P. Santangelo	.15	.07
❑	353	David Segui	.15	.07
❑	354	Dave Silvestri	.15	.07
❑	355	Ugueth Urbina	.15	.07
❑	356	Rondell White	.25	.11
❑	357	Edgardo Alfonzo	.25	.11
❑	358	Carlos Baerga	.15	.07
❑	359	Tim Bogar	.15	.07
❑	360	Rico Brogna	.15	.07
❑	361	Alvaro Espinoza	.15	.07
❑	362	Carl Everett	.25	.11
❑	363	John Franco	.25	.11
❑	364	Bernard Gilkey	.15	.07
❑	365	Todd Hundley	.15	.07
❑	366	Butch Huskey	.15	.07
❑	367	Jason Isringhausen	.15	.07
❑	368	Bobby Jones	.15	.07
❑	369	Lance Johnson	.15	.07
❑	370	Brent Mayne	.15	.07
❑	371	Alex Ochoa	.15	.07
❑	372	Rey Ordonez	.15	.07
❑	373	Ron Blazier	.15	.07
❑	374	Ricky Bottalico	.15	.07
❑	375	David Doster	.15	.07
❑	376	Lenny Dykstra	.25	.11
❑	377	Jim Eisenreich	.15	.07
❑	378	Bobby Estalella	.15	.07
❑	379	Gregg Jefferies	.15	.07
❑	380	Kevin Jordan	.15	.07
❑	381	Ricardo Jordan	.15	.07
❑	382	Mickey Morandini	.15	.07
❑	383	Ricky Otero	.15	.07
❑	384	Benito Santiago	.15	.07
❑	385	Gene Schall	.15	.07
❑	386	Curt Schilling	.60	.25
❑	387	Kevin Sefcik	.15	.07
❑	388	Kevin Stocker	.15	.07
❑	389	Jermaine Allensworth	.15	.07
❑	390	Jay Bell	.25	.11
❑	391	Jason Christiansen	.15	.07
❑	392	Francisco Cordova	.15	.07
❑	393	Mark Johnson	.15	.07
❑	394	Jason Kendall	.25	.11
❑	395	Jeff King	.15	.07
❑	396	Jon Lieber	.15	.07
❑	397	Nelson Liriano	.15	.07
❑	398	Esteban Loaiza	.15	.07
❑	399	Al Martin	.15	.07
❑	400	Orlando Merced	.15	.07
❑	401	Ramon Morel	.15	.07
❑	402	Luis Alicea	.15	.07
❑	403	Alan Benes	.15	.07
❑	404	Andy Benes	.15	.07
❑	405	Terry Bradshaw	.15	.07
❑	406	Royce Clayton	.15	.07
❑	407	Dennis Eckersley	.25	.11
❑	408	Gary Gaetti	.25	.11
❑	409	Mike Gallego	.15	.07
❑	410	Ron Gant	.15	.07
❑	411	Brian Jordan	.25	.11
❑	412	Ray Lankford	.15	.07
❑	413	John Mabry	.15	.07
❑	414	Willie McGee	.25	.11
❑	415	Tom Pagnozzi	.15	.07
❑	416	Ozzie Smith	.75	.35
❑	417	Todd Stottlemyre	.15	.07
❑	418	Mark Sweeney	.15	.07
❑	419	Andy Ashby	.15	.07
❑	420	Ken Caminiti	.25	.11
❑	421	Archi Cianfrocco	.15	.07
❑	422	Steve Finley	.25	.11
❑	423	Chris Gomez	.15	.07
❑	424	Tony Gwynn	1.25	.55
❑	425	Joey Hamilton	.15	.07
❑	426	Rickey Henderson	1.25	.55
❑	427	Trevor Hoffman	.25	.11
❑	428	Brian Johnson	.15	.07
❑	429	Wally Joyner	.25	.11
❑	430	Scott Livingstone	.15	.07
❑	431	Jody Reed	.15	.07
❑	432	Craig Shipley	.15	.07
❑	433	Fernando Valenzuela	.25	.11
❑	434	Greg Vaughn	.25	.11
❑	435	Rich Aurilia	.25	.11
❑	436	Kim Batiste	.15	.07
❑	437	Jose Bautista	.15	.07
❑	438	Rod Beck	.15	.07
❑	439	Marvin Benard	.15	.07
❑	440	Barry Bonds	1.50	.70
❑	441	Shawon Dunston	.15	.07
❑	442	Shawn Estes	.25	.11
❑	443	Osvaldo Fernandez	.15	.07
❑	444	Stan Javier	.15	.07
❑	445	David McCarty	.15	.07
❑	446	Bill Mueller RC	.40	.18
❑	447	Steve Scarsone	.15	.07
❑	448	Robby Thompson	.15	.07
❑	449	Rick Wilkins	.15	.07
❑	450	Matt Williams	.40	.18

1998 Pacific

			MINT	NRMT
		COMPLETE SET (450)	60.00	27.00
❑	1	Luis Alicea	.15	.07
❑	2	Garret Anderson	.25	.11
❑	3	Jason Dickson	.15	.07
❑	4	Gary DiSarcina	.15	.07

	Card	Player	Mint	NrMt
❑	5	Jim Edmonds	.40	.18
❑	6	Darin Erstad	.60	.25
❑	7	Chuck Finley	.25	.11
❑	8	Shigetoshi Hasegawa	.25	.11
❑	9	Rickey Henderson	1.25	.55
❑	10	Dave Hollins	.15	.07
❑	11	Mark Langston	.15	.07
❑	12	Orlando Palmeiro	.15	.07
❑	13	Troy Percival	.15	.07
❑	14	Tony Phillips	.15	.07
❑	15	Tim Salmon	.25	.11
❑	16	Allen Watson	.15	.07
❑	17	Roberto Alomar	.60	.25
❑	18	Brady Anderson	.25	.11
❑	19	Harold Baines	.25	.11
❑	20	Armando Benitez	.15	.07
❑	21	Geronimo Berroa	.15	.07
❑	22	Mike Bordick	.15	.07
❑	23	Eric Davis	.25	.11
❑	24	Scott Erickson	.15	.07
❑	25	Chris Hoiles	.15	.07
❑	26	Jimmy Key	.25	.11
❑	27	Aaron Ledesma	.15	.07
❑	28	Mike Mussina	.60	.25
❑	29	Randy Myers	.25	.11
❑	30	Jesse Orosco	.15	.07
❑	31	Rafael Palmeiro	.60	.25
❑	32	Jeff Reboulet	.15	.07
❑	33	Cal Ripken	2.50	1.10
❑	34	B.J. Surhoff	.25	.11
❑	35	Steve Avery	.15	.07
❑	36	Darren Bragg	.15	.07
❑	37	Wil Cordero	.15	.07
❑	38	Jeff Frye	.15	.07
❑	39	Nomar Garciaparra	1.50	.70
❑	40	Tom Gordon	.25	.11
❑	41	Bill Haselman	.15	.07
❑	42	Scott Hatteberg	.15	.07
❑	43	Butch Henry	.15	.07
❑	44	Reggie Jefferson	.15	.07
❑	45	Tim Naehring	.15	.07
❑	46	Troy O'Leary	.15	.07
❑	47	Jeff Suppan	.15	.07
❑	48	John Valentin	.15	.07
❑	49	Mo Vaughn	.25	.11
❑	50	Tim Wakefield	.15	.07
❑	51	James Baldwin	.15	.07
❑	52	Albert Belle	.25	.11
❑	53	Tony Castillo	.15	.07
❑	54	Doug Drabek	.15	.07
❑	55	Ray Durham	.25	.11
❑	56	Jorge Fabregas	.15	.07
❑	57	Ozzie Guillen	.15	.07
❑	58	Matt Karchner	.15	.07
❑	59	Norberto Martin	.15	.07
❑	60	Dave Martinez	.15	.07
❑	61	Lyle Mouton	.15	.07
❑	62	Jaime Navarro	.15	.07
❑	63	Frank Thomas	.75	.35
❑	64	Mario Valdez	.15	.07
❑	65	Robin Ventura	.25	.11
❑	66	Sandy Alomar Jr.	.25	.11
❑	67	Paul Assenmacher	.15	.07
❑	68	Tony Fernandez	.15	.07
❑	69	Brian Giles	.25	.11
❑	70	Marquis Grissom	.15	.07
❑	71	Orel Hershiser	.25	.11

❑ 72 Mike Jackson .15 .07
❑ 73 David Justice .25 .11
❑ 74 Albie Lopez .15 .07
❑ 75 Jose Mesa .15 .07
❑ 76 Charles Nagy .15 .07
❑ 77 Chad Ogea .15 .07
❑ 78 Manny Ramirez .75 .35
❑ 79 Jim Thome .60 .25
❑ 80 Omar Vizquel .25 .11
❑ 81 Matt Williams .40 .18
❑ 82 Jaret Wright .15 .07
❑ 83 Willie Blair .15 .07
❑ 84 Raul Casanova .15 .07
❑ 85 Tony Clark .25 .11
❑ 86 Deivi Cruz .15 .07
❑ 87 Damion Easley .15 .07
❑ 88 Travis Fryman .25 .11
❑ 89 Bobby Higginson .25 .11
❑ 90 Brian L. Hunter .15 .07
❑ 91 Todd Jones .15 .07
❑ 92 Dan Miceli .15 .07
❑ 93 Brian Moehler .15 .07
❑ 94 Mel Nieves .15 .07
❑ 95 Jody Reed .15 .07
❑ 96 Justin Thompson .15 .07
❑ 97 Bubba Trammell .15 .07
❑ 98 Kevin Appier .25 .11
❑ 99 Jay Bell .25 .11
❑ 100 Yamil Benitez .15 .07
❑ 101 Johnny Damon .25 .11
❑ 102 Chili Davis .25 .11
❑ 103 Jermaine Dye .25 .11
❑ 104 Jed Hansen .15 .07
❑ 105 Jeff King .15 .07
❑ 106 Mike Macfarlane .15 .07
❑ 107 Felix Martinez .15 .07
❑ 108 Jeff Montgomery .15 .07
❑ 109 Jose Offerman .15 .07
❑ 110 Dean Palmer .25 .11
❑ 111 Hipolito Pichardo .15 .07
❑ 112 Jose Rosado .15 .07
❑ 113 Jeromy Burnitz .25 .11
❑ 114 Jeff Cirillo .25 .11
❑ 115 Cal Eldred .15 .07
❑ 116 John Jaha .25 .11
❑ 117 Doug Jones .15 .07
❑ 118 Scott Karl .15 .07
❑ 119 Jesse Levis .15 .07
❑ 120 Mark Loretta .15 .07
❑ 121 Ben McDonald .15 .07
❑ 122 Jose Mercedes .15 .07
❑ 123 Matt Mieske .15 .07
❑ 124 Dave Nilsson .15 .07
❑ 125 Jose Valentin .15 .07
❑ 126 Fernando Vina .15 .07
❑ 127 Gerald Williams .15 .07
❑ 128 Rick Aguilera .15 .07
❑ 129 Rich Becker .15 .07
❑ 130 Ron Coomer .15 .07
❑ 131 Marty Cordova .15 .07
❑ 132 Eddie Guardado .15 .07
❑ 133 LaTroy Hawkins .15 .07
❑ 134 Denny Hocking .15 .07
❑ 135 Chuck Knoblauch .25 .11
❑ 136 Matt Lawton .15 .07
❑ 137 Pat Meares .15 .07
❑ 138 Paul Molitor .60 .25
❑ 139 David Ortiz .25 .11
❑ 140 Brad Radke .25 .11
❑ 141 Terry Steinbach .15 .07
❑ 142 Bob Tewksbury .15 .07
❑ 143 Javier Valentin .15 .07
❑ 144 Wade Boggs .60 .25
❑ 145 David Cone .25 .11
❑ 146 Chad Curtis .15 .07
❑ 147 Cecil Fielder .25 .11
❑ 148 Joe Girardi .15 .07
❑ 149 Dwight Gooden .15 .07
❑ 150 Hideki Irabu .15 .07
❑ 151 Derek Jeter 2.50 1.10
❑ 152 Tino Martinez .25 .11
❑ 153 Ramiro Mendoza .15 .07
❑ 154 Paul O'Neill .60 .25
❑ 155 Andy Pettitte .25 .11
❑ 156 Jorge Posada .25 .11
❑ 157 Mariano Rivera .25 .11
❑ 158 Rey Sanchez .15 .07
❑ 159 Luis Sojo .15 .07
❑ 160 David Wells .25 .11
❑ 161 Bernie Williams .60 .25
❑ 162 Rafael Bournigal .15 .07
❑ 163 Scott Brosius .25 .11
❑ 164 Jose Canseco .60 .25
❑ 165 Jason Giambi .60 .25
❑ 166 Ben Grieve .25 .11
❑ 167 Dave Magadan .15 .07
❑ 168 Brent Mayne .15 .07
❑ 169 Jason McDonald .15 .07
❑ 170 Izzy Molina .15 .07
❑ 171 Ariel Prieto .15 .07
❑ 172 Carlos Reyes .15 .07
❑ 173 Scott Spiezio .15 .07
❑ 174 Matt Stairs .15 .07
❑ 175 Bill Taylor .15 .07
❑ 176 Dave Telgheder .15 .07
❑ 177 Steve Wojciechowski .15 .07
❑ 178 Rich Amaral .15 .07
❑ 179 Bobby Ayala .15 .07
❑ 180 Jay Buhner .25 .11
❑ 181 Rafael Carmona .15 .07
❑ 182 Ken Cloude .15 .07
❑ 183 Joey Cora .15 .07
❑ 184 Russ Davis .15 .07
❑ 185 Jeff Fassero .15 .07
❑ 186 Ken Griffey Jr. 2.00 .90
❑ 187 Raul Ibanez .15 .07
❑ 188 Randy Johnson .75 .35
❑ 189 Roberto Kelly .15 .07
❑ 190 Edgar Martinez .40 .18
❑ 191 Jamie Moyer .15 .07
❑ 192 Omar Olivares .15 .07
❑ 193 Alex Rodriguez 1.50 .70
❑ 194 Heathcliff Slocumb .15 .07
❑ 195 Paul Sorrento .15 .07
❑ 196 Dan Wilson .15 .07
❑ 197 Scott Bailes .15 .07
❑ 198 John Burkett .15 .07
❑ 199 Domingo Cedeno .15 .07
❑ 200 Will Clark .60 .25
❑ 201 Hanley Frias RC .15 .07
❑ 202 Juan Gonzalez .60 .25
❑ 203 Tom Goodwin .15 .07
❑ 204 Rusty Greer .25 .11
❑ 205 Wilson Heredia .15 .07
❑ 206 Darren Oliver .15 .07
❑ 207 Bill Ripken .15 .07
❑ 208 Ivan Rodriguez .60 .25
❑ 209 Lee Stevens .15 .07
❑ 210 Fernando Tatis .15 .07
❑ 211 John Wetteland .25 .11
❑ 212 Bobby Witt .15 .07
❑ 213 Jacob Brumfield .15 .07
❑ 214 Joe Carter .25 .11
❑ 215 Roger Clemens 1.50 .70
❑ 216 Felipe Crespo .15 .07
❑ 217 Jose Cruz Jr. .25 .11
❑ 218 Carlos Delgado .60 .25
❑ 219 Mariano Duncan .15 .07
❑ 220 Carlos Garcia .15 .07
❑ 221 Alex Gonzalez .15 .07
❑ 222 Juan Guzman .15 .07
❑ 223 Pat Hentgen .15 .07
❑ 224 Orlando Merced .15 .07
❑ 225 Tomas Perez .15 .07
❑ 226 Paul Quantrill .15 .07
❑ 227 Benito Santiago .15 .07
❑ 228 Woody Williams .15 .07
❑ 229 Rafael Belliard .15 .07
❑ 230 Jeff Blauser .15 .07
❑ 231 Pedro Borbon .15 .07
❑ 232 Tom Glavine .60 .25
❑ 233 Tony Graffanino .15 .07
❑ 234 Andruw Jones .60 .25
❑ 235 Chipper Jones 1.25 .55
❑ 236 Ryan Klesko .25 .11
❑ 237 Mark Lemke .15 .07
❑ 238 Kenny Lofton .25 .11
❑ 239 Javier Lopez .25 .11
❑ 240 Fred McGriff .40 .18
❑ 241 Greg Maddux 1.50 .70
❑ 242 Denny Neagle .15 .07
❑ 243 John Smoltz .25 .11
❑ 244 Michael Tucker .15 .07
❑ 245 Mark Wohlers .15 .07
❑ 246 Manny Alexander .15 .07
❑ 247 Miguel Batista .15 .07
❑ 248 Mark Clark .15 .07
❑ 249 Doug Glanville .15 .07
❑ 250 Jeremi Gonzalez .15 .07
❑ 251 Mark Grace .60 .25
❑ 252 Jose Hernandez .15 .07
❑ 253 Lance Johnson .15 .07
❑ 254 Brooks Kieschnick .15 .07
❑ 255 Kevin Orie .15 .07
❑ 256 Ryne Sandberg .75 .35
❑ 257 Scott Servais .15 .07
❑ 258 Sammy Sosa 1.25 .55
❑ 259 Kevin Tapani .15 .07
❑ 260 Ramon Tatis .15 .07
❑ 261 Bret Boone .25 .11
❑ 262 Dave Burba .15 .07
❑ 263 Brook Fordyce .15 .07
❑ 264 Willie Greene .15 .07
❑ 265 Barry Larkin .60 .25
❑ 266 Pedro A. Martinez .15 .07
❑ 267 Hal Morris .15 .07
❑ 268 Joe Oliver .15 .07
❑ 269 Eduardo Perez .15 .07
❑ 270 Pokey Reese .15 .07
❑ 271 Felix Rodriguez .15 .07
❑ 272 Deion Sanders .25 .11
❑ 273 Reggie Sanders .15 .07
❑ 274 Jeff Shaw .15 .07
❑ 275 Scott Sullivan .15 .07
❑ 276 Brett Tomko .15 .07
❑ 277 Roger Bailey .15 .07
❑ 278 Dante Bichette .25 .11
❑ 279 Ellis Burks .25 .11
❑ 280 Vinny Castilla .25 .11
❑ 281 Frank Castillo .15 .07
❑ 282 Mike DeJean RC .15 .07
❑ 283 Andres Galarraga .40 .18
❑ 284 Darren Holmes .15 .07
❑ 285 Kirt Manwaring .15 .07
❑ 286 Quinton McCracken .15 .07
❑ 287 Neifi Perez .15 .07
❑ 288 Steve Reed .15 .07
❑ 289 John Thomson .15 .07
❑ 290 Larry Walker .40 .18
❑ 291 Walt Weiss .25 .11
❑ 292 Kurt Abbott .15 .07
❑ 293 Antonio Alfonseca .15 .07
❑ 294 Moises Alou .25 .11
❑ 295 Alex Arias .15 .07
❑ 296 Bobby Bonilla .25 .11
❑ 297 Kevin Brown .40 .18
❑ 298 Craig Counsell .15 .07
❑ 299 Darren Daulton .25 .11
❑ 300 Jim Eisenreich .15 .07
❑ 301 Alex Fernandez .15 .07
❑ 302 Felix Heredia .15 .07
❑ 303 Livan Hernandez .15 .07
❑ 304 Charles Johnson .25 .11
❑ 305 Al Leiter .25 .11
❑ 306 Robb Nen .15 .07
❑ 307 Edgar Renteria .15 .07
❑ 308 Gary Sheffield .25 .11
❑ 309 Devon White .15 .07
❑ 310 Bob Abreu .25 .11
❑ 311 Brad Ausmus .15 .07
❑ 312 Jeff Bagwell .75 .35
❑ 313 Derek Bell .15 .07
❑ 314 Sean Berry .15 .07
❑ 315 Craig Biggio .40 .18
❑ 316 Ramon Garcia .15 .07
❑ 317 Luis Gonzalez .60 .25
❑ 318 Ricky Gutierrez .15 .07
❑ 319 Mike Hampton .25 .11
❑ 320 Richard Hidalgo .25 .11
❑ 321 Thomas Howard .15 .07
❑ 322 Darryl Kile .25 .11
❑ 323 Jose Lima .15 .07
❑ 324 Shane Reynolds .15 .07
❑ 325 Bill Spiers .15 .07
❑ 326 Tom Candiotti .15 .07
❑ 327 Roger Cedeno .15 .07
❑ 328 Greg Gagne .15 .07
❑ 329 Karim Garcia .15 .07

❑ 330 Wilton Guerrero	.15	.07
❑ 331 Todd Hollandsworth	.15	.07
❑ 332 Eric Karros	.25	.11
❑ 333 Ramon Martinez	.15	.07
❑ 334 Raul Mondesi	.25	.11
❑ 335 Otis Nixon	.15	.07
❑ 336 Hideo Nomo	.60	.25
❑ 337 Antonio Osuna	.15	.07
❑ 338 Chan Ho Park	.25	.11
❑ 339 Mike Piazza	1.50	.70
❑ 340 Dennis Reyes	.15	.07
❑ 341 Ismael Valdes	.15	.07
❑ 342 Todd Worrell	.15	.07
❑ 343 Todd Zeile	.25	.11
❑ 344 Darrin Fletcher	.15	.07
❑ 345 Mark Grudzielanek	.15	.07
❑ 346 Vladimir Guerrero	.75	.35
❑ 347 Dustin Hermanson	.15	.07
❑ 348 Mike Lansing	.15	.07
❑ 349 Pedro Martinez	.75	.35
❑ 350 Ryan McGuire	.15	.07
❑ 351 Jose Paniagua	.15	.07
❑ 352 Carlos Perez	.15	.07
❑ 353 Henry Rodriguez	.15	.07
❑ 354 F.P. Santangelo	.15	.07
❑ 355 David Segui	.15	.07
❑ 356 Ugueth Urbina	.15	.07
❑ 357 Marc Valdes	.15	.07
❑ 358 Jose Vidro	.25	.11
❑ 359 Rondell White	.25	.11
❑ 360 Juan Acevedo	.15	.07
❑ 361 Edgardo Alfonzo	.25	.11
❑ 362 Carlos Baerga	.15	.07
❑ 363 Carl Everett	.25	.11
❑ 364 John Franco	.25	.11
❑ 365 Bernard Gilkey	.15	.07
❑ 366 Todd Hundley	.15	.07
❑ 367 Butch Huskey	.15	.07
❑ 368 Bobby Jones	.15	.07
❑ 369 T.Kashiwada RC	.15	.07
❑ 370 Greg McMichael	.15	.07
❑ 371 Brian McRae	.15	.07
❑ 372 Alex Ochoa	.15	.07
❑ 373 John Olerud	.25	.11
❑ 374 Rey Ordonez	.15	.07
❑ 375 Turk Wendell	.15	.07
❑ 376 Ricky Bottalico	.15	.07
❑ 377 Rico Brogna	.15	.07
❑ 378 Len Dykstra	.25	.11
❑ 379 Bobby Estalella	.15	.07
❑ 380 Wayne Gomes	.15	.07
❑ 381 Tyler Green	.15	.07
❑ 382 Gregg Jefferies	.15	.07
❑ 383 Mark Leiter	.15	.07
❑ 384 Mike Lieberthal	.25	.11
❑ 385 Mickey Morandini	.15	.07
❑ 386 Scott Rolen	.60	.25
❑ 387 Curt Schilling	.60	.25
❑ 388 Kevin Stocker	.15	.07
❑ 389 Danny Tartabull	.15	.07
❑ 390 Jermaine Allensworth	.15	.07
❑ 391 Adrian Brown	.15	.07
❑ 392 Jason Christiansen	.15	.07
❑ 393 Steve Cooke	.15	.07
❑ 394 Francisco Cordova	.15	.07
❑ 395 Jose Guillen	.15	.07
❑ 396 Jason Kendall	.25	.11
❑ 397 Jon Lieber	.15	.07
❑ 398 Esteban Loaiza	.15	.07
❑ 399 Al Martin	.15	.07
❑ 400 Kevin Polcovich	.15	.07
❑ 401 Joe Randa	.15	.07
❑ 402 Ricardo Rincon	.15	.07
❑ 403 Tony Womack	.15	.07
❑ 404 Kevin Young	.25	.11
❑ 405 Andy Benes	.15	.07
❑ 406 Royce Clayton	.15	.07
❑ 407 Delino DeShields	.15	.07
❑ 408 Mike Difelice RC	.15	.07
❑ 409 Dennis Eckersley	.25	.11
❑ 410 John Frascatore	.15	.07
❑ 411 Gary Gaetti	.25	.11
❑ 412 Ron Gant	.25	.11
❑ 413 Brian Jordan	.25	.11
❑ 414 Ray Lankford	.15	.07
❑ 415 Willie McGee	.25	.11
❑ 416 Mark McGwire	2.50	1.10
❑ 417 Matt Morris	.25	.11
❑ 418 Luis Ordaz	.15	.07
❑ 419 Todd Stottlemyre	.15	.07
❑ 420 Andy Ashby	.15	.07
❑ 421 Jim Bruske	.15	.07
❑ 422 Ken Caminiti	.25	.11
❑ 423 Will Cunnane	.15	.07
❑ 424 Steve Finley	.25	.11
❑ 425 John Flaherty	.15	.07
❑ 426 Chris Gomez	.15	.07
❑ 427 Tony Gwynn	1.25	.55
❑ 428 Joey Hamilton	.15	.07
❑ 429 Carlos Hernandez	.15	.07
❑ 430 Sterling Hitchcock	.15	.07
❑ 431 Trevor Hoffman	.25	.11
❑ 432 Wally Joyner	.25	.11
❑ 433 Greg Vaughn	.25	.11
❑ 434 Quilvio Veras	.15	.07
❑ 435 Wilson Alvarez	.15	.07
❑ 436 Rod Beck	.15	.07
❑ 437 Barry Bonds	1.50	.70
❑ 438 Jacob Cruz	.15	.07
❑ 439 Shawn Estes	.25	.11
❑ 440 Darryl Hamilton	.15	.07
❑ 441 Roberto Hernandez	.15	.07
❑ 442 Glenallen Hill	.15	.07
❑ 443 Stan Javier	.15	.07
❑ 444 Brian Johnson	.15	.07
❑ 445 Jeff Kent	.40	.18
❑ 446 Bill Mueller	.15	.07
❑ 447 Kirk Rueter	.15	.07
❑ 448 J.T. Snow	.25	.11
❑ 449 Julian Tavarez	.15	.07
❑ 450 Jose Vizcaino	.15	.07

1999 Pacific

	MINT	NRMT
COMPLETE SET (500)	80.00	36.00
❑ 1 Garret Anderson	.25	.11
❑ 2 Jason Dickson	.15	.07
❑ 3 Gary DiSarcina	.15	.07
❑ 4 Jim Edmonds	.40	.18
❑ 5 Darin Erstad	.60	.25
❑ 6 Chuck Finley	.25	.11
❑ 7 Shigetoshi Hasegawa	.15	.07
❑ 8 Ken Hill	.15	.07
❑ 9 Dave Hollins	.15	.07
❑ 10 Phil Nevin	.25	.11
❑ 11 Troy Percival	.15	.07
❑ 12 Tim Salmon *	.25	.11
❑ 12A Tim Salmon Headshot	.25	.11
❑ 13 Brian Anderson	.15	.07
❑ 14 Tony Batista	.25	.11
❑ 15 Jay Bell	.25	.11
❑ 16 Andy Benes	.15	.07
❑ 17 Yamil Benitez	.15	.07
❑ 18 Omar Daal	.15	.07
❑ 19 David Dellucci	.15	.07
❑ 20 Karim Garcia	.15	.07
❑ 21 Bernard Gilkey	.15	.07
❑ 22 Travis Lee *	.15	.07
❑ 22A Travis Lee Headshot	.15	.07
❑ 23 Aaron Small	.15	.07
❑ 24 Kelly Stinnett	.15	.07
❑ 25 Devon White	.15	.07
❑ 26 Matt Williams	.40	.18
❑ 27 Bruce Chen *	.15	.07
❑ 27A Bruce Chen Headshot	.15	.07
❑ 28 Andres Galarraga *	.40	.18
❑ 28A A.Galarraga Headshot	.40	.18
❑ 29 Tom Glavine	.60	.25
❑ 30 Ozzie Guillen	.15	.07
❑ 31 Andruw Jones	.60	.25
❑ 32 Chipper Jones *	1.25	.55
❑ 32A C.Jones Headshot	1.50	.70
❑ 33 Ryan Klesko	.25	.11
❑ 34 George Lombard	.15	.07
❑ 35 Javy Lopez	.25	.11
❑ 36 Greg Maddux *	1.50	.70
❑ 36A G.Maddux Headshot	1.50	.70
❑ 37 Marty Malloy *	.15	.07
❑ 37A M.Malloy Headshot	.15	.07
❑ 38 Dennis Martinez	.25	.11
❑ 39 Kevin Millwood	.15	.07
❑ 40 Alex Rodriguez *	1.50	.70
❑ 40A Alex Rodriguez Headshot	1.50	.70
❑ 41 Denny Neagle	.15	.07
❑ 42 John Smoltz	.25	.11
❑ 43 Michael Tucker	.15	.07
❑ 44 Walt Weiss	.15	.07
❑ 45 Roberto Alomar *	.60	.25
❑ 45A R.Alomar Headshot	.60	.25
❑ 46 Brady Anderson	.25	.11
❑ 47 Harold Baines	.25	.11
❑ 48 Mike Burdick	.15	.07
❑ 49 Danny Clyburn *	.15	.07
❑ 49A D.Clyburn Headshot	.15	.07
❑ 50 Eric Davis	.25	.11
❑ 51 Scott Erickson	.15	.07
❑ 52 Chris Hoiles	.15	.07
❑ 53 Jimmy Key	.15	.07
❑ 54 Ryan Minor *	.15	.07
❑ 54A Ryan Minor Headshot	.15	.07
❑ 55 Mike Mussina	.60	.25
❑ 56 Jesse Orosco	.15	.07
❑ 57 Rafael Palmeiro *	.60	.25
❑ 57A R.Palmeiro Headshot	.60	.25
❑ 58 Sidney Ponson	.15	.07
❑ 59 Arthur Rhodes	.15	.07
❑ 60 Cal Ripken *	2.50	1.10
❑ 60A Cal Ripken Headshot	2.50	1.10
❑ 61 B.J. Surhoff	.25	.11
❑ 62 Steve Avery	.15	.07
❑ 63 Darren Bragg	.15	.07
❑ 64 Dennis Eckersley	.25	.11
❑ 65 Nomar Garciaparra *	1.50	.70
❑ 65A Nomar Garciaparra Headshot	1.50	.70
❑ 66 Sammy Sosa *	1.25	.55
❑ 66A S.Sosa Headshot	1.25	.55
❑ 67 Tom Gordon	.15	.07
❑ 68 Reggie Jefferson	.15	.07
❑ 69 Darren Lewis	.15	.07
❑ 70 Mark McGwire *	2.50	1.10
❑ 70A M.McGwire Headshot	2.50	1.10
❑ 71 Pedro Martinez	.75	.35
❑ 72 Troy O'Leary	.15	.07
❑ 73 Bret Saberhagen	.25	.11
❑ 74 Mike Stanley	.15	.07
❑ 75 John Valentin	.15	.07
❑ 76 Jason Varitek	.25	.11
❑ 77 Mo Vaughn	.25	.11
❑ 78 Tim Wakefield	.15	.07
❑ 79 Manny Alexander	.15	.07
❑ 80 Rod Beck	.15	.07
❑ 81 Brant Brown	.15	.07
❑ 82 Mark Clark	.15	.07
❑ 83 Gary Gaetti	.15	.07
❑ 84 Mark Grace	.60	.25
❑ 85 Jose Hernandez	.15	.07
❑ 86 Lance Johnson	.15	.07
❑ 87 Jason Maxwell *	.15	.07
❑ 87A J.Maxwell Headshot	.15	.07
❑ 88 Mickey Morandini	.15	.07
❑ 89 Terry Mulholland	.15	.07
❑ 90 Henry Rodriguez	.15	.07
❑ 91 Scott Servais	.15	.07
❑ 92 Kevin Tapani	.15	.07
❑ 93 Pedro Valdes	.15	.07
❑ 94 Kerry Wood	.60	.25

❑ 95 Jeff Abbott .15 .07
❑ 96 James Baldwin .15 .07
❑ 97 Albert Belle .25 .11
❑ 98 Mike Cameron .25 .11
❑ 99 Mike Caruso .15 .07
❑ 100 Wil Cordero .15 .07
❑ 101 Ray Durham .25 .11
❑ 102 Jaime Navarro .15 .07
❑ 103 Greg Norton .15 .07
❑ 104 Maggio Ordonez .40 .18
❑ 105 Mike Sirotka .15 .07
❑ 106 Frank Thomas * .75 .35
❑ 106A F.Thomas Headshot .. 1.00 .45
❑ 107 Robin Ventura .25 .11
❑ 108 Craig Wilson .15 .07
❑ 109 Aaron Boone .15 .07
❑ 110 Bret Boone .25 .11
❑ 111 Sean Casey .40 .18
❑ 112 Pete Harnisch .15 .07
❑ 113 John Hudek .15 .07
❑ 114 Barry Larkin .60 .25
❑ 115 Eduardo Perez .15 .07
❑ 116 Mike Remlinger .15 .07
❑ 117 Reggie Sanders .15 .07
❑ 118 Chris Stynes .15 .07
❑ 119 Eddie Taubensee .15 .07
❑ 120 Brett Tomko .15 .07
❑ 121 Pat Watkins .15 .07
❑ 122 Dmitri Young .25 .11
❑ 123 Sandy Alomar Jr. .25 .11
❑ 124 Dave Burba .15 .07
❑ 125 Bartolo Colon .25 .11
❑ 126 Joey Cora .15 .07
❑ 127 Brian Giles .25 .11
❑ 128 Dwight Gooden .25 .11
❑ 129 Mike Jackson .15 .07
❑ 130 David Justice .25 .11
❑ 131 Kenny Lofton .25 .11
❑ 132 Charles Nagy .15 .07
❑ 133 Chad Ogea .15 .07
❑ 134 Manny Ramirez * .75 .35
❑ 134A M.Ramirez Headshot .. .75 .35
❑ 135 Richie Sexson .25 .11
❑ 136 Jim Thome * .60 .25
❑ 136A J.Thome Headshot .60 .25
❑ 137 Omar Vizquel .25 .11
❑ 138 Jaret Wright .15 .07
❑ 139 Pedro Astacio .15 .07
❑ 140 Jason Bates .15 .07
❑ 141 Dante Bichette * .25 .11
❑ 141A Dante Bichette Headshot .25 .11
❑ 142 Vinny Castilla * .25 .11
❑ 142A V.Castilla Headshot .25 .11
❑ 143 Edgard Clemente * .15 .07
❑ 143A Edgard Clemente Headshot .15 .07
❑ 144 Derrick Gibson * .15 .07
❑ 144A D. Gibson Headshot .15 .07
❑ 145 Curtis Goodwin .15 .07
❑ 146 Todd Helton * .75 .35
❑ 146A T.Helton Headshot .75 .35
❑ 147 Bobby Jones .15 .07
❑ 148 Darryl Kile .25 .11
❑ 149 Mike Lansing .15 .07
❑ 150 Chuck McElroy .15 .07
❑ 151 Neifi Perez .15 .07
❑ 152 Jeff Reed .15 .07
❑ 153 John Thomson .15 .07
❑ 154 Larry Walker * .40 .18
❑ 154A L.Walker Headshot .40 .18
❑ 155 Jamey Wright .15 .07
❑ 156 Kimera Bartee .15 .07
❑ 157 Geronimo Berroa .15 .07
❑ 158 Raul Casanova .15 .07
❑ 159 Frank Catalanotto .15 .07
❑ 160 Tony Clark .25 .11
❑ 161 Deivi Cruz .15 .07
❑ 162 Damion Easley .15 .07
❑ 163 Juan Encarnacion .25 .11
❑ 164 Luis Gonzalez .60 .25
❑ 165 Seth Greisinger .15 .07
❑ 166 Bob Higginson .25 .11
❑ 167 Brian L.Hunter .15 .07
❑ 168 Todd Jones .15 .07
❑ 169 Justin Thompson .15 .07
❑ 170 Antonio Alfonseca .15 .07
❑ 171 Dave Berg .15 .07
❑ 172 John Cangelosi .15 .07
❑ 173 Craig Counsell .15 .07
❑ 174 Todd Dunwoody .15 .07
❑ 175 Cliff Floyd .25 .11
❑ 176 Alex Gonzalez .15 .07
❑ 177 Livan Hernandez .15 .07
❑ 178 Ryan Jackson .15 .07
❑ 179 Mark Kotsay .15 .07
❑ 180 Derrek Lee .25 .11
❑ 181 Matt Mantei .15 .07
❑ 182 Brian Meadows .15 .07
❑ 183 Edgar Renteria .15 .07
❑ 184 Moises Alou * .25 .11
❑ 184A M.Alou Headshot .25 .11
❑ 185 Brad Ausmus .15 .07
❑ 186 Jeff Bagwell * .75 .35
❑ 186A J.Bagwell Headshot .75 .35
❑ 187 Derek Bell .15 .07
❑ 188 Sean Berry .15 .07
❑ 189 Craig Biggio .40 .18
❑ 190 Carl Everett .25 .11
❑ 191 Ricky Gutierrez .15 .07
❑ 192 Mike Hampton .25 .11
❑ 193 Doug Henry .15 .07
❑ 194 Richard Hidalgo .25 .11
❑ 195 Randy Johnson .75 .35
❑ 196 Russ Johnson * .15 .07
❑ 196A R.Johnson Headshot .. .15 .07
❑ 197 Shane Reynolds .15 .07
❑ 198 Bill Spiers .15 .07
❑ 199 Kevin Appier .25 .11
❑ 200 Tim Belcher .15 .07
❑ 201 Jeff Conine .15 .07
❑ 202 Johnny Damon .25 .11
❑ 203 Jermaine Dye .25 .11
❑ 204 Jeremy Giambi * .15 .07
❑ 204A Je. Giambi Headshot .. .15 .07
❑ 205 Jeff King .15 .07
❑ 206 Shane Mack .15 .07
❑ 207 Jeff Montgomery .15 .07
❑ 208 Hal Morris .15 .07
❑ 209 Jose Offerman .15 .07
❑ 210 Dean Palmer .25 .11
❑ 211 Jose Rosado .15 .07
❑ 212 Glendon Rusch .15 .07
❑ 213 Larry Sutton .15 .07
❑ 214 Mike Sweeney .25 .11
❑ 215 Bobby Bonilla .25 .11
❑ 216 Alex Cora .15 .07
❑ 217 Darren Dreifort .15 .07
❑ 218 Mark Grudzielanek .15 .07
❑ 219 Todd Hollandsworth .15 .07
❑ 220 Trenidad Hubbard .15 .07
❑ 221 Charles Johnson .25 .11
❑ 222 Eric Karros .25 .11
❑ 223 Matt Luke .15 .07
❑ 224 Ramon Martinez .15 .07
❑ 225 Raul Mondesi .25 .11
❑ 226 Chan Ho Park .25 .11
❑ 227 Jeff Shaw .15 .07
❑ 228 Gary Sheffield .25 .11
❑ 229 Eric Young .15 .07
❑ 230 Jeromy Burnitz .25 .11
❑ 231 Jeff Cirillo .25 .11
❑ 232 Marquis Grissom .15 .07
❑ 233 Bobby Hughes .15 .07
❑ 234 John Jaha .15 .07
❑ 235 Geoff Jenkins .25 .11
❑ 236 Scott Karl .15 .07
❑ 237 Mark Loretta .15 .07
❑ 238 Mike Matheny .15 .07
❑ 239 Mike Myers .15 .07
❑ 240 Dave Nilsson .15 .07
❑ 241 Bob Wickman .15 .07
❑ 242 Jose Valentin .15 .07
❑ 243 Fernando Vina .15 .07
❑ 244 Rick Aguilera .15 .07
❑ 245 Ron Coomer .15 .07
❑ 246 Marty Cordova .15 .07
❑ 247 Denny Hocking .15 .07
❑ 248 Matt Lawton .25 .11
❑ 249 Pat Meares .15 .07
❑ 250 Paul Molitor * .60 .25
❑ 250A P.Molitor Headshot .60 .25
❑ 251 Otis Nixon .15 .07
❑ 252 Alex Ochoa .15 .07
❑ 253 David Ortiz .25 .11
❑ 254 A.J. Pierzynski .15 .07
❑ 255 Brad Radke .25 .11
❑ 256 Terry Steinbach .15 .07
❑ 257 Bob Tewksbury .15 .07
❑ 258 Todd Walker .15 .07
❑ 259 Shane Andrews .15 .07
❑ 260 Shayne Bennett .15 .07
❑ 261 Orlando Cabrera .15 .07
❑ 262 Brad Fullmer .25 .11
❑ 263 Vladimir Guerrero .75 .35
❑ 264 Wilton Guerrero .15 .07
❑ 265 Dustin Hermanson .15 .07
❑ 266 Terry Jones RC .15 .07
❑ 267 Steve Kline .15 .07
❑ 268 Carl Pavano .15 .07
❑ 269 F.P. Santangelo .15 .07
❑ 270 Fernando Seguignol * .15 .07
❑ 270A Fernando Seguignol Headshot .15 .07
❑ 271 Ugueth Urbina .15 .07
❑ 272 Jose Vidro .25 .11
❑ 273 Chris Widger .15 .07
❑ 274 Edgardo Alfonzo .25 .11
❑ 275 Carlos Baerga .15 .07
❑ 276 John Franco .25 .11
❑ 277 Todd Hundley .15 .07
❑ 278 Butch Huskey .15 .07
❑ 279 Bobby Jones .15 .07
❑ 280 Al Leiter .25 .11
❑ 281 Greg McMichael .15 .07
❑ 282 Brian McRae .15 .07
❑ 283 Hideo Nomo .60 .25
❑ 284 John Olerud .25 .11
❑ 285 Rey Ordonez .15 .07
❑ 286 Mike Piazza * 1.50 .70
❑ 286A M.Piazza Headshot 1.50 .70
❑ 287 Turk Wendell .15 .07
❑ 288 Masato Yoshii .25 .11
❑ 289 David Cone .25 .11
❑ 290 Chad Curtis .15 .07
❑ 291 Joe Girardi .15 .07
❑ 292 Orlando Hernandez .25 .11
❑ 293 Hideki Irabu * .15 .07
❑ 293A H.Irabu Headshot .15 .07
❑ 294 Derek Jeter * 2.50 1.10
❑ 294A D.Jeter Headshot 2.50 1.10
❑ 295 Chuck Knoblauch .25 .11
❑ 296 Mike Lowell * .25 .11
❑ 296A M.Lowell Headshot .25 .11
❑ 297 Tino Martinez .25 .11
❑ 298 Ramiro Mendoza .15 .07
❑ 299 Paul O'Neill .60 .25
❑ 300 Andy Pettitte .25 .11
❑ 301 Jorge Posada .25 .11
❑ 302 Tim Raines .25 .11
❑ 303 Mariano Rivera .25 .11
❑ 304 David Wells .25 .11
❑ 305 Bernie Williams * .60 .25
❑ 305A Bernie Williams Headshot .60 .25
❑ 306 Mike Blowers .15 .07
❑ 307 Tom Candiotti .15 .07
❑ 308 Eric Chavez * .25 .11
❑ 308A E.Chavez Headshot .25 .11
❑ 309 Ryan Christenson .15 .07
❑ 310 Jason Giambi .60 .25
❑ 311 Ben Grieve * .25 .11
❑ 311A Ben Grieve Headshot .. .25 .11
❑ 312 Rickey Henderson 1.25 .55
❑ 313 A.J. Hinch .15 .07
❑ 314 Jason McDonald .15 .07
❑ 315 Bip Roberts .15 .07
❑ 316 Kenny Rogers .15 .07
❑ 317 Scott Spiezio .15 .07
❑ 318 Matt Stairs .15 .07
❑ 319 Miguel Tejada .25 .11
❑ 320 Bob Abreu .25 .11
❑ 321 Alex Arias .15 .07
❑ 322 Gary Bennett RC .15 .07
❑ 322A Gary Bennett RC Headshot .15 .07
❑ 323 Ricky Bottalico .15 .07
❑ 324 Rico Brogna .15 .07

❑ 325 Bobby Estalella .15 .07
❑ 326 Doug Glanville .15 .07
❑ 327 Kevin Jordan .15 .07
❑ 328 Mark Leiter .15 .07
❑ 329 Wendell Magee .15 .07
❑ 330 Mark Portugal .15 .07
❑ 331 Desi Relaford .15 .07
❑ 332 Scott Rolen .60 .25
❑ 333 Curt Schilling .60 .25
❑ 334 Kevin Sefcik .15 .07
❑ 335 Adrian Brown .15 .07
❑ 336 Emil Brown .15 .07
❑ 337 Lou Collier .15 .07
❑ 338 Francisco Cordova .15 .07
❑ 339 Freddy Garcia .15 .07
❑ 340 Jose Guillen .15 .07
❑ 341 Jason Kendall .25 .11
❑ 342 Al Martin .15 .07
❑ 343 Abraham Nunez .15 .07
❑ 344 Aramis Ramirez .25 .11
❑ 345 Ricardo Rincon .15 .07
❑ 346 Jason Schmidt .15 .07
❑ 347 Turner Ward .15 .07
❑ 348 Tony Womack .15 .07
❑ 349 Kevin Young .25 .11
❑ 350 Juan Acevedo .15 .07
❑ 351 Delino DeShields .15 .07
❑ 352 J.D. Drew * .60 .25
❑ 352A J.D. Drew Headshot .60 .25
❑ 353 Ron Gant .25 .11
❑ 354 Brian Jordan .25 .11
❑ 355 Ray Lankford .15 .07
❑ 356 Eli Marrero .15 .07
❑ 357 Kent Mercker .15 .07
❑ 358 Matt Morris .25 .11
❑ 359 Luis Ordaz .15 .07
❑ 360 Donovan Osborne .15 .07
❑ 361 Placido Polanco .15 .07
❑ 362 Fernando Tatis .15 .07
❑ 363 Andy Ashby .15 .07
❑ 364 Kevin Brown .40 .18
❑ 365 Ken Caminiti .25 .11
❑ 366 Steve Finley .25 .11
❑ 367 Chris Gomez .15 .07
❑ 368 Tony Gwynn * 1.25 .55
❑ 368A T.Gwynn Headshot 1.25 .55
❑ 369 Joey Hamilton .15 .07
❑ 370 Carlos Hernandez .15 .07
❑ 371 Trevor Hoffman .25 .11
❑ 372 Wally Joyner .25 .11
❑ 373 Jim Leyritz .15 .07
❑ 374 Ruben Rivera .15 .07
❑ 375 Greg Vaughn .25 .11
❑ 376 Quilvio Veras .15 .07
❑ 377 Rich Aurilia .25 .11
❑ 378 Barry Bonds * 1.50 .70
❑ 378A B.Bonds Headshot 1.25 .55
❑ 379 Ellis Burks .25 .11
❑ 380 Joe Carter .25 .11
❑ 381 Stan Javier .15 .07
❑ 382 Brian Johnson .15 .07
❑ 383 Jeff Kent .40 .18
❑ 384 Jose Mesa .15 .07
❑ 385 Bill Mueller .15 .07
❑ 386 Robb Nen .15 .07
❑ 387 Armando Rios * .15 .07
❑ 387A A.Rios Headshot .15 .07
❑ 388 Kirk Rueter .15 .07
❑ 389 Rey Sanchez .15 .07
❑ 390 J.T. Snow .25 .11
❑ 391 David Bell .15 .07
❑ 392 Jay Buhner .25 .11
❑ 393 Ken Cloude .15 .07
❑ 394 Russ Davis .15 .07
❑ 395 Jeff Fassero .15 .07
❑ 396 Ken Griffey Jr. * 2.00 .90
❑ 396A Ken Griffey Jr. Headshot 2.00 .90
❑ 397 Giomar Guevara RC .15 .07
❑ 398 Carlos Guillen .15 .07
❑ 399 Edgar Martinez .40 .18
❑ 400 Shane Monahan .15 .07
❑ 401 Jamie Moyer .15 .07
❑ 402 David Segui .15 .07
❑ 403 Makoto Suzuki .15 .07
❑ 404 Mike Timlin .15 .07
❑ 405 Dan Wilson .15 .07
❑ 406 Wilson Alvarez .15 .07
❑ 407 Rolando Arrojo .15 .07
❑ 408 Wade Boggs .60 .25
❑ 409 Miguel Cairo .15 .07
❑ 410 Roberto Hernandez .15 .07
❑ 411 Mike Kelly .15 .07
❑ 412 Aaron Ledesma .15 .07
❑ 413 Albie Lopez .15 .07
❑ 414 Dave Martinez .15 .07
❑ 415 Quinton McCracken .15 .07
❑ 416 Fred McGriff .40 .18
❑ 417 Bryan Rekar .15 .07
❑ 418 Paul Sorrento .15 .07
❑ 419 Randy Winn .15 .07
❑ 420 John Burkett .15 .07
❑ 421 Will Clark .60 .25
❑ 422 Royce Clayton .15 .07
❑ 423 Juan Gonzalez * .60 .25
❑ 423A Juan Gonzalez Headshot .60 .25
❑ 424 Tom Goodwin .15 .07
❑ 425 Rusty Greer .25 .11
❑ 426 Rick Helling .15 .07
❑ 427 Roberto Kelly .15 .07
❑ 428 Mark McLemore .15 .07
❑ 429 Ivan Rodriguez * .60 .25
❑ 429A Ivan Rodriguez Headshot .60 .25
❑ 430 Aaron Sele .25 .11
❑ 431 Lee Stevens .15 .07
❑ 432 Todd Stottlemyre .15 .07
❑ 433 John Wetteland .25 .11
❑ 434 Todd Zeile .25 .11
❑ 435 Jose Canseco * .60 .25
❑ 435A J.Canseco Headshot .60 .25
❑ 436 Roger Clemens * 1.50 .70
❑ 436A R.Clemens Headshot 1.50 .70
❑ 437 Felipe Crespo .15 .07
❑ 438 Jose Cruz Jr. .25 .11
❑ 439 Carlos Delgado .60 .25
❑ 440 Tom Evans * .15 .07
❑ 440A T.Evans Headshot .15 .07
❑ 441 Tony Fernandez .15 .07
❑ 442 Darrin Fletcher .15 .07
❑ 443 Alex Gonzalez .15 .07
❑ 444 Shawn Green .60 .25
❑ 445 Roy Halladay .15 .07
❑ 446 Pat Hentgen .15 .07
❑ 447 Juan Samuel .15 .07
❑ 448 Benito Santiago .15 .07
❑ 449 Shannon Stewart .25 .11
❑ 450 Woody Williams .15 .07
❑ NNO Tony Gwynn Sample 2.00 .90

2000 Pacific

	MINT	NRMT
COMPLETE SET (500)	100.00	45.00

❑ 1 Garret Anderson .25 .11
❑ 2 Tim Belcher .15 .07
❑ 3 Gary DiSarcina .15 .07
❑ 4 Trent Durrington .15 .07
❑ 5 Jim Edmonds .40 .18
❑ 6 Darin Erstad ACTION .60 .25
❑ 6A Darin Erstad POR .60 .25
❑ 7 Chuck Finley .25 .11
❑ 8 Troy Glaus .60 .25
❑ 9 Todd Greene .15 .07
❑ 10 Bret Hemphill .15 .07
❑ 11 Ken Hill .15 .07
❑ 12 Ramon Ortiz .25 .11
❑ 13 Troy Percival .15 .07
❑ 14 Mark Petkovsek .15 .07
❑ 15 Tim Salmon .25 .11
❑ 16 Mo Vaughn ACTION .25 .11
❑ 16A Mo Vaughn POR .25 .11
❑ 17 Jay Bell .25 .11
❑ 18 Omar Daal .15 .07
❑ 19 Erubiel Durazo .25 .11
❑ 20 Steve Finley .25 .11
❑ 21 Bernard Gilkey .15 .07
❑ 22 Luis Gonzalez .60 .25
❑ 23 Randy Johnson .75 .35
❑ 24 Byung-Hyun Kim .25 .11
❑ 25 Travis Lee .15 .07
❑ 26 Matt Mantei .15 .07
❑ 27 Armando Reynoso .15 .07
❑ 28 Rob Ryan .15 .07
❑ 29 Kelly Stinnett .15 .07
❑ 30 Todd Stottlemyre .15 .07
❑ 31 Matt Williams ACTION .40 .18
❑ 31A Matt Williams POR .40 .18
❑ 32 Tony Womack .15 .07
❑ 33 Bret Boone .25 .11
❑ 34 Andres Galarraga .40 .18
❑ 35 Tom Glavine .60 .25
❑ 36 Ozzie Guillen .15 .07
❑ 37 Andruw Jones ACTION .60 .25
❑ 37A Andruw Jones POR .60 .25
❑ 38 Chipper Jones ACTION 1.25 .55
❑ 38A Chipper Jones POR 1.50 .70
❑ 39 Brian Jordan .25 .11
❑ 40 Ryan Klesko .25 .11
❑ 41 Javy Lopez .25 .11
❑ 42 Greg Maddux ACTION 1.50 .70
❑ 42A Greg Maddux POR 1.50 .70
❑ 43 Kevin Millwood .15 .07
❑ 44 John Rocker .25 .11
❑ 45 Randall Simon .15 .07
❑ 46 John Smoltz .25 .11
❑ 47 Gerald Williams .15 .07
❑ 48 Brady Anderson .25 .11
❑ 49 Albert Belle ACTION .25 .11
❑ 49A Albert Belle POR .25 .11
❑ 50 Mike Bordick .15 .07
❑ 51 Will Clark .60 .25
❑ 52 Jeff Conine .15 .07
❑ 53 Delino DeShields .15 .07
❑ 54 Jerry Hairston Jr. .15 .07
❑ 55 Charles Johnson .25 .11
❑ 56 Eugene Kingsale .15 .07
❑ 57 Ryan Minor .15 .07
❑ 58 Mike Mussina .60 .25
❑ 59 Sidney Ponson .15 .07
❑ 60 Cal Ripken ACTION 2.50 1.10
❑ 60A Cal Ripken POR 2.50 1.10
❑ 61 B.J. Surhoff .25 .11
❑ 62 Mike Timlin .15 .07
❑ 63 Rod Beck .15 .07
❑ 64 N.Garciaparra ACTION 1.50 .70
❑ 64A N.Garciaparra POR 1.50 .70
❑ 65 Tom Gordon .15 .07
❑ 66 Butch Huskey .15 .07
❑ 67 Derek Lowe .15 .07
❑ 68 P.Martinez ACTION .75 .35
❑ 68A Pedro Martinez POR .75 .35
❑ 69 Trot Nixon .25 .11
❑ 70 Jose Offerman .15 .07
❑ 71 Troy O'Leary .15 .07
❑ 72 Pat Rapp .15 .07
❑ 73 Donnie Sadler .15 .07
❑ 74 Mike Stanley .15 .07
❑ 75 John Valentin .15 .07
❑ 76 Jason Varitek .25 .11
❑ 77 Wilton Veras .15 .07
❑ 78 Tim Wakefield .15 .07
❑ 79 Rick Aguilera .25 .11
❑ 80 Manny Alexander .15 .07
❑ 81 Roosevelt Brown .15 .07
❑ 82 Mark Grace .60 .25
❑ 83 Glenallen Hill .15 .07
❑ 84 Lance Johnson .15 .07

❑ 85	Jon Lieber	.15	.07
❑ 86	Cole Liniak	.15	.07
❑ 87	Chad Meyers	.15	.07
❑ 88	Mickey Morandini	.15	.07
❑ 89	Jose Nieves	.15	.07
❑ 90	Henry Rodriguez	.15	.07
❑ 91	Sammy Sosa ACTION	1.25	.55
❑ 91A	Sammy Sosa POR	1.25	.55
❑ 92	Kevin Tapani	.15	.07
❑ 93	Kerry Wood	.60	.25
❑ 94	Mike Caruso	.15	.07
❑ 95	Ray Durham	.25	.11
❑ 96	Brook Fordyce	.15	.07
❑ 97	Bobby Howry	.15	.07
❑ 98	Paul Konerko	.25	.11
❑ 99	Carlos Lee	.25	.11
❑ 100	Aaron Myette	.25	.11
❑ 101	Greg Norton	.15	.07
❑ 102	Magglio Ordonez	.25	.11
❑ 103	Jim Parque	.15	.07
❑ 104	Liu Rodriguez	.15	.07
❑ 105	Chris Singleton	.15	.07
❑ 106	Mike Sirotka	.15	.07
❑ 107	F.Thomas ACTION	.75	.35
❑ 107A	Frank Thomas POR	1.00	.45
❑ 108	Kip Wells	.25	.11
❑ 109	Aaron Boone	.15	.07
❑ 110	Mike Cameron	.25	.11
❑ 111	Sean Casey ACTION	.40	.18
❑ 111A	Sean Casey POR	.40	.18
❑ 112	Jeffrey Hammonds	.15	.07
❑ 113	Pete Harnisch	.15	.07
❑ 114	Barry Larkin ACTION	.60	.25
❑ 114A	Barry Larkin POR	.60	.25
❑ 115	Jason LaRue	.15	.07
❑ 116	Denny Neagle	.15	.07
❑ 117	Pokey Reese	.15	.07
❑ 118	Scott Sullivan	.15	.07
❑ 119	Eddie Taubensee	.15	.07
❑ 120	Greg Vaughn	.25	.11
❑ 121	Scott Williamson	.15	.07
❑ 122	Dmitri Young	.25	.11
❑ 123	R.Alomar ACTION	.60	.25
❑ 123A	R.Alomar POR	.60	.25
❑ 124	Sandy Alomar Jr.	.15	.07
❑ 125	Harold Baines	.25	.11
❑ 126	Russell Branyan	.25	.11
❑ 127	Dave Burba	.15	.07
❑ 128	Bartolo Colon	.25	.11
❑ 129	Travis Fryman	.25	.11
❑ 130	Mike Jackson	.15	.07
❑ 131	David Justice	.25	.11
❑ 132	Kenny Lofton ACTION	.25	.11
❑ 132A	Kenny Lofton POR	.25	.11
❑ 133	Charles Nagy	.15	.07
❑ 134	M.Ramirez ACTION	.75	.35
❑ 134A	Manny Ramirez POR	.75	.35
❑ 135	Dave Roberts	.15	.07
❑ 136	Richie Sexson	.25	.11
❑ 137	Jim Thome	.60	.25
❑ 138	Omar Vizquel	.25	.11
❑ 139	Jaret Wright	.15	.07
❑ 140	Pedro Astacio	.15	.07
❑ 141	Dante Bichette	.25	.11
❑ 142	Brian Bohanon	.15	.07
❑ 143	Vinny Castilla ACTION	.25	.11
❑ 143A	Vinny Castilla POR	.25	.11
❑ 144	Edgard Clemente	.15	.07
❑ 145	Derrick Gibson	.15	.07
❑ 146	Todd Helton	.75	.35
❑ 147	Darryl Kile	.25	.11
❑ 148	Mike Lansing	.15	.07
❑ 149	Kirt Manwaring	.15	.07
❑ 150	Neifi Perez	.15	.07
❑ 151	Ben Petrick	.15	.07
❑ 152	Juan Sosa RC	.25	.11
❑ 153	Dave Veres	.15	.07
❑ 154	Larry Walker ACTION	.40	.18
❑ 154A	Larry Walker POR	.40	.18
❑ 155	Brad Ausmus	.15	.07
❑ 156	Dave Borkowski	.15	.07
❑ 157	Tony Clark	.25	.11
❑ 158	Francisco Cordero	.15	.07
❑ 159	Deivi Cruz	.15	.07
❑ 160	Damion Easley	.15	.07
❑ 161	Juan Encarnacion	.25	.11
❑ 162	Robert Fick	.15	.07
❑ 163	Bobby Higginson	.15	.07
❑ 164	Gabe Kapler	.25	.11
❑ 165	Brian Moehler	.15	.07
❑ 166	Dean Palmer	.25	.11
❑ 167	Luis Polonia	.15	.07
❑ 168	Justin Thompson	.15	.07
❑ 169	Jeff Weaver	.25	.11
❑ 170	Antonio Alfonseca	.15	.07
❑ 171	Bruce Aven	.15	.07
❑ 172	A.J. Burnett	.25	.11
❑ 173	Luis Castillo	.15	.07
❑ 174	Ramon Castro	.15	.07
❑ 175	Ryan Dempster	.25	.11
❑ 176	Alex Fernandez	.15	.07
❑ 177	Cliff Floyd	.25	.11
❑ 178	Amaury Garcia	.15	.07
❑ 179	Alex Gonzalez	.15	.07
❑ 180	Mark Kotsay	.15	.07
❑ 181	Mike Lowell	.15	.07
❑ 182	Brian Meadows	.15	.07
❑ 183	Kevin Orie	.15	.07
❑ 184	Julio Ramirez	.15	.07
❑ 185	Preston Wilson	.25	.11
❑ 186	Moises Alou	.25	.11
❑ 187	Jeff Bagwell ACTION	.75	.35
❑ 187A	Jeff Bagwell POR	.75	.35
❑ 188	Glen Barker	.15	.07
❑ 189	Derek Bell	.15	.07
❑ 190	Craig Biggio ACTION	.40	.18
❑ 190A	Craig Biggio POR	.40	.18
❑ 191	Ken Caminiti	.25	.11
❑ 192	Scott Elarton	.15	.07
❑ 193	Carl Everett	.25	.11
❑ 194	Mike Hampton	.25	.11
❑ 195	Carlos E. Hernandez	.15	.07
❑ 196	Richard Hidalgo	.25	.11
❑ 197	Jose Lima	.15	.07
❑ 198	Shane Reynolds	.15	.07
❑ 199	Bill Spiers	.15	.07
❑ 200	Billy Wagner	.15	.07
❑ 201	C. Beltran ACTION	.25	.11
❑ 201A	Carlos Beltran POR	.25	.11
❑ 202	Dermal Brown	.15	.07
❑ 203	Johnny Damon	.25	.11
❑ 204	Jermaine Dye	.25	.11
❑ 205	Carlos Febles	.15	.07
❑ 206	Jeremy Giambi	.15	.07
❑ 207	Mark Quinn	.25	.11
❑ 208	Joe Randa	.15	.07
❑ 209	Dan Reichert	.15	.07
❑ 210	Jose Rosado	.15	.07
❑ 211	Rey Sanchez	.15	.07
❑ 212	Jeff Suppan	.15	.07
❑ 213	Mike Sweeney	.25	.11
❑ 214	Kevin Brown ACTION	.25	.11
❑ 214A	Kevin Brown POR	.25	.11
❑ 215	Darren Dreifort	.15	.07
❑ 216	Eric Gagne	.15	.07
❑ 217	Mark Grudzielanek	.15	.07
❑ 218	Todd Hollandsworth	.15	.07
❑ 219	Todd Hundley	.15	.07
❑ 220	Eric Karros	.25	.11
❑ 221	Raul Mondesi	.25	.11
❑ 222	Chan Ho Park	.25	.11
❑ 223	Jeff Shaw	.15	.07
❑ 224	G.Sheffield ACTION	.25	.11
❑ 224A	Gary Sheffield POR	.25	.11
❑ 225	Ismael Valdes	.15	.07
❑ 226	Devon White	.15	.07
❑ 227	Eric Young	.15	.07
❑ 228	Kevin Barker	.15	.07
❑ 229	Ron Belliard	.15	.07
❑ 230	J.Burnitz ACTION	.25	.11
❑ 230A	Jeromy Burnitz POR	.25	.11
❑ 231	Jeff Cirillo	.25	.11
❑ 232	Marquis Grissom	.15	.07
❑ 233	Geoff Jenkins	.25	.11
❑ 234	Mark Loretta	.15	.07
❑ 235	David Nilsson	.15	.07
❑ 236	Hideo Nomo	.60	.25
❑ 237	Alex Ochoa	.15	.07
❑ 238	Kyle Peterson	.15	.07
❑ 239	Fernando Vina	.15	.07
❑ 240	Bob Wickman	.15	.07
❑ 241	Steve Woodard	.15	.07
❑ 242	Chad Allen	.15	.07
❑ 243	Ron Coomer	.15	.07
❑ 244	Marty Cordova	.15	.07
❑ 245	Cristian Guzman	.25	.11
❑ 246	Denny Hocking	.15	.07
❑ 247	Jacque Jones	.25	.11
❑ 248	Corey Koskie	.25	.11
❑ 249	Matt Lawton	.15	.07
❑ 250	Joe Mays	.25	.11
❑ 251	Eric Milton	.25	.11
❑ 252	Brad Radke	.25	.11
❑ 253	Mark Redman	.15	.07
❑ 254	Terry Steinbach	.15	.07
❑ 255	Todd Walker	.15	.07
❑ 256	Tony Armas Jr.	.25	.11
❑ 257	Michael Barrett	.15	.07
❑ 258	Peter Bergeron	.15	.07
❑ 259	Geoff Blum	.15	.07
❑ 260	Orlando Cabrera	.15	.07
❑ 261	Trace Coquillette RC	.25	.11
❑ 262	Brad Fullmer	.25	.11
❑ 263	V.Guerrero ACTION	.75	.35
❑ 263A	V.Guerrero POR	1.00	.45
❑ 264	Wilton Guerrero	.15	.07
❑ 265	Dustin Hermanson	.15	.07
❑ 266	Manny Martinez RC	.25	.11
❑ 267	Ryan McGuire	.15	.07
❑ 268	Ugueth Urbina	.15	.07
❑ 269	Jose Vidro	.25	.11
❑ 270	Rondell White	.25	.11
❑ 271	Chris Widger	.15	.07
❑ 272	Edgardo Alfonzo	.25	.11
❑ 273	Armando Benitez	.25	.11
❑ 274	Roger Cedeno	.15	.07
❑ 275	Dennis Cook	.15	.07
❑ 276	Octavio Dotel	.15	.07
❑ 277	John Franco	.25	.11
❑ 278	Darryl Hamilton	.15	.07
❑ 279	Rickey Henderson	1.25	.55
❑ 280	Orel Hershiser	.25	.11
❑ 281	Al Leiter	.15	.07
❑ 282	John Olerud ACTION	.25	.11
❑ 282A	John Olerud POR	.25	.11
❑ 283	Rey Ordonez	.15	.07
❑ 284	Mike Piazza ACTION	1.50	.70
❑ 284A	Mike Piazza POR	1.50	.70
❑ 285	Kenny Rogers	.15	.07
❑ 286	Jorge Toca	.15	.07
❑ 287	Robin Ventura	.40	.18
❑ 288	Scott Brosius	.25	.11
❑ 289	R.Clemens ACTION	1.50	.70
❑ 289A	Roger Clemens POR	1.50	.70
❑ 290	David Cone	.25	.11
❑ 291	Chili Davis	.25	.11
❑ 292	Orlando Hernandez	.25	.11
❑ 293	Hideki Irabu	.15	.07
❑ 294	Derek Jeter ACTION	2.50	1.10
❑ 294A	Derek Jeter POR	2.50	1.10
❑ 295	Chuck Knoblauch	.25	.11
❑ 296	Ricky Ledee	.15	.07
❑ 297	Jim Leyritz	.15	.07
❑ 298	Tino Martinez	.25	.11
❑ 299	Paul O'Neill	.60	.25
❑ 300	Andy Pettitte	.25	.11
❑ 301	Jorge Posada	.25	.11
❑ 302	Mariano Rivera	.25	.11
❑ 303	Alfonso Soriano	.60	.25
❑ 304	B.Williams ACTION	.60	.25
❑ 304A	Bernie Williams POR	.60	.25
❑ 305	Ed Yarnall	.15	.07
❑ 306	Kevin Appier	.15	.07
❑ 307	Rich Becker	.15	.07
❑ 308	Eric Chavez	.25	.11
❑ 309	Jason Giambi	.60	.25
❑ 310	Ben Grieve	.25	.11
❑ 311	Ramon Hernandez	.15	.07
❑ 312	Tim Hudson	.60	.25
❑ 313	John Jaha	.15	.07
❑ 314	Doug Jones	.15	.07
❑ 315	Omar Olivares	.15	.07
❑ 316	Mike Oquist	.15	.07
❑ 317	Matt Stairs	.15	.07
❑ 318	Miguel Tejada	.25	.11
❑ 319	Randy Velarde	.15	.07
❑ 320	Bob Abreu	.25	.11
❑ 321	Marlon Anderson	.15	.07

❑ 322 Alex Arias .15 .07
❑ 323 Rico Brogna .15 .07
❑ 324 Paul Byrd .15 .07
❑ 325 Ron Gant .25 .11
❑ 326 Doug Glanville .15 .07
❑ 327 Wayne Gomes .15 .07
❑ 328 Mike Lieberthal .25 .11
❑ 329 Robert Person .15 .07
❑ 330 Desi Relaford .15 .07
❑ 331 Scott Rolen ACTION .60 .25
❑ 331A Scott Rolen POR .60 .25
❑ 332 Curt Schilling ACTION .60 .25
❑ 332A Curt Schilling POR .60 .25
❑ 333 Kris Benson .25 .11
❑ 334 Adrian Brown .15 .07
❑ 335 Brant Brown .15 .07
❑ 336 Brian Giles .25 .11
❑ 337 Chad Hermansen .15 .07
❑ 338 Jason Kendall .25 .11
❑ 339 Al Martin .15 .07
❑ 340 Pat Meares .15 .07
❑ 341 W.Morris ACTION .15 .07
❑ 341A Warren Morris POR .15 .07
❑ 342 Todd Ritchie .15 .07
❑ 343 Jason Schmidt .15 .07
❑ 344 Ed Sprague .15 .07
❑ 345 Mike Williams .15 .07
❑ 346 Kevin Young .15 .07
❑ 347 Rick Ankiel .60 .25
❑ 348 Ricky Bottalico .15 .07
❑ 349 Kent Bottenfield .15 .07
❑ 350 Darren Bragg .15 .07
❑ 351 Eric Davis .25 .11
❑ 352 J.D. Drew ACTION .60 .25
❑ 352A J.D. Drew POR .60 .25
❑ 353 Adam Kennedy .15 .07
❑ 354 Ray Lankford .15 .07
❑ 355 Joe McEwing .15 .07
❑ 356 M.McGwire ACTION 2.50 1.10
❑ 356A Mark McGwire POR 2.50 1.10
❑ 357 Matt Morris .25 .11
❑ 358 Darren Oliver .15 .07
❑ 359 Edgar Renteria .15 .07
❑ 360 Fernando Tatis .15 .07
❑ 361 Andy Ashby .15 .07
❑ 362 Ben Davis .25 .11
❑ 363 Tony Gwynn ACTION 1.25 .55
❑ 363A Tony Gwynn POR 1.25 .55
❑ 364 Sterling Hitchcock .15 .07
❑ 365 Trevor Hoffman .25 .11
❑ 366 Damian Jackson .15 .07
❑ 367 Wally Joyner .25 .11
❑ 368 Dave Magadan .15 .07
❑ 369 Gary Matthews Jr. .15 .07
❑ 370 Phil Nevin .25 .11
❑ 371 Eric Owens .15 .07
❑ 372 Ruben Rivera .15 .07
❑ 373 R.Sanders ACTION .15 .07
❑ 373A Reggie Sanders POR .15 .07
❑ 374 Quilvio Veras .15 .07
❑ 375 Rich Aurilia .25 .11
❑ 376 Marvin Benard .15 .07
❑ 377 Barry Bonds ACTION 1.50 .70
❑ 377A Barry Bonds POR 1.25 .55
❑ 378 Ellis Burks .25 .11
❑ 379 Shawn Estes .25 .11
❑ 380 Livan Hernandez .15 .07
❑ 381 Jeff Kent ACTION .40 .18
❑ 381A Jeff Kent POR .40 .18
❑ 382 Brent Mayne .15 .07
❑ 383 Bill Mueller .15 .07
❑ 384 Calvin Murray .15 .07
❑ 385 Robb Nen .15 .07
❑ 386 Russ Ortiz .25 .11
❑ 387 Kirk Rueter .15 .07
❑ 388 J.T. Snow .25 .11
❑ 389 David Bell .15 .07
❑ 390 Jay Buhner .25 .11
❑ 391 Russ Davis .15 .07
❑ 392 Freddy Garcia ACTION .40 .18
❑ 392A Freddy Garcia POR .40 .18
❑ 393 K.Griffey Jr. ACTION 2.00 .90
❑ 393A Ken Griffey Jr. POR 2.00 .90
❑ 394 Carlos Guillen .15 .07
❑ 395 John Halama .15 .07
❑ 396 Brian L.Hunter .15 .07
❑ 397 Ryan Jackson .15 .07
❑ 398 Edgar Martinez .40 .18
❑ 399 Gil Meche .15 .07
❑ 400 Jose Mesa .15 .07
❑ 401 Jamie Moyer .15 .07
❑ 402 A.Rodriguez ACTION 1.50 .70
❑ 402A Alex Rodriguez POR 1.50 .70
❑ 403 Dan Wilson .15 .07
❑ 404 Wilson Alvarez .15 .07
❑ 405 Rolando Arrojo .15 .07
❑ 406 Wade Boggs ACTION .60 .25
❑ 406A Wade Boggs POR .60 .25
❑ 407 Miguel Cairo .15 .07
❑ 408 Jose Canseco ACTION .60 .25
❑ 408A Jose Canseco POR .75 .35
❑ 409 John Flaherty .15 .07
❑ 410 Jose Guillen .15 .07
❑ 411 Roberto Hernandez .15 .07
❑ 412 Terrell Lowery .15 .07
❑ 413 Dave Martinez .15 .07
❑ 414 Quinton McCracken .15 .07
❑ 415 Fred McGriff ACTION .40 .18
❑ 415A Fred McGriff POR .40 .18
❑ 416 Ryan Rupe .15 .07
❑ 417 Kevin Stocker .15 .07
❑ 418 Bubba Trammell .15 .07
❑ 419 Royce Clayton .15 .07
❑ 420 J.Gonzalez ACTION .60 .25
❑ 420A Juan Gonzalez POR .60 .25
❑ 421 Tom Goodwin .15 .07
❑ 422 Rusty Greer .25 .11
❑ 423 Rick Helling .15 .07
❑ 424 Roberto Kelly .15 .07
❑ 425 Ruben Mateo .25 .11
❑ 426 Mark McLemore .15 .07
❑ 427 Mike Morgan .15 .07
❑ 428 Rafael Palmeiro .60 .25
❑ 429 I.Rodriguez ACTION .60 .25
❑ 429A Ivan Rodriguez POR .60 .25
❑ 430 Aaron Sele .25 .11
❑ 431 Lee Stevens .15 .07
❑ 432 John Wetteland .25 .11
❑ 433 Todd Zeile .25 .11
❑ 434 Jeff Zimmerman .15 .07
❑ 435 Tony Batista .25 .11
❑ 436 Casey Blake .15 .07
❑ 437 Homer Bush .15 .07
❑ 438 Chris Carpenter .15 .07
❑ 439 Jose Cruz Jr. .25 .11
❑ 440 C.Delgado ACTION .60 .25
❑ 440A Carlos Delgado POR .60 .25
❑ 441 Tony Fernandez .15 .07
❑ 442 Darrin Fletcher .15 .07
❑ 443 Alex Gonzalez .15 .07
❑ 444 Shawn Green ACTION .60 .25
❑ 444A Shawn Green POR .60 .25
❑ 445 Roy Halladay .15 .07
❑ 446 Billy Koch .15 .07
❑ 447 David Segui .15 .07
❑ 448 Shannon Stewart .25 .11
❑ 449 David Wells .25 .11
❑ 450 Vernon Wells .25 .11
❑ SAMP T.Gwynn Sample 1.00 .45

2001 Pacific

	MINT	NRMT
COMPLETE SET (500)	100.00	45.00

❑ 1 Garret Anderson .25 .11
❑ 2 Gary DiSarcina .15 .07
❑ 3 Darin Erstad .60 .25
❑ 4 Seth Etherton .15 .07
❑ 5 Ron Gant .15 .07
❑ 6 Troy Glaus .60 .25
❑ 7 Shigetoshi Hasegawa .25 .11
❑ 8 Adam Kennedy .15 .07
❑ 9 Ben Molina .15 .07
❑ 10 Ramon Ortiz .25 .11
❑ 11 Troy Percival .15 .07
❑ 12 Tim Salmon .25 .11
❑ 13 Scott Schoeneweis .15 .07
❑ 14 Mo Vaughn .25 .11
❑ 15 Jarrod Washburn .15 .07
❑ 16 Brian Anderson .15 .07
❑ 17 Danny Bautista .15 .07
❑ 18 Jay Bell .25 .11
❑ 19 Greg Colbrunn .15 .07
❑ 20 Erubiel Durazo .15 .07
❑ 21 Steve Finley .25 .11
❑ 22 Luis Gonzalez .60 .25
❑ 23 Randy Johnson .75 .35
❑ 24 Byung-Hyun Kim .25 .11
❑ 25 Matt Mantei .15 .07
❑ 26 Armando Reynoso .15 .07
❑ 27 Todd Stottlemyre .15 .07
❑ 28 Matt Williams .40 .18
❑ 29 Tony Womack .15 .07
❑ 30 Andy Ashby .15 .07
❑ 31 Bobby Bonilla .25 .11
❑ 32 Rafael Furcal .25 .11
❑ 33 Andres Galarraga .40 .18
❑ 34 Tom Glavine .60 .25
❑ 35 Andruw Jones .60 .25
❑ 36 Chipper Jones 1.25 .55
❑ 37 Brian Jordan .25 .11
❑ 38 Wally Joyner .25 .11
❑ 39 Keith Lockhart .15 .07
❑ 40 Javy Lopez .25 .11
❑ 41 Greg Maddux 1.50 .70
❑ 42 Kevin Millwood .15 .07
❑ 43 John Rocker .25 .11
❑ 44 Reggie Sanders .15 .07
❑ 45 John Smoltz .25 .11
❑ 46 B.J. Surhoff .25 .11
❑ 47 Quilvio Veras .15 .07
❑ 48 Walt Weiss .15 .07
❑ 49 Brady Anderson .25 .11
❑ 50 Albert Belle .25 .11
❑ 51 Jeff Conine .15 .07
❑ 52 Delino DeShields .15 .07
❑ 53 Brook Fordyce .15 .07
❑ 54 Jerry Hairston Jr. .15 .07
❑ 55 Mark Lewis .15 .07
❑ 56 Luis Matos .15 .07
❑ 57 Melvin Mora .15 .07
❑ 58 Mike Mussina .60 .25
❑ 59 Chris Richard .15 .07
❑ 60 Cal Ripken 2.50 1.10
❑ 61 Manny Alexander .15 .07
❑ 62 Rolando Arrojo .15 .07
❑ 63 Midre Cummings .15 .07
❑ 64 Carl Everett .25 .11
❑ 65 Nomar Garciaparra 1.50 .70
❑ 66 Mike Lansing .15 .07
❑ 67 Darren Lewis .15 .07
❑ 68 Derek Lowe .15 .07
❑ 69 Pedro Martinez .75 .35
❑ 70 Ramon Martinez .15 .07
❑ 71 Trot Nixon .25 .11
❑ 72 Troy O'Leary .15 .07
❑ 73 Jose Offerman .15 .07
❑ 74 Tomo Ohka .25 .11
❑ 75 Jason Varitek .25 .11
❑ 76 Rick Aguilera .15 .07
❑ 77 Shane Andrews .15 .07
❑ 78 Brant Brown .15 .07
❑ 79 Damon Buford .15 .07
❑ 80 Joe Girardi .15 .07
❑ 81 Mark Grace .60 .25
❑ 82 Willie Greene .15 .07
❑ 83 Ricky Gutierrez .15 .07
❑ 84 Jon Lieber .15 .07
❑ 85 Sammy Sosa 1.25 .55

❑	86	Kevin Tapani	.15	.07
❑	87	Rondell White	.25	.11
❑	88	Kerry Wood	.60	.25
❑	89	Eric Young	.15	.07
❑	90	Harold Baines	.25	.11
❑	91	James Baldwin	.15	.07
❑	92	Ray Durham	.25	.11
❑	93	Cal Eldred	.15	.07
❑	94	Keith Foulke	.15	.07
❑	95	Charles Johnson	.25	.11
❑	96	Paul Konerko	.25	.11
❑	97	Carlos Lee	.25	.11
❑	98	Magglio Ordonez	.25	.11
❑	99	Jim Parque	.15	.07
❑	100	Herbert Perry	.15	.07
❑	101	Chris Singleton	.15	.07
❑	102	Mike Sirotka	.15	.07
❑	103	Frank Thomas	.75	.35
❑	104	Jose Valentin	.15	.07
❑	105	Rob Bell	.15	.07
❑	106	Aaron Boone	.15	.07
❑	107	Sean Casey	.40	.18
❑	108	Danny Graves	.15	.07
❑	109	Ken Griffey Jr.	2.00	.90
❑	110	Pete Harnisch	.15	.07
❑	111	Brian Hunter	.15	.07
❑	112	Barry Larkin	.60	.25
❑	113	Pokey Reese	.15	.07
❑	114	Benito Santiago	.15	.07
❑	115	Chris Stynes	.15	.07
❑	116	Michael Tucker	.15	.07
❑	117	Ron Villone	.15	.07
❑	118	Scott Williamson	.15	.07
❑	119	Dmitri Young	.25	.11
❑	120	Roberto Alomar	.60	.25
❑	121	Sandy Alomar Jr.	.25	.11
❑	122	Russell Branyan	.25	.11
❑	123	Dave Burba	.15	.07
❑	124	Bartolo Colon	.25	.11
❑	125	Wil Cordero	.15	.07
❑	126	Einar Diaz	.15	.07
❑	127	Chuck Finley	.25	.11
❑	128	Travis Fryman	.25	.11
❑	129	Kenny Lofton	.25	.11
❑	130	Charles Nagy	.15	.07
❑	131	Manny Ramirez	.75	.35
❑	132	David Segui	.15	.07
❑	133	Jim Thome	.60	.25
❑	134	Omar Vizquel	.25	.11
❑	135	Brian Bohanon	.15	.07
❑	136	Jeff Cirillo	.25	.11
❑	137	Jeff Frye	.15	.07
❑	138	Jeffrey Hammonds	.15	.07
❑	139	Todd Helton	.75	.35
❑	140	Todd Hollandsworth	.15	.07
❑	141	Jose Jimenez	.15	.07
❑	142	Brent Mayne	.15	.07
❑	143	Neifi Perez	.15	.07
❑	144	Ben Petrick	.15	.07
❑	145	Juan Pierre	.25	.11
❑	146	Larry Walker	.40	.18
❑	147	Todd Walker	.15	.07
❑	148	Masato Yoshii	.15	.07
❑	149	Brad Ausmus	.15	.07
❑	150	Rich Becker	.15	.07
❑	151	Tony Clark	.25	.11
❑	152	Deivi Cruz	.15	.07
❑	153	Damion Easley	.15	.07
❑	154	Juan Encarnacion	.25	.11
❑	155	Robert Fick	.15	.07
❑	156	Juan Gonzalez	.60	.25
❑	157	Bobby Higginson	.25	.11
❑	158	Todd Jones	.15	.07
❑	159	Wendell Magee Jr.	.15	.07
❑	160	Brian Moehler	.15	.07
❑	161	Hideo Nomo	.60	.25
❑	162	Dean Palmer	.25	.11
❑	163	Jeff Weaver	.25	.11
❑	164	Antonio Alfonseca	.15	.07
❑	165	Dave Berg	.15	.07
❑	166	A.J. Burnett	.25	.11
❑	167	Luis Castillo	.15	.07
❑	168	Ryan Dempster	.25	.11
❑	169	Cliff Floyd	.25	.11
❑	170	Alex Gonzalez	.15	.07
❑	171	Mark Kotsay	.15	.07
❑	172	Derrek Lee	.25	.11
❑	173	Mike Lowell	.25	.11
❑	174	Mike Redmond	.15	.07
❑	175	Henry Rodriguez	.15	.07
❑	176	Jesus Sanchez	.15	.07
❑	177	Preston Wilson	.25	.11
❑	178	Moises Alou	.25	.11
❑	179	Jeff Bagwell	.75	.35
❑	180	Glen Barker	.15	.07
❑	181	Lance Berkman	.60	.25
❑	182	Craig Biggio	.40	.18
❑	183	Tim Bogar	.15	.07
❑	184	Ken Caminiti	.25	.11
❑	185	Roger Cedeno	.15	.07
❑	186	Scott Elarton	.15	.07
❑	187	Tony Eusebio	.15	.07
❑	188	Richard Hidalgo	.25	.11
❑	189	Jose Lima	.15	.07
❑	190	Mitch Meluskey	.15	.07
❑	191	Shane Reynolds	.15	.07
❑	192	Bill Spiers	.15	.07
❑	193	Billy Wagner	.15	.07
❑	194	Daryle Ward	.15	.07
❑	195	Carlos Beltran	.25	.11
❑	196	Ricky Bottalico	.15	.07
❑	197	Johnny Damon	.25	.11
❑	198	Jermaine Dye	.25	.11
❑	199	Jorge Fabregas	.15	.07
❑	200	David McCarty	.15	.07
❑	201	Mark Quinn	.25	.11
❑	202	Joe Randa	.15	.07
❑	203	Jeff Reboulet	.15	.07
❑	204	Rey Sanchez	.15	.07
❑	205	Blake Stein	.15	.07
❑	206	Jeff Suppan	.15	.07
❑	207	Mac Suzuki	.15	.07
❑	208	Mike Sweeney	.25	.11
❑	209	Greg Zaun	.15	.07
❑	210	Adrian Beltre	.25	.11
❑	211	Kevin Brown	.25	.11
❑	212	Alex Cora	.15	.07
❑	213	Darren Dreifort	.15	.07
❑	214	Tom Goodwin	.15	.07
❑	215	Shawn Green	.60	.25
❑	216	Mark Grudzielanek	.15	.07
❑	217	Todd Hundley	.15	.07
❑	218	Eric Karros	.25	.11
❑	219	Chad Kreuter	.15	.07
❑	220	Jim Leyritz	.15	.07
❑	221	Chan Ho Park	.25	.11
❑	222	Jeff Shaw	.15	.07
❑	223	Gary Sheffield	.25	.11
❑	224	Devon White	.15	.07
❑	225	Ron Belliard	.15	.07
❑	226	Henry Blanco	.15	.07
❑	227	Jeromy Burnitz	.25	.11
❑	228	Jeff D'Amico	.15	.07
❑	229	Marquis Grissom	.15	.07
❑	230	Charlie Hayes	.15	.07
❑	231	Jimmy Haynes	.15	.07
❑	232	Tyler Houston	.15	.07
❑	233	Geoff Jenkins	.25	.11
❑	234	Mark Loretta	.15	.07
❑	235	James Mouton	.15	.07
❑	236	Richie Sexson	.25	.11
❑	237	Jamey Wright	.15	.07
❑	238	Jay Canizaro	.15	.07
❑	239	Ron Coomer	.15	.07
❑	240	Cristian Guzman	.25	.11
❑	241	Denny Hocking	.15	.07
❑	242	Torii Hunter	.25	.11
❑	243	Jacque Jones	.25	.11
❑	244	Corey Koskie	.25	.11
❑	245	Matt Lawton	.25	.11
❑	246	Matt LeCroy	.15	.07
❑	247	Eric Milton	.25	.11
❑	248	David Ortiz	.25	.11
❑	249	Brad Radke	.25	.11
❑	250	Mark Redman	.15	.07
❑	251	Michael Barrett	.15	.07
❑	252	Peter Bergeron	.15	.07
❑	253	Milton Bradley	.15	.07
❑	254	Orlando Cabrera	.15	.07
❑	255	Vladimir Guerrero	.75	.35
❑	256	Wilton Guerrero	.15	.07
❑	257	Dustin Hermanson	.15	.07
❑	258	Hideki Irabu	.15	.07
❑	259	Fernando Seguignol	.15	.07
❑	260	Lee Stevens	.15	.07
❑	261	Andy Tracy	.15	.07
❑	262	Javier Vazquez	.25	.11
❑	263	Jose Vidro	.25	.11
❑	264	Edgardo Alfonzo	.25	.11
❑	265	Derek Bell	.15	.07
❑	266	Armando Benitez	.15	.07
❑	267	Mike Bordick	.15	.07
❑	268	John Franco	.25	.11
❑	269	Darryl Hamilton	.15	.07
❑	270	Mike Hampton	.25	.11
❑	271	Lenny Harris	.15	.07
❑	272	Al Leiter	.25	.11
❑	273	Joe McEwing	.15	.07
❑	274	Rey Ordonez	.15	.07
❑	275	Jay Payton	.15	.07
❑	276	Mike Piazza	1.50	.70
❑	277	Glendon Rusch	.15	.07
❑	278	Bubba Trammell	.15	.07
❑	279	Robin Ventura	.25	.11
❑	280	Todd Zeile	.25	.11
❑	281	Scott Brosius	.25	.11
❑	282	Jose Canseco	.60	.25
❑	283	Roger Clemens	1.50	.70
❑	284	David Cone	.25	.11
❑	285	Dwight Gooden	.25	.11
❑	286	Orlando Hernandez	.25	.11
❑	287	Glenallen Hill	.15	.07
❑	288	Derek Jeter	2.50	1.10
❑	289	David Justice	.25	.11
❑	290	Chuck Knoblauch	.25	.11
❑	291	Tino Martinez	.25	.11
❑	292	Denny Neagle	.15	.07
❑	293	Paul O'Neill	.60	.25
❑	294	Andy Pettitte	.25	.11
❑	295	Jorge Posada	.25	.11
❑	296	Mariano Rivera	.25	.11
❑	297	Luis Sojo	.15	.07
❑	298	Jose Vizcaino	.15	.07
❑	299	Bernie Williams	.60	.25
❑	300	Kevin Appier	.25	.11
❑	301	Eric Chavez	.25	.11
❑	302	Ryan Christenson	.15	.07
❑	303	Jason Giambi	.60	.25
❑	304	Jeremy Giambi	.15	.07
❑	305	Ben Grieve	.25	.11
❑	306	Gil Heredia	.15	.07
❑	307	Ramon Hernandez	.15	.07
❑	308	Tim Hudson	.60	.25
❑	309	Jason Isringhausen	.15	.07
❑	310	Terrence Long	.25	.11
❑	311	Mark Mulder	.40	.18
❑	312	Adam Piatt	.25	.11
❑	313	Matt Stairs	.15	.07
❑	314	Miguel Tejada	.25	.11
❑	315	Randy Velarde	.15	.07
❑	316	Alex Arias	.15	.07
❑	317	Pat Burrell	.25	.11
❑	318	Omar Daal	.15	.07
❑	319	Travis Lee	.15	.07
❑	320	Mike Lieberthal	.25	.11
❑	321	Randy Wolf	.15	.07
❑	322	Bobby Abreu	.25	.11
❑	323	Jeff Brantley	.15	.07
❑	324	Bruce Chen	.15	.07
❑	325	Doug Glanville	.15	.07
❑	326	Kevin Jordan	.15	.07
❑	327	Robert Person	.15	.07
❑	328	Scott Rolen	.60	.25
❑	329	Jimmy Anderson	.15	.07
❑	330	Mike Benjamin	.15	.07
❑	331	Kris Benson	.25	.11
❑	332	Adrian Brown	.15	.07
❑	333	Brian Giles	.25	.11
❑	334	Jason Kendall	.25	.11
❑	335	Pat Meares	.15	.07
❑	336	Warren Morris	.15	.07
❑	337	Aramis Ramirez	.25	.11
❑	338	Todd Ritchie	.15	.07
❑	339	Jason Schmidt	.15	.07
❑	340	John VanderWal	.15	.07
❑	341	Mike Williams	.15	.07
❑	342	Enrique Wilson	.15	.07
❑	343	Kevin Young	.15	.07

❑ 344 Rick Ankiel .40 .18
❑ 345 Andy Benes .15 .07
❑ 346 Will Clark .60 .25
❑ 347 Eric Davis .25 .11
❑ 348 J.D. Drew .60 .25
❑ 349 Shawon Dunston .15 .07
❑ 350 Jim Edmonds .40 .18
❑ 351 Pat Hentgen .15 .07
❑ 352 Darryl Kile .25 .11
❑ 353 Ray Lankford .15 .07
❑ 354 Mike Matheny .15 .07
❑ 355 Mark McGwire 2.50 1.10
❑ 356 Craig Paquette .15 .07
❑ 357 Edgar Renteria .15 .07
❑ 358 Garrett Stephenson .15 .07
❑ 359 Fernando Tatis .15 .07
❑ 360 Dave Veres .15 .07
❑ 361 Fernando Vina .15 .07
❑ 362 Bret Boone .25 .11
❑ 363 Matt Clement .15 .07
❑ 364 Ben Davis .25 .11
❑ 365 Adam Eaton .25 .11
❑ 366 Wiki Gonzalez .15 .07
❑ 367 Tony Gwynn 1.25 .55
❑ 368 Damian Jackson .15 .07
❑ 369 Ryan Klesko .25 .11
❑ 370 John Mabry .15 .07
❑ 371 Dave Magadan .15 .07
❑ 372 Phil Nevin .25 .11
❑ 373 Eric Owens .15 .07
❑ 374 Desi Relaford .15 .07
❑ 375 Ruben Rivera .15 .07
❑ 376 Woody Williams .15 .07
❑ 377 Rich Aurilia .25 .11
❑ 378 Marvin Benard .15 .07
❑ 379 Barry Bonds 1.50 .70
❑ 380 Ellis Burks .25 .11
❑ 381 Bobby Estalella .15 .07
❑ 382 Shawn Estes .25 .11
❑ 383 Mark Gardner .15 .07
❑ 384 Livan Hernandez .15 .07
❑ 385 Jeff Kent .40 .18
❑ 386 Bill Mueller .15 .07
❑ 387 Robb Nen .15 .07
❑ 388 Russ Ortiz .15 .07
❑ 389 Armando Rios .15 .07
❑ 390 Kirk Rueter .15 .07
❑ 391 J.T. Snow .25 .11
❑ 392 David Bell .15 .07
❑ 393 Jay Buhner .25 .11
❑ 394 Mike Cameron .25 .11
❑ 395 Freddy Garcia .25 .11
❑ 396 Carlos Guillen .15 .07
❑ 397 John Halama .15 .07
❑ 398 Rickey Henderson 1.25 .55
❑ 399 Al Martin .15 .07
❑ 400 Edgar Martinez .40 .18
❑ 401 Mark McLemore .15 .07
❑ 402 Jamie Moyer .15 .07
❑ 403 John Olerud .25 .11
❑ 404 Joe Oliver .15 .07
❑ 405 Alex Rodriguez 1.50 .70
❑ 406 Kazuhiro Sasaki .60 .25
❑ 407 Aaron Sele .25 .11
❑ 408 Dan Wilson .15 .07
❑ 409 Miguel Cairo .15 .07
❑ 410 Vinny Castilla .25 .11
❑ 411 Steve Cox .15 .07
❑ 412 John Flaherty .15 .07
❑ 413 Jose Guillen .15 .07
❑ 414 Roberto Hernandez .15 .07
❑ 415 Russ Johnson .15 .07
❑ 416 Felix Martinez .15 .07
❑ 417 Fred McGriff .40 .18
❑ 418 Greg Vaughn .25 .11
❑ 419 Gerald Williams .15 .07
❑ 420 Luis Alicea .15 .07
❑ 421 Frank Catalanotto .15 .07
❑ 422 Royce Clayton .15 .07
❑ 423 Chad Curtis .15 .07
❑ 424 Rusty Greer .25 .11
❑ 425 Bill Haselman .15 .07
❑ 426 Rick Helling .15 .07
❑ 427 Gabe Kapler .25 .11
❑ 428 Mike Lamb .15 .07
❑ 429 Ricky Ledee .15 .07
❑ 430 Ruben Mateo .25 .11
❑ 431 Rafael Palmeiro .60 .25
❑ 432 Ivan Rodriguez .60 .25
❑ 433 Kenny Rogers .15 .07
❑ 434 John Wetteland .25 .11
❑ 435 Jeff Zimmerman .15 .07
❑ 436 Tony Batista .25 .11
❑ 437 Homer Bush .15 .07
❑ 438 Chris Carpenter .15 .07
❑ 439 Marty Cordova .15 .07
❑ 440 Jose Cruz Jr. .25 .11
❑ 441 Carlos Delgado .60 .25
❑ 442 Darrin Fletcher .15 .07
❑ 443 Brad Fullmer .25 .11
❑ 444 Alex Gonzalez .15 .07
❑ 445 Billy Koch .15 .07
❑ 446 Raul Mondesi .25 .11
❑ 447 Mickey Morandini .15 .07
❑ 448 Shannon Stewart .25 .11
❑ 449 Steve Trachsel .15 .07
❑ 450 David Wells .25 .11
❑ 451 Juan Alvarez .15 .07
❑ 452 Shawn Wooten .15 .07
❑ 453 Ismael Villegas .15 .07
❑ 454 Carlos Casimiro .15 .07
❑ 455 Morgan Burkhart .15 .07
❑ 456 Paxton Crawford .15 .07
❑ 457 Dernell Stenson .15 .07
❑ 458 Ross Gload .15 .07
❑ 459 Raul Gonzalez .15 .07
❑ 460 Corey Patterson .25 .11
❑ 461 Julio Zuleta .15 .07
❑ 462 Rocky Biddle .15 .07
❑ 463 Joe Crede .25 .11
❑ 464 Matt Ginter .25 .11
❑ 465 Aaron Myette .15 .07
❑ 466 Mike Bell .15 .07
❑ 467 Travis Dawkins .15 .07
❑ 468 Mark Watson .15 .07
❑ 469 Elvis Pena .15 .07
❑ 470 Eric Munson .25 .11
❑ 471 Pablo Ozuna .15 .07
❑ 472 Frank Charles .15 .07
❑ 473 Mike Judd .15 .07
❑ 474 Hector Ramirez .15 .07
❑ 475 Jack Cressend .15 .07
❑ 476 Talmadge Nunnari .15 .07
❑ 477 Jorge Toca .15 .07
❑ 478 Alfonso Soriano .60 .25
❑ 479 Jay Tessmer .15 .07
❑ 480 Jake Westbrook .15 .07
❑ 481 Eric Byrnes .15 .07
❑ 482 Jose Ortiz 1.00 .45
❑ 483 Tike Redman .15 .07
❑ 484 Domingo Guzman .15 .07
❑ 485 Rodrigo Lopez .15 .07
❑ 486 Xavier Nady .40 .18
❑ 487 Pedro Feliz .15 .07
❑ 488 Damon Minor .15 .07
❑ 489 Ryan Vogelsong .25 .11
❑ 490 Joel Pineiro .60 .25
❑ 491 Justin Brunette .15 .07
❑ 492 Keith McDonald .15 .07
❑ 493 Aubrey Huff .15 .07
❑ 494 Kenny Kelly .25 .11
❑ 495 Damian Rolls .15 .07
❑ 496 John Bale .15 .07
❑ 497 Pasqual Coco .15 .07
❑ 498 Matt DeWitt .15 .07
❑ 499 Leo Estrella .15 .07
❑ 500 Josh Phelps .25 .11

2000 Pacific Private Stock

	MINT	NRMT
COMPLETE SET (150)	150.00	70.00
COMP.SET w/o SP's (125)	50.00	22.00
COMMON CARD (1-150)	.25	.11
COMMON SP PROSPECT	5.00	2.20

❑ 1 Darin Erstad 1.00 .45
❑ 2 Troy Glaus 1.00 .45
❑ 3 Tim Salmon .40 .18
❑ 4 Mo Vaughn .40 .18

❑ 5 Jay Bell .40 .18
❑ 6 Luis Gonzalez 1.00 .45
❑ 7 Randy Johnson 1.25 .55
❑ 8 Matt Williams .60 .25
❑ 9 Andruw Jones 1.00 .45
❑ 10 Chipper Jones 2.00 .90
❑ 11 Brian Jordan .40 .18
❑ 12 Greg Maddux 2.50 1.10
❑ 13 Kevin Millwood .25 .11
❑ 14 Albert Belle .40 .18
❑ 15 Mike Mussina 1.00 .45
❑ 16 Cal Ripken 4.00 1.80
❑ 17 B.J. Surhoff .40 .18
❑ 18 Nomar Garciaparra 2.50 1.10
❑ 19 Butch Huskey .25 .11
❑ 20 Pedro Martinez 1.25 .55
❑ 21 Troy O'Leary .25 .11
❑ 22 Mark Grace 1.00 .45
❑ 23 Bo Porter SP 5.00 2.20
❑ 24 Henry Rodriguez .25 .11
❑ 25 Sammy Sosa 2.00 .90
❑ 26 Kerry Wood 1.00 .45
❑ 27 Jason Dellaero SP 5.00 2.20
❑ 28 Ray Durham .40 .18
❑ 29 Paul Konerko .40 .18
❑ 30 Carlos Lee .40 .18
❑ 31 Magglio Ordonez .40 .18
❑ 32 Frank Thomas 1.25 .55
❑ 33 Mike Cameron .40 .18
❑ 34 Sean Casey .60 .25
❑ 35 Barry Larkin 1.00 .45
❑ 36 Greg Vaughn .40 .18
❑ 37 Roberto Alomar 1.00 .45
❑ 38 Russell Branyan SP 5.00 2.20
❑ 39 Kenny Lofton .40 .18
❑ 40 Manny Ramirez 1.25 .55
❑ 41 Richie Sexson .40 .18
❑ 42 Jim Thome 1.00 .45
❑ 43 Omar Vizquel .40 .18
❑ 44 Pedro Astacio .25 .11
❑ 45 Vinny Castilla .40 .18
❑ 46 Todd Helton 1.25 .55
❑ 47 Ben Petrick SP 5.00 2.20
❑ 48 Juan Sosa SP RC 5.00 2.20
❑ 49 Larry Walker .60 .25
❑ 50 Tony Clark .40 .18
❑ 51 Damion Easley .25 .11
❑ 52 Juan Encarnacion .40 .18
❑ 53 Robert Fick SP 5.00 2.20
❑ 54 Dean Palmer .40 .18
❑ 55 A.J. Burnett SP 5.00 2.20
❑ 56 Luis Castillo .25 .11
❑ 57 Alex Gonzalez .25 .11
❑ 58 Julio Ramirez SP 5.00 2.20
❑ 59 Preston Wilson .40 .18
❑ 60 Jeff Bagwell 1.25 .55
❑ 61 Craig Biggio .60 .25
❑ 62 Ken Caminiti .40 .18
❑ 63 Carl Everett .40 .18
❑ 64 Mike Hampton .40 .18
❑ 65 Billy Wagner .25 .11
❑ 66 Carlos Beltran .40 .18
❑ 67 Dermal Brown SP 5.00 2.20
❑ 68 Jermaine Dye .40 .18
❑ 69 Carlos Febles .25 .11
❑ 70 Mark Quinn SP 5.00 2.20
❑ 71 Mike Sweeney .40 .18

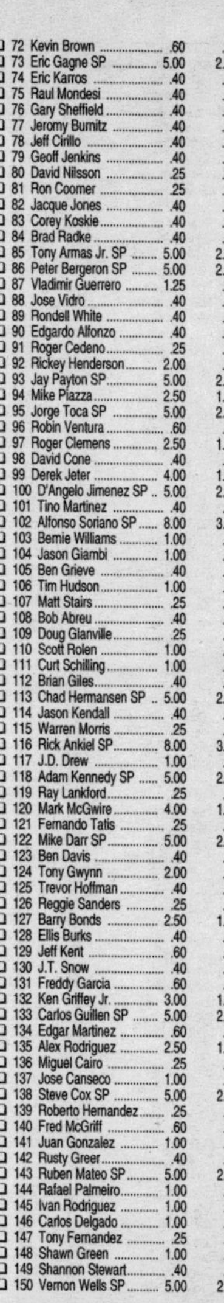

		MINT	NRMT
❑ 72	Kevin Brown	.60	.25
❑ 73	Eric Gagne SP	5.00	2.20
❑ 74	Eric Karros	.40	.18
❑ 75	Raul Mondesi	.40	.18
❑ 76	Gary Sheffield	.40	.18
❑ 77	Jeromy Burnitz	.40	.18
❑ 78	Jeff Cirillo	.40	.18
❑ 79	Geoff Jenkins	.40	.18
❑ 80	David Nilsson	.25	.11
❑ 81	Ron Coomer	.25	.11
❑ 82	Jacque Jones	.40	.18
❑ 83	Corey Koskie	.40	.18
❑ 84	Brad Radke	.40	.18
❑ 85	Tony Armas Jr. SP	5.00	2.20
❑ 86	Peter Bergeron SP	5.00	2.20
❑ 87	Vladimir Guerrero	1.25	.55
❑ 88	Jose Vidro	.40	.18
❑ 89	Rondell White	.40	.18
❑ 90	Edgardo Alfonzo	.40	.18
❑ 91	Roger Cedeno	.25	.11
❑ 92	Rickey Henderson	2.00	.90
❑ 93	Jay Payton SP	5.00	2.20
❑ 94	Mike Piazza	2.50	1.10
❑ 95	Jorge Toca SP	5.00	2.20
❑ 96	Robin Ventura	.60	.25
❑ 97	Roger Clemens	2.50	1.10
❑ 98	David Cone	.40	.18
❑ 99	Derek Jeter	4.00	1.80
❑ 100	D'Angelo Jimenez SP	5.00	2.20
❑ 101	Tino Martinez	.40	.18
❑ 102	Alfonso Soriano SP	8.00	3.60
❑ 103	Bernie Williams	1.00	.45
❑ 104	Jason Giambi	1.00	.45
❑ 105	Ben Grieve	.40	.18
❑ 106	Tim Hudson	1.00	.45
❑ 107	Matt Stairs	.25	.11
❑ 108	Bob Abreu	.40	.18
❑ 109	Doug Glanville	.25	.11
❑ 110	Scott Rolen	1.00	.45
❑ 111	Curt Schilling	1.00	.45
❑ 112	Brian Giles	.40	.18
❑ 113	Chad Hermansen SP	5.00	2.20
❑ 114	Jason Kendall	.40	.18
❑ 115	Warren Morris	.25	.11
❑ 116	Rick Ankiel SP	8.00	3.60
❑ 117	J.D. Drew	1.00	.45
❑ 118	Adam Kennedy SP	5.00	2.20
❑ 119	Ray Lankford	.25	.11
❑ 120	Mark McGwire	4.00	1.80
❑ 121	Fernando Tatis	.25	.11
❑ 122	Mike Darr SP	5.00	2.20
❑ 123	Ben Davis	.40	.18
❑ 124	Tony Gwynn	2.00	.90
❑ 125	Trevor Hoffman	.40	.18
❑ 126	Reggie Sanders	.25	.11
❑ 127	Barry Bonds	2.50	1.10
❑ 128	Ellis Burks	.40	.18
❑ 129	Jeff Kent	.60	.25
❑ 130	J.T. Snow	.40	.18
❑ 131	Freddy Garcia	.60	.25
❑ 132	Ken Griffey Jr.	3.00	1.35
❑ 133	Carlos Guillen SP	5.00	2.20
❑ 134	Edgar Martinez	.60	.25
❑ 135	Alex Rodriguez	2.50	1.10
❑ 136	Miguel Cairo	.25	.11
❑ 137	Jose Canseco	1.00	.45
❑ 138	Steve Cox SP	5.00	2.20
❑ 139	Roberto Hernandez	.25	.11
❑ 140	Fred McGriff	.60	.25
❑ 141	Juan Gonzalez	1.00	.45
❑ 142	Rusty Greer	.40	.18
❑ 143	Ruben Mateo SP	5.00	2.20
❑ 144	Rafael Palmeiro	1.00	.45
❑ 145	Ivan Rodriguez	1.00	.45
❑ 146	Carlos Delgado	1.00	.45
❑ 147	Tony Fernandez	.25	.11
❑ 148	Shawn Green	1.00	.45
❑ 149	Shannon Stewart	.40	.18
❑ 150	Vernon Wells SP	5.00	2.20

2001 Pacific Private Stock

		MINT	NRMT
COMPLETE SET (150)		150.00	70.00

		MINT	NRMT
COMP.SET w/o SP's (125)		50.00	22.00
❑ 1	Darin Erstad	1.00	.45
❑ 2	Troy Glaus	1.00	.45
❑ 3	Tim Salmon	.40	.18
❑ 4	Mo Vaughn	.40	.18
❑ 5	Steve Finley	.40	.18
❑ 6	Luis Gonzalez	1.00	.45
❑ 7	Randy Johnson	1.25	.55
❑ 8	Matt Williams	.60	.25
❑ 9	Rafael Furcal	.40	.18
❑ 10	Andres Galarraga	.60	.25
❑ 11	Tom Glavine	1.00	.45
❑ 12	Andruw Jones	1.00	.45
❑ 13	Chipper Jones	2.00	.90
❑ 14	Greg Maddux	2.50	1.10
❑ 15	B.J. Surhoff	.40	.18
❑ 16	Brady Anderson	.40	.18
❑ 17	Albert Belle	.40	.18
❑ 18	Mike Mussina	1.00	.45
❑ 19	Cal Ripken	4.00	1.80
❑ 20	Carl Everett	.40	.18
❑ 21	Nomar Garciaparra	2.50	1.10
❑ 22	Pedro Martinez	1.25	.55
❑ 23	Mark Grace	1.00	.45
❑ 24	Sammy Sosa	2.00	.90
❑ 25	Kerry Wood	1.00	.45
❑ 26	Carlos Lee	.40	.18
❑ 27	Magglio Ordonez	.40	.18
❑ 28	Frank Thomas	1.25	.55
❑ 29	Sean Casey	.60	.25
❑ 30	Ken Griffey Jr.	3.00	1.35
❑ 31	Barry Larkin	1.00	.45
❑ 32	Pokey Reese	.25	.11
❑ 33	Roberto Alomar	1.00	.45
❑ 34	Kenny Lofton	.40	.18
❑ 35	Manny Ramirez	1.25	.55
❑ 36	Jim Thome	1.00	.45
❑ 37	Omar Vizquel	.40	.18
❑ 38	Jeff Cirillo	.40	.18
❑ 39	Jeffrey Hammonds	.25	.11
❑ 40	Todd Helton	1.25	.55
❑ 41	Larry Walker	.60	.25
❑ 42	Tony Clark	.40	.18
❑ 43	Juan Encarnacion	.40	.18
❑ 44	Juan Gonzalez	1.00	.45
❑ 45	Hideo Nomo	1.00	.45
❑ 46	Cliff Floyd	.40	.18
❑ 47	Derek Lee	.25	.11
❑ 48	Henry Rodriguez	.25	.11
❑ 49	Preston Wilson	.40	.18
❑ 50	Jeff Bagwell	1.25	.55
❑ 51	Craig Biggio	.60	.25
❑ 52	Richard Hidalgo	.40	.18
❑ 53	Moises Alou	.40	.18
❑ 54	Carlos Beltran	.40	.18
❑ 55	Johnny Damon	.40	.18
❑ 56	Jermaine Dye	.40	.18
❑ 57	Mac Suzuki	.25	.11
❑ 58	Mike Sweeney	.40	.18
❑ 59	Adrian Beltre	.40	.18
❑ 60	Kevin Brown	.40	.18
❑ 61	Shawn Green	1.00	.45
❑ 62	Eric Karros	.40	.18
❑ 63	Chan Ho Park	.40	.18
❑ 64	Gary Sheffield	.40	.18
❑ 65	Jeromy Burnitz	.40	.18
❑ 66	Geoff Jenkins	.40	.18
❑ 67	Richie Sexson	.40	.18
❑ 68	Jacque Jones	.40	.18
❑ 69	Matt Lawton	.40	.18
❑ 70	Eric Milton	.40	.18
❑ 71	Vladimir Guerrero	1.25	.55
❑ 72	Jose Vidro	.40	.18
❑ 73	Edgardo Alfonzo	.40	.18
❑ 74	Mike Hampton	.40	.18
❑ 75	Mike Piazza	2.50	1.10
❑ 76	Robin Ventura	.40	.18
❑ 77	Jose Canseco	1.00	.45
❑ 78	Roger Clemens	2.50	1.10
❑ 79	Derek Jeter	4.00	1.80
❑ 80	David Justice	.40	.18
❑ 81	Jorge Posada	.40	.18
❑ 82	Bernie Williams	1.00	.45
❑ 83	Jason Giambi	1.00	.45
❑ 84	Ben Grieve	.40	.18
❑ 85	Tim Hudson	1.00	.45
❑ 86	Terrence Long	.40	.18
❑ 87	Miguel Tejada	.40	.18
❑ 88	Bob Abreu	.40	.18
❑ 89	Pat Burrell	.40	.18
❑ 90	Mike Lieberthal	.40	.18
❑ 91	Scott Rolen	1.00	.45
❑ 92	Kris Benson	.40	.18
❑ 93	Brian Giles	.40	.18
❑ 94	Jason Kendall	.40	.18
❑ 95	Aramis Ramirez	.40	.18
❑ 96	Rick Ankiel	.60	.25
❑ 97	Will Clark	1.00	.45
❑ 98	J.D. Drew	1.00	.45
❑ 99	Jim Edmonds	.60	.25
❑ 100	Mark McGwire	4.00	1.80
❑ 101	Fernando Tatis	.25	.11
❑ 102	Adam Eaton	.40	.18
❑ 103	Tony Gwynn	2.00	.90
❑ 104	Phil Nevin	.40	.18
❑ 105	Eric Owens	.25	.11
❑ 106	Barry Bonds	2.50	1.10
❑ 107	Jeff Kent	.60	.25
❑ 108	J.T. Snow	.40	.18
❑ 109	Rickey Henderson	2.00	.90
❑ 110	Edgar Martinez	.60	.25
❑ 111	John Olerud	.40	.18
❑ 112	Alex Rodriguez	2.50	1.10
❑ 113	Kazuhiro Sasaki	1.00	.45
❑ 114	Vinny Castilla	.40	.18
❑ 115	Fred McGriff	.60	.25
❑ 116	Greg Vaughn	.40	.18
❑ 117	Gabe Kapler	.40	.18
❑ 118	Ruben Mateo	.40	.18
❑ 119	Rafael Palmeiro	1.00	.45
❑ 120	Ivan Rodriguez	1.00	.45
❑ 121	Tony Batista	.40	.18
❑ 122	Jose Cruz Jr.	.40	.18
❑ 123	Carlos Delgado	1.00	.45
❑ 124	Shannon Stewart	.40	.18
❑ 125	David Wells	.40	.18
❑ 126	Shawn Wooten SP	5.00	2.20
❑ 127	George Lombard SP	5.00	2.20
❑ 128	Morgan Burkhart SP	5.00	2.20
❑ 129	Ross Gload SP	5.00	2.20
❑ 130	Corey Patterson SP	8.00	3.60
❑ 131	Julio Zuleta SP	5.00	2.20
❑ 132	Joe Crede SP	8.00	3.60
❑ 133	Matt Ginter SP	5.00	2.20
❑ 134	Travis Dawkins SP	5.00	2.20
❑ 135	Eric Munson SP	8.00	3.60
❑ 136	Dee Brown SP	5.00	2.20
❑ 137	Luke Prokopec SP	8.00	3.60
❑ 138	Timo Perez SP	5.00	2.20
❑ 139	Alfonso Soriano SP	10.00	4.50
❑ 140	Jake Westbrook SP	5.00	2.20
❑ 141	Eric Byrnes SP	5.00	2.20
❑ 142	Adam Hyzdu SP	5.00	2.20
❑ 143	Jimmy Rollins SP	8.00	3.60
❑ 144	Xavier Nady SP	8.00	3.60
❑ 145	Ryan Vogelsong SP	5.00	2.20
❑ 146	Joel Pineiro SP	10.00	4.50
❑ 147	Aubrey Huff SP	5.00	2.20
❑ 148	Kenny Kelly SP	5.00	2.20
❑ 149	Josh Phelps SP	8.00	3.60
❑ 150	Vernon Wells SP	8.00	3.60

1992 Pinnacle

	MINT	NRMT
COMPLETE SET (620)	40.00	18.00
COMPLETE SERIES 1 (310)	25.00	11.00
COMPLETE SERIES 2 (310)	15.00	6.75

No.	Player	MINT	NRMT
❑ 1	Frank Thomas	.50	.23
❑ 2	Benito Santiago	.10	.05
❑ 3	Carlos Baerga	.10	.05
❑ 4	Cecil Fielder	.15	.07
❑ 5	Barry Larkin	.40	.18
❑ 6	Ozzie Smith	.50	.23
❑ 7	Willie McGee	.15	.07
❑ 8	Paul Molitor	.40	.18
❑ 9	Andy Van Slyke	.15	.07
❑ 10	Ryne Sandberg	.50	.23
❑ 11	Kevin Seitzer	.10	.05
❑ 12	Len Dykstra	.15	.07
❑ 13	Edgar Martinez	.25	.11
❑ 14	Ruben Sierra	.10	.05
❑ 15	Howard Johnson	.10	.05
❑ 16	Dave Henderson	.10	.05
❑ 17	Devon White	.10	.05
❑ 18	Terry Pendleton	.15	.07
❑ 19	Steve Finley	.15	.07
❑ 20	Kirby Puckett	1.00	.45
❑ 21	Orel Hershiser	.15	.07
❑ 22	Hal Morris	.10	.05
❑ 23	Don Mattingly	1.00	.45
❑ 24	Delino DeShields	.10	.05
❑ 25	Dennis Eckersley	.15	.07
❑ 26	Ellis Burks	.15	.07
❑ 27	Jay Buhner	.15	.07
❑ 28	Matt Williams	.25	.11
❑ 29	Lou Whitaker	.15	.07
❑ 30	Alex Fernandez	.10	.05
❑ 31	Albert Belle	.15	.07
❑ 32	Todd Zeile	.10	.05
❑ 33	Tony Pena	.10	.05
❑ 34	Jay Bell	.15	.07
❑ 35	Rafael Palmeiro	.40	.18
❑ 36	Wes Chamberlain	.10	.05
❑ 37	George Bell	.10	.05
❑ 38	Robin Yount	.40	.18
❑ 39	Vince Coleman	.10	.05
❑ 40	Bruce Hurst	.10	.05
❑ 41	Harold Baines	.15	.07
❑ 42	Chuck Finley	.15	.07
❑ 43	Ken Caminiti	.15	.07
❑ 44	Ben McDonald	.10	.05
❑ 45	Roberto Alomar	.40	.18
❑ 46	Chili Davis	.15	.07
❑ 47	Bill Doran	.10	.05
❑ 48	Jerald Clark	.10	.05
❑ 49	Jose Lind	.10	.05
❑ 50	Nolan Ryan	2.00	.90
❑ 51	Phil Plantier	.10	.05
❑ 52	Gary DiSarcina	.10	.05
❑ 53	Kevin Bass	.10	.05
❑ 54	Pat Kelly	.10	.05
❑ 55	Mark Wohlers	.10	.05
❑ 56	Walt Weiss	.10	.05
❑ 57	Lenny Harris	.10	.05
❑ 58	Ivan Calderon	.10	.05
❑ 59	Harold Reynolds	.10	.05
❑ 60	George Brett	.75	.35
❑ 61	Gregg Olson	.10	.05
❑ 62	Orlando Merced	.10	.05
❑ 63	Steve Decker	.10	.05
❑ 64	John Franco	.15	.07
❑ 65	Greg Maddux	1.00	.45
❑ 66	Alex Cole	.10	.05
❑ 67	Dave Hollins	.10	.05
❑ 68	Kent Hrbek	.15	.07
❑ 69	Tom Pagnozzi	.10	.05
❑ 70	Jeff Bagwell	.75	.35
❑ 71	Jim Gantner	.10	.05
❑ 72	Matt Nokes	.10	.05
❑ 73	Brian Harper	.10	.05
❑ 74	Andy Benes	.10	.05
❑ 75	Tom Glavine	.40	.18
❑ 76	Terry Steinbach	.10	.05
❑ 77	Dennis Martinez	.15	.07
❑ 78	John Olerud	.15	.07
❑ 79	Ozzie Guillen	.10	.05
❑ 80	Darryl Strawberry	.15	.07
❑ 81	Gary Gaetti	.15	.07
❑ 82	Dave Righetti	.15	.07
❑ 83	Chris Hoiles	.10	.05
❑ 84	Andujar Cedeno	.10	.05
❑ 85	Jack Clark	.15	.07
❑ 86	David Howard	.10	.05
❑ 87	Bill Gullickson	.10	.05
❑ 88	Bernard Gilkey	.10	.05
❑ 89	Kevin Elster	.10	.05
❑ 90	Kevin Maas	.10	.05
❑ 91	Mark Lewis	.10	.05
❑ 92	Greg Vaughn	.15	.07
❑ 93	Bret Barberie	.10	.05
❑ 94	Dave Smith	.10	.05
❑ 95	Roger Clemens	1.00	.45
❑ 96	Doug Drabek	.10	.05
❑ 97	Omar Vizquel	.15	.07
❑ 98	Jose Guzman	.10	.05
❑ 99	Juan Samuel	.10	.05
❑ 100	Dave Justice	.15	.07
❑ 101	Tom Browning	.10	.05
❑ 102	Mark Gubicza	.10	.05
❑ 103	Mickey Morandini	.10	.05
❑ 104	Ed Whitson	.10	.05
❑ 105	Lance Parrish	.15	.07
❑ 106	Scott Erickson	.10	.05
❑ 107	Jack McDowell	.10	.05
❑ 108	Dave Stieb	.10	.05
❑ 109	Mike Moore	.10	.05
❑ 110	Travis Fryman	.15	.07
❑ 111	Dwight Gooden	.15	.07
❑ 112	Fred McGriff	.25	.11
❑ 113	Alan Trammell	.25	.11
❑ 114	Roberto Kelly	.10	.05
❑ 115	Andre Dawson	.25	.11
❑ 116	Bill Landrum	.10	.05
❑ 117	Brian McRae	.10	.05
❑ 118	B.J. Surhoff	.15	.07
❑ 119	Chuck Knoblauch	.15	.07
❑ 120	Steve Olin	.10	.05
❑ 121	Robin Ventura	.15	.07
❑ 122	Will Clark	.40	.18
❑ 123	Tino Martinez	.15	.07
❑ 124	Dale Murphy	.40	.18
❑ 125	Pete O'Brien	.10	.05
❑ 126	Ray Lankford	.10	.05
❑ 127	Juan Gonzalez	.40	.18
❑ 128	Ron Gant	.10	.05
❑ 129	Marquis Grissom	.10	.05
❑ 130	Jose Canseco	.40	.18
❑ 131	Mike Greenwell	.10	.05
❑ 132	Mark Langston	.10	.05
❑ 133	Brett Butler	.15	.07
❑ 134	Kelly Gruber	.10	.05
❑ 135	Chris Sabo	.10	.05
❑ 136	Mark Grace	.40	.18
❑ 137	Tony Fernandez	.10	.05
❑ 138	Glenn Davis	.10	.05
❑ 139	Pedro Munoz	.10	.05
❑ 140	Craig Biggio	.25	.11
❑ 141	Pete Schourek	.10	.05
❑ 142	Mike Boddicker	.10	.05
❑ 143	Robby Thompson	.10	.05
❑ 144	Mel Hall	.10	.05
❑ 145	Bryan Harvey	.10	.05
❑ 146	Mike LaValliere	.10	.05
❑ 147	John Kruk	.15	.07
❑ 148	Joe Carter	.15	.07
❑ 149	Greg Olson	.10	.05
❑ 150	Julio Franco	.15	.07
❑ 151	Darryl Hamilton	.10	.05
❑ 152	Felix Fermin	.10	.05
❑ 153	Jose Offerman	.10	.05
❑ 154	Paul O'Neill	.40	.18
❑ 155	Tommy Greene	.10	.05
❑ 156	Ivan Rodriguez	.60	.25
❑ 157	Dave Stewart	.15	.07
❑ 158	Jeff Reardon	.15	.07
❑ 159	Felix Jose	.10	.05
❑ 160	Doug Dascenzo	.10	.05
❑ 161	Tim Wallach	.10	.05
❑ 162	Dan Plesac	.10	.05
❑ 163	Luis Gonzalez	.40	.18
❑ 164	Mike Henneman	.10	.05
❑ 165	Mike Devereaux	.10	.05
❑ 166	Luis Polonia	.10	.05
❑ 167	Mike Sharperson	.10	.05
❑ 168	Chris Donnels	.10	.05
❑ 169	Greg W. Harris	.10	.05
❑ 170	Deion Sanders	.15	.07
❑ 171	Mike Schooler	.10	.05
❑ 172	Jose DeJesus	.10	.05
❑ 173	Jeff Montgomery	.10	.05
❑ 174	Milt Cuyler	.10	.05
❑ 175	Wade Boggs	.40	.18
❑ 176	Kevin Tapani	.10	.05
❑ 177	Bill Spiers	.10	.05
❑ 178	Tim Raines	.15	.07
❑ 179	Randy Milligan	.10	.05
❑ 180	Rob Dibble	.10	.05
❑ 181	Kirt Manwaring	.10	.05
❑ 182	Pascual Perez	.10	.05
❑ 183	Juan Guzman	.10	.05
❑ 184	John Smiley	.10	.05
❑ 185	David Segui	.10	.05
❑ 186	Omar Olivares	.10	.05
❑ 187	Joe Slusarski	.10	.05
❑ 188	Erik Hanson	.10	.05
❑ 189	Mark Portugal	.10	.05
❑ 190	Walt Terrell	.10	.05
❑ 191	John Smoltz	.15	.07
❑ 192	Wilson Alvarez	.10	.05
❑ 193	Jimmy Key	.15	.07
❑ 194	Larry Walker	.25	.11
❑ 195	Lee Smith	.15	.07
❑ 196	Pete Harnisch	.10	.05
❑ 197	Mike Harkey	.10	.05
❑ 198	Frank Tanana	.10	.05
❑ 199	Terry Mulholland	.10	.05
❑ 200	Cal Ripken	1.50	.70
❑ 201	Dave Magadan	.10	.05
❑ 202	Bud Black	.10	.05
❑ 203	Terry Shumpert	.10	.05
❑ 204	Mike Mussina	.60	.25
❑ 205	Mo Vaughn	.15	.07
❑ 206	Steve Farr	.10	.05
❑ 207	Darrin Jackson	.10	.05
❑ 208	Jerry Browne	.10	.05
❑ 209	Jeff Russell	.10	.05
❑ 210	Mike Scioscia	.10	.05
❑ 211	Rick Aguilera	.15	.07
❑ 212	Jaime Navarro	.10	.05
❑ 213	Randy Tomlin	.10	.05
❑ 214	Bobby Thigpen	.10	.05
❑ 215	Mark Gardner	.10	.05
❑ 216	Norm Charlton	.10	.05
❑ 217	Mark McGwire	1.50	.70
❑ 218	Skeeter Barnes	.10	.05
❑ 219	Bob Tewksbury	.10	.05
❑ 220	Junior Felix	.10	.05
❑ 221	Sam Horn	.10	.05
❑ 222	Jody Reed	.10	.05
❑ 223	Luis Sojo	.10	.05
❑ 224	Jerome Walton	.10	.05
❑ 225	Darryl Kile	.15	.07
❑ 226	Mickey Tettleton	.10	.05
❑ 227	Dan Pasqua	.10	.05
❑ 228	Jim Gott	.10	.05
❑ 229	Bernie Williams	.40	.18
❑ 230	Shane Mack	.10	.05
❑ 231	Steve Avery	.10	.05
❑ 232	Dave Valle	.10	.05
❑ 233	Mark Leonard	.10	.05

❑ 234 Spike Owen .10 .05
❑ 235 Gary Sheffield .15 .07
❑ 236 Steve Chitren .10 .05
❑ 237 Zane Smith .10 .05
❑ 238 Tom Gordon .10 .05
❑ 239 Jose Oquendo .10 .05
❑ 240 Todd Stottlemyre .10 .05
❑ 241 Darren Daulton .15 .07
❑ 242 Tim Naehring .10 .05
❑ 243 Tony Phillips .10 .05
❑ 244 Shawon Dunston .10 .05
❑ 245 Manuel Lee .10 .05
❑ 246 Mike Pagliarulo .10 .05
❑ 247 Jim Thome .40 .18
❑ 248 Luis Mercedes .10 .05
❑ 249 Cal Eldred .10 .05
❑ 250 Derek Bell .15 .07
❑ 251 Arthur Rhodes .10 .05
❑ 252 Scott Cooper .10 .05
❑ 253 Roberto Hernandez .10 .05
❑ 254 Mo Sanford .10 .05
❑ 255 Scott Servais .10 .05
❑ 256 Eric Karros .15 .07
❑ 257 Andy Mota .10 .05
❑ 258 Keith Mitchell .10 .05
❑ 259 Joel Johnston .10 .05
❑ 260 John Wehner .10 .05
❑ 261 Gino Minutelli .10 .05
❑ 262 Greg Gagne .10 .05
❑ 263 Stan Royer .10 .05
❑ 264 Carlos Garcia .10 .05
❑ 265 Andy Ashby .10 .05
❑ 266 Kim Batiste .10 .05
❑ 267 Julio Valera .10 .05
❑ 268 Royce Clayton .10 .05
❑ 269 Gary Scott .10 .05
❑ 270 Kirk Dressendorfer .10 .05
❑ 271 Sean Berry .10 .05
❑ 272 Lance Dickson .10 .05
❑ 273 Rob Maurer .10 .05
❑ 274 Scott Brosius RC .50 .23
❑ 275 Dave Fleming .10 .05
❑ 276 Lenny Webster .10 .05
❑ 277 Mike Humphreys .10 .05
❑ 278 Freddie Benavides .10 .05
❑ 279 Harvey Pulliam .10 .05
❑ 280 Jeff Carter .10 .05
❑ 281 Jim Abbott I .40 .18
Nolan Ryan
❑ 282 Wade Boggs I .50 .23
George Brett
❑ 283 Ken Griffey Jr. I .60 .25
Rickey Henderson
❑ 284 Wally Joyner .15 .07
Dale Murphy
❑ 285 Chuck Knoblauch I .15 .07
Ozzie Smith
❑ 286 Robin Ventura I .50 .23
Lou Gehrig
❑ 287 Robin Yount SIDE .15 .07
❑ 288 Bob Tewksbury SIDE .10 .05
❑ 289 Kirby Puckett SIDE .50 .23
❑ 290 Kenny Lofton SIDE .15 .07
❑ 291 Jack McDowell SIDE .10 .05
❑ 292 John Burkett SIDE .10 .05
❑ 293 Dwight Smith SIDE .10 .05
❑ 294 Nolan Ryan SIDE 1.00 .45
❑ 295 M.Ramirez DP RC 5.00 2.20
❑ 296 Cliff Floyd RC DP UER 1.25 .55
(Throws right, not left as indicated on back)
❑ 297 Al Shirley DP RC .10 .05
❑ 298 Brian Barber DP RC .10 .05
❑ 299 Jon Farrell DP RC .10 .05
❑ 300 Scott Ruffcorn DP RC .10 .05
❑ 301 Tyrone Hill DP RC .10 .05
❑ 302 Benji Gil DP RC .10 .05
❑ 303 Tyler Green DP RC .10 .05
❑ 304 Allen Watson DP RC .10 .05
❑ 305 Jay Buhner SH .10 .05
❑ 306 Roberto Alomar SH .15 .07
❑ 307 Chuck Knoblauch SH .10 .05
❑ 308 Darryl Strawberry SH .10 .05
❑ 309 Danny Tartabull SH .10 .05
❑ 310 Bobby Bonilla SH .10 .05
❑ 311 Mike Felder .10 .05
❑ 312 Storm Davis .10 .05
❑ 313 Tim Teufel .10 .05
❑ 314 Tom Brunansky .10 .05
❑ 315 Rex Hudler .10 .05
❑ 316 Dave Otto .10 .05
❑ 317 Jeff King .10 .05
❑ 318 Dan Gladden .10 .05
❑ 319 Bill Pecota .10 .05
❑ 320 Franklin Stubbs .10 .05
❑ 321 Gary Carter .25 .11
❑ 322 Melido Perez .10 .05
❑ 323 Eric Davis .15 .07
❑ 324 Greg Myers .10 .05
❑ 325 Pete Incaviglia .10 .05
❑ 326 Von Hayes .10 .05
❑ 327 Greg Swindell .10 .05
❑ 328 Steve Sax .10 .05
❑ 329 Chuck McElroy .10 .05
❑ 330 Gregg Jefferies .10 .05
❑ 331 Joe Oliver .10 .05
❑ 332 Paul Faries .10 .05
❑ 333 David West .10 .05
❑ 334 Craig Grebeck .10 .05
❑ 335 Chris Hammond .10 .05
❑ 336 Billy Ripken .10 .05
❑ 337 Scott Sanderson .10 .05
❑ 338 Dick Schofield .10 .05
❑ 339 Bob Milacki .10 .05
❑ 340 Kevin Reimer .10 .05
❑ 341 Jose DeLeon .10 .05
❑ 342 Henry Cotto .10 .05
❑ 343 Daryl Boston .10 .05
❑ 344 Kevin Gross .10 .05
❑ 345 Milt Thompson .10 .05
❑ 346 Luis Rivera .10 .05
❑ 347 Al Osuna .10 .05
❑ 348 Rob Deer .10 .05
❑ 349 Tim Leary .10 .05
❑ 350 Mike Stanton .10 .05
❑ 351 Dean Palmer .15 .07
❑ 352 Trevor Wilson .10 .05
❑ 353 Mark Eichhorn .10 .05
❑ 354 Scott Aldred .10 .05
❑ 355 Mark Whiten .10 .05
❑ 356 Leo Gomez .10 .05
❑ 357 Rafael Belliard .10 .05
❑ 358 Carlos Quintana .10 .05
❑ 359 Mark Davis .10 .05
❑ 360 Chris Nabholz .10 .05
❑ 361 Carlton Fisk .40 .18
❑ 362 Joe Orsulak .10 .05
❑ 363 Eric Anthony .10 .05
❑ 364 Greg Hibbard .10 .05
❑ 365 Scott Leius .10 .05
❑ 366 Hensley Meulens .10 .05
❑ 367 Chris Bosio .10 .05
❑ 368 Brian Downing .10 .05
❑ 369 Sammy Sosa .75 .35
❑ 370 Stan Belinda .10 .05
❑ 371 Joe Grahe .10 .05
❑ 372 Luis Salazar .10 .05
❑ 373 Lance Johnson .10 .05
❑ 374 Kal Daniels .10 .05
❑ 375 Dave Winfield .40 .18
❑ 376 Brook Jacoby .10 .05
❑ 377 Mariano Duncan .10 .05
❑ 378 Ron Darling .10 .05
❑ 379 Randy Johnson .50 .23
❑ 380 Chito Martinez .10 .05
❑ 381 Andres Galarraga .25 .11
❑ 382 Willie Randolph .15 .07
❑ 383 Charles Nagy .10 .05
❑ 384 Tim Belcher .10 .05
❑ 385 Duane Ward .10 .05
❑ 386 Vicente Palacios .10 .05
❑ 387 Mike Gallego .10 .05
❑ 388 Rich DeLucia .10 .05
❑ 389 Scott Radinsky .10 .05
❑ 390 Damon Berryhill .10 .05
❑ 391 Kirk McCaskill .10 .05
❑ 392 Pedro Guerrero .15 .07
❑ 393 Kevin Mitchell .10 .05
❑ 394 Dickie Thon .10 .05
❑ 395 Bobby Bonilla .15 .07
❑ 396 Bill Wegman .10 .05
❑ 397 Dave Martinez .10 .05
❑ 398 Rick Sutcliffe .15 .07
❑ 399 Larry Andersen .10 .05
❑ 400 Tony Gwynn .75 .35
❑ 401 Rickey Henderson .75 .35
❑ 402 Greg Cadaret .10 .05
❑ 403 Keith Miller .10 .05
❑ 404 Bip Roberts .10 .05
❑ 405 Kevin Brown .15 .07
❑ 406 Mitch Williams .10 .05
❑ 407 Frank Viola .15 .07
❑ 408 Darren Lewis .10 .05
❑ 409 Bob Welch .10 .05
❑ 410 Bob Walk .10 .05
❑ 411 Todd Frohwirth .10 .05
❑ 412 Brian Hunter .10 .05
❑ 413 Ron Karkovice .10 .05
❑ 414 Mike Morgan .10 .05
❑ 415 Joe Hesketh .10 .05
❑ 416 Don Slaught .10 .05
❑ 417 Tom Henke .10 .05
❑ 418 Kurt Stillwell .10 .05
❑ 419 Hector Villaneuva .10 .05
❑ 420 Glenallen Hill .10 .05
❑ 421 Pat Borders .10 .05
❑ 422 Charlie Hough .15 .07
❑ 423 Charlie Leibrandt .10 .05
❑ 424 Eddie Murray .40 .18
❑ 425 Jesse Barfield .10 .05
❑ 426 Mark Lemke .10 .05
❑ 427 Kevin McReynolds .10 .05
❑ 428 Gilberto Reyes .10 .05
❑ 429 Ramon Martinez .10 .05
❑ 430 Steve Buechele .10 .05
❑ 431 David Wells .15 .07
❑ 432 Kyle Abbott .10 .05
❑ 433 John Habyan .10 .05
❑ 434 Kevin Appier .15 .07
❑ 435 Gene Larkin .10 .05
❑ 436 Sandy Alomar Jr. .15 .07
❑ 437 Mike Jackson .10 .05
❑ 438 Todd Benzinger .10 .05
❑ 439 Teddy Higuera .10 .05
❑ 440 Reggie Sanders .10 .05
❑ 441 Mark Carreon .10 .05
❑ 442 Bret Saberhagen .15 .07
❑ 443 Gene Nelson .10 .05
❑ 444 Jay Howell .10 .05
❑ 445 Roger McDowell .10 .05
❑ 446 Sid Bream .10 .05
❑ 447 Mackey Sasser .10 .05
❑ 448 Bill Swift .10 .05
❑ 449 Hubie Brooks .10 .05
❑ 450 David Cone .15 .07
❑ 451 Bobby Witt .10 .05
❑ 452 Brady Anderson .15 .07
❑ 453 Lee Stevens .10 .05
❑ 454 Luis Aquino .10 .05
❑ 455 Carney Lansford .15 .07
❑ 456 Carlos Hernandez .10 .05
❑ 457 Danny Jackson .10 .05
❑ 458 Gerald Young .10 .05
❑ 459 Tom Candiotti .10 .05
❑ 460 Billy Hatcher .10 .05
❑ 461 John Wetteland .15 .07
❑ 462 Mike Bordick .10 .05
❑ 463 Don Robinson .10 .05
❑ 464 Jeff Johnson .10 .05
❑ 465 Lonnie Smith .10 .05
❑ 466 Paul Assenmacher .10 .05
❑ 467 Alvin Davis .10 .05
❑ 468 Jim Eisenreich .10 .05
❑ 469 Brent Mayne .10 .05
❑ 470 Jeff Brantley .10 .05
❑ 471 Tim Burke .10 .05
❑ 472 Pat Mahomes RC .10 .05
❑ 473 Ryan Bowen .10 .05
❑ 474 Bryn Smith .10 .05
❑ 475 Mike Flanagan .10 .05
❑ 476 Reggie Jefferson .10 .05
❑ 477 Jeff Blauser .10 .05
❑ 478 Craig Lefferts .10 .05
❑ 479 Todd Worrell .10 .05
❑ 480 Scott Scudder .10 .05
❑ 481 Kirk Gibson .15 .07
❑ 482 Kenny Rogers .10 .05
❑ 483 Jack Morris .15 .07

No.	Player	Mint	NrMt
484	Russ Swan	.10	.05
485	Mike Huff	.10	.05
486	Ken Hill	.10	.05
487	Geronimo Pena	.10	.05
488	Charlie O'Brien	.10	.05
489	Mike Maddux	.10	.05
490	Scott Livingstone	.10	.05
491	Carl Willis	.10	.05
492	Kelly Downs	.10	.05
493	Dennis Cook	.10	.05
494	Joe Magrane	.10	.05
495	Bob Kipper	.10	.05
496	Jose Mesa	.10	.05
497	Charlie Hayes	.10	.05
498	Joe Girardi	.10	.05
499	Doug Jones	.10	.05
500	Barry Bonds	1.00	.45
501	Bill Krueger	.10	.05
502	Glenn Braggs	.10	.05
503	Eric King	.10	.05
504	Frank Castillo	.10	.05
505	Mike Gardiner	.10	.05
506	Cory Snyder	.10	.05
507	Steve Howe	.10	.05
508	Jose Rijo	.10	.05
509	Sid Fernandez	.10	.05
510	Archi Cianfrocco RC	.10	.05
511	Mark Guthrie	.10	.05
512	Bob Ojeda	.10	.05
513	John Doherty RC	.10	.05
514	Dante Bichette	.15	.07
515	Juan Berenguer	.10	.05
516	Jeff M. Robinson	.10	.05
517	Mike Macfarlane	.10	.05
518	Matt Young	.10	.05
519	Otis Nixon	.10	.05
520	Brian Holman	.10	.05
521	Chris Haney	.10	.05
522	Jeff Kent RC	3.00	1.35
523	Chad Curtis RC	.15	.07
524	Vince Horsman	.10	.05
525	Rod Nichols	.10	.05
526	Peter Hoy	.10	.05
527	Shawn Boskie	.10	.05
528	Alejandro Pena	.10	.05
529	Dave Burba	.10	.05
530	Ricky Jordan	.10	.05
531	Dave Silvestri	.10	.05
532	John Patterson UER (Listed as being born in 1960; should be 1967)	.10	.05
533	Jeff Branson	.10	.05
534	Derrick May	.10	.05
535	Esteban Beltre	.10	.05
536	Jose Melendez	.10	.05
537	Wally Joyner	.15	.07
538	Eddie Taubensee RC	.15	.07
539	Jim Abbott	.15	.07
540	Brian Williams RC	.10	.05
541	Donovan Osborne	.10	.05
542	Patrick Lennon	.10	.05
543	Mike Groppuso RC	.10	.05
544	Jarvis Brown	.10	.05
545	Shawn Livsey RC	.10	.05
546	Jeff Ware	.10	.05
547	Danny Tartabull	.10	.05
548	Bobby Jones RC	.15	.07
549	Ken Griffey Jr.	1.25	.55
550	Rey Sanchez RC	.15	.07
551	Pedro Astacio RC	.15	.07
552	Juan Guerrero	.10	.05
553	Jacob Brumfield	.10	.05
554	Ben Rivera	.10	.05
555	Brian Jordan RC	1.00	.45
556	Denny Neagle	.15	.07
557	Cliff Brantley	.10	.05
558	Anthony Young	.10	.05
559	John Vander Wal	.10	.05
560	Monty Fariss	.10	.05
561	Russ Springer RC	.10	.05
562	Pat Listach RC	.15	.07
563	Pat Hentgen	.10	.05
564	Andy Stankiewicz	.10	.05
565	Mike Perez	.10	.05
566	Mike Bielecki	.10	.05
567	Butch Henry RC	.10	.05
568	Dave Nilsson	.10	.05
569	Scott Hatteberg RC	.10	.05
570	Ruben Amaro	.10	.05
571	Todd Hundley	.10	.05
572	Moises Alou	.15	.07
573	Hector Fajardo RC	.10	.05
574	Todd Van Poppel	.10	.05
575	Willie Banks	.10	.05
576	Bob Zupcic RC	.10	.05
577	J.J. Johnson RC	.10	.05
578	John Burkett	.10	.05
579	Trever Miller RC	.10	.05
580	Scott Bankhead	.10	.05
581	Rich Amaral	.10	.05
582	Kenny Lofton	.40	.18
583	Matt Stairs RC	.15	.07
584	Don Mattingly Rod Carew IDOLS	.40	.18
585	Steve Avery Jack Morris IDOLS	.10	.05
586	Roberto Alomar Sandy Alomar SR. IDOLS	.15	.07
587	Scott Sanderson Catfish Hunter IDOLS	.15	.07
588	Dave Justice Willie Stargell IDOLS	.15	.07
589	Rex Hudler Roger Staubach IDOLS	.40	.18
590	David Cone Jackie Gleason IDOLS	.15	.07
591	Tony Gwynn Willie Davis IDOLS	.40	.18
592	Orel Hershiser SIDE	.10	.05
593	John Wetteland SIDE	.10	.05
594	Tom Glavine SIDE	.15	.07
595	Randy Johnson SIDE	.25	.11
596	Jim Gott SIDE	.10	.05
597	Donald Harris	.10	.05
598	Shawn Hare RC	.10	.05
599	Chris Gardner	.10	.05
600	Rusty Meacham	.10	.05
601	Benito Santiago	.10	.05
602	Eric Davis SHADE	.10	.05
603	Jose Lind SHADE	.10	.05
604	Dave Justice SHADE	.15	.07
605	Tim Raines SHADE	.10	.05
606	Randy Tomlin GRIP	.10	.05
607	Jack McDowell GRIP	.10	.05
608	Greg Maddux GRIP	.40	.18
609	Charles Nagy GRIP	.10	.05
610	Tom Candiotti GRIP	.10	.05
611	David Cone GRIP	.10	.05
612	Steve Avery GRIP	.10	.05
613	Rod Beck GRIP RC	.40	.18
614	R. Henderson TECH	.40	.18
615	Benito Santiago TECH	.10	.05
616	Ruben Sierra TECH	.10	.05
617	Ryne Sandberg TECH	.25	.11
618	Nolan Ryan TECH	1.00	.45
619	Brett Butler TECH	.10	.05
620	Dave Justice TECH	.15	.07

1993 Pinnacle

	MINT	NRMT
COMPLETE SET (620)	45.00	20.00
COMPLETE SERIES 1 (310)	15.00	6.75
COMPLETE SERIES 2 (310)	30.00	13.50

No.	Player	Mint	NrMt
1	Gary Sheffield	.25	.11
2	Cal Eldred	.15	.07
3	Larry Walker	.40	.18
4	Deion Sanders	.25	.11
5	Dave Fleming	.15	.07
6	Carlos Baerga	.15	.07
7	Bernie Williams	.60	.25
8	John Kruk	.25	.11
9	Jimmy Key	.25	.11
10	Jeff Bagwell	.75	.35
11	Jim Abbott	.25	.11
12	Terry Steinbach	.15	.07
13	Bob Tewksbury	.15	.07
14	Eric Karros	.25	.11
15	Ryne Sandberg	.75	.35
16	Will Clark	.60	.25
17	Edgar Martinez	.40	.18
18	Eddie Murray	.60	.25
19	Andy Van Slyke	.25	.11
20	Cal Ripken Jr.	2.50	1.10
21	Ivan Rodriguez	.60	.25
22	Barry Larkin	.60	.25
23	Don Mattingly	1.50	.70
24	Gregg Jefferies	.15	.07
25	Roger Clemens	1.50	.70
26	Cecil Fielder	.25	.11
27	Kent Hrbek	.25	.11
28	Robin Ventura	.25	.11
29	Rickey Henderson	1.25	.55
30	Roberto Alomar	.60	.25
31	Luis Polonia	.15	.07
32	Andujar Cedeno	.15	.07
33	Pat Listach	.15	.07
34	Mark Grace	.60	.25
35	Otis Nixon	.15	.07
36	Felix Jose	.15	.07
37	Mike Sharperson	.15	.07
38	Dennis Martinez	.25	.11
39	Willie McGee	.25	.11
40	Kenny Lofton	.25	.11
41	Randy Johnson	.75	.35
42	Andy Benes	.15	.07
43	Bobby Bonilla	.25	.11
44	Mike Mussina	.60	.25
45	Len Dykstra	.25	.11
46	Ellis Burks	.25	.11
47	Chris Sabo	.15	.07
48	Jay Bell	.25	.11
49	Jose Canseco	.60	.25
50	Craig Biggio	.40	.18
51	Wally Joyner	.25	.11
52	Mickey Tettleton	.15	.07
53	Tim Raines	.25	.11
54	Brian Harper	.15	.07
55	Rene Gonzales	.15	.07
56	Mark Langston	.15	.07
57	Jack Morris	.25	.11
58	Mark McGwire	2.50	1.10
59	Ken Caminiti	.25	.11
60	Terry Pendleton	.25	.11
61	Dave Nilsson	.15	.07
62	Tom Pagnozzi	.15	.07
63	Mike Morgan	.15	.07
64	Darryl Strawberry	.25	.11
65	Charles Nagy	.15	.07
66	Ken Hill	.15	.07
67	Matt Williams	.40	.18
68	Jay Buhner	.25	.11
69	Vince Coleman	.15	.07
70	Brady Anderson	.25	.11
71	Fred McGriff	.40	.18
72	Ben McDonald	.15	.07
73	Terry Mulholland	.15	.07
74	Randy Tomlin	.15	.07
75	Nolan Ryan	3.00	1.35
76	Frank Viola UER (Card incorrectly states he has a surgically repaired elbow)	.25	.11
77	Jose Rijo	.15	.07
78	Shane Mack	.15	.07
79	Travis Fryman	.25	.11
80	Jack McDowell	.15	.07
81	Mark Gubicza	.15	.07
82	Matt Nokes	.15	.07

❑	83	Bert Blyleven	.25	.11
❑	84	Eric Anthony	.15	.07
❑	85	Mike Bordick	.15	.07
❑	86	John Olerud	.25	.11
❑	87	B.J. Surhoff	.25	.11
❑	88	Bernard Gilkey	.15	.07
❑	89	Shawon Dunston	.15	.07
❑	90	Tom Glavine	.60	.25
❑	91	Brett Butler	.25	.11
❑	92	Moises Alou	.25	.11
❑	93	Albert Belle	.25	.11
❑	94	Darren Lewis	.15	.07
❑	95	Omar Vizquel	.25	.11
❑	96	Dwight Gooden	.25	.11
❑	97	Gregg Olson	.15	.07
❑	98	Tony Gwynn	1.25	.55
❑	99	Darren Daulton	.25	.11
❑	100	Dennis Eckersley	.25	.11
❑	101	Rob Dibble	.15	.07
❑	102	Mike Greenwell	.15	.07
❑	103	Jose Lind	.15	.07
❑	104	Julio Franco	.25	.11
❑	105	Tom Gordon	.15	.07
❑	106	Scott Livingstone	.15	.07
❑	107	Chuck Knoblauch	.25	.11
❑	108	Frank Thomas	.75	.35
❑	109	Melido Perez	.15	.07
❑	110	Ken Griffey Jr.	2.00	.90
❑	111	Harold Baines	.25	.11
❑	112	Gary Gaetti	.25	.11
❑	113	Pete Harnisch	.15	.07
❑	114	David Wells	.25	.11
❑	115	Charlie Leibrandt	.15	.07
❑	116	Ray Lankford	.15	.07
❑	117	Kevin Seitzer	.15	.07
❑	118	Robin Yount	.60	.25
❑	119	Lenny Harris	.15	.07
❑	120	Chris James	.15	.07
❑	121	Delino DeShields	.15	.07
❑	122	Kirt Manwaring	.15	.07
❑	123	Glenallen Hill	.15	.07
❑	124	Hensley Meulens	.15	.07
❑	125	Darrin Jackson	.15	.07
❑	126	Todd Hundley	.15	.07
❑	127	Dave Hollins	.15	.07
❑	128	Sam Horn	.15	.07
❑	129	Roberto Hernandez	.15	.07
❑	130	Vicente Palacios	.15	.07
❑	131	George Brett	1.25	.55
❑	132	Dave Martinez	.15	.07
❑	133	Kevin Appier	.25	.11
❑	134	Pat Kelly	.15	.07
❑	135	Pedro Munoz	.15	.07
❑	136	Mark Carreon	.15	.07
❑	137	Lance Johnson	.15	.07
❑	138	Devon White	.15	.07
❑	139	Julio Valera	.15	.07
❑	140	Eddie Taubensee	.15	.07
❑	141	Willie Wilson	.15	.07
❑	142	Stan Belinda	.15	.07
❑	143	John Smoltz	.25	.11
❑	144	Darryl Hamilton	.15	.07
❑	145	Sammy Sosa	1.25	.55
❑	146	Carlos Hernandez	.15	.07
❑	147	Tom Candiotti	.15	.07
❑	148	Mike Felder	.15	.07
❑	149	Rusty Meacham	.15	.07
❑	150	Ivan Calderon	.15	.07
❑	151	Pete O'Brien	.15	.07
❑	152	Erik Hanson	.15	.07
❑	153	Billy Ripken	.15	.07
❑	154	Kurt Stillwell	.15	.07
❑	155	Jeff Kent	.60	.25
❑	156	Mickey Morandini	.15	.07
❑	157	Randy Milligan	.15	.07
❑	158	Reggie Sanders	.15	.07
❑	159	Luis Rivera	.15	.07
❑	160	Orlando Merced	.15	.07
❑	161	Dean Palmer	.25	.11
❑	162	Mike Perez	.15	.07
❑	163	Scott Erickson	.15	.07
❑	164	Kevin McReynolds	.15	.07
❑	165	Kevin Maas	.15	.07
❑	166	Ozzie Guillen	.15	.07
❑	167	Rob Deer	.15	.07
❑	168	Danny Tartabull	.15	.07
❑	169	Lee Stevens	.15	.07
❑	170	Dave Henderson	.15	.07
❑	171	Derek Bell	.15	.07
❑	172	Steve Finley	.25	.11
❑	173	Greg Olson	.15	.07
❑	174	Geronimo Pena	.15	.07
❑	175	Paul Quantrill	.15	.07
❑	176	Steve Buechele	.15	.07
❑	177	Kevin Gross	.15	.07
❑	178	Tim Wallach	.15	.07
❑	179	Dave Valle	.15	.07
❑	180	Dave Silvestri	.15	.07
❑	181	Bud Black	.15	.07
❑	182	Henry Rodriguez	.15	.07
❑	183	Tim Teufel	.15	.07
❑	184	Mark McLemore	.15	.07
❑	185	Bret Saberhagen	.25	.11
❑	186	Chris Hoiles	.15	.07
❑	187	Ricky Jordan	.15	.07
❑	188	Don Slaught	.15	.07
❑	189	Mo Vaughn	.25	.11
❑	190	Joe Oliver	.15	.07
❑	191	Juan Gonzalez	.60	.25
❑	192	Scott Leius	.15	.07
❑	193	Milt Cuyler	.15	.07
❑	194	Chris Haney	.15	.07
❑	195	Ron Karkovice	.15	.07
❑	196	Steve Farr	.15	.07
❑	197	John Orton	.15	.07
❑	198	Kelly Gruber	.15	.07
❑	199	Ron Darling	.15	.07
❑	200	Ruben Sierra	.15	.07
❑	201	Chuck Finley	.25	.11
❑	202	Mike Moore	.15	.07
❑	203	Pat Borders	.15	.07
❑	204	Sid Bream	.15	.07
❑	205	Todd Zeile	.15	.07
❑	206	Rick Wilkins	.15	.07
❑	207	Jim Gantner	.15	.07
❑	208	Frank Castillo	.15	.07
❑	209	Dave Hansen	.15	.07
❑	210	Trevor Wilson	.15	.07
❑	211	Sandy Alomar Jr.	.25	.11
❑	212	Sean Berry	.15	.07
❑	213	Tino Martinez	.25	.11
❑	214	Chito Martinez	.15	.07
❑	215	Dan Walters	.15	.07
❑	216	John Franco	.25	.11
❑	217	Glenn Davis	.15	.07
❑	218	Mariano Duncan	.15	.07
❑	219	Mike LaValliere	.15	.07
❑	220	Rafael Palmeiro	.60	.25
❑	221	Jack Clark	.25	.11
❑	222	Hal Morris	.15	.07
❑	223	Ed Sprague	.15	.07
❑	224	John Valentin	.15	.07
❑	225	Sam Militello	.15	.07
❑	226	Bob Wickman	.15	.07
❑	227	Damion Easley	.15	.07
❑	228	John Jaha	.15	.07
❑	229	Bob Ayrault	.15	.07
❑	230	Mo Sanford	.15	.07
❑	231	Walt Weiss	.15	.07
❑	232	Dante Bichette	.25	.11
❑	233	Steve Decker	.15	.07
❑	234	Jerald Clark	.15	.07
❑	235	Bryan Harvey	.15	.07
❑	236	Joe Girardi	.15	.07
❑	237	Dave Magadan	.15	.07
❑	238	David Nied	.15	.07
❑	239	Eric Wedge RC	.15	.07
❑	240	Rico Brogna	.15	.07
❑	241	J.T. Bruett	.15	.07
❑	242	Jonathan Hurst	.15	.07
❑	243	Bret Boone	.25	.11
❑	244	Manny Alexander	.15	.07
❑	245	Scooter Tucker	.15	.07
❑	246	Troy Neel	.15	.07
❑	247	Eddie Zosky	.15	.07
❑	248	Melvin Nieves	.15	.07
❑	249	Ryan Thompson	.15	.07
❑	250	Shawn Barton RC	.15	.07
❑	251	Ryan Klesko	.25	.11
❑	252	Mike Piazza	3.00	1.35
❑	253	Steve Hosey	.15	.07
❑	254	Shane Reynolds	.15	.07
❑	255	Dan Wilson	.25	.11
❑	256	Tom Marsh	.15	.07
❑	257	Barry Manuel	.15	.07
❑	258	Paul Miller	.15	.07
❑	259	Pedro Martinez	1.50	.70
❑	260	Steve Cooke	.15	.07
❑	261	Johnny Guzman	.15	.07
❑	262	Mike Butcher	.15	.07
❑	263	Bien Figueroa	.15	.07
❑	264	Rich Rowland	.15	.07
❑	265	Shawn Jeter	.15	.07
❑	266	Gerald Williams	.15	.07
❑	267	Derek Parks	.15	.07
❑	268	Henry Mercedes	.15	.07
❑	269	David Hulse RC	.15	.07
❑	270	Tim Pugh RC	.15	.07
❑	271	William Suero	.15	.07
❑	272	Ozzie Canseco	.15	.07
❑	273	Fernando Ramsey RC	.15	.07
❑	274	Bernardo Brito	.15	.07
❑	275	Dave Mlicki	.15	.07
❑	276	Tim Salmon	.25	.11
❑	277	Mike Raczka	.15	.07
❑	278	Ken Ryan RC	.15	.07
❑	279	Rafael Bournigal	.15	.07
❑	280	Wil Cordero	.15	.07
❑	281	Billy Ashley	.15	.07
❑	282	Paul Wagner	.15	.07
❑	283	Blas Minor	.15	.07
❑	284	Rick Trlicek	.15	.07
❑	285	Willie Greene	.15	.07
❑	286	Ted Wood	.15	.07
❑	287	Phil Clark	.15	.07
❑	288	Jesse Levis	.15	.07
❑	289	Tony Gwynn NT	.60	.25
❑	290	Nolan Ryan NT	1.50	.70
❑	291	Dennis Martinez NT	.15	.07
❑	292	Eddie Murray NT	.25	.11
❑	293	Robin Yount NT	.25	.11
❑	294	George Brett NT	.60	.25
❑	295	Dave Winfield NT	.25	.11
❑	296	Bert Blyleven NT	.15	.07
❑	297	Jeff Bagwell Carl Yastrzemski	.60	.25
❑	298	John Smoltz Jack Morris	.25	.11
❑	299	Larry Walker Mike Bossy	.40	.18
❑	300	Gary Sheffield Barry Larkin	.25	.11
❑	301	Ivan Rodriguez Carlton Fisk	.40	.18
❑	302	Delino DeShields Malcolm X	.60	.25
❑	303	Tim Salmon Dwight Evans	.25	.11
❑	304	Bernard Gilkey HH	.15	.07
❑	305	Cal Ripken Jr. HH	1.25	.55
❑	306	Barry Larkin HH	.25	.11
❑	307	Kent Hrbek HH	.15	.07
❑	308	Rickey Henderson HH	.60	.25
❑	309	Darryl Strawberry HH	.15	.07
❑	310	John Franco HH	.15	.07
❑	311	Todd Stottlemyre	.15	.07
❑	312	Luis Gonzalez	.60	.25
❑	313	Tommy Greene	.15	.07
❑	314	Randy Velarde	.15	.07
❑	315	Steve Avery	.15	.07
❑	316	Jose Oquendo	.15	.07
❑	317	Rey Sanchez	.15	.07
❑	318	Greg Vaughn	.25	.11
❑	319	Orel Hershiser	.25	.11
❑	320	Paul Sorrento	.15	.07
❑	321	Royce Clayton	.15	.07
❑	322	John Vander Wal	.15	.07
❑	323	Henry Cotto	.15	.07
❑	324	Pete Schourek	.15	.07
❑	325	David Segui	.15	.07
❑	326	Arthur Rhodes	.15	.07
❑	327	Bruce Hurst	.15	.07
❑	328	Wes Chamberlain	.15	.07
❑	329	Ozzie Smith	.75	.35
❑	330	Scott Cooper	.15	.07
❑	331	Felix Fermin	.15	.07
❑	332	Mike Macfarlane	.15	.07
❑	333	Dan Gladden	.15	.07

❑ 334 Kevin Tapani .15 .07
❑ 335 Steve Sax .15 .07
❑ 336 Jeff Montgomery .15 .07
❑ 337 Gary DiSarcina .15 .07
❑ 338 Lance Blankenship .15 .07
❑ 339 Brian Williams .15 .07
❑ 340 Duane Ward .15 .07
❑ 341 Chuck McElroy .15 .07
❑ 342 Joe Magrane .15 .07
❑ 343 Jaime Navarro .15 .07
❑ 344 Dave Justice .25 .11
❑ 345 Jose Offerman .15 .07
❑ 346 Marquis Grissom .15 .07
❑ 347 Bill Swift .15 .07
❑ 348 Jim Thome .60 .25
❑ 349 Archi Cianfrocco .15 .07
❑ 350 Anthony Young .15 .07
❑ 351 Leo Gomez .15 .07
❑ 352 Bill Gullickson .15 .07
❑ 353 Alan Trammell .40 .18
❑ 354 Dan Pasqua .15 .07
❑ 355 Jeff King .15 .07
❑ 356 Kevin Brown .25 .11
❑ 357 Tim Belcher .15 .07
❑ 358 Bip Roberts .15 .07
❑ 359 Brent Mayne .15 .07
❑ 360 Rheal Cormier .15 .07
❑ 361 Mark Guthrie .15 .07
❑ 362 Craig Grebeck .15 .07
❑ 363 Andy Stankiewicz .15 .07
❑ 364 Juan Guzman .15 .07
❑ 365 Bobby Witt .15 .07
❑ 366 Mark Portugal .15 .07
❑ 367 Brian McRae .15 .07
❑ 368 Mark Lemke .15 .07
❑ 369 Bill Wegman .15 .07
❑ 370 Donovan Osborne .15 .07
❑ 371 Derrick May .15 .07
❑ 372 Carl Willis .15 .07
❑ 373 Chris Nabholz .15 .07
❑ 374 Mark Lewis .15 .07
❑ 375 John Burkett .15 .07
❑ 376 Luis Mercedes .15 .07
❑ 377 Ramon Martinez .15 .07
❑ 378 Kyle Abbott .15 .07
❑ 379 Mark Wohlers .15 .07
❑ 380 Bob Walk .15 .07
❑ 381 Kenny Rogers .15 .07
❑ 382 Tim Naehring .15 .07
❑ 383 Alex Fernandez .15 .07
❑ 384 Keith Miller .15 .07
❑ 385 Mike Henneman .15 .07
❑ 386 Rick Aguilera .15 .07
❑ 387 George Bell .15 .07
❑ 388 Mike Gallego .15 .07
❑ 389 Howard Johnson .15 .07
❑ 390 Kim Batiste .15 .07
❑ 391 Jerry Browne .15 .07
❑ 392 Damon Berryhill .15 .07
❑ 393 Ricky Bones .15 .07
❑ 394 Omar Olivares .15 .07
❑ 395 Mike Harkey .15 .07
❑ 396 Pedro Astacio .15 .07
❑ 397 John Wetteland .25 .11
❑ 398 Rod Beck .15 .07
❑ 399 Thomas Howard .15 .07
❑ 400 Mike Devereaux .15 .07
❑ 401 Tim Wakefield .15 .07
❑ 402 Curt Schilling .60 .25
❑ 403 Zane Smith .15 .07
❑ 404 Bob Zupcic .15 .07
❑ 405 Tom Browning .15 .07
❑ 406 Tony Phillips .15 .07
❑ 407 John Doherty .15 .07
❑ 408 Pat Mahomes .15 .07
❑ 409 John Habyan .15 .07
❑ 410 Steve Olin .15 .07
❑ 411 Chad Curtis .15 .07
❑ 412 Joe Grahe .15 .07
❑ 413 John Patterson .15 .07
❑ 414 Brian Hunter .15 .07
❑ 415 Doug Henry .15 .07
❑ 416 Lee Smith .25 .11
❑ 417 Bob Scanlan .15 .07
❑ 418 Kent Mercker .15 .07
❑ 419 Mel Rojas .15 .07
❑ 420 Mark Whiten .15 .07
❑ 421 Carlton Fisk .60 .25
❑ 422 Candy Maldonado .15 .07
❑ 423 Doug Drabek .15 .07
❑ 424 Wade Boggs .60 .25
❑ 425 Mark Davis .15 .07
❑ 426 Kirby Puckett 1.50 .70
❑ 427 Joe Carter .25 .11
❑ 428 Paul Molitor .60 .25
❑ 429 Eric Davis .25 .11
❑ 430 Darryl Kile .25 .11
❑ 431 Jeff Parrett .15 .07
❑ 432 Jeff Blauser .15 .07
❑ 433 Dan Plesac .15 .07
❑ 434 Andres Galarraga .40 .18
❑ 435 Jim Gott .15 .07
❑ 436 Jose Mesa .15 .07
❑ 437 Ben Rivera .15 .07
❑ 438 Dave Winfield .60 .25
❑ 439 Norm Charlton .15 .07
❑ 440 Chris Bosio .15 .07
❑ 441 Wilson Alvarez .15 .07
❑ 442 Dave Stewart .25 .11
❑ 443 Doug Jones .15 .07
❑ 444 Jeff Russell .15 .07
❑ 445 Ron Gant .15 .07
❑ 446 Paul O'Neill .60 .25
❑ 447 Charlie Hayes .15 .07
❑ 448 Joe Hesketh .15 .07
❑ 449 Chris Hammond .15 .07
❑ 450 Hipolito Pichardo .15 .07
❑ 451 Scott Radinsky .15 .07
❑ 452 Bobby Thigpen .15 .07
❑ 453 Xavier Hernandez .15 .07
❑ 454 Lonnie Smith .15 .07
❑ 455 Jamie Arnold DP RC .15 .07
❑ 456 B.J. Wallace DP .15 .07
❑ 457 Derek Jeter DP RC 20.00 9.00
❑ 458 Jason Kendall DP RC 2.00 .90
❑ 459 Rick Helling DP .15 .07
❑ 460 Derek Wallace DP RC .15 .07
❑ 461 Sean Lowe DP RC .15 .07
❑ 462 S. Stewart DP RC 2.00 .90
❑ 463 Benji Grigsby DP RC .15 .07
❑ 464 T. Steverson DP RC .15 .07
❑ 465 Dan Serafini DP RC .15 .07
❑ 466 Michael Tucker DP .15 .07
❑ 467 Chris Roberts DP .15 .07
❑ 468 Pete Janicki DP RC .15 .07
❑ 469 Jeff Schmidt DP RC .15 .07
❑ 470 Don Mattingly NT .75 .35
❑ 471 Cal Ripken Jr. NT 1.25 .55
❑ 472 Jack Morris NT .15 .07
❑ 473 Terry Pendleton NT .15 .07
❑ 474 Dennis Eckersley NT .15 .07
❑ 475 Carlton Fisk NT .25 .11
❑ 476 Wade Boggs NT .25 .11
❑ 477 Len Dykstra .25 .11
Ken Stabler
❑ 478 Danny Tartabull .15 .07
Jose Tartabull
❑ 479 Jeff Conine .25 .11
Dale Murphy
❑ 480 Gregg Jefferies .15 .07
Ron Cey
❑ 481 Paul Molitor .40 .18
Harmon Killebrew
❑ 482 John Valentin .15 .07
Dave Concepcion
❑ 483 Alex Arias .25 .11
Dave Winfield
❑ 484 Barry Bonds HH .75 .35
❑ 485 Doug Drabek HH .15 .07
❑ 486 Dave Winfield HH .25 .11
❑ 487 Brett Butler HH .15 .07
❑ 488 Harold Baines HH .15 .07
❑ 489 David Cone HH .15 .07
❑ 490 Willie McGee HH .15 .07
❑ 491 Robby Thompson .15 .07
❑ 492 Pete Incaviglia .15 .07
❑ 493 Manuel Lee .15 .07
❑ 494 Rafael Belliard .15 .07
❑ 495 Scott Fletcher .15 .07
❑ 496 Jeff Frye .15 .07
❑ 497 Andre Dawson .40 .18
❑ 498 Mike Scioscia .15 .07
❑ 499 Spike Owen .15 .07
❑ 500 Sid Fernandez .15 .07
❑ 501 Joe Orsulak .15 .07
❑ 502 Benito Santiago .15 .07
❑ 503 Dale Murphy .40 .18
❑ 504 Barry Bonds 1.50 .70
❑ 505 Jose Guzman .15 .07
❑ 506 Tony Pena .15 .07
❑ 507 Greg Swindell .15 .07
❑ 508 Mike Pagliarulo .15 .07
❑ 509 Lou Whitaker .25 .11
❑ 510 Greg Gagne .15 .07
❑ 511 Butch Henry .15 .07
❑ 512 Jeff Brantley .15 .07
❑ 513 Jack Armstrong .15 .07
❑ 514 Danny Jackson .15 .07
❑ 515 Junior Felix .15 .07
❑ 516 Milt Thompson .15 .07
❑ 517 Greg Maddux 1.50 .70
❑ 518 Eric Young .15 .07
❑ 519 Jody Reed .15 .07
❑ 520 Roberto Kelly .15 .07
❑ 521 Darren Holmes .15 .07
❑ 522 Craig Lefferts .15 .07
❑ 523 Charlie Hough .25 .11
❑ 524 Bo Jackson .25 .11
❑ 525 Bill Spiers .15 .07
❑ 526 Orestes Destrade .15 .07
❑ 527 Greg Hibbard .15 .07
❑ 528 Roger McDowell .15 .07
❑ 529 Cory Snyder .15 .07
❑ 530 Harold Reynolds .15 .07
❑ 531 Kevin Reimer .15 .07
❑ 532 Rick Sutcliffe .25 .11
❑ 533 Tony Fernandez .15 .07
❑ 534 Tom Brunansky .15 .07
❑ 535 Jeff Reardon .25 .11
❑ 536 Chili Davis .25 .11
❑ 537 Bob Ojeda .15 .07
❑ 538 Greg Colbrunn .15 .07
❑ 539 Phil Plantier .15 .07
❑ 540 Brian Jordan .25 .11
❑ 541 Pete Smith .15 .07
❑ 542 Frank Tanana .15 .07
❑ 543 John Smiley .15 .07
❑ 544 David Cone .25 .11
❑ 545 Daryl Boston .15 .07
❑ 546 Tom Henke .15 .07
❑ 547 Bill Krueger .15 .07
❑ 548 Freddie Benavides .15 .07
❑ 549 Randy Myers .15 .07
❑ 550 Reggie Jefferson .15 .07
❑ 551 Kevin Mitchell .15 .07
❑ 552 Dave Stieb .15 .07
❑ 553 Bret Barberie .15 .07
❑ 554 Tim Crews .15 .07
❑ 555 Doug Dascenzo .15 .07
❑ 556 Alex Cole .15 .07
❑ 557 Jeff Innis .15 .07
❑ 558 Carlos Garcia .15 .07
❑ 559 Steve Howe .15 .07
❑ 560 Kirk McCaskill .15 .07
❑ 561 Frank Seminara .15 .07
❑ 562 Cris Carpenter .15 .07
❑ 563 Mike Stanley .15 .07
❑ 564 Carlos Quintana .15 .07
❑ 565 Mitch Williams .15 .07
❑ 566 Juan Bell .15 .07
❑ 567 Eric Fox .15 .07
❑ 568 Al Leiter .25 .11
❑ 569 Mike Stanton .15 .07
❑ 570 Scott Kamieniecki .15 .07
❑ 571 Ryan Bowen .15 .07
❑ 572 Andy Ashby .15 .07
❑ 573 Bob Welch .15 .07
❑ 574 Scott Sanderson .15 .07
❑ 575 Joe Kmak .15 .07
❑ 576 Scott Pose RC .15 .07
❑ 577 Ricky Gutierrez .15 .07
❑ 578 Mike Trombley .15 .07
❑ 579 Sterling Hitchcock RC .25 .11
❑ 580 Rodney Bolton .15 .07
❑ 581 Tyler Green .15 .07
❑ 582 Tim Costo .15 .07
❑ 583 Tim Laker RC .15 .07
❑ 584 Steve Reed RC .15 .07

No.	Player	MINT	NRMT
585	Tom Kramer RC	.15	.07
586	Robb Nen	.15	.07
587	Jim Tatum RC	.15	.07
588	Frank Bolick	.15	.07
589	Kevin Young	.25	.11
590	Matt Whiteside RC	.15	.07
591	Cesar Hernandez	.15	.07
592	Mike Mohler RC	.15	.07
593	Alan Embree	.15	.07
594	Terry Jorgensen	.15	.07
595	John Cummings RC	.15	.07
596	Domingo Martinez RC	.15	.07
597	Benji Gil	.15	.07
598	Todd Pratt RC	.25	.11
599	Rene Arocha RC	.25	.11
600	Dennis Moeller	.15	.07
601	Jeff Conine	.15	.07
602	Trevor Hoffman	.25	.11
603	Daniel Smith	.15	.07
604	Lee Tinsley	.15	.07
605	Dan Peltier	.15	.07
606	Billy Brewer	.15	.07
607	Matt Walbeck RC	.15	.07
608	Richie Lewis RC	.15	.07
609	J.T. Snow RC	.75	.35
610	Pat Gomez RC	.15	.07
611	Phil Hiatt	.15	.07
612	Alex Arias	.15	.07
613	Kevin Rogers	.15	.07
614	Al Martin	.15	.07
615	Greg Gohr	.15	.07
616	Graeme Lloyd RC	.25	.11
617	Kent Bottenfield	.15	.07
618	Chuck Carr	.15	.07
619	Darrell Sherman RC	.15	.07
620	Mike Lansing RC	.25	.11

1994 Pinnacle

	MINT	NRMT
COMPLETE SET (540)	20.00	9.00
COMPLETE SERIES 1 (270)	10.00	4.50
COMPLETE SERIES 2 (270)	10.00	4.50

No.	Player	MINT	NRMT
1	Frank Thomas	.60	.25
2	Carlos Baerga	.12	.05
3	Sammy Sosa	1.00	.45
4	Tony Gwynn	1.00	.45
5	John Olerud	.20	.09
6	Ryne Sandberg	.60	.25
7	Moises Alou	.20	.09
8	Steve Avery	.12	.05
9	Tim Salmon	.20	.09
10	Cecil Fielder	.20	.09
11	Greg Maddux	1.25	.55
12	Barry Larkin	.50	.23
13	Mike Devereaux	.12	.05
14	Charlie Hayes	.12	.05
15	Albert Belle	.20	.09
16	Andy Van Slyke	.20	.09
17	Mo Vaughn	.20	.09
18	Brian McRae	.12	.05
19	Cal Eldred	.12	.05
20	Craig Biggio	.30	.14
21	Kirby Puckett	1.25	.55
22	Derek Bell	.12	.05
23	Don Mattingly	1.25	.55
24	John Burkett	.12	.05
25	Roger Clemens	1.25	.55
26	Barry Bonds	1.25	.55
27	Paul Molitor	.50	.23
28	Mike Piazza	1.50	.70
29	Robin Ventura	.20	.09
30	Jeff Conine	.12	.05
31	Wade Boggs	.50	.23
32	Dennis Eckersley	.20	.09
33	Bobby Bonilla	.20	.09
34	Lenny Dykstra	.20	.09
35	Manny Alexander	.12	.05
36	Ray Lankford	.12	.05
37	Greg Vaughn	.20	.09
38	Chuck Finley	.20	.09
39	Todd Benzinger	.12	.05
40	Dave Justice	.20	.09
41	Rob Dibble	.12	.05
42	Tom Henke	.12	.05
43	David Nied	.12	.05
44	Sandy Alomar Jr.	.20	.09
45	Pete Harnisch	.12	.05
46	Jeff Russell	.12	.05
47	Terry Mulholland	.12	.05
48	Kevin Appier	.20	.09
49	Randy Tomlin	.12	.05
50	Cal Ripken Jr.	2.00	.90
51	Andy Benes	.12	.05
52	Jimmy Key	.20	.09
53	Kirt Manwaring	.12	.05
54	Kevin Tapani	.12	.05
55	Jose Guzman	.12	.05
56	Todd Stottlemyre	.12	.05
57	Jack McDowell	.12	.05
58	Orel Hershiser	.20	.09
59	Chris Hammond	.12	.05
60	Chris Nabholz	.12	.05
61	Ruben Sierra	.12	.05
62	Dwight Gooden	.20	.09
63	John Kruk	.20	.09
64	Omar Vizquel	.20	.09
65	Tim Naehring	.12	.05
66	Dwight Smith	.12	.05
67	Mickey Tettleton	.12	.05
68	J.T. Snow	.20	.09
69	Greg McMichael	.12	.05
70	Kevin Mitchell	.12	.05
71	Kevin Brown	.20	.09
72	Scott Cooper	.12	.05
73	Jim Thome	.50	.23
74	Joe Girardi	.12	.05
75	Eric Anthony	.12	.05
76	Orlando Merced	.12	.05
77	Felix Jose	.12	.05
78	Tommy Greene	.12	.05
79	Bernard Gilkey	.12	.05
80	Phil Plantier	.12	.05
81	Danny Tartabull	.12	.05
82	Trevor Wilson	.12	.05
83	Chuck Knoblauch	.20	.09
84	Rick Wilkins	.12	.05
85	Devon White	.12	.05
86	Lance Johnson	.12	.05
87	Eric Karros	.20	.09
88	Gary Sheffield	.20	.09
89	Wil Cordero	.12	.05
90	Ron Darling	.12	.05
91	Darren Daulton	.20	.09
92	Joe Orsulak	.12	.05
93	Steve Cooke	.12	.05
94	Darryl Hamilton	.12	.05
95	Aaron Sele	.20	.09
96	John Doherty	.12	.05
97	Gary DiSarcina	.12	.05
98	Jeff Blauser	.12	.05
99	John Smiley	.12	.05
100	Ken Griffey Jr.	1.50	.70
101	Dean Palmer	.20	.09
102	Felix Fermin	.12	.05
103	Jerald Clark	.12	.05
104	Doug Drabek	.12	.05
105	Curt Schilling	.50	.23
106	Jeff Montgomery	.12	.05
107	Rene Arocha	.12	.05
108	Carlos Garcia	.12	.05
109	Wally Whitehurst	.12	.05
110	Jim Abbott	.20	.09
111	Royce Clayton	.12	.05
112	Chris Hoiles	.12	.05
113	Mike Morgan	.12	.05
114	Joe Magrane	.12	.05
115	Tom Candiotti	.12	.05
116	Ron Karkovice	.12	.05
117	Ryan Bowen	.12	.05
118	Rod Beck	.12	.05
119	John Wetteland	.20	.09
120	Terry Steinbach	.12	.05
121	Dave Hollins	.12	.05
122	Jeff Kent	.30	.14
123	Ricky Bones	.12	.05
124	Brian Jordan	.20	.09
125	Chad Kreuter	.12	.05
126	John Valentin	.12	.05
127	Hilly Hathaway	.12	.05
128	Wilson Alvarez	.12	.05
129	Tino Martinez	.20	.09
130	Rodney Bolton	.12	.05
131	David Segui	.12	.05
132	Wayne Kirby	.12	.05
133	Eric Young	.12	.05
134	Scott Servais	.12	.05
135	Scott Radinsky	.12	.05
136	Bret Barberie	.12	.05
137	John Roper	.12	.05
138	Ricky Gutierrez	.12	.05
139	Bernie Williams	.50	.23
140	Bud Black	.12	.05
141	Jose Vizcaino	.12	.05
142	Gerald Williams	.12	.05
143	Duane Ward	.12	.05
144	Danny Jackson	.12	.05
145	Allen Watson	.12	.05
146	Scott Fletcher	.12	.05
147	Delino DeShields	.12	.05
148	Shane Mack	.12	.05
149	Jim Eisenreich	.12	.05
150	Troy Neel	.12	.05
151	Jay Bell	.20	.09
152	B.J. Surhoff	.20	.09
153	Mark Whiten	.12	.05
154	Mike Henneman	.12	.05
155	Todd Hundley	.12	.05
156	Greg Myers	.12	.05
157	Ryan Klesko	.20	.09
158	Dave Fleming	.12	.05
159	Mickey Morandini	.12	.05
160	Blas Minor	.12	.05
161	Reggie Jefferson	.12	.05
162	David Hulse	.12	.05
163	Greg Swindell	.12	.05
164	Roberto Hernandez	.12	.05
165	Brady Anderson	.20	.09
166	Jack Armstrong	.12	.05
167	Phil Clark	.12	.05
168	Melido Perez	.12	.05
169	Darren Lewis	.12	.05
170	Sam Horn	.12	.05
171	Mike Harkey	.12	.05
172	Juan Guzman	.12	.05
173	Bob Natal	.12	.05
174	Deion Sanders	.20	.09
175	Carlos Quintana	.12	.05
176	Mel Rojas	.12	.05
177	Willie Banks	.12	.05
178	Ben Rivera	.12	.05
179	Kenny Lofton	.20	.09
180	Leo Gomez	.12	.05
181	Roberto Mejia	.12	.05
182	Mike Perez	.12	.05
183	Travis Fryman	.20	.09
184	Ben McDonald	.12	.05
185	Steve Frey	.12	.05
186	Kevin Young	.12	.05
187	Dave Magadan	.12	.05
188	Bobby Munoz	.12	.05
189	Pat Rapp	.12	.05
190	Jose Offerman	.12	.05
191	Vinny Castilla	.20	.09
192	Ivan Calderon	.12	.05
193	Ken Caminiti	.20	.09
194	Benji Gil	.12	.05
195	Chuck Carr	.12	.05
196	Derrick May	.12	.05

❑ 197	Pat Kelly	.12	.05
❑ 198	Jeff Brantley	.12	.05
❑ 199	Jose Lind	.12	.05
❑ 200	Steve Buechele	.12	.05
❑ 201	Wes Chamberlain	.12	.05
❑ 202	Eduardo Perez	.12	.05
❑ 203	Bret Saberhagen	.20	.09
❑ 204	Gregg Jefferies	.12	.05
❑ 205	Darrin Fletcher	.12	.05
❑ 206	Kent Hrbek	.20	.09
❑ 207	Kim Batiste	.12	.05
❑ 208	Jeff King	.12	.05
❑ 209	Donovan Osborne	.12	.05
❑ 210	Dave Nilsson	.12	.05
❑ 211	Al Martin	.12	.05
❑ 212	Mike Moore	.12	.05
❑ 213	Sterling Hitchcock	.12	.05
❑ 214	Geronimo Pena	.12	.05
❑ 215	Kevin Higgins	.12	.05
❑ 216	Norm Charlton	.12	.05
❑ 217	Don Slaught	.12	.05
❑ 218	Mitch Williams	.12	.05
❑ 219	Derek Lilliquist	.12	.05
❑ 220	Armando Reynoso	.12	.05
❑ 221	Kenny Rogers	.12	.05
❑ 222	Doug Jones	.12	.05
❑ 223	Luis Aquino	.12	.05
❑ 224	Mike Oquist	.12	.05
❑ 225	Darryl Scott	.12	.05
❑ 226	Kurt Abbott RC	.20	.09
❑ 227	Andy Tomberlin	.12	.05
❑ 228	Norberto Martin	.12	.05
❑ 229	Pedro Castellano	.12	.05
❑ 230	Curtis Pride RC	.20	.09
❑ 231	Jeff McNeely	.12	.05
❑ 232	Scott Lydy	.12	.05
❑ 233	Darren Oliver RC	.20	.09
❑ 234	Danny Bautista	.12	.05
❑ 235	Butch Huskey	.12	.05
❑ 236	Chipper Jones	1.00	.45
❑ 237	Eddie Zambrano RC	.12	.05
❑ 238	Domingo Jean	.12	.05
❑ 239	Javier Lopez	.20	.09
❑ 240	Nigel Wilson	.12	.05
❑ 241	Drew Denson	.12	.05
❑ 242	Raul Mondesi	.20	.09
❑ 243	Luis Ortiz	.12	.05
❑ 244	Manny Ramirez	.75	.35
❑ 245	Greg Blosser	.12	.05
❑ 246	Rondell White	.20	.09
❑ 247	Steve Karsay	.12	.05
❑ 248	Scott Stahoviak	.12	.05
❑ 249	Jose Valentin	.12	.05
❑ 250	Marc Newfield	.12	.05
❑ 251	Keith Kessinger	.12	.05
❑ 252	Carl Everett	.20	.09
❑ 253	John O'Donoghue	.12	.05
❑ 254	Turk Wendell	.12	.05
❑ 255	Scott Ruffcorn	.12	.05
❑ 256	Tony Tarasco	.12	.05
❑ 257	Andy Cook	.12	.05
❑ 258	Matt Mieske	.12	.05
❑ 259	Luis Lopez	.12	.05
❑ 260	Ramon Caraballo	.12	.05
❑ 261	Salomon Torres	.12	.05
❑ 262	Brooks Kieschnick RC	.12	.05
❑ 263	Daron Kirkreit	.12	.05
❑ 264	Bill Wagner RC	.40	.18
❑ 265	Matt Drews RC	.12	.05
❑ 266	Scott Christman RC	.12	.05
❑ 267	Torii Hunter RC	.60	.25
❑ 268	Jamey Wright RC	.20	.09
❑ 269	Jeff Granger	.12	.05
❑ 270	Trot Nixon RC	1.00	.45
❑ 271	Randy Myers	.12	.05
❑ 272	Trevor Hoffman	.20	.09
❑ 273	Bob Wickman	.12	.05
❑ 274	Willie McGee	.20	.09
❑ 275	Hipolito Pichardo	.12	.05
❑ 276	Bobby Witt	.12	.05
❑ 277	Gregg Olson	.12	.05
❑ 278	Randy Johnson	.60	.25
❑ 279	Robb Nen	.12	.05
❑ 280	Paul O'Neill	.50	.23
❑ 281	Lou Whitaker	.20	.09
❑ 282	Chad Curtis	.12	.05
❑ 283	Doug Henry	.12	.05
❑ 284	Tom Glavine	.50	.23
❑ 285	Mike Greenwell	.12	.05
❑ 286	Roberto Kelly	.12	.05
❑ 287	Roberto Alomar	.50	.23
❑ 288	Charlie Hough	.20	.09
❑ 289	Alex Fernandez	.12	.05
❑ 290	Jeff Bagwell	.60	.25
❑ 291	Wally Joyner	.20	.09
❑ 292	Andujar Cedeno	.12	.05
❑ 293	Rick Aguilera	.12	.05
❑ 294	Darryl Strawberry	.20	.09
❑ 295	Mike Mussina	.50	.23
❑ 296	Jeff Gardner	.12	.05
❑ 297	Chris Gwynn	.12	.05
❑ 298	Matt Williams	.30	.14
❑ 299	Brent Gates	.12	.05
❑ 300	Mark McGwire	2.00	.90
❑ 301	Jim Deshaies	.12	.05
❑ 302	Edgar Martinez	.30	.14
❑ 303	Danny Darwin	.12	.05
❑ 304	Pat Meares	.12	.05
❑ 305	Benito Santiago	.12	.05
❑ 306	Jose Canseco	.50	.23
❑ 307	Jim Gott	.12	.05
❑ 308	Paul Sorrento	.12	.05
❑ 309	Scott Kamieniecki	.12	.05
❑ 310	Larry Walker	.30	.14
❑ 311	Mark Langston	.12	.05
❑ 312	John Jaha	.12	.05
❑ 313	Stan Javier	.12	.05
❑ 314	Hal Morris	.12	.05
❑ 315	Robby Thompson	.12	.05
❑ 316	Pat Hentgen	.12	.05
❑ 317	Tom Gordon	.12	.05
❑ 318	Joey Cora	.12	.05
❑ 319	Luis Alicea	.12	.05
❑ 320	Andre Dawson	.30	.14
❑ 321	Darryl Kile	.20	.09
❑ 322	Jose Rijo	.12	.05
❑ 323	Luis Gonzalez	.50	.23
❑ 324	Billy Ashley	.12	.05
❑ 325	David Cone	.20	.09
❑ 326	Bill Swift	.12	.05
❑ 327	Phil Hiatt	.12	.05
❑ 328	Craig Paquette	.12	.05
❑ 329	Bob Welch	.12	.05
❑ 330	Tony Phillips	.12	.05
❑ 331	Archi Cianfrocco	.12	.05
❑ 332	Dave Winfield	.50	.23
❑ 333	David McCarty	.12	.05
❑ 334	Al Leiter	.20	.09
❑ 335	Tom Browning	.12	.05
❑ 336	Mark Grace	.50	.23
❑ 337	Jose Mesa	.12	.05
❑ 338	Mike Stanley	.12	.05
❑ 339	Roger McDowell	.12	.05
❑ 340	Damion Easley	.12	.05
❑ 341	Angel Miranda	.12	.05
❑ 342	John Smoltz	.20	.09
❑ 343	Jay Buhner	.20	.09
❑ 344	Bryan Harvey	.12	.05
❑ 345	Joe Carter	.20	.09
❑ 346	Dante Bichette	.20	.09
❑ 347	Jason Bere	.12	.05
❑ 348	Frank Viola	.20	.09
❑ 349	Ivan Rodriguez	.50	.23
❑ 350	Juan Gonzalez	.50	.23
❑ 351	Steve Finley	.20	.09
❑ 352	Mike Felder	.12	.05
❑ 353	Ramon Martinez	.12	.05
❑ 354	Greg Gagne	.12	.05
❑ 355	Ken Hill	.12	.05
❑ 356	Pedro Munoz	.12	.05
❑ 357	Todd Van Poppel	.12	.05
❑ 358	Marquis Grissom	.12	.05
❑ 359	Milt Cuyler	.12	.05
❑ 360	Reggie Sanders	.12	.05
❑ 361	Scott Erickson	.12	.05
❑ 362	Billy Hatcher	.12	.05
❑ 363	Gene Harris	.12	.05
❑ 364	Rene Gonzales	.12	.05
❑ 365	Kevin Rogers	.12	.05
❑ 366	Eric Plunk	.12	.05
❑ 367	Todd Zeile	.12	.05
❑ 368	John Franco	.20	.09
❑ 369	Brett Butler	.20	.09
❑ 370	Bill Spiers	.12	.05
❑ 371	Terry Pendleton	.20	.09
❑ 372	Chris Bosio	.12	.05
❑ 373	Orestes Destrade	.12	.05
❑ 374	Dave Stewart	.20	.09
❑ 375	Darren Holmes	.12	.05
❑ 376	Doug Strange	.12	.05
❑ 377	Brian Turang	.12	.05
❑ 378	Carl Willis	.12	.05
❑ 379	Mark McLemore	.12	.05
❑ 380	Bobby Jones	.12	.05
❑ 381	Scott Sanders	.12	.05
❑ 382	Kirk Rueter	.12	.05
❑ 383	Randy Velarde	.12	.05
❑ 384	Fred McGriff	.30	.14
❑ 385	Charles Nagy	.12	.05
❑ 386	Rich Amaral	.12	.05
❑ 387	Geronimo Berroa	.12	.05
❑ 388	Eric Davis	.20	.09
❑ 389	Ozzie Smith	.60	.25
❑ 390	Alex Arias	.12	.05
❑ 391	Brad Ausmus	.12	.05
❑ 392	Cliff Floyd	.20	.09
❑ 393	Roger Salkeld	.12	.05
❑ 394	Jim Edmonds	.50	.23
❑ 395	Jeromy Burnitz	.20	.09
❑ 396	Dave Staton	.12	.05
❑ 397	Rob Butler	.12	.05
❑ 398	Marcos Armas	.12	.05
❑ 399	Darrell Whitmore	.12	.05
❑ 400	Ryan Thompson	.12	.05
❑ 401	Ross Powell RC	.12	.05
❑ 402	Joe Oliver	.12	.05
❑ 403	Paul Carey	.12	.05
❑ 404	Bob Hamelin	.12	.05
❑ 405	Chris Turner	.12	.05
❑ 406	Nate Minchey	.12	.05
❑ 407	Lonnie Maclin RC	.12	.05
❑ 408	Harold Baines	.20	.09
❑ 409	Brian Williams	.12	.05
❑ 410	Johnny Ruffin	.12	.05
❑ 411	Julian Tavarez RC	.20	.09
❑ 412	Mark Hutton	.12	.05
❑ 413	Carlos Delgado	.75	.35
❑ 414	Chris Gomez	.12	.05
❑ 415	Mike Hampton	.20	.09
❑ 416	Alex Diaz RC	.12	.05
❑ 417	Jeffrey Hammonds	.20	.09
❑ 418	Jayhawk Owens	.12	.05
❑ 419	J.R. Phillips	.12	.05
❑ 420	Cory Bailey RC	.12	.05
❑ 421	Denny Hocking	.12	.05
❑ 422	Jon Shave	.12	.05
❑ 423	Damon Buford	.12	.05
❑ 424	Troy O'Leary	.12	.05
❑ 425	Tripp Cromer	.12	.05
❑ 426	Albie Lopez	.12	.05
❑ 427	Tony Fernandez	.12	.05
❑ 428	Ozzie Guillen	.12	.05
❑ 429	Alan Trammell	.30	.14
❑ 430	John Wasdin RC	.12	.05
❑ 431	Marc Valdes	.12	.05
❑ 432	Brian Anderson RC	.20	.09
❑ 433	Matt Brunson RC	.12	.05
❑ 434	Wayne Gomes RC	.12	.05
❑ 435	Jay Powell RC	.12	.05
❑ 436	Kirk Presley RC	.12	.05
❑ 437	Jon Ratliff RC	.12	.05
❑ 438	Derrek Lee RC	.40	.18
❑ 439	Tom Pagnozzi	.12	.05
❑ 440	Kent Mercker	.12	.05
❑ 441	Phil Leftwich RC	.12	.05
❑ 442	Jamie Moyer	.12	.05
❑ 443	John Flaherty	.12	.05
❑ 444	Mark Wohlers	.12	.05
❑ 445	Jose Bautista	.12	.05
❑ 446	Andres Galarraga	.30	.14
❑ 447	Mark Lemke	.12	.05
❑ 448	Tim Wakefield	.12	.05
❑ 449	Pat Listach	.12	.05
❑ 450	Rickey Henderson	1.00	.45
❑ 451	Mike Gallego	.12	.05
❑ 452	Bob Tewksbury	.12	.05
❑ 453	Kirk Gibson	.20	.09
❑ 454	Pedro Astacio	.12	.05

Card	MINT	NRMT
❑ 455 Mike Lansing	.12	.05
❑ 456 Sean Berry	.12	.05
❑ 457 Bob Walk	.12	.05
❑ 458 Chili Davis	.20	.09
❑ 459 Ed Sprague	.12	.05
❑ 460 Kevin Stocker	.12	.05
❑ 461 Mike Stanton	.12	.05
❑ 462 Tim Raines	.20	.09
❑ 463 Mike Bordick	.12	.05
❑ 464 David Wells	.20	.09
❑ 465 Tim Laker	.12	.05
❑ 466 Cory Snyder	.12	.05
❑ 467 Alex Cole	.12	.05
❑ 468 Pete Incaviglia	.12	.05
❑ 469 Roger Pavlik	.12	.05
❑ 470 Greg W. Harris	.12	.05
❑ 471 Xavier Hernandez	.12	.05
❑ 472 Erik Hanson	.12	.05
❑ 473 Jesse Orosco	.12	.05
❑ 474 Greg Colbrunn	.12	.05
❑ 475 Harold Reynolds	.12	.05
❑ 476 Greg A. Harris	.12	.05
❑ 477 Pat Borders	.12	.05
❑ 478 Melvin Nieves	.12	.05
❑ 479 Mariano Duncan	.12	.05
❑ 480 Greg Hibbard	.12	.05
❑ 481 Tim Pugh	.12	.05
❑ 482 Bobby Ayala	.12	.05
❑ 483 Sid Fernandez	.12	.05
❑ 484 Tim Wallach	.12	.05
❑ 485 Randy Milligan	.12	.05
❑ 486 Walt Weiss	.12	.05
❑ 487 Matt Walbeck	.12	.05
❑ 488 Mike Macfarlane	.12	.05
❑ 489 Jerry Browne	.12	.05
❑ 490 Chris Sabo	.12	.05
❑ 491 Tim Belcher	.12	.05
❑ 492 Spike Owen	.12	.05
❑ 493 Rafael Palmeiro	.50	.23
❑ 494 Brian Harper	.12	.05
❑ 495 Eddie Murray	.50	.23
❑ 496 Ellis Burks	.20	.09
❑ 497 Karl Rhodes	.12	.05
❑ 498 Otis Nixon	.12	.05
❑ 499 Lee Smith	.20	.09
❑ 500 Bip Roberts	.12	.05
❑ 501 Pedro Martinez	.75	.35
❑ 502 Brian Hunter	.12	.05
❑ 503 Tyler Green	.12	.05
❑ 504 Bruce Hurst	.12	.05
❑ 505 Alex Gonzalez	.12	.05
❑ 506 Mark Portugal	.12	.05
❑ 507 Bob Ojeda	.12	.05
❑ 508 Dave Henderson	.12	.05
❑ 509 Bo Jackson	.20	.09
❑ 510 Bret Boone	.20	.09
❑ 511 Mark Eichhorn	.12	.05
❑ 512 Luis Polonia	.12	.05
❑ 513 Will Clark	.50	.23
❑ 514 Dave Valle	.12	.05
❑ 515 Dan Wilson	.12	.05
❑ 516 Dennis Martinez	.20	.09
❑ 517 Jim Leyritz	.12	.05
❑ 518 Howard Johnson	.12	.05
❑ 519 Jody Reed	.12	.05
❑ 520 Julio Franco	.20	.09
❑ 521 Jeff Reardon	.20	.09
❑ 522 Willie Greene	.12	.05
❑ 523 Shawon Dunston	.12	.05
❑ 524 Keith Mitchell	.12	.05
❑ 525 Rick Helling	.12	.05
❑ 526 Mark Kiefer	.12	.05
❑ 527 Chan Ho Park RC	1.00	.45
❑ 528 Tony Longmire	.12	.05
❑ 529 Rich Becker	.12	.05
❑ 530 Tim Hyers RC	.12	.05
❑ 531 Darrin Jackson	.12	.05
❑ 532 Jack Morris	.20	.09
❑ 533 Rick White	.12	.05
❑ 534 Mike Kelly	.12	.05
❑ 535 James Mouton	.12	.05
❑ 536 Steve Trachsel	.12	.05
❑ 537 Tony Eusebio	.12	.05
❑ 538 Kelly Stinnett RC	.20	.09
❑ 539 Paul Spoljaric	.12	.05
❑ 540 Darren Dreifort	.12	.05
❑ SR1 Carlos Delgado Super Rookie	6.00	2.70

1995 Pinnacle

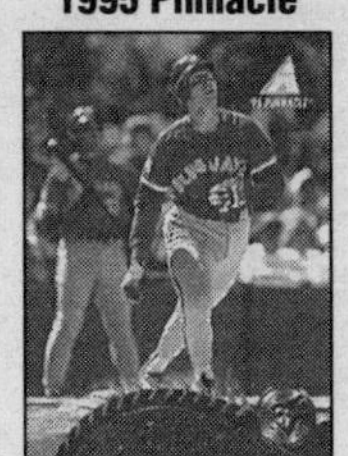

	MINT	NRMT
COMPLETE SET (450)	30.00	13.50
COMPLETE SERIES 1 (225)	15.00	6.75
COMPLETE SERIES 2 (225)	15.00	6.75

Card	MINT	NRMT
❑ 1 Jeff Bagwell	.60	.25
❑ 2 Roger Clemens	1.25	.55
❑ 3 Mark Whiten	.12	.05
❑ 4 Shawon Dunston	.12	.05
❑ 5 Bobby Bonilla	.20	.09
❑ 6 Kevin Tapani	.12	.05
❑ 7 Eric Karros	.20	.09
❑ 8 Cliff Floyd	.20	.09
❑ 9 Pat Kelly	.12	.05
❑ 10 Jeffrey Hammonds	.12	.05
❑ 11 Jeff Conine	.12	.05
❑ 12 Fred McGriff	.30	.14
❑ 13 Chris Bosio	.12	.05
❑ 14 Mike Mussina	.50	.23
❑ 15 Danny Bautista	.12	.05
❑ 16 Mickey Morandini	.12	.05
❑ 17 Chuck Finley	.20	.09
❑ 18 Jim Thome	.50	.23
❑ 19 Luis Ortiz	.12	.05
❑ 20 Walt Weiss	.12	.05
❑ 21 Don Mattingly	1.25	.55
❑ 22 Bob Hamelin	.12	.05
❑ 23 Melido Perez	.12	.05
❑ 24 Keith Mitchell	.12	.05
❑ 25 John Smoltz	.20	.09
❑ 26 Hector Carrasco	.12	.05
❑ 27 Pat Hentgen	.12	.05
❑ 28 Derrick May	.12	.05
❑ 29 Mike Kingery	.12	.05
❑ 30 Chuck Carr	.12	.05
❑ 31 Billy Ashley	.12	.05
❑ 32 Todd Hundley	.12	.05
❑ 33 Luis Gonzalez	.50	.23
❑ 34 Marquis Grissom	.12	.05
❑ 35 Jeff King	.12	.05
❑ 36 Eddie Williams	.12	.05
❑ 37 Tom Pagnozzi	.12	.05
❑ 38 Chris Hoiles	.12	.05
❑ 39 Sandy Alomar Jr.	.20	.09
❑ 40 Mike Greenwell	.12	.05
❑ 41 Lance Johnson	.12	.05
❑ 42 Junior Felix	.12	.05
❑ 43 Felix Jose	.12	.05
❑ 44 Scott Leius	.12	.05
❑ 45 Ruben Sierra	.12	.05
❑ 46 Kevin Seitzer	.12	.05
❑ 47 Wade Boggs	.50	.23
❑ 48 Reggie Jefferson	.12	.05
❑ 49 Jose Canseco	.50	.23
❑ 50 David Justice	.20	.09
❑ 51 John Smiley	.12	.05
❑ 52 Joe Carter	.20	.09
❑ 53 Rick Wilkins	.12	.05
❑ 54 Ellis Burks	.20	.09
❑ 55 Dave Weathers	.12	.05
❑ 56 Pedro Astacio	.12	.05
❑ 57 Ryan Thompson	.12	.05
❑ 58 James Mouton	.12	.05
❑ 59 Mel Rojas	.12	.05
❑ 60 Orlando Merced	.12	.05
❑ 61 Matt Williams	.30	.14
❑ 62 Bernard Gilkey	.12	.05
❑ 63 J.R. Phillips	.12	.05
❑ 64 Lee Smith	.20	.09
❑ 65 Jim Edmonds	.30	.14
❑ 66 Darrin Jackson	.12	.05
❑ 67 Scott Cooper	.12	.05
❑ 68 Ron Karkovice	.12	.05
❑ 69 Chris Gomez	.12	.05
❑ 70 Kevin Appier	.20	.09
❑ 71 Bobby Jones	.12	.05
❑ 72 Doug Drabek	.12	.05
❑ 73 Matt Mieske	.12	.05
❑ 74 Sterling Hitchcock	.12	.05
❑ 75 John Valentin	.12	.05
❑ 76 Reggie Sanders	.12	.05
❑ 77 Wally Joyner	.20	.09
❑ 78 Turk Wendell	.12	.05
❑ 79 Charlie Hayes	.12	.05
❑ 80 Bret Barberie	.12	.05
❑ 81 Troy Neel	.12	.05
❑ 82 Ken Caminiti	.20	.09
❑ 83 Milt Thompson	.12	.05
❑ 84 Paul Sorrento	.12	.05
❑ 85 Trevor Hoffman	.20	.09
❑ 86 Jay Bell	.20	.09
❑ 87 Mark Portugal	.12	.05
❑ 88 Sid Fernandez	.12	.05
❑ 89 Charles Nagy	.12	.05
❑ 90 Jeff Montgomery	.12	.05
❑ 91 Chuck Knoblauch	.20	.09
❑ 92 Jeff Frye	.12	.05
❑ 93 Tony Gwynn	1.00	.45
❑ 94 John Olerud	.20	.09
❑ 95 David Nied	.12	.05
❑ 96 Chris Hammond	.12	.05
❑ 97 Edgar Martinez	.30	.14
❑ 98 Kevin Stocker	.12	.05
❑ 99 Jeff Fassero	.12	.05
❑ 100 Curt Schilling	.50	.23
❑ 101 Dave Clark	.12	.05
❑ 102 Delino DeShields	.12	.05
❑ 103 Leo Gomez	.12	.05
❑ 104 Dave Hollins	.12	.05
❑ 105 Tim Naehring	.12	.05
❑ 106 Otis Nixon	.12	.05
❑ 107 Ozzie Guillen	.12	.05
❑ 108 Jose Lind	.12	.05
❑ 109 Stan Javier	.12	.05
❑ 110 Greg Vaughn	.20	.09
❑ 111 Chipper Jones	1.00	.45
❑ 112 Ed Sprague	.12	.05
❑ 113 Mike Macfarlane	.12	.05
❑ 114 Steve Finley	.20	.09
❑ 115 Ken Hill	.12	.05
❑ 116 Carlos Garcia	.12	.05
❑ 117 Lou Whitaker	.20	.09
❑ 118 Todd Zeile	.12	.05
❑ 119 Gary Sheffield	.20	.09
❑ 120 Ben McDonald	.12	.05
❑ 121 Pete Harnisch	.12	.05
❑ 122 Ivan Rodriguez	.50	.23
❑ 123 Wilson Alvarez	.12	.05
❑ 124 Travis Fryman	.20	.09
❑ 125 Pedro Munoz	.12	.05
❑ 126 Mark Lemke	.12	.05
❑ 127 Jose Valentin	.12	.05
❑ 128 Ken Griffey Jr.	1.50	.70
❑ 129 Omar Vizquel	.20	.09
❑ 130 Milt Cuyler	.12	.05
❑ 131 Steve Trachsel	.12	.05
❑ 132 Alex Rodriguez	1.50	.70
❑ 133 Garret Anderson	.20	.09
❑ 134 Armando Benitez	.20	.09
❑ 135 Shawn Green	.50	.23
❑ 136 Jorge Fabregas	.12	.05
❑ 137 Orlando Miller	.12	.05
❑ 138 Rikkert Faneyte	.12	.05
❑ 139 Ismael Valdes	.12	.05
❑ 140 Jose Oliva	.12	.05
❑ 141 Aaron Small	.12	.05
❑ 142 Tim Davis	.12	.05
❑ 143 Ricky Bottalico	.12	.05
❑ 144 Mike Matheny	.12	.05

❑ 145 Roberto Petagine .12 .05
❑ 146 Fausto Cruz .12 .05
❑ 147 Bryce Florie .12 .05
❑ 148 Jose Lima .12 .05
❑ 149 John Hudek .12 .05
❑ 150 Duane Singleton .12 .05
❑ 151 John Mabry .12 .05
❑ 152 Robert Eenhoorn .12 .05
❑ 153 Jon Lieber .12 .05
❑ 154 Garey Ingram .12 .05
❑ 155 Paul Shuey .12 .05
❑ 156 Mike Lieberthal .20 .09
❑ 157 Steve Dunn .12 .05
❑ 158 Charles Johnson .20 .09
❑ 159 Ernie Young .12 .05
❑ 160 Jose Martinez .12 .05
❑ 161 Kurt Miller .12 .05
❑ 162 Joey Eischen .12 .05
❑ 163 Dave Stevens .12 .05
❑ 164 Brian L.Hunter .12 .05
❑ 165 Jeff Cirillo .20 .09
❑ 166 Mark Smith .12 .05
❑ 167 M. Christensen RC .12 .05
❑ 168 C.J. Nitkowski .12 .05
❑ 169 A. Williamson RC .12 .05
❑ 170 Paul Konerko .50 .23
❑ 171 Scott Elarton RC .50 .23
❑ 172 Jacob Shumate .12 .05
❑ 173 Terrence Long .50 .23
❑ 174 Mark Johnson RC .20 .09
❑ 175 Ben Grieve .50 .23
❑ 176 Jayson Peterson RC .12 .05
❑ 177 Checklist .12 .05
❑ 178 Checklist .12 .05
❑ 179 Checklist .12 .05
❑ 180 Checklist .12 .05
❑ 181 Brian Anderson .12 .05
❑ 182 Steve Buechele .12 .05
❑ 183 Mark Clark .12 .05
❑ 184 Cecil Fielder .20 .09
❑ 185 Steve Avery .12 .05
❑ 186 Devon White .20 .09
❑ 187 Craig Shipley .12 .05
❑ 188 Brady Anderson .20 .09
❑ 189 Kenny Lofton .20 .09
❑ 190 Alex Cole .12 .05
❑ 191 Brent Gates .12 .05
❑ 192 Dean Palmer .20 .09
❑ 193 Alex Gonzalez .12 .05
❑ 194 Steve Cooke .12 .05
❑ 195 Ray Lankford .12 .05
❑ 196 Mark McGwire 2.00 .90
❑ 197 Marc Newfield .12 .05
❑ 198 Pat Rapp .12 .05
❑ 199 Darren Lewis .12 .05
❑ 200 Carlos Baerga .12 .05
❑ 201 Rickey Henderson 1.00 .45
❑ 202 Kurt Abbott .12 .05
❑ 203 Kirt Manwaring .12 .05
❑ 204 Cal Ripken 2.00 .90
❑ 205 Darren Daulton .20 .09
❑ 206 Greg Colbrunn .12 .05
❑ 207 Darryl Hamilton .12 .05
❑ 208 Bo Jackson .20 .09
❑ 209 Tony Phillips .12 .05
❑ 210 Geronimo Berroa .12 .05
❑ 211 Rich Becker .12 .05
❑ 212 Tony Tarasco .12 .05
❑ 213 Karl Rhodes .12 .05
❑ 214 Phil Plantier .12 .05
❑ 215 J.T. Snow .20 .09
❑ 216 Mo Vaughn .20 .09
❑ 217 Greg Gagne .12 .05
❑ 218 Ricky Bones .12 .05
❑ 219 Mike Bordick .12 .05
❑ 220 Chad Curtis .12 .05
❑ 221 Royce Clayton .12 .05
❑ 222 Roberto Alomar .50 .23
❑ 223 Jose Rijo .12 .05
❑ 224 Ryan Klesko .20 .09
❑ 225 Mark Langston .12 .05
❑ 226 Frank Thomas .60 .25
❑ 227 Juan Gonzalez .50 .23
❑ 228 Ron Gant .12 .05
❑ 229 Javier Lopez .20 .09
❑ 230 Sammy Sosa 1.00 .45
❑ 231 Kevin Brown .20 .09
❑ 232 Gary DiSarcina .12 .05
❑ 233 Albert Belle .20 .09
❑ 234 Jay Buhner .20 .09
❑ 235 Pedro Martinez .60 .25
❑ 236 Bob Tewksbury .12 .05
❑ 237 Mike Piazza 1.25 .55
❑ 238 Darryl Kile .20 .09
❑ 239 Bryan Harvey .12 .05
❑ 240 Andres Galarraga .30 .14
❑ 241 Jeff Blauser .12 .05
❑ 242 Jeff Kent .30 .14
❑ 243 Bobby Munoz .12 .05
❑ 244 Greg Maddux 1.25 .55
❑ 245 Paul O'Neill .50 .23
❑ 246 Lenny Dykstra .20 .09
❑ 247 Todd Van Poppel .12 .05
❑ 248 Bernie Williams .50 .23
❑ 249 Glenallen Hill .12 .05
❑ 250 Duane Ward .12 .05
❑ 251 Dennis Eckersley .20 .09
❑ 252 Pat Mahomes .12 .05
❑ 253 Rusty Greer .20 .09
❑ 254 Roberto Kelly .12 .05
❑ 255 Randy Myers .12 .05
❑ 256 Scott Ruffcorn .12 .05
❑ 257 Robin Ventura .20 .09
❑ 258 Eduardo Perez .12 .05
❑ 259 Aaron Sele .20 .09
❑ 260 Paul Molitor .50 .23
❑ 261 Juan Guzman .12 .05
❑ 262 Darren Oliver .12 .05
❑ 263 Mike Stanley .12 .05
❑ 264 Tom Glavine .50 .23
❑ 265 Rico Brogna .12 .05
❑ 266 Craig Biggio .30 .14
❑ 267 Darrell Whitmore .12 .05
❑ 268 Jimmy Key .20 .09
❑ 269 Will Clark .50 .23
❑ 270 David Cone .20 .09
❑ 271 Brian Jordan .20 .09
❑ 272 Barry Bonds 1.25 .55
❑ 273 Danny Tartabull .12 .05
❑ 274 Ramon J.Martinez .12 .05
❑ 275 Al Martin .12 .05
❑ 276 Fred McGriff SM .20 .09
❑ 277 Carlos Delgado SM .20 .09
❑ 278 Juan Gonzalez SM .20 .09
❑ 279 Shawn Green SM .20 .09
❑ 280 Carlos Baerga SM .12 .05
❑ 281 Cliff Floyd SM .12 .05
❑ 282 Ozzie Smith SM .30 .14
❑ 283 Alex Rodriguez SM .75 .35
❑ 284 Kenny Lofton SM .12 .05
❑ 285 Dave Justice SM .12 .05
❑ 286 Tim Salmon SM .12 .05
❑ 287 Manny Ramirez SM .30 .14
❑ 288 Will Clark SM .20 .09
❑ 289 Garret Anderson SM .12 .05
❑ 290 Billy Ashley SM .12 .05
❑ 291 Tony Gwynn SM .50 .23
❑ 292 Raul Mondesi SM .12 .05
❑ 293 Rafael Palmeiro SM .20 .09
❑ 294 Matt Williams SM .20 .09
❑ 295 Don Mattingly SM .60 .25
❑ 296 Kirby Puckett SM .60 .25
❑ 297 Paul Molitor SM .20 .09
❑ 298 Albert Belle SM .12 .05
❑ 299 Barry Bonds SM .60 .25
❑ 300 Mike Piazza SM .60 .25
❑ 301 Jeff Bagwell SM .30 .14
❑ 302 Frank Thomas SM .30 .14
❑ 303 Chipper Jones SM .50 .23
❑ 304 Ken Griffey Jr. SM .75 .35
❑ 305 Cal Ripken Jr. SM 1.00 .45
❑ 306 Eric Anthony .12 .05
❑ 307 Todd Benzinger .12 .05
❑ 308 Jacob Brumfield .12 .05
❑ 309 Wes Chamberlain .12 .05
❑ 310 Tino Martinez .20 .09
❑ 311 Roberto Mejia .12 .05
❑ 312 Jose Offerman .12 .05
❑ 313 David Segui .12 .05
❑ 314 Eric Young .12 .05
❑ 315 Rey Sanchez .12 .05
❑ 316 Raul Mondesi .20 .09
❑ 317 Bret Boone .20 .09
❑ 318 Andre Dawson .30 .14
❑ 319 Brian McRae .12 .05
❑ 320 Dave Nilsson .12 .05
❑ 321 Moises Alou .20 .09
❑ 322 Don Slaught .12 .05
❑ 323 Dave McCarty .12 .05
❑ 324 Mike Huff .12 .05
❑ 325 Rick Aguilera .12 .05
❑ 326 Rod Beck .12 .05
❑ 327 Kenny Rogers .12 .05
❑ 328 Andy Benes .12 .05
❑ 329 Allen Watson .12 .05
❑ 330 Randy Johnson .60 .25
❑ 331 Willie Greene .12 .05
❑ 332 Hal Morris .12 .05
❑ 333 Ozzie Smith .60 .25
❑ 334 Jason Bere .12 .05
❑ 335 Scott Erickson .12 .05
❑ 336 Dante Bichette .20 .09
❑ 337 Willie Banks .12 .05
❑ 338 Eric Davis .20 .09
❑ 339 Rondell White .20 .09
❑ 340 Kirby Puckett 1.25 .55
❑ 341 Deion Sanders .20 .09
❑ 342 Eddie Murray .50 .23
❑ 343 Mike Harkey .12 .05
❑ 344 Joey Hamilton .12 .05
❑ 345 Roger Salkeld .12 .05
❑ 346 Wil Cordero .12 .05
❑ 347 John Wetteland .20 .09
❑ 348 Geronimo Pena .12 .05
❑ 349 Kirk Gibson .20 .09
❑ 350 Manny Ramirez .60 .25
❑ 351 Wm.VanLandingham .12 .05
❑ 352 B.J. Surhoff .20 .09
❑ 353 Ken Ryan .12 .05
❑ 354 Terry Steinbach .12 .05
❑ 355 Bret Saberhagen .20 .09
❑ 356 John Jaha .12 .05
❑ 357 Joe Girardi .12 .05
❑ 358 Steve Karsay .12 .05
❑ 359 Alex Fernandez .12 .05
❑ 360 Salomon Torres .12 .05
❑ 361 John Burkett .12 .05
❑ 362 Derek Bell .12 .05
❑ 363 Tom Henke .12 .05
❑ 364 Gregg Jefferies .12 .05
❑ 365 Jack McDowell .12 .05
❑ 366 Andujar Cedeno .12 .05
❑ 367 Dave Winfield .50 .23
❑ 368 Carl Everett .20 .09
❑ 369 Danny Jackson .12 .05
❑ 370 Jeromy Burnitz .20 .09
❑ 371 Mark Grace .50 .23
❑ 372 Larry Walker .30 .14
❑ 373 Bill Swift .12 .05
❑ 374 Dennis Martinez .20 .09
❑ 375 Mickey Tettleton .12 .05
❑ 376 Mel Nieves .12 .05
❑ 377 Cal Eldred .12 .05
❑ 378 Orel Hershiser .20 .09
❑ 379 David Wells .20 .09
❑ 380 Gary Gaetti .20 .09
❑ 381 Jeromy Burnitz .20 .09
❑ 382 Barry Larkin .50 .23
❑ 383 Jason Jacome .12 .05
❑ 384 Tim Wallach .12 .05
❑ 385 Robby Thompson .12 .05
❑ 386 Frank Viola .20 .09
❑ 387 Dave Stewart .20 .09
❑ 388 Bip Roberts .12 .05
❑ 389 Ron Darling .12 .05
❑ 390 Carlos Delgado .50 .23
❑ 391 Tim Salmon .20 .09
❑ 392 Alan Trammell .30 .14
❑ 393 Kevin Foster .12 .05
❑ 394 Jim Abbott .20 .09
❑ 395 John Kruk .20 .09
❑ 396 Andy Van Slyke .20 .09
❑ 397 Dave Magadan .12 .05
❑ 398 Rafael Palmeiro .50 .23
❑ 399 Mike Devereaux .12 .05
❑ 400 Benito Santiago .12 .05
❑ 401 Brett Butler .20 .09
❑ 402 John Franco .20 .09

❑ 403 Matt Walbeck .12 .05
❑ 404 Terry Pendleton .20 .09
❑ 405 Chris Sabo .12 .05
❑ 406 Andrew Lorraine .12 .05
❑ 407 Dan Wilson .12 .05
❑ 408 Mike Lansing .12 .05
❑ 409 Ray McDavid .12 .05
❑ 410 Shane Andrews .12 .05
❑ 411 Tom Gordon .12 .05
❑ 412 Chad Ogea .12 .05
❑ 413 James Baldwin .12 .05
❑ 414 Russ Davis .12 .05
❑ 415 Ray Holbert .12 .05
❑ 416 Ray Durham .20 .09
❑ 417 Matt Nokes .12 .05
❑ 418 Rod Henderson .12 .05
❑ 419 Gabe White .12 .05
❑ 420 Todd Hollandsworth .12 .05
❑ 421 Midre Cummings .12 .05
❑ 422 Harold Baines .20 .09
❑ 423 Troy Percival .12 .05
❑ 424 Joe Vitiello .12 .05
❑ 425 Andy Ashby .12 .05
❑ 426 Michael Tucker .12 .05
❑ 427 Mark Gubicza .12 .05
❑ 428 Jim Bullinger .12 .05
❑ 429 Jose Malave .12 .05
❑ 430 Pete Schourek .12 .05
❑ 431 Bobby Ayala .12 .05
❑ 432 Marvin Freeman .12 .05
❑ 433 Pat Listach .12 .05
❑ 434 Eddie Taubensee .12 .05
❑ 435 Steve Howe .12 .05
❑ 436 Kent Mercker .12 .05
❑ 437 Hector Fajardo .12 .05
❑ 438 Scott Kamieniecki .12 .05
❑ 439 Robb Nen .12 .05
❑ 440 Mike Kelly .12 .05
❑ 441 Tom Candiotti .12 .05
❑ 442 Albie Lopez .12 .05
❑ 443 Jeff Granger .12 .05
❑ 444 Rich Aude .12 .05
❑ 445 Luis Polonia .12 .05
❑ 446 Frank Thomas CL .30 .14
❑ 447 Ken Griffey Jr. CL .75 .35
❑ 448 Mike Piazza CL .60 .25
❑ 449 Jeff Bagwell CL .30 .14
❑ 450 Jeff Bagwell CL .50 .23
Frank Thomas
Ken Griffey Jr.
Mike Piazza

1996 Pinnacle

	MINT	NRMT
COMPLETE SET (400)	30.00	13.50
COMPLETE SERIES 1 (200)	15.00	6.75
COMPLETE SERIES 2 (200)	15.00	6.75

❑ 1 Greg Maddux 1.00 .45
❑ 2 Bill Pulsipher .10 .05
❑ 3 Dante Bichette .15 .07
❑ 4 Mike Piazza 1.00 .45
❑ 5 Garret Anderson .15 .07
❑ 6 Steve Finley .15 .07
❑ 7 Andy Benes .10 .05
❑ 8 Chuck Knoblauch .15 .07
❑ 9 Tom Gordon .10 .05
❑ 10 Jeff Bagwell .50 .23
❑ 11 Wil Cordero .10 .05
❑ 12 John Mabry .10 .05
❑ 13 Jeff Frye .10 .05
❑ 14 Travis Fryman .15 .07
❑ 15 John Wetteland .15 .07
❑ 16 Jason Bates .10 .05
❑ 17 Danny Tartabull .10 .05
❑ 18 Charles Nagy .10 .05
❑ 19 Robin Ventura .15 .07
❑ 20 Reggie Sanders .10 .05
❑ 21 Dave Clark .10 .05
❑ 22 Jaime Navarro .10 .05
❑ 23 Joey Hamilton .10 .05
❑ 24 Al Leiter .15 .07
❑ 25 Deion Sanders .15 .07
❑ 26 Tim Salmon .15 .07
❑ 27 Tino Martinez .15 .07
❑ 28 Mike Greenwell .10 .05
❑ 29 Phil Plantier .10 .05
❑ 30 Bobby Bonilla .15 .07
❑ 31 Kenny Rogers .10 .05
❑ 32 Chili Davis .15 .07
❑ 33 Joe Carter .15 .07
❑ 34 Mike Mussina .40 .18
❑ 35 Matt Mieske .10 .05
❑ 36 Jose Canseco .40 .18
❑ 37 Brad Radke .15 .07
❑ 38 Juan Gonzalez .40 .18
❑ 39 David Segui .10 .05
❑ 40 Alex Fernandez .10 .05
❑ 41 Jeff Kent .25 .11
❑ 42 Todd Zeile .10 .05
❑ 43 Darryl Strawberry .15 .07
❑ 44 Jose Rijo .10 .05
❑ 45 Ramon Martinez .10 .05
❑ 46 Manny Ramirez .50 .23
❑ 47 Gregg Jefferies .10 .05
❑ 48 Bryan Rekar .10 .05
❑ 49 Jeff King .10 .05
❑ 50 John Olerud .15 .07
❑ 51 Marc Newfield .10 .05
❑ 52 Charles Johnson .15 .07
❑ 53 Robby Thompson .10 .05
❑ 54 Brian L. Hunter .10 .05
❑ 55 Mike Blowers .10 .05
❑ 56 Keith Lockhart .10 .05
❑ 57 Ray Lankford .10 .05
❑ 58 Tim Wallach .10 .05
❑ 59 Ivan Rodriguez .40 .18
❑ 60 Ed Sprague .10 .05
❑ 61 Paul Molitor .40 .18
❑ 62 Eric Karros .15 .07
❑ 63 Glenallen Hill .10 .05
❑ 64 Jay Bell .15 .07
❑ 65 Tom Pagnozzi .10 .05
❑ 66 Greg Colbrunn .10 .05
❑ 67 Edgar Martinez .25 .11
❑ 68 Paul Sorrento .10 .05
❑ 69 Kirt Manwaring .10 .05
❑ 70 Pete Schourek .10 .05
❑ 71 Orlando Merced .10 .05
❑ 72 Shawon Dunston .10 .05
❑ 73 Ricky Bottalico .10 .05
❑ 74 Brady Anderson .15 .07
❑ 75 Steve Ontiveros .10 .05
❑ 76 Jim Abbott .15 .07
❑ 77 Carl Everett .15 .07
❑ 78 Mo Vaughn .15 .07
❑ 79 Pedro Martinez .50 .23
❑ 80 Harold Baines .15 .07
❑ 81 Alan Trammell .25 .11
❑ 82 Steve Avery .10 .05
❑ 83 Jeff Cirillo .15 .07
❑ 84 John Valentin .10 .05
❑ 85 Bernie Williams .40 .18
❑ 86 Andre Dawson .25 .11
❑ 87 Dave Winfield .40 .18
❑ 88 B.J. Surhoff .15 .07
❑ 89 Jeff Blauser .10 .05
❑ 90 Barry Larkin .40 .18
❑ 91 Cliff Floyd .15 .07
❑ 92 Sammy Sosa .75 .35
❑ 93 Andres Galarraga .25 .11
❑ 94 Dave Nilsson .10 .05
❑ 95 James Mouton .10 .05
❑ 96 Marquis Grissom .10 .05
❑ 97 Matt Williams .25 .11
❑ 98 John Jaha .10 .05
❑ 99 Don Mattingly 1.00 .45
❑ 100 Tim Naehring .10 .05
❑ 101 Kevin Appier .15 .07
❑ 102 Bobby Higginson .15 .07
❑ 103 Andy Pettitte .15 .07
❑ 104 Ozzie Smith .50 .23
❑ 105 Kenny Lofton .15 .07
❑ 106 Ken Caminiti .15 .07
❑ 107 Walt Weiss .10 .05
❑ 108 Jack McDowell .10 .05
❑ 109 Brian McRae .10 .05
❑ 110 Gary Gaetti .15 .07
❑ 111 Curtis Goodwin .10 .05
❑ 112 Dennis Martinez .15 .07
❑ 113 Omar Vizquel .15 .07
❑ 114 Chipper Jones .75 .35
❑ 115 Mark Gubicza .10 .05
❑ 116 Ruben Sierra .10 .05
❑ 117 Eddie Murray .40 .18
❑ 118 Chad Curtis .10 .05
❑ 119 Hal Morris .10 .05
❑ 120 Ben McDonald .10 .05
❑ 121 Marty Cordova .10 .05
❑ 122 Ken Griffey Jr. UER 1.25 .55
Card says Ken homered from
both sides
He is only a left hitter
❑ 123 Gary Sheffield .15 .07
❑ 124 Charlie Hayes .10 .05
❑ 125 Shawn Green .40 .18
❑ 126 Jason Giambi .40 .18
❑ 127 Mark Langston .10 .05
❑ 128 Mark Whiten .10 .05
❑ 129 Greg Vaughn .15 .07
❑ 130 Mark McGwire 1.50 .70
❑ 131 Hideo Nomo .50 .23
❑ 132 Eric Karros .40 .18
Mike Piazza
Raul Mondesi
Hideo Nomo
❑ 133 Jason Bere .10 .05
❑ 134 Ken Griffey Jr. NAT .60 .25
❑ 135 Frank Thomas NAT .25 .11
❑ 136 Cal Ripken NAT .75 .35
❑ 137 Albert Belle NAT .15 .07
❑ 138 Mike Piazza NAT .50 .23
❑ 139 Dante Bichette NAT .10 .05
❑ 140 Sammy Sosa NAT .40 .18
❑ 141 Mo Vaughn NAT .10 .05
❑ 142 Tim Salmon NAT .10 .05
❑ 143 Reggie Sanders NAT .10 .05
❑ 144 Cecil Fielder NAT .10 .05
❑ 145 Jim Edmonds NAT .15 .07
❑ 146 Rafael Palmeiro NAT .15 .07
❑ 147 Edgar Martinez NAT .15 .07
❑ 148 Barry Bonds NAT .50 .23
❑ 149 Manny Ramirez NAT .25 .11
❑ 150 Larry Walker NAT .10 .05
❑ 151 Jeff Bagwell NAT .25 .11
❑ 152 Ron Gant NAT .10 .05
❑ 153 Andres Galarraga NAT .15 .07
❑ 154 Eddie Murray NAT .15 .07
❑ 155 Kirby Puckett NAT .50 .23
❑ 156 Will Clark NAT .15 .07
❑ 157 Don Mattingly NAT .50 .23
❑ 158 Mark McGwire NAT .75 .35
❑ 159 Dean Palmer NAT .10 .05
❑ 160 Matt Williams NAT .15 .07
❑ 161 Fred McGriff NAT .15 .07
❑ 162 Joe Carter NAT .10 .05
❑ 163 Juan Gonzalez NAT .15 .07
❑ 164 Alex Ochoa .10 .05
❑ 165 Ruben Rivera .10 .05
❑ 166 Tony Clark .15 .07
❑ 167 Brian Barber .10 .05
❑ 168 Matt Lawton RC .50 .23
❑ 169 Terrell Wade .10 .05
❑ 170 Johnny Damon .15 .07
❑ 171 Derek Jeter 1.50 .70
❑ 172 Phil Nevin .15 .07
❑ 173 Robert Perez .10 .05
❑ 174 C.J. Nitkowski .10 .05
❑ 175 Joe Vitiello .10 .05

	No.	Player	Mint	NrMt
❑	176	Roger Cedeno	.10	.05
❑	177	Ron Coomer	.10	.05
❑	178	Chris Widger	.10	.05
❑	179	Jimmy Haynes	.10	.05
❑	180	Mike Sweeney RC	1.50	.70
❑	181	Howard Battle	.10	.05
❑	182	John Wasdin	.10	.05
❑	183	Jim Pittsley	.10	.05
❑	184	Bob Wolcott	.10	.05
❑	185	LaTroy Hawkins	.10	.05
❑	186	Nigel Wilson	.10	.05
❑	187	Dustin Hermanson	.10	.05
❑	188	Chris Snopek	.10	.05
❑	189	Mariano Rivera	.15	.07
❑	190	Jose Herrera	.10	.05
❑	191	Chris Stynes	.10	.05
❑	192	Larry Thomas	.10	.05
❑	193	David Bell	.10	.05
❑	194	Frank Thomas CL	.25	.11
❑	195	Ken Griffey Jr. CL	.60	.25
❑	196	Cal Ripken CL	.75	.35
❑	197	Jeff Bagwell CL	.25	.11
❑	198	Mike Piazza CL	.50	.23
❑	199	Barry Bonds CL	.50	.23
❑	200	Garret Anderson CL Chipper Jones	.40	.18
❑	201	Frank Thomas	.50	.23
❑	202	Michael Tucker	.10	.05
❑	203	Kirby Puckett	1.00	.45
❑	204	Alex Gonzalez	.10	.05
❑	205	Tony Gwynn	.75	.35
❑	206	Moises Alou	.15	.07
❑	207	Albert Belle	.15	.07
❑	208	Barry Bonds	1.00	.45
❑	209	Fred McGriff	.25	.11
❑	210	Dennis Eckersley	.15	.07
❑	211	Craig Biggio	.25	.11
❑	212	David Cone	.15	.07
❑	213	Will Clark	.40	.18
❑	214	Cal Ripken	1.50	.70
❑	215	Wade Boggs	.40	.18
❑	216	Pete Schourek	.10	.05
❑	217	Darren Daulton	.15	.07
❑	218	Carlos Baerga	.10	.05
❑	219	Larry Walker	.25	.11
❑	220	Denny Neagle	.15	.07
❑	221	Jim Edmonds	.25	.11
❑	222	Lee Smith	.15	.07
❑	223	Jason Isringhausen	.15	.07
❑	224	Jay Buhner	.15	.07
❑	225	John Olerud	.15	.07
❑	226	Jeff Conine	.10	.05
❑	227	Dean Palmer	.15	.07
❑	228	Jim Abbott	.15	.07
❑	229	Raul Mondesi	.15	.07
❑	230	Tom Glavine	.40	.18
❑	231	Kevin Seitzer	.10	.05
❑	232	Lenny Dykstra	.15	.07
❑	233	Brian Jordan	.15	.07
❑	234	Rondell White	.15	.07
❑	235	Bret Boone	.15	.07
❑	236	Randy Johnson	.50	.23
❑	237	Paul O'Neill	.40	.18
❑	238	Jim Thome	.40	.18
❑	239	Edgardo Alfonzo	.15	.07
❑	240	Terry Pendleton	.15	.07
❑	241	Harold Baines	.15	.07
❑	242	Roberto Alomar	.40	.18
❑	243	Mark Grace	.40	.18
❑	244	Derek Bell	.10	.05
❑	245	Vinny Castilla	.15	.07
❑	246	Cecil Fielder	.15	.07
❑	247	Roger Clemens	1.00	.45
❑	248	Orel Hershiser	.15	.07
❑	249	J.T. Snow	.15	.07
❑	250	Rafael Palmeiro	.40	.18
❑	251	Bret Saberhagen	.15	.07
❑	252	Todd Hollandsworth	.10	.05
❑	253	Ryan Klesko	.15	.07
❑	254	Greg Maddux HH	.50	.23
❑	255	Ken Griffey Jr. HH	.60	.25
❑	256	Hideo Nomo HH	.15	.07
❑	257	Frank Thomas HH	.25	.11
❑	258	Cal Ripken HH	.75	.35
❑	259	Jeff Bagwell HH	.25	.11
❑	260	Barry Bonds HH	.50	.23
❑	261	Mo Vaughn HH	.10	.05
❑	262	Albert Belle HH	.15	.07
❑	263	Sammy Sosa HH	.40	.18
❑	264	Reggie Sanders HH	.10	.05
❑	265	Mike Piazza HH	.50	.23
❑	266	Chipper Jones HH	.40	.18
❑	267	Tony Gwynn HH	.40	.18
❑	268	Kirby Puckett HH	.50	.23
❑	269	Wade Boggs HH	.15	.07
❑	270	Will Clark HH	.15	.07
❑	271	Gary Sheffield HH	.10	.05
❑	272	Dante Bichette HH	.10	.05
❑	273	Randy Johnson HH	.25	.11
❑	274	Matt Williams HH	.15	.07
❑	275	Alex Rodriguez HH	1.00	.45
❑	276	Tim Salmon HH	.10	.05
❑	277	Johnny Damon HH	.10	.05
❑	278	Manny Ramirez HH	.25	.11
❑	279	Derek Jeter HH	.75	.35
❑	280	Eddie Murray HH	.15	.07
❑	281	Ozzie Smith HH	.25	.11
❑	282	Garret Anderson HH	.10	.05
❑	283	Raul Mondesi HH	.10	.05
❑	284	Terry Steinbach	.10	.05
❑	285	Carlos Garcia	.10	.05
❑	286	Dave Justice	.15	.07
❑	287	Eric Anthony	.10	.05
❑	288	Benji Gil	.10	.05
❑	289	Bob Hamelin	.10	.05
❑	290	Dwayne Hosey	.10	.05
❑	291	Andy Pettitte HH	.10	.05
❑	292	Rod Beck	.10	.05
❑	293	Shane Andrews	.10	.05
❑	294	Julian Tavarez	.10	.05
❑	295	Willie Greene	.10	.05
❑	296	Ismael Valdes	.10	.05
❑	297	Glenallen Hill	.10	.05
❑	298	Troy Percival	.10	.05
❑	299	Ray Durham	.15	.07
❑	300	Jeff Conine 300	.10	.05
❑	301	Ken Griffey Jr. 300	.60	.25
❑	302	Will Clark 300	.15	.07
❑	303	Mike Greenwell 300	.10	.05
❑	304	Carlos Baerga 300	.10	.05
❑	305A	Paul Molitor 300	.15	.07
❑	305B	Jeff Bagwell 300	.25	.11
❑	306	Mark Grace 300	.15	.07
❑	307	Don Mattingly 300	.50	.23
❑	308	Hal Morris 300	.10	.05
❑	309	Butch Huskey	.10	.05
❑	310	Ozzie Guillen	.10	.05
❑	311	Erik Hanson	.10	.05
❑	312	Kenny Lofton 300	.10	.05
❑	313	Edgar Martinez 300	.15	.07
❑	314	Kurt Abbott	.10	.05
❑	315	John Smoltz	.15	.07
❑	316	Ariel Prieto	.10	.05
❑	317	Mark Carreon	.10	.05
❑	318	Kirby Puckett 300	.50	.23
❑	319	Carlos Perez	.10	.05
❑	320	Gary DiSarcina	.10	.05
❑	321	Trevor Hoffman	.15	.07
❑	322	Mike Piazza 300	.50	.23
❑	323	Frank Thomas 300	.25	.11
❑	324	Juan Acevedo	.10	.05
❑	325	Bip Roberts	.10	.05
❑	326	Javier Lopez	.15	.07
❑	327	Benito Santiago	.10	.05
❑	328	Mark Lewis	.10	.05
❑	329	Royce Clayton	.10	.05
❑	330	Tom Gordon	.10	.05
❑	331	Ben McDonald	.10	.05
❑	332	Dan Wilson	.10	.05
❑	333	Ron Gant	.10	.05
❑	334	Wade Boggs 300	.15	.07
❑	335	Paul Molitor	.40	.18
❑	336	Tony Gwynn 300	.40	.18
❑	337	Sean Berry	.10	.05
❑	338	Rickey Henderson	.75	.35
❑	339	Wil Cordero	.10	.05
❑	340	Kent Mercker	.10	.05
❑	341	Kenny Rogers	.10	.05
❑	342	Ryne Sandberg	.50	.23
❑	343	Charlie Hayes	.10	.05
❑	344	Andy Benes	.10	.05
❑	345	Sterling Hitchcock	.10	.05
❑	346	Bernard Gilkey	.10	.05
❑	347	Julio Franco	.15	.07
❑	348	Ken Hill	.10	.05
❑	349	Russ Davis	.10	.05
❑	350	Mike Blowers	.10	.05
❑	351	B.J. Surhoff	.15	.07
❑	352	Lance Johnson	.10	.05
❑	353	Darryl Hamilton	.10	.05
❑	354	Shawon Dunston	.10	.05
❑	355	Rick Aguilera	.10	.05
❑	356	Danny Tartabull	.10	.05
❑	357	Todd Stottlemyre	.10	.05
❑	358	Mike Bordick	.10	.05
❑	359	Jack McDowell	.10	.05
❑	360	Todd Zeile	.10	.05
❑	361	Tino Martinez	.15	.07
❑	362	Greg Gagne	.10	.05
❑	363	Mike Kelly	.10	.05
❑	364	Tim Raines	.15	.07
❑	365	Ernie Young	.10	.05
❑	366	Mike Stanley	.10	.05
❑	367	Wally Joyner	.15	.07
❑	368	Karim Garcia	.10	.05
❑	369	Paul Wilson	.10	.05
❑	370	Sal Fasano	.10	.05
❑	371	Jason Schmidt	.10	.05
❑	372	Livan Hernandez RC	.50	.23
❑	373	George Arias	.10	.05
❑	374	Steve Gibralter	.10	.05
❑	375	Jermaine Dye	.15	.07
❑	376	Jason Kendall	.15	.07
❑	377	Brooks Kieschnick	.10	.05
❑	378	Jeff Ware	.10	.05
❑	379	Alan Benes	.10	.05
❑	380	Rey Ordonez	.10	.05
❑	381	Jay Powell	.10	.05
❑	382	O. Fernandez RC	.10	.05
❑	383	Wilton Guerrero RC	.15	.07
❑	384	Eric Owens	.10	.05
❑	385	George Williams RC	.10	.05
❑	386	Chan Ho Park	.15	.07
❑	387	Jeff Suppan	.10	.05
❑	388	F.P. Santangelo RC	.10	.05
❑	389	Terry Adams	.10	.05
❑	390	Bob Abreu	.40	.18
❑	391	Quinton McCracken	.10	.05
❑	392	Mike Busby RC	.10	.05
❑	393	Cal Ripken CL	.75	.35
❑	394	Ken Griffey Jr. CL	.60	.25
❑	395	Frank Thomas CL	.25	.11
❑	396	Chipper Jones CL	.40	.18
❑	397	Greg Maddux CL	.50	.23
❑	398	Mike Piazza CL	.50	.23
❑	399	Ken Griffey Jr CL Cal Ripken Jr. Chipper Jones Frank Thomas Greg Maddux Mike Piazza	.25	.11
❑	CR1	Cal Ripken Tribute	15.00	6.75

1997 Pinnacle

		MINT	NRMT
COMPLETE SET (200)		20.00	9.00
❑ 1	Cecil Fielder	.25	.11
❑ 2	Garret Anderson	.25	.11

No.	Player	MINT	NRMT
3	Charles Nagy	.15	.07
4	Darryl Hamilton	.15	.07
5	Greg Myers	.15	.07
6	Eric Davis	.25	.11
7	Jeff Frye	.15	.07
8	Marquis Grissom	.15	.07
9	Curt Schilling	.60	.25
10	Jeff Fassero	.15	.07
11	Alan Benes	.15	.07
12	Orlando Miller	.15	.07
13	Alex Fernandez	.15	.07
14	Andy Pettitte	.25	.11
15	Andre Dawson	.40	.18
16	Mark Grudzielanek	.15	.07
17	Joe Vitiello	.15	.07
18	Juan Gonzalez	.60	.25
19	Mark Whiten	.15	.07
20	Lance Johnson	.15	.07
21	Trevor Hoffman	.25	.11
22	Marc Newfield	.15	.07
23	Jim Eisenreich	.15	.07
24	Joe Carter	.25	.11
25	Jose Canseco	.60	.25
26	Bill Swift	.15	.07
27	Ellis Burks	.25	.11
28	Ben McDonald	.15	.07
29	Edgar Martinez	.40	.18
30	Jamie Moyer	.15	.07
31	Chan Ho Park	.25	.11
32	Carlos Delgado	.60	.25
33	Kevin Mitchell	.15	.07
34	Carlos Garcia	.15	.07
35	Darryl Strawberry	.25	.11
36	Jim Thome	.60	.25
37	Jose Offerman	.15	.07
38	Ryan Klesko	.25	.11
39	Ruben Sierra	.15	.07
40	Devon White	.25	.11
41	Brian Jordan	.25	.11
42	Tony Gwynn	1.25	.55
43	Rafael Palmeiro	.60	.25
44	Dante Bichette	.25	.11
45	Scott Stahoviak	.15	.07
46	Roger Cedeno	.15	.07
47	Ivan Rodriguez	.60	.25
48	Bob Abreu	.25	.11
49	Darryl Kile	.25	.11
50	Darren Dreifort	.15	.07
51	Shawon Dunston	.15	.07
52	Mark McGwire	2.50	1.10
53	Tim Salmon	.25	.11
54	Gene Schall	.15	.07
55	Roger Clemens	1.50	.70
56	Rondell White	.25	.11
57	Ed Sprague	.15	.07
58	Craig Paquette	.15	.07
59	David Segui	.15	.07
60	Jaime Navarro	.15	.07
61	Tom Glavine	.60	.25
62	Jeff Brantley	.15	.07
63	Kimera Bartee	.15	.07
64	Fernando Vina	.15	.07
65	Eddie Murray	.60	.25
66	Lenny Dykstra	.25	.11
67	Kevin Elster	.15	.07
68	Vinny Castilla	.25	.11
69	Mike Fetters	.15	.07
70	Brett Butler	.25	.11
71	Robby Thompson	.15	.07
72	Reggie Jefferson	.15	.07
73	Todd Hundley	.15	.07
74	Jeff King	.15	.07
75	Ernie Young	.15	.07
76	Jeff Bagwell	.75	.35
77	Dan Wilson	.15	.07
78	Paul Molitor	.60	.25
79	Kevin Seitzer	.15	.07
80	Kevin Brown	.25	.11
81	Ron Gant	.15	.07
82	Dwight Gooden	.25	.11
83	Todd Stottlemyre	.15	.07
84	Ken Caminiti	.25	.11
85	James Baldwin	.15	.07
86	Jermaine Dye	.25	.11
87	Harold Baines	.25	.11
88	Pat Hentgen	.15	.07
89	Frank Rodriguez	.15	.07
90	Mark Johnson	.15	.07
91	Jason Kendall	.25	.11
92	Alex Rodriguez	1.50	.70
93	Alan Trammell	.40	.18
94	Scott Brosius	.25	.11
95	Delino DeShields	.15	.07
96	Chipper Jones	1.25	.55
97	Barry Bonds	1.50	.70
98	Brady Anderson	.25	.11
99	Ryne Sandberg	.75	.35
100	Albert Belle	.25	.11
101	Jeff Cirillo	.25	.11
102	Frank Thomas	.75	.35
103	Mike Piazza	1.50	.70
104	Rickey Henderson	1.25	.55
105	Rey Ordonez	.15	.07
106	Mark Grace	.60	.25
107	Terry Steinbach	.15	.07
108	Ray Durham	.25	.11
109	Barry Larkin	.60	.25
110	Tony Clark	.25	.11
111	Bernie Williams	.60	.25
112	John Smoltz	.25	.11
113	Moises Alou	.25	.11
114	Alex Gonzalez	.15	.07
115	Rico Brogna	.15	.07
116	Eric Karros	.25	.11
117	Jeff Conine	.15	.07
118	Todd Hollandsworth	.15	.07
119	Troy Percival	.15	.07
120	Paul Wilson	.15	.07
121	Orel Hershiser	.25	.11
122	Ozzie Smith	.75	.35
123	Dave Hollins	.15	.07
124	Ken Hill	.15	.07
125	Rick Wilkins	.15	.07
126	Scott Servais	.15	.07
127	Fernando Valenzuela	.25	.11
128	Mariano Rivera	.25	.11
129	Mark Loretta	.15	.07
130	Shane Reynolds	.15	.07
131	Darren Oliver	.15	.07
132	Steve Trachsel	.15	.07
133	Darren Bragg	.15	.07
134	Jason Dickson	.15	.07
135	Darrin Fletcher	.15	.07
136	Gary Gaetti	.25	.11
137	Joey Cora	.15	.07
138	Terry Pendleton	.25	.11
139	Derek Jeter	2.50	1.10
140	Danny Tartabull	.15	.07
141	John Flaherty	.15	.07
142	B.J. Surhoff	.25	.11
143	Mike Sweeney	.25	.11
144	Chad Mottola	.15	.07
145	Andujar Cedeno	.15	.07
146	Tim Belcher	.15	.07
147	Mark Thompson	.15	.07
148	Rafael Bournigal	.15	.07
149	Marty Cordova	.15	.07
150	Osvaldo Fernandez	.15	.07
151	Mike Stanley	.15	.07
152	Ricky Bottalico	.15	.07
153	Donne Wall	.15	.07
154	Omar Vizquel	.25	.11
155	Mike Mussina	.60	.25
156	Brant Brown	.15	.07
157	F.P. Santangelo	.15	.07
158	Ryan Hancock	.15	.07
159	Jeff D'Amico	.15	.07
160	Luis Castillo	.15	.07
161	Darin Erstad	.60	.25
162	Ugueth Urbina	.15	.07
163	Andruw Jones	.75	.35
164	Steve Gibralter	.15	.07
165	Robin Jennings	.15	.07
166	Mike Cameron	.25	.11
167	George Arias	.15	.07
168	Chris Stynes	.15	.07
169	Justin Thompson	.15	.07
170	Jamey Wright	.15	.07
171	Todd Walker	.15	.07
172	Nomar Garciaparra	1.50	.70
173	Jose Paniagua	.15	.07
174	Marvin Benard	.15	.07
175	Rocky Coppinger	.15	.07
176	Quinton McCracken	.15	.07
177	Amaury Telemaco	.15	.07
178	Neifi Perez	.15	.07
179	Todd Greene	.15	.07
180	Jason Thompson	.15	.07
181	Wilton Guerrero	.15	.07
182	Edgar Renteria	.15	.07
183	Billy Wagner	.15	.07
184	Alex Ochoa	.15	.07
185	Dmitri Young	.25	.11
186	Kenny Lofton CT	.25	.11
187	Andres Galarraga CT	.40	.18
188	Chuck Knoblauch CT	.25	.11
189	Greg Maddux CT	1.50	.70
190	Mo Vaughn CT	.25	.11
191	Cal Ripken CT	2.50	1.10
192	Hideo Nomo CT	.60	.25
193	Ken Griffey Jr. CT	2.00	.90
194	Sammy Sosa CT	1.25	.55
195	Jay Buhner CT	.25	.11
196	Manny Ramirez CT	.75	.35
197	Matt Williams CT	.40	.18
198	Andruw Jones CL	.75	.35
199	Darin Erstad CL	.25	.11
200	Trey Beamon CL	.15	.07

1998 Pinnacle

	MINT	NRMT
COMPLETE SET (200)	25.00	11.00

No.	Player	MINT	NRMT
1	Tony Gwynn	1.25	.55
2	Pedro Martinez	.75	.35
3	Kenny Lofton	.25	.11
4	Curt Schilling	.60	.25
5	Shawn Estes	.25	.11
6	Tom Glavine	.60	.25
7	Mike Piazza	1.50	.70
8	Ray Lankford	.15	.07
9	Barry Larkin	.60	.25
10	Tony Womack	.15	.07
11	Jeff Blauser	.15	.07
12	Rod Beck	.15	.07
13	Larry Walker	.40	.18
14	Greg Maddux	1.50	.70
15	Mark Grace	.60	.25
16	Ken Caminiti	.25	.11
17	Bobby Jones	.15	.07
18	Chipper Jones	1.25	.55
19	Javier Lopez	.25	.11
20	Moises Alou	.25	.11
21	Royce Clayton	.15	.07
22	Darryl Kile	.25	.11
23	Barry Bonds	1.50	.70
24	Steve Finley	.25	.11
25	Andres Galarraga	.40	.18
26	Denny Neagle	.15	.07
27	Todd Hundley	.15	.07
28	Jeff Bagwell	.75	.35
29	Andy Pettitte	.25	.11
30	Darin Erstad	.60	.25
31	Carlos Delgado	.60	.25
32	Matt Williams	.40	.18
33	Will Clark	.60	.25
34	Vinny Castilla	.25	.11
35	Brad Radke	.25	.11
36	John Olerud	.25	.11

❑ 37 Andruw Jones .60 .25
❑ 38 Jason Giambi .60 .25
❑ 39 Scott Rolen .60 .25
❑ 40 Gary Sheffield .25 .11
❑ 41 Jimmy Key .25 .11
❑ 42 Kevin Appier .25 .11
❑ 43 Wade Boggs .60 .25
❑ 44 Hideo Nomo .60 .25
❑ 45 Manny Ramirez .75 .35
❑ 46 Wilton Guerrero .15 .07
❑ 47 Travis Fryman .25 .11
❑ 48 Chili Davis .25 .11
❑ 49 Jeromy Burnitz .25 .11
❑ 50 Craig Biggio .40 .18
❑ 51 Tim Salmon .25 .11
❑ 52 Jose Cruz Jr. .25 .11
❑ 53 Sammy Sosa 1.25 .55
❑ 54 Hideki Irabu .15 .07
❑ 55 Chan Ho Park .25 .11
❑ 56 Robin Ventura .25 .11
❑ 57 Jose Guillen .15 .07
❑ 58 Deion Sanders .25 .11
❑ 59 Jose Canseco .60 .25
❑ 60 Jay Buhner .25 .11
❑ 61 Rafael Palmeiro .60 .25
❑ 62 Vladimir Guerrero .75 .35
❑ 63 Mark McGwire 2.50 1.10
❑ 64 Derek Jeter 2.50 1.10
❑ 65 Bobby Bonilla .25 .11
❑ 66 Raul Mondesi .25 .11
❑ 67 Paul Molitor .60 .25
❑ 68 Joe Carter .25 .11
❑ 69 Marquis Grissom .15 .07
❑ 70 Juan Gonzalez .60 .25
❑ 71 Kevin Orie .15 .07
❑ 72 Rusty Greer .25 .11
❑ 73 Henry Rodriguez .15 .07
❑ 74 Fernando Tatis .15 .07
❑ 75 John Valentin .15 .07
❑ 76 Matt Morris .25 .11
❑ 77 Ray Durham .25 .11
❑ 78 Geronimo Berroa .15 .07
❑ 79 Scott Brosius .25 .11
❑ 80 Willie Greene .15 .07
❑ 81 Rondell White .25 .11
❑ 82 Doug Drabek .15 .07
❑ 83 Derek Bell .15 .07
❑ 84 Butch Huskey .15 .07
❑ 85 Doug Jones .15 .07
❑ 86 Jeff Kent .40 .18
❑ 87 Jim Edmonds .40 .18
❑ 88 Mark McLemore .15 .07
❑ 89 Todd Zeile .25 .11
❑ 90 Edgardo Alfonzo .25 .11
❑ 91 Carlos Baerga .15 .07
❑ 92 Jorge Fabregas .15 .07
❑ 93 Alan Benes .15 .07
❑ 94 Troy Percival .15 .07
❑ 95 Edgar Renteria .15 .07
❑ 96 Jeff Fassero .15 .07
❑ 97 Reggie Sanders .15 .07
❑ 98 Dean Palmer .25 .11
❑ 99 J.T. Snow .25 .11
❑ 100 Dave Nilsson .15 .07
❑ 101 Dan Wilson .15 .07
❑ 102 Robb Nen .15 .07
❑ 103 Damion Easley .15 .07
❑ 104 Kevin Foster .15 .07
❑ 105 Jose Offerman .15 .07
❑ 106 Steve Cooke .15 .07
❑ 107 Matt Stairs .15 .07
❑ 108 Darryl Hamilton .15 .07
❑ 109 Steve Karsay .15 .07
❑ 110 Gary DiSarcina .15 .07
❑ 111 Dante Bichette .25 .11
❑ 112 Billy Wagner .15 .07
❑ 113 David Segui .15 .07
❑ 114 Bobby Higginson .25 .11
❑ 115 Jeffrey Hammonds .15 .07
❑ 116 Kevin Brown .25 .11
❑ 117 Paul Sorrento .15 .07
❑ 118 Mark Leiter .15 .07
❑ 119 Charles Nagy .15 .07
❑ 120 Danny Patterson .15 .07
❑ 121 Brian McRae .15 .07
❑ 122 Jay Bell .25 .11
❑ 123 Jamie Moyer .15 .07
❑ 124 Carl Everett .25 .11
❑ 125 Greg Colbrunn .15 .07
❑ 126 Jason Kendall .25 .11
❑ 127 Luis Sojo .15 .07
❑ 128 Mike Lieberthal .25 .11
❑ 129 Reggie Jefferson .15 .07
❑ 130 Cal Eldred .15 .07
❑ 131 Orel Hershiser .25 .11
❑ 132 Doug Glanville .15 .07
❑ 133 Willie Blair .15 .07
❑ 134 Neifi Perez .15 .07
❑ 135 Sean Berry .15 .07
❑ 136 Chuck Finley .25 .11
❑ 137 Alex Gonzalez .15 .07
❑ 138 Dennis Eckersley .25 .11
❑ 139 Kenny Rogers .15 .07
❑ 140 Troy O'Leary .15 .07
❑ 141 Roger Bailey .15 .07
❑ 142 Yamil Benitez .15 .07
❑ 143 Wally Joyner .25 .11
❑ 144 Bobby Witt .15 .07
❑ 145 Pete Schourek .15 .07
❑ 146 Terry Steinbach .15 .07
❑ 147 B.J. Surhoff .25 .11
❑ 148 Esteban Loaiza .15 .07
❑ 149 Heathcliff Slocumb .15 .07
❑ 150 Ed Sprague .15 .07
❑ 151 Gregg Jefferies .15 .07
❑ 152 Scott Erickson .15 .07
❑ 153 Jaime Navarro .15 .07
❑ 154 David Wells .25 .11
❑ 155 Alex Fernandez .15 .07
❑ 156 Tim Belcher .15 .07
❑ 157 Mark Grudzielanek .15 .07
❑ 158 Scott Hatteberg .15 .07
❑ 159 Paul Konerko .25 .11
❑ 160 Ben Grieve .25 .11
❑ 161 Abraham Nunez .15 .07
❑ 162 Shannon Stewart .25 .11
❑ 163 Jaret Wright .15 .07
❑ 164 Derrek Lee .25 .11
❑ 165 Todd Dunwoody .15 .07
❑ 166 Steve Woodard .15 .07
❑ 167 Ryan McGuire .15 .07
❑ 168 Jeremi Gonzalez .15 .07
❑ 169 Mark Kotsay .25 .11
❑ 170 Brett Tomko .15 .07
❑ 171 Bobby Estalella .15 .07
❑ 172 Livan Hernandez .15 .07
❑ 173 Todd Helton .75 .35
❑ 174 Garrett Stephenson .15 .07
❑ 175 Pokey Reese .15 .07
❑ 176 Tony Saunders .15 .07
❑ 177 Antone Williamson .15 .07
❑ 178 Bartolo Colon .25 .11
❑ 179 Karim Garcia .15 .07
❑ 180 Juan Encarnacion .25 .11
❑ 181 Jacob Cruz .15 .07
❑ 182 Alex Rodriguez FV 1.50 .70
❑ 183 Cal Ripken FV 2.00 .90
Roberto Alomar
❑ 184 Roger Clemens FV 1.50 .70
❑ 185 Derek Jeter FV 2.50 1.10
❑ 186 Frank Thomas FV 1.00 .45
❑ 187 Ken Griffey Jr. FV 2.00 .90
❑ 188 Mark McGwire GJ 2.50 1.10
❑ 189 Tino Martinez GJ .15 .07
❑ 190 Larry Walker GJ .40 .18
❑ 191 Brady Anderson GJ .15 .07
❑ 192 Jeff Bagwell GJ .40 .18
❑ 193 Ken Griffey Jr. GJ 2.00 .90
❑ 194 Chipper Jones GJ 1.25 .55
❑ 195 Ray Lankford GJ .15 .07
❑ 196 Jim Thome GJ .25 .11
❑ 197 Nomar Garciaparra GJ 1.50 .70
❑ 198 AS HR Contestants .40 .18
Brady Anderson
Jeff Bagwell
Nomar Garciaparra
Ken Griffey Jr.
Chipper Jones
Ray Lankford
Tino Martinez
Mark McGwire
Jim Thome
Larry Walker
❑ 199 Tino Martinez CL .15 .07
❑ 200 Jacobs Field CL .15 .07

2001 Playoff Absolute Memorabilia

	MINT	NRMT
COMP.SET w/o SP's (150)	40.00	18.00
COMMON CARD (1-150)	.75	.35
COMMON RPM (151-200)	12.00	5.50

❑ 1 Alex Rodriguez 5.00 2.20
❑ 2 Barry Bonds 5.00 2.20
❑ 3 Cal Ripken 8.00 3.60
❑ 4 Chipper Jones 4.00 1.80
❑ 5 Derek Jeter 8.00 3.60
❑ 6 Troy Glaus 2.00 .90
❑ 7 Frank Thomas 2.50 1.10
❑ 8 Greg Maddux 5.00 2.20
❑ 9 Ivan Rodriguez 2.00 .90
❑ 10 Jeff Bagwell 2.50 1.10
❑ 11 Ryan Dempster .75 .35
❑ 12 Todd Helton 2.50 1.10
❑ 13 Ken Griffey Jr. 6.00 2.70
❑ 14 Manny Ramirez 2.50 1.10
❑ 15 Mark McGwire 8.00 3.60
❑ 16 Mike Piazza 5.00 2.20
❑ 17 Nomar Garciaparra 5.00 2.20
❑ 18 Pedro Martinez 2.50 1.10
❑ 19 Randy Johnson 2.50 1.10
❑ 20 Rick Ankiel 1.25 .55
❑ 21 Rickey Henderson 4.00 1.80
❑ 22 Roger Clemens 5.00 2.20
❑ 23 Sammy Sosa 4.00 1.80
❑ 24 Tony Gwynn 4.00 1.80
❑ 25 Vladimir Guerrero 2.50 1.10
❑ 26 Kazuhiro Sasaki 2.00 .90
❑ 27 Roberto Alomar 2.00 .90
❑ 28 Barry Zito 2.00 .90
❑ 29 Pat Burrell .75 .35
❑ 30 Harold Baines .75 .35
❑ 31 Carlos Delgado 2.00 .90
❑ 32 J.D. Drew 2.00 .90
❑ 33 Jim Edmonds 1.25 .55
❑ 34 Darin Erstad 2.00 .90
❑ 35 Jason Giambi 2.00 .90
❑ 36 Tom Glavine 2.00 .90
❑ 37 Juan Gonzalez 2.00 .90
❑ 38 Mark Grace 2.00 .90
❑ 39 Shawn Green 2.00 .90
❑ 40 Tim Hudson 2.00 .90
❑ 41 Andruw Jones 2.00 .90
❑ 42 David Justice .75 .35
❑ 43 Jeff Kent 1.25 .55
❑ 44 Barry Larkin 2.00 .90
❑ 45 Rafael Furcal .75 .35
❑ 46 Mike Mussina 2.00 .90
❑ 47 Hideo Nomo 2.00 .90
❑ 48 Rafael Palmeiro 2.00 .90
❑ 49 Adam Piatt .75 .35
❑ 50 Scott Rolen 2.00 .90
❑ 51 Gary Sheffield .75 .35
❑ 52 Bernie Williams 2.00 .90
❑ 53 Bob Abreu .75 .35
❑ 54 Edgardo Alfonzo .75 .35
❑ 55 Edgar Renteria .75 .35
❑ 56 Phil Nevin .75 .35

❑ 57 Craig Biggio 1.25 .55
❑ 58 Andres Galarraga 1.25 .55
❑ 59 Edgar Martinez 1.25 .55
❑ 60 Fred McGriff 1.25 .55
❑ 61 Magglio Ordonez .75 .35
❑ 62 Jim Thome 2.00 .90
❑ 63 Matt Williams 1.25 .55
❑ 64 Kerry Wood 2.00 .90
❑ 65 Moises Alou .75 .35
❑ 66 Brady Anderson .75 .35
❑ 67 Garret Anderson .75 .35
❑ 68 Russell Branyan .75 .35
❑ 69 Tony Batista .75 .35
❑ 70 Vernon Wells .75 .35
❑ 71 Carlos Beltran .75 .35
❑ 72 Adrian Beltre .75 .35
❑ 73 Kris Benson .75 .35
❑ 74 Lance Berkman 2.00 .90
❑ 75 Kevin Brown .75 .35
❑ 76 Dee Brown .75 .35
❑ 77 Jeromy Burnitz .75 .35
❑ 78 Timo Perez .75 .35
❑ 79 Sean Casey 1.25 .55
❑ 80 Luis Castillo .75 .35
❑ 81 Eric Chavez .75 .35
❑ 82 Jeff Cirillo .75 .35
❑ 83 Bartolo Colon .75 .35
❑ 84 David Cone .75 .35
❑ 85 Freddy Garcia .75 .35
❑ 86 Johnny Damon .75 .35
❑ 87 Ray Durham .75 .35
❑ 88 Jermaine Dye .75 .35
❑ 89 Juan Encarnacion .75 .35
❑ 90 Terrence Long .75 .35
❑ 91 Carl Everett .75 .35
❑ 92 Steve Finley .75 .35
❑ 93 Cliff Floyd .75 .35
❑ 94 Brad Fullmer .75 .35
❑ 95 Brian Giles .75 .35
❑ 96 Luis Gonzalez 2.00 .90
❑ 97 Rusty Greer .75 .35
❑ 98 Jeffrey Hammonds .75 .35
❑ 99 Mike Hampton .75 .35
❑ 100 Orlando Hernandez .75 .35
❑ 101 Richard Hidalgo .75 .35
❑ 102 Geoff Jenkins .75 .35
❑ 103 Jacque Jones .75 .35
❑ 104 Brian Jordan .75 .35
❑ 105 Gabe Kapler .75 .35
❑ 106 Eric Karros .75 .35
❑ 107 Jason Kendall .75 .35
❑ 108 Adam Kennedy .75 .35
❑ 109 Deion Sanders .75 .35
❑ 110 Ryan Klesko .75 .35
❑ 111 Chuck Knoblauch .75 .35
❑ 112 Paul Konerko .75 .35
❑ 113 Carlos Lee .75 .35
❑ 114 Kenny Lofton .75 .35
❑ 115 Javy Lopez .75 .35
❑ 116 Tino Martinez .75 .35
❑ 117 Ruben Mateo .75 .35
❑ 118 Kevin Millwood .75 .35
❑ 119 Jimmy Rollins .75 .35
❑ 120 Raul Mondesi .75 .35
❑ 121 Trot Nixon .75 .35
❑ 122 John Olerud .75
.35❑ 123 Paul O' Neill 2.00 .90
❑ 124 Chan Ho Park .75 .35
❑ 125 Andy Pettitte .75 .35
❑ 126 Jorge Posada .75 .35
❑ 127 Mark Quinn .75 .35
❑ 128 Aramis Ramirez .75 .35
❑ 129 Mariano Rivera .75 .35
❑ 130 Tim Salmon .75 .35
❑ 131 Curt Schilling 2.00 .90
❑ 132 Richie Sexson .75 .35
❑ 133 John Smoltz .75 .35
❑ 134 J.T. Snow .75 .35
❑ 135 Jay Payton .75 .35
❑ 136 Shannon Stewart .75 .35
❑ 137 B.J. Surhoff .75 .35
❑ 138 Mike Sweeney .75 .35
❑ 139 Fernando Tatis .75 .35
❑ 140 Miguel Tejada .75 .35
❑ 141 Jason Varitek .75 .35
❑ 142 Greg Vaughn .75 .35
❑ 143 Mo Vaughn .75 .35
❑ 144 Robin Ventura .75 .35
❑ 145 Jose Vidro .75 .35
❑ 146 Omar Vizquel .75 .35
❑ 147 Larry Walker 1.25 .55
❑ 148 David Wells .75 .35
❑ 149 Rondell White .75 .35
❑ 150 Preston Wilson .75 .35
❑ 151 Eddie Oropesa RPM 15.00 6.75
❑ 152 Cory Aldridge RPM RC 12.00 5.50
❑ 153 Wilmy Caceres RPM RC 12.00 5.50
❑ 154 Josh Beckett RPM 25.00 11.00
❑ 155 Wilson Betemit RPM RC 30.00 13.50
❑ 156 Jason Michaels RPM RC 12.00 5.50
❑ 157 Albert Pujols RPM RC 80.00 36.00
❑ 158 Andres Torres RPM RC 12.00 5.50
❑ 159 Jack Wilson RPM RC 12.00 5.50
❑ 160 Alex Escobar RPM 12.00 5.50
❑ 161 Ben Sheets RPM 15.00 6.75
❑ 162 Rafael Soriano RPM RC 15.00 6.75
❑ 163 Nate Frese RPM RC 12.00 5.50
❑ 164 C. Garcia RPM EXCH 12.00 5.50
❑ 165 Brandon Larson RPM RC 12.00 5.50
❑ 166 Alexis Gomez RPM RC 12.00 5.50
❑ 167 Jason Hart RPM 15.00 6.75
❑ 168 Nick Johnson RPM 12.00 5.50
❑ 169 D. Mendez RPM EXCH 12.00 5.50
❑ 170 Christian Parker RPM RC 12.00 5.50
❑ 171 Jackson Melian RPM 12.00 5.50
❑ 172 Jack Cust RPM 12.00 5.50
❑ 173 A. Hernandez RPM EXCH 12.00 5.50
❑ 174 Joe Crede RPM 12.00 5.50
❑ 175 Jose Mieses RPM RC 12.00 5.50
❑ 176 Roy Oswalt RPM 25.00 11.00
❑ 177 Eric Munson RPM 12.00 5.50
❑ 178 Xavier Nady RPM 15.00 6.75
❑ 179 H. Ramirez RPM RC 12.00 5.50
❑ 180 Abraham Nunez RPM 12.00 5.50
❑ 181 Jose Ortiz RPM 15.00 6.75
❑ 182 Jeremy Owens RPM RC 12.00 5.50
❑ 183 Claudio Vargas RPM RC 12.00 5.50
❑ 184 Marcus Giles RPM 12.00 5.50
❑ 185 Aubrey Huff RPM 12.00 5.50
❑ 186 C.C. Sabathia RPM 15.00 6.75
❑ 187 Adam Dunn RPM 40.00 18.00
❑ 188 A. Pettyjohn RPM EXCH 15.00 6.75
❑ 189 Elpidio Guzman RPM RC 12.00 5.50
❑ 190 Jay Gibbons RPM RC 15.00 6.75
❑ 191 Wilkin Ruan RPM RC 12.00 5.50
❑ 192 Tsuyoshi Shinjo RPM RC 30.00 13.50
❑ 193 Alfonso Soriano RPM 25.00 11.00
❑ 194 Corey Patterson RPM 12.00 5.50
❑ 195 Ichiro Suzuki RPM RC 180.00 80.00
❑ 196 B. Sylvester RPM EXCH 12.00 5.50
❑ 197 Juan Uribe RPM RC 20.00 9.00
❑ 198 Johnny Estrada RPM RC 20.00 9.00
❑ 199 C. Valderrama RPM RC 12.00 5.50
❑ 200 Matt White RPM EXCH 12.00 5.50

1988 Score

	MINT	NRMT
COMPLETE SET (660)	10.00	4.50
COMP.FACT.SET (660)	12.00	5.50

❑ 1 Don Mattingly .50 .23
❑ 2 Wade Boggs .20 .09
❑ 3 Tim Raines .10 .05
❑ 4 Andre Dawson .15 .07
❑ 5 Mark McGwire 2.00 .90
❑ 6 Kevin Seitzer .10 .05
❑ 7 Wally Joyner .15 .07
❑ 8 Jesse Barfield .05 .02
❑ 9 Pedro Guerrero .05 .02
❑ 10 Eric Davis .10 .05
❑ 11 George Brett .40 .18
❑ 12 Ozzie Smith .25 .11
❑ 13 Rickey Henderson .40 .18
❑ 14 Jim Rice .10 .05
❑ 15 Matt Nokes RC* .05 .02
❑ 16 Mike Schmidt .40 .18
❑ 17 Dave Parker .10 .05
❑ 18 Eddie Murray .20 .09
❑ 19 Andres Galarraga .15 .07
❑ 20 Tony Fernandez .05 .02
❑ 21 Kevin McReynolds .05 .02
❑ 22 B.J. Surhoff .10 .05
❑ 23 Pat Tabler .05 .02
❑ 24 Kirby Puckett .50 .23
❑ 25 Benny Santiago .05 .02
❑ 26 Ryne Sandberg .25 .11
❑ 27 Kelly Downs .10 .05
(Will Clark in background, out of focus)
❑ 28 Jose Cruz .05 .02
❑ 29 Pete O'Brien .05 .02
❑ 30 Mark Langston .05 .02
❑ 31 Lee Smith .10 .05
❑ 32 Juan Samuel .05 .02
❑ 33 Kevin Bass .05 .02
❑ 34 R.J. Reynolds .05 .02
❑ 35 Steve Sax .05 .02
❑ 36 John Kruk .10 .05
❑ 37 Alan Trammell .15 .07
❑ 38 Chris Bosio .05 .02
❑ 39 Brook Jacoby .05 .02
❑ 40 Willie McGee UER .10 .05
(Excited misspelled as excitd)
❑ 41 Dave Magadan .05 .02
❑ 42 Fred Lynn .05 .02
❑ 43 Kent Hrbek .10 .05
❑ 44 Brian Downing .05 .02
❑ 45 Jose Canseco .30 .14
❑ 46 Jim Presley .05 .02
❑ 47 Mike Stanley .10 .05
❑ 48 Tony Pena .05 .02
❑ 49 David Cone .10 .05
❑ 50 Rick Sutcliffe .10 .05
❑ 51 Doug Drabek .05 .02
❑ 52 Bill Doran .05 .02
❑ 53 Mike Scioscia .05 .02
❑ 54 Candy Maldonado .05 .02
❑ 55 Dave Winfield .20 .09
❑ 56 Lou Whitaker .10 .05
❑ 57 Tom Henke .05 .02
❑ 58 Ken Gerhart .05 .02
❑ 59 Glenn Braggs .05 .02
❑ 60 Julio Franco .05 .02
❑ 61 Charlie Leibrandt .05 .02
❑ 62 Gary Gaetti .10 .05
❑ 63 Bob Boone .10 .05
❑ 64 Luis Polonia RC* .05 .02
❑ 65 Dwight Evans .10 .05
❑ 66 Phil Bradley .05 .02
❑ 67 Mike Boddicker .05 .02
❑ 68 Vince Coleman .05 .02
❑ 69 Howard Johnson .05 .02
❑ 70 Tim Wallach .05 .02
❑ 71 Keith Moreland .05 .02
❑ 72 Barry Larkin .20 .09
❑ 73 Alan Ashby .05 .02
❑ 74 Rick Rhoden .05 .02
❑ 75 Darrell Evans .10 .05
❑ 76 Dave Stieb .05 .02
❑ 77 Dan Plesac .05 .02
❑ 78 Will Clark UER .25 .11
(Born 3/17/64, should be 3/13/64)
❑ 79 Frank White .10 .05
❑ 80 Joe Carter .20 .09
❑ 81 Mike Witt .05 .02
❑ 82 Terry Steinbach .10 .05
❑ 83 Alvin Davis .05 .02
❑ 84 Tommy Herr .10 .05

(Will Clark shown sliding into second)
❑ 85 Vance Law .05 .02
❑ 86 Kal Daniels .05 .02
❑ 87 Rick Honeycutt UER .05 .02
(Wrong years for stats on back)
❑ 88 Alfredo Griffin .05 .02
❑ 89 Bret Saberhagen .10 .05
❑ 90 Bert Blyleven .10 .05
❑ 91 Jeff Reardon .10 .05
❑ 92 Cory Snyder .05 .02
❑ 93A Greg Walker ERR 2.00 .90
(93 of 66)
❑ 93B Greg Walker COR .05 .02
(93 of 660)
❑ 94 Joe Magrane RC* .05 .02
❑ 95 Rob Deer .05 .02
❑ 96 Ray Knight .05 .02
❑ 97 Casey Candaele .05 .02
❑ 98 John Cerutti .05 .02
❑ 99 Buddy Bell .10 .05
❑ 100 Jack Clark .10 .05
❑ 101 Eric Bell .05 .02
❑ 102 Willie Wilson .05 .02
❑ 103 Dave Schmidt .05 .02
❑ 104 Dennis Eckersley UER .10 .05
(Complete games stats are wrong)
❑ 105 Don Sutton .20 .09
❑ 106 Danny Tartabull .05 .02
❑ 107 Fred McGriff .20 .09
❑ 108 Les Straker .05 .02
❑ 109 Lloyd Moseby .05 .02
❑ 110 Roger Clemens .50 .23
❑ 111 Glenn Hubbard .05 .02
❑ 112 Ken Williams RC .05 .02
❑ 113 Ruben Sierra .05 .02
❑ 114 Stan Jefferson .05 .02
❑ 115 Milt Thompson .05 .02
❑ 116 Bobby Bonilla .10 .05
❑ 117 Wayne Tolleson .05 .02
❑ 118 Matt Williams RC .75 .35
❑ 119 Chet Lemon .05 .02
❑ 120 Dale Sveum .05 .02
❑ 121 Dennis Boyd .05 .02
❑ 122 Brett Butler .10 .05
❑ 123 Terry Kennedy .05 .02
❑ 124 Jack Howell .05 .02
❑ 125 Curt Young .05 .02
❑ 126A Dave Valle ERR .10 .05
(Misspelled Dale on card front)
❑ 126B Dave Valle COR .05 .02
❑ 127 Curt Wilkerson .05 .02
❑ 128 Tim Teufel .05 .02
❑ 129 Ozzie Virgil .05 .02
❑ 130 Brian Fisher .05 .02
❑ 131 Lance Parrish .05 .02
❑ 132 Tom Browning .05 .02
❑ 133A Larry Andersen ERR .10 .05
(Misspelled Anderson on card front)
❑ 133B Larry Andersen COR .05 .02
❑ 134A Bob Brenly ERR .10 .05
(Misspelled Brenley on card front)
❑ 134B Bob Brenly COR .05 .02
❑ 135 Mike Marshall .05 .02
❑ 136 Gerald Perry .05 .02
❑ 137 Bobby Meacham .05 .02
❑ 138 Larry Herndon .05 .02
❑ 139 Fred Manrique .05 .02
❑ 140 Charlie Hough .10 .05
❑ 141 Ron Darling .05 .02
❑ 142 Herm Winningham .05 .02
❑ 143 Mike Diaz .05 .02
❑ 144 Mike Jackson RC* .10 .05
❑ 145 Denny Walling .05 .02
❑ 146 Robby Thompson .05 .02
❑ 147 Franklin Stubbs .05 .02
❑ 148 Albert Hall .05 .02
❑ 149 Bobby Witt .05 .02
❑ 150 Lance McCullers .05 .02
❑ 151 Scott Bradley .05 .02
❑ 152 Mark McLemore .05 .02
❑ 153 Tim Laudner .05 .02
❑ 154 Greg Swindell .05 .02
❑ 155 Marty Barrett .05 .02
❑ 156 Mike Heath .05 .02
❑ 157 Gary Ward .05 .02
❑ 158A Lee Mazzilli ERR .10 .05
(Misspelled Mazilli on card front)
❑ 158B Lee Mazzilli COR .05 .02
❑ 159 Tom Foley .05 .02
❑ 160 Robin Yount .20 .09
❑ 161 Steve Bedrosian .05 .02
❑ 162 Bob Walk .05 .02
❑ 163 Nick Esasky .05 .02
❑ 164 Ken Caminiti RC .50 .23
❑ 165 Jose Uribe .05 .02
❑ 166 Dave Anderson .05 .02
❑ 167 Ed Whitson .05 .02
❑ 168 Ernie Whitt .05 .02
❑ 169 Cecil Cooper .10 .05
❑ 170 Mike Pagliarulo .05 .02
❑ 171 Pat Sheridan .05 .02
❑ 172 Chris Bando .05 .02
❑ 173 Lee Lacy .05 .02
❑ 174 Steve Lombardozzi .05 .02
❑ 175 Mike Greenwell .05 .02
❑ 176 Greg Minton .05 .02
❑ 177 Moose Haas .05 .02
❑ 178 Mike Kingery .05 .02
❑ 179 Greg A. Harris .05 .02
❑ 180 Bo Jackson .20 .09
❑ 181 Carmelo Martinez .05 .02
❑ 182 Alex Trevino .05 .02
❑ 183 Ron Oester .05 .02
❑ 184 Danny Darwin .05 .02
❑ 185 Mike Krukow .05 .02
❑ 186 Rafael Palmeiro .40 .18
❑ 187 Tim Burke .05 .02
❑ 188 Roger McDowell .05 .02
❑ 189 Garry Templeton .05 .02
❑ 190 Terry Pendleton .10 .05
❑ 191 Larry Parrish .05 .02
❑ 192 Rey Quinones .05 .02
❑ 193 Joaquin Andujar .05 .02
❑ 194 Tom Brunansky .05 .02
❑ 195 Donnie Moore .05 .02
❑ 196 Dan Pasqua .05 .02
❑ 197 Jim Gantner .05 .02
❑ 198 Mark Eichhorn .05 .02
❑ 199 John Grubb .05 .02
❑ 200 Bill Ripken RC* .05 .02
❑ 201 Sam Horn RC .05 .02
❑ 202 Todd Worrell .10 .05
❑ 203 Terry Leach .05 .02
❑ 204 Garth Iorg .05 .02
❑ 205 Brian Dayett .05 .02
❑ 206 Bo Diaz .05 .02
❑ 207 Craig Reynolds .05 .02
❑ 208 Brian Holton .05 .02
❑ 209 Marvell Wynne UER .05 .02
(Misspelled Marvelle on card front)
❑ 210 Dave Concepcion .10 .05
❑ 211 Mike Davis .05 .02
❑ 212 Devon White .10 .05
❑ 213 Mickey Brantley .05 .02
❑ 214 Greg Gagne .05 .02
❑ 215 Oddibe McDowell .05 .02
❑ 216 Jimmy Key .10 .05
❑ 217 Dave Bergman .05 .02
❑ 218 Calvin Schiraldi .05 .02
❑ 219 Larry Sheets .05 .02
❑ 220 Mike Easler .05 .02
❑ 221 Kurt Stillwell .05 .02
❑ 222 Chuck Jackson .05 .02
❑ 223 Dave Martinez .05 .02
❑ 224 Tim Leary .05 .02
❑ 225 Steve Garvey .15 .07
❑ 226 Greg Mathews .05 .02
❑ 227 Doug Sisk .05 .02
❑ 228 Dave Henderson .05 .02
(Wearing Red Sox uniform; Red Sox logo on back)
❑ 229 Jimmy Dwyer .05 .02
❑ 230 Larry Owen .05 .02
❑ 231 Andre Thornton .10 .05
❑ 232 Mark Salas .05 .02
❑ 233 Tom Brookens .05 .02
❑ 234 Greg Brock .05 .02
❑ 235 Rance Mulliniks .05 .02
❑ 236 Bob Brower .05 .02
❑ 237 Joe Niekro .05 .02
❑ 238 Scott Bankhead .05 .02
❑ 239 Doug DeCinces .05 .02
❑ 240 Tommy John .10 .05
❑ 241 Rich Gedman .05 .02
❑ 242 Ted Power .05 .02
❑ 243 Dave Meads .05 .02
❑ 244 Jim Sundberg .05 .02
❑ 245 Ken Oberkfell .05 .02
❑ 246 Jimmy Jones .05 .02
❑ 247 Ken Landreaux .05 .02
❑ 248 Jose Oquendo .05 .02
❑ 249 John Mitchell .05 .02
❑ 250 Don Baylor .10 .05
❑ 251 Scott Fletcher .05 .02
❑ 252 Al Newman .05 .02
❑ 253 Carney Lansford .10 .05
❑ 254 Johnny Ray .05 .02
❑ 255 Gary Pettis .05 .02
❑ 256 Ken Phelps .05 .02
❑ 257 Rick Leach .05 .02
❑ 258 Tim Stoddard .05 .02
❑ 259 Ed Romero .05 .02
❑ 260 Sid Bream .05 .02
❑ 261A T.Niedenfuer ERR .10 .05
Misspelled Neidenfuer on card front
❑ 261B T.Niedenfuer COR .05 .02
❑ 262 Rick Dempsey .05 .02
❑ 263 Lonnie Smith .05 .02
❑ 264 Bob Forsch .05 .02
❑ 265 Barry Bonds 1.50 .70
❑ 266 Willie Randolph .10 .05
❑ 267 Mike Ramsey .05 .02
❑ 268 Don Slaught .05 .02
❑ 269 Mickey Tettleton .05 .02
❑ 270 Jerry Reuss .05 .02
❑ 271 Marc Sullivan .05 .02
❑ 272 Jim Morrison .05 .02
❑ 273 Steve Balboni .05 .02
❑ 274 Dick Schofield .05 .02
❑ 275 John Tudor .05 .02
❑ 276 Gene Larkin RC* .05 .02
❑ 277 Harold Reynolds .10 .05
❑ 278 Jerry Browne .05 .02
❑ 279 Willie Upshaw .05 .02
❑ 280 Ted Higuera .05 .02
❑ 281 Terry McGriff .05 .02
❑ 282 Terry Puhl .05 .02
❑ 283 Mark Wasinger .05 .02
❑ 284 Luis Salazar .05 .02
❑ 285 Ted Simmons .10 .05
❑ 286 John Shelby .05 .02
❑ 287 John Smiley RC* .10 .05
❑ 288 Curt Ford .05 .02
❑ 289 Steve Crawford .05 .02
❑ 290 Dan Quisenberry .05 .02
❑ 291 Alan Wiggins .05 .02
❑ 292 Randy Bush .05 .02
❑ 293 John Candelaria .05 .02
❑ 294 Tony Phillips .05 .02
❑ 295 Mike Morgan .05 .02
❑ 296 Bill Wegman .05 .02
❑ 297A Terry Francona ERR .10 .05
(Misspelled Franconia on card front)
❑ 297B Terry Francona COR .05 .02
❑ 298 Mickey Hatcher .05 .02
❑ 299 Andres Thomas .05 .02
❑ 300 Bob Stanley .05 .02
❑ 301 Al Pedrique .05 .02
❑ 302 Jim Lindeman .05 .02
❑ 303 Wally Backman .05 .02
❑ 304 Paul O'Neill .20 .09
❑ 305 Hubie Brooks .05 .02
❑ 306 Steve Buechele .05 .02
❑ 307 Bobby Thigpen .05 .02
❑ 308 George Hendrick .05 .02
❑ 309 John Moses .05 .02
❑ 310 Ron Guidry .05 .02
❑ 311 Bill Schroeder .05 .02

312	Jose Nunez	.05	.02
313	Bud Black	.05	.02
314	Joe Sambito	.05	.02
315	Scott McGregor	.05	.02
316	Rafael Santana	.05	.02
317	Frank Williams	.05	.02
318	Mike Fitzgerald	.05	.02
319	Rick Mahler	.05	.02
320	Jim Gott	.05	.02
321	Mariano Duncan	.05	.02
322	Jose Guzman	.05	.02
323	Lee Guetterman	.05	.02
324	Dan Gladden	.05	.02
325	Gary Carter	.15	.07
326	Tracy Jones	.05	.02
327	Floyd Youmans	.05	.02
328	Bill Dawley	.05	.02
329	Paul Noce	.05	.02
330	Angel Salazar	.05	.02
331	Goose Gossage	.15	.07
332	George Frazier	.05	.02
333	Ruppert Jones	.05	.02
334	Billy Joe Robidoux	.05	.02
335	Mike Scott	.05	.02
336	Randy Myers	.15	.07
337	Bob Sebra	.05	.02
338	Eric Show	.05	.02
339	Mitch Williams	.05	.02
340	Paul Molitor	.20	.09
341	Gus Polidor	.05	.02
342	Steve Trout	.05	.02
343	Jerry Don Gleaton	.05	.02
344	Bob Knepper	.05	.02
345	Mitch Webster	.05	.02
346	John Morris	.05	.02
347	Andy Hawkins	.05	.02
348	Dave Leiper	.05	.02
349	Ernest Riles	.05	.02
350	Dwight Gooden	.10	.05
351	Dave Righetti	.05	.02
352	Pat Dodson	.05	.02
353	John Habyan	.05	.02
354	Jim Deshaies	.05	.02
355	Butch Wynegar	.05	.02
356	Bryn Smith	.05	.02
357	Matt Young	.05	.02
358	Tom Pagnozzi RC	.05	.02
359	Floyd Rayford	.05	.02
360	Darryl Strawberry	.10	.05
361	Sal Butera	.05	.02
362	Domingo Ramos	.05	.02
363	Chris Brown	.05	.02
364	Jose Gonzalez	.05	.02
365	Dave Smith	.05	.02
366	Andy McGaffigan	.05	.02
367	Stan Javier	.05	.02
368	Henry Cotto	.05	.02
369	Mike Birkbeck	.05	.02
370	Len Dykstra	.10	.05
371	Dave Collins	.05	.02
372	Spike Owen	.05	.02
373	Geno Petralli	.05	.02
374	Ron Karkovice	.05	.02
375	Shane Rawley	.05	.02
376	DeWayne Buice	.05	.02
377	Bill Pecota RC*	.05	.02
378	Leon Durham	.05	.02
379	Ed Olwine	.05	.02
380	Bruce Hurst	.05	.02
381	Bob McClure	.05	.02
382	Mark Thurmond	.05	.02
383	Buddy Biancalana	.05	.02
384	Tim Conroy	.05	.02
385	Tony Gwynn	.40	.18
386	Greg Gross	.05	.02
387	Barry Lyons	.05	.02
388	Mike Felder	.05	.02
389	Pat Clements	.05	.02
390	Ken Griffey	.10	.05
391	Mark Davis	.05	.02
392	Jose Rijo	.05	.02
393	Mike Young	.05	.02
394	Willie Fraser	.05	.02
395	Dion James	.05	.02
396	Steve Shields	.05	.02
397	Randy St.Claire	.05	.02
398	Danny Jackson	.05	.02
399	Cecil Fielder	.15	.07
400	Keith Hernandez	.10	.05
401	Don Carman	.05	.02
402	Chuck Crim	.05	.02
403	Rob Woodward	.05	.02
404	Junior Ortiz	.05	.02
405	Glenn Wilson	.05	.02
406	Ken Howell	.05	.02
407	Jeff Kunkel	.05	.02
408	Jeff Reed	.05	.02
409	Chris James	.05	.02
410	Zane Smith	.05	.02
411	Ken Dixon	.05	.02
412	Ricky Horton	.05	.02
413	Frank DiPino	.05	.02
414	Shane Mack	.05	.02
415	Danny Cox	.05	.02
416	Andy Van Slyke	.10	.05
417	Danny Heep	.05	.02
418	John Cangelosi	.05	.02
419A	J.Christensen ERR Christiansen on card front	.10	.05
419B	J.Christensen COR	.05	.02
420	Joey Cora RC	.20	.09
421	Mike LaValliere	.05	.02
422	Kelly Gruber	.05	.02
423	Bruce Benedict	.05	.02
424	Len Matuszek	.05	.02
425	Kent Tekulve	.05	.02
426	Rafael Ramirez	.05	.02
427	Mike Flanagan	.05	.02
428	Mike Gallego	.05	.02
429	Juan Castillo	.05	.02
430	Neal Heaton	.05	.02
431	Phil Garner	.05	.02
432	Mike Dunne	.05	.02
433	Wallace Johnson	.05	.02
434	Jack O'Connor	.05	.02
435	Steve Jeltz	.05	.02
436	Donell Nixon	.05	.02
437	Jack Lazorko	.05	.02
438	Keith Comstock	.05	.02
439	Jeff D. Robinson	.05	.02
440	Graig Nettles	.10	.05
441	Mel Hall	.05	.02
442	Gerald Young	.05	.02
443	Gary Redus	.05	.02
444	Charlie Moore	.05	.02
445	Bill Madlock	.10	.05
446	Mark Clear	.05	.02
447	Greg Booker	.05	.02
448	Rick Schu	.05	.02
449	Ron Kittle	.05	.02
450	Dale Murphy	.20	.09
451	Bob Dernier	.05	.02
452	Dale Mohorcic	.05	.02
453	Rafael Belliard	.05	.02
454	Charlie Puleo	.05	.02
455	Dwayne Murphy	.05	.02
456	Jim Eisenreich	.20	.09
457	David Palmer	.05	.02
458	Dave Stewart	.10	.05
459	Pascual Perez	.05	.02
460	Glenn Davis	.05	.02
461	Dan Petry	.05	.02
462	Jim Winn	.05	.02
463	Darrell Miller	.05	.02
464	Mike Moore	.05	.02
465	Mike LaCoss	.05	.02
466	Steve Farr	.05	.02
467	Jerry Mumphrey	.05	.02
468	Kevin Gross	.05	.02
469	Bruce Bochy	.05	.02
470	Orel Hershiser	.10	.05
471	Eric King	.05	.02
472	Ellis Burks RC	.40	.18
473	Darren Daulton	.10	.05
474	Mookie Wilson	.10	.05
475	Frank Viola	.05	.02
476	Ron Robinson	.05	.02
477	Bob Melvin	.05	.02
478	Jeff Musselman	.05	.02
479	Charlie Kerfeld	.05	.02
480	Richard Dotson	.05	.02
481	Kevin Mitchell	.10	.05
482	Gary Roenicke	.05	.02
483	Tim Flannery	.05	.02
484	Rich Yett	.05	.02
485	Pete Incaviglia	.05	.02
486	Rick Cerone	.05	.02
487	Tony Armas	.05	.02
488	Jerry Reed	.05	.02
489	Dave Lopes	.10	.05
490	Frank Tanana	.05	.02
491	Mike Loynd	.05	.02
492	Bruce Ruffin	.05	.02
493	Chris Speier	.05	.02
494	Tom Hume	.05	.02
495	Jesse Orosco	.05	.02
496	Robbie Wine UER (Misspelled Robby on card front)	.05	.02
497	Jeff Montgomery RC	.20	.09
498	Jeff Dedmon	.05	.02
499	Luis Aguayo	.05	.02
500	Reggie Jackson (Oakland A's)	.20	.09
501	Reggie Jackson (Baltimore Orioles)	.20	.09
502	Reggie Jackson (New York Yankees)	.20	.09
503	Reggie Jackson (California Angels)	.20	.09
504	Reggie Jackson (Oakland A's)	.20	.09
505	Billy Hatcher	.05	.02
506	Ed Lynch	.05	.02
507	Willie Hernandez	.05	.02
508	Jose DeLeon	.05	.02
509	Joel Youngblood	.05	.02
510	Bob Welch	.05	.02
511	Steve Ontiveros	.05	.02
512	Randy Ready	.05	.02
513	Juan Nieves	.05	.02
514	Jeff Russell	.05	.02
515	Von Hayes	.05	.02
516	Mark Gubicza	.05	.02
517	Ken Dayley	.05	.02
518	Don Aase	.05	.02
519	Rick Reuschel	.05	.02
520	Mike Henneman RC*	.10	.05
521	Rick Aguilera	.10	.05
522	Jay Howell	.05	.02
523	Ed Correa	.05	.02
524	Manny Trillo	.05	.02
525	Kirk Gibson	.10	.05
526	Wally Ritchie	.05	.02
527	Al Nipper	.05	.02
528	Atlee Hammaker	.05	.02
529	Shawon Dunston	.05	.02
530	Jim Clancy	.05	.02
531	Tom Paciorek	.10	.05
532	Joel Skinner	.05	.02
533	Scott Garrelts	.05	.02
534	Tom O'Malley	.05	.02
535	John Franco	.10	.05
536	Paul Kilgus	.05	.02
537	Darrell Porter	.05	.02
538	Walt Terrell	.05	.02
539	Bill Long	.05	.02
540	George Bell	.05	.02
541	Jeff Sellers	.05	.02
542	Joe Boever	.05	.02
543	Steve Howe	.05	.02
544	Scott Sanderson	.05	.02
545	Jack Morris	.10	.05
546	Todd Benzinger RC*	.05	.02
547	Steve Henderson	.05	.02
548	Eddie Milner	.05	.02
549	Jeff M. Robinson	.05	.02
550	Cal Ripken	.75	.35
551	Jody Davis	.05	.02
552	Kirk McCaskill	.05	.02
553	Craig Lefferts	.05	.02
554	Darnell Coles	.05	.02
555	Phil Niekro	.20	.09
556	Mike Aldrete	.05	.02
557	Pat Perry	.05	.02
558	Juan Agosto	.05	.02
559	Rob Murphy	.05	.02

❑ 560 Dennis Rasmussen .... .05 .02
❑ 561 Manny Lee .... .05 .02
❑ 562 Jeff Blauser RC .... .20 .09
❑ 563 Bob Ojeda .... .05 .02
❑ 564 Dave Dravecky .... .10 .05
❑ 565 Gene Garber .... .05 .02
❑ 566 Ron Roenicke .... .05 .02
❑ 567 Tommy Hinzo .... .05 .02
❑ 568 Eric Nolte .... .05 .02
❑ 569 Ed Hearn .... .05 .02
❑ 570 Mark Davidson .... .05 .02
❑ 571 Jim Walewander .... .05 .02
❑ 572 Donnie Hill UER .... .05 .02
(84 Stolen Base
total listed as 7)
❑ 573 Jamie Moyer .... .10 .05
❑ 574 Ken Schrom .... .05 .02
❑ 575 Nolan Ryan .... 1.00 .45
❑ 576 Jim Acker .... .05 .02
❑ 577 Jamie Quirk .... .05 .02
❑ 578 Jay Aldrich .... .05 .02
❑ 579 Claudell Washington ...... .05 .02
❑ 580 Jeff Leonard .... .05 .02
❑ 581 Carmen Castillo .... .05 .02
❑ 582 Daryl Boston .... .05 .02
❑ 583 Jeff DeWillis .... .05 .02
❑ 584 John Marzano .... .05 .02
❑ 585 Bill Gullickson .... .05 .02
❑ 586 Andy Allanson .... .05 .02
❑ 587 Lee Tunnell UER .... .05 .02
(1987 stat line
reads .4.84 ERA)
❑ 588 Gene Nelson .... .05 .02
❑ 589 Dave LaPoint .... .05 .02
❑ 590 Harold Baines .... .10 .05
❑ 591 Bill Buckner .... .10 .05
❑ 592 Carlton Fisk .... .20 .09
❑ 593 Rick Manning .... .05 .02
❑ 594 Doug Jones RC .... .20 .09
❑ 595 Tom Candiotti .... .05 .02
❑ 596 Steve Lake .... .05 .02
❑ 597 Jose Lind RC .... .05 .02
❑ 598 Ross Jones .... .05 .02
❑ 599 Gary Matthews .... .05 .02
❑ 600 Fernando Valenzuela .... .10 .05
❑ 601 Dennis Martinez .... .10 .05
❑ 602 Les Lancaster .... .05 .02
❑ 603 Ozzie Guillen .... .05 .02
❑ 604 Tony Bernazard .... .05 .02
❑ 605 Chili Davis .... .15 .07
❑ 606 Roy Smalley .... .05 .02
❑ 607 Ivan Calderon .... .05 .02
❑ 608 Jay Tibbs .... .05 .02
❑ 609 Guy Hoffman .... .05 .02
❑ 610 Doyle Alexander .... .05 .02
❑ 611 Mike Bielecki .... .05 .02
❑ 612 Shawn Hillegas .... .05 .02
❑ 613 Keith Atherton .... .05 .02
❑ 614 Eric Plunk .... .05 .02
❑ 615 Sid Fernandez .... .05 .02
❑ 616 Dennis Lamp .... .05 .02
❑ 617 Dave Engle .... .05 .02
❑ 618 Harry Spilman .... .05 .02
❑ 619 Don Robinson .... .05 .02
❑ 620 John Farrell .... .05 .02
❑ 621 Nelson Liriano .... .05 .02
❑ 622 Floyd Bannister .... .05 .02
❑ 623 Randy Milligan RC .... .05 .02
❑ 624 Kevin Elster .... .05 .02
❑ 625 Jody Reed RC .... .10 .05
❑ 626 Shawn Abner .... .05 .02
❑ 627 Kirt Manwaring RC .... .05 .02
❑ 628 Pete Stanicek .... .05 .02
❑ 629 Rob Ducey .... .05 .02
❑ 630 Steve Kiefer .... .05 .02
❑ 631 Gary Thurman .... .05 .02
❑ 632 Darrel Akerfelds .... .05 .02
❑ 633 Dave Clark .... .05 .02
❑ 634 Roberto Kelly RC .... .20 .09
❑ 635 Keith Hughes .... .05 .02
❑ 636 John Davis .... .05 .02
❑ 637 Mike Devereaux RC ...... .10 .05
❑ 638 Tom Glavine RC .... 1.25 .55
❑ 639 Keith A. Miller RC .... .05 .02
❑ 640 Chris Gwynn RC UER .... .10 .05
(Wrong batting and
throwing on back)
❑ 641 Tim Crews RC .... .05 .02
❑ 642 Mackey Sasser RC .... .05 .02
❑ 643 Vicente Palacios .... .05 .02
❑ 644 Kevin Romine .... .05 .02
❑ 645 Gregg Jefferies RC .... .20 .09
❑ 646 Jeff Treadway RC .... .05 .02
❑ 647 Ron Gant RC .... .25 .11
❑ 648 Mark McGwire .... 1.00 .45
Matt Nokes
Rookie Sluggers
❑ 649 Eric Davis .... .10 .05
Tim Raines
Speed and Power
❑ 650 Don Mattingly .... .15 .07
Jack Clark
❑ 651 Tony Fernandez .... .25 .11
Alan Trammell
Cal Ripken
❑ 652 Vince Coleman HL .... .05 .02
100 Stolen Bases
❑ 653 Kirby Puckett HL .... .25 .11
10 Hits in a Row
❑ 654 Benito Santiago HL .... .05 .02
Hitting Streak
❑ 655 Juan Nieves HL .... .05 .02
No Hitter
❑ 656 Steve Bedrosian HL ...... .05 .02
Saves Record
❑ 657 Mike Schmidt HL .... .15 .07
500 Homers
❑ 658 Don Mattingly HL .... .15 .07
Home Run Streak
❑ 659 Mark McGwire HL .... 1.00 .45
Rookie HR Record
❑ 660 Paul Molitor HL .... .15 .07
Hitting Streak

1988 Score Rookie/Traded

	MINT	NRMT
COMP.FACT.SET (110)	40.00	18.00

❑ 1T Jack Clark .... .75 .35
❑ 2T Danny Jackson .... .25 .11
❑ 3T Brett Butler .... .75 .35
❑ 4T Kurt Stillwell .... .25 .11
❑ 5T Tom Brunansky .... .25 .11
❑ 6T Dennis Lamp .... .25 .11
❑ 7T Jose DeLeon .... .25 .11
❑ 8T Tom Herr .... .25 .11
❑ 9T Keith Moreland .... .25 .11
❑ 10T Kirk Gibson .... 2.00 .90
❑ 11T Bud Black .... .25 .11
❑ 12T Rafael Ramirez .... .25 .11
❑ 13T Luis Salazar .... .25 .11
❑ 14T Goose Gossage .... 1.25 .55
❑ 15T Bob Welch .... .25 .11
❑ 16T Vance Law .... .25 .11
❑ 17T Ray Knight .... .25 .11
❑ 18T Dan Quisenberry .... .25 .11
❑ 19T Don Slaught .... .25 .11
❑ 20T Lee Smith .... .75 .35
❑ 21T Rick Cerone .... .25 .11
❑ 22T Pat Tabler .... .25 .11
❑ 23T Larry McWilliams .... .25 .11
❑ 24T Ricky Horton .... .25 .11
❑ 25T Graig Nettles .... .75 .35
❑ 26T Dan Petry .... .25 .11
❑ 27T Jose Rijo .... .25 .11
❑ 28T Chili Davis .... 1.25 .55
❑ 29T Dickie Thon .... .25 .11
❑ 30T Mackey Sasser .... .25 .11
❑ 31T Mickey Tettleton .... .25 .11
❑ 32T Rick Dempsey .... .25 .11
❑ 33T Ron Hassey .... .25 .11
❑ 34T Phil Bradley .... .25 .11
❑ 35T Jay Howell .... .25 .11
❑ 36T Bill Buckner .... .75 .35
❑ 37T Alfredo Griffin .... .25 .11
❑ 38T Gary Pettis .... .25 .11
❑ 39T Calvin Schiraldi .... .25 .11
❑ 40T John Candelaria .... .25 .11
❑ 41T Joe Orsulak .... .25 .11
❑ 42T Willie Upshaw .... .25 .11
❑ 43T Herm Winningham .... .25 .11
❑ 44T Ron Kittle .... .25 .11
❑ 45T Bob Dernier .... .25 .11
❑ 46T Steve Balboni .... .25 .11
❑ 47T Steve Shields .... .25 .11
❑ 48T Henry Cotto .... .25 .11
❑ 49T Dave Henderson .... .25 .11
❑ 50T Dave Parker .... .75 .35
❑ 51T Mike Young .... .25 .11
❑ 52T Mark Salas .... .25 .11
❑ 53T Mike Davis .... .25 .11
❑ 54T Rafael Santana .... .25 .11
❑ 55T Don Baylor .... .75 .35
❑ 56T Dan Pasqua .... .25 .11
❑ 57T Ernest Riles .... .25 .11
❑ 58T Glenn Hubbard .... .25 .11
❑ 59T Mike Smithson .... .25 .11
❑ 60T Richard Dotson .... .25 .11
❑ 61T Jerry Reuss .... .25 .11
❑ 62T Mike Jackson .... .75 .35
❑ 63T Floyd Bannister .... .25 .11
❑ 64T Jesse Orosco .... .25 .11
❑ 65T Larry Parrish .... .25 .11
❑ 66T Jeff Bittiger .... .25 .11
❑ 67T Ray Hayward .... .25 .11
❑ 68T Ricky Jordan XRC .... .75 .35
❑ 69T Tommy Gregg .... .25 .11
❑ 70T Brady Anderson XRC .. 2.00 .90
❑ 71T Jeff Montgomery .... 2.00 .90
❑ 72T Darryl Hamilton XRC ...... .75 .35
❑ 73T Cecil Espy .... .25 .11
❑ 74T Greg Briley XRC .... .25 .11
❑ 75T Joey Meyer .... .25 .11
❑ 76T Mike Macfarlane XRC .... .25 .11
❑ 77T Oswald Peraza .... .25 .11
❑ 78T Jack Armstrong XRC ...... .25 .11
❑ 79T Don Heinkel .... .25 .11
❑ 80T Mark Grace XRC 8.00 3.60
❑ 81T Steve Curry .... .25 .11
❑ 82T Damon Berryhill XRC .... .25 .11
❑ 83T Steve Ellsworth .... .25 .11
❑ 84T Pete Smith XRC* .... .25 .11
❑ 85T Jack McDowell XRC .... 2.00 .90
❑ 86T Rob Dibble XRC .... .75 .35
❑ 87T Bryan Harvey UER .... .75 .35
(Games Pitched 47,
Innings 5) XRC
❑ 88T John Dopson .... .25 .11
❑ 89T Dave Gallagher .... .25 .11
❑ 90T Todd Stottlemyre XRC 2.00 .90
❑ 91T Mike Schooler .... .25 .11
❑ 92T Don Gordon .... .25 .11
❑ 93T Sil Campusano .... .25 .11
❑ 94T Jeff Pico .... .25 .11
❑ 95T Jay Buhner XRC 3.00 1.35
❑ 96T Nelson Santovenia .... .25 .11
❑ 97T Al Leiter XRC* .... 2.00 .90
❑ 98T Luis Alicea XRC .... .75 .35
❑ 99T Pat Borders XRC .... .75 .35
❑ 100T Chris Sabo XRC .... .75 .35
❑ 101T Tim Belcher .... .75 .35
❑ 102T Walt Weiss XRC* .... .75 .35
❑ 103T Craig Biggio XRC 10.00 4.50
❑ 104T Don August .... .25 .11
❑ 105T Roberto Alomar XRC 20.00 9.00
❑ 106T Todd Burns .... .25 .11
❑ 107T John Costello .... .25 .11
❑ 108T Melido Perez XRC* ...... .25 .11

❑ 109T	Darrin Jackson XRC	.25	.11
❑ 110T	O.Destrade XRC	.75	.35

1989 Score

	MINT	NRMT
COMPLETE SET (660)	8.00	3.60
COMP.FACT.SET (660)	10.00	4.50

		MINT	NRMT
❑ 1	Jose Canseco	.20	.09
❑ 2	Andre Dawson	.15	.07
❑ 3	Mark McGwire UER	1.00	.45
❑ 4	Benito Santiago	.05	.02
❑ 5	Rick Reuschel	.05	.02
❑ 6	Fred McGriff	.20	.09
❑ 7	Kal Daniels	.05	.02
❑ 8	Gary Gaetti	.10	.05
❑ 9	Ellis Burks	.15	.07
❑ 10	Darryl Strawberry	.10	.05
❑ 11	Julio Franco	.05	.02
❑ 12	Lloyd Moseby	.05	.02
❑ 13	Jeff Pico	.05	.02
❑ 14	Johnny Ray	.05	.02
❑ 15	Cal Ripken	.75	.35
❑ 16	Dick Schofield	.05	.02
❑ 17	Mel Hall	.05	.02
❑ 18	Bill Ripken	.05	.02
❑ 19	Brook Jacoby	.05	.02
❑ 20	Kirby Puckett	.50	.23
❑ 21	Bill Doran	.05	.02
❑ 22	Pete O'Brien	.05	.02
❑ 23	Matt Nokes	.05	.02
❑ 24	Brian Fisher	.05	.02
❑ 25	Jack Clark	.05	.02
❑ 26	Gary Pettis	.05	.02
❑ 27	Dave Valle	.05	.02
❑ 28	Willie Wilson	.05	.02
❑ 29	Curt Young	.05	.02
❑ 30	Dale Murphy	.20	.09
❑ 31	Barry Larkin	.20	.09
❑ 32	Dave Stewart	.10	.05
❑ 33	Mike LaValliere	.05	.02
❑ 34	Glenn Hubbard	.05	.02
❑ 35	Ryne Sandberg	.25	.11
❑ 36	Tony Pena	.05	.02
❑ 37	Greg Walker	.05	.02
❑ 38	Von Hayes	.05	.02
❑ 39	Kevin Mitchell	.10	.05
❑ 40	Tim Raines	.10	.05
❑ 41	Keith Hernandez	.10	.05
❑ 42	Keith Moreland	.05	.02
❑ 43	Ruben Sierra	.05	.02
❑ 44	Chet Lemon	.05	.02
❑ 45	Willie Randolph	.10	.05
❑ 46	Andy Allanson	.05	.02
❑ 47	Candy Maldonado	.05	.02
❑ 48	Sid Bream	.05	.02
❑ 49	Denny Walling	.05	.02
❑ 50	Dave Winfield	.20	.09
❑ 51	Alvin Davis	.05	.02
❑ 52	Cory Snyder	.05	.02
❑ 53	Hubie Brooks	.05	.02
❑ 54	Chili Davis	.10	.05
❑ 55	Kevin Seitzer	.05	.02
❑ 56	Jose Uribe	.05	.02
❑ 57	Tony Fernandez	.05	.02
❑ 58	Tim Teufel	.05	.02
❑ 59	Oddibe McDowell	.05	.02
❑ 60	Les Lancaster	.05	.02
❑ 61	Billy Hatcher	.05	.02
❑ 62	Dan Gladden	.05	.02
❑ 63	Marty Barrett	.05	.02
❑ 64	Nick Esasky	.05	.02
❑ 65	Wally Joyner	.10	.05
❑ 66	Mike Greenwell	.05	.02
❑ 67	Ken Williams	.05	.02
❑ 68	Bob Horner	.05	.02
❑ 69	Steve Sax	.05	.02
❑ 70	Rickey Henderson	.40	.18
❑ 71	Mitch Webster	.05	.02
❑ 72	Rob Deer	.05	.02
❑ 73	Jim Presley	.05	.02
❑ 74	Albert Hall	.05	.02
❑ 75	George Brett COR (At age 35)	.40	.18
❑ 75A	George Brett ERR (At age 33)	.75	.35
❑ 76	Brian Downing	.05	.02
❑ 77	Dave Martinez	.05	.02
❑ 78	Scott Fletcher	.05	.02
❑ 79	Phil Bradley	.05	.02
❑ 80	Ozzie Smith	.25	.11
❑ 81	Larry Sheets	.05	.02
❑ 82	Mike Aldrete	.05	.02
❑ 83	Darnell Coles	.05	.02
❑ 84	Len Dykstra	.10	.05
❑ 85	Jim Rice	.10	.05
❑ 86	Jeff Treadway	.05	.02
❑ 87	Jose Lind	.05	.02
❑ 88	Willie McGee	.10	.05
❑ 89	Mickey Brantley	.05	.02
❑ 90	Tony Gwynn	.40	.18
❑ 91	R.J. Reynolds	.05	.02
❑ 92	Milt Thompson	.05	.02
❑ 93	Kevin McReynolds	.05	.02
❑ 94	Eddie Murray UER ('86 batting .205, should be .305)	.20	.09
❑ 95	Lance Parrish	.05	.02
❑ 96	Ron Kittle	.05	.02
❑ 97	Gerald Young	.05	.02
❑ 98	Ernie Whitt	.05	.02
❑ 99	Jeff Reed	.05	.02
❑ 100	Don Mattingly	.50	.23
❑ 101	Gerald Perry	.05	.02
❑ 102	Vance Law	.05	.02
❑ 103	John Shelby	.05	.02
❑ 104	Chris Sabo RC*	.05	.02
❑ 105	Danny Tartabull	.05	.02
❑ 106	Glenn Wilson	.05	.02
❑ 107	Mark Davidson	.05	.02
❑ 108	Dave Parker	.10	.05
❑ 109	Eric Davis	.10	.05
❑ 110	Alan Trammell	.15	.07
❑ 111	Ozzie Virgil	.05	.02
❑ 112	Frank Tanana	.05	.02
❑ 113	Rafael Ramirez	.05	.02
❑ 114	Dennis Martinez	.10	.05
❑ 115	Jose DeLeon	.05	.02
❑ 116	Bob Ojeda	.05	.02
❑ 117	Doug Drabek	.05	.02
❑ 118	Andy Hawkins	.05	.02
❑ 119	Greg Maddux	.60	.25
❑ 120	Cecil Fielder UER (Reversed Photo on back)	.10	.05
❑ 121	Mike Scioscia	.05	.02
❑ 122	Dan Petry	.05	.02
❑ 123	Terry Kennedy	.05	.02
❑ 124	Kelly Downs	.05	.02
❑ 125	Greg Gross UER (Gregg on back)	.05	.02
❑ 126	Fred Lynn	.05	.02
❑ 127	Barry Bonds	.75	.35
❑ 128	Harold Baines	.10	.05
❑ 129	Doyle Alexander	.05	.02
❑ 130	Kevin Elster	.05	.02
❑ 131	Mike Heath	.05	.02
❑ 132	Teddy Higuera	.05	.02
❑ 133	Charlie Leibrandt	.05	.02
❑ 134	Tim Laudner	.05	.02
❑ 135A	Ray Knight ERR (Reverse negative)	.20	.09
❑ 135B	Ray Knight COR	.05	.02
❑ 136	Howard Johnson	.05	.02
❑ 137	Terry Pendleton	.10	.05
❑ 138	Andy McGaffigan	.05	.02
❑ 139	Ken Oberkfell	.05	.02
❑ 140	Butch Wynegar	.05	.02
❑ 141	Rob Murphy	.05	.02
❑ 142	Rich Renteria	.05	.02
❑ 143	Jose Guzman	.05	.02
❑ 144	Andres Galarraga	.15	.07
❑ 145	Ricky Horton	.05	.02
❑ 146	Frank DiPino	.05	.02
❑ 147	Glenn Braggs	.05	.02
❑ 148	John Kruk	.10	.05
❑ 149	Mike Schmidt	.40	.18
❑ 150	Lee Smith	.10	.05
❑ 151	Robin Yount	.20	.09
❑ 152	Mark Eichhorn	.05	.02
❑ 153	DeWayne Buice	.05	.02
❑ 154	B.J. Surhoff	.10	.05
❑ 155	Vince Coleman	.05	.02
❑ 156	Tony Phillips	.05	.02
❑ 157	Willie Fraser	.05	.02
❑ 158	Lance McCullers	.05	.02
❑ 159	Greg Gagne	.05	.02
❑ 160	Jesse Barfield	.05	.02
❑ 161	Mark Langston	.05	.02
❑ 162	Kurt Stillwell	.05	.02
❑ 163	Dion James	.05	.02
❑ 164	Glenn Davis	.05	.02
❑ 165	Walt Weiss	.05	.02
❑ 166	Dave Concepcion	.10	.05
❑ 167	Alfredo Griffin	.05	.02
❑ 168	Don Heinkel	.05	.02
❑ 169	Luis Rivera	.05	.02
❑ 170	Shane Rawley	.05	.02
❑ 171	Darrell Evans	.10	.05
❑ 172	Robby Thompson	.05	.02
❑ 173	Jody Davis	.05	.02
❑ 174	Andy Van Slyke	.10	.05
❑ 175	Wade Boggs UER (Bio says .364, should be .356)	.20	.09
❑ 176	Garry Templeton ('85 stats off-centered)	.05	.02
❑ 177	Gary Redus	.05	.02
❑ 178	Craig Lefferts	.05	.02
❑ 179	Carney Lansford	.10	.05
❑ 180	Ron Darling	.05	.02
❑ 181	Kirk McCaskill	.05	.02
❑ 182	Tony Armas	.05	.02
❑ 183	Steve Farr	.05	.02
❑ 184	Tom Brunansky	.05	.02
❑ 185	B.Harvey RC UER '87 games 47, should be 3	.05	.02
❑ 186	Mike Marshall	.05	.02
❑ 187	Bo Diaz	.05	.02
❑ 188	Willie Upshaw	.05	.02
❑ 189	Mike Pagliarulo	.05	.02
❑ 190	Mike Krukow	.05	.02
❑ 191	Tommy Herr	.05	.02
❑ 192	Jim Pankovits	.05	.02
❑ 193	Dwight Evans	.10	.05
❑ 194	Kelly Gruber	.05	.02
❑ 195	Bobby Bonilla	.10	.05
❑ 196	Wallace Johnson	.05	.02
❑ 197	Dave Stieb	.05	.02
❑ 198	Pat Borders RC*	.10	.05
❑ 199	Rafael Palmeiro	.25	.11
❑ 200	Dwight Gooden	.10	.05
❑ 201	Pete Incaviglia	.05	.02
❑ 202	Chris James	.05	.02
❑ 203	Marvell Wynne	.05	.02
❑ 204	Pat Sheridan	.05	.02
❑ 205	Don Baylor	.10	.05
❑ 206	Paul O'Neill	.20	.09
❑ 207	Pete Smith	.05	.02
❑ 208	Mark McLemore	.05	.02
❑ 209	Henry Cotto	.05	.02
❑ 210	Kirk Gibson	.10	.05
❑ 211	Claudell Washington	.05	.02
❑ 212	Randy Bush	.05	.02
❑ 213	Joe Carter	.15	.07
❑ 214	Bill Buckner	.10	.05
❑ 215	Bert Blyleven UER (Wrong birth year)	.10	.05

❑ 216 Brett Butler .10 .05
❑ 217 Lee Mazzilli .05 .02
❑ 218 Spike Owen .05 .02
❑ 219 Bill Swift .05 .02
❑ 220 Tim Wallach .05 .02
❑ 221 David Cone .10 .05
❑ 222 Don Carman .05 .02
❑ 223 Rich Gossage .10 .05
❑ 224 Bob Walk .05 .02
❑ 225 Dave Righetti .05 .02
❑ 226 Kevin Bass .05 .02
❑ 227 Kevin Gross .05 .02
❑ 228 Tim Burke .05 .02
❑ 229 Rick Mahler .05 .02
❑ 230 Lou Whitaker UER .10 .05
(252 games in '85,
should be 152)
❑ 231 Luis Alicea RC* .05 .02
❑ 232 Roberto Alomar .30 .14
❑ 233 Bob Boone .10 .05
❑ 234 Dickie Thon .05 .02
❑ 235 Shawon Dunston .05 .02
❑ 236 Pete Stanicek .05 .02
❑ 237 Craig Biggio RC .75 .35
(Inconsistent design,
portrait on front)
❑ 238 Dennis Boyd .05 .02
❑ 239 Tom Candiotti .05 .02
❑ 240 Gary Carter .15 .07
❑ 241 Mike Stanley .05 .02
❑ 242 Ken Phelps .05 .02
❑ 243 Chris Bosio .05 .02
❑ 244 Les Straker .05 .02
❑ 245 Dave Smith .05 .02
❑ 246 John Candelaria .05 .02
❑ 247 Joe Orsulak .05 .02
❑ 248 Storm Davis .05 .02
❑ 249 Floyd Bannister UER .05 .02
(ML Batting Record)
❑ 250 Jack Morris .10 .05
❑ 251 Bret Saberhagen .10 .05
❑ 252 Tom Niedenfuer .05 .02
❑ 253 Neal Heaton .05 .02
❑ 254 Eric Show .05 .02
❑ 255 Juan Samuel .05 .02
❑ 256 Dale Sveum .05 .02
❑ 257 Jim Gott .05 .02
❑ 258 Scott Garrelts .05 .02
❑ 259 Larry McWilliams .05 .02
❑ 260 Steve Bedrosian .05 .02
❑ 261 Jack Howell .05 .02
❑ 262 Jay Tibbs .05 .02
❑ 263 Jamie Moyer .05 .02
❑ 264 Doug Sisk .05 .02
❑ 265 Todd Worrell .05 .02
❑ 266 John Farrell .05 .02
❑ 267 Dave Collins .05 .02
❑ 268 Sid Fernandez .05 .02
❑ 269 Tom Brookens .05 .02
❑ 270 Shane Mack .05 .02
❑ 271 Paul Kilgus .05 .02
❑ 272 Chuck Crim .05 .02
❑ 273 Bob Knepper .05 .02
❑ 274 Mike Moore .05 .02
❑ 275 Guillermo Hernandez .05 .02
❑ 276 Dennis Eckersley .15 .07
❑ 277 Graig Nettles .10 .05
❑ 278 Rich Dotson .05 .02
❑ 279 Larry Herndon .05 .02
❑ 280 Gene Larkin .05 .02
❑ 281 Roger McDowell .05 .02
❑ 282 Greg Swindell .05 .02
❑ 283 Juan Agosto .05 .02
❑ 284 Jeff M. Robinson .05 .02
❑ 285 Mike Dunne .05 .02
❑ 286 Greg Mathews .05 .02
❑ 287 Kent Tekulve .05 .02
❑ 288 Jerry Mumphrey .05 .02
❑ 289 Jack McDowell .10 .05
❑ 290 Frank Viola .05 .02
❑ 291 Mark Gubicza .05 .02
❑ 292 Dave Schmidt .05 .02
❑ 293 Mike Henneman .05 .02
❑ 294 Jimmy Jones .05 .02
❑ 295 Charlie Hough .10 .05
❑ 296 Rafael Santana .05 .02
❑ 297 Chris Speier .05 .02
❑ 298 Mike Witt .05 .02
❑ 299 Pascual Perez .05 .02
❑ 300 Nolan Ryan 1.00 .45
❑ 301 Mitch Williams .05 .02
❑ 302 Mookie Wilson .10 .05
❑ 303 Mackey Sasser .05 .02
❑ 304 John Cerutti .05 .02
❑ 305 Jeff Reardon .10 .05
❑ 306 Randy Myers UER .10 .05
(6 hits in '87,
should be 61)
❑ 307 Greg Brock .05 .02
❑ 308 Bob Welch .05 .02
❑ 309 Jeff D. Robinson .05 .02
❑ 310 Harold Reynolds .05 .02
❑ 311 Jim Walewander .05 .02
❑ 312 Dave Magadan .05 .02
❑ 313 Jim Gantner .05 .02
❑ 314 Walt Terrell .05 .02
❑ 315 Wally Backman .05 .02
❑ 316 Luis Salazar .05 .02
❑ 317 Rick Rhoden .05 .02
❑ 318 Tom Henke .05 .02
❑ 319 Mike Macfarlane RC* .05 .02
❑ 320 Dan Plesac .05 .02
❑ 321 Calvin Schiraldi .05 .02
❑ 322 Stan Javier .05 .02
❑ 323 Devon White .10 .05
❑ 324 Scott Bradley .05 .02
❑ 325 Bruce Hurst .05 .02
❑ 326 Manny Lee .05 .02
❑ 327 Rick Aguilera .10 .05
❑ 328 Bruce Ruffin .05 .02
❑ 329 Ed Whitson .05 .02
❑ 330 Bo Jackson .15 .07
❑ 331 Ivan Calderon .05 .02
❑ 332 Mickey Hatcher .05 .02
❑ 333 Barry Jones .05 .02
❑ 334 Ron Hassey .05 .02
❑ 335 Bill Wegman .05 .02
❑ 336 Damon Berryhill .05 .02
❑ 337 Steve Ontiveros .05 .02
❑ 338 Dan Pasqua .05 .02
❑ 339 Bill Pecota .05 .02
❑ 340 Greg Cadaret .05 .02
❑ 341 Scott Bankhead .05 .02
❑ 342 Ron Guidry .10 .05
❑ 343 Danny Heep .05 .02
❑ 344 Bob Brower .05 .02
❑ 345 Rich Gedman .05 .02
❑ 346 Nelson Santovenia .05 .02
❑ 347 George Bell .05 .02
❑ 348 Ted Power .05 .02
❑ 349 Mark Grant .05 .02
❑ 350 Roger Clemens COR .50 .23
(78 career wins)
❑ 350A Roger Clemens ERR 1.25 .55
(778 career wins)
❑ 351 Bill Long .05 .02
❑ 352 Jay Bell .15 .07
❑ 353 Steve Balboni .05 .02
❑ 354 Bob Kipper .05 .02
❑ 355 Steve Jeltz .05 .02
❑ 356 Jesse Orosco .05 .02
❑ 357 Bob Dernier .05 .02
❑ 358 Mickey Tettleton .05 .02
❑ 359 Duane Ward .05 .02
❑ 360 Darrin Jackson .05 .02
❑ 361 Rey Quinones .05 .02
❑ 362 Mark Grace .20 .09
❑ 363 Steve Lake .05 .02
❑ 364 Pat Perry .05 .02
❑ 365 Terry Steinbach .10 .05
❑ 366 Alan Ashby .05 .02
❑ 367 Jeff Montgomery .10 .05
❑ 368 Steve Buechele .05 .02
❑ 369 Chris Brown .05 .02
❑ 370 Orel Hershiser .10 .05
❑ 371 Todd Benzinger .05 .02
❑ 372 Ron Gant .10 .05
❑ 373 Paul Assenmacher .05 .02
❑ 374 Joey Meyer .05 .02
❑ 375 Neil Allen .05 .02
❑ 376 Mike Davis .05 .02
❑ 377 Jeff Parrett .05 .02
❑ 378 Jay Howell .05 .02
❑ 379 Rafael Belliard .05 .02
❑ 380 Luis Polonia UER .05 .02
(2 triples in '87,
should be 10)
❑ 381 Keith Atherton .05 .02
❑ 382 Kent Hrbek .10 .05
❑ 383 Bob Stanley .05 .02
❑ 384 Dave LaPoint .05 .02
❑ 385 Rance Mulliniks .05 .02
❑ 386 Melido Perez .05 .02
❑ 387 Doug Jones .05 .02
❑ 388 Steve Lyons .05 .02
❑ 389 Alejandro Pena .05 .02
❑ 390 Frank White .10 .05
❑ 391 Pat Tabler .05 .02
❑ 392 Eric Plunk .05 .02
❑ 393 Mike Maddux .05 .02
❑ 394 Allan Anderson .05 .02
❑ 395 Bob Brenly .05 .02
❑ 396 Rick Cerone .05 .02
❑ 397 Scott Terry .05 .02
❑ 398 Mike Jackson .05 .02
❑ 399 Bobby Thigpen UER .05 .02
(Bio says 37 saves in
'88, should be 34)
❑ 400 Don Sutton .20 .09
❑ 401 Cecil Espy .05 .02
❑ 402 Junior Ortiz .05 .02
❑ 403 Mike Smithson .05 .02
❑ 404 Bud Black .05 .02
❑ 405 Tom Foley .05 .02
❑ 406 Andres Thomas .05 .02
❑ 407 Rick Sutcliffe .10 .05
❑ 408 Brian Harper .05 .02
❑ 409 John Smiley .05 .02
❑ 410 Juan Nieves .05 .02
❑ 411 Shawn Abner .05 .02
❑ 412 Wes Gardner .05 .02
❑ 413 Darren Daulton .10 .05
❑ 414 Juan Berenguer .05 .02
❑ 415 Charles Hudson .05 .02
❑ 416 Rick Honeycutt .05 .02
❑ 417 Greg Booker .05 .02
❑ 418 Tim Belcher .05 .02
❑ 419 Don August .05 .02
❑ 420 Dale Mohorcic .05 .02
❑ 421 Steve Lombardozzi .05 .02
❑ 422 Atlee Hammaker .05 .02
❑ 423 Jerry Don Gleaton .05 .02
❑ 424 Scott Bailes .05 .02
❑ 425 Bruce Sutter .05 .02
❑ 426 Randy Ready .05 .02
❑ 427 Jerry Reed .05 .02
❑ 428 Bryn Smith .05 .02
❑ 429 Tim Leary .05 .02
❑ 430 Mark Clear .05 .02
❑ 431 Terry Leach .05 .02
❑ 432 John Moses .05 .02
❑ 433 Ozzie Guillen .05 .02
❑ 434 Gene Nelson .05 .02
❑ 435 Gary Ward .05 .02
❑ 436 Luis Aguayo .05 .02
❑ 437 Fernando Valenzuela .10 .05
❑ 438 Jeff Russell UER .05 .02
(Saves total does
not add up correctly)
❑ 439 Cecilio Guante .05 .02
❑ 440 Don Robinson .05 .02
❑ 441 Rick Anderson .05 .02
❑ 442 Tom Glavine .20 .09
❑ 443 Daryl Boston .05 .02
❑ 444 Joe Price .05 .02
❑ 445 Stewart Cliburn .05 .02
❑ 446 Manny Trillo .05 .02
❑ 447 Joel Skinner .05 .02
❑ 448 Charlie Puleo .05 .02
❑ 449 Carlton Fisk .20 .09
❑ 450 Will Clark .20 .09
❑ 451 Otis Nixon .05 .02
❑ 452 Rick Schu .05 .02
❑ 453 Todd Stottlemyre UER .15 .07
(ML Batting Record)
❑ 454 Tim Birtsas .05 .02
❑ 455 Dave Gallagher .05 .02
❑ 456 Barry Lyons .05 .02

❑ 457 Fred Manrique .05 .02
❑ 458 Ernest Riles .05 .02
❑ 459 Doug Jennings .05 .02
❑ 460 Joe Magrane .05 .02
❑ 461 Jamie Quirk .05 .02
❑ 462 Jack Armstrong RC* .05 .02
❑ 463 Bobby Witt .05 .02
❑ 464 Keith A. Miller .05 .02
❑ 465 Todd Burns .05 .02
❑ 466 John Dopson .05 .02
❑ 467 Rich Yett .05 .02
❑ 468 Craig Reynolds .05 .02
❑ 469 Dave Bergman .05 .02
❑ 470 Rex Hudler .05 .02
❑ 471 Eric King .05 .02
❑ 472 Joaquin Andujar .05 .02
❑ 473 Sil Campusano .05 .02
❑ 474 Terry Mulholland .05 .02
❑ 475 Mike Flanagan .05 .02
❑ 476 Greg A. Harris .05 .02
❑ 477 Tommy John .10 .05
❑ 478 Dave Anderson .05 .02
❑ 479 Fred Toliver .05 .02
❑ 480 Jimmy Key .10 .05
❑ 481 Donell Nixon .05 .02
❑ 482 Mark Portugal .05 .02
❑ 483 Tom Pagnozzi .05 .02
❑ 484 Jeff Kunkel .05 .02
❑ 485 Frank Williams .05 .02
❑ 486 Jody Reed .05 .02
❑ 487 Roberto Kelly .10 .05
❑ 488 Shawn Hillegas UER .05 .02
(165 innings in '87,
should be 165.2)
❑ 489 Jerry Reuss .05 .02
❑ 490 Mark Davis .05 .02
❑ 491 Jeff Sellers .05 .02
❑ 492 Zane Smith .05 .02
❑ 493 Al Newman .05 .02
❑ 494 Mike Young .05 .02
❑ 495 Larry Parrish .05 .02
❑ 496 Herm Winningham .05 .02
❑ 497 Carmen Castillo .05 .02
❑ 498 Joe Hesketh .05 .02
❑ 499 Darrell Miller .05 .02
❑ 500 Mike LaCoss .05 .02
❑ 501 Charlie Lea .05 .02
❑ 502 Bruce Benedict .05 .02
❑ 503 Chuck Finley .10 .05
❑ 504 Brad Wellman .05 .02
❑ 505 Tim Crews .05 .02
❑ 506 Ken Gerhart .05 .02
❑ 507A Brian Holton ERR .05 .02
(Born 1/25/65 Denver,
should be 11/29/59
in McKeesport)
❑ 507B Brian Holton COR 2.00 .90
❑ 508 Dennis Lamp .05 .02
❑ 509 Bobby Meacham UER .05 .02
('84 games 099)
❑ 510 Tracy Jones .05 .02
❑ 511 Mike R. Fitzgerald .05 .02
❑ 512 Jeff Bittiger .05 .02
❑ 513 Tim Flannery .05 .02
❑ 514 Ray Hayward .05 .02
❑ 515 Dave Leiper .05 .02
❑ 516 Rod Scurry .05 .02
❑ 517 Carmelo Martinez .05 .02
❑ 518 Curtis Wilkerson .05 .02
❑ 519 Stan Jefferson .05 .02
❑ 520 Dan Quisenberry .05 .02
❑ 521 Lloyd McClendon .05 .02
❑ 522 Steve Trout .05 .02
❑ 523 Larry Andersen .05 .02
❑ 524 Don Aase .05 .02
❑ 525 Bob Forsch .05 .02
❑ 526 Geno Petralli .05 .02
❑ 527 Angel Salazar .05 .02
❑ 528 Mike Schooler .05 .02
❑ 529 Jose Oquendo .05 .02
❑ 530 Jay Buhner UER .10 .05
(Wearing 43 on front,
listed as 34 on back)
❑ 531 Tom Bolton .05 .02
❑ 532 Al Nipper .05 .02
❑ 533 Dave Henderson .05 .02
❑ 534 John Costello .05 .02
❑ 535 Donnie Moore .05 .02
❑ 536 Mike Laga .05 .02
❑ 537 Mike Gallego .05 .02
❑ 538 Jim Clancy .05 .02
❑ 539 Joel Youngblood .05 .02
❑ 540 Rick Leach .05 .02
❑ 541 Kevin Romine .05 .02
❑ 542 Mark Salas .05 .02
❑ 543 Greg Minton .05 .02
❑ 544 Dave Palmer .05 .02
❑ 545 Dwayne Murphy UER .05 .02
(Game-sinning)
❑ 546 Jim Deshaies .05 .02
❑ 547 Don Gordon .05 .02
❑ 548 Ricky Jordan RC* .10 .05
❑ 549 Mike Boddicker .05 .02
❑ 550 Mike Scott .05 .02
❑ 551 Jeff Ballard .05 .02
❑ 552A Jose Rijo ERR .20 .09
(Uniform listed as
27 on back)
❑ 552B Jose Rijo COR .20 .09
(Uniform listed as
24 on back)
❑ 553 Danny Darwin .05 .02
❑ 554 Tom Browning .05 .02
❑ 555 Danny Jackson .05 .02
❑ 556 Rick Dempsey .05 .02
❑ 557 Jeffrey Leonard .05 .02
❑ 558 Jeff Musselman .05 .02
❑ 559 Ron Robinson .05 .02
❑ 560 John Tudor .05 .02
❑ 561 Don Slaught UER .05 .02
(237 games in 1987)
❑ 562 Dennis Rasmussen .05 .02
❑ 563 Brady Anderson RC .40 .18
❑ 564 Pedro Guerrero .05 .02
❑ 565 Paul Molitor .20 .09
❑ 566 Terry Clark .05 .02
❑ 567 Terry Puhl .05 .02
❑ 568 Mike Campbell .05 .02
❑ 569 Paul Mirabella .05 .02
❑ 570 Jeff Hamilton .05 .02
❑ 571 Oswald Peraza .05 .02
❑ 572 Bob McClure .05 .02
❑ 573 Jose Bautista .05 .02
❑ 574 Alex Trevino .05 .02
❑ 575 John Franco .10 .05
❑ 576 Mark Parent .05 .02
❑ 577 Nelson Liriano .05 .02
❑ 578 Steve Shields .05 .02
❑ 579 Odell Jones .05 .02
❑ 580 Al Leiter .20 .09
❑ 581 Dave Stapleton .05 .02
❑ 582 World Series '88 .10 .05
Orel Hershiser
Jose Canseco
Kirk Gibson
Dave Stewart
❑ 583 Donnie Hill .05 .02
❑ 584 Chuck Jackson .05 .02
❑ 585 Rene Gonzales .05 .02
❑ 586 Tracy Woodson .05 .02
❑ 587 Jim Adduci .05 .02
❑ 588 Mario Soto .05 .02
❑ 589 Jeff Blauser .10 .05
❑ 590 Jim Traber .05 .02
❑ 591 Jon Perlman .05 .02
❑ 592 Mark Williamson .05 .02
❑ 593 Dave Meads .05 .02
❑ 594 Jim Eisenreich .05 .02
❑ 595A Paul Gibson P1 1.00 .45
❑ 595B Paul Gibson P2 .05 .02
(Airbrushed leg on
player in background)
❑ 596 Mike Birkbeck .05 .02
❑ 597 Terry Francona .10 .05
❑ 598 Paul Zuvella .05 .02
❑ 599 Franklin Stubbs .05 .02
❑ 600 Gregg Jefferies .10 .05
❑ 601 John Cangelosi .05 .02
❑ 602 Mike Sharperson .05 .02
❑ 603 Mike Diaz .05 .02
❑ 604 Gary Varsho .05 .02
❑ 605 Terry Blocker .05 .02
❑ 606 Charlie O'Brien .05 .02
❑ 607 Jim Eppard .05 .02
❑ 608 John Davis .05 .02
❑ 609 Ken Griffey Sr. .10 .05
❑ 610 Buddy Bell .10 .05
❑ 611 Ted Simmons UER .10 .05
('78 stats Cardinal)
❑ 612 Matt Williams .15 .07
❑ 613 Danny Cox .05 .02
❑ 614 Al Pedrique .05 .02
❑ 615 Ron Oester .05 .02
❑ 616 John Smoltz RC .40 .18
❑ 617 Bob Melvin .05 .02
❑ 618 Rob Dibble RC* .10 .05
❑ 619 Kirt Manwaring .05 .02
❑ 620 Felix Fermin .05 .02
❑ 621 Doug Dascenzo .05 .02
❑ 622 Bill Brennan .05 .02
❑ 623 Carlos Quintana RC .05 .02
❑ 624 Mike Harkey RC UER .05 .02
(13 and 31 walks
in '88, should
be 35 and 33)
❑ 625 Gary Sheffield RC 1.25 .55
❑ 626 Tom Prince .05 .02
❑ 627 Steve Searcy .05 .02
❑ 628 Charlie Hayes RC .20 .09
(Listed as outfielder)
❑ 629 Felix Jose RC UER .05 .02
(Modesto misspelled
as Modesta)
❑ 630 Sandy Alomar Jr. RC .25 .11
(Inconsistent design,
portrait on front)
❑ 631 Derek Lilliquist RC .05 .02
❑ 632 Geronimo Berroa .05 .02
❑ 633 Luis Medina .05 .02
❑ 634 Tom Gordon RC UER .20 .09
Height 6'0"
❑ 635 Ramon Martinez RC .25 .11
❑ 636 Craig Worthington .05 .02
❑ 637 Edgar Martinez .15 .07
❑ 638 Chad Kreuter RC .05 .02
❑ 639 Ron Jones .05 .02
❑ 640 Van Snider .05 .02
❑ 641 Lance Blankenship RC .05 .02
❑ 642 Dwight Smith RC UER .10 .05
(10 HR's in '87,
should be 18)
❑ 643 Cameron Drew .05 .02
❑ 644 Jerald Clark RC .05 .02
❑ 645 Randy Johnson RC 2.50 1.10
❑ 646 Norm Charlton RC .10 .05
❑ 647 Todd Frohwirth UER .05 .02
(Southpaw on back)
❑ 648 Luis De Los Santos .05 .02
❑ 649 Tim Jones .05 .02
❑ 650 Dave West RC UER .05 .02
ML hits 3
should be 6
❑ 651 Bob Milacki .05 .02
❑ 652 Wrigley Field HL .10 .05
(Let There Be Lights)
❑ 653 Orel Hershiser HL .10 .05
(The Streak)
❑ 654A W.Boggs HL ERR .20 .09
Wade Whacks 'Em
("seaason" on back
❑ 654B W.Boggs HL COR .10 .05
Wade Whacks 'Em
❑ 655 Jose Canseco HL .10 .05
(One of a Kind)
❑ 656 Doug Jones HL .05 .02
(Doug Sets Saves)
❑ 657 Rickey Henderson HL .20 .09
(Rickey Rocks 'Em)
❑ 658 Tom Browning HL .05 .02
(Tom Perfect Pitches)
❑ 659 Mike Greenwell HL .05 .02
(Greenwell Gamers)
❑ 660 Boston Red Sox HL .05 .02
(Joe Morgan MG,
Sox Sock 'Em)

1989 Score Rookie/Traded

	MINT	NRMT
COMP.FACT.SET (110)	25.00	11.00
❑ 1T Rafael Palmeiro	.50	.23
❑ 2T Nolan Ryan	4.00	1.80
❑ 3T Jack Clark	.10	.05
❑ 4T Dave LaPoint	.10	.05
❑ 5T Mike Moore	.10	.05
❑ 6T Pete O'Brien	.10	.05
❑ 7T Jeffrey Leonard	.10	.05
❑ 8T Rob Murphy	.10	.05
❑ 9T Tom Herr	.10	.05
❑ 10T Claudell Washington	.10	.05
❑ 11T Mike Pagliarulo	.10	.05
❑ 12T Steve Lake	.10	.05
❑ 13T Spike Owen	.10	.05
❑ 14T Andy Hawkins	.10	.05
❑ 15T Todd Benzinger	.10	.05
❑ 16T Mookie Wilson	.20	.09
❑ 17T Bert Blyleven	.20	.09
❑ 18T Jeff Treadway	.10	.05
❑ 19T Bruce Hurst	.10	.05
❑ 20T Steve Sax	.10	.05
❑ 21T Juan Samuel	.10	.05
❑ 22T Jesse Barfield	.10	.05
❑ 23T Carmen Castillo	.10	.05
❑ 24T Terry Leach	.10	.05
❑ 25T Mark Langston	.10	.05
❑ 26T Eric King	.10	.05
❑ 27T Steve Balboni	.10	.05
❑ 28T Len Dykstra	.20	.09
❑ 29T Keith Moreland	.10	.05
❑ 30T Terry Kennedy	.10	.05
❑ 31T Eddie Murray	.40	.18
❑ 32T Mitch Williams	.10	.05
❑ 33T Jeff Parrett	.10	.05
❑ 34T Wally Backman	.10	.05
❑ 35T Julio Franco	.10	.05
❑ 36T Lance Parrish	.10	.05
❑ 37T Nick Esasky	.10	.05
❑ 38T Luis Polonia	.10	.05
❑ 39T Kevin Gross	.10	.05
❑ 40T John Dopson	.10	.05
❑ 41T Willie Randolph	.20	.09
❑ 42T Jim Clancy	.10	.05
❑ 43T Tracy Jones	.10	.05
❑ 44T Phil Bradley	.10	.05
❑ 45T Milt Thompson	.10	.05
❑ 46T Chris James	.10	.05
❑ 47T Scott Fletcher	.10	.05
❑ 48T Kal Daniels	.10	.05
❑ 49T Steve Bedrosian	.10	.05
❑ 50T Rickey Henderson	.75	.35
❑ 51T Dion James	.10	.05
❑ 52T Tim Leary	.10	.05
❑ 53T Roger McDowell	.10	.05
❑ 54T Mel Hall	.10	.05
❑ 55T Dickie Thon	.10	.05
❑ 56T Zane Smith	.10	.05
❑ 57T Danny Heep	.10	.05
❑ 58T Bob McClure	.10	.05
❑ 59T Brian Holton	.10	.05
❑ 60T Randy Ready	.10	.05
❑ 61T Bob Melvin	.10	.05
❑ 62T Harold Baines	.20	.09
❑ 63T Lance McCullers	.10	.05
❑ 64T Jody Davis	.10	.05
❑ 65T Darrell Evans	.20	.09
❑ 66T Joel Youngblood	.10	.05
❑ 67T Frank Viola	.10	.05
❑ 68T Mike Aldrete	.10	.05
❑ 69T Greg Cadaret	.10	.05
❑ 70T John Kruk	.20	.09
❑ 71T Pat Sheridan	.10	.05
❑ 72T Oddibe McDowell	.10	.05
❑ 73T Tom Brookens	.10	.05
❑ 74T Bob Boone	.20	.09
❑ 75T Walt Terrell	.10	.05
❑ 76T Joel Skinner	.10	.05
❑ 77T Randy Johnson	3.00	1.35
❑ 78T Felix Fermin	.10	.05
❑ 79T Rick Mahler	.10	.05
❑ 80T Richard Dotson	.10	.05
❑ 81T Cris Carpenter RC*	.10	.05
❑ 82T Bill Spiers RC	.10	.05
❑ 83T Junior Felix RC	.10	.05
❑ 84T Joe Girardi RC	.40	.18
❑ 85T Jerome Walton	.40	.18
❑ 86T Greg Litton	.10	.05
❑ 87T Greg W.Harris RC	.10	.05
❑ 88T Jim Abbott RC*	.40	.18
❑ 89T Kevin Brown	1.00	.45
❑ 90T John Wetteland RC	.50	.23
❑ 91T Gary Wayne	.10	.05
❑ 92T Rich Monteleone	.10	.05
❑ 93T Bob Geren	.10	.05
❑ 94T Clay Parker	.10	.05
❑ 95T Steve Finley RC	1.25	.55
❑ 96T Gregg Olson RC	.40	.18
❑ 97T Ken Patterson	.10	.05
❑ 98T Ken Hill RC	.40	.18
❑ 99T Scott Scudder RC	.10	.05
❑ 100T Ken Griffey Jr. RC !	15.00	6.75
❑ 101T Jeff Brantley RC	.30	.14
❑ 102T Donn Pall	.10	.05
❑ 103T Carlos Martinez RC	.10	.05
❑ 104T Joe Oliver RC	.20	.09
❑ 105T Omar Vizquel RC	1.25	.55
❑ 106T Joey Belle RC	3.00	1.35
❑ 107T Kenny Rogers RC	.40	.18
❑ 108T Mark Carreon	.10	.05
❑ 109T Rolando Roomes	.10	.05
❑ 110T Pete Harnisch RC	.50	.23

1990 Score

	MINT	NRMT
COMPLETE SET (704)	12.00	5.50
COMP.RETAIL SET (704)	15.00	6.75
COMP.HOBBY SET (714)	20.00	9.00
❑ 1 Don Mattingly	.50	.23
❑ 2 Cal Ripken	.75	.35
❑ 3 Dwight Evans	.10	.05
❑ 4 Barry Bonds	.50	.23
❑ 5 Kevin McReynolds	.05	.02
❑ 6 Ozzie Guillen	.05	.02
❑ 7 Terry Kennedy	.05	.02
❑ 8 Bryan Harvey	.05	.02
❑ 9 Alan Trammell	.15	.07
❑ 10 Cory Snyder	.05	.02
❑ 11 Jody Reed	.05	.02
❑ 12 Roberto Alomar	.20	.09
❑ 13 Pedro Guerrero	.05	.02
❑ 14 Gary Redus	.05	.02
❑ 15 Marty Barrett	.05	.02
❑ 16 Ricky Jordan	.05	.02
❑ 17 Joe Magrane	.05	.02
❑ 18 Sid Fernandez	.05	.02
❑ 19 Richard Dotson	.05	.02
❑ 20 Jack Clark	.10	.05
❑ 21 Bob Walk	.05	.02
❑ 22 Ron Karkovice	.05	.02
❑ 23 Lenny Harris	.05	.02
❑ 24 Phil Bradley	.05	.02
❑ 25 Andres Galarraga	.15	.07
❑ 26 Brian Downing	.05	.02
❑ 27 Dave Martinez	.05	.02
❑ 28 Eric King	.05	.02
❑ 29 Barry Lyons	.05	.02
❑ 30 Dave Schmidt	.05	.02
❑ 31 Mike Boddicker	.05	.02
❑ 32 Tom Foley	.05	.02
❑ 33 Brady Anderson	.20	.09
❑ 34 Jim Presley	.05	.02
❑ 35 Lance Parrish	.05	.02
❑ 36 Von Hayes	.05	.02
❑ 37 Lee Smith	.10	.05
❑ 38 Herm Winningham	.05	.02
❑ 39 Alejandro Pena	.05	.02
❑ 40 Mike Scott	.05	.02
❑ 41 Joe Orsulak	.05	.02
❑ 42 Rafael Ramirez	.05	.02
❑ 43 Gerald Young	.05	.02
❑ 44 Dick Schofield	.05	.02
❑ 45 Dave Smith	.05	.02
❑ 46 Dave Magadan	.05	.02
❑ 47 Dennis Martinez	.10	.05
❑ 48 Greg Minton	.05	.02
❑ 49 Milt Thompson	.05	.02
❑ 50 Orel Hershiser	.10	.05
❑ 51 Bip Roberts	.05	.02
❑ 52 Jerry Browne	.05	.02
❑ 53 Bob Ojeda	.05	.02
❑ 54 Fernando Valenzuela	.10	.05
❑ 55 Matt Nokes	.05	.02
❑ 56 Brook Jacoby	.05	.02
❑ 57 Frank Tanana	.05	.02
❑ 58 Scott Fletcher	.05	.02
❑ 59 Ron Oester	.05	.02
❑ 60 Bob Boone	.10	.05
❑ 61 Dan Gladden	.05	.02
❑ 62 Darnell Coles	.05	.02
❑ 63 Gregg Olson	.10	.05
❑ 64 Todd Burns	.05	.02
❑ 65 Todd Benzinger	.05	.02
❑ 66 Dale Murphy	.20	.09
❑ 67 Mike Flanagan	.05	.02
❑ 68 Jose Oquendo	.05	.02
❑ 69 Cecil Espy	.05	.02
❑ 70 Chris Sabo	.05	.02
❑ 71 Shane Rawley	.05	.02
❑ 72 Tom Brunansky	.05	.02
❑ 73 Vance Law	.05	.02
❑ 74 B.J. Surhoff	.10	.05
❑ 75 Lou Whitaker	.10	.05
❑ 76 Ken Caminiti UER Euclid and Ohio should be Hanford and California	.10	.05
❑ 77 Nelson Liriano	.05	.02
❑ 78 Tommy Gregg	.05	.02
❑ 79 Don Slaught	.05	.02
❑ 80 Eddie Murray	.20	.09
❑ 81 Joe Boever	.05	.02
❑ 82 Charlie Leibrandt	.05	.02
❑ 83 Jose Lind	.05	.02
❑ 84 Tony Phillips	.05	.02
❑ 85 Mitch Webster	.05	.02
❑ 86 Dan Plesac	.05	.02
❑ 87 Rick Mahler	.05	.02
❑ 88 Steve Lyons	.05	.02
❑ 89 Tony Fernandez	.05	.02
❑ 90 Ryne Sandberg	.25	.11
❑ 91 Nick Esasky	.05	.02
❑ 92 Luis Salazar	.05	.02
❑ 93 Pete Incaviglia	.05	.02
❑ 94 Ivan Calderon	.05	.02
❑ 95 Jeff Treadway	.05	.02
❑ 96 Kurt Stillwell	.05	.02

❑ 97 Gary Sheffield .10 .05
❑ 98 Jeffrey Leonard .05 .02
❑ 99 Andres Thomas .05 .02
❑ 100 Roberto Kelly .05 .02
❑ 101 Alvaro Espinoza .05 .02
❑ 102 Greg Gagne .05 .02
❑ 103 John Farrell .05 .02
❑ 104 Willie Wilson .05 .02
❑ 105 Glenn Braggs .05 .02
❑ 106 Chet Lemon .05 .02
❑ 107A Jamie Moyer ERR .05 .02
(Scintilating)
❑ 107B Jamie Moyer COR .10 .05
(Scintillating)
❑ 108 Chuck Crim .05 .02
❑ 109 Dave Valle .05 .02
❑ 110 Walt Weiss .05 .02
❑ 111 Larry Sheets .05 .02
❑ 112 Don Robinson .05 .02
❑ 113 Danny Heep .05 .02
❑ 114 Carmelo Martinez .05 .02
❑ 115 Dave Gallagher .05 .02
❑ 116 Mike LaValliere .05 .02
❑ 117 Bob McClure .05 .02
❑ 118 Rene Gonzales .05 .02
❑ 119 Mark Parent .05 .02
❑ 120 Wally Joyner .10 .05
❑ 121 Mark Gubicza .05 .02
❑ 122 Tony Pena .05 .02
❑ 123 Carmen Castillo .05 .02
❑ 124 Howard Johnson .05 .02
❑ 125 Steve Sax .05 .02
❑ 126 Tim Belcher .05 .02
❑ 127 Tim Burke .05 .02
❑ 128 Al Newman .05 .02
❑ 129 Dennis Rasmussen .05 .02
❑ 130 Doug Jones .05 .02
❑ 131 Fred Lynn .05 .02
❑ 132 Jeff Hamilton .05 .02
❑ 133 German Gonzalez .05 .02
❑ 134 John Morris .05 .02
❑ 135 Dave Parker .10 .05
❑ 136 Gary Pettis .05 .02
❑ 137 Dennis Boyd .05 .02
❑ 138 Candy Maldonado .05 .02
❑ 139 Rick Cerone .05 .02
❑ 140 George Brett .40 .18
❑ 141 Dave Clark .05 .02
❑ 142 Dickie Thon .05 .02
❑ 143 Junior Ortiz .05 .02
❑ 144 Don August .05 .02
❑ 145 Gary Gaetti .10 .05
❑ 146 Kirt Manwaring .05 .02
❑ 147 Jeff Reed .05 .02
❑ 148 Jose Alvarez .05 .02
❑ 149 Mike Schooler .05 .02
❑ 150 Mark Grace .20 .09
❑ 151 Geronimo Berroa .05 .02
❑ 152 Barry Jones .05 .02
❑ 153 Geno Petralli .05 .02
❑ 154 Jim Deshaies .05 .02
❑ 155 Barry Larkin .20 .09
❑ 156 Alfredo Griffin .05 .02
❑ 157 Tom Henke .05 .02
❑ 158 Mike Jeffcoat .05 .02
❑ 159 Bob Welch .05 .02
❑ 160 Julio Franco .05 .02
❑ 161 Henry Cotto .05 .02
❑ 162 Terry Steinbach .05 .02
❑ 163 Damon Berryhill .05 .02
❑ 164 Tim Crews .05 .02
❑ 165 Tom Browning .05 .02
❑ 166 Fred Manrique .05 .02
❑ 167 Harold Reynolds .05 .02
❑ 168A Ron Hassey ERR .05 .02
(27 on back)
❑ 168B Ron Hassey COR .50 .23
(24 on back)
❑ 169 Shawon Dunston .05 .02
❑ 170 Bobby Bonilla .10 .05
❑ 171 Tommy Herr .05 .02
❑ 172 Mike Heath .05 .02
❑ 173 Rich Gedman .05 .02
❑ 174 Bill Ripken .05 .02
❑ 175 Pete O'Brien .05 .02
❑ 176A L.McClendon ERR
Uniform number on
back listed as 1
❑ 176B L.McClendon COR .05 .02
Uniform number on
back listed as 10
❑ 177 Brian Holton .05 .02
❑ 178 Jeff Blauser .05 .02
❑ 179 Jim Eisenreich .05 .02
❑ 180 Bert Blyleven .10 .05
❑ 181 Rob Murphy .05 .02
❑ 182 Bill Doran .05 .02
❑ 183 Curt Ford .05 .02
❑ 184 Mike Henneman .05 .02
❑ 185 Eric Davis .10 .05
❑ 186 Lance McCullers .05 .02
❑ 187 Steve Davis .05 .02
❑ 188 Bill Wegman .05 .02
❑ 189 Brian Harper .05 .02
❑ 190 Mike Moore .05 .02
❑ 191 Dale Mohorcic .05 .02
❑ 192 Tim Wallach .05 .02
❑ 193 Keith Hernandez .10 .05
❑ 194 Dave Righetti .05 .02
❑ 195A B.Saberhagen ERR .10 .05
Joke
❑ 195B B.Saberhagen COR .10 .05
Joker
❑ 196 Paul Kilgus .05 .02
❑ 197 Bud Black .05 .02
❑ 198 Juan Samuel .05 .02
❑ 199 Kevin Seitzer .05 .02
❑ 200 Darryl Strawberry .10 .05
❑ 201 Dave Stieb .10 .05
❑ 202 Charlie Hough .10 .05
❑ 203 Jack Morris .10 .05
❑ 204 Rance Mulliniks .05 .02
❑ 205 Alvin Davis .05 .02
❑ 206 Jack Howell .05 .02
❑ 207 Ken Patterson .05 .02
❑ 208 Terry Pendleton .10 .05
❑ 209 Craig Lefferts .05 .02
❑ 210 Kevin Brown UER .20 .09
(First mention of '89
Rangers should be '88)
❑ 211 Dan Petry .05 .02
❑ 212 Dave Leiper .05 .02
❑ 213 Daryl Boston .05 .02
❑ 214 Kevin Hickey .05 .02
❑ 215 Mike Krukow .05 .02
❑ 216 Terry Francona .10 .05
❑ 217 Kirk McCaskill .05 .02
❑ 218 Scott Bailes .05 .02
❑ 219 Bob Forsch .05 .02
❑ 220A Mike Aldrete ERR .05 .02
(25 on back)
❑ 220B Mike Aldrete COR .10 .05
(24 on back)
❑ 221 Steve Buechele .05 .02
❑ 222 Jesse Barfield .05 .02
❑ 223 Juan Berenguer .05 .02
❑ 224 Andy McGaffigan .05 .02
❑ 225 Pete Smith .05 .02
❑ 226 Mike Witt .05 .02
❑ 227 Jay Howell .05 .02
❑ 228 Scott Bradley .05 .02
❑ 229 Jerome Walton .05 .02
❑ 230 Greg Swindell .05 .02
❑ 231 Atlee Hammaker .05 .02
❑ 232A Mike Devereaux ERR .05 .02
(RF on front)
❑ 232B M.Devereaux COR .50 .23
CF on front
❑ 233 Ken Hill .10 .05
❑ 234 Craig Worthington .05 .02
❑ 235 Scott Terry .05 .02
❑ 236 Brett Butler .10 .05
❑ 237 Doyle Alexander .05 .02
❑ 238 Dave Anderson .05 .02
❑ 239 Bob Milacki .05 .02
❑ 240 Dwight Smith .05 .02
❑ 241 Otis Nixon .05 .02
❑ 242 Pat Tabler .05 .02
❑ 243 Derek Lilliquist .05 .02
❑ 244 Danny Tartabull .05 .02
❑ 245 Wade Boggs .20 .09
❑ 246 Scott Garrelts .05 .02
(Should say Relief
Pitcher on front)
❑ 247 Spike Owen .05 .02
❑ 248 Norm Charlton .05 .02
❑ 249 Gerald Perry .05 .02
❑ 250 Nolan Ryan 1.00 .45
❑ 251 Kevin Gross .05 .02
❑ 252 Randy Milligan .05 .02
❑ 253 Mike LaCoss .05 .02
❑ 254 Dave Bergman .05 .02
❑ 255 Tony Gwynn .40 .18
❑ 256 Felix Fermin .05 .02
❑ 257 Greg W. Harris .05 .02
❑ 258 Junior Felix .05 .02
❑ 259 Mark Davis .05 .02
❑ 260 Vince Coleman .05 .02
❑ 261 Paul Gibson .05 .02
❑ 262 Mitch Williams .05 .02
❑ 263 Jeff Russell .05 .02
❑ 264 Omar Vizquel .20 .09
❑ 265 Andre Dawson .15 .07
❑ 266 Storm Davis .05 .02
❑ 267 Guillermo Hernandez .05 .02
❑ 268 Mike Felder .05 .02
❑ 269 Tom Candiotti .05 .02
❑ 270 Bruce Hurst .05 .02
❑ 271 Fred McGriff .20 .09
❑ 272 Glenn Davis .05 .02
❑ 273 John Franco .10 .05
❑ 274 Rich Yett .05 .02
❑ 275 Craig Biggio .15 .07
❑ 276 Gene Larkin .05 .02
❑ 277 Rob Dibble .05 .02
❑ 278 Randy Bush .05 .02
❑ 279 Kevin Bass .05 .02
❑ 280A Bo Jackson ERR .20 .09
(Watham)
❑ 280B Bo Jackson COR .10 .05
(Wathan)
❑ 281 Wally Backman .05 .02
❑ 282 Larry Andersen .05 .02
❑ 283 Chris Bosio .05 .02
❑ 284 Juan Agosto .05 .02
❑ 285 Ozzie Smith .25 .11
❑ 286 George Bell .05 .02
❑ 287 Rex Hudler .05 .02
❑ 288 Pat Borders .05 .02
❑ 289 Danny Jackson .05 .02
❑ 290 Carlton Fisk .20 .09
❑ 291 Tracy Jones .05 .02
❑ 292 Allan Anderson .05 .02
❑ 293 Johnny Ray .05 .02
❑ 294 Lee Guetterman .05 .02
❑ 295 Paul O'Neill .20 .09
❑ 296 Carney Lansford .10 .05
❑ 297 Tom Brookens .05 .02
❑ 298 Claudell Washington .05 .02
❑ 299 Hubie Brooks .05 .02
❑ 300 Will Clark .20 .09
❑ 301 Kenny Rogers .10 .05
❑ 302 Darrell Evans .10 .05
❑ 303 Greg Briley .05 .02
❑ 304 Donn Pall .05 .02
❑ 305 Teddy Higuera .05 .02
❑ 306 Dan Pasqua .05 .02
❑ 307 Dave Winfield .20 .09
❑ 308 Dennis Powell .05 .02
❑ 309 Jose DeLeon .05 .02
❑ 310 Roger Clemens UER .50 .23
(Dominate, should
say dominant)
❑ 311 Melido Perez .05 .02
❑ 312 Devon White .05 .02
❑ 313 Dwight Gooden .10 .05
❑ 314 Carlos Martinez .05 .02
❑ 315 Dennis Eckersley .15 .07
❑ 316 Clay Parker UER .05 .02
(Height 6'11")
❑ 317 Rick Honeycutt .05 .02
❑ 318 Tim Laudner .05 .02
❑ 319 Joe Carter .10 .05
❑ 320 Robin Yount .20 .09
❑ 321 Felix Jose .05 .02
❑ 322 Mickey Tettleton .05 .02
❑ 323 Mike Gallego .05 .02
❑ 324 Edgar Martinez .15 .07

- ❑ 325 Dave Henderson .05 .02
- ❑ 326 Chili Davis .10 .05
- ❑ 327 Steve Balboni .05 .02
- ❑ 328 Jody Davis .05 .02
- ❑ 329 Shawn Hillegas .05 .02
- ❑ 330 Jim Abbott .15 .07
- ❑ 331 John Dopson .05 .02
- ❑ 332 Mark Williamson .05 .02
- ❑ 333 Jeff D. Robinson .05 .02
- ❑ 334 John Smiley .05 .02
- ❑ 335 Bobby Thigpen .05 .02
- ❑ 336 Garry Templeton .05 .02
- ❑ 337 Marvell Wynne .05 .02
- ❑ 338A Ken Griffey Sr. ERR .10 .05 (Uniform number on back listed as 25)
- ❑ 338B Ken Griffey Sr. COR .50 .23 (Uniform number on back listed as 30)
- ❑ 339 Steve Finley .10 .05
- ❑ 340 Ellis Burks .15 .07
- ❑ 341 Frank Williams .05 .02
- ❑ 342 Mike Morgan .05 .02
- ❑ 343 Kevin Mitchell .05 .02
- ❑ 344 Joel Youngblood .05 .02
- ❑ 345 Mike Greenwell .05 .02
- ❑ 346 Glenn Wilson .05 .02
- ❑ 347 John Costello .05 .02
- ❑ 348 Wes Gardner .05 .02
- ❑ 349 Jeff Ballard .05 .02
- ❑ 350 Mark Thurmond UER .05 .02 (ERA is 192, should be 1.92)
- ❑ 351 Randy Myers .10 .05
- ❑ 352 Shawn Abner .05 .02
- ❑ 353 Jesse Orosco .05 .02
- ❑ 354 Greg Walker .05 .02
- ❑ 355 Pete Harnisch .05 .02
- ❑ 356 Steve Farr .05 .02
- ❑ 357 Dave LaPoint .05 .02
- ❑ 358 Willie Fraser .05 .02
- ❑ 359 Mickey Hatcher .05 .02
- ❑ 360 Rickey Henderson .40 .18
- ❑ 361 Mike Fitzgerald .05 .02
- ❑ 362 Bill Schroeder .05 .02
- ❑ 363 Mark Carreon .05 .02
- ❑ 364 Ron Jones .05 .02
- ❑ 365 Jeff Montgomery .10 .05
- ❑ 366 Bill Krueger .05 .02
- ❑ 367 John Cangelosi .05 .02
- ❑ 368 Jose Gonzalez .05 .02
- ❑ 369 Greg Hibbard RC .05 .02
- ❑ 370 John Smoltz .10 .05
- ❑ 371 Jeff Brantley .05 .02
- ❑ 372 Frank White .10 .05
- ❑ 373 Ed Whitson .05 .02
- ❑ 374 Willie McGee .10 .05
- ❑ 375 Jose Canseco .20 .09
- ❑ 376 Randy Ready .05 .02
- ❑ 377 Don Aase .05 .02
- ❑ 378 Tony Armas .05 .02
- ❑ 379 Steve Bedrosian .05 .02
- ❑ 380 Chuck Finley .10 .05
- ❑ 381 Kent Hrbek .10 .05
- ❑ 382 Jim Gantner .05 .02
- ❑ 383 Mel Hall .05 .02
- ❑ 384 Mike Marshall .05 .02
- ❑ 385 Mark McGwire .75 .35
- ❑ 386 Wayne Tolleson .05 .02
- ❑ 387 Brian Holman .05 .02
- ❑ 388 John Wetteland .20 .09
- ❑ 389 Darren Daulton .10 .05
- ❑ 390 Rob Deer .05 .02
- ❑ 391 John Moses .05 .02
- ❑ 392 Todd Worrell .05 .02
- ❑ 393 Chuck Cary .05 .02
- ❑ 394 Stan Javier .05 .02
- ❑ 395 Willie Randolph .10 .05
- ❑ 396 Bill Buckner .05 .02
- ❑ 397 Robby Thompson .05 .02
- ❑ 398 Mike Scioscia .05 .02
- ❑ 399 Lonnie Smith .05 .02
- ❑ 400 Kirby Puckett .50 .23
- ❑ 401 Mark Langston .05 .02
- ❑ 402 Danny Darwin .05 .02
- ❑ 403 Greg Maddux .50 .23
- ❑ 404 Lloyd Moseby .05 .02
- ❑ 405 Rafael Palmeiro .20 .09
- ❑ 406 Chad Kreuter .05 .02
- ❑ 407 Jimmy Key .10 .05
- ❑ 408 Tim Birtsas .05 .02
- ❑ 409 Tim Raines .10 .05
- ❑ 410 Dave Stewart .10 .05
- ❑ 411 Eric Yelding .05 .02
- ❑ 412 Kent Anderson .05 .02
- ❑ 413 Les Lancaster .05 .02
- ❑ 414 Rick Dempsey .05 .02
- ❑ 415 Randy Johnson .40 .18
- ❑ 416 Gary Carter .15 .07
- ❑ 417 Rolando Roomes .05 .02
- ❑ 418 Dan Schatzeder .05 .02
- ❑ 419 Bryn Smith .05 .02
- ❑ 420 Ruben Sierra .05 .02
- ❑ 421 Steve Jeltz .05 .02
- ❑ 422 Ken Oberkfell .05 .02
- ❑ 423 Sid Bream .05 .02
- ❑ 424 Jim Clancy .05 .02
- ❑ 425 Kelly Gruber .05 .02
- ❑ 426 Rick Leach .05 .02
- ❑ 427 Len Dykstra .10 .05
- ❑ 428 Jeff Pico .05 .02
- ❑ 429 John Cerutti .05 .02
- ❑ 430 David Cone .10 .05
- ❑ 431 Jeff Kunkel .05 .02
- ❑ 432 Luis Aquino .05 .02
- ❑ 433 Ernie Whitt .05 .02
- ❑ 434 Bo Diaz .05 .02
- ❑ 435 Steve Lake .05 .02
- ❑ 436 Pat Perry .05 .02
- ❑ 437 Mike Davis .05 .02
- ❑ 438 Cecilio Guante .05 .02
- ❑ 439 Duane Ward .05 .02
- ❑ 440 Andy Van Slyke .10 .05
- ❑ 441 Gene Nelson .05 .02
- ❑ 442 Luis Polonia .05 .02
- ❑ 443 Kevin Elster .05 .02
- ❑ 444 Keith Moreland .05 .02
- ❑ 445 Roger McDowell .05 .02
- ❑ 446 Ron Darling .05 .02
- ❑ 447 Ernest Riles .05 .02
- ❑ 448 Mookie Wilson .10 .05
- ❑ 449A Billy Spiers ERR .20 .09 (No birth year)
- ❑ 449B Billy Spiers COR .05 .02 (Born in 1966)
- ❑ 450 Rick Sutcliffe .10 .05
- ❑ 451 Nelson Santovenia .05 .02
- ❑ 452 Andy Allanson .05 .02
- ❑ 453 Bob Melvin .05 .02
- ❑ 454 Benito Santiago .05 .02
- ❑ 455 Jose Uribe .05 .02
- ❑ 456 Bill Landrum .05 .02
- ❑ 457 Bobby Witt .05 .02
- ❑ 458 Kevin Romine .05 .02
- ❑ 459 Lee Mazzilli .05 .02
- ❑ 460 Paul Molitor .20 .09
- ❑ 461 Ramon Martinez .05 .02
- ❑ 462 Frank DiPino .05 .02
- ❑ 463 Walt Terrell .05 .02
- ❑ 464 Bob Geren .05 .02
- ❑ 465 Rick Reuschel .05 .02
- ❑ 466 Mark Grant .05 .02
- ❑ 467 John Kruk .10 .05
- ❑ 468 Gregg Jefferies .10 .05
- ❑ 469 R.J. Reynolds .05 .02
- ❑ 470 Harold Baines .10 .05
- ❑ 471 Dennis Lamp .05 .02
- ❑ 472 Tom Gordon .10 .05
- ❑ 473 Terry Puhl .05 .02
- ❑ 474 Curt Wilkerson .05 .02
- ❑ 475 Dan Quisenberry .05 .02
- ❑ 476 Oddibe McDowell .05 .02
- ❑ 477A Zane Smith ERR .05 .02 (Career ERA .393)
- ❑ 477B Zane Smith COR .05 .02 (career ERA 3.93)
- ❑ 478 Franklin Stubbs .05 .02
- ❑ 479 Wallace Johnson .05 .02
- ❑ 480 Jay Tibbs .05 .02
- ❑ 481 Tom Glavine .20 .09
- ❑ 482 Manny Lee .05 .02
- ❑ 483 Joe Hesketh UER .05 .02 (Says Rookiess on back, should say Rookies)
- ❑ 484 Mike Bielecki .05 .02
- ❑ 485 Greg Brock .05 .02
- ❑ 486 Pascual Perez .05 .02
- ❑ 487 Kirk Gibson .10 .05
- ❑ 488 Scott Sanderson .05 .02
- ❑ 489 Domingo Ramos .05 .02
- ❑ 490 Kal Daniels .05 .02
- ❑ 491A David Wells ERR .50 .23 (Reverse negative photo on card back)
- ❑ 491B David Wells COR .10 .05
- ❑ 492 Jerry Reed .05 .02
- ❑ 493 Eric Show .05 .02
- ❑ 494 Mike Pagliarulo .05 .02
- ❑ 495 Ron Robinson .05 .02
- ❑ 496 Brad Komminsk .05 .02
- ❑ 497 Greg Litton .05 .02
- ❑ 498 Chris James .05 .02
- ❑ 499 Luis Quinones .05 .02
- ❑ 500 Frank Viola .05 .02
- ❑ 501 Tim Teufel UER .05 .02 (Twins '85, the s is lower case, should be upper case)
- ❑ 502 Terry Leach .05 .02
- ❑ 503 Matt Williams UER .15 .07 (Wearing 10 on front, listed as 9 on back)
- ❑ 504 Tim Leary .05 .02
- ❑ 505 Doug Drabek .05 .02
- ❑ 506 Mariano Duncan .05 .02
- ❑ 507 Charlie Hayes .05 .02
- ❑ 508 Joey Belle .20 .09
- ❑ 509 Pat Sheridan .05 .02
- ❑ 510 Mackey Sasser .05 .02
- ❑ 511 Jose Rijo .05 .02
- ❑ 512 Mike Smithson .05 .02
- ❑ 513 Gary Ward .05 .02
- ❑ 514 Dion James .05 .02
- ❑ 515 Jim Gott .05 .02
- ❑ 516 Drew Hall .05 .02
- ❑ 517 Doug Bair .05 .02
- ❑ 518 Scott Scudder .05 .02
- ❑ 519 Rick Aguilera .10 .05
- ❑ 520 Rafael Belliard .05 .02
- ❑ 521 Jay Buhner .10 .05
- ❑ 522 Jeff Reardon .10 .05
- ❑ 523 Steve Rosenberg .05 .02
- ❑ 524 Randy Velarde .05 .02
- ❑ 525 Jeff Musselman .05 .02
- ❑ 526 Bill Long .05 .02
- ❑ 527 Gary Wayne .05 .02
- ❑ 528 Dave Johnson (P) .05 .02
- ❑ 529 Ron Kittle .05 .02
- ❑ 530 Erik Hanson UER .05 .02 (5th line on back says seson, should say season)
- ❑ 531 Steve Wilson .05 .02
- ❑ 532 Joey Meyer .05 .02
- ❑ 533 Curt Young .05 .02
- ❑ 534 Kelly Downs .05 .02
- ❑ 535 Joe Girardi .15 .07
- ❑ 536 Lance Blankenship .05 .02
- ❑ 537 Greg Mathews .05 .02
- ❑ 538 Donell Nixon .05 .02
- ❑ 539 Mark Knudson .05 .02
- ❑ 540 Jeff Wetherby .05 .02
- ❑ 541 Darrin Jackson .05 .02
- ❑ 542 Terry Mulholland .05 .02
- ❑ 543 Eric Hetzel .05 .02
- ❑ 544 Rick Reed RC .25 .11
- ❑ 545 Dennis Cook .05 .02
- ❑ 546 Mike Jackson .05 .02
- ❑ 547 Brian Fisher .05 .02
- ❑ 548 Gene Harris .05 .02
- ❑ 549 Jeff King .05 .02
- ❑ 550 Dave Dravecky .20 .09
- ❑ 551 Randy Kutcher .05 .02
- ❑ 552 Mark Portugal .05 .02
- ❑ 553 Jim Corsi .05 .02
- ❑ 554 Todd Stottlemyre .10 .05
- ❑ 555 Scott Bankhead .05 .02
- ❑ 556 Ken Dayley .05 .02

❑ 557 Rick Wrona .05 .02
❑ 558 Sammy Sosa RC 5.00 2.20
❑ 559 Keith Miller .05 .02
❑ 560 Ken Griffey Jr. 1.25 .55
❑ 561A R.Sandberg HL ERR 5.00 2.20
Position on front
listed as 3B
❑ 561B R.Sandberg HL COR .20 .09
❑ 562 Billy Hatcher .05 .02
❑ 563 Jay Bell .10 .05
❑ 564 Jack Daugherty .05 .02
❑ 565 Rich Monteleone .05 .02
❑ 566 Bo Jackson AS-MVP .10 .05
❑ 567 Tony Fossas .05 .02
❑ 568 Roy Smith .05 .02
❑ 569 Jaime Navarro .05 .02
❑ 570 Lance Johnson .05 .02
❑ 571 Mike Dyer .05 .02
❑ 572 Kevin Ritz .05 .02
❑ 573 Dave West .05 .02
❑ 574 Gary Mielke .05 .02
❑ 575 Scott Lusader .05 .02
❑ 576 Joe Oliver .05 .02
❑ 577 Sandy Alomar Jr. .10 .05
❑ 578 Andy Benes UER .05 .02
(Extra comma between
day and year)
❑ 579 Tim Jones .05 .02
❑ 580 Randy McCament .05 .02
❑ 581 Curt Schilling 1.00 .45
❑ 582 John Orton RC .05 .02
❑ 583A Milt Cuyler RC ERR .50 .23
(998 games)
❑ 583B Milt Cuyler RC COR .05 .02
(98 games; the extra 9
was ghosted out and
may still be visible)
❑ 584 Eric Anthony RC .05 .02
❑ 585 Greg Vaughn .20 .09
❑ 586 Deion Sanders .20 .09
❑ 587 Jose DeJesus .05 .02
❑ 588 Chip Hale .05 .02
❑ 589 John Olerud RC .50 .23
❑ 590 Steve Olin RC .10 .05
❑ 591 Marquis Grissom RC .10 .05
❑ 592 Moises Alou RC .50 .23
❑ 593 Mark Lemke .05 .02
❑ 594 Dean Palmer RC .40 .18
❑ 595 Robin Ventura .20 .09
❑ 596 Tino Martinez .20 .09
❑ 597 Mike Huff .05 .02
❑ 598 Scott Hemond RC .05 .02
❑ 599 Wally Whitehurst .05 .02
❑ 600 Todd Zeile .10 .05
❑ 601 Glenallen Hill .05 .02
❑ 602 Hal Morris .05 .02
❑ 603 Juan Bell .05 .02
❑ 604 Bobby Rose .05 .02
❑ 605 Matt Merullo .05 .02
❑ 606 Kevin Maas RC .10 .05
❑ 607 Randy Nosek .05 .02
❑ 608A Billy Bates .05 .02
(Text mentions 12
triples in tenth line)
❑ 608B Billy Bates .05 .02
(Text has no mention
of triples)
❑ 609 Mike Stanton RC .05 .02
❑ 610 Mauro Gozzo .05 .02
❑ 611 Charles Nagy .05 .02
❑ 612 Scott Coolbaugh .05 .02
❑ 613 Jose Vizcaino RC .15 .07
❑ 614 Greg Smith .05 .02
❑ 615 Jeff Huson RC .05 .02
❑ 616 Mickey Weston .05 .02
❑ 617 John Pawlowski .05 .02
❑ 618A Joe Skalski ERR .05 .02
(27 on back)
❑ 618B Joe Skalski COR .50 .23
(67 on back)
❑ 619 Bernie Williams RC 1.00 .45
❑ 620 Shawn Holman .05 .02
❑ 621 Gary Eave .05 .02
❑ 622 Darrin Fletcher UER .10 .05
(Elmherst, should
be Elmhurst)
❑ 623 Pat Combs .05 .02
❑ 624 Mike Blowers RC .10 .05
❑ 625 Kevin Appier .15 .07
❑ 626 Pat Austin .05 .02
❑ 627 Kelly Mann .05 .02
❑ 628 Matt Kinzer .05 .02
❑ 629 Chris Hammond RC .05 .02
❑ 630 Dean Wilkins .05 .02
❑ 631 Larry Walker RC UER .60 .25
(Uniform number 55 on
front and 33 on back;
Home is Maple Ridge,
not Maple River)
❑ 632 Blaine Beatty .05 .02
❑ 633A Tommy Barrett ERR .05 .02
(29 on back)
❑ 633B Tommy Barrett COR .50 .23
(14 on back)
❑ 634 Stan Belinda RC .05 .02
❑ 635 Mike (Tex) Smith .05 .02
❑ 636 Hensley Meulens .05 .02
❑ 637 J.Gonzalez RC UER 2.00 .90
Sarasots on back,
should be Sarasota
❑ 638 Lenny Webster RC .05 .02
❑ 639 Mark Gardner RC .05 .02
❑ 640 Tommy Greene RC .05 .02
❑ 641 Mike Hartley .05 .02
❑ 642 Phil Stephenson .05 .02
❑ 643 Kevin Mmahat .05 .02
❑ 644 Ed Whited .05 .02
❑ 645 Delino DeShields RC .20 .09
❑ 646 Kevin Blankenship .05 .02
❑ 647 Paul Sorrento RC .15 .07
❑ 648 Mike Roesler .05 .02
❑ 649 Jason Grimsley RC .05 .02
❑ 650 Dave Justice RC .60 .25
❑ 651 Scott Cooper RC .05 .02
❑ 652 Dave Eiland .05 .02
❑ 653 Mike Munoz .05 .02
❑ 654 Jeff Fischer .05 .02
❑ 655 Terry Jorgensen .05 .02
❑ 656 George Canale .05 .02
❑ 657 Brian DuBois UER .05 .02
(Misspelled Dubois
on card)
❑ 658 Carlos Quintana .05 .02
❑ 659 Luis de los Santos .05 .02
❑ 660 Jerald Clark .05 .02
❑ 661 Donald Harris DC .05 .02
❑ 662 Paul Coleman DC RC .05 .02
❑ 663 Frank Thomas DC RC 2.00 .90
❑ 664 Brent Mayne DC RC .05 .02
❑ 665 Eddie Zosky DC RC .05 .02
❑ 666 Steve Hosey DC RC .05 .02
❑ 667 Scott Bryant DC .05 .02
❑ 668 Tom Goodwin DC RC .20 .09
❑ 669 Cal Eldred DC RC .10 .05
❑ 670 E.Cunningham DC RC .05 .02
❑ 671 Alan Zinter DC RC .05 .02
❑ 672 C.Knoblauch DC RC .40 .18
❑ 673 Kyle Abbott DC .05 .02
❑ 674 Roger Salkeld DC RC .05 .02
❑ 675 M.Vaughn DC RC .40 .18
❑ 676 Keith(Kiki) Jones DC .05 .02
❑ 677 Tyler Houston DC RC .15 .07
❑ 678 Jeff Jackson DC RC .05 .02
❑ 679 Greg Gohr DC RC .05 .02
❑ 680 Ben McDonald DC RC .10 .05
❑ 681 Greg Blosser DC RC .05 .02
❑ 682 W.Greene RC DC UER .10 .05
Name spelled as Green
❑ 683A W.Boggs DT ERR .10 .05
Text says 215 hits in
'89, should be 205
❑ 683B W.Boggs DT COR .10 .05
Text says 205 hits in '89
❑ 684 Will Clark DT .10 .05
❑ 685 Tony Gwynn DT UER .20 .09
(Text reads battling
instead of batting)
❑ 686 Rickey Henderson DT .20 .09
❑ 687 Bo Jackson DT .10 .05
❑ 688 Mark Langston DT .05 .02
❑ 689 Barry Larkin DT .10 .05
❑ 690 Kirby Puckett DT .25 .11
❑ 691 Ryne Sandberg DT .20 .09
❑ 692 Mike Scott DT .05 .02
❑ 693A Terry Steinbach DT .05 .02
ERR (cathers)
❑ 693B Terry Steinbach DT .05 .02
COR (catchers)
❑ 694 Bobby Thigpen DT .05 .02
❑ 695 Mitch Williams DT .05 .02
❑ 696 Nolan Ryan HL .20 .09
❑ 697 Bo Jackson FB/BB .50 .23
❑ 698 Rickey Henderson .20 .09
ALCS-MVP
❑ 699 Will Clark .10 .05
NLCS-MVP
❑ 700 WS Games 1/2 .10 .05
(Dave Stewart
Mike Moore)
❑ 701 Lights Out: .20 .09
Candlestick
5:04pm (10/17/89)
❑ 702 WS Game 3 .20 .09
Bashers Blast Giants
(Carney Lansford,
Rickey Henderson,
Jose Canseco,
Dave Henderson)
❑ 703 WS Game 4/Wrap-up .05 .02
A's Sweep Battle of
of the Bay
(A's Celebrate)
❑ 704 Wade Boggs HL .10 .05
Wade Raps 200

1990 Score Rookie/Traded

	MINT	NRMT
COMP.FACT.SET (110)	4.00	1.80

❑ 1T Dave Winfield .20 .09
❑ 2T Kevin Bass .05 .02
❑ 3T Nick Esasky .05 .02
❑ 4T Mitch Webster .05 .02
❑ 5T Pascual Perez .05 .02
❑ 6T Gary Pettis .05 .02
❑ 7T Tony Pena .05 .02
❑ 8T Candy Maldonado .05 .02
❑ 9T Cecil Fielder .10 .05
❑ 10T Carmelo Martinez .05 .02
❑ 11T Mark Langston .05 .02
❑ 12T Dave Parker .10 .05
❑ 13T Don Slaught .05 .02
❑ 14T Tony Phillips .05 .02
❑ 15T John Franco .10 .05
❑ 16T Randy Myers .10 .05
❑ 17T Jeff Reardon .10 .05
❑ 18T Sandy Alomar Jr. .10 .05
❑ 19T Joe Carter .10 .05
❑ 20T Fred Lynn .05 .02
❑ 21T Storm Davis .05 .02
❑ 22T Craig Lefferts .05 .02
❑ 23T Pete O'Brien .05 .02
❑ 24T Dennis Boyd .05 .02
❑ 25T Lloyd Moseby .05 .02
❑ 26T Mark Davis .05 .02
❑ 27T Tim Leary .05 .02
❑ 28T Gerald Perry .05 .02
❑ 29T Don Aase .05 .02

❑ 30T Ernie Whitt .05 .02
❑ 31T Dale Murphy .20 .09
❑ 32T Alejandro Pena .05 .02
❑ 33T Juan Samuel .05 .02
❑ 34T Hubie Brooks .05 .02
❑ 35T Gary Carter .15 .07
❑ 36T Jim Presley .05 .02
❑ 37T Wally Backman .05 .02
❑ 38T Matt Nokes .05 .02
❑ 39T Dan Petry .05 .02
❑ 40T Franklin Stubbs .05 .02
❑ 41T Jeff Huson .05 .02
❑ 42T Billy Hatcher .05 .02
❑ 43T Terry Leach .05 .02
❑ 44T Phil Bradley .05 .02
❑ 45T Claudell Washington .05 .02
❑ 46T Luis Polonia .05 .02
❑ 47T Daryl Boston .05 .02
❑ 48T Lee Smith .10 .05
❑ 49T Tom Brunansky .05 .02
❑ 50T Mike Witt .05 .02
❑ 51T Willie Randolph .10 .05
❑ 52T Stan Javier .05 .02
❑ 53T Brad Komminsk .05 .02
❑ 54T John Candelaria .05 .02
❑ 55T Bryn Smith .05 .02
❑ 56T Glenn Braggs .05 .02
❑ 57T Keith Hernandez .10 .05
❑ 58T Ken Oberkfell .05 .02
❑ 59T Steve Jeltz .05 .02
❑ 60T Chris James .05 .02
❑ 61T Scott Sanderson .05 .02
❑ 62T Bill Long .05 .02
❑ 63T Rick Cerone .05 .02
❑ 64T Scott Bailes .05 .02
❑ 65T Larry Sheets .05 .02
❑ 66T Junior Ortiz .05 .02
❑ 67T Francisco Cabrera .05 .02
❑ 68T Gary DiSarcina RC .15 .07
❑ 69T Greg Olson .05 .02
❑ 70T Beau Allred .05 .02
❑ 71T Oscar Azocar .05 .02
❑ 72T Kent Mercker RC .05 .02
❑ 73T John Burkett .05 .02
❑ 74T Carlos Baerga RC .10 .05
❑ 75T Dave Hollins RC .20 .09
❑ 76T Todd Hundley RC .20 .09
❑ 77T Rick Parker .05 .02
❑ 78T Steve Cummings .05 .02
❑ 79T Bill Sampen .05 .02
❑ 80T Jerry Kutzler .05 .02
❑ 81T Derek Bell RC .25 .11
❑ 82T Kevin Tapani RC .20 .09
❑ 83T Jim Leyritz RC .10 .05
❑ 84T Ray Lankford RC .25 .11
❑ 85T Wayne Edwards .05 .02
❑ 86T Frank Thomas 2.00 .90
❑ 87T Tim Naehring RC .10 .05
❑ 88T Willie Blair RC .05 .02
❑ 89T Alan Mills RC .05 .02
❑ 90T Scott Radinsky RC .05 .02
❑ 91T Howard Farmer .05 .02
❑ 92T Julio Machado .05 .02
❑ 93T Rafael Valdez .05 .02
❑ 94T Shawn Boskie RC .05 .02
❑ 95T David Segui RC .25 .11
❑ 96T Chris Hoiles RC .20 .09
❑ 97T D.J. Dozier RC .10 .05
❑ 98T Hector Villanueva .05 .02
❑ 99T Eric Gunderson .05 .02
❑ 100T Eric Lindros 1.00 .45
❑ 101T Dave Otto .05 .02
❑ 102T Dana Kiecker .05 .02
❑ 103T Tim Drummond .05 .02
❑ 104T Mickey Pina .05 .02
❑ 105T Craig Grebeck RC .05 .02
❑ 106T Bernard Gilkey RC .10 .05
❑ 107T Tim Layana .05 .02
❑ 108T Scott Chiamparino .05 .02
❑ 109T Steve Avery .05 .02
❑ 110T Terry Shumpert .05 .02

1991 Score

	MINT	NRMT
COMPLETE SET (893)	10.00	4.50
COMP.FACT.SET (900)	20.00	9.00

❑ 1 Jose Canseco .20 .09
❑ 2 Ken Griffey Jr. .75 .35
❑ 3 Ryne Sandberg .25 .11
❑ 4 Nolan Ryan 1.00 .45
❑ 5 Bo Jackson .10 .05
❑ 6 Bret Saberhagen UER .05 .02
(In bio, missed misspelled as mised)
❑ 7 Will Clark .20 .09
❑ 8 Ellis Burks .10 .05
❑ 9 Joe Carter .10 .05
❑ 10 Rickey Henderson .40 .18
❑ 11 Ozzie Guillen .05 .02
❑ 12 Wade Boggs .20 .09
❑ 13 Jerome Walton .05 .02
❑ 14 John Franco .10 .05
❑ 15 Ricky Jordan UER .05 .02
(League misspelled as legue)
❑ 16 Wally Backman .05 .02
❑ 17 Rob Dibble .05 .02
❑ 18 Glenn Braggs .05 .02
❑ 19 Cory Snyder .05 .02
❑ 20 Kal Daniels .05 .02
❑ 21 Mark Langston .05 .02
❑ 22 Kevin Gross .05 .02
❑ 23 Don Mattingly UER .50 .23
(First line, ' is missing from Yankee)
❑ 24 Dave Righetti .10 .05
❑ 25 Roberto Alomar .20 .09
❑ 26 Robby Thompson .05 .02
❑ 27 Jack McDowell .05 .02
❑ 28 Bip Roberts UER .05 .02
(Bio reads playd)
❑ 29 Jay Howell .05 .02
❑ 30 Dave Stieb UER .05 .02
(17 wins in bio, 18 in stats)
❑ 31 Johnny Ray .05 .02
❑ 32 Steve Sax .05 .02
❑ 33 Terry Mulholland .05 .02
❑ 34 Lee Guetterman .05 .02
❑ 35 Tim Raines .10 .05
❑ 36 Scott Fletcher .05 .02
❑ 37 Lance Parrish .10 .05
❑ 38 Tony Phillips UER .05 .02
(Born 4/15 should be 4/25)
❑ 39 Todd Stottlemyre .05 .02
❑ 40 Alan Trammell .15 .07
❑ 41 Todd Burns .05 .02
❑ 42 Mookie Wilson .10 .05
❑ 43 Chris Bosio .05 .02
❑ 44 Jeffrey Leonard .05 .02
❑ 45 Doug Jones .05 .02
❑ 46 Mike Scott UER .05 .02
(In first line, dominate should read dominating)
❑ 47 Andy Hawkins .05 .02
❑ 48 Harold Reynolds .05 .02
❑ 49 Paul Molitor .20 .09
❑ 50 John Farrell .05 .02
❑ 51 Danny Darwin .05 .02
❑ 52 Jeff Blauser .05 .02
❑ 53 John Tudor UER .05 .02
(41 wins in '81)
❑ 54 Milt Thompson .05 .02
❑ 55 Dave Justice .20 .09
❑ 56 Greg Olson .05 .02
❑ 57 Willie Blair .05 .02
❑ 58 Rick Parker .05 .02
❑ 59 Shawn Boskie .05 .02
❑ 60 Kevin Tapani .05 .02
❑ 61 Dave Hollins .05 .02
❑ 62 Scott Radinsky .05 .02
❑ 63 Francisco Cabrera .05 .02
❑ 64 Tim Layana .05 .02
❑ 65 Jim Leyritz .05 .02
❑ 66 Wayne Edwards .05 .02
❑ 67 Lee Stevens .05 .02
❑ 68 Bill Sampen UER .05 .02
(Fourth line, long is spelled along)
❑ 69 Craig Grebeck UER .05 .02
(Born in Cerritos, not Johnstown)
❑ 70 John Burkett .05 .02
❑ 71 Hector Villanueva .05 .02
❑ 72 Oscar Azocar .05 .02
❑ 73 Alan Mills .05 .02
❑ 74 Carlos Baerga .05 .02
❑ 75 Charles Nagy .05 .02
❑ 76 Tim Drummond .05 .02
❑ 77 Dana Kiecker .05 .02
❑ 78 Tom Edens .05 .02
❑ 79 Kent Mercker .05 .02
❑ 80 Steve Avery .05 .02
❑ 81 Lee Smith .10 .05
❑ 82 Dave Martinez .05 .02
❑ 83 Dave Winfield .20 .09
❑ 84 Bill Spiers .05 .02
❑ 85 Dan Pasqua .05 .02
❑ 86 Randy Milligan .05 .02
❑ 87 Tracy Jones .05 .02
❑ 88 Greg Myers .05 .02
❑ 89 Keith Hernandez .10 .05
❑ 90 Todd Benzinger .05 .02
❑ 91 Mike Jackson .05 .02
❑ 92 Mike Stanley .05 .02
❑ 93 Candy Maldonado .05 .02
❑ 94 John Kruk UER .10 .05
(No decimal point before 1990 BA)
❑ 95 Cal Ripken UER .75 .35
(Genius spelled genuis)
❑ 96 Willie Fraser .05 .02
❑ 97 Mike Felder .05 .02
❑ 98 Bill Landrum .05 .02
❑ 99 Chuck Crim .05 .02
❑ 100 Chuck Finley .10 .05
❑ 101 Kirt Manwaring .05 .02
❑ 102 Jaime Navarro .05 .02
❑ 103 Dickie Thon .05 .02
❑ 104 Brian Downing .05 .02
❑ 105 Jim Abbott .10 .05
❑ 106 Tom Brookens .05 .02
❑ 107 Darryl Hamilton UER .05 .02
(Bio info is for Jeff Hamilton)
❑ 108 Bryan Harvey .05 .02
❑ 109 Greg A. Harris UER .05 .02
(Shown pitching lefty, bio says righty)
❑ 110 Greg Swindell .05 .02
❑ 111 Juan Berenguer .05 .02
❑ 112 Mike Heath .05 .02
❑ 113 Scott Bradley .05 .02
❑ 114 Jack Morris .10 .05
❑ 115 Barry Jones .05 .02
❑ 116 Kevin Romine .05 .02
❑ 117 Garry Templeton .05 .02
❑ 118 Scott Sanderson .05 .02
❑ 119 Roberto Kelly .05 .02
❑ 120 George Brett .40 .18
❑ 121 Oddibe McDowell .05 .02
❑ 122 Jim Acker .05 .02
❑ 123 Bill Swift UER .05 .02
(Born 12/27/61, should be 10/27)

❑ 124 Eric King .05 .02
❑ 125 Jay Buhner .10 .05
❑ 126 Matt Young .05 .02
❑ 127 Alvaro Espinoza .05 .02
❑ 128 Greg Hibbard .05 .02
❑ 129 Jeff M. Robinson .05 .02
❑ 130 Mike Greenwell .05 .02
❑ 131 Dion James .05 .02
❑ 132 Donn Pall UER .05 .02
(1988 ERA in stats 0.00)
❑ 133 Lloyd Moseby .05 .02
❑ 134 Randy Velarde .05 .02
❑ 135 Allan Anderson .05 .02
❑ 136 Mark Davis .05 .02
❑ 137 Eric Davis .10 .05
❑ 138 Phil Stephenson .05 .02
❑ 139 Felix Fermin .05 .02
❑ 140 Pedro Guerrero .10 .05
❑ 141 Charlie Hough .10 .05
❑ 142 Mike Henneman .05 .02
❑ 143 Jeff Montgomery .05 .02
❑ 144 Lenny Harris .05 .02
❑ 145 Bruce Hurst .05 .02
❑ 146 Eric Anthony .05 .02
❑ 147 Paul Assenmacher .05 .02
❑ 148 Jesse Barfield .05 .02
❑ 149 Carlos Quintana .05 .02
❑ 150 Dave Stewart .10 .05
❑ 151 Roy Smith .05 .02
❑ 152 Paul Gibson .05 .02
❑ 153 Mickey Hatcher .05 .02
❑ 154 Jim Eisenreich .05 .02
❑ 155 Kenny Rogers .05 .02
❑ 156 Dave Schmidt .05 .02
❑ 157 Lance Johnson .05 .02
❑ 158 Dave West .05 .02
❑ 159 Steve Balboni .05 .02
❑ 160 Jeff Brantley .05 .02
❑ 161 Craig Biggio .15 .07
❑ 162 Brook Jacoby .05 .02
❑ 163 Dan Gladden .05 .02
❑ 164 Jeff Reardon UER .10 .05
(Total IP shown as
943.2, should be 943.1)
❑ 165 Mark Carreon .05 .02
❑ 166 Mel Hall .05 .02
❑ 167 Gary Mielke .05 .02
❑ 168 Cecil Fielder .10 .05
❑ 169 Darrin Jackson .05 .02
❑ 170 Rick Aguilera .10 .05
❑ 171 Walt Weiss .05 .02
❑ 172 Steve Farr .05 .02
❑ 173 Jody Reed .05 .02
❑ 174 Mike Jeffcoat .05 .02
❑ 175 Mark Grace .20 .09
❑ 176 Larry Sheets .05 .02
❑ 177 Bill Gullickson .05 .02
❑ 178 Chris Gwynn .05 .02
❑ 179 Melido Perez .05 .02
❑ 180 Sid Fernandez UER .05 .02
(779 runs in 1990)
❑ 181 Tim Burke .05 .02
❑ 182 Gary Pettis .05 .02
❑ 183 Rob Murphy .05 .02
❑ 184 Craig Lefferts .05 .02
❑ 185 Howard Johnson .05 .02
❑ 186 Ken Caminiti .10 .05
❑ 187 Tim Belcher .05 .02
❑ 188 Greg Cadaret .05 .02
❑ 189 Matt Williams .15 .07
❑ 190 Dave Magadan .05 .02
❑ 191 Geno Petralli .05 .02
❑ 192 Jeff D. Robinson .05 .02
❑ 193 Jim Deshaies .05 .02
❑ 194 Willie Randolph .10 .05
❑ 195 George Bell .05 .02
❑ 196 Hubie Brooks .05 .02
❑ 197 Tom Gordon .05 .02
❑ 198 Mike Fitzgerald .05 .02
❑ 199 Mike Pagliarulo .05 .02
❑ 200 Kirby Puckett .50 .23
❑ 201 Shawon Dunston .05 .02
❑ 202 Dennis Boyd .05 .02
❑ 203 Junior Felix UER .05 .02
(Text has him in NL)
❑ 204 Alejandro Pena .05 .02
❑ 205 Pete Smith .05 .02
❑ 206 Tom Glavine UER .20 .09
(Lefty spelled leftie)
❑ 207 Luis Salazar .05 .02
❑ 208 John Smoltz .10 .05
❑ 209 Doug Dascenzo .05 .02
❑ 210 Tim Wallach .05 .02
❑ 211 Greg Gagne .05 .02
❑ 212 Mark Gubicza .05 .02
❑ 213 Mark Parent .05 .02
❑ 214 Ken Oberkfell .05 .02
❑ 215 Gary Carter .15 .07
❑ 216 Rafael Palmeiro .20 .09
❑ 217 Tom Niedenfuer .05 .02
❑ 218 Dave LaPoint .05 .02
❑ 219 Jeff Treadway .05 .02
❑ 220 Mitch Williams UER .05 .02
('89 ERA shown as 2.76,
should be 2.64)
❑ 221 Jose DeLeon .05 .02
❑ 222 Mike LaValliere .05 .02
❑ 223 Darrel Akerfelds .05 .02
❑ 224A Kent Anderson ERR .10 .05
(First line, flachy
should read flashy)
❑ 224B Kent Anderson COR .10 .05
(Corrected in
factory sets)
❑ 225 Dwight Evans .10 .05
❑ 226 Gary Redus .05 .02
❑ 227 Paul O'Neill .20 .09
❑ 228 Marty Barrett .05 .02
❑ 229 Tom Browning .05 .02
❑ 230 Terry Pendleton .10 .05
❑ 231 Jack Armstrong .05 .02
❑ 232 Mike Boddicker .05 .02
❑ 233 Neal Heaton .05 .02
❑ 234 Marquis Grissom .05 .02
❑ 235 Bert Blyleven .10 .05
❑ 236 Curt Young .05 .02
❑ 237 Don Carman .05 .02
❑ 238 Charlie Hayes .05 .02
❑ 239 Mark Knudson .05 .02
❑ 240 Todd Zeile .05 .02
❑ 241 Larry Walker UER .15 .07
(Maple River, should
be Maple Ridge)
❑ 242 Jerald Clark .05 .02
❑ 243 Jeff Ballard .05 .02
❑ 244 Jeff King .05 .02
❑ 245 Tom Brunansky .05 .02
❑ 246 Darren Daulton .10 .05
❑ 247 Scott Terry .05 .02
❑ 248 Rob Deer .05 .02
❑ 249 Brady Anderson UER .10 .05
(1990 Hagerstown 1 hit,
should say 13 hits)
❑ 250 Len Dykstra .10 .05
❑ 251 Greg W. Harris .05 .02
❑ 252 Mike Hartley .05 .02
❑ 253 Joey Cora .05 .02
❑ 254 Ivan Calderon .05 .02
❑ 255 Ted Power .05 .02
❑ 256 Sammy Sosa .50 .23
❑ 257 Steve Buechele .05 .02
❑ 258 Mike Devereaux UER .05 .02
(No comma between
city and state)
❑ 259 Brad Komminsk UER .05 .02
(Last text line,
Ba should be BA)
❑ 260 Ted Higuera .05 .02
❑ 261 Shawn Abner .05 .02
❑ 262 Dave Valle .05 .02
❑ 263 Jeff Huson .05 .02
❑ 264 Edgar Martinez .15 .07
❑ 265 Carlton Fisk .20 .09
❑ 266 Steve Finley .10 .05
❑ 267 John Wetteland .10 .05
❑ 268 Kevin Appier .10 .05
❑ 269 Steve Lyons .05 .02
❑ 270 Mickey Tettleton .05 .02
❑ 271 Luis Rivera .05 .02
❑ 272 Steve Jeltz .05 .02
❑ 273 R.J. Reynolds .05 .02
❑ 274 Carlos Martinez .05 .02
❑ 275 Dan Plesac .05 .02
❑ 276 Mike Morgan UER .05 .02
(Total IP shown as
1149.1, should be 1149)
❑ 277 Jeff Russell .05 .02
❑ 278 Pete Incaviglia .05 .02
❑ 279 Kevin Seitzer UER .05 .02
(Bio has 200 hits twice
and .300 four times,
should be once and
three times)
❑ 280 Bobby Thigpen .05 .02
❑ 281 Stan Javier UER .05 .02
(Born 1/9,
should say 9/1)
❑ 282 Henry Cotto .05 .02
❑ 283 Gary Wayne .05 .02
❑ 284 Shane Mack .05 .02
❑ 285 Brian Holman .05 .02
❑ 286 Gerald Perry .05 .02
❑ 287 Steve Crawford .05 .02
❑ 288 Nelson Liriano .05 .02
❑ 289 Don Aase .05 .02
❑ 290 Randy Johnson .30 .14
❑ 291 Harold Baines .10 .05
❑ 292 Kent Hrbek .10 .05
❑ 293A Les Lancaster ERR .05 .02
(No comma between
Dallas and Texas)
❑ 293B Les Lancaster COR .05 .02
(Corrected in
factory sets)
❑ 294 Jeff Musselman .05 .02
❑ 295 Kurt Stillwell .05 .02
❑ 296 Stan Belinda .05 .02
❑ 297 Lou Whitaker .10 .05
❑ 298 Glenn Wilson .05 .02
❑ 299 Omar Vizquel UER .10 .05
(Born 5/15, should be
4/24, there is a decimal
before GP total for '90)
❑ 300 Ramon Martinez .05 .02
❑ 301 Dwight Smith .05 .02
❑ 302 Tim Crews .05 .02
❑ 303 Lance Blankenship .05 .02
❑ 304 Sid Bream .05 .02
❑ 305 Rafael Ramirez .05 .02
❑ 306 Steve Wilson .05 .02
❑ 307 Mackey Sasser .05 .02
❑ 308 Franklin Stubbs .05 .02
❑ 309 Jack Daugherty UER .05 .02
(Born 6/3/60,
should say July)
❑ 310 Eddie Murray .20 .09
❑ 311 Bob Welch .05 .02
❑ 312 Brian Harper .05 .02
❑ 313 Lance McCullers .05 .02
❑ 314 Dave Smith .05 .02
❑ 315 Bobby Bonilla .10 .05
❑ 316 Jerry Don Gleaton .05 .02
❑ 317 Greg Maddux .50 .23
❑ 318 Keith Miller .05 .02
❑ 319 Mark Portugal .05 .02
❑ 320 Robin Ventura .10 .05
❑ 321 Bob Ojeda .05 .02
❑ 322 Mike Harkey .05 .02
❑ 323 Jay Bell .10 .05
❑ 324 Mark McGwire .75 .35
❑ 325 Gary Gaetti .10 .05
❑ 326 Jeff Pico .05 .02
❑ 327 Kevin McReynolds .05 .02
❑ 328 Frank Tanana .05 .02
❑ 329 Eric Yelding UER .05 .02
(Listed as 6'3"
should be 5'11")
❑ 330 Barry Bonds .50 .23
❑ 331 Brian McRae RC UER .10 .05
(No comma between
city and state)
❑ 332 Pedro Munoz RC .05 .02
❑ 333 Daryl Irvine .05 .02
❑ 334 Chris Hoiles .05 .02
❑ 335 Thomas Howard .05 .02
❑ 336 Jeff Schulz .05 .02
❑ 337 Jeff Manto .05 .02
❑ 338 Beau Allred .05 .02

❑ 339 Mike Bordick RC .50 .23
❑ 340 Todd Hundley .05 .02
❑ 341 Jim Vatcher UER .05 .02
(Height 6'9", should be 5'9")
❑ 342 Luis Sojo .05 .02
❑ 343 Jose Offerman UER .05 .02
(Born 1969, should say 1968)
❑ 344 Pete Coachman .05 .02
❑ 345 Mike Benjamin .05 .02
❑ 346 Ozzie Canseco .05 .02
❑ 347 Tim McIntosh .05 .02
❑ 348 Phil Plantier RC .05 .02
❑ 349 Terry Shumpert .05 .02
❑ 350 Darren Lewis .05 .02
❑ 351 David Walsh .05 .02
❑ 352A Scott Chiamparino .10 .05
ERR (Bats left, should be right)
❑ 352B Scott Chiamparino .10 .05
COR (corrected in factory sets)
❑ 353 Julio Valera .05 .02
UER (Progressed misspelled as progessed)
❑ 354 Anthony Telford .05 .02
❑ 355 Kevin Wickander .05 .02
❑ 356 Tim Naehring .05 .02
❑ 357 Jim Poole .05 .02
❑ 358 Mark Whiten UER .05 .02
(Shown hitting lefty, bio says righty)
❑ 359 Terry Wells .05 .02
❑ 360 Rafael Valdez .05 .02
❑ 361 Mel Stottlemyre Jr. .05 .02
❑ 362 David Segui .05 .02
❑ 363 Paul Abbott RC .10 .05
❑ 364 Steve Howard .05 .02
❑ 365 Karl Rhodes .05 .02
❑ 366 Rafael Novoa .05 .02
❑ 367 Joe Grahe RC .05 .02
❑ 368 Darren Reed .05 .02
❑ 369 Jeff McKnight .05 .02
❑ 370 Scott Leius .05 .02
❑ 371 Mark Dewey .05 .02
❑ 372 Mark Lee UER .05 .02
(Shown hitting lefty, bio says righty, born in Dakota, should say North Dakota)
❑ 373 Rosario Rodriguez .05 .02
(Shown hitting lefty, bio says righty) UER
❑ 374 Chuck McElroy .05 .02
❑ 375 Mike Bell .05 .02
❑ 376 Mickey Morandini .05 .02
❑ 377 Bill Haselman .05 .02
❑ 378 Dave Pavlas .05 .02
❑ 379 Derrick May .05 .02
❑ 380 J.Burnitz FDP RC .50 .23
❑ 381 Donald Peters FDP .05 .02
❑ 382 Alex Fernandez FDP .05 .02
❑ 383 Mike Mussina FDP RC 2.00 .90
❑ 384 Dan Smith FDP RC .05 .02
❑ 385 L.Dickson FDP RC .05 .02
❑ 386 Carl Everett FDP RC .50 .23
❑ 387 Tom Nevers FDP RC .05 .02
❑ 388 Adam Hyzdu FDP RC .05 .02
❑ 389 T.Van Poppel FDP RC .05 .02
❑ 390 R.White FDP RC .40 .18
❑ 391 M.Newfield FDP RC .05 .02
❑ 392 Julio Franco AS .05 .02
❑ 393 Wade Boggs AS .10 .05
❑ 394 Ozzie Guillen AS .05 .02
❑ 395 Cecil Fielder AS .05 .02
❑ 396 Ken Griffey Jr. AS .40 .18
❑ 397 Rickey Henderson AS .20 .09
❑ 398 Jose Canseco AS .10 .05
❑ 399 Roger Clemens AS .25 .11
❑ 400 Sandy Alomar Jr. AS .05 .02
❑ 401 Bobby Thigpen AS .05 .02
❑ 402 Bobby Bonilla MB .05 .02
❑ 403 Eric Davis MB .05 .02
❑ 404 Fred McGriff MB .10 .05
❑ 405 Glenn Davis MB .05 .02
❑ 406 Kevin Mitchell MB .05 .02
❑ 407 Rob Dibble KM .05 .02
❑ 408 Ramon Martinez KM .05 .02
❑ 409 David Cone KM .05 .02
❑ 410 Bobby Witt KM .05 .02
❑ 411 Mark Langston KM .05 .02
❑ 412 Bo Jackson RIF .05 .02
❑ 413 Shawon Dunston RIF .05 .02
UER (In the baseball, should say in baseball)
❑ 414 Jesse Barfield RIF .05 .02
❑ 415 Ken Caminiti RIF .05 .02
❑ 416 Benito Santiago RIF .05 .02
❑ 417 Nolan Ryan HL .50 .23
❑ 418 B.Thigpen HL UER .05 .02
Back refers to Hal McRae Jr., should say Brian McRae
❑ 419 Ramon Martinez HL .05 .02
❑ 420 Bo Jackson HL .05 .02
❑ 421 Carlton Fisk HL .10 .05
❑ 422 Jimmy Key .10 .05
❑ 423 Junior Noboa .05 .02
❑ 424 Al Newman .05 .02
❑ 425 Pat Borders .05 .02
❑ 426 Von Hayes .05 .02
❑ 427 Tim Teufel .05 .02
❑ 428 Eric Plunk UER .05 .02
(Text says Eric's had, no apostrophe needed)
❑ 429 John Moses .05 .02
❑ 430 Mike Witt .05 .02
❑ 431 Otis Nixon .05 .02
❑ 432 Tony Fernandez .05 .02
❑ 433 Rance Mulliniks .05 .02
❑ 434 Dan Petry .05 .02
❑ 435 Bob Geren .05 .02
❑ 436 Steve Frey .05 .02
❑ 437 Jamie Moyer .05 .02
❑ 438 Junior Ortiz .05 .02
❑ 439 Tom O'Malley .05 .02
❑ 440 Pat Combs .05 .02
❑ 441 Jose Canseco DT .20 .09
❑ 442 Alfredo Griffin .05 .02
❑ 443 Andres Galarraga .15 .07
❑ 444 Bryn Smith .05 .02
❑ 445 Andre Dawson .15 .07
❑ 446 Juan Samuel .05 .02
❑ 447 Mike Aldrete .05 .02
❑ 448 Ron Gant .05 .02
❑ 449 Fernando Valenzuela .10 .05
❑ 450 Vince Coleman UER .05 .02
(Should say topped majors in steals four times, not three times)
❑ 451 Kevin Mitchell .05 .02
❑ 452 Spike Owen .05 .02
❑ 453 Mike Bielecki .05 .02
❑ 454 Dennis Martinez .10 .05
❑ 455 Brett Butler .10 .05
❑ 456 Ron Darling .05 .02
❑ 457 Dennis Rasmussen .05 .02
❑ 458 Ken Howell .05 .02
❑ 459 Steve Bedrosian .05 .02
❑ 460 Frank Viola .10 .05
❑ 461 Jose Lind .05 .02
❑ 462 Chris Sabo .05 .02
❑ 463 Dante Bichette .10 .05
❑ 464 Rick Mahler .05 .02
❑ 465 John Smiley .05 .02
❑ 466 Devon White .05 .02
❑ 467 John Orton .05 .02
❑ 468 Mike Stanton .05 .02
❑ 469 Billy Hatcher .05 .02
❑ 470 Wally Joyner .10 .05
❑ 471 Gene Larkin .05 .02
❑ 472 Doug Drabek .05 .02
❑ 473 Gary Sheffield .10 .05
❑ 474 David Wells .10 .05
❑ 475 Andy Van Slyke .10 .05
❑ 476 Mike Gallego .05 .02
❑ 477 B.J. Surhoff .10 .05
❑ 478 Gene Nelson .05 .02
❑ 479 Mariano Duncan .05 .02
❑ 480 Fred McGriff .15 .07
❑ 481 Jerry Browne .05 .02
❑ 482 Alvin Davis .05 .02
❑ 483 Bill Wegman .05 .02
❑ 484 Dave Parker .10 .05
❑ 485 Dennis Eckersley .10 .05
❑ 486 Erik Hanson UER .05 .02
(Basketball misspelled as baseketball)
❑ 487 Bill Ripken .05 .02
❑ 488 Tom Candiotti .05 .02
❑ 489 Mike Schooler .05 .02
❑ 490 Gregg Olson .05 .02
❑ 491 Chris James .05 .02
❑ 492 Pete Harnisch .05 .02
❑ 493 Julio Franco .10 .05
❑ 494 Greg Briley .05 .02
❑ 495 Ruben Sierra .05 .02
❑ 496 Steve Olin .05 .02
❑ 497 Mike Fetters .05 .02
❑ 498 Mark Williamson .05 .02
❑ 499 Bob Tewksbury .05 .02
❑ 500 Tony Gwynn .40 .18
❑ 501 Randy Myers .05 .02
❑ 502 Keith Comstock .05 .02
❑ 503 C.Worthington UER .05 .02
DeCinces misspelled DiCinces on back
❑ 504 Mark Eichhorn UER .05 .02
(Stats incomplete, doesn't have '89 Braves stint)
❑ 505 Barry Larkin .20 .09
❑ 506 Dave Johnson .05 .02
❑ 507 Bobby Witt .05 .02
❑ 508 Joe Orsulak .05 .02
❑ 509 Pete O'Brien .05 .02
❑ 510 Brad Arnsberg .05 .02
❑ 511 Storm Davis .05 .02
❑ 512 Bob Milacki .05 .02
❑ 513 Bill Pecota .05 .02
❑ 514 Glenallen Hill .05 .02
❑ 515 Danny Tartabull .05 .02
❑ 516 Mike Moore .05 .02
❑ 517 Ron Robinson UER .05 .02
(577 K's in 1990)
❑ 518 Mark Gardner .05 .02
❑ 519 Rick Wrona .05 .02
❑ 520 Mike Scioscia .05 .02
❑ 521 Frank Wills .05 .02
❑ 522 Greg Brock .05 .02
❑ 523 Jack Clark .10 .05
❑ 524 Bruce Ruffin .05 .02
❑ 525 Robin Yount .20 .09
❑ 526 Tom Foley .05 .02
❑ 527 Pat Perry .05 .02
❑ 528 Greg Vaughn .10 .05
❑ 529 Wally Whitehurst .05 .02
❑ 530 Norm Charlton .05 .02
❑ 531 Marvell Wynne .05 .02
❑ 532 Jim Gantner .05 .02
❑ 533 Greg Litton .05 .02
❑ 534 Manny Lee .05 .02
❑ 535 Scott Bailes .05 .02
❑ 536 Charlie Leibrandt .05 .02
❑ 537 Roger McDowell .05 .02
❑ 538 Andy Benes .05 .02
❑ 539 Rick Honeycutt .05 .02
❑ 540 Dwight Gooden .10 .05
❑ 541 Scott Garrelts .05 .02
❑ 542 Dave Clark .05 .02
❑ 543 Lonnie Smith .05 .02
❑ 544 Rick Reuschel .05 .02
❑ 545 Delino DeShields UER .10 .05
(Rockford misspelled as Rock Ford in '88)
❑ 546 Mike Sharperson .05 .02
❑ 547 Mike Kingery .05 .02
❑ 548 Terry Kennedy .05 .02
❑ 549 David Cone .10 .05
❑ 550 Orel Hershiser .10 .05
❑ 551 Matt Nokes .05 .02
❑ 552 Eddie Williams .05 .02
❑ 553 Frank DiPino .05 .02
❑ 554 Fred Lynn .05 .02
❑ 555 Alex Cole .05 .02
❑ 556 Terry Leach .05 .02
❑ 557 Chet Lemon .05 .02

❑ 558 Paul Mirabella .05 .02
❑ 559 Bill Long .05 .02
❑ 560 Phil Bradley .05 .02
❑ 561 Duane Ward .05 .02
❑ 562 Dave Bergman .05 .02
❑ 563 Eric Show .05 .02
❑ 564 Xavier Hernandez .05 .02
❑ 565 Jeff Parrett .05 .02
❑ 566 Chuck Cary .05 .02
❑ 567 Ken Hill .05 .02
❑ 568 Bob Welch Hand .05 .02
(Complement should be compliment) UER
❑ 569 John Mitchell .05 .02
❑ 570 Travis Fryman .10 .05
❑ 571 Derek Lilliquist .05 .02
❑ 572 Steve Lake .05 .02
❑ 573 John Barfield .05 .02
❑ 574 Randy Bush .05 .02
❑ 575 Joe Magrane .05 .02
❑ 576 Eddie Diaz .05 .02
❑ 577 Casey Candaele .05 .02
❑ 578 Jesse Orosco .05 .02
❑ 579 Tom Henke .05 .02
❑ 580 Rick Cerone UER .05 .02
(Actually his third go-round with Yankees)
❑ 581 Drew Hall .05 .02
❑ 582 Tony Castillo .05 .02
❑ 583 Jimmy Jones .05 .02
❑ 584 Rick Reed .05 .02
❑ 585 Joe Girardi .05 .02
❑ 586 Jeff Gray .05 .02
❑ 587 Luis Polonia .05 .02
❑ 588 Joe Klink .05 .02
❑ 589 Rex Hudler .05 .02
❑ 590 Kirk McCaskill .05 .02
❑ 591 Juan Agosto .05 .02
❑ 592 Wes Gardner .05 .02
❑ 593 Rich Rodriguez .05 .02
❑ 594 Mitch Webster .05 .02
❑ 595 Kelly Gruber .05 .02
❑ 596 Dale Mohorcic .05 .02
❑ 597 Willie McGee .10 .05
❑ 598 Bill Krueger .05 .02
❑ 599 Bob Walk UER .05 .02
(Cards says he's 33, but actually he's 34)
❑ 600 Kevin Maas .05 .02
❑ 601 Danny Jackson .05 .02
❑ 602 Craig McMurtry UER .05 .02
(Anonymously misspelled anonimously)
❑ 603 Curtis Wilkerson .05 .02
❑ 604 Adam Peterson .05 .02
❑ 605 Sam Horn .05 .02
❑ 606 Tommy Gregg .05 .02
❑ 607 Ken Dayley .05 .02
❑ 608 Carmelo Castillo .05 .02
❑ 609 John Shelby .05 .02
❑ 610 Don Slaught .05 .02
❑ 611 Calvin Schiraldi .05 .02
❑ 612 Dennis Lamp .05 .02
❑ 613 Andres Thomas .05 .02
❑ 614 Jose Gonzalez .05 .02
❑ 615 Randy Ready .05 .02
❑ 616 Kevin Bass .05 .02
❑ 617 Mike Marshall .05 .02
❑ 618 Daryl Boston .05 .02
❑ 619 Andy McGaffigan .05 .02
❑ 620 Joe Oliver .05 .02
❑ 621 Jim Gott .05 .02
❑ 622 Jose Oquendo .05 .02
❑ 623 Jose DeJesus .05 .02
❑ 624 Mike Brumley .05 .02
❑ 625 John Olerud .15 .07
❑ 626 Ernest Riles .05 .02
❑ 627 Gene Harris .05 .02
❑ 628 Jose Uribe .05 .02
❑ 629 Darnell Coles .05 .02
❑ 630 Carney Lansford .10 .05
❑ 631 Tim Leary .05 .02
❑ 632 Tim Hulett .05 .02
❑ 633 Kevin Elster .05 .02
❑ 634 Tony Fossas .05 .02
❑ 635 Francisco Oliveras .05 .02
❑ 636 Bob Patterson .05 .02
❑ 637 Gary Ward .05 .02
❑ 638 Rene Gonzales .05 .02
❑ 639 Don Robinson .05 .02
❑ 640 Darryl Strawberry .10 .05
❑ 641 Dave Anderson .05 .02
❑ 642 Scott Scudder .05 .02
❑ 643 Reggie Harris UER .05 .02
(Hepatitis misspelled as hepititis)
❑ 644 Dave Henderson .05 .02
❑ 645 Ben McDonald .05 .02
❑ 646 Bob Kipper .05 .02
❑ 647 Hal Morris UER .05 .02
(It's should be its)
❑ 648 Tim Birtsas .05 .02
❑ 649 Steve Searcy .05 .02
❑ 650 Dale Murphy .20 .09
❑ 651 Ron Oester .05 .02
❑ 652 Mike LaCoss .05 .02
❑ 653 Ron Jones .05 .02
❑ 654 Kelly Downs .05 .02
❑ 655 Roger Clemens .50 .23
❑ 656 Herm Winningham .05 .02
❑ 657 Trevor Wilson .05 .02
❑ 658 Jose Rijo .05 .02
❑ 659 Dann Bilardello UER .05 .02
(Bio has 13 games, 1 hit, and 32 AB, stats show 19, 2, and 37)
❑ 660 Gregg Jefferies .05 .02
❑ 661 Doug Drabek AS UER .05 .02
(Through is misspelled though)
❑ 662 Randy Myers AS .05 .02
❑ 663 Benny Santiago AS .05 .02
❑ 664 Will Clark AS .10 .05
❑ 665 Ryne Sandberg AS .15 .07
❑ 666 Barry Larkin AS UER .10 .05
(Line 13, coolly misspelled cooly)
❑ 667 Matt Williams AS .10 .05
❑ 668 Barry Bonds AS .25 .11
❑ 669 Eric Davis AS .05 .02
❑ 670 Bobby Bonilla AS .05 .02
❑ 671 C.Jones FDP RC 3.00 1.35
❑ 672 E.Christopherson RC FDP .05 .02
❑ 673 R.Beckett FDP RC .05 .02
❑ 674 S.Andrews FDP RC .10 .05
❑ 675 Steve Karsay FDP RC .10 .05
❑ 676 Aaron Holbert FDP RC .05 .02
❑ 677 D.Osborne FDP RC .10 .05
❑ 678 Todd Ritchie FDP RC .10 .05
❑ 679 Ron Walden FDP RC .05 .02
❑ 680 Tim Costo FDP RC .05 .02
❑ 681 Dan Wilson FDP RC .10 .05
❑ 682 Kurt Miller FDP RC .05 .02
❑ 683 M.Lieberthal FDP RC .50 .23
❑ 684 Roger Clemens KM .25 .11
❑ 685 Dwight Gooden KM .05 .02
❑ 686 Nolan Ryan KM .50 .23
❑ 687 Frank Viola KM .05 .02
❑ 688 Erik Hanson KM .05 .02
❑ 689 Matt Williams MB .10 .05
❑ 690 J.Canseco MB UER .10 .05
Mammoth misspelled as monmouth
❑ 691 Darryl Strawberry MB .05 .02
❑ 692 Bo Jackson MB .05 .02
❑ 693 Cecil Fielder MB .05 .02
❑ 694 Sandy Alomar Jr. RF .05 .02
❑ 695 Cory Snyder RF .05 .02
❑ 696 Eric Davis RF .05 .02
❑ 697 Ken Griffey Jr. RF .40 .18
❑ 698 A.Van Slyke RF UER .05 .02
Line 2, outfielders does not need
❑ 699 Mark Langston NH .05 .02
Mike Witt
❑ 700 Randy Johnson NH .15 .07
❑ 701 Nolan Ryan NH .50 .23
❑ 702 Dave Stewart NH .05 .02
❑ 703 F.Valenzuela NH .05 .02
❑ 704 Andy Hawkins NH .05 .02
❑ 705 Melido Perez NH .05 .02
❑ 706 Terry Mulholland NH .05 .02
❑ 707 Dave Stieb NH .05 .02
❑ 708 Brian Barnes RC .05 .02
❑ 709 Bernard Gilkey .05 .02
❑ 710 Steve Decker .05 .02
❑ 711 Paul Faries .05 .02
❑ 712 Paul Marak .05 .02
❑ 713 Wes Chamberlain RC .05 .02
❑ 714 Kevin Belcher .05 .02
❑ 715 Dan Boone UER .05 .02
(IP adds up to 101, but card has 101.2)
❑ 716 Steve Adkins .05 .02
❑ 717 Geronimo Pena .05 .02
❑ 718 Howard Farmer .05 .02
❑ 719 Mark Leonard .05 .02
❑ 720 Tom Lampkin .05 .02
❑ 721 Mike Gardiner .05 .02
❑ 722 Jeff Conine RC .10 .05
❑ 723 Efrain Valdez .05 .02
❑ 724 Chuck Malone .05 .02
❑ 725 Leo Gomez .05 .02
❑ 726 Paul McClellan .05 .02
❑ 727 Mark Leiter RC .05 .02
❑ 728 Rich DeLucia UER .05 .02
(Line 2, all told is written alltold)
❑ 729 Mel Rojas .05 .02
❑ 730 Hector Wagner .05 .02
❑ 731 Ray Lankford .10 .05
❑ 732 Turner Ward RC .10 .05
❑ 733 Gerald Alexander .05 .02
❑ 734 Scott Anderson .05 .02
❑ 735 Tony Perezchica .05 .02
❑ 736 Jimmy Kremers .05 .02
❑ 737 American Flag .20 .09
(Pray for Peace)
❑ 738 Mike York .05 .02
❑ 739 Mike Rochford .05 .02
❑ 740 Scott Aldred .05 .02
❑ 741 Rico Brogna .05 .02
❑ 742 Dave Burba RC .10 .05
❑ 743 Ray Stephens .05 .02
❑ 744 Eric Gunderson .05 .02
❑ 745 Troy Afenir .05 .02
❑ 746 Jeff Shaw .05 .02
❑ 747 Orlando Merced RC .05 .02
❑ 748 O.Olivares UER RC .10 .05
Line 9, league is misspelled legaue
❑ 749 Jerry Kutzler .05 .02
❑ 750 Mo Vaughn UER .10 .05
(44 SB's in 1990)
❑ 751 Matt Stark .05 .02
❑ 752 Randy Hennis .05 .02
❑ 753 Andujar Cedeno .05 .02
❑ 754 Kelvin Torve .05 .02
❑ 755 Joe Kraemer .05 .02
❑ 756 Phil Clark RC .05 .02
❑ 757 Ed Vosberg .05 .02
❑ 758 Mike Perez RC .05 .02
❑ 759 Scott Lewis .05 .02
❑ 760 Steve Chitren .05 .02
❑ 761 Ray Young .05 .02
❑ 762 Andres Santana .05 .02
❑ 763 Rodney McCray .05 .02
❑ 764 Sean Berry UER RC .10 .05
(Name misspelled Barry on card front)
❑ 765 Brent Mayne .05 .02
❑ 766 Mike Simms .05 .02
❑ 767 Glenn Sutko .05 .02
❑ 768 Gary DiSarcina .05 .02
❑ 769 George Brett HL .20 .09
❑ 770 Cecil Fielder HL .05 .02
❑ 771 Jim Presley .05 .02
❑ 772 John Dopson .05 .02
❑ 773 Bo Jackson Breaker .05 .02
❑ 774 Brent Knackert UER .05 .02
(Born in 1954, shown throwing righty, but bio says lefty)
❑ 775 Bill Doran UER .05 .02
(Reds in NL East)
❑ 776 Dick Schofield .05 .02
❑ 777 Nelson Santovenia .05 .02

❑ 778 Mark Guthrie .05 .02
❑ 779 Mark Lemke .05 .02
❑ 780 Terry Steinbach .05 .02
❑ 781 Tom Bolton .05 .02
❑ 782 Randy Tomlin RC .05 .02
❑ 783 Jeff Kunkel .05 .02
❑ 784 Felix Jose .05 .02
❑ 785 Rick Sutcliffe .10 .05
❑ 786 John Cerutti .05 .02
❑ 787 Jose Vizcaino UER .05 .02
(Offerman, not Opperman)
❑ 788 Curt Schilling .20 .09
❑ 789 Ed Whitson .05 .02
❑ 790 Tony Pena .05 .02
❑ 791 John Candelaria .05 .02
❑ 792 Carmelo Martinez .05 .02
❑ 793 Sandy Alomar Jr. UER .10 .05
(Indian's should say Indians')
❑ 794 Jim Neidlinger .05 .02
❑ 795 Barry Larkin WS and Chris Sabo .10 .05
❑ 796 Paul Sorrento .05 .02
❑ 797 Tom Pagnozzi .05 .02
❑ 798 Tino Martinez .10 .05
❑ 799 Scott Ruskin UER .05 .02
(Text says first three seasons but lists averages for four)
❑ 800 Kirk Gibson .10 .05
❑ 801 Walt Terrell .05 .02
❑ 802 John Russell .05 .02
❑ 803 Chili Davis .10 .05
❑ 804 Chris Nabholz .05 .02
❑ 805 Juan Gonzalez .25 .11
❑ 806 Ron Hassey .05 .02
❑ 807 Todd Worrell .05 .02
❑ 808 Tommy Greene .05 .02
❑ 809 Joel Skinner UER .05 .02
(Joel, not Bob, was drafted in 1979)
❑ 810 Benito Santiago .05 .02
❑ 811 Pat Tabler UER .05 .02
(Line 3, always misspelled alway)
❑ 812 Scott Erickson UER .05 .02
(Record spelled rcord)
❑ 813 Moises Alou .10 .05
❑ 814 Dale Sveum .05 .02
❑ 815 R.Sandberg MANYR .15 .07
❑ 816 Rick Dempsey .05 .02
❑ 817 Scott Bankhead .05 .02
❑ 818 Jason Grimsley .05 .02
❑ 819 Doug Jennings .05 .02
❑ 820 Tom Herr .05 .02
❑ 821 Rob Ducey .05 .02
❑ 822 Luis Quinones .05 .02
❑ 823 Greg Minton .05 .02
❑ 824 Mark Grant .05 .02
❑ 825 Ozzie Smith UER .25 .11
(Shortstop misspelled shortsop)
❑ 826 Dave Eiland .05 .02
❑ 827 Danny Heep .05 .02
❑ 828 Hensley Meulens .05 .02
❑ 829 Charlie O'Brien .05 .02
❑ 830 Glenn Davis .05 .02
❑ 831 John Marzano UER .05 .02
(International misspelled Internaional)
❑ 832 Steve Ontiveros .05 .02
❑ 833 Ron Karkovice .05 .02
❑ 834 Jerry Goff .05 .02
❑ 835 Ken Griffey Sr. .10 .05
❑ 836 Kevin Reimer .05 .02
❑ 837 Randy Kutcher UER .05 .02
(Infectious misspelled infectous)
❑ 838 Mike Blowers .05 .02
❑ 839 Mike Macfarlane .05 .02
❑ 840 Frank Thomas UER .30 .14
(1989 Sarasota stats, 15 games but 188 AB)
❑ 841 The Griffeys .60 .25
Ken Griffey Jr.
Ken Griffey Sr.
❑ 842 Jack Howell .05 .02
❑ 843 Goose Gozzo .05 .02
❑ 844 Gerald Young .05 .02
❑ 845 Zane Smith .05 .02
❑ 846 Kevin Brown .10 .05
❑ 847 Sil Campusano .05 .02
❑ 848 Larry Andersen .05 .02
❑ 849 Cal Ripken FRAN .40 .18
❑ 850 Roger Clemens FRAN .25 .11
❑ 851 S.Alomar Jr. FRAN .05 .02
❑ 852 Alan Trammell FRAN .10 .05
❑ 853 George Brett FRAN .20 .09
❑ 854 Robin Yount FRAN .10 .05
❑ 855 Kirby Puckett FRAN .25 .11
❑ 856 Don Mattingly FRAN .25 .11
❑ 857 R.Henderson FRAN .20 .09
❑ 858 Ken Griffey Jr. FRAN .40 .18
❑ 859 Ruben Sierra FRAN .05 .02
❑ 860 John Olerud FRAN .10 .05
❑ 861 Dave Justice FRAN .10 .05
❑ 862 Ryne Sandberg FRAN .15 .07
❑ 863 Eric Davis FRAN .05 .02
❑ 864 D.Strawberry FRAN .05 .02
❑ 865 Tim Wallach FRAN .05 .02
❑ 866 Dwight Gooden FRAN .05 .02
❑ 867 Len Dykstra FRAN .05 .02
❑ 868 Barry Bonds FRAN .25 .11
❑ 869 Todd Zeile FRAN UER .05 .02
(Powerful misspelled as poweful)
❑ 870 Benito Santiago FRAN .05 .02
❑ 871 Will Clark FRAN .10 .05
❑ 872 Craig Biggio FRAN .10 .05
❑ 873 Wally Joyner FRAN .05 .02
❑ 874 Frank Thomas FRAN .15 .07
❑ 875 R.Henderson MVP .20 .09
❑ 876 Barry Bonds MVP .25 .11
❑ 877 Bob Welch CY .05 .02
❑ 878 Doug Drabek CY .05 .02
❑ 879 S.Alomar Jr. ROY .05 .02
❑ 880 Dave Justice ROY .10 .05
❑ 881 Damon Berryhill .05 .02
❑ 882 Frank Viola DT .05 .02
❑ 883 Dave Stewart DT .05 .02
❑ 884 Doug Jones DT .05 .02
❑ 885 Randy Myers DT .05 .02
❑ 886 Will Clark DT .10 .05
❑ 887 Roberto Alomar DT .10 .05
❑ 888 Barry Larkin DT .10 .05
❑ 889 Wade Boggs DT .20 .09
❑ 890 Rickey Henderson DT .40 .18
❑ 891 Kirby Puckett DT .50 .23
❑ 892 Ken Griffey Jr DT .75 .35
❑ 893 Benny Santiago DT .05 .02

1991 Score Rookie/Traded

	MINT	NRMT
COMP.FACT.SET (110)	8.00	3.60

❑ 1T Bo Jackson .10 .05
❑ 2T Mike Flanagan .05 .02
❑ 3T Pete Incaviglia .05 .02
❑ 4T Jack Clark .10 .05
❑ 5T Hubie Brooks .05 .02
❑ 6T Ivan Calderon .05 .02
❑ 7T Glenn Davis .05 .02
❑ 8T Wally Backman .05 .02
❑ 9T Dave Smith .05 .02
❑ 10T Tim Raines .10 .05
❑ 11T Joe Carter .10 .05
❑ 12T Sid Bream .05 .02
❑ 13T George Bell .05 .02
❑ 14T Steve Bedrosian .05 .02
❑ 15T Willie Wilson .05 .02
❑ 16T Darryl Strawberry .10 .05
❑ 17T Danny Jackson .05 .02
❑ 18T Kirk Gibson .10 .05
❑ 19T Willie McGee .10 .05
❑ 20T Junior Felix .05 .02
❑ 21T Steve Farr .05 .02
❑ 22T Pat Tabler .05 .02
❑ 23T Brett Butler .10 .05
❑ 24T Danny Darwin .05 .02
❑ 25T Mickey Tettleton .05 .02
❑ 26T Gary Carter .15 .07
❑ 27T Mitch Williams .05 .02
❑ 28T Candy Maldonado .05 .02
❑ 29T Otis Nixon .05 .02
❑ 30T Brian Downing .05 .02
❑ 31T Tom Candiotti .05 .02
❑ 32T John Candelaria .05 .02
❑ 33T Rob Murphy .05 .02
❑ 34T Deion Sanders .10 .05
❑ 35T Willie Randolph .10 .05
❑ 36T Pete Harnisch .05 .02
❑ 37T Dante Bichette .10 .05
❑ 38T Garry Templeton .05 .02
❑ 39T Gary Gaetti .10 .05
❑ 40T John Cerutti .05 .02
❑ 41T Rick Cerone .05 .02
❑ 42T Mike Pagliarulo .05 .02
❑ 43T Ron Hassey .05 .02
❑ 44T Roberto Alomar .25 .11
❑ 45T Mike Boddicker .05 .02
❑ 46T Bud Black .05 .02
❑ 47T Rob Deer .05 .02
❑ 48T Devon White .05 .02
❑ 49T Luis Sojo .05 .02
❑ 50T Terry Pendleton .10 .05
❑ 51T Kevin Gross .05 .02
❑ 52T Mike Huff .05 .02
❑ 53T Dave Righetti .10 .05
❑ 54T Matt Young .05 .02
❑ 55T Earnest Riles .05 .02
❑ 56T Bill Gullickson .05 .02
❑ 57T Vince Coleman .05 .02
❑ 58T Fred McGriff .15 .07
❑ 59T Franklin Stubbs .05 .02
❑ 60T Eric King .05 .02
❑ 61T Cory Snyder .05 .02
❑ 62T Dwight Evans .10 .05
❑ 63T Gerald Perry .05 .02
❑ 64T Eric Show .05 .02
❑ 65T Shawn Hillegas .05 .02
❑ 66T Tony Fernandez .05 .02
❑ 67T Tim Teufel .05 .02
❑ 68T Mitch Webster .05 .02
❑ 69T Mike Heath .05 .02
❑ 70T Chili Davis .10 .05
❑ 71T Larry Andersen .05 .02
❑ 72T Gary Varsho .05 .02
❑ 73T Juan Berenguer .05 .02
❑ 74T Jack Morris .10 .05
❑ 75T Barry Jones .05 .02
❑ 76T Rafael Belliard .05 .02
❑ 77T Steve Buechele .05 .02
❑ 78T Scott Sanderson .05 .02
❑ 79T Bob Ojeda .05 .02
❑ 80T Curt Schilling .25 .11
❑ 81T Brian Drahman .05 .02
❑ 82T Ivan Rodriguez RC 2.00 .90
❑ 83T David Howard .05 .02
❑ 84T H.Slocumb RC .10 .05
❑ 85T Mike Timlin RC .10 .05
❑ 86T Darryl Kile .10 .05
❑ 87T Pete Schourek RC .05 .02
❑ 88T Bruce Walton .05 .02
❑ 89T Al Osuna RC .05 .02
❑ 90T Gary Scott RC .05 .02
❑ 91T Doug Simons .05 .02
❑ 92T Chris Jones RC .05 .02
❑ 93T Chuck Knoblauch .10 .05

		MINT	NRMT
❑ 94T	Dana Allison RC	.05	.02
❑ 95T	Erik Pappas	.05	.02
❑ 96T	Jeff Bagwell RC	2.50	1.10
❑ 97T	K.Dressendorfer RC	.05	.02
❑ 98T	Freddie Benavides	.05	.02
❑ 99T	Luis Gonzalez RC	2.00	.90
❑ 100T	Wade Taylor	.05	.02
❑ 101T	Ed Sprague	.05	.02
❑ 102T	Bob Scanlan	.05	.02
❑ 103T	Rick Wilkins RC	.05	.02
❑ 104T	Chris Donnels	.05	.02
❑ 105T	Joe Slusarski	.05	.02
❑ 106T	Mark Lewis	.05	.02
❑ 107T	Pat Kelly RC	.05	.02
❑ 108T	John Briscoe	.05	.02
❑ 109T	Luis Lopez RC	.05	.02
❑ 110T	Jeff Johnson	.05	.02

1992 Score

	MINT	NRMT
COMPLETE SET (893)	15.00	6.75
COMP.FACT.SET (910)	20.00	9.00
COMPLETE SERIES 1 (442)	8.00	3.60
COMPLETE SERIES 2 (451)	8.00	3.60

		MINT	NRMT
❑ 1	Ken Griffey Jr.	.60	.25
❑ 2	Nolan Ryan	1.00	.45
❑ 3	Will Clark	.20	.09
❑ 4	Dave Justice	.10	.05
❑ 5	Dave Henderson	.05	.02
❑ 6	Bret Saberhagen	.10	.05
❑ 7	Fred McGriff	.15	.07
❑ 8	Erik Hanson	.05	.02
❑ 9	Darryl Strawberry	.10	.05
❑ 10	Dwight Gooden	.10	.05
❑ 11	Juan Gonzalez	.20	.09
❑ 12	Mark Langston	.05	.02
❑ 13	Lonnie Smith	.05	.02
❑ 14	Jeff Montgomery	.05	.02
❑ 15	Roberto Alomar	.20	.09
❑ 16	Delino DeShields	.05	.02
❑ 17	Steve Bedrosian	.05	.02
❑ 18	Terry Pendleton	.10	.05
❑ 19	Mark Carreon	.05	.02
❑ 20	Mark McGwire	.75	.35
❑ 21	Roger Clemens	.50	.23
❑ 22	Chuck Crim	.05	.02
❑ 23	Don Mattingly	.50	.23
❑ 24	Dickie Thon	.05	.02
❑ 25	Ron Gant	.05	.02
❑ 26	Milt Cuyler	.05	.02
❑ 27	Mike Macfarlane	.05	.02
❑ 28	Dan Gladden	.05	.02
❑ 29	Melido Perez	.05	.02
❑ 30	Willie Randolph	.10	.05
❑ 31	Albert Belle	.10	.05
❑ 32	Dave Winfield	.20	.09
❑ 33	Jimmy Jones	.05	.02
❑ 34	Kevin Gross	.05	.02
❑ 35	Andres Galarraga	.15	.07
❑ 36	Mike Devereaux	.05	.02
❑ 37	Chris Bosio	.05	.02
❑ 38	Mike LaValliere	.05	.02
❑ 39	Gary Gaetti	.10	.05
❑ 40	Felix Jose	.05	.02
❑ 41	Alvaro Espinoza	.05	.02
❑ 42	Rick Aguilera	.10	.05
❑ 43	Mike Gallego	.05	.02
❑ 44	Eric Davis	.10	.05
❑ 45	George Bell	.05	.02
❑ 46	Tom Brunansky	.05	.02
❑ 47	Steve Farr	.05	.02
❑ 48	Duane Ward	.05	.02
❑ 49	David Wells	.10	.05
❑ 50	Cecil Fielder	.10	.05
❑ 51	Walt Weiss	.05	.02
❑ 52	Todd Zeile	.05	.02
❑ 53	Doug Jones	.05	.02
❑ 54	Bob Walk	.05	.02
❑ 55	Rafael Palmeiro	.20	.09
❑ 56	Rob Deer	.05	.02
❑ 57	Paul O'Neill	.20	.09
❑ 58	Jeff Reardon	.10	.05
❑ 59	Randy Ready	.05	.02
❑ 60	Scott Erickson	.05	.02
❑ 61	Paul Molitor	.20	.09
❑ 62	Jack McDowell	.05	.02
❑ 63	Jim Acker	.05	.02
❑ 64	Jay Buhner	.10	.05
❑ 65	Travis Fryman	.10	.05
❑ 66	Marquis Grissom	.05	.02
❑ 67	Mike Harkey	.05	.02
❑ 68	Luis Polonia	.05	.02
❑ 69	Ken Caminiti	.10	.05
❑ 70	Chris Sabo	.05	.02
❑ 71	Gregg Olson	.05	.02
❑ 72	Carlton Fisk	.20	.09
❑ 73	Juan Samuel	.05	.02
❑ 74	Todd Stottlemyre	.05	.02
❑ 75	Andre Dawson	.15	.07
❑ 76	Alvin Davis	.05	.02
❑ 77	Bill Doran	.05	.02
❑ 78	B.J. Surhoff	.10	.05
❑ 79	Kirk McCaskill	.05	.02
❑ 80	Dale Murphy	.20	.09
❑ 81	Jose DeLeon	.05	.02
❑ 82	Alex Fernandez	.05	.02
❑ 83	Ivan Calderon	.05	.02
❑ 84	Brent Mayne	.05	.02
❑ 85	Jody Reed	.05	.02
❑ 86	Randy Tomlin	.05	.02
❑ 87	Randy Milligan	.05	.02
❑ 88	Pascual Perez	.05	.02
❑ 89	Hensley Meulens	.05	.02
❑ 90	Joe Carter	.10	.05
❑ 91	Mike Moore	.05	.02
❑ 92	Ozzie Guillen	.05	.02
❑ 93	Shawn Hillegas	.05	.02
❑ 94	Chili Davis	.10	.05
❑ 95	Vince Coleman	.05	.02
❑ 96	Jimmy Key	.10	.05
❑ 97	Billy Ripken	.05	.02
❑ 98	Dave Smith	.05	.02
❑ 99	Tom Bolton	.05	.02
❑ 100	Barry Larkin	.20	.09
❑ 101	Kenny Rogers	.05	.02
❑ 102	Mike Boddicker	.05	.02
❑ 103	Kevin Elster	.05	.02
❑ 104	Ken Hill	.05	.02
❑ 105	Charlie Leibrandt	.05	.02
❑ 106	Pat Combs	.05	.02
❑ 107	Hubie Brooks	.05	.02
❑ 108	Julio Franco	.10	.05
❑ 109	Vicente Palacios	.05	.02
❑ 110	Kal Daniels	.05	.02
❑ 111	Bruce Hurst	.05	.02
❑ 112	Willie McGee	.10	.05
❑ 113	Ted Power	.05	.02
❑ 114	Milt Thompson	.05	.02
❑ 115	Doug Drabek	.05	.02
❑ 116	Rafael Belliard	.05	.02
❑ 117	Scott Garrelts	.05	.02
❑ 118	Terry Mulholland	.05	.02
❑ 119	Jay Howell	.05	.02
❑ 120	Danny Jackson	.05	.02
❑ 121	Scott Ruskin	.05	.02
❑ 122	Robin Ventura	.10	.05
❑ 123	Bip Roberts	.05	.02
❑ 124	Jeff Russell	.05	.02
❑ 125	Hal Morris	.05	.02
❑ 126	Teddy Higuera	.05	.02
❑ 127	Luis Sojo	.05	.02
❑ 128	Carlos Baerga	.05	.02
❑ 129	Jeff Ballard	.05	.02
❑ 130	Tom Gordon	.05	.02
❑ 131	Sid Bream	.05	.02
❑ 132	Rance Mulliniks	.05	.02
❑ 133	Andy Benes	.05	.02
❑ 134	Mickey Tettleton	.05	.02
❑ 135	Rich DeLucia	.05	.02
❑ 136	Tom Pagnozzi	.05	.02
❑ 137	Harold Baines	.10	.05
❑ 138	Danny Darwin	.05	.02
❑ 139	Kevin Bass	.05	.02
❑ 140	Chris Nabholz	.05	.02
❑ 141	Pete O'Brien	.05	.02
❑ 142	Jeff Treadway	.05	.02
❑ 143	Mickey Morandini	.05	.02
❑ 144	Eric King	.05	.02
❑ 145	Danny Tartabull	.05	.02
❑ 146	Lance Johnson	.05	.02
❑ 147	Casey Candaele	.05	.02
❑ 148	Felix Fermin	.05	.02
❑ 149	Rich Rodriguez	.05	.02
❑ 150	Dwight Evans	.10	.05
❑ 151	Joe Klink	.05	.02
❑ 152	Kevin Reimer	.05	.02
❑ 153	Orlando Merced	.05	.02
❑ 154	Mel Hall	.05	.02
❑ 155	Randy Myers	.05	.02
❑ 156	Greg A. Harris	.05	.02
❑ 157	Jeff Brantley	.05	.02
❑ 158	Jim Eisenreich	.05	.02
❑ 159	Luis Rivera	.05	.02
❑ 160	Cris Carpenter	.05	.02
❑ 161	Bruce Ruffin	.05	.02
❑ 162	Omar Vizquel	.10	.05
❑ 163	Gerald Alexander	.05	.02
❑ 164	Mark Guthrie	.05	.02
❑ 165	Scott Lewis	.05	.02
❑ 166	Bill Sampen	.05	.02
❑ 167	Dave Anderson	.05	.02
❑ 168	Kevin McReynolds	.05	.02
❑ 169	Jose Vizcaino	.05	.02
❑ 170	Bob Geren	.05	.02
❑ 171	Mike Morgan	.05	.02
❑ 172	Jim Gott	.05	.02
❑ 173	Mike Pagliarulo	.05	.02
❑ 174	Mike Jeffcoat	.05	.02
❑ 175	Craig Lefferts	.05	.02
❑ 176	Steve Finley	.10	.05
❑ 177	Wally Backman	.05	.02
❑ 178	Kent Mercker	.05	.02
❑ 179	John Cerutti	.05	.02
❑ 180	Jay Bell	.10	.05
❑ 181	Dale Sveum	.05	.02
❑ 182	Greg Gagne	.05	.02
❑ 183	Donnie Hill	.05	.02
❑ 184	Rex Hudler	.05	.02
❑ 185	Pat Kelly	.05	.02
❑ 186	Jeff D. Robinson	.05	.02
❑ 187	Jeff Gray	.05	.02
❑ 188	Jerry Willard	.05	.02
❑ 189	Carlos Quintana	.05	.02
❑ 190	Dennis Eckersley	.10	.05
❑ 191	Kelly Downs	.05	.02
❑ 192	Gregg Jefferies	.05	.02
❑ 193	Darrin Fletcher	.05	.02
❑ 194	Mike Jackson	.05	.02
❑ 195	Eddie Murray	.20	.09
❑ 196	Bill Landrum	.05	.02
❑ 197	Eric Yelding	.05	.02
❑ 198	Devon White	.05	.02
❑ 199	Larry Walker	.15	.07
❑ 200	Ryne Sandberg	.25	.11
❑ 201	Dave Magadan	.05	.02
❑ 202	Steve Chitren	.05	.02
❑ 203	Scott Fletcher	.05	.02
❑ 204	Dwayne Henry	.05	.02
❑ 205	Scott Coolbaugh	.05	.02
❑ 206	Tracy Jones	.05	.02
❑ 207	Von Hayes	.05	.02
❑ 208	Bob Melvin	.05	.02
❑ 209	Scott Scudder	.05	.02
❑ 210	Luis Gonzalez	.20	.09
❑ 211	Scott Sanderson	.05	.02
❑ 212	Chris Donnels	.05	.02
❑ 213	Heathcliff Slocumb	.05	.02
❑ 214	Mike Timlin	.05	.02

❑ 215 Brian Harper .05 .02
❑ 216 Juan Berenguer UER .05 .02
(Decimal point missing in IP total)
❑ 217 Mike Henneman .05 .02
❑ 218 Bill Spiers .05 .02
❑ 219 Scott Terry .05 .02
❑ 220 Frank Viola .10 .05
❑ 221 Mark Eichhorn .05 .02
❑ 222 Ernest Riles .05 .02
❑ 223 Ray Lankford .05 .02
❑ 224 Pete Harnisch .05 .02
❑ 225 Bobby Bonilla .10 .05
❑ 226 Mike Scioscia .05 .02
❑ 227 Joel Skinner .05 .02
❑ 228 Brian Holman .05 .02
❑ 229 Gilberto Reyes .05 .02
❑ 230 Matt Williams .15 .07
❑ 231 Jaime Navarro .05 .02
❑ 232 Jose Rijo .05 .02
❑ 233 Atlee Hammaker .05 .02
❑ 234 Tim Teufel .05 .02
❑ 235 John Kruk .10 .05
❑ 236 Kurt Stillwell .05 .02
❑ 237 Dan Pasqua .05 .02
❑ 238 Tim Crews .05 .02
❑ 239 Dave Gallagher .05 .02
❑ 240 Leo Gomez .05 .02
❑ 241 Steve Avery .05 .02
❑ 242 Bill Gullickson .05 .02
❑ 243 Mark Portugal .05 .02
❑ 244 Lee Guetterman .05 .02
❑ 245 Benito Santiago .05 .02
❑ 246 Jim Gantner .05 .02
❑ 247 Robby Thompson .05 .02
❑ 248 Terry Shumpert .05 .02
❑ 249 Mike Bell .05 .02
❑ 250 Harold Reynolds .05 .02
❑ 251 Mike Felder .05 .02
❑ 252 Bill Pecota .05 .02
❑ 253 Bill Krueger .05 .02
❑ 254 Alfredo Griffin .05 .02
❑ 255 Lou Whitaker .10 .05
❑ 256 Roy Smith .05 .02
❑ 257 Jerald Clark .05 .02
❑ 258 Sammy Sosa .40 .18
❑ 259 Tim Naehring .05 .02
❑ 260 Dave Righetti .10 .05
❑ 261 Paul Gibson .05 .02
❑ 262 Chris James .05 .02
❑ 263 Larry Andersen .05 .02
❑ 264 Storm Davis .05 .02
❑ 265 Jose Lind .05 .02
❑ 266 Greg Hibbard .05 .02
❑ 267 Norm Charlton .05 .02
❑ 268 Paul Kilgus .05 .02
❑ 269 Greg Maddux .50 .23
❑ 270 Ellis Burks .10 .05
❑ 271 Frank Tanana .05 .02
❑ 272 Gene Larkin .05 .02
❑ 273 Ron Hassey .05 .02
❑ 274 Jeff M. Robinson .05 .02
❑ 275 Steve Howe .05 .02
❑ 276 Daryl Boston .05 .02
❑ 277 Mark Lee .05 .02
❑ 278 Jose Segura .05 .02
❑ 279 Lance Blankenship .05 .02
❑ 280 Don Slaught .05 .02
❑ 281 Russ Swan .05 .02
❑ 282 Bob Tewksbury .05 .02
❑ 283 Geno Petralli .05 .02
❑ 284 Shane Mack .05 .02
❑ 285 Bob Scanlan .05 .02
❑ 286 Tim Leary .05 .02
❑ 287 John Smoltz .10 .05
❑ 288 Pat Borders .05 .02
❑ 289 Mark Davidson .05 .02
❑ 290 Sam Horn .05 .02
❑ 291 Lenny Harris .05 .02
❑ 292 Franklin Stubbs .05 .02
❑ 293 Thomas Howard .05 .02
❑ 294 Steve Lyons .05 .02
❑ 295 Francisco Oliveras .05 .02
❑ 296 Terry Leach .05 .02
❑ 297 Barry Jones .05 .02
❑ 298 Lance Parrish .10 .05
❑ 299 Wally Whitehurst .05 .02
❑ 300 Bob Welch .05 .02
❑ 301 Charlie Hayes .05 .02
❑ 302 Charlie Hough .10 .05
❑ 303 Gary Redus .05 .02
❑ 304 Scott Bradley .05 .02
❑ 305 Jose Oquendo .05 .02
❑ 306 Pete Incaviglia .05 .02
❑ 307 Marvin Freeman .05 .02
❑ 308 Gary Pettis .05 .02
❑ 309 Joe Slusarski .05 .02
❑ 310 Kevin Seitzer .05 .02
❑ 311 Jeff Reed .05 .02
❑ 312 Pat Tabler .05 .02
❑ 313 Mike Maddux .05 .02
❑ 314 Bob Milacki .05 .02
❑ 315 Eric Anthony .05 .02
❑ 316 Dante Bichette .10 .05
❑ 317 Steve Decker .05 .02
❑ 318 Jack Clark .10 .05
❑ 319 Doug Dascenzo .05 .02
❑ 320 Scott Leius .05 .02
❑ 321 Jim Lindeman .05 .02
❑ 322 Bryan Harvey .05 .02
❑ 323 Spike Owen .05 .02
❑ 324 Roberto Kelly .05 .02
❑ 325 Stan Belinda .05 .02
❑ 326 Joey Cora .05 .02
❑ 327 Jeff Innis .05 .02
❑ 328 Willie Wilson .05 .02
❑ 329 Juan Agosto .05 .02
❑ 330 Charles Nagy .05 .02
❑ 331 Scott Bailes .05 .02
❑ 332 Pete Schourek .05 .02
❑ 333 Mike Flanagan .05 .02
❑ 334 Omar Olivares .05 .02
❑ 335 Dennis Lamp .05 .02
❑ 336 Tommy Greene .05 .02
❑ 337 Randy Velarde .05 .02
❑ 338 Tom Lampkin .05 .02
❑ 339 John Russell .05 .02
❑ 340 Bob Kipper .05 .02
❑ 341 Todd Burns .05 .02
❑ 342 Ron Jones .05 .02
❑ 343 Dave Valle .05 .02
❑ 344 Mike Heath .05 .02
❑ 345 John Olerud .10 .05
❑ 346 Gerald Young .05 .02
❑ 347 Ken Patterson .05 .02
❑ 348 Les Lancaster .05 .02
❑ 349 Steve Crawford .05 .02
❑ 350 John Candelaria .05 .02
❑ 351 Mike Aldrete .05 .02
❑ 352 Mariano Duncan .05 .02
❑ 353 Julio Machado .05 .02
❑ 354 Ken Williams .05 .02
❑ 355 Walt Terrell .05 .02
❑ 356 Mitch Williams .05 .02
❑ 357 Al Newman .05 .02
❑ 358 Bud Black .05 .02
❑ 359 Joe Hesketh .05 .02
❑ 360 Paul Assenmacher .05 .02
❑ 361 Bo Jackson .10 .05
❑ 362 Jeff Blauser .05 .02
❑ 363 Mike Brumley .05 .02
❑ 364 Jim Deshaies .05 .02
❑ 365 Brady Anderson .10 .05
❑ 366 Chuck McElroy .05 .02
❑ 367 Matt Merullo .05 .02
❑ 368 Tim Belcher .05 .02
❑ 369 Luis Aquino .05 .02
❑ 370 Joe Oliver .05 .02
❑ 371 Greg Swindell .05 .02
❑ 372 Lee Stevens .05 .02
❑ 373 Mark Knudson .05 .02
❑ 374 Bill Wegman .05 .02
❑ 375 Jerry Don Gleaton .05 .02
❑ 376 Pedro Guerrero .10 .05
❑ 377 Randy Bush .05 .02
❑ 378 Greg W. Harris .05 .02
❑ 379 Eric Plunk .05 .02
❑ 380 Jose DeJesus .05 .02
❑ 381 Bobby Witt .05 .02
❑ 382 Curtis Wilkerson .05 .02
❑ 383 Gene Nelson .05 .02
❑ 384 Wes Chamberlain .05 .02
❑ 385 Tom Henke .05 .02
❑ 386 Mark Lemke .05 .02
❑ 387 Greg Briley .05 .02
❑ 388 Rafael Ramirez .05 .02
❑ 389 Tony Fossas .05 .02
❑ 390 Henry Cotto .05 .02
❑ 391 Tim Hulett .05 .02
❑ 392 Dean Palmer .10 .05
❑ 393 Glenn Braggs .05 .02
❑ 394 Mark Salas .05 .02
❑ 395 Rusty Meacham .05 .02
❑ 396 Andy Ashby .05 .02
❑ 397 Jose Melendez .05 .02
❑ 398 Warren Newson .05 .02
❑ 399 Frank Castillo .05 .02
❑ 400 Chito Martinez .05 .02
❑ 401 Bernie Williams .20 .09
❑ 402 Derek Bell .10 .05
❑ 403 Javier Ortiz .05 .02
❑ 404 Tim Sherrill .05 .02
❑ 405 Rob MacDonald .05 .02
❑ 406 Phil Plantier .05 .02
❑ 407 Troy Afenir .05 .02
❑ 408 Gino Minutelli .05 .02
❑ 409 Reggie Jefferson .05 .02
❑ 410 Mike Remlinger .05 .02
❑ 411 Carlos Rodriguez .05 .02
❑ 412 Joe Redfield .05 .02
❑ 413 Alonzo Powell .05 .02
❑ 414 S.Livingstone UER .05 .02
(Travis Fryman, not Woodie, should be referenced on back
❑ 415 Scott Kamieniecki .05 .02
❑ 416 Tim Spehr .05 .02
❑ 417 Brian Hunter .05 .02
❑ 418 Ced Landrum .05 .02
❑ 419 Bret Barberie .05 .02
❑ 420 Kevin Morton .05 .02
❑ 421 Doug Henry RC .05 .02
❑ 422 Doug Piatt .05 .02
❑ 423 Pat Rice .05 .02
❑ 424 Juan Guzman .05 .02
❑ 425 Nolan Ryan NH .50 .23
❑ 426 Tommy Greene NH .05 .02
❑ 427 Bob Milacki and .05 .02
Mike Flanagan NH
(Mark Williamson and Gregg Olson)
❑ 428 Wilson Alvarez NH .05 .02
❑ 429 Otis Nixon HL .05 .02
❑ 430 Rickey Henderson HL .20 .09
❑ 431 Cecil Fielder AS .05 .02
❑ 432 Julio Franco AS .05 .02
❑ 433 Cal Ripken AS .40 .18
❑ 434 Wade Boggs AS .10 .05
❑ 435 Joe Carter AS .05 .02
❑ 436 Ken Griffey Jr. AS .50 .23
❑ 437 Ruben Sierra AS .05 .02
❑ 438 Scott Erickson AS .05 .02
❑ 439 Tom Henke AS .05 .02
❑ 440 Terry Steinbach AS .05 .02
❑ 441 Rickey Henderson DT .40 .18
❑ 442 Ryne Sandberg DT .25 .11
❑ 443 Otis Nixon .05 .02
❑ 444 Scott Radinsky .05 .02
❑ 445 Mark Grace .20 .09
❑ 446 Tony Pena .05 .02
❑ 447 Billy Hatcher .05 .02
❑ 448 Glenallen Hill .05 .02
❑ 449 Chris Gwynn .05 .02
❑ 450 Tom Glavine .20 .09
❑ 451 John Habyan .05 .02
❑ 452 Al Osuna .05 .02
❑ 453 Tony Phillips .05 .02
❑ 454 Greg Cadaret .05 .02
❑ 455 Rob Dibble .05 .02
❑ 456 Rick Honeycutt .05 .02
❑ 457 Jerome Walton .05 .02
❑ 458 Mookie Wilson .10 .05
❑ 459 Mark Gubicza .05 .02
❑ 460 Craig Biggio .15 .07
❑ 461 Dave Cochrane .05 .02
❑ 462 Keith Miller .05 .02
❑ 463 Alex Cole .05 .02
❑ 464 Pete Smith .05 .02

- ❑ 465 Brett Butler .10 .05
- ❑ 466 Jeff Huson .05 .02
- ❑ 467 Steve Lake .05 .02
- ❑ 468 Lloyd Moseby .05 .02
- ❑ 469 Tim McIntosh .05 .02
- ❑ 470 Dennis Martinez .10 .05
- ❑ 471 Greg Myers .05 .02
- ❑ 472 Mackey Sasser .05 .02
- ❑ 473 Junior Ortiz .05 .02
- ❑ 474 Greg Olson .05 .02
- ❑ 475 Steve Sax .05 .02
- ❑ 476 Ricky Jordan .05 .02
- ❑ 477 Max Venable .05 .02
- ❑ 478 Brian McRae .05 .02
- ❑ 479 Doug Simons .05 .02
- ❑ 480 Rickey Henderson .40 .18
- ❑ 481 Gary Varsho .05 .02
- ❑ 482 Carl Willis .05 .02
- ❑ 483 Rick Wilkins .05 .02
- ❑ 484 Donn Pall .05 .02
- ❑ 485 Edgar Martinez .15 .07
- ❑ 486 Tom Foley .05 .02
- ❑ 487 Mark Williamson .05 .02
- ❑ 488 Jack Armstrong .05 .02
- ❑ 489 Gary Carter .15 .07
- ❑ 490 Ruben Sierra .05 .02
- ❑ 491 Gerald Perry .05 .02
- ❑ 492 Rob Murphy .05 .02
- ❑ 493 Zane Smith .05 .02
- ❑ 494 Darryl Kile .10 .05
- ❑ 495 Kelly Gruber .05 .02
- ❑ 496 Jerry Browne .05 .02
- ❑ 497 Darryl Hamilton .05 .02
- ❑ 498 Mike Stanton .05 .02
- ❑ 499 Mark Leonard .05 .02
- ❑ 500 Jose Canseco .20 .09
- ❑ 501 Dave Martinez .05 .02
- ❑ 502 Jose Guzman .05 .02
- ❑ 503 Terry Kennedy .05 .02
- ❑ 504 Ed Sprague .05 .02
- ❑ 505 Frank Thomas UER .25 .11 (His Gulf Coast League stats are wrong)
- ❑ 506 Darren Daulton .10 .05
- ❑ 507 Kevin Tapani .05 .02
- ❑ 508 Luis Salazar .05 .02
- ❑ 509 Paul Faries .05 .02
- ❑ 510 Sandy Alomar Jr. .10 .05
- ❑ 511 Jeff King .05 .02
- ❑ 512 Gary Thurman .05 .02
- ❑ 513 Chris Hammond .05 .02
- ❑ 514 Pedro Munoz .05 .02
- ❑ 515 Alan Trammell .15 .07
- ❑ 516 Geronimo Pena .05 .02
- ❑ 517 Rodney McCray UER .05 .02 (Stole 6 bases in 1990, not 5; career totals are correct at 7)
- ❑ 518 Manny Lee .05 .02
- ❑ 519 Junior Felix .05 .02
- ❑ 520 Kirk Gibson .10 .05
- ❑ 521 Darrin Jackson .05 .02
- ❑ 522 John Burkett .05 .02
- ❑ 523 Jeff Johnson .05 .02
- ❑ 524 Jim Corsi .05 .02
- ❑ 525 Robin Yount .20 .09
- ❑ 526 Jamie Quirk .05 .02
- ❑ 527 Bob Ojeda .05 .02
- ❑ 528 Mark Lewis .05 .02
- ❑ 529 Bryn Smith .05 .02
- ❑ 530 Kent Hrbek .10 .05
- ❑ 531 Dennis Boyd .05 .02
- ❑ 532 Ron Karkovice .05 .02
- ❑ 533 Don August .05 .02
- ❑ 534 Todd Frohwirth .05 .02
- ❑ 535 Wally Joyner .10 .05
- ❑ 536 Dennis Rasmussen .05 .02
- ❑ 537 Andy Allanson .05 .02
- ❑ 538 Rich Gossage .10 .05
- ❑ 539 John Marzano .05 .02
- ❑ 540 Cal Ripken .75 .35
- ❑ 541 Bill Swift UER .05 .02 (Brewers logo on front)
- ❑ 542 Kevin Appier .10 .05
- ❑ 543 Dave Bergman .05 .02
- ❑ 544 Bernard Gilkey .05 .02
- ❑ 545 Mike Greenwell .05 .02
- ❑ 546 Jose Uribe .05 .02
- ❑ 547 Jesse Orosco .05 .02
- ❑ 548 Bob Patterson .05 .02
- ❑ 549 Mike Stanley .05 .02
- ❑ 550 Howard Johnson .05 .02
- ❑ 551 Joe Orsulak .05 .02
- ❑ 552 Dick Schofield .05 .02
- ❑ 553 Dave Hollins .05 .02
- ❑ 554 David Segui .05 .02
- ❑ 555 Barry Bonds .50 .23
- ❑ 556 Mo Vaughn .10 .05
- ❑ 557 Craig Wilson .05 .02
- ❑ 558 Bobby Rose .05 .02
- ❑ 559 Rod Nichols .05 .02
- ❑ 560 Len Dykstra .10 .05
- ❑ 561 Craig Grebeck .05 .02
- ❑ 562 Darren Lewis .05 .02
- ❑ 563 Todd Benzinger .05 .02
- ❑ 564 Ed Whitson .05 .02
- ❑ 565 Jesse Barfield .05 .02
- ❑ 566 Lloyd McClendon .05 .02
- ❑ 567 Dan Plesac .05 .02
- ❑ 568 Danny Cox .05 .02
- ❑ 569 Skeeter Barnes .05 .02
- ❑ 570 Bobby Thigpen .05 .02
- ❑ 571 Deion Sanders .10 .05
- ❑ 572 Chuck Knoblauch .10 .05
- ❑ 573 Matt Nokes .05 .02
- ❑ 574 Herm Winningham .05 .02
- ❑ 575 Tom Candiotti .05 .02
- ❑ 576 Jeff Bagwell .40 .18
- ❑ 577 Brook Jacoby .05 .02
- ❑ 578 Chico Walker .05 .02
- ❑ 579 Brian Downing .05 .02
- ❑ 580 Dave Stewart .10 .05
- ❑ 581 Francisco Cabrera .05 .02
- ❑ 582 Rene Gonzales .05 .02
- ❑ 583 Stan Javier .05 .02
- ❑ 584 Randy Johnson .25 .11
- ❑ 585 Chuck Finley .10 .05
- ❑ 586 Mark Gardner .05 .02
- ❑ 587 Mark Whiten .05 .02
- ❑ 588 Garry Templeton .05 .02
- ❑ 589 Gary Sheffield .10 .05
- ❑ 590 Ozzie Smith .25 .11
- ❑ 591 Candy Maldonado .05 .02
- ❑ 592 Mike Sharperson .05 .02
- ❑ 593 Carlos Martinez .05 .02
- ❑ 594 Scott Bankhead .05 .02
- ❑ 595 Tim Wallach .05 .02
- ❑ 596 Tino Martinez .10 .05
- ❑ 597 Roger McDowell .05 .02
- ❑ 598 Cory Snyder .05 .02
- ❑ 599 Andujar Cedeno .05 .02
- ❑ 600 Kirby Puckett .50 .23
- ❑ 601 Rick Parker .05 .02
- ❑ 602 Todd Hundley .05 .02
- ❑ 603 Greg Litton .05 .02
- ❑ 604 Dave Johnson .05 .02
- ❑ 605 John Franco .10 .05
- ❑ 606 Mike Fetters .05 .02
- ❑ 607 Luis Alicea .05 .02
- ❑ 608 Trevor Wilson .05 .02
- ❑ 609 Rob Ducey .05 .02
- ❑ 610 Ramon Martinez .05 .02
- ❑ 611 Dave Burba .05 .02
- ❑ 612 Dwight Smith .05 .02
- ❑ 613 Kevin Maas .05 .02
- ❑ 614 John Costello .05 .02
- ❑ 615 Glenn Davis .05 .02
- ❑ 616 Shawn Abner .05 .02
- ❑ 617 Scott Hemond .05 .02
- ❑ 618 Tom Prince .05 .02
- ❑ 619 Wally Ritchie .05 .02
- ❑ 620 Jim Abbott .10 .05
- ❑ 621 Charlie O'Brien .05 .02
- ❑ 622 Jack Daugherty .05 .02
- ❑ 623 Tommy Gregg .05 .02
- ❑ 624 Jeff Shaw .05 .02
- ❑ 625 Tony Gwynn .40 .18
- ❑ 626 Mark Leiter .05 .02
- ❑ 627 Jim Clancy .05 .02
- ❑ 628 Tim Layana .05 .02
- ❑ 629 Jeff Schaefer .05 .02
- ❑ 630 Lee Smith .10 .05
- ❑ 631 Wade Taylor .05 .02
- ❑ 632 Mike Simms .05 .02
- ❑ 633 Terry Steinbach .05 .02
- ❑ 634 Shawon Dunston .05 .02
- ❑ 635 Tim Raines .10 .05
- ❑ 636 Kirt Manwaring .05 .02
- ❑ 637 Warren Cromartie .05 .02
- ❑ 638 Luis Quinones .05 .02
- ❑ 639 Greg Vaughn .10 .05
- ❑ 640 Kevin Mitchell .05 .02
- ❑ 641 Chris Hoiles .05 .02
- ❑ 642 Tom Browning .05 .02
- ❑ 643 Mitch Webster .05 .02
- ❑ 644 Steve Olin .05 .02
- ❑ 645 Tony Fernandez .05 .02
- ❑ 646 Juan Bell .05 .02
- ❑ 647 Joe Boever .05 .02
- ❑ 648 Carney Lansford .10 .05
- ❑ 649 Mike Benjamin .05 .02
- ❑ 650 George Brett .40 .18
- ❑ 651 Tim Burke .05 .02
- ❑ 652 Jack Morris .10 .05
- ❑ 653 Orel Hershiser .10 .05
- ❑ 654 Mike Schooler .05 .02
- ❑ 655 Andy Van Slyke .10 .05
- ❑ 656 Dave Stieb .05 .02
- ❑ 657 Dave Clark .05 .02
- ❑ 658 Ben McDonald .05 .02
- ❑ 659 John Smiley .05 .02
- ❑ 660 Wade Boggs .20 .09
- ❑ 661 Eric Bullock .05 .02
- ❑ 662 Eric Show .05 .02
- ❑ 663 Lenny Webster .05 .02
- ❑ 664 Mike Huff .05 .02
- ❑ 665 Rick Sutcliffe .10 .05
- ❑ 666 Jeff Manto .05 .02
- ❑ 667 Mike Fitzgerald .05 .02
- ❑ 668 Matt Young .05 .02
- ❑ 669 Dave West .05 .02
- ❑ 670 Mike Hartley .05 .02
- ❑ 671 Curt Schilling .20 .09
- ❑ 672 Brian Bohanon .05 .02
- ❑ 673 Cecil Espy .05 .02
- ❑ 674 Joe Grahe .05 .02
- ❑ 675 Sid Fernandez .05 .02
- ❑ 676 Edwin Nunez .05 .02
- ❑ 677 Hector Villanueva .05 .02
- ❑ 678 Sean Berry .05 .02
- ❑ 679 Dave Eiland .05 .02
- ❑ 680 David Cone .10 .05
- ❑ 681 Mike Bordick .05 .02
- ❑ 682 Tony Castillo .05 .02
- ❑ 683 John Barfield .05 .02
- ❑ 684 Jeff Hamilton .05 .02
- ❑ 685 Ken Dayley .05 .02
- ❑ 686 Carmelo Martinez .05 .02
- ❑ 687 Mike Capel .05 .02
- ❑ 688 Scott Chiamparino .05 .02
- ❑ 689 Rich Gedman .05 .02
- ❑ 690 Rich Monteleone .05 .02
- ❑ 691 Alejandro Pena .05 .02
- ❑ 692 Oscar Azocar .05 .02
- ❑ 693 Jim Poole .05 .02
- ❑ 694 Mike Gardiner .05 .02
- ❑ 695 Steve Buechele .05 .02
- ❑ 696 Rudy Seanez .05 .02
- ❑ 697 Paul Abbott .05 .02
- ❑ 698 Steve Searcy .05 .02
- ❑ 699 Jose Offerman .05 .02
- ❑ 700 Ivan Rodriguez .25 .11
- ❑ 701 Joe Girardi .05 .02
- ❑ 702 Tony Perezchica .05 .02
- ❑ 703 Paul McClellan .05 .02
- ❑ 704 David Howard .05 .02
- ❑ 705 Dan Petry .05 .02
- ❑ 706 Jack Howell .05 .02
- ❑ 707 Jose Mesa .05 .02
- ❑ 708 Randy St. Claire .05 .02
- ❑ 709 Kevin Brown .10 .05
- ❑ 710 Ron Darling .05 .02
- ❑ 711 Jason Grimsley .05 .02
- ❑ 712 John Orton .05 .02
- ❑ 713 Shawn Boskie .05 .02
- ❑ 714 Pat Clements .05 .02
- ❑ 715 Brian Barnes .05 .02
- ❑ 716 Luis Lopez .05 .02

❑ 717 Bob McClure .05 .02
❑ 718 Mark Davis .05 .02
❑ 719 Dann Bilardello .05 .02
❑ 720 Tom Edens .05 .02
❑ 721 Willie Fraser .05 .02
❑ 722 Curt Young .05 .02
❑ 723 Neal Heaton .05 .02
❑ 724 Craig Worthington .05 .02
❑ 725 Mel Rojas .05 .02
❑ 726 Daryl Irvine .05 .02
❑ 727 Roger Mason .05 .02
❑ 728 Kirk Dressendorfer .05 .02
❑ 729 Scott Aldred .05 .02
❑ 730 Willie Blair .05 .02
❑ 731 Allan Anderson .05 .02
❑ 732 Dana Kiecker .05 .02
❑ 733 Jose Gonzalez .05 .02
❑ 734 Brian Drahman .05 .02
❑ 735 Brad Komminsk .05 .02
❑ 736 Arthur Rhodes .05 .02
❑ 737 Terry Mathews .05 .02
❑ 738 Jeff Fassero .05 .02
❑ 739 Mike Magnante RC .05 .02
❑ 740 Kip Gross .05 .02
❑ 741 Jim Hunter .05 .02
❑ 742 Jose Mota .05 .02
❑ 743 Joe Bitker .05 .02
❑ 744 Tim Mauser .05 .02
❑ 745 Ramon Garcia .05 .02
❑ 746 Rod Beck RC .20 .09
❑ 747 Jim Austin .05 .02
❑ 748 Keith Mitchell .05 .02
❑ 749 Wayne Rosenthal .05 .02
❑ 750 Bryan Hickerson RC .05 .02
❑ 751 Bruce Egloff .05 .02
❑ 752 John Wehner .05 .02
❑ 753 Darren Holmes .05 .02
❑ 754 Dave Hansen .05 .02
❑ 755 Mike Mussina .30 .14
❑ 756 Anthony Young .05 .02
❑ 757 Ron Tingley .05 .02
❑ 758 Ricky Bones .05 .02
❑ 759 Mark Wohlers .05 .02
❑ 760 Wilson Alvarez .05 .02
❑ 761 Harvey Pulliam .05 .02
❑ 762 Ryan Bowen .05 .02
❑ 763 Terry Bross .05 .02
❑ 764 Joel Johnston .05 .02
❑ 765 Terry McDaniel .05 .02
❑ 766 Esteban Beltre .05 .02
❑ 767 Rob Maurer .05 .02
❑ 768 Ted Wood .05 .02
❑ 769 Mo Sanford .05 .02
❑ 770 Jeff Carter .05 .02
❑ 771 Gil Heredia RC .10 .05
❑ 772 Monty Fariss .05 .02
❑ 773 Will Clark AS .10 .05
❑ 774 Ryne Sandberg AS .15 .07
❑ 775 Barry Larkin AS .10 .05
❑ 776 Howard Johnson AS .05 .02
❑ 777 Barry Bonds AS .25 .11
❑ 778 Brett Butler AS .05 .02
❑ 779 Tony Gwynn AS .20 .09
❑ 780 Ramon Martinez AS .05 .02
❑ 781 Lee Smith AS .05 .02
❑ 782 Mike Scioscia AS .05 .02
❑ 783 D.Martinez HL UER .05 .02
Card has both 13th and 15th perfect game in Major League history
❑ 784 Dennis Martinez NH .05 .02
❑ 785 Mark Gardner NH .05 .02
❑ 786 Bret Saberhagen NH .05 .02
❑ 787 Kent Mercker NH .05 .02
Mark Wohlers
Alejandro Pena
❑ 788 Cal Ripken MVP .40 .18
❑ 789 Terry Pendleton MVP .05 .02
❑ 790 Roger Clemens CY .25 .11
❑ 791 Tom Glavine CY .10 .05
❑ 792 C.Knoblauch ROY .05 .02
❑ 793 Jeff Bagwell ROY .15 .07
❑ 794 Cal Ripken MANYR .40 .18
❑ 795 David Cone HL .05 .02
❑ 796 Kirby Puckett HL .25 .11
❑ 797 Steve Avery HL .05 .02
❑ 798 Jack Morris HL .05 .02
❑ 799 Allen Watson DC RC .05 .02
❑ 800 M.Ramirez DC RC 2.50 1.10
❑ 801 Cliff Floyd DC RC 1.00 .45
❑ 802 Al Shirley DC RC .05 .02
❑ 803 Brian Barber DC RC .05 .02
❑ 804 Jon Farrell DC RC .05 .02
❑ 805 Brent Gates DC RC .05 .02
❑ 806 Scott Ruffcorn DC RC .05 .02
❑ 807 Tyrone Hill DC RC .05 .02
❑ 808 Benji Gil DC RC .05 .02
❑ 809 Aaron Sele DC RC .50 .23
❑ 810 Tyler Green DC RC .05 .02
❑ 811 Chris Jones .05 .02
❑ 812 Steve Wilson .05 .02
❑ 813 Freddie Benavides .05 .02
❑ 814 Don Wakamatsu .05 .02
❑ 815 Mike Humphreys .05 .02
❑ 816 Scott Servais .05 .02
❑ 817 Rico Rossy .05 .02
❑ 818 John Ramos .05 .02
❑ 819 Rob Mallicoat .05 .02
❑ 820 Milt Hill .05 .02
❑ 821 Carlos Garcia .05 .02
❑ 822 Stan Royer .05 .02
❑ 823 Jeff Plympton .05 .02
❑ 824 Braulio Castillo .05 .02
❑ 825 David Haas .05 .02
❑ 826 Luis Mercedes .05 .02
❑ 827 Eric Karros .10 .05
❑ 828 Shawn Hare RC .05 .02
❑ 829 Reggie Sanders .05 .02
❑ 830 Tom Goodwin .05 .02
❑ 831 Dan Gakeler .05 .02
❑ 832 Stacy Jones .05 .02
❑ 833 Kim Batiste .05 .02
❑ 834 Cal Eldred .05 .02
❑ 835 Chris George .05 .02
❑ 836 Wayne Housie .05 .02
❑ 837 Mike Ignasiak .05 .02
❑ 838 Josias Manzanillo RC .05 .02
❑ 839 Jim Olander .05 .02
❑ 840 Gary Cooper .05 .02
❑ 841 Royce Clayton .05 .02
❑ 842 Hector Fajardo RC .05 .02
❑ 843 Blaine Beatty .05 .02
❑ 844 Jorge Pedre .05 .02
❑ 845 Kenny Lofton .20 .09
❑ 846 Scott Brosius RC .50 .23
❑ 847 Chris Cron .05 .02
❑ 848 Denis Boucher .05 .02
❑ 849 Kyle Abbott .05 .02
❑ 850 Bob Zupcic RC .05 .02
❑ 851 Rheal Cormier .05 .02
❑ 852 Jim Lewis .05 .02
❑ 853 Anthony Telford .05 .02
❑ 854 Cliff Brantley .05 .02
❑ 855 Kevin Campbell .05 .02
❑ 856 Craig Shipley .05 .02
❑ 857 Chuck Carr .05 .02
❑ 858 Tony Eusebio .10 .05
❑ 859 Jim Thome .20 .09
❑ 860 Vinny Castilla RC .50 .23
❑ 861 Dann Howitt .05 .02
❑ 862 Kevin Ward .05 .02
❑ 863 Steve Wapnick .05 .02
❑ 864 Rod Brewer RC .05 .02
❑ 865 Todd Van Poppel .05 .02
❑ 866 Jose Hernandez RC .05 .02
❑ 867 Amalio Carreno .05 .02
❑ 868 Calvin Jones .05 .02
❑ 869 Jeff Gardner .05 .02
❑ 870 Jarvis Brown .05 .02
❑ 871 Eddie Taubensee RC .10 .05
❑ 872 Andy Mota .05 .02
❑ 873 Chris Haney .05 .02
❑ 874 Roberto Hernandez .05 .02
❑ 875 Laddie Renfroe .05 .02
❑ 876 Scott Cooper .05 .02
❑ 877 Armando Reynoso RC .10 .05
❑ 878 Ty Cobb MEMO .25 .11
❑ 879 Babe Ruth MEMO .40 .18
❑ 880 Honus Wagner MEMO .20 .09
❑ 881 Lou Gehrig MEMO .25 .11
❑ 882 Satchel Paige MEMO .20 .09
❑ 883 Will Clark DT .10 .05
❑ 884 Cal Ripken DT 2.00 .90
❑ 885 Wade Boggs DT .10 .05
❑ 886 Kirby Puckett DT .50 .23
❑ 887 Tony Gwynn DT .20 .09
❑ 888 Craig Biggio DT .10 .05
❑ 889 Scott Erickson DT .05 .02
❑ 890 Tom Glavine DT .10 .05
❑ 891 Rob Dibble DT .05 .02
❑ 892 Mitch Williams DT .05 .02
❑ 893 Frank Thomas DT .15 .07
❑ X672 C.Knoblauch AU 50.00 22.00
1990 Score card, autographed with special hologram on back

1992 Score Rookie/Traded

	MINT	NRMT
COMP.FACT.SET (110)	10.00	4.50

❑ 1T Gary Sheffield .30 .14
❑ 2T Kevin Seitzer .20 .09
❑ 3T Danny Tartabull .20 .09
❑ 4T Steve Sax .20 .09
❑ 5T Bobby Bonilla .30 .14
❑ 6T Frank Viola .30 .14
❑ 7T Dave Winfield .75 .35
❑ 8T Rick Sutcliffe .30 .14
❑ 9T Jose Canseco .75 .35
❑ 10T Greg Swindell .20 .09
❑ 11T Eddie Murray .75 .35
❑ 12T Randy Myers .20 .09
❑ 13T Wally Joyner .30 .14
❑ 14T Kenny Lofton 1.00 .45
❑ 15T Jack Morris .30 .14
❑ 16T Charlie Hayes .20 .09
❑ 17T Pete Incaviglia .20 .09
❑ 18T Kevin Mitchell .20 .09
❑ 19T Kurt Stillwell .20 .09
❑ 20T Bret Saberhagen .30 .14
❑ 21T Steve Buechele .20 .09
❑ 22T John Smiley .20 .09
❑ 23T Sammy Sosa 1.00 .45
❑ 24T George Bell .20 .09
❑ 25T Curt Schilling .75 .35
❑ 26T Dick Schofield .20 .09
❑ 27T David Cone .30 .14
❑ 28T Dan Gladden .20 .09
❑ 29T Kirk McCaskill .20 .09
❑ 30T Mike Gallego .20 .09
❑ 31T Kevin McReynolds .20 .09
❑ 32T Bill Swift .20 .09
❑ 33T Dave Martinez .20 .09
❑ 34T Storm Davis .20 .09
❑ 35T Willie Randolph .30 .14
❑ 36T Melido Perez .20 .09
❑ 37T Mark Carreon .20 .09
❑ 38T Doug Jones .20 .09
❑ 39T Gregg Jefferies .20 .09
❑ 40T Mike Jackson .20 .09
❑ 41T Dickie Thon .20 .09
❑ 42T Eric King .20 .09
❑ 43T Herm Winningham .20 .09
❑ 44T Derek Lilliquist .20 .09
❑ 45T Dave Anderson .20 .09
❑ 46T Jeff Reardon .30 .14
❑ 47T Scott Bankhead .20 .09

❑ 48T Cory Snyder .20 .09
❑ 49T Al Newman .20 .09
❑ 50T Keith Miller .20 .09
❑ 51T Dave Burba .20 .09
❑ 52T Bill Pecota .20 .09
❑ 53T Chuck Crim .20 .09
❑ 54T Mariano Duncan .20 .09
❑ 55T Dave Gallagher .20 .09
❑ 56T Chris Gwynn .20 .09
❑ 57T Scott Ruskin .20 .09
❑ 58T Jack Armstrong .20 .09
❑ 59T Gary Carter .50 .23
❑ 60T Andres Galarraga .50 .23
❑ 61T Ken Hill .20 .09
❑ 62T Eric Davis .30 .14
❑ 63T Ruben Sierra .20 .09
❑ 64T Darrin Fletcher .20 .09
❑ 65T Tim Belcher .20 .09
❑ 66T Mike Morgan .20 .09
❑ 67T Scott Scudder .20 .09
❑ 68T Tom Candiotti .20 .09
❑ 69T Hubie Brooks .20 .09
❑ 70T Kal Daniels .20 .09
❑ 71T Bruce Ruffin .20 .09
❑ 72T Billy Hatcher .20 .09
❑ 73T Bob Melvin .20 .09
❑ 74T Lee Guetterman .20 .09
❑ 75T Rene Gonzales .20 .09
❑ 76T Kevin Bass .20 .09
❑ 77T Tom Bolton .20 .09
❑ 78T John Wetteland .30 .14
❑ 79T Bip Roberts .20 .09
❑ 80T Pat Listach RC .30 .14
❑ 81T John Doherty RC .20 .09
❑ 82T Sam Militello .20 .09
❑ 83T Brian Jordan RC 1.00 .45
❑ 84T Jeff Kent RC 5.00 2.20
❑ 85T Dave Fleming .20 .09
❑ 86T Jeff Tackett .20 .09
❑ 87T Chad Curtis RC .30 .14
❑ 88T Eric Fox RC .20 .09
❑ 89T Denny Neagle .30 .14
❑ 90T Donovan Osborne .20 .09
❑ 91T Carlos Hernandez .20 .09
❑ 92T Tim Wakefield RC .30 .14
❑ 93T Tim Salmon 1.00 .45
❑ 94T Dave Nilsson .20 .09
❑ 95T Mike Perez .20 .09
❑ 96T Pat Hentgen .20 .09
❑ 97T Frank Seminara RC .20 .09
❑ 98T Ruben Amaro .20 .09
❑ 99T Archi Cianfrocco RC .20 .09
❑ 100T Andy Stankiewicz .20 .09
❑ 101T Jim Bullinger .20 .09
❑ 102T Pat Mahomes RC .20 .09
❑ 103T Hipolito Pichardo RC .20 .09
❑ 104T Bret Boone 1.00 .45
❑ 105T John Vander Wal .20 .09
❑ 106T Vince Horsman .20 .09
❑ 107T James Austin .20 .09
❑ 108T Brian Williams RC .20 .09
❑ 109T Dan Walters .20 .09
❑ 110T Wil Cordero .20 .09

1993 Score

	MINT	NRMT
COMPLETE SET (660)	40.00	18.00

❑ 1 Ken Griffey Jr. 1.25 .55
❑ 2 Gary Sheffield .15 .07
❑ 3 Frank Thomas .50 .23
❑ 4 Ryne Sandberg .50 .23
❑ 5 Larry Walker .25 .11
❑ 6 Cal Ripken Jr. 1.50 .70
❑ 7 Roger Clemens 1.00 .45
❑ 8 Bobby Bonilla .15 .07
❑ 9 Carlos Baerga .10 .05
❑ 10 Darren Daulton .15 .07
❑ 11 Travis Fryman .15 .07
❑ 12 Andy Van Slyke .15 .07
❑ 13 Jose Canseco .40 .18
❑ 14 Roberto Alomar .40 .18
❑ 15 Tom Glavine .40 .18
❑ 16 Barry Larkin .40 .18
❑ 17 Gregg Jefferies .10 .05
❑ 18 Craig Biggio .25 .11
❑ 19 Shane Mack .10 .05
❑ 20 Brett Butler .15 .07
❑ 21 Dennis Eckersley .15 .07
❑ 22 Will Clark .40 .18
❑ 23 Don Mattingly 1.00 .45
❑ 24 Tony Gwynn .75 .35
❑ 25 Ivan Rodriguez .40 .18
❑ 26 Shawon Dunston .10 .05
❑ 27 Mike Mussina .40 .18
❑ 28 Marquis Grissom .10 .05
❑ 29 Charles Nagy .10 .05
❑ 30 Len Dykstra .15 .07
❑ 31 Cecil Fielder .15 .07
❑ 32 Jay Bell .15 .07
❑ 33 B.J. Surhoff .15 .07
❑ 34 Bob Tewksbury .10 .05
❑ 35 Danny Tartabull .10 .05
❑ 36 Terry Pendleton .15 .07
❑ 37 Jack Morris .15 .07
❑ 38 Hal Morris .10 .05
❑ 39 Luis Polonia .10 .05
❑ 40 Ken Caminiti .15 .07
❑ 41 Robin Ventura .15 .07
❑ 42 Darryl Strawberry .15 .07
❑ 43 Wally Joyner .15 .07
❑ 44 Fred McGriff .25 .11
❑ 45 Kevin Tapani .10 .05
❑ 46 Matt Williams .25 .11
❑ 47 Robin Yount .40 .18
❑ 48 Ken Hill .10 .05
❑ 49 Edgar Martinez .25 .11
❑ 50 Mark Grace .40 .18
❑ 51 Juan Gonzalez .40 .18
❑ 52 Curt Schilling .40 .18
❑ 53 Dwight Gooden .15 .07
❑ 54 Chris Hoiles .10 .05
❑ 55 Frank Viola .15 .07
❑ 56 Ray Lankford .10 .05
❑ 57 George Brett .75 .35
❑ 58 Kenny Lofton .15 .07
❑ 59 Nolan Ryan 2.00 .90
❑ 60 Mickey Tettleton .10 .05
❑ 61 John Smoltz .15 .07
❑ 62 Howard Johnson .10 .05
❑ 63 Eric Karros .15 .07
❑ 64 Rick Aguilera .10 .05
❑ 65 Steve Finley .15 .07
❑ 66 Mark Langston .10 .05
❑ 67 Bill Swift .10 .05
❑ 68 John Olerud .15 .07
❑ 69 Kevin McReynolds .10 .05
❑ 70 Jack McDowell .10 .05
❑ 71 Rickey Henderson .75 .35
❑ 72 Brian Harper .10 .05
❑ 73 Mike Morgan .10 .05
❑ 74 Rafael Palmeiro .40 .18
❑ 75 Dennis Martinez .15 .07
❑ 76 Tino Martinez .15 .07
❑ 77 Eddie Murray .40 .18
❑ 78 Ellis Burks .15 .07
❑ 79 John Kruk .15 .07
❑ 80 Gregg Olson .10 .05
❑ 81 Bernard Gilkey .10 .05
❑ 82 Milt Cuyler .10 .05
❑ 83 Mike LaValliere .10 .05
❑ 84 Albert Belle .15 .07
❑ 85 Bip Roberts .10 .05
❑ 86 Melido Perez .10 .05
❑ 87 Otis Nixon .10 .05
❑ 88 Bill Spiers .10 .05
❑ 89 Jeff Bagwell .50 .23
❑ 90 Orel Hershiser .15 .07
❑ 91 Andy Benes .10 .05
❑ 92 Devon White .10 .05
❑ 93 Willie McGee .15 .07
❑ 94 Ozzie Guillen .10 .05
❑ 95 Ivan Calderon .10 .05
❑ 96 Keith Miller .10 .05
❑ 97 Steve Buechele .10 .05
❑ 98 Kent Hrbek .15 .07
❑ 99 Dave Hollins .10 .05
❑ 100 Mike Bordick .10 .05
❑ 101 Randy Tomlin .10 .05
❑ 102 Omar Vizquel .15 .07
❑ 103 Lee Smith .15 .07
❑ 104 Leo Gomez .10 .05
❑ 105 Jose Rijo .10 .05
❑ 106 Mark Whiten .10 .05
❑ 107 Dave Justice .15 .07
❑ 108 Eddie Taubensee .10 .05
❑ 109 Lance Johnson .10 .05
❑ 110 Felix Jose .10 .05
❑ 111 Mike Harkey .10 .05
❑ 112 Randy Milligan .10 .05
❑ 113 Anthony Young .10 .05
❑ 114 Rico Brogna .10 .05
❑ 115 Bret Saberhagen .15 .07
❑ 116 Sandy Alomar Jr. .15 .07
❑ 117 Terry Mulholland .10 .05
❑ 118 Darryl Hamilton .10 .05
❑ 119 Todd Zeile .10 .05
❑ 120 Bernie Williams .40 .18
❑ 121 Zane Smith .10 .05
❑ 122 Derek Bell .10 .05
❑ 123 Deion Sanders .15 .07
❑ 124 Luis Sojo .10 .05
❑ 125 Joe Oliver .10 .05
❑ 126 Craig Grebeck .10 .05
❑ 127 Andujar Cedeno .10 .05
❑ 128 Brian McRae .10 .05
❑ 129 Jose Offerman .10 .05
❑ 130 Pedro Munoz .10 .05
❑ 131 Bud Black .10 .05
❑ 132 Mo Vaughn .15 .07
❑ 133 Bruce Hurst .10 .05
❑ 134 Dave Henderson .10 .05
❑ 135 Tom Pagnozzi .10 .05
❑ 136 Erik Hanson .10 .05
❑ 137 Orlando Merced .10 .05
❑ 138 Dean Palmer .15 .07
❑ 139 John Franco .15 .07
❑ 140 Brady Anderson .15 .07
❑ 141 Ricky Jordan .10 .05
❑ 142 Jeff Blauser .10 .05
❑ 143 Sammy Sosa .75 .35
❑ 144 Bob Walk .10 .05
❑ 145 Delino DeShields .10 .05
❑ 146 Kevin Brown .15 .07
❑ 147 Mark Lemke .10 .05
❑ 148 Chuck Knoblauch .15 .07
❑ 149 Chris Sabo .10 .05
❑ 150 Bobby Witt .10 .05
❑ 151 Luis Gonzalez .40 .18
❑ 152 Ron Karkovice .10 .05
❑ 153 Jeff Brantley .10 .05
❑ 154 Kevin Appier .15 .07
❑ 155 Darrin Jackson .10 .05
❑ 156 Kelly Gruber .10 .05
❑ 157 Royce Clayton .10 .05
❑ 158 Chuck Finley .15 .07
❑ 159 Jeff King .10 .05
❑ 160 Greg Vaughn .15 .07
❑ 161 Geronimo Pena .10 .05
❑ 162 Steve Farr .10 .05
❑ 163 Jose Oquendo .10 .05
❑ 164 Mark Lewis .10 .05
❑ 165 John Wetteland .15 .07
❑ 166 Mike Henneman .10 .05
❑ 167 Todd Hundley .10 .05
❑ 168 Wes Chamberlain .10 .05
❑ 169 Steve Avery .10 .05
❑ 170 Mike Devereaux .10 .05
❑ 171 Reggie Sanders .10 .05
❑ 172 Jay Buhner .15 .07

❑ 173	Eric Anthony	.10	.05
❑ 174	John Burkett	.10	.05
❑ 175	Tom Candiotti	.10	.05
❑ 176	Phil Plantier	.10	.05
❑ 177	Doug Henry	.10	.05
❑ 178	Scott Leius	.10	.05
❑ 179	Kirt Manwaring	.10	.05
❑ 180	Jeff Parrett	.10	.05
❑ 181	Don Slaught	.10	.05
❑ 182	Scott Radinsky	.10	.05
❑ 183	Luis Alicea	.10	.05
❑ 184	Tom Gordon	.10	.05
❑ 185	Rick Wilkins	.10	.05
❑ 186	Todd Stottlemyre	.10	.05
❑ 187	Moises Alou	.15	.07
❑ 188	Joe Grahe	.10	.05
❑ 189	Jeff Kent	.40	.18
❑ 190	Bill Wegman	.10	.05
❑ 191	Kim Batiste	.10	.05
❑ 192	Matt Nokes	.10	.05
❑ 193	Mark Wohlers	.10	.05
❑ 194	Paul Sorrento	.10	.05
❑ 195	Chris Hammond	.10	.05
❑ 196	Scott Livingstone	.10	.05
❑ 197	Doug Jones	.10	.05
❑ 198	Scott Cooper	.10	.05
❑ 199	Ramon Martinez	.10	.05
❑ 200	Dave Valle	.10	.05
❑ 201	Mariano Duncan	.10	.05
❑ 202	Ben McDonald	.10	.05
❑ 203	Darren Lewis	.10	.05
❑ 204	Kenny Rogers	.10	.05
❑ 205	Manuel Lee	.10	.05
❑ 206	Scott Erickson	.10	.05
❑ 207	Dan Gladden	.10	.05
❑ 208	Bob Welch	.10	.05
❑ 209	Greg Olson	.10	.05
❑ 210	Dan Pasqua	.10	.05
❑ 211	Tim Wallach	.10	.05
❑ 212	Jeff Montgomery	.10	.05
❑ 213	Derrick May	.10	.05
❑ 214	Ed Sprague	.10	.05
❑ 215	David Haas	.10	.05
❑ 216	Darrin Fletcher	.10	.05
❑ 217	Brian Jordan	.15	.07
❑ 218	Jaime Navarro	.10	.05
❑ 219	Randy Velarde	.10	.05
❑ 220	Ron Gant	.10	.05
❑ 221	Paul Quantrill	.10	.05
❑ 222	Damion Easley	.10	.05
❑ 223	Charlie Hough	.15	.07
❑ 224	Brad Brink	.10	.05
❑ 225	Barry Manuel	.10	.05
❑ 226	Kevin Koslofski	.10	.05
❑ 227	Ryan Thompson	.10	.05
❑ 228	Mike Munoz	.10	.05
❑ 229	Dan Wilson	.15	.07
❑ 230	Peter Hoy	.10	.05
❑ 231	Pedro Astacio	.10	.05
❑ 232	Matt Stairs	.10	.05
❑ 233	Jeff Reboulet	.10	.05
❑ 234	Manny Alexander	.10	.05
❑ 235	Willie Banks	.10	.05
❑ 236	John Jaha	.10	.05
❑ 237	Scooter Tucker	.10	.05
❑ 238	Russ Springer	.10	.05
❑ 239	Paul Miller	.10	.05
❑ 240	Dan Peltier	.10	.05
❑ 241	Ozzie Canseco	.10	.05
❑ 242	Ben Rivera	.10	.05
❑ 243	John Valentin	.10	.05
❑ 244	Henry Rodriguez	.10	.05
❑ 245	Derek Parks	.10	.05
❑ 246	Carlos Garcia	.10	.05
❑ 247	Tim Pugh RC	.10	.05
❑ 248	Melvin Nieves	.10	.05
❑ 249	Rich Amaral	.10	.05
❑ 250	Willie Greene	.10	.05
❑ 251	Tim Scott	.10	.05
❑ 252	Dave Silvestri	.10	.05
❑ 253	Rob Mallicoat	.10	.05
❑ 254	Donald Harris	.10	.05
❑ 255	Craig Colbert	.10	.05
❑ 256	Jose Guzman	.10	.05
❑ 257	Domingo Martinez RC	.10	.05
❑ 258	William Suero	.10	.05
❑ 259	Juan Guerrero	.10	.05
❑ 260	J.T. Snow RC	.50	.23
❑ 261	Tony Pena	.10	.05
❑ 262	Tim Fortugno	.10	.05
❑ 263	Tom Marsh	.10	.05
❑ 264	Kurt Knudsen	.10	.05
❑ 265	Tim Costo	.10	.05
❑ 266	Steve Shifflett	.10	.05
❑ 267	Billy Ashley	.10	.05
❑ 268	Jerry Nielsen	.10	.05
❑ 269	Pete Young	.10	.05
❑ 270	Johnny Guzman	.10	.05
❑ 271	Greg Colbrunn	.10	.05
❑ 272	Jeff Nelson	.10	.05
❑ 273	Kevin Young	.15	.07
❑ 274	Jeff Frye	.10	.05
❑ 275	J.T. Bruett	.10	.05
❑ 276	Todd Pratt RC	.15	.07
❑ 277	Mike Butcher	.10	.05
❑ 278	John Flaherty	.10	.05
❑ 279	John Patterson	.10	.05
❑ 280	Eric Hillman	.10	.05
❑ 281	Bien Figueroa	.10	.05
❑ 282	Shane Reynolds	.10	.05
❑ 283	Rich Rowland	.10	.05
❑ 284	Steve Foster	.10	.05
❑ 285	Dave Mlicki	.10	.05
❑ 286	Mike Piazza	2.00	.90
❑ 287	Mike Trombley	.10	.05
❑ 288	Jim Pena	.10	.05
❑ 289	Bob Ayrault	.10	.05
❑ 290	Henry Mercedes	.10	.05
❑ 291	Bob Wickman	.10	.05
❑ 292	Jacob Brumfield	.10	.05
❑ 293	David Hulse RC	.10	.05
❑ 294	Ryan Klesko	.15	.07
❑ 295	Doug Linton	.10	.05
❑ 296	Steve Cooke	.10	.05
❑ 297	Eddie Zosky	.10	.05
❑ 298	Gerald Williams	.10	.05
❑ 299	Jonathan Hurst	.10	.05
❑ 300	Larry Carter	.10	.05
❑ 301	William Pennyfeather	.10	.05
❑ 302	Cesar Hernandez	.10	.05
❑ 303	Steve Hosey	.10	.05
❑ 304	Blas Minor	.10	.05
❑ 305	Jeff Grotewald	.10	.05
❑ 306	Bernardo Brito	.10	.05
❑ 307	Rafael Bournigal	.10	.05
❑ 308	Jeff Branson	.10	.05
❑ 309	Tom Quinlan RC	.10	.05
❑ 310	Pat Gomez RC	.10	.05
❑ 311	Sterling Hitchcock RC	.15	.07
❑ 312	Kent Bottenfield	.10	.05
❑ 313	Alan Trammell	.25	.11
❑ 314	Cris Colon	.10	.05
❑ 315	Paul Wagner	.10	.05
❑ 316	Matt Maysey	.10	.05
❑ 317	Mike Stanton	.10	.05
❑ 318	Rick Trlicek	.10	.05
❑ 319	Kevin Rogers	.10	.05
❑ 320	Mark Clark	.10	.05
❑ 321	Pedro Martinez	1.00	.45
❑ 322	Al Martin	.10	.05
❑ 323	Mike Macfarlane	.10	.05
❑ 324	Rey Sanchez	.10	.05
❑ 325	Roger Pavlik	.10	.05
❑ 326	Troy Neel	.10	.05
❑ 327	Kerry Woodson	.10	.05
❑ 328	Wayne Kirby	.10	.05
❑ 329	Ken Ryan RC	.10	.05
❑ 330	Jesse Levis	.10	.05
❑ 331	James Austin	.10	.05
❑ 332	Dan Walters	.10	.05
❑ 333	Brian Williams	.10	.05
❑ 334	Wil Cordero	.10	.05
❑ 335	Bret Boone	.15	.07
❑ 336	Hipolito Pichardo	.10	.05
❑ 337	Pat Mahomes	.10	.05
❑ 338	Andy Stankiewicz	.10	.05
❑ 339	Jim Bullinger	.10	.05
❑ 340	Archi Cianfrocco	.10	.05
❑ 341	Ruben Amaro	.10	.05
❑ 342	Frank Seminara	.10	.05
❑ 343	Pat Hentgen	.10	.05
❑ 344	Dave Nilsson	.10	.05
❑ 345	Mike Perez	.10	.05
❑ 346	Tim Salmon	.15	.07
❑ 347	Tim Wakefield	.10	.05
❑ 348	Carlos Hernandez	.10	.05
❑ 349	Donovan Osborne	.10	.05
❑ 350	Denny Neagle	.15	.07
❑ 351	Sam Militello	.10	.05
❑ 352	Eric Fox	.10	.05
❑ 353	John Doherty	.10	.05
❑ 354	Chad Curtis	.10	.05
❑ 355	Jeff Tackett	.10	.05
❑ 356	Dave Fleming	.10	.05
❑ 357	Pat Listach	.10	.05
❑ 358	Kevin Wickander	.10	.05
❑ 359	John Vander Wal	.10	.05
❑ 360	Arthur Rhodes	.10	.05
❑ 361	Bob Scanlan	.10	.05
❑ 362	Bob Zupcic	.10	.05
❑ 363	Mel Rojas	.10	.05
❑ 364	Jim Thome	.40	.18
❑ 365	Bill Pecota	.10	.05
❑ 366	Mark Carreon	.10	.05
❑ 367	Mitch Williams	.10	.05
❑ 368	Cal Eldred	.10	.05
❑ 369	Stan Belinda	.10	.05
❑ 370	Pat Kelly	.10	.05
❑ 371	Rheal Cormier	.10	.05
❑ 372	Juan Guzman	.10	.05
❑ 373	Damon Berryhill	.10	.05
❑ 374	Gary DiSarcina	.10	.05
❑ 375	Norm Charlton	.10	.05
❑ 376	Roberto Hernandez	.10	.05
❑ 377	Scott Kamieniecki	.10	.05
❑ 378	Rusty Meacham	.10	.05
❑ 379	Kurt Stillwell	.10	.05
❑ 380	Lloyd McClendon	.10	.05
❑ 381	Mark Leonard	.10	.05
❑ 382	Jerry Browne	.10	.05
❑ 383	Glenn Davis	.10	.05
❑ 384	Randy Johnson	.50	.23
❑ 385	Mike Greenwell	.10	.05
❑ 386	Scott Chiamparino	.10	.05
❑ 387	George Bell	.10	.05
❑ 388	Steve Olin	.10	.05
❑ 389	Chuck McElroy	.10	.05
❑ 390	Mark Gardner	.10	.05
❑ 391	Rod Beck	.10	.05
❑ 392	Dennis Rasmussen	.10	.05
❑ 393	Charlie Leibrandt	.10	.05
❑ 394	Julio Franco	.15	.07
❑ 395	Pete Harnisch	.10	.05
❑ 396	Sid Bream	.10	.05
❑ 397	Milt Thompson	.10	.05
❑ 398	Glenallen Hill	.10	.05
❑ 399	Chico Walker	.10	.05
❑ 400	Alex Cole	.10	.05
❑ 401	Trevor Wilson	.10	.05
❑ 402	Jeff Conine	.10	.05
❑ 403	Kyle Abbott	.10	.05
❑ 404	Tom Browning	.10	.05
❑ 405	Jerald Clark	.10	.05
❑ 406	Vince Horsman	.10	.05
❑ 407	Kevin Mitchell	.10	.05
❑ 408	Pete Smith	.10	.05
❑ 409	Jeff Innis	.10	.05
❑ 410	Mike Timlin	.10	.05
❑ 411	Charlie Hayes	.10	.05
❑ 412	Alex Fernandez	.10	.05
❑ 413	Jeff Russell	.10	.05
❑ 414	Jody Reed	.10	.05
❑ 415	Mickey Morandini	.10	.05
❑ 416	Darnell Coles	.10	.05
❑ 417	Xavier Hernandez	.10	.05
❑ 418	Steve Sax	.10	.05
❑ 419	Joe Girardi	.10	.05
❑ 420	Mike Fetters	.10	.05
❑ 421	Danny Jackson	.10	.05
❑ 422	Jim Gott	.10	.05
❑ 423	Tim Belcher	.10	.05
❑ 424	Jose Mesa	.10	.05
❑ 425	Junior Felix	.10	.05
❑ 426	Thomas Howard	.10	.05
❑ 427	Julio Valera	.10	.05
❑ 428	Dante Bichette	.15	.07
❑ 429	Mike Sharperson	.10	.05
❑ 430	Darryl Kile	.15	.07

❑ 431 Lonnie Smith .10 .05
❑ 432 Monty Fariss .10 .05
❑ 433 Reggie Jefferson .10 .05
❑ 434 Bob McClure .10 .05
❑ 435 Craig Lefferts .10 .05
❑ 436 Duane Ward .10 .05
❑ 437 Shawn Abner .10 .05
❑ 438 Roberto Kelly .10 .05
❑ 439 Paul O'Neill .40 .18
❑ 440 Alan Mills .10 .05
❑ 441 Roger Mason .10 .05
❑ 442 Gary Pettis .10 .05
❑ 443 Steve Lake .10 .05
❑ 444 Gene Larkin .10 .05
❑ 445 Larry Andersen .10 .05
❑ 446 Doug Dascenzo .10 .05
❑ 447 Daryl Boston .10 .05
❑ 448 John Candelaria .10 .05
❑ 449 Storm Davis .10 .05
❑ 450 Tom Edens .10 .05
❑ 451 Mike Maddux .10 .05
❑ 452 Tim Naehring .10 .05
❑ 453 John Orton .10 .05
❑ 454 Joey Cora .10 .05
❑ 455 Chuck Crim .10 .05
❑ 456 Dan Plesac .10 .05
❑ 457 Mike Bielecki .10 .05
❑ 458 Terry Jorgensen .10 .05
❑ 459 John Habyan .10 .05
❑ 460 Pete O'Brien .10 .05
❑ 461 Jeff Treadway .10 .05
❑ 462 Frank Castillo .10 .05
❑ 463 Jimmy Jones .10 .05
❑ 464 Tommy Greene .10 .05
❑ 465 Tracy Woodson .10 .05
❑ 466 Rich Rodriguez .10 .05
❑ 467 Joe Hesketh .10 .05
❑ 468 Greg Myers .10 .05
❑ 469 Kirk McCaskill .10 .05
❑ 470 Ricky Bones .10 .05
❑ 471 Lenny Webster .10 .05
❑ 472 Francisco Cabrera .10 .05
❑ 473 Turner Ward .10 .05
❑ 474 Dwayne Henry .10 .05
❑ 475 Al Osuna .10 .05
❑ 476 Craig Wilson .10 .05
❑ 477 Chris Nabholz .10 .05
❑ 478 Rafael Belliard .10 .05
❑ 479 Terry Leach .10 .05
❑ 480 Tim Teufel .10 .05
❑ 481 Dennis Eckersley AW .10 .05
❑ 482 Barry Bonds AW .50 .23
❑ 483 Dennis Eckersley AW .10 .05
❑ 484 Greg Maddux AW .50 .23
❑ 485 Pat Listach AW .10 .05
❑ 486 Eric Karros AW .10 .05
❑ 487 Jamie Arnold DP RC .10 .05
❑ 488 B.J. Wallace DP .10 .05
❑ 489 Derek Jeter DP RC 15.00 6.75
❑ 490 Jason Kendall DP RC 1.25 .55
❑ 491 Rick Helling DP .10 .05
❑ 492 Derek Wallace DP RC .10 .05
❑ 493 Sean Lowe DP RC .10 .05
❑ 494 S.Stewart DP RC 1.25 .55
❑ 495 Benji Grigsby DP RC .10 .05
❑ 496 T.Steverson DP RC .10 .05
❑ 497 Dan Serafini DP RC .10 .05
❑ 498 Michael Tucker DP .10 .05
❑ 499 Chris Roberts DP .10 .05
❑ 500 Pete Janicki DP RC .10 .05
❑ 501 Jeff Schmidt DP RC .10 .05
❑ 502 Edgar Martinez AS .15 .07
❑ 503 Omar Vizquel AS .15 .07
❑ 504 Ken Griffey Jr. AS .60 .25
❑ 505 Kirby Puckett AS .50 .23
❑ 506 Joe Carter AS .10 .05
❑ 507 Ivan Rodriguez AS .15 .07
❑ 508 Jack Morris AS .10 .05
❑ 509 Dennis Eckersley AS .10 .05
❑ 510 Frank Thomas AS .25 .11
❑ 511 Roberto Alomar AS .15 .07
❑ 512 Mickey Morandini AS .10 .05
❑ 513 Dennis Eckersley HL .10 .05
❑ 514 Jeff Reardon HL .10 .05
❑ 515 Danny Tartabull HL .10 .05
❑ 516 Bip Roberts HL .10 .05
❑ 517 George Brett HL .40 .18
❑ 518 Robin Yount HL .15 .07
❑ 519 Kevin Gross HL .10 .05
❑ 520 Ed Sprague WS .10 .05
❑ 521 Dave Winfield WS .15 .07
❑ 522 Ozzie Smith AS .25 .11
❑ 523 Barry Bonds AS .50 .23
❑ 524 Andy Van Slyke AS .10 .05
❑ 525 Tony Gwynn AS .40 .18
❑ 526 Darren Daulton AS .10 .05
❑ 527 Greg Maddux AS .50 .23
❑ 528 Fred McGriff AS .25 .11
❑ 529 Lee Smith AS .10 .05
❑ 530 Ryne Sandberg AS .25 .11
❑ 531 Gary Sheffield AS .10 .05
❑ 532 Ozzie Smith DT .25 .11
❑ 533 Kirby Puckett DT .50 .23
❑ 534 Gary Sheffield DT .10 .05
❑ 535 Andy Van Slyke DT .10 .05
❑ 536 Ken Griffey Jr. DT .60 .25
❑ 537 Ivan Rodriguez DT .15 .07
❑ 538 Charles Nagy DT .10 .05
❑ 539 Tom Glavine DT .15 .07
❑ 540 Dennis Eckersley DT .10 .05
❑ 541 Frank Thomas DT .25 .11
❑ 542 Roberto Alomar DT .15 .07
❑ 543 Sean Berry .10 .05
❑ 544 Mike Schooler .10 .05
❑ 545 Chuck Carr .10 .05
❑ 546 Lenny Harris .10 .05
❑ 547 Gary Scott .10 .05
❑ 548 Derek Lilliquist .10 .05
❑ 549 Brian Hunter .10 .05
❑ 550 Kirby Puckett MOY .50 .23
❑ 551 Jim Eisenreich .10 .05
❑ 552 Andre Dawson .25 .11
❑ 553 David Nied .10 .05
❑ 554 Spike Owen .10 .05
❑ 555 Greg Gagne .10 .05
❑ 556 Sid Fernandez .10 .05
❑ 557 Mark McGwire 1.50 .70
❑ 558 Bryan Harvey .10 .05
❑ 559 Harold Reynolds .10 .05
❑ 560 Barry Bonds 1.00 .45
❑ 561 Eric Wedge RC .10 .05
❑ 562 Ozzie Smith .50 .23
❑ 563 Rick Sutcliffe .15 .07
❑ 564 Jeff Reardon .15 .07
❑ 565 Alex Arias .10 .05
❑ 566 Greg Swindell .10 .05
❑ 567 Brook Jacoby .10 .05
❑ 568 Pete Incaviglia .10 .05
❑ 569 Butch Henry .10 .05
❑ 570 Eric Davis .15 .07
❑ 571 Kevin Seitzer .10 .05
❑ 572 Tony Fernandez .10 .05
❑ 573 Steve Reed RC .10 .05
❑ 574 Cory Snyder .10 .05
❑ 575 Joe Carter .15 .07
❑ 576 Greg Maddux 1.00 .45
❑ 577 Bert Blyleven UER .15 .07
(Should say 3701 career strikeouts)
❑ 578 Kevin Bass .10 .05
❑ 579 Carlton Fisk .40 .18
❑ 580 Doug Drabek .10 .05
❑ 581 Mark Gubicza .10 .05
❑ 582 Bobby Thigpen .10 .05
❑ 583 Chili Davis .15 .07
❑ 584 Scott Bankhead .10 .05
❑ 585 Harold Baines .15 .07
❑ 586 Eric Young .10 .05
❑ 587 Lance Parrish .15 .07
❑ 588 Juan Bell .10 .05
❑ 589 Bob Ojeda .10 .05
❑ 590 Joe Orsulak .10 .05
❑ 591 Benito Santiago .10 .05
❑ 592 Wade Boggs .40 .18
❑ 593 Robby Thompson .10 .05
❑ 594 Eric Plunk .10 .05
❑ 595 Hensley Meulens .10 .05
❑ 596 Lou Whitaker .15 .07
❑ 597 Dale Murphy .25 .11
❑ 598 Paul Molitor .40 .18
❑ 599 Greg W. Harris .10 .05
❑ 600 Darren Holmes .10 .05
❑ 601 Dave Martinez .10 .05
❑ 602 Tom Henke .10 .05
❑ 603 Mike Benjamin .10 .05
❑ 604 Rene Gonzales .10 .05
❑ 605 Roger McDowell .10 .05
❑ 606 Kirby Puckett 1.00 .45
❑ 607 Randy Myers .10 .05
❑ 608 Ruben Sierra .10 .05
❑ 609 Wilson Alvarez .10 .05
❑ 610 David Segui .10 .05
❑ 611 Juan Samuel .10 .05
❑ 612 Tom Brunansky .10 .05
❑ 613 Willie Randolph .15 .07
❑ 614 Tony Phillips .10 .05
❑ 615 Candy Maldonado .10 .05
❑ 616 Chris Bosio .10 .05
❑ 617 Bret Barberie .10 .05
❑ 618 Scott Sanderson .10 .05
❑ 619 Ron Darling .10 .05
❑ 620 Dave Winfield .40 .18
❑ 621 Mike Felder .10 .05
❑ 622 Greg Hibbard .10 .05
❑ 623 Mike Scioscia .10 .05
❑ 624 John Smiley .10 .05
❑ 625 Alejandro Pena .10 .05
❑ 626 Terry Steinbach .10 .05
❑ 627 Freddie Benavides .10 .05
❑ 628 Kevin Reimer .10 .05
❑ 629 Braulio Castillo .10 .05
❑ 630 Dave Stieb .10 .05
❑ 631 Dave Magadan .10 .05
❑ 632 Scott Fletcher .10 .05
❑ 633 Cris Carpenter .10 .05
❑ 634 Kevin Maas .10 .05
❑ 635 Todd Worrell .10 .05
❑ 636 Rob Deer .10 .05
❑ 637 Dwight Smith .10 .05
❑ 638 Chito Martinez .10 .05
❑ 639 Jimmy Key .15 .07
❑ 640 Greg A. Harris .10 .05
❑ 641 Mike Moore .10 .05
❑ 642 Pat Borders .10 .05
❑ 643 Bill Gullickson .10 .05
❑ 644 Gary Gaetti .15 .07
❑ 645 David Howard .10 .05
❑ 646 Jim Abbott .15 .07
❑ 647 Willie Wilson .10 .05
❑ 648 David Wells .15 .07
❑ 649 Andres Galarraga .25 .11
❑ 650 Vince Coleman .10 .05
❑ 651 Rob Dibble .10 .05
❑ 652 Frank Tanana .10 .05
❑ 653 Steve Decker .10 .05
❑ 654 David Cone .15 .07
❑ 655 Jack Armstrong .10 .05
❑ 656 Dave Stewart .15 .07
❑ 657 Billy Hatcher .10 .05
❑ 658 Tim Raines .15 .07
❑ 659 Walt Weiss .10 .05
❑ 660 Jose Lind .10 .05

1994 Score

	MINT	NRMT
COMPLETE SET (660)	24.00	11.00
COMPLETE SERIES 1 (330)	12.00	5.50
COMPLETE SERIES 2 (330)	12.00	5.50

❑ 1	Barry Bonds	1.00	.45
❑ 2	John Olerud	.15	.07
❑ 3	Ken Griffey Jr.	1.25	.55
❑ 4	Jeff Bagwell	.50	.23
❑ 5	John Burkett	.10	.05
❑ 6	Jack McDowell	.10	.05
❑ 7	Albert Belle	.15	.07
❑ 8	Andres Galarraga	.25	.11
❑ 9	Mike Mussina	.40	.18
❑ 10	Will Clark	.40	.18
❑ 11	Travis Fryman	.15	.07
❑ 12	Tony Gwynn	.75	.35
❑ 13	Robin Yount	.40	.18
❑ 14	Dave Magadan	.10	.05
❑ 15	Paul O'Neill	.40	.18
❑ 16	Ray Lankford	.10	.05
❑ 17	Damion Easley	.10	.05
❑ 18	Andy Van Slyke	.15	.07
❑ 19	Brian McRae	.10	.05
❑ 20	Ryne Sandberg	.50	.23
❑ 21	Kirby Puckett	1.00	.45
❑ 22	Dwight Gooden	.15	.07
❑ 23	Don Mattingly	1.00	.45
❑ 24	Kevin Mitchell	.10	.05
❑ 25	Roger Clemens	1.00	.45
❑ 26	Eric Karros	.15	.07
❑ 27	Juan Gonzalez	.40	.18
❑ 28	John Kruk	.15	.07
❑ 29	Gregg Jefferies	.10	.05
❑ 30	Tom Glavine	.40	.18
❑ 31	Ivan Rodriguez	.40	.18
❑ 32	Jay Bell	.15	.07
❑ 33	Randy Johnson	.50	.23
❑ 34	Darren Daulton	.15	.07
❑ 35	Rickey Henderson	.75	.35
❑ 36	Eddie Murray	.40	.18
❑ 37	Brian Harper	.10	.05
❑ 38	Delino DeShields	.10	.05
❑ 39	Jose Lind	.10	.05
❑ 40	Benito Santiago	.10	.05
❑ 41	Frank Thomas	.50	.23
❑ 42	Mark Grace	.40	.18
❑ 43	Roberto Alomar	.40	.18
❑ 44	Andy Benes	.10	.05
❑ 45	Luis Polonia	.10	.05
❑ 46	Brett Butler	.15	.07
❑ 47	Terry Steinbach	.10	.05
❑ 48	Craig Biggio	.25	.11
❑ 49	Greg Vaughn	.15	.07
❑ 50	Charlie Hayes	.10	.05
❑ 51	Mickey Tettleton	.10	.05
❑ 52	Jose Rijo	.10	.05
❑ 53	Carlos Baerga	.10	.05
❑ 54	Jeff Blauser	.10	.05
❑ 55	Leo Gomez	.10	.05
❑ 56	Bob Tewksbury	.10	.05
❑ 57	Mo Vaughn	.15	.07
❑ 58	Orlando Merced	.10	.05
❑ 59	Tino Martinez	.15	.07
❑ 60	Lenny Dykstra	.15	.07
❑ 61	Jose Canseco	.40	.18
❑ 62	Tony Fernandez	.10	.05
❑ 63	Donovan Osborne	.10	.05
❑ 64	Ken Hill	.10	.05
❑ 65	Kent Hrbek	.15	.07
❑ 66	Bryan Harvey	.10	.05
❑ 67	Wally Joyner	.15	.07
❑ 68	Derrick May	.10	.05
❑ 69	Lance Johnson	.10	.05
❑ 70	Willie McGee	.15	.07
❑ 71	Mark Langston	.10	.05
❑ 72	Terry Pendleton	.15	.07
❑ 73	Joe Carter	.15	.07
❑ 74	Barry Larkin	.40	.18
❑ 75	Jimmy Key	.15	.07
❑ 76	Joe Girardi	.10	.05
❑ 77	B.J. Surhoff	.15	.07
❑ 78	Pete Harnisch	.10	.05
❑ 79	Lou Whitaker UER	.15	.07
	(Milt Cuyler		
	pictured on front)		
❑ 80	Cory Snyder	.10	.05
❑ 81	Kenny Lofton	.15	.07
❑ 82	Fred McGriff	.25	.11
❑ 83	Mike Greenwell	.10	.05
❑ 84	Mike Perez	.10	.05

❑ 85	Cal Ripken	1.50	.70
❑ 86	Don Slaught	.10	.05
❑ 87	Omar Vizquel	.15	.07
❑ 88	Curt Schilling	.40	.18
❑ 89	Chuck Knoblauch	.15	.07
❑ 90	Moises Alou	.15	.07
❑ 91	Greg Gagne	.10	.05
❑ 92	Bret Saberhagen	.15	.07
❑ 93	Ozzie Guillen	.10	.05
❑ 94	Matt Williams	.25	.11
❑ 95	Chad Curtis	.10	.05
❑ 96	Mike Harkey	.10	.05
❑ 97	Devon White	.10	.05
❑ 98	Walt Weiss	.10	.05
❑ 99	Kevin Brown	.15	.07
❑ 100	Gary Sheffield	.15	.07
❑ 101	Wade Boggs	.40	.18
❑ 102	Orel Hershiser	.15	.07
❑ 103	Tony Phillips	.10	.05
❑ 104	Andujar Cedeno	.10	.05
❑ 105	Bill Spiers	.10	.05
❑ 106	Otis Nixon	.10	.05
❑ 107	Felix Fermin	.10	.05
❑ 108	Bip Roberts	.10	.05
❑ 109	Dennis Eckersley	.15	.07
❑ 110	Dante Bichette	.15	.07
❑ 111	Ben McDonald	.10	.05
❑ 112	Jim Poole	.10	.05
❑ 113	John Dopson	.10	.05
❑ 114	Rob Dibble	.10	.05
❑ 115	Jeff Treadway	.10	.05
❑ 116	Ricky Jordan	.10	.05
❑ 117	Mike Henneman	.10	.05
❑ 118	Willie Blair	.10	.05
❑ 119	Doug Henry	.10	.05
❑ 120	Gerald Perry	.10	.05
❑ 121	Greg Myers	.10	.05
❑ 122	John Franco	.15	.07
❑ 123	Roger Mason	.10	.05
❑ 124	Chris Hammond	.10	.05
❑ 125	Hubie Brooks	.10	.05
❑ 126	Kent Mercker	.10	.05
❑ 127	Jim Abbott	.15	.07
❑ 128	Kevin Bass	.10	.05
❑ 129	Rick Aguilera	.10	.05
❑ 130	Mitch Webster	.10	.05
❑ 131	Eric Plunk	.10	.05
❑ 132	Mark Carreon	.10	.05
❑ 133	Dave Stewart	.15	.07
❑ 134	Willie Wilson	.10	.05
❑ 135	Dave Fleming	.10	.05
❑ 136	Jeff Tackett	.10	.05
❑ 137	Geno Petralli	.10	.05
❑ 138	Gene Harris	.10	.05
❑ 139	Scott Bankhead	.10	.05
❑ 140	Trevor Wilson	.10	.05
❑ 141	Alvaro Espinoza	.10	.05
❑ 142	Ryan Bowen	.10	.05
❑ 143	Mike Moore	.10	.05
❑ 144	Bill Pecota	.10	.05
❑ 145	Jaime Navarro	.10	.05
❑ 146	Jack Daugherty	.10	.05
❑ 147	Bob Wickman	.10	.05
❑ 148	Chris Jones	.10	.05
❑ 149	Todd Stottlemyre	.10	.05
❑ 150	Brian Williams	.10	.05
❑ 151	Chuck Finley	.15	.07
❑ 152	Lenny Harris	.10	.05
❑ 153	Alex Fernandez	.10	.05
❑ 154	Candy Maldonado	.10	.05
❑ 155	Jeff Montgomery	.10	.05
❑ 156	David West	.10	.05
❑ 157	Mark Williamson	.10	.05
❑ 158	Milt Thompson	.10	.05
❑ 159	Ron Darling	.10	.05
❑ 160	Stan Belinda	.10	.05
❑ 161	Henry Cotto	.10	.05
❑ 162	Mel Rojas	.10	.05
❑ 163	Doug Strange	.10	.05
❑ 164	Rene Arocha	.10	.05
❑ 165	Tim Hulett	.10	.05
❑ 166	Steve Avery	.10	.05
❑ 167	Jim Thome	.40	.18
❑ 168	Tom Browning	.10	.05
❑ 169	Mario Diaz	.10	.05
❑ 170	Steve Reed	.10	.05

❑ 171	Scott Livingstone	.10	.05
❑ 172	Chris Donnels	.10	.05
❑ 173	John Jaha	.10	.05
❑ 174	Carlos Hernandez	.10	.05
❑ 175	Dion James	.10	.05
❑ 176	Bud Black	.10	.05
❑ 177	Tony Castillo	.10	.05
❑ 178	Jose Guzman	.10	.05
❑ 179	Torey Lovullo	.10	.05
❑ 180	John Vander Wal	.10	.05
❑ 181	Mike LaValliere	.10	.05
❑ 182	Sid Fernandez	.10	.05
❑ 183	Brent Mayne	.10	.05
❑ 184	Terry Mulholland	.10	.05
❑ 185	Willie Banks	.10	.05
❑ 186	Steve Cooke	.10	.05
❑ 187	Brent Gates	.10	.05
❑ 188	Erik Pappas	.10	.05
❑ 189	Bill Haselman	.10	.05
❑ 190	Fernando Valenzuela	.15	.07
❑ 191	Gary Redus	.10	.05
❑ 192	Danny Darwin	.10	.05
❑ 193	Mark Portugal	.10	.05
❑ 194	Derek Lilliquist	.10	.05
❑ 195	Charlie O'Brien	.10	.05
❑ 196	Matt Nokes	.10	.05
❑ 197	Danny Sheaffer	.10	.05
❑ 198	Bill Gullickson	.10	.05
❑ 199	Alex Arias	.10	.05
❑ 200	Mike Fetters	.10	.05
❑ 201	Brian Jordan	.15	.07
❑ 202	Joe Grahe	.10	.05
❑ 203	Tom Candiotti	.10	.05
❑ 204	Jeremy Hernandez	.10	.05
❑ 205	Mike Stanton	.10	.05
❑ 206	David Howard	.10	.05
❑ 207	Darren Holmes	.10	.05
❑ 208	Rick Honeycutt	.10	.05
❑ 209	Danny Jackson	.10	.05
❑ 210	Rich Amaral	.10	.05
❑ 211	Blas Minor	.10	.05
❑ 212	Kenny Rogers	.10	.05
❑ 213	Jim Leyritz	.10	.05
❑ 214	Mike Morgan	.10	.05
❑ 215	Dan Gladden	.10	.05
❑ 216	Randy Velarde	.10	.05
❑ 217	Mitch Williams	.10	.05
❑ 218	Hipolito Pichardo	.10	.05
❑ 219	Dave Burba	.10	.05
❑ 220	Wilson Alvarez	.10	.05
❑ 221	Bob Zupcic	.10	.05
❑ 222	Francisco Cabrera	.10	.05
❑ 223	Julio Valera	.10	.05
❑ 224	Paul Assenmacher	.10	.05
❑ 225	Jeff Branson	.10	.05
❑ 226	Todd Frohwirth	.10	.05
❑ 227	Armando Reynoso	.10	.05
❑ 228	Rich Rowland	.10	.05
❑ 229	Freddie Benavides	.10	.05
❑ 230	Wayne Kirby	.10	.05
❑ 231	Darryl Kile	.15	.07
❑ 232	Skeeter Barnes	.10	.05
❑ 233	Ramon Martinez	.10	.05
❑ 234	Tom Gordon	.10	.05
❑ 235	Dave Gallagher	.10	.05
❑ 236	Ricky Bones	.10	.05
❑ 237	Larry Andersen	.10	.05
❑ 238	Pat Meares	.10	.05
❑ 239	Zane Smith	.10	.05
❑ 240	Tim Leary	.10	.05
❑ 241	Phil Clark	.10	.05
❑ 242	Danny Cox	.10	.05
❑ 243	Mike Jackson	.10	.05
❑ 244	Mike Gallego	.10	.05
❑ 245	Lee Smith	.15	.07
❑ 246	Todd Jones	.10	.05
❑ 247	Steve Bedrosian	.10	.05
❑ 248	Troy Neel	.10	.05
❑ 249	Jose Bautista	.10	.05
❑ 250	Steve Frey	.10	.05
❑ 251	Jeff Reardon	.15	.07
❑ 252	Stan Javier	.10	.05
❑ 253	Mo Sanford	.10	.05
❑ 254	Steve Sax	.10	.05
❑ 255	Luis Aquino	.10	.05
❑ 256	Domingo Jean	.10	.05

❑	257	Scott Servais	.10	.05
❑	258	Brad Pennington	.10	.05
❑	259	Dave Hansen	.10	.05
❑	260	Rich Gossage	.15	.07
❑	261	Jeff Fassero	.10	.05
❑	262	Junior Ortiz	.10	.05
❑	263	Anthony Young	.10	.05
❑	264	Chris Bosio	.10	.05
❑	265	Ruben Amaro	.10	.05
❑	266	Mark Eichhorn	.10	.05
❑	267	Dave Clark	.10	.05
❑	268	Gary Thurman	.10	.05
❑	269	Les Lancaster	.10	.05
❑	270	Jamie Moyer	.10	.05
❑	271	Ricky Gutierrez	.10	.05
❑	272	Greg A. Harris	.10	.05
❑	273	Mike Benjamin	.10	.05
❑	274	Gene Nelson	.10	.05
❑	275	Damon Berryhill	.10	.05
❑	276	Scott Radinsky	.10	.05
❑	277	Mike Aldrete	.10	.05
❑	278	Jerry DiPoto	.10	.05
❑	279	Chris Haney	.10	.05
❑	280	Richie Lewis	.10	.05
❑	281	Jarvis Brown	.10	.05
❑	282	Juan Bell	.10	.05
❑	283	Joe Klink	.10	.05
❑	284	Graeme Lloyd	.10	.05
❑	285	Casey Candaele	.10	.05
❑	286	Bob MacDonald	.10	.05
❑	287	Mike Sharperson	.10	.05
❑	288	Gene Larkin	.10	.05
❑	289	Brian Barnes	.10	.05
❑	290	David McCarty	.10	.05
❑	291	Jeff Innis	.10	.05
❑	292	Bob Patterson	.10	.05
❑	293	Ben Rivera	.10	.05
❑	294	John Habyan	.10	.05
❑	295	Rich Rodriguez	.10	.05
❑	296	Edwin Nunez	.10	.05
❑	297	Rod Brewer	.10	.05
❑	298	Mike Timlin	.10	.05
❑	299	Jesse Orosco	.10	.05
❑	300	Gary Gaetti	.15	.07
❑	301	Todd Benzinger	.10	.05
❑	302	Jeff Nelson	.10	.05
❑	303	Rafael Belliard	.10	.05
❑	304	Matt Whiteside	.10	.05
❑	305	Vinny Castilla	.15	.07
❑	306	Matt Turner	.10	.05
❑	307	Eduardo Perez	.10	.05
❑	308	Joel Johnston	.10	.05
❑	309	Chris Gomez	.10	.05
❑	310	Pat Rapp	.10	.05
❑	311	Jim Tatum	.10	.05
❑	312	Kirk Rueter	.10	.05
❑	313	John Flaherty	.10	.05
❑	314	Tom Kramer	.10	.05
❑	315	Mark Whiten	.10	.05
❑	316	Chris Bosio	.10	.05
❑	317	Baltimore Orioles CL	.10	.05
❑	318	Bos.Red Sox CL UER Viola listed as 316; should be 331	.10	.05
❑	319	California Angels CL	.10	.05
❑	320	Chicago White Sox CL	.10	.05
❑	321	Cleveland Indians CL	.10	.05
❑	322	Detroit Tigers CL	.10	.05
❑	323	KC Royals CL	.10	.05
❑	324	Milw. Brewers CL	.10	.05
❑	325	Minnesota Twins CL	.10	.05
❑	326	New York Yankees CL	.10	.05
❑	327	Oakland Athletics CL	.10	.05
❑	328	Seattle Mariners CL	.10	.05
❑	329	Texas Rangers CL	.10	.05
❑	330	Toronto Blue Jays CL	.10	.05
❑	331	Frank Viola	.15	.07
❑	332	Ron Gant	.10	.05
❑	333	Charles Nagy	.10	.05
❑	334	Roberto Kelly	.10	.05
❑	335	Brady Anderson	.15	.07
❑	336	Alex Cole	.10	.05
❑	337	Alan Trammell	.25	.11
❑	338	Derek Bell	.10	.05
❑	339	Bernie Williams	.40	.18
❑	340	Jose Offerman	.10	.05
❑	341	Bill Wegman	.10	.05
❑	342	Ken Caminiti	.15	.07
❑	343	Pat Borders	.10	.05
❑	344	Kirt Manwaring	.10	.05
❑	345	Chili Davis	.15	.07
❑	346	Steve Buechele	.10	.05
❑	347	Robin Ventura	.15	.07
❑	348	Teddy Higuera	.10	.05
❑	349	Jerry Browne	.10	.05
❑	350	Scott Kamieniecki	.10	.05
❑	351	Kevin Tapani	.10	.05
❑	352	Marquis Grissom	.10	.05
❑	353	Jay Buhner	.15	.07
❑	354	Dave Hollins	.10	.05
❑	355	Dan Wilson	.10	.05
❑	356	Bob Walk	.10	.05
❑	357	Chris Hoiles	.10	.05
❑	358	Todd Zeile	.10	.05
❑	359	Kevin Appier	.15	.07
❑	360	Chris Sabo	.10	.05
❑	361	David Segui	.10	.05
❑	362	Jerald Clark	.10	.05
❑	363	Tony Pena	.10	.05
❑	364	Steve Finley	.15	.07
❑	365	Roger Pavlik	.10	.05
❑	366	John Smoltz	.15	.07
❑	367	Scott Fletcher	.10	.05
❑	368	Jody Reed	.10	.05
❑	369	David Wells	.15	.07
❑	370	Jose Vizcaino	.10	.05
❑	371	Pat Listach	.10	.05
❑	372	Orestes Destrade	.10	.05
❑	373	Danny Tartabull	.10	.05
❑	374	Greg W. Harris	.10	.05
❑	375	Juan Guzman	.10	.05
❑	376	Larry Walker	.25	.11
❑	377	Gary DiSarcina	.10	.05
❑	378	Bobby Bonilla	.15	.07
❑	379	Tim Raines	.15	.07
❑	380	Tommy Greene	.10	.05
❑	381	Chris Gwynn	.10	.05
❑	382	Jeff King	.10	.05
❑	383	Shane Mack	.10	.05
❑	384	Ozzie Smith	.50	.23
❑	385	Eddie Zambrano RC	.10	.05
❑	386	Mike Devereaux	.10	.05
❑	387	Erik Hanson	.10	.05
❑	388	Scott Cooper	.10	.05
❑	389	Dean Palmer	.15	.07
❑	390	John Wetteland	.15	.07
❑	391	Reggie Jefferson	.10	.05
❑	392	Mark Lemke	.10	.05
❑	393	Cecil Fielder	.15	.07
❑	394	Reggie Sanders	.10	.05
❑	395	Darryl Hamilton	.10	.05
❑	396	Daryl Boston	.10	.05
❑	397	Pat Kelly	.10	.05
❑	398	Joe Orsulak	.10	.05
❑	399	Ed Sprague	.10	.05
❑	400	Eric Anthony	.10	.05
❑	401	Scott Sanderson	.10	.05
❑	402	Jim Gott	.10	.05
❑	403	Ron Karkovice	.10	.05
❑	404	Phil Plantier	.10	.05
❑	405	David Cone	.15	.07
❑	406	Robby Thompson	.10	.05
❑	407	Dave Winfield	.40	.18
❑	408	Dwight Smith	.10	.05
❑	409	Ruben Sierra	.10	.05
❑	410	Jack Armstrong	.10	.05
❑	411	Mike Felder	.10	.05
❑	412	Wil Cordero	.10	.05
❑	413	Julio Franco	.15	.07
❑	414	Howard Johnson	.10	.05
❑	415	Mark McLemore	.10	.05
❑	416	Pete Incaviglia	.10	.05
❑	417	John Valentin	.10	.05
❑	418	Tim Wakefield	.10	.05
❑	419	Jose Mesa	.10	.05
❑	420	Bernard Gilkey	.10	.05
❑	421	Kirk Gibson	.15	.07
❑	422	Dave Justice	.15	.07
❑	423	Tom Brunansky	.10	.05
❑	424	John Smiley	.10	.05
❑	425	Kevin Maas	.10	.05
❑	426	Doug Drabek	.10	.05
❑	427	Paul Molitor	.40	.18
❑	428	Darryl Strawberry	.15	.07
❑	429	Tim Naehring	.10	.05
❑	430	Bill Swift	.10	.05
❑	431	Ellis Burks	.15	.07
❑	432	Greg Hibbard	.10	.05
❑	433	Felix Jose	.10	.05
❑	434	Bret Barberie	.10	.05
❑	435	Pedro Munoz	.10	.05
❑	436	Darrin Fletcher	.10	.05
❑	437	Bobby Witt	.10	.05
❑	438	Wes Chamberlain	.10	.05
❑	439	Mackey Sasser	.10	.05
❑	440	Mark Whiten	.10	.05
❑	441	Harold Reynolds	.10	.05
❑	442	Greg Olson	.10	.05
❑	443	Billy Hatcher	.10	.05
❑	444	Joe Oliver	.10	.05
❑	445	Sandy Alomar Jr.	.15	.07
❑	446	Tim Wallach	.10	.05
❑	447	Karl Rhodes	.10	.05
❑	448	Royce Clayton	.10	.05
❑	449	Cal Eldred	.10	.05
❑	450	Rick Wilkins	.10	.05
❑	451	Mike Stanley	.10	.05
❑	452	Charlie Hough	.15	.07
❑	453	Jack Morris	.15	.07
❑	454	Jon Ratliff RC	.10	.05
❑	455	Rene Gonzales	.10	.05
❑	456	Eddie Taubensee	.10	.05
❑	457	Roberto Hernandez	.10	.05
❑	458	Todd Hundley	.10	.05
❑	459	Mike Macfarlane	.10	.05
❑	460	Mickey Morandini	.10	.05
❑	461	Scott Erickson	.10	.05
❑	462	Lonnie Smith	.10	.05
❑	463	Dave Henderson	.10	.05
❑	464	Ryan Klesko	.15	.07
❑	465	Edgar Martinez	.25	.11
❑	466	Tom Pagnozzi	.10	.05
❑	467	Charlie Leibrandt	.10	.05
❑	468	Brian Anderson RC	.15	.07
❑	469	Harold Baines	.15	.07
❑	470	Tim Belcher	.10	.05
❑	471	Andre Dawson	.25	.11
❑	472	Eric Young	.10	.05
❑	473	Paul Sorrento	.10	.05
❑	474	Luis Gonzalez	.40	.18
❑	475	Rob Deer	.10	.05
❑	476	Mike Piazza	1.25	.55
❑	477	Kevin Reimer	.10	.05
❑	478	Jeff Gardner	.10	.05
❑	479	Melido Perez	.10	.05
❑	480	Darren Lewis	.10	.05
❑	481	Duane Ward	.10	.05
❑	482	Rey Sanchez	.10	.05
❑	483	Mark Lewis	.10	.05
❑	484	Jeff Conine	.10	.05
❑	485	Joey Cora	.10	.05
❑	486	Trot Nixon RC	.75	.35
❑	487	Kevin McReynolds	.10	.05
❑	488	Mike Lansing	.10	.05
❑	489	Mike Pagliarulo	.10	.05
❑	490	Mariano Duncan	.10	.05
❑	491	Mike Bordick	.10	.05
❑	492	Kevin Young	.10	.05
❑	493	Dave Valle	.10	.05
❑	494	Wayne Gomes RC	.10	.05
❑	495	Rafael Palmeiro	.40	.18
❑	496	Deion Sanders	.15	.07
❑	497	Rick Sutcliffe	.15	.07
❑	498	Randy Milligan	.10	.05
❑	499	Carlos Quintana	.10	.05
❑	500	Chris Turner	.10	.05
❑	501	Thomas Howard	.10	.05
❑	502	Greg Swindell	.10	.05
❑	503	Chad Kreuter	.10	.05
❑	504	Eric Davis	.15	.07
❑	505	Dickie Thon	.10	.05
❑	506	Matt Drews RC	.10	.05
❑	507	Spike Owen	.10	.05
❑	508	Rod Beck	.10	.05
❑	509	Pat Hentgen	.10	.05
❑	510	Sammy Sosa	.75	.35
❑	511	J.T. Snow	.15	.07
❑	512	Chuck Carr	.10	.05

	Card	Player	Mint	Nrmt
❑	513	Bo Jackson	.15	.07
❑	514	Dennis Martinez	.15	.07
❑	515	Phil Hiatt	.10	.05
❑	516	Jeff Kent	.25	.11
❑	517	Brooks Kieschnick RC	.10	.05
❑	518	Kirk Presley RC	.10	.05
❑	519	Kevin Seitzer	.10	.05
❑	520	Carlos Garcia	.10	.05
❑	521	Mike Blowers	.10	.05
❑	522	Luis Alicea	.10	.05
❑	523	David Hulse	.10	.05
❑	524	Greg Maddux UER (career strikeout totals listed as 113; should be 1134)	1.00	.45
❑	525	Gregg Olson	.10	.05
❑	526	Hal Morris	.10	.05
❑	527	Daron Kirkreit	.10	.05
❑	528	David Nied	.10	.05
❑	529	Jeff Russell	.10	.05
❑	530	Kevin Gross	.10	.05
❑	531	John Doherty	.10	.05
❑	532	Matt Brunson RC	.10	.05
❑	533	Dave Nilsson	.10	.05
❑	534	Randy Myers	.10	.05
❑	535	Steve Farr	.10	.05
❑	536	Billy Wagner RC	.40	.18
❑	537	Darnell Coles	.10	.05
❑	538	Frank Tanana	.10	.05
❑	539	Tim Salmon	.15	.07
❑	540	Kim Batiste	.10	.05
❑	541	George Bell	.10	.05
❑	542	Tom Henke	.10	.05
❑	543	Sam Horn	.10	.05
❑	544	Doug Jones	.10	.05
❑	545	Scott Leius	.10	.05
❑	546	Al Martin	.10	.05
❑	547	Bob Welch	.10	.05
❑	548	Scott Christman RC	.10	.05
❑	549	Norm Charlton	.10	.05
❑	550	Mark McGwire	1.50	.70
❑	551	Greg McMichael	.10	.05
❑	552	Tim Costo	.10	.05
❑	553	Rodney Bolton	.10	.05
❑	554	Pedro Martinez	.60	.25
❑	555	Marc Valdes	.10	.05
❑	556	Darrell Whitmore	.10	.05
❑	557	Tim Bogar	.10	.05
❑	558	Steve Karsay	.10	.05
❑	559	Danny Bautista	.10	.05
❑	560	Jeffrey Hammonds	.15	.07
❑	561	Aaron Sele	.15	.07
❑	562	Russ Springer	.10	.05
❑	563	Jason Bere	.10	.05
❑	564	Billy Brewer	.10	.05
❑	565	Sterling Hitchcock	.10	.05
❑	566	Bobby Munoz	.10	.05
❑	567	Craig Paquette	.10	.05
❑	568	Bret Boone	.15	.07
❑	569	Dan Peltier	.10	.05
❑	570	Jeromy Burnitz	.15	.07
❑	571	John Wasdin RC	.10	.05
❑	572	Chipper Jones	.75	.35
❑	573	Jamey Wright RC	.15	.07
❑	574	Jeff Granger	.10	.05
❑	575	Jay Powell RC	.10	.05
❑	576	Ryan Thompson	.10	.05
❑	577	Lou Frazier	.10	.05
❑	578	Paul Wagner	.10	.05
❑	579	Brad Ausmus	.10	.05
❑	580	Jack Voigt	.10	.05
❑	581	Kevin Rogers	.10	.05
❑	582	Damon Buford	.10	.05
❑	583	Paul Quantrill	.10	.05
❑	584	Marc Newfield	.10	.05
❑	585	Derrek Lee RC	.40	.18
❑	586	Shane Reynolds	.10	.05
❑	587	Cliff Floyd	.15	.07
❑	588	Jeff Schwarz	.10	.05
❑	589	Ross Powell RC	.10	.05
❑	590	Gerald Williams	.10	.05
❑	591	Mike Trombley	.10	.05
❑	592	Ken Ryan	.10	.05
❑	593	John O'Donoghue	.10	.05
❑	594	Rod Correia	.10	.05
❑	595	Darrell Sherman	.10	.05
❑	596	Steve Scarsone	.10	.05
❑	597	Sherman Obando	.10	.05
❑	598	Kurt Abbott RC	.15	.07
❑	599	Dave Telgheder	.10	.05
❑	600	Rick Trlicek	.10	.05
❑	601	Carl Everett	.15	.07
❑	602	Luis Ortiz	.10	.05
❑	603	Larry Luebbers	.10	.05
❑	604	Kevin Roberson	.10	.05
❑	605	Butch Huskey	.10	.05
❑	606	Benji Gil	.10	.05
❑	607	Todd Van Poppel	.10	.05
❑	608	Mark Hutton	.10	.05
❑	609	Chip Hale	.10	.05
❑	610	Matt Maysey	.10	.05
❑	611	Scott Ruffcorn	.10	.05
❑	612	Hilly Hathaway	.10	.05
❑	613	Allen Watson	.10	.05
❑	614	Carlos Delgado	.60	.25
❑	615	Roberto Mejia	.10	.05
❑	616	Turk Wendell	.10	.05
❑	617	Tony Tarasco	.10	.05
❑	618	Raul Mondesi	.15	.07
❑	619	Kevin Stocker	.10	.05
❑	620	Javier Lopez	.15	.07
❑	621	Keith Kessinger	.10	.05
❑	622	Bob Hamelin	.10	.05
❑	623	John Roper	.10	.05
❑	624	Lenny Dykstra WS	.10	.05
❑	625	Joe Carter WS	.10	.05
❑	626	Jim Abbott HL	.10	.05
❑	627	Lee Smith HL	.10	.05
❑	628	Ken Griffey Jr. HL	.60	.25
❑	629	Dave Winfield HL	.15	.07
❑	630	Darryl Kile HL	.10	.05
❑	631	F.Thomas AL MVP	.25	.11
❑	632	Barry Bonds NL MVP	.50	.23
❑	633	Jack McDowell AL CY	.10	.05
❑	634	Greg Maddux NL CY	.50	.23
❑	635	Tim Salmon AL ROY	.10	.05
❑	636	Mike Piazza NL ROY	.60	.25
❑	637	Brian Turang RC	.10	.05
❑	638	Rondell White	.15	.07
❑	639	Nigel Wilson	.10	.05
❑	640	Torii Hunter RC	.60	.25
❑	641	Salomon Torres	.10	.05
❑	642	Kevin Higgins	.10	.05
❑	643	Eric Wedge	.10	.05
❑	644	Roger Salkeld	.10	.05
❑	645	Manny Ramirez	.60	.25
❑	646	Jeff McNeely	.10	.05
❑	647	Atlanta Braves CL	.10	.05
❑	648	Chicago Cubs CL	.10	.05
❑	649	Cincinnati Reds CL	.10	.05
❑	650	Colorado Rockies CL	.10	.05
❑	651	Florida Marlins CL	.10	.05
❑	652	Houston Astros CL	.10	.05
❑	653	L.A. Dodgers CL	.10	.05
❑	654	Montreal Expos CL	.10	.05
❑	655	New York Mets CL	.10	.05
❑	656	Phi. Phillies CL	.10	.05
❑	657	Pittsburgh Pirates CL	.10	.05
❑	658	St. Louis Cardinals CL	.10	.05
❑	659	San Diego Padres CL	.10	.05
❑	660	S.F. Giants CL	.10	.05

1994 Score Rookie/Traded

	Card	Player	MINT	NRMT
		COMPLETE SET (165)	15.00	6.75
❑	RT1	Will Clark	.60	.25
❑	RT2	Lee Smith	.25	.11
❑	RT3	Bo Jackson	.25	.11
❑	RT4	Ellis Burks	.25	.11
❑	RT5	Eddie Murray	.60	.25
❑	RT6	Delino DeShields	.15	.07
❑	RT7	Erik Hanson	.15	.07
❑	RT8	Rafael Palmeiro	.60	.25
❑	RT9	Luis Polonia	.15	.07
❑	RT10	Omar Vizquel	.25	.11
❑	RT11	Kurt Abbott	.25	.11
❑	RT12	Vince Coleman	.15	.07
❑	RT13	Rickey Henderson	1.25	.55
❑	RT14	Terry Mulholland	.15	.07
❑	RT15	Greg Hibbard	.15	.07
❑	RT16	Walt Weiss	.15	.07
❑	RT17	Chris Sabo	.15	.07
❑	RT18	Dave Henderson	.15	.07
❑	RT19	Rick Sutcliffe	.25	.11
❑	RT20	Harold Reynolds	.15	.07
❑	RT21	Jack Morris	.25	.11
❑	RT22	Dan Wilson	.15	.07
❑	RT23	Dave Magadan	.15	.07
❑	RT24	Dennis Martinez	.25	.11
❑	RT25	Wes Chamberlain	.15	.07
❑	RT26	Otis Nixon	.15	.07
❑	RT27	Eric Anthony	.15	.07
❑	RT28	Randy Milligan	.15	.07
❑	RT29	Julio Franco	.25	.11
❑	RT30	Kevin McReynolds	.15	.07
❑	RT31	Anthony Young	.15	.07
❑	RT32	Brian Harper	.15	.07
❑	RT33	Gene Harris	.15	.07
❑	RT34	Eddie Taubensee	.15	.07
❑	RT35	David Segui	.15	.07
❑	RT36	Stan Javier	.15	.07
❑	RT37	Felix Fermin	.15	.07
❑	RT38	Darrin Jackson	.15	.07
❑	RT39	Tony Fernandez	.15	.07
❑	RT40	Jose Vizcaino	.15	.07
❑	RT41	Willie Banks	.15	.07
❑	RT42	Brian Hunter	.15	.07
❑	RT43	Reggie Jefferson	.15	.07
❑	RT44	Junior Felix	.15	.07
❑	RT45	Jack Armstrong	.15	.07
❑	RT46	Bip Roberts	.15	.07
❑	RT47	Jerry Browne	.15	.07
❑	RT48	Marvin Freeman	.15	.07
❑	RT49	Jody Reed	.15	.07
❑	RT50	Alex Cole	.15	.07
❑	RT51	Sid Fernandez	.15	.07
❑	RT52	Pete Smith	.15	.07
❑	RT53	Xavier Hernandez	.15	.07
❑	RT54	Scott Sanderson	.15	.07
❑	RT55	Turner Ward	.15	.07
❑	RT56	Rex Hudler	.15	.07
❑	RT57	Deion Sanders	.25	.11
❑	RT58	Sid Bream	.15	.07
❑	RT59	Tony Pena	.15	.07
❑	RT60	Bret Boone	.25	.11
❑	RT61	Bobby Ayala	.15	.07
❑	RT62	Pedro Martinez	1.00	.45
❑	RT63	Howard Johnson	.15	.07
❑	RT64	Mark Portugal	.15	.07
❑	RT65	Roberto Kelly	.15	.07
❑	RT66	Spike Owen	.15	.07
❑	RT67	Jeff Treadway	.15	.07
❑	RT68	Mike Harkey	.15	.07
❑	RT69	Doug Jones	.15	.07
❑	RT70	Steve Farr	.15	.07
❑	RT71	Billy Taylor RC	.25	.11
❑	RT72	Manny Ramirez	1.00	.45
❑	RT73	Bob Hamelin	.15	.07
❑	RT74	Steve Karsay	.15	.07
❑	RT75	Ryan Klesko	.25	.11
❑	RT76	Cliff Floyd	.25	.11
❑	RT77	Jeffrey Hammonds	.25	.11
❑	RT78	Javier Lopez	.25	.11
❑	RT79	Roger Salkeld	.15	.07
❑	RT80	Hector Carrasco	.15	.07
❑	RT81	Gerald Williams	.15	.07
❑	RT82	Raul Mondesi	.25	.11
❑	RT83	Sterling Hitchcock	.15	.07

Card	Player	Mint	Nrmt
❑ RT84	Danny Bautista	.15	.07
❑ RT85	Chris Turner	.15	.07
❑ RT86	Shane Reynolds	.15	.07
❑ RT87	Rondell White	.25	.11
❑ RT88	Salomon Torres	.15	.07
❑ RT89	Turk Wendell	.15	.07
❑ RT90	Tony Tarasco	.15	.07
❑ RT91	Shawn Green	.75	.35
❑ RT92	Greg Colbrunn	.15	.07
❑ RT93	Eddie Zambrano	.15	.07
❑ RT94	Rich Becker	.15	.07
❑ RT95	Chris Gomez	.15	.07
❑ RT96	John Patterson	.15	.07
❑ RT97	Derek Parks	.15	.07
❑ RT98	Rich Rowland	.15	.07
❑ RT99	James Mouton	.15	.07
❑ RT100	Tim Hyers RC	.15	.07
❑ RT101	Jose Valentin	.15	.07
❑ RT102	Carlos Delgado	1.00	.45
❑ RT103	Robert Eenhoorn	.15	.07
❑ RT104	John Hudek RC	.15	.07
❑ RT105	Domingo Cedeno	.15	.07
❑ RT106	Denny Hocking	.15	.07
❑ RT107	Greg Pirkl	.15	.07
❑ RT108	Mark Smith	.15	.07
❑ RT109	Paul Shuey	.15	.07
❑ RT110	Jorge Fabregas	.15	.07
❑ RT111	Rikkert Faneyte RC	.15	.07
❑ RT112	Rob Butler	.15	.07
❑ RT113	Darren Oliver RC	.25	.11
❑ RT114	Troy O'Leary	.15	.07
❑ RT115	Scott Brow	.15	.07
❑ RT116	Tony Eusebio	.15	.07
❑ RT117	Carlos Reyes	.15	.07
❑ RT118	J.R. Phillips	.15	.07
❑ RT119	Alex Diaz	.15	.07
❑ RT120	Charles Johnson	.25	.11
❑ RT121	Nate Minchey	.15	.07
❑ RT122	Scott Sanders	.15	.07
❑ RT123	Daryl Boston	.15	.07
❑ RT124	Joey Hamilton	.15	.07
❑ RT125	Brian Anderson	.25	.11
❑ RT126	Dan Miceli	.15	.07
❑ RT127	Tom Brunansky	.15	.07
❑ RT128	Dave Staton	.15	.07
❑ RT129	Mike Oquist	.15	.07
❑ RT130	John Mabry RC	.15	.07
❑ RT131	Norberto Martin	.15	.07
❑ RT132	Hector Fajardo	.15	.07
❑ RT133	Mark Hutton	.15	.07
❑ RT134	Fernando Vina	.15	.07
❑ RT135	Lee Tinsley	.15	.07
❑ RT136	Chan Ho Park RC	1.25	.55
❑ RT137	Paul Spoljaric	.15	.07
❑ RT138	Matias Carrillo	.15	.07
❑ RT139	Mark Kiefer	.15	.07
❑ RT140	Stan Royer	.15	.07
❑ RT141	Bryan Eversgerd	.15	.07
❑ RT142	Brian L. Hunter	.15	.07
❑ RT143	Joe Hall	.15	.07
❑ RT144	Johnny Ruffin	.15	.07
❑ RT145	Alex Gonzalez	.15	.07
❑ RT146	Keith Lockhart RC	.25	.11
❑ RT147	Tom Marsh	.15	.07
❑ RT148	Tony Longmire	.15	.07
❑ RT149	Keith Mitchell	.15	.07
❑ RT150	Melvin Nieves	.15	.07
❑ RT151	Kelly Stinnett RC	.25	.11
❑ RT152	Miguel Jimenez	.15	.07
❑ RT153	Jeff Juden	.15	.07
❑ RT154	Matt Walbeck	.15	.07
❑ RT155	Marc Newfield	.15	.07
❑ RT156	Matt Mieske	.15	.07
❑ RT157	Marcus Moore	.15	.07
❑ RT158	Jose Lima RC SP	5.00	2.20
❑ RT159	Mike Kelly	.15	.07
❑ RT160	Jim Edmonds	.60	.25
❑ RT161	Steve Trachsel	.15	.07
❑ RT162	Greg Blosser	.15	.07
❑ RT163	Marc Acre RC	.15	.07
❑ RT164	AL Checklist	.15	.07
❑ RT165	NL Checklist	.15	.07
❑ HC1	Alex Rodriguez Call-Up Redemption	250.00	110.00
❑ NNO	Sept. Call-Up Trade EXP	2.00	.90

1995 Score

	MINT	NRMT
COMPLETE SET (605)	24.00	11.00
COMPLETE SERIES 1 (330)	12.00	5.50
COMPLETE SERIES 2 (275)	12.00	5.50

Card	Player	Mint	Nrmt
❑ 1	Frank Thomas	.50	.23
❑ 2	Roberto Alomar	.40	.18
❑ 3	Cal Ripken	1.50	.70
❑ 4	Jose Canseco	.40	.18
❑ 5	Matt Williams	.25	.11
❑ 6	Esteban Beltre	.10	.05
❑ 7	Domingo Cedeno	.10	.05
❑ 8	John Valentin	.10	.05
❑ 9	Glenallen Hill	.10	.05
❑ 10	Rafael Belliard	.10	.05
❑ 11	Randy Myers	.10	.05
❑ 12	Mo Vaughn	.15	.07
❑ 13	Hector Carrasco	.10	.05
❑ 14	Chili Davis	.15	.07
❑ 15	Dante Bichette	.15	.07
❑ 16	Darrin Jackson	.10	.05
❑ 17	Mike Piazza	1.00	.45
❑ 18	Junior Felix	.10	.05
❑ 19	Moises Alou	.15	.07
❑ 20	Mark Gubicza	.10	.05
❑ 21	Bret Saberhagen	.15	.07
❑ 22	Lenny Dykstra	.15	.07
❑ 23	Steve Howe	.10	.05
❑ 24	Mark Dewey	.10	.05
❑ 25	Brian Harper	.10	.05
❑ 26	Ozzie Smith	.50	.23
❑ 27	Scott Erickson	.10	.05
❑ 28	Tony Gwynn	.75	.35
❑ 29	Bob Welch	.10	.05
❑ 30	Barry Bonds	1.00	.45
❑ 31	Leo Gomez	.10	.05
❑ 32	Greg Maddux	1.00	.45
❑ 33	Mike Greenwell	.10	.05
❑ 34	Sammy Sosa	.75	.35
❑ 35	Darnell Coles	.10	.05
❑ 36	Tommy Greene	.10	.05
❑ 37	Will Clark	.40	.18
❑ 38	Steve Ontiveros	.10	.05
❑ 39	Stan Javier	.10	.05
❑ 40	Bip Roberts	.10	.05
❑ 41	Paul O'Neill	.40	.18
❑ 42	Bill Haselman	.10	.05
❑ 43	Shane Mack	.10	.05
❑ 44	Orlando Merced	.10	.05
❑ 45	Kevin Seitzer	.10	.05
❑ 46	Trevor Hoffman	.15	.07
❑ 47	Greg Gagne	.10	.05
❑ 48	Jeff Kent	.25	.11
❑ 49	Tony Phillips	.10	.05
❑ 50	Ken Hill	.10	.05
❑ 51	Carlos Baerga	.10	.05
❑ 52	Henry Rodriguez	.10	.05
❑ 53	Scott Sanderson	.10	.05
❑ 54	Jeff Conine	.10	.05
❑ 55	Chris Turner	.10	.05
❑ 56	Ken Caminiti	.15	.07
❑ 57	Harold Baines	.15	.07
❑ 58	Charlie Hayes	.10	.05
❑ 59	Roberto Kelly	.10	.05
❑ 60	John Olerud	.15	.07
❑ 61	Tim Davis	.10	.05
❑ 62	Rich Rowland	.10	.05
❑ 63	Rey Sanchez	.10	.05
❑ 64	Junior Ortiz	.10	.05
❑ 65	Ricky Gutierrez	.10	.05
❑ 66	Rex Hudler	.10	.05
❑ 67	Johnny Ruffin	.10	.05
❑ 68	Jay Buhner	.15	.07
❑ 69	Tom Pagnozzi	.10	.05
❑ 70	Julio Franco	.15	.07
❑ 71	Eric Young	.10	.05
❑ 72	Mike Bordick	.10	.05
❑ 73	Don Slaught	.10	.05
❑ 74	Goose Gossage	.15	.07
❑ 75	Lonnie Smith	.10	.05
❑ 76	Jimmy Key	.15	.07
❑ 77	Dave Hollins	.10	.05
❑ 78	Mickey Tettleton	.10	.05
❑ 79	Luis Gonzalez	.40	.18
❑ 80	Dave Winfield	.40	.18
❑ 81	Ryan Thompson	.10	.05
❑ 82	Felix Jose	.10	.05
❑ 83	Rusty Meacham	.10	.05
❑ 84	Darryl Hamilton	.10	.05
❑ 85	John Wetteland	.15	.07
❑ 86	Tom Brunansky	.10	.05
❑ 87	Mark Lemke	.10	.05
❑ 88	Spike Owen	.10	.05
❑ 89	Shawon Dunston	.10	.05
❑ 90	Wilson Alvarez	.10	.05
❑ 91	Lee Smith	.15	.07
❑ 92	Scott Kamieniecki	.10	.05
❑ 93	Jacob Brumfield	.10	.05
❑ 94	Kirk Gibson	.15	.07
❑ 95	Joe Girardi	.10	.05
❑ 96	Mike Macfarlane	.10	.05
❑ 97	Greg Colbrunn	.10	.05
❑ 98	Ricky Bones	.10	.05
❑ 99	Delino DeShields	.10	.05
❑ 100	Pat Meares	.10	.05
❑ 101	Jeff Fassero	.10	.05
❑ 102	Jim Leyritz	.10	.05
❑ 103	Gary Redus	.10	.05
❑ 104	Terry Steinbach	.10	.05
❑ 105	Kevin McReynolds	.10	.05
❑ 106	Felix Fermin	.10	.05
❑ 107	Danny Jackson	.10	.05
❑ 108	Chris James	.10	.05
❑ 109	Jeff King	.10	.05
❑ 110	Pat Hentgen	.10	.05
❑ 111	Gerald Perry	.10	.05
❑ 112	Tim Raines	.15	.07
❑ 113	Eddie Williams	.10	.05
❑ 114	Jamie Moyer	.10	.05
❑ 115	Bud Black	.10	.05
❑ 116	Chris Gomez	.10	.05
❑ 117	Luis Lopez	.10	.05
❑ 118	Roger Clemens	1.00	.45
❑ 119	Javier Lopez	.15	.07
❑ 120	Dave Nilsson	.10	.05
❑ 121	Karl Rhodes	.10	.05
❑ 122	Rick Aguilera	.10	.05
❑ 123	Tony Fernandez	.10	.05
❑ 124	Bernie Williams	.40	.18
❑ 125	James Mouton	.10	.05
❑ 126	Mark Langston	.10	.05
❑ 127	Mike Lansing	.10	.05
❑ 128	Tino Martinez	.15	.07
❑ 129	Joe Orsulak	.10	.05
❑ 130	David Hulse	.10	.05
❑ 131	Pete Incaviglia	.10	.05
❑ 132	Mark Clark	.10	.05
❑ 133	Tony Eusebio	.10	.05
❑ 134	Chuck Finley	.15	.07
❑ 135	Lou Frazier	.10	.05
❑ 136	Craig Grebeck	.10	.05
❑ 137	Kelly Stinnett	.10	.05
❑ 138	Paul Shuey	.10	.05
❑ 139	David Nied	.10	.05
❑ 140	Billy Brewer	.10	.05
❑ 141	Dave Weathers	.10	.05
❑ 142	Scott Leius	.10	.05
❑ 143	Brian Jordan	.15	.07
❑ 144	Melido Perez	.10	.05
❑ 145	Tony Tarasco	.10	.05
❑ 146	Dan Wilson	.10	.05
❑ 147	Rondell White	.15	.07

❑ 148	Mike Henneman	.10	.05
❑ 149	Brian Johnson	.10	.05
❑ 150	Tom Henke	.10	.05
❑ 151	John Patterson	.10	.05
❑ 152	Bobby Witt	.10	.05
❑ 153	Eddie Taubensee	.10	.05
❑ 154	Pat Borders	.10	.05
❑ 155	Ramon Martinez	.10	.05
❑ 156	Mike Kingery	.10	.05
❑ 157	Zane Smith	.10	.05
❑ 158	Benito Santiago	.10	.05
❑ 159	Matias Carrillo	.10	.05
❑ 160	Scott Brosius	.15	.07
❑ 161	Dave Clark	.10	.05
❑ 162	Mark McLemore	.10	.05
❑ 163	Curt Schilling	.40	.18
❑ 164	J.T. Snow	.15	.07
❑ 165	Rod Beck	.10	.05
❑ 166	Scott Fletcher	.10	.05
❑ 167	Bob Tewksbury	.10	.05
❑ 168	Mike LaValliere	.10	.05
❑ 169	Dave Hansen	.10	.05
❑ 170	Pedro Martinez	.50	.23
❑ 171	Kirk Rueter	.10	.05
❑ 172	Jose Lind	.10	.05
❑ 173	Luis Alicea	.10	.05
❑ 174	Mike Moore	.10	.05
❑ 175	Andy Ashby	.10	.05
❑ 176	Jody Reed	.10	.05
❑ 177	Darryl Kile	.15	.07
❑ 178	Carl Willis	.10	.05
❑ 179	Jeromy Burnitz	.15	.07
❑ 180	Mike Gallego	.10	.05
❑ 181	Bill VanLandingham	.10	.05
❑ 182	Sid Fernandez	.10	.05
❑ 183	Kim Batiste	.10	.05
❑ 184	Greg Myers	.10	.05
❑ 185	Steve Avery	.10	.05
❑ 186	Steve Farr	.10	.05
❑ 187	Robb Nen	.10	.05
❑ 188	Dan Pasqua	.10	.05
❑ 189	Bruce Ruffin	.10	.05
❑ 190	Jose Valentin	.10	.05
❑ 191	Willie Banks	.10	.05
❑ 192	Mike Aldrete	.10	.05
❑ 193	Randy Milligan	.10	.05
❑ 194	Steve Karsay	.10	.05
❑ 195	Mike Stanley	.10	.05
❑ 196	Jose Mesa	.10	.05
❑ 197	Tom Browning	.10	.05
❑ 198	John Vander Wal	.10	.05
❑ 199	Kevin Brown	.15	.07
❑ 200	Mike Oquist	.10	.05
❑ 201	Greg Swindell	.10	.05
❑ 202	Eddie Zambrano	.10	.05
❑ 203	Joe Boever	.10	.05
❑ 204	Gary Varsho	.10	.05
❑ 205	Chris Gwynn	.10	.05
❑ 206	David Howard	.10	.05
❑ 207	Jerome Walton	.10	.05
❑ 208	Danny Darwin	.10	.05
❑ 209	Darryl Strawberry	.15	.07
❑ 210	Todd Van Poppel	.10	.05
❑ 211	Scott Livingstone	.10	.05
❑ 212	Dave Fleming	.10	.05
❑ 213	Todd Worrell	.10	.05
❑ 214	Carlos Delgado	.40	.18
❑ 215	Bill Pecota	.10	.05
❑ 216	Jim Lindeman	.10	.05
❑ 217	Rick White	.10	.05
❑ 218	Jose Oquendo	.10	.05
❑ 219	Tony Castillo	.10	.05
❑ 220	Fernando Vina	.10	.05
❑ 221	Jeff Bagwell	.50	.23
❑ 222	Randy Johnson	.50	.23
❑ 223	Albert Belle	.15	.07
❑ 224	Chuck Carr	.10	.05
❑ 225	Mark Leiter	.10	.05
❑ 226	Hal Morris	.10	.05
❑ 227	Robin Ventura	.15	.07
❑ 228	Mike Munoz	.10	.05
❑ 229	Jim Thome	.40	.18
❑ 230	Mario Diaz	.10	.05
❑ 231	John Doherty	.10	.05
❑ 232	Bobby Jones	.10	.05
❑ 233	Raul Mondesi	.15	.07
❑ 234	Ricky Jordan	.10	.05
❑ 235	John Jaha	.10	.05
❑ 236	Carlos Garcia	.10	.05
❑ 237	Kirby Puckett	1.00	.45
❑ 238	Orel Hershiser	.15	.07
❑ 239	Don Mattingly	1.00	.45
❑ 240	Sid Bream	.10	.05
❑ 241	Brent Gates	.10	.05
❑ 242	Tony Longmire	.10	.05
❑ 243	Robby Thompson	.10	.05
❑ 244	Rick Sutcliffe	.15	.07
❑ 245	Dean Palmer	.15	.07
❑ 246	Marquis Grissom	.10	.05
❑ 247	Paul Molitor	.40	.18
❑ 248	Mark Carreon	.10	.05
❑ 249	Jack Voigt	.10	.05
❑ 250	Greg McMichael UER (photo on front is Mike Stanton)	.10	.05
❑ 251	Damon Berryhill	.10	.05
❑ 252	Brian Dorsett	.10	.05
❑ 253	Jim Edmonds	.25	.11
❑ 254	Barry Larkin	.40	.18
❑ 255	Jack McDowell	.10	.05
❑ 256	Wally Joyner	.15	.07
❑ 257	Eddie Murray	.40	.18
❑ 258	Lenny Webster	.10	.05
❑ 259	Milt Cuyler	.10	.05
❑ 260	Todd Benzinger	.10	.05
❑ 261	Vince Coleman	.10	.05
❑ 262	Todd Stottlemyre	.10	.05
❑ 263	Turner Ward	.10	.05
❑ 264	Ray Lankford	.10	.05
❑ 265	Matt Walbeck	.10	.05
❑ 266	Deion Sanders	.15	.07
❑ 267	Gerald Williams	.10	.05
❑ 268	Jim Gott	.10	.05
❑ 269	Jeff Frye	.10	.05
❑ 270	Jose Rijo	.10	.05
❑ 271	Dave Justice	.15	.07
❑ 272	Ismael Valdes	.10	.05
❑ 273	Ben McDonald	.10	.05
❑ 274	Darren Lewis	.10	.05
❑ 275	Graeme Lloyd	.10	.05
❑ 276	Luis Ortiz	.10	.05
❑ 277	Julian Tavarez	.10	.05
❑ 278	Mark Dalesandro	.10	.05
❑ 279	Brett Merriman	.10	.05
❑ 280	Ricky Bottalico	.10	.05
❑ 281	Robert Eenhoorn	.10	.05
❑ 282	Rikkert Faneyte	.10	.05
❑ 283	Mike Kelly	.10	.05
❑ 284	Mark Smith	.10	.05
❑ 285	Turk Wendell	.10	.05
❑ 286	Greg Blosser	.10	.05
❑ 287	Garey Ingram	.10	.05
❑ 288	Jorge Fabregas	.10	.05
❑ 289	Blaise Ilsley	.10	.05
❑ 290	Joe Hall	.10	.05
❑ 291	Orlando Miller	.10	.05
❑ 292	Jose Lima	.10	.05
❑ 293	Greg O'Halloran RC	.10	.05
❑ 294	Mark Kiefer	.10	.05
❑ 295	Jose Oliva	.10	.05
❑ 296	Rich Becker	.10	.05
❑ 297	Brian L. Hunter	.10	.05
❑ 298	Dave Silvestri	.10	.05
❑ 299	Armando Benitez	.15	.07
❑ 300	Darren Dreifort	.10	.05
❑ 301	John Mabry	.10	.05
❑ 302	Greg Pirkl	.10	.05
❑ 303	J.R. Phillips	.10	.05
❑ 304	Shawn Green	.40	.18
❑ 305	Roberto Petagine	.10	.05
❑ 306	Keith Lockhart	.10	.05
❑ 307	Jonathan Hurst	.10	.05
❑ 308	Paul Spoljaric	.10	.05
❑ 309	Mike Lieberthal	.15	.07
❑ 310	Garret Anderson	.15	.07
❑ 311	John Johnstone	.10	.05
❑ 312	Alex Rodriguez	1.25	.55
❑ 313	Kent Mercker HL	.10	.05
❑ 314	John Valentin HL	.10	.05
❑ 315	Kenny Rogers HL	.10	.05
❑ 316	Fred McGriff HL	.15	.07
❑ 317	Team Checklists	.10	.05
❑ 318	Team Checklists	.10	.05
❑ 319	Team Checklists	.10	.05
❑ 320	Team Checklists	.10	.05
❑ 321	Team Checklists	.10	.05
❑ 322	Team Checklists	.10	.05
❑ 323	Team Checklists	.10	.05
❑ 324	Team Checklists	.10	.05
❑ 325	Team Checklists	.10	.05
❑ 326	Team Checklists	.10	.05
❑ 327	Team Checklists	.10	.05
❑ 328	Team Checklists	.10	.05
❑ 329	Team Checklists	.10	.05
❑ 330	Team Checklists	.10	.05
❑ 331	Pedro Munoz	.10	.05
❑ 332	Ryan Klesko	.15	.07
❑ 333	Andre Dawson	.25	.11
❑ 334	Derrick May	.10	.05
❑ 335	Aaron Sele	.15	.07
❑ 336	Kevin Mitchell	.10	.05
❑ 337	Steve Trachsel	.10	.05
❑ 338	Andres Galarraga	.25	.11
❑ 339	Terry Pendleton	.15	.07
❑ 340	Gary Sheffield	.15	.07
❑ 341	Travis Fryman	.15	.07
❑ 342	Bo Jackson	.15	.07
❑ 343	Gary Gaetti	.15	.07
❑ 344	Brett Butler	.15	.07
❑ 345	B.J. Surhoff	.15	.07
❑ 346	Larry Walker	.25	.11
❑ 347	Kevin Tapani	.10	.05
❑ 348	Rick Wilkins	.10	.05
❑ 349	Wade Boggs	.40	.18
❑ 350	Mariano Duncan	.10	.05
❑ 351	Ruben Sierra	.10	.05
❑ 352	Andy Van Slyke	.15	.07
❑ 353	Reggie Jefferson	.10	.05
❑ 354	Gregg Jefferies	.10	.05
❑ 355	Tim Naehring	.10	.05
❑ 356	John Roper	.10	.05
❑ 357	Joe Carter	.15	.07
❑ 358	Kurt Abbott	.10	.05
❑ 359	Lenny Harris	.10	.05
❑ 360	Lance Johnson	.10	.05
❑ 361	Brian Anderson	.10	.05
❑ 362	Jim Eisenreich	.10	.05
❑ 363	Jerry Browne	.10	.05
❑ 364	Mark Grace	.40	.18
❑ 365	Devon White	.15	.07
❑ 366	Reggie Sanders	.10	.05
❑ 367	Ivan Rodriguez	.40	.18
❑ 368	Kirt Manwaring	.10	.05
❑ 369	Pat Kelly	.10	.05
❑ 370	Ellis Burks	.15	.07
❑ 371	Charles Nagy	.10	.05
❑ 372	Kevin Bass	.10	.05
❑ 373	Lou Whitaker	.15	.07
❑ 374	Rene Arocha	.10	.05
❑ 375	Derek Parks	.10	.05
❑ 376	Mark Whiten	.10	.05
❑ 377	Mark McGwire	1.50	.70
❑ 378	Doug Drabek	.10	.05
❑ 379	Greg Vaughn	.15	.07
❑ 380	Al Martin	.10	.05
❑ 381	Ron Darling	.10	.05
❑ 382	Tim Wallach	.10	.05
❑ 383	Alan Trammell	.25	.11
❑ 384	Randy Velarde	.10	.05
❑ 385	Chris Sabo	.10	.05
❑ 386	Wil Cordero	.10	.05
❑ 387	Darrin Fletcher	.10	.05
❑ 388	David Segui	.10	.05
❑ 389	Steve Buechele	.10	.05
❑ 390	Dave Gallagher	.10	.05
❑ 391	Thomas Howard	.10	.05
❑ 392	Chad Curtis	.10	.05
❑ 393	Cal Eldred	.10	.05
❑ 394	Jason Bere	.10	.05
❑ 395	Bret Barberie	.10	.05
❑ 396	Paul Sorrento	.10	.05
❑ 397	Steve Finley	.15	.07
❑ 398	Cecil Fielder	.15	.07
❑ 399	Eric Karros	.15	.07
❑ 400	Jeff Montgomery	.10	.05
❑ 401	Cliff Floyd	.15	.07
❑ 402	Matt Mieske	.10	.05
❑ 403	Brian Hunter	.10	.05
❑ 404	Alex Cole	.10	.05

❑ 405 Kevin Stocker .10 .05
❑ 406 Eric Davis .15 .07
❑ 407 Marvin Freeman .10 .05
❑ 408 Dennis Eckersley .15 .07
❑ 409 Todd Zeile .10 .05
❑ 410 Keith Mitchell .10 .05
❑ 411 Andy Benes .10 .05
❑ 412 Juan Bell .10 .05
❑ 413 Royce Clayton .10 .05
❑ 414 Ed Sprague .10 .05
❑ 415 Mike Mussina .40 .18
❑ 416 Todd Hundley .10 .05
❑ 417 Pat Listach .10 .05
❑ 418 Joe Oliver .10 .05
❑ 419 Rafael Palmeiro .40 .18
❑ 420 Tim Salmon .15 .07
❑ 421 Brady Anderson .15 .07
❑ 422 Kenny Lofton .15 .07
❑ 423 Craig Biggio .25 .11
❑ 424 Bobby Bonilla .15 .07
❑ 425 Kenny Rogers .10 .05
❑ 426 Derek Bell .10 .05
❑ 427 Scott Cooper .10 .05
❑ 428 Ozzie Guillen .10 .05
❑ 429 Omar Vizquel .15 .07
❑ 430 Phil Plantier .10 .05
❑ 431 Chuck Knoblauch .15 .07
❑ 432 Darren Daulton .15 .07
❑ 433 Bob Hamelin .10 .05
❑ 434 Tom Glavine .40 .18
❑ 435 Walt Weiss .10 .05
❑ 436 Jose Vizcaino .10 .05
❑ 437 Ken Griffey Jr. 1.25 .55
❑ 438 Jay Bell .15 .07
❑ 439 Juan Gonzalez .40 .18
❑ 440 Jeff Blauser .10 .05
❑ 441 Rickey Henderson .75 .35
❑ 442 Bobby Ayala .10 .05
❑ 443 David Cone .15 .07
❑ 444 Pedro Martinez .50 .23
❑ 445 Manny Ramirez .50 .23
❑ 446 Mark Portugal .10 .05
❑ 447 Damion Easley .10 .05
❑ 448 Gary DiSarcina .10 .05
❑ 449 Roberto Hernandez .10 .05
❑ 450 Jeffrey Hammonds .10 .05
❑ 451 Jeff Treadway .10 .05
❑ 452 Jim Abbott .15 .07
❑ 453 Carlos Rodriguez .10 .05
❑ 454 Joey Cora .10 .05
❑ 455 Bret Boone .15 .07
❑ 456 Danny Tartabull .10 .05
❑ 457 John Franco .15 .07
❑ 458 Roger Salkeld .10 .05
❑ 459 Fred McGriff .25 .11
❑ 460 Pedro Astacio .10 .05
❑ 461 Jon Lieber .10 .05
❑ 462 Luis Polonia .10 .05
❑ 463 Geronimo Pena .10 .05
❑ 464 Tom Gordon .10 .05
❑ 465 Brad Ausmus .10 .05
❑ 466 Willie McGee .15 .07
❑ 467 Doug Jones .10 .05
❑ 468 John Smoltz .15 .07
❑ 469 Troy Neel .10 .05
❑ 470 Luis Sojo .10 .05
❑ 471 John Smiley .10 .05
❑ 472 Rafael Bournigal .10 .05
❑ 473 Bill Taylor .10 .05
❑ 474 Juan Guzman .10 .05
❑ 475 Dave Magadan .10 .05
❑ 476 Mike Devereaux .10 .05
❑ 477 Andujar Cedeno .10 .05
❑ 478 Edgar Martinez .25 .11
❑ 479 Milt Thompson .10 .05
❑ 480 Allen Watson .10 .05
❑ 481 Ron Karkovice .10 .05
❑ 482 Joey Hamilton .10 .05
❑ 483 Vinny Castilla .15 .07
❑ 484 Tim Belcher .10 .05
❑ 485 Bernard Gilkey .10 .05
❑ 486 Scott Servais .10 .05
❑ 487 Cory Snyder .10 .05
❑ 488 Mel Rojas .10 .05
❑ 489 Carlos Reyes .10 .05
❑ 490 Chip Hale .10 .05
❑ 491 Bill Swift .10 .05
❑ 492 Pat Rapp .10 .05
❑ 493 Brian McRae .10 .05
❑ 494 Mickey Morandini .10 .05
❑ 495 Tony Pena .10 .05
❑ 496 Danny Bautista .10 .05
❑ 497 Armando Reynoso .10 .05
❑ 498 Ken Ryan .10 .05
❑ 499 Billy Ripken .10 .05
❑ 500 Pat Mahomes .10 .05
❑ 501 Mark Acre .10 .05
❑ 502 Geronimo Berroa .10 .05
❑ 503 Norberto Martin .10 .05
❑ 504 Chad Kreuter .10 .05
❑ 505 Howard Johnson .10 .05
❑ 506 Eric Anthony .10 .05
❑ 507 Mark Wohlers .10 .05
❑ 508 Scott Sanders .10 .05
❑ 509 Pete Harnisch .10 .05
❑ 510 Wes Chamberlain .10 .05
❑ 511 Tom Candiotti .10 .05
❑ 512 Albie Lopez .10 .05
❑ 513 Denny Neagle .15 .07
❑ 514 Sean Berry .10 .05
❑ 515 Billy Hatcher .10 .05
❑ 516 Todd Jones .10 .05
❑ 517 Wayne Kirby .10 .05
❑ 518 Butch Henry .10 .05
❑ 519 Sandy Alomar Jr. .15 .07
❑ 520 Kevin Appier .15 .07
❑ 521 Roberto Mejia .10 .05
❑ 522 Steve Cooke .10 .05
❑ 523 Terry Shumpert .10 .05
❑ 524 Mike Jackson .10 .05
❑ 525 Kent Mercker .10 .05
❑ 526 David Wells .15 .07
❑ 527 Juan Samuel .10 .05
❑ 528 Salomon Torres .10 .05
❑ 529 Duane Ward .10 .05
❑ 530 Rob Dibble .10 .05
❑ 531 Mike Blowers .10 .05
❑ 532 Mark Eichhorn .10 .05
❑ 533 Alex Diaz .10 .05
❑ 534 Dan Miceli .10 .05
❑ 535 Jeff Branson .10 .05
❑ 536 Dave Stevens .10 .05
❑ 537 Charlie O'Brien .10 .05
❑ 538 Shane Reynolds .10 .05
❑ 539 Rich Amaral .10 .05
❑ 540 Rusty Greer .15 .07
❑ 541 Alex Arias .10 .05
❑ 542 Eric Plunk .10 .05
❑ 543 John Hudek .10 .05
❑ 544 Kirk McCaskill .10 .05
❑ 545 Jeff Reboulet .10 .05
❑ 546 Sterling Hitchcock .10 .05
❑ 547 Warren Newson .10 .05
❑ 548 Bryan Harvey .10 .05
❑ 549 Mike Huff .10 .05
❑ 550 Lance Parrish .15 .07
❑ 551 Ken Griffey Jr. HIT .60 .25
❑ 552 Matt Williams HIT .15 .07
❑ 553 R.Alomar HIT UER .15 .07
Card says he's a NL All-Star
He plays in the AL
❑ 554 Jeff Bagwell HIT .25 .11
❑ 555 Dave Justice HIT .10 .05
❑ 556 Cal Ripken Jr. HIT .75 .35
❑ 557 Albert Belle HIT .10 .05
❑ 558 Mike Piazza HIT .50 .23
❑ 559 Kirby Puckett HIT .50 .23
❑ 560 Wade Boggs HIT .15 .07
❑ 561 Tony Gwynn HIT UER .40 .18
card has him winning AL batting titles
he's played whole career in the NL
❑ 562 Barry Bonds HIT .50 .23
❑ 563 Mo Vaughn HIT .10 .05
❑ 564 Don Mattingly HIT .50 .23
❑ 565 Carlos Baerga HIT .10 .05
❑ 566 Paul Molitor HIT .15 .07
❑ 567 Raul Mondesi HIT .10 .05
❑ 568 Manny Ramirez HIT .25 .11
❑ 569 Alex Rodriguez HIT .60 .25
❑ 570 Will Clark HIT .15 .07
❑ 571 Frank Thomas HIT .25 .11
❑ 572 Moises Alou HIT .10 .05
❑ 573 Jeff Conine HIT .10 .05
❑ 574 Joe Ausanio .10 .05
❑ 575 Charles Johnson .15 .07
❑ 576 Ernie Young .10 .05
❑ 577 Jeff Granger .10 .05
❑ 578 Robert Perez .10 .05
❑ 579 Melvin Nieves .10 .05
❑ 580 Gar Finnvold .10 .05
❑ 581 Duane Singleton .10 .05
❑ 582 Chan Ho Park .15 .07
❑ 583 Fausto Cruz .10 .05
❑ 584 Dave Staton .10 .05
❑ 585 Denny Hocking .10 .05
❑ 586 Nate Minchey .10 .05
❑ 587 Marc Newfield .10 .05
❑ 588 Jayhawk Owens UER .10 .05
Front Photo is Jim Tatum
❑ 589 Darren Bragg .10 .05
❑ 590 Kevin King .10 .05
❑ 591 Kurt Miller .10 .05
❑ 592 Aaron Small .10 .05
❑ 593 Troy O'Leary .10 .05
❑ 594 Phil Stidham .10 .05
❑ 595 Steve Dunn .10 .05
❑ 596 Cory Bailey .10 .05
❑ 597 Alex Gonzalez .10 .05
❑ 598 Jim Bowie RC .10 .05
❑ 599 Jeff Cirillo .15 .07
❑ 600 Mark Hutton .10 .05
❑ 601 Russ Davis .10 .05
❑ 602 Checklist .10 .05
❑ 603 Checklist .10 .05
❑ 604 Checklist .10 .05
❑ 605 Checklist .10 .05
❑ RG1 R.Klesko Rook.Great. 1.00 .45
❑ SG1 Ryan Klesko AU6100 10.00 4.50
❑ NNO Trade Hall of Gold 1.00 .45

1996 Score

	MINT	NRMT
COMPLETE SET (517)	24.00	11.00
COMPLETE SERIES 1 (275)	12.00	5.50
COMPLETE SERIES 2 (242)	12.00	5.50

❑ 1 Will Clark .40 .18
❑ 2 Rich Becker .10 .05
❑ 3 Ryan Klesko .15 .07
❑ 4 Jim Edmonds .25 .11
❑ 5 Barry Larkin .40 .18
❑ 6 Jim Thome .40 .18
❑ 7 Raul Mondesi .15 .07
❑ 8 Don Mattingly 1.00 .45
❑ 9 Jeff Conine .10 .05
❑ 10 Rickey Henderson .75 .35
❑ 11 Chad Curtis .10 .05
❑ 12 Darren Daulton .15 .07
❑ 13 Larry Walker .25 .11
❑ 14 Carlos Garcia .10 .05
❑ 15 Carlos Baerga .10 .05
❑ 16 Tony Gwynn .75 .35
❑ 17 Jon Nunnally .10 .05
❑ 18 Deion Sanders .15 .07
❑ 19 Mark Grace .40 .18
❑ 20 Alex Rodriguez 1.00 .45
❑ 21 Frank Thomas .50 .23
❑ 22 Brian Jordan .15 .07
❑ 23 J.T. Snow .15 .07

❑ 24 Shawn Green .40 .18
❑ 25 Tim Wakefield .10 .05
❑ 26 Curtis Goodwin .10 .05
❑ 27 John Smoltz .15 .07
❑ 28 Devon White .15 .07
❑ 29 Johnny Damon .15 .07
❑ 30 Tim Salmon .25 .11
❑ 31 Rafael Palmeiro .40 .18
❑ 32 Bernard Gilkey .10 .05
❑ 33 John Valentin .10 .05
❑ 34 Randy Johnson .50 .23
❑ 35 Garret Anderson .15 .07
❑ 36 Rikkert Faneyte .10 .05
❑ 37 Ray Durham .15 .07
❑ 38 Bip Roberts .10 .05
❑ 39 Jaime Navarro .10 .05
❑ 40 Mark Johnson .10 .05
❑ 41 Darren Lewis .10 .05
❑ 42 Tyler Green .10 .05
❑ 43 Bill Pulsipher .10 .05
❑ 44 Jason Giambi .40 .18
❑ 45 Kevin Ritz .10 .05
❑ 46 Jack McDowell .10 .05
❑ 47 Felipe Lira .10 .05
❑ 48 Rico Brogna .10 .05
❑ 49 Terry Pendleton .15 .07
❑ 50 Rondell White .15 .07
❑ 51 Andre Dawson .25 .11
❑ 52 Kirby Puckett 1.00 .45
❑ 53 Wally Joyner .15 .07
❑ 54 B.J. Surhoff .15 .07
❑ 55 Randy Velarde .10 .05
❑ 56 Greg Vaughn .15 .07
❑ 57 Roberto Alomar .40 .18
❑ 58 David Justice .15 .07
❑ 59 Kevin Seitzer .10 .05
❑ 60 Cal Ripken 1.50 .70
❑ 61 Ozzie Smith .50 .23
❑ 62 Mo Vaughn .15 .07
❑ 63 Ricky Bones .10 .05
❑ 64 Gary DiSarcina .10 .05
❑ 65 Matt Williams .25 .11
❑ 66 Wilson Alvarez .10 .05
❑ 67 Lenny Dykstra .15 .07
❑ 68 Brian McRae .10 .05
❑ 69 Todd Stottlemyre .10 .05
❑ 70 Bret Boone .15 .07
❑ 71 Sterling Hitchcock .10 .05
❑ 72 Albert Belle .15 .07
❑ 73 Todd Hundley .10 .05
❑ 74 Vinny Castilla .15 .07
❑ 75 Moises Alou .15 .07
❑ 76 Cecil Fielder .15 .07
❑ 77 Brad Radke .15 .07
❑ 78 Quilvio Veras .10 .05
❑ 79 Eddie Murray .40 .18
❑ 80 James Mouton .10 .05
❑ 81 Pat Listach .10 .05
❑ 82 Mark Gubicza .10 .05
❑ 83 Dave Winfield .40 .18
❑ 84 Fred McGriff .25 .11
❑ 85 Darryl Hamilton .10 .05
❑ 86 Jeffrey Hammonds .10 .05
❑ 87 Pedro Munoz .10 .05
❑ 88 Craig Biggio .25 .11
❑ 89 Cliff Floyd .15 .07
❑ 90 Tim Naehring .10 .05
❑ 91 Brett Butler .15 .07
❑ 92 Kevin Foster .10 .05
❑ 93 Pat Kelly .10 .05
❑ 94 John Smiley .10 .05
❑ 95 Terry Steinbach .10 .05
❑ 96 Orel Hershiser .15 .07
❑ 97 Darrin Fletcher .10 .05
❑ 98 Walt Weiss .10 .05
❑ 99 John Wetteland .15 .07
❑ 100 Alan Trammell .25 .11
❑ 101 Steve Avery .10 .05
❑ 102 Tony Eusebio .10 .05
❑ 103 Sandy Alomar Jr. .15 .07
❑ 104 Joe Girardi .10 .05
❑ 105 Rick Aguilera .10 .05
❑ 106 Tony Tarasco .10 .05
❑ 107 Chris Hammond .10 .05
❑ 108 Mike Macfarlane .10 .05
❑ 109 Doug Drabek .10 .05
❑ 110 Derek Bell .10 .05
❑ 111 Ed Sprague .10 .05
❑ 112 Todd Hollandsworth .10 .05
❑ 113 Otis Nixon .10 .05
❑ 114 Keith Lockhart .10 .05
❑ 115 Donovan Osborne .10 .05
❑ 116 Dave Magadan .10 .05
❑ 117 Edgar Martinez .25 .11
❑ 118 Chuck Carr .10 .05
❑ 119 J.R. Phillips .10 .05
❑ 120 Sean Bergman .10 .05
❑ 121 Andujar Cedeno .10 .05
❑ 122 Eric Young .10 .05
❑ 123 Al Martin .10 .05
❑ 124 Mark Lemke .10 .05
❑ 125 Jim Eisenreich .10 .05
❑ 126 Benito Santiago .10 .05
❑ 127 Ariel Prieto .10 .05
❑ 128 Jim Bullinger .10 .05
❑ 129 Russ Davis .10 .05
❑ 130 Jim Abbott .15 .07
❑ 131 Jason Isringhausen .15 .07
❑ 132 Carlos Perez .10 .05
❑ 133 David Segui .10 .05
❑ 134 Troy O'Leary .10 .05
❑ 135 Pat Meares .10 .05
❑ 136 Chris Hoiles .10 .05
❑ 137 Ismael Valdes .10 .05
❑ 138 Jose Oliva .10 .05
❑ 139 Carlos Delgado .40 .18
❑ 140 Tom Goodwin .10 .05
❑ 141 Bob Tewksbury .10 .05
❑ 142 Chris Gomez .10 .05
❑ 143 Jose Oquendo .10 .05
❑ 144 Mark Lewis .10 .05
❑ 145 Salomon Torres .10 .05
❑ 146 Luis Gonzalez .40 .18
❑ 147 Mark Carreon .10 .05
❑ 148 Lance Johnson .10 .05
❑ 149 Melvin Nieves .10 .05
❑ 150 Lee Smith .15 .07
❑ 151 Jacob Brumfield .10 .05
❑ 152 Armando Benitez .10 .05
❑ 153 Curt Schilling .40 .18
❑ 154 Javier Lopez .15 .07
❑ 155 Frank Rodriguez .10 .05
❑ 156 Alex Gonzalez .10 .05
❑ 157 Todd Worrell .10 .05
❑ 158 Benji Gil .10 .05
❑ 159 Greg Gagne .10 .05
❑ 160 Tom Henke .10 .05
❑ 161 Randy Myers .10 .05
❑ 162 Joey Cora .10 .05
❑ 163 Scott Ruffcorn .10 .05
❑ 164 W. VanLandingham .10 .05
❑ 165 Tony Phillips .10 .05
❑ 166 Eddie Williams .10 .05
❑ 167 Bobby Bonilla .15 .07
❑ 168 Denny Neagle .15 .07
❑ 169 Troy Percival .10 .05
❑ 170 Billy Ashley .10 .05
❑ 171 Andy Van Slyke .15 .07
❑ 172 Jose Offerman .10 .05
❑ 173 Mark Parent .10 .05
❑ 174 Edgardo Alfonzo .15 .07
❑ 175 Trevor Hoffman .15 .07
❑ 176 David Cone .15 .07
❑ 177 Dan Wilson .10 .05
❑ 178 Steve Ontiveros .10 .05
❑ 179 Dean Palmer .15 .07
❑ 180 Mike Kelly .10 .05
❑ 181 Jim Leyritz .10 .05
❑ 182 Ron Karkovice .10 .05
❑ 183 Kevin Brown .15 .07
❑ 184 Jose Valentin .10 .05
❑ 185 Jorge Fabregas .10 .05
❑ 186 Jose Mesa .10 .05
❑ 187 Brent Mayne .10 .05
❑ 188 Carl Everett .15 .07
❑ 189 Paul Sorrento .10 .05
❑ 190 Pete Schourek .10 .05
❑ 191 Scott Kamieniecki .10 .05
❑ 192 Roberto Hernandez .10 .05
❑ 193 Randy Johnson RR .25 .11
❑ 194 Greg Maddux RR .50 .23
❑ 195 Hideo Nomo RR .15 .07
❑ 196 David Cone RR .10 .05
❑ 197 Mike Mussina RR .15 .07
❑ 198 Andy Benes RR .10 .05
❑ 199 Kevin Appier RR .10 .05
❑ 200 John Smoltz RR .10 .05
❑ 201 John Wetteland RR .10 .05
❑ 202 Mark Wohlers RR .10 .05
❑ 203 Stan Belinda .10 .05
❑ 204 Brian Anderson .10 .05
❑ 205 Mike Devereaux .10 .05
❑ 206 Mark Wohlers .10 .05
❑ 207 Omar Vizquel .15 .07
❑ 208 Jose Rijo .10 .05
❑ 209 Willie Blair .10 .05
❑ 210 Jamie Moyer .10 .05
❑ 211 Craig Shipley .10 .05
❑ 212 Shane Reynolds .10 .05
❑ 213 Chad Fonville .10 .05
❑ 214 Jose Vizcaino .10 .05
❑ 215 Sid Fernandez .10 .05
❑ 216 Andy Ashby .10 .05
❑ 217 Frank Castillo .10 .05
❑ 218 Kevin Tapani .10 .05
❑ 219 Kent Mercker .10 .05
❑ 220 Karim Garcia .10 .05
❑ 221 Antonio Osuna .10 .05
❑ 222 Tim Unroe .10 .05
❑ 223 Johnny Damon .15 .07
❑ 224 LaTroy Hawkins .10 .05
❑ 225 Mariano Rivera .15 .07
❑ 226 Jose Alberro .10 .05
❑ 227 Angel Martinez .10 .05
❑ 228 Jason Schmidt .10 .05
❑ 229 Tony Clark .15 .07
❑ 230 Kevin Jordan UER .10 .05
Ricky Jordan pictured on both sides
❑ 231 Mark Thompson .10 .05
❑ 232 Jim Dougherty .10 .05
❑ 233 Roger Cedeno .10 .05
❑ 234 Ugueth Urbina .10 .05
❑ 235 Ricky Otero .10 .05
❑ 236 Mark Smith .10 .05
❑ 237 Brian Barber .10 .05
❑ 238 Kevin Flora .10 .05
❑ 239 Joe Rosselli .10 .05
❑ 240 Derek Jeter 1.50 .70
❑ 241 Michael Tucker .10 .05
❑ 242 Ben Blomdahl .10 .05
❑ 243 Joe Vitiello .10 .05
❑ 244 Todd Steverson .10 .05
❑ 245 James Baldwin .10 .05
❑ 246 Alan Embree .10 .05
❑ 247 Shannon Penn .10 .05
❑ 248 Chris Stynes .10 .05
❑ 249 Oscar Munoz .10 .05
❑ 250 Jose Herrera .10 .05
❑ 251 Scott Sullivan .10 .05
❑ 252 Reggie Williams .10 .05
❑ 253 Mark Grudzielanek .10 .05
❑ 254 Steve Rodriguez .10 .05
❑ 255 Terry Bradshaw .10 .05
❑ 256 F.P. Santangelo .10 .05
❑ 257 Lyle Mouton .10 .05
❑ 258 George Williams .10 .05
❑ 259 Larry Thomas .10 .05
❑ 260 Rudy Pemberton .10 .05
❑ 261 Jim Pittsley .10 .05
❑ 262 Les Norman .10 .05
❑ 263 Ruben Rivera .10 .05
❑ 264 Cesar Devarez .10 .05
❑ 265 Greg Zaun .10 .05
❑ 266 Dustin Hermanson .10 .05
❑ 267 John Frascatore .10 .05
❑ 268 Joe Randa .10 .05
❑ 269 Jeff Bagwell CL .25 .11
❑ 270 Mike Piazza CL .50 .23
❑ 271 Dante Bichette CL .10 .05
❑ 272 Frank Thomas CL .25 .11
❑ 273 Ken Griffey Jr. CL .60 .25
❑ 274 Cal Ripken CL .75 .35
❑ 275 Greg Maddux CL .15 .07
Albert Belle
❑ 276 Greg Maddux 1.00 .45
❑ 277 Pedro Martinez .50 .23
❑ 278 Bobby Higginson .15 .07
❑ 279 Ray Lankford .10 .05

	No.	Player	Mint	Nrmt
❑	280	Shawon Dunston	.10	.05
❑	281	Gary Sheffield	.15	.07
❑	282	Ken Griffey Jr.	1.25	.55
❑	283	Paul Molitor	.40	.18
❑	284	Kevin Appier	.15	.07
❑	285	Chuck Knoblauch	.15	.07
❑	286	Alex Fernandez	.10	.05
❑	287	Steve Finley	.15	.07
❑	288	Jeff Blauser	.10	.05
❑	289	Charles Johnson	.15	.07
❑	290	John Franco	.15	.07
❑	291	Mark Langston	.10	.05
❑	292	Bret Saberhagen	.15	.07
❑	293	John Mabry	.10	.05
❑	294	Ramon Martinez	.10	.05
❑	295	Mike Blowers	.10	.05
❑	296	Paul O'Neill	.40	.18
❑	297	Dave Nilsson	.10	.05
❑	298	Dante Bichette	.15	.07
❑	299	Marty Cordova	.10	.05
❑	300	Jay Bell	.15	.07
❑	301	Mike Mussina	.40	.18
❑	302	Ivan Rodriguez	.40	.18
❑	303	Jose Canseco	.40	.18
❑	304	Jeff Bagwell	.50	.23
❑	305	Manny Ramirez	.50	.23
❑	306	Dennis Martinez	.15	.07
❑	307	Charlie Hayes	.10	.05
❑	308	Joe Carter	.15	.07
❑	309	Travis Fryman	.15	.07
❑	310	Mark McGwire	1.50	.70
❑	311	Reggie Sanders UER Photo on front is John Roper	.10	.05
❑	312	Julian Tavarez	.10	.05
❑	313	Jeff Montgomery	.10	.05
❑	314	Andy Benes	.10	.05
❑	315	John Jaha	.10	.05
❑	316	Jeff Kent	.25	.11
❑	317	Mike Piazza	1.00	.45
❑	318	Erik Hanson	.10	.05
❑	319	Kenny Rogers	.10	.05
❑	320	Hideo Nomo	.50	.23
❑	321	Gregg Jefferies	.10	.05
❑	322	Chipper Jones	.75	.35
❑	323	Jay Buhner	.15	.07
❑	324	Dennis Eckersley	.15	.07
❑	325	Kenny Lofton	.15	.07
❑	326	Robin Ventura	.15	.07
❑	327	Tom Glavine	.40	.18
❑	328	Tim Salmon	.15	.07
❑	329	Andres Galarraga	.25	.11
❑	330	Hal Morris	.10	.05
❑	331	Brady Anderson	.15	.07
❑	332	Chili Davis	.15	.07
❑	333	Roger Clemens	1.00	.45
❑	334	Marquis Grissom	.10	.05
❑	335	Mike Greenwell UER Name spelled Jeff on Front	.10	.05
❑	336	Sammy Sosa	.75	.35
❑	337	Ron Gant	.10	.05
❑	338	Ken Caminiti	.15	.07
❑	339	Danny Tartabull	.10	.05
❑	340	Barry Bonds	1.00	.45
❑	341	Ben McDonald	.10	.05
❑	342	Ruben Sierra	.10	.05
❑	343	Bernie Williams	.40	.18
❑	344	Wil Cordero	.10	.05
❑	345	Wade Boggs	.40	.18
❑	346	Gary Gaetti	.15	.07
❑	347	Greg Colbrunn	.10	.05
❑	348	Juan Gonzalez	.40	.18
❑	349	Marc Newfield	.10	.05
❑	350	Charles Nagy	.10	.05
❑	351	Robby Thompson	.10	.05
❑	352	Roberto Petagine	.10	.05
❑	353	Darryl Strawberry	.15	.07
❑	354	Tino Martinez	.15	.07
❑	355	Eric Karros	.15	.07
❑	356	Cal Ripken SS	.75	.35
❑	357	Cecil Fielder SS	.10	.05
❑	358	Kirby Puckett SS	.50	.23
❑	359	Jim Edmonds SS	.15	.07
❑	360	Matt Williams SS	.15	.07
❑	361	Alex Rodriguez SS	.50	.23
❑	362	Barry Larkin SS	.15	.07
❑	363	Rafael Palmeiro SS	.15	.07
❑	364	David Cone SS	.10	.05
❑	365	Roberto Alomar SS	.15	.07
❑	366	Eddie Murray SS	.15	.07
❑	367	Randy Johnson SS	.25	.11
❑	368	Ryan Klesko SS	.10	.05
❑	369	Raul Mondesi SS	.10	.05
❑	370	Mo Vaughn SS	.10	.05
❑	371	Will Clark SS	.15	.07
❑	372	Carlos Baerga SS	.10	.05
❑	373	Frank Thomas SS	.25	.11
❑	374	Larry Walker SS	.10	.05
❑	375	Garret Anderson SS	.10	.05
❑	376	Edgar Martinez SS	.15	.07
❑	377	Don Mattingly SS	.50	.23
❑	378	Tony Gwynn SS	.40	.18
❑	379	Albert Belle SS	.15	.07
❑	380	J.Isringhausen SS	.10	.05
❑	381	Ruben Rivera SS	.10	.05
❑	382	Johnny Damon SS	.10	.05
❑	383	Karim Garcia SS	.10	.05
❑	384	Derek Jeter SS	.75	.35
❑	385	David Justice SS	.10	.05
❑	386	Royce Clayton	.10	.05
❑	387	Mark Whiten	.10	.05
❑	388	Mickey Tettleton	.10	.05
❑	389	Steve Trachsel	.10	.05
❑	390	Danny Bautista	.10	.05
❑	391	Midre Cummings	.10	.05
❑	392	Scott Leius	.10	.05
❑	393	Manny Alexander	.10	.05
❑	394	Brent Gates	.10	.05
❑	395	Rey Sanchez	.10	.05
❑	396	Andy Pettitte	.15	.07
❑	397	Jeff Cirillo	.15	.07
❑	398	Kurt Abbott	.10	.05
❑	399	Lee Tinsley	.10	.05
❑	400	Paul Assenmacher	.10	.05
❑	401	Scott Erickson	.10	.05
❑	402	Todd Zeile	.10	.05
❑	403	Tom Pagnozzi	.10	.05
❑	404	Ozzie Guillen	.10	.05
❑	405	Jeff Frye	.10	.05
❑	406	Kirt Manwaring	.10	.05
❑	407	Chad Ogea	.10	.05
❑	408	Harold Baines	.15	.07
❑	409	Jason Bere	.10	.05
❑	410	Chuck Finley	.15	.07
❑	411	Jeff Fassero	.10	.05
❑	412	Joey Hamilton	.10	.05
❑	413	John Olerud	.15	.07
❑	414	Kevin Stocker	.10	.05
❑	415	Eric Anthony	.10	.05
❑	416	Aaron Sele	.15	.07
❑	417	Chris Bosio	.10	.05
❑	418	Michael Mimbs	.10	.05
❑	419	Orlando Miller	.10	.05
❑	420	Stan Javier	.10	.05
❑	421	Matt Mieske	.10	.05
❑	422	Jason Bates	.10	.05
❑	423	Orlando Merced	.10	.05
❑	424	John Flaherty	.10	.05
❑	425	Reggie Jefferson	.10	.05
❑	426	Scott Stahoviak	.10	.05
❑	427	John Burkett	.10	.05
❑	428	Rod Beck	.10	.05
❑	429	Bill Swift	.10	.05
❑	430	Scott Cooper	.10	.05
❑	431	Mel Rojas	.10	.05
❑	432	Todd Van Poppel	.10	.05
❑	433	Bobby Jones	.10	.05
❑	434	Mike Harkey	.10	.05
❑	435	Sean Berry	.10	.05
❑	436	Glenallen Hill	.10	.05
❑	437	Ryan Thompson	.10	.05
❑	438	Luis Alicea	.10	.05
❑	439	Esteban Loaiza	.10	.05
❑	440	Jeff Reboulet	.10	.05
❑	441	Vince Coleman	.10	.05
❑	442	Ellis Burks	.15	.07
❑	443	Allen Battle	.10	.05
❑	444	Jimmy Key	.15	.07
❑	445	Ricky Bottalico	.10	.05
❑	446	Delino DeShields	.10	.05
❑	447	Albie Lopez	.10	.05
❑	448	Mark Petkovsek	.10	.05
❑	449	Tim Raines	.15	.07
❑	450	Bryan Harvey	.10	.05
❑	451	Pat Hentgen	.10	.05
❑	452	Tim Laker	.10	.05
❑	453	Tom Gordon	.10	.05
❑	454	Phil Plantier	.10	.05
❑	455	Ernie Young	.10	.05
❑	456	Pete Harnisch	.10	.05
❑	457	Roberto Kelly	.10	.05
❑	458	Mark Portugal	.10	.05
❑	459	Mark Leiter	.10	.05
❑	460	Tony Pena	.10	.05
❑	461	Roger Pavlik	.10	.05
❑	462	Jeff King	.10	.05
❑	463	Bryan Rekar	.10	.05
❑	464	Al Leiter	.15	.07
❑	465	Phil Nevin	.15	.07
❑	466	Jose Lima	.10	.05
❑	467	Mike Stanley	.10	.05
❑	468	David McCarty	.10	.05
❑	469	Herb Perry	.10	.05
❑	470	Geronimo Berroa	.10	.05
❑	471	David Wells	.15	.07
❑	472	Vaughn Eshelman	.10	.05
❑	473	Greg Swindell	.10	.05
❑	474	Steve Sparks	.10	.05
❑	475	Luis Sojo	.10	.05
❑	476	Derrick May	.10	.05
❑	477	Joe Oliver	.10	.05
❑	478	Alex Arias	.10	.05
❑	479	Brad Ausmus	.10	.05
❑	480	Gabe White	.10	.05
❑	481	Pat Rapp	.10	.05
❑	482	Damon Buford	.10	.05
❑	483	Turk Wendell	.10	.05
❑	484	Jeff Brantley	.10	.05
❑	485	Curtis Leskanic	.10	.05
❑	486	Robb Nen	.10	.05
❑	487	Lou Whitaker	.15	.07
❑	488	Melido Perez	.10	.05
❑	489	Luis Polonia	.10	.05
❑	490	Scott Brosius	.15	.07
❑	491	Robert Perez	.10	.05
❑	492	Mike Sweeney RC	1.50	.70
❑	493	Mark Loretta	.10	.05
❑	494	Alex Ochoa	.10	.05
❑	495	Matt Lawton RC	.50	.23
❑	496	Shawn Estes	.15	.07
❑	497	John Wasdin	.10	.05
❑	498	Marc Kroon	.10	.05
❑	499	Chris Snopek	.10	.05
❑	500	Jeff Suppan	.10	.05
❑	501	Terrell Wade	.10	.05
❑	502	Marvin Benard RC	.15	.07
❑	503	Chris Widger	.10	.05
❑	504	Quinton McCracken	.10	.05
❑	505	Bob Wolcott	.10	.05
❑	506	C.J. Nitkowski	.10	.05
❑	507	Aaron Ledesma	.10	.05
❑	508	Scott Hatteberg	.10	.05
❑	509	Jimmy Haynes	.10	.05
❑	510	Howard Battle	.10	.05
❑	511	Marty Cordova CL	.10	.05
❑	512	Randy Johnson CL	.25	.11
❑	513	Mo Vaughn CL	.10	.05
❑	514	Chan Ho Park CL	.10	.05
❑	515	Greg Maddux CL	.50	.23
❑	516	Barry Larkin CL	.15	.07
❑	517	Tom Glavine CL	.15	.07
❑	NNO	Cal Ripken 2131	20.00	9.00

1997 Score

	MINT	NRMT
COMPLETE SET (551)	40.00	18.00
COMP.FACT.SET (551)	40.00	18.00
COMPLETE SERIES 1 (330)	15.00	6.75
COMPLETE SERIES 2 (221)	25.00	11.00

	No.	Player	Mint	Nrmt
❑	1	Jeff Bagwell	.50	.23
❑	2	Mickey Tettleton	.10	.05
❑	3	Johnny Damon	.15	.07
❑	4	Jeff Conine	.10	.05
❑	5	Bernie Williams	.40	.18
❑	6	Will Clark	.40	.18
❑	7	Ryan Klesko	.15	.07
❑	8	Cecil Fielder	.15	.07

❑ 9 Paul Wilson .10 .05
❑ 10 Gregg Jefferies .10 .05
❑ 11 Chili Davis .15 .07
❑ 12 Albert Belle .15 .07
❑ 13 Ken Hill .10 .05
❑ 14 Cliff Floyd .15 .07
❑ 15 Jaime Navarro .10 .05
❑ 16 Ismael Valdes .10 .05
❑ 17 Jeff King .10 .05
❑ 18 Chris Bosio .10 .05
❑ 19 Reggie Sanders .10 .05
❑ 20 Darren Daulton .15 .07
❑ 21 Ken Caminiti .15 .07
❑ 22 Mike Piazza 1.00 .45
❑ 23 Chad Mottola .10 .05
❑ 24 Darin Erstad .40 .18
❑ 25 Dante Bichette .15 .07
❑ 26 Frank Thomas .50 .23
❑ 27 Ben McDonald .10 .05
❑ 28 Raul Casanova .10 .05
❑ 29 Kevin Ritz .10 .05
❑ 30 Garret Anderson .15 .07
❑ 31 Jason Kendall .15 .07
❑ 32 Billy Wagner .10 .05
❑ 33 Dave Justice .15 .07
❑ 34 Marty Cordova .10 .05
❑ 35 Derek Jeter 1.50 .70
❑ 36 Trevor Hoffman .15 .07
❑ 37 Geronimo Berroa .10 .05
❑ 38 Walt Weiss .10 .05
❑ 39 Kirt Manwaring .10 .05
❑ 40 Alex Gonzalez .10 .05
❑ 41 Sean Berry .10 .05
❑ 42 Kevin Appier .15 .07
❑ 43 Rusty Greer .15 .07
❑ 44 Pete Incaviglia .10 .05
❑ 45 Rafael Palmeiro .40 .18
❑ 46 Eddie Murray .40 .18
❑ 47 Moises Alou .15 .07
❑ 48 Mark Lewis .10 .05
❑ 49 Hal Morris .10 .05
❑ 50 Edgar Renteria .10 .05
❑ 51 Rickey Henderson .75 .35
❑ 52 Pat Listach .10 .05
❑ 53 John Wasdin .10 .05
❑ 54 James Baldwin .10 .05
❑ 55 Brian Jordan .15 .07
❑ 56 Edgar Martinez .25 .11
❑ 57 Wil Cordero .10 .05
❑ 58 Danny Tartabull .10 .05
❑ 59 Keith Lockhart .10 .05
❑ 60 Rico Brogna .10 .05
❑ 61 Ricky Bottalico .10 .05
❑ 62 Terry Pendleton .15 .07
❑ 63 Bret Boone .15 .07
❑ 64 Charlie Hayes .10 .05
❑ 65 Marc Newfield .10 .05
❑ 66 Sterling Hitchcock .10 .05
❑ 67 Roberto Alomar .40 .18
❑ 68 John Jaha .10 .05
❑ 69 Greg Colbrunn .10 .05
❑ 70 Sal Fasano .10 .05
❑ 71 Brooks Kieschnick .10 .05
❑ 72 Pedro Martinez .50 .23
❑ 73 Kevin Elster .10 .05
❑ 74 Ellis Burks .15 .07
❑ 75 Chuck Finley .15 .07
❑ 76 John Olerud .15 .07
❑ 77 Jay Bell .15 .07
❑ 78 Allen Watson .10 .05
❑ 79 Darryl Strawberry .15 .07
❑ 80 Orlando Miller .10 .05
❑ 81 Jose Herrera .10 .05
❑ 82 Andy Pettitte .15 .07
❑ 83 Juan Guzman .10 .05
❑ 84 Alan Benes .10 .05
❑ 85 Jack McDowell .10 .05
❑ 86 Ugueth Urbina .10 .05
❑ 87 Rocky Coppinger .10 .05
❑ 88 Jeff Cirillo .15 .07
❑ 89 Tom Glavine .40 .18
❑ 90 Robby Thompson .10 .05
❑ 91 Barry Bonds 1.00 .45
❑ 92 Carlos Delgado .40 .18
❑ 93 Mo Vaughn .15 .07
❑ 94 Ryne Sandberg .50 .23
❑ 95 Alex Rodriguez 1.00 .45
❑ 96 Brady Anderson .15 .07
❑ 97 Scott Brosius .15 .07
❑ 98 Dennis Eckersley .15 .07
❑ 99 Brian McRae .10 .05
❑ 100 Rey Ordonez .10 .05
❑ 101 John Valentin .10 .05
❑ 102 Brett Butler .15 .07
❑ 103 Eric Karros .15 .07
❑ 104 Harold Baines .15 .07
❑ 105 Javier Lopez .15 .07
❑ 106 Alan Trammell .25 .11
❑ 107 Jim Thome .40 .18
❑ 108 Frank Rodriguez .10 .05
❑ 109 Bernard Gilkey .10 .05
❑ 110 Reggie Jefferson .10 .05
❑ 111 Scott Stahoviak .10 .05
❑ 112 Steve Gibralter .10 .05
❑ 113 Todd Hollandsworth .10 .05
❑ 114 Ruben Rivera .10 .05
❑ 115 Dennis Martinez .15 .07
❑ 116 Mariano Rivera .15 .07
❑ 117 John Smoltz .15 .07
❑ 118 John Mabry .10 .05
❑ 119 Tom Gordon .10 .05
❑ 120 Alex Ochoa .10 .05
❑ 121 Jamey Wright .10 .05
❑ 122 Dave Nilsson .10 .05
❑ 123 Bobby Bonilla .15 .07
❑ 124 Al Leiter .15 .07
❑ 125 Rick Aguilera .10 .05
❑ 126 Jeff Brantley .10 .05
❑ 127 Kevin Brown .15 .07
❑ 128 George Arias .10 .05
❑ 129 Darren Oliver .10 .05
❑ 130 Bill Pulsipher .10 .05
❑ 131 Roberto Hernandez .10 .05
❑ 132 Delino DeShields .10 .05
❑ 133 Mark Grudzielanek .10 .05
❑ 134 John Wetteland .15 .07
❑ 135 Carlos Baerga .10 .05
❑ 136 Paul Sorrento .10 .05
❑ 137 Leo Gomez .10 .05
❑ 138 Andy Ashby .10 .05
❑ 139 Julio Franco .15 .07
❑ 140 Brian Hunter .10 .05
❑ 141 Jermaine Dye .15 .07
❑ 142 Tony Clark .15 .07
❑ 143 Ruben Sierra .10 .05
❑ 144 Donovan Osborne .10 .05
❑ 145 Mark McLemore .10 .05
❑ 146 Terry Steinbach .10 .05
❑ 147 Bob Wells .10 .05
❑ 148 Chan Ho Park .15 .07
❑ 149 Tim Salmon .15 .07
❑ 150 Paul O'Neill .40 .18
❑ 151 Cal Ripken 1.50 .70
❑ 152 Wally Joyner .15 .07
❑ 153 Omar Vizquel .15 .07
❑ 154 Mike Mussina .40 .18
❑ 155 Andres Galarraga .25 .11
❑ 156 Ken Griffey Jr. 1.25 .55
❑ 157 Kenny Lofton .15 .07
❑ 158 Ray Durham .15 .07
❑ 159 Hideo Nomo .40 .18
❑ 160 Ozzie Guillen .10 .05
❑ 161 Roger Pavlik .10 .05
❑ 162 Manny Ramirez .50 .23
❑ 163 Mark Lemke .10 .05
❑ 164 Mike Stanley .10 .05
❑ 165 Chuck Knoblauch .15 .07
❑ 166 Kimera Bartee .10 .05
❑ 167 Wade Boggs .40 .18
❑ 168 Jay Buhner .15 .07
❑ 169 Eric Young .10 .05
❑ 170 Jose Canseco .40 .18
❑ 171 Dwight Gooden .15 .07
❑ 172 Fred McGriff .25 .11
❑ 173 Sandy Alomar Jr. .15 .07
❑ 174 Andy Benes .10 .05
❑ 175 Dean Palmer .15 .07
❑ 176 Larry Walker .25 .11
❑ 177 Charles Nagy .10 .05
❑ 178 David Cone .15 .07
❑ 179 Mark Grace .40 .18
❑ 180 Robin Ventura .15 .07
❑ 181 Roger Clemens 1.00 .45
❑ 182 Bobby Witt .10 .05
❑ 183 Vinny Castilla .15 .07
❑ 184 Gary Sheffield .15 .07
❑ 185 Dan Wilson .10 .05
❑ 186 Roger Cedeno .10 .05
❑ 187 Mark McGwire 1.50 .70
❑ 188 Darren Bragg .10 .05
❑ 189 Quinton McCracken .10 .05
❑ 190 Randy Myers .10 .05
❑ 191 Jeromy Burnitz .15 .07
❑ 192 Randy Johnson .50 .23
❑ 193 Chipper Jones .75 .35
❑ 194 Greg Vaughn .15 .07
❑ 195 Travis Fryman .15 .07
❑ 196 Tim Naehring .10 .05
❑ 197 B.J. Surhoff .15 .07
❑ 198 Juan Gonzalez .40 .18
❑ 199 Terrell Wade .10 .05
❑ 200 Jeff Frye .10 .05
❑ 201 Joey Cora .10 .05
❑ 202 Raul Mondesi .15 .07
❑ 203 Ivan Rodriguez .40 .18
❑ 204 Armando Reynoso .10 .05
❑ 205 Jeffrey Hammonds .10 .05
❑ 206 Darren Dreifort .10 .05
❑ 207 Kevin Seitzer .10 .05
❑ 208 Tino Martinez .15 .07
❑ 209 Jim Bruske .10 .05
❑ 210 Jeff Suppan .10 .05
❑ 211 Mark Carreon .10 .05
❑ 212 Wilson Alvarez .10 .05
❑ 213 John Burkett .10 .05
❑ 214 Tony Phillips .10 .05
❑ 215 Greg Maddux 1.00 .45
❑ 216 Mark Whiten .10 .05
❑ 217 Curtis Pride .10 .05
❑ 218 Lyle Mouton .10 .05
❑ 219 Todd Hundley .10 .05
❑ 220 Greg Gagne .10 .05
❑ 221 Rich Amaral .10 .05
❑ 222 Tom Goodwin .10 .05
❑ 223 Chris Hoiles .10 .05
❑ 224 Jayhawk Owens .10 .05
❑ 225 Kenny Rogers .10 .05
❑ 226 Mike Greenwell .10 .05
❑ 227 Mark Wohlers .10 .05
❑ 228 Henry Rodriguez .10 .05
❑ 229 Robert Perez .10 .05
❑ 230 Jeff Kent .25 .11
❑ 231 Darryl Hamilton .10 .05
❑ 232 Alex Fernandez .10 .05
❑ 233 Ron Karkovice .10 .05
❑ 234 Jimmy Haynes .10 .05
❑ 235 Craig Biggio .25 .11
❑ 236 Ray Lankford .10 .05
❑ 237 Lance Johnson .10 .05
❑ 238 Matt Williams .25 .11
❑ 239 Chad Curtis .10 .05
❑ 240 Mark Thompson .10 .05
❑ 241 Jason Giambi .40 .18
❑ 242 Barry Larkin .40 .18
❑ 243 Paul Molitor .40 .18
❑ 244 Sammy Sosa .75 .35
❑ 245 Kevin Tapani .10 .05
❑ 246 Marquis Grissom .10 .05
❑ 247 Joe Carter .15 .07

- ❑ 248 Ramon Martinez .10 .05
- ❑ 249 Tony Gwynn .75 .35
- ❑ 250 Andy Fox .10 .05
- ❑ 251 Troy O'Leary .10 .05
- ❑ 252 Warren Newson .10 .05
- ❑ 253 Troy Percival .10 .05
- ❑ 254 Jamie Moyer .10 .05
- ❑ 255 Danny Graves .10 .05
- ❑ 256 David Wells .15 .07
- ❑ 257 Todd Zeile .10 .05
- ❑ 258 Raul Ibanez .10 .05
- ❑ 259 Tyler Houston .10 .05
- ❑ 260 LaTroy Hawkins .10 .05
- ❑ 261 Joey Hamilton .10 .05
- ❑ 262 Mike Sweeney .15 .07
- ❑ 263 Brant Brown .10 .05
- ❑ 264 Pat Hentgen .10 .05
- ❑ 265 Mark Johnson .10 .05
- ❑ 266 Robb Nen .10 .05
- ❑ 267 Justin Thompson .10 .05
- ❑ 268 Ron Gant .10 .05
- ❑ 269 Jeff D'Amico .10 .05
- ❑ 270 Shawn Estes .15 .07
- ❑ 271 Derek Bell .10 .05
- ❑ 272 Fernando Valenzuela .15 .07
- ❑ 273 Tom Pagnozzi .10 .05
- ❑ 274 John Burke .10 .05
- ❑ 275 Ed Sprague .10 .05
- ❑ 276 F.P. Santangelo .10 .05
- ❑ 277 Todd Greene .10 .05
- ❑ 278 Butch Huskey .10 .05
- ❑ 279 Steve Finley .15 .07
- ❑ 280 Eric Davis .15 .07
- ❑ 281 Shawn Green .40 .18
- ❑ 282 Al Martin .10 .05
- ❑ 283 Michael Tucker .10 .05
- ❑ 284 Shane Reynolds .10 .05
- ❑ 285 Matt Mieske .10 .05
- ❑ 286 Jose Rosado .10 .05
- ❑ 287 Mark Langston .10 .05
- ❑ 288 Ralph Milliard .10 .05
- ❑ 289 Mike Lansing .10 .05
- ❑ 290 Scott Servais .10 .05
- ❑ 291 Royce Clayton .10 .05
- ❑ 292 Mike Grace .10 .05
- ❑ 293 James Mouton .10 .05
- ❑ 294 Charles Johnson .15 .07
- ❑ 295 Gary Gaetti .15 .07
- ❑ 296 Kevin Mitchell .10 .05
- ❑ 297 Carlos Garcia .10 .05
- ❑ 298 Desi Relaford .10 .05
- ❑ 299 Jason Thompson .10 .05
- ❑ 300 Osvaldo Fernandez .10 .05
- ❑ 301 Fernando Vina .10 .05
- ❑ 302 Jose Offerman .10 .05
- ❑ 303 Yamil Benitez .10 .05
- ❑ 304 J.T. Snow .15 .07
- ❑ 305 Rafael Bournigal .10 .05
- ❑ 306 Jason Isringhausen .10 .05
- ❑ 307 Bobby Higginson .15 .07
- ❑ 308 Nerio Rodriguez RC .10 .05
- ❑ 309 Brian Giles RC 1.50 .70
- ❑ 310 Andruw Jones .50 .23
- ❑ 311 Tony Graffanino .10 .05
- ❑ 312 Arquimedez Pozo .10 .05
- ❑ 313 Jermaine Allensworth .10 .05
- ❑ 314 Jeff Darwin .10 .05
- ❑ 315 George Williams .10 .05
- ❑ 316 Karim Garcia .10 .05
- ❑ 317 Trey Beamon .10 .05
- ❑ 318 Mac Suzuki .10 .05
- ❑ 319 Robin Jennings .10 .05
- ❑ 320 Danny Patterson .10 .05
- ❑ 321 Damon Mashore .10 .05
- ❑ 322 Wendell Magee .10 .05
- ❑ 323 Dax Jones .10 .05
- ❑ 324 Kevin Brown .15 .07
- ❑ 325 Marvin Benard .10 .05
- ❑ 326 Mike Cameron .15 .07
- ❑ 327 Marcus Jensen .10 .05
- ❑ 328 Eddie Murray CL .15 .07
- ❑ 329 Paul Molitor CL .15 .07
- ❑ 330 Todd Hundley CL .10 .05
- ❑ 331 Norm Charlton .10 .05
- ❑ 332 Bruce Ruffin .10 .05
- ❑ 333 John Wetteland .15 .07
- ❑ 334 Marquis Grissom .10 .05
- ❑ 335 Sterling Hitchcock .10 .05
- ❑ 336 John Olerud .15 .07
- ❑ 337 David Wells .15 .07
- ❑ 338 Chili Davis .15 .07
- ❑ 339 Mark Lewis .10 .05
- ❑ 340 Kenny Lofton .15 .07
- ❑ 341 Alex Fernandez .10 .05
- ❑ 342 Ruben Sierra .10 .05
- ❑ 343 Delino DeShields .10 .05
- ❑ 344 John Wasdin .10 .05
- ❑ 345 Dennis Martinez .15 .07
- ❑ 346 Kevin Elster .10 .05
- ❑ 347 Bobby Bonilla .15 .07
- ❑ 348 Jaime Navarro .10 .05
- ❑ 349 Chad Curtis .10 .05
- ❑ 350 Terry Steinbach .10 .05
- ❑ 351 Ariel Prieto .10 .05
- ❑ 352 Jeff Kent .25 .11
- ❑ 353 Carlos Garcia .10 .05
- ❑ 354 Mark Whiten .10 .05
- ❑ 355 Todd Zeile .10 .05
- ❑ 356 Eric Davis .15 .07
- ❑ 357 Greg Colbrunn .10 .05
- ❑ 358 Moises Alou .15 .07
- ❑ 359 Allen Watson .10 .05
- ❑ 360 Jose Canseco .40 .18
- ❑ 361 Matt Williams .25 .11
- ❑ 362 Jeff King .10 .05
- ❑ 363 Darryl Hamilton .10 .05
- ❑ 364 Mark Clark .10 .05
- ❑ 365 J.T. Snow .15 .07
- ❑ 366 Kevin Mitchell .10 .05
- ❑ 367 Orlando Miller .10 .05
- ❑ 368 Rico Brogna .10 .05
- ❑ 369 Mike James .10 .05
- ❑ 370 Brad Ausmus .10 .05
- ❑ 371 Darryl Kile .15 .07
- ❑ 372 Edgardo Alfonzo .15 .07
- ❑ 373 Julian Tavarez .10 .05
- ❑ 374 Darren Lewis .10 .05
- ❑ 375 Steve Karsay .10 .05
- ❑ 376 Lee Stevens .10 .05
- ❑ 377 Albie Lopez .10 .05
- ❑ 378 Orel Hershiser .15 .07
- ❑ 379 Lee Smith .15 .07
- ❑ 380 Rick Helling .10 .05
- ❑ 381 Carlos Perez .10 .05
- ❑ 382 Tony Tarasco .10 .05
- ❑ 383 Melvin Nieves .10 .05
- ❑ 384 Benji Gil .10 .05
- ❑ 385 Devon White .15 .07
- ❑ 386 Armando Benitez .10 .05
- ❑ 387 Bill Swift .10 .05
- ❑ 388 John Smiley .10 .05
- ❑ 389 Midre Cummings .10 .05
- ❑ 390 Tim Belcher .10 .05
- ❑ 391 Tim Raines .15 .07
- ❑ 392 Todd Worrell .10 .05
- ❑ 393 Quilvio Veras .10 .05
- ❑ 394 Matt Lawton .15 .07
- ❑ 395 Aaron Sele .15 .07
- ❑ 396 Bip Roberts .10 .05
- ❑ 397 Denny Neagle .15 .07
- ❑ 398 Tyler Green .10 .05
- ❑ 399 Hipolito Pichardo .10 .05
- ❑ 400 Scott Erickson .10 .05
- ❑ 401 Bobby Jones .10 .05
- ❑ 402 Jim Edmonds .25 .11
- ❑ 403 Chad Ogea .10 .05
- ❑ 404 Cal Eldred .10 .05
- ❑ 405 Pat Listach .10 .05
- ❑ 406 Todd Stottlemyre .10 .05
- ❑ 407 Phil Nevin .15 .07
- ❑ 408 Otis Nixon .10 .05
- ❑ 409 Billy Ashley .10 .05
- ❑ 410 Jimmy Key .15 .07
- ❑ 411 Mike Timlin .10 .05
- ❑ 412 Joe Vitiello .10 .05
- ❑ 413 Rondell White .15 .07
- ❑ 414 Jeff Fassero .10 .05
- ❑ 415 Rex Hudler .10 .05
- ❑ 416 Curt Schilling .40 .18
- ❑ 417 Rich Becker .10 .05
- ❑ 418 W.Van Landingham .10 .05
- ❑ 419 Chris Snopek .10 .05
- ❑ 420 David Segui .10 .05
- ❑ 421 Eddie Murray .40 .18
- ❑ 422 Shane Andrews .10 .05
- ❑ 423 Gary DiSarcina .10 .05
- ❑ 424 Brian Hunter .10 .05
- ❑ 425 Willie Greene .10 .05
- ❑ 426 Felipe Crespo .10 .05
- ❑ 427 Jason Bates .10 .05
- ❑ 428 Albert Belle .15 .07
- ❑ 429 Rey Sanchez .10 .05
- ❑ 430 Roger Clemens 1.00 .45
- ❑ 431 Deion Sanders .15 .07
- ❑ 432 Ernie Young .10 .05
- ❑ 433 Jay Bell .15 .07
- ❑ 434 Jeff Blauser .10 .05
- ❑ 435 Lenny Dykstra .15 .07
- ❑ 436 Chuck Carr .10 .05
- ❑ 437 Russ Davis .10 .05
- ❑ 438 Carl Everett .15 .07
- ❑ 439 Damion Easley .10 .05
- ❑ 440 Pat Kelly .10 .05
- ❑ 441 Pat Rapp .10 .05
- ❑ 442 Dave Justice .15 .07
- ❑ 443 Graeme Lloyd .10 .05
- ❑ 444 Damon Buford .10 .05
- ❑ 445 Jose Valentin .10 .05
- ❑ 446 Jason Schmidt .10 .05
- ❑ 447 Dave Martinez .10 .05
- ❑ 448 Danny Tartabull .10 .05
- ❑ 449 Jose Vizcaino .10 .05
- ❑ 450 Steve Avery .10 .05
- ❑ 451 Mike Devereaux .10 .05
- ❑ 452 Jim Eisenreich .10 .05
- ❑ 453 Mark Leiter .10 .05
- ❑ 454 Roberto Kelly .10 .05
- ❑ 455 Benito Santiago .10 .05
- ❑ 456 Steve Trachsel .10 .05
- ❑ 457 Gerald Williams .10 .05
- ❑ 458 Pete Schourek .10 .05
- ❑ 459 Esteban Loaiza .10 .05
- ❑ 460 Mel Rojas .10 .05
- ❑ 461 Tim Wakefield .10 .05
- ❑ 462 Tony Fernandez .10 .05
- ❑ 463 Doug Drabek .10 .05
- ❑ 464 Joe Girardi .10 .05
- ❑ 465 Mike Bordick .10 .05
- ❑ 466 Jim Leyritz .10 .05
- ❑ 467 Erik Hanson .10 .05
- ❑ 468 Michael Tucker .10 .05
- ❑ 469 Tony Womack RC .40 .18
- ❑ 470 Doug Glanville .10 .05
- ❑ 471 Rudy Pemberton .10 .05
- ❑ 472 Keith Lockhart .10 .05
- ❑ 473 Nomar Garciaparra 1.00 .45
- ❑ 474 Scott Rolen .40 .18
- ❑ 475 Jason Dickson .10 .05
- ❑ 476 Glendon Rusch .10 .05
- ❑ 477 Todd Walker .10 .05
- ❑ 478 Dmitri Young .15 .07
- ❑ 479 Rod Myers .10 .05
- ❑ 480 Wilton Guerrero .10 .05
- ❑ 481 Jorge Posada .15 .07
- ❑ 482 Brant Brown .10 .05
- ❑ 483 Bubba Trammell RC .15 .07
- ❑ 484 Jose Guillen .10 .05
- ❑ 485 Scott Spiezio .10 .05
- ❑ 486 Bob Abreu .15 .07
- ❑ 487 Chris Holt .10 .05
- ❑ 488 Deivi Cruz RC .50 .23
- ❑ 489 Vladimir Guerrero .60 .25
- ❑ 490 Julio Santana .10 .05
- ❑ 491 Ray Montgomery RC .10 .05
- ❑ 492 Kevin Orie .10 .05
- ❑ 493 Todd Hundley GY .10 .05
- ❑ 494 Tim Salmon GY .10 .05
- ❑ 495 Albert Belle GY .15 .07
- ❑ 496 Manny Ramirez GY .25 .11
- ❑ 497 Rafael Palmeiro GY .15 .07
- ❑ 498 Juan Gonzalez GY .15 .07
- ❑ 499 Ken Griffey Jr. GY .60 .25
- ❑ 500 Andruw Jones GY .25 .11
- ❑ 501 Mike Piazza GY .50 .23
- ❑ 502 Jeff Bagwell GY .25 .11
- ❑ 503 Bernie Williams GY .15 .07
- ❑ 504 Barry Bonds GY .50 .23
- ❑ 505 Ken Caminiti GY .10 .05

	Player	MINT	NRMT
❑ 506	Darin Erstad GY	.15	.07
❑ 507	Alex Rodriguez GY	.50	.23
❑ 508	Frank Thomas GY	.25	.11
❑ 509	Chipper Jones GY	.40	.18
❑ 510	Mo Vaughn GY	.10	.05
❑ 511	Mark McGwire GY	.75	.35
❑ 512	Fred McGriff GY	.15	.07
❑ 513	Jay Buhner GY	.10	.05
❑ 514	Gary Sheffield GY	.10	.05
❑ 515	Jim Thome GY	.15	.07
❑ 516	Dean Palmer GY	.10	.05
❑ 517	Henry Rodriguez GY	.10	.05
❑ 518	Andy Pettitte RF	.10	.05
❑ 519	Mike Mussina RF	.15	.07
❑ 520	Greg Maddux RF	.50	.23
❑ 521	John Smoltz RF	.10	.05
❑ 522	Hideo Nomo RF	.15	.07
❑ 523	Troy Percival RF	.10	.05
❑ 524	John Wetteland RF	.10	.05
❑ 525	Roger Clemens RF	.50	.23
❑ 526	Charles Nagy RF	.10	.05
❑ 527	Mariano Rivera RF	.10	.05
❑ 528	Tom Glavine RF	.15	.07
❑ 529	Randy Johnson RF	.25	.11
❑ 530	J.Isringhausen RF	.10	.05
❑ 531	Alex Fernandez RF	.10	.05
❑ 532	Kevin Brown RF	.10	.05
❑ 533	Chuck Knoblauch TG	.10	.05
❑ 534	Rusty Greer TG	.10	.05
❑ 535	Tony Gwynn TG	.40	.18
❑ 536	Ryan Klesko TG	.10	.05
❑ 537	Ryne Sandberg TG	.25	.11
❑ 538	Barry Larkin TG	.15	.07
❑ 539	Will Clark TG	.15	.07
❑ 540	Kenny Lofton TG	.10	.05
❑ 541	Paul Molitor TG	.15	.07
❑ 542	Roberto Alomar TG	.15	.07
❑ 543	Rey Ordonez TG	.10	.05
❑ 544	Jason Giambi TG	.15	.07
❑ 545	Derek Jeter TG	.75	.35
❑ 546	Cal Ripken TG	.75	.35
❑ 547	Ivan Rodriguez TG	.15	.07
❑ 548	Ken Griffey Jr. CL	.60	.25
❑ 549	Frank Thomas CL	.25	.11
❑ 550	Mike Piazza CL	.50	.23
❑ 551A	Hideki Irabu SP	2.50	1.10
❑ 551B	Hideki Irabu Japenese SP	2.50	1.10

1998 Score

		MINT	NRMT
COMPLETE SET (270)		50.00	22.00
❑ 1	Andruw Jones	.40	.18
❑ 2	Dan Wilson	.10	.05
❑ 3	Hideo Nomo	.40	.18
❑ 4	Chuck Carr	.10	.05
❑ 5	Barry Bonds	1.00	.45
❑ 6	Jack McDowell	.10	.05
❑ 7	Albert Belle	.15	.07
❑ 8	Francisco Cordova	.10	.05
❑ 9	Greg Maddux	1.00	.45
❑ 10	Alex Rodriguez	1.00	.45
❑ 11	Steve Avery	.10	.05
❑ 12	Chuck McElroy	.10	.05
❑ 13	Larry Walker	.25	.11
❑ 14	Hideki Irabu	.10	.05
❑ 15	Roberto Alomar	.40	.18
❑ 16	Neifi Perez	.10	.05
❑ 17	Jim Thome	.40	.18
❑ 18	Rickey Henderson	.75	.35
❑ 19	Andres Galarraga	.25	.11
❑ 20	Jeff Fassero	.10	.05
❑ 21	Kevin Young	.15	.07
❑ 22	Derek Jeter	1.50	.70
❑ 23	Andy Benes	.10	.05
❑ 24	Mike Piazza	1.00	.45
❑ 25	Todd Stottlemyre	.10	.05
❑ 26	Michael Tucker	.10	.05
❑ 27	Denny Neagle	.10	.05
❑ 28	Javier Lopez	.15	.07
❑ 29	Aaron Sele	.15	.07
❑ 30	Ryan Klesko	.15	.07
❑ 31	Dennis Eckersley	.15	.07
❑ 32	Quinton McCracken	.10	.05
❑ 33	Brian Anderson	.10	.05
❑ 34	Ken Griffey Jr.	1.25	.55
❑ 35	Shawn Estes	.15	.07
❑ 36	Tim Wakefield	.10	.05
❑ 37	Jimmy Key	.15	.07
❑ 38	Jeff Bagwell	.50	.23
❑ 39	Edgardo Alfonzo	.15	.07
❑ 40	Mike Cameron	.15	.07
❑ 41	Mark McGwire	1.50	.70
❑ 42	Tino Martinez	.15	.07
❑ 43	Cal Ripken	1.50	.70
❑ 44	Curtis Goodwin	.10	.05
❑ 45	Bobby Ayala	.10	.05
❑ 46	Sandy Alomar Jr.	.15	.07
❑ 47	Bobby Jones	.10	.05
❑ 48	Omar Vizquel	.15	.07
❑ 49	Roger Clemens	1.00	.45
❑ 50	Tony Gwynn	.75	.35
❑ 51	Chipper Jones	.75	.35
❑ 52	Ron Coomer	.10	.05
❑ 53	Dmitri Young	.15	.07
❑ 54	Brian Giles	.15	.07
❑ 55	Steve Finley	.15	.07
❑ 56	David Cone	.15	.07
❑ 57	Andy Pettitte	.15	.07
❑ 58	Wilton Guerrero	.10	.05
❑ 59	Deion Sanders	.15	.07
❑ 60	Carlos Delgado	.40	.18
❑ 61	Jason Giambi	.40	.18
❑ 62	Ozzie Guillen	.10	.05
❑ 63	Jay Bell	.15	.07
❑ 64	Barry Larkin	.40	.18
❑ 65	Sammy Sosa	.75	.35
❑ 66	Bernie Williams	.40	.18
❑ 67	Terry Steinbach	.10	.05
❑ 68	Scott Rolen	.40	.18
❑ 69	Melvin Nieves	.10	.05
❑ 70	Craig Biggio	.25	.11
❑ 71	Todd Greene	.10	.05
❑ 72	Greg Gagne	.10	.05
❑ 73	Shigetoshi Hasegawa	.15	.07
❑ 74	Mark McLemore	.10	.05
❑ 75	Darren Bragg	.10	.05
❑ 76	Brett Butler	.15	.07
❑ 77	Ron Gant	.15	.07
❑ 78	Mike Difelice RC	.10	.05
❑ 79	Charles Nagy	.10	.05
❑ 80	Scott Hatteberg	.10	.05
❑ 81	Brady Anderson	.15	.07
❑ 82	Jay Buhner	.15	.07
❑ 83	Todd Hollandsworth	.10	.05
❑ 84	Geronimo Berroa	.10	.05
❑ 85	Jeff Suppan	.10	.05
❑ 86	Pedro Martinez	.50	.23
❑ 87	Roger Cedeno	.10	.05
❑ 88	Ivan Rodriguez	.40	.18
❑ 89	Jaime Navarro	.10	.05
❑ 90	Chris Hoiles	.10	.05
❑ 91	Nomar Garciaparra	1.00	.45
❑ 92	Rafael Palmeiro	.40	.18
❑ 93	Darin Erstad	.40	.18
❑ 94	Kenny Lofton	.15	.07
❑ 95	Mike Timlin	.10	.05
❑ 96	Chris Clemons	.10	.05
❑ 97	Vinny Castilla	.15	.07
❑ 98	Charlie Hayes	.10	.05
❑ 99	Lyle Mouton	.10	.05
❑ 100	Jason Dickson	.10	.05
❑ 101	Justin Thompson	.10	.05
❑ 102	Pat Kelly	.10	.05
❑ 103	Chan Ho Park	.15	.07
❑ 104	Ray Lankford	.10	.05
❑ 105	Frank Thomas	.50	.23
❑ 106	Jermaine Allensworth	.10	.05
❑ 107	Doug Drabek	.10	.05
❑ 108	Todd Hundley	.10	.05
❑ 109	Carl Everett	.15	.07
❑ 110	Edgar Martinez	.25	.11
❑ 111	Robin Ventura	.15	.07
❑ 112	John Wetteland	.15	.07
❑ 113	Mariano Rivera	.15	.07
❑ 114	Jose Rosado	.10	.05
❑ 115	Ken Caminiti	.15	.07
❑ 116	Paul O'Neill	.40	.18
❑ 117	Tim Salmon	.15	.07
❑ 118	Eduardo Perez	.10	.05
❑ 119	Mike Jackson	.10	.05
❑ 120	John Smoltz	.15	.07
❑ 121	Brant Brown	.10	.05
❑ 122	John Mabry	.10	.05
❑ 123	Chuck Knoblauch	.15	.07
❑ 124	Reggie Sanders	.10	.05
❑ 125	Ken Hill	.10	.05
❑ 126	Mike Mussina	.40	.18
❑ 127	Chad Curtis	.10	.05
❑ 128	Todd Worrell	.10	.05
❑ 129	Chris Widger	.10	.05
❑ 130	Damon Mashore	.10	.05
❑ 131	Kevin Brown	.25	.11
❑ 132	Bip Roberts	.10	.05
❑ 133	Tim Naehring	.10	.05
❑ 134	Dave Martinez	.10	.05
❑ 135	Jeff Blauser	.10	.05
❑ 136	David Justice	.15	.07
❑ 137	Dave Hollins	.10	.05
❑ 138	Pat Hentgen	.10	.05
❑ 139	Darren Daulton	.15	.07
❑ 140	Ramon Martinez	.10	.05
❑ 141	Raul Casanova	.10	.05
❑ 142	Tom Glavine	.40	.18
❑ 143	J.T. Snow	.15	.07
❑ 144	Tony Graffanino	.10	.05
❑ 145	Randy Johnson	.50	.23
❑ 146	Orlando Merced	.10	.05
❑ 147	Jeff Juden	.10	.05
❑ 148	Darryl Kile	.15	.07
❑ 149	Ray Durham	.15	.07
❑ 150	Alex Fernandez	.10	.05
❑ 151	Joey Cora	.10	.05
❑ 152	Royce Clayton	.10	.05
❑ 153	Randy Myers	.15	.07
❑ 154	Charles Johnson	.15	.07
❑ 155	Alan Benes	.10	.05
❑ 156	Mike Bordick	.10	.05
❑ 157	Heathcliff Slocumb	.10	.05
❑ 158	Roger Bailey	.10	.05
❑ 159	Reggie Jefferson	.10	.05
❑ 160	Ricky Bottalico	.10	.05
❑ 161	Scott Erickson	.10	.05
❑ 162	Matt Williams	.25	.11
❑ 163	Robb Nen	.10	.05
❑ 164	Matt Stairs	.10	.05
❑ 165	Ismael Valdes	.10	.05
❑ 166	Lee Stevens	.10	.05
❑ 167	Gary DiSarcina	.10	.05
❑ 168	Brad Radke	.15	.07
❑ 169	Mike Lansing	.10	.05
❑ 170	Armando Benitez	.10	.05
❑ 171	Mike James	.10	.05
❑ 172	Russ Davis	.10	.05
❑ 173	Lance Johnson	.10	.05
❑ 174	Joey Hamilton	.10	.05
❑ 175	John Valentin	.10	.05
❑ 176	David Segui	.10	.05
❑ 177	David Wells	.15	.07
❑ 178	Delino DeShields	.10	.05
❑ 179	Eric Karros	.15	.07
❑ 180	Jim Leyritz	.10	.05
❑ 181	Raul Mondesi	.15	.07
❑ 182	Travis Fryman	.15	.07
❑ 183	Todd Zeile	.15	.07
❑ 184	Brian Jordan	.15	.07
❑ 185	Rey Ordonez	.10	.05
❑ 186	Jim Edmonds	.25	.11

❑ 187 Terrell Wade	.10	.05
❑ 188 Marquis Grissom	.10	.05
❑ 189 Chris Snopek	.10	.05
❑ 190 Shane Reynolds	.10	.05
❑ 191 Jeff Frye	.10	.05
❑ 192 Paul Sorrento	.10	.05
❑ 193 James Baldwin	.10	.05
❑ 194 Brian McRae	.10	.05
❑ 195 Fred McGriff	.25	.11
❑ 196 Troy Percival	.10	.05
❑ 197 Rich Amaral	.10	.05
❑ 198 Juan Guzman	.10	.05
❑ 199 Cecil Fielder	.15	.07
❑ 200 Willie Blair	.10	.05
❑ 201 Chili Davis	.15	.07
❑ 202 Gary Gaetti	.15	.07
❑ 203 B.J. Surhoff	.15	.07
❑ 204 Steve Cooke	.10	.05
❑ 205 Chuck Finley	.15	.07
❑ 206 Jeff Kent	.25	.11
❑ 207 Ben McDonald	.10	.05
❑ 208 Jeffrey Hammonds	.10	.05
❑ 209 Tom Goodwin	.10	.05
❑ 210 Billy Ashley	.10	.05
❑ 211 Wil Cordero	.10	.05
❑ 212 Shawon Dunston	.10	.05
❑ 213 Tony Phillips	.10	.05
❑ 214 Jamie Moyer	.10	.05
❑ 215 John Jaha	.15	.07
❑ 216 Troy O'Leary	.10	.05
❑ 217 Brad Ausmus	.10	.05
❑ 218 Garret Anderson	.15	.07
❑ 219 Wilson Alvarez	.10	.05
❑ 220 Kent Mercker	.10	.05
❑ 221 Wade Boggs	.40	.18
❑ 222 Mark Wohlers	.10	.05
❑ 223 Kevin Appier	.15	.07
❑ 224 Tony Fernandez	.10	.05
❑ 225 Ugueth Urbina	.10	.05
❑ 226 Gregg Jefferies	.10	.05
❑ 227 Mo Vaughn	.15	.07
❑ 228 Arthur Rhodes	.10	.05
❑ 229 Jorge Fabregas	.10	.05
❑ 230 Mark Gardner	.10	.05
❑ 231 Shane Mack	.10	.05
❑ 232 Jorge Posada	.15	.07
❑ 233 Jose Cruz Jr.	.15	.07
❑ 234 Paul Konerko	.15	.07
❑ 235 Derrek Lee	.15	.07
❑ 236 Steve Woodard	.10	.05
❑ 237 Todd Dunwoody	.10	.05
❑ 238 Fernando Tatis	.10	.05
❑ 239 Jacob Cruz	.10	.05
❑ 240 Pokey Reese	.10	.05
❑ 241 Mark Kotsay	.15	.07
❑ 242 Matt Morris	.15	.07
❑ 243 Antone Williamson	.10	.05
❑ 244 Ben Grieve	.15	.07
❑ 245 Ryan McGuire	.10	.05
❑ 246 Lou Collier	.10	.05
❑ 247 Shannon Stewart	.15	.07
❑ 248 Brett Tomko	.10	.05
❑ 249 Bobby Estalella	.10	.05
❑ 250 Livan Hernandez	.10	.05
❑ 251 Todd Helton	.50	.23
❑ 252 Jaret Wright	.10	.05
❑ 253 Darryl Hamilton IM	.10	.05
❑ 254 Stan Javier IM	.10	.05
❑ 255 Glenallen Hill IM	.10	.05
❑ 256 Mark Gardner IM	.10	.05
❑ 257 Cal Ripken IM	.75	.35
❑ 258 Mike Mussina IM	.15	.07
❑ 259 Mike Piazza IM	.50	.23
❑ 260 Sammy Sosa IM	.40	.18
❑ 261 Todd Hundley IM	.10	.05
❑ 262 Eric Karros IM	.10	.05
❑ 263 Denny Neagle IM	.10	.05
❑ 264 Jeromy Burnitz IM	.10	.05
❑ 265 Greg Maddux IM	.50	.23
❑ 266 Tony Clark IM	.15	.07
❑ 267 Vladimir Guerrero IM	.25	.11
❑ 268 Cal Ripken CL UER	.75	.35
❑ 269 Ken Griffey Jr. CL	.60	.25
❑ 270 Mark McGwire CL	.75	.35
❑ NNO CL Regular Issue	.10	.05
❑ NNO CL All-Star Edition	.25	.11

1998 Score Rookie Traded

	MINT	NRMT
COMPLETE SET (270)	40.00	18.00
COMMON SP (1-50)	.25	.11
COMMON CARD (51-270)	.10	.05
❑ 1 Tony Clark	.30	.14
❑ 2 Juan Gonzalez	.60	.25
❑ 3 Frank Thomas	.75	.35
❑ 4 Greg Maddux	1.50	.70
❑ 5 Barry Larkin	.60	.25
❑ 6 Derek Jeter	2.50	1.10
❑ 7 Randy Johnson	.75	.35
❑ 8 Roger Clemens	1.50	.70
❑ 9 Tony Gwynn	1.25	.55
❑ 10 Barry Bonds	1.50	.70
❑ 11 Jim Edmonds	.40	.18
❑ 12 Bernie Williams	.60	.25
❑ 13 Ken Griffey Jr.	2.00	.90
❑ 14 Tim Salmon	.30	.14
❑ 15 Mo Vaughn	.30	.14
❑ 16 David Justice	.30	.14
❑ 17 Jose Cruz Jr.	.30	.14
❑ 18 Andruw Jones	.60	.25
❑ 19 Sammy Sosa	1.25	.55
❑ 20 Jeff Bagwell	.75	.35
❑ 21 Scott Rolen	.60	.25
❑ 22 Darin Erstad	.60	.25
❑ 23 Andy Pettitte	.30	.14
❑ 24 Mike Mussina	.60	.25
❑ 25 Mark McGwire	2.50	1.10
❑ 26 Hideo Nomo	.60	.25
❑ 27 Chipper Jones	1.25	.55
❑ 28 Cal Ripken	2.50	1.10
❑ 29 Chuck Knoblauch	.30	.14
❑ 30 Alex Rodriguez	1.50	.70
❑ 31 Jim Thome	.60	.25
❑ 32 Mike Piazza	1.50	.70
❑ 33 Ivan Rodriguez	.60	.25
❑ 34 Roberto Alomar	.60	.25
❑ 35 Nomar Garciaparra	1.50	.70
❑ 36 Albert Belle	.30	.14
❑ 37 Vladimir Guerrero	.75	.35
❑ 38 Raul Mondesi	.30	.14
❑ 39 Larry Walker	.40	.18
❑ 40 Manny Ramirez	.75	.35
❑ 41 Tino Martinez	.30	.14
❑ 42 Craig Biggio	.40	.18
❑ 43 Jay Buhner	.30	.14
❑ 44 Kenny Lofton	.30	.14
❑ 45 Pedro Martinez	.75	.35
❑ 46 Edgar Martinez	.40	.18
❑ 47 Gary Sheffield	.30	.14
❑ 48 Jose Guillen	.25	.11
❑ 49 Ken Caminiti	.30	.14
❑ 50 Bobby Higginson	.30	.14
❑ 51 Alan Benes	.10	.05
❑ 52 Shawn Green	.40	.18
❑ 53 Ron Coomer	.10	.05
❑ 54 Charles Nagy	.10	.05
❑ 55 Steve Karsay	.10	.05
❑ 56 Matt Morris	.15	.07
❑ 57 Bobby Jones	.10	.05
❑ 58 Jason Kendall	.15	.07
❑ 59 Jeff Conine	.10	.05
❑ 60 Joe Girardi	.10	.05
❑ 61 Mark Kotsay	.15	.07
❑ 62 Eric Karros	.15	.07
❑ 63 Bartolo Colon	.15	.07
❑ 64 Mariano Rivera	.15	.07
❑ 65 Alex Gonzalez	.10	.05
❑ 66 Scott Spiezio	.10	.05
❑ 67 Luis Castillo	.10	.05
❑ 68 Joey Cora	.10	.05
❑ 69 Mark McLemore	.10	.05
❑ 70 Reggie Jefferson	.10	.05
❑ 71 Lance Johnson	.10	.05
❑ 72 Damian Jackson	.10	.05
❑ 73 Jeff D'Amico	.10	.05
❑ 74 David Ortiz	.15	.07
❑ 75 J.T. Snow	.15	.07
❑ 76 Todd Hundley	.10	.05
❑ 77 Billy Wagner	.10	.05
❑ 78 Vinny Castilla	.15	.07
❑ 79 Ismael Valdes	.10	.05
❑ 80 Neifi Perez	.10	.05
❑ 81 Derek Bell	.10	.05
❑ 82 Ryan Klesko	.15	.07
❑ 83 Rey Ordonez	.10	.05
❑ 84 Carlos Garcia	.10	.05
❑ 85 Curt Schilling	.40	.18
❑ 86 Robin Ventura	.15	.07
❑ 87 Pat Hentgen	.10	.05
❑ 88 Glendon Rusch	.10	.05
❑ 89 Hideki Irabu	.10	.05
❑ 90 Antone Williamson	.10	.05
❑ 91 Denny Neagle	.10	.05
❑ 92 Kevin Orie	.10	.05
❑ 93 Reggie Sanders	.10	.05
❑ 94 Brady Anderson	.15	.07
❑ 95 Andy Benes	.10	.05
❑ 96 John Valentin	.10	.05
❑ 97 Bobby Bonilla	.15	.07
❑ 98 Walt Weiss	.10	.05
❑ 99 Robin Jennings	.10	.05
❑ 100 Marty Cordova	.10	.05
❑ 101 Brad Ausmus	.10	.05
❑ 102 Brian Rose	.10	.05
❑ 103 Calvin Maduro	.10	.05
❑ 104 Raul Casanova	.10	.05
❑ 105 Jeff King	.10	.05
❑ 106 Sandy Alomar Jr.	.15	.07
❑ 107 Tim Naehring	.10	.05
❑ 108 Mike Cameron	.15	.07
❑ 109 Omar Vizquel	.15	.07
❑ 110 Brad Radke	.15	.07
❑ 111 Jeff Fassero	.10	.05
❑ 112 Deivi Cruz	.10	.05
❑ 113 Dave Hollins	.10	.05
❑ 114 Dean Palmer	.15	.07
❑ 115 Esteban Loaiza	.10	.05
❑ 116 Brian Giles	.15	.07
❑ 117 Steve Finley	.15	.07
❑ 118 Jose Canseco	.60	.25
❑ 119 Al Martin	.10	.05
❑ 120 Eric Young	.10	.05
❑ 121 Curtis Goodwin	.10	.05
❑ 122 Ellis Burks	.15	.07
❑ 123 Mike Hampton	.15	.07
❑ 124 Lou Collier	.10	.05
❑ 125 John Olerud	.15	.07
❑ 126 Ramon Martinez	.10	.05
❑ 127 Todd Dunwoody	.10	.05
❑ 128 Jermaine Allensworth	.10	.05
❑ 129 Eduardo Perez	.10	.05
❑ 130 Dante Bichette	.15	.07
❑ 131 Edgar Renteria	.10	.05
❑ 132 Bob Abreu	.15	.07
❑ 133 Rondell White	.15	.07
❑ 134 Michael Coleman	.10	.05
❑ 135 Jason Giambi	.40	.18
❑ 136 Brant Brown	.10	.05
❑ 137 Michael Tucker	.10	.05
❑ 138 Dave Nilsson	.10	.05
❑ 139 Benito Santiago	.10	.05
❑ 140 Ray Durham	.15	.07
❑ 141 Jeff Kent	.25	.11
❑ 142 Matt Stairs	.10	.05
❑ 143 Kevin Young	.15	.07
❑ 144 Eric Davis	.15	.07
❑ 145 John Wetteland	.15	.07
❑ 146 Esteban Yan RC	.25	.11

147	Wilton Guerrero	.10	.05
148	Moises Alou	.15	.07
149	Edgardo Alfonzo	.15	.07
150	Andy Ashby	.10	.05
151	Todd Walker	.10	.05
152	Jermaine Dye	.15	.07
153	Brian Hunter	.10	.05
154	Shawn Estes	.15	.07
155	Bernard Gilkey	.10	.05
156	Tony Womack	.10	.05
157	John Smoltz	.15	.07
158	Delino DeShields	.10	.05
159	Jacob Cruz	.10	.05
160	Javier Valentin	.10	.05
161	Chris Hoiles	.10	.05
162	Garret Anderson	.15	.07
163	Dan Wilson	.10	.05
164	Paul O'Neill	.40	.18
165	Matt Williams	.25	.11
166	Travis Fryman	.15	.07
167	Javier Lopez	.15	.07
168	Ray Lankford	.10	.05
169	Bobby Estalella	.10	.05
170	Henry Rodriguez	.10	.05
171	Quinton McCracken	.10	.05
172	Jaret Wright	.10	.05
173	Darryl Kile	.15	.07
174	Wade Boggs	.60	.25
175	Orel Hershiser	.15	.07
176	B.J. Surhoff	.15	.07
177	Fernando Tatis	.10	.05
178	Carlos Delgado	.40	.18
179	Jorge Fabregas	.10	.05
180	Tony Saunders	.10	.05
181	Devon White	.10	.05
182	Dmitri Young	.15	.07
183	Ryan McGuire	.10	.05
184	Mark Bellhorn	.10	.05
185	Joe Carter	.15	.07
186	Kevin Stocker	.10	.05
187	Mike Lansing	.10	.05
188	Jason Dickson	.10	.05
189	Charles Johnson	.15	.07
190	Will Clark	.40	.18
191	Shannon Stewart	.15	.07
192	Johnny Damon	.15	.07
193	Todd Greene	.10	.05
194	Carlos Baerga	.10	.05
195	David Cone	.15	.07
196	Pokey Reese	.10	.05
197	Livan Hernandez	.10	.05
198	Tom Glavine	.40	.18
199	Geronimo Berroa	.10	.05
200	Darryl Hamilton	.10	.05
201	Terry Steinbach	.10	.05
202	Robb Nen	.10	.05
203	Ron Gant	.15	.07
204	Rafael Palmeiro	.40	.18
205	Rickey Henderson	.75	.35
206	Justin Thompson	.10	.05
207	Jeff Suppan	.10	.05
208	Kevin Brown	.25	.11
209	Jimmy Key	.15	.07
210	Brian Jordan	.15	.07
211	Aaron Sele	.15	.07
212	Fred McGriff	.25	.11
213	Jay Bell	.15	.07
214	Andres Galarraga	.25	.11
215	Mark Grace	.40	.18
216	Brett Tomko	.10	.05
217	Francisco Cordova	.10	.05
218	Rusty Greer	.15	.07
219	Bubba Trammell	.10	.05
220	Derrek Lee	.15	.07
221	Brian Anderson	.10	.05
222	Mark Grudzielanek	.10	.05
223	Marquis Grissom	.10	.05
224	Gary DiSarcina	.10	.05
225	Jim Leyritz	.10	.05
226	Jeffrey Hammonds	.10	.05
227	Karim Garcia	.10	.05
228	Chan Ho Park	.15	.07
229	Brooks Kieschnick	.10	.05
230	Trey Beamon	.10	.05
231	Kevin Appier	.15	.07
232	Wally Joyner	.15	.07
233	Richie Sexson	.15	.07
234	Frank Catalanotto RC	.40	.18
235	Rafael Medina	.10	.05
236	Travis Lee	.15	.07
237	Eli Marrero	.10	.05
238	Carl Pavano	.10	.05
239	Enrique Wilson	.10	.05
240	Richard Hidalgo	.15	.07
241	Todd Helton	.50	.23
242	Ben Grieve	.15	.07
243	Mario Valdez	.10	.05
244	Magglio Ordonez RC	1.25	.55
245	Juan Encarnacion	.15	.07
246	Russell Branyan	.15	.07
247	Sean Casey	.25	.11
248	Abraham Nunez	.10	.05
249	Brad Fullmer	.15	.07
250	Paul Konerko	.15	.07
251	Miguel Tejada	.25	.11
252	Mike Lowell RC	.50	.23
253	Ken Griffey Jr. ST	.60	.25
254	Frank Thomas ST	.25	.11
255	Alex Rodriguez ST	.50	.23
256	Jose Cruz Jr. ST	.10	.05
257	Jeff Bagwell ST	.25	.11
258	Chipper Jones ST	.40	.18
259	Mo Vaughn ST	.15	.07
260	Nomar Garciaparra ST	.50	.23
261	Jim Thome ST	.15	.07
262	Derek Jeter ST	.75	.35
263	Mike Piazza ST	.50	.23
264	Tony Gwynn ST	.40	.18
265	Scott Rolen ST	.40	.18
266	Andruw Jones ST	.15	.07
267	Cal Ripken ST	.75	.35
268	Checklist 1	.10	.05
269	Checklist 2	.10	.05
270	Checklist 3	.10	.05
S250	Paul Konerko AU500	10.00	4.50

1993 SP

	MINT	NRMT
COMPLETE SET (290)	150.00	70.00
COMMON CARD (1-270)	.40	.18
FOIL PROSPECTS (271-290)	1.00	.45

1	Roberto Alomar AS	1.50	.70
2	Wade Boggs AS	1.50	.70
3	Joe Carter AS	.40	.18
4	Ken Griffey Jr. AS	5.00	2.20
5	Mark Langston AS	.40	.18
6	John Olerud AS	.60	.25
7	Kirby Puckett AS	4.00	1.80
8	Cal Ripken Jr. AS	6.00	2.70
9	Ivan Rodriguez AS	1.50	.70
10	Barry Bonds AS	4.00	1.80
11	Darren Daulton AS	.60	.25
12	Marquis Grissom AS	.40	.18
13	David Justice AS	.60	.25
14	John Kruk AS	.60	.25
15	Barry Larkin AS	1.50	.70
16	Terry Mulholland AS	.40	.18
17	Ryne Sandberg AS	2.00	.90
18	Gary Sheffield AS	.60	.25
19	Chad Curtis	.40	.18
20	Chili Davis	.60	.25
21	Gary DiSarcina	.40	.18
22	Damion Easley	.40	.18
23	Chuck Finley	.60	.25
24	Luis Polonia	.40	.18
25	Tim Salmon	.60	.25
26	J.T. Snow RC	2.00	.90
27	Russ Springer	.40	.18
28	Jeff Bagwell	2.00	.90
29	Craig Biggio	1.00	.45
30	Ken Caminiti	.60	.25
31	Andujar Cedeno	.40	.18
32	Doug Drabek	.40	.18
33	Steve Finley	.60	.25
34	Luis Gonzalez	1.50	.70
35	Pete Harnisch	.40	.18
36	Darryl Kile	.60	.25
37	Mike Bordick	.40	.18
38	Dennis Eckersley	.60	.25
39	Brent Gates	.40	.18
40	Rickey Henderson	3.00	1.35
41	Mark McGwire	6.00	2.70
42	Craig Paquette	.40	.18
43	Ruben Sierra	.40	.18
44	Terry Steinbach	.40	.18
45	Todd Van Poppel	.40	.18
46	Pat Borders	.40	.18
47	Tony Fernandez	.40	.18
48	Juan Guzman	.40	.18
49	Pat Hentgen	.40	.18
50	Paul Molitor	1.50	.70
51	Jack Morris	.60	.25
52	Ed Sprague	.40	.18
53	Duane Ward	.40	.18
54	Devon White	.40	.18
55	Steve Avery	.40	.18
56	Jeff Blauser	.40	.18
57	Ron Gant	.40	.18
58	Tom Glavine	1.50	.70
59	Greg Maddux	4.00	1.80
60	Fred McGriff	1.00	.45
61	Terry Pendleton	.60	.25
62	Deion Sanders	.60	.25
63	John Smoltz	.60	.25
64	Cal Eldred	.40	.18
65	Darryl Hamilton	.40	.18
66	John Jaha	.40	.18
67	Pat Listach	.40	.18
68	Jaime Navarro	.40	.18
69	Kevin Reimer	.40	.18
70	B.J. Surhoff	.60	.25
71	Greg Vaughn	.60	.25
72	Robin Yount	1.50	.70
73	Rene Arocha RC	.60	.25
74	Bernard Gilkey	.40	.18
75	Gregg Jefferies	.40	.18
76	Ray Lankford	.40	.18
77	Tom Pagnozzi	.40	.18
78	Lee Smith	.60	.25
79	Ozzie Smith	2.00	.90
80	Bob Tewksbury	.40	.18
81	Mark Whiten	.40	.18
82	Steve Buechele	.40	.18
83	Mark Grace	1.50	.70
84	Jose Guzman	.40	.18
85	Derrick May	.40	.18
86	Mike Morgan	.40	.18
87	Randy Myers	.40	.18
88	Kevin Roberson RC	.40	.18
89	Sammy Sosa	3.00	1.35
90	Rick Wilkins	.40	.18
91	Brett Butler	.60	.25
92	Eric Davis	.60	.25
93	Orel Hershiser	.60	.25
94	Eric Karros	.60	.25
95	Ramon Martinez	.40	.18
96	Raul Mondesi	.60	.25
97	Jose Offerman	.40	.18
98	Mike Piazza	8.00	3.60
99	Darryl Strawberry	.60	.25
100	Moises Alou	.60	.25
101	Wil Cordero	.40	.18
102	Delino DeShields	.40	.18
103	Darrin Fletcher	.40	.18
104	Ken Hill	.40	.18
105	Mike Lansing RC	.60	.25
106	Dennis Martinez	.60	.25
107	Larry Walker	1.00	.45

❑ 108 John Wetteland .60 .25
❑ 109 Rod Beck .40 .18
❑ 110 John Burkett .40 .18
❑ 111 Will Clark 1.50 .70
❑ 112 Royce Clayton .40 .18
❑ 113 Darren Lewis .40 .18
❑ 114 Willie McGee .60 .25
❑ 115 Bill Swift .40 .18
❑ 116 Robby Thompson .40 .18
❑ 117 Matt Williams 1.00 .45
❑ 118 Sandy Alomar Jr. .60 .25
❑ 119 Carlos Baerga .40 .18
❑ 120 Albert Belle .60 .25
❑ 121 Reggie Jefferson .40 .18
❑ 122 Wayne Kirby .40 .18
❑ 123 Kenny Lofton .60 .25
❑ 124 Carlos Martinez .40 .18
❑ 125 Charles Nagy .40 .18
❑ 126 Paul Sorrento .40 .18
❑ 127 Rich Amaral .40 .18
❑ 128 Jay Buhner .60 .25
❑ 129 Norm Charlton .40 .18
❑ 130 Dave Fleming .40 .18
❑ 131 Erik Hanson .40 .18
❑ 132 Randy Johnson 2.00 .90
❑ 133 Edgar Martinez 1.00 .45
❑ 134 Tino Martinez .60 .25
❑ 135 Omar Vizquel .60 .25
❑ 136 Bret Barberie .40 .18
❑ 137 Chuck Carr .40 .18
❑ 138 Jeff Conine .40 .18
❑ 139 Orestes Destrade .40 .18
❑ 140 Chris Hammond .40 .18
❑ 141 Bryan Harvey .40 .18
❑ 142 Benito Santiago .40 .18
❑ 143 Walt Weiss .40 .18
❑ 144 Darrell Whitmore RC .40 .18
❑ 145 Tim Bogar RC .40 .18
❑ 146 Bobby Bonilla .60 .25
❑ 147 Jeromy Burnitz .60 .25
❑ 148 Vince Coleman .40 .18
❑ 149 Dwight Gooden .60 .25
❑ 150 Todd Hundley .40 .18
❑ 151 Howard Johnson .40 .18
❑ 152 Eddie Murray 1.50 .70
❑ 153 Bret Saberhagen .60 .25
❑ 154 Brady Anderson .60 .25
❑ 155 Mike Devereaux .40 .18
❑ 156 Jeffrey Hammonds .60 .25
❑ 157 Chris Hoiles .40 .18
❑ 158 Ben McDonald .40 .18
❑ 159 Mark McLemore .40 .18
❑ 160 Mike Mussina 1.50 .70
❑ 161 Gregg Olson .40 .18
❑ 162 David Segui .40 .18
❑ 163 Derek Bell .40 .18
❑ 164 Andy Benes .40 .18
❑ 165 Archi Cianfrocco .40 .18
❑ 166 Ricky Gutierrez .40 .18
❑ 167 Tony Gwynn 3.00 1.35
❑ 168 Gene Harris .40 .18
❑ 169 Trevor Hoffman .60 .25
❑ 170 Ray McDavid RC .40 .18
❑ 171 Phil Plantier .40 .18
❑ 172 Mariano Duncan .40 .18
❑ 173 Len Dykstra .60 .25
❑ 174 Tommy Greene .40 .18
❑ 175 Dave Hollins .40 .18
❑ 176 Pete Incaviglia .40 .18
❑ 177 Mickey Morandini .40 .18
❑ 178 Curt Schilling 1.50 .70
❑ 179 Kevin Stocker .40 .18
❑ 180 Mitch Williams .40 .18
❑ 181 Stan Belinda .40 .18
❑ 182 Jay Bell .60 .25
❑ 183 Steve Cooke .40 .18
❑ 184 Carlos Garcia .40 .18
❑ 185 Jeff King .40 .18
❑ 186 Orlando Merced .40 .18
❑ 187 Don Slaught .40 .18
❑ 188 Andy Van Slyke .60 .25
❑ 189 Kevin Young .60 .25
❑ 190 Kevin Brown .60 .25
❑ 191 Jose Canseco 1.50 .70
❑ 192 Julio Franco .60 .25
❑ 193 Benji Gil .40 .18
❑ 194 Juan Gonzalez 1.50 .70
❑ 195 Tom Henke .40 .18
❑ 196 Rafael Palmeiro 1.50 .70
❑ 197 Dean Palmer .60 .25
❑ 198 Nolan Ryan 8.00 3.60
❑ 199 Roger Clemens 4.00 1.80
❑ 200 Scott Cooper .40 .18
❑ 201 Andre Dawson 1.00 .45
❑ 202 Mike Greenwell .40 .18
❑ 203 Carlos Quintana .40 .18
❑ 204 Jeff Russell .40 .18
❑ 205 Aaron Sele .60 .25
❑ 206 Mo Vaughn .60 .25
❑ 207 Frank Viola .60 .25
❑ 208 Rob Dibble .40 .18
❑ 209 Roberto Kelly .40 .18
❑ 210 Kevin Mitchell .40 .18
❑ 211 Hal Morris .40 .18
❑ 212 Joe Oliver .40 .18
❑ 213 Jose Rijo .40 .18
❑ 214 Bip Roberts .40 .18
❑ 215 Chris Sabo .40 .18
❑ 216 Reggie Sanders .40 .18
❑ 217 Dante Bichette .60 .25
❑ 218 Jerald Clark .40 .18
❑ 219 Alex Cole .40 .18
❑ 220 Andres Galarraga 1.00 .45
❑ 221 Joe Girardi .40 .18
❑ 222 Charlie Hayes .40 .18
❑ 223 Roberto Mejia RC .40 .18
❑ 224 Armando Reynoso .40 .18
❑ 225 Eric Young .40 .18
❑ 226 Kevin Appier .60 .25
❑ 227 George Brett 3.00 1.35
❑ 228 David Cone .60 .25
❑ 229 Phil Hiatt .40 .18
❑ 230 Felix Jose .40 .18
❑ 231 Wally Joyner .60 .25
❑ 232 Mike Macfarlane .40 .18
❑ 233 Brian McRae .40 .18
❑ 234 Jeff Montgomery .40 .18
❑ 235 Rob Deer .40 .18
❑ 236 Cecil Fielder .60 .25
❑ 237 Travis Fryman .60 .25
❑ 238 Mike Henneman .40 .18
❑ 239 Tony Phillips .40 .18
❑ 240 Mickey Tettleton .40 .18
❑ 241 Alan Trammell 1.00 .45
❑ 242 David Wells .60 .25
❑ 243 Lou Whitaker .60 .25
❑ 244 Rick Aguilera .40 .18
❑ 245 Scott Erickson .40 .18
❑ 246 Brian Harper .40 .18
❑ 247 Kent Hrbek .60 .25
❑ 248 Chuck Knoblauch .60 .25
❑ 249 Shane Mack .40 .18
❑ 250 David McCarty .40 .18
❑ 251 Pedro Munoz .40 .18
❑ 252 Dave Winfield 1.50 .70
❑ 253 Alex Fernandez .40 .18
❑ 254 Ozzie Guillen .40 .18
❑ 255 Bo Jackson .60 .25
❑ 256 Lance Johnson .40 .18
❑ 257 Ron Karkovice .40 .18
❑ 258 Jack McDowell .40 .18
❑ 259 Tim Raines .60 .25
❑ 260 Frank Thomas 2.00 .90
❑ 261 Robin Ventura .60 .25
❑ 262 Jim Abbott .60 .25
❑ 263 Steve Farr .40 .18
❑ 264 Jimmy Key .60 .25
❑ 265 Don Mattingly 4.00 1.80
❑ 266 Paul O'Neill 1.50 .70
❑ 267 Mike Stanley .40 .18
❑ 268 Danny Tartabull .40 .18
❑ 269 Bob Wickman .40 .18
❑ 270 Bernie Williams 1.50 .70
❑ 271 Jason Bere FOIL 1.00 .45
❑ 272 R.Cedeno FOIL RC 2.00 .90
❑ 273 J.Damon FOIL RC 8.00 3.60
❑ 274 Russ Davis FOIL RC 2.00 .90
❑ 275 Carlos Delgado FOIL 5.00 2.20
❑ 276 Carl Everett FOIL 2.00 .90
❑ 277 Cliff Floyd FOIL 2.00 .90
❑ 278 Alex Gonzalez FOIL 1.00 .45
❑ 279 Derek Jeter FOIL RC 120.00 55.00
❑ 280 Chipper Jones FOIL 5.00 2.20
❑ 281 Javier Lopez FOIL 2.00 .90
❑ 282 Chad Mottola FOIL RC 1.00 .45
❑ 283 Marc Newfield FOIL 1.00 .45
❑ 284 Eduardo Perez FOIL 1.00 .45
❑ 285 Manny Ramirez FOIL 8.00 3.60
❑ 286 T.Steverson FOIL RC 1.00 .45
❑ 287 Michael Tucker FOIL 1.00 .45
❑ 288 Allen Watson FOIL 1.00 .45
❑ 289 Rondell White FOIL 2.00 .90
❑ 290 Dmitri Young FOIL 2.00 .90

1994 SP

	MINT	NRMT
COMPLETE SET (200)	120.00	55.00
COMMON FOIL (1-20)	.50	.23
COMMON CARD (21-200)	.20	.09

❑ 1 Mike Bell FOIL RC .50 .23
❑ 2 D.J. Boston FOIL RC .50 .23
❑ 3 Johnny Damon FOIL .75 .35
❑ 4 Brad Fullmer FOIL RC 4.00 1.80
❑ 5 Joey Hamilton FOIL .50 .23
❑ 6 T.Hollandsworth FOIL .50 .23
❑ 7 Brian L. Hunter FOIL .50 .23
❑ 8 L.Hawkins FOIL RC .75 .35
❑ 9 B.Kieschnick FOIL RC .50 .23
❑ 10 Derrek Lee FOIL RC 2.00 .90
❑ 11 Trot Nixon FOIL RC 5.00 2.20
❑ 12 Alex Ochoa FOIL .50 .23
❑ 13 Chan Ho Park FOIL RC 5.00 2.20
❑ 14 Kirk Presley FOIL RC .50 .23
❑ 15 A.Rodriguez FOIL RC 80.00 36.00
❑ 16 Jose Silva FOIL RC .50 .23
❑ 17 Terrell Wade FOIL RC .50 .23
❑ 18 Billy Wagner FOIL RC 2.00 .90
❑ 19 G.Williams FOIL RC .50 .23
❑ 20 Preston Wilson FOIL 2.00 .90
❑ 21 Brian Anderson RC .30 .14
❑ 22 Chad Curtis .20 .09
❑ 23 Chili Davis .30 .14
❑ 24 Bo Jackson .30 .14
❑ 25 Mark Langston .20 .09
❑ 26 Tim Salmon .30 .14
❑ 27 Jeff Bagwell 1.00 .45
❑ 28 Craig Biggio .50 .23
❑ 29 Ken Caminiti .30 .14
❑ 30 Doug Drabek .20 .09
❑ 31 John Hudek RC .20 .09
❑ 32 Greg Swindell .20 .09
❑ 33 Brent Gates .20 .09
❑ 34 Rickey Henderson 1.50 .70
❑ 35 Steve Karsay .20 .09
❑ 36 Mark McGwire 3.00 1.35
❑ 37 Ruben Sierra .20 .09
❑ 38 Terry Steinbach .20 .09
❑ 39 Roberto Alomar .75 .35
❑ 40 Joe Carter .30 .14
❑ 41 Carlos Delgado 1.25 .55
❑ 42 Alex Gonzalez .20 .09
❑ 43 Juan Guzman .20 .09
❑ 44 Paul Molitor .75 .35
❑ 45 John Olerud .30 .14
❑ 46 Devon White .20 .09
❑ 47 Steve Avery .20 .09
❑ 48 Jeff Blauser .20 .09
❑ 49 Tom Glavine .75 .35

No.	Player	MINT	NRMT
50	David Justice	.30	.14
51	Roberto Kelly	.20	.09
52	Ryan Klesko	.30	.14
53	Javier Lopez	.30	.14
54	Greg Maddux	2.00	.90
55	Fred McGriff	.50	.23
56	Ricky Bones	.20	.09
57	Cal Eldred	.20	.09
58	Brian Harper	.20	.09
59	Pat Listach	.20	.09
60	B.J. Surhoff	.30	.14
61	Greg Vaughn	.30	.14
62	Bernard Gilkey	.20	.09
63	Gregg Jefferies	.20	.09
64	Ray Lankford	.20	.09
65	Ozzie Smith	1.00	.45
66	Bob Tewksbury	.20	.09
67	Mark Whiten	.20	.09
68	Todd Zeile	.20	.09
69	Mark Grace	.75	.35
70	Randy Myers	.20	.09
71	Ryne Sandberg	1.00	.45
72	Sammy Sosa	1.50	.70
73	Steve Trachsel	.20	.09
74	Rick Wilkins	.20	.09
75	Brett Butler	.30	.14
76	Delino DeShields	.20	.09
77	Orel Hershiser	.30	.14
78	Eric Karros	.30	.14
79	Raul Mondesi	.30	.14
80	Mike Piazza	2.50	1.10
81	Tim Wallach	.20	.09
82	Moises Alou	.30	.14
83	Cliff Floyd	.30	.14
84	Marquis Grissom	.20	.09
85	Pedro Martinez	1.25	.55
86	Larry Walker	.50	.23
87	John Wetteland	.30	.14
88	Rondell White	.30	.14
89	Rod Beck	.20	.09
90	Barry Bonds	2.00	.90
91	John Burkett	.20	.09
92	Royce Clayton	.20	.09
93	Billy Swift	.20	.09
94	Robby Thompson	.20	.09
95	Matt Williams	.50	.23
96	Carlos Baerga	.20	.09
97	Albert Belle	.30	.14
98	Kenny Lofton	.30	.14
99	Dennis Martinez	.30	.14
100	Eddie Murray	.75	.35
101	Manny Ramirez	1.25	.55
102	Eric Anthony	.20	.09
103	Chris Bosio	.20	.09
104	Jay Buhner	.30	.14
105	Ken Griffey Jr.	2.50	1.10
106	Randy Johnson	1.00	.45
107	Edgar Martinez	.50	.23
108	Chuck Carr	.20	.09
109	Jeff Conine	.20	.09
110	Carl Everett	.30	.14
111	Chris Hammond	.20	.09
112	Bryan Harvey	.20	.09
113	Charles Johnson	.30	.14
114	Gary Sheffield	.30	.14
115	Bobby Bonilla	.30	.14
116	Dwight Gooden	.30	.14
117	Todd Hundley	.20	.09
118	Bobby Jones	.20	.09
119	Jeff Kent	.50	.23
120	Bret Saberhagen	.30	.14
121	Jeffrey Hammonds	.30	.14
122	Chris Hoiles	.20	.09
123	Ben McDonald	.20	.09
124	Mike Mussina	.75	.35
125	Rafael Palmeiro	.75	.35
126	Cal Ripken Jr.	3.00	1.35
127	Lee Smith	.30	.14
128	Derek Bell	.20	.09
129	Andy Benes	.20	.09
130	Tony Gwynn	1.50	.70
131	Trevor Hoffman	.30	.14
132	Phil Plantier	.20	.09
133	Bip Roberts	.20	.09
134	Darren Daulton	.30	.14
135	Lenny Dykstra	.30	.14
136	Dave Hollins	.20	.09
137	Danny Jackson	.20	.09
138	John Kruk	.30	.14
139	Kevin Stocker	.20	.09
140	Jay Bell	.30	.14
141	Carlos Garcia	.20	.09
142	Jeff King	.20	.09
143	Orlando Merced	.20	.09
144	Andy Van Slyke	.30	.14
145	Rick White	.20	.09
146	Jose Canseco	.75	.35
147	Will Clark	.75	.35
148	Juan Gonzalez	.75	.35
149	Rick Helling	.20	.09
150	Dean Palmer	.30	.14
151	Ivan Rodriguez	.75	.35
152	Roger Clemens	2.00	.90
153	Scott Cooper	.20	.09
154	Andre Dawson	.50	.23
155	Mike Greenwell	.20	.09
156	Aaron Sele	.30	.14
157	Mo Vaughn	.30	.14
158	Bret Boone	.30	.14
159	Barry Larkin	.75	.35
160	Kevin Mitchell	.20	.09
161	Jose Rijo	.20	.09
162	Deion Sanders	.30	.14
163	Reggie Sanders	.20	.09
164	Dante Bichette	.30	.14
165	Ellis Burks	.30	.14
166	Andres Galarraga	.50	.23
167	Charlie Hayes	.20	.09
168	David Nied	.20	.09
169	Walt Weiss	.20	.09
170	Kevin Appier	.30	.14
171	David Cone	.30	.14
172	Jeff Granger	.20	.09
173	Felix Jose	.20	.09
174	Wally Joyner	.30	.14
175	Brian McRae	.20	.09
176	Cecil Fielder	.30	.14
177	Travis Fryman	.30	.14
178	Mike Henneman	.20	.09
179	Tony Phillips	.20	.09
180	Mickey Tettleton	.20	.09
181	Alan Trammell	.50	.23
182	Rick Aguilera	.20	.09
183	Rich Becker	.20	.09
184	Scott Erickson	.20	.09
185	Chuck Knoblauch	.30	.14
186	Kirby Puckett	2.00	.90
187	Dave Winfield	.75	.35
188	Wilson Alvarez	.20	.09
189	Jason Bere	.20	.09
190	Alex Fernandez	.20	.09
191	Julio Franco	.30	.14
192	Jack McDowell	.20	.09
193	Frank Thomas	1.00	.45
194	Robin Ventura	.30	.14
195	Jim Abbott	.30	.14
196	Wade Boggs	.75	.35
197	Jimmy Key	.30	.14
198	Don Mattingly	2.00	.90
199	Paul O'Neill	.75	.35
200	Danny Tartabull	.20	.09
P24	Ken Griffey Jr. Promo	2.50	1.10

1995 SP

	MINT	NRMT
COMPLETE SET (207)	40.00	18.00
COMMON CARD (1-207)	.20	.09
FOIL PROSPECTS (5-24)	.25	.11

No.	Player	MINT	NRMT
1	Cal Ripken Salute	3.00	1.35
2	Nolan Ryan Salute	4.00	1.80
3	George Brett Salute	1.50	.70
4	Mike Schmidt Salute	1.25	.55
5	Dustin Hermanson FOIL	.25	.11
6	Antonio Osuna FOIL	.25	.11
7	M.Grudzielanek FOIL RC	.30	.14
8	Ray Durham FOIL	.30	.14
9	Ugueth Urbina FOIL	.25	.11
10	Ruben Rivera FOIL	.25	.11
11	Curtis Goodwin FOIL	.25	.11
12	Jimmy Hurst FOIL	.25	.11
13	Jose Malave FOIL	.25	.11
14	Hideo Nomo FOIL RC	3.00	1.35
15	Juan Acevedo RC FOIL	.25	.11
16	Tony Clark FOIL	.30	.14
17	Jim Pittsley FOIL	.25	.11
18	Freddy A. Garcia RC FOIL	.25	.11
19	Carlos Perez RC FOIL	.30	.14
20	R.Casanova FOIL RC	.25	.11
21	Quilvio Veras FOIL	.25	.11
22	Edgardo Alfonzo FOIL	.75	.35
23	Marty Cordova FOIL	.25	.11
24	C.J. Nitkowski FOIL	.25	.11
25	Wade Boggs CL	.30	.14
26	Dave Winfield CL	.30	.14
27	Eddie Murray CL	.30	.14
28	David Justice	.30	.14
29	Marquis Grissom	.20	.09
30	Fred McGriff	.50	.23
31	Greg Maddux	2.00	.90
32	Tom Glavine	.75	.35
33	Steve Avery	.20	.09
34	Chipper Jones	1.50	.70
35	Sammy Sosa	1.50	.70
36	Jaime Navarro	.20	.09
37	Randy Myers	.20	.09
38	Mark Grace	.75	.35
39	Todd Zeile	.20	.09
40	Brian McRae	.20	.09
41	Reggie Sanders	.20	.09
42	Ron Gant	.20	.09
43	Deion Sanders	.30	.14
44	Bret Boone	.30	.14
45	Barry Larkin	.75	.35
46	Jose Rijo	.20	.09
47	Jason Bates	.20	.09
48	Andres Galarraga	.50	.23
49	Bill Swift	.20	.09
50	Larry Walker	.50	.23
51	Vinny Castilla	.30	.14
52	Dante Bichette	.30	.14
53	Jeff Conine	.20	.09
54	John Burkett	.20	.09
55	Gary Sheffield	.30	.14
56	Andre Dawson	.50	.23
57	Terry Pendleton	.30	.14
58	Charles Johnson	.30	.14
59	Brian L. Hunter	.20	.09
60	Jeff Bagwell	1.00	.45
61	Craig Biggio	.50	.23
62	Phil Nevin	.30	.14
63	Doug Drabek	.20	.09
64	Derek Bell	.20	.09
65	Raul Mondesi	.30	.14
66	Eric Karros	.30	.14
67	Roger Cedeno	.20	.09
68	Delino DeShields	.20	.09
69	Ramon Martinez	.20	.09
70	Mike Piazza	2.00	.90
71	Billy Ashley	.20	.09
72	Jeff Fassero	.20	.09
73	Shane Andrews	.20	.09
74	Wil Cordero	.20	.09
75	Tony Tarasco	.20	.09
76	Rondell White	.30	.14
77	Pedro Martinez	1.00	.45
78	Moises Alou	.30	.14
79	Rico Brogna	.20	.09
80	Bobby Bonilla	.30	.14
81	Jeff Kent	.50	.23

❑ 82 Brett Butler .30 .14
❑ 83 Bobby Jones .20 .09
❑ 84 Bill Pulsipher .20 .09
❑ 85 Bret Saberhagen .30 .14
❑ 86 Gregg Jefferies .20 .09
❑ 87 Lenny Dykstra .30 .14
❑ 88 Dave Hollins .20 .09
❑ 89 Charlie Hayes .20 .09
❑ 90 Darren Daulton .30 .14
❑ 91 Curt Schilling .75 .35
❑ 92 Heathcliff Slocumb .20 .09
❑ 93 Carlos Garcia .20 .09
❑ 94 Denny Neagle .30 .14
❑ 95 Jay Bell .30 .14
❑ 96 Orlando Merced .20 .09
❑ 97 Dave Clark .20 .09
❑ 98 Bernard Gilkey .20 .09
❑ 99 Scott Cooper .20 .09
❑ 100 Ozzie Smith 1.00 .45
❑ 101 Tom Henke .20 .09
❑ 102 Ken Hill .20 .09
❑ 103 Brian Jordan .30 .14
❑ 104 Ray Lankford .20 .09
❑ 105 Tony Gwynn 1.50 .70
❑ 106 Andy Benes .20 .09
❑ 107 Ken Caminiti .30 .14
❑ 108 Steve Finley .30 .14
❑ 109 Joey Hamilton .20 .09
❑ 110 Bip Roberts .20 .09
❑ 111 Eddie Williams .20 .09
❑ 112 Rod Beck .20 .09
❑ 113 Matt Williams .50 .23
❑ 114 Glenallen Hill .20 .09
❑ 115 Barry Bonds 2.00 .90
❑ 116 Robby Thompson .20 .09
❑ 117 Mark Portugal .20 .09
❑ 118 Brady Anderson .30 .14
❑ 119 Mike Mussina .75 .35
❑ 120 Rafael Palmeiro .75 .35
❑ 121 Chris Hoiles .20 .09
❑ 122 Harold Baines .30 .14
❑ 123 Jeffrey Hammonds .20 .09
❑ 124 Tim Naehring .20 .09
❑ 125 Mo Vaughn .30 .14
❑ 126 Mike Macfarlane .20 .09
❑ 127 Roger Clemens 2.00 .90
❑ 128 John Valentin .20 .09
❑ 129 Aaron Sele .30 .14
❑ 130 Jose Canseco .75 .35
❑ 131 J.T. Snow .30 .14
❑ 132 Mark Langston .20 .09
❑ 133 Chili Davis .30 .14
❑ 134 Chuck Finley .30 .14
❑ 135 Tim Salmon .30 .14
❑ 136 Tony Phillips .20 .09
❑ 137 Jason Bere .20 .09
❑ 138 Robin Ventura .30 .14
❑ 139 Tim Raines .30 .14
❑ 140 Frank Thomas COR 1.00 .45
❑ 140A Frank Thomas ERR 5.00 2.20
❑ 141 Alex Fernandez .20 .09
❑ 142 Jim Abbott .30 .14
❑ 143 Wilson Alvarez .20 .09
❑ 144 Carlos Baerga .20 .09
❑ 145 Albert Belle .30 .14
❑ 146 Jim Thome .75 .35
❑ 147 Dennis Martinez .30 .14
❑ 148 Eddie Murray .75 .35
❑ 149 Dave Winfield .75 .35
❑ 150 Kenny Lofton .50 .23
❑ 151 Manny Ramirez 1.00 .45
❑ 152 Chad Curtis .20 .09
❑ 153 Lou Whitaker .30 .14
❑ 154 Alan Trammell .50 .23
❑ 155 Cecil Fielder .30 .14
❑ 156 Kirk Gibson .30 .14
❑ 157 Michael Tucker .20 .09
❑ 158 Jon Nunnally .20 .09
❑ 159 Wally Joyner .30 .14
❑ 160 Kevin Appier .30 .14
❑ 161 Jeff Montgomery .20 .09
❑ 162 Greg Gagne .20 .09
❑ 163 Ricky Bones .20 .09
❑ 164 Cal Eldred .20 .09
❑ 165 Greg Vaughn .30 .14
❑ 166 Kevin Seitzer .20 .09
❑ 167 Jose Valentin .20 .09
❑ 168 Joe Oliver .20 .09
❑ 169 Rick Aguilera .20 .09
❑ 170 Kirby Puckett 2.00 .90
❑ 171 Scott Stahoviak .20 .09
❑ 172 Kevin Tapani .20 .09
❑ 173 Chuck Knoblauch .30 .14
❑ 174 Rich Becker .20 .09
❑ 175 Don Mattingly 2.00 .90
❑ 176 Jack McDowell .20 .09
❑ 177 Jimmy Key .30 .14
❑ 178 Paul O'Neill .75 .35
❑ 179 John Wetteland .30 .14
❑ 180 Wade Boggs .75 .35
❑ 181 Derek Jeter 3.00 1.35
❑ 182 Rickey Henderson 1.50 .70
❑ 183 Terry Steinbach .20 .09
❑ 184 Ruben Sierra .20 .09
❑ 185 Mark McGwire 3.00 1.35
❑ 186 Todd Stottlemyre .20 .09
❑ 187 Dennis Eckersley .30 .14
❑ 188 Alex Rodriguez 2.50 1.10
❑ 189 Randy Johnson 1.00 .45
❑ 190 Ken Griffey Jr. 2.50 1.10
❑ 191 Tino Martinez UER .30 .14
Mike Blowers pictured on back
❑ 192 Jay Buhner .30 .14
❑ 193 Edgar Martinez .50 .23
❑ 194 Mickey Tettleton .20 .09
❑ 195 Juan Gonzalez .75 .35
❑ 196 Benji Gil .20 .09
❑ 197 Dean Palmer .30 .14
❑ 198 Ivan Rodriguez .75 .35
❑ 199 Kenny Rogers .20 .09
❑ 200 Will Clark .75 .35
❑ 201 Roberto Alomar .75 .35
❑ 202 David Cone .30 .14
❑ 203 Paul Molitor .75 .35
❑ 204 Shawn Green .75 .35
❑ 205 Joe Carter .30 .14
❑ 206 Alex Gonzalez .20 .09
❑ 207 Pat Hentgen .20 .09
❑ P100 K.Griffey Jr. Promo 3.00 1.35
❑ AU190 Ken Griffey Jr. AU 200.00 90.00

1996 SP

	MINT	NRMT
COMPLETE SET (188)	40.00	18.00

❑ 1 Rey Ordonez FOIL .20 .09
❑ 2 George Arias FOIL .20 .09
❑ 3 Osvaldo Fernandez FOIL .20 .09
❑ 4 Darin Erstad FOIL RC 10.00 4.50
❑ 5 Paul Wilson FOIL .20 .09
❑ 6 Richard Hidalgo FOIL .30 .14
❑ 7 Justin Thompson FOIL .20 .09
❑ 8 Jimmy Haynes FOIL .20 .09
❑ 9 Edgar Renteria FOIL .20 .09
❑ 10 Ruben Rivera FOIL .20 .09
❑ 11 Chris Snopek FOIL .20 .09
❑ 12 Billy Wagner FOIL .20 .09
❑ 13 Mike Grace FOIL RC .20 .09
❑ 14 Todd Greene FOIL .20 .09
❑ 15 Karim Garcia FOIL .20 .09
❑ 16 John Wasdin FOIL .20 .09
❑ 17 Jason Kendall FOIL .30 .14
❑ 18 Bob Abreu FOIL .75 .35
❑ 19 Jermaine Dye FOIL .30 .14
❑ 20 Jason Schmidt FOIL .20 .09
❑ 21 Javy Lopez .30 .14
❑ 22 Ryan Klesko .30 .14
❑ 23 Tom Glavine .75 .35
❑ 24 John Smoltz .30 .14
❑ 25 Greg Maddux 2.00 .90
❑ 26 Chipper Jones 1.50 .70
❑ 27 Fred McGriff .50 .23
❑ 28 David Justice .30 .14
❑ 29 Roberto Alomar .75 .35
❑ 30 Cal Ripken 3.00 1.35
❑ 31 B.J. Surhoff .20 .09
❑ 32 Bobby Bonilla .30 .14
❑ 33 Mike Mussina .75 .35
❑ 34 Randy Myers .20 .09
❑ 35 Rafael Palmeiro .75 .35
❑ 36 Brady Anderson .30 .14
❑ 37 Tim Naehring .20 .09
❑ 38 Jose Canseco .75 .35
❑ 39 Roger Clemens 2.00 .90
❑ 40 Mo Vaughn .30 .14
❑ 41 Jose Valentin .20 .09
❑ 42 Kevin Mitchell .20 .09
❑ 43 Chili Davis .30 .14
❑ 44 Garret Anderson .30 .14
❑ 45 Tim Salmon .30 .14
❑ 46 Chuck Finley .30 .14
❑ 47 Troy Percival .20 .09
❑ 48 Jim Abbott .30 .14
❑ 49 J.T. Snow .30 .14
❑ 50 Jim Edmonds .50 .23
❑ 51 Sammy Sosa 1.50 .70
❑ 52 Brian McRae .20 .09
❑ 53 Ryne Sandberg 1.00 .45
❑ 54 Jaime Navarro .20 .09
❑ 55 Mark Grace .50 .23
❑ 56 Harold Baines .30 .14
❑ 57 Robin Ventura .30 .14
❑ 58 Tony Phillips .20 .09
❑ 59 Alex Fernandez .20 .09
❑ 60 Frank Thomas 1.00 .45
❑ 61 Ray Durham .30 .14
❑ 62 Bret Boone .30 .14
❑ 63 Reggie Sanders .20 .09
❑ 64 Pete Schourek .20 .09
❑ 65 Barry Larkin .75 .35
❑ 66 John Smiley .20 .09
❑ 67 Carlos Baerga .20 .09
❑ 68 Jim Thome .75 .35
❑ 69 Eddie Murray .75 .35
❑ 70 Albert Belle .30 .14
❑ 71 Dennis Martinez .30 .14
❑ 72 Jack McDowell .20 .09
❑ 73 Kenny Lofton .30 .14
❑ 74 Manny Ramirez 1.00 .45
❑ 75 Dante Bichette .30 .14
❑ 76 Vinny Castilla .30 .14
❑ 77 Andres Galarraga .50 .23
❑ 78 Walt Weiss .20 .09
❑ 79 Ellis Burks .30 .14
❑ 80 Larry Walker .50 .23
❑ 81 Cecil Fielder .30 .14
❑ 82 Melvin Nieves .20 .09
❑ 83 Travis Fryman .30 .14
❑ 84 Chad Curtis .20 .09
❑ 85 Alan Trammell .50 .23
❑ 86 Gary Sheffield .30 .14
❑ 87 Charles Johnson .30 .14
❑ 88 Andre Dawson .50 .23
❑ 89 Jeff Conine .20 .09
❑ 90 Greg Colbrunn .20 .09
❑ 91 Derek Bell .20 .09
❑ 92 Brian L.Hunter .20 .09
❑ 93 Doug Drabek .20 .09
❑ 94 Craig Biggio .50 .23
❑ 95 Jeff Bagwell 1.00 .45
❑ 96 Kevin Appier .30 .14
❑ 97 Jeff Montgomery .20 .09
❑ 98 Michael Tucker .20 .09
❑ 99 Bip Roberts .20 .09
❑ 100 Johnny Damon .30 .14
❑ 101 Eric Karros .30 .14
❑ 102 Raul Mondesi .30 .14
❑ 103 Ramon Martinez .20 .09
❑ 104 Ismael Valdes .20 .09

		MINT	NRMT
❑	105 Mike Piazza	2.00	.90
❑	106 Hideo Nomo	1.00	.45
❑	107 Chan Ho Park	.30	.14
❑	108 Ben McDonald	.20	.09
❑	109 Kevin Seitzer	.20	.09
❑	110 Greg Vaughn	.30	.14
❑	111 Jose Valentin	.20	.09
❑	112 Rick Aguilera	.20	.09
❑	113 Marty Cordova	.20	.09
❑	114 Brad Radke	.30	.14
❑	115 Kirby Puckett	2.00	.90
❑	116 Chuck Knoblauch	.30	.14
❑	117 Paul Molitor	.75	.35
❑	118 Pedro Martinez	1.00	.45
❑	119 Mike Lansing	.20	.09
❑	120 Rondell White	.30	.14
❑	121 Moises Alou	.30	.14
❑	122 Mark Grudzielanek	.20	.09
❑	123 Jeff Fassero	.20	.09
❑	124 Rico Brogna	.20	.09
❑	125 Jason Isringhausen	.30	.14
❑	126 Jeff Kent	.50	.23
❑	127 Bernard Gilkey	.20	.09
❑	128 Todd Hundley	.20	.09
❑	129 David Cone	.30	.14
❑	130 Andy Pettitte	.30	.14
❑	131 Wade Boggs	.75	.35
❑	132 Paul O'Neill	.75	.35
❑	133 Ruben Sierra	.20	.09
❑	134 John Wetteland	.30	.14
❑	135 Derek Jeter	3.00	1.35
❑	136 Geronimo Berroa	.20	.09
❑	137 Terry Steinbach	.20	.09
❑	138 Ariel Prieto	.20	.09
❑	139 Scott Brosius	.30	.14
❑	140 Mark McGwire	3.00	1.35
❑	141 Lenny Dykstra	.30	.14
❑	142 Todd Zeile	.20	.09
❑	143 Benito Santiago	.20	.09
❑	144 Mickey Morandini	.20	.09
❑	145 Gregg Jefferies	.20	.09
❑	146 Denny Neagle	.30	.14
❑	147 Orlando Merced	.20	.09
❑	148 Charlie Hayes	.20	.09
❑	149 Carlos Garcia	.20	.09
❑	150 Jay Bell	.30	.14
❑	151 Ray Lankford	.20	.09
❑	152 Alan Benes Andy Benes	.20	.09
❑	153 Dennis Eckersley	.30	.14
❑	154 Gary Gaetti	.30	.14
❑	155 Ozzie Smith	1.00	.45
❑	156 Ron Gant	.20	.09
❑	157 Brian Jordan	.30	.14
❑	158 Ken Caminiti	.30	.14
❑	159 Rickey Henderson	1.50	.70
❑	160 Tony Gwynn	1.50	.70
❑	161 Wally Joyner	.30	.14
❑	162 Andy Ashby	.20	.09
❑	163 Steve Finley	.30	.14
❑	164 Glenallen Hill	.20	.09
❑	165 Matt Williams	.50	.23
❑	166 Barry Bonds	2.00	.90
❑	167 W. VanLandingham	.20	.09
❑	168 Rod Beck	.20	.09
❑	169 Randy Johnson	1.00	.45
❑	170 Ken Griffey Jr.	2.50	1.10
❑	171 Alex Rodriguez	2.00	.90
❑	172 Edgar Martinez	.50	.23
❑	173 Jay Buhner	.30	.14
❑	174 Russ Davis	.20	.09
❑	175 Juan Gonzalez	.75	.35
❑	176 Mickey Tettleton	.20	.09
❑	177 Will Clark	.75	.35
❑	178 Ken Hill	.20	.09
❑	179 Dean Palmer	.30	.14
❑	180 Ivan Rodriguez	.75	.35
❑	181 Carlos Delgado	.75	.35
❑	182 Alex Gonzalez	.20	.09
❑	183 Shawn Green	.75	.35
❑	184 Juan Guzman	.20	.09
❑	185 Joe Carter	.30	.14
❑	186 Hideo Nomo CL UER Checklist lists Livan Hernandez as #4	.30	.14
❑	187 Cal Ripken CL	1.50	.70
❑	188 Ken Griffey Jr. CL	1.25	.55

1997 SP

		MINT	NRMT
	COMPLETE SET (184)	50.00	22.00
❑	1 Andruw Jones FOIL	1.00	.45
❑	2 Kevin Orie FOIL	.20	.09
❑	3 Nomar Garciaparra FOIL	2.00	.90
❑	4 Jose Guillen FOIL	.20	.09
❑	5 Todd Walker FOIL	.20	.09
❑	6 Derrick Gibson FOIL	.20	.09
❑	7 Aaron Boone FOIL	.20	.09
❑	8 Bartolo Colon FOIL	.30	.14
❑	9 Derrek Lee FOIL	.30	.14
❑	10 Vladimir Guerrero FOIL	1.25	.55
❑	11 Wilton Guerrero FOIL	.20	.09
❑	12 Luis Castillo FOIL	.20	.09
❑	13 Jason Dickson FOIL	.20	.09
❑	14 B.Trammell FOIL RC	.30	.14
❑	15 Jose Cruz Jr. FOIL RC	2.00	.90
❑	16 Eddie Murray	.75	.35
❑	17 Darin Erstad	.75	.35
❑	18 Garret Anderson	.30	.14
❑	19 Jim Edmonds	.50	.23
❑	20 Tim Salmon	.30	.14
❑	21 Chuck Finley	.30	.14
❑	22 John Smoltz	.30	.14
❑	23 Greg Maddux	2.00	.90
❑	24 Kenny Lofton	.30	.14
❑	25 Chipper Jones	1.50	.70
❑	26 Ryan Klesko	.30	.14
❑	27 Javy Lopez	.30	.14
❑	28 Fred McGriff	.50	.23
❑	29 Roberto Alomar	.75	.35
❑	30 Rafael Palmeiro	.75	.35
❑	31 Mike Mussina	.75	.35
❑	32 Brady Anderson	.30	.14
❑	33 Rocky Coppinger	.20	.09
❑	34 Cal Ripken	3.00	1.35
❑	35 Mo Vaughn	.30	.14
❑	36 Steve Avery	.20	.09
❑	37 Tom Gordon	.20	.09
❑	38 Tim Naehring	.20	.09
❑	39 Troy O'Leary	.20	.09
❑	40 Sammy Sosa	1.50	.70
❑	41 Brian McRae	.20	.09
❑	42 Mel Rojas	.20	.09
❑	43 Ryne Sandberg	1.00	.45
❑	44 Mark Grace	.75	.35
❑	45 Albert Belle	.30	.14
❑	46 Robin Ventura	.30	.14
❑	47 Roberto Hernandez	.20	.09
❑	48 Ray Durham	.30	.14
❑	49 Harold Baines	.30	.14
❑	50 Frank Thomas	1.00	.45
❑	51 Bret Boone	.30	.14
❑	52 Reggie Sanders	.20	.09
❑	53 Deion Sanders	.30	.14
❑	54 Hal Morris	.20	.09
❑	55 Barry Larkin	.75	.35
❑	56 Jim Thome	.75	.35
❑	57 Marquis Grissom	.20	.09
❑	58 David Justice	.30	.14
❑	59 Charles Nagy	.20	.09
❑	60 Manny Ramirez	1.00	.45
❑	61 Matt Williams	.50	.23
❑	62 Jack McDowell	.20	.09
❑	63 Vinny Castilla	.30	.14
❑	64 Dante Bichette	.30	.14
❑	65 Andres Galarraga	.50	.23
❑	66 Ellis Burks	.30	.14
❑	67 Larry Walker	.50	.23
❑	68 Eric Young	.20	.09
❑	69 Brian L. Hunter	.20	.09
❑	70 Travis Fryman	.30	.14
❑	71 Tony Clark	.30	.14
❑	72 Bobby Higginson	.30	.14
❑	73 Melvin Nieves	.20	.09
❑	74 Jeff Conine	.20	.09
❑	75 Gary Sheffield	.30	.14
❑	76 Moises Alou	.30	.14
❑	77 Edgar Renteria	.20	.09
❑	78 Alex Fernandez	.20	.09
❑	79 Charles Johnson	.30	.14
❑	80 Bobby Bonilla	.30	.14
❑	81 Darryl Kile	.30	.14
❑	82 Derek Bell	.20	.09
❑	83 Shane Reynolds	.20	.09
❑	84 Craig Biggio	.50	.23
❑	85 Jeff Bagwell	1.00	.45
❑	86 Billy Wagner	.20	.09
❑	87 Chili Davis	.30	.14
❑	88 Kevin Appier	.30	.14
❑	89 Jay Bell	.30	.14
❑	90 Johnny Damon	.30	.14
❑	91 Jeff King	.20	.09
❑	92 Hideo Nomo	.75	.35
❑	93 Todd Hollandsworth	.20	.09
❑	94 Eric Karros	.30	.14
❑	95 Mike Piazza	2.00	.90
❑	96 Ramon Martinez	.20	.09
❑	97 Todd Worrell	.20	.09
❑	98 Raul Mondesi	.30	.14
❑	99 Dave Nilsson	.20	.09
❑	100 John Jaha	.20	.09
❑	101 Jose Valentin	.20	.09
❑	102 Jeff Cirillo	.30	.14
❑	103 Jeff D'Amico	.20	.09
❑	104 Ben McDonald	.20	.09
❑	105 Paul Molitor	.75	.35
❑	106 Rich Becker	.20	.09
❑	107 Frank Rodriguez	.20	.09
❑	108 Marty Cordova	.20	.09
❑	109 Terry Steinbach	.20	.09
❑	110 Chuck Knoblauch	.30	.14
❑	111 Mark Grudzielanek	.20	.09
❑	112 Mike Lansing	.20	.09
❑	113 Pedro Martinez	1.00	.45
❑	114 Henry Rodriguez	.20	.09
❑	115 Rondell White	.30	.14
❑	116 Rey Ordonez	.20	.09
❑	117 Carlos Baerga	.20	.09
❑	118 Lance Johnson	.20	.09
❑	119 Bernard Gilkey	.20	.09
❑	120 Todd Hundley	.20	.09
❑	121 John Franco	.30	.14
❑	122 Bernie Williams	.75	.35
❑	123 David Cone	.30	.14
❑	124 Cecil Fielder	.30	.14
❑	125 Derek Jeter	3.00	1.35
❑	126 Tino Martinez	.30	.14
❑	127 Mariano Rivera	.30	.14
❑	128 Andy Pettitte	.30	.14
❑	129 Wade Boggs	.75	.35
❑	130 Mark McGwire	3.00	1.35
❑	131 Jose Canseco	.75	.35
❑	132 Geronimo Berroa	.20	.09
❑	133 Jason Giambi	.75	.35
❑	134 Ernie Young	.20	.09
❑	135 Scott Rolen	.75	.35
❑	136 Ricky Bottalico	.20	.09
❑	137 Curt Schilling	.75	.35
❑	138 Gregg Jefferies	.20	.09
❑	139 Mickey Morandini	.20	.09
❑	140 Jason Kendall	.30	.14
❑	141 Kevin Elster	.20	.09
❑	142 Al Martin	.20	.09
❑	143 Joe Randa	.20	.09
❑	144 Jason Schmidt	.20	.09
❑	145 Ray Lankford	.20	.09
❑	146 Brian Jordan	.30	.14
❑	147 Andy Benes	.20	.09
❑	148 Alan Benes	.20	.09
❑	149 Gary Gaetti	.30	.14

❑ 150 Ron Gant	.20	.09
❑ 151 Dennis Eckersley	.30	.14
❑ 152 Rickey Henderson	1.50	.70
❑ 153 Joey Hamilton	.20	.09
❑ 154 Ken Caminiti	.30	.14
❑ 155 Tony Gwynn	1.50	.70
❑ 156 Steve Finley	.30	.14
❑ 157 Trevor Hoffman	.30	.14
❑ 158 Greg Vaughn	.30	.14
❑ 159 J.T.Snow	.30	.14
❑ 160 Barry Bonds	2.00	.90
❑ 161 Glenallen Hill	.20	.09
❑ 162 Bill Van Landingham	.20	.09
❑ 163 Jeff Kent	.50	.23
❑ 164 Jay Buhner	.30	.14
❑ 165 Ken Griffey Jr.	2.50	1.10
❑ 166 Alex Rodriguez	2.00	.90
❑ 167 Randy Johnson	1.00	.45
❑ 168 Edgar Martinez	.50	.23
❑ 169 Dan Wilson	.20	.09
❑ 170 Ivan Rodriguez	.75	.35
❑ 171 Roger Pavlik	.20	.09
❑ 172 Will Clark	.75	.35
❑ 173 Dean Palmer	.30	.14
❑ 174 Rusty Greer	.30	.14
❑ 175 Juan Gonzalez	.75	.35
❑ 176 John Wetteland	.30	.14
❑ 177 Joe Carter	.30	.14
❑ 178 Ed Sprague	.20	.09
❑ 179 Carlos Delgado	.75	.35
❑ 180 Roger Clemens	2.00	.90
❑ 181 Juan Guzman	.20	.09
❑ 182 Pat Hentgen	.20	.09
❑ 183 Ken Griffey Jr. CL	1.25	.55
❑ 184 Hideki Irabu RC	.30	.14

1998 SP Authentic

	MINT	NRMT
COMPLETE SET (198)	50.00	22.00
❑ 1 Travis Lee FOIL	.30	.14
❑ 2 Mike Caruso FOIL	.20	.09
❑ 3 Kerry Wood FOIL	1.50	.70
❑ 4 Mark Kotsay FOIL	.30	.14
❑ 5 M.Ordonez FOIL RC	8.00	3.60
❑ 6 Scott Elarton FOIL	.20	.09
❑ 7 Carl Pavano FOIL	.20	.09
❑ 8 A.J. Hinch FOIL	.20	.09
❑ 9 Rolando Arrojo FOIL RC	1.00	.45
❑ 10 Ben Grieve FOIL	.30	.14
❑ 11 Gabe Alvarez FOIL	.20	.09
❑ 12 Mike Kinkade FOIL RC	.30	.14
❑ 13 Bruce Chen FOIL	.20	.09
❑ 14 Juan Encarnacion FOIL	.30	.14
❑ 15 Todd Helton FOIL	1.00	.45
❑ 16 Aaron Boone FOIL	.20	.09
❑ 17 Sean Casey FOIL	.50	.23
❑ 18 R.Hernandez FOIL	.20	.09
❑ 19 Daryle Ward FOIL	.20	.09
❑ 20 Paul Konerko FOIL	.30	.14
❑ 21 David Ortiz FOIL	.30	.14
❑ 22 Derrek Lee FOIL	.30	.14
❑ 23 Brad Fullmer FOIL	.30	.14
❑ 24 Javier Vazquez FOIL	.30	.14
❑ 25 Miguel Tejada FOIL	.50	.23
❑ 26 Dave Dellucci FOIL RC	.20	.09
❑ 27 Alex Gonzalez FOIL	.20	.09
❑ 28 Matt Clement FOIL	.30	.14
❑ 29 Masato Yoshii FOIL RC	1.00	.45
❑ 30 Russell Branyan FOIL	.30	.14
❑ 31 Chuck Finley	.30	.14
❑ 32 Jim Edmonds	.50	.23
❑ 33 Darin Erstad	.75	.35
❑ 34 Jason Dickson	.20	.09
❑ 35 Tim Salmon	.30	.14
❑ 36 Cecil Fielder	.30	.14
❑ 37 Todd Greene	.20	.09
❑ 38 Andy Benes	.20	.09
❑ 39 Jay Bell	.30	.14
❑ 40 Matt Williams	.50	.23
❑ 41 Brian Anderson	.20	.09
❑ 42 Karim Garcia	.20	.09
❑ 43 Javy Lopez	.30	.14
❑ 44 Tom Glavine	.75	.35
❑ 45 Greg Maddux	2.00	.90
❑ 46 Andruw Jones	.75	.35
❑ 47 Chipper Jones	1.50	.70
❑ 48 Ryan Klesko	.30	.14
❑ 49 John Smoltz	.30	.14
❑ 50 Andres Galarraga	.50	.23
❑ 51 Rafael Palmeiro	.75	.35
❑ 52 Mike Mussina	.75	.35
❑ 53 Roberto Alomar	.75	.35
❑ 54 Joe Carter	.30	.14
❑ 55 Cal Ripken	3.00	1.35
❑ 56 Brady Anderson	.30	.14
❑ 57 Mo Vaughn	.30	.14
❑ 58 John Valentin	.20	.09
❑ 59 Dennis Eckersley	.30	.14
❑ 60 Nomar Garciaparra	2.00	.90
❑ 61 Pedro Martinez	1.00	.45
❑ 62 Jeff Blauser	.20	.09
❑ 63 Kevin Orie	.20	.09
❑ 64 Henry Rodriguez	.20	.09
❑ 65 Mark Grace	.75	.35
❑ 66 Albert Belle	.30	.14
❑ 67 Mike Cameron	.30	.14
❑ 68 Robin Ventura	.30	.14
❑ 69 Frank Thomas	1.00	.45
❑ 70 Barry Larkin	.75	.35
❑ 71 Brett Tomko	.20	.09
❑ 72 Willie Greene	.20	.09
❑ 73 Reggie Sanders	.20	.09
❑ 74 Sandy Alomar Jr.	.30	.14
❑ 75 Kenny Lofton	.30	.14
❑ 76 Jaret Wright	.20	.09
❑ 77 David Justice	.30	.14
❑ 78 Omar Vizquel	.30	.14
❑ 79 Manny Ramirez	1.00	.45
❑ 80 Jim Thome	.75	.35
❑ 81 Travis Fryman	.30	.14
❑ 82 Neifi Perez	.20	.09
❑ 83 Mike Lansing	.20	.09
❑ 84 Vinny Castilla	.30	.14
❑ 85 Larry Walker	.50	.23
❑ 86 Dante Bichette	.30	.14
❑ 87 Darryl Kile	.30	.14
❑ 88 Justin Thompson	.20	.09
❑ 89 Damion Easley	.20	.09
❑ 90 Tony Clark	.30	.14
❑ 91 Bobby Higginson	.30	.14
❑ 92 Brian Hunter	.20	.09
❑ 93 Edgar Renteria	.20	.09
❑ 94 Craig Counsell	.20	.09
❑ 95 Mike Piazza	2.00	.90
❑ 96 Livan Hernandez	.20	.09
❑ 97 Todd Zeile	.30	.14
❑ 98 Richard Hidalgo	.30	.14
❑ 99 Moises Alou	.30	.14
❑ 100 Jeff Bagwell	1.00	.45
❑ 101 Mike Hampton	.30	.14
❑ 102 Craig Biggio	.50	.23
❑ 103 Dean Palmer	.30	.14
❑ 104 Tim Belcher	.20	.09
❑ 105 Jeff King	.20	.09
❑ 106 Jeff Conine	.20	.09
❑ 107 Johnny Damon	.30	.14
❑ 108 Hideo Nomo	.75	.35
❑ 109 Raul Mondesi	.30	.14
❑ 110 Gary Sheffield	.30	.14
❑ 111 Ramon Martinez	.20	.09
❑ 112 Chan Ho Park	.30	.14
❑ 113 Eric Young	.20	.09
❑ 114 Charles Johnson	.30	.14
❑ 115 Eric Karros	.30	.14
❑ 116 Bobby Bonilla	.30	.14
❑ 117 Jeromy Burnitz	.30	.14
❑ 118 Cal Eldred	.20	.09
❑ 119 Jeff D'Amico	.20	.09
❑ 120 Marquis Grissom	.20	.09
❑ 121 Dave Nilsson	.20	.09
❑ 122 Brad Radke	.30	.14
❑ 123 Marty Cordova	.20	.09
❑ 124 Ron Coomer	.20	.09
❑ 125 Paul Molitor	.75	.35
❑ 126 Todd Walker	.20	.09
❑ 127 Rondell White	.30	.14
❑ 128 Mark Grudzielanek	.20	.09
❑ 129 Carlos Perez	.20	.09
❑ 130 Vladimir Guerrero	1.00	.45
❑ 131 Dustin Hermanson	.20	.09
❑ 132 Butch Huskey	.20	.09
❑ 133 John Franco	.30	.14
❑ 134 Rey Ordonez	.20	.09
❑ 135 Todd Hundley	.20	.09
❑ 136 Edgardo Alfonzo	.30	.14
❑ 137 Bobby Jones	.20	.09
❑ 138 John Olerud	.30	.14
❑ 139 Chili Davis	.30	.14
❑ 140 Tino Martinez	.30	.14
❑ 141 Andy Pettitte	.30	.14
❑ 142 Chuck Knoblauch	.30	.14
❑ 143 Bernie Williams	.75	.35
❑ 144 David Cone	.30	.14
❑ 145 Derek Jeter	3.00	1.35
❑ 146 Paul O'Neill	.75	.35
❑ 147 Rickey Henderson	1.50	.70
❑ 148 Jason Giambi	.75	.35
❑ 149 Kenny Rogers	.20	.09
❑ 150 Scott Rolen	.75	.35
❑ 151 Curt Schilling	.75	.35
❑ 152 Ricky Bottalico	.20	.09
❑ 153 Mike Lieberthal	.30	.14
❑ 154 Francisco Cordova	.20	.09
❑ 155 Jose Guillen	.20	.09
❑ 156 Jason Schmidt	.20	.09
❑ 157 Jason Kendall	.30	.14
❑ 158 Kevin Young	.30	.14
❑ 159 Delino DeShields	.20	.09
❑ 160 Mark McGwire	3.00	1.35
❑ 161 Ray Lankford	.20	.09
❑ 162 Brian Jordan	.30	.14
❑ 163 Ron Gant	.30	.14
❑ 164 Todd Stottlemyre	.20	.09
❑ 165 Ken Caminiti	.30	.14
❑ 166 Kevin Brown	.50	.23
❑ 167 Trevor Hoffman	.30	.14
❑ 168 Steve Finley	.30	.14
❑ 169 Wally Joyner	.30	.14
❑ 170 Tony Gwynn	1.50	.70
❑ 171 Shawn Estes	.30	.14
❑ 172 J.T. Snow	.30	.14
❑ 173 Jeff Kent	.50	.23
❑ 174 Robb Nen	.20	.09
❑ 175 Barry Bonds	2.00	.90
❑ 176 Randy Johnson	1.00	.45
❑ 177 Edgar Martinez	.50	.23
❑ 178 Jay Buhner	.30	.14
❑ 179 Alex Rodriguez	2.00	.90
❑ 180 Ken Griffey Jr.	2.50	1.10
❑ 181 Ken Cloude	.20	.09
❑ 182 Wade Boggs	.75	.35
❑ 183 Tony Saunders	.20	.09
❑ 184 Wilson Alvarez	.20	.09
❑ 185 Fred McGriff	.50	.23
❑ 186 Roberto Hernandez	.20	.09
❑ 187 Kevin Stocker	.20	.09
❑ 188 Fernando Tatis	.20	.09
❑ 189 Will Clark	.75	.35
❑ 190 Juan Gonzalez	.75	.35
❑ 191 Rusty Greer	.30	.14
❑ 192 Ivan Rodriguez	.75	.35
❑ 193 Jose Canseco	.75	.35
❑ 194 Carlos Delgado	.75	.35
❑ 195 Roger Clemens	2.00	.90
❑ 196 Pat Hentgen	.20	.09
❑ 197 Randy Myers	.30	.14
❑ 198 Ken Griffey Jr. CL	1.25	.55
❑ S123 K.Griffey Jr. Sample	3.00	1.35

1999 SP Authentic

	MINT	NRMT
COMP.SET w/o SP's (90)	25.00	11.00
COMMON CARD (1-90)	.20	.09
COMMON FW (91-120)	10.00	4.50
COMMON STR (121-135)	4.00	1.80

❑ 1 Mo Vaughn	.30	.14
❑ 2 Jim Edmonds	.50	.23
❑ 3 Darin Erstad	.75	.35
❑ 4 Travis Lee	.20	.09
❑ 5 Matt Williams	.50	.23
❑ 6 Randy Johnson	1.00	.45
❑ 7 Chipper Jones	1.50	.70
❑ 8 Greg Maddux	2.00	.90
❑ 9 Andruw Jones	.75	.35
❑ 10 Andres Galarraga	.50	.23
❑ 11 Tom Glavine	.75	.35
❑ 12 Cal Ripken	3.00	1.35
❑ 13 Brady Anderson	.30	.14
❑ 14 Albert Belle	.30	.14
❑ 15 Nomar Garciaparra	2.00	.90
❑ 16 Donnie Sadler	.20	.09
❑ 17 Pedro Martinez	1.00	.45
❑ 18 Sammy Sosa	1.50	.70
❑ 19 Kerry Wood	.75	.35
❑ 20 Mark Grace	.75	.35
❑ 21 Mike Caruso	.20	.09
❑ 22 Frank Thomas	1.00	.45
❑ 23 Paul Konerko	.30	.14
❑ 24 Sean Casey	.50	.23
❑ 25 Barry Larkin	.75	.35
❑ 26 Kenny Lofton	.30	.14
❑ 27 Manny Ramirez	1.00	.45
❑ 28 Jim Thome	.75	.35
❑ 29 Bartolo Colon	.30	.14
❑ 30 Jaret Wright	.20	.09
❑ 31 Larry Walker	.50	.23
❑ 32 Todd Helton	1.00	.45
❑ 33 Tony Clark	.30	.14
❑ 34 Dean Palmer	.30	.14
❑ 35 Mark Kotsay	.20	.09
❑ 36 Cliff Floyd	.30	.14
❑ 37 Ken Caminiti	.30	.14
❑ 38 Craig Biggio	.50	.23
❑ 39 Jeff Bagwell	1.00	.45
❑ 40 Moises Alou	.30	.14
❑ 41 Johnny Damon	.30	.14
❑ 42 Larry Sutton	.20	.09
❑ 43 Kevin Brown	.50	.23
❑ 44 Gary Sheffield	.30	.14
❑ 45 Raul Mondesi	.30	.14
❑ 46 Jeromy Burnitz	.30	.14
❑ 47 Jeff Cirillo	.30	.14
❑ 48 Todd Walker	.20	.09
❑ 49 David Ortiz	.30	.14
❑ 50 Brad Radke	.30	.14
❑ 51 Vladimir Guerrero	1.00	.45
❑ 52 Rondell White	.30	.14
❑ 53 Brad Fullmer	.30	.14
❑ 54 Mike Piazza	2.00	.90
❑ 55 Robin Ventura	.30	.14
❑ 56 John Olerud	.30	.14
❑ 57 Derek Jeter	3.00	1.35
❑ 58 Tino Martinez	.30	.14
❑ 59 Bernie Williams	.75	.35
❑ 60 Roger Clemens	2.00	.90
❑ 61 Ben Grieve	.30	.14
❑ 62 Miguel Tejada	.30	.14
❑ 63 A.J. Hinch	.20	.09
❑ 64 Scott Rolen	.75	.35
❑ 65 Curt Schilling	.75	.35
❑ 66 Doug Glanville	.20	.09
❑ 67 Aramis Ramirez	.30	.14
❑ 68 Tony Womack	.20	.09
❑ 69 Jason Kendall	.30	.14
❑ 70 Tony Gwynn	1.50	.70
❑ 71 Wally Joyner	.30	.14
❑ 72 Greg Vaughn	.30	.14
❑ 73 Barry Bonds	2.00	.90
❑ 74 Ellis Burks	.30	.14
❑ 75 Jeff Kent	.50	.23
❑ 76 Ken Griffey Jr.	2.50	1.10
❑ 77 Alex Rodriguez	2.00	.90
❑ 78 Edgar Martinez	.50	.23
❑ 79 Mark McGwire	3.00	1.35
❑ 80 Eli Marrero	.20	.09
❑ 81 Matt Morris	.30	.14
❑ 82 Rolando Arrojo	.20	.09
❑ 83 Quinton McCracken	.20	.09
❑ 84 Jose Canseco	.75	.35
❑ 85 Ivan Rodriguez	.75	.35
❑ 86 Juan Gonzalez	.75	.35
❑ 87 Royce Clayton	.20	.09
❑ 88 Shawn Green	.75	.35
❑ 89 Jose Cruz Jr.	.30	.14
❑ 90 Carlos Delgado	.75	.35
❑ 91 Troy Glaus FW	20.00	9.00
❑ 92 George Lombard FW	10.00	4.50
❑ 93 Ryan Minor FW	10.00	4.50
❑ 94 Calvin Pickering FW	10.00	4.50
❑ 95 Jin Ho Cho FW	10.00	4.50
❑ 96 Russ Branyan FW	10.00	4.50
❑ 97 Derrick Gibson FW	10.00	4.50
❑ 98 Gabe Kapler FW	10.00	4.50
❑ 99 Matt Anderson FW	10.00	4.50
❑ 100 Preston Wilson FW	10.00	4.50
❑ 101 Alex Gonzalez FW	10.00	4.50
❑ 102 Carlos Beltran FW	10.00	4.50
❑ 103 Dee Brown FW	10.00	4.50
❑ 104 Jeremy Giambi FW	10.00	4.50
❑ 105 Angel Pena FW	10.00	4.50
❑ 106 Geoff Jenkins FW	10.00	4.50
❑ 107 Corey Koskie FW	10.00	4.50
❑ 108 A.J. Pierzynski FW	10.00	4.50
❑ 109 Michael Barrett FW	10.00	4.50
❑ 110 F.Seguignol FW	10.00	4.50
❑ 111 Mike Kinkade FW	10.00	4.50
❑ 112 Ricky Ledee FW	10.00	4.50
❑ 113 Mike Lowell FW	10.00	4.50
❑ 114 Eric Chavez FW	10.00	4.50
❑ 115 Matt Clement FW	10.00	4.50
❑ 116 Shane Monahan FW	10.00	4.50
❑ 117 J.D. Drew FW	20.00	9.00
❑ 118 Bubba Trammell FW	10.00	4.50
❑ 119 Kevin Witt FW	10.00	4.50
❑ 120 Roy Halladay FW	10.00	4.50
❑ 121 Mark McGwire STR	15.00	6.75
❑ 122 Mark McGwire STR Sammy Sosa	12.00	5.50
❑ 123 Sammy Sosa STR	8.00	3.60
❑ 124 Ken Griffey Jr. STR	12.00	5.50
❑ 125 Cal Ripken STR	15.00	6.75
❑ 126 Juan Gonzalez STR	4.00	1.80
❑ 127 Kerry Wood STR	4.00	1.80
❑ 128 Trevor Hoffman STR	4.00	1.80
❑ 129 Barry Bonds STR	10.00	4.50
❑ 130 Alex Rodriguez STR	10.00	4.50
❑ 131 Ben Grieve STR	4.00	1.80
❑ 132 Tom Glavine STR	4.00	1.80
❑ 133 David Wells STR	4.00	1.80
❑ 134 Mike Piazza STR	10.00	4.50
❑ 135 Scott Brosius STR	4.00	1.80

2000 SP Authentic

	MINT	NRMT
COMPLETE SET (194)	900.00	400.00
COMP.BASIC SET (135)	500.00	220.00
COMP.UPDATE SET (59)	400.00	180.00
COMP.BASIC w/o SP's (90)	25.00	11.00
COMP.UPDATE w/o SP'S (30)	10.00	4.50
COMMON CARD (1-90)	.20	.09

COMMON SUP (91-105)	4.00	1.80
COMMON FW (106-135)	10.00	4.50
COMMON FW (136-164)	10.00	4.50
COMMON CARD (166-195)	.30	.14

❑ 1 Mo Vaughn	.30	.14
❑ 2 Troy Glaus	.75	.35
❑ 3 Jason Giambi	.75	.35
❑ 4 Tim Hudson	.75	.35
❑ 5 Eric Chavez	.30	.14
❑ 6 Shannon Stewart	.30	.14
❑ 7 Raul Mondesi	.30	.14
❑ 8 Carlos Delgado	.75	.35
❑ 9 Jose Canseco	.75	.35
❑ 10 Vinny Castilla	.30	.14
❑ 11 Greg Vaughn	.30	.14
❑ 12 Manny Ramirez	1.00	.45
❑ 13 Roberto Alomar	.75	.35
❑ 14 Jim Thome	.75	.35
❑ 15 Richie Sexson	.30	.14
❑ 16 Alex Rodriguez	2.00	.90
❑ 17 Freddy Garcia	.50	.23
❑ 18 John Olerud	.30	.14
❑ 19 Albert Belle	.30	.14
❑ 20 Cal Ripken	3.00	1.35
❑ 21 Mike Mussina	.75	.35
❑ 22 Ivan Rodriguez	.75	.35
❑ 23 Gabe Kapler	.30	.14
❑ 24 Rafael Palmeiro	.75	.35
❑ 25 Nomar Garciaparra	2.00	.90
❑ 26 Pedro Martinez	1.00	.45
❑ 27 Carl Everett	.30	.14
❑ 28 Carlos Beltran	.30	.14
❑ 29 Jermaine Dye	.30	.14
❑ 30 Juan Gonzalez	.75	.35
❑ 31 Dean Palmer	.30	.14
❑ 32 Corey Koskie	.30	.14
❑ 33 Jacque Jones	.30	.14
❑ 34 Frank Thomas	1.00	.45
❑ 35 Paul Konerko	.30	.14
❑ 36 Magglio Ordonez	.30	.14
❑ 37 Bernie Williams	.75	.35
❑ 38 Derek Jeter	3.00	1.35
❑ 39 Roger Clemens	2.00	.90
❑ 40 Mariano Rivera	.30	.14
❑ 41 Jeff Bagwell	1.00	.45
❑ 42 Craig Biggio	.50	.23
❑ 43 Jose Lima	.20	.09
❑ 44 Moises Alou	.30	.14
❑ 45 Chipper Jones	1.50	.70
❑ 46 Greg Maddux	2.00	.90
❑ 47 Andruw Jones	.75	.35
❑ 48 Andres Galarraga	.50	.23
❑ 49 Jeromy Burnitz	.30	.14
❑ 50 Geoff Jenkins	.30	.14
❑ 51 Mark McGwire	3.00	1.35
❑ 52 Fernando Tatis	.20	.09
❑ 53 J.D. Drew	.75	.35
❑ 54 Sammy Sosa	1.50	.70
❑ 55 Kerry Wood	.75	.35
❑ 56 Mark Grace	.75	.35
❑ 57 Matt Williams	.50	.23
❑ 58 Randy Johnson	1.00	.45
❑ 59 Erubiel Durazo	.30	.14
❑ 60 Gary Sheffield	.30	.14
❑ 61 Kevin Brown	.50	.23
❑ 62 Shawn Green	.75	.35

❑	63 Vladimir Guerrero	1.00	.45
❑	64 Michael Barrett	.20	.09
❑	65 Barry Bonds	2.00	.90
❑	66 Jeff Kent	.50	.23
❑	67 Russ Ortiz	.20	.09
❑	68 Preston Wilson	.30	.14
❑	69 Mike Lowell	.30	.14
❑	70 Mike Piazza	2.00	.90
❑	71 Mike Hampton	.30	.14
❑	72 Robin Ventura	.30	.14
❑	73 Edgardo Alfonzo	.30	.14
❑	74 Tony Gwynn	1.50	.70
❑	75 Ryan Klesko	.30	.14
❑	76 Trevor Hoffman	.30	.14
❑	77 Scott Rolen	.75	.35
❑	78 Bob Abreu	.30	.14
❑	79 Mike Lieberthal	.30	.14
❑	80 Curt Schilling	.75	.35
❑	81 Jason Kendall	.30	.14
❑	82 Brian Giles	.30	.14
❑	83 Kris Benson	.30	.14
❑	84 Ken Griffey Jr.	2.50	1.10
❑	85 Sean Casey	.50	.23
❑	86 Pokey Reese	.20	.09
❑	87 Barry Larkin	.75	.35
❑	88 Larry Walker	.50	.23
❑	89 Todd Helton	1.00	.45
❑	90 Jeff Cirillo	.30	.14
❑	91 Ken Griffey Jr. SUP	12.00	5.50
❑	92 Mark McGwire SUP	15.00	6.75
❑	93 Chipper Jones SUP	8.00	3.60
❑	94 Derek Jeter SUP	15.00	6.75
❑	95 Shawn Green SUP	4.00	1.80
❑	96 Pedro Martinez SUP	5.00	2.20
❑	97 Mike Piazza SUP	10.00	4.50
❑	98 Alex Rodriguez SUP	10.00	4.50
❑	99 Jeff Bagwell SUP	5.00	2.20
❑	100 Cal Ripken SUP	15.00	6.75
❑	101 Sammy Sosa SUP	8.00	3.60
❑	102 Barry Bonds SUP	10.00	4.50
❑	103 Jose Canseco SUP	4.00	1.80
❑	104 N.Garciaparra SUP	10.00	4.50
❑	105 Ivan Rodriguez SUP	4.00	1.80
❑	106 Rick Ankiel FW	15.00	6.75
❑	107 Pat Burrell FW	15.00	6.75
❑	108 Vernon Wells FW	10.00	4.50
❑	109 Nick Johnson FW	15.00	6.75
❑	110 Kip Wells FW	10.00	4.50
❑	111 Matt Riley FW	10.00	4.50
❑	112 Alfonso Soriano FW	15.00	6.75
❑	113 Josh Beckett FW	20.00	9.00
❑	114 Danys Baez FW RC	12.00	5.50
❑	115 Travis Dawkins FW	10.00	4.50
❑	116 Eric Gagne FW	10.00	4.50
❑	117 Mike Lamb FW RC	10.00	4.50
❑	118 Eric Munson FW	10.00	4.50
❑	119 W.Rodriguez FW RC	10.00	4.50
❑	120 K.Sasaki FW RC	25.00	11.00
❑	121 Chad Hutchinson FW	10.00	4.50
❑	122 Peter Bergeron FW	10.00	4.50
❑	123 W.Serrano FW RC	10.00	4.50
❑	124 Tony Armas Jr. FW	10.00	4.50
❑	125 Ramon Ortiz FW	10.00	4.50
❑	126 Adam Kennedy FW	10.00	4.50
❑	127 Joe Crede FW	10.00	4.50
❑	128 Roosevelt Brown FW	10.00	4.50
❑	129 Mark Mulder FW	15.00	6.75
❑	130 Brad Penny FW	10.00	4.50
❑	131 Terrence Long FW	10.00	4.50
❑	132 Ruben Mateo FW	10.00	4.50
❑	133 Wily Mo Pena FW	15.00	6.75
❑	134 Rafael Furcal FW	15.00	6.75
❑	135 M.Encarnacion FW	10.00	4.50
❑	136 Barry Zito FW RC	30.00	13.50
❑	137 Aaron McNeal FW RC	10.00	4.50
❑	138 Timo Perez FW RC	10.00	4.50
❑	139 Sun Woo Kim FW RC	10.00	4.50
❑	140 Xavier Nady FW RC	25.00	11.00
❑	141 M.Wheatland FW RC	10.00	4.50
❑	142 B.Abernathy FW RC	10.00	4.50
❑	143 Cory Vance FW RC	10.00	4.50
❑	144 Scott Heard FW RC	10.00	4.50
❑	145 Mike Meyers FW RC	10.00	4.50
❑	146 Ben Diggins FW RC	12.00	5.50
❑	147 Luis Matos FW RC	10.00	4.50
❑	148 Ben Sheets FW RC	25.00	11.00
❑	149 K.Ainsworth FW RC	12.00	5.50
❑	150 Dave Krynzel FW RC	12.00	5.50
❑	151 Alex Cabrera FW RC	10.00	4.50
❑	152 Mike Tonis FW RC	12.00	5.50
❑	153 Dane Sardinha FW RC	10.00	4.50
❑	154 Keith Ginter FW RC	12.00	5.50
❑	155 D.Espinosa FW RC	12.00	5.50
❑	156 Joe Torres FW RC	12.00	5.50
❑	157 Daylan Holt FW RC	10.00	4.50
❑	158 Koyie Hill FW RC	10.00	4.50
❑	159 B.Wilkerson FW RC	10.00	4.50
❑	160 Juan Pierre FW RC	12.00	5.50
❑	161 Matt Ginter FW RC	10.00	4.50
❑	162 Dane Artman FW RC	10.00	4.50
❑	163 Jon Rauch FW RC	15.00	6.75
❑	164 Sean Burnett FW RC	10.00	4.50
❑	165 Does Not Exist		
❑	166 Darin Erstad	1.25	.55
❑	167 Ben Grieve	.50	.23
❑	168 David Wells	.50	.23
❑	169 Fred McGriff	.75	.35
❑	170 Bob Wickman	.30	.14
❑	171 Al Martin	.30	.14
❑	172 Melvin Mora	.30	.14
❑	173 Ricky Ledee	.30	.14
❑	174 Dante Bichette	.50	.23
❑	175 Mike Sweeney	.50	.23
❑	176 Bobby Higginson	.50	.23
❑	177 Matt Lawton	.50	.23
❑	178 Charles Johnson	.50	.23
❑	179 David Justice	.50	.23
❑	180 Richard Hidalgo	.50	.23
❑	181 B.J. Surhoff	.50	.23
❑	182 Richie Sexson	.50	.23
❑	183 Jim Edmonds	.75	.35
❑	184 Rondell White	.50	.23
❑	185 Curt Schilling	1.25	.55
❑	186 Tom Goodwin	.30	.14
❑	187 Jose Vidro	.50	.23
❑	188 Ellis Burks	.50	.23
❑	189 Henry Rodriguez	.30	.14
❑	190 Mike Bordick	.30	.14
❑	191 Eric Owens	.30	.14
❑	192 Travis Lee	.30	.14
❑	193 Kevin Young	.30	.14
❑	194 Aaron Boone	.30	.14
❑	195 Todd Hollandsworth	.30	.14
❑	SPA K.Griffey Jr. Sample	2.50	1.10

2001 SP Authentic

		MINT	NRMT
	COMP.BASIC w/o SP's (90)	25.00	11.00
	COMMON CARD (1-90)	.30	.14
	COMMON FW (91-135)	10.00	4.50
	COMMON SS (136-180)	5.00	2.20
❑	1 Troy Glaus	.75	.35
❑	2 Darin Erstad	.75	.35
❑	3 Jason Giambi	.75	.35
❑	4 Tim Hudson	.75	.35
❑	5 Eric Chavez	.30	.14
❑	6 Miguel Tejada	.30	.14
❑	7 Jose Ortiz	.50	.23
❑	8 Carlos Delgado	.75	.35
❑	9 Tony Batista	.30	.14
❑	10 Raul Mondesi	.30	.14
❑	11 Aubrey Huff	.30	.14
❑	12 Greg Vaughn	.30	.14
❑	13 Roberto Alomar	.75	.35
❑	14 Juan Gonzalez	.75	.35
❑	15 Jim Thome	.75	.35
❑	16 Omar Vizquel	.30	.14
❑	17 Edgar Martinez	.50	.23
❑	18 Freddy Garcia	.30	.14
❑	19 Cal Ripken	3.00	1.35
❑	20 Ivan Rodriguez	.75	.35
❑	21 Rafael Palmeiro	.75	.35
❑	22 Alex Rodriguez	2.00	.90
❑	23 Manny Ramirez	1.00	.45
❑	24 Pedro Martinez	1.00	.45
❑	25 Nomar Garciaparra	2.00	.90
❑	26 Mike Sweeney	.30	.14
❑	27 Jermaine Dye	.30	.14
❑	28 Bobby Higginson	.30	.14
❑	29 Dean Palmer	.30	.14
❑	30 Matt Lawton	.30	.14
❑	31 Eric Milton	.30	.14
❑	32 Frank Thomas	1.00	.45
❑	33 Magglio Ordonez	.30	.14
❑	34 David Wells	.30	.14
❑	35 Paul Konerko	.30	.14
❑	36 Derek Jeter	3.00	1.35
❑	37 Bernie Williams	.75	.35
❑	38 Roger Clemens	2.00	.90
❑	39 Mike Mussina	.75	.35
❑	40 Jorge Posada	.30	.14
❑	41 Jeff Bagwell	1.00	.45
❑	42 Richard Hidalgo	.30	.14
❑	43 Craig Biggio	.50	.23
❑	44 Greg Maddux	2.00	.90
❑	45 Chipper Jones	1.50	.70
❑	46 Andruw Jones	.75	.35
❑	47 Rafael Furcal	.30	.14
❑	48 Tom Glavine	.75	.35
❑	49 Jeromy Burnitz	.30	.14
❑	50 Jeffrey Hammonds	.30	.14
❑	51 Mark McGwire	3.00	1.35
❑	52 Jim Edmonds	.50	.23
❑	53 Rick Ankiel	.50	.23
❑	54 J.D. Drew	.75	.35
❑	55 Sammy Sosa	1.50	.70
❑	56 Corey Patterson	.30	.14
❑	57 Kerry Wood	.75	.35
❑	58 Randy Johnson	.75	.35
❑	59 Luis Gonzalez	.75	.35
❑	60 Curt Schilling	.75	.35
❑	61 Gary Sheffield	.30	.14
❑	62 Shawn Green	.75	.35
❑	63 Kevin Brown	.30	.14
❑	64 Vladimir Guerrero	1.00	.45
❑	65 Jose Vidro	.30	.14
❑	66 Barry Bonds	2.00	.90
❑	67 Jeff Kent	.50	.23
❑	68 Livan Hernandez	.30	.14
❑	69 Preston Wilson	.30	.14
❑	70 Charles Johnson	.30	.14
❑	71 Ryan Dempster	.30	.14
❑	72 Mike Piazza	2.00	.90
❑	73 Al Leiter	.30	.14
❑	74 Edgardo Alfonzo	.30	.14
❑	75 Robin Ventura	.30	.14
❑	76 Tony Gwynn	1.50	.70
❑	77 Phil Nevin	.30	.14
❑	78 Trevor Hoffman	.30	.14
❑	79 Scott Rolen	.75	.35
❑	80 Pat Burrell	.30	.14
❑	81 Bob Abreu	.30	.14
❑	82 Jason Kendall	.30	.14
❑	83 Brian Giles	.30	.14
❑	84 Kris Benson	.30	.14
❑	85 Ken Griffey Jr.	2.50	1.10
❑	86 Barry Larkin	.75	.35
❑	87 Sean Casey	.50	.23
❑	88 Todd Helton	1.00	.45
❑	89 Mike Hampton	.30	.14
❑	90 Larry Walker	.50	.23
❑	91 Ichiro Suzuki FW RC	200.00	90.00
❑	92 Wilson Betemit FW RC	30.00	13.50
❑	93 Adrian Hernandez FW RC	10.00	4.50
❑	94 Juan Uribe FW RC	15.00	6.75
❑	95 Travis Hafner FW RC	12.00	5.50
❑	96 Morgan Ensberg FW RC	15.00	6.75
❑	97 Sean Douglass FW RC	10.00	4.50

Card	Mint	NrMt
❑ 98 Juan Diaz FW RC	10.00	4.50
❑ 99 Erick Almonte FW RC	10.00	4.50
❑ 100 Ryan Freel FW RC	10.00	4.50
❑ 101 Elpidio Guzman FW RC	10.00	4.50
❑ 102 Christian Parker FW RC	10.00	4.50
❑ 103 Josh Fogg FW RC	10.00	4.50
❑ 104 Bert Snow FW RC	10.00	4.50
❑ 105 Horacio Ramirez FW RC	10.00	4.50
❑ 106 R. Rodriguez FW RC	12.00	5.50
❑ 107 Tyler Walker FW RC	10.00	4.50
❑ 108 Jose Mieses FW RC	10.00	4.50
❑ 109 Billy Sylvester FW RC	10.00	4.50
❑ 110 Martin Vargas FW RC	10.00	4.50
❑ 111 Andres Torres FW RC	10.00	4.50
❑ 112 Greg Miller FW RC	10.00	4.50
❑ 113 Alexis Gomez FW RC	10.00	4.50
❑ 114 Grant Balfour FW RC	10.00	4.50
❑ 115 Henry Mateo FW RC	10.00	4.50
❑ 116 Esix Snead FW RC	10.00	4.50
❑ 117 Jackson Melian FW RC	10.00	4.50
❑ 118 Nate Teut FW RC	10.00	4.50
❑ 119 Tsuyoshi Shinjo FW RC	25.00	11.00
❑ 120 C. Valderrama FW RC	10.00	4.50
❑ 121 Johnny Estrada FW RC	15.00	6.75
❑ 122 Jason Michaels FW RC	10.00	4.50
❑ 123 William Ortega FW RC	10.00	4.50
❑ 124 Jason Smith FW RC	10.00	4.50
❑ 125 Brian Lawrence FW RC	10.00	4.50
❑ 126 Albert Pujols FW RC	125.00	55.00
❑ 127 Wilkin Ruan FW RC	10.00	4.50
❑ 128 Josh Towers FW RC	15.00	6.75
❑ 129 Kris Keller FW RC	10.00	4.50
❑ 130 Nick Maness FW RC	10.00	4.50
❑ 131 Jack Wilson FW RC	10.00	4.50
❑ 132 B. Duckworth FW RC	20.00	9.00
❑ 133 Mike Penney FW RC	10.00	4.50
❑ 134 Jay Gibbons FW RC	12.00	5.50
❑ 135 Cesar Crespo FW RC	10.00	4.50
❑ 136 Ken Griffey Jr. SS	15.00	6.75
❑ 137 Mark McGwire SS	20.00	9.00
❑ 138 Derek Jeter SS	20.00	9.00
❑ 139 Alex Rodriguez SS	12.00	5.50
❑ 140 Sammy Sosa SS	10.00	4.50
❑ 141 Carlos Delgado SS	5.00	2.20
❑ 142 Cal Ripken SS	20.00	9.00
❑ 143 Pedro Martinez SS	6.00	2.70
❑ 144 Frank Thomas SS	6.00	2.70
❑ 145 Juan Gonzalez SS	5.00	2.20
❑ 146 Troy Glaus SS	5.00	2.20
❑ 147 Jason Giambi SS	5.00	2.20
❑ 148 Ivan Rodriguez SS	5.00	2.20
❑ 149 Chipper Jones SS	10.00	4.50
❑ 150 Vladimir Guerrero SS	6.00	2.70
❑ 151 Mike Piazza SS	12.00	5.50
❑ 152 Jeff Bagwell SS	6.00	2.70
❑ 153 Randy Johnson SS	6.00	2.70
❑ 154 Todd Helton SS	6.00	2.70
❑ 155 Gary Sheffield SS	5.00	2.20
❑ 156 Tony Gwynn SS	10.00	4.50
❑ 157 Barry Bonds SS	12.00	5.50
❑ 158 Nomar Garciaparra SS	12.00	5.50
❑ 159 Bernie Williams SS	5.00	2.20
❑ 160 Greg Vaughn SS	5.00	2.20
❑ 161 David Wells SS	5.00	2.20
❑ 162 Roberto Alomar SS	5.00	2.20
❑ 163 Jermaine Dye SS	5.00	2.20
❑ 164 Rafael Palmeiro SS	5.00	2.20
❑ 165 Andruw Jones SS	5.00	2.20
❑ 166 Preston Wilson SS	5.00	2.20
❑ 167 Edgardo Alfonzo SS	5.00	2.20
❑ 168 Pat Burrell SS	5.00	2.20
❑ 169 Jim Edmonds SS	5.00	2.20
❑ 170 Mike Hampton SS	5.00	2.20
❑ 171 Jeff Kent SS	5.00	2.20
❑ 172 Kevin Brown SS	5.00	2.20
❑ 173 Manny Ramirez SS	6.00	2.70
❑ 174 Magglio Ordonez SS	5.00	2.20
❑ 175 Roger Clemens SS	12.00	5.50
❑ 176 Jim Thome SS	5.00	2.20
❑ 177 Barry Zito SS	5.00	2.20
❑ 178 Brian Giles SS	5.00	2.20
❑ 179 Rick Ankiel SS	5.00	2.20
❑ 180 Corey Patterson SS	5.00	2.20

2001 SP Game Bat Edition

	MINT	NRMT
COMPLETE SET (90)	80.00	36.00
❑ 1 Troy Glaus	2.00	.90
❑ 2 Darin Erstad	2.00	.90
❑ 3 Mo Vaughn	.75	.35
❑ 4 Jason Giambi	2.00	.90
❑ 5 Ben Grieve	.75	.35
❑ 6 Eric Chavez	.75	.35
❑ 7 Carlos Delgado	2.00	.90
❑ 8 Tony Batista	.75	.35
❑ 9 Shannon Stewart	.75	.35
❑ 10 Jose Cruz Jr.	.75	.35
❑ 11 Fred McGriff	1.25	.55
❑ 12 Greg Vaughn	.75	.35
❑ 13 Roberto Alomar	2.00	.90
❑ 14 Manny Ramirez	2.50	1.10
❑ 15 Jim Thome	2.00	.90
❑ 16 Russell Branyan	.75	.35
❑ 17 Alex Rodriguez	5.00	2.20
❑ 18 John Olerud	.75	.35
❑ 19 Edgar Martinez	1.25	.55
❑ 20 Cal Ripken	8.00	3.60
❑ 21 Albert Belle	.75	.35
❑ 22 Ivan Rodriguez	2.00	.90
❑ 23 Rafael Palmeiro	2.00	.90
❑ 24 Nomar Garciaparra	5.00	2.20
❑ 25 Carl Everett	.75	.35
❑ 26 Dante Bichette	.75	.35
❑ 27 Mike Sweeney	.75	.35
❑ 28 Jermaine Dye	.75	.35
❑ 29 Carlos Beltran	.75	.35
❑ 30 Juan Gonzalez	2.00	.90
❑ 31 Dean Palmer	.75	.35
❑ 32 Bobby Higginson	.75	.35
❑ 33 Matt Lawton	.75	.35
❑ 34 Jacque Jones	.75	.35
❑ 35 Frank Thomas	2.50	1.10
❑ 36 Magglio Ordonez	.75	.35
❑ 37 Paul Konerko	.75	.35
❑ 38 Carlos Lee	.75	.35
❑ 39 Bernie Williams	2.00	.90
❑ 40 Derek Jeter	8.00	3.60
❑ 41 Paul O'Neill	2.00	.90
❑ 42 Jose Canseco	2.00	.90
❑ 43 Ken Caminiti	.75	.35
❑ 44 Jeff Bagwell	2.50	1.10
❑ 45 Craig Biggio	1.25	.55
❑ 46 Richard Hidalgo	.75	.35
❑ 47 Andruw Jones	2.00	.90
❑ 48 Chipper Jones	4.00	1.80
❑ 49 Andres Galarraga	1.25	.55
❑ 50 B.J. Surhoff	.75	.35
❑ 51 Jeromy Burnitz	.75	.35
❑ 52 Geoff Jenkins	.75	.35
❑ 53 Richie Sexson	.75	.35
❑ 54 Mark McGwire	8.00	3.60
❑ 55 Jim Edmonds	1.25	.55
❑ 56 J.D. Drew	2.00	.90
❑ 57 Fernando Tatis	.75	.35
❑ 58 Sammy Sosa	4.00	1.80
❑ 59 Mark Grace	2.00	.90
❑ 60 Eric Young	.75	.35
❑ 61 Matt Williams	.75	.35
❑ 62 Luis Gonzalez	2.00	.90
❑ 63 Steve Finley	.75	.35
❑ 64 Shawn Green	2.00	.90
❑ 65 Gary Sheffield	.75	.35
❑ 66 Eric Karros	.75	.35
❑ 67 Vladimir Guerrero	2.50	1.10
❑ 68 Jose Vidro	.75	.35
❑ 69 Barry Bonds	5.00	2.20
❑ 70 Jeff Kent	1.25	.55
❑ 71 Preston Wilson	.75	.35
❑ 72 Mike Lowell	.75	.35
❑ 73 Luis Castillo	.75	.35
❑ 74 Mike Piazza	5.00	2.20
❑ 75 Robin Ventura	.75	.35
❑ 76 Edgardo Alfonzo	.75	.35
❑ 77 Tony Gwynn	4.00	1.80
❑ 78 Eric Owens	.75	.35
❑ 79 Ryan Klesko	.75	.35
❑ 80 Scott Rolen	2.00	.90
❑ 81 Bobby Abreu	.75	.35
❑ 82 Pat Burrell	.75	.35
❑ 83 Brian Giles	.75	.35
❑ 84 Jason Kendall	.75	.35
❑ 85 Aaron Boone	.75	.35
❑ 86 Ken Griffey Jr.	6.00	2.70
❑ 87 Barry Larkin	2.00	.90
❑ 88 Todd Helton	2.50	1.10
❑ 89 Larry Walker	1.25	.55
❑ 90 Jeffrey Hammonds	.75	.35

2001 SP Game Bat Milestone

	MINT	NRMT
COMP.SET w/o SP's (90)	80.00	36.00
COMMON CARD (1-90)	.75	.35
COMMON BAT (91-96)	15.00	6.75
❑ 1 Troy Glaus	2.00	.90
❑ 2 Darin Erstad	2.00	.90
❑ 3 Jason Giambi	2.00	.90
❑ 4 Jermaine Dye	.75	.35
❑ 5 Eric Chavez	.75	.35
❑ 6 Carlos Delgado	2.00	.90
❑ 7 Raul Mondesi	.75	.35
❑ 8 Shannon Stewart	.75	.35
❑ 9 Greg Vaughn	.75	.35
❑ 10 Aubrey Huff	.75	.35
❑ 11 Juan Gonzalez	2.00	.90
❑ 12 Roberto Alomar	2.00	.90
❑ 13 Jim Thome	2.00	.90
❑ 14 Omar Vizquel	.75	.35
❑ 15 Mike Cameron	.75	.35
❑ 16 Edgar Martinez	1.25	.55
❑ 17 John Olerud	.75	.35
❑ 18 Bret Boone	.75	.35
❑ 19 Cal Ripken	8.00	3.60
❑ 20 Tony Batista	.75	.35
❑ 21 Alex Rodriguez	5.00	2.20
❑ 22 Ivan Rodriguez	2.00	.90
❑ 23 Rafael Palmeiro	2.00	.90
❑ 24 Manny Ramirez	2.50	1.10
❑ 25 Pedro Martinez	2.50	1.10
❑ 26 Nomar Garciaparra	5.00	2.20
❑ 27 Carl Everett	.75	.35
❑ 28 Mike Sweeney	.75	.35
❑ 29 Neifi Perez	.75	.35
❑ 30 Mark Quinn	.75	.35
❑ 31 Bobby Higginson	.75	.35

❑ 32 Tony Clark	.75	.35
❑ 33 Doug Mientkiewicz	.75	.35
❑ 34 Cristian Guzman	.75	.35
❑ 35 Joe Mays	.75	.35
❑ 36 David Ortiz	.75	.35
❑ 37 Frank Thomas	2.50	1.10
❑ 38 Magglio Ordonez	.75	.35
❑ 39 Carlos Lee	.75	.35
❑ 40 Alfonso Soriano	2.00	.90
❑ 41 Bernie Williams	2.00	.90
❑ 42 Derek Jeter	8.00	3.60
❑ 43 Roger Clemens	5.00	2.20
❑ 44 Jeff Bagwell	2.50	1.10
❑ 45 Richard Hidalgo	.75	.35
❑ 46 Moises Alou	.75	.35
❑ 47 Chipper Jones	4.00	1.80
❑ 48 Greg Maddux	5.00	2.20
❑ 49 Rafael Furcal	.75	.35
❑ 50 Andruw Jones	2.00	.90
❑ 51 Jeromy Burnitz	.75	.35
❑ 52 Geoff Jenkins	.75	.35
❑ 53 Richie Sexson	.75	.35
❑ 54 Edgar Renteria	.75	.35
❑ 55 Mark McGwire	8.00	3.60
❑ 56 Jim Edmonds	1.25	.55
❑ 57 J.D. Drew	2.00	.90
❑ 58 Sammy Sosa	4.00	1.80
❑ 59 Bill Mueller	.75	.35
❑ 60 Luis Gonzalez	2.00	.90
❑ 61 Randy Johnson	2.50	1.10
❑ 62 Gary Sheffield	.75	.35
❑ 63 Shawn Green	2.00	.90
❑ 64 Kevin Brown	.75	.35
❑ 65 Vladimir Guerrero	2.50	1.10
❑ 66 Jose Vidro	.75	.35
❑ 67 Fernando Tatis	.75	.35
❑ 68 Barry Bonds	5.00	2.20
❑ 69 Jeff Kent	1.25	.55
❑ 70 Rich Aurilia	.75	.35
❑ 71 Preston Wilson	.75	.35
❑ 72 Charles Johnson	.75	.35
❑ 73 Cliff Floyd	.75	.35
❑ 74 Mike Piazza	5.00	2.20
❑ 75 Matt Lawton	.75	.35
❑ 76 Edgardo Alfonzo	.75	.35
❑ 77 Tony Gwynn	4.00	1.80
❑ 78 Phil Nevin	.75	.35
❑ 79 Scott Rolen	2.00	.90
❑ 80 Pat Burrell	.75	.35
❑ 81 Bobby Abreu	.75	.35
❑ 82 Brian Giles	.75	.35
❑ 83 Jason Kendall	.75	.35
❑ 84 Aramis Ramirez	.75	.35
❑ 85 Sean Casey	1.25	.55
❑ 86 Ken Griffey Jr.	6.00	2.70
❑ 87 Barry Larkin	2.00	.90
❑ 88 Todd Helton	2.50	1.10
❑ 89 Mike Hampton	.75	.35
❑ 90 Larry Walker	1.25	.55
❑ 91 Ichiro Suzuki BAT RC	250.00	110.00
❑ 92 Albert Pujols BAT RC	100.00	45.00
❑ 93 Tsuyoshi Shinjo BAT RC	50.00	22.00
❑ 94 Jack Wilson BAT RC	15.00	6.75
❑ 95 Donaldo Mendez BAT RC	15.00	6.75
❑ 96 Junior Spivey BAT RC	15.00	6.75

2001 SP Game-Used Edition

	MINT	NRMT
fCOMP.SET w/o SP's (60)	80.00	36.00
COMMON CARD (61-90)	15.00	6.75
❑ 1 Garret Anderson	1.00	.45
❑ 2 Troy Glaus	2.50	1.10
❑ 3 Darin Erstad	2.50	1.10
❑ 4 Jason Giambi	2.50	1.10
❑ 5 Tim Hudson	2.50	1.10
❑ 6 Johnny Damon	1.00	.45
❑ 7 Carlos Delgado	2.50	1.10
❑ 8 Greg Vaughn	1.00	.45
❑ 9 Juan Gonzalez	2.50	1.10
❑ 10 Roberto Alomar	2.50	1.10
❑ 11 Jim Thome	2.50	1.10
❑ 12 Edgar Martinez	1.50	.70

❑ 13 Cal Ripken	10.00	4.50
❑ 14 Andres Galarraga	1.50	.70
❑ 15 Alex Rodriguez	6.00	2.70
❑ 16 Rafael Palmeiro	2.50	1.10
❑ 17 Ivan Rodriguez	2.50	1.10
❑ 18 Manny Ramirez	3.00	1.35
❑ 19 Nomar Garciaparra	6.00	2.70
❑ 20 Pedro Martinez	3.00	1.35
❑ 21 Jermaine Dye	1.00	.45
❑ 22 Dean Palmer	1.00	.45
❑ 23 Matt Lawton	1.00	.45
❑ 24 Frank Thomas	3.00	1.35
❑ 25 David Wells	1.00	.45
❑ 26 Magglio Ordonez	1.00	.45
❑ 27 Derek Jeter	10.00	4.50
❑ 28 Bernie Williams	2.50	1.10
❑ 29 Roger Clemens	6.00	2.70
❑ 30 Jeff Bagwell	3.00	1.35
❑ 31 Richard Hidalgo	1.00	.45
❑ 32 Chipper Jones	5.00	2.20
❑ 33 Andruw Jones	2.50	1.10
❑ 34 Greg Maddux	6.00	2.70
❑ 35 Jeffrey Hammonds	1.00	.45
❑ 36 Mark McGwire	10.00	4.50
❑ 37 Jim Edmonds	1.50	.70
❑ 38 Sammy Sosa	5.00	2.20
❑ 39 Corey Patterson	1.00	.45
❑ 40 Randy Johnson	3.00	1.35
❑ 41 Luis Gonzalez	2.50	1.10
❑ 42 Gary Sheffield	1.00	.45
❑ 43 Shawn Green	2.50	1.10
❑ 44 Kevin Brown	1.00	.45
❑ 45 Vladimir Guerrero	3.00	1.35
❑ 46 Barry Bonds	6.00	2.70
❑ 47 Jeff Kent	1.50	.70
❑ 48 Preston Wilson	1.00	.45
❑ 49 Charles Johnson	1.00	.45
❑ 50 Mike Piazza	6.00	2.70
❑ 51 Edgardo Alfonzo	1.00	.45
❑ 52 Tony Gwynn	5.00	2.20
❑ 53 Scott Rolen	2.50	1.10
❑ 54 Pat Burrell	1.00	.45
❑ 55 Brian Giles	1.00	.45
❑ 56 Jason Kendall	1.00	.45
❑ 57 Ken Griffey Jr.	8.00	3.60
❑ 58 Mike Hampton	1.00	.45
❑ 59 Todd Helton	3.00	1.35
❑ 60 Larry Walker	1.50	.70
❑ 61 Wilson Betemit RC	40.00	18.00
❑ 62 Travis Hafner RC	20.00	9.00
❑ 63 Ichiro Suzuki RC	250.00	110.00
❑ 64 Juan Diaz RC	15.00	6.75
❑ 65 Morgan Ensberg RC	25.00	11.00
❑ 66 Horacio Ramirez RC	15.00	6.75
❑ 67 Ricardo Rodriguez RC	20.00	9.00
❑ 68 Sean Douglass RC	15.00	6.75
❑ 69 Brandon Duckworth RC	30.00	13.50
❑ 70 Jackson Melian RC	15.00	6.75
❑ 71 Adrian Hernandez RC	15.00	6.75
❑ 72 Kyle Kessel RC	15.00	6.75
❑ 73 Jason Michaels RC	15.00	6.75
❑ 74 Esix Snead RC	15.00	6.75
❑ 75 Jason Smith RC	15.00	6.75
❑ 76 Tyler Walker RC	15.00	6.75
❑ 77 Juan Uribe RC	25.00	11.00
❑ 78 Adam Pettyjohn RC	15.00	6.75
❑ 79 Tsuyoshi Shinjo RC	40.00	18.00
❑ 80 Mike Penney RC	15.00	6.75
❑ 81 Josh Towers RC	25.00	11.00
❑ 82 Erick Almonte RC	20.00	9.00
❑ 83 Ryan Freel RC	15.00	6.75
❑ 84 Juan Pena	15.00	6.75
❑ 85 Albert Pujols RC	120.00	55.00
❑ 86 Henry Mateo RC	15.00	6.75
❑ 87 Greg Miller RC	15.00	6.75
❑ 88 Jose Mieses RC	15.00	6.75
❑ 89 Jack Wilson RC	15.00	6.75
❑ 90 Carlos Valderrama RC	15.00	6.75

2001 SP Legendary Cuts

	MINT	NRMT
COMPLETE SET (90)	40.00	18.00
❑ 1 Al Simmons	.25	.11
❑ 2 Jimmie Foxx	.60	.25
❑ 3 Mickey Cochrane	.40	.18
❑ 4 Phil Niekro	.40	.18
❑ 5 Eddie Mathews	.60	.25
❑ 6 Gary Matthews	.25	.11
❑ 7 Hank Aaron	1.50	.70
❑ 8 Joe Adcock	.25	.11
❑ 9 Warren Spahn	.60	.25
❑ 10 George Sisler	.25	.11
❑ 11 Stan Musial	1.25	.55
❑ 12 Dizzy Dean	.60	.25
❑ 13 Frankie Frisch	.25	.11
❑ 14 Harvey Haddix	.25	.11
❑ 15 Johnny Mize	.40	.18
❑ 16 Ken Boyer	.25	.11
❑ 17 Rogers Hornsby	.60	.25
❑ 18 Cap Anson	.60	.25
❑ 19 Andre Dawson	.40	.18
❑ 20 Billy Williams	.40	.18
❑ 21 Billy Herman	.25	.11
❑ 22 Hack Wilson	.40	.18
❑ 23 Ron Santo	.40	.18
❑ 24 Ryne Sandberg	.75	.35
❑ 25 Ernie Banks	.75	.35
❑ 26 Burleigh Grimes	.25	.11
❑ 27 Don Drysdale	.60	.25
❑ 28 Gil Hodges	.60	.25
❑ 29 Jackie Robinson	1.25	.55
❑ 30 Tommy Lasorda	.25	.11
❑ 31 Pee Wee Reese	.60	.25
❑ 32 Roy Campanella	.75	.35
❑ 33 Tommy Davis	.25	.11
❑ 34 Branch Rickey	.25	.11
❑ 35 Leo Durocher	.40	.18
❑ 36 Walt Alston	.25	.11
❑ 37 Bill Terry	.25	.11
❑ 38 Carl Hubbell	.40	.18
❑ 39 Eddie Stanky	.25	.11
❑ 40 George Kelly	.25	.11
❑ 41 Mel Ott	.60	.25
❑ 42 Juan Marichal	.40	.18
❑ 43 Rube Marquard	.25	.11
❑ 44 Travis Jackson	.25	.11
❑ 45 Bob Feller	.60	.25
❑ 46 Earl Averill	.25	.11
❑ 47 Elmer Flick	.25	.11
❑ 48 Ken Keltner	.25	.11
❑ 49 Lou Boudreau	.40	.18
❑ 50 Early Wynn	.40	.18
❑ 51 Satchel Paige	.75	.35

❑ 52 Ron Hunt	.25	.11
❑ 53 Tom Seaver	.75	.35
❑ 54 Richie Ashburn	.60	.25
❑ 55 Mike Schmidt	1.25	.55
❑ 56 Honus Wagner	1.00	.45
❑ 57 Lloyd Waner	.40	.18
❑ 58 Max Carey	.25	.11
❑ 59 Paul Waner	.40	.18
❑ 60 Roberto Clemente	2.00	.90
❑ 61 Nolan Ryan	3.00	1.35
❑ 62 Bobby Doerr	.40	.18
❑ 63 Carlton Fisk	.60	.25
❑ 64 Joe Cronin	.25	.11
❑ 65 Joe Wood	.25	.11
❑ 66 Tony Conigliaro	.40	.18
❑ 67 Edd Roush	.25	.11
❑ 68 Johnny VanderMeer	.25	.11
❑ 69 Walter Johnson	.60	.25
❑ 70 Charlie Gehringer	.25	.11
❑ 71 Al Kaline	.75	.35
❑ 72 Ty Cobb	1.50	.70
❑ 73 Tony Oliva	.25	.11
❑ 74 Luke Appling	.25	.11
❑ 75 Minnie Minoso	.25	.11
❑ 76 Nellie Fox	.40	.18
❑ 77 Joe Jackson	1.50	.70
❑ 78 Babe Ruth	3.00	1.35
❑ 79 Bill Dickey	.40	.18
❑ 80 Elston Howard	.25	.11
❑ 81 Joe DiMaggio	2.00	.90
❑ 82 Lefty Gomez	.60	.25
❑ 83 Lou Gehrig	2.00	.90
❑ 84 Mickey Mantle	3.00	1.35
❑ 85 Reggie Jackson	.75	.35
❑ 86 Roger Maris	1.25	.55
❑ 87 Whitey Ford	.60	.25
❑ 88 Waite Hoyt	.25	.11
❑ 89 Yogi Berra	.75	.35
❑ 90 Casey Stengel	.60	.25

1996 SPx

	MINT	NRMT
COMPLETE SET (60)	60.00	27.00
❑ 1 Greg Maddux	4.00	1.80
❑ 2 Chipper Jones	3.00	1.35
❑ 3 Fred McGriff	1.00	.45
❑ 4 Tom Glavine	1.50	.70
❑ 5 Cal Ripken	6.00	2.70
❑ 6 Roberto Alomar	1.50	.70
❑ 7 Rafael Palmeiro	1.50	.70
❑ 8 Jose Canseco	1.50	.70
❑ 9 Roger Clemens	4.00	1.80
❑ 10 Mo Vaughn	.60	.25
❑ 11 Jim Edmonds	1.00	.45
❑ 12 Tim Salmon	.60	.25
❑ 13 Sammy Sosa	3.00	1.35
❑ 14 Ryne Sandberg	2.00	.90
❑ 15 Mark Grace	1.50	.70
❑ 16 Frank Thomas	2.00	.90
❑ 17 Barry Larkin	1.50	.70
❑ 18 Kenny Lofton	.60	.25
❑ 19 Albert Belle	.60	.25
❑ 20 Eddie Murray	1.50	.70
❑ 21 Manny Ramirez	2.00	.90
❑ 22 Dante Bichette	.60	.25
❑ 23 Larry Walker	1.00	.45
❑ 24 Vinny Castilla	.60	.25
❑ 25 Andres Galarraga	1.00	.45
❑ 26 Cecil Fielder	.60	.25
❑ 27 Gary Sheffield	.60	.25
❑ 28 Craig Biggio	1.00	.45
❑ 29 Jeff Bagwell	2.00	.90
❑ 30 Derek Bell	.60	.25
❑ 31 Johnny Damon	.60	.25
❑ 32 Eric Karros	.60	.25
❑ 33 Mike Piazza	4.00	1.80
❑ 34 Raul Mondesi	.60	.25
❑ 35 Hideo Nomo	2.00	.90
❑ 36 Kirby Puckett	4.00	1.80
❑ 37 Paul Molitor	1.50	.70
❑ 38 Marty Cordova	.60	.25
❑ 39 Rondell White	.60	.25
❑ 40 Jason Isringhausen	.60	.25
❑ 41 Paul Wilson	.60	.25
❑ 42 Rey Ordonez	.60	.25
❑ 43 Derek Jeter	6.00	2.70
❑ 44 Wade Boggs	1.50	.70
❑ 45 Mark McGwire	6.00	2.70
❑ 46 Jason Kendall	.60	.25
❑ 47 Ron Gant	.60	.25
❑ 48 Ozzie Smith	2.00	.90
❑ 49 Tony Gwynn	3.00	1.35
❑ 50 Ken Caminiti	.60	.25
❑ 51 Barry Bonds	4.00	1.80
❑ 52 Matt Williams	1.00	.45
❑ 53 Osvaldo Fernandez	.60	.25
❑ 54 Jay Buhner	.60	.25
❑ 55 Ken Griffey Jr.	5.00	2.20
❑ 56 Randy Johnson	2.00	.90
❑ 57 Alex Rodriguez	4.00	1.80
❑ 58 Juan Gonzalez	1.50	.70
❑ 59 Joe Carter	.60	.25
❑ 60 Carlos Delgado	1.50	.70
❑ KG1 K.Griffey Jr. Comm.	8.00	3.60
❑ MP1 Mike Piazza Trib.	6.00	2.70
❑ KGA1 Ken Griffey Jr. Auto.	200.00	90.00
❑ MPA1 Mike Piazza Auto.	120.00	55.00

1997 SPx

	MINT	NRMT
COMPLETE SET (50)	60.00	27.00
❑ 1 Eddie Murray	1.25	.55
❑ 2 Darin Erstad	1.25	.55
❑ 3 Tim Salmon	.50	.23
❑ 4 Andruw Jones	1.50	.70
❑ 5 Chipper Jones	2.50	1.10
❑ 6 John Smoltz	.50	.23
❑ 7 Greg Maddux	3.00	1.35
❑ 8 Kenny Lofton	.50	.23
❑ 9 Roberto Alomar	1.25	.55
❑ 10 Rafael Palmeiro	1.25	.55
❑ 11 Brady Anderson	.50	.23
❑ 12 Cal Ripken	5.00	2.20
❑ 13 Nomar Garciaparra	3.00	1.35
❑ 14 Mo Vaughn	.50	.23
❑ 15 Ryne Sandberg	1.50	.70
❑ 16 Sammy Sosa	2.50	1.10
❑ 17 Frank Thomas	1.50	.70
❑ 18 Albert Belle	.50	.23
❑ 19 Barry Larkin	1.25	.55
❑ 20 Deion Sanders	.50	.23
❑ 21 Manny Ramirez	1.50	.70
❑ 22 Jim Thome	1.25	.55
❑ 23 Dante Bichette	.50	.23
❑ 24 Andres Galarraga	.75	.35
❑ 25 Larry Walker	.75	.35
❑ 26 Gary Sheffield	.50	.23
❑ 27 Jeff Bagwell	1.50	.70
❑ 28 Raul Mondesi	.50	.23
❑ 29 Hideo Nomo	1.25	.55
❑ 30 Mike Piazza	3.00	1.35
❑ 31 Paul Molitor	1.25	.55
❑ 32 Todd Walker	.50	.23
❑ 33 Vladimir Guerrero	2.00	.90
❑ 34 Todd Hundley	.50	.23
❑ 35 Andy Pettitte	.50	.23
❑ 36 Derek Jeter	5.00	2.20
❑ 37 Jose Canseco	1.25	.55
❑ 38 Mark McGwire	5.00	2.20
❑ 39 Scott Rolen	1.25	.55
❑ 40 Ron Gant	.50	.23
❑ 41 Ken Caminiti	.50	.23
❑ 42 Tony Gwynn	2.50	1.10
❑ 43 Barry Bonds	3.00	1.35
❑ 44 Jay Buhner	.50	.23
❑ 45 Ken Griffey Jr.	4.00	1.80
❑ 46 Alex Rodriguez	3.00	1.35
❑ 47 Jose Cruz Jr. RC	3.00	1.35
❑ 48 Juan Gonzalez	1.25	.55
❑ 49 Ivan Rodriguez	1.25	.55
❑ 50 Roger Clemens	3.00	1.35
❑ S45 Ken Griffey Jr. SAMPLE	2.50	1.10

1998 SPx Finite

	MINT	NRMT
COMP.YM SER.1 (30)	60.00	27.00
COMMON YM (1-30)	.75	.35
COMP.PE SER.1 (20)	150.00	70.00
COMMON PE (31-50)	2.00	.90
COMP.BASIC SER.1 (90)	100.00	45.00
COMMON CARD (51-140)	.50	.23
COMP.SF SER.1 (30)	120.00	55.00
COMMON SF (141-170)	1.00	.45
COMP.HG SER.1 (10)	200.00	90.00
COMMON HG (171-180)	10.00	4.50
COMP.YM SER.2 (30)	120.00	55.00
COMMON YM (181-210)	1.50	.70
COMP.PP SER.2 (30)	100.00	45.00
COMMON PP (211-240)	1.00	.45
COMP.BASIC SER.2 (90)	60.00	27.00
COMMON CARD (241-330)	.50	.23
COMP.TW SER.2 (20)	40.00	18.00
COMMON TW (331-350)	1.25	.55
COMP.CG SER.2 (10)	200.00	90.00
COMMON CG (351-360)	8.00	3.60
❑ 1 Nomar Garciaparra YM	8.00	3.60
❑ 2 Miguel Tejada YM	2.00	.90
❑ 3 Mike Cameron YM	1.25	.55
❑ 4 Ken Cloude YM	.75	.35
❑ 5 Jaret Wright YM	.75	.35
❑ 6 Mark Kotsay YM	1.25	.55
❑ 7 Craig Counsell YM	.75	.35
❑ 8 Jose Guillen YM	.75	.35
❑ 9 Neifi Perez YM	.75	.35
❑ 10 Jose Cruz Jr. YM	1.25	.55
❑ 11 Brett Tomko YM	.75	.35
❑ 12 Matt Morris YM	1.25	.55
❑ 13 Justin Thompson YM	.75	.35
❑ 14 Jeremi Gonzalez YM	.75	.35
❑ 15 Scott Rolen YM	3.00	1.35

❑ 16 Vladimir Guerrero YM 4.00 1.80
❑ 17 Brad Fullmer YM 1.25 .55
❑ 18 Brian Giles YM 1.25 .55
❑ 19 Todd Dunwoody YM .75 .35
❑ 20 Ben Grieve YM 1.25 .55
❑ 21 Juan Encarnacion YM 1.25 .55
❑ 22 Aaron Boone YM .75 .35
❑ 23 Richie Sexson YM 1.25 .55
❑ 24 Richard Hidalgo YM 1.25 .55
❑ 25 Andruw Jones YM 3.00 1.35
❑ 26 Todd Helton YM 4.00 1.80
❑ 27 Paul Konerko YM 1.25 .55
❑ 28 Dante Powell YM .75 .35
❑ 29 Eli Marrero YM .75 .35
❑ 30 Derek Jeter YM 12.00 5.50
❑ 31 Mike Piazza PE 12.00 5.50
❑ 32 Tony Clark PE 2.50 1.10
❑ 33 Larry Walker PE 3.00 1.35
❑ 34 Jim Thome PE 5.00 2.20
❑ 35 Juan Gonzalez PE 5.00 2.20
❑ 36 Jeff Bagwell PE 6.00 2.70
❑ 37 Jay Buhner PE 2.50 1.10
❑ 38 Tim Salmon PE 2.50 1.10
❑ 39 Albert Belle PE 2.50 1.10
❑ 40 Mark McGwire PE 20.00 9.00
❑ 41 Sammy Sosa PE 10.00 4.50
❑ 42 Mo Vaughn PE 2.50 1.10
❑ 43 Manny Ramirez PE 6.00 2.70
❑ 44 Tino Martinez PE 2.50 1.10
❑ 45 Frank Thomas PE 6.00 2.70
❑ 46 Nomar Garciaparra PE 12.00 5.50
❑ 47 Alex Rodriguez PE 12.00 5.50
❑ 48 Chipper Jones PE 10.00 4.50
❑ 49 Barry Bonds PE 12.00 5.50
❑ 50 Ken Griffey Jr. PE 15.00 6.75
❑ 51 Jason Dickson .50 .23
❑ 52 Jim Edmonds 3.00 1.35
❑ 53 Darin Erstad 2.00 .90
❑ 54 Tim Salmon .75 .35
❑ 55 Chipper Jones 4.00 1.80
❑ 56 Ryan Klesko .75 .35
❑ 57 Tom Glavine 2.00 .90
❑ 58 Denny Neagle .50 .23
❑ 59 John Smoltz .75 .35
❑ 60 Javy Lopez .75 .35
❑ 61 Roberto Alomar 2.00 .90
❑ 62 Rafael Palmeiro 2.00 .90
❑ 63 Mike Mussina 2.00 .90
❑ 64 Cal Ripken 8.00 3.60
❑ 65 Mo Vaughn .75 .35
❑ 66 Tim Naehring .50 .23
❑ 67 John Valentin .50 .23
❑ 68 Mark Grace 2.00 .90
❑ 69 Kevin Orie .50 .23
❑ 70 Sammy Sosa 4.00 1.80
❑ 71 Albert Belle .75 .35
❑ 72 Frank Thomas 2.50 1.10
❑ 73 Robin Ventura .75 .35
❑ 74 David Justice .75 .35
❑ 75 Kenny Lofton .75 .35
❑ 76 Omar Vizquel .75 .35
❑ 77 Manny Ramirez 2.50 1.10
❑ 78 Jim Thome 2.00 .90
❑ 79 Dante Bichette .75 .35
❑ 80 Larry Walker 1.25 .55
❑ 81 Vinny Castilla .75 .35
❑ 82 Ellis Burks .75 .35
❑ 83 Bobby Higginson .75 .35
❑ 84 Brian Hunter .50 .23
❑ 85 Tony Clark .75 .35
❑ 86 Mike Hampton .75 .35
❑ 87 Jeff Bagwell 2.50 1.10
❑ 88 Craig Biggio 1.25 .55
❑ 89 Derek Bell .75 .35
❑ 90 Mike Piazza 5.00 2.20
❑ 91 Ramon Martinez .50 .23
❑ 92 Raul Mondesi .75 .35
❑ 93 Hideo Nomo 2.00 .90
❑ 94 Eric Karros .75 .35
❑ 95 Paul Molitor 2.00 .90
❑ 96 Marty Cordova .50 .23
❑ 97 Brad Radke .75 .35
❑ 98 Mark Grudzielanek .50 .23
❑ 99 Carlos Perez .50 .23
❑ 100 Rondell White .75 .35
❑ 101 Todd Hundley .50 .23
❑ 102 Edgardo Alfonzo .75 .35
❑ 103 John Franco .75 .35
❑ 104 John Olerud .75 .35
❑ 105 Tino Martinez .75 .35
❑ 106 David Cone .75 .35
❑ 107 Paul O'Neill 2.00 .90
❑ 108 Andy Pettitte .75 .35
❑ 109 Bernie Williams 2.00 .90
❑ 110 Rickey Henderson 4.00 1.80
❑ 111 Jason Giambi 2.00 .90
❑ 112 Matt Stairs .50 .23
❑ 113 Gregg Jefferies .50 .23
❑ 114 Rico Brogna .50 .23
❑ 115 Curt Schilling 2.00 .90
❑ 116 Jason Schmidt .50 .23
❑ 117 Jose Guillen .50 .23
❑ 118 Kevin Young .75 .35
❑ 119 Ray Lankford .50 .23
❑ 120 Mark McGwire 8.00 3.60
❑ 121 Delino DeShields .50 .23
❑ 122 Ken Caminiti .75 .35
❑ 123 Tony Gwynn 4.00 1.80
❑ 124 Trevor Hoffman .75 .35
❑ 125 Barry Bonds 5.00 2.20
❑ 126 Jeff Kent 1.25 .55
❑ 127 Shawn Estes .75 .35
❑ 128 J.T. Snow .75 .35
❑ 129 Jay Buhner .75 .35
❑ 130 Ken Griffey Jr. 6.00 2.70
❑ 131 Dan Wilson .50 .23
❑ 132 Edgar Martinez 1.25 .55
❑ 133 Alex Rodriguez 5.00 2.20
❑ 134 Rusty Greer .75 .35
❑ 135 Juan Gonzalez .75 .35
❑ 136 Fernando Tatis .50 .23
❑ 137 Ivan Rodriguez 3.00 1.35
❑ 138 Carlos Delgado 2.00 .90
❑ 139 Pat Hentgen .50 .23
❑ 140 Roger Clemens 5.00 2.20
❑ 141 Chipper Jones SF 5.00 2.20
❑ 142 Greg Maddux SF 6.00 2.70
❑ 143 Rafael Palmeiro SF 2.50 1.10
❑ 144 Mike Mussina SF 2.50 1.10
❑ 145 Cal Ripken SF 10.00 4.50
❑ 146 Nomar Garciaparra SF 6.00 2.70
❑ 147 Mo Vaughn SF 1.00 .45
❑ 148 Sammy Sosa SF 5.00 2.20
❑ 149 Albert Belle SF 1.00 .45
❑ 150 Frank Thomas SF 3.00 1.35
❑ 151 Jim Thome SF 2.50 1.10
❑ 152 Kenny Lofton SF 1.00 .45
❑ 153 Manny Ramirez SF 3.00 1.35
❑ 154 Larry Walker SF 1.50 .70
❑ 155 Jeff Bagwell SF 3.00 1.35
❑ 156 Craig Biggio SF 1.50 .70
❑ 157 Mike Piazza SF 6.00 2.70
❑ 158 Paul Molitor SF 2.50 1.10
❑ 159 Derek Jeter SF 10.00 4.50
❑ 160 Tino Martinez SF 1.00 .45
❑ 161 Curt Schilling SF 2.50 1.10
❑ 162 Mark McGwire SF 10.00 4.50
❑ 163 Tony Gwynn SF 5.00 2.20
❑ 164 Barry Bonds SF 6.00 2.70
❑ 165 Ken Griffey Jr. SF 8.00 3.60
❑ 166 Randy Johnson SF 3.00 1.35
❑ 167 Alex Rodriguez SF 6.00 2.70
❑ 168 Juan Gonzalez SF 2.50 1.10
❑ 169 Ivan Rodriguez SF 3.00 1.35
❑ 170 Roger Clemens SF 6.00 2.70
❑ 171 Greg Maddux HG 20.00 9.00
❑ 172 Cal Ripken HG 30.00 13.50
❑ 173 Frank Thomas HG 10.00 4.50
❑ 174 Jeff Bagwell HG 10.00 4.50
❑ 175 Mike Piazza HG 20.00 9.00
❑ 176 Mark McGwire HG 30.00 13.50
❑ 177 Barry Bonds HG 20.00 9.00
❑ 178 Ken Griffey Jr. HG 25.00 11.00
❑ 179 Alex Rodriguez HG 20.00 9.00
❑ 180 Roger Clemens HG 20.00 9.00
❑ 181 Mike Caruso YM 1.50 .70
❑ 182 David Ortiz YM 2.00 .90
❑ 183 Gabe Alvarez YM 1.50 .70
❑ 184 G.Matthews Jr. YM RC 1.50 .70
❑ 185 Kerry Wood YM 4.00 1.80
❑ 186 Carl Pavano YM 1.50 .70
❑ 187 Alex Gonzalez YM 1.50 .70
❑ 188 Masato Yoshii YM RC 5.00 2.20
❑ 189 Larry Sutton YM 1.50 .70
❑ 190 Russell Branyan YM 2.00 .90
❑ 191 Bruce Chen YM 1.50 .70
❑ 192 R. Arrojo YM RC 5.00 2.20
❑ 193 R.Christenson YM RC 1.50 .70
❑ 194 Cliff Politte YM 1.50 .70
❑ 195 A.J. Hinch YM 1.50 .70
❑ 196 Kevin Witt YM 1.50 .70
❑ 197 Daryle Ward YM 1.50 .70
❑ 198 Corey Koskie YM RC 10.00 4.50
❑ 199 Mike Lowell YM RC 8.00 3.60
❑ 200 Travis Lee YM 2.00 .90
❑ 201 K.Millwood YM RC 6.00 2.70
❑ 202 Robert Smith YM 1.50 .70
❑ 203 M.Ordonez YM RC 15.00 6.75
❑ 204 Eric Milton YM 2.00 .90
❑ 205 Geoff Jenkins YM 2.00 .90
❑ 206 Rich Butler YM RC 1.50 .70
❑ 207 Mike Kinkade YM RC 2.00 .90
❑ 208 Braden Looper YM 1.50 .70
❑ 209 Matt Clement YM 2.00 .90
❑ 210 Derrek Lee YM 2.00 .90
❑ 211 Randy Johnson PP 3.00 1.35
❑ 212 John Smoltz PP 1.00 .45
❑ 213 Roger Clemens PP 6.00 2.70
❑ 214 Curt Schilling PP 2.50 1.10
❑ 215 Pedro Martinez PP 3.00 1.35
❑ 216 Vinny Castilla PP 1.00 .45
❑ 217 Jose Cruz Jr. PP 1.00 .45
❑ 218 Jim Thome PP 2.50 1.10
❑ 219 Alex Rodriguez PP 6.00 2.70
❑ 220 Frank Thomas PP 3.00 1.35
❑ 221 Tim Salmon PP 1.00 .45
❑ 222 Larry Walker PP 1.50 .70
❑ 223 Albert Belle PP 1.00 .45
❑ 224 Manny Ramirez PP 3.00 1.35
❑ 225 Mark McGwire PP 10.00 4.50
❑ 226 Mo Vaughn PP 1.00 .45
❑ 227 Andres Galarraga PP 1.50 .70
❑ 228 Scott Rolen PP 2.50 1.10
❑ 229 Travis Lee PP 1.00 .45
❑ 230 Mike Piazza PP 6.00 2.70
❑ 231 N.Garciaparra PP 6.00 2.70
❑ 232 Andruw Jones PP 2.50 1.10
❑ 233 Barry Bonds PP 6.00 2.70
❑ 234 Jeff Bagwell PP 3.00 1.35
❑ 235 Juan Gonzalez PP 2.50 1.10
❑ 236 Tino Martinez PP 1.00 .45
❑ 237 Vladimir Guerrero PP 3.00 1.35
❑ 238 Rafael Palmeiro PP 2.50 1.10
❑ 239 Russell Branyan PP 1.00 .45
❑ 240 Ken Griffey Jr. PP 8.00 3.60
❑ 241 Cecil Fielder .75 .35
❑ 242 Chuck Finley .75 .35
❑ 243 Jay Bell .75 .35
❑ 244 Andy Benes .50 .23
❑ 245 Matt Williams 1.25 .55
❑ 246 Brian Anderson .50 .23
❑ 247 Dave Dellucci RC .50 .23
❑ 248 Andres Galarraga 1.25 .55
❑ 249 Andruw Jones 2.00 .90
❑ 250 Greg Maddux 5.00 2.20
❑ 251 Brady Anderson .75 .35
❑ 252 Joe Carter .75 .35
❑ 253 Eric Davis .75 .35
❑ 254 Pedro Martinez 2.50 1.10
❑ 255 Nomar Garciaparra 5.00 2.20
❑ 256 Dennis Eckersley .75 .35
❑ 257 Henry Rodriguez .50 .23
❑ 258 Jeff Blauser .50 .23
❑ 259 Jaime Navarro .50 .23
❑ 260 Ray Durham .75 .35
❑ 261 Chris Stynes .50 .23
❑ 262 Willie Greene .50 .23
❑ 263 Reggie Sanders .50 .23
❑ 264 Bret Boone .75 .35
❑ 265 Barry Larkin 2.00 .90
❑ 266 Travis Fryman .75 .35
❑ 267 Charles Nagy .50 .23
❑ 268 Sandy Alomar Jr. .75 .35
❑ 269 Darryl Kile .75 .35
❑ 270 Mike Lansing .50 .23
❑ 271 Pedro Astacio .50 .23
❑ 272 Damion Easley .50 .23
❑ 273 Joe Randa .50 .23

	Card	Player	Mint	NrMt
❑	274	Luis Gonzalez	2.00	.90
❑	275	Mike Piazza	5.00	2.20
❑	276	Todd Zeile	.75	.35
❑	277	Edgar Renteria	.50	.23
❑	278	Livan Hernandez	.50	.23
❑	279	Cliff Floyd	.75	.35
❑	280	Moises Alou	.75	.35
❑	281	Billy Wagner	.50	.23
❑	282	Jeff King	.50	.23
❑	283	Hal Morris	.50	.23
❑	284	Johnny Damon	.75	.35
❑	285	Dean Palmer	.75	.35
❑	286	Tim Belcher	.50	.23
❑	287	Eric Young	.50	.23
❑	288	Bobby Bonilla	.75	.35
❑	289	Gary Sheffield	.75	.35
❑	290	Chan Ho Park	.75	.35
❑	291	Charles Johnson	.75	.35
❑	292	Jeff Cirillo	.75	.35
❑	293	Jeromy Burnitz	.75	.35
❑	294	Jose Valentin	.50	.23
❑	295	Marquis Grissom	.50	.23
❑	296	Todd Walker	.50	.23
❑	297	Terry Steinbach	.50	.23
❑	298	Rick Aguilera	.50	.23
❑	299	Vladimir Guerrero	2.50	1.10
❑	300	Rey Ordonez	.50	.23
❑	301	Butch Huskey	.50	.23
❑	302	Bernard Gilkey	.50	.23
❑	303	Mariano Rivera	.75	.35
❑	304	Chuck Knoblauch	.75	.35
❑	305	Derek Jeter	8.00	3.60
❑	306	Ricky Bottalico	.50	.23
❑	307	Bob Abreu	.75	.35
❑	308	Scott Rolen	2.00	.90
❑	309	Al Martin	.50	.23
❑	310	Jason Kendall	.75	.35
❑	311	Brian Jordan	.75	.35
❑	312	Ron Gant	.75	.35
❑	313	Todd Stottlemyre	.50	.23
❑	314	Greg Vaughn	.75	.35
❑	315	Kevin Brown	1.25	.55
❑	316	Wally Joyner	.75	.35
❑	317	Robb Nen	.50	.23
❑	318	Orel Hershiser	.75	.35
❑	319	Russ Davis	.50	.23
❑	320	Randy Johnson	2.50	1.10
❑	321	Quinton McCracken	.50	.23
❑	322	Tony Saunders	.50	.23
❑	323	Wilson Alvarez	.50	.23
❑	324	Wade Boggs	2.00	.90
❑	325	Fred McGriff	1.25	.55
❑	326	Lee Stevens	.50	.23
❑	327	John Wetteland	.75	.35
❑	328	Jose Canseco	2.00	.90
❑	329	Randy Myers	.75	.35
❑	330	Jose Cruz Jr.	.75	.35
❑	331	Matt Williams TW	3.00	1.35
❑	332	Andres Galarraga TW	3.00	1.35
❑	333	Walt Weiss TW	2.00	.90
❑	334	Joe Carter TW	2.00	.90
❑	335	Pedro Martinez TW	6.00	2.70
❑	336	Henry Rodriguez TW	1.25	.55
❑	337	Travis Fryman TW	2.00	.90
❑	338	Darryl Kile TW	2.00	.90
❑	339	Mike Lansing TW	1.25	.55
❑	340	Mike Piazza TW	12.00	5.50
❑	341	Moises Alou TW	2.00	.90
❑	342	Charles Johnson TW	2.00	.90
❑	343	Chuck Knoblauch TW	2.00	.90
❑	344	Rickey Henderson TW	10.00	4.50
❑	345	Kevin Brown TW	3.00	1.35
❑	346	Orel Hershiser TW	2.00	.90
❑	347	Wade Boggs TW	5.00	2.20
❑	348	Fred McGriff TW	3.00	1.35
❑	349	Jose Canseco TW	5.00	2.20
❑	350	Gary Sheffield TW	2.00	.90
❑	351	Travis Lee CG	8.00	3.60
❑	352	N.Garciaparra CG	20.00	9.00
❑	353	Frank Thomas CG	10.00	4.50
❑	354	Cal Ripken CG	30.00	13.50
❑	355	Mark McGwire CG	30.00	13.50
❑	356	Mike Piazza CG	20.00	9.00
❑	357	Alex Rodriguez CG	20.00	9.00
❑	358	Barry Bonds CG	20.00	9.00
❑	359	Tony Gwynn CG	15.00	6.75
❑	360	Ken Griffey Jr. CG	25.00	11.00

1999 SPx

	MINT	NRMT
COMPLETE SET (120)	400.00	180.00
COMP.SET w/o SP's (80)	40.00	18.00
COMMON MCGWIRE (1-10)	2.00	.90
COMMON CARD (11-80)	.25	.11
COMMON SP (81-120)	10.00	4.50

	Card	Player	Mint	NrMt
❑	1	Mark McGwire 61	4.00	1.80
❑	2	Mark McGwire 62	4.00	1.80
❑	3	Mark McGwire 63	2.00	.90
❑	4	Mark McGwire 64	2.00	.90
❑	5	Mark McGwire 65	2.00	.90
❑	6	Mark McGwire 66	2.00	.90
❑	7	Mark McGwire 67	2.00	.90
❑	8	Mark McGwire 68	2.00	.90
❑	9	Mark McGwire 69	2.00	.90
❑	10	Mark McGwire 70	5.00	2.20
❑	11	Mo Vaughn	.40	.18
❑	12	Darin Erstad	1.00	.45
❑	13	Travis Lee	.25	.11
❑	14	Randy Johnson	1.25	.55
❑	15	Matt Williams	.60	.25
❑	16	Chipper Jones	2.00	.90
❑	17	Greg Maddux	2.50	1.10
❑	18	Andruw Jones	1.00	.45
❑	19	Andres Galarraga	.60	.25
❑	20	Cal Ripken	4.00	1.80
❑	21	Albert Belle	.40	.18
❑	22	Mike Mussina	1.00	.45
❑	23	Nomar Garciaparra	2.50	1.10
❑	24	Pedro Martinez	1.25	.55
❑	25	John Valentin	.25	.11
❑	26	Kerry Wood	1.00	.45
❑	27	Sammy Sosa	2.00	.90
❑	28	Mark Grace	1.00	.45
❑	29	Frank Thomas	1.25	.55
❑	30	Mike Caruso	.25	.11
❑	31	Barry Larkin	1.00	.45
❑	32	Sean Casey	.60	.25
❑	33	Jim Thome	1.00	.45
❑	34	Kenny Lofton	.40	.18
❑	35	Manny Ramirez	1.25	.55
❑	36	Larry Walker	.60	.25
❑	37	Todd Helton	1.25	.55
❑	38	Vinny Castilla	.40	.18
❑	39	Tony Clark	.40	.18
❑	40	Derrek Lee	.40	.18
❑	41	Mark Kotsay	.25	.11
❑	42	Jeff Bagwell	1.25	.55
❑	43	Craig Biggio	.60	.25
❑	44	Moises Alou	.40	.18
❑	45	Larry Sutton	.25	.11
❑	46	Johnny Damon	.40	.18
❑	47	Gary Sheffield	.40	.18
❑	48	Raul Mondesi	.40	.18
❑	49	Jeromy Burnitz	.40	.18
❑	50	Todd Walker	.25	.11
❑	51	David Ortiz	.40	.18
❑	52	Vladimir Guerrero	1.25	.55
❑	53	Rondell White	.40	.18
❑	54	Mike Piazza	2.50	1.10
❑	55	Derek Jeter	4.00	1.80
❑	56	Tino Martinez	.40	.18
❑	57	Roger Clemens	2.50	1.10
❑	58	Ben Grieve	.40	.18
❑	59	A.J. Hinch	.25	.11
❑	60	Scott Rolen	1.00	.45
❑	61	Doug Glanville	.25	.11
❑	62	Aramis Ramirez	.40	.18
❑	63	Jose Guillen	.25	.11
❑	64	Tony Gwynn	2.00	.90
❑	65	Greg Vaughn	.40	.18
❑	66	Ruben Rivera	.25	.11
❑	67	Barry Bonds	2.50	1.10
❑	68	J.T. Snow	.40	.18
❑	69	Alex Rodriguez	2.50	1.10
❑	70	Ken Griffey Jr.	3.00	1.35
❑	71	Jay Buhner	.40	.18
❑	72	Mark McGwire	4.00	1.80
❑	73	Fernando Tatis	.25	.11
❑	74	Quinton McCracken	.25	.11
❑	75	Wade Boggs	1.00	.45
❑	76	Ivan Rodriguez	1.00	.45
❑	77	Juan Gonzalez	1.00	.45
❑	78	Rafael Palmeiro	1.00	.45
❑	79	Jose Cruz Jr.	.40	.18
❑	80	Carlos Delgado	1.00	.45
❑	81	Troy Glaus SP	25.00	11.00
❑	82	Vladimir Nunez SP	10.00	4.50
❑	83	George Lombard SP	10.00	4.50
❑	84	Bruce Chen SP	10.00	4.50
❑	85	Ryan Minor SP	10.00	4.50
❑	86	Calvin Pickering SP	10.00	4.50
❑	87	Jin Ho Cho SP	10.00	4.50
❑	88	Russ Branyan SP	10.00	4.50
❑	89	Derrick Gibson SP	10.00	4.50
❑	90	Gabe Kapler SP AU	25.00	11.00
❑	91	Matt Anderson SP	10.00	4.50
❑	92	Robert Fick SP	10.00	4.50
❑	93	Juan Encarnacion SP	10.00	4.50
❑	94	Preston Wilson SP	10.00	4.50
❑	95	Alex Gonzalez SP	10.00	4.50
❑	96	Carlos Beltran SP	10.00	4.50
❑	97	Jeremy Giambi SP	10.00	4.50
❑	98	Dee Brown SP	10.00	4.50
❑	99	Adrian Beltre SP	10.00	4.50
❑	100	Alex Cora SP	10.00	4.50
❑	101	Angel Pena SP	10.00	4.50
❑	102	Geoff Jenkins SP	10.00	4.50
❑	103	Ronnie Belliard SP	10.00	4.50
❑	104	Corey Koskie SP	10.00	4.50
❑	105	A.J. Pierzynski SP	10.00	4.50
❑	106	Michael Barrett SP	10.00	4.50
❑	107	Fern.Seguignol SP	10.00	4.50
❑	108	Mike Kinkade SP	10.00	4.50
❑	109	Mike Lowell SP	10.00	4.50
❑	110	Ricky Ledee SP	10.00	4.50
❑	111	Eric Chavez SP	10.00	4.50
❑	112	Abraham Nunez SP	10.00	4.50
❑	113	Matt Clement SP	10.00	4.50
❑	114	Ben Davis SP	10.00	4.50
❑	115	Mike Darr SP	10.00	4.50
❑	116	Ramon E.Martinez SP RC	10.00	4.50
❑	117	Carlos Guillen SP	10.00	4.50
❑	118	Shane Monahan SP	10.00	4.50
❑	119	J.D. Drew SP AU	60.00	27.00
❑	120	Kevin Witt SP	10.00	4.50
❑	24EAST	K.Griffey Jr. Sample	2.50	1.10

2000 SPx

	MINT	NRMT
COMPLETE SET (196)	1500.00	700.00
COMP.BASIC SET (120)	800.00	350.00
COMP.UPDATE SET (76)	700.00	325.00
COMP.BASIC w/o SP's (90)	30.00	13.50
COMP.UPDATE w/o SP's (30)	10.00	4.50
COMMON CARD (1-90)	.25	.11
COMMON CARD (91-120)	20.00	9.00
COMMON (121-135/182-196)	10.00	4.50
COMMON CARD (136-151)	15.00	6.75
COMMON CARD (152-181)	.40	.18

	MINT	NRMT
❑ 1 Troy Glaus	1.00	.45
❑ 2 Mo Vaughn	.40	.18
❑ 3 Ramon Ortiz	.40	.18
❑ 4 Jeff Bagwell	1.25	.55
❑ 5 Moises Alou	.40	.18
❑ 6 Craig Biggio	.60	.25
❑ 7 Jose Lima	.25	.11
❑ 8 Jason Giambi	1.00	.45
❑ 9 John Jaha	.25	.11
❑ 10 Matt Stairs	.25	.11
❑ 11 Chipper Jones	2.00	.90
❑ 12 Greg Maddux	2.50	1.10
❑ 13 Andres Galarraga	.60	.25
❑ 14 Andruw Jones	1.00	.45
❑ 15 Jeromy Burnitz	.40	.18
❑ 16 Ron Belliard	.25	.11
❑ 17 Carlos Delgado	1.00	.45
❑ 18 David Wells	.40	.18
❑ 19 Tony Batista	.40	.18
❑ 20 Shannon Stewart	.40	.18
❑ 21 Sammy Sosa	2.00	.90
❑ 22 Mark Grace	1.00	.45
❑ 23 Henry Rodriguez	.25	.11
❑ 24 Mark McGwire	4.00	1.80
❑ 25 J.D. Drew	1.00	.45
❑ 26 Luis Gonzalez	1.00	.45
❑ 27 Randy Johnson	1.25	.55
❑ 28 Matt Williams	.60	.25
❑ 29 Steve Finley	.40	.18
❑ 30 Shawn Green	1.00	.45
❑ 31 Kevin Brown	.60	.25
❑ 32 Gary Sheffield	.40	.18
❑ 33 Jose Canseco	1.00	.45
❑ 34 Greg Vaughn	.40	.18
❑ 35 Vladimir Guerrero	1.25	.55
❑ 36 Michael Barrett	.25	.11
❑ 37 Russ Ortiz	.40	.18
❑ 38 Barry Bonds	2.50	1.10
❑ 39 Jeff Kent	.60	.25
❑ 40 Richie Sexson	.40	.18
❑ 41 Manny Ramirez	1.25	.55
❑ 42 Jim Thome	1.00	.45
❑ 43 Roberto Alomar	1.00	.45
❑ 44 Edgar Martinez	.60	.25
❑ 45 Alex Rodriguez	2.50	1.10
❑ 46 John Olerud	.40	.18
❑ 47 Alex Gonzalez	.25	.11
❑ 48 Cliff Floyd	.40	.18
❑ 49 Mike Piazza	2.50	1.10
❑ 50 Al Leiter	.25	.11
❑ 51 Robin Ventura	.60	.25
❑ 52 Edgardo Alfonzo	.40	.18
❑ 53 Albert Belle	.40	.18
❑ 54 Cal Ripken	4.00	1.80
❑ 55 B.J. Surhoff	.40	.18
❑ 56 Tony Gwynn	2.00	.90
❑ 57 Trevor Hoffman	.40	.18
❑ 58 Brian Giles	.40	.18
❑ 59 Jason Kendall	.40	.18
❑ 60 Kris Benson	.40	.18
❑ 61 Bob Abreu	.40	.18
❑ 62 Scott Rolen	1.00	.45
❑ 63 Curt Schilling	1.00	.45
❑ 64 Mike Lieberthal	.40	.18
❑ 65 Sean Casey	.60	.25
❑ 66 Dante Bichette	.40	.18
❑ 67 Ken Griffey Jr.	3.00	1.35
❑ 68 Pokey Reese	.25	.11
❑ 69 Mike Sweeney	.40	.18
❑ 70 Carlos Febles	.25	.11
❑ 71 Ivan Rodriguez	1.00	.45
❑ 72 Ruben Mateo	.40	.18
❑ 73 Rafael Palmeiro	1.00	.45
❑ 74 Larry Walker	.60	.25
❑ 75 Todd Helton	1.25	.55
❑ 76 Nomar Garciaparra	2.50	1.10
❑ 77 Pedro Martinez	1.25	.55
❑ 78 Troy O'Leary	.25	.11
❑ 79 Jacque Jones	.40	.18
❑ 80 Corey Koskie	.40	.18
❑ 81 Juan Gonzalez	1.00	.45
❑ 82 Dean Palmer	.40	.18
❑ 83 Juan Encarnacion	.40	.18
❑ 84 Frank Thomas	1.25	.55
❑ 85 Magglio Ordonez	.40	.18
❑ 86 Paul Konerko	.40	.18
❑ 87 Bernie Williams	1.00	.45
❑ 88 Derek Jeter	4.00	1.80
❑ 89 Roger Clemens	2.50	1.10
❑ 90 Orlando Hernandez	.40	.18
❑ 91 Vernon Wells/1500 AU	20.00	9.00
❑ 92 Rick Ankiel/1500 AU	50.00	22.00
❑ 93 Eric Chavez/1500 AU	25.00	11.00
❑ 94 A.Soriano/1500 AU	50.00	22.00
❑ 95 Eric Gagne/1500 AU	20.00	9.00
❑ 96 Rob Bell/1500 AU	20.00	9.00
❑ 97 Matt Riley/1500 AU	20.00	9.00
❑ 98 Josh Beckett/1500 AU	60.00	27.00
❑ 99 Ben Petrick/1500 AU	20.00	9.00
❑ 100 Rob Ramsay/1500 AU	20.00	9.00
❑ 101 S.Williamson/1500 AU	20.00	9.00
❑ 102 Doug Davis/1500 AU	20.00	9.00
❑ 103 E.Munson/1500 AU*	25.00	11.00
❑ 104 Pat Burrell/500 AU	100.00	45.00
❑ 105 Jim Morris/1500 AU	20.00	9.00
❑ 106 Gabe Kapler/500 AU	40.00	18.00
❑ 107 Lance Berkman/1000	25.00	11.00
❑ 108 E.Durazo/1500 AU	20.00	9.00
❑ 109 Tim Hudson/1500 AU	50.00	22.00
❑ 110 Ben Davis/1500 AU*	20.00	9.00
❑ 111 N.Johnson/1500 AU	30.00	13.50
❑ 112 O.Dotel/1500 AU	20.00	9.00
❑ 113 Jerry Hairston/1000	20.00	9.00
❑ 114 Ruben Mateo/1000	20.00	9.00
❑ 115 Chris Singleton/1000	20.00	9.00
❑ 116 Bruce Chen/1500 AU	20.00	9.00
❑ 117 Derrick Gibson/1000	20.00	9.00
❑ 118 Carlos Beltran/500 AU	40.00	18.00
❑ 119 F.Garcia/1500 AU	25.00	11.00
❑ 120 P.Wilson/1500 AU	20.00	9.00
❑ 121 B.Wilkerson/1600 RC	12.00	5.50
❑ 122 Roy Oswalt/1600 RC	60.00	27.00
❑ 123 W.Serrano/1600 RC	10.00	4.50
❑ 124 Sean Burnett/1600 RC	12.00	5.50
❑ 125 Alex Cabrera/1600 RC	12.00	5.50
❑ 126 Timo Perez/1600 RC	10.00	4.50
❑ 127 Juan Pierre/1600 RC	15.00	6.75
❑ 128 Daylan Holt/1600 RC	10.00	4.50
❑ 129 T.Ohka/1600 RC	12.00	5.50
❑ 130 K.Sasaki/1600 RC	20.00	9.00
❑ 131 K.Ainsworth/1600 RC	15.00	6.75
❑ 132 B.Abernathy/1600 RC	12.00	5.50
❑ 133 Danys Baez/1600 RC	12.00	5.50
❑ 134 Brad Cresse/1600 RC	20.00	9.00
❑ 135 R.Franklin/1600 RC	10.00	4.50
❑ 136 M.Lamb/1500 AU RC	15.00	6.75
❑ 137 David Espinosa 1500 AU RC	25.00	11.00
❑ 138 Matt Wheatland 1500 AU RC	20.00	9.00
❑ 139 X.Nady/1500 AU RC	40.00	18.00
❑ 140 S.Heard/1500 AU RC	20.00	9.00
❑ 141 P.Coco/1500 AU RC	15.00	6.75
Card erroneously numbered 54 instead of 141		
❑ 142 J.Miller/1500 AU RC	15.00	6.75
❑ 143 D.Krynzel/1500 AU RC	25.00	11.00
❑ 144 Dane Sardinha 1500 AU RC	20.00	9.00
❑ 145 B.Sheets/1500 AU RC	40.00	18.00
❑ 146 L.Estrella/1500 AU RC	15.00	6.75
❑ 147 Ben Diggins 1500 AU RC	25.00	11.00
❑ 148 B.Zito/1500 AU RC	50.00	22.00
❑ 149 J.Torres/1500 AU RC	25.00	11.00
❑ 150 Mike Meyers 1500 AU RC	15.00	6.75
❑ 151 K.Wilson/1500 AU RC	15.00	6.75
❑ 152 Darin Erstad	1.50	.70
❑ 153 Richard Hidalgo	.60	.25
❑ 154 Eric Chavez	.60	.25
❑ 155 B.J. Surhoff	.60	.25
❑ 156 Richie Sexson	.60	.25
❑ 157 Raul Mondesi	.60	.25
❑ 158 Rondell White	.60	.25
❑ 159 Jim Edmonds	1.00	.45
❑ 160 Curt Schilling	1.50	.70
❑ 161 Tom Goodwin	.40	.18
❑ 162 Fred McGriff	1.00	.45
❑ 163 Jose Vidro	.60	.25
❑ 164 Ellis Burks	.60	.25
❑ 165 David Segui	.40	.18
❑ 166 Aaron Sele	.60	.25
❑ 167 Henry Rodriguez	.40	.18
❑ 168 Mike Bordick	.40	.18
❑ 169 Mike Mussina	1.50	.70
❑ 170 Ryan Klesko	.60	.25
❑ 171 Kevin Young	.40	.18
❑ 172 Travis Lee	.40	.18
❑ 173 Aaron Boone	.40	.18
❑ 174 Jermaine Dye	.60	.25
❑ 175 Ricky Ledee	.40	.18
❑ 176 Jeffrey Hammonds	.40	.18
❑ 177 Carl Everett	.60	.25
❑ 178 Matt Lawton	.60	.25
❑ 179 Bobby Higginson	.60	.25
❑ 180 Charles Johnson	.60	.25
❑ 181 David Justice	.60	.25
❑ 182 Joey Nation/1600 RC	10.00	4.50
❑ 183 Rico Washington 1600 RC	10.00	4.50
❑ 184 Luis Matos/1600 RC	10.00	4.50
❑ 185 C.Wakeland/1600 RC	10.00	4.50
❑ 186 SW Kim/1600 RC	12.00	5.50
❑ 187 Keith Ginter/1600 RC	15.00	6.75
❑ 188 G.Guzman/1600 RC	10.00	4.50
❑ 189 J.Spurgeon/1600 RC	10.00	4.50
❑ 190 Jace Brewer/1600 RC	10.00	4.50
❑ 191 J.Guzman/1600 RC	10.00	4.50
❑ 192 Ross Gload/1600 RC	10.00	4.50
❑ 193 P.Crawford/1600 RC	10.00	4.50
❑ 194 R.Kohlmeier/1600 RC	10.00	4.50
❑ 195 Julio Zuleta/1600 RC	10.00	4.50
❑ 196 Matt Ginter/1600 RC	10.00	4.50

2001 SPx

	MINT	NRMT
COMP.BASIC w/o SP's (90)	30.00	13.50
COMMON CARD (1-90)	.40	.18
COMMON YS (91-120)	10.00	4.50
COMMON JSY (121-135)	15.00	6.75
COMMON JSY AU (136-150)	20.00	9.00

	MINT	NRMT
❑ 1 Darin Erstad	1.00	.45
❑ 2 Troy Glaus	1.00	.45
❑ 3 Mo Vaughn	.40	.18
❑ 4 Johnny Damon	.40	.18
❑ 5 Jason Giambi	1.00	.45
❑ 6 Tim Hudson	1.00	.45
❑ 7 Miguel Tejada	.40	.18
❑ 8 Carlos Delgado	1.00	.45
❑ 9 Raul Mondesi	.40	.18
❑ 10 Tony Batista	.40	.18
❑ 11 Ben Grieve	.40	.18
❑ 12 Greg Vaughn	.40	.18
❑ 13 Juan Gonzalez	1.00	.45
❑ 14 Jim Thome	1.00	.45

❑ 15 Roberto Alomar 1.00 .45
❑ 16 John Olerud .40 .18
❑ 17 Edgar Martinez .60 .25
❑ 18 Albert Belle .40 .18
❑ 19 Cal Ripken 4.00 1.80
❑ 20 Ivan Rodriguez 1.00 .45
❑ 21 Rafael Palmeiro 1.00 .45
❑ 22 Alex Rodriguez 2.50 1.10
❑ 23 Nomar Garciaparra 2.50 1.10
❑ 24 Pedro Martinez 1.25 .55
❑ 25 Manny Ramirez 1.25 .55
❑ 26 Jermaine Dye .40 .18
❑ 27 Mark Quinn .40 .18
❑ 28 Carlos Beltran .40 .18
❑ 29 Tony Clark .40 .18
❑ 30 Bobby Higginson .40 .18
❑ 31 Eric Milton .40 .18
❑ 32 Matt Lawton .40 .18
❑ 33 Frank Thomas 1.25 .55
❑ 34 Magglio Ordonez .40 .18
❑ 35 Ray Durham .40 .18
❑ 36 David Wells .40 .18
❑ 37 Derek Jeter 4.00 1.80
❑ 38 Bernie Williams 1.00 .45
❑ 39 Roger Clemens UER 2.50 1.10
Wrong uniform number on card
❑ 40 David Justice .40 .18
❑ 41 Jeff Bagwell 1.25 .55
❑ 42 Richard Hidalgo .40 .18
❑ 43 Moises Alou .40 .18
❑ 44 Chipper Jones 2.00 .90
❑ 45 Andruw Jones 1.00 .45
❑ 46 Greg Maddux 2.50 1.10
❑ 47 Rafael Furcal .40 .18
❑ 48 Jeromy Burnitz .40 .18
❑ 49 Geoff Jenkins .40 .18
❑ 50 Mark McGwire 4.00 1.80
❑ 51 Jim Edmonds .60 .25
❑ 52 Rick Ankiel .60 .25
❑ 53 Edgar Renteria .40 .18
❑ 54 Sammy Sosa 2.00 .90
❑ 55 Kerry Wood 1.00 .45
❑ 56 Rondell White .40 .18
❑ 57 Randy Johnson 1.25 .55
❑ 58 Steve Finley .40 .18
❑ 59 Matt Williams .60 .25
❑ 60 Luis Gonzalez 1.00 .45
❑ 61 Kevin Brown .40 .18
❑ 62 Gary Sheffield .40 .18
❑ 63 Shawn Green 1.00 .45
❑ 64 Vladimir Guerrero 1.25 .55
❑ 65 Jose Vidro .40 .18
❑ 66 Barry Bonds 2.50 1.10
❑ 67 Jeff Kent .60 .25
❑ 68 Livan Hernandez .40 .18
❑ 69 Preston Wilson .40 .18
❑ 70 Charles Johnson .40 .18
❑ 71 Cliff Floyd .40 .18
❑ 72 Mike Piazza 2.50 1.10
❑ 73 Edgardo Alfonzo .40 .18
❑ 74 Jay Payton .40 .18
❑ 75 Robin Ventura .40 .18
❑ 76 Tony Gwynn 2.00 .90
❑ 77 Phil Nevin .40 .18
❑ 78 Ryan Klesko .40 .18
❑ 79 Scott Rolen 1.00 .45
❑ 80 Pat Burrell .40 .18
❑ 81 Bob Abreu .40 .18
❑ 82 Brian Giles .40 .18
❑ 83 Kris Benson .40 .18
❑ 84 Jason Kendall .40 .18
❑ 85 Ken Griffey Jr. 3.00 1.35
❑ 86 Barry Larkin 1.00 .45
❑ 87 Sean Casey .60 .25
❑ 88 Todd Helton 1.25 .55
❑ 89 Larry Walker .60 .25
❑ 90 Mike Hampton .40 .18
❑ 91 Billy Sylvester YS RC 10.00 4.50
❑ 92 Josh Towers YS RC 20.00 9.00
❑ 93 Zach Day YS RC 15.00 6.75
❑ 94 Martin Vargas YS RC 10.00 4.50
❑ 95 Adam Pettyjohn YS RC 15.00 6.75
❑ 96 Andres Torres YS RC 10.00 4.50
❑ 97 Kris Keller YS RC 10.00 4.50
❑ 98 Blaine Neal YS RC 10.00 4.50
❑ 99 Kyle Kessel YS RC 10.00 4.50
❑ 100 Greg Miller YS RC 15.00 6.75
❑ 101 Shawn Sonnier YS 10.00 4.50
❑ 102 Alexis Gomez YS RC 15.00 6.75
❑ 103 Grant Balfour YS RC 10.00 4.50
❑ 104 Henry Mateo YS RC 10.00 4.50
❑ 105 Wilken Ruan YS RC 15.00 6.75
❑ 106 Nick Maness YS RC 10.00 4.50
❑ 107 Jason Michaels YS RC 10.00 4.50
❑ 108 Esix Snead YS RC 10.00 4.50
❑ 109 William Ortega YS RC 10.00 4.50
❑ 110 David Elder YS RC 10.00 4.50
❑ 111 Jackson Melian YS RC 10.00 4.50
❑ 112 Nate Teut YS RC 10.00 4.50
❑ 113 Jason Smith YS RC 10.00 4.50
❑ 114 Mike Penney YS RC 10.00 4.50
❑ 115 Jose Mieses YS RC 10.00 4.50
❑ 116 Juan Pena YS 10.00 4.50
❑ 117 Brian Lawrence YS RC 10.00 4.50
❑ 118 Jeremy Owens YS RC 10.00 4.50
❑ 119 C. Valderrama YS RC 10.00 4.50
❑ 120 Rafael Soriano YS RC 15.00 6.75
❑ 121 Horacio Ramirez JSY RC 15.00 6.75
❑ 122 R. Rodriguez JSY RC 15.00 6.75
❑ 123 Juan Diaz JSY RC 15.00 6.75
❑ 124 Donnie Bridges JSY 15.00 6.75
❑ 125 Tyler Walker JSY RC 15.00 6.75
❑ 126 Erick Almonte JSY RC 15.00 6.75
❑ 127 Jesus Colome JSY 15.00 6.75
❑ 128 Ryan Freel JSY RC 15.00 6.75
❑ 129 Elpidio Guzman JSY RC 10.00 4.50
❑ 130 Jack Cust JSY 15.00 6.75
❑ 131 Eric Hinske JSY RC 20.00 9.00
❑ 132 Josh Fogg JSY RC 15.00 6.75
❑ 133 Juan Uribe JSY RC 20.00 9.00
❑ 134 Bert Snow JSY RC 15.00 6.75
❑ 135 Pedro Feliz JSY 15.00 6.75
❑ 136 W. Betemit JSY AU RC 50.00 22.00
❑ 137 S. Douglass JSY AU RC 20.00 9.00
❑ 138 Dernell Stenson JSY AU 20.00 9.00
❑ 139 Brandon Inge JSY AU 25.00 11.00
❑ 140 M. Ensberg JSY AU RC 25.00 11.00
❑ 141 Brian Cole JSY AU 20.00 9.00
❑ 142 A. Hernandez JSY AU RC 20.00 9.00
❑ 143 B.Duckworth JSY AU RC 40.00 18.00
❑ 144 Jack Wilson JSY AU RC 20.00 9.00
❑ 145 Travis Hafner JSY AU RC 25.00 11.00
❑ 146 Carlos Pena JSY AU 25.00 11.00
❑ 147 Corey Patterson JSY AU 30.00 13.50
❑ 148 Xavier Nady JSY AU 25.00 11.00
❑ 149 Jason Hart JSY AU 25.00 11.00
❑ 150 Ichiro Suzuki JSY AU RC 800.00 350.00

1991 Stadium Club

	MINT	NRMT
COMPLETE SET (600)	60.00	27.00
COMPLETE SERIES 1 (300)	40.00	18.00
COMPLETE SERIES 2 (300)	20.00	9.00

❑ 1 Dave Stewart TUX .40 .18
❑ 2 Wally Joyner .40 .18
❑ 3 Shawon Dunston .25 .11
❑ 4 Darren Daulton .40 .18
❑ 5 Will Clark 1.00 .45
❑ 6 Sammy Sosa 2.50 1.10
❑ 7 Dan Plesac .25 .11
❑ 8 Marquis Grissom .25 .11
❑ 9 Erik Hanson .25 .11
❑ 10 Geno Petralli .25 .11
❑ 11 Jose Rijo .25 .11
❑ 12 Carlos Quintana .25 .11
❑ 13 Junior Ortiz .25 .11
❑ 14 Bob Walk .25 .11
❑ 15 Mike Macfarlane .25 .11
❑ 16 Eric Yelding .25 .11
❑ 17 Bryn Smith .25 .11
❑ 18 Bip Roberts .25 .11
❑ 19 Mike Scioscia .25 .11
❑ 20 Mark Williamson .25 .11
❑ 21 Don Mattingly 2.50 1.10
❑ 22 John Franco .40 .18
❑ 23 Chet Lemon .25 .11
❑ 24 Tom Henke .25 .11
❑ 25 Jerry Browne .25 .11
❑ 26 Dave Justice 1.00 .45
❑ 27 Mark Langston .25 .11
❑ 28 Damon Berryhill .25 .11
❑ 29 Kevin Bass .25 .11
❑ 30 Scott Fletcher .25 .11
❑ 31 Moises Alou .40 .18
❑ 32 Dave Valle .25 .11
❑ 33 Jody Reed .25 .11
❑ 34 Dave West .25 .11
❑ 35 Kevin McReynolds .25 .11
❑ 36 Pat Combs .25 .11
❑ 37 Eric Davis .40 .18
❑ 38 Bret Saberhagen .40 .18
❑ 39 Stan Javier .25 .11
❑ 40 Chuck Cary .25 .11
❑ 41 Tony Phillips .25 .11
❑ 42 Lee Smith .40 .18
❑ 43 Tim Teufel .25 .11
❑ 44 Lance Dickson RC .25 .11
❑ 45 Greg Litton .25 .11
❑ 46 Ted Higuera .25 .11
❑ 47 Edgar Martinez .60 .25
❑ 48 Steve Avery .25 .11
❑ 49 Walt Weiss .25 .11
❑ 50 David Segui .25 .11
❑ 51 Andy Benes .25 .11
❑ 52 Karl Rhodes .25 .11
❑ 53 Neal Heaton .25 .11
❑ 54 Danny Gladden .25 .11
❑ 55 Luis Rivera .25 .11
❑ 56 Kevin Brown .40 .18
❑ 57 Frank Thomas 1.50 .70
❑ 58 Terry Mulholland .25 .11
❑ 59 Dick Schofield .25 .11
❑ 60 Ron Darling .25 .11
❑ 61 Sandy Alomar Jr. .40 .18
❑ 62 Dave Stieb .25 .11
❑ 63 Alan Trammell .60 .25
❑ 64 Matt Nokes .25 .11
❑ 65 Lenny Harris .25 .11
❑ 66 Milt Thompson .25 .11
❑ 67 Storm Davis .25 .11
❑ 68 Joe Oliver .25 .11
❑ 69 Andres Galarraga .60 .25
❑ 70 Ozzie Guillen .25 .11
❑ 71 Ken Howell .25 .11
❑ 72 Garry Templeton .25 .11
❑ 73 Derrick May .25 .11
❑ 74 Xavier Hernandez .25 .11
❑ 75 Dave Parker .40 .18
❑ 76 Rick Aguilera .40 .18
❑ 77 Robby Thompson .25 .11
❑ 78 Pete Incaviglia .25 .11
❑ 79 Bob Welch .25 .11
❑ 80 Randy Milligan .25 .11
❑ 81 Chuck Finley .40 .18
❑ 82 Alvin Davis .25 .11
❑ 83 Tim Naehring .25 .11
❑ 84 Jay Bell .40 .18
❑ 85 Joe Magrane .25 .11
❑ 86 Howard Johnson .25 .11
❑ 87 Jack McDowell .25 .11
❑ 88 Kevin Seitzer .25 .11
❑ 89 Bruce Ruffin .25 .11
❑ 90 Fernando Valenzuela .40 .18
❑ 91 Terry Kennedy .25 .11
❑ 92 Barry Larkin 1.00 .45
❑ 93 Larry Walker .60 .25
❑ 94 Luis Salazar .25 .11
❑ 95 Gary Sheffield .40 .18

❑ 96 Bobby Witt .25 .11
❑ 97 Lonnie Smith .25 .11
❑ 98 Bryan Harvey .25 .11
❑ 99 Mookie Wilson .40 .18
❑ 100 Dwight Gooden .40 .18
❑ 101 Lou Whitaker .40 .18
❑ 102 Ron Karkovice .25 .11
❑ 103 Jesse Barfield .25 .11
❑ 104 Jose DeJesus .25 .11
❑ 105 Benito Santiago .25 .11
❑ 106 Brian Holman .25 .11
❑ 107 Rafael Ramirez .25 .11
❑ 108 Ellis Burks .40 .18
❑ 109 Mike Bielecki .25 .11
❑ 110 Kirby Puckett 2.50 1.10
❑ 111 Terry Shumpert .25 .11
❑ 112 Chuck Crim .25 .11
❑ 113 Todd Benzinger .25 .11
❑ 114 Brian Barnes RC .25 .11
❑ 115 Carlos Baerga .25 .11
❑ 116 Kal Daniels .25 .11
❑ 117 Dave Johnson .25 .11
❑ 118 Andy Van Slyke .40 .18
❑ 119 John Burkett .25 .11
❑ 120 Rickey Henderson 2.00 .90
❑ 121 Tim Jones .25 .11
❑ 122 Daryl Irvine .25 .11
❑ 123 Ruben Sierra .25 .11
❑ 124 Jim Abbott .40 .18
❑ 125 Daryl Boston .25 .11
❑ 126 Greg Maddux 2.50 1.10
❑ 127 Von Hayes .25 .11
❑ 128 Mike Fitzgerald .25 .11
❑ 129 Wayne Edwards .25 .11
❑ 130 Greg Briley .25 .11
❑ 131 Rob Dibble .25 .11
❑ 132 Gene Larkin .25 .11
❑ 133 David Wells .40 .18
❑ 134 Steve Balboni .25 .11
❑ 135 Greg Vaughn .40 .18
❑ 136 Mark Davis .25 .11
❑ 137 Dave Rhode .25 .11
❑ 138 Eric Show .25 .11
❑ 139 Bobby Bonilla .40 .18
❑ 140 Dana Kiecker .25 .11
❑ 141 Gary Pettis .25 .11
❑ 142 Dennis Boyd .25 .11
❑ 143 Mike Benjamin .25 .11
❑ 144 Luis Polonia .25 .11
❑ 145 Doug Jones .25 .11
❑ 146 Al Newman .25 .11
❑ 147 Alex Fernandez .25 .11
❑ 148 Bill Doran .25 .11
❑ 149 Kevin Elster .25 .11
❑ 150 Len Dykstra .40 .18
❑ 151 Mike Gallego .25 .11
❑ 152 Tim Belcher .25 .11
❑ 153 Jay Buhner .40 .18
❑ 154 Ozzie Smith UER 1.25 .55
(Rookie card is 1979,
but card back says '78)
❑ 155 Jose Canseco 1.00 .45
❑ 156 Gregg Olson .25 .11
❑ 157 Charlie O'Brien .25 .11
❑ 158 Frank Tanana .25 .11
❑ 159 George Brett 2.00 .90
❑ 160 Jeff Huson .25 .11
❑ 161 Kevin Tapani .25 .11
❑ 162 Jerome Walton .25 .11
❑ 163 Charlie Hayes .25 .11
❑ 164 Chris Bosio .25 .11
❑ 165 Chris Sabo .25 .11
❑ 166 Lance Parrish .40 .18
❑ 167 Don Robinson .25 .11
❑ 168 Manny Lee .25 .11
❑ 169 Dennis Rasmussen .25 .11
❑ 170 Wade Boggs 1.00 .45
❑ 171 Bob Geren .25 .11
❑ 172 Mackey Sasser .25 .11
❑ 173 Julio Franco .40 .18
❑ 174 Otis Nixon .25 .11
❑ 175 Bert Blyleven .40 .18
❑ 176 Craig Biggio .60 .25
❑ 177 Eddie Murray 1.00 .45
❑ 178 Randy Tomlin RC .25 .11
❑ 179 Tino Martinez .40 .18
❑ 180 Carlton Fisk 1.00 .45
❑ 181 Dwight Smith .25 .11
❑ 182 Scott Garrelts .25 .11
❑ 183 Jim Gantner .25 .11
❑ 184 Dickie Thon .25 .11
❑ 185 John Farrell .25 .11
❑ 186 Cecil Fielder .40 .18
❑ 187 Glenn Braggs .25 .11
❑ 188 Allan Anderson .25 .11
❑ 189 Kurt Stillwell .25 .11
❑ 190 Jose Oquendo .25 .11
❑ 191 Joe Orsulak .25 .11
❑ 192 Ricky Jordan .25 .11
❑ 193 Kelly Downs .25 .11
❑ 194 Delino DeShields .40 .18
❑ 195 Omar Vizquel .40 .18
❑ 196 Mark Carreon .25 .11
❑ 197 Mike Harkey .25 .11
❑ 198 Jack Howell .25 .11
❑ 199 Lance Johnson .25 .11
❑ 200 Nolan Ryan TUX 5.00 2.20
❑ 201 John Marzano .25 .11
❑ 202 Doug Drabek .25 .11
❑ 203 Mark Lemke .25 .11
❑ 204 Steve Sax .25 .11
❑ 205 Greg Harris .25 .11
❑ 206 B.J. Surhoff .40 .18
❑ 207 Todd Burns .25 .11
❑ 208 Jose Gonzalez .25 .11
❑ 209 Mike Scott .25 .11
❑ 210 Dave Magadan .25 .11
❑ 211 Dante Bichette .40 .18
❑ 212 Trevor Wilson .25 .11
❑ 213 Hector Villanueva .25 .11
❑ 214 Dan Pasqua .25 .11
❑ 215 Greg Colbrunn RC .40 .18
❑ 216 Mike Jeffcoat .25 .11
❑ 217 Harold Reynolds .25 .11
❑ 218 Paul O'Neill 1.00 .45
❑ 219 Mark Guthrie .25 .11
❑ 220 Barry Bonds 2.50 1.10
❑ 221 Jimmy Key .40 .18
❑ 222 Billy Ripken .25 .11
❑ 223 Tom Pagnozzi .25 .11
❑ 224 Bo Jackson .40 .18
❑ 225 Sid Fernandez .25 .11
❑ 226 Mike Marshall .25 .11
❑ 227 John Kruk .40 .18
❑ 228 Mike Fetters .25 .11
❑ 229 Eric Anthony .25 .11
❑ 230 Ryne Sandberg 1.25 .55
❑ 231 Carney Lansford .40 .18
❑ 232 Melido Perez .25 .11
❑ 233 Jose Lind .25 .11
❑ 234 Darryl Hamilton .25 .11
❑ 235 Tom Browning .25 .11
❑ 236 Spike Owen .25 .11
❑ 237 Juan Gonzalez 2.50 1.10
❑ 238 Felix Fermin .25 .11
❑ 239 Keith Miller .25 .11
❑ 240 Mark Gubicza .25 .11
❑ 241 Kent Anderson .25 .11
❑ 242 Alvaro Espinoza .25 .11
❑ 243 Dale Murphy 1.00 .45
❑ 244 Orel Hershiser .40 .18
❑ 245 Paul Molitor 1.00 .45
❑ 246 Eddie Whitson .25 .11
❑ 247 Joe Girardi .25 .11
❑ 248 Kent Hrbek .40 .18
❑ 249 Bill Sampen .25 .11
❑ 250 Kevin Mitchell .25 .11
❑ 251 Mariano Duncan .25 .11
❑ 252 Scott Bradley .25 .11
❑ 253 Mike Greenwell .25 .11
❑ 254 Tom Gordon .25 .11
❑ 255 Todd Zeile .25 .11
❑ 256 Bobby Thigpen .25 .11
❑ 257 Gregg Jefferies .25 .11
❑ 258 Kenny Rogers .25 .11
❑ 259 Shane Mack .25 .11
❑ 260 Zane Smith .25 .11
❑ 261 Mitch Williams .25 .11
❑ 262 Jim Deshaies .25 .11
❑ 263 Dave Winfield 1.00 .45
❑ 264 Ben McDonald .25 .11
❑ 265 Randy Ready .25 .11
❑ 266 Pat Borders .25 .11
❑ 267 Jose Uribe .25 .11
❑ 268 Derek Lilliquist .25 .11
❑ 269 Greg Brock .25 .11
❑ 270 Ken Griffey Jr. 4.00 1.80
❑ 271 Jeff Gray .25 .11
❑ 272 Danny Tartabull .25 .11
❑ 273 Dennis Martinez .40 .18
❑ 274 Robin Ventura .40 .18
❑ 275 Randy Myers .25 .11
❑ 276 Jack Daugherty .25 .11
❑ 277 Greg Gagne .25 .11
❑ 278 Jay Howell .25 .11
❑ 279 Mike LaValliere .25 .11
❑ 280 Rex Hudler .25 .11
❑ 281 Mike Simms .25 .11
❑ 282 Kevin Maas .25 .11
❑ 283 Jeff Ballard .25 .11
❑ 284 Dave Henderson .25 .11
❑ 285 Pete O'Brien .25 .11
❑ 286 Brook Jacoby .25 .11
❑ 287 Mike Henneman .25 .11
❑ 288 Greg Olson .25 .11
❑ 289 Greg Myers .25 .11
❑ 290 Mark Grace 1.00 .45
❑ 291 Shawn Abner .25 .11
❑ 292 Frank Viola .40 .18
❑ 293 Lee Stevens .25 .11
❑ 294 Jason Grimsley .25 .11
❑ 295 Matt Williams .60 .25
❑ 296 Ron Robinson .25 .11
❑ 297 Tom Brunansky .25 .11
❑ 298 Checklist 1-100 .25 .11
❑ 299 Checklist 101-200 .25 .11
❑ 300 Checklist 201-300 .25 .11
❑ 301 Darryl Strawberry .40 .18
❑ 302 Bud Black .25 .11
❑ 303 Harold Baines .40 .18
❑ 304 Roberto Alomar 1.00 .45
❑ 305 Norm Charlton .25 .11
❑ 306 Gary Thurman .25 .11
❑ 307 Mike Felder .25 .11
❑ 308 Tony Gwynn 2.00 .90
❑ 309 Roger Clemens 2.50 1.10
❑ 310 Andre Dawson .60 .25
❑ 311 Scott Radinsky .25 .11
❑ 312 Bob Melvin .25 .11
❑ 313 Kirk McCaskill .25 .11
❑ 314 Pedro Guerrero .40 .18
❑ 315 Walt Terrell .25 .11
❑ 316 Sam Horn .25 .11
❑ 317 W.Chamberlain RC UER .25 .11
Card listed as 1989
Debut card, should be 1990
❑ 318 Pedro Munoz RC .25 .11
❑ 319 Roberto Kelly .25 .11
❑ 320 Mark Portugal .25 .11
❑ 321 Tim McIntosh .25 .11
❑ 322 Jesse Orosco .25 .11
❑ 323 Gary Green .25 .11
❑ 324 Greg Harris .25 .11
❑ 325 Hubie Brooks .25 .11
❑ 326 Chris Nabholz .25 .11
❑ 327 Terry Pendleton .40 .18
❑ 328 Eric King .25 .11
❑ 329 Chili Davis .40 .18
❑ 330 Anthony Telford .25 .11
❑ 331 Kelly Gruber .25 .11
❑ 332 Dennis Eckersley .40 .18
❑ 333 Mel Hall .25 .11
❑ 334 Bob Kipper .25 .11
❑ 335 Willie McGee .40 .18
❑ 336 Steve Olin .25 .11
❑ 337 Steve Buechele .25 .11
❑ 338 Scott Leius .25 .11
❑ 339 Hal Morris .25 .11
❑ 340 Jose Offerman .25 .11
❑ 341 Kent Mercker .25 .11
❑ 342 Ken Griffey Sr. .40 .18
❑ 343 Pete Harnisch .25 .11
❑ 344 Kirk Gibson .40 .18
❑ 345 Dave Smith .25 .11
❑ 346 Dave Martinez .25 .11
❑ 347 Atlee Hammaker .25 .11
❑ 348 Brian Downing .25 .11
❑ 349 Todd Hundley .25 .11

❑ 350 Candy Maldonado .25 .11
❑ 351 Dwight Evans .40 .18
❑ 352 Steve Searcy .25 .11
❑ 353 Gary Gaetti .40 .18
❑ 354 Jeff Reardon .40 .18
❑ 355 Travis Fryman .40 .18
❑ 356 Dave Righetti .40 .18
❑ 357 Fred McGriff .60 .25
❑ 358 Don Slaught .25 .11
❑ 359 Gene Nelson .25 .11
❑ 360 Billy Spiers .25 .11
❑ 361 Lee Guetterman .25 .11
❑ 362 Darren Lewis .25 .11
❑ 363 Duane Ward .25 .11
❑ 364 Lloyd Moseby .25 .11
❑ 365 John Smoltz .40 .18
❑ 366 Felix Jose .25 .11
❑ 367 David Cone .40 .18
❑ 368 Wally Backman .25 .11
❑ 369 Jeff Montgomery .25 .11
❑ 370 Rich Garces RC .25 .11
❑ 371 Billy Hatcher .25 .11
❑ 372 Bill Swift .25 .11
❑ 373 Jim Eisenreich .25 .11
❑ 374 Rob Ducey .25 .11
❑ 375 Tim Crews .25 .11
❑ 376 Steve Finley .40 .18
❑ 377 Jeff Blauser .25 .11
❑ 378 Willie Wilson .25 .11
❑ 379 Gerald Perry .25 .11
❑ 380 Jose Mesa .25 .11
❑ 381 Pat Kelly RC .25 .11
❑ 382 Matt Merullo .25 .11
❑ 383 Ivan Calderon .25 .11
❑ 384 Scott Chiamparino .25 .11
❑ 385 Lloyd McClendon .25 .11
❑ 386 Dave Bergman .25 .11
❑ 387 Ed Sprague .25 .11
❑ 388 Jeff Bagwell RC 4.00 1.80
❑ 389 Brett Butler .40 .18
❑ 390 Larry Andersen .25 .11
❑ 391 Glenn Davis .25 .11
❑ 392 Alex Cole UER .25 .11
(Front photo actually Otis Nixon)
❑ 393 Mike Heath .25 .11
❑ 394 Danny Darwin .25 .11
❑ 395 Steve Lake .25 .11
❑ 396 Tim Layana .25 .11
❑ 397 Terry Leach .25 .11
❑ 398 Bill Wegman .25 .11
❑ 399 Mark McGwire 4.00 1.80
❑ 400 Mike Boddicker .25 .11
❑ 401 Steve Howe .25 .11
❑ 402 Bernard Gilkey .25 .11
❑ 403 Thomas Howard .25 .11
❑ 404 Rafael Belliard .25 .11
❑ 405 Tom Candiotti .25 .11
❑ 406 Rene Gonzales .25 .11
❑ 407 Chuck McElroy .25 .11
❑ 408 Paul Sorrento .25 .11
❑ 409 Randy Johnson 1.50 .70
❑ 410 Brady Anderson .40 .18
❑ 411 Dennis Cook .25 .11
❑ 412 Mickey Tettleton .25 .11
❑ 413 Mike Stanton .25 .11
❑ 414 Ken Oberkfell .25 .11
❑ 415 Rick Honeycutt .25 .11
❑ 416 Nelson Santovenia .25 .11
❑ 417 Bob Tewksbury .25 .11
❑ 418 Brent Mayne .25 .11
❑ 419 Steve Farr .25 .11
❑ 420 Phil Stephenson .25 .11
❑ 421 Jeff Russell .25 .11
❑ 422 Chris James .25 .11
❑ 423 Tim Leary .25 .11
❑ 424 Gary Carter .60 .25
❑ 425 Glenallen Hill .25 .11
❑ 426 Matt Young UER .25 .11
(Card mentions 83T/Tr as RC, but 84T shown)
❑ 427 Sid Bream .25 .11
❑ 428 Greg Swindell .25 .11
❑ 429 Scott Aldred .25 .11
❑ 430 Cal Ripken 4.00 1.80
❑ 431 Bill Landrum .25 .11
❑ 432 Earnest Riles .25 .11
❑ 433 Danny Jackson .25 .11
❑ 434 Casey Candaele .25 .11
❑ 435 Ken Hill .25 .11
❑ 436 Jaime Navarro .25 .11
❑ 437 Lance Blankenship .25 .11
❑ 438 Randy Velarde .25 .11
❑ 439 Frank DiPino .25 .11
❑ 440 Carl Nichols .25 .11
❑ 441 Jeff M. Robinson .25 .11
❑ 442 Deion Sanders .40 .18
❑ 443 Vicente Palacios .25 .11
❑ 444 Devon White .25 .11
❑ 445 John Cerutti .25 .11
❑ 446 Tracy Jones .25 .11
❑ 447 Jack Morris .40 .18
❑ 448 Mitch Webster .25 .11
❑ 449 Bob Ojeda .25 .11
❑ 450 Oscar Azocar .25 .11
❑ 451 Luis Aquino .25 .11
❑ 452 Mark Whiten .25 .11
❑ 453 Stan Belinda .25 .11
❑ 454 Ron Gant .25 .11
❑ 455 Jose DeLeon .25 .11
❑ 456 Mark Salas UER .25 .11
(Back has 85T photo, but calls it 86T)
❑ 457 Junior Felix .25 .11
❑ 458 Wally Whitehurst .25 .11
❑ 459 Phil Plantier RC .25 .11
❑ 460 Juan Berenguer .25 .11
❑ 461 Franklin Stubbs .25 .11
❑ 462 Joe Boever .25 .11
❑ 463 Tim Wallach .25 .11
❑ 464 Mike Moore .25 .11
❑ 465 Albert Belle .40 .18
❑ 466 Mike Witt .25 .11
❑ 467 Craig Worthington .25 .11
❑ 468 Jerald Clark .25 .11
❑ 469 Scott Terry .25 .11
❑ 470 Milt Cuyler .25 .11
❑ 471 John Smiley .25 .11
❑ 472 Charles Nagy .25 .11
❑ 473 Alan Mills .25 .11
❑ 474 John Russell .25 .11
❑ 475 Bruce Hurst .25 .11
❑ 476 Andujar Cedeno .25 .11
❑ 477 Dave Eiland .25 .11
❑ 478 Brian McRae RC .40 .18
❑ 479 Mike LaCoss .25 .11
❑ 480 Chris Gwynn .25 .11
❑ 481 Jamie Moyer .25 .11
❑ 482 John Olerud .60 .25
❑ 483 Efrain Valdez .25 .11
❑ 484 Sil Campusano .25 .11
❑ 485 Pascual Perez .25 .11
❑ 486 Gary Redus .25 .11
❑ 487 Andy Hawkins .25 .11
❑ 488 Cory Snyder .25 .11
❑ 489 Chris Hoiles .25 .11
❑ 490 Ron Hassey .25 .11
❑ 491 Gary Wayne .25 .11
❑ 492 Mark Lewis .25 .11
❑ 493 Scott Coolbaugh .25 .11
❑ 494 Gerald Young .25 .11
❑ 495 Juan Samuel .25 .11
❑ 496 Willie Fraser .25 .11
❑ 497 Jeff Treadway .25 .11
❑ 498 Vince Coleman .25 .11
❑ 499 Cris Carpenter .25 .11
❑ 500 Jack Clark .40 .18
❑ 501 Kevin Appier .40 .18
❑ 502 Rafael Palmeiro 1.00 .45
❑ 503 Hensley Meulens .25 .11
❑ 504 George Bell .25 .11
❑ 505 Tony Pena .25 .11
❑ 506 Roger McDowell .25 .11
❑ 507 Luis Sojo .25 .11
❑ 508 Mike Schooler .25 .11
❑ 509 Robin Yount 1.00 .45
❑ 510 Jack Armstrong .25 .11
❑ 511 Rick Cerone .25 .11
❑ 512 Curt Wilkerson .25 .11
❑ 513 Joe Carter .40 .18
❑ 514 Tim Burke .25 .11
❑ 515 Tony Fernandez .25 .11
❑ 516 Ramon Martinez .25 .11
❑ 517 Tim Hulett .25 .11
❑ 518 Terry Steinbach .25 .11
❑ 519 Pete Smith .25 .11
❑ 520 Ken Caminiti .40 .18
❑ 521 Shawn Boskie .25 .11
❑ 522 Mike Pagliarulo .25 .11
❑ 523 Tim Raines .40 .18
❑ 524 Alfredo Griffin .25 .11
❑ 525 Henry Cotto .25 .11
❑ 526 Mike Stanley .25 .11
❑ 527 Charlie Leibrandt .25 .11
❑ 528 Jeff King .25 .11
❑ 529 Eric Plunk .25 .11
❑ 530 Tom Lampkin .25 .11
❑ 531 Steve Bedrosian .25 .11
❑ 532 Tom Herr .25 .11
❑ 533 Craig Lefferts .25 .11
❑ 534 Jeff Reed .25 .11
❑ 535 Mickey Morandini .25 .11
❑ 536 Greg Cadaret .25 .11
❑ 537 Ray Lankford .40 .18
❑ 538 John Candelaria .25 .11
❑ 539 Rob Deer .25 .11
❑ 540 Brad Arnsberg .25 .11
❑ 541 Mike Sharperson .25 .11
❑ 542 Jeff D. Robinson .25 .11
❑ 543 Mo Vaughn 1.00 .45
❑ 544 Jeff Parrett .25 .11
❑ 545 Willie Randolph .40 .18
❑ 546 Herm Winningham .25 .11
❑ 547 Jeff Innis .25 .11
❑ 548 Chuck Knoblauch .40 .18
❑ 549 Tommy Greene UER .25 .11
(Born in North Carolina, not South Carolina)
❑ 550 Jeff Hamilton .25 .11
❑ 551 Barry Jones .25 .11
❑ 552 Ken Dayley .25 .11
❑ 553 Rick Dempsey .25 .11
❑ 554 Greg Smith .25 .11
❑ 555 Mike Devereaux .25 .11
❑ 556 Keith Comstock .25 .11
❑ 557 Paul Faries .25 .11
❑ 558 Tom Glavine 1.00 .45
❑ 559 Craig Grebeck .25 .11
❑ 560 Scott Erickson .25 .11
❑ 561 Joel Skinner .25 .11
❑ 562 Mike Morgan .25 .11
❑ 563 Dave Gallagher .25 .11
❑ 564 Todd Stottlemyre .25 .11
❑ 565 Rich Rodriguez .25 .11
❑ 566 Craig Wilson .25 .11
❑ 567 Jeff Brantley .25 .11
❑ 568 Scott Kamieniecki RC .25 .11
❑ 569 Steve Decker RC .25 .11
❑ 570 Juan Agosto .25 .11
❑ 571 Tommy Gregg .25 .11
❑ 572 Kevin Wickander .25 .11
❑ 573 Jamie Quirk UER .25 .11
(Rookie card is 1976, but card back is 1990)
❑ 574 Jerry Don Gleaton .25 .11
❑ 575 Chris Hammond .25 .11
❑ 576 Luis Gonzalez RC 4.00 1.80
❑ 577 Russ Swan .25 .11
❑ 578 Jeff Conine RC .40 .18
❑ 579 Charlie Hough .40 .18
❑ 580 Jeff Kunkel .25 .11
❑ 581 Darrel Akerfelds .25 .11
❑ 582 Jeff Manto .25 .11
❑ 583 Alejandro Pena .25 .11
❑ 584 Mark Davidson .25 .11
❑ 585 Bob MacDonald RC .25 .11
❑ 586 Paul Assenmacher .25 .11
❑ 587 Dan Wilson RC .40 .18
❑ 588 Tom Bolton .25 .11
❑ 589 Brian Harper .25 .11
❑ 590 John Habyan .25 .11
❑ 591 John Orton .25 .11
❑ 592 Mark Gardner .25 .11
❑ 593 Turner Ward RC .40 .18
❑ 594 Bob Patterson .25 .11
❑ 595 Ed Nunez .25 .11
❑ 596 Gary Scott RC UER .25 .11
(Major League Batting

Record should be
Minor League)
❑ 597 Scott Bankhead .25 .11
❑ 598 Checklist 301-400 .25 .11
❑ 599 Checklist 401-500 .25 .11
❑ 600 Checklist 501-600 .25 .11

1992 Stadium Club Dome

	MINT	NRMT
COMP.FACT.SET (200)	25.00	11.00

❑ 1 Terry Adams RC .10 .05
❑ 2 Tommy Adams RC .10 .05
❑ 3 Rick Aguilera .15 .07
❑ 4 Ron Allen RC .10 .05
❑ 5 Roberto Alomar .40 .18
❑ 6 Sandy Alomar Jr. .15 .07
❑ 7 Greg Anthony RC .10 .05
❑ 8 James Austin RC .10 .05
❑ 9 Steve Avery .10 .05
❑ 10 Harold Baines .15 .07
❑ 11 Brian Barber RC .10 .05
❑ 12 Jon Barnes RC .10 .05
❑ 13 George Bell .10 .05
❑ 14 Doug Bennett RC .10 .05
❑ 15 Sean Bergman RC .10 .05
❑ 16 Craig Biggio .25 .11
❑ 17 Bill Bliss RC .10 .05
❑ 18 Wade Boggs .40 .18
❑ 19 Bobby Bonilla .15 .07
❑ 20 Russell Brock RC .10 .05
❑ 21 Tarrik Brock RC .10 .05
❑ 22 Tom Browning .10 .05
❑ 23 Brett Butler .15 .07
❑ 24 Ivan Calderon .10 .05
❑ 25 Joe Carter .15 .07
❑ 26 Joe Caruso RC .10 .05
❑ 27 Dan Cholowsky RC .10 .05
❑ 28 Will Clark .40 .18
❑ 29 Roger Clemens 1.00 .45
❑ 30 Shawn Curran RC .10 .05
❑ 31 Chris Curtis RC .10 .05
❑ 32 Chili Davis .15 .07
❑ 33 Andre Dawson .25 .11
❑ 34 Joe DeBerry RC .10 .05
❑ 35 John Dettmer .10 .05
❑ 36 Rob Dibble .10 .05
❑ 37 John Donati RC .10 .05
❑ 38 Dave Doorneweerd RC .10 .05
❑ 39 Darren Dreifort .15 .07
❑ 40 Mike Durant RC .10 .05
❑ 41 Chris Durkin RC .10 .05
❑ 42 Dennis Eckersley .15 .07
❑ 43 Brian Edmondson RC .10 .05
❑ 44 Vaughn Eshelman RC .10 .05
❑ 45 Shawn Estes RC 1.00 .45
❑ 46 Jorge Fabregas RC .10 .05
❑ 47 Jon Farrell RC .10 .05
❑ 48 Cecil Fielder .15 .07
❑ 49 Carlton Fisk .40 .18
❑ 50 Tim Flannelly RC .10 .05
❑ 51 Cliff Floyd RC 2.00 .90
❑ 52 Julio Franco .15 .07
❑ 53 Greg Gagne .10 .05
❑ 54 Chris Gambs RC .10 .05
❑ 55 Ron Gant .10 .05
❑ 56 Brent Gates RC .10 .05
❑ 57 Dwayne Gerald RC .10 .05
❑ 58 Jason Giambi 4.00 1.80
❑ 59 Benji Gil RC .10 .05
❑ 60 Mark Gipner RC .10 .05
❑ 61 Danny Gladden .10 .05
❑ 62 Tom Glavine .40 .18
❑ 63 Jimmy Gonzalez RC .10 .05
❑ 64 Jeff Granger .10 .05
❑ 65 Dan Grapenthien RC .10 .05
❑ 66 Dennis Gray RC .10 .05
❑ 67 Shawn Green RC 6.00 2.70
❑ 68 Tyler Green RC .10 .05
❑ 69 Todd Greene .10 .05
❑ 70 Ken Griffey Jr. 1.25 .55
❑ 71 Kelly Gruber .10 .05
❑ 72 Ozzie Guillen .10 .05
❑ 73 Tony Gwynn .75 .35
❑ 74 Shane Halter RC .10 .05
❑ 75 Jeffrey Hammonds .15 .07
❑ 76 Larry Hanlon RC .10 .05
❑ 77 Pete Harnisch .10 .05
❑ 78 Mike Harrison RC .10 .05
❑ 79 Bryan Harvey .10 .05
❑ 80 Scott Hatteberg RC .10 .05
❑ 81 Rick Helling .10 .05
❑ 82 Dave Henderson .10 .05
❑ 83 Rickey Henderson .75 .35
❑ 84 Tyrone Hill RC .10 .05
❑ 85 T.Hollandsworth RC 1.00 .45
❑ 86 Brian Holliday RC .10 .05
❑ 87 Terry Horn RC .10 .05
❑ 88 Jeff Hostetler RC .10 .05
❑ 89 Kent Hrbek .15 .07
❑ 90 Mark Hubbard RC .10 .05
❑ 91 Charles Johnson .15 .07
❑ 92 Howard Johnson .10 .05
❑ 93 Todd Johnson .10 .05
❑ 94 Bobby Jones RC .15 .07
❑ 95 Dan Jones RC .10 .05
❑ 96 Felix Jose .10 .05
❑ 97 David Justice .15 .07
❑ 98 Jimmy Key .15 .07
❑ 99 Marc Kroon RC .10 .05
❑ 100 John Kruk .15 .07
❑ 101 Mark Langston .10 .05
❑ 102 Barry Larkin .40 .18
❑ 103 Mike LaValliere .10 .05
❑ 104 Scott Leius .10 .05
❑ 105 Mark Lemke .10 .05
❑ 106 Donnie Leshnock .10 .05
❑ 107 Jimmy Lewis RC .10 .05
❑ 108 Shane Livesy RC .10 .05
❑ 109 Ryan Long RC .10 .05
❑ 110 Trevor Mallory RC .10 .05
❑ 111 Dennis Martinez .15 .07
❑ 112 Justin Mashore RC .10 .05
❑ 113 Jason McDonald .10 .05
❑ 114 Jack McDowell .10 .05
❑ 115 Tom McKinnon RC .10 .05
❑ 116 Billy McMillon .10 .05
❑ 117 Buck McNabb RC .10 .05
❑ 118 Jim Mecir RC .10 .05
❑ 119 Dan Melendez .10 .05
❑ 120 Shawn Miller RC .10 .05
❑ 121 Trever Miller RC .10 .05
❑ 122 Paul Molitor .40 .18
❑ 123 Vincent Moore RC .10 .05
❑ 124 Mike Morgan .10 .05
❑ 125 Jack Morris WS .10 .05
❑ 126 Jack Morris AS .10 .05
❑ 127 Sean Mulligan RC .10 .05
❑ 128 Eddie Murray AS .40 .18
❑ 129 Mike Neill RC .15 .07
❑ 130 Phil Nevin 1.00 .45
❑ 131 Mark O'Brien RC .10 .05
❑ 132 Alex Ochoa RC .15 .07
❑ 133 Chad Ogea RC .10 .05
❑ 134 Greg Olson .10 .05
❑ 135 Paul O'Neill .40 .18
❑ 136 Jared Osentowski RC .10 .05
❑ 137 Mike Pagliarulo .10 .05
❑ 138 Rafael Palmeiro .40 .18
❑ 139 Rodney Pedraza RC .10 .05
❑ 140 Tony Phillips (P) .10 .05
❑ 141 Scott Pisciotta RC .10 .05
❑ 142 C.Pritchett RC .10 .05
❑ 143 Jason Pruitt RC .10 .05
❑ 144 K.Puckett WS UER 1.00 .45
Championship series
AB and BA is wrong
❑ 145 Kirby Puckett AS 1.00 .45
❑ 146 Manny Ramirez RC 8.00 3.60
❑ 147 Eddie Ramos RC .10 .05
❑ 148 Mark Ratekin RC .10 .05
❑ 149 Jeff Reardon .15 .07
❑ 150 Sean Rees RC .10 .05
❑ 151 Pokey Reese RC .75 .35
❑ 152 Desmond Relaford RC .15 .07
❑ 153 Eric Richardson RC .10 .05
❑ 154 Cal Ripken 1.50 .70
❑ 155 Chris Roberts .10 .05
❑ 156 Mike Robertson RC .10 .05
❑ 157 Steve Rodriguez .10 .05
❑ 158 Mike Rossiter RC .10 .05
❑ 159 Scott Ruffcorn RC .10 .05
❑ 160 Chris Sabo .10 .05
❑ 161 Juan Samuel .10 .05
❑ 162 Ryne Sandberg UER .50 .23
(On 5th line, prior
misspelled as prilor)
❑ 163 Scott Sanderson .10 .05
❑ 164 Benny Santiago .10 .05
❑ 165 Gene Schall RC .10 .05
❑ 166 Chad Schoenvogel RC .10 .05
❑ 167 Chris Seelbach RC .10 .05
❑ 168 Aaron Sele RC 1.00 .45
❑ 169 Basil Shabazz RC .10 .05
❑ 170 Al Shirley RC .10 .05
❑ 171 Paul Shuey .10 .05
❑ 172 Ruben Sierra .10 .05
❑ 173 John Smiley .10 .05
❑ 174 Lee Smith .15 .07
❑ 175 Ozzie Smith .50 .23
❑ 176 Tim Smith RC .10 .05
❑ 177 Zane Smith .10 .05
❑ 178 John Smoltz .15 .07
❑ 179 Scott Stahoviak RC .10 .05
❑ 180 Kennie Steenstra .10 .05
❑ 181 Kevin Stocker RC .15 .07
❑ 182 Chris Stynes RC .15 .07
❑ 183 Danny Tartabull .10 .05
❑ 184 Brien Taylor RC .15 .07
❑ 185 Todd Taylor .10 .05
❑ 186 Larry Thomas RC .10 .05
❑ 187 Ozzie Timmons RC .10 .05
(See also 188)
❑ 188 David Tuttle UER .10 .05
(Mistakenly numbered
as 187 on card)
❑ 189 Andy Van Slyke .15 .07
❑ 190 Frank Viola .15 .07
❑ 191 Michael Walkden RC .10 .05
❑ 192 Jeff Ware .10 .05
❑ 193 Allen Watson RC .10 .05
❑ 194 Steve Whitaker RC .10 .05
❑ 195 Jerry Willard .10 .05
❑ 196 Craig Wilson .10 .05
❑ 197 Chris Wimmer .10 .05
❑ 198 S.Wojciechowski RC .10 .05
❑ 199 Joel Wolfe RC .10 .05
❑ 200 Ivan Zweig .10 .05

1992 Stadium Club

	MINT	NRMT
COMPLETE SET (900)	45.00	20.00
COMPLETE SERIES 1 (300)	15.00	6.75
COMPLETE SERIES 2 (300)	15.00	6.75
COMPLETE SERIES 3 (300)	15.00	6.75
❑ 1 Cal Ripken UER (Misspelled Ripkin on card back)	1.50	.70
❑ 2 Eric Yelding	.10	.05
❑ 3 Geno Petralli	.10	.05
❑ 4 Wally Backman	.10	.05
❑ 5 Milt Cuyler	.10	.05
❑ 6 Kevin Bass	.10	.05
❑ 7 Dante Bichette	.15	.07
❑ 8 Ray Lankford	.10	.05
❑ 9 Mel Hall	.10	.05
❑ 10 Joe Carter	.15	.07
❑ 11 Juan Samuel	.10	.05
❑ 12 Jeff Montgomery	.10	.05
❑ 13 Glenn Braggs	.10	.05
❑ 14 Henry Cotto	.10	.05
❑ 15 Deion Sanders	.15	.07
❑ 16 Dick Schofield	.10	.05
❑ 17 David Cone	.15	.07
❑ 18 Chili Davis	.15	.07
❑ 19 Tom Foley	.10	.05
❑ 20 Ozzie Guillen	.10	.05
❑ 21 Luis Salazar	.10	.05
❑ 22 Terry Steinbach	.10	.05
❑ 23 Chris James	.10	.05
❑ 24 Jeff King	.10	.05
❑ 25 Carlos Quintana	.10	.05
❑ 26 Mike Maddux	.10	.05
❑ 27 Tommy Greene	.10	.05
❑ 28 Jeff Russell	.10	.05
❑ 29 Steve Finley	.15	.07
❑ 30 Mike Flanagan	.10	.05
❑ 31 Darren Lewis	.10	.05
❑ 32 Mark Lee	.10	.05
❑ 33 Willie Fraser	.10	.05
❑ 34 Mike Henneman	.10	.05
❑ 35 Kevin Maas	.10	.05
❑ 36 Dave Hansen	.10	.05
❑ 37 Erik Hanson	.10	.05
❑ 38 Bill Doran	.10	.05
❑ 39 Mike Boddicker	.10	.05
❑ 40 Vince Coleman	.10	.05
❑ 41 Devon White	.10	.05
❑ 42 Mark Gardner	.10	.05
❑ 43 Scott Lewis	.10	.05
❑ 44 Juan Berenguer	.10	.05
❑ 45 Carney Lansford	.15	.07
❑ 46 Curt Wilkerson	.10	.05
❑ 47 Shane Mack	.10	.05
❑ 48 Bip Roberts	.10	.05
❑ 49 Greg A. Harris	.10	.05
❑ 50 Ryne Sandberg	.50	.23
❑ 51 Mark Whiten	.10	.05
❑ 52 Jack McDowell	.10	.05
❑ 53 Jimmy Jones	.10	.05
❑ 54 Steve Lake	.10	.05
❑ 55 Bud Black	.10	.05
❑ 56 Dave Valle	.10	.05
❑ 57 Kevin Reimer	.10	.05
❑ 58 Rich Gedman UER (Wrong BARS chart used)	.10	.05
❑ 59 Travis Fryman	.15	.07
❑ 60 Steve Avery	.10	.05
❑ 61 Francisco de la Rosa	.10	.05
❑ 62 Scott Hemond	.10	.05
❑ 63 Hal Morris	.10	.05
❑ 64 Hensley Meulens	.10	.05
❑ 65 Frank Castillo	.10	.05
❑ 66 Gene Larkin	.10	.05
❑ 67 Jose DeLeon	.10	.05
❑ 68 Al Osuna	.10	.05
❑ 69 Dave Cochrane	.10	.05
❑ 70 Robin Ventura	.15	.07
❑ 71 John Cerutti	.10	.05
❑ 72 Kevin Gross	.10	.05
❑ 73 Ivan Calderon	.10	.05
❑ 74 Mike Macfarlane	.10	.05
❑ 75 Stan Belinda	.10	.05
❑ 76 Shawn Hillegas	.10	.05
❑ 77 Pat Borders	.10	.05
❑ 78 Jim Vatcher	.10	.05
❑ 79 Bobby Rose	.10	.05
❑ 80 Roger Clemens	1.00	.45
❑ 81 Craig Worthington	.10	.05
❑ 82 Jeff Treadway	.10	.05
❑ 83 Jamie Quirk	.10	.05
❑ 84 Randy Bush	.10	.05
❑ 85 Anthony Young	.10	.05
❑ 86 Trevor Wilson	.10	.05
❑ 87 Jaime Navarro	.10	.05
❑ 88 Les Lancaster	.10	.05
❑ 89 Pat Kelly	.10	.05
❑ 90 Alvin Davis	.10	.05
❑ 91 Larry Andersen	.10	.05
❑ 92 Rob Deer	.10	.05
❑ 93 Mike Sharperson	.10	.05
❑ 94 Lance Parrish	.15	.07
❑ 95 Cecil Espy	.10	.05
❑ 96 Tim Spehr	.10	.05
❑ 97 Dave Stieb	.10	.05
❑ 98 Terry Mulholland	.10	.05
❑ 99 Dennis Boyd	.10	.05
❑ 100 Barry Larkin	.40	.18
❑ 101 Ryan Bowen	.10	.05
❑ 102 Felix Fermin	.10	.05
❑ 103 Luis Alicea	.10	.05
❑ 104 Tim Hulett	.10	.05
❑ 105 Rafael Belliard	.10	.05
❑ 106 Mike Gallego	.10	.05
❑ 107 Dave Righetti	.15	.07
❑ 108 Jeff Schaefer	.10	.05
❑ 109 Ricky Bones	.10	.05
❑ 110 Scott Erickson	.10	.05
❑ 111 Matt Nokes	.10	.05
❑ 112 Bob Scanlan	.10	.05
❑ 113 Tom Candiotti	.10	.05
❑ 114 Sean Berry	.10	.05
❑ 115 Kevin Morton	.10	.05
❑ 116 Scott Fletcher	.10	.05
❑ 117 B.J. Surhoff	.15	.07
❑ 118 Dave Magadan UER (Born Tampa, not Tamps)	.10	.05
❑ 119 Bill Gullickson	.10	.05
❑ 120 Marquis Grissom	.10	.05
❑ 121 Lenny Harris	.10	.05
❑ 122 Wally Joyner	.15	.07
❑ 123 Kevin Brown	.15	.07
❑ 124 Braulio Castillo	.10	.05
❑ 125 Eric King	.10	.05
❑ 126 Mark Portugal	.10	.05
❑ 127 Calvin Jones	.10	.05
❑ 128 Mike Heath	.10	.05
❑ 129 Todd Van Poppel	.10	.05
❑ 130 Benny Santiago	.10	.05
❑ 131 Gary Thurman	.10	.05
❑ 132 Joe Girardi	.10	.05
❑ 133 Dave Eiland	.10	.05
❑ 134 Orlando Merced	.10	.05
❑ 135 Joe Orsulak	.10	.05
❑ 136 John Burkett	.10	.05
❑ 137 Ken Dayley	.10	.05
❑ 138 Ken Hill	.10	.05
❑ 139 Walt Terrell	.10	.05
❑ 140 Mike Scioscia	.10	.05
❑ 141 Junior Felix	.10	.05
❑ 142 Ken Caminiti	.15	.07
❑ 143 Carlos Baerga	.10	.05
❑ 144 Tony Fossas	.10	.05
❑ 145 Craig Grebeck	.10	.05
❑ 146 Scott Bradley	.10	.05
❑ 147 Kent Mercker	.10	.05
❑ 148 Derrick May	.10	.05
❑ 149 Jerald Clark	.10	.05
❑ 150 George Brett	.75	.35
❑ 151 Luis Quinones	.10	.05
❑ 152 Mike Pagliarulo	.10	.05
❑ 153 Jose Guzman	.10	.05
❑ 154 Charlie O'Brien	.10	.05
❑ 155 Darren Holmes	.10	.05
❑ 156 Joe Boever	.10	.05
❑ 157 Rich Monteleone	.10	.05
❑ 158 Reggie Harris	.10	.05
❑ 159 Roberto Alomar	.40	.18
❑ 160 Robby Thompson	.10	.05
❑ 161 Chris Hoiles	.10	.05
❑ 162 Tom Pagnozzi	.10	.05
❑ 163 Omar Vizquel	.15	.07
❑ 164 John Candelaria	.10	.05
❑ 165 Terry Shumpert	.10	.05
❑ 166 Andy Mota	.10	.05
❑ 167 Scott Bailes	.10	.05
❑ 168 Jeff Blauser	.10	.05
❑ 169 Steve Olin	.10	.05
❑ 170 Doug Drabek	.10	.05
❑ 171 Dave Bergman	.10	.05
❑ 172 Eddie Whitson	.10	.05
❑ 173 Gilberto Reyes	.10	.05
❑ 174 Mark Grace	.40	.18
❑ 175 Paul O'Neill	.40	.18
❑ 176 Greg Cadaret	.10	.05
❑ 177 Mark Williamson	.10	.05
❑ 178 Casey Candaele	.10	.05
❑ 179 Candy Maldonado	.10	.05
❑ 180 Lee Smith	.15	.07
❑ 181 Harold Reynolds	.10	.05
❑ 182 David Justice	.15	.07
❑ 183 Lenny Webster	.10	.05
❑ 184 Donn Pall	.10	.05
❑ 185 Gerald Alexander	.10	.05
❑ 186 Jack Clark	.15	.07
❑ 187 Stan Javier	.10	.05
❑ 188 Ricky Jordan	.10	.05
❑ 189 Franklin Stubbs	.10	.05
❑ 190 Dennis Eckersley	.15	.07
❑ 191 Danny Tartabull	.10	.05
❑ 192 Pete O'Brien	.10	.05
❑ 193 Mark Lewis	.10	.05
❑ 194 Mike Felder	.10	.05
❑ 195 Mickey Tettleton	.10	.05
❑ 196 Dwight Smith	.10	.05
❑ 197 Shawn Abner	.10	.05
❑ 198 Jim Leyritz UER (Career totals less than 1991 totals)	.10	.05
❑ 199 Mike Devereaux	.10	.05
❑ 200 Craig Biggio	.25	.11
❑ 201 Kevin Elster	.10	.05
❑ 202 Rance Mulliniks	.10	.05
❑ 203 Tony Fernandez	.10	.05
❑ 204 Allan Anderson	.10	.05
❑ 205 Herm Winningham	.10	.05
❑ 206 Tim Jones	.10	.05
❑ 207 Ramon Martinez	.10	.05
❑ 208 Teddy Higuera	.10	.05
❑ 209 John Kruk	.15	.07
❑ 210 Jim Abbott	.15	.07
❑ 211 Dean Palmer	.15	.07
❑ 212 Mark Davis	.10	.05
❑ 213 Jay Buhner	.15	.07
❑ 214 Jesse Barfield	.10	.05
❑ 215 Kevin Mitchell	.10	.05
❑ 216 Mike LaValliere	.10	.05
❑ 217 Mark Wohlers	.10	.05
❑ 218 Dave Henderson	.10	.05
❑ 219 Dave Smith	.10	.05
❑ 220 Albert Belle	.15	.07
❑ 221 Spike Owen	.10	.05
❑ 222 Jeff Gray	.10	.05
❑ 223 Paul Gibson	.10	.05
❑ 224 Bobby Thigpen	.10	.05
❑ 225 Mike Mussina	.60	.25
❑ 226 Darrin Jackson	.10	.05
❑ 227 Luis Gonzalez	.40	.18
❑ 228 Greg Briley	.10	.05
❑ 229 Brent Mayne	.10	.05
❑ 230 Paul Molitor	.40	.18
❑ 231 Al Leiter	.15	.07
❑ 232 Andy Van Slyke	.15	.07
❑ 233 Ron Tingley	.10	.05
❑ 234 Bernard Gilkey	.10	.05
❑ 235 Kent Hrbek	.15	.07
❑ 236 Eric Karros	.15	.07
❑ 237 Randy Velarde	.10	.05
❑ 238 Andy Allanson	.10	.05
❑ 239 Willie McGee	.15	.07
❑ 240 Juan Gonzalez	.40	.18
❑ 241 Karl Rhodes	.10	.05
❑ 242 Luis Mercedes	.10	.05
❑ 243 Bill Swift	.10	.05
❑ 244 Tommy Gregg	.10	.05
❑ 245 David Howard	.10	.05
❑ 246 Dave Hollins	.10	.05

❑ 247 Kip Gross .10 .05
❑ 248 Walt Weiss .10 .05
❑ 249 Mackey Sasser .10 .05
❑ 250 Cecil Fielder .15 .07
❑ 251 Jerry Browne .10 .05
❑ 252 Doug Dascenzo .10 .05
❑ 253 Darryl Hamilton .10 .05
❑ 254 Dann Bilardello .10 .05
❑ 255 Luis Rivera .10 .05
❑ 256 Larry Walker .25 .11
❑ 257 Ron Karkovice .10 .05
❑ 258 Bob Tewksbury .10 .05
❑ 259 Jimmy Key .15 .07
❑ 260 Bernie Williams .40 .18
❑ 261 Gary Wayne .10 .05
❑ 262 Mike Simms UER .10 .05
(Reversed negative)
❑ 263 John Orton .10 .05
❑ 264 Marvin Freeman .10 .05
❑ 265 Mike Jeffcoat .10 .05
❑ 266 Roger Mason .10 .05
❑ 267 Edgar Martinez .25 .11
❑ 268 Henry Rodriguez .10 .05
❑ 269 Sam Horn .10 .05
❑ 270 Brian McRae .10 .05
❑ 271 Kirt Manwaring .10 .05
❑ 272 Mike Bordick .10 .05
❑ 273 Chris Sabo .10 .05
❑ 274 Jim Olander .10 .05
❑ 275 Greg W. Harris .10 .05
❑ 276 Dan Gakeler .10 .05
❑ 277 Bill Sampen .10 .05
❑ 278 Joel Skinner .10 .05
❑ 279 Curt Schilling .40 .18
❑ 280 Dale Murphy .40 .18
❑ 281 Lee Stevens .10 .05
❑ 282 Lonnie Smith .10 .05
❑ 283 Manuel Lee .10 .05
❑ 284 Shawn Boskie .10 .05
❑ 285 Kevin Seitzer .10 .05
❑ 286 Stan Royer .10 .05
❑ 287 John Dopson .10 .05
❑ 288 Scott Bullett RC .10 .05
❑ 289 Ken Patterson .10 .05
❑ 290 Todd Hundley .10 .05
❑ 291 Tim Leary .10 .05
❑ 292 Brett Butler .15 .07
❑ 293 Gregg Olson .10 .05
❑ 294 Jeff Brantley .10 .05
❑ 295 Brian Holman .10 .05
❑ 296 Brian Harper .10 .05
❑ 297 Brian Bohanon .10 .05
❑ 298 Checklist 1-100 .10 .05
❑ 299 Checklist 101-200 .10 .05
❑ 300 Checklist 201-300 .10 .05
❑ 301 Frank Thomas .50 .23
❑ 302 Lloyd McClendon .10 .05
❑ 303 Brady Anderson .15 .07
❑ 304 Julio Valera .10 .05
❑ 305 Mike Aldrete .10 .05
❑ 306 Joe Oliver .10 .05
❑ 307 Todd Stottlemyre .10 .05
❑ 308 Rey Sanchez RC .15 .07
❑ 309 Gary Sheffield UER .15 .07
(Listed as 5'1", should be 5'11")
❑ 310 Andujar Cedeno .10 .05
❑ 311 Kenny Rogers .10 .05
❑ 312 Bruce Hurst .10 .05
❑ 313 Mike Schooler .10 .05
❑ 314 Mike Benjamin .10 .05
❑ 315 Chuck Finley .15 .07
❑ 316 Mark Lemke .10 .05
❑ 317 Scott Livingstone .10 .05
❑ 318 Chris Nabholz .10 .05
❑ 319 Mike Humphreys .10 .05
❑ 320 Pedro Guerrero .15 .07
❑ 321 Willie Banks .10 .05
❑ 322 Tom Goodwin .10 .05
❑ 323 Hector Wagner .10 .05
❑ 324 Wally Ritchie .10 .05
❑ 325 Mo Vaughn .15 .07
❑ 326 Joe Klink .10 .05
❑ 327 Cal Eldred .10 .05
❑ 328 Daryl Boston .10 .05
❑ 329 Mike Huff .10 .05
❑ 330 Jeff Bagwell .75 .35
❑ 331 Bob Milacki .10 .05
❑ 332 Tom Prince .10 .05
❑ 333 Pat Tabler .10 .05
❑ 334 Ced Landrum .10 .05
❑ 335 Reggie Jefferson .10 .05
❑ 336 Mo Sanford .10 .05
❑ 337 Kevin Ritz .10 .05
❑ 338 Gerald Perry .10 .05
❑ 339 Jeff Hamilton .10 .05
❑ 340 Tim Wallach .10 .05
❑ 341 Jeff Huson .10 .05
❑ 342 Jose Melendez .10 .05
❑ 343 Willie Wilson .10 .05
❑ 344 Mike Stanton .10 .05
❑ 345 Joel Johnston .10 .05
❑ 346 Lee Guetterman .10 .05
❑ 347 Francisco Oliveras .10 .05
❑ 348 Dave Burba .10 .05
❑ 349 Tim Crews .10 .05
❑ 350 Scott Leius .10 .05
❑ 351 Danny Cox .10 .05
❑ 352 Wayne Housie .10 .05
❑ 353 Chris Donnels .10 .05
❑ 354 Chris George .10 .05
❑ 355 Gerald Young .10 .05
❑ 356 Roberto Hernandez .10 .05
❑ 357 Neal Heaton .10 .05
❑ 358 Todd Frohwirth .10 .05
❑ 359 Jose Vizcaino .10 .05
❑ 360 Jim Thome .40 .18
❑ 361 Craig Wilson .10 .05
❑ 362 Dave Haas .10 .05
❑ 363 Billy Hatcher .10 .05
❑ 364 John Barfield .10 .05
❑ 365 Luis Aquino .10 .05
❑ 366 Charlie Leibrandt .10 .05
❑ 367 Howard Farmer .10 .05
❑ 368 Bryn Smith .10 .05
❑ 369 Mickey Morandini .10 .05
❑ 370 Jose Canseco .40 .18
(See also 597)
❑ 371 Jose Uribe .10 .05
❑ 372 Bob MacDonald .10 .05
❑ 373 Luis Sojo .10 .05
❑ 374 Craig Shipley .10 .05
❑ 375 Scott Bankhead .10 .05
❑ 376 Greg Gagne .10 .05
❑ 377 Scott Cooper .10 .05
❑ 378 Jose Offerman .10 .05
❑ 379 Bill Spiers .10 .05
❑ 380 John Smiley .10 .05
❑ 381 Jeff Carter .10 .05
❑ 382 Heathcliff Slocumb .10 .05
❑ 383 Jeff Tackett .10 .05
❑ 384 John Kiely .10 .05
❑ 385 John Vander Wal .10 .05
❑ 386 Omar Olivares .10 .05
❑ 387 Ruben Sierra .10 .05
❑ 388 Tom Gordon .10 .05
❑ 389 Charles Nagy .10 .05
❑ 390 Dave Stewart .15 .07
❑ 391 Pete Harnisch .10 .05
❑ 392 Tim Burke .10 .05
❑ 393 Roberto Kelly .10 .05
❑ 394 Freddie Benavides .10 .05
❑ 395 Tom Glavine .40 .18
❑ 396 Wes Chamberlain .10 .05
❑ 397 Eric Gunderson .10 .05
❑ 398 Dave West .10 .05
❑ 399 Ellis Burks .15 .07
❑ 400 Ken Griffey Jr. 1.25 .55
❑ 401 Thomas Howard .10 .05
❑ 402 Juan Guzman .10 .05
❑ 403 Mitch Webster .10 .05
❑ 404 Matt Merullo .10 .05
❑ 405 Steve Buechele .10 .05
❑ 406 Danny Jackson .10 .05
❑ 407 Felix Jose .10 .05
❑ 408 Doug Piatt .10 .05
❑ 409 Jim Eisenreich .10 .05
❑ 410 Bryan Harvey .10 .05
❑ 411 Jim Austin .10 .05
❑ 412 Jim Poole .10 .05
❑ 413 Glenallen Hill .10 .05
❑ 414 Gene Nelson .10 .05
❑ 415 Ivan Rodriguez .60 .25
❑ 416 Frank Tanana .10 .05
❑ 417 Steve Decker .10 .05
❑ 418 Jason Grimsley .10 .05
❑ 419 Tim Layana .10 .05
❑ 420 Don Mattingly 1.00 .45
❑ 421 Jerome Walton .10 .05
❑ 422 Rob Ducey .10 .05
❑ 423 Andy Benes .10 .05
❑ 424 John Marzano .10 .05
❑ 425 Gene Harris .10 .05
❑ 426 Tim Raines .15 .07
❑ 427 Bret Barberie .10 .05
❑ 428 Harvey Pulliam .10 .05
❑ 429 Cris Carpenter .10 .05
❑ 430 Howard Johnson .10 .05
❑ 431 Orel Hershiser .15 .07
❑ 432 Brian Hunter .10 .05
❑ 433 Kevin Tapani .10 .05
❑ 434 Rick Reed .10 .05
❑ 435 Ron Witmeyer RC .10 .05
❑ 436 Gary Gaetti .15 .07
❑ 437 Alex Cole .10 .05
❑ 438 Chito Martinez .10 .05
❑ 439 Greg Litton .10 .05
❑ 440 Julio Franco .15 .07
❑ 441 Mike Munoz .10 .05
❑ 442 Erik Pappas .10 .05
❑ 443 Pat Combs .10 .05
❑ 444 Lance Johnson .10 .05
❑ 445 Ed Sprague .10 .05
❑ 446 Mike Greenwell .10 .05
❑ 447 Milt Thompson .10 .05
❑ 448 Mike Magnante RC .10 .05
❑ 449 Chris Haney .10 .05
❑ 450 Robin Yount .40 .18
❑ 451 Rafael Ramirez .10 .05
❑ 452 Gino Minutelli .10 .05
❑ 453 Tom Lampkin .10 .05
❑ 454 Tony Perezchica .10 .05
❑ 455 Dwight Gooden .15 .07
❑ 456 Mark Guthrie .10 .05
❑ 457 Jay Howell .10 .05
❑ 458 Gary DiSarcina .10 .05
❑ 459 John Smoltz .15 .07
❑ 460 Will Clark .40 .18
❑ 461 Dave Otto .10 .05
❑ 462 Rob Maurer .10 .05
❑ 463 Dwight Evans .15 .07
❑ 464 Tom Brunansky .10 .05
❑ 465 Shawn Hare RC .10 .05
❑ 466 Geronimo Pena .10 .05
❑ 467 Alex Fernandez .10 .05
❑ 468 Greg Myers .10 .05
❑ 469 Jeff Fassero .10 .05
❑ 470 Len Dykstra .15 .07
❑ 471 Jeff Johnson .10 .05
❑ 472 Russ Swan .10 .05
❑ 473 Archie Corbin .10 .05
❑ 474 Chuck McElroy .10 .05
❑ 475 Mark McGwire 1.50 .70
❑ 476 Wally Whitehurst .10 .05
❑ 477 Tim McIntosh .10 .05
❑ 478 Sid Bream .10 .05
❑ 479 Jeff Juden .10 .05
❑ 480 Carlton Fisk .40 .18
❑ 481 Jeff Plympton .10 .05
❑ 482 Carlos Martinez .10 .05
❑ 483 Jim Gott .10 .05
❑ 484 Bob McClure .10 .05
❑ 485 Tim Teufel .10 .05
❑ 486 Vicente Palacios .10 .05
❑ 487 Jeff Reed .10 .05
❑ 488 Tony Phillips .10 .05
❑ 489 Mel Rojas .10 .05
❑ 490 Ben McDonald .10 .05
❑ 491 Andres Santana .10 .05
❑ 492 Chris Beasley .10 .05
❑ 493 Mike Timlin .10 .05
❑ 494 Brian Downing .10 .05
❑ 495 Kirk Gibson .15 .07
❑ 496 Scott Sanderson .10 .05
❑ 497 Nick Esasky .10 .05
❑ 498 Johnny Guzman RC .10 .05
❑ 499 Mitch Williams .10 .05
❑ 500 Kirby Puckett 1.00 .45

❑ 501 Mike Harkey .10 .05
❑ 502 Jim Gantner .10 .05
❑ 503 Bruce Egloff .10 .05
❑ 504 Josias Manzanillo RC .10 .05
❑ 505 Delino DeShields .10 .05
❑ 506 Rheal Cormier .10 .05
❑ 507 Jay Bell .15 .07
❑ 508 Rich Rowland RC .10 .05
❑ 509 Scott Servais .10 .05
❑ 510 Terry Pendleton .15 .07
❑ 511 Rich DeLucia .10 .05
❑ 512 Warren Newson .10 .05
❑ 513 Paul Faries .10 .05
❑ 514 Kal Daniels .10 .05
❑ 515 Jarvis Brown .10 .05
❑ 516 Rafael Palmeiro .40 .18
❑ 517 Kelly Downs .10 .05
❑ 518 Steve Chitren .10 .05
❑ 519 Moises Alou .15 .07
❑ 520 Wade Boggs .40 .18
❑ 521 Pete Schourek .10 .05
❑ 522 Scott Terry .10 .05
❑ 523 Kevin Appier .15 .07
❑ 524 Gary Redus .10 .05
❑ 525 George Bell .10 .05
❑ 526 Jeff Kaiser .10 .05
❑ 527 Alvaro Espinoza .10 .05
❑ 528 Luis Polonia .10 .05
❑ 529 Darren Daulton .15 .07
❑ 530 Norm Charlton .10 .05
❑ 531 John Olerud .15 .07
❑ 532 Dan Plesac .10 .05
❑ 533 Billy Ripken .10 .05
❑ 534 Rod Nichols .10 .05
❑ 535 Joey Cora .10 .05
❑ 536 Harold Baines .15 .07
❑ 537 Bob Ojeda .10 .05
❑ 538 Mark Leonard .10 .05
❑ 539 Danny Darwin .10 .05
❑ 540 Shawon Dunston .10 .05
❑ 541 Pedro Munoz .10 .05
❑ 542 Mark Gubicza .10 .05
❑ 543 Kevin Baez .10 .05
❑ 544 Todd Zeile .10 .05
❑ 545 Don Slaught .10 .05
❑ 546 Tony Eusebio .15 .07
❑ 547 Alonzo Powell .10 .05
❑ 548 Gary Pettis .10 .05
❑ 549 Brian Barnes .10 .05
❑ 550 Lou Whitaker .15 .07
❑ 551 Keith Mitchell .10 .05
❑ 552 Oscar Azocar .10 .05
❑ 553 Stu Cole RC .10 .05
❑ 554 Steve Wapnick .10 .05
❑ 555 Derek Bell .15 .07
❑ 556 Luis Lopez .10 .05
❑ 557 Anthony Telford .10 .05
❑ 558 Tim Mauser .10 .05
❑ 559 Glen Sutko .10 .05
❑ 560 Darryl Strawberry .15 .07
❑ 561 Tom Bolton .10 .05
❑ 562 Cliff Young .10 .05
❑ 563 Bruce Walton .10 .05
❑ 564 Chico Walker .10 .05
❑ 565 John Franco .15 .07
❑ 566 Paul McClellan .10 .05
❑ 567 Paul Abbott .10 .05
❑ 568 Gary Varsho .10 .05
❑ 569 Carlos Maldonado RC .10 .05
❑ 570 Kelly Gruber .10 .05
❑ 571 Jose Oquendo .10 .05
❑ 572 Steve Frey .10 .05
❑ 573 Tino Martinez .15 .07
❑ 574 Bill Haselman .10 .05
❑ 575 Eric Anthony .10 .05
❑ 576 John Habyan .10 .05
❑ 577 Jeff McNeely .10 .05
❑ 578 Chris Bosio .10 .05
❑ 579 Joe Grahe .10 .05
❑ 580 Fred McGriff .25 .11
❑ 581 Rick Honeycutt .10 .05
❑ 582 Matt Williams .25 .11
❑ 583 Cliff Brantley .10 .05
❑ 584 Rob Dibble .10 .05
❑ 585 Skeeter Barnes .10 .05
❑ 586 Greg Hibbard .10 .05
❑ 587 Randy Milligan .10 .05
❑ 588 Checklist 301-400 .10 .05
❑ 589 Checklist 401-500 .10 .05
❑ 590 Checklist 501-600 .10 .05
❑ 591 Frank Thomas MC .25 .11
❑ 592 David Justice MC .15 .07
❑ 593 Roger Clemens MC .50 .23
❑ 594 Steve Avery MC .10 .05
❑ 595 Cal Ripken MC .75 .35
❑ 596 Barry Larkin MC UER .15 .07
(Ranked in AL, should be NL)
❑ 597 J.Canseco MC UER .15 .07
Mistakenly numbered 370 on card back
❑ 598 Will Clark MC .15 .07
❑ 599 Cecil Fielder MC .10 .05
❑ 600 Ryne Sandberg MC .25 .11
❑ 601 Chuck Knoblauch MC .10 .05
❑ 602 Dwight Gooden MC .10 .05
❑ 603 Ken Griffey Jr. MC 1.00 .45
❑ 604 Barry Bonds MC .50 .23
❑ 605 Nolan Ryan MC .75 .35
❑ 606 Jeff Bagwell MC .25 .11
❑ 607 Robin Yount MC .15 .07
❑ 608 Bobby Bonilla MC .10 .05
❑ 609 George Brett MC .40 .18
❑ 610 Howard Johnson MC .10 .05
❑ 611 Esteban Beltre .10 .05
❑ 612 Mike Christopher .10 .05
❑ 613 Troy Afenir .10 .05
❑ 614 Mariano Duncan .10 .05
❑ 615 Doug Henry RC .10 .05
❑ 616 Doug Jones .10 .05
❑ 617 Alvin Davis .10 .05
❑ 618 Craig Lefferts .10 .05
❑ 619 Kevin McReynolds .10 .05
❑ 620 Barry Bonds 1.00 .45
❑ 621 Turner Ward .10 .05
❑ 622 Joe Magrane .10 .05
❑ 623 Mark Parent .10 .05
❑ 624 Tom Browning .10 .05
❑ 625 John Smiley .10 .05
❑ 626 Steve Wilson .10 .05
❑ 627 Mike Gallego .10 .05
❑ 628 Sammy Sosa .75 .35
❑ 629 Rico Rossy .10 .05
❑ 630 Royce Clayton .10 .05
❑ 631 Clay Parker .10 .05
❑ 632 Pete Smith .10 .05
❑ 633 Jeff McKnight .10 .05
❑ 634 Jack Daugherty .10 .05
❑ 635 Steve Sax .10 .05
❑ 636 Joe Hesketh .10 .05
❑ 637 Vince Horsman .10 .05
❑ 638 Eric King .10 .05
❑ 639 Joe Boever .10 .05
❑ 640 Jack Morris .15 .07
❑ 641 Arthur Rhodes .10 .05
❑ 642 Bob Melvin .10 .05
❑ 643 Rick Wilkins .10 .05
❑ 644 Scott Scudder .10 .05
❑ 645 Bip Roberts .10 .05
❑ 646 Julio Valera .10 .05
❑ 647 Kevin Campbell .10 .05
❑ 648 Steve Searcy .10 .05
❑ 649 Scott Kamieniecki .10 .05
❑ 650 Kurt Stillwell .10 .05
❑ 651 Bob Welch .10 .05
❑ 652 Andres Galarraga .25 .11
❑ 653 Mike Jackson .10 .05
❑ 654 Bo Jackson .15 .07
❑ 655 Sid Fernandez .10 .05
❑ 656 Mike Bielecki .10 .05
❑ 657 Jeff Reardon .15 .07
❑ 658 Wayne Rosenthal .10 .05
❑ 659 Eric Bullock .10 .05
❑ 660 Eric Davis .15 .07
❑ 661 Randy Tomlin .10 .05
❑ 662 Tom Edens .10 .05
❑ 663 Rob Murphy .10 .05
❑ 664 Leo Gomez .10 .05
❑ 665 Greg Maddux 1.00 .45
❑ 666 Greg Vaughn .15 .07
❑ 667 Wade Taylor .10 .05
❑ 668 Brad Arnsberg .10 .05
❑ 669 Mike Moore .10 .05
❑ 670 Mark Langston .10 .05
❑ 671 Barry Jones .10 .05
❑ 672 Bill Landrum .10 .05
❑ 673 Greg Swindell .10 .05
❑ 674 Wayne Edwards .10 .05
❑ 675 Greg Olson .10 .05
❑ 676 Bill Pulsipher RC .10 .05
❑ 677 Bobby Witt .10 .05
❑ 678 Mark Carreon .10 .05
❑ 679 Patrick Lennon .10 .05
❑ 680 Ozzie Smith .50 .23
❑ 681 John Briscoe .10 .05
❑ 682 Matt Young .10 .05
❑ 683 Jeff Conine .10 .05
❑ 684 Phil Stephenson .10 .05
❑ 685 Ron Darling .10 .05
❑ 686 Bryan Hickerson RC .10 .05
❑ 687 Dale Sveum .10 .05
❑ 688 Kirk McCaskill .10 .05
❑ 689 Rich Amaral .10 .05
❑ 690 Danny Tartabull .10 .05
❑ 691 Donald Harris .10 .05
❑ 692 Doug Davis .10 .05
❑ 693 John Farrell .10 .05
❑ 694 Paul Gibson .10 .05
❑ 695 Kenny Lofton .40 .18
❑ 696 Mike Fetters .10 .05
❑ 697 Rosario Rodriguez .10 .05
❑ 698 Chris Jones .10 .05
❑ 699 Jeff Manto .10 .05
❑ 700 Rick Sutcliffe .15 .07
❑ 701 Scott Bankhead .10 .05
❑ 702 Donnie Hill .10 .05
❑ 703 Todd Worrell .10 .05
❑ 704 Rene Gonzales .10 .05
❑ 705 Rick Cerone .10 .05
❑ 706 Tony Pena .10 .05
❑ 707 Paul Sorrento .10 .05
❑ 708 Gary Scott .10 .05
❑ 709 Junior Noboa .10 .05
❑ 710 Wally Joyner .15 .07
❑ 711 Charlie Hayes .10 .05
❑ 712 Rich Rodriguez .10 .05
❑ 713 Rudy Seanez .10 .05
❑ 714 Jim Bullinger .10 .05
❑ 715 Jeff M. Robinson .10 .05
❑ 716 Jeff Branson .10 .05
❑ 717 Andy Ashby .10 .05
❑ 718 Dave Burba .10 .05
❑ 719 Rich Gossage .15 .07
❑ 720 Randy Johnson .50 .23
❑ 721 David Wells .15 .07
❑ 722 Paul Kilgus .10 .05
❑ 723 Dave Martinez .10 .05
❑ 724 Denny Neagle .15 .07
❑ 725 Andy Stankiewicz .10 .05
❑ 726 Rick Aguilera .15 .07
❑ 727 Junior Ortiz .10 .05
❑ 728 Storm Davis .10 .05
❑ 729 Don Robinson .10 .05
❑ 730 Ron Gant .10 .05
❑ 731 Paul Assenmacher .10 .05
❑ 732 Mike Gardiner .10 .05
❑ 733 Milt Hill .10 .05
❑ 734 Jeremy Hernandez RC .10 .05
❑ 735 Ken Hill .10 .05
❑ 736 Xavier Hernandez .10 .05
❑ 737 Gregg Jefferies .10 .05
❑ 738 Dick Schofield .10 .05
❑ 739 Ron Robinson .10 .05
❑ 740 Sandy Alomar Jr. .15 .07
❑ 741 Mike Stanley .10 .05
❑ 742 Butch Henry RC .10 .05
❑ 743 Floyd Bannister .10 .05
❑ 744 Brian Drahman .10 .05
❑ 745 Dave Winfield .40 .18
❑ 746 Bob Walk .10 .05
❑ 747 Chris James .10 .05
❑ 748 Don Prybylinski RC .10 .05
❑ 749 Dennis Rasmussen .10 .05
❑ 750 Rickey Henderson .75 .35
❑ 751 Chris Hammond .10 .05
❑ 752 Bob Kipper .10 .05
❑ 753 Dave Rohde .10 .05
❑ 754 Hubie Brooks .10 .05

❑ 755 Bret Saberhagen	.15	.07
❑ 756 Jeff D. Robinson	.10	.05
❑ 757 Pat Listach RC	.15	.07
❑ 758 Bill Wegman	.10	.05
❑ 759 John Wetteland	.15	.07
❑ 760 Phil Plantier	.10	.05
❑ 761 Wilson Alvarez	.10	.05
❑ 762 Scott Aldred	.10	.05
❑ 763 Armando Reynoso RC	.15	.07
❑ 764 Todd Benzinger	.10	.05
❑ 765 Kevin Mitchell	.10	.05
❑ 766 Gary Sheffield	.15	.07
❑ 767 Allan Anderson	.10	.05
❑ 768 Rusty Meacham	.10	.05
❑ 769 Rick Parker	.10	.05
❑ 770 Nolan Ryan	2.00	.90
❑ 771 Jeff Ballard	.10	.05
❑ 772 Cory Snyder	.10	.05
❑ 773 Denis Boucher	.10	.05
❑ 774 Jose Gonzalez	.10	.05
❑ 775 Juan Guerrero	.10	.05
❑ 776 Ed Nunez	.10	.05
❑ 777 Scott Ruskin	.10	.05
❑ 778 Terry Leach	.10	.05
❑ 779 Carl Willis	.10	.05
❑ 780 Bobby Bonilla	.15	.07
❑ 781 Duane Ward	.10	.05
❑ 782 Joe Slusarski	.10	.05
❑ 783 David Segui	.10	.05
❑ 784 Kirk Gibson	.15	.07
❑ 785 Frank Viola	.15	.07
❑ 786 Keith Miller	.10	.05
❑ 787 Mike Morgan	.10	.05
❑ 788 Kim Batiste	.10	.05
❑ 789 Sergio Valdez	.10	.05
❑ 790 Eddie Taubensee RC	.15	.07
❑ 791 Jack Armstrong	.10	.05
❑ 792 Scott Fletcher	.10	.05
❑ 793 Steve Farr	.10	.05
❑ 794 Dan Pasqua	.10	.05
❑ 795 Eddie Murray	.40	.18
❑ 796 John Morris	.10	.05
❑ 797 Francisco Cabrera	.10	.05
❑ 798 Mike Perez	.10	.05
❑ 799 Ted Wood	.10	.05
❑ 800 Jose Rijo	.10	.05
❑ 801 Danny Gladden	.10	.05
❑ 802 Archi Cianfrocco RC	.10	.05
❑ 803 Monty Fariss	.10	.05
❑ 804 Roger McDowell	.10	.05
❑ 805 Randy Myers	.10	.05
❑ 806 Kirk Dressendorfer	.10	.05
❑ 807 Zane Smith	.10	.05
❑ 808 Glenn Davis	.10	.05
❑ 809 Torey Lovullo	.10	.05
❑ 810 Andre Dawson	.25	.11
❑ 811 Bill Pecota	.10	.05
❑ 812 Ted Power	.10	.05
❑ 813 Willie Blair	.10	.05
❑ 814 Dave Fleming	.10	.05
❑ 815 Chris Gwynn	.10	.05
❑ 816 Jody Reed	.10	.05
❑ 817 Mark Dewey	.10	.05
❑ 818 Kyle Abbott	.10	.05
❑ 819 Tom Henke	.10	.05
❑ 820 Kevin Seitzer	.10	.05
❑ 821 Al Newman	.10	.05
❑ 822 Tim Sherrill	.10	.05
❑ 823 Chuck Crim	.10	.05
❑ 824 Darren Reed	.10	.05
❑ 825 Tony Gwynn	.75	.35
❑ 826 Steve Foster	.10	.05
❑ 827 Steve Howe	.10	.05
❑ 828 Brook Jacoby	.10	.05
❑ 829 Rodney McCray	.10	.05
❑ 830 Chuck Knoblauch	.15	.07
❑ 831 John Wehner	.10	.05
❑ 832 Scott Garrelts	.10	.05
❑ 833 Alejandro Pena	.10	.05
❑ 834 Jeff Parrett UER (Kentucky)	.10	.05
❑ 835 Juan Bell	.10	.05
❑ 836 Lance Dickson	.10	.05
❑ 837 Darryl Kile	.15	.07
❑ 838 Efrain Valdez	.10	.05
❑ 839 Bob Zupcic RC	.10	.05
❑ 840 George Bell	.10	.05
❑ 841 Dave Gallagher	.10	.05
❑ 842 Tim Belcher	.10	.05
❑ 843 Jeff Shaw	.10	.05
❑ 844 Mike Fitzgerald	.10	.05
❑ 845 Gary Carter	.25	.11
❑ 846 John Russell	.10	.05
❑ 847 Eric Hillman RC	.10	.05
❑ 848 Mike Witt	.10	.05
❑ 849 Curt Wilkerson	.10	.05
❑ 850 Alan Trammell	.25	.11
❑ 851 Rex Hudler	.10	.05
❑ 852 Mike Walkden RC	.10	.05
❑ 853 Kevin Ward	.10	.05
❑ 854 Tim Naehring	.10	.05
❑ 855 Bill Swift	.10	.05
❑ 856 Damon Berryhill	.10	.05
❑ 857 Mark Eichhorn	.10	.05
❑ 858 Hector Villanueva	.10	.05
❑ 859 Jose Lind	.10	.05
❑ 860 Dennis Martinez	.15	.07
❑ 861 Bill Krueger	.10	.05
❑ 862 Mike Kingery	.10	.05
❑ 863 Jeff Innis	.10	.05
❑ 864 Derek Lilliquist	.10	.05
❑ 865 Reggie Sanders	.10	.05
❑ 866 Ramon Garcia	.10	.05
❑ 867 Bruce Ruffin	.10	.05
❑ 868 Dickie Thon	.10	.05
❑ 869 Melido Perez	.10	.05
❑ 870 Ruben Amaro	.10	.05
❑ 871 Alan Mills	.10	.05
❑ 872 Matt Sinatro	.10	.05
❑ 873 Eddie Zosky	.10	.05
❑ 874 Pete Incaviglia	.10	.05
❑ 875 Tom Candiotti	.10	.05
❑ 876 Bob Patterson	.10	.05
❑ 877 Neal Heaton	.10	.05
❑ 878 Terrel Hansen RC	.10	.05
❑ 879 Dave Eiland	.10	.05
❑ 880 Von Hayes	.10	.05
❑ 881 Tim Scott	.10	.05
❑ 882 Otis Nixon	.10	.05
❑ 883 Herm Winningham	.10	.05
❑ 884 Dion James	.10	.05
❑ 885 Dave Wainhouse	.10	.05
❑ 886 Frank DiPino	.10	.05
❑ 887 Dennis Cook	.10	.05
❑ 888 Jose Mesa	.10	.05
❑ 889 Mark Leiter	.10	.05
❑ 890 Willie Randolph	.15	.07
❑ 891 Craig Colbert	.10	.05
❑ 892 Dwayne Henry	.10	.05
❑ 893 Jim Lindeman	.10	.05
❑ 894 Charlie Hough	.15	.07
❑ 895 Gil Heredia RC	.15	.07
❑ 896 Scott Chiamparino	.10	.05
❑ 897 Lance Blankenship	.10	.05
❑ 898 Checklist 601-700	.10	.05
❑ 899 Checklist 701-800	.10	.05
❑ 900 Checklist 801-900	.10	.05

1993 Stadium Club Murphy

	MINT	NRMT
COMP.FACT.SET (212)	80.00	36.00
COMPLETE SET (200)	25.00	11.00
❑ 1 Dave Winfield	.25	.11
❑ 2 Juan Guzman	.15	.07
❑ 3 Tony Gwynn	1.25	.55
❑ 4 Chris Roberts	.15	.07
❑ 5 Benny Santiago	.15	.07
❑ 6 Sherard Clinkscales RC	.15	.07
❑ 7 Jon Nunnally RC	.15	.07
❑ 8 Chuck Knoblauch	.25	.11
❑ 9 Bob Wolcott RC	.15	.07
❑ 10 Steve Rodriguez	.15	.07
❑ 11 Mark Williams RC	.15	.07
❑ 12 Danny Clyburn RC	.15	.07
❑ 13 Darren Dreifort	.25	.11
❑ 14 Andy Van Slyke	.25	.11
❑ 15 Wade Boggs	.60	.25
❑ 16 Scott Patton RC	.15	.07
❑ 17 Gary Sheffield	.25	.11
❑ 18 Ron Villone	.15	.07
❑ 19 Roberto Alomar	.60	.25
❑ 20 Marc Valdes	.15	.07
❑ 21 Daron Kirkreit	.15	.07
❑ 22 Jeff Granger	.15	.07
❑ 23 Levon Largusa RC	.15	.07
❑ 24 Jimmy Key	.25	.11
❑ 25 Kevin Pearson RC	.15	.07
❑ 26 Michael Moore RC	.15	.07
❑ 27 Preston Wilson RC	8.00	3.60
❑ 28 Kirby Puckett	1.50	.70
❑ 29 Tim Crabtree RC	.15	.07
❑ 30 Bip Roberts	.15	.07
❑ 31 Kelly Gruber	.15	.07
❑ 32 Tony Fernandez	.15	.07
❑ 33 Jason Angel RC	.15	.07
❑ 34 Calvin Murray	.15	.07
❑ 35 Chad McConnell	.15	.07
❑ 36 Jason Moler	.15	.07
❑ 37 Mark Lemke	.15	.07
❑ 38 Tom Knauss RC	.15	.07
❑ 39 Larry Mitchell RC	.15	.07
❑ 40 Doug Mirabelli RC	.15	.07
❑ 41 Everett Stull II RC	.15	.07
❑ 42 Chris Wimmer	.15	.07
❑ 43 Dan Serafini RC	.15	.07
❑ 44 Ryne Sandberg	.75	.35
❑ 45 Steve Lyons RC	.15	.07
❑ 46 Ryan Freeburg RC	.15	.07
❑ 47 Ruben Sierra	.15	.07
❑ 48 David Mysel RC	.15	.07
❑ 49 Joe Hamilton RC	.15	.07
❑ 50 Steve Rodriguez	.15	.07
❑ 51 Tim Wakefield	.15	.07
❑ 52 Scott Gentile RC	.15	.07
❑ 53 Doug Jones	.15	.07
❑ 54 Willie Brown RC	.15	.07
❑ 55 Chad Mottola RC	.15	.07
❑ 56 Ken Griffey Jr.	2.00	.90
❑ 57 Jon Lieber RC	4.00	1.80
❑ 58 Dennis Martinez	.25	.11
❑ 59 Joe Petcka RC	.15	.07
❑ 60 Benji Simonton RC	.15	.07
❑ 61 Brett Backlund RC	.15	.07
❑ 62 Damon Berryhill	.15	.07
❑ 63 Juan Guzman	.15	.07
❑ 64 Doug Hecker RC	.15	.07
❑ 65 Jamie Arnold RC	.15	.07
❑ 66 Bob Tewksbury	.15	.07
❑ 67 Tim Leger RC	.15	.07
❑ 68 Todd Etler RC	.15	.07
❑ 69 Lloyd McClendon	.15	.07
❑ 70 Kurt Ehmann RC	.15	.07
❑ 71 Rick Magdaleno RC	.15	.07
❑ 72 Tom Pagnozzi	.15	.07
❑ 73 Jeffrey Hammonds	.25	.11
❑ 74 Joe Carter	.25	.11
❑ 75 Chris Holt RC	.25	.11
❑ 76 Charles Johnson	1.00	.45
❑ 77 Bob Walk	.15	.07
❑ 78 Fred McGriff	.40	.18
❑ 79 Tom Evans RC	.15	.07
❑ 80 Scott Klingenbeck RC	.15	.07
❑ 81 Chad McConnell	.15	.07
❑ 82 Chris Eddy RC	.15	.07
❑ 83 Phil Nevin	.25	.11
❑ 84 John Kruk	.25	.11

	Player	MINT	NRMT
❑ 85	Tony Sheffield RC	.15	.07
❑ 86	John Smoltz	.25	.11
❑ 87	Trevor Humphry RC	.15	.07
❑ 88	Charles Nagy	.15	.07
❑ 89	Sean Runyan RC	.15	.07
❑ 90	Mike Gulan RC	.15	.07
❑ 91	Darren Daulton	.25	.11
❑ 92	Otis Nixon	.15	.07
❑ 93	Nomar Garciaparra	15.00	6.75
❑ 94	Larry Walker	.15	.07
❑ 95	Hut Smith RC	.15	.07
❑ 96	Rick Helling	.15	.07
❑ 97	Roger Clemens	1.50	.70
❑ 98	Ron Gant	.15	.07
❑ 99	Kenny Felder RC	.15	.07
❑ 100	Steve Murphy RC	.15	.07
❑ 101	Mike Smith RC	.15	.07
❑ 102	Terry Pendleton	.25	.11
❑ 103	Tim Davis	.15	.07
❑ 104	Jeff Patzke RC	.15	.07
❑ 105	Craig Wilson	.15	.07
❑ 106	Tom Glavine	.60	.25
❑ 107	Mark Langston	.15	.07
❑ 108	Mark Thompson RC	.15	.07
❑ 109	Eric Owens RC	1.00	.45
❑ 110	Keith Johnson RC	.15	.07
❑ 111	Robin Ventura	.25	.11
❑ 112	Ed Sprague	.15	.07
❑ 113	Jeff Schmidt RC	.15	.07
❑ 114	Don Wengert RC	.15	.07
❑ 115	Craig Biggio	.40	.18
❑ 116	Kenny Carlyle RC	.15	.07
❑ 117	Derek Jeter RC	40.00	18.00
❑ 118	Manuel Lee	.15	.07
❑ 119	Jeff Haas RC	.15	.07
❑ 120	Roger Bailey RC	.15	.07
❑ 121	Sean Lowe RC	.15	.07
❑ 122	Rick Aguilera	.15	.07
❑ 123	Sandy Alomar Jr.	.25	.11
❑ 124	Derek Wallace RC	.15	.07
❑ 125	B.J. Wallace	.15	.07
❑ 126	Greg Maddux	1.50	.70
❑ 127	Tim Moore RC	.15	.07
❑ 128	Lee Smith	.25	.11
❑ 129	Todd Steverson RC	.15	.07
❑ 130	Chris Widger RC	.25	.11
❑ 131	Paul Molitor	.60	.25
❑ 132	Chris Smith RC	.15	.07
❑ 133	Chris Gomez RC	.25	.11
❑ 134	Jimmy Baron RC	.15	.07
❑ 135	John Smoltz	.25	.11
❑ 136	Pat Borders	.15	.07
❑ 137	Donnie Leshnock	.15	.07
❑ 138	Gus Gandarillos RC	.15	.07
❑ 139	Will Clark	.60	.25
❑ 140	Ryan Luzinski RC	.15	.07
❑ 141	Cal Ripken	2.50	1.10
❑ 142	B.J. Wallace	.15	.07
❑ 143	Trey Beamon RC	.15	.07
❑ 144	Norm Charlton	.15	.07
❑ 145	Mike Mussina	.60	.25
❑ 146	Billy Owens RC	.15	.07
❑ 147	Ozzie Smith	.75	.35
❑ 148	Jason Kendall RC	8.00	3.60
❑ 149	Mike Matthews RC	.15	.07
❑ 150	David Spykstra RC	.15	.07
❑ 151	Benji Grigsby RC	.15	.07
❑ 152	Sean Smith RC	.15	.07
❑ 153	Mark McGwire	2.50	1.10
❑ 154	David Cone	.25	.11
❑ 155	Shon Walker RC	.15	.07
❑ 156	Jason Giambi	1.50	.70
❑ 157	Jack McDowell	.15	.07
❑ 158	Paxton Briley RC	.15	.07
❑ 159	Edgar Martinez	.40	.18
❑ 160	Brian Sackinsky RC	.15	.07
❑ 161	Barry Bonds	1.50	.70
❑ 162	Roberto Kelly	.15	.07
❑ 163	Jeff Alkire	.15	.07
❑ 164	Mike Sharperson	.15	.07
❑ 165	Jamie Taylor RC	.15	.07
❑ 166	John Saffer RC	.15	.07
❑ 167	Jerry Browne	.15	.07
❑ 168	Travis Fryman	.25	.11
❑ 169	Brady Anderson	.25	.11
❑ 170	Chris Roberts	.15	.07
❑ 171	Lloyd Peever RC	.15	.07
❑ 172	Francisco Cabrera	.15	.07
❑ 173	Ramiro Martinez RC	.15	.07
❑ 174	Jeff Alkire	.15	.07
❑ 175	Ivan Rodriguez	.60	.25
❑ 176	Kevin Brown	.25	.11
❑ 177	Chad Roper RC	.15	.07
❑ 178	Rod Henderson RC	.15	.07
❑ 179	Dennis Eckersley	.25	.11
❑ 180	Shannon Stewart RC	8.00	3.60
❑ 181	DeShawn Warren RC	.15	.07
❑ 182	Lonnie Smith	.15	.07
❑ 183	Willie Adams	.15	.07
❑ 184	Jeff Montgomery	.15	.07
❑ 185	Damon Hollins RC	.15	.07
❑ 186	Byron Mathews RC	.15	.07
❑ 187	Harold Baines	.25	.11
❑ 188	Rick Greene	.15	.07
❑ 189	Carlos Baerga	.15	.07
❑ 190	Brandon Cromer RC	.15	.07
❑ 191	Roberto Alomar	.60	.25
❑ 192	Rich Ireland RC	.15	.07
❑ 193	S.Montgomery RC	.15	.07
❑ 194	Brant Brown RC	.25	.11
❑ 195	Ritchie Moody RC	.15	.07
❑ 196	Michael Tucker	.15	.07
❑ 197	Jason Varitek	1.00	.45
❑ 198	David Manning RC	.15	.07
❑ 199	Marquis Riley RC	.15	.07
❑ 200	Jason Giambi	1.50	.70

1993 Stadium Club

	MINT	NRMT
COMPLETE SET (750)	50.00	22.00
COMPLETE SERIES 1 (300)	15.00	6.75
COMPLETE SERIES 2 (300)	20.00	9.00
COMPLETE SERIES 3 (150)	15.00	6.75

	Player	MINT	NRMT
❑ 1	Pat Borders	.15	.07
❑ 2	Greg Maddux	1.50	.70
❑ 3	Daryl Boston	.15	.07
❑ 4	Bob Ayrault	.15	.07
❑ 5	Tony Phillips IF	.15	.07
❑ 6	Damion Easley	.15	.07
❑ 7	Kip Gross	.15	.07
❑ 8	Jim Thome	.60	.25
❑ 9	Tim Belcher	.15	.07
❑ 10	Gary Wayne	.15	.07
❑ 11	Sam Militello	.15	.07
❑ 12	Mike Magnante	.15	.07
❑ 13	Tim Wakefield	.15	.07
❑ 14	Tim Hulett	.15	.07
❑ 15	Rheal Cormier	.15	.07
❑ 16	Juan Guerrero	.15	.07
❑ 17	Rich Gossage	.25	.11
❑ 18	Tim Laker RC	.15	.07
❑ 19	Darrin Jackson	.15	.07
❑ 20	Jack Clark	.25	.11
❑ 21	Roberto Hernandez	.15	.07
❑ 22	Dean Palmer	.25	.11
❑ 23	Harold Reynolds	.15	.07
❑ 24	Dan Plesac	.15	.07
❑ 25	Brent Mayne	.15	.07
❑ 26	Pat Hentgen	.15	.07
❑ 27	Luis Sojo	.15	.07
❑ 28	Ron Gant	.15	.07
❑ 29	Paul Gibson	.15	.07
❑ 30	Bip Roberts	.15	.07
❑ 31	Mickey Tettleton	.15	.07
❑ 32	Randy Velarde	.15	.07
❑ 33	Brian McRae	.15	.07
❑ 34	Wes Chamberlain	.15	.07
❑ 35	Wayne Kirby	.15	.07
❑ 36	Rey Sanchez	.15	.07
❑ 37	Jesse Orosco	.15	.07
❑ 38	Mike Stanton	.15	.07
❑ 39	Royce Clayton	.15	.07
❑ 40	Cal Ripken UER	2.50	1.10
	(Place of birth Havre de Grave; should be Havre de Grace)		
❑ 41	John Dopson	.15	.07
❑ 42	Gene Larkin	.15	.07
❑ 43	Tim Raines	.25	.11
❑ 44	Randy Myers	.15	.07
❑ 45	Clay Parker	.15	.07
❑ 46	Mike Scioscia	.15	.07
❑ 47	Pete Incaviglia	.15	.07
❑ 48	Todd Van Poppel	.15	.07
❑ 49	Ray Lankford	.15	.07
❑ 50	Eddie Murray	.60	.25
❑ 51	Barry Bonds COR	1.50	.70
❑ 51A	Barry Bonds ERR	1.50	.70
	(Missing four stars over name to indicate NL MVP)		
❑ 52	Gary Thurman	.15	.07
❑ 53	Bob Wickman	.15	.07
❑ 54	Joey Cora	.15	.07
❑ 55	Kenny Rogers	.15	.07
❑ 56	Mike Devereaux	.15	.07
❑ 57	Kevin Seitzer	.15	.07
❑ 58	Rafael Belliard	.15	.07
❑ 59	David Wells	.25	.11
❑ 60	Mark Clark	.15	.07
❑ 61	Carlos Baerga	.15	.07
❑ 62	Scott Brosius	.25	.11
❑ 63	Jeff Grotewold	.15	.07
❑ 64	Rick Wrona	.15	.07
❑ 65	Kurt Knudsen	.15	.07
❑ 66	Lloyd McClendon	.15	.07
❑ 67	Omar Vizquel	.25	.11
❑ 68	Jose Vizcaino	.15	.07
❑ 69	Rob Ducey	.15	.07
❑ 70	Casey Candaele	.15	.07
❑ 71	Ramon Martinez	.15	.07
❑ 72	Todd Hundley	.15	.07
❑ 73	John Marzano	.15	.07
❑ 74	Derek Parks	.15	.07
❑ 75	Jack McDowell	.15	.07
❑ 76	Tim Scott	.15	.07
❑ 77	Mike Mussina	.60	.25
❑ 78	Delino DeShields	.15	.07
❑ 79	Chris Bosio	.15	.07
❑ 80	Mike Bordick	.15	.07
❑ 81	Rod Beck	.15	.07
❑ 82	Ted Power	.15	.07
❑ 83	John Kruk	.25	.11
❑ 84	Steve Shifflett	.15	.07
❑ 85	Danny Tartabull	.15	.07
❑ 86	Mike Greenwell	.15	.07
❑ 87	Jose Melendez	.15	.07
❑ 88	Craig Wilson	.15	.07
❑ 89	Melvin Nieves	.15	.07
❑ 90	Ed Sprague	.15	.07
❑ 91	Willie McGee	.25	.11
❑ 92	Joe Orsulak	.15	.07
❑ 93	Jeff King	.15	.07
❑ 94	Dan Pasqua	.15	.07
❑ 95	Brian Harper	.15	.07
❑ 96	Joe Oliver	.15	.07
❑ 97	Shane Turner	.15	.07
❑ 98	Lenny Harris	.15	.07
❑ 99	Jeff Parrett	.15	.07
❑ 100	Luis Polonia	.15	.07
❑ 101	Kent Bottenfield	.15	.07
❑ 102	Albert Belle	.25	.11
❑ 103	Mike Maddux	.15	.07
❑ 104	Randy Tomlin	.15	.07
❑ 105	Andy Stankiewicz	.15	.07
❑ 106	Rico Rossy	.15	.07
❑ 107	Joe Hesketh	.15	.07
❑ 108	Dennis Powell	.15	.07
❑ 109	Derrick May	.15	.07
❑ 110	Pete Harnisch	.15	.07

No.	Player	Mint	Nr Mint
111	Kent Mercker	.15	.07
112	Scott Fletcher	.15	.07
113	Rex Hudler	.15	.07
114	Chico Walker	.15	.07
115	Rafael Palmeiro	.60	.25
116	Mark Leiter	.15	.07
117	Pedro Munoz	.15	.07
118	Jim Bullinger	.15	.07
119	Ivan Calderon	.15	.07
120	Mike Timlin	.15	.07
121	Rene Gonzales	.15	.07
122	Greg Vaughn	.25	.11
123	Mike Flanagan	.15	.07
124	Mike Hartley	.15	.07
125	Jeff Montgomery	.15	.07
126	Mike Gallego	.15	.07
127	Don Slaught	.15	.07
128	Charlie O'Brien	.15	.07
129	Jose Offerman (Can be found with home town missing on back)	.15	.07
130	Mark Wohlers	.15	.07
131	Eric Fox	.15	.07
132	Doug Strange	.15	.07
133	Jeff Frye	.15	.07
134	Wade Boggs UER (Redundantly lists lefty breakdown)	.60	.25
135	Lou Whitaker	.25	.11
136	Craig Grebeck	.15	.07
137	Rich Rodriguez	.15	.07
138	Jay Bell	.25	.11
139	Felix Fermin	.15	.07
140	Dennis Martinez	.25	.11
141	Eric Anthony	.15	.07
142	Roberto Alomar	.60	.25
143	Darren Lewis	.15	.07
144	Mike Blowers	.15	.07
145	Scott Bankhead	.15	.07
146	Jeff Reboulet	.15	.07
147	Frank Viola	.25	.11
148	Bill Pecota	.15	.07
149	Carlos Hernandez	.15	.07
150	Bobby Witt	.15	.07
151	Sid Bream	.15	.07
152	Todd Zeile	.15	.07
153	Dennis Cook	.15	.07
154	Brian Bohanon	.15	.07
155	Pat Kelly	.15	.07
156	Milt Cuyler	.15	.07
157	Juan Bell	.15	.07
158	Randy Milligan	.15	.07
159	Mark Gardner	.15	.07
160	Pat Tabler	.15	.07
161	Jeff Reardon	.25	.11
162	Ken Patterson	.15	.07
163	Bobby Bonilla	.25	.11
164	Tony Pena	.15	.07
165	Greg Swindell	.15	.07
166	Kirk McCaskill	.15	.07
167	Doug Drabek	.15	.07
168	Franklin Stubbs	.15	.07
169	Ron Tingley	.15	.07
170	Willie Banks	.15	.07
171	Sergio Valdez	.15	.07
172	Mark Lemke	.15	.07
173	Robin Yount	.60	.25
174	Storm Davis	.15	.07
175	Dan Walters	.15	.07
176	Steve Farr	.15	.07
177	Curt Wilkerson	.15	.07
178	Luis Alicea	.15	.07
179	Russ Swan	.15	.07
180	Mitch Williams	.15	.07
181	Wilson Alvarez	.15	.07
182	Carl Willis	.15	.07
183	Craig Biggio	.40	.18
184	Sean Berry	.15	.07
185	Trevor Wilson	.15	.07
186	Jeff Tackett	.15	.07
187	Ellis Burks	.25	.11
188	Jeff Branson	.15	.07
189	Matt Nokes	.15	.07
190	John Smiley	.15	.07
191	Danny Gladden	.15	.07
192	Mike Boddicker	.15	.07
193	Roger Pavlik	.15	.07
194	Paul Sorrento	.15	.07
195	Vince Coleman	.15	.07
196	Gary DiSarcina	.15	.07
197	Rafael Bournigal	.15	.07
198	Mike Schooler	.15	.07
199	Scott Ruskin	.15	.07
200	Frank Thomas	.75	.35
201	Kyle Abbott	.15	.07
202	Mike Perez	.15	.07
203	Andre Dawson	.40	.18
204	Bill Swift	.15	.07
205	Alejandro Pena	.15	.07
206	Dave Winfield	.60	.25
207	Andujar Cedeno	.15	.07
208	Terry Steinbach	.15	.07
209	Chris Hammond	.15	.07
210	Todd Burns	.15	.07
211	Hipolito Pichardo	.15	.07
212	John Kiely	.15	.07
213	Tim Teufel	.15	.07
214	Lee Guetterman	.15	.07
215	Geronimo Pena	.15	.07
216	Brett Butler	.25	.11
217	Bryan Hickerson	.15	.07
218	Rick Trlicek	.15	.07
219	Lee Stevens	.15	.07
220	Roger Clemens	1.50	.70
221	Carlton Fisk	.60	.25
222	Chili Davis	.25	.11
223	Walt Terrell	.15	.07
224	Jim Eisenreich	.15	.07
225	Ricky Bones	.15	.07
226	Henry Rodriguez	.15	.07
227	Ken Hill	.15	.07
228	Rick Wilkins	.15	.07
229	Ricky Jordan	.15	.07
230	Bernard Gilkey	.15	.07
231	Tim Fortugno	.15	.07
232	Geno Petralli	.15	.07
233	Jose Rijo	.15	.07
234	Jim Leyritz	.15	.07
235	Kevin Campbell	.15	.07
236	Al Osuna	.15	.07
237	Pete Smith	.15	.07
238	Pete Schourek	.15	.07
239	Moises Alou	.25	.11
240	Donn Pall	.15	.07
241	Denny Neagle	.25	.11
242	Dan Peltier	.15	.07
243	Scott Scudder	.15	.07
244	Juan Guzman	.15	.07
245	Dave Burba	.15	.07
246	Rick Sutcliffe	.25	.11
247	Tony Fossas	.15	.07
248	Mike Munoz	.15	.07
249	Tim Salmon	.25	.11
250	Rob Murphy	.15	.07
251	Roger McDowell	.15	.07
252	Lance Parrish	.25	.11
253	Cliff Brantley	.15	.07
254	Scott Leius	.15	.07
255	Carlos Martinez	.15	.07
256	Vince Horsman	.15	.07
257	Oscar Azocar	.15	.07
258	Craig Shipley	.15	.07
259	Ben McDonald	.15	.07
260	Jeff Brantley	.15	.07
261	Damon Berryhill	.15	.07
262	Joe Grahe	.15	.07
263	Dave Hansen	.15	.07
264	Rich Amaral	.15	.07
265	Tim Pugh RC	.15	.07
266	Dion James	.15	.07
267	Frank Tanana	.15	.07
268	Stan Belinda	.15	.07
269	Jeff Kent	.60	.25
270	Bruce Ruffin	.15	.07
271	Xavier Hernandez	.15	.07
272	Darrin Fletcher	.15	.07
273	Tino Martinez	.25	.11
274	Benny Santiago	.15	.07
275	Scott Radinsky	.15	.07
276	Mariano Duncan	.15	.07
277	Kenny Lofton	.25	.11
278	Dwight Smith	.15	.07
279	Joe Carter	.25	.11
280	Tim Jones	.15	.07
281	Jeff Huson	.15	.07
282	Phil Plantier	.15	.07
283	Kirby Puckett	1.50	.70
284	Johnny Guzman	.15	.07
285	Mike Morgan	.15	.07
286	Chris Sabo	.15	.07
287	Matt Williams	.40	.18
288	Checklist 1-100	.15	.07
289	Checklist 101-200	.15	.07
290	Checklist 201-300	.15	.07
291	Dennis Eckersley MC	.15	.07
292	Eric Karros MC	.15	.07
293	Pat Listach MC	.15	.07
294	Andy Van Slyke MC	.15	.07
295	Robin Ventura MC	.15	.07
296	Tom Glavine MC	.25	.11
297	J.Gonzalez MC UER (Misspelled Gonzales)	.25	.11
298	Travis Fryman MC	.15	.07
299	Larry Walker MC	.15	.07
300	Gary Sheffield MC	.15	.07
301	Chuck Finley	.25	.11
302	Luis Gonzalez	.60	.25
303	Darryl Hamilton	.15	.07
304	Bien Figueroa	.15	.07
305	Ron Darling	.15	.07
306	Jonathan Hurst	.15	.07
307	Mike Sharperson	.15	.07
308	Mike Christopher	.15	.07
309	Marvin Freeman	.15	.07
310	Jay Buhner	.25	.11
311	Butch Henry	.15	.07
312	Greg W. Harris	.15	.07
313	Darren Daulton	.25	.11
314	Chuck Knoblauch	.25	.11
315	Greg A. Harris	.15	.07
316	John Franco	.25	.11
317	John Wehner	.15	.07
318	Donald Harris	.15	.07
319	Benny Santiago	.15	.07
320	Larry Walker	.40	.18
321	Randy Knorr	.15	.07
322	Ramon Martinez RC	.15	.07
323	Mike Stanley	.15	.07
324	Bill Wegman	.15	.07
325	Tom Candiotti	.15	.07
326	Glenn Davis	.15	.07
327	Chuck Crim	.15	.07
328	Scott Livingstone	.15	.07
329	Eddie Taubensee	.15	.07
330	George Bell	.15	.07
331	Edgar Martinez	.40	.18
332	Paul Assenmacher	.15	.07
333	Steve Hosey	.15	.07
334	Mo Vaughn	.25	.11
335	Bret Saberhagen	.25	.11
336	Mike Trombley	.15	.07
337	Mark Lewis	.15	.07
338	Terry Pendleton	.25	.11
339	Dave Hollins	.15	.07
340	Jeff Conine	.15	.07
341	Bob Tewksbury	.15	.07
342	Billy Ashley	.15	.07
343	Zane Smith	.15	.07
344	John Wetteland	.25	.11
345	Chris Hoiles	.15	.07
346	Frank Castillo	.15	.07
347	Bruce Hurst	.15	.07
348	Kevin McReynolds	.15	.07
349	Dave Henderson	.15	.07
350	Ryan Bowen	.15	.07
351	Sid Fernandez	.15	.07
352	Mark Whiten	.15	.07
353	Nolan Ryan	3.00	1.35
354	Rick Aguilera	.15	.07
355	Mark Langston	.15	.07
356	Jack Morris	.25	.11
357	Rob Deer	.15	.07
358	Dave Fleming	.15	.07
359	Lance Johnson	.15	.07
360	Joe Millette	.15	.07
361	Wil Cordero	.15	.07
362	Chito Martinez	.15	.07
363	Scott Servais	.15	.07

❑ 364 Bernie Williams .60 .25
❑ 365 Pedro Martinez 1.50 .70
❑ 366 Ryne Sandberg .75 .35
❑ 367 Brad Ausmus .15 .07
❑ 368 Scott Cooper .15 .07
❑ 369 Rob Dibble .15 .07
❑ 370 Walt Weiss .15 .07
❑ 371 Mark Davis .15 .07
❑ 372 Orlando Merced .15 .07
❑ 373 Mike Jackson .15 .07
❑ 374 Kevin Appier .25 .11
❑ 375 Esteban Beltre .15 .07
❑ 376 Joe Slusarski .15 .07
❑ 377 William Suero .15 .07
❑ 378 Pete O'Brien .15 .07
❑ 379 Alan Embree .15 .07
❑ 380 Lenny Webster .15 .07
❑ 381 Eric Davis .25 .11
❑ 382 Duane Ward .15 .07
❑ 383 John Habyan .15 .07
❑ 384 Jeff Bagwell .75 .35
❑ 385 Ruben Amaro .15 .07
❑ 386 Julio Valera .15 .07
❑ 387 Robin Ventura .25 .11
❑ 388 Archi Cianfrocco .15 .07
❑ 389 Skeeter Barnes .15 .07
❑ 390 Tim Costo .15 .07
❑ 391 Luis Mercedes .15 .07
❑ 392 Jeremy Hernandez .15 .07
❑ 393 Shawon Dunston .15 .07
❑ 394 Andy Van Slyke .25 .11
❑ 395 Kevin Maas .15 .07
❑ 396 Kevin Brown .25 .11
❑ 397 J.T. Bruett .15 .07
❑ 398 Darryl Strawberry .25 .11
❑ 399 Tom Pagnozzi .15 .07
❑ 400 Sandy Alomar Jr. .25 .11
❑ 401 Keith Miller .15 .07
❑ 402 Rich DeLucia .15 .07
❑ 403 Shawn Abner .15 .07
❑ 404 Howard Johnson .15 .07
❑ 405 Mike Benjamin .15 .07
❑ 406 Roberto Mejia RC .15 .07
❑ 407 Mike Butcher .15 .07
❑ 408 Deion Sanders UER .25 .11
(Braves on front and Yankees on back)
❑ 409 Todd Stottlemyre .15 .07
❑ 410 Scott Kamieniecki .15 .07
❑ 411 Doug Jones .15 .07
❑ 412 John Burkett .15 .07
❑ 413 Lance Blankenship .15 .07
❑ 414 Jeff Parrett .15 .07
❑ 415 Barry Larkin .60 .25
❑ 416 Alan Trammell .40 .18
❑ 417 Mark Kiefer .15 .07
❑ 418 Gregg Olson .15 .07
❑ 419 Mark Grace .60 .25
❑ 420 Shane Mack .15 .07
❑ 421 Bob Walk .15 .07
❑ 422 Curt Schilling .60 .25
❑ 423 Erik Hanson .15 .07
❑ 424 George Brett 1.25 .55
❑ 425 Reggie Jefferson .15 .07
❑ 426 Mark Portugal .15 .07
❑ 427 Ron Karkovice .15 .07
❑ 428 Matt Young .15 .07
❑ 429 Troy Neel .15 .07
❑ 430 Hector Fajardo .15 .07
❑ 431 Dave Righetti .25 .11
❑ 432 Pat Listach .15 .07
❑ 433 Jeff Innis .15 .07
❑ 434 Bob MacDonald .15 .07
❑ 435 Brian Jordan .25 .11
❑ 436 Jeff Blauser .15 .07
❑ 437 Mike Myers RC .15 .07
❑ 438 Frank Seminara .15 .07
❑ 439 Rusty Meacham .15 .07
❑ 440 Greg Briley .15 .07
❑ 441 Derek Lilliquist .15 .07
❑ 442 John Vander Wal .15 .07
❑ 443 Scott Erickson .15 .07
❑ 444 Bob Scanlan .15 .07
❑ 445 Todd Frohwirth .15 .07
❑ 446 Tom Goodwin .15 .07
❑ 447 William Pennyfeather .15 .07
❑ 448 Travis Fryman .25 .11
❑ 449 Mickey Morandini .15 .07
❑ 450 Greg Olson .15 .07
❑ 451 Trevor Hoffman .25 .11
❑ 452 Dave Magadan .15 .07
❑ 453 Shawn Jeter .15 .07
❑ 454 Andres Galarraga .40 .18
❑ 455 Ted Wood .15 .07
❑ 456 Freddie Benavides .15 .07
❑ 457 Junior Felix .15 .07
❑ 458 Alex Cole .15 .07
❑ 459 John Orton .15 .07
❑ 460 Eddie Zosky .15 .07
❑ 461 Dennis Eckersley .25 .11
❑ 462 Lee Smith .25 .11
❑ 463 John Smoltz .25 .11
❑ 464 Ken Caminiti .25 .11
❑ 465 Melido Perez .15 .07
❑ 466 Tom Marsh .15 .07
❑ 467 Jeff Nelson .15 .07
❑ 468 Jesse Levis .15 .07
❑ 469 Chris Nabholz .15 .07
❑ 470 Mike Macfarlane .15 .07
❑ 471 Reggie Sanders .15 .07
❑ 472 Chuck McElroy .15 .07
❑ 473 Kevin Gross .15 .07
❑ 474 Matt Whiteside RC .15 .07
❑ 475 Cal Eldred .15 .07
❑ 476 Dave Gallagher .15 .07
❑ 477 Len Dykstra .25 .11
❑ 478 Mark McGwire 2.50 1.10
❑ 479 David Segui .15 .07
❑ 480 Mike Henneman .15 .07
❑ 481 Bret Barberie .15 .07
❑ 482 Steve Sax .15 .07
❑ 483 Dave Valle .15 .07
❑ 484 Danny Darwin .15 .07
❑ 485 Devon White .15 .07
❑ 486 Eric Plunk .15 .07
❑ 487 Jim Gott .15 .07
❑ 488 Scooter Tucker .15 .07
❑ 489 Omar Olivares .15 .07
❑ 490 Greg Myers .15 .07
❑ 491 Brian Hunter .15 .07
❑ 492 Kevin Tapani .15 .07
❑ 493 Rich Monteleone .15 .07
❑ 494 Steve Buechele .15 .07
❑ 495 Bo Jackson .25 .11
❑ 496 Mike LaValliere .15 .07
❑ 497 Mark Leonard .15 .07
❑ 498 Daryl Boston .15 .07
❑ 499 Jose Canseco .60 .25
❑ 500 Brian Barnes .15 .07
❑ 501 Randy Johnson .75 .35
❑ 502 Tim McIntosh .15 .07
❑ 503 Cecil Fielder .25 .11
❑ 504 Derek Bell .15 .07
❑ 505 Kevin Koslofski .15 .07
❑ 506 Darren Holmes .15 .07
❑ 507 Brady Anderson .25 .11
❑ 508 John Valentin .15 .07
❑ 509 Jerry Browne .15 .07
❑ 510 Fred McGriff .40 .18
❑ 511 Pedro Astacio .15 .07
❑ 512 Gary Gaetti .25 .11
❑ 513 John Burke RC .15 .07
❑ 514 Dwight Gooden .25 .11
❑ 515 Thomas Howard .15 .07
❑ 516 D.Whitmore RC UER .15 .07
11 games played in 1992; should be 121
❑ 517 Ozzie Guillen .15 .07
❑ 518 Darryl Kile .25 .11
❑ 519 Rich Rowland .15 .07
❑ 520 Carlos Delgado 1.25 .55
❑ 521 Doug Henry .15 .07
❑ 522 Greg Colbrunn .15 .07
❑ 523 Tom Gordon .15 .07
❑ 524 Ivan Rodriguez .60 .25
❑ 525 Kent Hrbek .25 .11
❑ 526 Eric Young .15 .07
❑ 527 Rod Brewer .15 .07
❑ 528 Eric Karros .25 .11
❑ 529 Marquis Grissom .15 .07
❑ 530 Rico Brogna .15 .07
❑ 531 Sammy Sosa 1.25 .55
❑ 532 Bret Boone .25 .11
❑ 533 Luis Rivera .15 .07
❑ 534 Hal Morris .15 .07
❑ 535 Monty Fariss .15 .07
❑ 536 Leo Gomez .15 .07
❑ 537 Wally Joyner .25 .11
❑ 538 Tony Gwynn 1.25 .55
❑ 539 Mike Williams .15 .07
❑ 540 Juan Gonzalez .60 .25
❑ 541 Ryan Klesko .25 .11
❑ 542 Ryan Thompson .15 .07
❑ 543 Chad Curtis .15 .07
❑ 544 Orel Hershiser .25 .11
❑ 545 Carlos Garcia .15 .07
❑ 546 Bob Welch .15 .07
❑ 547 Vinny Castilla .25 .11
❑ 548 Ozzie Smith .75 .35
❑ 549 Luis Salazar .15 .07
❑ 550 Mark Guthrie .15 .07
❑ 551 Charles Nagy .15 .07
❑ 552 Alex Fernandez .15 .07
❑ 553 Mel Rojas .15 .07
❑ 554 Orestes Destrade .15 .07
❑ 555 Mark Gubicza .15 .07
❑ 556 Steve Finley .25 .11
❑ 557 Don Mattingly 1.50 .70
❑ 558 Rickey Henderson 1.25 .55
❑ 559 Tommy Greene .15 .07
❑ 560 Arthur Rhodes .15 .07
❑ 561 Alfredo Griffin .15 .07
❑ 562 Will Clark .60 .25
❑ 563 Bob Zupcic .15 .07
❑ 564 Chuck Carr .15 .07
❑ 565 Henry Cotto .15 .07
❑ 566 Billy Spiers .15 .07
❑ 567 Jack Armstrong .15 .07
❑ 568 Kurt Stillwell .15 .07
❑ 569 David McCarty .15 .07
❑ 570 Joe Vitiello .15 .07
❑ 571 Gerald Williams .15 .07
❑ 572 Dale Murphy .40 .18
❑ 573 Scott Aldred .15 .07
❑ 574 Bill Gullickson .15 .07
❑ 575 Bobby Thigpen .15 .07
❑ 576 Glenallen Hill .15 .07
❑ 577 Dwayne Henry .15 .07
❑ 578 Calvin Jones .15 .07
❑ 579 Al Martin .15 .07
❑ 580 Ruben Sierra .15 .07
❑ 581 Andy Benes .15 .07
❑ 582 Anthony Young .15 .07
❑ 583 Shawn Boskie .15 .07
❑ 584 Scott Pose RC .15 .07
❑ 585 Mike Piazza 3.00 1.35
❑ 586 Donovan Osborne .15 .07
❑ 587 James Austin .15 .07
❑ 588 Checklist 301-400 .15 .07
❑ 589 Checklist 401-500 .15 .07
❑ 590 Checklist 501-600 .15 .07
❑ 591 Ken Griffey Jr. MC 1.00 .45
❑ 592 Ivan Rodriguez MC .25 .11
❑ 593 Carlos Baerga MC .15 .07
❑ 594 Fred McGriff MC .25 .11
❑ 595 Mark McGwire MC 1.25 .55
❑ 596 Roberto Alomar MC .25 .11
❑ 597 Kirby Puckett MC .75 .35
❑ 598 Marquis Grissom MC .15 .07
❑ 599 John Smoltz MC .15 .07
❑ 600 Ryne Sandberg MC .40 .18
❑ 601 Wade Boggs .60 .25
❑ 602 Jeff Reardon .25 .11
❑ 603 Billy Ripken .15 .07
❑ 604 Bryan Harvey .15 .07
❑ 605 Carlos Quintana .15 .07
❑ 606 Greg Hibbard .15 .07
❑ 607 Ellis Burks .25 .11
❑ 608 Greg Swindell .15 .07
❑ 609 Dave Winfield .60 .25
❑ 610 Charlie Hough .25 .11
❑ 611 Chili Davis .25 .11
❑ 612 Jody Reed .15 .07
❑ 613 Mark Williamson .15 .07
❑ 614 Phil Plantier .15 .07
❑ 615 Jim Abbott .25 .11
❑ 616 Dante Bichette .25 .11
❑ 617 Mark Eichhorn .15 .07

❑ 618 Gary Sheffield .25 .11
❑ 619 Richie Lewis RC .15 .07
❑ 620 Joe Girardi .15 .07
❑ 621 Jaime Navarro .15 .07
❑ 622 Willie Wilson .15 .07
❑ 623 Scott Fletcher .15 .07
❑ 624 Bud Black .15 .07
❑ 625 Tom Brunansky .15 .07
❑ 626 Steve Avery .15 .07
❑ 627 Paul Molitor .60 .25
❑ 628 Gregg Jefferies .15 .07
❑ 629 Dave Stewart .25 .11
❑ 630 Javier Lopez .25 .11
❑ 631 Greg Gagne .15 .07
❑ 632 Roberto Kelly .15 .07
❑ 633 Mike Fetters .15 .07
❑ 634 Ozzie Canseco .15 .07
❑ 635 Jeff Russell .15 .07
❑ 636 Pete Incaviglia .15 .07
❑ 637 Tom Henke .15 .07
❑ 638 Chipper Jones 1.50 .70
❑ 639 Jimmy Key .25 .11
❑ 640 Dave Martinez .15 .07
❑ 641 Dave Stieb .15 .07
❑ 642 Milt Thompson .15 .07
❑ 643 Alan Mills .15 .07
❑ 644 Tony Fernandez .15 .07
❑ 645 Randy Bush .15 .07
❑ 646 Joe Magrane .15 .07
❑ 647 Ivan Calderon .15 .07
❑ 648 Jose Guzman .15 .07
❑ 649 John Olerud .25 .11
❑ 650 Tom Glavine .60 .25
❑ 651 Julio Franco .25 .11
❑ 652 Armando Reynoso .15 .07
❑ 653 Felix Jose .15 .07
❑ 654 Ben Rivera .15 .07
❑ 655 Andre Dawson .40 .18
❑ 656 Mike Harkey .15 .07
❑ 657 Kevin Seitzer .15 .07
❑ 658 Lonnie Smith .15 .07
❑ 659 Norm Charlton .15 .07
❑ 660 David Justice .25 .11
❑ 661 Fernando Valenzuela .25 .11
❑ 662 Dan Wilson .25 .11
❑ 663 Mark Gardner .15 .07
❑ 664 Doug Dascenzo .15 .07
❑ 665 Greg Maddux 1.50 .70
❑ 666 Harold Baines .25 .11
❑ 667 Randy Myers .15 .07
❑ 668 Harold Reynolds .15 .07
❑ 669 Candy Maldonado .15 .07
❑ 670 Al Leiter .25 .11
❑ 671 Jerald Clark .15 .07
❑ 672 Doug Drabek .15 .07
❑ 673 Kirk Gibson .25 .11
❑ 674 Steve Reed RC .15 .07
❑ 675 Mike Felder .15 .07
❑ 676 Ricky Gutierrez .15 .07
❑ 677 Spike Owen .15 .07
❑ 678 Otis Nixon .15 .07
❑ 679 Scott Sanderson .15 .07
❑ 680 Mark Carreon .15 .07
❑ 681 Troy Percival .25 .11
❑ 682 Kevin Stocker .15 .07
❑ 683 Jim Converse RC .15 .07
❑ 684 Barry Bonds 1.50 .70
❑ 685 Greg Gohr .15 .07
❑ 686 Tim Wallach .15 .07
❑ 687 Matt Mieske .15 .07
❑ 688 Robby Thompson .15 .07
❑ 689 Brien Taylor .15 .07
❑ 690 Kirt Manwaring .15 .07
❑ 691 Mike Lansing RC .25 .11
❑ 692 Steve Decker .15 .07
❑ 693 Mike Moore .15 .07
❑ 694 Kevin Mitchell .15 .07
❑ 695 Phil Hiatt .15 .07
❑ 696 Tony Tarasco RC .15 .07
❑ 697 Benji Gil .15 .07
❑ 698 Jeff Juden .15 .07
❑ 699 Kevin Reimer .15 .07
❑ 700 Andy Ashby .15 .07
❑ 701 John Jaha .15 .07
❑ 702 Tim Bogar RC .15 .07
❑ 703 David Cone .25 .11
❑ 704 Willie Greene .15 .07
❑ 705 David Hulse RC .15 .07
❑ 706 Cris Carpenter .15 .07
❑ 707 Ken Griffey Jr. 2.00 .90
❑ 708 Steve Bedrosian .15 .07
❑ 709 Dave Nilsson .15 .07
❑ 710 Paul Wagner .15 .07
❑ 711 B.J. Surhoff .25 .11
❑ 712 Rene Arocha RC .25 .11
❑ 713 Manuel Lee .15 .07
❑ 714 Brian Williams .15 .07
❑ 715 Sherman Obando RC .15 .07
❑ 716 Terry Mulholland .15 .07
❑ 717 Paul O'Neill .60 .25
❑ 718 David Nied .15 .07
❑ 719 J.T. Snow RC .75 .35
❑ 720 Nigel Wilson .15 .07
❑ 721 Mike Bielecki .15 .07
❑ 722 Kevin Young .25 .11
❑ 723 Charlie Leibrandt .15 .07
❑ 724 Frank Bolick .15 .07
❑ 725 Jon Shave RC .15 .07
❑ 726 Steve Cooke .15 .07
❑ 727 Domingo Martinez RC .15 .07
❑ 728 Todd Worrell .15 .07
❑ 729 Jose Lind .15 .07
❑ 730 Jim Tatum RC .15 .07
❑ 731 Mike Hampton .60 .25
❑ 732 Mike Draper .15 .07
❑ 733 Henry Mercedes .15 .07
❑ 734 John Johnstone RC .15 .07
❑ 735 Mitch Webster .15 .07
❑ 736 Russ Springer .15 .07
❑ 737 Rob Natal .15 .07
❑ 738 Steve Howe .15 .07
❑ 739 Darrell Sherman RC .15 .07
❑ 740 Pat Mahomes .15 .07
❑ 741 Alex Arias .15 .07
❑ 742 Damon Buford .15 .07
❑ 743 Charlie Hayes .15 .07
❑ 744 Guillermo Velasquez .15 .07
❑ 745 CL 601-750 UER .15 .07
650 Tom Glavine
❑ 746 Frank Thomas MC .40 .18
❑ 747 Barry Bonds MC .75 .35
❑ 748 Roger Clemens MC .75 .35
❑ 749 Joe Carter MC .15 .07
❑ 750 Greg Maddux MC .75 .35

1994 Stadium Club

	MINT	NRMT
COMPLETE SET (720)	55.00	25.00
COMPLETE SERIES 1 (270)	20.00	9.00
COMPLETE SERIES 2 (270)	20.00	9.00
COMPLETE SERIES 3 (180)	15.00	6.75

❑ 1 Robin Yount .60 .25
❑ 2 Rick Wilkins .15 .07
❑ 3 Steve Scarsone .15 .07
❑ 4 Gary Sheffield .25 .11
❑ 5 George Brett UER 1.25 .55
(birthdate listed as 1963; should be 1953)
❑ 6 Al Martin .15 .07
❑ 7 Joe Oliver .15 .07
❑ 8 Stan Belinda .15 .07
❑ 9 Denny Hocking .15 .07
❑ 10 Roberto Alomar .60 .25
❑ 11 Luis Polonia .15 .07
❑ 12 Scott Hemond .15 .07
❑ 13 Jody Reed .15 .07
❑ 14 Mel Rojas .15 .07
❑ 15 Junior Ortiz .15 .07
❑ 16 Harold Baines .25 .11
❑ 17 Brad Pennington .15 .07
❑ 18 Jay Bell .25 .11
❑ 19 Tom Henke .15 .07
❑ 20 Jeff Branson .15 .07
❑ 21 Roberto Mejia .15 .07
❑ 22 Pedro Munoz .15 .07
❑ 23 Matt Nokes .15 .07
❑ 24 Jack McDowell .15 .07
❑ 25 Cecil Fielder .25 .11
❑ 26 Tony Fossas .15 .07
❑ 27 Jim Eisenreich .15 .07
❑ 28 Anthony Young .15 .07
❑ 29 Chuck Carr .15 .07
❑ 30 Jeff Treadway .15 .07
❑ 31 Chris Nabholz .15 .07
❑ 32 Tom Candiotti .15 .07
❑ 33 Mike Maddux .15 .07
❑ 34 Nolan Ryan 3.00 1.35
❑ 35 Luis Gonzalez .60 .25
❑ 36 Tim Salmon .25 .11
❑ 37 Mark Whiten .15 .07
❑ 38 Roger McDowell .15 .07
❑ 39 Royce Clayton .15 .07
❑ 40 Troy Neel .15 .07
❑ 41 Mike Harkey .15 .07
❑ 42 Darrin Fletcher .15 .07
❑ 43 Wayne Kirby .15 .07
❑ 44 Rich Amaral .15 .07
❑ 45 Robb Nen UER .15 .07
(Nenn on back)
❑ 46 Tim Teufel .15 .07
❑ 47 Steve Cooke .15 .07
❑ 48 Jeff McNeely .15 .07
❑ 49 Jeff Montgomery .15 .07
❑ 50 Skeeter Barnes .15 .07
❑ 51 Scott Stahoviak .15 .07
❑ 52 Pat Kelly .15 .07
❑ 53 Brady Anderson .25 .11
❑ 54 Mariano Duncan .15 .07
❑ 55 Brian Bohanon .15 .07
❑ 56 Jerry Spradlin .15 .07
❑ 57 Ron Karkovice .15 .07
❑ 58 Jeff Gardner .15 .07
❑ 59 Bobby Bonilla .25 .11
❑ 60 Tino Martinez .25 .11
❑ 61 Todd Benzinger .15 .07
❑ 62 Steve Trachsel .15 .07
❑ 63 Brian Jordan .25 .11
❑ 64 Steve Bedrosian .15 .07
❑ 65 Brent Gates .15 .07
❑ 66 Shawn Green .75 .35
❑ 67 Sean Berry .15 .07
❑ 68 Joe Klink .15 .07
❑ 69 Fernando Valenzuela .25 .11
❑ 70 Andy Tomberlin .15 .07
❑ 71 Tony Pena .15 .07
❑ 72 Eric Young .15 .07
❑ 73 Chris Gomez .15 .07
❑ 74 Paul O'Neill .60 .25
❑ 75 Ricky Gutierrez .15 .07
❑ 76 Brad Holman .15 .07
❑ 77 Lance Painter .15 .07
❑ 78 Mike Butcher .15 .07
❑ 79 Sid Bream .15 .07
❑ 80 Sammy Sosa 1.25 .55
❑ 81 Felix Fermin .15 .07
❑ 82 Todd Hundley .15 .07
❑ 83 Kevin Higgins .15 .07
❑ 84 Todd Pratt .15 .07
❑ 85 Ken Griffey Jr. 2.00 .90
❑ 86 John O'Donoghue .15 .07
❑ 87 Rick Renteria .15 .07
❑ 88 John Burkett .15 .07
❑ 89 Jose Vizcaino .15 .07
❑ 90 Kevin Seitzer .15 .07
❑ 91 Bobby Witt .15 .07
❑ 92 Chris Turner .15 .07
❑ 93 Omar Vizquel .25 .11
❑ 94 David Justice .25 .11

❑ 95 David Segui .15 .07
❑ 96 Dave Hollins .15 .07
❑ 97 Doug Strange .15 .07
❑ 98 Jerald Clark .15 .07
❑ 99 Mike Moore .15 .07
❑ 100 Joey Cora .15 .07
❑ 101 Scott Kamieniecki .15 .07
❑ 102 Andy Benes .15 .07
❑ 103 Chris Bosio .15 .07
❑ 104 Rey Sanchez .15 .07
❑ 105 John Jaha .15 .07
❑ 106 Otis Nixon .15 .07
❑ 107 Rickey Henderson 1.25 .55
❑ 108 Jeff Bagwell .75 .35
❑ 109 Gregg Jefferies .15 .07
❑ 110 Roberto Alomar .25 .11
Paul Molitor
John Olerud
❑ 111 Ron Gant .15 .07
David Justice
Fred McGriff
❑ 112 Juan Gonzalez .25 .11
Rafael Palmeiro
Dean Palmer
❑ 113 Greg Swindell .15 .07
❑ 114 Bill Haselman .15 .07
❑ 115 Phil Plantier .15 .07
❑ 116 Ivan Rodriguez .60 .25
❑ 117 Kevin Tapani .15 .07
❑ 118 Mike LaValliere .15 .07
❑ 119 Tim Costo .15 .07
❑ 120 Mickey Morandini .15 .07
❑ 121 Brett Butler .25 .11
❑ 122 Tom Pagnozzi .15 .07
❑ 123 Ron Gant .15 .07
❑ 124 Damion Easley .15 .07
❑ 125 Dennis Eckersley .25 .11
❑ 126 Matt Mieske .15 .07
❑ 127 Cliff Floyd .25 .11
❑ 128 Julian Tavarez RC .25 .11
❑ 129 Arthur Rhodes .15 .07
❑ 130 Dave West .15 .07
❑ 131 Tim Naehring .15 .07
❑ 132 Freddie Benavides .15 .07
❑ 133 Paul Assenmacher .15 .07
❑ 134 David McCarty .15 .07
❑ 135 Jose Lind .15 .07
❑ 136 Reggie Sanders .15 .07
❑ 137 Don Slaught .15 .07
❑ 138 Andujar Cedeno .15 .07
❑ 139 Rob Deer .15 .07
❑ 140 Mike Piazza UER 2.00 .90
(listed as outfielder)
❑ 141 Moises Alou .25 .11
❑ 142 Tom Foley .15 .07
❑ 143 Benito Santiago .15 .07
❑ 144 Sandy Alomar Jr. .25 .11
❑ 145 Carlos Hernandez .15 .07
❑ 146 Luis Alicea .15 .07
❑ 147 Tom Lampkin .15 .07
❑ 148 Ryan Klesko .25 .11
❑ 149 Juan Guzman .15 .07
❑ 150 Scott Servais .15 .07
❑ 151 Tony Gwynn 1.25 .55
❑ 152 Tim Wakefield .15 .07
❑ 153 David Nied .15 .07
❑ 154 Chris Haney .15 .07
❑ 155 Danny Bautista .15 .07
❑ 156 Randy Velarde .15 .07
❑ 157 Darrin Jackson .15 .07
❑ 158 J.R. Phillips .15 .07
❑ 159 Greg Gagne .15 .07
❑ 160 Luis Aquino .15 .07
❑ 161 John Vander Wal .15 .07
❑ 162 Randy Myers .15 .07
❑ 163 Ted Power .15 .07
❑ 164 Scott Brosius .25 .11
❑ 165 Len Dykstra .25 .11
❑ 166 Jacob Brumfield .15 .07
❑ 167 Bo Jackson .25 .11
❑ 168 Eddie Taubensee .15 .07
❑ 169 Carlos Baerga .15 .07
❑ 170 Tim Bogar .15 .07
❑ 171 Jose Canseco .60 .25
❑ 172 Greg Blosser UER .15 .07
(Gregg on front)
❑ 173 Chili Davis .25 .11
❑ 174 Randy Knorr .15 .07
❑ 175 Mike Perez .15 .07
❑ 176 Henry Rodriguez .15 .07
❑ 177 Brian Turang RC .15 .07
❑ 178 Roger Pavlik .15 .07
❑ 179 Aaron Sele .25 .11
❑ 180 Fred McGriff .40 .18
Gary Sheffield
❑ 181 J.T. Snow .25 .11
Tim Salmon
❑ 182 Roberto Hernandez .15 .07
❑ 183 Jeff Reboulet .15 .07
❑ 184 John Doherty .15 .07
❑ 185 Danny Sheaffer .15 .07
❑ 186 Bip Roberts .15 .07
❑ 187 Dennis Martinez .25 .11
❑ 188 Darryl Hamilton .15 .07
❑ 189 Eduardo Perez .15 .07
❑ 190 Pete Harnisch .15 .07
❑ 191 Rich Gossage .25 .11
❑ 192 Mickey Tettleton .15 .07
❑ 193 Lenny Webster .15 .07
❑ 194 Lance Johnson .15 .07
❑ 195 Don Mattingly 1.50 .70
❑ 196 Gregg Olson .15 .07
❑ 197 Mark Gubicza .15 .07
❑ 198 Scott Fletcher .15 .07
❑ 199 Jon Shave .15 .07
❑ 200 Tim Mauser .15 .07
❑ 201 Jeromy Burnitz .25 .11
❑ 202 Rob Dibble .15 .07
❑ 203 Will Clark .60 .25
❑ 204 Steve Buechele .15 .07
❑ 205 Brian Williams .15 .07
❑ 206 Carlos Garcia .15 .07
❑ 207 Mark Clark .15 .07
❑ 208 Rafael Palmeiro .60 .25
❑ 209 Eric Davis .25 .11
❑ 210 Pat Meares .15 .07
❑ 211 Chuck Finley .25 .11
❑ 212 Jason Bere .15 .07
❑ 213 Gary DiSarcina .15 .07
❑ 214 Tony Fernandez .15 .07
❑ 215 B.J. Surhoff .25 .11
❑ 216 Lee Guetterman .15 .07
❑ 217 Tim Wallach .15 .07
❑ 218 Kirt Manwaring .15 .07
❑ 219 Albert Belle .25 .11
❑ 220 Dwight Gooden .25 .11
❑ 221 Archi Cianfrocco .15 .07
❑ 222 Terry Mulholland .15 .07
❑ 223 Hipolito Pichardo .15 .07
❑ 224 Kent Hrbek .25 .11
❑ 225 Craig Grebeck .15 .07
❑ 226 Todd Jones .15 .07
❑ 227 Mike Bordick .15 .07
❑ 228 John Olerud .25 .11
❑ 229 Jeff Blauser .15 .07
❑ 230 Alex Arias .15 .07
❑ 231 Bernard Gilkey .15 .07
❑ 232 Denny Neagle .25 .11
❑ 233 Pedro Borbon .15 .07
❑ 234 Dick Schofield .15 .07
❑ 235 Matias Carrillo .15 .07
❑ 236 Juan Bell .15 .07
❑ 237 Mike Hampton .25 .11
❑ 238 Barry Bonds 1.50 .70
❑ 239 Cris Carpenter .15 .07
❑ 240 Eric Karros .25 .11
❑ 241 Greg McMichael .15 .07
❑ 242 Pat Hentgen .15 .07
❑ 243 Tim Pugh .15 .07
❑ 244 Vinny Castilla .25 .11
❑ 245 Charlie Hough .25 .11
❑ 246 Bobby Munoz .15 .07
❑ 247 Kevin Baez .15 .07
❑ 248 Todd Frohwirth .15 .07
❑ 249 Charlie Hayes .15 .07
❑ 250 Mike Macfarlane .15 .07
❑ 251 Danny Darwin .15 .07
❑ 252 Ben Rivera .15 .07
❑ 253 Dave Henderson .15 .07
❑ 254 Steve Avery .15 .07
❑ 255 Tim Belcher .15 .07
❑ 256 Dan Plesac .15 .07
❑ 257 Jim Thome .60 .25
❑ 258 Albert Belle HR .25 .11
❑ 259 Barry Bonds HR .75 .35
❑ 260 Ron Gant HR .15 .07
❑ 261 Juan Gonzalez HR .25 .11
❑ 262 Ken Griffey Jr. HR 1.00 .45
❑ 263 David Justice HR .15 .07
❑ 264 Fred McGriff HR .25 .11
❑ 265 Rafael Palmeiro HR .25 .11
❑ 266 Mike Piazza HR 1.00 .45
❑ 267 Frank Thomas HR .40 .18
❑ 268 Matt Williams HR .25 .11
❑ 269 Checklist 1-135 .15 .07
❑ 270 Checklist 136-270 .15 .07
❑ 271 Mike Stanley .15 .07
❑ 272 Tony Tarasco .15 .07
❑ 273 Teddy Higuera .15 .07
❑ 274 Ryan Thompson .15 .07
❑ 275 Rick Aguilera .15 .07
❑ 276 Ramon Martinez .15 .07
❑ 277 Orlando Merced .15 .07
❑ 278 Guillermo Velasquez .15 .07
❑ 279 Mark Hutton .15 .07
❑ 280 Larry Walker .40 .18
❑ 281 Kevin Gross .15 .07
❑ 282 Jose Offerman .15 .07
❑ 283 Jim Leyritz .15 .07
❑ 284 Jamie Moyer .15 .07
❑ 285 Frank Thomas .75 .35
❑ 286 Derek Bell .15 .07
❑ 287 Derrick May .15 .07
❑ 288 Dave Winfield .60 .25
❑ 289 Curt Schilling .60 .25
❑ 290 Carlos Quintana .15 .07
❑ 291 Bob Natal .15 .07
❑ 292 David Cone .25 .11
❑ 293 Al Osuna .15 .07
❑ 294 Bob Hamelin .15 .07
❑ 295 Chad Curtis .15 .07
❑ 296 Danny Jackson .15 .07
❑ 297 Bob Welch .15 .07
❑ 298 Felix Jose .15 .07
❑ 299 Jay Buhner .25 .11
❑ 300 Joe Carter .25 .11
❑ 301 Kenny Lofton .25 .11
❑ 302 Kirk Rueter .15 .07
❑ 303 Kim Batiste .15 .07
❑ 304 Mike Morgan .15 .07
❑ 305 Pat Borders .15 .07
❑ 306 Rene Arocha .15 .07
❑ 307 Ruben Sierra .15 .07
❑ 308 Steve Finley .25 .11
❑ 309 Travis Fryman .25 .11
❑ 310 Zane Smith .15 .07
❑ 311 Willie Wilson .15 .07
❑ 312 Trevor Hoffman .25 .11
❑ 313 Terry Pendleton .25 .11
❑ 314 Salomon Torres .15 .07
❑ 315 Robin Ventura .25 .11
❑ 316 Randy Tomlin .15 .07
❑ 317 Dave Stewart .25 .11
❑ 318 Mike Benjamin .15 .07
❑ 319 Matt Turner .15 .07
❑ 320 Manny Ramirez 1.00 .45
❑ 321 Kevin Young .15 .07
❑ 322 Ken Caminiti .25 .11
❑ 323 Joe Girardi .15 .07
❑ 324 Jeff McKnight .15 .07
❑ 325 Gene Harris .15 .07
❑ 326 Devon White .15 .07
❑ 327 Darryl Kile .25 .11
❑ 328 Craig Paquette .15 .07
❑ 329 Cal Eldred .15 .07
❑ 330 Bill Swift .15 .07
❑ 331 Alan Trammell .40 .18
❑ 332 Armando Reynoso .15 .07
❑ 333 Brent Mayne .15 .07
❑ 334 Chris Donnels .15 .07
❑ 335 Darryl Strawberry .25 .11
❑ 336 Dean Palmer .25 .11
❑ 337 Frank Castillo .15 .07
❑ 338 Jeff King .15 .07
❑ 339 John Franco .25 .11
❑ 340 Kevin Appier .25 .11
❑ 341 Lance Blankenship .15 .07
❑ 342 Mark McLemore .15 .07

❑ 343 Pedro Astacio .15 .07
❑ 344 Rich Batchelor .15 .07
❑ 345 Ryan Bowen .15 .07
❑ 346 Terry Steinbach .15 .07
❑ 347 Troy O'Leary .15 .07
❑ 348 Willie Blair .15 .07
❑ 349 Wade Boggs .60 .25
❑ 350 Tim Raines .25 .11
❑ 351 Scott Livingstone .15 .07
❑ 352 Rod Correia .15 .07
❑ 353 Ray Lankford .15 .07
❑ 354 Pat Listach .15 .07
❑ 355 Milt Thompson .15 .07
❑ 356 Miguel Jimenez .15 .07
❑ 357 Marc Newfield .15 .07
❑ 358 Mark McGwire 2.50 1.10
❑ 359 Kirby Puckett 1.50 .70
❑ 360 Kent Mercker .15 .07
❑ 361 John Kruk .25 .11
❑ 362 Jeff Kent .40 .18
❑ 363 Hal Morris .15 .07
❑ 364 Edgar Martinez .40 .18
❑ 365 Dave Magadan .15 .07
❑ 366 Dante Bichette .25 .11
❑ 367 Chris Hammond .15 .07
❑ 368 Bret Saberhagen .25 .11
❑ 369 Billy Ripken .15 .07
❑ 370 Bill Gullickson .15 .07
❑ 371 Andre Dawson .40 .18
❑ 372 Roberto Kelly .15 .07
❑ 373 Cal Ripken 2.50 1.10
❑ 374 Craig Biggio .40 .18
❑ 375 Dan Pasqua .15 .07
❑ 376 Dave Nilsson .15 .07
❑ 377 Duane Ward .15 .07
❑ 378 Greg Vaughn .25 .11
❑ 379 Jeff Fassero .15 .07
❑ 380 Jerry DiPoto .15 .07
❑ 381 John Patterson .15 .07
❑ 382 Kevin Brown .25 .11
❑ 383 Kevin Roberson .15 .07
❑ 384 Joe Orsulak .15 .07
❑ 385 Hilly Hathaway .15 .07
❑ 386 Mike Greenwell .15 .07
❑ 387 Orestes Destrade .15 .07
❑ 388 Mike Gallego .15 .07
❑ 389 Ozzie Guillen .15 .07
❑ 390 Raul Mondesi .25 .11
❑ 391 Scott Lydy .15 .07
❑ 392 Tom Urbani .15 .07
❑ 393 Wil Cordero .15 .07
❑ 394 Tony Longmire .15 .07
❑ 395 Todd Zeile .15 .07
❑ 396 Scott Cooper .15 .07
❑ 397 Ryne Sandberg .75 .35
❑ 398 Ricky Bones .15 .07
❑ 399 Phil Clark .15 .07
❑ 400 Orel Hershiser .25 .11
❑ 401 Mike Henneman .15 .07
❑ 402 Mark Lemke .15 .07
❑ 403 Mark Grace .60 .25
❑ 404 Ken Ryan .15 .07
❑ 405 John Smoltz .25 .11
❑ 406 Jeff Conine .15 .07
❑ 407 Greg Harris .15 .07
❑ 408 Doug Drabek .15 .07
❑ 409 Dave Fleming .15 .07
❑ 410 Danny Tartabull .15 .07
❑ 411 Chad Kreuter .15 .07
❑ 412 Brad Ausmus .15 .07
❑ 413 Ben McDonald .15 .07
❑ 414 Barry Larkin .60 .25
❑ 415 Bret Barberie .15 .07
❑ 416 Chuck Knoblauch .25 .11
❑ 417 Ozzie Smith .75 .35
❑ 418 Ed Sprague .15 .07
❑ 419 Matt Williams .40 .18
❑ 420 Jeremy Hernandez .15 .07
❑ 421 Jose Bautista .15 .07
❑ 422 Kevin Mitchell .15 .07
❑ 423 Manuel Lee .15 .07
❑ 424 Mike Devereaux .15 .07
❑ 425 Omar Olivares .15 .07
❑ 426 Rafael Belliard .15 .07
❑ 427 Richie Lewis .15 .07
❑ 428 Ron Darling .15 .07
❑ 429 Shane Mack .15 .07
❑ 430 Tim Hulett .15 .07
❑ 431 Wally Joyner .25 .11
❑ 432 Wes Chamberlain .15 .07
❑ 433 Tom Browning .15 .07
❑ 434 Scott Radinsky .15 .07
❑ 435 Rondell White .25 .11
❑ 436 Rod Beck .15 .07
❑ 437 Rheal Cormier .15 .07
❑ 438 Randy Johnson .75 .35
❑ 439 Pete Schourek .15 .07
❑ 440 Mo Vaughn .25 .11
❑ 441 Mike Timlin .15 .07
❑ 442 Mark Langston .15 .07
❑ 443 Lou Whitaker .25 .11
❑ 444 Kevin Stocker .15 .07
❑ 445 Ken Hill .15 .07
❑ 446 John Wetteland .25 .11
❑ 447 J.T. Snow .25 .11
❑ 448 Erik Pappas .15 .07
❑ 449 David Hulse .15 .07
❑ 450 Darren Daulton .25 .11
❑ 451 Chris Hoiles .15 .07
❑ 452 Bryan Harvey .15 .07
❑ 453 Darren Lewis .15 .07
❑ 454 Andres Galarraga .40 .18
❑ 455 Joe Hesketh .15 .07
❑ 456 Jose Valentin .15 .07
❑ 457 Dan Peltier .15 .07
❑ 458 Joe Boever .15 .07
❑ 459 Kevin Rogers .15 .07
❑ 460 Craig Shipley .15 .07
❑ 461 Alvaro Espinoza .15 .07
❑ 462 Wilson Alvarez .15 .07
❑ 463 Cory Snyder .15 .07
❑ 464 Candy Maldonado .15 .07
❑ 465 Blas Minor .15 .07
❑ 466 Rod Bolton .15 .07
❑ 467 Kenny Rogers .15 .07
❑ 468 Greg Myers .15 .07
❑ 469 Jimmy Key .25 .11
❑ 470 Tony Castillo .15 .07
❑ 471 Mike Stanton .15 .07
❑ 472 Deion Sanders .25 .11
❑ 473 Tito Navarro .15 .07
❑ 474 Mike Gardiner .15 .07
❑ 475 Steve Reed .15 .07
❑ 476 John Roper .15 .07
❑ 477 Mike Trombley .15 .07
❑ 478 Charles Nagy .15 .07
❑ 479 Larry Casian .15 .07
❑ 480 Eric Hillman .15 .07
❑ 481 Bill Wertz .15 .07
❑ 482 Jeff Schwarz .15 .07
❑ 483 John Valentin .15 .07
❑ 484 Carl Willis .15 .07
❑ 485 Gary Gaetti .25 .11
❑ 486 Bill Pecota .15 .07
❑ 487 John Smiley .15 .07
❑ 488 Mike Mussina .60 .25
❑ 489 Mike Ignasiak .15 .07
❑ 490 Billy Brewer .15 .07
❑ 491 Jack Voigt .15 .07
❑ 492 Mike Munoz .15 .07
❑ 493 Lee Tinsley .15 .07
❑ 494 Bob Wickman .15 .07
❑ 495 Roger Salkeld .15 .07
❑ 496 Thomas Howard .15 .07
❑ 497 Mark Davis .15 .07
❑ 498 Dave Clark .15 .07
❑ 499 Turk Wendell .15 .07
❑ 500 Rafael Bournigal .15 .07
❑ 501 Chip Hale .15 .07
❑ 502 Matt Whiteside .15 .07
❑ 503 Brian Koelling .15 .07
❑ 504 Jeff Reed .15 .07
❑ 505 Paul Wagner .15 .07
❑ 506 Torey Lovullo .15 .07
❑ 507 Curt Leskanic .15 .07
❑ 508 Derek Lilliquist .15 .07
❑ 509 Joe Magrane .15 .07
❑ 510 Mackey Sasser .15 .07
❑ 511 Lloyd McClendon .15 .07
❑ 512 Jayhawk Owens .15 .07
❑ 513 Woody Williams .15 .07
❑ 514 Gary Redus .15 .07
❑ 515 Tim Spehr .15 .07
❑ 516 Jim Abbott .25 .11
❑ 517 Lou Frazier .15 .07
❑ 518 Erik Plantenberg RC .15 .07
❑ 519 Tim Worrell .15 .07
❑ 520 Brian McRae .15 .07
❑ 521 Chan Ho Park RC 1.25 .55
❑ 522 Mark Wohlers .15 .07
❑ 523 Geronimo Pena .15 .07
❑ 524 Andy Ashby .15 .07
❑ 525 Tim Raines .15 .07
Andre Dawson TALE
❑ 526 Paul Molitor TALE .25 .11
❑ 527 Joe Carter DL .15 .07
❑ 528 F.Thomas DL UER .40 .18
listed as third in RBI in
1993; was actually second
❑ 529 Ken Griffey Jr. DL 1.00 .45
❑ 530 David Justice DL .15 .07
❑ 531 Gregg Jefferies DL .15 .07
❑ 532 Barry Bonds DL .75 .35
❑ 533 John Kruk QS .15 .07
❑ 534 Roger Clemens QS .75 .35
❑ 535 Cecil Fielder QS .15 .07
❑ 536 Ruben Sierra QS .15 .07
❑ 537 Tony Gwynn QS .60 .25
❑ 538 Tom Glavine QS .25 .11
❑ 539 CL 271-405 UER .15 .07
number on back is 269
❑ 540 CL 406-540 UER .15 .07
numbered 270 on back
❑ 541 Ozzie Smith ATL .40 .18
❑ 542 Eddie Murray ATL .25 .11
❑ 543 Lee Smith ATL .15 .07
❑ 544 Greg Maddux 1.50 .70
❑ 545 Denis Boucher .15 .07
❑ 546 Mark Gardner .15 .07
❑ 547 Bo Jackson .25 .11
❑ 548 Eric Anthony .15 .07
❑ 549 Delino DeShields .15 .07
❑ 550 Turner Ward .15 .07
❑ 551 Scott Sanderson .15 .07
❑ 552 Hector Carrasco .15 .07
❑ 553 Tony Phillips .15 .07
❑ 554 Melido Perez .15 .07
❑ 555 Mike Felder .15 .07
❑ 556 Jack Morris .25 .11
❑ 557 Rafael Palmeiro .60 .25
❑ 558 Shane Reynolds .15 .07
❑ 559 Pete Incaviglia .15 .07
❑ 560 Greg Harris .15 .07
❑ 561 Matt Walbeck .15 .07
❑ 562 Todd Van Poppel .15 .07
❑ 563 Todd Stottlemyre .15 .07
❑ 564 Ricky Bones .15 .07
❑ 565 Mike Jackson .15 .07
❑ 566 Kevin McReynolds .15 .07
❑ 567 Melvin Nieves .15 .07
❑ 568 Juan Gonzalez .60 .25
❑ 569 Frank Viola .25 .11
❑ 570 Vince Coleman .15 .07
❑ 571 Brian Anderson RC .25 .11
❑ 572 Omar Vizquel .25 .11
❑ 573 Bernie Williams .60 .25
❑ 574 Tom Glavine .60 .25
❑ 575 Mitch Williams .15 .07
❑ 576 Shawon Dunston .15 .07
❑ 577 Mike Lansing .15 .07
❑ 578 Greg Pirkl .15 .07
❑ 579 Sid Fernandez .15 .07
❑ 580 Doug Jones .15 .07
❑ 581 Walt Weiss .15 .07
❑ 582 Tim Belcher .15 .07
❑ 583 Alex Fernandez .15 .07
❑ 584 Alex Cole .15 .07
❑ 585 Greg Cadaret .15 .07
❑ 586 Bob Tewksbury .15 .07
❑ 587 Dave Hansen .15 .07
❑ 588 Kurt Abbott RC .25 .11
❑ 589 Rick White RC .15 .07
❑ 590 Kevin Bass .15 .07
❑ 591 Geronimo Berroa .15 .07
❑ 592 Jaime Navarro .15 .07
❑ 593 Steve Farr .15 .07
❑ 594 Jack Armstrong .15 .07
❑ 595 Steve Howe .15 .07

❑ 596 Jose Rijo .15 .07
❑ 597 Otis Nixon .15 .07
❑ 598 Robby Thompson .15 .07
❑ 599 Kelly Stinnett RC .25 .11
❑ 600 Carlos Delgado 1.00 .45
❑ 601 Brian Johnson RC .15 .07
❑ 602 Gregg Olson .15 .07
❑ 603 Jim Edmonds .60 .25
❑ 604 Mike Blowers .15 .07
❑ 605 Lee Smith .25 .11
❑ 606 Pat Rapp .15 .07
❑ 607 Mike Magnante .15 .07
❑ 608 Karl Rhodes .15 .07
❑ 609 Jeff Juden .15 .07
❑ 610 Rusty Meacham .15 .07
❑ 611 Pedro Martinez .75 .35
❑ 612 Todd Worrell .15 .07
❑ 613 Stan Javier .15 .07
❑ 614 Mike Hampton .25 .11
❑ 615 Jose Guzman .15 .07
❑ 616 Xavier Hernandez .15 .07
❑ 617 David Wells .25 .11
❑ 618 John Habyan .15 .07
❑ 619 Chris Nabholz .15 .07
❑ 620 Bobby Jones .15 .07
❑ 621 Chris James .15 .07
❑ 622 Ellis Burks .25 .11
❑ 623 Erik Hanson .15 .07
❑ 624 Pat Meares .15 .07
❑ 625 Harold Reynolds .15 .07
❑ 626 Bob Hamelin RR .15 .07
❑ 627 Manny Ramirez RR .40 .18
❑ 628 Ryan Klesko RR .15 .07
❑ 629 Carlos Delgado RR .60 .25
❑ 630 Javier Lopez RR .25 .11
❑ 631 Steve Karsay RR .15 .07
❑ 632 Rick Helling RR .15 .07
❑ 633 Steve Trachsel RR .15 .07
❑ 634 Hector Carrasco RR .15 .07
❑ 635 Andy Stankiewicz .15 .07
❑ 636 Paul Sorrento .15 .07
❑ 637 Scott Erickson .15 .07
❑ 638 Chipper Jones 1.25 .55
❑ 639 Luis Polonia .15 .07
❑ 640 Howard Johnson .15 .07
❑ 641 John Dopson .15 .07
❑ 642 Jody Reed .15 .07
❑ 643 Lonnie Smith UER .15 .07
Card numbered 543
❑ 644 Mark Portugal .15 .07
❑ 645 Paul Molitor .60 .25
❑ 646 Paul Assenmacher .15 .07
❑ 647 Hubie Brooks .15 .07
❑ 648 Gary Wayne .15 .07
❑ 649 Sean Berry .15 .07
❑ 650 Roger Clemens 1.50 .70
❑ 651 Brian L. Hunter .15 .07
❑ 652 Wally Whitehurst .15 .07
❑ 653 Allen Watson .15 .07
❑ 654 Rickey Henderson 1.25 .55
❑ 655 Sid Bream .15 .07
❑ 656 Dan Wilson .15 .07
❑ 657 Ricky Jordan .15 .07
❑ 658 Sterling Hitchcock .15 .07
❑ 659 Darrin Jackson .15 .07
❑ 660 Junior Felix .15 .07
❑ 661 Tom Brunansky .15 .07
❑ 662 Jose Vizcaino .15 .07
❑ 663 Mark Leiter .15 .07
❑ 664 Gil Heredia .15 .07
❑ 665 Fred McGriff .40 .18
❑ 666 Will Clark .60 .25
❑ 667 Al Leiter .25 .11
❑ 668 James Mouton .15 .07
❑ 669 Billy Bean .15 .07
❑ 670 Scott Leius .15 .07
❑ 671 Bret Boone .25 .11
❑ 672 Darren Holmes .15 .07
❑ 673 Dave Weathers .15 .07
❑ 674 Eddie Murray .60 .25
❑ 675 Felix Fermin .15 .07
❑ 676 Chris Sabo .15 .07
❑ 677 Billy Spiers .15 .07
❑ 678 Aaron Sele .25 .11
❑ 679 Juan Samuel .15 .07
❑ 680 Julio Franco .25 .11
❑ 681 Heathcliff Slocumb .15 .07
❑ 682 Dennis Martinez .25 .11
❑ 683 Jerry Browne .15 .07
❑ 684 Pedro Martinez RC .15 .07
❑ 685 Rex Hudler .15 .07
❑ 686 Willie McGee .25 .11
❑ 687 Andy Van Slyke .25 .11
❑ 688 Pat Mahomes .15 .07
❑ 689 Dave Henderson .15 .07
❑ 690 Tony Eusebio .15 .07
❑ 691 Rick Sutcliffe .25 .11
❑ 692 Willie Banks .15 .07
❑ 693 Alan Mills .15 .07
❑ 694 Jeff Treadway .15 .07
❑ 695 Alex Gonzalez .15 .07
❑ 696 David Segui .15 .07
❑ 697 Rick Helling .15 .07
❑ 698 Bip Roberts .15 .07
❑ 699 Jeff Cirillo RC 2.00 .90
❑ 700 Terry Mulholland .15 .07
❑ 701 Marvin Freeman .15 .07
❑ 702 Jason Bere .15 .07
❑ 703 Javier Lopez .25 .11
❑ 704 Greg Hibbard .15 .07
❑ 705 Tommy Greene .15 .07
❑ 706 Marquis Grissom .15 .07
❑ 707 Brian Harper .15 .07
❑ 708 Steve Karsay .15 .07
❑ 709 Jeff Brantley .15 .07
❑ 710 Jeff Russell .15 .07
❑ 711 Bryan Hickerson .15 .07
❑ 712 Jim Pittsley RC .15 .07
❑ 713 Bobby Ayala .15 .07
❑ 714 John Smoltz .25 .11
❑ 715 Jose Rijo .15 .07
❑ 716 Greg Maddux .75 .35
❑ 717 Matt Williams .25 .11
❑ 718 Frank Thomas .40 .18
❑ 719 Ryne Sandberg .40 .18
❑ 720 Checklist .15 .07

1994 Stadium Club Draft Picks

	MINT	NRMT
COMPLETE SET (90)	20.00	9.00

❑ 1 Jacob Shumate XRC .15 .07
❑ 2 C.J. Nitkowski XRC .15 .07
❑ 3 Doug Million XRC .15 .07
❑ 4 Matt Smith XRC .15 .07
❑ 5 Kevin Lovinger XRC .15 .07
❑ 6 Alberto Castillo XRC .15 .07
❑ 7 Mike Russell XRC .15 .07
❑ 8 Dan Lock XRC .15 .07
❑ 9 Tom Szimanski XRC .15 .07
❑ 10 Aaron Boone XRC 1.00 .45
❑ 11 Jayson Peterson XRC .15 .07
❑ 12 Mark Johnson XRC .15 .07
❑ 13 Cade Gaspar XRC .15 .07
❑ 14 George Lombard XRC .50 .23
❑ 15 Russ Johnson .15 .07
❑ 16 Travis Miller XRC .15 .07
❑ 17 Jay Payton XRC 1.00 .45
❑ 18 Brian Buchanan XRC .15 .07
❑ 19 Jacob Cruz XRC .50 .23
❑ 20 Gary Rath XRC .15 .07
❑ 21 Ramon Castro XRC .15 .07
❑ 22 Tommy Davis XRC .15 .07
❑ 23 Tony Terry XRC .15 .07
❑ 24 Jerry Whittaker XRC .15 .07
❑ 25 Mike Darr XRC .50 .23
❑ 26 Doug Webb XRC .15 .07
❑ 27 Jason Camilli XRC .15 .07
❑ 28 Brad Rigby XRC .15 .07
❑ 29 Ryan Nye XRC .15 .07
❑ 30 Carl Dale XRC .15 .07
❑ 31 Andy Taulbee XRC .15 .07
❑ 32 Trey Moore XRC .15 .07
❑ 33 John Crowther XRC .15 .07
❑ 34 Joe Giuliano XRC .15 .07
❑ 35 Brian Rose XRC .50 .23
❑ 36 Paul Failla XRC .15 .07
❑ 37 Brian Meadows XRC .15 .07
❑ 38 Oscar Robles XRC .15 .07
❑ 39 Mike Metcalfe XRC .15 .07
❑ 40 Larry Barnes XRC .15 .07
❑ 41 Paul Ottavinia XRC .15 .07
❑ 42 Chris McBride XRC .15 .07
❑ 43 Ricky Stone XRC .15 .07
❑ 44 Billy Blythe XRC .15 .07
❑ 45 Eddie Priest XRC .15 .07
❑ 46 Scott Forster XRC .15 .07
❑ 47 Eric Pickett XRC .15 .07
❑ 48 Matt Beaumont .15 .07
❑ 49 Darrell Nicholas XRC .15 .07
❑ 50 Mike A. Hampton XRC .15 .07
❑ 51 Paul O'Malley XRC .15 .07
❑ 52 Steve Shoemaker XRC .15 .07
❑ 53 Jason Sikes XRC .15 .07
❑ 54 Bryan Farson XRC .15 .07
❑ 55 Yates Hall XRC .15 .07
❑ 56 Troy Brohawn XRC .15 .07
❑ 57 Dan Hower XRC .15 .07
❑ 58 Clay Caruthers XRC .15 .07
❑ 59 Pepe McNeal XRC .15 .07
❑ 60 Ray Ricken XRC .15 .07
❑ 61 Scott Shores XRC .15 .07
❑ 62 Eddie Brooks XRC .15 .07
❑ 63 Dave Kauflin XRC .15 .07
❑ 64 David Meyer XRC .15 .07
❑ 65 Geoff Blum XRC .50 .23
❑ 66 Roy Marsh XRC .15 .07
❑ 67 Ryan Beeney XRC .15 .07
❑ 68 Derek Dukart XRC .15 .07
❑ 69 Nomar Garciaparra 8.00 3.60
❑ 70 Jason Kelly XRC .15 .07
❑ 71 Jesse Ibarra XRC .15 .07
❑ 72 Bucky Buckles XRC .15 .07
❑ 73 Mark Little XRC .15 .07
❑ 74 Heath Murray XRC .15 .07
❑ 75 Greg Morris XRC .15 .07
❑ 76 Mike Halperlin XRC .15 .07
❑ 77 Wes Helms XRC 1.00 .45
❑ 78 Ray Brown XRC .15 .07
❑ 79 Kevin L.Brown XRC .50 .23
❑ 80 Paul Konerko XRC 2.00 .90
❑ 81 Mike Thurman XRC .15 .07
❑ 82 Paul Wilson .15 .07
❑ 83 Terrence Long XRC 2.00 .90
❑ 84 Ben Grieve XRC 2.00 .90
❑ 85 Mark Farris XRC .15 .07
❑ 86 Bret Wagner .15 .07
❑ 87 Dustin Hermanson .50 .23
❑ 88 Kevin Witt XRC .50 .23
❑ 89 Corey Pointer XRC .15 .07
❑ 90 Tim Grieve XRC .15 .07

1995 Stadium Club

	MINT	NRMT
COMPLETE SET (630)	60.00	27.00
COMPLETE SERIES 1 (270)	25.00	11.00
COMPLETE SERIES 2 (225)	20.00	9.00
COMPLETE SERIES 3 (135)	15.00	6.75

❑ 1 Cal Ripken 2.50 1.10
❑ 2 Bo Jackson .25 .11
❑ 3 Bryan Harvey .15 .07
❑ 4 Curt Schilling .60 .25
❑ 5 Bruce Ruffin .15 .07
❑ 6 Travis Fryman .25 .11
❑ 7 Jim Abbott .25 .11
❑ 8 David McCarty .15 .07

❑ 9 Gary Gaetti	.25	.11
❑ 10 Roger Clemens	1.50	.70
❑ 11 Carlos Garcia	.15	.07
❑ 12 Lee Smith	.25	.11
❑ 13 Bobby Ayala	.15	.07
❑ 14 Charles Nagy	.15	.07
❑ 15 Lou Frazier	.15	.07
❑ 16 Rene Arocha	.15	.07
❑ 17 Carlos Delgado	.60	.25
❑ 18 Steve Finley	.25	.11
❑ 19 Ryan Klesko	.25	.11
❑ 20 Cal Eldred	.15	.07
❑ 21 Rey Sanchez	.15	.07
❑ 22 Ken Hill	.15	.07
❑ 23 Benito Santiago	.15	.07
❑ 24 Julian Tavarez	.15	.07
❑ 25 Jose Vizcaino	.15	.07
❑ 26 Andy Benes	.15	.07
❑ 27 Mariano Duncan	.15	.07
❑ 28 Checklist A	.15	.07
❑ 29 Shawon Dunston	.15	.07
❑ 30 Rafael Palmeiro	.60	.25
❑ 31 Dean Palmer	.25	.11
❑ 32 Andres Galarraga	.40	.18
❑ 33 Joey Cora	.15	.07
❑ 34 Mickey Tettleton	.15	.07
❑ 35 Barry Larkin	.60	.25
❑ 36 Carlos Baerga	.15	.07
❑ 37 Orel Hershiser	.25	.11
❑ 38 Jody Reed	.15	.07
❑ 39 Paul Molitor	.60	.25
❑ 40 Jim Edmonds	.40	.18
❑ 41 Bob Tewksbury	.15	.07
❑ 42 John Patterson	.15	.07
❑ 43 Ray McDavid	.15	.07
❑ 44 Zane Smith	.15	.07
❑ 45 Bret Saberhagen SE	.15	.07
❑ 46 Greg Maddux SE	.75	.35
❑ 47 Frank Thomas SE	.40	.18
❑ 48 Carlos Baerga SE	.15	.07
❑ 49 Billy Spiers	.15	.07
❑ 50 Stan Javier	.15	.07
❑ 51 Rex Hudler	.15	.07
❑ 52 Denny Hocking	.15	.07
❑ 53 Todd Worrell	.15	.07
❑ 54 Mark Clark	.15	.07
❑ 55 Hipolito Pichardo	.15	.07
❑ 56 Bob Wickman	.15	.07
❑ 57 Raul Mondesi	.25	.11
❑ 58 Steve Cooke	.15	.07
❑ 59 Rod Beck	.15	.07
❑ 60 Tim Davis	.15	.07
❑ 61 Jeff Kent	.40	.18
❑ 62 John Valentin	.15	.07
❑ 63 Alex Arias	.15	.07
❑ 64 Steve Reed	.15	.07
❑ 65 Ozzie Smith	.75	.35
❑ 66 Terry Pendleton	.25	.11
❑ 67 Kenny Rogers	.15	.07
❑ 68 Vince Coleman	.15	.07
❑ 69 Tom Pagnozzi	.15	.07
❑ 70 Roberto Alomar	.60	.25
❑ 71 Darrin Jackson	.15	.07
❑ 72 Dennis Eckersley	.25	.11
❑ 73 Jay Buhner	.25	.11
❑ 74 Darren Lewis	.15	.07
❑ 75 Dave Weathers	.15	.07
❑ 76 Matt Walbeck	.15	.07
❑ 77 Brad Ausmus	.15	.07
❑ 78 Danny Bautista	.15	.07
❑ 79 Bob Hamelin	.15	.07
❑ 80 Steve Trachsel	.15	.07
❑ 81 Ken Ryan	.15	.07
❑ 82 Chris Turner	.15	.07
❑ 83 David Segui	.15	.07
❑ 84 Ben McDonald	.15	.07
❑ 85 Wade Boggs	.60	.25
❑ 86 John Vander Wal	.15	.07
❑ 87 Sandy Alomar Jr.	.25	.11
❑ 88 Ron Karkovice	.15	.07
❑ 89 Doug Jones	.15	.07
❑ 90 Gary Sheffield	.25	.11
❑ 91 Ken Caminiti	.25	.11
❑ 92 Chris Bosio	.15	.07
❑ 93 Kevin Tapani	.15	.07
❑ 94 Walt Weiss	.15	.07
❑ 95 Erik Hanson	.15	.07
❑ 96 Ruben Sierra	.15	.07
❑ 97 Nomar Garciaparra	3.00	1.35
❑ 98 Terrence Long	.60	.25
❑ 99 Jacob Shumate	.15	.07
❑ 100 Paul Wilson	.15	.07
❑ 101 Kevin Witt	.15	.07
❑ 102 Paul Konerko	.60	.25
❑ 103 Ben Grieve	.60	.25
❑ 104 Mark Johnson RC	.25	.11
❑ 105 Cade Gaspar RC	.15	.07
❑ 106 Mark Farris RC	.15	.07
❑ 107 Dustin Hermanson	.15	.07
❑ 108 Scott Elarton RC	.50	.23
❑ 109 Doug Million	.15	.07
❑ 110 Matt Smith RC	.15	.07
❑ 111 Brian Buchanan RC	.15	.07
❑ 112 Jayson Peterson RC	.15	.07
❑ 113 Bret Wagner RC	.15	.07
❑ 114 C.J. Nitkowski RC	.15	.07
❑ 115 Ramon Castro RC	.25	.11
❑ 116 Rafael Bournigal	.15	.07
❑ 117 Jeff Fassero	.15	.07
❑ 118 Bobby Bonilla	.25	.11
❑ 119 Ricky Gutierrez	.15	.07
❑ 120 Roger Pavlik	.15	.07
❑ 121 Mike Greenwell	.15	.07
❑ 122 Deion Sanders	.25	.11
❑ 123 Charlie Hayes	.15	.07
❑ 124 Paul O'Neill	.60	.25
❑ 125 Jay Bell	.25	.11
❑ 126 Royce Clayton	.15	.07
❑ 127 Willie Banks	.15	.07
❑ 128 Mark Wohlers	.15	.07
❑ 129 Todd Jones	.15	.07
❑ 130 Todd Stottlemyre	.15	.07
❑ 131 Will Clark	.60	.25
❑ 132 Wilson Alvarez	.15	.07
❑ 133 Chili Davis	.25	.11
❑ 134 Dave Burba	.15	.07
❑ 135 Chris Hoiles	.15	.07
❑ 136 Jeff Blauser	.15	.07
❑ 137 Jeff Reboulet	.15	.07
❑ 138 Bret Saberhagen	.25	.11
❑ 139 Kirk Rueter	.15	.07
❑ 140 Dave Nilsson	.15	.07
❑ 141 Pat Borders	.15	.07
❑ 142 Ron Darling	.15	.07
❑ 143 Derek Bell	.15	.07
❑ 144 Dave Hollins	.15	.07
❑ 145 Juan Gonzalez	.60	.25
❑ 146 Andre Dawson	.40	.18
❑ 147 Jim Thome	.60	.25
❑ 148 Larry Walker	.40	.18
❑ 149 Mike Piazza	1.50	.70
❑ 150 Mike Perez	.15	.07
❑ 151 Steve Avery	.15	.07
❑ 152 Dan Wilson	.15	.07
❑ 153 Andy Van Slyke	.25	.11
❑ 154 Junior Felix	.15	.07
❑ 155 Jack McDowell	.15	.07
❑ 156 Danny Tartabull	.15	.07
❑ 157 Willie Blair	.15	.07
❑ 158 Wm.VanLandingham	.15	.07
❑ 159 Robb Nen	.15	.07
❑ 160 Lee Tinsley	.15	.07
❑ 161 Ismael Valdes	.15	.07
❑ 162 Juan Guzman	.15	.07
❑ 163 Scott Servais	.15	.07
❑ 164 Cliff Floyd	.25	.11
❑ 165 Allen Watson	.15	.07
❑ 166 Eddie Taubensee	.15	.07
❑ 167 Scott Hemond	.15	.07
❑ 168 Jeff Tackett	.15	.07
❑ 169 Chad Curtis	.15	.07
❑ 170 Rico Brogna	.15	.07
❑ 171 Luis Polonia	.15	.07
❑ 172 Checklist B	.15	.07
❑ 173 Lance Johnson	.15	.07
❑ 174 Sammy Sosa	1.25	.55
❑ 175 Mike Macfarlane	.15	.07
❑ 176 Darryl Hamilton	.15	.07
❑ 177 Rick Aguilera	.15	.07
❑ 178 Dave West	.15	.07
❑ 179 Mike Gallego	.15	.07
❑ 180 Marc Newfield	.15	.07
❑ 181 Steve Buechele	.15	.07
❑ 182 David Wells	.25	.11
❑ 183 Tom Glavine	.60	.25
❑ 184 Joe Girardi	.15	.07
❑ 185 Craig Biggio	.40	.18
❑ 186 Eddie Murray	.60	.25
❑ 187 Kevin Gross	.15	.07
❑ 188 Sid Fernandez	.15	.07
❑ 189 John Franco	.25	.11
❑ 190 Bernard Gilkey	.15	.07
❑ 191 Matt Williams	.40	.18
❑ 192 Darrin Fletcher	.15	.07
❑ 193 Jeff Conine	.15	.07
❑ 194 Ed Sprague	.15	.07
❑ 195 Eduardo Perez	.15	.07
❑ 196 Scott Livingstone	.15	.07
❑ 197 Ivan Rodriguez	.60	.25
❑ 198 Orlando Merced	.15	.07
❑ 199 Ricky Bones	.15	.07
❑ 200 Javier Lopez	.25	.11
❑ 201 Miguel Jimenez	.15	.07
❑ 202 Terry McGriff	.15	.07
❑ 203 Mike Lieberthal	.25	.11
❑ 204 David Cone	.25	.11
❑ 205 Todd Hundley	.15	.07
❑ 206 Ozzie Guillen	.15	.07
❑ 207 Alex Cole	.15	.07
❑ 208 Tony Phillips	.15	.07
❑ 209 Jim Eisenreich	.15	.07
❑ 210 Greg Vaughn BES	.15	.07
❑ 211 Barry Larkin BES	.25	.11
❑ 212 Don Mattingly BES	.75	.35
❑ 213 Mark Grace BES	.25	.11
❑ 214 Jose Canseco BES	.25	.11
❑ 215 Joe Carter BES	.15	.07
❑ 216 David Cone BES	.15	.07
❑ 217 Sandy Alomar Jr. BES	.15	.07
❑ 218 Al Martin BES	.15	.07
❑ 219 Roberto Kelly BES	.15	.07
❑ 220 Paul Sorrento	.15	.07
❑ 221 Tony Fernandez	.15	.07
❑ 222 Stan Belinda	.15	.07
❑ 223 Mike Stanley	.15	.07
❑ 224 Doug Drabek	.15	.07
❑ 225 Todd Van Poppel	.15	.07
❑ 226 Matt Mieske	.15	.07
❑ 227 Tino Martinez	.25	.11
❑ 228 Andy Ashby	.15	.07
❑ 229 Midre Cummings	.15	.07
❑ 230 Jeff Frye	.15	.07
❑ 231 Hal Morris	.15	.07
❑ 232 Jose Lind	.15	.07
❑ 233 Shawn Green	.60	.25
❑ 234 Rafael Belliard	.15	.07
❑ 235 Randy Myers	.15	.07
❑ 236 Frank Thomas CE	.40	.18
❑ 237 Darren Daulton CE	.15	.07
❑ 238 Sammy Sosa CE	.60	.25
❑ 239 Cal Ripken CE	1.25	.55
❑ 240 Jeff Bagwell CE	.40	.18
❑ 241 Ken Griffey Jr.	2.00	.90
❑ 242 Brett Butler	.25	.11
❑ 243 Derrick May	.15	.07
❑ 244 Pat Listach	.15	.07
❑ 245 Mike Bordick	.15	.07
❑ 246 Mark Langston	.15	.07
❑ 247 Randy Velarde	.15	.07

❑ 248 Julio Franco .25 .11
❑ 249 Chuck Knoblauch .25 .11
❑ 250 Bill Gullickson .15 .07
❑ 251 Dave Henderson .15 .07
❑ 252 Bret Boone .25 .11
❑ 253 Al Martin .15 .07
❑ 254 Armando Benitez .25 .11
❑ 255 Wil Cordero .15 .07
❑ 256 Al Leiter .25 .11
❑ 257 Luis Gonzalez .60 .25
❑ 258 Charlie O'Brien .15 .07
❑ 259 Tim Wallach .15 .07
❑ 260 Scott Sanders .15 .07
❑ 261 Tom Henke .15 .07
❑ 262 Otis Nixon .15 .07
❑ 263 Darren Daulton .25 .11
❑ 264 Manny Ramirez .75 .35
❑ 265 Bret Barberie .15 .07
❑ 266 Mel Rojas .15 .07
❑ 267 John Burkett .15 .07
❑ 268 Brady Anderson .25 .11
❑ 269 John Roper .15 .07
❑ 270 Shane Reynolds .15 .07
❑ 271 Barry Bonds 1.50 .70
❑ 272 Alex Fernandez .15 .07
❑ 273 Brian McRae .15 .07
❑ 274 Todd Zeile .15 .07
❑ 275 Greg Swindell .15 .07
❑ 276 Johnny Ruffin .15 .07
❑ 277 Troy Neel .15 .07
❑ 278 Eric Karros .25 .11
❑ 279 John Hudek .15 .07
❑ 280 Thomas Howard .15 .07
❑ 281 Joe Carter .25 .11
❑ 282 Mike Devereaux .15 .07
❑ 283 Butch Henry .15 .07
❑ 284 Reggie Jefferson .15 .07
❑ 285 Mark Lemke .15 .07
❑ 286 Jeff Montgomery .15 .07
❑ 287 Ryan Thompson .15 .07
❑ 288 Paul Shuey .15 .07
❑ 289 Mark McGwire 2.50 1.10
❑ 290 Bernie Williams .60 .25
❑ 291 Mickey Morandini .15 .07
❑ 292 Scott Leius .15 .07
❑ 293 David Hulse .15 .07
❑ 294 Greg Gagne .15 .07
❑ 295 Moises Alou .25 .11
❑ 296 Geronimo Berroa .15 .07
❑ 297 Eddie Zambrano .15 .07
❑ 298 Alan Trammell .40 .18
❑ 299 Don Slaught .15 .07
❑ 300 Jose Rijo .15 .07
❑ 301 Joe Ausanio .15 .07
❑ 302 Tim Raines .25 .11
❑ 303 Melido Perez .15 .07
❑ 304 Kent Mercker .15 .07
❑ 305 James Mouton .15 .07
❑ 306 Luis Lopez .15 .07
❑ 307 Mike Kingery .15 .07
❑ 308 Willie Greene .15 .07
❑ 309 Cecil Fielder .25 .11
❑ 310 Scott Kamieniecki .15 .07
❑ 311 Mike Greenwell BES .15 .07
❑ 312 Bobby Bonilla BES .15 .07
❑ 313 A.Galarraga BES .25 .11
❑ 314 Cal Ripken BES 1.25 .55
❑ 315 Matt Williams BES .25 .11
❑ 316 Tom Pagnozzi BES .15 .07
❑ 317 Len Dykstra BES .15 .07
❑ 318 Frank Thomas BES .40 .18
❑ 319 Kirby Puckett BES .75 .35
❑ 320 Mike Piazza BES .75 .35
❑ 321 Jason Jacome .15 .07
❑ 322 Brian Hunter .15 .07
❑ 323 Brent Gates .15 .07
❑ 324 Jim Converse .15 .07
❑ 325 Damion Easley .15 .07
❑ 326 Dante Bichette .25 .11
❑ 327 Kurt Abbott .15 .07
❑ 328 Scott Cooper .15 .07
❑ 329 Mike Henneman .15 .07
❑ 330 Orlando Miller .15 .07
❑ 331 John Kruk .25 .11
❑ 332 Jose Oliva .15 .07
❑ 333 Reggie Sanders .15 .07
❑ 334 Omar Vizquel .25 .11
❑ 335 Devon White .25 .11
❑ 336 Mike Morgan .15 .07
❑ 337 J.R. Phillips .15 .07
❑ 338 Gary DiSarcina .15 .07
❑ 339 Joey Hamilton .15 .07
❑ 340 Randy Johnson .75 .35
❑ 341 Jim Leyritz .15 .07
❑ 342 Bobby Jones .15 .07
❑ 343 Jaime Navarro .15 .07
❑ 344 Bip Roberts .15 .07
❑ 345 Steve Karsay .15 .07
❑ 346 Kevin Stocker .15 .07
❑ 347 Jose Canseco .60 .25
❑ 348 Bill Wegman .15 .07
❑ 349 Rondell White .25 .11
❑ 350 Mo Vaughn .25 .11
❑ 351 Joe Orsulak .15 .07
❑ 352 Pat Meares .15 .07
❑ 353 Albie Lopez .15 .07
❑ 354 Edgar Martinez .40 .18
❑ 355 Brian Jordan .25 .11
❑ 356 Tommy Greene .15 .07
❑ 357 Chuck Carr .15 .07
❑ 358 Pedro Astacio .15 .07
❑ 359 Russ Davis .15 .07
❑ 360 Chris Hammond .15 .07
❑ 361 Gregg Jefferies .15 .07
❑ 362 Shane Mack .15 .07
❑ 363 Fred McGriff .40 .18
❑ 364 Pat Rapp .15 .07
❑ 365 Bill Swift .15 .07
❑ 366 Checklist .15 .07
❑ 367 Robin Ventura .25 .11
❑ 368 Bobby Witt .15 .07
❑ 369 Karl Rhodes .15 .07
❑ 370 Eddie Williams .15 .07
❑ 371 John Jaha .15 .07
❑ 372 Steve Howe .15 .07
❑ 373 Leo Gomez .15 .07
❑ 374 Hector Fajardo .15 .07
❑ 375 Jeff Bagwell .75 .35
❑ 376 Mark Acre .15 .07
❑ 377 Wayne Kirby .15 .07
❑ 378 Mark Portugal .15 .07
❑ 379 Jesus Tavarez .15 .07
❑ 380 Jim Lindeman .15 .07
❑ 381 Don Mattingly 1.50 .70
❑ 382 Trevor Hoffman .25 .11
❑ 383 Chris Gomez .15 .07
❑ 384 Garret Anderson .25 .11
❑ 385 Bobby Munoz .15 .07
❑ 386 Jon Lieber .15 .07
❑ 387 Rick Helling .15 .07
❑ 388 Marvin Freeman .15 .07
❑ 389 Juan Castillo .15 .07
❑ 390 Jeff Cirillo .25 .11
❑ 391 Sean Berry .15 .07
❑ 392 Hector Carrasco .15 .07
❑ 393 Mark Grace .60 .25
❑ 394 Pat Kelly .15 .07
❑ 395 Tim Naehring .15 .07
❑ 396 Greg Pirkl .15 .07
❑ 397 John Smoltz .25 .11
❑ 398 Robby Thompson .15 .07
❑ 399 Rick White .15 .07
❑ 400 Frank Thomas .75 .35
❑ 401 Jeff Conine CS .15 .07
❑ 402 Jose Valentin CS .15 .07
❑ 403 Carlos Baerga CS .15 .07
❑ 404 Rick Aguilera CS .15 .07
❑ 405 Wilson Alvarez CS .15 .07
❑ 406 Juan Gonzalez CS .25 .11
❑ 407 Barry Larkin CS .25 .11
❑ 408 Ken Hill CS .15 .07
❑ 409 Chuck Carr CS .15 .07
❑ 410 Tim Raines CS .15 .07
❑ 411 Bryan Eversgerd .15 .07
❑ 412 Phil Plantier .15 .07
❑ 413 Josias Manzanillo .15 .07
❑ 414 Roberto Kelly .15 .07
❑ 415 Rickey Henderson 1.25 .55
❑ 416 John Smiley .15 .07
❑ 417 Kevin Brown .25 .11
❑ 418 Jimmy Key .25 .11
❑ 419 Wally Joyner .25 .11
❑ 420 Roberto Hernandez .15 .07
❑ 421 Felix Fermin .15 .07
❑ 422 Checklist .15 .07
❑ 423 Greg Vaughn .25 .11
❑ 424 Ray Lankford .15 .07
❑ 425 Greg Maddux 1.50 .70
❑ 426 Mike Mussina .60 .25
❑ 427 Geronimo Pena .15 .07
❑ 428 David Nied .15 .07
❑ 429 Scott Erickson .15 .07
❑ 430 Kevin Mitchell .15 .07
❑ 431 Mike Lansing .15 .07
❑ 432 Brian Anderson .15 .07
❑ 433 Jeff King .15 .07
❑ 434 Ramon Martinez .15 .07
❑ 435 Kevin Seitzer .15 .07
❑ 436 Salomon Torres .15 .07
❑ 437 Brian L.Hunter .15 .07
❑ 438 Melvin Nieves .15 .07
❑ 439 Mike Kelly .15 .07
❑ 440 Marquis Grissom .15 .07
❑ 441 Chuck Finley .25 .11
❑ 442 Len Dykstra .25 .11
❑ 443 Ellis Burks .25 .11
❑ 444 Harold Baines .25 .11
❑ 445 Kevin Appier .25 .11
❑ 446 David Justice .25 .11
❑ 447 Darryl Kile .25 .11
❑ 448 John Olerud .25 .11
❑ 449 Greg McMichael .15 .07
❑ 450 Kirby Puckett 1.50 .70
❑ 451 Jose Valentin .15 .07
❑ 452 Rick Wilkins .15 .07
❑ 453 Arthur Rhodes .15 .07
❑ 454 Pat Hentgen .15 .07
❑ 455 Tom Gordon .15 .07
❑ 456 Tom Candiotti .15 .07
❑ 457 Jason Bere .15 .07
❑ 458 Wes Chamberlain .15 .07
❑ 459 Greg Colbrunn .15 .07
❑ 460 John Doherty .15 .07
❑ 461 Kevin Foster .15 .07
❑ 462 Mark Whiten .15 .07
❑ 463 Terry Steinbach .15 .07
❑ 464 Aaron Sele .25 .11
❑ 465 Kirt Manwaring .15 .07
❑ 466 Darren Hall .15 .07
❑ 467 Delino DeShields .15 .07
❑ 468 Andujar Cedeno .15 .07
❑ 469 Billy Ashley .15 .07
❑ 470 Kenny Lofton .25 .11
❑ 471 Pedro Munoz .15 .07
❑ 472 John Wetteland .25 .11
❑ 473 Tim Salmon .25 .11
❑ 474 Denny Neagle .25 .11
❑ 475 Tony Gwynn 1.25 .55
❑ 476 Vinny Castilla .25 .11
❑ 477 Steve Dreyer .15 .07
❑ 478 Jeff Shaw .15 .07
❑ 479 Chad Ogea .15 .07
❑ 480 Scott Ruffcorn .15 .07
❑ 481 Lou Whitaker .25 .11
❑ 482 J.T. Snow .25 .11
❑ 483 Rich Rowland .15 .07
❑ 484 Denny Martinez .25 .11
❑ 485 Pedro Martinez .75 .35
❑ 486 Rusty Greer .25 .11
❑ 487 Dave Fleming .15 .07
❑ 488 John Dettmer .15 .07
❑ 489 Albert Belle .25 .11
❑ 490 Ravelo Manzanillo .15 .07
❑ 491 Henry Rodriguez .15 .07
❑ 492 Andrew Lorraine .15 .07
❑ 493 Dwayne Hosey .15 .07
❑ 494 Mike Blowers .15 .07
❑ 495 Turner Ward .15 .07
❑ 496 Fred McGriff EC .25 .11
❑ 497 Sammy Sosa EC .60 .25
❑ 498 Barry Larkin EC .25 .11
❑ 499 Andres Galarraga EC .25 .11
❑ 500 Gary Sheffield EC .15 .07
❑ 501 Jeff Bagwell EC .40 .18
❑ 502 Mike Piazza EC .75 .35
❑ 503 Moises Alou EC .15 .07
❑ 504 Bobby Bonilla EC .15 .07
❑ 505 Darren Daulton EC .15 .07

❑ 506 Jeff King EC .15 .07
❑ 507 Ray Lankford EC .15 .07
❑ 508 Tony Gwynn EC .60 .25
❑ 509 Barry Bonds EC .75 .35
❑ 510 Cal Ripken EC 1.25 .55
❑ 511 Mo Vaughn EC .15 .07
❑ 512 Tim Salmon EC .15 .07
❑ 513 Frank Thomas EC .40 .18
❑ 514 Albert Belle EC .15 .07
❑ 515 Cecil Fielder EC .15 .07
❑ 516 Kevin Appier EC .15 .07
❑ 517 Greg Vaughn EC .15 .07
❑ 518 Kirby Puckett EC .75 .35
❑ 519 Paul O'Neill EC .60 .25
❑ 520 Ruben Sierra EC .15 .07
❑ 521 Ken Griffey Jr. EC 1.00 .45
❑ 522 Will Clark EC .25 .11
❑ 523 Joe Carter EC .15 .07
❑ 524 Antonio Osuna .15 .07
❑ 525 Glenallen Hill .15 .07
❑ 526 Alex Gonzalez .15 .07
❑ 527 Dave Stewart .25 .11
❑ 528 Ron Gant .15 .07
❑ 529 Jason Bates .15 .07
❑ 530 Mike Macfarlane .15 .07
❑ 531 Esteban Loaiza .15 .07
❑ 532 Joe Randa .15 .07
❑ 533 Dave Winfield .60 .25
❑ 534 Danny Darwin .15 .07
❑ 535 Pete Harnisch .15 .07
❑ 536 Joey Cora .15 .07
❑ 537 Jaime Navarro .15 .07
❑ 538 Marty Cordova .15 .07
❑ 539 Andujar Cedeno .15 .07
❑ 540 Mickey Tettleton .15 .07
❑ 541 Andy Van Slyke .25 .11
❑ 542 Carlos Perez RC .25 .11
❑ 543 Chipper Jones 1.25 .55
❑ 544 Tony Fernandez .15 .07
❑ 545 Tom Henke .15 .07
❑ 546 Pat Borders .15 .07
❑ 547 Chad Curtis .15 .07
❑ 548 Ray Durham .25 .11
❑ 549 Joe Oliver .15 .07
❑ 550 Jose Mesa .15 .07
❑ 551 Steve Finley .25 .11
❑ 552 Otis Nixon .15 .07
❑ 553 Jacob Brumfield .15 .07
❑ 554 Bill Swift .15 .07
❑ 555 Quilvio Veras .15 .07
❑ 556 Hideo Nomo RC UER .. 2.00 .90
Wins and IP totals reversed
❑ 557 Joe Vitiello .15 .07
❑ 558 Mike Perez .15 .07
❑ 559 Charlie Hayes .15 .07
❑ 560 Brad Radke RC 2.50 1.10
❑ 561 Darren Bragg .15 .07
❑ 562 Orel Hershiser .25 .11
❑ 563 Edgardo Alfonzo .60 .25
❑ 564 Doug Jones .15 .07
❑ 565 Andy Pettitte .25 .11
❑ 566 Benito Santiago .15 .07
❑ 567 John Burkett .15 .07
❑ 568 Brad Clontz .15 .07
❑ 569 Jim Abbott .25 .11
❑ 570 Joe Rosselli .15 .07
❑ 571 Mark Grudzielanek RC .. .25 .11
❑ 572 Dustin Hermanson .15 .07
❑ 573 Benji Gil .15 .07
❑ 574 Mark Whiten .15 .07
❑ 575 Mike Ignasiak .15 .07
❑ 576 Kevin Ritz .15 .07
❑ 577 Paul Quantrill .15 .07
❑ 578 Andre Dawson .40 .18
❑ 579 Jerald Clark .15 .07
❑ 580 Frank Rodriguez .15 .07
❑ 581 Mark Kiefer .15 .07
❑ 582 Trevor Wilson .15 .07
❑ 583 Gary Wilson RC .15 .07
❑ 584 Andy Stankiewicz .15 .07
❑ 585 Felipe Lira .15 .07
❑ 586 Mike Mimbs RC .15 .07
❑ 587 Jon Nunnally .15 .07
❑ 588 Tomas Perez RC .15 .07
❑ 589 Checklist .15 .07
❑ 590 Todd Hollandsworth .15 .07
❑ 591 Roberto Petagine .15 .07
❑ 592 Mariano Rivera .25 .11
❑ 593 Mark McLemore .15 .07
❑ 594 Bobby Witt .15 .07
❑ 595 Jose Offerman .15 .07
❑ 596 J.Christiansen RC .15 .07
❑ 597 Jeff Manto .15 .07
❑ 598 Jim Dougherty RC .15 .07
❑ 599 Juan Acevedo RC .15 .07
❑ 600 Troy O'Leary .15 .07
❑ 601 Ron Villone .15 .07
❑ 602 Tripp Cromer .15 .07
❑ 603 Steve Scarsone .15 .07
❑ 604 Lance Parrish .25 .11
❑ 605 Ozzie Timmons .15 .07
❑ 606 Ray Holbert .15 .07
❑ 607 Tony Phillips .15 .07
❑ 608 Phil Plantier .15 .07
❑ 609 Shane Andrews .15 .07
❑ 610 Heathcliff Slocumb .15 .07
❑ 611 Bobby Higginson RC .... 1.25 .55
❑ 612 Bob Tewksbury .15 .07
❑ 613 Terry Pendleton .25 .11
❑ 614 Scott Cooper TA .15 .07
❑ 615 John Wetteland TA .15 .07
❑ 616 Ken Hill TA .15 .07
❑ 617 Marquis Grissom TA .15 .07
❑ 618 Larry Walker TA .15 .07
❑ 619 Derek Bell TA .15 .07
❑ 620 David Cone TA .15 .07
❑ 621 Ken Caminiti TA .15 .07
❑ 622 Jack McDowell TA .15 .07
❑ 623 Vaughn Eshelman TA .15 .07
❑ 624 Brian McRae TA .15 .07
❑ 625 Gregg Jefferies TA .15 .07
❑ 626 Kevin Brown TA .15 .07
❑ 627 Lee Smith TA .15 .07
❑ 628 Tony Tarasco TA .15 .07
❑ 629 Brett Butler TA .15 .07
❑ 630 Jose Canseco TA .25 .11

1996 Stadium Club

	MINT	NRMT
COMPLETE SET (450)	90.00	40.00
COMP.CEREAL SET (454)	90.00	40.00
COMPLETE SERIES 1 (225)	50.00	22.00
COMPLETE SERIES 2 (225)	40.00	18.00
COMMON (1-180/271-450)	.15	.07
COMMON TSC SP (181-270)	.25	.11

❑ 1 Hideo Nomo .75 .35
❑ 2 Paul Molitor .60 .25
❑ 3 Garret Anderson .25 .11
❑ 4 Jose Mesa .15 .07
❑ 5 Vinny Castilla .25 .11
❑ 6 Mike Mussina .60 .25
❑ 7 Ray Durham .25 .11
❑ 8 Jack McDowell .15 .07
❑ 9 Juan Gonzalez .60 .25
❑ 10 Chipper Jones 1.25 .55
❑ 11 Deion Sanders .25 .11
❑ 12 Rondell White .25 .11
❑ 13 Tom Henke .15 .07
❑ 14 Derek Bell .15 .07
❑ 15 Randy Myers .15 .07
❑ 16 Randy Johnson .75 .35
❑ 17 Len Dykstra .25 .11
❑ 18 Bill Pulsipher .15 .07
❑ 19 Greg Colbrunn .15 .07
❑ 20 David Wells .25 .11
❑ 21 Chad Curtis .15 .07
❑ 22 Roberto Hernandez SP .. 5.00 2.20
❑ 23 Kirby Puckett 1.50 .70
❑ 24 Joe Vitiello .15 .07
❑ 25 Roger Clemens 1.50 .70
❑ 26 Al Martin .15 .07
❑ 27 Chad Ogea .15 .07
❑ 28 David Segui .15 .07
❑ 29 Joey Hamilton .15 .07
❑ 30 Dan Wilson .15 .07
❑ 31 Chad Fonville .15 .07
❑ 32 Bernard Gilkey .15 .07
❑ 33 Kevin Seitzer .15 .07
❑ 34 Shawn Green .60 .25
❑ 35 Rick Aguilera .15 .07
❑ 36 Gary DiSarcina .15 .07
❑ 37 Jaime Navarro .15 .07
❑ 38 Doug Jones .15 .07
❑ 39 Brent Gates .15 .07
❑ 40 Dean Palmer .25 .11
❑ 41 Pat Rapp .15 .07
❑ 42 Tony Clark .25 .11
❑ 43 Bill Swift .15 .07
❑ 44 Randy Velarde .15 .07
❑ 45 Matt Williams .40 .18
❑ 46 John Mabry .15 .07
❑ 47 Mike Fetters .15 .07
❑ 48 Orlando Miller .15 .07
❑ 49 Tom Glavine .60 .25
❑ 50 Delino DeShields .15 .07
❑ 51 Scott Erickson .15 .07
❑ 52 Andy Van Slyke .25 .11
❑ 53 Jim Bullinger .15 .07
❑ 54 Lyle Mouton .15 .07
❑ 55 Bret Saberhagen .25 .11
❑ 56 Benito Santiago .15 .07
❑ 57 Dan Miceli .15 .07
❑ 58 Carl Everett .25 .11
❑ 59 Rod Beck .15 .07
❑ 60 Phil Nevin .25 .11
❑ 61 Jason Giambi .60 .25
❑ 62 Paul Menhart .15 .07
❑ 63 Eric Karros .25 .11
❑ 64 Allen Watson .15 .07
❑ 65 Jeff Cirillo .25 .11
❑ 66 Lee Smith .25 .11
❑ 67 Sean Berry .15 .07
❑ 68 Luis Sojo .15 .07
❑ 69 Jeff Montgomery .15 .07
❑ 70 Todd Hundley .15 .07
❑ 71 John Burkett .15 .07
❑ 72 Mark Gubicza .15 .07
❑ 73 Don Mattingly 1.00 .45
❑ 74 Jeff Brantley .15 .07
❑ 75 Matt Walbeck .15 .07
❑ 76 Steve Parris .15 .07
❑ 77 Ken Caminiti .25 .11
❑ 78 Kirt Manwaring .15 .07
❑ 79 Greg Vaughn .25 .11
❑ 80 Pedro Martinez .75 .35
❑ 81 Benji Gil .15 .07
❑ 82 Heathcliff Slocumb .15 .07
❑ 83 Joe Girardi .15 .07
❑ 84 Sean Bergman .15 .07
❑ 85 Matt Karchner .15 .07
❑ 86 Butch Huskey .15 .07
❑ 87 Mike Morgan .15 .07
❑ 88 Todd Worrell .15 .07
❑ 89 Mike Bordick .15 .07
❑ 90 Bip Roberts .15 .07
❑ 91 Mike Hampton .25 .11
❑ 92 Troy O'Leary .15 .07
❑ 93 Wally Joyner .25 .11
❑ 94 Dave Stevens .15 .07
❑ 95 Cecil Fielder .25 .11
❑ 96 Wade Boggs .60 .25
❑ 97 Hal Morris .15 .07
❑ 98 Mickey Tettleton .15 .07
❑ 99 Jeff Kent .40 .18
❑ 100 Denny Martinez .25 .11
❑ 101 Luis Gonzalez .60 .25
❑ 102 John Jaha .15 .07
❑ 103 Javier Lopez .25 .11

❑	104	Mark McGwire	2.50	1.10
❑	105	Ken Griffey Jr.	2.00	.90
❑	106	Darren Daulton	.25	.11
❑	107	Bryan Rekar	.15	.07
❑	108	Mike Macfarlane	.15	.07
❑	109	Gary Gaetti	.25	.11
❑	110	Shane Reynolds	.15	.07
❑	111	Pat Meares	.15	.07
❑	112	Jason Schmidt	.15	.07
❑	113	Otis Nixon	.15	.07
❑	114	John Franco	.25	.11
❑	115	Marc Newfield	.15	.07
❑	116	Andy Benes	.15	.07
❑	117	Ozzie Guillen	.15	.07
❑	118	Brian Jordan	.25	.11
❑	119	Terry Pendleton	.25	.11
❑	120	Chuck Finley	.25	.11
❑	121	Scott Stahoviak	.15	.07
❑	122	Sid Fernandez	.15	.07
❑	123	Derek Jeter	2.50	1.10
❑	124	John Smiley	.15	.07
❑	125	David Bell	.15	.07
❑	126	Brett Butler	.25	.11
❑	127	Doug Drabek	.15	.07
❑	128	J.T. Snow	.25	.11
❑	129	Joe Carter	.25	.11
❑	130	Dennis Eckersley	.25	.11
❑	131	Marty Cordova	.15	.07
❑	132	Greg Maddux	1.50	.70
❑	133	Tom Goodwin	.15	.07
❑	134	Andy Ashby	.15	.07
❑	135	Paul Sorrento	.15	.07
❑	136	Ricky Bones	.15	.07
❑	137	Shawon Dunston	.15	.07
❑	138	Moises Alou	.25	.11
❑	139	Mickey Morandini	.15	.07
❑	140	Ramon Martinez	.15	.07
❑	141	Royce Clayton	.15	.07
❑	142	Brad Ausmus	.15	.07
❑	143	Kenny Rogers	.15	.07
❑	144	Tim Naehring	.15	.07
❑	145	Chris Gomez	.15	.07
❑	146	Bobby Bonilla	.25	.11
❑	147	Wilson Alvarez	.15	.07
❑	148	Johnny Damon	.25	.11
❑	149	Pat Hentgen	.15	.07
❑	150	Andres Galarraga	.40	.18
❑	151	David Cone	.25	.11
❑	152	Lance Johnson	.15	.07
❑	153	Carlos Garcia	.15	.07
❑	154	Doug Johns	.15	.07
❑	155	Midre Cummings	.15	.07
❑	156	Steve Sparks	.15	.07
❑	157	Sandy Martinez	.15	.07
❑	158	Wm. Van Landingham	.15	.07
❑	159	David Justice	.25	.11
❑	160	Mark Grace	.60	.25
❑	161	Robb Nen	.15	.07
❑	162	Mike Greenwell	.15	.07
❑	163	Brad Radke	.25	.11
❑	164	Edgardo Alfonzo	.25	.11
❑	165	Mark Leiter	.15	.07
❑	166	Walt Weiss	.15	.07
❑	167	Mel Rojas	.15	.07
❑	168	Bret Boone	.25	.11
❑	169	Ricky Bottalico	.15	.07
❑	170	Bobby Higginson	.25	.11
❑	171	Trevor Hoffman	.25	.11
❑	172	Jay Bell	.25	.11
❑	173	Gabe White	.15	.07
❑	174	Curtis Goodwin	.15	.07
❑	175	Tyler Green	.15	.07
❑	176	Roberto Alomar	.60	.25
❑	177	Sterling Hitchcock	.15	.07
❑	178	Ryan Klesko	.25	.11
❑	179	Donne Wall	.15	.07
❑	180	Brian McRae	.15	.07
❑	181	Will Clark TSC SP	.75	.35
❑	182	F.Thomas TSC SP	1.00	.45
❑	183	Jeff Bagwell TSC SP	1.00	.45
❑	184	Mo Vaughn TSC SP	.40	.18
❑	185	Tino Martinez TSC SP	.40	.18
❑	186	Craig Biggio TSC SP	.50	.23
❑	187	C. Knoblauch TSC SP	.40	.18
❑	188	Carlos Baerga TSC SP	.25	.11
❑	189	Quilvio Veras TSC SP	.25	.11
❑	190	Luis Alicea TSC SP	.25	.11
❑	191	Jim Thome TSC SP	.75	.35
❑	192	Mike Blowers TSC SP	.25	.11
❑	193	R.Ventura TSC SP	.40	.18
❑	194	Jeff King TSC SP	.25	.11
❑	195	Tony Phillips TSC SP	.25	.11
❑	196	John Valentin TSC SP	.25	.11
❑	197	Barry Larkin TSC SP	.75	.35
❑	198	Cal Ripken TSC SP	3.00	1.35
❑	199	Omar Vizquel TSC SP	.40	.18
❑	200	Kurt Abbott TSC SP	.25	.11
❑	201	Albert Belle TSC SP	.40	.18
❑	202	Barry Bonds TSC SP	2.00	.90
❑	203	Ron Gant TSC SP	.25	.11
❑	204	D.Bichette TSC SP	.40	.18
❑	205	Jeff Conine TSC SP	.25	.11
❑	206	Jim Edmonds TSC SP UER Greg Myers pictured on front	.50	.23
❑	207	Stan Javier TSC SP	.25	.11
❑	208	Kenny Lofton TSC SP	.40	.18
❑	209	Ray Lankford TSC SP	.25	.11
❑	210	B.Williams TSC SP	.75	.35
❑	211	Jay Buhner TSC SP	.40	.18
❑	212	Paul O'Neill TSC SP	.75	.35
❑	213	Tim Salmon TSC SP	.40	.18
❑	214	R.Sanders TSC SP	.25	.11
❑	215	M.Ramirez TSC SP	1.00	.45
❑	216	Mike Piazza TSC SP	2.00	.90
❑	217	Mike Stanley TSC SP	.25	.11
❑	218	Tony Eusebio TSC SP	.25	.11
❑	219	Chris Hoiles TSC SP	.25	.11
❑	220	R.Karkovice TSC SP	.25	.11
❑	221	E.Martinez TSC SP	.50	.23
❑	222	Chili Davis TSC SP	.40	.18
❑	223	Jose Canseco TSC SP	.60	.25
❑	224	Eddie Murray TSC SP	.75	.35
❑	225	G.Berroa TSC SP	.25	.11
❑	226	C.Jones TSC SP	1.50	.70
❑	227	G.Anderson TSC SP	.40	.18
❑	228	M.Cordova TSC SP	.25	.11
❑	229	Jon Nunnally TSC SP	.25	.11
❑	230	Brian L.Hunter TSC SP	.25	.11
❑	231	Shawn Green TSC SP	.75	.35
❑	232	Ray Durham TSC SP	.40	.18
❑	233	Alex Gonzalez TSC SP	.25	.11
❑	234	B.Higginson TSC SP	.40	.18
❑	235	R.Johnson TSC SP	1.00	.45
❑	236	Al Leiter TSC SP	.40	.18
❑	237	Tom Glavine TSC SP	.75	.35
❑	238	Kenny Rogers TSC SP	.25	.11
❑	239	M.Hampton TSC SP	.40	.18
❑	240	David Wells TSC SP	.40	.18
❑	241	Jim Abbott TSC SP	.40	.18
❑	242	Denny Neagle TSC SP	.40	.18
❑	243	W.Alvarez TSC SP	.25	.11
❑	244	John Smiley TSC SP	.25	.11
❑	245	Greg Maddux TSC SP	2.00	.90
❑	246	Andy Ashby TSC SP	.25	.11
❑	247	Hideo Nomo TSC SP	1.00	.45
❑	248	Pat Rapp TSC SP	.25	.11
❑	249	T.Wakefield TSC SP	.25	.11
❑	250	John Smoltz TSC SP	.40	.18
❑	251	J.Hamilton TSC SP	.25	.11
❑	252	Frank Castillo TSC SP	.25	.11
❑	253	D.Martinez TSC SP	.40	.18
❑	254	J.Navarro TSC SP	.25	.11
❑	255	Karim Garcia TSC SP	.25	.11
❑	256	Bob Abreu TSC SP	.60	.25
❑	257	Butch Huskey TSC SP	.25	.11
❑	258	Ruben Rivera TSC SP	.25	.11
❑	259	J.Damon TSC SP	.40	.18
❑	260	Derek Jeter TSC SP	3.00	1.35
❑	261	D. Eckersley TSC SP	.40	.18
❑	262	Jose Mesa TSC SP	.25	.11
❑	263	Tom Henke TSC SP	.25	.11
❑	264	Rick Aguilera TSC SP	.25	.11
❑	265	Randy Myers TSC SP	.25	.11
❑	266	John Franco TSC SP	.40	.18
❑	267	Jeff Brantley TSC SP	.25	.11
❑	268	J.Wetteland TSC SP	.40	.18
❑	269	Mark Wohlers TSC SP	.25	.11
❑	270	Rod Beck TSC SP	.25	.11
❑	271	Barry Larkin	.60	.25
❑	272	Paul O'Neill	.60	.25
❑	273	Bobby Jones	.15	.07
❑	274	Will Clark	.60	.25
❑	275	Steve Avery	.15	.07
❑	276	Jim Edmonds	.40	.18
❑	277	John Olerud	.25	.11
❑	278	Carlos Perez	.15	.07
❑	279	Chris Hoiles	.15	.07
❑	280	Jeff Conine	.15	.07
❑	281	Jim Eisenreich	.15	.07
❑	282	Jason Jacome	.15	.07
❑	283	Ray Lankford	.15	.07
❑	284	John Wasdin	.15	.07
❑	285	Frank Thomas	.75	.35
❑	286	Jason Isringhausen	.25	.11
❑	287	Glenallen Hill	.15	.07
❑	288	Esteban Loaiza	.15	.07
❑	289	Bernie Williams	.60	.25
❑	290	Curtis Leskanic	.15	.07
❑	291	Scott Cooper	.15	.07
❑	292	Curt Schilling	.60	.25
❑	293	Eddie Murray	.60	.25
❑	294	Rick Krivda	.15	.07
❑	295	Domingo Cedeno	.15	.07
❑	296	Jeff Fassero	.15	.07
❑	297	Albert Belle	.25	.11
❑	298	Craig Biggio	.40	.18
❑	299	Fernando Vina	.15	.07
❑	300	Edgar Martinez	.40	.18
❑	301	Tony Gwynn	1.25	.55
❑	302	Felipe Lira	.15	.07
❑	303	Mo Vaughn	.25	.11
❑	304	Alex Fernandez	.15	.07
❑	305	Keith Lockhart	.15	.07
❑	306	Roger Pavlik	.15	.07
❑	307	Lee Tinsley	.15	.07
❑	308	Omar Vizquel	.25	.11
❑	309	Scott Servais	.15	.07
❑	310	Danny Tartabull	.15	.07
❑	311	Chili Davis	.25	.11
❑	312	Cal Eldred	.15	.07
❑	313	Roger Cedeno	.15	.07
❑	314	Chris Hammond	.15	.07
❑	315	Rusty Greer	.25	.11
❑	316	Brady Anderson	.25	.11
❑	317	Ron Villone	.15	.07
❑	318	Mark Carreon	.15	.07
❑	319	Larry Walker	.40	.18
❑	320	Pete Harnisch	.15	.07
❑	321	Robin Ventura	.25	.11
❑	322	Tim Belcher	.15	.07
❑	323	Tony Tarasco	.15	.07
❑	324	Juan Guzman	.15	.07
❑	325	Kenny Lofton	.25	.11
❑	326	Kevin Foster	.15	.07
❑	327	Wil Cordero	.15	.07
❑	328	Troy Percival	.15	.07
❑	329	Turk Wendell	.15	.07
❑	330	Thomas Howard	.15	.07
❑	331	Carlos Baerga	.15	.07
❑	332	B.J. Surhoff	.25	.11
❑	333	Jay Buhner	.25	.11
❑	334	Andujar Cedeno	.15	.07
❑	335	Jeff King	.15	.07
❑	336	Dante Bichette	.25	.11
❑	337	Alan Trammell	.40	.18
❑	338	Scott Leius	.15	.07
❑	339	Chris Snopek	.15	.07
❑	340	Roger Bailey	.15	.07
❑	341	Jacob Brumfield	.15	.07
❑	342	Jose Canseco	.60	.25
❑	343	Rafael Palmeiro	.60	.25
❑	344	Quilvio Veras	.15	.07
❑	345	Darrin Fletcher	.15	.07
❑	346	Carlos Delgado	.60	.25
❑	347	Tony Eusebio	.15	.07
❑	348	Ismael Valdes	.15	.07
❑	349	Terry Steinbach	.15	.07
❑	350	Orel Hershiser	.25	.11
❑	351	Kurt Abbott	.15	.07
❑	352	Jody Reed	.15	.07
❑	353	David Howard	.15	.07
❑	354	Ruben Sierra	.15	.07
❑	355	John Ericks	.15	.07
❑	356	Buck Showalter MG	.15	.07
❑	357	Jim Thome	.60	.25
❑	358	Geronimo Berroa	.15	.07
❑	359	Robby Thompson	.15	.07

❑ 360 Jose Vizcaino .15 .07
❑ 361 Jeff Frye .15 .07
❑ 362 Kevin Appier .25 .11
❑ 363 Pat Kelly .15 .07
❑ 364 Ron Gant .15 .07
❑ 365 Luis Alicea .15 .07
❑ 366 Armando Benitez .15 .07
❑ 367 Rico Brogna .15 .07
❑ 368 Manny Ramirez .75 .35
❑ 369 Mike Lansing .15 .07
❑ 370 Sammy Sosa 1.25 .55
❑ 371 Don Wengert .15 .07
❑ 372 Dave Nilsson .15 .07
❑ 373 Sandy Alomar Jr. .25 .11
❑ 374 Joey Cora .15 .07
❑ 375 Larry Thomas .15 .07
❑ 376 John Valentin .15 .07
❑ 377 Kevin Ritz .15 .07
❑ 378 Steve Finley .25 .11
❑ 379 Frank Rodriguez .15 .07
❑ 380 Ivan Rodriguez .60 .25
❑ 381 Alex Ochoa .15 .07
❑ 382 Mark Lemke .15 .07
❑ 383 Scott Brosius .25 .11
❑ 384 James Mouton .15 .07
❑ 385 Mark Langston .15 .07
❑ 386 Ed Sprague .15 .07
❑ 387 Joe Oliver .15 .07
❑ 388 Steve Ontiveros .15 .07
❑ 389 Rey Sanchez .15 .07
❑ 390 Mike Henneman .15 .07
❑ 391 Jose Valentin .15 .07
❑ 392 Tom Candiotti .15 .07
❑ 393 Damon Buford .15 .07
❑ 394 Erik Hanson .15 .07
❑ 395 Mark Smith .15 .07
❑ 396 Pete Schourek .15 .07
❑ 397 John Flaherty .15 .07
❑ 398 Dave Martinez .15 .07
❑ 399 Tommy Greene .15 .07
❑ 400 Gary Sheffield .25 .11
❑ 401 Glenn Dishman .15 .07
❑ 402 Barry Bonds 1.50 .70
❑ 403 Tom Pagnozzi .15 .07
❑ 404 Todd Stottlemyre .15 .07
❑ 405 Tim Salmon .25 .11
❑ 406 John Hudek .15 .07
❑ 407 Fred McGriff .40 .18
❑ 408 Orlando Merced .15 .07
❑ 409 Brian Barber .15 .07
❑ 410 Ryan Thompson .15 .07
❑ 411 Mariano Rivera .25 .11
❑ 412 Eric Young .15 .07
❑ 413 Chris Bosio .15 .07
❑ 414 Chuck Knoblauch .25 .11
❑ 415 Jamie Moyer .15 .07
❑ 416 Chan Ho Park .25 .11
❑ 417 Mark Portugal .15 .07
❑ 418 Tim Raines .25 .11
❑ 419 Antonio Osuna .15 .07
❑ 420 Todd Zeile .15 .07
❑ 421 Steve Wojciechowski .15 .07
❑ 422 Marquis Grissom .15 .07
❑ 423 Norm Charlton .15 .07
❑ 424 Cal Ripken 2.50 1.10
❑ 425 Gregg Jefferies .15 .07
❑ 426 Mike Stanton .15 .07
❑ 427 Tony Fernandez .15 .07
❑ 428 Jose Rijo .15 .07
❑ 429 Jeff Bagwell .75 .35
❑ 430 Raul Mondesi .25 .11
❑ 431 Travis Fryman .25 .11
❑ 432 Ron Karkovice .15 .07
❑ 433 Alan Benes .15 .07
❑ 434 Tony Phillips .15 .07
❑ 435 Reggie Sanders .15 .07
❑ 436 Andy Pettitte .25 .11
❑ 437 Matt Lawton RC .75 .35
❑ 438 Jeff Blauser .15 .07
❑ 439 Michael Tucker .15 .07
❑ 440 Mark Loretta .15 .07
❑ 441 Charlie Hayes .15 .07
❑ 442 Mike Piazza 1.50 .70
❑ 443 Shane Andrews .15 .07
❑ 444 Jeff Suppan .15 .07
❑ 445 Steve Rodriguez .15 .07
❑ 446 Mike Matheny .15 .07
❑ 447 Trenidad Hubbard .15 .07
❑ 448 Denny Hocking .15 .07
❑ 449 Mark Grudzielanek .15 .07
❑ 450 Joe Randa .15 .07

1997 Stadium Club

	MINT	NRMT
COMPLETE SET (390)	90.00	40.00
COMPLETE SERIES 1 (195)	50.00	22.00
COMPLETE SERIES 2 (195)	40.00	18.00
COMMON (1-180/196-375)	.15	.07
COM.SP (181-195/376-390)	.50	.23

❑ 1 Chipper Jones 1.25 .55
❑ 2 Gary Sheffield .25 .11
❑ 3 Kenny Lofton .25 .11
❑ 4 Brian Jordan .25 .11
❑ 5 Mark McGwire 2.50 1.10
❑ 6 Charles Nagy .15 .07
❑ 7 Tim Salmon .25 .11
❑ 8 Cal Ripken 2.50 1.10
❑ 9 Jeff Conine .15 .07
❑ 10 Paul Molitor .60 .25
❑ 11 Mariano Rivera .25 .11
❑ 12 Pedro Martinez .75 .35
❑ 13 Jeff Bagwell .75 .35
❑ 14 Bobby Bonilla .25 .11
❑ 15 Barry Bonds 1.50 .70
❑ 16 Ryan Klesko .25 .11
❑ 17 Barry Larkin .60 .25
❑ 18 Jim Thome .60 .25
❑ 19 Jay Buhner .25 .11
❑ 20 Juan Gonzalez .60 .25
❑ 21 Mike Mussina .60 .25
❑ 22 Kevin Appier .25 .11
❑ 23 Eric Karros .25 .11
❑ 24 Steve Finley .25 .11
❑ 25 Ed Sprague .15 .07
❑ 26 Bernard Gilkey .15 .07
❑ 27 Tony Phillips .15 .07
❑ 28 Henry Rodriguez .15 .07
❑ 29 John Smoltz .25 .11
❑ 30 Dante Bichette .25 .11
❑ 31 Mike Piazza 1.50 .70
❑ 32 Paul O'Neill .60 .25
❑ 33 Billy Wagner .15 .07
❑ 34 Reggie Sanders .15 .07
❑ 35 John Jaha .15 .07
❑ 36 Eddie Murray .60 .25
❑ 37 Eric Young .15 .07
❑ 38 Roberto Hernandez .15 .07
❑ 39 Pat Hentgen .15 .07
❑ 40 Sammy Sosa 1.25 .55
❑ 41 Todd Hundley .15 .07
❑ 42 Mo Vaughn .25 .11
❑ 43 Robin Ventura .25 .11
❑ 44 Mark Grudzielanek .15 .07
❑ 45 Shane Reynolds .15 .07
❑ 46 Andy Pettitte .25 .11
❑ 47 Fred McGriff .40 .18
❑ 48 Rey Ordonez .15 .07
❑ 49 Will Clark .60 .25
❑ 50 Ken Griffey Jr. 2.00 .90
❑ 51 Todd Worrell .15 .07
❑ 52 Rusty Greer .25 .11
❑ 53 Mark Grace .60 .25
❑ 54 Tom Glavine .60 .25
❑ 55 Derek Jeter 2.50 1.10
❑ 56 Rafael Palmeiro .60 .25
❑ 57 Bernie Williams .60 .25
❑ 58 Marty Cordova .15 .07
❑ 59 Andres Galarraga .40 .18
❑ 60 Ken Caminiti .25 .11
❑ 61 Garret Anderson .25 .11
❑ 62 Denny Martinez .25 .11
❑ 63 Mike Greenwell .15 .07
❑ 64 David Segui .15 .07
❑ 65 Julio Franco .25 .11
❑ 66 Rickey Henderson 1.25 .55
❑ 67 Ozzie Guillen .15 .07
❑ 68 Pete Harnisch .15 .07
❑ 69 Chan Ho Park .25 .11
❑ 70 Harold Baines .25 .11
❑ 71 Mark Clark .15 .07
❑ 72 Steve Avery .15 .07
❑ 73 Brian Hunter .15 .07
❑ 74 Pedro Astacio .15 .07
❑ 75 Jack McDowell .15 .07
❑ 76 Gregg Jefferies .15 .07
❑ 77 Jason Kendall .25 .11
❑ 78 Todd Walker .15 .07
❑ 79 B.J. Surhoff .25 .11
❑ 80 Moises Alou .25 .11
❑ 81 Fernando Vina .15 .07
❑ 82 Darryl Strawberry .25 .11
❑ 83 Jose Rosado .15 .07
❑ 84 Chris Gomez .15 .07
❑ 85 Chili Davis .25 .11
❑ 86 Alan Benes .15 .07
❑ 87 Todd Hollandsworth .15 .07
❑ 88 Jose Vizcaino .15 .07
❑ 89 Edgardo Alfonzo .25 .11
❑ 90 Ruben Rivera .15 .07
❑ 91 Donovan Osborne .15 .07
❑ 92 Doug Glanville .15 .07
❑ 93 Gary DiSarcina .15 .07
❑ 94 Brooks Kieschnick .15 .07
❑ 95 Bobby Jones .15 .07
❑ 96 Raul Casanova .15 .07
❑ 97 Jermaine Allensworth .15 .07
❑ 98 Kenny Rogers .15 .07
❑ 99 Mark McLemore .15 .07
❑ 100 Jeff Fassero .15 .07
❑ 101 Sandy Alomar Jr. .25 .11
❑ 102 Chuck Finley .25 .11
❑ 103 Eric Owens .15 .07
❑ 104 Billy McMillon .15 .07
❑ 105 Dwight Gooden .25 .11
❑ 106 Sterling Hitchcock .15 .07
❑ 107 Doug Drabek .15 .07
❑ 108 Paul Wilson .15 .07
❑ 109 Chris Snopek .15 .07
❑ 110 Al Leiter .25 .11
❑ 111 Bob Tewksbury .15 .07
❑ 112 Todd Greene .15 .07
❑ 113 Jose Valentin .15 .07
❑ 114 Delino DeShields .15 .07
❑ 115 Mike Bordick .15 .07
❑ 116 Pat Meares .15 .07
❑ 117 Mariano Duncan .15 .07
❑ 118 Steve Trachsel .15 .07
❑ 119 Luis Castillo .15 .07
❑ 120 Andy Benes .15 .07
❑ 121 Donne Wall .15 .07
❑ 122 Alex Gonzalez .15 .07
❑ 123 Dan Wilson .15 .07
❑ 124 Omar Vizquel .25 .11
❑ 125 Devon White .25 .11
❑ 126 Darryl Hamilton .15 .07
❑ 127 Orlando Merced .15 .07
❑ 128 Royce Clayton .15 .07
❑ 129 W.VanLandingham .15 .07
❑ 130 Terry Steinbach .15 .07
❑ 131 Jeff Blauser .15 .07
❑ 132 Jeff Cirillo .25 .11
❑ 133 Roger Pavlik .15 .07
❑ 134 Danny Tartabull .15 .07
❑ 135 Jeff Montgomery .15 .07
❑ 136 Bobby Higginson .25 .11
❑ 137 Mike Grace .15 .07
❑ 138 Kevin Elster .15 .07
❑ 139 Brian Giles RC 2.50 1.10

❑ 140 Rod Beck .15 .07
❑ 141 Ismael Valdes .15 .07
❑ 142 Scott Brosius .25 .11
❑ 143 Mike Fetters .15 .07
❑ 144 Gary Gaetti .25 .11
❑ 145 Mike Lansing .15 .07
❑ 146 Glenallen Hill .15 .07
❑ 147 Shawn Green .60 .25
❑ 148 Mel Rojas .15 .07
❑ 149 Joey Cora .15 .07
❑ 150 John Smiley .15 .07
❑ 151 Marvin Benard .15 .07
❑ 152 Curt Schilling .60 .25
❑ 153 Dave Nilsson .15 .07
❑ 154 Edgar Renteria .15 .07
❑ 155 Joey Hamilton .15 .07
❑ 156 Carlos Garcia .15 .07
❑ 157 Nomar Garciaparra 1.50 .70
❑ 158 Kevin Ritz .15 .07
❑ 159 Keith Lockhart .15 .07
❑ 160 Justin Thompson .15 .07
❑ 161 Terry Adams .15 .07
❑ 162 Jamey Wright .15 .07
❑ 163 Otis Nixon .15 .07
❑ 164 Michael Tucker .15 .07
❑ 165 Mike Stanley .15 .07
❑ 166 Ben McDonald .15 .07
❑ 167 John Mabry .15 .07
❑ 168 Troy O'Leary .15 .07
❑ 169 Mel Nieves .15 .07
❑ 170 Bret Boone .25 .11
❑ 171 Mike Timlin .15 .07
❑ 172 Scott Rolen .60 .25
❑ 173 Reggie Jefferson .15 .07
❑ 174 Neifi Perez .15 .07
❑ 175 Brian McRae .15 .07
❑ 176 Tom Goodwin .15 .07
❑ 177 Aaron Sele .25 .11
❑ 178 Benito Santiago .15 .07
❑ 179 Frank Rodriguez .15 .07
❑ 180 Eric Davis .25 .11
❑ 181 A.Jones 2000 SP 1.50 .70
❑ 182 Todd Walker 2000 SP .50 .23
❑ 183 Wes Helms 2000 SP .60 .25
❑ 184 Nelson Figueroa .50 .23
2000 SP RC
❑ 185 V. Guerrero 2000 SP 2.00 .90
❑ 186 B.McMillon 2000 SP .50 .23
❑ 187 Todd Helton 2000 SP 2.00 .90
❑ 188 Nomar Garciaparra 3.00 1.35
2000 SP
❑ 189 K. Maeda 2000 SP .50 .23
❑ 190 R.Branyan 2000 SP .60 .25
❑ 191 G.Rusch 2000 SP .50 .23
❑ 192 B.Colon 2000 SP .60 .25
❑ 193 Scott Rolen 2000 SP 1.25 .55
❑ 194 A. Echevarria 2000 SP .50 .23
❑ 195 Bob Abreu 2000 SP .60 .25
❑ 196 Greg Maddux 1.50 .70
❑ 197 Joe Carter .25 .11
❑ 198 Alex Ochoa .15 .07
❑ 199 Ellis Burks .25 .11
❑ 200 Ivan Rodriguez .60 .25
❑ 201 Marquis Grissom .15 .07
❑ 202 Trevor Hoffman .25 .11
❑ 203 Matt Williams .40 .18
❑ 204 Carlos Delgado .60 .25
❑ 205 Ramon Martinez .15 .07
❑ 206 Chuck Knoblauch .25 .11
❑ 207 Juan Guzman .15 .07
❑ 208 Derek Bell .15 .07
❑ 209 Roger Clemens 1.50 .70
❑ 210 Vladimir Guerrero 1.00 .45
❑ 211 Cecil Fielder .25 .11
❑ 212 Hideo Nomo .60 .25
❑ 213 Frank Thomas .75 .35
❑ 214 Greg Vaughn .25 .11
❑ 215 Javy Lopez .25 .11
❑ 216 Raul Mondesi .25 .11
❑ 217 Wade Boggs .60 .25
❑ 218 Carlos Baerga .15 .07
❑ 219 Tony Gwynn 1.25 .55
❑ 220 Tino Martinez .25 .11
❑ 221 Vinny Castilla .25 .11
❑ 222 Lance Johnson .15 .07
❑ 223 David Justice .25 .11
❑ 224 Rondell White .25 .11
❑ 225 Dean Palmer .25 .11
❑ 226 Jim Edmonds .40 .18
❑ 227 Albert Belle .25 .11
❑ 228 Alex Fernandez .15 .07
❑ 229 Ryne Sandberg .75 .35
❑ 230 Jose Mesa .15 .07
❑ 231 David Cone .25 .11
❑ 232 Troy Percival .15 .07
❑ 233 Edgar Martinez .40 .18
❑ 234 Jose Canseco .60 .25
❑ 235 Kevin Brown .25 .11
❑ 236 Ray Lankford .15 .07
❑ 237 Karim Garcia .15 .07
❑ 238 J.T. Snow .25 .11
❑ 239 Dennis Eckersley .25 .11
❑ 240 Roberto Alomar .60 .25
❑ 241 John Valentin .15 .07
❑ 242 Ron Gant .15 .07
❑ 243 Geronimo Berroa .15 .07
❑ 244 Manny Ramirez .75 .35
❑ 245 Travis Fryman .25 .11
❑ 246 Denny Neagle .25 .11
❑ 247 Randy Johnson .75 .35
❑ 248 Darin Erstad .60 .25
❑ 249 Mark Wohlers .15 .07
❑ 250 Ken Hill .15 .07
❑ 251 Larry Walker .40 .18
❑ 252 Craig Biggio .40 .18
❑ 253 Brady Anderson .25 .11
❑ 254 John Wetteland .25 .11
❑ 255 Andruw Jones .75 .35
❑ 256 Turk Wendell .15 .07
❑ 257 Jason Isringhausen .15 .07
❑ 258 Jaime Navarro .15 .07
❑ 259 Sean Berry .15 .07
❑ 260 Albie Lopez .15 .07
❑ 261 Jay Bell .25 .11
❑ 262 Bobby Witt .15 .07
❑ 263 Tony Clark .25 .11
❑ 264 Tim Wakefield .15 .07
❑ 265 Brad Radke .25 .11
❑ 266 Tim Belcher .15 .07
❑ 267 Nerio Rodriguez RC .15 .07
❑ 268 Roger Cedeno .15 .07
❑ 269 Tim Naehring .15 .07
❑ 270 Kevin Tapani .15 .07
❑ 271 Joe Randa .15 .07
❑ 272 Randy Myers .15 .07
❑ 273 Dave Burba .15 .07
❑ 274 Mike Sweeney .25 .11
❑ 275 Danny Graves .15 .07
❑ 276 Chad Mottola .15 .07
❑ 277 Ruben Sierra .15 .07
❑ 278 Norm Charlton .15 .07
❑ 279 Scott Servais .15 .07
❑ 280 Jacob Cruz .15 .07
❑ 281 Mike Macfarlane .15 .07
❑ 282 Rich Becker .15 .07
❑ 283 Shannon Stewart .25 .11
❑ 284 Gerald Williams .15 .07
❑ 285 Jody Reed .15 .07
❑ 286 Jeff D'Amico .15 .07
❑ 287 Walt Weiss .15 .07
❑ 288 Jim Leyritz .15 .07
❑ 289 Francisco Cordova .15 .07
❑ 290 F.P. Santangelo .15 .07
❑ 291 Scott Erickson .15 .07
❑ 292 Hal Morris .15 .07
❑ 293 Ray Durham .25 .11
❑ 294 Andy Ashby .15 .07
❑ 295 Darryl Kile .25 .11
❑ 296 Jose Paniagua .15 .07
❑ 297 Mickey Tettleton .15 .07
❑ 298 Joe Girardi .15 .07
❑ 299 Rocky Coppinger .15 .07
❑ 300 Bob Abreu .25 .11
❑ 301 John Olerud .25 .11
❑ 302 Paul Shuey .15 .07
❑ 303 Jeff Brantley .15 .07
❑ 304 Bob Wells .15 .07
❑ 305 Kevin Seitzer .15 .07
❑ 306 Shawon Dunston .15 .07
❑ 307 Jose Herrera .15 .07
❑ 308 Butch Huskey .15 .07
❑ 309 Jose Offerman .15 .07
❑ 310 Rick Aguilera .15 .07
❑ 311 Greg Gagne .15 .07
❑ 312 John Burkett .15 .07
❑ 313 Mark Thompson .15 .07
❑ 314 Alvaro Espinoza .15 .07
❑ 315 Todd Stottlemyre .15 .07
❑ 316 Al Martin .15 .07
❑ 317 James Baldwin .15 .07
❑ 318 Cal Eldred .15 .07
❑ 319 Sid Fernandez .15 .07
❑ 320 Mickey Morandini .15 .07
❑ 321 Robb Nen .15 .07
❑ 322 Mark Lemke .15 .07
❑ 323 Pete Schourek .15 .07
❑ 324 Marcus Jensen .15 .07
❑ 325 Rich Aurilia .25 .11
❑ 326 Jeff King .15 .07
❑ 327 Scott Stahoviak .15 .07
❑ 328 Ricky Otero .15 .07
❑ 329 Antonio Osuna .15 .07
❑ 330 Chris Hoiles .15 .07
❑ 331 Luis Gonzalez .60 .25
❑ 332 Wil Cordero .15 .07
❑ 333 Johnny Damon .25 .11
❑ 334 Mark Langston .15 .07
❑ 335 Orlando Miller .15 .07
❑ 336 Jason Giambi .60 .25
❑ 337 Damian Jackson .15 .07
❑ 338 David Wells .25 .11
❑ 339 Bip Roberts .15 .07
❑ 340 Matt Ruebel .15 .07
❑ 341 Tom Candiotti .15 .07
❑ 342 Wally Joyner .25 .11
❑ 343 Jimmy Key .25 .11
❑ 344 Tony Batista .25 .11
❑ 345 Paul Sorrento .15 .07
❑ 346 Ron Karkovice .15 .07
❑ 347 Wilson Alvarez .15 .07
❑ 348 John Flaherty .15 .07
❑ 349 Rey Sanchez .15 .07
❑ 350 John Vander Wal .15 .07
❑ 351 Jermaine Dye .25 .11
❑ 352 Mike Hampton .25 .11
❑ 353 Greg Colbrunn .15 .07
❑ 354 Heathcliff Slocumb .15 .07
❑ 355 Ricky Bottalico .15 .07
❑ 356 Marty Janzen .15 .07
❑ 357 Orel Hershiser .25 .11
❑ 358 Rex Hudler .15 .07
❑ 359 Amaury Telemaco .15 .07
❑ 360 Darrin Fletcher .15 .07
❑ 361 Brant Brown UER .15 .07
Card numbered 351
❑ 362 Russ Davis .15 .07
❑ 363 Allen Watson .15 .07
❑ 364 Mike Lieberthal .25 .11
❑ 365 Dave Stevens .15 .07
❑ 366 Jay Powell .15 .07
❑ 367 Tony Fossas .15 .07
❑ 368 Bob Wolcott .15 .07
❑ 369 Mark Loretta .15 .07
❑ 370 Shawn Estes .25 .11
❑ 371 Sandy Martinez .15 .07
❑ 372 Wendell Magee Jr. .15 .07
❑ 373 John Franco .25 .11
❑ 374 Tom Pagnozzi UER .15 .07
misnumbered as 274
❑ 375 Willie Adams .15 .07
❑ 376 Chipper Jones SS SP 2.50 1.10
❑ 377 Mo Vaughn SS SP .60 .25
❑ 378 Frank Thomas SS SP 1.50 .70
❑ 379 Albert Belle SS SP .60 .25
❑ 380 A.Galarraga SS SP .75 .35
❑ 381 Gary Sheffield SS SP .60 .25
❑ 382 Jeff Bagwell SS SP 1.50 .70
❑ 383 Mike Piazza SS SP 3.00 1.35
❑ 384 Mark McGwire SS SP 5.00 2.20
❑ 385 Ken Griffey Jr. SS SP 4.00 1.80
❑ 386 Barry Bonds SS SP 3.00 1.35
❑ 387 Juan Gonzalez SS SP 1.25 .55
❑ 388 B.Anderson SS SP .60 .25
❑ 389 Ken Caminiti SS SP .60 .25
❑ 390 Jay Buhner SS SP .60 .25

1998 Stadium Club

	MINT	NRMT
COMPLETE SET (400)	80.00	36.00
COMPLETE SERIES 1 (200)	40.00	18.00
COMPLETE SERIES 2 (200)	40.00	18.00

	Player	MINT	NRMT
❑ 1	Chipper Jones	1.25	.55
❑ 2	Frank Thomas	.75	.35
❑ 3	Vladimir Guerrero	.75	.35
❑ 4	Ellis Burks	.25	.11
❑ 5	John Franco	.25	.11
❑ 6	Paul Molitor	.60	.25
❑ 7	Rusty Greer	.25	.11
❑ 8	Todd Hundley	.15	.07
❑ 9	Brett Tomko	.15	.07
❑ 10	Eric Karros	.25	.11
❑ 11	Mike Cameron	.25	.11
❑ 12	Jim Edmonds	.40	.18
❑ 13	Bernie Williams	.60	.25
❑ 14	Denny Neagle	.15	.07
❑ 15	Jason Dickson	.15	.07
❑ 16	Sammy Sosa	1.25	.55
❑ 17	Brian Jordan	.25	.11
❑ 18	Jose Vidro	.25	.11
❑ 19	Scott Spiezio	.15	.07
❑ 20	Jay Buhner	.25	.11
❑ 21	Jim Thome	.60	.25
❑ 22	Sandy Alomar Jr.	.25	.11
❑ 23	Livan Hernandez	.15	.07
❑ 24	Roberto Alomar	.60	.25
❑ 25	Chris Gomez	.15	.07
❑ 26	John Wetteland	.25	.11
❑ 27	Willie Greene	.15	.07
❑ 28	Gregg Jefferies	.15	.07
❑ 29	Johnny Damon	.25	.11
❑ 30	Barry Larkin	.60	.25
❑ 31	Chuck Knoblauch	.25	.11
❑ 32	Mo Vaughn	.25	.11
❑ 33	Tony Clark	.25	.11
❑ 34	Marty Cordova	.15	.07
❑ 35	Vinny Castilla	.25	.11
❑ 36	Jeff King	.15	.07
❑ 37	Reggie Jefferson	.15	.07
❑ 38	Mariano Rivera	.25	.11
❑ 39	Jermaine Allensworth	.15	.07
❑ 40	Livan Hernandez	.15	.07
❑ 41	Heathcliff Slocumb	.15	.07
❑ 42	Jacob Cruz	.15	.07
❑ 43	Barry Bonds	1.50	.70
❑ 44	Dave Magadan	.15	.07
❑ 45	Chan Ho Park	.25	.11
❑ 46	Jeremi Gonzalez	.15	.07
❑ 47	Jeff Cirillo	.25	.11
❑ 48	Delino DeShields	.15	.07
❑ 49	Craig Biggio	.40	.18
❑ 50	Benito Santiago	.15	.07
❑ 51	Mark Clark	.15	.07
❑ 52	Fernando Vina	.15	.07
❑ 53	F.P. Santangelo	.15	.07
❑ 54	Pep Harris	.15	.07
❑ 55	Edgar Renteria	.15	.07
❑ 56	Jeff Bagwell	.75	.35
❑ 57	Jimmy Key	.25	.11
❑ 58	Bartolo Colon	.25	.11
❑ 59	Curt Schilling	.60	.25
❑ 60	Steve Finley	.25	.11
❑ 61	Andy Ashby	.15	.07
❑ 62	John Burkett	.15	.07
❑ 63	Orel Hershiser	.25	.11
❑ 64	Pokey Reese	.15	.07
❑ 65	Scott Servais	.15	.07
❑ 66	Todd Jones	.15	.07
❑ 67	Javy Lopez	.25	.11
❑ 68	Robin Ventura	.25	.11
❑ 69	Miguel Tejada	.40	.18
❑ 70	Raul Casanova	.15	.07
❑ 71	Reggie Sanders	.15	.07
❑ 72	Edgardo Alfonzo	.25	.11
❑ 73	Dean Palmer	.25	.11
❑ 74	Todd Stottlemyre	.15	.07
❑ 75	David Wells	.25	.11
❑ 76	Troy Percival	.15	.07
❑ 77	Albert Belle	.25	.11
❑ 78	Pat Hentgen	.15	.07
❑ 79	Brian Hunter	.15	.07
❑ 80	Richard Hidalgo	.25	.11
❑ 81	Darren Oliver	.15	.07
❑ 82	Mark Wohlers	.15	.07
❑ 83	Cal Ripken	2.50	1.10
❑ 84	Hideo Nomo	.60	.25
❑ 85	Derrek Lee	.25	.11
❑ 86	Stan Javier	.15	.07
❑ 87	Rey Ordonez	.15	.07
❑ 88	Randy Johnson	.75	.35
❑ 89	Jeff Kent	.40	.18
❑ 90	Brian McRae	.15	.07
❑ 91	Manny Ramirez	.75	.35
❑ 92	Trevor Hoffman	.25	.11
❑ 93	Doug Glanville	.15	.07
❑ 94	Todd Walker	.15	.07
❑ 95	Andy Benes	.15	.07
❑ 96	Jason Schmidt	.15	.07
❑ 97	Mike Matheny	.15	.07
❑ 98	Tim Naehring	.15	.07
❑ 99	Keith Lockhart	.15	.07
❑ 100	Jose Rosado	.15	.07
❑ 101	Roger Clemens	1.50	.70
❑ 102	Pedro Astacio	.15	.07
❑ 103	Mark Bellhorn	.15	.07
❑ 104	Paul O'Neill	.60	.25
❑ 105	Darin Erstad	.60	.25
❑ 106	Mike Lieberthal	.25	.11
❑ 107	Wilson Alvarez	.15	.07
❑ 108	Mike Mussina	.60	.25
❑ 109	George Williams	.15	.07
❑ 110	Cliff Floyd	.25	.11
❑ 111	Shawn Estes	.25	.11
❑ 112	Mark Grudzielanek	.15	.07
❑ 113	Tony Gwynn	1.25	.55
❑ 114	Alan Benes	.15	.07
❑ 115	Terry Steinbach	.15	.07
❑ 116	Greg Maddux	1.50	.70
❑ 117	Andy Pettitte	.25	.11
❑ 118	Dave Nilsson	.15	.07
❑ 119	Deivi Cruz	.15	.07
❑ 120	Carlos Delgado	.60	.25
❑ 121	Scott Hatteberg	.15	.07
❑ 122	John Olerud	.25	.11
❑ 123	Todd Dunwoody	.15	.07
❑ 124	Garret Anderson	.25	.11
❑ 125	Royce Clayton	.15	.07
❑ 126	Dante Powell	.15	.07
❑ 127	Tom Glavine	.60	.25
❑ 128	Gary DiSarcina	.15	.07
❑ 129	Terry Adams	.15	.07
❑ 130	Raul Mondesi	.25	.11
❑ 131	Dan Wilson	.15	.07
❑ 132	Al Martin	.15	.07
❑ 133	Mickey Morandini	.15	.07
❑ 134	Rafael Palmeiro	.60	.25
❑ 135	Juan Encarnacion	.25	.11
❑ 136	Jim Pittsley	.15	.07
❑ 137	Magglio Ordonez RC	2.00	.90
❑ 138	Will Clark	.60	.25
❑ 139	Todd Helton	.75	.35
❑ 140	Kelvim Escobar	.15	.07
❑ 141	Esteban Loaiza	.15	.07
❑ 142	John Jaha	.25	.11
❑ 143	Jeff Fassero	.15	.07
❑ 144	Harold Baines	.25	.11
❑ 145	Butch Huskey	.15	.07
❑ 146	Pat Meares	.15	.07
❑ 147	Brian Giles	.25	.11
❑ 148	Ramiro Mendoza	.15	.07
❑ 149	John Smoltz	.25	.11
❑ 150	Felix Martinez	.15	.07
❑ 151	Jose Valentin	.15	.07
❑ 152	Brad Rigby	.15	.07
❑ 153	Ed Sprague	.15	.07
❑ 154	Mike Hampton	.25	.11
❑ 155	Carlos Perez	.15	.07
❑ 156	Ray Lankford	.15	.07
❑ 157	Bobby Bonilla	.25	.11
❑ 158	Bill Mueller	.15	.07
❑ 159	Jeffrey Hammonds	.15	.07
❑ 160	Charles Nagy	.15	.07
❑ 161	Rich Loiselle RC	.15	.07
❑ 162	Al Leiter	.25	.11
❑ 163	Larry Walker	.40	.18
❑ 164	Chris Hoiles	.15	.07
❑ 165	Jeff Montgomery	.15	.07
❑ 166	Francisco Cordova	.15	.07
❑ 167	James Baldwin	.15	.07
❑ 168	Mark McLemore	.15	.07
❑ 169	Kevin Appier	.25	.11
❑ 170	Jamey Wright	.15	.07
❑ 171	Nomar Garciaparra	1.50	.70
❑ 172	Matt Franco	.15	.07
❑ 173	Armando Benitez	.15	.07
❑ 174	Jeromy Burnitz	.25	.11
❑ 175	Ismael Valdes	.15	.07
❑ 176	Lance Johnson	.15	.07
❑ 177	Paul Sorrento	.15	.07
❑ 178	Rondell White	.25	.11
❑ 179	Kevin Elster	.15	.07
❑ 180	Jason Giambi	.60	.25
❑ 181	Carlos Baerga	.15	.07
❑ 182	Russ Davis	.15	.07
❑ 183	Ryan McGuire	.15	.07
❑ 184	Eric Young	.15	.07
❑ 185	Ron Gant	.25	.11
❑ 186	Manny Alexander	.15	.07
❑ 187	Scott Karl	.15	.07
❑ 188	Brady Anderson	.25	.11
❑ 189	Randall Simon	.15	.07
❑ 190	Tim Belcher	.15	.07
❑ 191	Jaret Wright	.15	.07
❑ 192	Dante Bichette	.25	.11
❑ 193	John Valentin	.15	.07
❑ 194	Darren Bragg	.15	.07
❑ 195	Mike Sweeney	.25	.11
❑ 196	Craig Counsell	.15	.07
❑ 197	Jaime Navarro	.15	.07
❑ 198	Todd Dunn	.15	.07
❑ 199	Ken Griffey Jr.	2.00	.90
❑ 200	Juan Gonzalez	.60	.25
❑ 201	Billy Wagner	.15	.07
❑ 202	Tino Martinez	.25	.11
❑ 203	Mark McGwire	2.50	1.10
❑ 204	Jeff D'Amico	.15	.07
❑ 205	Rico Brogna	.15	.07
❑ 206	Todd Hollandsworth	.15	.07
❑ 207	Chad Curtis	.15	.07
❑ 208	Tom Goodwin	.15	.07
❑ 209	Neifi Perez	.15	.07
❑ 210	Derek Bell	.15	.07
❑ 211	Quilvio Veras	.15	.07
❑ 212	Greg Vaughn	.25	.11
❑ 213	Kirk Rueter	.15	.07
❑ 214	Arthur Rhodes	.15	.07
❑ 215	Cal Eldred	.15	.07
❑ 216	Bill Taylor	.15	.07
❑ 217	Todd Greene	.15	.07
❑ 218	Mario Valdez	.15	.07
❑ 219	Ricky Bottalico	.15	.07
❑ 220	Frank Rodriguez	.15	.07
❑ 221	Rich Becker	.15	.07
❑ 222	Roberto Duran RC	.25	.11
❑ 223	Ivan Rodriguez	.60	.25
❑ 224	Mike Jackson	.15	.07
❑ 225	Deion Sanders	.25	.11
❑ 226	Tony Womack	.15	.07
❑ 227	Mark Kotsay	.25	.11
❑ 228	Steve Trachsel	.15	.07
❑ 229	Ryan Klesko	.25	.11
❑ 230	Ken Cloude	.15	.07
❑ 231	Luis Gonzalez	.60	.25
❑ 232	Gary Gaetti	.25	.11
❑ 233	Michael Tucker	.15	.07

	#	Player	MINT	NRMT
❑	234	Shawn Green	.60	.25
❑	235	Ariel Prieto	.15	.07
❑	236	Kirt Manwaring	.15	.07
❑	237	Omar Vizquel	.25	.11
❑	238	Matt Beech	.15	.07
❑	239	Justin Thompson	.15	.07
❑	240	Bret Boone	.25	.11
❑	241	Derek Jeter	2.50	1.10
❑	242	Ken Caminiti	.25	.11
❑	243	Jose Offerman	.15	.07
❑	244	Kevin Tapani	.15	.07
❑	245	Jason Kendall	.25	.11
❑	246	Jose Guillen	.15	.07
❑	247	Mike Bordick	.15	.07
❑	248	Dustin Hermanson	.15	.07
❑	249	Darrin Fletcher	.15	.07
❑	250	Dave Hollins	.15	.07
❑	251	Ramon Martinez	.15	.07
❑	252	Hideki Irabu	.15	.07
❑	253	Mark Grace	.60	.25
❑	254	Jason Isringhausen	.15	.07
❑	255	Jose Cruz Jr.	.25	.11
❑	256	Brian Johnson	.15	.07
❑	257	Brad Ausmus	.15	.07
❑	258	Andruw Jones	.60	.25
❑	259	Doug Jones	.15	.07
❑	260	Jeff Shaw	.15	.07
❑	261	Chuck Finley	.25	.11
❑	262	Gary Sheffield	.25	.11
❑	263	David Segui	.15	.07
❑	264	John Smiley	.15	.07
❑	265	Tim Salmon	.25	.11
❑	266	J.T. Snow	.25	.11
❑	267	Alex Fernandez	.15	.07
❑	268	Matt Stairs	.15	.07
❑	269	B.J. Surhoff	.25	.11
❑	270	Keith Foulke	.15	.07
❑	271	Edgar Martinez	.40	.18
❑	272	Shannon Stewart	.25	.11
❑	273	Eduardo Perez	.15	.07
❑	274	Wally Joyner	.25	.11
❑	275	Kevin Young	.25	.11
❑	276	Eli Marrero	.15	.07
❑	277	Brad Radke	.25	.11
❑	278	Jamie Moyer	.15	.07
❑	279	Joe Girardi	.15	.07
❑	280	Troy O'Leary	.15	.07
❑	281	Jeff Frye	.15	.07
❑	282	Jose Offerman	.15	.07
❑	283	Scott Erickson	.15	.07
❑	284	Sean Berry	.15	.07
❑	285	Shigetoshi Hasegawa	.25	.11
❑	286	Felix Heredia	.15	.07
❑	287	Willie McGee	.25	.11
❑	288	Alex Rodriguez	1.50	.70
❑	289	Ugueth Urbina	.15	.07
❑	290	Jon Lieber	.15	.07
❑	291	Fernando Tatis	.15	.07
❑	292	Chris Stynes	.15	.07
❑	293	Bernard Gilkey	.15	.07
❑	294	Joey Hamilton	.15	.07
❑	295	Matt Karchner	.15	.07
❑	296	Paul Wilson	.15	.07
❑	297	Damion Easley	.15	.07
❑	298	Kevin Millwood RC	.60	.25
❑	299	Ellis Burks	.25	.11
❑	300	Jerry DiPoto	.15	.07
❑	301	Jermaine Dye	.25	.11
❑	302	Travis Lee	.25	.11
❑	303	Ron Coomer	.15	.07
❑	304	Matt Williams	.40	.18
❑	305	Bobby Higginson	.25	.11
❑	306	Jorge Fabregas	.15	.07
❑	307	Jon Nunnally	.15	.07
❑	308	Jay Bell	.25	.11
❑	309	Jason Schmidt	.15	.07
❑	310	Andy Benes	.15	.07
❑	311	Sterling Hitchcock	.15	.07
❑	312	Jeff Suppan	.15	.07
❑	313	Shane Reynolds	.15	.07
❑	314	Willie Blair	.15	.07
❑	315	Scott Rolen	.60	.25
❑	316	Wilson Alvarez	.15	.07
❑	317	David Justice	.25	.11
❑	318	Fred McGriff	.40	.18
❑	319	Bobby Jones	.15	.07
❑	320	Wade Boggs	.60	.25
❑	321	Tim Wakefield	.15	.07
❑	322	Tony Saunders	.15	.07
❑	323	David Cone	.25	.11
❑	324	Roberto Hernandez	.15	.07
❑	325	Jose Canseco	.60	.25
❑	326	Kevin Stocker	.15	.07
❑	327	Gerald Williams	.15	.07
❑	328	Quinton McCracken	.15	.07
❑	329	Mark Gardner	.15	.07
❑	330	Ben Grieve	.25	.11
❑	331	Kevin Brown	.40	.18
❑	332	Mike Lowell	.60	.25
❑	333	Jed Hansen	.15	.07
❑	334	Abraham Nunez	.15	.07
❑	335	John Thomson	.15	.07
❑	336	Masato Yoshii RC	.50	.23
❑	337	Mike Piazza	1.50	.70
❑	338	Brad Fullmer	.25	.11
❑	339	Ray Durham	.25	.11
❑	340	Kerry Wood	.60	.25
❑	341	Kevin Polcovich	.15	.07
❑	342	Russ Johnson	.15	.07
❑	343	Darryl Hamilton	.15	.07
❑	344	David Ortiz	.25	.11
❑	345	Kevin Orie	.15	.07
❑	346	Mike Caruso	.15	.07
❑	347	Juan Guzman	.15	.07
❑	348	Ruben Rivera	.15	.07
❑	349	Rick Aguilera	.15	.07
❑	350	Bobby Estalella	.15	.07
❑	351	Bobby Witt	.15	.07
❑	352	Paul Konerko	.25	.11
❑	353	Matt Morris	.25	.11
❑	354	Carl Pavano	.15	.07
❑	355	Todd Zeile	.25	.11
❑	356	Kevin Brown TR	.40	.18
❑	357	Alex Gonzalez	.15	.07
❑	358	Chuck Knoblauch TR	.25	.11
❑	359	Joey Cora	.15	.07
❑	360	Mike Lansing TR	.15	.07
❑	361	Adrian Beltre	.25	.11
❑	362	Dennis Eckersley TR	.25	.11
❑	363	A.J. Hinch	.15	.07
❑	364	Kenny Lofton TR	.25	.11
❑	365	Alex Gonzalez	.15	.07
❑	366	Henry Rodriguez TR	.15	.07
❑	367	Mike Stoner RC	.15	.07
❑	368	Darryl Kile TR	.25	.11
❑	369	Kevin McGlinchy	.15	.07
❑	370	Walt Weiss TR	.15	.07
❑	371	Kris Benson	.25	.11
❑	372	Cecil Fielder TR	.25	.11
❑	373	Dermal Brown	.15	.07
❑	374	Rod Beck TR	.15	.07
❑	375	Eric Milton	.25	.11
❑	376	Travis Fryman TR	.25	.11
❑	377	Preston Wilson	.25	.11
❑	378	Chili Davis TR	.25	.11
❑	379	Travis Lee	.25	.11
❑	380	Jim Leyritz TR	.15	.07
❑	381	Vernon Wells	.40	.18
❑	382	Joe Carter TR	.25	.11
❑	383	J.J. Davis	.25	.11
❑	384	Marquis Grissom TR	.15	.07
❑	385	Mike Cuddyer RC	1.00	.45
❑	386	Rickey Henderson TR	1.25	.55
❑	387	Chris Enochs RC	.25	.11
❑	388	Andres Galarraga TR	.40	.18
❑	389	Jason Dellaero	.15	.07
❑	390	Robb Nen TR	.15	.07
❑	391	Mark Mangum	.15	.07
❑	392	Jeff Blauser TR	.15	.07
❑	393	Adam Kennedy	.15	.07
❑	394	Bob Abreu TR	.25	.11
❑	395	Jack Cust RC	1.25	.55
❑	396	Jose Vizcaino TR	.15	.07
❑	397	Jon Garland	.15	.07
❑	398	Pedro Martinez TR	.75	.35
❑	399	Aaron Akin	.15	.07
❑	400	Jeff Conine TR	.15	.07
❑	NNO	Cal Ripken Sound Chip 1	15.00	6.75
❑	NNO	Cal Ripken Sound Chip 2	15.00	6.75

1999 Stadium Club

	MINT	NRMT
COMPLETE SET (355)	125.00	55.00
COMPLETE SERIES 1 (170)	65.00	29.00
COMP.SER.1 w/o SP's (150)	25.00	11.00
COMPLETE SERIES 2 (185)	60.00	27.00
COMP.SER.2 w/o SP's (165)	25.00	11.00
COMMON CARD (1-140/161-170)	.15	.07
COMMON CARD (171-335)	.15	.07
COMM.SP (141-160/336-355)	1.00	.45

	#	Player	MINT	NRMT
❑	1	Alex Rodriguez	1.50	.70
❑	2	Chipper Jones	1.25	.55
❑	3	Rusty Greer	.25	.11
❑	4	Jim Edmonds	.40	.18
❑	5	Ron Gant	.25	.11
❑	6	Kevin Polcovich	.15	.07
❑	7	Darryl Strawberry	.25	.11
❑	8	Bill Mueller	.15	.07
❑	9	Vinny Castilla	.25	.11
❑	10	Wade Boggs	.60	.25
❑	11	Jose Lima	.15	.07
❑	12	Darren Dreifort	.15	.07
❑	13	Jay Bell	.25	.11
❑	14	Ben Grieve	.25	.11
❑	15	Shawn Green	.60	.25
❑	16	Andres Galarraga	.40	.18
❑	17	Bartolo Colon	.25	.11
❑	18	Francisco Cordova	.15	.07
❑	19	Paul O'Neill	.60	.25
❑	20	Trevor Hoffman	.25	.11
❑	21	Darren Oliver	.15	.07
❑	22	John Franco	.25	.11
❑	23	Eli Marrero	.15	.07
❑	24	Roberto Hernandez	.15	.07
❑	25	Craig Biggio	.40	.18
❑	26	Brad Fullmer	.25	.11
❑	27	Scott Erickson	.15	.07
❑	28	Tom Gordon	.15	.07
❑	29	Brian Hunter	.15	.07
❑	30	Raul Mondesi	.25	.11
❑	31	Rick Reed	.15	.07
❑	32	Jose Canseco	.60	.25
❑	33	Robb Nen	.15	.07
❑	34	Turner Ward	.15	.07
❑	35	Orlando Hernandez	.25	.11
❑	36	Jeff Shaw	.15	.07
❑	37	Matt Lawton	.25	.11
❑	38	David Wells	.25	.11
❑	39	Bob Abreu	.25	.11
❑	40	Jeromy Burnitz	.25	.11
❑	41	Deivi Cruz	.15	.07
❑	42	Derek Bell	.15	.07
❑	43	Rico Brogna	.15	.07
❑	44	Dmitri Young	.25	.11
❑	45	Chuck Knoblauch	.25	.11
❑	46	Johnny Damon	.25	.11
❑	47	Brian Meadows	.15	.07
❑	48	Jeremi Gonzalez	.15	.07
❑	49	Gary DiSarcina	.15	.07
❑	50	Frank Thomas	.75	.35
❑	51	F.P. Santangelo	.15	.07
❑	52	Tom Candiotti	.15	.07
❑	53	Shane Reynolds	.15	.07
❑	54	Rod Beck	.15	.07
❑	55	Rey Ordonez	.15	.07
❑	56	Todd Helton	.75	.35

❑	57	Mickey Morandini	.15	.07
❑	58	Jorge Posada	.25	.11
❑	59	Mike Mussina	.60	.25
❑	60	Al Leiter	.25	.11
❑	61	David Segui	.15	.07
❑	62	Brian McRae	.15	.07
❑	63	Fred McGriff	.40	.18
❑	64	Brett Tomko	.15	.07
❑	65	Derek Jeter	2.50	1.10
❑	66	Sammy Sosa	1.25	.55
❑	67	Kenny Rogers	.15	.07
❑	68	Dave Nilsson	.15	.07
❑	69	Eric Young	.15	.07
❑	70	Mark McGwire	2.50	1.10
❑	71	Kenny Lofton	.25	.11
❑	72	Tom Glavine	.60	.25
❑	73	Joey Hamilton	.15	.07
❑	74	John Valentin	.15	.07
❑	75	Mariano Rivera	.25	.11
❑	76	Ray Durham	.25	.11
❑	77	Tony Clark	.25	.11
❑	78	Livan Hernandez	.15	.07
❑	79	Rickey Henderson	1.25	.55
❑	80	Vladimir Guerrero	.75	.35
❑	81	J.T. Snow	.25	.11
❑	82	Juan Guzman	.15	.07
❑	83	Darryl Hamilton	.15	.07
❑	84	Matt Anderson	.15	.07
❑	85	Travis Lee	.15	.07
❑	86	Joe Randa	.15	.07
❑	87	Dave Dellucci	.15	.07
❑	88	Moises Alou	.25	.11
❑	89	Alex Gonzalez	.15	.07
❑	90	Tony Womack	.15	.07
❑	91	Neifi Perez	.15	.07
❑	92	Travis Fryman	.25	.11
❑	93	Masato Yoshii	.25	.11
❑	94	Woody Williams	.15	.07
❑	95	Ray Lankford	.15	.07
❑	96	Roger Clemens	1.50	.70
❑	97	Dustin Hermanson	.15	.07
❑	98	Joe Carter	.25	.11
❑	99	Jason Schmidt	.15	.07
❑	100	Greg Maddux	1.50	.70
❑	101	Kevin Tapani	.15	.07
❑	102	Charles Johnson	.25	.11
❑	103	Derrek Lee	.25	.11
❑	104	Pete Harnisch	.15	.07
❑	105	Dante Bichette	.25	.11
❑	106	Scott Brosius	.25	.11
❑	107	Mike Caruso	.15	.07
❑	108	Eddie Taubensee	.15	.07
❑	109	Jeff Fassero	.15	.07
❑	110	Marquis Grissom	.15	.07
❑	111	Jose Hernandez	.15	.07
❑	112	Chan Ho Park	.25	.11
❑	113	Wally Joyner	.25	.11
❑	114	Bobby Estalella	.15	.07
❑	115	Pedro Martinez	.75	.35
❑	116	Shawn Estes	.25	.11
❑	117	Walt Weiss	.15	.07
❑	118	John Mabry	.15	.07
❑	119	Brian Johnson	.15	.07
❑	120	Jim Thome	.60	.25
❑	121	Bill Spiers	.15	.07
❑	122	John Olerud	.25	.11
❑	123	Jeff King	.15	.07
❑	124	Tim Belcher	.15	.07
❑	125	John Wetteland	.25	.11
❑	126	Tony Gwynn	1.25	.55
❑	127	Brady Anderson	.25	.11
❑	128	Randy Winn	.15	.07
❑	129	Andy Fox	.15	.07
❑	130	Eric Karros	.25	.11
❑	131	Kevin Millwood	.15	.07
❑	132	Andy Benes	.15	.07
❑	133	Andy Ashby	.15	.07
❑	134	Ron Coomer	.15	.07
❑	135	Juan Gonzalez	.60	.25
❑	136	Randy Johnson	.75	.35
❑	137	Aaron Sele	.25	.11
❑	138	Edgardo Alfonzo	.25	.11
❑	139	B.J. Surhoff	.25	.11
❑	140	Jose Vizcaino	.15	.07
❑	141	Chad Moeller SP RC	1.00	.45
❑	142	Mike Zywica SP RC	1.00	.45
❑	143	Angel Pena SP	1.00	.45
❑	144	Nick Johnson SP RC	5.00	2.20
❑	145	G. Chiaramonte SP RC	1.00	.45
❑	146	Kit Pellow SP RC	3.00	1.35
❑	147	C.Andrews SP RC	1.00	.45
❑	148	Jerry Hairston Jr. SP	1.25	.55
❑	149	Jason Tyner SP RC	1.00	.45
❑	150	Chip Ambres SP RC	1.25	.55
❑	151	Pat Burrell SP RC	5.00	2.20
❑	152	Josh McKinley SP RC	1.00	.45
❑	153	Choo Freeman SP RC	1.25	.55
❑	154	Rick Elder SP RC	2.00	.90
❑	155	Eric Valent SP RC	2.00	.90
❑	156	J.Winchester SP RC	1.00	.45
❑	157	Mike Nannini SP RC	1.50	.70
❑	158	Mamon Tucker SP RC	1.00	.45
❑	159	Nate Bump SP RC	1.00	.45
❑	160	Andy Brown SP RC	1.25	.55
❑	161	Troy Glaus	.60	.25
❑	162	Adrian Beltre	.25	.11
❑	163	Mitch Meluskey	.15	.07
❑	164	Alex Gonzalez	.15	.07
❑	165	George Lombard	.15	.07
❑	166	Eric Chavez	.25	.11
❑	167	Ruben Mateo	.25	.11
❑	168	Calvin Pickering	.15	.07
❑	169	Gabe Kapler	.25	.11
❑	170	Bruce Chen	.15	.07
❑	171	Darin Erstad	.60	.25
❑	172	Sandy Alomar Jr.	.25	.11
❑	173	Miguel Cairo	.15	.07
❑	174	Jason Kendall	.25	.11
❑	175	Cal Ripken	2.50	1.10
❑	176	Darryl Kile	.25	.11
❑	177	David Cone	.25	.11
❑	178	Mike Sweeney	.25	.11
❑	179	Royce Clayton	.15	.07
❑	180	Curt Schilling	.60	.25
❑	181	Barry Larkin	.60	.25
❑	182	Eric Milton	.25	.11
❑	183	Ellis Burks	.25	.11
❑	184	A.J. Hinch	.15	.07
❑	185	Garret Anderson	.25	.11
❑	186	Sean Bergman	.15	.07
❑	187	Shannon Stewart	.25	.11
❑	188	Bernard Gilkey	.15	.07
❑	189	Jeff Blauser	.15	.07
❑	190	Andruw Jones	.60	.25
❑	191	Omar Daal	.15	.07
❑	192	Jeff Kent	.40	.18
❑	193	Mark Kotsay	.15	.07
❑	194	Dave Burba	.15	.07
❑	195	Bobby Higginson	.25	.11
❑	196	Hideki Irabu	.15	.07
❑	197	Jamie Moyer	.15	.07
❑	198	Doug Glanville	.15	.07
❑	199	Quinton McCracken	.15	.07
❑	200	Ken Griffey Jr.	2.00	.90
❑	201	Mike Lieberthal	.25	.11
❑	202	Carl Everett	.25	.11
❑	203	Omar Vizquel	.25	.11
❑	204	Mike Lansing	.15	.07
❑	205	Manny Ramirez	.75	.35
❑	206	Ryan Klesko	.25	.11
❑	207	Jeff Montgomery	.15	.07
❑	208	Chad Curtis	.15	.07
❑	209	Rick Helling	.15	.07
❑	210	Justin Thompson	.15	.07
❑	211	Tom Goodwin	.15	.07
❑	212	Todd Dunwoody	.15	.07
❑	213	Kevin Young	.25	.11
❑	214	Tony Saunders	.15	.07
❑	215	Gary Sheffield	.25	.11
❑	216	Jaret Wright	.15	.07
❑	217	Quilvio Veras	.15	.07
❑	218	Marty Cordova	.15	.07
❑	219	Tino Martinez	.25	.11
❑	220	Scott Rolen	.60	.25
❑	221	Fernando Tatis	.15	.07
❑	222	Damion Easley	.15	.07
❑	223	Aramis Ramirez	.25	.11
❑	224	Brad Radke	.25	.11
❑	225	Nomar Garciaparra	1.50	.70
❑	226	Magglio Ordonez	.40	.18
❑	227	Andy Pettitte	.25	.11
❑	228	David Ortiz	.25	.11
❑	229	Todd Jones	.15	.07
❑	230	Larry Walker	.40	.18
❑	231	Tim Wakefield	.15	.07
❑	232	Jose Guillen	.15	.07
❑	233	Gregg Olson	.15	.07
❑	234	Ricky Gutierrez	.15	.07
❑	235	Todd Walker	.15	.07
❑	236	Abraham Nunez	.15	.07
❑	237	Sean Casey	.40	.18
❑	238	Greg Norton	.15	.07
❑	239	Bret Saberhagen	.25	.11
❑	240	Bernie Williams	.60	.25
❑	241	Tim Salmon	.25	.11
❑	242	Jason Giambi	.60	.25
❑	243	Fernando Vina	.15	.07
❑	244	Darrin Fletcher	.15	.07
❑	245	Greg Vaughn	.25	.11
❑	246	Dennis Reyes	.15	.07
❑	247	Hideo Nomo	.60	.25
❑	248	Kevin Stocker	.15	.07
❑	249	Mike Hampton	.25	.11
❑	250	Kerry Wood	.60	.25
❑	251	Ismael Valdes	.15	.07
❑	252	Pat Hentgen	.15	.07
❑	253	Scott Spiezio	.15	.07
❑	254	Chuck Finley	.25	.11
❑	255	Troy Glaus	.60	.25
❑	256	Bobby Jones	.15	.07
❑	257	Wayne Gomes	.15	.07
❑	258	Rondell White	.25	.11
❑	259	Todd Zeile	.25	.11
❑	260	Matt Williams	.40	.18
❑	261	Henry Rodriguez	.15	.07
❑	262	Matt Stairs	.15	.07
❑	263	Jose Valentin	.15	.07
❑	264	David Justice	.25	.11
❑	265	Javy Lopez	.25	.11
❑	266	Matt Morris	.25	.11
❑	267	Steve Trachsel	.15	.07
❑	268	Edgar Martinez	.40	.18
❑	269	Al Martin	.15	.07
❑	270	Ivan Rodriguez	.60	.25
❑	271	Carlos Delgado	.60	.25
❑	272	Mark Grace	.60	.25
❑	273	Ugueth Urbina	.15	.07
❑	274	Jay Buhner	.25	.11
❑	275	Mike Piazza	1.50	.70
❑	276	Rick Aguilera	.15	.07
❑	277	Javier Valentin	.15	.07
❑	278	Brian Anderson	.15	.07
❑	279	Cliff Floyd	.25	.11
❑	280	Barry Bonds	1.50	.70
❑	281	Troy O'Leary	.15	.07
❑	282	Seth Greisinger	.15	.07
❑	283	Mark Grudzielanek	.15	.07
❑	284	Jose Cruz Jr.	.25	.11
❑	285	Jeff Bagwell	.75	.35
❑	286	John Smoltz	.25	.11
❑	287	Jeff Cirillo	.25	.11
❑	288	Richie Sexson	.25	.11
❑	289	Charles Nagy	.15	.07
❑	290	Pedro Martinez	.75	.35
❑	291	Juan Encarnacion	.25	.11
❑	292	Phil Nevin	.25	.11
❑	293	Terry Steinbach	.15	.07
❑	294	Miguel Tejada	.25	.11
❑	295	Dan Wilson	.15	.07
❑	296	Chris Peters	.15	.07
❑	297	Brian Moehler	.15	.07
❑	298	Jason Christiansen	.15	.07
❑	299	Kelly Stinnett	.15	.07
❑	300	Dwight Gooden	.25	.11
❑	301	Randy Velarde	.15	.07
❑	302	Kirt Manwaring	.15	.07
❑	303	Jeff Abbott	.15	.07
❑	304	Dave Hollins	.15	.07
❑	305	Kerry Ligtenberg	.15	.07
❑	306	Aaron Boone	.15	.07
❑	307	Carlos Hernandez	.15	.07
❑	308	Mike Difelice	.15	.07
❑	309	Brian Meadows	.15	.07
❑	310	Tim Bogar	.15	.07
❑	311	Greg Vaughn TR	.25	.11
❑	312	Brant Brown TR	.15	.07
❑	313	Steve Finley TR	.25	.11
❑	314	Bret Boone TR	.25	.11

Card		
❑ 315 Albert Belle TR	.25	.11
❑ 316 Robin Ventura TR	.25	.11
❑ 317 Eric Davis TR	.25	.11
❑ 318 Todd Hundley TR	.15	.07
❑ 319 Roger Clemens TR	.75	.35
❑ 320 Kevin Brown TR	.40	.18
❑ 321 Jose Offerman TR	.15	.07
❑ 322 Brian Jordan TR	.25	.11
❑ 323 Mike Cameron TR	.25	.11
❑ 324 Bobby Bonilla TR	.25	.11
❑ 325 Roberto Alomar TR	.60	.25
❑ 326 Ken Caminiti TR	.25	.11
❑ 327 Todd Stottlemyre TR	.15	.07
❑ 328 Randy Johnson TR	.60	.25
❑ 329 Luis Gonzalez TR	.60	.25
❑ 330 Rafael Palmeiro TR	.60	.25
❑ 331 Devon White TR	.15	.07
❑ 332 Will Clark TR	.60	.25
❑ 333 Dean Palmer TR	.25	.11
❑ 334 Gregg Jefferies TR	.15	.07
❑ 335 Mo Vaughn TR	.25	.11
❑ 336 Brad Lidge SP RC	1.00	.45
❑ 337 Chris George SP RC	2.00	.90
❑ 338 Austin Kearns SP RC	6.00	2.70
❑ 339 Matt Belisle SP RC	1.25	.55
❑ 340 Nate Cornejo SP RC	3.00	1.35
❑ 341 Matt Holliday SP RC	1.50	.70
❑ 342 J.M. Gold SP RC	1.00	.45
❑ 343 Matt Roney SP RC	1.00	.45
❑ 344 Seth Etherton SP RC	1.00	.45
❑ 345 Adam Everett SP RC	1.25	.55
❑ 346 Marlon Anderson SP	1.00	.45
❑ 347 Ron Belliard SP	1.00	.45
❑ 348 F.Seguignol SP	1.00	.45
❑ 349 Michael Barrett SP	1.00	.45
❑ 350 Dernell Stenson SP	1.00	.45
❑ 351 Ryan Anderson SP	1.25	.55
❑ 352 Ramon Hernandez SP	1.00	.45
❑ 353 Jeremy Giambi SP	1.00	.45
❑ 354 Ricky Ledee SP	1.00	.45
❑ 355 Carlos Lee SP	1.25	.55

2000 Stadium Club

	MINT	NRMT
COMPLETE SET (250)	250.00	110.00
COMP.SET w/o SP'S (200)	30.00	13.50
COMMON CARD (1-200)	.15	.07
COMMON SP (201-250)	3.00	1.35

Card		
❑ 1 Nomar Garciaparra	1.50	.70
❑ 2 Brian Jordan	.25	.11
❑ 3 Mark Grace	.60	.25
❑ 4 Jeromy Burnitz	.25	.11
❑ 5 Shane Reynolds	.15	.07
❑ 6 Alex Gonzalez	.15	.07
❑ 7 Jose Offerman	.15	.07
❑ 8 Orlando Hernandez	.25	.11
❑ 9 Mike Caruso	.15	.07
❑ 10 Tony Clark	.25	.11
❑ 11 Sean Casey	.40	.18
❑ 12 Johnny Damon	.25	.11
❑ 13 Dante Bichette	.25	.11
❑ 14 Kevin Young	.15	.07
❑ 15 Juan Gonzalez	.60	.25
❑ 16 Chipper Jones	1.25	.55
❑ 17 Quilvio Veras	.15	.07
❑ 18 Trevor Hoffman	.25	.11
❑ 19 Roger Cedeno	.15	.07
❑ 20 Ellis Burks	.25	.11
❑ 21 Richie Sexson	.25	.11
❑ 22 Gary Sheffield	.25	.11
❑ 23 Delino DeShields	.15	.07
❑ 24 Wade Boggs	.60	.25
❑ 25 Ray Lankford	.15	.07
❑ 26 Kevin Appier	.15	.07
❑ 27 Roy Halladay	.15	.07
❑ 28 Harold Baines	.25	.11
❑ 29 Todd Zeile	.25	.11
❑ 30 Barry Larkin	.60	.25
❑ 31 Ron Coomer	.15	.07
❑ 32 Jorge Posada	.25	.11
❑ 33 Magglio Ordonez	.25	.11
❑ 34 Brian Giles	.25	.11
❑ 35 Jeff Kent	.40	.18
❑ 36 Henry Rodriguez	.15	.07
❑ 37 Fred McGriff	.40	.18
❑ 38 Shawn Green	.60	.25
❑ 39 Derek Bell	.15	.07
❑ 40 Ben Grieve	.25	.11
❑ 41 Dave Nilsson	.15	.07
❑ 42 Mo Vaughn	.25	.11
❑ 43 Rondell White	.25	.11
❑ 44 Doug Glanville	.15	.07
❑ 45 Paul O'Neill	.60	.25
❑ 46 Carlos Lee	.25	.11
❑ 47 Vinny Castilla	.25	.11
❑ 48 Mike Sweeney	.25	.11
❑ 49 Rico Brogna	.15	.07
❑ 50 Alex Rodriguez	1.50	.70
❑ 51 Luis Castillo	.15	.07
❑ 52 Kevin Brown	.40	.18
❑ 53 Jose Vidro	.25	.11
❑ 54 John Smoltz	.25	.11
❑ 55 Garret Anderson	.25	.11
❑ 56 Matt Stairs	.15	.07
❑ 57 Omar Vizquel	.25	.11
❑ 58 Tom Goodwin	.15	.07
❑ 59 Scott Brosius	.25	.11
❑ 60 Robin Ventura	.40	.18
❑ 61 B.J. Surhoff	.25	.11
❑ 62 Andy Ashby	.15	.07
❑ 63 Chris Widger	.15	.07
❑ 64 Tim Hudson	.60	.25
❑ 65 Javy Lopez	.25	.11
❑ 66 Tim Salmon	.25	.11
❑ 67 Warren Morris	.15	.07
❑ 68 John Wetteland	.25	.11
❑ 69 Gabe Kapler	.25	.11
❑ 70 Bernie Williams	.60	.25
❑ 71 Rickey Henderson	1.25	.55
❑ 72 Andruw Jones	.60	.25
❑ 73 Eric Young	.15	.07
❑ 74 Bob Abreu	.25	.11
❑ 75 David Cone	.25	.11
❑ 76 Rusty Greer	.25	.11
❑ 77 Ron Belliard	.15	.07
❑ 78 Troy Glaus	.60	.25
❑ 79 Mike Hampton	.25	.11
❑ 80 Miguel Tejada	.25	.11
❑ 81 Jeff Cirillo	.25	.11
❑ 82 Todd Hundley	.15	.07
❑ 83 Roberto Alomar	.75	.35
❑ 84 Charles Johnson	.25	.11
❑ 85 Rafael Palmeiro	.60	.25
❑ 86 Doug Mientkiewicz	.40	.18
❑ 87 Mariano Rivera	.25	.11
❑ 88 Neifi Perez	.15	.07
❑ 89 Jermaine Dye	.25	.11
❑ 90 Ivan Rodriguez	.60	.25
❑ 91 Jay Buhner	.25	.11
❑ 92 Pokey Reese	.15	.07
❑ 93 John Olerud	.25	.11
❑ 94 Brady Anderson	.25	.11
❑ 95 Manny Ramirez	.75	.35
❑ 96 Keith Osik RC	.15	.07
❑ 97 Mickey Morandini	.15	.07
❑ 98 Matt Williams	.40	.18
❑ 99 Eric Karros	.25	.11
❑ 100 Ken Griffey Jr.	2.00	.90
❑ 101 Bret Boone	.25	.11
❑ 102 Ryan Klesko	.25	.11
❑ 103 Craig Biggio	.40	.18
❑ 104 John Jaha	.15	.07
❑ 105 Vladimir Guerrero	.75	.35
❑ 106 Devon White	.15	.07
❑ 107 Tony Womack	.15	.07
❑ 108 Marvin Benard	.15	.07
❑ 109 Kenny Lofton	.25	.11
❑ 110 Preston Wilson	.25	.11
❑ 111 Al Leiter	.15	.07
❑ 112 Reggie Sanders	.15	.07
❑ 113 Scott Williamson	.15	.07
❑ 114 Deivi Cruz	.15	.07
❑ 115 Carlos Beltran	.25	.11
❑ 116 Ray Durham	.25	.11
❑ 117 Ricky Ledee	.15	.07
❑ 118 Torii Hunter	.25	.11
❑ 119 John Valentin	.15	.07
❑ 120 Scott Rolen	.60	.25
❑ 121 Jason Kendall	.25	.11
❑ 122 Dave Martinez	.15	.07
❑ 123 Jim Thome	.60	.25
❑ 124 David Bell	.15	.07
❑ 125 Jose Canseco	.60	.25
❑ 126 Jose Lima	.15	.07
❑ 127 Carl Everett	.25	.11
❑ 128 Kevin Millwood	.15	.07
❑ 129 Bill Spiers	.15	.07
❑ 130 Omar Daal	.15	.07
❑ 131 Miguel Cairo	.15	.07
❑ 132 Mark Grudzielanek	.15	.07
❑ 133 David Justice	.25	.11
❑ 134 Russ Ortiz	.25	.11
❑ 135 Mike Piazza	1.50	.70
❑ 136 Brian Meadows	.15	.07
❑ 137 Tony Gwynn	1.25	.55
❑ 138 Cal Ripken	2.50	1.10
❑ 139 Kris Benson	.25	.11
❑ 140 Larry Walker	.40	.18
❑ 141 Cristian Guzman	.25	.11
❑ 142 Tino Martinez	.25	.11
❑ 143 Chris Singleton	.15	.07
❑ 144 Lee Stevens	.15	.07
❑ 145 Rey Ordonez	.15	.07
❑ 146 Russ Davis	.15	.07
❑ 147 J.T. Snow	.25	.11
❑ 148 Luis Gonzalez	.60	.25
❑ 149 Marquis Grissom	.15	.07
❑ 150 Greg Maddux	1.50	.70
❑ 151 Fernando Tatis	.15	.07
❑ 152 Jason Giambi	.60	.25
❑ 153 Carlos Delgado	.60	.25
❑ 154 Joe McEwing	.15	.07
❑ 155 Raul Mondesi	.25	.11
❑ 156 Rich Aurilia	.25	.11
❑ 157 Alex Fernandez	.15	.07
❑ 158 Albert Belle	.25	.11
❑ 159 Pat Meares	.15	.07
❑ 160 Mike Lieberthal	.25	.11
❑ 161 Mike Cameron	.25	.11
❑ 162 Juan Encarnacion	.25	.11
❑ 163 Chuck Knoblauch	.25	.11
❑ 164 Pedro Martinez	.75	.35
❑ 165 Randy Johnson	.75	.35
❑ 166 Shannon Stewart	.25	.11
❑ 167 Jeff Bagwell	.75	.35
❑ 168 Edgar Renteria	.15	.07
❑ 169 Barry Bonds	1.50	.70
❑ 170 Steve Finley	.25	.11
❑ 171 Brian Hunter	.15	.07
❑ 172 Tom Glavine	.60	.25
❑ 173 Mark Kotsay	.15	.07
❑ 174 Tony Fernandez	.15	.07
❑ 175 Sammy Sosa	1.25	.55
❑ 176 Geoff Jenkins	.25	.11
❑ 177 Adrian Beltre	.25	.11
❑ 178 Jay Bell	.25	.11
❑ 179 Mike Bordick	.15	.07
❑ 180 Ed Sprague	.15	.07
❑ 181 Dave Roberts	.15	.07
❑ 182 Greg Vaughn	.25	.11
❑ 183 Brian Daubach	.25	.11
❑ 184 Damion Easley	.15	.07
❑ 185 Carlos Febles	.15	.07
❑ 186 Kevin Tapani	.15	.07
❑ 187 Frank Thomas	.75	.35
❑ 188 Roger Clemens	1.50	.70
❑ 189 Mike Benjamin	.15	.07
❑ 190 Curt Schilling	.60	.25

❑ 191 Edgardo Alfonzo .25 .11
❑ 192 Mike Mussina .60 .25
❑ 193 Todd Helton .75 .35
❑ 194 Todd Jones .15 .07
❑ 195 Dean Palmer .25 .11
❑ 196 John Flaherty .15 .07
❑ 197 Derek Jeter 2.50 1.10
❑ 198 Todd Walker .15 .07
❑ 199 Brad Ausmus .15 .07
❑ 200 Mark McGwire 2.50 1.10
❑ 201 Erubiel Durazo SP 3.00 1.35
❑ 202 Nick Johnson SP 5.00 2.20
❑ 203 Ruben Mateo SP 3.00 1.35
❑ 204 Lance Berkman SP 5.00 2.20
❑ 205 Pat Burrell SP 5.00 2.20
❑ 206 Pablo Ozuna SP 3.00 1.35
❑ 207 Roosevelt Brown SP 3.00 1.35
❑ 208 Alfonso Soriano SP 5.00 2.20
❑ 209 A.J. Burnett SP 3.00 1.35
❑ 210 Rafael Furcal SP 5.00 2.20
❑ 211 Scott Morgan SP 3.00 1.35
❑ 212 Adam Piatt SP 4.00 1.80
❑ 213 Dee Brown SP 3.00 1.35
❑ 214 Corey Patterson SP 5.00 2.20
❑ 215 Mickey Lopez SP 3.00 1.35
❑ 216 Rob Ryan SP 3.00 1.35
❑ 217 Sean Burroughs SP 5.00 2.20
❑ 218 Jack Cust SP 3.00 1.35
❑ 219 John Patterson SP 3.00 1.35
❑ 220 Kit Pellow SP 3.00 1.35
❑ 221 Chad Hermansen SP 3.00 1.35
❑ 222 Daryle Ward SP 3.00 1.35
❑ 223 Jayson Werth SP 3.00 1.35
❑ 224 Jason Standridge SP 3.00 1.35
❑ 225 Mark Mulder SP 5.00 2.20
❑ 226 Peter Bergeron SP 3.00 1.35
❑ 227 Willi Mo Pena SP 5.00 2.20
❑ 228 Aramis Ramirez SP 3.00 1.35
❑ 229 John Sneed SP RC 3.00 1.35
❑ 230 Wilton Veras SP 3.00 1.35
❑ 231 Josh Hamilton SP 6.00 2.70
❑ 232 Eric Munson SP 3.00 1.35
❑ 233 Bobby Bradley SP RC 5.00 2.20
❑ 234 Larry Bigbie SP RC 4.00 1.80
❑ 235 B.J. Garbe SP RC 6.00 2.70
❑ 236 Brett Myers SP RC 4.00 1.80
❑ 237 Jason Stumm SP RC 4.00 1.80
❑ 238 Corey Myers SP RC 3.00 1.35
❑ 239 R.Christianson SP RC 5.00 2.20
❑ 240 David Walling SP 3.00 1.35
❑ 241 Josh Girdley SP 3.00 1.35
❑ 242 Omar Ortiz SP 3.00 1.35
❑ 243 Jason Jennings SP 3.00 1.35
❑ 244 Kyle Snyder SP 3.00 1.35
❑ 245 Jay Gehrke SP 3.00 1.35
❑ 246 Mike Paradis SP 3.00 1.35
❑ 247 Chance Caple SP RC 3.00 1.35
❑ 248 B.Christensen SP RC 3.00 1.35
❑ 249 Brad Baker SP RC 5.00 2.20
❑ 250 R.Asadoorian SP RC 5.00 2.20

2001 Stadium Club

	MINT	NRMT
COMPLETE SET (200)	120.00	55.00
COMP.SET w/o SP's (175)	25.00	11.00
COMMON CARD (1-150)	.15	.07
COMMON SP (151-200)	3.00	1.35

❑ 1 Nomar Garciaparra 1.50 .70
❑ 2 Chipper Jones 1.25 .55
❑ 3 Jeff Bagwell .75 .35
❑ 4 Chad Kreuter .15 .07
❑ 5 Randy Johnson .75 .35
❑ 6 Mike Hampton .25 .11
❑ 7 Barry Larkin .60 .25
❑ 8 Bernie Williams .60 .25
❑ 9 Chris Singleton .15 .07
❑ 10 Larry Walker .40 .18
❑ 11 Brad Ausmus .15 .07
❑ 12 Ron Coomer .15 .07
❑ 13 Edgardo Alfonzo .25 .11
❑ 14 Delino DeShields .15 .07
❑ 15 Tony Gwynn 1.25 .55
❑ 16 Andruw Jones .60 .25
❑ 17 Raul Mondesi .25 .11
❑ 18 Troy Glaus .60 .25
❑ 19 Ben Grieve .25 .11
❑ 20 Sammy Sosa 1.25 .55
❑ 21 Fernando Vina .25 .11
❑ 22 Jeromy Burnitz .25 .11
❑ 23 Jay Bell .25 .11
❑ 24 Pete Harnisch .15 .07
❑ 25 Barry Bonds 1.50 .70
❑ 26 Eric Karros .25 .11
❑ 27 Alex Gonzalez .15 .07
❑ 28 Mike Lieberthal .25 .11
❑ 29 Juan Encarnacion .25 .11
❑ 30 Derek Jeter 2.50 1.10
❑ 31 Luis Sojo .15 .07
❑ 32 Eric Milton .25 .11
❑ 33 Aaron Boone .15 .07
❑ 34 Roberto Alomar .60 .25
❑ 35 John Olerud .25 .11
❑ 36 Orlando Cabrera .15 .07
❑ 37 Shawn Green .60 .25
❑ 38 Roger Cedeno .15 .07
❑ 39 Garret Anderson .25 .11
❑ 40 Jim Thome .60 .25
❑ 41 Gabe Kapler .25 .11
❑ 42 Mo Vaughn .25 .11
❑ 43 Sean Casey .40 .18
❑ 44 Preston Wilson .25 .11
❑ 45 Javy Lopez .25 .11
❑ 46 Ryan Klesko .25 .11
❑ 47 Ray Durham .25 .11
❑ 48 Dean Palmer .25 .11
❑ 49 Jorge Posada .25 .11
❑ 50 Alex Rodriguez 1.50 .70
❑ 51 Tom Glavine .60 .25
❑ 52 Ray Lankford .15 .07
❑ 53 Jose Canseco .60 .25
❑ 54 Tim Salmon .25 .11
❑ 55 Cal Ripken 2.50 1.10
❑ 56 Bob Abreu .25 .11
❑ 57 Robin Ventura .25 .11
❑ 58 Damion Easley .15 .07
❑ 59 Paul O'Neill .60 .25
❑ 60 Ivan Rodriguez .60 .25
❑ 61 Carl Everett .25 .11
❑ 62 Doug Glanville .15 .07
❑ 63 Jeff Kent .40 .18
❑ 64 Jay Buhner .25 .11
❑ 65 Cliff Floyd .25 .11
❑ 66 Rick Ankiel .40 .18
❑ 67 Mark Grace .60 .25
❑ 68 Brian Jordan .25 .11
❑ 69 Craig Biggio .40 .18
❑ 70 Carlos Delgado .60 .25
❑ 71 Brad Radke .25 .11
❑ 72 Greg Maddux 1.50 .70
❑ 73 Al Leiter .25 .11
❑ 74 Pokey Reese .15 .07
❑ 75 Todd Helton .75 .35
❑ 76 Mariano Rivera .25 .11
❑ 77 Shane Spencer .15 .07
❑ 78 Jason Kendall .25 .11
❑ 79 Chuck Knoblauch .25 .11
❑ 80 Scott Rolen .60 .25
❑ 81 Jose Offerman .15 .07
❑ 82 J.T. Snow .25 .11
❑ 83 Pat Meares .15 .07
❑ 84 Quilvio Veras .15 .07
❑ 85 Edgar Renteria .15 .07
❑ 86 Luis Matos .15 .07
❑ 87 Adrian Beltre .25 .11
❑ 88 Luis Gonzalez .60 .25
❑ 89 Rickey Henderson 1.25 .55
❑ 90 Brian Giles .25 .11
❑ 91 Carlos Febles .15 .07
❑ 92 Tino Martinez .25 .11
❑ 93 Magglio Ordonez .25 .11
❑ 94 Rafael Furcal .25 .11
❑ 95 Mike Mussina .60 .25
❑ 96 Gary Sheffield .25 .11
❑ 97 Kenny Lofton .25 .11
❑ 98 Fred McGriff .40 .18
❑ 99 Ken Caminiti .25 .11
❑ 100 Mark McGwire 2.50 1.10
❑ 101 Tom Goodwin .15 .07
❑ 102 Mark Grudzielanek .15 .07
❑ 103 Derek Bell .15 .07
❑ 104 Mike Lowell .25 .11
❑ 105 Jeff Cirillo .25 .11
❑ 106 Orlando Hernandez .25 .11
❑ 107 Jose Valentin .15 .07
❑ 108 Warren Morris .15 .07
❑ 109 Mike Williams .15 .07
❑ 110 Greg Vaughn .25 .11
❑ 111 Jose Vidro .25 .11
❑ 112 Omar Vizquel .25 .11
❑ 113 Vinny Castilla .25 .11
❑ 114 Gregg Jefferies .15 .07
❑ 115 Kevin Brown .25 .11
❑ 116 Shannon Stewart .25 .11
❑ 117 Marquis Grissom .15 .07
❑ 118 Manny Ramirez .75 .35
❑ 119 Albert Belle .25 .11
❑ 120 Bret Boone .25 .11
❑ 121 Johnny Damon .25 .11
❑ 122 Juan Gonzalez .60 .25
❑ 123 David Justice .25 .11
❑ 124 Jeffrey Hammonds .15 .07
❑ 125 Ken Griffey Jr. 2.00 .90
❑ 126 Mike Sweeney .25 .11
❑ 127 Tony Clark .25 .11
❑ 128 Todd Zeile .25 .11
❑ 129 Mark Johnson .15 .07
❑ 130 Matt Williams .40 .18
❑ 131 Geoff Jenkins .25 .11
❑ 132 Jason Giambi .60 .25
❑ 133 Steve Finley .25 .11
❑ 134 Derek Lee .25 .11
❑ 135 Royce Clayton .15 .07
❑ 136 Joe Randa .25 .11
❑ 137 Rafael Palmeiro .60 .25
❑ 138 Kevin Young .15 .07
❑ 139 Mike Redmond .15 .07
❑ 140 Vladimir Guerrero .75 .35
❑ 141 Greg Vaughn .25 .11
❑ 142 Jermaine Dye .25 .11
❑ 143 Roger Clemens 1.50 .70
❑ 144 Denny Hocking .15 .07
❑ 145 Frank Thomas .75 .35
❑ 146 Carlos Beltran .25 .11
❑ 147 Eric Young .15 .07
❑ 148 Pat Burrell .25 .11
❑ 149 Pedro Martinez .75 .35
❑ 150 Mike Piazza 1.50 .70
❑ 151 Adrian Gonzalez .75 .35
❑ 152 Adam Johnson .50 .23
❑ 153 Luis Montanez SP RC 8.00 3.60
❑ 154 Mike Stodolka .50 .23
❑ 155 Phil Dumatrait .50 .23
❑ 156 Sean Burnett SP 3.00 1.35
❑ 157 Dominic Rich SP RC 4.00 1.80
❑ 158 Adam Wainwright 1.00 .45
❑ 159 Scott Thorman .50 .23
❑ 160 Scott Heard SP 3.00 1.35
❑ 161 Chad Petty SP RC 4.00 1.80
❑ 162 Matt Wheatland .50 .23
❑ 163 Bryan Digby .50 .23
❑ 164 Rocco Baldelli 1.00 .45
❑ 165 Grady Sizemore .50 .23
❑ 166 Brian Sellier SP RC 3.00 1.35
❑ 167 Rick Brosseau SP RC 4.00 1.80
❑ 168 Shawn Fagan SP RC 4.00 1.80
❑ 169 Sean Smith SP 3.00 1.35
❑ 170 Chris Bass SP RC 4.00 1.80
❑ 171 Corey Patterson .50 .23
❑ 172 Sean Burroughs 1.00 .45

❑ 173 Ben Petrick	.50	.23
❑ 174 Mike Glendenning	.50	.23
❑ 175 Barry Zito	1.00	.45
❑ 176 Milton Bradley	.50	.23
❑ 177 Bobby Bradley	.50	.23
❑ 178 Jason Hart	.75	.35
❑ 179 Ryan Anderson	.50	.23
❑ 180 Ben Sheets	.40	.18
❑ 181 Adam Everett	.50	.23
❑ 182 Alfonso Soriano	1.00	.45
❑ 183 Josh Hamilton	1.00	.45
❑ 184 Eric Munson	.50	.23
❑ 185 Chin-Feng Chen	.75	.35
❑ 186 Tim Christman SP RC	3.00	1.35
❑ 187 J.R. House SP	6.00	2.70
❑ 188 B.Parker SP RC	3.00	1.35
❑ 189 Sean Fesh SP RC	3.00	1.35
❑ 190 Joel Pineiro SP	5.00	2.20
❑ 191 Oscar Ramirez SP RC	3.00	1.35
❑ 192 Alex Santos SP RC	3.00	1.35
❑ 193 Eddy Reyes SP RC	3.00	1.35
❑ 194 Mike Jacobs SP RC	3.00	1.35
❑ 195 Erick Almonte SP RC	4.00	1.80
❑ 196 B.Claussen SP RC	4.00	1.80
❑ 197 Kris Keller SP RC	4.00	1.80
❑ 198 Wilson Betemit SP RC	12.00	5.50
❑ 199 Andy Phillips SP RC	4.00	1.80
❑ 200 A.Pettyjohn SP RC	4.00	1.80

2002 Stadium Club

	MINT	NRMT
COMP.SET w/o SP's (100)	25.00	11.00
COMMON CARD (1-100)	.15	.07
COMMON CARD (101-125)	10.00	4.50

❑ 1 Pedro Martinez	.75	.35
❑ 2 Derek Jeter	2.50	1.10
❑ 3 Chipper Jones	1.25	.55
❑ 4 Roberto Alomar	.60	.25
❑ 5 Albert Pujols	1.50	.70
❑ 6 Bret Boone	.25	.11
❑ 7 Alex Rodriguez	1.50	.70
❑ 8 Jose Cruz Jr.	.25	.11
❑ 9 Mike Hampton	.25	.11
❑ 10 Vladimir Guerrero	.75	.35
❑ 11 Jim Edmonds	.40	.18
❑ 12 Luis Gonzalez	.60	.25
❑ 13 Jeff Kent	.40	.18
❑ 14 Mike Piazza	1.50	.70
❑ 15 Ben Sheets	.25	.11
❑ 16 Tsuyoshi Shinjo	.40	.18
❑ 17 Pat Burrell	.25	.11
❑ 18 Jermaine Dye	.25	.11
❑ 19 Rafael Furcal	.25	.11
❑ 20 Randy Johnson	.75	.35
❑ 21 Carlos Delgado	.60	.25
❑ 22 Roger Clemens	1.50	.70
❑ 23 Eric Chavez	.25	.11
❑ 24 Nomar Garciaparra	1.50	.70
❑ 25 Ivan Rodriguez	.60	.25
❑ 26 Juan Gonzalez	.60	.25
❑ 27 Reggie Sanders	.25	.11
❑ 28 Jeff Bagwell	.75	.35
❑ 29 Kazuhiro Sasaki	.60	.25
❑ 30 Larry Walker	.40	.18
❑ 31 Ben Grieve	.25	.11
❑ 32 David Justice	.25	.11
❑ 33 David Wells	.25	.11
❑ 34 Kevin Brown	.25	.11
❑ 35 Miguel Tejada	.25	.11
❑ 36 Jorge Posada	.25	.11
❑ 37 Javy Lopez	.25	.11
❑ 38 Cliff Floyd	.25	.11
❑ 39 Carlos Lee	.25	.11
❑ 40 Manny Ramirez	.75	.35
❑ 41 Jim Thome	.60	.25
❑ 42 Pokey Reese	.15	.07
❑ 43 Scott Rolen	.60	.25
❑ 44 Richie Sexson	.25	.11
❑ 45 Dean Palmer	.25	.11
❑ 46 Rafael Palmeiro	.60	.25
❑ 47 Alfonso Soriano	.60	.25
❑ 48 Craig Biggio	.40	.18
❑ 49 Troy Glaus	.60	.25
❑ 50 Andruw Jones	.60	.25
❑ 51 Ichiro Suzuki	2.50	1.10
❑ 52 Kenny Lofton	.25	.11
❑ 53 Hideo Nomo	.60	.25
❑ 54 Magglio Ordonez	.25	.11
❑ 55 Brad Penny	.25	.11
❑ 56 Omar Vizquel	.25	.11
❑ 57 Mike Sweeney	.25	.11
❑ 58 Gary Sheffield	.25	.11
❑ 59 Ken Griffey Jr.	2.00	.90
❑ 60 Curt Schilling	.60	.25
❑ 61 Bobby Higginson	.25	.11
❑ 62 Terrence Long	.25	.11
❑ 63 Moises Alou	.25	.11
❑ 64 Sandy Alomar Jr.	.25	.11
❑ 65 Cristian Guzman	.25	.11
❑ 66 Sammy Sosa	1.25	.55
❑ 67 Jose Vidro	.25	.11
❑ 68 Edgar Martinez	.40	.18
❑ 69 Jason Giambi	.60	.25
❑ 70 Mark McGwire	2.50	1.10
❑ 71 Barry Bonds	1.50	.70
❑ 72 Greg Vaughn	.25	.11
❑ 73 Phil Nevin	.25	.11
❑ 74 Jason Kendall	.25	.11
❑ 75 Greg Maddux	1.50	.70
❑ 76 Jeromy Burnitz	.25	.11
❑ 77 Mike Mussina	.60	.25
❑ 78 Johnny Damon	.25	.11
❑ 79 Shawn Green	.60	.25
❑ 80 Jimmy Rollins	.25	.11
❑ 81 Edgardo Alfonzo	.25	.11
❑ 82 Barry Larkin	.60	.25
❑ 83 Raul Mondesi	.25	.11
❑ 84 Preston Wilson	.25	.11
❑ 85 Mike Lieberthal	.25	.11
❑ 86 J.D. Drew	.60	.25
❑ 87 Ryan Klesko	.25	.11
❑ 88 David Segui	.15	.07
❑ 89 Derek Bell	.15	.07
❑ 90 Bernie Williams	.60	.25
❑ 91 Doug Mientkiewicz	.25	.11
❑ 92 Rich Aurilia	.25	.11
❑ 93 Ellis Burks	.25	.11
❑ 94 Placido Polanco	.15	.07
❑ 95 Darin Erstad	.60	.25
❑ 96 Brian Giles	.25	.11
❑ 97 Geoff Jenkins	.25	.11
❑ 98 Kerry Wood	.60	.25
❑ 99 Mariano Rivera	.25	.11
❑ 100 Todd Helton	.75	.35
❑ 101 Adam Dunn FS	15.00	6.75
❑ 102 Grant Balfour FS	10.00	4.50
❑ 103 Jae Seo FS	10.00	4.50
❑ 104 Hank Blalock FS	15.00	6.75
❑ 105 Chris George FS	10.00	4.50
❑ 106 Jack Cust FS	10.00	4.50
❑ 107 Juan Cruz FS	10.00	4.50
❑ 108 Adrian Gonzalez FS	15.00	6.75
❑ 109 Nick Johnson FS	10.00	4.50
❑ 110 Jeff DaVanon FS	10.00	4.50
❑ 111 Juan Diaz FS	10.00	4.50
❑ 112 Brandon Duckworth FS	10.00	4.50
❑ 113 Jason Lane FS	10.00	4.50
❑ 114 Seung Song FS	10.00	4.50
❑ 115 Morgan Ensberg FS	10.00	4.50
❑ 116 Marlyn Tisdale FY RC	15.00	6.75
❑ 117 Jason Botts FY RC	10.00	4.50
❑ 118 Henry Pichardo FY RC	15.00	6.75
❑ 119 John Rodriguez FY RC	15.00	6.75
❑ 120 Mike Peeples FY RC	10.00	4.50
❑ 121 Rob Bowen EFY RC	20.00	9.00
❑ 122 Jeremy Affeldt EFY	10.00	4.50
❑ 123 Jorge Buret EFY RC	10.00	4.50
❑ 124 Manny Ravelo EFY RC	15.00	6.75
❑ 125 Eudy Lajara EFY RC	15.00	6.75
❑ NNO B. Bonds AU Ball EXCH	100.00	45.00

2000 Stadium Club Chrome

	MINT	NRMT
COMPLETE SET (250)	150.00	70.00

❑ 1 Nomar Garciaparra	5.00	2.20
❑ 2 Brian Jordan	.75	.35
❑ 3 Mark Grace	2.00	.90
❑ 4 Jeromy Burnitz	.75	.35
❑ 5 Shane Reynolds	.50	.23
❑ 6 Alex Gonzalez	.50	.23
❑ 7 Jose Offerman	.50	.23
❑ 8 Orlando Hernandez	.75	.35
❑ 9 Mike Caruso	.50	.23
❑ 10 Tony Clark	.75	.35
❑ 11 Sean Casey	1.25	.55
❑ 12 Johnny Damon	.75	.35
❑ 13 Dante Bichette	.75	.35
❑ 14 Kevin Young	.50	.23
❑ 15 Juan Gonzalez	2.00	.90
❑ 16 Chipper Jones	4.00	1.80
❑ 17 Quilvio Veras	.50	.23
❑ 18 Trevor Hoffman	.75	.35
❑ 19 Roger Cedeno	.50	.23
❑ 20 Ellis Burks	.75	.35
❑ 21 Richie Sexson	.75	.35
❑ 22 Gary Sheffield	.75	.35
❑ 23 Delino DeShields	.50	.23
❑ 24 Wade Boggs	2.00	.90
❑ 25 Ray Lankford	.50	.23
❑ 26 Kevin Appier	.50	.23
❑ 27 Roy Halladay	.50	.23
❑ 28 Harold Baines	.75	.35
❑ 29 Todd Zeile	.75	.35
❑ 30 Barry Larkin	2.00	.90
❑ 31 Ron Coomer	.50	.23
❑ 32 Jorge Posada	.75	.35
❑ 33 Magglio Ordonez	.75	.35
❑ 34 Brian Giles	.75	.35
❑ 35 Jeff Kent	1.25	.55
❑ 36 Henry Rodriguez	.50	.23
❑ 37 Fred McGriff	1.25	.55
❑ 38 Shawn Green	2.00	.90
❑ 39 Derek Bell	.50	.23
❑ 40 Ben Grieve	.75	.35
❑ 41 Dave Nilsson	.50	.23
❑ 42 Mo Vaughn	.75	.35
❑ 43 Rondell White	.75	.35
❑ 44 Doug Glanville	.50	.23
❑ 45 Paul O'Neill	2.00	.90
❑ 46 Carlos Lee	.75	.35
❑ 47 Vinny Castilla	.75	.35
❑ 48 Mike Sweeney	.75	.35
❑ 49 Rico Brogna	.50	.23
❑ 50 Alex Rodriguez	5.00	2.20
❑ 51 Luis Castillo	.50	.23
❑ 52 Kevin Brown	1.25	.55
❑ 53 Jose Vidro	.75	.35

❑ 54 John Smoltz	.75	.35
❑ 55 Garret Anderson	.75	.35
❑ 56 Matt Stairs	.50	.23
❑ 57 Omar Vizquel	.75	.35
❑ 58 Tom Goodwin	.50	.23
❑ 59 Scott Brosius	.75	.35
❑ 60 Robin Ventura	1.25	.55
❑ 61 B.J. Surhoff	.75	.35
❑ 62 Andy Ashby	.50	.23
❑ 63 Chris Widger	.50	.23
❑ 64 Tim Hudson	2.00	.90
❑ 65 Javy Lopez	.75	.35
❑ 66 Tim Salmon	.75	.35
❑ 67 Warren Morris	.50	.23
❑ 68 John Wetteland	.75	.35
❑ 69 Gabe Kapler	.75	.35
❑ 70 Bernie Williams	2.00	.90
❑ 71 Rickey Henderson	4.00	1.80
❑ 72 Andruw Jones	2.00	.90
❑ 73 Eric Young	.50	.23
❑ 74 Bob Abreu	.75	.35
❑ 75 David Cone	.75	.35
❑ 76 Rusty Greer	.75	.35
❑ 77 Ron Belliard	.50	.23
❑ 78 Troy Glaus	2.00	.90
❑ 79 Mike Hampton	.75	.35
❑ 80 Miguel Tejada	.75	.35
❑ 81 Jeff Cirillo	.75	.35
❑ 82 Todd Hundley	.50	.23
❑ 83 Roberto Alomar	2.00	.90
❑ 84 Charles Johnson	.75	.35
❑ 85 Rafael Palmeiro	2.00	.90
❑ 86 Doug Mientkiewicz	1.25	.55
❑ 87 Mariano Rivera	.75	.35
❑ 88 Neifi Perez	.50	.23
❑ 89 Jermaine Dye	.75	.35
❑ 90 Ivan Rodriguez	2.00	.90
❑ 91 Jay Buhner	.75	.35
❑ 92 Pokey Reese	.50	.23
❑ 93 John Olerud	.75	.35
❑ 94 Brady Anderson	.75	.35
❑ 95 Manny Ramirez	2.50	1.10
❑ 96 Keith Osik RC	.50	.23
❑ 97 Mickey Morandini	.50	.23
❑ 98 Matt Williams	1.25	.55
❑ 99 Eric Karros	.75	.35
❑ 100 Ken Griffey Jr.	6.00	2.70
❑ 101 Bret Boone	.75	.35
❑ 102 Ryan Klesko	.75	.35
❑ 103 Craig Biggio	1.25	.55
❑ 104 John Jaha	.50	.23
❑ 105 Vladimir Guerrero	2.00	.90
❑ 106 Devon White	.50	.23
❑ 107 Tony Womack	.50	.23
❑ 108 Marvin Benard	.50	.23
❑ 109 Kenny Lofton	.75	.35
❑ 110 Preston Wilson	.75	.35
❑ 111 Al Leiter	.50	.23
❑ 112 Reggie Sanders	.50	.23
❑ 113 Scott Williamson	.50	.23
❑ 114 Deivi Cruz	.50	.23
❑ 115 Carlos Beltran	.75	.35
❑ 116 Ray Durham	.75	.35
❑ 117 Ricky Ledee	.50	.23
❑ 118 Torii Hunter	.75	.35
❑ 119 John Valentin	.50	.23
❑ 120 Scott Rolen	2.00	.90
❑ 121 Jason Kendall	.75	.35
❑ 122 Dave Martinez	.50	.23
❑ 123 Jim Thome	2.00	.90
❑ 124 David Bell	.50	.23
❑ 125 Jose Canseco	2.00	.90
❑ 126 Jose Lima	.50	.23
❑ 127 Carl Everett	.75	.35
❑ 128 Kevin Millwood	.50	.23
❑ 129 Bill Spiers	.50	.23
❑ 130 Omar Daal	.50	.23
❑ 131 Miguel Cairo	.50	.23
❑ 132 Mark Grudzielanek	.50	.23
❑ 133 David Justice	.75	.35
❑ 134 Russ Ortiz	.75	.35
❑ 135 Mike Piazza	5.00	2.20
❑ 136 Brian Meadows	.50	.23
❑ 137 Tony Gwynn	4.00	1.80
❑ 138 Cal Ripken	8.00	3.60
❑ 139 Kris Benson	.75	.35
❑ 140 Larry Walker	1.25	.55
❑ 141 Cristian Guzman	.75	.35
❑ 142 Tino Martinez	.75	.35
❑ 143 Chris Singleton	.50	.23
❑ 144 Lee Stevens	.50	.23
❑ 145 Rey Ordonez	.50	.23
❑ 146 Russ Davis	.50	.23
❑ 147 J.T. Snow	.75	.35
❑ 148 Luis Gonzalez	2.00	.90
❑ 149 Marquis Grissom	.50	.23
❑ 150 Greg Maddux	5.00	2.20
❑ 151 Fernando Tatis	.50	.23
❑ 152 Jason Giambi	2.00	.90
❑ 153 Carlos Delgado	2.00	.90
❑ 154 Joe McEwing	.50	.23
❑ 155 Raul Mondesi	.75	.35
❑ 156 Rich Aurilia	.75	.35
❑ 157 Alex Fernandez	.50	.23
❑ 158 Albert Belle	.75	.35
❑ 159 Pat Meares	.50	.23
❑ 160 Mike Lieberthal	.75	.35
❑ 161 Mike Cameron	.75	.35
❑ 162 Juan Encarnacion	.75	.35
❑ 163 Chuck Knoblauch	.75	.35
❑ 164 Pedro Martinez	2.50	1.10
❑ 165 Randy Johnson	2.50	1.10
❑ 166 Shannon Stewart	.75	.35
❑ 167 Jeff Bagwell	2.50	1.10
❑ 168 Edgar Renteria	.50	.23
❑ 169 Barry Bonds	5.00	2.20
❑ 170 Steve Finley	.75	.35
❑ 171 Brian Hunter	.50	.23
❑ 172 Tom Glavine	2.00	.90
❑ 173 Mark Kotsay	.50	.23
❑ 174 Tony Fernandez	.50	.23
❑ 175 Sammy Sosa	4.00	1.80
❑ 176 Geoff Jenkins	.75	.35
❑ 177 Adrian Beltre	.75	.35
❑ 178 Jay Bell	.75	.35
❑ 179 Mike Bordick	.50	.23
❑ 180 Ed Sprague	.50	.23
❑ 181 Dave Roberts	.50	.23
❑ 182 Greg Vaughn	.75	.35
❑ 183 Brian Daubach	.75	.35
❑ 184 Damion Easley	.50	.23
❑ 185 Carlos Febles	.50	.23
❑ 186 Kevin Tapani	.50	.23
❑ 187 Frank Thomas	2.50	1.10
❑ 188 Roger Clemens	5.00	2.20
❑ 189 Mike Benjamin	.50	.23
❑ 190 Curt Schilling	2.00	.90
❑ 191 Edgardo Alfonzo	.75	.35
❑ 192 Mike Mussina	2.00	.90
❑ 193 Todd Helton	2.50	1.10
❑ 194 Todd Jones	.50	.23
❑ 195 Dean Palmer	.75	.35
❑ 196 John Flaherty	.50	.23
❑ 197 Derek Jeter	8.00	3.60
❑ 198 Todd Walker	.50	.23
❑ 199 Brad Ausmus	.50	.23
❑ 200 Mark McGwire	8.00	3.60
❑ 201 Erubiel Durazo	.75	.35
❑ 202 Nick Johnson	2.00	.90
❑ 203 Ruben Mateo	.75	.35
❑ 204 Lance Berkman	2.00	.90
❑ 205 Pat Burrell	2.00	.90
❑ 206 Pablo Ozuna	.50	.23
❑ 207 Roosevelt Brown	.50	.23
❑ 208 Alfonso Soriano	2.00	.90
❑ 209 A.J. Burnett	.75	.35
❑ 210 Rafael Furcal	2.00	.90
❑ 211 Scott Morgan	.50	.23
❑ 212 Adam Piatt	1.25	.55
❑ 213 Dee Brown	.50	.23
❑ 214 Corey Patterson	2.00	.90
❑ 215 Mickey Lopez	.50	.23
❑ 216 Rob Ryan	.50	.23
❑ 217 Sean Burroughs	2.00	.90
❑ 218 Jack Cust	.75	.35
❑ 219 John Patterson	.50	.23
❑ 220 Kit Pellow	.50	.23
❑ 221 Chad Hermansen	.50	.23
❑ 222 Daryle Ward	.50	.23
❑ 223 Jayson Werth	.50	.23
❑ 224 Jason Standridge	.50	.23
❑ 225 Mark Mulder	2.00	.90
❑ 226 Peter Bergeron	.50	.23
❑ 227 Willi Mo Pena	2.00	.90
❑ 228 Aramis Ramirez	.75	.35
❑ 229 John Sneed RC	2.00	.90
❑ 230 Wilton Veras	.50	.23
❑ 231 Josh Hamilton	2.50	1.10
❑ 232 Eric Munson	.75	.35
❑ 233 Bobby Bradley RC	2.50	1.10
❑ 234 Larry Bigbie RC	2.00	.90
❑ 235 B.J. Garbe RC	3.00	1.35
❑ 236 Brett Myers RC	2.00	.90
❑ 237 Jason Stumm RC	2.00	.90
❑ 238 Corey Myers RC	1.50	.70
❑ 239 Ryan Christianson RC	2.50	1.10
❑ 240 David Walling	.50	.23
❑ 241 Josh Girdley	.50	.23
❑ 242 Omar Ortiz	.50	.23
❑ 243 Jason Jennings	.75	.35
❑ 244 Kyle Snyder	.50	.23
❑ 245 Jay Gehrke	.50	.23
❑ 246 Mike Paradis	.50	.23
❑ 247 Chance Caple RC	1.50	.70
❑ 248 Ben Christensen RC	1.25	.55
❑ 249 Brad Baker RC	2.50	1.10
❑ 250 Rick Asadoorian RC	2.50	1.10

1991 Studio

	MINT	NRMT
COMPLETE SET (264)	15.00	6.75
❑ 1 Glenn Davis	.10	.05
❑ 2 Dwight Evans	.15	.07
❑ 3 Leo Gomez	.10	.05
❑ 4 Chris Hoiles	.10	.05
❑ 5 Sam Horn	.10	.05
❑ 6 Ben McDonald	.10	.05
❑ 7 Randy Milligan	.10	.05
❑ 8 Gregg Olson	.10	.05
❑ 9 Cal Ripken	1.50	.70
❑ 10 David Segui	.10	.05
❑ 11 Wade Boggs	.40	.18
❑ 12 Ellis Burks	.15	.07
❑ 13 Jack Clark	.15	.07
❑ 14 Roger Clemens	1.00	.45
❑ 15 Mike Greenwell	.10	.05
❑ 16 Tim Naehring	.10	.05
❑ 17 Tony Pena	.10	.05
❑ 18 Phil Plantier RC	.10	.05
❑ 19 Jeff Reardon	.15	.07
❑ 20 Mo Vaughn	.15	.07
❑ 21 Jimmie Reese CO	.15	.07
❑ 22 Jim Abbott UER (Born in 1967, not 1969)	.15	.07
❑ 23 Bert Blyleven	.15	.07
❑ 24 Chuck Finley	.15	.07
❑ 25 Gary Gaetti	.15	.07
❑ 26 Wally Joyner	.15	.07
❑ 27 Mark Langston	.10	.05
❑ 28 Kirk McCaskill	.10	.05
❑ 29 Lance Parrish	.15	.07
❑ 30 Dave Winfield	.40	.18
❑ 31 Alex Fernandez	.10	.05
❑ 32 Carlton Fisk	.40	.18
❑ 33 Scott Fletcher	.10	.05
❑ 34 Greg Hibbard	.10	.05
❑ 35 Charlie Hough	.15	.07
❑ 36 Jack McDowell	.10	.05

❑ 37 Tim Raines .15 .07
❑ 38 Sammy Sosa 1.00 .45
❑ 39 Bobby Thigpen .10 .05
❑ 40 Frank Thomas .60 .25
❑ 41 Sandy Alomar Jr. .15 .07
❑ 42 John Farrell .10 .05
❑ 43 Glenallen Hill .10 .05
❑ 44 Brook Jacoby .10 .05
❑ 45 Chris James .10 .05
❑ 46 Doug Jones .10 .05
❑ 47 Eric King .10 .05
❑ 48 Mark Lewis .10 .05
❑ 49 Greg Swindell UER .10 .05
(Photo actually
Turner Ward)
❑ 50 Mark Whiten .10 .05
❑ 51 Milt Cuyler .10 .05
❑ 52 Rob Deer .10 .05
❑ 53 Cecil Fielder .15 .07
❑ 54 Travis Fryman .15 .07
❑ 55 Bill Gullickson .10 .05
❑ 56 Lloyd Moseby .10 .05
❑ 57 Frank Tanana .10 .05
❑ 58 Mickey Tettleton .10 .05
❑ 59 Alan Trammell .25 .11
❑ 60 Lou Whitaker .15 .07
❑ 61 Mike Boddicker .10 .05
❑ 62 George Brett .75 .35
❑ 63 Jeff Conine RC .15 .07
❑ 64 Warren Cromartie .10 .05
❑ 65 Storm Davis .10 .05
❑ 66 Kirk Gibson .15 .07
❑ 67 Mark Gubicza .10 .05
❑ 68 Brian McRae RC .15 .07
❑ 69 Bret Saberhagen .15 .07
❑ 70 Kurt Stillwell .10 .05
❑ 71 Tim McIntosh .10 .05
❑ 72 Candy Maldonado .10 .05
❑ 73 Paul Molitor .40 .18
❑ 74 Willie Randolph .15 .07
❑ 75 Ron Robinson .10 .05
❑ 76 Gary Sheffield .15 .07
❑ 77 Franklin Stubbs .10 .05
❑ 78 B.J. Surhoff .15 .07
❑ 79 Greg Vaughn .15 .07
❑ 80 Robin Yount .40 .18
❑ 81 Rick Aguilera .15 .07
❑ 82 Steve Bedrosian .10 .05
❑ 83 Scott Erickson .10 .05
❑ 84 Greg Gagne .10 .05
❑ 85 Dan Gladden .10 .05
❑ 86 Brian Harper .10 .05
❑ 87 Kent Hrbek .15 .07
❑ 88 Shane Mack .10 .05
❑ 89 Jack Morris .15 .07
❑ 90 Kirby Puckett 1.00 .45
❑ 91 Jesse Barfield .10 .05
❑ 92 Steve Farr .10 .05
❑ 93 Steve Howe .10 .05
❑ 94 Roberto Kelly .10 .05
❑ 95 Tim Leary .10 .05
❑ 96 Kevin Maas .10 .05
❑ 97 Don Mattingly 1.00 .45
❑ 98 Hensley Meulens .10 .05
❑ 99 Scott Sanderson .10 .05
❑ 100 Steve Sax .10 .05
❑ 101 Jose Canseco .40 .18
❑ 102 Dennis Eckersley .15 .07
❑ 103 Dave Henderson .10 .05
❑ 104 Rickey Henderson .75 .35
❑ 105 Rick Honeycutt .10 .05
❑ 106 Mark McGwire 1.50 .70
❑ 107 Dave Stewart UER .15 .07
(No-hitter against
Toronto, not Texas)
❑ 108 Eric Show .10 .05
❑ 109 Todd Van Poppel RC .10 .05
❑ 110 Bob Welch .10 .05
❑ 111 Alvin Davis .10 .05
❑ 112 Ken Griffey Jr. 1.50 .70
❑ 113 Ken Griffey Sr. .15 .07
❑ 114 Erik Hanson UER .10 .05
(Misspelled Eric)
❑ 115 Brian Holman .10 .05
❑ 116 Randy Johnson .60 .25
❑ 117 Edgar Martinez .25 .11
❑ 118 Tino Martinez .15 .07
❑ 119 Harold Reynolds .10 .05
❑ 120 David Valle .10 .05
❑ 121 Kevin Belcher .10 .05
❑ 122 Scott Chiamparino .10 .05
❑ 123 Julio Franco .15 .07
❑ 124 Juan Gonzalez .50 .23
❑ 125 Rich Gossage .15 .07
❑ 126 Jeff Kunkel .10 .05
❑ 127 Rafael Palmeiro .40 .18
❑ 128 Nolan Ryan 2.00 .90
❑ 129 Ruben Sierra .10 .05
❑ 130 Bobby Witt .10 .05
❑ 131 Roberto Alomar .40 .18
❑ 132 Tom Candiotti .10 .05
❑ 133 Joe Carter .15 .07
❑ 134 Ken Dayley .10 .05
❑ 135 Kelly Gruber .10 .05
❑ 136 John Olerud .25 .11
❑ 137 Dave Stieb .10 .05
❑ 138 Turner Ward RC .15 .07
❑ 139 Devon White .10 .05
❑ 140 Mookie Wilson .15 .07
❑ 141 Steve Avery .10 .05
❑ 142 Sid Bream .10 .05
❑ 143 Nick Esasky UER .10 .05
(Homers abbreviated RH)
❑ 144 Ron Gant .10 .05
❑ 145 Tom Glavine .40 .18
❑ 146 David Justice .40 .18
❑ 147 Kelly Mann .10 .05
❑ 148 Terry Pendleton .15 .07
❑ 149 John Smoltz .15 .07
❑ 150 Jeff Treadway .10 .05
❑ 151 George Bell .10 .05
❑ 152 Shawn Boskie .10 .05
❑ 153 Andre Dawson .25 .11
❑ 154 Lance Dickson RC .10 .05
❑ 155 Shawon Dunston .10 .05
❑ 156 Joe Girardi .10 .05
❑ 157 Mark Grace .40 .18
❑ 158 Ryne Sandberg .50 .23
❑ 159 Gary Scott RC .10 .05
❑ 160 Dave Smith .10 .05
❑ 161 Tom Browning .10 .05
❑ 162 Eric Davis .15 .07
❑ 163 Rob Dibble .10 .05
❑ 164 Mariano Duncan .10 .05
❑ 165 Chris Hammond .10 .05
❑ 166 Billy Hatcher .10 .05
❑ 167 Barry Larkin .40 .18
❑ 168 Hal Morris .10 .05
❑ 169 Paul O'Neill .40 .18
❑ 170 Chris Sabo .10 .05
❑ 171 Eric Anthony .10 .05
❑ 172 Jeff Bagwell RC 3.00 1.35
❑ 173 Craig Biggio .25 .11
❑ 174 Ken Caminiti .15 .07
❑ 175 Jim Deshaies .10 .05
❑ 176 Steve Finley .15 .07
❑ 177 Pete Harnisch .10 .05
❑ 178 Darryl Kile .15 .07
❑ 179 Curt Schilling .40 .18
❑ 180 Mike Scott .10 .05
❑ 181 Brett Butler .15 .07
❑ 182 Gary Carter .25 .11
❑ 183 Orel Hershiser .15 .07
❑ 184 Ramon Martinez .10 .05
❑ 185 Eddie Murray .40 .18
❑ 186 Jose Offerman .10 .05
❑ 187 Bob Ojeda .10 .05
❑ 188 Juan Samuel .10 .05
❑ 189 Mike Scioscia .10 .05
❑ 190 Darryl Strawberry .15 .07
❑ 191 Moises Alou .15 .07
❑ 192 Brian Barnes .10 .05
❑ 193 Oil Can Boyd .10 .05
❑ 194 Ivan Calderon .10 .05
❑ 195 Delino DeShields .15 .07
❑ 196 Mike Fitzgerald .10 .05
❑ 197 Andres Galarraga .25 .11
❑ 198 Marquis Grissom .10 .05
❑ 199 Bill Sampen .10 .05
❑ 200 Tim Wallach .10 .05
❑ 201 Daryl Boston .10 .05
❑ 202 Vince Coleman .10 .05
❑ 203 John Franco .15 .07
❑ 204 Dwight Gooden .15 .07
❑ 205 Tom Herr .10 .05
❑ 206 Gregg Jefferies .10 .05
❑ 207 Howard Johnson .10 .05
❑ 208 Dave Magadan UER .10 .05
(Born 1862,
should be 1962)
❑ 209 Kevin McReynolds .10 .05
❑ 210 Frank Viola .15 .07
❑ 211 Wes Chamberlain RC .10 .05
❑ 212 Darren Daulton .15 .07
❑ 213 Len Dykstra .15 .07
❑ 214 Charlie Hayes .10 .05
❑ 215 Ricky Jordan .10 .05
❑ 216 Steve Lake .10 .05
(Pictured with parrot
on his shoulder)
❑ 217 Roger McDowell .10 .05
❑ 218 Mickey Morandini .10 .05
❑ 219 Terry Mulholland .10 .05
❑ 220 Dale Murphy .40 .18
❑ 221 Jay Bell .15 .07
❑ 222 Barry Bonds 1.00 .45
❑ 223 Bobby Bonilla .15 .07
❑ 224 Doug Drabek .10 .05
❑ 225 Bill Landrum .10 .05
❑ 226 Mike LaValliere .10 .05
❑ 227 Jose Lind .10 .05
❑ 228 Don Slaught .10 .05
❑ 229 John Smiley .10 .05
❑ 230 Andy Van Slyke .15 .07
❑ 231 Bernard Gilkey .10 .05
❑ 232 Pedro Guerrero .15 .07
❑ 233 Rex Hudler .10 .05
❑ 234 Ray Lankford .15 .07
❑ 235 Joe Magrane .10 .05
❑ 236 Jose Oquendo .10 .05
❑ 237 Lee Smith .15 .07
❑ 238 Ozzie Smith .50 .23
❑ 239 Milt Thompson .10 .05
❑ 240 Todd Zeile .10 .05
❑ 241 Larry Andersen .10 .05
❑ 242 Andy Benes .10 .05
❑ 243 Paul Faries .10 .05
❑ 244 Tony Fernandez .10 .05
❑ 245 Tony Gwynn .75 .35
❑ 246 Atlee Hammaker .10 .05
❑ 247 Fred McGriff .25 .11
❑ 248 Bip Roberts .10 .05
❑ 249 Bentio Santiago .10 .05
❑ 250 Ed Whitson .10 .05
❑ 251 Dave Anderson .10 .05
❑ 252 Mike Benjamin .10 .05
❑ 253 John Burkett UER .10 .05
(Front photo actually
Trevor Wilson)
❑ 254 Will Clark .40 .18
❑ 255 Scott Garrelts .10 .05
❑ 256 Willie McGee .15 .07
❑ 257 Kevin Mitchell .10 .05
❑ 258 Dave Righetti .15 .07
❑ 259 Matt Williams .25 .11
❑ 260 Bud Black .10 .05
Steve Decker
❑ 261 S.Anderson MG CL .15 .07
❑ 262 Tom Lasorda MG CL .25 .11
❑ 263 Tony LaRussa MG CL .15 .07
❑ NNO Title Card .10 .05

1992 Studio

	MINT	NRMT
COMPLETE SET (264)	15.00	6.75

❑ 1 Steve Avery .05 .02
❑ 2 Sid Bream .05 .02
❑ 3 Ron Gant .05 .02
❑ 4 Tom Glavine .30 .14
❑ 5 David Justice .10 .05
❑ 6 Mark Lemke .05 .02
❑ 7 Greg Olson .05 .02
❑ 8 Terry Pendleton .10 .05
❑ 9 Deion Sanders .10 .05
❑ 10 John Smoltz .10 .05
❑ 11 Doug Dascenzo .05 .02

❑	12	Andre Dawson	.20	.09
❑	13	Joe Girardi	.05	.02
❑	14	Mark Grace	.30	.14
❑	15	Greg Maddux	.75	.35
❑	16	Chuck McElroy	.05	.02
❑	17	Mike Morgan	.05	.02
❑	18	Ryne Sandberg	.40	.18
❑	19	Gary Scott	.05	.02
❑	20	Sammy Sosa	.60	.25
❑	21	Norm Charlton	.05	.02
❑	22	Rob Dibble	.05	.02
❑	23	Barry Larkin	.30	.14
❑	24	Hal Morris	.05	.02
❑	25	Paul O'Neill	.30	.14
❑	26	Jose Rijo	.05	.02
❑	27	Bip Roberts	.05	.02
❑	28	Chris Sabo	.05	.02
❑	29	Reggie Sanders	.05	.02
❑	30	Greg Swindell	.05	.02
❑	31	Jeff Bagwell	.60	.25
❑	32	Craig Biggio	.20	.09
❑	33	Ken Caminiti	.10	.05
❑	34	Andujar Cedeno	.05	.02
❑	35	Steve Finley	.10	.05
❑	36	Pete Harnisch	.05	.02
❑	37	Butch Henry RC	.05	.02
❑	38	Doug Jones	.05	.02
❑	39	Darryl Kile	.10	.05
❑	40	Eddie Taubensee RC	.10	.05
❑	41	Brett Butler	.10	.05
❑	42	Tom Candiotti	.05	.02
❑	43	Eric Davis	.10	.05
❑	44	Orel Hershiser	.10	.05
❑	45	Eric Karros	.10	.05
❑	46	Ramon Martinez	.05	.02
❑	47	Jose Offerman	.05	.02
❑	48	Mike Scioscia	.05	.02
❑	49	Mike Sharperson	.05	.02
❑	50	Darryl Strawberry	.10	.05
❑	51	Bret Barberie	.05	.02
❑	52	Ivan Calderon	.05	.02
❑	53	Gary Carter	.20	.09
❑	54	Delino DeShields	.05	.02
❑	55	Marquis Grissom	.05	.02
❑	56	Ken Hill	.05	.02
❑	57	Dennis Martinez	.10	.05
❑	58	Spike Owen	.05	.02
❑	59	Larry Walker	.20	.09
❑	60	Tim Wallach	.05	.02
❑	61	Bobby Bonilla	.10	.05
❑	62	Tim Burke	.05	.02
❑	63	Vince Coleman	.05	.02
❑	64	John Franco	.10	.05
❑	65	Dwight Gooden	.10	.05
❑	66	Todd Hundley	.05	.02
❑	67	Howard Johnson	.05	.02
❑	68	Eddie Murray UER (He's not all-time switch homer leader, but he has most games with homers from both sides)	.30	.14
❑	69	Bret Saberhagen	.10	.05
❑	70	Anthony Young	.05	.02
❑	71	Kim Batiste	.05	.02
❑	72	Wes Chamberlain	.05	.02
❑	73	Darren Daulton	.10	.05
❑	74	Mariano Duncan	.05	.02
❑	75	Len Dykstra	.10	.05
❑	76	John Kruk	.10	.05
❑	77	Mickey Morandini	.05	.02
❑	78	Terry Mulholland	.05	.02
❑	79	Dale Murphy	.30	.14
❑	80	Mitch Williams	.05	.02
❑	81	Jay Bell	.10	.05
❑	82	Barry Bonds	.75	.35
❑	83	Steve Buechele	.05	.02
❑	84	Doug Drabek	.05	.02
❑	85	Mike LaValliere	.05	.02
❑	86	Jose Lind	.05	.02
❑	87	Denny Neagle	.10	.05
❑	88	Randy Tomlin	.05	.02
❑	89	Andy Van Slyke	.10	.05
❑	90	Gary Varsho	.05	.02
❑	91	Pedro Guerrero	.10	.05
❑	92	Rex Hudler	.05	.02
❑	93	Brian Jordan RC	.75	.35
❑	94	Felix Jose	.05	.02
❑	95	Donovan Osborne	.05	.02
❑	96	Tom Pagnozzi	.05	.02
❑	97	Lee Smith	.10	.05
❑	98	Ozzie Smith	.40	.18
❑	99	Todd Worrell	.05	.02
❑	100	Todd Zeile	.05	.02
❑	101	Andy Benes	.05	.02
❑	102	Jerald Clark	.05	.02
❑	103	Tony Fernandez	.05	.02
❑	104	Tony Gwynn	.60	.25
❑	105	Greg W. Harris	.05	.02
❑	106	Fred McGriff	.20	.09
❑	107	Benito Santiago	.05	.02
❑	108	Gary Sheffield	.10	.05
❑	109	Kurt Stillwell	.05	.02
❑	110	Tim Teufel	.05	.02
❑	111	Kevin Bass	.05	.02
❑	112	Jeff Brantley	.05	.02
❑	113	John Burkett	.05	.02
❑	114	Will Clark	.30	.14
❑	115	Royce Clayton	.05	.02
❑	116	Mike Jackson	.05	.02
❑	117	Darren Lewis	.05	.02
❑	118	Bill Swift	.05	.02
❑	119	Robby Thompson	.05	.02
❑	120	Matt Williams	.20	.09
❑	121	Brady Anderson	.10	.05
❑	122	Glenn Davis	.05	.02
❑	123	Mike Devereaux	.05	.02
❑	124	Chris Hoiles	.05	.02
❑	125	Sam Horn	.05	.02
❑	126	Ben McDonald	.05	.02
❑	127	Mike Mussina	.50	.23
❑	128	Gregg Olson	.05	.02
❑	129	Cal Ripken Jr.	1.25	.55
❑	130	Rick Sutcliffe	.10	.05
❑	131	Wade Boggs	.30	.14
❑	132	Roger Clemens	.75	.35
❑	133	Greg A. Harris	.05	.02
❑	134	Tim Naehring	.05	.02
❑	135	Tony Pena	.05	.02
❑	136	Phil Plantier	.05	.02
❑	137	Jeff Reardon	.10	.05
❑	138	Jody Reed	.05	.02
❑	139	Mo Vaughn	.10	.05
❑	140	Frank Viola	.10	.05
❑	141	Jim Abbott	.10	.05
❑	142	Hubie Brooks	.05	.02
❑	143	Chad Curtis RC	.10	.05
❑	144	Gary DiSarcina	.05	.02
❑	145	Chuck Finley	.10	.05
❑	146	Bryan Harvey	.05	.02
❑	147	Von Hayes	.05	.02
❑	148	Mark Langston	.05	.02
❑	149	Lance Parrish	.10	.05
❑	150	Lee Stevens	.05	.02
❑	151	George Bell	.05	.02
❑	152	Alex Fernandez	.05	.02
❑	153	Greg Hibbard	.05	.02
❑	154	Lance Johnson	.05	.02
❑	155	Kirk McCaskill	.05	.02
❑	156	Tim Raines	.10	.05
❑	157	Steve Sax	.05	.02
❑	158	Bobby Thigpen	.05	.02
❑	159	Frank Thomas	.40	.18
❑	160	Robin Ventura	.10	.05
❑	161	Sandy Alomar Jr.	.10	.05
❑	162	Jack Armstrong	.05	.02
❑	163	Carlos Baerga	.05	.02
❑	164	Albert Belle	.10	.05
❑	165	Alex Cole	.05	.02
❑	166	Glenallen Hill	.05	.02
❑	167	Mark Lewis	.05	.02
❑	168	Kenny Lofton	.30	.14
❑	169	Paul Sorrento	.05	.02
❑	170	Mark Whiten	.05	.02
❑	171	Milt Cuyler	.05	.02
❑	172	Rob Deer	.05	.02
❑	173	Cecil Fielder	.10	.05
❑	174	Travis Fryman	.10	.05
❑	175	Mike Henneman	.05	.02
❑	176	Tony Phillips	.05	.02
❑	177	Frank Tanana	.05	.02
❑	178	Mickey Tettleton	.05	.02
❑	179	Alan Trammell	.20	.09
❑	180	Lou Whitaker	.10	.05
❑	181	George Brett	.60	.25
❑	182	Tom Gordon	.05	.02
❑	183	Mark Gubicza	.05	.02
❑	184	Gregg Jefferies	.05	.02
❑	185	Wally Joyner	.10	.05
❑	186	Brent Mayne	.05	.02
❑	187	Brian McRae	.05	.02
❑	188	Kevin McReynolds	.05	.02
❑	189	Keith Miller	.05	.02
❑	190	Jeff Montgomery	.05	.02
❑	191	Dante Bichette	.10	.05
❑	192	Ricky Bones	.05	.02
❑	193	Scott Fletcher	.05	.02
❑	194	Paul Molitor	.30	.14
❑	195	Jaime Navarro	.05	.02
❑	196	Franklin Stubbs	.05	.02
❑	197	B.J. Surhoff	.10	.05
❑	198	Greg Vaughn	.10	.05
❑	199	Bill Wegman	.05	.02
❑	200	Robin Yount	.30	.14
❑	201	Rick Aguilera	.10	.05
❑	202	Scott Erickson	.05	.02
❑	203	Greg Gagne	.05	.02
❑	204	Brian Harper	.05	.02
❑	205	Kent Hrbek	.10	.05
❑	206	Scott Leius	.05	.02
❑	207	Shane Mack	.05	.02
❑	208	Pat Mahomes RC	.05	.02
❑	209	Kirby Puckett	.75	.35
❑	210	John Smiley	.05	.02
❑	211	Mike Gallego	.05	.02
❑	212	Charlie Hayes	.05	.02
❑	213	Pat Kelly	.05	.02
❑	214	Roberto Kelly	.05	.02
❑	215	Kevin Maas	.05	.02
❑	216	Don Mattingly	.75	.35
❑	217	Matt Nokes	.05	.02
❑	218	Melido Perez	.05	.02
❑	219	Scott Sanderson	.05	.02
❑	220	Danny Tartabull	.05	.02
❑	221	Harold Baines	.10	.05
❑	222	Jose Canseco	.30	.14
❑	223	Dennis Eckersley	.10	.05
❑	224	Dave Henderson	.05	.02
❑	225	Carney Lansford	.10	.05
❑	226	Mark McGwire	1.25	.55
❑	227	Mike Moore	.05	.02
❑	228	Randy Ready	.05	.02
❑	229	Terry Steinbach	.05	.02
❑	230	Dave Stewart	.10	.05
❑	231	Jay Buhner	.10	.05
❑	232	Ken Griffey Jr.	1.00	.45
❑	233	Erik Hanson	.05	.02
❑	234	Randy Johnson	.40	.18
❑	235	Edgar Martinez	.20	.09
❑	236	Tino Martinez	.10	.05
❑	237	Kevin Mitchell	.05	.02
❑	238	Pete O'Brien	.05	.02
❑	239	Harold Reynolds	.05	.02
❑	240	David Valle	.05	.02
❑	241	Julio Franco	.10	.05
❑	242	Juan Gonzalez	.30	.14
❑	243	Jose Guzman	.05	.02
❑	244	Rafael Palmeiro	.30	.14
❑	245	Dean Palmer	.10	.05
❑	246	Ivan Rodriguez	.50	.23

		MINT	NRMT
❑ 247	Jeff Russell	.05	.02
❑ 248	Nolan Ryan	1.50	.70
❑ 249	Ruben Sierra	.05	.02
❑ 250	Dickie Thon	.05	.02
❑ 251	Roberto Alomar	.30	.14
❑ 252	Derek Bell	.10	.05
❑ 253	Pat Borders	.05	.02
❑ 254	Joe Carter	.10	.05
❑ 255	Kelly Gruber	.05	.02
❑ 256	Juan Guzman	.05	.02
❑ 257	Jack Morris	.10	.05
❑ 258	John Olerud	.10	.05
❑ 259	Devon White	.05	.02
❑ 260	Dave Winfield	.30	.14
❑ 261	Checklist	.05	.02
❑ 262	Checklist	.05	.02
❑ 263	Checklist	.05	.02
❑ 264	History Card	.05	.02

1993 Studio

		MINT	NRMT
COMPLETE SET (220)		20.00	9.00
❑ 1	Dennis Eckersley	.20	.09
❑ 2	Chad Curtis	.10	.05
❑ 3	Eric Anthony	.10	.05
❑ 4	Roberto Alomar	.50	.23
❑ 5	Steve Avery	.10	.05
❑ 6	Cal Eldred	.10	.05
❑ 7	Bernard Gilkey	.10	.05
❑ 8	Steve Buechele	.10	.05
❑ 9	Brett Butler	.20	.09
❑ 10	Terry Mulholland	.10	.05
❑ 11	Moises Alou	.20	.09
❑ 12	Barry Bonds	1.25	.55
❑ 13	Sandy Alomar Jr.	.20	.09
❑ 14	Chris Bosio	.10	.05
❑ 15	Scott Sanderson	.10	.05
❑ 16	Bobby Bonilla	.20	.09
❑ 17	Brady Anderson	.20	.09
❑ 18	Derek Bell	.10	.05
❑ 19	Wes Chamberlain	.10	.05
❑ 20	Jay Bell	.20	.09
❑ 21	Kevin Brown	.20	.09
❑ 22	Roger Clemens	1.25	.55
❑ 23	Roberto Kelly	.10	.05
❑ 24	Dante Bichette	.20	.09
❑ 25	George Brett	1.00	.45
❑ 26	Rob Deer	.10	.05
❑ 27	Brian Harper	.10	.05
❑ 28	George Bell	.10	.05
❑ 29	Jim Abbott	.20	.09
❑ 30	Dave Henderson	.10	.05
❑ 31	Wade Boggs	.50	.23
❑ 32	Chili Davis	.20	.09
❑ 33	Ellis Burks	.20	.09
❑ 34	Jeff Bagwell	.60	.25
❑ 35	Kent Hrbek	.20	.09
❑ 36	Pat Borders	.10	.05
❑ 37	Cecil Fielder	.20	.09
❑ 38	Sid Bream	.10	.05
❑ 39	Greg Gagne	.10	.05
❑ 40	Darryl Hamilton	.10	.05
❑ 41	Jerald Clark	.10	.05
❑ 42	Mark Grace	.50	.23
❑ 43	Barry Larkin	.50	.23
❑ 44	John Burkett	.10	.05
❑ 45	Scott Cooper	.10	.05
❑ 46	Mike Lansing RC	.20	.09
❑ 47	Jose Canseco	.50	.23
❑ 48	Will Clark	.50	.23
❑ 49	Carlos Garcia	.10	.05
❑ 50	Carlos Baerga	.10	.05
❑ 51	Darren Daulton	.20	.09
❑ 52	Jay Buhner	.20	.09
❑ 53	Andy Benes	.10	.05
❑ 54	Jeff Conine	.10	.05
❑ 55	Mike Devereaux	.10	.05
❑ 56	Vince Coleman	.10	.05
❑ 57	Terry Steinbach	.10	.05
❑ 58	J.T. Snow RC	.60	.25
❑ 59	Greg Swindell	.10	.05
❑ 60	Devon White	.10	.05
❑ 61	John Smoltz	.20	.09
❑ 62	Todd Zeile	.10	.05
❑ 63	Rick Wilkins	.10	.05
❑ 64	Tim Wallach	.10	.05
❑ 65	John Wetteland	.20	.09
❑ 66	Matt Williams	.30	.14
❑ 67	Paul Sorrento	.10	.05
❑ 68	David Valle	.10	.05
❑ 69	Walt Weiss	.10	.05
❑ 70	John Franco	.20	.09
❑ 71	Nolan Ryan	2.50	1.10
❑ 72	Frank Viola	.20	.09
❑ 73	Chris Sabo	.10	.05
❑ 74	David Nied	.10	.05
❑ 75	Kevin McReynolds	.10	.05
❑ 76	Lou Whitaker	.20	.09
❑ 77	Dave Winfield	.50	.23
❑ 78	Robin Ventura	.20	.09
❑ 79	Spike Owen	.10	.05
❑ 80	Cal Ripken Jr.	2.00	.90
❑ 81	Dan Walters	.10	.05
❑ 82	Mitch Williams	.10	.05
❑ 83	Tim Wakefield	.10	.05
❑ 84	Rickey Henderson	1.00	.45
❑ 85	Gary DiSarcina	.10	.05
❑ 86	Craig Biggio	.30	.14
❑ 87	Joe Carter	.20	.09
❑ 88	Ron Gant	.10	.05
❑ 89	John Jaha	.10	.05
❑ 90	Gregg Jefferies	.10	.05
❑ 91	Jose Guzman	.10	.05
❑ 92	Eric Karros	.20	.09
❑ 93	Wil Cordero	.10	.05
❑ 94	Royce Clayton	.10	.05
❑ 95	Albert Belle	.20	.09
❑ 96	Ken Griffey Jr.	1.50	.70
❑ 97	Orestes Destrade	.10	.05
❑ 98	Tony Fernandez	.10	.05
❑ 99	Leo Gomez	.10	.05
❑ 100	Tony Gwynn	1.00	.45
❑ 101	Len Dykstra	.20	.09
❑ 102	Jeff King	.10	.05
❑ 103	Julio Franco	.20	.09
❑ 104	Andre Dawson	.30	.14
❑ 105	Randy Milligan	.10	.05
❑ 106	Alex Cole	.10	.05
❑ 107	Phil Hiatt	.10	.05
❑ 108	Travis Fryman	.20	.09
❑ 109	Chuck Knoblauch	.20	.09
❑ 110	Bo Jackson	.20	.09
❑ 111	Pat Kelly	.10	.05
❑ 112	Bret Saberhagen	.20	.09
❑ 113	Ruben Sierra	.10	.05
❑ 114	Tim Salmon	.20	.09
❑ 115	Doug Jones	.10	.05
❑ 116	Ed Sprague	.10	.05
❑ 117	Terry Pendleton	.20	.09
❑ 118	Robin Yount	.50	.23
❑ 119	Mark Whiten	.10	.05
❑ 120	Checklist 1-110	.10	.05
❑ 121	Sammy Sosa	1.00	.45
❑ 122	Darryl Strawberry	.20	.09
❑ 123	Larry Walker	.30	.14
❑ 124	Robby Thompson	.10	.05
❑ 125	Carlos Martinez	.10	.05
❑ 126	Edgar Martinez	.30	.14
❑ 127	Benito Santiago	.10	.05
❑ 128	Howard Johnson	.10	.05
❑ 129	Harold Reynolds	.10	.05
❑ 130	Craig Shipley	.10	.05
❑ 131	Curt Schilling	.50	.23
❑ 132	Andy Van Slyke	.20	.09
❑ 133	Ivan Rodriguez	.50	.23
❑ 134	Mo Vaughn	.20	.09
❑ 135	Bip Roberts	.10	.05
❑ 136	Charlie Hayes	.10	.05
❑ 137	Brian McRae	.10	.05
❑ 138	Mickey Tettleton	.10	.05
❑ 139	Frank Thomas	.60	.25
❑ 140	Paul O'Neill	.50	.23
❑ 141	Mark McGwire	2.00	.90
❑ 142	Damion Easley	.10	.05
❑ 143	Ken Caminiti	.20	.09
❑ 144	Juan Guzman	.10	.05
❑ 145	Tom Glavine	.50	.23
❑ 146	Pat Listach	.10	.05
❑ 147	Lee Smith	.20	.09
❑ 148	Derrick May	.10	.05
❑ 149	Ramon Martinez	.10	.05
❑ 150	Delino DeShields	.10	.05
❑ 151	Kirt Manwaring	.10	.05
❑ 152	Reggie Jefferson	.10	.05
❑ 153	Randy Johnson	.60	.25
❑ 154	Dave Magadan	.10	.05
❑ 155	Dwight Gooden	.20	.09
❑ 156	Chris Hoiles	.10	.05
❑ 157	Fred McGriff	.30	.14
❑ 158	Dave Hollins	.10	.05
❑ 159	Al Martin	.10	.05
❑ 160	Juan Gonzalez	.50	.23
❑ 161	Mike Greenwell	.10	.05
❑ 162	Kevin Mitchell	.10	.05
❑ 163	Andres Galarraga	.30	.14
❑ 164	Wally Joyner	.20	.09
❑ 165	Kirk Gibson	.20	.09
❑ 166	Pedro Munoz	.10	.05
❑ 167	Ozzie Guillen	.10	.05
❑ 168	Jimmy Key	.20	.09
❑ 169	Kevin Seitzer	.10	.05
❑ 170	Luis Polonia	.10	.05
❑ 171	Luis Gonzalez	.50	.23
❑ 172	Paul Molitor	.50	.23
❑ 173	David Justice	.20	.09
❑ 174	B.J. Surhoff	.20	.09
❑ 175	Ray Lankford	.10	.05
❑ 176	Ryne Sandberg	.60	.25
❑ 177	Jody Reed	.10	.05
❑ 178	Marquis Grissom	.10	.05
❑ 179	Willie McGee	.20	.09
❑ 180	Kenny Lofton	.20	.09
❑ 181	Junior Felix	.10	.05
❑ 182	Jose Offerman	.10	.05
❑ 183	John Kruk	.20	.09
❑ 184	Orlando Merced	.10	.05
❑ 185	Rafael Palmeiro	.50	.23
❑ 186	Billy Hatcher	.10	.05
❑ 187	Joe Oliver	.10	.05
❑ 188	Joe Girardi	.10	.05
❑ 189	Jose Lind	.10	.05
❑ 190	Harold Baines	.20	.09
❑ 191	Mike Pagliarulo	.10	.05
❑ 192	Lance Johnson	.10	.05
❑ 193	Don Mattingly	1.25	.55
❑ 194	Doug Drabek	.10	.05
❑ 195	John Olerud	.20	.09
❑ 196	Greg Maddux	1.25	.55
❑ 197	Greg Vaughn	.20	.09
❑ 198	Tom Pagnozzi	.10	.05
❑ 199	Willie Wilson	.10	.05
❑ 200	Jack McDowell	.10	.05
❑ 201	Mike Piazza	2.50	1.10
❑ 202	Mike Mussina	.50	.23
❑ 203	Charles Nagy	.10	.05
❑ 204	Tino Martinez	.20	.09
❑ 205	Charlie Hough	.20	.09
❑ 206	Todd Hundley	.10	.05
❑ 207	Gary Sheffield	.20	.09
❑ 208	Mickey Morandini	.10	.05
❑ 209	Don Slaught	.10	.05
❑ 210	Dean Palmer	.20	.09
❑ 211	Jose Rijo	.10	.05
❑ 212	Vinny Castilla	.20	.09
❑ 213	Tony Phillips	.10	.05
❑ 214	Kirby Puckett	1.25	.55
❑ 215	Tim Raines	.20	.09
❑ 216	Otis Nixon	.10	.05

❑ 217 Ozzie Smith	.60	.25
❑ 218 Jose Vizcaino	.10	.05
❑ 219 Randy Tomlin	.10	.05
❑ 220 Checklist 111-220	.10	.05

1994 Studio

	MINT	NRMT
COMPLETE SET (220)	15.00	6.75
❑ 1 Dennis Eckersley	.25	.11
❑ 2 Brent Gates	.15	.07
❑ 3 Rickey Henderson	1.25	.55
❑ 4 Mark McGwire	2.50	1.10
❑ 5 Troy Neel	.15	.07
❑ 6 Ruben Sierra	.15	.07
❑ 7 Terry Steinbach	.15	.07
❑ 8 Chad Curtis	.15	.07
❑ 9 Chili Davis	.25	.11
❑ 10 Gary DiSarcina	.15	.07
❑ 11 Damion Easley	.15	.07
❑ 12 Bo Jackson	.25	.11
❑ 13 Mark Langston	.15	.07
❑ 14 Eduardo Perez	.15	.07
❑ 15 Tim Salmon	.25	.11
❑ 16 Jeff Bagwell	.75	.35
❑ 17 Craig Biggio	.40	.18
❑ 18 Ken Caminiti	.25	.11
❑ 19 Andujar Cedeno	.15	.07
❑ 20 Doug Drabek	.15	.07
❑ 21 Steve Finley	.25	.11
❑ 22 Luis Gonzalez	.60	.25
❑ 23 Darryl Kile	.25	.11
❑ 24 Roberto Alomar	.60	.25
❑ 25 Pat Borders	.15	.07
❑ 26 Joe Carter	.25	.11
❑ 27 Carlos Delgado	1.00	.45
❑ 28 Pat Hentgen	.15	.07
❑ 29 Paul Molitor	.60	.25
❑ 30 John Olerud	.25	.11
❑ 31 Ed Sprague	.15	.07
❑ 32 Devon White	.15	.07
❑ 33 Steve Avery	.15	.07
❑ 34 Tom Glavine	.60	.25
❑ 35 David Justice	.25	.11
❑ 36 Roberto Kelly	.15	.07
❑ 37 Ryan Klesko	.25	.11
❑ 38 Javier Lopez	.25	.11
❑ 39 Greg Maddux	1.50	.70
❑ 40 Fred McGriff	.40	.18
❑ 41 Terry Pendleton	.25	.11
❑ 42 Ricky Bones	.15	.07
❑ 43 Darryl Hamilton	.15	.07
❑ 44 Brian Harper	.15	.07
❑ 45 John Jaha	.15	.07
❑ 46 Dave Nilsson	.15	.07
❑ 47 Kevin Seitzer	.15	.07
❑ 48 Greg Vaughn	.25	.11
❑ 49 Turner Ward	.15	.07
❑ 50 Bernard Gilkey	.15	.07
❑ 51 Gregg Jefferies	.15	.07
❑ 52 Ray Lankford	.15	.07
❑ 53 Tom Pagnozzi	.15	.07
❑ 54 Ozzie Smith	.75	.35
❑ 55 Bob Tewksbury	.15	.07
❑ 56 Mark Whiten	.15	.07
❑ 57 Todd Zeile	.15	.07
❑ 58 Steve Buechele	.15	.07
❑ 59 Shawon Dunston	.15	.07
❑ 60 Mark Grace	.60	.25
❑ 61 Derrick May	.15	.07
❑ 62 Karl Rhodes	.15	.07
❑ 63 Ryne Sandberg	.75	.35
❑ 64 Sammy Sosa	1.25	.55
❑ 65 Rick Wilkins	.15	.07
❑ 66 Brett Butler	.25	.11
❑ 67 Delino DeShields	.15	.07
❑ 68 Orel Hershiser	.25	.11
❑ 69 Eric Karros	.25	.11
❑ 70 Raul Mondesi	.25	.11
❑ 71 Jose Offerman	.15	.07
❑ 72 Mike Piazza	2.00	.90
❑ 73 Tim Wallach	.15	.07
❑ 74 Moises Alou	.25	.11
❑ 75 Sean Berry	.15	.07
❑ 76 Wil Cordero	.15	.07
❑ 77 Cliff Floyd	.25	.11
❑ 78 Marquis Grissom	.15	.07
❑ 79 Ken Hill	.15	.07
❑ 80 Larry Walker	.40	.18
❑ 81 John Wetteland	.25	.11
❑ 82 Rod Beck	.15	.07
❑ 83 Barry Bonds	1.50	.70
❑ 84 Royce Clayton	.15	.07
❑ 85 Darren Lewis	.15	.07
❑ 86 Willie McGee	.25	.11
❑ 87 Bill Swift	.15	.07
❑ 88 Robby Thompson	.15	.07
❑ 89 Matt Williams	.40	.18
❑ 90 Sandy Alomar Jr.	.25	.11
❑ 91 Carlos Baerga	.15	.07
❑ 92 Albert Belle	.25	.11
❑ 93 Kenny Lofton	.25	.11
❑ 94 Eddie Murray	.60	.25
❑ 95 Manny Ramirez	1.00	.45
❑ 96 Paul Sorrento	.15	.07
❑ 97 Jim Thome	.60	.25
❑ 98 Rich Amaral	.15	.07
❑ 99 Eric Anthony	.15	.07
❑ 100 Jay Buhner	.25	.11
❑ 101 Ken Griffey Jr.	2.00	.90
❑ 102 Randy Johnson	.75	.35
❑ 103 Edgar Martinez	.40	.18
❑ 104 Tino Martinez	.25	.11
❑ 105 Kurt Abbott RC	.25	.11
❑ 106 Bret Barberie	.15	.07
❑ 107 Chuck Carr	.15	.07
❑ 108 Jeff Conine	.15	.07
❑ 109 Chris Hammond	.15	.07
❑ 110 Bryan Harvey	.15	.07
❑ 111 Benito Santiago	.15	.07
❑ 112 Gary Sheffield	.25	.11
❑ 113 Bobby Bonilla	.25	.11
❑ 114 Dwight Gooden	.25	.11
❑ 115 Todd Hundley	.15	.07
❑ 116 Bobby Jones	.15	.07
❑ 117 Jeff Kent	.40	.18
❑ 118 Kevin McReynolds	.15	.07
❑ 119 Bret Saberhagen	.25	.11
❑ 120 Ryan Thompson	.15	.07
❑ 121 Harold Baines	.25	.11
❑ 122 Mike Devereaux	.15	.07
❑ 123 Jeffrey Hammonds	.25	.11
❑ 124 Ben McDonald	.15	.07
❑ 125 Mike Mussina	.60	.25
❑ 126 Rafael Palmeiro	.60	.25
❑ 127 Cal Ripken Jr.	2.50	1.10
❑ 128 Lee Smith	.25	.11
❑ 129 Brad Ausmus	.15	.07
❑ 130 Derek Bell	.15	.07
❑ 131 Andy Benes	.15	.07
❑ 132 Tony Gwynn	1.25	.55
❑ 133 Trevor Hoffman	.25	.11
❑ 134 Scott Livingstone	.15	.07
❑ 135 Phil Plantier	.15	.07
❑ 136 Darren Daulton	.25	.11
❑ 137 Mariano Duncan	.15	.07
❑ 138 Lenny Dykstra	.25	.11
❑ 139 Dave Hollins	.15	.07
❑ 140 Pete Incaviglia	.15	.07
❑ 141 Danny Jackson	.15	.07
❑ 142 John Kruk	.25	.11
❑ 143 Kevin Stocker	.15	.07
❑ 144 Jay Bell	.25	.11
❑ 145 Carlos Garcia	.15	.07
❑ 146 Jeff King	.15	.07
❑ 147 Al Martin	.15	.07
❑ 148 Orlando Merced	.15	.07
❑ 149 Don Slaught	.15	.07
❑ 150 Andy Van Slyke	.25	.11
❑ 151 Kevin Brown	.25	.11
❑ 152 Jose Canseco	.60	.25
❑ 153 Will Clark	.60	.25
❑ 154 Juan Gonzalez	.60	.25
❑ 155 David Hulse	.15	.07
❑ 156 Dean Palmer	.25	.11
❑ 157 Ivan Rodriguez	.60	.25
❑ 158 Kenny Rogers	.15	.07
❑ 159 Roger Clemens	1.50	.70
❑ 160 Scott Cooper	.15	.07
❑ 161 Andre Dawson	.40	.18
❑ 162 Mike Greenwell	.15	.07
❑ 163 Otis Nixon	.15	.07
❑ 164 Aaron Sele	.25	.11
❑ 165 John Valentin	.15	.07
❑ 166 Mo Vaughn	.25	.11
❑ 167 Bret Boone	.25	.11
❑ 168 Barry Larkin	.60	.25
❑ 169 Kevin Mitchell	.15	.07
❑ 170 Hal Morris	.15	.07
❑ 171 Jose Rijo	.15	.07
❑ 172 Deion Sanders	.25	.11
❑ 173 Reggie Sanders	.15	.07
❑ 174 John Smiley	.15	.07
❑ 175 Dante Bichette	.25	.11
❑ 176 Ellis Burks	.25	.11
❑ 177 Andres Galarraga	.40	.18
❑ 178 Joe Girardi	.15	.07
❑ 179 Charlie Hayes	.15	.07
❑ 180 Roberto Mejia	.15	.07
❑ 181 Walt Weiss	.15	.07
❑ 182 David Cone	.25	.11
❑ 183 Gary Gaetti	.25	.11
❑ 184 Greg Gagne	.15	.07
❑ 185 Felix Jose	.15	.07
❑ 186 Wally Joyner	.25	.11
❑ 187 Mike Macfarlane	.15	.07
❑ 188 Brian McRae	.15	.07
❑ 189 Eric Davis	.25	.11
❑ 190 Cecil Fielder	.25	.11
❑ 191 Travis Fryman	.25	.11
❑ 192 Tony Phillips	.15	.07
❑ 193 Mickey Tettleton	.15	.07
❑ 194 Alan Trammell	.40	.18
❑ 195 Lou Whitaker	.25	.11
❑ 196 Kent Hrbek	.25	.11
❑ 197 Chuck Knoblauch	.25	.11
❑ 198 Shane Mack	.15	.07
❑ 199 Pat Meares	.15	.07
❑ 200 Kirby Puckett	1.50	.70
❑ 201 Matt Walbeck	.15	.07
❑ 202 Dave Winfield	.60	.25
❑ 203 Wilson Alvarez	.15	.07
❑ 204 Alex Fernandez	.15	.07
❑ 205 Julio Franco	.25	.11
❑ 206 Ozzie Guillen	.15	.07
❑ 207 Jack McDowell	.15	.07
❑ 208 Tim Raines	.25	.11
❑ 209 Frank Thomas	.75	.35
❑ 210 Robin Ventura	.25	.11
❑ 211 Jim Abbott	.25	.11
❑ 212 Wade Boggs	.60	.25
❑ 213 Pat Kelly	.15	.07
❑ 214 Jimmy Key	.25	.11
❑ 215 Don Mattingly	1.50	.70
❑ 216 Paul O'Neill	.60	.25
❑ 217 Mike Stanley	.15	.07
❑ 218 Danny Tartabull	.15	.07
❑ 219 Checklist	.15	.07
❑ 220 Checklist	.15	.07

1995 Studio

	MINT	NRMT
COMPLETE SET (200)	60.00	27.00
❑ 1 Frank Thomas	1.00	.45
❑ 2 Jeff Bagwell	1.00	.45
❑ 3 Don Mattingly	2.00	.90
❑ 4 Mike Piazza	2.00	.90

❑ 5 Ken Griffey Jr. 2.50 1.10
❑ 6 Greg Maddux 2.00 .90
❑ 7 Barry Bonds 2.00 .90
❑ 8 Cal Ripken Jr. 3.00 1.35
❑ 9 Jose Canseco .75 .35
❑ 10 Paul Molitor .75 .35
❑ 11 Kenny Lofton .30 .14
❑ 12 Will Clark .75 .35
❑ 13 Tim Salmon .30 .14
❑ 14 Joe Carter .30 .14
❑ 15 Albert Belle .30 .14
❑ 16 Roger Clemens 2.00 .90
❑ 17 Roberto Alomar .75 .35
❑ 18 Alex Rodriguez 2.50 1.10
❑ 19 Raul Mondesi .30 .14
❑ 20 Deion Sanders .30 .14
❑ 21 Juan Gonzalez .75 .35
❑ 22 Kirby Puckett 2.00 .90
❑ 23 Fred McGriff .50 .23
❑ 24 Matt Williams .50 .23
❑ 25 Tony Gwynn 1.50 .70
❑ 26 Cliff Floyd .30 .14
❑ 27 Travis Fryman .30 .14
❑ 28 Shawn Green .75 .35
❑ 29 Mike Mussina .75 .35
❑ 30 Bob Hamelin .20 .09
❑ 31 David Justice .30 .14
❑ 32 Manny Ramirez 1.00 .45
❑ 33 David Cone .30 .14
❑ 34 Marquis Grissom .20 .09
❑ 35 Moises Alou .30 .14
❑ 36 Carlos Baerga .20 .09
❑ 37 Barry Larkin .75 .35
❑ 38 Robin Ventura .30 .14
❑ 39 Mo Vaughn .30 .14
❑ 40 Jeffrey Hammonds .20 .09
❑ 41 Ozzie Smith 1.00 .45
❑ 42 Andres Galarraga .50 .23
❑ 43 Carlos Delgado .75 .35
❑ 44 Lenny Dykstra .30 .14
❑ 45 Cecil Fielder .30 .14
❑ 46 Wade Boggs .75 .35
❑ 47 Gregg Jefferies .20 .09
❑ 48 Randy Johnson 1.00 .45
❑ 49 Rafael Palmeiro .75 .35
❑ 50 Craig Biggio .50 .23
❑ 51 Steve Avery .20 .09
❑ 52 Ricky Bottalico .20 .09
❑ 53 Chris Gomez .20 .09
❑ 54 Carlos Garcia .20 .09
❑ 55 Brian Anderson .20 .09
❑ 56 Wilson Alvarez .20 .09
❑ 57 Roberto Kelly .20 .09
❑ 58 Larry Walker .50 .23
❑ 59 Dean Palmer .30 .14
❑ 60 Rick Aguilera .20 .09
❑ 61 Javier Lopez .30 .14
❑ 62 Shawon Dunston .20 .09
❑ 63 Wm. VanLandingham .20 .09
❑ 64 Jeff Kent .50 .23
❑ 65 David McCarty .20 .09
❑ 66 Armando Benitez .30 .14
❑ 67 Brett Butler .30 .14
❑ 68 Bernard Gilkey .20 .09
❑ 69 Joey Hamilton .20 .09
❑ 70 Chad Curtis .20 .09
❑ 71 Dante Bichette .30 .14
❑ 72 Chuck Carr .20 .09
❑ 73 Pedro Martinez 1.00 .45
❑ 74 Ramon Martinez .20 .09
❑ 75 Rondell White .30 .14
❑ 76 Alex Fernandez .20 .09
❑ 77 Dennis Martinez .30 .14
❑ 78 Sammy Sosa 1.50 .70
❑ 79 Bernie Williams .75 .35
❑ 80 Lou Whitaker .30 .14
❑ 81 Kurt Abbott .20 .09
❑ 82 Tino Martinez .30 .14
❑ 83 Willie Greene .20 .09
❑ 84 Garret Anderson .30 .14
❑ 85 Jose Rijo .20 .09
❑ 86 Jeff Montgomery .20 .09
❑ 87 Mark Langston .20 .09
❑ 88 Reggie Sanders .20 .09
❑ 89 Rusty Greer .30 .14
❑ 90 Delino DeShields .20 .09
❑ 91 Jason Bere .20 .09
❑ 92 Lee Smith .30 .14
❑ 93 Devon White .30 .14
❑ 94 John Wetteland .30 .14
❑ 95 Luis Gonzalez .75 .35
❑ 96 Greg Vaughn .30 .14
❑ 97 Lance Johnson .20 .09
❑ 98 Alan Trammell .50 .23
❑ 99 Bret Saberhagen .30 .14
❑ 100 Jack McDowell .20 .09
❑ 101 Trevor Hoffman .30 .14
❑ 102 Dave Nilsson .20 .09
❑ 103 Bryan Harvey .20 .09
❑ 104 Chuck Knoblauch .30 .14
❑ 105 Bobby Bonilla .30 .14
❑ 106 Hal Morris .20 .09
❑ 107 Mark Whiten .20 .09
❑ 108 Phil Plantier .20 .09
❑ 109 Ryan Klesko .30 .14
❑ 110 Greg Gagne .20 .09
❑ 111 Ruben Sierra .20 .09
❑ 112 J.R. Phillips .20 .09
❑ 113 Terry Steinbach .20 .09
❑ 114 Jay Buhner .30 .14
❑ 115 Ken Caminiti .30 .14
❑ 116 Gary DiSarcina .20 .09
❑ 117 Ivan Rodriguez .75 .35
❑ 118 Bip Roberts .20 .09
❑ 119 Jay Bell .30 .14
❑ 120 Ken Hill .20 .09
❑ 121 Mike Greenwell .20 .09
❑ 122 Rick Wilkins .20 .09
❑ 123 Rickey Henderson 1.50 .70
❑ 124 Dave Hollins .20 .09
❑ 125 Terry Pendleton .30 .14
❑ 126 Rich Becker .20 .09
❑ 127 Billy Ashley .20 .09
❑ 128 Derek Bell .20 .09
❑ 129 Dennis Eckersley .30 .14
❑ 130 Andujar Cedeno .20 .09
❑ 131 John Jaha .20 .09
❑ 132 Chuck Finley .30 .14
❑ 133 Steve Finley .30 .14
❑ 134 Danny Tartabull .20 .09
❑ 135 Jeff Conine .20 .09
❑ 136 Jon Lieber .20 .09
❑ 137 Jim Abbott .30 .14
❑ 138 Steve Trachsel .20 .09
❑ 139 Bret Boone .30 .14
❑ 140 Charles Johnson .30 .14
❑ 141 Mark McGwire 3.00 1.35
❑ 142 Eddie Murray .75 .35
❑ 143 Doug Drabek .20 .09
❑ 144 Steve Cooke .20 .09
❑ 145 Kevin Seitzer .20 .09
❑ 146 Rod Beck .20 .09
❑ 147 Eric Karros .30 .14
❑ 148 Tim Raines .30 .14
❑ 149 Joe Girardi .20 .09
❑ 150 Aaron Sele .30 .14
❑ 151 Robby Thompson .20 .09
❑ 152 Chan Ho Park .30 .14
❑ 153 Ellis Burks .30 .14
❑ 154 Brian McRae .20 .09
❑ 155 Jimmy Key .30 .14
❑ 156 Rico Brogna .20 .09
❑ 157 Ozzie Guillen .20 .09
❑ 158 Chili Davis .30 .14
❑ 159 Darren Daulton .30 .14
❑ 160 Chipper Jones 1.50 .70
❑ 161 Walt Weiss .20 .09
❑ 162 Paul O'Neill .75 .35
❑ 163 Al Martin .20 .09
❑ 164 John Valentin .20 .09
❑ 165 Tim Wallach .20 .09
❑ 166 Scott Erickson .20 .09
❑ 167 Ryan Thompson .20 .09
❑ 168 Todd Zeile .20 .09
❑ 169 Scott Cooper .20 .09
❑ 170 Matt Mieske .20 .09
❑ 171 Allen Watson .20 .09
❑ 172 Brian L.Hunter .20 .09
❑ 173 Kevin Stocker .20 .09
❑ 174 Cal Eldred .20 .09
❑ 175 Tony Phillips .20 .09
❑ 176 Ben McDonald .20 .09
❑ 177 Mark Grace .75 .35
❑ 178 Midre Cummings .20 .09
❑ 179 Orlando Merced .20 .09
❑ 180 Jeff King .20 .09
❑ 181 Gary Sheffield .30 .14
❑ 182 Tom Glavine .75 .35
❑ 183 Edgar Martinez .50 .23
❑ 184 Steve Karsay .20 .09
❑ 185 Pat Listach .20 .09
❑ 186 Wil Cordero .20 .09
❑ 187 Brady Anderson .30 .14
❑ 188 Bobby Jones .20 .09
❑ 189 Andy Benes .20 .09
❑ 190 Ray Lankford .20 .09
❑ 191 John Doherty .20 .09
❑ 192 Wally Joyner .30 .14
❑ 193 Jim Thome .75 .35
❑ 194 Royce Clayton .20 .09
❑ 195 John Olerud .30 .14
❑ 196 Steve Buechele .20 .09
❑ 197 Harold Baines .30 .14
❑ 198 Geronimo Berroa .20 .09
❑ 199 Checklist .20 .09
❑ 200 Checklist .20 .09

1996 Studio

	MINT	NRMT
COMPLETE SET (150)	15.00	6.75

❑ 1 Cal Ripken 2.00 .90
❑ 2 Alex Gonzalez .12 .05
❑ 3 Roger Cedeno .12 .05
❑ 4 Todd Hollandsworth .12 .05
❑ 5 Gregg Jefferies .12 .05
❑ 6 Ryne Sandberg .60 .25
❑ 7 Eric Karros .20 .09
❑ 8 Jeff Conine .12 .05
❑ 9 Rafael Palmeiro .50 .23
❑ 10 Bip Roberts .12 .05
❑ 11 Roger Clemens 1.25 .55
❑ 12 Tom Glavine .50 .23
❑ 13 Jason Giambi .50 .23
❑ 14 Rey Ordonez .12 .05
❑ 15 Chan Ho Park .20 .09
❑ 16 Vinny Castilla .20 .09
❑ 17 Butch Huskey .12 .05
❑ 18 Greg Maddux 1.25 .55
❑ 19 Bernard Gilkey .12 .05

❑	20 Marquis Grissom	.12	.05
❑	21 Chuck Knoblauch	.20	.09
❑	22 Ozzie Smith	.60	.25
❑	23 Garret Anderson	.20	.09
❑	24 J.T. Snow	.20	.09
❑	25 John Valentin	.12	.05
❑	26 Barry Larkin	.50	.23
❑	27 Bobby Bonilla	.20	.09
❑	28 Todd Zeile	.12	.05
❑	29 Roberto Alomar	.50	.23
❑	30 Ramon Martinez	.12	.05
❑	31 Jeff King	.12	.05
❑	32 Dennis Eckersley	.20	.09
❑	33 Derek Jeter	2.00	.90
❑	34 Edgar Martinez	.30	.14
❑	35 Geronimo Berroa	.12	.05
❑	36 Hal Morris	.12	.05
❑	37 Troy Percival	.12	.05
❑	38 Jason Isringhausen	.20	.09
❑	39 Greg Vaughn	.20	.09
❑	40 Robin Ventura	.20	.09
❑	41 Craig Biggio	.30	.14
❑	42 Will Clark	.50	.23
❑	43 Sammy Sosa	1.00	.45
❑	44 Bernie Williams	.50	.23
❑	45 Kenny Lofton	.20	.09
❑	46 Wade Boggs	.50	.23
❑	47 Javy Lopez	.20	.09
❑	48 Reggie Sanders	.12	.05
❑	49 Jeff Bagwell	.60	.25
❑	50 Fred McGriff	.30	.14
❑	51 Charles Johnson	.20	.09
❑	52 Darren Daulton	.20	.09
❑	53 Jose Canseco	.50	.23
❑	54 Cecil Fielder	.20	.09
❑	55 Hideo Nomo	.60	.25
❑	56 Tim Salmon	.20	.09
❑	57 Carlos Delgado	.50	.23
❑	58 David Cone	.20	.09
❑	59 Tim Raines	.20	.09
❑	60 Lyle Mouton	.12	.05
❑	61 Wally Joyner	.20	.09
❑	62 Bret Boone	.20	.09
❑	63 Raul Mondesi	.20	.09
❑	64 Gary Sheffield	.20	.09
❑	65 Alex Rodriguez	1.25	.55
❑	66 Russ Davis	.12	.05
❑	67 Checklist	.12	.05
❑	68 Marty Cordova	.12	.05
❑	69 Ruben Sierra	.12	.05
❑	70 Jose Mesa	.12	.05
❑	71 Matt Williams	.30	.14
❑	72 Chipper Jones	1.00	.45
❑	73 Randy Johnson	.60	.25
❑	74 Kirby Puckett	1.25	.55
❑	75 Jim Edmonds	.30	.14
❑	76 Barry Bonds	1.25	.55
❑	77 David Segui	.12	.05
❑	78 Larry Walker	.30	.14
❑	79 Jason Kendall	.20	.09
❑	80 Mike Piazza	1.25	.55
❑	81 Brian L.Hunter	.12	.05
❑	82 Julio Franco	.20	.09
❑	83 Jay Bell	.20	.09
❑	84 Kevin Seitzer	.12	.05
❑	85 John Smoltz	.20	.09
❑	86 Joe Carter	.20	.09
❑	87 Ray Durham	.20	.09
❑	88 Carlos Baerga	.12	.05
❑	89 Ron Gant	.12	.05
❑	90 Orlando Merced	.12	.05
❑	91 Lee Smith	.20	.09
❑	92 Pedro Martinez	.60	.25
❑	93 Frank Thomas	.60	.25
❑	94 Al Martin	.12	.05
❑	95 Chad Curtis	.12	.05
❑	96 Eddie Murray	.50	.23
❑	97 Rusty Greer	.20	.09
❑	98 Jay Buhner	.20	.09
❑	99 Rico Brogna	.12	.05
❑	100 Todd Hundley	.12	.05
❑	101 Moises Alou	.20	.09
❑	102 Chili Davis	.20	.09
❑	103 Ismael Valdes	.12	.05
❑	104 Mo Vaughn	.20	.09
❑	105 Juan Gonzalez	.50	.23
❑	106 Mark Grudzielanek	.12	.05
❑	107 Derek Bell	.12	.05
❑	108 Shawn Green	.50	.23
❑	109 David Justice	.20	.09
❑	110 Paul O'Neill	.50	.23
❑	111 Kevin Appier	.20	.09
❑	112 Ray Lankford	.12	.05
❑	113 Travis Fryman	.20	.09
❑	114 Manny Ramirez	.60	.25
❑	115 Brooks Kieschnick	.12	.05
❑	116 Ken Griffey Jr.	1.50	.70
❑	117 Jeffrey Hammonds	.12	.05
❑	118 Mark McGwire	2.00	.90
❑	119 Denny Neagle	.20	.09
❑	120 Quilvio Veras	.12	.05
❑	121 Alan Benes	.12	.05
❑	122 Rondell White	.20	.09
❑	123 Osvaldo Fernandez RC	.12	.05
❑	124 Andres Galarraga	.30	.14
❑	125 Johnny Damon	.20	.09
❑	126 Lenny Dykstra	.20	.09
❑	127 Jason Schmidt	.12	.05
❑	128 Mike Mussina	.50	.23
❑	129 Ken Caminiti	.20	.09
❑	130 Michael Tucker	.12	.05
❑	131 LaTroy Hawkins	.12	.05
❑	132 Checklist	.12	.05
❑	133 Delino DeShields	.12	.05
❑	134 Dave Nilsson	.12	.05
❑	135 Jack McDowell	.12	.05
❑	136 Joey Hamilton	.12	.05
❑	137 Dante Bichette	.20	.09
❑	138 Paul Molitor	.50	.23
❑	139 Ivan Rodriguez	.50	.23
❑	140 Mark Grace	.50	.23
❑	141 Paul Wilson	.12	.05
❑	142 Orel Hershiser	.20	.09
❑	143 Albert Belle	.20	.09
❑	144 Tino Martinez	.20	.09
❑	145 Tony Gwynn	1.00	.45
❑	146 George Arias	.12	.05
❑	147 Brian Jordan	.20	.09
❑	148 Brian McRae	.12	.05
❑	149 Rickey Henderson	1.00	.45
❑	150 Ryan Klesko	.20	.09

1997 Studio

		MINT	NRMT
	COMPLETE SET (165)	60.00	27.00
❑	1 Frank Thomas	.75	.35
❑	2 Gary Sheffield	.25	.11
❑	3 Jason Isringhausen	.15	.07
❑	4 Ron Gant	.15	.07
❑	5 Andy Pettitte	.25	.11
❑	6 Todd Hollandsworth	.15	.07
❑	7 Troy Percival	.15	.07
❑	8 Mark McGwire	2.50	1.10
❑	9 Barry Larkin	.60	.25
❑	10 Ken Caminiti	.25	.11
❑	11 Paul Molitor	.60	.25
❑	12 Travis Fryman	.25	.11
❑	13 Kevin Brown	.25	.11
❑	14 Robin Ventura	.25	.11
❑	15 Andres Galarraga	.40	.18
❑	16 Ken Griffey Jr.	2.00	.90
❑	17 Roger Clemens	1.50	.70
❑	18 Alan Benes	.15	.07
❑	19 Dave Justice	.25	.11
❑	20 Damon Buford	.15	.07
❑	21 Mike Piazza	1.50	.70
❑	22 Ray Durham	.25	.11
❑	23 Billy Wagner	.15	.07
❑	24 Dean Palmer	.25	.11
❑	25 David Cone	.25	.11
❑	26 Ruben Sierra	.15	.07
❑	27 Henry Rodriguez	.15	.07
❑	28 Ray Lankford	.15	.07
❑	29 Jamey Wright	.15	.07
❑	30 Brady Anderson	.25	.11
❑	31 Tino Martinez	.25	.11
❑	32 Manny Ramirez	.75	.35
❑	33 Jeff Conine	.15	.07
❑	34 Dante Bichette	.25	.11
❑	35 Jose Canseco	.60	.25
❑	36 Mo Vaughn	.25	.11
❑	37 Sammy Sosa	1.25	.55
❑	38 Mark Grudzielanek	.15	.07
❑	39 Mike Mussina	.60	.25
❑	40 Bill Pulsipher	.15	.07
❑	41 Ryne Sandberg	.75	.35
❑	42 Rickey Henderson	1.25	.55
❑	43 Alex Rodriguez	1.50	.70
❑	44 Eddie Murray	.60	.25
❑	45 Ernie Young	.15	.07
❑	46 Joey Hamilton	.15	.07
❑	47 Wade Boggs	.60	.25
❑	48 Rusty Greer	.25	.11
❑	49 Carlos Delgado	.60	.25
❑	50 Ellis Burks	.25	.11
❑	51 Cal Ripken	2.50	1.10
❑	52 Alex Fernandez	.15	.07
❑	53 Wally Joyner	.25	.11
❑	54 James Baldwin	.15	.07
❑	55 Juan Gonzalez	.60	.25
❑	56 John Smoltz	.25	.11
❑	57 Omar Vizquel	.25	.11
❑	58 Shane Reynolds	.15	.07
❑	59 Barry Bonds	1.50	.70
❑	60 Jason Kendall	.25	.11
❑	61 Marty Cordova	.15	.07
❑	62 Charles Johnson	.25	.11
❑	63 John Jaha	.15	.07
❑	64 Chan Ho Park	.25	.11
❑	65 Jermaine Allensworth	.15	.07
❑	66 Mark Grace	.60	.25
❑	67 Tim Salmon	.25	.11
❑	68 Edgar Martinez	.40	.18
❑	69 Marquis Grissom	.15	.07
❑	70 Craig Biggio	.40	.18
❑	71 Bobby Higginson	.25	.11
❑	72 Kevin Seitzer	.15	.07
❑	73 Hideo Nomo	.60	.25
❑	74 Dennis Eckersley	.25	.11
❑	75 Bobby Bonilla	.25	.11
❑	76 Dwight Gooden	.25	.11
❑	77 Jeff Cirillo	.25	.11
❑	78 Brian McRae	.15	.07
❑	79 Chipper Jones	1.25	.55
❑	80 Jeff Fassero	.15	.07
❑	81 Fred McGriff	.40	.18
❑	82 Garret Anderson	.25	.11
❑	83 Eric Karros	.25	.11
❑	84 Derek Bell	.15	.07
❑	85 Kenny Lofton	.25	.11
❑	86 John Mabry	.15	.07
❑	87 Pat Hentgen	.15	.07
❑	88 Greg Maddux	1.50	.70
❑	89 Jason Giambi	.60	.25
❑	90 Al Martin	.15	.07
❑	91 Derek Jeter	2.50	1.10
❑	92 Rey Ordonez	.15	.07
❑	93 Will Clark	.60	.25
❑	94 Kevin Appier	.25	.11
❑	95 Roberto Alomar	.60	.25
❑	96 Joe Carter	.25	.11
❑	97 Bernie Williams	.60	.25
❑	98 Albert Belle	.25	.11
❑	99 Greg Vaughn	.25	.11
❑	100 Tony Clark	.25	.11
❑	101 Matt Williams	.40	.18
❑	102 Jeff Bagwell	.75	.35
❑	103 Reggie Sanders	.15	.07

No.	Player	MINT	NRMT
104	Mariano Rivera	.25	.11
105	Larry Walker	.40	.18
106	Shawn Green	.60	.25
107	Alex Ochoa	.15	.07
108	Ivan Rodriguez	.60	.25
109	Eric Young	.15	.07
110	Javier Lopez	.25	.11
111	Brian Hunter	.15	.07
112	Raul Mondesi SP	5.00	2.20
113	Randy Johnson	.75	.35
114	Tony Phillips	.15	.07
115	Carlos Garcia	.15	.07
116	Moises Alou	.25	.11
117	Paul O'Neill	.60	.25
118	Jim Thome	.60	.25
119	Jermaine Dye	.25	.11
120	Wilson Alvarez	.15	.07
121	Rondell White	.25	.11
122	Michael Tucker	.15	.07
123	Mike Lansing	.15	.07
124	Tony Gwynn	1.25	.55
125	Ryan Klesko	.25	.11
126	Jim Edmonds	.40	.18
127	Chuck Knoblauch	.25	.11
128	Rafael Palmeiro	.60	.25
129	Jay Buhner	.25	.11
130	Tom Glavine	.60	.25
131	Julio Franco	.25	.11
132	Cecil Fielder	.25	.11
133	Paul Wilson SP	4.00	1.80
134	Deion Sanders	.25	.11
135	Alex Gonzalez	.15	.07
136	Charles Nagy	.15	.07
137	Andy Ashby SP	4.00	1.80
138	Edgar Renteria	.15	.07
139	Pedro Martinez	.75	.35
140	Brian Jordan	.25	.11
141	Todd Hundley	.15	.07
142	Marc Newfield	.15	.07
143	Darryl Strawberry	.25	.11
144	Dan Wilson	.15	.07
145	Brian Giles RC	2.50	1.10
146	F.P. Santangelo	.15	.07
147	Shannon Stewart SP	5.00	2.20
148	Scott Spiezio	.15	.07
149	Andruw Jones	.75	.35
150	Karim Garcia	.15	.07
151	Vladimir Guerrero	1.00	.45
152	George Arias	.15	.07
153	Brooks Kieschnick	.15	.07
154	Todd Walker	.15	.07
155	Scott Rolen	.60	.25
156	Todd Greene	.15	.07
157	Dmitri Young	.25	.11
158	Ruben Rivera	.15	.07
159	Bartolo Colon	.25	.11
160	Nomar Garciaparra	1.50	.70
161	Bob Abreu SP	5.00	2.20
162	Darin Erstad	.60	.25
163	Ken Griffey Jr. CL	1.00	.45
164	Frank Thomas CL	.40	.18
165	Alex Rodriguez CL	.75	.35

1998 Studio

	MINT	NRMT
COMPLETE SET (220)	50.00	22.00

No.	Player	MINT	NRMT
1	Tony Clark	.25	.11
2	Jose Cruz Jr.	.25	.11
3	Ivan Rodriguez	.60	.25
4	Mo Vaughn	.25	.11
5	Kenny Lofton	.25	.11
6	Will Clark	.60	.25
7	Barry Larkin	.60	.25
8	Jay Bell	.25	.11
9	Kevin Young	.25	.11
10	Francisco Cordova	.15	.07
11	Justin Thompson	.15	.07
12	Paul Molitor	.60	.25
13	Jeff Bagwell	.75	.35
14	Jose Canseco	.60	.25
15	Scott Rolen	.60	.25
16	Wilton Guerrero	.15	.07
17	Shannon Stewart	.25	.11
18	Hideki Irabu	.15	.07
19	Michael Tucker	.15	.07
20	Joe Carter	.25	.11
21	Gabe Alvarez	.15	.07
22	Ricky Ledee	.15	.07
23	Karim Garcia	.15	.07
24	Eli Marrero	.15	.07
25	Scott Elarton	.15	.07
26	Mario Valdez	.15	.07
27	Ben Grieve	.25	.11
28	Paul Konerko	.25	.11
29	Esteban Yan RC	.40	.18
30	Esteban Loaiza	.15	.07
31	Delino DeShields	.15	.07
32	Bernie Williams	.60	.25
33	Joe Randa	.15	.07
34	Randy Johnson	.75	.35
35	Brett Tomko	.15	.07
36	Todd Erdos RC	.25	.11
37	Bobby Higginson	.25	.11
38	Jason Kendall	.25	.11
39	Ray Lankford	.15	.07
40	Mark Grace	.60	.25
41	Andy Pettitte	.25	.11
42	Alex Rodriguez	1.50	.70
43	Hideo Nomo	.60	.25
44	Sammy Sosa	1.25	.55
45	J.T. Snow	.25	.11
46	Jason Varitek	.25	.11
47	Vinny Castilla	.25	.11
48	Neifi Perez	.15	.07
49	Todd Walker	.15	.07
50	Mike Cameron	.25	.11
51	Jeffrey Hammonds	.15	.07
52	Deivi Cruz	.15	.07
53	Brian Hunter	.15	.07
54	Al Martin	.15	.07
55	Ron Coomer	.15	.07
56	Chan Ho Park	.25	.11
57	Pedro Martinez	.75	.35
58	Darin Erstad	.60	.25
59	Albert Belle	.25	.11
60	Nomar Garciaparra	1.50	.70
61	Tony Gwynn	1.25	.55
62	Mike Piazza	1.50	.70
63	Todd Helton	.75	.35
64	David Ortiz	.25	.11
65	Todd Dunwoody	.15	.07
66	Orlando Cabrera	.15	.07
67	Ken Cloude	.15	.07
68	Andy Benes	.15	.07
69	Mariano Rivera	.25	.11
70	Cecil Fielder	.25	.11
71	Brian Jordan	.25	.11
72	Darryl Kile	.25	.11
73	Reggie Jefferson	.15	.07
74	Shawn Estes	.25	.11
75	Bobby Bonilla	.25	.11
76	Denny Neagle	.15	.07
77	Robin Ventura	.25	.11
78	Omar Vizquel	.25	.11
79	Craig Biggio	.40	.18
80	Moises Alou	.25	.11
81	Garret Anderson	.25	.11
82	Eric Karros	.25	.11
83	Dante Bichette	.25	.11
84	Charles Johnson	.25	.11
85	Rusty Greer	.25	.11
86	Travis Fryman	.25	.11
87	Fernando Tatis	.15	.07
88	Wilson Alvarez	.15	.07
89	Carl Pavano	.15	.07
90	Brian Rose	.15	.07
91	Geoff Jenkins	.25	.11
92	Maggio Ordonez RC	2.00	.90
93	David Segui	.15	.07
94	David Cone	.25	.11
95	John Smoltz	.25	.11
96	Jim Thome	.60	.25
97	Gary Sheffield	.25	.11
98	Barry Bonds	1.50	.70
99	Andres Galarraga	.40	.18
100	Brad Fullmer	.25	.11
101	Bobby Estalella	.15	.07
102	Enrique Wilson	.15	.07
103	Frank Catalanotto RC	.60	.25
104	Mike Lowell RC	.75	.35
105	Kevin Orie	.15	.07
106	Matt Morris	.25	.11
107	Pokey Reese	.15	.07
108	Shawn Green	.60	.25
109	Tony Womack	.15	.07
110	Ken Caminiti	.25	.11
111	Roberto Alomar	.60	.25
112	Ken Griffey Jr.	2.00	.90
113	Cal Ripken	2.50	1.10
114	Lou Collier	.15	.07
115	Larry Walker	.40	.18
116	Fred McGriff	.40	.18
117	Jim Edmonds	.40	.18
118	Edgar Martinez	.40	.18
119	Matt Williams	.40	.18
120	Ismael Valdes	.15	.07
121	Bartolo Colon	.25	.11
122	Jeff Cirillo	.25	.11
123	Steve Woodard	.15	.07
124	Kevin Millwood RC	.60	.25
125	Derrick Gibson	.15	.07
126	Jacob Cruz	.15	.07
127	Russell Branyan	.25	.11
128	Sean Casey	.40	.18
129	Derrek Lee	.25	.11
130	Paul O'Neill	.60	.25
131	Brad Radke	.25	.11
132	Kevin Appier	.25	.11
133	John Olerud	.25	.11
134	Alan Benes	.15	.07
135	Todd Greene	.15	.07
136	Carlos Mendoza RC	.25	.11
137	Wade Boggs	.60	.25
138	Jose Guillen	.15	.07
139	Tino Martinez	.25	.11
140	Aaron Boone	.15	.07
141	Abraham Nunez	.15	.07
142	Preston Wilson	.25	.11
143	Randall Simon	.15	.07
144	Dennis Reyes	.15	.07
145	Mark Kotsay	.25	.11
146	Richard Hidalgo	.25	.11
147	Travis Lee	.25	.11
148	Hanley Frias RC	.15	.07
149	Ruben Rivera	.15	.07
150	Rafael Medina	.15	.07
151	Dave Nilsson	.15	.07
152	Curt Schilling	.60	.25
153	Brady Anderson	.25	.11
154	Carlos Delgado	.60	.25
155	Jason Giambi	.60	.25
156	Pat Hentgen	.15	.07
157	Tom Glavine	.60	.25
158	Ryan Klesko	.25	.11
159	Chipper Jones	1.25	.55
160	Juan Gonzalez	.60	.25
161	Mark McGwire	2.50	1.10
162	Vladimir Guerrero	.75	.35
163	Derek Jeter	2.50	1.10
164	Manny Ramirez	.75	.35
165	Mike Mussina	.60	.25
166	Rafael Palmeiro	.60	.25
167	Henry Rodriguez	.15	.07
168	Jeff Suppan	.15	.07
169	Eric Milton	.25	.11
170	Scott Spiezio	.15	.07
171	Wilson Delgado	.15	.07
172	Bubba Trammell	.15	.07

❑ 173 Ellis Burks	.25	.11
❑ 174 Jason Dickson	.15	.07
❑ 175 Butch Huskey	.15	.07
❑ 176 Edgardo Alfonzo	.25	.11
❑ 177 Eric Young	.15	.07
❑ 178 Marquis Grissom	.15	.07
❑ 179 Lance Johnson	.15	.07
❑ 180 Kevin Brown	.40	.18
❑ 181 Sandy Alomar Jr.	.25	.11
❑ 182 Todd Hundley	.15	.07
❑ 183 Rondell White	.25	.11
❑ 184 Javier Lopez	.25	.11
❑ 185 Damian Jackson	.15	.07
❑ 186 Raul Mondesi	.25	.11
❑ 187 Rickey Henderson	1.25	.55
❑ 188 David Justice	.25	.11
❑ 189 Jay Buhner	.25	.11
❑ 190 Jaret Wright	.15	.07
❑ 191 Miguel Tejada	.40	.18
❑ 192 Ron Wright	.15	.07
❑ 193 Livan Hernandez	.15	.07
❑ 194 A.J. Hinch	.15	.07
❑ 195 Richie Sexson	.25	.11
❑ 196 Bob Abreu	.25	.11
❑ 197 Louis Castillo	.15	.07
❑ 198 Michael Coleman	.15	.07
❑ 199 Greg Maddux	1.50	.70
❑ 200 Frank Thomas	.75	.35
❑ 201 Andruw Jones	.60	.25
❑ 202 Roger Clemens	1.50	.70
❑ 203 Tim Salmon	.25	.11
❑ 204 Chuck Knoblauch	.25	.11
❑ 205 Wes Helms	.15	.07
❑ 206 Juan Encarnacion	.25	.11
❑ 207 Russ Davis	.15	.07
❑ 208 John Valentin	.15	.07
❑ 209 Tony Saunders	.15	.07
❑ 210 Mike Sweeney	.25	.11
❑ 211 Steve Finley	.25	.11
❑ 212 Dave Dellucci RC	.15	.07
❑ 213 Edgar Renteria	.15	.07
❑ 214 Jeremi Gonzalez	.15	.07
❑ CL1 Jeff Bagwell CL	.60	.25
❑ CL2 Mike Piazza CL	.75	.35
❑ CL3 Greg Maddux CL	.75	.35
❑ CL4 Cal Ripken CL	1.25	.55
❑ CL5 Frank Thomas CL	.40	.18
❑ CL6 Ken Griffey Jr. CL	1.00	.45

2001 Studio

	MINT	NRMT
COMP.SET w/o SP's (150)	50.00	22.00
COMMON CARD (1-150)	.75	.35
COMMON CARD (151-200)	10.00	4.50

❑ 1 Alex Rodriguez	5.00	2.20
❑ 2 Barry Bonds	5.00	2.20
❑ 3 Cal Ripken	8.00	3.60
❑ 4 Chipper Jones	4.00	1.80
❑ 5 Derek Jeter	8.00	3.60
❑ 6 Troy Glaus	2.00	.90
❑ 7 Frank Thomas	2.50	1.10
❑ 8 Greg Maddux	5.00	2.20
❑ 9 Ivan Rodriguez	2.00	.90
❑ 10 Jeff Bagwell	2.50	1.10
❑ 11 Mark Quinn	.75	.35
❑ 12 Todd Helton	2.50	1.10
❑ 13 Ken Griffey Jr.	6.00	2.70
❑ 14 Manny Ramirez	2.50	1.10
❑ 15 Mark McGwire	8.00	3.60
❑ 16 Mike Piazza	5.00	2.20
❑ 17 Nomar Garciaparra	5.00	2.20
❑ 18 Robin Ventura	.75	.35
❑ 19 Aramis Ramirez	.75	.35
❑ 20 J.T. Snow	.75	.35
❑ 21 Pat Burrell	.75	.35
❑ 22 Curt Schilling	2.00	.90
❑ 23 Carlos Delgado	2.00	.90
❑ 24 J.D. Drew	2.00	.90
❑ 25 Cliff Floyd	.75	.35
❑ 26 Brian Jordan	.75	.35
❑ 27 Roberto Alomar	2.00	.90
❑ 28 Barry Zito	2.00	.90
❑ 29 Harold Baines	.75	.35
❑ 30 Brad Penny	.75	.35
❑ 31 Jose Cruz Jr.	.75	.35
❑ 32 Andy Pettitte	.75	.35
❑ 33 Jim Edmonds	1.25	.55
❑ 34 Darin Erstad	2.00	.90
❑ 35 Jason Giambi	2.00	.90
❑ 36 Tom Glavine	2.00	.90
❑ 37 Juan Gonzalez	2.00	.90
❑ 38 Mark Grace	2.00	.90
❑ 39 Shawn Green	2.00	.90
❑ 40 Tim Hudson	2.00	.90
❑ 41 Andruw Jones	2.00	.90
❑ 42 Jeff Kent	1.25	.55
❑ 43 Barry Larkin	2.00	.90
❑ 44 Rafael Furcal	.75	.35
❑ 45 Mike Mussina	2.00	.90
❑ 46 Hideo Nomo	2.00	.90
❑ 47 Rafael Palmeiro	2.00	.90
❑ 48 Scott Rolen	2.00	.90
❑ 49 Gary Sheffield	.75	.35
❑ 50 Bernie Williams	2.00	.90
❑ 51 Bob Abreu	.75	.35
❑ 52 Edgardo Alfonzo	.75	.35
❑ 53 Edgar Martinez	1.25	.55
❑ 54 Magglio Ordonez	.75	.35
❑ 55 Kerry Wood	2.00	.90
❑ 56 Matt Morris	.75	.35
❑ 57 Lance Berkman	2.00	.90
❑ 58 Kevin Brown	.75	.35
❑ 59 Sean Casey	1.25	.55
❑ 60 Eric Chavez	.75	.35
❑ 61 Bartolo Colon	.75	.35
❑ 62 Johnny Damon	.75	.35
❑ 63 Jermaine Dye	.75	.35
❑ 64 Juan Encarnacion	.75	.35
❑ 65 Carl Everett	.75	.35
❑ 66 Brian Giles	.75	.35
❑ 67 Mike Hampton	.75	.35
❑ 68 Richard Hidalgo	.75	.35
❑ 69 Geoff Jenkins	.75	.35
❑ 70 Jacque Jones	.75	.35
❑ 71 Jason Kendall	.75	.35
❑ 72 Ryan Klesko	.75	.35
❑ 73 Chan Ho Park	.75	.35
❑ 74 Richie Sexson	.75	.35
❑ 75 Mike Sweeney	.75	.35
❑ 76 Fernando Tatis	.75	.35
❑ 77 Miguel Tejada	.75	.35
❑ 78 Jose Vidro	.75	.35
❑ 79 Larry Walker	2.00	.90
❑ 80 Preston Wilson	.75	.35
❑ 81 Craig Biggio	1.25	.55
❑ 82 Fred McGriff	1.25	.55
❑ 83 Jim Thome	2.00	.90
❑ 84 Garret Anderson	.75	.35
❑ 85 Mark Mulder	1.25	.55
❑ 86 Tony Batista	.75	.35
❑ 87 Terrence Long	.75	.35
❑ 88 Brad Fullmer	.75	.35
❑ 89 Rusty Greer	.75	.35
❑ 90 Orlando Hernandez	.75	.35
❑ 91 Gabe Kapler	.75	.35
❑ 92 Paul Konerko	.75	.35
❑ 93 Carlos Lee	.75	.35
❑ 94 Kenny Lofton	.75	.35
❑ 95 Raul Mondesi	.75	.35
❑ 96 Jorge Posada	.75	.35
❑ 97 Tim Salmon	.75	.35
❑ 98 Greg Vaughn	.75	.35
❑ 99 Mo Vaughn	.75	.35
❑ 100 Omar Vizquel	.75	.35
❑ 101 Ben Grieve	.75	.35
❑ 102 Luis Gonzalez	2.00	.90
❑ 103 Ray Durham	.75	.35
❑ 104 Ryan Dempster	.75	.35
❑ 105 Eric Karros	.75	.35
❑ 106 David Justice	.75	.35
❑ 107 Pedro Martinez	2.50	1.10
❑ 108 Randy Johnson	2.50	1.10
❑ 109 Rick Ankiel	1.25	.55
❑ 110 Rickey Henderson	4.00	1.80
❑ 111 Roger Clemens	5.00	2.20
❑ 112 Sammy Sosa	4.00	1.80
❑ 113 Tony Gwynn	4.00	1.80
❑ 114 Vladimir Guerrero	2.50	1.10
❑ 115 Kazuhiro Sasaki	2.00	.90
❑ 116 Phil Nevin	.75	.35
❑ 117 Ruben Mateo	.75	.35
❑ 118 Shannon Stewart	.75	.35
❑ 119 Matt Williams	1.25	.55
❑ 120 Tino Martinez	.75	.35
❑ 121 Ken Caminiti	.75	.35
❑ 122 Edgar Renteria	.75	.35
❑ 123 Charles Johnson	.75	.35
❑ 124 Aaron Sele	.75	.35
❑ 125 Javy Lopez	.75	.35
❑ 126 Mariano Rivera	.75	.35
❑ 127 Shea Hillenbrand	.75	.35
❑ 128 Jeff D'Amico	.75	.35
❑ 129 Brady Anderson	.75	.35
❑ 130 Kevin Millwood	.75	.35
❑ 131 Trot Nixon	.75	.35
❑ 132 Mike Lieberthal	.75	.35
❑ 133 Juan Pierre	.75	.35
❑ 134 Russ Ortiz	.75	.35
❑ 135 Jose Macias	.75	.35
❑ 136 John Smoltz	.75	.35
❑ 137 Jason Varitek	.75	.35
❑ 138 Dean Palmer	.75	.35
❑ 139 Jeff Cirillo	.75	.35
❑ 140 Paul O'Neill	2.00	.90
❑ 141 Andres Galarraga	1.25	.55
❑ 142 David Wells	.75	.35
❑ 143 Brad Radke	.75	.35
❑ 144 Wade Miller	.75	.35
❑ 145 John Olerud	.75	.35
❑ 146 Moises Alou	.75	.35
❑ 147 Carlos Beltran	.75	.35
❑ 148 Jeromy Burnitz	.75	.35
❑ 149 Steve Finley	.75	.35
❑ 150 Joe Mays	.75	.35
❑ 151 Alex Escobar ROO	10.00	4.50
❑ 152 Johnny Estrada ROO RC	20.00	9.00
❑ 153 Pedro Feliz ROO	10.00	4.50
❑ 154 Nate Frese ROO RC	10.00	4.50
❑ 155 Dee Brown ROO	10.00	4.50
❑ 156 Brandon Larson ROO RC	10.00	4.50
❑ 157 Alexis Gomez ROO RC	10.00	4.50
❑ 158 Jason Hart ROO	15.00	6.75
❑ 159 C.C. Sabathia ROO	15.00	6.75
❑ 160 Josh Towers ROO RC	20.00	9.00
❑ 161 Christian Parker ROO RC	10.00	4.50
❑ 162 Jackson Melian ROO RC	10.00	4.50
❑ 163 Joe Kennedy ROO RC	15.00	6.75
❑ 164 A. Hernandez ROO RC	10.00	4.50
❑ 165 Jimmy Rollins ROO	10.00	4.50
❑ 166 Jose Mieses ROO RC	10.00	4.50
❑ 167 Roy Oswalt ROO	20.00	9.00
❑ 168 Eric Munson ROO	10.00	4.50
❑ 169 Xavier Nady ROO	15.00	6.75
❑ 170 H. Ramirez ROO RC	10.00	4.50
❑ 171 Abraham Nunez ROO	10.00	4.50
❑ 172 Jose Ortiz ROO	15.00	6.75
❑ 173 Jeremy Owens ROO RC	10.00	4.50
❑ 174 Claudio Vargas ROO RC	10.00	4.50
❑ 175 Corey Patterson ROO	10.00	4.50
❑ 176 Carlos Pena ROO	10.00	4.50
❑ 177 Bud Smith ROO RC	40.00	18.00
❑ 178 Adam Dunn ROO	30.00	13.50
❑ 179 Adam Pettyjohn ROO RC	10.00	4.50
❑ 180 Elpidio Guzman ROO RC	10.00	4.50
❑ 181 Jay Gibbons ROO RC	15.00	6.75
❑ 182 Wilkin Ruan ROO RC	10.00	4.50
❑ 183 Tsuyoshi Shinjo ROO RC	30.00	13.50
❑ 184 Alfonso Soriano ROO	20.00	9.00

❑ 185 Marcus Giles ROO	10.00	4.50
❑ 186 Ichiro Suzuki ROO RC	200.00	90.00
❑ 187 Juan Uribe ROO RC	20.00	9.00
❑ 188 David Williams ROO RC	15.00	6.75
❑ 189 C. Valderrama ROO RC	10.00	4.50
❑ 190 Matt White ROO RC	10.00	4.50
❑ 191 Albert Pujols ROO RC	80.00	36.00
❑ 192 D. Mendez ROO RC	10.00	4.50
❑ 193 Cory Aldridge ROO RC	10.00	4.50
❑ 194 Endy Chavez ROO RC	10.00	4.50
❑ 195 Josh Beckett ROO	20.00	9.00
❑ 196 Wilson Betemit ROO RC	30.00	13.50
❑ 197 Ben Sheets ROO	15.00	6.75
❑ 198 Andres Torres ROO RC	10.00	4.50
❑ 199 Aubrey Huff ROO	10.00	4.50
❑ 200 Jack Wilson ROO RC	10.00	4.50

1952 Topps

	NRMT	VG-E
COMP.MASTER SET (487)	80000.00	36000.00
COMPLETE SET (407)	65000.00	29200.00
COMMON CARD (1-80)	60.00	27.00
COMMON CARD (81-250)	40.00	18.00
COMMON CARD (251-310)	50.00	22.00
COMMON CARD (311-407)	250.00	110.00
WRAPPER (1-CENT)	250.00	110.00
WRAPPER (5-CENT)	100.00	45.00

Card	NRMT	VG-E
❑ 1 Andy Pafko	3000.00	300.00
❑ 1A Andy Pafko Black	3000.00	1350.00
❑ 2 Pete Runnels RC	250.00	110.00
❑ 2A Pete Runnells RC Black	250.00	110.00
❑ 3 Hank Thompson	70.00	32.00
❑ 3A Hank Thompson Black	70.00	32.00
❑ 4 Don Lenhardt	60.00	27.00
❑ 4A Don Lenhardt Black	60.00	27.00
❑ 5 Larry Jansen	70.00	32.00
❑ 5A Larry Jansen Black	70.00	32.00
❑ 6 Grady Hatton	60.00	27.00
❑ 6A Grady Hatton Black	60.00	27.00
❑ 7 Wayne Terwilliger	60.00	27.00
❑ 7A Wayne Terwilliger Black	60.00	27.00
❑ 8 Fred Marsh	60.00	27.00
❑ 8A Fred Marsh Black	60.00	27.00
❑ 9 Robert Hogue	60.00	27.00
❑ 9A Robert Hogue Black	60.00	27.00
❑ 10 Al Rosen	70.00	32.00
❑ 10A Al Rosen Black	70.00	32.00
❑ 11 Phil Rizzuto	350.00	160.00
❑ 11A Phil Rizzuto Black	350.00	160.00
❑ 12 Monty Basgall	60.00	27.00
❑ 12A Monty Basgall Black	60.00	27.00
❑ 13 Johnny Wyrostek	60.00	27.00
❑ 13A Johnny Wyrostek Black	60.00	27.00
❑ 14 Bob Elliott	70.00	32.00
❑ 14A Bob Elliott Black	70.00	32.00
❑ 15 Johnny Pesky	70.00	32.00
❑ 15A Johnny Pesky Black	70.00	32.00
❑ 16 Gene Hermanski	60.00	27.00
❑ 16A Gene Hermanski Black	60.00	27.00
❑ 17 Jim Hegan	70.00	32.00
❑ 17A Jim Hegan Black	70.00	32.00
❑ 18 Merrill Combs	60.00	27.00
❑ 18A Merrill Combs Black	60.00	27.00
❑ 19 Johnny Bucha	60.00	27.00
❑ 19A Johnny Bucha Black	60.00	27.00
❑ 20 Billy Loes RC	125.00	55.00
❑ 20A Billy Loes RC Black	125.00	55.00
❑ 21 Ferris Fain	70.00	32.00
❑ 21A Ferris Fain Black	70.00	32.00
❑ 22 Dom DiMaggio	100.00	45.00
❑ 22A Dom DiMaggio Black	100.00	45.00
❑ 23 Billy Goodman	70.00	32.00
❑ 23A Billy Goodman Black	70.00	32.00
❑ 24 Luke Easter	80.00	36.00
❑ 24A Luke Easter Black	80.00	36.00
❑ 25 Johnny Groth	60.00	27.00
❑ 25A Johnny Groth Black	60.00	27.00
❑ 26 Monte Irvin	125.00	55.00
❑ 26A Monte Irvin Black	125.00	55.00
❑ 27 Sam Jethroe	70.00	32.00
❑ 27A Sam Jethroe Black	70.00	32.00
❑ 28 Jerry Priddy	60.00	27.00
❑ 28A Jerry Priddy Black	60.00	27.00
❑ 29 Ted Kluszewski	125.00	55.00
❑ 29A Ted Kluszewski Black	125.00	55.00
❑ 30 Mel Parnell	70.00	32.00
❑ 30A Mel Parnell Black	70.00	32.00
❑ 31 Gus Zernial Posed with seven baseballs	80.00	36.00
❑ 31A Gus Zernial Black Posed with seven baseballs	80.00	36.00
❑ 32 Eddie Robinson	60.00	27.00
❑ 32A Eddie Robinson Black	60.00	27.00
❑ 33 Warren Spahn	250.00	110.00
❑ 33A Warren Spahn Black	250.00	110.00
❑ 34 Elmer Valo	60.00	27.00
❑ 34A Elmer Valo Black	60.00	27.00
❑ 35 Hank Sauer	70.00	32.00
❑ 35A Hank Sauer Black	70.00	32.00
❑ 36 Gil Hodges	250.00	110.00
❑ 36A Gil Hodges Black	250.00	110.00
❑ 37 Duke Snider	400.00	180.00
❑ 37A Duke Snider Black	400.00	180.00
❑ 38 Wally Westlake	60.00	27.00
❑ 38A Wally Westlake Black	60.00	27.00
❑ 39 Dizzy Trout	70.00	32.00
❑ 39A Dizzy Trout Black	70.00	32.00
❑ 40 Irv Noren	70.00	32.00
❑ 40A Irv Noren Black	70.00	32.00
❑ 41 Bob Wellman	60.00	27.00
❑ 41A Bob Wellman Black	60.00	27.00
❑ 42 Lou Kretlow	60.00	27.00
❑ 42A Lou Kretlow Black	60.00	27.00
❑ 43 Ray Scarborough	60.00	27.00
❑ 43A Ray Scarbourough Black	60.00	27.00
❑ 44 Con Dempsey	60.00	27.00
❑ 44A Con Dempsey Black	60.00	27.00
❑ 45 Eddie Joost	60.00	27.00
❑ 45A Eddie Joost Black	60.00	27.00
❑ 46 Gordon Goldsberry	60.00	27.00
❑ 46A Gordon Goldsberry Black	60.00	27.00
❑ 47 Willie Jones	70.00	32.00
❑ 47A Willie Jones Black	70.00	32.00
❑ 48A Joe Page ERR Bio for Sain Black Back	400.00	180.00
❑ 48B Joe Page COR Black Back	125.00	55.00
❑ 48C Joe Page COR Red Back	125.00	55.00
❑ 49A John Sain ERR Bio for Page Black Back	400.00	180.00
❑ 49B John Sain COR Black Back	125.00	55.00
❑ 49C John Sain COR Red Back	125.00	55.00
❑ 50 Marv Rickert	60.00	27.00
❑ 50A Marv Richert Black	60.00	27.00
❑ 51 Jim Russell	60.00	27.00
❑ 51A Jim Russell Black	60.00	27.00
❑ 52 Don Mueller	70.00	32.00
❑ 52A Don Mueller Black	70.00	32.00
❑ 53 Chris Van Cuyk	60.00	27.00
❑ 53A Chris Van Cuyk Black	60.00	27.00
❑ 54 Leo Kiely	60.00	27.00
❑ 54A Leo Kiely Black	60.00	27.00
❑ 55 Ray Boone	80.00	36.00
❑ 55A Ray Boone Black	80.00	36.00
❑ 56 Tommy Glaviano	60.00	27.00
❑ 56A Tommy Glaviano Black	60.00	27.00
❑ 57 Ed Lopat	100.00	45.00
❑ 57A Ed Lopat Black	100.00	45.00
❑ 58 Bob Mahoney	60.00	27.00
❑ 58A Bob Mahoney Black	60.00	27.00
❑ 59 Robin Roberts	175.00	80.00
❑ 59A Robin Roberts Black	175.00	80.00
❑ 60 Sid Hudson	60.00	27.00
❑ 60A Sid Hudson Black	60.00	27.00
❑ 61 Tookie Gilbert	60.00	27.00
❑ 61A Tookie Gilbert Black	60.00	27.00
❑ 62 Chuck Stobbs	60.00	27.00
❑ 62A Chuck Stobbs Black	60.00	27.00
❑ 63 Howie Pollet	60.00	27.00
❑ 63A Howie Pollet Black	60.00	27.00
❑ 64 Roy Sievers	70.00	32.00
❑ 64A Roy Sievers Black	70.00	32.00
❑ 65 Enos Slaughter	175.00	80.00
❑ 65A Enos Slaughter Black	175.00	80.00
❑ 66 Preacher Roe	100.00	45.00
❑ 66A Preacher Roe Black	100.00	45.00
❑ 67 Allie Reynolds	100.00	45.00
❑ 67A Allie Reynolds Black	100.00	45.00
❑ 68 Cliff Chambers	60.00	27.00
❑ 68A Cliff Chambers Black	60.00	27.00
❑ 69 Virgil Stallcup	60.00	27.00
❑ 69A Virgil Stallcup Black	60.00	27.00
❑ 70 Al Zarilla	60.00	27.00
❑ 70A Al Zarilla Black	60.00	27.00
❑ 71 Tom Upton	60.00	27.00
❑ 71A Tom Upton Black	60.00	27.00
❑ 72 Karl Olson	60.00	27.00
❑ 72A Karl Olson Black	60.00	27.00
❑ 73 Bill Werle	60.00	27.00
❑ 73A Bill Werle Black	60.00	27.00
❑ 74 Andy Hansen	60.00	27.00
❑ 74A Andy Hansen Black	60.00	27.00
❑ 75 Wes Westrum	70.00	32.00
❑ 75A Wes Westrum Black	70.00	32.00
❑ 76 Eddie Stanky	70.00	32.00
❑ 76A Eddie Stanky Black	70.00	32.00
❑ 77 Bob Kennedy	70.00	32.00
❑ 77A Bob Kennedy Black	70.00	32.00
❑ 78 Ellis Kinder	60.00	27.00
❑ 78A Ellis Kinder Black	60.00	27.00
❑ 79 Gerry Staley	60.00	27.00
❑ 79A Gerry Staley Black	60.00	27.00
❑ 80 Herman Wehmeier	80.00	36.00
❑ 80A Herman Wehmeier Black	80.00	36.00
❑ 81 Vernon Law	80.00	36.00
❑ 82 Duane Pillette	40.00	18.00
❑ 83 Billy Johnson	40.00	18.00
❑ 84 Vern Stephens	50.00	22.00
❑ 85 Bob Kuzava	50.00	22.00
❑ 86 Ted Gray	40.00	18.00
❑ 87 Dale Coogan	40.00	18.00
❑ 88 Bob Feller	250.00	110.00
❑ 89 Johnny Lipon	40.00	18.00
❑ 90 Mickey Grasso	40.00	18.00
❑ 91 Red Schoendienst	100.00	45.00
❑ 92 Dale Mitchell	50.00	22.00
❑ 93 Al Sima	40.00	18.00
❑ 94 Sam Mele	40.00	18.00
❑ 95 Ken Holcombe	40.00	18.00
❑ 96 Willard Marshall	40.00	18.00
❑ 97 Earl Torgeson	40.00	18.00
❑ 98 Billy Pierce	50.00	22.00
❑ 99 Gene Woodling	60.00	27.00
❑ 100 Del Rice	40.00	18.00
❑ 101 Max Lanier	40.00	18.00
❑ 102 Bill Kennedy	40.00	18.00
❑ 103 Cliff Mapes	40.00	18.00
❑ 104 Don Kolloway	40.00	18.00
❑ 105 Johnny Pramesa	40.00	18.00
❑ 106 Mickey Vernon	60.00	27.00
❑ 107 Connie Ryan	40.00	18.00
❑ 108 Jim Konstanty	60.00	27.00
❑ 109 Ted Wilks	40.00	18.00
❑ 110 Dutch Leonard	40.00	18.00
❑ 111 Peanuts Lowrey	40.00	18.00
❑ 112 Hank Majeski	40.00	18.00
❑ 113 Dick Sisler	50.00	22.00
❑ 114 Willard Ramsdell	40.00	18.00
❑ 115 Red Munger	40.00	18.00
❑ 116 Carl Scheib	40.00	18.00
❑ 117 Sherm Lollar	50.00	22.00
❑ 118 Ken Raffensberger	40.00	18.00
❑ 119 Mickey McDermott	40.00	18.00

❑ 120 Bob Chakales 40.00 18.00
❑ 121 Gus Niarhos 40.00 18.00
❑ 122 Jackie Jensen 80.00 36.00
❑ 123 Eddie Yost 50.00 22.00
❑ 124 Monte Kennedy 40.00 18.00
❑ 125 Bill Rigney 40.00 18.00
❑ 126 Fred Hutchinson 50.00 22.00
❑ 127 Paul Minner 40.00 18.00
❑ 128 Don Bollweg 40.00 18.00
❑ 129 Johnny Mize 150.00 70.00
❑ 130 Sheldon Jones 40.00 18.00
❑ 131 Morrie Martin 40.00 18.00
❑ 132 Clyde Kluttz 40.00 18.00
❑ 133 Al Widmar 40.00 18.00
❑ 134 Joe Tipton 40.00 18.00
❑ 135 Dixie Howell 40.00 18.00
❑ 136 Johnny Schmitz 40.00 18.00
❑ 137 Roy McMillan RC 50.00 22.00
❑ 138 Bill MacDonald 40.00 18.00
❑ 139 Ken Wood 40.00 18.00
❑ 140 Johnny Antonelli 60.00 27.00
❑ 141 Clint Hartung 40.00 18.00
❑ 142 Harry Perkowski 40.00 18.00
❑ 143 Les Moss 40.00 18.00
❑ 144 Ed Blake 40.00 18.00
❑ 145 Joe Haynes 40.00 18.00
❑ 146 Frank House 40.00 18.00
❑ 147 Bob Young 40.00 18.00
❑ 148 Johnny Klippstein 40.00 18.00
❑ 149 Dick Kryhoski 40.00 18.00
❑ 150 Ted Beard 40.00 18.00
❑ 151 Wally Post RC 50.00 22.00
❑ 152 Al Evans 40.00 18.00
❑ 153 Bob Rush 40.00 18.00
❑ 154 Joe Muir 40.00 18.00
❑ 155 Frank Overmire 40.00 18.00
❑ 156 Frank Hiller 40.00 18.00
❑ 157 Bob Usher 40.00 18.00
❑ 158 Eddie Waitkus 40.00 18.00
❑ 159 Saul Rogovin 40.00 18.00
❑ 160 Owen Friend 40.00 18.00
❑ 161 Bud Byerly 40.00 18.00
❑ 162 Del Crandall 50.00 22.00
❑ 163 Stan Rojek 40.00 18.00
❑ 164 Walt Dubiel 40.00 18.00
❑ 165 Eddie Kazak 40.00 18.00
❑ 166 Paul LaPalme 40.00 18.00
❑ 167 Bill Howerton 40.00 18.00
❑ 168 Charlie Silvera RC 60.00 27.00
❑ 169 Howie Judson 40.00 18.00
❑ 170 Gus Bell 50.00 22.00
❑ 171 Ed Erautt 40.00 18.00
❑ 172 Eddie Miksis 40.00 18.00
❑ 173 Roy Smalley 40.00 18.00
❑ 174 Clarence Marshall 50.00 22.00
❑ 175 Billy Martin RC 450.00 200.00
❑ 176 Hank Edwards 40.00 18.00
❑ 177 Bill Wight 40.00 18.00
❑ 178 Cass Michaels 40.00 18.00
❑ 179 Frank Smith 40.00 18.00
❑ 180 Charlie Maxwell RC 50.00 22.00
❑ 181 Bob Swift 40.00 18.00
❑ 182 Billy Hitchcock 40.00 18.00
❑ 183 Erv Dusak 40.00 18.00
❑ 184 Bob Ramazzotti 40.00 18.00
❑ 185 Bill Nicholson 50.00 22.00
❑ 186 Walt Masterson 40.00 18.00
❑ 187 Bob Miller 40.00 18.00
❑ 188 Clarence Podbielan 40.00 18.00
❑ 189 Pete Reiser 60.00 27.00
❑ 190 Don Johnson 40.00 18.00
❑ 191 Yogi Berra 700.00 325.00
❑ 192 Myron Ginsberg 40.00 18.00
❑ 193 Harry Simpson 50.00 22.00
❑ 194 Joe Hatton 40.00 18.00
❑ 195 Minnie Minoso RC 150.00 70.00
❑ 196 Solly Hemus RC 60.00 27.00
❑ 197 George Strickland 40.00 18.00
❑ 198 Phil Haugstad 40.00 18.00
❑ 199 George Zuverink 40.00 18.00
❑ 200 Ralph Houk RC 80.00 36.00
❑ 201 Alex Kellner 40.00 18.00
❑ 202 Joe Collins RC 60.00 27.00
❑ 203 Curt Simmons 60.00 27.00
❑ 204 Ron Northey 40.00 18.00
❑ 205 Clyde King 60.00 27.00
❑ 206 Joe Ostrowski 40.00 18.00
❑ 207 Mickey Harris 40.00 18.00
❑ 208 Marlin Stuart 40.00 18.00
❑ 209 Howie Fox 40.00 18.00
❑ 210 Dick Fowler 40.00 18.00
❑ 211 Ray Coleman 40.00 18.00
❑ 212 Ned Garver 40.00 18.00
❑ 213 Nippy Jones 40.00 18.00
❑ 214 Johnny Hopp 50.00 22.00
❑ 215 Hank Bauer 80.00 36.00
❑ 216 Richie Ashburn 200.00 90.00
❑ 217 Snuffy Stirnweiss 50.00 22.00
❑ 218 Clyde McCullough 40.00 18.00
❑ 219 Bobby Shantz 60.00 27.00
❑ 220 Joe Presko 40.00 18.00
❑ 221 Granny Hamner 40.00 18.00
❑ 222 Hoot Evers 40.00 18.00
❑ 223 Del Ennis 50.00 22.00
❑ 224 Bruce Edwards 40.00 18.00
❑ 225 Frank Baumholtz 40.00 18.00
❑ 226 Dave Philley 40.00 18.00
❑ 227 Joe Garagiola 80.00 36.00
❑ 228 Al Brazle 40.00 18.00
❑ 229 Gene Bearden UER 40.00 18.00
(Misspelled Beardon)
❑ 230 Matt Batts 40.00 18.00
❑ 231 Sam Zoldak 40.00 18.00
❑ 232 Billy Cox 50.00 22.00
❑ 233 Bob Friend RC 80.00 36.00
❑ 234 Steve Souchock 40.00 18.00
❑ 235 Walt Dropo 40.00 18.00
❑ 236 Ed Fitzgerald 40.00 18.00
❑ 237 Jerry Coleman 60.00 27.00
❑ 238 Art Houtteman 40.00 18.00
❑ 239 Rocky Bridges 50.00 22.00
❑ 240 Jack Phillips 40.00 18.00
❑ 241 Tommy Byrne 40.00 18.00
❑ 242 Tom Poholsky 40.00 18.00
❑ 243 Larry Doby 80.00 36.00
❑ 244 Vic Wertz 40.00 18.00
❑ 245 Sherry Robertson 40.00 18.00
❑ 246 George Kell 80.00 36.00
❑ 247 Randy Gumpert 40.00 18.00
❑ 248 Frank Shea 40.00 18.00
❑ 249 Bobby Adams 40.00 18.00
❑ 250 Carl Erskine 100.00 45.00
❑ 251 Chico Carrasquel 50.00 22.00
❑ 252 Vern Bickford 50.00 22.00
❑ 253 Johnny Berardino 100.00 45.00
❑ 254 Joe Dobson 50.00 22.00
❑ 255 Clyde Vollmer 50.00 22.00
❑ 256 Pete Suder 50.00 22.00
❑ 257 Bobby Avila 60.00 27.00
❑ 258 Steve Gromek 60.00 27.00
❑ 259 Bob Addis 50.00 22.00
❑ 260 Pete Castiglione 50.00 22.00
❑ 261 Willie Mays 2500.00 1100.00
❑ 262 Virgil Trucks 60.00 27.00
❑ 263 Harry Brecheen 60.00 27.00
❑ 264 Roy Hartsfield 50.00 22.00
❑ 265 Chuck Diering 50.00 22.00
❑ 266 Murry Dickson 50.00 22.00
❑ 267 Sid Gordon 60.00 27.00
❑ 268 Bob Lemon 150.00 70.00
❑ 269 Willard Nixon 50.00 22.00
❑ 270 Lou Brissie 50.00 22.00
❑ 271 Jim Delsing 60.00 27.00
❑ 272 Mike Garcia 75.00 34.00
❑ 273 Erv Palica 50.00 22.00
❑ 274 Ralph Branca 125.00 55.00
❑ 275 Pat Mullin 50.00 22.00
❑ 276 Jim Wilson 50.00 22.00
❑ 277 Early Wynn 150.00 70.00
❑ 278 Allie Clark 50.00 22.00
❑ 279 Eddie Stewart 50.00 22.00
❑ 280 Cloyd Boyer 75.00 34.00
❑ 281 Tommy Brown SP 75.00 34.00
❑ 282 Birdie Tebbetts SP 75.00 34.00
❑ 283 Phil Masi SP 60.00 27.00
❑ 284 Hank Arft SP 60.00 27.00
❑ 285 Cliff Fannin SP 60.00 27.00
❑ 286 Joe DeMaestri SP 60.00 27.00
❑ 287 Steve Bilko SP 60.00 27.00
❑ 288 Chet Nichols SP 75.00 34.00
❑ 289 Tommy Holmes SP 90.00 40.00
❑ 290 Joe Astroth SP 60.00 27.00
❑ 291 Gil Coan SP 60.00 27.00
❑ 292 Floyd Baker SP 60.00 27.00
❑ 293 Sibby Sisti SP 60.00 27.00
❑ 294 Walker Cooper SP 60.00 27.00
❑ 295 Phil Cavarretta SP 75.00 34.00
❑ 296 Red Rolfe MG SP 60.00 27.00
❑ 297 Andy Seminick SP 60.00 27.00
❑ 298 Bob Ross SP 60.00 27.00
❑ 299 Ray Murray SP 75.00 34.00
❑ 300 Barney McCosky SP 75.00 34.00
❑ 301 Bob Porterfield 50.00 22.00
❑ 302 Max Surkont 50.00 22.00
❑ 303 Harry Dorish 50.00 22.00
❑ 304 Sam Dente 50.00 22.00
❑ 305 Paul Richards MG 60.00 27.00
❑ 306 Lou Sleater 50.00 22.00
❑ 307 Frank Campos 50.00 22.00
❑ 308 Luis Aloma 50.00 22.00
❑ 309 Jim Busby 60.00 27.00
❑ 310 George Metkovich 90.00 40.00
❑ 311 Mickey Mantle 18000.00 8100.00
❑ 312 Jackie Robinson DP 2000.00 900.00
❑ 313 Bobby Thomson DP 300.00 135.00
❑ 314 Roy Campanella 2200.00 1000.00
❑ 315 Leo Durocher MG 600.00 275.00
❑ 316 Dave Williams RC 300.00 135.00
❑ 317 Conrado Marrero 300.00 135.00
❑ 318 Harold Gregg 300.00 135.00
❑ 319 Al Walker 250.00 110.00
❑ 320 John Rutherford RC 300.00 135.00
❑ 321 Joe Black RC 350.00 160.00
❑ 322 Randy Jackson 300.00 135.00
❑ 323 Bubba Church 250.00 110.00
❑ 324 Warren Hacker 250.00 110.00
❑ 325 Bill Serena 300.00 135.00
❑ 326 George Shuba RC 400.00 180.00
❑ 327 Al Wilson 250.00 110.00
❑ 328 Bob Borkowski 300.00 135.00
❑ 329 Ike Delock 300.00 135.00
❑ 330 Turk Lown 300.00 135.00
❑ 331 Tom Morgan 300.00 135.00
❑ 332 Anthony Bartirome 300.00 135.00
❑ 333 Pee Wee Reese 1600.00 700.00
❑ 334 Wilmer Mizell RC 300.00 135.00
❑ 335 Ted Lepcio 250.00 110.00
❑ 336 Dave Koslo 250.00 110.00
❑ 337 Jim Hearn 300.00 135.00
❑ 338 Sal Yvars 300.00 135.00
❑ 339 Russ Meyer 300.00 135.00
❑ 340 Bob Hooper 300.00 135.00
❑ 341 Hal Jeffcoat 300.00 135.00
❑ 342 Clem Labine RC 400.00 180.00
❑ 343 Dick Gernert 250.00 110.00
❑ 344 Ewell Blackwell 300.00 135.00
❑ 345 Sammy White 250.00 110.00
❑ 346 George Spencer 250.00 110.00
❑ 347 Joe Adcock 300.00 135.00
❑ 348 Robert Kelly 250.00 110.00
❑ 349 Bob Cain 300.00 135.00
❑ 350 Cal Abrams 300.00 135.00
❑ 351 Alvin Dark 300.00 135.00
❑ 352 Karl Drews 300.00 135.00
❑ 353 Bobby Del Greco 300.00 135.00
❑ 354 Fred Hatfield 300.00 135.00
❑ 355 Bobby Morgan 300.00 135.00
❑ 356 Toby Atwell 300.00 135.00
❑ 357 Smoky Burgess 300.00 135.00
❑ 358 John Kucab 300.00 135.00
❑ 359 Dee Fondy 250.00 110.00
❑ 360 George Crowe RC 300.00 135.00
❑ 361 William Posedel CO 250.00 110.00
❑ 362 Ken Heintzelman 300.00 135.00
❑ 363 Dick Rozek 300.00 135.00
❑ 364 Clyde Sukeforth CO 300.00 135.00
❑ 365 Cookie Lavagetto CO 350.00 160.00
❑ 366 Dave Madison 250.00 110.00
❑ 367 Ben Thorpe 300.00 135.00
❑ 368 Ed Wright 300.00 135.00
❑ 369 Dick Groat RC 350.00 160.00
❑ 370 Billy Hoeft RC 300.00 135.00
❑ 371 Bobby Hofman 250.00 110.00
❑ 372 Gil McDougald RC 450.00 200.00
❑ 373 Jim Turner RC CO 400.00 180.00
❑ 374 John Benton 250.00 110.00
❑ 375 John Merson 250.00 110.00
❑ 376 Faye Throneberry 250.00 110.00

	NRMT	VG-E
❑ 377 Chuck Dressen MG	350.00	160.00
❑ 378 Leroy Fusselman	300.00	135.00
❑ 379 Joe Rossi	250.00	110.00
❑ 380 Clem Koshorek	250.00	110.00
❑ 381 Milton Stock CO	300.00	135.00
❑ 382 Sam Jones RC	350.00	160.00
❑ 383 Del Wilber	250.00	110.00
❑ 384 Frank Crosetti CO	450.00	200.00
❑ 385 H.Franks CO RC	250.00	110.00
❑ 386 John Yuhas	300.00	135.00
❑ 387 Billy Meyer MG	250.00	110.00
❑ 388 Bob Chipman	250.00	110.00
❑ 389 Ben Wade	300.00	135.00
❑ 390 Glenn Nelson	300.00	135.00
❑ 391 B.Chapman UER CO Photo actually Sam Chapman	250.00	110.00
❑ 392 Hoyt Wilhelm RC	750.00	350.00
❑ 393 Ebba St.Claire	300.00	135.00
❑ 394 Billy Herman CO	400.00	180.00
❑ 395 Jake Pitler CO	300.00	135.00
❑ 396 Dick Williams RC	400.00	180.00
❑ 397 Forrest Main	250.00	110.00
❑ 398 Hal Rice	250.00	110.00
❑ 399 Jim Fridley	250.00	110.00
❑ 400 Bill Dickey CO	1000.00	450.00
❑ 401 Bob Schultz	300.00	135.00
❑ 402 Earl Harrist	300.00	135.00
❑ 403 Bill Miller	300.00	135.00
❑ 404 Dick Brodowski	300.00	135.00
❑ 405 Eddie Pellagrini	300.00	135.00
❑ 406 Joe Nuxhall RC	400.00	180.00
❑ 407 Eddie Mathews RC	8000.00	2000.00

1953 Topps

	NRMT	VG-E
COMPLETE SET (274)	13500.00	6100.00
COMMON CARD (1-165)	30.00	13.50
COMMON CARD (166-220)	25.00	11.00
COMMON DP (1-220)	15.00	6.75
COMMON CARD (221-280)	100.00	45.00
NOT ISSUED (253/261/267)		
NOT ISSUED (268/271/275)		
WRAP.(1-CENT, DATED)	200.00	90.00
WRAP.(1-CENT,NO DATE)	300.00	135.00
WRAP.(5-CENT, DATED)	400.00	180.00
WRAP.(5-CENT,NO DATE)	350.00	160.00

	NRMT	VG-E
❑ 1 Jackie Robinson DP	700.00	190.00
❑ 2 Luke Easter DP	20.00	9.00
❑ 3 George Crowe	40.00	18.00
❑ 4 Ben Wade	30.00	13.50
❑ 5 Joe Dobson	30.00	13.50
❑ 6 Sam Jones	40.00	18.00
❑ 7 Bob Borkowski DP	15.00	6.75
❑ 8 Clem Koshorek DP	15.00	6.75
❑ 9 Joe Collins	60.00	27.00
❑ 10 Smoky Burgess SP	70.00	32.00
❑ 11 Sal Yvars	30.00	13.50
❑ 12 Howie Judson DP	15.00	6.75
❑ 13 Conrado Marrero DP	15.00	6.75
❑ 14 Clem Labine DP	20.00	9.00
❑ 15 Bobo Newsom DP	20.00	9.00
❑ 16 Peanuts Lowrey DP	15.00	6.75
❑ 17 Billy Hitchcock	30.00	13.50
❑ 18 Ted Lepcio DP	15.00	6.75
❑ 19 Mel Parnell DP	20.00	9.00
❑ 20 Hank Thompson	40.00	18.00
❑ 21 Billy Johnson	30.00	13.50
❑ 22 Howie Fox	30.00	13.50
❑ 23 Toby Atwell DP	15.00	6.75
❑ 24 Ferris Fain	40.00	18.00
❑ 25 Ray Boone	40.00	18.00
❑ 26 Dale Mitchell DP	20.00	9.00
❑ 27 Roy Campanella DP	200.00	90.00
❑ 28 Eddie Pellagrini	30.00	13.50
❑ 29 Hal Jeffcoat	30.00	13.50
❑ 30 Willard Nixon	30.00	13.50
❑ 31 Ewell Blackwell	60.00	27.00
❑ 32 Clyde Vollmer	30.00	13.50
❑ 33 Bob Kennedy DP	15.00	6.75
❑ 34 George Shuba	40.00	18.00
❑ 35 Irv Noren DP	15.00	6.75
❑ 36 Johnny Groth DP	15.00	6.75
❑ 37 Eddie Mathews DP	150.00	70.00
❑ 38 Jim Hearn DP	15.00	6.75
❑ 39 Eddie Miksis	30.00	13.50
❑ 40 John Lipon	30.00	13.50
❑ 41 Enos Slaughter	80.00	36.00
❑ 42 Gus Zernial DP	20.00	9.00
❑ 43 Gil McDougald	60.00	27.00
❑ 44 Ellis Kinder SP	35.00	16.00
❑ 45 Grady Hatton DP	15.00	6.75
❑ 46 Johnny Klippstein DP	15.00	6.75
❑ 47 Bubba Church DP	15.00	6.75
❑ 48 Bob Del Greco DP	15.00	6.75
❑ 49 Faye Throneberry DP	15.00	6.75
❑ 50 Chuck Dressen MG DP	20.00	9.00
❑ 51 Frank Campos DP	15.00	6.75
❑ 52 Ted Gray DP	15.00	6.75
❑ 53 Sherm Lollar DP	20.00	9.00
❑ 54 Bob Feller DP	125.00	55.00
❑ 55 Maurice McDermott DP	15.00	6.75
❑ 56 Gerry Staley DP	15.00	6.75
❑ 57 Carl Scheib	30.00	13.50
❑ 58 George Metkovich	30.00	13.50
❑ 59 Karl Drews DP	15.00	6.75
❑ 60 Cloyd Boyer DP	15.00	6.75
❑ 61 Early Wynn SP	110.00	50.00
❑ 62 Monte Irvin DP	35.00	16.00
❑ 63 Gus Niarhos DP	15.00	6.75
❑ 64 Dave Philley	30.00	13.50
❑ 65 Earl Harrist	30.00	13.50
❑ 66 Minnie Minoso	60.00	27.00
❑ 67 Roy Sievers DP	20.00	9.00
❑ 68 Del Rice	30.00	13.50
❑ 69 Dick Brodowski	30.00	13.50
❑ 70 Ed Yuhas	30.00	13.50
❑ 71 Tony Bartirome	30.00	13.50
❑ 72 F.Hutchinson MG SP	50.00	22.00
❑ 73 Eddie Robinson	30.00	13.50
❑ 74 Joe Rossi	30.00	13.50
❑ 75 Mike Garcia	40.00	18.00
❑ 76 Pee Wee Reese	175.00	80.00
❑ 77 Johnny Mize DP	80.00	36.00
❑ 78 Red Schoendienst	80.00	36.00
❑ 79 Johnny Wyrostek	30.00	13.50
❑ 80 Jim Hegan	40.00	18.00
❑ 81 Joe Black SP	70.00	32.00
❑ 82 Mickey Mantle	3000.00	1350.00
❑ 83 Howie Pollet	30.00	13.50
❑ 84 Bob Hooper DP	15.00	6.75
❑ 85 Bobby Morgan DP	15.00	6.75
❑ 86 Billy Martin	125.00	55.00
❑ 87 Ed Lopat	60.00	27.00
❑ 88 Willie Jones DP	15.00	6.75
❑ 89 Chuck Stobbs DP	15.00	6.75
❑ 90 Hank Edwards DP	15.00	6.75
❑ 91 Ebba St.Claire DP	15.00	6.75
❑ 92 Paul Minner DP	15.00	6.75
❑ 93 Hal Rice DP	15.00	6.75
❑ 94 Bill Kennedy DP	15.00	6.75
❑ 95 Willard Marshall DP	15.00	6.75
❑ 96 Virgil Trucks	40.00	18.00
❑ 97 Don Kolloway DP	15.00	6.75
❑ 98 Cal Abrams DP	15.00	6.75
❑ 99 Dave Madison	30.00	13.50
❑ 100 Bill Miller	30.00	13.50
❑ 101 Ted Wilks	30.00	13.50
❑ 102 Connie Ryan DP	15.00	6.75
❑ 103 Joe Astroth DP	15.00	6.75
❑ 104 Yogi Berra	300.00	135.00
❑ 105 Joe Nuxhall DP	20.00	9.00
❑ 106 Johnny Antonelli	40.00	18.00
❑ 107 Danny O'Connell DP	15.00	6.75
❑ 108 Bob Porterfield DP	15.00	6.75
❑ 109 Alvin Dark	60.00	27.00
❑ 110 Herman Wehmeier DP	15.00	6.75
❑ 111 Hank Sauer DP	15.00	6.75
❑ 112 Ned Garver DP	15.00	6.75
❑ 113 Jerry Priddy	30.00	13.50
❑ 114 Phil Rizzuto	175.00	80.00
❑ 115 George Spencer	30.00	13.50
❑ 116 Frank Smith DP	15.00	6.75
❑ 117 Sid Gordon DP	15.00	6.75
❑ 118 Gus Bell DP	20.00	9.00
❑ 119 Johnny Sain SP	50.00	22.00
❑ 120 Davey Williams	40.00	18.00
❑ 121 Walt Dropo	40.00	18.00
❑ 122 Elmer Valo	30.00	13.50
❑ 123 Tommy Byrne DP	15.00	6.75
❑ 124 Sibby Sisti DP	15.00	6.75
❑ 125 Dick Williams DP	25.00	11.00
❑ 126 Bill Connelly DP	15.00	6.75
❑ 127 Clint Courtney DP	15.00	6.75
❑ 128 Wilmer Mizell DP (Inconsistent design, logo on front with black birds)	20.00	9.00
❑ 129 Keith Thomas	30.00	13.50
❑ 130 Turk Lown DP	15.00	6.75
❑ 131 Harry Byrd DP	15.00	6.75
❑ 132 Tom Morgan	30.00	13.50
❑ 133 Gil Coan	30.00	13.50
❑ 134 Rube Walker	40.00	18.00
❑ 135 Al Rosen DP	25.00	11.00
❑ 136 Ken Heintzelman DP	15.00	6.75
❑ 137 John Rutherford DP	15.00	6.75
❑ 138 George Kell	80.00	36.00
❑ 139 Sammy White	30.00	13.50
❑ 140 Tommy Glaviano	30.00	13.50
❑ 141 Allie Reynolds DP	25.00	11.00
❑ 142 Vic Wertz	40.00	18.00
❑ 143 Billy Pierce	60.00	27.00
❑ 144 Bob Schultz DP	15.00	6.75
❑ 145 Harry Dorish DP	15.00	6.75
❑ 146 Granny Hamner	30.00	13.50
❑ 147 Warren Spahn	150.00	70.00
❑ 148 Mickey Grasso	30.00	13.50
❑ 149 Dom DiMaggio DP	35.00	16.00
❑ 150 Harry Simpson DP	15.00	6.75
❑ 151 Hoyt Wilhelm	80.00	36.00
❑ 152 Bob Adams DP	15.00	6.75
❑ 153 Andy Seminick DP	15.00	6.75
❑ 154 Dick Groat	40.00	18.00
❑ 155 Dutch Leonard	30.00	13.50
❑ 156 Jim Rivera DP	20.00	9.00
❑ 157 Bob Addis DP	15.00	6.75
❑ 158 Johnny Logan RC	40.00	18.00
❑ 159 Wayne Terwilliger DP	15.00	6.75
❑ 160 Bob Young	30.00	13.50
❑ 161 Vern Bickford DP	15.00	6.75
❑ 162 Ted Kluszewski	60.00	27.00
❑ 163 Fred Hatfield DP	15.00	6.75
❑ 164 Frank Shea DP	15.00	6.75
❑ 165 Billy Hoeft	30.00	13.50
❑ 166 Billy Hunter	25.00	11.00
❑ 167 Art Schult	25.00	11.00
❑ 168 Willard Schmidt	25.00	11.00
❑ 169 Dizzy Trout	30.00	13.50
❑ 170 Bill Werle	25.00	11.00
❑ 171 Bill Glynn	25.00	11.00
❑ 172 Rip Repulski	25.00	11.00
❑ 173 Preston Ward	25.00	11.00
❑ 174 Billy Loes	30.00	13.50
❑ 175 Ron Kline	25.00	11.00
❑ 176 Don Hoak RC	40.00	18.00
❑ 177 Jim Dyck	25.00	11.00
❑ 178 Jim Waugh	25.00	11.00
❑ 179 Gene Hermanski	25.00	11.00
❑ 180 Virgil Stallcup	25.00	11.00
❑ 181 Al Zarilla	25.00	11.00
❑ 182 Bobby Hofman	25.00	11.00

Card	NRMT	VG-E
❑ 183 Stu Miller RC	40.00	18.00
❑ 184 Hal Brown	25.00	11.00
❑ 185 Jim Pendleton	25.00	11.00
❑ 186 Charlie Bishop	25.00	11.00
❑ 187 Jim Fridley	25.00	11.00
❑ 188 Andy Carey RC	40.00	18.00
❑ 189 Ray Jablonski	25.00	11.00
❑ 190 Dixie Walker CO	30.00	13.50
❑ 191 Ralph Kiner	80.00	36.00
❑ 192 Wally Westlake	25.00	11.00
❑ 193 Mike Clark	25.00	11.00
❑ 194 Eddie Kazak	25.00	11.00
❑ 195 Ed McGhee	25.00	11.00
❑ 196 Bob Keegan	25.00	11.00
❑ 197 Del Crandall	40.00	18.00
❑ 198 Forrest Main	25.00	11.00
❑ 199 Marion Fricano	25.00	11.00
❑ 200 Gordon Goldsberry	25.00	11.00
❑ 201 Paul LaPalme	25.00	11.00
❑ 202 Carl Sawatski	25.00	11.00
❑ 203 Cliff Fannin	25.00	11.00
❑ 204 Dick Bokelman	25.00	11.00
❑ 205 Vern Benson	25.00	11.00
❑ 206 Ed Bailey RC	30.00	13.50
❑ 207 Whitey Ford	175.00	80.00
❑ 208 Jim Wilson	25.00	11.00
❑ 209 Jim Greengrass	25.00	11.00
❑ 210 Bob Cerv RC	40.00	18.00
❑ 211 J.W. Porter	25.00	11.00
❑ 212 Jack Dittmer	25.00	11.00
❑ 213 Ray Scarborough	25.00	11.00
❑ 214 Bill Bruton RC	40.00	18.00
❑ 215 Gene Conley RC	30.00	13.50
❑ 216 Jim Hughes	25.00	11.00
❑ 217 Murray Wall	25.00	11.00
❑ 218 Les Fusselman	25.00	11.00
❑ 219 Pete Runnels UER (Photo actually Don Johnson)	30.00	13.50
❑ 220 Satchel Paige UER (Misspelled Satchell on card front)	600.00	275.00
❑ 221 Bob Milliken	100.00	45.00
❑ 222 Vic Janowicz DP RC	60.00	27.00
❑ 223 Johnny O'Brien DP	50.00	22.00
❑ 224 Lou Sleater DP	50.00	22.00
❑ 225 Bobby Shantz	120.00	55.00
❑ 226 Ed Erautt	100.00	45.00
❑ 227 Morrie Martin	100.00	45.00
❑ 228 Hal Newhouser	150.00	70.00
❑ 229 Rocky Krsnich	100.00	45.00
❑ 230 Johnny Lindell DP	50.00	22.00
❑ 231 Solly Hemus DP	50.00	22.00
❑ 232 Dick Kokos	100.00	45.00
❑ 233 Al Aber	100.00	45.00
❑ 234 Ray Murray DP	50.00	22.00
❑ 235 John Hetki DP	50.00	22.00
❑ 236 Harry Perkowski DP	50.00	22.00
❑ 237 Bud Podbielan DP	50.00	22.00
❑ 238 Cal Hogue DP	50.00	22.00
❑ 239 Jim Delsing	100.00	45.00
❑ 240 Fred Marsh	100.00	45.00
❑ 241 Al Sima DP	50.00	22.00
❑ 242 Charlie Silvera	120.00	55.00
❑ 243 Carlos Bernier DP	50.00	22.00
❑ 244 Willie Mays	2700.00	1200.00
❑ 245 Bill Norman CO	100.00	45.00
❑ 246 Roy Face DP RC	80.00	36.00
❑ 247 Mike Sandlock DP	50.00	22.00
❑ 248 Gene Stephens DP	50.00	22.00
❑ 249 Eddie O'Brien	100.00	45.00
❑ 250 Bob Wilson	100.00	45.00
❑ 251 Sid Hudson	100.00	45.00
❑ 252 Hank Foiles	100.00	45.00
❑ 253 Does not exist		
❑ 254 Preacher Roe DP	80.00	36.00
❑ 255 Dixie Howell	100.00	45.00
❑ 256 Les Peden	100.00	45.00
❑ 257 Bob Boyd	100.00	45.00
❑ 258 Jim Gilliam RC	300.00	135.00
❑ 259 Roy McMillan DP	50.00	22.00
❑ 260 Sam Calderone	100.00	45.00
❑ 261 Does not exist		
❑ 262 Bob Oldis	100.00	45.00
❑ 263 Johnny Podres RC	300.00	135.00
❑ 264 Gene Woodling DP	60.00	27.00
❑ 265 Jackie Jensen	120.00	55.00
❑ 266 Bob Cain	100.00	45.00
❑ 267 Does not exist		
❑ 268 Does not exist		
❑ 269 Duane Pillette	100.00	45.00
❑ 270 Vern Stephens	120.00	55.00
❑ 271 Does not exist		
❑ 272 Bill Antonello	100.00	45.00
❑ 273 Harvey Haddix RC	150.00	70.00
❑ 274 John Riddle CO	100.00	45.00
❑ 275 Does not exist		
❑ 276 Ken Raffensberger	100.00	45.00
❑ 277 Don Lund	100.00	45.00
❑ 278 Willie Miranda	100.00	45.00
❑ 279 Joe Coleman DP	50.00	22.00
❑ 280 Milt Bolling RC	350.00	57.50

1954 Topps

	NRMT	VG-E
COMPLETE SET (250)	7500.00	3400.00
COMMON (1-50/76-250)	15.00	6.75
COMMON CARD (51-75)	25.00	11.00
WRAP.(1-CENT, DATED)	200.00	90.00
WRAP.(1-CENT, UNDAT)	150.00	70.00
WRAP.(5-CENT, DATED)	300.00	135.00
WRAP.(5-CENT, UNDAT)	250.00	110.00

Card	NRMT	VG-E
❑ 1 Ted Williams	800.00	275.00
❑ 2 Gus Zernial	25.00	11.00
❑ 3 Monte Irvin	50.00	22.00
❑ 4 Hank Sauer	25.00	11.00
❑ 5 Ed Lopat	25.00	11.00
❑ 6 Pete Runnels	25.00	11.00
❑ 7 Ted Kluszewski	50.00	22.00
❑ 8 Bob Young	15.00	6.75
❑ 9 Harvey Haddix	25.00	11.00
❑ 10 Jackie Robinson	300.00	135.00
❑ 11 Paul Leslie Smith	15.00	6.75
❑ 12 Del Crandall	25.00	11.00
❑ 13 Billy Martin	80.00	36.00
❑ 14 Preacher Roe	25.00	11.00
❑ 15 Al Rosen	25.00	11.00
❑ 16 Vic Janowicz	25.00	11.00
❑ 17 Phil Rizzuto	100.00	45.00
❑ 18 Walt Dropo	25.00	11.00
❑ 19 Johnny Lipon (Orioles Team Name on Front, White Sox team on Back, Wearing a Red Sox cap)	15.00	6.75
❑ 20 Warren Spahn	80.00	36.00
❑ 21 Bobby Shantz	25.00	11.00
❑ 22 Jim Greengrass	15.00	6.75
❑ 23 Luke Easter	25.00	11.00
❑ 24 Granny Hamner	15.00	6.75
❑ 25 Harvey Kuenn RC	40.00	18.00
❑ 26 Ray Jablonski	15.00	6.75
❑ 27 Ferris Fain	25.00	11.00
❑ 28 Paul Minner	15.00	6.75
❑ 29 Jim Hegan	25.00	11.00
❑ 30 Eddie Mathews	80.00	36.00
❑ 31 Johnny Klippstein	15.00	6.75
❑ 32 Duke Snider	175.00	80.00
❑ 33 Johnny Schmitz	15.00	6.75
❑ 34 Jim Rivera	15.00	6.75
❑ 35 Jim Gilliam	50.00	22.00
❑ 36 Hoyt Wilhelm	50.00	22.00
❑ 37 Whitey Ford	125.00	55.00
❑ 38 Eddie Stanky MG	25.00	11.00
❑ 39 Sherm Lollar	25.00	11.00
❑ 40 Mel Parnell	25.00	11.00
❑ 41 Willie Jones	15.00	6.75
❑ 42 Don Mueller	25.00	11.00
❑ 43 Dick Groat	25.00	11.00
❑ 44 Ned Garver	15.00	6.75
❑ 45 Richie Ashburn	80.00	36.00
❑ 46 Ken Raffensberger	15.00	6.75
❑ 47 Ellis Kinder	15.00	6.75
❑ 48 Billy Hunter	25.00	11.00
❑ 49 Ray Murray	15.00	6.75
❑ 50 Yogi Berra	200.00	90.00
❑ 51 Johnny Lindell	25.00	11.00
❑ 52 Vic Power RC	30.00	13.50
❑ 53 Jack Dittmer	25.00	11.00
❑ 54 Vern Stephens	30.00	13.50
❑ 55 Phil Cavarretta MG	30.00	13.50
❑ 56 Willie Miranda	25.00	11.00
❑ 57 Luis Aloma	25.00	11.00
❑ 58 Bob Wilson	25.00	11.00
❑ 59 Gene Conley	30.00	13.50
❑ 60 Frank Baumholtz	25.00	11.00
❑ 61 Bob Cain	25.00	11.00
❑ 62 Eddie Robinson	25.00	11.00
❑ 63 Johnny Pesky	30.00	13.50
❑ 64 Hank Thompson	25.00	11.00
❑ 65 Bob Swift CO	25.00	11.00
❑ 66 Ted Lepcio	25.00	11.00
❑ 67 Jim Willis	25.00	11.00
❑ 68 Sam Calderone	25.00	11.00
❑ 69 Bud Podbielan	25.00	11.00
❑ 70 Larry Doby	60.00	27.00
❑ 71 Frank Smith	25.00	11.00
❑ 72 Preston Ward	25.00	11.00
❑ 73 Wayne Terwilliger	25.00	11.00
❑ 74 Bill Taylor	25.00	11.00
❑ 75 Fred Haney MG	25.00	11.00
❑ 76 Bob Scheffing CO	15.00	6.75
❑ 77 Ray Boone	25.00	11.00
❑ 78 Ted Kazanski	15.00	6.75
❑ 79 Andy Pafko	25.00	11.00
❑ 80 Jackie Jensen	25.00	11.00
❑ 81 Dave Hoskins	15.00	6.75
❑ 82 Milt Bolling	15.00	6.75
❑ 83 Joe Collins	25.00	11.00
❑ 84 Dick Cole	15.00	6.75
❑ 85 Bob Turley RC	40.00	18.00
❑ 86 Billy Herman CO	25.00	11.00
❑ 87 Roy Face	25.00	11.00
❑ 88 Matt Batts	15.00	6.75
❑ 89 Howie Pollet	15.00	6.75
❑ 90 Willie Mays	500.00	220.00
❑ 91 Bob Oldis	15.00	6.75
❑ 92 Wally Westlake	15.00	6.75
❑ 93 Sid Hudson	15.00	6.75
❑ 94 Ernie Banks RC	800.00	350.00
❑ 95 Hal Rice	15.00	6.75
❑ 96 Charlie Silvera	25.00	11.00
❑ 97 Jerald Hal Lane	15.00	6.75
❑ 98 Joe Black	40.00	18.00
❑ 99 Bobby Hofman	15.00	6.75
❑ 100 Bob Keegan	15.00	6.75
❑ 101 Gene Woodling	25.00	11.00
❑ 102 Gil Hodges	80.00	36.00
❑ 103 Jim Lemon RC	15.00	6.75
❑ 104 Mike Sandlock	15.00	6.75
❑ 105 Andy Carey	25.00	11.00
❑ 106 Dick Kokos	15.00	6.75
❑ 107 Duane Pillette	15.00	6.75
❑ 108 Thornton Kipper	15.00	6.75
❑ 109 Bill Bruton	25.00	11.00
❑ 110 Harry Dorish	15.00	6.75
❑ 111 Jim Delsing	15.00	6.75
❑ 112 Bill Renna	15.00	6.75
❑ 113 Bob Boyd	15.00	6.75
❑ 114 Dean Stone	15.00	6.75
❑ 115 Rip Repulski	15.00	6.75
❑ 116 Steve Bilko	15.00	6.75
❑ 117 Solly Hemus	15.00	6.75
❑ 118 Carl Scheib	15.00	6.75
❑ 119 Johnny Antonelli	25.00	11.00
❑ 120 Roy McMillan	25.00	11.00
❑ 121 Clem Labine	25.00	11.00
❑ 122 Johnny Logan	25.00	11.00
❑ 123 Bobby Adams	15.00	6.75

	No.	Player	NRMT	VG-E
❑	124	Marion Fricano	15.00	6.75
❑	125	Harry Perkowski	15.00	6.75
❑	126	Ben Wade	15.00	6.75
❑	127	Steve O'Neill MG	15.00	6.75
❑	128	Hank Aaron RC	1500.00	700.00
❑	129	Forrest Jacobs	15.00	6.75
❑	130	Hank Bauer	25.00	11.00
❑	131	Reno Bertoia	25.00	11.00
❑	132	Tommy Lasorda RC	200.00	90.00
❑	133	Del Baker CO	15.00	6.75
❑	134	Cal Hogue	15.00	6.75
❑	135	Joe Presko	15.00	6.75
❑	136	Connie Ryan	15.00	6.75
❑	137	Wally Moon RC	40.00	18.00
❑	138	Bob Borkowski	15.00	6.75
❑	139	The O'Briens Johnny O'Brien Eddie O'Brien	50.00	22.00
❑	140	Tom Wright	15.00	6.75
❑	141	Joey Jay RC	25.00	11.00
❑	142	Tom Poholsky	15.00	6.75
❑	143	Rollie Hemsley CO	15.00	6.75
❑	144	Bill Werle	15.00	6.75
❑	145	Elmer Valo	15.00	6.75
❑	146	Don Johnson	15.00	6.75
❑	147	Johnny Riddle CO	15.00	6.75
❑	148	Bob Trice	15.00	6.75
❑	149	Al Robertson	15.00	6.75
❑	150	Dick Kryhoski	15.00	6.75
❑	151	Alex Grammas	15.00	6.75
❑	152	Michael Blyzka	15.00	6.75
❑	153	Al Walker	25.00	11.00
❑	154	Mike Fornieles	15.00	6.75
❑	155	Bob Kennedy	25.00	11.00
❑	156	Joe Coleman	25.00	11.00
❑	157	Don Lenhardt	25.00	11.00
❑	158	Peanuts Lowrey	15.00	6.75
❑	159	Dave Philley	15.00	6.75
❑	160	Ralph Kress CO	15.00	6.75
❑	161	John Hetki	15.00	6.75
❑	162	Herman Wehmeier	15.00	6.75
❑	163	Frank House	15.00	6.75
❑	164	Stu Miller	25.00	11.00
❑	165	Jim Pendleton	15.00	6.75
❑	166	Johnny Podres	40.00	18.00
❑	167	Don Lund	15.00	6.75
❑	168	Morrie Martin	25.00	11.00
❑	169	Jim Hughes	40.00	18.00
❑	170	Dusty Rhodes RC	25.00	11.00
❑	171	Leo Kiely	15.00	6.75
❑	172	Harold Brown	15.00	6.75
❑	173	Jack Harshman	15.00	6.75
❑	174	Tom Qualters	15.00	6.75
❑	175	Frank Leja RC	25.00	11.00
❑	176	Robert Keely CO	15.00	6.75
❑	177	Bob Milliken	15.00	6.75
❑	178	Bill Glynn UER Spelled Gylnn on the front	15.00	6.75
❑	179	Gair Allie	15.00	6.75
❑	180	Wes Westrum	25.00	11.00
❑	181	Mel Roach	15.00	6.75
❑	182	Chuck Harmon	15.00	6.75
❑	183	Earle Combs CO	25.00	11.00
❑	184	Ed Bailey	15.00	6.75
❑	185	Chuck Stobbs	15.00	6.75
❑	186	Karl Olson	15.00	6.75
❑	187	Heinie Manush CO	25.00	11.00
❑	188	Dave Jolly	15.00	6.75
❑	189	Bob Ross	15.00	6.75
❑	190	Ray Herbert	15.00	6.75
❑	191	John(Dick) Schofield RC	25.00	11.00
❑	192	Ellis Deal CO	15.00	6.75
❑	193	Johnny Hopp CO	25.00	11.00
❑	194	Bill Sarni	15.00	6.75
❑	195	Billy Consolo RC	15.00	6.75
❑	196	Stan Jok	15.00	6.75
❑	197	Lynwood Rowe CO ("Schoolboy")	25.00	11.00
❑	198	Carl Sawatski	15.00	6.75
❑	199	Glenn(Rocky) Nelson	15.00	6.75
❑	200	Larry Jansen	25.00	11.00
❑	201	Al Kaline RC	700.00	325.00
❑	202	Bob Purkey RC	25.00	11.00
❑	203	Harry Brecheen CO	25.00	11.00
❑	204	Angel Scull	15.00	6.75
❑	205	Johnny Sain	40.00	18.00
❑	206	Ray Crone	15.00	6.75
❑	207	Tom Oliver CO	15.00	6.75
❑	208	Grady Hatton	15.00	6.75
❑	209	Chuck Thompson	15.00	6.75
❑	210	Bob Buhl RC	25.00	11.00
❑	211	Don Hoak	25.00	11.00
❑	212	Bob Micelotta	15.00	6.75
❑	213	Johnny Fitzpatrick CO	15.00	6.75
❑	214	Arnie Portocarrero	15.00	6.75
❑	215	Ed McGhee	25.00	11.00
❑	216	Al Sima	15.00	6.75
❑	217	Paul Schreiber CO	15.00	6.75
❑	218	Fred Marsh	15.00	6.75
❑	219	Chuck Kress	15.00	6.75
❑	220	Ruben Gomez	25.00	11.00
❑	221	Dick Brodowski	15.00	6.75
❑	222	Bill Wilson	15.00	6.75
❑	223	Joe Haynes CO	15.00	6.75
❑	224	Dick Weik	15.00	6.75
❑	225	Don Liddle	15.00	6.75
❑	226	Jehosie Heard	25.00	11.00
❑	227	Colonel Mills CO	15.00	6.75
❑	228	Gene Hermanski	15.00	6.75
❑	229	Bob Talbot	15.00	6.75
❑	230	Bob Kuzava	25.00	11.00
❑	231	Roy Smalley	15.00	6.75
❑	232	Lou Limmer	15.00	6.75
❑	233	Augie Galan CO	15.00	6.75
❑	234	Jerry Lynch RC	15.00	6.75
❑	235	Vern Law	25.00	11.00
❑	236	Paul Penson	15.00	6.75
❑	237	Mike Ryba CO	15.00	6.75
❑	238	Al Aber	15.00	6.75
❑	239	Bill Skowron RC	100.00	45.00
❑	240	Sam Mele	25.00	11.00
❑	241	Robert Miller	15.00	6.75
❑	242	Curt Roberts	15.00	6.75
❑	243	Ray Blades CO	15.00	6.75
❑	244	Leroy Wheat	15.00	6.75
❑	245	Roy Sievers	25.00	11.00
❑	246	Howie Fox	15.00	6.75
❑	247	Ed Mayo CO	15.00	6.75
❑	248	Al Smith RC	25.00	11.00
❑	249	Wilmer Mizell	25.00	11.00
❑	250	Ted Williams	800.00	325.00

1955 Topps

	NRMT	VG-E
COMPLETE SET (206)	7200.00	3200.00
COMMON CARD (1-150)	12.00	5.50
COMMON CARD (151-160)	20.00	9.00
COMMON CARD (161-210)	30.00	13.50
WRAP.(1-CENT, DATED)	150.00	70.00
WRAP.(1-CENT, UNDAT)	50.00	22.00
WRAP.(5-CENT, DATED)	150.00	70.00
WRAP.(5-CENT, UNDAT)	100.00	45.00

	No.	Player	NRMT	VG-E
❑	1	Dusty Rhodes	75.00	15.00
❑	2	Ted Williams	600.00	275.00
❑	3	Art Fowler	15.00	6.75
❑	4	Al Kaline	150.00	70.00
❑	5	Jim Gilliam	40.00	18.00
❑	6	Stan Hack MG	25.00	11.00
❑	7	Jim Hegan	15.00	6.75
❑	8	Harold Smith	12.00	5.50
❑	9	Robert Miller	12.00	5.50
❑	10	Bob Keegan	12.00	5.50
❑	11	Ferris Fain	15.00	6.75
❑	12	Vernon(Jake) Thies	12.00	5.50
❑	13	Fred Marsh	12.00	5.50
❑	14	Jim Finigan	12.00	5.50
❑	15	Jim Pendleton	12.00	5.50
❑	16	Roy Sievers	15.00	6.75
❑	17	Bobby Hofman	12.00	5.50
❑	18	Russ Kemmerer	12.00	5.50
❑	19	Billy Herman CO	15.00	6.75
❑	20	Andy Carey	15.00	6.75
❑	21	Alex Grammas	12.00	5.50
❑	22	Bill Skowron	40.00	18.00
❑	23	Jack Parks	12.00	5.50
❑	24	Hal Newhouser	40.00	18.00
❑	25	Johnny Podres	25.00	11.00
❑	26	Dick Groat	15.00	6.75
❑	27	Billy Gardner	15.00	6.75
❑	28	Ernie Banks	175.00	80.00
❑	29	Herman Wehmeier	12.00	5.50
❑	30	Vic Power	15.00	6.75
❑	31	Warren Spahn	100.00	45.00
❑	32	Warren McGhee	12.00	5.50
❑	33	Tom Qualters	12.00	5.50
❑	34	Wayne Terwilliger	12.00	5.50
❑	35	Dave Jolly	12.00	5.50
❑	36	Leo Kiely	12.00	5.50
❑	37	Joe Cunningham RC	15.00	6.75
❑	38	Bob Turley	15.00	6.75
❑	39	Bill Glynn	12.00	5.50
❑	40	Don Hoak	15.00	6.75
❑	41	Chuck Stobbs	12.00	5.50
❑	42	John(Windy) McCall	12.00	5.50
❑	43	Harvey Haddix	15.00	6.75
❑	44	Harold Valentine	12.00	5.50
❑	45	Hank Sauer	15.00	6.75
❑	46	Ted Kazanski	12.00	5.50
❑	47	Hank Aaron UER (Birth incorrectly listed as 2/10)	350.00	160.00
❑	48	Bob Kennedy	15.00	6.75
❑	49	J.W. Porter	12.00	5.50
❑	50	Jackie Robinson	350.00	160.00
❑	51	Jim Hughes	15.00	6.75
❑	52	Bill Tremel	12.00	5.50
❑	53	Bill Taylor	12.00	5.50
❑	54	Lou Limmer	12.00	5.50
❑	55	Rip Repulski	12.00	5.50
❑	56	Ray Jablonski	12.00	5.50
❑	57	Billy O'Dell	12.00	5.50
❑	58	Jim Rivera	12.00	5.50
❑	59	Gair Allie	12.00	5.50
❑	60	Dean Stone	12.00	5.50
❑	61	Forrest Jacobs	12.00	5.50
❑	62	Thornton Kipper	12.00	5.50
❑	63	Joe Collins	15.00	6.75
❑	64	Gus Triandos RC	15.00	6.75
❑	65	Ray Boone	15.00	6.75
❑	66	Ron Jackson	12.00	5.50
❑	67	Wally Moon	15.00	6.75
❑	68	Jim Davis	12.00	5.50
❑	69	Ed Bailey	15.00	6.75
❑	70	Al Rosen	15.00	6.75
❑	71	Ruben Gomez	12.00	5.50
❑	72	Karl Olson	12.00	5.50
❑	73	Jack Shepard	12.00	5.50
❑	74	Bob Borkowski	12.00	5.50
❑	75	Sandy Amoros RC	40.00	18.00
❑	76	Howie Pollet	12.00	5.50
❑	77	Arnie Portocarrero	12.00	5.50
❑	78	Gordon Jones	12.00	5.50
❑	79	Clyde(Danny) Schell	12.00	5.50
❑	80	Bob Grim RC	15.00	6.75
❑	81	Gene Conley	15.00	6.75
❑	82	Chuck Harmon	12.00	5.50
❑	83	Tom Brewer	12.00	5.50
❑	84	Camilo Pascual RC	15.00	6.75
❑	85	Don Mossi RC	25.00	11.00
❑	86	Bill Wilson	12.00	5.50
❑	87	Frank House	12.00	5.50
❑	88	Bob Skinner RC	15.00	6.75
❑	89	Joe Frazier	15.00	6.75
❑	90	Karl Spooner RC	15.00	6.75
❑	91	Milt Bolling	12.00	5.50
❑	92	Don Zimmer RC	25.00	11.00
❑	93	Steve Bilko	12.00	5.50

Card	NRMT	VG-E
❑ 94 Reno Bertoia	12.00	5.50
❑ 95 Preston Ward	12.00	5.50
❑ 96 Chuck Bishop	12.00	5.50
❑ 97 Carlos Paula	12.00	5.50
❑ 98 John Riddle CO	12.00	5.50
❑ 99 Frank Leja	12.00	5.50
❑ 100 Monte Irvin	40.00	18.00
❑ 101 Johnny Gray	12.00	5.50
❑ 102 Wally Westlake	12.00	5.50
❑ 103 Chuck White	12.00	5.50
❑ 104 Jack Harshman	12.00	5.50
❑ 105 Chuck Diering	12.00	5.50
❑ 106 Frank Sullivan	12.00	5.50
❑ 107 Curt Roberts	12.00	5.50
❑ 108 Al Walker	15.00	6.75
❑ 109 Ed Lopat	15.00	6.75
❑ 110 Gus Zernial	15.00	6.75
❑ 111 Bob Milliken	15.00	6.75
❑ 112 Nelson King	12.00	5.50
❑ 113 Harry Brecheen CO	15.00	6.75
❑ 114 Louis Ortiz	12.00	5.50
❑ 115 Ellis Kinder	12.00	5.50
❑ 116 Tom Hurd	12.00	5.50
❑ 117 Mel Roach	12.00	5.50
❑ 118 Bob Purkey	12.00	5.50
❑ 119 Bob Lennon	12.00	5.50
❑ 120 Ted Kluszewski	75.00	34.00
❑ 121 Bill Renna	12.00	5.50
❑ 122 Carl Sawatski	12.00	5.50
❑ 123 Sandy Koufax RC	800.00	350.00
❑ 124 Harmon Killebrew RC	250.00	110.00
❑ 125 Ken Boyer RC	60.00	27.00
❑ 126 Dick Hall	12.00	5.50
❑ 127 Dale Long RC	15.00	6.75
❑ 128 Ted Lepcio	12.00	5.50
❑ 129 Elvin Tappe	15.00	6.75
❑ 130 Mayo Smith MG	12.00	5.50
❑ 131 Grady Hatton	12.00	5.50
❑ 132 Bob Trice	12.00	5.50
❑ 133 Dave Hoskins	12.00	5.50
❑ 134 Joey Jay	15.00	6.75
❑ 135 Johnny O'Brien	15.00	6.75
❑ 136 Veston(Bunky)Stewart	12.00	5.50
❑ 137 Harry Elliott	12.00	5.50
❑ 138 Ray Herbert	12.00	5.50
❑ 139 Steve Kraly	12.00	5.50
❑ 140 Mel Parnell	15.00	6.75
❑ 141 Tom Wright	12.00	5.50
❑ 142 Jerry Lynch	15.00	6.75
❑ 143 John(Dick) Schofield	15.00	6.75
❑ 144 John(Joe) Amalfitano RC	12.00	5.50
❑ 145 Elmer Valo	12.00	5.50
❑ 146 Dick Donovan RC	12.00	5.50
❑ 147 Hugh Pepper	12.00	5.50
❑ 148 Hector Brown	12.00	5.50
❑ 149 Ray Crone	12.00	5.50
❑ 150 Mike Higgins MG	12.00	5.50
❑ 151 Ralph Kress CO	20.00	9.00
❑ 152 Harry Agganis RC	80.00	36.00
❑ 153 Bud Podbielan	25.00	11.00
❑ 154 Willie Miranda	20.00	9.00
❑ 155 Eddie Mathews	125.00	55.00
❑ 156 Joe Black	50.00	22.00
❑ 157 Robert Miller	20.00	9.00
❑ 158 Tommy Carroll	25.00	11.00
❑ 159 Johnny Schmitz	20.00	9.00
❑ 160 Ray Narleski RC	20.00	9.00
❑ 161 Chuck Tanner RC	40.00	18.00
❑ 162 Joe Coleman	30.00	13.50
❑ 163 Faye Throneberry	30.00	13.50
❑ 164 Roberto Clemente RC	2000.00	900.00
❑ 165 Don Johnson	30.00	13.50
❑ 166 Hank Bauer	75.00	34.00
❑ 167 Thomas Casagrande	30.00	13.50
❑ 168 Duane Pillette	30.00	13.50
❑ 169 Bob Oldis	40.00	18.00
❑ 170 Jim Pearce DP	15.00	6.75
❑ 171 Dick Brodowski	30.00	13.50
❑ 172 Frank Baumholtz DP	15.00	6.75
❑ 173 Bob Kline	30.00	13.50
❑ 174 Rudy Minarcin	30.00	13.50
❑ 175 Does not exist		
❑ 176 Norm Zauchin	30.00	13.50
❑ 177 Al Robertson	30.00	13.50
❑ 178 Bobby Adams	30.00	13.50
❑ 179 Jim Bolger	30.00	13.50
❑ 180 Clem Labine	60.00	27.00
❑ 181 Roy McMillan	40.00	18.00
❑ 182 Humberto Robinson	30.00	13.50
❑ 183 Anthony Jacobs	30.00	13.50
❑ 184 Harry Perkowski DP	15.00	6.75
❑ 185 Don Ferrarese	30.00	13.50
❑ 186 Does not exist		
❑ 187 Gil Hodges	150.00	70.00
❑ 188 Charlie Silvera DP	15.00	6.75
❑ 189 Phil Rizzuto	150.00	70.00
❑ 190 Gene Woodling	40.00	18.00
❑ 191 Eddie Stanky MG	40.00	18.00
❑ 192 Jim Delsing	40.00	18.00
❑ 193 Johnny Sain	60.00	27.00
❑ 194 Willie Mays	500.00	220.00
❑ 195 Ed Roebuck RC	60.00	27.00
❑ 196 Gale Wade	30.00	13.50
❑ 197 Al Smith	60.00	27.00
❑ 198 Yogi Berra	250.00	110.00
❑ 199 Odbert Hamric	60.00	27.00
❑ 200 Jackie Jensen	60.00	27.00
❑ 201 Sherman Lollar	30.00	13.50
❑ 202 Jim Owens	30.00	13.50
❑ 203 Does not exist		
❑ 204 Frank Smith	30.00	13.50
❑ 205 Gene Freese RC	40.00	18.00
❑ 206 Pete Daley	30.00	13.50
❑ 207 Billy Consolo	30.00	13.50
❑ 208 Ray Moore	40.00	18.00
❑ 209 Does not exist		
❑ 210 Duke Snider	500.00	150.00

1956 Topps

	NRMT	VG-E
COMPLETE SET (340)	7000.00	3200.00
COMMON CARD (1-100)	10.00	4.50
COMMON CARD (101-180)	12.00	5.50
COMMON CARD (261-340)	12.00	5.50
COMMON CARD (181-260)	15.00	6.75
WRAP.(1-CENT)	250.00	110.00
WRAP.(1-CENT, REPEAT)	100.00	45.00
WRAPPER (5-CENT)	200.00	90.00

Card	NRMT	VG-E
❑ 1 W.Harridge PRES RC	100.00	28.00
❑ 2 Warren Giles PRES RC DP	40.00	18.00
❑ 3 Elmer Valo	15.00	6.75
❑ 4 Carlos Paula	15.00	6.75
❑ 5 Ted Williams	400.00	180.00
❑ 6 Ray Boone	25.00	11.00
❑ 7 Ron Negray	10.00	4.50
❑ 8 Walter Alston MG RC	40.00	18.00
❑ 9 Ruben Gomez DP	9.00	4.00
❑ 10 Warren Spahn	80.00	36.00
❑ 11A Chicago Cubs (Centered)	30.00	13.50
❑ 11B Cubs Team (Dated 1955)	80.00	36.00
❑ 11C Cubs Team (Name at far left)	30.00	13.50
❑ 12 Andy Carey	15.00	6.75
❑ 13 Roy Face	15.00	6.75
❑ 14 Ken Boyer DP	15.00	6.75
❑ 15 Ernie Banks DP	90.00	40.00
❑ 16 Hector Lopez RC	15.00	6.75
❑ 17 Gene Conley	15.00	6.75
❑ 18 Dick Donovan	10.00	4.50
❑ 19 Chuck Diering DP	10.00	4.50
❑ 20 Al Kaline	100.00	45.00
❑ 21 Joe Collins DP	15.00	6.75
❑ 22 Jim Finigan	10.00	4.50
❑ 23 Fred Marsh	10.00	4.50
❑ 24 Dick Groat	15.00	6.75
❑ 25 Ted Kluszewski	75.00	34.00
❑ 26 Grady Hatton	10.00	4.50
❑ 27 Nelson Burbrink DP	10.00	4.50
❑ 28 Bobby Hofman	10.00	4.50
❑ 29 Jack Harshman	10.00	4.50
❑ 30 Jackie Robinson DP	200.00	90.00
❑ 31 Hank Aaron UER DP (Small photo actually Willie Mays)	300.00	135.00
❑ 32 Frank House	10.00	4.50
❑ 33 Roberto Clemente	375.00	170.00
❑ 34 Tom Brewer DP	10.00	4.50
❑ 35 Al Rosen	15.00	6.75
❑ 36 Rudy Minarcin	15.00	6.75
❑ 37 Alex Grammas	10.00	4.50
❑ 38 Bob Kennedy	15.00	6.75
❑ 39 Don Mossi	15.00	6.75
❑ 40 Bob Turley	15.00	6.75
❑ 41 Hank Sauer	15.00	6.75
❑ 42 Sandy Amoros	25.00	11.00
❑ 43 Ray Moore	10.00	4.50
❑ 44 Windy McCall	10.00	4.50
❑ 45 Gus Zernial	15.00	6.75
❑ 46 Gene Freese DP	9.00	4.00
❑ 47 Art Fowler	10.00	4.50
❑ 48 Jim Hegan	15.00	6.75
❑ 49 Pedro Ramos	10.00	4.50
❑ 50 Dusty Rhodes DP	15.00	6.75
❑ 51 Ernie Oravetz	10.00	4.50
❑ 52 Bob Grim DP	15.00	6.75
❑ 53 Arnie Portocarrero	10.00	4.50
❑ 54 Bob Keegan	10.00	4.50
❑ 55 Wally Moon	15.00	6.75
❑ 56 Dale Long	15.00	6.75
❑ 57 Duke Maas	10.00	4.50
❑ 58 Ed Roebuck	25.00	11.00
❑ 59 Jose Santiago	10.00	4.50
❑ 60 Mayo Smith MG DP	9.00	4.00
❑ 61 Bill Skowron	25.00	11.00
❑ 62 Hal Smith	15.00	6.75
❑ 63 Roger Craig RC	40.00	18.00
❑ 64 Luis Arroyo RC	10.00	4.50
❑ 65 Johnny O'Brien	15.00	6.75
❑ 66 Bob Speake DP	10.00	4.50
❑ 67 Vic Power	15.00	6.75
❑ 68 Chuck Stobbs	10.00	4.50
❑ 69 Chuck Tanner	15.00	6.75
❑ 70 Jim Rivera	10.00	4.50
❑ 71 Frank Sullivan	10.00	4.50
❑ 72A Phillies Team (Centered)	30.00	13.50
❑ 72B Phillies Team (Dated 1955)	80.00	36.00
❑ 72C Phillies Team DP (Name at far left)	30.00	13.50
❑ 73 Wayne Terwilliger	10.00	4.50
❑ 74 Jim King	10.00	4.50
❑ 75 Roy Sievers DP	15.00	6.75
❑ 76 Ray Crone	10.00	4.50
❑ 77 Harvey Haddix	15.00	6.75
❑ 78 Herman Wehmeier	10.00	4.50
❑ 79 Sandy Koufax	350.00	160.00
❑ 80 Gus Triandos DP	9.00	4.00
❑ 81 Wally Westlake	10.00	4.50
❑ 82 Bill Renna DP	10.00	4.50
❑ 83 Karl Spooner	15.00	6.75
❑ 84 Babe Birrer	10.00	4.50
❑ 85A Cleveland Indians (Centered)	30.00	13.50
❑ 85B Indians Team (Dated 1955)	80.00	36.00
❑ 85C Indians Team (Name at far left)	30.00	13.50
❑ 86 Ray Jablonski DP	9.00	4.00
❑ 87 Dean Stone	10.00	4.50
❑ 88 Johnny Kucks RC	15.00	6.75
❑ 89 Norm Zauchin	10.00	4.50
❑ 90A Cincinnati Redlegs Team (Centered)	30.00	13.50
❑ 90B Reds Team (Dated 1955)	80.00	36.00

❑ 90C Reds Team 30.00 13.50
(Name at far left)
❑ 91 Gail Harris 10.00 4.50
❑ 92 Bob(Red) Wilson 10.00 4.50
❑ 93 George Susce 10.00 4.50
❑ 94 Ron Kline 10.00 4.50
❑ 95A Milwaukee Braves 40.00 18.00
Team (Centered)
❑ 95B Braves Team 80.00 36.00
(Dated 1955)
❑ 95C Braves Team 40.00 18.00
(Name at far left)
❑ 96 Bill Tremel 10.00 4.50
❑ 97 Jerry Lynch 15.00 6.75
❑ 98 Camilo Pascual 15.00 6.75
❑ 99 Don Zimmer 25.00 11.00
❑ 100A Baltimore Orioles 35.00 16.00
Team (centered)
❑ 100B Orioles Team 80.00 36.00
(Dated 1955)
❑ 100C Orioles Team 35.00 16.00
(Name at far left)
❑ 101 Roy Campanella 150.00 70.00
❑ 102 Jim Davis 12.00 5.50
❑ 103 Willie Miranda 12.00 5.50
❑ 104 Bob Lennon 12.00 5.50
❑ 105 Al Smith 12.00 5.50
❑ 106 Joe Astroth 12.00 5.50
❑ 107 Eddie Mathews 80.00 36.00
❑ 108 Laurin Pepper 12.00 5.50
❑ 109 Enos Slaughter 40.00 18.00
❑ 110 Yogi Berra 150.00 70.00
❑ 111 Boston Red Sox 35.00 16.00
Team Card
❑ 112 Dee Fondy 12.00 5.50
❑ 113 Phil Rizzuto 125.00 55.00
❑ 114 Jim Owens 15.00 6.75
❑ 115 Jackie Jensen 15.00 6.75
❑ 116 Eddie O'Brien 12.00 5.50
❑ 117 Virgil Trucks 15.00 6.75
❑ 118 Nellie Fox 60.00 27.00
❑ 119 Larry Jackson RC 15.00 6.75
❑ 120 Richie Ashburn 60.00 27.00
❑ 121 Pittsburgh Pirates 35.00 16.00
Team Card
❑ 122 Willard Nixon 12.00 5.50
❑ 123 Roy McMillan 15.00 6.75
❑ 124 Don Kaiser 12.00 5.50
❑ 125 Minnie Minoso 40.00 18.00
❑ 126 Jim Brady 12.00 5.50
❑ 127 Willie Jones 15.00 6.75
❑ 128 Eddie Yost 15.00 6.75
❑ 129 Jake Martin 12.00 5.50
❑ 130 Willie Mays 300.00 135.00
❑ 131 Bob Roselli 12.00 5.50
❑ 132 Bobby Avila 12.00 5.50
❑ 133 Ray Narleski 12.00 5.50
❑ 134 St. Louis Cardinals 35.00 16.00
Team Card
❑ 135 Mickey Mantle 1400.00 650.00
❑ 136 Johnny Logan 15.00 6.75
❑ 137 Al Silvera 12.00 5.50
❑ 138 Johnny Antonelli 15.00 6.75
❑ 139 Tommy Carroll 15.00 6.75
❑ 140 Herb Score RC 60.00 27.00
❑ 141 Joe Frazier 12.00 5.50
❑ 142 Gene Baker 12.00 5.50
❑ 143 Jim Piersall 15.00 6.75
❑ 144 Leroy Powell 12.00 5.50
❑ 145 Gil Hodges 60.00 27.00
❑ 146 Washington Nationals 35.00 16.00
Team Card
❑ 147 Earl Torgeson 12.00 5.50
❑ 148 Alvin Dark 15.00 6.75
❑ 149 Dixie Howell 12.00 5.50
❑ 150 Duke Snider 125.00 55.00
❑ 151 Spook Jacobs 15.00 6.75
❑ 152 Billy Hoeft 15.00 6.75
❑ 153 Frank Thomas 15.00 6.75
❑ 154 Dave Pope 12.00 5.50
❑ 155 Harvey Kuenn 15.00 6.75
❑ 156 Wes Westrum 15.00 6.75
❑ 157 Dick Brodowski 12.00 5.50
❑ 158 Wally Post 15.00 6.75
❑ 159 Clint Courtney 12.00 5.50
❑ 160 Billy Pierce 15.00 6.75
❑ 161 Joe DeMaestri 12.00 5.50
❑ 162 Dave(Gus) Bell 15.00 6.75
❑ 163 Gene Woodling 15.00 6.75
❑ 164 Harmon Killebrew 100.00 45.00
❑ 165 Red Schoendienst 40.00 18.00
❑ 166 Brooklyn Dodgers 200.00 90.00
Team Card
❑ 167 Harry Dorish 12.00 5.50
❑ 168 Sammy White 12.00 5.50
❑ 169 Bob Nelson 12.00 5.50
❑ 170 Bill Virdon 15.00 6.75
❑ 171 Jim Wilson 12.00 5.50
❑ 172 Frank Torre RC 15.00 6.75
❑ 173 Johnny Podres 25.00 11.00
❑ 174 Glen Gorbous 12.00 5.50
❑ 175 Del Crandall 15.00 6.75
❑ 176 Alex Kellner 12.00 5.50
❑ 177 Hank Bauer 25.00 11.00
❑ 178 Joe Black 15.00 6.75
❑ 179 Harry Chiti 12.00 5.50
❑ 180 Robin Roberts 50.00 22.00
❑ 181 Billy Martin 60.00 27.00
❑ 182 Paul Minner 15.00 6.75
❑ 183 Stan Lopata 20.00 9.00
❑ 184 Don Bessent 20.00 9.00
❑ 185 Bill Bruton 20.00 9.00
❑ 186 Ron Jackson 15.00 6.75
❑ 187 Early Wynn 50.00 22.00
❑ 188 Chicago White Sox 50.00 22.00
Team Card
❑ 189 Ned Garver 15.00 6.75
❑ 190 Carl Furillo 30.00 13.50
❑ 191 Frank Lary 20.00 9.00
❑ 192 Smoky Burgess 20.00 9.00
❑ 193 Wilmer Mizell 20.00 9.00
❑ 194 Monte Irvin 30.00 13.50
❑ 195 George Kell 30.00 13.50
❑ 196 Tom Poholsky 15.00 6.75
❑ 197 Granny Hamner 15.00 6.75
❑ 198 Ed Fitzgerald 15.00 6.75
❑ 199 Hank Thompson 20.00 9.00
❑ 200 Bob Feller 100.00 45.00
❑ 201 Rip Repulski 15.00 6.75
❑ 202 Jim Hearn 15.00 6.75
❑ 203 Bill Tuttle 15.00 6.75
❑ 204 Art Swanson 15.00 6.75
❑ 205 Whitey Lockman 20.00 9.00
❑ 206 Erv Palica 15.00 6.75
❑ 207 Jim Small 15.00 6.75
❑ 208 Elston Howard 60.00 27.00
❑ 209 Max Surkont 15.00 6.75
❑ 210 Mike Garcia 20.00 9.00
❑ 211 Murry Dickson 15.00 6.75
❑ 212 Johnny Temple 15.00 6.75
❑ 213 Detroit Tigers 60.00 27.00
Team Card
❑ 214 Bob Rush 15.00 6.75
❑ 215 Tommy Byrne 20.00 9.00
❑ 216 Jerry Schoonmaker 15.00 6.75
❑ 217 Billy Klaus 15.00 6.75
❑ 218 Joe Nuxhall UER 20.00 9.00
(Misspelled Nuxall)
❑ 219 Lew Burdette 20.00 9.00
❑ 220 Del Ennis 20.00 9.00
❑ 221 Bob Friend 20.00 9.00
❑ 222 Dave Philley 15.00 6.75
❑ 223 Randy Jackson 15.00 6.75
❑ 224 Bud Podbielan 15.00 6.75
❑ 225 Gil McDougald 50.00 22.00
❑ 226 New York Giants 75.00 34.00
Team Card
❑ 227 Russ Meyer 15.00 6.75
❑ 228 Mickey Vernon 20.00 9.00
❑ 229 Harry Brecheen CO 20.00 9.00
❑ 230 Chico Carrasquel 15.00 6.75
❑ 231 Bob Hale 15.00 6.75
❑ 232 Toby Atwell 15.00 6.75
❑ 233 Carl Erskine 30.00 13.50
❑ 234 Pete Runnels 15.00 6.75
❑ 235 Don Newcombe 50.00 22.00
❑ 236 Kansas City Athletics 35.00 16.00
Team Card
❑ 237 Jose Valdivielso 15.00 6.75
❑ 238 Walt Dropo 20.00 9.00
❑ 239 Harry Simpson 15.00 6.75
❑ 240 Whitey Ford 125.00 55.00
❑ 241 Don Mueller UER 20.00 9.00
(6~ tall)
❑ 242 Hershell Freeman 15.00 6.75
❑ 243 Sherm Lollar 20.00 9.00
❑ 244 Bob Buhl 30.00 13.50
❑ 245 Billy Goodman 20.00 9.00
❑ 246 Tom Gorman 15.00 6.75
❑ 247 Bill Sarni 15.00 6.75
❑ 248 Bob Porterfield 15.00 6.75
❑ 249 Johnny Klippstein 15.00 6.75
❑ 250 Larry Doby 30.00 13.50
❑ 251 New York Yankees .. 250.00 110.00
Team Card UER
(Don Larsen misspelled
as Larson on front)
❑ 252 Vern Law 20.00 9.00
❑ 253 Irv Noren 30.00 13.50
❑ 254 George Crowe 15.00 6.75
❑ 255 Bob Lemon 50.00 22.00
❑ 256 Tom Hurd 15.00 6.75
❑ 257 Bobby Thomson 30.00 13.50
❑ 258 Art Ditmar 15.00 6.75
❑ 259 Sam Jones 20.00 9.00
❑ 260 Pee Wee Reese 125.00 55.00
❑ 261 Bobby Shantz 15.00 6.75
❑ 262 Howie Pollet 12.00 5.50
❑ 263 Bob Miller 12.00 5.50
❑ 264 Ray Monzant 12.00 5.50
❑ 265 Sandy Consuegra 12.00 5.50
❑ 266 Don Ferrarese 12.00 5.50
❑ 267 Bob Nieman 12.00 5.50
❑ 268 Dale Mitchell 15.00 6.75
❑ 269 Jack Meyer 12.00 5.50
❑ 270 Billy Loes 15.00 6.75
❑ 271 Foster Castleman 12.00 5.50
❑ 272 Danny O'Connell 12.00 5.50
❑ 273 Walker Cooper 12.00 5.50
❑ 274 Frank Baumholtz 12.00 5.50
❑ 275 Jim Greengrass 12.00 5.50
❑ 276 George Zuverink 12.00 5.50
❑ 277 Daryl Spencer 12.00 5.50
❑ 278 Chet Nichols 12.00 5.50
❑ 279 Johnny Groth 12.00 5.50
❑ 280 Jim Gilliam 40.00 18.00
❑ 281 Art Houtteman 12.00 5.50
❑ 282 Warren Hacker 12.00 5.50
❑ 283 Hal Smith RC 15.00 6.75
❑ 284 Ike Delock 12.00 5.50
❑ 285 Eddie Miksis 12.00 5.50
❑ 286 Bill Wight 12.00 5.50
❑ 287 Bobby Adams 12.00 5.50
❑ 288 Bob Cerv 40.00 18.00
❑ 289 Hal Jeffcoat 12.00 5.50
❑ 290 Curt Simmons 15.00 6.75
❑ 291 Frank Kellert 12.00 5.50
❑ 292 Luis Aparicio RC 150.00 70.00
❑ 293 Stu Miller 25.00 11.00
❑ 294 Ernie Johnson 15.00 6.75
❑ 295 Clem Labine 15.00 6.75
❑ 296 Andy Seminick 12.00 5.50
❑ 297 Bob Skinner 15.00 6.75
❑ 298 Johnny Schmitz 12.00 5.50
❑ 299 Charlie Neal 40.00 18.00
❑ 300 Vic Wertz 15.00 6.75
❑ 301 Marv Grissom 12.00 5.50
❑ 302 Eddie Robinson 12.00 5.50
❑ 303 Jim Dyck 12.00 5.50
❑ 304 Frank Malzone 15.00 6.75
❑ 305 Brooks Lawrence 12.00 5.50
❑ 306 Curt Roberts 12.00 5.50
❑ 307 Hoyt Wilhelm 40.00 18.00
❑ 308 Chuck Harmon 12.00 5.50
❑ 309 Don Blasingame RC .. 15.00 6.75
❑ 310 Steve Gromek 12.00 5.50
❑ 311 Hal Naragon 12.00 5.50
❑ 312 Andy Pafko 15.00 6.75
❑ 313 Gene Stephens 12.00 5.50
❑ 314 Hobie Landrith 12.00 5.50
❑ 315 Milt Bolling 12.00 5.50
❑ 316 Jerry Coleman 15.00 6.75
❑ 317 Al Aber 12.00 5.50
❑ 318 Fred Hatfield 12.00 5.50
❑ 319 Jack Crimian 12.00 5.50
❑ 320 Joe Adcock 15.00 6.75
❑ 321 Jim Konstanty 15.00 6.75
❑ 322 Karl Olson 12.00 5.50

❑ 323 Willard Schmidt	12.00	5.50
❑ 324 Rocky Bridges	15.00	6.75
❑ 325 Don Liddle	12.00	5.50
❑ 326 Connie Johnson	12.00	5.50
❑ 327 Bob Wiesler	12.00	5.50
❑ 328 Preston Ward	12.00	5.50
❑ 329 Lou Berberet	12.00	5.50
❑ 330 Jim Busby	15.00	6.75
❑ 331 Dick Hall	12.00	5.50
❑ 332 Don Larsen	60.00	27.00
❑ 333 Rube Walker	12.00	5.50
❑ 334 Bob Miller	15.00	6.75
❑ 335 Don Hoak	15.00	6.75
❑ 336 Ellis Kinder	12.00	5.50
❑ 337 Bobby Morgan	12.00	5.50
❑ 338 Jim Delsing	12.00	5.50
❑ 339 Rance Pless	12.00	5.50
❑ 340 Mickey McDermott	60.00	12.00
❑ NNO Checklist 2/4	275.00	90.00
❑ NNO Checklist 1/3	275.00	90.00

1957 Topps

	NRMT	VG-E
COMPLETE SET (407)	7000.00	3200.00
COMMON CARD (1-88)	10.00	4.50
COMMON CARD (89-176)	8.00	3.60
COMMON CARD (177-264)	8.00	3.60
COMMON CARD (265-352)	20.00	9.00
COMMON CARD (353-407)	8.00	3.60
COMMON DP (265-352)	13.00	5.75
WRAPPER (1-CENT)	300.00	135.00
WRAPPER (5-CENT)	200.00	90.00

❑ 1 Ted Williams	500.00	150.00
❑ 2 Yogi Berra	135.00	60.00
❑ 3 Dale Long	20.00	9.00
❑ 4 Johnny Logan	20.00	9.00
❑ 5 Sal Maglie	20.00	9.00
❑ 6 Hector Lopez	15.00	6.75
❑ 7 Luis Aparicio	30.00	13.50
❑ 8 Don Mossi	15.00	6.75
❑ 9 Johnny Temple	15.00	6.75
❑ 10 Willie Mays	225.00	100.00
❑ 11 George Zuverink	10.00	4.50
❑ 12 Dick Groat	20.00	9.00
❑ 13 Wally Burnette	10.00	4.50
❑ 14 Bob Nieman	10.00	4.50
❑ 15 Robin Roberts	30.00	13.50
❑ 16 Walt Moryn	10.00	4.50
❑ 17 Billy Gardner	10.00	4.50
❑ 18 Don Drysdale RC	225.00	100.00
❑ 19 Bob Wilson	10.00	4.50
❑ 20 Hank Aaron UER (Reverse negative photo on front)	250.00	110.00
❑ 21 Frank Sullivan	10.00	4.50
❑ 22 Jerry Snyder UER (Photo actually Ed Fitzgerald)	10.00	4.50
❑ 23 Sherm Lollar	15.00	6.75
❑ 24 Bill Mazeroski RC	75.00	34.00
❑ 25 Whitey Ford	100.00	45.00
❑ 26 Bob Boyd	10.00	4.50
❑ 27 Ted Kazanski	10.00	4.50
❑ 28 Gene Conley	15.00	6.75
❑ 29 Whitey Herzog RC	30.00	13.50
❑ 30 Pee Wee Reese	75.00	34.00
❑ 31 Ron Northey	10.00	4.50
❑ 32 Hershell Freeman	10.00	4.50
❑ 33 Jim Small	10.00	4.50
❑ 34 Tom Sturdivant	15.00	6.75
❑ 35 Frank Robinson RC	200.00	90.00
❑ 36 Bob Grim	10.00	4.50
❑ 37 Frank Torre	15.00	6.75
❑ 38 Nellie Fox	50.00	22.00
❑ 39 Al Worthington	10.00	4.50
❑ 40 Early Wynn	30.00	13.50
❑ 41 Hal W. Smith	10.00	4.50
❑ 42 Dee Fondy	10.00	4.50
❑ 43 Connie Johnson	10.00	4.50
❑ 44 Joe DeMaestri	10.00	4.50
❑ 45 Carl Furillo	30.00	13.50
❑ 46 Robert J. Miller	10.00	4.50
❑ 47 Don Blasingame	10.00	4.50
❑ 48 Bill Bruton	15.00	6.75
❑ 49 Daryl Spencer	10.00	4.50
❑ 50 Herb Score	30.00	13.50
❑ 51 Clint Courtney	10.00	4.50
❑ 52 Lee Walls	10.00	4.50
❑ 53 Clem Labine	20.00	9.00
❑ 54 Elmer Valo	10.00	4.50
❑ 55 Ernie Banks	125.00	55.00
❑ 56 Dave Sisler	10.00	4.50
❑ 57 Jim Lemon	15.00	6.75
❑ 58 Ruben Gomez	10.00	4.50
❑ 59 Dick Williams	15.00	6.75
❑ 60 Billy Hoeft	15.00	6.75
❑ 61 Dusty Rhodes	15.00	6.75
❑ 62 Billy Martin	50.00	22.00
❑ 63 Ike Delock	10.00	4.50
❑ 64 Pete Runnels	15.00	6.75
❑ 65 Wally Moon	15.00	6.75
❑ 66 Brooks Lawrence	10.00	4.50
❑ 67 Chico Carrasquel	10.00	4.50
❑ 68 Ray Crone	10.00	4.50
❑ 69 Roy McMillan	15.00	6.75
❑ 70 Richie Ashburn	50.00	22.00
❑ 71 Murry Dickson	10.00	4.50
❑ 72 Bill Tuttle	10.00	4.50
❑ 73 George Crowe	10.00	4.50
❑ 74 Vito Valentinetti	10.00	4.50
❑ 75 Jimmy Piersall	15.00	6.75
❑ 76 Roberto Clemente	300.00	135.00
❑ 77 Paul Foytack	10.00	4.50
❑ 78 Vic Wertz	15.00	6.75
❑ 79 Lindy McDaniel RC	15.00	6.75
❑ 80 Gil Hodges	50.00	22.00
❑ 81 Herman Wehmeier	10.00	4.50
❑ 82 Elston Howard	30.00	13.50
❑ 83 Lou Skizas	10.00	4.50
❑ 84 Moe Drabowsky	15.00	6.75
❑ 85 Larry Doby	30.00	13.50
❑ 86 Bill Sarni	10.00	4.50
❑ 87 Tom Gorman	10.00	4.50
❑ 88 Harvey Kuenn	15.00	6.75
❑ 89 Roy Sievers	15.00	6.75
❑ 90 Warren Spahn	90.00	40.00
❑ 91 Mack Burk	8.00	3.60
❑ 92 Mickey Vernon	15.00	6.75
❑ 93 Hal Jeffcoat	8.00	3.60
❑ 94 Bobby Del Greco	8.00	3.60
❑ 95 Mickey Mantle	1000.00	450.00
❑ 96 Hank Aguirre	8.00	3.60
❑ 97 New York Yankees Team Card	90.00	40.00
❑ 98 Alvin Dark	15.00	6.75
❑ 99 Bob Keegan	8.00	3.60
❑ 100 League Presidents Warren Giles Will Harridge	15.00	6.75
❑ 101 Chuck Stobbs	8.00	3.60
❑ 102 Ray Boone	15.00	6.75
❑ 103 Joe Nuxhall	15.00	6.75
❑ 104 Hank Foiles	8.00	3.60
❑ 105 Johnny Antonelli	15.00	6.75
❑ 106 Ray Moore	8.00	3.60
❑ 107 Jim Rivera	8.00	3.60
❑ 108 Tommy Byrne	15.00	6.75
❑ 109 Hank Thompson	8.00	3.60
❑ 110 Bill Virdon	15.00	6.75
❑ 111 Hal R. Smith	8.00	3.60
❑ 112 Tom Brewer	8.00	3.60
❑ 113 Wilmer Mizell	15.00	6.75
❑ 114 Milwaukee Braves Team Card	20.00	9.00
❑ 115 Jim Gilliam	15.00	6.75
❑ 116 Mike Fornieles	8.00	3.60
❑ 117 Joe Adcock	20.00	9.00
❑ 118 Bob Porterfield	8.00	3.60
❑ 119 Stan Lopata	8.00	3.60
❑ 120 Bob Lemon	30.00	13.50
❑ 121 Clete Boyer RC	30.00	13.50
❑ 122 Ken Boyer	20.00	9.00
❑ 123 Steve Ridzik	8.00	3.60
❑ 124 Dave Philley	8.00	3.60
❑ 125 Al Kaline	100.00	45.00
❑ 126 Bob Wiesler	8.00	3.60
❑ 127 Bob Buhl	15.00	6.75
❑ 128 Ed Bailey	15.00	6.75
❑ 129 Saul Rogovin	8.00	3.60
❑ 130 Don Newcombe	20.00	9.00
❑ 131 Milt Bolling	8.00	3.60
❑ 132 Art Ditmar	15.00	6.75
❑ 133 Del Crandall	15.00	6.75
❑ 134 Don Kaiser	8.00	3.60
❑ 135 Bill Skowron	20.00	9.00
❑ 136 Jim Hegan	15.00	6.75
❑ 137 Bob Rush	8.00	3.60
❑ 138 Minnie Minoso	20.00	9.00
❑ 139 Lou Kretlow	8.00	3.60
❑ 140 Frank Thomas	15.00	6.75
❑ 141 Al Aber	8.00	3.60
❑ 142 Charley Thompson	8.00	3.60
❑ 143 Andy Pafko	15.00	6.75
❑ 144 Ray Narleski	8.00	3.60
❑ 145 Al Smith	8.00	3.60
❑ 146 Don Ferrarese	8.00	3.60
❑ 147 Al Walker	8.00	3.60
❑ 148 Don Mueller	15.00	6.75
❑ 149 Bob Kennedy	15.00	6.75
❑ 150 Bob Friend	15.00	6.75
❑ 151 Willie Miranda	8.00	3.60
❑ 152 Jack Harshman	8.00	3.60
❑ 153 Karl Olson	8.00	3.60
❑ 154 Red Schoendienst	30.00	13.50
❑ 155 Jim Brosnan	15.00	6.75
❑ 156 Gus Triandos	15.00	6.75
❑ 157 Wally Post	15.00	6.75
❑ 158 Curt Simmons	15.00	6.75
❑ 159 Solly Drake	8.00	3.60
❑ 160 Billy Pierce	15.00	6.75
❑ 161 Pittsburgh Pirates Team Card	15.00	6.75
❑ 162 Jack Meyer	8.00	3.60
❑ 163 Sammy White	8.00	3.60
❑ 164 Tommy Carroll	8.00	3.60
❑ 165 Ted Kluszewski	90.00	40.00
❑ 166 Roy Face	15.00	6.75
❑ 167 Vic Power	15.00	6.75
❑ 168 Frank Lary	15.00	6.75
❑ 169 Herb Plews	8.00	3.60
❑ 170 Duke Snider	125.00	55.00
❑ 171 Boston Red Sox Team Card	15.00	6.75
❑ 172 Gene Woodling	15.00	6.75
❑ 173 Roger Craig	15.00	6.75
❑ 174 Willie Jones	8.00	3.60
❑ 175 Don Larsen	30.00	13.50
❑ 176A Gene Baker ERR (Misspelled Bakep on card back)	350.00	160.00
❑ 176B Gene Baker COR	15.00	6.75
❑ 177 Eddie Yost	15.00	6.75
❑ 178 Don Bessent	8.00	3.60
❑ 179 Ernie Oravetz	8.00	3.60
❑ 180 Gus Bell	15.00	6.75
❑ 181 Dick Donovan	8.00	3.60
❑ 182 Hobie Landrith	8.00	3.60
❑ 183 Chicago Cubs Team Card	15.00	6.75
❑ 184 Tito Francona RC	8.00	3.60
❑ 185 Johnny Kucks	15.00	6.75
❑ 186 Jim King	15.00	6.75
❑ 187 Virgil Trucks	15.00	6.75
❑ 188 Felix Mantilla RC	15.00	6.75
❑ 189 Willard Nixon	8.00	3.60
❑ 190 Randy Jackson	8.00	3.60
❑ 191 Joe Margoneri	8.00	3.60
❑ 192 Jerry Coleman	15.00	6.75

	No.	Card	Price	Price
❑	193	Del Rice	8.00	3.60
❑	194	Hal Brown	8.00	3.60
❑	195	Bobby Avila	8.00	3.60
❑	196	Larry Jackson	15.00	6.75
❑	197	Hank Sauer	15.00	6.75
❑	198	Detroit Tigers Team Card	15.00	6.75
❑	199	Vern Law	15.00	6.75
❑	200	Gil McDougald	15.00	6.75
❑	201	Sandy Amoros	15.00	6.75
❑	202	Dick Gernert	8.00	3.60
❑	203	Hoyt Wilhelm	30.00	13.50
❑	204	Kansas City Athletics Team Card	15.00	6.75
❑	205	Charlie Maxwell	15.00	6.75
❑	206	Willard Schmidt	8.00	3.60
❑	207	Gordon(Billy) Hunter	8.00	3.60
❑	208	Lou Burdette	15.00	6.75
❑	209	Bob Skinner	15.00	6.75
❑	210	Roy Campanella	150.00	70.00
❑	211	Camilo Pascual	15.00	6.75
❑	212	Rocky Colavito RC !	150.00	70.00
❑	213	Les Moss	8.00	3.60
❑	214	Philadelphia Phillies Team Card	15.00	6.75
❑	215	Enos Slaughter	30.00	13.50
❑	216	Marv Grissom	8.00	3.60
❑	217	Gene Stephens	8.00	3.60
❑	218	Ray Jablonski	8.00	3.60
❑	219	Tom Acker	8.00	3.60
❑	220	Jackie Jensen	20.00	9.00
❑	221	Dixie Howell	8.00	3.60
❑	222	Alex Grammas	8.00	3.60
❑	223	Frank House	8.00	3.60
❑	224	Marv Blaylock	8.00	3.60
❑	225	Harry Simpson	8.00	3.60
❑	226	Preston Ward	8.00	3.60
❑	227	Gerry Staley	8.00	3.60
❑	228	Smoky Burgess UER (Misspelled Smokey on card back)	15.00	6.75
❑	229	George Susce	8.00	3.60
❑	230	George Kell	30.00	13.50
❑	231	Solly Hemus	8.00	3.60
❑	232	Whitey Lockman	15.00	6.75
❑	233	Art Fowler	8.00	3.60
❑	234	Dick Cole	8.00	3.60
❑	235	Tom Poholsky	8.00	3.60
❑	236	Joe Ginsberg	8.00	3.60
❑	237	Foster Castleman	8.00	3.60
❑	238	Eddie Robinson	8.00	3.60
❑	239	Tom Morgan	8.00	3.60
❑	240	Hank Bauer	15.00	6.75
❑	241	Joe Lonnett	8.00	3.60
❑	242	Charlie Neal	15.00	6.75
❑	243	St. Louis Cardinals Team Card	15.00	6.75
❑	244	Billy Loes	15.00	6.75
❑	245	Rip Repulski	8.00	3.60
❑	246	Jose Valdivielso	8.00	3.60
❑	247	Turk Lown	8.00	3.60
❑	248	Jim Finigan	8.00	3.60
❑	249	Dave Pope	8.00	3.60
❑	250	Eddie Mathews	50.00	22.00
❑	251	Baltimore Orioles Team Card	15.00	6.75
❑	252	Carl Erskine	15.00	6.75
❑	253	Gus Zernial	15.00	6.75
❑	254	Ron Negray	8.00	3.60
❑	255	Charlie Silvera	15.00	6.75
❑	256	Ron Kline	8.00	3.60
❑	257	Walt Dropo	8.00	3.60
❑	258	Steve Gromek	8.00	3.60
❑	259	Eddie O'Brien	8.00	3.60
❑	260	Del Ennis	15.00	6.75
❑	261	Bob Chakales	8.00	3.60
❑	262	Bobby Thomson	15.00	6.75
❑	263	George Strickland	8.00	3.60
❑	264	Bob Turley	15.00	6.75
❑	265	Harvey Haddix DP	13.00	5.75
❑	266	Ken Kuhn DP	13.00	5.75
❑	267	Danny Kravitz	20.00	9.00
❑	268	Jack Collum	20.00	9.00
❑	269	Bob Cerv	30.00	13.50
❑	270	Washington Senators Team Card	60.00	27.00
❑	271	Danny O'Connell DP	13.00	5.75
❑	272	Bobby Shantz	30.00	13.50
❑	273	Jim Davis	20.00	9.00
❑	274	Don Hoak	15.00	6.75
❑	275	Cleveland Indians Team Card UER (Text on back credits Tribe with winning AL title in '28. The Yankees won that year.)	60.00	27.00
❑	276	Jim Pyburn	20.00	9.00
❑	277	Johnny Podres DP	45.00	20.00
❑	278	Fred Hatfield DP	13.00	5.75
❑	279	Bob Thurman	20.00	9.00
❑	280	Alex Kellner	20.00	9.00
❑	281	Gail Harris	20.00	9.00
❑	282	Jack Dittmer DP	13.00	5.75
❑	283	Wes Covington DP	13.00	5.75
❑	284	Don Zimmer	45.00	20.00
❑	285	Ned Garver	20.00	9.00
❑	286	Bobby Richardson RC	125.00	55.00
❑	287	Sam Jones	20.00	9.00
❑	288	Ted Lepcio	20.00	9.00
❑	289	Jim Bolger DP	13.00	5.75
❑	290	Andy Carey DP	40.00	18.00
❑	291	Windy McCall	20.00	9.00
❑	292	Billy Klaus	20.00	9.00
❑	293	Ted Abernathy	20.00	9.00
❑	294	Rocky Bridges DP	13.00	5.75
❑	295	Joe Collins DP	40.00	18.00
❑	296	Johnny Klippstein	20.00	9.00
❑	297	Jack Crimian	20.00	9.00
❑	298	Irv Noren DP	13.00	5.75
❑	299	Chuck Harmon	20.00	9.00
❑	300	Mike Garcia	30.00	13.50
❑	301	Sammy Esposito DP	20.00	9.00
❑	302	Sandy Koufax DP	300.00	135.00
❑	303	Billy Goodman	30.00	13.50
❑	304	Joe Cunningham	30.00	13.50
❑	305	Chico Fernandez	20.00	9.00
❑	306	Darrell Johnson DP	13.00	5.75
❑	307	Jack D. Phillips DP	13.00	5.75
❑	308	Dick Hall	20.00	9.00
❑	309	Jim Busby DP	13.00	5.75
❑	310	Max Surkont DP	13.00	5.75
❑	311	Al Pilarcik DP	13.00	5.75
❑	312	Tony Kubek DP RC	90.00	40.00
❑	313	Mel Parnell	15.00	6.75
❑	314	Ed Bouchee DP	13.00	5.75
❑	315	Lou Berberet DP	13.00	5.75
❑	316	Billy O'Dell	20.00	9.00
❑	317	New York Giants Team Card	75.00	34.00
❑	318	Mickey McDermott	20.00	9.00
❑	319	Gino Cimoli RC	20.00	9.00
❑	320	Neil Chrisley	20.00	9.00
❑	321	John(Red) Murff	20.00	9.00
❑	322	Cincinnati Reds Team Card	75.00	34.00
❑	323	Wes Westrum	30.00	13.50
❑	324	Brooklyn Dodgers Team Card	125.00	55.00
❑	325	Frank Bolling	20.00	9.00
❑	326	Pedro Ramos	20.00	9.00
❑	327	Jim Pendleton	20.00	9.00
❑	328	Brooks Robinson RC	400.00	180.00
❑	329	Chicago White Sox Team Card	60.00	27.00
❑	330	Jim Wilson	20.00	9.00
❑	331	Ray Katt	20.00	9.00
❑	332	Bob Bowman	20.00	9.00
❑	333	Ernie Johnson	20.00	9.00
❑	334	Jerry Schoonmaker	20.00	9.00
❑	335	Granny Hamner	20.00	9.00
❑	336	Haywood Sullivan RC	40.00	18.00
❑	337	Rene Valdes	20.00	9.00
❑	338	Jim Bunning RC	125.00	55.00
❑	339	Bob Speake	20.00	9.00
❑	340	Bill Wight	20.00	9.00
❑	341	Don Gross	20.00	9.00
❑	342	Gene Mauch	30.00	13.50
❑	343	Taylor Phillips	15.00	6.75
❑	344	Paul LaPalme	20.00	9.00
❑	345	Paul Smith	20.00	9.00
❑	346	Dick Littlefield	20.00	9.00
❑	347	Hal Naragon	20.00	9.00
❑	348	Jim Hearn	20.00	9.00
❑	349	Nellie King	20.00	9.00
❑	350	Eddie Miksis	20.00	9.00
❑	351	Dave Hillman	20.00	9.00
❑	352	Ellis Kinder	20.00	9.00
❑	353	Cal Neeman	8.00	3.60
❑	354	W. (Rip) Coleman	8.00	3.60
❑	355	Frank Malzone	15.00	6.75
❑	356	Faye Throneberry	8.00	3.60
❑	357	Earl Torgeson	8.00	3.60
❑	358	Jerry Lynch	15.00	6.75
❑	359	Tom Cheney	8.00	3.60
❑	360	Johnny Groth	8.00	3.60
❑	361	Curt Barclay	8.00	3.60
❑	362	Roman Mejias	15.00	6.75
❑	363	Eddie Kasko	8.00	3.60
❑	364	Cal McLish	15.00	6.75
❑	365	Ozzie Virgil	8.00	3.60
❑	366	Ken Lehman	8.00	3.60
❑	367	Ed Fitzgerald	8.00	3.60
❑	368	Bob Purkey	8.00	3.60
❑	369	Milt Graff	8.00	3.60
❑	370	Warren Hacker	8.00	3.60
❑	371	Bob Lennon	8.00	3.60
❑	372	Norm Zauchin	8.00	3.60
❑	373	Pete Whisenant	8.00	3.60
❑	374	Don Cardwell	8.00	3.60
❑	375	Jim Landis	15.00	6.75
❑	376	Don Elston	8.00	3.60
❑	377	Andre Rodgers	8.00	3.60
❑	378	Elmer Singleton	8.00	3.60
❑	379	Don Lee	8.00	3.60
❑	380	Walker Cooper	8.00	3.60
❑	381	Dean Stone	8.00	3.60
❑	382	Jim Brideweser	8.00	3.60
❑	383	Juan Pizarro	8.00	3.60
❑	384	Bobby G. Smith	8.00	3.60
❑	385	Art Houtteman	8.00	3.60
❑	386	Lyle Luttrell	8.00	3.60
❑	387	Jack Sanford RC	15.00	6.75
❑	388	Pete Daley	8.00	3.60
❑	389	Dave Jolly	8.00	3.60
❑	390	Reno Bertoia	8.00	3.60
❑	391	Ralph Terry RC	15.00	6.75
❑	392	Chuck Tanner	15.00	6.75
❑	393	Raul Sanchez	8.00	3.60
❑	394	Luis Arroyo	15.00	6.75
❑	395	Bubba Phillips	8.00	3.60
❑	396	Casey Wise	8.00	3.60
❑	397	Roy Smalley	8.00	3.60
❑	398	Al Cicotte	15.00	6.75
❑	399	Billy Consolo	8.00	3.60
❑	400	Dodgers' Sluggers Carl Furillo Gil Hodges Roy Campanella Duke Snider	250.00	110.00
❑	401	Earl Battey RC	15.00	6.75
❑	402	Jim Pisoni	8.00	3.60
❑	403	Dick Hyde	8.00	3.60
❑	404	Harry Anderson	8.00	3.60
❑	405	Duke Maas	8.00	3.60
❑	406	Bob Hale	8.00	3.60
❑	407	Yankee Power Hitters Mickey Mantle Yogi Berra	500.00	150.00
❑	CC1	Contest Card Saturday, May 4th Boston Red Sox vs. Cleveland Indians Cincinnati Redlegs vs. New York Giants	90.00	22.00
❑	CC2	Contest Card Saturday, May 25th Detroit Tigers vs. Kansas City Athletics Pittsburgh Pirates vs. Philadelphia Phillies	90.00	22.00
❑	CC3	Contest Card Saturday, June 22nd Brooklyn Dodgers vs. St. Louis Cardinals Chicago White Sox vs. New York Yankees	120.00	30.00
❑	CC4	Contest Card Saturday, July 19th Milwaukee Braves	120.00	30.00

Card	NRMT	VG-E
vs. New York Giants		
Baltimore Orioles		
vs. Kansas City Athletics		
❑ NNO Checklist 1/2	250.00	75.00
Bazooka Back		
❑ NNO Checklist 1/2	250.00	75.00
Blony Back		
❑ NNO Checklist 2/3	400.00	100.00
Bazooka Back		
❑ NNO Checklist 2/3	400.00	100.00
Blony Back		
❑ NNO Checklist 3/4	750.00	170.00
Bazooka Back		
❑ NNO Checklist 3/4	750.00	170.00
Blony Back		
❑ NNO Checklist 4/5	900.00	200.00
Bazooka Back		
❑ NNO Checklist 4/5	900.00	200.00
Blony Back		
❑ NNO Lucky Penny Charm and Key Chain offer card	100.00	45.00

1958 Topps

	NRMT	VG-E
COMP. MASTER SET (534)	12000.00	5400.00
COMPLETE SET (494)	4800.00	2200.00
COMMON CARD (1-110)	12.00	5.50
COMMON CARD (111-495)	8.00	3.60
WRAPPER (1-CENT)	100.00	45.00
WRAPPER (5-CENT)	125.00	55.00

Card	NRMT	VG-E
❑ 1 Ted Williams	500.00	180.00
❑ 2A Bob Lemon	30.00	13.50
❑ 2B Bob Lemon YT	60.00	27.00
❑ 3 Alex Kellner	12.00	5.50
❑ 4 Hank Foiles	12.00	5.50
❑ 5 Willie Mays	225.00	100.00
❑ 6 George Zuverink	12.00	5.50
❑ 7 Dale Long	15.00	6.75
❑ 8A Eddie Kasko	12.00	5.50
❑ 8B Eddie Kasko YL	45.00	20.00
❑ 9 Hank Bauer	20.00	9.00
❑ 10 Lou Burdette	20.00	9.00
❑ 11A Jim Rivera	12.00	5.50
❑ 11B Jim Rivera YT	45.00	20.00
❑ 12 George Crowe	12.00	5.50
❑ 13A Billy Hoeft	12.00	5.50
❑ 13B Billy Hoeft YL	45.00	20.00
❑ 14 Rip Repulski	12.00	5.50
❑ 15 Jim Lemon	15.00	6.75
❑ 16 Charlie Neal	15.00	6.75
❑ 17 Felix Mantilla	12.00	5.50
❑ 18 Frank Sullivan	12.00	5.50
❑ 19 New York Giants Team Card (Checklist on back)	40.00	8.00
❑ 20A Gil McDougald	20.00	9.00
❑ 20B Gil McDougald YL	60.00	27.00
❑ 21 Curt Barclay	12.00	5.50
❑ 22 Hal Naragon	12.00	5.50
❑ 23A Bill Tuttle	12.00	5.50
❑ 23B Bill Tuttle YL	45.00	20.00
❑ 24A Hobie Landrith	12.00	5.50
❑ 24B Hobie Landrith YL	45.00	20.00
❑ 25 Don Drysdale	75.00	34.00
❑ 26 Ron Jackson	12.00	5.50
❑ 27 Bud Freeman	12.00	5.50
❑ 28 Jim Busby	12.00	5.50
❑ 29 Ted Lepcio	12.00	5.50
❑ 30A Hank Aaron	200.00	90.00
❑ 30B Hank Aaron YL	500.00	220.00
❑ 31 Tex Clevenger	12.00	5.50
❑ 32A J.W. Porter	12.00	5.50
❑ 32B J.W. Porter YL	45.00	20.00
❑ 33A Cal Neeman	12.00	5.50
❑ 33B Cal Neeman YT	45.00	20.00
❑ 34 Bob Thurman	12.00	5.50
❑ 35A Don Mossi	15.00	6.75
❑ 35B Don Mossi YT	45.00	20.00
❑ 36 Ted Kazanski	12.00	5.50
❑ 37 M.McCormick UER RC Photo actually Ray Monzant	15.00	6.75
❑ 38 Dick Gernert	12.00	5.50
❑ 39 Bob Martyn	12.00	5.50
❑ 40 George Kell	30.00	13.50
❑ 41 Dave Hillman	12.00	5.50
❑ 42 John Roseboro RC	30.00	13.50
❑ 43 Sal Maglie	15.00	6.75
❑ 44 Washington Senators Team Card (Checklist on back)	20.00	4.00
❑ 45 Dick Groat	15.00	6.75
❑ 46A Lou Sleater	12.00	5.50
❑ 46B Lou Sleater YL	45.00	20.00
❑ 47 Roger Maris RC	400.00	180.00
❑ 48 Chuck Harmon	12.00	5.50
❑ 49 Smoky Burgess	15.00	6.75
❑ 50A Billy Pierce	15.00	6.75
❑ 50B Billy Pierce YT	45.00	20.00
❑ 51 Del Rice	12.00	5.50
❑ 52A Roberto Clemente	300.00	135.00
❑ 52B Roberto Clemente YT	500.00	220.00
❑ 53A Morrie Martin	12.00	5.50
❑ 53B Morrie Martin YL	45.00	20.00
❑ 54 Norm Siebern RC	20.00	9.00
❑ 55 Chico Carrasquel	12.00	5.50
❑ 56 Bill Fischer	12.00	5.50
❑ 57A Tim Thompson	12.00	5.50
❑ 57B Tim Thompson YL	45.00	20.00
❑ 58A Art Schult	12.00	5.50
❑ 58B Art Schult YT	45.00	20.00
❑ 59 Dave Sisler	12.00	5.50
❑ 60A Del Ennis	15.00	6.75
❑ 60B Del Ennis YL	45.00	20.00
❑ 61A Darrell Johnson	12.00	5.50
❑ 61B Darrell Johnson YL	45.00	20.00
❑ 62 Joe DeMaestri	12.00	5.50
❑ 63 Joe Nuxhall	15.00	6.75
❑ 64 Joe Lonnett	12.00	5.50
❑ 65A Von McDaniel RC	12.00	5.50
❑ 65B Von McDaniel YL RC	45.00	20.00
❑ 66 Lee Walls	12.00	5.50
❑ 67 Joe Ginsberg	12.00	5.50
❑ 68 Daryl Spencer	12.00	5.50
❑ 69 Wally Burnette	12.00	5.50
❑ 70A Al Kaline	100.00	45.00
❑ 70B Al Kaline YL	250.00	110.00
❑ 71 Dodgers Team (Checklist on back)	60.00	12.00
❑ 72 Bud Byerly	12.00	5.50
❑ 73 Pete Daley	12.00	5.50
❑ 74 Roy Face	15.00	6.75
❑ 75 Gus Bell	15.00	6.75
❑ 76A Dick Farrell	12.00	5.50
❑ 76B Dick Farrell YT	45.00	20.00
❑ 77A Don Zimmer	15.00	6.75
❑ 77B Don Zimmer YT	45.00	20.00
❑ 78A Ernie Johnson	15.00	6.75
❑ 78B Ernie Johnson YL	45.00	20.00
❑ 79A Dick Williams	15.00	6.75
❑ 79B Dick Williams YT	45.00	20.00
❑ 80 Dick Drott	12.00	5.50
❑ 81A Steve Boros RC	12.00	5.50
❑ 81B Steve Boros YT RC	45.00	20.00
❑ 82 Ron Kline	12.00	5.50
❑ 83 Bob Hazle RC	12.00	5.50
❑ 84 Billy O'Dell	12.00	5.50
❑ 85A Luis Aparicio	30.00	13.50
❑ 85B Luis Aparicio YT	75.00	34.00
❑ 86 Valmy Thomas	12.00	5.50
❑ 87 Johnny Kucks	12.00	5.50
❑ 88 Duke Snider	75.00	34.00
❑ 89 Billy Klaus	12.00	5.50
❑ 90 Robin Roberts	30.00	13.50
❑ 91 Chuck Tanner	15.00	6.75
❑ 92A Clint Courtney	12.00	5.50
❑ 92B Clint Courtney YL	45.00	20.00
❑ 93 Sandy Amoros	15.00	6.75
❑ 94 Bob Skinner	15.00	6.75
❑ 95 Frank Bolling	12.00	5.50
❑ 96 Joe Durham	12.00	5.50
❑ 97A Larry Jackson	12.00	5.50
❑ 97B Larry Jackson YL	45.00	20.00
❑ 98A Billy Hunter	12.00	5.50
❑ 98B Billy Hunter YL	45.00	20.00
❑ 99 Bobby Adams	12.00	5.50
❑ 100A Early Wynn	30.00	13.50
❑ 100B Early Wynn YT	75.00	34.00
❑ 101A Bobby Richardson	30.00	13.50
❑ 101B B.Richardson YL	60.00	27.00
❑ 102 George Strickland	12.00	5.50
❑ 103 Jerry Lynch	15.00	6.75
❑ 104 Jim Pendleton	12.00	5.50
❑ 105 Billy Gardner	12.00	5.50
❑ 106 Dick Schofield	15.00	6.75
❑ 107 Ossie Virgil	12.00	5.50
❑ 108A Jim Landis	12.00	5.50
❑ 108B Jim Landis YT	45.00	20.00
❑ 109 Herb Plews	12.00	5.50
❑ 110 Johnny Logan	15.00	6.75
❑ 111 Stu Miller	10.00	4.50
❑ 112 Gus Zernial	10.00	4.50
❑ 113 Jerry Walker RC	8.00	3.60
❑ 114 Irv Noren	10.00	4.50
❑ 115 Jim Bunning	30.00	13.50
❑ 116 Dave Philley	8.00	3.60
❑ 117 Frank Torre	10.00	4.50
❑ 118 Harvey Haddix	10.00	4.50
❑ 119 Harry Chiti	8.00	3.60
❑ 120 Johnny Podres	10.00	4.50
❑ 121 Eddie Miksis	8.00	3.60
❑ 122 Walt Moryn	8.00	3.60
❑ 123 Dick Tomanek	8.00	3.60
❑ 124 Bobby Usher	8.00	3.60
❑ 125 Alvin Dark	10.00	4.50
❑ 126 Stan Palys	8.00	3.60
❑ 127 Tom Sturdivant	10.00	4.50
❑ 128 Willie Kirkland	8.00	3.60
❑ 129 Jim Derrington	8.00	3.60
❑ 130 Jackie Jensen	10.00	4.50
❑ 131 Bob Henrich	8.00	3.60
❑ 132 Vern Law	10.00	4.50
❑ 133 Russ Nixon RC	8.00	3.60
❑ 134 Philadelphia Phillies Team Card (Checklist on back)	15.00	3.00
❑ 135 Mike(Moe)Drabowsky	10.00	4.50
❑ 136 Jim Finigan	8.00	3.60
❑ 137 Russ Kemmerer	8.00	3.60
❑ 138 Earl Torgeson	8.00	3.60
❑ 139 George Brunet	8.00	3.60
❑ 140 Wes Covington	10.00	4.50
❑ 141 Ken Lehman	8.00	3.60
❑ 142 Enos Slaughter	25.00	11.00
❑ 143 Billy Muffett RC	8.00	3.60
❑ 144 Bobby Morgan	8.00	3.60
❑ 145 Never issued		
❑ 146 Dick Gray	8.00	3.60
❑ 147 Don McMahon RC	8.00	3.60
❑ 148 Billy Consolo	8.00	3.60
❑ 149 Tom Acker	8.00	3.60
❑ 150 Mickey Mantle	800.00	350.00
❑ 151 Buddy Pritchard	8.00	3.60
❑ 152 Johnny Antonelli	10.00	4.50
❑ 153 Les Moss	8.00	3.60
❑ 154 Harry Byrd	8.00	3.60
❑ 155 Hector Lopez	10.00	4.50
❑ 156 Dick Hyde	8.00	3.60
❑ 157 Dee Fondy	8.00	3.60
❑ 158 Cleveland Indians Team Card (Checklist on back)	15.00	3.00
❑ 159 Taylor Phillips	8.00	3.60
❑ 160 Don Hoak	10.00	4.50
❑ 161 Don Larsen	15.00	6.75
❑ 162 Gil Hodges	40.00	18.00
❑ 163 Jim Wilson	8.00	3.60

	Card	NrMt	VgE
❑	164 Bob Taylor	8.00	3.60
❑	165 Bob Nieman	8.00	3.60
❑	166 Danny O'Connell	8.00	3.60
❑	167 Frank Baumann	8.00	3.60
❑	168 Joe Cunningham	8.00	3.60
❑	169 Ralph Terry	10.00	4.50
❑	170 Vic Wertz	10.00	4.50
❑	171 Harry Anderson	8.00	3.60
❑	172 Don Gross	8.00	3.60
❑	173 Eddie Yost	8.00	3.60
❑	174 Athletics Team (Checklist on back)	15.00	3.00
❑	175 Marv Throneberry RC	15.00	6.75
❑	176 Bob Buhl	10.00	4.50
❑	177 Al Smith	8.00	3.60
❑	178 Ted Kluszewski	25.00	11.00
❑	179 Willie Miranda	8.00	3.60
❑	180 Lindy McDaniel	10.00	4.50
❑	181 Willie Jones	8.00	3.60
❑	182 Joe Caffie	8.00	3.60
❑	183 Dave Jolly	8.00	3.60
❑	184 Elvin Tappe	8.00	3.60
❑	185 Ray Boone	10.00	4.50
❑	186 Jack Meyer	8.00	3.60
❑	187 Sandy Koufax	225.00	100.00
❑	188 Milt Bolling UER (Photo actually Lou Berberet)	8.00	3.60
❑	189 George Susce	8.00	3.60
❑	190 Red Schoendienst	25.00	11.00
❑	191 Art Ceccarelli	8.00	3.60
❑	192 Milt Graff	8.00	3.60
❑	193 Jerry Lumpe RC	8.00	3.60
❑	194 Roger Craig	10.00	4.50
❑	195 Whitey Lockman	10.00	4.50
❑	196 Mike Garcia	10.00	4.50
❑	197 Haywood Sullivan	10.00	4.50
❑	198 Bill Virdon	10.00	4.50
❑	199 Don Blasingame	8.00	3.60
❑	200 Bob Keegan	8.00	3.60
❑	201 Jim Bolger	8.00	3.60
❑	202 Woody Held RC	8.00	3.60
❑	203 Al Walker	8.00	3.60
❑	204 Leo Kiely	8.00	3.60
❑	205 Johnny Temple	10.00	4.50
❑	206 Bob Shaw RC	8.00	3.60
❑	207 Solly Hemus	8.00	3.60
❑	208 Cal McLish	8.00	3.60
❑	209 Bob Anderson	8.00	3.60
❑	210 Wally Moon	10.00	4.50
❑	211 Pete Burnside	8.00	3.60
❑	212 Bubba Phillips	8.00	3.60
❑	213 Red Wilson	8.00	3.60
❑	214 Willard Schmidt	8.00	3.60
❑	215 Jim Gilliam	15.00	6.75
❑	216 St. Louis Cardinals Team Card (Checklist on back)	15.00	3.00
❑	217 Jack Harshman	8.00	3.60
❑	218 Dick Rand	8.00	3.60
❑	219 Camilo Pascual	10.00	4.50
❑	220 Tom Brewer	8.00	3.60
❑	221 Jerry Kindall RC	8.00	3.60
❑	222 Bud Daley	8.00	3.60
❑	223 Andy Pafko	10.00	4.50
❑	224 Bob Grim	10.00	4.50
❑	225 Billy Goodman	10.00	4.50
❑	226 Bob Smith	8.00	3.60
❑	227 Gene Stephens	8.00	3.60
❑	228 Duke Maas	8.00	3.60
❑	229 Frank Zupo	8.00	3.60
❑	230 Richie Ashburn	40.00	18.00
❑	231 Lloyd Merritt	8.00	3.60
❑	232 Reno Bertoia	8.00	3.60
❑	233 Mickey Vernon	10.00	4.50
❑	234 Carl Sawatski	8.00	3.60
❑	235 Tom Gorman	8.00	3.60
❑	236 Ed Fitzgerald	8.00	3.60
❑	237 Bill Wight	8.00	3.60
❑	238 Bill Mazeroski	30.00	13.50
❑	239 Chuck Stobbs	8.00	3.60
❑	240 Bill Skowron	25.00	11.00
❑	241 Dick Littlefield	8.00	3.60
❑	242 Johnny Klippstein	8.00	3.60
❑	243 Larry Raines	8.00	3.60
❑	244 Don Demeter	8.00	3.60
❑	245 Frank Lary	10.00	4.50
❑	246 New York Yankees Team Card (Checklist on back)	100.00	20.00
❑	247 Casey Wise	8.00	3.60
❑	248 Herman Wehmeier	8.00	3.60
❑	249 Ray Moore	8.00	3.60
❑	250 Roy Sievers	10.00	4.50
❑	251 Warren Hacker	8.00	3.60
❑	252 Bob Trowbridge	8.00	3.60
❑	253 Don Mueller	10.00	4.50
❑	254 Alex Grammas	8.00	3.60
❑	255 Bob Turley	10.00	4.50
❑	256 Chicago White Sox Team Card (Checklist on back)	15.00	3.00
❑	257 Hal Smith	8.00	3.60
❑	258 Carl Erskine	15.00	6.75
❑	259 Al Pilarcik	8.00	3.60
❑	260 Frank Malzone	10.00	4.50
❑	261 Turk Lown	8.00	3.60
❑	262 Johnny Groth	8.00	3.60
❑	263 Eddie Bressoud	10.00	4.50
❑	264 Jack Sanford	10.00	4.50
❑	265 Pete Runnels	10.00	4.50
❑	266 Connie Johnson	8.00	3.60
❑	267 Sherm Lollar	10.00	4.50
❑	268 Granny Hamner	8.00	3.60
❑	269 Paul Smith	8.00	3.60
❑	270 Warren Spahn	60.00	27.00
❑	271 Billy Martin	40.00	18.00
❑	272 Ray Crone	8.00	3.60
❑	273 Hal Smith	8.00	3.60
❑	274 Rocky Bridges	8.00	3.60
❑	275 Elston Howard	15.00	6.75
❑	276 Bobby Avila	8.00	3.60
❑	277 Virgil Trucks	10.00	4.50
❑	278 Mack Burk	8.00	3.60
❑	279 Bob Boyd	8.00	3.60
❑	280 Jim Piersall	10.00	4.50
❑	281 Sammy Taylor	8.00	3.60
❑	282 Paul Foytack	8.00	3.60
❑	283 Ray Shearer	8.00	3.60
❑	284 Ray Katt	8.00	3.60
❑	285 Frank Robinson	100.00	45.00
❑	286 Gino Cimoli	8.00	3.60
❑	287 Sam Jones	10.00	4.50
❑	288 Harmon Killebrew	90.00	40.00
❑	289 Lou Burdette Bobby Shantz	10.00	4.50
❑	290 Dick Donovan	8.00	3.60
❑	291 Don Landrum	8.00	3.60
❑	292 Ned Garver	8.00	3.60
❑	293 Gene Freese	8.00	3.60
❑	294 Hal Jeffcoat	8.00	3.60
❑	295 Minnie Minoso	25.00	11.00
❑	296 Ryne Duren RC	15.00	6.75
❑	297 Don Buddin	8.00	3.60
❑	298 Jim Hearn	8.00	3.60
❑	299 Harry Simpson	8.00	3.60
❑	300 Will Harridge PRES Warren Giles	15.00	6.75
❑	301 Randy Jackson	8.00	3.60
❑	302 Mike Baxes	8.00	3.60
❑	303 Neil Chrisley	8.00	3.60
❑	304 Harvey Kuenn Al Kaline	25.00	11.00
❑	305 Clem Labine	10.00	4.50
❑	306 Whammy Douglas	8.00	3.60
❑	307 Brooks Robinson	100.00	45.00
❑	308 Paul Giel	10.00	4.50
❑	309 Gail Harris	8.00	3.60
❑	310 Ernie Banks	100.00	45.00
❑	311 Bob Purkey	8.00	3.60
❑	312 Boston Red Sox Team Card (Checklist on back)	15.00	3.00
❑	313 Bob Rush	8.00	3.60
❑	314 Duke Snider Walt Alston MG	50.00	22.00
❑	315 Bob Friend	10.00	4.50
❑	316 Tito Francona	10.00	4.50
❑	317 Albie Pearson	10.00	4.50
❑	318 Frank House	8.00	3.60
❑	319 Lou Skizas	8.00	3.60
❑	320 Whitey Ford	60.00	27.00
❑	321 Sluggers Supreme Ted Kluszewski Ted Williams	75.00	34.00
❑	322 Harding Peterson	10.00	4.50
❑	323 Elmer Valo	8.00	3.60
❑	324 Hoyt Wilhelm	25.00	11.00
❑	325 Joe Adcock	10.00	4.50
❑	326 Bob Miller	8.00	3.60
❑	327 Chicago Cubs Team Card (Checklist on back)	15.00	3.00
❑	328 Ike Delock	8.00	3.60
❑	329 Bob Cerv	10.00	4.50
❑	330 Ed Bailey	10.00	4.50
❑	331 Pedro Ramos	8.00	3.60
❑	332 Jim King	8.00	3.60
❑	333 Andy Carey	10.00	4.50
❑	334 Bob Friend Billy Pierce	10.00	4.50
❑	335 Ruben Gomez	8.00	3.60
❑	336 Bert Hamric	8.00	3.60
❑	337 Hank Aguirre	8.00	3.60
❑	338 Walt Dropo	10.00	4.50
❑	339 Fred Hatfield	8.00	3.60
❑	340 Don Newcombe	15.00	6.75
❑	341 Pittsburgh Pirates Team Card (Checklist on back)	15.00	3.00
❑	342 Jim Brosnan	10.00	4.50
❑	343 Orlando Cepeda RC	100.00	45.00
❑	344 Bob Porterfield	8.00	3.60
❑	345 Jim Hegan	10.00	4.50
❑	346 Steve Bilko	8.00	3.60
❑	347 Don Rudolph	8.00	3.60
❑	348 Chico Fernandez	8.00	3.60
❑	349 Murry Dickson	8.00	3.60
❑	350 Ken Boyer	25.00	11.00
❑	351 Braves Fence Busters Del Crandall Eddie Mathews Hank Aaron Joe Adcock	40.00	18.00
❑	352 Herb Score	15.00	6.75
❑	353 Stan Lopata	8.00	3.60
❑	354 Art Ditmar	10.00	4.50
❑	355 Bill Bruton	10.00	4.50
❑	356 Bob Malkmus	8.00	3.60
❑	357 Danny McDevitt	8.00	3.60
❑	358 Gene Baker	8.00	3.60
❑	359 Billy Loes	10.00	4.50
❑	360 Roy McMillan	10.00	4.50
❑	361 Mike Fornieles	8.00	3.60
❑	362 Ray Jablonski	8.00	3.60
❑	363 Don Elston	8.00	3.60
❑	364 Earl Battey	8.00	3.60
❑	365 Tom Morgan	8.00	3.60
❑	366 Gene Green	8.00	3.60
❑	367 Jack Urban	8.00	3.60
❑	368 Rocky Colavito	50.00	22.00
❑	369 Ralph Lumenti	8.00	3.60
❑	370 Yogi Berra	100.00	45.00
❑	371 Marty Keough	8.00	3.60
❑	372 Don Cardwell	8.00	3.60
❑	373 Joe Pignatano	8.00	3.60
❑	374 Brooks Lawrence	8.00	3.60
❑	375 Pee Wee Reese	75.00	34.00
❑	376 Charley Rabe	8.00	3.60
❑	377A Milwaukee Braves Team Card (Alphabetical)	15.00	6.75
❑	377B Milwaukee Team numerical checklist	100.00	20.00
❑	378 Hank Sauer	10.00	4.50
❑	379 Ray Herbert	8.00	3.60
❑	380 Charlie Maxwell	10.00	4.50
❑	381 Hal Brown	8.00	3.60
❑	382 Al Cicotte	8.00	3.60
❑	383 Lou Berberet	8.00	3.60
❑	384 John Goryl	8.00	3.60
❑	385 Wilmer Mizell	10.00	4.50
❑	386 Birdie's Sluggers Ed Bailey Birdie Tebbetts MG Frank Robinson	15.00	6.75
❑	387 Wally Post	10.00	4.50
❑	388 Billy Moran	8.00	3.60

❏ 389 Bill Taylor 8.00 3.60
❏ 390 Del Crandall 10.00 4.50
❏ 391 Dave Melton 8.00 3.60
❏ 392 Bennie Daniels 8.00 3.60
❏ 393 Tony Kubek 30.00 13.50
❏ 394 Jim Grant RC 8.00 3.60
❏ 395 Willard Nixon 8.00 3.60
❏ 396 Dutch Dotterer 8.00 3.60
❏ 397A Detroit Tigers 15.00 6.75
Team Card
(Alphabetical)
❏ 397B Detroit Team 100.00 20.00
numerical checklist
❏ 398 Gene Woodling 10.00 4.50
❏ 399 Marv Grissom 8.00 3.60
❏ 400 Nellie Fox 30.00 13.50
❏ 401 Don Bessent 8.00 3.60
❏ 402 Bobby Gene Smith 8.00 3.60
❏ 403 Steve Korcheck 8.00 3.60
❏ 404 Curt Simmons 10.00 4.50
❏ 405 Ken Aspromonte 8.00 3.60
❏ 406 Vic Power 10.00 4.50
❏ 407 Carlton Willey 10.00 4.50
❏ 408A Baltimore Orioles 15.00 6.75
Team Card
(Alphabetical)
❏ 408B Baltimore Team 100.00 20.00
numerical checklist
❏ 409 Frank Thomas 10.00 4.50
❏ 410 Murray Wall 8.00 3.60
❏ 411 Tony Taylor RC 10.00 4.50
❏ 412 Gerry Staley 8.00 3.60
❏ 413 Jim Davenport RC 8.00 3.60
❏ 414 Sammy White 8.00 3.60
❏ 415 Bob Bowman 8.00 3.60
❏ 416 Foster Castleman 8.00 3.60
❏ 417 Carl Furillo 15.00 6.75
❏ 418 Mickey Mantle 300.00 135.00
Hank Aaron
❏ 419 Bobby Shantz 10.00 4.50
❏ 420 Vada Pinson RC 40.00 18.00
❏ 421 Dixie Howell 8.00 3.60
❏ 422 Norm Zauchin 8.00 3.60
❏ 423 Phil Clark 8.00 3.60
❏ 424 Larry Doby 25.00 11.00
❏ 425 Sammy Esposito 8.00 3.60
❏ 426 Johnny O'Brien 10.00 4.50
❏ 427 Al Worthington 8.00 3.60
❏ 428A Cincinnati Reds 15.00 6.75
Team Card
(Alphabetical)
❏ 428B Cincinnati Team 100.00 20.00
numerical checklist
❏ 429 Gus Triandos 10.00 4.50
❏ 430 Bobby Thomson 10.00 4.50
❏ 431 Gene Conley 10.00 4.50
❏ 432 John Powers 8.00 3.60
❏ 433A Pancho Herrer ERR 650.00 300.00
❏ 433B Pancho Herrera COR 10.00 4.50
❏ 434 Harvey Kuenn 10.00 4.50
❏ 435 Ed Roebuck 10.00 4.50
❏ 436 Willie Mays 75.00 34.00
Duke Snider
❏ 437 Bob Speake 8.00 3.60
❏ 438 Whitey Herzog 10.00 4.50
❏ 439 Ray Narleski 8.00 3.60
❏ 440 Eddie Mathews 50.00 22.00
❏ 441 Jim Marshall 10.00 4.50
❏ 442 Phil Paine 8.00 3.60
❏ 443 Billy Harrell SP 20.00 9.00
❏ 444 Danny Kravitz 8.00 3.60
❏ 445 Bob Smith 8.00 3.60
❏ 446 Carroll Hardy SP 20.00 9.00
❏ 447 Ray Monzant 8.00 3.60
❏ 448 Charlie Lau RC 10.00 4.50
❏ 449 Gene Fodge 8.00 3.60
❏ 450 Preston Ward SP 20.00 9.00
❏ 451 Joe Taylor 8.00 3.60
❏ 452 Roman Mejias 8.00 3.60
❏ 453 Tom Qualters 8.00 3.60
❏ 454 Harry Hanebrink 8.00 3.60
❏ 455 Hal Griggs 8.00 3.60
❏ 456 Dick Brown 8.00 3.60
❏ 457 Milt Pappas RC 10.00 4.50
❏ 458 Julio Becquer 8.00 3.60
❏ 459 Ron Blackburn 8.00 3.60
❏ 460 Chuck Essegian 8.00 3.60
❏ 461 Ed Mayer 8.00 3.60
❏ 462 Gary Geiger SP 20.00 9.00
❏ 463 Vito Valentinetti 8.00 3.60
❏ 464 Curt Flood RC 30.00 13.50
❏ 465 Arnie Portocarrero 8.00 3.60
❏ 466 Pete Whisenant 8.00 3.60
❏ 467 Glen Hobbie 8.00 3.60
❏ 468 Bob Schmidt 8.00 3.60
❏ 469 Don Ferrarese 8.00 3.60
❏ 470 R.C. Stevens 8.00 3.60
❏ 471 Lenny Green 8.00 3.60
❏ 472 Joey Jay 10.00 4.50
❏ 473 Bill Renna 8.00 3.60
❏ 474 Roman Semproch 8.00 3.60
❏ 475 Fred Haney AS MG 25.00 7.50
Casey Stengel AS MG
Checklist back
❏ 476 Stan Musial AS TP 50.00 22.00
❏ 477 Bill Skowron AS 10.00 4.50
❏ 478 Johnny Temple AS UER 8.00 3.60
Card says record vs American League
Temple was NL AS
❏ 479 Nellie Fox AS 15.00 6.75
❏ 480 Eddie Mathews AS 25.00 11.00
❏ 481 Frank Malzone AS 8.00 3.60
❏ 482 Ernie Banks AS 40.00 18.00
❏ 483 Luis Aparicio AS 15.00 6.75
❏ 484 Frank Robinson AS 30.00 13.50
❏ 485 Ted Williams AS 125.00 55.00
❏ 486 Willie Mays AS 50.00 22.00
❏ 487 Mickey Mantle AS TP 175.00 80.00
❏ 488 Hank Aaron AS 60.00 27.00
❏ 489 Jackie Jensen AS 10.00 4.50
❏ 490 Ed Bailey AS 8.00 3.60
❏ 491 Sherm Lollar AS 8.00 3.60
❏ 492 Bob Friend AS 8.00 3.60
❏ 493 Bob Turley AS 10.00 4.50
❏ 494 Warren Spahn AS 25.00 11.00
❏ 495 Herb Score AS 15.00 3.00
❏ xx Contest Cards 40.00 18.00

1959 Topps

	NRMT	VG-E
COMPLETE SET (572)	4500.00	2000.00
COMMON CARD (1-110)	6.00	2.70
COMMON CARD (111-506)	4.00	1.80
COMMON CARD (507-572)	16.00	7.25
WRAPPER (1-CENT)	125.00	55.00
WRAPPER (5-CENT)	100.00	45.00

❏ 1 Ford Frick COMM RC 60.00 16.50
❏ 2 Eddie Yost 8.00 3.60
❏ 3 Don McMahon 8.00 3.60
❏ 4 Albie Pearson 8.00 3.60
❏ 5 Dick Donovan 8.00 3.60
❏ 6 Alex Grammas 6.00 2.70
❏ 7 Al Pilarcik 6.00 2.70
❏ 8 Phillies Team 75.00 15.00
(Checklist on back)
❏ 9 Paul Giel 8.00 3.60
❏ 10 Mickey Mantle 700.00 325.00
❏ 11 Billy Hunter 8.00 3.60
❏ 12 Vern Law 8.00 3.60
❏ 13 Dick Gernert 6.00 2.70
❏ 14 Pete Whisenant 6.00 2.70
❏ 15 Dick Drott 6.00 2.70
❏ 16 Joe Pignatano 6.00 2.70
❏ 17 Frank Thomas 8.00 3.60
Danny Murtaugh MG
Ted Kluszewski
❏ 18 Jack Urban 6.00 2.70
❏ 19 Eddie Bressoud 6.00 2.70
❏ 20 Duke Snider 60.00 27.00
❏ 21 Connie Johnson 6.00 2.70
❏ 22 Al Smith 8.00 3.60
❏ 23 Murry Dickson 8.00 3.60
❏ 24 Red Wilson 6.00 2.70
❏ 25 Don Hoak 8.00 3.60
❏ 26 Chuck Stobbs 6.00 2.70
❏ 27 Andy Pafko 8.00 3.60
❏ 28 Al Worthington 6.00 2.70
❏ 29 Jim Bolger 6.00 2.70
❏ 30 Nellie Fox 30.00 13.50
❏ 31 Ken Lehman 6.00 2.70
❏ 32 Don Buddin 6.00 2.70
❏ 33 Ed Fitzgerald 6.00 2.70
❏ 34 Al Kaline 20.00 9.00
Charley Maxwell
❏ 35 Ted Kluszewski 12.00 5.50
❏ 36 Hank Aguirre 6.00 2.70
❏ 37 Gene Green 6.00 2.70
❏ 38 Morrie Martin 6.00 2.70
❏ 39 Ed Bouchee 6.00 2.70
❏ 40A Warren Spahn ERR 75.00 34.00
(Born 1931)
❏ 40B Warren Spahn ERR 100.00 45.00
(Born 1931, but three
is partially obscured)
❏ 40C Warren Spahn COR 60.00 27.00
(Born 1921)
❏ 41 Bob Martyn 6.00 2.70
❏ 42 Murray Wall 6.00 2.70
❏ 43 Steve Bilko 6.00 2.70
❏ 44 Vito Valentinetti 6.00 2.70
❏ 45 Andy Carey 8.00 3.60
❏ 46 Bill R. Henry 6.00 2.70
❏ 47 Jim Finigan 6.00 2.70
❏ 48 Orioles Team 24.00 4.80
(Checklist on back)
❏ 49 Bill Hall 6.00 2.70
❏ 50 Willie Mays 125.00 55.00
❏ 51 Rip Coleman 6.00 2.70
❏ 52 Coot Veal 6.00 2.70
❏ 53 Stan Williams RC 8.00 3.60
❏ 54 Mel Roach 6.00 2.70
❏ 55 Tom Brewer 6.00 2.70
❏ 56 Carl Sawatski 6.00 2.70
❏ 57 Al Cicotte 6.00 2.70
❏ 58 Eddie Miksis 6.00 2.70
❏ 59 Irv Noren 8.00 3.60
❏ 60 Bob Turley 8.00 3.60
❏ 61 Dick Brown 6.00 2.70
❏ 62 Tony Taylor 8.00 3.60
❏ 63 Jim Hearn 6.00 2.70
❏ 64 Joe DeMaestri 6.00 2.70
❏ 65 Frank Torre 8.00 3.60
❏ 66 Joe Ginsberg 6.00 2.70
❏ 67 Brooks Lawrence 6.00 2.70
❏ 68 Dick Schofield 8.00 3.60
❏ 69 Giants Team 24.00 4.80
(Checklist on back)
❏ 70 Harvey Kuenn 8.00 3.60
❏ 71 Don Bessent 6.00 2.70
❏ 72 Bill Renna 6.00 2.70
❏ 73 Ron Jackson 8.00 3.60
❏ 74 Jim Lemon 8.00 3.60
Cookie Lavagetto MG
Roy Sievers
❏ 75 Sam Jones 8.00 3.60
❏ 76 Bobby Richardson 20.00 9.00
❏ 77 John Goryl 6.00 2.70
❏ 78 Pedro Ramos 6.00 2.70
❏ 79 Harry Chiti 6.00 2.70
❏ 80 Minnie Minoso 12.00 5.50
❏ 81 Hal Jeffcoat 6.00 2.70
❏ 82 Bob Boyd 6.00 2.70
❏ 83 Bob Smith 6.00 2.70
❏ 84 Reno Bertoia 6.00 2.70
❏ 85 Harry Anderson 6.00 2.70
❏ 86 Bob Keegan 8.00 3.60
❏ 87 Danny O'Connell 6.00 2.70

❑ 88 Herb Score 12.00 5.50
❑ 89 Billy Gardner 6.00 2.70
❑ 90 Bill Skowron 12.00 5.50
❑ 91 Herb Moford 6.00 2.70
❑ 92 Dave Philley 6.00 2.70
❑ 93 Julio Becquer 6.00 2.70
❑ 94 White Sox Team 40.00 8.00
(Checklist on back)
❑ 95 Carl Willey 6.00 2.70
❑ 96 Lou Berberet 6.00 2.70
❑ 97 Jerry Lynch 8.00 3.60
❑ 98 Arnie Portocarrero 6.00 2.70
❑ 99 Ted Kazanski 6.00 2.70
❑ 100 Bob Cerv 8.00 3.60
❑ 101 Alex Kellner 6.00 2.70
❑ 102 Felipe Alou RC 30.00 13.50
❑ 103 Billy Goodman 8.00 3.60
❑ 104 Del Rice 8.00 3.60
❑ 105 Lee Walls 6.00 2.70
❑ 106 Hal Woodeshick 6.00 2.70
❑ 107 Norm Larker 8.00 3.60
❑ 108 Zack Monroe 8.00 3.60
❑ 109 Bob Schmidt 6.00 2.70
❑ 110 George Witt 8.00 3.60
❑ 111 Redlegs Team 15.00 3.00
(Checklist on back)
❑ 112 Billy Consolo 4.00 1.80
❑ 113 Taylor Phillips 4.00 1.80
❑ 114 Earl Battey 8.00 3.60
❑ 115 Mickey Vernon 8.00 3.60
❑ 116 Bob Allison RP RC 12.00 5.50
❑ 117 J.Blanchard RP RC 12.00 5.50
❑ 118 John Buzhardt RP 5.00 2.20
❑ 119 John Callison RP RC 12.00 5.50
❑ 120 Chuck Coles RP 5.00 2.20
❑ 121 Bob Conley RP 5.00 2.20
❑ 122 Bennie Daniels RP 5.00 2.20
❑ 123 Don Dillard RP 5.00 2.20
❑ 124 Dan Dobbek RP 5.00 2.20
❑ 125 Ron Fairly RP RC 12.00 5.50
❑ 126 Ed Haas RP 5.00 2.20
❑ 127 Kent Hadley RP 5.00 2.20
❑ 128 Bob Hartman RP 5.00 2.20
❑ 129 Frank Herrera RP 5.00 2.20
❑ 130 Lou Jackson RP 5.00 2.20
❑ 131 Deron Johnson RP RC 12.00 5.50
❑ 132 Don Lee RP 5.00 2.20
❑ 133 Bob Lillis RP RC 5.00 2.20
❑ 134 Jim McDaniel RP 5.00 2.20
❑ 135 Gene Oliver RP 5.00 2.20
❑ 136 Jim O'Toole RP RC 5.00 2.20
❑ 137 Dick Ricketts RP 5.00 2.20
❑ 138 John Romano RP RC 5.00 2.20
❑ 139 Ed Sadowski RP 5.00 2.20
❑ 140 Charlie Secrest RP 5.00 2.20
❑ 141 Joe Shipley RP 5.00 2.20
❑ 142 Dick Stigman RP 5.00 2.20
❑ 143 Willie Tasby RP RC 5.00 2.20
❑ 144 Jerry Walker RP 5.00 2.20
❑ 145 Dom Zanni RP 5.00 2.20
❑ 146 Jerry Zimmerman RP 5.00 2.20
❑ 147 Cubs Clubbers 30.00 13.50
Dale Long
Ernie Banks
Walt Moryn
❑ 148 Mike McCormick 8.00 3.60
❑ 149 Jim Bunning 20.00 9.00
❑ 150 Stan Musial 125.00 55.00
❑ 151 Bob Malkmus 4.00 1.80
❑ 152 Johnny Klippstein 4.00 1.80
❑ 153 Jim Marshall 4.00 1.80
❑ 154 Ray Herbert 4.00 1.80
❑ 155 Enos Slaughter 20.00 9.00
❑ 156 Ace Hurlers 12.00 5.50
Billy Pierce
Robin Roberts
❑ 157 Felix Mantilla 4.00 1.80
❑ 158 Walt Dropo 4.00 1.80
❑ 159 Bob Shaw 8.00 3.60
❑ 160 Dick Groat 8.00 3.60
❑ 161 Frank Baumann 4.00 1.80
❑ 162 Bobby G. Smith 4.00 1.80
❑ 163 Sandy Koufax 150.00 70.00
❑ 164 Johnny Groth 4.00 1.80
❑ 165 Bill Bruton 4.00 1.80
❑ 166 Destruction Crew 30.00 13.50
Minnie Minoso
Rocky Colavito
(Misspelled Colovito
on card back)
Larry Doby
❑ 167 Duke Maas 4.00 1.80
❑ 168 Carroll Hardy 4.00 1.80
❑ 169 Ted Abernathy 4.00 1.80
❑ 170 Gene Woodling 8.00 3.60
❑ 171 Willard Schmidt 4.00 1.80
❑ 172 Athletics Team 15.00 3.00
(Checklist on back)
❑ 173 Bill Monbouquette 8.00 3.60
❑ 174 Jim Pendleton 4.00 1.80
❑ 175 Dick Farrell 8.00 3.60
❑ 176 Preston Ward 4.00 1.80
❑ 177 John Briggs 4.00 1.80
❑ 178 Ruben Amaro RC 12.00 5.50
❑ 179 Don Rudolph 4.00 1.80
❑ 180 Yogi Berra 75.00 34.00
❑ 181 Bob Porterfield 4.00 1.80
❑ 182 Milt Graff 4.00 1.80
❑ 183 Stu Miller 8.00 3.60
❑ 184 Harvey Haddix 8.00 3.60
❑ 185 Jim Busby 4.00 1.80
❑ 186 Mudcat Grant 8.00 3.60
❑ 187 Bubba Phillips 8.00 3.60
❑ 188 Juan Pizarro 4.00 1.80
❑ 189 Neil Chrisley 4.00 1.80
❑ 190 Bill Virdon 8.00 3.60
❑ 191 Russ Kemmerer 4.00 1.80
❑ 192 Charlie Beamon 4.00 1.80
❑ 193 Sammy Taylor 4.00 1.80
❑ 194 Jim Brosnan 8.00 3.60
❑ 195 Rip Repulski 4.00 1.80
❑ 196 Billy Moran 4.00 1.80
❑ 197 Ray Semproch 4.00 1.80
❑ 198 Jim Davenport 8.00 3.60
❑ 199 Leo Kiely 4.00 1.80
❑ 200 W.Giles NL PRES 8.00 3.60
❑ 201 Tom Acker 4.00 1.80
❑ 202 Roger Maris 125.00 55.00
❑ 203 Ossie Virgil 4.00 1.80
❑ 204 Casey Wise 4.00 1.80
❑ 205 Don Larsen 8.00 3.60
❑ 206 Carl Furillo 12.00 5.50
❑ 207 George Strickland 4.00 1.80
❑ 208 Willie Jones 4.00 1.80
❑ 209 Lenny Green 4.00 1.80
❑ 210 Ed Bailey 4.00 1.80
❑ 211 Bob Blaylock 4.00 1.80
❑ 212 Hank Aaron 75.00 34.00
Eddie Mathews
❑ 213 Jim Rivera 8.00 3.60
❑ 214 Marcelino Solis 4.00 1.80
❑ 215 Jim Lemon 8.00 3.60
❑ 216 Andre Rodgers 4.00 1.80
❑ 217 Carl Erskine 12.00 5.50
❑ 218 Roman Mejias 4.00 1.80
❑ 219 George Zuverink 4.00 1.80
❑ 220 Frank Malzone 8.00 3.60
❑ 221 Bob Bowman 4.00 1.80
❑ 222 Bobby Shantz 8.00 3.60
❑ 223 Cardinals Team 15.00 3.00
(Checklist on back)
❑ 224 Claude Osteen RC 8.00 3.60
❑ 225 Johnny Logan 8.00 3.60
❑ 226 Art Ceccarelli 4.00 1.80
❑ 227 Hal W. Smith 4.00 1.80
❑ 228 Don Gross 4.00 1.80
❑ 229 Vic Power 8.00 3.60
❑ 230 Bill Fischer 4.00 1.80
❑ 231 Ellis Burton 4.00 1.80
❑ 232 Eddie Kasko 4.00 1.80
❑ 233 Paul Foytack 4.00 1.80
❑ 234 Chuck Tanner 8.00 3.60
❑ 235 Valmy Thomas 4.00 1.80
❑ 236 Ted Bowsfield 4.00 1.80
❑ 237 Run Preventers 12.00 5.50
Gil McDougald
Bob Turley
Bobby Richardson
❑ 238 Gene Baker 4.00 1.80
❑ 239 Bob Trowbridge 4.00 1.80
❑ 240 Hank Bauer 12.00 5.50
❑ 241 Billy Muffett 4.00 1.80
❑ 242 Ron Samford 4.00 1.80
❑ 243 Marv Grissom 4.00 1.80
❑ 244 Ted Gray 4.00 1.80
❑ 245 Ned Garver 4.00 1.80
❑ 246 J.W. Porter 4.00 1.80
❑ 247 Don Ferrarese 4.00 1.80
❑ 248 Red Sox Team 15.00 3.00
(Checklist on back)
❑ 249 Bobby Adams 4.00 1.80
❑ 250 Billy O'Dell 4.00 1.80
❑ 251 Clete Boyer 12.00 5.50
❑ 252 Ray Boone 8.00 3.60
❑ 253 Seth Morehead 4.00 1.80
❑ 254 Zeke Bella 4.00 1.80
❑ 255 Del Ennis 8.00 3.60
❑ 256 Jerry Davie 4.00 1.80
❑ 257 Leon Wagner RC 8.00 3.60
❑ 258 Fred Kipp 4.00 1.80
❑ 259 Jim Pisoni 4.00 1.80
❑ 260 Early Wynn UER 20.00 9.00
1957 Cleevland
❑ 261 Gene Stephens 4.00 1.80
❑ 262 Johnny Podres 12.00 5.50
Clem Labine
Don Drysdale
❑ 263 Bud Daley 4.00 1.80
❑ 264 Chico Carrasquel 4.00 1.80
❑ 265 Ron Kline 4.00 1.80
❑ 266 Woody Held 4.00 1.80
❑ 267 John Romonosky 4.00 1.80
❑ 268 Tito Francona 8.00 3.60
❑ 269 Jack Meyer 4.00 1.80
❑ 270 Gil Hodges 30.00 13.50
❑ 271 Orlando Pena 4.00 1.80
❑ 272 Jerry Lumpe 4.00 1.80
❑ 273 Joey Jay 8.00 3.60
❑ 274 Jerry Kindall 8.00 3.60
❑ 275 Jack Sanford 8.00 3.60
❑ 276 Pete Daley 4.00 1.80
❑ 277 Turk Lown 8.00 3.60
❑ 278 Chuck Essegian 4.00 1.80
❑ 279 Ernie Johnson 4.00 1.80
❑ 280 Frank Bolling 4.00 1.80
❑ 281 Walt Craddock 4.00 1.80
❑ 282 R.C. Stevens 4.00 1.80
❑ 283 Russ Heman 4.00 1.80
❑ 284 Steve Korcheck 4.00 1.80
❑ 285 Joe Cunningham 4.00 1.80
❑ 286 Dean Stone 4.00 1.80
❑ 287 Don Zimmer 12.00 5.50
❑ 288 Dutch Dotterer 4.00 1.80
❑ 289 Johnny Kucks 8.00 3.60
❑ 290 Wes Covington 4.00 1.80
❑ 291 Pedro Ramos 4.00 1.80
Camilo Pascual
❑ 292 Dick Williams 8.00 3.60
❑ 293 Ray Moore 4.00 1.80
❑ 294 Hank Foiles 4.00 1.80
❑ 295 Billy Martin 30.00 13.50
❑ 296 Ernie Broglio RC 4.00 1.80
❑ 297 Jackie Brandt 4.00 1.80
❑ 298 Tex Clevenger 4.00 1.80
❑ 299 Billy Klaus 4.00 1.80
❑ 300 Richie Ashburn 30.00 13.50
❑ 301 Earl Averill 4.00 1.80
❑ 302 Don Mossi 8.00 3.60
❑ 303 Marty Keough 4.00 1.80
❑ 304 Cubs Team 15.00 3.00
(Checklist on back)
❑ 305 Curt Raydon 4.00 1.80
❑ 306 Jim Gilliam 8.00 3.60
❑ 307 Curt Barclay 4.00 1.80
❑ 308 Norm Siebern 4.00 1.80
❑ 309 Sal Maglie 8.00 3.60
❑ 310 Luis Aparicio 20.00 9.00
❑ 311 Norm Zauchin 4.00 1.80
❑ 312 Don Newcombe 8.00 3.60
❑ 313 Frank House 4.00 1.80
❑ 314 Don Cardwell 4.00 1.80
❑ 315 Joe Adcock 8.00 3.60
❑ 316A Ralph Lumenti UER 4.00 1.80
(Option)
(Photo actually
Camilo Pascual)
❑ 316B Ralph Lumenti UER 80.00 36.00
(No option)

(Photo actually
Camilo Pascual)
❑ 317 Willie Mays 75.00 34.00
Richie Ashburn
❑ 318 Rocky Bridges 4.00 1.80
❑ 319 Dave Hillman 4.00 1.80
❑ 320 Bob Skinner 8.00 3.60
❑ 321A Bob Giallombardo 8.00 3.60
(Option)
❑ 321B Bob Giallombardo 80.00 36.00
(No option)
❑ 322A Harry Hanebrink 8.00 3.60
(Traded)
❑ 322B Harry Hanebrink 80.00 36.00
(No trade)
❑ 323 Frank Sullivan 4.00 1.80
❑ 324 Don Demeter 4.00 1.80
❑ 325 Ken Boyer 12.00 5.50
❑ 326 Marv Throneberry 8.00 3.60
❑ 327 Gary Bell 4.00 1.80
❑ 328 Lou Skizas 4.00 1.80
❑ 329 Tigers Team 15.00 3.00
(Checklist on back)
❑ 330 Gus Triandos 8.00 3.60
❑ 331 Steve Boros 4.00 1.80
❑ 332 Ray Monzant 4.00 1.80
❑ 333 Harry Simpson 4.00 1.80
❑ 334 Glen Hobbie 4.00 1.80
❑ 335 Johnny Temple 8.00 3.60
❑ 336A Billy Loes 8.00 3.60
(With traded line)
❑ 336B Billy Loes 80.00 36.00
(No trade)
❑ 337 George Crowe 4.00 1.80
❑ 338 Sparky Anderson RC 60.00 27.00
❑ 339 Roy Face 8.00 3.60
❑ 340 Roy Sievers 8.00 3.60
❑ 341 Tom Qualters 4.00 1.80
❑ 342 Ray Jablonski 4.00 1.80
❑ 343 Billy Hoeft 4.00 1.80
❑ 344 Russ Nixon 4.00 1.80
❑ 345 Gil McDougald 12.00 5.50
❑ 346 Dave Sisler 4.00 1.80
Tom Brewer
❑ 347 Bob Buhl 4.00 1.80
❑ 348 Ted Lepcio 4.00 1.80
❑ 349 Hoyt Wilhelm 20.00 9.00
❑ 350 Ernie Banks 75.00 34.00
❑ 351 Earl Torgeson 4.00 1.80
❑ 352 Robin Roberts 20.00 9.00
❑ 353 Curt Flood 8.00 3.60
❑ 354 Pete Burnside 4.00 1.80
❑ 355 Jimmy Piersall 8.00 3.60
❑ 356 Bob Mabe 4.00 1.80
❑ 357 Dick Stuart RC 8.00 3.60
❑ 358 Ralph Terry 8.00 3.60
❑ 359 Bill White RC 20.00 9.00
❑ 360 Al Kaline 60.00 27.00
❑ 361 Willard Nixon 4.00 1.80
❑ 362A Dolan Nichols 4.00 1.80
(With option line)
❑ 362B Dolan Nichols 80.00 36.00
(No option)
❑ 363 Bobby Avila 4.00 1.80
❑ 364 Danny McDevitt 4.00 1.80
❑ 365 Gus Bell 8.00 3.60
❑ 366 Humberto Robinson 4.00 1.80
❑ 367 Cal Neeman 4.00 1.80
❑ 368 Don Mueller 8.00 3.60
❑ 369 Dick Tomanek 4.00 1.80
❑ 370 Pete Runnels 8.00 3.60
❑ 371 Dick Brodowski 4.00 1.80
❑ 372 Jim Hegan 8.00 3.60
❑ 373 Herb Plews 4.00 1.80
❑ 374 Art Ditmar 8.00 3.60
❑ 375 Bob Nieman 4.00 1.80
❑ 376 Hal Naragon 4.00 1.80
❑ 377 John Antonelli 8.00 3.60
❑ 378 Gail Harris 4.00 1.80
❑ 379 Bob Miller 4.00 1.80
❑ 380 Hank Aaron 125.00 55.00
❑ 381 Mike Baxes 4.00 1.80
❑ 382 Curt Simmons 8.00 3.60
❑ 383 Words of Wisdom 12.00 5.50
Don Larsen
Casey Stengel MG
❑ 384 Dave Sisler 4.00 1.80
❑ 385 Sherm Lollar 8.00 3.60
❑ 386 Jim Delsing 4.00 1.80
❑ 387 Don Drysdale 50.00 22.00
❑ 388 Bob Will 4.00 1.80
❑ 389 Joe Nuxhall 8.00 3.60
❑ 390 Orlando Cepeda 20.00 9.00
❑ 391 Milt Pappas 8.00 3.60
❑ 392 Whitey Herzog 8.00 3.60
❑ 393 Frank Lary 8.00 3.60
❑ 394 Randy Jackson 4.00 1.80
❑ 395 Elston Howard 12.00 5.50
❑ 396 Bob Rush 4.00 1.80
❑ 397 Senators Team 15.00 3.00
(Checklist on back)
❑ 398 Wally Post 8.00 3.60
❑ 399 Larry Jackson 4.00 1.80
❑ 400 Jackie Jensen 8.00 3.60
❑ 401 Ron Blackburn 4.00 1.80
❑ 402 Hector Lopez 8.00 3.60
❑ 403 Clem Labine 8.00 3.60
❑ 404 Hank Sauer 8.00 3.60
❑ 405 Roy McMillan 8.00 3.60
❑ 406 Solly Drake 4.00 1.80
❑ 407 Moe Drabowsky 8.00 3.60
❑ 408 Nellie Fox 35.00 16.00
Luis Aparicio
❑ 409 Gus Zernial 8.00 3.60
❑ 410 Billy Pierce 8.00 3.60
❑ 411 Whitey Lockman 8.00 3.60
❑ 412 Stan Lopata 4.00 1.80
❑ 413 Camilo Pascual UER 8.00 3.60
(Listed as Camillo
on front and Pasqual
on back)
❑ 414 Dale Long 8.00 3.60
❑ 415 Bill Mazeroski 12.00 5.50
❑ 416 Haywood Sullivan 8.00 3.60
❑ 417 Virgil Trucks 8.00 3.60
❑ 418 Gino Cimoli 4.00 1.80
❑ 419 Braves Team 15.00 3.00
(Checklist on back)
❑ 420 Rocky Colavito 30.00 13.50
❑ 421 Herman Wehmeier 4.00 1.80
❑ 422 Hobie Landrith 4.00 1.80
❑ 423 Bob Grim 8.00 3.60
❑ 424 Ken Aspromonte 4.00 1.80
❑ 425 Del Crandall 8.00 3.60
❑ 426 Gerry Staley 8.00 3.60
❑ 427 Charlie Neal 8.00 3.60
❑ 428 Ron Kline 4.00 1.80
Bob Friend
Vernon Law
Roy Face
❑ 429 Bobby Thomson 8.00 3.60
❑ 430 Whitey Ford 60.00 27.00
❑ 431 Whammy Douglas 4.00 1.80
❑ 432 Smoky Burgess 8.00 3.60
❑ 433 Billy Harrell 4.00 1.80
❑ 434 Hal Griggs 4.00 1.80
❑ 435 Frank Robinson 50.00 22.00
❑ 436 Granny Hamner 4.00 1.80
❑ 437 Ike Delock 4.00 1.80
❑ 438 Sammy Esposito 4.00 1.80
❑ 439 Brooks Robinson 50.00 22.00
❑ 440 Lou Burdette 8.00 3.60
(Posing as if
lefthanded)
❑ 441 John Roseboro 8.00 3.60
❑ 442 Ray Narleski 4.00 1.80
❑ 443 Daryl Spencer 4.00 1.80
❑ 444 Ron Hansen RC 8.00 3.60
❑ 445 Cal McLish 4.00 1.80
❑ 446 Rocky Nelson 4.00 1.80
❑ 447 Bob Anderson 4.00 1.80
❑ 448 Vada Pinson UER 12.00 5.50
(Born: 8/8/38
should be 8/11/38)
❑ 449 Tom Gorman 4.00 1.80
❑ 450 Eddie Mathews 35.00 16.00
❑ 451 Jimmy Constable 4.00 1.80
❑ 452 Chico Fernandez 4.00 1.80
❑ 453 Les Moss 4.00 1.80
❑ 454 Phil Clark 4.00 1.80
❑ 455 Larry Doby 12.00 5.50
❑ 456 Jerry Casale 4.00 1.80
❑ 457 Dodgers Team 30.00 6.00
(Checklist on back)
❑ 458 Gordon Jones 4.00 1.80
❑ 459 Bill Tuttle 4.00 1.80
❑ 460 Bob Friend 8.00 3.60
❑ 461 Mickey Mantle HL 125.00 55.00
❑ 462 Rocky Colavito HL 12.00 5.50
❑ 463 Al Kaline HL 30.00 13.50
❑ 464 Willie Mays HL 40.00 18.00
54 World Series Catch
❑ 465 Roy Sievers HL 8.00 3.60
❑ 466 Billy Pierce HL 8.00 3.60
❑ 467 Hank Aaron HL 40.00 18.00
❑ 468 Duke Snider HL 20.00 9.00
❑ 469 Ernie Banks HL 20.00 9.00
❑ 470 Stan Musial HL 30.00 13.50
3,000 Hits
❑ 471 Tom Sturdivant 4.00 1.80
❑ 472 Gene Freese 4.00 1.80
❑ 473 Mike Fornieles 4.00 1.80
❑ 474 Moe Thacker 4.00 1.80
❑ 475 Jack Harshman 4.00 1.80
❑ 476 Indians Team 15.00 3.00
(Checklist on back)
❑ 477 Barry Latman 4.00 1.80
❑ 478 Roberto Clemente 225.00 100.00
❑ 479 Lindy McDaniel 8.00 3.60
❑ 480 Red Schoendienst 12.00 5.50
❑ 481 Charlie Maxwell 8.00 3.60
❑ 482 Russ Meyer 4.00 1.80
❑ 483 Clint Courtney 4.00 1.80
❑ 484 Willie Kirkland 4.00 1.80
❑ 485 Ryne Duren 8.00 3.60
❑ 486 Sammy White 4.00 1.80
❑ 487 Hal Brown 4.00 1.80
❑ 488 Walt Moryn 4.00 1.80
❑ 489 John Powers 4.00 1.80
❑ 490 Frank Thomas 8.00 3.60
❑ 491 Don Blasingame 4.00 1.80
❑ 492 Gene Conley 8.00 3.60
❑ 493 Jim Landis 8.00 3.60
❑ 494 Don Pavletich 4.00 1.80
❑ 495 Johnny Podres 12.00 5.50
❑ 496 W.Terwilliger UER 4.00 1.80
Athlftics on front
❑ 497 Hal R. Smith 4.00 1.80
❑ 498 Dick Hyde 4.00 1.80
❑ 499 Johnny O'Brien 8.00 3.60
❑ 500 Vic Wertz 8.00 3.60
❑ 501 Bob Tiefenauer 4.00 1.80
❑ 502 Alvin Dark 8.00 3.60
❑ 503 Jim Owens 4.00 1.80
❑ 504 Ossie Alvarez 4.00 1.80
❑ 505 Tony Kubek 12.00 5.50
❑ 506 Bob Purkey 4.00 1.80
❑ 507 Bob Hale 16.00 7.25
❑ 508 Art Fowler 16.00 7.25
❑ 509 Norm Cash RC 80.00 36.00
❑ 510 Yankees Team 125.00 25.00
(Checklist on back)
❑ 511 George Susce 16.00 7.25
❑ 512 George Altman 16.00 7.25
❑ 513 Tommy Carroll 16.00 7.25
❑ 514 Bob Gibson RC 250.00 110.00
❑ 515 Harmon Killebrew 125.00 55.00
❑ 516 Mike Garcia 20.00 9.00
❑ 517 Joe Koppe 16.00 7.25
❑ 518 Mike Cueller UER RC 30.00 13.50
Sic, Cuellar
❑ 519 Pete Runnels 20.00 9.00
Dick Gernert
Frank Malzone
❑ 520 Don Elston 16.00 7.25
❑ 521 Gary Geiger 16.00 7.25
❑ 522 Gene Snyder 16.00 7.25
❑ 523 Harry Bright 16.00 7.25
❑ 524 Larry Osborne 16.00 7.25
❑ 525 Jim Coates 20.00 9.00
❑ 526 Bob Speake 16.00 7.25
❑ 527 Solly Hemus 16.00 7.25
❑ 528 Pirates Team 75.00 15.00
(Checklist on back)
❑ 529 G.Bamberger RC 20.00 9.00
❑ 530 Wally Moon 20.00 9.00
❑ 531 Ray Webster 16.00 7.25
❑ 532 Mark Freeman 16.00 7.25

No.	Card	NRMT	VG-E
❑ 533	Darrell Johnson	20.00	9.00
❑ 534	Faye Throneberry	16.00	7.25
❑ 535	Ruben Gomez	16.00	7.25
❑ 536	Danny Kravitz	16.00	7.25
❑ 537	Rudolph Arias	16.00	7.25
❑ 538	Chick King	16.00	7.25
❑ 539	Gary Blaylock	16.00	7.25
❑ 540	Willie Miranda	16.00	7.25
❑ 541	Bob Thurman	16.00	7.25
❑ 542	Jim Perry RC	30.00	13.50
❑ 543	Bob Skinner	150.00	70.00
	Bill Virdon		
	Roberto Clemente		
❑ 544	Lee Tate	16.00	7.25
❑ 545	Tom Morgan	16.00	7.25
❑ 546	Al Schroll	16.00	7.25
❑ 547	Jim Baxes	16.00	7.25
❑ 548	Elmer Singleton	16.00	7.25
❑ 549	Howie Nunn	16.00	7.25
❑ 550	Roy Campanella	150.00	70.00
	(Symbol of Courage)		
❑ 551	Fred Haney AS MG	16.00	7.25
❑ 552	Casey Stengel AS MG	30.00	13.50
❑ 553	Orlando Cepeda AS	30.00	13.50
❑ 554	Bill Skowron AS	20.00	9.00
❑ 555	Bill Mazeroski AS	30.00	13.50
❑ 556	Nellie Fox AS	40.00	18.00
❑ 557	Ken Boyer AS	30.00	13.50
❑ 558	Frank Malzone AS	16.00	7.25
❑ 559	Ernie Banks AS	60.00	27.00
❑ 560	Luis Aparicio AS	40.00	18.00
❑ 561	Hank Aaron AS	125.00	55.00
❑ 562	Al Kaline AS	60.00	27.00
❑ 563	Willie Mays AS	125.00	55.00
❑ 564	Mickey Mantle AS	250.00	110.00
❑ 565	Wes Covington AS	20.00	9.00
❑ 566	Roy Sievers AS	16.00	7.25
❑ 567	Del Crandall AS	16.00	7.25
❑ 568	Gus Triandos AS	16.00	7.25
❑ 569	Bob Friend AS	16.00	7.25
❑ 570	Bob Turley AS	16.00	7.25
❑ 571	Warren Spahn AS	40.00	18.00
❑ 572	Billy Pierce AS	40.00	13.00

1960 Topps

	NRMT	VG-E
COMPLETE SET (572)	3500.00	1600.00
COMMON CARD (1-440)	4.00	1.80
COMMON CARD (441-506)	7.00	3.10
COMMON CARD (507-572)	16.00	7.25
WRAPPER (1-CENT)	900.00	400.00
WRAP. (1-CENT REPEAT)	500.00	220.00
WRAPPER (5-CENT)	40.00	18.00

No.	Card	NRMT	VG-E
❑ 1	Early Wynn	35.00	8.75
❑ 2	Roman Mejias	4.00	1.80
❑ 3	Joe Adcock	6.00	2.70
❑ 4	Bob Purkey	4.00	1.80
❑ 5	Wally Moon	6.00	2.70
❑ 6	Lou Berberet	4.00	1.80
❑ 7	Master and Mentor	25.00	11.00
	Willie Mays		
	Bill Rigney MG		
❑ 8	Bud Daley	4.00	1.80
❑ 9	Faye Throneberry	4.00	1.80
❑ 10	Ernie Banks	50.00	22.00
❑ 11	Norm Siebern	4.00	1.80
❑ 12	Milt Pappas	6.00	2.70
❑ 13	Wally Post	6.00	2.70
❑ 14	Jim Grant	6.00	2.70
❑ 15	Pete Runnels	6.00	2.70
❑ 16	Ernie Broglio	6.00	2.70
❑ 17	Johnny Callison	6.00	2.70
❑ 18	Dodgers Team	50.00	10.00
	(Checklist on back)		
❑ 19	Felix Mantilla	4.00	1.80
❑ 20	Roy Face	6.00	2.70
❑ 21	Dutch Dotterer	4.00	1.80
❑ 22	Rocky Bridges	4.00	1.80
❑ 23	Eddie Fisher	4.00	1.80
❑ 24	Dick Gray	4.00	1.80
❑ 25	Roy Sievers	6.00	2.70
❑ 26	Wayne Terwilliger	4.00	1.80
❑ 27	Dick Drott	4.00	1.80
❑ 28	Brooks Robinson	50.00	22.00
❑ 29	Clem Labine	6.00	2.70
❑ 30	Tito Francona	4.00	1.80
❑ 31	Sammy Esposito	4.00	1.80
❑ 32	Sophomore Stalwarts	4.00	1.80
	Jim O'Toole		
	Vada Pinson		
❑ 33	Tom Morgan	4.00	1.80
❑ 34	Sparky Anderson	15.00	6.75
❑ 35	Whitey Ford	50.00	22.00
❑ 36	Russ Nixon	4.00	1.80
❑ 37	Bill Bruton	4.00	1.80
❑ 38	Jerry Casale	4.00	1.80
❑ 39	Earl Averill	4.00	1.80
❑ 40	Joe Cunningham	4.00	1.80
❑ 41	Barry Latman	4.00	1.80
❑ 42	Hobie Landrith	4.00	1.80
❑ 43	Senators Team	10.00	2.00
	(Checklist on back)		
❑ 44	Bobby Locke	4.00	1.80
❑ 45	Roy McMillan	6.00	2.70
❑ 46	Jerry Fisher	4.00	1.80
❑ 47	Don Zimmer	6.00	2.70
❑ 48	Hal W. Smith	4.00	1.80
❑ 49	Curt Raydon	4.00	1.80
❑ 50	Al Kaline	50.00	22.00
❑ 51	Jim Coates	6.00	2.70
❑ 52	Dave Philley	4.00	1.80
❑ 53	Jackie Brandt	4.00	1.80
❑ 54	Mike Fornieles	4.00	1.80
❑ 55	Bill Mazeroski	15.00	6.75
❑ 56	Steve Korcheck	4.00	1.80
❑ 57	Win Savers	4.00	1.80
	Turk Lown		
	Gerry Staley		
❑ 58	Gino Cimoli	4.00	1.80
❑ 58A	Gino Cimoli		
	Cardinals Team Logo		
❑ 59	Juan Pizarro	4.00	1.80
❑ 60	Gus Triandos	6.00	2.70
❑ 61	Eddie Kasko	4.00	1.80
❑ 62	Roger Craig	6.00	2.70
❑ 63	George Strickland	4.00	1.80
❑ 64	Jack Meyer	4.00	1.80
❑ 65	Elston Howard	6.00	2.70
❑ 66	Bob Trowbridge	4.00	1.80
❑ 67	Jose Pagan	4.00	1.80
❑ 68	Dave Hillman	4.00	1.80
❑ 69	Billy Goodman	6.00	2.70
❑ 70	Lew Burdette	6.00	2.70
❑ 71	Marty Keough	4.00	1.80
❑ 72	Tigers Team	25.00	5.00
	(Checklist on back)		
❑ 73	Bob Gibson	50.00	22.00
❑ 74	Walt Moryn	4.00	1.80
❑ 75	Vic Power	6.00	2.70
❑ 76	Bill Fischer	4.00	1.80
❑ 77	Hank Foiles	4.00	1.80
❑ 78	Bob Grim	4.00	1.80
❑ 79	Walt Dropo	4.00	1.80
❑ 80	Johnny Antonelli	6.00	2.70
❑ 81	Russ Snyder	4.00	1.80
❑ 82	Ruben Gomez	4.00	1.80
❑ 83	Tony Kubek	15.00	6.75
❑ 84	Hal R. Smith	4.00	1.80
❑ 85	Frank Lary	6.00	2.70
❑ 86	Dick Gernert	4.00	1.80
❑ 87	John Romonosky	4.00	1.80
❑ 88	John Roseboro	6.00	2.70
❑ 89	Hal Brown	4.00	1.80
❑ 90	Bobby Avila	4.00	1.80
❑ 91	Bennie Daniels	4.00	1.80
❑ 92	Whitey Herzog	6.00	2.70
❑ 93	Art Schult	4.00	1.80
❑ 94	Leo Kiely	4.00	1.80
❑ 95	Frank Thomas	6.00	2.70
❑ 96	Ralph Terry	6.00	2.70
❑ 97	Ted Lepcio	4.00	1.80
❑ 98	Gordon Jones	4.00	1.80
❑ 99	Lenny Green	4.00	1.80
❑ 100	Nellie Fox	20.00	9.00
❑ 101	Bob Miller	4.00	1.80
❑ 102	Kent Hadley	4.00	1.80
❑ 102A	Kent Hadley		
	Athletics Team Logo		
❑ 103	Dick Farrell	6.00	2.70
❑ 104	Dick Schofield	6.00	2.70
❑ 105	Larry Sherry RC	6.00	2.70
❑ 106	Billy Gardner	4.00	1.80
❑ 107	Carlton Willey	4.00	1.80
❑ 108	Pete Daley	4.00	1.80
❑ 109	Clete Boyer	15.00	6.75
❑ 110	Cal McLish	4.00	1.80
❑ 111	Vic Wertz	6.00	2.70
❑ 112	Jack Harshman	4.00	1.80
❑ 113	Bob Skinner	4.00	1.80
❑ 114	Ken Aspromonte	4.00	1.80
❑ 115	Fork and Knuckler	6.00	2.70
	Roy Face		
	Hoyt Wilhelm		
❑ 116	Jim Rivera	4.00	1.80
❑ 117	Tom Borland RP	4.00	1.80
❑ 118	Bob Bruce RP	4.00	1.80
❑ 119	Chico Cardenas RP	6.00	2.70
❑ 120	Duke Carmel RP	4.00	1.80
❑ 121	Camilo Carreon RP	4.00	1.80
❑ 122	Don Dillard RP	4.00	1.80
❑ 123	Dan Dobbek RP	4.00	1.80
❑ 124	Jim Donohue RP	4.00	1.80
❑ 125	Dick Ellsworth RP RC	6.00	2.70
❑ 126	Chuck Estrada RP RC	4.00	1.80
❑ 127	Ron Hansen RP	6.00	2.70
❑ 128	Bill Harris RP	4.00	1.80
❑ 129	Bob Hartman RP	4.00	1.80
❑ 130	Frank Herrera RP	4.00	1.80
❑ 131	Ed Hobaugh RP	4.00	1.80
❑ 132	Frank Howard RP RC	25.00	11.00
❑ 133	Manuel Javier RC RP	6.00	2.70
	(Sic, Julian)		
❑ 134	Deron Johnson RP	6.00	2.70
❑ 135	Ken Johnson RP	4.00	1.80
❑ 136	Jim Kaat RP RC	40.00	18.00
❑ 137	Lou Klimchock RP	4.00	1.80
❑ 138	Art Mahaffey RP	15.00	6.75
❑ 139	Carl Mathias RP	4.00	1.80
❑ 140	Julio Navarro RP RC	4.00	1.80
❑ 141	Jim Proctor RP	4.00	1.80
❑ 142	Bill Short RP	4.00	1.80
❑ 143	Al Spangler RP	4.00	1.80
❑ 144	Al Stieglitz RP	4.00	1.80
❑ 145	Jim Umbricht RP	4.00	1.80
❑ 146	Ted Wieand RP	4.00	1.80
❑ 147	Bob Will RP	4.00	1.80
❑ 148	C.Yastrzemski RP RC	150.00	70.00
❑ 149	Bob Nieman	4.00	1.80
❑ 150	Billy Pierce	6.00	2.70
❑ 151	Giants Team	10.00	2.00
	(Checklist on back)		
❑ 152	Gail Harris	4.00	1.80
❑ 153	Bobby Thomson	6.00	2.70
❑ 154	Jim Davenport	6.00	2.70
❑ 155	Charlie Neal	6.00	2.70
❑ 156	Art Ceccarelli	4.00	1.80
❑ 157	Rocky Nelson	6.00	2.70
❑ 158	Wes Covington	6.00	2.70
❑ 159	Jim Piersall	6.00	2.70
❑ 160	Rival All-Stars	150.00	70.00
	Mickey Mantle		
	Ken Boyer		
❑ 161	Ray Narleski	4.00	1.80
❑ 162	Sammy Taylor	4.00	1.80
❑ 163	Hector Lopez	6.00	2.70
❑ 164	Reds Team	10.00	2.00
	(Checklist on back)		
❑ 165	Jack Sanford	6.00	2.70

❑ 166 Chuck Essegian 4.00 1.80
❑ 167 Valmy Thomas 4.00 1.80
❑ 168 Alex Grammas 4.00 1.80
❑ 169 Jake Striker 4.00 1.80
❑ 170 Del Crandall 6.00 2.70
❑ 171 Johnny Groth 4.00 1.80
❑ 172 Willie Kirkland 4.00 1.80
❑ 173 Billy Martin 20.00 9.00
❑ 174 Indians Team 10.00 2.00
(Checklist on back)
❑ 175 Pedro Ramos 4.00 1.80
❑ 176 Vada Pinson 6.00 2.70
❑ 177 Johnny Kucks 4.00 1.80
❑ 178 Woody Held 4.00 1.80
❑ 179 Rip Coleman 4.00 1.80
❑ 180 Harry Simpson 4.00 1.80
❑ 181 Billy Loes 6.00 2.70
❑ 182 Glen Hobbie 4.00 1.80
❑ 183 Eli Grba 4.00 1.80
❑ 184 Gary Geiger 4.00 1.80
❑ 185 Jim Owens 4.00 1.80
❑ 186 Dave Sisler 4.00 1.80
❑ 187 Jay Hook 4.00 1.80
❑ 188 Dick Williams 6.00 2.70
❑ 189 Don McMahon 4.00 1.80
❑ 190 Gene Woodling 6.00 2.70
❑ 191 Johnny Klippstein 4.00 1.80
❑ 192 Danny O'Connell 4.00 1.80
❑ 193 Dick Hyde 4.00 1.80
❑ 194 Bobby Gene Smith 4.00 1.80
❑ 195 Lindy McDaniel 6.00 2.70
❑ 196 Andy Carey 6.00 2.70
❑ 197 Ron Kline 4.00 1.80
❑ 198 Jerry Lynch 6.00 2.70
❑ 199 Dick Donovan 6.00 2.70
❑ 200 Willie Mays 100.00 45.00
❑ 201 Larry Osborne 4.00 1.80
❑ 202 Fred Kipp 4.00 1.80
❑ 203 Sammy White 4.00 1.80
❑ 204 Ryne Duren 6.00 2.70
❑ 205 Johnny Logan 6.00 2.70
❑ 206 Claude Osteen 6.00 2.70
❑ 207 Bob Boyd 4.00 1.80
❑ 208 White Sox Team 10.00 2.00
(Checklist on back)
❑ 209 Ron Blackburn 4.00 1.80
❑ 210 Harmon Killebrew 25.00 11.00
❑ 211 Taylor Phillips 4.00 1.80
❑ 212 Walter Alston MG 10.00 4.50
❑ 213 Chuck Dressen MG 6.00 2.70
❑ 214 Jimmy Dykes MG 6.00 2.70
❑ 215 Bob Elliott MG 6.00 2.70
❑ 216 Joe Gordon MG 6.00 2.70
❑ 217 Charlie Grimm MG 6.00 2.70
❑ 218 Solly Hemus MG 4.00 1.80
❑ 219 Fred Hutchinson MG 6.00 2.70
❑ 220 Billy Jurges MG 4.00 1.80
❑ 221 Cookie Lavagetto MG 4.00 1.80
❑ 222 Al Lopez MG 10.00 4.50
❑ 223 Danny Murtaugh MG 6.00 2.70
❑ 224 Paul Richards MG 6.00 2.70
❑ 225 Bill Rigney MG 4.00 1.80
❑ 226 Eddie Sawyer MG 4.00 1.80
❑ 227 Casey Stengel MG 15.00 6.75
❑ 228 Ernie Johnson 6.00 2.70
❑ 229 Joe M. Morgan 4.00 1.80
❑ 230 Mound Magicians 10.00 4.50
Lou Burdette
Warren Spahn
Bob Buhl
❑ 231 Hal Naragon 4.00 1.80
❑ 232 Jim Busby 4.00 1.80
❑ 233 Don Elston 4.00 1.80
❑ 234 Don Demeter 4.00 1.80
❑ 235 Gus Bell 6.00 2.70
❑ 236 Dick Ricketts 4.00 1.80
❑ 237 Elmer Valo 4.00 1.80
❑ 238 Danny Kravitz 4.00 1.80
❑ 239 Joe Shipley 4.00 1.80
❑ 240 Luis Aparicio 15.00 6.75
❑ 241 Albie Pearson 6.00 2.70
❑ 242 Cardinals Team 10.00 2.00
(Checklist on back)
❑ 243 Bubba Phillips 4.00 1.80
❑ 244 Hal Griggs 4.00 1.80
❑ 245 Eddie Yost 6.00 2.70
❑ 246 Lee Maye 6.00 2.70
❑ 247 Gil McDougald 10.00 4.50
❑ 248 Del Rice 4.00 1.80
❑ 249 Earl Wilson RC 6.00 2.70
❑ 250 Stan Musial 100.00 45.00
❑ 251 Bob Malkmus 4.00 1.80
❑ 252 Ray Herbert 4.00 1.80
❑ 253 Eddie Bressoud 4.00 1.80
❑ 254 Arnie Portocarrero 4.00 1.80
❑ 255 Jim Gilliam 6.00 2.70
❑ 256 Dick Brown 4.00 1.80
❑ 257 Gordy Coleman RC 4.00 1.80
❑ 258 Dick Groat 6.00 2.70
❑ 259 George Altman 4.00 1.80
❑ 260 Power Plus 15.00 6.75
Rocky Colavito
Tito Francona
❑ 261 Pete Burnside 4.00 1.80
❑ 262 Hank Bauer 6.00 2.70
❑ 263 Darrell Johnson 4.00 1.80
❑ 264 Robin Roberts 15.00 6.75
❑ 265 Rip Repulski 4.00 1.80
❑ 266 Joey Jay 6.00 2.70
❑ 267 Jim Marshall 4.00 1.80
❑ 268 Al Worthington 4.00 1.80
❑ 269 Gene Green 4.00 1.80
❑ 270 Bob Turley 6.00 2.70
❑ 271 Julio Becquer 4.00 1.80
❑ 272 Fred Green 6.00 2.70
❑ 273 Neil Chrisley 4.00 1.80
❑ 274 Tom Acker 4.00 1.80
❑ 275 Curt Flood 6.00 2.70
❑ 276 Ken McBride 4.00 1.80
❑ 277 Harry Bright 4.00 1.80
❑ 278 Stan Williams 6.00 2.70
❑ 279 Chuck Tanner 6.00 2.70
❑ 280 Frank Sullivan 4.00 1.80
❑ 281 Ray Boone 6.00 2.70
❑ 282 Joe Nuxhall 6.00 2.70
❑ 283 John Blanchard 6.00 2.70
❑ 284 Don Gross 4.00 1.80
❑ 285 Harry Anderson 4.00 1.80
❑ 286 Ray Semproch 4.00 1.80
❑ 287 Felipe Alou 6.00 2.70
❑ 288 Bob Mabe 4.00 1.80
❑ 289 Willie Jones 4.00 1.80
❑ 290 Jerry Lumpe 4.00 1.80
❑ 291 Bob Keegan 4.00 1.80
❑ 292 Dodger Backstops 6.00 2.70
Joe Pignatano
John Roseboro
❑ 293 Gene Conley 6.00 2.70
❑ 294 Tony Taylor 6.00 2.70
❑ 295 Gil Hodges 25.00 11.00
❑ 296 Nelson Chittum 4.00 1.80
❑ 297 Reno Bertoia 4.00 1.80
❑ 298 George Witt 4.00 1.80
❑ 299 Earl Torgeson 4.00 1.80
❑ 300 Hank Aaron 100.00 45.00
❑ 301 Jerry Davie 4.00 1.80
❑ 302 Phillies Team 10.00 2.00
(Checklist on back)
❑ 303 Billy O'Dell 4.00 1.80
❑ 304 Joe Ginsberg 4.00 1.80
❑ 305 Richie Ashburn 20.00 9.00
❑ 306 Frank Baumann 4.00 1.80
❑ 307 Gene Oliver 4.00 1.80
❑ 308 Dick Hall 4.00 1.80
❑ 309 Bob Hale 4.00 1.80
❑ 310 Frank Malzone 6.00 2.70
❑ 311 Raul Sanchez 4.00 1.80
❑ 312 Charley Lau 6.00 2.70
❑ 313 Turk Lown 4.00 1.80
❑ 314 Chico Fernandez 4.00 1.80
❑ 315 Bobby Shantz 10.00 4.50
❑ 316 Willie McCovey RC 125.00 55.00
❑ 317 Pumpsie Green 6.00 2.70
❑ 318 Jim Baxes 6.00 2.70
❑ 319 Joe Koppe 6.00 2.70
❑ 320 Bob Allison 6.00 2.70
❑ 321 Ron Fairly 6.00 2.70
❑ 322 Willie Tasby 6.00 2.70
❑ 323 John Romano 6.00 2.70
❑ 324 Jim Perry 6.00 2.70
❑ 325 Jim O'Toole 6.00 2.70
❑ 326 Roberto Clemente 175.00 80.00
❑ 327 Ray Sadecki RC 4.00 1.80
❑ 328 Earl Battey 4.00 1.80
❑ 329 Zack Monroe 4.00 1.80
❑ 330 Harvey Kuenn 6.00 2.70
❑ 331 Henry Mason 4.00 1.80
❑ 332 Yankees Team 75.00 15.00
(Checklist on back)
❑ 333 Danny McDevitt 4.00 1.80
❑ 334 Ted Abernathy 4.00 1.80
❑ 335 Red Schoendienst 15.00 6.75
❑ 336 Ike Delock 4.00 1.80
❑ 337 Cal Neeman 4.00 1.80
❑ 338 Ray Monzant 4.00 1.80
❑ 339 Harry Chiti 4.00 1.80
❑ 340 Harvey Haddix 6.00 2.70
❑ 341 Carroll Hardy 4.00 1.80
❑ 342 Casey Wise 4.00 1.80
❑ 343 Sandy Koufax 125.00 55.00
❑ 344 Clint Courtney 4.00 1.80
❑ 345 Don Newcombe 6.00 2.70
❑ 346 J.C. Martin UER 6.00 2.70
(Face actually
Gary Peters)
❑ 347 Ed Bouchee 4.00 1.80
❑ 348 Barry Shetrone 4.00 1.80
❑ 349 Moe Drabowsky 6.00 2.70
❑ 350 Mickey Mantle 450.00 200.00
❑ 351 Don Nottebart 4.00 1.80
❑ 352 Cincy Clouters 10.00 4.50
Gus Bell
Frank Robinson
Jerry Lynch
❑ 353 Don Larsen 6.00 2.70
❑ 354 Bob Lillis 4.00 1.80
❑ 355 Bill White 6.00 2.70
❑ 356 Joe Amalfitano 4.00 1.80
❑ 357 Al Schroll 4.00 1.80
❑ 358 Joe DeMaestri 4.00 1.80
❑ 359 Buddy Gilbert 4.00 1.80
❑ 360 Herb Score 6.00 2.70
❑ 361 Bob Oldis 6.00 2.70
❑ 362 Russ Kemmerer 4.00 1.80
❑ 363 Gene Stephens 4.00 1.80
❑ 364 Paul Foytack 4.00 1.80
❑ 365 Minnie Minoso 10.00 4.50
❑ 366 Dallas Green RC 10.00 4.50
❑ 367 Bill Tuttle 4.00 1.80
❑ 368 Daryl Spencer 4.00 1.80
❑ 369 Billy Hoeft 4.00 1.80
❑ 370 Bill Skowron 10.00 4.50
❑ 371 Bud Byerly 4.00 1.80
❑ 372 Frank House 4.00 1.80
❑ 373 Don Hoak 6.00 2.70
❑ 374 Bob Buhl 6.00 2.70
❑ 375 Dale Long 10.00 4.50
❑ 376 John Briggs 4.00 1.80
❑ 377 Roger Maris 100.00 45.00
❑ 378 Stu Miller 6.00 2.70
❑ 379 Red Wilson 4.00 1.80
❑ 380 Bob Shaw 4.00 1.80
❑ 381 Braves Team 10.00 2.00
(Checklist on back)
❑ 382 Ted Bowsfield 4.00 1.80
❑ 383 Leon Wagner 4.00 1.80
❑ 384 Don Cardwell 4.00 1.80
❑ 385 Charlie Neal WS 6.00 2.70
❑ 386 Charlie Neal WS 6.00 2.70
❑ 387 Carl Furillo WS 6.00 2.70
❑ 388 Gil Hodges WS 10.00 4.50
❑ 389 Luis Aparicio WS 12.00 5.50
Maury Wills
❑ 390 World Series Game 6 6.00 2.70
❑ 391 WS Summary 6.00 2.70
The Champs Celebrate
❑ 392 Tex Clevenger 4.00 1.80
❑ 393 Smoky Burgess 6.00 2.70
❑ 394 Norm Larker 6.00 2.70
❑ 395 Hoyt Wilhelm 15.00 6.75
❑ 396 Steve Bilko 4.00 1.80
❑ 397 Don Blasingame 4.00 1.80
❑ 398 Mike Cuellar 6.00 2.70
❑ 399 Young Hill Stars 6.00 2.70
Milt Pappas
Jack Fisher
Jerry Walker
❑ 400 Rocky Colavito 20.00 9.00

☐ 401 Bob Duliba 4.00 1.80
☐ 402 Dick Stuart 15.00 6.75
☐ 403 Ed Sadowski 4.00 1.80
☐ 404 Bob Rush 4.00 1.80
☐ 405 Bobby Richardson 15.00 6.75
☐ 406 Billy Klaus 4.00 1.80
☐ 407 Gary Peters RC UER 6.00 2.70
(Face actually
J.C. Martin)
☐ 408 Carl Furillo 10.00 4.50
☐ 409 Ron Samford 4.00 1.80
☐ 410 Sam Jones 6.00 2.70
☐ 411 Ed Bailey 4.00 1.80
☐ 412 Bob Anderson 4.00 1.80
☐ 413 Athletics Team 10.00 2.00
(Checklist on back)
☐ 414 Don Williams 4.00 1.80
☐ 415 Bob Cerv 4.00 1.80
☐ 416 Humberto Robinson 4.00 1.80
☐ 417 Chuck Cottier RC 4.00 1.80
☐ 418 Don Mossi 6.00 2.70
☐ 419 George Crowe 4.00 1.80
☐ 420 Eddie Mathews 40.00 18.00
☐ 421 Duke Maas 4.00 1.80
☐ 422 John Powers 4.00 1.80
☐ 423 Ed Fitzgerald 4.00 1.80
☐ 424 Pete Whisenant 4.00 1.80
☐ 425 Johnny Podres 6.00 2.70
☐ 426 Ron Jackson 4.00 1.80
☐ 427 Al Grunwald 4.00 1.80
☐ 428 Al Smith 4.00 1.80
☐ 429 AL Kings 10.00 4.50
Nellie Fox
Harvey Kuenn
☐ 430 Art Ditmar 4.00 1.80
☐ 431 Andre Rodgers 4.00 1.80
☐ 432 Chuck Stobbs 4.00 1.80
☐ 433 Irv Noren 4.00 1.80
☐ 434 Brooks Lawrence 6.00 2.70
☐ 435 Gene Freese 4.00 1.80
☐ 436 Marv Throneberry 6.00 2.70
☐ 437 Bob Friend 6.00 2.70
☐ 438 Jim Coker 4.00 1.80
☐ 439 Tom Brewer 4.00 1.80
☐ 440 Jim Lemon 6.00 2.70
☐ 441 Gary Bell 10.00 4.50
☐ 442 Joe Pignatano 7.00 3.10
☐ 443 Charlie Maxwell 7.00 3.10
☐ 444 Jerry Kindall 7.00 3.10
☐ 445 Warren Spahn 50.00 22.00
☐ 446 Ellis Burton 7.00 3.10
☐ 447 Ray Moore 7.00 3.10
☐ 448 Jim Gentile RC 15.00 6.75
☐ 449 Jim Brosnan 7.00 3.10
☐ 450 Orlando Cepeda 25.00 11.00
☐ 451 Curt Simmons 7.00 3.10
☐ 452 Ray Webster 7.00 3.10
☐ 453 Vern Law 25.00 11.00
☐ 454 Hal Woodeshick 7.00 3.10
☐ 455 Baltimore Coaches 7.00 3.10
Eddie Robinson
Harry Brecheen
Luman Harris
☐ 456 Red Sox Coaches 10.00 4.50
Rudy York
Billy Herman
Sal Maglie
Del Baker
☐ 457 Cubs Coaches 7.00 3.10
Charlie Root
Lou Klein
Elvin Tappe
☐ 458 White Sox Coaches 7.00 3.10
Johnny Cooney
Don Gutteridge
Tony Cuccinello
Ray Berres
☐ 459 Reds Coaches 7.00 3.10
Reggie Otero
Cot Deal
Wally Moses
☐ 460 Indians Coaches 15.00 6.75
Mel Harder
Jo-Jo White
Bob Lemon
Ralph(Red) Kress
☐ 461 Tigers Coaches 10.00 4.50
Tom Ferrick
Luke Appling
Billy Hitchcock
☐ 462 Athletics Coaches 7.00 3.10
Fred Fitzsimmons
Don Heffner
Walker Cooper
☐ 463 Dodgers Coaches 7.00 3.10
Bobby Bragan
Pete Reiser
Joe Becker
Greg Mulleavy
☐ 464 Braves Coaches 7.00 3.10
Bob Scheffing
Whitlow Wyatt
Andy Pafko
George Myatt
☐ 465 Yankees Coaches 25.00 11.00
Bill Dickey
Ralph Houk
Frank Crosetti
Ed Lopat
☐ 466 Phillies Coaches 7.00 3.10
Ken Silvestri
Dick Carter
Andy Cohen
☐ 467 Pirates Coaches 7.00 3.10
Mickey Vernon
Frank Oceak
Sam Narron
Bill Burwell
☐ 468 Cardinals Coaches 7.00 3.10
Johnny Keane
Howie Pollet
Ray Katt
Harry Walker
☐ 469 Giants Coaches 7.00 3.10
Wes Westrum
Salty Parker
Bill Posedel
☐ 470 Senators Coaches 7.00 3.10
Bob Swift
Ellis Clary
Sam Mele
☐ 471 Ned Garver 7.00 3.10
☐ 472 Alvin Dark 7.00 3.10
☐ 473 Al Cicotte 7.00 3.10
☐ 474 Haywood Sullivan 7.00 3.10
☐ 475 Don Drysdale 40.00 18.00
☐ 476 Lou Johnson 7.00 3.10
☐ 477 Don Ferrarese 7.00 3.10
☐ 478 Frank Torre 7.00 3.10
☐ 479 Georges Maranda 7.00 3.10
☐ 480 Yogi Berra 75.00 34.00
☐ 481 Wes Stock 7.00 3.10
☐ 482 Frank Bolling 7.00 3.10
☐ 483 Camilo Pascual 7.00 3.10
☐ 484 Pirates Team 40.00 8.00
(Checklist on back)
☐ 485 Ken Boyer 15.00 6.75
☐ 486 Bobby Del Greco 7.00 3.10
☐ 487 Tom Sturdivant 7.00 3.10
☐ 488 Norm Cash 25.00 11.00
☐ 489 Steve Ridzik 7.00 3.10
☐ 490 Frank Robinson 50.00 22.00
☐ 491 Mel Roach 7.00 3.10
☐ 492 Larry Jackson 7.00 3.10
☐ 493 Duke Snider 50.00 22.00
☐ 494 Orioles Team 25.00 5.00
(Checklist on back)
☐ 495 Sherm Lollar 7.00 3.10
☐ 496 Bill Virdon 10.00 4.50
☐ 497 John Tsitouris 7.00 3.10
☐ 498 Al Pilarcik 7.00 3.10
☐ 499 Johnny James 10.00 4.50
☐ 500 Johnny Temple 7.00 3.10
☐ 501 Bob Schmidt 7.00 3.10
☐ 502 Jim Bunning 25.00 11.00
☐ 503 Don Lee 7.00 3.10
☐ 504 Seth Morehead 7.00 3.10
☐ 505 Ted Kluszewski 25.00 11.00
☐ 506 Lee Walls 7.00 3.10
☐ 507 Dick Stigman 16.00 7.25
☐ 508 Billy Consolo 16.00 7.25
☐ 509 Tommy Davis RC 25.00 11.00
☐ 510 Gerry Staley 16.00 7.25
☐ 511 Ken Walters 16.00 7.25
☐ 512 Joe Gibbon 16.00 7.25
☐ 513 Chicago Cubs 30.00 6.00
Team Card
(Checklist on back)
☐ 514 Steve Barber RC 16.00 7.25
☐ 515 Stan Lopata 16.00 7.25
☐ 516 Marty Kutyna 16.00 7.25
☐ 517 Charlie James 25.00 11.00
☐ 518 Tony Gonzalez 16.00 7.25
☐ 519 Ed Roebuck 16.00 7.25
☐ 520 Don Buddin 16.00 7.25
☐ 521 Mike Lee 16.00 7.25
☐ 522 Ken Hunt 30.00 13.50
☐ 523 Clay Dalrymple 16.00 7.25
☐ 524 Bill Henry 16.00 7.25
☐ 525 Marv Breeding 16.00 7.25
☐ 526 Paul Giel 25.00 11.00
☐ 527 Jose Valdivielso 25.00 11.00
☐ 528 Ben Johnson 16.00 7.25
☐ 529 Norm Sherry RC 20.00 9.00
☐ 530 Mike McCormick 16.00 7.25
☐ 531 Sandy Amoros 20.00 9.00
☐ 532 Mike Garcia 20.00 9.00
☐ 533 Lu Clinton 16.00 7.25
☐ 534 Ken MacKenzie 16.00 7.25
☐ 535 Whitey Lockman 16.00 7.25
☐ 536 Wynn Hawkins 16.00 7.25
☐ 537 Boston Red Sox 30.00 6.00
Team Card
(Checklist on back)
☐ 538 Frank Barnes 16.00 7.25
☐ 539 Gene Baker 16.00 7.25
☐ 540 Jerry Walker 16.00 7.25
☐ 541 Tony Curry 16.00 7.25
☐ 542 Ken Hamlin 16.00 7.25
☐ 543 Elio Chacon 16.00 7.25
☐ 544 Bill Monbouquette 20.00 9.00
☐ 545 Carl Sawatski 16.00 7.25
☐ 546 Hank Aguirre 16.00 7.25
☐ 547 Bob Aspromonte 20.00 9.00
☐ 548 Don Mincher 16.00 7.25
☐ 549 John Buzhardt 16.00 7.25
☐ 550 Jim Landis 16.00 7.25
☐ 551 Ed Rakow 16.00 7.25
☐ 552 Walt Bond 16.00 7.25
☐ 553 Bill Skowron AS 20.00 9.00
☐ 554 Willie McCovey AS 35.00 16.00
☐ 555 Nellie Fox AS 30.00 13.50
☐ 556 Charlie Neal AS 16.00 7.25
☐ 557 Frank Malzone AS 16.00 7.25
☐ 558 Eddie Mathews AS 35.00 16.00
☐ 559 Luis Aparicio AS 30.00 13.50
☐ 560 Ernie Banks AS 60.00 27.00
☐ 561 Al Kaline AS 60.00 27.00
☐ 562 Joe Cunningham AS 16.00 7.25
☐ 563 Mickey Mantle AS 250.00 110.00
☐ 564 Willie Mays AS 100.00 45.00
☐ 565 Roger Maris AS 100.00 45.00
☐ 566 Hank Aaron AS 100.00 45.00
☐ 567 Sherm Lollar AS 16.00 7.25
☐ 568 Del Crandall AS 16.00 7.25
☐ 569 Camilo Pascual AS 16.00 7.25
☐ 570 Don Drysdale AS 35.00 16.00
☐ 571 Billy Pierce AS 16.00 7.25
☐ 572 Johnny Antonelli AS 30.00 9.00
☐ NNO Iron-on team transfer 4.00 1.80

1961 Topps

	NRMT	VG-E
COMPLETE SET (587)	4800.00	2200.00
COMMON CARD (1-370)	3.00	1.35
COMMON CARD (371-446)	4.00	1.80
COMMON CARD (447-522)	7.00	3.10
COMMON CARD (523-589)	30.00	13.50
NOT ISSUED (587/588)		
WRAPPER (1-CENT)	200.00	90.00
WRAP.(1-CENT, REPEAT)	100.00	45.00
WRAPPER (5-CENT)	40.00	18.00

☐ 1 Dick Groat 30.00 6.00
☐ 2 Roger Maris 175.00 80.00
☐ 3 John Buzhardt 3.00 1.35
☐ 4 Lenny Green 3.00 1.35

❑ 5 John Romano 3.00 1.35
❑ 6 Ed Roebuck 3.00 1.35
❑ 7 White Sox Team 8.00 3.60
❑ 8 Dick Williams 6.00 2.70
❑ 9 Bob Purkey 3.00 1.35
❑ 10 Brooks Robinson 50.00 22.00
❑ 11 Curt Simmons 6.00 2.70
❑ 12 Moe Thacker 3.00 1.35
❑ 13 Chuck Cottier 3.00 1.35
❑ 14 Don Mossi 6.00 2.70
❑ 15 Willie Kirkland 3.00 1.35
❑ 16 Billy Muffett 3.00 1.35
❑ 17 Checklist 1 10.00 2.00
❑ 18 Jim Grant 6.00 2.70
❑ 19 Clete Boyer 8.00 3.60
❑ 20 Robin Roberts 15.00 6.75
❑ 21 Zorro Versalles 8.00 3.60
UER RC
First name should
be Zoilo
❑ 22 Clem Labine 6.00 2.70
❑ 23 Don Demeter 3.00 1.35
❑ 24 Ken Johnson 6.00 2.70
❑ 25 Reds' Heavy Artillery 8.00 3.60
Vada Pinson
Gus Bell
Frank Robinson
❑ 26 Wes Stock 3.00 1.35
❑ 27 Jerry Kindall 3.00 1.35
❑ 28 Hector Lopez 6.00 2.70
❑ 29 Don Nottebart 3.00 1.35
❑ 30 Nellie Fox 15.00 6.75
❑ 31 Bob Schmidt 3.00 1.35
❑ 32 Ray Sadecki 3.00 1.35
❑ 33 Gary Geiger 3.00 1.35
❑ 34 Wynn Hawkins 3.00 1.35
❑ 35 Ron Santo RC 40.00 18.00
❑ 36 Jack Kralick 3.00 1.35
❑ 37 Charley Maxwell 6.00 2.70
❑ 38 Bob Lillis 3.00 1.35
❑ 39 Leo Posada 3.00 1.35
❑ 40 Bob Turley 6.00 2.70
❑ 41 NL Batting Leaders 35.00 16.00
Dick Groat
Norm Larker
Willie Mays
Roberto Clemente
❑ 42 AL Batting Leaders 8.00 3.60
Pete Runnels
Al Smith
Minnie Minoso
Bill Skowron
❑ 43 NL Home Run Leaders 30.00 13.50
Ernie Banks
Hank Aaron
Ed Mathews
Ken Boyer
❑ 44 AL Home Run Leaders 80.00 36.00
Mickey Mantle
Roger Maris
Jim Lemon
Rocky Colavito
❑ 45 NL ERA Leaders 8.00 3.60
Mike McCormick
Ernie Broglio
Don Drysdale
Bob Friend
Stan Williams
❑ 46 AL ERA Leaders 8.00 3.60
Frank Baumann
Jim Bunning
Art Ditmar
Hal Brown
❑ 47 NL Pitching Leaders 8.00 3.60
Ernie Broglio
Warren Spahn
Vern Law
Lou Burdette
❑ 48 AL Pitching Leaders 8.00 3.60
Chuck Estrada
Jim Perry UER
(Listed as an Oriole)
Bud Daley
Art Ditmar
Frank Lary
Milt Pappas
❑ 49 NL Strikeout Leaders 20.00 9.00
Don Drysdale
Sandy Koufax
Sam Jones
Ernie Broglio
❑ 50 AL Strikeout Leaders 8.00 3.60
Jim Bunning
Pedro Ramos
Early Wynn
Frank Lary
❑ 51 Detroit Tigers 8.00 3.60
Team Card
❑ 52 George Crowe 3.00 1.35
❑ 53 Russ Nixon 3.00 1.35
❑ 54 Earl Francis 3.00 1.35
❑ 55 Jim Davenport 6.00 2.70
❑ 56 Russ Kemmerer 3.00 1.35
❑ 57 Marv Throneberry 6.00 2.70
❑ 58 Joe Schaffernoth 3.00 1.35
❑ 59 Jim Woods 3.00 1.35
❑ 60 Woody Held 3.00 1.35
❑ 61 Ron Piche 3.00 1.35
❑ 62 Al Pilarcik 3.00 1.35
❑ 63 Jim Kaat 8.00 3.60
❑ 64 Alex Grammas 3.00 1.35
❑ 65 Ted Kluszewski 8.00 3.60
❑ 66 Bill Henry 3.00 1.35
❑ 67 Ossie Virgil 3.00 1.35
❑ 68 Deron Johnson 6.00 2.70
❑ 69 Earl Wilson 6.00 2.70
❑ 70 Bill Virdon 6.00 2.70
❑ 71 Jerry Adair 3.00 1.35
❑ 72 Stu Miller 6.00 2.70
❑ 73 Al Spangler 3.00 1.35
❑ 74 Joe Pignatano 3.00 1.35
❑ 75 Lindy Shows Larry 6.00 2.70
Lindy McDaniel
Larry Jackson
❑ 76 Harry Anderson 3.00 1.35
❑ 77 Dick Stigman 3.00 1.35
❑ 78 Lee Walls 6.00 2.70
❑ 79 Joe Ginsberg 3.00 1.35
❑ 80 Harmon Killebrew 20.00 9.00
❑ 81 Tracy Stallard 3.00 1.35
❑ 82 Joe Christopher 3.00 1.35
❑ 83 Bob Bruce 3.00 1.35
❑ 84 Lee Maye 3.00 1.35
❑ 85 Jerry Walker 3.00 1.35
❑ 86 Los Angeles Dodgers 8.00 3.60
Team Card
❑ 87 Joe Amalfitano 3.00 1.35
❑ 88 Richie Ashburn 15.00 6.75
❑ 89 Billy Martin 15.00 6.75
❑ 90 Gerry Staley 3.00 1.35
❑ 91 Walt Moryn 3.00 1.35
❑ 92 Hal Naragon 3.00 1.35
❑ 93 Tony Gonzalez 3.00 1.35
❑ 94 Johnny Kucks 3.00 1.35
❑ 95 Norm Cash 8.00 3.60
❑ 96 Billy O'Dell 3.00 1.35
❑ 97 Jerry Lynch 6.00 2.70
❑ 98A Checklist 2 10.00 2.00
(Red "Checklist"
98 black on white)
❑ 98B Checklist 2 10.00 2.00
(Yellow "Checklist"
98 black on white)
❑ 98C Checklist 2 10.00 2.00
(Yellow "Checklist"
98 white on black
no copyright)
❑ 99 Don Buddin UER 3.00 1.35
(66 HR's)
❑ 100 Harvey Haddix 6.00 2.70
❑ 101 Bubba Phillips 3.00 1.35
❑ 102 Gene Stephens 3.00 1.35
❑ 103 Ruben Amaro 3.00 1.35
❑ 104 John Blanchard 8.00 3.60
❑ 105 Carl Willey 3.00 1.35
❑ 106 Whitey Herzog 3.00 1.35
❑ 107 Seth Morehead 3.00 1.35
❑ 108 Dan Dobbek 3.00 1.35
❑ 109 Johnny Podres 8.00 3.60
❑ 110 Vada Pinson 8.00 3.60
❑ 111 Jack Meyer 3.00 1.35
❑ 112 Chico Fernandez 3.00 1.35
❑ 113 Mike Fornieles 3.00 1.35
❑ 114 Hobie Landrith 3.00 1.35
❑ 115 Johnny Antonelli 6.00 2.70
❑ 116 Joe DeMaestri 3.00 1.35
❑ 117 Dale Long 6.00 2.70
❑ 118 Chris Cannizzaro 3.00 1.35
❑ 119 A's Big Armor 6.00 2.70
Norm Siebern
Hank Bauer
Jerry Lumpe
❑ 120 Eddie Mathews 30.00 13.50
❑ 121 Eli Grba 6.00 2.70
❑ 122 Chicago Cubs 8.00 3.60
Team Card
❑ 123 Billy Gardner 3.00 1.35
❑ 124 J.C. Martin 3.00 1.35
❑ 125 Steve Barber 3.00 1.35
❑ 126 Dick Stuart 6.00 2.70
❑ 127 Ron Kline 3.00 1.35
❑ 128 Rip Repulski 3.00 1.35
❑ 129 Ed Hobaugh 3.00 1.35
❑ 130 Norm Larker 3.00 1.35
❑ 131 Paul Richards MG 6.00 2.70
❑ 132 Al Lopez MG 8.00 3.60
❑ 133 Ralph Houk MG 6.00 2.70
❑ 134 Mickey Vernon MG 6.00 2.70
❑ 135 Fred Hutchinson MG 6.00 2.70
❑ 136 Walter Alston MG 8.00 3.60
❑ 137 Chuck Dressen MG 6.00 2.70
❑ 138 Danny Murtaugh MG 6.00 2.70
❑ 139 Solly Hemus MG 6.00 2.70
❑ 140 Gus Triandos 6.00 2.70
❑ 141 Billy Williams RC 60.00 27.00
❑ 142 Luis Arroyo 6.00 2.70
❑ 143 Russ Snyder 3.00 1.35
❑ 144 Jim Coker 3.00 1.35
❑ 145 Bob Buhl 6.00 2.70
❑ 146 Marty Keough 3.00 1.35
❑ 147 Ed Rakow 3.00 1.35
❑ 148 Julian Javier 6.00 2.70
❑ 149 Bob Oldis 3.00 1.35
❑ 150 Willie Mays 100.00 45.00
❑ 151 Jim Donohue 3.00 1.35
❑ 152 Earl Torgeson 3.00 1.35
❑ 153 Don Lee 3.00 1.35
❑ 154 Bobby Del Greco 3.00 1.35
❑ 155 Johnny Temple 6.00 2.70
❑ 156 Ken Hunt 6.00 2.70
❑ 157 Cal McLish 3.00 1.35
❑ 158 Pete Daley 3.00 1.35
❑ 159 Orioles Team 8.00 3.60
❑ 160 Whitey Ford UER 50.00 22.00
Incorrectly listed
as 5'0" tall
❑ 161 Sherman Jones UER 3.00 1.35
(Photo actually
Eddie Fisher)
❑ 162 Jay Hook 3.00 1.35
❑ 163 Ed Sadowski 3.00 1.35
❑ 164 Felix Mantilla 3.00 1.35
❑ 165 Gino Cimoli 3.00 1.35
❑ 166 Danny Kravitz 3.00 1.35
❑ 167 San Francisco Giants 8.00 3.60
Team Card
❑ 168 Tommy Davis 8.00 3.60
❑ 169 Don Elston 3.00 1.35
❑ 170 Al Smith 3.00 1.35

❑	171	Paul Foytack	3.00	1.35
❑	172	Don Dillard	3.00	1.35
❑	173	Beantown Bombers	6.00	2.70
		Frank Malzone		
		Vic Wertz		
		Jackie Jensen		
❑	174	Ray Semproch	3.00	1.35
❑	175	Gene Freese	3.00	1.35
❑	176	Ken Aspromonte	3.00	1.35
❑	177	Don Larsen	6.00	2.70
❑	178	Bob Nieman	3.00	1.35
❑	179	Joe Koppe	3.00	1.35
❑	180	Bobby Richardson	12.00	5.50
❑	181	Fred Green	3.00	1.35
❑	182	Dave Nicholson	3.00	1.35
❑	183	Andre Rodgers	3.00	1.35
❑	184	Steve Bilko	6.00	2.70
❑	185	Herb Score	6.00	2.70
❑	186	Elmer Valo	6.00	2.70
❑	187	Billy Klaus	3.00	1.35
❑	188	Jim Marshall	3.00	1.35
❑	189A	Checklist 3	10.00	2.00
		(Copyright symbol almost adjacent to 263 Ken Hamlin)		
❑	189B	Checklist 3	10.00	2.00
		(Copyright symbol adjacent to 264 Glen Hobbie)		
❑	190	Stan Williams	6.00	2.70
❑	191	Mike de la Hoz	3.00	1.35
❑	192	Dick Brown	3.00	1.35
❑	193	Gene Conley	6.00	2.70
❑	194	Gordy Coleman	6.00	2.70
❑	195	Jerry Casale	3.00	1.35
❑	196	Ed Bouchee	3.00	1.35
❑	197	Dick Hall	3.00	1.35
❑	198	Carl Sawatski	3.00	1.35
❑	199	Bob Boyd	3.00	1.35
❑	200	Warren Spahn	40.00	18.00
❑	201	Pete Whisenant	3.00	1.35
❑	202	Al Neiger	3.00	1.35
❑	203	Eddie Bressoud	3.00	1.35
❑	204	Bob Skinner	6.00	2.70
❑	205	Billy Pierce	6.00	2.70
❑	206	Gene Green	3.00	1.35
❑	207	Dodger Southpaws	30.00	13.50
		Sandy Koufax		
		Johnny Podres		
❑	208	Larry Osborne	3.00	1.35
❑	209	Ken McBride	3.00	1.35
❑	210	Pete Runnels	6.00	2.70
❑	211	Bob Gibson	40.00	18.00
❑	212	Haywood Sullivan	6.00	2.70
❑	213	Bill Stafford	3.00	1.35
❑	214	Danny Murphy	6.00	2.70
❑	215	Gus Bell	6.00	2.70
❑	216	Ted Bowsfield	3.00	1.35
❑	217	Mel Roach	3.00	1.35
❑	218	Hal Brown	3.00	1.35
❑	219	Gene Mauch MG	6.00	2.70
❑	220	Alvin Dark MG	6.00	2.70
❑	221	Mike Higgins MG	3.00	1.35
❑	222	Jimmy Dykes MG	6.00	2.70
❑	223	Bob Scheffing MG	3.00	1.35
❑	224	Joe Gordon MG	6.00	2.70
❑	225	Bill Rigney MG	6.00	2.70
❑	226	Cookie Lavagetto MG	6.00	2.70
❑	227	Juan Pizarro	3.00	1.35
❑	228	New York Yankees	60.00	27.00
		Team Card		
❑	229	Rudy Hernandez	3.00	1.35
❑	230	Don Hoak	6.00	2.70
❑	231	Dick Drott	3.00	1.35
❑	232	Bill White	6.00	2.70
❑	233	Joey Jay	6.00	2.70
❑	234	Ted Lepcio	3.00	1.35
❑	235	Camilo Pascual	6.00	2.70
❑	236	Don Gile	3.00	1.35
❑	237	Billy Loes	6.00	2.70
❑	238	Jim Gilliam	6.00	2.70
❑	239	Dave Sisler	3.00	1.35
❑	240	Ron Hansen	3.00	1.35
❑	241	Al Cicotte	3.00	1.35
❑	242	Hal Smith	3.00	1.35
❑	243	Frank Lary	6.00	2.70
❑	244	Chico Cardenas	6.00	2.70
❑	245	Joe Adcock	6.00	2.70
❑	246	Bob Davis	3.00	1.35
❑	247	Billy Goodman	6.00	2.70
❑	248	Ed Keegan	3.00	1.35
❑	249	Cincinnati Reds	8.00	3.60
		Team Card		
❑	250	Buc Hill Aces	6.00	2.70
		Vern Law		
		Roy Face		
❑	251	Bill Bruton	3.00	1.35
❑	252	Bill Short	3.00	1.35
❑	253	Sammy Taylor	3.00	1.35
❑	254	Ted Sadowski	6.00	2.70
❑	255	Vic Power	6.00	2.70
❑	256	Billy Hoeft	3.00	1.35
❑	257	Carroll Hardy	3.00	1.35
❑	258	Jack Sanford	6.00	2.70
❑	259	John Schaive	3.00	1.35
❑	260	Don Drysdale	30.00	13.50
❑	261	Charlie Lau	6.00	2.70
❑	262	Tony Curry	3.00	1.35
❑	263	Ken Hamlin	3.00	1.35
❑	264	Glen Hobbie	3.00	1.35
❑	265	Tony Kubek	12.00	5.50
❑	266	Lindy McDaniel	6.00	2.70
❑	267	Norm Siebern	3.00	1.35
❑	268	Ike Delock	3.00	1.35
❑	269	Harry Chiti	3.00	1.35
❑	270	Bob Friend	6.00	2.70
❑	271	Jim Landis	3.00	1.35
❑	272	Tom Morgan	3.00	1.35
❑	273A	Checklist 4	16.00	3.20
		(Copyright symbol adjacent to 336 Don Mincher)		
❑	273B	Checklist 4	10.00	2.00
		(Copyright symbol adjacent to 339 Gene Baker)		
❑	274	Gary Bell	3.00	1.35
❑	275	Gene Woodling	6.00	2.70
❑	276	Ray Rippelmeyer	3.00	1.35
❑	277	Hank Foiles	3.00	1.35
❑	278	Don McMahon	3.00	1.35
❑	279	Jose Pagan	3.00	1.35
❑	280	Frank Howard	8.00	3.60
❑	281	Frank Sullivan	3.00	1.35
❑	282	Faye Throneberry	3.00	1.35
❑	283	Bob Anderson	3.00	1.35
❑	284	Dick Gernert	3.00	1.35
❑	285	Sherm Lollar	6.00	2.70
❑	286	George Witt	3.00	1.35
❑	287	Carl Yastrzemski	50.00	22.00
❑	288	Albie Pearson	6.00	2.70
❑	289	Ray Moore	3.00	1.35
❑	290	Stan Musial	100.00	45.00
❑	291	Tex Clevenger	3.00	1.35
❑	292	Jim Baumer	3.00	1.35
❑	293	Tom Sturdivant	3.00	1.35
❑	294	Don Blasingame	3.00	1.35
❑	295	Milt Pappas	6.00	2.70
❑	296	Wes Covington	6.00	2.70
❑	297	Athletics Team	8.00	3.60
❑	298	Jim Golden	3.00	1.35
❑	299	Clay Dalrymple	3.00	1.35
❑	300	Mickey Mantle	400.00	180.00
❑	301	Chet Nichols	3.00	1.35
❑	302	Al Heist	3.00	1.35
❑	303	Gary Peters	6.00	2.70
❑	304	Rocky Nelson	3.00	1.35
❑	305	Mike McCormick	6.00	2.70
❑	306	Bill Virdon WS	9.00	4.00
❑	307	Mickey Mantle WS	80.00	36.00
❑	308	B.Richardson WS	12.00	5.50
❑	309	Gino Cimoli WS	9.00	4.00
❑	310	Roy Face WS	9.00	4.00
❑	311	Whitey Ford WS	16.00	7.25
❑	312	Bill Mazeroski WS	20.00	9.00
		Mazeroski Homer Wins it		
❑	313	WS Summary	16.00	7.25
		Pirates Celebrate		
❑	314	Bob Miller	3.00	1.35
❑	315	Earl Battey	6.00	2.70
❑	316	Bobby Gene Smith	3.00	1.35
❑	317	Jim Brewer	3.00	1.35
❑	318	Danny O'Connell	3.00	1.35
❑	319	Valmy Thomas	3.00	1.35
❑	320	Lou Burdette	6.00	2.70
❑	321	Marv Breeding	3.00	1.35
❑	322	Bill Kunkel	6.00	2.70
❑	323	Sammy Esposito	3.00	1.35
❑	324	Hank Aguirre	3.00	1.35
❑	325	Wally Moon	6.00	2.70
❑	326	Dave Hillman	3.00	1.35
❑	327	Matty Alou RC	12.00	5.50
❑	328	Jim O'Toole	6.00	2.70
❑	329	Julio Becquer	3.00	1.35
❑	330	Rocky Colavito	20.00	9.00
❑	331	Ned Garver	3.00	1.35
❑	332	Dutch Dotterer UER	3.00	1.35
		(Photo actually Tommy Dotterer Dutch's brother)		
❑	333	Fritz Brickell	3.00	1.35
❑	334	Walt Bond	3.00	1.35
❑	335	Frank Bolling	3.00	1.35
❑	336	Don Mincher	6.00	2.70
❑	337	Al's Aces	8.00	3.60
		Early Wynn		
		Al Lopez		
		Herb Score		
❑	338	Don Landrum	3.00	1.35
❑	339	Gene Baker	3.00	1.35
❑	340	Vic Wertz	6.00	2.70
❑	341	Jim Owens	3.00	1.35
❑	342	Clint Courtney	3.00	1.35
❑	343	Earl Robinson	3.00	1.35
❑	344	Sandy Koufax	100.00	45.00
❑	345	Jimmy Piersall	8.00	3.60
❑	346	Howie Nunn	3.00	1.35
❑	347	St. Louis Cardinals	8.00	3.60
		Team Card		
❑	348	Steve Boros	3.00	1.35
❑	349	Danny McDevitt	3.00	1.35
❑	350	Ernie Banks	40.00	18.00
❑	351	Jim King	3.00	1.35
❑	352	Bob Shaw	3.00	1.35
❑	353	Howie Bedell	3.00	1.35
❑	354	Billy Harrell	6.00	2.70
❑	355	Bob Allison	8.00	3.60
❑	356	Ryne Duren	3.00	1.35
❑	357	Daryl Spencer	3.00	1.35
❑	358	Earl Averill	6.00	2.70
❑	359	Dallas Green	3.00	1.35
❑	360	Frank Robinson	40.00	18.00
❑	361A	Checklist 5	16.00	3.20
		(No ad on back)		
❑	361B	Checklist 5	16.00	3.20
		(Special Feature ad on back)		
❑	362	Frank Funk	3.00	1.35
❑	363	John Roseboro	6.00	2.70
❑	364	Moe Drabowsky	6.00	2.70
❑	365	Jerry Lumpe	3.00	1.35
❑	366	Eddie Fisher	3.00	1.35
❑	367	Jim Rivera	3.00	1.35
❑	368	Bennie Daniels	3.00	1.35
❑	369	Dave Philley	3.00	1.35
❑	370	Roy Face	6.00	2.70
❑	371	Bill Skowron SP	50.00	22.00
❑	372	Bob Hendley	4.00	1.80
❑	373	Boston Red Sox	8.00	3.60
		Team Card		
❑	374	Paul Giel	4.00	1.80
❑	375	Ken Boyer	12.00	5.50
❑	376	Mike Roarke RC	6.00	2.70
❑	377	Ruben Gomez	4.00	1.80
❑	378	Wally Post	6.00	2.70
❑	379	Bobby Shantz	4.00	1.80
❑	380	Minnie Minoso	8.00	3.60
❑	381	Dave Wickersham	4.00	1.80
❑	382	Frank Thomas	6.00	2.70
❑	383	Frisco First Liners	6.00	2.70
		Mike McCormick		
		Jack Sanford		
		Billy O'Dell		
❑	384	Chuck Essegian	4.00	1.80
❑	385	Jim Perry	6.00	2.70
❑	386	Joe Hicks	4.00	1.80
❑	387	Duke Maas	4.00	1.80
❑	388	Roberto Clemente	135.00	60.00

- ❑ 389 Ralph Terry 6.00 2.70
- ❑ 390 Del Crandall 8.00 3.60
- ❑ 391 Winston Brown 4.00 1.80
- ❑ 392 Reno Bertoia 4.00 1.80
- ❑ 393 Batter Bafflers 4.00 1.80
  Don Cardwell
  Glen Hobbie
- ❑ 394 Ken Walters 4.00 1.80
- ❑ 395 Chuck Estrada 6.00 2.70
- ❑ 396 Bob Aspromonte 4.00 1.80
- ❑ 397 Hal Woodeshick 4.00 1.80
- ❑ 398 Hank Bauer 6.00 2.70
- ❑ 399 Cliff Cook 4.00 1.80
- ❑ 400 Vern Law 6.00 2.70
- ❑ 401 Babe Ruth HL 60.00 27.00
  60th HR
- ❑ 402 Don Larsen HL SP 25.00 11.00
  WS Perfect Game
- ❑ 403 Joe Oeschger HL 7.00 3.10
  Leon Cadore
  26 Inning Tie
- ❑ 404 Rogers Hornsby HL.... 12.00 5.50
  .424 Season BA
- ❑ 405 Lou Gehrig HL........ 75.00 34.00
  Consecutive Game Streak
- ❑ 406 Mickey Mantle HL 100.00 45.00
  565 foot HR
- ❑ 407 Jack Chesbro HL........ 7.00 3.10
  41 victories
- ❑ 408 C. Mathewson HL SP 20.00 9.00
  267 Strikeouts
- ❑ 409 Walter Johnson SL 12.00 5.50
  3 Shutouts in 4 days
- ❑ 410 Harvey Haddix HL........ 7.00 3.10
  12 Perfect Innings
- ❑ 411 Tony Taylor 6.00 2.70
- ❑ 412 Larry Sherry 6.00 2.70
- ❑ 413 Eddie Yost 6.00 2.70
- ❑ 414 Dick Donovan 6.00 2.70
- ❑ 415 Hank Aaron 100.00 45.00
- ❑ 416 Dick Howser RC 8.00 3.60
- ❑ 417 Juan Marichal SP RC 100.00 45.00
- ❑ 418 Ed Bailey 6.00 2.70
- ❑ 419 Tom Borland 4.00 1.80
- ❑ 420 Ernie Broglio 6.00 2.70
- ❑ 421 Ty Cline SP 18.00 8.00
- ❑ 422 Bud Daley 4.00 1.80
- ❑ 423 Charlie Neal SP........ 18.00 8.00
- ❑ 424 Turk Lown 4.00 1.80
- ❑ 425 Yogi Berra 80.00 36.00
- ❑ 426 Milwaukee Braves...... 12.00 5.50
  Team Card
  (Back numbered 463)
- ❑ 427 Dick Ellsworth 6.00 2.70
- ❑ 428 Ray Barker SP 18.00 8.00
- ❑ 429 Al Kaline 50.00 22.00
- ❑ 430 Bill Mazeroski SP 50.00 22.00
- ❑ 431 Chuck Stobbs 4.00 1.80
- ❑ 432 Coot Veal 6.00 2.70
- ❑ 433 Art Mahaffey 4.00 1.80
- ❑ 434 Tom Brewer 4.00 1.80
- ❑ 435 Orlando Cepeda UER 12.00 5.50
  (San Francis on
  card front)
- ❑ 436 Jim Maloney SP RC .. 20.00 9.00
- ❑ 437A Checklist 6 .... 16.00 3.20
  440 Louis Aparicio
- ❑ 437B Checklist 6 .... 16.00 3.20
  440 Luis Aparicio
- ❑ 438 Curt Flood 8.00 3.60
- ❑ 439 Phil Regan RC 6.00 2.70
- ❑ 440 Luis Aparicio 12.00 5.50
- ❑ 441 Dick Bertell 4.00 1.80
- ❑ 442 Gordon Jones 4.00 1.80
- ❑ 443 Duke Snider 40.00 18.00
- ❑ 444 Joe Nuxhall 6.00 2.70
- ❑ 445 Frank Malzone 6.00 2.70
- ❑ 446 Bob Taylor 4.00 1.80
- ❑ 447 Harry Bright 7.00 3.10
- ❑ 448 Del Rice 15.00 6.75
- ❑ 449 Bob Bolin 7.00 3.10
- ❑ 450 Jim Lemon 7.00 3.10
- ❑ 451 Power for Ernie 7.00 3.10
  Daryl Spencer
  Bill White
  Ernie Broglio
- ❑ 452 Bob Allen 7.00 3.10
- ❑ 453 Dick Schofield 7.00 3.10
- ❑ 454 Pumpsie Green 7.00 3.10
- ❑ 455 Early Wynn 15.00 6.75
- ❑ 456 Hal Bevan 7.00 3.10
- ❑ 457 Johnny James 7.00 3.10
  (Listed as Angel,
  but wearing Yankee
  uniform and cap)
- ❑ 458 Willie Tasby 7.00 3.10
- ❑ 459 Terry Fox 10.00 4.50
- ❑ 460 Gil Hodges 25.00 11.00
- ❑ 461 Smoky Burgess 15.00 6.75
- ❑ 462 Lou Klimchock 7.00 3.10
- ❑ 463 Jack Fisher 7.00 3.10
  (See also 426)
- ❑ 464 Lee Thomas RC 10.00 4.50
  (Pictured with Yankee
  cap but listed as
  Los Angeles Angel)
- ❑ 465 Roy McMillan 15.00 6.75
- ❑ 466 Ron Moeller 7.00 3.10
- ❑ 467 Cleveland Indians 12.00 5.50
  Team Card
- ❑ 468 John Callison 10.00 4.50
- ❑ 469 Ralph Lumenti 7.00 3.10
- ❑ 470 Roy Sievers 10.00 4.50
- ❑ 471 Phil Rizzuto MVP 25.00 11.00
- ❑ 472 Yogi Berra MVP 50.00 22.00
- ❑ 473 Bob Shantz MVP 8.00 3.60
- ❑ 474 Al Rosen MVP 10.00 4.50
- ❑ 475 Mickey Mantle MVP 175.00 80.00
- ❑ 476 Jackie Jensen MVP.... 10.00 4.50
- ❑ 477 Nellie Fox MVP 15.00 6.75
- ❑ 478 Roger Maris MVP 60.00 27.00
- ❑ 479 Jim Konstanty MVP...... 8.00 3.60
- ❑ 480 Roy Campanella MVP 40.00 18.00
- ❑ 481 Hank Sauer MVP 8.00 3.60
- ❑ 482 Willie Mays MVP 50.00 22.00
- ❑ 483 Don Newcombe MVP 10.00 4.50
- ❑ 484 Hank Aaron MVP 50.00 22.00
- ❑ 485 Ernie Banks MVP 40.00 18.00
- ❑ 486 Dick Groat MVP 10.00 4.50
- ❑ 487 Gene Oliver 7.00 3.10
- ❑ 488 Joe McClain 10.00 4.50
- ❑ 489 Walt Dropo 7.00 3.10
- ❑ 490 Jim Bunning 25.00 11.00
- ❑ 491 Philadelphia Phillies .. 12.00 5.50
  Team Card
- ❑ 492 Ron Fairly 10.00 4.50
- ❑ 493 Don Zimmer UER 10.00 4.50
  (Brooklyn A.L.)
- ❑ 494 Tom Cheney 15.00 6.75
- ❑ 495 Elston Howard 10.00 4.50
- ❑ 496 Ken MacKenzie 7.00 3.10
- ❑ 497 Willie Jones 7.00 3.10
- ❑ 498 Ray Herbert 7.00 3.10
- ❑ 499 Chuck Schilling 7.00 3.10
- ❑ 500 Harvey Kuenn 10.00 4.50
- ❑ 501 John DeMerit 7.00 3.10
- ❑ 502 Clarence Coleman RC 10.00 4.50
- ❑ 503 Tito Francona 7.00 3.10
- ❑ 504 Billy Consolo 7.00 3.10
- ❑ 505 Red Schoendienst...... 15.00 6.75
- ❑ 506 Willie Davis RC 15.00 6.75
- ❑ 507 Pete Burnside 7.00 3.10
- ❑ 508 Rocky Bridges 7.00 3.10
- ❑ 509 Camilo Carreon 7.00 3.10
- ❑ 510 Art Ditmar 7.00 3.10
- ❑ 511 Joe M. Morgan 7.00 3.10
- ❑ 512 Bob Will 7.00 3.10
- ❑ 513 Jim Brosnan 7.00 3.10
- ❑ 514 Jake Wood 7.00 3.10
- ❑ 515 Jackie Brandt 7.00 3.10
- ❑ 516 Checklist 7 .... 16.00 3.20
- ❑ 517 Willie McCovey 40.00 18.00
- ❑ 518 Andy Carey 7.00 3.10
- ❑ 519 Jim Pagliaroni 7.00 3.10
- ❑ 520 Joe Cunningham 7.00 3.10
- ❑ 521 Brother Battery 7.00 3.10
  Norm Sherry
  Larry Sherry
- ❑ 522 Dick Farrell UER 15.00 6.75
  (Phillies cap but
  listed on Dodgers)
- ❑ 523 Joe Gibbon 30.00 13.50
- ❑ 524 Johnny Logan 30.00 13.50
- ❑ 525 Ron Perranoski RC 60.00 27.00
- ❑ 526 R.C. Stevens 30.00 13.50
- ❑ 527 Gene Leek 30.00 13.50
- ❑ 528 Pedro Ramos 30.00 13.50
- ❑ 529 Bob Roselli 30.00 13.50
- ❑ 530 Bob Malkmus 30.00 13.50
- ❑ 531 Jim Coates 50.00 22.00
- ❑ 532 Bob Hale 30.00 13.50
- ❑ 533 Jack Curtis 30.00 13.50
- ❑ 534 Eddie Kasko 40.00 18.00
- ❑ 535 Larry Jackson 30.00 13.50
- ❑ 536 Bill Tuttle 30.00 13.50
- ❑ 537 Bobby Locke 30.00 13.50
- ❑ 538 Chuck Hiller 30.00 13.50
- ❑ 539 Johnny Klippstein 30.00 13.50
- ❑ 540 Jackie Jensen 40.00 18.00
- ❑ 541 Roland Sheldon RC .. 40.00 18.00
- ❑ 542 Minnesota Twins 60.00 27.00
  Team Card
- ❑ 543 Roger Craig 40.00 18.00
- ❑ 544 George Thomas 50.00 22.00
- ❑ 545 Hoyt Wilhelm 50.00 22.00
- ❑ 546 Marty Kutyna 30.00 13.50
- ❑ 547 Leon Wagner 30.00 13.50
- ❑ 548 Ted Wills 30.00 13.50
- ❑ 549 Hal R. Smith 30.00 13.50
- ❑ 550 Frank Baumann 30.00 13.50
- ❑ 551 George Altman 30.00 13.50
- ❑ 552 Jim Archer 30.00 13.50
- ❑ 553 Bill Fischer 30.00 13.50
- ❑ 554 Pittsburgh Pirates 70.00 32.00
  Team Card
- ❑ 555 Sam Jones 30.00 13.50
- ❑ 556 Ken R. Hunt 30.00 13.50
- ❑ 557 Jose Valdivielso 30.00 13.50
- ❑ 558 Don Ferrarese 30.00 13.50
- ❑ 559 Jim Gentile 60.00 27.00
- ❑ 560 Barry Latman 40.00 18.00
- ❑ 561 Charley James 30.00 13.50
- ❑ 562 Bill Monbouquette 30.00 13.50
- ❑ 563 Bob Cerv 60.00 27.00
- ❑ 564 Don Cardwell 30.00 13.50
- ❑ 565 Felipe Alou 50.00 22.00
- ❑ 566 Paul Richards AS MG 30.00 13.50
- ❑ 567 D.Murtaugh AS MG.... 30.00 13.50
- ❑ 568 Bill Skowron AS........ 50.00 22.00
- ❑ 569 Frank Herrera AS 40.00 18.00
- ❑ 570 Nellie Fox AS 60.00 27.00
- ❑ 571 Bill Mazeroski AS 50.00 22.00
- ❑ 572 Brooks Robinson AS.. 80.00 36.00
- ❑ 573 Ken Boyer AS 50.00 22.00
- ❑ 574 Luis Aparicio AS 60.00 27.00
- ❑ 575 Ernie Banks AS........ 80.00 36.00
- ❑ 576 Roger Maris AS........ 175.00 80.00
- ❑ 577 Hank Aaron AS 150.00 70.00
- ❑ 578 Mickey Mantle AS 400.00 180.00
- ❑ 579 Willie Mays AS 150.00 70.00
- ❑ 580 Al Kaline AS 80.00 36.00
- ❑ 581 Frank Robinson AS.... 80.00 36.00
- ❑ 582 Earl Battey AS........ 30.00 13.50
- ❑ 583 Del Crandall AS........ 30.00 13.50
- ❑ 584 Jim Perry AS 30.00 13.50
- ❑ 585 Bob Friend AS........ 30.00 13.50
- ❑ 586 Whitey Ford AS........ 100.00 45.00
- ❑ 589 Warren Spahn AS.... 100.00 30.00

1962 Topps

	NRMT	VG-E
COMP. MASTER SET (689)	10000.00	5000.00
COMPLETE SET (598)	4600.00	2100.00
COMMON CARD (1-370)	5.00	2.20
COMMON CARD (371-446)	6.00	2.70
COMMON CARD (447-522)	12.00	5.50
COMMON CARD (523-598)	20.00	9.00
WRAPPER (1-CENT)	100.00	45.00
WRAPPER (5-CENT)	30.00	13.50
❑ 1 Roger Maris	300.00	75.00
❑ 2 Jim Brosnan	5.00	2.20
❑ 3 Pete Runnels	5.00	2.20
❑ 4 John DeMerit	8.00	3.60
❑ 5 Sandy Koufax UER	135.00	60.00
Struck ou 18		
❑ 6 Marv Breeding	5.00	2.20
❑ 7 Frank Thomas	10.00	4.50
❑ 8 Ray Herbert	5.00	2.20
❑ 9 Jim Davenport	8.00	3.60
❑ 10 Roberto Clemente	175.00	80.00
❑ 11 Tom Morgan	5.00	2.20
❑ 12 Harry Craft MG	8.00	3.60
❑ 13 Dick Howser	8.00	3.60
❑ 14 Bill White	8.00	3.60
❑ 15 Dick Donovan	5.00	2.20
❑ 16 Darrell Johnson	5.00	2.20
❑ 17 Johnny Callison	8.00	3.60
❑ 18 Managers' Dream	175.00	80.00
Mickey Mantle		
Willie Mays		
❑ 19 Ray Washburn	5.00	2.20
❑ 20 Rocky Colavito	15.00	6.75
❑ 21 Jim Kaat	8.00	3.60
❑ 22A Checklist 1 ERR	12.00	2.40
(121-176 on back)		
❑ 22B Checklist 1 COR	12.00	2.40
❑ 23 Norm Larker	5.00	2.20
❑ 24 Tigers Team	10.00	4.50
❑ 25 Ernie Banks	50.00	22.00
❑ 26 Chris Cannizzaro	8.00	3.60
❑ 27 Chuck Cottier	5.00	2.20
❑ 28 Minnie Minoso	10.00	4.50
❑ 29 Casey Stengel MG	20.00	9.00
❑ 30 Eddie Mathews	40.00	18.00
❑ 31 Tom Tresh RC	15.00	6.75
❑ 32 John Roseboro	8.00	3.60
❑ 33 Don Larsen	8.00	3.60
❑ 34 Johnny Temple	8.00	3.60
❑ 35 Don Schwall	10.00	4.50
❑ 36 Don Leppert	5.00	2.20
❑ 37 Tribe Hill Trio	5.00	2.20
Barry Latman		
Dick Stigman		
Jim Perry		
❑ 38 Gene Stephens	5.00	2.20
❑ 39 Joe Koppe	5.00	2.20
❑ 40 Orlando Cepeda	15.00	6.75
❑ 41 Cliff Cook	5.00	2.20
❑ 42 Jim King	5.00	2.20
❑ 43 Los Angeles Dodgers	10.00	4.50
Team Card		
❑ 44 Don Taussig	5.00	2.20
❑ 45 Brooks Robinson	50.00	22.00
❑ 46 Jack Baldschun	5.00	2.20
❑ 47 Bob Will	5.00	2.20
❑ 48 Ralph Terry	8.00	3.60
❑ 49 Hal Jones	5.00	2.20
❑ 50 Stan Musial	100.00	45.00
❑ 51 AL Batting Leaders	8.00	3.60
Norm Cash		
Jim Piersall		
Al Kaline		
Elston Howard		
❑ 52 NL Batting Leaders	20.00	9.00
Roberto Clemente		
Vada Pinson		
Ken Boyer		
Wally Moon		
❑ 53 AL Home Run Leaders	100.00	45.00
Roger Maris		
Mickey Mantle		
Jim Gentile		
Harmon Killebrew		
❑ 54 NL Home Run Leaders	20.00	9.00
Orlando Cepeda		
Willie Mays		
Frank Robinson		
❑ 55 AL ERA Leaders	8.00	3.60
Dick Donovan		
Bill Stafford		
Don Mossi		
Milt Pappas		
❑ 56 NL ERA Leaders	8.00	3.60
Warren Spahn		
Jim O'Toole		
Curt Simmons		
Mike McCormick		
❑ 57 AL Wins Leaders	8.00	3.60
Whitey Ford		
Frank Lary		
Steve Barber		
Jim Bunning		
❑ 58 NL Wins Leaders	8.00	3.60
Warren Spahn		
Joe Jay		
Jim O'Toole		
❑ 59 AL Strikeout Leaders	8.00	3.60
Camilo Pascual		
Whitey Ford		
Jim Bunning		
Juan Pizzaro		
❑ 60 NL Strikeout Leaders	20.00	9.00
Sandy Koufax		
Stan Williams		
Don Drysdale		
Jim O'Toole		
❑ 61 Cardinals Team	10.00	4.50
❑ 62 Steve Boros	5.00	2.20
❑ 63 Tony Cloninger RC	8.00	3.60
❑ 64 Russ Snyder	5.00	2.20
❑ 65 Bobby Richardson	10.00	4.50
❑ 66 Cuno Barragan	5.00	2.20
❑ 67 Harvey Haddix	8.00	3.60
❑ 68 Ken Hunt	5.00	2.20
❑ 69 Phil Ortega	5.00	2.20
❑ 70 Harmon Killebrew	25.00	11.00
❑ 71 Dick LeMay	5.00	2.20
❑ 72 Bob's Pupils	5.00	2.20
Steve Boros		
Bob Scheffing MG		
Jake Wood		
❑ 73 Nellie Fox	20.00	9.00
❑ 74 Bob Lillis	8.00	3.60
❑ 75 Milt Pappas	8.00	3.60
❑ 76 Howie Bedell	5.00	2.20
❑ 77 Tony Taylor	8.00	3.60
❑ 78 Gene Green	5.00	2.20
❑ 79 Ed Hobaugh	5.00	2.20
❑ 80 Vada Pinson	8.00	3.60
❑ 81 Jim Pagliaroni	5.00	2.20
❑ 82 Deron Johnson	8.00	3.60
❑ 83 Larry Jackson	5.00	2.20
❑ 84 Lenny Green	5.00	2.20
❑ 85 Gil Hodges	20.00	9.00
❑ 86 Donn Clendenon RC	8.00	3.60
❑ 87 Mike Roarke	5.00	2.20
❑ 88 Ralph Houk MG	8.00	3.60
(Berra in background)		
❑ 89 Barney Schultz	5.00	2.20
❑ 90 Jimmy Piersall	8.00	3.60
❑ 91 J.C. Martin	5.00	2.20
❑ 92 Sam Jones	5.00	2.20
❑ 93 John Blanchard	8.00	3.60
❑ 94 Jay Hook	8.00	3.60
❑ 95 Don Hoak	8.00	3.60
❑ 96 Eli Grba	5.00	2.20
❑ 97 Tito Francona	5.00	2.20
❑ 98 Checklist 2	12.00	2.40
❑ 99 John (Boog) Powell RC	30.00	13.50
❑ 100 Warren Spahn	40.00	18.00
❑ 101 Carroll Hardy	5.00	2.20
❑ 102 Al Schroll	5.00	2.20
❑ 103 Don Blasingame	5.00	2.20
❑ 104 Ted Savage	5.00	2.20
❑ 105 Don Mossi	8.00	3.60
❑ 106 Carl Sawatski	5.00	2.20
❑ 107 Mike McCormick	8.00	3.60
❑ 108 Willie Davis	8.00	3.60
❑ 109 Bob Shaw	5.00	2.20
❑ 110 Bill Skowron	8.00	3.60
❑ 110A Bill Skowron	8.00	3.60
Green Tint		
❑ 111 Dallas Green	8.00	3.60
❑ 111A Dallas Green	8.00	3.60
Green Tint		
❑ 112 Hank Foiles	5.00	2.20
❑ 112A Hank Foiles	5.00	2.20
Green Tint		
❑ 113 Chicago White Sox	10.00	4.50
Team Card		
❑ 113A Chicago White Sox	10.00	4.50
Team Card		
Green Tint		
❑ 114 Howie Koplitz	5.00	2.20
❑ 114A Howie Koplitz	5.00	2.20
Green Tint		
❑ 115 Bob Skinner	8.00	3.60
❑ 115A Bob Skinner	8.00	3.60
Green Tint		
❑ 116 Herb Score	8.00	3.60
❑ 116A Herb Score	8.00	3.60
Green Tint		
❑ 117 Gary Geiger	8.00	3.60
❑ 117A Gary Geiger	8.00	3.60
Green Tint		
❑ 118 Julian Javier	8.00	3.60
❑ 118A Julian Javier	8.00	3.60
Green Tint		
❑ 119 Danny Murphy	5.00	2.20
❑ 119A Danny Murphy	5.00	2.20
Green Tint		
❑ 120 Bob Purkey	5.00	2.20
❑ 120A Bob Purkey	5.00	2.20
Green Tint		
❑ 121 Billy Hitchcock MG	5.00	2.20
❑ 121A Billy Hitchcock	5.00	2.20
Green Tint		
❑ 122 Norm Bass	5.00	2.20
❑ 122A Norm Bass	5.00	2.20
Green Tint		
❑ 123 Mike de la Hoz	5.00	2.20
❑ 123A Mike de la Hoz	5.00	2.20
Green Tint		
❑ 124 Bill Pleis	5.00	2.20
❑ 124A Bill Pleis	5.00	2.20
Green Tint		
❑ 125 Gene Woodling	8.00	3.60
❑ 125A Gene Woodling	8.00	3.60
Green Tint		
❑ 126 Al Cicotte	5.00	2.20
❑ 126A Al Cicotte	5.00	2.20
Green Tint		
❑ 127 Pride of A's	5.00	2.20
Norm Siebern		
Hank Bauer MG		
Jerry Lumpe		
❑ 127A Pride of A's	5.00	2.20
Norm Siebern		
Hank Bauer MG		
Jerry Lumpe		
Green Tint		
❑ 128 Art Fowler	5.00	2.20
❑ 128A Art Fowler	5.00	2.20
Green Tint		
❑ 129A Lee Walls	5.00	2.20
(Facing right)		
❑ 129B Lee Walls	30.00	13.50
(Facing left)		
❑ 130 Frank Bolling	5.00	2.20
❑ 130A Frank Bolling	5.00	2.20
Green Tint		
❑ 131 Pete Richert	5.00	2.20
❑ 131A Pete Richert	5.00	2.20
Green Tint		
❑ 132A Angels Team	10.00	4.50
(Without photo)		
❑ 132B Angels Team	30.00	13.50
(With photo)		
❑ 133 Felipe Alou	8.00	3.60
❑ 133A Felipe Alou	8.00	3.60
Green Tint		
❑ 134A Billy Hoeft	5.00	2.20
(Facing right)		
❑ 134B Billy Hoeft	30.00	13.50
(Facing straight)		
❑ 135 Babe Ruth Special 1	20.00	9.00
Babe as a Boy		

❑ 135A Babe Ruth Special .. 20.00 9.00
Base as a Boy
❑ 136 Babe Ruth Special 2 .. 20.00 9.00
Jacob Ruppert OWN
Babe Joins Yanks
❑ 136A Babe Ruth Special .. 20.00 9.00
Jacob Ruppert OWN
Babe Joins Yanks
Green Tint
❑ 137 Babe Ruth Special 3 .. 20.00 9.00
With Miller Huggins
❑ 137A Babe Ruth Special .. 20.00 9.00
With Miller Huggins
Green Tint
❑ 138 Babe Ruth Special 4 .. 20.00 9.00
Famous Slugger
❑ 138A Babe Ruth Special .. 20.00 9.00
Famous Slugger
Green Tint
❑ 139A Babe Ruth Special 5 30.00 13.50
Babe Hits 60
❑ 139B Hal Reniff PORT RC 15.00 6.75
❑ 139C Hal Reniff RC 65.00 29.00
Pitching
❑ 140 Babe Ruth Special 6 .. 60.00 27.00
With Lou Gehrig
❑ 140A Babe Ruth Special .. 60.00 27.00
Lou Gehrig
Green Tint
❑ 141 Babe Ruth Special 7 .. 20.00 9.00
Twilight Years
❑ 141A Babe Ruth Special .. 20.00 9.00
Twilight Years
Green Tint
❑ 142 Babe Ruth Special 8 .. 20.00 9.00
Coaching Dodgers
❑ 142A Babe Ruth Special .. 20.00 9.00
Coaching Dodgers
Green Tint
❑ 143 Babe Ruth Special 9 .. 20.00 9.00
Greatest Sports Hero
❑ 143A Babe Ruth Special .. 20.00 9.00
Greatest Sports Hero
Green Tint
❑ 144 Babe Ruth Special 10 20.00 9.00
Farewell Speech
❑ 144A Babe Ruth Special .. 20.00 9.00
Babe Ruth Special
Farewell Speech
❑ 145 Barry Latman............... 5.00 2.20
❑ 145A Barry Latman 5.00 2.20
Green Tint
❑ 146 Don Demeter............... 5.00 2.20
❑ 146A Don Demeter 5.00 2.20
Green Tint
❑ 147A Bill Kunkel PORT 5.00 2.20
❑ 147B Bill Kunkel............... 30.00 13.50
(Pitching pose)
❑ 148 Wally Post.................... 5.00 2.20
❑ 148A Wally Post................. 5.00 2.20
Green Tint
❑ 149 Bob Duliba.................... 5.00 2.20
❑ 149A Bob Duliba 5.00 2.20
Green Tint
❑ 150 Al Kaline 50.00 22.00
❑ 150A Al Kaline 50.00 22.00
Green Tint
❑ 151 Johnny Klippstein 5.00 2.20
❑ 151A Johnny Klippstein 5.00 2.20
Green Tint
❑ 152 Mickey Vernon MG 8.00 3.60
❑ 152A Mickey Vernon MG 8.00 3.60
Green Tint
❑ 153 Pumpsie Green 6.00 2.70
❑ 153A Pumpsie Green.......... 6.00 2.70
Green Tint
❑ 154 Lee Thomas 6.00 2.70
❑ 154A Lee Thomas 6.00 2.70
Green Tint
❑ 155 Stu Miller...................... 6.00 2.70
❑ 155A Stu Miller.................... 6.00 2.70
Green Tint
❑ 156 Merritt Ranew 5.00 2.20
❑ 156A Merritt Ranew 5.00 2.20
Green Tint
❑ 157 Wes Covington 8.00 3.60
❑ 157A Wes Covington 8.00 3.60
Green Tint
❑ 158 Braves Team............. 10.00 4.50
❑ 158A Braves Team 15.00 6.75
Green Tint
❑ 159 Hal Reniff RC 8.00 3.60
❑ 160 Dick Stuart................... 8.00 3.60
❑ 160A Dick Stuart 8.00 3.60
Green Tint
❑ 161 Frank Baumann........... 5.00 2.20
❑ 161A Frank Baumann 5.00 2.20
Green Tint
❑ 162 Sammy Drake 5.00 2.20
❑ 162A Solly Drake 5.00 2.20
Green Tint
❑ 163 Hot Corner Guard 8.00 3.60
Billy Gardner
Cletis Boyer
❑ 163A Hot Corner Guard 8.00 3.60
Billy Gardner
Clete Boyer
Green Tint
❑ 164 Hal Naragon 5.00 2.20
❑ 164A Hal Naragon 5.00 2.20
Green Tint
❑ 165 Jackie Brandt 5.00 2.20
❑ 165A Jackie Brandt 5.00 2.20
Green Tint
❑ 166 Don Lee....................... 5.00 2.20
❑ 166A Don Lee 5.00 2.20
Green Tint
❑ 167 Tim McCarver RC 30.00 13.50
❑ 167A Tim McCarver RC 30.00 13.50
Green Tint
❑ 168 Leo Posada................. 5.00 2.20
❑ 168A Leo Posada............... 5.00 2.20
Green Tint
❑ 169 Bob Cerv 10.00 4.50
❑ 169A Bob Cerv................. 10.00 4.50
Green Tint
❑ 170 Ron Santo................. 15.00 6.75
❑ 170A Ron Santo............... 15.00 6.75
Green Tint
❑ 171 Dave Sisler 5.00 2.20
❑ 171A Dave Sisler 5.00 2.20
Green Tint
❑ 172 Fred Hutchinson MG 8.00 3.60
❑ 172A Fred Hutchinson MG.. 8.00 3.60
Green Tint
❑ 173 Chico Fernandez.......... 5.00 2.20
❑ 173A Chico Fernandez 5.00 2.20
Green Tint
❑ 174A Carl Willey................. 5.00 2.20
(Capless)
❑ 174B Carl Willey.............. 30.00 13.50
(With cap)
❑ 175 Frank Howard 10.00 4.50
❑ 175A Frank Howard 10.00 4.50
Green Tint
❑ 176A Eddie Yost PORT 5.00 2.20
❑ 176B Eddie Yost BATTING 30.00 13.50
❑ 177 Bobby Shantz 8.00 3.60
❑ 177A Bobby Shantz 8.00 3.60
Green Tint
❑ 178 Camilo Carreon........... 5.00 2.20
❑ 178A Camilo Carreon......... 5.00 2.20
Green Tint
❑ 179 Tom Sturdivant 5.00 2.20
❑ 179A Tom Sturdivant 5.00 2.20
Green Tint
❑ 180 Bob Allison 10.00 4.50
❑ 180A Bob Allison 10.00 4.50
Greent Tint
❑ 181 Paul Brown 5.00 2.20
❑ 181A Paul Brown 5.00 2.20
Green Tint
❑ 182 Bob Nieman 5.00 2.20
❑ 182A Bob Nieman 5.00 2.20
Green Tint
❑ 183 Roger Craig................. 8.00 3.60
❑ 183A Roger Craig 8.00 3.60
Green Tint
❑ 184 Haywood Sullivan 8.00 3.60
❑ 184A Haywood Sullivan 8.00 3.60
Green Tint
❑ 185 Roland Sheldon......... 10.00 4.50
❑ 185A Roland Sheldon 10.00 4.50
Green Tint
❑ 186 Mack Jones.................. 5.00 2.20
❑ 186A Mack Jones............... 5.00 2.20
Green Tint
❑ 187 Gene Conley 5.00 2.20
❑ 187A Gene Conley............. 5.00 2.20
Green Tint
❑ 188 Chuck Hiller................. 5.00 2.20
❑ 188A Chuck Hiller 5.00 2.20
Green Tint
❑ 189 Dick Hall 5.00 2.20
❑ 189A Dick Hall 5.00 2.20
Green Tint
❑ 190A Wally Moon PORT 5.00 2.20
❑ 190B W.Moon BATTING .. 30.00 13.50
❑ 191 Jim Brewer 5.00 2.20
❑ 191A Jim Brewer 5.00 2.20
Green Tint
❑ 192A Checklist 3 .... 12.00 2.40
(Without comma)
❑ 192B Checklist 3 .... 16.00 3.20
(Comma after
Checklist)
❑ 193 Eddie Kasko 5.00 2.20
❑ 193A Eddie Kasko 5.00 2.20
Green Tint
❑ 194 Dean Chance RC 8.00 3.60
❑ 194A Dean Chance RC 8.00 3.60
Green Tint
❑ 195 Joe Cunningham.......... 5.00 2.20
❑ 195A Joe Cunningham........ 5.00 2.20
Green Tint
❑ 196 Terry Fox..................... 5.00 2.20
❑ 196A Terry Fox 5.00 2.20
Green Tint
❑ 197 Daryl Spencer 5.00 2.20
❑ 198 Johnny Keane MG 5.00 2.20
❑ 199 Gaylord Perry RC 80.00 36.00
❑ 200 Mickey Mantle 500.00 220.00
❑ 201 Ike Delock 5.00 2.20
❑ 202 Carl Warwick 5.00 2.20
❑ 203 Jack Fisher 5.00 2.20
❑ 204 Johnny Weekly 5.00 2.20
❑ 205 Gene Freese 5.00 2.20
❑ 206 Senators Team 10.00 4.50
❑ 207 Pete Burnside 5.00 2.20
❑ 208 Billy Martin................. 20.00 9.00
❑ 209 Jim Fregosi RC 15.00 6.75
❑ 210 Roy Face..................... 8.00 3.60
❑ 211 Midway Masters 5.00 2.20
Frank Bolling
Roy McMillan
❑ 212 Jim Owens 5.00 2.20
❑ 213 Richie Ashburn 20.00 9.00
❑ 214 Dom Zanni.................. 5.00 2.20
❑ 215 Woody Held................. 5.00 2.20
❑ 216 Ron Kline..................... 5.00 2.20
❑ 217 Walter Alston MG 10.00 4.50
❑ 218 Joe Torre RC............. 40.00 18.00
❑ 219 Al Downing RC 8.00 3.60
❑ 220 Roy Sievers................. 8.00 3.60
❑ 221 Bill Short 5.00 2.20
❑ 222 Jerry Zimmerman 5.00 2.20
❑ 223 Alex Grammas 5.00 2.20
❑ 224 Don Rudolph 5.00 2.20
❑ 225 Frank Malzone 8.00 3.60
❑ 226 San Francisco Giants 10.00 4.50
Team Card
❑ 227 Bob Tiefenauer 5.00 2.20
❑ 228 Dale Long 10.00 4.50
❑ 229 Jesus McFarlane......... 5.00 2.20
❑ 230 Camilo Pascual........... 8.00 3.60
❑ 231 Ernie Bowman............. 5.00 2.20
❑ 232 World Series Game 1 10.00 4.50
Yanks win opener
❑ 233 Joey Jay WS 10.00 4.50
❑ 234 Roger Maris WS 25.00 11.00
❑ 235 Whitey Ford WS 15.00 6.75
sets new mark
❑ 236 World Series Game 5 10.00 4.50
Yanks crush Reds
❑ 237 WS Summary 10.00 4.50
Yanks celebrate
❑ 238 Norm Sherry 5.00 2.20
❑ 239 Cecil Butler 5.00 2.20

❑ 240 George Altman 5.00 2.20
❑ 241 Johnny Kucks 5.00 2.20
❑ 242 Mel McGaha MG 5.00 2.20
❑ 243 Robin Roberts 15.00 6.75
❑ 244 Don Gile 5.00 2.20
❑ 245 Ron Hansen 5.00 2.20
❑ 246 Art Ditmar 5.00 2.20
❑ 247 Joe Pignatano 5.00 2.20
❑ 248 Bob Aspromonte 8.00 3.60
❑ 249 Ed Keegan 5.00 2.20
❑ 250 Norm Cash 10.00 4.50
❑ 251 New York Yankees 50.00 22.00
Team Card
❑ 252 Earl Francis 5.00 2.20
❑ 253 Harry Chiti MG 5.00 2.20
❑ 254 Gordon Windhorn 5.00 2.20
❑ 255 Juan Pizarro 5.00 2.20
❑ 256 Elio Chacon 8.00 3.60
❑ 257 Jack Spring 5.00 2.20
❑ 258 Marty Keough 5.00 2.20
❑ 259 Lou Klimchock 5.00 2.20
❑ 260 Billy Pierce 8.00 3.60
❑ 261 George Alusik 5.00 2.20
❑ 262 Bob Schmidt 5.00 2.20
❑ 263 The Right Pitch 5.00 2.20
Bob Purkey
Jim Turner CO
Joe Jay
❑ 264 Dick Ellsworth 8.00 3.60
❑ 265 Joe Adcock 8.00 3.60
❑ 266 John Anderson 5.00 2.20
❑ 267 Dan Dobbek 5.00 2.20
❑ 268 Ken McBride 5.00 2.20
❑ 269 Bob Oldis 5.00 2.20
❑ 270 Dick Groat 8.00 3.60
❑ 271 Ray Rippelmeyer 5.00 2.20
❑ 272 Earl Robinson 5.00 2.20
❑ 273 Gary Bell 5.00 2.20
❑ 274 Sammy Taylor 5.00 2.20
❑ 275 Norm Siebern 5.00 2.20
❑ 276 Hal Kolstad 5.00 2.20
❑ 277 Checklist 4 16.00 3.20
❑ 278 Ken Johnson 8.00 3.60
❑ 279 Hobie Landrith UER 8.00 3.60
(Wrong birthdate)
❑ 280 Johnny Podres 8.00 3.60
❑ 281 Jake Gibbs 10.00 4.50
❑ 282 Dave Hillman 5.00 2.20
❑ 283 Charlie Smith 5.00 2.20
❑ 284 Ruben Amaro 5.00 2.20
❑ 285 Curt Simmons 8.00 3.60
❑ 286 Al Lopez MG 10.00 4.50
❑ 287 George Witt 5.00 2.20
❑ 288 Billy Williams 30.00 13.50
❑ 289 Mike Krsnich 5.00 2.20
❑ 290 Jim Gentile 8.00 3.60
❑ 291 Hal Stowe 5.00 2.20
❑ 292 Jerry Kindall 5.00 2.20
❑ 293 Bob Miller 8.00 3.60
❑ 294 Phillies Team 10.00 4.50
❑ 295 Vern Law 8.00 3.60
❑ 296 Ken Hamlin 5.00 2.20
❑ 297 Ron Perranoski 8.00 3.60
❑ 298 Bill Tuttle 5.00 2.20
❑ 299 Don Wert 5.00 2.20
❑ 300 Willie Mays 150.00 70.00
❑ 301 Galen Cisco RC 5.00 2.20
❑ 302 Johnny Edwards 5.00 2.20
❑ 303 Frank Torre 8.00 3.60
❑ 304 Dick Farrell 8.00 3.60
❑ 305 Jerry Lumpe 5.00 2.20
❑ 306 Redbird Rippers 5.00 2.20
Lindy McDaniel
Larry Jackson
❑ 307 Jim Grant 8.00 3.60
❑ 308 Neil Chrisley 8.00 3.60
❑ 309 Moe Morhardt 5.00 2.20
❑ 310 Whitey Ford 50.00 22.00
❑ 311 Tony Kubek IA 8.00 3.60
❑ 312 Warren Spahn IA 15.00 6.75
❑ 313 Roger Maris IA 75.00 34.00
Blasts 61th
❑ 314 Rocky Colavito IA 8.00 3.60
❑ 315 Whitey Ford IA 15.00 6.75
❑ 316 Harmon Killebrew IA 15.00 6.75
❑ 317 Stan Musial IA 20.00 9.00
❑ 318 Mickey Mantle IA 125.00 55.00
❑ 319 Mike McCormick IA 5.00 2.20
❑ 320 Hank Aaron 150.00 70.00
❑ 321 Lee Stange 5.00 2.20
❑ 322 Alvin Dark MG 8.00 3.60
❑ 323 Don Landrum 5.00 2.20
❑ 324 Joe McClain 5.00 2.20
❑ 325 Luis Aparicio 15.00 6.75
❑ 326 Tom Parsons 5.00 2.20
❑ 327 Ozzie Virgil 5.00 2.20
❑ 328 Ken Walters 5.00 2.20
❑ 329 Bob Bolin 5.00 2.20
❑ 330 John Romano 5.00 2.20
❑ 331 Moe Drabowsky 8.00 3.60
❑ 332 Don Buddin 5.00 2.20
❑ 333 Frank Cipriani 5.00 2.20
❑ 334 Boston Red Sox 10.00 4.50
Team Card
❑ 335 Bill Bruton 5.00 2.20
❑ 336 Billy Muffett 5.00 2.20
❑ 337 Jim Marshall 8.00 3.60
❑ 338 Billy Gardner 5.00 2.20
❑ 339 Jose Valdivielso 5.00 2.20
❑ 340 Don Drysdale 50.00 22.00
❑ 341 Mike Hershberger 5.00 2.20
❑ 342 Ed Rakow 5.00 2.20
❑ 343 Albie Pearson 8.00 3.60
❑ 344 Ed Bauta 5.00 2.20
❑ 345 Chuck Schilling 5.00 2.20
❑ 346 Jack Kralick 5.00 2.20
❑ 347 Chuck Hinton 5.00 2.20
❑ 348 Larry Burright 8.00 3.60
❑ 349 Paul Foytack 5.00 2.20
❑ 350 Frank Robinson 50.00 22.00
❑ 351 Braves' Backstops 8.00 3.60
Joe Torre
Del Crandall
❑ 352 Frank Sullivan 5.00 2.20
❑ 353 Bill Mazeroski 15.00 6.75
❑ 354 Roman Mejias 8.00 3.60
❑ 355 Steve Barber 5.00 2.20
❑ 356 Tom Haller RC 5.00 2.20
❑ 357 Jerry Walker 5.00 2.20
❑ 358 Tommy Davis 8.00 3.60
❑ 359 Bobby Locke 5.00 2.20
❑ 360 Yogi Berra 80.00 36.00
❑ 361 Bob Hendley 5.00 2.20
❑ 362 Ty Cline 5.00 2.20
❑ 363 Bob Roselli 5.00 2.20
❑ 364 Ken Hunt 5.00 2.20
❑ 365 Charlie Neal 8.00 3.60
❑ 366 Phil Regan 8.00 3.60
❑ 367 Checklist 5 16.00 3.20
❑ 368 Bob Tillman 5.00 2.20
❑ 369 Ted Bowsfield 5.00 2.20
❑ 370 Ken Boyer 10.00 4.50
❑ 371 Earl Battey 6.00 2.70
❑ 372 Jack Curtis 6.00 2.70
❑ 373 Al Heist 6.00 2.70
❑ 374 Gene Mauch MG 10.00 4.50
❑ 375 Ron Fairly 10.00 4.50
❑ 376 Bud Daley 8.00 3.60
❑ 377 John Orsino 6.00 2.70
❑ 378 Bennie Daniels 6.00 2.70
❑ 379 Chuck Essegian 6.00 2.70
❑ 380 Lou Burdette 10.00 4.50
❑ 381 Chico Cardenas 10.00 4.50
❑ 382 Dick Williams 8.00 3.60
❑ 383 Ray Sadecki 6.00 2.70
❑ 384 K.C. Athletics 10.00 4.50
Team Card
❑ 385 Early Wynn 15.00 6.75
❑ 386 Don Mincher 8.00 3.60
❑ 387 Lou Brock RC 125.00 55.00
❑ 388 Ryne Duren 8.00 3.60
❑ 389 Smoky Burgess 10.00 4.50
❑ 390 Orlando Cepeda AS 10.00 4.50
❑ 391 Bill Mazeroski AS 10.00 4.50
❑ 392 Ken Boyer AS UER 8.00 3.60
Batting Average mistakenly
listed as .392
❑ 393 Roy McMillan AS 6.00 2.70
❑ 394 Hank Aaron AS 50.00 22.00
❑ 395 Willie Mays AS 50.00 22.00
❑ 396 Frank Robinson AS 15.00 6.75
❑ 397 John Roseboro AS 6.00 2.70
❑ 398 Don Drysdale AS 15.00 6.75
❑ 399 Warren Spahn AS 15.00 6.75
❑ 400 Elston Howard 10.00 4.50
❑ 401 AL/NL Homer Kings 60.00 27.00
Roger Maris
Orlando Cepeda
❑ 402 Gino Cimoli 6.00 2.70
❑ 403 Chet Nichols 6.00 2.70
❑ 404 Tim Harkness 8.00 3.60
❑ 405 Jim Perry 8.00 3.60
❑ 406 Bob Taylor 6.00 2.70
❑ 407 Hank Aguirre 6.00 2.70
❑ 408 Gus Bell 8.00 3.60
❑ 409 Pittsburgh Pirates 10.00 4.50
Team Card
❑ 410 Al Smith 6.00 2.70
❑ 411 Danny O'Connell 6.00 2.70
❑ 412 Charlie James 6.00 2.70
❑ 413 Matty Alou 10.00 4.50
❑ 414 Joe Gaines 6.00 2.70
❑ 415 Bill Virdon 10.00 4.50
❑ 416 Bob Scheffing MG 6.00 2.70
❑ 417 Joe Azcue 6.00 2.70
❑ 418 Andy Carey 6.00 2.70
❑ 419 Bob Bruce 8.00 3.60
❑ 420 Gus Triandos 8.00 3.60
❑ 421 Ken MacKenzie 8.00 3.60
❑ 422 Steve Bilko 6.00 2.70
❑ 423 Rival League 10.00 4.50
Relief Aces:
Roy Face
Hoyt Wilhelm
❑ 424 Al McBean RC 6.00 2.70
❑ 425 Carl Yastrzemski 125.00 55.00
❑ 426 Bob Farley 6.00 2.70
❑ 427 Jake Wood 6.00 2.70
❑ 428 Joe Hicks 6.00 2.70
❑ 429 Billy O'Dell 6.00 2.70
❑ 430 Tony Kubek 15.00 6.75
❑ 431 Bob Rodgers RC 8.00 3.60
❑ 432 Jim Pendleton 6.00 2.70
❑ 433 Jim Archer 6.00 2.70
❑ 434 Clay Dalrymple 6.00 2.70
❑ 435 Larry Sherry 8.00 3.60
❑ 436 Felix Mantilla 8.00 3.60
❑ 437 Ray Moore 6.00 2.70
❑ 438 Dick Brown 6.00 2.70
❑ 439 Jerry Buchek 6.00 2.70
❑ 440 Joey Jay 6.00 2.70
❑ 441 Checklist 6 16.00 7.25
❑ 442 Wes Stock 6.00 2.70
❑ 443 Del Crandall 8.00 3.60
❑ 444 Ted Wills 6.00 2.70
❑ 445 Vic Power 8.00 3.60
❑ 446 Don Elston 6.00 2.70
❑ 447 Willie Kirkland 12.00 5.50
❑ 448 Joe Gibbon 12.00 5.50
❑ 449 Jerry Adair 12.00 5.50
❑ 450 Jim O'Toole 15.00 6.75
❑ 451 Jose Tartabull RC 15.00 6.75
❑ 452 Earl Averill Jr. 12.00 5.50
❑ 453 Cal McLish 12.00 5.50
❑ 454 Floyd Robinson 12.00 5.50
❑ 455 Luis Arroyo 15.00 6.75
❑ 456 Joe Amalfitano 15.00 6.75
❑ 457 Lou Clinton 12.00 5.50
❑ 458A Bob Buhl 15.00 6.75
(Braves emblem
on cap)
❑ 458B Bob Buhl 50.00 22.00
(No emblem on cap)
❑ 459 Ed Bailey 12.00 5.50
❑ 460 Jim Bunning 20.00 9.00
❑ 461 Ken Hubbs RC 35.00 16.00
❑ 462A Willie Tasby 12.00 5.50
(Senators emblem
on cap)
❑ 462B Willie Tasby 50.00 22.00
(No emblem on cap)
❑ 463 Hank Bauer MG 15.00 6.75
❑ 464 Al Jackson RC 12.00 5.50
❑ 465 Reds Team 20.00 9.00
❑ 466 Norm Cash AS 15.00 6.75
❑ 467 Chuck Schilling AS 12.00 5.50
❑ 468 Brooks Robinson AS 25.00 11.00
❑ 469 Luis Aparicio AS 15.00 6.75

❑ 470 Al Kaline AS 25.00 11.00
❑ 471 Mickey Mantle AS 200.00 90.00
❑ 472 Rocky Colavito AS 15.00 6.75
❑ 473 Elston Howard AS 15.00 6.75
❑ 474 Frank Lary AS 12.00 5.50
❑ 475 Whitey Ford AS 15.00 6.75
❑ 476 Orioles Team............. 20.00 9.00
❑ 477 Andre Rodgers 12.00 5.50
❑ 478 Don Zimmer 20.00 9.00
(Shown with Mets cap,
but listed as with
Cincinnati)
❑ 479 Joel Horlen RC 12.00 5.50
❑ 480 Harvey Kuenn 15.00 6.75
❑ 481 Vic Wertz.................... 15.00 6.75
❑ 482 Sam Mele MG 12.00 5.50
❑ 483 Don McMahon............ 12.00 5.50
❑ 484 Dick Schofield 12.00 5.50
❑ 485 Pedro Ramos 12.00 5.50
❑ 486 Jim Gilliam.................. 15.00 6.75
❑ 487 Jerry Lynch 12.00 5.50
❑ 488 Hal Brown 12.00 5.50
❑ 489 Julio Gotay 12.00 5.50
❑ 490 Clete Boyer UER........ 15.00 6.75
Reversed Negative
❑ 491 Leon Wagner............. 12.00 5.50
❑ 492 Hal W. Smith.............. 15.00 6.75
❑ 493 Danny McDevitt.......... 12.00 5.50
❑ 494 Sammy White 12.00 5.50
❑ 495 Don Cardwell.............. 12.00 5.50
❑ 496 Wayne Causey 12.00 5.50
❑ 497 Ed Bouchee................ 15.00 6.75
❑ 498 Jim Donohue.............. 12.00 5.50
❑ 499 Zoilo Versalles............ 15.00 6.75
❑ 500 Duke Snider 60.00 27.00
❑ 501 Claude Osteen 15.00 6.75
❑ 502 Hector Lopez.............. 15.00 6.75
❑ 503 Danny Murtaugh MG .. 15.00 6.75
❑ 504 Eddie Bressoud.......... 12.00 5.50
❑ 505 Juan Marichal 40.00 18.00
❑ 506 Charlie Maxwell.......... 15.00 6.75
❑ 507 Ernie Broglio 15.00 6.75
❑ 508 Gordy Coleman.......... 15.00 6.75
❑ 509 Dave Giusti RC 15.00 6.75
❑ 510 Jim Lemon.................. 12.00 5.50
❑ 511 Bubba Phillips 12.00 5.50
❑ 512 Mike Fornieles............ 12.00 5.50
❑ 513 Whitey Herzog............ 15.00 6.75
❑ 514 Sherm Lollar 15.00 6.75
❑ 515 Stan Williams 15.00 6.75
❑ 516A Checklist 7 .... 16.00 3.20
White Boxes
❑ 516B Checklist 7 .... 16.00 7.25
Yellow Boxes
❑ 517 Dave Wickersham...... 12.00 5.50
❑ 518 Lee Maye 12.00 5.50
❑ 519 Bob Johnson 12.00 5.50
❑ 520 Bob Friend.................. 15.00 6.75
❑ 521 Jacke Davis UER 12.00 5.50
(Listed as OF on
front and P on back)
❑ 522 Lindy McDaniel 15.00 6.75
❑ 523 Russ Nixon SP 30.00 13.50
❑ 524 Howie Nunn SP.......... 30.00 13.50
❑ 525 George Thomas 20.00 9.00
❑ 526 Hal Woodeshick SP .. 30.00 13.50
❑ 527 Dick McAuliffe RC 30.00 13.50
❑ 528 Turk Lown 20.00 9.00
❑ 529 John Schaive SP........ 30.00 13.50
❑ 530 Bob Gibson SP 125.00 55.00
❑ 531 Bobby G. Smith 20.00 9.00
❑ 532 Dick Stigman.............. 20.00 9.00
❑ 533 Charley Lau SP.......... 30.00 13.50
❑ 534 Tony Gonzalez SP 30.00 13.50
❑ 535 Ed Roebuck................ 20.00 9.00
❑ 536 Dick Gernert 20.00 9.00
❑ 537 Cleveland Indians 50.00 22.00
Team Card
❑ 538 Jack Sanford.............. 20.00 9.00
❑ 539 Billy Moran 20.00 9.00
❑ 540 Jim Landis SP............ 30.00 13.50
❑ 541 Don Nottebart SP 30.00 13.50
❑ 542 Dave Philley 20.00 9.00
❑ 543 Bob Allen SP.............. 30.00 13.50
❑ 544 Willie McCovey SP .. 125.00 55.00
❑ 545 Hoyt Wilhelm SP 50.00 22.00
❑ 546 Moe Thacker SP 30.00 13.50
❑ 547 Don Ferrarese............ 20.00 9.00
❑ 548 Bobby Del Greco........ 20.00 9.00
❑ 549 Bill Rigney MG SP...... 30.00 13.50
❑ 550 Art Mahaffey SP 30.00 13.50
❑ 551 Harry Bright................ 20.00 9.00
❑ 552 Chicago Cubs SP 50.00 22.00
Team Card
❑ 553 Jim Coates 30.00 13.50
❑ 554 Bubba Morton SP 30.00 13.50
❑ 555 John Buzhardt SP...... 30.00 13.50
❑ 556 Al Spangler 20.00 9.00
❑ 557 Bob Anderson SP 30.00 13.50
❑ 558 John Goryl.................. 20.00 9.00
❑ 559 Mike Higgins MG........ 20.00 9.00
❑ 560 Chuck Estrada SP...... 30.00 13.50
❑ 561 Gene Oliver SP 30.00 13.50
❑ 562 Bill Henry.................... 20.00 9.00
❑ 563 Ken Aspromonte 20.00 9.00
❑ 564 Bob Grim.................... 20.00 9.00
❑ 565 Jose Pagan 20.00 9.00
❑ 566 Marty Kutyna SP 30.00 13.50
❑ 567 Tracy Stallard SP 30.00 13.50
❑ 568 Jim Golden 20.00 9.00
❑ 569 Ed Sadowski SP 30.00 13.50
❑ 570 Bill Stafford SP 30.00 13.50
❑ 571 Billy Klaus SP 30.00 13.50
❑ 572 Bob G. Miller SP 30.00 13.50
❑ 573 Johnny Logan 20.00 9.00
❑ 574 Dean Stone 20.00 9.00
❑ 575 Red Schoendienst SP 50.00 22.00
❑ 576 Russ Kemmerer SP .. 30.00 13.50
❑ 577 Dave Nicholson SP 30.00 13.50
❑ 578 Jim Duffalo 20.00 9.00
❑ 579 Jim Schaffer SP 30.00 13.50
❑ 580 Bill Monbouquette 20.00 9.00
❑ 581 Mel Roach.................. 20.00 9.00
❑ 582 Ron Piche 20.00 9.00
❑ 583 Larry Osborne 20.00 9.00
❑ 584 Minnesota Twins SP .. 60.00 27.00
Team Card
❑ 585 Glen Hobbie SP 30.00 13.50
❑ 586 Sammy Esposito SP .. 30.00 13.50
❑ 587 Frank Funk SP 30.00 13.50
❑ 588 Birdie Tebbetts MG 20.00 9.00
❑ 589 Bob Turley.................. 30.00 13.50
❑ 590 Curt Flood 30.00 13.50
❑ 591 Rookie Pitchers SP 70.00 32.00
Sam McDowell RC
Ron Taylor
Ron Nischwitz
Art Quirk
Dick Radatz
❑ 592 Rookie Pitchers SP 70.00 32.00
Dan Pfister
Bo Belinsky
Dave Stenhouse
Jim Bouton RC
Joe Bonikowski
❑ 593 Rookie Pitchers SP 50.00 22.00
Jack Lamabe
Craig Anderson
Jack Hamilton
Bob Moorhead
Bob Veale
❑ 594 Rookie Catchers SP .. 75.00 34.00
Doc Edwards
Ken Retzer
Bob Uecker RC
Doug Camilli
Don Pavletich
❑ 595 Rookie Infielders SP .. 50.00 22.00
Bob Sadowski
Felix Torres
Marlan Coughtry
Ed Charles
❑ 596 Rookie Infielders SP .. 70.00 32.00
Bernie Allen
Joe Pepitone RC
Phil Linz
Rich Rollins
❑ 597 Rookie Infielders SP .. 50.00 22.00
Jim McKnight
Rod Kanehl
Amado Samuel
Denis Menke RC
❑ 598 Rookie Outfielders SP 80.00 23.00
Al Luplow
Manny Jimenez
Howie Goss
Jim Hickman
Ed Olivares

1963 Topps

	NRMT	VG-E
COMPLETE SET (576)	5000.00	2200.00
COMMON CARD (1-196)..........	4.00	1.80
COMMON CARD (197-283)......	5.00	2.20
COMMON CARD (284-370)......	5.00	2.20
COMMON CARD (371-446)......	5.00	2.20
COMMON CARD (447-522)....	25.00	11.00
COMMON CARD (523-576)....	15.00	6.75
WRAPPER (1-CENT)............	40.00	18.00
WRAPPER (5-CENT)............	30.00	13.50

❑ 1 NL Batting Leaders 40.00 8.00
Tommy Davis
Frank Robinson
Stan Musial
Hank Aaron
Bill White
❑ 2 AL Batting Leaders 50.00 22.00
Pete Runnels
Mickey Mantle
Floyd Robinson
Norm Siebern
Chuck Hinton
❑ 3 NL Home Run Leaders .. 40.00 18.00
Willie Mays
Hank Aaron
Frank Robinson
Orlando Cepeda
Ernie Banks
❑ 4 AL Home Run Leaders .. 20.00 9.00
Harmon Killebrew
Norm Cash
Rocky Colavito
Roger Maris
Jim Gentile
Leon Wagner
❑ 5 NL ERA Leaders 25.00 11.00
Sandy Koufax
Bob Shaw
Bob Purkey
Bob Gibson
Don Drysdale
❑ 6 AL ERA Leaders 10.00 4.50
Hank Aguirre
Robin Roberts
Whitey Ford
Eddie Fisher
Dean Chance
❑ 7 NL Pitching Leaders 10.00 4.50
Don Drysdale
Jack Sanford
Bob Purkey
Billy O'Dell
Art Mahaffey
Joe Jay
❑ 8 AL Pitching Leaders 8.00 3.60
Ralph Terry
Dick Donovan
Ray Herbert

Jim Bunning
Camilo Pascual
❑ 9 NL Strikeout Leaders 30.00 13.50
Don Drysdale
Sandy Koufax
Bob Gibson
Billy O'Dell
Dick Farrell
❑ 10 AL Strikeout Leaders...... 8.00 3.60
Camilo Pascual
Jim Bunning
Ralph Terry
Juan Pizarro
Jim Kaat
❑ 11 Lee Walls 4.00 1.80
❑ 12 Steve Barber 4.00 1.80
❑ 13 Philadelphia Phillies 8.00 3.60
Team Card
❑ 14 Pedro Ramos 4.00 1.80
❑ 15 Ken Hubbs UER 10.00 4.50
(No position listed
on front of card)
❑ 16 Al Smith 4.00 1.80
❑ 17 Ryne Duren 8.00 3.60
❑ 18 Buc Blasters 80.00 36.00
Smoky Burgess
Dick Stuart
Bob Clemente
Bob Skinner
❑ 19 Pete Burnside 4.00 1.80
❑ 20 Tony Kubek 10.00 4.50
❑ 21 Marty Keough 4.00 1.80
❑ 22 Curt Simmons 8.00 3.60
❑ 23 Ed Lopat MG 8.00 3.60
❑ 24 Bob Bruce 4.00 1.80
❑ 25 Al Kaline 45.00 20.00
❑ 26 Ray Moore 4.00 1.80
❑ 27 Choo Choo Coleman...... 8.00 3.60
❑ 28 Mike Fornieles 4.00 1.80
❑ 29A 1962 Rookie Stars 10.00 4.50
Sammy Ellis
Ray Culp
John Boozer
Jesse Gonder
❑ 29B 1963 Rookie Stars 4.00 1.80
Sammy Ellis
Ray Culp
John Boozer
Jesse Gonder
❑ 30 Harvey Kuenn 8.00 3.60
❑ 31 Cal Koonce 4.00 1.80
❑ 32 Tony Gonzalez 4.00 1.80
❑ 33 Bo Belinsky 8.00 3.60
❑ 34 Dick Schofield 4.00 1.80
❑ 35 John Buzhardt 4.00 1.80
❑ 36 Jerry Kindall 4.00 1.80
❑ 37 Jerry Lynch 4.00 1.80
❑ 38 Bud Daley 8.00 3.60
❑ 39 Angels Team 8.00 3.60
❑ 40 Vic Power 8.00 3.60
❑ 41 Charley Lau 8.00 3.60
❑ 42 Stan Williams 8.00 3.60
(Listed as Yankee on
card but LA cap)
❑ 43 Veteran Masters 8.00 3.60
Casey Stengel MG
Gene Woodling
❑ 44 Terry Fox 4.00 1.80
❑ 45 Bob Aspromonte 4.00 1.80
❑ 46 Tommie Aaron RC 8.00 3.60
❑ 47 Don Lock 4.00 1.80
❑ 48 Birdie Tebbetts MG 8.00 3.60
❑ 49 Dal Maxvill RC 8.00 3.60
❑ 50 Billy Pierce 8.00 3.60
❑ 51 George Alusik 4.00 1.80
❑ 52 Chuck Schilling 4.00 1.80
❑ 53 Joe Moeller 8.00 3.60
❑ 54A 1962 Rookie Stars 15.00 6.75
Nelson Mathews
Harry Fanok
Jack Cullen
Dave DeBusschere RC
❑ 54B 1963 Rookie Stars 8.00 3.60
Nelson Mathews
Harry Fanok
Jack Cullen
Dave DeBusschere RC
❑ 55 Bill Virdon 8.00 3.60
❑ 56 Dennis Bennett 4.00 1.80
❑ 57 Billy Moran 4.00 1.80
❑ 58 Bob Will 4.00 1.80
❑ 59 Craig Anderson 4.00 1.80
❑ 60 Elston Howard 8.00 3.60
❑ 61 Ernie Bowman 4.00 1.80
❑ 62 Bob Hendley 4.00 1.80
❑ 63 Reds Team 8.00 3.60
❑ 64 Dick McAuliffe 8.00 3.60
❑ 65 Jackie Brandt 4.00 1.80
❑ 66 Mike Joyce 4.00 1.80
❑ 67 Ed Charles 4.00 1.80
❑ 68 Friendly Foes 25.00 11.00
Duke Snider
Gil Hodges
❑ 69 Bud Zipfel 4.00 1.80
❑ 70 Jim O'Toole 8.00 3.60
❑ 71 Bobby Wine 8.00 3.60
❑ 72 Johnny Romano 4.00 1.80
❑ 73 Bobby Bragan MG RC .. 8.00 3.60
❑ 74 Denny Lemaster 4.00 1.80
❑ 75 Bob Allison 8.00 3.60
❑ 76 Earl Wilson 8.00 3.60
❑ 77 Al Spangler 4.00 1.80
❑ 78 Marv Throneberry 8.00 3.60
❑ 79 Checklist 1 .... 12.00 2.40
❑ 80 Jim Gilliam 8.00 3.60
❑ 81 Jim Schaffer 4.00 1.80
❑ 82 Ed Rakow 4.00 1.80
❑ 83 Charley James 4.00 1.80
❑ 84 Ron Kline 4.00 1.80
❑ 85 Tom Haller 8.00 3.60
❑ 86 Charley Maxwell 8.00 3.60
❑ 87 Bob Veale 8.00 3.60
❑ 88 Ron Hansen 4.00 1.80
❑ 89 Dick Stigman 4.00 1.80
❑ 90 Gordy Coleman 8.00 3.60
❑ 91 Dallas Green 8.00 3.60
❑ 92 Hector Lopez 8.00 3.60
❑ 93 Galen Cisco 4.00 1.80
❑ 94 Bob Schmidt 4.00 1.80
❑ 95 Larry Jackson 4.00 1.80
❑ 96 Lou Clinton 4.00 1.80
❑ 97 Bob Duliba 4.00 1.80
❑ 98 George Thomas 4.00 1.80
❑ 99 Jim Umbricht 4.00 1.80
❑ 100 Joe Cunningham 4.00 1.80
❑ 101 Joe Gibbon 4.00 1.80
❑ 102A Checklist 2 .... 12.00 2.40
(Red on yellow)
❑ 102B Checklist 2 .... 12.00 2.40
(White on red)
❑ 103 Chuck Essegian 4.00 1.80
❑ 104 Lew Krausse 4.00 1.80
❑ 105 Ron Fairly 8.00 3.60
❑ 106 Bobby Bolin 4.00 1.80
❑ 107 Jim Hickman 8.00 3.60
❑ 108 Hoyt Wilhelm 10.00 4.50
❑ 109 Lee Maye 4.00 1.80
❑ 110 Rich Rollins 8.00 3.60
❑ 111 Al Jackson 4.00 1.80
❑ 112 Dick Brown 4.00 1.80
❑ 113 Don Landrum UER 4.00 1.80
(Photo actually
Ron Santo)
❑ 114 Dan Osinski 4.00 1.80
❑ 115 Carl Yastrzemski 40.00 18.00
❑ 116 Jim Brosnan 8.00 3.60
❑ 117 Jacke Davis 4.00 1.80
❑ 118 Sherm Lollar 4.00 1.80
❑ 119 Bob Lillis 4.00 1.80
❑ 120 Roger Maris 80.00 36.00
❑ 121 Jim Hannan 4.00 1.80
❑ 122 Julio Gotay 4.00 1.80
❑ 123 Frank Howard 8.00 3.60
❑ 124 Dick Howser 8.00 3.60
❑ 125 Robin Roberts 15.00 6.75
❑ 126 Bob Uecker 15.00 6.75
❑ 127 Bill Tuttle 4.00 1.80
❑ 128 Matty Alou 8.00 3.60
❑ 129 Gary Bell 4.00 1.80
❑ 130 Dick Groat 8.00 3.60
❑ 131 Washington Senators .. 8.00 3.60
Team Card
❑ 132 Jack Hamilton 4.00 1.80
❑ 133 Gene Freese 4.00 1.80
❑ 134 Bob Scheffing MG 4.00 1.80
❑ 135 Richie Ashburn 20.00 9.00
❑ 136 Ike Delock 4.00 1.80
❑ 137 Mack Jones 4.00 1.80
❑ 138 Pride of NL 70.00 32.00
Willie Mays
Stan Musial
❑ 139 Earl Averill 4.00 1.80
❑ 140 Frank Lary 8.00 3.60
❑ 141 Manny Mota RC 8.00 3.60
❑ 142 Whitey Ford WS 10.00 4.50
❑ 143 Jack Sanford WS 8.00 3.60
❑ 144 Roger Maris WS 15.00 6.75
❑ 145 Chuck Hiller WS 8.00 3.60
❑ 146 Tom Tresh WS 8.00 3.60
❑ 147 Billy Pierce WS 8.00 3.60
❑ 148 Ralph Terry WS 8.00 3.60
❑ 149 Marv Breeding 4.00 1.80
❑ 150 Johnny Podres 8.00 3.60
❑ 151 Pirates Team 8.00 3.60
❑ 152 Ron Nischwitz 4.00 1.80
❑ 153 Hal Smith 4.00 1.80
❑ 154 Walter Alston MG 8.00 3.60
❑ 155 Bill Stafford 4.00 1.80
❑ 156 Roy McMillan 8.00 3.60
❑ 157 Diego Segui RC 8.00 3.60
❑ 158 Rookie Stars 8.00 3.60
Rogelio Alvares
Dave Roberts
Tommy Harper RC
Bob Saverine
❑ 159 Jim Pagliaroni 4.00 1.80
❑ 160 Juan Pizarro 4.00 1.80
❑ 161 Frank Torre 8.00 3.60
❑ 162 Twins Team 8.00 3.60
❑ 163 Don Larsen 8.00 3.60
❑ 164 Bubba Morton 4.00 1.80
❑ 165 Jim Kaat 8.00 3.60
❑ 166 Johnny Keane MG 4.00 1.80
❑ 167 Jim Fregosi 8.00 3.60
❑ 168 Russ Nixon 4.00 1.80
❑ 169 Rookie Stars 25.00 11.00
Dick Egan
Julio Navarro
Tommie Sisk
Gaylord Perry
❑ 170 Joe Adcock 8.00 3.60
❑ 171 Steve Hamilton 4.00 1.80
❑ 172 Gene Oliver 4.00 1.80
❑ 173 Bombers' Best 150.00 70.00
Tom Tresh
Mickey Mantle
Bobby Richardson
❑ 174 Larry Burright 4.00 1.80
❑ 175 Bob Buhl 8.00 3.60
❑ 176 Jim King 4.00 1.80
❑ 177 Bubba Phillips 4.00 1.80
❑ 178 Johnny Edwards 4.00 1.80
❑ 179 Ron Piche 4.00 1.80
❑ 180 Bill Skowron 8.00 3.60
❑ 181 Sammy Esposito 4.00 1.80
❑ 182 Albie Pearson 8.00 3.60
❑ 183 Joe Pepitone 8.00 3.60
❑ 184 Vern Law 8.00 3.60
❑ 185 Chuck Hiller 4.00 1.80
❑ 186 Jerry Zimmerman 4.00 1.80
❑ 187 Willie Kirkland 4.00 1.80
❑ 188 Eddie Bressoud 4.00 1.80
❑ 189 Dave Giusti 8.00 3.60
❑ 190 Minnie Minoso 8.00 3.60
❑ 191 Checklist 3 .... 12.00 2.40
❑ 192 Clay Dalrymple 4.00 1.80
❑ 193 Andre Rodgers 4.00 1.80
❑ 194 Joe Nuxhall 8.00 3.60
❑ 195 Manny Jimenez 4.00 1.80
❑ 196 Doug Camilli 4.00 1.80
❑ 197 Roger Craig 8.00 3.60
❑ 198 Lenny Green 5.00 2.20
❑ 199 Joe Amalfitano 5.00 2.20
❑ 200 Mickey Mantle 500.00 220.00
❑ 201 Cecil Butler 5.00 2.20
❑ 202 Boston Red Sox 8.00 3.60
Team Card
❑ 203 Chico Cardenas 8.00 3.60

❑ 204 Don Nottebart 5.00 2.20
❑ 205 Luis Aparicio 15.00 6.75
❑ 206 Ray Washburn 5.00 2.20
❑ 207 Ken Hunt 5.00 2.20
❑ 208 Rookie Stars 5.00 2.20
Ron Herbel
John Miller
Wally Wolf
Ron Taylor
❑ 209 Hobie Landrith 5.00 2.20
❑ 210 Sandy Koufax 150.00 70.00
❑ 211 Fred Whitfield 5.00 2.20
❑ 212 Glen Hobbie 5.00 2.20
❑ 213 Billy Hitchcock MG 5.00 2.20
❑ 214 Orlando Pena 5.00 2.20
❑ 215 Bob Skinner 8.00 3.60
❑ 216 Gene Conley 8.00 3.60
❑ 217 Joe Christopher 5.00 2.20
❑ 218 Tiger Twirlers 8.00 3.60
Frank Lary
Don Mossi
Jim Bunning
❑ 219 Chuck Cottier 5.00 2.20
❑ 220 Camilo Pascual 8.00 3.60
❑ 221 Cookie Rojas RC 8.00 3.60
❑ 222 Cubs Team 8.00 3.60
❑ 223 Eddie Fisher 5.00 2.20
❑ 224 Mike Roarke 5.00 2.20
❑ 225 Joey Jay 5.00 2.20
❑ 226 Julian Javier 8.00 3.60
❑ 227 Jim Grant 8.00 3.60
❑ 228 Rookie Stars 50.00 22.00
Max Alvis
Bob Bailey
Tony Oliva
(Listed as Pedro)
Ed Kranepool RC
❑ 229 Willie Davis 8.00 3.60
❑ 230 Pete Runnels 8.00 3.60
❑ 231 Eli Grba UER 5.00 2.20
(Large photo is
Ryne Duren)
❑ 232 Frank Malzone 8.00 3.60
❑ 233 Casey Stengel MG 20.00 9.00
❑ 234 Dave Nicholson 5.00 2.20
❑ 235 Billy O'Dell 5.00 2.20
❑ 236 Bill Bryan 5.00 2.20
❑ 237 Jim Coates 8.00 3.60
❑ 238 Lou Johnson 5.00 2.20
❑ 239 Harvey Haddix 8.00 3.60
❑ 240 Rocky Colavito 15.00 6.75
❑ 241 Bob Smith 5.00 2.20
❑ 242 Power Plus 60.00 27.00
Ernie Banks
Hank Aaron
❑ 243 Don Leppert 5.00 2.20
❑ 244 John Tsitouris 5.00 2.20
❑ 245 Gil Hodges 20.00 9.00
❑ 246 Lee Stange 5.00 2.20
❑ 247 Yankees Team 50.00 22.00
❑ 248 Tito Francona 5.00 2.20
❑ 249 Leo Burke 5.00 2.20
❑ 250 Stan Musial 100.00 45.00
❑ 251 Jack Lamabe 5.00 2.20
❑ 252 Ron Santo 10.00 4.50
❑ 253 Rookie Stars 5.00 2.20
Len Gabrielson
Pete Jernigan
John Wojcik
Deacon Jones
❑ 254 Mike Hershberger 5.00 2.20
❑ 255 Bob Shaw 5.00 2.20
❑ 256 Jerry Lumpe 5.00 2.20
❑ 257 Hank Aguirre 5.00 2.20
❑ 258 Alvin Dark MG 8.00 3.60
❑ 259 Johnny Logan 8.00 3.60
❑ 260 Jim Gentile 8.00 3.60
❑ 261 Bob Miller 5.00 2.20
❑ 262 Ellis Burton 5.00 2.20
❑ 263 Dave Stenhouse 5.00 2.20
❑ 264 Phil Linz 5.00 2.20
❑ 265 Vada Pinson 8.00 3.60
❑ 266 Bob Allen 5.00 2.20
❑ 267 Carl Sawatski 5.00 2.20
❑ 268 Don Demeter 5.00 2.20
❑ 269 Don Mincher 5.00 2.20
❑ 270 Felipe Alou 8.00 3.60
❑ 271 Dean Stone 5.00 2.20
❑ 272 Danny Murphy 5.00 2.20
❑ 273 Sammy Taylor 5.00 2.20
❑ 274 Checklist 4 12.00 2.40
❑ 275 Eddie Mathews 30.00 13.50
❑ 276 Barry Shetrone 5.00 2.20
❑ 277 Dick Farrell 5.00 2.20
❑ 278 Chico Fernandez 5.00 2.20
❑ 279 Wally Moon 8.00 3.60
❑ 280 Bob Rodgers 5.00 2.20
❑ 281 Tom Sturdivant 5.00 2.20
❑ 282 Bobby Del Greco 5.00 2.20
❑ 283 Roy Sievers 8.00 3.60
❑ 284 Dave Sisler 5.00 2.20
❑ 285 Dick Stuart 8.00 3.60
❑ 286 Stu Miller 8.00 3.60
❑ 287 Dick Bertell 5.00 2.20
❑ 288 Chicago White Sox 10.00 4.50
Team Card
❑ 289 Hal Brown 5.00 2.20
❑ 290 Bill White 8.00 3.60
❑ 291 Don Rudolph 5.00 2.20
❑ 292 Pumpsie Green 8.00 3.60
❑ 293 Bill Pleis 5.00 2.20
❑ 294 Bill Rigney MG 5.00 2.20
❑ 295 Ed Roebuck 5.00 2.20
❑ 296 Doc Edwards 5.00 2.20
❑ 297 Jim Golden 5.00 2.20
❑ 298 Don Dillard 5.00 2.20
❑ 299 Rookie Stars 8.00 3.60
Dave Morehead
Bob Dustal
Tom Butters
Dan Schneider
❑ 300 Willie Mays 150.00 70.00
❑ 301 Bill Fischer 5.00 2.20
❑ 302 Whitey Herzog 8.00 3.60
❑ 303 Earl Francis 5.00 2.20
❑ 304 Harry Bright 5.00 2.20
❑ 305 Don Hoak 5.00 2.20
❑ 306 Star Receivers 10.00 4.50
Earl Battey
Elston Howard
❑ 307 Chet Nichols 5.00 2.20
❑ 308 Camilo Carreon 5.00 2.20
❑ 309 Jim Brewer 5.00 2.20
❑ 310 Tommy Davis 8.00 3.60
❑ 311 Joe McClain 5.00 2.20
❑ 312 Houston Colts 25.00 11.00
Team Card
❑ 313 Ernie Broglio 5.00 2.20
❑ 314 John Goryl 5.00 2.20
❑ 315 Ralph Terry 8.00 3.60
❑ 316 Norm Sherry 8.00 3.60
❑ 317 Sam McDowell 8.00 3.60
❑ 318 Gene Mauch MG 8.00 3.60
❑ 319 Joe Gaines 5.00 2.20
❑ 320 Warren Spahn 60.00 27.00
❑ 321 Gino Cimoli 5.00 2.20
❑ 322 Bob Turley 8.00 3.60
❑ 323 Bill Mazeroski 15.00 6.75
❑ 324 Rookie Stars 8.00 3.60
George Williams
Pete Ward
Phil Roof
Vic Davalillo
❑ 325 Jack Sanford 5.00 2.20
❑ 326 Hank Foiles 5.00 2.20
❑ 327 Paul Foytack 5.00 2.20
❑ 328 Dick Williams 8.00 3.60
❑ 329 Lindy McDaniel 8.00 3.60
❑ 330 Chuck Hinton 5.00 2.20
❑ 331 Series Foes 8.00 3.60
Bill Stafford
Bill Pierce
❑ 332 Joel Horlen 8.00 3.60
❑ 333 Carl Warwick 5.00 2.20
❑ 334 Wynn Hawkins 5.00 2.20
❑ 335 Leon Wagner 5.00 2.20
❑ 336 Ed Bauta 5.00 2.20
❑ 337 Dodgers Team 25.00 11.00
❑ 338 Russ Kemmerer 5.00 2.20
❑ 339 Ted Bowsfield 5.00 2.20
❑ 340 Yogi Berra P/CO 80.00 36.00
❑ 341 Jack Baldschun 5.00 2.20
❑ 342 Gene Woodling 8.00 3.60
❑ 343 Johnny Pesky MG 8.00 3.60
❑ 344 Don Schwall 5.00 2.20
❑ 345 Brooks Robinson 60.00 27.00
❑ 346 Billy Hoeft 5.00 2.20
❑ 347 Joe Torre 15.00 6.75
❑ 348 Vic Wertz 8.00 3.60
❑ 349 Zoilo Versalles 8.00 3.60
❑ 350 Bob Purkey 5.00 2.20
❑ 351 Al Luplow 5.00 2.20
❑ 352 Ken Johnson 5.00 2.20
❑ 353 Billy Williams 30.00 13.50
❑ 354 Dom Zanni 5.00 2.20
❑ 355 Dean Chance 8.00 3.60
❑ 356 John Schaive 5.00 2.20
❑ 357 George Altman 5.00 2.20
❑ 358 Milt Pappas 8.00 3.60
❑ 359 Haywood Sullivan 8.00 3.60
❑ 360 Don Drysdale 60.00 27.00
❑ 361 Clete Boyer 10.00 4.50
❑ 362 Checklist 5 12.00 2.40
❑ 363 Dick Radatz 8.00 3.60
❑ 364 Howie Goss 5.00 2.20
❑ 365 Jim Bunning 20.00 9.00
❑ 366 Tony Taylor 8.00 3.60
❑ 367 Tony Cloninger 5.00 2.20
❑ 368 Ed Bailey 5.00 2.20
❑ 369 Jim Lemon 5.00 2.20
❑ 370 Dick Donovan 5.00 2.20
❑ 371 Rod Kanehl 8.00 3.60
❑ 372 Don Lee 5.00 2.20
❑ 373 Jim Campbell 5.00 2.20
❑ 374 Claude Osteen 8.00 3.60
❑ 375 Ken Boyer 15.00 6.75
❑ 376 John Wyatt 5.00 2.20
❑ 377 Baltimore Orioles 10.00 4.50
Team Card
❑ 378 Bill Henry 5.00 2.20
❑ 379 Bob Anderson 5.00 2.20
❑ 380 Ernie Banks UER 80.00 36.00
(Back has career Major
and Minor, but he
never played in Minors)
❑ 381 Frank Baumann 5.00 2.20
❑ 382 Ralph Houk MG 10.00 4.50
❑ 383 Pete Richert 5.00 2.20
❑ 384 Bob Tillman 5.00 2.20
❑ 385 Art Mahaffey 5.00 2.20
❑ 386 Rookie Stars 5.00 2.20
Ed Kirkpatrick
John Bateman RC RC
Larry Bearnarth
Garry Roggenburk
❑ 387 Al McBean 5.00 2.20
❑ 388 Jim Davenport 8.00 3.60
❑ 389 Frank Sullivan 5.00 2.20
❑ 390 Hank Aaron 125.00 55.00
❑ 391 Bill Dailey 5.00 2.20
❑ 392 Tribe Thumpers 5.00 2.20
Johnny Romano
Tito Francona
❑ 393 Ken MacKenzie 8.00 3.60
❑ 394 Tim McCarver 15.00 6.75
❑ 395 Don McMahon 5.00 2.20
❑ 396 Joe Koppe 5.00 2.20
❑ 397 Kansas City Athletics 10.00 4.50
Team Card
❑ 398 Boog Powell 25.00 11.00
❑ 399 Dick Ellsworth 5.00 2.20
❑ 400 Frank Robinson 60.00 27.00
❑ 401 Jim Bouton 15.00 6.75
❑ 402 Mickey Vernon MG 8.00 3.60
❑ 403 Ron Perranoski 8.00 3.60
❑ 404 Bob Oldis 5.00 2.20
❑ 405 Floyd Robinson 5.00 2.20
❑ 406 Howie Koplitz 5.00 2.20
❑ 407 Rookie Stars 8.00 3.60
Frank Kostro
Chico Ruiz
Larry Elliot
Dick Simpson
❑ 408 Billy Gardner 5.00 2.20
❑ 409 Roy Face 8.00 3.60
❑ 410 Earl Battey 5.00 2.20
❑ 411 Jim Constable 5.00 2.20
❑ 412 Dodger Big Three 50.00 22.00

Johnny Podres
Don Drysdale
Sandy Koufax
❑ 413 Jerry Walker 5.00 2.20
❑ 414 Ty Cline 5.00 2.20
❑ 415 Bob Gibson 60.00 27.00
❑ 416 Alex Grammas 5.00 2.20
❑ 417 Giants Team 10.00 4.50
❑ 418 John Orsino 5.00 2.20
❑ 419 Tracy Stallard 5.00 2.20
❑ 420 Bobby Richardson 15.00 6.75
❑ 421 Tom Morgan 5.00 2.20
❑ 422 Fred Hutchinson MG 8.00 3.60
❑ 423 Ed Hobaugh 5.00 2.20
❑ 424 Charlie Smith 5.00 2.20
❑ 425 Smoky Burgess 8.00 3.60
❑ 426 Barry Latman 5.00 2.20
❑ 427 Bernie Allen 5.00 2.20
❑ 428 Carl Boles 5.00 2.20
❑ 429 Lou Burdette 8.00 3.60
❑ 430 Norm Siebern 5.00 2.20
❑ 431A Checklist 6 12.00 2.40
(White on red)
❑ 431B Checklist 6 30.00 6.00
(Black on orange)
❑ 432 Roman Mejias 5.00 2.20
❑ 433 Denis Menke 5.00 2.20
❑ 434 John Callison 8.00 3.60
❑ 435 Woody Held 5.00 2.20
❑ 436 Tim Harkness 8.00 3.60
❑ 437 Bill Bruton 5.00 2.20
❑ 438 Wes Stock 5.00 2.20
❑ 439 Don Zimmer 8.00 3.60
❑ 440 Juan Marichal 30.00 13.50
❑ 441 Lee Thomas 8.00 3.60
❑ 442 J.C. Hartman 5.00 2.20
❑ 443 Jimmy Piersall 8.00 3.60
❑ 444 Jim Maloney 8.00 3.60
❑ 445 Norm Cash 10.00 4.50
❑ 446 Whitey Ford 60.00 27.00
❑ 447 Felix Mantilla 25.00 11.00
❑ 448 Jack Kralick 25.00 11.00
❑ 449 Jose Tartabull 25.00 11.00
❑ 450 Bob Friend 30.00 13.50
❑ 451 Indians Team 40.00 18.00
❑ 452 Barney Schultz 25.00 11.00
❑ 453 Jake Wood 25.00 11.00
❑ 454A Art Fowler 25.00 11.00
(Card number on white background)
❑ 454B Art Fowler 30.00 13.50
(Card number on orange background)
❑ 455 Ruben Amaro 25.00 11.00
❑ 456 Jim Coker 25.00 11.00
❑ 457 Tex Clevenger 25.00 11.00
❑ 458 Al Lopez MG 30.00 13.50
❑ 459 Dick LeMay 25.00 11.00
❑ 460 Del Crandall 30.00 13.50
❑ 461 Norm Bass 25.00 11.00
❑ 462 Wally Post 25.00 11.00
❑ 463 Joe Schaffernoth 25.00 11.00
❑ 464 Ken Aspromonte 25.00 11.00
❑ 465 Chuck Estrada 25.00 11.00
❑ 466 Rookie Stars SP 60.00 27.00
Nate Oliver
Tony Martinez
Bill Freehan RC
Jerry Robinson
❑ 467 Phil Ortega 25.00 11.00
❑ 468 Carroll Hardy 30.00 13.50
❑ 469 Jay Hook 30.00 13.50
❑ 470 Tom Tresh SP 60.00 27.00
❑ 471 Ken Retzer 25.00 11.00
❑ 472 Lou Brock 80.00 36.00
❑ 473 New York Mets Team Card 100.00 45.00
❑ 474 Jack Fisher 25.00 11.00
❑ 475 Gus Triandos 30.00 13.50
❑ 476 Frank Funk 25.00 11.00
❑ 477 Donn Clendenon 30.00 13.50
❑ 478 Paul Brown 25.00 11.00
❑ 479 Ed Brinkman 25.00 11.00
❑ 480 Bill Monbouquette 25.00 11.00
❑ 481 Bob Taylor 25.00 11.00
❑ 482 Felix Torres 25.00 11.00
❑ 483 Jim Owens UER 25.00 11.00
(Stat column for Wins has an R instead)
❑ 484 Dale Long SP 30.00 13.50
❑ 485 Jim Landis 25.00 11.00
❑ 486 Ray Sadecki 25.00 11.00
❑ 487 John Roseboro 30.00 13.50
❑ 488 Jerry Adair 25.00 11.00
❑ 489 Paul Toth 25.00 11.00
❑ 490 Willie McCovey 100.00 45.00
❑ 491 Harry Craft MG 25.00 11.00
❑ 492 Dave Wickersham 25.00 11.00
❑ 493 Walt Bond 25.00 11.00
❑ 494 Phil Regan 25.00 11.00
❑ 495 Frank Thomas SP 30.00 13.50
❑ 496 Rookie Stars 30.00 13.50
Steve Dalkowski RC
Fred Newman
Jack Smith
Carl Bouldin
❑ 497 Bennie Daniels 25.00 11.00
❑ 498 Eddie Kasko 25.00 11.00
❑ 499 J.C. Martin 25.00 11.00
❑ 500 Harmon Killebrew SP 150.00 70.00
❑ 501 Joe Azcue 25.00 11.00
❑ 502 Daryl Spencer 25.00 11.00
❑ 503 Braves Team 40.00 18.00
❑ 504 Bob Johnson 25.00 11.00
❑ 505 Curt Flood 40.00 18.00
❑ 506 Gene Green 25.00 11.00
❑ 507 Roland Sheldon 30.00 13.50
❑ 508 Ted Savage 25.00 11.00
❑ 509A Checklist 7 30.00 6.00
(Copyright centered)
❑ 509B Checklist 7 30.00 6.00
(Copyright to right)
❑ 510 Ken McBride 25.00 11.00
❑ 511 Charlie Neal 30.00 13.50
❑ 512 Cal McLish 25.00 11.00
❑ 513 Gary Geiger 25.00 11.00
❑ 514 Larry Osborne 25.00 11.00
❑ 515 Don Elston 25.00 11.00
❑ 516 Purnell Goldy 25.00 11.00
❑ 517 Hal Woodeshick 25.00 11.00
❑ 518 Don Blasingame 25.00 11.00
❑ 519 Claude Raymond RC 25.00 11.00
❑ 520 Orlando Cepeda 40.00 18.00
❑ 521 Dan Pfister 25.00 11.00
❑ 522 Rookie Stars 30.00 13.50
Mel Nelson
Gary Peters
Jim Roland
Art Quirk
❑ 523 Bill Kunkel 15.00 6.75
❑ 524 Cardinals Team 30.00 13.50
❑ 525 Nellie Fox 50.00 22.00
❑ 526 Dick Hall 15.00 6.75
❑ 527 Ed Sadowski 15.00 6.75
❑ 528 Carl Willey 15.00 6.75
❑ 529 Wes Covington 15.00 6.75
❑ 530 Don Mossi 20.00 9.00
❑ 531 Sam Mele MG 15.00 6.75
❑ 532 Steve Boros 15.00 6.75
❑ 533 Bobby Shantz 20.00 9.00
❑ 534 Ken Walters 15.00 6.75
❑ 535 Jim Perry 20.00 9.00
❑ 536 Norm Larker 15.00 6.75
❑ 537 Rookie Stars 850.00 375.00
Pedro Gonzalez
Ken McMullen
Al Weis
Pete Rose RC
❑ 538 George Brunet 15.00 6.75
❑ 539 Wayne Causey 15.00 6.75
❑ 540 Roberto Clemente 300.00 135.00
❑ 541 Ron Moeller 15.00 6.75
❑ 542 Lou Klimchock 15.00 6.75
❑ 543 Russ Snyder 15.00 6.75
❑ 544 Rookie Stars 50.00 22.00
Duke Carmel
Bill Haas
Rusty Staub RC
Dick Phillips
❑ 545 Jose Pagan 15.00 6.75
❑ 546 Hal Reniff 20.00 9.00
❑ 547 Gus Bell 15.00 6.75
❑ 548 Tom Satriano 15.00 6.75
❑ 549 Rookie Stars 15.00 6.75
Marcelino Lopez
Pete Lovrich
Paul Ratliff
Elmo Plaskett
❑ 550 Duke Snider 80.00 36.00
❑ 551 Billy Klaus 15.00 6.75
❑ 552 Detroit Tigers Team Card 50.00 22.00
❑ 553 Rookie Stars 125.00 55.00
Brock Davis
Jim Gosger
Willie Stargell RC
John Herrnstein
❑ 554 Hank Fischer 15.00 6.75
❑ 555 John Blanchard 20.00 9.00
❑ 556 Al Worthington 15.00 6.75
❑ 557 Cuno Barragan 15.00 6.75
❑ 558 Rookie Stars 20.00 9.00
Bill Faul
Ron Hunt RC
Al Moran
Bob Lipski
❑ 559 Danny Murtaugh MG 15.00 6.75
❑ 560 Ray Herbert 15.00 6.75
❑ 561 Mike De La Hoz 15.00 6.75
❑ 562 Rookie Stars 30.00 13.50
Randy Cardinal
Dave McNally RC
Ken Rowe
Don Rowe
❑ 563 Mike McCormick 15.00 6.75
❑ 564 George Banks 15.00 6.75
❑ 565 Larry Sherry 15.00 6.75
❑ 566 Cliff Cook 15.00 6.75
❑ 567 Jim Duffalo 15.00 6.75
❑ 568 Bob Sadowski 15.00 6.75
❑ 569 Luis Arroyo 20.00 9.00
❑ 570 Frank Bolling 15.00 6.75
❑ 571 Johnny Klippstein 15.00 6.75
❑ 572 Jack Spring 15.00 6.75
❑ 573 Coot Veal 15.00 6.75
❑ 574 Hal Kolstad 15.00 6.75
❑ 575 Don Cardwell 15.00 6.75
❑ 576 Johnny Temple 30.00 11.00

1964 Topps

	NRMT	VG-E
COMPLETE SET (587)	3000.00	1350.00
COMMON CARD (1-196)	3.00	1.35
COMMON CARD (197-370)	4.00	1.80
COMMON CARD (371-522)	7.00	3.10
COMMON CARD (523-587)	16.00	7.25
WRAPPER (1-CENT)	100.00	45.00
WRAP.(1-CENT, REPEAT)	125.00	55.00
WRAPPER (5-CENT)	30.00	13.50
WRAPPER (5-CENT, COIN)	40.00	18.00

❑ 1 NL ERA Leaders 30.00 9.00
Sandy Koufax
Dick Ellsworth
Bob Friend
❑ 2 AL ERA Leaders 8.00 3.60
Gary Peters
Juan Pizarro
Camilo Pascual

❑ 3 NL Pitching Leaders 20.00 9.00
Sandy Koufax
Juan Marichal
Warren Spahn
Jim Maloney
❑ 4 AL Pitching Leaders 8.00 3.60
Whitey Ford
Camilo Pascual
Jim Bouton
❑ 5 NL Strikeout Leaders 15.00 6.75
Sandy Koufax
Jim Maloney
Don Drysdale
❑ 6 AL Strikeout Leaders........ 8.00 3.60
Camilo Pascual
Jim Bunning
Dick Stigman
❑ 7 NL Batting Leaders 20.00 9.00
Tommy Davis
Roberto Clemente
Dick Groat
Hank Aaron
❑ 8 AL Batting Leaders 15.00 6.75
Carl Yastrzemski
Al Kaline
Rich Rollins
❑ 9 NL Home Run Leaders .. 30.00 13.50
Hank Aaron
Willie McCovey
Willie Mays
Orlando Cepeda
❑ 10 AL Home Run Leaders .. 8.00 3.60
Harmon Killebrew
Dick Stuart
Bob Allison
❑ 11 NL RBI Leaders............ 15.00 6.75
Hank Aaron
Ken Boyer
Bill White
❑ 12 AL RBI Leaders.............. 8.00 3.60
Dick Stuart
Al Kaline
Harmon Killebrew
❑ 13 Hoyt Wilhelm................ 12.00 5.50
❑ 14 Dodgers Rookies............ 3.00 1.35
Dick Nen RC
Nick Willhite
❑ 15 Zoilo Versalles................ 6.00 2.70
❑ 16 John Boozer 3.00 1.35
❑ 17 Willie Kirkland 3.00 1.35
❑ 18 Billy O'Dell...................... 3.00 1.35
❑ 19 Don Wert......................... 3.00 1.35
❑ 20 Bob Friend....................... 6.00 2.70
❑ 21 Yogi Berra MG 35.00 16.00
❑ 22 Jerry Adair...................... 3.00 1.35
❑ 23 Chris Zachary 3.00 1.35
❑ 24 Carl Sawatski 3.00 1.35
❑ 25 Bill Monbouquette 3.00 1.35
❑ 26 Gino Cimoli 3.00 1.35
❑ 27 New York Mets 8.00 3.60
Team Card
❑ 28 Claude Osteen 6.00 2.70
❑ 29 Lou Brock 35.00 16.00
❑ 30 Ron Perranoski 6.00 2.70
❑ 31 Dave Nicholson 3.00 1.35
❑ 32 Dean Chance 6.00 2.70
❑ 33 Reds Rookies 6.00 2.70
Sammy Ellis
Mel Queen
❑ 34 Jim Perry......................... 6.00 2.70
❑ 35 Eddie Mathews 20.00 9.00
❑ 36 Hal Reniff 3.00 1.35
❑ 37 Smoky Burgess 6.00 2.70
❑ 38 Jim Wynn RC 8.00 3.60
❑ 39 Hank Aguirre 3.00 1.35
❑ 40 Dick Groat 6.00 2.70
❑ 41 Friendly Foes 8.00 3.60
Willie McCovey
Leon Wagner
❑ 42 Moe Drabowsky 6.00 2.70
❑ 43 Roy Sievers..................... 6.00 2.70
❑ 44 Duke Carmel 3.00 1.35
❑ 45 Milt Pappas 6.00 2.70
❑ 46 Ed Brinkman 3.00 1.35
❑ 47 Giants Rookies 6.00 2.70
Jesus Alou RC
Ron Herbel
❑ 48 Bob Perry 3.00 1.35
❑ 49 Bill Henry........................ 3.00 1.35
❑ 50 Mickey Mantle 300.00 135.00
❑ 51 Pete Richert 3.00 1.35
❑ 52 Chuck Hinton.................. 3.00 1.35
❑ 53 Denis Menke 3.00 1.35
❑ 54 Sam Mele MG 3.00 1.35
❑ 55 Ernie Banks................. 35.00 16.00
❑ 56 Hal Brown 3.00 1.35
❑ 57 Tim Harkness 6.00 2.70
❑ 58 Don Demeter.................. 6.00 2.70
❑ 59 Ernie Broglio 3.00 1.35
❑ 60 Frank Malzone 6.00 2.70
❑ 61 Angel Backstops 6.00 2.70
Bob Rodgers
Ed Sadowski
❑ 62 Ted Savage..................... 3.00 1.35
❑ 63 John Orsino.................... 3.00 1.35
❑ 64 Ted Abernathy................ 3.00 1.35
❑ 65 Felipe Alou 6.00 2.70
❑ 66 Eddie Fisher 3.00 1.35
❑ 67 Tigers Team 6.00 2.70
❑ 68 Willie Davis 6.00 2.70
❑ 69 Clete Boyer 6.00 2.70
❑ 70 Joe Torre......................... 8.00 3.60
❑ 71 Jack Spring 3.00 1.35
❑ 72 Chico Cardenas 6.00 2.70
❑ 73 Jimmie Hall 8.00 3.60
❑ 74 Pirates Rookies.............. 3.00 1.35
Bob Priddy
Tom Butters
❑ 75 Wayne Causey 3.00 1.35
❑ 76 Checklist 1.................... 10.00 2.00
❑ 77 Jerry Walker 3.00 1.35
❑ 78 Merritt Ranew 3.00 1.35
❑ 79 Bob Heffner.................... 3.00 1.35
❑ 80 Vada Pinson 8.00 3.60
❑ 81 All-Star Vets 12.00 5.50
Nellie Fox
Harmon Killebrew
❑ 82 Jim Davenport................ 6.00 2.70
❑ 83 Gus Triandos.................. 6.00 2.70
❑ 84 Carl Willey...................... 3.00 1.35
❑ 85 Pete Ward 3.00 1.35
❑ 86 Al Downing 6.00 2.70
❑ 87 St. Louis Cardinals 6.00 2.70
Team Card
❑ 88 John Roseboro 6.00 2.70
❑ 89 Boog Powell 6.00 2.70
❑ 90 Earl Battey...................... 3.00 1.35
❑ 91 Bob Bailey...................... 6.00 2.70
❑ 92 Steve Ridzik 3.00 1.35
❑ 93 Gary Geiger.................... 3.00 1.35
❑ 94 Braves Rookies.............. 3.00 1.35
Jim Britton
Larry Maxie
❑ 95 George Altman 3.00 1.35
❑ 96 Bob Buhl 6.00 2.70
❑ 97 Jim Fregosi 6.00 2.70
❑ 98 Bill Bruton 3.00 1.35
❑ 99 Al Stanek........................ 3.00 1.35
❑ 100 Elston Howard.............. 6.00 2.70
❑ 101 Walt Alston MG............ 8.00 3.60
❑ 102 Checklist 2................ 10.00 2.00
❑ 103 Curt Flood 6.00 2.70
❑ 104 Art Mahaffey 6.00 2.70
❑ 105 Woody Held.................. 3.00 1.35
❑ 106 Joe Nuxhall 6.00 2.70
❑ 107 White Sox Rookies 3.00 1.35
Bruce Howard
Frank Kreutzer
❑ 108 John Wyatt 3.00 1.35
❑ 109 Rusty Staub.................. 6.00 2.70
❑ 110 Albie Pearson 6.00 2.70
❑ 111 Don Elston.................... 3.00 1.35
❑ 112 Bob Tillman 3.00 1.35
❑ 113 Grover Powell 6.00 2.70
❑ 114 Don Lock...................... 3.00 1.35
❑ 115 Frank Bolling 3.00 1.35
❑ 116 Twins Rookies............ 12.00 5.50
Jay Ward
Tony Oliva
❑ 117 Earl Francis.................. 3.00 1.35
❑ 118 John Blanchard 6.00 2.70
❑ 119 Gary Kolb 3.00 1.35
❑ 120 Don Drysdale 20.00 9.00
❑ 121 Pete Runnels................ 6.00 2.70
❑ 122 Don McMahon.............. 3.00 1.35
❑ 123 Jose Pagan 3.00 1.35
❑ 124 Orlando Pena 3.00 1.35
❑ 125 Pete Rose 150.00 70.00
❑ 126 Russ Snyder 3.00 1.35
❑ 127 Angels Rookies 3.00 1.35
Aubrey Gatewood
Dick Simpson
❑ 128 Mickey Lolich RC 20.00 9.00
❑ 129 Amado Samuel 3.00 1.35
❑ 130 Gary Peters 6.00 2.70
❑ 131 Steve Boros.................. 3.00 1.35
❑ 132 Braves Team................ 6.00 2.70
❑ 133 Jim Grant...................... 6.00 2.70
❑ 134 Don Zimmer 6.00 2.70
❑ 135 Johnny Callison............ 6.00 2.70
❑ 136 Sandy Koufax WS 20.00 9.00
strikes out 15
❑ 137 Willie Davis WS............ 8.00 3.60
❑ 138 Ron Fairly WS 8.00 3.60
❑ 139 Frank Howard WS........ 8.00 3.60
❑ 140 WS Summary 8.00 3.60
Dodgers celebrate
❑ 141 Danny Murtaugh MG.... 6.00 2.70
❑ 142 John Bateman.............. 3.00 1.35
❑ 143 Bubba Phillips 3.00 1.35
❑ 144 Al Worthington.............. 3.00 1.35
❑ 145 Norm Siebern 3.00 1.35
❑ 146 Indians Rookies.......... 30.00 13.50
Tommy John RC
Bob Chance
❑ 147 Ray Sadecki 3.00 1.35
❑ 148 J.C. Martin.................... 3.00 1.35
❑ 149 Paul Foytack 3.00 1.35
❑ 150 Willie Mays 100.00 45.00
❑ 151 Athletics Team 6.00 2.70
❑ 152 Denny Lemaster 3.00 1.35
❑ 153 Dick Williams................ 6.00 2.70
❑ 154 Dick Tracewski RC 6.00 2.70
❑ 155 Duke Snider 30.00 13.50
❑ 156 Bill Dailey 3.00 1.35
❑ 157 Gene Mauch MG.......... 6.00 2.70
❑ 158 Ken Johnson 3.00 1.35
❑ 159 Charlie Dees 3.00 1.35
❑ 160 Ken Boyer 6.00 2.70
❑ 161 Dave McNally 6.00 2.70
❑ 162 Hitting Area 6.00 2.70
Dick Sisler CO
Vada Pinson
❑ 163 Donn Clendenon 6.00 2.70
❑ 164 Bud Daley 3.00 1.35
❑ 165 Jerry Lumpe 3.00 1.35
❑ 166 Marty Keough 3.00 1.35
❑ 167 Senators Rookies 30.00 13.50
Mike Brumley
Lou Piniella RC
❑ 168 Al Weis 3.00 1.35
❑ 169 Del Crandall 6.00 2.70
❑ 170 Dick Radatz.................. 6.00 2.70
❑ 171 Ty Cline........................ 3.00 1.35
❑ 172 Indians Team 6.00 2.70
❑ 173 Ryne Duren 6.00 2.70
❑ 174 Doc Edwards................ 3.00 1.35
❑ 175 Billy Williams 12.00 5.50
❑ 176 Tracy Stallard 3.00 1.35
❑ 177 Harmon Killebrew 20.00 9.00
❑ 178 Hank Bauer MG 6.00 2.70
❑ 179 Carl Warwick................ 3.00 1.35
❑ 180 Tommy Davis 6.00 2.70
❑ 181 Dave Wickersham........ 3.00 1.35
❑ 182 Sox Sockers 15.00 6.75
Carl Yastrzemski
Chuck Schilling
❑ 183 Ron Taylor.................... 3.00 1.35
❑ 184 Al Luplow...................... 3.00 1.35
❑ 185 Jim O'Toole 6.00 2.70
❑ 186 Roman Mejias 3.00 1.35
❑ 187 Ed Roebuck.................. 3.00 1.35
❑ 188 Checklist 3.................. 10.00 2.00
❑ 189 Bob Hendley 3.00 1.35
❑ 190 Bobby Richardson........ 8.00 3.60
❑ 191 Clay Dalrymple 6.00 2.70
❑ 192 Cubs Rookies 3.00 1.35
John Boccabella

Billy Cowan
❑ 193 Jerry Lynch 3.00 1.35
❑ 194 John Goryl 3.00 1.35
❑ 195 Floyd Robinson 3.00 1.35
❑ 196 Jim Gentile 3.00 1.35
❑ 197 Frank Lary 6.00 2.70
❑ 198 Len Gabrielson 4.00 1.80
❑ 199 Joe Azcue 4.00 1.80
❑ 200 Sandy Koufax 100.00 45.00
❑ 201 Orioles Rookies 6.00 2.70
Sam Bowens
Wally Bunker
❑ 202 Galen Cisco 6.00 2.70
❑ 203 John Kennedy 6.00 2.70
❑ 204 Matty Alou 6.00 2.70
❑ 205 Nellie Fox 12.00 5.50
❑ 206 Steve Hamilton 6.00 2.70
❑ 207 Fred Hutchinson MG 6.00 2.70
❑ 208 Wes Covington 6.00 2.70
❑ 209 Bob Allen 4.00 1.80
❑ 210 Carl Yastrzemski 40.00 18.00
❑ 211 Jim Coker 4.00 1.80
❑ 212 Pete Lovrich 4.00 1.80
❑ 213 Angels Team 6.00 2.70
❑ 214 Ken McMullen 6.00 2.70
❑ 215 Ray Herbert 4.00 1.80
❑ 216 Mike de la Hoz 4.00 1.80
❑ 217 Jim King 4.00 1.80
❑ 218 Hank Fischer 4.00 1.80
❑ 219 Young Aces 6.00 2.70
Al Downing
Jim Bouton
❑ 220 Dick Ellsworth 6.00 2.70
❑ 221 Bob Saverine 4.00 1.80
❑ 222 Billy Pierce 6.00 2.70
❑ 223 George Banks 4.00 1.80
❑ 224 Tommie Sisk 4.00 1.80
❑ 225 Roger Maris 60.00 27.00
❑ 226 Colts Rookies 6.00 2.70
Jerry Grote RC
Larry Yellen
❑ 227 Barry Latman 4.00 1.80
❑ 228 Felix Mantilla 4.00 1.80
❑ 229 Charley Lau 6.00 2.70
❑ 230 Brooks Robinson 40.00 18.00
❑ 231 Dick Calmus 4.00 1.80
❑ 232 Al Lopez MG 6.00 2.70
❑ 233 Hal Smith 4.00 1.80
❑ 234 Gary Bell 4.00 1.80
❑ 235 Ron Hunt 4.00 1.80
❑ 236 Bill Faul 4.00 1.80
❑ 237 Cubs Team 6.00 2.70
❑ 238 Roy McMillan 6.00 2.70
❑ 239 Herm Starrette 4.00 1.80
❑ 240 Bill White 6.00 2.70
❑ 241 Jim Owens 4.00 1.80
❑ 242 Harvey Kuenn 6.00 2.70
❑ 243 Phillies Rookies 30.00 13.50
Richie Allen RC
John Herrnstein
❑ 244 Tony LaRussa RC 30.00 13.50
❑ 245 Dick Stigman 4.00 1.80
❑ 246 Manny Mota 6.00 2.70
❑ 247 Dave DeBusschere 6.00 2.70
❑ 248 Johnny Pesky MG 6.00 2.70
❑ 249 Doug Camilli 4.00 1.80
❑ 250 Al Kaline 40.00 18.00
❑ 251 Choo Choo Coleman 6.00 2.70
❑ 252 Ken Aspromonte 4.00 1.80
❑ 253 Wally Post 6.00 2.70
❑ 254 Don Hoak 6.00 2.70
❑ 255 Lee Thomas 6.00 2.70
❑ 256 Johnny Weekly 4.00 1.80
❑ 257 San Francisco Giants 6.00 2.70
Team Card
❑ 258 Garry Roggenburk 4.00 1.80
❑ 259 Harry Bright 4.00 1.80
❑ 260 Frank Robinson 40.00 18.00
❑ 261 Jim Hannan 4.00 1.80
❑ 262 Cards Rookies 8.00 3.60
Mike Shannon RC
Harry Fanok
❑ 263 Chuck Estrada 4.00 1.80
❑ 264 Jim Landis 4.00 1.80
❑ 265 Jim Bunning 12.00 5.50
❑ 266 Gene Freese 4.00 1.80
❑ 267 Wilbur Wood RC 6.00 2.70
❑ 268 Bill's Got It 6.00 2.70
Danny Murtaugh MG
Bill Virdon
❑ 269 Ellis Burton 4.00 1.80
❑ 270 Rich Rollins 6.00 2.70
❑ 271 Bob Sadowski 4.00 1.80
❑ 272 Jake Wood 4.00 1.80
❑ 273 Mel Nelson 4.00 1.80
❑ 274 Checklist 4 .... 10.00 2.00
❑ 275 John Tsitouris 4.00 1.80
❑ 276 Jose Tartabull 6.00 2.70
❑ 277 Ken Retzer 4.00 1.80
❑ 278 Bobby Shantz 6.00 2.70
❑ 279 Joe Koppe UER 4.00 1.80
(Glove on wrong hand)
❑ 280 Juan Marichal 12.00 5.50
❑ 281 Yankees Rookies 6.00 2.70
Jake Gibbs
Tom Metcalf
❑ 282 Bob Bruce 4.00 1.80
❑ 283 Tom McCraw RC 4.00 1.80
❑ 284 Dick Schofield 4.00 1.80
❑ 285 Robin Roberts 12.00 5.50
❑ 286 Don Landrum 4.00 1.80
❑ 287 Red Sox Rookies 50.00 22.00
Tony Conigliaro RC
Bill Spanswick
❑ 288 Al Moran 4.00 1.80
❑ 289 Frank Funk 4.00 1.80
❑ 290 Bob Allison 6.00 2.70
❑ 291 Phil Ortega 4.00 1.80
❑ 292 Mike Roarke 4.00 1.80
❑ 293 Phillies Team 6.00 2.70
❑ 294 Ken L. Hunt 4.00 1.80
❑ 295 Roger Craig 6.00 2.70
❑ 296 Ed Kirkpatrick 4.00 1.80
❑ 297 Ken MacKenzie 4.00 1.80
❑ 298 Harry Craft MG 4.00 1.80
❑ 299 Bill Stafford 4.00 1.80
❑ 300 Hank Aaron 100.00 45.00
❑ 301 Larry Brown 4.00 1.80
❑ 302 Dan Pfister 4.00 1.80
❑ 303 Jim Campbell 4.00 1.80
❑ 304 Bob Johnson 4.00 1.80
❑ 305 Jack Lamabe 4.00 1.80
❑ 306 Giant Gunners 40.00 18.00
Willie Mays
Orlando Cepeda
❑ 307 Joe Gibbon 4.00 1.80
❑ 308 Gene Stephens 4.00 1.80
❑ 309 Paul Toth 4.00 1.80
❑ 310 Jim Gilliam 6.00 2.70
❑ 311 Tom Brown RC 6.00 2.70
❑ 312 Tigers Rookies 4.00 1.80
Fritz Fisher
Fred Gladding
❑ 313 Chuck Hiller 4.00 1.80
❑ 314 Jerry Buchek 4.00 1.80
❑ 315 Bo Belinsky 6.00 2.70
❑ 316 Gene Oliver 4.00 1.80
❑ 317 Al Smith 4.00 1.80
❑ 318 Minnesota Twins 6.00 2.70
Team Card
❑ 319 Paul Brown 4.00 1.80
❑ 320 Rocky Colavito 12.00 5.50
❑ 321 Bob Lillis 4.00 1.80
❑ 322 George Brunet 4.00 1.80
❑ 323 John Buzhardt 4.00 1.80
❑ 324 Casey Stengel MG 15.00 6.75
❑ 325 Hector Lopez 6.00 2.70
❑ 326 Ron Brand 4.00 1.80
❑ 327 Don Blasingame 4.00 1.80
❑ 328 Bob Shaw 4.00 1.80
❑ 329 Russ Nixon 4.00 1.80
❑ 330 Tommy Harper 6.00 2.70
❑ 331 AL Bombers 150.00 70.00
Roger Maris
Norm Cash
Mickey Mantle
Al Kaline
❑ 332 Ray Washburn 4.00 1.80
❑ 333 Billy Moran 4.00 1.80
❑ 334 Lew Krausse 4.00 1.80
❑ 335 Don Mossi 6.00 2.70
❑ 336 Andre Rodgers 4.00 1.80
❑ 337 Dodgers Rookies 6.00 2.70
Al Ferrara
Jeff Torborg RC
❑ 338 Jack Kralick 4.00 1.80
❑ 339 Walt Bond 4.00 1.80
❑ 340 Joe Cunningham 4.00 1.80
❑ 341 Jim Roland 4.00 1.80
❑ 342 Willie Stargell 30.00 13.50
❑ 343 Senators Team 6.00 2.70
❑ 344 Phil Linz 6.00 2.70
❑ 345 Frank Thomas 8.00 3.60
❑ 346 Joey Jay 4.00 1.80
❑ 347 Bobby Wine 6.00 2.70
❑ 348 Ed Lopat MG 6.00 2.70
❑ 349 Art Fowler 4.00 1.80
❑ 350 Willie McCovey 25.00 11.00
❑ 351 Dan Schneider 4.00 1.80
❑ 352 Eddie Bressoud 4.00 1.80
❑ 353 Wally Moon 6.00 2.70
❑ 354 Dave Giusti 4.00 1.80
❑ 355 Vic Power 6.00 2.70
❑ 356 Reds Rookies 6.00 2.70
Bill McCool
Chico Ruiz
❑ 357 Charley James 4.00 1.80
❑ 358 Ron Kline 4.00 1.80
❑ 359 Jim Schaffer 4.00 1.80
❑ 360 Joe Pepitone 12.00 5.50
❑ 361 Jay Hook 4.00 1.80
❑ 362 Checklist 5 .... 10.00 2.00
❑ 363 Dick McAuliffe 6.00 2.70
❑ 364 Joe Gaines 4.00 1.80
❑ 365 Cal McLish 6.00 2.70
❑ 366 Nelson Mathews 4.00 1.80
❑ 367 Fred Whitfield 4.00 1.80
❑ 368 White Sox Rookies 6.00 2.70
Fritz Ackley
Don Buford RC
❑ 369 Jerry Zimmerman 4.00 1.80
❑ 370 Hal Woodeshick 4.00 1.80
❑ 371 Frank Howard 8.00 3.60
❑ 372 Howie Koplitz 7.00 3.10
❑ 373 Pirates Team 12.00 5.50
❑ 374 Bobby Bolin 7.00 3.10
❑ 375 Ron Santo 10.00 4.50
❑ 376 Dave Morehead 7.00 3.10
❑ 377 Bob Skinner 7.00 3.10
❑ 378 Braves Rookies 10.00 4.50
Woody Woodward RC
Jack Smith
❑ 379 Tony Gonzalez 7.00 3.10
❑ 380 Whitey Ford 40.00 18.00
❑ 381 Bob Taylor 7.00 3.10
❑ 382 Wes Stock 7.00 3.10
❑ 383 Bill Rigney MG 7.00 3.10
❑ 384 Ron Hansen 7.00 3.10
❑ 385 Curt Simmons 10.00 4.50
❑ 386 Lenny Green 7.00 3.10
❑ 387 Terry Fox 7.00 3.10
❑ 388 A's Rookies 10.00 4.50
John O'Donoghue RC
George Williams
❑ 389 Jim Umbricht 10.00 4.50
(Card back mentions
his death)
❑ 390 Orlando Cepeda 25.00 11.00
❑ 391 Sam McDowell 10.00 4.50
❑ 392 Jim Pagliaroni 7.00 3.10
❑ 393 Casey Teaches 15.00 6.75
Casey Stengel MG
Ed Kranepool
❑ 394 Bob Miller 7.00 3.10
❑ 395 Tom Tresh 10.00 4.50
❑ 396 Dennis Bennett 7.00 3.10
❑ 397 Chuck Cottier 7.00 3.10
❑ 398 Mets Rookies 10.00 4.50
Bill Haas
Dick Smith
❑ 399 Jackie Brandt 7.00 3.10
❑ 400 Warren Spahn 40.00 18.00
❑ 401 Charlie Maxwell 7.00 3.10
❑ 402 Tom Sturdivant 7.00 3.10
❑ 403 Reds Team 12.00 5.50
❑ 404 Tony Martinez 7.00 3.10
❑ 405 Ken McBride 7.00 3.10
❑ 406 Al Spangler 7.00 3.10

❑ 407 Bill Freehan 10.00 4.50
❑ 408 Cubs Rookies 7.00 3.10
Jim Stewart
Fred Burdette
❑ 409 Bill Fischer 7.00 3.10
❑ 410 Dick Stuart 10.00 4.50
❑ 411 Lee Walls 7.00 3.10
❑ 412 Ray Culp 10.00 4.50
❑ 413 Johnny Keane MG 7.00 3.10
❑ 414 Jack Sanford 7.00 3.10
❑ 415 Tony Kubek 15.00 6.75
❑ 416 Lee Maye 7.00 3.10
❑ 417 Don Cardwell 7.00 3.10
❑ 418 Orioles Rookies 10.00 4.50
Darold Knowles
Les Narum
❑ 419 Ken Harrelson RC 15.00 6.75
❑ 420 Jim Maloney 10.00 4.50
❑ 421 Camilo Carreon 7.00 3.10
❑ 422 Jack Fisher 7.00 3.10
❑ 423 Tops in NL 125.00 55.00
Hank Aaron
Willie Mays
❑ 424 Dick Bertell 7.00 3.10
❑ 425 Norm Cash 10.00 4.50
❑ 426 Bob Rodgers 7.00 3.10
❑ 427 Don Rudolph 7.00 3.10
❑ 428 Red Sox Rookies 7.00 3.10
Archie Skeen
Pete Smith
(Back states Archie
has retired)
❑ 429 Tim McCarver 10.00 4.50
❑ 430 Juan Pizarro 7.00 3.10
❑ 431 George Alusik 7.00 3.10
❑ 432 Ruben Amaro 10.00 4.50
❑ 433 Yankees Team 40.00 22.00
❑ 434 Don Nottebart 7.00 3.10
❑ 435 Vic Davalillo 7.00 3.10
❑ 436 Charlie Neal 10.00 4.50
❑ 437 Ed Bailey 7.00 3.10
❑ 438 Checklist 6 16.00 3.20
❑ 439 Harvey Haddix 10.00 4.50
❑ 440 R.Clemente UER 250.00 110.00
1960 Pittsburfh
❑ 441 Bob Duliba 7.00 3.10
❑ 442 Pumpsie Green 10.00 4.50
❑ 443 Chuck Dressen MG 10.00 4.50
❑ 444 Larry Jackson 7.00 3.10
❑ 445 Bill Skowron 10.00 4.50
❑ 446 Julian Javier 15.00 6.75
❑ 447 Ted Bowsfield 7.00 3.10
❑ 448 Cookie Rojas 10.00 4.50
❑ 449 Deron Johnson 10.00 4.50
❑ 450 Steve Barber 7.00 3.10
❑ 451 Joe Amalfitano 7.00 3.10
❑ 452 Giants Rookies 10.00 4.50
Gil Garrido
Jim Ray Hart RC
❑ 453 Frank Baumann 7.00 3.10
❑ 454 Tommie Aaron 10.00 4.50
❑ 455 Bernie Allen 7.00 3.10
❑ 456 Dodgers Rookies 10.00 4.50
Wes Parker RC
John Werhas
❑ 457 Jesse Gonder 7.00 3.10
❑ 458 Ralph Terry 10.00 4.50
❑ 459 Red Sox Rookies 7.00 3.10
Pete Charton
Dalton Jones
❑ 460 Bob Gibson 40.00 18.00
❑ 461 George Thomas 7.00 3.10
❑ 462 Birdie Tebbetts MG 7.00 3.10
❑ 463 Don Leppert 7.00 3.10
❑ 464 Dallas Green 15.00 6.75
❑ 465 Mike Hershberger 7.00 3.10
❑ 466 A's Rookies 10.00 4.50
Dick Green
Aurelio Monteagudo
❑ 467 Bob Aspromonte 7.00 3.10
❑ 468 Gaylord Perry 40.00 18.00
❑ 469 Cubs Rookies 10.00 4.50
Fred Norman
Sterling Slaughter
❑ 470 Jim Bouton 10.00 4.50
❑ 471 Gates Brown RC 10.00 4.50
❑ 472 Vern Law 10.00 4.50
❑ 473 Baltimore Orioles 12.00 5.50
Team Card
❑ 474 Larry Sherry 10.00 4.50
❑ 475 Ed Charles 7.00 3.10
❑ 476 Braves Rookies 15.00 6.75
Rico Carty RC
Dick Kelley
❑ 477 Mike Joyce 7.00 3.10
❑ 478 Dick Howser 10.00 4.50
❑ 479 Cardinals Rookies 7.00 3.10
Dave Bakenhaster
Johnny Lewis
❑ 480 Bob Purkey 7.00 3.10
❑ 481 Chuck Schilling 7.00 3.10
❑ 482 Phillies Rookies 10.00 4.50
John Briggs
Danny Cater
❑ 483 Fred Valentine 7.00 3.10
❑ 484 Bill Pleis 7.00 3.10
❑ 485 Tom Haller 7.00 3.10
❑ 486 Bob Kennedy MG 7.00 3.10
❑ 487 Mike McCormick 10.00 4.50
❑ 488 Yankees Rookies 15.00 6.75
Pete Mikkelsen
Bob Meyer
❑ 489 Julio Navarro 7.00 3.10
❑ 490 Ron Fairly 10.00 4.50
❑ 491 Ed Rakow 7.00 3.10
❑ 492 Colts Rookies 7.00 3.10
Jim Beauchamp RC
Mike White
❑ 493 Don Lee 7.00 3.10
❑ 494 Al Jackson 7.00 3.10
❑ 495 Bill Virdon 10.00 4.50
❑ 496 White Sox Team 12.00 5.50
❑ 497 Jeoff Long 7.00 3.10
❑ 498 Dave Stenhouse 7.00 3.10
❑ 499 Indians Rookies 7.00 3.10
Chico Salmon
Gordon Seyfried
❑ 500 Camilo Pascual 10.00 4.50
❑ 501 Bob Veale 10.00 4.50
❑ 502 Angels Rookies 7.00 3.10
Bobby Knoop RC
Bob Lee
❑ 503 Earl Wilson 7.00 3.10
❑ 504 Claude Raymond 7.00 3.10
❑ 505 Stan Williams 7.00 3.10
❑ 506 Bobby Bragan MG 7.00 3.10
❑ 507 Johnny Edwards 7.00 3.10
❑ 508 Diego Segui 7.00 3.10
❑ 509 Pirates Rookies 10.00 4.50
Gene Alley RC
Orlando McFarlane
❑ 510 Lindy McDaniel 10.00 4.50
❑ 511 Lou Jackson 10.00 4.50
❑ 512 Tigers Rookies 15.00 6.75
Willie Horton RC
Joe Sparma
❑ 513 Don Larsen 10.00 4.50
❑ 514 Jim Hickman 10.00 4.50
❑ 515 Johnny Romano 7.00 3.10
❑ 516 Twins Rookies 7.00 3.10
Jerry Arrigo
Dwight Siebler
❑ 517A Checklist 7 ERR 25.00 5.00
(Incorrect numbering
sequence on back)
❑ 517B Checklist 7 COR 16.00 3.20
(Correct numbering
on back)
❑ 518 Carl Bouldin 7.00 3.10
❑ 519 Charlie Smith 7.00 3.10
❑ 520 Jack Baldschun 10.00 4.50
❑ 521 Tom Satriano 7.00 3.10
❑ 522 Bob Tiefenauer 7.00 3.10
❑ 523 Lou Burdette UER 20.00 9.00
(Pitching lefty)
❑ 524 Reds Rookies 16.00 7.25
Jim Dickson
Bobby Klaus
❑ 525 Al McBean 16.00 7.25
❑ 526 Lou Clinton 16.00 7.25
❑ 527 Larry Bearnarth 16.00 7.25
❑ 528 A's Rookies 20.00 9.00
Dave Duncan RC
Tommie Reynolds
❑ 529 Alvin Dark MG 20.00 9.00
❑ 530 Leon Wagner 16.00 7.25
❑ 531 Los Angeles Dodgers 25.00 11.00
Team Card
❑ 532 Twins Rookies 16.00 7.25
Bud Bloomfield
(Bloomfield photo
actually Jay Ward)
Joe Nossek RC
❑ 533 Johnny Klippstein 16.00 7.25
❑ 534 Gus Bell 16.00 7.25
❑ 535 Phil Regan 16.00 7.25
❑ 536 Mets Rookies 16.00 7.25
Larry Elliot
John Stephenson
❑ 537 Dan Osinski 16.00 7.25
❑ 538 Minnie Minoso 20.00 9.00
❑ 539 Roy Face 20.00 9.00
❑ 540 Luis Aparicio 40.00 18.00
❑ 541 Braves Rookies 80.00 36.00
Phil Roof
Phil Niekro RC
❑ 542 Don Mincher 16.00 7.25
❑ 543 Bob Uecker 40.00 18.00
❑ 544 Colts Rookies 16.00 7.25
Steve Hertz
Joe Hoerner
❑ 545 Max Alvis 16.00 7.25
❑ 546 Joe Christopher 16.00 7.25
❑ 547 Gil Hodges MG 30.00 13.50
❑ 548 NL Rookies 20.00 9.00
Wayne Schurr
Paul Speckenbach
❑ 549 Joe Moeller 16.00 7.25
❑ 550 Ken Hubbs MEM 40.00 18.00
❑ 551 Billy Hoeft 16.00 7.25
❑ 552 Indians Rookies 16.00 7.25
Tom Kelley
Sonny Siebert
❑ 553 Jim Brewer 16.00 7.25
❑ 554 Hank Foiles 16.00 7.25
❑ 555 Lee Stange 16.00 7.25
❑ 556 Mets Rookies 16.00 7.25
Steve Dillon
Ron Locke
❑ 557 Leo Burke 16.00 7.25
❑ 558 Don Schwall 16.00 7.25
❑ 559 Dick Phillips 16.00 7.25
❑ 560 Dick Farrell 16.00 7.25
❑ 561 Phillies Rookies UER 20.00 9.00
Dave Bennett
(19 ... is 18)
Rick Wise RC
❑ 562 Pedro Ramos 16.00 7.25
❑ 563 Dal Maxvill 20.00 9.00
❑ 564 AL Rookies 20.00 9.00
Joe McCabe
Jerry McNertney
❑ 565 Stu Miller 16.00 7.25
❑ 566 Ed Kranepool 20.00 9.00
❑ 567 Jim Kaat 20.00 9.00
❑ 568 NL Rookies 16.00 7.25
Phil Gagliano
Cap Peterson
❑ 569 Fred Newman 16.00 7.25
❑ 570 Bill Mazeroski 40.00 18.00
❑ 571 Gene Conley 16.00 7.25
❑ 572 AL Rookies 16.00 7.25
Dave Gray
Dick Egan
❑ 573 Jim Duffalo 16.00 7.25
❑ 574 Manny Jimenez 16.00 7.25
❑ 575 Tony Cloninger 16.00 7.25
❑ 576 Mets Rookies 16.00 7.25
Jerry Hinsley
Bill Wakefield
❑ 577 Gordy Coleman 16.00 7.25
❑ 578 Glen Hobbie 16.00 7.25
❑ 579 Red Sox Team 25.00 11.00
❑ 580 Johnny Podres 20.00 9.00
❑ 581 Yankees Rookies 20.00 9.00
Pedro Gonzalez
Archie Moore
❑ 582 Rod Kanehl 20.00 9.00

Card	NRMT	VG-E
❑ 583 Tito Francona	16.00	7.25
❑ 584 Joel Horlen	16.00	7.25
❑ 585 Tony Taylor	20.00	9.00
❑ 586 Jimmy Piersall	20.00	9.00
❑ 587 Bennie Daniels	20.00	8.00

1965 Topps

	NRMT	VG-E
COMPLETE SET (598)	3500.00	1600.00
COMMON CARD (1-196)	2.00	.90
COMMON CARD (197-283)	2.50	1.10
COMMON CARD (284-370)	4.00	1.80
COMMON CARD (371-598)	7.00	3.10
WRAPPER (1-CENT)	125.00	55.00
WRAPPER (5-CENT)	100.00	45.00

Card	NRMT	VG-E
❑ 1 AL Batting Leaders	20.00	6.00
Tony Oliva		
Elston Howard		
Brooks Robinson		
❑ 2 NL Batting Leaders	25.00	11.00
Roberto Clemente		
Hank Aaron		
Rico Carty		
❑ 3 AL Home Run Leaders	50.00	22.00
Harmon Killebrew		
Mickey Mantle		
Boog Powell		
❑ 4 NL Home Run Leaders	15.00	6.75
Willie Mays		
Billy Williams		
Jim Ray Hart		
Orlando Cepeda		
Johnny Callison		
❑ 5 AL RBI Leaders	40.00	18.00
Brooks Robinson		
Harmon Killebrew		
Mickey Mantle		
Dick Stuart		
❑ 6 NL RBI Leaders	12.00	5.50
Ken Boyer		
Willie Mays		
Ron Santo		
❑ 7 AL ERA Leaders	5.00	2.20
Dean Chance		
Joel Horlen		
❑ 8 NL ERA Leaders	20.00	9.00
Sandy Koufax		
Don Drysdale		
❑ 9 AL Pitching Leaders	5.00	2.20
Dean Chance		
Gary Peters		
Dave Wickersham		
Juan Pizarro		
Wally Bunker		
❑ 10 NL Pitching Leaders	5.00	2.20
Larry Jackson		
Ray Sadecki		
Juan Marichal		
❑ 11 AL Strikeout Leaders	5.00	2.20
Al Downing		
Dean Chance		
Camilo Pascual		
❑ 12 NL Strikeout Leaders	10.00	4.50
Bob Veale		
Don Drysdale		
Bob Gibson		
❑ 13 Pedro Ramos	4.00	1.80
❑ 14 Len Gabrielson	2.00	.90
❑ 15 Robin Roberts	10.00	4.50
❑ 16 Houston Rookie DP	60.00	27.00
Joe Morgan RC		
Sonny Jackson		
❑ 17 Johnny Romano	2.00	.90
❑ 18 Bill McCool	2.00	.90
❑ 19 Gates Brown	4.00	1.80
❑ 20 Jim Bunning	10.00	4.50
❑ 21 Don Blasingame	2.00	.90
❑ 22 Charlie Smith	2.00	.90
❑ 23 Bob Tiefenauer	2.00	.90
❑ 24 Minnesota Twins	6.00	2.70
Team Card		
❑ 25 Al McBean	2.00	.90
❑ 26 Bobby Knoop	2.00	.90
❑ 27 Dick Bertell	2.00	.90
❑ 28 Barney Schultz	2.00	.90
❑ 29 Felix Mantilla	2.00	.90
❑ 30 Jim Bouton	6.00	2.70
❑ 31 Mike White	2.00	.90
❑ 32 Herman Franks MG	2.00	.90
❑ 33 Jackie Brandt	2.00	.90
❑ 34 Cal Koonce	2.00	.90
❑ 35 Ed Charles	2.00	.90
❑ 36 Bobby Wine	2.00	.90
❑ 37 Fred Gladding	2.00	.90
❑ 38 Jim King	2.00	.90
❑ 39 Gerry Arrigo	2.00	.90
❑ 40 Frank Howard	6.00	2.70
❑ 41 White Sox Rookies	2.00	.90
Bruce Howard		
Marv Staehle		
❑ 42 Earl Wilson	4.00	1.80
❑ 43 Mike Shannon	4.00	1.80
(Name in red, other		
Cardinals in yellow)		
❑ 44 Wade Blasingame	2.00	.90
❑ 45 Roy McMillan	4.00	1.80
❑ 46 Bob Lee	2.00	.90
❑ 47 Tommy Harper	4.00	1.80
❑ 48 Claude Raymond	4.00	1.80
❑ 49 Orioles Rookies	4.00	1.80
Curt Blefary RC		
John Miller		
❑ 50 Juan Marichal	10.00	4.50
❑ 51 Bill Bryan	2.00	.90
❑ 52 Ed Roebuck	2.00	.90
❑ 53 Dick McAuliffe	4.00	1.80
❑ 54 Joe Gibbon	2.00	.90
❑ 55 Tony Conigliaro	15.00	6.75
❑ 56 Ron Kline	2.00	.90
❑ 57 Cardinals Team	6.00	2.70
❑ 58 Fred Talbot	2.00	.90
❑ 59 Nate Oliver	2.00	.90
❑ 60 Jim O'Toole	4.00	1.80
❑ 61 Chris Cannizzaro	2.00	.90
❑ 62 Jim Kaat UER DP	6.00	2.70
(Misspelled Katt)		
❑ 63 Ty Cline	2.00	.90
❑ 64 Lou Burdette	4.00	1.80
❑ 65 Tony Kubek	10.00	4.50
❑ 66 Bill Rigney MG	2.00	.90
❑ 67 Harvey Haddix	4.00	1.80
❑ 68 Del Crandall	4.00	1.80
❑ 69 Bill Virdon	4.00	1.80
❑ 70 Bill Skowron	6.00	2.70
❑ 71 John O'Donoghue	2.00	.90
❑ 72 Tony Gonzalez	2.00	.90
❑ 73 Dennis Ribant	2.00	.90
❑ 74 Red Sox Rookies	10.00	4.50
Rico Petrocelli RC		
Jerry Stephenson		
❑ 75 Deron Johnson	4.00	1.80
❑ 76 Sam McDowell	6.00	2.70
❑ 77 Doug Camilli	2.00	.90
❑ 78 Dal Maxvill	2.00	.90
❑ 79A Checklist 1	10.00	2.00
(61 Cannizzaro)		
❑ 79B Checklist 1	10.00	2.00
(61 C.Cannizzaro)		
❑ 80 Turk Farrell	2.00	.90
❑ 81 Don Buford	4.00	1.80
❑ 82 Braves Rookies	6.00	2.70
Santos Alomar RC		
John Braun		
❑ 83 George Thomas	2.00	.90
❑ 84 Ron Herbel	2.00	.90
❑ 85 Willie Smith	2.00	.90
❑ 86 Les Narum	2.00	.90
❑ 87 Nelson Mathews	2.00	.90
❑ 88 Jack Lamabe	2.00	.90
❑ 89 Mike Hershberger	2.00	.90
❑ 90 Rich Rollins	4.00	1.80
❑ 91 Cubs Team	6.00	2.70
❑ 92 Dick Howser	4.00	1.80
❑ 93 Jack Fisher	2.00	.90
❑ 94 Charlie Lau	4.00	1.80
❑ 95 Bill Mazeroski DP	6.00	2.70
❑ 96 Sonny Siebert	4.00	1.80
❑ 97 Pedro Gonzalez	2.00	.90
❑ 98 Bob Miller	2.00	.90
❑ 99 Gil Hodges MG	6.00	2.70
❑ 100 Ken Boyer	10.00	4.50
❑ 101 Fred Newman	2.00	.90
❑ 102 Steve Boros	2.00	.90
❑ 103 Harvey Kuenn	4.00	1.80
❑ 104 Checklist 2	10.00	2.00
❑ 105 Chico Salmon	2.00	.90
❑ 106 Gene Oliver	2.00	.90
❑ 107 Phillies Rookies	4.00	1.80
Pat Corrales RC		
Costen Shockley		
❑ 108 Don Mincher	2.00	.90
❑ 109 Walt Bond	2.00	.90
❑ 110 Ron Santo	6.00	2.70
❑ 111 Lee Thomas	4.00	1.80
❑ 112 Derrell Griffith	2.00	.90
❑ 113 Steve Barber	2.00	.90
❑ 114 Jim Hickman	4.00	1.80
❑ 115 Bobby Richardson	10.00	4.50
❑ 116 Cardinals Rookies	4.00	1.80
Dave Dowling		
Bob Tolan RC		
❑ 117 Wes Stock	2.00	.90
❑ 118 Hal Lanier	4.00	1.80
❑ 119 John Kennedy	2.00	.90
❑ 120 Frank Robinson	35.00	16.00
❑ 121 Gene Alley	4.00	1.80
❑ 122 Bill Pleis	2.00	.90
❑ 123 Frank Thomas	4.00	1.80
❑ 124 Tom Satriano	2.00	.90
❑ 125 Juan Pizarro	2.00	.90
❑ 126 Dodgers Team	6.00	2.70
❑ 127 Frank Lary	2.00	.90
❑ 128 Vic Davalillo	2.00	.90
❑ 129 Bennie Daniels	2.00	.90
❑ 130 Al Kaline	35.00	16.00
❑ 131 Johnny Keane MG	2.00	.90
❑ 132 Mike Shannon WS	10.00	4.50
❑ 133 Mel Stottlemyre WS	6.00	2.70
❑ 134 Mickey Mantle WS	80.00	36.00
Mantle's Clutch HR		
❑ 135 Ken Boyer WS	10.00	4.50
❑ 136 Tim McCarver WS	6.00	2.70
❑ 137 Jim Bouton WS	6.00	2.70
❑ 138 Bob Gibson WS	12.00	5.50
❑ 139 WS Summary	6.00	2.70
Cards celebrate		
❑ 140 Dean Chance	4.00	1.80
❑ 141 Charlie James	2.00	.90
❑ 142 Bill Monbouquette	2.00	.90
❑ 143 Pirates Rookies	2.00	.90
John Gelnar		
Jerry May		
❑ 144 Ed Kranepool	4.00	1.80
❑ 145 Luis Tiant RC	10.00	4.50
❑ 146 Ron Hansen	2.00	.90
❑ 147 Dennis Bennett	2.00	.90
❑ 148 Willie Kirkland	2.00	.90
❑ 149 Wayne Schurr	2.00	.90
❑ 150 Brooks Robinson	40.00	18.00
❑ 151 Athletics Team	6.00	2.70
❑ 152 Phil Ortega	2.00	.90
❑ 153 Norm Cash	6.00	2.70
❑ 154 Bob Humphreys	2.00	.90
❑ 155 Roger Maris	60.00	27.00
❑ 156 Bob Sadowski	2.00	.90
❑ 157 Zoilo Versalles	4.00	1.80
❑ 158 Dick Sisler	2.00	.90
❑ 159 Jim Duffalo	2.00	.90

❑ 160 R.Clemente UER...... 175.00 80.00
1960 Pittsburfh
❑ 161 Frank Baumann........... 2.00 .90
❑ 162 Russ Nixon .... 2.00 .90
❑ 163 Johnny Briggs .... 2.00 .90
❑ 164 Al Spangler .... 2.00 .90
❑ 165 Dick Ellsworth .... 2.00 .90
❑ 166 Indians Rookies........... 4.00 1.80
George Culver
Tommie Agee RC
❑ 167 Bill Wakefield.............. 2.00 .90
❑ 168 Dick Green .... 2.00 .90
❑ 169 Dave Vineyard............ 2.00 .90
❑ 170 Hank Aaron 100.00 45.00
❑ 171 Jim Roland .... 2.00 .90
❑ 172 Jimmy Piersall 6.00 2.70
❑ 173 Detroit Tigers.............. 6.00 2.70
Team Card
❑ 174 Joey Jay .... 2.00 .90
❑ 175 Bob Aspromonte .... 2.00 .90
❑ 176 Willie McCovey 20.00 9.00
❑ 177 Pete Mikkelsen .... 2.00 .90
❑ 178 Dalton Jones .... 2.00 .90
❑ 179 Hal Woodeshick .... 2.00 .90
❑ 180 Bob Allison 4.00 1.80
❑ 181 Senators Rookies .... 2.00 .90
Don Loun
Joe McCabe
❑ 182 Mike de la Hoz .... 2.00 .90
❑ 183 Dave Nicholson........... 2.00 .90
❑ 184 John Boozer .... 2.00 .90
❑ 185 Max Alvis.................... 2.00 .90
❑ 186 Billy Cowan .... 2.00 .90
❑ 187 Casey Stengel MG 15.00 6.75
❑ 188 Sam Bowens............... 2.00 .90
❑ 189 Checklist 3................ 10.00 2.00
❑ 190 Bill White 6.00 2.70
❑ 191 Phil Regan.................. 4.00 1.80
❑ 192 Jim Coker .... 2.00 .90
❑ 193 Gaylord Perry 15.00 6.75
❑ 194 Rookie Stars .... 2.00 .90
Bill Kelso
Rick Reichardt
❑ 195 Bob Veale 4.00 1.80
❑ 196 Ron Fairly 4.00 1.80
❑ 197 Diego Segui................ 2.50 1.10
❑ 198 Smoky Burgess........... 4.00 1.80
❑ 199 Bob Heffner................ 2.50 1.10
❑ 200 Joe Torre.................... 6.00 2.70
❑ 201 Twins Rookies............ 4.00 1.80
Sandy Valdespino
Cesar Tovar RC
❑ 202 Leo Burke 2.50 1.10
❑ 203 Dallas Green 4.00 1.80
❑ 204 Russ Snyder 2.50 1.10
❑ 205 Warren Spahn........... 30.00 13.50
❑ 206 Willie Horton 4.00 1.80
❑ 207 Pete Rose 125.00 55.00
❑ 208 Tommy John 6.00 2.70
❑ 209 Pirates Team.............. 6.00 2.70
❑ 210 Jim Fregosi 4.00 1.80
❑ 211 Steve Ridzik 2.50 1.10
❑ 212 Ron Brand.................. 2.50 1.10
❑ 213 Jim Davenport............. 2.50 1.10
❑ 214 Bob Purkey 2.50 1.10
❑ 215 Pete Ward 2.50 1.10
❑ 216 Al Worthington............ 2.50 1.10
❑ 217 Walter Alston MG 6.00 2.70
❑ 218 Dick Schofield 2.50 1.10
❑ 219 Bob Meyer.................. 2.50 1.10
❑ 220 Billy Williams 10.00 4.50
❑ 221 John Tsitouris 2.50 1.10
❑ 222 Bob Tillman 2.50 1.10
❑ 223 Dan Osinski................ 2.50 1.10
❑ 224 Bob Chance 2.50 1.10
❑ 225 Bo Belinsky 4.00 1.80
❑ 226 Yankees Rookies 6.00 2.70
Elvio Jimenez
Jake Gibbs
❑ 227 Bobby Klaus 2.50 1.10
❑ 228 Jack Sanford 2.50 1.10
❑ 229 Lou Clinton 2.50 1.10
❑ 230 Ray Sadecki 2.50 1.10
❑ 231 Jerry Adair................. 2.50 1.10
❑ 232 Steve Blass RC 4.00 1.80
❑ 233 Don Zimmer 4.00 1.80
❑ 234 White Sox Team 6.00 2.70
❑ 235 Chuck Hinton.............. 2.50 1.10
❑ 236 Denny McLain RC...... 25.00 11.00
❑ 237 Bernie Allen................ 2.50 1.10
❑ 238 Joe Moeller 2.50 1.10
❑ 239 Doc Edwards.............. 2.50 1.10
❑ 240 Bob Bruce 2.50 1.10
❑ 241 Mack Jones................ 2.50 1.10
❑ 242 George Brunet............ 2.50 1.10
❑ 243 Reds Rookies 4.00 1.80
Ted Davidson
Tommy Helms RC
❑ 244 Lindy McDaniel 4.00 1.80
❑ 245 Joe Pepitone 6.00 2.70
❑ 246 Tom Butters................ 4.00 1.80
❑ 247 Wally Moon 4.00 1.80
❑ 248 Gus Triandos.............. 4.00 1.80
❑ 249 Dave McNally 4.00 1.80
❑ 250 Willie Mays 100.00 45.00
❑ 251 Billy Herman MG......... 4.00 1.80
❑ 252 Pete Richert 2.50 1.10
❑ 253 Danny Cater 2.50 1.10
❑ 254 Roland Sheldon........... 2.50 1.10
❑ 255 Camilo Pascual 4.00 1.80
❑ 256 Tito Francona 2.50 1.10
❑ 257 Jim Wynn 4.00 1.80
❑ 258 Larry Bearnarth 2.50 1.10
❑ 259 Tigers Rookies 6.00 2.70
Jim Northrup RC
Ray Oyler
❑ 260 Don Drysdale 20.00 9.00
❑ 261 Duke Carmel 2.50 1.10
❑ 262 Bud Daley 2.50 1.10
❑ 263 Marty Keough 2.50 1.10
❑ 264 Bob Buhl 4.00 1.80
❑ 265 Jim Pagliaroni 2.50 1.10
❑ 266 Bert Campaneris RC.. 10.00 4.50
❑ 267 Senators Team 6.00 2.70
❑ 268 Ken McBride 2.50 1.10
❑ 269 Frank Bolling 2.50 1.10
❑ 270 Milt Pappas 4.00 1.80
❑ 271 Don Wert 4.00 1.80
❑ 272 Chuck Schilling 2.50 1.10
❑ 273 Checklist 4................ 10.00 2.00
❑ 274 Lum Harris MG 2.50 1.10
❑ 275 Dick Groat 6.00 2.70
❑ 276 Hoyt Wilhelm 10.00 4.50
❑ 277 Johnny Lewis 2.50 1.10
❑ 278 Ken Retzer 2.50 1.10
❑ 279 Dick Tracewski 2.50 1.10
❑ 280 Dick Stuart.................. 4.00 1.80
❑ 281 Bill Stafford 2.50 1.10
❑ 282 Giants Rookies 40.00 18.00
Dick Estelle
Masanori Murakami RC
❑ 283 Fred Whitfield 2.50 1.10
❑ 284 Nick Willhite............... 4.00 1.80
❑ 285 Ron Hunt.................... 4.00 1.80
❑ 286 Athletics Rookies......... 4.00 1.80
Jim Dickson
Aurelio Monteagudo
❑ 287 Gary Kolb 4.00 1.80
❑ 288 Jack Hamilton 4.00 1.80
❑ 289 Gordy Coleman........... 6.00 2.70
❑ 290 Wally Bunker.............. 6.00 2.70
❑ 291 Jerry Lynch 4.00 1.80
❑ 292 Larry Yellen 4.00 1.80
❑ 293 Angels Team 6.00 2.70
❑ 294 Tim McCarver 10.00 4.50
❑ 295 Dick Radatz................ 6.00 2.70
❑ 296 Tony Taylor 6.00 2.70
❑ 297 Dave DeBusschere 10.00 4.50
❑ 298 Jim Stewart 4.00 1.80
❑ 299 Jerry Zimmerman 4.00 1.80
❑ 300 Sandy Koufax 100.00 45.00
❑ 301 Birdie Tebbetts MG 6.00 2.70
❑ 302 Al Stanek.................... 4.00 1.80
❑ 303 John Orsino................ 4.00 1.80
❑ 304 Dave Stenhouse 4.00 1.80
❑ 305 Rico Carty 6.00 2.70
❑ 306 Bubba Phillips 4.00 1.80
❑ 307 Barry Latman.............. 4.00 1.80
❑ 308 Mets Rookies 6.00 2.70
Cleon Jones RC
Tom Parsons
❑ 309 Steve Hamilton 6.00 2.70
❑ 310 Johnny Callison........... 6.00 2.70
❑ 311 Orlando Pena 4.00 1.80
❑ 312 Joe Nuxhall 4.00 1.80
❑ 313 Jim Schaffer 4.00 1.80
❑ 314 Sterling Slaughter 4.00 1.80
❑ 315 Frank Malzone 6.00 2.70
❑ 316 Reds Team 6.00 2.70
❑ 317 Don McMahon............. 4.00 1.80
❑ 318 Matty Alou 6.00 2.70
❑ 319 Ken McMullen 4.00 1.80
❑ 320 Bob Gibson 50.00 22.00
❑ 321 Rusty Staub.............. 10.00 4.50
❑ 322 Rick Wise 6.00 2.70
❑ 323 Hank Bauer MG 6.00 2.70
❑ 324 Bobby Locke 4.00 1.80
❑ 325 Donn Clendenon 6.00 2.70
❑ 326 Dwight Siebler 4.00 1.80
❑ 327 Denis Menke 4.00 1.80
❑ 328 Eddie Fisher 4.00 1.80
❑ 329 Hawk Taylor 4.00 1.80
❑ 330 Whitey Ford.............. 40.00 18.00
❑ 331 Dodgers Rookies......... 6.00 2.70
Al Ferrara
John Purdin
❑ 332 Ted Abernathy............. 4.00 1.80
❑ 333 Tom Reynolds............. 4.00 1.80
❑ 334 Vic Roznovsky............. 4.00 1.80
❑ 335 Mickey Lolich.............. 6.00 2.70
❑ 336 Woody Held................ 4.00 1.80
❑ 337 Mike Cuellar 6.00 2.70
❑ 338 Philadelphia Phillies 6.00 2.70
Team Card
❑ 339 Ryne Duren................ 6.00 2.70
❑ 340 Tony Oliva 20.00 9.00
❑ 341 Bob Bolin.................... 4.00 1.80
❑ 342 Bob Rodgers 6.00 2.70
❑ 343 Mike McCormick 6.00 2.70
❑ 344 Wes Parker 6.00 2.70
❑ 345 Floyd Robinson 4.00 1.80
❑ 346 Bobby Bragan MG........ 4.00 1.80
❑ 347 Roy Face.................... 6.00 2.70
❑ 348 George Banks 4.00 1.80
❑ 349 Larry Miller 4.00 1.80
❑ 350 Mickey Mantle 450.00 200.00
❑ 351 Jim Perry.................... 6.00 2.70
❑ 352 Alex Johnson RC 6.00 2.70
❑ 353 Jerry Lumpe 4.00 1.80
❑ 354 Cubs Rookies 4.00 1.80
Billy Ott
Jack Warner
❑ 355 Vada Pinson 10.00 4.50
❑ 356 Bill Spanswick 4.00 1.80
❑ 357 Carl Warwick.............. 4.00 1.80
❑ 358 Albie Pearson 6.00 2.70
❑ 359 Ken Johnson 4.00 1.80
❑ 360 Orlando Cepeda 15.00 6.75
❑ 361 Checklist 5............... 12.00 2.40
❑ 362 Don Schwall 4.00 1.80
❑ 363 Bob Johnson 4.00 1.80
❑ 364 Galen Cisco................ 4.00 1.80
❑ 365 Jim Gentile 6.00 2.70
❑ 366 Dan Schneider 4.00 1.80
❑ 367 Leon Wagner.............. 4.00 1.80
❑ 368 White Sox Rookies 6.00 2.70
Ken Berry
Joel Gibson
❑ 369 Phil Linz..................... 6.00 2.70
❑ 370 Tommy Davis 6.00 2.70
❑ 371 Frank Kreutzer 7.00 3.10
❑ 372 Clay Dalrymple 7.00 3.10
❑ 373 Curt Simmons 7.00 3.10
❑ 374 Angels Rookies 7.00 3.10
Jose Cardenal RC
Dick Simpson
❑ 375 Dave Wickersham........ 7.00 3.10
❑ 376 Jim Landis.................. 7.00 3.10
❑ 377 Willie Stargell 25.00 11.00
❑ 378 Chuck Estrada............. 7.00 3.10
❑ 379 Giants Team 7.00 3.10
❑ 380 Rocky Colavito 25.00 11.00
❑ 381 Al Jackson.................. 7.00 3.10
❑ 382 J.C. Martin.................. 7.00 3.10
❑ 383 Felipe Alou 15.00 6.75
❑ 384 Johnny Klippstein 7.00 3.10
❑ 385 Carl Yastrzemski 60.00 27.00
❑ 386 Cubs Rookies 7.00 3.10

Paul Jaeckel
Fred Norman
❑ 387 Johnny Podres 15.00 6.75
❑ 388 John Blanchard 15.00 6.75
❑ 389 Don Larsen 15.00 6.75
❑ 390 Bill Freehan 15.00 6.75
❑ 391 Mel McGaha MG 7.00 3.10
❑ 392 Bob Friend 15.00 6.75
❑ 393 Ed Kirkpatrick 7.00 3.10
❑ 394 Jim Hannan 7.00 3.10
❑ 395 Jim Ray Hart 7.00 3.10
❑ 396 Frank Bertaina 7.00 3.10
❑ 397 Jerry Buchek 7.00 3.10
❑ 398 Reds Rookies 15.00 6.75
Dan Neville
Art Shamsky
❑ 399 Ray Herbert 7.00 3.10
❑ 400 Harmon Killebrew 50.00 22.00
❑ 401 Carl Willey 7.00 3.10
❑ 402 Joe Amalfitano 7.00 3.10
❑ 403 Boston Red Sox 7.00 3.10
Team Card
❑ 404 Stan Williams 7.00 3.10
(Listed as Indian
but Yankee cap)
❑ 405 John Roseboro 20.00 9.00
❑ 406 Ralph Terry 15.00 6.75
❑ 407 Lee Maye 7.00 3.10
❑ 408 Larry Sherry 7.00 3.10
❑ 409 Astros Rookies 15.00 6.75
Jim Beauchamp
Larry Dierker RC
❑ 410 Luis Aparicio 25.00 11.00
❑ 411 Roger Craig 15.00 6.75
❑ 412 Bob Bailey 7.00 3.10
❑ 413 Hal Reniff 7.00 3.10
❑ 414 Al Lopez MG 15.00 6.75
❑ 415 Curt Flood 15.00 6.75
❑ 416 Jim Brewer 7.00 3.10
❑ 417 Ed Brinkman 7.00 3.10
❑ 418 Johnny Edwards 7.00 3.10
❑ 419 Ruben Amaro 7.00 3.10
❑ 420 Larry Jackson 7.00 3.10
❑ 421 Twins Rookies 7.00 3.10
Gary Dotter
Jay Ward
❑ 422 Aubrey Gatewood 7.00 3.10
❑ 423 Jesse Gonder 7.00 3.10
❑ 424 Gary Bell 7.00 3.10
❑ 425 Wayne Causey 7.00 3.10
❑ 426 Braves Team 7.00 3.10
❑ 427 Bob Saverine 7.00 3.10
❑ 428 Bob Shaw 7.00 3.10
❑ 429 Don Demeter 7.00 3.10
❑ 430 Gary Peters 7.00 3.10
❑ 431 Cards Rookies 15.00 6.75
Nelson Briles RC
Wayne Spiezio
❑ 432 Jim Grant 15.00 6.75
❑ 433 John Bateman 7.00 3.10
❑ 434 Dave Morehead 7.00 3.10
❑ 435 Willie Davis 15.00 6.75
❑ 436 Don Elston 7.00 3.10
❑ 437 Chico Cardenas 15.00 6.75
❑ 438 Harry Walker MG 7.00 3.10
❑ 439 Moe Drabowsky 15.00 6.75
❑ 440 Tom Tresh 15.00 6.75
❑ 441 Denny Lemaster 7.00 3.10
❑ 442 Vic Power 7.00 3.10
❑ 443 Checklist 6 .... 12.00 2.40
❑ 444 Bob Hendley 7.00 3.10
❑ 445 Don Lock 7.00 3.10
❑ 446 Art Mahaffey 7.00 3.10
❑ 447 Julian Javier 15.00 6.75
❑ 448 Lee Stange 7.00 3.10
❑ 449 Mets Rookies 15.00 6.75
Jerry Hinsley
Gary Kroll
❑ 450 Elston Howard 15.00 6.75
❑ 451 Jim Owens 7.00 3.10
❑ 452 Gary Geiger 7.00 3.10
❑ 453 Dodgers Rookies 15.00 6.75
Willie Crawford
John Werhas
❑ 454 Ed Rakow 7.00 3.10
❑ 455 Norm Siebern 7.00 3.10
❑ 456 Bill Henry 7.00 3.10
❑ 457 Bob Kennedy MG 15.00 6.75
❑ 458 John Buzhardt 7.00 3.10
❑ 459 Frank Kostro 7.00 3.10
❑ 460 Richie Allen 40.00 18.00
❑ 461 Braves Rookies 50.00 22.00
Clay Carroll RC
Phil Niekro
❑ 462 Lew Krausse UER 7.00 3.10
(Photo actually
Pete Lovrich)
❑ 463 Manny Mota 15.00 6.75
❑ 464 Ron Piche 7.00 3.10
❑ 465 Tom Haller 15.00 6.75
❑ 466 Senators Rookies 7.00 3.10
Pete Craig
Dick Nen
❑ 467 Ray Washburn 7.00 3.10
❑ 468 Larry Brown 7.00 3.10
❑ 469 Don Nottebart 7.00 3.10
❑ 470 Yogi Berra P/CO 50.00 22.00
❑ 471 Billy Hoeft 7.00 3.10
❑ 472 Don Pavletich UER 7.00 3.10
Listed as a pitcher
❑ 473 Orioles Rookies 15.00 6.75
Paul Blair
Dave Johnson RC
❑ 474 Cookie Rojas 15.00 6.75
❑ 475 Clete Boyer 15.00 6.75
❑ 476 Billy O'Dell 7.00 3.10
❑ 477 Cards Rookies 175.00 80.00
Fritz Ackley
Steve Carlton RC
❑ 478 Wilbur Wood 15.00 6.75
❑ 479 Ken Harrelson 15.00 6.75
❑ 480 Joel Horlen 7.00 3.10
❑ 481 Cleveland Indians 10.00 4.50
Team Card
❑ 482 Bob Priddy 7.00 3.10
❑ 483 George Smith 7.00 3.10
❑ 484 Ron Perranoski 20.00 9.00
❑ 485 Nellie Fox P/CO 25.00 11.00
❑ 486 Angels Rookies 7.00 3.10
Tom Egan
Pat Rogan
❑ 487 Woody Woodward 15.00 6.75
❑ 488 Ted Wills 7.00 3.10
❑ 489 Gene Mauch MG 15.00 6.75
❑ 490 Earl Battey 7.00 3.10
❑ 491 Tracy Stallard 7.00 3.10
❑ 492 Gene Freese 7.00 3.10
❑ 493 Tigers Rookies 7.00 3.10
Bill Roman
Bruce Brubaker
❑ 494 Jay Ritchie 7.00 3.10
❑ 495 Joe Christopher 7.00 3.10
❑ 496 Joe Cunningham 7.00 3.10
❑ 497 Giants Rookies 15.00 6.75
Ken Henderson
Jack Hiatt
❑ 498 Gene Stephens 7.00 3.10
❑ 499 Stu Miller 15.00 6.75
❑ 500 Eddie Mathews 40.00 18.00
❑ 501 Indians Rookies 7.00 3.10
Ralph Gagliano
Jim Rittwage
❑ 502 Don Cardwell 7.00 3.10
❑ 503 Phil Gagliano 7.00 3.10
❑ 504 Jerry Grote 15.00 6.75
❑ 505 Ray Culp 7.00 3.10
❑ 506 Sam Mele MG 7.00 3.10
❑ 507 Sammy Ellis 7.00 3.10
❑ 508 Checklist 7 .... 12.00 2.40
❑ 509 Red Sox Rookies 7.00 3.10
Bob Guindon
Gerry Vezendy
❑ 510 Ernie Banks 80.00 36.00
❑ 511 Ron Locke 7.00 3.10
❑ 512 Cap Peterson 7.00 3.10
❑ 513 New York Yankees 40.00 18.00
Team Card
❑ 514 Joe Azcue 7.00 3.10
❑ 515 Vern Law 15.00 6.75
❑ 516 Al Weis 7.00 3.10
❑ 517 Angels Rookies 15.00 6.75
Paul Schaal
Jack Warner
❑ 518 Ken Rowe 7.00 3.10
❑ 519 Bob Uecker UER 30.00 13.50
(Posing as a left-
handed batter)
❑ 520 Tony Cloninger 7.00 3.10
❑ 521 Phillies Rookies 7.00 3.10
Dave Bennett
Morrie Stevens
❑ 522 Hank Aguirre 7.00 3.10
❑ 523 Mike Brumley SP 12.00 5.50
❑ 524 Dave Giusti SP 12.00 5.50
❑ 525 Eddie Bressoud 7.00 3.10
❑ 526 Athletics Rookies SP .. 80.00 36.00
Rene Lachemann
Johnny Odom
Jim Hunter RC UER
(Tim on back)
Skip Lockwood
❑ 527 Jeff Torborg SP 12.00 5.50
❑ 528 George Altman 7.00 3.10
❑ 529 Jerry Fosnow SP 12.00 5.50
❑ 530 Jim Maloney 15.00 6.75
❑ 531 Chuck Hiller 7.00 3.10
❑ 532 Hector Lopez 15.00 6.75
❑ 533 Mets Rookies SP 25.00 11.00
Dan Napoleon
Ron Swoboda RC
Tug McGraw RC
Jim Bethke
❑ 534 John Herrnstein 7.00 3.10
❑ 535 Jack Kralick SP 12.00 5.50
❑ 536 Andre Rodgers SP 12.00 5.50
❑ 537 Angels Rookies 7.00 3.10
Marcelino Lopez
Phil Roof
Rudy May RC
❑ 538 C.Dressen SP MG 12.00 5.50
❑ 539 Herm Starrette 7.00 3.10
❑ 540 Lou Brock SP 50.00 22.00
❑ 541 White Sox Rookies 7.00 3.10
Greg Bollo
Bob Locker
❑ 542 Lou Klimchock 7.00 3.10
❑ 543 Ed Connolly SP 12.00 5.50
❑ 544 Howie Reed 7.00 3.10
❑ 545 Jesus Alou SP 14.00 6.25
❑ 546 Indians Rookies 7.00 3.10
Bill Davis
Mike Hedlund
Ray Barker
Floyd Weaver
❑ 547 Jake Wood SP 12.00 5.50
❑ 548 Dick Stigman 7.00 3.10
❑ 549 Cubs Rookies SP 20.00 9.00
Roberto Pena
Glenn Beckert RC
❑ 550 M.Stottlemyre RC SP 30.00 13.50
❑ 551 New York Mets SP 30.00 13.50
Team Card
❑ 552 Julio Gotay 7.00 3.10
❑ 553 Astros Rookies 7.00 3.10
Dan Coombs
Gene Ratliff
Jack McClure
❑ 554 Chico Ruiz SP 12.00 5.50
❑ 555 Jack Baldschun SP 12.00 5.50
❑ 556 Red Schoendienst 24.00 11.00
SP MG
❑ 557 Jose Santiago 7.00 3.10
❑ 558 Tommie Sisk 7.00 3.10
❑ 559 Ed Bailey SP 12.00 5.50
❑ 560 Boog Powell SP 24.00 11.00
❑ 561 Dodgers Rookies 15.00 6.75
Dennis Daboll
Mike Kekich
Hector Valle
Jim Lefebvre RC
❑ 562 Billy Moran 7.00 3.10
❑ 563 Julio Navarro 7.00 3.10
❑ 564 Mel Nelson 7.00 3.10
❑ 565 Ernie Broglio SP 12.00 5.50
❑ 566 Yankees Rookies SP 12.00 5.50
Gil Blanco
Ross Moschitto
Art Lopez

	No.	Player	NRMT	VG-E
❑	567	Tommie Aaron	7.00	3.10
❑	568	Ron Taylor SP	12.00	5.50
❑	569	Gino Cimoli SP	12.00	5.50
❑	570	Claude Osteen SP	15.00	6.75
❑	571	Ossie Virgil SP	12.00	5.50
❑	572	Baltimore Orioles SP	25.00	11.00
		Team Card		
❑	573	Red Sox Rookies SP	24.00	11.00
		Jim Lonborg RC		
		Gerry Moses		
		Bill Schlesinger		
		Mike Ryan		
❑	574	Roy Sievers	15.00	6.75
❑	575	Jose Pagan	7.00	3.10
❑	576	Terry Fox SP	12.00	5.50
❑	577	AL Rookie Stars SP	12.00	5.50
		Darold Knowles		
		Don Buschhorn		
		Richie Scheinblum		
❑	578	Camilo Carreon SP	12.00	5.50
❑	579	Dick Smith SP	12.00	5.50
❑	580	Jimmie Hall SP	12.00	5.50
❑	581	NL Rookie Stars SP	80.00	36.00
		Tony Perez RC		
		Dave Ricketts		
		Kevin Collins		
❑	582	Bob Schmidt SP	12.00	5.50
❑	583	Wes Covington SP	12.00	5.50
❑	584	Harry Bright	15.00	6.75
❑	585	Hank Fischer	7.00	3.10
❑	586	Tom McCraw SP	12.00	5.50
❑	587	Joe Sparma	7.00	3.10
❑	588	Lenny Green	7.00	3.10
❑	589	Giants Rookies SP	12.00	5.50
		Frank Linzy		
		Bob Schroder		
❑	590	John Wyatt	7.00	3.10
❑	591	Bob Skinner SP	12.00	5.50
❑	592	Frank Bork SP	12.00	5.50
❑	593	Tigers Rookies SP	12.00	5.50
		Jackie Moore RC		
		John Sullivan		
❑	594	Joe Gaines	7.00	3.10
❑	595	Don Lee	7.00	3.10
❑	596	Don Landrum SP	12.00	5.50
❑	597	Twins Rookies	7.00	3.10
		Joe Nossek		
		John Sevcik		
		Dick Reese		
❑	598	Al Downing SP	24.00	7.25

1966 Topps

	NRMT	VG-E
COMPLETE SET (598)	4000.00	1800.00
COMMON CARD (1-109)	1.50	.70
COMMON CARD (110-283)	2.00	.90
COMMON CARD (284-370)	3.00	1.35
COMMON CARD (371-446)	5.00	2.20
COMMON CARD (447-522)	9.00	4.00
COMMON CARD (523-598)	15.00	6.75
COMMON SP (523-598)	30.00	13.50
WRAPPER (5-CENT)	25.00	11.00

	No.	Player	NRMT	VG-E
❑	1	Willie Mays	150.00	47.50
❑	2	Ted Abernathy	1.50	.70
❑	3	Sam Mele MG	1.50	.70
❑	4	Ray Culp	1.50	.70
❑	5	Jim Fregosi	4.00	1.80
❑	6	Chuck Schilling	1.50	.70
❑	7	Tracy Stallard	1.50	.70
❑	8	Floyd Robinson	1.50	.70
❑	9	Clete Boyer	4.00	1.80
❑	10	Tony Cloninger	1.50	.70
❑	11	Senators Rookies	1.50	.70
		Brant Alyea		
		Pete Craig		
❑	12	John Tsitouris	1.50	.70
❑	13	Lou Johnson	4.00	1.80
❑	14	Norm Siebern	1.50	.70
❑	15	Vern Law	4.00	1.80
❑	16	Larry Brown	1.50	.70
❑	17	John Stephenson	1.50	.70
❑	18	Roland Sheldon	1.50	.70
❑	19	San Francisco Giants	5.00	2.20
		Team Card		
❑	20	Willie Horton	4.00	1.80
❑	21	Don Nottebart	1.50	.70
❑	22	Joe Nossek	1.50	.70
❑	23	Jack Sanford	1.50	.70
❑	24	Don Kessinger RC	6.00	2.70
❑	25	Pete Ward	1.50	.70
❑	26	Ray Sadecki	1.50	.70
❑	27	Orioles Rookies	1.50	.70
		Darold Knowles		
		Andy Etchebarren		
❑	28	Phil Niekro	20.00	9.00
❑	29	Mike Brumley	1.50	.70
❑	30	Pete Rose DP	50.00	22.00
❑	31	Jack Cullen	4.00	1.80
❑	32	Adolfo Phillips	1.50	.70
❑	33	Jim Pagliaroni	1.50	.70
❑	34	Checklist 1	8.00	1.60
❑	35	Ron Swoboda	4.00	1.80
❑	36	Jim Hunter UER	20.00	9.00
		Stats say 1963 and 1964		
		should be 1964 and 1965		
❑	37	Billy Herman MG	4.00	1.80
❑	38	Ron Nischwitz	1.50	.70
❑	39	Ken Henderson	1.50	.70
❑	40	Jim Grant	1.50	.70
❑	41	Don LeJohn	1.50	.70
❑	42	Aubrey Gatewood	1.50	.70
❑	43A	Don Landrum	4.00	1.80
		(Dark button on pants		
		showing)		
❑	43B	Don Landrum	20.00	9.00
		(Button on pants		
		partially airbrushed)		
❑	43C	Don Landrum	4.00	1.80
		(Button on pants		
		not showing)		
❑	44	Indians Rookies	1.50	.70
		Bill Davis		
		Tom Kelley		
❑	45	Jim Gentile	4.00	1.80
❑	46	Howie Koplitz	1.50	.70
❑	47	J.C. Martin	1.50	.70
❑	48	Paul Blair	4.00	1.80
❑	49	Woody Woodward	4.00	1.80
❑	50	Mickey Mantle DP	250.00	110.00
❑	51	Gordon Richardson	1.50	.70
❑	52	Power Plus	4.00	1.80
		Wes Covington		
		Johnny Callison		
❑	53	Bob Duliba	1.50	.70
❑	54	Jose Pagan	1.50	.70
❑	55	Ken Harrelson	4.00	1.80
❑	56	Sandy Valdespino	1.50	.70
❑	57	Jim Lefebvre	4.00	1.80
❑	58	Dave Wickersham	1.50	.70
❑	59	Reds Team	5.00	2.20
❑	60	Curt Flood	6.00	2.70
❑	61	Bob Bolin	1.50	.70
❑	62A	Merritt Ranew	4.00	1.80
		(With sold line)		
❑	62B	Merritt Ranew	30.00	13.50
		(Without sold line)		
❑	63	Jim Stewart	1.50	.70
❑	64	Bob Bruce	1.50	.70
❑	65	Leon Wagner	1.50	.70
❑	66	Al Weis	1.50	.70
❑	67	Mets Rookies	4.00	1.80
		Cleon Jones		
		Dick Selma		
❑	68	Hal Reniff	1.50	.70
❑	69	Ken Hamlin	1.50	.70
❑	70	Carl Yastrzemski	30.00	13.50
❑	71	Frank Carpin	1.50	.70
❑	72	Tony Perez	25.00	11.00
❑	73	Jerry Zimmerman	1.50	.70
❑	74	Don Mossi	4.00	1.80
❑	75	Tommy Davis	4.00	1.80
❑	76	Red Schoendienst MG	4.00	1.80
❑	77	John Orsino	1.50	.70
❑	78	Frank Linzy	1.50	.70
❑	79	Joe Pepitone	4.00	1.80
❑	80	Richie Allen	6.00	2.70
❑	81	Ray Oyler	1.50	.70
❑	82	Bob Hendley	1.50	.70
❑	83	Albie Pearson	4.00	1.80
❑	84	Braves Rookies	1.50	.70
		Jim Beauchamp		
		Dick Kelley		
❑	85	Eddie Fisher	1.50	.70
❑	86	John Bateman	1.50	.70
❑	87	Dan Napoleon	1.50	.70
❑	88	Fred Whitfield	1.50	.70
❑	89	Ted Davidson	1.50	.70
❑	90	Luis Aparicio	8.00	3.60
❑	91A	Bob Uecker TR	10.00	4.50
❑	91B	Bob Uecker NTR	40.00	18.00
❑	92	Yankees Team	14.00	6.25
❑	93	Jim Lonborg	4.00	1.80
❑	94	Matty Alou	4.00	1.80
❑	95	Pete Richert	1.50	.70
❑	96	Felipe Alou	4.00	1.80
❑	97	Jim Merritt	1.50	.70
❑	98	Don Demeter	1.50	.70
❑	99	Buc Belters	6.00	2.70
		Willie Stargell		
		Donn Clendenon		
❑	100	Sandy Koufax	75.00	34.00
❑	101A	Checklist 2	16.00	3.20
		(115 W. Spahn) ERR		
❑	101B	Checklist 2	10.00	2.00
		(115 Bill Henry) COR		
❑	102	Ed Kirkpatrick	1.50	.70
❑	103A	Dick Groat TR	4.00	1.80
❑	103B	Dick Groat NTR	40.00	18.00
❑	104A	Alex Johnson TR	4.00	1.80
❑	104B	Alex Johnson NTR	30.00	13.50
❑	105	Milt Pappas	4.00	1.80
❑	106	Rusty Staub	4.00	1.80
❑	107	A's Rookies	1.50	.70
		Larry Stahl		
		Ron Tompkins		
❑	108	Bobby Klaus	1.50	.70
❑	109	Ralph Terry	4.00	1.80
❑	110	Ernie Banks	30.00	13.50
❑	111	Gary Peters	2.00	.90
❑	112	Manny Mota	4.00	1.80
❑	113	Hank Aguirre	2.00	.90
❑	114	Jim Gosger	2.00	.90
❑	115	Bill Henry	2.00	.90
❑	116	Walter Alston MG	6.00	2.70
❑	117	Jake Gibbs	4.00	1.80
❑	118	Mike McCormick	4.00	1.80
❑	119	Art Shamsky	2.00	.90
❑	120	Harmon Killebrew	15.00	6.75
❑	121	Ray Herbert	2.00	.90
❑	122	Joe Gaines	2.00	.90
❑	123	Pirates Rookies	2.00	.90
		Frank Bork		
		Jerry May		
❑	124	Tug McGraw	4.00	1.80
❑	125	Lou Brock	20.00	9.00
❑	126	Jim Palmer RC UER	100.00	45.00
		Described as a		
		lefthander on		
		card back		
❑	127	Ken Berry	2.00	.90
❑	128	Jim Landis	2.00	.90
❑	129	Jack Kralick	2.00	.90
❑	130	Joe Torre	6.00	2.70
❑	131	Angels Team	5.00	2.20
❑	132	Orlando Cepeda	8.00	3.60

❑ 133 Don McMahon 2.00 .90
❑ 134 Wes Parker 4.00 1.80
❑ 135 Dave Morehead 2.00 .90
❑ 136 Woody Held 2.00 .90
❑ 137 Pat Corrales 4.00 1.80
❑ 138 Roger Repoz 2.00 .90
❑ 139 Cubs Rookies 2.00 .90
Byron Browne
Don Young
❑ 140 Jim Maloney 4.00 1.80
❑ 141 Tom McCraw 2.00 .90
❑ 142 Don Dennis 2.00 .90
❑ 143 Jose Tartabull 4.00 1.80
❑ 144 Don Schwall 2.00 .90
❑ 145 Bill Freehan 4.00 1.80
❑ 146 George Altman 2.00 .90
❑ 147 Lum Harris MG 2.00 .90
❑ 148 Bob Johnson 2.00 .90
❑ 149 Dick Nen 2.00 .90
❑ 150 Rocky Colavito 8.00 3.60
❑ 151 Gary Wagner 2.00 .90
❑ 152 Frank Malzone 4.00 1.80
❑ 153 Rico Carty 4.00 1.80
❑ 154 Chuck Hiller 2.00 .90
❑ 155 Marcelino Lopez 2.00 .90
❑ 156 Double Play Combo 2.00 .90
Dick Schofield
Hal Lanier
❑ 157 Rene Lachemann 2.00 .90
❑ 158 Jim Brewer 2.00 .90
❑ 159 Chico Ruiz 2.00 .90
❑ 160 Whitey Ford 25.00 11.00
❑ 161 Jerry Lumpe 2.00 .90
❑ 162 Lee Maye 2.00 .90
❑ 163 Tito Francona 2.00 .90
❑ 164 White Sox Rookies 4.00 1.80
Tommie Agee
Marv Staehle
❑ 165 Don Lock 2.00 .90
❑ 166 Chris Krug 2.00 .90
❑ 167 Boog Powell 6.00 2.70
❑ 168 Dan Osinski 2.00 .90
❑ 169 Duke Sims 2.00 .90
❑ 170 Cookie Rojas 4.00 1.80
❑ 171 Nick Willhite 2.00 .90
❑ 172 Mets Team 5.00 2.20
❑ 173 Al Spangler 2.00 .90
❑ 174 Ron Taylor 2.00 .90
❑ 175 Bert Campaneris 4.00 1.80
❑ 176 Jim Davenport 2.00 .90
❑ 177 Hector Lopez 2.00 .90
❑ 178 Bob Tillman 2.00 .90
❑ 179 Cards Rookies 4.00 1.80
Dennis Aust
Bob Tolan
❑ 180 Vada Pinson 4.00 1.80
❑ 181 Al Worthington 2.00 .90
❑ 182 Jerry Lynch 2.00 .90
❑ 183A Checklist 3 8.00 1.60
(Large print
on front)
❑ 183B Checklist 3 8.00 1.60
(Small print
on front)
❑ 184 Denis Menke 2.00 .90
❑ 185 Bob Buhl 4.00 1.80
❑ 186 Ruben Amaro 2.00 .90
❑ 187 Chuck Dressen MG 4.00 1.80
❑ 188 Al Luplow 2.00 .90
❑ 189 John Roseboro 4.00 1.80
❑ 190 Jimmie Hall 2.00 .90
❑ 191 Darrell Sutherland 2.00 .90
❑ 192 Vic Power 4.00 1.80
❑ 193 Dave McNally 4.00 1.80
❑ 194 Senators Team 5.00 2.20
❑ 195 Joe Morgan 15.00 6.75
❑ 196 Don Pavletich 2.00 .90
❑ 197 Sonny Siebert 2.00 .90
❑ 198 Mickey Stanley RC 6.00 2.70
❑ 199 Chisox Clubbers 4.00 1.80
Bill Skowron
Johnny Romano
Floyd Robinson
❑ 200 Eddie Mathews 15.00 6.75
❑ 201 Jim Dickson 2.00 .90
❑ 202 Clay Dalrymple 2.00 .90
❑ 203 Jose Santiago 2.00 .90
❑ 204 Cubs Team 5.00 2.20
❑ 205 Tom Tresh 4.00 1.80
❑ 206 Al Jackson 2.00 .90
❑ 207 Frank Quilici 2.00 .90
❑ 208 Bob Miller 2.00 .90
❑ 209 Tigers Rookies 4.00 1.80
Fritz Fisher
John Hiller RC
❑ 210 Bill Mazeroski 8.00 3.60
❑ 211 Frank Kreutzer 2.00 .90
❑ 212 Ed Kranepool 4.00 1.80
❑ 213 Fred Newman 2.00 .90
❑ 214 Tommy Harper 4.00 1.80
❑ 215 NL Batting Leaders 50.00 22.00
Bob Clemente
Hank Aaron
Willie Mays
❑ 216 AL Batting Leaders 5.00 2.20
Tony Oliva
Carl Yastrzemski
Vic Davalillo
❑ 217 NL HR Leaders 20.00 9.00
Willie Mays
Willie McCovey
Billy Williams
❑ 218 AL HR Leaders 5.00 2.20
Tony Conigliaro
Norm Cash
Willie Horton
❑ 219 NL RBI Leaders 12.00 5.50
Deron Johnson
Frank Robinson
Willie Mays
❑ 220 AL RBI Leaders 5.00 2.20
Rocky Colavito
Willie Horton
Tony Oliva
❑ 221 NL ERA Leaders 12.00 5.50
Sandy Koufax
Juan Marichal
Vern Law
❑ 222 AL ERA Leaders 5.00 2.20
Sam McDowell
Eddie Fisher
Sonny Siebert
❑ 223 NL Pitching Leaders 12.00 5.50
Sandy Koufax
Tony Cloninger
Don Drysdale
❑ 224 AL Pitching Leaders 5.00 2.20
Jim Grant
Mel Stottlemyre
Jim Kaat
❑ 225 NL Strikeout Leaders 12.00 5.50
Sandy Koufax
Bob Veale
Bob Gibson
❑ 226 AL Strikeout Leaders 5.00 2.20
Sam McDowell
Mickey Lolich
Dennis McLain
Sonny Siebert
❑ 227 Russ Nixon 2.00 .90
❑ 228 Larry Dierker 4.00 1.80
❑ 229 Hank Bauer MG 4.00 1.80
❑ 230 Johnny Callison 4.00 1.80
❑ 231 Floyd Weaver 2.00 .90
❑ 232 Glenn Beckert 4.00 1.80
❑ 233 Dom Zanni 2.00 .90
❑ 234 Yankees Rookies 8.00 3.60
Rich Beck
Roy White RC
❑ 235 Don Cardwell 2.00 .90
❑ 236 Mike Hershberger 2.00 .90
❑ 237 Billy O'Dell 2.00 .90
❑ 238 Dodgers Team 5.00 2.20
❑ 239 Orlando Pena 2.00 .90
❑ 240 Earl Battey 2.00 .90
❑ 241 Dennis Ribant 2.00 .90
❑ 242 Jesus Alou 2.00 .90
❑ 243 Nelson Briles 4.00 1.80
❑ 244 Astros Rookies 2.00 .90
Chuck Harrison
Sonny Jackson
❑ 245 John Buzhardt 2.00 .90
❑ 246 Ed Bailey 2.00 .90
❑ 247 Carl Warwick 2.00 .90
❑ 248 Pete Mikkelsen 2.00 .90
❑ 249 Bill Rigney MG 2.00 .90
❑ 250 Sammy Ellis 2.00 .90
❑ 251 Ed Brinkman 2.00 .90
❑ 252 Denny Lemaster 2.00 .90
❑ 253 Don Wert 2.00 .90
❑ 254 Phillies Rookies 70.00 32.00
Ferguson Jenkins RC
Bill Sorrell
❑ 255 Willie Stargell 20.00 9.00
❑ 256 Lew Krausse 2.00 .90
❑ 257 Jeff Torborg 4.00 1.80
❑ 258 Dave Giusti 2.00 .90
❑ 259 Boston Red Sox 5.00 2.20
Team Card
❑ 260 Bob Shaw 2.00 .90
❑ 261 Ron Hansen 2.00 .90
❑ 262 Jack Hamilton 2.00 .90
❑ 263 Tom Egan 2.00 .90
❑ 264 Twins Rookies 2.00 .90
Andy Kosco
Ted Uhlaender
❑ 265 Stu Miller 4.00 1.80
❑ 266 Pedro Gonzalez UER 2.00 .90
(Misspelled Gonzales
on card back)
❑ 267 Joe Sparma 2.00 .90
❑ 268 John Blanchard 2.00 .90
❑ 269 Don Heffner MG 2.00 .90
❑ 270 Claude Osteen 4.00 1.80
❑ 271 Hal Lanier 2.00 .90
❑ 272 Jack Baldschun 2.00 .90
❑ 273 Astro Aces 4.00 1.80
Bob Aspromonte
Rusty Staub
❑ 274 Buster Narum 2.00 .90
❑ 275 Tim McCarver 4.00 1.80
❑ 276 Jim Bouton 4.00 1.80
❑ 277 George Thomas 2.00 .90
❑ 278 Cal Koonce 2.00 .90
❑ 279A Checklist 4 8.00 1.60
(Player's cap black)
❑ 279B Checklist 4 8.00 1.60
(Player's cap red)
❑ 280 Bobby Knoop 2.00 .90
❑ 281 Bruce Howard 2.00 .90
❑ 282 Johnny Lewis 2.00 .90
❑ 283 Jim Perry 4.00 1.80
❑ 284 Bobby Wine 3.00 1.35
❑ 285 Luis Tiant 5.00 2.20
❑ 286 Gary Geiger 3.00 1.35
❑ 287 Jack Aker 3.00 1.35
❑ 288 Dodgers Rookies 50.00 22.00
Bill Singer
Don Sutton RC
❑ 289 Larry Sherry 3.00 1.35
❑ 290 Ron Santo 5.00 2.20
❑ 291 Moe Drabowsky 5.00 2.20
❑ 292 Jim Coker 3.00 1.35
❑ 293 Mike Shannon 5.00 2.20
❑ 294 Steve Ridzik 3.00 1.35
❑ 295 Jim Ray Hart 5.00 2.20
❑ 296 Johnny Keane MG 5.00 2.20
❑ 297 Jim Owens 3.00 1.35
❑ 298 Rico Petrocelli 5.00 2.20
❑ 299 Lou Burdette 5.00 2.20
❑ 300 Bob Clemente 150.00 70.00
❑ 301 Greg Bollo 3.00 1.35
❑ 302 Ernie Bowman 3.00 1.35
❑ 303 Cleveland Indians 5.00 2.20
Team Card
❑ 304 John Herrnstein 3.00 1.35
❑ 305 Camilo Pascual 5.00 2.20
❑ 306 Ty Cline 3.00 1.35
❑ 307 Clay Carroll 5.00 2.20
❑ 308 Tom Haller 5.00 2.20
❑ 309 Diego Segui 3.00 1.35
❑ 310 Frank Robinson 40.00 18.00
❑ 311 Reds Rookies 5.00 2.20
Tommy Helms
Dick Simpson
❑ 312 Bob Saverine 3.00 1.35
❑ 313 Chris Zachary 3.00 1.35
❑ 314 Hector Valle 3.00 1.35

❑	315	Norm Cash	5.00	2.20
❑	316	Jack Fisher	3.00	1.35
❑	317	Dalton Jones	3.00	1.35
❑	318	Harry Walker MG	3.00	1.35
❑	319	Gene Freese	3.00	1.35
❑	320	Bob Gibson	25.00	11.00
❑	321	Rick Reichardt	3.00	1.35
❑	322	Bill Faul	3.00	1.35
❑	323	Ray Barker	3.00	1.35
❑	324	John Boozer	3.00	1.35
❑	325	Vic Davalillo	3.00	1.35
❑	326	Braves Team	5.00	2.20
❑	327	Bernie Allen	3.00	1.35
❑	328	Jerry Grote	5.00	2.20
❑	329	Pete Charton	3.00	1.35
❑	330	Ron Fairly	5.00	2.20
❑	331	Ron Herbel	3.00	1.35
❑	332	Bill Bryan	3.00	1.35
❑	333	Senators Rookies	3.00	1.35
		Joe Coleman RC		
		Jim French		
❑	334	Marty Keough	3.00	1.35
❑	335	Juan Pizarro	3.00	1.35
❑	336	Gene Alley	5.00	2.20
❑	337	Fred Gladding	3.00	1.35
❑	338	Dal Maxvill	3.00	1.35
❑	339	Del Crandall	5.00	2.20
❑	340	Dean Chance	5.00	2.20
❑	341	Wes Westrum MG	5.00	2.20
❑	342	Bob Humphreys	3.00	1.35
❑	343	Joe Christopher	3.00	1.35
❑	344	Steve Blass	5.00	2.20
❑	345	Bob Allison	5.00	2.20
❑	346	Mike de la Hoz	3.00	1.35
❑	347	Phil Regan	5.00	2.20
❑	348	Orioles Team	8.00	3.60
❑	349	Cap Peterson	3.00	1.35
❑	350	Mel Stottlemyre	8.00	3.60
❑	351	Fred Valentine	3.00	1.35
❑	352	Bob Aspromonte	3.00	1.35
❑	353	Al McBean	3.00	1.35
❑	354	Smoky Burgess	5.00	2.20
❑	355	Wade Blasingame	3.00	1.35
❑	356	Red Sox Rookies	3.00	1.35
		Owen Johnson		
		Ken Sanders		
❑	357	Gerry Arrigo	3.00	1.35
❑	358	Charlie Smith	3.00	1.35
❑	359	Johnny Briggs	3.00	1.35
❑	360	Ron Hunt	3.00	1.35
❑	361	Tom Satriano	3.00	1.35
❑	362	Gates Brown	5.00	2.20
❑	363	Checklist 5	10.00	2.00
❑	364	Nate Oliver	3.00	1.35
❑	365	Roger Maris UER	50.00	22.00
		Wrong birth year listed on card		
❑	366	Wayne Causey	3.00	1.35
❑	367	Mel Nelson	3.00	1.35
❑	368	Charlie Lau	5.00	2.20
❑	369	Jim King	3.00	1.35
❑	370	Chico Cardenas	3.00	1.35
❑	371	Lee Stange	5.00	2.20
❑	372	Harvey Kuenn	8.00	3.60
❑	373	Giants Rookies	8.00	3.60
		Jack Hiatt		
		Dick Estelle		
❑	374	Bob Locker	5.00	2.20
❑	375	Donn Clendenon	8.00	3.60
❑	376	Paul Schaal	5.00	2.20
❑	377	Turk Farrell	5.00	2.20
❑	378	Dick Tracewski	5.00	2.20
❑	379	Cardinal Team	10.00	4.50
❑	380	Tony Conigliaro	10.00	4.50
❑	381	Hank Fischer	5.00	2.20
❑	382	Phil Roof	5.00	2.20
❑	383	Jackie Brandt	5.00	2.20
❑	384	Al Downing	8.00	3.60
❑	385	Ken Boyer	10.00	4.50
❑	386	Gil Hodges MG	8.00	3.60
❑	387	Howie Reed	5.00	2.20
❑	388	Don Mincher	5.00	2.20
❑	389	Jim O'Toole	8.00	3.60
❑	390	Brooks Robinson	50.00	22.00
❑	391	Chuck Hinton	5.00	2.20
❑	392	Cubs Rookies	8.00	3.60
		Bill Hands		
		Randy Hundley RC		
❑	393	George Brunet	5.00	2.20
❑	394	Ron Brand	5.00	2.20
❑	395	Len Gabrielson	5.00	2.20
❑	396	Jerry Stephenson	5.00	2.20
❑	397	Bill White	8.00	3.60
❑	398	Danny Cater	5.00	2.20
❑	399	Ray Washburn	5.00	2.20
❑	400	Zoilo Versalles	8.00	3.60
❑	401	Ken McMullen	5.00	2.20
❑	402	Jim Hickman	5.00	2.20
❑	403	Fred Talbot	5.00	2.20
❑	404	Pittsburgh Pirates	10.00	4.50
		Team Card		
❑	405	Elston Howard	8.00	3.60
❑	406	Joey Jay	5.00	2.20
❑	407	John Kennedy	5.00	2.20
❑	408	Lee Thomas	8.00	3.60
❑	409	Billy Hoeft	5.00	2.20
❑	410	Al Kaline	40.00	18.00
❑	411	Gene Mauch MG	5.00	2.20
❑	412	Sam Bowens	5.00	2.20
❑	413	Johnny Romano	5.00	2.20
❑	414	Dan Coombs	5.00	2.20
❑	415	Max Alvis	5.00	2.20
❑	416	Phil Ortega	5.00	2.20
❑	417	Angels Rookies	5.00	2.20
		Jim McGlothlin		
		Ed Sukla		
❑	418	Phil Gagliano	5.00	2.20
❑	419	Mike Ryan	5.00	2.20
❑	420	Juan Marichal	15.00	6.75
❑	421	Roy McMillan	8.00	3.60
❑	422	Ed Charles	5.00	2.20
❑	423	Ernie Broglio	5.00	2.20
❑	424	Reds Rookies	10.00	4.50
		Lee May RC		
		Darrell Osteen		
❑	425	Bob Veale	8.00	3.60
❑	426	White Sox Team	10.00	4.50
❑	427	John Miller	5.00	2.20
❑	428	Sandy Alomar	5.00	2.20
❑	429	Bill Monbouquette	5.00	2.20
❑	430	Don Drysdale	20.00	9.00
❑	431	Walt Bond	5.00	2.20
❑	432	Bob Heffner	5.00	2.20
❑	433	Alvin Dark MG	8.00	3.60
❑	434	Willie Kirkland	5.00	2.20
❑	435	Jim Bunning	15.00	6.75
❑	436	Julian Javier	8.00	3.60
❑	437	Al Stanek	5.00	2.20
❑	438	Willie Smith	5.00	2.20
❑	439	Pedro Ramos	5.00	2.20
❑	440	Deron Johnson	8.00	3.60
❑	441	Tommie Sisk	5.00	2.20
❑	442	Orioles Rookies	5.00	2.20
		Ed Barnowski		
		Eddie Watt		
❑	443	Bill Wakefield	5.00	2.20
❑	444	Checklist 6	10.00	2.00
❑	445	Jim Kaat	10.00	4.50
❑	446	Mack Jones	5.00	2.20
❑	447	Dick Ellsworth UER	15.00	6.75
		(Photo actually		
		Ken Hubbs)		
❑	448	Eddie Stanky MG	9.00	4.00
❑	449	Joe Moeller	9.00	4.00
❑	450	Tony Oliva	15.00	6.75
❑	451	Barry Latman	9.00	4.00
❑	452	Joe Azcue	9.00	4.00
❑	453	Ron Kline	9.00	4.00
❑	454	Jerry Buchek	9.00	4.00
❑	455	Mickey Lolich	15.00	6.75
❑	456	Red Sox Rookies	9.00	4.00
		Darrell Brandon		
		Joe Foy		
❑	457	Joe Gibbon	9.00	4.00
❑	458	Manny Jiminez	9.00	4.00
❑	459	Bill McCool	9.00	4.00
❑	460	Curt Blefary	9.00	4.00
❑	461	Roy Face	15.00	6.75
❑	462	Bob Rodgers	9.00	4.00
❑	463	Philadelphia Phillies	15.00	6.75
		Team Card		
❑	464	Larry Bearnarth	9.00	4.00
❑	465	Don Buford	9.00	4.00
❑	466	Ken Johnson	9.00	4.00
❑	467	Vic Roznovsky	9.00	4.00
❑	468	Johnny Podres	15.00	6.75
❑	469	Yankees Rookies	30.00	13.50
		Bobby Murcer RC		
		Dooley Womack		
❑	470	Sam McDowell	15.00	6.75
❑	471	Bob Skinner	9.00	4.00
❑	472	Terry Fox	9.00	4.00
❑	473	Rich Rollins	9.00	4.00
❑	474	Dick Schofield	9.00	4.00
❑	475	Dick Radatz	9.00	4.00
❑	476	Bobby Bragan MG	9.00	4.00
❑	477	Steve Barber	9.00	4.00
❑	478	Tony Gonzalez	9.00	4.00
❑	479	Jim Hannan	9.00	4.00
❑	480	Dick Stuart	9.00	4.00
❑	481	Bob Lee	9.00	4.00
❑	482	Cubs Rookies	9.00	4.00
		John Boccabella		
		Dave Dowling		
❑	483	Joe Nuxhall	9.00	4.00
❑	484	Wes Covington	9.00	4.00
❑	485	Bob Bailey	9.00	4.00
❑	486	Tommy John	15.00	6.75
❑	487	Al Ferrara	9.00	4.00
❑	488	George Banks	9.00	4.00
❑	489	Curt Simmons	9.00	4.00
❑	490	Bobby Richardson	25.00	11.00
❑	491	Dennis Bennett	9.00	4.00
❑	492	Athletics Team	15.00	6.75
❑	493	Johnny Klippstein	9.00	4.00
❑	494	Gordy Coleman	9.00	4.00
❑	495	Dick McAuliffe	15.00	6.75
❑	496	Lindy McDaniel	9.00	4.00
❑	497	Chris Cannizzaro	9.00	4.00
❑	498	Pirates Rookies	9.00	4.00
		Luke Walker		
		Woody Fryman		
❑	499	Wally Bunker	9.00	4.00
❑	500	Hank Aaron	125.00	55.00
❑	501	John O'Donoghue	9.00	4.00
❑	502	Lenny Green UER	9.00	4.00
		(Born: aJn. 6, 1933)		
❑	503	Steve Hamilton	15.00	6.75
❑	504	Grady Hatton MG	9.00	4.00
❑	505	Jose Cardenal	9.00	4.00
❑	506	Bo Belinsky	15.00	6.75
❑	507	Johnny Edwards	9.00	4.00
❑	508	Steve Hargan RC	9.00	4.00
❑	509	Jake Wood	9.00	4.00
❑	510	Hoyt Wilhelm	15.00	6.75
❑	511	Giants Rookies	9.00	4.00
		Bob Barton		
		Tito Fuentes RC		
❑	512	Dick Stigman	9.00	4.00
❑	513	Camilo Carreon	9.00	4.00
❑	514	Hal Woodeshick	9.00	4.00
❑	515	Frank Howard	15.00	6.75
❑	516	Eddie Bressoud	9.00	4.00
❑	517A	Checklist 7	16.00	3.20
		529 White Sox Rookies		
		544 Cardinals Rookies		
❑	517B	Checklist 7	16.00	3.20
		529 W. Sox Rookies		
		544 Cards Rookies		
❑	518	Braves Rookies	9.00	4.00
		Herb Hippauf		
		Arnie Umbach		
❑	519	Bob Friend	15.00	6.75
❑	520	Jim Wynn	15.00	6.75
❑	521	John Wyatt	9.00	4.00
❑	522	Phil Linz	9.00	4.00
❑	523	Bob Sadowski	15.00	6.75
❑	524	Giants Rookies SP	30.00	13.50
		Ollie Brown		
		Don Mason		
❑	525	Gary Bell SP	30.00	13.50
❑	526	Twins Team SP	100.00	45.00
❑	527	Julio Navarro	15.00	6.75
❑	528	Jesse Gonder SP	30.00	13.50
❑	529	White Sox Rookies	15.00	6.75
		Lee Elia		
		Dennis Higgins		
		Bill Voss		
❑	530	Robin Roberts	50.00	22.00

❑ 531 Joe Cunningham 15.00 6.75
❑ 532 A.Monteagudo SP 30.00 13.50
❑ 533 Jerry Adair SP 30.00 13.50
❑ 534 Mets Rookies 15.00 6.75
Dave Eilers
Rob Gardner
❑ 535 Willie Davis SP 40.00 18.00
❑ 536 Dick Egan 15.00 6.75
❑ 537 Herman Franks MG 15.00 6.75
❑ 538 Bob Allen SP 30.00 13.50
❑ 539 Astros Rookies 25.00 11.00
Bill Heath
Carroll Sembera
❑ 540 Denny McLain SP 60.00 27.00
❑ 541 Gene Oliver SP 30.00 13.50
❑ 542 George Smith 15.00 6.75
❑ 543 Roger Craig SP 30.00 13.50
❑ 544 Cardinals Rookies SP 30.00 13.50
Joe Hoerner
George Kernek
Jimy Williams UER
(Misspelled Jimmy
on card)
❑ 545 Dick Green SP 30.00 13.50
❑ 546 Dwight Siebler 25.00 11.00
❑ 547 Horace Clarke RC SP 40.00 18.00
❑ 548 Gary Kroll SP 30.00 13.50
❑ 549 Senators Rookies 15.00 6.75
Al Closter
Casey Cox
❑ 550 Willie McCovey SP .. 100.00 45.00
❑ 551 Bob Purkey SP 30.00 13.50
❑ 552 Birdie Tebbetts 30.00 13.50
MG SP
❑ 553 Rookie Stars 15.00 6.75
Pat Garrett
Jackie Warner
❑ 554 Jim Northrup SP 30.00 13.50
❑ 555 Ron Perranoski SP 30.00 13.50
❑ 556 Mel Queen SP 30.00 13.50
❑ 557 Felix Mantilla SP 30.00 13.50
❑ 558 Red Sox Rookies 20.00 9.00
Guido Grilli
Pete Magrini
George Scott RC
❑ 559 Roberto Pena SP 30.00 13.50
❑ 560 Joel Horlen 8.00 3.60
❑ 561 C.C. Coleman SP 30.00 13.50
❑ 562 Russ Snyder 25.00 11.00
❑ 563 Twins Rookies 15.00 6.75
Pete Cimino
Cesar Tovar
❑ 564 Bob Chance SP 30.00 13.50
❑ 565 Jimmy Piersall SP 40.00 18.00
❑ 566 Mike Cuellar SP 30.00 13.50
❑ 567 Dick Howser SP 40.00 18.00
❑ 568 Athletics Rookies 15.00 6.75
Paul Lindblad
Ron Stone
❑ 569 Orlando McFarlane SP 30.00 13.50
❑ 570 Art Mahaffey SP 30.00 13.50
❑ 571 Dave Roberts SP 30.00 13.50
❑ 572 Bob Priddy 15.00 6.75
❑ 573 Derrell Griffith 15.00 6.75
❑ 574 Mets Rookies 15.00 6.75
Bill Hepler
Bill Murphy
❑ 575 Earl Wilson 15.00 6.75
❑ 576 Dave Nicholson SP 30.00 13.50
❑ 577 Jack Lamabe SP 30.00 13.50
❑ 578 Chi Chi Olivo SP 30.00 13.50
❑ 579 Orioles Rookies 20.00 9.00
Frank Bertaina
Gene Brabender
Dave Johnson
❑ 580 Billy Williams SP 60.00 27.00
❑ 581 Tony Martinez 15.00 6.75
❑ 582 Garry Roggenburk 15.00 6.75
❑ 583 Tigers Team SP UER 125.00 55.00
(Text on back states Tigers
finished third in 1966 instead
of fourth.)
❑ 584 Yankees Rookies 15.00 6.75
Frank Fernandez
Fritz Peterson
❑ 585 Tony Taylor 25.00 11.00
❑ 586 Claude Raymond SP .. 30.00 13.50
❑ 587 Dick Bertell 15.00 6.75
❑ 588 Athletics Rookies 15.00 6.75
Chuck Dobson
Ken Suarez
❑ 589 Lou Klimchock SP 30.00 13.50
❑ 590 Bill Skowron SP 40.00 18.00
❑ 591 NL Rookies SP 40.00 18.00
Bart Shirley
Grant Jackson RC
❑ 592 Andre Rodgers 15.00 6.75
❑ 593 Doug Camilli SP 30.00 13.50
❑ 594 Chico Salmon 15.00 6.75
❑ 595 Larry Jackson 15.00 6.75
❑ 596 Astros Rookies SP 30.00 13.50
Nate Colbert RC
Greg Sims
❑ 597 John Sullivan 15.00 6.75
❑ 598 Gaylord Perry SP 175.00 50.00

1967 Topps

	NRMT	VG-E
COMPLETE SET (609)	4600.00	2100.00
COMMON CARD (1-109)	1.50	.70
COMMON CARD (110-283)	2.00	.90
COMMON CARD (284-370)	2.50	1.10
COMMON CARD (371-457)	4.00	1.80
COMMON CARD (458-533)	6.00	2.70
COMMON CARD (534-609)	16.00	7.25
COMMON DP (534-609)	9.00	4.00
WRAPPER (5-CENT)	25.00	11.00

❑ 1 The Champs DP 25.00 7.50
Frank Robinson
Hank Bauer MG
Brooks Robinson
❑ 2 Jack Hamilton .... 1.50 .70
❑ 3 Duke Sims .... 1.50 .70
❑ 4 Hal Lanier .... 1.50 .70
❑ 5 Whitey Ford UER 20.00 9.00
(1953 listed as
1933 in stats on back)
❑ 6 Dick Simpson .... 1.50 .70
❑ 7 Don McMahon .... 1.50 .70
❑ 8 Chuck Harrison .... 1.50 .70
❑ 9 Ron Hansen .... 1.50 .70
❑ 10 Matty Alou 4.00 1.80
❑ 11 Barry Moore .... 1.50 .70
❑ 12 Dodgers Rookies 4.00 1.80
Jim Campanis
Bill Singer
❑ 13 Joe Sparma .... 1.50 .70
❑ 14 Phil Linz 4.00 1.80
❑ 15 Earl Battey .... 1.50 .70
❑ 16 Bill Hands .... 1.50 .70
❑ 17 Jim Gosger .... 1.50 .70
❑ 18 Gene Oliver .... 1.50 .70
❑ 19 Jim McGlothlin .... 1.50 .70
❑ 20 Orlando Cepeda 8.00 3.60
❑ 21 Dave Bristol MG .... 1.50 .70
❑ 22 Gene Brabender .... 1.50 .70
❑ 23 Larry Elliot .... 1.50 .70
❑ 24 Bob Allen .... 1.50 .70
❑ 25 Elston Howard 4.00 1.80
❑ 26A Bob Priddy NTR 30.00 13.50
❑ 26B Bob Priddy TR 4.00 1.80
❑ 27 Bob Saverine .... 1.50 .70
❑ 28 Barry Latman .... 1.50 .70
❑ 29 Tom McCraw .... 1.50 .70
❑ 30 Al Kaline DP 20.00 9.00
❑ 31 Jim Brewer .... 1.50 .70
❑ 32 Bob Bailey 4.00 1.80
❑ 33 Athletic Rookies 6.00 2.70
Sal Bando RC
Randy Schwartz
❑ 34 Pete Cimino .... 1.50 .70
❑ 35 Rico Carty 4.00 1.80
❑ 36 Bob Tillman .... 1.50 .70
❑ 37 Rick Wise 4.00 1.80
❑ 38 Bob Johnson .... 1.50 .70
❑ 39 Curt Simmons 4.00 1.80
❑ 40 Rick Reichardt .... 1.50 .70
❑ 41 Joe Hoerner .... 1.50 .70
❑ 42 Mets Team 10.00 4.50
❑ 43 Chico Salmon .... 1.50 .70
❑ 44 Joe Nuxhall 4.00 1.80
❑ 45 Roger Maris 50.00 22.00
❑ 45A Roger Maris 1000.00 450.00
Yankees listed as team
Blank Back
❑ 46 Lindy McDaniel 4.00 1.80
❑ 47 Ken McMullen .... 1.50 .70
❑ 48 Bill Freehan 4.00 1.80
❑ 49 Roy Face 4.00 1.80
❑ 50 Tony Oliva 6.00 2.70
❑ 51 Astros Rookies .... 1.50 .70
Dave Adlesh
Wes Bales
❑ 52 Dennis Higgins .... 1.50 .70
❑ 53 Clay Dalrymple .... 1.50 .70
❑ 54 Dick Green .... 1.50 .70
❑ 55 Don Drysdale 16.00 7.25
❑ 56 Jose Tartabull 4.00 1.80
❑ 57 Pat Jarvis RC 4.00 1.80
❑ 58A Paul Schaal 20.00 9.00
Green Bat
❑ 58B Paul Schaal .... 1.50 .70
Normal Colored Bat
❑ 59 Ralph Terry 4.00 1.80
❑ 60 Luis Aparicio 8.00 3.60
❑ 61 Gordy Coleman 4.00 1.80
❑ 62 Frank Robinson CL 8.00 1.60
❑ 63 Cards' Clubbers 8.00 3.60
Lou Brock
Curt Flood
❑ 64 Fred Valentine .... 1.50 .70
❑ 65 Tom Haller 4.00 1.80
❑ 66 Manny Mota 4.00 1.80
❑ 67 Ken Berry .... 1.50 .70
❑ 68 Bob Buhl 4.00 1.80
❑ 69 Vic Davalillo .... 1.50 .70
❑ 70 Ron Santo 6.00 2.70
❑ 71 Camilo Pascual 4.00 1.80
❑ 72 Tigers Rookies .... 1.50 .70
George Korince
(Photo actually
James Murray Brown)
John (Tom) Matchick
❑ 73 Rusty Staub 6.00 2.70
❑ 74 Wes Stock .... 1.50 .70
❑ 75 George Scott 4.00 1.80
❑ 76 Jim Barbieri .... 1.50 .70
❑ 77 Dooley Womack 4.00 1.80
❑ 78 Pat Corrales 4.00 1.80
❑ 79 Bubba Morton .... 1.50 .70
❑ 80 Jim Maloney 4.00 1.80
❑ 81 Eddie Stanky MG 4.00 1.80
❑ 82 Steve Barber .... 1.50 .70
❑ 83 Ollie Brown .... 1.50 .70
❑ 84 Tommie Sisk .... 1.50 .70
❑ 85 Johnny Callison 4.00 1.80
❑ 86A Mike McCormick NTR 30.00 13.50
(Senators on front
and Senators on back)
❑ 86B Mike McCormick TR 4.00 1.80
(Traded line
at end of bio;
Senators on front,
but Giants on back)
❑ 87 George Altman .... 1.50 .70
❑ 88 Mickey Lolich 4.00 1.80
❑ 89 Felix Millan 4.00 1.80
❑ 90 Jim Nash .... 1.50 .70

❑ 91 Johnny Lewis .... 1.50 .70
❑ 92 Ray Washburn .... 1.50 .70
❑ 93 Yankees Rookies 4.00 1.80
Stan Bahnsen RC
Bobby Murcer
❑ 94 Ron Fairly 4.00 1.80
❑ 95 Sonny Siebert .... 1.50 .70
❑ 96 Art Shamsky .... 1.50 .70
❑ 97 Mike Cuellar 4.00 1.80
❑ 98 Rich Rollins .... 1.50 .70
❑ 99 Lee Stange .... 1.50 .70
❑ 100 Frank Robinson DP 14.00 6.25
❑ 101 Ken Johnson .... 1.50 .70
❑ 102 Philadelphia Phillies 4.00 1.80
Team Card
❑ 103 Mickey Mantle CL 20.00 4.00
❑ 104 Minnie Rojas .... 1.50 .70
❑ 105 Ken Boyer 6.00 2.70
❑ 106 Randy Hundley 4.00 1.80
❑ 107 Joel Horlen .... 1.50 .70
❑ 108 Alex Johnson 4.00 1.80
❑ 109 Tribe Thumpers 6.00 2.70
Rocky Colavito
Leon Wagner
❑ 110 Jack Aker 4.00 1.80
❑ 111 John Kennedy .... 2.00 .90
❑ 112 Dave Wickersham .... 2.00 .90
❑ 113 Dave Nicholson .... 2.00 .90
❑ 114 Jack Baldschun .... 2.00 .90
❑ 115 Paul Casanova .... 2.00 .90
❑ 116 Herman Franks MG ...... 2.00 .90
❑ 117 Darrell Brandon .... 2.00 .90
❑ 118 Bernie Allen .... 2.00 .90
❑ 119 Wade Blasingame .... 2.00 .90
❑ 120 Floyd Robinson .... 2.00 .90
❑ 121 Eddie Bressoud .... 2.00 .90
❑ 122 George Brunet .... 2.00 .90
❑ 123 Pirates Rookies 4.00 1.80
Jim Price
Luke Walker
❑ 124 Jim Stewart .... 2.00 .90
❑ 125 Moe Drabowsky 4.00 1.80
❑ 126 Tony Taylor .... 2.00 .90
❑ 127 John O'Donoghue .... 2.00 .90
❑ 128 Ed Spiezio .... 2.00 .90
❑ 129 Phil Roof .... 2.00 .90
❑ 130 Phil Regan 4.00 1.80
❑ 131 Yankees Team 10.00 4.50
❑ 132 Ozzie Virgil .... 2.00 .90
❑ 133 Ron Kline .... 2.00 .90
❑ 134 Gates Brown 6.00 2.70
❑ 135 Deron Johnson 4.00 1.80
❑ 136 Carroll Sembera .... 2.00 .90
❑ 137 Twins Rookies .... 2.00 .90
Ron Clark
Jim Ollum
❑ 138 Dick Kelley .... 2.00 .90
❑ 139 Dalton Jones 4.00 1.80
❑ 140 Willie Stargell 20.00 9.00
❑ 141 John Miller .... 2.00 .90
❑ 142 Jackie Brandt .... 2.00 .90
❑ 143 Sox Sockers .... 2.00 .90
Pete Ward
Don Buford
❑ 144 Bill Hepler .... 2.00 .90
❑ 145 Larry Brown .... 2.00 .90
❑ 146 Steve Carlton 50.00 22.00
❑ 147 Tom Egan .... 2.00 .90
❑ 148 Adolfo Phillips .... 2.00 .90
❑ 149 Joe Moeller .... 2.00 .90
❑ 150 Mickey Mantle 250.00 110.00
❑ 151 Moe Drabowsky WS 4.00 1.80
❑ 152 Jim Palmer WS 8.00 3.60
❑ 153 Paul Blair WS 4.00 1.80
❑ 154 Brooks Robinson WS .. 4.00 1.80
Dave McNally
❑ 155 WS Summary 4.00 1.80
Winners celebrate
❑ 156 Ron Herbel .... 2.00 .90
❑ 157 Danny Cater .... 2.00 .90
❑ 158 Jimmie Coker .... 2.00 .90
❑ 159 Bruce Howard .... 2.00 .90
❑ 160 Willie Davis 4.00 1.80
❑ 161 Dick Williams MG 4.00 1.80
❑ 162 Billy O'Dell .... 2.00 .90
❑ 163 Vic Roznovsky .... 2.00 .90
❑ 164 Dwight Siebler UER .... 2.00 .90
(Last line of stats
shows 1960 Minnesota)
❑ 165 Cleon Jones 4.00 1.80
❑ 166 Eddie Mathews 15.00 6.75
❑ 167 Senators Rookies .... 2.00 .90
Joe Coleman
Tim Cullen
❑ 168 Ray Culp .... 2.00 .90
❑ 169 Horace Clarke 4.00 1.80
❑ 170 Dick McAuliffe 4.00 1.80
❑ 171 Cal Koonce .... 2.00 .90
❑ 172 Bill Heath .... 2.00 .90
❑ 173 St. Louis Cardinals 4.00 1.80
Team Card
❑ 174 Dick Radatz 4.00 1.80
❑ 175 Bobby Knoop .... 2.00 .90
❑ 176 Sammy Ellis .... 2.00 .90
❑ 177 Tito Fuentes 4.00 1.80
❑ 178 John Buzhardt .... 2.00 .90
❑ 179 Braves Rookies 4.00 1.80
Charles Vaughan
Cecil Upshaw
❑ 180 Curt Blefary .... 2.00 .90
❑ 181 Terry Fox .... 2.00 .90
❑ 182 Ed Charles .... 2.00 .90
❑ 183 Jim Pagliaroni .... 2.00 .90
❑ 184 George Thomas .... 2.00 .90
❑ 185 Ken Holtzman RC 4.00 1.80
❑ 186 Mets Maulers 4.00 1.80
Ed Kranepool
Ron Swoboda
❑ 187 Pedro Ramos .... 2.00 .90
❑ 188 Ken Harrelson 4.00 1.80
❑ 189 Chuck Hinton .... 2.00 .90
❑ 190 Turk Farrell .... 2.00 .90
❑ 191A Willie Mays CL 10.00 2.00
214 Tom Kelley
❑ 191B Willie Mays CL 12.00 2.40
214 Dick Kelley
❑ 192 Fred Gladding .... 2.00 .90
❑ 193 Jose Cardenal 4.00 1.80
❑ 194 Bob Allison 4.00 1.80
❑ 195 Al Jackson .... 2.00 .90
❑ 196 Johnny Romano .... 2.00 .90
❑ 197 Ron Perranoski 4.00 1.80
❑ 198 Chuck Hiller .... 2.00 .90
❑ 199 Billy Hitchcock MG ...... 2.00 .90
❑ 200 Willie Mays UER 80.00 36.00
('63 Sna Francisco
on card back stats)
❑ 201 Hal Reniff 4.00 1.80
❑ 202 Johnny Edwards .... 2.00 .90
❑ 203 Al McBean .... 2.00 .90
❑ 204 Orioles Rookies 6.00 2.70
Mike Epstein
Tom Phoebus
❑ 205 Dick Groat 4.00 1.80
❑ 206 Dennis Bennett .... 2.00 .90
❑ 207 John Orsino .... 2.00 .90
❑ 208 Jack Lamabe .... 2.00 .90
❑ 209 Joe Nossek .... 2.00 .90
❑ 210 Bob Gibson 20.00 9.00
❑ 211 Twins Team 4.00 1.80
❑ 212 Chris Zachary .... 2.00 .90
❑ 213 Jay Johnstone RC 4.00 1.80
❑ 214 Dick Kelley .... 2.00 .90
❑ 215 Ernie Banks 20.00 9.00
❑ 216 Bengal Belters 8.00 3.60
Norm Cash
Al Kaline
❑ 217 Rob Gardner .... 2.00 .90
❑ 218 Wes Parker 4.00 1.80
❑ 219 Clay Carroll 4.00 1.80
❑ 220 Jim Ray Hart 4.00 1.80
❑ 221 Woody Fryman 4.00 1.80
❑ 222 Reds Rookies 4.00 1.80
Darrell Osteen
Lee May
❑ 223 Mike Ryan 4.00 1.80
❑ 224 Walt Bond .... 2.00 .90
❑ 225 Mel Stottlemyre 6.00 2.70
❑ 226 Julian Javier 4.00 1.80
❑ 227 Paul Lindblad .... 2.00 .90
❑ 228 Gil Hodges MG 6.00 2.70
❑ 229 Larry Jackson .... 2.00 .90
❑ 230 Boog Powell 6.00 2.70
❑ 231 John Bateman .... 2.00 .90
❑ 232 Don Buford .... 2.00 .90
❑ 233 AL ERA Leaders 4.00 1.80
Gary Peters
Joel Horlen
Steve Hargan
❑ 234 NL ERA Leaders 15.00 6.75
Sandy Koufax
Mike Cuellar
Juan Marichal
❑ 235 AL Pitching Leaders 6.00 2.70
Jim Kaat
Denny McLain
Earl Wilson
❑ 236 NL Pitching Leaders .. 25.00 11.00
Sandy Koufax
Juan Marichal
Bob Gibson
Gaylord Perry
❑ 237 AL Strikeout Leaders.... 6.00 2.70
Sam McDowell
Jim Kaat
Earl Wilson
❑ 238 NL Strikeout Leaders 12.00 5.50
Sandy Koufax
Jim Bunning
Bob Veale
❑ 239 AL Batting Leaders 9.00 4.00
Frank Robinson
Tony Oliva
Al Kaline
❑ 240 NL Batting Leaders 6.00 2.70
Matty Alou
Felipe Alou
Rico Carty
❑ 241 AL RBI Leaders 9.00 4.00
Frank Robinson
Harmon Killebrew
Boog Powell
❑ 242 NL RBI Leaders 25.00 11.00
Hank Aaron
Bob Clemente
Richie Allen
❑ 243 AL HR Leaders 9.00 4.00
Frank Robinson
Harmon Killebrew
Boog Powell
❑ 244 NL HR Leaders 20.00 9.00
Hank Aaron
Richie Allen
Willie Mays
❑ 245 Curt Flood 6.00 2.70
❑ 246 Jim Perry 4.00 1.80
❑ 247 Jerry Lumpe .... 2.00 .90
❑ 248 Gene Mauch MG 4.00 1.80
❑ 249 Nick Willhite .... 2.00 .90
❑ 250 Hank Aaron UER 80.00 36.00
(Second 1961 in stats
should be 1962)
❑ 251 Woody Held .... 2.00 .90
❑ 252 Bob Bolin .... 2.00 .90
❑ 253 Indians Rookies .... 2.00 .90
Bill Davis
Gus Gil
❑ 254 Milt Pappas 4.00 1.80
(No facsimile auto-
graph on card front)
❑ 255 Frank Howard 4.00 1.80
❑ 256 Bob Hendley .... 2.00 .90
❑ 257 Charlie Smith .... 2.00 .90
❑ 258 Lee Maye .... 2.00 .90
❑ 259 Don Dennis .... 2.00 .90
❑ 260 Jim Lefebvre 4.00 1.80
❑ 261 John Wyatt .... 2.00 .90
❑ 262 Athletics Team 4.00 1.80
❑ 263 Hank Aguirre .... 2.00 .90
❑ 264 Ron Swoboda 4.00 1.80
❑ 265 Lou Burdette 4.00 1.80
❑ 266 Pitt Power 4.00 1.80
Willie Stargell
Donn Clendenon
❑ 267 Don Schwall .... 2.00 .90
❑ 268 Johnny Briggs .... 2.00 .90
❑ 269 Don Nottebart .... 2.00 .90
❑ 270 Zoilo Versalles .... 2.00 .90

❑ 271 Eddie Watt .... 2.00 .90
❑ 272 Cubs Rookies 4.00 1.80
Bill Connors RC
Dave Dowling
❑ 273 Dick Lines .... 2.00 .90
❑ 274 Bob Aspromonte .... 2.00 .90
❑ 275 Fred Whitfield .... 2.00 .90
❑ 276 Bruce Brubaker .... 2.00 .90
❑ 277 Steve Whitaker 6.00 2.70
❑ 278 Jim Kaat CL 8.00 1.60
❑ 279 Frank Linzy .... 2.00 .90
❑ 280 Tony Conigliaro 8.00 3.60
❑ 281 Bob Rodgers .... 2.00 .90
❑ 282 John Odom .... 2.00 .90
❑ 283 Gene Alley 4.00 1.80
❑ 284 Johnny Podres 4.00 1.80
❑ 285 Lou Brock 20.00 9.00
❑ 286 Wayne Causey 2.50 1.10
❑ 287 Mets Rookies 2.50 1.10
Greg Goossen
Bart Shirley
❑ 288 Denny Lemaster 2.50 1.10
❑ 289 Tom Tresh 5.00 2.20
❑ 290 Bill White 5.00 2.20
❑ 291 Jim Hannan 2.50 1.10
❑ 292 Don Pavletich 2.50 1.10
❑ 293 Ed Kirkpatrick 2.50 1.10
❑ 294 Walter Alston MG 8.00 3.60
❑ 295 Sam McDowell 5.00 2.20
❑ 296 Glenn Beckert 5.00 2.20
❑ 297 Dave Morehead 5.00 2.20
❑ 298 Ron Davis 2.50 1.10
❑ 299 Norm Siebern 2.50 1.10
❑ 300 Jim Kaat 5.00 2.20
❑ 301 Jesse Gonder 2.50 1.10
❑ 302 Orioles Team 8.00 3.60
❑ 303 Gil Blanco 2.50 1.10
❑ 304 Phil Gagliano 2.50 1.10
❑ 305 Earl Wilson 5.00 2.20
❑ 306 Bud Harrelson RC 5.00 2.20
❑ 307 Jim Beauchamp 2.50 1.10
❑ 308 Al Downing 5.00 2.20
❑ 309 Hurlers Beware 5.00 2.20
Johnny Callison
Richie Allen
❑ 310 Gary Peters 2.50 1.10
❑ 311 Ed Brinkman 2.50 1.10
❑ 312 Don Mincher 2.50 1.10
❑ 313 Bob Lee 2.50 1.10
❑ 314 Red Sox Rookies 8.00 3.60
Mike Andrews
Reggie Smith RC
❑ 315 Billy Williams 15.00 6.75
❑ 316 Jack Kralick 2.50 1.10
❑ 317 Cesar Tovar 2.50 1.10
❑ 318 Dave Giusti 2.50 1.10
❑ 319 Paul Blair 5.00 2.20
❑ 320 Gaylord Perry 15.00 6.75
❑ 321 Mayo Smith MG 2.50 1.10
❑ 322 Jose Pagan 2.50 1.10
❑ 323 Mike Hershberger 2.50 1.10
❑ 324 Hal Woodeshick 2.50 1.10
❑ 325 Chico Cardenas 5.00 2.20
❑ 326 Bob Uecker 10.00 4.50
❑ 327 California Angels 8.00 3.60
Team Card
❑ 328 Clete Boyer UER 5.00 2.20
(Stats only go up
through 1965)
❑ 329 Charlie Lau 5.00 2.20
❑ 330 Claude Osteen 5.00 2.20
❑ 331 Joe Foy 5.00 2.20
❑ 332 Jesus Alou 2.50 1.10
❑ 333 Ferguson Jenkins 20.00 9.00
❑ 334 Twin Terrors 10.00 4.50
Bob Allison
Harmon Killebrew
❑ 335 Bob Veale 5.00 2.20
❑ 336 Joe Azcue 2.50 1.10
❑ 337 Joe Morgan 15.00 6.75
❑ 338 Bob Locker 2.50 1.10
❑ 339 Chico Ruiz 2.50 1.10
❑ 340 Joe Pepitone 8.00 3.60
❑ 341 Giants Rookies 2.50 1.10
Dick Dietz
Bill Sorrell

❑ 342 Hank Fischer 2.50 1.10
❑ 343 Tom Satriano 2.50 1.10
❑ 344 Ossie Chavarria 2.50 1.10
❑ 345 Stu Miller 5.00 2.20
❑ 346 Jim Hickman 2.50 1.10
❑ 347 Grady Hatton MG 2.50 1.10
❑ 348 Tug McGraw 5.00 2.20
❑ 349 Bob Chance 2.50 1.10
❑ 350 Joe Torre 8.00 3.60
❑ 351 Vern Law 5.00 2.20
❑ 352 Ray Oyler 2.50 1.10
❑ 353 Bill McCool 2.50 1.10
❑ 354 Cubs Team 8.00 3.60
❑ 355 Carl Yastrzemski 50.00 22.00
❑ 356 Larry Jaster 2.50 1.10
❑ 357 Bill Skowron 5.00 2.20
❑ 358 Ruben Amaro 2.50 1.10
❑ 359 Dick Ellsworth 2.50 1.10
❑ 360 Leon Wagner 2.50 1.10
❑ 361 Roberto Clemente CL 15.00 3.00
❑ 362 Darold Knowles 2.50 1.10
❑ 363 Dave Johnson 5.00 2.20
❑ 364 Claude Raymond 2.50 1.10
❑ 365 John Roseboro 5.00 2.20
❑ 366 Andy Kosco 2.50 1.10
❑ 367 Angels Rookies 2.50 1.10
Bill Kelso
Don Wallace
❑ 368 Jack Hiatt 2.50 1.10
❑ 369 Jim Hunter 15.00 6.75
❑ 370 Tommy Davis 5.00 2.20
❑ 371 Jim Lonborg 8.00 3.60
❑ 372 Mike de la Hoz 4.00 1.80
❑ 373 W.S. Rookies DP 4.00 1.80
Duane Josephson
Fred Klages
❑ 374A Mel Queen ERR DP 20.00 9.00
(Incomplete stat
line on back)
❑ 374B Mel Queen COR DP .. 4.00 1.80
(Complete stat
line on back)
❑ 375 Jake Gibbs 8.00 3.60
❑ 376 Don Lock DP 4.00 1.80
❑ 377 Luis Tiant 8.00 3.60
❑ 378 Detroit Tigers 8.00 3.60
Team Card UER
(Willie Horton with
262 RBI's in 1966)
❑ 379 Jerry May DP 4.00 1.80
❑ 380 Dean Chance DP 4.00 1.80
❑ 381 Dick Schofield DP 4.00 1.80
❑ 382 Dave McNally 8.00 3.60
❑ 383 Ken Henderson DP 4.00 1.80
❑ 384 Cardinals Rookies 4.00 1.80
Jim Cosman
Dick Hughes
❑ 385 Jim Fregosi 8.00 3.60
(Batting wrong)
❑ 386 Dick Selma DP 4.00 1.80
❑ 387 Cap Peterson DP 4.00 1.80
❑ 388 Arnold Earley DP 4.00 1.80
❑ 389 Alvin Dark MG DP 8.00 3.60
❑ 390 Jim Wynn DP 8.00 3.60
❑ 391 Wilbur Wood DP 8.00 3.60
❑ 392 Tommy Harper DP 8.00 3.60
❑ 393 Jim Bouton DP 8.00 3.60
❑ 394 Jake Wood DP 4.00 1.80
❑ 395 Chris Short 8.00 3.60
❑ 396 Atlanta Aces 4.00 1.80
Denis Menke
Tony Cloninger
❑ 397 Willie Smith DP 4.00 1.80
❑ 398 Jeff Torborg 8.00 3.60
❑ 399 Al Worthington DP 4.00 1.80
❑ 400 Bob Clemente DP 100.00 45.00
❑ 401 Jim Coates 4.00 1.80
❑ 402A Phillies Rookies DP 20.00 9.00
Grant Jackson
Billy Wilson
Incomplete stat line
❑ 402B Phillies Rookies DP .. 8.00 3.60
Grant Jackson
Billy Wilson
❑ 403 Dick Nen 4.00 1.80
❑ 404 Nelson Briles 8.00 3.60

❑ 405 Russ Snyder 4.00 1.80
❑ 406 Lee Elia DP 4.00 1.80
❑ 407 Reds Team 8.00 3.60
❑ 408 Jim Northrup DP 8.00 3.60
❑ 409 Ray Sadecki 4.00 1.80
❑ 410 Lou Johnson DP 4.00 1.80
❑ 411 Dick Howser DP 4.00 1.80
❑ 412 Astros Rookies 8.00 3.60
Norm Miller
Doug Rader RC
❑ 413 Jerry Grote 4.00 1.80
❑ 414 Casey Cox 4.00 1.80
❑ 415 Sonny Jackson 4.00 1.80
❑ 416 Roger Repoz 4.00 1.80
❑ 417A Bob Bruce ERR DP 30.00 13.50
(RBAVES on back)
❑ 417B Bob Bruce COR DP .. 4.00 1.80
❑ 418 Sam Mele MG 4.00 1.80
❑ 419 Don Kessinger DP 8.00 3.60
❑ 420 Denny McLain 12.00 5.50
❑ 421 Dal Maxvill DP 4.00 1.80
❑ 422 Hoyt Wilhelm 15.00 6.75
❑ 423 Fence Busters DP 25.00 11.00
Willie Mays
Willie McCovey
❑ 424 Pedro Gonzalez 4.00 1.80
❑ 425 Pete Mikkelsen 4.00 1.80
❑ 426 Lou Clinton 4.00 1.80
❑ 427A R.Gomez ERR DP .. 20.00 9.00
Incomplete stat
line on back
❑ 427B R.Gomez COR DP 4.00 1.80
Complete stat
line on back
❑ 428 Dodgers Rookies DP 8.00 3.60
Tom Hutton RC
Gene Michael
❑ 429 Garry Roggenburk DP .. 4.00 1.80
❑ 430 Pete Rose 80.00 36.00
❑ 431 Ted Uhlaender 4.00 1.80
❑ 432 Jimmie Hall DP 4.00 1.80
❑ 433 Al Luplow DP 4.00 1.80
❑ 434 Eddie Fisher DP 4.00 1.80
❑ 435 Mack Jones DP 4.00 1.80
❑ 436 Pete Ward 4.00 1.80
❑ 437 Senators Team 8.00 3.60
❑ 438 Chuck Dobson 4.00 1.80
❑ 439 Byron Browne 4.00 1.80
❑ 440 Steve Hargan 4.00 1.80
❑ 441 Jim Davenport 4.00 1.80
❑ 442 Yankees Rookies DP .. 8.00 3.60
Bill Robinson RC
Joe Verbanic
❑ 443 Tito Francona DP 4.00 1.80
❑ 444 George Smith 4.00 1.80
❑ 445 Don Sutton 25.00 11.00
❑ 446 Russ Nixon DP 4.00 1.80
❑ 447A Bo Belinsky ERR DP 5.00 2.20
(Incomplete stat
line on back)
❑ 447B Bo Belinsky COR DP 8.00 3.60
(Complete stat
line on back)
❑ 448 Harry Walker DP MG .. 4.00 1.80
❑ 449 Orlando Pena 4.00 1.80
❑ 450 Richie Allen 8.00 3.60
❑ 451 Fred Newman DP 4.00 1.80
❑ 452 Ed Kranepool 8.00 3.60
❑ 453 A.Monteagudo DP 4.00 1.80
❑ 454A Juan Marichal CL 12.00 2.40
Missing left ear
❑ 454B Juan Marichal CL 12.00 2.40
left ear showing
❑ 455 Tommie Agee 8.00 3.60
❑ 456 Phil Niekro 15.00 6.75
❑ 457 Andy Etchebarren DP .. 8.00 3.60
❑ 458 Lee Thomas 6.00 2.70
❑ 459 Senators Rookies 6.00 2.70
Dick Bosman RC
Pete Craig
❑ 460 Harmon Killebrew 60.00 27.00
❑ 461 Bob Miller 12.00 5.50
❑ 462 Bob Barton 6.00 2.70
❑ 463 Hill Aces 12.00 5.50
Sam McDowell
Sonny Siebert

❑ 464 Dan Coombs	6.00	2.70
❑ 465 Willie Horton	12.00	5.50
❑ 466 Bobby Wine	6.00	2.70
❑ 467 Jim O'Toole	6.00	2.70
❑ 468 Ralph Houk MG	6.00	2.70
❑ 469 Len Gabrielson	6.00	2.70
❑ 470 Bob Shaw	6.00	2.70
❑ 471 Rene Lachemann	6.00	2.70
❑ 472 Rookies Pirates	6.00	2.70
John Gelnar		
George Spriggs		
❑ 473 Jose Santiago	6.00	2.70
❑ 474 Bob Tolan	6.00	2.70
❑ 475 Jim Palmer	80.00	36.00
❑ 476 Tony Perez SP	60.00	27.00
❑ 477 Braves Team	15.00	6.75
❑ 478 Bob Humphreys	6.00	2.70
❑ 479 Gary Bell	6.00	2.70
❑ 480 Willie McCovey	40.00	18.00
❑ 481 Leo Durocher MG	20.00	9.00
❑ 482 Bill Monbouquette	6.00	2.70
❑ 483 Jim Landis	6.00	2.70
❑ 484 Jerry Adair	6.00	2.70
❑ 485 Tim McCarver	25.00	11.00
❑ 486 Twins Rookies	6.00	2.70
Rich Reese		
Bill Whitby		
❑ 487 Tommie Reynolds	6.00	2.70
❑ 488 Gerry Arrigo	6.00	2.70
❑ 489 Doug Clemens	6.00	2.70
❑ 490 Tony Cloninger	6.00	2.70
❑ 491 Sam Bowens	6.00	2.70
❑ 492 Pittsburgh Pirates	15.00	6.75
Team Card		
❑ 493 Phil Ortega	6.00	2.70
❑ 494 Bill Rigney MG	6.00	2.70
❑ 495 Fritz Peterson	6.00	2.70
❑ 496 Orlando McFarlane	6.00	2.70
❑ 497 Ron Campbell	6.00	2.70
❑ 498 Larry Dierker	12.00	5.50
❑ 499 Indians Rookies	6.00	2.70
George Culver		
Jose Vidal		
❑ 500 Juan Marichal	25.00	11.00
❑ 501 Jerry Zimmerman	6.00	2.70
❑ 502 Derrell Griffith	6.00	2.70
❑ 503 Los Angeles Dodgers	20.00	9.00
Team Card		
❑ 504 Orlando Martinez	6.00	2.70
❑ 505 Tommy Helms	12.00	5.50
❑ 506 Smoky Burgess	6.00	2.70
❑ 507 Orioles Rookies	6.00	2.70
Ed Barnowski		
Larry Haney RC		
❑ 508 Dick Hall	6.00	2.70
❑ 509 Jim King	6.00	2.70
❑ 510 Bill Mazeroski	25.00	11.00
❑ 511 Don Wert	6.00	2.70
❑ 512 Red Schoendienst MG	25.00	11.00
❑ 513 Marcelino Lopez	6.00	2.70
❑ 514 John Werhas	6.00	2.70
❑ 515 Bert Campaneris	12.00	5.50
❑ 516 Giants Team	15.00	6.75
❑ 517 Fred Talbot	12.00	5.50
❑ 518 Denis Menke	6.00	2.70
❑ 519 Ted Davidson	6.00	2.70
❑ 520 Max Alvis	6.00	2.70
❑ 521 Bird Bombers	12.00	5.50
Boog Powell		
Curt Blefary		
❑ 522 John Stephenson	6.00	2.70
❑ 523 Jim Merritt	6.00	2.70
❑ 524 Felix Mantilla	6.00	2.70
❑ 525 Ron Hunt	6.00	2.70
❑ 526 Tigers Rookies	6.00	2.70
Pat Dobson RC		
George Korince		
(See 67T-72)		
❑ 527 Dennis Ribant	6.00	2.70
❑ 528 Rico Petrocelli	20.00	9.00
❑ 529 Gary Wagner	6.00	2.70
❑ 530 Felipe Alou	12.00	5.50
❑ 531 Brooks Robinson CL	14.00	2.80
❑ 532 Jim Hicks	6.00	2.70
❑ 533 Jack Fisher	6.00	2.70
❑ 534 Hank Bauer MG DP	9.00	4.00
❑ 535 Donn Clendenon	25.00	11.00
❑ 536 Cubs Rookies	50.00	22.00
Joe Niekro RC		
Paul Popovich		
❑ 537 Chuck Estrada DP	9.00	4.00
❑ 538 J.C. Martin	16.00	7.25
❑ 539 Dick Egan DP	9.00	4.00
❑ 540 Norm Cash	50.00	22.00
❑ 541 Joe Gibbon	16.00	7.25
❑ 542 Athletics Rookies DP	15.00	6.75
Rick Monday RC		
Tony Pierce		
❑ 543 Dan Schneider	16.00	7.25
❑ 544 Cleveland Indians	30.00	13.50
Team Card		
❑ 545 Jim Grant	25.00	11.00
❑ 546 Woody Woodward	25.00	11.00
❑ 547 Red Sox Rookies DP	9.00	4.00
Russ Gibson		
Bill Rohr		
❑ 548 Tony Gonzalez DP	9.00	4.00
❑ 549 Jack Sanford	16.00	7.25
❑ 550 Vada Pinson DP	10.00	4.50
❑ 551 Doug Camilli DP	9.00	4.00
❑ 552 Ted Savage	25.00	11.00
❑ 553 Yankees Rookies	40.00	18.00
Mike Hegan RC		
Thad Tillotson		
❑ 554 Andre Rodgers DP	9.00	4.00
❑ 555 Don Cardwell	25.00	11.00
❑ 556 Al Weis DP	9.00	4.00
❑ 557 Al Ferrara	25.00	11.00
❑ 558 Orioles Rookies	50.00	22.00
Mark Belanger RC		
Bill Dillman		
❑ 559 Dick Tracewski DP	9.00	4.00
❑ 560 Jim Bunning	60.00	27.00
❑ 561 Sandy Alomar	40.00	18.00
❑ 562 Steve Blass DP	9.00	4.00
❑ 563 Joe Adcock	40.00	18.00
❑ 564 Astros Rookies DP	9.00	4.00
Alonzo Harris		
Aaron Pointer		
❑ 565 Lew Krausse	25.00	11.00
❑ 566 Gary Geiger DP	9.00	4.00
❑ 567 Steve Hamilton	40.00	18.00
❑ 568 John Sullivan	40.00	18.00
❑ 569 AL Rookies DP	200.00	90.00
Rod Carew RC		
Hank Allen		
❑ 570 Maury Wills	90.00	40.00
❑ 571 Larry Sherry	25.00	11.00
❑ 572 Don Demeter	25.00	11.00
❑ 573 Chicago White Sox	30.00	13.50
Team Card UER		
(Indians team		
stats on back)		
❑ 574 Jerry Buchek	25.00	11.00
❑ 575 Dave Boswell	16.00	7.25
❑ 576 NL Rookies	40.00	18.00
Ramon Hernandez		
Norm Gigon RC		
❑ 577 Bill Short	16.00	7.25
❑ 578 John Boccabella	16.00	7.25
❑ 579 Bill Henry	16.00	7.25
❑ 580 Rocky Colavito	125.00	55.00
❑ 581 Mets Rookies	500.00	220.00
Bill Denehy		
Tom Seaver RC		
❑ 582 Jim Owens DP	9.00	4.00
❑ 583 Ray Barker	40.00	18.00
❑ 584 Jimmy Piersall	40.00	18.00
❑ 585 Wally Bunker	25.00	11.00
❑ 586 Manny Jimenez	16.00	7.25
❑ 587 NL Rookies	40.00	18.00
Don Shaw		
Gary Sutherland RC		
❑ 588 Johnny Klippstein DP	9.00	4.00
❑ 589 Dave Ricketts DP	9.00	4.00
❑ 590 Pete Richert	16.00	7.25
❑ 591 Ty Cline	25.00	11.00
❑ 592 NL Rookies	25.00	11.00
Jim Shellenback		
Ron Willis RC		
❑ 593 Wes Westrum MG	50.00	22.00
❑ 594 Dan Osinski	40.00	18.00
❑ 595 Cookie Rojas	25.00	11.00
❑ 596 Galen Cisco DP	9.00	4.00
❑ 597 Ted Abernathy	16.00	7.25
❑ 598 White Sox Rookies	25.00	11.00
Walt Williams		
Ed Stroud		
❑ 599 Bob Duliba DP	9.00	4.00
❑ 600 Brooks Robinson	250.00	110.00
❑ 601 Bill Bryan DP	9.00	4.00
❑ 602 Juan Pizarro	40.00	18.00
❑ 603 Athletics Rookies	25.00	11.00
Tim Talton		
Ramon Webster		
❑ 604 Red Sox Team	125.00	55.00
❑ 605 Mike Shannon	50.00	22.00
❑ 606 Ron Taylor	25.00	11.00
❑ 607 Mickey Stanley	50.00	22.00
❑ 608 Cubs Rookies DP	9.00	4.00
Rich Nye		
John Upham		
❑ 609 Tommy John	80.00	27.00

1968 Topps

	NRMT	VG-E
COMPLETE SET (598)	3000.00	1350.00
COMMON CARD (1-457)	1.75	.80
COMMON CARD (458-598)	3.50	1.55
WRAPPER (5-CENT)	25.00	11.00
❑ 1 NL Batting Leaders	30.00	12.00
Roberto Clemente		
Tony Gonzalez		
Matty Alou		
❑ 2 AL Batting Leaders	14.00	6.25
Carl Yastrzemski		
Frank Robinson		
Al Kaline		
❑ 3 NL RBI Leaders	20.00	9.00
Orlando Cepeda		
Roberto Clemente		
Hank Aaron		
❑ 4 AL RBI Leaders	14.00	6.25
Carl Yastrzemski		
Harmon Killebrew		
Frank Robinson		
❑ 5 NL Home Run Leaders	8.00	3.60
Hank Aaron		
Jim Wynn		
Ron Santo		
Willie McCovey		
❑ 6 AL Home Run Leaders	8.00	3.60
Carl Yastrzemski		
Harmon Killebrew		
Frank Howard		
❑ 7 NL ERA Leaders	4.00	1.80
Phil Niekro		
Jim Bunning		
Chris Short		
❑ 8 AL ERA Leaders	4.00	1.80
Joel Horlen		
Gary Peters		
Sonny Siebert		
❑ 9 NL Pitching Leaders	4.00	1.80
Mike McCormick		
Ferguson Jenkins		
Jim Bunning		
Claude Osteen		

Card	Player	Price 1	Price 2
❑ 10A	AL Pitching Leaders	4.00	1.80
	Jim Lonborg ERR		
	(Misspelled Lonberg		
	on card back)		
	Earl Wilson		
	Dean Chance		
❑ 10B	AL Pitching Leaders	4.00	1.80
	Jim Lonborg COR		
	Earl Wilson		
	Dean Chance		
❑ 11	NL Strikeout Leaders	6.00	2.70
	Jim Bunning		
	Ferguson Jenkins		
	Gaylord Perry		
❑ 12	AL Strikeout Leaders	4.00	1.80
	Jim Lonborg UER		
	(Misspelled Longberg		
	on card back)		
	Sam McDowell		
	Dean Chance		
❑ 13	Chuck Hartenstein	1.75	.80
❑ 14	Jerry McNertney	1.75	.80
❑ 15	Ron Hunt	1.75	.80
❑ 16	Indians Rookies	6.00	2.70
	Lou Piniella		
	Richie Scheinblum		
❑ 17	Dick Hall	1.75	.80
❑ 18	Mike Hershberger	1.75	.80
❑ 19	Juan Pizarro	1.75	.80
❑ 20	Brooks Robinson	25.00	11.00
❑ 21	Ron Davis	1.75	.80
❑ 22	Pat Dobson	4.00	1.80
❑ 23	Chico Cardenas	4.00	1.80
❑ 24	Bobby Locke	1.75	.80
❑ 25	Julian Javier	4.00	1.80
❑ 26	Darrell Brandon	1.75	.80
❑ 27	Gil Hodges MG	8.00	3.60
❑ 28	Ted Uhlaender	1.75	.80
❑ 29	Joe Verbanic	1.75	.80
❑ 30	Joe Torre	6.00	2.70
❑ 31	Ed Stroud	1.75	.80
❑ 32	Joe Gibbon	1.75	.80
❑ 33	Pete Ward	1.75	.80
❑ 34	Al Ferrara	1.75	.80
❑ 35	Steve Hargan	1.75	.80
❑ 36	Pirates Rookies	4.00	1.80
	Bob Moose		
	Bob Robertson		
❑ 37	Billy Williams	8.00	3.60
❑ 38	Tony Pierce	1.75	.80
❑ 39	Cookie Rojas	4.00	1.80
❑ 40	Denny McLain	8.00	3.60
❑ 41	Julio Gotay	1.75	.80
❑ 42	Larry Haney	1.75	.80
❑ 43	Gary Bell	1.75	.80
❑ 44	Frank Kostro	1.75	.80
❑ 45	Tom Seaver	50.00	22.00
❑ 46	Dave Ricketts	1.75	.80
❑ 47	Ralph Houk MG	4.00	1.80
❑ 48	Ted Davidson	1.75	.80
❑ 49A	Eddie Brinkman	1.75	.80
	(White team name)		
❑ 49B	Eddie Brinkman	50.00	22.00
	(Yellow team name)		
❑ 50	Willie Mays	60.00	27.00
❑ 51	Bob Locker	1.75	.80
❑ 52	Hawk Taylor	1.75	.80
❑ 53	Gene Alley	4.00	1.80
❑ 54	Stan Williams	4.00	1.80
❑ 55	Felipe Alou	4.00	1.80
❑ 56	Orioles Rookies	1.75	.80
	Dave Leonhard		
	Dave May RC		
❑ 57	Dan Schneider	1.75	.80
❑ 58	Eddie Mathews	15.00	6.75
❑ 59	Don Lock	1.75	.80
❑ 60	Ken Holtzman	4.00	1.80
❑ 61	Reggie Smith	4.00	1.80
❑ 62	Chuck Dobson	1.75	.80
❑ 63	Dick Kenworthy	1.75	.80
❑ 64	Jim Merritt	1.75	.80
❑ 65	John Roseboro	4.00	1.80
❑ 66A	Casey Cox	1.75	.80
	(White team name)		
❑ 66B	Casey Cox	100.00	45.00
	(Yellow team name)		
❑ 67	Jim Kaat CL	6.00	1.20
❑ 68	Ron Willis	1.75	.80
❑ 69	Tom Tresh	4.00	1.80
❑ 70	Bob Veale	4.00	1.80
❑ 71	Vern Fuller	1.75	.80
❑ 72	Tommy John	6.00	2.70
❑ 73	Jim Ray Hart	4.00	1.80
❑ 74	Milt Pappas	4.00	1.80
❑ 75	Don Mincher	1.75	.80
❑ 76	Braves Rookies	4.00	1.80
	Jim Britton		
	Ron Reed		
❑ 77	Don Wilson	4.00	1.80
❑ 78	Jim Northrup	6.00	2.70
❑ 79	Ted Kubiak	1.75	.80
❑ 80	Rod Carew	50.00	22.00
❑ 81	Larry Jackson	1.75	.80
❑ 82	Sam Bowens	1.75	.80
❑ 83	John Stephenson	1.75	.80
❑ 84	Bob Tolan	4.00	1.80
❑ 85	Gaylord Perry	8.00	3.60
❑ 86	Willie Stargell	8.00	3.60
❑ 87	Dick Williams MG	4.00	1.80
❑ 88	Phil Regan	4.00	1.80
❑ 89	Jake Gibbs	4.00	1.80
❑ 90	Vada Pinson	4.00	1.80
❑ 91	Jim Ollom	1.75	.80
❑ 92	Ed Kranepool	4.00	1.80
❑ 93	Tony Cloninger	1.75	.80
❑ 94	Lee Maye	1.75	.80
❑ 95	Bob Aspromonte	1.75	.80
❑ 96	Senator Rookies	1.75	.80
	Frank Coggins		
	Dick Nold		
❑ 97	Tom Phoebus	1.75	.80
❑ 98	Gary Sutherland	1.75	.80
❑ 99	Rocky Colavito	8.00	3.60
❑ 100	Bob Gibson	25.00	11.00
❑ 101	Glenn Beckert	4.00	1.80
❑ 102	Jose Cardenal	4.00	1.80
❑ 103	Don Sutton	8.00	3.60
❑ 104	Dick Dietz	1.75	.80
❑ 105	Al Downing	4.00	1.80
❑ 106	Dalton Jones	1.75	.80
❑ 107A	Juan Marichal CL	6.00	1.20
	Tan wide mesh		
❑ 107B	Juan Marichal CL	6.00	1.20
	Brown fine mesh		
❑ 108	Don Pavletich	1.75	.80
❑ 109	Bert Campaneris	4.00	1.80
❑ 110	Hank Aaron	60.00	27.00
❑ 111	Rich Reese	1.75	.80
❑ 112	Woody Fryman	1.75	.80
❑ 113	Tigers Rookies	4.00	1.80
	Tom Matchick		
	Daryl Patterson		
❑ 114	Ron Swoboda	4.00	1.80
❑ 115	Sam McDowell	4.00	1.80
❑ 116	Ken McMullen	1.75	.80
❑ 117	Larry Jaster	1.75	.80
❑ 118	Mark Belanger	4.00	1.80
❑ 119	Ted Savage	1.75	.80
❑ 120	Mel Stottlemyre	4.00	1.80
❑ 121	Jimmie Hall	1.75	.80
❑ 122	Gene Mauch MG	4.00	1.80
❑ 123	Jose Santiago	1.75	.80
❑ 124	Nate Oliver	1.75	.80
❑ 125	Joel Horlen	1.75	.80
❑ 126	Bobby Etheridge	1.75	.80
❑ 127	Paul Lindblad	1.75	.80
❑ 128	Astros Rookies	1.75	.80
	Tom Dukes		
	Alonzo Harris		
❑ 129	Mickey Stanley	6.00	2.70
❑ 130	Tony Perez	8.00	3.60
❑ 131	Frank Bertaina	1.75	.80
❑ 132	Bud Harrelson	4.00	1.80
❑ 133	Fred Whitfield	1.75	.80
❑ 134	Pat Jarvis	1.75	.80
❑ 135	Paul Blair	4.00	1.80
❑ 136	Randy Hundley	4.00	1.80
❑ 137	Twins Team	4.00	1.80
❑ 138	Ruben Amaro	1.75	.80
❑ 139	Chris Short	4.00	1.80
❑ 140	Tony Conigliaro	8.00	3.60
❑ 141	Dal Maxvill	1.75	.80
❑ 142	White Sox Rookies	1.75	.80
	Buddy Bradford		
	Bill Voss		
❑ 143	Pete Cimino	1.75	.80
❑ 144	Joe Morgan	12.00	5.50
❑ 145	Don Drysdale	12.00	5.50
❑ 146	Sal Bando	4.00	1.80
❑ 147	Frank Linzy	1.75	.80
❑ 148	Dave Bristol MG	1.75	.80
❑ 149	Bob Saverine	1.75	.80
❑ 150	Roberto Clemente	75.00	34.00
❑ 151	Lou Brock WS	10.00	4.50
❑ 152	Carl Yastrzemski WS	10.00	4.50
❑ 153	Nellie Briles WS	5.00	2.20
❑ 154	Bob Gibson WS	10.00	4.50
❑ 155	Jim Lonborg WS	5.00	2.20
❑ 156	Rico Petrocelli WS	5.00	2.20
❑ 157	World Series Game 7	5.00	2.20
	St. Louis wins it		
❑ 158	WS Summary	5.00	2.20
	Cardinals celebrate		
❑ 159	Don Kessinger	4.00	1.80
❑ 160	Earl Wilson	4.00	1.80
❑ 161	Norm Miller	1.75	.80
❑ 162	Cards Rookies	4.00	1.80
	Hal Gilson		
	Mike Torrez		
❑ 163	Gene Brabender	1.75	.80
❑ 164	Ramon Webster	1.75	.80
❑ 165	Tony Oliva	6.00	2.70
❑ 166	Claude Raymond	1.75	.80
❑ 167	Elston Howard	6.00	2.70
❑ 168	Dodgers Team	4.00	1.80
❑ 169	Bob Bolin	1.75	.80
❑ 170	Jim Fregosi	4.00	1.80
❑ 171	Don Nottebart	1.75	.80
❑ 172	Walt Williams	1.75	.80
❑ 173	John Boozer	1.75	.80
❑ 174	Bob Tillman	1.75	.80
❑ 175	Maury Wills	6.00	2.70
❑ 176	Bob Allen	1.75	.80
❑ 177	Mets Rookies	700.00	325.00
	Jerry Koosman RC		
	Nolan Ryan RC		
❑ 178	Don Wert	4.00	1.80
❑ 179	Bill Stoneman	1.75	.80
❑ 180	Curt Flood	6.00	2.70
❑ 181	Jerry Zimmerman	1.75	.80
❑ 182	Dave Giusti	1.75	.80
❑ 183	Bob Kennedy MG	4.00	1.80
❑ 184	Lou Johnson	4.00	1.80
❑ 185	Tom Haller	1.75	.80
❑ 186	Eddie Watt	1.75	.80
❑ 187	Sonny Jackson	1.75	.80
❑ 188	Cap Peterson	1.75	.80
❑ 189	Bill Landis	1.75	.80
❑ 190	Bill White	4.00	1.80
❑ 191	Dan Frisella	1.75	.80
❑ 192A	Carl Yastrzemski CL	8.00	1.60
	Special Baseball Playing Card		
❑ 192B	Carl Yastrzemski CL	8.00	1.60
	Special Baseball		
	Playing Card Game		
❑ 193	Jack Hamilton	1.75	.80
❑ 194	Don Buford	1.75	.80
❑ 195	Joe Pepitone	4.00	1.80
❑ 196	Gary Nolan	4.00	1.80
❑ 197	Larry Brown	1.75	.80
❑ 198	Roy Face	4.00	1.80
❑ 199	A's Rookies	1.75	.80
	Roberto Rodriquez		
	Darrell Osteen		
❑ 200	Orlando Cepeda	8.00	3.60
❑ 201	Mike Marshall RC	4.00	1.80
❑ 202	Adolfo Phillips	1.75	.80
❑ 203	Dick Kelley	1.75	.80
❑ 204	Andy Etchebarren	1.75	.80
❑ 205	Juan Marichal	8.00	3.60
❑ 206	Cal Ermer MG	1.75	.80
❑ 207	Carroll Sembera	1.75	.80
❑ 208	Willie Davis	4.00	1.80
❑ 209	Tim Cullen	1.75	.80
❑ 210	Gary Peters	1.75	.80
❑ 211	J.C. Martin	1.75	.80
❑ 212	Dave Morehead	1.75	.80
❑ 213	Chico Ruiz	1.75	.80

	No.	Card	NrMT	VG-E
❑	214	Yankees Rookies	4.00	1.80
		Stan Bahnsen		
		Frank Fernandez		
❑	215	Jim Bunning	8.00	3.60
❑	216	Bubba Morton	1.75	.80
❑	217	Dick Farrell	1.75	.80
❑	218	Ken Suarez	1.75	.80
❑	219	Rob Gardner	1.75	.80
❑	220	Harmon Killebrew	15.00	6.75
❑	221	Braves Team	4.00	1.80
❑	222	Jim Hardin	1.75	.80
❑	223	Ollie Brown	1.75	.80
❑	224	Jack Aker	1.75	.80
❑	225	Richie Allen	6.00	2.70
❑	226	Jimmie Price	1.75	.80
❑	227	Joe Hoerner	1.75	.80
❑	228	Dodgers Rookies	4.00	1.80
		Jack Billingham		
		Jim Fairey		
❑	229	Fred Klages	1.75	.80
❑	230	Pete Rose	50.00	22.00
❑	231	Dave Baldwin	1.75	.80
❑	232	Denis Menke	1.75	.80
❑	233	George Scott	4.00	1.80
❑	234	Bill Monbouquette	1.75	.80
❑	235	Ron Santo	8.00	3.60
❑	236	Tug McGraw	6.00	2.70
❑	237	Alvin Dark MG	4.00	1.80
❑	238	Tom Satriano	1.75	.80
❑	239	Bill Henry	1.75	.80
❑	240	Al Kaline	25.00	11.00
❑	241	Felix Millan	1.75	.80
❑	242	Moe Drabowsky	4.00	1.80
❑	243	Rich Rollins	1.75	.80
❑	244	John Donaldson	1.75	.80
❑	245	Tony Gonzalez	1.75	.80
❑	246	Fritz Peterson	4.00	1.80
❑	247	Reds Rookies	125.00	55.00
		Johnny Bench RC		
		Ron Tompkins		
❑	248	Fred Valentine	1.75	.80
❑	249	Bill Singer	1.75	.80
❑	250	Carl Yastrzemski	30.00	13.50
❑	251	Manny Sanguillen RC	6.00	2.70
❑	252	Angels Team	4.00	1.80
❑	253	Dick Hughes	1.75	.80
❑	254	Cleon Jones	4.00	1.80
❑	255	Dean Chance	4.00	1.80
❑	256	Norm Cash	6.00	2.70
❑	257	Phil Niekro	8.00	3.60
❑	258	Cubs Rookies	1.75	.80
		Jose Arcia		
		Bill Schlesinger		
❑	259	Ken Boyer	6.00	2.70
❑	260	Jim Wynn	4.00	1.80
❑	261	Dave Duncan	4.00	1.80
❑	262	Rick Wise	4.00	1.80
❑	263	Horace Clarke	4.00	1.80
❑	264	Ted Abernathy	1.75	.80
❑	265	Tommy Davis	4.00	1.80
❑	266	Paul Popovich	1.75	.80
❑	267	Herman Franks MG	1.75	.80
❑	268	Bob Humphreys	1.75	.80
❑	269	Bob Tiefenauer	1.75	.80
❑	270	Matty Alou	4.00	1.80
❑	271	Bobby Knoop	1.75	.80
❑	272	Ray Culp	1.75	.80
❑	273	Dave Johnson	4.00	1.80
❑	274	Mike Cuellar	4.00	1.80
❑	275	Tim McCarver	6.00	2.70
❑	276	Jim Roland	1.75	.80
❑	277	Jerry Buchek	1.75	.80
❑	278	Orlando Cepeda CL	6.00	1.20
❑	279	Bill Hands	1.75	.80
❑	280	Mickey Mantle	250.00	110.00
❑	281	Jim Campanis	1.75	.80
❑	282	Rick Monday	4.00	1.80
❑	283	Mel Queen	1.75	.80
❑	284	Johnny Briggs	1.75	.80
❑	285	Dick McAuliffe	6.00	2.70
❑	286	Cecil Upshaw	1.75	.80
❑	287	White Sox Rookies	1.75	.80
		Mickey Abarbanel		
		Cisco Carlos		
❑	288	Dave Wickersham	1.75	.80
❑	289	Woody Held	1.75	.80
❑	290	Willie McCovey	12.00	5.50
❑	291	Dick Lines	1.75	.80
❑	292	Art Shamsky	1.75	.80
❑	293	Bruce Howard	1.75	.80
❑	294	Red Schoendienst MG	6.00	2.70
❑	295	Sonny Siebert	1.75	.80
❑	296	Byron Browne	1.75	.80
❑	297	Russ Gibson	1.75	.80
❑	298	Jim Brewer	1.75	.80
❑	299	Gene Michael	4.00	1.80
❑	300	Rusty Staub	4.00	1.80
❑	301	Twins Rookies	1.75	.80
		George Mitterwald		
		Rick Renick		
❑	302	Gerry Arrigo	1.75	.80
❑	303	Dick Green	4.00	1.80
❑	304	Sandy Valdespino	1.75	.80
❑	305	Minnie Rojas	1.75	.80
❑	306	Mike Ryan	1.75	.80
❑	307	John Hiller	4.00	1.80
❑	308	Pirates Team	4.00	1.80
❑	309	Ken Henderson	1.75	.80
❑	310	Luis Aparicio	8.00	3.60
❑	311	Jack Lamabe	1.75	.80
❑	312	Curt Blefary	1.75	.80
❑	313	Al Weis	1.75	.80
❑	314	Red Sox Rookies	1.75	.80
		Bill Rohr		
		George Spriggs		
❑	315	Zoilo Versalles	1.75	.80
❑	316	Steve Barber	1.75	.80
❑	317	Ron Brand	1.75	.80
❑	318	Chico Salmon	1.75	.80
❑	319	George Culver	1.75	.80
❑	320	Frank Howard	4.00	1.80
❑	321	Leo Durocher MG	6.00	2.70
❑	322	Dave Boswell	1.75	.80
❑	323	Deron Johnson	4.00	1.80
❑	324	Jim Nash	1.75	.80
❑	325	Manny Mota	4.00	1.80
❑	326	Dennis Ribant	1.75	.80
❑	327	Tony Taylor	4.00	1.80
❑	328	Angels Rookies	1.75	.80
		Chuck Vinson		
		Jim Weaver		
❑	329	Duane Josephson	1.75	.80
❑	330	Roger Maris	50.00	22.00
❑	331	Dan Osinski	1.75	.80
❑	332	Doug Rader	4.00	1.80
❑	333	Ron Herbel	1.75	.80
❑	334	Orioles Team	4.00	1.80
❑	335	Bob Allison	4.00	1.80
❑	336	John Purdin	1.75	.80
❑	337	Bill Robinson	4.00	1.80
❑	338	Bob Johnson	1.75	.80
❑	339	Rich Nye	1.75	.80
❑	340	Max Alvis	1.75	.80
❑	341	Jim Lemon MG	1.75	.80
❑	342	Ken Johnson	1.75	.80
❑	343	Jim Gosger	1.75	.80
❑	344	Donn Clendenon	4.00	1.80
❑	345	Bob Hendley	1.75	.80
❑	346	Jerry Adair	1.75	.80
❑	347	George Brunet	1.75	.80
❑	348	Phillies Rookies	1.75	.80
		Larry Colton		
		Dick Thoenen		
❑	349	Ed Spiezio	4.00	1.80
❑	350	Hoyt Wilhelm	8.00	3.60
❑	351	Bob Barton	1.75	.80
❑	352	Jackie Hernandez	1.75	.80
❑	353	Mack Jones	1.75	.80
❑	354	Pete Richert	1.75	.80
❑	355	Ernie Banks	25.00	11.00
❑	356A	Ken Holtzman CL	6.00	1.20
		Head centered within circle		
❑	356B	Ken Holtzman	6.00	1.20
		Head shifted right within circle		
❑	357	Len Gabrielson	1.75	.80
❑	358	Mike Epstein	1.75	.80
❑	359	Joe Moeller	1.75	.80
❑	360	Willie Horton	6.00	2.70
❑	361	Harmon Killebrew AS	8.00	3.60
❑	362	Orlando Cepeda AS	6.00	2.70
❑	363	Rod Carew AS	8.00	3.60
❑	364	Joe Morgan AS	8.00	3.60
❑	365	Brooks Robinson AS	8.00	3.60
❑	366	Ron Santo AS	5.00	2.20
❑	367	Jim Fregosi AS	5.00	2.20
❑	368	Gene Alley AS	5.00	2.20
❑	369	Carl Yastrzemski AS	10.00	4.50
❑	370	Hank Aaron AS	20.00	9.00
❑	371	Tony Oliva AS	6.00	2.70
❑	372	Lou Brock AS	8.00	3.60
❑	373	Frank Robinson AS	8.00	3.60
❑	374	Bob Clemente AS	30.00	13.50
❑	375	Bill Freehan AS	5.00	2.20
❑	376	Tim McCarver AS	5.00	2.20
❑	377	Joel Horlen AS	5.00	2.20
❑	378	Bob Gibson AS	8.00	3.60
❑	379	Gary Peters AS	5.00	2.20
❑	380	Ken Holtzman AS	5.00	2.20
❑	381	Boog Powell	4.00	1.80
❑	382	Ramon Hernandez	1.75	.80
❑	383	Steve Whitaker	1.75	.80
❑	384	Reds Rookies	6.00	2.70
		Bill Henry		
		Hal McRae RC		
❑	385	Jim Hunter	10.00	4.50
❑	386	Greg Goossen	1.75	.80
❑	387	Joe Foy	1.75	.80
❑	388	Ray Washburn	1.75	.80
❑	389	Jay Johnstone	4.00	1.80
❑	390	Bill Mazeroski	8.00	3.60
❑	391	Bob Priddy	1.75	.80
❑	392	Grady Hatton MG	1.75	.80
❑	393	Jim Perry	4.00	1.80
❑	394	Tommie Aaron	6.00	2.70
❑	395	Camilo Pascual	4.00	1.80
❑	396	Bobby Wine	1.75	.80
❑	397	Vic Davalillo	1.75	.80
❑	398	Jim Grant	1.75	.80
❑	399	Ray Oyler	4.00	1.80
❑	400A	Mike McCormick	4.00	1.80
		(Yellow letters)		
❑	400B	Mike McCormick	150.00	70.00
		(Team name in white letters)		
❑	401	Mets Team	4.00	1.80
❑	402	Mike Hegan	4.00	1.80
❑	403	John Buzhardt	1.75	.80
❑	404	Floyd Robinson	1.75	.80
❑	405	Tommy Helms	4.00	1.80
❑	406	Dick Ellsworth	1.75	.80
❑	407	Gary Kolb	1.75	.80
❑	408	Steve Carlton	30.00	13.50
❑	409	Orioles Rookies	1.75	.80
		Frank Peters		
		Ron Stone		
❑	410	Ferguson Jenkins	10.00	4.50
❑	411	Ron Hansen	1.75	.80
❑	412	Clay Carroll	4.00	1.80
❑	413	Tom McCraw	1.75	.80
❑	414	Mickey Lolich	8.00	3.60
❑	415	Johnny Callison	4.00	1.80
❑	416	Bill Rigney MG	1.75	.80
❑	417	Willie Crawford	1.75	.80
❑	418	Eddie Fisher	1.75	.80
❑	419	Jack Hiatt	1.75	.80
❑	420	Cesar Tovar	1.75	.80
❑	421	Ron Taylor	1.75	.80
❑	422	Rene Lachemann	1.75	.80
❑	423	Fred Gladding	1.75	.80
❑	424	Chicago White Sox	4.00	1.80
		Team Card		
❑	425	Jim Maloney	4.00	1.80
❑	426	Hank Allen	1.75	.80
❑	427	Dick Calmus	1.75	.80
❑	428	Vic Roznovsky	1.75	.80
❑	429	Tommie Sisk	1.75	.80
❑	430	Rico Petrocelli	4.00	1.80
❑	431	Dooley Womack	1.75	.80
❑	432	Indians Rookies	1.75	.80
		Bill Davis		
		Jose Vidal		
❑	433	Bob Rodgers	1.75	.80
❑	434	Ricardo Joseph	1.75	.80
❑	435	Ron Perranoski	4.00	1.80
❑	436	Hal Lanier	1.75	.80
❑	437	Don Cardwell	1.75	.80
❑	438	Lee Thomas	4.00	1.80

❑ 439 Lum Harris MG 1.75 .80
❑ 440 Claude Osteen 4.00 1.80
❑ 441 Alex Johnson 4.00 1.80
❑ 442 Dick Bosman 1.75 .80
❑ 443 Joe Azcue 1.75 .80
❑ 444 Jack Fisher 1.75 .80
❑ 445 Mike Shannon 4.00 1.80
❑ 446 Ron Kline 1.75 .80
❑ 447 Tigers Rookies 4.00 1.80
George Korince
Fred Lasher
❑ 448 Gary Wagner 1.75 .80
❑ 449 Gene Oliver 1.75 .80
❑ 450 Jim Kaat 6.00 2.70
❑ 451 Al Spangler 1.75 .80
❑ 452 Jesus Alou 1.75 .80
❑ 453 Sammy Ellis 1.75 .80
❑ 454A Frank Robinson CL 8.00 1.60
Cap complete within circle
❑ 454B Frank Robinson CL 8.00 1.60
Cap partially within circle
❑ 455 Rico Carty 4.00 1.80
❑ 456 John O'Donoghue 1.75 .80
❑ 457 Jim Lefebvre 4.00 1.80
❑ 458 Lew Krausse 6.00 2.70
❑ 459 Dick Simpson 3.50 1.55
❑ 460 Jim Lonborg 6.00 2.70
❑ 461 Chuck Hiller 3.50 1.55
❑ 462 Barry Moore 3.50 1.55
❑ 463 Jim Schaffer 3.50 1.55
❑ 464 Don McMahon 3.50 1.55
❑ 465 Tommie Agee 10.00 4.50
❑ 466 Bill Dillman 3.50 1.55
❑ 467 Dick Howser 10.00 4.50
❑ 468 Larry Sherry 3.50 1.55
❑ 469 Ty Cline 3.50 1.55
❑ 470 Bill Freehan 10.00 4.50
❑ 471 Orlando Pena 3.50 1.55
❑ 472 Walter Alston MG 6.00 2.70
❑ 473 Al Worthington 3.50 1.55
❑ 474 Paul Schaal 3.50 1.55
❑ 475 Joe Niekro 6.00 2.70
❑ 476 Woody Woodward 3.50 1.55
❑ 477 Philadelphia Phillies 7.00 3.10
Team Card
❑ 478 Dave McNally 6.00 2.70
❑ 479 Phil Gagliano 6.00 2.70
❑ 480 Manager's Dream 80.00 36.00
Tony Oliva
Chico Cardenas
Bob Clemente
❑ 481 John Wyatt 3.50 1.55
❑ 482 Jose Pagan 3.50 1.55
❑ 483 Darold Knowles 3.50 1.55
❑ 484 Phil Roof 3.50 1.55
❑ 485 Ken Berry 6.00 2.70
❑ 486 Cal Koonce 3.50 1.55
❑ 487 Lee May 10.00 4.50
❑ 488 Dick Tracewski 6.00 2.70
❑ 489 Wally Bunker 3.50 1.55
❑ 490 Super Stars 175.00 80.00
Harmon Killebrew
Willie Mays
Mickey Mantle
❑ 491 Denny Lemaster 3.50 1.55
❑ 492 Jeff Torborg 6.00 2.70
❑ 493 Jim McGlothlin 3.50 1.55
❑ 494 Ray Sadecki 3.50 1.55
❑ 495 Leon Wagner 3.50 1.55
❑ 496 Steve Hamilton 6.00 2.70
❑ 497 Cardinals Team 7.00 3.10
❑ 498 Bill Bryan 6.00 2.70
❑ 499 Steve Blass 6.00 2.70
❑ 500 Frank Robinson 30.00 13.50
❑ 501 John Odom 6.00 2.70
❑ 502 Mike Andrews 3.50 1.55
❑ 503 Al Jackson 6.00 2.70
❑ 504 Russ Snyder 3.50 1.55
❑ 505 Joe Sparma 10.00 4.50
❑ 506 Clarence Jones RC 3.50 1.55
❑ 507 Wade Blasingame 3.50 1.55
❑ 508 Duke Sims 3.50 1.55
❑ 509 Dennis Higgins 3.50 1.55
❑ 510 Ron Fairly 10.00 4.50
❑ 511 Bill Kelso 3.50 1.55
❑ 512 Grant Jackson 3.50 1.55
❑ 513 Hank Bauer MG 6.00 2.70
❑ 514 Al McBean 3.50 1.55
❑ 515 Russ Nixon 3.50 1.55
❑ 516 Pete Mikkelsen 3.50 1.55
❑ 517 Diego Segui 6.00 2.70
❑ 518A Clete Boyer CL ERR 12.00 2.40
539 AL Rookies
❑ 518B Clete Boyer CL COR 12.00 2.40
539 ML Rookies
❑ 519 Jerry Stephenson 3.50 1.55
❑ 520 Lou Brock 25.00 11.00
❑ 521 Don Shaw 3.50 1.55
❑ 522 Wayne Causey 3.50 1.55
❑ 523 John Tsitouris 3.50 1.55
❑ 524 Andy Kosco 6.00 2.70
❑ 525 Jim Davenport 3.50 1.55
❑ 526 Bill Denehy 3.50 1.55
❑ 527 Tito Francona 3.50 1.55
❑ 528 Tigers Team 60.00 27.00
❑ 529 Bruce Von Hoff 3.50 1.55
❑ 530 Bird Belters 40.00 18.00
Brooks Robinson
Frank Robinson
❑ 531 Chuck Hinton 3.50 1.55
❑ 532 Luis Tiant 6.00 2.70
❑ 533 Wes Parker 6.00 2.70
❑ 534 Bob Miller 6.00 2.70
❑ 535 Danny Cater 6.00 2.70
❑ 536 Bill Short 3.50 1.55
❑ 537 Norm Siebern 6.00 2.70
❑ 538 Manny Jimenez 6.00 2.70
❑ 539 Major League Rookies 3.50 1.55
Jim Ray
Mike Ferraro
❑ 540 Nelson Briles 6.00 2.70
❑ 541 Sandy Alomar 6.00 2.70
❑ 542 John Boccabella 3.50 1.55
❑ 543 Bob Lee 3.50 1.55
❑ 544 Mayo Smith MG 12.00 5.50
❑ 545 Lindy McDaniel 6.00 2.70
❑ 546 Roy White 6.00 2.70
❑ 547 Dan Coombs 3.50 1.55
❑ 548 Bernie Allen 3.50 1.55
❑ 549 Orioles Rookies 3.50 1.55
Curt Motton
Roger Nelson
❑ 550 Clete Boyer 6.00 2.70
❑ 551 Darrell Sutherland 3.50 1.55
❑ 552 Ed Kirkpatrick 3.50 1.55
❑ 553 Hank Aguirre 3.50 1.55
❑ 554 A's Team 10.00 4.50
❑ 555 Jose Tartabull 6.00 2.70
❑ 556 Dick Selma 3.50 1.55
❑ 557 Frank Quilici 6.00 2.70
❑ 558 Johnny Edwards 3.50 1.55
❑ 559 Pirates Rookies 3.50 1.55
Carl Taylor
Luke Walker
❑ 560 Paul Casanova 3.50 1.55
❑ 561 Lee Elia 3.50 1.55
❑ 562 Jim Bouton 6.00 2.70
❑ 563 Ed Charles 3.50 1.55
❑ 564 Eddie Stanky MG 6.00 2.70
❑ 565 Larry Dierker 6.00 2.70
❑ 566 Ken Harrelson 6.00 2.70
❑ 567 Clay Dalrymple 3.50 1.55
❑ 568 Willie Smith 3.50 1.55
❑ 569 NL Rookies 3.50 1.55
Ivan Murrell
Les Rohr
❑ 570 Rick Reichardt 3.50 1.55
❑ 571 Tony LaRussa 12.00 5.50
❑ 572 Don Bosch 3.50 1.55
❑ 573 Joe Coleman 3.50 1.55
❑ 574 Cincinnati Reds 10.00 4.50
Team Card
❑ 575 Jim Palmer 40.00 18.00
❑ 576 Dave Adlesh 3.50 1.55
❑ 577 Fred Talbot 3.50 1.55
❑ 578 Orlando Martinez 3.50 1.55
❑ 579 NL Rookies 10.00 4.50
Larry Hisle RC
Mike Lum
❑ 580 Bob Bailey 3.50 1.55
❑ 581 Garry Roggenburk 3.50 1.55
❑ 582 Jerry Grote 10.00 4.50
❑ 583 Gates Brown 10.00 4.50
❑ 584 Larry Shepard MG 3.50 1.55
❑ 585 Wilbur Wood 6.00 2.70
❑ 586 Jim Pagliaroni 6.00 2.70
❑ 587 Roger Repoz 3.50 1.55
❑ 588 Dick Schofield 3.50 1.55
❑ 589 Twins Rookies 3.50 1.55
Ron Clark
Moe Ogier
❑ 590 Tommy Harper 6.00 2.70
❑ 591 Dick Nen 3.50 1.55
❑ 592 John Bateman 3.50 1.55
❑ 593 Lee Stange 3.50 1.55
❑ 594 Phil Linz 6.00 2.70
❑ 595 Phil Ortega 3.50 1.55
❑ 596 Charlie Smith 3.50 1.55
❑ 597 Bill McCool 3.50 1.55
❑ 598 Jerry May 6.00 1.85

1969 Topps

	NRMT	VG-E
COMP. MASTER SET (695)	5000.00	2200.00
COMPLETE SET (664)	2200.00	1000.00
COMMON (1-218/328-512)	1.50	.70
COMMON CARD (219-327)	2.50	1.10
COMMON CARD (513-588)	2.00	.90
COMMON CARD (589-664)	3.00	1.35
WRAPPER (5-CENT)	20.00	9.00

❑ 1 AL Batting Leaders 15.00 5.25
Carl Yastrzemski
Danny Cater
Tony Oliva
❑ 2 NL Batting Leaders 7.00 3.10
Pete Rose
Matty Alou
Felipe Alou
❑ 3 AL RBI Leaders 3.50 1.55
Ken Harrelson
Frank Howard
Jim Northrup
❑ 4 NL RBI Leaders 6.00 2.70
Willie McCovey
Ron Santo
Billy Williams
❑ 5 AL Home Run Leaders 3.50 1.55
Frank Howard
Willie Horton
Ken Harrelson
❑ 6 NL Home Run Leaders 6.00 2.70
Willie McCovey
Richie Allen
Ernie Banks
❑ 7 AL ERA Leaders 3.50 1.55
Luis Tiant
Sam McDowell
Dave McNally
❑ 8 NL ERA Leaders 6.00 2.70
Bob Gibson
Bobby Bolin
Bob Veale
❑ 9 AL Pitching Leaders 3.50 1.55
Denny McLain
Dave McNally
Luis Tiant
Mel Stottlemyre
❑ 10 NL Pitching Leaders 7.00 3.10

	Juan Marichal		
	Bob Gibson		
	Fergie Jenkins		
❑ 11	AL Strikeout Leaders	3.50	1.55
	Sam McDowell		
	Denny McLain		
	Luis Tiant		
❑ 12	NL Strikeout Leaders	4.00	1.80
	Bob Gibson		
	Fergie Jenkins		
	Bill Singer		
❑ 13	Mickey Stanley	2.50	1.10
❑ 14	Al McBean	1.50	.70
❑ 15	Boog Powell	4.00	1.80
❑ 16	Giants Rookies	1.50	.70
	Cesar Gutierrez		
	Rich Robertson		
❑ 17	Mike Marshall	2.50	1.10
❑ 18	Dick Schofield	1.50	.70
❑ 19	Ken Suarez	1.50	.70
❑ 20	Ernie Banks	20.00	9.00
❑ 21	Jose Santiago	1.50	.70
❑ 22	Jesus Alou	2.50	1.10
❑ 23	Lew Krausse	1.50	.70
❑ 24	Walt Alston MG	4.00	1.80
❑ 25	Roy White	2.50	1.10
❑ 26	Clay Carroll	2.50	1.10
❑ 27	Bernie Allen	1.50	.70
❑ 28	Mike Ryan	1.50	.70
❑ 29	Dave Morehead	1.50	.70
❑ 30	Bob Allison	2.50	1.10
❑ 31	Mets Rookies	2.50	1.10
	Gary Gentry RC		
	Amos Otis		
❑ 32	Sammy Ellis	1.50	.70
❑ 33	Wayne Causey	1.50	.70
❑ 34	Gary Peters	1.50	.70
❑ 35	Joe Morgan	10.00	4.50
❑ 36	Luke Walker	1.50	.70
❑ 37	Curt Motton	1.50	.70
❑ 38	Zoilo Versalles	2.50	1.10
❑ 39	Dick Hughes	1.50	.70
❑ 40	Mayo Smith MG	1.50	.70
❑ 41	Bob Barton	1.50	.70
❑ 42	Tommy Harper	2.50	1.10
❑ 43	Joe Niekro	2.50	1.10
❑ 44	Danny Cater	1.50	.70
❑ 45	Maury Wills	2.50	1.10
❑ 46	Fritz Peterson	2.50	1.10
❑ 47A	Paul Popovich	1.50	.70
	(No helmet emblem)		
❑ 47B	Paul Popovich	25.00	11.00
	(C emblem on helmet)		
❑ 48	Brant Alyea	1.50	.70
❑ 49A	Royals Rookies ERR	25.00	11.00
	Steve Jones		
	E. Rodriquez		
❑ 49B	Royals Rookies COR	1.50	.70
	Steve Jones		
	E. Rodriguez		
❑ 50	Roberto Clemente UER	60.00	27.00
	Bats Right listed twice		
❑ 51	Woody Fryman	1.50	.70
❑ 52	Mike Andrews	1.50	.70
❑ 53	Sonny Jackson	1.50	.70
❑ 54	Cisco Carlos	1.50	.70
❑ 55	Jerry Grote	2.50	1.10
❑ 56	Rich Reese	1.50	.70
❑ 57	Denny McLain CL	6.00	1.20
❑ 58	Fred Gladding	1.50	.70
❑ 59	Jay Johnstone	2.50	1.10
❑ 60	Nelson Briles	2.50	1.10
❑ 61	Jimmie Hall	1.50	.70
❑ 62	Chico Salmon	1.50	.70
❑ 63	Jim Hickman	2.50	1.10
❑ 64	Bill Monbouquette	1.50	.70
❑ 65	Willie Davis	2.50	1.10
❑ 66	Orioles Rookies	1.50	.70
	Mike Adamson		
	Merv Rettenmund		
❑ 67	Bill Stoneman	2.50	1.10
❑ 68	Dave Duncan	2.50	1.10
❑ 69	Steve Hamilton	2.50	1.10
❑ 70	Tommy Helms	2.50	1.10
❑ 71	Steve Whitaker	2.50	1.10
❑ 72	Ron Taylor	1.50	.70
❑ 73	Johnny Briggs	1.50	.70
❑ 74	Preston Gomez MG	2.50	1.10
❑ 75	Luis Aparicio	6.00	2.70
❑ 76	Norm Miller	1.50	.70
❑ 77A	Ron Perranoski	2.50	1.10
	(No emblem on cap)		
❑ 77B	Ron Perranoski	25.00	11.00
	(LA on cap)		
❑ 78	Tom Satriano	1.50	.70
❑ 79	Milt Pappas	2.50	1.10
❑ 80	Norm Cash	2.50	1.10
❑ 81	Mel Queen	1.50	.70
❑ 82	Pirates Rookies	8.00	3.60
	Rich Hebner		
	Al Oliver RC		
❑ 83	Mike Ferraro	2.50	1.10
❑ 84	Bob Humphreys	1.50	.70
❑ 85	Lou Brock	20.00	9.00
❑ 86	Pete Richert	1.50	.70
❑ 87	Horace Clarke	2.50	1.10
❑ 88	Rich Nye	1.50	.70
❑ 89	Russ Gibson	1.50	.70
❑ 90	Jerry Koosman	2.50	1.10
❑ 91	Alvin Dark MG	2.50	1.10
❑ 92	Jack Billingham	2.50	1.10
❑ 93	Joe Foy	2.50	1.10
❑ 94	Hank Aguirre	1.50	.70
❑ 95	Johnny Bench	50.00	22.00
❑ 96	Denny Lemaster	1.50	.70
❑ 97	Buddy Bradford	1.50	.70
❑ 98	Dave Giusti	1.50	.70
❑ 99A	Twins Rookies	15.00	6.75
	Danny Morris		
	Graig Nettles RC		
	(No loop)		
❑ 99B	Twins Rookies	15.00	6.75
	Danny Morris		
	Graig Nettles RC		
	(Errant loop in		
	upper left corner		
	of obverse)		
❑ 100	Hank Aaron	40.00	18.00
❑ 101	Daryl Patterson	1.50	.70
❑ 102	Jim Davenport	1.50	.70
❑ 103	Roger Repoz	1.50	.70
❑ 104	Steve Blass	2.50	1.10
❑ 105	Rick Monday	2.50	1.10
❑ 106	Jim Hannan	1.50	.70
❑ 107A	Bob Gibson CL ERR	6.00	1.20
	161 Jim Purdin		
❑ 107B	Bob Gibson CL COR	7.50	1.50
	161 John Purdin		
❑ 108	Tony Taylor	2.50	1.10
❑ 109	Jim Lonborg	2.50	1.10
❑ 110	Mike Shannon	2.50	1.10
❑ 111	Johnny Morris	1.50	.70
❑ 112	J.C. Martin	2.50	1.10
❑ 113	Dave May	1.50	.70
❑ 114	Yankees Rookies	2.50	1.10
	Alan Closter		
	John Cumberland		
❑ 115	Bill Hands	1.50	.70
❑ 116	Chuck Harrison	1.50	.70
❑ 117	Jim Fairey	1.50	.70
❑ 118	Stan Williams	1.50	.70
❑ 119	Doug Rader	2.50	1.10
❑ 120	Pete Rose	30.00	13.50
❑ 121	Joe Grzenda	1.50	.70
❑ 122	Ron Fairly	2.50	1.10
❑ 123	Wilbur Wood	2.50	1.10
❑ 124	Hank Bauer MG	2.50	1.10
❑ 125	Ray Sadecki	1.50	.70
❑ 126	Dick Tracewski	1.50	.70
❑ 127	Kevin Collins	2.50	1.10
❑ 128	Tommie Aaron	2.50	1.10
❑ 129	Bill McCool	1.50	.70
❑ 130	Carl Yastrzemski	20.00	9.00
❑ 131	Chris Cannizzaro	1.50	.70
❑ 132	Dave Baldwin	1.50	.70
❑ 133	Johnny Callison	2.50	1.10
❑ 134	Jim Weaver	1.50	.70
❑ 135	Tommy Davis	2.50	1.10
❑ 136	Cards Rookies	1.50	.70
	Steve Huntz		
	Mike Torrez		
❑ 137	Wally Bunker	1.50	.70
❑ 138	John Bateman	1.50	.70
❑ 139	Andy Kosco	1.50	.70
❑ 140	Jim Lefebvre	2.50	1.10
❑ 141	Bill Dillman	1.50	.70
❑ 142	Woody Woodward	1.50	.70
❑ 143	Joe Nossek	1.50	.70
❑ 144	Bob Hendley	2.50	1.10
❑ 145	Max Alvis	1.50	.70
❑ 146	Jim Perry	2.50	1.10
❑ 147	Leo Durocher MG	4.00	1.80
❑ 148	Lee Stange	1.50	.70
❑ 149	Ollie Brown	2.50	1.10
❑ 150	Denny McLain	4.00	1.80
❑ 151A	Clay Dalrymple	1.50	.70
	Portrait, Orioles		
❑ 151B	Clay Dalrymple	15.00	6.75
	Catching, Phillies		
❑ 152	Tommie Sisk	1.50	.70
❑ 153	Ed Brinkman	1.50	.70
❑ 154	Jim Britton	1.50	.70
❑ 155	Pete Ward	1.50	.70
❑ 156	Houston Rookies	1.50	.70
	Hal Gilson		
	Leon McFadden		
❑ 157	Bob Rodgers	2.50	1.10
❑ 158	Joe Gibbon	1.50	.70
❑ 159	Jerry Adair	1.50	.70
❑ 160	Vada Pinson	2.50	1.10
❑ 161	John Purdin	1.50	.70
❑ 162	Bob Gibson WS	8.00	3.60
	Fans 17		
❑ 163	Willie Horton WS	6.00	2.70
❑ 164	Tim McCarver WS	12.00	5.50
	Roger Maris		
❑ 165	Lou Brock WS	8.00	3.60
❑ 166	Al Kaline WS	8.00	3.60
❑ 167	Jim Northrup WS	6.00	2.70
❑ 168	Mickey Lolich WS	8.00	3.60
	Bob Gibson		
❑ 169	Dick McAuliffe WS	6.00	2.70
	Denny McLain		
	Willie Horton		
❑ 170	Frank Howard	2.50	1.10
❑ 171	Glenn Beckert	2.50	1.10
❑ 172	Jerry Stephenson	1.50	.70
❑ 173	White Sox Rookies	1.50	.70
	Bob Christian		
	Gerry Nyman		
❑ 174	Grant Jackson	1.50	.70
❑ 175	Jim Bunning	6.00	2.70
❑ 176	Joe Azcue	1.50	.70
❑ 177	Ron Reed	1.50	.70
❑ 178	Ray Oyler	2.50	1.10
❑ 179	Don Pavletich	1.50	.70
❑ 180	Willie Horton	2.50	1.10
❑ 181	Mel Nelson	1.50	.70
❑ 182	Bill Rigney MG	1.50	.70
❑ 183	Don Shaw	1.50	.70
❑ 184	Roberto Pena	1.50	.70
❑ 185	Tom Phoebus	1.50	.70
❑ 186	Johnny Edwards	1.50	.70
❑ 187	Leon Wagner	1.50	.70
❑ 188	Rick Wise	2.50	1.10
❑ 189	Red Sox Rookies	1.50	.70
	Joe Lahoud		
	John Thibodeau		
❑ 190	Willie Mays	60.00	27.00
❑ 191	Lindy McDaniel	2.50	1.10
❑ 192	Jose Pagan	1.50	.70
❑ 193	Don Cardwell	2.50	1.10
❑ 194	Ted Uhlaender	1.50	.70
❑ 195	John Odom	1.50	.70
❑ 196	Lum Harris MG	1.50	.70
❑ 197	Dick Selma	1.50	.70
❑ 198	Willie Smith	1.50	.70
❑ 199	Jim French	1.50	.70
❑ 200	Bob Gibson	12.00	5.50
❑ 201	Russ Snyder	1.50	.70
❑ 202	Don Wilson	2.50	1.10
❑ 203	Dave Johnson	2.50	1.10
❑ 204	Jack Hiatt	1.50	.70
❑ 205	Rick Reichardt	1.50	.70
❑ 206	Phillies Rookies	2.50	1.10
	Larry Hisle		
	Barry Lersch		
❑ 207	Roy Face	2.50	1.10

❑ 208A Donn Clendenon 2.50 1.10
Houston
❑ 208B Donn Clendenon 15.00 6.75
Expos
❑ 209 Larry Haney UER 1.50 .70
(Reverse negative)
❑ 210 Felix Millan 1.50 .70
❑ 211 Galen Cisco 1.50 .70
❑ 212 Tom Tresh 2.50 1.10
❑ 213 Gerry Arrigo 1.50 .70
❑ 214 Checklist 3 6.00 1.20
With 69T deckle CL
on back (no player)
❑ 215 Rico Petrocelli 2.50 1.10
❑ 216 Don Sutton 6.00 2.70
❑ 217 John Donaldson 1.50 .70
❑ 218 John Roseboro 2.50 1.10
❑ 219 Freddie Patek RC 4.00 1.80
❑ 220 Sam McDowell 4.00 1.80
❑ 221 Art Shamsky 4.00 1.80
❑ 222 Duane Josephson 2.50 1.10
❑ 223 Tom Dukes 4.00 1.80
❑ 224 Angels Rookies 2.50 1.10
Bill Harrelson
Steve Kealey
❑ 225 Don Kessinger 4.00 1.80
❑ 226 Bruce Howard 2.50 1.10
❑ 227 Frank Johnson 2.50 1.10
❑ 228 Dave Leonhard 2.50 1.10
❑ 229 Don Lock 2.50 1.10
❑ 230 Rusty Staub UER 4.00 1.80
For 1966 stats, Houston spelled
Huoston
❑ 231 Pat Dobson 4.00 1.80
❑ 232 Dave Ricketts 2.50 1.10
❑ 233 Steve Barber 4.00 1.80
❑ 234 Dave Bristol MG 2.50 1.10
❑ 235 Jim Hunter 10.00 4.50
❑ 236 Manny Mota 4.00 1.80
❑ 237 Bobby Cox RC 10.00 4.50
❑ 238 Ken Johnson 2.50 1.10
❑ 239 Bob Taylor 4.00 1.80
❑ 240 Ken Harrelson 4.00 1.80
❑ 241 Jim Brewer 2.50 1.10
❑ 242 Frank Kostro 2.50 1.10
❑ 243 Ron Kline 2.50 1.10
❑ 244 Indians Rookies 4.00 1.80
Ray Fosse RC
George Woodson
❑ 245 Ed Charles 4.00 1.80
❑ 246 Joe Coleman 2.50 1.10
❑ 247 Gene Oliver 2.50 1.10
❑ 248 Bob Priddy 2.50 1.10
❑ 249 Ed Spiezio 4.00 1.80
❑ 250 Frank Robinson 20.00 9.00
❑ 251 Ron Herbel 2.50 1.10
❑ 252 Chuck Cottier 2.50 1.10
❑ 253 Jerry Johnson 2.50 1.10
❑ 254 Joe Schultz MG 4.00 1.80
❑ 255 Steve Carlton 30.00 13.50
❑ 256 Gates Brown 4.00 1.80
❑ 257 Jim Ray 2.50 1.10
❑ 258 Jackie Hernandez 4.00 1.80
❑ 259 Bill Short 2.50 1.10
❑ 260 Reggie Jackson RC 250.00 110.00
❑ 261 Bob Johnson 2.50 1.10
❑ 262 Mike Kekich 4.00 1.80
❑ 263 Jerry May 2.50 1.10
❑ 264 Bill Landis 2.50 1.10
❑ 265 Chico Cardenas 4.00 1.80
❑ 266 Dodger Rookies 4.00 1.80
Tom Hutton
Alan Foster
❑ 267 Vicente Romo 2.50 1.10
❑ 268 Al Spangler 2.50 1.10
❑ 269 Al Weis 4.00 1.80
❑ 270 Mickey Lolich 4.00 1.80
❑ 271 Larry Stahl 4.00 1.80
❑ 272 Ed Stroud 2.50 1.10
❑ 273 Ron Willis 2.50 1.10
❑ 274 Clyde King MG 2.50 1.10
❑ 275 Vic Davalillo 2.50 1.10
❑ 276 Gary Wagner 2.50 1.10
❑ 277 Elrod Hendricks RC 2.50 1.10
❑ 278 Gary Geiger UER 2.50 1.10
(Batting wrong)
❑ 279 Roger Nelson 4.00 1.80
❑ 280 Alex Johnson 4.00 1.80
❑ 281 Ted Kubiak 2.50 1.10
❑ 282 Pat Jarvis 2.50 1.10
❑ 283 Sandy Alomar 4.00 1.80
❑ 284 Expos Rookies 4.00 1.80
Jerry Robertson
Mike Wegener
❑ 285 Don Mincher 4.00 1.80
❑ 286 Dock Ellis RC 4.00 1.80
❑ 287 Jose Tartabull 4.00 1.80
❑ 288 Ken Holtzman 4.00 1.80
❑ 289 Bart Shirley 2.50 1.10
❑ 290 Jim Kaat 4.00 1.80
❑ 291 Vern Fuller 2.50 1.10
❑ 292 Al Downing 4.00 1.80
❑ 293 Dick Dietz 2.50 1.10
❑ 294 Jim Lemon MG 2.50 1.10
❑ 295 Tony Perez 12.00 5.50
❑ 296 Andy Messersmith RC 4.00 1.80
❑ 297 Deron Johnson 2.50 1.10
❑ 298 Dave Nicholson 4.00 1.80
❑ 299 Mark Belanger 4.00 1.80
❑ 300 Felipe Alou 4.00 1.80
❑ 301 Darrell Brandon 4.00 1.80
❑ 302 Jim Pagliaroni 2.50 1.10
❑ 303 Cal Koonce 4.00 1.80
❑ 304 Padres Rookies 6.00 2.70
Bill Davis
Clarence Gaston RC
❑ 305 Dick McAuliffe 4.00 1.80
❑ 306 Jim Grant 4.00 1.80
❑ 307 Gary Kolb 2.50 1.10
❑ 308 Wade Blasingame 2.50 1.10
❑ 309 Walt Williams 2.50 1.10
❑ 310 Tom Haller 2.50 1.10
❑ 311 Sparky Lyle RC 10.00 4.50
❑ 312 Lee Elia 2.50 1.10
❑ 313 Bill Robinson 4.00 1.80
❑ 314 Don Drysdale CL 6.00 1.20
❑ 315 Eddie Fisher 2.50 1.10
❑ 316 Hal Lanier 2.50 1.10
❑ 317 Bruce Look 2.50 1.10
❑ 318 Jack Fisher 2.50 1.10
❑ 319 Ken McMullen UER 2.50 1.10
(Headings on back
are for a pitcher)
❑ 320 Dal Maxvill 2.50 1.10
❑ 321 Jim McAndrew 4.00 1.80
❑ 322 Jose Vidal 4.00 1.80
❑ 323 Larry Miller 2.50 1.10
❑ 324 Tiger Rookies 4.00 1.80
Les Cain
Dave Campbell RC
❑ 325 Jose Cardenal 4.00 1.80
❑ 326 Gary Sutherland 4.00 1.80
❑ 327 Willie Crawford 2.50 1.10
❑ 328 Joel Horlen 1.50 .70
❑ 329 Rick Joseph 1.50 .70
❑ 330 Tony Conigliaro 4.00 1.80
❑ 331 Braves Rookies 2.50 1.10
Gil Garrido
Tom House RC
❑ 332 Fred Talbot 1.50 .70
❑ 333 Ivan Murrell 1.50 .70
❑ 334 Phil Roof 1.50 .70
❑ 335 Bill Mazeroski 6.00 2.70
❑ 336 Jim Roland 1.50 .70
❑ 337 Marty Martinez 1.50 .70
❑ 338 Del Unser 1.50 .70
❑ 339 Reds Rookies 1.50 .70
Steve Mingori
Jose Pena
❑ 340 Dave McNally 2.50 1.10
❑ 341 Dave Adlesh 1.50 .70
❑ 342 Bubba Morton 1.50 .70
❑ 343 Dan Frisella 1.50 .70
❑ 344 Tom Matchick 1.50 .70
❑ 345 Frank Linzy 1.50 .70
❑ 346 Wayne Comer 1.50 .70
❑ 347 Randy Hundley 2.50 1.10
❑ 348 Steve Hargan 1.50 .70
❑ 349 Dick Williams MG 2.50 1.10
❑ 350 Richie Allen 4.00 1.80
❑ 351 Carroll Sembera 1.50 .70
❑ 352 Paul Schaal 2.50 1.10
❑ 353 Jeff Torborg 2.50 1.10
❑ 354 Nate Oliver 1.50 .70
❑ 355 Phil Niekro 6.00 2.70
❑ 356 Frank Quilici 1.50 .70
❑ 357 Carl Taylor 1.50 .70
❑ 358 Athletics Rookies 1.50 .70
George Lauzerique
Roberto Rodriquez
❑ 359 Dick Kelley 1.50 .70
❑ 360 Jim Wynn 2.50 1.10
❑ 361 Gary Holman 1.50 .70
❑ 362 Jim Maloney 2.50 1.10
❑ 363 Russ Nixon 1.50 .70
❑ 364 Tommie Agee 4.00 1.80
❑ 365 Jim Fregosi 2.50 1.10
❑ 366 Bo Belinsky 2.50 1.10
❑ 367 Lou Johnson 2.50 1.10
❑ 368 Vic Roznovsky 1.50 .70
❑ 369 Bob Skinner MG 2.50 1.10
❑ 370 Juan Marichal 8.00 3.60
❑ 371 Sal Bando 2.50 1.10
❑ 372 Adolfo Phillips 1.50 .70
❑ 373 Fred Lasher 1.50 .70
❑ 374 Bob Tillman 1.50 .70
❑ 375 Harmon Killebrew 15.00 6.75
❑ 376 Royals Rookies 1.50 .70
Mike Fiore
Jim Rooker RC
❑ 377 Gary Bell 2.50 1.10
❑ 378 Jose Herrera 1.50 .70
❑ 379 Ken Boyer 2.50 1.10
❑ 380 Stan Bahnsen 2.50 1.10
❑ 381 Ed Kranepool 2.50 1.10
❑ 382 Pat Corrales 2.50 1.10
❑ 383 Casey Cox 1.50 .70
❑ 384 Larry Shepard MG 1.50 .70
❑ 385 Orlando Cepeda 6.00 2.70
❑ 386 Jim McGlothlin 1.50 .70
❑ 387 Bobby Klaus 1.50 .70
❑ 388 Tom McCraw 1.50 .70
❑ 389 Dan Coombs 1.50 .70
❑ 390 Bill Freehan 2.50 1.10
❑ 391 Ray Culp 1.50 .70
❑ 392 Bob Burda 1.50 .70
❑ 393 Gene Brabender 2.50 1.10
❑ 394 Pilots Rookies 6.00 2.70
Lou Piniella
Marv Staehle
❑ 395 Chris Short 1.50 .70
❑ 396 Jim Campanis 1.50 .70
❑ 397 Chuck Dobson 1.50 .70
❑ 398 Tito Francona 1.50 .70
❑ 399 Bob Bailey 2.50 1.10
❑ 400 Don Drysdale 16.00 7.25
❑ 401 Jake Gibbs 2.50 1.10
❑ 402 Ken Boswell 2.50 1.10
❑ 403 Bob Miller 1.50 .70
❑ 404 Cubs Rookies 2.50 1.10
Vic LaRose
Gary Ross
❑ 405 Lee May 2.50 1.10
❑ 406 Phil Ortega 1.50 .70
❑ 407 Tom Egan 1.50 .70
❑ 408 Nate Colbert 1.50 .70
❑ 409 Bob Moose 1.50 .70
❑ 410 Al Kaline 25.00 11.00
❑ 411 Larry Dierker 2.50 1.10
❑ 412 Mickey Mantle CL DP 15.00 3.00
❑ 413 Roland Sheldon 2.50 1.10
❑ 414 Duke Sims 1.50 .70
❑ 415 Ray Washburn 1.50 .70
❑ 416 Willie McCovey AS 7.00 3.10
❑ 417 Ken Harrelson AS 3.00 1.35
❑ 418 Tommy Helms AS 3.00 1.35
❑ 419 Rod Carew AS 10.00 4.50
❑ 420 Ron Santo AS 4.00 1.80
❑ 421 Brooks Robinson AS 7.00 3.10
❑ 422 Don Kessinger AS 3.00 1.35
❑ 423 Bert Campaneris AS 4.00 1.80
❑ 424 Pete Rose AS 14.00 6.25
❑ 425 Carl Yastrzemski AS 10.00 4.50
❑ 426 Curt Flood AS 4.00 1.80
❑ 427 Tony Oliva AS 4.00 1.80
❑ 428 Lou Brock AS 6.00 2.70
❑ 429 Willie Horton AS 3.00 1.35
❑ 430 Johnny Bench AS 10.00 4.50

❑ 431 Bill Freehan AS 4.00 1.80
❑ 432 Bob Gibson AS 6.00 2.70
❑ 433 Denny McLain AS 3.00 1.35
❑ 434 Jerry Koosman AS 3.00 1.35
❑ 435 Sam McDowell AS 2.50 1.10
❑ 436 Gene Alley 2.50 1.10
❑ 437 Luis Alcaraz 1.50 .70
❑ 438 Gary Waslewski 1.50 .70
❑ 439 White Sox Rookies 1.50 .70
Ed Herrmann
Dan Lazar
❑ 440A Willie McCovey 15.00 6.75
❑ 440B Willie McCovey WL 100.00 45.00
(McCovey white)
❑ 441A Dennis Higgins 1.50 .70
❑ 441B Dennis Higgins WL 25.00 11.00
(Higgins white)
❑ 442 Ty Cline 1.50 .70
❑ 443 Don Wert 1.50 .70
❑ 444A Joe Moeller 1.50 .70
❑ 444B Joe Moeller WL 25.00 11.00
(Moeller white)
❑ 445 Bobby Knoop 1.50 .70
❑ 446 Claude Raymond 1.50 .70
❑ 447A Ralph Houk MG 2.50 1.10
❑ 447B Ralph Houk WL 25.00 11.00
MG (Houk white)
❑ 448 Bob Tolan 2.50 1.10
❑ 449 Paul Lindblad 1.50 .70
❑ 450 Billy Williams 7.00 3.10
❑ 451A Rich Rollins 2.50 1.10
❑ 451B Rich Rollins WL 25.00 11.00
(Rich and 3B white)
❑ 452A Al Ferrara 1.50 .70
❑ 452B Al Ferrara WL 25.00 11.00
(Al and OF white)
❑ 453 Mike Cuellar 2.50 1.10
❑ 454A Phillies Rookies 2.50 1.10
Larry Colton
Don Money
❑ 454B Phillies Rookies WL 25.00 11.00
Larry Colton
Don Money
(Names in white)
❑ 455 Sonny Siebert 1.50 .70
❑ 456 Bud Harrelson 2.50 1.10
❑ 457 Dalton Jones 1.50 .70
❑ 458 Curt Blefary 1.50 .70
❑ 459 Dave Boswell 1.50 .70
❑ 460 Joe Torre 4.00 1.80
❑ 461A Mike Epstein 1.50 .70
❑ 461B Mike Epstein WL 25.00 11.00
(Epstein white)
❑ 462 Red Schoendienst 2.50 1.10
MG
❑ 463 Dennis Ribant 1.50 .70
❑ 464A Dave Marshall 1.50 .70
❑ 464B Dave Marshall WL 25.00 11.00
(Marshall white)
❑ 465 Tommy John 4.00 1.80
❑ 466 John Boccabella 2.50 1.10
❑ 467 Tommie Reynolds 1.50 .70
❑ 468A Pirates Rookies 1.50 .70
Bruce Dal Canton
Bob Robertson
❑ 468B Pirates Rookies WL 25.00 11.00
Bruce Dal Canton
Bob Robertson
(Names in white)
❑ 469 Chico Ruiz 1.50 .70
❑ 470A Mel Stottlemyre 2.50 1.10
❑ 470B Mel Stottlemyre WL 30.00 13.50
(Stottlemyre white)
❑ 471A Ted Savage 1.50 .70
❑ 471B Ted Savage WL 25.00 11.00
(Savage white)
❑ 472 Jim Price 1.50 .70
❑ 473A Jose Arcia 1.50 .70
❑ 473B Jose Arcia WL 25.00 11.00
(Jose and 2B white)
❑ 474 Tom Murphy 1.50 .70
❑ 475 Tim McCarver 4.00 1.80
❑ 476A Boston Rookies 3.00 1.35
Ken Brett RC
Gerry Moses
❑ 476B Boston Rookies WL 30.00 13.50
Ken Brett RC
Gerry Moses
(Names in white)
❑ 477 Jeff James 1.50 .70
❑ 478 Don Buford 1.50 .70
❑ 479 Richie Scheinblum 1.50 .70
❑ 480 Tom Seaver 70.00 32.00
❑ 481 Bill Melton 2.50 1.10
❑ 482A Jim Gosger 1.50 .70
❑ 482B Jim Gosger WL 25.00 11.00
(Jim and OF white)
❑ 483 Ted Abernathy 1.50 .70
❑ 484 Joe Gordon MG 2.50 1.10
❑ 485A Gaylord Perry 10.00 4.50
❑ 485B Gaylord Perry WL 85.00 38.00
(Perry white)
❑ 486A Paul Casanova 1.50 .70
❑ 486B Paul Casanova WL 25.00 11.00
(Casanova white)
❑ 487 Denis Menke 1.50 .70
❑ 488 Joe Sparma 1.50 .70
❑ 489 Clete Boyer 2.50 1.10
❑ 490 Matty Alou 2.50 1.10
❑ 491A Twins Rookies 1.50 .70
Jerry Crider
George Mitterwald
❑ 491B Twins Rookies WL 25.00 11.00
Jerry Crider
George Mitterwald
(Names in white)
❑ 492 Tony Cloninger 1.50 .70
❑ 493A Wes Parker 2.50 1.10
❑ 493B Wes Parker WL 25.00 11.00
(Parker white)
❑ 494 Ken Berry 1.50 .70
❑ 495 Bert Campaneris 2.50 1.10
❑ 496 Larry Jaster 1.50 .70
❑ 497 Julian Javier 2.50 1.10
❑ 498 Juan Pizarro 2.50 1.10
❑ 499 Astro Rookies 1.50 .70
Don Bryant
Steve Shea
❑ 500A Mickey Mantle UER 300.00 135.00
(No Topps copy-
right on card back)
❑ 500B Mickey Mantle WL 1200.00 550.00
(Mantle in white;
no Topps copyright
on card back) UER
❑ 501A Tony Gonzalez 2.50 1.10
❑ 501B Tony Gonzalez WL 25.00 11.00
(Tony and OF white)
❑ 502 Minnie Rojas 1.50 .70
❑ 503 Larry Brown 1.50 .70
❑ 504 Brooks Robinson CL 7.00 1.40
❑ 505A Bobby Bolin 1.50 .70
❑ 505B Bobby Bolin WL 25.00 11.00
(Bolin white)
❑ 506 Paul Blair 2.50 1.10
❑ 507 Cookie Rojas 2.50 1.10
❑ 508 Moe Drabowsky 2.50 1.10
❑ 509 Manny Sanguillen 2.50 1.10
❑ 510 Rod Carew 40.00 18.00
❑ 511A Diego Segui 2.50 1.10
❑ 511B Diego Segui WL 25.00 11.00
(Diego and P white)
❑ 512 Cleon Jones 2.50 1.10
❑ 513 Camilo Pascual 3.00 1.35
❑ 514 Mike Lum 2.00 .90
❑ 515 Dick Green 2.00 .90
❑ 516 Earl Weaver RC MG 20.00 9.00
❑ 517 Mike McCormick 3.00 1.35
❑ 518 Fred Whitfield 2.00 .90
❑ 519 Yankees Rookies 2.00 .90
Jerry Kenney
Len Boehmer
❑ 520 Bob Veale 3.00 1.35
❑ 521 George Thomas 2.00 .90
❑ 522 Joe Hoerner 2.00 .90
❑ 523 Bob Chance 2.00 .90
❑ 524 Expos Rookies 3.00 1.35
Jose Laboy
Floyd Wicker
❑ 525 Earl Wilson 3.00 1.35
❑ 526 Hector Torres 2.00 .90
❑ 527 Al Lopez MG 5.00 2.20
❑ 528 Claude Osteen 3.00 1.35
❑ 529 Ed Kirkpatrick 3.00 1.35
❑ 530 Cesar Tovar 2.00 .90
❑ 531 Dick Farrell 2.00 .90
❑ 532 Bird Hill Aces 3.00 1.35
Tom Phoebus
Jim Hardin
Dave McNally
Mike Cuellar
❑ 533 Nolan Ryan 250.00 110.00
❑ 534 Jerry McNertney 3.00 1.35
❑ 535 Phil Regan 3.00 1.35
❑ 536 Padres Rookies 2.00 .90
Danny Breeden
Dave Roberts
❑ 537 Mike Paul 2.00 .90
❑ 538 Charlie Smith 2.00 .90
❑ 539 Ted Shows How 12.00 5.50
Mike Epstein
Ted Williams MG
❑ 540 Curt Flood 3.00 1.35
❑ 541 Joe Verbanic 2.00 .90
❑ 542 Bob Aspromonte 2.00 .90
❑ 543 Fred Newman 2.00 .90
❑ 544 Tigers Rookies 2.00 .90
Mike Kilkenny
Ron Woods
❑ 545 Willie Stargell 12.00 5.50
❑ 546 Jim Nash 2.00 .90
❑ 547 Billy Martin MG 5.00 2.20
❑ 548 Bob Locker 2.00 .90
❑ 549 Ron Brand 2.00 .90
❑ 550 Brooks Robinson 30.00 13.50
❑ 551 Wayne Granger 2.00 .90
❑ 552 Dodgers Rookies 3.00 1.35
Ted Sizemore RC
Bill Sudakis
❑ 553 Ron Davis 2.00 .90
❑ 554 Frank Bertaina 2.00 .90
❑ 555 Jim Ray Hart 3.00 1.35
❑ 556 A's Stars 3.00 1.35
Sal Bando
Bert Campaneris
Danny Cater
❑ 557 Frank Fernandez 2.00 .90
❑ 558 Tom Burgmeier 3.00 1.35
❑ 559 Cardinals Rookies 2.00 .90
Joe Hague
Jim Hicks
❑ 560 Luis Tiant 3.00 1.35
❑ 561 Ron Clark 2.00 .90
❑ 562 Bob Watson RC 8.00 3.60
❑ 563 Marty Pattin 3.00 1.35
❑ 564 Gil Hodges MG 10.00 4.50
❑ 565 Hoyt Wilhelm 8.00 3.60
❑ 566 Ron Hansen 2.00 .90
❑ 567 Pirates Rookies 2.00 .90
Elvio Jimenez
Jim Shellenback
❑ 568 Cecil Upshaw 2.00 .90
❑ 569 Billy Harris 1.50 .70
❑ 570 Ron Santo 8.00 3.60
❑ 571 Cap Peterson 2.00 .90
❑ 572 Giants Heroes 16.00 7.25
Willie McCovey
Juan Marichal
❑ 573 Jim Palmer 30.00 13.50
❑ 574 George Scott 3.00 1.35
❑ 575 Bill Singer 3.00 1.35
❑ 576 Phillies Rookies 2.00 .90
Ron Stone
Bill Wilson
❑ 577 Mike Hegan 3.00 1.35
❑ 578 Don Bosch 2.00 .90
❑ 579 Dave Nelson 2.00 .90
❑ 580 Jim Northrup 3.00 1.35
❑ 581 Gary Nolan 3.00 1.35
❑ 582A Tony Oliva CL 6.00 1.20
White circle on back
❑ 582B Tony Oliva CL 7.50 1.50
Red circle on back
❑ 583 Clyde Wright 2.00 .90
❑ 584 Don Mason 2.00 .90
❑ 585 Ron Swoboda 3.00 1.35
❑ 586 Tim Cullen 2.00 .90
❑ 587 Joe Rudi RC 8.00 3.60

❑ 588 Bill White 3.00 1.35
❑ 589 Joe Pepitone 5.00 2.20
❑ 590 Rico Carty 5.00 2.20
❑ 591 Mike Hedlund 3.00 1.35
❑ 592 Padres Rookies 5.00 2.20
Rafael Robles
Al Santorini
❑ 593 Don Nottebart 3.00 1.35
❑ 594 Dooley Womack 3.00 1.35
❑ 595 Lee Maye 3.00 1.35
❑ 596 Chuck Hartenstein 3.00 1.35
❑ 597 A.L. Rookies 40.00 18.00
Bob Floyd
Larry Burchart
Rollie Fingers RC
❑ 598 Ruben Amaro 3.00 1.35
❑ 599 John Boozer 3.00 1.35
❑ 600 Tony Oliva 8.00 3.60
❑ 601 Tug McGraw 8.00 3.60
❑ 602 Cubs Rookies 5.00 2.20
Alec Distaso
Don Young
Jim Qualls
❑ 603 Joe Keough 3.00 1.35
❑ 604 Bobby Etheridge 3.00 1.35
❑ 605 Dick Ellsworth 3.00 1.35
❑ 606 Gene Mauch MG 5.00 2.20
❑ 607 Dick Bosman 3.00 1.35
❑ 608 Dick Simpson 3.00 1.35
❑ 609 Phil Gagliano 3.00 1.35
❑ 610 Jim Hardin 3.00 1.35
❑ 611 Braves Rookies 5.00 2.20
Bob Didier
Walt Hriniak RC
Gary Neibauer
❑ 612 Jack Aker 5.00 2.20
❑ 613 Jim Beauchamp 3.00 1.35
❑ 614 Houston Rookies 3.00 1.35
Tom Griffin
Skip Guinn
❑ 615 Len Gabrielson 3.00 1.35
❑ 616 Don McMahon 3.00 1.35
❑ 617 Jesse Gonder 3.00 1.35
❑ 618 Ramon Webster 3.00 1.35
❑ 619 Royals Rookies 5.00 2.20
Bill Butler
Pat Kelly
Juan Rios
❑ 620 Dean Chance 5.00 2.20
❑ 621 Bill Voss 3.00 1.35
❑ 622 Dan Osinski 3.00 1.35
❑ 623 Hank Allen 3.00 1.35
❑ 624 NL Rookies 5.00 2.20
Darrel Chaney
Duffy Dyer RC
Terry Harmon
❑ 625 Mack Jones UER 5.00 2.20
(Batting wrong)
❑ 626 Gene Michael 5.00 2.20
❑ 627 George Stone 3.00 1.35
❑ 628 Red Sox Rookies 5.00 2.20
Bill Conigliaro RC
Syd O'Brien
Fred Wenz
❑ 629 Jack Hamilton 3.00 1.35
❑ 630 Bobby Bonds RC 30.00 13.50
❑ 631 John Kennedy 5.00 2.20
❑ 632 Jon Warden 3.00 1.35
❑ 633 Harry Walker MG 3.00 1.35
❑ 634 Andy Etchebarren 3.00 1.35
❑ 635 George Culver 3.00 1.35
❑ 636 Woody Held 3.00 1.35
❑ 637 Padres Rookies 5.00 2.20
Jerry DaVanon
Frank Reberger
Clay Kirby
❑ 638 Ed Sprague RC 3.00 1.35
❑ 639 Barry Moore 3.00 1.35
❑ 640 Ferguson Jenkins 20.00 9.00
❑ 641 NL Rookies 5.00 2.20
Bobby Darwin
John Miller
Tommy Dean
❑ 642 John Hiller 3.00 1.35
❑ 643 Billy Cowan 3.00 1.35
❑ 644 Chuck Hinton 3.00 1.35
❑ 645 George Brunet 3.00 1.35
❑ 646 Expos Rookies 5.00 2.20
Dan McGinn
Carl Morton
❑ 647 Dave Wickersham 3.00 1.35
❑ 648 Bobby Wine 5.00 2.20
❑ 649 Al Jackson 3.00 1.35
❑ 650 Ted Williams MG 20.00 9.00
❑ 651 Gus Gil 5.00 2.20
❑ 652 Eddie Watt 3.00 1.35
❑ 653 A.Rodriguez RC UER .. 5.00 2.20
Photo actually
Angels' batboy
❑ 654 White Sox Rookies 5.00 2.20
Carlos May RC
Don Secrist
Rich Morales
❑ 655 Mike Hershberger 3.00 1.35
❑ 656 Dan Schneider 3.00 1.35
❑ 657 Bobby Murcer 8.00 3.60
❑ 658 AL Rookies 3.00 1.35
Tom Hall
Bill Burbach
Jim Miles
❑ 659 Johnny Podres 5.00 2.20
❑ 660 Reggie Smith 5.00 2.20
❑ 661 Jim Merritt 3.00 1.35
❑ 662 Royals Rookies 5.00 2.20
Dick Drago
George Spriggs
Bob Oliver
❑ 663 Dick Radatz 5.00 2.20
❑ 664 Ron Hunt 5.00 1.35

1970 Topps

	NRMT	VG-E
COMPLETE SET (720)	1800.00	800.00
COMMON CARD (1-372)	1.00	.45
COMMON CARD (373-459)	1.50	.70
COMMON CARD (460-546)	2.00	.90
COMMON CARD (547-633)	4.00	1.80
COMMON CARD (634-720)	10.00	4.50
WRAPPER (10-CENT)	20.00	9.00

❑ 1 New York Mets 30.00 9.50
Team Card
❑ 2 Diego Segui .... 2.00 .90
❑ 3 Darrel Chaney .... 1.00 .45
❑ 4 Tom Egan .... 1.00 .45
❑ 5 Wes Parker .... 2.00 .90
❑ 6 Grant Jackson .... 1.00 .45
❑ 7 Indians Rookies .... 1.00 .45
Gary Boyd
Russ Nagelson
❑ 8 Jose Martinez .... 1.00 .45
❑ 9 Checklist 1 .... 12.00 2.40
❑ 10 Carl Yastrzemski 15.00 6.75
❑ 11 Nate Colbert .... 1.00 .45
❑ 12 John Hiller .... 1.00 .45
❑ 13 Jack Hiatt .... 1.00 .45
❑ 14 Hank Allen .... 1.00 .45
❑ 15 Larry Dierker .... 2.00 .90
❑ 16 Charlie Metro MG .... 1.00 .45
❑ 17 Hoyt Wilhelm 6.00 2.70
❑ 18 Carlos May .... 2.00 .90
❑ 19 John Boccabella .... 1.00 .45
❑ 20 Dave McNally .... 2.00 .90
❑ 21 A's Rookies 6.00 2.70
Vida Blue RC
Gene Tenace RC
❑ 22 Ray Washburn .... 1.00 .45
❑ 23 Bill Robinson .... 2.00 .90
❑ 24 Dick Selma .... 1.00 .45
❑ 25 Cesar Tovar .... 1.00 .45
❑ 26 Tug McGraw 4.00 1.80
❑ 27 Chuck Hinton .... 1.00 .45
❑ 28 Billy Wilson .... 1.00 .45
❑ 29 Sandy Alomar .... 2.00 .90
❑ 30 Matty Alou .... 2.00 .90
❑ 31 Marty Pattin .... 2.00 .90
❑ 32 Harry Walker MG .... 1.00 .45
❑ 33 Don Wert .... 1.00 .45
❑ 34 Willie Crawford .... 1.00 .45
❑ 35 Joel Horlen .... 1.00 .45
❑ 36 Red Rookies .... 2.00 .90
Danny Breeden
Bernie Carbo
❑ 37 Dick Drago .... 1.00 .45
❑ 38 Mack Jones .... 1.00 .45
❑ 39 Mike Nagy .... 1.00 .45
❑ 40 Rich Allen .... 2.00 .90
❑ 41 George Lauzerique .... 1.00 .45
❑ 42 Tito Fuentes .... 1.00 .45
❑ 43 Jack Aker .... 1.00 .45
❑ 44 Roberto Pena .... 1.00 .45
❑ 45 Dave Johnson .... 2.00 .90
❑ 46 Ken Rudolph .... 1.00 .45
❑ 47 Bob Miller .... 1.00 .45
❑ 48 Gil Garrido .... 1.00 .45
❑ 49 Tim Cullen .... 1.00 .45
❑ 50 Tommie Agee .... 2.00 .90
❑ 51 Bob Christian .... 1.00 .45
❑ 52 Bruce Dal Canton .... 1.00 .45
❑ 53 John Kennedy .... 1.00 .45
❑ 54 Jeff Torborg .... 2.00 .90
❑ 55 John Odom .... 1.00 .45
❑ 56 Phillies Rookies .... 1.00 .45
Joe Lis
Scott Reid
❑ 57 Pat Kelly .... 1.00 .45
❑ 58 Dave Marshall .... 1.00 .45
❑ 59 Dick Ellsworth .... 1.00 .45
❑ 60 Jim Wynn .... 2.00 .90
❑ 61 NL Batting Leaders 12.00 5.50
Pete Rose
Bob Clemente
Cleon Jones
❑ 62 AL Batting Leaders 4.00 1.80
Rod Carew
Reggie Smith
Tony Oliva
❑ 63 NL RBI Leaders 4.00 1.80
Willie McCovey
Ron Santo
Tony Perez
❑ 64 AL RBI Leaders 6.00 2.70
Harmon Killebrew
Boog Powell
Reggie Jackson
❑ 65 NL Home Run Leaders .. 6.00 2.70
Willie McCovey
Hank Aaron
Lee May
❑ 66 AL Home Run Leaders .. 6.00 2.70
Harmon Killebrew
Frank Howard
Reggie Jackson
❑ 67 NL ERA Leaders 6.00 2.70
Juan Marichal
Steve Carlton
Bob Gibson
❑ 68 AL ERA Leaders .... 2.00 .90
Dick Bosman
Jim Palmer
Mike Cuellar
❑ 69 NL Pitching Leaders 6.00 2.70
Tom Seaver
Phil Niekro
Fergie Jenkins
Juan Marichal
❑ 70 AL Pitching Leaders .... 2.00 .90
Dennis McLain
Mike Cuellar

Dave Boswell
Dave McNally
Jim Perry
Mel Stottlemyre
❏ 71 NL Strikeout Leaders 4.00 1.80
Fergie Jenkins
Bob Gibson
Bill Singer
❏ 72 AL Strikeout Leaders...... 2.00 .90
Sam McDowell
Mickey Lolich
Andy Messersmith
❏ 73 Wayne Granger.............. 1.00 .45
❏ 74 Angels Rookies .... 1.00 .45
Greg Washburn
Wally Wolf
❏ 75 Jim Kaat .... 2.00 .90
❏ 76 Carl Taylor...................... 1.00 .45
❏ 77 Frank Linzy .... 1.00 .45
❏ 78 Joe Lahoud .... 1.00 .45
❏ 79 Clay Kirby .... 1.00 .45
❏ 80 Don Kessinger................. 2.00 .90
❏ 81 Dave May .... 1.00 .45
❏ 82 Frank Fernandez............. 1.00 .45
❏ 83 Don Cardwell.................. 1.00 .45
❏ 84 Paul Casanova .... 1.00 .45
❏ 85 Max Alvis......................... 1.00 .45
❏ 86 Lum Harris MG .... 1.00 .45
❏ 87 Steve Renko .... 1.00 .45
❏ 88 Pilots Rookies .... 2.00 .90
Miguel Fuentes
Dick Baney
❏ 89 Juan Rios .... 1.00 .45
❏ 90 Tim McCarver .... 2.00 .90
❏ 91 Rich Morales .... 1.00 .45
❏ 92 George Culver................. 1.00 .45
❏ 93 Rick Renick .... 1.00 .45
❏ 94 Freddie Patek .... 2.00 .90
❏ 95 Earl Wilson .... 2.00 .90
❏ 96 Cardinals Rookies .... 2.00 .90
Leron Lee
Jerry Reuss RC
❏ 97 Joe Moeller .... 1.00 .45
❏ 98 Gates Brown .... 2.00 .90
❏ 99 Bobby Pfeil .... 1.00 .45
❏ 100 Mel Stottlemyre .... 2.00 .90
❏ 101 Bobby Floyd .... 1.00 .45
❏ 102 Joe Rudi .... 2.00 .90
❏ 103 Frank Reberger............. 1.00 .45
❏ 104 Gerry Moses .... 1.00 .45
❏ 105 Tony Gonzalez .... 1.00 .45
❏ 106 Darold Knowles............. 1.00 .45
❏ 107 Bobby Etheridge .... 1.00 .45
❏ 108 Tom Burgmeier .... 1.00 .45
❏ 109 Expos Rookies .... 1.00 .45
Garry Jestadt
Carl Morton
❏ 110 Bob Moose .... 1.00 .45
❏ 111 Mike Hegan................... 2.00 .90
❏ 112 Dave Nelson .... 1.00 .45
❏ 113 Jim Ray .... 1.00 .45
❏ 114 Gene Michael .... 1.00 .45
❏ 115 Alex Johnson................ 2.00 .90
❏ 116 Sparky Lyle .... 2.00 .90
❏ 117 Don Young .... 1.00 .45
❏ 118 George Mitterwald........ 1.00 .45
❏ 119 Chuck Taylor................ 1.00 .45
❏ 120 Sal Bando .... 2.00 .90
❏ 121 Orioles Rookies .... 1.00 .45
Fred Beene
Terry Crowley
❏ 122 George Stone .... 1.00 .45
❏ 123 Don Gutteridge MG...... 1.00 .45
❏ 124 Larry Jaster .... 1.00 .45
❏ 125 Deron Johnson .... 1.00 .45
❏ 126 Marty Martinez .... 1.00 .45
❏ 127 Joe Coleman .... 1.00 .45
❏ 128A Checklist 2 ERR 6.00 1.20
(226 R Perranoski)
❏ 128B Checklist 2 COR 6.00 1.20
(226 R. Perranoski)
❏ 129 Jimmie Price .... 1.00 .45
❏ 130 Ollie Brown .... 1.00 .45
❏ 131 Dodgers Rookies.......... 1.00 .45
Ray Lamb
Bob Stinson

❏ 132 Jim McGlothlin.............. 1.00 .45
❏ 133 Clay Carroll .... 1.00 .45
❏ 134 Danny Walton .... 1.00 .45
❏ 135 Dick Dietz .... 1.00 .45
❏ 136 Steve Hargan .... 1.00 .45
❏ 137 Art Shamsky .... 1.00 .45
❏ 138 Joe Foy .... 1.00 .45
❏ 139 Rich Nye .... 1.00 .45
❏ 140 Reggie Jackson.......... 50.00 22.00
❏ 141 Pirates Rookies............ 2.00 .90
Dave Cash RC
Johnny Jeter
❏ 142 Fritz Peterson .... 1.00 .45
❏ 143 Phil Gagliano................ 1.00 .45
❏ 144 Ray Culp .... 1.00 .45
❏ 145 Rico Carty .... 2.00 .90
❏ 146 Danny Murphy.............. 1.00 .45
❏ 147 Angel Hermoso .... 1.00 .45
❏ 148 Earl Weaver MG 4.00 1.80
❏ 149 Billy Champion .... 1.00 .45
❏ 150 Harmon Killebrew 8.00 3.60
❏ 151 Dave Roberts .... 1.00 .45
❏ 152 Ike Brown .... 1.00 .45
❏ 153 Gary Gentry.................. 1.00 .45
❏ 154 Senators Rookies .... 1.00 .45
Jim Miles
Jan Dukes
❏ 155 Denis Menke .... 1.00 .45
❏ 156 Eddie Fisher .... 1.00 .45
❏ 157 Manny Mota .... 2.00 .90
❏ 158 Jerry McNertney .... 2.00 .90
❏ 159 Tommy Helms.............. 2.00 .90
❏ 160 Phil Niekro................... 6.00 2.70
❏ 161 Richie Scheinblum ...... 1.00 .45
❏ 162 Jerry Johnson .... 1.00 .45
❏ 163 Syd O'Brien .... 1.00 .45
❏ 164 Ty Cline .... 1.00 .45
❏ 165 Ed Kirkpatrick .... 1.00 .45
❏ 166 Al Oliver........................ 4.00 1.80
❏ 167 Bill Burbach .... 1.00 .45
❏ 168 Dave Watkins .... 1.00 .45
❏ 169 Tom Hall .... 1.00 .45
❏ 170 Billy Williams 6.00 2.70
❏ 171 Jim Nash .... 1.00 .45
❏ 172 Braves Rookies............ 2.00 .90
Garry Hill
Ralph Garr RC
❏ 173 Jim Hicks...................... 1.00 .45
❏ 174 Ted Sizemore .... 2.00 .90
❏ 175 Dick Bosman .... 1.00 .45
❏ 176 Jim Ray Hart .... 2.00 .90
❏ 177 Jim Northrup .... 2.00 .90
❏ 178 Denny Lemaster .... 1.00 .45
❏ 179 Ivan Murrell .... 1.00 .45
❏ 180 Tommy John .... 2.00 .90
❏ 181 Sparky Anderson MG .. 6.00 2.70
❏ 182 Dick Hall .... 1.00 .45
❏ 183 Jerry Grote .... 1.00 .45
❏ 184 Ray Fosse .... 1.00 .45
❏ 185 Don Mincher .... 2.00 .90
❏ 186 Rick Joseph.................. 1.00 .45
❏ 187 Mike Hedlund .... 1.00 .45
❏ 188 Manny Sanguillen .... 2.00 .90
❏ 189 Yankees Rookies 60.00 27.00
Thurman Munson RC
Dave McDonald
❏ 190 Joe Torre...................... 4.00 1.80
❏ 191 Vicente Romo .... 1.00 .45
❏ 192 Jim Qualls .... 1.00 .45
❏ 193 Mike Wegener.............. 1.00 .45
❏ 194 Chuck Manuel .... 1.00 .45
❏ 195 Tom Seaver NLCS 15.00 6.75
❏ 196 Ken Boswell NLCS ...... 2.00 .90
❏ 197 Nolan Ryan NLCS...... 30.00 13.50
❏ 198 NL Playoff Summary .. 15.00 6.75
Mets celebrate
(Nolan Ryan)
❏ 199 Mike Cuellar ALCS ...... 2.00 .90
❏ 200 Boog Powell ALCS 4.00 1.80
❏ 201 Boog Powell ALCS ...... 2.00 .90
Andy Etchebarren)
❏ 202 AL Playoff Summary .... 2.00 .90
Orioles celebrate
❏ 203 Rudy May .... 1.00 .45
❏ 204 Len Gabrielson .... 1.00 .45
❏ 205 Bert Campaneris .... 2.00 .90

❏ 206 Clete Boyer .... 2.00 .90
❏ 207 Tigers Rookies .... 1.00 .45
Norman McRae
Bob Reed
❏ 208 Fred Gladding .... 1.00 .45
❏ 209 Ken Suarez .... 1.00 .45
❏ 210 Juan Marichal 6.00 2.70
❏ 211 Ted Williams MG........ 15.00 6.75
❏ 212 Al Santorini .... 1.00 .45
❏ 213 Andy Etchebarren .... 1.00 .45
❏ 214 Ken Boswell .... 1.00 .45
❏ 215 Reggie Smith............... 2.00 .90
❏ 216 Chuck Hartenstein....... 1.00 .45
❏ 217 Ron Hansen .... 1.00 .45
❏ 218 Ron Stone.................... 1.00 .45
❏ 219 Jerry Kenney .... 1.00 .45
❏ 220 Steve Carlton 15.00 6.75
❏ 221 Ron Brand.................... 1.00 .45
❏ 222 Jim Rooker .... 2.00 .90
❏ 223 Nate Oliver .... 1.00 .45
❏ 224 Steve Barber .... 2.00 .90
❏ 225 Lee May .... 2.00 .90
❏ 226 Ron Perranoski .... 1.00 .45
❏ 227 Astros Rookies .... 2.00 .90
John Mayberry RC
Bob Watkins
❏ 228 Aurelio Rodriguez .... 1.00 .45
❏ 229 Rich Robertson .... 1.00 .45
❏ 230 Brooks Robinson........ 15.00 6.75
❏ 231 Luis Tiant..................... 2.00 .90
❏ 232 Bob Didier .... 1.00 .45
❏ 233 Lew Krausse .... 1.00 .45
❏ 234 Tommy Dean............... 1.00 .45
❏ 235 Mike Epstein .... 1.00 .45
❏ 236 Bob Veale .... 2.00 .90
❏ 237 Russ Gibson .... 1.00 .45
❏ 238 Jose Laboy .... 1.00 .45
❏ 239 Ken Berry .... 1.00 .45
❏ 240 Ferguson Jenkins 6.00 2.70
❏ 241 Royals Rookies .... 1.00 .45
Al Fitzmorris
Scott Northey
❏ 242 Walter Alston MG 4.00 1.80
❏ 243 Joe Sparma................. 1.00 .45
❏ 244A Checklist 3 .... 6.00 1.20
(Red bat on front)
❏ 244B Checklist 3 .... 6.00 1.20
(Brown bat on front)
❏ 245 Leo Cardenas .... 1.00 .45
❏ 246 Jim McAndrew............. 1.00 .45
❏ 247 Lou Klimchock............. 1.00 .45
❏ 248 Jesus Alou................... 1.00 .45
❏ 249 Bob Locker .... 1.00 .45
❏ 250 Willie McCovey UER.. 10.00 4.50
(1963 San Francisci)
❏ 251 Dick Schofield .... 1.00 .45
❏ 252 Lowell Palmer .... 1.00 .45
❏ 253 Ron Woods .... 1.00 .45
❏ 254 Camilo Pascual .... 1.00 .45
❏ 255 Jim Spencer .... 1.00 .45
❏ 256 Vic Davalillo................. 1.00 .45
❏ 257 Dennis Higgins .... 1.00 .45
❏ 258 Paul Popovich .... 1.00 .45
❏ 259 Tommie Reynolds .... 1.00 .45
❏ 260 Claude Osteen .... 1.00 .45
❏ 261 Curt Motton .... 1.00 .45
❏ 262 Padres Rookies........... 1.00 .45
Jerry Morales
Jim Williams
❏ 263 Duane Josephson .... 1.00 .45
❏ 264 Rich Hebner .... 1.00 .45
❏ 265 Randy Hundley .... 1.00 .45
❏ 266 Wally Bunker............... 1.00 .45
❏ 267 Twins Rookies............. 1.00 .45
Herman Hill
Paul Ratliff
❏ 268 Claude Raymond .... 1.00 .45
❏ 269 Cesar Gutierrez........... 1.00 .45
❏ 270 Chris Short .... 1.00 .45
❏ 271 Greg Goossen............. 1.00 .45
❏ 272 Hector Torres .... 1.00 .45
❏ 273 Ralph Houk MG........... 2.00 .90
❏ 274 Gerry Arrigo................. 1.00 .45
❏ 275 Duke Sims................... 1.00 .45
❏ 276 Ron Hunt...................... 1.00 .45
❏ 277 Paul Doyle................... 1.00 .45

❑ 278 Tommie Aaron 1.00 .45
❑ 279 Bill Lee RC 2.00 .90
❑ 280 Donn Clendenon 1.00 .45
❑ 281 Casey Cox 1.00 .45
❑ 282 Steve Huntz 1.00 .45
❑ 283 Angel Bravo 1.00 .45
❑ 284 Jack Baldschun 1.00 .45
❑ 285 Paul Blair 2.00 .90
❑ 286 Dodgers Rookies 6.00 2.70
Jack Jenkins
Bill Buckner RC
❑ 287 Fred Talbot 1.00 .45
❑ 288 Larry Hisle 2.00 .90
❑ 289 Gene Brabender 1.00 .45
❑ 290 Rod Carew 18.00 8.00
❑ 291 Leo Durocher MG 4.00 1.80
❑ 292 Eddie Leon 1.00 .45
❑ 293 Bob Bailey 2.00 .90
❑ 294 Jose Azcue 1.00 .45
❑ 295 Cecil Upshaw 1.00 .45
❑ 296 Woody Woodward 1.00 .45
❑ 297 Curt Blefary 1.00 .45
❑ 298 Ken Henderson 1.00 .45
❑ 299 Buddy Bradford 1.00 .45
❑ 300 Tom Seaver 30.00 13.50
❑ 301 Chico Salmon 1.00 .45
❑ 302 Jeff James 1.00 .45
❑ 303 Brant Alyea 1.00 .45
❑ 304 Bill Russell RC 6.00 2.70
❑ 305 Don Buford WS 4.00 1.80
❑ 306 Donn Clendenon WS 4.00 1.80
❑ 307 Tommie Agee WS 4.00 1.80
❑ 308 J.C. Martin WS 4.00 1.80
❑ 309 Jerry Koosman WS 4.00 1.80
❑ 310 WS Summary 6.00 2.70
Mets whoop it up
❑ 311 Dick Green 1.00 .45
❑ 312 Mike Torrez 1.00 .45
❑ 313 Mayo Smith MG 1.00 .45
❑ 314 Bill McCool 1.00 .45
❑ 315 Luis Aparicio 6.00 2.70
❑ 316 Skip Guinn 1.00 .45
❑ 317 Red Sox Rookies 1.00 .45
Billy Conigliaro
Luis Alvarado
❑ 318 Willie Smith 1.00 .45
❑ 319 Clay Dalrymple 1.00 .45
❑ 320 Jim Maloney 2.00 .90
❑ 321 Lou Piniella 2.00 .90
❑ 322 Luke Walker 1.00 .45
❑ 323 Wayne Comer 1.00 .45
❑ 324 Tony Taylor 2.00 .90
❑ 325 Dave Boswell 1.00 .45
❑ 326 Bill Voss 1.00 .45
❑ 327 Hal King 1.00 .45
❑ 328 George Brunet 1.00 .45
❑ 329 Chris Cannizzaro 1.00 .45
❑ 330 Lou Brock 10.00 4.50
❑ 331 Chuck Dobson 1.00 .45
❑ 332 Bobby Wine 1.00 .45
❑ 333 Bobby Murcer 2.00 .90
❑ 334 Phil Regan 2.00 .90
❑ 335 Bill Freehan 2.00 .90
❑ 336 Del Unser 1.00 .45
❑ 337 Mike McCormick 2.00 .90
❑ 338 Paul Schaal 1.00 .45
❑ 339 Johnny Edwards 1.00 .45
❑ 340 Tony Conigliaro 4.00 1.80
❑ 341 Bill Sudakis 1.00 .45
❑ 342 Wilbur Wood 2.00 .90
❑ 343A Checklist 4 6.00 1.20
(Red bat on front)
❑ 343B Checklist 4 6.00 1.20
(Brown bat on front)
❑ 344 Marcelino Lopez 1.00 .45
❑ 345 Al Ferrara 1.00 .45
❑ 346 Red Schoendienst MG 2.00 .90
❑ 347 Russ Snyder 1.00 .45
❑ 348 Mets Rookies 2.00 .90
Mike Jorgensen
Jesse Hudson
❑ 349 Steve Hamilton 1.00 .45
❑ 350 Roberto Clemente 60.00 27.00
❑ 351 Tom Murphy 1.00 .45
❑ 352 Bob Barton 1.00 .45
❑ 353 Stan Williams 1.00 .45
❑ 354 Amos Otis 2.00 .90
❑ 355 Doug Rader 1.00 .45
❑ 356 Fred Lasher 1.00 .45
❑ 357 Bob Burda 1.00 .45
❑ 358 Pedro Borbon RC 2.00 .90
❑ 359 Phil Roof 1.00 .45
❑ 360 Curt Flood 2.00 .90
❑ 361 Ray Jarvis 1.00 .45
❑ 362 Joe Hague 1.00 .45
❑ 363 Tom Shopay 1.00 .45
❑ 364 Dan McGinn 1.00 .45
❑ 365 Zoilo Versalles 1.00 .45
❑ 366 Barry Moore 1.00 .45
❑ 367 Mike Lum 1.00 .45
❑ 368 Ed Herrmann 1.00 .45
❑ 369 Alan Foster 1.00 .45
❑ 370 Tommy Harper 2.00 .90
❑ 371 Rod Gaspar 1.00 .45
❑ 372 Dave Giusti 1.50 .70
❑ 373 Roy White 2.00 .90
❑ 374 Tommie Sisk 1.50 .70
❑ 375 Johnny Callison 2.00 .90
❑ 376 Lefty Phillips MG 1.50 .70
❑ 377 Bill Butler 1.00 .45
❑ 378 Jim Davenport 1.50 .70
❑ 379 Tom Tischinski 1.50 .70
❑ 380 Tony Perez 6.00 2.70
❑ 381 Athletics Rookies 1.50 .70
Bobby Brooks
Mike Olivo
❑ 382 Jack DiLauro 1.50 .70
❑ 383 Mickey Stanley 2.00 .90
❑ 384 Gary Neibauer 1.50 .70
❑ 385 George Scott 2.00 .90
❑ 386 Bill Dillman 1.50 .70
❑ 387 Baltimore Orioles 3.00 1.35
Team Card
❑ 388 Byron Browne 1.50 .70
❑ 389 Jim Shellenback 1.50 .70
❑ 390 Willie Davis 2.00 .90
❑ 391 Larry Brown 1.50 .70
❑ 392 Walt Hriniak 2.00 .90
❑ 393 John Gelnar 1.50 .70
❑ 394 Gil Hodges MG 4.00 1.80
❑ 395 Walt Williams 1.50 .70
❑ 396 Steve Blass 2.00 .90
❑ 397 Roger Repoz 1.50 .70
❑ 398 Bill Stoneman 1.50 .70
❑ 399 New York Yankees 3.00 1.35
Team Card
❑ 400 Denny McLain 4.00 1.80
❑ 401 Giants Rookies 1.50 .70
John Harrell
Bernie Williams
❑ 402 Ellie Rodriguez 1.50 .70
❑ 403 Jim Bunning 6.00 2.70
❑ 404 Rich Reese 1.50 .70
❑ 405 Bill Hands 1.50 .70
❑ 406 Mike Andrews 1.50 .70
❑ 407 Bob Watson 2.00 .90
❑ 408 Paul Lindblad 1.50 .70
❑ 409 Bob Tolan 2.00 .90
❑ 410 Boog Powell 4.00 1.80
❑ 411 Los Angeles Dodgers 3.00 1.35
Team Card
❑ 412 Larry Burchart 1.50 .70
❑ 413 Sonny Jackson 1.50 .70
❑ 414 Paul Edmondson 1.50 .70
❑ 415 Julian Javier 2.00 .90
❑ 416 Joe Verbanic 1.50 .70
❑ 417 John Bateman 1.50 .70
❑ 418 John Donaldson 1.50 .70
❑ 419 Ron Taylor 1.50 .70
❑ 420 Ken McMullen 2.00 .90
❑ 421 Pat Dobson 2.00 .90
❑ 422 Royals Team 3.00 1.35
❑ 423 Jerry May 1.50 .70
❑ 424 Mike Kilkenny 1.50 .70
(Inconsistent design
card number in
white circle)
❑ 425 Bobby Bonds 6.00 2.70
❑ 426 Bill Rigney MG 1.50 .70
❑ 427 Fred Norman 1.50 .70
❑ 428 Don Buford 1.50 .70
❑ 429 Cubs Rookies 1.50 .70
Randy Bobb
Jim Cosman
❑ 430 Andy Messersmith 2.00 .90
❑ 431 Ron Swoboda 2.00 .90
❑ 432A Checklist 5 6.00 1.20
(Baseball in
yellow letters)
❑ 432B Checklist 5 6.00 1.20
(Baseball in
white letters)
❑ 433 Ron Bryant 1.50 .70
❑ 434 Felipe Alou 2.00 .90
❑ 435 Nelson Briles 2.00 .90
❑ 436 Philadelphia Phillies 3.00 1.35
Team Card
❑ 437 Danny Cater 1.50 .70
❑ 438 Pat Jarvis 1.50 .70
❑ 439 Lee Maye 1.50 .70
❑ 440 Bill Mazeroski 6.00 2.70
❑ 441 John O'Donoghue 1.50 .70
❑ 442 Gene Mauch MG 2.00 .90
❑ 443 Al Jackson 1.50 .70
❑ 444 White Sox Rookies 1.50 .70
Billy Farmer
John Matias
❑ 445 Vada Pinson 2.00 .90
❑ 446 Billy Grabarkewitz 1.50 .70
❑ 447 Lee Stange 1.50 .70
❑ 448 Houston Astros 3.00 1.35
Team Card
❑ 449 Jim Palmer 12.00 5.50
❑ 450 Willie McCovey AS 6.00 2.70
❑ 451 Boog Powell AS 4.00 1.80
❑ 452 Felix Millan AS 2.00 .90
❑ 453 Rod Carew AS 6.00 2.70
❑ 454 Ron Santo AS 4.00 1.80
❑ 455 Brooks Robinson AS 6.00 2.70
❑ 456 Don Kessinger AS 2.00 .90
❑ 457 Rico Petrocelli AS 4.00 1.80
❑ 458 Pete Rose AS 14.00 6.25
❑ 459 Reggie Jackson AS 12.00 5.50
❑ 460 Matty Alou AS 3.00 1.35
❑ 461 Carl Yastrzemski AS 10.00 4.50
❑ 462 Hank Aaron AS 15.00 6.75
❑ 463 Frank Robinson AS 7.00 3.10
❑ 464 Johnny Bench AS 15.00 6.75
❑ 465 Bill Freehan AS 3.00 1.35
❑ 466 Juan Marichal AS 5.00 2.20
❑ 467 Denny McLain AS 3.00 1.35
❑ 468 Jerry Koosman AS 3.00 1.35
❑ 469 Sam McDowell AS 3.00 1.35
❑ 470 Willie Stargell 10.00 4.50
❑ 471 Chris Zachary 2.00 .90
❑ 472 Braves Team 3.50 1.55
❑ 473 Don Bryant 2.00 .90
❑ 474 Dick Kelley 2.00 .90
❑ 475 Dick McAuliffe 3.00 1.35
❑ 476 Don Shaw 2.00 .90
❑ 477 Orioles Rookies 2.00 .90
Al Severinsen
Roger Freed
❑ 478 Bobby Heise 2.00 .90
❑ 479 Dick Woodson 2.00 .90
❑ 480 Glenn Beckert 3.00 1.35
❑ 481 Jose Tartabull 3.00 1.35
❑ 482 Tom Hilgendorf 2.00 .90
❑ 483 Gail Hopkins 2.00 .90
❑ 484 Gary Nolan 3.00 1.35
❑ 485 Jay Johnstone 3.00 1.35
❑ 486 Terry Harmon 2.00 .90
❑ 487 Cisco Carlos 2.00 .90
❑ 488 J.C. Martin 2.00 .90
❑ 489 Eddie Kasko MG 2.00 .90
❑ 490 Bill Singer 3.00 1.35
❑ 491 Graig Nettles 5.00 2.20
❑ 492 Astros Rookies 2.00 .90
Keith Lampard
Scipio Spinks
❑ 493 Lindy McDaniel 3.00 1.35
❑ 494 Larry Stahl 2.00 .90
❑ 495 Dave Morehead 2.00 .90
❑ 496 Steve Whitaker 2.00 .90
❑ 497 Eddie Watt 2.00 .90
❑ 498 Al Weis 2.00 .90
❑ 499 Skip Lockwood 3.00 1.35
❑ 500 Hank Aaron 50.00 22.00

❑ 501	Chicago White Sox Team Card	3.50	1.55
❑ 502	Rollie Fingers	10.00	4.50
❑ 503	Dal Maxvill	2.00	.90
❑ 504	Don Pavletich	2.00	.90
❑ 505	Ken Holtzman	3.00	1.35
❑ 506	Ed Stroud	2.00	.90
❑ 507	Pat Corrales	3.00	1.35
❑ 508	Joe Niekro	3.00	1.35
❑ 509	Montreal Expos Team Card	3.50	1.55
❑ 510	Tony Oliva	5.00	2.20
❑ 511	Joe Hoerner	2.00	.90
❑ 512	Billy Harris	2.00	.90
❑ 513	Preston Gomez MG	2.00	.90
❑ 514	Steve Hovley	2.00	.90
❑ 515	Don Wilson	3.00	1.35
❑ 516	Yankees Rookies John Ellis Jim Lyttle	2.00	.90
❑ 517	Joe Gibbon	2.00	.90
❑ 518	Bill Melton	2.00	.90
❑ 519	Don McMahon	2.00	.90
❑ 520	Willie Horton	3.00	1.35
❑ 521	Cal Koonce	2.00	.90
❑ 522	Angels Team	3.50	1.55
❑ 523	Jose Pena	2.00	.90
❑ 524	Alvin Dark MG	3.00	1.35
❑ 525	Jerry Adair	2.00	.90
❑ 526	Ron Herbel	2.00	.90
❑ 527	Don Bosch	2.00	.90
❑ 528	Elrod Hendricks	2.00	.90
❑ 529	Bob Aspromonte	2.00	.90
❑ 530	Bob Gibson	14.00	6.25
❑ 531	Ron Clark	2.00	.90
❑ 532	Danny Murtaugh MG	3.00	1.35
❑ 533	Buzz Stephen	2.00	.90
❑ 534	Minnesota Twins Team Card	3.50	1.55
❑ 535	Andy Kosco	2.00	.90
❑ 536	Mike Kekich	2.00	.90
❑ 537	Joe Morgan	10.00	4.50
❑ 538	Bob Humphreys	2.00	.90
❑ 539	Phillies Rookies Denny Doyle Larry Bowa RC	8.00	3.60
❑ 540	Gary Peters	2.00	.90
❑ 541	Bill Heath	2.00	.90
❑ 542	Checklist 6	6.00	1.20
❑ 543	Clyde Wright	2.00	.90
❑ 544	Cincinnati Reds Team Card	3.50	1.55
❑ 545	Ken Harrelson	3.00	1.35
❑ 546	Ron Reed	2.00	.90
❑ 547	Rick Monday	6.00	2.70
❑ 548	Howie Reed	4.00	1.80
❑ 549	St. Louis Cardinals Team Card	6.00	2.70
❑ 550	Frank Howard	6.00	2.70
❑ 551	Dock Ellis	6.00	2.70
❑ 552	Royals Rookies Don O'Riley Dennis Paepke Fred Rico	4.00	1.80
❑ 553	Jim Lefebvre	6.00	2.70
❑ 554	Tom Timmermann	4.00	1.80
❑ 555	Orlando Cepeda	12.00	5.50
❑ 556	Dave Bristol MG	6.00	2.70
❑ 557	Ed Kranepool	6.00	2.70
❑ 558	Vern Fuller	4.00	1.80
❑ 559	Tommy Davis	6.00	2.70
❑ 560	Gaylord Perry	12.00	5.50
❑ 561	Tom McCraw	4.00	1.80
❑ 562	Ted Abernathy	4.00	1.80
❑ 563	Boston Red Sox Team Card	6.00	2.70
❑ 564	Johnny Briggs	4.00	1.80
❑ 565	Jim Hunter	12.00	5.50
❑ 566	Gene Alley	6.00	2.70
❑ 567	Bob Oliver	4.00	1.80
❑ 568	Stan Bahnsen	6.00	2.70
❑ 569	Cookie Rojas	6.00	2.70
❑ 570	Jim Fregosi White Chevy Pick-Up in Background	6.00	2.70
❑ 571	Jim Brewer	4.00	1.80
❑ 572	Frank Quilici	4.00	1.80
❑ 573	Padres Rookies Mike Corkins Rafael Robles Ron Slocum	4.00	1.80
❑ 574	Bobby Bolin	6.00	2.70
❑ 575	Cleon Jones	6.00	2.70
❑ 576	Milt Pappas	6.00	2.70
❑ 577	Bernie Allen	4.00	1.80
❑ 578	Tom Griffin	4.00	1.80
❑ 579	Detroit Tigers Team Card	6.00	2.70
❑ 580	Pete Rose	50.00	22.00
❑ 581	Tom Satriano	4.00	1.80
❑ 582	Mike Paul	4.00	1.80
❑ 583	Hal Lanier	4.00	1.80
❑ 584	Al Downing	6.00	2.70
❑ 585	Rusty Staub	8.00	3.60
❑ 586	Rickey Clark	4.00	1.80
❑ 587	Jose Arcia	4.00	1.80
❑ 588A	Checklist 7 ERR (666 Adolfo)	8.00	1.60
❑ 588B	Checklist 7 COR (666 Adolpho)	6.00	1.20
❑ 589	Joe Keough	4.00	1.80
❑ 590	Mike Cuellar	6.00	2.70
❑ 591	Mike Ryan UER (Pitching Record header on card back)	4.00	1.80
❑ 592	Daryl Patterson	4.00	1.80
❑ 593	Chicago Cubs Team Card	8.00	3.60
❑ 594	Jake Gibbs	4.00	1.80
❑ 595	Maury Wills	8.00	3.60
❑ 596	Mike Hershberger	6.00	2.70
❑ 597	Sonny Siebert	4.00	1.80
❑ 598	Joe Pepitone	6.00	2.70
❑ 599	Senators Rookies Dick Stelmaszek Gene Martin Dick Such	4.00	1.80
❑ 600	Willie Mays	70.00	32.00
❑ 601	Pete Richert	4.00	1.80
❑ 602	Ted Savage	4.00	1.80
❑ 603	Ray Oyler	4.00	1.80
❑ 604	Clarence Gaston	6.00	2.70
❑ 605	Rick Wise	6.00	2.70
❑ 606	Chico Ruiz	4.00	1.80
❑ 607	Gary Waslewski	4.00	1.80
❑ 608	Pittsburgh Pirates Team Card	6.00	2.70
❑ 609	Buck Martinez RC (Inconsistent design card number in white circle)	6.00	2.70
❑ 610	Jerry Koosman	8.00	3.60
❑ 611	Norm Cash	6.00	2.70
❑ 612	Jim Hickman	6.00	2.70
❑ 613	Dave Baldwin	6.00	2.70
❑ 614	Mike Shannon	6.00	2.70
❑ 615	Mark Belanger	6.00	2.70
❑ 616	Jim Merritt	4.00	1.80
❑ 617	Jim French	4.00	1.80
❑ 618	Billy Wynne	4.00	1.80
❑ 619	Norm Miller	4.00	1.80
❑ 620	Jim Perry	6.00	2.70
❑ 621	Braves Rookies Mike McQueen Darrell Evans RC Rick Kester	12.00	5.50
❑ 622	Don Sutton	12.00	5.50
❑ 623	Horace Clarke	6.00	2.70
❑ 624	Clyde King MG	4.00	1.80
❑ 625	Dean Chance	4.00	1.80
❑ 626	Dave Ricketts	4.00	1.80
❑ 627	Gary Wagner	4.00	1.80
❑ 628	Wayne Garrett	4.00	1.80
❑ 629	Merv Rettenmund	4.00	1.80
❑ 630	Ernie Banks	50.00	22.00
❑ 631	Oakland Athletics Team Card	6.00	2.70
❑ 632	Gary Sutherland	4.00	1.80
❑ 633	Roger Nelson	4.00	1.80
❑ 634	Bud Harrelson	15.00	6.75
❑ 635	Bob Allison	15.00	6.75
❑ 636	Jim Stewart	10.00	4.50
❑ 637	Cleveland Indians Team Card	12.00	5.50
❑ 638	Frank Bertaina	10.00	4.50
❑ 639	Dave Campbell	10.00	4.50
❑ 640	Al Kaline	50.00	22.00
❑ 641	Al McBean	10.00	4.50
❑ 642	Angels Rookies Greg Garrett Gordon Lund Jarvis Tatum	10.00	4.50
❑ 643	Jose Pagan	10.00	4.50
❑ 644	Gerry Nyman	10.00	4.50
❑ 645	Don Money	15.00	6.75
❑ 646	Jim Britton	10.00	4.50
❑ 647	Tom Matchick	10.00	4.50
❑ 648	Larry Haney	10.00	4.50
❑ 649	Jimmie Hall	10.00	4.50
❑ 650	Sam McDowell	15.00	6.75
❑ 651	Jim Gosger	10.00	4.50
❑ 652	Rich Rollins	15.00	6.75
❑ 653	Moe Drabowsky	10.00	4.50
❑ 654	NL Rookies Oscar Gamble RC Boots Day Angel Mangual	15.00	6.75
❑ 655	John Roseboro	15.00	6.75
❑ 656	Jim Hardin	10.00	4.50
❑ 657	San Diego Padres Team Card	12.00	5.50
❑ 658	Ken Tatum	10.00	4.50
❑ 659	Pete Ward	10.00	4.50
❑ 660	Johnny Bench	80.00	36.00
❑ 661	Jerry Robertson	10.00	4.50
❑ 662	Frank Lucchesi MG	10.00	4.50
❑ 663	Tito Francona	10.00	4.50
❑ 664	Bob Robertson	10.00	4.50
❑ 665	Jim Lonborg	15.00	6.75
❑ 666	Adolpho Phillips	10.00	4.50
❑ 667	Bob Meyer	15.00	6.75
❑ 668	Bob Tillman	10.00	4.50
❑ 669	White Sox Rookies Bart Johnson Dan Lazar Mickey Scott	10.00	4.50
❑ 670	Ron Santo	15.00	6.75
❑ 671	Jim Campanis	10.00	4.50
❑ 672	Leon McFadden	10.00	4.50
❑ 673	Ted Uhlaender	10.00	4.50
❑ 674	Dave Leonhard	10.00	4.50
❑ 675	Jose Cardenal	15.00	6.75
❑ 676	Washington Senators Team Card	12.00	5.50
❑ 677	Woodie Fryman	10.00	4.50
❑ 678	Dave Duncan	15.00	6.75
❑ 679	Ray Sadecki	10.00	4.50
❑ 680	Rico Petrocelli	15.00	6.75
❑ 681	Bob Garibaldi	10.00	4.50
❑ 682	Dalton Jones	10.00	4.50
❑ 683	Reds Rookies Vern Geishert Hal McRae Wayne Simpson	15.00	6.75
❑ 684	Jack Fisher	10.00	4.50
❑ 685	Tom Haller	10.00	4.50
❑ 686	Jackie Hernandez	10.00	4.50
❑ 687	Bob Priddy	10.00	4.50
❑ 688	Ted Kubiak	15.00	6.75
❑ 689	Frank Tepedino	10.00	4.50
❑ 690	Ron Fairly	15.00	6.75
❑ 691	Joe Grzenda	10.00	4.50
❑ 692	Duffy Dyer	10.00	4.50
❑ 693	Bob Johnson	10.00	4.50
❑ 694	Gary Ross	10.00	4.50
❑ 695	Bobby Knoop	10.00	4.50
❑ 696	San Francisco Giants Team Card	12.00	5.50
❑ 697	Jim Hannan	10.00	4.50
❑ 698	Tom Tresh	15.00	6.75
❑ 699	Hank Aguirre	10.00	4.50
❑ 700	Frank Robinson	50.00	22.00
❑ 701	Jack Billingham	10.00	4.50
❑ 702	AL Rookies Bob Johnson Ron Klimkowski Bill Zepp	10.00	4.50
❑ 703	Lou Marone	10.00	4.50
❑ 704	Frank Baker	10.00	4.50

❑ 705 Tony Cloninger UER .. 10.00 4.50
(Batter headings
on card back)
❑ 706 John McNamara MG .. 10.00 4.50
❑ 707 Kevin Collins 10.00 4.50
❑ 708 Jose Santiago 10.00 4.50
❑ 709 Mike Fiore 10.00 4.50
❑ 710 Felix Millan 10.00 4.50
❑ 711 Ed Brinkman 10.00 4.50
❑ 712 Nolan Ryan 225.00 100.00
❑ 713 Seattle Pilots 25.00 11.00
Team Card
❑ 714 Al Spangler 10.00 4.50
❑ 715 Mickey Lolich 15.00 6.75
❑ 716 Cardinals Rookies 15.00 6.75
Sal Campisi
Reggie Cleveland
Santiago Guzman
❑ 717 Tom Phoebus 10.00 4.50
❑ 718 Ed Spiezio 10.00 4.50
❑ 719 Jim Roland 10.00 4.50
❑ 720 Rick Reichardt 15.00 5.00

1971 Topps

	NRMT	VG-E
COMPLETE SET (752)	2000.00	900.00
COMMON CARD (1-393)	1.50	.70
COMMON CARD (394-523)	2.50	1.10
COMMON CARD (524-643)	4.00	1.80
COMMON CARD (644-752)	8.00	3.60
COMMON SP (644-752)	12.00	5.50
WRAPPER (10-CENT)	15.00	6.75

❑ 1 Baltimore Orioles 20.00 6.75
Team Card
❑ 2 Dock Ellis .... 1.50 .70
❑ 3 Dick McAuliffe .... 2.00 .90
❑ 4 Vic Davalillo .... 1.50 .70
❑ 5 Thurman Munson 25.00 11.00
❑ 6 Ed Spiezio .... 1.50 .70
❑ 7 Jim Holt .... 1.50 .70
❑ 8 Mike McQueen .... 1.50 .70
❑ 9 George Scott .... 2.00 .90
❑ 10 Claude Osteen .... 1.50 .70
❑ 11 Elliott Maddox .... 1.50 .70
❑ 12 Johnny Callison .... 1.50 .70
❑ 13 White Sox Rookies .... 1.50 .70
Charlie Brinkman
Dick Moloney
❑ 14 Dave Concepcion RC .. 15.00 6.75
❑ 15 Andy Messersmith .... 2.00 .90
❑ 16 Ken Singleton RC 4.00 1.80
❑ 17 Billy Sorrell .... 1.50 .70
❑ 18 Norm Miller .... 1.50 .70
❑ 19 Skip Pitlock .... 1.50 .70
❑ 20 Reggie Jackson 30.00 13.50
❑ 21 Dan McGinn .... 1.50 .70
❑ 22 Phil Roof .... 1.50 .70
❑ 23 Oscar Gamble .... 1.50 .70
❑ 24 Rich Hand .... 1.50 .70
❑ 25 Clarence Gaston .... 2.00 .90
❑ 26 Bert Blyleven RC 8.00 3.60
❑ 27 Pirates Rookies .... 1.50 .70
Fred Cambria
Gene Clines
❑ 28 Ron Klimkowski .... 1.50 .70
❑ 29 Don Buford .... 1.50 .70
❑ 30 Phil Niekro 6.00 2.70
❑ 31 Eddie Kasko MG .... 1.50 .70
❑ 32 Jerry DaVanon .... 1.50 .70
❑ 33 Del Unser .... 1.50 .70
❑ 34 Sandy Vance .... 1.50 .70
❑ 35 Lou Piniella .... 2.00 .90
❑ 36 Dean Chance .... 1.50 .70
❑ 37 Rich McKinney .... 1.50 .70
❑ 38 Jim Colborn .... 1.50 .70
❑ 39 Tiger Rookies .... 1.50 .70
Lerrin LaGrow
Gene Lamont RC
❑ 40 Lee May .... 2.00 .90
❑ 41 Rick Austin .... 1.50 .70
❑ 42 Boots Day .... 1.50 .70
❑ 43 Steve Kealey .... 1.50 .70
❑ 44 Johnny Edwards .... 1.50 .70
❑ 45 Jim Hunter 6.00 2.70
❑ 46 Dave Campbell .... 1.50 .70
❑ 47 Johnny Jeter .... 1.50 .70
❑ 48 Dave Baldwin .... 1.50 .70
❑ 49 Don Money .... 1.50 .70
❑ 50 Willie McCovey 8.00 3.60
❑ 51 Steve Kline .... 1.50 .70
❑ 52 Braves Rookies .... 1.50 .70
Oscar Brown
Earl Williams RC
❑ 53 Paul Blair .... 2.00 .90
❑ 54 Checklist 1 .... 11.00 2.20
❑ 55 Steve Carlton 15.00 6.75
❑ 56 Duane Josephson .... 1.50 .70
❑ 57 Von Joshua .... 1.50 .70
❑ 58 Bill Lee .... 2.00 .90
❑ 59 Gene Mauch MG .... 2.00 .90
❑ 60 Dick Bosman .... 1.50 .70
❑ 61 AL Batting Leaders 4.00 1.80
Alex Johnson
Carl Yastrzemski
Tony Oliva
❑ 62 NL Batting Leaders .... 2.00 .90
Rico Carty
Joe Torre
Manny Sanguillen
❑ 63 AL RBI Leaders 4.00 1.80
Frank Howard
Tony Conigliaro
Boog Powell
❑ 64 NL RBI Leaders 6.00 2.70
Johnny Bench
Tony Perez
Billy Williams
❑ 65 AL HR Leaders 4.00 1.80
Frank Howard
Harmon Killebrew
Carl Yastrzemski
❑ 66 NL HR Leaders 6.00 2.70
Johnny Bench
Billy Williams
Tony Perez
❑ 67 AL ERA Leaders 4.00 1.80
Diego Segui
Jim Palmer
Clyde Wright
❑ 68 NL ERA Leaders 4.00 1.80
Tom Seaver
Wayne Simpson
Luke Walker
❑ 69 AL Pitching Leaders .... 2.00 .90
Mike Cuellar
Dave McNally
Jim Perry
❑ 70 NL Pitching Leaders 6.00 2.70
Bob Gibson
Gaylord Perry
Fergie Jenkins
❑ 71 AL Strikeout Leaders .... 2.00 .90
Sam McDowell
Mickey Lolich
Bob Johnson
❑ 72 NL Strikeout Leaders 6.00 2.70
Tom Seaver
Bob Gibson
Fergie Jenkins
❑ 73 George Brunet .... 1.50 .70
❑ 74 Twins Rookies .... 1.50 .70
Pete Hamm
Jim Nettles
❑ 75 Gary Nolan .... 2.00 .90
❑ 76 Ted Savage .... 1.50 .70
❑ 77 Mike Compton .... 1.50 .70
❑ 78 Jim Spencer .... 1.50 .70
❑ 79 Wade Blasingame .... 1.50 .70
❑ 80 Bill Melton .... 1.50 .70
❑ 81 Felix Millan .... 1.50 .70
❑ 82 Casey Cox .... 1.50 .70
❑ 83 Met Rookies .... 1.50 .70
Tim Foli RC
Randy Bobb
❑ 84 Marcel Lachemann RC .. 1.50 .70
❑ 85 Billy Grabarkewitz .... 1.50 .70
❑ 86 Mike Kilkenny .... 1.50 .70
❑ 87 Jack Heidemann .... 1.50 .70
❑ 88 Hal King .... 1.50 .70
❑ 89 Ken Brett .... 1.50 .70
❑ 90 Joe Pepitone .... 2.00 .90
❑ 91 Bob Lemon MG .... 2.00 .90
❑ 92 Fred Wenz .... 1.50 .70
❑ 93 Senators Rookies .... 1.50 .70
Norm McRae
Denny Riddleberger
❑ 94 Don Hahn .... 1.50 .70
❑ 95 Luis Tiant .... 2.00 .90
❑ 96 Joe Hague .... 1.50 .70
❑ 97 Floyd Wicker .... 1.50 .70
❑ 98 Joe Decker .... 1.50 .70
❑ 99 Mark Belanger .... 2.00 .90
❑ 100 Pete Rose 40.00 18.00
❑ 101 Les Cain .... 1.50 .70
❑ 102 Astros Rookies .... 2.00 .90
Ken Forsch
Larry Howard
❑ 103 Rich Severson .... 1.50 .70
❑ 104 Dan Frisella .... 1.50 .70
❑ 105 Tony Conigliaro .... 2.00 .90
❑ 106 Tom Dukes .... 1.50 .70
❑ 107 Roy Foster .... 1.50 .70
❑ 108 John Cumberland .... 1.50 .70
❑ 109 Steve Hovley .... 1.50 .70
❑ 110 Bill Mazeroski 6.00 2.70
❑ 111 Yankee Rookies .... 1.50 .70
Loyd Colson
Bobby Mitchell
❑ 112 Manny Mota .... 2.00 .90
❑ 113 Jerry Crider .... 1.50 .70
❑ 114 Billy Conigliaro .... 2.00 .90
❑ 115 Donn Clendenon .... 2.00 .90
❑ 116 Ken Sanders .... 1.50 .70
❑ 117 Ted Simmons RC 8.00 3.60
❑ 118 Cookie Rojas .... 2.00 .90
❑ 119 Frank Lucchesi MG .... 1.50 .70
❑ 120 Willie Horton .... 2.00 .90
❑ 121 Cubs Rookies .... 1.50 .70
Jim Dunegan
Roe Skidmore
❑ 122 Eddie Watt .... 1.50 .70
❑ 123A Checklist 2 .... 11.00 2.20
(Card number
at bottom right)
❑ 123B Checklist 2 .... 11.00 2.20
(Card number
centered)
❑ 124 Don Gullett RC .... 2.00 .90
❑ 125 Ray Fosse .... 1.50 .70
❑ 126 Danny Coombs .... 1.50 .70
❑ 127 Danny Thompson .... 2.00 .90
❑ 128 Frank Johnson .... 1.50 .70
❑ 129 Aurelio Monteagudo .... 1.50 .70
❑ 130 Denis Menke .... 1.50 .70
❑ 131 Curt Blefary .... 1.50 .70
❑ 132 Jose Laboy .... 1.50 .70
❑ 133 Mickey Lolich .... 2.00 .90
❑ 134 Jose Arcia .... 1.50 .70
❑ 135 Rick Monday .... 2.00 .90
❑ 136 Duffy Dyer .... 1.50 .70
❑ 137 Marcelino Lopez .... 1.50 .70
❑ 138 Phillies Rookies .... 2.00 .90
Joe Lis
Willie Montanez
❑ 139 Paul Casanova .... 1.50 .70
❑ 140 Gaylord Perry 6.00 2.70
❑ 141 Frank Quilici .... 1.50 .70
❑ 142 Mack Jones .... 1.50 .70

❑ 143 Steve Blass	2.00	.90
❑ 144 Jackie Hernandez	1.50	.70
❑ 145 Bill Singer	2.00	.90
❑ 146 Ralph Houk MG	2.00	.90
❑ 147 Bob Priddy	1.50	.70
❑ 148 John Mayberry	2.00	.90
❑ 149 Mike Hershberger	1.50	.70
❑ 150 Sam McDowell	2.00	.90
❑ 151 Tommy Davis	2.00	.90
❑ 152 Angels Rookies	1.50	.70
Lloyd Allen		
Winston Llenas		
❑ 153 Gary Ross	1.50	.70
❑ 154 Cesar Gutierrez	1.50	.70
❑ 155 Ken Henderson	1.50	.70
❑ 156 Bart Johnson	1.50	.70
❑ 157 Bob Bailey	2.00	.90
❑ 158 Jerry Reuss	2.00	.90
❑ 159 Jarvis Tatum	1.50	.70
❑ 160 Tom Seaver	25.00	11.00
❑ 161 Coin Checklist	11.00	2.20
❑ 162 Jack Billingham	1.50	.70
❑ 163 Buck Martinez	2.00	.90
❑ 164 Reds Rookies	2.00	.90
Frank Duffy		
Milt Wilcox		
❑ 165 Cesar Tovar	1.50	.70
❑ 166 Joe Hoerner	1.50	.70
❑ 167 Tom Grieve RC	2.00	.90
❑ 168 Bruce Dal Canton	1.50	.70
❑ 169 Ed Herrmann	1.50	.70
❑ 170 Mike Cuellar	2.00	.90
❑ 171 Bobby Wine	1.50	.70
❑ 172 Duke Sims	1.50	.70
❑ 173 Gil Garrido	1.50	.70
❑ 174 Dave LaRoche	1.50	.70
❑ 175 Jim Hickman	1.50	.70
❑ 176 Red Sox Rookies	2.00	.90
Bob Montgomery RC		
Doug Griffin		
❑ 177 Hal McRae	2.00	.90
❑ 178 Dave Duncan	1.50	.70
❑ 179 Mike Corkins	1.50	.70
❑ 180 Al Kaline UER	20.00	9.00
(Home instead		
of Birth)		
❑ 181 Hal Lanier	1.50	.70
❑ 182 Al Downing	2.00	.90
❑ 183 Gil Hodges MG	4.00	1.80
❑ 184 Stan Bahnsen	1.50	.70
❑ 185 Julian Javier	2.00	.90
❑ 186 Bob Spence	1.50	.70
❑ 187 Ted Abernathy	1.50	.70
❑ 188 Dodgers Rookies	6.00	2.70
Bob Valentine RC		
Mike Strahler		
❑ 189 George Mitterwald	1.50	.70
❑ 190 Bob Tolan	2.00	.90
❑ 191 Mike Andrews	1.50	.70
❑ 192 Billy Wilson	1.50	.70
❑ 193 Bob Grich RC	4.00	1.80
❑ 194 Mike Lum	1.50	.70
❑ 195 Boog Powell ALCS	2.00	.90
❑ 196 Dave McNally ALCS	2.00	.90
❑ 197 Jim Palmer ALCS	4.00	1.80
❑ 198 AL Playoff Summary	2.00	.90
Orioles celebrate		
❑ 199 Ty Cline NLCS	2.00	.90
❑ 200 Bobby Tolan NLCS	2.00	.90
❑ 201 Ty Cline NLCS	2.00	.90
❑ 202 NL Playoff Summary	2.00	.90
Reds celebrate		
❑ 203 Larry Gura	2.00	.90
❑ 204 Brewers Rookies	1.50	.70
Bernie Smith		
George Kopacz		
❑ 205 Gerry Moses	1.50	.70
❑ 206 Checklist 3	11.00	2.20
❑ 207 Alan Foster	1.50	.70
❑ 208 Billy Martin MG	4.00	1.80
❑ 209 Steve Renko	1.50	.70
❑ 210 Rod Carew	15.00	6.75
❑ 211 Phil Hennigan	1.50	.70
❑ 212 Rich Hebner	2.00	.90
❑ 213 Frank Baker	1.50	.70
❑ 214 Al Ferrara	1.50	.70
❑ 215 Diego Segui	1.50	.70
❑ 216 Cards Rookies	1.50	.70
Reggie Cleveland		
Luis Melendez		
❑ 217 Ed Stroud	1.50	.70
❑ 218 Tony Cloninger	1.50	.70
❑ 219 Elrod Hendricks	1.50	.70
❑ 220 Ron Santo	4.00	1.80
❑ 221 Dave Morehead	1.50	.70
❑ 222 Bob Watson	2.00	.90
❑ 223 Cecil Upshaw	1.50	.70
❑ 224 Alan Gallagher	1.50	.70
❑ 225 Gary Peters	1.50	.70
❑ 226 Bill Russell	2.00	.90
❑ 227 Floyd Weaver	1.50	.70
❑ 228 Wayne Garrett	1.50	.70
❑ 229 Jim Hannan	1.50	.70
❑ 230 Willie Stargell	8.00	3.60
❑ 231 Indians Rookies	1.50	.70
Vince Colbert		
John Lowenstein RC		
❑ 232 John Strohmayer	1.50	.70
❑ 233 Larry Bowa	2.00	.90
❑ 234 Jim Lyttle	1.50	.70
❑ 235 Nate Colbert	1.50	.70
❑ 236 Bob Humphreys	1.50	.70
❑ 237 Cesar Cedeno RC	2.00	.90
❑ 238 Chuck Dobson	1.50	.70
❑ 239 Red Schoendienst MG	2.00	.90
❑ 240 Clyde Wright	1.50	.70
❑ 241 Dave Nelson	1.50	.70
❑ 242 Jim Ray	1.50	.70
❑ 243 Carlos May	2.00	.90
❑ 244 Bob Tillman	1.50	.70
❑ 245 Jim Kaat	2.00	.90
❑ 246 Tony Taylor	2.00	.90
❑ 247 Royals Rookies	2.00	.90
Jerry Cram		
Paul Splittorff		
❑ 248 Hoyt Wilhelm	6.00	2.70
❑ 249 Chico Salmon	1.50	.70
❑ 250 Johnny Bench	25.00	11.00
❑ 251 Frank Reberger	1.50	.70
❑ 252 Eddie Leon	1.50	.70
❑ 253 Bill Sudakis	1.50	.70
❑ 254 Cal Koonce	1.50	.70
❑ 255 Bob Robertson	2.00	.90
❑ 256 Tony Gonzalez	1.50	.70
❑ 257 Nelson Briles	2.00	.90
❑ 258 Dick Green	1.50	.70
❑ 259 Dave Marshall	1.50	.70
❑ 260 Tommy Harper	2.00	.90
❑ 261 Darold Knowles	1.50	.70
❑ 262 Padres Rookies	1.50	.70
Jim Williams		
Dave Robinson		
❑ 263 John Ellis	1.50	.70
❑ 264 Joe Morgan	8.00	3.60
❑ 265 Jim Northrup	2.00	.90
❑ 266 Bill Stoneman	1.50	.70
❑ 267 Rich Morales	1.50	.70
❑ 268 Philadelphia Phillies	4.00	1.80
Team Card		
❑ 269 Gail Hopkins	1.50	.70
❑ 270 Rico Carty	2.00	.90
❑ 271 Bill Zepp	1.50	.70
❑ 272 Tommy Helms	2.00	.90
❑ 273 Pete Richert	1.50	.70
❑ 274 Ron Slocum	1.50	.70
❑ 275 Vada Pinson	2.00	.90
❑ 276 Giants Rookies	8.00	3.60
Mike Davison		
George Foster RC		
❑ 277 Gary Waslewski	1.50	.70
❑ 278 Jerry Grote	1.50	.70
❑ 279 Lefty Phillips MG	1.50	.70
❑ 280 Ferguson Jenkins	6.00	2.70
❑ 281 Danny Walton	1.50	.70
❑ 282 Jose Pagan	1.50	.70
❑ 283 Dick Such	1.50	.70
❑ 284 Jim Gosger	1.50	.70
❑ 285 Sal Bando	2.00	.90
❑ 286 Jerry McNertney	1.50	.70
❑ 287 Mike Fiore	1.50	.70
❑ 288 Joe Moeller	1.50	.70
❑ 289 Chicago White Sox	4.00	1.80
Team Card		
❑ 290 Tony Oliva	4.00	1.80
❑ 291 George Culver	1.50	.70
❑ 292 Jay Johnstone	2.00	.90
❑ 293 Pat Corrales	2.00	.90
❑ 294 Steve Dunning	1.50	.70
❑ 295 Bobby Bonds	4.00	1.80
❑ 296 Tom Timmermann	1.50	.70
❑ 297 Johnny Briggs	1.50	.70
❑ 298 Jim Nelson	1.50	.70
❑ 299 Ed Kirkpatrick	1.50	.70
❑ 300 Brooks Robinson	20.00	9.00
❑ 301 Earl Wilson	1.50	.70
❑ 302 Phil Gagliano	1.50	.70
❑ 303 Lindy McDaniel	2.00	.90
❑ 304 Ron Brand	1.50	.70
❑ 305 Reggie Smith	2.00	.90
❑ 306 Jim Nash	1.50	.70
❑ 307 Don Wert	1.50	.70
❑ 308 St. Louis Cardinals	4.00	1.80
Team Card		
❑ 309 Dick Ellsworth	1.50	.70
❑ 310 Tommie Agee	2.00	.90
❑ 311 Lee Stange	1.50	.70
❑ 312 Harry Walker MG	1.50	.70
❑ 313 Tom Hall	1.50	.70
❑ 314 Jeff Torborg	2.00	.90
❑ 315 Ron Fairly	2.00	.90
❑ 316 Fred Scherman	1.50	.70
❑ 317 Athletic Rookies	1.50	.70
Jim Driscoll		
Angel Mangual		
❑ 318 Rudy May	1.50	.70
❑ 319 Ty Cline	1.50	.70
❑ 320 Dave McNally	2.00	.90
❑ 321 Tom Matchick	1.50	.70
❑ 322 Jim Beauchamp	1.50	.70
❑ 323 Billy Champion	1.50	.70
❑ 324 Graig Nettles	2.00	.90
❑ 325 Juan Marichal	6.00	2.70
❑ 326 Richie Scheinblum	1.50	.70
❑ 327 Boog Powell WS	2.00	.90
❑ 328 Don Buford WS	2.00	.90
❑ 329 Frank Robinson WS	4.00	1.80
❑ 330 World Series Game 4	2.00	.90
Reds stay alive		
❑ 331 Brooks Robinson WS	6.00	2.70
commits robbery		
❑ 332 WS Summary	2.00	.90
Orioles celebrate		
❑ 333 Clay Kirby	1.50	.70
❑ 334 Roberto Pena	1.50	.70
❑ 335 Jerry Koosman	2.00	.90
❑ 336 Detroit Tigers	4.00	1.80
Team Card		
❑ 337 Jesus Alou	1.50	.70
❑ 338 Gene Tenace	2.00	.90
❑ 339 Wayne Simpson	1.50	.70
❑ 340 Rico Petrocelli	2.00	.90
❑ 341 Steve Garvey RC	30.00	13.50
❑ 342 Frank Tepedino	1.50	.70
❑ 343 Pirates Rookies	1.50	.70
Ed Acosta		
Milt May RC		
❑ 344 Ellie Rodriguez	1.50	.70
❑ 345 Joel Horlen	1.50	.70
❑ 346 Lum Harris MG	1.50	.70
❑ 347 Ted Uhlaender	1.50	.70
❑ 348 Fred Norman	1.50	.70
❑ 349 Rich Reese	1.50	.70
❑ 350 Billy Williams	6.00	2.70
❑ 351 Jim Shellenback	1.50	.70
❑ 352 Denny Doyle	1.50	.70
❑ 353 Carl Taylor	1.50	.70
❑ 354 Don McMahon	1.50	.70
❑ 355 Bud Harrelson	4.00	1.80
(Nolan Ryan in photo)		
❑ 356 Bob Locker	1.50	.70
❑ 357 Cincinnati Reds	4.00	1.80
Team Card		
❑ 358 Danny Cater	1.50	.70
❑ 359 Ron Reed	1.50	.70
❑ 360 Jim Fregosi	2.00	.90
❑ 361 Don Sutton	6.00	2.70
❑ 362 Orioles Rookies	1.50	.70
Mike Adamson		

	Roger Freed		
❑ 363	Mike Nagy	1.50	.70
❑ 364	Tommy Dean	1.50	.70
❑ 365	Bob Johnson	1.50	.70
❑ 366	Ron Stone	1.50	.70
❑ 367	Dalton Jones	1.50	.70
❑ 368	Bob Veale	2.00	.90
❑ 369	Checklist 4	11.00	2.20
❑ 370	Joe Torre	4.00	1.80
❑ 371	Jack Hiatt	1.50	.70
❑ 372	Lew Krausse	1.50	.70
❑ 373	Tom McCraw	1.50	.70
❑ 374	Clete Boyer	2.00	.90
❑ 375	Steve Hargan	1.50	.70
❑ 376	Expos Rookies	1.50	.70
	Clyde Mashore		
	Ernie McAnally		
❑ 377	Greg Garrett	1.50	.70
❑ 378	Tito Fuentes	1.50	.70
❑ 379	Wayne Granger	1.50	.70
❑ 380	Ted Williams MG	12.00	5.50
❑ 381	Fred Gladding	1.50	.70
❑ 382	Jake Gibbs	1.50	.70
❑ 383	Rod Gaspar	1.50	.70
❑ 384	Rollie Fingers	6.00	2.70
❑ 385	Maury Wills	4.00	1.80
❑ 386	Boston Red Sox	2.00	.90
	Team Card		
❑ 387	Ron Herbel	1.50	.70
❑ 388	Al Oliver	4.00	1.80
❑ 389	Ed Brinkman	1.50	.70
❑ 390	Glenn Beckert	2.00	.90
❑ 391	Twins Rookies	2.00	.90
	Steve Brye		
	Cotton Nash		
❑ 392	Grant Jackson	1.50	.70
❑ 393	Merv Rettenmund	2.00	.90
❑ 394	Clay Carroll	2.50	1.10
❑ 395	Roy White	4.00	1.80
❑ 396	Dick Schofield	2.50	1.10
❑ 397	Alvin Dark MG	4.00	1.80
❑ 398	Howie Reed	2.50	1.10
❑ 399	Jim French	2.50	1.10
❑ 400	Hank Aaron	50.00	22.00
❑ 401	Tom Murphy	2.50	1.10
❑ 402	Los Angeles Dodgers	6.00	2.70
	Team Card		
❑ 403	Joe Coleman	2.50	1.10
❑ 404	Astros Rookies	2.50	1.10
	Buddy Harris		
	Roger Metzger		
❑ 405	Leo Cardenas	2.50	1.10
❑ 406	Ray Sadecki	2.50	1.10
❑ 407	Joe Rudi	4.00	1.80
❑ 408	Rafael Robles	2.50	1.10
❑ 409	Don Pavletich	2.50	1.10
❑ 410	Ken Holtzman	4.00	1.80
❑ 411	George Spriggs	2.50	1.10
❑ 412	Jerry Johnson	2.50	1.10
❑ 413	Pat Kelly	2.50	1.10
❑ 414	Woodie Fryman	2.50	1.10
❑ 415	Mike Hegan	2.50	1.10
❑ 416	Gene Alley	2.50	1.10
❑ 417	Dick Hall	2.50	1.10
❑ 418	Adolfo Phillips	2.50	1.10
❑ 419	Ron Hansen	2.50	1.10
❑ 420	Jim Merritt	2.50	1.10
❑ 421	John Stephenson	2.50	1.10
❑ 422	Frank Bertaina	2.50	1.10
❑ 423	Tigers Rookies	2.50	1.10
	Dennis Saunders		
	Tim Marting		
❑ 424	Roberto Rodriquez	2.50	1.10
❑ 425	Doug Rader	2.50	1.10
❑ 426	Chris Cannizzaro	2.50	1.10
❑ 427	Bernie Allen	2.50	1.10
❑ 428	Jim McAndrew	2.50	1.10
❑ 429	Chuck Hinton	2.50	1.10
❑ 430	Wes Parker	4.00	1.80
❑ 431	Tom Burgmeier	2.50	1.10
❑ 432	Bob Didier	2.50	1.10
❑ 433	Skip Lockwood	2.50	1.10
❑ 434	Gary Sutherland	2.50	1.10
❑ 435	Jose Cardenal	4.00	1.80
❑ 436	Wilbur Wood	4.00	1.80
❑ 437	Danny Murtaugh MG	4.00	1.80
❑ 438	Mike McCormick	4.00	1.80
❑ 439	Phillies Rookies	6.00	2.70
	Greg Luzinski RC		
	Scott Reid		
❑ 440	Bert Campaneris	4.00	1.80
❑ 441	Milt Pappas	4.00	1.80
❑ 442	California Angels	4.00	1.80
	Team Card		
❑ 443	Rich Robertson	2.50	1.10
❑ 444	Jimmie Price	2.50	1.10
❑ 445	Art Shamsky	2.50	1.10
❑ 446	Bobby Bolin	2.50	1.10
❑ 447	Cesar Geronimo	4.00	1.80
❑ 448	Dave Roberts	2.50	1.10
❑ 449	Brant Alyea	2.50	1.10
❑ 450	Bob Gibson	15.00	6.75
❑ 451	Joe Keough	2.50	1.10
❑ 452	John Boccabella	2.50	1.10
❑ 453	Terry Crowley	2.50	1.10
❑ 454	Mike Paul	2.50	1.10
❑ 455	Don Kessinger	4.00	1.80
❑ 456	Bob Meyer	2.50	1.10
❑ 457	Willie Smith	2.50	1.10
❑ 458	White Sox Rookies	2.50	1.10
	Ron Lolich		
	Dave Lemonds		
❑ 459	Jim Lefebvre	2.50	1.10
❑ 460	Fritz Peterson	2.50	1.10
❑ 461	Jim Ray Hart	4.00	1.80
❑ 462	Washington Senators	6.00	2.70
	Team Card		
❑ 463	Tom Kelley	2.50	1.10
❑ 464	Aurelio Rodriguez	2.50	1.10
❑ 465	Tim McCarver	6.00	2.70
❑ 466	Ken Berry	2.50	1.10
❑ 467	Al Santorini	2.50	1.10
❑ 468	Frank Fernandez	2.50	1.10
❑ 469	Bob Aspromonte	2.50	1.10
❑ 470	Bob Oliver	2.50	1.10
❑ 471	Tom Griffin	2.50	1.10
❑ 472	Ken Rudolph	2.50	1.10
❑ 473	Gary Wagner	2.50	1.10
❑ 474	Jim Fairey	2.50	1.10
❑ 475	Ron Perranoski	2.50	1.10
❑ 476	Dal Maxvill	2.50	1.10
❑ 477	Earl Weaver MG	6.00	2.70
❑ 478	Bernie Carbo	2.50	1.10
❑ 479	Dennis Higgins	2.50	1.10
❑ 480	Manny Sanguillen	4.00	1.80
❑ 481	Daryl Patterson	2.50	1.10
❑ 482	San Diego Padres	6.00	2.70
	Team Card		
❑ 483	Gene Michael	4.00	1.80
❑ 484	Don Wilson	2.50	1.10
❑ 485	Ken McMullen	2.50	1.10
❑ 486	Steve Huntz	2.50	1.10
❑ 487	Paul Schaal	2.50	1.10
❑ 488	Jerry Stephenson	2.50	1.10
❑ 489	Luis Alvarado	2.50	1.10
❑ 490	Deron Johnson	4.00	1.80
❑ 491	Jim Hardin	2.50	1.10
❑ 492	Ken Boswell	2.50	1.10
❑ 493	Dave May	2.50	1.10
❑ 494	Braves Rookies	4.00	1.80
	Ralph Garr		
	Rick Kester		
❑ 495	Felipe Alou	4.00	1.80
❑ 496	Woody Woodward	2.50	1.10
❑ 497	Horacio Pina	2.50	1.10
❑ 498	John Kennedy	2.50	1.10
❑ 499	Checklist 5	11.00	2.20
❑ 500	Jim Perry	4.00	1.80
❑ 501	Andy Etchebarren	2.50	1.10
❑ 502	Chicago Cubs	6.00	2.70
	Team Card		
❑ 503	Gates Brown	4.00	1.80
❑ 504	Ken Wright	2.50	1.10
❑ 505	Ollie Brown	2.50	1.10
❑ 506	Bobby Knoop	2.50	1.10
❑ 507	George Stone	2.50	1.10
❑ 508	Roger Repoz	2.50	1.10
❑ 509	Jim Grant	2.50	1.10
❑ 510	Ken Harrelson	4.00	1.80
❑ 511	Chris Short	4.00	1.80
	(Pete Rose leading off second)		
❑ 512	Red Sox Rookies	2.50	1.10
	Dick Mills		
	Mike Garman		
❑ 513	Nolan Ryan	150.00	70.00
❑ 514	Ron Woods	2.50	1.10
❑ 515	Carl Morton	2.50	1.10
❑ 516	Ted Kubiak	2.50	1.10
❑ 517	Charlie Fox MG	2.50	1.10
❑ 518	Joe Grzenda	2.50	1.10
❑ 519	Willie Crawford	2.50	1.10
❑ 520	Tommy John	6.00	2.70
❑ 521	Leron Lee	2.50	1.10
❑ 522	Minnesota Twins	6.00	2.70
	Team Card		
❑ 523	John Odom	2.50	1.10
❑ 524	Mickey Stanley	6.00	2.70
❑ 525	Ernie Banks	50.00	22.00
❑ 526	Ray Jarvis	4.00	1.80
❑ 527	Cleon Jones	6.00	2.70
❑ 528	Wally Bunker	4.00	1.80
❑ 529	NL Rookie Infielders	6.00	2.70
	Enzo Hernandez		
	Bill Buckner		
	Marty Perez		
❑ 530	Carl Yastrzemski	30.00	13.50
❑ 531	Mike Torrez	4.00	1.80
❑ 532	Bill Rigney MG	4.00	1.80
❑ 533	Mike Ryan	4.00	1.80
❑ 534	Luke Walker	4.00	1.80
❑ 535	Curt Flood	6.00	2.70
❑ 536	Claude Raymond	6.00	2.70
❑ 537	Tom Egan	4.00	1.80
❑ 538	Angel Bravo	4.00	1.80
❑ 539	Larry Brown	4.00	1.80
❑ 540	Larry Dierker	6.00	2.70
❑ 541	Bob Burda	4.00	1.80
❑ 542	Bob Miller	4.00	1.80
❑ 543	New York Yankees	10.00	4.50
	Team Card		
❑ 544	Vida Blue	6.00	2.70
❑ 545	Dick Dietz	4.00	1.80
❑ 546	John Matias	4.00	1.80
❑ 547	Pat Dobson	6.00	2.70
❑ 548	Don Mason	4.00	1.80
❑ 549	Jim Brewer	6.00	2.70
❑ 550	Harmon Killebrew	25.00	11.00
❑ 551	Frank Linzy	4.00	1.80
❑ 552	Buddy Bradford	4.00	1.80
❑ 553	Kevin Collins	4.00	1.80
❑ 554	Lowell Palmer	4.00	1.80
❑ 555	Walt Williams	4.00	1.80
❑ 556	Jim McGlothlin	4.00	1.80
❑ 557	Tom Satriano	4.00	1.80
❑ 558	Hector Torres	4.00	1.80
❑ 559	AL Rookie Pitchers	4.00	1.80
	Terry Cox		
	Bill Gogolewski		
	Gary Jones		
❑ 560	Rusty Staub	6.00	2.70
❑ 561	Syd O'Brien	4.00	1.80
❑ 562	Dave Giusti	4.00	1.80
❑ 563	San Francisco Giants	8.00	3.60
	Team Card		
❑ 564	Al Fitzmorris	4.00	1.80
❑ 565	Jim Wynn	6.00	2.70
❑ 566	Tim Cullen	4.00	1.80
❑ 567	Walt Alston MG	6.00	2.70
❑ 568	Sal Campisi	4.00	1.80
❑ 569	Ivan Murrell	4.00	1.80
❑ 570	Jim Palmer	30.00	13.50
❑ 571	Ted Sizemore	4.00	1.80
❑ 572	Jerry Kenney	4.00	1.80
❑ 573	Ed Kranepool	6.00	2.70
❑ 574	Jim Bunning	8.00	3.60
❑ 575	Bill Freehan	6.00	2.70
❑ 576	Cubs Rookies	4.00	1.80
	Adrian Garrett		
	Brock Davis		
	Garry Jestadt		
❑ 577	Jim Lonborg	6.00	2.70
❑ 578	Ron Hunt	4.00	1.80
❑ 579	Marty Pattin	4.00	1.80
❑ 580	Tony Perez	20.00	9.00
❑ 581	Roger Nelson	4.00	1.80
❑ 582	Dave Cash	6.00	2.70
❑ 583	Ron Cook	4.00	1.80
❑ 584	Cleveland Indians	8.00	3.60

	No.	Card	NRMT	VG-E
		Team Card		
❑	585	Willie Davis	6.00	2.70
❑	586	Dick Woodson	4.00	1.80
❑	587	Sonny Jackson	4.00	1.80
❑	588	Tom Bradley	4.00	1.80
❑	589	Bob Barton	4.00	1.80
❑	590	Alex Johnson	6.00	2.70
❑	591	Jackie Brown	4.00	1.80
❑	592	Randy Hundley	6.00	2.70
❑	593	Jack Aker	4.00	1.80
❑	594	Cards Rookies	6.00	2.70
		Bob Chlupsa		
		Bob Stinson		
		Al Hrabosky RC		
❑	595	Dave Johnson	6.00	2.70
❑	596	Mike Jorgensen	4.00	1.80
❑	597	Ken Suarez	4.00	1.80
❑	598	Rick Wise	6.00	2.70
❑	599	Norm Cash	6.00	2.70
❑	600	Willie Mays	100.00	45.00
❑	601	Ken Tatum	4.00	1.80
❑	602	Marty Martinez	4.00	1.80
❑	603	Pittsburgh Pirates	8.00	3.60
		Team Card		
❑	604	John Gelnar	4.00	1.80
❑	605	Orlando Cepeda	8.00	3.60
❑	606	Chuck Taylor	4.00	1.80
❑	607	Paul Ratliff	4.00	1.80
❑	608	Mike Wegener	4.00	1.80
❑	609	Leo Durocher MG	8.00	3.60
❑	610	Amos Otis	6.00	2.70
❑	611	Tom Phoebus	4.00	1.80
❑	612	Indians Rookies	4.00	1.80
		Lou Camilli		
		Ted Ford		
		Steve Mingori		
❑	613	Pedro Borbon	4.00	1.80
❑	614	Billy Cowan	4.00	1.80
❑	615	Mel Stottlemyre	6.00	2.70
❑	616	Larry Hisle	6.00	2.70
❑	617	Clay Dalrymple	4.00	1.80
❑	618	Tug McGraw	6.00	2.70
❑	619A	Checklist 6 ERR	11.00	2.20
		(No copyright)		
❑	619B	Checklist 6 COR	6.00	1.20
		(Copyright on back)		
❑	620	Frank Howard	6.00	2.70
❑	621	Ron Bryant	4.00	1.80
❑	622	Joe Lahoud	4.00	1.80
❑	623	Pat Jarvis	4.00	1.80
❑	624	Oakland Athletics	8.00	3.60
		Team Card		
❑	625	Lou Brock	30.00	13.50
❑	626	Freddie Patek	6.00	2.70
❑	627	Steve Hamilton	4.00	1.80
❑	628	John Bateman	4.00	1.80
❑	629	John Hiller	6.00	2.70
❑	630	Roberto Clemente	125.00	55.00
❑	631	Eddie Fisher	4.00	1.80
❑	632	Darrel Chaney	4.00	1.80
❑	633	AL Rookie Outfielders	4.00	1.80
		Bobby Brooks		
		Pete Koegel		
		Scott Northey		
❑	634	Phil Regan	6.00	2.70
❑	635	Bobby Murcer	6.00	2.70
❑	636	Denny Lemaster	4.00	1.80
❑	637	Dave Bristol MG	4.00	1.80
❑	638	Stan Williams	4.00	1.80
❑	639	Tom Haller	4.00	1.80
❑	640	Frank Robinson	40.00	18.00
❑	641	New York Mets	15.00	6.75
		Team Card		
❑	642	Jim Roland	4.00	1.80
❑	643	Rick Reichardt	6.00	2.70
❑	644	Jim Stewart SP	12.00	5.50
❑	645	Jim Maloney SP	15.00	6.75
❑	646	Bobby Floyd SP	12.00	5.50
❑	647	Juan Pizarro	8.00	3.60
❑	648	Mets Rookies SP	25.00	11.00
		Rich Folkers		
		Ted Martinez		
		John Matlack RC		
❑	649	Sparky Lyle SP	15.00	6.75
❑	650	Rich Allen SP	30.00	13.50
❑	651	Jerry Robertson SP	12.00	5.50
❑	652	Atlanta Braves	12.00	5.50
		Team Card		
❑	653	Russ Snyder SP	12.00	5.50
❑	654	Don Shaw SP	12.00	5.50
❑	655	Mike Epstein SP	12.00	5.50
❑	656	Gerry Nyman SP	12.00	5.50
❑	657	Jose Azcue	8.00	3.60
❑	658	Paul Lindblad SP	12.00	5.50
❑	659	Byron Browne SP	12.00	5.50
❑	660	Ray Culp	8.00	3.60
❑	661	Chuck Tanner MG SP	15.00	6.75
❑	662	Mike Hedlund SP	12.00	5.50
❑	663	Marv Staehle	8.00	3.60
❑	664	Rookie Pitchers SP	12.00	5.50
		Archie Reynolds		
		Bob Reynolds		
		Ken Reynolds		
❑	665	Ron Swoboda SP	15.00	6.75
❑	666	Gene Brabender SP	12.00	5.50
❑	667	Pete Ward	8.00	3.60
❑	668	Gary Neibauer	8.00	3.60
❑	669	Ike Brown SP	12.00	5.50
❑	670	Bill Hands	8.00	3.60
❑	671	Bill Voss SP	12.00	5.50
❑	672	Ed Crosby SP	12.00	5.50
❑	673	Gerry Janeski SP	12.00	5.50
❑	674	Montreal Expos	12.00	5.50
		Team Card		
❑	675	Dave Boswell	8.00	3.60
❑	676	Tommie Reynolds	8.00	3.60
❑	677	Jack DiLauro SP	12.00	5.50
❑	678	George Thomas	8.00	3.60
❑	679	Don O'Riley	8.00	3.60
❑	680	Don Mincher SP	12.00	5.50
❑	681	Bill Butler	8.00	3.60
❑	682	Terry Harmon	8.00	3.60
❑	683	Bill Burbach SP	12.00	5.50
❑	684	Curt Motton	8.00	3.60
❑	685	Moe Drabowsky	8.00	3.60
❑	686	Chico Ruiz SP	12.00	5.50
❑	687	Ron Taylor SP	12.00	5.50
❑	688	S.Anderson MG SP	30.00	13.50
❑	689	Frank Baker	8.00	3.60
❑	690	Bob Moose	8.00	3.60
❑	691	Bobby Heise	8.00	3.60
❑	692	AL Rookie Pitchers SP	12.00	5.50
		Hal Haydel		
		Rogelio Moret		
		Wayne Twitchell		
❑	693	Jose Pena SP	12.00	5.50
❑	694	Rick Renick SP	12.00	5.50
❑	695	Joe Niekro	12.00	5.50
❑	696	Jerry Morales	8.00	3.60
❑	697	Rickey Clark SP	12.00	5.50
❑	698	M. Brewers SP	20.00	9.00
		Team Card		
❑	699	Jim Britton	8.00	3.60
❑	700	Boog Powell SP	25.00	11.00
❑	701	Bob Garibaldi	8.00	3.60
❑	702	Milt Ramirez	8.00	3.60
❑	703	Mike Kekich	8.00	3.60
❑	704	J.C. Martin SP	12.00	5.50
❑	705	Dick Selma SP	12.00	5.50
❑	706	Joe Foy SP	12.00	5.50
❑	707	Fred Lasher	8.00	3.60
❑	708	Russ Nagelson SP	12.00	5.50
❑	709	Rookie Outfielders SP	80.00	36.00
		Dusty Baker RC		
		Don Baylor RC		
		Tom Paciorek		
❑	710	Sonny Siebert	8.00	3.60
❑	711	Larry Stahl SP	12.00	5.50
❑	712	Jose Martinez	8.00	3.60
❑	713	Mike Marshall SP	15.00	6.75
❑	714	Dick Williams MG SP	15.00	6.75
❑	715	Horace Clarke SP	15.00	6.75
❑	716	Dave Leonhard	8.00	3.60
❑	717	Tommie Aaron SP	12.00	5.50
❑	718	Billy Wynne	8.00	3.60
❑	719	Jerry May SP	12.00	5.50
❑	720	Matty Alou	12.00	5.50
❑	721	John Morris	8.00	3.60
❑	722	Houston Astros SP	20.00	9.00
		Team Card		
❑	723	Vicente Romo SP	12.00	5.50
❑	724	Tom Tischinski SP	12.00	5.50
❑	725	Gary Gentry SP	12.00	5.50
❑	726	Paul Popovich	8.00	3.60
❑	727	Ray Lamb SP	12.00	5.50
❑	728	NL Rookie Outfielders	8.00	3.60
		Wayne Redmond		
		Keith Lampard		
		Bernie Williams		
❑	729	Dick Billings	8.00	3.60
❑	730	Jim Rooker	8.00	3.60
❑	731	Jim Qualls SP	12.00	5.50
❑	732	Bob Reed	8.00	3.60
❑	733	Lee Maye SP	12.00	5.50
❑	734	Rob Gardner SP	12.00	5.50
❑	735	Mike Shannon SP	15.00	6.75
❑	736	Mel Queen SP	12.00	5.50
❑	737	P.Gomez SP MG	12.00	5.50
❑	738	Russ Gibson SP	12.00	5.50
❑	739	Barry Lersch SP	12.00	5.50
❑	740	Luis Aparicio SP UER	30.00	13.50
		(Led AL in steals		
		from 1965 to 1964,		
		should be 1956 to 1964)		
❑	741	Skip Guinn	8.00	3.60
❑	742	Kansas City Royals	12.00	5.50
		Team Card		
❑	743	John O'Donoghue SP	12.00	5.50
❑	744	Chuck Manuel SP	12.00	5.50
❑	745	Sandy Alomar SP	12.00	5.50
❑	746	Andy Kosco	8.00	3.60
❑	747	NL Rookie Pitchers	8.00	3.60
		Al Severinsen		
		Scipio Spinks		
		Balor Moore		
❑	748	John Purdin SP	12.00	5.50
❑	749	Ken Szotkiewicz	8.00	3.60
❑	750	Denny McLain SP	25.00	11.00
❑	751	Al Weis SP	15.00	6.75
❑	752	Dick Drago	12.00	2.90

1972 Topps

	NRMT	VG-E
COMPLETE SET (787)	1600.00	700.00
COMMON CARD (1-132)	.60	.25
COMMON CARD (133-263)	1.00	.45
COMMON CARD (264-394)	1.25	.55
COMMON CARD (395-525)	1.50	.70
COMMON CARD (526-656)	4.00	1.80
COMMON CARD (657-787)	12.00	5.50
WRAPPER (10-CENT)	15.00	6.75

	No.	Card	NRMT	VG-E
❑	1	Pittsburgh Pirates	8.00	2.90
		Team Card		
❑	2	Ray Culp	.60	.25
❑	3	Bob Tolan	.60	.25
❑	4	Checklist 1-132	6.00	1.20
❑	5	John Bateman	.60	.25
❑	6	Fred Scherman	.60	.25
❑	7	Enzo Hernandez	.60	.25
❑	8	Ron Swoboda	1.25	.55
❑	9	Stan Williams	.60	.25
❑	10	Amos Otis	1.25	.55
❑	11	Bobby Valentine	1.25	.55
❑	12	Jose Cardenal	.60	.25
❑	13	Joe Grzenda	.60	.25
❑	14	Phillies Rookies	.60	.25
		Pete Koegel		
		Mike Anderson		

Wayne Twitchell
❑ 15 Walt Williams .60 .25
❑ 16 Mike Jorgensen .60 .25
❑ 17 Dave Duncan .60 .25
❑ 18A Juan Pizarro .60 .25
(Yellow underline
C and S of Cubs)
❑ 18B Juan Pizarro 5.00 2.20
(Green underline
C and S of Cubs)
❑ 19 Billy Cowan .60 .25
❑ 20 Don Wilson .60 .25
❑ 21 Atlanta Braves 1.50 .70
Team Card
❑ 22 Rob Gardner .60 .25
❑ 23 Ted Kubiak .60 .25
❑ 24 Ted Ford .60 .25
❑ 25 Bill Singer .60 .25
❑ 26 Andy Etchebarren .60 .25
❑ 27 Bob Johnson .60 .25
❑ 28 Twins Rookies .60 .25
Bob Gebhard
Steve Brye
Hal Haydel
❑ 29A Bill Bonham .60 .25
(Yellow underline
C and S of Cubs)
❑ 29B Bill Bonham 5.00 2.20
(Green underline
C and S of Cubs)
❑ 30 Rico Petrocelli 1.25 .55
❑ 31 Cleon Jones 1.25 .55
❑ 32 Cleon Jones IA .60 .25
❑ 33 Billy Martin MG 4.00 1.80
❑ 34 Billy Martin IA 2.50 1.10
❑ 35 Jerry Johnson .60 .25
❑ 36 Jerry Johnson IA .60 .25
❑ 37 Carl Yastrzemski 10.00 4.50
❑ 38 Carl Yastrzemski IA 6.00 2.70
❑ 39 Bob Barton .60 .25
❑ 40 Bob Barton IA .60 .25
❑ 41 Tommy Davis 1.25 .55
❑ 42 Tommy Davis IA .60 .25
❑ 43 Rick Wise 1.25 .55
❑ 44 Rick Wise IA .60 .25
❑ 45A Glenn Beckert 1.25 .55
(Yellow underline
C and S of Cubs)
❑ 45B Glenn Beckert 5.00 2.20
(Green underline
C and S of Cubs)
❑ 46 Glenn Beckert IA .60 .25
❑ 47 John Ellis .60 .25
❑ 48 John Ellis IA .60 .25
❑ 49 Willie Mays 30.00 13.50
❑ 50 Willie Mays IA 14.00 6.25
❑ 51 Harmon Killebrew 7.00 3.10
❑ 52 Harmon Killebrew IA 4.00 1.80
❑ 53 Bud Harrelson 1.25 .55
❑ 54 Bud Harrelson IA .60 .25
❑ 55 Clyde Wright .60 .25
❑ 56 Rich Chiles .60 .25
❑ 57 Bob Oliver .60 .25
❑ 58 Ernie McAnally .60 .25
❑ 59 Fred Stanley .60 .25
❑ 60 Manny Sanguillen 1.25 .55
❑ 61 Cubs Rookies 1.25 .55
Burt Hooton RC
Gene Hiser
Earl Stephenson
❑ 62 Angel Mangual .60 .25
❑ 63 Duke Sims .60 .25
❑ 64 Pete Broberg .60 .25
❑ 65 Cesar Cedeno 1.25 .55
❑ 66 Ray Corbin .60 .25
❑ 67 Red Schoendienst MG 1.25 .55
❑ 68 Jim York .60 .25
❑ 69 Roger Freed .60 .25
❑ 70 Mike Cuellar 1.25 .55
❑ 71 California Angels 1.50 .70
Team Card
❑ 72 Bruce Kison RC .60 .25
❑ 73 Steve Huntz .60 .25
❑ 74 Cecil Upshaw .60 .25
❑ 75 Bert Campaneris 1.25 .55
❑ 76 Don Carrithers .60 .25
❑ 77 Ron Theobald .60 .25
❑ 78 Steve Arlin .60 .25
❑ 79 Red Sox Rookies 50.00 22.00
Mike Garman
Cecil Cooper RC
Carlton Fisk RC
❑ 80 Tony Perez 4.00 1.80
❑ 81 Mike Hedlund .60 .25
❑ 82 Ron Woods .60 .25
❑ 83 Dalton Jones .60 .25
❑ 84 Vince Colbert .60 .25
❑ 85 NL Batting Leaders 2.50 1.10
Joe Torre
Ralph Garr
Glenn Beckert
❑ 86 AL Batting Leaders 2.50 1.10
Tony Oliva
Bobby Murcer
Merv Rettenmund
❑ 87 NL RBI Leaders 4.00 1.80
Joe Torre
Willie Stargell
Hank Aaron
❑ 88 AL RBI Leaders 4.00 1.80
Harmon Killebrew
Frank Robinson
Reggie Smith
❑ 89 NL Home Run Leaders 2.50 1.10
Willie Stargell
Hank Aaron
Lee May
❑ 90 AL Home Run Leaders 2.50 1.10
Bill Melton
Norm Cash
Reggie Jackson
❑ 91 NL ERA Leaders 2.50 1.10
Tom Seaver
Dave Roberts UER
(Photo actually
Danny Coombs)
Don Wilson
❑ 92 AL ERA Leaders 2.50 1.10
Vida Blue
Wilbur Wood
Jim Palmer
❑ 93 NL Pitching Leaders 4.00 1.80
Fergie Jenkins
Steve Carlton
Al Downing
Tom Seaver
❑ 94 AL Pitching Leaders 2.50 1.10
Mickey Lolich
Vida Blue
Wilbur Wood
❑ 95 NL Strikeout Leaders 4.00 1.80
Tom Seaver
Fergie Jenkins
Bill Stoneman
❑ 96 AL Strikeout Leaders 2.50 1.10
Mickey Lolich
Vida Blue
Joe Coleman
❑ 97 Tom Kelley .60 .25
❑ 98 Chuck Tanner MG 1.25 .55
❑ 99 Ross Grimsley .60 .25
❑ 100 Frank Robinson 8.00 3.60
❑ 101 Astros Rookies 1.50 .70
Bill Greif
J.R. Richard RC
Ray Busse
❑ 102 Lloyd Allen .60 .25
❑ 103 Checklist 133-263 6.00 1.20
❑ 104 Toby Harrah RC 1.25 .55
❑ 105 Gary Gentry .60 .25
❑ 106 Milwaukee Brewers 1.50 .70
Team Card
❑ 107 Jose Cruz RC 1.25 .55
❑ 108 Gary Waslewski .60 .25
❑ 109 Jerry May .60 .25
❑ 110 Ron Hunt .60 .25
❑ 111 Jim Grant .60 .25
❑ 112 Greg Luzinski 1.25 .55
❑ 113 Rogelio Moret .60 .25
❑ 114 Bill Buckner 1.25 .55
❑ 115 Jim Fregosi 1.25 .55
❑ 116 Ed Farmer .60 .25
❑ 117A Cleo James .60 .25
(Yellow underline
C and S of Cubs)
❑ 117B Cleo James 5.00 2.20
(Green underline
C and S of Cubs)
❑ 118 Skip Lockwood .60 .25
❑ 119 Marty Perez .60 .25
❑ 120 Bill Freehan 1.25 .55
❑ 121 Ed Sprague .60 .25
❑ 122 Larry Biittner .60 .25
❑ 123 Ed Acosta .60 .25
❑ 124 Yankees Rookies .60 .25
Alan Closter
Rusty Torres
Roger Hambright
❑ 125 Dave Cash 1.25 .55
❑ 126 Bart Johnson .60 .25
❑ 127 Duffy Dyer .60 .25
❑ 128 Eddie Watt .60 .25
❑ 129 Charlie Fox MG .60 .25
❑ 130 Bob Gibson 8.00 3.60
❑ 131 Jim Nettles .60 .25
❑ 132 Joe Morgan 6.00 2.70
❑ 133 Joe Keough 1.00 .45
❑ 134 Carl Morton 1.00 .45
❑ 135 Vada Pinson 2.00 .90
❑ 136 Darrel Chaney 1.00 .45
❑ 137 Dick Williams MG 2.00 .90
❑ 138 Mike Kekich 1.00 .45
❑ 139 Tim McCarver 2.00 .90
❑ 140 Pat Dobson 2.00 .90
❑ 141 Mets Rookies 2.00 .90
Buzz Capra
Lee Stanton
Jon Matlack
❑ 142 Chris Chambliss RC 4.00 1.80
❑ 143 Garry Jestadt 1.00 .45
❑ 144 Marty Pattin 1.00 .45
❑ 145 Don Kessinger 2.00 .90
❑ 146 Steve Kealey 1.00 .45
❑ 147 Dave Kingman RC 6.00 2.70
❑ 148 Dick Billings 1.00 .45
❑ 149 Gary Neibauer 1.00 .45
❑ 150 Norm Cash 2.00 .90
❑ 151 Jim Brewer 1.00 .45
❑ 152 Gene Clines 1.00 .45
❑ 153 Rick Auerbach 1.00 .45
❑ 154 Ted Simmons 4.00 1.80
❑ 155 Larry Dierker 2.00 .90
❑ 156 Minnesota Twins 2.00 .90
Team Card
❑ 157 Don Gullett 1.00 .45
❑ 158 Jerry Kenney 1.00 .45
❑ 159 John Boccabella 1.00 .45
❑ 160 Andy Messersmith 2.00 .90
❑ 161 Brock Davis 1.00 .45
❑ 162 Brewers Rookies UER 2.00 .90
Jerry Bell
Darrell Porter RC
Bob Reynolds
(Porter and Bell
photos switched)
❑ 163 Tug McGraw 2.00 .90
❑ 164 Tug McGraw IA 2.00 .90
❑ 165 Chris Speier RC 2.00 .90
❑ 166 Chris Speier IA 2.00 .90
❑ 167 Deron Johnson 1.00 .45
❑ 168 Deron Johnson IA 1.00 .45
❑ 169 Vida Blue 2.00 .90
❑ 170 Vida Blue IA 2.00 .90
❑ 171 Darrell Evans 2.00 .90
❑ 172 Darrell Evans IA 2.00 .90
❑ 173 Clay Kirby 1.00 .45
❑ 174 Clay Kirby IA 1.00 .45
❑ 175 Tom Haller 1.00 .45
❑ 176 Tom Haller IA 1.00 .45
❑ 177 Paul Schaal 1.00 .45
❑ 178 Paul Schaal IA 1.00 .45
❑ 179 Dock Ellis 1.00 .45
❑ 180 Dock Ellis IA 1.00 .45
❑ 181 Ed Kranepool 2.00 .90
❑ 182 Ed Kranepool IA 1.00 .45
❑ 183 Bill Melton 1.00 .45
❑ 184 Bill Melton IA 1.00 .45
❑ 185 Ron Bryant 1.00 .45

❑ 186 Ron Bryant IA 1.00 .45
❑ 187 Gates Brown 1.00 .45
❑ 188 Frank Lucchesi MG 1.00 .45
❑ 189 Gene Tenace 2.00 .90
❑ 190 Dave Giusti 1.00 .45
❑ 191 Jeff Burroughs RC 2.00 .90
❑ 192 Chicago Cubs 2.00 .90
Team Card
❑ 193 Kurt Bevacqua 1.00 .45
❑ 194 Fred Norman 1.00 .45
❑ 195 Orlando Cepeda 6.00 2.70
❑ 196 Mel Queen 1.00 .45
❑ 197 Johnny Briggs 1.00 .45
❑ 198 Dodgers Rookies 6.00 2.70
Charlie Hough RC
Bob O'Brien
Mike Strahler
❑ 199 Mike Fiore 1.00 .45
❑ 200 Lou Brock 7.00 3.10
❑ 201 Phil Roof 1.00 .45
❑ 202 Scipio Spinks 1.00 .45
❑ 203 Ron Blomberg 1.00 .45
❑ 204 Tommy Helms 1.00 .45
❑ 205 Dick Drago 1.00 .45
❑ 206 Dal Maxvill 1.00 .45
❑ 207 Tom Egan 1.00 .45
❑ 208 Milt Pappas 2.00 .90
❑ 209 Joe Rudi 2.00 .90
❑ 210 Denny McLain 2.00 .90
❑ 211 Gary Sutherland 1.00 .45
❑ 212 Grant Jackson 1.00 .45
❑ 213 Angels Rookies 1.00 .45
Billy Parker
Art Kusnyer
Tom Silverio
❑ 214 Mike McQueen 1.00 .45
❑ 215 Alex Johnson 2.00 .90
❑ 216 Joe Niekro 2.00 .90
❑ 217 Roger Metzger 1.00 .45
❑ 218 Eddie Kasko MG 1.00 .45
❑ 219 Rennie Stennett 2.00 .90
❑ 220 Jim Perry 2.00 .90
❑ 221 NL Playoffs 2.00 .90
Bucs champs
❑ 222 Br. Robinson ALCS 4.00 1.80
❑ 223 Dave McNally WS 2.00 .90
❑ 224 Dave Johnson WS 2.00 .90
Mark Belanger
❑ 225 Manny Sanguillen WS 2.00 .90
❑ 226 Roberto Clemente WS 8.00 3.60
❑ 227 Nellie Briles WS 2.00 .90
❑ 228 Frank Robinson WS 2.00 .90
Manny Sanguillen
❑ 229 Steve Blass WS 2.00 .90
❑ 230 WS Summary 2.00 .90
Pirates celebrate
❑ 231 Casey Cox 1.00 .45
❑ 232 Giants Rookies 1.00 .45
Chris Arnold
Jim Barr
Dave Rader
❑ 233 Jay Johnstone 2.00 .90
❑ 234 Ron Taylor 1.00 .45
❑ 235 Merv Rettenmund 1.00 .45
❑ 236 Jim McGlothlin 1.00 .45
❑ 237 New York Yankees 2.00 .90
Team Card
❑ 238 Leron Lee 1.00 .45
❑ 239 Tom Timmermann 1.00 .45
❑ 240 Rich Allen 2.00 .90
❑ 241 Rollie Fingers 6.00 2.70
❑ 242 Don Mincher 2.00 .90
❑ 243 Frank Linzy 1.00 .45
❑ 244 Steve Braun 1.00 .45
❑ 245 Tommie Agee 2.00 .90
❑ 246 Tom Burgmeier 1.00 .45
❑ 247 Milt May 1.00 .45
❑ 248 Tom Bradley 1.00 .45
❑ 249 Harry Walker MG 1.00 .45
❑ 250 Boog Powell 2.00 .90
❑ 251 Checklist 264-394 6.00 1.20
❑ 252 Ken Reynolds 1.00 .45
❑ 253 Sandy Alomar 2.00 .90
❑ 254 Boots Day 1.00 .45
❑ 255 Jim Lonborg 2.00 .90
❑ 256 George Foster 2.00 .90
❑ 257 Tigers Rookies 1.00 .45
Jim Foor
Tim Hosley
Paul Jata
❑ 258 Randy Hundley 2.00 .90
❑ 259 Sparky Lyle 2.00 .90
❑ 260 Ralph Garr 2.00 .90
❑ 261 Steve Mingori 1.00 .45
❑ 262 San Diego Padres 2.00 .90
Team Card
❑ 263 Felipe Alou 2.00 .90
❑ 264 Tommy John 2.00 .90
❑ 265 Wes Parker 2.00 .90
❑ 266 Bobby Bolin 1.25 .55
❑ 267 Dave Concepcion 4.00 1.80
❑ 268 A's Rookies 1.25 .55
Dwain Anderson
Chris Floethe
❑ 269 Don Hahn 1.25 .55
❑ 270 Jim Palmer 8.00 3.60
❑ 271 Ken Rudolph 1.25 .55
❑ 272 Mickey Rivers RC 2.00 .90
❑ 273 Bobby Floyd 1.25 .55
❑ 274 Al Severinsen 1.25 .55
❑ 275 Cesar Tovar 1.25 .55
❑ 276 Gene Mauch MG 2.00 .90
❑ 277 Elliott Maddox 1.25 .55
❑ 278 Dennis Higgins 1.25 .55
❑ 279 Larry Brown 1.25 .55
❑ 280 Willie McCovey 7.00 3.10
❑ 281 Bill Parsons 1.25 .55
❑ 282 Houston Astros 2.00 .90
Team Card
❑ 283 Darrell Brandon 1.25 .55
❑ 284 Ike Brown 1.25 .55
❑ 285 Gaylord Perry 6.00 2.70
❑ 286 Gene Alley 2.00 .90
❑ 287 Jim Hardin 1.25 .55
❑ 288 Johnny Jeter 1.25 .55
❑ 289 Syd O'Brien 1.25 .55
❑ 290 Sonny Siebert 1.25 .55
❑ 291 Hal McRae 2.00 .90
❑ 292 Hal McRae IA 2.00 .90
❑ 293 Dan Frisella 1.25 .55
❑ 294 Dan Frisella IA 1.25 .55
❑ 295 Dick Dietz 1.25 .55
❑ 296 Dick Dietz IA 1.25 .55
❑ 297 Claude Osteen 2.00 .90
❑ 298 Claude Osteen IA 1.25 .55
❑ 299 Hank Aaron 40.00 18.00
❑ 300 Hank Aaron IA 20.00 9.00
❑ 301 George Mitterwald 1.25 .55
❑ 302 George Mitterwald IA 1.25 .55
❑ 303 Joe Pepitone 2.00 .90
❑ 304 Joe Pepitone IA 1.25 .55
❑ 305 Ken Boswell 1.25 .55
❑ 306 Ken Boswell IA 1.25 .55
❑ 307 Steve Renko 1.25 .55
❑ 308 Steve Renko IA 1.25 .55
❑ 309 Roberto Clemente 60.00 27.00
❑ 310 Roberto Clemente IA 30.00 13.50
❑ 311 Clay Carroll 1.25 .55
❑ 312 Clay Carroll IA 1.25 .55
❑ 313 Luis Aparicio 6.00 2.70
❑ 314 Luis Aparicio IA 2.00 .90
❑ 315 Paul Splittorff 1.25 .55
❑ 316 Cardinals Rookies 2.00 .90
Jim Bibby
Jorge Roque
Santiago Guzman
❑ 317 Rich Hand 1.25 .55
❑ 318 Sonny Jackson 1.25 .55
❑ 319 Aurelio Rodriguez 1.25 .55
❑ 320 Steve Blass 2.00 .90
❑ 321 Joe Lahoud 1.25 .55
❑ 322 Jose Pena 1.25 .55
❑ 323 Earl Weaver MG 4.00 1.80
❑ 324 Mike Ryan 1.25 .55
❑ 325 Mel Stottlemyre 2.00 .90
❑ 326 Pat Kelly 1.25 .55
❑ 327 Steve Stone RC 2.00 .90
❑ 328 Boston Red Sox 2.00 .90
Team Card
❑ 329 Roy Foster 1.25 .55
❑ 330 Jim Hunter 6.00 2.70
❑ 331 Stan Swanson 1.25 .55
❑ 332 Buck Martinez 1.25 .55
❑ 333 Steve Barber 1.25 .55
❑ 334 Rangers Rookies 1.25 .55
Bill Fahey
Jim Mason
Tom Ragland
❑ 335 Bill Hands 1.25 .55
❑ 336 Marty Martinez 1.25 .55
❑ 337 Mike Kilkenny 1.25 .55
❑ 338 Bob Grich 2.00 .90
❑ 339 Ron Cook 1.25 .55
❑ 340 Roy White 2.00 .90
❑ 341 Joe Torre KP 1.25 .55
❑ 342 Wilbur Wood KP 1.25 .55
❑ 343 Willie Stargell KP 2.00 .90
❑ 344 Dave McNally KP 1.25 .55
❑ 345 Rick Wise KP 1.25 .55
❑ 346 Jim Fregosi KP 1.25 .55
❑ 347 Tom Seaver KP 4.00 1.80
❑ 348 Sal Bando KP 1.25 .55
❑ 349 Al Fitzmorris 1.25 .55
❑ 350 Frank Howard 2.00 .90
❑ 351 Braves Rookies 2.00 .90
Tom House
Rick Kester
Jimmy Britton
❑ 352 Dave LaRoche 1.25 .55
❑ 353 Art Shamsky 1.25 .55
❑ 354 Tom Murphy 1.25 .55
❑ 355 Bob Watson 2.00 .90
❑ 356 Gerry Moses 1.25 .55
❑ 357 Woody Fryman 1.25 .55
❑ 358 Sparky Anderson MG 4.00 1.80
❑ 359 Don Pavletich 1.25 .55
❑ 360 Dave Roberts 1.25 .55
❑ 361 Mike Andrews 1.25 .55
❑ 362 New York Mets 2.00 .90
Team Card
❑ 363 Ron Klimkowski 1.25 .55
❑ 364 Johnny Callison 2.00 .90
❑ 365 Dick Bosman 2.00 .90
❑ 366 Jimmy Rosario 1.25 .55
❑ 367 Ron Perranoski 1.25 .55
❑ 368 Danny Thompson 1.25 .55
❑ 369 Jim Lefebvre 2.00 .90
❑ 370 Don Buford 1.25 .55
❑ 371 Denny Lemaster 1.25 .55
❑ 372 Royals Rookies 1.25 .55
Lance Clemons
Monty Montgomery
❑ 373 John Mayberry 2.00 .90
❑ 374 Jack Heidemann 1.25 .55
❑ 375 Reggie Cleveland 1.25 .55
❑ 376 Andy Kosco 1.25 .55
❑ 377 Terry Harmon 1.25 .55
❑ 378 Checklist 395-525 6.00 1.20
❑ 379 Ken Berry 1.25 .55
❑ 380 Earl Williams 1.25 .55
❑ 381 Chicago White Sox 2.00 .90
Team Card
❑ 382 Joe Gibbon 1.25 .55
❑ 383 Brant Alyea 1.25 .55
❑ 384 Dave Campbell 2.00 .90
❑ 385 Mickey Stanley 2.00 .90
❑ 386 Jim Colborn 1.25 .55
❑ 387 Horace Clarke 2.00 .90
❑ 388 Charlie Williams 1.25 .55
❑ 389 Bill Rigney MG 1.25 .55
❑ 390 Willie Davis 2.00 .90
❑ 391 Ken Sanders 1.25 .55
❑ 392 Pirates Rookies 2.00 .90
Fred Cambria
Richie Zisk
❑ 393 Curt Motton 1.25 .55
❑ 394 Ken Forsch 2.00 .90
❑ 395 Matty Alou 2.00 .90
❑ 396 Paul Lindblad 1.50 .70
❑ 397 Philadelphia Phillies 2.00 .90
Team Card
❑ 398 Larry Hisle 2.00 .90
❑ 399 Milt Wilcox 2.00 .90
❑ 400 Tony Oliva 4.00 1.80
❑ 401 Jim Nash 1.50 .70
❑ 402 Bobby Heise 1.50 .70
❑ 403 John Cumberland 1.50 .70
❑ 404 Jeff Torborg 2.00 .90

❑ 405 Ron Fairly 2.00 .90
❑ 406 George Hendrick RC 2.00 .90
❑ 407 Chuck Taylor 1.50 .70
❑ 408 Jim Northrup 2.00 .90
❑ 409 Frank Baker 1.50 .70
❑ 410 Ferguson Jenkins 6.00 2.70
❑ 411 Bob Montgomery 1.50 .70
❑ 412 Dick Kelley 1.50 .70
❑ 413 White Sox Rookies 1.50 .70
Don Eddy
Dave Lemonds
❑ 414 Bob Miller 1.50 .70
❑ 415 Cookie Rojas 2.00 .90
❑ 416 Johnny Edwards 1.50 .70
❑ 417 Tom Hall 1.50 .70
❑ 418 Tom Shopay 1.50 .70
❑ 419 Jim Spencer 1.50 .70
❑ 420 Steve Carlton 18.00 8.00
❑ 421 Ellie Rodriguez 1.50 .70
❑ 422 Ray Lamb 1.50 .70
❑ 423 Oscar Gamble 2.00 .90
❑ 424 Bill Gogolewski 1.50 .70
❑ 425 Ken Singleton 2.00 .90
❑ 426 Ken Singleton IA 1.50 .70
❑ 427 Tito Fuentes 1.50 .70
❑ 428 Tito Fuentes IA 1.50 .70
❑ 429 Bob Robertson 1.50 .70
❑ 430 Bob Robertson IA 1.50 .70
❑ 431 Clarence Gaston 2.00 .90
❑ 432 Clarence Gaston IA 2.00 .90
❑ 433 Johnny Bench 25.00 11.00
❑ 434 Johnny Bench IA 15.00 6.75
❑ 435 Reggie Jackson 30.00 13.50
❑ 436 Reggie Jackson IA 12.00 5.50
❑ 437 Maury Wills 2.00 .90
❑ 438 Maury Wills IA 2.00 .90
❑ 439 Billy Williams 6.00 2.70
❑ 440 Billy Williams IA 4.00 1.80
❑ 441 Thurman Munson 15.00 6.75
❑ 442 Thurman Munson IA 8.00 3.60
❑ 443 Ken Henderson 1.50 .70
❑ 444 Ken Henderson IA 1.50 .70
❑ 445 Tom Seaver 30.00 13.50
❑ 446 Tom Seaver IA 15.00 6.75
❑ 447 Willie Stargell 8.00 3.60
❑ 448 Willie Stargell IA 4.00 1.80
❑ 449 Bob Lemon MG 2.00 .90
❑ 450 Mickey Lolich 2.00 .90
❑ 451 Tony LaRussa 4.00 1.80
❑ 452 Ed Herrmann 1.50 .70
❑ 453 Barry Lersch 1.50 .70
❑ 454 Oakland A's 2.00 .90
Team Card
❑ 455 Tommy Harper 2.00 .90
❑ 456 Mark Belanger 2.00 .90
❑ 457 Padres Rookies 1.50 .70
Darcy Fast
Derrel Thomas
Mike Ivie
❑ 458 Aurelio Monteagudo 1.50 .70
❑ 459 Rick Renick 1.50 .70
❑ 460 Al Downing 1.50 .70
❑ 461 Tim Cullen 1.50 .70
❑ 462 Rickey Clark 1.50 .70
❑ 463 Bernie Carbo 1.50 .70
❑ 464 Jim Roland 1.50 .70
❑ 465 Gil Hodges MG 4.00 1.80
❑ 466 Norm Miller 1.50 .70
❑ 467 Steve Kline 1.50 .70
❑ 468 Richie Scheinblum 1.50 .70
❑ 469 Ron Herbel 1.50 .70
❑ 470 Ray Fosse 1.50 .70
❑ 471 Luke Walker 1.50 .70
❑ 472 Phil Gagliano 1.50 .70
❑ 473 Dan McGinn 1.50 .70
❑ 474 Orioles Rookies 15.00 6.75
Don Baylor
Roric Harrison
Johnny Oates RC
❑ 475 Gary Nolan 2.00 .90
❑ 476 Lee Richard 1.50 .70
❑ 477 Tom Phoebus 1.50 .70
❑ 478 Checklist 526-656 6.00 1.20
❑ 479 Don Shaw 1.50 .70
❑ 480 Lee May 2.00 .90
❑ 481 Billy Conigliaro 2.00 .90
❑ 482 Joe Hoerner 1.50 .70
❑ 483 Ken Suarez 1.50 .70
❑ 484 Lum Harris MG 1.50 .70
❑ 485 Phil Regan 2.00 .90
❑ 486 John Lowenstein 1.50 .70
❑ 487 Detroit Tigers 2.00 .90
Team Card
❑ 488 Mike Nagy 1.50 .70
❑ 489 Expos Rookies 1.50 .70
Terry Humphrey
Keith Lampard
❑ 490 Dave McNally 2.00 .90
❑ 491 Lou Piniella KP 2.00 .90
❑ 492 Mel Stottlemyre KP 2.00 .90
❑ 493 Bob Bailey KP 2.00 .90
❑ 494 Willie Horton KP 2.00 .90
❑ 495 Bill Melton KP 2.00 .90
❑ 496 Bud Harrelson KP 2.00 .90
❑ 497 Jim Perry KP 2.00 .90
❑ 498 Brooks Robinson KP 4.00 1.80
❑ 499 Vicente Romo 1.50 .70
❑ 500 Joe Torre 4.00 1.80
❑ 501 Pete Hamm 1.50 .70
❑ 502 Jackie Hernandez 1.50 .70
❑ 503 Gary Peters 1.50 .70
❑ 504 Ed Spiezio 1.50 .70
❑ 505 Mike Marshall 2.00 .90
❑ 506 Indians Rookies 1.50 .70
Terry Ley
Jim Moyer
Dick Tidrow
❑ 507 Fred Gladding 1.50 .70
❑ 508 Elrod Hendricks 1.50 .70
❑ 509 Don McMahon 1.50 .70
❑ 510 Ted Williams MG 12.00 5.50
❑ 511 Tony Taylor 2.00 .90
❑ 512 Paul Popovich 1.50 .70
❑ 513 Lindy McDaniel 2.00 .90
❑ 514 Ted Sizemore 1.50 .70
❑ 515 Bert Blyleven 4.00 1.80
❑ 516 Oscar Brown 1.50 .70
❑ 517 Ken Brett 1.50 .70
❑ 518 Wayne Garrett 1.50 .70
❑ 519 Ted Abernathy 1.50 .70
❑ 520 Larry Bowa 2.00 .90
❑ 521 Alan Foster 1.50 .70
❑ 522 Los Angeles Dodgers 2.00 .90
Team Card
❑ 523 Chuck Dobson 1.50 .70
❑ 524 Reds Rookies 1.50 .70
Ed Armbrister
Mel Behney
❑ 525 Carlos May 2.00 .90
❑ 526 Bob Bailey 6.00 2.70
❑ 527 Dave Leonhard 4.00 1.80
❑ 528 Ron Stone 4.00 1.80
❑ 529 Dave Nelson 6.00 2.70
❑ 530 Don Sutton 12.00 5.50
❑ 531 Freddie Patek 6.00 2.70
❑ 532 Fred Kendall 4.00 1.80
❑ 533 Ralph Houk MG 6.00 2.70
❑ 534 Jim Hickman 6.00 2.70
❑ 535 Ed Brinkman 4.00 1.80
❑ 536 Doug Rader 6.00 2.70
❑ 537 Bob Locker 4.00 1.80
❑ 538 Charlie Sands 4.00 1.80
❑ 539 Terry Forster RC 6.00 2.70
❑ 540 Felix Millan 4.00 1.80
❑ 541 Roger Repoz 4.00 1.80
❑ 542 Jack Billingham 4.00 1.80
❑ 543 Duane Josephson 4.00 1.80
❑ 544 Ted Martinez 4.00 1.80
❑ 545 Wayne Granger 4.00 1.80
❑ 546 Joe Hague 4.00 1.80
❑ 547 Cleveland Indians 8.00 3.60
Team Card
❑ 548 Frank Reberger 4.00 1.80
❑ 549 Dave May 4.00 1.80
❑ 550 Brooks Robinson 25.00 11.00
❑ 551 Ollie Brown 4.00 1.80
❑ 552 Ollie Brown IA 4.00 1.80
❑ 553 Wilbur Wood 6.00 2.70
❑ 554 Wilbur Wood IA 4.00 1.80
❑ 555 Ron Santo 8.00 3.60
❑ 556 Ron Santo IA 6.00 2.70
❑ 557 John Odom 4.00 1.80
❑ 558 John Odom IA 4.00 1.80
❑ 559 Pete Rose 50.00 22.00
❑ 560 Pete Rose IA 20.00 9.00
❑ 561 Leo Cardenas 4.00 1.80
❑ 562 Leo Cardenas IA 4.00 1.80
❑ 563 Ray Sadecki 4.00 1.80
❑ 564 Ray Sadecki IA 4.00 1.80
❑ 565 Reggie Smith 6.00 2.70
❑ 566 Reggie Smith IA 4.00 1.80
❑ 567 Juan Marichal 12.00 5.50
❑ 568 Juan Marichal IA 6.00 2.70
❑ 569 Ed Kirkpatrick 4.00 1.80
❑ 570 Ed Kirkpatrick IA 4.00 1.80
❑ 571 Nate Colbert 4.00 1.80
❑ 572 Nate Colbert IA 4.00 1.80
❑ 573 Fritz Peterson 4.00 1.80
❑ 574 Fritz Peterson IA 4.00 1.80
❑ 575 Al Oliver 8.00 3.60
❑ 576 Leo Durocher MG 6.00 2.70
❑ 577 Mike Paul 6.00 2.70
❑ 578 Billy Grabarkewitz 4.00 1.80
❑ 579 Doyle Alexander RC 6.00 2.70
❑ 580 Lou Piniella 6.00 2.70
❑ 581 Wade Blasingame 4.00 1.80
❑ 582 Montreal Expos 8.00 3.60
Team Card
❑ 583 Darold Knowles 4.00 1.80
❑ 584 Jerry McNertney 4.00 1.80
❑ 585 George Scott 6.00 2.70
❑ 586 Denis Menke 4.00 1.80
❑ 587 Billy Wilson 4.00 1.80
❑ 588 Jim Holt 4.00 1.80
❑ 589 Hal Lanier 4.00 1.80
❑ 590 Graig Nettles 8.00 3.60
❑ 591 Paul Casanova 4.00 1.80
❑ 592 Lew Krausse 4.00 1.80
❑ 593 Rich Morales 4.00 1.80
❑ 594 Jim Beauchamp 4.00 1.80
❑ 595 Nolan Ryan 100.00 55.00
❑ 596 Manny Mota 6.00 2.70
❑ 597 Jim Magnuson 4.00 1.80
❑ 598 Hal King 6.00 2.70
❑ 599 Billy Champion 4.00 1.80
❑ 600 Al Kaline 25.00 11.00
❑ 601 George Stone 4.00 1.80
❑ 602 Dave Bristol MG 4.00 1.80
❑ 603 Jim Ray 4.00 1.80
❑ 604A Checklist 657-787 12.00 2.40
(Copyright on back
bottom right)
❑ 604B Checklist 657-787 12.00 2.40
(Copyright on back
bottom left)
❑ 605 Nelson Briles 6.00 2.70
❑ 606 Luis Melendez 4.00 1.80
❑ 607 Frank Duffy 4.00 1.80
❑ 608 Mike Corkins 4.00 1.80
❑ 609 Tom Grieve 6.00 2.70
❑ 610 Bill Stoneman 6.00 2.70
❑ 611 Rich Reese 4.00 1.80
❑ 612 Joe Decker 4.00 1.80
❑ 613 Mike Ferraro 4.00 1.80
❑ 614 Ted Uhlaender 4.00 1.80
❑ 615 Steve Hargan 4.00 1.80
❑ 616 Joe Ferguson RC 6.00 2.70
❑ 617 Kansas City Royals 8.00 3.60
Team Card
❑ 618 Rich Robertson 4.00 1.80
❑ 619 Rich McKinney 4.00 1.80
❑ 620 Phil Niekro 12.00 5.50
❑ 621 Comm. Award 8.00 3.60
❑ 622 MVP Award 8.00 3.60
❑ 623 Cy Young Award 8.00 3.60
❑ 624 Minor League Player 8.00 3.60
of the Year
❑ 625 Rookie of the Year 8.00 3.60
❑ 626 Babe Ruth Award 8.00 3.60
❑ 627 Moe Drabowsky 4.00 1.80
❑ 628 Terry Crowley 4.00 1.80
❑ 629 Paul Doyle 4.00 1.80
❑ 630 Rich Hebner 6.00 2.70
❑ 631 John Strohmayer 4.00 1.80
❑ 632 Mike Hegan 4.00 1.80
❑ 633 Jack Hiatt 4.00 1.80
❑ 634 Dick Woodson 4.00 1.80
❑ 635 Don Money 6.00 2.70

Card	NRMT	VG-E
❑ 636 Bill Lee	6.00	2.70
❑ 637 Preston Gomez MG	4.00	1.80
❑ 638 Ken Wright	4.00	1.80
❑ 639 J.C. Martin	4.00	1.80
❑ 640 Joe Coleman	4.00	1.80
❑ 641 Mike Lum	4.00	1.80
❑ 642 Dennis Riddleberger	4.00	1.80
❑ 643 Russ Gibson	4.00	1.80
❑ 644 Bernie Allen	4.00	1.80
❑ 645 Jim Maloney	6.00	2.70
❑ 646 Chico Salmon	4.00	1.80
❑ 647 Bob Moose	4.00	1.80
❑ 648 Jim Lyttle	4.00	1.80
❑ 649 Pete Richert	4.00	1.80
❑ 650 Sal Bando	6.00	2.70
❑ 651 Cincinnati Reds	8.00	3.60
Team Card		
❑ 652 Marcelino Lopez	4.00	1.80
❑ 653 Jim Fairey	4.00	1.80
❑ 654 Horacio Pina	6.00	2.70
❑ 655 Jerry Grote	4.00	1.80
❑ 656 Rudy May	4.00	1.80
❑ 657 Bobby Wine	12.00	5.50
❑ 658 Steve Dunning	12.00	5.50
❑ 659 Bob Aspromonte	12.00	5.50
❑ 660 Paul Blair	15.00	6.75
❑ 661 Bill Virdon MG	12.00	5.50
❑ 662 Stan Bahnsen	12.00	5.50
❑ 663 Fran Healy	15.00	6.75
❑ 664 Bobby Knoop	12.00	5.50
❑ 665 Chris Short	12.00	5.50
❑ 666 Hector Torres	12.00	5.50
❑ 667 Ray Newman	12.00	5.50
❑ 668 Texas Rangers	30.00	13.50
Team Card		
❑ 669 Willie Crawford	12.00	5.50
❑ 670 Ken Holtzman	15.00	6.75
❑ 671 Donn Clendenon	15.00	6.75
❑ 672 Archie Reynolds	12.00	5.50
❑ 673 Dave Marshall	12.00	5.50
❑ 674 John Kennedy	12.00	5.50
❑ 675 Pat Jarvis	12.00	5.50
❑ 676 Danny Cater	12.00	5.50
❑ 677 Ivan Murrell	12.00	5.50
❑ 678 Steve Luebber	12.00	5.50
❑ 679 Astros Rookies	12.00	5.50
Bob Fenwick		
Bob Stinson		
❑ 680 Dave Johnson	15.00	6.75
❑ 681 Bobby Pfeil	12.00	5.50
❑ 682 Mike McCormick	15.00	6.75
❑ 683 Steve Hovley	12.00	5.50
❑ 684 Hal Breeden	12.00	5.50
❑ 685 Joel Horlen	12.00	5.50
❑ 686 Steve Garvey	40.00	18.00
❑ 687 Del Unser	12.00	5.50
❑ 688 St. Louis Cardinals	20.00	9.00
Team Card		
❑ 689 Eddie Fisher	12.00	5.50
❑ 690 Willie Montanez	15.00	6.75
❑ 691 Curt Blefary	12.00	5.50
❑ 692 Curt Blefary IA	12.00	5.50
❑ 693 Alan Gallagher	12.00	5.50
❑ 694 Alan Gallagher IA	12.00	5.50
❑ 695 Rod Carew	50.00	22.00
❑ 696 Rod Carew IA	30.00	13.50
❑ 697 Jerry Koosman	15.00	6.75
❑ 698 Jerry Koosman IA	15.00	6.75
❑ 699 Bobby Murcer	15.00	6.75
❑ 700 Bobby Murcer IA	15.00	6.75
❑ 701 Jose Pagan	12.00	5.50
❑ 702 Jose Pagan IA	12.00	5.50
❑ 703 Doug Griffin	12.00	5.50
❑ 704 Doug Griffin IA	12.00	5.50
❑ 705 Pat Corrales	15.00	6.75
❑ 706 Pat Corrales IA	12.00	5.50
❑ 707 Tim Foli	12.00	5.50
❑ 708 Tim Foli IA	12.00	5.50
❑ 709 Jim Kaat	15.00	6.75
❑ 710 Jim Kaat IA	15.00	6.75
❑ 711 Bobby Bonds	20.00	9.00
❑ 712 Bobby Bonds IA	15.00	6.75
❑ 713 Gene Michael	20.00	9.00
❑ 714 Gene Michael IA	15.00	6.75
❑ 715 Mike Epstein	12.00	5.50
❑ 716 Jesus Alou	12.00	5.50
❑ 717 Bruce Dal Canton	12.00	5.50
❑ 718 Del Rice MG	12.00	5.50
❑ 719 Cesar Geronimo	12.00	5.50
❑ 720 Sam McDowell	15.00	6.75
❑ 721 Eddie Leon	12.00	5.50
❑ 722 Bill Sudakis	12.00	5.50
❑ 723 Al Santorini	12.00	5.50
❑ 724 AL Rookie Pitchers	12.00	5.50
John Curtis		
Rich Hinton		
Mickey Scott RC		
❑ 725 Dick McAuliffe	15.00	6.75
❑ 726 Dick Selma	12.00	5.50
❑ 727 Jose Laboy	12.00	5.50
❑ 728 Gail Hopkins	12.00	5.50
❑ 729 Bob Veale	15.00	6.75
❑ 730 Rick Monday	15.00	6.75
❑ 731 Baltimore Orioles	20.00	9.00
Team Card		
❑ 732 George Culver	12.00	5.50
❑ 733 Jim Ray Hart	15.00	6.75
❑ 734 Bob Burda	12.00	5.50
❑ 735 Diego Segui	12.00	5.50
❑ 736 Bill Russell	15.00	6.75
❑ 737 Len Randle	15.00	6.75
❑ 738 Jim Merritt	12.00	5.50
❑ 739 Don Mason	12.00	5.50
❑ 740 Rico Carty	15.00	6.75
❑ 741 Rookie First Basemen	15.00	6.75
Tom Hutton		
John Milner		
Rick Miller RC		
❑ 742 Jim Rooker	12.00	5.50
❑ 743 Cesar Gutierrez	12.00	5.50
❑ 744 Jim Slaton	12.00	5.50
❑ 745 Julian Javier	15.00	6.75
❑ 746 Lowell Palmer	12.00	5.50
❑ 747 Jim Stewart	12.00	5.50
❑ 748 Phil Hennigan	12.00	5.50
❑ 749 Walter Alston MG	20.00	9.00
❑ 750 Willie Horton	15.00	6.75
❑ 751 Steve Carlton TR	40.00	18.00
❑ 752 Joe Morgan TR	45.00	20.00
❑ 753 Denny McLain TR	20.00	9.00
❑ 754 Frank Robinson TR	45.00	20.00
❑ 755 Jim Fregosi TR	15.00	6.75
❑ 756 Rick Wise TR	15.00	6.75
❑ 757 Jose Cardenal TR	15.00	6.75
❑ 758 Gil Garrido	12.00	5.50
❑ 759 Chris Cannizzaro	12.00	5.50
❑ 760 Bill Mazeroski	25.00	11.00
❑ 761 Rookie Outfielders	25.00	11.00
Ben Oglivie		
Ron Cey RC		
Bernie Williams		
❑ 762 Wayne Simpson	12.00	5.50
❑ 763 Ron Hansen	12.00	5.50
❑ 764 Dusty Baker	20.00	9.00
❑ 765 Ken McMullen	12.00	5.50
❑ 766 Steve Hamilton	12.00	5.50
❑ 767 Tom McCraw	15.00	6.75
❑ 768 Denny Doyle	12.00	5.50
❑ 769 Jack Aker	12.00	5.50
❑ 770 Jim Wynn	15.00	6.75
❑ 771 San Francisco Giants	20.00	9.00
Team Card		
❑ 772 Ken Tatum	12.00	5.50
❑ 773 Ron Brand	12.00	5.50
❑ 774 Luis Alvarado	12.00	5.50
❑ 775 Jerry Reuss	15.00	6.75
❑ 776 Bill Voss	12.00	5.50
❑ 777 Hoyt Wilhelm	25.00	11.00
❑ 778 Twins Rookies	20.00	9.00
Vic Albury		
Rick Dempsey RC		
Jim Strickland		
❑ 779 Tony Cloninger	12.00	5.50
❑ 780 Dick Green	12.00	5.50
❑ 781 Jim McAndrew	12.00	5.50
❑ 782 Larry Stahl	12.00	5.50
❑ 783 Les Cain	12.00	5.50
❑ 784 Ken Aspromonte	12.00	5.50
❑ 785 Vic Davalillo	12.00	5.50
❑ 786 Chuck Brinkman	12.00	5.50
❑ 787 Ron Reed	15.00	5.25

1973 Topps

	NRMT	VG-E
COMPLETE SET (660)	700.00	325.00
COMMON CARD (1-264)	.50	.23
COMMON CARD (265-396)	.75	.35
COMMON CARD (397-528)	1.25	.55
COMMON CARD (529-660)	3.50	1.55
WRAPPER (10-CENT, BAT)	15.00	6.75
WRAPPER (10-CENT)	15.00	6.75
❑ 1 All-Time HR Leaders	40.00	11.50
Babe Ruth 714		
Hank Aaron 673		
Willie Mays 654		
❑ 2 Rich Hebner	1.50	.70
❑ 3 Jim Lonborg	1.50	.70
❑ 4 John Milner	.50	.23
❑ 5 Ed Brinkman	.50	.23
❑ 6 Mac Scarce	.50	.23
❑ 7 Texas Rangers	2.00	.90
Team Card		
❑ 8 Tom Hall	.50	.23
❑ 9 Johnny Oates	.50	.23
❑ 10 Don Sutton	4.00	1.80
❑ 11 Chris Chambliss	1.50	.70
❑ 12A Padres Leaders	3.00	1.35
Don Zimmer MG		
Dave Garcia CO		
Johnny Podres CO		
Bob Skinner CO		
Whitey Wietelmann CO		
(Podres no right ear)		
❑ 12B Padres Leaders	.75	.35
(Podres has right ear)		
❑ 13 George Hendrick	1.50	.70
❑ 14 Sonny Siebert	.50	.23
❑ 15 Ralph Garr	1.50	.70
❑ 16 Steve Braun	.50	.23
❑ 17 Fred Gladding	.50	.23
❑ 18 Leroy Stanton	.50	.23
❑ 19 Tim Foli	.50	.23
❑ 20 Stan Bahnsen	.50	.23
❑ 21 Randy Hundley	1.50	.70
❑ 22 Ted Abernathy	.50	.23
❑ 23 Dave Kingman	1.50	.70
❑ 24 Al Santorini	.50	.23
❑ 25 Roy White	1.50	.70
❑ 26 Pittsburgh Pirates	2.00	.90
Team Card		
❑ 27 Bill Gogolewski	.50	.23
❑ 28 Hal McRae	1.50	.70
❑ 29 Tony Taylor	1.50	.70
❑ 30 Tug McGraw	1.50	.70
❑ 31 Buddy Bell RC	2.50	1.10
❑ 32 Fred Norman	.50	.23
❑ 33 Jim Breazeale	.50	.23
❑ 34 Pat Dobson	.50	.23
❑ 35 Willie Davis	1.50	.70
❑ 36 Steve Barber	.50	.23
❑ 37 Bill Robinson	1.50	.70
❑ 38 Mike Epstein	.50	.23
❑ 39 Dave Roberts	.50	.23
❑ 40 Reggie Smith	1.50	.70
❑ 41 Tom Walker	.50	.23
❑ 42 Mike Andrews	.50	.23
❑ 43 Randy Moffitt	.50	.23
❑ 44 Rick Monday	1.50	.70

	No.	Card	Price	Price
❑	45	Ellie Rodriguez UER	.50	.23
		(Photo actually John Felske)		
❑	46	Lindy McDaniel	1.50	.70
❑	47	Luis Melendez	.50	.23
❑	48	Paul Splittorff	.50	.23
❑	49A	Twins Leaders	3.00	1.35
		Frank Quilici MG		
		Vern Morgan CO		
		Bob Rodgers CO		
		Ralph Rowe CO		
		Al Worthington CO		
		(Solid backgrounds)		
❑	49B	Twins Leaders	.75	.35
		(Natural backgrounds)		
❑	50	Roberto Clemente	50.00	22.00
❑	51	Chuck Seelbach	.50	.23
❑	52	Denis Menke	.50	.23
❑	53	Steve Dunning	.50	.23
❑	54	Checklist 1-132	3.00	.60
❑	55	Jon Matlack	1.50	.70
❑	56	Merv Rettenmund	.50	.23
❑	57	Derrel Thomas	.50	.23
❑	58	Mike Paul	.50	.23
❑	59	Steve Yeager RC	1.50	.70
❑	60	Ken Holtzman	1.50	.70
❑	61	Batting Leaders	2.50	1.10
		Billy Williams		
		Rod Carew		
❑	62	Home Run Leaders	2.50	1.10
		Johnny Bench		
		Dick Allen		
❑	63	RBI Leaders	2.50	1.10
		Johnny Bench		
		Dick Allen		
❑	64	Stolen Base Leaders	1.50	.70
		Lou Brock		
		Bert Campaneris		
❑	65	ERA Leaders	1.50	.70
		Steve Carlton		
		Luis Tiant		
❑	66	Victory Leaders	1.50	.70
		Steve Carlton		
		Gaylord Perry		
		Wilbur Wood		
❑	67	Strikeout Leaders	30.00	13.50
		Steve Carlton		
		Nolan Ryan		
❑	68	Leading Firemen	1.50	.70
		Clay Carroll		
		Sparky Lyle		
❑	69	Phil Gagliano	.50	.23
❑	70	Milt Pappas	1.50	.70
❑	71	Johnny Briggs	.50	.23
❑	72	Ron Reed	.50	.23
❑	73	Ed Herrmann	.50	.23
❑	74	Billy Champion	.50	.23
❑	75	Vada Pinson	1.50	.70
❑	76	Doug Rader	.50	.23
❑	77	Mike Torrez	1.50	.70
❑	78	Richie Scheinblum	.50	.23
❑	79	Jim Willoughby	.50	.23
❑	80	Tony Oliva UER	2.50	1.10
		(Minnseota on front)		
❑	81A	Cubs Leaders	1.50	.70
		Whitey Lockman MG		
		Hank Aguirre CO		
		Ernie Banks CO		
		Larry Jansen CO		
		Pete Reiser CO		
		(Solid backgrounds)		
❑	81B	Cubs Leaders	1.50	.70
		(Natural backgrounds)		
❑	82	Fritz Peterson	.50	.23
❑	83	Leron Lee	.50	.23
❑	84	Rollie Fingers	4.00	1.80
❑	85	Ted Simmons	1.50	.70
❑	86	Tom McCraw	.50	.23
❑	87	Ken Boswell	.50	.23
❑	88	Mickey Stanley	1.50	.70
❑	89	Jack Billingham	.50	.23
❑	90	Brooks Robinson	7.00	3.10
❑	91	Los Angeles Dodgers	2.00	.90
		Team Card		
❑	92	Jerry Bell	.50	.23
❑	93	Jesus Alou	.50	.23
❑	94	Dick Billings	.50	.23
❑	95	Steve Blass	1.50	.70
❑	96	Doug Griffin	.50	.23
❑	97	Willie Montanez	1.50	.70
❑	98	Dick Woodson	.50	.23
❑	99	Carl Taylor	.50	.23
❑	100	Hank Aaron	25.00	11.00
❑	101	Ken Henderson	.50	.23
❑	102	Rudy May	.50	.23
❑	103	Celerino Sanchez	.50	.23
❑	104	Reggie Cleveland	.50	.23
❑	105	Carlos May	.50	.23
❑	106	Terry Humphrey	.50	.23
❑	107	Phil Hennigan	.50	.23
❑	108	Bill Russell	1.50	.70
❑	109	Doyle Alexander	1.50	.70
❑	110	Bob Watson	1.50	.70
❑	111	Dave Nelson	.50	.23
❑	112	Gary Ross	.50	.23
❑	113	Jerry Grote	.50	.23
❑	114	Lynn McGlothen	.50	.23
❑	115	Ron Santo	1.50	.70
❑	116A	Yankees Leaders	3.00	1.35
		Ralph Houk MG		
		Jim Hegan CO		
		Elston Howard CO		
		Dick Howser CO		
		Jim Turner CO		
		(Solid backgrounds)		
❑	116B	Yankees Leaders	.75	.35
		(Natural backgrounds)		
❑	117	Ramon Hernandez	.50	.23
❑	118	John Mayberry	1.50	.70
❑	119	Larry Bowa	1.50	.70
❑	120	Joe Coleman	.50	.23
❑	121	Dave Rader	.50	.23
❑	122	Jim Strickland	.50	.23
❑	123	Sandy Alomar	1.50	.70
❑	124	Jim Hardin	.50	.23
❑	125	Ron Fairly	1.50	.70
❑	126	Jim Brewer	.50	.23
❑	127	Milwaukee Brewers	2.00	.90
		Team Card		
❑	128	Ted Sizemore	.50	.23
❑	129	Terry Forster	1.50	.70
❑	130	Pete Rose	20.00	9.00
❑	131A	Red Sox Leaders	3.00	1.35
		Eddie Kasko MG		
		Doug Camilli CO		
		Don Lenhardt CO		
		Eddie Popowski CO		
		(No right ear)		
		Lee Stange CO		
❑	131B	Red Sox Leaders	1.50	.70
		(Popowski has right ear showing)		
❑	132	Matty Alou	1.50	.70
❑	133	Dave Roberts	.50	.23
❑	134	Milt Wilcox	.50	.23
❑	135	Lee May UER	1.50	.70
		(Career average .000)		
❑	136A	Orioles Leaders	2.00	.90
		Earl Weaver MG		
		George Bamberger CO		
		Jim Frey CO		
		Billy Hunter CO		
		George Staller CO		
		(Orange backgrounds)		
❑	136B	Orioles Leaders	3.00	1.35
		(Dark pale backgrounds)		
❑	137	Jim Beauchamp	.50	.23
❑	138	Horacio Pina	.50	.23
❑	139	Carmen Fanzone	.50	.23
❑	140	Lou Piniella	2.50	1.10
❑	141	Bruce Kison	.50	.23
❑	142	Thurman Munson	6.00	2.70
❑	143	John Curtis	.50	.23
❑	144	Marty Perez	.50	.23
❑	145	Bobby Bonds	2.50	1.10
❑	146	Woodie Fryman	.50	.23
❑	147	Mike Anderson	.50	.23
❑	148	Dave Goltz	.50	.23
❑	149	Ron Hunt	.50	.23
❑	150	Wilbur Wood	1.50	.70
❑	151	Wes Parker	1.50	.70
❑	152	Dave May	.50	.23
❑	153	Al Hrabosky	1.50	.70
❑	154	Jeff Torborg	1.50	.70
❑	155	Sal Bando	1.50	.70
❑	156	Cesar Geronimo	.50	.23
❑	157	Denny Riddleberger	.50	.23
❑	158	Houston Astros	2.00	.90
		Team Card		
❑	159	Clarence Gaston	1.50	.70
❑	160	Jim Palmer	7.00	3.10
❑	161	Ted Martinez	.50	.23
❑	162	Pete Broberg	.50	.23
❑	163	Vic Davalillo	.50	.23
❑	164	Monty Montgomery	.50	.23
❑	165	Luis Aparicio	4.00	1.80
❑	166	Terry Harmon	.50	.23
❑	167	Steve Stone	1.50	.70
❑	168	Jim Northrup	1.50	.70
❑	169	Ron Schueler RC	1.50	.70
❑	170	Harmon Killebrew	5.00	2.20
❑	171	Bernie Carbo	.50	.23
❑	172	Steve Kline	.50	.23
❑	173	Hal Breeden	.50	.23
❑	174	Rich Gossage RC	6.00	2.70
❑	175	Frank Robinson	7.00	3.10
❑	176	Chuck Taylor	.50	.23
❑	177	Bill Plummer	.50	.23
❑	178	Don Rose	.50	.23
❑	179A	A's Leaders	4.00	1.80
		Dick Williams MG		
		Jerry Adair CO		
		Vern Hoscheit CO		
		Irv Noren CO		
		Wes Stock CO		
		(Hoscheit left ear showing)		
❑	179B	A's Leaders	1.50	.70
		(Hoscheit left ear not showing)		
❑	180	Ferguson Jenkins	4.00	1.80
❑	181	Jack Brohamer	.50	.23
❑	182	Mike Caldwell	1.50	.70
❑	183	Don Buford	.50	.23
❑	184	Jerry Koosman	1.50	.70
❑	185	Jim Wynn	1.50	.70
❑	186	Bill Fahey	.50	.23
❑	187	Luke Walker	.50	.23
❑	188	Cookie Rojas	1.50	.70
❑	189	Greg Luzinski	2.50	1.10
❑	190	Bob Gibson	7.00	3.10
❑	191	Detroit Tigers	2.50	1.10
		Team Card		
❑	192	Pat Jarvis	.50	.23
❑	193	Carlton Fisk	10.00	4.50
❑	194	Jorge Orta	.50	.23
❑	195	Clay Carroll	.50	.23
❑	196	Ken McMullen	.50	.23
❑	197	Ed Goodson	.50	.23
❑	198	Horace Clarke	.50	.23
❑	199	Bert Blyleven	2.50	1.10
❑	200	Billy Williams	4.00	1.80
❑	201	G. Hendrick ALCS	1.50	.70
❑	202	George Foster NLCS	1.50	.70
❑	203	Gene Tenace WS	1.50	.70
❑	204	World Series Game 2	1.50	.70
		A's two straight		
❑	205	Tony Perez WS	2.50	1.10
❑	206	Gene Tenace WS	1.50	.70
❑	207	Blue Moon Odom WS	1.50	.70
❑	208	Johnny Bench WS6	5.00	2.20
❑	209	Bert Campaneris WS	1.50	.70
❑	210	W.S. Summary	.50	.23
		World champions: A's Win		
❑	211	Balor Moore	.50	.23
❑	212	Joe Lahoud	.50	.23
❑	213	Steve Garvey	5.00	2.20
❑	214	Dave Hamilton	.50	.23
❑	215	Dusty Baker	2.50	1.10
❑	216	Toby Harrah	1.50	.70
❑	217	Don Wilson	.50	.23
❑	218	Aurelio Rodriguez	.50	.23
❑	219	St. Louis Cardinals	2.50	1.10
		Team Card		
❑	220	Nolan Ryan	60.00	27.00
❑	221	Fred Kendall	.50	.23

❑ 222 Rob Gardner .50 .23
❑ 223 Bud Harrelson 1.50 .70
❑ 224 Bill Lee 1.50 .70
❑ 225 Al Oliver 1.50 .70
❑ 226 Ray Fosse .50 .23
❑ 227 Wayne Twitchell .50 .23
❑ 228 Bobby Darwin .50 .23
❑ 229 Roric Harrison .50 .23
❑ 230 Joe Morgan 6.00 2.70
❑ 231 Bill Parsons .50 .23
❑ 232 Ken Singleton 1.50 .70
❑ 233 Ed Kirkpatrick .50 .23
❑ 234 Bill North .50 .23
❑ 235 Jim Hunter 4.00 1.80
❑ 236 Tito Fuentes .50 .23
❑ 237A Braves Leaders 1.50 .70
Eddie Mathews MG
Lew Burdette CO
Jim Busby CO
Roy Hartsfield CO
Ken Silvestri CO
(Burdette right ear
showing)
❑ 237B Braves Leaders 3.00 1.35
(Burdette right ear
not showing)
❑ 238 Tony Muser .50 .23
❑ 239 Pete Richert .50 .23
❑ 240 Bobby Murcer 1.50 .70
❑ 241 Dwain Anderson .50 .23
❑ 242 George Culver .50 .23
❑ 243 California Angels 2.50 1.10
Team Card
❑ 244 Ed Acosta .50 .23
❑ 245 Carl Yastrzemski 8.00 3.60
❑ 246 Ken Sanders .50 .23
❑ 247 Del Unser .50 .23
❑ 248 Jerry Johnson .50 .23
❑ 249 Larry Biittner .50 .23
❑ 250 Manny Sanguillen 1.50 .70
❑ 251 Roger Nelson .50 .23
❑ 252A Giants Leaders 4.00 1.80
Charlie Fox MG
Joe Amalfitano CO
Andy Gilbert CO
Don McMahon CO
John McNamara CO
(Orange backgrounds)
❑ 252B Giants Leaders 1.50 .70
(Dark pale
backgrounds)
❑ 253 Mark Belanger 1.50 .70
❑ 254 Bill Stoneman .50 .23
❑ 255 Reggie Jackson 15.00 6.75
❑ 256 Chris Zachary .50 .23
❑ 257A Mets Leaders 2.50 1.10
Yogi Berra MG
Roy McMillan CO
Joe Pignatano CO
Rube Walker CO
Eddie Yost CO
(Orange backgrounds)
❑ 257B Mets Leaders 5.00 2.20
(Dark pale
backgrounds)
❑ 258 Tommy John 1.50 .70
❑ 259 Jim Holt .50 .23
❑ 260 Gary Nolan 1.50 .70
❑ 261 Pat Kelly .50 .23
❑ 262 Jack Aker .50 .23
❑ 263 George Scott 1.50 .70
❑ 264 Checklist 133-264 3.00 .60
❑ 265 Gene Michael 1.50 .70
❑ 266 Mike Lum .75 .35
❑ 267 Lloyd Allen .75 .35
❑ 268 Jerry Morales .75 .35
❑ 269 Tim McCarver 1.50 .70
❑ 270 Luis Tiant 1.50 .70
❑ 271 Tom Hutton .75 .35
❑ 272 Ed Farmer .75 .35
❑ 273 Chris Speier .75 .35
❑ 274 Darold Knowles .75 .35
❑ 275 Tony Perez 4.00 1.80
❑ 276 Joe Lovitto .75 .35
❑ 277 Bob Miller .75 .35
❑ 278 Baltimore Orioles 1.50 .70
Team Card
❑ 279 Mike Strahler .75 .35
❑ 280 Al Kaline 7.00 3.10
❑ 281 Mike Jorgensen .75 .35
❑ 282 Steve Hovley .75 .35
❑ 283 Ray Sadecki .75 .35
❑ 284 Glenn Borgmann .75 .35
❑ 285 Don Kessinger .75 .35
❑ 286 Frank Linzy .75 .35
❑ 287 Eddie Leon .75 .35
❑ 288 Gary Gentry .75 .35
❑ 289 Bob Oliver .75 .35
❑ 290 Cesar Cedeno 1.50 .70
❑ 291 Rogelio Moret .75 .35
❑ 292 Jose Cruz 1.50 .70
❑ 293 Bernie Allen .75 .35
❑ 294 Steve Arlin .75 .35
❑ 295 Bert Campaneris 1.50 .70
❑ 296 Reds Leaders 2.50 1.10
Sparky Anderson MG
Alex Grammas CO
Ted Kluszewski CO
George Scherger CO
Larry Shepard CO
❑ 297 Walt Williams .75 .35
❑ 298 Ron Bryant .75 .35
❑ 299 Ted Ford .75 .35
❑ 300 Steve Carlton 10.00 4.50
❑ 301 Billy Grabarkewitz .75 .35
❑ 302 Terry Crowley .75 .35
❑ 303 Nelson Briles .75 .35
❑ 304 Duke Sims .75 .35
❑ 305 Willie Mays 40.00 18.00
❑ 306 Tom Burgmeier .75 .35
❑ 307 Boots Day .75 .35
❑ 308 Skip Lockwood .75 .35
❑ 309 Paul Popovich .75 .35
❑ 310 Dick Allen 1.50 .70
❑ 311 Joe Decker .75 .35
❑ 312 Oscar Brown .75 .35
❑ 313 Jim Ray .75 .35
❑ 314 Ron Swoboda 1.50 .70
❑ 315 John Odom .75 .35
❑ 316 San Diego Padres 1.50 .70
Team Card
❑ 317 Danny Cater .75 .35
❑ 318 Jim McGlothlin .75 .35
❑ 319 Jim Spencer .75 .35
❑ 320 Lou Brock 7.00 3.10
❑ 321 Rich Hinton .75 .35
❑ 322 Garry Maddox RC 1.50 .70
❑ 323 Tigers Leaders 1.50 .70
Billy Martin MG
Art Fowler CO
Charlie Silvera CO
Dick Tracewski CO
❑ 324 Al Downing .75 .35
❑ 325 Boog Powell 1.50 .70
❑ 326 Darrell Brandon .75 .35
❑ 327 John Lowenstein .75 .35
❑ 328 Bill Bonham .75 .35
❑ 329 Ed Kranepool 1.50 .70
❑ 330 Rod Carew 7.00 3.10
❑ 331 Carl Morton .75 .35
❑ 332 John Felske .75 .35
❑ 333 Gene Clines .75 .35
❑ 334 Freddie Patek .75 .35
❑ 335 Bob Tolan .75 .35
❑ 336 Tom Bradley .75 .35
❑ 337 Dave Duncan .75 .35
❑ 338 Checklist 265-396 3.00 .60
❑ 339 Dick Tidrow .75 .35
❑ 340 Nate Colbert .75 .35
❑ 341 Jim Palmer KP 2.50 1.10
❑ 342 Sam McDowell KP .75 .35
❑ 343 Bobby Murcer KP .75 .35
❑ 344 Jim Hunter KP 2.50 1.10
❑ 345 Chris Speier KP .75 .35
❑ 346 Gaylord Perry KP 1.50 .70
❑ 347 Kansas City Royals 1.50 .70
Team Card
❑ 348 Rennie Stennett .75 .35
❑ 349 Dick McAuliffe .75 .35
❑ 350 Tom Seaver 12.00 5.50
❑ 351 Jimmy Stewart .75 .35
❑ 352 Don Stanhouse .75 .35
❑ 353 Steve Brye .75 .35
❑ 354 Billy Parker .75 .35
❑ 355 Mike Marshall 1.50 .70
❑ 356 White Sox Leaders 4.00 1.80
Chuck Tanner MG
Joe Lonnett CO
Jim Mahoney CO
Al Monchak CO
Johnny Sain CO
❑ 357 Ross Grimsley .75 .35
❑ 358 Jim Nettles .75 .35
❑ 359 Cecil Upshaw .75 .35
❑ 360 Joe Rudi UER 1.50 .70
(Photo actually
Gene Tenace)
❑ 361 Fran Healy .75 .35
❑ 362 Eddie Watt .75 .35
❑ 363 Jackie Hernandez .75 .35
❑ 364 Rick Wise .75 .35
❑ 365 Rico Petrocelli 1.50 .70
❑ 366 Brock Davis .75 .35
❑ 367 Burt Hooton .75 .35
❑ 368 Bill Buckner 1.50 .70
❑ 369 Lerrin LaGrow .75 .35
❑ 370 Willie Stargell 5.00 2.20
❑ 371 Mike Kekich .75 .35
❑ 372 Oscar Gamble .75 .35
❑ 373 Clyde Wright .75 .35
❑ 374 Darrell Evans 1.50 .70
❑ 375 Larry Dierker 1.50 .70
❑ 376 Frank Duffy .75 .35
❑ 377 Expos Leaders 4.00 1.80
Gene Mauch MG
Dave Bristol CO
Larry Doby CO
Cal McLish CO
Jerry Zimmerman CO
❑ 378 Len Randle .75 .35
❑ 379 Cy Acosta .75 .35
❑ 380 Johnny Bench 12.00 5.50
❑ 381 Vicente Romo .75 .35
❑ 382 Mike Hegan .75 .35
❑ 383 Diego Segui .75 .35
❑ 384 Don Baylor 4.00 1.80
❑ 385 Jim Perry 1.50 .70
❑ 386 Don Money .75 .35
❑ 387 Jim Barr .75 .35
❑ 388 Ben Oglivie 1.50 .70
❑ 389 New York Mets 4.00 1.80
Team Card
❑ 390 Mickey Lolich 1.50 .70
❑ 391 Lee Lacy RC .75 .35
❑ 392 Dick Drago .75 .35
❑ 393 Jose Cardenal .75 .35
❑ 394 Sparky Lyle 1.50 .70
❑ 395 Roger Metzger .75 .35
❑ 396 Grant Jackson .75 .35
❑ 397 Dave Cash 1.25 .55
❑ 398 Rich Hand 1.25 .55
❑ 399 George Foster 2.00 .90
❑ 400 Gaylord Perry 5.00 2.20
❑ 401 Clyde Mashore 1.25 .55
❑ 402 Jack Hiatt 1.25 .55
❑ 403 Sonny Jackson 1.25 .55
❑ 404 Chuck Brinkman 1.25 .55
❑ 405 Cesar Tovar 1.25 .55
❑ 406 Paul Lindblad 1.25 .55
❑ 407 Felix Millan 1.25 .55
❑ 408 Jim Colborn 1.25 .55
❑ 409 Ivan Murrell 1.25 .55
❑ 410 Willie McCovey 6.00 2.70
(Bench behind plate)
❑ 411 Ray Corbin 1.25 .55
❑ 412 Manny Mota 2.00 .90
❑ 413 Tom Timmermann 1.25 .55
❑ 414 Ken Rudolph 1.25 .55
❑ 415 Marty Pattin 1.25 .55
❑ 416 Paul Schaal 1.25 .55
❑ 417 Scipio Spinks 1.25 .55
❑ 418 Bob Grich 2.00 .90
❑ 419 Casey Cox 1.25 .55
❑ 420 Tommie Agee 1.25 .55
❑ 421A Angels Leaders 1.50 .70
Bobby Winkles MG
Tom Morgan CO
Salty Parker CO

Jimmie Reese CO
John Roseboro CO
(Orange backgrounds)
❑ 421B Angels Leaders 3.00 1.35
(Dark pale
backgrounds)
❑ 422 Bob Robertson .... 1.25 .55
❑ 423 Johnny Jeter .... 1.25 .55
❑ 424 Denny Doyle .... 1.25 .55
❑ 425 Alex Johnson .... 1.25 .55
❑ 426 Dave LaRoche .... 1.25 .55
❑ 427 Rick Auerbach .... 1.25 .55
❑ 428 Wayne Simpson .... 1.25 .55
❑ 429 Jim Fairey .... 1.25 .55
❑ 430 Vida Blue .... 2.00 .90
❑ 431 Gerry Moses .... 1.25 .55
❑ 432 Dan Frisella .... 1.25 .55
❑ 433 Willie Horton .... 2.00 .90
❑ 434 San Francisco Giants .. 3.00 1.35
Team Card
❑ 435 Rico Carty .... 2.00 .90
❑ 436 Jim McAndrew .... 1.25 .55
❑ 437 John Kennedy .... 1.25 .55
❑ 438 Enzo Hernandez .... 1.25 .55
❑ 439 Eddie Fisher .... 1.25 .55
❑ 440 Glenn Beckert .... 1.25 .55
❑ 441 Gail Hopkins .... 1.25 .55
❑ 442 Dick Dietz .... 1.25 .55
❑ 443 Danny Thompson .... 1.25 .55
❑ 444 Ken Brett .... 1.25 .55
❑ 445 Ken Berry .... 1.25 .55
❑ 446 Jerry Reuss .... 2.00 .90
❑ 447 Joe Hague .... 1.25 .55
❑ 448 John Hiller .... 1.25 .55
❑ 449A Indians Leaders 4.00 1.80
Ken Aspromonte MG
Rocky Colavito CO
Joe Lutz CO
Warren Spahn CO
(Spahn's right
ear pointed)
❑ 449B Indians Leaders 4.00 1.80
(Spahn's right
ear round)
❑ 450 Joe Torre 3.00 1.35
❑ 451 John Vukovich .... 1.25 .55
❑ 452 Paul Casanova .... 1.25 .55
❑ 453 Checklist 397-528 .... 3.00 .60
❑ 454 Tom Haller .... 1.25 .55
❑ 455 Bill Melton .... 1.25 .55
❑ 456 Dick Green .... 1.25 .55
❑ 457 John Strohmayer .... 1.25 .55
❑ 458 Jim Mason .... 1.25 .55
❑ 459 Jimmy Howarth .... 1.25 .55
❑ 460 Bill Freehan .... 2.00 .90
❑ 461 Mike Corkins .... 1.25 .55
❑ 462 Ron Blomberg .... 1.25 .55
❑ 463 Ken Tatum .... 1.25 .55
❑ 464 Chicago Cubs 3.00 1.35
Team Card
❑ 465 Dave Giusti .... 1.25 .55
❑ 466 Jose Arcia .... 1.25 .55
❑ 467 Mike Ryan .... 1.25 .55
❑ 468 Tom Griffin .... 1.25 .55
❑ 469 Dan Monzon .... 1.25 .55
❑ 470 Mike Cuellar .... 2.00 .90
❑ 471 Ty Cobb ATL 10.00 4.50
4191 Hits
❑ 472 Lou Gehrig ATL 15.00 6.75
23 Grand Slams
❑ 473 Hank Aaron ATL 10.00 4.50
6172 Total Bases
❑ 474 Babe Ruth ATL 20.00 9.00
2209 RBI
❑ 475 Ty Cobb ATL 8.00 3.60
.367 Batting Average
❑ 476 Walter Johnson ATL 3.00 1.35
113 Shutouts
❑ 477 Cy Young ATL 3.00 1.35
511 Victories
❑ 478 Walter Johnson ATL 3.00 1.35
3508 Strikeouts
❑ 479 Hal Lanier .... 1.25 .55
❑ 480 Juan Marichal 5.00 2.20
❑ 481 Chicago White Sox 3.00 1.35
Team Card

❑ 482 Rick Reuschel RC 3.00 1.35
❑ 483 Dal Maxvill .... 1.25 .55
❑ 484 Ernie McAnally .... 1.25 .55
❑ 485 Norm Cash .... 2.00 .90
❑ 486A Phillies Leaders .... 1.50 .70
Danny Ozark MG
Carroll Beringer CO
Billy DeMars CO
Ray Rippelmeyer CO
Bobby Wine CO
(Orange backgrounds)
❑ 486B Phillies Leaders 3.00 1.35
(Dark pale
backgrounds)
❑ 487 Bruce Dal Canton .... 1.25 .55
❑ 488 Dave Campbell .... 2.00 .90
❑ 489 Jeff Burroughs .... 2.00 .90
❑ 490 Claude Osteen .... 1.25 .55
❑ 491 Bob Montgomery .... 1.25 .55
❑ 492 Pedro Borbon .... 1.25 .55
❑ 493 Duffy Dyer .... 1.25 .55
❑ 494 Rich Morales .... 1.25 .55
❑ 495 Tommy Helms .... 1.25 .55
❑ 496 Ray Lamb .... 1.25 .55
❑ 497A Cardinals Leaders .... 2.00 .90
Red Schoendienst MG
Vern Benson CO
George Kissell CO
Barney Schultz CO
(Orange backgrounds)
❑ 497B Cardinals Leaders 3.00 1.35
(Dark pale
backgrounds)
❑ 498 Graig Nettles 3.00 1.35
❑ 499 Bob Moose .... 1.25 .55
❑ 500 Oakland A's 3.00 1.35
Team Card
❑ 501 Larry Gura .... 1.25 .55
❑ 502 Bobby Valentine 3.00 1.35
❑ 503 Phil Niekro 5.00 2.20
❑ 504 Earl Williams .... 1.25 .55
❑ 505 Bob Bailey .... 1.25 .55
❑ 506 Bart Johnson .... 1.25 .55
❑ 507 Darrel Chaney .... 1.25 .55
❑ 508 Gates Brown .... 1.25 .55
❑ 509 Jim Nash .... 1.25 .55
❑ 510 Amos Otis .... 2.00 .90
❑ 511 Sam McDowell .... 2.00 .90
❑ 512 Dalton Jones .... 1.25 .55
❑ 513 Dave Marshall .... 1.25 .55
❑ 514 Jerry Kenney .... 1.25 .55
❑ 515 Andy Messersmith .... 2.00 .90
❑ 516 Danny Walton .... 1.25 .55
❑ 517A Pirates Leaders .... 1.50 .70
Bill Virdon MG
Don Leppert CO
Bill Mazeroski CO
Dave Ricketts CO
Mel Wright CO
(Mazeroski has
no right ear)
❑ 517B Pirates Leaders 3.00 1.35
(Mazeroski has
right ear)
❑ 518 Bob Veale .... 1.25 .55
❑ 519 Johnny Edwards .... 1.25 .55
❑ 520 Mel Stottlemyre .... 2.00 .90
❑ 521 Atlanta Braves 3.00 1.35
Team Card
❑ 522 Leo Cardenas .... 1.25 .55
❑ 523 Wayne Granger .... 1.25 .55
❑ 524 Gene Tenace .... 2.00 .90
❑ 525 Jim Fregosi .... 2.00 .90
❑ 526 Ollie Brown .... 1.25 .55
❑ 527 Dan McGinn .... 1.25 .55
❑ 528 Paul Blair .... 1.25 .55
❑ 529 Milt May 3.50 1.55
❑ 530 Jim Kaat 5.00 2.20
❑ 531 Ron Woods 3.50 1.55
❑ 532 Steve Mingori 3.50 1.55
❑ 533 Larry Stahl 3.50 1.55
❑ 534 Dave Lemonds 3.50 1.55
❑ 535 Johnny Callison 5.00 2.20
❑ 536 Philadelphia Phillies 6.00 2.70
Team Card
❑ 537 Bill Slayback 3.50 1.55

❑ 538 Jim Ray Hart 5.00 2.20
❑ 539 Tom Murphy 3.50 1.55
❑ 540 Cleon Jones 5.00 2.20
❑ 541 Bob Bolin 3.50 1.55
❑ 542 Pat Corrales 5.00 2.20
❑ 543 Alan Foster 3.50 1.55
❑ 544 Von Joshua 3.50 1.55
❑ 545 Orlando Cepeda 8.00 3.60
❑ 546 Jim York 3.50 1.55
❑ 547 Bobby Heise 3.50 1.55
❑ 548 Don Durham 3.50 1.55
❑ 549 Rangers Leaders 5.00 2.20
Whitey Herzog MG
Chuck Estrada CO
Chuck Hiller CO
Jackie Moore CO
❑ 550 Dave Johnson 5.00 2.20
❑ 551 Mike Kilkenny 3.50 1.55
❑ 552 J.C. Martin 3.50 1.55
❑ 553 Mickey Scott 3.50 1.55
❑ 554 Dave Concepcion 5.00 2.20
❑ 555 Bill Hands 3.50 1.55
❑ 556 New York Yankees 8.00 3.60
Team Card
❑ 557 Bernie Williams 3.50 1.55
❑ 558 Jerry May 3.50 1.55
❑ 559 Barry Lersch 3.50 1.55
❑ 560 Frank Howard 5.00 2.20
❑ 561 Jim Geddes 3.50 1.55
❑ 562 Wayne Garrett 3.50 1.55
❑ 563 Larry Haney 3.50 1.55
❑ 564 Mike Thompson 3.50 1.55
❑ 565 Jim Hickman 3.50 1.55
❑ 566 Lew Krausse 3.50 1.55
❑ 567 Bob Fenwick 3.50 1.55
❑ 568 Ray Newman 3.50 1.55
❑ 569 Dodgers Leaders 5.00 2.20
Walt Alston MG
Red Adams CO
Monty Basgall CO
Jim Gilliam CO
Tom Lasorda CO
❑ 570 Bill Singer 5.00 2.20
❑ 571 Rusty Torres 3.50 1.55
❑ 572 Gary Sutherland 3.50 1.55
❑ 573 Fred Beene 3.50 1.55
❑ 574 Bob Didier 3.50 1.55
❑ 575 Dock Ellis 3.50 1.55
❑ 576 Montreal Expos 6.00 2.70
Team Card
❑ 577 Eric Soderholm 3.50 1.55
❑ 578 Ken Wright 3.50 1.55
❑ 579 Tom Grieve 5.00 2.20
❑ 580 Joe Pepitone 5.00 2.20
❑ 581 Steve Kealey 3.50 1.55
❑ 582 Darrell Porter 5.00 2.20
❑ 583 Bill Grief 3.50 1.55
❑ 584 Chris Arnold 3.50 1.55
❑ 585 Joe Niekro 5.00 2.20
❑ 586 Bill Sudakis 3.50 1.55
❑ 587 Rich McKinney 3.50 1.55
❑ 588 Checklist 529-660 .... 20.00 4.00
❑ 589 Ken Forsch 3.50 1.55
❑ 590 Deron Johnson 5.00 2.20
❑ 591 Mike Hedlund 3.50 1.55
❑ 592 John Boccabella 3.50 1.55
❑ 593 Royals Leaders 3.50 1.55
Jack McKeon MG
Galen Cisco CO
Harry Dunlop CO
Charlie Lau CO
❑ 594 Vic Harris 3.50 1.55
❑ 595 Don Gullett 5.00 2.20
❑ 596 Boston Red Sox 6.00 2.70
Team Card
❑ 597 Mickey Rivers 5.00 2.20
❑ 598 Phil Roof 3.50 1.55
❑ 599 Ed Crosby 3.50 1.55
❑ 600 Dave McNally 5.00 2.20
❑ 601 Rookie Catchers 5.00 2.20
Sergio Robles
George Pena
Rick Stelmaszek
❑ 602 Rookie Pitchers 5.00 2.20
Mel Behney
Ralph Garcia

Doug Rau
❑ 603 Rookie 3rd Basemen 5.00 2.20
Terry Hughes
Bill McNulty
Ken Reitz
❑ 604 Rookie Pitchers 5.00 2.20
Jesse Jefferson
Dennis O'Toole
Bob Strampe
❑ 605 Rookie 1st Basemen 5.00 2.20
Enos Cabell RC
Pat Bourque
Gonzalo Marquez
❑ 606 Rookie Outfielders 5.00 2.20
Gary Matthews RC
Tom Paciorek
Jorge Roque
❑ 607 Rookie Shortstops 5.00 2.20
Pepe Frias
Ray Busse
Mario Guerrero
❑ 608 Rookie Pitchers 5.00 2.20
Steve Busby RC
Dick Colpaert
George Medich
❑ 609 Rookie 2nd Basemen .. 5.00 2.20
Larvell Blanks
Pedro Garcia
Dave Lopes RC
❑ 610 Rookie Pitchers 5.00 2.20
Jimmy Freeman
Charlie Hough
Hank Webb
❑ 611 Rookie Outfielders 5.00 2.20
Rich Coggins
Jim Wohlford
Richie Zisk
❑ 612 Rookie Pitchers 5.00 2.20
Steve Lawson
Bob Reynolds
Brent Strom
❑ 613 Rookie Catchers 15.00 6.75
Bob Boone RC
Skip Jutze
Mike Ivie
❑ 614 Rookie Outfielders 18.00 8.00
Al Bumbry
Dwight Evans RC
Charlie Spikes
❑ 615 Rookie 3rd Basemen 200.00 90.00
Ron Cey
John Hilton
Mike Schmidt RC
❑ 616 Rookie Pitchers 5.00 2.20
Norm Angelini
Steve Blateric
Mike Garman
❑ 617 Rich Chiles 3.50 1.55
❑ 618 Andy Etchebarren 3.50 1.55
❑ 619 Billy Wilson 3.50 1.55
❑ 620 Tommy Harper 5.00 2.20
❑ 621 Joe Ferguson 5.00 2.20
❑ 622 Larry Hisle 5.00 2.20
❑ 623 Steve Renko 3.50 1.55
❑ 624 Astros Leaders 5.00 2.20
Leo Durocher MG
Preston Gomez CO
Grady Hatton CO
Hub Kittle CO
Jim Owens CO
❑ 625 Angel Mangual 3.50 1.55
❑ 626 Bob Barton 3.50 1.55
❑ 627 Luis Alvarado 3.50 1.55
❑ 628 Jim Slaton 3.50 1.55
❑ 629 Cleveland Indians 6.00 2.70
Team Card
❑ 630 Denny McLain 8.00 3.60
❑ 631 Tom Matchick 3.50 1.55
❑ 632 Dick Selma 3.50 1.55
❑ 633 Ike Brown 3.50 1.55
❑ 634 Alan Closter 3.50 1.55
❑ 635 Gene Alley 5.00 2.20
❑ 636 Rickey Clark 3.50 1.55
❑ 637 Norm Miller 3.50 1.55
❑ 638 Ken Reynolds 3.50 1.55
❑ 639 Willie Crawford 3.50 1.55
❑ 640 Dick Bosman 3.50 1.55
❑ 641 Cincinnati Reds 6.00 2.70
Team Card
❑ 642 Jose Laboy 3.50 1.55
❑ 643 Al Fitzmorris 3.50 1.55
❑ 644 Jack Heidemann 3.50 1.55
❑ 645 Bob Locker 3.50 1.55
❑ 646 Brewers Leaders 3.50 1.55
Del Crandall MG
Harvey Kuenn CO
Joe Nossek CO
Bob Shaw CO
Jim Walton CO
❑ 647 George Stone 3.50 1.55
❑ 648 Tom Egan 3.50 1.55
❑ 649 Rich Folkers 3.50 1.55
❑ 650 Felipe Alou 5.00 2.20
❑ 651 Don Carrithers 3.50 1.55
❑ 652 Ted Kubiak 3.50 1.55
❑ 653 Joe Hoerner 3.50 1.55
❑ 654 Minnesota Twins 6.00 2.70
Team Card
❑ 655 Clay Kirby 3.50 1.55
❑ 656 John Ellis 3.50 1.55
❑ 657 Bob Johnson 3.50 1.55
❑ 658 Elliott Maddox 3.50 1.55
❑ 659 Jose Pagan 3.50 1.55
❑ 660 Fred Scherman 5.00 1.95

1974 Topps

	NRMT	VG-E
COMPLETE SET (660)	400.00	180.00
COMP.FACT.SET (660)	600.00	275.00
WRAPPERS (10-CENTS)	10.00	4.50

❑ 1 Hank Aaron 40.00 12.00
All-Time Home Run King
(Complete ML record)
❑ 2 Aaron Special 54-57 .... 8.00 3.60
(Records on back)
❑ 3 Aaron Special 58-61 .... 8.00 3.60
(Memorable homers)
❑ 4 Aaron Special 62-65 .... 8.00 3.60
(Life in ML's 1954-63)
❑ 5 Aaron Special 66-69 .... 8.00 3.60
(Life in ML's 1964-73)
❑ 6 Aaron Special 70-73 .... 8.00 3.60
(Milestone homers)
❑ 7 Jim Hunter 4.00 1.80
❑ 8 George Theodore .... .50 .23
❑ 9 Mickey Lolich .... 1.00 .45
❑ 10 Johnny Bench 15.00 6.75
❑ 11 Jim Bibby .... .50 .23
❑ 12 Dave May .... .50 .23
❑ 13 Tom Hilgendorf .... .50 .23
❑ 14 Paul Popovich .... .50 .23
❑ 15 Joe Torre .... 2.00 .90
❑ 16 Baltimore Orioles .... 1.00 .45
Team Card
❑ 17 Doug Bird .... .50 .23
❑ 18 Gary Thomasson .... .50 .23
❑ 19 Gerry Moses .... .50 .23
❑ 20 Nolan Ryan 40.00 18.00
❑ 21 Bob Gallagher .... .50 .23
❑ 22 Cy Acosta .... .50 .23
❑ 23 Craig Robinson .... .50 .23
❑ 24 John Hiller .... 1.00 .45
❑ 25 Ken Singleton .... 1.00 .45
❑ 26 Bill Campbell .... .50 .23
❑ 27 George Scott .... 1.00 .45
❑ 28 Manny Sanguillen .... 1.00 .45
❑ 29 Phil Niekro 3.00 1.35
❑ 30 Bobby Bonds .... 2.00 .90
❑ 31 Astros Leaders .... 1.00 .45
Preston Gomez MG
Roger Craig CO
Hub Kittle CO
Grady Hatton CO
Bob Lillis CO
❑ 32A Johnny Grubb SD .... 1.00 .45
❑ 32B Johnny Grubb WASH .. 4.00 1.80
❑ 33 Don Newhauser .... .50 .23
❑ 34 Andy Kosco .... .50 .23
❑ 35 Gaylord Perry 3.00 1.35
❑ 36 St. Louis Cardinals .... 1.00 .45
Team Card
❑ 37 Dave Sells .... .50 .23
❑ 38 Don Kessinger .... 1.00 .45
❑ 39 Ken Suarez .... .50 .23
❑ 40 Jim Palmer 6.00 2.70
❑ 41 Bobby Floyd .... .50 .23
❑ 42 Claude Osteen .... 1.00 .45
❑ 43 Jim Wynn .... 1.00 .45
❑ 44 Mel Stottlemyre .... 1.00 .45
❑ 45 Dave Johnson .... 1.00 .45
❑ 46 Pat Kelly .... .50 .23
❑ 47 Dick Ruthven .... .50 .23
❑ 48 Dick Sharon .... .50 .23
❑ 49 Steve Renko .... .50 .23
❑ 50 Rod Carew 8.00 3.60
❑ 51 Bobby Heise .... .50 .23
❑ 52 Al Oliver .... .50 .23
❑ 53A Fred Kendall SD .... 1.00 .45
❑ 53B Fred Kendall WASH 4.00 1.80
❑ 54 Elias Sosa .... .50 .23
❑ 55 Frank Robinson 6.00 2.70
❑ 56 New York Mets .... 1.00 .45
Team Card
❑ 57 Darold Knowles .... .50 .23
❑ 58 Charlie Spikes .... .50 .23
❑ 59 Ross Grimsley .... .50 .23
❑ 60 Lou Brock 6.00 2.70
❑ 61 Luis Aparicio 3.00 1.35
❑ 62 Bob Locker .... .50 .23
❑ 63 Bill Sudakis .... .50 .23
❑ 64 Doug Rau .... .50 .23
❑ 65 Amos Otis .... 1.00 .45
❑ 66 Sparky Lyle .... 1.00 .45
❑ 67 Tommy Helms .... .50 .23
❑ 68 Grant Jackson .... .50 .23
❑ 69 Del Unser .... .50 .23
❑ 70 Dick Allen .... 2.00 .90
❑ 71 Dan Frisella .... .50 .23
❑ 72 Aurelio Rodriguez .... .50 .23
❑ 73 Mike Marshall .... 2.00 .90
❑ 74 Minnesota Twins .... 1.00 .45
Team Card
❑ 75 Jim Colborn .... .50 .23
❑ 76 Mickey Rivers .... 1.00 .45
❑ 77A Rich Troedson SD 4.00 1.80
❑ 77B Rich Troedson WASH .. 1.00 .45
❑ 78 Giants Leaders .... 1.00 .45
Charlie Fox MG
John McNamara CO
Joe Amalfitano CO
Andy Gilbert CO
Don McMahon CO
❑ 79 Gene Tenace .... 1.00 .45
❑ 80 Tom Seaver 12.00 5.50
❑ 81 Frank Duffy .... .50 .23
❑ 82 Dave Giusti .... .50 .23
❑ 83 Orlando Cepeda 3.00 1.35
❑ 84 Rick Wise .... .50 .23
❑ 85 Joe Morgan 6.00 2.70
❑ 86 Joe Ferguson .... 1.00 .45
❑ 87 Fergie Jenkins 3.00 1.35
❑ 88 Freddie Patek .... 1.00 .45
❑ 89 Jackie Brown .... .50 .23
❑ 90 Bobby Murcer .... 1.00 .45
❑ 91 Ken Forsch .... .50 .23
❑ 92 Paul Blair .... 1.00 .45
❑ 93 Rod Gilbreath .... .50 .23
❑ 94 Detroit Tigers .... 1.00 .45

	Card		
	Team Card		
❑ 95	Steve Carlton	8.00	3.60
❑ 96	Jerry Hairston	.50	.23
❑ 97	Bob Bailey	.50	.23
❑ 98	Bert Blyleven	2.00	.90
❑ 99	Brewers Leaders	1.00	.45
	Del Crandall MG		
	Harvey Kuenn CO		
	Joe Nossek CO		
	Jim Walton CO		
	Al Widmar CO		
❑ 100	Willie Stargell	4.00	1.80
❑ 101	Bobby Valentine	1.00	.45
❑ 102A	Bill Greif SD	1.00	.45
❑ 102B	Bill Greif WASH	4.00	1.80
❑ 103	Sal Bando	1.00	.45
❑ 104	Ron Bryant	.50	.23
❑ 105	Carlton Fisk	10.00	4.50
❑ 106	Harry Parker	.50	.23
❑ 107	Alex Johnson	.50	.23
❑ 108	Al Hrabosky	1.00	.45
❑ 109	Bob Grich	1.00	.45
❑ 110	Billy Williams	3.00	1.35
❑ 111	Clay Carroll	.50	.23
❑ 112	Dave Lopes	2.00	.90
❑ 113	Dick Drago	.50	.23
❑ 114	Angels Team	1.00	.45
❑ 115	Willie Horton	1.00	.45
❑ 116	Jerry Reuss	1.00	.45
❑ 117	Ron Blomberg	.50	.23
❑ 118	Bill Lee	1.00	.45
❑ 119	Phillies Leaders	1.00	.45
	Danny Ozark MG		
	Ray Ripplemeyer CO		
	Bobby Wine CO		
	Carroll Beringer CO		
	Billy DeMars CO		
❑ 120	Wilbur Wood	.50	.23
❑ 121	Larry Lintz	.50	.23
❑ 122	Jim Holt	.50	.23
❑ 123	Nelson Briles	1.00	.45
❑ 124	Bobby Coluccio	.50	.23
❑ 125A	Nate Colbert SD	1.00	.45
❑ 125B	Nate Colbert WASH	4.00	1.80
❑ 126	Checklist 1-132	3.00	.60
❑ 127	Tom Paciorek	1.00	.45
❑ 128	John Ellis	.50	.23
❑ 129	Chris Speier	.50	.23
❑ 130	Reggie Jackson	15.00	6.75
❑ 131	Bob Boone	2.00	.90
❑ 132	Felix Millan	.50	.23
❑ 133	David Clyde	1.00	.45
❑ 134	Denis Menke	.50	.23
❑ 135	Roy White	1.00	.45
❑ 136	Rick Reuschel	1.00	.45
❑ 137	Al Bumbry	1.00	.45
❑ 138	Eddie Brinkman	.50	.23
❑ 139	Aurelio Monteagudo	.50	.23
❑ 140	Darrell Evans	2.00	.90
❑ 141	Pat Bourque	.50	.23
❑ 142	Pedro Garcia	.50	.23
❑ 143	Dick Woodson	.50	.23
❑ 144	Dodgers Leaders	2.00	.90
	Walter Alston MG		
	Tom Lasorda CO		
	Jim Gilliam CO		
	Red Adams CO		
	Monty Basgall CO		
❑ 145	Dock Ellis	.50	.23
❑ 146	Ron Fairly	1.00	.45
❑ 147	Bart Johnson	.50	.23
❑ 148A	Dave Hilton SD	1.00	.45
❑ 148B	Dave Hilton WASH	4.00	1.80
❑ 149	Mac Scarce	.50	.23
❑ 150	John Mayberry	1.00	.45
❑ 151	Diego Segui	.50	.23
❑ 152	Oscar Gamble	1.00	.45
❑ 153	Jon Matlack	1.00	.45
❑ 154	Houston Astros	1.00	.45
	Team Card		
❑ 155	Bert Campaneris	1.00	.45
❑ 156	Randy Moffitt	.50	.23
❑ 157	Vic Harris	.50	.23
❑ 158	Jack Billingham	.50	.23
❑ 159	Jim Ray Hart	1.00	.45
❑ 160	Brooks Robinson	8.00	3.60
❑ 161	Ray Burris UER	1.00	.45
	(Card number is		
	printed sideways)		
❑ 162	Bill Freehan	1.00	.45
❑ 163	Ken Berry	.50	.23
❑ 164	Tom House	.50	.23
❑ 165	Willie Davis	1.00	.45
❑ 166	Royals Leaders	1.00	.45
	Jack McKeon MG		
	Charlie Lau CO		
	Harry Dunlop CO		
	Galen Cisco CO		
❑ 167	Luis Tiant	2.00	.90
❑ 168	Danny Thompson	.50	.23
❑ 169	Steve Rogers	2.00	.90
❑ 170	Bill Melton	.50	.23
❑ 171	Eduardo Rodriguez	.50	.23
❑ 172	Gene Clines	.50	.23
❑ 173A	Randy Jones SD RC	2.00	.90
❑ 173B	Randy Jones WASH	5.00	2.20
❑ 174	Bill Robinson	1.00	.45
❑ 175	Reggie Cleveland	.50	.23
❑ 176	John Lowenstein	.50	.23
❑ 177	Dave Roberts	.50	.23
❑ 178	Garry Maddox	1.00	.45
❑ 179	Mets Leaders	5.00	2.20
	Yogi Berra MG		
	Rube Walker CO		
	Eddie Yost CO		
	Roy McMillan CO		
	Joe Pignatano CO		
❑ 180	Ken Holtzman	1.00	.45
❑ 181	Cesar Geronimo	.50	.23
❑ 182	Lindy McDaniel	1.00	.45
❑ 183	Johnny Oates	1.00	.45
❑ 184	Texas Rangers	1.00	.45
	Team Card		
❑ 185	Jose Cardenal	.50	.23
❑ 186	Fred Scherman	.50	.23
❑ 187	Don Baylor	2.00	.90
❑ 188	Rudy Meoli	.50	.23
❑ 189	Jim Brewer	.50	.23
❑ 190	Tony Oliva	2.00	.90
❑ 191	Al Fitzmorris	.50	.23
❑ 192	Mario Guerrero	.50	.23
❑ 193	Tom Walker	.50	.23
❑ 194	Darrell Porter	1.00	.45
❑ 195	Carlos May	.50	.23
❑ 196	Jim Fregosi	1.00	.45
❑ 197A	Vicente Romo SD	1.00	.45
❑ 197B	V.Romo WASH	4.00	1.80
❑ 198	Dave Cash	.50	.23
❑ 199	Mike Kekich	.50	.23
❑ 200	Cesar Cedeno	1.00	.45
❑ 201	Batting Leaders	5.00	2.20
	Rod Carew		
	Pete Rose		
❑ 202	Home Run Leaders	5.00	2.20
	Reggie Jackson		
	Willie Stargell		
❑ 203	RBI Leaders	5.00	2.20
	Reggie Jackson		
	Willie Stargell		
❑ 204	Stolen Base Leaders	2.00	.90
	Tommy Harper		
	Lou Brock		
❑ 205	Victory Leaders	1.00	.45
	Wilbur Wood		
	Ron Bryant		
❑ 206	ERA Leaders	5.00	2.20
	Jim Palmer		
	Tom Seaver		
❑ 207	Strikeout Leaders	12.00	5.50
	Nolan Ryan		
	Tom Seaver		
❑ 208	Firemen Leaders	1.00	.45
	John Hiller		
	Mike Marshall		
❑ 209	Ted Sizemore	.50	.23
❑ 210	Bill Singer	.50	.23
❑ 211	Chicago Cubs	1.00	.45
	Team Card		
❑ 212	Rollie Fingers	3.00	1.35
❑ 213	Dave Rader	.50	.23
❑ 214	Billy Grabarkewitz	.50	.23
❑ 215	Al Kaline UER	10.00	4.50
	(No copyright on back)		
❑ 216	Ray Sadecki	.50	.23
❑ 217	Tim Foli	.50	.23
❑ 218	Johnny Briggs	.50	.23
❑ 219	Doug Griffin	.50	.23
❑ 220	Don Sutton	3.00	1.35
❑ 221	White Sox Leaders	1.00	.45
	Chuck Tanner MG		
	Jim Mahoney CO		
	Alex Monchak CO		
	Johnny Sain CO		
	Joe Lonnett CO		
❑ 222	Ramon Hernandez	.50	.23
❑ 223	Jeff Burroughs	2.00	.90
❑ 224	Roger Metzger	.50	.23
❑ 225	Paul Splittorff	.50	.23
❑ 226A	San Diego Padres	2.00	.90
	Team Card San Diego Variation		
❑ 226B	San Diego Padres	8.00	3.60
	Team Card Washington Variation		
❑ 227	Mike Lum	.50	.23
❑ 228	Ted Kubiak	.50	.23
❑ 229	Fritz Peterson	.50	.23
❑ 230	Tony Perez	4.00	1.80
❑ 231	Dick Tidrow	.50	.23
❑ 232	Steve Brye	.50	.23
❑ 233	Jim Barr	.50	.23
❑ 234	John Milner	.50	.23
❑ 235	Dave McNally	1.00	.45
❑ 236	Cardinals Leaders	2.00	.90
	Red Schoendienst MG		
	Barney Schultz CO		
	George Kissell CO		
	Johnny Lewis CO		
	Vern Benson CO		
❑ 237	Ken Brett	.50	.23
❑ 238	Fran Healy HOR	2.00	.90
	(Munson sliding		
	in background)		
❑ 239	Bill Russell	1.00	.45
❑ 240	Joe Coleman	.50	.23
❑ 241A	Glenn Beckert SD	1.00	.45
❑ 241B	G.Beckert WASH	4.00	1.80
❑ 242	Bill Gogolewski	.50	.23
❑ 243	Bob Oliver	.50	.23
❑ 244	Carl Morton	.50	.23
❑ 245	Cleon Jones	.50	.23
❑ 246	Oakland Athletics	2.00	.90
	Team Card		
❑ 247	Rick Miller	.50	.23
❑ 248	Tom Hall	.50	.23
❑ 249	George Mitterwald	.50	.23
❑ 250A	Willie McCovey SD	6.00	2.70
❑ 250B	W.McCovey WASH	25.00	11.00
❑ 251	Graig Nettles	2.00	.90
❑ 252	Dave Parker RC	10.00	4.50
❑ 253	John Boccabella	.50	.23
❑ 254	Stan Bahnsen	.50	.23
❑ 255	Larry Bowa	1.00	.45
❑ 256	Tom Griffin	.50	.23
❑ 257	Buddy Bell	2.00	.90
❑ 258	Jerry Morales	.50	.23
❑ 259	Bob Reynolds	.50	.23
❑ 260	Ted Simmons	2.00	.90
❑ 261	Jerry Bell	.50	.23
❑ 262	Ed Kirkpatrick	.50	.23
❑ 263	Checklist 133-264	3.00	.60
❑ 264	Joe Rudi	1.00	.45
❑ 265	Tug McGraw	2.00	.90
❑ 266	Jim Northrup	1.00	.45
❑ 267	Andy Messersmith	1.00	.45
❑ 268	Tom Grieve	1.00	.45
❑ 269	Bob Johnson	.50	.23
❑ 270	Ron Santo	2.00	.90
❑ 271	Bill Hands	.50	.23
❑ 272	Paul Casanova	.50	.23
❑ 273	Checklist 265-396	3.00	.60
❑ 274	Fred Beene	.50	.23
❑ 275	Ron Hunt	.50	.23
❑ 276	Angels Leaders	1.00	.45
	Bobby Winkles MG		
	John Roseboro CO		
	Tom Morgan CO		
	Jimmie Reese CO		
	Salty Parker CO		
❑ 277	Gary Nolan	1.00	.45

❑ 278	Cookie Rojas	1.00	.45
❑ 279	Jim Crawford	.50	.23
❑ 280	Carl Yastrzemski	12.00	5.50
❑ 281	San Francisco Giants Team Card	1.00	.45
❑ 282	Doyle Alexander	1.00	.45
❑ 283	Mike Schmidt	20.00	9.00
❑ 284	Dave Duncan	1.00	.45
❑ 285	Reggie Smith	1.00	.45
❑ 286	Tony Muser	.50	.23
❑ 287	Clay Kirby	.50	.23
❑ 288	Gorman Thomas RC	2.00	.90
❑ 289	Rick Auerbach	.50	.23
❑ 290	Vida Blue	1.00	.45
❑ 291	Don Hahn	.50	.23
❑ 292	Chuck Seelbach	.50	.23
❑ 293	Milt May	.50	.23
❑ 294	Steve Foucault	.50	.23
❑ 295	Rick Monday	1.00	.45
❑ 296	Ray Corbin	.50	.23
❑ 297	Hal Breeden	.50	.23
❑ 298	Roric Harrison	.50	.23
❑ 299	Gene Michael	1.00	.45
❑ 300	Pete Rose	25.00	11.00
❑ 301	Bob Montgomery	.50	.23
❑ 302	Rudy May	.50	.23
❑ 303	George Hendrick	1.00	.45
❑ 304	Don Wilson	.50	.23
❑ 305	Tito Fuentes	.50	.23
❑ 306	Orioles Leaders	2.00	.90
	Earl Weaver MG		
	Jim Frey CO		
	George Bamberger CO		
	Billy Hunter CO		
	George Staller CO		
❑ 307	Luis Melendez	.50	.23
❑ 308	Bruce Dal Canton	.50	.23
❑ 309A	Dave Roberts SD	1.00	.45
❑ 309B	Dave Roberts WASH	6.00	2.70
❑ 310	Terry Forster	1.00	.45
❑ 311	Jerry Grote	.50	.23
❑ 312	Deron Johnson	1.00	.45
❑ 313	Barry Lersch	.50	.23
❑ 314	Milwaukee Brewers Team Card	1.00	.45
❑ 315	Ron Cey	2.00	.90
❑ 316	Jim Perry	1.00	.45
❑ 317	Richie Zisk	1.00	.45
❑ 318	Jim Merritt	.50	.23
❑ 319	Randy Hundley	1.00	.45
❑ 320	Dusty Baker	2.00	.90
❑ 321	Steve Braun	.50	.23
❑ 322	Ernie McAnally	.50	.23
❑ 323	Richie Scheinblum	.50	.23
❑ 324	Steve Kline	.50	.23
❑ 325	Tommy Harper	2.00	.90
❑ 326	Reds Leaders	3.00	1.35
	Sparky Anderson MG		
	Larry Shepard CO		
	George Scherger CO		
	Alex Grammas CO		
	Ted Kluszewski CO		
❑ 327	Tom Timmermann	.50	.23
❑ 328	Skip Jutze	.50	.23
❑ 329	Mark Belanger	1.00	.45
❑ 330	Juan Marichal	4.00	1.80
❑ 331	All-Star Catchers	5.00	2.20
	Carlton Fisk		
	Johnny Bench		
❑ 332	All-Star 1B	8.00	3.60
	Dick Allen		
	Hank Aaron		
❑ 333	All-Star 2B	4.00	1.80
	Rod Carew		
	Joe Morgan		
❑ 334	All-Star 3B	3.00	1.35
	Brooks Robinson		
	Ron Santo		
❑ 335	All-Star SS	1.00	.45
	Bert Campaneris		
	Chris Speier		
❑ 336	All-Star LF	5.00	2.20
	Bobby Murcer		
	Pete Rose		
❑ 337	All-Star CF	1.00	.45
	Amos Otis		
	Cesar Cedeno		
❑ 338	All-Star RF	5.00	2.20
	Reggie Jackson		
	Billy Williams		
❑ 339	All-Star Pitchers	3.00	1.35
	Jim Hunter		
	Rick Wise		
❑ 340	Thurman Munson	8.00	3.60
❑ 341	Dan Driessen RC	1.00	.45
❑ 342	Jim Lonborg	1.00	.45
❑ 343	Royals Team	1.00	.45
❑ 344	Mike Caldwell	.50	.23
❑ 345	Bill North	.50	.23
❑ 346	Ron Reed	.50	.23
❑ 347	Sandy Alomar	1.00	.45
❑ 348	Pete Richert	.50	.23
❑ 349	John Vukovich	.50	.23
❑ 350	Bob Gibson	6.00	2.70
❑ 351	Dwight Evans	3.00	1.35
❑ 352	Bill Stoneman	.50	.23
❑ 353	Rich Coggins	.50	.23
❑ 354	Cubs Leaders	1.00	.45
	Whitey Lockman MG		
	J.C. Martin CO		
	Hank Aguirre CO		
	Al Spangler CO		
	Jim Marshall CO		
❑ 355	Dave Nelson	.50	.23
❑ 356	Jerry Koosman	1.00	.45
❑ 357	Buddy Bradford	.50	.23
❑ 358	Dal Maxvill	.50	.23
❑ 359	Brent Strom	.50	.23
❑ 360	Greg Luzinski	2.00	.90
❑ 361	Don Carrithers	.50	.23
❑ 362	Hal King	.50	.23
❑ 363	New York Yankees Team Card	2.00	.90
❑ 364A	Cito Gaston SD	2.00	.90
❑ 364B	Cito Gaston WASH	8.00	3.60
❑ 365	Steve Busby	.50	.23
❑ 366	Larry Hisle	1.00	.45
❑ 367	Norm Cash	2.00	.90
❑ 368	Manny Mota	1.00	.45
❑ 369	Paul Lindblad	.50	.23
❑ 370	Bob Watson	1.00	.45
❑ 371	Jim Slaton	.50	.23
❑ 372	Ken Reitz	.50	.23
❑ 373	John Curtis	.50	.23
❑ 374	Marty Perez	.50	.23
❑ 375	Earl Williams	.50	.23
❑ 376	Jorge Orta	.50	.23
❑ 377	Ron Woods	.50	.23
❑ 378	Burt Hooton	1.00	.45
❑ 379	Rangers Leaders	2.00	.90
	Billy Martin MG		
	Frank Lucchesi CO		
	Art Fowler CO		
	Charlie Silvera CO		
	Jackie Moore CO		
❑ 380	Bud Harrelson	1.00	.45
❑ 381	Charlie Sands	.50	.23
❑ 382	Bob Moose	.50	.23
❑ 383	Philadelphia Phillies Team Card	1.00	.45
❑ 384	Chris Chambliss	1.00	.45
❑ 385	Don Gullett	1.00	.45
❑ 386	Gary Matthews	2.00	.90
❑ 387A	Rich Morales SD	1.00	.45
❑ 387B	Rich Morales WASH	6.00	2.70
❑ 388	Phil Roof	.50	.23
❑ 389	Gates Brown	.50	.23
❑ 390	Lou Piniella	2.00	.90
❑ 391	Billy Champion	.50	.23
❑ 392	Dick Green	.50	.23
❑ 393	Orlando Pena	.50	.23
❑ 394	Ken Henderson	.50	.23
❑ 395	Doug Rader	.50	.23
❑ 396	Tommy Davis	1.00	.45
❑ 397	George Stone	.50	.23
❑ 398	Duke Sims	.50	.23
❑ 399	Mike Paul	.50	.23
❑ 400	Harmon Killebrew	6.00	2.70
❑ 401	Elliott Maddox	.50	.23
❑ 402	Jim Rooker	.50	.23
❑ 403	Red Sox Leaders	1.00	.45
	Darrell Johnson MG		
	Eddie Popowski CO		
	Lee Stange CO		
	Don Zimmer CO		
	Don Bryant CO		
❑ 404	Jim Howarth	.50	.23
❑ 405	Ellie Rodriguez	.50	.23
❑ 406	Steve Arlin	.50	.23
❑ 407	Jim Wohlford	.50	.23
❑ 408	Charlie Hough	1.00	.45
❑ 409	Ike Brown	.50	.23
❑ 410	Pedro Borbon	.50	.23
❑ 411	Frank Baker	.50	.23
❑ 412	Chuck Taylor	.50	.23
❑ 413	Don Money	1.00	.45
❑ 414	Checklist 397-528	3.00	.60
❑ 415	Gary Gentry	.50	.23
❑ 416	Chicago White Sox Team Card	1.00	.45
❑ 417	Rich Folkers	.50	.23
❑ 418	Walt Williams	.50	.23
❑ 419	Wayne Twitchell	.50	.23
❑ 420	Ray Fosse	.50	.23
❑ 421	Dan Fife	.50	.23
❑ 422	Gonzalo Marquez	.50	.23
❑ 423	Fred Stanley	.50	.23
❑ 424	Jim Beauchamp	.50	.23
❑ 425	Pete Broberg	.50	.23
❑ 426	Rennie Stennett	.50	.23
❑ 427	Bobby Bolin	.50	.23
❑ 428	Gary Sutherland	.50	.23
❑ 429	Dick Lange	.50	.23
❑ 430	Matty Alou	1.00	.45
❑ 431	Gene Garber RC	1.00	.45
❑ 432	Chris Arnold	.50	.23
❑ 433	Lerrin LaGrow	.50	.23
❑ 434	Ken McMullen	.50	.23
❑ 435	Dave Concepcion	2.00	.90
❑ 436	Don Hood	.50	.23
❑ 437	Jim Lyttle	.50	.23
❑ 438	Ed Herrmann	.50	.23
❑ 439	Norm Miller	.50	.23
❑ 440	Jim Kaat	2.00	.90
❑ 441	Tom Ragland	.50	.23
❑ 442	Alan Foster	.50	.23
❑ 443	Tom Hutton	.50	.23
❑ 444	Vic Davalillo	.50	.23
❑ 445	George Medich	.50	.23
❑ 446	Len Randle	.50	.23
❑ 447	Twins Leaders	1.00	.45
	Frank Quilici MG		
	Ralph Rowe CO		
	Bob Rodgers CO		
	Vern Morgan CO		
❑ 448	Ron Hodges	.50	.23
❑ 449	Tom McCraw	.50	.23
❑ 450	Rich Hebner	1.00	.45
❑ 451	Tommy John	2.00	.90
❑ 452	Gene Hiser	.50	.23
❑ 453	Balor Moore	.50	.23
❑ 454	Kurt Bevacqua	.50	.23
❑ 455	Tom Bradley	.50	.23
❑ 456	Dave Winfield RC	40.00	18.00
❑ 457	Chuck Goggin	.50	.23
❑ 458	Jim Ray	.50	.23
❑ 459	Cincinnati Reds Team Card	2.00	.90
❑ 460	Boog Powell	2.00	.90
❑ 461	John Odom	.50	.23
❑ 462	Luis Alvarado	.50	.23
❑ 463	Pat Dobson	.50	.23
❑ 464	Jose Cruz	2.00	.90
❑ 465	Dick Bosman	.50	.23
❑ 466	Dick Billings	.50	.23
❑ 467	Winston Llenas	.50	.23
❑ 468	Pepe Frias	.50	.23
❑ 469	Joe Decker	.50	.23
❑ 470	Reggie Jackson ALCS	5.00	2.20
❑ 471	Jon Matlack NLCS	1.00	.45
❑ 472	Darold Knowles WS1	1.00	.45
❑ 473	Willie Mays WS	8.00	3.60
❑ 474	Bert Campaneris WS3	1.00	.45
❑ 475	Rusty Staub WS4	1.00	.45
❑ 476	Cleon Jones WS5	1.00	.45
❑ 477	Reggie Jackson WS	5.00	2.20
❑ 478	Bert Campaneris WS7	1.00	.45
❑ 479	WS Summary	1.00	.45

A's celebrate; win
2nd consecutive
championship
❑ 480 Willie Crawford .50 .23
❑ 481 Jerry Terrell .50 .23
❑ 482 Bob Didier .50 .23
❑ 483 Atlanta Braves 1.00 .45
Team Card
❑ 484 Carmen Fanzone .50 .23
❑ 485 Felipe Alou 2.00 .90
❑ 486 Steve Stone 1.00 .45
❑ 487 Ted Martinez .50 .23
❑ 488 Andy Etchebarren .50 .23
❑ 489 Pirates Leaders 1.00 .45
Danny Murtaugh MG
Don Osborn CO
Don Leppert CO
Bill Mazeroski CO
Bob Skinner CO
❑ 490 Vada Pinson 2.00 .90
❑ 491 Roger Nelson .50 .23
❑ 492 Mike Rogodzinski .50 .23
❑ 493 Joe Hoerner .50 .23
❑ 494 Ed Goodson .50 .23
❑ 495 Dick McAuliffe 1.00 .45
❑ 496 Tom Murphy .50 .23
❑ 497 Bobby Mitchell .50 .23
❑ 498 Pat Corrales .50 .23
❑ 499 Rusty Torres .50 .23
❑ 500 Lee May 1.00 .45
❑ 501 Eddie Leon .50 .23
❑ 502 Dave LaRoche .50 .23
❑ 503 Eric Soderholm .50 .23
❑ 504 Joe Niekro 1.00 .45
❑ 505 Bill Buckner 1.00 .45
❑ 506 Ed Farmer .50 .23
❑ 507 Larry Stahl .50 .23
❑ 508 Montreal Expos 1.00 .45
Team Card
❑ 509 Jesse Jefferson .50 .23
❑ 510 Wayne Garrett .50 .23
❑ 511 Toby Harrah 1.00 .45
❑ 512 Joe Lahoud .50 .23
❑ 513 Jim Campanis .50 .23
❑ 514 Paul Schaal .50 .23
❑ 515 Willie Montanez .50 .23
❑ 516 Horacio Pina .50 .23
❑ 517 Mike Hegan .50 .23
❑ 518 Derrel Thomas .50 .23
❑ 519 Bill Sharp .50 .23
❑ 520 Tim McCarver 2.00 .90
❑ 521 Indians Leaders 1.00 .45
Ken Aspromonte MG
Clay Bryant CO
Tony Pacheco CO
❑ 522 J.R. Richard 2.00 .90
❑ 523 Cecil Cooper 2.00 .90
❑ 524 Bill Plummer .50 .23
❑ 525 Clyde Wright .50 .23
❑ 526 Frank Tepedino .50 .23
❑ 527 Bobby Darwin .50 .23
❑ 528 Bill Bonham .50 .23
❑ 529 Horace Clarke 1.00 .45
❑ 530 Mickey Stanley 1.00 .45
❑ 531 Expos Leaders 1.00 .45
Gene Mauch MG
Dave Bristol CO
Cal McLish CO
Larry Doby CO
Jerry Zimmerman CO
❑ 532 Skip Lockwood .50 .23
❑ 533 Mike Phillips .50 .23
❑ 534 Eddie Watt .50 .23
❑ 535 Bob Tolan .50 .23
❑ 536 Duffy Dyer .50 .23
❑ 537 Steve Mingori .50 .23
❑ 538 Cesar Tovar .50 .23
❑ 539 Lloyd Allen .50 .23
❑ 540 Bob Robertson .50 .23
❑ 541 Cleveland Indians 1.00 .45
Team Card
❑ 542 Rich Gossage 2.00 .90
❑ 543 Danny Cater .50 .23
❑ 544 Ron Schueler .50 .23
❑ 545 Billy Conigliaro 1.00 .45
❑ 546 Mike Corkins .50 .23
❑ 547 Glenn Borgmann .50 .23
❑ 548 Sonny Siebert .50 .23
❑ 549 Mike Jorgensen .50 .23
❑ 550 Sam McDowell 1.00 .45
❑ 551 Von Joshua .50 .23
❑ 552 Denny Doyle .50 .23
❑ 553 Jim Willoughby .50 .23
❑ 554 Tim Johnson .50 .23
❑ 555 Woodie Fryman .50 .23
❑ 556 Dave Campbell .50 .23
❑ 557 Jim McGlothlin .50 .23
❑ 558 Bill Fahey .50 .23
❑ 559 Darrel Chaney .50 .23
❑ 560 Mike Cuellar 1.00 .45
❑ 561 Ed Kranepool 1.00 .45
❑ 562 Jack Aker .50 .23
❑ 563 Hal McRae 1.00 .45
❑ 564 Mike Ryan .50 .23
❑ 565 Milt Wilcox .50 .23
❑ 566 Jackie Hernandez .50 .23
❑ 567 Boston Red Sox 1.00 .45
Team Card
❑ 568 Mike Torrez 1.00 .45
❑ 569 Rick Dempsey 1.00 .45
❑ 570 Ralph Garr 1.00 .45
❑ 571 Rich Hand .50 .23
❑ 572 Enzo Hernandez .50 .23
❑ 573 Mike Adams .50 .23
❑ 574 Bill Parsons .50 .23
❑ 575 Steve Garvey 3.00 1.35
❑ 576 Scipio Spinks .50 .23
❑ 577 Mike Sadek .50 .23
❑ 578 Ralph Houk MG 1.00 .45
❑ 579 Cecil Upshaw .50 .23
❑ 580 Jim Spencer .50 .23
❑ 581 Fred Norman .50 .23
❑ 582 Bucky Dent RC 4.00 1.80
❑ 583 Marty Pattin .50 .23
❑ 584 Ken Rudolph .50 .23
❑ 585 Merv Rettenmund .50 .23
❑ 586 Jack Brohamer .50 .23
❑ 587 Larry Christenson .50 .23
❑ 588 Hal Lanier .50 .23
❑ 589 Boots Day .50 .23
❑ 590 Roger Moret .50 .23
❑ 591 Sonny Jackson .50 .23
❑ 592 Ed Bane .50 .23
❑ 593 Steve Yeager 1.00 .45
❑ 594 Leroy Stanton .50 .23
❑ 595 Steve Blass .50 .23
❑ 596 Rookie Pitchers .50 .23
Wayne Garland
Fred Holdsworth
Mark Littell
Dick Pole
❑ 597 Rookie Shortstops 1.00 .45
Dave Chalk
John Gamble
Pete MacKanin
Manny Trillo RC
❑ 598 Rookie Outfielders 10.00 4.50
Dave Augustine
Ken Griffey RC
Steve Ontiveros
Jim Tyrone
❑ 599A Rookie Pitchers WAS 2.00 .90
Ron Diorio
Dave Freisleben
Frank Riccelli
Greg Shanahan
❑ 599B Rookie Pitchers SD 3.00 1.35
(SD in large print)
❑ 599C Rookie Pitchers SD 6.00 2.70
(SD in small print)
❑ 600 Rookie Infielders 5.00 2.20
Ron Cash
Jim Cox
Bill Madlock RC
Reggie Sanders
❑ 601 Rookie Outfielders 3.00 1.35
Ed Armbrister
Rich Bladt
Brian Downing RC
Bake McBride
❑ 602 Rookie Pitchers 1.00 .45
Glen Abbott
Rick Henninger
Craig Swan
Dan Vossler
❑ 603 Rookie Catchers 1.00 .45
Barry Foote
Tom Lundstedt
Charlie Moore RC
Sergio Robles
❑ 604 Rookie Infielders 5.00 2.20
Terry Hughes
John Knox
Andre Thornton
Frank White RC
❑ 605 Rookie Pitchers 4.00 1.80
Vic Albury
Ken Frailing
Kevin Kobel
Frank Tanana RC
❑ 606 Rookie Outfielders 1.00 .45
Jim Fuller
Wilbur Howard
Tommy Smith
Otto Velez
❑ 607 Rookie Shortstops 1.00 .45
Leo Foster
Tom Heintzelman
Dave Rosello
Frank Taveras RC
❑ 608A Rookie Pitchers ERR 2.00 .90
Bob Apodaco (sic)
Dick Baney
John D'Acquisto
Mike Wallace
❑ 608B Rookie Pitchers COR 1.00 .45
Bob Apodaca
Dick Baney
John D'Acquisto
Mike Wallace
❑ 609 Rico Petrocelli 1.00 .45
❑ 610 Dave Kingman 2.00 .90
❑ 611 Rich Stelmaszek .50 .23
❑ 612 Luke Walker .50 .23
❑ 613 Dan Monzon .50 .23
❑ 614 Adrian Devine .50 .23
❑ 615 Johnny Jeter UER .50 .23
(Misspelled Johnnie
on card back)
❑ 616 Larry Gura .50 .23
❑ 617 Ted Ford .50 .23
❑ 618 Jim Mason .50 .23
❑ 619 Mike Anderson .50 .23
❑ 620 Al Downing .50 .23
❑ 621 Bernie Carbo .50 .23
❑ 622 Phil Gagliano .50 .23
❑ 623 Celerino Sanchez .50 .23
❑ 624 Bob Miller .50 .23
❑ 625 Ollie Brown .50 .23
❑ 626 Pittsburgh Pirates 1.00 .45
Team Card
❑ 627 Carl Taylor .50 .23
❑ 628 Ivan Murrell .50 .23
❑ 629 Rusty Staub 2.00 .90
❑ 630 Tommie Agee 1.00 .45
❑ 631 Steve Barber .50 .23
❑ 632 George Culver .50 .23
❑ 633 Dave Hamilton .50 .23
❑ 634 Braves Leaders 2.00 .90
Eddie Mathews MG
Herm Starrette CO
Connie Ryan CO
Jim Busby CO
Ken Silvestri CO
❑ 635 Johnny Edwards .50 .23
❑ 636 Dave Goltz .50 .23
❑ 637 Checklist 529-660 3.00 .60
❑ 638 Ken Sanders .50 .23
❑ 639 Joe Lovitto .50 .23
❑ 640 Milt Pappas 1.00 .45
❑ 641 Chuck Brinkman .50 .23
❑ 642 Terry Harmon .50 .23
❑ 643 Dodgers Team 1.00 .45
❑ 644 Wayne Granger .50 .23
❑ 645 Ken Boswell .50 .23
❑ 646 George Foster 2.00 .90
❑ 647 Juan Beniquez .50 .23
❑ 648 Terry Crowley .50 .23

	NRMT	VG-E
❑ 649 Fernando Gonzalez	.50	.23
❑ 650 Mike Epstein	.50	.23
❑ 651 Leron Lee	.50	.23
❑ 652 Gail Hopkins	.50	.23
❑ 653 Bob Stinson	.50	.23
❑ 654A Jesus Alou ERR (No position)	1.00	.45
❑ 654B Jesus Alou COR (Outfield)	4.00	1.80
❑ 655 Mike Tyson	.50	.23
❑ 656 Adrian Garrett	.50	.23
❑ 657 Jim Shellenback	.50	.23
❑ 658 Lee Lacy	.50	.23
❑ 659 Joe Lis	.50	.23
❑ 660 Larry Dierker	2.00	.50

1974 Topps Traded

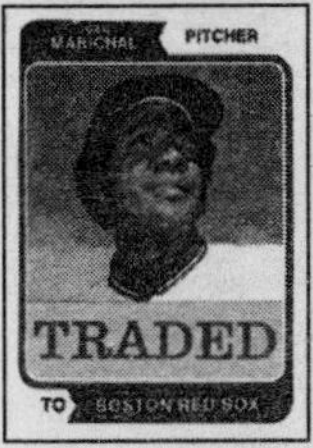

	NRMT	VG-E
COMPLETE SET (44)	20.00	9.00
❑ 23T Craig Robinson	.50	.23
❑ 42T Claude Osteen	.75	.35
❑ 43T Jim Wynn	.75	.35
❑ 51T Bobby Heise	.50	.23
❑ 59T Ross Grimsley	.50	.23
❑ 62T Bob Locker	.50	.23
❑ 63T Bill Sudakis	.50	.23
❑ 73T Mike Marshall	.75	.35
❑ 123T Nelson Briles	.75	.35
❑ 139T Aurelio Monteagudo	.50	.23
❑ 151T Diego Segui	.50	.23
❑ 165T Willie Davis	.75	.35
❑ 175T Reggie Cleveland	.50	.23
❑ 182T Lindy McDaniel	.75	.35
❑ 186T Fred Scherman	.50	.23
❑ 249T George Mitterwald	.50	.23
❑ 262T Ed Kirkpatrick	.50	.23
❑ 269T Bob Johnson	.50	.23
❑ 270T Ron Santo	1.00	.45
❑ 313T Barry Lersch	.50	.23
❑ 319T Randy Hundley	.75	.35
❑ 330T Juan Marichal	2.00	.90
❑ 348T Pete Richert	.50	.23
❑ 373T John Curtis	.50	.23
❑ 390T Lou Piniella	1.00	.45
❑ 428T Gary Sutherland	.50	.23
❑ 454T Kurt Bevacqua	.50	.23
❑ 458T Jim Ray	.50	.23
❑ 485T Felipe Alou	1.00	.45
❑ 486T Steve Stone	.75	.35
❑ 496T Tom Murphy	.50	.23
❑ 516T Horacio Pina	.50	.23
❑ 534T Eddie Watt	.50	.23
❑ 538T Cesar Tovar	.50	.23
❑ 544T Ron Schueler	.50	.23
❑ 579T Cecil Upshaw	.50	.23
❑ 585T Merv Rettenmund	.50	.23
❑ 612T Luke Walker	.50	.23
❑ 616T Larry Gura	.75	.35
❑ 618T Jim Mason	.50	.23
❑ 630T Tommie Agee	.75	.35
❑ 648T Terry Crowley	.50	.23
❑ 649T Fernando Gonzalez	.50	.23
❑ NNO Traded Checklist	1.50	.30

1975 Topps

	NRMT	VG-E
COMPLETE SET (660)	600.00	275.00
WRAPPER (15-CENT)	8.00	3.60
❑ 1 Hank Aaron RB Sets Homer Mark	30.00	10.00
❑ 2 Lou Brock RB 118 Stolen Bases	3.00	1.35
❑ 3 Bob Gibson RB 3000th Strikeout	3.00	1.35
❑ 4 Al Kaline RB 3000 Hit Club	6.00	2.70
❑ 5 Nolan Ryan RB Fans 300 for 3rd Year in a Row	15.00	6.75
❑ 6 Mike Marshall HL Hurls 106 Games	1.00	.45
❑ 7 Steve Busby HL Dick Bosman Nolan Ryan	8.00	3.60
❑ 8 Rogelio Moret	.50	.23
❑ 9 Frank Tepedino	.50	.23
❑ 10 Willie Davis	1.00	.45
❑ 11 Bill Melton	.50	.23
❑ 12 David Clyde	.50	.23
❑ 13 Gene Locklear RC	1.00	.45
❑ 14 Milt Wilcox	.50	.23
❑ 15 Jose Cardenal	1.00	.45
❑ 16 Frank Tanana	2.00	.90
❑ 17 Dave Concepcion	2.00	.90
❑ 18 Tigers: Team/Mgr. Ralph Houk (Checklist back)	2.00	.40
❑ 19 Jerry Koosman	1.00	.45
❑ 20 Thurman Munson	8.00	3.60
❑ 21 Rollie Fingers	3.00	1.35
❑ 22 Dave Cash	.50	.23
❑ 23 Bill Russell	1.00	.45
❑ 24 Al Fitzmorris	.50	.23
❑ 25 Lee May	1.00	.45
❑ 26 Dave McNally	1.00	.45
❑ 27 Ken Reitz	.50	.23
❑ 28 Tom Murphy	.50	.23
❑ 29 Dave Parker	3.00	1.35
❑ 30 Bert Blyleven	2.00	.90
❑ 31 Dave Rader	.50	.23
❑ 32 Reggie Cleveland	.50	.23
❑ 33 Dusty Baker	2.00	.90
❑ 34 Steve Renko	.50	.23
❑ 35 Ron Santo	1.00	.45
❑ 36 Joe Lovitto	.50	.23
❑ 37 Dave Freisleben	.50	.23
❑ 38 Buddy Bell	2.00	.90
❑ 39 Andre Thornton	1.00	.45
❑ 40 Bill Singer	.50	.23
❑ 41 Cesar Geronimo	1.00	.45
❑ 42 Joe Coleman	.50	.23
❑ 43 Cleon Jones	1.00	.45
❑ 44 Pat Dobson	.50	.23
❑ 45 Joe Rudi	1.00	.45
❑ 46 Phillies: Team/Mgr. Danny Ozark UER (Checklist back) (Terry Harmon listed as 339 instead of 399)	2.00	.40
❑ 47 Tommy John	2.00	.90
❑ 48 Freddie Patek	1.00	.45
❑ 49 Larry Dierker	1.00	.45
❑ 50 Brooks Robinson	8.00	3.60
❑ 51 Bob Forsch RC	1.00	.45
❑ 52 Darrell Porter	1.00	.45
❑ 53 Dave Giusti	.50	.23
❑ 54 Eric Soderholm	.50	.23
❑ 55 Bobby Bonds	2.00	.90
❑ 56 Rick Wise	1.00	.45
❑ 57 Dave Johnson	1.00	.45
❑ 58 Chuck Taylor	.50	.23
❑ 59 Ken Henderson	.50	.23
❑ 60 Fergie Jenkins	3.00	1.35
❑ 61 Dave Winfield	15.00	6.75
❑ 62 Fritz Peterson	.50	.23
❑ 63 Steve Swisher	.50	.23
❑ 64 Dave Chalk	.50	.23
❑ 65 Don Gullett	1.00	.45
❑ 66 Willie Horton	1.00	.45
❑ 67 Tug McGraw	1.00	.45
❑ 68 Ron Blomberg	.50	.23
❑ 69 John Odom	.50	.23
❑ 70 Mike Schmidt	20.00	9.00
❑ 71 Charlie Hough	1.00	.45
❑ 72 Royals: Team/Mgr. Jack McKeon (Checklist back)	2.00	.40
❑ 73 J.R. Richard	1.00	.45
❑ 74 Mark Belanger	1.00	.45
❑ 75 Ted Simmons	2.00	.90
❑ 76 Ed Sprague	.50	.23
❑ 77 Richie Zisk	1.00	.45
❑ 78 Ray Corbin	.50	.23
❑ 79 Gary Matthews	1.00	.45
❑ 80 Carlton Fisk	8.00	3.60
❑ 81 Ron Reed	.50	.23
❑ 82 Pat Kelly	.50	.23
❑ 83 Jim Merritt	.50	.23
❑ 84 Enzo Hernandez	.50	.23
❑ 85 Bill Bonham	.50	.23
❑ 86 Joe Lis	.50	.23
❑ 87 George Foster	2.00	.90
❑ 88 Tom Egan	.50	.23
❑ 89 Jim Ray	.50	.23
❑ 90 Rusty Staub	2.00	.90
❑ 91 Dick Green	.50	.23
❑ 92 Cecil Upshaw	.50	.23
❑ 93 Dave Lopes	2.00	.90
❑ 94 Jim Lonborg	1.00	.45
❑ 95 John Mayberry	1.00	.45
❑ 96 Mike Cosgrove	.50	.23
❑ 97 Earl Williams	.50	.23
❑ 98 Rich Folkers	.50	.23
❑ 99 Mike Hegan	.50	.23
❑ 100 Willie Stargell	4.00	1.80
❑ 101 Expos: Team/Mgr. Gene Mauch (Checklist back)	2.00	.40
❑ 102 Joe Decker	.50	.23
❑ 103 Rick Miller	.50	.23
❑ 104 Bill Madlock	2.00	.90
❑ 105 Buzz Capra	.50	.23
❑ 106 Mike Hargrove RC UER Gastonia At-bats are wrong	3.00	1.35
❑ 107 Jim Barr	.50	.23
❑ 108 Tom Hall	.50	.23
❑ 109 George Hendrick	1.00	.45
❑ 110 Wilbur Wood	.50	.23
❑ 111 Wayne Garrett	.50	.23
❑ 112 Larry Hardy	.50	.23
❑ 113 Elliott Maddox	.50	.23
❑ 114 Dick Lange	.50	.23
❑ 115 Joe Ferguson	.50	.23
❑ 116 Lerrin LaGrow	.50	.23
❑ 117 Orioles: Team/Mgr. Earl Weaver (Checklist back)	3.00	.60
❑ 118 Mike Anderson	.50	.23
❑ 119 Tommy Helms	.50	.23
❑ 120 Steve Busby UER (Photo actually Fran Healy)	1.00	.45
❑ 121 Bill North	.50	.23
❑ 122 Al Hrabosky	1.00	.45
❑ 123 Johnny Briggs	.50	.23
❑ 124 Jerry Reuss	1.00	.45

❑	125	Ken Singleton	1.00	.45
❑	126	Checklist 1-132	3.00	.60
❑	127	Glenn Borgmann	.50	.23
❑	128	Bill Lee	1.00	.45
❑	129	Rick Monday	1.00	.45
❑	130	Phil Niekro	3.00	1.35
❑	131	Toby Harrah	1.00	.45
❑	132	Randy Moffitt	.50	.23
❑	133	Dan Driessen	1.00	.45
❑	134	Ron Hodges	.50	.23
❑	135	Charlie Spikes	.50	.23
❑	136	Jim Mason	.50	.23
❑	137	Terry Forster	1.00	.45
❑	138	Del Unser	.50	.23
❑	139	Horacio Pina	.50	.23
❑	140	Steve Garvey	3.00	1.35
❑	141	Mickey Stanley	1.00	.45
❑	142	Bob Reynolds	.50	.23
❑	143	Cliff Johnson	1.00	.45
❑	144	Jim Wohlford	.50	.23
❑	145	Ken Holtzman	1.00	.45
❑	146	Padres: Team/Mgr.	2.00	.40
		John McNamara		
		(Checklist back)		
❑	147	Pedro Garcia	.50	.23
❑	148	Jim Rooker	.50	.23
❑	149	Tim Foli	.50	.23
❑	150	Bob Gibson	6.00	2.70
❑	151	Steve Brye	.50	.23
❑	152	Mario Guerrero	.50	.23
❑	153	Rick Reuschel	1.00	.45
❑	154	Mike Lum	.50	.23
❑	155	Jim Bibby	.50	.23
❑	156	Dave Kingman	2.00	.90
❑	157	Pedro Borbon	1.00	.45
❑	158	Jerry Grote	.50	.23
❑	159	Steve Arlin	.50	.23
❑	160	Graig Nettles	2.00	.90
❑	161	Stan Bahnsen	.50	.23
❑	162	Willie Montanez	.50	.23
❑	163	Jim Brewer	.50	.23
❑	164	Mickey Rivers	1.00	.45
❑	165	Doug Rader	1.00	.45
❑	166	Woodie Fryman	.50	.23
❑	167	Rich Coggins	.50	.23
❑	168	Bill Greif	.50	.23
❑	169	Cookie Rojas	1.00	.45
❑	170	Bert Campaneris	1.00	.45
❑	171	Ed Kirkpatrick	.50	.23
❑	172	Red Sox: Team/Mgr.	3.00	.60
		Darrell Johnson		
		(Checklist back)		
❑	173	Steve Rogers	1.00	.45
❑	174	Bake McBride	1.00	.45
❑	175	Don Money	1.00	.45
❑	176	Burt Hooton	1.00	.45
❑	177	Vic Correll	.50	.23
❑	178	Cesar Tovar	.50	.23
❑	179	Tom Bradley	.50	.23
❑	180	Joe Morgan	6.00	2.70
❑	181	Fred Beene	.50	.23
❑	182	Don Hahn	.50	.23
❑	183	Mel Stottlemyre	1.00	.45
❑	184	Jorge Orta	.50	.23
❑	185	Steve Carlton	8.00	3.60
❑	186	Willie Crawford	.50	.23
❑	187	Denny Doyle	.50	.23
❑	188	Tom Griffin	.50	.23
❑	189	1951 MVP's	4.00	1.80
		Larry (Yogi) Berra		
		Roy Campanella		
		(Campy never issued)		
❑	190	1952 MVP's	2.00	.90
		Bobby Shantz		
		Hank Sauer		
❑	191	1953 MVP's	2.00	.90
		Al Rosen		
		Roy Campanella		
❑	192	1954 MVP's	4.00	1.80
		Yogi Berra		
		Willie Mays		
❑	193	1955 MVP's UER	3.00	1.35
		Yogi Berra		
		Roy Campanella		
		(Campy card never		
		issued, pictured		
		with LA cap)		
❑	194	1956 MVP's	10.00	4.50
		Mickey Mantle		
		Don Newcombe		
❑	195	1957 MVP's	12.00	5.50
		Mickey Mantle		
		Hank Aaron		
❑	196	1958 MVP's	2.00	.90
		Jackie Jensen		
		Ernie Banks		
❑	197	1959 MVP's	2.00	.90
		Nellie Fox		
		Ernie Banks		
❑	198	1960 MVP's	2.00	.90
		Roger Maris		
		Dick Groat		
❑	199	1961 MVP's	3.00	1.35
		Roger Maris		
		Frank Robinson		
❑	200	1962 MVP's	10.00	4.50
		Mickey Mantle		
		Maury Wills		
		(Wills never issued)		
❑	201	1963 MVP's	2.00	.90
		Elston Howard		
		Sandy Koufax		
❑	202	1964 MVP's	2.00	.90
		Brooks Robinson		
		Ken Boyer		
❑	203	1965 MVP's	2.00	.90
		Zoilo Versalles		
		Willie Mays		
❑	204	1966 MVP's	6.00	2.70
		Frank Robinson		
		Bob Clemente		
❑	205	1967 MVP's	2.00	.90
		Carl Yastrzemski		
		Orlando Cepeda		
❑	206	1968 MVP's UER	2.00	.90
		Denny McLain		
		Bob Gibson		
		On the back McLain is spelled McClain		
❑	207	1969 MVP's	2.00	.90
		Harmon Killebrew		
		Willie McCovey		
❑	208	1970 MVP's	2.00	.90
		Boog Powell		
		Johnny Bench		
❑	209	1971 MVP's	2.00	.90
		Vida Blue		
		Joe Torre		
❑	210	1972 MVP's	2.00	.90
		Rich Allen		
		Johnny Bench		
❑	211	1973 MVP's	5.00	2.20
		Reggie Jackson		
		Pete Rose		
❑	212	1974 MVP's	2.00	.90
		Jeff Burroughs		
		Steve Garvey		
❑	213	Oscar Gamble	1.00	.45
❑	214	Harry Parker	.50	.23
❑	215	Bobby Valentine	1.00	.45
❑	216	Giants: Team/Mgr.	2.00	.40
		Wes Westrum		
		(Checklist back)		
❑	217	Lou Piniella	2.00	.90
❑	218	Jerry Johnson	.50	.23
❑	219	Ed Herrmann	.50	.23
❑	220	Don Sutton	3.00	1.35
❑	221	Aurelio Rodriguez	.50	.23
❑	222	Dan Spillner	.50	.23
❑	223	Robin Yount RC	50.00	22.00
❑	224	Ramon Hernandez	.50	.23
❑	225	Bob Grich	1.00	.45
❑	226	Bill Campbell	.50	.23
❑	227	Bob Watson	1.00	.45
❑	228	George Brett RC	80.00	36.00
❑	229	Barry Foote	.50	.23
❑	230	Jim Hunter	4.00	1.80
❑	231	Mike Tyson	.50	.23
❑	232	Diego Segui	.50	.23
❑	233	Billy Grabarkewitz	.50	.23
❑	234	Tom Grieve	1.00	.45
❑	235	Jack Billingham	1.00	.45
❑	236	Angels: Team/Mgr.	2.00	.40
		Dick Williams		
		(Checklist back)		
❑	237	Carl Morton	.50	.23
❑	238	Dave Duncan	.50	.23
❑	239	George Stone	.50	.23
❑	240	Garry Maddox	1.00	.45
❑	241	Dick Tidrow	.50	.23
❑	242	Jay Johnstone	1.00	.45
❑	243	Jim Kaat	2.00	.90
❑	244	Bill Buckner	1.00	.45
❑	245	Mickey Lolich	2.00	.90
❑	246	Cardinals: Team/Mgr.	2.00	.40
		Red Schoendienst		
		(Checklist back)		
❑	247	Enos Cabell	.50	.23
❑	248	Randy Jones	2.00	.90
❑	249	Danny Thompson	.50	.23
❑	250	Ken Brett	.50	.23
❑	251	Fran Healy	.50	.23
❑	252	Fred Scherman	.50	.23
❑	253	Jesus Alou	.50	.23
❑	254	Mike Torrez	1.00	.45
❑	255	Dwight Evans	2.00	.90
❑	256	Billy Champion	.50	.23
❑	257	Checklist: 133-264	3.00	.60
❑	258	Dave LaRoche	.50	.23
❑	259	Len Randle	.50	.23
❑	260	Johnny Bench	15.00	6.75
❑	261	Andy Hassler	.50	.23
❑	262	Rowland Office	.50	.23
❑	263	Jim Perry	1.00	.45
❑	264	John Milner	.50	.23
❑	265	Ron Bryant	.50	.23
❑	266	Sandy Alomar	1.00	.45
❑	267	Dick Ruthven	.50	.23
❑	268	Hal McRae	1.00	.45
❑	269	Doug Rau	.50	.23
❑	270	Ron Fairly	1.00	.45
❑	271	Gerry Moses	.50	.23
❑	272	Lynn McGlothen	.50	.23
❑	273	Steve Braun	.50	.23
❑	274	Vicente Romo	.50	.23
❑	275	Paul Blair	1.00	.45
❑	276	White Sox Team/Mgr.	2.00	.40
		Chuck Tanner		
		(Checklist back)		
❑	277	Frank Taveras	.50	.23
❑	278	Paul Lindblad	.50	.23
❑	279	Milt May	.50	.23
❑	280	Carl Yastrzemski	12.00	5.50
❑	281	Jim Slaton	.50	.23
❑	282	Jerry Morales	.50	.23
❑	283	Steve Foucault	.50	.23
❑	284	Ken Griffey	4.00	1.80
❑	285	Ellie Rodriguez	.50	.23
❑	286	Mike Jorgensen	.50	.23
❑	287	Roric Harrison	.50	.23
❑	288	Bruce Ellingsen	.50	.23
❑	289	Ken Rudolph	.50	.23
❑	290	Jon Matlack	.50	.23
❑	291	Bill Sudakis	.50	.23
❑	292	Ron Schueler	.50	.23
❑	293	Dick Sharon	.50	.23
❑	294	Geoff Zahn	.50	.23
❑	295	Vada Pinson	2.00	.90
❑	296	Alan Foster	.50	.23
❑	297	Craig Kusick	.50	.23
❑	298	Johnny Grubb	.50	.23
❑	299	Bucky Dent	2.00	.90
❑	300	Reggie Jackson	15.00	6.75
❑	301	Dave Roberts	.50	.23
❑	302	Rick Burleson	1.00	.45
❑	303	Grant Jackson	.50	.23
❑	304	Pirates: Team/Mgr.	2.00	.40
		Danny Murtaugh		
		(Checklist back)		
❑	305	Jim Colborn	.50	.23
❑	306	Batting Leaders	2.00	.90
		Rod Carew		
		Ralph Garr		
❑	307	Home Run Leaders	4.00	1.80
		Dick Allen		
		Mike Schmidt		
❑	308	RBI Leaders	2.00	.90
		Jeff Burroughs		

Johnny Bench
- ❑ 309 Stolen Base Leaders 2.00 .90
  Bill North
  Lou Brock
- ❑ 310 Victory Leaders 2.00 .90
  Jim Hunter
  Fergie Jenkins
  Andy Messersmith
  Phil Niekro
- ❑ 311 ERA Leaders 2.00 .90
  Jim Hunter
  Buzz Capra
- ❑ 312 Strikeout Leaders 12.00 5.50
  Nolan Ryan
  Steve Carlton
- ❑ 313 Firemen Leaders 1.00 .45
  Terry Forster
  Mike Marshall
- ❑ 314 Buck Martinez .50 .23
- ❑ 315 Don Kessinger 1.00 .45
- ❑ 316 Jackie Brown .50 .23
- ❑ 317 Joe Lahoud .50 .23
- ❑ 318 Ernie McAnally .50 .23
- ❑ 319 Johnny Oates 1.00 .45
- ❑ 320 Pete Rose 30.00 13.50
- ❑ 321 Rudy May .50 .23
- ❑ 322 Ed Goodson .50 .23
- ❑ 323 Fred Holdsworth .50 .23
- ❑ 324 Ed Kranepool 1.00 .45
- ❑ 325 Tony Oliva 2.00 .90
- ❑ 326 Wayne Twitchell .50 .23
- ❑ 327 Jerry Hairston .50 .23
- ❑ 328 Sonny Siebert .50 .23
- ❑ 329 Ted Kubiak .50 .23
- ❑ 330 Mike Marshall 1.00 .45
- ❑ 331 Indians: Team/Mgr. 2.00 .40
  Frank Robinson
  (Checklist back)
- ❑ 332 Fred Kendall .50 .23
- ❑ 333 Dick Drago .50 .23
- ❑ 334 Greg Gross .50 .23
- ❑ 335 Jim Palmer 6.00 2.70
- ❑ 336 Rennie Stennett .50 .23
- ❑ 337 Kevin Kobel .50 .23
- ❑ 338 Rich Stelmaszek .50 .23
- ❑ 339 Jim Fregosi 1.00 .45
- ❑ 340 Paul Splittorff .50 .23
- ❑ 341 Hal Breeden .50 .23
- ❑ 342 Leroy Stanton .50 .23
- ❑ 343 Danny Frisella .50 .23
- ❑ 344 Ben Oglivie 1.00 .45
- ❑ 345 Clay Carroll 1.00 .45
- ❑ 346 Bobby Darwin .50 .23
- ❑ 347 Mike Caldwell .50 .23
- ❑ 348 Tony Muser .50 .23
- ❑ 349 Ray Sadecki .50 .23
- ❑ 350 Bobby Murcer 1.00 .45
- ❑ 351 Bob Boone 2.00 .90
- ❑ 352 Darold Knowles .50 .23
- ❑ 353 Luis Melendez .50 .23
- ❑ 354 Dick Bosman .50 .23
- ❑ 355 Chris Cannizzaro .50 .23
- ❑ 356 Rico Petrocelli 1.00 .45
- ❑ 357 Ken Forsch UER .50 .23
  Forsch is misspelled in blurb
- ❑ 358 Al Bumbry 1.00 .45
- ❑ 359 Paul Popovich .50 .23
- ❑ 360 George Scott 1.00 .45
- ❑ 361 Dodgers: Team/Mgr. 2.00 .40
  Walter Alston
  (Checklist back)
- ❑ 362 Steve Hargan .50 .23
- ❑ 363 Carmen Fanzone .50 .23
- ❑ 364 Doug Bird .50 .23
- ❑ 365 Bob Bailey .50 .23
- ❑ 366 Ken Sanders .50 .23
- ❑ 367 Craig Robinson .50 .23
- ❑ 368 Vic Albury .50 .23
- ❑ 369 Merv Rettenmund .50 .23
- ❑ 370 Tom Seaver 12.00 5.50
- ❑ 371 Gates Brown .50 .23
- ❑ 372 John D'Acquisto .50 .23
- ❑ 373 Bill Sharp .50 .23
- ❑ 374 Eddie Watt .50 .23
- ❑ 375 Roy White 1.00 .45
- ❑ 376 Steve Yeager 1.00 .45
- ❑ 377 Tom Hilgendorf .50 .23
- ❑ 378 Derrel Thomas .50 .23
- ❑ 379 Bernie Carbo .50 .23
- ❑ 380 Sal Bando 1.00 .45
- ❑ 381 John Curtis .50 .23
- ❑ 382 Don Baylor 2.00 .90
- ❑ 383 Jim York .50 .23
- ❑ 384 Brewers: Team/Mgr. 2.00 .40
  Del Crandall
  (Checklist back)
- ❑ 385 Dock Ellis .50 .23
- ❑ 386 Checklist: 265-396 UER 3.00 .60
  Dick Sharon's name is misspelled
- ❑ 387 Jim Spencer .50 .23
- ❑ 388 Steve Stone 1.00 .45
- ❑ 389 Tony Solaita .50 .23
- ❑ 390 Ron Cey 2.00 .90
- ❑ 391 Don DeMola .50 .23
- ❑ 392 Bruce Bochte 1.00 .45
- ❑ 393 Gary Gentry .50 .23
- ❑ 394 Larvell Blanks .50 .23
- ❑ 395 Bud Harrelson 1.00 .45
- ❑ 396 Fred Norman 1.00 .45
- ❑ 397 Bill Freehan 1.00 .45
- ❑ 398 Elias Sosa .50 .23
- ❑ 399 Terry Harmon .50 .23
- ❑ 400 Dick Allen 2.00 .90
- ❑ 401 Mike Wallace .50 .23
- ❑ 402 Bob Tolan .50 .23
- ❑ 403 Tom Buskey .50 .23
- ❑ 404 Ted Sizemore .50 .23
- ❑ 405 John Montague .50 .23
- ❑ 406 Bob Gallagher .50 .23
- ❑ 407 Herb Washington RC 2.00 .90
- ❑ 408 Clyde Wright UER .50 .23
  Listed with wrong 1974 team
- ❑ 409 Bob Robertson .50 .23
- ❑ 410 Mike Cueller UER 1.00 .45
  Sic, Cuellar
- ❑ 411 George Mitterwald .50 .23
- ❑ 412 Bill Hands .50 .23
- ❑ 413 Marty Pattin .50 .23
- ❑ 414 Manny Mota 1.00 .45
- ❑ 415 John Hiller 1.00 .45
- ❑ 416 Larry Lintz .50 .23
- ❑ 417 Skip Lockwood .50 .23
- ❑ 418 Leo Foster .50 .23
- ❑ 419 Dave Goltz .50 .23
- ❑ 420 Larry Bowa 2.00 .90
- ❑ 421 Mets: Team/Mgr. 3.00 .60
  Yogi Berra
  (Checklist back)
- ❑ 422 Brian Downing 1.00 .45
- ❑ 423 Clay Kirby .50 .23
- ❑ 424 John Lowenstein .50 .23
- ❑ 425 Tito Fuentes .50 .23
- ❑ 426 George Medich .50 .23
- ❑ 427 Clarence Gaston 1.00 .45
- ❑ 428 Dave Hamilton .50 .23
- ❑ 429 Jim Dwyer .50 .23
- ❑ 430 Luis Tiant 2.00 .90
- ❑ 431 Rod Gilbreath .50 .23
- ❑ 432 Ken Berry .50 .23
- ❑ 433 Larry Demery .50 .23
- ❑ 434 Bob Locker .50 .23
- ❑ 435 Dave Nelson .50 .23
- ❑ 436 Ken Frailing .50 .23
- ❑ 437 Al Cowens 1.00 .45
- ❑ 438 Don Carrithers .50 .23
- ❑ 439 Ed Brinkman .50 .23
- ❑ 440 Andy Messersmith 1.00 .45
- ❑ 441 Bobby Heise .50 .23
- ❑ 442 Maximino Leon .50 .23
- ❑ 443 Twins: Team/Mgr. 2.00 .40
  Frank Quilici
  (Checklist back)
- ❑ 444 Gene Garber 1.00 .45
- ❑ 445 Felix Millan .50 .23
- ❑ 446 Bart Johnson .50 .23
- ❑ 447 Terry Crowley .50 .23
- ❑ 448 Frank Duffy .50 .23
- ❑ 449 Charlie Williams .50 .23
- ❑ 450 Willie McCovey 6.00 2.70
- ❑ 451 Rick Dempsey 1.00 .45
- ❑ 452 Angel Mangual .50 .23
- ❑ 453 Claude Osteen 1.00 .45
- ❑ 454 Doug Griffin .50 .23
- ❑ 455 Don Wilson .50 .23
- ❑ 456 Bob Coluccio .50 .23
- ❑ 457 Mario Mendoza .50 .23
- ❑ 458 Ross Grimsley .50 .23
- ❑ 459 1974 AL Champs 1.00 .45
  A's over Orioles
  (Second base action
  pictured)
- ❑ 460 Steve Garvey NLCS 2.00 .90
  Frank Taveras
- ❑ 461 Reggie Jackson WS 5.00 2.20
- ❑ 462 World Series Game 2 1.00 .45
  (Dodger dugout)
- ❑ 463 Rollie Fingers WS 2.00 .90
- ❑ 464 World Series Game 4 1.00 .45
  (A's batter)
- ❑ 465 Joe Rudi WS5 1.00 .45
- ❑ 466 WS Summary 2.00 .90
  A's do it again;
  win third straight
  A's group picture
- ❑ 467 Ed Halicki .50 .23
- ❑ 468 Bobby Mitchell .50 .23
- ❑ 469 Tom Dettore .50 .23
- ❑ 470 Jeff Burroughs 1.00 .45
- ❑ 471 Bob Stinson .50 .23
- ❑ 472 Bruce Dal Canton .50 .23
- ❑ 473 Ken McMullen .50 .23
- ❑ 474 Luke Walker .50 .23
- ❑ 475 Darrell Evans 1.00 .45
- ❑ 476 Ed Figueroa .50 .23
- ❑ 477 Tom Hutton .50 .23
- ❑ 478 Tom Burgmeier .50 .23
- ❑ 479 Ken Boswell .50 .23
- ❑ 480 Carlos May .50 .23
- ❑ 481 Will McEnaney 1.00 .45
- ❑ 482 Tom McCraw .50 .23
- ❑ 483 Steve Ontiveros .50 .23
- ❑ 484 Glenn Beckert 1.00 .45
- ❑ 485 Sparky Lyle 1.00 .45
- ❑ 486 Ray Fosse .50 .23
- ❑ 487 Astros: Team/Mgr. 2.00 .40
  Preston Gomez
  (Checklist back)
- ❑ 488 Bill Travers .50 .23
- ❑ 489 Cecil Cooper 2.00 .90
- ❑ 490 Reggie Smith 1.00 .45
- ❑ 491 Doyle Alexander 1.00 .45
- ❑ 492 Rich Hebner 1.00 .45
- ❑ 493 Don Stanhouse .50 .23
- ❑ 494 Pete LaCock .50 .23
- ❑ 495 Nelson Briles 1.00 .45
- ❑ 496 Pepe Frias .50 .23
- ❑ 497 Jim Nettles .50 .23
- ❑ 498 Al Downing .50 .23
- ❑ 499 Marty Perez .50 .23
- ❑ 500 Nolan Ryan 50.00 22.00
- ❑ 501 Bill Robinson 1.00 .45
- ❑ 502 Pat Bourque .50 .23
- ❑ 503 Fred Stanley .50 .23
- ❑ 504 Buddy Bradford .50 .23
- ❑ 505 Chris Speier .50 .23
- ❑ 506 Leron Lee .50 .23
- ❑ 507 Tom Carroll .50 .23
- ❑ 508 Bob Hansen .50 .23
- ❑ 509 Dave Hilton .50 .23
- ❑ 510 Vida Blue 1.00 .45
- ❑ 511 Rangers: Team/Mgr. 2.00 .40
  Billy Martin
  (Checklist back)
- ❑ 512 Larry Milbourne .50 .23
- ❑ 513 Dick Pole .50 .23
- ❑ 514 Jose Cruz 2.00 .90
- ❑ 515 Manny Sanguillen 1.00 .45
- ❑ 516 Don Hood .50 .23
- ❑ 517 Checklist: 397-528 3.00 .60
- ❑ 518 Leo Cardenas .50 .23
- ❑ 519 Jim Todd .50 .23
- ❑ 520 Amos Otis 1.00 .45
- ❑ 521 Dennis Blair .50 .23
- ❑ 522 Gary Sutherland .50 .23
- ❑ 523 Tom Paciorek 1.00 .45
- ❑ 524 John Doherty .50 .23
- ❑ 525 Tom House .50 .23
- ❑ 526 Larry Hisle 1.00 .45

❑ 527 Mac Scarce .50 .23
❑ 528 Eddie Leon .50 .23
❑ 529 Gary Thomasson .50 .23
❑ 530 Gaylord Perry 3.00 1.35
❑ 531 Reds: Team/Mgr. 5.00 1.00
Sparky Anderson
(Checklist back)
❑ 532 Gorman Thomas 1.00 .45
❑ 533 Rudy Meoli .50 .23
❑ 534 Alex Johnson .50 .23
❑ 535 Gene Tenace 1.00 .45
❑ 536 Bob Moose .50 .23
❑ 537 Tommy Harper 1.00 .45
❑ 538 Duffy Dyer .50 .23
❑ 539 Jesse Jefferson .50 .23
❑ 540 Lou Brock 6.00 2.70
❑ 541 Roger Metzger .50 .23
❑ 542 Pete Broberg .50 .23
❑ 543 Larry Biittner .50 .23
❑ 544 Steve Mingori .50 .23
❑ 545 Billy Williams 3.00 1.35
❑ 546 John Knox .50 .23
❑ 547 Von Joshua .50 .23
❑ 548 Charlie Sands .50 .23
❑ 549 Bill Butler .50 .23
❑ 550 Ralph Garr 1.00 .45
❑ 551 Larry Christenson .50 .23
❑ 552 Jack Brohamer .50 .23
❑ 553 John Boccabella .50 .23
❑ 554 Rich Gossage 2.00 .90
❑ 555 Al Oliver 2.00 .90
❑ 556 Tim Johnson .50 .23
❑ 557 Larry Gura .50 .23
❑ 558 Dave Roberts .50 .23
❑ 559 Bob Montgomery .50 .23
❑ 560 Tony Perez 4.00 1.80
❑ 561 A's: Team/Mgr. 2.00 .40
Alvin Dark
(Checklist back)
❑ 562 Gary Nolan 1.00 .45
❑ 563 Wilbur Howard .50 .23
❑ 564 Tommy Davis 1.00 .45
❑ 565 Joe Torre 2.00 .90
❑ 566 Ray Burris .50 .23
❑ 567 Jim Sundberg RC 2.00 .90
❑ 568 Dale Murray .50 .23
❑ 569 Frank White 1.00 .45
❑ 570 Jim Wynn 1.00 .45
❑ 571 Dave Lemanczyk .50 .23
❑ 572 Roger Nelson .50 .23
❑ 573 Orlando Pena .50 .23
❑ 574 Tony Taylor 1.00 .45
❑ 575 Gene Clines .50 .23
❑ 576 Phil Roof .50 .23
❑ 577 John Morris .50 .23
❑ 578 Dave Tomlin .50 .23
❑ 579 Skip Pitlock .50 .23
❑ 580 Frank Robinson 6.00 2.70
❑ 581 Darrel Chaney .50 .23
❑ 582 Eduardo Rodriguez .50 .23
❑ 583 Andy Etchebarren .50 .23
❑ 584 Mike Garman .50 .23
❑ 585 Chris Chambliss 1.00 .45
❑ 586 Tim McCarver 2.00 .90
❑ 587 Chris Ward .50 .23
❑ 588 Rick Auerbach .50 .23
❑ 589 Braves: Team/Mgr. 2.00 .40
Clyde King
(Checklist back)
❑ 590 Cesar Cedeno 1.00 .45
❑ 591 Glenn Abbott .50 .23
❑ 592 Balor Moore .50 .23
❑ 593 Gene Lamont .50 .23
❑ 594 Jim Fuller .50 .23
❑ 595 Joe Niekro 1.00 .45
❑ 596 Ollie Brown .50 .23
❑ 597 Winston Llenas .50 .23
❑ 598 Bruce Kison .50 .23
❑ 599 Nate Colbert .50 .23
❑ 600 Rod Carew 8.00 3.60
❑ 601 Juan Beniquez .50 .23
❑ 602 John Vukovich .50 .23
❑ 603 Lew Krausse .50 .23
❑ 604 Oscar Zamora .50 .23
❑ 605 John Ellis .50 .23
❑ 606 Bruce Miller .50 .23
❑ 607 Jim Holt .50 .23
❑ 608 Gene Michael 1.00 .45
❑ 609 Elrod Hendricks .50 .23
❑ 610 Ron Hunt .50 .23
❑ 611 Yankees: Team/Mgr. 2.00 .40
Bill Virdon
(Checklist back)
❑ 612 Terry Hughes .50 .23
❑ 613 Bill Parsons .50 .23
❑ 614 Rookie Pitchers 1.00 .45
Jack Kucek
Dyar Miller
Vern Ruhle
Paul Siebert
❑ 615 Rookie Pitchers 2.00 .90
Pat Darcy
Dennis Leonard RC
Tom Underwood
Hank Webb
❑ 616 Rookie Outfielders 15.00 6.75
Dave Augustine
Pepe Mangual
Jim Rice RC
John Scott
❑ 617 Rookie Infielders 2.00 .90
Mike Cubbage
Doug DeCinces RC
Reggie Sanders
Manny Trillo
❑ 618 Rookie Pitchers 1.00 .45
Jamie Easterly
Tom Johnson
Scott McGregor RC
Rick Rhoden
❑ 619 Rookie Outfielders 1.00 .45
Benny Ayala
Nyls Nyman
Tommy Smith
Jerry Turner
❑ 620 Rookie Catcher/OF 15.00 6.75
Gary Carter RC
Marc Hill
Danny Meyer
Leon Roberts
❑ 621 Rookie Pitchers 2.00 .90
John Denny RC
Rawly Eastwick
Jim Kern
Juan Veintidos
❑ 622 Rookie Outfielders 8.00 3.60
Ed Armbrister
Fred Lynn RC
Tom Poquette
Terry Whitfield UER
(Listed as Ney York)
❑ 623 Rookie Infielders 6.00 2.70
Phil Garner
Keith Hernandez RC UER
(Sic, bats right)
Bob Sheldon
Tom Veryzer
❑ 624 Rookie Pitchers 1.00 .45
Doug Konieczny
Gary Lavelle
Jim Otten
Eddie Solomon
❑ 625 Boog Powell 2.00 .90
❑ 626 Larry Haney UER .50 .23
Photo actually
Dave Duncan
❑ 627 Tom Walker .50 .23
❑ 628 Ron LeFlore RC 1.00 .45
❑ 629 Joe Hoerner .50 .23
❑ 630 Greg Luzinski 2.00 .90
❑ 631 Lee Lacy .50 .23
❑ 632 Morris Nettles .50 .23
❑ 633 Paul Casanova .50 .23
❑ 634 Cy Acosta .50 .23
❑ 635 Chuck Dobson .50 .23
❑ 636 Charlie Moore .50 .23
❑ 637 Ted Martinez .50 .23
❑ 638 Cubs: Team/Mgr. 2.00 .40
Jim Marshall
(Checklist back)
❑ 639 Steve Kline .50 .23
❑ 640 Harmon Killebrew 6.00 2.70
❑ 641 Jim Northrup .50 .23
❑ 642 Mike Phillips .50 .23
❑ 643 Brent Strom .50 .23
❑ 644 Bill Fahey .50 .23
❑ 645 Danny Cater .50 .23
❑ 646 Checklist: 529-660 3.00 .60
❑ 647 Cl. Washington RC 2.00 .90
❑ 648 Dave Pagan .50 .23
❑ 649 Jack Heidemann .50 .23
❑ 650 Dave May .50 .23
❑ 651 John Morlan .50 .23
❑ 652 Lindy McDaniel 1.00 .45
❑ 653 Lee Richard UER .50 .23
(Listed as Richards
on card front)
❑ 654 Jerry Terrell .50 .23
❑ 655 Rico Carty 1.00 .45
❑ 656 Bill Plummer .50 .23
❑ 657 Bob Oliver .50 .23
❑ 658 Vic Harris .50 .23
❑ 659 Bob Apodaca .50 .23
❑ 660 Hank Aaron 30.00 9.00

1976 Topps

	NRMT	VG-E
COMPLETE SET (660)	300.00	135.00

❑ 1 Hank Aaron RB 15.00 4.70
2262 Career RBIs
❑ 2 Bobby Bonds RB 1.50 .70
Most leadoff HR's 32;
plus three seasons
30 homers/30 steals
❑ 3 Mickey Lolich RB .75 .35
Most Lefthanded Strikeouts: 2679
❑ 4 Dave Lopes RB .75 .35
Most Consecutive SB's: 38
❑ 5 Tom Seaver RB 5.00 2.20
Most Consecutive seasons
with 200 Strikeouts
❑ 6 Rennie Stennett RB .75 .35
7 Hits in a 9 inning game
❑ 7 Jim Umbarger .40 .18
❑ 8 Tito Fuentes .40 .18
❑ 9 Paul Lindblad .40 .18
❑ 10 Lou Brock 5.00 2.20
❑ 11 Jim Hughes .40 .18
❑ 12 Richie Zisk .75 .35
❑ 13 John Wockenfuss .40 .18
❑ 14 Gene Garber .75 .35
❑ 15 George Scott .75 .35
❑ 16 Bob Apodaca .40 .18
❑ 17 New York Yankees 1.50 .30
Team Card;
Billy Martin MG
(Checklist back)
❑ 18 Dale Murray .40 .18
❑ 19 George Brett 30.00 13.50
❑ 20 Bob Watson .75 .35
❑ 21 Dave LaRoche .40 .18
❑ 22 Bill Russell .75 .35
❑ 23 Brian Downing .40 .18
❑ 24 Cesar Geronimo .75 .35
❑ 25 Mike Torrez .75 .35
❑ 26 Andre Thornton .75 .35
❑ 27 Ed Figueroa .40 .18
❑ 28 Dusty Baker 1.50 .70

❑ 29 Rick Burleson .75 .35
❑ 30 John Montefusco .75 .35
❑ 31 Len Randle .40 .18
❑ 32 Danny Frisella .40 .18
❑ 33 Bill North .40 .18
❑ 34 Mike Garman .40 .18
❑ 35 Tony Oliva 1.50 .70
❑ 36 Frank Taveras .40 .18
❑ 37 John Hiller .75 .35
❑ 38 Garry Maddox .75 .35
❑ 39 Pete Broberg .40 .18
❑ 40 Dave Kingman 1.50 .70
❑ 41 Tippy Martinez .75 .35
❑ 42 Barry Foote .40 .18
❑ 43 Paul Splittorff .40 .18
❑ 44 Doug Rader .75 .35
❑ 45 Boog Powell 1.50 .70
❑ 46 Los Angeles Dodgers 1.50 .30
Team Card;
Walter Alston MG
(Checklist back)
❑ 47 Jesse Jefferson .40 .18
❑ 48 Dave Concepcion 1.50 .70
❑ 49 Dave Duncan .40 .18
❑ 50 Fred Lynn 1.50 .70
❑ 51 Ray Burris .40 .18
❑ 52 Dave Chalk .40 .18
❑ 53 Mike Beard .40 .18
❑ 54 Dave Rader .40 .18
❑ 55 Gaylord Perry 2.50 1.10
❑ 56 Bob Tolan .40 .18
❑ 57 Phil Garner .75 .35
❑ 58 Ron Reed .40 .18
❑ 59 Larry Hisle .75 .35
❑ 60 Jerry Reuss .75 .35
❑ 61 Ron LeFlore .75 .35
❑ 62 Johnny Oates .75 .35
❑ 63 Bobby Darwin .40 .18
❑ 64 Jerry Koosman .75 .35
❑ 65 Chris Chambliss .75 .35
❑ 66 Gus Bell FS .75 .35
Buddy Bell
❑ 67 Ray Boone FS .75 .35
Bob Boone
❑ 68 Joe Coleman FS .40 .18
Joe Coleman Jr.
❑ 69 Jim Hegan FS .40 .18
Mike Hegan
❑ 70 Roy Smalley FS .75 .35
Roy Smalley Jr.
❑ 71 Steve Rogers .75 .35
❑ 72 Hal McRae .75 .35
❑ 73 Baltimore Orioles 1.50 .30
Team Card;
Earl Weaver MG
(Checklist back)
❑ 74 Oscar Gamble .75 .35
❑ 75 Larry Dierker .75 .35
❑ 76 Willie Crawford .40 .18
❑ 77 Pedro Borbon .75 .35
❑ 78 Cecil Cooper .75 .35
❑ 79 Jerry Morales .40 .18
❑ 80 Jim Kaat 1.50 .70
❑ 81 Darrell Evans .75 .35
❑ 82 Von Joshua .40 .18
❑ 83 Jim Spencer .40 .18
❑ 84 Brent Strom .40 .18
❑ 85 Mickey Rivers .75 .35
❑ 86 Mike Tyson .40 .18
❑ 87 Tom Burgmeier .40 .18
❑ 88 Duffy Dyer .40 .18
❑ 89 Vern Ruhle .40 .18
❑ 90 Sal Bando .75 .35
❑ 91 Tom Hutton .40 .18
❑ 92 Eduardo Rodriguez .40 .18
❑ 93 Mike Phillips .40 .18
❑ 94 Jim Dwyer .40 .18
❑ 95 Brooks Robinson 6.00 2.70
❑ 96 Doug Bird .40 .18
❑ 97 Wilbur Howard .40 .18
❑ 98 Dennis Eckersley RC 25.00 11.00
❑ 99 Lee Lacy .40 .18
❑ 100 Jim Hunter 3.00 1.35
❑ 101 Pete LaCock .40 .18
❑ 102 Jim Willoughby .40 .18
❑ 103 Biff Pocoroba .40 .18
❑ 104 Cincinnati Reds 2.50 .50
Team Card;
Sparky Anderson MG
(Checklist back)
❑ 105 Gary Lavelle .40 .18
❑ 106 Tom Grieve .40 .18
❑ 107 Dave Roberts .40 .18
❑ 108 Don Kirkwood .40 .18
❑ 109 Larry Lintz .40 .18
❑ 110 Carlos May .40 .18
❑ 111 Danny Thompson .40 .18
❑ 112 Kent Tekulve RC 1.50 .70
❑ 113 Gary Sutherland .40 .18
❑ 114 Jay Johnstone .75 .35
❑ 115 Ken Holtzman .75 .35
❑ 116 Charlie Moore .40 .18
❑ 117 Mike Jorgensen .40 .18
❑ 118 Boston Red Sox 1.50 .30
Team Card;
Darrell Johnson MG
(Checklist back)
❑ 119 Checklist 1-132 1.50 .30
❑ 120 Rusty Staub .75 .35
❑ 121 Tony Solaita .40 .18
❑ 122 Mike Cosgrove .40 .18
❑ 123 Walt Williams .40 .18
❑ 124 Doug Rau .40 .18
❑ 125 Don Baylor 1.50 .70
❑ 126 Tom Dettore .40 .18
❑ 127 Larvell Blanks .40 .18
❑ 128 Ken Griffey Sr. 2.50 1.10
❑ 129 Andy Etchebarren .40 .18
❑ 130 Luis Tiant 1.50 .70
❑ 131 Bill Stein .40 .18
❑ 132 Don Hood .40 .18
❑ 133 Gary Matthews .75 .35
❑ 134 Mike Ivie .40 .18
❑ 135 Bake McBride .75 .35
❑ 136 Dave Goltz .40 .18
❑ 137 Bill Robinson .75 .35
❑ 138 Lerrin LaGrow .40 .18
❑ 139 Gorman Thomas .75 .35
❑ 140 Vida Blue .75 .35
❑ 141 Larry Parrish RC 1.50 .70
❑ 142 Dick Drago .40 .18
❑ 143 Jerry Grote .40 .18
❑ 144 Al Fitzmorris .40 .18
❑ 145 Larry Bowa .75 .35
❑ 146 George Medich .40 .18
❑ 147 Houston Astros 1.50 .30
Team Card;
Bill Virdon MG
(Checklist back)
❑ 148 Stan Thomas .40 .18
❑ 149 Tommy Davis .75 .35
❑ 150 Steve Garvey 2.50 1.10
❑ 151 Bill Bonham .40 .18
❑ 152 Leroy Stanton .40 .18
❑ 153 Buzz Capra .40 .18
❑ 154 Bucky Dent .75 .35
❑ 155 Jack Billingham .75 .35
❑ 156 Rico Carty .75 .35
❑ 157 Mike Caldwell .40 .18
❑ 158 Ken Reitz .40 .18
❑ 159 Jerry Terrell .40 .18
❑ 160 Dave Winfield 10.00 4.50
❑ 161 Bruce Kison .40 .18
❑ 162 Jack Pierce .40 .18
❑ 163 Jim Slaton .40 .18
❑ 164 Pepe Mangual .40 .18
❑ 165 Gene Tenace .75 .35
❑ 166 Skip Lockwood .40 .18
❑ 167 Freddie Patek .75 .35
❑ 168 Tom Hilgendorf .40 .18
❑ 169 Graig Nettles 1.50 .70
❑ 170 Rick Wise .40 .18
❑ 171 Greg Gross .40 .18
❑ 172 Texas Rangers 1.50 .30
Team Card;
Frank Lucchesi MG
(Checklist back)
❑ 173 Steve Swisher .40 .18
❑ 174 Charlie Hough .75 .35
❑ 175 Ken Singleton .75 .35
❑ 176 Dick Lange .40 .18
❑ 177 Marty Perez .40 .18
❑ 178 Tom Buskey .40 .18
❑ 179 George Foster 1.50 .70
❑ 180 Rich Gossage 1.50 .70
❑ 181 Willie Montanez .40 .18
❑ 182 Harry Rasmussen .40 .18
❑ 183 Steve Braun .40 .18
❑ 184 Bill Greif .40 .18
❑ 185 Dave Parker 1.50 .70
❑ 186 Tom Walker .40 .18
❑ 187 Pedro Garcia .40 .18
❑ 188 Fred Scherman .40 .18
❑ 189 Claudell Washington .75 .35
❑ 190 Jon Matlack .40 .18
❑ 191 NL Batting Leaders .75 .35
Bill Madlock
Ted Simmons
Manny Sanguillen
❑ 192 AL Batting Leaders 2.50 1.10
Rod Carew
Fred Lynn
Thurman Munson
❑ 193 NL HR Leaders 3.00 1.35
Mike Schmidt
Dave Kingman
Greg Luzinski
❑ 194 AL HR Leaders 3.00 1.35
Reggie Jackson
George Scott
John Mayberry
❑ 195 NL RBI Leaders 1.50 .70
Greg Luzinski
Johnny Bench
Tony Perez
❑ 196 AL RBI Leaders .75 .35
George Scott
John Mayberry
Fred Lynn
❑ 197 NL SB Leaders 1.50 .70
Dave Lopes
Joe Morgan
Lou Brock
❑ 198 AL SB Leaders .75 .35
Mickey Rivers
Claudell Washington
Amos Otis
❑ 199 NL Victory Leaders 2.50 1.10
Tom Seaver
Randy Jones
Andy Messersmith
❑ 200 AL Victory Leaders 1.50 .70
Jim Hunter
Jim Palmer
Vida Blue
❑ 201 NL ERA Leaders 1.50 .70
Randy Jones
Andy Messersmith
Tom Seaver
❑ 202 AL ERA Leaders 3.00 1.35
Jim Palmer
Jim Hunter
Dennis Eckersley
❑ 203 NL Strikeout Leaders 2.50 1.10
Tom Seaver
John Montefusco
Andy Messersmith
❑ 204 AL Strikeout Leaders .75 .35
Frank Tanana
Bert Blyleven
Gaylord Perry
❑ 205 Leading Firemen .75 .35
Al Hrabosky
Rich Gossage
❑ 206 Manny Trillo .40 .18
❑ 207 Andy Hassler .40 .18
❑ 208 Mike Lum .40 .18
❑ 209 Alan Ashby .75 .35
❑ 210 Lee May .75 .35
❑ 211 Clay Carroll .75 .35
❑ 212 Pat Kelly .40 .18
❑ 213 Dave Heaverlo .40 .18
❑ 214 Eric Soderholm .40 .18
❑ 215 Reggie Smith .75 .35
❑ 216 Montreal Expos 1.50 .30
Team Card;
Karl Kuehl MG
(Checklist back)

❑ 217 Dave Freisleben .40 .18
❑ 218 John Knox .40 .18
❑ 219 Tom Murphy .40 .18
❑ 220 Manny Sanguillen .75 .35
❑ 221 Jim Todd .40 .18
❑ 222 Wayne Garrett .40 .18
❑ 223 Ollie Brown .40 .18
❑ 224 Jim York .40 .18
❑ 225 Roy White .75 .35
❑ 226 Jim Sundberg .75 .35
❑ 227 Oscar Zamora .40 .18
❑ 228 John Hale .40 .18
❑ 229 Jerry Remy .40 .18
❑ 230 Carl Yastrzemski 10.00 4.50
❑ 231 Tom House .40 .18
❑ 232 Frank Duffy .40 .18
❑ 233 Grant Jackson .40 .18
❑ 234 Mike Sadek .40 .18
❑ 235 Bert Blyleven 1.50 .70
❑ 236 Kansas City Royals 1.50 .30
Team Card;
Whitey Herzog MG
(Checklist back)
❑ 237 Dave Hamilton .40 .18
❑ 238 Larry Biittner .40 .18
❑ 239 John Curtis .40 .18
❑ 240 Pete Rose 25.00 11.00
❑ 241 Hector Torres .40 .18
❑ 242 Dan Meyer .40 .18
❑ 243 Jim Rooker .40 .18
❑ 244 Bill Sharp .40 .18
❑ 245 Felix Millan .40 .18
❑ 246 Cesar Tovar .40 .18
❑ 247 Terry Harmon .40 .18
❑ 248 Dick Tidrow .40 .18
❑ 249 Cliff Johnson .75 .35
❑ 250 Fergie Jenkins 2.50 1.10
❑ 251 Rick Monday .75 .35
❑ 252 Tim Nordbrook .40 .18
❑ 253 Bill Buckner .75 .35
❑ 254 Rudy Meoli .40 .18
❑ 255 Fritz Peterson .40 .18
❑ 256 Rowland Office .40 .18
❑ 257 Ross Grimsley .40 .18
❑ 258 Nyls Nyman .40 .18
❑ 259 Darrel Chaney .40 .18
❑ 260 Steve Busby .40 .18
❑ 261 Gary Thomasson .40 .18
❑ 262 Checklist 133-264 1.50 .30
❑ 263 Lyman Bostock RC 1.50 .70
❑ 264 Steve Renko .40 .18
❑ 265 Willie Davis .75 .35
❑ 266 Alan Foster .40 .18
❑ 267 Aurelio Rodriguez .40 .18
❑ 268 Del Unser .40 .18
❑ 269 Rick Austin .40 .18
❑ 270 Willie Stargell 3.00 1.35
❑ 271 Jim Lonborg .75 .35
❑ 272 Rick Dempsey .75 .35
❑ 273 Joe Niekro .75 .35
❑ 274 Tommy Harper .75 .35
❑ 275 Rick Manning .40 .18
❑ 276 Mickey Scott .40 .18
❑ 277 Chicago Cubs 1.50 .30
Team Card;
Jim Marshall MG
(Checklist back)
❑ 278 Bernie Carbo .40 .18
❑ 279 Roy Howell .40 .18
❑ 280 Burt Hooton .75 .35
❑ 281 Dave May .40 .18
❑ 282 Dan Osborn .40 .18
❑ 283 Merv Rettenmund .40 .18
❑ 284 Steve Ontiveros .40 .18
❑ 285 Mike Cuellar .75 .35
❑ 286 Jim Wohlford .40 .18
❑ 287 Pete Mackanin .40 .18
❑ 288 Bill Campbell .40 .18
❑ 289 Enzo Hernandez .40 .18
❑ 290 Ted Simmons .75 .35
❑ 291 Ken Sanders .40 .18
❑ 292 Leon Roberts .40 .18
❑ 293 Bill Castro .40 .18
❑ 294 Ed Kirkpatrick .40 .18
❑ 295 Dave Cash .40 .18
❑ 296 Pat Dobson .40 .18
❑ 297 Roger Metzger .40 .18
❑ 298 Dick Bosman .40 .18
❑ 299 Champ Summers .40 .18
❑ 300 Johnny Bench 12.00 5.50
❑ 301 Jackie Brown .40 .18
❑ 302 Rick Miller .40 .18
❑ 303 Steve Foucault .40 .18
❑ 304 California Angels 1.50 .30
Team Card;
Dick Williams MG
(Checklist back)
❑ 305 Andy Messersmith .75 .35
❑ 306 Rod Gilbreath .40 .18
❑ 307 Al Bumbry .75 .35
❑ 308 Jim Barr .40 .18
❑ 309 Bill Melton .40 .18
❑ 310 Randy Jones .75 .35
❑ 311 Cookie Rojas .75 .35
❑ 312 Don Carrithers .40 .18
❑ 313 Dan Ford .40 .18
❑ 314 Ed Kranepool .40 .18
❑ 315 Al Hrabosky .75 .35
❑ 316 Robin Yount 15.00 6.75
❑ 317 John Candelaria RC 1.50 .70
❑ 318 Bob Boone 1.50 .70
❑ 319 Larry Gura .40 .18
❑ 320 Willie Horton .75 .35
❑ 321 Jose Cruz 1.50 .70
❑ 322 Glenn Abbott .40 .18
❑ 323 Rob Sperring .40 .18
❑ 324 Jim Bibby .40 .18
❑ 325 Tony Perez 3.00 1.35
❑ 326 Dick Pole .40 .18
❑ 327 Dave Moates .40 .18
❑ 328 Carl Morton .40 .18
❑ 329 Joe Ferguson .40 .18
❑ 330 Nolan Ryan 25.00 11.00
❑ 331 San Diego Padres 1.50 .30
Team Card;
John McNamara MG
(Checklist back)
❑ 332 Charlie Williams .40 .18
❑ 333 Bob Coluccio .40 .18
❑ 334 Dennis Leonard .75 .35
❑ 335 Bob Grich .75 .35
❑ 336 Vic Albury .40 .18
❑ 337 Bud Harrelson .75 .35
❑ 338 Bob Bailey .40 .18
❑ 339 John Denny .75 .35
❑ 340 Jim Rice 4.00 1.80
❑ 341 Lou Gehrig ATG 12.00 5.50
❑ 342 Rogers Hornsby ATG 3.00 1.35
❑ 343 Pie Traynor ATG 1.50 .70
❑ 344 Honus Wagner ATG 5.00 2.20
❑ 345 Babe Ruth ATG 15.00 6.75
❑ 346 Ty Cobb ATG 12.00 5.50
❑ 347 Ted Williams ATG 12.00 5.50
❑ 348 Mickey Cochrane ATG 1.50 .70
❑ 349 Walter Johnson ATG 5.00 2.20
❑ 350 Lefty Grove ATG 1.50 .70
❑ 351 Randy Hundley .75 .35
❑ 352 Dave Giusti .40 .18
❑ 353 Sixto Lezcano .75 .35
❑ 354 Ron Blomberg .40 .18
❑ 355 Steve Carlton 6.00 2.70
❑ 356 Ted Martinez .40 .18
❑ 357 Ken Forsch .40 .18
❑ 358 Buddy Bell .75 .35
❑ 359 Rick Reuschel .75 .35
❑ 360 Jeff Burroughs .75 .35
❑ 361 Detroit Tigers 1.50 .30
Team Card;
Ralph Houk MG
(Checklist back)
❑ 362 Will McEnaney .75 .35
❑ 363 Dave Collins RC .75 .35
❑ 364 Elias Sosa .40 .18
❑ 365 Carlton Fisk 6.00 2.70
❑ 366 Bobby Valentine .75 .35
❑ 367 Bruce Miller .40 .18
❑ 368 Wilbur Wood .40 .18
❑ 369 Frank White .75 .35
❑ 370 Ron Cey .75 .35
❑ 371 Elrod Hendricks .40 .18
❑ 372 Rick Baldwin .40 .18
❑ 373 Johnny Briggs .40 .18
❑ 374 Dan Warthen .40 .18
❑ 375 Ron Fairly .75 .35
❑ 376 Rich Hebner .75 .35
❑ 377 Mike Hegan .40 .18
❑ 378 Steve Stone .75 .35
❑ 379 Ken Boswell .40 .18
❑ 380 Bobby Bonds 1.50 .70
❑ 381 Denny Doyle .40 .18
❑ 382 Matt Alexander .40 .18
❑ 383 John Ellis .40 .18
❑ 384 Philadelphia Phillies 1.50 .30
Team Card;
Danny Ozark MG
(Checklist back)
❑ 385 Mickey Lolich .75 .35
❑ 386 Ed Goodson .40 .18
❑ 387 Mike Miley .40 .18
❑ 388 Stan Perzanowski .40 .18
❑ 389 Glenn Adams .40 .18
❑ 390 Don Gullett .75 .35
❑ 391 Jerry Hairston .40 .18
❑ 392 Checklist 265-396 1.50 .30
❑ 393 Paul Mitchell .40 .18
❑ 394 Fran Healy .40 .18
❑ 395 Jim Wynn .75 .35
❑ 396 Bill Lee .40 .18
❑ 397 Tim Foli .40 .18
❑ 398 Dave Tomlin .40 .18
❑ 399 Luis Melendez .40 .18
❑ 400 Rod Carew 6.00 2.70
❑ 401 Ken Brett .40 .18
❑ 402 Don Money .75 .35
❑ 403 Geoff Zahn .40 .18
❑ 404 Enos Cabell .40 .18
❑ 405 Rollie Fingers 2.50 1.10
❑ 406 Ed Herrmann .40 .18
❑ 407 Tom Underwood .40 .18
❑ 408 Charlie Spikes .40 .18
❑ 409 Dave Lemanczyk .40 .18
❑ 410 Ralph Garr .75 .35
❑ 411 Bill Singer .40 .18
❑ 412 Toby Harrah .75 .35
❑ 413 Pete Varney .40 .18
❑ 414 Wayne Garland .40 .18
❑ 415 Vada Pinson 1.50 .70
❑ 416 Tommy John 1.50 .70
❑ 417 Gene Clines .40 .18
❑ 418 Jose Morales RC .40 .18
❑ 419 Reggie Cleveland .40 .18
❑ 420 Joe Morgan 5.00 2.20
❑ 421 Oakland A's 1.50 .30
Team Card;
(No MG on front;
checklist back)
❑ 422 Johnny Grubb .40 .18
❑ 423 Ed Halicki .40 .18
❑ 424 Phil Roof .40 .18
❑ 425 Rennie Stennett .40 .18
❑ 426 Bob Forsch .40 .18
❑ 427 Kurt Bevacqua .40 .18
❑ 428 Jim Crawford .40 .18
❑ 429 Fred Stanley .40 .18
❑ 430 Jose Cardenal .75 .35
❑ 431 Dick Ruthven .40 .18
❑ 432 Tom Veryzer .40 .18
❑ 433 Rick Waits .40 .18
❑ 434 Morris Nettles .40 .18
❑ 435 Phil Niekro 2.50 1.10
❑ 436 Bill Fahey .40 .18
❑ 437 Terry Forster .40 .18
❑ 438 Doug DeCinces .75 .35
❑ 439 Rick Rhoden .75 .35
❑ 440 John Mayberry .75 .35
❑ 441 Gary Carter 4.00 1.80
❑ 442 Hank Webb .40 .18
❑ 443 San Francisco Giants 1.50 .30
Team Card;
(No MG on front;
checklist back)
❑ 444 Gary Nolan .75 .35
❑ 445 Rico Petrocelli .75 .35
❑ 446 Larry Haney .40 .18
❑ 447 Gene Locklear .75 .35
❑ 448 Tom Johnson .40 .18
❑ 449 Bob Robertson .40 .18
❑ 450 Jim Palmer 5.00 2.20

❑ 451 Buddy Bradford .40 .18
❑ 452 Tom Hausman .40 .18
❑ 453 Lou Piniella 1.50 .70
❑ 454 Tom Griffin .40 .18
❑ 455 Dick Allen 1.50 .70
❑ 456 Joe Coleman .40 .18
❑ 457 Ed Crosby .40 .18
❑ 458 Earl Williams .40 .18
❑ 459 Jim Brewer .40 .18
❑ 460 Cesar Cedeno .75 .35
❑ 461 NL and AL Champs .75 .35
Reds sweep Bucs,
Bosox surprise A's
❑ 462 '75 World Series .75 .35
Reds Champs
❑ 463 Steve Hargan .40 .18
❑ 464 Ken Henderson .40 .18
❑ 465 Mike Marshall .75 .35
❑ 466 Bob Stinson .40 .18
❑ 467 Woodie Fryman .40 .18
❑ 468 Jesus Alou .40 .18
❑ 469 Rawly Eastwick .75 .35
❑ 470 Bobby Murcer .75 .35
❑ 471 Jim Burton .40 .18
❑ 472 Bob Davis .40 .18
❑ 473 Paul Blair .75 .35
❑ 474 Ray Corbin .40 .18
❑ 475 Joe Rudi .75 .35
❑ 476 Bob Moose .40 .18
❑ 477 Cleveland Indians 1.50 .30
Team Card;
Frank Robinson MG
(Checklist back)
❑ 478 Lynn McGlothen .40 .18
❑ 479 Bobby Mitchell .40 .18
❑ 480 Mike Schmidt 15.00 6.75
❑ 481 Rudy May .40 .18
❑ 482 Tim Hosley .40 .18
❑ 483 Mickey Stanley .40 .18
❑ 484 Eric Raich .40 .18
❑ 485 Mike Hargrove .75 .35
❑ 486 Bruce Dal Canton .40 .18
❑ 487 Leron Lee .40 .18
❑ 488 Claude Osteen .75 .35
❑ 489 Skip Jutze .40 .18
❑ 490 Frank Tanana .75 .35
❑ 491 Terry Crowley .40 .18
❑ 492 Marty Pattin .40 .18
❑ 493 Derrel Thomas .40 .18
❑ 494 Craig Swan .75 .35
❑ 495 Nate Colbert .40 .18
❑ 496 Juan Beniquez .40 .18
❑ 497 Joe McIntosh .40 .18
❑ 498 Glenn Borgmann .40 .18
❑ 499 Mario Guerrero .40 .18
❑ 500 Reggie Jackson 12.00 5.50
❑ 501 Billy Champion .40 .18
❑ 502 Tim McCarver 1.50 .70
❑ 503 Elliott Maddox .40 .18
❑ 504 Pittsburgh Pirates 1.50 .30
Team Card;
Danny Murtaugh MG
(Checklist back)
❑ 505 Mark Belanger .75 .35
❑ 506 George Mitterwald .40 .18
❑ 507 Ray Bare .40 .18
❑ 508 Duane Kuiper .40 .18
❑ 509 Bill Hands .40 .18
❑ 510 Amos Otis .75 .35
❑ 511 Jamie Easterley .40 .18
❑ 512 Ellie Rodriguez .40 .18
❑ 513 Bart Johnson .40 .18
❑ 514 Dan Driessen .75 .35
❑ 515 Steve Yeager .75 .35
❑ 516 Wayne Granger .40 .18
❑ 517 John Milner .40 .18
❑ 518 Doug Flynn .40 .18
❑ 519 Steve Brye .40 .18
❑ 520 Willie McCovey 5.00 2.20
❑ 521 Jim Colborn .40 .18
❑ 522 Ted Sizemore .40 .18
❑ 523 Bob Montgomery .40 .18
❑ 524 Pete Falcone .40 .18
❑ 525 Billy Williams 2.50 1.10
❑ 526 Checklist 397-528 1.50 .30
❑ 527 Mike Anderson .40 .18
❑ 528 Dock Ellis .40 .18
❑ 529 Deron Johnson .75 .35
❑ 530 Don Sutton 2.50 1.10
❑ 531 New York Mets 1.50 .30
Team Card;
Joe Frazier MG
(Checklist back)
❑ 532 Milt May .40 .18
❑ 533 Lee Richard .40 .18
❑ 534 Stan Bahnsen .40 .18
❑ 535 Dave Nelson .40 .18
❑ 536 Mike Thompson .40 .18
❑ 537 Tony Muser .40 .18
❑ 538 Pat Darcy .40 .18
❑ 539 John Balaz .75 .35
❑ 540 Bill Freehan .75 .35
❑ 541 Steve Mingori .40 .18
❑ 542 Keith Hernandez 1.50 .70
❑ 543 Wayne Twitchell .40 .18
❑ 544 Pepe Frias .40 .18
❑ 545 Sparky Lyle .75 .35
❑ 546 Dave Rosello .40 .18
❑ 547 Roric Harrison .40 .18
❑ 548 Manny Mota .75 .35
❑ 549 Randy Tate .40 .18
❑ 550 Hank Aaron 25.00 11.00
❑ 551 Jerry DaVanon .40 .18
❑ 552 Terry Humphrey .40 .18
❑ 553 Randy Moffitt .40 .18
❑ 554 Ray Fosse .40 .18
❑ 555 Dyar Miller .40 .18
❑ 556 Minnesota Twins 1.50 .30
Team Card;
Gene Mauch MG
(Checklist back)
❑ 557 Dan Spillner .40 .18
❑ 558 Clarence Gaston .75 .35
❑ 559 Clyde Wright .40 .18
❑ 560 Jorge Orta .40 .18
❑ 561 Tom Carroll .40 .18
❑ 562 Adrian Garrett .40 .18
❑ 563 Larry Demery .40 .18
❑ 564 Bubble Gum Champ 1.50 .70
Kurt Bevacqua
❑ 565 Tug McGraw .75 .35
❑ 566 Ken McMullen .40 .18
❑ 567 George Stone .40 .18
❑ 568 Rob Andrews .40 .18
❑ 569 Nelson Briles .75 .35
❑ 570 George Hendrick .75 .35
❑ 571 Don DeMola .40 .18
❑ 572 Rich Coggins .40 .18
❑ 573 Bill Travers .40 .18
❑ 574 Don Kessinger .75 .35
❑ 575 Dwight Evans 1.50 .70
❑ 576 Maximino Leon .40 .18
❑ 577 Marc Hill .40 .18
❑ 578 Ted Kubiak .40 .18
❑ 579 Clay Kirby .40 .18
❑ 580 Bert Campaneris .75 .35
❑ 581 St. Louis Cardinals 1.50 .30
Team Card;
Red Schoendienst MG
(Checklist back)
❑ 582 Mike Kekich .40 .18
❑ 583 Tommy Helms .40 .18
❑ 584 Stan Wall .40 .18
❑ 585 Joe Torre 1.50 .70
❑ 586 Ron Schueler .40 .18
❑ 587 Leo Cardenas .40 .18
❑ 588 Kevin Kobel .40 .18
❑ 589 Rookie Pitchers 1.50 .70
Santo Alcala
Mike Flanagan RC
Joe Pactwa
Pablo Torrealba
❑ 590 Rookie Outfielders .75 .35
Henry Cruz
Chet Lemon RC
Ellis Valentine
Terry Whitfield
❑ 591 Rookie Pitchers .75 .35
Steve Grilli
Craig Mitchell
Jose Sosa
George Throop
❑ 592 Rookie Infielders 6.00 2.70
Willie Randolph RC
Dave McKay
Jerry Royster
Roy Staiger
❑ 593 Rookie Pitchers .75 .35
Larry Anderson
Ken Crosby
Mark Littell
Butch Metzger
❑ 594 Rookie Catchers/OF .75 .35
Andy Merchant
Ed Ott
Royle Stillman
Jerry White
❑ 595 Rookie Pitchers .75 .35
Art DeFillipis
Randy Lerch
Sid Monge
Steve Barr
❑ 596 Rookie Infielders .75 .35
Craig Reynolds
Lamar Johnson
Johnnie LeMaster
Jerry Manuel
❑ 597 Rookie Pitchers .75 .35
Don Aase
Jack Kucek
Frank LaCorte
Mike Pazik
❑ 598 Rookie Outfielders .75 .35
Hector Cruz
Jamie Quirk
Jerry Turner
Joe Wallis
❑ 599 Rookie Pitchers 6.00 2.70
Rob Dressler
Ron Guidry RC
Bob McClure
Pat Zachry
❑ 600 Tom Seaver 10.00 4.50
❑ 601 Ken Rudolph .40 .18
❑ 602 Doug Konieczny .40 .18
❑ 603 Jim Holt .40 .18
❑ 604 Joe Lovitto .40 .18
❑ 605 Al Downing .40 .18
❑ 606 Milwaukee Brewers 1.50 .30
Team Card;
Alex Grammas MG
(Checklist back)
❑ 607 Rich Hinton .40 .18
❑ 608 Vic Correll .40 .18
❑ 609 Fred Norman .75 .35
❑ 610 Greg Luzinski 1.50 .70
❑ 611 Rich Folkers .40 .18
❑ 612 Joe Lahoud .40 .18
❑ 613 Tim Johnson .40 .18
❑ 614 Fernando Arroyo .40 .18
❑ 615 Mike Cubbage .40 .18
❑ 616 Buck Martinez .40 .18
❑ 617 Darold Knowles .40 .18
❑ 618 Jack Brohamer .40 .18
❑ 619 Bill Butler .40 .18
❑ 620 Al Oliver .75 .35
❑ 621 Tom Hall .40 .18
❑ 622 Rick Auerbach .40 .18
❑ 623 Bob Allietta .40 .18
❑ 624 Tony Taylor .75 .35
❑ 625 J.R. Richard .75 .35
❑ 626 Bob Sheldon .40 .18
❑ 627 Bill Plummer .40 .18
❑ 628 John D'Acquisto .40 .18
❑ 629 Sandy Alomar .75 .35
❑ 630 Chris Speier .40 .18
❑ 631 Atlanta Braves 1.50 .30
Team Card;
Dave Bristol MG
(Checklist back)
❑ 632 Rogelio Moret .40 .18
❑ 633 John Stearns RC .75 .35
❑ 634 Larry Christenson .40 .18
❑ 635 Jim Fregosi .75 .35
❑ 636 Joe Decker .40 .18
❑ 637 Bruce Bochte .40 .18
❑ 638 Doyle Alexander .75 .35
❑ 639 Fred Kendall .40 .18

	NRMT	VG-E
❑ 640 Bill Madlock	1.50	.70
❑ 641 Tom Paciorek	.75	.35
❑ 642 Dennis Blair	.40	.18
❑ 643 Checklist 529-660	1.50	.30
❑ 644 Tom Bradley	.40	.18
❑ 645 Darrell Porter	.75	.35
❑ 646 John Lowenstein	.40	.18
❑ 647 Ramon Hernandez	.40	.18
❑ 648 Al Cowens	.40	.18
❑ 649 Dave Roberts	.40	.18
❑ 650 Thurman Munson	6.00	2.70
❑ 651 John Odom	.40	.18
❑ 652 Ed Armbrister	.40	.18
❑ 653 Mike Norris	.75	.35
❑ 654 Doug Griffin	.40	.18
❑ 655 Mike Vail	.40	.18
❑ 656 Chicago White Sox Team Card; Chuck Tanner MG (Checklist back)	1.50	.30
❑ 657 Roy Smalley RC	.75	.35
❑ 658 Jerry Johnson	.40	.18
❑ 659 Ben Oglivie	.75	.35
❑ 660 Dave Lopes	1.50	.30

1976 Topps Traded

	NRMT	VG-E
COMPLETE SET (44)	30.00	13.50
❑ 27T Ed Figueroa	.40	.18
❑ 28T Dusty Baker	1.50	.70
❑ 44T Doug Rader	.75	.35
❑ 58T Ron Reed	.40	.18
❑ 74T Oscar Gamble	1.50	.70
❑ 80T Jim Kaat	1.50	.70
❑ 83T Jim Spencer	.40	.18
❑ 85T Mickey Rivers	.75	.35
❑ 99T Lee Lacy	.40	.18
❑ 120T Rusty Staub	.75	.35
❑ 127T Larvell Blanks	.40	.18
❑ 146T George Medich	.40	.18
❑ 158T Ken Reitz	.40	.18
❑ 208T Mike Lum	.40	.18
❑ 211T Clay Carroll	.40	.18
❑ 231T Tom House	.40	.18
❑ 250T Fergie Jenkins	3.00	1.35
❑ 259T Darrel Chaney	.40	.18
❑ 292T Leon Roberts	.40	.18
❑ 296T Pat Dobson	.40	.18
❑ 309T Bill Melton	.40	.18
❑ 338T Bob Bailey	.40	.18
❑ 380T Bobby Bonds	1.50	.70
❑ 383T John Ellis	.40	.18
❑ 385T Mickey Lolich	.75	.35
❑ 401T Ken Brett	.40	.18
❑ 410T Ralph Garr	.40	.18
❑ 411T Bill Singer	.40	.18
❑ 428T Jim Crawford	.40	.18
❑ 434T Morris Nettles	.40	.18
❑ 464T Ken Henderson	.40	.18
❑ 497T Joe McIntosh	.40	.18
❑ 524T Pete Falcone	.40	.18
❑ 527T Mike Anderson	.40	.18
❑ 528T Dock Ellis	.40	.18
❑ 532T Milt May	.40	.18
❑ 554T Ray Fosse	.40	.18
❑ 579T Clay Kirby	.40	.18
❑ 583T Tommy Helms	.40	.18
❑ 592T Willie Randolph	5.00	2.20
❑ 618T Jack Brohamer	.40	.18
❑ 632T Rogelio Moret	.40	.18
❑ 649T Dave Roberts	.40	.18
❑ NNO Traded Checklist	2.00	.40

1977 Topps

	NRMT	VG-E
COMPLETE SET (660)	250.00	110.00
❑ 1 Batting Leaders George Brett Bill Madlock	8.00	2.30
❑ 2 Home Run Leaders Graig Nettles Mike Schmidt	2.50	1.10
❑ 3 RBI Leaders Lee May George Foster	1.50	.70
❑ 4 Stolen Base Leaders Bill North Dave Lopes	.75	.35
❑ 5 Victory Leaders Jim Palmer Randy Jones	1.50	.70
❑ 6 Strikeout Leaders Nolan Ryan Tom Seaver	15.00	6.75
❑ 7 ERA Leaders Mark Fidrych John Denny	.75	.35
❑ 8 Firemen Leaders Bill Campbell Rawly Eastwick	.75	.35
❑ 9 Doug Rader	.30	.14
❑ 10 Reggie Jackson	10.00	4.50
❑ 11 Rob Dressler	.30	.14
❑ 12 Larry Haney	.30	.14
❑ 13 Luis Gomez	.30	.14
❑ 14 Tommy Smith	.30	.14
❑ 15 Don Gullett	.75	.35
❑ 16 Bob Jones	.30	.14
❑ 17 Steve Stone	.75	.35
❑ 18 Indians Team/Mgr. Frank Robinson (Checklist back)	1.50	.30
❑ 19 John D'Acquisto	.30	.14
❑ 20 Graig Nettles	1.50	.70
❑ 21 Ken Forsch	.30	.14
❑ 22 Bill Freehan	.75	.35
❑ 23 Dan Driessen	.30	.14
❑ 24 Carl Morton	.30	.14
❑ 25 Dwight Evans	1.50	.70
❑ 26 Ray Sadecki	.30	.14
❑ 27 Bill Buckner	.75	.35
❑ 28 Woodie Fryman	.30	.14
❑ 29 Bucky Dent	.75	.35
❑ 30 Greg Luzinski	1.50	.70
❑ 31 Jim Todd	.30	.14
❑ 32 Checklist 1-132	1.50	.30
❑ 33 Wayne Garland	.30	.14
❑ 34 Angels Team/Mgr. Norm Sherry (Checklist back)	1.50	.30
❑ 35 Rennie Stennett	.30	.14
❑ 36 John Ellis	.30	.14
❑ 37 Steve Hargan	.30	.14
❑ 38 Craig Kusick	.30	.14
❑ 39 Tom Griffin	.30	.14
❑ 40 Bobby Murcer	.75	.35
❑ 41 Jim Kern	.30	.14
❑ 42 Jose Cruz	.75	.35
❑ 43 Ray Bare	.30	.14
❑ 44 Bud Harrelson	.75	.35
❑ 45 Rawly Eastwick	.30	.14
❑ 46 Buck Martinez	.30	.14
❑ 47 Lynn McGlothen	.30	.14
❑ 48 Tom Paciorek	.75	.35
❑ 49 Grant Jackson	.30	.14
❑ 50 Ron Cey	.75	.35
❑ 51 Brewers Team/Mgr. Alex Grammas (Checklist back)	1.50	.30
❑ 52 Ellis Valentine	.30	.14
❑ 53 Paul Mitchell	.30	.14
❑ 54 Sandy Alomar	.75	.35
❑ 55 Jeff Burroughs	.75	.35
❑ 56 Rudy May	.30	.14
❑ 57 Marc Hill	.30	.14
❑ 58 Chet Lemon	.75	.35
❑ 59 Larry Christenson	.30	.14
❑ 60 Jim Rice	2.50	1.10
❑ 61 Manny Sanguillen	.75	.35
❑ 62 Eric Raich	.30	.14
❑ 63 Tito Fuentes	.30	.14
❑ 64 Larry Biittner	.30	.14
❑ 65 Skip Lockwood	.30	.14
❑ 66 Roy Smalley	.75	.35
❑ 67 Joaquin Andujar RC	.75	.35
❑ 68 Bruce Bochte	.30	.14
❑ 69 Jim Crawford	.30	.14
❑ 70 Johnny Bench	10.00	4.50
❑ 71 Dock Ellis	.30	.14
❑ 72 Mike Anderson	.30	.14
❑ 73 Charlie Williams	.30	.14
❑ 74 A's Team/Mgr. Jack McKeon (Checklist back)	1.50	.30
❑ 75 Dennis Leonard	.75	.35
❑ 76 Tim Foli	.30	.14
❑ 77 Dyar Miller	.30	.14
❑ 78 Bob Davis	.30	.14
❑ 79 Don Money	.75	.35
❑ 80 Andy Messersmith	.75	.35
❑ 81 Juan Beniquez	.30	.14
❑ 82 Jim Rooker	.30	.14
❑ 83 Kevin Bell	.30	.14
❑ 84 Ollie Brown	.30	.14
❑ 85 Duane Kuiper	.30	.14
❑ 86 Pat Zachry	.30	.14
❑ 87 Glenn Borgmann	.30	.14
❑ 88 Stan Wall	.30	.14
❑ 89 Butch Hobson RC	.75	.35
❑ 90 Cesar Cedeno	.75	.35
❑ 91 John Verhoeven	.30	.14
❑ 92 Dave Rosello	.30	.14
❑ 93 Tom Poquette	.30	.14
❑ 94 Craig Swan	.30	.14
❑ 95 Keith Hernandez	.75	.35
❑ 96 Lou Piniella	.75	.35
❑ 97 Dave Heaverlo	.30	.14
❑ 98 Milt May	.30	.14
❑ 99 Tom Hausman	.30	.14
❑ 100 Joe Morgan	4.00	1.80
❑ 101 Dick Bosman	.30	.14
❑ 102 Jose Morales	.30	.14
❑ 103 Mike Bacsik	.30	.14
❑ 104 Omar Moreno	.75	.35
❑ 105 Steve Yeager	.75	.35
❑ 106 Mike Flanagan	.75	.35
❑ 107 Bill Melton	.30	.14
❑ 108 Alan Foster	.30	.14
❑ 109 Jorge Orta	.30	.14
❑ 110 Steve Carlton	5.00	2.20
❑ 111 Rico Petrocelli	.75	.35
❑ 112 Bill Greif	.30	.14
❑ 113 Blue Jays Leaders Roy Hartsfield MG Don Leppert CO Bob Miller CO Jackie Moore CO Harry Warner CO	1.50	.30

	(Checklist back)		
114	Bruce Dal Canton	.30	.14
115	Rick Manning	.30	.14
116	Joe Niekro	.75	.35
117	Frank White	.75	.35
118	Rick Jones	.30	.14
119	John Stearns	.30	.14
120	Rod Carew	5.00	2.20
121	Gary Nolan	.30	.14
122	Ben Oglivie	.75	.35
123	Fred Stanley	.30	.14
124	George Mitterwald	.30	.14
125	Bill Travers	.30	.14
126	Rod Gilbreath	.30	.14
127	Ron Fairly	.75	.35
128	Tommy John	1.50	.70
129	Mike Sadek	.30	.14
130	Al Oliver	.75	.35
131	Orlando Ramirez	.30	.14
132	Chip Lang	.30	.14
133	Ralph Garr	.75	.35
134	Padres Team/Mgr.	1.50	.30
	John McNamara		
	(Checklist back)		
135	Mark Belanger	.75	.35
136	Jerry Mumphrey	.75	.35
137	Jeff Terpko	.30	.14
138	Bob Stinson	.30	.14
139	Fred Norman	.30	.14
140	Mike Schmidt	12.00	5.50
141	Mark Littell	.30	.14
142	Steve Dillard	.30	.14
143	Ed Herrmann	.30	.14
144	Bruce Sutter RC	3.00	1.35
145	Tom Veryzer	.30	.14
146	Dusty Baker	1.50	.70
147	Jackie Brown	.30	.14
148	Fran Healy	.30	.14
149	Mike Cubbage	.30	.14
150	Tom Seaver	8.00	3.60
151	Johnny LeMaster	.30	.14
152	Gaylord Perry	2.50	1.10
153	Ron Jackson	.30	.14
154	Dave Giusti	.30	.14
155	Joe Rudi	.75	.35
156	Pete Mackanin	.30	.14
157	Ken Brett	.30	.14
158	Ted Kubiak	.30	.14
159	Bernie Carbo	.30	.14
160	Will McEnaney	.30	.14
161	Garry Templeton RC	1.50	.70
162	Mike Cuellar	.75	.35
163	Dave Hilton	.30	.14
164	Tug McGraw	.75	.35
165	Jim Wynn	.75	.35
166	Bill Campbell	.30	.14
167	Rich Hebner	.75	.35
168	Charlie Spikes	.30	.14
169	Darold Knowles	.30	.14
170	Thurman Munson	5.00	2.20
171	Ken Sanders	.30	.14
172	John Milner	.30	.14
173	Chuck Scrivener	.30	.14
174	Nelson Briles	.75	.35
175	Butch Wynegar	.75	.35
176	Bob Robertson	.30	.14
177	Bart Johnson	.30	.14
178	Bombo Rivera	.30	.14
179	Paul Hartzell	.30	.14
180	Dave Lopes	.75	.35
181	Ken McMullen	.30	.14
182	Dan Spillner	.30	.14
183	Cardinals Team/Mgr.	1.50	.30
	Vern Rapp		
	(Checklist back)		
184	Bo McLaughlin	.30	.14
185	Sixto Lezcano	.30	.14
186	Doug Flynn	.30	.14
187	Dick Pole	.30	.14
188	Bob Tolan	.30	.14
189	Rick Dempsey	.75	.35
190	Ray Burris	.30	.14
191	Doug Griffin	.30	.14
192	Clarence Gaston	.75	.35
193	Larry Gura	.30	.14
194	Gary Matthews	.75	.35
195	Ed Figueroa	.30	.14
196	Len Randle	.30	.14
197	Ed Ott	.30	.14
198	Wilbur Wood	.30	.14
199	Pepe Frias	.30	.14
200	Frank Tanana	.75	.35
201	Ed Kranepool	.30	.14
202	Tom Johnson	.30	.14
203	Ed Armbrister	.30	.14
204	Jeff Newman	.30	.14
205	Pete Falcone	.30	.14
206	Boog Powell	1.50	.70
207	Glenn Abbott	.30	.14
208	Checklist 133-264	1.50	.30
209	Rob Andrews	.30	.14
210	Fred Lynn	.75	.15
211	Giants Team/Mgr.	1.50	.70
	Joe Altobelli		
	(Checklist back)		
212	Jim Mason	.30	.14
213	Maximino Leon	.30	.14
214	Darrell Porter	.75	.35
215	Butch Metzger	.30	.14
216	Doug DeCinces	.75	.35
217	Tom Underwood	.30	.14
218	John Wathan RC	.30	.14
219	Joe Coleman	.30	.14
220	Chris Chambliss	.75	.35
221	Bob Bailey	.30	.14
222	Francisco Barrios	.30	.14
223	Earl Williams	.30	.14
224	Rusty Torres	.30	.14
225	Bob Apodaca	.30	.14
226	Leroy Stanton	.75	.35
227	Joe Sambito	.30	.14
228	Twins Team/Mgr.	1.50	.30
	Gene Mauch		
	(Checklist back)		
229	Don Kessinger	.75	.35
230	Vida Blue	.75	.35
231	George Brett RB	8.00	3.60
	Most consecutive games		
	3 or more hits		
232	Minnie Minoso RB	.75	.35
	Oldest to hit safely		
233	Jose Morales RB	.30	.14
	Most pinch-hits season		
234	Nolan Ryan RB	15.00	6.75
	Most seasons, 300 strikeouts		
235	Cecil Cooper	.75	.35
236	Tom Buskey	.30	.14
237	Gene Clines	.30	.14
238	Tippy Martinez	.30	.14
239	Bill Plummer	.30	.14
240	Ron LeFlore	.75	.35
241	Dave Tomlin	.30	.14
242	Ken Henderson	.30	.14
243	Ron Reed	.30	.14
244	John Mayberry	.75	.35
	(Cartoon mentions		
	T206 Wagner)		
245	Rick Rhoden	.75	.35
246	Mike Vail	.30	.14
247	Chris Knapp	.30	.14
248	Wilbur Howard	.30	.14
249	Pete Redfern	.30	.14
250	Bill Madlock	.75	.35
251	Tony Muser	.30	.14
252	Dale Murray	.30	.14
253	John Hale	.30	.14
254	Doyle Alexander	.30	.14
255	George Scott	.75	.35
256	Joe Hoerner	.30	.14
257	Mike Miley	.30	.14
258	Luis Tiant	.75	.35
259	Mets Team/Mgr.	1.50	.30
	Joe Frazier		
	(Checklist back)		
260	J.R. Richard	.75	.35
261	Phil Garner	.75	.35
262	Al Cowens	.30	.14
263	Mike Marshall	.75	.35
264	Tom Hutton	.30	.14
265	Mark Fidrych RC	3.00	1.35
266	Derrel Thomas	.30	.14
267	Ray Fosse	.30	.14
268	Rick Sawyer	.30	.14
269	Joe Lis	.30	.14
270	Dave Parker	1.50	.70
271	Terry Forster	.30	.14
272	Lee Lacy	.30	.14
273	Eric Soderholm	.30	.14
274	Don Stanhouse	.30	.14
275	Mike Hargrove	.75	.35
276	C.Chambliss ALCS	1.50	.70
	homer decides it		
277	Pete Rose NLCS	5.00	2.20
278	Danny Frisella	.30	.14
279	Joe Wallis	.30	.14
280	Jim Hunter	2.50	1.10
281	Roy Staiger	.30	.14
282	Sid Monge	.30	.14
283	Jerry DaVanon	.30	.14
284	Mike Norris	.30	.14
285	Brooks Robinson	5.00	2.20
286	Johnny Grubb	.30	.06
287	Reds Team/Mgr.	1.50	.70
	Sparky Anderson		
	(Checklist back)		
288	Bob Montgomery	.30	.14
289	Gene Garber	.75	.35
290	Amos Otis	.75	.35
291	Jason Thompson RC	.75	.35
292	Rogelio Moret	.30	.14
293	Jack Brohamer	.30	.14
294	George Medich	.30	.14
295	Gary Carter	2.50	1.10
296	Don Hood	.30	.14
297	Ken Reitz	.30	.14
298	Charlie Hough	.75	.35
299	Otto Velez	.75	.35
300	Jerry Koosman	.75	.35
301	Toby Harrah	.75	.35
302	Mike Garman	.30	.14
303	Gene Tenace	.75	.35
304	Jim Hughes	.30	.14
305	Mickey Rivers	.75	.35
306	Rick Waits	.30	.14
307	Gary Sutherland	.30	.14
308	Gene Pentz	.30	.14
309	Red Sox Team/Mgr.	1.50	.30
	Don Zimmer		
	(Checklist back)		
310	Larry Bowa	.75	.35
311	Vern Ruhle	.30	.14
312	Rob Belloir	.30	.14
313	Paul Blair	.75	.35
314	Steve Mingori	.30	.14
315	Dave Chalk	.30	.14
316	Steve Rogers	.30	.14
317	Kurt Bevacqua	.30	.14
318	Duffy Dyer	.30	.14
319	Rich Gossage	1.50	.70
320	Ken Griffey	1.50	.70
321	Dave Goltz	.30	.14
322	Bill Russell	.75	.35
323	Larry Lintz	.30	.14
324	John Curtis	.30	.14
325	Mike Ivie	.30	.14
326	Jesse Jefferson	.30	.14
327	Astros Team/Mgr.	1.50	.30
	Bill Virdon		
	(Checklist back)		
328	Tommy Boggs	.30	.14
329	Ron Hodges	.30	.14
330	George Hendrick	.75	.35
331	Jim Colborn	.30	.14
332	Elliott Maddox	.30	.14
333	Paul Reuschel	.30	.14
334	Bill Stein	.30	.14
335	Bill Robinson	.75	.35
336	Denny Doyle	.30	.14
337	Ron Schueler	.30	.14
338	Dave Duncan	.30	.14
339	Adrian Devine	.30	.14
340	Hal McRae	.75	.35
341	Joe Kerrigan	.30	.14
342	Jerry Remy	.30	.14
343	Ed Halicki	.30	.14
344	Brian Downing	.75	.35
345	Reggie Smith	.75	.35
346	Bill Singer	.30	.14

❑ 347 George Foster 1.50 .70
❑ 348 Brent Strom .30 .14
❑ 349 Jim Holt .30 .14
❑ 350 Larry Dierker .75 .35
❑ 351 Jim Sundberg .75 .35
❑ 352 Mike Phillips .30 .14
❑ 353 Stan Thomas .30 .14
❑ 354 Pirates Team/Mgr. 1.50 .30
Chuck Tanner
(Checklist back)
❑ 355 Lou Brock 4.00 1.80
❑ 356 Checklist 265-396 1.50 .30
❑ 357 Tim McCarver 1.50 .70
❑ 358 Tom House .30 .14
❑ 359 Willie Randolph 1.50 .70
❑ 360 Rick Monday .75 .35
❑ 361 Eduardo Rodriguez .30 .14
❑ 362 Tommy Davis .75 .35
❑ 363 Dave Roberts .30 .14
❑ 364 Vic Correll .30 .14
❑ 365 Mike Torrez .75 .35
❑ 366 Ted Sizemore .30 .14
❑ 367 Dave Hamilton .30 .14
❑ 368 Mike Jorgensen .30 .14
❑ 369 Terry Humphrey .30 .14
❑ 370 John Montefusco .30 .14
❑ 371 Royals Team/Mgr. 1.50 .30
Whitey Herzog
(Checklist back)
❑ 372 Rich Folkers .30 .14
❑ 373 Bert Campaneris .75 .35
❑ 374 Kent Tekulve .75 .35
❑ 375 Larry Hisle .75 .35
❑ 376 Nino Espinosa .30 .14
❑ 377 Dave McKay .30 .14
❑ 378 Jim Umbarger .30 .14
❑ 379 Larry Cox .30 .14
❑ 380 Lee May .75 .35
❑ 381 Bob Forsch .30 .14
❑ 382 Charlie Moore .30 .14
❑ 383 Stan Bahnsen .30 .14
❑ 384 Darrel Chaney .30 .14
❑ 385 Dave LaRoche .30 .14
❑ 386 Manny Mota .75 .35
❑ 387 Yankees Team/Mgr. 2.50 .50
Billy Martin
(Checklist back)
❑ 388 Terry Harmon .30 .14
❑ 389 Ken Kravec .30 .14
❑ 390 Dave Winfield 6.00 2.70
❑ 391 Dan Warthen .30 .14
❑ 392 Phil Roof .30 .14
❑ 393 John Lowenstein .30 .14
❑ 394 Bill Laxton .30 .14
❑ 395 Manny Trillo .30 .14
❑ 396 Tom Murphy .30 .14
❑ 397 Larry Herndon RC .75 .35
❑ 398 Tom Burgmeier .30 .14
❑ 399 Bruce Boisclair .30 .14
❑ 400 Steve Garvey 2.50 1.10
❑ 401 Mickey Scott .30 .14
❑ 402 Tommy Helms .30 .14
❑ 403 Tom Grieve .75 .35
❑ 404 Eric Rasmussen .30 .14
❑ 405 Claudell Washington .75 .35
❑ 406 Tim Johnson .30 .14
❑ 407 Dave Freisleben .30 .14
❑ 408 Cesar Tovar .30 .14
❑ 409 Pete Broberg .30 .14
❑ 410 Willie Montanez .30 .14
❑ 411 Joe Morgan WS 2.50 1.10
Johnny Bench
❑ 412 Johnny Bench WS 2.50 1.10
❑ 413 WS Summary .75 .35
Cincy wins 2nd
straight series
❑ 414 Tommy Harper .75 .35
❑ 415 Jay Johnstone .75 .35
❑ 416 Chuck Hartenstein .30 .14
❑ 417 Wayne Garrett .30 .14
❑ 418 White Sox Team/Mgr. 1.50 .30
Bob Lemon
(Checklist back)
❑ 419 Steve Swisher .30 .14
❑ 420 Rusty Staub 1.50 .70
❑ 421 Doug Rau .30 .14
❑ 422 Freddie Patek .75 .35
❑ 423 Gary Lavelle .30 .14
❑ 424 Steve Brye .30 .14
❑ 425 Joe Torre 1.50 .70
❑ 426 Dick Drago .30 .14
❑ 427 Dave Rader .30 .14
❑ 428 Rangers Team/Mgr. 1.50 .30
Frank Lucchesi
(Checklist back)
❑ 429 Ken Boswell .30 .14
❑ 430 Fergie Jenkins 2.50 1.10
❑ 431 Dave Collins UER .75 .35
(Photo actually
Bobby Jones)
❑ 432 Buzz Capra .30 .14
❑ 433 Nate Colbert TBC .30 .14
(5 HR, 13 RBI)
❑ 434 Carl Yastrzemski TBC 1.50 .70
'67 Triple Crown
❑ 435 Maury Wills TBC .75 .35
104 steals
❑ 436 Bob Keegan TBC .30 .14
Majors' only no-hitter
❑ 437 Ralph Kiner TBC 1.50 .70
Leads NL in HR's
7th straight year
❑ 438 Marty Perez .30 .14
❑ 439 Gorman Thomas .75 .35
❑ 440 Jon Matlack .30 .14
❑ 441 Larvell Blanks .30 .14
❑ 442 Braves Team/Mgr. 1.50 .30
Dave Bristol
(Checklist back)
❑ 443 Lamar Johnson .30 .14
❑ 444 Wayne Twitchell .30 .14
❑ 445 Ken Singleton .75 .35
❑ 446 Bill Bonham .30 .14
❑ 447 Jerry Turner .30 .14
❑ 448 Ellie Rodriguez .30 .14
❑ 449 Al Fitzmorris .30 .14
❑ 450 Pete Rose 20.00 9.00
❑ 451 Checklist 397-528 1.50 .30
❑ 452 Mike Caldwell .30 .14
❑ 453 Pedro Garcia .30 .14
❑ 454 Andy Etchebarren .30 .14
❑ 455 Rick Wise .30 .14
❑ 456 Leon Roberts .30 .14
❑ 457 Steve Luebber .30 .14
❑ 458 Leo Foster .30 .14
❑ 459 Steve Foucault .30 .14
❑ 460 Willie Stargell 2.50 1.10
❑ 461 Dick Tidrow .30 .14
❑ 462 Don Baylor 1.50 .70
❑ 463 Jamie Quirk .30 .14
❑ 464 Randy Moffitt .30 .14
❑ 465 Rico Carty .75 .35
❑ 466 Fred Holdsworth .30 .14
❑ 467 Phillies Team/Mgr. 1.50 .30
Danny Ozark
(Checklist back)
❑ 468 Ramon Hernandez .30 .14
❑ 469 Pat Kelly .30 .14
❑ 470 Ted Simmons .75 .35
❑ 471 Del Unser .30 .14
❑ 472 Rookie Pitchers .30 .14
Don Aase
Bob McClure
Gil Patterson
Dave Wehrmeister
❑ 473 Rookie Outfielders 20.00 9.00
Andre Dawson RC
Gene Richards
John Scott
Denny Walling
❑ 474 Rookie Shortstops .75 .35
Bob Bailor
Kiko Garcia
Craig Reynolds
Alex Taveras
❑ 475 Rookie Pitchers .75 .35
Chris Batton
Rick Camp
Scott McGregor
Manny Sarmiento
❑ 476 Rookie Catchers 20.00 9.00
Gary Alexander
Rick Cerone
Dale Murphy RC
Kevin Pasley
❑ 477 Rookie Infielders .75 .35
Doug Ault
Rich Dauer
Orlando Gonzalez
Phil Mankowski
❑ 478 Rookie Pitchers .75 .35
Jim Gideon
Leon Hooten
Dave Johnson
Mark Lemongello
❑ 479 Rookie Outfielders .75 .35
Brian Asselstine
Wayne Gross
Sam Mejias
Alvis Woods
❑ 480 Carl Yastrzemski 8.00 3.60
❑ 481 Roger Metzger .30 .14
❑ 482 Tony Solaita .30 .14
❑ 483 Richie Zisk .30 .14
❑ 484 Burt Hooton .75 .35
❑ 485 Roy White .75 .35
❑ 486 Ed Bane .30 .14
❑ 487 Rookie Pitchers .75 .35
Larry Anderson
Ed Glynn
Joe Henderson
Greg Terlecky
❑ 488 Rookie Outfielders 3.00 1.35
Jack Clark RC
Ruppert Jones
Lee Mazzilli
Dan Thomas
❑ 489 Rookie Pitchers .75 .35
Len Barker RC
Randy Lerch
Greg Minton
Mike Overy
❑ 490 Rookie Shortstops .75 .35
Billy Almon
Mickey Klutts
Tommy McMillan
Mark Wagner
❑ 491 Rookie Pitchers 5.00 2.20
Mike Dupree
Dennis Martinez RC
Craig Mitchell
Bob Sykes
❑ 492 Rookie Outfielders .75 .35
Tony Armas
Steve Kemp RC
Carlos Lopez
Gary Woods
❑ 493 Rookie Pitchers .75 .35
Mike Krukow
Jim Otten
Gary Wheelock
Mike Willis
❑ 494 Rookie Infielders 1.50 .70
Juan Bernhardt
Mike Champion
Jim Gantner RC
Bump Wills
❑ 495 Al Hrabosky .30 .14
❑ 496 Gary Thomasson .30 .14
❑ 497 Clay Carroll .30 .14
❑ 498 Sal Bando .75 .35
❑ 499 Pablo Torrealba .30 .14
❑ 500 Dave Kingman 1.50 .70
❑ 501 Jim Bibby .30 .14
❑ 502 Randy Hundley .30 .14
❑ 503 Bill Lee .30 .14
❑ 504 Dodgers Team/Mgr. 1.50 .30
Tom Lasorda
(Checklist back)
❑ 505 Oscar Gamble .75 .35
❑ 506 Steve Grilli .30 .14
❑ 507 Mike Hegan .30 .14
❑ 508 Dave Pagan .30 .14
❑ 509 Cookie Rojas .75 .35
❑ 510 John Candelaria .30 .14
❑ 511 Bill Fahey .30 .14
❑ 512 Jack Billingham .30 .14
❑ 513 Jerry Terrell .30 .14

❑ 514	Cliff Johnson	.30	.14
❑ 515	Chris Speier	.30	.14
❑ 516	Bake McBride	.75	.35
❑ 517	Pete Vuckovich RC	.75	.35
❑ 518	Cubs Team/Mgr.	1.50	.30
	Herman Franks		
	(Checklist back)		
❑ 519	Don Kirkwood	.30	.14
❑ 520	Garry Maddox	.30	.14
❑ 521	Bob Grich	.75	.35
❑ 522	Enzo Hernandez	.30	.14
❑ 523	Rollie Fingers	2.50	1.10
❑ 524	Rowland Office	.30	.14
❑ 525	Dennis Eckersley	5.00	2.20
❑ 526	Larry Parrish	.75	.35
❑ 527	Dan Meyer	.75	.35
❑ 528	Bill Castro	.30	.14
❑ 529	Jim Essian	.30	.14
❑ 530	Rick Reuschel	.75	.35
❑ 531	Lyman Bostock	.75	.35
❑ 532	Jim Willoughby	.30	.14
❑ 533	Mickey Stanley	.30	.14
❑ 534	Paul Splittorff	.30	.14
❑ 535	Cesar Geronimo	.30	.14
❑ 536	Vic Albury	.30	.14
❑ 537	Dave Roberts	.30	.14
❑ 538	Frank Taveras	.30	.14
❑ 539	Mike Wallace	.30	.14
❑ 540	Bob Watson	.75	.35
❑ 541	John Denny	.75	.35
❑ 542	Frank Duffy	.30	.14
❑ 543	Ron Blomberg	.30	.14
❑ 544	Gary Ross	.30	.14
❑ 545	Bob Boone	.75	.35
❑ 546	Orioles Team/Mgr.	1.50	.30
	Earl Weaver		
	(Checklist back)		
❑ 547	Willie McCovey	4.00	1.80
❑ 548	Joel Youngblood	.30	.14
❑ 549	Jerry Royster	.30	.14
❑ 550	Randy Jones	.30	.14
❑ 551	Bill North	.30	.14
❑ 552	Pepe Mangual	.30	.14
❑ 553	Jack Heidemann	.30	.14
❑ 554	Bruce Kimm	.30	.14
❑ 555	Dan Ford	.30	.14
❑ 556	Doug Bird	.30	.14
❑ 557	Jerry White	.30	.14
❑ 558	Elias Sosa	.30	.14
❑ 559	Alan Bannister	.30	.14
❑ 560	Dave Concepcion	1.50	.70
❑ 561	Pete LaCock	.30	.14
❑ 562	Checklist 529-660	1.50	.30
❑ 563	Bruce Kison	.30	.14
❑ 564	Alan Ashby	.75	.35
❑ 565	Mickey Lolich	.75	.35
❑ 566	Rick Miller	.30	.14
❑ 567	Enos Cabell	.30	.14
❑ 568	Carlos May	.30	.14
❑ 569	Jim Lonborg	.75	.35
❑ 570	Bobby Bonds	1.50	.70
❑ 571	Darrell Evans	.75	.35
❑ 572	Ross Grimsley	.30	.14
❑ 573	Joe Ferguson	.30	.14
❑ 574	Aurelio Rodriguez	.30	.14
❑ 575	Dick Ruthven	.30	.14
❑ 576	Fred Kendall	.30	.14
❑ 577	Jerry Augustine	.30	.14
❑ 578	Bob Randall	.30	.14
❑ 579	Don Carrithers	.30	.14
❑ 580	George Brett	15.00	6.75
❑ 581	Pedro Borbon	.30	.14
❑ 582	Ed Kirkpatrick	.30	.14
❑ 583	Paul Lindblad	.30	.14
❑ 584	Ed Goodson	.30	.14
❑ 585	Rick Burleson	.75	.35
❑ 586	Steve Renko	.30	.14
❑ 587	Rick Baldwin	.30	.14
❑ 588	Dave Moates	.30	.14
❑ 589	Mike Cosgrove	.30	.14
❑ 590	Buddy Bell	.75	.35
❑ 591	Chris Arnold	.30	.14
❑ 592	Dan Briggs	.30	.14
❑ 593	Dennis Blair	.30	.14
❑ 594	Biff Pocoroba	.30	.14
❑ 595	John Hiller	.30	.14

❑ 596	Jerry Martin	.30	.14
❑ 597	Mariners Leaders	1.50	.30
	Darrell Johnson MG		
	Don Bryant CO		
	Jim Busby CO		
	Vada Pinson CO		
	Wes Stock CO		
	(Checklist back)		
❑ 598	Sparky Lyle	.75	.35
❑ 599	Mike Tyson	.30	.14
❑ 600	Jim Palmer	4.00	1.80
❑ 601	Mike Lum	.30	.14
❑ 602	Andy Hassler	.30	.14
❑ 603	Willie Davis	.75	.35
❑ 604	Jim Slaton	.30	.14
❑ 605	Felix Millan	.30	.14
❑ 606	Steve Braun	.30	.14
❑ 607	Larry Demery	.30	.14
❑ 608	Roy Howell	.30	.14
❑ 609	Jim Barr	.30	.14
❑ 610	Jose Cardenal	.75	.35
❑ 611	Dave Lemanczyk	.30	.14
❑ 612	Barry Foote	.30	.14
❑ 613	Reggie Cleveland	.30	.14
❑ 614	Greg Gross	.30	.14
❑ 615	Phil Niekro	2.50	1.10
❑ 616	Tommy Sandt	.30	.14
❑ 617	Bobby Darwin	.30	.14
❑ 618	Pat Dobson	.30	.14
❑ 619	Johnny Oates	.75	.35
❑ 620	Don Sutton	2.50	1.10
❑ 621	Tigers Team/Mgr.	1.50	.30
	Ralph Houk		
	(Checklist back)		
❑ 622	Jim Wohlford	.30	.14
❑ 623	Jack Kucek	.30	.14
❑ 624	Hector Cruz	.30	.14
❑ 625	Ken Holtzman	.75	.35
❑ 626	Al Bumbry	.75	.35
❑ 627	Bob Myrick	.30	.14
❑ 628	Mario Guerrero	.30	.14
❑ 629	Bobby Valentine	.30	.14
❑ 630	Bert Blyleven	1.50	.70
❑ 631	George Brett	6.00	2.70
	Ken Brett		
❑ 632	Bob Forsch	.75	.35
	Ken Forsch		
❑ 633	Lee May	.75	.35
	Carlos May		
❑ 634	Paul Reuschel	.75	.35
	Rick Reuschel UER		
	(Photos switched)		
❑ 635	Robin Yount	8.00	3.60
❑ 636	Santo Alcala	.30	.14
❑ 637	Alex Johnson	.30	.14
❑ 638	Jim Kaat	1.50	.70
❑ 639	Jerry Morales	.30	.14
❑ 640	Carlton Fisk	5.00	2.20
❑ 641	Dan Larson	.30	.14
❑ 642	Willie Crawford	.30	.14
❑ 643	Mike Pazik	.30	.14
❑ 644	Matt Alexander	.30	.14
❑ 645	Jerry Reuss	.75	.35
❑ 646	Andres Mora	.30	.14
❑ 647	Expos Team/Mgr.	1.50	.30
	Dick Williams		
	(Checklist back)		
❑ 648	Jim Spencer	.30	.14
❑ 649	Dave Cash	.30	.14
❑ 650	Nolan Ryan	30.00	13.50
❑ 651	Von Joshua	.30	.14
❑ 652	Tom Walker	.30	.14
❑ 653	Diego Segui	.75	.35
❑ 654	Ron Pruitt	.30	.14
❑ 655	Tony Perez	2.50	1.10
❑ 656	Ron Guidry	1.50	.70
❑ 657	Mick Kelleher	.30	.14
❑ 658	Marty Pattin	.30	.14
❑ 659	Merv Rettenmund	.30	.14
❑ 660	Willie Horton	1.50	.30

1978 Topps

	NRMT	VG-E
COMPLETE SET (726)	200.00	90.00
COMMON CARD (1-726)	.25	.11

	COMMON CARD DP	.15	.07
❑ 1	Lou Brock RB	3.00	.90
	Most lifetime steals		
❑ 2	Sparky Lyle RB	.60	.25
	Most career games pure relief		
❑ 3	Willie McCovey RB	2.50	1.10
	Most times 2 HR's in inning		
❑ 4	Brooks Robinson RB	2.50	1.10
	Most consecutive		
	seasons with one club		
❑ 5	Pete Rose RB	8.00	3.60
	Most lifetime switch-hitter hits		
❑ 6	Nolan Ryan RB	15.00	6.75
	Most games 10 or more strikeouts		
❑ 7	Reggie Jackson RB	4.00	1.80
	Most homers,		
	one World Series		
❑ 8	Mike Sadek	.25	.11
❑ 9	Doug DeCinces	.60	.25
❑ 10	Phil Niekro	2.50	1.10
❑ 11	Rick Manning	.25	.11
❑ 12	Don Aase	.25	.11
❑ 13	Art Howe RC	.60	.25
❑ 14	Lerrin LaGrow	.25	.11
❑ 15	Tony Perez DP	1.25	.55
❑ 16	Roy White	.60	.25
❑ 17	Mike Krukow	.25	.11
❑ 18	Bob Grich	.60	.25
❑ 19	Darrell Porter	.60	.25
❑ 20	Pete Rose DP	12.00	5.50
❑ 21	Steve Kemp	.25	.11
❑ 22	Charlie Hough	.60	.25
❑ 23	Bump Wills	.25	.11
❑ 24	Don Money DP	.15	.07
❑ 25	Jon Matlack	.25	.11
❑ 26	Rich Hebner	.60	.25
❑ 27	Geoff Zahn	.25	.11
❑ 28	Ed Ott	.25	.11
❑ 29	Bob Lacey	.25	.11
❑ 30	George Hendrick	.60	.25
❑ 31	Glenn Abbott	.25	.11
❑ 32	Garry Templeton	.60	.25
❑ 33	Dave Lemanczyk	.25	.11
❑ 34	Willie McCovey	3.00	1.35
❑ 35	Sparky Lyle	.60	.25
❑ 36	Eddie Murray RC	80.00	36.00
❑ 37	Rick Waits	.25	.11
❑ 38	Willie Montanez	.25	.11
❑ 39	Floyd Bannister RC	.25	.11
❑ 40	Carl Yastrzemski	6.00	2.70
❑ 41	Burt Hooton	.60	.25
❑ 42	Jorge Orta	.25	.11
❑ 43	Bill Atkinson	.25	.11
❑ 44	Toby Harrah	.60	.25
❑ 45	Mark Fidrych	2.50	1.10
❑ 46	Al Cowens	.25	.11
❑ 47	Jack Billingham	.25	.11
❑ 48	Don Baylor	1.25	.55
❑ 49	Ed Kranepool	.60	.25
❑ 50	Rick Reuschel	.60	.25
❑ 51	Charlie Moore DP	.15	.07
❑ 52	Jim Lonborg	.25	.11
❑ 53	Phil Garner DP	.25	.11
❑ 54	Tom Johnson	.25	.11
❑ 55	Mitchell Page	.25	.11
❑ 56	Randy Jones	.25	.11

❑ 57 Dan Meyer .25 .11
❑ 58 Bob Forsch .25 .11
❑ 59 Otto Velez .25 .11
❑ 60 Thurman Munson 4.00 1.80
❑ 61 Larvell Blanks .25 .11
❑ 62 Jim Barr .25 .11
❑ 63 Don Zimmer MG .60 .25
❑ 64 Gene Pentz .25 .11
❑ 65 Ken Singleton .60 .25
❑ 66 Chicago White Sox 1.25 .25
Team Card
(Checklist back)
❑ 67 Claudell Washington .60 .25
❑ 68 Steve Foucault DP .15 .07
❑ 69 Mike Vail .25 .11
❑ 70 Rich Gossage 1.25 .55
❑ 71 Terry Humphrey .25 .11
❑ 72 Andre Dawson 4.00 1.80
❑ 73 Andy Hassler .25 .11
❑ 74 Checklist 1-121 1.25 .25
❑ 75 Dick Ruthven .25 .11
❑ 76 Steve Ontiveros .25 .11
❑ 77 Ed Kirkpatrick .25 .11
❑ 78 Pablo Torrealba .25 .11
❑ 79 Da.Johnson DP MG .15 .07
❑ 80 Ken Griffey Sr. 1.25 .55
❑ 81 Pete Redfern .25 .11
❑ 82 San Francisco Giants 1.25 .25
Team Card
(Checklist back)
❑ 83 Bob Montgomery .25 .11
❑ 84 Kent Tekulve .60 .25
❑ 85 Ron Fairly .60 .25
❑ 86 Dave Tomlin .25 .11
❑ 87 John Lowenstein .25 .11
❑ 88 Mike Phillips .25 .11
❑ 89 Ken Clay .25 .11
❑ 90 Larry Bowa 1.25 .55
❑ 91 Oscar Zamora .25 .11
❑ 92 Adrian Devine .25 .11
❑ 93 Bobby Cox DP .25 .11
❑ 94 Chuck Scrivener .25 .11
❑ 95 Jamie Quirk .25 .11
❑ 96 Baltimore Orioles 1.25 .25
Team Card
(Checklist back)
❑ 97 Stan Bahnsen .25 .11
❑ 98 Jim Essian .60 .25
❑ 99 Willie Hernandez RC 1.25 .55
❑ 100 George Brett 15.00 6.75
❑ 101 Sid Monge .25 .11
❑ 102 Matt Alexander .25 .11
❑ 103 Tom Murphy .25 .11
❑ 104 Lee Lacy .25 .11
❑ 105 Reggie Cleveland .25 .11
❑ 106 Bill Plummer .25 .11
❑ 107 Ed Halicki .25 .11
❑ 108 Von Joshua .25 .11
❑ 109 Joe Torre MG .60 .25
❑ 110 Richie Zisk .25 .11
❑ 111 Mike Tyson .25 .11
❑ 112 Houston Astros 1.25 .25
Team Card
(Checklist back)
❑ 113 Don Carrithers .25 .11
❑ 114 Paul Blair .60 .25
❑ 115 Gary Nolan .25 .11
❑ 116 Tucker Ashford .25 .11
❑ 117 John Montague .25 .11
❑ 118 Terry Harmon .25 .11
❑ 119 Dennis Martinez 2.50 1.10
❑ 120 Gary Carter 2.50 1.10
❑ 121 Alvis Woods .25 .11
❑ 122 Dennis Eckersley 3.00 1.35
❑ 123 Manny Trillo .25 .11
❑ 124 Dave Rozema .25 .11
❑ 125 George Scott .60 .25
❑ 126 Paul Moskau .25 .11
❑ 127 Chet Lemon .60 .25
❑ 128 Bill Russell .60 .25
❑ 129 Jim Colborn .25 .11
❑ 130 Jeff Burroughs .60 .25
❑ 131 Bert Blyleven 1.25 .55
❑ 132 Enos Cabell .25 .11
❑ 133 Jerry Augustine .25 .11
❑ 134 Steve Henderson .25 .11
❑ 135 Ron Guidry DP 1.25 .55
❑ 136 Ted Sizemore .25 .11
❑ 137 Craig Kusick .25 .11
❑ 138 Larry Demery .25 .11
❑ 139 Wayne Gross .25 .11
❑ 140 Rollie Fingers 2.50 1.10
❑ 141 Ruppert Jones .25 .11
❑ 142 John Montefusco .25 .11
❑ 143 Keith Hernandez .60 .25
❑ 144 Jesse Jefferson .25 .11
❑ 145 Rick Monday .60 .25
❑ 146 Doyle Alexander .25 .11
❑ 147 Lee Mazzilli .25 .11
❑ 148 Andre Thornton .60 .25
❑ 149 Dale Murray .25 .11
❑ 150 Bobby Bonds 1.25 .55
❑ 151 Milt Wilcox .25 .11
❑ 152 Ivan DeJesus .25 .11
❑ 153 Steve Stone .60 .25
❑ 154 Cecil Cooper DP .25 .11
❑ 155 Butch Hobson .25 .11
❑ 156 Andy Messersmith .60 .25
❑ 157 Pete LaCock DP .15 .07
❑ 158 Joaquin Andujar .60 .25
❑ 159 Lou Piniella .60 .25
❑ 160 Jim Palmer 3.00 1.35
❑ 161 Bob Boone 1.25 .55
❑ 162 Paul Thormodsgard .25 .11
❑ 163 Bill North .25 .11
❑ 164 Bob Owchinko .25 .11
❑ 165 Rennie Stennett .25 .11
❑ 166 Carlos Lopez .25 .11
❑ 167 Tim Foli .25 .11
❑ 168 Reggie Smith .60 .25
❑ 169 Jerry Johnson .25 .11
❑ 170 Lou Brock 3.00 1.35
❑ 171 Pat Zachry .25 .11
❑ 172 Mike Hargrove .60 .25
❑ 173 Robin Yount UER 5.00 2.20
(Played for Newark
in 1973, not 1971)
❑ 174 Wayne Garland .25 .11
❑ 175 Jerry Morales .25 .11
❑ 176 Milt May .25 .11
❑ 177 Gene Garber DP .25 .11
❑ 178 Dave Chalk .25 .11
❑ 179 Dick Tidrow .25 .11
❑ 180 Dave Concepcion 1.25 .55
❑ 181 Ken Forsch .25 .11
❑ 182 Jim Spencer .25 .11
❑ 183 Doug Bird .25 .11
❑ 184 Checklist 122-242 1.25 .25
❑ 185 Ellis Valentine .25 .11
❑ 186 Bob Stanley DP .25 .11
❑ 187 Jerry Royster DP .15 .07
❑ 188 Al Bumbry .60 .25
❑ 189 Tom Lasorda MG 2.50 1.10
❑ 190 John Candelaria .60 .25
❑ 191 Rodney Scott .25 .11
❑ 192 San Diego Padres 1.25 .25
Team Card
(Checklist back)
❑ 193 Rich Chiles .25 .11
❑ 194 Derrel Thomas .25 .11
❑ 195 Larry Dierker .60 .25
❑ 196 Bob Bailor .25 .11
❑ 197 Nino Espinosa .25 .11
❑ 198 Ron Pruitt .25 .11
❑ 199 Craig Reynolds .25 .11
❑ 200 Reggie Jackson 8.00 3.60
❑ 201 Batting Leaders 1.25 .55
Dave Parker
Rod Carew
❑ 202 HR Leaders DP .60 .25
George Foster
Jim Rice
❑ 203 RBI Leaders .60 .25
George Foster
Larry Hisle
❑ 204 SB Leaders DP .25 .11
Frank Taveras
Freddie Patek
❑ 205 Victory Leaders 2.50 1.10
Steve Carlton
Dave Goltz
Dennis Leonard
Jim Palmer
❑ 206 Strikeout Leaders DP 6.00 2.70
Phil Niekro
Nolan Ryan
❑ 207 ERA Leaders DP .60 .25
John Candelaria
Frank Tanana
❑ 208 Firemen Leaders 1.25 .55
Rollie Fingers
Bill Campbell
❑ 209 Dock Ellis .25 .11
❑ 210 Jose Cardenal .25 .11
❑ 211 Earl Weaver MG DP 1.25 .55
❑ 212 Mike Caldwell .25 .11
❑ 213 Alan Bannister .25 .11
❑ 214 California Angels 1.25 .25
Team Card
(Checklist back)
❑ 215 Darrell Evans .60 .25
❑ 216 Mike Paxton .25 .11
❑ 217 Rod Gilbreath .25 .11
❑ 218 Marty Pattin .25 .11
❑ 219 Mike Cubbage .25 .11
❑ 220 Pedro Borbon .25 .11
❑ 221 Chris Speier .25 .11
❑ 222 Jerry Martin .25 .11
❑ 223 Bruce Kison .25 .11
❑ 224 Jerry Tabb .25 .11
❑ 225 Don Gullett DP .25 .11
❑ 226 Joe Ferguson .25 .11
❑ 227 Al Fitzmorris .25 .11
❑ 228 Manny Mota DP .25 .11
❑ 229 Leo Foster .25 .11
❑ 230 Al Hrabosky .25 .11
❑ 231 Wayne Nordhagen .25 .11
❑ 232 Mickey Stanley .25 .11
❑ 233 Dick Pole .25 .11
❑ 234 Herman Franks MG .25 .11
❑ 235 Tim McCarver .60 .25
❑ 236 Terry Whitfield .25 .11
❑ 237 Rich Dauer .25 .11
❑ 238 Juan Beniquez .25 .11
❑ 239 Dyar Miller .25 .11
❑ 240 Gene Tenace .60 .25
❑ 241 Pete Vuckovich .60 .25
❑ 242 Barry Bonnell DP .15 .07
❑ 243 Bob McClure .25 .11
❑ 244 Montreal Expos .60 .12
Team Card DP
(Checklist back)
❑ 245 Rick Burleson .60 .25
❑ 246 Dan Driessen .25 .11
❑ 247 Larry Christenson .25 .11
❑ 248 Frank White DP .60 .25
❑ 249 Dave Goltz DP .15 .07
❑ 250 Graig Nettles DP .60 .25
❑ 251 Don Kirkwood .25 .11
❑ 252 Steve Swisher DP .15 .07
❑ 253 Jim Kern .25 .11
❑ 254 Dave Collins .60 .25
❑ 255 Jerry Reuss .60 .25
❑ 256 Joe Altobelli MG .25 .11
❑ 257 Hector Cruz .25 .11
❑ 258 John Hiller .25 .11
❑ 259 Los Angeles Dodgers 1.25 .25
Team Card
(Checklist back)
❑ 260 Bert Campaneris .60 .25
❑ 261 Tim Hosley .25 .11
❑ 262 Rudy May .25 .11
❑ 263 Danny Walton .25 .11
❑ 264 Jamie Easterly .25 .11
❑ 265 Sal Bando DP .60 .25
❑ 266 Bob Shirley .25 .11
❑ 267 Doug Ault .25 .11
❑ 268 Gil Flores .25 .11
❑ 269 Wayne Twitchell .25 .11
❑ 270 Carlton Fisk 4.00 1.80
❑ 271 Randy Lerch DP .15 .07
❑ 272 Royle Stillman .25 .11
❑ 273 Fred Norman .25 .11
❑ 274 Freddie Patek .60 .25
❑ 275 Dan Ford .25 .11
❑ 276 Bill Bonham DP .15 .07
❑ 277 Bruce Boisclair .25 .11
❑ 278 Enrique Romo .25 .11

❑	279	Bill Virdon MG	.25	.11
❑	280	Buddy Bell	.60	.25
❑	281	Eric Rasmussen DP	.15	.07
❑	282	New York Yankees Team Card (Checklist back)	2.50	.50
❑	283	Omar Moreno	.25	.11
❑	284	Randy Moffitt	.25	.11
❑	285	Steve Yeager DP	.60	.25
❑	286	Ben Oglivie	.60	.25
❑	287	Kiko Garcia	.25	.11
❑	288	Dave Hamilton	.25	.11
❑	289	Checklist 243-363	1.25	.25
❑	290	Willie Horton	.60	.25
❑	291	Gary Ross	.25	.11
❑	292	Gene Richards	.25	.11
❑	293	Mike Willis	.25	.11
❑	294	Larry Parrish	.60	.25
❑	295	Bill Lee	.25	.11
❑	296	Biff Pocoroba	.25	.11
❑	297	Warren Brusstar DP	.15	.07
❑	298	Tony Armas	.60	.25
❑	299	Whitey Herzog MG	.60	.25
❑	300	Joe Morgan	3.00	1.35
❑	301	Buddy Schultz	.25	.11
❑	302	Chicago Cubs Team Card (Checklist back)	1.25	.25
❑	303	Sam Hinds	.25	.11
❑	304	John Milner	.25	.11
❑	305	Rico Carty	.60	.25
❑	306	Joe Niekro	.60	.25
❑	307	Glenn Borgmann	.25	.11
❑	308	Jim Rooker	.25	.11
❑	309	Cliff Johnson	.25	.11
❑	310	Don Sutton	2.50	1.10
❑	311	Jose Baez DP	.15	.07
❑	312	Greg Minton	.25	.11
❑	313	Andy Etchebarren	.25	.11
❑	314	Paul Lindblad	.25	.11
❑	315	Mark Belanger	.60	.25
❑	316	Henry Cruz DP	.15	.07
❑	317	Dave Johnson	.25	.11
❑	318	Tom Griffin	.25	.11
❑	319	Alan Ashby	.25	.11
❑	320	Fred Lynn	.60	.25
❑	321	Santo Alcala	.25	.11
❑	322	Tom Paciorek	.60	.25
❑	323	Jim Fregosi DP	.25	.11
❑	324	Vern Rapp MG	.25	.11
❑	325	Bruce Sutter	1.25	.55
❑	326	Mike Lum DP	.15	.07
❑	327	Rick Langford DP	.15	.07
❑	328	Milwaukee Brewers Team Card (Checklist back)	1.25	.25
❑	329	John Verhoeven	.25	.11
❑	330	Bob Watson	.60	.25
❑	331	Mark Littell	.25	.11
❑	332	Duane Kuiper	.25	.11
❑	333	Jim Todd	.25	.11
❑	334	John Stearns	.25	.11
❑	335	Bucky Dent	.60	.25
❑	336	Steve Busby	.25	.11
❑	337	Tom Grieve	.60	.25
❑	338	Dave Heaverlo	.25	.11
❑	339	Mario Guerrero	.25	.11
❑	340	Bake McBride	.60	.25
❑	341	Mike Flanagan	.60	.25
❑	342	Aurelio Rodriguez	.25	.11
❑	343	John Wathan DP	.15	.07
❑	344	Sam Ewing	.25	.11
❑	345	Luis Tiant	.60	.25
❑	346	Larry Biittner	.25	.11
❑	347	Terry Forster	.25	.11
❑	348	Del Unser	.25	.11
❑	349	Rick Camp DP	.15	.07
❑	350	Steve Garvey	2.50	1.10
❑	351	Jeff Torborg	.60	.25
❑	352	Tony Scott	.25	.11
❑	353	Doug Bair	.25	.11
❑	354	Cesar Geronimo	.25	.11
❑	355	Bill Travers	.25	.11
❑	356	New York Mets Team Card (Checklist back)	1.25	.25
❑	357	Tom Poquette	.25	.11
❑	358	Mark Lemongello	.25	.11
❑	359	Marc Hill	.25	.11
❑	360	Mike Schmidt	10.00	4.50
❑	361	Chris Knapp	.25	.11
❑	362	Dave May	.25	.11
❑	363	Bob Randall	.25	.11
❑	364	Jerry Turner	.25	.11
❑	365	Ed Figueroa	.25	.11
❑	366	Larry Milbourne DP	.15	.07
❑	367	Rick Dempsey	.60	.25
❑	368	Balor Moore	.25	.11
❑	369	Tim Nordbrook	.25	.11
❑	370	Rusty Staub	1.25	.55
❑	371	Ray Burris	.25	.11
❑	372	Brian Asselstine	.25	.11
❑	373	Jim Willoughby	.25	.11
❑	374	Jose Morales	.25	.11
❑	375	Tommy John	1.25	.55
❑	376	Jim Wohlford	.25	.11
❑	377	Manny Sarmiento	.25	.11
❑	378	Bobby Winkles MG	.25	.11
❑	379	Skip Lockwood	.25	.11
❑	380	Ted Simmons	.60	.25
❑	381	Philadelphia Phillies Team Card (Checklist back)	1.25	.25
❑	382	Joe Lahoud	.25	.11
❑	383	Mario Mendoza	.25	.11
❑	384	Jack Clark	1.25	.55
❑	385	Tito Fuentes	.25	.11
❑	386	Bob Gorinski	.25	.11
❑	387	Ken Holtzman	.60	.25
❑	388	Bill Fahey DP	.15	.07
❑	389	Julio Gonzalez	.25	.11
❑	390	Oscar Gamble	.60	.25
❑	391	Larry Haney	.25	.11
❑	392	Billy Almon	.25	.11
❑	393	Tippy Martinez	.60	.25
❑	394	Roy Howell DP	.15	.07
❑	395	Jim Hughes	.25	.11
❑	396	Bob Stinson DP	.15	.07
❑	397	Greg Gross	.25	.11
❑	398	Don Hood	.25	.11
❑	399	Pete Mackanin	.25	.11
❑	400	Nolan Ryan	30.00	13.50
❑	401	Sparky Anderson MG	.60	.25
❑	402	Dave Campbell	.25	.11
❑	403	Bud Harrelson	.60	.25
❑	404	Detroit Tigers Team Card (Checklist back)	1.25	.25
❑	405	Rawly Eastwick	.25	.11
❑	406	Mike Jorgensen	.25	.11
❑	407	Odell Jones	.25	.11
❑	408	Joe Zdeb	.25	.11
❑	409	Ron Schueler	.25	.11
❑	410	Bill Madlock	.60	.25
❑	411	AL Champs Willie Randolph	.60	.25
❑	412	NL Champs Davey Lopes	.60	.25
❑	413	World Series Reggie Jackson	4.00	1.80
❑	414	Darold Knowles DP	.15	.07
❑	415	Ray Fosse	.25	.11
❑	416	Jack Brohamer	.25	.11
❑	417	Mike Garman DP	.15	.07
❑	418	Tony Muser	.25	.11
❑	419	Jerry Garvin	.25	.11
❑	420	Greg Luzinski	1.25	.55
❑	421	Junior Moore	.25	.11
❑	422	Steve Braun	.25	.11
❑	423	Dave Rosello	.25	.11
❑	424	Boston Red Sox Team Card (Checklist back)	1.25	.25
❑	425	Steve Rogers DP	.25	.11
❑	426	Fred Kendall	.25	.11
❑	427	Mario Soto RC	.60	.25
❑	428	Joel Youngblood	.25	.11
❑	429	Mike Barlow	.25	.11
❑	430	Al Oliver	.60	.25
❑	431	Butch Metzger	.25	.11
❑	432	Terry Bulling	.25	.11
❑	433	Fernando Gonzalez	.25	.11
❑	434	Mike Norris	.25	.11
❑	435	Checklist 364-484	1.25	.25
❑	436	Vic Harris DP	.15	.07
❑	437	Bo McLaughlin	.25	.11
❑	438	John Ellis	.25	.11
❑	439	Ken Kravec	.25	.11
❑	440	Dave Lopes	.60	.25
❑	441	Larry Gura	.25	.11
❑	442	Elliott Maddox	.25	.11
❑	443	Darrel Chaney	.25	.11
❑	444	Roy Hartsfield MG	.25	.11
❑	445	Mike Ivie	.25	.11
❑	446	Tug McGraw	.60	.25
❑	447	Leroy Stanton	.25	.11
❑	448	Bill Castro	.25	.11
❑	449	Tim Blackwell DP	.15	.07
❑	450	Tom Seaver	6.00	2.70
❑	451	Minnesota Twins Team Card (Checklist back)	1.25	.25
❑	452	Jerry Mumphrey	.25	.11
❑	453	Doug Flynn	.25	.11
❑	454	Dave LaRoche	.25	.11
❑	455	Bill Robinson	.60	.25
❑	456	Vern Ruhle	.25	.11
❑	457	Bob Bailey	.25	.11
❑	458	Jeff Newman	.25	.11
❑	459	Charlie Spikes	.25	.11
❑	460	Jim Hunter	2.50	1.10
❑	461	Rob Andrews DP	.15	.07
❑	462	Rogelio Moret	.25	.11
❑	463	Kevin Bell	.25	.11
❑	464	Jerry Grote	.25	.11
❑	465	Hal McRae	.60	.25
❑	466	Dennis Blair	.25	.11
❑	467	Alvin Dark MG	.60	.25
❑	468	Warren Cromartie RC	.60	.25
❑	469	Rick Cerone	.60	.25
❑	470	J.R. Richard	.60	.25
❑	471	Roy Smalley	.60	.25
❑	472	Ron Reed	.25	.11
❑	473	Bill Buckner	.60	.25
❑	474	Jim Slaton	.25	.11
❑	475	Gary Matthews	.60	.25
❑	476	Bill Stein	.25	.11
❑	477	Doug Capilla	.25	.11
❑	478	Jerry Remy	.25	.11
❑	479	St. Louis Cardinals Team Card (Checklist back)	1.25	.25
❑	480	Ron LeFlore	.60	.25
❑	481	Jackson Todd	.25	.11
❑	482	Rick Miller	.25	.11
❑	483	Ken Macha	.25	.11
❑	484	Jim Norris	.25	.11
❑	485	Chris Chambliss	.60	.25
❑	486	John Curtis	.25	.11
❑	487	Jim Tyrone	.25	.11
❑	488	Dan Spillner	.25	.11
❑	489	Rudy Meoli	.25	.11
❑	490	Amos Otis	.60	.25
❑	491	Scott McGregor	.60	.25
❑	492	Jim Sundberg	.60	.25
❑	493	Steve Renko	.25	.11
❑	494	Chuck Tanner MG	.60	.25
❑	495	Dave Cash	.25	.11
❑	496	Jim Clancy DP	.15	.07
❑	497	Glenn Adams	.25	.11
❑	498	Joe Sambito	.25	.11
❑	499	Seattle Mariners Team Card (Checklist back)	1.25	.25
❑	500	George Foster	1.25	.55
❑	501	Dave Roberts	.25	.11
❑	502	Pat Rockett	.25	.11
❑	503	Ike Hampton	.25	.11
❑	504	Roger Freed	.25	.11
❑	505	Felix Millan	.25	.11
❑	506	Ron Blomberg	.25	.11
❑	507	Willie Crawford	.25	.11
❑	508	Johnny Oates	.60	.25
❑	509	Brent Strom	.25	.11
❑	510	Willie Stargell	2.50	1.10
❑	511	Frank Duffy	.25	.11
❑	512	Larry Herndon	.25	.11
❑	513	Barry Foote	.25	.11

❏ 514	Rob Sperring	.25	.11
❏ 515	Tim Corcoran	.25	.11
❏ 516	Gary Beare	.25	.11
❏ 517	Andres Mora	.25	.11
❏ 518	Tommy Boggs DP	.15	.07
❏ 519	Brian Downing	.60	.25
❏ 520	Larry Hisle	.25	.11
❏ 521	Steve Staggs	.25	.11
❏ 522	Dick Williams MG	.60	.25
❏ 523	Donnie Moore	.25	.11
❏ 524	Bernie Carbo	.25	.11
❏ 525	Jerry Terrell	.25	.11
❏ 526	Cincinnati Reds Team Card (Checklist back)	1.25	.25
❏ 527	Vic Correll	.25	.11
❏ 528	Rob Picciolo	.25	.11
❏ 529	Paul Hartzell	.25	.11
❏ 530	Dave Winfield	4.00	1.80
❏ 531	Tom Underwood	.25	.11
❏ 532	Skip Jutze	.25	.11
❏ 533	Sandy Alomar	.60	.25
❏ 534	Wilbur Howard	.25	.11
❏ 535	Checklist 485-605	1.25	.25
❏ 536	Roric Harrison	.25	.11
❏ 537	Bruce Bochte	.25	.11
❏ 538	Johnny LeMaster	.25	.11
❏ 539	Vic Davalillo DP	.15	.07
❏ 540	Steve Carlton	4.00	1.80
❏ 541	Larry Cox	.25	.11
❏ 542	Tim Johnson	.25	.11
❏ 543	Larry Harlow DP	.15	.07
❏ 544	Len Randle DP	.15	.07
❏ 545	Bill Campbell	.25	.11
❏ 546	Ted Martinez	.25	.11
❏ 547	John Scott	.25	.11
❏ 548	Billy Hunter DP MG	.15	.07
❏ 549	Joe Kerrigan	.25	.11
❏ 550	John Mayberry	.60	.25
❏ 551	Atlanta Braves Team Card (Checklist back)	1.25	.25
❏ 552	Francisco Barrios	.25	.11
❏ 553	Terry Puhl	.60	.25
❏ 554	Joe Coleman	.25	.11
❏ 555	Butch Wynegar	.25	.11
❏ 556	Ed Armbrister	.25	.11
❏ 557	Tony Solaita	.25	.11
❏ 558	Paul Mitchell	.25	.11
❏ 559	Phil Mankowski	.25	.11
❏ 560	Dave Parker	1.25	.55
❏ 561	Charlie Williams	.25	.11
❏ 562	Glenn Burke	.25	.11
❏ 563	Dave Rader	.25	.11
❏ 564	Mick Kelleher	.25	.11
❏ 565	Jerry Koosman	.60	.25
❏ 566	Merv Rettenmund	.25	.11
❏ 567	Dick Drago	.25	.11
❏ 568	Tom Hutton	.25	.11
❏ 569	Lary Sorensen	.25	.11
❏ 570	Dave Kingman	1.25	.55
❏ 571	Buck Martinez	.25	.11
❏ 572	Rick Wise	.25	.11
❏ 573	Luis Gomez	.25	.11
❏ 574	Bob Lemon MG	1.25	.55
❏ 575	Pat Dobson	.25	.11
❏ 576	Sam Mejias	.25	.11
❏ 577	Oakland A's Team Card (Checklist back)	1.25	.25
❏ 578	Buzz Capra	.25	.11
❏ 579	Rance Mulliniks	.25	.11
❏ 580	Rod Carew	4.00	1.80
❏ 581	Lynn McGlothen	.25	.11
❏ 582	Fran Healy	.25	.11
❏ 583	George Medich	.25	.11
❏ 584	John Hale	.25	.11
❏ 585	Woodie Fryman DP	.15	.07
❏ 586	Ed Goodson	.25	.11
❏ 587	John Urrea	.25	.11
❏ 588	Jim Mason	.25	.11
❏ 589	Bob Knepper	.25	.11
❏ 590	Bobby Murcer	.60	.25
❏ 591	George Zeber	.25	.11
❏ 592	Bob Apodaca	.25	.11
❏ 593	Dave Skaggs	.25	.11
❏ 594	Dave Freisleben	.25	.11
❏ 595	Sixto Lezcano	.25	.11
❏ 596	Gary Wheelock	.25	.11
❏ 597	Steve Dillard	.25	.11
❏ 598	Eddie Solomon	.25	.11
❏ 599	Gary Woods	.25	.11
❏ 600	Frank Tanana	.60	.25
❏ 601	Gene Mauch MG	.60	.25
❏ 602	Eric Soderholm	.25	.11
❏ 603	Will McEnaney	.25	.11
❏ 604	Earl Williams	.25	.11
❏ 605	Rick Rhoden	.60	.25
❏ 606	Pittsburgh Pirates Team Card (Checklist back)	1.25	.25
❏ 607	Fernando Arroyo	.25	.11
❏ 608	Johnny Grubb	.25	.11
❏ 609	John Denny	.25	.11
❏ 610	Garry Maddox	.60	.25
❏ 611	Pat Scanlon	.25	.11
❏ 612	Ken Henderson	.25	.11
❏ 613	Marty Perez	.25	.11
❏ 614	Joe Wallis	.25	.11
❏ 615	Clay Carroll	.25	.11
❏ 616	Pat Kelly	.25	.11
❏ 617	Joe Nolan	.25	.11
❏ 618	Tommy Helms	.25	.11
❏ 619	Thad Bosley DP	.15	.07
❏ 620	Willie Randolph	1.25	.55
❏ 621	Craig Swan DP	.15	.07
❏ 622	Champ Summers	.25	.11
❏ 623	Eduardo Rodriguez	.25	.11
❏ 624	Gary Alexander DP	.15	.07
❏ 625	Jose Cruz	.60	.25
❏ 626	Toronto Blue Jays Team Card DP (Checklist back)	1.25	.25
❏ 627	David Johnson	.25	.11
❏ 628	Ralph Garr	.60	.25
❏ 629	Don Stanhouse	.25	.11
❏ 630	Ron Cey	1.25	.55
❏ 631	Danny Ozark MG	.25	.11
❏ 632	Rowland Office	.25	.11
❏ 633	Tom Veryzer	.25	.11
❏ 634	Len Barker	.25	.11
❏ 635	Joe Rudi	.60	.25
❏ 636	Jim Bibby	.25	.11
❏ 637	Duffy Dyer	.25	.11
❏ 638	Paul Splittorff	.25	.11
❏ 639	Gene Clines	.25	.11
❏ 640	Lee May DP	.25	.11
❏ 641	Doug Rau	.25	.11
❏ 642	Denny Doyle	.25	.11
❏ 643	Tom House	.25	.11
❏ 644	Jim Dwyer	.25	.11
❏ 645	Mike Torrez	.60	.25
❏ 646	Rick Auerbach DP	.15	.07
❏ 647	Steve Dunning	.25	.11
❏ 648	Gary Thomasson	.25	.11
❏ 649	Moose Haas	.25	.11
❏ 650	Cesar Cedeno	.60	.25
❏ 651	Doug Rader	.25	.11
❏ 652	Checklist 606-726	1.25	.25
❏ 653	Ron Hodges DP	.15	.07
❏ 654	Pepe Frias	.25	.11
❏ 655	Lyman Bostock	.60	.25
❏ 656	Dave Garcia MG	.25	.11
❏ 657	Bombo Rivera	.25	.11
❏ 658	Manny Sanguillen	.60	.25
❏ 659	Texas Rangers Team Card (Checklist back)	1.25	.25
❏ 660	Jason Thompson	.60	.25
❏ 661	Grant Jackson	.25	.11
❏ 662	Paul Dade	.25	.11
❏ 663	Paul Reuschel	.25	.11
❏ 664	Fred Stanley	.25	.11
❏ 665	Dennis Leonard	.60	.25
❏ 666	Billy Smith	.25	.11
❏ 667	Jeff Byrd	.25	.11
❏ 668	Dusty Baker	1.25	.55
❏ 669	Pete Falcone	.25	.11
❏ 670	Jim Rice	1.25	.55
❏ 671	Gary Lavelle	.25	.11
❏ 672	Don Kessinger	.60	.25
❏ 673	Steve Brye	.25	.11
❏ 674	Ray Knight RC	2.50	1.10
❏ 675	Jay Johnstone	.60	.25
❏ 676	Bob Myrick	.25	.11
❏ 677	Ed Herrmann	.25	.11
❏ 678	Tom Burgmeier	.25	.11
❏ 679	Wayne Garrett	.25	.11
❏ 680	Vida Blue	.60	.25
❏ 681	Rob Belloir	.25	.11
❏ 682	Ken Brett	.25	.11
❏ 683	Mike Champion	.25	.11
❏ 684	Ralph Houk MG	.60	.25
❏ 685	Frank Taveras	.25	.11
❏ 686	Gaylord Perry	2.50	1.10
❏ 687	Julio Cruz	.25	.11
❏ 688	George Mitterwald	.25	.11
❏ 689	Cleveland Indians Team Card (Checklist back)	1.25	.25
❏ 690	Mickey Rivers	.60	.25
❏ 691	Ross Grimsley	.25	.11
❏ 692	Ken Reitz	.25	.11
❏ 693	Lamar Johnson	.25	.11
❏ 694	Elias Sosa	.25	.11
❏ 695	Dwight Evans	1.25	.55
❏ 696	Steve Mingori	.25	.11
❏ 697	Roger Metzger	.25	.11
❏ 698	Juan Bernhardt	.25	.11
❏ 699	Jackie Brown	.25	.11
❏ 700	Johnny Bench	8.00	3.60
❏ 701	Rookie Pitchers Tom Hume Larry Landreth Steve McCatty Bruce Taylor	.60	.25
❏ 702	Rookie Catchers Bill Nahorodny Kevin Pasley Rick Sweet Don Werner	.60	.25
❏ 703	Rookie Pitchers DP Larry Andersen Tim Jones Mickey Mahler Jack Morris RC	5.00	2.20
❏ 704	Rookie 2nd Basemen Garth Iorg Dave Oliver Sam Perlozzo Lou Whitaker RC	8.00	3.60
❏ 705	Rookie Outfielders Dave Bergman Miguel Dilone Clint Hurdle Willie Norwood	1.25	.55
❏ 706	Rookie 1st Basemen Wayne Cage Ted Cox Pat Putnam Dave Revering	.60	.25
❏ 707	Rookie Shortstops Mickey Klutts Paul Molitor RC Alan Trammell RC U.L. Washington	80.00	36.00
❏ 708	Rookie Catchers Bo Diaz Dale Murphy Lance Parrish RC Ernie Whitt	4.00	1.80
❏ 709	Rookie Pitchers Steve Burke Matt Keough Lance Rautzhan Dan Schatzeder	.60	.25
❏ 710	Rookie Outfielders Dell Alston Rick Bosetti Mike Easler Keith Smith	1.25	.55
❏ 711	Rookie Pitchers DP Cardell Camper Dennis Lamp Craig Mitchell Roy Thomas	.25	.11
❏ 712	Bobby Valentine	.60	.25
❏ 713	Bob Davis	.25	.11

Card	NRMT	VG-E
❑ 714 Mike Anderson	.25	.11
❑ 715 Jim Kaat	1.25	.55
❑ 716 Clarence Gaston	.60	.25
❑ 717 Nelson Briles	.25	.11
❑ 718 Ron Jackson	.25	.11
❑ 719 Randy Elliott	.25	.11
❑ 720 Fergie Jenkins	2.50	1.10
❑ 721 Billy Martin MG	1.25	.55
❑ 722 Pete Broberg	.25	.11
❑ 723 John Wockenfuss	.25	.11
❑ 724 Kansas City Royals Team Card (Checklist back)	1.25	.25
❑ 725 Kurt Bevacqua	.25	.11
❑ 726 Wilbur Wood	1.25	.30

1979 Topps

	NRMT	VG-E
COMPLETE SET (726)	150.00	70.00
COMMON CARD (1-726)	.25	.11
COMMON CARD DP	.10	.05

Card	NRMT	VG-E
❑ 1 Batting Leaders Rod Carew Dave Parker	2.50	.50
❑ 2 Home Run Leaders Jim Rice George Foster	1.00	.45
❑ 3 RBI Leaders Jim Rice George Foster	1.00	.45
❑ 4 Stolen Base Leaders Ron LeFlore Omar Moreno	.50	.23
❑ 5 Victory Leaders Ron Guidry Gaylord Perry	.50	.23
❑ 6 Strikeout Leaders Nolan Ryan J.R. Richard	5.00	2.20
❑ 7 ERA Leaders Ron Guidry Craig Swan	.50	.23
❑ 8 Leading Firemen Rich Gossage Rollie Fingers	1.00	.45
❑ 9 Dave Campbell	.25	.11
❑ 10 Lee May	.50	.23
❑ 11 Marc Hill	.25	.11
❑ 12 Dick Drago	.25	.11
❑ 13 Paul Dade	.25	.11
❑ 14 Rafael Landestoy	.25	.11
❑ 15 Ross Grimsley	.25	.11
❑ 16 Fred Stanley	.25	.11
❑ 17 Donnie Moore	.25	.11
❑ 18 Tony Solaita	.25	.11
❑ 19 Larry Gura DP	.10	.05
❑ 20 Joe Morgan DP	2.00	.90
❑ 21 Kevin Kobel	.25	.11
❑ 22 Mike Jorgensen	.25	.11
❑ 23 Terry Forster	.25	.11
❑ 24 Paul Molitor	12.00	5.50
❑ 25 Steve Carlton	3.00	1.35
❑ 26 Jamie Quirk	.25	.11
❑ 27 Dave Goltz	.25	.11
❑ 28 Steve Brye	.25	.11
❑ 29 Rick Langford	.25	.11
❑ 30 Dave Winfield	4.00	1.80
❑ 31 Tom House DP	.10	.05
❑ 32 Jerry Mumphrey	.25	.11
❑ 33 Dave Rozema	.25	.11
❑ 34 Rob Andrews	.25	.11
❑ 35 Ed Figueroa	.25	.11
❑ 36 Alan Ashby	.25	.11
❑ 37 Joe Kerrigan DP	.10	.05
❑ 38 Bernie Carbo	.25	.11
❑ 39 Dale Murphy	3.00	1.35
❑ 40 Dennis Eckersley	2.00	.90
❑ 41 Twins Team/Mgr. Gene Mauch (Checklist back)	1.00	.20
❑ 42 Ron Blomberg	.25	.11
❑ 43 Wayne Twitchell	.25	.11
❑ 44 Kurt Bevacqua	.25	.11
❑ 45 Al Hrabosky	.25	.11
❑ 46 Ron Hodges	.25	.11
❑ 47 Fred Norman	.25	.11
❑ 48 Merv Rettenmund	.25	.11
❑ 49 Vern Ruhle	.25	.11
❑ 50 Steve Garvey DP	1.00	.45
❑ 51 Ray Fosse DP	.10	.05
❑ 52 Randy Lerch	.25	.11
❑ 53 Mick Kelleher	.25	.11
❑ 54 Dell Alston DP	.10	.05
❑ 55 Willie Stargell	2.00	.90
❑ 56 John Hale	.25	.11
❑ 57 Eric Rasmussen	.25	.11
❑ 58 Bob Randall DP	.10	.05
❑ 59 John Denny DP	.25	.11
❑ 60 Mickey Rivers	.50	.23
❑ 61 Bo Diaz	.25	.11
❑ 62 Randy Moffitt	.25	.11
❑ 63 Jack Brohamer	.25	.11
❑ 64 Tom Underwood	.25	.11
❑ 65 Mark Belanger	.50	.23
❑ 66 Tigers Team/Mgr. Les Moss (Checklist back)	1.00	.20
❑ 67 Jim Mason DP	.10	.05
❑ 68 Joe Niekro DP	.25	.11
❑ 69 Elliott Maddox	.25	.11
❑ 70 John Candelaria	.50	.23
❑ 71 Brian Downing	.50	.23
❑ 72 Steve Mingori	.25	.11
❑ 73 Ken Henderson	.25	.11
❑ 74 Shane Rawley	.25	.11
❑ 75 Steve Yeager	.50	.23
❑ 76 Warren Cromartie	.50	.23
❑ 77 Dan Briggs DP	.10	.05
❑ 78 Elias Sosa	.25	.11
❑ 79 Ted Cox	.25	.11
❑ 80 Jason Thompson	.50	.23
❑ 81 Roger Erickson	.25	.11
❑ 82 Mets Team/Mgr. Joe Torre (Checklist back)	1.00	.20
❑ 83 Fred Kendall	.25	.11
❑ 84 Greg Minton	.25	.11
❑ 85 Gary Matthews	.50	.23
❑ 86 Rodney Scott	.25	.11
❑ 87 Pete Falcone	.25	.11
❑ 88 Bob Molinaro	.25	.11
❑ 89 Dick Tidrow	.25	.11
❑ 90 Bob Boone	1.00	.45
❑ 91 Terry Crowley	.25	.11
❑ 92 Jim Bibby	.25	.11
❑ 93 Phil Mankowski	.25	.11
❑ 94 Len Barker	.25	.11
❑ 95 Robin Yount	5.00	2.20
❑ 96 Indians Team/Mgr. Jeff Torborg (Checklist back)	1.00	.20
❑ 97 Sam Mejias	.25	.11
❑ 98 Ray Burris	.25	.11
❑ 99 John Wathan	.50	.23
❑ 100 Tom Seaver DP	4.00	1.80
❑ 101 Roy Howell	.25	.11
❑ 102 Mike Anderson	.25	.11
❑ 103 Jim Todd	.25	.11
❑ 104 Johnny Oates DP	.25	.11
❑ 105 Rick Camp DP	.10	.05
❑ 106 Frank Duffy	.25	.11
❑ 107 Jesus Alou DP	.10	.05
❑ 108 Eduardo Rodriguez	.25	.11
❑ 109 Joel Youngblood	.25	.11
❑ 110 Vida Blue	.50	.23
❑ 111 Roger Freed	.25	.11
❑ 112 Phillies Team/Mgr. Danny Ozark (Checklist back)	1.00	.20
❑ 113 Pete Redfern	.25	.11
❑ 114 Cliff Johnson	.25	.11
❑ 115 Nolan Ryan	20.00	9.00
❑ 116 Ozzie Smith RC	80.00	36.00
❑ 117 Grant Jackson	.25	.11
❑ 118 Bud Harrelson	.50	.23
❑ 119 Don Stanhouse	.25	.11
❑ 120 Jim Sundberg	.50	.23
❑ 121 Checklist 1-121 DP	.50	.10
❑ 122 Mike Paxton	.25	.11
❑ 123 Lou Whitaker	2.50	1.10
❑ 124 Dan Schatzeder	.25	.11
❑ 125 Rick Burleson	.25	.11
❑ 126 Doug Bair	.25	.11
❑ 127 Thad Bosley	.25	.11
❑ 128 Ted Martinez	.25	.11
❑ 129 Marty Pattin DP	.10	.05
❑ 130 Bob Watson DP	.25	.11
❑ 131 Jim Clancy	.25	.11
❑ 132 Rowland Office	.25	.11
❑ 133 Bill Castro	.25	.11
❑ 134 Alan Bannister	.25	.11
❑ 135 Bobby Murcer	.50	.23
❑ 136 Jim Kaat	.50	.23
❑ 137 Larry Wolfe DP	.10	.05
❑ 138 Mark Lee	.25	.11
❑ 139 Luis Pujols	.25	.11
❑ 140 Don Gullett	.50	.23
❑ 141 Tom Paciorek	.50	.23
❑ 142 Charlie Williams	.25	.11
❑ 143 Tony Scott	.25	.11
❑ 144 Sandy Alomar	.25	.11
❑ 145 Rick Rhoden	.25	.11
❑ 146 Duane Kuiper	.25	.11
❑ 147 Dave Hamilton	.25	.11
❑ 148 Bruce Boisclair	.25	.11
❑ 149 Manny Sarmiento	.25	.11
❑ 150 Wayne Cage	.25	.11
❑ 151 John Hiller	.25	.11
❑ 152 Rick Cerone	.25	.11
❑ 153 Dennis Lamp	.25	.11
❑ 154 Jim Gantner DP	.25	.11
❑ 155 Dwight Evans	1.00	.45
❑ 156 Buddy Solomon	.25	.11
❑ 157 U.L. Washington UER (Sic, bats left, should be right)	.25	.11
❑ 158 Joe Sambito	.25	.11
❑ 159 Roy White	.50	.23
❑ 160 Mike Flanagan	1.00	.45
❑ 161 Barry Foote	.25	.11
❑ 162 Tom Johnson	.25	.11
❑ 163 Glenn Burke	.25	.11
❑ 164 Mickey Lolich	.50	.23
❑ 165 Frank Taveras	.25	.11
❑ 166 Leon Roberts	.25	.11
❑ 167 Roger Metzger DP	.10	.05
❑ 168 Dave Freisleben	.25	.11
❑ 169 Bill Nahorodny	.25	.11
❑ 170 Don Sutton	2.00	.90
❑ 171 Gene Clines	.25	.11
❑ 172 Mike Bruhert	.25	.11
❑ 173 John Lowenstein	.25	.11
❑ 174 Rick Auerbach	.25	.11
❑ 175 George Hendrick	1.00	.45
❑ 176 Aurelio Rodriguez	.25	.11
❑ 177 Ron Reed	.25	.11
❑ 178 Alvis Woods	.25	.11
❑ 179 Jim Beattie DP	.25	.11
❑ 180 Larry Hisle	.25	.11
❑ 181 Mike Garman	.25	.11
❑ 182 Tim Johnson	.25	.11
❑ 183 Paul Splittorff	.25	.11
❑ 184 Darrel Chaney	.25	.11
❑ 185 Mike Torrez	.50	.23
❑ 186 Eric Soderholm	.25	.11
❑ 187 Mark Lemongello	.25	.11
❑ 188 Pat Kelly	.25	.11
❑ 189 Eddie Whitson RC	.25	.11

❑ 190 Ron Cey .50 .23
❑ 191 Mike Norris .25 .11
❑ 192 Cardinals Team/Mgr. 1.00 .20
Ken Boyer
(Checklist back)
❑ 193 Glenn Adams .25 .11
❑ 194 Randy Jones .25 .11
❑ 195 Bill Madlock .50 .23
❑ 196 Steve Kemp DP .25 .11
❑ 197 Bob Apodaca .25 .11
❑ 198 Johnny Grubb .25 .11
❑ 199 Larry Milbourne .25 .11
❑ 200 Johnny Bench DP 5.00 2.20
❑ 201 Mike Edwards RB .25 .11
Most unassisted DP's,
second base
❑ 202 Ron Guidry RB 1.00 .45
Most strikeouts, lefthander nine
innings
❑ 203 J.R. Richard RB .25 .11
Most strikeouts, season, righthander
❑ 204 Pete Rose RB 5.00 2.20
Most hits NL season
❑ 205 John Stearns RB .25 .11
Most SB's by
catcher, season
❑ 206 Sammy Stewart RB .25 .11
7 straight SO's,
first ML game
❑ 207 Dave Lemanczyk .25 .11
❑ 208 Clarence Gaston .25 .11
❑ 209 Reggie Cleveland .25 .11
❑ 210 Larry Bowa .50 .23
❑ 211 Denny Martinez 2.00 .90
❑ 212 Carney Lansford RC 1.00 .45
❑ 213 Bill Travers .25 .11
❑ 214 Red Sox Team/Mgr. 1.00 .20
Don Zimmer
(Checklist back)
❑ 215 Willie McCovey 2.50 1.10
❑ 216 Wilbur Wood .25 .11
❑ 217 Steve Dillard .25 .11
❑ 218 Dennis Leonard .50 .23
❑ 219 Roy Smalley .50 .23
❑ 220 Cesar Geronimo .25 .11
❑ 221 Jesse Jefferson .25 .11
❑ 222 Bob Beall .25 .11
❑ 223 Kent Tekulve .50 .23
❑ 224 Dave Revering .25 .11
❑ 225 Rich Gossage 1.00 .45
❑ 226 Ron Pruitt .25 .11
❑ 227 Steve Stone .50 .23
❑ 228 Vic Davalillo .25 .11
❑ 229 Doug Flynn .25 .11
❑ 230 Bob Forsch .25 .11
❑ 231 John Wockenfuss .25 .11
❑ 232 Jimmy Sexton .25 .11
❑ 233 Paul Mitchell .25 .11
❑ 234 Toby Harrah .50 .23
❑ 235 Steve Rogers .25 .11
❑ 236 Jim Dwyer .25 .11
❑ 237 Billy Smith .25 .11
❑ 238 Balor Moore .25 .11
❑ 239 Willie Horton .50 .23
❑ 240 Rick Reuschel .50 .23
❑ 241 Checklist 122-242 DP .50 .10
❑ 242 Pablo Torrealba .25 .11
❑ 243 Buck Martinez DP .10 .05
❑ 244 Pirates Team/Mgr. 1.00 .20
Chuck Tanner
(Checklist back)
❑ 245 Jeff Burroughs .50 .23
❑ 246 Darrell Jackson .25 .11
❑ 247 Tucker Ashford DP .10 .05
❑ 248 Pete LaCock .25 .11
❑ 249 Paul Thormodsgard .25 .11
❑ 250 Willie Randolph .50 .23
❑ 251 Jack Morris 2.00 .90
❑ 252 Bob Stinson .25 .11
❑ 253 Rick Wise .25 .11
❑ 254 Luis Gomez .25 .11
❑ 255 Tommy John 1.00 .45
❑ 256 Mike Sadek .25 .11
❑ 257 Adrian Devine .25 .11
❑ 258 Mike Phillips .25 .11
❑ 259 Reds Team/Mgr. 1.00 .20
Sparky Anderson
(Checklist back)
❑ 260 Richie Zisk .25 .11
❑ 261 Mario Guerrero .25 .11
❑ 262 Nelson Briles .25 .11
❑ 263 Oscar Gamble .50 .23
❑ 264 Don Robinson RC .25 .11
❑ 265 Don Money .25 .11
❑ 266 Jim Willoughby .25 .11
❑ 267 Joe Rudi .50 .23
❑ 268 Julio Gonzalez .25 .11
❑ 269 Woodie Fryman .25 .11
❑ 270 Butch Hobson .50 .23
❑ 271 Rawly Eastwick .25 .11
❑ 272 Tim Corcoran .25 .11
❑ 273 Jerry Terrell .25 .11
❑ 274 Willie Norwood .25 .11
❑ 275 Junior Moore .25 .11
❑ 276 Jim Colborn .25 .11
❑ 277 Tom Grieve .50 .23
❑ 278 Andy Messersmith .50 .23
❑ 279 Jerry Grote DP .10 .05
❑ 280 Andre Thornton .50 .23
❑ 281 Vic Correll DP .10 .05
❑ 282 Blue Jays Team/Mgr. .50 .10
Roy Hartsfield
(Checklist back)
❑ 283 Ken Kravec .25 .11
❑ 284 Johnnie LeMaster .25 .11
❑ 285 Bobby Bonds 1.00 .45
❑ 286 Duffy Dyer .25 .11
❑ 287 Andres Mora .25 .11
❑ 288 Milt Wilcox .25 .11
❑ 289 Jose Cruz 1.00 .45
❑ 290 Dave Lopes .50 .23
❑ 291 Tom Griffin .25 .11
❑ 292 Don Reynolds .25 .11
❑ 293 Jerry Garvin .25 .11
❑ 294 Pepe Frias .25 .11
❑ 295 Mitchell Page .25 .11
❑ 296 Preston Hanna .25 .11
❑ 297 Ted Sizemore .25 .11
❑ 298 Rich Gale .25 .11
❑ 299 Steve Ontiveros .25 .11
❑ 300 Rod Carew 3.00 1.35
❑ 301 Tom Hume .25 .11
❑ 302 Braves Team/Mgr. 1.00 .20
Bobby Cox
(Checklist back)
❑ 303 Lary Sorensen DP .10 .05
❑ 304 Steve Swisher .25 .11
❑ 305 Willie Montanez .25 .11
❑ 306 Floyd Bannister .25 .11
❑ 307 Larvell Blanks .25 .11
❑ 308 Bert Blyleven 1.00 .45
❑ 309 Ralph Garr .50 .23
❑ 310 Thurman Munson 3.00 1.35
❑ 311 Gary Lavelle .25 .11
❑ 312 Bob Robertson .25 .11
❑ 313 Dyar Miller .25 .11
❑ 314 Larry Harlow .25 .11
❑ 315 Jon Matlack .25 .11
❑ 316 Milt May .25 .11
❑ 317 Jose Cardenal .50 .23
❑ 318 Bob Welch RC 2.00 .90
❑ 319 Wayne Garrett .25 .11
❑ 320 Carl Yastrzemski 5.00 2.20
❑ 321 Gaylord Perry 2.00 .90
❑ 322 Danny Goodwin .25 .11
❑ 323 Lynn McGlothen .25 .11
❑ 324 Mike Tyson .25 .11
❑ 325 Cecil Cooper .50 .23
❑ 326 Pedro Borbon .25 .11
❑ 327 Art Howe DP .25 .11
❑ 328 A's Team/Mgr. 1.00 .20
Jack McKeon
Checklist back
❑ 329 Joe Coleman .25 .11
❑ 330 George Brett 10.00 4.50
❑ 331 Mickey Mahler .25 .11
❑ 332 Gary Alexander .25 .11
❑ 333 Chet Lemon .50 .23
❑ 334 Craig Swan .25 .11
❑ 335 Chris Chambliss .50 .23
❑ 336 Bobby Thompson .25 .11
❑ 337 John Montague .25 .11
❑ 338 Vic Harris .25 .11
❑ 339 Ron Jackson .25 .11
❑ 340 Jim Palmer 2.50 1.10
❑ 341 Willie Upshaw .50 .23
❑ 342 Dave Roberts .25 .11
❑ 343 Ed Glynn .25 .11
❑ 344 Jerry Royster .25 .11
❑ 345 Tug McGraw .50 .23
❑ 346 Bill Buckner .50 .23
❑ 347 Doug Rau .25 .11
❑ 348 Andre Dawson 3.00 1.35
❑ 349 Jim Wright .25 .11
❑ 350 Garry Templeton .50 .23
❑ 351 Wayne Nordhagen DP .10 .05
❑ 352 Steve Renko .25 .11
❑ 353 Checklist 243-363 1.00 .20
❑ 354 Bill Bonham .25 .11
❑ 355 Lee Mazzilli .25 .11
❑ 356 Giants Team/Mgr. 1.00 .20
Joe Altobelli
(Checklist back)
❑ 357 Jerry Augustine .25 .11
❑ 358 Alan Trammell 3.00 1.35
❑ 359 Dan Spillner DP .10 .05
❑ 360 Amos Otis .50 .23
❑ 361 Tom Dixon .25 .11
❑ 362 Mike Cubbage .25 .11
❑ 363 Craig Skok .25 .11
❑ 364 Gene Richards .25 .11
❑ 365 Sparky Lyle .50 .23
❑ 366 Juan Bernhardt .25 .11
❑ 367 Dave Skaggs .25 .11
❑ 368 Don Aase .25 .11
❑ 369A Bump Wills ERR 3.00 1.35
(Blue Jays)
❑ 369B Bump Wills COR 3.00 1.35
(Rangers)
❑ 370 Dave Kingman 1.00 .45
❑ 371 Jeff Holly .25 .11
❑ 372 Lamar Johnson .25 .11
❑ 373 Lance Rautzhan .25 .11
❑ 374 Ed Herrmann .25 .11
❑ 375 Bill Campbell .25 .11
❑ 376 Gorman Thomas .50 .23
❑ 377 Paul Moskau .25 .11
❑ 378 Rob Picciolo DP .10 .05
❑ 379 Dale Murray .25 .11
❑ 380 John Mayberry .50 .23
❑ 381 Astros Team/Mgr. 1.00 .20
Bill Virdon
(Checklist back)
❑ 382 Jerry Martin .25 .11
❑ 383 Phil Garner .50 .23
❑ 384 Tommy Boggs .25 .11
❑ 385 Dan Ford .25 .11
❑ 386 Francisco Barrios .25 .11
❑ 387 Gary Thomasson .25 .11
❑ 388 Jack Billingham .25 .11
❑ 389 Joe Zdeb .25 .11
❑ 390 Rollie Fingers 2.00 .90
❑ 391 Al Oliver .50 .23
❑ 392 Doug Ault .25 .11
❑ 393 Scott McGregor .50 .23
❑ 394 Randy Stein .25 .11
❑ 395 Dave Cash .25 .11
❑ 396 Bill Plummer .25 .11
❑ 397 Sergio Ferrer .25 .11
❑ 398 Ivan DeJesus .25 .11
❑ 399 David Clyde .25 .11
❑ 400 Jim Rice 1.00 .45
❑ 401 Ray Knight .50 .23
❑ 402 Paul Hartzell .25 .11
❑ 403 Tim Foli .25 .11
❑ 404 White Sox Team/Mgr 1.00 .20
Don Kessinger
(Checklist back)
❑ 405 Butch Wynegar DP .10 .05
❑ 406 Joe Wallis DP .10 .05
❑ 407 Pete Vuckovich .50 .23
❑ 408 Charlie Moore DP .10 .05
❑ 409 Willie Wilson RC 1.00 .45
❑ 410 Darrell Evans 1.00 .45
❑ 411 George Sisler ATL 2.50 1.10
Ty Cobb
❑ 412 Hack Wilson ATL 2.50 1.10
Hank Aaron

❑ 413 Roger Maris ATL 4.00 1.80
Hank Aaron
❑ 414 Rogers Hornsby ATL 2.50 1.10
Ty Cobb
❑ 415 Lou Brock ATL 1.00 .45
❑ 416 Jack Chesbro ATL .50 .23
Cy Young
❑ 417 Nolan Ryan ATL DP 5.00 2.20
Walter Johnson
❑ 418 D.Leonard ATL DP .25 .11
Walter Johnson
❑ 419 Dick Ruthven .25 .11
❑ 420 Ken Griffey Sr. .50 .23
❑ 421 Doug DeCinces .50 .23
❑ 422 Ruppert Jones .25 .11
❑ 423 Bob Montgomery .25 .11
❑ 424 Angels Team/Mgr. 1.00 .20
Jim Fregosi
(Checklist back)
❑ 425 Rick Manning .25 .11
❑ 426 Chris Speier .25 .11
❑ 427 Andy Replogle .25 .11
❑ 428 Bobby Valentine .50 .23
❑ 429 John Urrea DP .10 .05
❑ 430 Dave Parker .50 .23
❑ 431 Glenn Borgmann .25 .11
❑ 432 Dave Heaverlo .25 .11
❑ 433 Larry Biittner .25 .11
❑ 434 Ken Clay .25 .11
❑ 435 Gene Tenace .50 .23
❑ 436 Hector Cruz .25 .11
❑ 437 Rick Williams .25 .11
❑ 438 Horace Speed .25 .11
❑ 439 Frank White .50 .23
❑ 440 Rusty Staub 1.00 .45
❑ 441 Lee Lacy .25 .11
❑ 442 Doyle Alexander .25 .11
❑ 443 Bruce Bochte .25 .11
❑ 444 Aurelio Lopez .25 .11
❑ 445 Steve Henderson .25 .11
❑ 446 Jim Lonborg .50 .23
❑ 447 Manny Sanguillen .50 .23
❑ 448 Moose Haas .25 .11
❑ 449 Bombo Rivera .25 .11
❑ 450 Dave Concepcion 1.00 .45
❑ 451 Royals Team/Mgr. 1.00 .20
Whitey Herzog
(Checklist back)
❑ 452 Jerry Morales .25 .11
❑ 453 Chris Knapp .25 .11
❑ 454 Len Randle .25 .11
❑ 455 Bill Lee DP .10 .05
❑ 456 Chuck Baker .25 .11
❑ 457 Bruce Sutter .50 .23
❑ 458 Jim Essian .25 .11
❑ 459 Sid Monge .25 .11
❑ 460 Graig Nettles 1.00 .45
❑ 461 Jim Barr DP .10 .05
❑ 462 Otto Velez .25 .11
❑ 463 Steve Comer .25 .11
❑ 464 Joe Nolan .25 .11
❑ 465 Reggie Smith .50 .23
❑ 466 Mark Littell .25 .11
❑ 467 Don Kessinger DP .25 .11
❑ 468 Stan Bahnsen DP .10 .05
❑ 469 Lance Parrish 1.00 .45
❑ 470 Garry Maddox DP .25 .11
❑ 471 Joaquin Andujar .50 .23
❑ 472 Craig Kusick .25 .11
❑ 473 Dave Roberts .25 .11
❑ 474 Dick Davis .25 .11
❑ 475 Dan Driessen .25 .11
❑ 476 Tom Poquette .25 .11
❑ 477 Bob Grich .50 .23
❑ 478 Juan Beniquez .25 .11
❑ 479 Padres Team/Mgr. 1.00 .20
Roger Craig
(Checklist back)
❑ 480 Fred Lynn .50 .23
❑ 481 Skip Lockwood .25 .11
❑ 482 Craig Reynolds .25 .11
❑ 483 Checklist 364-484 DP .50 .10
❑ 484 Rick Waits .25 .11
❑ 485 Bucky Dent .50 .23
❑ 486 Bob Knepper .25 .11
❑ 487 Miguel Dilone .25 .11
❑ 488 Bob Owchinko .25 .11
❑ 489 Larry Cox UER .25 .11
(Photo actually
Dave Rader)
❑ 490 Al Cowens .25 .11
❑ 491 Tippy Martinez .25 .11
❑ 492 Bob Bailor .25 .11
❑ 493 Larry Christenson .25 .11
❑ 494 Jerry White .25 .11
❑ 495 Tony Perez 2.00 .90
❑ 496 Barry Bonnell DP .10 .05
❑ 497 Glenn Abbott .25 .11
❑ 498 Rich Chiles .25 .11
❑ 499 Rangers Team/Mgr. 1.00 .20
Pat Corrales
(Checklist back)
❑ 500 Ron Guidry .50 .23
❑ 501 Junior Kennedy .25 .11
❑ 502 Steve Braun .25 .11
❑ 503 Terry Humphrey .25 .11
❑ 504 Larry McWilliams .25 .11
❑ 505 Ed Kranepool .25 .11
❑ 506 John D'Acquisto .25 .11
❑ 507 Tony Armas .50 .23
❑ 508 Charlie Hough .50 .23
❑ 509 Mario Mendoza UER .25 .11
(Career BA .278,
should say .204)
❑ 510 Ted Simmons 1.00 .45
❑ 511 Paul Reuschel DP .10 .05
❑ 512 Jack Clark .50 .23
❑ 513 Dave Johnson .50 .23
❑ 514 Mike Proly .25 .11
❑ 515 Enos Cabell .25 .11
❑ 516 Champ Summers DP .10 .05
❑ 517 Al Bumbry .50 .23
❑ 518 Jim Umbarger .25 .11
❑ 519 Ben Oglivie .50 .23
❑ 520 Gary Carter 2.00 .90
❑ 521 Sam Ewing .25 .11
❑ 522 Ken Holtzman .50 .23
❑ 523 John Milner .25 .11
❑ 524 Tom Burgmeier .25 .11
❑ 525 Freddie Patek .25 .11
❑ 526 Dodgers Team/Mgr. 1.00 .20
Tom Lasorda
(Checklist back)
❑ 527 Lerrin LaGrow .25 .11
❑ 528 Wayne Gross DP .10 .05
❑ 529 Brian Asselstine .25 .11
❑ 530 Frank Tanana .50 .23
❑ 531 Fernando Gonzalez .25 .11
❑ 532 Buddy Schultz .25 .11
❑ 533 Leroy Stanton .25 .11
❑ 534 Ken Forsch .25 .11
❑ 535 Ellis Valentine .25 .11
❑ 536 Jerry Reuss .50 .23
❑ 537 Tom Veryzer .25 .11
❑ 538 Mike Ivie DP .10 .05
❑ 539 John Ellis .25 .11
❑ 540 Greg Luzinski .50 .23
❑ 541 Jim Slaton .25 .11
❑ 542 Rick Bosetti .25 .11
❑ 543 Kiko Garcia .25 .11
❑ 544 Fergie Jenkins 2.00 .90
❑ 545 John Stearns .25 .11
❑ 546 Bill Russell .50 .23
❑ 547 Clint Hurdle .25 .11
❑ 548 Enrique Romo .25 .11
❑ 549 Bob Bailey .25 .11
❑ 550 Sal Bando .50 .23
❑ 551 Cubs Team/Mgr. 1.00 .20
Herman Franks
(Checklist back)
❑ 552 Jose Morales .25 .11
❑ 553 Denny Walling .25 .11
❑ 554 Matt Keough .25 .11
❑ 555 Biff Pocoroba .25 .11
❑ 556 Mike Lum .25 .11
❑ 557 Ken Brett .25 .11
❑ 558 Jay Johnstone .50 .23
❑ 559 Greg Pryor .25 .11
❑ 560 John Montefusco .25 .11
❑ 561 Ed Ott .25 .11
❑ 562 Dusty Baker 1.00 .45
❑ 563 Roy Thomas .25 .11
❑ 564 Jerry Turner .25 .11
❑ 565 Rico Carty .50 .23
❑ 566 Nino Espinosa .25 .11
❑ 567 Richie Hebner .50 .23
❑ 568 Carlos Lopez .25 .11
❑ 569 Bob Sykes .25 .11
❑ 570 Cesar Cedeno .50 .23
❑ 571 Darrell Porter .50 .23
❑ 572 Rod Gilbreath .25 .11
❑ 573 Jim Kern .25 .11
❑ 574 Claudell Washington .50 .23
❑ 575 Luis Tiant .50 .23
❑ 576 Mike Parrott .25 .11
❑ 577 Brewers Team/Mgr. 1.00 .20
George Bamberger
(Checklist back)
❑ 578 Pete Broberg .25 .11
❑ 579 Greg Gross .25 .11
❑ 580 Ron Fairly .50 .23
❑ 581 Darold Knowles .25 .11
❑ 582 Paul Blair .50 .23
❑ 583 Julio Cruz .25 .11
❑ 584 Jim Rooker .25 .11
❑ 585 Hal McRae 1.00 .45
❑ 586 Bob Horner RC 1.00 .45
❑ 587 Ken Reitz .25 .11
❑ 588 Tom Murphy .25 .11
❑ 589 Terry Whitfield .25 .11
❑ 590 J.R. Richard .50 .23
❑ 591 Mike Hargrove .50 .23
❑ 592 Mike Krukow .25 .11
❑ 593 Rick Dempsey .50 .23
❑ 594 Bob Shirley .25 .11
❑ 595 Phil Niekro 2.00 .90
❑ 596 Jim Wohlford .25 .11
❑ 597 Bob Stanley .25 .11
❑ 598 Mark Wagner .25 .11
❑ 599 Jim Spencer .25 .11
❑ 600 George Foster .50 .23
❑ 601 Dave LaRoche .25 .11
❑ 602 Checklist 485-605 1.00 .20
❑ 603 Rudy May .25 .11
❑ 604 Jeff Newman .25 .11
❑ 605 Rick Monday DP .25 .11
❑ 606 Expos Team/Mgr. 1.00 .20
Dick Williams
(Checklist back)
❑ 607 Omar Moreno .25 .11
❑ 608 Dave McKay .25 .11
❑ 609 Silvio Martinez .25 .11
❑ 610 Mike Schmidt 8.00 3.60
❑ 611 Jim Norris .25 .11
❑ 612 Rick Honeycutt RC .50 .23
❑ 613 Mike Edwards .25 .11
❑ 614 Willie Hernandez .50 .23
❑ 615 Ken Singleton .50 .23
❑ 616 Billy Almon .25 .11
❑ 617 Terry Puhl .25 .11
❑ 618 Jerry Remy .25 .11
❑ 619 Ken Landreaux .50 .23
❑ 620 Bert Campaneris .50 .23
❑ 621 Pat Zachry .25 .11
❑ 622 Dave Collins .50 .23
❑ 623 Bob McClure .25 .11
❑ 624 Larry Herndon .25 .11
❑ 625 Mark Fidrych 2.00 .90
❑ 626 Yankees Team/Mgr. 1.00 .20
Bob Lemon
(Checklist back)
❑ 627 Gary Serum .25 .11
❑ 628 Del Unser .25 .11
❑ 629 Gene Garber .50 .23
❑ 630 Bake McBride .50 .23
❑ 631 Jorge Orta .25 .11
❑ 632 Don Kirkwood .25 .11
❑ 633 Rob Wilfong DP .10 .05
❑ 634 Paul Lindblad .25 .11
❑ 635 Don Baylor 1.00 .45
❑ 636 Wayne Garland .25 .11
❑ 637 Bill Robinson .50 .23
❑ 638 Al Fitzmorris .25 .11
❑ 639 Manny Trillo .25 .11
❑ 640 Eddie Murray 12.00 5.50
❑ 641 Bobby Castillo .25 .11
❑ 642 Wilbur Howard DP .10 .05
❑ 643 Tom Hausman .25 .11

❑ 644 Manny Mota .50 .23
❑ 645 George Scott DP .25 .11
❑ 646 Rick Sweet .25 .11
❑ 647 Bob Lacey .25 .11
❑ 648 Lou Piniella .50 .23
❑ 649 John Curtis .25 .11
❑ 650 Pete Rose 12.00 5.50
❑ 651 Mike Caldwell .25 .11
❑ 652 Stan Papi .25 .11
❑ 653 Warren Brusstar DP .10 .05
❑ 654 Rick Miller .25 .11
❑ 655 Jerry Koosman .50 .23
❑ 656 Hosken Powell .25 .11
❑ 657 George Medich .25 .11
❑ 658 Taylor Duncan .25 .11
❑ 659 Mariners Team/Mgr. 1.00 .20
Darrell Johnson
(Checklist back)
❑ 660 Ron LeFlore DP .25 .11
❑ 661 Bruce Kison .25 .11
❑ 662 Kevin Bell .25 .11
❑ 663 Mike Vail .25 .11
❑ 664 Doug Bird .25 .11
❑ 665 Lou Brock 2.50 1.10
❑ 666 Rich Dauer .25 .11
❑ 667 Don Hood .25 .11
❑ 668 Bill North .25 .11
❑ 669 Checklist 606-726 1.00 .20
❑ 670 Jim Hunter DP 1.00 .45
❑ 671 Joe Ferguson DP .10 .05
❑ 672 Ed Halicki .25 .11
❑ 673 Tom Hutton .25 .11
❑ 674 Dave Tomlin .25 .11
❑ 675 Tim McCarver 1.00 .45
❑ 676 Johnny Sutton .25 .11
❑ 677 Larry Parrish .50 .23
❑ 678 Geoff Zahn .25 .11
❑ 679 Derrel Thomas .25 .11
❑ 680 Carlton Fisk 3.00 1.35
❑ 681 John Henry Johnson .25 .11
❑ 682 Dave Chalk .25 .11
❑ 683 Dan Meyer DP .10 .05
❑ 684 Jamie Easterly DP .10 .05
❑ 685 Sixto Lezcano .25 .11
❑ 686 Ron Schueler DP .10 .05
❑ 687 Rennie Stennett .25 .11
❑ 688 Mike Willis .25 .11
❑ 689 Orioles Team/Mgr. 1.00 .20
Earl Weaver
(Checklist back)
❑ 690 Buddy Bell DP .25 .11
❑ 691 Dock Ellis DP .10 .05
❑ 692 Mickey Stanley .25 .11
❑ 693 Dave Rader .25 .11
❑ 694 Burt Hooton .50 .23
❑ 695 Keith Hernandez 1.00 .45
❑ 696 Andy Hassler .25 .11
❑ 697 Dave Bergman .25 .11
❑ 698 Bill Stein .25 .11
❑ 699 Hal Dues .25 .11
❑ 700 Reggie Jackson DP 5.00 2.20
❑ 701 Orioles Prospects .50 .23
Mark Corey
John Flinn
Sammy Stewart
❑ 702 Red Sox Prospects .50 .23
Joel Finch
Garry Hancock
Allen Ripley
❑ 703 Angels Prospects .50 .23
Jim Anderson
Dave Frost
Bob Slater
❑ 704 White Sox Prospects .50 .23
Ross Baumgarten
Mike Colbern
Mike Squires
❑ 705 Indians Prospects 1.00 .45
Alfredo Griffin
Tim Norrid
Dave Oliver
❑ 706 Tigers Prospects .50 .23
Dave Stegman
Dave Tobik
Kip Young
❑ 707 Royals Prospects 1.00 .45
Randy Bass
Jim Gaudet
Randy McGilberry
❑ 708 Brewers Prospects 1.00 .45
Kevin Bass
Eddie Romero
Ned Yost
❑ 709 Twins Prospects .50 .23
Sam Perlozzo
Rick Sofield
Kevin Stanfield
❑ 710 Yankees Prospects .50 .23
Brian Doyle
Mike Heath
Dave Rajsich
❑ 711 A's Prospects 1.00 .45
Dwayne Murphy
Bruce Robinson
Alan Wirth
❑ 712 Mariners Prospects .50 .23
Bud Anderson
Greg Biercevicz
Byron McLaughlin
❑ 713 Rangers Prospects 1.00 .45
Danny Darwin
Pat Putnam
Billy Sample
❑ 714 Blue Jays Prospects .50 .23
Victor Cruz
Pat Kelly
Ernie Whitt
❑ 715 Braves Prospects 1.00 .45
Bruce Benedict
Glenn Hubbard
Larry Whisenton
❑ 716 Cubs Prospects .50 .23
Dave Geisel
Karl Pagel
Scot Thompson
❑ 717 Reds Prospects .50 .23
Mike LaCoss
Ron Oester
Harry Spilman
❑ 718 Astros Prospects .50 .23
Bruce Bochy
Mike Fischlin
Don Pisker
❑ 719 Dodgers Prospects 1.00 .45
Pedro Guerrero
Rudy Law
Joe Simpson
❑ 720 Expos Prospects 1.00 .45
Jerry Fry
Jerry Pirtle
Scott Sanderson
❑ 721 Mets Prospects .50 .23
Juan Berenguer
Dwight Bernard
Dan Norman
❑ 722 Phillies Prospects 1.00 .45
Jim Morrison
Lonnie Smith
Jim Wright
❑ 723 Pirates Prospects .50 .23
Dale Berra
Eugenio Cotes
Ben Wiltbank
❑ 724 Cardinals Prospects 1.00 .45
Tom Bruno
George Frazier
Terry Kennedy
❑ 725 Padres Prospects .50 .23
Jim Beswick
Steve Mura
Broderick Perkins
❑ 726 Giants Prospects .50 .10
Greg Johnston
Joe Strain
John Tamargo

1980 Topps

	NRMT	VG-E
COMPLETE SET (726)	120.00	55.00
COMMON CARD (1-726)	.25	.11
COMMON CARD DP	.10	.05

❑ 1 Lou Brock HL 2.50 .50
Carl Yastrzemski
Enter 3000 hit circle
❑ 2 Willie McCovey HL .75 .35
512th homer sets new
mark for NL lefties
❑ 3 Manny Mota HL .25 .11
All-time pinch-hits, 145
❑ 4 Pete Rose HL 3.00 1.35
Career Record 10th season
with 200 or more hits
❑ 5 Garry Templeton HL .40 .18
First with 100 hits
from each side of plate
❑ 6 Del Unser HL .40 .18
3 consecutive
pinch homers
❑ 7 Mike Lum .25 .11
❑ 8 Craig Swan .25 .11
❑ 9 Steve Braun .25 .11
❑ 10 Dennis Martinez 1.25 .55
❑ 11 Jimmy Sexton .25 .11
❑ 12 John Curtis DP .10 .05
❑ 13 Ron Pruitt .25 .11
❑ 14 Dave Cash .25 .11
❑ 15 Bill Campbell .25 .11
❑ 16 Jerry Narron .25 .11
❑ 17 Bruce Sutter .75 .35
❑ 18 Ron Jackson .25 .11
❑ 19 Balor Moore .25 .11
❑ 20 Dan Ford .25 .11
❑ 21 Manny Sarmiento .25 .11
❑ 22 Pat Putnam .25 .11
❑ 23 Derrel Thomas .25 .11
❑ 24 Jim Slaton .25 .11
❑ 25 Lee Mazzilli .40 .18
❑ 26 Marty Pattin .25 .11
❑ 27 Del Unser .25 .11
❑ 28 Bruce Kison .25 .11
❑ 29 Mark Wagner .25 .11
❑ 30 Vida Blue .75 .35
❑ 31 Jay Johnstone .40 .18
❑ 32 Julio Cruz DP .10 .05
❑ 33 Tony Scott .25 .11
❑ 34 Jeff Newman DP .10 .05
❑ 35 Luis Tiant .40 .18
❑ 36 Rusty Torres .25 .11
❑ 37 Kiko Garcia .25 .11
❑ 38 Dan Spillner DP .10 .05
❑ 39 Rowland Office .25 .11
❑ 40 Carlton Fisk 2.00 .90
❑ 41 Rangers Team/Mgr. .75 .15
Pat Corrales
(Checklist back)
❑ 42 David Palmer .25 .11
❑ 43 Bombo Rivera .25 .11
❑ 44 Bill Fahey .25 .11
❑ 45 Frank White .75 .35
❑ 46 Rico Carty .40 .18
❑ 47 Bill Bonham DP .10 .05
❑ 48 Rick Miller .25 .11
❑ 49 Mario Guerrero .25 .11
❑ 50 J.R. Richard .40 .18
❑ 51 Joe Ferguson DP .10 .05
❑ 52 Warren Brusstar .25 .11
❑ 53 Ben Oglivie .40 .18
❑ 54 Dennis Lamp .25 .11

❑ 55 Bill Madlock .40 .18
❑ 56 Bobby Valentine .40 .18
❑ 57 Pete Vuckovich .25 .11
❑ 58 Doug Flynn .25 .11
❑ 59 Eddy Putman .25 .11
❑ 60 Bucky Dent .40 .18
❑ 61 Gary Serum .25 .11
❑ 62 Mike Ivie .25 .11
❑ 63 Bob Stanley .25 .11
❑ 64 Joe Nolan .25 .11
❑ 65 Al Bumbry .40 .18
❑ 66 Royals Team/Mgr. .75 .15
Jim Frey
(Checklist back)
❑ 67 Doyle Alexander .25 .11
❑ 68 Larry Harlow .25 .11
❑ 69 Rick Williams .25 .11
❑ 70 Gary Carter 1.25 .55
❑ 71 John Milner DP .10 .05
❑ 72 Fred Howard DP .10 .05
❑ 73 Dave Collins .25 .11
❑ 74 Sid Monge .25 .11
❑ 75 Bill Russell .40 .18
❑ 76 John Stearns .25 .11
❑ 77 Dave Stieb RC 1.25 .55
❑ 78 Ruppert Jones .25 .11
❑ 79 Bob Owchinko .25 .11
❑ 80 Ron LeFlore .40 .18
❑ 81 Ted Sizemore .25 .11
❑ 82 Astros Team/Mgr. .75 .15
Bill Virdon
(Checklist back)
❑ 83 Steve Trout .25 .11
❑ 84 Gary Lavelle .25 .11
❑ 85 Ted Simmons .40 .18
❑ 86 Dave Hamilton .25 .11
❑ 87 Pepe Frias .25 .11
❑ 88 Ken Landreaux .25 .11
❑ 89 Don Hood .25 .11
❑ 90 Manny Trillo .40 .18
❑ 91 Rick Dempsey .40 .18
❑ 92 Rick Rhoden .25 .11
❑ 93 Dave Roberts DP .10 .05
❑ 94 Neil Allen .40 .18
❑ 95 Cecil Cooper .40 .18
❑ 96 A's Team/Mgr. .75 .15
Jim Marshall
(Checklist back)
❑ 97 Bill Lee .40 .18
❑ 98 Jerry Terrell .25 .11
❑ 99 Victor Cruz .25 .11
❑ 100 Johnny Bench 4.00 1.80
❑ 101 Aurelio Lopez .25 .11
❑ 102 Rich Dauer .25 .11
❑ 103 Bill Caudill .25 .11
❑ 104 Manny Mota .40 .18
❑ 105 Frank Tanana .40 .18
❑ 106 Jeff Leonard RC .75 .35
❑ 107 Francisco Barrios .25 .11
❑ 108 Bob Horner .40 .18
❑ 109 Bill Travers .25 .11
❑ 110 Fred Lynn DP .40 .18
❑ 111 Bob Knepper .25 .11
❑ 112 White Sox Team/Mgr. .75 .15
Tony LaRussa
(Checklist back)
❑ 113 Geoff Zahn .25 .11
❑ 114 Juan Beniquez .25 .11
❑ 115 Sparky Lyle .40 .18
❑ 116 Larry Cox .25 .11
❑ 117 Dock Ellis .25 .11
❑ 118 Phil Garner .40 .18
❑ 119 Sammy Stewart .25 .11
❑ 120 Greg Luzinski .40 .18
❑ 121 Checklist 1-121 .75 .15
❑ 122 Dave Rosello DP .10 .05
❑ 123 Lynn Jones .25 .11
❑ 124 Dave Lemanczyk .25 .11
❑ 125 Tony Perez 1.25 .55
❑ 126 Dave Tomlin .25 .11
❑ 127 Gary Thomasson .25 .11
❑ 128 Tom Burgmeier .25 .11
❑ 129 Craig Reynolds .25 .11
❑ 130 Amos Otis .40 .18
❑ 131 Paul Mitchell .25 .11
❑ 132 Biff Pocoroba .25 .11
❑ 133 Jerry Turner .25 .11
❑ 134 Matt Keough .25 .11
❑ 135 Bill Buckner .40 .18
❑ 136 Dick Ruthven .25 .11
❑ 137 John Castino .25 .11
❑ 138 Ross Baumgarten .25 .11
❑ 139 Dane Iorg .25 .11
❑ 140 Rich Gossage .75 .35
❑ 141 Gary Alexander .25 .11
❑ 142 Phil Huffman .25 .11
❑ 143 Bruce Bochte DP .10 .05
❑ 144 Steve Comer .25 .11
❑ 145 Darrell Evans .40 .18
❑ 146 Bob Welch .40 .18
❑ 147 Terry Puhl .25 .11
❑ 148 Manny Sanguillen .40 .18
❑ 149 Tom Hume .25 .11
❑ 150 Jason Thompson .25 .11
❑ 151 Tom Hausman DP .10 .05
❑ 152 John Fulgham .25 .11
❑ 153 Tim Blackwell .25 .11
❑ 154 Lary Sorensen .25 .11
❑ 155 Jerry Remy .25 .11
❑ 156 Tony Brizzolara .25 .11
❑ 157 Willie Wilson DP .40 .18
❑ 158 Rob Picciolo DP .10 .05
❑ 159 Ken Clay .25 .11
❑ 160 Eddie Murray 5.00 2.20
❑ 161 Larry Christenson .25 .11
❑ 162 Bob Randall .25 .11
❑ 163 Steve Swisher .25 .11
❑ 164 Greg Pryor .25 .11
❑ 165 Omar Moreno .25 .11
❑ 166 Glenn Abbott .25 .11
❑ 167 Jack Clark .40 .18
❑ 168 Rick Waits .25 .11
❑ 169 Luis Gomez .25 .11
❑ 170 Burt Hooton .25 .11
❑ 171 Fernando Gonzalez .25 .11
❑ 172 Ron Hodges .25 .11
❑ 173 John Henry Johnson .25 .11
❑ 174 Ray Knight .40 .18
❑ 175 Rick Reuschel .40 .18
❑ 176 Champ Summers .25 .11
❑ 177 Dave Heaverlo .25 .11
❑ 178 Tim McCarver .75 .35
❑ 179 Ron Davis .25 .11
❑ 180 Warren Cromartie .25 .11
❑ 181 Moose Haas .25 .11
❑ 182 Ken Reitz .25 .11
❑ 183 Jim Anderson DP .10 .05
❑ 184 Steve Renko DP .10 .05
❑ 185 Hal McRae .40 .18
❑ 186 Junior Moore .25 .11
❑ 187 Alan Ashby .25 .11
❑ 188 Terry Crowley .25 .11
❑ 189 Kevin Kobel .25 .11
❑ 190 Buddy Bell .40 .18
❑ 191 Ted Martinez .25 .11
❑ 192 Braves Team/Mgr. .75 .15
Bobby Cox
(Checklist back)
❑ 193 Dave Goltz .25 .11
❑ 194 Mike Easler .25 .11
❑ 195 John Montefusco .25 .11
❑ 196 Lance Parrish .40 .18
❑ 197 Byron McLaughlin .25 .11
❑ 198 Dell Alston DP .10 .05
❑ 199 Mike LaCoss .25 .11
❑ 200 Jim Rice .40 .18
❑ 201 Batting Leaders .75 .35
Keith Hernandez
Fred Lynn
❑ 202 Home Run Leaders .75 .35
Dave Kingman
Gorman Thomas
❑ 203 RBI Leaders 1.25 .55
Dave Winfield
Don Baylor
❑ 204 Stolen Base Leaders .40 .18
Omar Moreno
Willie Wilson
❑ 205 Victory Leaders .75 .35
Joe Niekro
Phil Niekro
Mike Flanagan
❑ 206 Strikeout Leaders 5.00 2.20
J.R. Richard
Nolan Ryan
❑ 207 ERA Leaders .75 .35
J.R. Richard
Ron Guidry
❑ 208 Wayne Cage .25 .11
❑ 209 Von Joshua .25 .11
❑ 210 Steve Carlton 2.00 .90
❑ 211 Dave Skaggs DP .10 .05
❑ 212 Dave Roberts .25 .11
❑ 213 Mike Jorgensen DP .10 .05
❑ 214 Angels Team/Mgr. .75 .15
Jim Fregosi
(Checklist back)
❑ 215 Sixto Lezcano .25 .11
❑ 216 Phil Mankowski .25 .11
❑ 217 Ed Halicki .25 .11
❑ 218 Jose Morales .25 .11
❑ 219 Steve Mingori .25 .11
❑ 220 Dave Concepcion .75 .35
❑ 221 Joe Cannon .25 .11
❑ 222 Ron Hassey .25 .11
❑ 223 Bob Sykes .25 .11
❑ 224 Willie Montanez .25 .11
❑ 225 Lou Piniella .75 .35
❑ 226 Bill Stein .25 .11
❑ 227 Len Barker .25 .11
❑ 228 Johnny Oates .40 .18
❑ 229 Jim Bibby .25 .11
❑ 230 Dave Winfield 2.50 1.10
❑ 231 Steve McCatty .25 .11
❑ 232 Alan Trammell 1.25 .55
❑ 233 LaRue Washington .25 .11
❑ 234 Vern Ruhle .25 .11
❑ 235 Andre Dawson 1.50 .70
❑ 236 Marc Hill .25 .11
❑ 237 Scott McGregor .25 .11
❑ 238 Rob Wilfong .25 .11
❑ 239 Don Aase .25 .11
❑ 240 Dave Kingman .75 .35
❑ 241 Checklist 122-242 .75 .15
❑ 242 Lamar Johnson .25 .11
❑ 243 Jerry Augustine .25 .11
❑ 244 Cardinals Team/Mgr. .75 .15
Ken Boyer
(Checklist back)
❑ 245 Phil Niekro 1.25 .55
❑ 246 Tim Foli DP .10 .05
❑ 247 Frank Riccelli .25 .11
❑ 248 Jamie Quirk .25 .11
❑ 249 Jim Clancy .25 .11
❑ 250 Jim Kaat .75 .35
❑ 251 Kip Young .25 .11
❑ 252 Ted Cox .25 .11
❑ 253 John Montague .25 .11
❑ 254 Paul Dade DP .10 .05
❑ 255 Dusty Baker DP .40 .18
❑ 256 Roger Erickson .25 .11
❑ 257 Larry Herndon .25 .11
❑ 258 Paul Moskau .25 .11
❑ 259 Mets Team/Mgr. .75 .15
Joe Torre
(Checklist back)
❑ 260 Al Oliver .75 .35
❑ 261 Dave Chalk .25 .11
❑ 262 Benny Ayala .25 .11
❑ 263 Dave LaRoche DP .10 .05
❑ 264 Bill Robinson .25 .11
❑ 265 Robin Yount 3.00 1.35
❑ 266 Bernie Carbo .25 .11
❑ 267 Dan Schatzeder .25 .11
❑ 268 Rafael Landestoy .25 .11
❑ 269 Dave Tobik .25 .11
❑ 270 Mike Schmidt DP 3.00 1.35
❑ 271 Dick Drago DP .40 .18
❑ 272 Ralph Garr .40 .18
❑ 273 Eduardo Rodriguez .25 .11
❑ 274 Dale Murphy 1.25 .55
❑ 275 Jerry Koosman .40 .18
❑ 276 Tom Veryzer .25 .11
❑ 277 Rick Bosetti .25 .11
❑ 278 Jim Spencer .25 .11
❑ 279 Rob Andrews .25 .11
❑ 280 Gaylord Perry 1.25 .55
❑ 281 Paul Blair .40 .18

❑	282	Mariners Team/Mgr.	.75	.15
		Darrell Johnson		
		(Checklist back)		
❑	283	John Ellis	.25	.11
❑	284	Larry Murray DP	.10	.05
❑	285	Don Baylor	.75	.35
❑	286	Darold Knowles DP	.10	.05
❑	287	John Lowenstein	.25	.11
❑	288	Dave Rozema	.25	.11
❑	289	Bruce Bochy	.25	.11
❑	290	Steve Garvey	1.25	.55
❑	291	Randy Scarberry	.25	.11
❑	292	Dale Berra	.25	.11
❑	293	Elias Sosa	.25	.11
❑	294	Charlie Spikes	.25	.11
❑	295	Larry Gura	.25	.11
❑	296	Dave Rader	.25	.11
❑	297	Tim Johnson	.25	.11
❑	298	Ken Holtzman	.40	.18
❑	299	Steve Henderson	.25	.11
❑	300	Ron Guidry	.40	.18
❑	301	Mike Edwards	.25	.11
❑	302	Dodgers Team/Mgr.	.75	.15
		Tom Lasorda		
		(Checklist back)		
❑	303	Bill Castro	.25	.11
❑	304	Butch Wynegar	.25	.11
❑	305	Randy Jones	.25	.11
❑	306	Denny Walling	.25	.11
❑	307	Rick Honeycutt	.25	.11
❑	308	Mike Hargrove	.40	.18
❑	309	Larry McWilliams	.25	.11
❑	310	Dave Parker	.75	.35
❑	311	Roger Metzger	.25	.11
❑	312	Mike Barlow	.25	.11
❑	313	Johnny Grubb	.25	.11
❑	314	Tim Stoddard	.25	.11
❑	315	Steve Kemp	.25	.11
❑	316	Bob Lacey	.25	.11
❑	317	Mike Anderson DP	.10	.05
❑	318	Jerry Reuss	.40	.18
❑	319	Chris Speier	.25	.11
❑	320	Dennis Eckersley	.75	.35
❑	321	Keith Hernandez	.40	.18
❑	322	Claudell Washington	.40	.18
❑	323	Mick Kelleher	.25	.11
❑	324	Tom Underwood	.25	.11
❑	325	Dan Driessen	.25	.11
❑	326	Bo McLaughlin	.25	.11
❑	327	Ray Fosse DP	.10	.05
❑	328	Twins Team/Mgr.	.75	.15
		Gene Mauch		
		(Checklist back)		
❑	329	Bert Roberge	.25	.11
❑	330	Al Cowens	.25	.11
❑	331	Richie Hebner	.40	.18
❑	332	Enrique Romo	.25	.11
❑	333	Jim Norris DP	.10	.05
❑	334	Jim Beattie	.25	.11
❑	335	Willie McCovey	1.50	.70
❑	336	George Medich	.25	.11
❑	337	Carney Lansford	.40	.18
❑	338	John Wockenfuss	.25	.11
❑	339	John D'Acquisto	.25	.11
❑	340	Ken Singleton	.40	.18
❑	341	Jim Essian	.25	.11
❑	342	Odell Jones	.25	.11
❑	343	Mike Vail	.25	.11
❑	344	Randy Lerch	.25	.11
❑	345	Larry Parrish	.40	.18
❑	346	Buddy Solomon	.25	.11
❑	347	Harry Chappas	.25	.11
❑	348	Checklist 243-363	.75	.15
❑	349	Jack Brohamer	.25	.11
❑	350	George Hendrick	.40	.18
❑	351	Bob Davis	.25	.11
❑	352	Dan Briggs	.25	.11
❑	353	Andy Hassler	.25	.11
❑	354	Rick Auerbach	.25	.11
❑	355	Gary Matthews	.40	.18
❑	356	Padres Team/Mgr.	.75	.15
		Jerry Coleman		
		(Checklist back)		
❑	357	Bob McClure	.25	.11
❑	358	Lou Whitaker	1.25	.55
❑	359	Randy Moffitt	.25	.11
❑	360	Darrell Porter DP	.25	.11
❑	361	Wayne Garland	.25	.11
❑	362	Danny Goodwin	.25	.11
❑	363	Wayne Gross	.25	.11
❑	364	Ray Burris	.25	.11
❑	365	Bobby Murcer	.40	.18
❑	366	Rob Dressler	.25	.11
❑	367	Billy Smith	.25	.11
❑	368	Willie Aikens	.25	.11
❑	369	Jim Kern	.25	.11
❑	370	Cesar Cedeno	.40	.18
❑	371	Jack Morris	.75	.35
❑	372	Joel Youngblood	.25	.11
❑	373	Dan Petry RC DP	.25	.11
❑	374	Jim Gantner	.40	.18
❑	375	Ross Grimsley	.25	.11
❑	376	Gary Allenson	.25	.11
❑	377	Junior Kennedy	.25	.11
❑	378	Jerry Mumphrey	.25	.11
❑	379	Kevin Bell	.25	.11
❑	380	Garry Maddox	.40	.18
❑	381	Cubs Team/Mgr.	.75	.15
		Preston Gomez		
		(Checklist back)		
❑	382	Dave Freisleben	.25	.11
❑	383	Ed Ott	.25	.11
❑	384	Joey McLaughlin	.25	.11
❑	385	Enos Cabell	.25	.11
❑	386	Darrell Jackson	.25	.11
❑	387A	Fred Stanley YL	2.00	.90
❑	387B	Fred Stanley	.25	.11
		(Red name on front)		
❑	388	Mike Paxton	.25	.11
❑	389	Pete LaCock	.25	.11
❑	390	Fergie Jenkins	1.25	.55
❑	391	Tony Armas DP	.25	.11
❑	392	Milt Wilcox	.25	.11
❑	393	Ozzie Smith	10.00	4.50
❑	394	Reggie Cleveland	.25	.11
❑	395	Ellis Valentine	.25	.11
❑	396	Dan Meyer	.25	.11
❑	397	Roy Thomas DP	.10	.05
❑	398	Barry Foote	.25	.11
❑	399	Mike Proly DP	.10	.05
❑	400	George Foster	.40	.18
❑	401	Pete Falcone	.25	.11
❑	402	Merv Rettenmund	.25	.11
❑	403	Pete Redfern DP	.10	.05
❑	404	Orioles Team/Mgr.	.75	.15
		Earl Weaver		
		(Checklist back)		
❑	405	Dwight Evans	.40	.18
❑	406	Paul Molitor	5.00	2.20
❑	407	Tony Solaita	.25	.11
❑	408	Bill North	.25	.11
❑	409	Paul Splittorff	.25	.11
❑	410	Bobby Bonds	.75	.35
❑	411	Frank LaCorte	.25	.11
❑	412	Thad Bosley	.25	.11
❑	413	Allen Ripley	.25	.11
❑	414	George Scott	.40	.18
❑	415	Bill Atkinson	.25	.11
❑	416	Tom Brookens	.25	.11
❑	417	Craig Chamberlain DP	.10	.05
❑	418	Roger Freed DP	.10	.05
❑	419	Vic Correll	.25	.11
❑	420	Butch Hobson	.25	.11
❑	421	Doug Bird	.25	.11
❑	422	Larry Milbourne	.25	.11
❑	423	Dave Frost	.25	.11
❑	424	Yankees Team/Mgr.	.75	.15
		Dick Howser		
		(Checklist back)		
❑	425	Mark Belanger	.40	.18
❑	426	Grant Jackson	.25	.11
❑	427	Tom Hutton DP	.10	.05
❑	428	Pat Zachry	.25	.11
❑	429	Duane Kuiper	.25	.11
❑	430	Larry Hisle DP	.10	.05
❑	431	Mike Krukow	.25	.11
❑	432	Willie Norwood	.25	.11
❑	433	Rich Gale	.25	.11
❑	434	Johnnie LeMaster	.25	.11
❑	435	Don Gullett	.40	.18
❑	436	Billy Almon	.25	.11
❑	437	Joe Niekro	.40	.18
❑	438	Dave Revering	.25	.11
❑	439	Mike Phillips	.25	.11
❑	440	Don Sutton	1.25	.55
❑	441	Eric Soderholm	.25	.11
❑	442	Jorge Orta	.25	.11
❑	443	Mike Parrott	.25	.11
❑	444	Alvis Woods	.25	.11
❑	445	Mark Fidrych	1.25	.55
❑	446	Duffy Dyer	.25	.11
❑	447	Nino Espinosa	.25	.11
❑	448	Jim Wohlford	.25	.11
❑	449	Doug Bair	.25	.11
❑	450	George Brett	8.00	3.60
❑	451	Indians Team/Mgr.	.40	.08
		Dave Garcia		
		(Checklist back)		
❑	452	Steve Dillard	.25	.11
❑	453	Mike Bacsik	.25	.11
❑	454	Tom Donohue	.25	.11
❑	455	Mike Torrez	.25	.11
❑	456	Frank Taveras	.25	.11
❑	457	Bert Blyleven	.75	.35
❑	458	Billy Sample	.25	.11
❑	459	Mickey Lolich DP	.25	.11
❑	460	Willie Randolph	.40	.18
❑	461	Dwayne Murphy	.25	.11
❑	462	Mike Sadek DP	.10	.05
❑	463	Jerry Royster	.25	.11
❑	464	John Denny	.25	.11
❑	465	Rick Monday	.25	.11
❑	466	Mike Squires	.25	.11
❑	467	Jesse Jefferson	.25	.11
❑	468	Aurelio Rodriguez	.25	.11
❑	469	Randy Niemann DP	.10	.05
❑	470	Bob Boone	.75	.35
❑	471	Hosken Powell DP	.10	.05
❑	472	Willie Hernandez	.40	.18
❑	473	Bump Wills	.25	.11
❑	474	Steve Busby	.25	.11
❑	475	Cesar Geronimo	.25	.11
❑	476	Bob Shirley	.25	.11
❑	477	Buck Martinez	.25	.11
❑	478	Gil Flores	.25	.11
❑	479	Expos Team/Mgr.	.75	.15
		Dick Williams		
		(Checklist back)		
❑	480	Bob Watson	.40	.18
❑	481	Tom Paciorek	.40	.18
❑	482	R.Henderson RC UER	70.00	32.00
		7 steals at Modesto,		
		should be at Fresno		
❑	483	Bo Diaz	.25	.11
❑	484	Checklist 364-484	.75	.15
❑	485	Mickey Rivers	.40	.18
❑	486	Mike Tyson DP	.10	.05
❑	487	Wayne Nordhagen	.25	.11
❑	488	Roy Howell	.25	.11
❑	489	Preston Hanna DP	.10	.05
❑	490	Lee May	.40	.18
❑	491	Steve Mura DP	.10	.05
❑	492	Todd Cruz	.25	.11
❑	493	Jerry Martin	.25	.11
❑	494	Craig Minetto	.25	.11
❑	495	Bake McBride	.25	.11
❑	496	Silvio Martinez	.25	.11
❑	497	Jim Mason	.25	.11
❑	498	Danny Darwin	.25	.11
❑	499	Giants Team/Mgr.	.75	.15
		Dave Bristol		
		(Checklist back)		
❑	500	Tom Seaver	3.00	1.35
❑	501	Rennie Stennett	.25	.11
❑	502	Rich Wortham DP	.10	.05
❑	503	Mike Cubbage	.25	.11
❑	504	Gene Garber	.40	.18
❑	505	Bert Campaneris	.40	.18
❑	506	Tom Buskey	.25	.11
❑	507	Leon Roberts	.25	.11
❑	508	U.L. Washington	.25	.11
❑	509	Ed Glynn	.25	.11
❑	510	Ron Cey	.75	.35
❑	511	Eric Wilkins	.25	.11
❑	512	Jose Cardenal	.25	.11
❑	513	Tom Dixon DP	.10	.05
❑	514	Steve Ontiveros	.25	.11
❑	515	Mike Caldwell UER	.25	.11

1979 loss total reads
96 instead of 6#

- ❑ 516 Hector Cruz .25 .11
- ❑ 517 Don Stanhouse .25 .11
- ❑ 518 Nelson Norman .25 .11
- ❑ 519 Steve Nicosia .25 .11
- ❑ 520 Steve Rogers .25 .11
- ❑ 521 Ken Brett .25 .11
- ❑ 522 Jim Morrison .25 .11
- ❑ 523 Ken Henderson .25 .11
- ❑ 524 Jim Wright DP .10 .05
- ❑ 525 Clint Hurdle .25 .11
- ❑ 526 Phillies Team/Mgr. .75 .15
  Dallas Green
  (Checklist back)
- ❑ 527 Doug Rau DP .10 .05
- ❑ 528 Adrian Devine .25 .11
- ❑ 529 Jim Barr .25 .11
- ❑ 530 Jim Sundberg DP .25 .11
- ❑ 531 Eric Rasmussen .25 .11
- ❑ 532 Willie Horton .40 .18
- ❑ 533 Checklist 485-605 .75 .15
- ❑ 534 Andre Thornton .40 .18
- ❑ 535 Bob Forsch .25 .11
- ❑ 536 Lee Lacy .25 .11
- ❑ 537 Alex Trevino .25 .11
- ❑ 538 Joe Strain .25 .11
- ❑ 539 Rudy May .25 .11
- ❑ 540 Pete Rose 8.00 3.60
- ❑ 541 Miguel Dilone .25 .11
- ❑ 542 Joe Coleman .25 .11
- ❑ 543 Pat Kelly .25 .11
- ❑ 544 Rick Sutcliffe RC .75 .35
- ❑ 545 Jeff Burroughs .40 .18
- ❑ 546 Rick Langford .25 .11
- ❑ 547 John Wathan .25 .11
- ❑ 548 Dave Rajsich .25 .11
- ❑ 549 Larry Wolfe .25 .11
- ❑ 550 Ken Griffey Sr. .75 .35
- ❑ 551 Pirates Team/Mgr. .75 .15
  Chuck Tanner
  (Checklist back)
- ❑ 552 Bill Nahorodny .25 .11
- ❑ 553 Dick Davis .25 .11
- ❑ 554 Art Howe .40 .18
- ❑ 555 Ed Figueroa .25 .11
- ❑ 556 Joe Rudi .40 .18
- ❑ 557 Mark Lee .25 .11
- ❑ 558 Alfredo Griffin .25 .11
- ❑ 559 Dale Murray .25 .11
- ❑ 560 Dave Lopes .40 .18
- ❑ 561 Eddie Whitson .25 .11
- ❑ 562 Joe Wallis .25 .11
- ❑ 563 Will McEnaney .25 .11
- ❑ 564 Rick Manning .25 .11
- ❑ 565 Dennis Leonard .40 .18
- ❑ 566 Bud Harrelson .40 .18
- ❑ 567 Skip Lockwood .25 .11
- ❑ 568 Gary Roenicke .40 .18
- ❑ 569 Terry Kennedy .40 .18
- ❑ 570 Roy Smalley .25 .11
- ❑ 571 Joe Sambito .25 .11
- ❑ 572 Jerry Morales DP .10 .05
- ❑ 573 Kent Tekulve .40 .18
- ❑ 574 Scot Thompson .25 .11
- ❑ 575 Ken Kravec .25 .11
- ❑ 576 Jim Dwyer .25 .11
- ❑ 577 Blue Jays Team/Mgr. .75 .15
  Bobby Mattick
  (Checklist back)
- ❑ 578 Scott Sanderson .40 .18
- ❑ 579 Charlie Moore .25 .11
- ❑ 580 Nolan Ryan 15.00 6.75
- ❑ 581 Bob Bailor .25 .11
- ❑ 582 Brian Doyle .25 .11
- ❑ 583 Bob Stinson .25 .11
- ❑ 584 Kurt Bevacqua .25 .11
- ❑ 585 Al Hrabosky .25 .11
- ❑ 586 Mitchell Page .25 .11
- ❑ 587 Garry Templeton .25 .11
- ❑ 588 Greg Minton .25 .11
- ❑ 589 Chet Lemon .40 .18
- ❑ 590 Jim Palmer 1.50 .70
- ❑ 591 Rick Cerone .25 .11
- ❑ 592 Jon Matlack .25 .11
- ❑ 593 Jesus Alou .25 .11
- ❑ 594 Dick Tidrow .25 .11
- ❑ 595 Don Money .25 .11
- ❑ 596 Rick Matula .25 .11
- ❑ 597 Tom Poquette .25 .11
- ❑ 598 Fred Kendall DP .10 .05
- ❑ 599 Mike Norris .25 .11
- ❑ 600 Reggie Jackson 4.00 1.80
- ❑ 601 Buddy Schultz .25 .11
- ❑ 602 Brian Downing .25 .11
- ❑ 603 Jack Billingham DP .10 .05
- ❑ 604 Glenn Adams .25 .11
- ❑ 605 Terry Forster .25 .11
- ❑ 606 Reds Team/Mgr. .75 .15
  John McNamara
  (Checklist back)
- ❑ 607 Woodie Fryman .25 .11
- ❑ 608 Alan Bannister .25 .11
- ❑ 609 Ron Reed .25 .11
- ❑ 610 Willie Stargell 1.25 .55
- ❑ 611 Jerry Garvin DP .10 .05
- ❑ 612 Cliff Johnson .25 .11
- ❑ 613 Randy Stein .25 .11
- ❑ 614 John Hiller .25 .11
- ❑ 615 Doug DeCinces .40 .18
- ❑ 616 Gene Richards .25 .11
- ❑ 617 Joaquin Andujar .40 .18
- ❑ 618 Bob Montgomery DP .40 .18
- ❑ 619 Sergio Ferrer .25 .11
- ❑ 620 Richie Zisk .25 .11
- ❑ 621 Bob Grich .40 .18
- ❑ 622 Mario Soto .25 .11
- ❑ 623 Gorman Thomas .40 .18
- ❑ 624 Lerrin LaGrow .25 .11
- ❑ 625 Chris Chambliss .40 .18
- ❑ 626 Tigers Team/Mgr. .75 .15
  Sparky Anderson
  (Checklist back)
- ❑ 627 Pedro Borbon .25 .11
- ❑ 628 Doug Capilla .25 .11
- ❑ 629 Jim Todd .25 .11
- ❑ 630 Larry Bowa .40 .18
- ❑ 631 Mark Littell .25 .11
- ❑ 632 Barry Bonnell .25 .11
- ❑ 633 Bob Apodaca .25 .11
- ❑ 634 Glenn Borgmann DP .10 .05
- ❑ 635 John Candelaria .40 .18
- ❑ 636 Toby Harrah .40 .18
- ❑ 637 Joe Simpson .25 .11
- ❑ 638 Mark Clear .25 .11
- ❑ 639 Larry Biittner .25 .11
- ❑ 640 Mike Flanagan .40 .18
- ❑ 641 Ed Kranepool .25 .11
- ❑ 642 Ken Forsch DP .10 .05
- ❑ 643 John Mayberry .40 .18
- ❑ 644 Charlie Hough .40 .18
- ❑ 645 Rick Burleson .25 .11
- ❑ 646 Checklist 606-726 .75 .15
- ❑ 647 Milt May .25 .11
- ❑ 648 Roy White .25 .11
- ❑ 649 Tom Griffin .25 .11
- ❑ 650 Joe Morgan 1.50 .70
- ❑ 651 Rollie Fingers 1.25 .55
- ❑ 652 Mario Mendoza .25 .11
- ❑ 653 Stan Bahnsen .25 .11
- ❑ 654 Bruce Boisclair DP .10 .05
- ❑ 655 Tug McGraw .40 .18
- ❑ 656 Larvell Blanks .25 .11
- ❑ 657 Dave Edwards .25 .11
- ❑ 658 Chris Knapp .25 .11
- ❑ 659 Brewers Team/Mgr. .75 .15
  George Bamberger
  (Checklist back)
- ❑ 660 Rusty Staub .40 .18
- ❑ 661 Orioles Rookies .40 .18
  Mark Corey
  Dave Ford
  Wayne Krenchicki
- ❑ 662 Red Sox Rookies .40 .18
  Joel Finch
  Mike O'Berry
  Chuck Rainey
- ❑ 663 Angels Rookies .75 .35
  Ralph Botting
  Bob Clark
  Dickie Thon
- ❑ 664 White Sox Rookies .40 .18
  Mike Colbern
  Guy Hoffman
  Dewey Robinson
- ❑ 665 Indians Rookies .75 .35
  Larry Andersen
  Bobby Cuellar
  Sandy Wihtol
- ❑ 666 Tigers Rookies .40 .18
  Mike Chris
  Al Greene
  Bruce Robbins
- ❑ 667 Royals Rookies .75 .35
  Renie Martin
  Bill Paschall
  Dan Quisenberry
- ❑ 668 Brewers Rookies .40 .18
  Danny Boitano
  Willie Mueller
  Lenn Sakata
- ❑ 669 Twins Rookies .40 .18
  Dan Graham
  Rick Sofield
  Gary Ward
- ❑ 670 Yankees Rookies .40 .18
  Bobby Brown
  Brad Gulden
  Darryl Jones
- ❑ 671 A's Rookies 1.25 .55
  Derek Bryant
  Brian Kingman
  Mike Morgan
- ❑ 672 Mariners Rookies .40 .18
  Charlie Beamon
  Rodney Craig
  Rafael Vasquez
- ❑ 673 Rangers Rookies .40 .18
  Brian Allard
  Jerry Don Gleaton
  Greg Mahlberg
- ❑ 674 Blue Jays Rookies .40 .18
  Butch Edge
  Pat Kelly
  Ted Wilborn
- ❑ 675 Braves Rookies .40 .18
  Bruce Benedict
  Larry Bradford
  Eddie Miller
- ❑ 676 Cubs Rookies .40 .18
  Dave Geisel
  Steve Macko
  Karl Pagel
- ❑ 677 Reds Rookies .40 .18
  Art DeFreites
  Frank Pastore
  Harry Spilman
- ❑ 678 Astros Rookies .40 .18
  Reggie Baldwin
  Alan Knicely
  Pete Ladd
- ❑ 679 Dodgers Rookies .75 .35
  Joe Beckwith
  Mickey Hatcher
  Dave Patterson
- ❑ 680 Expos Rookies .75 .35
  Tony Bernazard
  Randy Miller
  John Tamargo
- ❑ 681 Mets Rookies .40 .18
  Dan Norman
  Jesse Orosco
  Mike Scott
- ❑ 682 Phillies Rookies .40 .18
  Ramon Aviles
  Dickie Noles
  Kevin Saucier
- ❑ 683 Pirates Rookies .40 .18
  Dorian Boyland
  Alberto Lois
  Harry Saferight
- ❑ 684 Cardinals Rookies .75 .35
  George Frazier
  Tom Herr
  Dan O'Brien
- ❑ 685 Padres Rookies .40 .18
  Tim Flannery
  Brian Greer

Jim Wilhelm		
❑ 686 Giants Rookies	.40	.18
Greg Johnston		
Dennis Littlejohn		
Phil Nastu		
❑ 687 Mike Heath DP	.10	.05
❑ 688 Steve Stone	.40	.18
❑ 689 Red Sox Team/Mgr.	.75	.15
Don Zimmer		
(Checklist back)		
❑ 690 Tommy John	.75	.35
❑ 691 Ivan DeJesus	.25	.11
❑ 692 Rawly Eastwick DP	.10	.05
❑ 693 Craig Kusick	.25	.11
❑ 694 Jim Rooker	.25	.11
❑ 695 Reggie Smith	.40	.18
❑ 696 Julio Gonzalez	.25	.11
❑ 697 David Clyde	.25	.11
❑ 698 Oscar Gamble	.40	.18
❑ 699 Floyd Bannister	.25	.11
❑ 700 Rod Carew DP	1.50	.70
❑ 701 Ken Oberkfell	.25	.11
❑ 702 Ed Farmer	.25	.11
❑ 703 Otto Velez	.25	.11
❑ 704 Gene Tenace	.40	.18
❑ 705 Freddie Patek	.25	.11
❑ 706 Tippy Martinez	.25	.11
❑ 707 Elliott Maddox	.25	.11
❑ 708 Bob Tolan	.25	.11
❑ 709 Pat Underwood	.25	.11
❑ 710 Graig Nettles	.75	.35
❑ 711 Bob Galasso	.25	.11
❑ 712 Rodney Scott	.25	.11
❑ 713 Terry Whitfield	.25	.11
❑ 714 Fred Norman	.25	.11
❑ 715 Sal Bando	.40	.18
❑ 716 Lynn McGlothen	.25	.11
❑ 717 Mickey Klutts DP	.10	.05
❑ 718 Greg Gross	.25	.11
❑ 719 Don Robinson	.40	.18
❑ 720 Carl Yastrzemski DP	2.00	.90
❑ 721 Paul Hartzell	.25	.11
❑ 722 Jose Cruz	.40	.18
❑ 723 Shane Rawley	.25	.11
❑ 724 Jerry White	.25	.11
❑ 725 Rick Wise	.25	.11
❑ 726 Steve Yeager	.75	.15

1981 Topps

	NRMT	VG-E
COMPLETE SET (726)	60.00	27.00
COMMON CARD (1-726)	.15	.07
COMMON CARD DP	.07	.03

❑ 1 Batting Leaders	2.50	1.10
George Brett		
Bill Buckner		
❑ 2 Home Run Leaders	1.50	.70
Reggie Jackson		
Ben Oglivie		
Mike Schmidt		
❑ 3 RBI Leaders	1.50	.70
Cecil Cooper		
Mike Schmidt		
❑ 4 Stolen Base Leaders	3.00	1.35
Rickey Henderson		
Ron LeFlore		
❑ 5 Victory Leaders	1.50	.70
Steve Stone		
Steve Carlton		
❑ 6 Strikeout Leaders	1.50	.70
Len Barker		
Steve Carlton		
❑ 7 ERA Leaders	.75	.35
Rudy May		
Don Sutton		
❑ 8 Leading Firemen	.75	.35
Dan Quisenberry		
Rollie Fingers		
Tom Hume		
❑ 9 Pete LaCock DP	.07	.03
❑ 10 Mike Flanagan	.40	.18
❑ 11 Jim Wohlford DP	.07	.03
❑ 12 Mark Clear	.15	.07
❑ 13 Joe Charboneau RC	1.50	.70
❑ 14 John Tudor RC	.40	.18
❑ 15 Larry Parrish	.15	.07
❑ 16 Ron Davis	.15	.07
❑ 17 Cliff Johnson	.15	.07
❑ 18 Glenn Adams	.15	.07
❑ 19 Jim Clancy	.15	.07
❑ 20 Jeff Burroughs	.15	.07
❑ 21 Ron Oester	.15	.07
❑ 22 Danny Darwin	.15	.07
❑ 23 Alex Trevino	.15	.07
❑ 24 Don Stanhouse	.15	.07
❑ 25 Sixto Lezcano	.15	.07
❑ 26 U.L. Washington	.15	.07
❑ 27 Champ Summers DP	.07	.03
❑ 28 Enrique Romo	.15	.07
❑ 29 Gene Tenace	.40	.18
❑ 30 Jack Clark	.40	.18
❑ 31 Checklist 1-121 DP	.15	.07
❑ 32 Ken Oberkfell	.15	.07
❑ 33 Rick Honeycutt	.15	.07
❑ 34 Aurelio Rodriguez	.15	.07
❑ 35 Mitchell Page	.15	.07
❑ 36 Ed Farmer	.15	.07
❑ 37 Gary Roenicke	.15	.07
❑ 38 Win Remmerswaal	.15	.07
❑ 39 Tom Veryzer	.15	.07
❑ 40 Tug McGraw	.40	.18
❑ 41 Ranger Rookies	.15	.07
Bob Babcock		
John Butcher		
Jerry Don Gleaton		
❑ 42 Jerry White DP	.07	.03
❑ 43 Jose Morales	.15	.07
❑ 44 Larry McWilliams	.15	.07
❑ 45 Enos Cabell	.15	.07
❑ 46 Rick Bosetti	.15	.07
❑ 47 Ken Brett	.15	.07
❑ 48 Dave Skaggs	.15	.07
❑ 49 Bob Shirley	.15	.07
❑ 50 Dave Lopes	.40	.18
❑ 51 Bill Robinson DP	.15	.07
❑ 52 Hector Cruz	.15	.07
❑ 53 Kevin Saucier	.15	.07
❑ 54 Ivan DeJesus	.15	.07
❑ 55 Mike Norris	.15	.07
❑ 56 Buck Martinez	.15	.07
❑ 57 Dave Roberts	.15	.07
❑ 58 Joel Youngblood	.15	.07
❑ 59 Dan Petry	.15	.07
❑ 60 Willie Randolph	.40	.18
❑ 61 Butch Wynegar	.15	.07
❑ 62 Joe Pettini	.15	.07
❑ 63 Steve Renko DP	.07	.03
❑ 64 Brian Asselstine	.15	.07
❑ 65 Scott McGregor	.15	.07
❑ 66 Royals Rookies	.15	.07
Manny Castillo		
Tim Ireland		
Mike Jones		
❑ 67 Ken Kravec	.15	.07
❑ 68 Matt Alexander DP	.07	.03
❑ 69 Ed Halicki	.15	.07
❑ 70 Al Oliver DP	.40	.18
❑ 71 Hal Dues	.15	.07
❑ 72 Barry Evans DP	.07	.03
❑ 73 Doug Bair	.15	.07
❑ 74 Mike Hargrove	.40	.18
❑ 75 Reggie Smith	.40	.18
❑ 76 Mario Mendoza	.15	.07
❑ 77 Mike Barlow	.15	.07
❑ 78 Steve Dillard	.15	.07
❑ 79 Bruce Robbins	.15	.07
❑ 80 Rusty Staub	.40	.18
❑ 81 Dave Stapleton	.15	.07
❑ 82 Astros Rookies DP	.15	.07
Danny Heep		
Alan Knicely		
Bobby Sprowl		
❑ 83 Mike Proly	.15	.07
❑ 84 Johnnie LeMaster	.15	.07
❑ 85 Mike Caldwell	.15	.07
❑ 86 Wayne Gross	.15	.07
❑ 87 Rick Camp	.15	.07
❑ 88 Joe Lefebvre	.15	.07
❑ 89 Darrell Jackson	.15	.07
❑ 90 Bake McBride	.15	.07
❑ 91 Tim Stoddard DP	.07	.03
❑ 92 Mike Easler	.15	.07
❑ 93 Ed Glynn DP	.07	.03
❑ 94 Harry Spilman DP	.07	.03
❑ 95 Jim Sundberg	.40	.18
❑ 96 A's Rookies	.15	.07
Dave Beard		
Ernie Camacho		
Pat Dempsey		
❑ 97 Chris Speier	.15	.07
❑ 98 Clint Hurdle	.15	.07
❑ 99 Eric Wilkins	.15	.07
❑ 100 Rod Carew	1.50	.70
❑ 101 Benny Ayala	.15	.07
❑ 102 Dave Tobik	.15	.07
❑ 103 Jerry Martin	.15	.07
❑ 104 Terry Forster	.15	.07
❑ 105 Jose Cruz	.40	.18
❑ 106 Don Money	.15	.07
❑ 107 Rich Wortham	.15	.07
❑ 108 Bruce Benedict	.15	.07
❑ 109 Mike Scott	.40	.18
❑ 110 Carl Yastrzemski	1.50	.70
❑ 111 Greg Minton	.15	.07
❑ 112 White Sox Rookies	.15	.07
Rusty Kuntz		
Fran Mullins		
Leo Sutherland		
❑ 113 Mike Phillips	.15	.07
❑ 114 Tom Underwood	.15	.07
❑ 115 Roy Smalley	.15	.07
❑ 116 Joe Simpson	.15	.07
❑ 117 Pete Falcone	.15	.07
❑ 118 Kurt Bevacqua	.15	.07
❑ 119 Tippy Martinez	.15	.07
❑ 120 Larry Bowa	.40	.18
❑ 121 Larry Harlow	.15	.07
❑ 122 John Denny	.15	.07
❑ 123 Al Cowens	.15	.07
❑ 124 Jerry Garvin	.15	.07
❑ 125 Andre Dawson	.75	.35
❑ 126 Charlie Leibrandt RC	.75	.35
❑ 127 Rudy Law	.15	.07
❑ 128 Gary Allenson DP	.07	.03
❑ 129 Art Howe	.40	.18
❑ 130 Larry Gura	.15	.07
❑ 131 Keith Moreland	.40	.18
❑ 132 Tommy Boggs	.15	.07
❑ 133 Jeff Cox	.15	.07
❑ 134 Steve Mura	.15	.07
❑ 135 Gorman Thomas	.40	.18
❑ 136 Doug Capilla	.15	.07
❑ 137 Hosken Powell	.15	.07
❑ 138 Rich Dotson DP	.15	.07
❑ 139 Oscar Gamble	.15	.07
❑ 140 Bob Forsch	.15	.07
❑ 141 Miguel Dilone	.15	.07
❑ 142 Jackson Todd	.15	.07
❑ 143 Dan Meyer	.15	.07
❑ 144 Allen Ripley	.15	.07
❑ 145 Mickey Rivers	.40	.18
❑ 146 Bobby Castillo	.15	.07
❑ 147 Dale Berra	.15	.07
❑ 148 Randy Niemann	.15	.07
❑ 149 Joe Nolan	.15	.07
❑ 150 Mark Fidrych	1.50	.70
❑ 151 Claudell Washington	.15	.07
❑ 152 John Urrea	.15	.07

❑ 153	Tom Poquette	.15	.07
❑ 154	Rick Langford	.15	.07
❑ 155	Chris Chambliss	.40	.18
❑ 156	Bob McClure	.15	.07
❑ 157	John Wathan	.15	.07
❑ 158	Fergie Jenkins	1.50	.70
❑ 159	Brian Doyle	.15	.07
❑ 160	Garry Maddox	.15	.07
❑ 161	Dan Graham	.15	.07
❑ 162	Doug Corbett	.15	.07
❑ 163	Bill Almon	.15	.07
❑ 164	LaMarr Hoyt RC	.40	.18
❑ 165	Tony Scott	.15	.07
❑ 166	Floyd Bannister	.15	.07
❑ 167	Terry Whitfield	.15	.07
❑ 168	Don Robinson DP	.07	.03
❑ 169	John Mayberry	.15	.07
❑ 170	Ross Grimsley	.15	.07
❑ 171	Gene Richards	.15	.07
❑ 172	Gary Woods	.15	.07
❑ 173	Bump Wills	.15	.07
❑ 174	Doug Rau	.15	.07
❑ 175	Dave Collins	.15	.07
❑ 176	Mike Krukow	.15	.07
❑ 177	Rick Peters	.15	.07
❑ 178	Jim Essian DP	.07	.03
❑ 179	Rudy May	.15	.07
❑ 180	Pete Rose	5.00	2.20
❑ 181	Elias Sosa	.15	.07
❑ 182	Bob Grich	.40	.18
❑ 183	Dick Davis DP	.07	.03
❑ 184	Jim Dwyer	.15	.07
❑ 185	Dennis Leonard	.15	.07
❑ 186	Wayne Nordhagen	.15	.07
❑ 187	Mike Parrott	.15	.07
❑ 188	Doug DeCinces	.40	.18
❑ 189	Craig Swan	.15	.07
❑ 190	Cesar Cedeno	.40	.18
❑ 191	Rick Sutcliffe	.40	.18
❑ 192	Braves Rookies	.40	.18
	Terry Harper		
	Ed Miller		
	Rafael Ramirez		
❑ 193	Pete Vuckovich	.40	.18
❑ 194	Rod Scurry	.15	.07
❑ 195	Rich Murray	.15	.07
❑ 196	Duffy Dyer	.15	.07
❑ 197	Jim Kern	.15	.07
❑ 198	Jerry Dybzinski	.15	.07
❑ 199	Chuck Rainey	.15	.07
❑ 200	George Foster	.40	.18
❑ 201	Johnny Bench RB	.75	.35
	Most homers catchers		
❑ 202	Steve Carlton RB	.75	.35
	Most strikeouts, lefthander, lifetime		
❑ 203	Bill Gullickson RB	.75	.35
	Most SO's, game, rookie		
❑ 204	Ron LeFlore RB	.40	.18
	Rodney Scott RB		
	Most stolen bases teammates, season		
❑ 205	Pete Rose RB	1.50	.70
	Most cons. seasons 600 or more at-bats		
❑ 206	Mike Schmidt RB	.75	.35
	Most homers, 3rd baseman, season		
❑ 207	Ozzie Smith RB	2.00	.90
	Most assists, season, shortstop		
❑ 208	Willie Wilson RB	.40	.18
	Most AB's season		
❑ 209	Dickie Thon DP	.40	.18
❑ 210	Jim Palmer	1.50	.70
❑ 211	Derrel Thomas	.15	.07
❑ 212	Steve Nicosia	.15	.07
❑ 213	Al Holland	.15	.07
❑ 214	Angels Rookies	.15	.07
	Ralph Botting		
	Jim Dorsey		
	John Harris		
❑ 215	Larry Hisle	.15	.07
❑ 216	John Henry Johnson	.15	.07
❑ 217	Rich Hebner	.15	.07
❑ 218	Paul Splittorff	.15	.07
❑ 219	Ken Landreaux	.15	.07
❑ 220	Tom Seaver	2.50	1.10
❑ 221	Bob Davis	.15	.07
❑ 222	Jorge Orta	.15	.07
❑ 223	Roy Lee Jackson	.15	.07
❑ 224	Pat Zachry	.15	.07
❑ 225	Ruppert Jones	.15	.07
❑ 226	Manny Sanguillen DP	.07	.03
❑ 227	Fred Martinez	.15	.07
❑ 228	Tom Paciorek	.40	.18
❑ 229	Rollie Fingers	1.50	.70
❑ 230	George Hendrick	.40	.18
❑ 231	Joe Beckwith	.15	.07
❑ 232	Mickey Klutts	.15	.07
❑ 233	Skip Lockwood	.15	.07
❑ 234	Lou Whitaker	1.50	.70
❑ 235	Scott Sanderson	.15	.07
❑ 236	Mike Ivie	.15	.07
❑ 237	Charlie Moore	.15	.07
❑ 238	Willie Hernandez	.40	.18
❑ 239	Rick Miller DP	.07	.03
❑ 240	Nolan Ryan	8.00	3.60
❑ 241	Checklist 122-242 DP	.15	.07
❑ 242	Chet Lemon	.15	.07
❑ 243	Sal Butera	.15	.07
❑ 244	Cardinals Rookies	.15	.07
	Tito Landrum		
	Al Olmsted		
	Andy Rincon		
❑ 245	Ed Figueroa	.15	.07
❑ 246	Ed Ott DP	.07	.03
❑ 247	Glenn Hubbard DP	.07	.03
❑ 248	Joey McLaughlin	.15	.07
❑ 249	Larry Cox	.15	.07
❑ 250	Ron Guidry	.40	.18
❑ 251	Tom Brookens	.15	.07
❑ 252	Victor Cruz	.15	.07
❑ 253	Dave Bergman	.15	.07
❑ 254	Ozzie Smith	5.00	2.20
❑ 255	Mark Littell	.15	.07
❑ 256	Bombo Rivera	.15	.07
❑ 257	Rennie Stennett	.15	.07
❑ 258	Joe Price	.15	.07
❑ 259	Mets Rookies	1.50	.70
	Juan Berenguer		
	Hubie Brooks RC		
	Mookie Wilson		
❑ 260	Ron Cey	.40	.18
❑ 261	Rickey Henderson	10.00	4.50
❑ 262	Sammy Stewart	.15	.07
❑ 263	Brian Downing	.40	.18
❑ 264	Jim Norris	.15	.07
❑ 265	John Candelaria	.40	.18
❑ 266	Tom Herr	.40	.18
❑ 267	Stan Bahnsen	.15	.07
❑ 268	Jerry Royster	.15	.07
❑ 269	Ken Forsch	.15	.07
❑ 270	Greg Luzinski	.40	.18
❑ 271	Bill Castro	.15	.07
❑ 272	Bruce Kimm	.15	.07
❑ 273	Stan Papi	.15	.07
❑ 274	Craig Chamberlain	.15	.07
❑ 275	Dwight Evans	.75	.35
❑ 276	Dan Spillner	.15	.07
❑ 277	Alfredo Griffin	.15	.07
❑ 278	Rick Sofield	.15	.07
❑ 279	Bob Knepper	.15	.07
❑ 280	Ken Griffey	.75	.35
❑ 281	Fred Stanley	.15	.07
❑ 282	Mariners Rookies	.15	.07
	Rick Anderson		
	Greg Biercevicz		
	Rodney Craig		
❑ 283	Billy Sample	.15	.07
❑ 284	Brian Kingman	.15	.07
❑ 285	Jerry Turner	.15	.07
❑ 286	Dave Frost	.15	.07
❑ 287	Lenn Sakata	.15	.07
❑ 288	Bob Clark	.15	.07
❑ 289	Mickey Hatcher	.40	.18
❑ 290	Bob Boone DP	.40	.18
❑ 291	Aurelio Lopez	.15	.07
❑ 292	Mike Squires	.15	.07
❑ 293	Charlie Lea	.15	.07
❑ 294	Mike Tyson DP	.07	.03
❑ 295	Hal McRae	.40	.18
❑ 296	Bill Nahorodny DP	.07	.03
❑ 297	Bob Bailor	.15	.07
❑ 298	Buddy Solomon	.15	.07
❑ 299	Elliott Maddox	.15	.07
❑ 300	Paul Molitor	3.00	1.35
❑ 301	Matt Keough	.15	.07
❑ 302	Dodgers Rookies	3.00	1.35
	Jack Perconte		
	Mike Scioscia		
	Fernando Valenzuela RC		
❑ 303	Johnny Oates	.40	.18
❑ 304	John Castino	.15	.07
❑ 305	Ken Clay	.15	.07
❑ 306	Juan Beniquez DP	.07	.03
❑ 307	Gene Garber	.15	.07
❑ 308	Rick Manning	.15	.07
❑ 309	Luis Salazar RC	.15	.07
❑ 310	Vida Blue DP	.15	.07
❑ 311	Freddie Patek	.15	.07
❑ 312	Rick Rhoden	.15	.07
❑ 313	Luis Pujols	.15	.07
❑ 314	Rich Dauer	.15	.07
❑ 315	Kirk Gibson RC	3.00	1.35
❑ 316	Craig Minetto	.15	.07
❑ 317	Lonnie Smith	.40	.18
❑ 318	Steve Yeager	.15	.07
❑ 319	Rowland Office	.15	.07
❑ 320	Tom Burgmeier	.15	.07
❑ 321	Leon Durham	.40	.18
❑ 322	Neil Allen	.15	.07
❑ 323	Jim Morrison DP	.07	.03
❑ 324	Mike Willis	.15	.07
❑ 325	Ray Knight	.40	.18
❑ 326	Biff Pocoroba	.15	.07
❑ 327	Moose Haas	.15	.07
❑ 328	Twins Rookies	.15	.07
	Dave Engle		
	Greg Johnston		
	Gary Ward		
❑ 329	Joaquin Andujar	.40	.18
❑ 330	Frank White	.40	.18
❑ 331	Dennis Lamp	.15	.07
❑ 332	Lee Lacy DP	.07	.03
❑ 333	Sid Monge	.15	.07
❑ 334	Dane Iorg	.15	.07
❑ 335	Rick Cerone	.15	.07
❑ 336	Eddie Whitson	.15	.07
❑ 337	Lynn Jones	.15	.07
❑ 338	Checklist 243-363	.75	.35
❑ 339	John Ellis	.15	.07
❑ 340	Bruce Kison	.15	.07
❑ 341	Dwayne Murphy	.15	.07
❑ 342	Eric Rasmussen DP	.07	.03
❑ 343	Frank Taveras	.15	.07
❑ 344	Byron McLaughlin	.15	.07
❑ 345	Warren Cromartie	.15	.07
❑ 346	Larry Christenson DP	.07	.03
❑ 347	Harold Baines RC	8.00	3.60
❑ 348	Bob Sykes	.15	.07
❑ 349	Glenn Hoffman	.15	.07
❑ 350	J.R. Richard	.40	.18
❑ 351	Otto Velez	.15	.07
❑ 352	Dick Tidrow DP	.07	.03
❑ 353	Terry Kennedy	.15	.07
❑ 354	Mario Soto	.15	.07
❑ 355	Bob Horner	.40	.18
❑ 356	Padres Rookies	.15	.07
	George Stablein		
	Craig Stimac		
	Tom Tellmann		
❑ 357	Jim Slaton	.15	.07
❑ 358	Mark Wagner	.15	.07
❑ 359	Tom Hausman	.15	.07
❑ 360	Willie Wilson	.40	.18
❑ 361	Joe Strain	.15	.07
❑ 362	Bo Diaz	.15	.07
❑ 363	Geoff Zahn	.15	.07
❑ 364	Mike Davis	.15	.07
❑ 365	Graig Nettles DP	.40	.18
❑ 366	Mike Ramsey	.15	.07
❑ 367	Dennis Martinez	.75	.35
❑ 368	Leon Roberts	.15	.07
❑ 369	Frank Tanana	.40	.18
❑ 370	Dave Winfield	1.50	.70
❑ 371	Charlie Hough	.40	.18
❑ 372	Jay Johnstone	.40	.18
❑ 373	Pat Underwood	.15	.07

❑ 374 Tommy Hutton .15 .07
❑ 375 Dave Concepcion .40 .18
❑ 376 Ron Reed .15 .07
❑ 377 Jerry Morales .15 .07
❑ 378 Dave Rader .15 .07
❑ 379 Lary Sorensen .15 .07
❑ 380 Willie Stargell 1.50 .70
❑ 381 Cubs Rookies .15 .07
Carlos Lezcano
Steve Macko
Randy Martz
❑ 382 Paul Mirabella .15 .07
❑ 383 Eric Soderholm DP .07 .03
❑ 384 Mike Sadek .15 .07
❑ 385 Joe Sambito .15 .07
❑ 386 Dave Edwards .15 .07
❑ 387 Phil Niekro 1.50 .70
❑ 388 Andre Thornton .40 .18
❑ 389 Marty Pattin .15 .07
❑ 390 Cesar Geronimo .15 .07
❑ 391 Dave Lemanczyk DP .07 .03
❑ 392 Lance Parrish .40 .18
❑ 393 Broderick Perkins .15 .07
❑ 394 Woodie Fryman .15 .07
❑ 395 Scot Thompson .15 .07
❑ 396 Bill Campbell .15 .07
❑ 397 Julio Cruz .15 .07
❑ 398 Ross Baumgarten .15 .07
❑ 399 Orioles Rookies 1.50 .70
Mike Boddicker RC
Mark Corey
Floyd Rayford
❑ 400 Reggie Jackson 2.00 .90
❑ 401 George Brett ALCS 2.00 .90
❑ 402 NL Champs .75 .35
Phillies squeak
past Astros
(Phillies celebrating)
❑ 403 Larry Bowa WS .75 .35
❑ 404 Tug McGraw WS .75 .35
❑ 405 Nino Espinosa .15 .07
❑ 406 Dickie Noles .15 .07
❑ 407 Ernie Whitt .15 .07
❑ 408 Fernando Arroyo .15 .07
❑ 409 Larry Herndon .15 .07
❑ 410 Bert Campaneris .40 .18
❑ 411 Terry Puhl .15 .07
❑ 412 Britt Burns .15 .07
❑ 413 Tony Bernazard .15 .07
❑ 414 John Pacella DP .07 .03
❑ 415 Ben Oglivie .40 .18
❑ 416 Gary Alexander .15 .07
❑ 417 Dan Schatzeder .15 .07
❑ 418 Bobby Brown .15 .07
❑ 419 Tom Hume .15 .07
❑ 420 Keith Hernandez .40 .18
❑ 421 Bob Stanley .15 .07
❑ 422 Dan Ford .15 .07
❑ 423 Shane Rawley .15 .07
❑ 424 Yankees Rookies .15 .07
Tim Lollar
Bruce Robinson
Dennis Werth
❑ 425 Al Bumbry .40 .18
❑ 426 Warren Brusstar .15 .07
❑ 427 John D'Acquisto .15 .07
❑ 428 John Stearns .15 .07
❑ 429 Mick Kelleher .15 .07
❑ 430 Jim Bibby .15 .07
❑ 431 Dave Roberts .15 .07
❑ 432 Len Barker .15 .07
❑ 433 Rance Mulliniks .15 .07
❑ 434 Roger Erickson .15 .07
❑ 435 Jim Spencer .15 .07
❑ 436 Gary Lucas .15 .07
❑ 437 Mike Heath DP .07 .03
❑ 438 John Montefusco .15 .07
❑ 439 Denny Walling .15 .07
❑ 440 Jerry Reuss .40 .18
❑ 441 Ken Reitz .15 .07
❑ 442 Ron Pruitt .15 .07
❑ 443 Jim Beattie DP .07 .03
❑ 444 Garth Iorg .15 .07
❑ 445 Ellis Valentine .15 .07
❑ 446 Checklist 364-484 .75 .35
❑ 447 Junior Kennedy DP .07 .03
❑ 448 Tim Corcoran .15 .07
❑ 449 Paul Mitchell .15 .07
❑ 450 Dave Kingman DP .40 .18
❑ 451 Indians Rookies .15 .07
Chris Bando
Tom Brennan
Sandy Wihtol
❑ 452 Renie Martin .15 .07
❑ 453 Rob Wilfong DP .40 .18
❑ 454 Andy Hassler .15 .07
❑ 455 Rick Burleson .15 .07
❑ 456 Jeff Reardon RC 1.50 .70
❑ 457 Mike Lum .15 .07
❑ 458 Randy Jones .15 .07
❑ 459 Greg Gross .15 .07
❑ 460 Rich Gossage .75 .35
❑ 461 Dave McKay .15 .07
❑ 462 Jack Brohamer .15 .07
❑ 463 Milt May .15 .07
❑ 464 Adrian Devine .15 .07
❑ 465 Bill Russell .40 .18
❑ 466 Bob Molinaro .15 .07
❑ 467 Dave Stieb .40 .18
❑ 468 John Wockenfuss .15 .07
❑ 469 Jeff Leonard .40 .18
❑ 470 Manny Trillo .15 .07
❑ 471 Mike Vail .15 .07
❑ 472 Dyar Miller DP .07 .03
❑ 473 Jose Cardenal .15 .07
❑ 474 Mike LaCoss .15 .07
❑ 475 Buddy Bell .40 .18
❑ 476 Jerry Koosman .40 .18
❑ 477 Luis Gomez .15 .07
❑ 478 Juan Eichelberger .15 .07
❑ 479 Expos Rookies 3.00 1.35
Tim Raines RC
Roberto Ramos
Bobby Pate
❑ 480 Carlton Fisk 1.50 .70
❑ 481 Bob Lacey DP .07 .03
❑ 482 Jim Gantner .40 .18
❑ 483 Mike Griffin RC .15 .07
❑ 484 Max Venable DP .07 .03
❑ 485 Garry Templeton .15 .07
❑ 486 Marc Hill .15 .07
❑ 487 Dewey Robinson .15 .07
❑ 488 Damaso Garcia .15 .07
❑ 489 John Littlefield .15 .07
Photo on card believed to be Mark Riggins
❑ 490 Eddie Murray 3.00 1.35
❑ 491 Gordy Pladson .15 .07
❑ 492 Barry Foote .15 .07
❑ 493 Dan Quisenberry .40 .18
❑ 494 Bob Walk RC .40 .18
❑ 495 Dusty Baker .75 .35
❑ 496 Paul Dade .15 .07
❑ 497 Fred Norman .15 .07
❑ 498 Pat Putnam .15 .07
❑ 499 Frank Pastore .15 .07
❑ 500 Jim Rice .40 .18
❑ 501 Tim Foli DP .40 .18
❑ 502 Giants Rookies .15 .07
Chris Bourjos
Al Hargesheimer
Mike Rowland
❑ 503 Steve McCatty .15 .07
❑ 504 Dale Murphy 1.50 .70
❑ 505 Jason Thompson .15 .07
❑ 506 Phil Huffman .15 .07
❑ 507 Jamie Quirk .15 .07
❑ 508 Rob Dressler .15 .07
❑ 509 Pete Mackanin .15 .07
❑ 510 Lee Mazzilli .15 .07
❑ 511 Wayne Garland .15 .07
❑ 512 Gary Thomasson .15 .07
❑ 513 Frank LaCorte .15 .07
❑ 514 George Riley .15 .07
❑ 515 Robin Yount 1.50 .70
❑ 516 Doug Bird .15 .07
❑ 517 Richie Zisk .15 .07
❑ 518 Grant Jackson .15 .07
❑ 519 John Tamargo DP .40 .18
❑ 520 Steve Stone .40 .18
❑ 521 Sam Mejias .15 .07
❑ 522 Mike Colbern .15 .07
❑ 523 John Fulgham .15 .07
❑ 524 Willie Aikens .15 .07
❑ 525 Mike Torrez .15 .07
❑ 526 Phillies Rookies .15 .07
Marty Bystrom
Jay Loviglio
Jim Wright
❑ 527 Danny Goodwin .15 .07
❑ 528 Gary Matthews .40 .18
❑ 529 Dave LaRoche .15 .07
❑ 530 Steve Garvey .75 .35
❑ 531 John Curtis .15 .07
❑ 532 Bill Stein .15 .07
❑ 533 Jesus Figueroa .15 .07
❑ 534 Dave Smith RC .40 .18
❑ 535 Omar Moreno .15 .07
❑ 536 Bob Owchinko DP .07 .03
❑ 537 Ron Hodges .15 .07
❑ 538 Tom Griffin .15 .07
❑ 539 Rodney Scott .15 .07
❑ 540 Mike Schmidt DP 2.00 .90
❑ 541 Steve Swisher .15 .07
❑ 542 Larry Bradford DP .07 .03
❑ 543 Terry Crowley .15 .07
❑ 544 Rich Gale .15 .07
❑ 545 Johnny Grubb .15 .07
❑ 546 Paul Moskau .15 .07
❑ 547 Mario Guerrero .15 .07
❑ 548 Dave Goltz .15 .07
❑ 549 Jerry Remy .15 .07
❑ 550 Tommy John .75 .35
❑ 551 Pirates Rookies 1.50 .70
Vance Law
Tony Pena
Pascual Perez RC
❑ 552 Steve Trout .15 .07
❑ 553 Tim Blackwell .15 .07
❑ 554 Bert Blyleven UER .75 .35
(1 is missing from
1980 on card back)
❑ 555 Cecil Cooper .40 .18
❑ 556 Jerry Mumphrey .15 .07
❑ 557 Chris Knapp .15 .07
❑ 558 Barry Bonnell .15 .07
❑ 559 Willie Montanez .15 .07
❑ 560 Joe Morgan 1.50 .70
❑ 561 Dennis Littlejohn .15 .07
❑ 562 Checklist 485-605 .75 .35
❑ 563 Jim Kaat .40 .18
❑ 564 Ron Hassey DP .07 .03
❑ 565 Burt Hooton .15 .07
❑ 566 Del Unser .15 .07
❑ 567 Mark Bomback .15 .07
❑ 568 Dave Revering .15 .07
❑ 569 Al Williams DP .07 .03
❑ 570 Ken Singleton .40 .18
❑ 571 Todd Cruz .15 .07
❑ 572 Jack Morris 1.50 .70
❑ 573 Phil Garner .40 .18
❑ 574 Bill Caudill .15 .07
❑ 575 Tony Perez 1.50 .70
❑ 576 Reggie Cleveland .15 .07
❑ 577 Blue Jays Rookies .15 .07
Luis Leal
Brian Milner
Ken Schrom
❑ 578 Bill Gullickson RC .75 .35
❑ 579 Tim Flannery .15 .07
❑ 580 Don Baylor .75 .35
❑ 581 Roy Howell .15 .07
❑ 582 Gaylord Perry 1.50 .70
❑ 583 Larry Milbourne .15 .07
❑ 584 Randy Lerch .15 .07
❑ 585 Amos Otis .40 .18
❑ 586 Silvio Martinez .15 .07
❑ 587 Jeff Newman .15 .07
❑ 588 Gary Lavelle .15 .07
❑ 589 Lamar Johnson .15 .07
❑ 590 Bruce Sutter .40 .18
❑ 591 John Lowenstein .15 .07
❑ 592 Steve Comer .15 .07
❑ 593 Steve Kemp .15 .07
❑ 594 Preston Hanna DP .07 .03
❑ 595 Butch Hobson .15 .07
❑ 596 Jerry Augustine .15 .07
❑ 597 Rafael Landestoy .15 .07

❑ 598 George Vukovich DP...... .07 .03
❑ 599 Dennis Kinney................ .15 .07
❑ 600 Johnny Bench 2.50 1.10
❑ 601 Don Aase .... .15 .07
❑ 602 Bobby Murcer .... .40 .18
❑ 603 John Verhoeven .... .15 .07
❑ 604 Rob Picciolo .... .15 .07
❑ 605 Don Sutton .... 1.50 .70
❑ 606 Reds Rookies DP .... .15 .07
Bruce Berenyi
Geoff Combe
Paul Householder
❑ 607 David Palmer.................. .15 .07
❑ 608 Greg Pryor...................... .15 .07
❑ 609 Lynn McGlothen .... .15 .07
❑ 610 Darrell Porter.................. .15 .07
❑ 611 Rick Matula DP .... .07 .03
❑ 612 Duane Kuiper .... .15 .07
❑ 613 Jim Anderson .... .15 .07
❑ 614 Dave Rozema .... .15 .07
❑ 615 Rick Dempsey................ .40 .18
❑ 616 Rick Wise .... .15 .07
❑ 617 Craig Reynolds .... .15 .07
❑ 618 John Milner .... .15 .07
❑ 619 Steve Henderson .... .15 .07
❑ 620 Dennis Eckersley .... 1.50 .70
❑ 621 Tom Donohue .... .15 .07
❑ 622 Randy Moffitt.................. .15 .07
❑ 623 Sal Bando .... .40 .18
❑ 624 Bob Welch...................... .40 .18
❑ 625 Bill Buckner .... .40 .18
❑ 626 Tigers Rookies .... .15 .07
Dave Steffen
Jerry Ujdur
Roger Weaver
❑ 627 Luis Tiant........................ .40 .18
❑ 628 Vic Correll .... .15 .07
❑ 629 Tony Armas..................... .40 .18
❑ 630 Steve Carlton .... 1.50 .70
❑ 631 Ron Jackson .... .15 .07
❑ 632 Alan Bannister................. .15 .07
❑ 633 Bill Lee .... .40 .18
❑ 634 Doug Flynn .... .15 .07
❑ 635 Bobby Bonds.................. .40 .18
❑ 636 Al Hrabosky.................... .15 .07
❑ 637 Jerry Narron .... .15 .07
❑ 638 Checklist 606-726 .... .75 .35
❑ 639 Carney Lansford .... .40 .18
❑ 640 Dave Parker .... .40 .18
❑ 641 Mark Belanger................. .40 .18
❑ 642 Vern Ruhle .... .15 .07
❑ 643 Lloyd Moseby .... .40 .18
❑ 644 Ramon Aviles DP .... .07 .03
❑ 645 Rick Reuschel .... .40 .18
❑ 646 Marvis Foley .... .15 .07
❑ 647 Dick Drago .... .15 .07
❑ 648 Darrell Evans.................. .40 .18
❑ 649 Manny Sarmiento .... .15 .07
❑ 650 Bucky Dent .... .40 .18
❑ 651 Pedro Guerrero .... .75 .35
❑ 652 John Montague .... .15 .07
❑ 653 Bill Fahey .... .15 .07
❑ 654 Ray Burris .... .15 .07
❑ 655 Dan Driessen .... .15 .07
❑ 656 Jon Matlack..................... .15 .07
❑ 657 Mike Cubbage DP.......... .07 .03
❑ 658 Milt Wilcox...................... .15 .07
❑ 659 Brewers Rookies............ .15 .07
John Flinn
Ed Romero
Ned Yost
❑ 660 Gary Carter .... .75 .35
❑ 661 Orioles Team/Mgr. .... .75 .35
Earl Weaver
❑ 662 Red Sox Team/Mgr. .... .75 .35
Ralph Houk
❑ 663 Angels Team/Mgr........... .75 .35
Jim Fregosi
❑ 664 White Sox Team/Mgr. ..... .75 .35
Tony LaRussa
❑ 665 Indians Team/Mgr. .... .75 .35
Dave Garcia
❑ 666 Tigers Team/Mgr. .... .75 .35
Sparky Anderson
❑ 667 Royals Team/Mgr........... .75 .35
Jim Frey
❑ 668 Brewers Team/Mgr.......... .75 .35
Bob Rodgers
❑ 669 Twins Team/Mgr. .... .75 .35
John Goryl
❑ 670 Yankees Team/Mgr. .... .75 .35
Gene Michael
❑ 671 A's Team/Mgr................. .75 .35
Billy Martin
❑ 672 Mariners Team/Mgr. .... .75 .35
Maury Wills
❑ 673 Rangers Team/Mgr. .... .75 .35
Don Zimmer
❑ 674 Blue Jays Team/Mgr. ..... .75 .35
Bobby Mattick
❑ 675 Braves Team/Mgr........... .75 .35
Bobby Cox
❑ 676 Cubs Team/Mgr. .... .75 .35
Joe Amalfitano
❑ 677 Reds Team/Mgr. .... .75 .35
John McNamara
❑ 678 Astros Team/Mgr. .... .75 .35
Bill Virdon
❑ 679 Dodgers Team/Mgr. .... .75 .35
Tom Lasorda
❑ 680 Expos Team/Mgr. .... .75 .35
Dick Williams
❑ 681 Mets Team/Mgr. .... .75 .35
Joe Torre
❑ 682 Phillies Team/Mgr. .... .75 .35
Dallas Green
❑ 683 Pirates Team/Mgr........... .75 .35
Chuck Tanner
❑ 684 Cardinals Team/Mgr....... .75 .35
Whitey Herzog
❑ 685 Padres Team/Mgr. .... .75 .35
Frank Howard
❑ 686 Giants Team/Mgr. .... .75 .35
Dave Bristol
❑ 687 Jeff Jones .... .15 .07
❑ 688 Kiko Garcia .... .15 .07
❑ 689 Red Sox Rookies .... 1.50 .70
Bruce Hurst RC
Keith MacWhorter
Reid Nichols
❑ 690 Bob Watson..................... .40 .18
❑ 691 Dick Ruthven.................. .15 .07
❑ 692 Lenny Randle .... .15 .07
❑ 693 Steve Howe.................... .40 .18
❑ 694 Bud Harrelson DP .... .15 .07
❑ 695 Kent Tekulve .... .40 .18
❑ 696 Alan Ashby .... .15 .07
❑ 697 Rick Waits....................... .15 .07
❑ 698 Mike Jorgensen.............. .15 .07
❑ 699 Glenn Abbott................... .15 .07
❑ 700 George Brett 4.00 1.80
❑ 701 Joe Rudi .... .40 .18
❑ 702 George Medich .... .15 .07
❑ 703 Alvis Woods .... .15 .07
❑ 704 Bill Travers DP .... .07 .03
❑ 705 Ted Simmons .... .40 .18
❑ 706 Dave Ford .... .15 .07
❑ 707 Dave Cash .... .15 .07
❑ 708 Doyle Alexander .... .15 .07
❑ 709 Alan Trammell DP .... .75 .35
❑ 710 Ron LeFlore DP .... .15 .07
❑ 711 Joe Ferguson .... .15 .07
❑ 712 Bill Bonham.................... .15 .07
❑ 713 Bill North .... .15 .07
❑ 714 Pete Redfern.................. .15 .07
❑ 715 Bill Madlock.................... .40 .18
❑ 716 Glenn Borgmann .... .15 .07
❑ 717 Jim Barr DP.................... .07 .03
❑ 718 Larry Biittner .... .15 .07
❑ 719 Sparky Lyle .... .40 .18
❑ 720 Fred Lynn .... .40 .18
❑ 721 Toby Harrah .... .40 .18
❑ 722 Joe Niekro....................... .40 .18
❑ 723 Bruce Bochte.................. .15 .07
❑ 724 Lou Piniella .... .40 .18
❑ 725 Steve Rogers .... .15 .07
❑ 726 Rick Monday .... .40 .18

1981 Topps Traded

	NRMT	VG-E
COMP.FACT.SET (132)..........	25.00	11.00

❑ 727 Danny Ainge XRC........ 5.00 2.20
❑ 728 Doyle Alexander .... .25 .11
❑ 729 Gary Alexander............. .25 .11
❑ 730 Bill Almon .... .25 .11
❑ 731 Joaquin Andujar .... 1.00 .45
❑ 732 Bob Bailor .... .25 .11
❑ 733 Juan Beniquez .... .25 .11
❑ 734 Dave Bergman .... .25 .11
❑ 735 Tony Bernazard.............. .25 .11
❑ 736 Larry Biittner .... .25 .11
❑ 737 Doug Bird .... .25 .11
❑ 738 Bert Blyleven .... 1.50 .70
❑ 739 Mark Bomback .... .25 .11
❑ 740 Bobby Bonds............... 1.00 .45
❑ 741 Rick Bosetti .... .25 .11
❑ 742 Hubie Brooks............... 1.00 .45
❑ 743 Rick Burleson .... .25 .11
❑ 744 Ray Burris .... .25 .11
❑ 745 Jeff Burroughs................ .25 .11
❑ 746 Enos Cabell.................... .25 .11
❑ 747 Ken Clay .... .25 .11
❑ 748 Mark Clear...................... .25 .11
❑ 749 Larry Cox........................ .25 .11
❑ 750 Hector Cruz .... .25 .11
❑ 751 Victor Cruz .... .25 .11
❑ 752 Mike Cubbage................ .25 .11
❑ 753 Dick Davis .... .25 .11
❑ 754 Brian Doyle .... .25 .11
❑ 755 Dick Drago .... .25 .11
❑ 756 Leon Durham .... 1.00 .45
❑ 757 Jim Dwyer .... .25 .11
❑ 758 Dave Edwards UER ...... .25 .11
No birthdate on card
❑ 759 Jim Essian...................... .25 .11
❑ 760 Bill Fahey .... .25 .11
❑ 761 Rollie Fingers 2.50 1.10
❑ 762 Carlton Fisk................. 5.00 2.20
❑ 763 Barry Foote .... .25 .11
❑ 764 Ken Forsch..................... .25 .11
❑ 765 Kiko Garcia .... .25 .11
❑ 766 Cesar Geronimo .... .25 .11
❑ 767 Gary Gray .... .25 .11
❑ 768 Mickey Hatcher .... 1.00 .45
❑ 769 Steve Henderson .... .25 .11
❑ 770 Marc Hill .... .25 .11
❑ 771 Butch Hobson .... .25 .11
❑ 772 Rick Honeycutt .... .25 .11
❑ 773 Roy Howell .... .25 .11
❑ 774 Mike Ivie .... .25 .11
❑ 775 Roy Lee Jackson............ .25 .11
❑ 776 Cliff Johnson.................. .25 .11
❑ 777 Randy Jones .... .25 .11
❑ 778 Ruppert Jones............... .25 .11
❑ 779 Mick Kelleher.................. .25 .11
❑ 780 Terry Kennedy................ .25 .11
❑ 781 Dave Kingman............. 1.50 .70
❑ 782 Bob Knepper .... .25 .11
❑ 783 Ken Kravec .... .25 .11
❑ 784 Bob Lacey .... .25 .11
❑ 785 Dennis Lamp.................. .25 .11
❑ 786 Rafael Landestoy .... .25 .11
❑ 787 Ken Landreaux .... .25 .11
❑ 788 Carney Lansford .... 1.00 .45

❑ 789 Dave LaRoche .25 .11
❑ 790 Joe Lefebvre .25 .11
❑ 791 Ron LeFlore 1.00 .45
❑ 792 Randy Lerch .25 .11
❑ 793 Sixto Lezcano .25 .11
❑ 794 John Littlefield .25 .11
❑ 795 Mike Lum .25 .11
❑ 796 Greg Luzinski 1.00 .45
❑ 797 Fred Lynn 1.00 .45
❑ 798 Jerry Martin .25 .11
❑ 799 Buck Martinez .25 .11
❑ 800 Gary Matthews 1.00 .45
❑ 801 Mario Mendoza .25 .11
❑ 802 Larry Milbourne .25 .11
❑ 803 Rick Miller .25 .11
❑ 804 John Montefusco .25 .11
❑ 805 Jerry Morales .25 .11
❑ 806 Jose Morales .25 .11
❑ 807 Joe Morgan 2.50 1.10
❑ 808 Jerry Mumphrey .25 .11
❑ 809 Gene Nelson .25 .11
❑ 810 Ed Ott .25 .11
❑ 811 Bob Owchinko .25 .11
❑ 812 Gaylord Perry 2.50 1.10
❑ 813 Mike Phillips .25 .11
❑ 814 Darrell Porter .25 .11
❑ 815 Mike Proly .25 .11
❑ 816 Tim Raines 5.00 2.20
❑ 817 Lenny Randle .25 .11
❑ 818 Doug Rau .25 .11
❑ 819 Jeff Reardon 2.50 1.10
❑ 820 Ken Reitz .25 .11
❑ 821 Steve Renko .25 .11
❑ 822 Rick Reuschel 1.00 .45
❑ 823 Dave Revering .25 .11
❑ 824 Dave Roberts .25 .11
❑ 825 Leon Roberts .25 .11
❑ 826 Joe Rudi 1.00 .45
❑ 827 Kevin Saucier .25 .11
❑ 828 Tony Scott .25 .11
❑ 829 Bob Shirley .25 .11
❑ 830 Ted Simmons 1.00 .45
❑ 831 Lary Sorensen .25 .11
❑ 832 Jim Spencer .25 .11
❑ 833 Harry Spilman .25 .11
❑ 834 Fred Stanley .25 .11
❑ 835 Rusty Staub 1.00 .45
❑ 836 Bill Stein .25 .11
❑ 837 Joe Strain .25 .11
❑ 838 Bruce Sutter 1.00 .45
❑ 839 Don Sutton 2.50 1.10
❑ 840 Steve Swisher .25 .11
❑ 841 Frank Tanana 1.00 .45
❑ 842 Gene Tenace 1.00 .45
❑ 843 Jason Thompson .25 .11
❑ 844 Dickie Thon 1.00 .45
❑ 845 Bill Travers .25 .11
❑ 846 Tom Underwood .25 .11
❑ 847 John Urrea .25 .11
❑ 848 Mike Vail .25 .11
❑ 849 Ellis Valentine .25 .11
❑ 850 Fernando Valenzuela 5.00 2.20
❑ 851 Pete Vuckovich 1.00 .45
❑ 852 Mark Wagner .25 .11
❑ 853 Bob Walk 1.00 .45
❑ 854 Claudell Washington .25 .11
❑ 855 Dave Winfield 5.00 2.20
❑ 856 Geoff Zahn .25 .11
❑ 857 Richie Zisk .25 .11
❑ 858 Checklist 727-858 .25 .11

1982 Topps

	NRMT	VG-E
COMPLETE SET (792)	100.00	45.00

❑ 1 Steve Carlton HL 1.25 .55
Sets new NL strikeout record
❑ 2 Ron Davis HL .15 .07
Fans 8 straight in relief
❑ 3 Tim Raines HL .60 .25
71 steals as rookie
❑ 4 Pete Rose HL .60 .25
Sets NL hit mark
❑ 5 Nolan Ryan HL 3.00 1.35
Pitches fifth no-hitter
❑ 6 Fernando Valenzuela HL .60 .25
8 shutouts as rookie
❑ 7 Scott Sanderson .15 .07
❑ 8 Rich Dauer .15 .07
❑ 9 Ron Guidry .30 .14
❑ 10 Ron Guidry SA .15 .07
❑ 11 Gary Alexander .15 .07
❑ 12 Moose Haas .15 .07
❑ 13 Lamar Johnson .15 .07
❑ 14 Steve Howe .15 .07
❑ 15 Ellis Valentine .15 .07
❑ 16 Steve Comer .15 .07
❑ 17 Darrell Evans .30 .14
❑ 18 Fernando Arroyo .15 .07
❑ 19 Ernie Whitt .15 .07
❑ 20 Garry Maddox .15 .07
❑ 22 Jim Beattie .15 .07
❑ 23 Willie Hernandez .30 .14
❑ 24 Dave Frost .15 .07
❑ 25 Jerry Remy .15 .07
❑ 26 Jorge Orta .15 .07
❑ 27 Tom Herr .30 .14
❑ 28 John Urrea .15 .07
❑ 29 Dwayne Murphy .15 .07
❑ 30 Tom Seaver 2.00 .90
❑ 31 Tom Seaver SA .60 .25
❑ 32 Gene Garber .15 .07
❑ 33 Jerry Morales .15 .07
❑ 34 Joe Sambito .15 .07
❑ 35 Willie Aikens .15 .07
❑ 36 Rangers TL .60 .25
BA: Al Oliver
Pitching: Doc Medich
❑ 37 Dan Graham .15 .07
❑ 38 Charlie Lea .15 .07
❑ 39 Lou Whitaker 1.25 .55
❑ 40 Dave Parker .30 .14
❑ 41 Dave Parker SA .15 .07
❑ 42 Rick Sofield .15 .07
❑ 43 Mike Cubbage .15 .07
❑ 44 Britt Burns .15 .07
❑ 45 Rick Cerone .15 .07
❑ 46 Jerry Augustine .15 .07
❑ 47 Jeff Leonard .15 .07
❑ 48 Bobby Castillo .15 .07
❑ 49 Alvis Woods .15 .07
❑ 50 Buddy Bell .30 .14
❑ 51 Cubs Rookies .60 .25
Jay Howell RC
Carlos Lezcano
Ty Waller
❑ 52 Larry Andersen .15 .07
❑ 53 Greg Gross .15 .07
❑ 54 Ron Hassey .15 .07
❑ 55 Rick Burleson .15 .07
❑ 56 Mark Littell .15 .07
❑ 57 Craig Reynolds .15 .07
❑ 58 John D'Acquisto .15 .07
❑ 59 Rich Gedman .30 .14
❑ 60 Tony Armas .15 .07
❑ 61 Tommy Boggs .15 .07
❑ 62 Mike Tyson .15 .07
❑ 63 Mario Soto .15 .07
❑ 64 Lynn Jones .15 .07
❑ 65 Terry Kennedy .15 .07
❑ 66 Astros TL 2.00 .90
BA: Art Howe
Pitching: Nolan Ryan
❑ 67 Rich Gale .15 .07
❑ 68 Roy Howell .15 .07
❑ 69 Al Williams .15 .07
❑ 70 Tim Raines 1.25 .55
❑ 71 Roy Lee Jackson .15 .07
❑ 72 Rick Auerbach .15 .07
❑ 73 Buddy Solomon .15 .07
❑ 74 Bob Clark .15 .07
❑ 75 Tommy John .60 .25
❑ 76 Greg Pryor .15 .07
❑ 77 Miguel Dilone .15 .07
❑ 78 George Medich .15 .07
❑ 79 Bob Bailor .15 .07
❑ 80 Jim Palmer 1.25 .55
❑ 81 Jim Palmer SA .60 .25
❑ 82 Bob Welch .30 .14
❑ 83 Yankees Rookies .60 .25
Steve Balboni RC
Andy McGaffigan
Andre Robertson
❑ 84 Rennie Stennett .15 .07
❑ 85 Lynn McGlothen .15 .07
❑ 86 Dane Iorg .15 .07
❑ 87 Matt Keough .15 .07
❑ 88 Biff Pocoroba .15 .07
❑ 89 Steve Henderson .15 .07
❑ 90 Nolan Ryan 6.00 2.70
❑ 91 Carney Lansford .30 .14
❑ 92 Brad Havens .15 .07
❑ 93 Larry Hisle .15 .07
❑ 94 Andy Hassler .15 .07
❑ 95 Ozzie Smith 2.50 1.10
❑ 96 Royals TL 1.25 .55
BA: George Brett
Pitching: Larry Gura
❑ 97 Paul Moskau .15 .07
❑ 98 Terry Bulling .15 .07
❑ 99 Barry Bonnell .15 .07
❑ 100 Mike Schmidt 2.50 1.10
❑ 101 Mike Schmidt SA .60 .25
❑ 102 Dan Briggs .15 .07
❑ 103 Bob Lacey .15 .07
❑ 104 Rance Mulliniks .15 .07
❑ 105 Kirk Gibson 1.25 .55
❑ 106 Enrique Romo .15 .07
❑ 107 Wayne Krenchicki .15 .07
❑ 108 Bob Sykes .15 .07
❑ 109 Dave Revering .15 .07
❑ 110 Carlton Fisk 1.25 .55
❑ 111 Carlton Fisk SA .60 .25
❑ 112 Billy Sample .15 .07
❑ 113 Steve McCatty .15 .07
❑ 114 Ken Landreaux .15 .07
❑ 115 Gaylord Perry 1.25 .55
❑ 116 Jim Wohlford .15 .07
❑ 117 Rawly Eastwick .15 .07
❑ 118 Expos Rookies .30 .14
Terry Francona
Brad Mills
Bryn Smith RC
❑ 119 Joe Pittman .15 .07
❑ 120 Gary Lucas .15 .07
❑ 121 Ed Lynch .15 .07
❑ 122 Jamie Easterly UER .15 .07
(Photo actually
Reggie Cleveland)
❑ 123 Danny Goodwin .15 .07
❑ 124 Reid Nichols .15 .07
❑ 125 Danny Ainge 1.50 .70
❑ 126 Braves TL .60 .25
BA: Claudell Washington
Pitching: Rick Mahler
❑ 127 Lonnie Smith .30 .14
❑ 128 Frank Pastore .15 .07
❑ 129 Checklist 1-132 .60 .25
❑ 130 Julio Cruz .15 .07
❑ 131 Stan Bahnsen .15 .07
❑ 132 Lee May .30 .14
❑ 133 Pat Underwood .15 .07
❑ 134 Dan Ford .15 .07
❑ 135 Andy Rincon .15 .07
❑ 136 Lenn Sakata .15 .07
❑ 137 George Cappuzzello .15 .07
❑ 138 Tony Pena .30 .14
❑ 139 Jeff Jones .15 .07

❑ 140 Ron LeFlore .30 .14
❑ 141 Indians Rookies .30 .14
Chris Bando
Tom Brennan
Von Hayes
❑ 142 Dave LaRoche .15 .07
❑ 143 Mookie Wilson .30 .14
❑ 144 Fred Breining .15 .07
❑ 145 Bob Horner .30 .14
❑ 146 Mike Griffin .15 .07
❑ 147 Denny Walling .15 .07
❑ 148 Mickey Klutts .15 .07
❑ 149 Pat Putnam .15 .07
❑ 150 Ted Simmons .30 .14
❑ 151 Dave Edwards .15 .07
❑ 152 Ramon Aviles .15 .07
❑ 153 Roger Erickson .15 .07
❑ 154 Dennis Werth .15 .07
❑ 155 Otto Velez .15 .07
❑ 156 Oakland A's TL 1.25 .55
BA: Rickey Henderson
Pitching: Steve McCatty
❑ 157 Steve Crawford .15 .07
❑ 158 Brian Downing .15 .07
❑ 159 Larry Biittner .15 .07
❑ 160 Luis Tiant .30 .14
❑ 161 Batting Leaders .30 .14
Bill Madlock
Carney Lansford
❑ 162 Home Run Leaders 1.25 .55
Mike Schmidt
Tony Armas
Dwight Evans
Bobby Grich
Eddie Murray
❑ 163 RBI Leaders 1.25 .55
Mike Schmidt
Eddie Murray
❑ 164 Stolen Base Leaders 1.25 .55
Tim Raines
Rickey Henderson
❑ 165 Victory Leaders .60 .25
Tom Seaver
Denny Martinez
Steve McCatty
Jack Morris
Pete Vuckovich
❑ 166 Strikeout Leaders .30 .14
Fernando Valenzuela
Len Barker
❑ 167 ERA Leaders 2.00 .90
Nolan Ryan
Steve McCatty
❑ 168 Leading Firemen .60 .25
Bruce Sutter
Rollie Fingers
❑ 169 Charlie Leibrandt .15 .07
❑ 170 Jim Bibby .15 .07
❑ 171 Giants Rookies 3.00 1.35
Bob Brenly
Chili Davis RC
Bob Tufts
❑ 172 Bill Gullickson .15 .07
❑ 173 Jamie Quirk .15 .07
❑ 174 Dave Ford .15 .07
❑ 175 Jerry Mumphrey .15 .07
❑ 176 Dewey Robinson .15 .07
❑ 177 John Ellis .15 .07
❑ 178 Dyar Miller .15 .07
❑ 179 Steve Garvey .60 .25
❑ 180 Steve Garvey SA .30 .14
❑ 181 Silvio Martinez .15 .07
❑ 182 Larry Herndon .15 .07
❑ 183 Mike Proly .15 .07
❑ 184 Mick Kelleher .15 .07
❑ 185 Phil Niekro 1.25 .55
❑ 186 Cardinals TL .60 .25
BA: Keith Hernandez
Pitching: Bob Forsch
❑ 187 Jeff Newman .15 .07
❑ 188 Randy Martz .15 .07
❑ 189 Glenn Hoffman .15 .07
❑ 190 J.R. Richard .30 .14
❑ 191 Tim Wallach RC .60 .25
❑ 192 Broderick Perkins .15 .07
❑ 193 Darrell Jackson .15 .07
❑ 194 Mike Vail .15 .07
❑ 195 Paul Molitor 1.50 .70
❑ 196 Willie Upshaw .15 .07
❑ 197 Shane Rawley .15 .07
❑ 198 Chris Speier .15 .07
❑ 199 Don Aase .15 .07
❑ 200 George Brett 2.50 1.10
❑ 201 George Brett SA 1.25 .55
❑ 202 Rick Manning .15 .07
❑ 203 Blue Jays Rookies .60 .25
Jesse Barfield RC
Brian Milner
Boomer Wells
❑ 204 Gary Roenicke .15 .07
❑ 205 Neil Allen .15 .07
❑ 206 Tony Bernazard .15 .07
❑ 207 Rod Scurry .15 .07
❑ 208 Bobby Murcer .30 .14
❑ 209 Gary Lavelle .15 .07
❑ 210 Keith Hernandez .30 .14
❑ 211 Dan Petry .15 .07
❑ 212 Mario Mendoza .15 .07
❑ 213 Dave Stewart RC 1.50 .70
❑ 214 Brian Asselstine .15 .07
❑ 215 Mike Krukow .15 .07
❑ 216 White Sox TL .60 .25
BA: Chet Lemon
Pitching: Dennis Lamp
❑ 217 Bo McLaughlin .15 .07
❑ 218 Dave Roberts .15 .07
❑ 219 John Curtis .15 .07
❑ 220 Manny Trillo .15 .07
❑ 221 Jim Slaton .15 .07
❑ 222 Butch Wynegar .15 .07
❑ 223 Lloyd Moseby .15 .07
❑ 224 Bruce Bochte .15 .07
❑ 225 Mike Torrez .15 .07
❑ 226 Checklist 133-264 .60 .25
❑ 227 Ray Burris .15 .07
❑ 228 Sam Mejias .15 .07
❑ 229 Geoff Zahn .15 .07
❑ 230 Willie Wilson .30 .14
❑ 231 Phillies Rookies .60 .25
Mark Davis RC
Bob Dernier
Ozzie Virgil
❑ 232 Terry Crowley .15 .07
❑ 233 Duane Kuiper .15 .07
❑ 234 Ron Hodges .15 .07
❑ 235 Mike Easler .15 .07
❑ 236 John Martin .15 .07
❑ 237 Rusty Kuntz .15 .07
❑ 238 Kevin Saucier .15 .07
❑ 239 Jon Matlack .15 .07
❑ 240 Bucky Dent .30 .14
❑ 241 Bucky Dent SA .15 .07
❑ 242 Milt May .15 .07
❑ 243 Bob Owchinko .15 .07
❑ 244 Rufino Linares .15 .07
❑ 245 Ken Reitz .15 .07
❑ 246 New York Mets TL .60 .25
BA: Hubie Brooks
Pitching: Mike Scott
❑ 247 Pedro Guerrero .30 .14
❑ 248 Frank LaCorte .15 .07
❑ 249 Tim Flannery .15 .07
❑ 250 Tug McGraw .30 .14
❑ 251 Fred Lynn .30 .14
❑ 252 Fred Lynn SA .15 .07
❑ 253 Chuck Baker .15 .07
❑ 254 Jorge Bell RC 1.25 .55
❑ 255 Tony Perez 1.25 .55
❑ 256 Tony Perez SA .60 .25
❑ 257 Larry Harlow .15 .07
❑ 258 Bo Diaz .15 .07
❑ 259 Rodney Scott .15 .07
❑ 260 Bruce Sutter .30 .14
❑ 261 Tigers Rookies UER .15 .07
Howard Bailey
Marty Castillo
Dave Rucker
(Rucker photo actually Roger Weaver)
❑ 262 Doug Bair .15 .07
❑ 263 Victor Cruz .15 .07
❑ 264 Dan Quisenberry .30 .14
❑ 265 Al Bumbry .15 .07
❑ 266 Rick Leach .15 .07
❑ 267 Kurt Bevacqua .15 .07
❑ 268 Rickey Keeton .15 .07
❑ 269 Jim Essian .15 .07
❑ 270 Rusty Staub .30 .14
❑ 271 Larry Bradford .15 .07
❑ 272 Bump Wills .15 .07
❑ 273 Doug Bird .15 .07
❑ 274 Bob Ojeda RC .60 .25
❑ 275 Bob Watson .30 .14
❑ 276 Angels TL .60 .25
BA: Rod Carew
Pitching: Ken Forsch
❑ 277 Terry Puhl .15 .07
❑ 278 John Littlefield .15 .07
❑ 279 Bill Russell .15 .07
❑ 280 Ben Oglivie .30 .14
❑ 281 John Verhoeven .15 .07
❑ 282 Ken Macha .15 .07
❑ 283 Brian Allard .15 .07
❑ 284 Bobby Grich .30 .14
❑ 285 Sparky Lyle .30 .14
❑ 286 Bill Fahey .15 .07
❑ 287 Alan Bannister .15 .07
❑ 288 Garry Templeton .15 .07
❑ 289 Bob Stanley .15 .07
❑ 290 Ken Singleton .30 .14
❑ 291 Pirates Rookies .30 .14
Vance Law
Bob Long
Johnny Ray
❑ 292 David Palmer .15 .07
❑ 293 Rob Picciolo .15 .07
❑ 294 Mike LaCoss .15 .07
❑ 295 Jason Thompson .15 .07
❑ 296 Bob Walk .15 .07
❑ 297 Clint Hurdle .15 .07
❑ 298 Danny Darwin .15 .07
❑ 299 Steve Trout .15 .07
❑ 300 Reggie Jackson 1.50 .70
❑ 301 Reggie Jackson SA .60 .25
❑ 302 Doug Flynn .15 .07
❑ 303 Bill Caudill .15 .07
❑ 304 Johnnie LeMaster .15 .07
❑ 305 Don Sutton 1.25 .55
❑ 306 Don Sutton SA .60 .25
❑ 307 Randy Bass RC .15 .07
❑ 308 Charlie Moore .15 .07
❑ 309 Pete Redfern .15 .07
❑ 310 Mike Hargrove .30 .14
❑ 311 Dodgers TL .60 .25
BA: Dusty Baker
Pitching: Burt Hooton
❑ 312 Lenny Randle .15 .07
❑ 313 John Harris .15 .07
❑ 314 Buck Martinez .15 .07
❑ 315 Burt Hooton .15 .07
❑ 316 Steve Braun .15 .07
❑ 317 Dick Ruthven .15 .07
❑ 318 Mike Heath .15 .07
❑ 319 Dave Rozema .15 .07
❑ 320 Chris Chambliss .30 .14
❑ 321 Chris Chambliss SA .15 .07
❑ 322 Garry Hancock .15 .07
❑ 323 Bill Lee .30 .14
❑ 324 Steve Dillard .15 .07
❑ 325 Jose Cruz .30 .14
❑ 326 Pete Falcone .15 .07
❑ 327 Joe Nolan .15 .07
❑ 328 Ed Farmer .15 .07
❑ 329 U.L. Washington .15 .07
❑ 330 Rick Wise .15 .07
❑ 331 Benny Ayala .15 .07
❑ 332 Don Robinson .15 .07
❑ 333 Brewers Rookies .15 .07
Frank DiPino
Marshall Edwards
Chuck Porter
❑ 334 Aurelio Rodriguez .15 .07
❑ 335 Jim Sundberg .15 .07
❑ 336 Mariners TL .60 .25
BA: Tom Paciorek
Pitching: Glenn Abbott
❑ 337 Pete Rose AS .60 .25
❑ 338 Dave Lopes AS .15 .07

❑ 339 Mike Schmidt AS .60 .25
❑ 340 Dave Concepcion AS .15 .07
❑ 341 Andre Dawson AS .30 .14
❑ 342A George Foster AS .30 .14
(With autograph)
❑ 342B George Foster AS 1.25 .55
(W/o autograph)
❑ 343 Dave Parker AS .15 .07
❑ 344 Gary Carter AS .30 .14
❑ 345 Fernando Valenzuela AS .60 .25
❑ 346 Tom Seaver AS ERR .. 1.25 .55
("t ed")
❑ 346B Tom Seaver AS COR 1.25 .55
("tied")
❑ 347 Bruce Sutter AS .15 .07
❑ 348 Derrel Thomas .15 .07
❑ 349 George Frazier .15 .07
❑ 350 Thad Bosley .15 .07
❑ 351 Reds Rookies .15 .07
Scott Brown
Geoff Combe
Paul Householder
❑ 352 Dick Davis .15 .07
❑ 353 Jack O'Connor .15 .07
❑ 354 Roberto Ramos .15 .07
❑ 355 Dwight Evans .60 .25
❑ 356 Denny Lewallyn .15 .07
❑ 357 Butch Hobson .15 .07
❑ 358 Mike Parrott .15 .07
❑ 359 Jim Dwyer .15 .07
❑ 360 Len Barker .15 .07
❑ 361 Rafael Landestoy .15 .07
❑ 362 Jim Wright UER .15 .07
(Wrong Jim Wright pictured)
❑ 363 Bob Molinaro .15 .07
❑ 364 Doyle Alexander .15 .07
❑ 365 Bill Madlock .30 .14
❑ 366 Padres TL .60 .25
BA: Luis Salazar
Pitching: Juan Eichelberger
❑ 367 Jim Kaat .30 .14
❑ 368 Alex Trevino .15 .07
❑ 369 Champ Summers .15 .07
❑ 370 Mike Norris .15 .07
❑ 371 Jerry Don Gleaton .15 .07
❑ 372 Luis Gomez .15 .07
❑ 373 Gene Nelson .15 .07
❑ 374 Tim Blackwell .15 .07
❑ 375 Dusty Baker .60 .25
❑ 376 Chris Welsh .15 .07
❑ 377 Kiko Garcia .15 .07
❑ 378 Mike Caldwell .15 .07
❑ 379 Rob Wilfong .15 .07
❑ 380 Dave Stieb .30 .14
❑ 381 Red Sox Rookies .30 .14
Bruce Hurst
Dave Schmidt
Julio Valdez
❑ 382 Joe Simpson .15 .07
❑ 383A Pascual Perez ERR 40.00 18.00
(No position on front)
❑ 383B Pascual Perez COR .30 .14
❑ 384 Keith Moreland .15 .07
❑ 385 Ken Forsch .15 .07
❑ 386 Jerry White .15 .07
❑ 387 Tom Veryzer .15 .07
❑ 388 Joe Rudi .15 .07
❑ 389 George Vukovich .15 .07
❑ 390 Eddie Murray 1.50 .70
❑ 391 Dave Tobik .15 .07
❑ 392 Rick Bosetti .15 .07
❑ 393 Al Hrabosky .15 .07
❑ 394 Checklist 265-396 .60 .25
❑ 395 Omar Moreno .15 .07
❑ 396 Twins TL .60 .25
BA: John Castino
Fernando Arroyo
❑ 397 Ken Brett .15 .07
❑ 398 Mike Squires .15 .07
❑ 399 Pat Zachry .15 .07
❑ 400 Johnny Bench 2.00 .90
❑ 401 Johnny Bench SA .60 .25
❑ 402 Bill Stein .15 .07
❑ 403 Jim Tracy .15 .07
❑ 404 Dickie Thon .15 .07
❑ 405 Rick Reuschel .30 .14
❑ 406 Al Holland .15 .07
❑ 407 Danny Boone .15 .07
❑ 408 Ed Romero .15 .07
❑ 409 Don Cooper .15 .07
❑ 410 Ron Cey .30 .14
❑ 411 Ron Cey SA .15 .07
❑ 412 Luis Leal .15 .07
❑ 413 Dan Meyer .15 .07
❑ 414 Elias Sosa .15 .07
❑ 415 Don Baylor .60 .25
❑ 416 Marty Bystrom .15 .07
❑ 417 Pat Kelly .15 .07
❑ 418 Rangers Rookies .15 .07
John Butcher
Bobby Johnson
Dave Schmidt
❑ 419 Steve Stone .30 .14
❑ 420 George Hendrick .15 .07
❑ 421 Mark Clear .15 .07
❑ 422 Cliff Johnson .15 .07
❑ 423 Stan Papi .15 .07
❑ 424 Bruce Benedict .15 .07
❑ 425 John Candelaria .15 .07
❑ 426 Orioles TL .60 .25
BA: Eddie Murray
Pitching: Sammy Stewart
❑ 427 Ron Oester .15 .07
❑ 428 LaMarr Hoyt .15 .07
❑ 429 John Wathan .15 .07
❑ 430 Vida Blue .30 .14
❑ 431 Vida Blue SA .15 .07
❑ 432 Mike Scott .30 .14
❑ 433 Alan Ashby .15 .07
❑ 434 Joe Lefebvre .15 .07
❑ 435 Robin Yount 1.25 .55
❑ 436 Joe Strain .15 .07
❑ 437 Juan Berenguer .15 .07
❑ 438 Pete Mackanin .15 .07
❑ 439 Dave Righetti RC 1.25 .55
❑ 440 Jeff Burroughs .15 .07
❑ 441 Astros Rookies .15 .07
Danny Heep
Billy Smith
Bobby Sprowl
❑ 442 Bruce Kison .15 .07
❑ 443 Mark Wagner .15 .07
❑ 444 Terry Forster .15 .07
❑ 445 Larry Parrish .15 .07
❑ 446 Wayne Garland .15 .07
❑ 447 Darrell Porter .30 .14
❑ 448 Darrell Porter SA .15 .07
❑ 449 Luis Aguayo .15 .07
❑ 450 Jack Morris .30 .14
❑ 451 Ed Miller .15 .07
❑ 452 Lee Smith RC 3.00 1.35
❑ 453 Art Howe .30 .14
❑ 454 Rick Langford .15 .07
❑ 455 Tom Burgmeier .15 .07
❑ 456 Chicago Cubs TL .60 .25
BA: Bill Buckner
Pitching: Randy Martz
❑ 457 Tim Stoddard .15 .07
❑ 458 Willie Montanez .15 .07
❑ 459 Bruce Berenyi .15 .07
❑ 460 Jack Clark .30 .14
❑ 461 Rich Dotson .15 .07
❑ 462 Dave Chalk .15 .07
❑ 463 Jim Kern .15 .07
❑ 464 Juan Bonilla .15 .07
❑ 465 Lee Mazzilli .15 .07
❑ 466 Randy Lerch .15 .07
❑ 467 Mickey Hatcher .15 .07
❑ 468 Floyd Bannister .15 .07
❑ 469 Ed Ott .15 .07
❑ 470 John Mayberry .15 .07
❑ 471 Royals Rookies .15 .07
Atlee Hammaker
Mike Jones
Darryl Motley
❑ 472 Oscar Gamble .15 .07
❑ 473 Mike Stanton .15 .07
❑ 474 Ken Oberkfell .15 .07
❑ 475 Alan Trammell .60 .25
❑ 476 Brian Kingman .15 .07
❑ 477 Steve Yeager .15 .07
❑ 478 Ray Searage .15 .07
❑ 479 Rowland Office .15 .07
❑ 480 Steve Carlton 1.25 .55
❑ 481 Steve Carlton SA .60 .25
❑ 482 Glenn Hubbard .15 .07
❑ 483 Gary Woods .15 .07
❑ 484 Ivan DeJesus .15 .07
❑ 485 Kent Tekulve .30 .14
❑ 486 Yankees TL .30 .14
BA: Jerry Mumphrey
Pitching: Tommy John
❑ 487 Bob McClure .15 .07
❑ 488 Ron Jackson .15 .07
❑ 489 Rick Dempsey .30 .14
❑ 490 Dennis Eckersley 1.25 .55
❑ 491 Checklist 397-528 .60 .25
❑ 492 Joe Price .15 .07
❑ 493 Chet Lemon .15 .07
❑ 494 Hubie Brooks .30 .14
❑ 495 Dennis Leonard .15 .07
❑ 496 Johnny Grubb .15 .07
❑ 497 Jim Anderson .15 .07
❑ 498 Dave Bergman .15 .07
❑ 499 Paul Mirabella .15 .07
❑ 500 Rod Carew 1.25 .55
❑ 501 Rod Carew SA .60 .25
❑ 502 Braves Rookies 1.50 .70
Steve Bedrosian UER
(Photo actually Larry Owen)
Brett Butler RC
Larry Owen
❑ 503 Julio Gonzalez .15 .07
❑ 504 Rick Peters .15 .07
❑ 505 Graig Nettles .30 .14
❑ 506 Graig Nettles SA .15 .07
❑ 507 Terry Harper .15 .07
❑ 508 Jody Davis .15 .07
❑ 509 Harry Spilman .15 .07
❑ 510 Fernando Valenzuela .. 1.25 .55
❑ 511 Ruppert Jones .15 .07
❑ 512 Jerry Dybzinski .15 .07
❑ 513 Rick Rhoden .15 .07
❑ 514 Joe Ferguson .15 .07
❑ 515 Larry Bowa .30 .14
❑ 516 Larry Bowa SA .15 .07
❑ 517 Mark Brouhard .15 .07
❑ 518 Garth Iorg .15 .07
❑ 519 Glenn Adams .15 .07
❑ 520 Mike Flanagan .30 .14
❑ 521 Bill Almon .15 .07
❑ 522 Chuck Rainey .15 .07
❑ 523 Gary Gray .15 .07
❑ 524 Tom Hausman .15 .07
❑ 525 Ray Knight .30 .14
❑ 526 Expos TL .60 .25
BA: Warren Cromartie
Pitching: Bill Gullickson
❑ 527 John Henry Johnson .15 .07
❑ 528 Matt Alexander .15 .07
❑ 529 Allen Ripley .15 .07
❑ 530 Dickie Noles .15 .07
❑ 531 A's Rookies .15 .07
Rich Bordi
Mark Budaska
Kelvin Moore
❑ 532 Toby Harrah .30 .14
❑ 533 Joaquin Andujar .30 .14
❑ 534 Dave McKay .15 .07
❑ 535 Lance Parrish .60 .25
❑ 536 Rafael Ramirez .15 .07
❑ 537 Doug Capilla .15 .07
❑ 538 Lou Piniella .30 .14
❑ 539 Vern Ruhle .15 .07
❑ 540 Andre Dawson .60 .25
❑ 541 Barry Evans .15 .07
❑ 542 Ned Yost .15 .07
❑ 543 Bill Robinson .15 .07
❑ 544 Larry Christenson .15 .07
❑ 545 Reggie Smith .30 .14
❑ 546 Reggie Smith SA .15 .07
❑ 547 Rod Carew AS 1.25 .55
❑ 548 Willie Randolph AS .30 .14
❑ 549 George Brett AS 1.25 .55

❑ 550	Bucky Dent AS	.15	.07
❑ 551	Reggie Jackson AS	.60	.25
❑ 552	Ken Singleton AS	.15	.07
❑ 553	Dave Winfield AS	.30	.14
❑ 554	Carlton Fisk AS	.60	.25
❑ 555	Scott McGregor AS	.15	.07
❑ 556	Jack Morris AS	.15	.07
❑ 557	Rich Gossage AS	.30	.14
❑ 558	John Tudor	.15	.07
❑ 559	Indians TL	.30	.14
	BA: Mike Hargrove		
	Pitching: Bert Blyleven		
❑ 560	Doug Corbett	.15	.07
❑ 561	Cardinals Rookies	.15	.07
	Glenn Brummer		
	Luis DeLeon		
	Gene Roof		
❑ 562	Mike O'Berry	.15	.07
❑ 563	Ross Baumgarten	.15	.07
❑ 564	Doug DeCinces	.30	.14
❑ 565	Jackson Todd	.15	.07
❑ 566	Mike Jorgensen	.15	.07
❑ 567	Bob Babcock	.15	.07
❑ 568	Joe Pettini	.15	.07
❑ 569	Willie Randolph	.30	.14
❑ 570	Willie Randolph SA	.30	.14
❑ 571	Glenn Abbott	.15	.07
❑ 572	Juan Beniquez	.15	.07
❑ 573	Rick Waits	.15	.07
❑ 574	Mike Ramsey	.15	.07
❑ 575	Al Cowens	.15	.07
❑ 576	Giants TL	.60	.25
	BA: Milt May		
	Pitching: Vida Blue		
❑ 577	Rick Monday	.15	.07
❑ 578	Shooty Babitt	.15	.07
❑ 579	Rick Mahler	.15	.07
❑ 580	Bobby Bonds	.30	.14
❑ 581	Ron Reed	.15	.07
❑ 582	Luis Pujols	.15	.07
❑ 583	Tippy Martinez	.15	.07
❑ 584	Hosken Powell	.15	.07
❑ 585	Rollie Fingers	1.25	.55
❑ 586	Rollie Fingers SA	.60	.25
❑ 587	Tim Lollar	.15	.07
❑ 588	Dale Berra	.15	.07
❑ 589	Dave Stapleton	.15	.07
❑ 590	Al Oliver	.30	.14
❑ 591	Al Oliver SA	.15	.07
❑ 592	Craig Swan	.15	.07
❑ 593	Billy Smith	.15	.07
❑ 594	Renie Martin	.15	.07
❑ 595	Dave Collins	.15	.07
❑ 596	Damaso Garcia	.15	.07
❑ 597	Wayne Nordhagen	.15	.07
❑ 598	Bob Galasso	.15	.07
❑ 599	White Sox Rookies	.15	.07
	Jay Loviglio		
	Reggie Patterson		
	Leo Sutherland		
❑ 600	Dave Winfield	1.25	.55
❑ 601	Sid Monge	.15	.07
❑ 602	Freddie Patek	.15	.07
❑ 603	Rich Hebner	.30	.14
❑ 604	Orlando Sanchez	.15	.07
❑ 605	Steve Rogers	.15	.07
❑ 606	Blue Jays TL	.60	.25
	BA: John Mayberry		
	Pitching: Dave Stieb		
❑ 607	Leon Durham	.15	.07
❑ 608	Jerry Royster	.15	.07
❑ 609	Rick Sutcliffe	.30	.14
❑ 610	Rickey Henderson	4.00	1.80
❑ 611	Joe Niekro	.30	.14
❑ 612	Gary Ward	.15	.07
❑ 613	Jim Gantner	.30	.14
❑ 614	Juan Eichelberger	.15	.07
❑ 615	Bob Boone	.30	.14
❑ 616	Bob Boone SA	.15	.07
❑ 617	Scott McGregor	.15	.07
❑ 618	Tim Foli	.15	.07
❑ 619	Bill Campbell	.15	.07
❑ 620	Ken Griffey	.30	.14
❑ 621	Ken Griffey SA	.15	.07
❑ 622	Dennis Lamp	.15	.07
❑ 623	Mets Rookies	.60	.25
	Ron Gardenhire		
	Terry Leach		
	Tim Leary RC		
❑ 624	Fergie Jenkins	1.25	.55
❑ 625	Hal McRae	.30	.14
❑ 626	Randy Jones	.15	.07
❑ 627	Enos Cabell	.15	.07
❑ 628	Bill Travers	.15	.07
❑ 629	John Wockenfuss	.15	.07
❑ 630	Joe Charboneau	.30	.14
❑ 631	Gene Tenace	.30	.14
❑ 632	Bryan Clark	.15	.07
❑ 633	Mitchell Page	.15	.07
❑ 634	Checklist 529-660	.60	.25
❑ 635	Ron Davis	.15	.07
❑ 636	Phillies TL	1.25	.55
	BA: Pete Rose		
	Pitching: Steve Carlton		
❑ 637	Rick Camp	.15	.07
❑ 638	John Milner	.15	.07
❑ 639	Ken Kravec	.15	.07
❑ 640	Cesar Cedeno	.30	.14
❑ 641	Steve Mura	.15	.07
❑ 642	Mike Scioscia	.30	.14
❑ 643	Pete Vuckovich	.15	.07
❑ 644	John Castino	.15	.07
❑ 645	Frank White	.30	.14
❑ 646	Frank White SA	.15	.07
❑ 647	Warren Brusstar	.15	.07
❑ 648	Jose Morales	.15	.07
❑ 649	Ken Clay	.15	.07
❑ 650	Carl Yastrzemski	1.25	.55
❑ 651	Carl Yastrzemski SA	.60	.25
❑ 652	Steve Nicosia	.15	.07
❑ 653	Angels Rookies	.60	.25
	Tom Brunansky RC		
	Luis Sanchez		
	Daryl Sconiers		
❑ 654	Jim Morrison	.15	.07
❑ 655	Joel Youngblood	.15	.07
❑ 656	Eddie Whitson	.15	.07
❑ 657	Tom Poquette	.15	.07
❑ 658	Tito Landrum	.15	.07
❑ 659	Fred Martinez	.15	.07
❑ 660	Dave Concepcion	.30	.14
❑ 661	Dave Concepcion SA	.15	.07
❑ 662	Luis Salazar	.15	.07
❑ 663	Hector Cruz	.15	.07
❑ 664	Dan Spillner	.15	.07
❑ 665	Jim Clancy	.15	.07
❑ 666	Tigers TL	.60	.25
	BA: Steve Kemp		
	Pitching: Dan Petry		
❑ 667	Jeff Reardon	.60	.25
❑ 668	Dale Murphy	1.25	.55
❑ 669	Larry Milbourne	.15	.07
❑ 670	Steve Kemp	.15	.07
❑ 671	Mike Davis	.15	.07
❑ 672	Bob Knepper	.15	.07
❑ 673	Keith Drumwright	.15	.07
❑ 674	Dave Goltz	.15	.07
❑ 675	Cecil Cooper	.30	.14
❑ 676	Sal Butera	.15	.07
❑ 677	Alfredo Griffin	.15	.07
❑ 678	Tom Paciorek	.30	.14
❑ 679	Sammy Stewart	.15	.07
❑ 680	Gary Matthews	.30	.14
❑ 681	Dodgers Rookies	1.25	.55
	Mike Marshall		
	Ron Roenicke		
	Steve Sax RC		
❑ 682	Jesse Jefferson	.15	.07
❑ 683	Phil Garner	.30	.14
❑ 684	Harold Baines	1.25	.55
❑ 685	Bert Blyleven	.60	.25
❑ 686	Gary Allenson	.15	.07
❑ 687	Greg Minton	.15	.07
❑ 688	Leon Roberts	.15	.07
❑ 689	Lary Sorensen	.15	.07
❑ 690	Dave Kingman	.30	.14
❑ 691	Dan Schatzeder	.15	.07
❑ 692	Wayne Gross	.15	.07
❑ 693	Cesar Geronimo	.15	.07
❑ 694	Dave Wehrmeister	.15	.07
❑ 695	Warren Cromartie	.15	.07
❑ 696	Pirates TL	.60	.25
	BA: Bill Madlock		
	Pitching: Eddie Solomon		
❑ 697	John Montefusco	.15	.07
❑ 698	Tony Scott	.15	.07
❑ 699	Dick Tidrow	.15	.07
❑ 700	George Foster	.30	.14
❑ 701	George Foster SA	.15	.07
❑ 702	Steve Renko	.15	.07
❑ 703	Brewers TL	.60	.25
	BA: Cecil Cooper		
	Pitching: Pete Vuckovich		
❑ 704	Mickey Rivers	.15	.07
❑ 705	Mickey Rivers SA	.15	.07
❑ 706	Barry Foote	.15	.07
❑ 707	Mark Bomback	.15	.07
❑ 708	Gene Richards	.15	.07
❑ 709	Don Money	.15	.07
❑ 710	Jerry Reuss	.30	.14
❑ 711	Mariners Rookies	.60	.25
	Dave Edler		
	Dave Henderson RC		
	Reggie Walton		
❑ 712	Dennis Martinez	.60	.25
❑ 713	Del Unser	.15	.07
❑ 714	Jerry Koosman	.30	.14
❑ 715	Willie Stargell	1.25	.55
❑ 716	Willie Stargell SA	.60	.25
❑ 717	Rick Miller	.15	.07
❑ 718	Charlie Hough	.30	.14
❑ 719	Jerry Narron	.15	.07
❑ 720	Greg Luzinski	.30	.14
❑ 721	Greg Luzinski SA	.15	.07
❑ 722	Jerry Martin	.15	.07
❑ 723	Junior Kennedy	.15	.07
❑ 724	Dave Rosello	.15	.07
❑ 725	Amos Otis	.30	.14
❑ 726	Amos Otis SA	.15	.07
❑ 727	Sixto Lezcano	.15	.07
❑ 728	Aurelio Lopez	.15	.07
❑ 729	Jim Spencer	.15	.07
❑ 730	Gary Carter	.60	.25
❑ 731	Padres Rookies	.15	.07
	Mike Armstrong		
	Doug Gwosdz		
	Fred Kuhaulua		
❑ 732	Mike Lum	.15	.07
❑ 733	Larry McWilliams	.15	.07
❑ 734	Mike Ivie	.15	.07
❑ 735	Rudy May	.15	.07
❑ 736	Jerry Turner	.15	.07
❑ 737	Reggie Cleveland	.15	.07
❑ 738	Dave Engle	.15	.07
❑ 739	Joey McLaughlin	.15	.07
❑ 740	Dave Lopes	.30	.14
❑ 741	Dave Lopes SA	.15	.07
❑ 742	Dick Drago	.15	.07
❑ 743	John Stearns	.15	.07
❑ 744	Mike Witt	.30	.14
❑ 745	Bake McBride	.15	.07
❑ 746	Andre Thornton	.15	.07
❑ 747	John Lowenstein	.15	.07
❑ 748	Marc Hill	.15	.07
❑ 749	Bob Shirley	.15	.07
❑ 750	Jim Rice	.30	.14
❑ 751	Rick Honeycutt	.15	.07
❑ 752	Lee Lacy	.15	.07
❑ 753	Tom Brookens	.15	.07
❑ 754	Joe Morgan	1.25	.55
❑ 755	Joe Morgan SA	.60	.25
❑ 756	Reds TL	.60	.25
	BA: Ken Griffey		
	Pitching: Tom Seaver		
❑ 757	Tom Underwood	.15	.07
❑ 758	Claudell Washington	.15	.07
❑ 759	Paul Splittorff	.15	.07
❑ 760	Bill Buckner	.30	.14
❑ 761	Dave Smith	.15	.07
❑ 762	Mike Phillips	.15	.07
❑ 763	Tom Hume	.15	.07
❑ 764	Steve Swisher	.15	.07
❑ 765	Gorman Thomas	.30	.14
❑ 766	Twins Rookies	1.50	.70
	Lenny Faedo		
	Kent Hrbek RC		
	Tim Laudner		
❑ 767	Roy Smalley	.15	.07

❑ 768 Jerry Garvin .... .15 .07
❑ 769 Richie Zisk .... .15 .07
❑ 770 Rich Gossage .... .60 .25
❑ 771 Rich Gossage SA .... .30 .14
❑ 772 Bert Campaneris .... .30 .14
❑ 773 John Denny .... .15 .07
❑ 774 Jay Johnstone .... .30 .14
❑ 775 Bob Forsch .... .15 .07
❑ 776 Mark Belanger .... .15 .07
❑ 777 Tom Griffin .... .15 .07
❑ 778 Kevin Hickey .... .15 .07
❑ 779 Grant Jackson .... .15 .07
❑ 780 Pete Rose 4.00 1.80
❑ 781 Pete Rose SA .... 1.25 .55
❑ 782 Frank Taveras .... .15 .07
❑ 783 Greg Harris RC .... .15 .07
❑ 784 Milt Wilcox .... .15 .07
❑ 785 Dan Driessen .... .15 .07
❑ 786 Red Sox TL .... .60 .25
BA: Carney Lansford
Pitching: Mike Torrez
❑ 787 Fred Stanley .... .15 .07
❑ 788 Woodie Fryman .... .15 .07
❑ 789 Checklist 661-792 .... .60 .25
❑ 790 Larry Gura .... .15 .07
❑ 791 Bobby Brown .... .15 .07
❑ 792 Frank Tanana .... .30 .14

1982 Topps Traded

	NRMT	VG-E
COMP.FACT.SET (132)	200.00	90.00

❑ 1T Doyle Alexander .... .50 .23
❑ 2T Jesse Barfield .... 1.00 .45
❑ 3T Ross Baumgarten .... .50 .23
❑ 4T Steve Bedrosian .... 1.00 .45
❑ 5T Mark Belanger .... 1.00 .45
❑ 6T Kurt Bevacqua .... .50 .23
❑ 7T Tim Blackwell .... .50 .23
❑ 8T Vida Blue .... 1.00 .45
❑ 9T Bob Boone .... 1.00 .45
❑ 10T Larry Bowa .... 1.00 .45
❑ 11T Dan Briggs .... .50 .23
❑ 12T Bobby Brown .... .50 .23
❑ 13T Tom Brunansky .... 1.00 .45
❑ 14T Jeff Burroughs .... .50 .23
❑ 15T Enos Cabell .... .50 .23
❑ 16T Bill Campbell .... .50 .23
❑ 17T Bobby Castillo .... .50 .23
❑ 18T Bill Caudill .... .50 .23
❑ 19T Cesar Cedeno .... 1.00 .45
❑ 20T Dave Collins .... .50 .23
❑ 21T Doug Corbett .... .50 .23
❑ 22T Al Cowens .... .50 .23
❑ 23T Chili Davis 8.00 3.60
❑ 24T Dick Davis .... .50 .23
❑ 25T Ron Davis .... .50 .23
❑ 26T Doug DeCinces .... 1.00 .45
❑ 27T Ivan DeJesus .... .50 .23
❑ 28T Bob Dernier .... .50 .23
❑ 29T Bo Diaz .... .50 .23
❑ 30T Roger Erickson .... .50 .23
❑ 31T Jim Essian .... .50 .23
❑ 32T Ed Farmer .... .50 .23
❑ 33T Doug Flynn .... .50 .23
❑ 34T Tim Foli .... .50 .23
❑ 35T Dan Ford .... .50 .23
❑ 36T George Foster .... 1.00 .45
❑ 37T Dave Frost .... .50 .23
❑ 38T Rich Gale .... .50 .23
❑ 39T Ron Gardenhire .... .50 .23
❑ 40T Ken Griffey .... 1.00 .45
❑ 41T Greg Harris .... .50 .23
❑ 42T Von Hayes .... 1.00 .45
❑ 43T Larry Herndon .... .50 .23
❑ 44T Kent Hrbek .... 2.00 .90
❑ 45T Mike Ivie .... .50 .23
❑ 46T Grant Jackson .... .50 .23
❑ 47T Reggie Jackson 8.00 3.60
❑ 48T Ron Jackson .... .50 .23
❑ 49T Fergie Jenkins 4.00 1.80
❑ 50T Lamar Johnson .... .50 .23
❑ 51T Randy Johnson .... .50 .23
❑ 52T Jay Johnstone .... 1.00 .45
❑ 53T Mick Kelleher .... .50 .23
❑ 54T Steve Kemp .... .50 .23
❑ 55T Junior Kennedy .... .50 .23
❑ 56T Jim Kern .... .50 .23
❑ 57T Ray Knight .... 1.00 .45
❑ 58T Wayne Krenchicki .... .50 .23
❑ 59T Mike Krukow .... .50 .23
❑ 60T Duane Kuiper .... .50 .23
❑ 61T Mike LaCoss .... .50 .23
❑ 62T Chet Lemon .... .50 .23
❑ 63T Sixto Lezcano .... .50 .23
❑ 64T Dave Lopes .... 1.00 .45
❑ 65T Jerry Martin .... .50 .23
❑ 66T Renie Martin .... .50 .23
❑ 67T John Mayberry .... .50 .23
❑ 68T Lee Mazzilli .... .50 .23
❑ 69T Bake McBride .... .50 .23
❑ 70T Dan Meyer .... .50 .23
❑ 71T Larry Milbourne .... .50 .23
❑ 72T Eddie Milner .... .50 .23
❑ 73T Sid Monge .... .50 .23
❑ 74T John Montefusco .... .50 .23
❑ 75T Jose Morales .... .50 .23
❑ 76T Keith Moreland .... .50 .23
❑ 77T Jim Morrison .... .50 .23
❑ 78T Rance Mulliniks .... .50 .23
❑ 79T Steve Mura .... .50 .23
❑ 80T Gene Nelson .... .50 .23
❑ 81T Joe Nolan .... .50 .23
❑ 82T Dickie Noles .... .50 .23
❑ 83T Al Oliver .... 1.00 .45
❑ 84T Jorge Orta .... .50 .23
❑ 85T Tom Paciorek .... 1.00 .45
❑ 86T Larry Parrish .... .50 .23
❑ 87T Jack Perconte .... .50 .23
❑ 88T Gaylord Perry 4.00 1.80
❑ 89T Rob Picciolo .... .50 .23
❑ 90T Joe Pittman .... .50 .23
❑ 91T Hosken Powell .... .50 .23
❑ 92T Mike Proly .... .50 .23
❑ 93T Greg Pryor .... .50 .23
❑ 94T Charlie Puleo .... .50 .23
❑ 95T Shane Rawley .... .50 .23
❑ 96T Johnny Ray .... 1.00 .45
❑ 97T Dave Revering .... .50 .23
❑ 98T Cal Ripken 150.00 70.00
❑ 99T Allen Ripley .... .50 .23
❑ 100T Bill Robinson .... .50 .23
❑ 101T Aurelio Rodriguez .... .50 .23
❑ 102T Joe Rudi .... .50 .23
❑ 103T Steve Sax 4.00 1.80
❑ 104T Dan Schatzeder .... .50 .23
❑ 105T Bob Shirley .... .50 .23
❑ 106T Eric Show .... 1.00 .45
❑ 107T Roy Smalley .... .50 .23
❑ 108T Lonnie Smith .... 1.00 .45
❑ 109T Ozzie Smith 15.00 6.75
❑ 110T Reggie Smith .... 1.00 .45
❑ 111T Lary Sorensen .... .50 .23
❑ 112T Elias Sosa .... .50 .23
❑ 113T Mike Stanton .... .50 .23
❑ 114T Steve Stroughter .... .50 .23
❑ 115T Champ Summers .... .50 .23
❑ 116T Rick Sutcliffe .... 1.00 .45
❑ 117T Frank Tanana .... 1.00 .45
❑ 118T Frank Taveras .... .50 .23
❑ 119T Garry Templeton .... .50 .23
❑ 120T Alex Trevino .... .50 .23
❑ 121T Jerry Turner .... .50 .23
❑ 122T Ed VandeBerg .... .50 .23
❑ 123T Tom Veryzer .... .50 .23
❑ 124T Ron Washington .... .50 .23
❑ 125T Bob Watson .... 1.00 .45
❑ 126T Dennis Werth .... .50 .23
❑ 127T Eddie Whitson .... .50 .23
❑ 128T Rob Wilfong .... .50 .23
❑ 129T Bump Wills .... .50 .23
❑ 130T Gary Woods .... .50 .23
❑ 131T Butch Wynegar .... .50 .23
❑ 132T Checklist: 1-132 .... .50 .23

1983 Topps

	NRMT	VG-E
COMPLETE SET (792)	100.00	45.00

❑ 1 Tony Armas RB .... .30 .14
❑ 2 Rickey Henderson RB ...... 1.25 .55
Sets modern SB record
❑ 3 Greg Minton RB .... .15 .07
269 1/3 homerless
innings streak
❑ 4 Lance Parrish RB .... .15 .07
❑ 5 Manny Trillo RB .... .15 .07
479 consecutive
errorless chances,
second baseman
❑ 6 John Wathan RB .... .15 .07
ML catcher steals, season
❑ 7 Gene Richards .... .15 .07
❑ 8 Steve Balboni .... .15 .07
❑ 9 Joey McLaughlin .... .15 .07
❑ 10 Gorman Thomas .... .15 .07
❑ 11 Billy Gardner MG .... .15 .07
❑ 12 Paul Mirabella .... .15 .07
❑ 13 Larry Herndon .... .15 .07
❑ 14 Frank LaCorte .... .15 .07
❑ 15 Ron Cey .... .30 .14
❑ 16 George Vukovich .... .15 .07
❑ 17 Kent Tekulve .... .30 .14
❑ 18 Kent Tekulve SV .... .15 .07
❑ 19 Oscar Gamble .... .15 .07
❑ 20 Carlton Fisk .... 1.25 .55
❑ 21 Baltimore Orioles TL .... .60 .25
BA: Eddie Murray
ERA: Jim Palmer
❑ 22 Randy Martz .... .15 .07
❑ 23 Mike Heath .... .15 .07
❑ 24 Steve Mura .... .15 .07
❑ 25 Hal McRae .... .30 .14
❑ 26 Jerry Royster .... .15 .07
❑ 27 Doug Corbett .... .15 .07
❑ 28 Bruce Bochte .... .15 .07
❑ 29 Randy Jones .... .15 .07
❑ 30 Jim Rice .... .30 .14
❑ 31 Bill Gullickson .... .15 .07
❑ 32 Dave Bergman .... .15 .07
❑ 33 Jack O'Connor .... .15 .07
❑ 34 Paul Householder .... .15 .07
❑ 35 Rollie Fingers .... 1.25 .55
❑ 36 Rollie Fingers SV .... .60 .25
❑ 37 Darrell Johnson MG .... .15 .07
❑ 38 Tim Flannery .... .15 .07
❑ 39 Terry Puhl .... .15 .07
❑ 40 Fernando Valenzuela ...... .60 .25
❑ 41 Jerry Turner .... .15 .07
❑ 42 Dale Murray .... .15 .07

Card	Player	Price 1	Price 2
❑ 43	Bob Dernier	.15	.07
❑ 44	Don Robinson	.15	.07
❑ 45	John Mayberry	.15	.07
❑ 46	Richard Dotson	.15	.07
❑ 47	Dave McKay	.15	.07
❑ 48	Lary Sorensen	.15	.07
❑ 49	Willie McGee RC	3.00	1.35
❑ 50	Bob Horner UER ('82 RBI total 7)	.15	.07
❑ 51	Chicago Cubs TL BA: Leon Durham ERA: Fergie Jenkins	.30	.14
❑ 52	Onix Concepcion	.15	.07
❑ 53	Mike Witt	.15	.07
❑ 54	Jim Maler	.15	.07
❑ 55	Mookie Wilson	.30	.14
❑ 56	Chuck Rainey	.15	.07
❑ 57	Tim Blackwell	.15	.07
❑ 58	Al Holland	.15	.07
❑ 59	Benny Ayala	.15	.07
❑ 60	Johnny Bench	2.00	.90
❑ 61	Johnny Bench SV	.60	.25
❑ 62	Bob McClure	.15	.07
❑ 63	Rick Monday	.15	.07
❑ 64	Bill Stein	.15	.07
❑ 65	Jack Morris	.30	.14
❑ 66	Bob Lillis MG	.15	.07
❑ 67	Sal Butera	.15	.07
❑ 68	Eric Show	.15	.07
❑ 69	Lee Lacy	.15	.07
❑ 70	Steve Carlton	1.25	.55
❑ 71	Steve Carlton SV	.60	.25
❑ 72	Tom Paciorek	.30	.14
❑ 73	Allen Ripley	.15	.07
❑ 74	Julio Gonzalez	.15	.07
❑ 75	Amos Otis	.30	.14
❑ 76	Rick Mahler	.15	.07
❑ 77	Hosken Powell	.15	.07
❑ 78	Bill Caudill	.15	.07
❑ 79	Mick Kelleher	.15	.07
❑ 80	George Foster	.30	.14
❑ 81	Yankees TL BA: Jerry Mumphrey ERA: Dave Righetti	.30	.14
❑ 82	Bruce Hurst	.15	.07
❑ 83	Ryne Sandberg RC	20.00	9.00
❑ 84	Milt May	.15	.07
❑ 85	Ken Singleton	.15	.07
❑ 86	Tom Hume	.15	.07
❑ 87	Joe Rudi	.15	.07
❑ 88	Jim Gantner	.15	.07
❑ 89	Leon Roberts	.15	.07
❑ 90	Jerry Reuss	.30	.14
❑ 91	Larry Milbourne	.15	.07
❑ 92	Mike LaCoss	.15	.07
❑ 93	John Castino	.15	.07
❑ 94	Dave Edwards	.15	.07
❑ 95	Alan Trammell	.60	.25
❑ 96	Dick Howser MG	.15	.07
❑ 97	Ross Baumgarten	.15	.07
❑ 98	Vance Law	.15	.07
❑ 99	Dickie Noles	.15	.07
❑ 100	Pete Rose	4.00	1.80
❑ 101	Pete Rose SV	1.25	.55
❑ 102	Dave Beard	.15	.07
❑ 103	Darrell Porter	.15	.07
❑ 104	Bob Walk	.15	.07
❑ 105	Don Baylor	.60	.25
❑ 106	Gene Nelson	.15	.07
❑ 107	Mike Jorgensen	.15	.07
❑ 108	Glenn Hoffman	.15	.07
❑ 109	Luis Leal	.15	.07
❑ 110	Ken Griffey	.30	.14
❑ 111	Montreal Expos TL BA: Al Oliver ERA: Steve Rogers	.30	.14
❑ 112	Bob Shirley	.15	.07
❑ 113	Ron Roenicke	.15	.07
❑ 114	Jim Slaton	.15	.07
❑ 115	Chili Davis	1.25	.55
❑ 116	Dave Schmidt	.15	.07
❑ 117	Alan Knicely	.15	.07
❑ 118	Chris Welsh	.15	.07
❑ 119	Tom Brookens	.15	.07
❑ 120	Len Barker	.15	.07
❑ 121	Mickey Hatcher	.15	.07
❑ 122	Jimmy Smith	.15	.07
❑ 123	George Frazier	.15	.07
❑ 124	Marc Hill	.15	.07
❑ 125	Leon Durham	.15	.07
❑ 126	Joe Torre MG	.30	.14
❑ 127	Preston Hanna	.15	.07
❑ 128	Mike Ramsey	.15	.07
❑ 129	Checklist: 1-132	.30	.14
❑ 130	Dave Stieb	.30	.14
❑ 131	Ed Ott	.15	.07
❑ 132	Todd Cruz	.15	.07
❑ 133	Jim Barr	.15	.07
❑ 134	Hubie Brooks	.30	.14
❑ 135	Dwight Evans	.30	.14
❑ 136	Willie Aikens	.15	.07
❑ 137	Woodie Fryman	.15	.07
❑ 138	Rick Dempsey	.30	.14
❑ 139	Bruce Berenyi	.15	.07
❑ 140	Willie Randolph	.30	.14
❑ 141	Indians TL BA: Toby Harrah ERA: Rick Sutcliffe	.30	.14
❑ 142	Mike Caldwell	.15	.07
❑ 143	Joe Pettini	.15	.07
❑ 144	Mark Wagner	.15	.07
❑ 145	Don Sutton	1.25	.55
❑ 146	Don Sutton SV	.60	.25
❑ 147	Rick Leach	.15	.07
❑ 148	Dave Roberts	.15	.07
❑ 149	Johnny Ray	.15	.07
❑ 150	Bruce Sutter	.30	.14
❑ 151	Bruce Sutter SV	.15	.07
❑ 152	Jay Johnstone	.30	.14
❑ 153	Jerry Koosman	.30	.14
❑ 154	Johnnie LeMaster	.15	.07
❑ 155	Dan Quisenberry	.30	.14
❑ 156	Billy Martin MG	.30	.14
❑ 157	Steve Bedrosian	.30	.14
❑ 158	Rob Wilfong	.15	.07
❑ 159	Mike Stanton	.15	.07
❑ 160	Dave Kingman	.60	.25
❑ 161	Dave Kingman SV	.30	.14
❑ 162	Mark Clear	.15	.07
❑ 163	Cal Ripken	12.00	5.50
❑ 164	David Palmer	.15	.07
❑ 165	Dan Driessen	.15	.07
❑ 166	John Pacella	.15	.07
❑ 167	Mark Brouhard	.15	.07
❑ 168	Juan Eichelberger	.15	.07
❑ 169	Doug Flynn	.15	.07
❑ 170	Steve Howe	.15	.07
❑ 171	Giants TL BA: Joe Morgan ERA: Bill Laskey	.60	.25
❑ 172	Vern Ruhle	.15	.07
❑ 173	Jim Morrison	.15	.07
❑ 174	Jerry Ujdur	.15	.07
❑ 175	Bo Diaz	.15	.07
❑ 176	Dave Righetti	.30	.14
❑ 177	Harold Baines	1.25	.55
❑ 178	Luis Tiant	.30	.14
❑ 179	Luis Tiant SV	.15	.07
❑ 180	Rickey Henderson	2.50	1.10
❑ 181	Terry Felton	.15	.07
❑ 182	Mike Fischlin	.15	.07
❑ 183	Ed VandeBerg	.15	.07
❑ 184	Bob Clark	.15	.07
❑ 185	Tim Lollar	.15	.07
❑ 186	Whitey Herzog MG	.30	.14
❑ 187	Terry Leach	.15	.07
❑ 188	Rick Miller	.15	.07
❑ 189	Dan Schatzeder	.15	.07
❑ 190	Cecil Cooper	.30	.14
❑ 191	Joe Price	.15	.07
❑ 192	Floyd Rayford	.15	.07
❑ 193	Harry Spilman	.15	.07
❑ 194	Cesar Geronimo	.15	.07
❑ 195	Bob Stoddard	.15	.07
❑ 196	Bill Fahey	.15	.07
❑ 197	Jim Eisenreich RC	1.25	.55
❑ 198	Kiko Garcia	.15	.07
❑ 199	Marty Bystrom	.15	.07
❑ 200	Rod Carew	1.25	.55
❑ 201	Rod Carew SV	.60	.25
❑ 202	Blue Jays TL BA: Damaso Garcia ERA: Dave Stieb	.30	.14
❑ 203	Mike Morgan	.15	.07
❑ 204	Junior Kennedy	.15	.07
❑ 205	Dave Parker	.30	.14
❑ 206	Ken Oberkfell	.15	.07
❑ 207	Rick Camp	.15	.07
❑ 208	Dan Meyer	.15	.07
❑ 209	Mike Moore RC	.30	.14
❑ 210	Jack Clark	.30	.14
❑ 211	John Denny	.15	.07
❑ 212	John Stearns	.15	.07
❑ 213	Tom Burgmeier	.15	.07
❑ 214	Jerry White	.15	.07
❑ 215	Mario Soto	.15	.07
❑ 216	Tony LaRussa MG	.30	.14
❑ 217	Tim Stoddard	.15	.07
❑ 218	Roy Howell	.15	.07
❑ 219	Mike Armstrong	.15	.07
❑ 220	Dusty Baker	.30	.14
❑ 221	Joe Niekro	.30	.14
❑ 222	Damaso Garcia	.15	.07
❑ 223	John Montefusco	.15	.07
❑ 224	Mickey Rivers	.15	.07
❑ 225	Enos Cabell	.15	.07
❑ 226	Enrique Romo	.15	.07
❑ 227	Chris Bando	.15	.07
❑ 228	Joaquin Andujar	.15	.07
❑ 229	Phillies TL BA: Bo Diaz ERA: Steve Carlton	.60	.25
❑ 230	Fergie Jenkins	1.25	.55
❑ 231	Fergie Jenkins SV	.60	.25
❑ 232	Tom Brunansky	.30	.14
❑ 233	Wayne Gross	.15	.07
❑ 234	Larry Andersen	.15	.07
❑ 235	Claudell Washington	.15	.07
❑ 236	Steve Renko	.15	.07
❑ 237	Dan Norman	.15	.07
❑ 238	Bud Black RC	.30	.14
❑ 239	Dave Stapleton	.15	.07
❑ 240	Rich Gossage	.60	.25
❑ 241	Rich Gossage SV	.30	.14
❑ 242	Joe Nolan	.15	.07
❑ 243	Duane Walker	.15	.07
❑ 244	Dwight Bernard	.15	.07
❑ 245	Steve Sax	.30	.14
❑ 246	G.Bamberger MG	.15	.07
❑ 247	Dave Smith	.15	.07
❑ 248	Bake McBride	.15	.07
❑ 249	Checklist: 133-264	.30	.14
❑ 250	Bill Buckner	.30	.14
❑ 251	Alan Wiggins	.15	.07
❑ 252	Luis Aguayo	.15	.07
❑ 253	Larry McWilliams	.15	.07
❑ 254	Rick Cerone	.15	.07
❑ 255	Gene Garber	.15	.07
❑ 256	Gene Garber SV	.15	.07
❑ 257	Jesse Barfield	.30	.14
❑ 258	Manny Castillo	.15	.07
❑ 259	Jeff Jones	.15	.07
❑ 260	Steve Kemp	.15	.07
❑ 261	Tigers TL BA: Larry Herndon ERA: Dan Petry	.30	.14
❑ 262	Ron Jackson	.15	.07
❑ 263	Renie Martin	.15	.07
❑ 264	Jamie Quirk	.15	.07
❑ 265	Joel Youngblood	.15	.07
❑ 266	Paul Boris	.15	.07
❑ 267	Terry Francona	.15	.07
❑ 268	Storm Davis RC	.15	.07
❑ 269	Ron Oester	.15	.07
❑ 270	Dennis Eckersley	1.25	.55
❑ 271	Ed Romero	.15	.07
❑ 272	Frank Tanana	.30	.14
❑ 273	Mark Belanger	.15	.07
❑ 274	Terry Kennedy	.15	.07
❑ 275	Ray Knight	.30	.14
❑ 276	Gene Mauch MG	.15	.07
❑ 277	Rance Mulliniks	.15	.07
❑ 278	Kevin Hickey	.15	.07
❑ 279	Greg Gross	.15	.07
❑ 280	Bert Blyleven	.60	.25
❑ 281	Andre Robertson	.15	.07
❑ 282	Reggie Smith (Ryne Sandberg	1.25	.55

ducking back)
❑ 283 Reggie Smith SV .15 .07
❑ 284 Jeff Lahti .15 .07
❑ 285 Lance Parrish .30 .14
❑ 286 Rick Langford .15 .07
❑ 287 Bobby Brown .15 .07
❑ 288 Joe Cowley .15 .07
❑ 289 Jerry Dybzinski .15 .07
❑ 290 Jeff Reardon .30 .14
❑ 291 Pirates TL .30 .14
BA: Bill Madlock
ERA: John Candelaria
❑ 292 Craig Swan .15 .07
❑ 293 Glenn Gulliver .15 .07
❑ 294 Dave Engle .15 .07
❑ 295 Jerry Remy .15 .07
❑ 296 Greg Harris .15 .07
❑ 297 Ned Yost .15 .07
❑ 298 Floyd Chiffer .15 .07
❑ 299 George Wright .15 .07
❑ 300 Mike Schmidt 2.50 1.10
❑ 301 Mike Schmidt SV 1.25 .55
❑ 302 Ernie Whitt .15 .07
❑ 303 Miguel Dilone .15 .07
❑ 304 Dave Rucker .15 .07
❑ 305 Larry Bowa .30 .14
❑ 306 Tom Lasorda MG .60 .25
❑ 307 Lou Piniella .30 .14
❑ 308 Jesus Vega .15 .07
❑ 309 Jeff Leonard .15 .07
❑ 310 Greg Luzinski .30 .14
❑ 311 Glenn Brummer .15 .07
❑ 312 Brian Kingman .15 .07
❑ 313 Gary Gray .15 .07
❑ 314 Ken Dayley .15 .07
❑ 315 Rick Burleson .15 .07
❑ 316 Paul Splittorff .15 .07
❑ 317 Gary Rajsich .15 .07
❑ 318 John Tudor .15 .07
❑ 319 Lenn Sakata .15 .07
❑ 320 Steve Rogers .15 .07
❑ 321 Brewers TL .60 .25
BA: Robin Yount
ERA: Pete Vuckovich
❑ 322 Dave Van Gorder .15 .07
❑ 323 Luis DeLeon .15 .07
❑ 324 Mike Marshall .15 .07
❑ 325 Von Hayes .30 .14
❑ 326 Garth Iorg .15 .07
❑ 327 Bobby Castillo .15 .07
❑ 328 Craig Reynolds .15 .07
❑ 329 Randy Niemann .15 .07
❑ 330 Buddy Bell .30 .14
❑ 331 Mike Krukow .15 .07
❑ 332 Glenn Wilson .30 .14
❑ 333 Dave LaRoche .15 .07
❑ 334 Dave LaRoche SV .15 .07
❑ 335 Steve Henderson .15 .07
❑ 336 Rene Lachemann MG .15 .07
❑ 337 Tito Landrum .15 .07
❑ 338 Bob Owchinko .15 .07
❑ 339 Terry Harper .15 .07
❑ 340 Larry Gura .15 .07
❑ 341 Doug DeCinces .30 .14
❑ 342 Atlee Hammaker .15 .07
❑ 343 Bob Bailor .15 .07
❑ 344 Roger LaFrancois .15 .07
❑ 345 Jim Clancy .15 .07
❑ 346 Joe Pittman .15 .07
❑ 347 Sammy Stewart .15 .07
❑ 348 Alan Bannister .15 .07
❑ 349 Checklist: 265-396 .30 .14
❑ 350 Robin Yount 1.25 .55
❑ 351 Reds TL .30 .14
BA: Cesar Cedeno
ERA: Mario Soto
❑ 352 Mike Scioscia .30 .14
❑ 353 Steve Comer .15 .07
❑ 354 Randy Johnson .15 .07
❑ 355 Jim Bibby .15 .07
❑ 356 Gary Woods .15 .07
❑ 357 Len Matuszek .15 .07
❑ 358 Jerry Garvin .15 .07
❑ 359 Dave Collins .15 .07
❑ 360 Nolan Ryan 6.00 2.70
❑ 361 Nolan Ryan SV 3.00 1.35
❑ 362 Bill Almon .15 .07
❑ 363 John Stuper .15 .07
❑ 364 Brett Butler 1.25 .55
❑ 365 Dave Lopes .30 .14
❑ 366 Dick Williams MG .15 .07
❑ 367 Bud Anderson .15 .07
❑ 368 Richie Zisk .15 .07
❑ 369 Jesse Orosco .15 .07
❑ 370 Gary Carter .60 .25
❑ 371 Mike Richardt .15 .07
❑ 372 Terry Crowley .15 .07
❑ 373 Kevin Saucier .15 .07
❑ 374 Wayne Krenchicki .15 .07
❑ 375 Pete Vuckovich .15 .07
❑ 376 Ken Landreaux .15 .07
❑ 377 Lee May .30 .14
❑ 378 Lee May SV .15 .07
❑ 379 Guy Sularz .15 .07
❑ 380 Ron Davis .15 .07
❑ 381 Red Sox TL .30 .14
BA: Jim Rice
ERA: Bob Stanley
❑ 382 Bob Knepper .15 .07
❑ 383 Ozzie Virgil .15 .07
❑ 384 Dave Dravecky RC 1.25 .55
❑ 385 Mike Easler .15 .07
❑ 386 Rod Carew AS .60 .25
❑ 387 Bob Grich AS .15 .07
❑ 388 George Brett AS 1.25 .55
❑ 389 Robin Yount AS .60 .25
❑ 390 Reggie Jackson AS .60 .25
❑ 391 Rickey Henderson AS 1.25 .55
❑ 392 Fred Lynn AS .15 .07
❑ 393 Carlton Fisk AS .60 .25
❑ 394 Pete Vuckovich AS .15 .07
❑ 395 Larry Gura AS .15 .07
❑ 396 Dan Quisenberry AS .15 .07
❑ 397 Pete Rose AS .60 .25
❑ 398 Manny Trillo AS .15 .07
❑ 399 Mike Schmidt AS .60 .25
❑ 400 Dave Concepcion AS .15 .07
❑ 401 Dale Murphy AS .60 .25
❑ 402 Andre Dawson AS .30 .14
❑ 403 Tim Raines AS .30 .14
❑ 404 Gary Carter AS .30 .14
❑ 405 Steve Rogers AS .15 .07
❑ 406 Steve Carlton AS .60 .25
❑ 407 Bruce Sutter AS .15 .07
❑ 408 Rudy May .15 .07
❑ 409 Marvis Foley .15 .07
❑ 410 Phil Niekro 1.25 .55
❑ 411 Phil Niekro SV .60 .25
❑ 412 Rangers TL .30 .14
BA: Buddy Bell
ERA: Charlie Hough
❑ 413 Matt Keough .15 .07
❑ 414 Julio Cruz .15 .07
❑ 415 Bob Forsch .15 .07
❑ 416 Joe Ferguson .15 .07
❑ 417 Tom Hausman .15 .07
❑ 418 Greg Pryor .15 .07
❑ 419 Steve Crawford .15 .07
❑ 420 Al Oliver .30 .14
❑ 421 Al Oliver SV .15 .07
❑ 422 George Cappuzzello .15 .07
❑ 423 Tom Lawless .15 .07
❑ 424 Jerry Augustine .15 .07
❑ 425 Pedro Guerrero .30 .14
❑ 426 Earl Weaver MG .60 .25
❑ 427 Roy Lee Jackson .15 .07
❑ 428 Champ Summers .15 .07
❑ 429 Eddie Whitson .15 .07
❑ 430 Kirk Gibson 1.25 .55
❑ 431 Gary Gaetti RC 1.25 .55
❑ 432 Porfirio Altamirano .15 .07
❑ 433 Dale Berra .15 .07
❑ 434 Dennis Lamp .15 .07
❑ 435 Tony Armas .15 .07
❑ 436 Bill Campbell .15 .07
❑ 437 Rick Sweet .15 .07
❑ 438 Dave LaPoint .15 .07
❑ 439 Rafael Ramirez .15 .07
❑ 440 Ron Guidry .30 .14
❑ 441 Astros TL .30 .14
BA: Ray Knight
ERA: Joe Niekro
❑ 442 Brian Downing .15 .07
❑ 443 Don Hood .15 .07
❑ 444 Wally Backman .15 .07
❑ 445 Mike Flanagan .30 .14
❑ 446 Reid Nichols .15 .07
❑ 447 Bryn Smith .15 .07
❑ 448 Darrell Evans .30 .14
❑ 449 Eddie Milner .15 .07
❑ 450 Ted Simmons .30 .14
❑ 451 Ted Simmons SV .15 .07
❑ 452 Lloyd Moseby .15 .07
❑ 453 Lamar Johnson .15 .07
❑ 454 Bob Welch .30 .14
❑ 455 Sixto Lezcano .15 .07
❑ 456 Lee Elia MG .15 .07
❑ 457 Milt Wilcox .15 .07
❑ 458 Ron Washington .15 .07
❑ 459 Ed Farmer .15 .07
❑ 460 Roy Smalley .15 .07
❑ 461 Steve Trout .15 .07
❑ 462 Steve Nicosia .15 .07
❑ 463 Gaylord Perry 1.25 .55
❑ 464 Gaylord Perry SV .60 .25
❑ 465 Lonnie Smith .15 .07
❑ 466 Tom Underwood .15 .07
❑ 467 Rufino Linares .15 .07
❑ 468 Dave Goltz .15 .07
❑ 469 Ron Gardenhire .15 .07
❑ 470 Greg Minton .15 .07
❑ 471 Kansas City Royals TL .30 .14
BA: Willie Wilson
ERA: Vida Blue
❑ 472 Gary Allenson .15 .07
❑ 473 John Lowenstein .15 .07
❑ 474 Ray Burris .15 .07
❑ 475 Cesar Cedeno .30 .14
❑ 476 Rob Picciolo .15 .07
❑ 477 Tom Niedenfuer .15 .07
❑ 478 Phil Garner .30 .14
❑ 479 Charlie Hough .30 .14
❑ 480 Toby Harrah .15 .07
❑ 481 Scot Thompson .15 .07
❑ 482 Tony Gwynn UER RC 40.00 18.00
No Topps logo under
card number on back
❑ 483 Lynn Jones .15 .07
❑ 484 Dick Ruthven .15 .07
❑ 485 Omar Moreno .15 .07
❑ 486 Clyde King MG .15 .07
❑ 487 Jerry Hairston .15 .07
❑ 488 Alfredo Griffin .15 .07
❑ 489 Tom Herr .30 .14
❑ 490 Jim Palmer 1.25 .55
❑ 491 Jim Palmer SV .60 .25
❑ 492 Paul Serna .15 .07
❑ 493 Steve McCatty .15 .07
❑ 494 Bob Brenly .15 .07
❑ 495 Warren Cromartie .15 .07
❑ 496 Tom Veryzer .15 .07
❑ 497 Rick Sutcliffe .30 .14
❑ 498 Wade Boggs RC 20.00 9.00
❑ 499 Jeff Little .15 .07
❑ 500 Reggie Jackson 1.50 .70
❑ 501 Reggie Jackson SV .60 .25
❑ 502 Atlanta Braves TL .30 .14
BA: Dale Murphy
ERA: Phil Niekro
❑ 503 Moose Haas .15 .07
❑ 504 Don Werner .15 .07
❑ 505 Garry Templeton .15 .07
❑ 506 Jim Gott RC .15 .07
❑ 507 Tony Scott .15 .07
❑ 508 Tom Filer .15 .07
❑ 509 Lou Whitaker .60 .25
❑ 510 Tug McGraw .30 .14
❑ 511 Tug McGraw SV .15 .07
❑ 512 Doyle Alexander .15 .07
❑ 513 Fred Stanley .15 .07
❑ 514 Rudy Law .15 .07
❑ 515 Gene Tenace .30 .14
❑ 516 Bill Virdon MG .15 .07
❑ 517 Gary Ward .15 .07
❑ 518 Bill Laskey .15 .07
❑ 519 Terry Bulling .15 .07
❑ 520 Fred Lynn .30 .14
❑ 521 Bruce Benedict .15 .07

❑	522 Pat Zachry	.15	.07
❑	523 Carney Lansford	.30	.14
❑	524 Tom Brennan	.15	.07
❑	525 Frank White	.30	.14
❑	526 Checklist: 397-528	.30	.14
❑	527 Larry Biittner	.15	.07
❑	528 Jamie Easterly	.15	.07
❑	529 Tim Laudner	.15	.07
❑	530 Eddie Murray	1.50	.70
❑	531 Oakland A's TL BA: Rickey Henderson ERA: Rick Langford	1.25	.55
❑	532 Dave Stewart	.30	.14
❑	533 Luis Salazar	.15	.07
❑	534 John Butcher	.15	.07
❑	535 Manny Trillo	.15	.07
❑	536 John Wockenfuss	.15	.07
❑	537 Rod Scurry	.15	.07
❑	538 Danny Heep	.15	.07
❑	539 Roger Erickson	.15	.07
❑	540 Ozzie Smith	2.00	.90
❑	541 Britt Burns	.15	.07
❑	542 Jody Davis	.15	.07
❑	543 Alan Fowlkes	.15	.07
❑	544 Larry Whisenton	.15	.07
❑	545 Floyd Bannister	.15	.07
❑	546 Dave Garcia MG	.15	.07
❑	547 Geoff Zahn	.15	.07
❑	548 Brian Giles	.15	.07
❑	549 Charlie Puleo	.15	.07
❑	550 Carl Yastrzemski	1.25	.55
❑	551 Carl Yastrzemski SV	.60	.25
❑	552 Tim Wallach	.30	.14
❑	553 Dennis Martinez	.30	.14
❑	554 Mike Vail	.15	.07
❑	555 Steve Yeager	.15	.07
❑	556 Willie Upshaw	.15	.07
❑	557 Rick Honeycutt	.15	.07
❑	558 Dickie Thon	.15	.07
❑	559 Pete Redfern	.15	.07
❑	560 Ron LeFlore	.15	.07
❑	561 Cardinals TL BA: Lonnie Smith ERA: Joaquin Andujar	.30	.14
❑	562 Dave Rozema	.15	.07
❑	563 Juan Bonilla	.15	.07
❑	564 Sid Monge	.15	.07
❑	565 Bucky Dent	.30	.14
❑	566 Manny Sarmiento	.15	.07
❑	567 Joe Simpson	.15	.07
❑	568 Willie Hernandez	.30	.14
❑	569 Jack Perconte	.15	.07
❑	570 Vida Blue	.30	.14
❑	571 Mickey Klutts	.15	.07
❑	572 Bob Watson	.30	.14
❑	573 Andy Hassler	.15	.07
❑	574 Glenn Adams	.15	.07
❑	575 Neil Allen	.15	.07
❑	576 Frank Robinson MG	.60	.25
❑	577 Luis Aponte	.15	.07
❑	578 David Green	.15	.07
❑	579 Rich Dauer	.15	.07
❑	580 Tom Seaver	2.00	.90
❑	581 Tom Seaver SV	.60	.25
❑	582 Marshall Edwards	.15	.07
❑	583 Terry Forster	.15	.07
❑	584 Dave Hostetler	.15	.07
❑	585 Jose Cruz	.30	.14
❑	586 Frank Viola RC	1.25	.55
❑	587 Ivan DeJesus	.15	.07
❑	588 Pat Underwood	.15	.07
❑	589 Alvis Woods	.15	.07
❑	590 Tony Pena	.15	.07
❑	591 White Sox TL BA: Greg Luzinski ERA: LaMarr Hoyt	.30	.14
❑	592 Shane Rawley	.15	.07
❑	593 Broderick Perkins	.15	.07
❑	594 Eric Rasmussen	.15	.07
❑	595 Tim Raines	1.25	.55
❑	596 Randy Johnson	.15	.07
❑	597 Mike Proly	.15	.07
❑	598 Dwayne Murphy	.15	.07
❑	599 Don Aase	.15	.07
❑	600 George Brett	2.50	1.10
❑	601 Ed Lynch	.15	.07
❑	602 Rich Gedman	.15	.07
❑	603 Joe Morgan	1.25	.55
❑	604 Joe Morgan SV	.60	.25
❑	605 Gary Roenicke	.15	.07
❑	606 Bobby Cox MG	.30	.14
❑	607 Charlie Leibrandt	.15	.07
❑	608 Don Money	.15	.07
❑	609 Danny Darwin	.15	.07
❑	610 Steve Garvey	.60	.25
❑	611 Bert Roberge	.15	.07
❑	612 Steve Swisher	.15	.07
❑	613 Mike Ivie	.15	.07
❑	614 Ed Glynn	.15	.07
❑	615 Garry Maddox	.15	.07
❑	616 Bill Nahorodny	.15	.07
❑	617 Butch Wynegar	.15	.07
❑	618 LaMarr Hoyt	.30	.14
❑	619 Keith Moreland	.15	.07
❑	620 Mike Norris	.15	.07
❑	621 New York Mets TL BA: Mookie Wilson ERA: Craig Swan	.30	.14
❑	622 Dave Edler	.15	.07
❑	623 Luis Sanchez	.15	.07
❑	624 Glenn Hubbard	.15	.07
❑	625 Ken Forsch	.15	.07
❑	626 Jerry Martin	.15	.07
❑	627 Doug Bair	.15	.07
❑	628 Julio Valdez	.15	.07
❑	629 Charlie Lea	.15	.07
❑	630 Paul Molitor	1.50	.70
❑	631 Tippy Martinez	.15	.07
❑	632 Alex Trevino	.15	.07
❑	633 Vicente Romo	.15	.07
❑	634 Max Venable	.15	.07
❑	635 Graig Nettles	.30	.14
❑	636 Graig Nettles SV	.15	.07
❑	637 Pat Corrales MG	.15	.07
❑	638 Dan Petry	.15	.07
❑	639 Art Howe	.30	.14
❑	640 Andre Thornton	.15	.07
❑	641 Billy Sample	.15	.07
❑	642 Checklist: 529-660	.30	.14
❑	643 Bump Wills	.15	.07
❑	644 Joe Lefebvre	.15	.07
❑	645 Bill Madlock	.30	.14
❑	646 Jim Essian	.15	.07
❑	647 Bobby Mitchell	.15	.07
❑	648 Jeff Burroughs	.15	.07
❑	649 Tommy Boggs	.15	.07
❑	650 George Hendrick	.15	.07
❑	651 Angels TL BA: Rod Carew ERA: Mike Witt	.60	.25
❑	652 Butch Hobson	.15	.07
❑	653 Ellis Valentine	.15	.07
❑	654 Bob Ojeda	.15	.07
❑	655 Al Bumbry	.15	.07
❑	656 Dave Frost	.15	.07
❑	657 Mike Gates	.15	.07
❑	658 Frank Pastore	.15	.07
❑	659 Charlie Moore	.15	.07
❑	660 Mike Hargrove	.30	.14
❑	661 Bill Russell	.15	.07
❑	662 Joe Sambito	.15	.07
❑	663 Tom O'Malley	.15	.07
❑	664 Bob Molinaro	.15	.07
❑	665 Jim Sundberg	.30	.14
❑	666 Sparky Anderson MG	.30	.14
❑	667 Dick Davis	.15	.07
❑	668 Larry Christenson	.15	.07
❑	669 Mike Squires	.15	.07
❑	670 Jerry Mumphrey	.15	.07
❑	671 Lenny Faedo	.15	.07
❑	672 Jim Kaat	.30	.14
❑	673 Jim Kaat SV	.15	.07
❑	674 Kurt Bevacqua	.15	.07
❑	675 Jim Beattie	.15	.07
❑	676 Biff Pocoroba	.15	.07
❑	677 Dave Revering	.15	.07
❑	678 Juan Beniquez	.15	.07
❑	679 Mike Scott	.30	.14
❑	680 Andre Dawson	.60	.25
❑	681 Dodgers Leaders BA: Pedro Guerrero ERA: Fernando Valenzuela	.30	.14
❑	682 Bob Stanley	.15	.07
❑	683 Dan Ford	.15	.07
❑	684 Rafael Landestoy	.15	.07
❑	685 Lee Mazzilli	.15	.07
❑	686 Randy Lerch	.15	.07
❑	687 U.L. Washington	.15	.07
❑	688 Jim Wohlford	.15	.07
❑	689 Ron Hassey	.15	.07
❑	690 Kent Hrbek	.30	.14
❑	691 Dave Tobik	.15	.07
❑	692 Denny Walling	.15	.07
❑	693 Sparky Lyle	.30	.14
❑	694 Sparky Lyle SV	.15	.07
❑	695 Ruppert Jones	.15	.07
❑	696 Chuck Tanner MG	.15	.07
❑	697 Barry Foote	.15	.07
❑	698 Tony Bernazard	.15	.07
❑	699 Lee Smith	1.25	.55
❑	700 Keith Hernandez	.30	.14
❑	701 Batting Leaders AL: Willie Wilson NL: Al Oliver	.30	.14
❑	702 Home Run Leaders AL: Reggie Jackson AL: Gorman Thomas NL: Dave Kingman	.60	.25
❑	703 RBI Leaders AL: Hal McRae NL: Dale Murphy NL: Al Oliver	.30	.14
❑	704 SB Leaders AL: Rickey Henderson NL: Tim Raines	1.25	.55
❑	705 Victory Leaders AL: LaMarr Hoyt NL: Steve Carlton	.60	.25
❑	706 Strikeout Leaders AL: Floyd Bannister NL: Steve Carlton	.60	.25
❑	707 ERA Leaders AL: Rick Sutcliffe NL: Steve Rogers	.30	.14
❑	708 Leading Firemen AL: Dan Quisenberry NL: Bruce Sutter	.30	.14
❑	709 Jimmy Sexton	.15	.07
❑	710 Willie Wilson	.30	.14
❑	711 Mariners TL BA: Bruce Bochte ERA: Jim Beattie	.30	.14
❑	712 Bruce Kison	.15	.07
❑	713 Ron Hodges	.15	.07
❑	714 Wayne Nordhagen	.15	.07
❑	715 Tony Perez	1.25	.55
❑	716 Tony Perez SV	.60	.25
❑	717 Scott Sanderson	.15	.07
❑	718 Jim Dwyer	.15	.07
❑	719 Rich Gale	.15	.07
❑	720 Dave Concepcion	.30	.14
❑	721 John Martin	.15	.07
❑	722 Jorge Orta	.15	.07
❑	723 Randy Moffitt	.15	.07
❑	724 Johnny Grubb	.15	.07
❑	725 Dan Spillner	.15	.07
❑	726 Harvey Kuenn MG	.15	.07
❑	727 Chet Lemon	.15	.07
❑	728 Ron Reed	.15	.07
❑	729 Jerry Morales	.15	.07
❑	730 Jason Thompson	.15	.07
❑	731 Al Williams	.15	.07
❑	732 Dave Henderson	.15	.07
❑	733 Buck Martinez	.15	.07
❑	734 Steve Braun	.15	.07
❑	735 Tommy John	.60	.25
❑	736 Tommy John SV	.30	.14
❑	737 Mitchell Page	.15	.07
❑	738 Tim Foli	.15	.07
❑	739 Rick Ownbey	.15	.07
❑	740 Rusty Staub	.30	.14
❑	741 Rusty Staub SV	.15	.07
❑	742 Padres TL BA: Terry Kennedy ERA: Tim Lollar	.30	.14
❑	743 Mike Torrez	.15	.07
❑	744 Brad Mills	.15	.07
❑	745 Scott McGregor	.15	.07

Card	NRMT	VG-E
❑ 746 John Wathan	.15	.07
❑ 747 Fred Breining	.15	.07
❑ 748 Derrel Thomas	.15	.07
❑ 749 Jon Matlack	.15	.07
❑ 750 Ben Oglivie	.15	.07
❑ 751 Brad Havens	.15	.07
❑ 752 Luis Pujols	.15	.07
❑ 753 Elias Sosa	.15	.07
❑ 754 Bill Robinson	.15	.07
❑ 755 John Candelaria	.15	.07
❑ 756 Russ Nixon MG	.15	.07
❑ 757 Rick Manning	.15	.07
❑ 758 Aurelio Rodriguez	.15	.07
❑ 759 Doug Bird	.15	.07
❑ 760 Dale Murphy	1.25	.55
❑ 761 Gary Lucas	.15	.07
❑ 762 Cliff Johnson	.15	.07
❑ 763 Al Cowens	.15	.07
❑ 764 Pete Falcone	.15	.07
❑ 765 Bob Boone	.30	.14
❑ 766 Barry Bonnell	.15	.07
❑ 767 Duane Kuiper	.15	.07
❑ 768 Chris Speier	.15	.07
❑ 769 Checklist: 661-792	.30	.14
❑ 770 Dave Winfield	1.25	.55
❑ 771 Twins TL BA: Kent Hrbek ERA: Bobby Castillo	.30	.14
❑ 772 Jim Kern	.15	.07
❑ 773 Larry Hisle	.15	.07
❑ 774 Alan Ashby	.15	.07
❑ 775 Burt Hooton	.15	.07
❑ 776 Larry Parrish	.15	.07
❑ 777 John Curtis	.15	.07
❑ 778 Rich Hebner	.30	.14
❑ 779 Rick Waits	.15	.07
❑ 780 Gary Matthews	.30	.14
❑ 781 Rick Rhoden	.15	.07
❑ 782 Bobby Murcer	.30	.14
❑ 783 Bobby Murcer SV	.15	.07
❑ 784 Jeff Newman	.15	.07
❑ 785 Dennis Leonard	.15	.07
❑ 786 Ralph Houk MG	.15	.07
❑ 787 Dick Tidrow	.15	.07
❑ 788 Dane Iorg	.15	.07
❑ 789 Bryan Clark	.15	.07
❑ 790 Bob Grich	.30	.14
❑ 791 Gary Lavelle	.15	.07
❑ 792 Chris Chambliss	.30	.14
❑ XX Game Insert Card	.10	.05

1983 Topps Traded

	NRMT	VG-E
COMP.FACT.SET (132)	30.00	13.50

Card	NRMT	VG-E
❑ 1T Neil Allen	.25	.11
❑ 2T Bill Almon	.25	.11
❑ 3T Joe Altobelli MG	.25	.11
❑ 4T Tony Armas	.25	.11
❑ 5T Doug Bair	.25	.11
❑ 6T Steve Baker	.25	.11
❑ 7T Floyd Bannister	.25	.11
❑ 8T Don Baylor	2.00	.90
❑ 9T Tony Bernazard	.25	.11
❑ 10T Larry Biittner	.25	.11
❑ 11T Dann Bilardello	.25	.11
❑ 12T Doug Bird	.25	.11
❑ 13T Steve Boros MG	.25	.11
❑ 14T Greg Brock	.25	.11
❑ 15T Mike C. Brown	.25	.11
❑ 16T Tom Burgmeier	.25	.11
❑ 17T Randy Bush	.25	.11
❑ 18T Bert Campaneris	1.00	.45
❑ 19T Ron Cey	1.00	.45
❑ 20T Chris Codiroli	.25	.11
❑ 21T Dave Collins	.25	.11
❑ 22T Terry Crowley	.25	.11
❑ 23T Julio Cruz	.25	.11
❑ 24T Mike Davis	.25	.11
❑ 25T Frank DiPino	.25	.11
❑ 26T Bill Doran XRC	1.00	.45
❑ 27T Jerry Dybzinski	.25	.11
❑ 28T Jamie Easterly	.25	.11
❑ 29T Juan Eichelberger	.25	.11
❑ 30T Jim Essian	.25	.11
❑ 31T Pete Falcone	.25	.11
❑ 32T Mike Ferraro MG	.25	.11
❑ 33T Terry Forster	.25	.11
❑ 34T Julio Franco XRC	4.00	1.80
❑ 35T Rich Gale	.25	.11
❑ 36T Kiko Garcia	.25	.11
❑ 37T Steve Garvey	2.00	.90
❑ 38T Johnny Grubb	.25	.11
❑ 39T Mel Hall XRC*	1.00	.45
❑ 40T Von Hayes	1.00	.45
❑ 41T Danny Heep	.25	.11
❑ 42T Steve Henderson	.25	.11
❑ 43T Keith Hernandez	2.00	.90
❑ 44T Leo Hernandez	.25	.11
❑ 45T Willie Hernandez	1.00	.45
❑ 46T Al Holland	.25	.11
❑ 47T Frank Howard MG	1.00	.45
❑ 48T Bobby Johnson	.25	.11
❑ 49T Cliff Johnson	.25	.11
❑ 50T Odell Jones	.25	.11
❑ 51T Mike Jorgensen	.25	.11
❑ 52T Bob Kearney	.25	.11
❑ 53T Steve Kemp	.25	.11
❑ 54T Matt Keough	.25	.11
❑ 55T Ron Kittle XRC*	2.00	.90
❑ 56T Mickey Klutts	.25	.11
❑ 57T Alan Knicely	.25	.11
❑ 58T Mike Krukow	.25	.11
❑ 59T Rafael Landestoy	.25	.11
❑ 60T Carney Lansford	1.00	.45
❑ 61T Joe Lefebvre	.25	.11
❑ 62T Bryan Little	.25	.11
❑ 63T Aurelio Lopez	.25	.11
❑ 64T Mike Madden	.25	.11
❑ 65T Rick Manning	.25	.11
❑ 66T Billy Martin MG	1.00	.45
❑ 67T Lee Mazzilli	.25	.11
❑ 68T Andy McGaffigan	.25	.11
❑ 69T Craig McMurtry	.25	.11
❑ 70T John McNamara MG	.25	.11
❑ 71T Orlando Mercado	.25	.11
❑ 72T Larry Milbourne	.25	.11
❑ 73T Randy Moffitt	.25	.11
❑ 74T Sid Monge	.25	.11
❑ 75T Jose Morales	.25	.11
❑ 76T Omar Moreno	.25	.11
❑ 77T Joe Morgan	2.00	.90
❑ 78T Mike Morgan	.25	.11
❑ 79T Dale Murray	.25	.11
❑ 80T Jeff Newman	.25	.11
❑ 81T Pete O'Brien XRC	1.00	.45
❑ 82T Jorge Orta	.25	.11
❑ 83T Alejandro Pena XRC	1.00	.45
❑ 84T Pascual Perez	.25	.11
❑ 85T Tony Perez	2.00	.90
❑ 86T Broderick Perkins	.25	.11
❑ 87T Tony Phillips XRC	2.00	.90
❑ 88T Charlie Puleo	.25	.11
❑ 89T Pat Putnam	.25	.11
❑ 90T Jamie Quirk	.25	.11
❑ 91T Doug Rader MG	.25	.11
❑ 92T Chuck Rainey	.25	.11
❑ 93T Bobby Ramos	.25	.11
❑ 94T Gary Redus XRC	1.00	.45
❑ 95T Steve Renko	.25	.11
❑ 96T Leon Roberts	.25	.11
❑ 97T Aurelio Rodriguez	.25	.11
❑ 98T Dick Ruthven	.25	.11
❑ 99T Daryl Sconiers	.25	.11
❑ 100T Mike Scott	1.00	.45
❑ 101T Tom Seaver	5.00	2.20
❑ 102T John Shelby	.25	.11
❑ 103T Bob Shirley	.25	.11
❑ 104T Joe Simpson	.25	.11
❑ 105T Doug Sisk	.25	.11
❑ 106T Mike Smithson	.25	.11
❑ 107T Elias Sosa	.25	.11
❑ 108T D.Strawberry XRC	10.00	4.50
❑ 109T Tom Tellmann	.25	.11
❑ 110T Gene Tenace	1.00	.45
❑ 111T Gorman Thomas	.25	.11
❑ 112T Dick Tidrow	.25	.11
❑ 113T Dave Tobik	.25	.11
❑ 114T Wayne Tolleson	.25	.11
❑ 115T Mike Torrez	.25	.11
❑ 116T Manny Trillo	.25	.11
❑ 117T Steve Trout	.25	.11
❑ 118T Lee Tunnell	.25	.11
❑ 119T Mike Vail	.25	.11
❑ 120T Ellis Valentine	.25	.11
❑ 121T Tom Veryzer	.25	.11
❑ 122T George Vukovich	.25	.11
❑ 123T Rick Waits	.25	.11
❑ 124T Greg Walker	1.00	.45
❑ 125T Chris Welsh	.25	.11
❑ 126T Len Whitehouse	.25	.11
❑ 127T Eddie Whitson	.25	.11
❑ 128T Jim Wohlford	.25	.11
❑ 129T Matt Young	.25	.11
❑ 130T Joel Youngblood	.25	.11
❑ 131T Pat Zachry	.25	.11
❑ 132T Checklist 1T-132T	.25	.11

1984 Topps

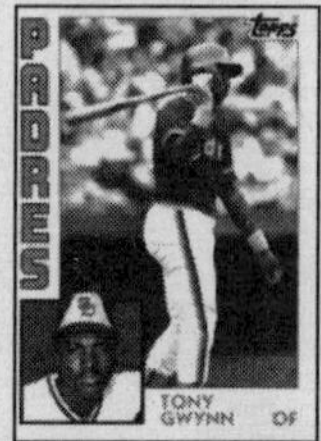

	NRMT	VG-E
COMPLETE SET (792)	40.00	18.00

Card	NRMT	VG-E
❑ 1 Steve Carlton HL 300th win and all-time SO king	.60	.25
❑ 2 Rickey Henderson HL 100 stolen bases three times	.60	.25
❑ 3 Dan Quisenberry HL Sets save record	.15	.07
❑ 4 Nolan Ryan HL Steve Carlton Gaylord Perry All surpass Johnson	1.00	.45
❑ 5 Dave Righetti HL Bob Forsch Mike Warren All pitch no-hitters	.25	.11
❑ 6 Johnny Bench HL Gaylord Perry Carl Yastrzemski Superstars retire	.60	.25
❑ 7 Gary Lucas	.15	.07
❑ 8 Don Mattingly RC	10.00	4.50
❑ 9 Jim Gott	.15	.07
❑ 10 Robin Yount	.60	.25
❑ 11 Minnesota Twins TL Kent Hrbek Ken Schrom	.25	.11
❑ 12 Billy Sample	.15	.07

❑ 13 Scott Holman .15 .07
❑ 14 Tom Brookens .25 .11
❑ 15 Burt Hooton .15 .07
❑ 16 Omar Moreno .15 .07
❑ 17 John Denny .15 .07
❑ 18 Dale Berra .15 .07
❑ 19 Ray Fontenot .15 .07
❑ 20 Greg Luzinski .25 .11
❑ 21 Joe Altobelli MG .15 .07
❑ 22 Bryan Clark .15 .07
❑ 23 Keith Moreland .15 .07
❑ 24 John Martin .15 .07
❑ 25 Glenn Hubbard .15 .07
❑ 26 Bud Black .15 .07
❑ 27 Daryl Sconiers .15 .07
❑ 28 Frank Viola .40 .18
❑ 29 Danny Heep .15 .07
❑ 30 Wade Boggs 1.50 .70
❑ 31 Andy McGaffigan .15 .07
❑ 32 Bobby Ramos .15 .07
❑ 33 Tom Burgmeier .15 .07
❑ 34 Eddie Milner .15 .07
❑ 35 Don Sutton .60 .25
❑ 36 Denny Walling .15 .07
❑ 37 Texas Rangers TL .25 .11
Buddy Bell
Rick Honeycutt
❑ 38 Luis DeLeon .15 .07
❑ 39 Garth Iorg .15 .07
❑ 40 Dusty Baker .25 .11
❑ 41 Tony Bernazard .15 .07
❑ 42 Johnny Grubb .15 .07
❑ 43 Ron Reed .15 .07
❑ 44 Jim Morrison .15 .07
❑ 45 Jerry Mumphrey .15 .07
❑ 46 Ray Smith .15 .07
❑ 47 Rudy Law .15 .07
❑ 48 Julio Franco .40 .18
❑ 49 John Stuper .15 .07
❑ 50 Chris Chambliss .25 .11
❑ 51 Jim Frey MG .15 .07
❑ 52 Paul Splittorff .15 .07
❑ 53 Juan Beniquez .15 .07
❑ 54 Jesse Orosco .15 .07
❑ 55 Dave Concepcion .25 .11
❑ 56 Gary Allenson .15 .07
❑ 57 Dan Schatzeder .15 .07
❑ 58 Max Venable .15 .07
❑ 59 Sammy Stewart .15 .07
❑ 60 Paul Molitor UER .60 .25
('83 stats .272, 613, 167; should be .270, 608, 164)
❑ 61 Chris Codiroli .15 .07
❑ 62 Dave Hostetler .15 .07
❑ 63 Ed VandeBerg .15 .07
❑ 64 Mike Scioscia .15 .07
❑ 65 Kirk Gibson .60 .25
❑ 66 Houston Astros TL 1.00 .45
Jose Cruz
Nolan Ryan
❑ 67 Gary Ward .15 .07
❑ 68 Luis Salazar .15 .07
❑ 69 Rod Scurry .15 .07
❑ 70 Gary Matthews .25 .11
❑ 71 Leo Hernandez .15 .07
❑ 72 Mike Squires .15 .07
❑ 73 Jody Davis .15 .07
❑ 74 Jerry Martin .15 .07
❑ 75 Bob Forsch .15 .07
❑ 76 Alfredo Griffin .15 .07
❑ 77 Brett Butler .40 .18
❑ 78 Mike Torrez .15 .07
❑ 79 Rob Wilfong .15 .07
❑ 80 Steve Rogers .15 .07
❑ 81 Billy Martin MG .25 .11
❑ 82 Doug Bird .15 .07
❑ 83 Richie Zisk .15 .07
❑ 84 Lenny Faedo .15 .07
❑ 85 Atlee Hammaker .15 .07
❑ 86 John Shelby .15 .07
❑ 87 Frank Pastore .15 .07
❑ 88 Rob Picciolo .15 .07
❑ 89 Mike Smithson .15 .07
❑ 90 Pedro Guerrero .25 .11
❑ 91 Dan Spillner .15 .07
❑ 92 Lloyd Moseby .15 .07
❑ 93 Bob Knepper .15 .07
❑ 94 Mario Ramirez .15 .07
❑ 95 Aurelio Lopez .25 .11
❑ 96 Kansas City Royals TL .25 .11
Hal McRae
Larry Gura
❑ 97 LaMarr Hoyt .15 .07
❑ 98 Steve Nicosia .15 .07
❑ 99 Craig Lefferts RC .15 .07
❑ 100 Reggie Jackson .75 .35
❑ 101 Porfirio Altamirano .15 .07
❑ 102 Ken Oberkfell .15 .07
❑ 103 Dwayne Murphy .15 .07
❑ 104 Ken Dayley .15 .07
❑ 105 Tony Armas .15 .07
❑ 106 Tim Stoddard .15 .07
❑ 107 Ned Yost .15 .07
❑ 108 Randy Moffitt .15 .07
❑ 109 Brad Wellman .15 .07
❑ 110 Ron Guidry .25 .11
❑ 111 Bill Virdon MG .15 .07
❑ 112 Tom Niedenfuer .15 .07
❑ 113 Kelly Paris .15 .07
❑ 114 Checklist 1-132 .25 .11
❑ 115 Andre Thornton .15 .07
❑ 116 George Bjorkman .15 .07
❑ 117 Tom Veryzer .15 .07
❑ 118 Charlie Hough .25 .11
❑ 119 John Wockenfuss .15 .07
❑ 120 Keith Hernandez .25 .11
❑ 121 Pat Sheridan .15 .07
❑ 122 Cecilio Guante .15 .07
❑ 123 Butch Wynegar .15 .07
❑ 124 Damaso Garcia .15 .07
❑ 125 Britt Burns .15 .07
❑ 126 Atlanta Braves TL .40 .18
Dale Murphy
Craig McMurtry
❑ 127 Mike Madden .15 .07
❑ 128 Rick Manning .15 .07
❑ 129 Bill Laskey .15 .07
❑ 130 Ozzie Smith .75 .35
❑ 131 Batting Leaders .60 .25
Bill Madlock
Wade Boggs
❑ 132 Home Run Leaders .60 .25
Mike Schmidt
Jim Rice
❑ 133 RBI Leaders .60 .25
Dale Murphy
Cecil Cooper
Jim Rice
❑ 134 Stolen Base Leaders .60 .25
Tim Raines
Rickey Henderson
❑ 135 Victory Leaders .60 .25
John Denny
LaMarr Hoyt
❑ 136 Strikeout Leaders .60 .25
Steve Carlton
Jack Morris
❑ 137 ERA Leaders .25 .11
Atlee Hammaker
Rick Honeycutt
❑ 138 Leading Firemen .25 .11
Al Holland
Dan Quisenberry
❑ 139 Bert Campaneris .25 .11
❑ 140 Storm Davis .15 .07
❑ 141 Pat Corrales MG .15 .07
❑ 142 Rich Gale .15 .07
❑ 143 Jose Morales .15 .07
❑ 144 Brian Harper RC .25 .11
❑ 145 Gary Lavelle .15 .07
❑ 146 Ed Romero .15 .07
❑ 147 Dan Petry .25 .11
❑ 148 Joe Lefebvre .15 .07
❑ 149 Jon Matlack .15 .07
❑ 150 Dale Murphy .60 .25
❑ 151 Steve Trout .15 .07
❑ 152 Glenn Brummer .15 .07
❑ 153 Dick Tidrow .15 .07
❑ 154 Dave Henderson .25 .11
❑ 155 Frank White .25 .11
❑ 156 Oakland A's TL .60 .25
Rickey Henderson
Tim Conroy
❑ 157 Gary Gaetti .40 .18
❑ 158 John Curtis .15 .07
❑ 159 Darryl Cias .15 .07
❑ 160 Mario Soto .15 .07
❑ 161 Junior Ortiz .15 .07
❑ 162 Bob Ojeda .15 .07
❑ 163 Lorenzo Gray .15 .07
❑ 164 Scott Sanderson .15 .07
❑ 165 Ken Singleton .15 .07
❑ 166 Jamie Nelson .15 .07
❑ 167 Marshall Edwards .15 .07
❑ 168 Juan Bonilla .15 .07
❑ 169 Larry Parrish .15 .07
❑ 170 Jerry Reuss .15 .07
❑ 171 Frank Robinson MG .40 .18
❑ 172 Frank DiPino .15 .07
❑ 173 Marvell Wynne .15 .07
❑ 174 Juan Berenguer .15 .07
❑ 175 Graig Nettles .25 .11
❑ 176 Lee Smith .60 .25
❑ 177 Jerry Hairston .15 .07
❑ 178 Bill Krueger RC .15 .07
❑ 179 Buck Martinez .15 .07
❑ 180 Manny Trillo .15 .07
❑ 181 Roy Thomas .15 .07
❑ 182 Darryl Strawberry RC 1.00 .45
❑ 183 Al Williams .15 .07
❑ 184 Mike O'Berry .15 .07
❑ 185 Sixto Lezcano .15 .07
❑ 186 Cardinal TL .25 .11
Lonnie Smith
John Stuper
❑ 187 Luis Aponte .15 .07
❑ 188 Bryan Little .15 .07
❑ 189 Tim Conroy .15 .07
❑ 190 Ben Oglivie .15 .07
❑ 191 Mike Boddicker .15 .07
❑ 192 Nick Esasky .15 .07
❑ 193 Darrell Brown .15 .07
❑ 194 Domingo Ramos .15 .07
❑ 195 Jack Morris .60 .25
❑ 196 Don Slaught .25 .11
❑ 197 Garry Hancock .15 .07
❑ 198 Bill Doran RC* .25 .11
❑ 199 Willie Hernandez .25 .11
❑ 200 Andre Dawson .40 .18
❑ 201 Bruce Kison .15 .07
❑ 202 Bobby Cox MG .25 .11
❑ 203 Matt Keough .15 .07
❑ 204 Bobby Meacham .15 .07
❑ 205 Greg Minton .15 .07
❑ 206 Andy Van Slyke RC .60 .25
❑ 207 Donnie Moore .15 .07
❑ 208 Jose Oquendo RC .25 .11
❑ 209 Manny Sarmiento .15 .07
❑ 210 Joe Morgan .60 .25
❑ 211 Rick Sweet .15 .07
❑ 212 Broderick Perkins .15 .07
❑ 213 Bruce Hurst .15 .07
❑ 214 Paul Householder .15 .07
❑ 215 Tippy Martinez .15 .07
❑ 216 White Sox TL .60 .25
Carlton Fisk
Richard Dotson
❑ 217 Alan Ashby .15 .07
❑ 218 Rick Waits .15 .07
❑ 219 Joe Simpson .15 .07
❑ 220 Fernando Valenzuela .25 .11
❑ 221 Cliff Johnson .15 .07
❑ 222 Rick Honeycutt .15 .07
❑ 223 Wayne Krenchicki .15 .07
❑ 224 Sid Monge .15 .07
❑ 225 Lee Mazzilli .15 .07
❑ 226 Juan Eichelberger .15 .07
❑ 227 Steve Braun .15 .07
❑ 228 John Rabb .15 .07
❑ 229 Paul Owens MG .15 .07
❑ 230 Rickey Henderson 1.25 .55
❑ 231 Gary Woods .15 .07
❑ 232 Tim Wallach .25 .11
❑ 233 Checklist 133-264 .25 .11
❑ 234 Rafael Ramirez .15 .07
❑ 235 Matt Young .15 .07
❑ 236 Ellis Valentine .15 .07

❑ 237 John Castino .15 .07
❑ 238 Reid Nichols .15 .07
❑ 239 Jay Howell .15 .07
❑ 240 Eddie Murray .60 .25
❑ 241 Bill Almon .15 .07
❑ 242 Alex Trevino .15 .07
❑ 243 Pete Ladd .15 .07
❑ 244 Candy Maldonado .15 .07
❑ 245 Rick Sutcliffe .25 .11
❑ 246 New York Mets TL .60 .25
Mookie Wilson
Tom Seaver
❑ 247 Onix Concepcion .15 .07
❑ 248 Bill Dawley .15 .07
❑ 249 Jay Johnstone .25 .11
❑ 250 Bill Madlock .25 .11
❑ 251 Tony Gwynn 3.00 1.35
❑ 252 Larry Christenson .15 .07
❑ 253 Jim Wohlford .15 .07
❑ 254 Shane Rawley .15 .07
❑ 255 Bruce Benedict .15 .07
❑ 256 Dave Geisel .15 .07
❑ 257 Julio Cruz .15 .07
❑ 258 Luis Sanchez .15 .07
❑ 259 Sparky Anderson MG .40 .18
❑ 260 Scott McGregor .15 .07
❑ 261 Bobby Brown .15 .07
❑ 262 Tom Candiotti RC .60 .25
❑ 263 Jack Fimple .15 .07
❑ 264 Doug Frobel .15 .07
❑ 265 Donnie Hill .15 .07
❑ 266 Steve Lubratich .15 .07
❑ 267 Carmelo Martinez .15 .07
❑ 268 Jack O'Connor .15 .07
❑ 269 Aurelio Rodriguez .15 .07
❑ 270 Jeff Russell RC .25 .11
❑ 271 Moose Haas .15 .07
❑ 272 Rick Dempsey .15 .07
❑ 273 Charlie Puleo .15 .07
❑ 274 Rick Monday .15 .07
❑ 275 Len Matuszek .15 .07
❑ 276 Angels TL .60 .25
Rod Carew
Geoff Zahn
❑ 277 Eddie Whitson .15 .07
❑ 278 Jorge Bell .40 .18
❑ 279 Ivan DeJesus .15 .07
❑ 280 Floyd Bannister .15 .07
❑ 281 Larry Milbourne .15 .07
❑ 282 Jim Barr .15 .07
❑ 283 Larry Biittner .15 .07
❑ 284 Howard Bailey .15 .07
❑ 285 Darrell Porter .15 .07
❑ 286 Lary Sorensen .15 .07
❑ 287 Warren Cromartie .15 .07
❑ 288 Jim Beattie .15 .07
❑ 289 Randy Johnson .15 .07
❑ 290 Dave Dravecky .25 .11
❑ 291 Chuck Tanner MG .15 .07
❑ 292 Tony Scott .15 .07
❑ 293 Ed Lynch .15 .07
❑ 294 U.L. Washington .15 .07
❑ 295 Mike Flanagan .15 .07
❑ 296 Jeff Newman .15 .07
❑ 297 Bruce Berenyi .15 .07
❑ 298 Jim Gantner .15 .07
❑ 299 John Butcher .15 .07
❑ 300 Pete Rose 2.00 .90
❑ 301 Frank LaCorte .15 .07
❑ 302 Barry Bonnell .15 .07
❑ 303 Marty Castillo .15 .07
❑ 304 Warren Brusstar .15 .07
❑ 305 Roy Smalley .15 .07
❑ 306 Dodgers TL .25 .11
Pedro Guerrero
Bob Welch
❑ 307 Bobby Mitchell .15 .07
❑ 308 Ron Hassey .15 .07
❑ 309 Tony Phillips RC .60 .25
❑ 310 Willie McGee .40 .18
❑ 311 Jerry Koosman .25 .11
❑ 312 Jorge Orta .15 .07
❑ 313 Mike Jorgensen .15 .07
❑ 314 Orlando Mercado .15 .07
❑ 315 Bobby Grich .25 .11
❑ 316 Mark Bradley .15 .07

❑ 317 Greg Pryor .15 .07
❑ 318 Bill Gullickson .15 .07
❑ 319 Al Bumbry .15 .07
❑ 320 Bob Stanley .15 .07
❑ 321 Harvey Kuenn MG .25 .11
❑ 322 Ken Schrom .15 .07
❑ 323 Alan Knicely .15 .07
❑ 324 Alejandro Pena RC* .25 .11
❑ 325 Darrell Evans .25 .11
❑ 326 Bob Kearney .15 .07
❑ 327 Ruppert Jones .15 .07
❑ 328 Vern Ruhle .15 .07
❑ 329 Pat Tabler .15 .07
❑ 330 John Candelaria .15 .07
❑ 331 Bucky Dent .25 .11
❑ 332 Kevin Gross RC .15 .07
❑ 333 Larry Herndon .25 .11
❑ 334 Chuck Rainey .15 .07
❑ 335 Don Baylor .40 .18
❑ 336 Seattle Mariners TL .25 .11
Pat Putnam
Matt Young
❑ 337 Kevin Hagen .15 .07
❑ 338 Mike Warren .15 .07
❑ 339 Roy Lee Jackson .15 .07
❑ 340 Hal McRae .25 .11
❑ 341 Dave Tobik .15 .07
❑ 342 Tim Foli .15 .07
❑ 343 Mark Davis .15 .07
❑ 344 Rick Miller .15 .07
❑ 345 Kent Hrbek .25 .11
❑ 346 Kurt Bevacqua .15 .07
❑ 347 Allan Ramirez .15 .07
❑ 348 Toby Harrah .25 .11
❑ 349 Bob L. Gibson .15 .07
❑ 350 George Foster .25 .11
❑ 351 Russ Nixon MG .15 .07
❑ 352 Dave Stewart .25 .11
❑ 353 Jim Anderson .15 .07
❑ 354 Jeff Burroughs .15 .07
❑ 355 Jason Thompson .15 .07
❑ 356 Glenn Abbott .15 .07
❑ 357 Ron Cey .25 .11
❑ 358 Bob Dernier .15 .07
❑ 359 Jim Acker .15 .07
❑ 360 Willie Randolph .25 .11
❑ 361 Dave Smith .15 .07
❑ 362 David Green .15 .07
❑ 363 Tim Laudner .15 .07
❑ 364 Scott Fletcher .15 .07
❑ 365 Steve Bedrosian .15 .07
❑ 366 Padres TL .25 .11
Terry Kennedy
Dave Dravecky
❑ 367 Jamie Easterly .15 .07
❑ 368 Hubie Brooks .15 .07
❑ 369 Steve McCatty .15 .07
❑ 370 Tim Raines .40 .18
❑ 371 Dave Gumpert .15 .07
❑ 372 Gary Roenicke .15 .07
❑ 373 Bill Scherrer .15 .07
❑ 374 Don Money .15 .07
❑ 375 Dennis Leonard .15 .07
❑ 376 Dave Anderson .15 .07
❑ 377 Danny Darwin .15 .07
❑ 378 Bob Brenly .15 .07
❑ 379 Checklist 265-396 .25 .11
❑ 380 Steve Garvey .40 .18
❑ 381 Ralph Houk MG .25 .11
❑ 382 Chris Nyman .15 .07
❑ 383 Terry Puhl .15 .07
❑ 384 Lee Tunnell .15 .07
❑ 385 Tony Perez .60 .25
❑ 386 George Hendrick AS .15 .07
❑ 387 Johnny Ray AS .15 .07
❑ 388 Mike Schmidt AS .40 .18
❑ 389 Ozzie Smith AS .60 .25
❑ 390 Tim Raines AS .25 .11
❑ 391 Dale Murphy AS .40 .18
❑ 392 Andre Dawson AS .25 .11
❑ 393 Gary Carter AS .25 .11
❑ 394 Steve Rogers AS .15 .07
❑ 395 Steve Carlton AS .40 .18
❑ 396 Jesse Orosco AS .15 .07
❑ 397 Eddie Murray AS .40 .18
❑ 398 Lou Whitaker AS .25 .11

❑ 399 George Brett AS .60 .25
❑ 400 Cal Ripken AS 2.00 .90
❑ 401 Jim Rice AS .15 .07
❑ 402 Dave Winfield AS .25 .11
❑ 403 Lloyd Moseby AS .15 .07
❑ 404 Ted Simmons AS .15 .07
❑ 405 LaMarr Hoyt AS .15 .07
❑ 406 Ron Guidry AS .15 .07
❑ 407 Dan Quisenberry AS .15 .07
❑ 408 Lou Piniella .25 .11
❑ 409 Juan Agosto .15 .07
❑ 410 Claudell Washington .15 .07
❑ 411 Houston Jimenez .15 .07
❑ 412 Doug Rader MG .15 .07
❑ 413 Spike Owen RC .25 .11
❑ 414 Mitchell Page .15 .07
❑ 415 Tommy John .40 .18
❑ 416 Dane Iorg .15 .07
❑ 417 Mike Armstrong .15 .07
❑ 418 Ron Hodges .15 .07
❑ 419 John Henry Johnson .15 .07
❑ 420 Cecil Cooper .25 .11
❑ 421 Charlie Lea .15 .07
❑ 422 Jose Cruz .25 .11
❑ 423 Mike Morgan .15 .07
❑ 424 Dann Bilardello .15 .07
❑ 425 Steve Howe .15 .07
❑ 426 Orioles TL 1.50 .70
Cal Ripken
Mike Boddicker
❑ 427 Rick Leach .15 .07
❑ 428 Fred Breining .15 .07
❑ 429 Randy Bush .15 .07
❑ 430 Rusty Staub .25 .11
❑ 431 Chris Bando .15 .07
❑ 432 Charles Hudson .15 .07
❑ 433 Rich Hebner .15 .07
❑ 434 Harold Baines .60 .25
❑ 435 Neil Allen .15 .07
❑ 436 Rick Peters .15 .07
❑ 437 Mike Proly .15 .07
❑ 438 Biff Pocoroba .15 .07
❑ 439 Bob Stoddard .15 .07
❑ 440 Steve Kemp .15 .07
❑ 441 Bob Lillis MG .15 .07
❑ 442 Byron McLaughlin .15 .07
❑ 443 Benny Ayala .15 .07
❑ 444 Steve Renko .15 .07
❑ 445 Jerry Remy .15 .07
❑ 446 Luis Pujols .15 .07
❑ 447 Tom Brunansky .25 .11
❑ 448 Ben Hayes .15 .07
❑ 449 Joe Pettini .15 .07
❑ 450 Gary Carter .40 .18
❑ 451 Bob Jones .15 .07
❑ 452 Chuck Porter .15 .07
❑ 453 Willie Upshaw .15 .07
❑ 454 Joe Beckwith .15 .07
❑ 455 Terry Kennedy .15 .07
❑ 456 Chicago Cubs TL .40 .18
Keith Moreland
Fergie Jenkins
❑ 457 Dave Rozema .15 .07
❑ 458 Kiko Garcia .15 .07
❑ 459 Kevin Hickey .15 .07
❑ 460 Dave Winfield .60 .25
❑ 461 Jim Maler .15 .07
❑ 462 Lee Lacy .15 .07
❑ 463 Dave Engle .15 .07
❑ 464 Jeff A. Jones .15 .07
❑ 465 Mookie Wilson .25 .11
❑ 466 Gene Garber .15 .07
❑ 467 Mike Ramsey .15 .07
❑ 468 Geoff Zahn .15 .07
❑ 469 Tom O'Malley .15 .07
❑ 470 Nolan Ryan 3.00 1.35
❑ 471 Dick Howser MG .15 .07
❑ 472 Mike G. Brown .15 .07
❑ 473 Jim Dwyer .15 .07
❑ 474 Greg Bargar .15 .07
❑ 475 Gary Redus RC* .15 .07
❑ 476 Tom Tellmann .15 .07
❑ 477 Rafael Landestoy .15 .07
❑ 478 Alan Bannister .15 .07
❑ 479 Frank Tanana .25 .11
❑ 480 Ron Kittle .15 .07

❑ 481	Mark Thurmond	.15	.07
❑ 482	Enos Cabell	.15	.07
❑ 483	Fergie Jenkins	.60	.25
❑ 484	Ozzie Virgil	.15	.07
❑ 485	Rick Rhoden	.15	.07
❑ 486	N.Y. Yankees TL	.60	.25
	Don Baylor		
	Ron Guidry		
❑ 487	Ricky Adams	.15	.07
❑ 488	Jesse Barfield	.25	.11
❑ 489	Dave Von Ohlen	.15	.07
❑ 490	Cal Ripken	4.00	1.80
❑ 491	Bobby Castillo	.15	.07
❑ 492	Tucker Ashford	.15	.07
❑ 493	Mike Norris	.15	.07
❑ 494	Chili Davis	.40	.18
❑ 495	Rollie Fingers	.60	.25
❑ 496	Terry Francona	.15	.07
❑ 497	Bud Anderson	.15	.07
❑ 498	Rich Gedman	.15	.07
❑ 499	Mike Witt	.15	.07
❑ 500	George Brett	1.25	.55
❑ 501	Steve Henderson	.15	.07
❑ 502	Joe Torre MG	.25	.11
❑ 503	Elias Sosa	.15	.07
❑ 504	Mickey Rivers	.15	.07
❑ 505	Pete Vuckovich	.15	.07
❑ 506	Ernie Whitt	.15	.07
❑ 507	Mike LaCoss	.15	.07
❑ 508	Mel Hall	.25	.11
❑ 509	Brad Havens	.15	.07
❑ 510	Alan Trammell	.40	.18
❑ 511	Marty Bystrom	.15	.07
❑ 512	Oscar Gamble	.15	.07
❑ 513	Dave Beard	.15	.07
❑ 514	Floyd Rayford	.15	.07
❑ 515	Gorman Thomas	.15	.07
❑ 516	Montreal Expos TL	.25	.11
	Al Oliver		
	Charlie Lea		
❑ 517	John Moses	.15	.07
❑ 518	Greg Walker	.25	.11
❑ 519	Ron Davis	.15	.07
❑ 520	Bob Boone	.25	.11
❑ 521	Pete Falcone	.15	.07
❑ 522	Dave Bergman	.15	.07
❑ 523	Glenn Hoffman	.15	.07
❑ 524	Carlos Diaz	.15	.07
❑ 525	Willie Wilson	.15	.07
❑ 526	Ron Oester	.15	.07
❑ 527	Checklist 397-528	.25	.11
❑ 528	Mark Brouhard	.15	.07
❑ 529	Keith Atherton	.15	.07
❑ 530	Dan Ford	.15	.07
❑ 531	Steve Boros MG	.15	.07
❑ 532	Eric Show	.15	.07
❑ 533	Ken Landreaux	.15	.07
❑ 534	Pete O'Brien RC*	.25	.11
❑ 535	Bo Diaz	.15	.07
❑ 536	Doug Bair	.15	.07
❑ 537	Johnny Ray	.15	.07
❑ 538	Kevin Bass	.15	.07
❑ 539	George Frazier	.15	.07
❑ 540	George Hendrick	.15	.07
❑ 541	Dennis Lamp	.15	.07
❑ 542	Duane Kuiper	.15	.07
❑ 543	Craig McMurtry	.15	.07
❑ 544	Cesar Geronimo	.15	.07
❑ 545	Bill Buckner	.25	.11
❑ 546	Indians TL	.25	.11
	Mike Hargrove		
	Lary Sorensen		
❑ 547	Mike Moore	.15	.07
❑ 548	Ron Jackson	.15	.07
❑ 549	Walt Terrell	.15	.07
❑ 550	Jim Rice	.25	.11
❑ 551	Scott Ullger	.15	.07
❑ 552	Ray Burris	.15	.07
❑ 553	Joe Nolan	.15	.07
❑ 554	Ted Power	.15	.07
❑ 555	Greg Brock	.15	.07
❑ 556	Joey McLaughlin	.15	.07
❑ 557	Wayne Tolleson	.15	.07
❑ 558	Mike Davis	.15	.07
❑ 559	Mike Scott	.25	.11
❑ 560	Carlton Fisk	.60	.25
❑ 561	Whitey Herzog MG	.25	.11
❑ 562	Manny Castillo	.15	.07
❑ 563	Glenn Wilson	.25	.11
❑ 564	Al Holland	.15	.07
❑ 565	Leon Durham	.15	.07
❑ 566	Jim Bibby	.15	.07
❑ 567	Mike Heath	.15	.07
❑ 568	Pete Filson	.15	.07
❑ 569	Bake McBride	.15	.07
❑ 570	Dan Quisenberry	.15	.07
❑ 571	Bruce Bochy	.15	.07
❑ 572	Jerry Royster	.15	.07
❑ 573	Dave Kingman	.40	.18
❑ 574	Brian Downing	.15	.07
❑ 575	Jim Clancy	.15	.07
❑ 576	Giants TL	.25	.11
	Jeff Leonard		
	Atlee Hammaker		
❑ 577	Mark Clear	.15	.07
❑ 578	Lenn Sakata	.15	.07
❑ 579	Bob James	.15	.07
❑ 580	Lonnie Smith	.15	.07
❑ 581	Jose DeLeon	.15	.07
❑ 582	Bob McClure	.15	.07
❑ 583	Derrel Thomas	.15	.07
❑ 584	Dave Schmidt	.15	.07
❑ 585	Dan Driessen	.15	.07
❑ 586	Joe Niekro	.25	.11
❑ 587	Von Hayes	.15	.07
❑ 588	Milt Wilcox	.15	.07
❑ 589	Mike Easler	.15	.07
❑ 590	Dave Stieb	.15	.07
❑ 591	Tony LaRussa MG	.25	.11
❑ 592	Andre Robertson	.15	.07
❑ 593	Jeff Lahti	.15	.07
❑ 594	Gene Richards	.15	.07
❑ 595	Jeff Reardon	.25	.11
❑ 596	Ryne Sandberg	2.00	.90
❑ 597	Rick Camp	.15	.07
❑ 598	Rusty Kuntz	.15	.07
❑ 599	Doug Sisk	.15	.07
❑ 600	Rod Carew	.60	.25
❑ 601	John Tudor	.15	.07
❑ 602	John Wathan	.15	.07
❑ 603	Renie Martin	.15	.07
❑ 604	John Lowenstein	.15	.07
❑ 605	Mike Caldwell	.15	.07
❑ 606	Blue Jays TL	.25	.11
	Lloyd Moseby		
	Dave Stieb		
❑ 607	Tom Hume	.15	.07
❑ 608	Bobby Johnson	.15	.07
❑ 609	Dan Meyer	.15	.07
❑ 610	Steve Sax	.25	.11
❑ 611	Chet Lemon	.15	.07
❑ 612	Harry Spilman	.15	.07
❑ 613	Greg Gross	.15	.07
❑ 614	Len Barker	.15	.07
❑ 615	Garry Templeton	.15	.07
❑ 616	Don Robinson	.15	.07
❑ 617	Rick Cerone	.15	.07
❑ 618	Dickie Noles	.15	.07
❑ 619	Jerry Dybzinski	.15	.07
❑ 620	Al Oliver	.25	.11
❑ 621	Frank Howard MG	.25	.11
❑ 622	Al Cowens	.15	.07
❑ 623	Ron Washington	.15	.07
❑ 624	Terry Harper	.15	.07
❑ 625	Larry Gura	.15	.07
❑ 626	Bob Clark	.15	.07
❑ 627	Dave LaPoint	.15	.07
❑ 628	Ed Jurak	.15	.07
❑ 629	Rick Langford	.15	.07
❑ 630	Ted Simmons	.25	.11
❑ 631	Dennis Martinez	.25	.11
❑ 632	Tom Foley	.15	.07
❑ 633	Mike Krukow	.15	.07
❑ 634	Mike Marshall	.15	.07
❑ 635	Dave Righetti	.25	.11
❑ 636	Pat Putnam	.15	.07
❑ 637	Phillies TL	.25	.11
	Gary Matthews		
	John Denny		
❑ 638	George Vukovich	.15	.07
❑ 639	Rick Lysander	.15	.07
❑ 640	Lance Parrish	.40	.18
❑ 641	Mike Richardt	.15	.07
❑ 642	Tom Underwood	.15	.07
❑ 643	Mike C. Brown	.15	.07
❑ 644	Tim Lollar	.15	.07
❑ 645	Tony Pena	.15	.07
❑ 646	Checklist 529-660	.25	.11
❑ 647	Ron Roenicke	.15	.07
❑ 648	Len Whitehouse	.15	.07
❑ 649	Tom Herr	.25	.11
❑ 650	Phil Niekro	.60	.25
❑ 651	John McNamara MG	.15	.07
❑ 652	Rudy May	.15	.07
❑ 653	Dave Stapleton	.15	.07
❑ 654	Bob Bailor	.15	.07
❑ 655	Amos Otis	.25	.11
❑ 656	Bryn Smith	.15	.07
❑ 657	Thad Bosley	.15	.07
❑ 658	Jerry Augustine	.15	.07
❑ 659	Duane Walker	.15	.07
❑ 660	Ray Knight	.25	.11
❑ 661	Steve Yeager	.15	.07
❑ 662	Tom Brennan	.15	.07
❑ 663	Johnnie LeMaster	.15	.07
❑ 664	Dave Stegman	.15	.07
❑ 665	Buddy Bell	.25	.11
❑ 666	Detroit Tigers TL	.60	.25
	Lou Whitaker		
	Jack Morris		
❑ 667	Vance Law	.15	.07
❑ 668	Larry McWilliams	.15	.07
❑ 669	Dave Lopes	.25	.11
❑ 670	Rich Gossage	.40	.18
❑ 671	Jamie Quirk	.15	.07
❑ 672	Ricky Nelson	.15	.07
❑ 673	Mike Walters	.15	.07
❑ 674	Tim Flannery	.15	.07
❑ 675	Pascual Perez	.15	.07
❑ 676	Brian Giles	.15	.07
❑ 677	Doyle Alexander	.15	.07
❑ 678	Chris Speier	.15	.07
❑ 679	Art Howe	.25	.11
❑ 680	Fred Lynn	.25	.11
❑ 681	Tom Lasorda MG	.40	.18
❑ 682	Dan Morogiello	.15	.07
❑ 683	Marty Barrett	.25	.11
❑ 684	Bob Shirley	.15	.07
❑ 685	Willie Aikens	.15	.07
❑ 686	Joe Price	.15	.07
❑ 687	Roy Howell	.15	.07
❑ 688	George Wright	.15	.07
❑ 689	Mike Fischlin	.15	.07
❑ 690	Jack Clark	.25	.11
❑ 691	Steve Lake	.15	.07
❑ 692	Dickie Thon	.15	.07
❑ 693	Alan Wiggins	.15	.07
❑ 694	Mike Stanton	.15	.07
❑ 695	Lou Whitaker	.60	.25
❑ 696	Pirates TL	.25	.11
	Bill Madlock		
	Rick Rhoden		
❑ 697	Dale Murray	.15	.07
❑ 698	Marc Hill	.15	.07
❑ 699	Dave Rucker	.15	.07
❑ 700	Mike Schmidt	1.25	.55
❑ 701	NL Active Batting	.60	.25
	Bill Madlock		
	Pete Rose		
	Dave Parker		
❑ 702	NL Active Hits	.60	.25
	Pete Rose		
	Rusty Staub		
	Tony Perez		
❑ 703	NL Active Home Run	.60	.25
	Mike Schmidt		
	Tony Perez		
	Dave Kingman		
❑ 704	NL Active RBI	.60	.25
	Tony Perez		
	Rusty Staub		
	Al Oliver		
❑ 705	NL Active Steals	.60	.25
	Joe Morgan		
	Cesar Cedeno		
	Larry Bowa		
❑ 706	NL Active Victory	.60	.25
	Steve Carlton		

Fergie Jenkins
Tom Seaver
❑ 707 NL Active Strikeout ...... 1.50 .70
Steve Carlton
Nolan Ryan
Tom Seaver
❑ 708 NL Active ERA ...... .60 .25
Tom Seaver
Steve Carlton
Steve Rogers
❑ 709 NL Active Save ...... .25 .11
Bruce Sutter
Tug McGraw
Gene Garber
❑ 710 AL Active Batting ...... .60 .25
Rod Carew
George Brett
Cecil Cooper
❑ 711 AL Active Hits ...... .60 .25
Rod Carew
Bert Campaneris
Reggie Jackson
❑ 712 AL Active Home Run ...... .60 .25
Reggie Jackson
Graig Nettles
Greg Luzinski
❑ 713 AL Active RBI ...... .60 .25
Reggie Jackson
Ted Simmons
Graig Nettles
❑ 714 AL Active Steals ...... .25 .11
Bert Campaneris
Dave Lopes
Omar Moreno
❑ 715 AL Active Victory ...... .60 .25
Jim Palmer
Don Sutton
Tommy John
❑ 716 AL Active Strikeout ...... .60 .25
Don Sutton
Bert Blyleven
Jerry Koosman
❑ 717 AL Active ERA ...... .60 .25
Jim Palmer
Rollie Fingers
Ron Guidry
❑ 718 AL Active Save ...... .60 .25
Rollie Fingers
Rich Gossage
Dan Quisenberry
❑ 719 Andy Hassler ...... .15 .07
❑ 720 Dwight Evans ...... .25 .11
❑ 721 Del Crandall MG ...... .15 .07
❑ 722 Bob Welch ...... .15 .07
❑ 723 Rich Dauer ...... .15 .07
❑ 724 Eric Rasmussen ...... .15 .07
❑ 725 Cesar Cedeno ...... .25 .11
❑ 726 Brewers TL ...... .25 .11
Ted Simmons
Moose Haas
❑ 727 Joel Youngblood ...... .15 .07
❑ 728 Tug McGraw ...... .25 .11
❑ 729 Gene Tenace ...... .25 .11
❑ 730 Bruce Sutter ...... .25 .11
❑ 731 Lynn Jones ...... .15 .07
❑ 732 Terry Crowley ...... .15 .07
❑ 733 Dave Collins ...... .15 .07
❑ 734 Odell Jones ...... .15 .07
❑ 735 Rick Burleson ...... .15 .07
❑ 736 Dick Ruthven ...... .15 .07
❑ 737 Jim Essian ...... .15 .07
❑ 738 Bill Schroeder ...... .15 .07
❑ 739 Bob Watson ...... .25 .11
❑ 740 Tom Seaver ...... 1.00 .45
❑ 741 Wayne Gross ...... .15 .07
❑ 742 Dick Williams MG ...... .25 .11
❑ 743 Don Hood ...... .15 .07
❑ 744 Jamie Allen ...... .15 .07
❑ 745 Dennis Eckersley ...... .60 .25
❑ 746 Mickey Hatcher ...... .15 .07
❑ 747 Pat Zachry ...... .15 .07
❑ 748 Jeff Leonard ...... .15 .07
❑ 749 Doug Flynn ...... .15 .07
❑ 750 Jim Palmer ...... .60 .25
❑ 751 Charlie Moore ...... .15 .07
❑ 752 Phil Garner ...... .25 .11
❑ 753 Doug Gwosdz ...... .15 .07
❑ 754 Kent Tekulve ...... .25 .11
❑ 755 Garry Maddox ...... .15 .07
❑ 756 Reds TL ...... .25 .11
Ron Oester
Mario Soto
❑ 757 Larry Bowa ...... .25 .11
❑ 758 Bill Stein ...... .15 .07
❑ 759 Richard Dotson ...... .15 .07
❑ 760 Bob Horner ...... .15 .07
❑ 761 John Montefusco ...... .15 .07
❑ 762 Rance Mulliniks ...... .15 .07
❑ 763 Craig Swan ...... .15 .07
❑ 764 Mike Hargrove ...... .25 .11
❑ 765 Ken Forsch ...... .15 .07
❑ 766 Mike Vail ...... .15 .07
❑ 767 Carney Lansford ...... .25 .11
❑ 768 Champ Summers ...... .15 .07
❑ 769 Bill Caudill ...... .15 .07
❑ 770 Ken Griffey ...... .25 .11
❑ 771 Billy Gardner MG ...... .15 .07
❑ 772 Jim Slaton ...... .15 .07
❑ 773 Todd Cruz ...... .15 .07
❑ 774 Tom Gorman ...... .15 .07
❑ 775 Dave Parker ...... .25 .11
❑ 776 Craig Reynolds ...... .15 .07
❑ 777 Tom Paciorek ...... .25 .11
❑ 778 Andy Hawkins ...... .15 .07
❑ 779 Jim Sundberg ...... .25 .11
❑ 780 Steve Carlton ...... .60 .25
❑ 781 Checklist 661-792 ...... .25 .11
❑ 782 Steve Balboni ...... .15 .07
❑ 783 Luis Leal ...... .15 .07
❑ 784 Leon Roberts ...... .15 .07
❑ 785 Joaquin Andujar ...... .15 .07
❑ 786 Red Sox TL ...... .40 .18
Wade Boggs
Bob Ojeda
❑ 787 Bill Campbell ...... .15 .07
❑ 788 Milt May ...... .15 .07
❑ 789 Bert Blyleven ...... .25 .11
❑ 790 Doug DeCinces ...... .15 .07
❑ 791 Terry Forster ...... .15 .07
❑ 792 Bill Russell ...... .15 .07

1984 Topps Traded

	NRMT	VG-E
COMP.FACT.SET (132)	30.00	13.50

❑ 1T Willie Aikens ...... .40 .18
❑ 2T Luis Aponte ...... .40 .18
❑ 3T Mike Armstrong ...... .40 .18
❑ 4T Bob Bailor ...... .40 .18
❑ 5T Dusty Baker ...... .60 .25
❑ 6T Steve Balboni ...... .40 .18
❑ 7T Alan Bannister ...... .40 .18
❑ 8T Dave Beard ...... .40 .18
❑ 9T Joe Beckwith ...... .40 .18
❑ 10T Bruce Berenyi ...... .40 .18
❑ 11T Dave Bergman ...... .40 .18
❑ 12T Tony Bernazard ...... .40 .18
❑ 13T Yogi Berra MG ...... 1.50 .70
❑ 14T Barry Bonnell ...... .40 .18
❑ 15T Phil Bradley ...... .60 .25
❑ 16T Fred Breining ...... .40 .18
❑ 17T Bill Buckner ...... .60 .25
❑ 18T Ray Burris ...... .40 .18
❑ 19T John Butcher ...... .40 .18
❑ 20T Brett Butler ...... 1.00 .45
❑ 21T Enos Cabell ...... .40 .18
❑ 22T Bill Campbell ...... .40 .18
❑ 23T Bill Caudill ...... .40 .18
❑ 24T Bob Clark ...... .40 .18
❑ 25T Bryan Clark ...... .40 .18
❑ 26T Jaime Cocanower ...... .40 .18
❑ 27T Ron Darling XRC* ...... 1.00 .45
❑ 28T Alvin Davis XRC ...... .60 .25
❑ 29T Ken Dayley ...... .40 .18
❑ 30T Jeff Dedmon ...... .40 .18
❑ 31T Bob Dernier ...... .40 .18
❑ 32T Carlos Diaz ...... .40 .18
❑ 33T Mike Easler ...... .40 .18
❑ 34T Dennis Eckersley ...... .60 .25
❑ 35T Jim Essian ...... .40 .18
❑ 36T Darrell Evans ...... .60 .25
❑ 37T Mike Fitzgerald ...... .40 .18
❑ 38T Tim Foli ...... .40 .18
❑ 39T George Frazier ...... .40 .18
❑ 40T Rich Gale ...... .40 .18
❑ 41T Barbaro Garbey ...... .40 .18
❑ 42T Dwight Gooden XRC 5.00 2.20
❑ 43T Rich Gossage ...... 1.00 .45
❑ 44T Wayne Gross ...... .40 .18
❑ 45T Mark Gubicza XRC ...... .60 .25
❑ 46T Jackie Gutierrez ...... .40 .18
❑ 47T Mel Hall ...... .60 .25
❑ 48T Toby Harrah ...... .60 .25
❑ 49T Ron Hassey ...... .40 .18
❑ 50T Rich Hebner ...... .40 .18
❑ 51T Willie Hernandez ...... .60 .25
❑ 52T Ricky Horton ...... .40 .18
❑ 53T Art Howe ...... .60 .25
❑ 54T Dane Iorg ...... .40 .18
❑ 55T Brook Jacoby ...... .60 .25
❑ 56T Mike Jeffcoat ...... .40 .18
❑ 57T Dave Johnson MG ...... .60 .25
❑ 58T Lynn Jones ...... .40 .18
❑ 59T Ruppert Jones ...... .40 .18
❑ 60T Mike Jorgensen ...... .40 .18
❑ 61T Bob Kearney ...... .40 .18
❑ 62T Jimmy Key XRC ...... 1.00 .45
❑ 63T Dave Kingman ...... 1.00 .45
❑ 64T Jerry Koosman ...... .60 .25
❑ 65T Wayne Krenchicki ...... .40 .18
❑ 66T Rusty Kuntz ...... .40 .18
❑ 67T Rene Lachemann MG ...... .40 .18
❑ 68T Frank LaCorte ...... .40 .18
❑ 69T Dennis Lamp ...... .40 .18
❑ 70T Mark Langston XRC ...... 1.00 .45
❑ 71T Rick Leach ...... .40 .18
❑ 72T Craig Lefferts ...... .60 .25
❑ 73T Gary Lucas ...... .40 .18
❑ 74T Jerry Martin ...... .40 .18
❑ 75T Carmelo Martinez ...... .40 .18
❑ 76T Mike Mason ...... .40 .18
❑ 77T Gary Matthews ...... .60 .25
❑ 78T Andy McGaffigan ...... .40 .18
❑ 79T Larry Milbourne ...... .40 .18
❑ 80T Sid Monge ...... .40 .18
❑ 81T Jackie Moore MG ...... .40 .18
❑ 82T Joe Morgan ...... 1.50 .70
❑ 83T Graig Nettles ...... .60 .25
❑ 84T Phil Niekro ...... 1.50 .70
❑ 85T Ken Oberkfell ...... .40 .18
❑ 86T Mike O'Berry ...... .40 .18
❑ 87T Al Oliver ...... .60 .25
❑ 88T Jorge Orta ...... .40 .18
❑ 89T Amos Otis ...... .60 .25
❑ 90T Dave Parker ...... .60 .25
❑ 91T Tony Perez ...... 1.50 .70
❑ 92T Gerald Perry ...... .60 .25
❑ 93T Gary Pettis ...... .40 .18
❑ 94T Rob Picciolo ...... .40 .18
❑ 95T Vern Rapp MG ...... .40 .18
❑ 96T Floyd Rayford ...... .40 .18
❑ 97T Randy Ready XRC ...... .60 .25
❑ 98T Ron Reed ...... .40 .18
❑ 99T Gene Richards ...... .40 .18
❑ 100T Jose Rijo XRC ...... 1.50 .70
❑ 101T Jeff D. Robinson ...... .40 .18
❑ 102T Ron Romanick ...... .40 .18
❑ 103T Pete Rose 5.00 2.20
❑ 104T B.Saberhagen XRC .. 3.00 1.35

❑ 105T Juan Samuel XRC*	1.00	.45
❑ 106T Scott Sanderson	.40	.18
❑ 107T Dick Schofield XRC*	.60	.25
❑ 108T Tom Seaver	2.50	1.10
❑ 109T Jim Slaton	.40	.18
❑ 110T Mike Smithson	.40	.18
❑ 111T Lary Sorensen	.40	.18
❑ 112T Tim Stoddard	.40	.18
❑ 113T Champ Summers	.40	.18
❑ 114T Jim Sundberg	.60	.25
❑ 115T Rick Sutcliffe	.60	.25
❑ 116T Craig Swan	.40	.18
❑ 117T Tim Teufel XRC*	.40	.18
❑ 118T Derrel Thomas	.40	.18
❑ 119T Gorman Thomas	.40	.18
❑ 120T Alex Trevino	.40	.18
❑ 121T Manny Trillo	.40	.18
❑ 122T John Tudor	.40	.18
❑ 123T Tom Underwood	.40	.18
❑ 124T Mike Vail	.40	.18
❑ 125T Tom Waddell	.40	.18
❑ 126T Gary Ward	.40	.18
❑ 127T Curtis Wilkerson	.40	.18
❑ 128T Frank Williams	.40	.18
❑ 129T Glenn Wilson	.40	.18
❑ 130T John Wockenfuss	.40	.18
❑ 131T Ned Yost	.40	.18
❑ 132T Checklist 1T-132T	.40	.18

1985 Topps

	NRMT	VG-E
COMPLETE SET (792)	120.00	55.00
COMP.FACT.SET (792)	200.00	90.00

Card	NRMT	VG-E
❑ 1 Carlton Fisk RB Longest game by catcher	.25	.11
❑ 2 Steve Garvey RB Consecutive error- less games, 1B	.25	.11
❑ 3 Dwight Gooden RB Most rookie strikeouts	.60	.25
❑ 4 Cliff Johnson RB Most pinch-hit homers	.15	.07
❑ 5 Joe Morgan RB Most homers 2B, lifetime	.25	.11
❑ 6 Pete Rose RB Most career singles	.40	.18
❑ 7 Nolan Ryan RB Most career strikeouts	1.50	.70
❑ 8 Juan Samuel RB Most SB's, rookie season	.15	.07
❑ 9 Bruce Sutter RB Most NL season saves	.15	.07
❑ 10 Don Sutton RB Most seasons 100 or more K's	.25	.11
❑ 11 Ralph Houk MG	.15	.07
❑ 12 Dave Lopes (Now with Cubs on card front)	.25	.11
❑ 13 Tim Lollar	.15	.07
❑ 14 Chris Bando	.15	.07
❑ 15 Jerry Koosman	.25	.11
❑ 16 Bobby Meacham	.15	.07
❑ 17 Mike Scott	.15	.07
❑ 18 Mickey Hatcher	.15	.07
❑ 19 George Frazier	.15	.07
❑ 20 Chet Lemon	.15	.07
❑ 21 Lee Tunnell	.15	.07
❑ 22 Duane Kuiper	.15	.07
❑ 23 Bret Saberhagen RC	.50	.23
❑ 24 Jesse Barfield	.15	.07
❑ 25 Steve Bedrosian	.15	.07
❑ 26 Roy Smalley	.15	.07
❑ 27 Bruce Berenyi	.15	.07
❑ 28 Dann Bilardello	.15	.07
❑ 29 Odell Jones	.15	.07
❑ 30 Cal Ripken	2.50	1.10
❑ 31 Terry Whitfield	.15	.07
❑ 32 Chuck Porter	.15	.07
❑ 33 Tito Landrum	.15	.07
❑ 34 Ed Nunez	.15	.07
❑ 35 Graig Nettles	.25	.11
❑ 36 Fred Breining	.15	.07
❑ 37 Reid Nichols	.15	.07
❑ 38 Jackie Moore MG	.15	.07
❑ 39 John Wockenfuss	.15	.07
❑ 40 Phil Niekro	.60	.25
❑ 41 Mike Fischlin	.15	.07
❑ 42 Luis Sanchez	.15	.07
❑ 43 Andre David	.15	.07
❑ 44 Dickie Thon	.15	.07
❑ 45 Greg Minton	.15	.07
❑ 46 Gary Woods	.15	.07
❑ 47 Dave Rozema	.15	.07
❑ 48 Tony Fernandez	.25	.11
❑ 49 Butch Davis	.15	.07
❑ 50 John Candelaria	.15	.07
❑ 51 Bob Watson	.25	.11
❑ 52 Jerry Dybzinski	.15	.07
❑ 53 Tom Gorman	.15	.07
❑ 54 Cesar Cedeno	.25	.11
❑ 55 Frank Tanana	.15	.07
❑ 56 Jim Dwyer	.15	.07
❑ 57 Pat Zachry	.15	.07
❑ 58 Orlando Mercado	.15	.07
❑ 59 Rick Waits	.15	.07
❑ 60 George Hendrick	.15	.07
❑ 61 Curt Kaufman	.15	.07
❑ 62 Mike Ramsey	.15	.07
❑ 63 Steve McCatty	.15	.07
❑ 64 Mark Bailey	.15	.07
❑ 65 Bill Buckner	.25	.11
❑ 66 Dick Williams MG	.25	.11
❑ 67 Rafael Santana	.15	.07
❑ 68 Von Hayes	.15	.07
❑ 69 Jim Winn	.15	.07
❑ 70 Don Baylor	.25	.11
❑ 71 Tim Laudner	.15	.07
❑ 72 Rick Sutcliffe	.25	.11
❑ 73 Rusty Kuntz	.15	.07
❑ 74 Mike Krukow	.15	.07
❑ 75 Willie Upshaw	.15	.07
❑ 76 Alan Bannister	.15	.07
❑ 77 Joe Beckwith	.15	.07
❑ 78 Scott Fletcher	.15	.07
❑ 79 Rick Mahler	.15	.07
❑ 80 Keith Hernandez	.25	.11
❑ 81 Lenn Sakata	.15	.07
❑ 82 Joe Price	.15	.07
❑ 83 Charlie Moore	.15	.07
❑ 84 Spike Owen	.15	.07
❑ 85 Mike Marshall	.15	.07
❑ 86 Don Aase	.15	.07
❑ 87 David Green	.15	.07
❑ 88 Bryn Smith	.15	.07
❑ 89 Jackie Gutierrez	.15	.07
❑ 90 Rich Gossage	.25	.11
❑ 91 Jeff Burroughs	.15	.07
❑ 92 Paul Owens MG	.15	.07
❑ 93 Don Schulze	.15	.07
❑ 94 Toby Harrah	.15	.07
❑ 95 Jose Cruz	.25	.11
❑ 96 Johnny Ray	.15	.07
❑ 97 Pete Filson	.15	.07
❑ 98 Steve Lake	.15	.07
❑ 99 Milt Wilcox	.15	.07
❑ 100 George Brett	1.25	.55
❑ 101 Jim Acker	.15	.07
❑ 102 Tommy Dunbar	.15	.07
❑ 103 Randy Lerch	.15	.07
❑ 104 Mike Fitzgerald	.15	.07
❑ 105 Ron Kittle	.15	.07
❑ 106 Pascual Perez	.15	.07
❑ 107 Tom Foley	.15	.07
❑ 108 Darnell Coles	.15	.07
❑ 109 Gary Roenicke	.15	.07
❑ 110 Alejandro Pena	.15	.07
❑ 111 Doug DeCinces	.15	.07
❑ 112 Tom Tellmann	.15	.07
❑ 113 Tom Herr	.15	.07
❑ 114 Bob James	.15	.07
❑ 115 Rickey Henderson	1.25	.55
❑ 116 Dennis Boyd	.15	.07
❑ 117 Greg Gross	.15	.07
❑ 118 Eric Show	.15	.07
❑ 119 Pat Corrales MG	.15	.07
❑ 120 Steve Kemp	.15	.07
❑ 121 Checklist: 1-132	.15	.07
❑ 122 Tom Brunansky	.25	.11
❑ 123 Dave Smith	.15	.07
❑ 124 Rich Hebner	.15	.07
❑ 125 Kent Tekulve	.15	.07
❑ 126 Ruppert Jones	.15	.07
❑ 127 Mark Gubicza RC*	.25	.11
❑ 128 Ernie Whitt	.15	.07
❑ 129 Gene Garber	.15	.07
❑ 130 Al Oliver	.25	.11
❑ 131 Buddy Bell FS Gus Bell	.25	.11
❑ 132 Dale Berra FS Yogi Berra	.25	.11
❑ 133 Bob Boone FS Ray Boone	.15	.07
❑ 134 Terry Francona FS Tito Francona	.15	.07
❑ 135 Terry Kennedy FS Bob Kennedy	.15	.07
❑ 136 Jeff Kunkel FS Bill Kunkel	.15	.07
❑ 137 Vance Law FS Vern Law	.25	.11
❑ 138 Dick Schofield FS Dick Schofield	.15	.07
❑ 139 Joel Skinner FS Bob Skinner	.15	.07
❑ 140 Roy Smalley Jr. FS Roy Smalley	.15	.07
❑ 141 Mike Stenhouse FS Dave Stenhouse	.15	.07
❑ 142 Steve Trout FS Dizzy Trout	.15	.07
❑ 143 Ozzie Virgil FS Ossie Virgil	.15	.07
❑ 144 Ron Gardenhire	.15	.07
❑ 145 Alvin Davis RC*	.25	.11
❑ 146 Gary Redus	.15	.07
❑ 147 Bill Swaggerty	.15	.07
❑ 148 Steve Yeager	.15	.07
❑ 149 Dickie Noles	.15	.07
❑ 150 Jim Rice	.25	.11
❑ 151 Moose Haas	.15	.07
❑ 152 Steve Braun	.15	.07
❑ 153 Frank LaCorte	.15	.07
❑ 154 Argenis Salazar	.15	.07
❑ 155 Yogi Berra MG	.40	.18
❑ 156 Craig Reynolds	.15	.07
❑ 157 Tug McGraw	.25	.11
❑ 158 Pat Tabler	.15	.07
❑ 159 Carlos Diaz	.15	.07
❑ 160 Lance Parrish	.25	.11
❑ 161 Ken Schrom	.15	.07
❑ 162 Benny Distefano	.15	.07
❑ 163 Dennis Eckersley	.60	.25
❑ 164 Jorge Orta	.15	.07
❑ 165 Dusty Baker	.25	.11
❑ 166 Keith Atherton	.15	.07
❑ 167 Rufino Linares	.15	.07
❑ 168 Garth Iorg	.15	.07
❑ 169 Dan Spillner	.15	.07
❑ 170 George Foster	.25	.11
❑ 171 Bill Stein	.15	.07
❑ 172 Jack Perconte	.15	.07
❑ 173 Mike Young	.15	.07
❑ 174 Rick Honeycutt	.15	.07
❑ 175 Dave Parker	.25	.11
❑ 176 Bill Schroeder	.15	.07
❑ 177 Dave Von Ohlen	.15	.07
❑ 178 Miguel Dilone	.15	.07

❑ 179 Tommy John .40 .18
❑ 180 Dave Winfield .60 .25
❑ 181 Roger Clemens RC 20.00 9.00
❑ 182 Tim Flannery .15 .07
❑ 183 Larry McWilliams .15 .07
❑ 184 Carmen Castillo .15 .07
❑ 185 Al Holland .15 .07
❑ 186 Bob Lillis MG .15 .07
❑ 187 Mike Walters .15 .07
❑ 188 Greg Pryor .15 .07
❑ 189 Warren Brusstar .15 .07
❑ 190 Rusty Staub .25 .11
❑ 191 Steve Nicosia .15 .07
❑ 192 Howard Johnson .25 .11
❑ 193 Jimmy Key RC .60 .25
❑ 194 Dave Stegman .15 .07
❑ 195 Glenn Hubbard .15 .07
❑ 196 Pete O'Brien .15 .07
❑ 197 Mike Warren .15 .07
❑ 198 Eddie Milner .15 .07
❑ 199 Dennis Martinez .25 .11
❑ 200 Reggie Jackson .75 .35
❑ 201 Burt Hooton .15 .07
❑ 202 Gorman Thomas .15 .07
❑ 203 Bob McClure .15 .07
❑ 204 Art Howe .15 .07
❑ 205 Steve Rogers .15 .07
❑ 206 Phil Garner .25 .11
❑ 207 Mark Clear .15 .07
❑ 208 Champ Summers .15 .07
❑ 209 Bill Campbell .15 .07
❑ 210 Gary Matthews .15 .07
❑ 211 Clay Christiansen .15 .07
❑ 212 George Vukovich .15 .07
❑ 213 Billy Gardner MG .25 .11
❑ 214 John Tudor .15 .07
❑ 215 Bob Brenly .15 .07
❑ 216 Jerry Don Gleaton .15 .07
❑ 217 Leon Roberts .15 .07
❑ 218 Doyle Alexander .15 .07
❑ 219 Gerald Perry .15 .07
❑ 220 Fred Lynn .25 .11
❑ 221 Ron Reed .15 .07
❑ 222 Hubie Brooks .15 .07
❑ 223 Tom Hume .15 .07
❑ 224 Al Cowens .15 .07
❑ 225 Mike Boddicker .15 .07
❑ 226 Juan Beniquez .15 .07
❑ 227 Danny Darwin .15 .07
❑ 228 Dion James .15 .07
❑ 229 Dave LaPoint .15 .07
❑ 230 Gary Carter .40 .18
❑ 231 Dwayne Murphy .15 .07
❑ 232 Dave Beard .15 .07
❑ 233 Ed Jurak .15 .07
❑ 234 Jerry Narron .15 .07
❑ 235 Garry Maddox .15 .07
❑ 236 Mark Thurmond .15 .07
❑ 237 Julio Franco .40 .18
❑ 238 Jose Rijo RC .40 .18
❑ 239 Tim Teufel .15 .07
❑ 240 Dave Stieb .25 .11
❑ 241 Jim Frey MG .15 .07
❑ 242 Greg Harris .15 .07
❑ 243 Barbaro Garbey .15 .07
❑ 244 Mike Jones .15 .07
❑ 245 Chili Davis .25 .11
❑ 246 Mike Norris .15 .07
❑ 247 Wayne Tolleson .15 .07
❑ 248 Terry Forster .15 .07
❑ 249 Harold Baines .25 .11
❑ 250 Jesse Orosco .15 .07
❑ 251 Brad Gulden .15 .07
❑ 252 Dan Ford .15 .07
❑ 253 Sid Bream RC .25 .11
❑ 254 Pete Vuckovich .15 .07
❑ 255 Lonnie Smith .15 .07
❑ 256 Mike Stanton .15 .07
❑ 257 Bryan Little UER .15 .07
Name spelled Brian on front
❑ 258 Mike C. Brown .15 .07
❑ 259 Gary Allenson .15 .07
❑ 260 Dave Righetti .25 .11
❑ 261 Checklist: 133-264 .15 .07
❑ 262 Greg Booker .15 .07
❑ 263 Mel Hall .15 .07
❑ 264 Joe Sambito .15 .07
❑ 265 Juan Samuel .15 .07
❑ 266 Frank Viola .25 .11
❑ 267 Henry Cotto RC .15 .07
❑ 268 Chuck Tanner MG .25 .11
❑ 269 Doug Baker .15 .07
❑ 270 Dan Quisenberry .25 .11
❑ 271 Tim Foli FDP68 .15 .07
❑ 272 Jeff Burroughs FDP69 .15 .07
❑ 273 Bill Almon FDP74 .15 .07
❑ 274 F.Bannister FDP76 .15 .07
❑ 275 Harold Baines FDP77 .15 .07
❑ 276 Bob Horner FDP78 .15 .07
❑ 277 Al Chambers FDP79 .15 .07
❑ 278 Darryl Strawberry FDP80 .25 .11
❑ 279 Mike Moore FDP81 .15 .07
❑ 280 S.Dunston FDP82 RC .50 .23
❑ 281 T.Belcher RC FDP83 .60 .25
❑ 282 Shawn Abner FDP84 .15 .07
❑ 283 Fran Mullins .15 .07
❑ 284 Marty Bystrom .15 .07
❑ 285 Dan Driessen .15 .07
❑ 286 Rudy Law .15 .07
❑ 287 Walt Terrell .15 .07
❑ 288 Jeff Kunkel .15 .07
❑ 289 Tom Underwood .15 .07
❑ 290 Cecil Cooper .25 .11
❑ 291 Bob Welch .15 .07
❑ 292 Brad Komminsk .15 .07
❑ 293 Curt Young .15 .07
❑ 294 Tom Nieto .15 .07
❑ 295 Joe Niekro .15 .07
❑ 296 Ricky Nelson .15 .07
❑ 297 Gary Lucas .15 .07
❑ 298 Marty Barrett .15 .07
❑ 299 Andy Hawkins .15 .07
❑ 300 Rod Carew .60 .25
❑ 301 John Montefusco .15 .07
❑ 302 Tim Corcoran .15 .07
❑ 303 Mike Jeffcoat .15 .07
❑ 304 Gary Gaetti .25 .11
❑ 305 Dale Berra .15 .07
❑ 306 Rick Reuschel .15 .07
❑ 307 Sparky Anderson MG .25 .11
❑ 308 John Wathan .15 .07
❑ 309 Mike Witt .15 .07
❑ 310 Manny Trillo .15 .07
❑ 311 Jim Gott .15 .07
❑ 312 Marc Hill .15 .07
❑ 313 Dave Schmidt .15 .07
❑ 314 Ron Oester .15 .07
❑ 315 Doug Sisk .15 .07
❑ 316 John Lowenstein .15 .07
❑ 317 Jack Lazorko .15 .07
❑ 318 Ted Simmons .25 .11
❑ 319 Jeff Jones .15 .07
❑ 320 Dale Murphy .60 .25
❑ 321 Ricky Horton .15 .07
❑ 322 Dave Stapleton .15 .07
❑ 323 Andy McGaffigan .15 .07
❑ 324 Bruce Bochy .15 .07
❑ 325 John Denny .15 .07
❑ 326 Kevin Bass .15 .07
❑ 327 Brook Jacoby .15 .07
❑ 328 Bob Shirley .15 .07
❑ 329 Ron Washington .15 .07
❑ 330 Leon Durham .15 .07
❑ 331 Bill Laskey .15 .07
❑ 332 Brian Harper .15 .07
❑ 333 Willie Hernandez .15 .07
❑ 334 Dick Howser MG .25 .11
❑ 335 Bruce Benedict .15 .07
❑ 336 Rance Mulliniks .15 .07
❑ 337 Billy Sample .15 .07
❑ 338 Britt Burns .15 .07
❑ 339 Danny Heep .15 .07
❑ 340 Robin Yount .60 .25
❑ 341 Floyd Rayford .15 .07
❑ 342 Ted Power .15 .07
❑ 343 Bill Russell .15 .07
❑ 344 Dave Henderson .15 .07
❑ 345 Charlie Lea .15 .07
❑ 346 Terry Pendleton RC .60 .25
❑ 347 Rick Langford .15 .07
❑ 348 Bob Boone .25 .11
❑ 349 Domingo Ramos .15 .07
❑ 350 Wade Boggs .60 .25
❑ 351 Juan Agosto .15 .07
❑ 352 Joe Morgan .60 .25
❑ 353 Julio Solano .15 .07
❑ 354 Andre Robertson .15 .07
❑ 355 Bert Blyleven .25 .11
❑ 356 Dave Meier .15 .07
❑ 357 Rich Bordi .15 .07
❑ 358 Tony Pena .15 .07
❑ 359 Pat Sheridan .15 .07
❑ 360 Steve Carlton .60 .25
❑ 361 Alfredo Griffin .15 .07
❑ 362 Craig McMurtry .15 .07
❑ 363 Ron Hodges .15 .07
❑ 364 Richard Dotson .15 .07
❑ 365 Danny Ozark MG .15 .07
❑ 366 Todd Cruz .15 .07
❑ 367 Keefe Cato .15 .07
❑ 368 Dave Bergman .15 .07
❑ 369 R.J. Reynolds .15 .07
❑ 370 Bruce Sutter .25 .11
❑ 371 Mickey Rivers .15 .07
❑ 372 Roy Howell .15 .07
❑ 373 Mike Moore .15 .07
❑ 374 Brian Downing .15 .07
❑ 375 Jeff Reardon .25 .11
❑ 376 Jeff Newman .15 .07
❑ 377 Checklist: 265-396 .15 .07
❑ 378 Alan Wiggins .15 .07
❑ 379 Charles Hudson .15 .07
❑ 380 Ken Griffey .25 .11
❑ 381 Roy Smith .15 .07
❑ 382 Denny Walling .15 .07
❑ 383 Rick Lysander .15 .07
❑ 384 Jody Davis .15 .07
❑ 385 Jose DeLeon .15 .07
❑ 386 Dan Gladden RC .25 .11
❑ 387 Buddy Biancalana .15 .07
❑ 388 Bert Roberge .15 .07
❑ 389 Rod Dedeaux OLY CO .25 .11
❑ 390 Sid Akins OLY .15 .07
❑ 391 Flavio Alfaro OLY .15 .07
❑ 392 Don August OLY .15 .07
❑ 393 S.Bankhead RC OLY .15 .07
❑ 394 Bob Caffrey OLY .15 .07
❑ 395 Mike Dunne OLY .25 .11
❑ 396 Gary Green OLY .15 .07
❑ 397 John Hoover OLY .15 .07
❑ 398 Shane Mack RC OLY .60 .25
❑ 399 John Marzano OLY .25 .11
❑ 400 O.McDowell RC OLY .25 .11
❑ 401 M.McGwire OLY RC 80.00 36.00
❑ 402 Pat Pacillo OLY .25 .11
❑ 403 Cory Snyder RC OLY .40 .18
❑ 404 Billy Swift OLY RC .40 .18
❑ 405 Tom Veryzer .15 .07
❑ 406 Len Whitehouse .15 .07
❑ 407 Bobby Ramos .15 .07
❑ 408 Sid Monge .15 .07
❑ 409 Brad Wellman .15 .07
❑ 410 Bob Horner .15 .07
❑ 411 Bobby Cox MG .15 .07
❑ 412 Bud Black .15 .07
❑ 413 Vance Law .15 .07
❑ 414 Gary Ward .15 .07
❑ 415 Ron Darling UER .25 .11
(No trivia answer)
❑ 416 Wayne Gross .15 .07
❑ 417 John Franco RC .60 .25
❑ 418 Ken Landreaux .15 .07
❑ 419 Mike Caldwell .15 .07
❑ 420 Andre Dawson .40 .18
❑ 421 Dave Rucker .15 .07
❑ 422 Carney Lansford .25 .11
❑ 423 Barry Bonnell .15 .07
❑ 424 Al Nipper .15 .07
❑ 425 Mike Hargrove .25 .11
❑ 426 Vern Ruhle .15 .07
❑ 427 Mario Ramirez .15 .07
❑ 428 Larry Andersen .15 .07
❑ 429 Rick Cerone .15 .07
❑ 430 Ron Davis .15 .07
❑ 431 U.L. Washington .15 .07
❑ 432 Thad Bosley .15 .07
❑ 433 Jim Morrison .15 .07

❑ 434 Gene Richards .15 .07
❑ 435 Dan Petry .15 .07
❑ 436 Willie Aikens .15 .07
❑ 437 Al Jones .15 .07
❑ 438 Joe Torre MG .40 .18
❑ 439 Junior Ortiz .15 .07
❑ 440 Fernando Valenzuela .25 .11
❑ 441 Duane Walker .15 .07
❑ 442 Ken Forsch .15 .07
❑ 443 George Wright .15 .07
❑ 444 Tony Phillips .15 .07
❑ 445 Tippy Martinez .15 .07
❑ 446 Jim Sundberg .15 .07
❑ 447 Jeff Lahti .15 .07
❑ 448 Derrel Thomas .15 .07
❑ 449 Phil Bradley .25 .11
❑ 450 Steve Garvey .40 .18
❑ 451 Bruce Hurst .15 .07
❑ 452 John Castino .15 .07
❑ 453 Tom Waddell .15 .07
❑ 454 Glenn Wilson .15 .07
❑ 455 Bob Knepper .15 .07
❑ 456 Tim Foli .15 .07
❑ 457 Cecilio Guante .15 .07
❑ 458 Randy Johnson .15 .07
❑ 459 Charlie Leibrandt .15 .07
❑ 460 Ryne Sandberg 1.25 .55
❑ 461 Marty Castillo .15 .07
❑ 462 Gary Lavelle .15 .07
❑ 463 Dave Collins .15 .07
❑ 464 Mike Mason .15 .07
❑ 465 Bobby Grich .25 .11
❑ 466 Tony LaRussa MG .40 .18
❑ 467 Ed Lynch .15 .07
❑ 468 Wayne Krenchicki .15 .07
❑ 469 Sammy Stewart .15 .07
❑ 470 Steve Sax .15 .07
❑ 471 Pete Ladd .15 .07
❑ 472 Jim Essian .15 .07
❑ 473 Tim Wallach .25 .11
❑ 474 Kurt Kepshire .15 .07
❑ 475 Andre Thornton .15 .07
❑ 476 Jeff Stone .15 .07
❑ 477 Bob Ojeda .15 .07
❑ 478 Kurt Bevacqua .15 .07
❑ 479 Mike Madden .15 .07
❑ 480 Lou Whitaker .40 .18
❑ 481 Dale Murray .15 .07
❑ 482 Harry Spilman .15 .07
❑ 483 Mike Smithson .15 .07
❑ 484 Larry Bowa .25 .11
❑ 485 Matt Young .15 .07
❑ 486 Steve Balboni .15 .07
❑ 487 Frank Williams .15 .07
❑ 488 Joel Skinner .15 .07
❑ 489 Bryan Clark .15 .07
❑ 490 Jason Thompson .15 .07
❑ 491 Rick Camp .15 .07
❑ 492 Dave Johnson MG .25 .11
❑ 493 Orel Hershiser RC .75 .35
❑ 494 Rich Dauer .15 .07
❑ 495 Mario Soto .15 .07
❑ 496 Donnie Scott .15 .07
❑ 497 Gary Pettis UER .15 .07
(Photo actually
Gary's little
brother Lynn)
❑ 498 Ed Romero .15 .07
❑ 499 Danny Cox .15 .07
❑ 500 Mike Schmidt 1.25 .55
❑ 501 Dan Schatzeder .15 .07
❑ 502 Rick Miller .15 .07
❑ 503 Tim Conroy .15 .07
❑ 504 Jerry Willard .15 .07
❑ 505 Jim Beattie .15 .07
❑ 506 Franklin Stubbs .15 .07
❑ 507 Ray Fontenot .15 .07
❑ 508 John Shelby .15 .07
❑ 509 Milt May .15 .07
❑ 510 Kent Hrbek .25 .11
❑ 511 Lee Smith .40 .18
❑ 512 Tom Brookens .15 .07
❑ 513 Lynn Jones .15 .07
❑ 514 Jeff Cornell .15 .07
❑ 515 Dave Concepcion .25 .11
❑ 516 Roy Lee Jackson .15 .07
❑ 517 Jerry Martin .15 .07
❑ 518 Chris Chambliss .25 .11
❑ 519 Doug Rader MG .15 .07
❑ 520 LaMarr Hoyt .15 .07
❑ 521 Rick Dempsey .15 .07
❑ 522 Paul Molitor .60 .25
❑ 523 Candy Maldonado .15 .07
❑ 524 Rob Wilfong .15 .07
❑ 525 Darrell Porter .15 .07
❑ 526 David Palmer .15 .07
❑ 527 Checklist: 397-528 .15 .07
❑ 528 Bill Krueger .15 .07
❑ 529 Rich Gedman .15 .07
❑ 530 Dave Dravecky .25 .11
❑ 531 Joe Lefebvre .15 .07
❑ 532 Frank DiPino .15 .07
❑ 533 Tony Bernazard .15 .07
❑ 534 Brian Dayett .15 .07
❑ 535 Pat Putnam .15 .07
❑ 536 Kirby Puckett RC 8.00 3.60
❑ 537 Don Robinson .15 .07
❑ 538 Keith Moreland .15 .07
❑ 539 Aurelio Lopez .15 .07
❑ 540 Claudell Washington .15 .07
❑ 541 Mark Davis .15 .07
❑ 542 Don Slaught .15 .07
❑ 543 Mike Squires .15 .07
❑ 544 Bruce Kison .15 .07
❑ 545 Lloyd Moseby .15 .07
❑ 546 Brent Gaff .15 .07
❑ 547 Pete Rose MG .40 .18
❑ 548 Larry Parrish .15 .07
❑ 549 Mike Scioscia .15 .07
❑ 550 Scott McGregor .15 .07
❑ 551 Andy Van Slyke .25 .11
❑ 552 Chris Codiroli .15 .07
❑ 553 Bob Clark .15 .07
❑ 554 Doug Flynn .15 .07
❑ 555 Bob Stanley .15 .07
❑ 556 Sixto Lezcano .15 .07
❑ 557 Len Barker .15 .07
❑ 558 Carmelo Martinez .15 .07
❑ 559 Jay Howell .15 .07
❑ 560 Bill Madlock .25 .11
❑ 561 Darryl Motley .15 .07
❑ 562 Houston Jimenez .15 .07
❑ 563 Dick Ruthven .15 .07
❑ 564 Alan Ashby .15 .07
❑ 565 Kirk Gibson .25 .11
❑ 566 Ed VandeBerg .15 .07
❑ 567 Joel Youngblood .15 .07
❑ 568 Cliff Johnson .15 .07
❑ 569 Ken Oberkfell .15 .07
❑ 570 Darryl Strawberry .60 .25
❑ 571 Charlie Hough .25 .11
❑ 572 Tom Paciorek .25 .11
❑ 573 Jay Tibbs .15 .07
❑ 574 Joe Altobelli MG .15 .07
❑ 575 Pedro Guerrero .25 .11
❑ 576 Jaime Cocanower .15 .07
❑ 577 Chris Speier .15 .07
❑ 578 Terry Francona .15 .07
❑ 579 Ron Romanick .15 .07
❑ 580 Dwight Evans .25 .11
❑ 581 Mark Wagner .15 .07
❑ 582 Ken Phelps .15 .07
❑ 583 Bobby Brown .15 .07
❑ 584 Kevin Gross .15 .07
❑ 585 Butch Wynegar .15 .07
❑ 586 Bill Scherrer .15 .07
❑ 587 Doug Frobel .15 .07
❑ 588 Bobby Castillo .15 .07
❑ 589 Bob Dernier .15 .07
❑ 590 Ray Knight .15 .07
❑ 591 Larry Herndon .15 .07
❑ 592 Jeff D. Robinson .15 .07
❑ 593 Rick Leach .15 .07
❑ 594 Curt Wilkerson .15 .07
❑ 595 Larry Gura .15 .07
❑ 596 Jerry Hairston .15 .07
❑ 597 Brad Lesley .15 .07
❑ 598 Jose Oquendo .15 .07
❑ 599 Storm Davis .15 .07
❑ 600 Pete Rose 1.50 .70
❑ 601 Tom Lasorda MG .40 .18
❑ 602 Jeff Dedmon .15 .07
❑ 603 Rick Manning .15 .07
❑ 604 Daryl Sconiers .15 .07
❑ 605 Ozzie Smith .75 .35
❑ 606 Rich Gale .15 .07
❑ 607 Bill Almon .15 .07
❑ 608 Craig Lefferts .15 .07
❑ 609 Broderick Perkins .15 .07
❑ 610 Jack Morris .25 .11
❑ 611 Ozzie Virgil .15 .07
❑ 612 Mike Armstrong .15 .07
❑ 613 Terry Puhl .15 .07
❑ 614 Al Williams .15 .07
❑ 615 Marvell Wynne .15 .07
❑ 616 Scott Sanderson .15 .07
❑ 617 Willie Wilson .15 .07
❑ 618 Pete Falcone .15 .07
❑ 619 Jeff Leonard .15 .07
❑ 620 Dwight Gooden RC .75 .35
❑ 621 Marvis Foley .15 .07
❑ 622 Luis Leal .15 .07
❑ 623 Greg Walker .15 .07
❑ 624 Benny Ayala .15 .07
❑ 625 Mark Langston RC .40 .18
❑ 626 German Rivera .15 .07
❑ 627 Eric Davis RC 1.00 .45
❑ 628 Rene Lachemann MG .15 .07
❑ 629 Dick Schofield .15 .07
❑ 630 Tim Raines .25 .11
❑ 631 Bob Forsch .15 .07
❑ 632 Bruce Bochte .15 .07
❑ 633 Glenn Hoffman .15 .07
❑ 634 Bill Dawley .15 .07
❑ 635 Terry Kennedy .15 .07
❑ 636 Shane Rawley .15 .07
❑ 637 Brett Butler .25 .11
❑ 638 Mike Pagliarulo .15 .07
❑ 639 Ed Hodge .15 .07
❑ 640 Steve Henderson .15 .07
❑ 641 Rod Scurry .15 .07
❑ 642 Dave Owen .15 .07
❑ 643 Johnny Grubb .15 .07
❑ 644 Mark Huismann .15 .07
❑ 645 Damaso Garcia .15 .07
❑ 646 Scot Thompson .15 .07
❑ 647 Rafael Ramirez .15 .07
❑ 648 Bob Jones .15 .07
❑ 649 Sid Fernandez .25 .11
❑ 650 Greg Luzinski .25 .11
❑ 651 Jeff Russell .15 .07
❑ 652 Joe Nolan .15 .07
❑ 653 Mark Brouhard .15 .07
❑ 654 Dave Anderson .15 .07
❑ 655 Joaquin Andujar .15 .07
❑ 656 Chuck Cottier MG .15 .07
❑ 657 Jim Slaton .15 .07
❑ 658 Mike Stenhouse .15 .07
❑ 659 Checklist: 529-660 .15 .07
❑ 660 Tony Gwynn 2.00 .90
❑ 661 Steve Crawford .15 .07
❑ 662 Mike Heath .15 .07
❑ 663 Luis Aguayo .15 .07
❑ 664 Steve Farr RC .25 .11
❑ 665 Don Mattingly 1.50 .70
❑ 666 Mike LaCoss .15 .07
❑ 667 Dave Engle .15 .07
❑ 668 Steve Trout .15 .07
❑ 669 Lee Lacy .15 .07
❑ 670 Tom Seaver 1.00 .45
❑ 671 Dane Iorg .15 .07
❑ 672 Juan Berenguer .15 .07
❑ 673 Buck Martinez .15 .07
❑ 674 Atlee Hammaker .15 .07
❑ 675 Tony Perez .60 .25
❑ 676 Albert Hall .15 .07
❑ 677 Wally Backman .15 .07
❑ 678 Joey McLaughlin .15 .07
❑ 679 Bob Kearney .15 .07
❑ 680 Jerry Reuss .15 .07
❑ 681 Ben Oglivie .15 .07
❑ 682 Doug Corbett .15 .07
❑ 683 Whitey Herzog MG .25 .11
❑ 684 Bill Doran .15 .07
❑ 685 Bill Caudill .15 .07
❑ 686 Mike Easler .15 .07
❑ 687 Bill Gullickson .15 .07
❑ 688 Len Matuszek .15 .07

	No.	Player	NRMT	VG-E
❑	689	Luis DeLeon	.15	.07
❑	690	Alan Trammell	.40	.18
❑	691	Dennis Rasmussen	.15	.07
❑	692	Randy Bush	.15	.07
❑	693	Tim Stoddard	.15	.07
❑	694	Joe Carter	.60	.25
❑	695	Rick Rhoden	.15	.07
❑	696	John Rabb	.15	.07
❑	697	Onix Concepcion	.15	.07
❑	698	Jorge Bell	.25	.11
❑	699	Donnie Moore	.15	.07
❑	700	Eddie Murray	.60	.25
❑	701	Eddie Murray AS	.25	.11
❑	702	Damaso Garcia AS	.15	.07
❑	703	George Brett AS	.60	.25
❑	704	Cal Ripken AS	1.50	.70
❑	705	Dave Winfield AS	.25	.11
❑	706	Rickey Henderson AS	.60	.25
❑	707	Tony Armas AS	.15	.07
❑	708	Lance Parrish AS	.15	.07
❑	709	Mike Boddicker AS	.15	.07
❑	710	Frank Viola AS	.15	.07
❑	711	Dan Quisenberry AS	.15	.07
❑	712	Keith Hernandez AS	.15	.07
❑	713	Ryne Sandberg AS	.60	.25
❑	714	Mike Schmidt AS	.40	.18
❑	715	Ozzie Smith AS	.40	.18
❑	716	Dale Murphy AS	.25	.11
❑	717	Tony Gwynn AS	1.25	.55
❑	718	Jeff Leonard AS	.15	.07
❑	719	Gary Carter AS	.25	.11
❑	720	Rick Sutcliffe AS	.15	.07
❑	721	Bob Knepper AS	.15	.07
❑	722	Bruce Sutter AS	.15	.07
❑	723	Dave Stewart	.25	.11
❑	724	Oscar Gamble	.15	.07
❑	725	Floyd Bannister	.15	.07
❑	726	Al Bumbry	.15	.07
❑	727	Frank Pastore	.15	.07
❑	728	Bob Bailor	.15	.07
❑	729	Don Sutton	.60	.25
❑	730	Dave Kingman	.25	.11
❑	731	Neil Allen	.15	.07
❑	732	John McNamara MG	.15	.07
❑	733	Tony Scott	.15	.07
❑	734	John Henry Johnson	.15	.07
❑	735	Garry Templeton	.15	.07
❑	736	Jerry Mumphrey	.15	.07
❑	737	Bo Diaz	.15	.07
❑	738	Omar Moreno	.15	.07
❑	739	Ernie Camacho	.15	.07
❑	740	Jack Clark	.25	.11
❑	741	John Butcher	.15	.07
❑	742	Ron Hassey	.15	.07
❑	743	Frank White	.25	.11
❑	744	Doug Bair	.15	.07
❑	745	Buddy Bell	.25	.11
❑	746	Jim Clancy	.15	.07
❑	747	Alex Trevino	.15	.07
❑	748	Lee Mazzilli	.15	.07
❑	749	Julio Cruz	.15	.07
❑	750	Rollie Fingers	.60	.25
❑	751	Kelvin Chapman	.15	.07
❑	752	Bob Owchinko	.15	.07
❑	753	Greg Brock	.15	.07
❑	754	Larry Milbourne	.15	.07
❑	755	Ken Singleton	.15	.07
❑	756	Rob Picciolo	.15	.07
❑	757	Willie McGee	.25	.11
❑	758	Ray Burris	.15	.07
❑	759	Jim Fanning MG	.15	.07
❑	760	Nolan Ryan	3.00	1.35
❑	761	Jerry Remy	.15	.07
❑	762	Eddie Whitson	.15	.07
❑	763	Kiko Garcia	.15	.07
❑	764	Jamie Easterly	.15	.07
❑	765	Willie Randolph	.25	.11
❑	766	Paul Mirabella	.15	.07
❑	767	Darrell Brown	.15	.07
❑	768	Ron Cey	.25	.11
❑	769	Joe Cowley	.15	.07
❑	770	Carlton Fisk	.60	.25
❑	771	Geoff Zahn	.15	.07
❑	772	Johnnie LeMaster	.15	.07
❑	773	Hal McRae	.25	.11
❑	774	Dennis Lamp	.15	.07
❑	775	Mookie Wilson	.25	.11
❑	776	Jerry Royster	.15	.07
❑	777	Ned Yost	.15	.07
❑	778	Mike Davis	.15	.07
❑	779	Nick Esasky	.15	.07
❑	780	Mike Flanagan	.15	.07
❑	781	Jim Gantner	.15	.07
❑	782	Tom Niedenfuer	.15	.07
❑	783	Mike Jorgensen	.15	.07
❑	784	Checklist: 661-792	.15	.07
❑	785	Tony Armas	.15	.07
❑	786	Enos Cabell	.15	.07
❑	787	Jim Wohlford	.15	.07
❑	788	Steve Comer	.15	.07
❑	789	Luis Salazar	.15	.07
❑	790	Ron Guidry	.25	.11
❑	791	Ivan DeJesus	.15	.07
❑	792	Darrell Evans	.25	.11

1985 Topps Traded

	No.	Player	NRMT	VG-E
		COMP.FACT.SET (132)	6.00	2.70
❑	1T	Don Aase	.15	.07
❑	2T	Bill Almon	.15	.07
❑	3T	Benny Ayala	.15	.07
❑	4T	Dusty Baker	.40	.18
❑	5T	George Bamberger MG	.15	.07
❑	6T	Dale Berra	.15	.07
❑	7T	Rich Bordi	.15	.07
❑	8T	Daryl Boston XRC*	.15	.07
❑	9T	Hubie Brooks	.15	.07
❑	10T	Chris Brown	.15	.07
❑	11T	Tom Browning XRC*	.40	.18
❑	12T	Al Bumbry	.15	.07
❑	13T	Ray Burris	.15	.07
❑	14T	Jeff Burroughs	.15	.07
❑	15T	Bill Campbell	.15	.07
❑	16T	Don Carman	.15	.07
❑	17T	Gary Carter	.75	.35
❑	18T	Bobby Castillo	.15	.07
❑	19T	Bill Caudill	.15	.07
❑	20T	Rick Cerone	.15	.07
❑	21T	Bryan Clark	.15	.07
❑	22T	Jack Clark	.40	.18
❑	23T	Pat Clements	.15	.07
❑	24T	Vince Coleman XRC	1.00	.45
❑	25T	Dave Collins	.15	.07
❑	26T	Danny Darwin	.15	.07
❑	27T	Jim Davenport MG	.15	.07
❑	28T	Jerry Davis	.15	.07
❑	29T	Brian Dayett	.15	.07
❑	30T	Ivan DeJesus	.15	.07
❑	31T	Ken Dixon	.15	.07
❑	32T	Mariano Duncan XRC	1.00	.45
❑	33T	John Felske MG	.15	.07
❑	34T	Mike Fitzgerald	.15	.07
❑	35T	Ray Fontenot	.15	.07
❑	36T	Greg Gagne XRC*	.40	.18
❑	37T	Oscar Gamble	.15	.07
❑	38T	Scott Garrelts	.15	.07
❑	39T	Bob L. Gibson	.15	.07
❑	40T	Jim Gott	.15	.07
❑	41T	David Green	.15	.07
❑	42T	Alfredo Griffin	.15	.07
❑	43T	Ozzie Guillen XRC	1.00	.45
❑	44T	Eddie Haas MG	.15	.07
❑	45T	Terry Harper	.15	.07
❑	46T	Toby Harrah	.15	.07
❑	47T	Greg Harris	.15	.07
❑	48T	Ron Hassey	.15	.07
❑	49T	Rickey Henderson	3.00	1.35
❑	50T	Steve Henderson	.15	.07
❑	51T	George Hendrick	.15	.07
❑	52T	Joe Hesketh	.15	.07
❑	53T	Teddy Higuera XRC	.40	.18
❑	54T	Donnie Hill	.15	.07
❑	55T	Al Holland	.15	.07
❑	56T	Burt Hooton	.15	.07
❑	57T	Jay Howell	.15	.07
❑	58T	Ken Howell	.15	.07
❑	59T	LaMarr Hoyt	.15	.07
❑	60T	Tim Hulett XRC*	.15	.07
❑	61T	Bob James	.15	.07
❑	62T	Steve Jeltz	.15	.07
❑	63T	Cliff Johnson	.15	.07
❑	64T	Howard Johnson	.40	.18
❑	65T	Ruppert Jones	.15	.07
❑	66T	Steve Kemp	.15	.07
❑	67T	Bruce Kison	.15	.07
❑	68T	Alan Knicely	.15	.07
❑	69T	Mike LaCoss	.15	.07
❑	70T	Lee Lacy	.15	.07
❑	71T	Dave LaPoint	.15	.07
❑	72T	Gary Lavelle	.15	.07
❑	73T	Vance Law	.15	.07
❑	74T	Johnnie LeMaster	.15	.07
❑	75T	Sixto Lezcano	.15	.07
❑	76T	Tim Lollar	.15	.07
❑	77T	Fred Lynn	.40	.18
❑	78T	Billy Martin MG	.40	.18
❑	79T	Ron Mathis	.15	.07
❑	80T	Len Matuszek	.15	.07
❑	81T	Gene Mauch MG	.40	.18
❑	82T	Oddibe McDowell	.40	.18
❑	83T	Roger McDowell XRC	.40	.18
❑	84T	John McNamara MG	.15	.07
❑	85T	Donnie Moore	.15	.07
❑	86T	Gene Nelson	.15	.07
❑	87T	Steve Nicosia	.15	.07
❑	88T	Al Oliver	.40	.18
❑	89T	Joe Orsulak XRC	.40	.18
❑	90T	Rob Picciolo	.15	.07
❑	91T	Chris Pittaro	.15	.07
❑	92T	Jim Presley	.40	.18
❑	93T	Rick Reuschel	.15	.07
❑	94T	Bert Roberge	.15	.07
❑	95T	Bob Rodgers MG	.15	.07
❑	96T	Jerry Royster	.15	.07
❑	97T	Dave Rozema	.15	.07
❑	98T	Dave Rucker	.15	.07
❑	99T	Vern Ruhle	.15	.07
❑	100T	Paul Runge	.15	.07
❑	101T	Mark Salas	.15	.07
❑	102T	Luis Salazar	.15	.07
❑	103T	Joe Sambito	.15	.07
❑	104T	Rick Schu	.15	.07
❑	105T	Donnie Scott	.15	.07
❑	106T	Larry Sheets	.15	.07
❑	107T	Don Slaught	.15	.07
❑	108T	Roy Smalley	.15	.07
❑	109T	Lonnie Smith	.15	.07
❑	110T	Nate Snell UER (Headings on back for a batter)	.15	.07
❑	111T	Chris Speier	.15	.07
❑	112T	Mike Stenhouse	.15	.07
❑	113T	Tim Stoddard	.15	.07
❑	114T	Jim Sundberg	.15	.07
❑	115T	Bruce Sutter	.40	.18
❑	116T	Don Sutton	1.00	.45
❑	117T	Kent Tekulve	.15	.07
❑	118T	Tom Tellmann	.15	.07
❑	119T	Walt Terrell	.15	.07
❑	120T	M.Tettleton XRC	1.00	.45
❑	121T	Derrel Thomas	.15	.07
❑	122T	Rich Thompson	.15	.07
❑	123T	Alex Trevino	.15	.07
❑	124T	John Tudor	.15	.07
❑	125T	Jose Uribe	.15	.07
❑	126T	Bobby Valentine MG	.15	.07
❑	127T	Dave Von Ohlen	.15	.07
❑	128T	U.L. Washington	.15	.07

	Card	Player	Price	Price
❑	129T	Earl Weaver MG	.75	.35
❑	130T	Eddie Whitson	.15	.07
❑	131T	Herm Winningham	.15	.07
❑	132T	Checklist 1-132	.15	.07

1986 Topps

	MINT	NRMT
COMPLETE SET (792)	30.00	13.50
COMP.FACT.SET (792)	50.00	22.00

	No.	Player	MINT	NRMT
❑	1	Pete Rose	1.25	.55
❑	2	Rose Special: '63-'66	.25	.11
❑	3	Rose Special: '67-'70	.25	.11
❑	4	Rose Special: '71-'74	.25	.11
❑	5	Rose Special: '75-'78	.25	.11
❑	6	Rose Special: '79-'82	.25	.11
❑	7	Rose Special: '83-'85	.25	.11
❑	8	Dwayne Murphy	.10	.05
❑	9	Roy Smith	.10	.05
❑	10	Tony Gwynn	.75	.35
❑	11	Bob Ojeda	.10	.05
❑	12	Jose Uribe	.10	.05
❑	13	Bob Kearney	.10	.05
❑	14	Julio Cruz	.10	.05
❑	15	Eddie Whitson	.10	.05
❑	16	Rick Schu	.10	.05
❑	17	Mike Stenhouse	.10	.05
❑	18	Brent Gaff	.10	.05
❑	19	Rich Hebner	.10	.05
❑	20	Lou Whitaker	.15	.07
❑	21	George Bamberger MG	.10	.05
❑	22	Duane Walker	.10	.05
❑	23	Manny Lee RC*	.10	.05
❑	24	Len Barker	.10	.05
❑	25	Willie Wilson	.10	.05
❑	26	Frank DiPino	.10	.05
❑	27	Ray Knight	.15	.07
❑	28	Eric Davis	.25	.11
❑	29	Tony Phillips	.10	.05
❑	30	Eddie Murray	.40	.18
❑	31	Jamie Easterly	.10	.05
❑	32	Steve Yeager	.10	.05
❑	33	Jeff Lahti	.10	.05
❑	34	Ken Phelps	.10	.05
❑	35	Jeff Reardon	.10	.05
❑	36	Lance Parrish TL	.15	.07
❑	37	Mark Thurmond	.10	.05
❑	38	Glenn Hoffman	.10	.05
❑	39	Dave Rucker	.10	.05
❑	40	Ken Griffey	.15	.07
❑	41	Brad Wellman	.10	.05
❑	42	Geoff Zahn	.10	.05
❑	43	Dave Engle	.10	.05
❑	44	Lance McCullers	.10	.05
❑	45	Damaso Garcia	.10	.05
❑	46	Billy Hatcher	.10	.05
❑	47	Juan Berenguer	.10	.05
❑	48	Bill Almon	.10	.05
❑	49	Rick Manning	.10	.05
❑	50	Dan Quisenberry	.10	.05
❑	51	Bobby Wine MG ERR Number of card on back is actually 57)	.10	.05
❑	52	Chris Welsh	.10	.05
❑	53	Len Dykstra RC	.75	.35
❑	54	John Franco	.40	.18
❑	55	Fred Lynn	.15	.07
❑	56	Tom Niedenfuer	.10	.05
❑	57	Bill Doran (See also 51)	.10	.05
❑	58	Bill Krueger	.10	.05
❑	59	Andre Thornton	.10	.05
❑	60	Dwight Evans	.15	.07
❑	61	Karl Best	.10	.05
❑	62	Bob Boone	.15	.07
❑	63	Ron Roenicke	.10	.05
❑	64	Floyd Bannister	.10	.05
❑	65	Dan Driessen	.10	.05
❑	66	Bob Forsch TL	.10	.05
❑	67	Carmelo Martinez	.10	.05
❑	68	Ed Lynch	.10	.05
❑	69	Luis Aguayo	.10	.05
❑	70	Dave Winfield	.40	.18
❑	71	Ken Schrom	.10	.05
❑	72	Shawon Dunston	.15	.07
❑	73	Randy O'Neal	.10	.05
❑	74	Rance Mulliniks	.10	.05
❑	75	Jose DeLeon	.10	.05
❑	76	Dion James	.10	.05
❑	77	Charlie Leibrandt	.10	.05
❑	78	Bruce Benedict	.10	.05
❑	79	Dave Schmidt	.10	.05
❑	80	Darryl Strawberry	.40	.18
❑	81	Gene Mauch MG	.15	.07
❑	82	Tippy Martinez	.10	.05
❑	83	Phil Garner	.15	.07
❑	84	Curt Young	.10	.05
❑	85	Tony Perez (Eric Davis also shown on card)	.40	.18
❑	86	Tom Waddell	.10	.05
❑	87	Candy Maldonado	.10	.05
❑	88	Tom Nieto	.10	.05
❑	89	Randy St.Claire	.10	.05
❑	90	Garry Templeton	.10	.05
❑	91	Steve Crawford	.10	.05
❑	92	Al Cowens	.10	.05
❑	93	Scot Thompson	.10	.05
❑	94	Rich Bordi	.10	.05
❑	95	Ozzie Virgil	.10	.05
❑	96	Jim Clancy TL	.10	.05
❑	97	Gary Gaetti	.15	.07
❑	98	Dick Ruthven	.10	.05
❑	99	Buddy Biancalana	.10	.05
❑	100	Nolan Ryan	2.00	.90
❑	101	Dave Bergman	.10	.05
❑	102	Joe Orsulak RC*	.10	.05
❑	103	Luis Salazar	.10	.05
❑	104	Sid Fernandez	.15	.07
❑	105	Gary Ward	.10	.05
❑	106	Ray Burris	.10	.05
❑	107	Rafael Ramirez	.10	.05
❑	108	Ted Power	.10	.05
❑	109	Len Matuszek	.10	.05
❑	110	Scott McGregor	.10	.05
❑	111	Roger Craig MG	.15	.07
❑	112	Bill Campbell	.10	.05
❑	113	U.L. Washington	.10	.05
❑	114	Mike C. Brown	.10	.05
❑	115	Jay Howell	.10	.05
❑	116	Brook Jacoby	.10	.05
❑	117	Bruce Kison	.10	.05
❑	118	Jerry Royster	.10	.05
❑	119	Barry Bonnell	.10	.05
❑	120	Steve Carlton	.40	.18
❑	121	Nelson Simmons	.10	.05
❑	122	Pete Filson	.10	.05
❑	123	Greg Walker	.10	.05
❑	124	Luis Sanchez	.10	.05
❑	125	Dave Lopes	.15	.07
❑	126	Mookie Wilson TL	.10	.05
❑	127	Jack Howell	.10	.05
❑	128	John Wathan	.10	.05
❑	129	Jeff Dedmon	.10	.05
❑	130	Alan Trammell	.25	.11
❑	131	Checklist: 1-132	.15	.07
❑	132	Razor Shines	.10	.05
❑	133	Andy McGaffigan	.10	.05
❑	134	Carney Lansford	.15	.07
❑	135	Joe Niekro	.10	.05
❑	136	Mike Hargrove	.15	.07
❑	137	Charlie Moore	.10	.05
❑	138	Mark Davis	.10	.05
❑	139	Daryl Boston	.10	.05
❑	140	John Candelaria	.10	.05
❑	141	Chuck Cottier MG See also 171	.10	.05
❑	142	Bob Jones	.10	.05
❑	143	Dave Van Gorder	.10	.05
❑	144	Doug Sisk	.10	.05
❑	145	Pedro Guerrero	.15	.07
❑	146	Jack Perconte	.10	.05
❑	147	Larry Sheets	.10	.05
❑	148	Mike Heath	.10	.05
❑	149	Brett Butler	.15	.07
❑	150	Joaquin Andujar	.10	.05
❑	151	Dave Stapleton	.10	.05
❑	152	Mike Morgan	.10	.05
❑	153	Ricky Adams	.10	.05
❑	154	Bert Roberge	.10	.05
❑	155	Bobby Grich	.15	.07
❑	156	Richard Dotson TL	.10	.05
❑	157	Ron Hassey	.10	.05
❑	158	Derrel Thomas	.10	.05
❑	159	Orel Hershiser UER (82 Alburquerque)	.40	.18
❑	160	Chet Lemon	.10	.05
❑	161	Lee Tunnell	.10	.05
❑	162	Greg Gagne	.10	.05
❑	163	Pete Ladd	.10	.05
❑	164	Steve Balboni	.10	.05
❑	165	Mike Davis	.10	.05
❑	166	Dickie Thon	.10	.05
❑	167	Zane Smith	.10	.05
❑	168	Jeff Burroughs	.10	.05
❑	169	George Wright	.10	.05
❑	170	Gary Carter	.25	.11
❑	171	Bob Rodgers MG ERR Number of card on back actually 141)	.10	.05
❑	172	Jerry Reed	.10	.05
❑	173	Wayne Gross	.10	.05
❑	174	Brian Snyder	.10	.05
❑	175	Steve Sax	.10	.05
❑	176	Jay Tibbs	.10	.05
❑	177	Joel Youngblood	.10	.05
❑	178	Ivan DeJesus	.10	.05
❑	179	Stu Cliburn	.10	.05
❑	180	Don Mattingly	1.00	.45
❑	181	Al Nipper	.10	.05
❑	182	Bobby Brown	.10	.05
❑	183	Larry Andersen	.10	.05
❑	184	Tim Laudner	.10	.05
❑	185	Rollie Fingers	.40	.18
❑	186	Jose Cruz TL	.10	.05
❑	187	Scott Fletcher	.10	.05
❑	188	Bob Dernier	.10	.05
❑	189	Mike Mason	.10	.05
❑	190	George Hendrick	.10	.05
❑	191	Wally Backman	.10	.05
❑	192	Milt Wilcox	.10	.05
❑	193	Daryl Sconiers	.10	.05
❑	194	Craig McMurtry	.10	.05
❑	195	Dave Concepcion	.15	.07
❑	196	Doyle Alexander	.10	.05
❑	197	Enos Cabell	.10	.05
❑	198	Ken Dixon	.10	.05
❑	199	Dick Howser MG	.15	.07
❑	200	Mike Schmidt	.75	.35
❑	201	Vince Coleman RB Most SB's rookie season	.15	.07
❑	202	Dwight Gooden RB Youngest 20 game winner	.15	.07
❑	203	Keith Hernandez RB Most game-winning RBI's	.10	.05
❑	204	Phil Niekro RB Oldest shutout pitcher	.15	.07
❑	205	Tony Perez RB Oldest grand slammer	.15	.07
❑	206	Pete Rose RB Most lifetime hits	.40	.18
❑	207	F.Valenzuela RB Most cons. innings start of season, no earned runs	.15	.07
❑	208	Ramon Romero	.10	.05
❑	209	Randy Ready	.10	.05
❑	210	Calvin Schiraldi	.10	.05

❑ 211 Ed Wojna .10 .05
❑ 212 Chris Speier .10 .05
❑ 213 Bob Shirley .10 .05
❑ 214 Randy Bush .10 .05
❑ 215 Frank White .15 .07
❑ 216 Dwayne Murphy TL .10 .05
❑ 217 Bill Scherrer .10 .05
❑ 218 Randy Hunt .10 .05
❑ 219 Dennis Lamp .10 .05
❑ 220 Bob Horner .10 .05
❑ 221 Dave Henderson .10 .05
❑ 222 Craig Gerber .10 .05
❑ 223 Atlee Hammaker .10 .05
❑ 224 Cesar Cedeno .15 .07
❑ 225 Ron Darling .10 .05
❑ 226 Lee Lacy .10 .05
❑ 227 Al Jones .10 .05
❑ 228 Tom Lawless .10 .05
❑ 229 Bill Gullickson .10 .05
❑ 230 Terry Kennedy .10 .05
❑ 231 Jim Frey MG .10 .05
❑ 232 Rick Rhoden .10 .05
❑ 233 Steve Lyons .10 .05
❑ 234 Doug Corbett .10 .05
❑ 235 Butch Wynegar .10 .05
❑ 236 Frank Eufemia .10 .05
❑ 237 Ted Simmons .15 .07
❑ 238 Larry Parrish .10 .05
❑ 239 Joel Skinner .10 .05
❑ 240 Tommy John .40 .18
❑ 241 Tony Fernandez .10 .05
❑ 242 Rich Thompson .10 .05
❑ 243 Johnny Grubb .10 .05
❑ 244 Craig Lefferts .10 .05
❑ 245 Jim Sundberg .10 .05
❑ 246 Steve Carlton TL .15 .07
❑ 247 Terry Harper .10 .05
❑ 248 Spike Owen .10 .05
❑ 249 Rob Deer .15 .07
❑ 250 Dwight Gooden .40 .18
❑ 251 Rich Dauer .10 .05
❑ 252 Bobby Castillo .10 .05
❑ 253 Dann Bilardello .10 .05
❑ 254 Ozzie Guillen RC* .25 .11
❑ 255 Tony Armas .10 .05
❑ 256 Kurt Kepshire .10 .05
❑ 257 Doug DeCinces .10 .05
❑ 258 Tim Burke .10 .05
❑ 259 Dan Pasqua .10 .05
❑ 260 Tony Pena .10 .05
❑ 261 Bobby Valentine MG .15 .07
❑ 262 Mario Ramirez .10 .05
❑ 263 Checklist: 133-264 .15 .07
❑ 264 Darren Daulton RC .75 .35
❑ 265 Ron Davis .10 .05
❑ 266 Keith Moreland .10 .05
❑ 267 Paul Molitor .40 .18
❑ 268 Mike Scott .10 .05
❑ 269 Dane Iorg .10 .05
❑ 270 Jack Morris .15 .07
❑ 271 Dave Collins .10 .05
❑ 272 Tim Tolman .10 .05
❑ 273 Jerry Willard .10 .05
❑ 274 Ron Gardenhire .10 .05
❑ 275 Charlie Hough .15 .07
❑ 276 Willie Randolph TL .15 .07
❑ 277 Jaime Cocanower .10 .05
❑ 278 Sixto Lezcano .10 .05
❑ 279 Al Pardo .10 .05
❑ 280 Tim Raines .15 .07
❑ 281 Steve Mura .10 .05
❑ 282 Jerry Mumphrey .10 .05
❑ 283 Mike Fischlin .10 .05
❑ 284 Brian Dayett .10 .05
❑ 285 Buddy Bell .15 .07
❑ 286 Luis DeLeon .10 .05
❑ 287 John Christensen .10 .05
❑ 288 Don Aase .10 .05
❑ 289 Johnnie LeMaster .10 .05
❑ 290 Carlton Fisk .40 .18
❑ 291 Tom Lasorda MG .25 .11
❑ 292 Chuck Porter .10 .05
❑ 293 Chris Chambliss .15 .07
❑ 294 Danny Cox .10 .05
❑ 295 Kirk Gibson .15 .07
❑ 296 Geno Petralli .10 .05
❑ 297 Tim Lollar .10 .05
❑ 298 Craig Reynolds .10 .05
❑ 299 Bryn Smith .10 .05
❑ 300 George Brett .75 .35
❑ 301 Dennis Rasmussen .10 .05
❑ 302 Greg Gross .10 .05
❑ 303 Curt Wardle .10 .05
❑ 304 Mike Gallego RC .15 .07
❑ 305 Phil Bradley .10 .05
❑ 306 Terry Kennedy TL .10 .05
❑ 307 Dave Sax .10 .05
❑ 308 Ray Fontenot .10 .05
❑ 309 John Shelby .10 .05
❑ 310 Greg Minton .10 .05
❑ 311 Dick Schofield .10 .05
❑ 312 Tom Filer .10 .05
❑ 313 Joe DeSa .10 .05
❑ 314 Frank Pastore .10 .05
❑ 315 Mookie Wilson .15 .07
❑ 316 Sammy Khalifa .10 .05
❑ 317 Ed Romero .10 .05
❑ 318 Terry Whitfield .10 .05
❑ 319 Rick Camp .10 .05
❑ 320 Jim Rice .15 .07
❑ 321 Earl Weaver MG .40 .18
❑ 322 Bob Forsch .10 .05
❑ 323 Jerry Davis .10 .05
❑ 324 Dan Schatzeder .10 .05
❑ 325 Juan Beniquez .10 .05
❑ 326 Kent Tekulve .10 .05
❑ 327 Mike Pagliarulo .10 .05
❑ 328 Pete O'Brien .10 .05
❑ 329 Kirby Puckett 1.25 .55
❑ 330 Rick Sutcliffe .15 .07
❑ 331 Alan Ashby .10 .05
❑ 332 Darryl Motley .10 .05
❑ 333 Tom Henke .15 .07
❑ 334 Ken Oberkfell .10 .05
❑ 335 Don Sutton .40 .18
❑ 336 Andre Thornton TL .15 .07
❑ 337 Darnell Coles .10 .05
❑ 338 Jorge Bell .15 .07
❑ 339 Bruce Berenyi .10 .05
❑ 340 Cal Ripken 1.50 .70
❑ 341 Frank Williams .10 .05
❑ 342 Gary Redus .10 .05
❑ 343 Carlos Diaz .10 .05
❑ 344 Jim Wohlford .10 .05
❑ 345 Donnie Moore .10 .05
❑ 346 Bryan Little .10 .05
❑ 347 Teddy Higuera RC* .15 .07
❑ 348 Cliff Johnson .10 .05
❑ 349 Mark Clear .10 .05
❑ 350 Jack Clark .15 .07
❑ 351 Chuck Tanner MG .10 .05
❑ 352 Harry Spilman .10 .05
❑ 353 Keith Atherton .10 .05
❑ 354 Tony Bernazard .10 .05
❑ 355 Lee Smith .25 .11
❑ 356 Mickey Hatcher .10 .05
❑ 357 Ed VandeBerg .10 .05
❑ 358 Rick Dempsey .10 .05
❑ 359 Mike LaCoss .10 .05
❑ 360 Lloyd Moseby .10 .05
❑ 361 Shane Rawley .10 .05
❑ 362 Tom Paciorek .15 .07
❑ 363 Terry Forster .10 .05
❑ 364 Reid Nichols .10 .05
❑ 365 Mike Flanagan .10 .05
❑ 366 Dave Concepcion TL .15 .07
❑ 367 Aurelio Lopez .10 .05
❑ 368 Greg Brock .10 .05
❑ 369 Al Holland .10 .05
❑ 370 Vince Coleman RC* .40 .18
❑ 371 Bill Stein .10 .05
❑ 372 Ben Oglivie .10 .05
❑ 373 Urbano Lugo .10 .05
❑ 374 Terry Francona .10 .05
❑ 375 Rich Gedman .10 .05
❑ 376 Bill Dawley .10 .05
❑ 377 Joe Carter .40 .18
❑ 378 Bruce Bochte .10 .05
❑ 379 Bobby Meacham .10 .05
❑ 380 LaMarr Hoyt .10 .05
❑ 381 Ray Miller MG .10 .05
❑ 382 Ivan Calderon RC* .15 .07
❑ 383 Chris Brown .10 .05
❑ 384 Steve Trout .10 .05
❑ 385 Cecil Cooper .15 .07
❑ 386 Cecil Fielder RC .75 .35
❑ 387 Steve Kemp .10 .05
❑ 388 Dickie Noles .10 .05
❑ 389 Glenn Davis .15 .07
❑ 390 Tom Seaver .60 .25
❑ 391 Julio Franco .15 .07
❑ 392 John Russell .10 .05
❑ 393 Chris Pittaro .10 .05
❑ 394 Checklist: 265-396 .15 .07
❑ 395 Scott Garrelts .10 .05
❑ 396 Dwight Evans TL .15 .07
❑ 397 Steve Buechele RC .15 .07
❑ 398 Earnie Riles .10 .05
❑ 399 Bill Swift .10 .05
❑ 400 Rod Carew .40 .18
❑ 401 Fernando Valenzuela TBC '81 .15 .07
❑ 402 Tom Seaver TBC '76 .15 .07
❑ 403 Willie Mays TBC '71 .25 .11
❑ 404 Frank Robinson TBC '66 .15 .07
❑ 405 Roger Maris TBC '61 .15 .07
❑ 406 Scott Sanderson .10 .05
❑ 407 Sal Butera .10 .05
❑ 408 Dave Smith .10 .05
❑ 409 Paul Runge .10 .05
❑ 410 Dave Kingman .15 .07
❑ 411 Sparky Anderson MG .25 .11
❑ 412 Jim Clancy .10 .05
❑ 413 Tim Flannery .10 .05
❑ 414 Tom Gorman .10 .05
❑ 415 Hal McRae .15 .07
❑ 416 Dennis Martinez .15 .07
❑ 417 R.J. Reynolds .10 .05
❑ 418 Alan Knicely .10 .05
❑ 419 Frank Wills .10 .05
❑ 420 Von Hayes .10 .05
❑ 421 David Palmer .10 .05
❑ 422 Mike Jorgensen .10 .05
❑ 423 Dan Spillner .10 .05
❑ 424 Rick Miller .10 .05
❑ 425 Larry McWilliams .10 .05
❑ 426 Charlie Moore TL .10 .05
❑ 427 Joe Cowley .10 .05
❑ 428 Max Venable .10 .05
❑ 429 Greg Booker .10 .05
❑ 430 Kent Hrbek .15 .07
❑ 431 George Frazier .10 .05
❑ 432 Mark Bailey .10 .05
❑ 433 Chris Codiroli .10 .05
❑ 434 Curt Wilkerson .10 .05
❑ 435 Bill Caudill .10 .05
❑ 436 Doug Flynn .10 .05
❑ 437 Rick Mahler .10 .05
❑ 438 Clint Hurdle .10 .05
❑ 439 Rick Honeycutt .10 .05
❑ 440 Alvin Davis .10 .05
❑ 441 Whitey Herzog MG .25 .11
❑ 442 Ron Robinson .10 .05
❑ 443 Bill Buckner .15 .07
❑ 444 Alex Trevino .10 .05
❑ 445 Bert Blyleven .15 .07
❑ 446 Lenn Sakata .10 .05
❑ 447 Jerry Don Gleaton .10 .05
❑ 448 Herm Winningham .10 .05
❑ 449 Rod Scurry .10 .05
❑ 450 Graig Nettles .15 .07
❑ 451 Mark Brown .10 .05
❑ 452 Bob Clark .10 .05
❑ 453 Steve Jeltz .10 .05
❑ 454 Burt Hooton .10 .05
❑ 455 Willie Randolph .15 .07
❑ 456 Dale Murphy TL .15 .07
❑ 457 Mickey Tettleton RC .15 .07
❑ 458 Kevin Bass .10 .05
❑ 459 Luis Leal .10 .05
❑ 460 Leon Durham .10 .05
❑ 461 Walt Terrell .10 .05
❑ 462 Domingo Ramos .10 .05
❑ 463 Jim Gott .10 .05
❑ 464 Ruppert Jones .10 .05
❑ 465 Jesse Orosco .10 .05
❑ 466 Tom Foley .10 .05

467	Bob James	.10	.05
468	Mike Scioscia	.10	.05
469	Storm Davis	.10	.05
470	Bill Madlock	.10	.05
471	Bobby Cox MG	.15	.07
472	Joe Hesketh	.10	.05
473	Mark Brouhard	.10	.05
474	John Tudor	.10	.05
475	Juan Samuel	.10	.05
476	Ron Mathis	.10	.05
477	Mike Easler	.10	.05
478	Andy Hawkins	.10	.05
479	Bob Melvin	.10	.05
480	Oddibe McDowell	.10	.05
481	Scott Bradley	.10	.05
482	Rick Lysander	.10	.05
483	George Vukovich	.10	.05
484	Donnie Hill	.10	.05
485	Gary Matthews	.10	.05
486	Bobby Grich TL	.10	.05
487	Bret Saberhagen	.15	.07
488	Lou Thornton	.10	.05
489	Jim Winn	.10	.05
490	Jeff Leonard	.10	.05
491	Pascual Perez	.10	.05
492	Kelvin Chapman	.10	.05
493	Gene Nelson	.10	.05
494	Gary Roenicke	.10	.05
495	Mark Langston	.10	.05
496	Jay Johnstone	.15	.07
497	John Stuper	.10	.05
498	Tito Landrum	.10	.05
499	Bob L. Gibson	.10	.05
500	Rickey Henderson	.75	.35
501	Dave Johnson MG	.15	.07
502	Glen Cook	.10	.05
503	Mike Fitzgerald	.10	.05
504	Denny Walling	.10	.05
505	Jerry Koosman	.15	.07
506	Bill Russell	.10	.05
507	Steve Ontiveros RC	.15	.07
508	Alan Wiggins	.10	.05
509	Ernie Camacho	.10	.05
510	Wade Boggs	.40	.18
511	Ed Nunez	.10	.05
512	Thad Bosley	.10	.05
513	Ron Washington	.10	.05
514	Mike Jones	.10	.05
515	Darrell Evans	.15	.07
516	Greg Minton TL	.10	.05
517	Milt Thompson RC	.15	.07
518	Buck Martinez	.10	.05
519	Danny Darwin	.10	.05
520	Keith Hernandez	.15	.07
521	Nate Snell	.10	.05
522	Bob Bailor	.10	.05
523	Joe Price	.10	.05
524	Darrell Miller	.10	.05
525	Marvell Wynne	.10	.05
526	Charlie Lea	.10	.05
527	Checklist: 397-528	.15	.07
528	Terry Pendleton	.15	.07
529	Marc Sullivan	.10	.05
530	Rich Gossage	.15	.07
531	Tony LaRussa MG	.15	.07
532	Don Carman	.10	.05
533	Billy Sample	.10	.05
534	Jeff Calhoun	.10	.05
535	Toby Harrah	.10	.05
536	Jose Rijo	.10	.05
537	Mark Salas	.10	.05
538	Dennis Eckersley	.40	.18
539	Glenn Hubbard	.10	.05
540	Dan Petry	.10	.05
541	Jorge Orta	.10	.05
542	Don Schulze	.10	.05
543	Jerry Narron	.10	.05
544	Eddie Milner	.10	.05
545	Jimmy Key	.40	.18
546	Dave Henderson TL	.10	.05
547	Roger McDowell RC*	.15	.07
548	Mike Young	.10	.05
549	Bob Welch	.10	.05
550	Tom Herr	.10	.05
551	Dave LaPoint	.10	.05
552	Marc Hill	.10	.05
553	Jim Morrison	.10	.05
554	Paul Householder	.10	.05
555	Hubie Brooks	.10	.05
556	John Denny	.10	.05
557	Gerald Perry	.10	.05
558	Tim Stoddard	.10	.05
559	Tommy Dunbar	.10	.05
560	Dave Righetti	.10	.05
561	Bob Lillis MG	.10	.05
562	Joe Beckwith	.10	.05
563	Alejandro Sanchez	.10	.05
564	Warren Brusstar	.10	.05
565	Tom Brunansky	.10	.05
566	Alfredo Griffin	.10	.05
567	Jeff Barkley	.10	.05
568	Donnie Scott	.10	.05
569	Jim Acker	.10	.05
570	Rusty Staub	.15	.07
571	Mike Jeffcoat	.10	.05
572	Paul Zuvella	.10	.05
573	Tom Hume	.10	.05
574	Ron Kittle	.10	.05
575	Mike Boddicker	.10	.05
576	Andre Dawson TL	.15	.07
577	Jerry Reuss	.10	.05
578	Lee Mazzilli	.10	.05
579	Jim Slaton	.10	.05
580	Willie McGee	.15	.07
581	Bruce Hurst	.10	.05
582	Jim Gantner	.10	.05
583	Al Bumbry	.10	.05
584	Brian Fisher	.10	.05
585	Garry Maddox	.10	.05
586	Greg Harris	.10	.05
587	Rafael Santana	.10	.05
588	Steve Lake	.10	.05
589	Sid Bream	.10	.05
590	Bob Knepper	.10	.05
591	Jackie Moore MG	.10	.05
592	Frank Tanana	.10	.05
593	Jesse Barfield	.10	.05
594	Chris Bando	.10	.05
595	Dave Parker	.15	.07
596	Onix Concepcion	.10	.05
597	Sammy Stewart	.10	.05
598	Jim Presley	.10	.05
599	Rick Aguilera RC	.40	.18
600	Dale Murphy	.40	.18
601	Gary Lucas	.10	.05
602	Mariano Duncan RC*	.40	.18
603	Bill Laskey	.10	.05
604	Gary Pettis	.10	.05
605	Dennis Boyd	.10	.05
606	Hal McRae TL	.15	.07
607	Ken Dayley	.10	.05
608	Bruce Bochy	.10	.05
609	Barbaro Garbey	.10	.05
610	Ron Guidry	.15	.07
611	Gary Woods	.10	.05
612	Richard Dotson	.10	.05
613	Roy Smalley	.10	.05
614	Rick Waits	.10	.05
615	Johnny Ray	.10	.05
616	Glenn Brummer	.10	.05
617	Lonnie Smith	.10	.05
618	Jim Pankovits	.10	.05
619	Danny Heep	.10	.05
620	Bruce Sutter	.15	.07
621	John Felske MG	.10	.05
622	Gary Lavelle	.10	.05
623	Floyd Rayford	.10	.05
624	Steve McCatty	.10	.05
625	Bob Brenly	.10	.05
626	Roy Thomas	.10	.05
627	Ron Oester	.10	.05
628	Kirk McCaskill RC	.15	.07
629	Mitch Webster	.10	.05
630	Fernando Valenzuela	.15	.07
631	Steve Braun	.10	.05
632	Dave Von Ohlen	.10	.05
633	Jackie Gutierrez	.10	.05
634	Roy Lee Jackson	.10	.05
635	Jason Thompson	.10	.05
636	Lee Smith TL	.15	.07
637	Rudy Law	.10	.05
638	John Butcher	.10	.05
639	Bo Diaz	.10	.05
640	Jose Cruz	.15	.07
641	Wayne Tolleson	.10	.05
642	Ray Searage	.10	.05
643	Tom Brookens	.10	.05
644	Mark Gubicza	.10	.05
645	Dusty Baker	.15	.07
646	Mike Moore	.10	.05
647	Mel Hall	.10	.05
648	Steve Bedrosian	.10	.05
649	Ronn Reynolds	.10	.05
650	Dave Stieb	.10	.05
651	Billy Martin MG	.15	.07
652	Tom Browning	.10	.05
653	Jim Dwyer	.10	.05
654	Ken Howell	.10	.05
655	Manny Trillo	.10	.05
656	Brian Harper	.10	.05
657	Juan Agosto	.10	.05
658	Rob Wilfong	.10	.05
659	Checklist: 529-660	.15	.07
660	Steve Garvey	.25	.11
661	Roger Clemens	1.50	.70
662	Bill Schroeder	.10	.05
663	Neil Allen	.10	.05
664	Tim Corcoran	.10	.05
665	Alejandro Pena	.10	.05
666	Charlie Hough TL	.15	.07
667	Tim Teufel	.10	.05
668	Cecilio Guante	.10	.05
669	Ron Cey	.15	.07
670	Willie Hernandez	.10	.05
671	Lynn Jones	.10	.05
672	Rob Picciolo	.10	.05
673	Ernie Whitt	.10	.05
674	Pat Tabler	.10	.05
675	Claudell Washington	.10	.05
676	Matt Young	.10	.05
677	Nick Esasky	.10	.05
678	Dan Gladden	.10	.05
679	Britt Burns	.10	.05
680	George Foster	.15	.07
681	Dick Williams MG	.15	.07
682	Junior Ortiz	.10	.05
683	Andy Van Slyke	.15	.07
684	Bob McClure	.10	.05
685	Tim Wallach	.10	.05
686	Jeff Stone	.10	.05
687	Mike Trujillo	.10	.05
688	Larry Herndon	.10	.05
689	Dave Stewart	.15	.07
690	Ryne Sandberg UER (No Topps logo on front)	.50	.23
691	Mike Madden	.10	.05
692	Dale Berra	.10	.05
693	Tom Tellmann	.10	.05
694	Garth Iorg	.10	.05
695	Mike Smithson	.10	.05
696	Bill Russell TL	.15	.07
697	Bud Black	.10	.05
698	Brad Komminsk	.10	.05
699	Pat Corrales MG	.10	.05
700	Reggie Jackson	.50	.23
701	Keith Hernandez AS	.10	.05
702	Tom Herr AS	.10	.05
703	Tim Wallach AS	.10	.05
704	Ozzie Smith AS	.25	.11
705	Dale Murphy AS	.15	.07
706	Pedro Guerrero AS	.10	.05
707	Willie McGee AS	.10	.05
708	Gary Carter AS	.15	.07
709	Dwight Gooden AS	.15	.07
710	John Tudor AS	.10	.05
711	Jeff Reardon AS	.10	.05
712	Don Mattingly AS	.40	.18
713	Damaso Garcia AS	.10	.05
714	George Brett AS	.40	.18
715	Cal Ripken AS	.40	.18
716	Rickey Henderson AS	.40	.18
717	Dave Winfield AS	.15	.07
718	George Bell AS	.10	.05
719	Carlton Fisk AS	.15	.07
720	Bret Saberhagen AS	.10	.05
721	Ron Guidry AS	.15	.07
722	Dan Quisenberry AS	.10	.05

❑ 723	Marty Bystrom	.10	.05
❑ 724	Tim Hulett	.10	.05
❑ 725	Mario Soto	.10	.05
❑ 726	Rick Dempsey TL	.15	.07
❑ 727	David Green	.10	.05
❑ 728	Mike Marshall	.10	.05
❑ 729	Jim Beattie	.10	.05
❑ 730	Ozzie Smith	.50	.23
❑ 731	Don Robinson	.10	.05
❑ 732	Floyd Youmans	.10	.05
❑ 733	Ron Romanick	.10	.05
❑ 734	Marty Barrett	.10	.05
❑ 735	Dave Dravecky	.15	.07
❑ 736	Glenn Wilson	.10	.05
❑ 737	Pete Vuckovich	.10	.05
❑ 738	Andre Robertson	.10	.05
❑ 739	Dave Rozema	.10	.05
❑ 740	Lance Parrish	.15	.07
❑ 741	Pete Rose MG	.40	.18
❑ 742	Frank Viola	.15	.07
❑ 743	Pat Sheridan	.10	.05
❑ 744	Lary Sorensen	.10	.05
❑ 745	Willie Upshaw	.10	.05
❑ 746	Denny Gonzalez	.10	.05
❑ 747	Rick Cerone	.10	.05
❑ 748	Steve Henderson	.10	.05
❑ 749	Ed Jurak	.10	.05
❑ 750	Gorman Thomas	.10	.05
❑ 751	Howard Johnson	.15	.07
❑ 752	Mike Krukow	.10	.05
❑ 753	Dan Ford	.10	.05
❑ 754	Pat Clements	.10	.05
❑ 755	Harold Baines	.25	.11
❑ 756	Rick Rhoden TL	.10	.05
❑ 757	Darrell Porter	.15	.07
❑ 758	Dave Anderson	.10	.05
❑ 759	Moose Haas	.10	.05
❑ 760	Andre Dawson	.25	.11
❑ 761	Don Slaught	.10	.05
❑ 762	Eric Show	.10	.05
❑ 763	Terry Puhl	.10	.05
❑ 764	Kevin Gross	.10	.05
❑ 765	Don Baylor	.25	.11
❑ 766	Rick Langford	.10	.05
❑ 767	Jody Davis	.10	.05
❑ 768	Vern Ruhle	.10	.05
❑ 769	Harold Reynolds RC	.40	.18
❑ 770	Vida Blue	.15	.07
❑ 771	John McNamara MG	.10	.05
❑ 772	Brian Downing	.10	.05
❑ 773	Greg Pryor	.10	.05
❑ 774	Terry Leach	.10	.05
❑ 775	Al Oliver	.15	.07
❑ 776	Gene Garber	.10	.05
❑ 777	Wayne Krenchicki	.10	.05
❑ 778	Jerry Hairston	.10	.05
❑ 779	Rick Reuschel	.10	.05
❑ 780	Robin Yount	.40	.18
❑ 781	Joe Nolan	.10	.05
❑ 782	Ken Landreaux	.10	.05
❑ 783	Ricky Horton	.10	.05
❑ 784	Alan Bannister	.10	.05
❑ 785	Bob Stanley	.10	.05
❑ 786	Mickey Hatcher TL	.10	.05
❑ 787	Vance Law	.10	.05
❑ 788	Marty Castillo	.10	.05
❑ 789	Kurt Bevacqua	.10	.05
❑ 790	Phil Niekro	.40	.18
❑ 791	Checklist: 661-792	.15	.07
❑ 792	Charles Hudson	.10	.05

1986 Topps Traded

		MINT	NRMT
COMP.FACT.SET (132)		30.00	13.50
❑ 1T	Andy Allanson	.10	.05
❑ 2T	Neil Allen	.10	.05
❑ 3T	Joaquin Andujar	.10	.05
❑ 4T	Paul Assenmacher	.10	.05
❑ 5T	Scott Bailes	.10	.05
❑ 6T	Don Baylor	.25	.11
❑ 7T	Steve Bedrosian	.10	.05
❑ 8T	Juan Beniquez	.10	.05
❑ 9T	Juan Berenguer	.10	.05
❑ 10T	Mike Bielecki	.10	.05

❑ 11T	Barry Bonds XRC	20.00	9.00
❑ 12T	Bobby Bonilla XRC	.50	.23
❑ 13T	Juan Bonilla	.10	.05
❑ 14T	Rich Bordi	.10	.05
❑ 15T	Steve Boros MG	.10	.05
❑ 16T	Rick Burleson	.10	.05
❑ 17T	Bill Campbell	.10	.05
❑ 18T	Tom Candiotti	.10	.05
❑ 19T	John Cangelosi	.10	.05
❑ 20T	Jose Canseco XRC	2.50	1.10
❑ 21T	Carmen Castillo	.10	.05
❑ 22T	Rick Cerone	.10	.05
❑ 23T	John Cerutti	.10	.05
❑ 24T	Will Clark XRC	1.00	.45
❑ 25T	Mark Clear	.10	.05
❑ 26T	Darnell Coles	.10	.05
❑ 27T	Dave Collins	.10	.05
❑ 28T	Tim Conroy	.10	.05
❑ 29T	Joe Cowley	.10	.05
❑ 30T	Joel Davis	.10	.05
❑ 31T	Rob Deer	.10	.05
❑ 32T	John Denny	.10	.05
❑ 33T	Mike Easler	.10	.05
❑ 34T	Mark Eichhorn	.10	.05
❑ 35T	Steve Farr	.10	.05
❑ 36T	Scott Fletcher	.10	.05
❑ 37T	Terry Forster	.10	.05
❑ 38T	Terry Francona	.10	.05
❑ 39T	Jim Fregosi MG	.10	.05
❑ 40T	Andres Galarraga XRC	1.00	.45
❑ 41T	Ken Griffey	.15	.07
❑ 42T	Bill Gullickson	.10	.05
❑ 43T	Jose Guzman XRC*	.10	.05
❑ 44T	Moose Haas	.10	.05
❑ 45T	Billy Hatcher	.10	.05
❑ 46T	Mike Heath	.10	.05
❑ 47T	Tom Hume	.10	.05
❑ 48T	Pete Incaviglia XRC	.40	.18
❑ 49T	Dane Iorg	.10	.05
❑ 50T	Bo Jackson XRC	1.00	.45
❑ 51T	Wally Joyner XRC	.40	.18
❑ 52T	Charlie Kerfeld	.10	.05
❑ 53T	Eric King	.10	.05
❑ 54T	Bob Kipper	.10	.05
❑ 55T	Wayne Krenchicki	.10	.05
❑ 56T	John Kruk XRC	.40	.18
❑ 57T	Mike LaCoss	.10	.05
❑ 58T	Pete Ladd	.10	.05
❑ 59T	Mike Laga	.10	.05
❑ 60T	Hal Lanier MG	.10	.05
❑ 61T	Dave LaPoint	.10	.05
❑ 62T	Rudy Law	.10	.05
❑ 63T	Rick Leach	.10	.05
❑ 64T	Tim Leary	.10	.05
❑ 65T	Dennis Leonard	.10	.05
❑ 66T	Jim Leyland MG XRC	.10	.05
❑ 67T	Steve Lyons	.10	.05
❑ 68T	Mickey Mahler	.10	.05
❑ 69T	Candy Maldonado	.10	.05
❑ 70T	Roger Mason XRC*	.10	.05
❑ 71T	Bob McClure	.10	.05
❑ 72T	Andy McGaffigan	.10	.05
❑ 73T	Gene Michael MG	.10	.05
❑ 74T	Kevin Mitchell XRC	.40	.18
❑ 75T	Omar Moreno	.10	.05
❑ 76T	Jerry Mumphrey	.10	.05
❑ 77T	Phil Niekro	.40	.18
❑ 78T	Randy Niemann	.10	.05
❑ 79T	Juan Nieves	.10	.05
❑ 80T	Otis Nixon XRC*	.15	.07
❑ 81T	Bob Ojeda	.10	.05
❑ 82T	Jose Oquendo	.10	.05
❑ 83T	Tom Paciorek	.15	.07
❑ 84T	David Palmer	.10	.05
❑ 85T	Frank Pastore	.10	.05
❑ 86T	Lou Piniella MG	.15	.07
❑ 87T	Dan Plesac	.10	.05
❑ 88T	Darrell Porter	.15	.07
❑ 89T	Rey Quinones	.10	.05
❑ 90T	Gary Redus	.10	.05
❑ 91T	Bip Roberts XRC	.40	.18
❑ 92T	Billy Joe Robidoux	.10	.05
❑ 93T	Jeff D. Robinson	.10	.05
❑ 94T	Gary Roenicke	.10	.05
❑ 95T	Ed Romero	.10	.05
❑ 96T	Argenis Salazar	.10	.05
❑ 97T	Joe Sambito	.10	.05
❑ 98T	Billy Sample	.10	.05
❑ 99T	Dave Schmidt	.10	.05
❑ 100T	Ken Schrom	.10	.05
❑ 101T	Tom Seaver	.60	.25
❑ 102T	Ted Simmons	.15	.07
❑ 103T	Sammy Stewart	.10	.05
❑ 104T	Kurt Stillwell	.10	.05
❑ 105T	Franklin Stubbs	.10	.05
❑ 106T	Dale Sveum	.10	.05
❑ 107T	Chuck Tanner MG	.10	.05
❑ 108T	D.Tartabull XRC**	.15	.07
❑ 109T	Tim Teufel	.10	.05
❑ 110T	Bob Tewksbury XRC	.15	.07
❑ 111T	Andres Thomas	.10	.05
❑ 112T	Milt Thompson	.10	.05
❑ 113T	R.Thompson XRC	.15	.07
❑ 114T	Jay Tibbs	.10	.05
❑ 115T	Wayne Tolleson	.10	.05
❑ 116T	Alex Trevino	.10	.05
❑ 117T	Manny Trillo	.10	.05
❑ 118T	Ed VandeBerg	.10	.05
❑ 119T	Ozzie Virgil	.10	.05
❑ 120T	Bob Walk	.10	.05
❑ 121T	Gene Walter	.10	.05
❑ 122T	Claudell Washington	.10	.05
❑ 123T	Bill Wegman XRC*	.10	.05
❑ 124T	Dick Williams MG	.15	.07
❑ 125T	Mitch Williams XRC	.15	.07
❑ 126T	Bobby Witt XRC	.25	.11
❑ 127T	Todd Worrell XRC*	.40	.18
❑ 128T	George Wright	.10	.05
❑ 129T	Ricky Wright	.10	.05
❑ 130T	Steve Yeager	.10	.05
❑ 131T	Paul Zuvella	.10	.05
❑ 132T	Checklist 1T-132T	.10	.05

1987 Topps

		MINT	NRMT
COMPLETE SET (792)		25.00	11.00
COMP.HOBBY SET (792)		40.00	18.00
COMP.X-MAS.SET (792)		40.00	18.00
❑ 1	Roger Clemens RB Most K's 9-inning game	.25	.11
❑ 2	Jim Deshaies RB Most cons. K's, start of game	.05	.02

❑ 3 Dwight Evans RB .10 .05
Earliest home run
❑ 4 Davey Lopes RB .05 .02
Most steals season, 40-year-old
❑ 5 Dave Righetti RB .05 .02
Most saves season
❑ 6 Ruben Sierra RB .10 .05
Youngest player to switch hit HR's, game
❑ 7 Todd Worrell RB .05 .02
Most saves rookie season
❑ 8 Terry Pendleton .10 .05
❑ 9 Jay Tibbs .05 .02
❑ 10 Cecil Cooper .10 .05
❑ 11 Indians Team .05 .02
(Mound conference)
❑ 12 Jeff Sellers .05 .02
❑ 13 Nick Esasky .05 .02
❑ 14 Dave Stewart .10 .05
❑ 15 Claudell Washington .05 .02
❑ 16 Pat Clements .05 .02
❑ 17 Pete O'Brien .05 .02
❑ 18 Dick Howser MG .05 .02
❑ 19 Matt Young .05 .02
❑ 20 Gary Carter .15 .07
❑ 21 Mark Davis .05 .02
❑ 22 Doug DeCinces .05 .02
❑ 23 Lee Smith .15 .07
❑ 24 Tony Walker .05 .02
❑ 25 Bert Blyleven .10 .05
❑ 26 Greg Brock .05 .02
❑ 27 Joe Cowley .05 .02
❑ 28 Rick Dempsey .10 .05
❑ 29 Jimmy Key .10 .05
❑ 30 Tim Raines .10 .05
❑ 31 Braves Team .05 .02
(Glenn Hubbard and Rafael Ramirez)
❑ 32 Tim Leary .05 .02
❑ 33 Andy Van Slyke .10 .05
❑ 34 Jose Rijo .05 .02
❑ 35 Sid Bream .05 .02
❑ 36 Eric King .05 .02
❑ 37 Marvell Wynne .05 .02
❑ 38 Dennis Leonard .05 .02
❑ 39 Marty Barrett .05 .02
❑ 40 Dave Righetti .05 .02
❑ 41 Bo Diaz .05 .02
❑ 42 Gary Redus .05 .02
❑ 43 Gene Michael MG .05 .02
❑ 44 Greg Harris .05 .02
❑ 45 Jim Presley .05 .02
❑ 46 Dan Gladden .05 .02
❑ 47 Dennis Powell .05 .02
❑ 48 Wally Backman .05 .02
❑ 49 Terry Harper .05 .02
❑ 50 Dave Smith .05 .02
❑ 51 Mel Hall .05 .02
❑ 52 Keith Atherton .05 .02
❑ 53 Ruppert Jones .05 .02
❑ 54 Bill Dawley .05 .02
❑ 55 Tim Wallach .05 .02
❑ 56 Brewers Team .05 .02
(Mound conference)
❑ 57 Scott Nielsen .05 .02
❑ 58 Thad Bosley .05 .02
❑ 59 Ken Dayley .05 .02
❑ 60 Tony Pena .05 .02
❑ 61 Bobby Thigpen RC .10 .05
❑ 62 Bobby Meacham .05 .02
❑ 63 Fred Toliver .05 .02
❑ 64 Harry Spilman .05 .02
❑ 65 Tom Browning .05 .02
❑ 66 Marc Sullivan .05 .02
❑ 67 Bill Swift .05 .02
❑ 68 Tony LaRussa MG .10 .05
❑ 69 Lonnie Smith .05 .02
❑ 70 Charlie Hough .10 .05
❑ 71 Mike Aldrete .05 .02
❑ 72 Walt Terrell .05 .02
❑ 73 Dave Anderson .05 .02
❑ 74 Dan Pasqua .05 .02
❑ 75 Ron Darling .05 .02
❑ 76 Rafael Ramirez .05 .02
❑ 77 Bryan Oelkers .05 .02
❑ 78 Tom Foley .05 .02
❑ 79 Juan Nieves .05 .02
❑ 80 Wally Joyner RC .20 .09
❑ 81 Padres Team .05 .02
(Andy Hawkins and Terry Kennedy)
❑ 82 Rob Murphy .05 .02
❑ 83 Mike Davis .05 .02
❑ 84 Steve Lake .05 .02
❑ 85 Kevin Bass .05 .02
❑ 86 Nate Snell .05 .02
❑ 87 Mark Salas .05 .02
❑ 88 Ed Wojna .05 .02
❑ 89 Ozzie Guillen .10 .05
❑ 90 Dave Stieb .05 .02
❑ 91 Harold Reynolds .10 .05
❑ 92A Urbano Lugo .20 .09
ERR (no trademark)
❑ 92B Urbano Lugo COR .05 .02
❑ 93 Jim Leyland MG RC* .10 .05
❑ 94 Calvin Schiraldi .05 .02
❑ 95 Oddibe McDowell .05 .02
❑ 96 Frank Williams .05 .02
❑ 97 Glenn Wilson .05 .02
❑ 98 Bill Scherrer .05 .02
❑ 99 Darryl Motley .05 .02
(Now with Braves on card front)
❑ 100 Steve Garvey .15 .07
❑ 101 Carl Willis RC .05 .02
❑ 102 Paul Zuvella .05 .02
❑ 103 Rick Aguilera .10 .05
❑ 104 Billy Sample .05 .02
❑ 105 Floyd Youmans .05 .02
❑ 106 Blue Jays Team .05 .02
(George Bell and Jesse Barfield)
❑ 107 John Butcher .05 .02
❑ 108 Jim Gantner UER .05 .02
(Brewers logo reversed)
❑ 109 R.J. Reynolds .05 .02
❑ 110 John Tudor .05 .02
❑ 111 Alfredo Griffin .05 .02
❑ 112 Alan Ashby .05 .02
❑ 113 Neil Allen .05 .02
❑ 114 Billy Beane .05 .02
❑ 115 Donnie Moore .05 .02
❑ 116 Bill Russell .05 .02
❑ 117 Jim Beattie .05 .02
❑ 118 Bobby Valentine MG .05 .02
❑ 119 Ron Robinson .05 .02
❑ 120 Eddie Murray .20 .09
❑ 121 Kevin Romine .05 .02
❑ 122 Jim Clancy .05 .02
❑ 123 John Kruk RC* .20 .09
❑ 124 Ray Fontenot .05 .02
❑ 125 Bob Brenly .05 .02
❑ 126 Mike Loynd .05 .02
❑ 127 Vance Law .05 .02
❑ 128 Checklist 1-132 .05 .02
❑ 129 Rick Cerone .05 .02
❑ 130 Dwight Gooden .15 .07
❑ 131 Pirates Team .05 .02
(Sid Bream and Tony Pena)
❑ 132 Paul Assenmacher .15 .07
❑ 133 Jose Oquendo .05 .02
❑ 134 Rich Yett .05 .02
❑ 135 Mike Easler .05 .02
❑ 136 Ron Romanick .05 .02
❑ 137 Jerry Willard .05 .02
❑ 138 Roy Lee Jackson .05 .02
❑ 139 Devon White RC .25 .11
❑ 140 Bret Saberhagen .10 .05
❑ 141 Herm Winningham .05 .02
❑ 142 Rick Sutcliffe .10 .05
❑ 143 Steve Boros MG .05 .02
❑ 144 Mike Scioscia .05 .02
❑ 145 Charlie Kerfeld .05 .02
❑ 146 Tracy Jones .05 .02
❑ 147 Randy Niemann .05 .02
❑ 148 Dave Collins .05 .02
❑ 149 Ray Searage .05 .02
❑ 150 Wade Boggs .20 .09
❑ 151 Mike LaCoss .05 .02
❑ 152 Toby Harrah .05 .02
❑ 153 Duane Ward RC* .10 .05
❑ 154 Tom O'Malley .05 .02
❑ 155 Eddie Whitson .05 .02
❑ 156 Mariners Team .05 .02
(Mound conference)
❑ 157 Danny Darwin .05 .02
❑ 158 Tim Teufel .05 .02
❑ 159 Ed Olwine .05 .02
❑ 160 Julio Franco .10 .05
❑ 161 Steve Ontiveros .05 .02
❑ 162 Mike LaValliere RC* .05 .02
❑ 163 Kevin Gross .05 .02
❑ 164 Sammy Khalifa .05 .02
❑ 165 Jeff Reardon .10 .05
❑ 166 Bob Boone .10 .05
❑ 167 Jim Deshaies RC* .05 .02
❑ 168 Lou Piniella MG .10 .05
❑ 169 Ron Washington .05 .02
❑ 170 Bo Jackson RC .40 .18
❑ 171 Chuck Cary .05 .02
❑ 172 Ron Oester .05 .02
❑ 173 Alex Trevino .05 .02
❑ 174 Henry Cotto .05 .02
❑ 175 Bob Stanley .05 .02
❑ 176 Steve Buechele .05 .02
❑ 177 Keith Moreland .05 .02
❑ 178 Cecil Fielder .15 .07
❑ 179 Bill Wegman .05 .02
❑ 180 Chris Brown .05 .02
❑ 181 Cardinals Team .05 .02
(Mound conference)
❑ 182 Lee Lacy .05 .02
❑ 183 Andy Hawkins .05 .02
❑ 184 Bobby Bonilla RC .25 .11
❑ 185 Roger McDowell .05 .02
❑ 186 Bruce Benedict .05 .02
❑ 187 Mark Huismann .05 .02
❑ 188 Tony Phillips .05 .02
❑ 189 Joe Hesketh .05 .02
❑ 190 Jim Sundberg .05 .02
❑ 191 Charles Hudson .05 .02
❑ 192 Cory Snyder .05 .02
❑ 193 Roger Craig MG .05 .02
❑ 194 Kirk McCaskill .05 .02
❑ 195 Mike Pagliarulo .05 .02
❑ 196 Randy O'Neal UER .05 .02
(Wrong ML career W-L totals)
❑ 197 Mark Bailey .05 .02
❑ 198 Lee Mazzilli .05 .02
❑ 199 Mariano Duncan .05 .02
❑ 200 Pete Rose .60 .25
❑ 201 John Cangelosi .05 .02
❑ 202 Ricky Wright .05 .02
❑ 203 Mike Kingery RC .05 .02
❑ 204 Sammy Stewart .05 .02
❑ 205 Graig Nettles .10 .05
❑ 206 Twins Team .05 .02
(Frank Viola and Tim Laudner)
❑ 207 George Frazier .05 .02
❑ 208 John Shelby .05 .02
❑ 209 Rick Schu .05 .02
❑ 210 Lloyd Moseby .05 .02
❑ 211 John Morris .05 .02
❑ 212 Mike Fitzgerald .05 .02
❑ 213 Randy Myers RC .20 .09
❑ 214 Omar Moreno .05 .02
❑ 215 Mark Langston .05 .02
❑ 216 B.J. Surhoff RC .40 .18
❑ 217 Chris Codiroli .05 .02
❑ 218 Sparky Anderson MG .10 .05
❑ 219 Cecilio Guante .05 .02
❑ 220 Joe Carter .20 .09
❑ 221 Vern Ruhle .05 .02
❑ 222 Denny Walling .05 .02
❑ 223 Charlie Leibrandt .05 .02
❑ 224 Wayne Tolleson .05 .02
❑ 225 Mike Smithson .05 .02
❑ 226 Max Venable .05 .02
❑ 227 Jamie Moyer RC .40 .18
❑ 228 Curt Wilkerson .05 .02
❑ 229 Mike Birkbeck .05 .02
❑ 230 Don Baylor .10 .05
❑ 231 Giants Team .05 .02

(Bob Brenly and
Jim Gott)
❑ 232 Reggie Williams .05 .02
❑ 233 Russ Morman .05 .02
❑ 234 Pat Sheridan .05 .02
❑ 235 Alvin Davis .05 .02
❑ 236 Tommy John .10 .05
❑ 237 Jim Morrison .05 .02
❑ 238 Bill Krueger .05 .02
❑ 239 Juan Espino .05 .02
❑ 240 Steve Balboni .05 .02
❑ 241 Danny Heep .05 .02
❑ 242 Rick Mahler .05 .02
❑ 243 Whitey Herzog MG .10 .05
❑ 244 Dickie Noles .05 .02
❑ 245 Willie Upshaw .05 .02
❑ 246 Jim Dwyer .05 .02
❑ 247 Jeff Reed .05 .02
❑ 248 Gene Walter .05 .02
❑ 249 Jim Pankovits .05 .02
❑ 250 Teddy Higuera .05 .02
❑ 251 Rob Wilfong .05 .02
❑ 252 Dennis Martinez .10 .05
❑ 253 Eddie Milner .05 .02
❑ 254 Bob Tewksbury RC* .10 .05
❑ 255 Juan Samuel .05 .02
❑ 256 Royals Team .15 .07
(George Brett and
Frank White)
❑ 257 Bob Forsch .05 .02
❑ 258 Steve Yeager .05 .02
❑ 259 Mike Greenwell RC .20 .09
❑ 260 Vida Blue .10 .05
❑ 261 Ruben Sierra RC .25 .11
❑ 262 Jim Winn .05 .02
❑ 263 Stan Javier .05 .02
❑ 264 Checklist 133-264 .05 .02
❑ 265 Darrell Evans .10 .05
❑ 266 Jeff Hamilton .05 .02
❑ 267 Howard Johnson .05 .02
❑ 268 Pat Corrales MG .10 .05
❑ 269 Cliff Speck .05 .02
❑ 270 Jody Davis .05 .02
❑ 271 Mike G. Brown .05 .02
❑ 272 Andres Galarraga .20 .09
❑ 273 Gene Nelson .05 .02
❑ 274 Jeff Hearron UER .05 .02
(Duplicate 1986
stat line on back)
❑ 275 LaMarr Hoyt .05 .02
❑ 276 Jackie Gutierrez .05 .02
❑ 277 Juan Agosto .05 .02
❑ 278 Gary Pettis .05 .02
❑ 279 Dan Plesac .05 .02
❑ 280 Jeff Leonard .05 .02
❑ 281 Reds Team .20 .09
(Pete Rose, Bo Diaz,
and Bill Gullickson)
❑ 282 Jeff Calhoun .05 .02
❑ 283 Doug Drabek RC* .20 .09
❑ 284 John Moses .05 .02
❑ 285 Dennis Boyd .05 .02
❑ 286 Mike Woodard .05 .02
❑ 287 Dave Von Ohlen .05 .02
❑ 288 Tito Landrum .05 .02
❑ 289 Bob Kipper .05 .02
❑ 290 Leon Durham .05 .02
❑ 291 Mitch Williams RC* .10 .05
❑ 292 Franklin Stubbs .05 .02
❑ 293 Bob Rodgers MG .05 .02
❑ 294 Steve Jeltz .05 .02
❑ 295 Len Dykstra .15 .07
❑ 296 Andres Thomas .05 .02
❑ 297 Don Schulze .05 .02
❑ 298 Larry Herndon .05 .02
❑ 299 Joel Davis .05 .02
❑ 300 Reggie Jackson .25 .11
❑ 301 Luis Aquino UER .05 .02
(No trademark
never corrected)
❑ 302 Bill Schroeder .05 .02
❑ 303 Juan Berenguer .05 .02
❑ 304 Phil Garner .05 .02
❑ 305 John Franco .10 .05
❑ 306 Red Sox Team .10 .05
(Tom Seaver,
John McNamara MG,
and Rich Gedman)
❑ 307 Lee Guetterman .05 .02
❑ 308 Don Slaught .05 .02
❑ 309 Mike Young .05 .02
❑ 310 Frank Viola .05 .02
❑ 311 Rickey Henderson .20 .09
TBC '82
❑ 312 Reggie Jackson .20 .09
TBC '77
❑ 313 Roberto Clemente .25 .11
TBC '72
❑ 314 Carl Yastrzemski UER .. .20 .09
TBC '67 (Sic, 112
RBI's on back)
❑ 315 Maury Wills TBC '62 .10 .05
❑ 316 Brian Fisher .05 .02
❑ 317 Clint Hurdle .05 .02
❑ 318 Jim Fregosi MG .05 .02
❑ 319 Greg Swindell RC .20 .09
❑ 320 Barry Bonds RC 10.00 4.50
❑ 321 Mike Laga .05 .02
❑ 322 Chris Bando .05 .02
❑ 323 Al Newman .05 .02
❑ 324 David Palmer .05 .02
❑ 325 Garry Templeton .05 .02
❑ 326 Mark Gubicza .05 .02
❑ 327 Dale Sveum .05 .02
❑ 328 Bob Welch .05 .02
❑ 329 Ron Roenicke .05 .02
❑ 330 Mike Scott .05 .02
❑ 331 Mets Team .10 .05
(Gary Carter and
Darryl Strawberry)
❑ 332 Joe Price .05 .02
❑ 333 Ken Phelps .05 .02
❑ 334 Ed Correa .05 .02
❑ 335 Candy Maldonado .05 .02
❑ 336 Allan Anderson .05 .02
❑ 337 Darrell Miller .05 .02
❑ 338 Tim Conroy .05 .02
❑ 339 Donnie Hill .05 .02
❑ 340 Roger Clemens .50 .23
❑ 341 Mike C. Brown .05 .02
❑ 342 Bob James .05 .02
❑ 343 Hal Lanier MG .05 .02
❑ 344A Joe Niekro .05 .02
(Copyright inside
righthand border)
❑ 344B Joe Niekro .05 .02
(Copyright outside
righthand border)
❑ 345 Andre Dawson .15 .07
❑ 346 Shawon Dunston .05 .02
❑ 347 Mickey Brantley .05 .02
❑ 348 Carmelo Martinez .05 .02
❑ 349 Storm Davis .05 .02
❑ 350 Keith Hernandez .10 .05
❑ 351 Gene Garber .05 .02
❑ 352 Mike Felder .05 .02
❑ 353 Ernie Camacho .05 .02
❑ 354 Jamie Quirk .05 .02
❑ 355 Don Carman .05 .02
❑ 356 White Sox Team .05 .02
(Mound conference)
❑ 357 Steve Fireovid .05 .02
❑ 358 Sal Butera .05 .02
❑ 359 Doug Corbett .05 .02
❑ 360 Pedro Guerrero .05 .02
❑ 361 Mark Thurmond .05 .02
❑ 362 Luis Quinones .05 .02
❑ 363 Jose Guzman .05 .02
❑ 364 Randy Bush .05 .02
❑ 365 Rick Rhoden .05 .02
❑ 366 Mark McGwire 5.00 2.20
❑ 367 Jeff Lahti .05 .02
❑ 368 John McNamara MG .05 .02
❑ 369 Brian Dayett .05 .02
❑ 370 Fred Lynn .10 .05
❑ 371 Mark Eichhorn .05 .02
❑ 372 Jerry Mumphrey .05 .02
❑ 373 Jeff Dedmon .05 .02
❑ 374 Glenn Hoffman .05 .02
❑ 375 Ron Guidry .10 .05
❑ 376 Scott Bradley .05 .02
❑ 377 John Henry Johnson .05 .02
❑ 378 Rafael Santana .05 .02
❑ 379 John Russell .05 .02
❑ 380 Rich Gossage .10 .05
❑ 381 Expos Team .05 .02
(Mound conference)
❑ 382 Rudy Law .05 .02
❑ 383 Ron Davis .05 .02
❑ 384 Johnny Grubb .05 .02
❑ 385 Orel Hershiser .10 .05
❑ 386 Dickie Thon .05 .02
❑ 387 T.R. Bryden .05 .02
❑ 388 Geno Petralli .05 .02
❑ 389 Jeff D. Robinson .05 .02
❑ 390 Gary Matthews .05 .02
❑ 391 Jay Howell .05 .02
❑ 392 Checklist 265-396 .05 .02
❑ 393 Pete Rose MG .15 .07
❑ 394 Mike Bielecki .05 .02
❑ 395 Damaso Garcia .05 .02
❑ 396 Tim Lollar .05 .02
❑ 397 Greg Walker .05 .02
❑ 398 Brad Havens .05 .02
❑ 399 Curt Ford .05 .02
❑ 400 George Brett .40 .18
❑ 401 Billy Joe Robidoux .05 .02
❑ 402 Mike Trujillo .05 .02
❑ 403 Jerry Royster .05 .02
❑ 404 Doug Sisk .05 .02
❑ 405 Brook Jacoby .05 .02
❑ 406 Yankees Team .20 .09
(Rickey Henderson and
Don Mattingly)
❑ 407 Jim Acker .05 .02
❑ 408 John Mizerock .05 .02
❑ 409 Milt Thompson .05 .02
❑ 410 Fernando Valenzuela .... .10 .05
❑ 411 Darnell Coles .05 .02
❑ 412 Eric Davis .15 .07
❑ 413 Moose Haas .05 .02
❑ 414 Joe Orsulak .05 .02
❑ 415 Bobby Witt RC .10 .05
❑ 416 Tom Nieto .05 .02
❑ 417 Pat Perry .05 .02
❑ 418 Dick Williams MG .10 .05
❑ 419 Mark Portugal RC* .10 .05
❑ 420 Will Clark RC .75 .35
❑ 421 Jose DeLeon .05 .02
❑ 422 Jack Howell .05 .02
❑ 423 Jaime Cocanower .05 .02
❑ 424 Chris Speier .05 .02
❑ 425 Tom Seaver UER .20 .09
Earned Runs amount is wrong
For 86 Red Sox and Career
Also the ERA is wrong for 86 and
career
❑ 426 Floyd Rayford .05 .02
❑ 427 Edwin Nunez .05 .02
❑ 428 Bruce Bochy .05 .02
❑ 429 Tim Pyznarski .05 .02
❑ 430 Mike Schmidt .40 .18
❑ 431 Dodgers Team .05 .02
(Mound conference)
❑ 432 Jim Slaton .05 .02
❑ 433 Ed Hearn .05 .02
❑ 434 Mike Fischlin .05 .02
❑ 435 Bruce Sutter .05 .02
❑ 436 Andy Allanson .05 .02
❑ 437 Ted Power .05 .02
❑ 438 Kelly Downs RC .05 .02
❑ 439 Karl Best .05 .02
❑ 440 Willie McGee .10 .05
❑ 441 Dave Leiper .05 .02
❑ 442 Mitch Webster .05 .02
❑ 443 John Felske MG .05 .02
❑ 444 Jeff Russell .05 .02
❑ 445 Dave Lopes .10 .05
❑ 446 Chuck Finley RC .40 .18
❑ 447 Bill Almon .05 .02
❑ 448 Chris Bosio RC .10 .05
❑ 449 Pat Dodson .05 .02
❑ 450 Kirby Puckett .50 .23
❑ 451 Joe Sambito .05 .02
❑ 452 Dave Henderson .05 .02
❑ 453 Scott Terry .05 .02
❑ 454 Luis Salazar .05 .02
❑ 455 Mike Boddicker .05 .02

❑ 456 A's Team .05 .02
(Mound conference)
❑ 457 Len Matuszek .05 .02
❑ 458 Kelly Gruber .05 .02
❑ 459 Dennis Eckersley .20 .09
❑ 460 Darryl Strawberry .15 .07
❑ 461 Craig McMurtry .05 .02
❑ 462 Scott Fletcher .05 .02
❑ 463 Tom Candiotti .05 .02
❑ 464 Butch Wynegar .05 .02
❑ 465 Todd Worrell .10 .05
❑ 466 Kal Daniels .05 .02
❑ 467 Randy St.Claire .05 .02
❑ 468 G.Bamberger MG .05 .02
❑ 469 Mike Diaz .05 .02
❑ 470 Dave Dravecky .10 .05
❑ 471 Ronn Reynolds .05 .02
❑ 472 Bill Doran .05 .02
❑ 473 Steve Farr .05 .02
❑ 474 Jerry Narron .05 .02
❑ 475 Scott Garrelts .05 .02
❑ 476 Danny Tartabull .05 .02
❑ 477 Ken Howell .05 .02
❑ 478 Tim Laudner .05 .02
❑ 479 Bob Sebra .05 .02
❑ 480 Jim Rice .10 .05
❑ 481 Phillies Team .05 .02
(Glenn Wilson
Juan Samuel and
Von Hayes)
❑ 482 Daryl Boston .05 .02
❑ 483 Dwight Lowry .05 .02
❑ 484 Jim Traber .05 .02
❑ 485 Tony Fernandez .05 .02
❑ 486 Otis Nixon .05 .02
❑ 487 Dave Gumpert .05 .02
❑ 488 Ray Knight .05 .02
❑ 489 Bill Gullickson .05 .02
❑ 490 Dale Murphy .20 .09
❑ 491 Ron Karkovice RC .10 .05
❑ 492 Mike Heath .05 .02
❑ 493 Tom Lasorda MG .10 .05
❑ 494 Barry Jones .05 .02
❑ 495 Gorman Thomas .05 .02
❑ 496 Bruce Bochte .05 .02
❑ 497 Dale Mohorcic .05 .02
❑ 498 Bob Kearney .05 .02
❑ 499 Bruce Ruffin .05 .02
❑ 500 Don Mattingly .50 .23
❑ 501 Craig Lefferts .05 .02
❑ 502 Dick Schofield .05 .02
❑ 503 Larry Andersen .05 .02
❑ 504 Mickey Hatcher .05 .02
❑ 505 Bryn Smith .05 .02
❑ 506 Orioles Team .05 .02
(Mound conference)
❑ 507 Dave L. Stapleton .05 .02
❑ 508 Scott Bankhead .05 .02
❑ 509 Enos Cabell .05 .02
❑ 510 Tom Henke .05 .02
❑ 511 Steve Lyons .05 .02
❑ 512 Dave Magadan RC .10 .05
❑ 513 Carmen Castillo .05 .02
❑ 514 Orlando Mercado .05 .02
❑ 515 Willie Hernandez .05 .02
❑ 516 Ted Simmons .10 .05
❑ 517 Mario Soto .05 .02
❑ 518 Gene Mauch MG .10 .05
❑ 519 Curt Young .05 .02
❑ 520 Jack Clark .10 .05
❑ 521 Rick Reuschel .05 .02
❑ 522 Checklist 397-528 .05 .02
❑ 523 Earnie Riles .05 .02
❑ 524 Bob Shirley .05 .02
❑ 525 Phil Bradley .05 .02
❑ 526 Roger Mason .05 .02
❑ 527 Jim Wohlford .05 .02
❑ 528 Ken Dixon .05 .02
❑ 529 Alvaro Espinoza RC .05 .02
❑ 530 Tony Gwynn .40 .18
❑ 531 Astros Team .10 .05
(Yogi Berra conference)
❑ 532 Jeff Stone .05 .02
❑ 533 Argenis Salazar .05 .02
❑ 534 Scott Sanderson .05 .02
❑ 535 Tony Armas .05 .02
❑ 536 Terry Mulholland RC .10 .05
❑ 537 Rance Mulliniks .05 .02
❑ 538 Tom Niedenfuer .05 .02
❑ 539 Reid Nichols .05 .02
❑ 540 Terry Kennedy .05 .02
❑ 541 Rafael Belliard RC .05 .02
❑ 542 Ricky Horton .05 .02
❑ 543 Dave Johnson MG .10 .05
❑ 544 Zane Smith .05 .02
❑ 545 Buddy Bell .10 .05
❑ 546 Mike Morgan .05 .02
❑ 547 Rob Deer .05 .02
❑ 548 Bill Mooneyham .05 .02
❑ 549 Bob Melvin .05 .02
❑ 550 Pete Incaviglia RC* .10 .05
❑ 551 Frank Wills .05 .02
❑ 552 Larry Sheets .05 .02
❑ 553 Mike Maddux .05 .02
❑ 554 Buddy Biancalana .05 .02
❑ 555 Dennis Rasmussen .05 .02
❑ 556 Angels Team .05 .02
(Rene Lachemann CO,
Mike Witt, and
Bob Boone)
❑ 557 John Cerutti .05 .02
❑ 558 Greg Gagne .05 .02
❑ 559 Lance McCullers .05 .02
❑ 560 Glenn Davis .05 .02
❑ 561 Rey Quinones .05 .02
❑ 562 Bryan Clutterbuck .05 .02
❑ 563 John Stefero .05 .02
❑ 564 Larry McWilliams .05 .02
❑ 565 Dusty Baker .10 .05
❑ 566 Tim Hulett .05 .02
❑ 567 Greg Mathews .05 .02
❑ 568 Earl Weaver MG .20 .09
❑ 569 Wade Rowdon .05 .02
❑ 570 Sid Fernandez .05 .02
❑ 571 Ozzie Virgil .05 .02
❑ 572 Pete Ladd .05 .02
❑ 573 Hal McRae .10 .05
❑ 574 Manny Lee .05 .02
❑ 575 Pat Tabler .05 .02
❑ 576 Frank Pastore .05 .02
❑ 577 Dann Bilardello .05 .02
❑ 578 Billy Hatcher .05 .02
❑ 579 Rick Burleson .05 .02
❑ 580 Mike Krukow .05 .02
❑ 581 Cubs Team .05 .02
(Ron Cey and
Steve Trout)
❑ 582 Bruce Berenyi .05 .02
❑ 583 Junior Ortiz .05 .02
❑ 584 Ron Kittle .05 .02
❑ 585 Scott Bailes .05 .02
❑ 586 Ben Oglivie .05 .02
❑ 587 Eric Plunk .05 .02
❑ 588 Wallace Johnson .05 .02
❑ 589 Steve Crawford .05 .02
❑ 590 Vince Coleman .05 .02
❑ 591 Spike Owen .05 .02
❑ 592 Chris Welsh .05 .02
❑ 593 Chuck Tanner MG .05 .02
❑ 594 Rick Anderson .05 .02
❑ 595 Keith Hernandez AS .05 .02
❑ 596 Steve Sax AS .05 .02
❑ 597 Mike Schmidt AS .15 .07
❑ 598 Ozzie Smith AS .15 .07
❑ 599 Tony Gwynn AS .20 .09
❑ 600 Dave Parker AS .05 .02
❑ 601 Darryl Strawberry AS .10 .05
❑ 602 Gary Carter AS .10 .05
❑ 603A D.Gooden AS .15 .07
ERR no trademark
❑ 603B D.Gooden AS COR .15 .07
❑ 604 F.Valenzuela AS .10 .05
❑ 605 Todd Worrell AS .10 .05
❑ 606 D.Mattingly AS COR .20 .09
❑ 606A Don Mattingly AS .75 .35
ERR (no trademark)
❑ 607 Tony Bernazard AS .05 .02
❑ 608 Wade Boggs AS .10 .05
❑ 609 Cal Ripken AS .20 .09
❑ 610 Jim Rice AS .05 .02
❑ 611 Kirby Puckett AS .20 .09
❑ 612 George Bell AS .05 .02
❑ 613 Lance Parrish AS UER .10 .05
(Pitcher heading
on back)
❑ 614 Roger Clemens AS .20 .09
❑ 615 Teddy Higuera AS .05 .02
❑ 616 Dave Righetti AS .05 .02
❑ 617 Al Nipper .05 .02
❑ 618 Tom Kelly MG .05 .02
❑ 619 Jerry Reed .05 .02
❑ 620 Jose Canseco .60 .25
❑ 621 Danny Cox .05 .02
❑ 622 Glenn Braggs RC .05 .02
❑ 623 Kurt Stillwell .05 .02
❑ 624 Tim Burke .05 .02
❑ 625 Mookie Wilson .10 .05
❑ 626 Joel Skinner .05 .02
❑ 627 Ken Oberkfell .05 .02
❑ 628 Bob Walk .05 .02
❑ 629 Larry Parrish .05 .02
❑ 630 John Candelaria .05 .02
❑ 631 Tigers Team .05 .02
(Mound conference)
❑ 632 Rob Woodward .05 .02
❑ 633 Jose Uribe .05 .02
❑ 634 Rafael Palmeiro RC 2.00 .90
❑ 635 Ken Schrom .05 .02
❑ 636 Darren Daulton .15 .07
❑ 637 Bip Roberts RC* .20 .09
❑ 638 Rich Bordi .05 .02
❑ 639 Gerald Perry .05 .02
❑ 640 Mark Clear .05 .02
❑ 641 Domingo Ramos .05 .02
❑ 642 Al Pulido .05 .02
❑ 643 Ron Shepherd .05 .02
❑ 644 John Denny .05 .02
❑ 645 Dwight Evans .10 .05
❑ 646 Mike Mason .05 .02
❑ 647 Tom Lawless .05 .02
❑ 648 Barry Larkin RC 1.00 .45
❑ 649 Mickey Tettleton .05 .02
❑ 650 Hubie Brooks .05 .02
❑ 651 Benny Distefano .05 .02
❑ 652 Terry Forster .05 .02
❑ 653 Kevin Mitchell RC* .15 .07
❑ 654 Checklist 529-660 .10 .05
❑ 655 Jesse Barfield .05 .02
❑ 656 Rangers Team .05 .02
(Bobby Valentine MG
and Ricky Wright)
❑ 657 Tom Waddell .05 .02
❑ 658 R.Thompson RC* .10 .05
❑ 659 Aurelio Lopez .05 .02
❑ 660 Bob Horner .05 .02
❑ 661 Lou Whitaker .10 .05
❑ 662 Frank DiPino .05 .02
❑ 663 Cliff Johnson .05 .02
❑ 664 Mike Marshall .05 .02
❑ 665 Rod Scurry .05 .02
❑ 666 Von Hayes .05 .02
❑ 667 Ron Hassey .05 .02
❑ 668 Juan Bonilla .05 .02
❑ 669 Bud Black .05 .02
❑ 670 Jose Cruz .10 .05
❑ 671A Ray Soff ERR .05 .02
(No D* before
copyright line)
❑ 671B Ray Soff COR .05 .02
(D* before
copyright line)
❑ 672 Chili Davis .15 .07
❑ 673 Don Sutton .20 .09
❑ 674 Bill Campbell .05 .02
❑ 675 Ed Romero .05 .02
❑ 676 Charlie Moore .05 .02
❑ 677 Bob Grich .10 .05
❑ 678 Carney Lansford .10 .05
❑ 679 Kent Hrbek .10 .05
❑ 680 Ryne Sandberg .25 .11
❑ 681 George Bell .05 .02
❑ 682 Jerry Reuss .05 .02
❑ 683 Gary Roenicke .05 .02
❑ 684 Kent Tekulve .05 .02
❑ 685 Jerry Hairston .05 .02
❑ 686 Doyle Alexander .05 .02
❑ 687 Alan Trammell .15 .07
❑ 688 Juan Beniquez .05 .02

❑ 689	Darrell Porter	.05	.02
❑ 690	Dane Iorg	.05	.02
❑ 691	Dave Parker	.10	.05
❑ 692	Frank White	.10	.05
❑ 693	Terry Puhl	.05	.02
❑ 694	Phil Niekro	.20	.09
❑ 695	Chico Walker	.05	.02
❑ 696	Gary Lucas	.05	.02
❑ 697	Ed Lynch	.05	.02
❑ 698	Ernie Whitt	.05	.02
❑ 699	Ken Landreaux	.05	.02
❑ 700	Dave Bergman	.05	.02
❑ 701	Willie Randolph	.10	.05
❑ 702	Greg Gross	.05	.02
❑ 703	Dave Schmidt	.05	.02
❑ 704	Jesse Orosco	.05	.02
❑ 705	Bruce Hurst	.05	.02
❑ 706	Rick Manning	.05	.02
❑ 707	Bob McClure	.05	.02
❑ 708	Scott McGregor	.05	.02
❑ 709	Dave Kingman	.10	.05
❑ 710	Gary Gaetti	.10	.05
❑ 711	Ken Griffey	.10	.05
❑ 712	Don Robinson	.05	.02
❑ 713	Tom Brookens	.05	.02
❑ 714	Dan Quisenberry	.05	.02
❑ 715	Bob Dernier	.05	.02
❑ 716	Rick Leach	.05	.02
❑ 717	Ed VandeBerg	.05	.02
❑ 718	Steve Carlton	.20	.09
❑ 719	Tom Hume	.05	.02
❑ 720	Richard Dotson	.05	.02
❑ 721	Tom Herr	.05	.02
❑ 722	Bob Knepper	.05	.02
❑ 723	Brett Butler	.10	.05
❑ 724	Greg Minton	.05	.02
❑ 725	George Hendrick	.05	.02
❑ 726	Frank Tanana	.05	.02
❑ 727	Mike Moore	.05	.02
❑ 728	Tippy Martinez	.05	.02
❑ 729	Tom Paciorek	.10	.05
❑ 730	Eric Show	.05	.02
❑ 731	Dave Concepcion	.10	.05
❑ 732	Manny Trillo	.05	.02
❑ 733	Bill Caudill	.05	.02
❑ 734	Bill Madlock	.10	.05
❑ 735	Rickey Henderson	.40	.18
❑ 736	Steve Bedrosian	.05	.02
❑ 737	Floyd Bannister	.05	.02
❑ 738	Jorge Orta	.05	.02
❑ 739	Chet Lemon	.05	.02
❑ 740	Rich Gedman	.05	.02
❑ 741	Paul Molitor	.20	.09
❑ 742	Andy McGaffigan	.05	.02
❑ 743	Dwayne Murphy	.05	.02
❑ 744	Roy Smalley	.05	.02
❑ 745	Glenn Hubbard	.05	.02
❑ 746	Bob Ojeda	.05	.02
❑ 747	Johnny Ray	.05	.02
❑ 748	Mike Flanagan	.05	.02
❑ 749	Ozzie Smith	.25	.11
❑ 750	Steve Trout	.05	.02
❑ 751	Garth Iorg	.05	.02
❑ 752	Dan Petry	.05	.02
❑ 753	Rick Honeycutt	.05	.02
❑ 754	Dave LaPoint	.05	.02
❑ 755	Luis Aguayo	.05	.02
❑ 756	Carlton Fisk	.20	.09
❑ 757	Nolan Ryan	1.00	.45
❑ 758	Tony Bernazard	.05	.02
❑ 759	Joel Youngblood	.05	.02
❑ 760	Mike Witt	.05	.02
❑ 761	Greg Pryor	.05	.02
❑ 762	Gary Ward	.05	.02
❑ 763	Tim Flannery	.05	.02
❑ 764	Bill Buckner	.10	.05
❑ 765	Kirk Gibson	.10	.05
❑ 766	Don Aase	.05	.02
❑ 767	Ron Cey	.10	.05
❑ 768	Dennis Lamp	.05	.02
❑ 769	Steve Sax	.05	.02
❑ 770	Dave Winfield	.20	.09
❑ 771	Shane Rawley	.05	.02
❑ 772	Harold Baines	.10	.05
❑ 773	Robin Yount	.20	.09
❑ 774	Wayne Krenchicki	.05	.02
❑ 775	Joaquin Andujar	.05	.02
❑ 776	Tom Brunansky	.05	.02
❑ 777	Chris Chambliss	.10	.05
❑ 778	Jack Morris	.10	.05
❑ 779	Craig Reynolds	.05	.02
❑ 780	Andre Thornton	.05	.02
❑ 781	Atlee Hammaker	.05	.02
❑ 782	Brian Downing	.05	.02
❑ 783	Willie Wilson	.10	.05
❑ 784	Cal Ripken	.75	.35
❑ 785	Terry Francona	.10	.05
❑ 786	Jimy Williams MG	.05	.02
❑ 787	Alejandro Pena	.05	.02
❑ 788	Tim Stoddard	.05	.02
❑ 789	Dan Schatzeder	.05	.02
❑ 790	Julio Cruz	.05	.02
❑ 791	Lance Parrish UER (No trademark, never corrected)	.10	.05
❑ 792	Checklist 661-792	.05	.02

1987 Topps Traded

		MINT	NRMT
COMP.FACT.SET (132)		8.00	3.60
❑ 1T	Bill Almon	.05	.02
❑ 2T	Scott Bankhead	.05	.02
❑ 3T	Eric Bell	.05	.02
❑ 4T	Juan Beniquez	.05	.02
❑ 5T	Juan Berenguer	.05	.02
❑ 6T	Greg Booker	.05	.02
❑ 7T	Thad Bosley	.05	.02
❑ 8T	Larry Bowa MG	.10	.05
❑ 9T	Greg Brock	.05	.02
❑ 10T	Bob Brower	.05	.02
❑ 11T	Jerry Browne	.05	.02
❑ 12T	Ralph Bryant	.05	.02
❑ 13T	DeWayne Buice	.05	.02
❑ 14T	Ellis Burks XRC	.50	.23
❑ 15T	Ivan Calderon	.05	.02
❑ 16T	Jeff Calhoun	.05	.02
❑ 17T	Casey Candaele	.05	.02
❑ 18T	John Cangelosi	.05	.02
❑ 19T	Steve Carlton	.20	.09
❑ 20T	Juan Castillo	.05	.02
❑ 21T	Rick Cerone	.05	.02
❑ 22T	Ron Cey	.10	.05
❑ 23T	John Christensen	.05	.02
❑ 24T	David Cone XRC	.75	.35
❑ 25T	Chuck Crim	.05	.02
❑ 26T	Storm Davis	.05	.02
❑ 27T	Andre Dawson	.15	.07
❑ 28T	Rick Dempsey	.10	.05
❑ 29T	Doug Drabek	.20	.09
❑ 30T	Mike Dunne	.05	.02
❑ 31T	Dennis Eckersley	.20	.09
❑ 32T	Lee Elia MG	.05	.02
❑ 33T	Brian Fisher	.05	.02
❑ 34T	Terry Francona	.10	.05
❑ 35T	Willie Fraser	.05	.02
❑ 36T	Billy Gardner MG	.05	.02
❑ 37T	Ken Gerhart	.05	.02
❑ 38T	Dan Gladden	.05	.02
❑ 39T	Jim Gott	.05	.02
❑ 40T	Cecilio Guante	.05	.02
❑ 41T	Albert Hall	.05	.02
❑ 42T	Terry Harper	.05	.02
❑ 43T	Mickey Hatcher	.05	.02
❑ 44T	Brad Havens	.05	.02
❑ 45T	Neal Heaton	.05	.02
❑ 46T	Mike Henneman XRC	.15	.07
❑ 47T	Donnie Hill	.05	.02
❑ 48T	Guy Hoffman	.05	.02
❑ 49T	Brian Holton	.05	.02
❑ 50T	Charles Hudson	.05	.02
❑ 51T	Danny Jackson	.05	.02
❑ 52T	Reggie Jackson	.25	.11
❑ 53T	Chris James XRC*	.05	.02
❑ 54T	Dion James	.05	.02
❑ 55T	Stan Jefferson	.05	.02
❑ 56T	Joe Johnson	.05	.02
❑ 57T	Terry Kennedy	.05	.02
❑ 58T	Mike Kingery	.05	.02
❑ 59T	Ray Knight	.05	.02
❑ 60T	Gene Larkin XRC	.05	.02
❑ 61T	Mike LaValliere	.05	.02
❑ 62T	Jack Lazorko	.05	.02
❑ 63T	Terry Leach	.05	.02
❑ 64T	Tim Leary	.05	.02
❑ 65T	Jim Lindeman	.05	.02
❑ 66T	Steve Lombardozzi	.05	.02
❑ 67T	Bill Long	.05	.02
❑ 68T	Barry Lyons	.05	.02
❑ 69T	Shane Mack	.10	.05
❑ 70T	Greg Maddux XRC	5.00	2.20
❑ 71T	Bill Madlock	.10	.05
❑ 72T	Joe Magrane XRC	.05	.02
❑ 73T	Dave Martinez XRC*	.10	.05
❑ 74T	Fred McGriff	.40	.18
❑ 75T	Mark McLemore XRC	.10	.05
❑ 76T	Kevin McReynolds	.05	.02
❑ 77T	Dave Meads	.05	.02
❑ 78T	Eddie Milner	.05	.02
❑ 79T	Greg Minton	.05	.02
❑ 80T	John Mitchell	.05	.02
❑ 81T	Kevin Mitchell	.15	.07
❑ 82T	Charlie Moore	.05	.02
❑ 83T	Jeff Musselman	.05	.02
❑ 84T	Gene Nelson	.05	.02
❑ 85T	Graig Nettles	.10	.05
❑ 86T	Al Newman	.05	.02
❑ 87T	Reid Nichols	.05	.02
❑ 88T	Tom Niedenfuer	.05	.02
❑ 89T	Joe Niekro	.05	.02
❑ 90T	Tom Nieto	.05	.02
❑ 91T	Matt Nokes XRC	.10	.05
❑ 92T	Dickie Noles	.05	.02
❑ 93T	Pat Pacillo	.05	.02
❑ 94T	Lance Parrish	.10	.05
❑ 95T	Tony Pena	.05	.02
❑ 96T	Luis Polonia XRC	.10	.05
❑ 97T	Randy Ready	.05	.02
❑ 98T	Jeff Reardon	.10	.05
❑ 99T	Gary Redus	.05	.02
❑ 100T	Jeff Reed	.05	.02
❑ 101T	Rick Rhoden	.05	.02
❑ 102T	Cal Ripken Sr. MG	.05	.02
❑ 103T	Wally Ritchie	.05	.02
❑ 104T	Jeff M. Robinson	.05	.02
❑ 105T	Gary Roenicke	.05	.02
❑ 106T	Jerry Royster	.05	.02
❑ 107T	Mark Salas	.05	.02
❑ 108T	Luis Salazar	.05	.02
❑ 109T	Benny Santiago XRC	.10	.05
❑ 110T	Dave Schmidt	.05	.02
❑ 111T	Kevin Seitzer XRC*	.20	.09
❑ 112T	John Shelby	.05	.02
❑ 113T	Steve Shields	.05	.02
❑ 114T	John Smiley XRC	.05	.02
❑ 115T	Chris Speier	.05	.02
❑ 116T	Mike Stanley XRC*	.20	.09
❑ 117T	Terry Steinbach XRC	.20	.09
❑ 118T	Les Straker	.05	.02
❑ 119T	Jim Sundberg	.05	.02
❑ 120T	Danny Tartabull	.05	.02
❑ 121T	Tom Trebelhorn MG	.05	.02
❑ 122T	Dave Valle XRC**	.05	.02
❑ 123T	Ed VandeBerg	.05	.02
❑ 124T	Andy Van Slyke	.10	.05
❑ 125T	Gary Ward	.05	.02
❑ 126T	Alan Wiggins	.05	.02
❑ 127T	Bill Wilkinson	.05	.02
❑ 128T	Frank Williams	.05	.02

❑ 129T	Matt Williams XRC	1.00	.45
❑ 130T	Jim Winn	.05	.02
❑ 131T	Matt Young	.05	.02
❑ 132T	Checklist 1T-132T	.05	.02

1988 Topps

	MINT	NRMT
COMPLETE SET (792)	15.00	6.75
COMP.FACT.SET (792)	20.00	9.00

		MINT	NRMT
❑ 1	Vince Coleman RB	.05	.02
	100 Steals for Third Cons. Season		
❑ 2	Don Mattingly RB	.15	.07
	Six Grand Slams		
❑ 3	Mark McGwire RB	1.00	.45
	Rookie Homer Record (No white spot)		
❑ 3A	Mark McGwire RB	.25	.11
	Rookie Homer Record (White spot behind left foot)		
❑ 4	Eddie Murray RB	.10	.05
	Switch Home Runs, Two Straight Games (No caption on front)		
❑ 4A	Eddie Murray RB	.40	.18
	Switch Home Runs, Two Straight Games (Caption in box on card front)		
❑ 5	Phil Niekro	.10	.05
	Joe Niekro RB Brothers Win Record		
❑ 6	Nolan Ryan RB	.20	.09
	11th 200 K's Season		
❑ 7	Benito Santiago RB	.05	.02
	34-Game Hitting Streak Rookie Record		
❑ 8	Kevin Elster	.05	.02
❑ 9	Andy Hawkins	.05	.02
❑ 10	Ryne Sandberg	.25	.11
❑ 11	Mike Young	.05	.02
❑ 12	Bill Schroeder	.05	.02
❑ 13	Andres Thomas	.05	.02
❑ 14	Sparky Anderson MG	.10	.05
❑ 15	Chili Davis	.15	.07
❑ 16	Kirk McCaskill	.05	.02
❑ 17	Ron Oester	.05	.02
❑ 18A	Al Leiter RC ERR	.20	.09
	(Photo actually Steve George, right ear visible)		
❑ 18B	Al Leiter RC COR	.40	.18
	(Left ear visible)		
❑ 19	Mark Davidson	.05	.02
❑ 20	Kevin Gross	.05	.02
❑ 21	Red Sox TL	.10	.05
	Wade Boggs and Spike Owen		
❑ 22	Greg Swindell	.05	.02
❑ 23	Ken Landreaux	.05	.02
❑ 24	Jim Deshaies	.05	.02
❑ 25	Andres Galarraga	.15	.07
❑ 26	Mitch Williams	.05	.02
❑ 27	R.J. Reynolds	.05	.02
❑ 28	Jose Nunez	.05	.02
❑ 29	Argenis Salazar	.05	.02
❑ 30	Sid Fernandez	.05	.02
❑ 31	Bruce Bochy	.05	.02
❑ 32	Mike Morgan	.05	.02
❑ 33	Rob Deer	.05	.02
❑ 34	Ricky Horton	.05	.02
❑ 35	Harold Baines	.10	.05
❑ 36	Jamie Moyer	.10	.05
❑ 37	Ed Romero	.05	.02
❑ 38	Jeff Calhoun	.05	.02
❑ 39	Gerald Perry	.05	.02
❑ 40	Orel Hershiser	.10	.05
❑ 41	Bob Melvin	.05	.02
❑ 42	Bill Landrum	.05	.02
❑ 43	Dick Schofield	.05	.02
❑ 44	Lou Piniella MG	.10	.05
❑ 45	Kent Hrbek	.10	.05
❑ 46	Darnell Coles	.05	.02
❑ 47	Joaquin Andujar	.05	.02
❑ 48	Alan Ashby	.05	.02
❑ 49	Dave Clark	.05	.02
❑ 50	Hubie Brooks	.05	.02
❑ 51	Orioles TL	.40	.18
	Eddie Murray and Cal Ripken		
❑ 52	Don Robinson	.05	.02
❑ 53	Curt Wilkerson	.05	.02
❑ 54	Jim Clancy	.05	.02
❑ 55	Phil Bradley	.05	.02
❑ 56	Ed Hearn	.05	.02
❑ 57	Tim Crews RC	.05	.02
❑ 58	Dave Magadan	.05	.02
❑ 59	Danny Cox	.05	.02
❑ 60	Rickey Henderson	.40	.18
❑ 61	Mark Knudson	.05	.02
❑ 62	Jeff Hamilton	.05	.02
❑ 63	Jimmy Jones	.05	.02
❑ 64	Ken Caminiti RC	.50	.23
❑ 65	Leon Durham	.05	.02
❑ 66	Shane Rawley	.05	.02
❑ 67	Ken Oberkfell	.05	.02
❑ 68	Dave Dravecky	.10	.05
❑ 69	Mike Hart	.05	.02
❑ 70	Roger Clemens	.50	.23
❑ 71	Gary Pettis	.05	.02
❑ 72	Dennis Eckersley	.10	.05
❑ 73	Randy Bush	.05	.02
❑ 74	Tom Lasorda MG	.20	.09
❑ 75	Joe Carter	.20	.09
❑ 76	Dennis Martinez	.10	.05
❑ 77	Tom O'Malley	.05	.02
❑ 78	Dan Petry	.05	.02
❑ 79	Ernie Whitt	.05	.02
❑ 80	Mark Langston	.05	.02
❑ 81	Reds TL	.05	.02
	Ron Robinson and John Franco		
❑ 82	Darrel Akerfelds	.05	.02
❑ 83	Jose Oquendo	.05	.02
❑ 84	Cecilio Guante	.05	.02
❑ 85	Howard Johnson	.05	.02
❑ 86	Ron Karkovice	.05	.02
❑ 87	Mike Mason	.05	.02
❑ 88	Earnie Riles	.05	.02
❑ 89	Gary Thurman	.05	.02
❑ 90	Dale Murphy	.20	.09
❑ 91	Joey Cora RC	.20	.09
❑ 92	Len Matuszek	.05	.02
❑ 93	Bob Sebra	.05	.02
❑ 94	Chuck Jackson	.05	.02
❑ 95	Lance Parrish	.05	.02
❑ 96	Todd Benzinger RC*	.05	.02
❑ 97	Scott Garrelts	.05	.02
❑ 98	Rene Gonzales RC	.05	.02
❑ 99	Chuck Finley	.15	.07
❑ 100	Jack Clark	.10	.05
❑ 101	Allan Anderson	.05	.02
❑ 102	Barry Larkin	.20	.09
❑ 103	Curt Young	.05	.02
❑ 104	Dick Williams MG	.10	.05
❑ 105	Jesse Orosco	.05	.02
❑ 106	Jim Walewander	.05	.02
❑ 107	Scott Bailes	.05	.02
❑ 108	Steve Lyons	.05	.02
❑ 109	Joel Skinner	.05	.02
❑ 110	Teddy Higuera	.05	.02
❑ 111	Expos TL	.05	.02
	Hubie Brooks and Vance Law		
❑ 112	Les Lancaster	.05	.02
❑ 113	Kelly Gruber	.05	.02
❑ 114	Jeff Russell	.05	.02
❑ 115	Johnny Ray	.05	.02
❑ 116	Jerry Don Gleaton	.05	.02
❑ 117	James Steels	.05	.02
❑ 118	Bob Welch	.05	.02
❑ 119	Robbie Wine	.05	.02
❑ 120	Kirby Puckett	.50	.23
❑ 121	Checklist 1-132	.05	.02
❑ 122	Tony Bernazard	.05	.02
❑ 123	Tom Candiotti	.05	.02
❑ 124	Ray Knight	.05	.02
❑ 125	Bruce Hurst	.05	.02
❑ 126	Steve Jeltz	.05	.02
❑ 127	Jim Gott	.05	.02
❑ 128	Johnny Grubb	.05	.02
❑ 129	Greg Minton	.05	.02
❑ 130	Buddy Bell	.10	.05
❑ 131	Don Schulze	.05	.02
❑ 132	Donnie Hill	.05	.02
❑ 133	Greg Mathews	.05	.02
❑ 134	Chuck Tanner MG	.10	.05
❑ 135	Dennis Rasmussen	.05	.02
❑ 136	Brian Dayett	.05	.02
❑ 137	Chris Bosio	.05	.02
❑ 138	Mitch Webster	.05	.02
❑ 139	Jerry Browne	.05	.02
❑ 140	Jesse Barfield	.05	.02
❑ 141	Royals TL	.20	.09
	George Brett and Bret Saberhagen		
❑ 142	Andy Van Slyke	.10	.05
❑ 143	Mickey Tettleton	.05	.02
❑ 144	Don Gordon	.05	.02
❑ 145	Bill Madlock	.10	.05
❑ 146	Donell Nixon	.05	.02
❑ 147	Bill Buckner	.10	.05
❑ 148	Carmelo Martinez	.05	.02
❑ 149	Ken Howell	.05	.02
❑ 150	Eric Davis	.10	.05
❑ 151	Bob Knepper	.05	.02
❑ 152	Jody Reed RC	.10	.05
❑ 153	John Habyan	.05	.02
❑ 154	Jeff Stone	.05	.02
❑ 155	Bruce Sutter	.10	.05
❑ 156	Gary Matthews	.05	.02
❑ 157	Atlee Hammaker	.05	.02
❑ 158	Tim Hulett	.05	.02
❑ 159	Brad Arnsberg	.05	.02
❑ 160	Willie McGee	.10	.05
❑ 161	Bryn Smith	.05	.02
❑ 162	Mark McLemore	.05	.02
❑ 163	Dale Mohorcic	.05	.02
❑ 164	Dave Johnson MG	.10	.05
❑ 165	Robin Yount	.20	.09
❑ 166	Rick Rodriquez	.05	.02
❑ 167	Rance Mulliniks	.05	.02
❑ 168	Barry Jones	.05	.02
❑ 169	Ross Jones	.05	.02
❑ 170	Rich Gossage	.10	.05
❑ 171	Cubs TL	.05	.02
	Shawon Dunston and Manny Trillo		
❑ 172	Lloyd McClendon RC	.05	.02
❑ 173	Eric Plunk	.05	.02
❑ 174	Phil Garner	.05	.02
❑ 175	Kevin Bass	.05	.02
❑ 176	Jeff Reed	.05	.02
❑ 177	Frank Tanana	.05	.02
❑ 178	Dwayne Henry	.05	.02
❑ 179	Charlie Puleo	.05	.02
❑ 180	Terry Kennedy	.05	.02
❑ 181	David Cone	.10	.05
❑ 182	Ken Phelps	.05	.02
❑ 183	Tom Lawless	.05	.02
❑ 184	Ivan Calderon	.05	.02
❑ 185	Rick Rhoden	.05	.02
❑ 186	Rafael Palmeiro	.40	.18
❑ 187	Steve Kiefer	.05	.02
❑ 188	John Russell	.05	.02
❑ 189	Wes Gardner	.05	.02
❑ 190	Candy Maldonado	.05	.02

❑ 191 John Cerutti .05 .02
❑ 192 Devon White .10 .05
❑ 193 Brian Fisher .05 .02
❑ 194 Tom Kelly MG .05 .02
❑ 195 Dan Quisenberry .05 .02
❑ 196 Dave Engle .05 .02
❑ 197 Lance McCullers .05 .02
❑ 198 Franklin Stubbs .05 .02
❑ 199 Dave Meads .05 .02
❑ 200 Wade Boggs .20 .09
❑ 201 Rangers TL .05 .02
Bobby Valentine MG
Pete O'Brien,
Pete Incaviglia and
Steve Buechele
❑ 202 Glenn Hoffman .05 .02
❑ 203 Fred Toliver .05 .02
❑ 204 Paul O'Neill .20 .09
❑ 205 Nelson Liriano .05 .02
❑ 206 Domingo Ramos .05 .02
❑ 207 John Mitchell .05 .02
❑ 208 Steve Lake .05 .02
❑ 209 Richard Dotson .05 .02
❑ 210 Willie Randolph .10 .05
❑ 211 Frank DiPino .05 .02
❑ 212 Greg Brock .05 .02
❑ 213 Albert Hall .05 .02
❑ 214 Dave Schmidt .05 .02
❑ 215 Von Hayes .05 .02
❑ 216 Jerry Reuss .05 .02
❑ 217 Harry Spilman .05 .02
❑ 218 Dan Schatzeder .05 .02
❑ 219 Mike Stanley .10 .05
❑ 220 Tom Henke .05 .02
❑ 221 Rafael Belliard .05 .02
❑ 222 Steve Farr .05 .02
❑ 223 Stan Jefferson .05 .02
❑ 224 Tom Trebelhorn MG .05 .02
❑ 225 Mike Scioscia .05 .02
❑ 226 Dave Lopes .10 .05
❑ 227 Ed Correa .05 .02
❑ 228 Wallace Johnson .05 .02
❑ 229 Jeff Musselman .05 .02
❑ 230 Pat Tabler .05 .02
❑ 231 Pirates TL .25 .11
Barry Bonds and
Bobby Bonilla
❑ 232 Bob James .05 .02
❑ 233 Rafael Santana .05 .02
❑ 234 Ken Dayley .05 .02
❑ 235 Gary Ward .05 .02
❑ 236 Ted Power .05 .02
❑ 237 Mike Heath .05 .02
❑ 238 Luis Polonia RC* .05 .02
❑ 239 Roy Smalley .05 .02
❑ 240 Lee Smith .10 .05
❑ 241 Damaso Garcia .05 .02
❑ 242 Tom Niedenfuer .05 .02
❑ 243 Mark Ryal .05 .02
❑ 244 Jeff D. Robinson .05 .02
❑ 245 Rich Gedman .05 .02
❑ 246 Mike Campbell .05 .02
❑ 247 Thad Bosley .05 .02
❑ 248 Storm Davis .05 .02
❑ 249 Mike Marshall .05 .02
❑ 250 Nolan Ryan 1.00 .45
❑ 251 Tom Foley .05 .02
❑ 252 Bob Brower .05 .02
❑ 253 Checklist 133-264 .05 .02
❑ 254 Lee Elia MG .05 .02
❑ 255 Mookie Wilson .10 .05
❑ 256 Ken Schrom .05 .02
❑ 257 Jerry Royster .05 .02
❑ 258 Ed Nunez .05 .02
❑ 259 Ron Kittle .05 .02
❑ 260 Vince Coleman .05 .02
❑ 261 Giants TL .05 .02
(Five players)
❑ 262 Drew Hall .05 .02
❑ 263 Glenn Braggs .05 .02
❑ 264 Les Straker .05 .02
❑ 265 Bo Diaz .05 .02
❑ 266 Paul Assenmacher .05 .02
❑ 267 Billy Bean .05 .02
❑ 268 Bruce Ruffin .05 .02
❑ 269 Ellis Burks RC .40 .18
❑ 270 Mike Witt .05 .02
❑ 271 Ken Gerhart .05 .02
❑ 272 Steve Ontiveros .05 .02
❑ 273 Garth Iorg .05 .02
❑ 274 Junior Ortiz .05 .02
❑ 275 Kevin Seitzer .10 .05
❑ 276 Luis Salazar .05 .02
❑ 277 Alejandro Pena .05 .02
❑ 278 Jose Cruz .05 .02
❑ 279 Randy St.Claire .05 .02
❑ 280 Pete Incaviglia .05 .02
❑ 281 Jerry Hairston .05 .02
❑ 282 Pat Perry .05 .02
❑ 283 Phil Lombardi .05 .02
❑ 284 Larry Bowa MG .05 .02
❑ 285 Jim Presley .05 .02
❑ 286 Chuck Crim .05 .02
❑ 287 Manny Trillo .05 .02
❑ 288 Pat Pacillo .05 .02
(Chris Sabo in
background of photo)
❑ 289 Dave Bergman .05 .02
❑ 290 Tony Fernandez .05 .02
❑ 291 Astros TL .05 .02
Billy Hatcher
and Kevin Bass
❑ 292 Carney Lansford .10 .05
❑ 293 Doug Jones RC .20 .09
❑ 294 Al Pedrique .05 .02
❑ 295 Bert Blyleven .10 .05
❑ 296 Floyd Rayford .05 .02
❑ 297 Zane Smith .05 .02
❑ 298 Milt Thompson .05 .02
❑ 299 Steve Crawford .05 .02
❑ 300 Don Mattingly .50 .23
❑ 301 Bud Black .05 .02
❑ 302 Jose Uribe .05 .02
❑ 303 Eric Show .05 .02
❑ 304 George Hendrick .05 .02
❑ 305 Steve Sax .05 .02
❑ 306 Billy Hatcher .05 .02
❑ 307 Mike Trujillo .05 .02
❑ 308 Lee Mazzilli .05 .02
❑ 309 Bill Long .05 .02
❑ 310 Tom Herr .05 .02
❑ 311 Scott Sanderson .05 .02
❑ 312 Joey Meyer .05 .02
❑ 313 Bob McClure .05 .02
❑ 314 Jimy Williams MG .05 .02
❑ 315 Dave Parker .10 .05
❑ 316 Jose Rijo .05 .02
❑ 317 Tom Nieto .05 .02
❑ 318 Mel Hall .05 .02
❑ 319 Mike Loynd .05 .02
❑ 320 Alan Trammell .15 .07
❑ 321 White Sox TL .10 .05
Harold Baines and
Carlton Fisk
❑ 322 Vicente Palacios .05 .02
❑ 323 Rick Leach .05 .02
❑ 324 Danny Jackson .05 .02
❑ 325 Glenn Hubbard .05 .02
❑ 326 Al Nipper .05 .02
❑ 327 Larry Sheets .05 .02
❑ 328 Greg Cadaret .05 .02
❑ 329 Chris Speier .05 .02
❑ 330 Eddie Whitson .05 .02
❑ 331 Brian Downing .05 .02
❑ 332 Jerry Reed .05 .02
❑ 333 Wally Backman .05 .02
❑ 334 Dave LaPoint .05 .02
❑ 335 Claudell Washington .05 .02
❑ 336 Ed Lynch .05 .02
❑ 337 Jim Gantner .05 .02
❑ 338 Brian Holton UER .05 .02
(1987 ERA .389,
should be 3.89)
❑ 339 Kurt Stillwell .05 .02
❑ 340 Jack Morris .10 .05
❑ 341 Carmen Castillo .05 .02
❑ 342 Larry Andersen .05 .02
❑ 343 Greg Gagne .05 .02
❑ 344 Tony LaRussa MG .10 .05
❑ 345 Scott Fletcher .05 .02
❑ 346 Vance Law .05 .02
❑ 347 Joe Johnson .05 .02
❑ 348 Jim Eisenreich .20 .09
❑ 349 Bob Walk .05 .02
❑ 350 Will Clark .25 .11
❑ 351 Cardinals TL .10 .05
Red Schoendienst CO
and Tony Pena
❑ 352 Bill Ripken RC* .05 .02
❑ 353 Ed Olwine .05 .02
❑ 354 Marc Sullivan .05 .02
❑ 355 Roger McDowell .05 .02
❑ 356 Luis Aguayo .05 .02
❑ 357 Floyd Bannister .05 .02
❑ 358 Rey Quinones .05 .02
❑ 359 Tim Stoddard .05 .02
❑ 360 Tony Gwynn .40 .18
❑ 361 Greg Maddux 1.00 .45
❑ 362 Juan Castillo .05 .02
❑ 363 Willie Fraser .05 .02
❑ 364 Nick Esasky .05 .02
❑ 365 Floyd Youmans .05 .02
❑ 366 Chet Lemon .05 .02
❑ 367 Tim Leary .05 .02
❑ 368 Gerald Young .05 .02
❑ 369 Greg Harris .05 .02
❑ 370 Jose Canseco .30 .14
❑ 371 Joe Hesketh .05 .02
❑ 372 Matt Williams RC .75 .35
❑ 373 Checklist 265-396 .05 .02
❑ 374 Doc Edwards MG .05 .02
❑ 375 Tom Brunansky .05 .02
❑ 376 Bill Wilkinson .05 .02
❑ 377 Sam Horn RC .05 .02
❑ 378 Todd Frohwirth .05 .02
❑ 379 Rafael Ramirez .05 .02
❑ 380 Joe Magrane RC* .05 .02
❑ 381 Angels TL .10 .05
Wally Joyner and
Jack Howell
❑ 382 Keith A. Miller RC .05 .02
❑ 383 Eric Bell .05 .02
❑ 384 Neil Allen .05 .02
❑ 385 Carlton Fisk .20 .09
❑ 386 Don Mattingly AS .15 .07
❑ 387 Willie Randolph AS .05 .02
❑ 388 Wade Boggs AS .10 .05
❑ 389 Alan Trammell AS .05 .02
❑ 390 George Bell AS .05 .02
❑ 391 Kirby Puckett AS .25 .11
❑ 392 Dave Winfield AS .20 .09
❑ 393 Matt Nokes AS .05 .02
❑ 394 Roger Clemens AS .25 .11
❑ 395 Jimmy Key AS .05 .02
❑ 396 Tom Henke AS .05 .02
❑ 397 Jack Clark AS .10 .05
❑ 398 Juan Samuel AS .05 .02
❑ 399 Tim Wallach AS .05 .02
❑ 400 Ozzie Smith AS .15 .07
❑ 401 Andre Dawson AS .10 .05
❑ 402 Tony Gwynn AS .20 .09
❑ 403 Tim Raines AS .10 .05
❑ 404 Benny Santiago AS .05 .02
❑ 405 Dwight Gooden AS .10 .05
❑ 406 Shane Rawley AS .05 .02
❑ 407 Steve Bedrosian AS .05 .02
❑ 408 Dion James .05 .02
❑ 409 Joel McKeon .05 .02
❑ 410 Tony Pena .05 .02
❑ 411 Wayne Tolleson .05 .02
❑ 412 Randy Myers .15 .07
❑ 413 John Christensen .05 .02
❑ 414 John McNamara MG .05 .02
❑ 415 Don Carman .05 .02
❑ 416 Keith Moreland .05 .02
❑ 417 Mark Ciardi .05 .02
❑ 418 Joel Youngblood .05 .02
❑ 419 Scott McGregor .05 .02
❑ 420 Wally Joyner .15 .07
❑ 421 Ed VandeBerg .05 .02
❑ 422 Dave Concepcion .10 .05
❑ 423 John Smiley RC* .10 .05
❑ 424 Dwayne Murphy .05 .02
❑ 425 Jeff Reardon .10 .05
❑ 426 Randy Ready .05 .02
❑ 427 Paul Kilgus .05 .02
❑ 428 John Shelby .05 .02
❑ 429 Tigers TL .05 .02

	Alan Trammell and		
	Kirk Gibson		
❑ 430	Glenn Davis	.05	.02
❑ 431	Casey Candaele	.05	.02
❑ 432	Mike Moore	.05	.02
❑ 433	Bill Pecota RC*	.05	.02
❑ 434	Rick Aguilera	.10	.05
❑ 435	Mike Pagliarulo	.05	.02
❑ 436	Mike Bielecki	.05	.02
❑ 437	Fred Manrique	.05	.02
❑ 438	Rob Ducey	.05	.02
❑ 439	Dave Martinez	.05	.02
❑ 440	Steve Bedrosian	.05	.02
❑ 441	Rick Manning	.05	.02
❑ 442	Tom Bolton	.05	.02
❑ 443	Ken Griffey	.10	.05
❑ 444	C.Ripken Sr. MG UER	.05	.02
	two copyrights		
❑ 445	Mike Krukow	.05	.02
❑ 446	Doug DeCinces	.05	.02
	(Now with Cardinals		
	on card front)		
❑ 447	Jeff Montgomery RC	.20	.09
❑ 448	Mike Davis	.05	.02
❑ 449	Jeff M. Robinson	.05	.02
❑ 450	Barry Bonds	1.50	.70
❑ 451	Keith Atherton	.05	.02
❑ 452	Willie Wilson	.05	.02
❑ 453	Dennis Powell	.05	.02
❑ 454	Marvell Wynne	.05	.02
❑ 455	Shawn Hillegas	.05	.02
❑ 456	Dave Anderson	.05	.02
❑ 457	Terry Leach	.05	.02
❑ 458	Ron Hassey	.05	.02
❑ 459	Yankees TL	.20	.09
	Dave Winfield and		
	Willie Randolph		
❑ 460	Ozzie Smith	.25	.11
❑ 461	Danny Darwin	.05	.02
❑ 462	Don Slaught	.05	.02
❑ 463	Fred McGriff	.20	.09
❑ 464	Jay Tibbs	.05	.02
❑ 465	Paul Molitor	.20	.09
❑ 466	Jerry Mumphrey	.05	.02
❑ 467	Don Aase	.05	.02
❑ 468	Darren Daulton	.10	.05
❑ 469	Jeff Dedmon	.05	.02
❑ 470	Dwight Evans	.10	.05
❑ 471	Donnie Moore	.05	.02
❑ 472	Robby Thompson	.05	.02
❑ 473	Joe Niekro	.05	.02
❑ 474	Tom Brookens	.05	.02
❑ 475	Pete Rose MG	.50	.23
❑ 476	Dave Stewart	.10	.05
❑ 477	Jamie Quirk	.05	.02
❑ 478	Sid Bream	.05	.02
❑ 479	Brett Butler	.10	.05
❑ 480	Dwight Gooden	.10	.05
❑ 481	Mariano Duncan	.05	.02
❑ 482	Mark Davis	.05	.02
❑ 483	Rod Booker	.05	.02
❑ 484	Pat Clements	.05	.02
❑ 485	Harold Reynolds	.10	.05
❑ 486	Pat Keedy	.05	.02
❑ 487	Jim Pankovits	.05	.02
❑ 488	Andy McGaffigan	.05	.02
❑ 489	Dodgers TL	.05	.02
	Pedro Guerrero and		
	Fernando Valenzuela		
❑ 490	Larry Parrish	.05	.02
❑ 491	B.J. Surhoff	.10	.05
❑ 492	Doyle Alexander	.05	.02
❑ 493	Mike Greenwell	.05	.02
❑ 494	Wally Ritchie	.05	.02
❑ 495	Eddie Murray	.20	.09
❑ 496	Guy Hoffman	.05	.02
❑ 497	Kevin Mitchell	.10	.05
❑ 498	Bob Boone	.10	.05
❑ 499	Eric King	.05	.02
❑ 500	Andre Dawson	.15	.07
❑ 501	Tim Birtsas	.05	.02
❑ 502	Dan Gladden	.05	.02
❑ 503	Junior Noboa	.05	.02
❑ 504	Bob Rodgers MG	.05	.02
❑ 505	Willie Upshaw	.05	.02
❑ 506	John Cangelosi	.05	.02
❑ 507	Mark Gubicza	.05	.02
❑ 508	Tim Teufel	.05	.02
❑ 509	Bill Dawley	.05	.02
❑ 510	Dave Winfield	.20	.09
❑ 511	Joel Davis	.05	.02
❑ 512	Alex Trevino	.05	.02
❑ 513	Tim Flannery	.05	.02
❑ 514	Pat Sheridan	.05	.02
❑ 515	Juan Nieves	.05	.02
❑ 516	Jim Sundberg	.05	.02
❑ 517	Ron Robinson	.05	.02
❑ 518	Greg Gross	.05	.02
❑ 519	Mariners TL	.05	.02
	Harold Reynolds and		
	Phil Bradley		
❑ 520	Dave Smith	.05	.02
❑ 521	Jim Dwyer	.05	.02
❑ 522	Bob Patterson	.05	.02
❑ 523	Gary Roenicke	.05	.02
❑ 524	Gary Lucas	.05	.02
❑ 525	Marty Barrett	.05	.02
❑ 526	Juan Berenguer	.05	.02
❑ 527	Steve Henderson	.05	.02
❑ 528A	Checklist 397-528	.20	.09
	ERR (455 S. Carlton)		
❑ 528B	Checklist 397-528	.10	.05
	COR (455 S. Hillegas)		
❑ 529	Tim Burke	.05	.02
❑ 530	Gary Carter	.15	.07
❑ 531	Rich Yett	.05	.02
❑ 532	Mike Kingery	.05	.02
❑ 533	John Farrell	.05	.02
❑ 534	John Wathan MG	.05	.02
❑ 535	Ron Guidry	.05	.02
❑ 536	John Morris	.05	.02
❑ 537	Steve Buechele	.05	.02
❑ 538	Bill Wegman	.05	.02
❑ 539	Mike LaValliere	.05	.02
❑ 540	Bret Saberhagen	.10	.05
❑ 541	Juan Beniquez	.05	.02
❑ 542	Paul Noce	.05	.02
❑ 543	Kent Tekulve	.05	.02
❑ 544	Jim Traber	.05	.02
❑ 545	Don Baylor	.10	.05
❑ 546	John Candelaria	.05	.02
❑ 547	Felix Fermin	.05	.02
❑ 548	Shane Mack	.05	.02
❑ 549	Braves TL	.05	.02
	Albert Hall,		
	Dale Murphy,		
	Ken Griffey		
	and Dion James		
❑ 550	Pedro Guerrero	.05	.02
❑ 551	Terry Steinbach	.10	.05
❑ 552	Mark Thurmond	.05	.02
❑ 553	Tracy Jones	.05	.02
❑ 554	Mike Smithson	.05	.02
❑ 555	Brook Jacoby	.05	.02
❑ 556	Stan Clarke	.05	.02
❑ 557	Craig Reynolds	.05	.02
❑ 558	Bob Ojeda	.05	.02
❑ 559	Ken Williams RC	.05	.02
❑ 560	Tim Wallach	.05	.02
❑ 561	Rick Cerone	.05	.02
❑ 562	Jim Lindeman	.05	.02
❑ 563	Jose Guzman	.05	.02
❑ 564	Frank Lucchesi MG	.05	.02
❑ 565	Lloyd Moseby	.05	.02
❑ 566	Charlie O'Brien	.05	.02
❑ 567	Mike Diaz	.05	.02
❑ 568	Chris Brown	.05	.02
❑ 569	Charlie Leibrandt	.05	.02
❑ 570	Jeffrey Leonard	.05	.02
❑ 571	Mark Williamson	.05	.02
❑ 572	Chris James	.05	.02
❑ 573	Bob Stanley	.05	.02
❑ 574	Graig Nettles	.10	.05
❑ 575	Don Sutton	.20	.09
❑ 576	Tommy Hinzo	.05	.02
❑ 577	Tom Browning	.05	.02
❑ 578	Gary Gaetti	.10	.05
❑ 579	Mets TL	.05	.02
	Gary Carter and		
	Kevin McReynolds		
❑ 580	Mark McGwire	2.00	.90
❑ 581	Tito Landrum	.05	.02
❑ 582	Mike Henneman RC*	.10	.05
❑ 583	Dave Valle	.05	.02
❑ 584	Steve Trout	.05	.02
❑ 585	Ozzie Guillen	.05	.02
❑ 586	Bob Forsch	.05	.02
❑ 587	Terry Puhl	.05	.02
❑ 588	Jeff Parrett	.05	.02
❑ 589	Geno Petralli	.05	.02
❑ 590	George Bell	.05	.02
❑ 591	Doug Drabek	.05	.02
❑ 592	Dale Sveum	.05	.02
❑ 593	Bob Tewksbury	.05	.02
❑ 594	Bobby Valentine MG	.10	.05
❑ 595	Frank White	.10	.05
❑ 596	John Kruk	.10	.05
❑ 597	Gene Garber	.05	.02
❑ 598	Lee Lacy	.05	.02
❑ 599	Calvin Schiraldi	.05	.02
❑ 600	Mike Schmidt	.40	.18
❑ 601	Jack Lazorko	.05	.02
❑ 602	Mike Aldrete	.05	.02
❑ 603	Rob Murphy	.05	.02
❑ 604	Chris Bando	.05	.02
❑ 605	Kirk Gibson	.10	.05
❑ 606	Moose Haas	.05	.02
❑ 607	Mickey Hatcher	.05	.02
❑ 608	Charlie Kerfeld	.05	.02
❑ 609	Twins TL	.10	.05
	Gary Gaetti and		
	Kent Hrbek		
❑ 610	Keith Hernandez	.10	.05
❑ 611	Tommy John	.10	.05
❑ 612	Curt Ford	.05	.02
❑ 613	Bobby Thigpen	.05	.02
❑ 614	Herm Winningham	.05	.02
❑ 615	Jody Davis	.05	.02
❑ 616	Jay Aldrich	.05	.02
❑ 617	Oddibe McDowell	.05	.02
❑ 618	Cecil Fielder	.15	.07
❑ 619	Mike Dunne	.05	.02
	(Inconsistent design,		
	black name on front)		
❑ 620	Cory Snyder	.05	.02
❑ 621	Gene Nelson	.05	.02
❑ 622	Kal Daniels	.05	.02
❑ 623	Mike Flanagan	.05	.02
❑ 624	Jim Leyland MG	.10	.05
❑ 625	Frank Viola	.05	.02
❑ 626	Glenn Wilson	.05	.02
❑ 627	Joe Boever	.05	.02
❑ 628	Dave Henderson	.05	.02
❑ 629	Kelly Downs	.05	.02
❑ 630	Darrell Evans	.10	.05
❑ 631	Jack Howell	.05	.02
❑ 632	Steve Shields	.05	.02
❑ 633	Barry Lyons	.05	.02
❑ 634	Jose DeLeon	.05	.02
❑ 635	Terry Pendleton	.10	.05
❑ 636	Charles Hudson	.05	.02
❑ 637	Jay Bell RC	.40	.18
❑ 638	Steve Balboni	.05	.02
❑ 639	Brewers TL	.05	.02
	Glenn Braggs		
	and Tony Muser CO		
❑ 640	Garry Templeton	.05	.02
	(Inconsistent design,		
	green border)		
❑ 641	Rick Honeycutt	.05	.02
❑ 642	Bob Dernier	.05	.02
❑ 643	Rocky Childress	.05	.02
❑ 644	Terry McGriff	.05	.02
❑ 645	Matt Nokes RC*	.05	.02
❑ 646	Checklist 529-660	.05	.02
❑ 647	Pascual Perez	.05	.02
❑ 648	Al Newman	.05	.02
❑ 649	DeWayne Buice	.05	.02
❑ 650	Cal Ripken	.75	.35
❑ 651	Mike Jackson RC*	.10	.05
❑ 652	Bruce Benedict	.05	.02
❑ 653	Jeff Sellers	.05	.02
❑ 654	Roger Craig MG	.10	.05
❑ 655	Len Dykstra	.10	.05
❑ 656	Lee Guetterman	.05	.02
❑ 657	Gary Redus	.05	.02
❑ 658	Tim Conroy	.05	.02
	(Inconsistent design,		

name in white)
❑ 659 Bobby Meacham .05 .02
❑ 660 Rick Reuschel .05 .02
❑ 661 Nolan Ryan TBC '83 .50 .23
❑ 662 Jim Rice TBC .05 .02
❑ 663 Ron Blomberg TBC .05 .02
❑ 664 Bob Gibson TBC '68 .25 .11
❑ 665 Stan Musial TBC '63 .25 .11
❑ 666 Mario Soto .05 .02
❑ 667 Luis Quinones .05 .02
❑ 668 Walt Terrell .05 .02
❑ 669 Phillies TL .05 .02
Lance Parrish
and Mike Ryan CO
❑ 670 Dan Plesac .05 .02
❑ 671 Tim Laudner .05 .02
❑ 672 John Davis .05 .02
❑ 673 Tony Phillips .05 .02
❑ 674 Mike Fitzgerald .05 .02
❑ 675 Jim Rice .10 .05
❑ 676 Ken Dixon .05 .02
❑ 677 Eddie Milner .05 .02
❑ 678 Jim Acker .05 .02
❑ 679 Darrell Miller .05 .02
❑ 680 Charlie Hough .10 .05
❑ 681 Bobby Bonilla .10 .05
❑ 682 Jimmy Key .10 .05
❑ 683 Julio Franco .05 .02
❑ 684 Hal Lanier MG .05 .02
❑ 685 Ron Darling .05 .02
❑ 686 Terry Francona .05 .02
❑ 687 Mickey Brantley .05 .02
❑ 688 Jim Winn .05 .02
❑ 689 Tom Pagnozzi RC .05 .02
❑ 690 Jay Howell .05 .02
❑ 691 Dan Pasqua .05 .02
❑ 692 Mike Birkbeck .05 .02
❑ 693 Benito Santiago .05 .02
❑ 694 Eric Nolte .05 .02
❑ 695 Shawon Dunston .05 .02
❑ 696 Duane Ward .05 .02
❑ 697 Steve Lombardozzi .05 .02
❑ 698 Brad Havens .05 .02
❑ 699 Padres TL .10 .05
Benito Santiago
and Tony Gwynn
❑ 700 George Brett .40 .18
❑ 701 Sammy Stewart .05 .02
❑ 702 Mike Gallego .05 .02
❑ 703 Bob Brenly .05 .02
❑ 704 Dennis Boyd .05 .02
❑ 705 Juan Samuel .05 .02
❑ 706 Rick Mahler .05 .02
❑ 707 Fred Lynn .05 .02
❑ 708 Gus Polidor .05 .02
❑ 709 George Frazier .05 .02
❑ 710 Darryl Strawberry .10 .05
❑ 711 Bill Gullickson .05 .02
❑ 712 John Moses .05 .02
❑ 713 Willie Hernandez .05 .02
❑ 714 Jim Fregosi MG .05 .02
❑ 715 Todd Worrell .10 .05
❑ 716 Lenn Sakata .05 .02
❑ 717 Jay Baller .05 .02
❑ 718 Mike Felder .05 .02
❑ 719 Denny Walling .05 .02
❑ 720 Tim Raines .10 .05
❑ 721 Pete O'Brien .05 .02
❑ 722 Manny Lee .05 .02
❑ 723 Bob Kipper .05 .02
❑ 724 Danny Tartabull .05 .02
❑ 725 Mike Boddicker .05 .02
❑ 726 Alfredo Griffin .05 .02
❑ 727 Greg Booker .05 .02
❑ 728 Andy Allanson .05 .02
❑ 729 Blue Jays TL .10 .05
George Bell and
Fred McGriff
❑ 730 John Franco .10 .05
❑ 731 Rick Schu .05 .02
❑ 732 David Palmer .05 .02
❑ 733 Spike Owen .05 .02
❑ 734 Craig Lefferts .05 .02
❑ 735 Kevin McReynolds .05 .02
❑ 736 Matt Young .05 .02
❑ 737 Butch Wynegar .05 .02
❑ 738 Scott Bankhead .05 .02
❑ 739 Daryl Boston .05 .02
❑ 740 Rick Sutcliffe .10 .05
❑ 741 Mike Easler .05 .02
❑ 742 Mark Clear .05 .02
❑ 743 Larry Herndon .05 .02
❑ 744 Whitey Herzog MG .10 .05
❑ 745 Bill Doran .05 .02
❑ 746 Gene Larkin RC* .05 .02
❑ 747 Bobby Witt .05 .02
❑ 748 Reid Nichols .05 .02
❑ 749 Mark Eichhorn .05 .02
❑ 750 Bo Jackson .20 .09
❑ 751 Jim Morrison .05 .02
❑ 752 Mark Grant .05 .02
❑ 753 Danny Heep .05 .02
❑ 754 Mike LaCoss .05 .02
❑ 755 Ozzie Virgil .05 .02
❑ 756 Mike Maddux .05 .02
❑ 757 John Marzano .05 .02
❑ 758 Eddie Williams RC .10 .05
❑ 759 A's TL UER 1.00 .45
Mark McGwire
and Jose Canseco
(two copyrights)
❑ 760 Mike Scott .05 .02
❑ 761 Tony Armas .05 .02
❑ 762 Scott Bradley .05 .02
❑ 763 Doug Sisk .05 .02
❑ 764 Greg Walker .05 .02
❑ 765 Neal Heaton .05 .02
❑ 766 Henry Cotto .05 .02
❑ 767 Jose Lind RC .05 .02
❑ 768 Dickie Noles .05 .02
(Now with Tigers
on card front)
❑ 769 Cecil Cooper .10 .05
❑ 770 Lou Whitaker .10 .05
❑ 771 Ruben Sierra .05 .02
❑ 772 Sal Butera .05 .02
❑ 773 Frank Williams .05 .02
❑ 774 Gene Mauch MG .10 .05
❑ 775 Dave Stieb .05 .02
❑ 776 Checklist 661-792 .05 .02
❑ 777 Lonnie Smith .05 .02
❑ 778A Keith Comstock ERR 2.00 .90
(White "Padres")
❑ 778B Keith Comstock COR .05 .02
(Blue "Padres")
❑ 779 Tom Glavine RC 1.25 .55
❑ 780 Fernando Valenzuela .10 .05
❑ 781 Keith Hughes .05 .02
❑ 782 Jeff Ballard .05 .02
❑ 783 Ron Roenicke .05 .02
❑ 784 Joe Sambito .05 .02
❑ 785 Alvin Davis .05 .02
❑ 786 Joe Price .05 .02
(Inconsistent design,
orange team name)
❑ 787 Bill Almon .05 .02
❑ 788 Ray Searage .05 .02
❑ 789 Indians' TL .10 .05
Joe Carter and
Cory Snyder
❑ 790 Dave Righetti .05 .02
❑ 791 Ted Simmons .10 .05
❑ 792 John Tudor .05 .02

1988 Topps Traded

	MINT	NRMT
COMP.FACT.SET (132)	10.00	4.50

❑ 1T Jim Abbott OLY XRC .50 .23
❑ 2T Juan Agosto .10 .05
❑ 3T Luis Alicea XRC .20 .09
❑ 4T Roberto Alomar XRC 3.00 1.35
❑ 5T Brady Anderson XRC 1.00 .45
❑ 6T Jack Armstrong XRC .10 .05
❑ 7T Don August .10 .05
❑ 8T Floyd Bannister .10 .05
❑ 9T Bret Barberie OLY XRC .20 .09
❑ 10T Jose Bautista .10 .05
❑ 11T Don Baylor .20 .09
❑ 12T Tim Belcher .20 .09
❑ 13T Buddy Bell .20 .09

❑ 14T Andy Benes OLY XRC .50 .23
❑ 15T Damon Berryhill XRC .10 .05
❑ 16T Bud Black .10 .05
❑ 17T Pat Borders XRC .20 .09
❑ 18T Phil Bradley .10 .05
❑ 19T J.Branson XRC OLY .20 .09
❑ 20T Tom Brunansky .10 .05
❑ 21T Jay Buhner XRC .75 .35
❑ 22T Brett Butler .20 .09
❑ 23T Jim Campanis OLY .10 .05
❑ 24T Sil Campusano .10 .05
❑ 25T John Candelaria .10 .05
❑ 26T Jose Cecena .10 .05
❑ 27T Rick Cerone .10 .05
❑ 28T Jack Clark .20 .09
❑ 29T Kevin Coffman .10 .05
❑ 30T Pat Combs XRC OLY .10 .05
❑ 31T Henry Cotto .10 .05
❑ 32T Chili Davis .30 .14
❑ 33T Mike Davis .10 .05
❑ 34T Jose DeLeon .10 .05
❑ 35T Richard Dotson .10 .05
❑ 36T Cecil Espy .10 .05
❑ 37T Tom Filer .10 .05
❑ 38T Mike Fiore OLY .10 .05
❑ 39T Ron Gant XRC .50 .23
❑ 40T Kirk Gibson .50 .23
❑ 41T Rich Gossage .20 .09
❑ 42T Mark Grace XRC 1.50 .70
❑ 43T Alfredo Griffin .10 .05
❑ 44T Ty Griffin OLY .10 .05
❑ 45T Bryan Harvey XRC .20 .09
❑ 46T Ron Hassey .10 .05
❑ 47T Ray Hayward .10 .05
❑ 48T Dave Henderson .10 .05
❑ 49T Tom Herr .10 .05
❑ 50T Bob Horner .10 .05
❑ 51T Ricky Horton .10 .05
❑ 52T Jay Howell .10 .05
❑ 53T Glenn Hubbard .10 .05
❑ 54T Jeff Innis .10 .05
❑ 55T Danny Jackson .10 .05
❑ 56T Darrin Jackson XRC* .20 .09
❑ 57T Roberto Kelly XRC* .50 .23
❑ 58T Ron Kittle .10 .05
❑ 59T Ray Knight .10 .05
❑ 60T Vance Law .10 .05
❑ 61T Jeffrey Leonard .10 .05
❑ 62T Mike Macfarlane XRC .10 .05
❑ 63T Scotti Madison .10 .05
❑ 64T Kirt Manwaring .10 .05
❑ 65T M.Marquess OLY CO .10 .05
❑ 66T T.Martinez OLY XRC 2.50 1.10
❑ 67T Billy Masse OLY XRC .10 .05
❑ 68T Jack McDowell XRC .50 .23
❑ 69T Jack McKeon MG .10 .05
❑ 70T Larry McWilliams .10 .05
❑ 71T M.Morandini OLY XRC .50 .23
❑ 72T Keith Moreland .10 .05
❑ 73T Mike Morgan .10 .05
❑ 74T C.Nagy OLY XRC .50 .23
❑ 75T Al Nipper .10 .05
❑ 76T Russ Nixon MG .10 .05
❑ 77T Jesse Orosco .10 .05
❑ 78T Joe Orsulak .10 .05
❑ 79T Dave Palmer .10 .05
❑ 80T Mark Parent .10 .05

❑ 81T Dave Parker .20 .09
❑ 82T Dan Pasqua .10 .05
❑ 83T Melido Perez XRC* .10 .05
❑ 84T Steve Peters .10 .05
❑ 85T Dan Petry .10 .05
❑ 86T Gary Pettis .10 .05
❑ 87T Jeff Pico .10 .05
❑ 88T Jim Poole XRC OLY .20 .09
❑ 89T Ted Power .10 .05
❑ 90T Rafael Ramirez .10 .05
❑ 91T Dennis Rasmussen .10 .05
❑ 92T Jose Rijo .10 .05
❑ 93T Ernie Riles .10 .05
❑ 94T Luis Rivera .10 .05
❑ 95T D.Robbins XRC OLY .10 .05
❑ 96T Frank Robinson MG .30 .14
❑ 97T Cookie Rojas MG .10 .05
❑ 98T Chris Sabo XRC .20 .09
❑ 99T Mark Salas .10 .05
❑ 100T Luis Salazar .10 .05
❑ 101T Rafael Santana .10 .05
❑ 102T Nelson Santovenia .10 .05
❑ 103T Mackey Sasser XRC .10 .05
❑ 104T Calvin Schiraldi .10 .05
❑ 105T Mike Schooler .10 .05
❑ 106T S.Servais XRC OLY .10 .05
❑ 107T D.Silvestri XRC OLY .10 .05
❑ 108T Don Slaught .10 .05
❑ 109T J.Slusarski XRC OLY .10 .05
❑ 110T Lee Smith .20 .09
❑ 111T Pete Smith XRC* .10 .05
❑ 112T Jim Snyder MG .10 .05
❑ 113T E.Sprague OLY XRC .50 .23
❑ 114T Pete Stanicek .10 .05
❑ 115T Kurt Stillwell .10 .05
❑ 116T T.Stottlemyre XRC .50 .23
❑ 117T Bill Swift .10 .05
❑ 118T Pat Tabler .10 .05
❑ 119T Scott Terry .10 .05
❑ 120T Mickey Tettleton .10 .05
❑ 121T Dickie Thon .10 .05
❑ 122T Jeff Treadway XRC* .10 .05
❑ 123T Willie Upshaw .10 .05
❑ 124T R.Ventura OLY XRC 3.00 1.35
❑ 125T Ron Washington .10 .05
❑ 126T Walt Weiss XRC* .50 .23
❑ 127T Bob Welch .10 .05
❑ 128T David Wells XRC 2.00 .90
❑ 129T Glenn Wilson .10 .05
❑ 130T Ted Wood XRC OLY .10 .05
❑ 131T Don Zimmer MG .20 .09
❑ 132T Checklist 1T-132T .10 .05

1989 Topps

	MINT	NRMT
COMPLETE SET (792)	15.00	6.75
COMP.FACT.SET (792)	20.00	9.00

❑ 1 George Bell RB .05 .02
Slams 3 Opening Day HR's
❑ 2 Wade Boggs RB .10 .05
200 Hits 6th Straight Season
❑ 3 Gary Carter RB .10 .05
Career Putouts Record
❑ 4 Andre Dawson RB .10 .05
Logs Double Figures
in HR and SB
❑ 5 Orel Hershiser RB .10 .05
59 Scoreless Innings
❑ 6 Doug Jones RB UER .05 .02
Earns His 15th
Straight Save
(Photo actually
Chris Codiroli)
❑ 7 Kevin McReynolds RB .05 .02
Steals 21 Without
Being Caught
❑ 8 Dave Eiland .05 .02
❑ 9 Tim Teufel .05 .02
❑ 10 Andre Dawson .15 .07
❑ 11 Bruce Sutter .05 .02
❑ 12 Dale Sveum .05 .02
❑ 13 Doug Sisk .05 .02
❑ 14 Tom Kelly MG .05 .02
❑ 15 Robby Thompson .05 .02
❑ 16 Ron Robinson .05 .02
❑ 17 Brian Downing .05 .02
❑ 18 Rick Rhoden .05 .02
❑ 19 Greg Gagne .05 .02
❑ 20 Steve Bedrosian .05 .02
❑ 21 Chicago White Sox TL .05 .02
Greg Walker
❑ 22 Tim Crews .05 .02
❑ 23 Mike Fitzgerald .05 .02
❑ 24 Larry Andersen .05 .02
❑ 25 Frank White .10 .05
❑ 26 Dale Mohorcic .05 .02
❑ 27A Orestes Destrade .05 .02
(F* next to copyright) RC*
❑ 27B Orestes Destrade .05 .02
(E*F* next to
copyright) RC*
❑ 28 Mike Moore .05 .02
❑ 29 Kelly Gruber .05 .02
❑ 30 Dwight Gooden .10 .05
❑ 31 Terry Francona .10 .05
❑ 32 Dennis Rasmussen .05 .02
❑ 33 B.J. Surhoff .10 .05
❑ 34 Ken Williams .05 .02
❑ 35 John Tudor UER .05 .02
(With Red Sox in '84,should be
Pirates)
❑ 36 Mitch Webster .05 .02
❑ 37 Bob Stanley .05 .02
❑ 38 Paul Runge .05 .02
❑ 39 Mike Maddux .05 .02
❑ 40 Steve Sax .05 .02
❑ 41 Terry Mulholland .05 .02
❑ 42 Jim Eppard .05 .02
❑ 43 Guillermo Hernandez .05 .02
❑ 44 Jim Snyder MG .05 .02
❑ 45 Kal Daniels .05 .02
❑ 46 Mark Portugal .05 .02
❑ 47 Carney Lansford .10 .05
❑ 48 Tim Burke .05 .02
❑ 49 Craig Biggio RC .75 .35
❑ 50 George Bell .05 .02
❑ 51 California Angels TL .05 .02
Mark McLemore
❑ 52 Bob Brenly .05 .02
❑ 53 Ruben Sierra .05 .02
❑ 54 Steve Trout .05 .02
❑ 55 Julio Franco .05 .02
❑ 56 Pat Tabler .05 .02
❑ 57 Alejandro Pena .05 .02
❑ 58 Lee Mazzilli .05 .02
❑ 59 Mark Davis .05 .02
❑ 60 Tom Brunansky .05 .02
❑ 61 Neil Allen .05 .02
❑ 62 Alfredo Griffin .05 .02
❑ 63 Mark Clear .05 .02
❑ 64 Alex Trevino .05 .02
❑ 65 Rick Reuschel .05 .02
❑ 66 Manny Trillo .05 .02
❑ 67 Dave Palmer .05 .02
❑ 68 Darrell Miller .05 .02
❑ 69 Jeff Ballard .05 .02
❑ 70 Mark McGwire 1.00 .45
❑ 71 Mike Boddicker .05 .02
❑ 72 John Moses .05 .02
❑ 73 Pascual Perez .05 .02
❑ 74 Nick Leyva MG .05 .02
❑ 75 Tom Henke .05 .02
❑ 76 Terry Blocker .05 .02
❑ 77 Doyle Alexander .05 .02
❑ 78 Jim Sundberg .05 .02
❑ 79 Scott Bankhead .05 .02
❑ 80 Cory Snyder .05 .02
❑ 81 Montreal Expos TL .10 .05
Tim Raines
❑ 82 Dave Leiper .05 .02
❑ 83 Jeff Blauser .10 .05
❑ 84 Bill Bene FDP .05 .02
❑ 85 Kevin McReynolds .05 .02
❑ 86 Al Nipper .05 .02
❑ 87 Larry Owen .05 .02
❑ 88 Darryl Hamilton RC* .05 .02
❑ 89 Dave LaPoint .05 .02
❑ 90 Vince Coleman UER .05 .02
(Wrong birth year)
❑ 91 Floyd Youmans .05 .02
❑ 92 Jeff Kunkel .05 .02
❑ 93 Ken Howell .05 .02
❑ 94 Chris Speier .05 .02
❑ 95 Gerald Young .05 .02
❑ 96 Rick Cerone .05 .02
❑ 97 Greg Mathews .05 .02
❑ 98 Larry Sheets .05 .02
❑ 99 Sherman Corbett .05 .02
❑ 100 Mike Schmidt .40 .18
❑ 101 Les Straker .05 .02
❑ 102 Mike Gallego .05 .02
❑ 103 Tim Birtsas .05 .02
❑ 104 Dallas Green MG .05 .02
❑ 105 Ron Darling .05 .02
❑ 106 Willie Upshaw .05 .02
❑ 107 Jose DeLeon .05 .02
❑ 108 Fred Manrique .05 .02
❑ 109 Hipolito Pena .05 .02
❑ 110 Paul Molitor .20 .09
❑ 111 Cincinnati Reds TL .05 .02
Eric Davis
(Swinging bat)
❑ 112 Jim Presley .05 .02
❑ 113 Lloyd Moseby .05 .02
❑ 114 Bob Kipper .05 .02
❑ 115 Jody Davis .05 .02
❑ 116 Jeff Montgomery .10 .05
❑ 117 Dave Anderson .05 .02
❑ 118 Checklist 1-132 .05 .02
❑ 119 Terry Puhl .05 .02
❑ 120 Frank Viola .05 .02
❑ 121 Garry Templeton .05 .02
❑ 122 Lance Johnson .10 .05
❑ 123 Spike Owen .05 .02
❑ 124 Jim Traber .05 .02
❑ 125 Mike Krukow .05 .02
❑ 126 Sid Bream .05 .02
❑ 127 Walt Terrell .05 .02
❑ 128 Milt Thompson .05 .02
❑ 129 Terry Clark .05 .02
❑ 130 Gerald Perry .05 .02
❑ 131 Dave Otto .05 .02
❑ 132 Curt Ford .05 .02
❑ 133 Bill Long .05 .02
❑ 134 Don Zimmer MG .05 .02
❑ 135 Jose Rijo .05 .02
❑ 136 Joey Meyer .05 .02
❑ 137 Geno Petralli .05 .02
❑ 138 Wallace Johnson .05 .02
❑ 139 Mike Flanagan .05 .02
❑ 140 Shawon Dunston .05 .02
❑ 141 Cleveland Indians TL .05 .02
Brook Jacoby
❑ 142 Mike Diaz .05 .02
❑ 143 Mike Campbell .05 .02
❑ 144 Jay Bell .15 .07
❑ 145 Dave Stewart .10 .05
❑ 146 Gary Pettis .05 .02
❑ 147 DeWayne Buice .05 .02
❑ 148 Bill Pecota .05 .02
❑ 149 Doug Dascenzo .05 .02
❑ 150 Fernando Valenzuela .10 .05
❑ 151 Terry McGriff .05 .02
❑ 152 Mark Thurmond .05 .02
❑ 153 Jim Pankovits .05 .02
❑ 154 Don Carman .05 .02
❑ 155 Marty Barrett .05 .02
❑ 156 Dave Gallagher .05 .02

❑ 157 Tom Glavine .20 .09
❑ 158 Mike Aldrete .05 .02
❑ 159 Pat Clements .05 .02
❑ 160 Jeffrey Leonard .05 .02
❑ 161 Gregg Olson RC FDP UER .20 .09
(Born Scribner, NE,
should be Omaha, NE
❑ 162 John Davis .05 .02
❑ 163 Bob Forsch .05 .02
❑ 164 Hal Lanier MG .05 .02
❑ 165 Mike Dunne .05 .02
❑ 166 Doug Jennings .05 .02
❑ 167 Steve Searcy FS .05 .02
❑ 168 Willie Wilson .05 .02
❑ 169 Mike Jackson .05 .02
❑ 170 Tony Fernandez .05 .02
❑ 171 Atlanta Braves TL .05 .02
Andres Thomas
❑ 172 Frank Williams .05 .02
❑ 173 Mel Hall .05 .02
❑ 174 Todd Burns .05 .02
❑ 175 John Shelby .05 .02
❑ 176 Jeff Parrett .05 .02
❑ 177 Monty Fariss FDP .05 .02
❑ 178 Mark Grant .05 .02
❑ 179 Ozzie Virgil .05 .02
❑ 180 Mike Scott .05 .02
❑ 181 Craig Worthington .05 .02
❑ 182 Bob McClure .05 .02
❑ 183 Oddibe McDowell .05 .02
❑ 184 John Costello .05 .02
❑ 185 Claudell Washington .05 .02
❑ 186 Pat Perry .05 .02
❑ 187 Darren Daulton .10 .05
❑ 188 Dennis Lamp .05 .02
❑ 189 Kevin Mitchell .10 .05
❑ 190 Mike Witt .05 .02
❑ 191 Sil Campusano .05 .02
❑ 192 Paul Mirabella .05 .02
❑ 193 Sparky Anderson MG .10 .05
UER (553 Salazer)
❑ 194 Greg W. Harris RC .05 .02
❑ 195 Ozzie Guillen .05 .02
❑ 196 Denny Walling .05 .02
❑ 197 Neal Heaton .05 .02
❑ 198 Danny Heep .05 .02
❑ 199 Mike Schooler RC* .05 .02
❑ 200 George Brett .40 .18
❑ 201 Blue Jays TL .05 .02
Kelly Gruber
❑ 202 Brad Moore .05 .02
❑ 203 Rob Ducey .05 .02
❑ 204 Brad Havens .05 .02
❑ 205 Dwight Evans .10 .05
❑ 206 Roberto Alomar .30 .14
❑ 207 Terry Leach .05 .02
❑ 208 Tom Pagnozzi .05 .02
❑ 209 Jeff Bittiger .05 .02
❑ 210 Dale Murphy .20 .09
❑ 211 Mike Pagliarulo .05 .02
❑ 212 Scott Sanderson .05 .02
❑ 213 Rene Gonzales .05 .02
❑ 214 Charlie O'Brien .05 .02
❑ 215 Kevin Gross .05 .02
❑ 216 Jack Howell .05 .02
❑ 217 Joe Price .05 .02
❑ 218 Mike LaValliere .05 .02
❑ 219 Jim Clancy .05 .02
❑ 220 Gary Gaetti .10 .05
❑ 221 Cecil Espy .05 .02
❑ 222 Mark Lewis FDP RC .10 .05
❑ 223 Jay Buhner .10 .05
❑ 224 Tony LaRussa MG .10 .05
❑ 225 Ramon Martinez RC .25 .11
❑ 226 Bill Doran .05 .02
❑ 227 John Farrell .05 .02
❑ 228 Nelson Santovenia .05 .02
❑ 229 Jimmy Key .10 .05
❑ 230 Ozzie Smith .25 .11
❑ 231 San Diego Padres TL .20 .09
Roberto Alomar
(Gary Carter at plate)
❑ 232 Ricky Horton .05 .02
❑ 233 Gregg Jefferies FS .10 .05
❑ 234 Tom Browning .05 .02
❑ 235 John Kruk .10 .05
❑ 236 Charles Hudson .05 .02
❑ 237 Glenn Hubbard .05 .02
❑ 238 Eric King .05 .02
❑ 239 Tim Laudner .05 .02
❑ 240 Greg Maddux .60 .25
❑ 241 Brett Butler .10 .05
❑ 242 Ed VandeBerg .05 .02
❑ 243 Bob Boone .10 .05
❑ 244 Jim Acker .05 .02
❑ 245 Jim Rice .10 .05
❑ 246 Rey Quinones .05 .02
❑ 247 Shawn Hillegas .05 .02
❑ 248 Tony Phillips .05 .02
❑ 249 Tim Leary .05 .02
❑ 250 Cal Ripken .75 .35
❑ 251 John Dopson .05 .02
❑ 252 Billy Hatcher .05 .02
❑ 253 Jose Alvarez .05 .02
❑ 254 Tom Lasorda MG .20 .09
❑ 255 Ron Guidry .10 .05
❑ 256 Benny Santiago .05 .02
❑ 257 Rick Aguilera .10 .05
❑ 258 Checklist 133-264 .05 .02
❑ 259 Larry McWilliams .05 .02
❑ 260 Dave Winfield .20 .09
❑ 261 St.Louis Cardinals TL .05 .02
Tom Brunansky
(With Luis Alicea)
❑ 262 Jeff Pico .05 .02
❑ 263 Mike Felder .05 .02
❑ 264 Rob Dibble RC* .10 .05
❑ 265 Kent Hrbek .10 .05
❑ 266 Luis Aquino .05 .02
❑ 267 Jeff M. Robinson .05 .02
❑ 268 N. Keith Miller .05 .02
❑ 269 Tom Bolton .05 .02
❑ 270 Wally Joyner .10 .05
❑ 271 Jay Tibbs .05 .02
❑ 272 Ron Hassey .05 .02
❑ 273 Jose Lind .05 .02
❑ 274 Mark Eichhorn .05 .02
❑ 275 Danny Tartabull UER .05 .02
(Born San Juan, PR
should be Miami, FL)
❑ 276 Paul Kilgus .05 .02
❑ 277 Mike Davis .05 .02
❑ 278 Andy McGaffigan .05 .02
❑ 279 Scott Bradley .05 .02
❑ 280 Bob Knepper .05 .02
❑ 281 Gary Redus .05 .02
❑ 282 Cris Carpenter RC* .05 .02
❑ 283 Andy Allanson .05 .02
❑ 284 Jim Leyland MG .10 .05
❑ 285 John Candelaria .05 .02
❑ 286 Darrin Jackson .05 .02
❑ 287 Juan Nieves .05 .02
❑ 288 Pat Sheridan .05 .02
❑ 289 Ernie Whitt .05 .02
❑ 290 John Franco .10 .05
❑ 291 New York Mets TL .10 .05
Darryl Strawberry
(With Keith Hernandez
and Kevin McReynolds)
❑ 292 Jim Corsi .05 .02
❑ 293 Glenn Wilson .05 .02
❑ 294 Juan Berenguer .05 .02
❑ 295 Scott Fletcher .05 .02
❑ 296 Ron Gant .10 .05
❑ 297 Oswald Peraza .05 .02
❑ 298 Chris James .05 .02
❑ 299 Steve Ellsworth .05 .02
❑ 300 Darryl Strawberry .10 .05
❑ 301 Charlie Leibrandt .05 .02
❑ 302 Gary Ward .05 .02
❑ 303 Felix Fermin .05 .02
❑ 304 Joel Youngblood .05 .02
❑ 305 Dave Smith .05 .02
❑ 306 Tracy Woodson .05 .02
❑ 307 Lance McCullers .05 .02
❑ 308 Ron Karkovice .05 .02
❑ 309 Mario Diaz .05 .02
❑ 310 Rafael Palmeiro .25 .11
❑ 311 Chris Bosio .05 .02
❑ 312 Tom Lawless .05 .02
❑ 313 Dennis Martinez .10 .05
❑ 314 Bobby Valentine MG .05 .02
❑ 315 Greg Swindell .05 .02
❑ 316 Walt Weiss .05 .02
❑ 317 Jack Armstrong RC* .05 .02
❑ 318 Gene Larkin .05 .02
❑ 319 Greg Booker .05 .02
❑ 320 Lou Whitaker .10 .05
❑ 321 Boston Red Sox TL .05 .02
Jody Reed
❑ 322 John Smiley .05 .02
❑ 323 Gary Thurman .05 .02
❑ 324 Bob Milacki .05 .02
❑ 325 Jesse Barfield .05 .02
❑ 326 Dennis Boyd .05 .02
❑ 327 Mark Lemke RC .15 .07
❑ 328 Rick Honeycutt .05 .02
❑ 329 Bob Melvin .05 .02
❑ 330 Eric Davis .10 .05
❑ 331 Curt Wilkerson .05 .02
❑ 332 Tony Armas .05 .02
❑ 333 Bob Ojeda .05 .02
❑ 334 Steve Lyons .05 .02
❑ 335 Dave Righetti .05 .02
❑ 336 Steve Balboni .05 .02
❑ 337 Calvin Schiraldi .05 .02
❑ 338 Jim Adduci .05 .02
❑ 339 Scott Bailes .05 .02
❑ 340 Kirk Gibson .10 .05
❑ 341 Jim Deshaies .05 .02
❑ 342 Tom Brookens .05 .02
❑ 343 Gary Sheffield FS RC 1.00 .45
❑ 344 Tom Trebelhorn MG .05 .02
❑ 345 Charlie Hough .10 .05
❑ 346 Rex Hudler .05 .02
❑ 347 John Cerutti .05 .02
❑ 348 Ed Hearn .05 .02
❑ 349 Ron Jones .05 .02
❑ 350 Andy Van Slyke .10 .05
❑ 351 San Fran. Giants TL .05 .02
Bob Melvin
(With Bill Fahey CO)
❑ 352 Rick Schu .05 .02
❑ 353 Marvell Wynne .05 .02
❑ 354 Larry Parrish .05 .02
❑ 355 Mark Langston .05 .02
❑ 356 Kevin Elster .05 .02
❑ 357 Jerry Reuss .05 .02
❑ 358 Ricky Jordan RC* .10 .05
❑ 359 Tommy John .10 .05
❑ 360 Ryne Sandberg .25 .11
❑ 361 Kelly Downs .05 .02
❑ 362 Jack Lazorko .05 .02
❑ 363 Rich Yett .05 .02
❑ 364 Rob Deer .05 .02
❑ 365 Mike Henneman .05 .02
❑ 366 Herm Winningham .05 .02
❑ 367 Johnny Paredes .05 .02
❑ 368 Brian Holton .05 .02
❑ 369 Ken Caminiti .10 .05
❑ 370 Dennis Eckersley .15 .07
❑ 371 Manny Lee .05 .02
❑ 372 Craig Lefferts .05 .02
❑ 373 Tracy Jones .05 .02
❑ 374 John Wathan MG .05 .02
❑ 375 Terry Pendleton .10 .05
❑ 376 Steve Lombardozzi .05 .02
❑ 377 Mike Smithson .05 .02
❑ 378 Checklist 265-396 .05 .02
❑ 379 Tim Flannery .05 .02
❑ 380 Rickey Henderson .40 .18
❑ 381 Baltimore Orioles TL .05 .02
Larry Sheets
❑ 382 John Smoltz RC .40 .18
❑ 383 Howard Johnson .05 .02
❑ 384 Mark Salas .05 .02
❑ 385 Von Hayes .05 .02
❑ 386 Andres Galarraga AS .05 .02
❑ 387 Ryne Sandberg AS .15 .07
❑ 388 Bobby Bonilla AS .10 .05
❑ 389 Ozzie Smith AS .15 .07
❑ 390 Darryl Strawberry AS .05 .02
❑ 391 Andre Dawson AS .10 .05
❑ 392 Andy Van Slyke AS .05 .02
❑ 393 Gary Carter AS .10 .05
❑ 394 Orel Hershiser AS .10 .05
❑ 395 Danny Jackson AS .05 .02
❑ 396 Kirk Gibson AS .10 .05

❑ 397 Don Mattingly AS .15 .07
❑ 398 Julio Franco AS .05 .02
❑ 399 Wade Boggs AS .10 .05
❑ 400 Alan Trammell AS .05 .02
❑ 401 Jose Canseco AS .10 .05
❑ 402 Mike Greenwell AS .05 .02
❑ 403 Kirby Puckett AS .25 .11
❑ 404 Bob Boone AS .05 .02
❑ 405 Roger Clemens AS .25 .11
❑ 406 Frank Viola AS .05 .02
❑ 407 Dave Winfield AS .10 .05
❑ 408 Greg Walker .05 .02
❑ 409 Ken Dayley .05 .02
❑ 410 Jack Clark .05 .02
❑ 411 Mitch Williams .05 .02
❑ 412 Barry Lyons .05 .02
❑ 413 Mike Kingery .05 .02
❑ 414 Jim Fregosi MG .05 .02
❑ 415 Rich Gossage .10 .05
❑ 416 Fred Lynn .05 .02
❑ 417 Mike LaCoss .05 .02
❑ 418 Bob Dernier .05 .02
❑ 419 Tom Filer .05 .02
❑ 420 Joe Carter .15 .07
❑ 421 Kirk McCaskill .05 .02
❑ 422 Bo Diaz .05 .02
❑ 423 Brian Fisher .05 .02
❑ 424 Luis Polonia UER .05 .02
(Wrong birthdate)
❑ 425 Jay Howell .05 .02
❑ 426 Dan Gladden .05 .02
❑ 427 Eric Show .05 .02
❑ 428 Craig Reynolds .05 .02
❑ 429 Minnesota Twins TL .05 .02
Greg Gagne
(Taking throw at 2nd)
❑ 430 Mark Gubicza .05 .02
❑ 431 Luis Rivera .05 .02
❑ 432 Chad Kreuter RC .05 .02
❑ 433 Albert Hall .05 .02
❑ 434 Ken Patterson .05 .02
❑ 435 Len Dykstra .10 .05
❑ 436 Bobby Meacham .05 .02
❑ 437 Andy Benes FDP RC .25 .11
❑ 438 Greg Gross .05 .02
❑ 439 Frank DiPino .05 .02
❑ 440 Bobby Bonilla .10 .05
❑ 441 Jerry Reed .05 .02
❑ 442 Jose Oquendo .05 .02
❑ 443 Rod Nichols .05 .02
❑ 444 Moose Stubing MG .05 .02
❑ 445 Matt Nokes .05 .02
❑ 446 Rob Murphy .05 .02
❑ 447 Donell Nixon .05 .02
❑ 448 Eric Plunk .05 .02
❑ 449 Carmelo Martinez .05 .02
❑ 450 Roger Clemens .50 .23
❑ 451 Mark Davidson .05 .02
❑ 452 Israel Sanchez .05 .02
❑ 453 Tom Prince .05 .02
❑ 454 Paul Assenmacher .05 .02
❑ 455 Johnny Ray .05 .02
❑ 456 Tim Belcher .05 .02
❑ 457 Mackey Sasser .05 .02
❑ 458 Donn Pall .05 .02
❑ 459 Seattle Mariners TL .05 .02
Dave Valle
❑ 460 Dave Stieb .05 .02
❑ 461 Buddy Bell .10 .05
❑ 462 Jose Guzman .05 .02
❑ 463 Steve Lake .05 .02
❑ 464 Bryn Smith .05 .02
❑ 465 Mark Grace .20 .09
❑ 466 Chuck Crim .05 .02
❑ 467 Jim Walewander .05 .02
❑ 468 Henry Cotto .05 .02
❑ 469 Jose Bautista .05 .02
❑ 470 Lance Parrish .05 .02
❑ 471 Steve Curry .05 .02
❑ 472 Brian Harper .05 .02
❑ 473 Don Robinson .05 .02
❑ 474 Bob Rodgers MG .05 .02
❑ 475 Dave Parker .10 .05
❑ 476 Jon Perlman .05 .02
❑ 477 Dick Schofield .05 .02
❑ 478 Doug Drabek .05 .02
❑ 479 Mike Macfarlane RC* .05 .02
❑ 480 Keith Hernandez .10 .05
❑ 481 Chris Brown .05 .02
❑ 482 Steve Peters .05 .02
❑ 483 Mickey Hatcher .05 .02
❑ 484 Steve Shields .05 .02
❑ 485 Hubie Brooks .05 .02
❑ 486 Jack McDowell .10 .05
❑ 487 Scott Lusader .05 .02
❑ 488 Kevin Coffman .05 .02
Now with Cubs
❑ 489 Phila. Phillies TL .10 .05
Mike Schmidt
❑ 490 Chris Sabo RC* .05 .02
❑ 491 Mike Birkbeck .05 .02
❑ 492 Alan Ashby .05 .02
❑ 493 Todd Benzinger .05 .02
❑ 494 Shane Rawley .05 .02
❑ 495 Candy Maldonado .05 .02
❑ 496 Dwayne Henry .05 .02
❑ 497 Pete Stanicek .05 .02
❑ 498 Dave Valle .05 .02
❑ 499 Don Heinkel .05 .02
❑ 500 Jose Canseco .20 .09
❑ 501 Vance Law .05 .02
❑ 502 Duane Ward .05 .02
❑ 503 Al Newman .05 .02
❑ 504 Bob Walk .05 .02
❑ 505 Pete Rose MG .50 .23
❑ 506 Kirt Manwaring .05 .02
❑ 507 Steve Farr .05 .02
❑ 508 Wally Backman .05 .02
❑ 509 Bud Black .05 .02
❑ 510 Bob Horner .05 .02
❑ 511 Richard Dotson .05 .02
❑ 512 Donnie Hill .05 .02
❑ 513 Jesse Orosco .05 .02
❑ 514 Chet Lemon .05 .02
❑ 515 Barry Larkin .20 .09
❑ 516 Eddie Whitson .05 .02
❑ 517 Greg Brock .05 .02
❑ 518 Bruce Ruffin .05 .02
❑ 519 New York Yankees TL .05 .02
Willie Randolph
❑ 520 Rick Sutcliffe .10 .05
❑ 521 Mickey Tettleton .05 .02
❑ 522 Randy Kramer .05 .02
❑ 523 Andres Thomas .05 .02
❑ 524 Checklist 397-528 .05 .02
❑ 525 Chili Davis .10 .05
❑ 526 Wes Gardner .05 .02
❑ 527 Dave Henderson .05 .02
❑ 528 Luis Medina .05 .02
(Lower left front
has white triangle)
❑ 529 Tom Foley .05 .02
❑ 530 Nolan Ryan 1.00 .45
❑ 531 Dave Hengel .05 .02
❑ 532 Jerry Browne .05 .02
❑ 533 Andy Hawkins .05 .02
❑ 534 Doc Edwards MG .05 .02
❑ 535 Todd Worrell UER .05 .02
(4 wins in '88,
should be 5)
❑ 536 Joel Skinner .05 .02
❑ 537 Pete Smith .05 .02
❑ 538 Juan Castillo .05 .02
❑ 539 Barry Jones .05 .02
❑ 540 Bo Jackson .15 .07
❑ 541 Cecil Fielder .10 .05
❑ 542 Todd Frohwirth .05 .02
❑ 543 Damon Berryhill .05 .02
❑ 544 Jeff Sellers .05 .02
❑ 545 Mookie Wilson .10 .05
❑ 546 Mark Williamson .05 .02
❑ 547 Mark McLemore .05 .02
❑ 548 Bobby Witt .05 .02
❑ 549 Chicago Cubs TL .05 .02
Jamie Moyer
(Pitching)
❑ 550 Orel Hershiser .10 .05
❑ 551 Randy Ready .05 .02
❑ 552 Greg Cadaret .05 .02
❑ 553 Luis Salazar .05 .02
❑ 554 Nick Esasky .05 .02
❑ 555 Bert Blyleven .10 .05
❑ 556 Bruce Fields .05 .02
❑ 557 Keith A. Miller .05 .02
❑ 558 Dan Pasqua .05 .02
❑ 559 Juan Agosto .05 .02
❑ 560 Tim Raines .10 .05
❑ 561 Luis Aguayo .05 .02
❑ 562 Danny Cox .05 .02
❑ 563 Bill Schroeder .05 .02
❑ 564 Russ Nixon MG .05 .02
❑ 565 Jeff Russell .05 .02
❑ 566 Al Pedrique .05 .02
❑ 567 David Wells UER .10 .05
(Complete Pitching
Recor)
❑ 568 Mickey Brantley .05 .02
❑ 569 German Jimenez .05 .02
❑ 570 Tony Gwynn UER .40 .18
('88 average should
be italicized as
league leader)
❑ 571 Billy Ripken .05 .02
❑ 572 Atlee Hammaker .05 .02
❑ 573 Jim Abbott FDP RC* .20 .09
❑ 574 Dave Clark .05 .02
❑ 575 Juan Samuel .05 .02
❑ 576 Greg Minton .05 .02
❑ 577 Randy Bush .05 .02
❑ 578 John Morris .05 .02
❑ 579 Houston Astros TL .05 .02
Glenn Davis
(Batting stance)
❑ 580 Harold Reynolds .05 .02
❑ 581 Gene Nelson .05 .02
❑ 582 Mike Marshall .05 .02
❑ 583 Paul Gibson .05 .02
❑ 584 Randy Velarde UER .05 .02
(Signed 1935,
should be 1985)
❑ 585 Harold Baines .10 .05
❑ 586 Joe Boever .05 .02
❑ 587 Mike Stanley .05 .02
❑ 588 Luis Alicea RC* .05 .02
❑ 589 Dave Meads .05 .02
❑ 590 Andres Galarraga .15 .07
❑ 591 Jeff Musselman .05 .02
❑ 592 John Cangelosi .05 .02
❑ 593 Drew Hall .05 .02
❑ 594 Jimy Williams MG .05 .02
❑ 595 Teddy Higuera .05 .02
❑ 596 Kurt Stillwell .05 .02
❑ 597 Terry Taylor .05 .02
❑ 598 Ken Gerhart .05 .02
❑ 599 Tom Candiotti .05 .02
❑ 600 Wade Boggs .20 .09
❑ 601 Dave Dravecky .10 .05
❑ 602 Devon White .10 .05
❑ 603 Frank Tanana .05 .02
❑ 604 Paul O'Neill .20 .09
❑ 605A Bob Welch ERR 2.00 .90
(Missing line on back
Complete M.L. Pitching Record
❑ 605B Bob Welch COR .05 .02
❑ 606 Rick Dempsey .05 .02
❑ 607 Willie Ansley FDP RC .05 .02
❑ 608 Phil Bradley .05 .02
❑ 609 Detroit Tigers TL .05 .02
Frank Tanana
(With Alan Trammell
and Mike Heath)
❑ 610 Randy Myers .10 .05
❑ 611 Don Slaught .05 .02
❑ 612 Dan Quisenberry .05 .02
❑ 613 Gary Varsho .05 .02
❑ 614 Joe Hesketh .05 .02
❑ 615 Robin Yount .20 .09
❑ 616 Steve Rosenberg .05 .02
❑ 617 Mark Parent .05 .02
❑ 618 Rance Mulliniks .05 .02
❑ 619 Checklist 529-660 .05 .02
❑ 620 Barry Bonds .75 .35
❑ 621 Rick Mahler .05 .02
❑ 622 Stan Javier .05 .02
❑ 623 Fred Toliver .05 .02
❑ 624 Jack McKeon MG .05 .02
❑ 625 Eddie Murray .20 .09
❑ 626 Jeff Reed .05 .02

❑ 627 Greg A. Harris .05 .02
❑ 628 Matt Williams .15 .07
❑ 629 Pete O'Brien .05 .02
❑ 630 Mike Greenwell .05 .02
❑ 631 Dave Bergman .05 .02
❑ 632 Bryan Harvey RC* .05 .02
❑ 633 Daryl Boston .05 .02
❑ 634 Marvin Freeman .05 .02
❑ 635 Willie Randolph .10 .05
❑ 636 Bill Wilkinson .05 .02
❑ 637 Carmen Castillo .05 .02
❑ 638 Floyd Bannister .05 .02
❑ 639 Oakland A's TL .05 .02
Walt Weiss
❑ 640 Willie McGee .10 .05
❑ 641 Curt Young .05 .02
❑ 642 Argenis Salazar .05 .02
❑ 643 Louie Meadows .05 .02
❑ 644 Lloyd McClendon .05 .02
❑ 645 Jack Morris .10 .05
❑ 646 Kevin Bass .05 .02
❑ 647 Randy Johnson RC 2.50 1.10
❑ 648 Sandy Alomar FS RC .25 .11
❑ 649 Stewart Cliburn .05 .02
❑ 650 Kirby Puckett .50 .23
❑ 651 Tom Niedenfuer .05 .02
❑ 652 Rich Gedman .05 .02
❑ 653 Tommy Barrett .05 .02
❑ 654 Whitey Herzog MG .05 .02
❑ 655 Dave Magadan .05 .02
❑ 656 Ivan Calderon .05 .02
❑ 657 Joe Magrane .05 .02
❑ 658 R.J. Reynolds .05 .02
❑ 659 Al Leiter .20 .09
❑ 660 Will Clark .20 .09
❑ 661 D.Gooden TBC84 .05 .02
❑ 662 Lou Brock TBC79 .20 .09
❑ 663 Hank Aaron TBC74 .20 .09
❑ 664 Gil Hodges TBC69 .15 .07
❑ 665A Tony Oliva TBC64 2.00 .90
ERR (fabricated card is enlarged version of Oliva's 64T card; Topps copyright missing)
❑ 665B Tony Oliva TBC64 .10 .05
COR (fabricated card)
❑ 666 Randy St.Claire .05 .02
❑ 667 Dwayne Murphy .05 .02
❑ 668 Mike Bielecki .05 .02
❑ 669 L.A. Dodgers TL .10 .05
Orel Hershiser (Mound conference with Mike Scioscia)
❑ 670 Kevin Seitzer .05 .02
❑ 671 Jim Gantner .05 .02
❑ 672 Allan Anderson .05 .02
❑ 673 Don Baylor .10 .05
❑ 674 Otis Nixon .05 .02
❑ 675 Bruce Hurst .05 .02
❑ 676 Ernie Riles .05 .02
❑ 677 Dave Schmidt .05 .02
❑ 678 Dion James .05 .02
❑ 679 Willie Fraser .05 .02
❑ 680 Gary Carter .15 .07
❑ 681 Jeff D. Robinson .05 .02
❑ 682 Rick Leach .05 .02
❑ 683 Jose Cecena .05 .02
❑ 684 Dave Johnson MG .05 .02
❑ 685 Jeff Treadway .05 .02
❑ 686 Scott Terry .05 .02
❑ 687 Alvin Davis .05 .02
❑ 688 Zane Smith .05 .02
❑ 689A Stan Jefferson .05 .02
(Pink triangle on front bottom left)
❑ 689B Stan Jefferson .05 .02
(Violet triangle on front bottom left)
❑ 690 Doug Jones .05 .02
❑ 691 Roberto Kelly UER .05 .02
(83 Oneonita)
❑ 692 Steve Ontiveros .05 .02
❑ 693 Pat Borders RC* .10 .05
❑ 694 Les Lancaster .05 .02
❑ 695 Carlton Fisk .20 .09
❑ 696 Don August .05 .02
❑ 697A Franklin Stubbs .05 .02
(Team name on front in white)
❑ 697B Franklin Stubbs .05 .02
(Team name on front in gray)
❑ 698 Keith Atherton .05 .02
❑ 699 Pittsburgh Pirates TL .05 .02
Al Pedrique (Tony Gwynn sliding)
❑ 700 Don Mattingly .50 .23
❑ 701 Storm Davis .05 .02
❑ 702 Jamie Quirk .05 .02
❑ 703 Scott Garrelts .05 .02
❑ 704 Carlos Quintana RC .05 .02
❑ 705 Terry Kennedy .05 .02
❑ 706 Pete Incaviglia .05 .02
❑ 707 Steve Jeltz .05 .02
❑ 708 Chuck Finley .10 .05
❑ 709 Tom Herr .05 .02
❑ 710 David Cone .10 .05
❑ 711 Candy Sierra .05 .02
❑ 712 Bill Swift .05 .02
❑ 713 Ty Griffin FDP .05 .02
❑ 714 Joe Morgan MG .05 .02
❑ 715 Tony Pena .05 .02
❑ 716 Wayne Tolleson .05 .02
❑ 717 Jamie Moyer .05 .02
❑ 718 Glenn Braggs .05 .02
❑ 719 Danny Darwin .05 .02
❑ 720 Tim Wallach .05 .02
❑ 721 Ron Tingley .05 .02
❑ 722 Todd Stottlemyre .15 .07
❑ 723 Rafael Belliard .05 .02
❑ 724 Jerry Don Gleaton .05 .02
❑ 725 Terry Steinbach .10 .05
❑ 726 Dickie Thon .05 .02
❑ 727 Joe Orsulak .05 .02
❑ 728 Charlie Puleo .05 .02
❑ 729 Texas Rangers TL .05 .02
Steve Buechele (Inconsistent design, team name on front surrounded by black, should be white)
❑ 730 Danny Jackson .05 .02
❑ 731 Mike Young .05 .02
❑ 732 Steve Buechele .05 .02
❑ 733 Randy Bockus .05 .02
❑ 734 Jody Reed .05 .02
❑ 735 Roger McDowell .05 .02
❑ 736 Jeff Hamilton .05 .02
❑ 737 Norm Charlton RC .10 .05
❑ 738 Darnell Coles .05 .02
❑ 739 Brook Jacoby .05 .02
❑ 740 Dan Plesac .05 .02
❑ 741 Ken Phelps .05 .02
❑ 742 Mike Harkey FS RC .05 .02
❑ 743 Mike Heath .05 .02
❑ 744 Roger Craig MG .05 .02
❑ 745 Fred McGriff .20 .09
❑ 746 G.Gonzalez UER .05 .02
Wrong birthdate
❑ 747 Wil Tejada .05 .02
❑ 748 Jimmy Jones .05 .02
❑ 749 Rafael Ramirez .05 .02
❑ 750 Bret Saberhagen .10 .05
❑ 751 Ken Oberkfell .05 .02
❑ 752 Jim Gott .05 .02
❑ 753 Jose Uribe .05 .02
❑ 754 Bob Brower .05 .02
❑ 755 Mike Scioscia .05 .02
❑ 756 Scott Medvin .05 .02
❑ 757 Brady Anderson RC .40 .18
❑ 758 Gene Walter .05 .02
❑ 759 Milw.Brewers TL .05 .02
Rob Deer
❑ 760 Lee Smith .10 .05
❑ 761 Dante Bichette RC .40 .18
❑ 762 Bobby Thigpen .05 .02
❑ 763 Dave Martinez .05 .02
❑ 764 Robin Ventura FDP RC .75 .35
❑ 765 Glenn Davis .05 .02
❑ 766 Cecilio Guante .05 .02
❑ 767 Mike Capel .05 .02
❑ 768 Bill Wegman .05 .02
❑ 769 Junior Ortiz .05 .02
❑ 770 Alan Trammell .15 .07
❑ 771 Ron Kittle .05 .02
❑ 772 Ron Oester .05 .02
❑ 773 Keith Moreland .05 .02
❑ 774 Frank Robinson MG .20 .09
❑ 775 Jeff Reardon .10 .05
❑ 776 Nelson Liriano .05 .02
❑ 777 Ted Power .05 .02
❑ 778 Bruce Benedict .05 .02
❑ 779 Craig McMurtry .05 .02
❑ 780 Pedro Guerrero .05 .02
❑ 781 Greg Briley .05 .02
❑ 782 Checklist 661-792 .05 .02
❑ 783 Trevor Wilson RC .05 .02
❑ 784 Steve Avery FDP RC .20 .09
❑ 785 Ellis Burks .15 .07
❑ 786 Melido Perez .05 .02
❑ 787 Dave West RC .05 .02
❑ 788 Mike Morgan .05 .02
❑ 789 Kansas City Royals TL .20 .09
Bo Jackson (Throwing)
❑ 790 Sid Fernandez .05 .02
❑ 791 Jim Lindeman .05 .02
❑ 792 Rafael Santana .05 .02

1989 Topps Traded

	MINT	NRMT
COMP.FACT.SET (132)	20.00	9.00

❑ 1T Don Aase .05 .02
❑ 2T Jim Abbott .20 .09
❑ 3T Kent Anderson .05 .02
❑ 4T Keith Atherton .05 .02
❑ 5T Wally Backman .05 .02
❑ 6T Steve Balboni .05 .02
❑ 7T Jesse Barfield .05 .02
❑ 8T Steve Bedrosian .05 .02
❑ 9T Todd Benzinger .05 .02
❑ 10T Geronimo Berroa .05 .02
❑ 11T Bert Blyleven .10 .05
❑ 12T Bob Boone .10 .05
❑ 13T Phil Bradley .05 .02
❑ 14T Jeff Brantley RC .15 .07
❑ 15T Kevin Brown .40 .18
❑ 16T Jerry Browne .05 .02
❑ 17T Chuck Cary .05 .02
❑ 18T Carmen Castillo .05 .02
❑ 19T Jim Clancy .05 .02
❑ 20T Jack Clark .05 .02
❑ 21T Bryan Clutterbuck .05 .02
❑ 22T Jody Davis .05 .02
❑ 23T Mike Devereaux .05 .02
❑ 24T Frank DiPino .05 .02
❑ 25T Benny Distefano .05 .02
❑ 26T John Dopson .05 .02
❑ 27T Len Dykstra .10 .05
❑ 28T Jim Eisenreich .05 .02
❑ 29T Nick Esasky .05 .02
❑ 30T Alvaro Espinoza .05 .02
❑ 31T Darrell Evans UER .10 .05
(Stat headings on back are for a pitcher)
❑ 32T Junior Felix RC .05 .02

❑ 33T Felix Fermin .05 .02
❑ 34T Julio Franco .05 .02
❑ 35T Terry Francona .10 .05
❑ 36T Cito Gaston MG .10 .05
❑ 37T Bob Geren UER .05 .02
(Photo actually Mike Fennell)
❑ 38T Tom Gordon RC .20 .09
❑ 39T Tommy Gregg .05 .02
❑ 40T Ken Griffey Sr. .10 .05
❑ 41T Ken Griffey Jr. RC 15.00 6.75
❑ 42T Kevin Gross .05 .02
❑ 43T Lee Guetterman .05 .02
❑ 44T Mel Hall .05 .02
❑ 45T Erik Hanson RC .10 .05
❑ 46T Gene Harris RC .05 .02
❑ 47T Andy Hawkins .05 .02
❑ 48T Rickey Henderson .40 .18
❑ 49T Tom Herr .05 .02
❑ 50T Ken Hill RC .20 .09
❑ 51T Brian Holman RC* .05 .02
❑ 52T Brian Holton .05 .02
❑ 53T Art Howe MG .05 .02
❑ 54T Ken Howell .05 .02
❑ 55T Bruce Hurst .05 .02
❑ 56T Chris James .05 .02
❑ 57T Randy Johnson 2.00 .90
❑ 58T Jimmy Jones .05 .02
❑ 59T Terry Kennedy .05 .02
❑ 60T Paul Kilgus .05 .02
❑ 61T Eric King .05 .02
❑ 62T Ron Kittle .05 .02
❑ 63T John Kruk .10 .05
❑ 64T Randy Kutcher .05 .02
❑ 65T Steve Lake .05 .02
❑ 66T Mark Langston .05 .02
❑ 67T Dave LaPoint .05 .02
❑ 68T Rick Leach .05 .02
❑ 69T Terry Leach .05 .02
❑ 70T Jim Lefebvre MG .05 .02
❑ 71T Al Leiter .20 .09
❑ 72T Jeffrey Leonard .05 .02
❑ 73T Derek Lilliquist RC .05 .02
❑ 74T Rick Mahler .05 .02
❑ 75T Tom McCarthy .05 .02
❑ 76T Lloyd McClendon .05 .02
❑ 77T Lance McCullers .05 .02
❑ 78T Oddibe McDowell .05 .02
❑ 79T Roger McDowell .05 .02
❑ 80T Larry McWilliams .05 .02
❑ 81T Randy Milligan .05 .02
❑ 82T Mike Moore .05 .02
❑ 83T Keith Moreland .05 .02
❑ 84T Mike Morgan .05 .02
❑ 85T Jamie Moyer .05 .02
❑ 86T Rob Murphy .05 .02
❑ 87T Eddie Murray .20 .09
❑ 88T Pete O'Brien .05 .02
❑ 89T Gregg Olson .20 .09
❑ 90T Steve Ontiveros .05 .02
❑ 91T Jesse Orosco .05 .02
❑ 92T Spike Owen .05 .02
❑ 93T Rafael Palmeiro .25 .11
❑ 94T Clay Parker .05 .02
❑ 95T Jeff Parrett .05 .02
❑ 96T Lance Parrish .05 .02
❑ 97T Dennis Powell .05 .02
❑ 98T Rey Quinones .05 .02
❑ 99T Doug Rader MG .05 .02
❑ 100T Willie Randolph .10 .05
❑ 101T Shane Rawley .05 .02
❑ 102T Randy Ready .05 .02
❑ 103T Bip Roberts .10 .05
❑ 104T Kenny Rogers RC .20 .09
❑ 105T Ed Romero .05 .02
❑ 106T Nolan Ryan 2.00 .90
❑ 107T Luis Salazar .05 .02
❑ 108T Juan Samuel .05 .02
❑ 109T Alex Sanchez .05 .02
❑ 110T Deion Sanders RC .50 .23
❑ 111T Steve Sax .05 .02
❑ 112T Rick Schu .05 .02
❑ 113T Dwight Smith RC .10 .05
❑ 114T Lonnie Smith .05 .02
❑ 115T Billy Spiers RC .05 .02
❑ 116T Kent Tekulve .05 .02
❑ 117T Walt Terrell .05 .02
❑ 118T Milt Thompson .05 .02
❑ 119T Dickie Thon .05 .02
❑ 120T Jeff Torborg MG .05 .02
❑ 121T Jeff Treadway .05 .02
❑ 122T Omar Vizquel RC .50 .23
❑ 123T Jerome Walton .20 .09
❑ 124T Gary Ward .05 .02
❑ 125T Claudell Washington .05 .02
❑ 126T Curt Wilkerson .05 .02
❑ 127T Eddie Williams .05 .02
❑ 128T Frank Williams .05 .02
❑ 129T Ken Williams .05 .02
❑ 130T Mitch Williams .05 .02
❑ 131T Steve Wilson .05 .02
❑ 132T Checklist 1T-132T .05 .02

1990 Topps

	MINT	NRMT
COMPLETE SET (792)	20.00	9.00
COMP.FACT.SET (792)	25.00	11.00
COMP.X-MAS.SET (792)	25.00	11.00

❑ 1 Nolan Ryan 1.00 .45
❑ 2 Nolan Ryan Salute .40 .18
New York Mets
❑ 3 Nolan Ryan Salute .40 .18
California Angels
❑ 4 Nolan Ryan Salute .40 .18
Houston Astros
❑ 5 Nolan Ryan Salute .40 .18
Texas Rangers UER
(Says Texas Stadium rather than Arlington Stadium)
❑ 6 Vince Coleman RB .05 .02
(50 consecutive SB's
❑ 7 Rickey Henderson RB .20 .09
(40 career leadoff HR's
❑ 8 Cal Ripken RB .20 .09
(20 or more homers for 8 consecutive years, record for shortstops)
❑ 9 Eric Plunk .05 .02
❑ 10 Barry Larkin .20 .09
❑ 11 Paul Gibson .05 .02
❑ 12 Joe Girardi .15 .07
❑ 13 Mark Williamson .05 .02
❑ 14 Mike Fetters RC .05 .02
❑ 15 Teddy Higuera .05 .02
❑ 16 Kent Anderson .05 .02
❑ 17 Kelly Downs .05 .02
❑ 18 Carlos Quintana .05 .02
❑ 19 Al Newman .05 .02
❑ 20 Mark Gubicza .05 .02
❑ 21 Jeff Torborg MG .05 .02
❑ 22 Bruce Ruffin .05 .02
❑ 23 Randy Velarde .05 .02
❑ 24 Joe Hesketh .05 .02
❑ 25 Willie Randolph .10 .05
❑ 26 Don Slaught .05 .02
❑ 27 Rick Leach .05 .02
❑ 28 Duane Ward .05 .02
❑ 29 John Cangelosi .05 .02
❑ 30 David Cone .10 .05
❑ 31 Henry Cotto .05 .02
❑ 32 John Farrell .05 .02
❑ 33 Greg Walker .05 .02
❑ 34 Tony Fossas .05 .02
❑ 35 Benito Santiago .05 .02
❑ 36 John Costello .05 .02
❑ 37 Domingo Ramos .05 .02
❑ 38 Wes Gardner .05 .02
❑ 39 Curt Ford .05 .02
❑ 40 Jay Howell .05 .02
❑ 41 Matt Williams .15 .07
❑ 42 Jeff M. Robinson .05 .02
❑ 43 Dante Bichette .20 .09
❑ 44 Roger Salkeld FDP RC .05 .02
❑ 45 Dave Parker UER .10 .05
(Born in Jackson, not Calhoun)
❑ 46 Rob Dibble .05 .02
❑ 47 Brian Harper .05 .02
❑ 48 Zane Smith .05 .02
❑ 49 Tom Lawless .05 .02
❑ 50 Glenn Davis .05 .02
❑ 51 Doug Rader MG .05 .02
❑ 52 Jack Daugherty .05 .02
❑ 53 Mike LaCoss .05 .02
❑ 54 Joel Skinner .05 .02
❑ 55 Darrell Evans UER .10 .05
(HR total should be 414, not 424)
❑ 56 Franklin Stubbs .05 .02
❑ 57 Greg Vaughn .20 .09
❑ 58 Keith Miller .05 .02
❑ 59 Ted Power .05 .02
❑ 60 George Brett .40 .18
❑ 61 Deion Sanders .20 .09
❑ 62 Ramon Martinez .05 .02
❑ 63 Mike Pagliarulo .05 .02
❑ 64 Danny Darwin .05 .02
❑ 65 Devon White .05 .02
❑ 66 Greg Litton .05 .02
❑ 67 Scott Sanderson .05 .02
❑ 68 Dave Henderson .05 .02
❑ 69 Todd Frohwirth .05 .02
❑ 70 Mike Greenwell .05 .02
❑ 71 Allan Anderson .05 .02
❑ 72 Jeff Huson RC .05 .02
❑ 73 Bob Milacki .05 .02
❑ 74 Jeff Jackson FDP RC .05 .02
❑ 75 Doug Jones .05 .02
❑ 76 Dave Valle .05 .02
❑ 77 Dave Bergman .05 .02
❑ 78 Mike Flanagan .05 .02
❑ 79 Ron Kittle .05 .02
❑ 80 Jeff Russell .05 .02
❑ 81 Bob Rodgers MG .05 .02
❑ 82 Scott Terry .05 .02
❑ 83 Hensley Meulens .05 .02
❑ 84 Ray Searage .05 .02
❑ 85 Juan Samuel .05 .02
❑ 86 Paul Kilgus .05 .02
❑ 87 Rick Luecken .05 .02
❑ 88 Glenn Braggs .05 .02
❑ 89 Clint Zavaras .05 .02
❑ 90 Jack Clark .10 .05
❑ 91 Steve Frey .05 .02
❑ 92 Mike Stanley .05 .02
❑ 93 Shawn Hillegas .05 .02
❑ 94 Herm Winningham .05 .02
❑ 95 Todd Worrell .05 .02
❑ 96 Jody Reed .05 .02
❑ 97 Curt Schilling 1.00 .45
❑ 98 Jose Gonzalez .05 .02
❑ 99 Rich Monteleone .05 .02
❑ 100 Will Clark .20 .09
❑ 101 Shane Rawley .05 .02
❑ 102 Stan Javier .05 .02
❑ 103 Marvin Freeman .05 .02
❑ 104 Bob Knepper .05 .02
❑ 105 Randy Myers .10 .05
❑ 106 Charlie O'Brien .05 .02
❑ 107 Fred Lynn .05 .02
❑ 108 Rod Nichols .05 .02
❑ 109 Roberto Kelly .05 .02
❑ 110 Tommy Helms MG .05 .02
❑ 111 Ed Whited .05 .02
❑ 112 Glenn Wilson .05 .02
❑ 113 Manny Lee .05 .02
❑ 114 Mike Bielecki .05 .02

❑	115	Tony Pena	.05	.02
❑	116	Floyd Bannister	.05	.02
❑	117	Mike Sharperson	.05	.02
❑	118	Erik Hanson	.05	.02
❑	119	Billy Hatcher	.05	.02
❑	120	John Franco	.10	.05
❑	121	Robin Ventura	.20	.09
❑	122	Shawn Abner	.05	.02
❑	123	Rich Gedman	.05	.02
❑	124	Dave Dravecky	.10	.05
❑	125	Kent Hrbek	.10	.05
❑	126	Randy Kramer	.05	.02
❑	127	Mike Devereaux	.05	.02
❑	128	Checklist 1	.05	.02
❑	129	Ron Jones	.05	.02
❑	130	Bert Blyleven	.10	.05
❑	131	Matt Nokes	.05	.02
❑	132	Lance Blankenship	.05	.02
❑	133	Ricky Horton	.05	.02
❑	134	E.Cunningham FDP RC	.05	.02
❑	135	Dave Magadan	.05	.02
❑	136	Kevin Brown	.20	.09
❑	137	Marty Pevey	.05	.02
❑	138	Al Leiter	.20	.09
❑	139	Greg Brock	.05	.02
❑	140	Andre Dawson	.15	.07
❑	141	John Hart MG	.05	.02
❑	142	Jeff Wetherby	.05	.02
❑	143	Rafael Belliard	.05	.02
❑	144	Bud Black	.05	.02
❑	145	Terry Steinbach	.05	.02
❑	146	Rob Richie	.05	.02
❑	147	Chuck Finley	.10	.05
❑	148	Edgar Martinez	.15	.07
❑	149	Steve Farr	.05	.02
❑	150	Kirk Gibson	.10	.05
❑	151	Rick Mahler	.05	.02
❑	152	Lonnie Smith	.05	.02
❑	153	Randy Milligan	.05	.02
❑	154	Mike Maddux	.05	.02
❑	155	Ellis Burks	.15	.07
❑	156	Ken Patterson	.05	.02
❑	157	Craig Biggio	.15	.07
❑	158	Craig Lefferts	.05	.02
❑	159	Mike Felder	.05	.02
❑	160	Dave Righetti	.05	.02
❑	161	Harold Reynolds	.05	.02
❑	162	Todd Zeile	.10	.05
❑	163	Phil Bradley	.05	.02
❑	164	Jeff Juden FDP RC	.05	.02
❑	165	Walt Weiss	.05	.02
❑	166	Bobby Witt	.05	.02
❑	167	Kevin Appier	.15	.07
❑	168	Jose Lind	.05	.02
❑	169	Richard Dotson	.05	.02
❑	170	George Bell	.05	.02
❑	171	Russ Nixon MG	.05	.02
❑	172	Tom Lampkin	.05	.02
❑	173	Tim Belcher	.05	.02
❑	174	Jeff Kunkel	.05	.02
❑	175	Mike Moore	.05	.02
❑	176	Luis Quinones	.05	.02
❑	177	Mike Henneman	.05	.02
❑	178	Chris James	.05	.02
❑	179	Brian Holton	.05	.02
❑	180	Tim Raines	.10	.05
❑	181	Juan Agosto	.05	.02
❑	182	Mookie Wilson	.10	.05
❑	183	Steve Lake	.05	.02
❑	184	Danny Cox	.05	.02
❑	185	Ruben Sierra	.05	.02
❑	186	Dave LaPoint	.05	.02
❑	187	Rick Wrona	.05	.02
❑	188	Mike Smithson	.05	.02
❑	189	Dick Schofield	.05	.02
❑	190	Rick Reuschel	.05	.02
❑	191	Pat Borders	.05	.02
❑	192	Don August	.05	.02
❑	193	Andy Benes	.05	.02
❑	194	Glenallen Hill	.05	.02
❑	195	Tim Burke	.05	.02
❑	196	Gerald Young	.05	.02
❑	197	Doug Drabek	.05	.02
❑	198	Mike Marshall	.05	.02
❑	199	Sergio Valdez	.05	.02
❑	200	Don Mattingly	.50	.23
❑	201	Cito Gaston MG	.05	.02
❑	202	Mike Macfarlane	.05	.02
❑	203	Mike Roesler	.05	.02
❑	204	Bob Dernier	.05	.02
❑	205	Mark Davis	.05	.02
❑	206	Nick Esasky	.05	.02
❑	207	Bob Ojeda	.05	.02
❑	208	Brook Jacoby	.05	.02
❑	209	Greg Mathews	.05	.02
❑	210	Ryne Sandberg	.25	.11
❑	211	John Cerutti	.05	.02
❑	212	Joe Orsulak	.05	.02
❑	213	Scott Bankhead	.05	.02
❑	214	Terry Francona	.10	.05
❑	215	Kirk McCaskill	.05	.02
❑	216	Ricky Jordan	.05	.02
❑	217	Don Robinson	.05	.02
❑	218	Wally Backman	.05	.02
❑	219	Donn Pall	.05	.02
❑	220	Barry Bonds	.50	.23
❑	221	Gary Mielke	.05	.02
❑	222	Kurt Stillwell UER (Graduate misspelled as gradute)	.05	.02
❑	223	Tommy Gregg	.05	.02
❑	224	Delino DeShields RC	.20	.09
❑	225	Jim Deshaies	.05	.02
❑	226	Mickey Hatcher	.05	.02
❑	227	Kevin Tapani RC	.20	.09
❑	228	Dave Martinez	.05	.02
❑	229	David Wells	.10	.05
❑	230	Keith Hernandez	.10	.05
❑	231	Jack McKeon MG	.05	.02
❑	232	Darnell Coles	.05	.02
❑	233	Ken Hill	.10	.05
❑	234	Mariano Duncan	.05	.02
❑	235	Jeff Reardon	.10	.05
❑	236	Hal Morris	.05	.02
❑	237	Kevin Ritz	.05	.02
❑	238	Felix Jose	.05	.02
❑	239	Eric Show	.05	.02
❑	240	Mark Grace	.20	.09
❑	241	Mike Krukow	.05	.02
❑	242	Fred Manrique	.05	.02
❑	243	Barry Jones	.05	.02
❑	244	Bill Schroeder	.05	.02
❑	245	Roger Clemens	.50	.23
❑	246	Jim Eisenreich	.05	.02
❑	247	Jerry Reed	.05	.02
❑	248	Dave Anderson	.05	.02
❑	249	Mike(Texas) Smith	.05	.02
❑	250	Jose Canseco	.20	.09
❑	251	Jeff Blauser	.05	.02
❑	252	Otis Nixon	.05	.02
❑	253	Mark Portugal	.05	.02
❑	254	Francisco Cabrera	.05	.02
❑	255	Bobby Thigpen	.05	.02
❑	256	Marvell Wynne	.05	.02
❑	257	Jose DeLeon	.05	.02
❑	258	Barry Lyons	.05	.02
❑	259	Lance McCullers	.05	.02
❑	260	Eric Davis	.10	.05
❑	261	Whitey Herzog MG	.10	.05
❑	262	Checklist 2	.05	.02
❑	263	Mel Stottlemyre Jr.	.05	.02
❑	264	Bryan Clutterbuck	.05	.02
❑	265	Pete O'Brien	.05	.02
❑	266	German Gonzalez	.05	.02
❑	267	Mark Davidson	.05	.02
❑	268	Rob Murphy	.05	.02
❑	269	Dickie Thon	.05	.02
❑	270	Dave Stewart	.10	.05
❑	271	Chet Lemon	.05	.02
❑	272	Bryan Harvey	.05	.02
❑	273	Bobby Bonilla	.10	.05
❑	274	Mauro Gozzo	.05	.02
❑	275	Mickey Tettleton	.05	.02
❑	276	Gary Thurman	.05	.02
❑	277	Lenny Harris	.05	.02
❑	278	Pascual Perez	.05	.02
❑	279	Steve Buechele	.05	.02
❑	280	Lou Whitaker	.10	.05
❑	281	Kevin Bass	.05	.02
❑	282	Derek Lilliquist	.05	.02
❑	283	Joey Belle	.20	.09
❑	284	Mark Gardner RC	.05	.02
❑	285	Willie McGee	.10	.05
❑	286	Lee Guetterman	.05	.02
❑	287	Vance Law	.05	.02
❑	288	Greg Briley	.05	.02
❑	289	Norm Charlton	.05	.02
❑	290	Robin Yount	.20	.09
❑	291	Dave Johnson MG	.10	.05
❑	292	Jim Gott	.05	.02
❑	293	Mike Gallego	.05	.02
❑	294	Craig McMurtry	.05	.02
❑	295	Fred McGriff	.20	.09
❑	296	Jeff Ballard	.05	.02
❑	297	Tommy Herr	.05	.02
❑	298	Dan Gladden	.05	.02
❑	299	Adam Peterson	.05	.02
❑	300	Bo Jackson	.10	.05
❑	301	Don Aase	.05	.02
❑	302	Marcus Lawton	.05	.02
❑	303	Rick Cerone	.05	.02
❑	304	Marty Clary	.05	.02
❑	305	Eddie Murray	.20	.09
❑	306	Tom Niedenfuer	.05	.02
❑	307	Bip Roberts	.05	.02
❑	308	Jose Guzman	.05	.02
❑	309	Eric Yelding	.05	.02
❑	310	Steve Bedrosian	.05	.02
❑	311	Dwight Smith	.05	.02
❑	312	Dan Quisenberry	.05	.02
❑	313	Gus Polidor	.05	.02
❑	314	Donald Harris FDP	.05	.02
❑	315	Bruce Hurst	.05	.02
❑	316	Carney Lansford	.10	.05
❑	317	Mark Guthrie	.05	.02
❑	318	Wallace Johnson	.05	.02
❑	319	Dion James	.05	.02
❑	320	Dave Stieb	.10	.05
❑	321	Joe Morgan MG	.05	.02
❑	322	Junior Ortiz	.05	.02
❑	323	Willie Wilson	.05	.02
❑	324	Pete Harnisch	.05	.02
❑	325	Robby Thompson	.05	.02
❑	326	Tom McCarthy	.05	.02
❑	327	Ken Williams	.05	.02
❑	328	Curt Young	.05	.02
❑	329	Oddibe McDowell	.05	.02
❑	330	Ron Darling	.05	.02
❑	331	Juan Gonzalez RC	2.00	.90
❑	332	Paul O'Neill	.20	.09
❑	333	Bill Wegman	.05	.02
❑	334	Johnny Ray	.05	.02
❑	335	Andy Hawkins	.05	.02
❑	336	Ken Griffey Jr.	1.50	.70
❑	337	Lloyd McClendon	.05	.02
❑	338	Dennis Lamp	.05	.02
❑	339	Dave Clark	.05	.02
❑	340	Fernando Valenzuela	.10	.05
❑	341	Tom Foley	.05	.02
❑	342	Alex Trevino	.05	.02
❑	343	Frank Tanana	.05	.02
❑	344	George Canale	.05	.02
❑	345	Harold Baines	.10	.05
❑	346	Jim Presley	.05	.02
❑	347	Junior Felix	.05	.02
❑	348	Gary Wayne	.05	.02
❑	349	Steve Finley	.10	.05
❑	350	Bret Saberhagen	.10	.05
❑	351	Roger Craig MG	.05	.02
❑	352	Bryn Smith	.05	.02
❑	353	Sandy Alomar Jr. (Not listed as Jr. on card front)	.10	.05
❑	354	Stan Belinda RC	.05	.02
❑	355	Marty Barrett	.05	.02
❑	356	Randy Ready	.05	.02
❑	357	Dave West	.05	.02
❑	358	Andres Thomas	.05	.02
❑	359	Jimmy Jones	.05	.02
❑	360	Paul Molitor	.20	.09
❑	361	Randy McCament	.05	.02
❑	362	Damon Berryhill	.05	.02
❑	363	Dan Petry	.05	.02
❑	364	Rolando Roomes	.05	.02
❑	365	Ozzie Guillen	.05	.02
❑	366	Mike Heath	.05	.02
❑	367	Mike Morgan	.05	.02
❑	368	Bill Doran	.05	.02

❑ 369 Todd Burns .05 .02
❑ 370 Tim Wallach .05 .02
❑ 371 Jimmy Key .10 .05
❑ 372 Terry Kennedy .05 .02
❑ 373 Alvin Davis .05 .02
❑ 374 Steve Cummings .05 .02
❑ 375 Dwight Evans .10 .05
❑ 376 Checklist 3 UER .05 .02
(Higuera misalphabet-
ized in Brewer list)
❑ 377 Mickey Weston .05 .02
❑ 378 Luis Salazar .05 .02
❑ 379 Steve Rosenberg .05 .02
❑ 380 Dave Winfield .20 .09
❑ 381 Frank Robinson MG .15 .07
❑ 382 Jeff Musselman .05 .02
❑ 383 John Morris .05 .02
❑ 384 Pat Combs .05 .02
❑ 385 Fred McGriff AS .10 .05
❑ 386 Julio Franco AS .05 .02
❑ 387 Wade Boggs AS .10 .05
❑ 388 Cal Ripken AS .40 .18
❑ 389 Robin Yount AS .10 .05
❑ 390 Ruben Sierra AS .05 .02
❑ 391 Kirby Puckett AS .20 .09
❑ 392 Carlton Fisk AS .10 .05
❑ 393 Bret Saberhagen AS .05 .02
❑ 394 Jeff Ballard AS .05 .02
❑ 395 Jeff Russell AS .05 .02
❑ 396 A.Bartlett Giamatti RC .20 .09
COMM MEM
❑ 397 Will Clark AS .10 .05
❑ 398 Ryne Sandberg AS .20 .09
❑ 399 Howard Johnson AS .05 .02
❑ 400 Ozzie Smith AS .20 .09
❑ 401 Kevin Mitchell AS .05 .02
❑ 402 Eric Davis AS .05 .02
❑ 403 Tony Gwynn AS .20 .09
❑ 404 Craig Biggio AS .10 .05
❑ 405 Mike Scott AS .05 .02
❑ 406 Joe Magrane AS .05 .02
❑ 407 Mark Davis AS .05 .02
❑ 408 Trevor Wilson .05 .02
❑ 409 Tom Brunansky .05 .02
❑ 410 Joe Boever .05 .02
❑ 411 Ken Phelps .05 .02
❑ 412 Jamie Moyer .05 .02
❑ 413 Brian DuBois .05 .02
❑ 414A Frank Thomas FDP 800.00 350.00
ERR (Name missing
on card front)
❑ 414B Frank Thomas COR RC 2.00 .90
❑ 415 Shawon Dunston .05 .02
❑ 416 Dave Johnson (P) .05 .02
❑ 417 Jim Gantner .05 .02
❑ 418 Tom Browning .05 .02
❑ 419 Beau Allred .05 .02
❑ 420 Carlton Fisk .20 .09
❑ 421 Greg Minton .05 .02
❑ 422 Pat Sheridan .05 .02
❑ 423 Fred Toliver .05 .02
❑ 424 Jerry Reuss .05 .02
❑ 425 Bill Landrum .05 .02
❑ 426 Jeff Hamilton UER .05 .02
(Stats say he fanned
197 times in 1987, but
he only had 147 at bats)
❑ 427 Carmen Castillo .05 .02
❑ 428 Steve Davis .05 .02
❑ 429 Tom Kelly MG .05 .02
❑ 430 Pete Incaviglia .05 .02
❑ 431 Randy Johnson .40 .18
❑ 432 Damaso Garcia .05 .02
❑ 433 Steve Olin RC .10 .05
❑ 434 Mark Carreon .05 .02
❑ 435 Kevin Seitzer .05 .02
❑ 436 Mel Hall .05 .02
❑ 437 Les Lancaster .05 .02
❑ 438 Greg Myers .05 .02
❑ 439 Jeff Parrett .05 .02
❑ 440 Alan Trammell .15 .07
❑ 441 Bob Kipper .05 .02
❑ 442 Jerry Browne .05 .02
❑ 443 Cris Carpenter .05 .02
❑ 444 Kyle Abbott FDP .05 .02
❑ 445 Danny Jackson .05 .02
❑ 446 Dan Pasqua .05 .02
❑ 447 Atlee Hammaker .05 .02
❑ 448 Greg Gagne .05 .02
❑ 449 Dennis Rasmussen .05 .02
❑ 450 Rickey Henderson .40 .18
❑ 451 Mark Lemke .05 .02
❑ 452 Luis DeLosSantos .05 .02
❑ 453 Jody Davis .05 .02
❑ 454 Jeff King .05 .02
❑ 455 Jeffrey Leonard .05 .02
❑ 456 Chris Gwynn .05 .02
❑ 457 Gregg Jefferies .10 .05
❑ 458 Bob McClure .05 .02
❑ 459 Jim Lefebvre MG .05 .02
❑ 460 Mike Scott .05 .02
❑ 461 Carlos Martinez .05 .02
❑ 462 Denny Walling .05 .02
❑ 463 Drew Hall .05 .02
❑ 464 Jerome Walton .05 .02
❑ 465 Kevin Gross .05 .02
❑ 466 Rance Mulliniks .05 .02
❑ 467 Juan Nieves .05 .02
❑ 468 Bill Ripken .05 .02
❑ 469 John Kruk .10 .05
❑ 470 Frank Viola .05 .02
❑ 471 Mike Brumley .05 .02
❑ 472 Jose Uribe .05 .02
❑ 473 Joe Price .05 .02
❑ 474 Rich Thompson .05 .02
❑ 475 Bob Welch .05 .02
❑ 476 Brad Komminsk .05 .02
❑ 477 Willie Fraser .05 .02
❑ 478 Mike LaValliere .05 .02
❑ 479 Frank White .10 .05
❑ 480 Sid Fernandez .05 .02
❑ 481 Garry Templeton .05 .02
❑ 482 Steve Carter .05 .02
❑ 483 Alejandro Pena .05 .02
❑ 484 Mike Fitzgerald .05 .02
❑ 485 John Candelaria .05 .02
❑ 486 Jeff Treadway .05 .02
❑ 487 Steve Searcy .05 .02
❑ 488 Ken Oberkfell .05 .02
❑ 489 Nick Leyva MG .05 .02
❑ 490 Dan Plesac .05 .02
❑ 491 Dave Cochrane .05 .02
❑ 492 Ron Oester .05 .02
❑ 493 Jason Grimsley RC .05 .02
❑ 494 Terry Puhl .05 .02
❑ 495 Lee Smith .10 .05
❑ 496 Cecil Espy UER .05 .02
('88 stats have 3
SB's, should be 33)
❑ 497 Dave Schmidt .05 .02
❑ 498 Rick Schu .05 .02
❑ 499 Bill Long .05 .02
❑ 500 Kevin Mitchell .05 .02
❑ 501 Matt Young .05 .02
❑ 502 Mitch Webster .05 .02
❑ 503 Randy St.Claire .05 .02
❑ 504 Tom O'Malley .05 .02
❑ 505 Kelly Gruber .05 .02
❑ 506 Tom Glavine .20 .09
❑ 507 Gary Redus .05 .02
❑ 508 Terry Leach .05 .02
❑ 509 Tom Pagnozzi .05 .02
❑ 510 Dwight Gooden .10 .05
❑ 511 Clay Parker .05 .02
❑ 512 Gary Pettis .05 .02
❑ 513 Mark Eichhorn .05 .02
❑ 514 Andy Allanson .05 .02
❑ 515 Len Dykstra .10 .05
❑ 516 Tim Leary .05 .02
❑ 517 Roberto Alomar .20 .09
❑ 518 Bill Krueger .05 .02
❑ 519 Bucky Dent MG .05 .02
❑ 520 Mitch Williams .05 .02
❑ 521 Craig Worthington .05 .02
❑ 522 Mike Dunne .05 .02
❑ 523 Jay Bell .10 .05
❑ 524 Daryl Boston .05 .02
❑ 525 Wally Joyner .10 .05
❑ 526 Checklist 4 .05 .02
❑ 527 Ron Hassey .05 .02
❑ 528 Kevin Wickander UER .05 .02
(Monthly scoreboard
strikeout total was 2.2,
that was his innings
pitched total)
❑ 529 Greg A. Harris .05 .02
❑ 530 Mark Langston .05 .02
❑ 531 Ken Caminiti .10 .05
❑ 532 Cecilio Guante .05 .02
❑ 533 Tim Jones .05 .02
❑ 534 Louie Meadows .05 .02
❑ 535 John Smoltz .10 .05
❑ 536 Bob Geren .05 .02
❑ 537 Mark Grant .05 .02
❑ 538 Bill Spiers UER .05 .02
(Photo actually
George Canale)
❑ 539 Neal Heaton .05 .02
❑ 540 Danny Tartabull .05 .02
❑ 541 Pat Perry .05 .02
❑ 542 Darren Daulton .10 .05
❑ 543 Nelson Liriano .05 .02
❑ 544 Dennis Boyd .05 .02
❑ 545 Kevin McReynolds .05 .02
❑ 546 Kevin Hickey .05 .02
❑ 547 Jack Howell .05 .02
❑ 548 Pat Clements .05 .02
❑ 549 Don Zimmer MG .05 .02
❑ 550 Julio Franco .05 .02
❑ 551 Tim Crews .05 .02
❑ 552 Mike(Miss.) Smith .05 .02
❑ 553 Scott Scudder UER .05 .02
(Cedar Rap1ds)
❑ 554 Jay Buhner .10 .05
❑ 555 Jack Morris .10 .05
❑ 556 Gene Larkin .05 .02
❑ 557 Jeff Innis .05 .02
❑ 558 Rafael Ramirez .05 .02
❑ 559 Andy McGaffigan .05 .02
❑ 560 Steve Sax .05 .02
❑ 561 Ken Dayley .05 .02
❑ 562 Chad Kreuter .05 .02
❑ 563 Alex Sanchez .05 .02
❑ 564 T.Houston FDP RC .15 .07
❑ 565 Scott Fletcher .05 .02
❑ 566 Mark Knudson .05 .02
❑ 567 Ron Gant .10 .05
❑ 568 John Smiley .05 .02
❑ 569 Ivan Calderon .05 .02
❑ 570 Cal Ripken .75 .35
❑ 571 Brett Butler .10 .05
❑ 572 Greg W. Harris .05 .02
❑ 573 Danny Heep .05 .02
❑ 574 Bill Swift .05 .02
❑ 575 Lance Parrish .05 .02
❑ 576 Mike Dyer .05 .02
❑ 577 Charlie Hayes .05 .02
❑ 578 Joe Magrane .05 .02
❑ 579 Art Howe MG .05 .02
❑ 580 Joe Carter .10 .05
❑ 581 Ken Griffey Sr. .10 .05
❑ 582 Rick Honeycutt .05 .02
❑ 583 Bruce Benedict .05 .02
❑ 584 Phil Stephenson .05 .02
❑ 585 Kal Daniels .05 .02
❑ 586 Edwin Nunez .05 .02
❑ 587 Lance Johnson .05 .02
❑ 588 Rick Rhoden .05 .02
❑ 589 Mike Aldrete .05 .02
❑ 590 Ozzie Smith .25 .11
❑ 591 Todd Stottlemyre .10 .05
❑ 592 R.J. Reynolds .05 .02
❑ 593 Scott Bradley .05 .02
❑ 594 Luis Sojo .05 .02
❑ 595 Greg Swindell .05 .02
❑ 596 Jose DeJesus .05 .02
❑ 597 Chris Bosio .05 .02
❑ 598 Brady Anderson .20 .09
❑ 599 Frank Williams .05 .02
❑ 600 Darryl Strawberry .10 .05
❑ 601 Luis Rivera .05 .02
❑ 602 Scott Garrelts .05 .02
❑ 603 Tony Armas .05 .02
❑ 604 Ron Robinson .05 .02
❑ 605 Mike Scioscia .05 .02
❑ 606 Storm Davis .05 .02
❑ 607 Steve Jeltz .05 .02
❑ 608 Eric Anthony RC .05 .02

❑ 609 Sparky Anderson MG .10 .05
❑ 610 Pedro Guerrero .05 .02
❑ 611 Walt Terrell .05 .02
❑ 612 Dave Gallagher .05 .02
❑ 613 Jeff Pico .05 .02
❑ 614 Nelson Santovenia .05 .02
❑ 615 Rob Deer .05 .02
❑ 616 Brian Holman .05 .02
❑ 617 Geronimo Berroa .05 .02
❑ 618 Ed Whitson .05 .02
❑ 619 Rob Ducey .05 .02
❑ 620 Tony Castillo .05 .02
❑ 621 Melido Perez .05 .02
❑ 622 Sid Bream .05 .02
❑ 623 Jim Corsi .05 .02
❑ 624 Darrin Jackson .05 .02
❑ 625 Roger McDowell .05 .02
❑ 626 Bob Melvin .05 .02
❑ 627 Jose Rijo .05 .02
❑ 628 Candy Maldonado .05 .02
❑ 629 Eric Hetzel .05 .02
❑ 630 Gary Gaetti .10 .05
❑ 631 John Wetteland .20 .09
❑ 632 Scott Lusader .05 .02
❑ 633 Dennis Cook .05 .02
❑ 634 Luis Polonia .05 .02
❑ 635 Brian Downing .05 .02
❑ 636 Jesse Orosco .05 .02
❑ 637 Craig Reynolds .05 .02
❑ 638 Jeff Montgomery .10 .05
❑ 639 Tony LaRussa MG .10 .05
❑ 640 Rick Sutcliffe .10 .05
❑ 641 Doug Strange .05 .02
❑ 642 Jack Armstrong .05 .02
❑ 643 Alfredo Griffin .05 .02
❑ 644 Paul Assenmacher .05 .02
❑ 645 Jose Oquendo .05 .02
❑ 646 Checklist 5 .05 .02
❑ 647 Rex Hudler .05 .02
❑ 648 Jim Clancy .05 .02
❑ 649 Dan Murphy RC .05 .02
❑ 650 Mike Witt .05 .02
❑ 651 Rafael Santana .05 .02
❑ 652 Mike Boddicker .05 .02
❑ 653 John Moses .05 .02
❑ 654 Paul Coleman FDP RC .05 .02
❑ 655 Gregg Olson .10 .05
❑ 656 Mackey Sasser .05 .02
❑ 657 Terry Mulholland .05 .02
❑ 658 Donell Nixon .05 .02
❑ 659 Greg Cadaret .05 .02
❑ 660 Vince Coleman .05 .02
❑ 661 Dick Howser TBC'85 .05 .02
UER (Seaver's 300th
on 7/11/85, should
be 8/4/85)
❑ 662 Mike Schmidt TBC'80 .20 .09
❑ 663 Fred Lynn TBC'75 .05 .02
❑ 664 Johnny Bench TBC'70 .20 .09
❑ 665 Sandy Koufax TBC'65 .25 .11
❑ 666 Brian Fisher .05 .02
❑ 667 Curt Wilkerson .05 .02
❑ 668 Joe Oliver .05 .02
❑ 669 Tom Lasorda MG .20 .09
❑ 670 Dennis Eckersley .15 .07
❑ 671 Bob Boone .10 .05
❑ 672 Roy Smith .05 .02
❑ 673 Joey Meyer .05 .02
❑ 674 Spike Owen .05 .02
❑ 675 Jim Abbott .15 .07
❑ 676 Randy Kutcher .05 .02
❑ 677 Jay Tibbs .05 .02
❑ 678 Kirt Manwaring UER .05 .02
('88 Phoenix stats
repeated)
❑ 679 Gary Ward .05 .02
❑ 680 Howard Johnson .05 .02
❑ 681 Mike Schooler .05 .02
❑ 682 Dann Bilardello .05 .02
❑ 683 Kenny Rogers .10 .05
❑ 684 Julio Machado .05 .02
❑ 685 Tony Fernandez .05 .02
❑ 686 Carmelo Martinez .05 .02
❑ 687 Tim Birtsas .05 .02
❑ 688 Milt Thompson .05 .02
❑ 689 Rich Yett .05 .02
❑ 690 Mark McGwire .75 .35
❑ 691 Chuck Cary .05 .02
❑ 692 Sammy Sosa RC 5.00 2.20
❑ 693 Calvin Schiraldi .05 .02
❑ 694 Mike Stanton RC .05 .02
❑ 695 Tom Henke .05 .02
❑ 696 B.J. Surhoff .10 .05
❑ 697 Mike Davis .05 .02
❑ 698 Omar Vizquel .20 .09
❑ 699 Jim Leyland MG .05 .02
❑ 700 Kirby Puckett .50 .23
❑ 701 Bernie Williams RC 1.00 .45
❑ 702 Tony Phillips .05 .02
❑ 703 Jeff Brantley .05 .02
❑ 704 Chip Hale .05 .02
❑ 705 Claudell Washington .05 .02
❑ 706 Geno Petralli .05 .02
❑ 707 Luis Aquino .05 .02
❑ 708 Larry Sheets .05 .02
❑ 709 Juan Berenguer .05 .02
❑ 710 Von Hayes .05 .02
❑ 711 Rick Aguilera .10 .05
❑ 712 Todd Benzinger .05 .02
❑ 713 Tim Drummond .05 .02
❑ 714 Marquis Grissom RC .10 .05
❑ 715 Greg Maddux .50 .23
❑ 716 Steve Balboni .05 .02
❑ 717 Ron Karkovice .05 .02
❑ 718 Gary Sheffield .10 .05
❑ 719 Wally Whitehurst .05 .02
❑ 720 Andres Galarraga .15 .07
❑ 721 Lee Mazzilli .05 .02
❑ 722 Felix Fermin .05 .02
❑ 723 Jeff D. Robinson .05 .02
❑ 724 Juan Bell .05 .02
❑ 725 Terry Pendleton .10 .05
❑ 726 Gene Nelson .05 .02
❑ 727 Pat Tabler .05 .02
❑ 728 Jim Acker .05 .02
❑ 729 Bobby Valentine MG .05 .02
❑ 730 Tony Gwynn .40 .18
❑ 731 Don Carman .05 .02
❑ 732 Ernest Riles .05 .02
❑ 733 John Dopson .05 .02
❑ 734 Kevin Elster .05 .02
❑ 735 Charlie Hough .10 .05
❑ 736 Rick Dempsey .05 .02
❑ 737 Chris Sabo .05 .02
❑ 738 Gene Harris .05 .02
❑ 739 Dale Sveum .05 .02
❑ 740 Jesse Barfield .05 .02
❑ 741 Steve Wilson .05 .02
❑ 742 Ernie Whitt .05 .02
❑ 743 Tom Candiotti .05 .02
❑ 744 Kelly Mann .05 .02
❑ 745 Hubie Brooks .05 .02
❑ 746 Dave Smith .05 .02
❑ 747 Randy Bush .05 .02
❑ 748 Doyle Alexander .05 .02
❑ 749 Mark Parent UER .05 .02
('87 BA .80,
should be .080)
❑ 750 Dale Murphy .20 .09
❑ 751 Steve Lyons .05 .02
❑ 752 Tom Gordon .10 .05
❑ 753 Chris Speier .05 .02
❑ 754 Bob Walk .05 .02
❑ 755 Rafael Palmeiro .20 .09
❑ 756 Ken Howell .05 .02
❑ 757 Larry Walker RC .60 .25
❑ 758 Mark Thurmond .05 .02
❑ 759 Tom Trebelhorn MG .05 .02
❑ 760 Wade Boggs .20 .09
❑ 761 Mike Jackson .05 .02
❑ 762 Doug Dascenzo .05 .02
❑ 763 Dennis Martinez .10 .05
❑ 764 Tim Teufel .05 .02
❑ 765 Chili Davis .10 .05
❑ 766 Brian Meyer .05 .02
❑ 767 Tracy Jones .05 .02
❑ 768 Chuck Crim .05 .02
❑ 769 Greg Hibbard RC .05 .02
❑ 770 Cory Snyder .05 .02
❑ 771 Pete Smith .05 .02
❑ 772 Jeff Reed .05 .02
❑ 773 Dave Leiper .05 .02
❑ 774 Ben McDonald RC .10 .05
❑ 775 Andy Van Slyke .10 .05
❑ 776 Charlie Leibrandt .05 .02
❑ 777 Tim Laudner .05 .02
❑ 778 Mike Jeffcoat .05 .02
❑ 779 Lloyd Moseby .05 .02
❑ 780 Orel Hershiser .10 .05
❑ 781 Mario Diaz .05 .02
❑ 782 Jose Alvarez .05 .02
❑ 783 Checklist 6 .05 .02
❑ 784 Scott Bailes .05 .02
❑ 785 Jim Rice .10 .05
❑ 786 Eric King .05 .02
❑ 787 Rene Gonzales .05 .02
❑ 788 Frank DiPino .05 .02
❑ 789 John Wathan MG .05 .02
❑ 790 Gary Carter .15 .07
❑ 791 Alvaro Espinoza .05 .02
❑ 792 Gerald Perry .05 .02
❑ XX George Bush PRES

1990 Topps Traded

	MINT	NRMT
COMPLETE SET (132)	2.50	1.10
COMP.FACT.SET (132)	3.00	1.35

❑ 1T Darrel Akerfelds .05 .02
❑ 2T Sandy Alomar Jr. .10 .05
❑ 3T Brad Arnsberg .05 .02
❑ 4T Steve Avery .05 .02
❑ 5T Wally Backman .05 .02
❑ 6T Carlos Baerga RC .10 .05
❑ 7T Kevin Bass .05 .02
❑ 8T Willie Blair RC .05 .02
❑ 9T Mike Blowers RC .10 .05
❑ 10T Shawn Boskie RC .05 .02
❑ 11T Daryl Boston .05 .02
❑ 12T Dennis Boyd .05 .02
❑ 13T Glenn Braggs .05 .02
❑ 14T Hubie Brooks .05 .02
❑ 15T Tom Brunansky .05 .02
❑ 16T John Burkett .05 .02
❑ 17T Casey Candaele .05 .02
❑ 18T John Candelaria .05 .02
❑ 19T Gary Carter .15 .07
❑ 20T Joe Carter .10 .05
❑ 21T Rick Cerone .05 .02
❑ 22T Scott Coolbaugh .05 .02
❑ 23T Bobby Cox MG .10 .05
❑ 24T Mark Davis .05 .02
❑ 25T Storm Davis .05 .02
❑ 26T Edgar Diaz .05 .02
❑ 27T Wayne Edwards .05 .02
❑ 28T Mark Eichhorn .05 .02
❑ 29T Scott Erickson RC .10 .05
❑ 30T Nick Esasky .05 .02
❑ 31T Cecil Fielder .10 .05
❑ 32T John Franco .10 .05
❑ 33T Travis Fryman RC .25 .11
❑ 34T Bill Gullickson .05 .02
❑ 35T Darryl Hamilton .05 .02
❑ 36T Mike Harkey .05 .02
❑ 37T Bud Harrelson MG .05 .02
❑ 38T Billy Hatcher .05 .02
❑ 39T Keith Hernandez .10 .05
❑ 40T Joe Hesketh .05 .02
❑ 41T Dave Hollins RC .20 .09

❑ 42T	Sam Horn	.05	.02
❑ 43T	Steve Howard	.05	.02
❑ 44T	Todd Hundley RC	.20	.09
❑ 45T	Jeff Huson	.05	.02
❑ 46T	Chris James	.05	.02
❑ 47T	Stan Javier	.05	.02
❑ 48T	Dave Justice RC	.75	.35
❑ 49T	Jeff Kaiser	.05	.02
❑ 50T	Dana Kiecker	.05	.02
❑ 51T	Joe Klink	.05	.02
❑ 52T	Brent Knackert RC	.05	.02
❑ 53T	Brad Komminsk	.05	.02
❑ 54T	Mark Langston	.05	.02
❑ 55T	Tim Layana	.05	.02
❑ 56T	Rick Leach	.05	.02
❑ 57T	Terry Leach	.05	.02
❑ 58T	Tim Leary	.05	.02
❑ 59T	Craig Lefferts	.05	.02
❑ 60T	Charlie Leibrandt	.05	.02
❑ 61T	Jim Leyritz RC	.10	.05
❑ 62T	Fred Lynn	.05	.02
❑ 63T	Kevin Maas RC	.10	.05
❑ 64T	Shane Mack	.05	.02
❑ 65T	Candy Maldonado	.05	.02
❑ 66T	Fred Manrique	.05	.02
❑ 67T	Mike Marshall	.05	.02
❑ 68T	Carmelo Martinez	.05	.02
❑ 69T	John Marzano	.05	.02
❑ 70T	Ben McDonald	.05	.02
❑ 71T	Jack McDowell	.05	.02
❑ 72T	John McNamara MG	.05	.02
❑ 73T	Orlando Mercado	.05	.02
❑ 74T	Stump Merrill MG	.05	.02
❑ 75T	Alan Mills RC	.05	.02
❑ 76T	Hal Morris	.05	.02
❑ 77T	Lloyd Moseby	.05	.02
❑ 78T	Randy Myers	.10	.05
❑ 79T	Tim Naehring RC	.10	.05
❑ 80T	Junior Noboa	.05	.02
❑ 81T	Matt Nokes	.05	.02
❑ 82T	Pete O'Brien	.05	.02
❑ 83T	John Olerud RC	.60	.25
❑ 84T	Greg Olson RC	.05	.02
❑ 85T	Junior Ortiz	.05	.02
❑ 86T	Dave Parker	.10	.05
❑ 87T	Rick Parker	.05	.02
❑ 88T	Bob Patterson	.05	.02
❑ 89T	Alejandro Pena	.05	.02
❑ 90T	Tony Pena	.05	.02
❑ 91T	Pascual Perez	.05	.02
❑ 92T	Gerald Perry	.05	.02
❑ 93T	Dan Petry	.05	.02
❑ 94T	Gary Pettis	.05	.02
❑ 95T	Tony Phillips	.05	.02
❑ 96T	Lou Piniella MG	.10	.05
❑ 97T	Luis Polonia	.05	.02
❑ 98T	Jim Presley	.05	.02
❑ 99T	Scott Radinsky RC	.05	.02
❑ 100T	Willie Randolph	.10	.05
❑ 101T	Jeff Reardon	.10	.05
❑ 102T	Greg Riddoch MG	.05	.02
❑ 103T	Jeff Robinson	.05	.02
❑ 104T	Ron Robinson	.05	.02
❑ 105T	Kevin Romine	.05	.02
❑ 106T	Scott Ruskin	.05	.02
❑ 107T	John Russell	.05	.02
❑ 108T	Bill Sampen	.05	.02
❑ 109T	Juan Samuel	.05	.02
❑ 110T	Scott Sanderson	.05	.02
❑ 111T	Jack Savage	.05	.02
❑ 112T	Dave Schmidt	.05	.02
❑ 113T	R.Schoendienst MG	.20	.09
❑ 114T	Terry Shumpert	.05	.02
❑ 115T	Matt Sinatro	.05	.02
❑ 116T	Don Slaught	.05	.02
❑ 117T	Bryn Smith	.05	.02
❑ 118T	Lee Smith	.10	.05
❑ 119T	Paul Sorrento RC	.15	.07
❑ 120T	Franklin Stubbs UER ('84 says '99 and has the same stats as '89, '83 stats are missing)	.05	.02
❑ 121T	Russ Swan RC	.05	.02
❑ 122T	Bob Tewksbury	.05	.02
❑ 123T	Wayne Tolleson	.05	.02
❑ 124T	John Tudor	.05	.02
❑ 125T	Randy Veres	.05	.02
❑ 126T	Hector Villanueva RC	.05	.02
❑ 127T	Mitch Webster	.05	.02
❑ 128T	Ernie Whitt	.05	.02
❑ 129T	Frank Wills	.05	.02
❑ 130T	Dave Winfield	.20	.09
❑ 131T	Matt Young	.05	.02
❑ 132T	Checklist 1T-132T	.05	.02

1991 Topps

	MINT	NRMT
COMPLETE SET (792)	20.00	9.00
COMP.FACT.SET (792)	30.00	13.50

❑ 1	Nolan Ryan	1.00	.45
❑ 2	George Brett RB Batting Title, 3 decades	.20	.09
❑ 3	Carlton Fisk RB Catcher HR Record	.10	.05
❑ 4	Kevin Maas RB Quickest to 10 HR's	.05	.02
❑ 5	Cal Ripken RB Most cons. errorless games	.40	.18
❑ 6	Nolan Ryan RB Oldest pitcher, no-hitter	.50	.23
❑ 7	Ryne Sandberg RB Most cons. errorless games	.15	.07
❑ 8	Bobby Thigpen RB Most saves, season	.05	.02
❑ 9	Darrin Fletcher	.05	.02
❑ 10	Gregg Olson	.05	.02
❑ 11	Roberto Kelly	.05	.02
❑ 12	Paul Assenmacher	.05	.02
❑ 13	Mariano Duncan	.05	.02
❑ 14	Dennis Lamp	.05	.02
❑ 15	Von Hayes	.05	.02
❑ 16	Mike Heath	.05	.02
❑ 17	Jeff Brantley	.05	.02
❑ 18	Nelson Liriano	.05	.02
❑ 19	Jeff D. Robinson	.05	.02
❑ 20	Pedro Guerrero	.10	.05
❑ 21	Joe Morgan MG	.05	.02
❑ 22	Storm Davis	.05	.02
❑ 23	Jim Gantner	.05	.02
❑ 24	Dave Martinez	.05	.02
❑ 25	Tim Belcher	.05	.02
❑ 26	Luis Sojo UER (Born in Barquisimento, not Carquis)	.05	.02
❑ 27	Bobby Witt	.05	.02
❑ 28	Alvaro Espinoza	.05	.02
❑ 29	Bob Walk	.05	.02
❑ 30	Gregg Jefferies	.05	.02
❑ 31	Colby Ward	.05	.02
❑ 32	Mike Simms	.05	.02
❑ 33	Barry Jones	.05	.02
❑ 34	Atlee Hammaker	.05	.02
❑ 35	Greg Maddux	.50	.23
❑ 36	Donnie Hill	.05	.02
❑ 37	Tom Bolton	.05	.02
❑ 38	Scott Bradley	.05	.02
❑ 39	Jim Neidlinger	.05	.02
❑ 40	Kevin Mitchell	.05	.02
❑ 41	Ken Dayley	.05	.02
❑ 42	Chris Hoiles	.05	.02
❑ 43	Roger McDowell	.05	.02
❑ 44	Mike Felder	.05	.02
❑ 45	Chris Sabo	.05	.02
❑ 46	Tim Drummond	.05	.02
❑ 47	Brook Jacoby	.05	.02
❑ 48	Dennis Boyd	.05	.02
❑ 49A	Pat Borders ERR (40 steals at Kinston in '86)	.20	.09
❑ 49B	Pat Borders COR (0 steals at Kinston in '86)	.05	.02
❑ 50	Bob Welch	.05	.02
❑ 51	Art Howe MG	.05	.02
❑ 52	Francisco Oliveras	.05	.02
❑ 53	Mike Sharperson UER (Born in 1961, not 1960)	.05	.02
❑ 54	Gary Mielke	.05	.02
❑ 55	Jeffrey Leonard	.05	.02
❑ 56	Jeff Parrett	.05	.02
❑ 57	Jack Howell	.05	.02
❑ 58	Mel Stottlemyre Jr.	.05	.02
❑ 59	Eric Yelding	.05	.02
❑ 60	Frank Viola	.10	.05
❑ 61	Stan Javier	.05	.02
❑ 62	Lee Guetterman	.05	.02
❑ 63	Milt Thompson	.05	.02
❑ 64	Tom Herr	.05	.02
❑ 65	Bruce Hurst	.05	.02
❑ 66	Terry Kennedy	.05	.02
❑ 67	Rick Honeycutt	.05	.02
❑ 68	Gary Sheffield	.10	.05
❑ 69	Steve Wilson	.05	.02
❑ 70	Ellis Burks	.10	.05
❑ 71	Jim Acker	.05	.02
❑ 72	Junior Ortiz	.05	.02
❑ 73	Craig Worthington	.05	.02
❑ 74	Shane Andrews RC	.10	.05
❑ 75	Jack Morris	.10	.05
❑ 76	Jerry Browne	.05	.02
❑ 77	Drew Hall	.05	.02
❑ 78	Geno Petralli	.05	.02
❑ 79	Frank Thomas	.40	.18
❑ 80A	Fernando Valenzuela ERR (104 earned runs in '90 tied for league lead)	.10	.05
❑ 80B	Fernando Valenzuela COR (104 earned runs in '90 led league, 20 CG's in 1986 now italicized)	.10	.05
❑ 81	Cito Gaston MG	.05	.02
❑ 82	Tom Glavine	.20	.09
❑ 83	Daryl Boston	.05	.02
❑ 84	Bob McClure	.05	.02
❑ 85	Jesse Barfield	.05	.02
❑ 86	Les Lancaster	.05	.02
❑ 87	Tracy Jones	.05	.02
❑ 88	Bob Tewksbury	.05	.02
❑ 89	Darren Daulton	.10	.05
❑ 90	Danny Tartabull	.05	.02
❑ 91	Greg Colbrunn RC	.10	.05
❑ 92	Danny Jackson	.05	.02
❑ 93	Ivan Calderon	.05	.02
❑ 94	John Dopson	.05	.02
❑ 95	Paul Molitor	.20	.09
❑ 96	Trevor Wilson	.05	.02
❑ 97A	Brady Anderson ERR (September, 2 RBI and 3 hits, should be 3 RBI and 14 hits	.10	.05
❑ 97B	Brady Anderson COR	.10	.05
❑ 98	Sergio Valdez	.05	.02
❑ 99	Chris Gwynn	.05	.02
❑ 100	Don Mattingly COR (101 hits in 1990)	.50	.23
❑ 100A	Don Mattingly ERR (10 hits in 1990)	1.00	.45
❑ 101	Rob Ducey	.05	.02
❑ 102	Gene Larkin	.05	.02
❑ 103	Tim Costo RC	.05	.02
❑ 104	Don Robinson	.05	.02
❑ 105	Kevin McReynolds	.05	.02
❑ 106	Ed Nunez	.05	.02
❑ 107	Luis Polonia	.05	.02
❑ 108	Matt Young	.05	.02
❑ 109	Greg Riddoch MG	.05	.02

❑ 110 Tom Henke .05 .02
❑ 111 Andres Thomas .05 .02
❑ 112 Frank DiPino .05 .02
❑ 113 Carl Everett RC .50 .23
❑ 114 Lance Dickson RC .05 .02
❑ 115 Hubie Brooks .05 .02
❑ 116 Mark Davis .05 .02
❑ 117 Dion James .05 .02
❑ 118 Tom Edens .05 .02
❑ 119 Carl Nichols .05 .02
❑ 120 Joe Carter .10 .05
❑ 121 Eric King .05 .02
❑ 122 Paul O'Neill .20 .09
❑ 123 Greg A. Harris .05 .02
❑ 124 Randy Bush .05 .02
❑ 125 Steve Bedrosian .05 .02
❑ 126 Bernard Gilkey .05 .02
❑ 127 Joe Price .05 .02
❑ 128 Travis Fryman .10 .05
(Front has SS
back has SS-3B)
❑ 129 Mark Eichhorn .05 .02
❑ 130 Ozzie Smith .25 .11
❑ 131A Checklist 1 ERR .20 .09
727 Phil Bradley
❑ 131B Checklist 1 COR .05 .02
717 Phil Bradley
❑ 132 Jamie Quirk .05 .02
❑ 133 Greg Briley .05 .02
❑ 134 Kevin Elster .05 .02
❑ 135 Jerome Walton .05 .02
❑ 136 Dave Schmidt .05 .02
❑ 137 Randy Ready .05 .02
❑ 138 Jamie Moyer .05 .02
❑ 139 Jeff Treadway .05 .02
❑ 140 Fred McGriff .15 .07
❑ 141 Nick Leyva MG .05 .02
❑ 142 Curt Wilkerson .05 .02
❑ 143 John Smiley .05 .02
❑ 144 Dave Henderson .05 .02
❑ 145 Lou Whitaker .10 .05
❑ 146 Dan Plesac .05 .02
❑ 147 Carlos Baerga .05 .02
❑ 148 Rey Palacios .05 .02
❑ 149 Al Osuna UER .05 .02
(Shown throwing right,
but bio says lefty)
❑ 150 Cal Ripken .75 .35
❑ 151 Tom Browning .05 .02
❑ 152 Mickey Hatcher .05 .02
❑ 153 Bryan Harvey .05 .02
❑ 154 Jay Buhner .10 .05
❑ 155A Dwight Evans ERR .20 .09
(Led league with
162 games in '82)
❑ 155B Dwight Evans COR .10 .05
(Tied for lead with
162 games in '82)
❑ 156 Carlos Martinez .05 .02
❑ 157 John Smoltz .10 .05
❑ 158 Jose Uribe .05 .02
❑ 159 Joe Boever .05 .02
❑ 160 Vince Coleman UER .05 .02
(Wrong birth year,
born 9/22/60)
❑ 161 Tim Leary .05 .02
❑ 162 Ozzie Canseco .05 .02
❑ 163 Dave Johnson .05 .02
❑ 164 Edgar Diaz .05 .02
❑ 165 Sandy Alomar Jr. .10 .05
❑ 166 Harold Baines .10 .05
❑ 167A R.Tomlin RC ERR .20 .09
Harriburg
❑ 167B R.Tomlin RC COR .05 .02
Harrisburg
❑ 168 John Olerud .15 .07
❑ 169 Luis Aquino .05 .02
❑ 170 Carlton Fisk .20 .09
❑ 171 Tony LaRussa MG .10 .05
❑ 172 Pete Incaviglia .05 .02
❑ 173 Jason Grimsley .05 .02
❑ 174 Ken Caminiti .10 .05
❑ 175 Jack Armstrong .05 .02
❑ 176 John Orton .05 .02
❑ 177 Reggie Harris .05 .02
❑ 178 Dave Valle .05 .02
❑ 179 Pete Harnisch .05 .02
❑ 180 Tony Gwynn .40 .18
❑ 181 Duane Ward .05 .02
❑ 182 Junior Noboa .05 .02
❑ 183 Clay Parker .05 .02
❑ 184 Gary Green .05 .02
❑ 185 Joe Magrane .05 .02
❑ 186 Rod Booker .05 .02
❑ 187 Greg Cadaret .05 .02
❑ 188 Damon Berryhill .05 .02
❑ 189 Daryl Irvine .05 .02
❑ 190 Matt Williams .15 .07
❑ 191 Willie Blair .05 .02
❑ 192 Rob Deer .05 .02
❑ 193 Felix Fermin .05 .02
❑ 194 Xavier Hernandez .05 .02
❑ 195 Wally Joyner .10 .05
❑ 196 Jim Vatcher .05 .02
❑ 197 Chris Nabholz .05 .02
❑ 198 R.J. Reynolds .05 .02
❑ 199 Mike Hartley .05 .02
❑ 200 Darryl Strawberry .10 .05
❑ 201 Tom Kelly MG .05 .02
❑ 202 Jim Leyritz .05 .02
❑ 203 Gene Harris .05 .02
❑ 204 Herm Winningham .05 .02
❑ 205 Mike Perez RC .05 .02
❑ 206 Carlos Quintana .05 .02
❑ 207 Gary Wayne .05 .02
❑ 208 Willie Wilson .05 .02
❑ 209 Ken Howell .05 .02
❑ 210 Lance Parrish .10 .05
❑ 211 Brian Barnes .05 .02
❑ 212 Steve Finley .10 .05
❑ 213 Frank Wills .05 .02
❑ 214 Joe Girardi .05 .02
❑ 215 Dave Smith .05 .02
❑ 216 Greg Gagne .05 .02
❑ 217 Chris Bosio .05 .02
❑ 218 Rick Parker .05 .02
❑ 219 Jack McDowell .05 .02
❑ 220 Tim Wallach .05 .02
❑ 221 Don Slaught .05 .02
❑ 222 Brian McRae RC .10 .05
❑ 223 Allan Anderson .05 .02
❑ 224 Juan Gonzalez .25 .11
❑ 225 Randy Johnson .30 .14
❑ 226 Alfredo Griffin .05 .02
❑ 227 Steve Avery UER .05 .02
(Pitched 13 games for
Durham in 1989, not 2)
❑ 228 Rex Hudler .05 .02
❑ 229 Rance Mulliniks .05 .02
❑ 230 Sid Fernandez .05 .02
❑ 231 Doug Rader MG .05 .02
❑ 232 Jose DeJesus .05 .02
❑ 233 Al Leiter .10 .05
❑ 234 Scott Erickson .05 .02
❑ 235 Dave Parker .10 .05
❑ 236A Frank Tanana ERR .10 .05
(Tied for lead with
269 K's in '75)
❑ 236B Frank Tanana COR .05 .02
(Led league with
269 K's in '75)
❑ 237 Rick Cerone .05 .02
❑ 238 Mike Dunne .05 .02
❑ 239 Darren Lewis .05 .02
❑ 240 Mike Scott .05 .02
❑ 241 Dave Clark UER .05 .02
(Career totals 19 HR
and 5 3B, should
be 22 and 3)
❑ 242 Mike LaCoss .05 .02
❑ 243 Lance Johnson .05 .02
❑ 244 Mike Jeffcoat .05 .02
❑ 245 Kal Daniels .05 .02
❑ 246 Kevin Wickander .05 .02
❑ 247 Jody Reed .05 .02
❑ 248 Tom Gordon .05 .02
❑ 249 Bob Melvin .05 .02
❑ 250 Dennis Eckersley .10 .05
❑ 251 Mark Lemke .05 .02
❑ 252 Mel Rojas .05 .02
❑ 253 Garry Templeton .05 .02
❑ 254 Shawn Boskie .05 .02
❑ 255 Brian Downing .05 .02
❑ 256 Greg Hibbard .05 .02
❑ 257 Tom O'Malley .05 .02
❑ 258 Chris Hammond .05 .02
❑ 259 Hensley Meulens .05 .02
❑ 260 Harold Reynolds .05 .02
❑ 261 Bud Harrelson MG .05 .02
❑ 262 Tim Jones .05 .02
❑ 263 Checklist 2 .05 .02
❑ 264 Dave Hollins .05 .02
❑ 265 Mark Gubicza .05 .02
❑ 266 Carmelo Castillo .05 .02
❑ 267 Mark Knudson .05 .02
❑ 268 Tom Brookens .05 .02
❑ 269 Joe Hesketh .05 .02
❑ 270 Mark McGwire COR .75 .35
(1987 Slugging Pctg.
listed as .618)
❑ 270A Mark McGwire ERR 1.50 .70
(1987 Slugging Pctg.
listed as 618)
❑ 271 Omar Olivares RC .10 .05
❑ 272 Jeff King .05 .02
❑ 273 Johnny Ray .05 .02
❑ 274 Ken Williams .05 .02
❑ 275 Alan Trammell .15 .07
❑ 276 Bill Swift .05 .02
❑ 277 Scott Coolbaugh .05 .02
❑ 278 Alex Fernandez UER .05 .02
(No '90 White Sox stats)
❑ 279A Jose Gonzalez ERR .05 .02
(Photo actually
Billy Bean)
❑ 279B Jose Gonzalez COR .05 .02
❑ 280 Bret Saberhagen .10 .05
❑ 281 Larry Sheets .05 .02
❑ 282 Don Carman .05 .02
❑ 283 Marquis Grissom .05 .02
❑ 284 Billy Spiers .05 .02
❑ 285 Jim Abbott .10 .05
❑ 286 Ken Oberkfell .05 .02
❑ 287 Mark Grant .05 .02
❑ 288 Derrick May .05 .02
❑ 289 Tim Birtsas .05 .02
❑ 290 Steve Sax .05 .02
❑ 291 John Wathan MG .05 .02
❑ 292 Bud Black .05 .02
❑ 293 Jay Bell .10 .05
❑ 294 Mike Moore .05 .02
❑ 295 Rafael Palmeiro .20 .09
❑ 296 Mark Williamson .05 .02
❑ 297 Manny Lee .05 .02
❑ 298 Omar Vizquel .10 .05
❑ 299 Scott Radinsky .05 .02
❑ 300 Kirby Puckett .50 .23
❑ 301 Steve Farr .05 .02
❑ 302 Tim Teufel .05 .02
❑ 303 Mike Boddicker .05 .02
❑ 304 Kevin Reimer .05 .02
❑ 305 Mike Scioscia .05 .02
❑ 306A Lonnie Smith ERR .20 .09
(136 games in '90)
❑ 306B Lonnie Smith COR .05 .02
(135 games in '90)
❑ 307 Andy Benes .05 .02
❑ 308 Tom Pagnozzi .05 .02
❑ 309 Norm Charlton .05 .02
❑ 310 Gary Carter .15 .07
❑ 311 Jeff Pico .05 .02
❑ 312 Charlie Hayes .05 .02
❑ 313 Ron Robinson .05 .02
❑ 314 Gary Pettis .05 .02
❑ 315 Roberto Alomar .20 .09
❑ 316 Gene Nelson .05 .02
❑ 317 Mike Fitzgerald .05 .02
❑ 318 Rick Aguilera .10 .05
❑ 319 Jeff McKnight .05 .02
❑ 320 Tony Fernandez .05 .02
❑ 321 Bob Rodgers MG .05 .02
❑ 322 Terry Shumpert .05 .02
❑ 323 Cory Snyder .05 .02
❑ 324A Ron Kittle ERR .20 .09
(Set another
standard ...)
❑ 324B Ron Kittle COR .05 .02
(Tied another

standard ...)
❑ 325 Brett Butler .10 .05
❑ 326 Ken Patterson .05 .02
❑ 327 Ron Hassey .05 .02
❑ 328 Walt Terrell .05 .02
❑ 329 Dave Justice UER .20 .09
(Drafted third round on card, should say fourth pick)
❑ 330 Dwight Gooden .10 .05
❑ 331 Eric Anthony .05 .02
❑ 332 Kenny Rogers .05 .02
❑ 333 C.Jones FDP RC 3.00 1.35
❑ 334 Todd Benzinger .05 .02
❑ 335 Mitch Williams .05 .02
❑ 336 Matt Nokes .05 .02
❑ 337A Keith Comstock ERR .20 .09
(Cubs logo on front)
❑ 337B Keith Comstock COR .05 .02
(Mariners logo on front)
❑ 338 Luis Rivera .05 .02
❑ 339 Larry Walker .15 .07
❑ 340 Ramon Martinez .05 .02
❑ 341 John Moses .05 .02
❑ 342 Mickey Morandini .05 .02
❑ 343 Jose Oquendo .05 .02
❑ 344 Jeff Russell .05 .02
❑ 345 Len Dykstra .10 .05
❑ 346 Jesse Orosco .05 .02
❑ 347 Greg Vaughn .10 .05
❑ 348 Todd Stottlemyre .05 .02
❑ 349 Dave Gallagher .05 .02
❑ 350 Glenn Davis .05 .02
❑ 351 Joe Torre MG .10 .05
❑ 352 Frank White .10 .05
❑ 353 Tony Castillo .05 .02
❑ 354 Sid Bream .05 .02
❑ 355 Chili Davis .10 .05
❑ 356 Mike Marshall .05 .02
❑ 357 Jack Savage .05 .02
❑ 358 Mark Parent .05 .02
❑ 359 Chuck Cary .05 .02
❑ 360 Tim Raines .10 .05
❑ 361 Scott Garrelts .05 .02
❑ 362 Hector Villenueva .05 .02
❑ 363 Rick Mahler .05 .02
❑ 364 Dan Pasqua .05 .02
❑ 365 Mike Schooler .05 .02
❑ 366A Checklist 3 ERR .20 .09
19 Carl Nichols
❑ 366B Checklist 3 COR .05 .02
119 Carl Nichols
❑ 367 Dave Walsh .05 .02
❑ 368 Felix Jose .05 .02
❑ 369 Steve Searcy .05 .02
❑ 370 Kelly Gruber .05 .02
❑ 371 Jeff Montgomery .05 .02
❑ 372 Spike Owen .05 .02
❑ 373 Darrin Jackson .05 .02
❑ 374 Larry Casian .05 .02
❑ 375 Tony Pena .05 .02
❑ 376 Mike Harkey .05 .02
❑ 377 Rene Gonzales .05 .02
❑ 378A Wilson Alvarez ERR .75 .35
('89 Port Charlotte and '90 Birmingham stat lines omitted)
❑ 378B Wilson Alvarez COR .05 .02
(Text still says 143 K's in 1988, whereas stats say 134)
❑ 379 Randy Velarde .05 .02
❑ 380 Willie McGee .10 .05
❑ 381 Jim Leyland MG .05 .02
❑ 382 Mackey Sasser .05 .02
❑ 383 Pete Smith .05 .02
❑ 384 Gerald Perry .05 .02
❑ 385 Mickey Tettleton .05 .02
❑ 386 Cecil Fielder AS .05 .02
❑ 387 Julio Franco AS .05 .02
❑ 388 Kelly Gruber AS .05 .02
❑ 389 Alan Trammell AS .10 .05
❑ 390 Jose Canseco AS .10 .05
❑ 391 Rickey Henderson AS .20 .09
❑ 392 Ken Griffey Jr. AS .40 .18
❑ 393 Carlton Fisk AS .10 .05
❑ 394 Bob Welch AS .05 .02
❑ 395 Chuck Finley AS .05 .02
❑ 396 Bobby Thigpen AS .05 .02
❑ 397 Eddie Murray AS .10 .05
❑ 398 Ryne Sandberg AS .15 .07
❑ 399 Matt Williams AS .10 .05
❑ 400 Barry Larkin AS .10 .05
❑ 401 Barry Bonds AS .25 .11
❑ 402 Darryl Strawberry AS .05 .02
❑ 403 Bobby Bonilla AS .05 .02
❑ 404 Mike Scioscia AS .05 .02
❑ 405 Doug Drabek AS .05 .02
❑ 406 Frank Viola AS .05 .02
❑ 407 John Franco AS .05 .02
❑ 408 Earnest Riles .05 .02
❑ 409 Mike Stanley .05 .02
❑ 410 Dave Righetti .10 .05
❑ 411 Lance Blankenship .05 .02
❑ 412 Dave Bergman .05 .02
❑ 413 Terry Mulholland .05 .02
❑ 414 Sammy Sosa .30 .14
❑ 415 Rick Sutcliffe .10 .05
❑ 416 Randy Milligan .05 .02
❑ 417 Bill Krueger .05 .02
❑ 418 Nick Esasky .05 .02
❑ 419 Jeff Reed .05 .02
❑ 420 Bobby Thigpen .05 .02
❑ 421 Alex Cole .05 .02
❑ 422 Rick Reuschel .05 .02
❑ 423 Rafael Ramirez UER .05 .02
(Born 1959, not 1958)
❑ 424 Calvin Schiraldi .05 .02
❑ 425 Andy Van Slyke .10 .05
❑ 426 Joe Grahe RC .05 .02
❑ 427 Rick Dempsey .05 .02
❑ 428 John Barfield .05 .02
❑ 429 Stump Merrill MG .05 .02
❑ 430 Gary Gaetti .10 .05
❑ 431 Paul Gibson .05 .02
❑ 432 Delino DeShields .10 .05
❑ 433 Pat Tabler .05 .02
❑ 434 Julio Machado .05 .02
❑ 435 Kevin Maas .05 .02
❑ 436 Scott Bankhead .05 .02
❑ 437 Doug Dascenzo .05 .02
❑ 438 Vicente Palacios .05 .02
❑ 439 Dickie Thon .05 .02
❑ 440 George Bell .05 .02
❑ 441 Zane Smith .05 .02
❑ 442 Charlie O'Brien .05 .02
❑ 443 Jeff Innis .05 .02
❑ 444 Glenn Braggs .05 .02
❑ 445 Greg Swindell .05 .02
❑ 446 Craig Grebeck .05 .02
❑ 447 John Burkett .05 .02
❑ 448 Craig Lefferts .05 .02
❑ 449 Juan Berenguer .05 .02
❑ 450 Wade Boggs .20 .09
❑ 451 Neal Heaton .05 .02
❑ 452 Bill Schroeder .05 .02
❑ 453 Lenny Harris .05 .02
❑ 454A Kevin Appier ERR .10 .05
('90 Omaha stat line omitted)
❑ 454B Kevin Appier COR .10 .05
❑ 455 Walt Weiss .05 .02
❑ 456 Charlie Leibrandt .05 .02
❑ 457 Todd Hundley .05 .02
❑ 458 Brian Holman .05 .02
❑ 459 T.Trebelhorn MG UER .05 .02
Pitching and batting columns switched
❑ 460 Dave Stieb .05 .02
❑ 461 Robin Ventura .10 .05
❑ 462 Steve Frey .05 .02
❑ 463 Dwight Smith .05 .02
❑ 464 Steve Buechele .05 .02
❑ 465 Ken Griffey Sr. .10 .05
❑ 466 Charles Nagy .05 .02
❑ 467 Dennis Cook .05 .02
❑ 468 Tim Hulett .05 .02
❑ 469 Chet Lemon .05 .02
❑ 470 Howard Johnson .05 .02
❑ 471 Mike Lieberthal RC .50 .23
❑ 472 Kirt Manwaring .05 .02
❑ 473 Curt Young .05 .02
❑ 474 Phil Plantier RC .05 .02
❑ 475 Ted Higuera .05 .02
❑ 476 Glenn Wilson .05 .02
❑ 477 Mike Fetters .05 .02
❑ 478 Kurt Stillwell .05 .02
❑ 479 Bob Patterson UER .05 .02
(Has a decimal point between 7 and 9)
❑ 480 Dave Magadan .05 .02
❑ 481 Eddie Whitson .05 .02
❑ 482 Tino Martinez .10 .05
❑ 483 Mike Aldrete .05 .02
❑ 484 Dave LaPoint .05 .02
❑ 485 Terry Pendleton .10 .05
❑ 486 Tommy Greene .05 .02
❑ 487 Rafael Belliard .05 .02
❑ 488 Jeff Manto .05 .02
❑ 489 Bobby Valentine MG .05 .02
❑ 490 Kirk Gibson .10 .05
❑ 491 Kurt Miller RC .05 .02
❑ 492 Ernie Whitt .05 .02
❑ 493 Jose Rijo .05 .02
❑ 494 Chris James .05 .02
❑ 495 Charlie Hough .10 .05
❑ 496 Marty Barrett .05 .02
❑ 497 Ben McDonald .05 .02
❑ 498 Mark Salas .05 .02
❑ 499 Melido Perez .05 .02
❑ 500 Will Clark .20 .09
❑ 501 Mike Bielecki .05 .02
❑ 502 Carney Lansford .10 .05
❑ 503 Roy Smith .05 .02
❑ 504 Julio Valera .05 .02
❑ 505 Chuck Finley .10 .05
❑ 506 Darnell Coles .05 .02
❑ 507 Steve Jeltz .05 .02
❑ 508 Mike York .05 .02
❑ 509 Glenallen Hill .05 .02
❑ 510 John Franco .10 .05
❑ 511 Steve Balboni .05 .02
❑ 512 Jose Mesa .05 .02
❑ 513 Jerald Clark .05 .02
❑ 514 Mike Stanton .05 .02
❑ 515 Alvin Davis .05 .02
❑ 516 Karl Rhodes .05 .02
❑ 517 Joe Oliver .05 .02
❑ 518 Cris Carpenter .05 .02
❑ 519 Sparky Anderson MG .10 .05
❑ 520 Mark Grace .20 .09
❑ 521 Joe Orsulak .05 .02
❑ 522 Stan Belinda .05 .02
❑ 523 Rodney McCray .05 .02
❑ 524 Darrel Akerfelds .05 .02
❑ 525 Willie Randolph .10 .05
❑ 526A Moises Alou ERR .50 .23
(37 runs in 2 games for '90 Pirates)
❑ 526B Moises Alou COR .10 .05
(0 runs in 2 games for '90 Pirates)
❑ 527A Checklist 4 ERR .20 .09
105 Keith Miller
719 Kevin McReynolds
❑ 527B Checklist 4 COR .05 .02
105 Kevin McReynolds
719 Keith Miller
❑ 528 Dennis Martinez .10 .05
❑ 529 Marc Newfield RC .05 .02
❑ 530 Roger Clemens .50 .23
❑ 531 Dave Rohde .05 .02
❑ 532 Kirk McCaskill .05 .02
❑ 533 Oddibe McDowell .05 .02
❑ 534 Mike Jackson .05 .02
❑ 535 Ruben Sierra UER .05 .02
(Back reads 100 Runs amd 100 RBI's)
❑ 536 Mike Witt .05 .02
❑ 537 Jose Lind .05 .02
❑ 538 Bip Roberts .05 .02
❑ 539 Scott Terry .05 .02
❑ 540 George Brett .40 .18
❑ 541 Domingo Ramos .05 .02
❑ 542 Rob Murphy .05 .02
❑ 543 Junior Felix .05 .02
❑ 544 Alejandro Pena .05 .02
❑ 545 Dale Murphy .20 .09

❑ 546 Jeff Ballard .05 .02
❑ 547 Mike Pagliarulo .05 .02
❑ 548 Jaime Navarro .05 .02
❑ 549 John McNamara MG .05 .02
❑ 550 Eric Davis .10 .05
❑ 551 Bob Kipper .05 .02
❑ 552 Jeff Hamilton .05 .02
❑ 553 Joe Klink .05 .02
❑ 554 Brian Harper .05 .02
❑ 555 Turner Ward RC .10 .05
❑ 556 Gary Ward .05 .02
❑ 557 Wally Whitehurst .05 .02
❑ 558 Otis Nixon .05 .02
❑ 559 Adam Peterson .05 .02
❑ 560 Greg Smith .05 .02
❑ 561 Tim McIntosh .05 .02
❑ 562 Jeff Kunkel .05 .02
❑ 563 Brent Knackert .05 .02
❑ 564 Dante Bichette .10 .05
❑ 565 Craig Biggio .15 .07
❑ 566 Craig Wilson .05 .02
❑ 567 Dwayne Henry .05 .02
❑ 568 Ron Karkovice .05 .02
❑ 569 Curt Schilling .20 .09
❑ 570 Barry Bonds .50 .23
❑ 571 Pat Combs .05 .02
❑ 572 Dave Anderson .05 .02
❑ 573 Rich Rodriguez UER .05 .02
(Stats say drafted 4th, but bio says 9th round)
❑ 574 John Marzano .05 .02
❑ 575 Robin Yount .20 .09
❑ 576 Jeff Kaiser .05 .02
❑ 577 Bill Doran .05 .02
❑ 578 Dave West .05 .02
❑ 579 Roger Craig MG .05 .02
❑ 580 Dave Stewart .10 .05
❑ 581 Luis Quinones .05 .02
❑ 582 Marty Clary .05 .02
❑ 583 Tony Phillips .05 .02
❑ 584 Kevin Brown .10 .05
❑ 585 Pete O'Brien .05 .02
❑ 586 Fred Lynn .05 .02
❑ 587 Jose Offerman UER .05 .02
(Text says he signed 7/24/86, but bio says 1988)
❑ 588 Mark Whiten .05 .02
❑ 589 Scott Ruskin .05 .02
❑ 590 Eddie Murray .20 .09
❑ 591 Ken Hill .05 .02
❑ 592 B.J. Surhoff .10 .05
❑ 593A Mike Walker ERR .20 .09
('90 Canton-Akron stat line omitted)
❑ 593B Mike Walker COR .05 .02
❑ 594 Rich Garces RC .05 .02
❑ 595 Bill Landrum .05 .02
❑ 596 Ronnie Walden RC .05 .02
❑ 597 Jerry Don Gleaton .05 .02
❑ 598 Sam Horn .05 .02
❑ 599A Greg Myers ERR .20 .09
('90 Syracuse stat line omitted)
❑ 599B Greg Myers COR .05 .02
❑ 600 Bo Jackson .10 .05
❑ 601 Bob Ojeda .05 .02
❑ 602 Casey Candaele .05 .02
❑ 603A W.Chamberlain RC ERR .20 .09
Photo actually Louie Meadows
❑ 603B Wes Chamberlain RC COR .05 .02
❑ 604 Billy Hatcher .05 .02
❑ 605 Jeff Reardon .10 .05
❑ 606 Jim Gott .05 .02
❑ 607 Edgar Martinez .15 .07
❑ 608 Todd Burns .05 .02
❑ 609 Jeff Torborg MG .05 .02
❑ 610 Andres Galarraga .15 .07
❑ 611 Dave Eiland .05 .02
❑ 612 Steve Lyons .05 .02
❑ 613 Eric Show .05 .02
❑ 614 Luis Salazar .05 .02
❑ 615 Bert Blyleven .10 .05
❑ 616 Todd Zeile .05 .02
❑ 617 Bill Wegman .05 .02
❑ 618 Sil Campusano .05 .02
❑ 619 David Wells .10 .05
❑ 620 Ozzie Guillen .05 .02
❑ 621 Ted Power .05 .02
❑ 622 Jack Daugherty .05 .02
❑ 623 Jeff Blauser .05 .02
❑ 624 Tom Candiotti .05 .02
❑ 625 Terry Steinbach .05 .02
❑ 626 Gerald Young .05 .02
❑ 627 Tim Layana .05 .02
❑ 628 Greg Litton .05 .02
❑ 629 Wes Gardner .05 .02
❑ 630 Dave Winfield .20 .09
❑ 631 Mike Morgan .05 .02
❑ 632 Lloyd Moseby .05 .02
❑ 633 Kevin Tapani .05 .02
❑ 634 Henry Cotto .05 .02
❑ 635 Andy Hawkins .05 .02
❑ 636 Geronimo Pena .05 .02
❑ 637 Bruce Ruffin .05 .02
❑ 638 Mike Macfarlane .05 .02
❑ 639 Frank Robinson MG .20 .09
❑ 640 Andre Dawson .15 .07
❑ 641 Mike Henneman .05 .02
❑ 642 Hal Morris .05 .02
❑ 643 Jim Presley .05 .02
❑ 644 Chuck Crim .05 .02
❑ 645 Juan Samuel .05 .02
❑ 646 Andujar Cedeno .05 .02
❑ 647 Mark Portugal .05 .02
❑ 648 Lee Stevens .05 .02
❑ 649 Bill Sampen .05 .02
❑ 650 Jack Clark .10 .05
❑ 651 Alan Mills .05 .02
❑ 652 Kevin Romine .05 .02
❑ 653 Anthony Telford .05 .02
❑ 654 Paul Sorrento .05 .02
❑ 655 Erik Hanson .05 .02
❑ 656A Checklist 5 ERR .20 .09
348 Vicente Palacios
381 Jose Lind
537 Mike LaValliere
665 Jim Leyland
❑ 656B Checklist 5 ERR .20 .09
433 Vicente Palacios
(Palacios should be 438)
537 Jose Lind
665 Mike LaValliere
381 Jim Leyland
❑ 656C Checklist 5 COR .20 .09
438 Vicente Palacios
537 Jose Lind
665 Mike LaValliere
381 Jim Leyland
❑ 657 Mike Kingery .05 .02
❑ 658 Scott Aldred .05 .02
❑ 659 Oscar Azocar .05 .02
❑ 660 Lee Smith .10 .05
❑ 661 Steve Lake .05 .02
❑ 662 Ron Dibble .05 .02
❑ 663 Greg Brock .05 .02
❑ 664 John Farrell .05 .02
❑ 665 Mike LaValliere .05 .02
❑ 666 Danny Darwin .05 .02
❑ 667 Kent Anderson .05 .02
❑ 668 Bill Long .05 .02
❑ 669 Lou Piniella MG .10 .05
❑ 670 Rickey Henderson .40 .18
❑ 671 Andy McGaffigan .05 .02
❑ 672 Shane Mack .05 .02
❑ 673 Greg Olson UER .05 .02
(6 RBI in '88 at Tidewater and 2 RBI in '87, should be 48 and 15)
❑ 674A Kevin Gross ERR .20 .09
(89 BB with Phillies in '88 tied for league lead)
❑ 674B Kevin Gross COR .05 .02
(89 BB with Phillies in '88 led league)
❑ 675 Tom Brunansky .05 .02
❑ 676 Scott Chiamparino .05 .02
❑ 677 Billy Ripken .05 .02
❑ 678 Mark Davidson .05 .02
❑ 679 Bill Bathe .05 .02
❑ 680 David Cone .10 .05
❑ 681 Jeff Schaefer .05 .02
❑ 682 Ray Lankford .10 .05
❑ 683 Derek Lilliquist .05 .02
❑ 684 Milt Cuyler .05 .02
❑ 685 Doug Drabek .05 .02
❑ 686 Mike Gallego .05 .02
❑ 687A John Cerutti ERR .20 .09
(4.46 ERA in '90)
❑ 687B John Cerutti COR .05 .02
(4.76 ERA in '90)
❑ 688 Rosario Rodriguez .05 .02
❑ 689 John Kruk .10 .05
❑ 690 Orel Hershiser .10 .05
❑ 691 Mike Blowers .05 .02
❑ 692A Efrain Valdez ERR .20 .09
(Born 6/11/66)
❑ 692B Efrain Valdez COR .05 .02
(Born 7/11/66 and two lines of text added)
❑ 693 Francisco Cabrera .05 .02
❑ 694 Randy Veres .05 .02
❑ 695 Kevin Seitzer .05 .02
❑ 696 Steve Olin .05 .02
❑ 697 Shawn Abner .05 .02
❑ 698 Mark Guthrie .05 .02
❑ 699 Jim Lefebvre MG .05 .02
❑ 700 Jose Canseco .20 .09
❑ 701 Pascual Perez .05 .02
❑ 702 Tim Naehring .05 .02
❑ 703 Juan Agosto .05 .02
❑ 704 Devon White .05 .02
❑ 705 Robby Thompson .05 .02
❑ 706A Brad Arnsberg ERR .20 .09
(68.2 IP in '90)
❑ 706B Brad Arnsberg COR .05 .02
(62.2 IP in '90)
❑ 707 Jim Eisenreich .05 .02
❑ 708 John Mitchell .05 .02
❑ 709 Matt Sinatro .05 .02
❑ 710 Kent Hrbek .10 .05
❑ 711 Jose DeLeon .05 .02
❑ 712 Ricky Jordan .05 .02
❑ 713 Scott Scudder .05 .02
❑ 714 Marvell Wynne .05 .02
❑ 715 Tim Burke .05 .02
❑ 716 Bob Geren .05 .02
❑ 717 Phil Bradley .05 .02
❑ 718 Steve Crawford .05 .02
❑ 719 Keith Miller .05 .02
❑ 720 Cecil Fielder .10 .05
❑ 721 Mark Lee .05 .02
❑ 722 Wally Backman .05 .02
❑ 723 Candy Maldonado .05 .02
❑ 724 David Segui .05 .02
❑ 725 Ron Gant .05 .02
❑ 726 Phil Stephenson .05 .02
❑ 727 Mookie Wilson .10 .05
❑ 728 Scott Sanderson .05 .02
❑ 729 Don Zimmer MG .10 .05
❑ 730 Barry Larkin .20 .09
❑ 731 Jeff Gray .05 .02
❑ 732 Franklin Stubbs .05 .02
❑ 733 Kelly Downs .05 .02
❑ 734 John Russell .05 .02
❑ 735 Ron Darling .05 .02
❑ 736 Dick Schofield .05 .02
❑ 737 Tim Crews .05 .02
❑ 738 Mel Hall .05 .02
❑ 739 Russ Swan .05 .02
❑ 740 Ryne Sandberg .25 .11
❑ 741 Jimmy Key .10 .05
❑ 742 Tommy Gregg .05 .02
❑ 743 Bryn Smith .05 .02
❑ 744 Nelson Santovenia .05 .02
❑ 745 Doug Jones .05 .02
❑ 746 John Shelby .05 .02
❑ 747 Tony Fossas .05 .02
❑ 748 Al Newman .05 .02
❑ 749 Greg W. Harris .05 .02
❑ 750 Bobby Bonilla .10 .05
❑ 751 Wayne Edwards .05 .02
❑ 752 Kevin Bass .05 .02
❑ 753 Paul Marak UER .05 .02

(Stats say drafted in Jan. but bio says May)
❑ 754 Bill Pecota .05 .02
❑ 755 Mark Langston .05 .02
❑ 756 Jeff Huson .05 .02
❑ 757 Mark Gardner .05 .02
❑ 758 Mike Devereaux .05 .02
❑ 759 Bobby Cox MG .05 .02
❑ 760 Benny Santiago .05 .02
❑ 761 Larry Andersen .05 .02
❑ 762 Mitch Webster .05 .02
❑ 763 Dana Kiecker .05 .02
❑ 764 Mark Carreon .05 .02
❑ 765 Shawon Dunston .05 .02
❑ 766 Jeff Robinson .05 .02
❑ 767 Dan Wilson RC .10 .05
❑ 768 Don Pall .05 .02
❑ 769 Tim Sherrill .05 .02
❑ 770 Jay Howell .05 .02
❑ 771 Gary Redus UER .05 .02
(Born in Tanner, should say Athens)
❑ 772 Kent Mercker UER .05 .02
(Born in Indianapolis, should say Dublin, Ohio)
❑ 773 Tom Foley .05 .02
❑ 774 Dennis Rasmussen .05 .02
❑ 775 Julio Franco .10 .05
❑ 776 Brent Mayne .05 .02
❑ 777 John Candelaria .05 .02
❑ 778 Dan Gladden .05 .02
❑ 779 Carmelo Martinez .05 .02
❑ 780A Randy Myers ERR .05 .02
(15 career losses)
❑ 780B Randy Myers COR .05 .02
(19 career losses)
❑ 781 Darryl Hamilton .05 .02
❑ 782 Jim Deshaies .05 .02
❑ 783 Joel Skinner .05 .02
❑ 784 Willie Fraser .05 .02
❑ 785 Scott Fletcher .05 .02
❑ 786 Eric Plunk .05 .02
❑ 787 Checklist 6 .05 .02
❑ 788 Bob Milacki .05 .02
❑ 789 Tom Lasorda MG .20 .09
❑ 790 Ken Griffey Jr. .75 .35
❑ 791 Mike Benjamin .05 .02
❑ 792 Mike Greenwell .05 .02

1991 Topps Traded

	MINT	NRMT
COMPLETE SET (132)	15.00	6.75
COMP.FACT.SET (132)	15.00	6.75

❑ 1T Juan Agosto .05 .02
❑ 2T Roberto Alomar .20 .09
❑ 3T Wally Backman .05 .02
❑ 4T Jeff Bagwell RC 2.50 1.10
❑ 5T Skeeter Barnes .05 .02
❑ 6T Steve Bedrosian .05 .02
❑ 7T Derek Bell .10 .05
❑ 8T George Bell .05 .02
❑ 9T Rafael Belliard .05 .02
❑ 10T Dante Bichette .10 .05
❑ 11T Bud Black .05 .02
❑ 12T Mike Boddicker .05 .02
❑ 13T Sid Bream .05 .02
❑ 14T Hubie Brooks .05 .02
❑ 15T Brett Butler .10 .05
❑ 16T Ivan Calderon .05 .02
❑ 17T John Candelaria .05 .02
❑ 18T Tom Candiotti .05 .02
❑ 19T Gary Carter .15 .07
❑ 20T Joe Carter .10 .05
❑ 21T Rick Cerone .05 .02
❑ 22T Jack Clark .10 .05
❑ 23T Vince Coleman .05 .02
❑ 24T Scott Coolbaugh .05 .02
❑ 25T Danny Cox .05 .02
❑ 26T Danny Darwin .05 .02
❑ 27T Chili Davis .10 .05
❑ 28T Glenn Davis .05 .02
❑ 29T Steve Decker .05 .02
❑ 30T Rob Deer .05 .02
❑ 31T Rich DeLucia .05 .02
❑ 32T John Dettmer USA RC .05 .02
❑ 33T Brian Downing .05 .02
❑ 34T D.Dreifort USA RC .50 .23
❑ 35T K.Dressendorfer RC .05 .02
❑ 36T Jim Essian MG .05 .02
❑ 37T Dwight Evans .10 .05
❑ 38T Steve Farr .05 .02
❑ 39T Jeff Fassero RC .10 .05
❑ 40T Junior Felix .05 .02
❑ 41T Tony Fernandez .05 .02
❑ 42T Steve Finley .10 .05
❑ 43T Jim Fregosi MG .05 .02
❑ 44T Gary Gaetti .10 .05
❑ 45T Jason Giambi USA RC 10.00 4.50
❑ 46T Kirk Gibson .10 .05
❑ 47T Leo Gomez .05 .02
❑ 48T Luis Gonzalez RC 2.00 .90
❑ 49T Jeff Granger USA RC .05 .02
❑ 50T Todd Greene USA RC .10 .05
❑ 51T J.Hammonds USA RC .50 .23
❑ 52T Mike Hargrove MG .05 .02
❑ 53T Pete Harnisch .05 .02
❑ 54T R.Helling RC USA UER .50 .23
Misspelled Hellings on card back
❑ 55T Glenallen Hill .05 .02
❑ 56T Charlie Hough .10 .05
❑ 57T Pete Incaviglia .05 .02
❑ 58T Bo Jackson .10 .05
❑ 59T Danny Jackson .05 .02
❑ 60T Reggie Jefferson .05 .02
❑ 61T C.Johnson USA RC .75 .35
❑ 62T Jeff Johnson .05 .02
❑ 63T T.Johnson USA RC .05 .02
❑ 64T Barry Jones .05 .02
❑ 65T Chris Jones RC .05 .02
❑ 66T Scott Kamieniecki RC .05 .02
❑ 67T Pat Kelly RC .05 .02
❑ 68T Darryl Kile .10 .05
❑ 69T Chuck Knoblauch .10 .05
❑ 70T Bill Krueger .05 .02
❑ 71T Scott Leius .05 .02
❑ 72T D.Leshnock USA RC .05 .02
❑ 73T Mark Lewis .05 .02
❑ 74T Candy Maldonado .05 .02
❑ 75T J.McDonald USA RC .10 .05
❑ 76T Willie McGee .10 .05
❑ 77T Fred McGriff .15 .07
❑ 78T B.McMillon USA RC .05 .02
❑ 79T Hal McRae MG .10 .05
❑ 80T D.Melendez USA RC .05 .02
❑ 81T Orlando Merced RC .05 .02
❑ 82T Jack Morris .10 .05
❑ 83T Phil Nevin USA RC 1.00 .45
❑ 84T Otis Nixon .05 .02
❑ 85T Johnny Oates MG .05 .02
❑ 86T Bob Ojeda .05 .02
❑ 87T Mike Pagliarulo .05 .02
❑ 88T Dean Palmer .10 .05
❑ 89T Dave Parker .10 .05
❑ 90T Terry Pendleton .10 .05
❑ 91T T.Phillips (P) USA RC .05 .02
❑ 92T Doug Piatt .05 .02
❑ 93T Ron Polk USA CO .05 .02
❑ 94T Tim Raines .10 .05
❑ 95T Willie Randolph .10 .05
❑ 96T Dave Righetti .10 .05
❑ 97T Ernie Riles .05 .02
❑ 98T C.Roberts USA RC .05 .02
❑ 99T Jeff D. Robinson .05 .02
❑ 100T Jeff M. Robinson .05 .02
❑ 101T Ivan Rodriguez RC 2.00 .90
❑ 102T S.Rodriguez USA RC .05 .02
❑ 103T Tom Runnells MG .05 .02
❑ 104T Scott Sanderson .05 .02
❑ 105T Bob Scanlan .05 .02
❑ 106T Pete Schourek RC .05 .02
❑ 107T Gary Scott .05 .02
❑ 108T Paul Shuey USA RC .10 .05
❑ 109T Doug Simons .05 .02
❑ 110T Dave Smith .05 .02
❑ 111T Cory Snyder .05 .02
❑ 112T Luis Sojo .05 .02
❑ 113T K.Steenstra USA RC .05 .02
❑ 114T Darryl Strawberry .10 .05
❑ 115T Franklin Stubbs .05 .02
❑ 116T Todd Taylor USA RC .05 .02
❑ 117T Wade Taylor .05 .02
❑ 118T Garry Templeton .05 .02
❑ 119T Mickey Tettleton .05 .02
❑ 120T Tim Teufel .05 .02
❑ 121T Mike Timlin RC .10 .05
❑ 122T David Tuttle USA RC .05 .02
❑ 123T Mo Vaughn .10 .05
❑ 124T Jeff Ware USA RC .05 .02
❑ 125T Devon White .05 .02
❑ 126T Mark Whiten .05 .02
❑ 127T Mitch Williams .05 .02
❑ 128T C.Wilson USA RC .05 .02
❑ 129T Willie Wilson .05 .02
❑ 130T C.Wimmer USA RC .05 .02
❑ 131T Ivan Zweig USA RC .05 .02
❑ 132T Checklist 1T-132T .05 .02

1992 Topps

	MINT	NRMT
COMPLETE SET (792)	30.00	13.50
COMP.FACT.SET (802)	40.00	18.00
COMP.HOLIDAY SET (811)	40.00	18.00

❑ 1 Nolan Ryan 1.00 .45
❑ 2 Ricky Henderson RB .20 .09
Most career SB's
(Some cards have print marks that show 1.991 on the front)
❑ 3 Jeff Reardon RB .05 .02
10 seasons, 20 or more saves
❑ 4 Nolan Ryan RB .50 .23
22 cons. 100 K seasons
❑ 5 Dave Winfield RB .10 .05
Oldest player, cycle
❑ 6 Brien Taylor RC .10 .05
❑ 7 Jim Olander .05 .02
❑ 8 Bryan Hickerson RC .05 .02
❑ 9 Jon Farrell RC .05 .02
❑ 10 Wade Boggs .20 .09
❑ 11 Jack McDowell .05 .02
❑ 12 Luis Gonzalez .20 .09
❑ 13 Mike Scioscia .05 .02
❑ 14 Wes Chamberlain .05 .02
❑ 15 Dennis Martinez .10 .05
❑ 16 Jeff Montgomery .05 .02
❑ 17 Randy Milligan .05 .02
❑ 18 Greg Cadaret .05 .02
❑ 19 Jamie Quirk .05 .02

❑ 20	Bip Roberts	.05	.02
❑ 21	Buck Rodgers MG	.05	.02
❑ 22	Bill Wegman	.05	.02
❑ 23	Chuck Knoblauch	.10	.05
❑ 24	Randy Myers	.05	.02
❑ 25	Ron Gant	.05	.02
❑ 26	Mike Bielecki	.05	.02
❑ 27	Juan Gonzalez	.20	.09
❑ 28	Mike Schooler	.05	.02
❑ 29	Mickey Tettleton	.05	.02
❑ 30	John Kruk	.10	.05
❑ 31	Bryn Smith	.05	.02
❑ 32	Chris Nabholz	.05	.02
❑ 33	Carlos Baerga	.05	.02
❑ 34	Jeff Juden	.05	.02
❑ 35	Dave Righetti	.10	.05
❑ 36	Scott Ruffcorn RC	.05	.02
❑ 37	Luis Polonia	.05	.02
❑ 38	Tom Candiotti	.05	.02
❑ 39	Greg Olson	.05	.02
❑ 40	Cal Ripken	2.00	.90
❑ 41	Craig Lefferts	.05	.02
❑ 42	Mike Macfarlane	.05	.02
❑ 43	Jose Lind	.05	.02
❑ 44	Rick Aguilera	.10	.05
❑ 45	Gary Carter	.15	.07
❑ 46	Steve Farr	.05	.02
❑ 47	Rex Hudler	.05	.02
❑ 48	Scott Scudder	.05	.02
❑ 49	Damon Berryhill	.05	.02
❑ 50	Ken Griffey Jr.	.60	.25
❑ 51	Tom Runnells MG	.05	.02
❑ 52	Juan Bell	.05	.02
❑ 53	Tommy Gregg	.05	.02
❑ 54	David Wells	.10	.05
❑ 55	Rafael Palmeiro	.20	.09
❑ 56	Charlie O'Brien	.05	.02
❑ 57	Donn Pall	.05	.02
❑ 58	1992 Prospects C	.20	.09
	Brad Ausmus RC		
	Jim Campanis Jr.		
	Dave Nilsson		
	Doug Robbins		
❑ 59	Mo Vaughn	.10	.05
❑ 60	Tony Fernandez	.05	.02
❑ 61	Paul O'Neill	.20	.09
❑ 62	Gene Nelson	.05	.02
❑ 63	Randy Ready	.05	.02
❑ 64	Bob Kipper	.05	.02
❑ 65	Willie McGee	.10	.05
❑ 66	Scott Stahoviak RC	.05	.02
❑ 67	Luis Salazar	.05	.02
❑ 68	Marvin Freeman	.05	.02
❑ 69	Kenny Lofton	.20	.09
❑ 70	Gary Gaetti	.10	.05
❑ 71	Erik Hanson	.05	.02
❑ 72	Eddie Zosky	.05	.02
❑ 73	Brian Barnes	.05	.02
❑ 74	Scott Leius	.05	.02
❑ 75	Bret Saberhagen	.10	.05
❑ 76	Mike Gallego	.05	.02
❑ 77	Jack Armstrong	.05	.02
❑ 78	Ivan Rodriguez	.25	.11
❑ 79	Jesse Orosco	.05	.02
❑ 80	David Justice	.10	.05
❑ 81	Ced Landrum	.05	.02
❑ 82	Doug Simons	.05	.02
❑ 83	Tommy Greene	.05	.02
❑ 84	Leo Gomez	.05	.02
❑ 85	Jose DeLeon	.05	.02
❑ 86	Steve Finley	.10	.05
❑ 87	Bob MacDonald	.05	.02
❑ 88	Darrin Jackson	.05	.02
❑ 89	Neal Heaton	.05	.02
❑ 90	Robin Yount	.20	.09
❑ 91	Jeff Reed	.05	.02
❑ 92	Lenny Harris	.05	.02
❑ 93	Reggie Jefferson	.05	.02
❑ 94	Sammy Sosa	.40	.18
❑ 95	Scott Bailes	.05	.02
❑ 96	Tom McKinnon RC	.05	.02
❑ 97	Luis Rivera	.05	.02
❑ 98	Mike Harkey	.05	.02
❑ 99	Jeff Treadway	.05	.02
❑ 100	Jose Canseco	.20	.09
❑ 101	Omar Vizquel	.10	.05
❑ 102	Scott Kamieniecki	.05	.02
❑ 103	Ricky Jordan	.05	.02
❑ 104	Jeff Ballard	.05	.02
❑ 105	Felix Jose	.05	.02
❑ 106	Mike Boddicker	.05	.02
❑ 107	Dan Pasqua	.05	.02
❑ 108	Mike Timlin	.05	.02
❑ 109	Roger Craig MG	.05	.02
❑ 110	Ryne Sandberg	.25	.11
❑ 111	Mark Carreon	.05	.02
❑ 112	Oscar Azocar	.05	.02
❑ 113	Mike Greenwell	.05	.02
❑ 114	Mark Portugal	.05	.02
❑ 115	Terry Pendleton	.10	.05
❑ 116	Willie Randolph	.10	.05
❑ 117	Scott Terry	.05	.02
❑ 118	Chili Davis	.10	.05
❑ 119	Mark Gardner	.05	.02
❑ 120	Alan Trammell	.15	.07
❑ 121	Derek Bell	.10	.05
❑ 122	Gary Varsho	.05	.02
❑ 123	Bob Ojeda	.05	.02
❑ 124	Shawn Livsey RC	.05	.02
❑ 125	Chris Hoiles	.05	.02
❑ 126	1992 Prospects 1B	.10	.05
	Ryan Klesko		
	John Jaha RC		
	Rico Brogna		
	Dave Staton		
❑ 127	Carlos Quintana	.05	.02
❑ 128	Kurt Stillwell	.05	.02
❑ 129	Melido Perez	.05	.02
❑ 130	Alvin Davis	.05	.02
❑ 131	Checklist 1-132	.05	.02
❑ 132	Eric Show	.05	.02
❑ 133	Rance Mulliniks	.05	.02
❑ 134	Darryl Kile	.10	.05
❑ 135	Von Hayes	.05	.02
❑ 136	Bill Doran	.05	.02
❑ 137	Jeff D. Robinson	.05	.02
❑ 138	Monty Fariss	.05	.02
❑ 139	Jeff Innis	.05	.02
❑ 140	Mark Grace UER	.20	.09
	(Home Calie., should be Calif.)		
❑ 141	Jim Leyland MG UER	.10	.05
	(No closed parenthesis after East in 1991)		
❑ 142	Todd Van Poppel	.05	.02
❑ 143	Paul Gibson	.05	.02
❑ 144	Bill Swift	.05	.02
❑ 145	Danny Tartabull	.05	.02
❑ 146	Al Newman	.05	.02
❑ 147	Cris Carpenter	.05	.02
❑ 148	Anthony Young	.05	.02
❑ 149	Brian Bohanon	.05	.02
❑ 150	Roger Clemens UER	.50	.23
	(League leading ERA in 1990 not italicized)		
❑ 151	Jeff Hamilton	.05	.02
❑ 152	Charlie Leibrandt	.05	.02
❑ 153	Ron Karkovice	.05	.02
❑ 154	Hensley Meulens	.05	.02
❑ 155	Scott Bankhead	.05	.02
❑ 156	Manny Ramirez RC	2.50	1.10
❑ 157	Keith Miller	.05	.02
❑ 158	Todd Frohwirth	.05	.02
❑ 159	Darrin Fletcher	.05	.02
❑ 160	Bobby Bonilla	.10	.05
❑ 161	Casey Candaele	.05	.02
❑ 162	Paul Faries	.05	.02
❑ 163	Dana Kiecker	.05	.02
❑ 164	Shane Mack	.05	.02
❑ 165	Mark Langston	.05	.02
❑ 166	Geronimo Pena	.05	.02
❑ 167	Andy Allanson	.05	.02
❑ 168	Dwight Smith	.05	.02
❑ 169	Chuck Crim	.05	.02
❑ 170	Alex Cole	.05	.02
❑ 171	Bill Plummer MG	.05	.02
❑ 172	Juan Berenguer	.05	.02
❑ 173	Brian Downing	.05	.02
❑ 174	Steve Frey	.05	.02
❑ 175	Orel Hershiser	.10	.05
❑ 176	Ramon Garcia	.05	.02
❑ 177	Dan Gladden	.05	.02
❑ 178	Jim Acker	.05	.02
❑ 179	1992 Prospects 2B	.05	.02
	Bobby DeJardin		
	Cesar Bernhardt		
	Armando Moreno		
	Andy Stankiewicz		
❑ 180	Kevin Mitchell	.05	.02
❑ 181	Hector Villanueva	.05	.02
❑ 182	Jeff Reardon	.10	.05
❑ 183	Brent Mayne	.05	.02
❑ 184	Jimmy Jones	.05	.02
❑ 185	Benito Santiago	.05	.02
❑ 186	Cliff Floyd RC	1.00	.45
❑ 187	Ernie Riles	.05	.02
❑ 188	Jose Guzman	.05	.02
❑ 189	Junior Felix	.05	.02
❑ 190	Glenn Davis	.05	.02
❑ 191	Charlie Hough	.10	.05
❑ 192	Dave Fleming	.05	.02
❑ 193	Omar Olivares	.05	.02
❑ 194	Eric Karros	.10	.05
❑ 195	David Cone	.10	.05
❑ 196	Frank Castillo	.05	.02
❑ 197	Glenn Braggs	.05	.02
❑ 198	Scott Aldred	.05	.02
❑ 199	Jeff Blauser	.05	.02
❑ 200	Len Dykstra	.10	.05
❑ 201	B.Showalter RC MG	.10	.05
❑ 202	Rick Honeycutt	.05	.02
❑ 203	Greg Myers	.05	.02
❑ 204	Trevor Wilson	.05	.02
❑ 205	Jay Howell	.05	.02
❑ 206	Luis Sojo	.05	.02
❑ 207	Jack Clark	.10	.05
❑ 208	Julio Machado	.05	.02
❑ 209	Lloyd McClendon	.05	.02
❑ 210	Ozzie Guillen	.05	.02
❑ 211	Jeremy Hernandez RC	.05	.02
❑ 212	Randy Velarde	.05	.02
❑ 213	Les Lancaster	.05	.02
❑ 214	Andy Mota	.05	.02
❑ 215	Rich Gossage	.10	.05
❑ 216	Brent Gates RC	.05	.02
❑ 217	Brian Harper	.05	.02
❑ 218	Mike Flanagan	.05	.02
❑ 219	Jerry Browne	.05	.02
❑ 220	Jose Rijo	.05	.02
❑ 221	Skeeter Barnes	.05	.02
❑ 222	Jaime Navarro	.05	.02
❑ 223	Mel Hall	.05	.02
❑ 224	Bret Barberie	.05	.02
❑ 225	Roberto Alomar	.20	.09
❑ 226	Pete Smith	.05	.02
❑ 227	Daryl Boston	.05	.02
❑ 228	Eddie Whitson	.05	.02
❑ 229	Shawn Boskie	.05	.02
❑ 230	Dick Schofield	.05	.02
❑ 231	Brian Drahman	.05	.02
❑ 232	John Smiley	.05	.02
❑ 233	Mitch Webster	.05	.02
❑ 234	Terry Steinbach	.05	.02
❑ 235	Jack Morris	.10	.05
❑ 236	Bill Pecota	.05	.02
❑ 237	Jose Hernandez RC	.05	.02
❑ 238	Greg Litton	.05	.02
❑ 239	Brian Holman	.05	.02
❑ 240	Andres Galarraga	.15	.07
❑ 241	Gerald Young	.05	.02
❑ 242	Mike Mussina	.30	.14
❑ 243	Alvaro Espinoza	.05	.02
❑ 244	Darren Daulton	.10	.05
❑ 245	John Smoltz	.10	.05
❑ 246	Jason Pruitt RC	.05	.02
❑ 247	Chuck Finley	.10	.05
❑ 248	Jim Gantner	.05	.02
❑ 249	Tony Fossas	.05	.02
❑ 250	Ken Griffey Sr.	.10	.05
❑ 251	Kevin Elster	.05	.02
❑ 252	Dennis Rasmussen	.05	.02
❑ 253	Terry Kennedy	.05	.02
❑ 254	Ryan Bowen	.05	.02
❑ 255	Robin Ventura	.10	.05
❑ 256	Mike Aldrete	.05	.02
❑ 257	Jeff Russell	.05	.02
❑ 258	Jim Lindeman	.05	.02
❑ 259	Ron Darling	.05	.02

❑ 260	Devon White	.05	.02
❑ 261	Tom Lasorda MG	.10	.05
❑ 262	Terry Lee	.05	.02
❑ 263	Bob Patterson	.05	.02
❑ 264	Checklist 133-264	.05	.02
❑ 265	Teddy Higuera	.05	.02
❑ 266	Roberto Kelly	.05	.02
❑ 267	Steve Bedrosian	.05	.02
❑ 268	Brady Anderson	.10	.05
❑ 269	Ruben Amaro	.05	.02
❑ 270	Tony Gwynn	.40	.18
❑ 271	Tracy Jones	.05	.02
❑ 272	Jerry Don Gleaton	.05	.02
❑ 273	Craig Grebeck	.05	.02
❑ 274	Bob Scanlan	.05	.02
❑ 275	Todd Zeile	.05	.02
❑ 276	Shawn Green RC	2.00	.90
❑ 277	Scott Chiamparino	.05	.02
❑ 278	Darryl Hamilton	.05	.02
❑ 279	Jim Clancy	.05	.02
❑ 280	Carlos Martinez	.05	.02
❑ 281	Kevin Appier	.10	.05
❑ 282	John Wehner	.05	.02
❑ 283	Reggie Sanders	.05	.02
❑ 284	Gene Larkin	.05	.02
❑ 285	Bob Welch	.05	.02
❑ 286	Gilberto Reyes	.05	.02
❑ 287	Pete Schourek	.05	.02
❑ 288	Andujar Cedeno	.05	.02
❑ 289	Mike Morgan	.05	.02
❑ 290	Bo Jackson	.10	.05
❑ 291	Phil Garner MG	.05	.02
❑ 292	Ray Lankford	.05	.02
❑ 293	Mike Henneman	.05	.02
❑ 294	Dave Valle	.05	.02
❑ 295	Alonzo Powell	.05	.02
❑ 296	Tom Brunansky	.05	.02
❑ 297	Kevin Brown	.10	.05
❑ 298	Kelly Gruber	.05	.02
❑ 299	Charles Nagy	.05	.02
❑ 300	Don Mattingly	.50	.23
❑ 301	Kirk McCaskill	.05	.02
❑ 302	Joey Cora	.05	.02
❑ 303	Dan Plesac	.05	.02
❑ 304	Joe Oliver	.05	.02
❑ 305	Tom Glavine	.20	.09
❑ 306	Al Shirley RC	.05	.02
❑ 307	Bruce Ruffin	.05	.02
❑ 308	Craig Shipley	.05	.02
❑ 309	Dave Martinez	.05	.02
❑ 310	Jose Mesa	.05	.02
❑ 311	Henry Cotto	.05	.02
❑ 312	Mike LaValliere	.05	.02
❑ 313	Kevin Tapani	.05	.02
❑ 314	Jeff Huson	.05	.02
	(Shows Jose Canseco		
	sliding into second)		
❑ 315	Juan Samuel	.05	.02
❑ 316	Curt Schilling	.20	.09
❑ 317	Mike Bordick	.05	.02
❑ 318	Steve Howe	.05	.02
❑ 319	Tony Phillips	.05	.02
❑ 320	George Bell	.05	.02
❑ 321	Lou Piniella MG	.10	.05
❑ 322	Tim Burke	.05	.02
❑ 323	Milt Thompson	.05	.02
❑ 324	Danny Darwin	.05	.02
❑ 325	Joe Orsulak	.05	.02
❑ 326	Eric King	.05	.02
❑ 327	Jay Buhner	.10	.05
❑ 328	Joel Johnston	.05	.02
❑ 329	Franklin Stubbs	.05	.02
❑ 330	Will Clark	.20	.09
❑ 331	Steve Lake	.05	.02
❑ 332	Chris Jones	.05	.02
❑ 333	Pat Tabler	.05	.02
❑ 334	Kevin Gross	.05	.02
❑ 335	Dave Henderson	.05	.02
❑ 336	Greg Anthony RC	.05	.02
❑ 337	Alejandro Pena	.05	.02
❑ 338	Shawn Abner	.05	.02
❑ 339	Tom Browning	.05	.02
❑ 340	Otis Nixon	.05	.02
❑ 341	Bob Geren	.05	.02
❑ 342	Tim Spehr	.05	.02
❑ 343	John Vander Wal	.05	.02
❑ 344	Jack Daugherty	.05	.02
❑ 345	Zane Smith	.05	.02
❑ 346	Rheal Cormier	.05	.02
❑ 347	Kent Hrbek	.10	.05
❑ 348	Rick Wilkins	.05	.02
❑ 349	Steve Lyons	.05	.02
❑ 350	Gregg Olson	.05	.02
❑ 351	Greg Riddoch MG	.05	.02
❑ 352	Ed Nunez	.05	.02
❑ 353	Braulio Castillo	.05	.02
❑ 354	Dave Bergman	.05	.02
❑ 355	Warren Newson	.05	.02
❑ 356	Luis Quinones	.05	.02
❑ 357	Mike Witt	.05	.02
❑ 358	Ted Wood	.05	.02
❑ 359	Mike Moore	.05	.02
❑ 360	Lance Parrish	.10	.05
❑ 361	Barry Jones	.05	.02
❑ 362	Javier Ortiz	.05	.02
❑ 363	John Candelaria	.05	.02
❑ 364	Glenallen Hill	.05	.02
❑ 365	Duane Ward	.05	.02
❑ 366	Checklist 265-396	.05	.02
❑ 367	Rafael Belliard	.05	.02
❑ 368	Bill Krueger	.05	.02
❑ 369	Steve Whitaker RC	.05	.02
❑ 370	Shawon Dunston	.05	.02
❑ 371	Dante Bichette	.10	.05
❑ 372	Kip Gross	.05	.02
❑ 373	Don Robinson	.05	.02
❑ 374	Bernie Williams	.20	.09
❑ 375	Bert Blyleven	.10	.05
❑ 376	Chris Donnels	.05	.02
❑ 377	Bob Zupcic RC	.05	.02
❑ 378	Joel Skinner	.05	.02
❑ 379	Steve Chitren	.05	.02
❑ 380	Barry Bonds	.50	.23
❑ 381	Sparky Anderson MG	.10	.05
❑ 382	Sid Fernandez	.05	.02
❑ 383	Dave Hollins	.05	.02
❑ 384	Mark Lee	.05	.02
❑ 385	Tim Wallach	.05	.02
❑ 386	Will Clark AS	.10	.05
❑ 387	Ryne Sandberg AS	.15	.07
❑ 388	Howard Johnson AS	.05	.02
❑ 389	Barry Larkin AS	.10	.05
❑ 390	Barry Bonds AS	.25	.11
❑ 391	Ron Gant AS	.05	.02
❑ 392	Bobby Bonilla AS	.05	.02
❑ 393	Craig Biggio AS	.10	.05
❑ 394	Dennis Martinez AS	.05	.02
❑ 395	Tom Glavine AS	.10	.05
❑ 396	Lee Smith AS	.05	.02
❑ 397	Cecil Fielder AS	.05	.02
❑ 398	Julio Franco AS	.05	.02
❑ 399	Wade Boggs AS	.10	.05
❑ 400	Cal Ripken AS	.40	.18
❑ 401	Jose Canseco AS	.20	.09
❑ 402	Joe Carter AS	.05	.02
❑ 403	Ruben Sierra AS	.05	.02
❑ 404	Matt Nokes AS	.05	.02
❑ 405	Roger Clemens AS	.25	.11
❑ 406	Jim Abbott AS	.05	.02
❑ 407	Bryan Harvey AS	.05	.02
❑ 408	Bob Milacki	.05	.02
❑ 409	Geno Petralli	.05	.02
❑ 410	Dave Stewart	.10	.05
❑ 411	Mike Jackson	.05	.02
❑ 412	Luis Aquino	.05	.02
❑ 413	Tim Teufel	.05	.02
❑ 414	Jeff Ware	.05	.02
❑ 415	Jim Deshaies	.05	.02
❑ 416	Ellis Burks	.10	.05
❑ 417	Allan Anderson	.05	.02
❑ 418	Alfredo Griffin	.05	.02
❑ 419	Wally Whitehurst	.05	.02
❑ 420	Sandy Alomar Jr.	.10	.05
❑ 421	Juan Agosto	.05	.02
❑ 422	Sam Horn	.05	.02
❑ 423	Jeff Fassero	.05	.02
❑ 424	Paul McClellan	.05	.02
❑ 425	Cecil Fielder	.10	.05
❑ 426	Tim Raines	.10	.05
❑ 427	Eddie Taubensee RC	.10	.05
❑ 428	Dennis Boyd	.05	.02
❑ 429	Tony LaRussa MG	.10	.05
❑ 430	Steve Sax	.05	.02
❑ 431	Tom Gordon	.05	.02
❑ 432	Billy Hatcher	.05	.02
❑ 433	Cal Eldred	.05	.02
❑ 434	Wally Backman	.05	.02
❑ 435	Mark Eichhorn	.05	.02
❑ 436	Mookie Wilson	.10	.05
❑ 437	Scott Servais	.05	.02
❑ 438	Mike Maddux	.05	.02
❑ 439	Chico Walker	.05	.02
❑ 440	Doug Drabek	.05	.02
❑ 441	Rob Deer	.05	.02
❑ 442	Dave West	.05	.02
❑ 443	Spike Owen	.05	.02
❑ 444	Tyrone Hill RC	.05	.02
❑ 445	Matt Williams	.15	.07
❑ 446	Mark Lewis	.05	.02
❑ 447	David Segui	.05	.02
❑ 448	Tom Pagnozzi	.05	.02
❑ 449	Jeff Johnson	.05	.02
❑ 450	Mark McGwire	.75	.35
❑ 451	Tom Henke	.05	.02
❑ 452	Wilson Alvarez	.05	.02
❑ 453	Gary Redus	.05	.02
❑ 454	Darren Holmes	.05	.02
❑ 455	Pete O'Brien	.05	.02
❑ 456	Pat Combs	.05	.02
❑ 457	Hubie Brooks	.05	.02
❑ 458	Frank Tanana	.05	.02
❑ 459	Tom Kelly MG	.05	.02
❑ 460	Andre Dawson	.15	.07
❑ 461	Doug Jones	.05	.02
❑ 462	Rich Rodriguez	.05	.02
❑ 463	Mike Simms	.05	.02
❑ 464	Mike Jeffcoat	.05	.02
❑ 465	Barry Larkin	.20	.09
❑ 466	Stan Belinda	.05	.02
❑ 467	Lonnie Smith	.05	.02
❑ 468	Greg Harris	.05	.02
❑ 469	Jim Eisenreich	.05	.02
❑ 470	Pedro Guerrero	.10	.05
❑ 471	Jose DeJesus	.05	.02
❑ 472	Rich Rowland RC	.05	.02
❑ 473	1992 Prospects 3B UER	.20	.09
	Frank Bolick		
	Craig Paquette		
	Tom Redington		
	Paul Russo		
	(Line around top border)		
❑ 474	Mike Rossiter RC	.05	.02
❑ 475	Robby Thompson	.05	.02
❑ 476	Randy Bush	.05	.02
❑ 477	Greg Hibbard	.05	.02
❑ 478	Dale Sveum	.05	.02
❑ 479	Chito Martinez	.05	.02
❑ 480	Scott Sanderson	.05	.02
❑ 481	Tino Martinez	.10	.05
❑ 482	Jimmy Key	.10	.05
❑ 483	Terry Shumpert	.05	.02
❑ 484	Mike Hartley	.05	.02
❑ 485	Chris Sabo	.05	.02
❑ 486	Bob Walk	.05	.02
❑ 487	John Cerutti	.05	.02
❑ 488	Scott Cooper	.05	.02
❑ 489	Bobby Cox MG	.10	.05
❑ 490	Julio Franco	.10	.05
❑ 491	Jeff Brantley	.05	.02
❑ 492	Mike Devereaux	.05	.02
❑ 493	Jose Offerman	.05	.02
❑ 494	Gary Thurman	.05	.02
❑ 495	Carney Lansford	.10	.05
❑ 496	Joe Grahe	.05	.02
❑ 497	Andy Ashby	.05	.02
❑ 498	Gerald Perry	.05	.02
❑ 499	Dave Otto	.05	.02
❑ 500	Vince Coleman	.05	.02
❑ 501	Rob Mallicoat	.05	.02
❑ 502	Greg Briley	.05	.02
❑ 503	Pascual Perez	.05	.02
❑ 504	Aaron Sele RC	.50	.23
❑ 505	Bobby Thigpen	.05	.02
❑ 506	Todd Benzinger	.05	.02
❑ 507	Candy Maldonado	.05	.02
❑ 508	Bill Gullickson	.05	.02
❑ 509	Doug Dascenzo	.05	.02
❑ 510	Frank Viola	.10	.05

❑	511	Kenny Rogers	.05	.02
❑	512	Mike Heath	.05	.02
❑	513	Kevin Bass	.05	.02
❑	514	Kim Batiste	.05	.02
❑	515	Delino DeShields	.05	.02
❑	516	Ed Sprague	.05	.02
❑	517	Jim Gott	.05	.02
❑	518	Jose Melendez	.05	.02
❑	519	Hal McRae MG	.10	.05
❑	520	Jeff Bagwell	.40	.18
❑	521	Joe Hesketh	.05	.02
❑	522	Milt Cuyler	.05	.02
❑	523	Shawn Hillegas	.05	.02
❑	524	Don Slaught	.05	.02
❑	525	Randy Johnson	.25	.11
❑	526	Doug Piatt	.05	.02
❑	527	Checklist 397-528	.05	.02
❑	528	Steve Foster	.05	.02
❑	529	Joe Girardi	.05	.02
❑	530	Jim Abbott	.10	.05
❑	531	Larry Walker	.15	.07
❑	532	Mike Huff	.05	.02
❑	533	Mackey Sasser	.05	.02
❑	534	Benji Gil RC	.05	.02
❑	535	Dave Stieb	.05	.02
❑	536	Willie Wilson	.05	.02
❑	537	Mark Leiter	.05	.02
❑	538	Jose Uribe	.05	.02
❑	539	Thomas Howard	.05	.02
❑	540	Ben McDonald	.05	.02
❑	541	Jose Tolentino	.05	.02
❑	542	Keith Mitchell	.05	.02
❑	543	Jerome Walton	.05	.02
❑	544	Cliff Brantley	.05	.02
❑	545	Andy Van Slyke	.10	.05
❑	546	Paul Sorrento	.05	.02
❑	547	Herm Winningham	.05	.02
❑	548	Mark Guthrie	.05	.02
❑	549	Joe Torre MG	.10	.05
❑	550	Darryl Strawberry	.10	.05
❑	551	1992 Prospects SS UER Wilfredo Cordero Chipper Jones Manny Alexander Alex Arias (No line around top border)	1.00	.45
❑	552	Dave Gallagher	.05	.02
❑	553	Edgar Martinez	.15	.07
❑	554	Donald Harris	.05	.02
❑	555	Frank Thomas	.25	.11
❑	556	Storm Davis	.05	.02
❑	557	Dickie Thon	.05	.02
❑	558	Scott Garrelts	.05	.02
❑	559	Steve Olin	.05	.02
❑	560	Rickey Henderson	.40	.18
❑	561	Jose Vizcaino	.05	.02
❑	562	Wade Taylor	.05	.02
❑	563	Pat Borders	.05	.02
❑	564	Jimmy Gonzalez RC	.05	.02
❑	565	Lee Smith	.10	.05
❑	566	Bill Sampen	.05	.02
❑	567	Dean Palmer	.10	.05
❑	568	Bryan Harvey	.05	.02
❑	569	Tony Pena	.05	.02
❑	570	Lou Whitaker	.10	.05
❑	571	Randy Tomlin	.05	.02
❑	572	Greg Vaughn	.10	.05
❑	573	Kelly Downs	.05	.02
❑	574	Steve Avery UER (Should be 13 games for Durham in 1989)	.05	.02
❑	575	Kirby Puckett	.50	.23
❑	576	Heathcliff Slocumb	.05	.02
❑	577	Kevin Seitzer	.05	.02
❑	578	Lee Guetterman	.05	.02
❑	579	Johnny Oates MG	.05	.02
❑	580	Greg Maddux	.50	.23
❑	581	Stan Javier	.05	.02
❑	582	Vicente Palacios	.05	.02
❑	583	Mel Rojas	.05	.02
❑	584	Wayne Rosenthal RC	.05	.02
❑	585	Lenny Webster	.05	.02
❑	586	Rod Nichols	.05	.02
❑	587	Mickey Morandini	.05	.02
❑	588	Russ Swan	.05	.02
❑	589	Mariano Duncan	.05	.02
❑	590	Howard Johnson	.05	.02
❑	591	1992 Prospects OF Jeromy Burnitz Jacob Brumfield Alan Cockrell D.J. Dozier	.10	.05
❑	592	Denny Neagle	.10	.05
❑	593	Steve Decker	.05	.02
❑	594	Brian Barber RC	.05	.02
❑	595	Bruce Hurst	.05	.02
❑	596	Kent Mercker	.05	.02
❑	597	Mike Magnante RC	.05	.02
❑	598	Jody Reed	.05	.02
❑	599	Steve Searcy	.05	.02
❑	600	Paul Molitor	.20	.09
❑	601	Dave Smith	.05	.02
❑	602	Mike Fetters	.05	.02
❑	603	Luis Mercedes	.05	.02
❑	604	Chris Gwynn	.05	.02
❑	605	Scott Erickson	.05	.02
❑	606	Brook Jacoby	.05	.02
❑	607	Todd Stottlemyre	.05	.02
❑	608	Scott Bradley	.05	.02
❑	609	Mike Hargrove MG	.10	.05
❑	610	Eric Davis	.10	.05
❑	611	Brian Hunter	.05	.02
❑	612	Pat Kelly	.05	.02
❑	613	Pedro Munoz	.05	.02
❑	614	Al Osuna	.05	.02
❑	615	Matt Merullo	.05	.02
❑	616	Larry Andersen	.05	.02
❑	617	Junior Ortiz	.05	.02
❑	618	1992 Prospects OF Cesar Hernandez Steve Hosey Jeff McNeely Dan Peltier	.05	.02
❑	619	Danny Jackson	.05	.02
❑	620	George Brett	.40	.18
❑	621	Dan Gakeler	.05	.02
❑	622	Steve Buechele	.05	.02
❑	623	Bob Tewksbury	.05	.02
❑	624	Shawn Estes RC	.50	.23
❑	625	Kevin McReynolds	.05	.02
❑	626	Chris Haney	.05	.02
❑	627	Mike Sharperson	.05	.02
❑	628	Mark Williamson	.05	.02
❑	629	Wally Joyner	.10	.05
❑	630	Carlton Fisk	.20	.09
❑	631	Armando Reynoso RC	.10	.05
❑	632	Felix Fermin	.05	.02
❑	633	Mitch Williams	.05	.02
❑	634	Manuel Lee	.05	.02
❑	635	Harold Baines	.10	.05
❑	636	Greg Harris	.05	.02
❑	637	Orlando Merced	.05	.02
❑	638	Chris Bosio	.05	.02
❑	639	Wayne Housie	.05	.02
❑	640	Xavier Hernandez	.05	.02
❑	641	David Howard	.05	.02
❑	642	Tim Crews	.05	.02
❑	643	Rick Cerone	.05	.02
❑	644	Terry Leach	.05	.02
❑	645	Deion Sanders	.10	.05
❑	646	Craig Wilson	.05	.02
❑	647	Marquis Grissom	.05	.02
❑	648	Scott Fletcher	.05	.02
❑	649	Norm Charlton	.05	.02
❑	650	Jesse Barfield	.05	.02
❑	651	Joe Slusarski	.05	.02
❑	652	Bobby Rose	.05	.02
❑	653	Dennis Lamp	.05	.02
❑	654	Allen Watson RC	.05	.02
❑	655	Brett Butler	.10	.05
❑	656	1992 Prospects OF Rudy Pemberton Henry Rodriguez Lee Tinsley RC Gerald Williams	.05	.02
❑	657	Dave Johnson	.05	.02
❑	658	Checklist 529-660	.05	.02
❑	659	Brian McRae	.05	.02
❑	660	Fred McGriff	.15	.07
❑	661	Bill Landrum	.05	.02
❑	662	Juan Guzman	.05	.02
❑	663	Greg Gagne	.05	.02
❑	664	Ken Hill	.05	.02
❑	665	Dave Haas	.05	.02
❑	666	Tom Foley	.05	.02
❑	667	Roberto Hernandez	.05	.02
❑	668	Dwayne Henry	.05	.02
❑	669	Jim Fregosi MG	.05	.02
❑	670	Harold Reynolds	.05	.02
❑	671	Mark Whiten	.05	.02
❑	672	Eric Plunk	.05	.02
❑	673	Todd Hundley	.05	.02
❑	674	Mo Sanford	.05	.02
❑	675	Bobby Witt	.05	.02
❑	676	1992 Prospects P Sam Militello Pat Mahomes RC Turk Wendell Roger Salkeld	.05	.02
❑	677	John Marzano	.05	.02
❑	678	Joe Klink	.05	.02
❑	679	Pete Incaviglia	.05	.02
❑	680	Dale Murphy	.20	.09
❑	681	Rene Gonzales	.05	.02
❑	682	Andy Benes	.05	.02
❑	683	Jim Poole	.05	.02
❑	684	Trever Miller RC	.05	.02
❑	685	Scott Livingstone	.05	.02
❑	686	Rich DeLucia	.05	.02
❑	687	Harvey Pulliam	.05	.02
❑	688	Tim Belcher	.05	.02
❑	689	Mark Lemke	.05	.02
❑	690	John Franco	.10	.05
❑	691	Walt Weiss	.05	.02
❑	692	Scott Ruskin	.05	.02
❑	693	Jeff King	.05	.02
❑	694	Mike Gardiner	.05	.02
❑	695	Gary Sheffield	.10	.05
❑	696	Joe Boever	.05	.02
❑	697	Mike Felder	.05	.02
❑	698	John Habyan	.05	.02
❑	699	Cito Gaston MG	.05	.02
❑	700	Ruben Sierra	.05	.02
❑	701	Scott Radinsky	.05	.02
❑	702	Lee Stevens	.05	.02
❑	703	Mark Wohlers	.05	.02
❑	704	Curt Young	.05	.02
❑	705	Dwight Evans	.10	.05
❑	706	Rob Murphy	.05	.02
❑	707	Gregg Jefferies	.05	.02
❑	708	Tom Bolton	.05	.02
❑	709	Chris James	.05	.02
❑	710	Kevin Maas	.05	.02
❑	711	Ricky Bones	.05	.02
❑	712	Curt Wilkerson	.05	.02
❑	713	Roger McDowell	.05	.02
❑	714	Pokey Reese RC	.40	.18
❑	715	Craig Biggio	.15	.07
❑	716	Kirk Dressendorfer	.05	.02
❑	717	Ken Dayley	.05	.02
❑	718	B.J. Surhoff	.10	.05
❑	719	Terry Mulholland	.05	.02
❑	720	Kirk Gibson	.10	.05
❑	721	Mike Pagliarulo	.05	.02
❑	722	Walt Terrell	.05	.02
❑	723	Jose Oquendo	.05	.02
❑	724	Kevin Morton	.05	.02
❑	725	Dwight Gooden	.10	.05
❑	726	Kirt Manwaring	.05	.02
❑	727	Chuck McElroy	.05	.02
❑	728	Dave Burba	.05	.02
❑	729	Art Howe MG	.05	.02
❑	730	Ramon Martinez	.05	.02
❑	731	Donnie Hill	.05	.02
❑	732	Nelson Santovenia	.05	.02
❑	733	Bob Melvin	.05	.02
❑	734	Scott Hatteberg RC	.05	.02
❑	735	Greg Swindell	.05	.02
❑	736	Lance Johnson	.05	.02
❑	737	Kevin Reimer	.05	.02
❑	738	Dennis Eckersley	.10	.05
❑	739	Rob Ducey	.05	.02
❑	740	Ken Caminiti	.10	.05
❑	741	Mark Gubicza	.05	.02
❑	742	Bill Spiers	.05	.02
❑	743	Darren Lewis	.05	.02
❑	744	Chris Hammond	.05	.02

		MINT	NRMT
❑ 745	Dave Magadan	.05	.02
❑ 746	Bernard Gilkey	.05	.02
❑ 747	Willie Banks	.05	.02
❑ 748	Matt Nokes	.05	.02
❑ 749	Jerald Clark	.05	.02
❑ 750	Travis Fryman	.10	.05
❑ 751	Steve Wilson	.05	.02
❑ 752	Billy Ripken	.05	.02
❑ 753	Paul Assenmacher	.05	.02
❑ 754	Charlie Hayes	.05	.02
❑ 755	Alex Fernandez	.05	.02
❑ 756	Gary Pettis	.05	.02
❑ 757	Rob Dibble	.05	.02
❑ 758	Tim Naehring	.05	.02
❑ 759	Jeff Torborg MG	.05	.02
❑ 760	Ozzie Smith	.25	.11
❑ 761	Mike Fitzgerald	.05	.02
❑ 762	John Burkett	.05	.02
❑ 763	Kyle Abbott	.05	.02
❑ 764	Tyler Green RC	.05	.02
❑ 765	Pete Harnisch	.05	.02
❑ 766	Mark Davis	.05	.02
❑ 767	Kal Daniels	.05	.02
❑ 768	Jim Thome	.20	.09
❑ 769	Jack Howell	.05	.02
❑ 770	Sid Bream	.05	.02
❑ 771	Arthur Rhodes	.05	.02
❑ 772	Garry Templeton UER (Stat heading in for pitchers)	.05	.02
❑ 773	Hal Morris	.05	.02
❑ 774	Bud Black	.05	.02
❑ 775	Ivan Calderon	.05	.02
❑ 776	Doug Henry RC	.05	.02
❑ 777	John Olerud	.10	.05
❑ 778	Tim Leary	.05	.02
❑ 779	Jay Bell	.10	.05
❑ 780	Eddie Murray	.20	.09
❑ 781	Paul Abbott	.05	.02
❑ 782	Phil Plantier	.05	.02
❑ 783	Joe Magrane	.05	.02
❑ 784	Ken Patterson	.05	.02
❑ 785	Albert Belle	.10	.05
❑ 786	Royce Clayton	.05	.02
❑ 787	Checklist 661-792	.05	.02
❑ 788	Mike Stanton	.05	.02
❑ 789	Bobby Valentine MG	.05	.02
❑ 790	Joe Carter	.10	.05
❑ 791	Danny Cox	.05	.02
❑ 792	Dave Winfield	.20	.09

1992 Topps Traded

	MINT	NRMT
COMP.FACT.SET (132)	100.00	45.00

		MINT	NRMT
❑ 1T	Willie Adams USA RC	.10	.05
❑ 2T	Jeff Alkire USA RC	.10	.05
❑ 3T	Felipe Alou MG	.15	.07
❑ 4T	Moises Alou	.15	.07
❑ 5T	Ruben Amaro	.10	.05
❑ 6T	Jack Armstrong	.10	.05
❑ 7T	Scott Bankhead	.10	.05
❑ 8T	Tim Belcher	.10	.05
❑ 9T	George Bell	.10	.05
❑ 10T	Freddie Benavides	.10	.05
❑ 11T	Todd Benzinger	.10	.05
❑ 12T	Joe Boever	.10	.05
❑ 13T	Ricky Bones	.10	.05
❑ 14T	Bobby Bonilla	.15	.07
❑ 15T	Hubie Brooks	.10	.05
❑ 16T	Jerry Browne	.10	.05
❑ 17T	Jim Bullinger	.10	.05
❑ 18T	Dave Burba	.10	.05
❑ 19T	Kevin Campbell	.10	.05
❑ 20T	Tom Candiotti	.10	.05
❑ 21T	Mark Carreon	.10	.05
❑ 22T	Gary Carter	.25	.11
❑ 23T	Archi Cianfrocco RC	.10	.05
❑ 24T	Phil Clark	.10	.05
❑ 25T	Chad Curtis RC	.15	.07
❑ 26T	Eric Davis	.15	.07
❑ 27T	Tim Davis USA RC	.10	.05
❑ 28T	Gary DiSarcina	.10	.05
❑ 29T	Darren Dreifort USA	.15	.07
❑ 30T	Mariano Duncan	.10	.05
❑ 31T	Mike Fitzgerald	.10	.05
❑ 32T	John Flaherty	.10	.05
❑ 33T	Darrin Fletcher	.10	.05
❑ 34T	Scott Fletcher	.10	.05
❑ 35T	R.Fraser CO USA RC	.10	.05
❑ 36T	Andres Galarraga	.25	.11
❑ 37T	Dave Gallagher	.10	.05
❑ 38T	Mike Gallego	.10	.05
❑ 39T	N.Garciaparra USA RC	60.00	27.00
❑ 40T	Jason Giambi USA	2.00	.90
❑ 41T	Danny Gladden	.10	.05
❑ 42T	Rene Gonzales	.10	.05
❑ 43T	Jeff Granger USA	.10	.05
❑ 44T	Rick Greene USA RC	.10	.05
❑ 45T	J.Hammonds USA	.15	.07
❑ 46T	Charlie Hayes	.10	.05
❑ 47T	Von Hayes	.10	.05
❑ 48T	Rick Helling USA	.10	.05
❑ 49T	Butch Henry RC	.10	.05
❑ 50T	Carlos Hernandez	.10	.05
❑ 51T	Ken Hill	.10	.05
❑ 52T	Butch Hobson	.10	.05
❑ 53T	Vince Horsman	.10	.05
❑ 54T	Pete Incaviglia	.10	.05
❑ 55T	Gregg Jefferies	.10	.05
❑ 56T	Charles Johnson USA	.15	.07
❑ 57T	Doug Jones	.10	.05
❑ 58T	Brian Jordan RC	3.00	1.35
❑ 59T	Wally Joyner	.15	.07
❑ 60T	D.Kirkreit USA RC	.10	.05
❑ 61T	Bill Krueger	.10	.05
❑ 62T	Gene Lamont MG	.10	.05
❑ 63T	Jim Lefebvre MG	.10	.05
❑ 64T	Danny Leon	.10	.05
❑ 65T	Pat Listach RC	.15	.07
❑ 66T	Kenny Lofton	.40	.18
❑ 67T	Dave Martinez	.10	.05
❑ 68T	Derrick May	.10	.05
❑ 69T	Kirk McCaskill	.10	.05
❑ 70T	C.McConnell USA RC	.10	.05
❑ 71T	Kevin McReynolds	.10	.05
❑ 72T	Rusty Meacham	.10	.05
❑ 73T	Keith Miller	.10	.05
❑ 74T	Kevin Mitchell	.10	.05
❑ 75T	Jason Moler USA RC	.10	.05
❑ 76T	Mike Morgan	.10	.05
❑ 77T	Jack Morris	.15	.07
❑ 78T	C.Murray USA RC	.10	.05
❑ 79T	Eddie Murray	.40	.18
❑ 80T	Randy Myers	.10	.05
❑ 81T	Denny Neagle	.15	.07
❑ 82T	Phil Nevin USA	.50	.23
❑ 83T	Dave Nilsson	.10	.05
❑ 84T	Junior Ortiz	.10	.05
❑ 85T	Donovan Osborne	.10	.05
❑ 86T	Bill Pecota	.10	.05
❑ 87T	Melido Perez	.10	.05
❑ 88T	Mike Perez	.10	.05
❑ 89T	Hipolito Pichardo RC	.10	.05
❑ 90T	Willie Randolph	.15	.07
❑ 91T	Darren Reed	.10	.05
❑ 92T	Bip Roberts	.10	.05
❑ 93T	Chris Roberts USA	.10	.05
❑ 94T	Steve Rodriguez USA	.10	.05
❑ 95T	Bruce Ruffin	.10	.05
❑ 96T	Scott Ruskin	.10	.05
❑ 97T	Bret Saberhagen	.15	.07
❑ 98T	Rey Sanchez RC	.15	.07
❑ 99T	Steve Sax	.10	.05
❑ 100T	Curt Schilling	.40	.18
❑ 101T	Dick Schofield	.10	.05
❑ 102T	Gary Scott	.10	.05
❑ 103T	Kevin Seitzer	.10	.05
❑ 104T	Frank Seminara RC	.10	.05
❑ 105T	Gary Sheffield	.15	.07
❑ 106T	John Smiley	.10	.05
❑ 107T	Cory Snyder	.10	.05
❑ 108T	Paul Sorrento	.10	.05
❑ 109T	Sammy Sosa	1.50	.70
❑ 110T	Matt Stairs RC	.40	.18
❑ 111T	Andy Stankiewicz	.10	.05
❑ 112T	Kurt Stillwell	.10	.05
❑ 113T	Rick Sutcliffe	.15	.07
❑ 114T	Bill Swift	.10	.05
❑ 115T	Jeff Tackett	.10	.05
❑ 116T	Danny Tartabull	.10	.05
❑ 117T	Eddie Taubensee	.15	.07
❑ 118T	Dickie Thon	.10	.05
❑ 119T	M.Tucker USA RC	.15	.07
❑ 120T	Scooter Tucker	.10	.05
❑ 121T	Marc Valdes USA RC	.10	.05
❑ 122T	Julio Valera	.10	.05
❑ 123T	J.Varitek USA RC	3.00	1.35
❑ 124T	Ron Villone USA RC	.10	.05
❑ 125T	Frank Viola	.15	.07
❑ 126T	B.J. Wallace USA RC	.10	.05
❑ 127T	Dan Walters	.10	.05
❑ 128T	Craig Wilson USA	.10	.05
❑ 129T	Chris Wimmer USA	.10	.05
❑ 130T	Dave Winfield	.40	.18
❑ 131T	Herm Winningham	.10	.05
❑ 132T	Checklist 1T-132T	.10	.05

1993 Topps

	MINT	NRMT
COMPLETE SET (825)	35.00	16.00
COMP.HOBBY.SET (847)	60.00	27.00
COMP.RETAIL.SET (838)	60.00	27.00
COMPLETE SERIES 1 (396)	20.00	9.00
COMPLETE SERIES 2 (429)	15.00	6.75

		MINT	NRMT
❑ 1	Robin Yount	.40	.18
❑ 2	Barry Bonds	1.00	.45
❑ 3	Ryne Sandberg	.50	.23
❑ 4	Roger Clemens	1.00	.45
❑ 5	Tony Gwynn	.75	.35
❑ 6	Jeff Tackett	.10	.05
❑ 7	Pete Incaviglia	.10	.05
❑ 8	Mark Wohlers	.10	.05
❑ 9	Kent Hrbek	.15	.07
❑ 10	Will Clark	.40	.18
❑ 11	Eric Karros	.15	.07
❑ 12	Lee Smith	.15	.07
❑ 13	Esteban Beltre	.10	.05
❑ 14	Greg Briley	.10	.05
❑ 15	Marquis Grissom	.10	.05
❑ 16	Dan Plesac	.10	.05
❑ 17	Dave Hollins	.10	.05
❑ 18	Terry Steinbach	.10	.05
❑ 19	Ed Nunez	.10	.05
❑ 20	Tim Salmon	.15	.07
❑ 21	Luis Salazar	.10	.05
❑ 22	Jim Eisenreich	.10	.05
❑ 23	Todd Stottlemyre	.10	.05
❑ 24	Tim Naehring	.10	.05
❑ 25	John Franco	.15	.07
❑ 26	Skeeter Barnes	.10	.05
❑ 27	Carlos Garcia	.10	.05
❑ 28	Joe Orsulak	.10	.05
❑ 29	Dwayne Henry	.10	.05
❑ 30	Fred McGriff	.25	.11
❑ 31	Derek Lilliquist	.10	.05
❑ 32	Don Mattingly	1.00	.45
❑ 33	B.J. Wallace	.10	.05
❑ 34	Juan Gonzalez	.40	.18
❑ 35	John Smoltz	.15	.07
❑ 36	Scott Servais	.10	.05
❑ 37	Lenny Webster	.10	.05
❑ 38	Chris James	.10	.05
❑ 39	Roger McDowell	.10	.05
❑ 40	Ozzie Smith	.50	.23
❑ 41	Alex Fernandez	.10	.05
❑ 42	Spike Owen	.10	.05
❑ 43	Ruben Amaro	.10	.05

	No.	Player	Nm-Mt	Ex-Mt
❑	44	Kevin Seitzer	.10	.05
❑	45	Dave Fleming	.10	.05
❑	46	Eric Fox	.10	.05
❑	47	Bob Scanlan	.10	.05
❑	48	Bert Blyleven	.15	.07
❑	49	Brian McRae	.10	.05
❑	50	Roberto Alomar	.40	.18
❑	51	Mo Vaughn	.15	.07
❑	52	Bobby Bonilla	.15	.07
❑	53	Frank Tanana	.10	.05
❑	54	Mike LaValliere	.10	.05
❑	55	Mark McLemore	.10	.05
❑	56	Chad Mottola RC	.10	.05
❑	57	Norm Charlton	.10	.05
❑	58	Jose Melendez	.10	.05
❑	59	Carlos Martinez	.10	.05
❑	60	Roberto Kelly	.10	.05
❑	61	Gene Larkin	.10	.05
❑	62	Rafael Belliard	.10	.05
❑	63	Al Osuna	.10	.05
❑	64	Scott Chiamparino	.10	.05
❑	65	Brett Butler	.15	.07
❑	66	John Burkett	.10	.05
❑	67	Felix Jose	.10	.05
❑	68	Omar Vizquel	.15	.07
❑	69	John Vander Wal	.10	.05
❑	70	Roberto Hernandez	.10	.05
❑	71	Ricky Bones	.10	.05
❑	72	Jeff Grotewold	.10	.05
❑	73	Mike Moore	.10	.05
❑	74	Steve Buechele	.10	.05
❑	75	Juan Guzman	.10	.05
❑	76	Kevin Appier	.15	.07
❑	77	Junior Felix	.10	.05
❑	78	Greg W. Harris	.10	.05
❑	79	Dick Schofield	.10	.05
❑	80	Cecil Fielder	.15	.07
❑	81	Lloyd McClendon	.10	.05
❑	82	David Segui	.10	.05
❑	83	Reggie Sanders	.10	.05
❑	84	Kurt Stillwell	.10	.05
❑	85	Sandy Alomar Jr.	.15	.07
❑	86	John Habyan	.10	.05
❑	87	Kevin Reimer	.10	.05
❑	88	Mike Stanton	.10	.05
❑	89	Eric Anthony	.10	.05
❑	90	Scott Erickson	.10	.05
❑	91	Craig Colbert	.10	.05
❑	92	Tom Pagnozzi	.10	.05
❑	93	Pedro Astacio	.10	.05
❑	94	Lance Johnson	.10	.05
❑	95	Larry Walker	.25	.11
❑	96	Russ Swan	.10	.05
❑	97	Scott Fletcher	.10	.05
❑	98	Derek Jeter RC	12.00	5.50
❑	99	Mike Williams	.10	.05
❑	100	Mark McGwire	1.50	.70
❑	101	Jim Bullinger	.10	.05
❑	102	Brian Hunter	.10	.05
❑	103	Jody Reed	.10	.05
❑	104	Mike Butcher	.10	.05
❑	105	Gregg Jefferies	.10	.05
❑	106	Howard Johnson	.10	.05
❑	107	John Kiely	.10	.05
❑	108	Jose Lind	.10	.05
❑	109	Sam Horn	.10	.05
❑	110	Barry Larkin	.40	.18
❑	111	Bruce Hurst	.10	.05
❑	112	Brian Barnes	.10	.05
❑	113	Thomas Howard	.10	.05
❑	114	Mel Hall	.10	.05
❑	115	Robby Thompson	.10	.05
❑	116	Mark Lemke	.10	.05
❑	117	Eddie Taubensee	.10	.05
❑	118	David Hulse RC	.10	.05
❑	119	Pedro Munoz	.10	.05
❑	120	Ramon Martinez	.10	.05
❑	121	Todd Worrell	.10	.05
❑	122	Joey Cora	.10	.05
❑	123	Moises Alou	.15	.07
❑	124	Franklin Stubbs	.10	.05
❑	125	Pete O'Brien	.10	.05
❑	126	Bob Ayrault	.10	.05
❑	127	Carney Lansford	.15	.07
❑	128	Kal Daniels	.10	.05
❑	129	Joe Grahe	.10	.05
❑	130	Jeff Montgomery	.10	.05
❑	131	Dave Winfield	.40	.18
❑	132	Preston Wilson RC	.75	.35
❑	133	Steve Wilson	.10	.05
❑	134	Lee Guetterman	.10	.05
❑	135	Mickey Tettleton	.10	.05
❑	136	Jeff King	.10	.05
❑	137	Alan Mills	.10	.05
❑	138	Joe Oliver	.10	.05
❑	139	Gary Gaetti	.15	.07
❑	140	Gary Sheffield	.15	.07
❑	141	Dennis Cook	.10	.05
❑	142	Charlie Hayes	.10	.05
❑	143	Jeff Huson	.10	.05
❑	144	Kent Mercker	.10	.05
❑	145	Eric Young	.10	.05
❑	146	Scott Leius	.10	.05
❑	147	Bryan Hickerson	.10	.05
❑	148	Steve Finley	.15	.07
❑	149	Rheal Cormier	.10	.05
❑	150	Frank Thomas UER (Categories leading league are italicized but not printed in red)	.50	.23
❑	151	Archi Cianfrocco	.10	.05
❑	152	Rich DeLucia	.10	.05
❑	153	Greg Vaughn	.15	.07
❑	154	Wes Chamberlain	.10	.05
❑	155	Dennis Eckersley	.15	.07
❑	156	Sammy Sosa	.75	.35
❑	157	Gary DiSarcina	.10	.05
❑	158	Kevin Koslofski	.10	.05
❑	159	Doug Linton	.10	.05
❑	160	Lou Whitaker	.15	.07
❑	161	Chad McConnell	.10	.05
❑	162	Joe Hesketh	.10	.05
❑	163	Tim Wakefield	.10	.05
❑	164	Leo Gomez	.10	.05
❑	165	Jose Rijo	.10	.05
❑	166	Tim Scott	.10	.05
❑	167	Steve Olin UER (Born 10/4/65 should say 10/10/65)	.10	.05
❑	168	Kevin Maas	.10	.05
❑	169	Kenny Rogers	.10	.05
❑	170	David Justice	.15	.07
❑	171	Doug Jones	.10	.05
❑	172	Jeff Reboulet	.10	.05
❑	173	Andres Galarraga	.25	.11
❑	174	Randy Velarde	.10	.05
❑	175	Kirk McCaskill	.10	.05
❑	176	Darren Lewis	.10	.05
❑	177	Lenny Harris	.10	.05
❑	178	Jeff Fassero	.10	.05
❑	179	Ken Griffey Jr.	1.25	.55
❑	180	Darren Daulton	.15	.07
❑	181	John Jaha	.10	.05
❑	182	Ron Darling	.10	.05
❑	183	Greg Maddux	1.00	.45
❑	184	Damion Easley	.10	.05
❑	185	Jack Morris	.15	.07
❑	186	Mike Magnante	.10	.05
❑	187	John Dopson	.10	.05
❑	188	Sid Fernandez	.10	.05
❑	189	Tony Phillips	.10	.05
❑	190	Doug Drabek	.10	.05
❑	191	Sean Lowe RC	.10	.05
❑	192	Bob Milacki	.10	.05
❑	193	Steve Foster	.10	.05
❑	194	Jerald Clark	.10	.05
❑	195	Pete Harnisch	.10	.05
❑	196	Pat Kelly	.10	.05
❑	197	Jeff Frye	.10	.05
❑	198	Alejandro Pena	.10	.05
❑	199	Junior Ortiz	.10	.05
❑	200	Kirby Puckett	1.00	.45
❑	201	Jose Uribe	.10	.05
❑	202	Mike Scioscia	.10	.05
❑	203	Bernard Gilkey	.10	.05
❑	204	Dan Pasqua	.10	.05
❑	205	Gary Carter	.25	.11
❑	206	Henry Cotto	.10	.05
❑	207	Paul Molitor	.40	.18
❑	208	Mike Hartley	.10	.05
❑	209	Jeff Parrett	.10	.05
❑	210	Mark Langston	.10	.05
❑	211	Doug Dascenzo	.10	.05
❑	212	Rick Reed	.10	.05
❑	213	Candy Maldonado	.10	.05
❑	214	Danny Darwin	.10	.05
❑	215	Pat Howell	.10	.05
❑	216	Mark Leiter	.10	.05
❑	217	Kevin Mitchell	.10	.05
❑	218	Ben McDonald	.10	.05
❑	219	Bip Roberts	.10	.05
❑	220	Benny Santiago	.10	.05
❑	221	Carlos Baerga	.10	.05
❑	222	Bernie Williams	.40	.18
❑	223	Roger Pavlik	.10	.05
❑	224	Sid Bream	.10	.05
❑	225	Matt Williams	.25	.11
❑	226	Willie Banks	.10	.05
❑	227	Jeff Bagwell	.50	.23
❑	228	Tom Goodwin	.10	.05
❑	229	Mike Perez	.10	.05
❑	230	Carlton Fisk	.40	.18
❑	231	John Wetteland	.15	.07
❑	232	Tino Martinez	.15	.07
❑	233	Rick Greene	.10	.05
❑	234	Tim McIntosh	.10	.05
❑	235	Mitch Williams	.10	.05
❑	236	Kevin Campbell	.10	.05
❑	237	Jose Vizcaino	.10	.05
❑	238	Chris Donnels	.10	.05
❑	239	Mike Boddicker	.10	.05
❑	240	John Olerud	.15	.07
❑	241	Mike Gardiner	.10	.05
❑	242	Charlie O'Brien	.10	.05
❑	243	Rob Deer	.10	.05
❑	244	Denny Neagle	.15	.07
❑	245	Chris Sabo	.10	.05
❑	246	Gregg Olson	.10	.05
❑	247	Frank Seminara UER (Acquired 12/3/98)	.10	.05
❑	248	Scott Scudder	.10	.05
❑	249	Tim Burke	.10	.05
❑	250	Chuck Knoblauch	.15	.07
❑	251	Mike Bielecki	.10	.05
❑	252	Xavier Hernandez	.10	.05
❑	253	Jose Guzman	.10	.05
❑	254	Cory Snyder	.10	.05
❑	255	Orel Hershiser	.15	.07
❑	256	Wil Cordero	.10	.05
❑	257	Luis Alicea	.10	.05
❑	258	Mike Schooler	.10	.05
❑	259	Craig Grebeck	.10	.05
❑	260	Duane Ward	.10	.05
❑	261	Bill Wegman	.10	.05
❑	262	Mickey Morandini	.10	.05
❑	263	Vince Horsman	.10	.05
❑	264	Paul Sorrento	.10	.05
❑	265	Andre Dawson	.25	.11
❑	266	Rene Gonzales	.10	.05
❑	267	Keith Miller	.10	.05
❑	268	Derek Bell	.10	.05
❑	269	Todd Steverson RC	.10	.05
❑	270	Frank Viola	.15	.07
❑	271	Wally Whitehurst	.10	.05
❑	272	Kurt Knudsen	.10	.05
❑	273	Dan Walters	.10	.05
❑	274	Rick Sutcliffe	.15	.07
❑	275	Andy Van Slyke	.15	.07
❑	276	Paul O'Neill	.40	.18
❑	277	Mark Whiten	.10	.05
❑	278	Chris Nabholz	.10	.05
❑	279	Todd Burns	.10	.05
❑	280	Tom Glavine	.40	.18
❑	281	Butch Henry	.10	.05
❑	282	Shane Mack	.10	.05
❑	283	Mike Jackson	.10	.05
❑	284	Henry Rodriguez	.10	.05
❑	285	Bob Tewksbury	.10	.05
❑	286	Ron Karkovice	.10	.05
❑	287	Mike Gallego	.10	.05
❑	288	Dave Cochrane	.10	.05
❑	289	Jesse Orosco	.10	.05
❑	290	Dave Stewart	.15	.07
❑	291	Tommy Greene	.10	.05
❑	292	Rey Sanchez	.10	.05
❑	293	Rob Ducey	.10	.05
❑	294	Brent Mayne	.10	.05
❑	295	Dave Stieb	.10	.05

❑ 296 Luis Rivera .10 .05
❑ 297 Jeff Innis .10 .05
❑ 298 Scott Livingstone .10 .05
❑ 299 Bob Patterson .10 .05
❑ 300 Cal Ripken 1.50 .70
❑ 301 Cesar Hernandez .10 .05
❑ 302 Randy Myers .10 .05
❑ 303 Brook Jacoby .10 .05
❑ 304 Melido Perez .10 .05
❑ 305 Rafael Palmeiro .40 .18
❑ 306 Damon Berryhill .10 .05
❑ 307 Dan Serafini RC .10 .05
❑ 308 Darryl Kile .15 .07
❑ 309 J.T. Bruett .10 .05
❑ 310 Dave Righetti .15 .07
❑ 311 Jay Howell .10 .05
❑ 312 Geronimo Pena .10 .05
❑ 313 Greg Hibbard .10 .05
❑ 314 Mark Gardner .10 .05
❑ 315 Edgar Martinez .25 .11
❑ 316 Dave Nilsson .10 .05
❑ 317 Kyle Abbott .10 .05
❑ 318 Willie Wilson .10 .05
❑ 319 Paul Assenmacher .10 .05
❑ 320 Tim Fortugno .10 .05
❑ 321 Rusty Meacham .10 .05
❑ 322 Pat Borders .10 .05
❑ 323 Mike Greenwell .10 .05
❑ 324 Willie Randolph .15 .07
❑ 325 Bill Gullickson .10 .05
❑ 326 Gary Varsho .10 .05
❑ 327 Tim Hulett .10 .05
❑ 328 Scott Ruskin .10 .05
❑ 329 Mike Maddux .10 .05
❑ 330 Danny Tartabull .10 .05
❑ 331 Kenny Lofton .15 .07
❑ 332 Geno Petralli .10 .05
❑ 333 Otis Nixon .10 .05
❑ 334 Jason Kendall RC 1.50 .70
❑ 335 Mark Portugal .10 .05
❑ 336 Mike Pagliarulo .10 .05
❑ 337 Kirt Manwaring .10 .05
❑ 338 Bob Ojeda .10 .05
❑ 339 Mark Clark .10 .05
❑ 340 John Kruk .15 .07
❑ 341 Mel Rojas .10 .05
❑ 342 Erik Hanson .10 .05
❑ 343 Doug Henry .10 .05
❑ 344 Jack McDowell .10 .05
❑ 345 Harold Baines .15 .07
❑ 346 Chuck McElroy .10 .05
❑ 347 Luis Sojo .10 .05
❑ 348 Andy Stankiewicz .10 .05
❑ 349 Hipolito Pichardo .10 .05
❑ 350 Joe Carter .15 .07
❑ 351 Ellis Burks .15 .07
❑ 352 Pete Schourek .10 .05
❑ 353 Bubby Groom .10 .05
❑ 354 Jay Bell .15 .07
❑ 355 Brady Anderson .15 .07
❑ 356 Freddie Benavides .10 .05
❑ 357 Phil Stephenson .10 .05
❑ 358 Kevin Wickander .10 .05
❑ 359 Mike Stanley .10 .05
❑ 360 Ivan Rodriguez .40 .18
❑ 361 Scott Bankhead .10 .05
❑ 362 Luis Gonzalez .40 .18
❑ 363 John Smiley .10 .05
❑ 364 Trevor Wilson .10 .05
❑ 365 Tom Candiotti .10 .05
❑ 366 Craig Wilson .10 .05
❑ 367 Steve Sax .10 .05
❑ 368 Delino DeShields .10 .05
❑ 369 Jaime Navarro .10 .05
❑ 370 Dave Valle .10 .05
❑ 371 Mariano Duncan .10 .05
❑ 372 Rod Nichols .10 .05
❑ 373 Mike Morgan .10 .05
❑ 374 Julio Valera .10 .05
❑ 375 Wally Joyner .15 .07
❑ 376 Tom Henke .10 .05
❑ 377 Herm Winningham .10 .05
❑ 378 Orlando Merced .10 .05
❑ 379 Mike Munoz .10 .05
❑ 380 Todd Hundley .10 .05
❑ 381 Mike Flanagan .10 .05
❑ 382 Tim Belcher .10 .05
❑ 383 Jerry Browne .10 .05
❑ 384 Mike Benjamin .10 .05
❑ 385 Jim Leyritz .10 .05
❑ 386 Ray Lankford .10 .05
❑ 387 Devon White .10 .05
❑ 388 Jeremy Hernandez .10 .05
❑ 389 Brian Harper .10 .05
❑ 390 Wade Boggs .40 .18
❑ 391 Derrick May .10 .05
❑ 392 Travis Fryman .15 .07
❑ 393 Ron Gant .10 .05
❑ 394 Checklist 1-132 .10 .05
❑ 395 CL 133-264 UER .10 .05
Eckerlsey
❑ 396 Checklist 265-396 .10 .05
❑ 397 George Brett .75 .35
❑ 398 Bobby Witt .10 .05
❑ 399 Daryl Boston .10 .05
❑ 400 Bo Jackson .15 .07
❑ 401 Fred McGriff .25 .11
Frank Thomas
❑ 402 Ryne Sandberg .15 .07
Carlos Baerga
❑ 403 Gary Sheffield .15 .07
Edgar Martinez
❑ 404 Barry Larkin .15 .07
Travis Fryman
❑ 405 Andy Van Slyke .50 .23
Ken Griffey Jr.
❑ 406 Larry Walker .25 .11
Kirby Puckett
❑ 407 Barry Bonds .50 .23
Joe Carter
❑ 408 Darren Daulton .15 .07
Brian Harper
❑ 409 Greg Maddux .50 .23
Roger Clemens
❑ 410 Tom Glavine .15 .07
Dave Fleming
❑ 411 Lee Smith .15 .07
Dennis Eckersley
❑ 412 Jamie McAndrew .10 .05
❑ 413 Pete Smith .10 .05
❑ 414 Juan Guerrero .10 .05
❑ 415 Todd Frohwirth .10 .05
❑ 416 Randy Tomlin .10 .05
❑ 417 B.J. Surhoff .15 .07
❑ 418 Jim Gott .10 .05
❑ 419 Mark Thompson RC .10 .05
❑ 420 Kevin Tapani .10 .05
❑ 421 Curt Schilling .40 .18
❑ 422 J.T. Snow RC .50 .23
❑ 423 1993 Prospects .15 .07
Ryan Klesko
Ivan Cruz
Bubba Smith
Larry Sutton
❑ 424 John Valentin .10 .05
❑ 425 Joe Girardi .10 .05
❑ 426 Nigel Wilson .10 .05
❑ 427 Bob MacDonald .10 .05
❑ 428 Todd Zeile .10 .05
❑ 429 Milt Cuyler .10 .05
❑ 430 Eddie Murray .40 .18
❑ 431 Rich Amaral .10 .05
❑ 432 Pete Young .10 .05
❑ 433 Roger Bailey RC and .10 .05
Tom Schmidt
❑ 434 Jack Armstrong .10 .05
❑ 435 Willie McGee .15 .07
❑ 436 Greg W. Harris .10 .05
❑ 437 Chris Hammond .10 .05
❑ 438 Ritchie Moody RC .10 .05
❑ 439 Bryan Harvey .10 .05
❑ 440 Ruben Sierra .10 .05
❑ 441 Don Lemon and .10 .05
Todd Pridy RC
❑ 442 Kevin McReynolds .10 .05
❑ 443 Terry Leach .10 .05
❑ 444 David Nied .10 .05
❑ 445 Dale Murphy .25 .11
❑ 446 Luis Mercedes .10 .05
❑ 447 Keith Shepherd RC .10 .05
❑ 448 Ken Caminiti .15 .07
❑ 449 James Austin .10 .05
❑ 450 Darryl Strawberry .15 .07
❑ 451 1993 Prospects .15 .07
Ramon Caraballo
Jon Shave RC
Brent Gates
Quinton McCracken
❑ 452 Bob Wickman .10 .05
❑ 453 Victor Cole .10 .05
❑ 454 John Johnstone RC .10 .05
❑ 455 Chili Davis .15 .07
❑ 456 Scott Taylor .10 .05
❑ 457 Tracy Woodson .10 .05
❑ 458 David Wells .15 .07
❑ 459 Derek Wallace RC .10 .05
❑ 460 Randy Johnson .50 .23
❑ 461 Steve Reed RC .10 .05
❑ 462 Felix Fermin .10 .05
❑ 463 Scott Aldred .10 .05
❑ 464 Greg Colbrunn .10 .05
❑ 465 Tony Fernandez .10 .05
❑ 466 Mike Felder .10 .05
❑ 467 Lee Stevens .10 .05
❑ 468 Matt Whiteside RC .10 .05
❑ 469 Dave Hansen .10 .05
❑ 470 Rob Dibble .10 .05
❑ 471 Dave Gallagher .10 .05
❑ 472 Chris Gwynn .10 .05
❑ 473 Dave Henderson .10 .05
❑ 474 Ozzie Guillen .10 .05
❑ 475 Jeff Reardon .15 .07
❑ 476 Mark Voisard and .10 .05
Will Scalzitti RC
❑ 477 Jimmy Jones .10 .05
❑ 478 Greg Cadaret .10 .05
❑ 479 Todd Pratt RC .15 .07
❑ 480 Pat Listach .10 .05
❑ 481 Ryan Luzinski RC .10 .05
❑ 482 Darren Reed .10 .05
❑ 483 Brian Griffiths RC .10 .05
❑ 484 John Wehner .10 .05
❑ 485 Glenn Davis .10 .05
❑ 486 Eric Wedge RC .10 .05
❑ 487 Jesse Hollins .10 .05
❑ 488 Manuel Lee .10 .05
❑ 489 Scott Fredrickson RC .10 .05
❑ 490 Omar Olivares .10 .05
❑ 491 Shawn Hare .10 .05
❑ 492 Tom Lampkin .10 .05
❑ 493 Jeff Nelson .10 .05
❑ 494 1993 Prospects .10 .05
Kevin Young
Adell Davenport
Eduardo Perez
Lou Lucca RC
❑ 495 Ken Hill .10 .05
❑ 496 Reggie Jefferson .10 .05
❑ 497 Matt Petersen and .10 .05
Willie Brown RC
❑ 498 Bud Black .10 .05
❑ 499 Chuck Crim .10 .05
❑ 500 Jose Canseco .40 .18
❑ 501 Johnny Oates MG .15 .07
Bobby Cox MG
❑ 502 Butch Hobson MG .10 .05
Jim Lefebvre MG
❑ 503 Buck Rodgers MG .15 .07
Tony Perez MG
❑ 504 Gene Lamont MG .15 .07
Don Baylor MG
❑ 505 Mike Hargrove MG .15 .07
Rene Lachemann MG
❑ 506 Sparky Anderson MG .15 .07
Art Howe MG
❑ 507 Hal McRae MG .15 .07
Tom Lasorda MG
❑ 508 Phil Garner MG .15 .07
Felipe Alou MG
❑ 509 Tom Kelly MG .10 .05
Jeff Torborg MG
❑ 510 Buck Showalter MG .15 .07
Jim Fregosi MG
❑ 511 Tony LaRussa MG .15 .07
Jim Leyland MG
❑ 512 Lou Piniella MG .15 .07
Joe Torre MG

❑ 513 Kevin Kennedy MG .... .10 .05
Jim Riggleman MG
❑ 514 Cito Gaston MG .... .10 .05
Dusty Baker MG
❑ 515 Greg Swindell .... .10 .05
❑ 516 Alex Arias .... .10 .05
❑ 517 Bill Pecota .... .10 .05
❑ 518 Benji Grigsby RC UER .. .10 .05
(Misspelled Bengi
on card front)
❑ 519 David Howard .... .10 .05
❑ 520 Charlie Hough .... .15 .07
❑ 521 Kevin Flora .... .10 .05
❑ 522 Shane Reynolds .... .10 .05
❑ 523 Doug Bochtler RC .... .10 .05
❑ 524 Chris Hoiles................... .10 .05
❑ 525 Scott Sanderson .... .10 .05
❑ 526 Mike Sharperson............ .10 .05
❑ 527 Mike Fetters .... .10 .05
❑ 528 Paul Quantrill................ .10 .05
❑ 529 1993 Prospects .... 1.00 .45
Dave Silvestri
Chipper Jones
Benji Gil
Jeff Patzke
❑ 530 Sterling Hitchcock RC .... .15 .07
❑ 531 Joe Millette .... .10 .05
❑ 532 Tom Brunansky .... .10 .05
❑ 533 Frank Castillo .... .10 .05
❑ 534 Randy Knorr .... .10 .05
❑ 535 Jose Oquendo.............. .10 .05
❑ 536 Dave Haas .... .10 .05
❑ 537 Jason Hutchins RC and .10 .05
Ryan Turner
❑ 538 Jimmy Baron RC........... .10 .05
❑ 539 Kerry Woodson .... .10 .05
❑ 540 Ivan Calderon .... .10 .05
❑ 541 Denis Boucher............... .10 .05
❑ 542 Royce Clayton............... .10 .05
❑ 543 Reggie Williams .... .10 .05
❑ 544 Steve Decker................. .10 .05
❑ 545 Dean Palmer .... .15 .07
❑ 546 Hal Morris .... .10 .05
❑ 547 Ryan Thompson .... .10 .05
❑ 548 Lance Blankenship .... .10 .05
❑ 549 Hensley Meulens........... .10 .05
❑ 550 Scott Radinsky .... .10 .05
❑ 551 Eric Young.................... .10 .05
❑ 552 Jeff Blauser .... .10 .05
❑ 553 Andujar Cedeno .... .10 .05
❑ 554 Arthur Rhodes............... .10 .05
❑ 555 Terry Mulholland .... .10 .05
❑ 556 Darryl Hamilton .... .10 .05
❑ 557 Pedro Martinez .... 1.00 .45
❑ 558 Ryan Whitman RC .... .10 .05
Mark Skeels
❑ 559 Jamie Arnold RC........... .10 .05
❑ 560 Zane Smith .... .10 .05
❑ 561 Matt Nokes .... .10 .05
❑ 562 Bob Zupcic .... .10 .05
❑ 563 Shawn Boskie .... .10 .05
❑ 564 Mike Timlin .... .10 .05
❑ 565 Jerald Clark.................. .10 .05
❑ 566 Rod Brewer................... .10 .05
❑ 567 Mark Carreon .... .10 .05
❑ 568 Andy Benes................... .10 .05
❑ 569 Shawn Barton RC .... .10 .05
❑ 570 Tim Wallach .... .10 .05
❑ 571 Dave Mlicki .... .10 .05
❑ 572 Trevor Hoffman .... .15 .07
❑ 573 John Patterson .... .10 .05
❑ 574 De Shawn Warren RC.... .10 .05
❑ 575 Monty Fariss .... .10 .05
❑ 576 1993 Prospects .... .15 .07
Darrell Sherman
Damon Buford
Cliff Floyd
Michael Moore
❑ 577 Tim Costo .... .10 .05
❑ 578 Dave Magadan .... .10 .05
❑ 579 Neil Garret and .... .10 .05
Jason Bates RC
❑ 580 Walt Weiss .... .10 .05
❑ 581 Chris Haney .... .10 .05
❑ 582 Shawn Abner................. .10 .05
❑ 583 Marvin Freeman .... .10 .05
❑ 584 Casey Candaele .... .10 .05
❑ 585 Ricky Jordan .... .10 .05
❑ 586 Jeff Tabaka RC .... .10 .05
❑ 587 Manny Alexander .... .10 .05
❑ 588 Mike Trombley.............. .10 .05
❑ 589 Carlos Hernandez .... .10 .05
❑ 590 Cal Eldred .... .10 .05
❑ 591 Alex Cole...................... .10 .05
❑ 592 Phil Plantier.................. .10 .05
❑ 593 Brett Merriman RC .... .10 .05
❑ 594 Jerry Nielsen .... .10 .05
❑ 595 Shawon Dunston........... .10 .05
❑ 596 Jimmy Key.................... .15 .07
❑ 597 Gerald Perry .... .10 .05
❑ 598 Rico Brogna .... .10 .05
❑ 599 Clemente Nunez and .... .10 .05
Daniel Robinson
❑ 600 Bret Saberhagen .... .15 .07
❑ 601 Craig Shipley................ .10 .05
❑ 602 Henry Mercedes .... .10 .05
❑ 603 Jim Thome .... .40 .18
❑ 604 Rod Beck...................... .10 .05
❑ 605 Chuck Finley .... .15 .07
❑ 606 J. Owens RC .... .10 .05
❑ 607 Dan Smith .... .10 .05
❑ 608 Bill Doran...................... .10 .05
❑ 609 Lance Parrish .... .15 .07
❑ 610 Dennis Martinez .... .15 .07
❑ 611 Tom Gordon .... .10 .05
❑ 612 Byron Mathews RC .... .10 .05
❑ 613 Joel Adamson RC .... .10 .05
❑ 614 Brian Williams .... .10 .05
❑ 615 Steve Avery.................. .10 .05
❑ 616 1993 Prospects .... .10 .05
Matt Mieske
Tracy Sanders
Midre Cummings RC
Ryan Freeburg
❑ 617 Craig Lefferts................ .10 .05
❑ 618 Tony Pena.................... .10 .05
❑ 619 Billy Spiers .... .10 .05
❑ 620 Todd Benzinger............. .10 .05
❑ 621 Mike Kotarski and .... .10 .05
Greg Boyd RC
❑ 622 Ben Rivera .... .10 .05
❑ 623 Al Martin .... .10 .05
❑ 624 Sam Militello UER .... .10 .05
(Profile says drafted
in 1988, bio says
drafted in 1990)
❑ 625 Rick Aguilera................ .10 .05
❑ 626 Dan Gladden................. .10 .05
❑ 627 Andres Berumen RC..... .10 .05
❑ 628 Kelly Gruber .... .10 .05
❑ 629 Cris Carpenter.............. .10 .05
❑ 630 Mark Grace .... .40 .18
❑ 631 Jeff Brantley .... .10 .05
❑ 632 Chris Widger RC .... .15 .07
❑ 633 Three Russians UER .... .10 .05
Rudolf Razjigaev
Eugneyi Puchkov
Ilya Bogatyrev
Bogatyrev is a shortstop,
card has pitching header
❑ 634 Mo Sanford .... .10 .05
❑ 635 Albert Belle .... .15 .07
❑ 636 Tim Teufel .... .10 .05
❑ 637 Greg Myers .... .10 .05
❑ 638 Brian Bohanon .... .10 .05
❑ 639 Mike Bordick .... .10 .05
❑ 640 Dwight Gooden .... .15 .07
❑ 641 Pat Leahy and .... .10 .05
Gavin Baugh RC
❑ 642 Milt Hill......................... .10 .05
❑ 643 Luis Aquino .... .10 .05
❑ 644 Dante Bichette.............. .15 .07
❑ 645 Bobby Thigpen .... .10 .05
❑ 646 Rich Scheid RC............. .10 .05
❑ 647 Brian Sackinsky RC ...... .10 .05
❑ 648 Ryan Hawblitzel .... .10 .05
❑ 649 Tom Marsh .... .10 .05
❑ 650 Terry Pendleton............ .15 .07
❑ 651 Rafael Bournigal .... .10 .05
❑ 652 Dave West.................... .10 .05
❑ 653 Steve Hosey .... .10 .05
❑ 654 Gerald Williams............ .10 .05
❑ 655 Scott Cooper .... .10 .05
❑ 656 Gary Scott .... .10 .05
❑ 657 Mike Harkey .... .10 .05
❑ 658 1993 Prospects .... .10 .05
Jeromy Burnitz
Melvin Nieves
Rich Becker
Shon Walker RC
❑ 659 Ed Sprague .... .10 .05
❑ 660 Alan Trammell .... .25 .11
❑ 661 Garvin Alston RCand .... .10 .05
Michael Case
❑ 662 Donovan Osborne .... .10 .05
❑ 663 Jeff Gardner .... .10 .05
❑ 664 Calvin Jones .... .10 .05
❑ 665 Darrin Fletcher .... .10 .05
❑ 666 Glenallen Hill .... .10 .05
❑ 667 Jim Rosenbohm RC ...... .10 .05
❑ 668 Scott Lewis .... .10 .05
❑ 669 Kip Yaughn RC .... .10 .05
❑ 670 Julio Franco.................. .15 .07
❑ 671 Dave Martinez .... .10 .05
❑ 672 Kevin Bass .... .10 .05
❑ 673 Todd Van Poppel .... .10 .05
❑ 674 Mark Gubicza .... .10 .05
❑ 675 Tim Raines .... .15 .07
❑ 676 Rudy Seanez................ .10 .05
❑ 677 Charlie Leibrandt.......... .10 .05
❑ 678 Randy Milligan.............. .10 .05
❑ 679 Kim Batiste .... .10 .05
❑ 680 Craig Biggio.................. .25 .11
❑ 681 Darren Holmes .... .10 .05
❑ 682 John Candelaria .... .10 .05
❑ 683 Jerry Stafford and .... .10 .05
Eddie Christian RC
❑ 684 Pat Mahomes .... .10 .05
❑ 685 Bob Walk...................... .10 .05
❑ 686 Russ Springer .... .10 .05
❑ 687 Tony Sheffield RC......... .10 .05
❑ 688 Dwight Smith .... .10 .05
❑ 689 Eddie Zosky .... .10 .05
❑ 690 Bien Figueroa .... .10 .05
❑ 691 Jim Tatum RC .... .10 .05
❑ 692 Chad Kreuter................ .10 .05
❑ 693 Rich Rodriguez .... .10 .05
❑ 694 Shane Turner .... .10 .05
❑ 695 Kent Bottenfield............ .10 .05
❑ 696 Jose Mesa.................... .10 .05
❑ 697 Darrell Whitmore RC..... .10 .05
❑ 698 Ted Wood .... .10 .05
❑ 699 Chad Curtis .... .10 .05
❑ 700 Nolan Ryan .... 2.00 .90
❑ 701 1993 Prospects .... 2.00 .90
Mike Piazza
Brook Fordyce
Carlos Delgado
Donnie Leshnock
❑ 702 Tim Pugh RC................ .10 .05
❑ 703 Jeff Kent .... .40 .18
❑ 704 Jon Goodrich and .... .10 .05
Danny Figueroa RC
❑ 705 Bob Welch.................... .10 .05
❑ 706 S.Clinkscales RC .... .10 .05
❑ 707 Donn Pall...................... .10 .05
❑ 708 Greg Olson .... .10 .05
❑ 709 Jeff Juden .... .10 .05
❑ 710 Mike Mussina .... .40 .18
❑ 711 Scott Chiamparino........ .10 .05
❑ 712 Stan Javier .... .10 .05
❑ 713 John Doherty .... .10 .05
❑ 714 Kevin Gross.................. .10 .05
❑ 715 Greg Gagne .... .10 .05
❑ 716 Steve Cooke .... .10 .05
❑ 717 Steve Farr .... .10 .05
❑ 718 Jay Buhner .... .15 .07
❑ 719 Butch Henry .... .10 .05
❑ 720 David Cone .... .15 .07
❑ 721 Rick Wilkins.................. .10 .05
❑ 722 Chuck Carr .... .10 .05
❑ 723 Kenny Felder RC.......... .10 .05
❑ 724 Guillermo Velasquez...... .10 .05
❑ 725 Billy Hatcher .... .10 .05
❑ 726 Mike Veneziale RC .... .10 .05
Ken Kendrena
❑ 727 Jonathan Hurst .... .10 .05
❑ 728 Steve Frey.................... .10 .05

❑ 729	Mark Leonard	.10	.05
❑ 730	Charles Nagy	.10	.05
❑ 731	Donald Harris	.10	.05
❑ 732	Travis Buckley RC	.10	.05
❑ 733	Tom Browning	.10	.05
❑ 734	Anthony Young	.10	.05
❑ 735	Steve Shifflett	.10	.05
❑ 736	Jeff Russell	.10	.05
❑ 737	Wilson Alvarez	.10	.05
❑ 738	Lance Painter RC	.10	.05
❑ 739	Dave Weathers	.10	.05
❑ 740	Len Dykstra	.15	.07
❑ 741	Mike Devereaux	.10	.05
❑ 742	1993 Prospects	.15	.07
	Rene Arocha		
	Alan Embree		
	Brien Taylor		
	Tim Crabtree		
❑ 743	Dave Landaker RC	.10	.05
❑ 744	Chris George	.10	.05
❑ 745	Eric Davis	.15	.07
❑ 746	Mark Strittmatter and	.10	.05
	Lamarr Rogers RC		
❑ 747	Carl Willis	.10	.05
❑ 748	Stan Belinda	.10	.05
❑ 749	Scott Kamieniecki	.10	.05
❑ 750	Rickey Henderson	.75	.35
❑ 751	Eric Hillman	.10	.05
❑ 752	Pat Hentgen	.10	.05
❑ 753	Jim Corsi	.10	.05
❑ 754	Brian Jordan	.15	.07
❑ 755	Bill Swift	.10	.05
❑ 756	Mike Henneman	.10	.05
❑ 757	Harold Reynolds	.10	.05
❑ 758	Sean Berry	.10	.05
❑ 759	Charlie Hayes	.10	.05
❑ 760	Luis Polonia	.10	.05
❑ 761	Darrin Jackson	.10	.05
❑ 762	Mark Lewis	.10	.05
❑ 763	Rob Maurer	.10	.05
❑ 764	Willie Greene	.10	.05
❑ 765	Vince Coleman	.10	.05
❑ 766	Todd Revenig	.10	.05
❑ 767	Rich Ireland RC	.10	.05
❑ 768	Mike Macfarlane	.10	.05
❑ 769	Francisco Cabrera	.10	.05
❑ 770	Robin Ventura	.15	.07
❑ 771	Kevin Ritz	.10	.05
❑ 772	Chito Martinez	.10	.05
❑ 773	Cliff Brantley	.10	.05
❑ 774	Curt Leskanic RC	.10	.05
❑ 775	Chris Bosio	.10	.05
❑ 776	Jose Offerman	.10	.05
❑ 777	Mark Guthrie	.10	.05
❑ 778	Don Slaught	.10	.05
❑ 779	Rich Monteleone	.10	.05
❑ 780	Jim Abbott	.15	.07
❑ 781	Jack Clark	.15	.07
❑ 782	Reynol Mendoza and	.10	.05
	Dan Roman RC		
❑ 783	Heathcliff Slocumb	.10	.05
❑ 784	Jeff Branson	.10	.05
❑ 785	Kevin Brown	.15	.07
❑ 786	1993 Prospects	.10	.05
	Mike Christopher		
	Ken Ryan		
	Aaron Taylor		
	Gus Gandarillas RC		
❑ 787	Mike Matthews RC	.10	.05
❑ 788	Mackey Sasser	.10	.05
❑ 789	Jeff Conine UER	.10	.05
	No inclusion of 1990		
	RBI stats in career total		
❑ 790	George Bell	.10	.05
❑ 791	Pat Rapp	.10	.05
❑ 792	Joe Boever	.10	.05
❑ 793	Jim Poole	.10	.05
❑ 794	Andy Ashby	.10	.05
❑ 795	Deion Sanders	.15	.07
❑ 796	Scott Brosius	.15	.07
❑ 797	Brad Pennington	.10	.05
❑ 798	Greg Blosser	.10	.05
❑ 799	Jim Edmonds RC	2.00	.90
❑ 800	Shawn Jeter	.10	.05
❑ 801	Jesse Levis	.10	.05
❑ 802	Phil Clark UER	.10	.05
	(Word "a" is missing in		
	sentence beginning		
	with "In 1992 ...")		
❑ 803	Ed Pierce RC	.10	.05
❑ 804	Jose Valentin RC	.50	.23
❑ 805	Terry Jorgensen	.10	.05
❑ 806	Mark Hutton	.10	.05
❑ 807	Troy Neel	.10	.05
❑ 808	Bret Boone	.15	.07
❑ 809	Cris Colon	.10	.05
❑ 810	Domingo Martinez RC	.10	.05
❑ 811	Javier Lopez	.15	.07
❑ 812	Matt Walbeck RC	.10	.05
❑ 813	Dan Wilson	.15	.07
❑ 814	Scooter Tucker	.10	.05
❑ 815	Billy Ashley	.10	.05
❑ 816	Tim Laker RC	.10	.05
❑ 817	Bobby Jones	.15	.07
❑ 818	Brad Brink	.10	.05
❑ 819	William Pennyfeather	.10	.05
❑ 820	Stan Royer	.10	.05
❑ 821	Doug Brocail	.10	.05
❑ 822	Kevin Rogers	.10	.05
❑ 823	Checklist 397-540	.10	.05
❑ 824	Checklist 541-691	.10	.05
❑ 825	Checklist 692-825	.10	.05

1993 Topps Traded

		MINT	NRMT
COMP.FACT.SET (132)		50.00	22.00
❑ 1T	Barry Bonds	1.00	.45
❑ 2T	Rich Renteria	.10	.05
❑ 3T	Aaron Sele	.15	.07
❑ 4T	C.Loewer USA RC	.15	.07
❑ 5T	Erik Pappas	.10	.05
❑ 6T	Greg McMichael RC	.10	.05
❑ 7T	Freddie Benavides	.10	.05
❑ 8T	Kirk Gibson	.15	.07
❑ 9T	Tony Fernandez	.10	.05
❑ 10T	Jay Gainer RC	.10	.05
❑ 11T	Orestes Destrade	.10	.05
❑ 12T	A.J. Hinch USA RC	.15	.07
❑ 13T	Bobby Munoz	.10	.05
❑ 14T	Tom Henke	.10	.05
❑ 15T	Rob Butler	.10	.05
❑ 16T	Gary Wayne	.10	.05
❑ 17T	David McCarty	.10	.05
❑ 18T	Walt Weiss	.10	.05
❑ 19T	Todd Helton USA RC	30.00	13.50
❑ 20T	Mark Whiten	.10	.05
❑ 21T	Ricky Gutierrez	.10	.05
❑ 22T	D.Hermanson USA RC	1.00	.45
❑ 23T	Sherman Obando RC	.10	.05
❑ 24T	Mike Piazza	2.00	.90
❑ 25T	Jeff Russell	.10	.05
❑ 26T	Jason Bere	.10	.05
❑ 27T	Jack Voigt RC	.10	.05
❑ 28T	Chris Bosio	.10	.05
❑ 29T	Phil Hiatt	.10	.05
❑ 30T	M.Beaumont USA RC	.10	.05
❑ 31T	Andres Galarraga	.25	.11
❑ 32T	Greg Swindell	.10	.05
❑ 33T	Vinny Castilla	.15	.07
❑ 34T	P.Clougherty RC USA	.10	.05
❑ 35T	Greg Briley	.10	.05
❑ 36T	Dallas Green MG	.10	.05
	Davey Johnson MG		
❑ 37T	Tyler Green	.10	.05
❑ 38T	Craig Paquette	.10	.05
❑ 39T	Danny Sheaffer RC	.10	.05
❑ 40T	Jim Converse RC	.10	.05
❑ 41T	Terry Harvey RC USA	.10	.05
❑ 42T	Phil Plantier	.10	.05
❑ 43T	Doug Saunders RC	.10	.05
❑ 44T	Benny Santiago	.10	.05
❑ 45T	Dante Powell USA RC	.15	.07
❑ 46T	Jeff Parrett	.10	.05
❑ 47T	Wade Boggs	.40	.18
❑ 48T	Paul Molitor	.40	.18
❑ 49T	Turk Wendell	.10	.05
❑ 50T	David Wells	.15	.07
❑ 51T	Gary Sheffield	.15	.07
❑ 52T	Kevin Young	.15	.07
❑ 53T	Nelson Liriano	.10	.05
❑ 54T	Greg Maddux	1.00	.45
❑ 55T	Derek Bell	.10	.05
❑ 56T	Matt Turner RC	.10	.05
❑ 57T	C.Nelson RC USA	.10	.05
❑ 58T	Mike Hampton	.40	.18
❑ 59T	Troy O'Leary RC	.40	.18
❑ 60T	Benji Gil	.10	.05
❑ 61T	Mitch Lyden RC	.10	.05
❑ 62T	J.T. Snow	.40	.18
❑ 63T	Damon Buford	.10	.05
❑ 64T	Gene Harris	.10	.05
❑ 65T	Randy Myers	.10	.05
❑ 66T	Felix Jose	.10	.05
❑ 67T	Todd Dunn USA RC	.10	.05
❑ 68T	Jimmy Key	.15	.07
❑ 69T	Pedro Castellano	.10	.05
❑ 70T	Mark Merila USA RC	.10	.05
❑ 71T	Rich Rodriguez	.10	.05
❑ 72T	Matt Mieske	.10	.05
❑ 73T	Pete Incaviglia	.10	.05
❑ 74T	Carl Everett	.15	.07
❑ 75T	Jim Abbott	.15	.07
❑ 76T	Luis Aquino	.10	.05
❑ 77T	Rene Arocha	.15	.07
❑ 78T	Jon Shave	.10	.05
❑ 79T	Todd Walker USA RC	2.00	.90
❑ 80T	Jack Armstrong	.10	.05
❑ 81T	Jeff Richardson	.10	.05
❑ 82T	Blas Minor	.10	.05
❑ 83T	Dave Winfield	.40	.18
❑ 84T	Paul O'Neill	.40	.18
❑ 85T	Steve Reich RC USA	.10	.05
❑ 86T	Chris Hammond	.10	.05
❑ 87T	Hilly Hathaway RC	.10	.05
❑ 88T	Fred McGriff	.25	.11
❑ 89T	Dave Telgheder RC	.10	.05
❑ 90T	Richie Lewis RC	.10	.05
❑ 91T	Brent Gates	.10	.05
❑ 92T	Andre Dawson	.25	.11
❑ 93T	Andy Barkett RC USA	.10	.05
❑ 94T	Doug Drabek	.10	.05
❑ 95T	Joe Klink	.10	.05
❑ 96T	Willie Blair	.10	.05
❑ 97T	D.Graves USA RC	1.00	.45
❑ 98T	Pat Meares RC	.15	.07
❑ 99T	Mike Lansing RC	.15	.07
❑ 100T	Marcos Armas RC	.10	.05
❑ 101T	D.Grass RC USA	.10	.05
❑ 102T	Chris Jones	.10	.05
❑ 103T	Ken Ryan RC	.10	.05
❑ 104T	Ellis Burks	.15	.07
❑ 105T	Roberto Kelly	.10	.05
❑ 106T	Dave Magadan	.10	.05
❑ 107T	Paul Wilson USA RC	.15	.07
❑ 108T	Rob Natal	.10	.05
❑ 109T	Paul Wagner	.10	.05
❑ 110T	Jeromy Burnitz	.15	.07
❑ 111T	Monty Fariss	.10	.05
❑ 112T	Kevin Mitchell	.10	.05
❑ 113T	Scott Pose RC	.10	.05
❑ 114T	Dave Stewart	.15	.07
❑ 115T	R.Johnson USA RC	.15	.07
❑ 116T	Armando Reynoso	.10	.05
❑ 117T	Geronimo Berroa	.10	.05
❑ 118T	Woody Williams RC	.15	.07
❑ 119T	Tim Bogar RC	.10	.05
❑ 120T	Bob Scafa RC USA	.10	.05
❑ 121T	Henry Cotto	.10	.05

No.	Player	MINT	NRMT
122T	Gregg Jefferies	.10	.05
123T	Norm Charlton	.10	.05
124T	B.Wagner USA RC	.10	.05
125T	David Cone	.15	.07
126T	Daryl Boston	.10	.05
127T	Tim Wallach	.10	.05
128T	Mike Martin USA RC	.10	.05
129T	John Cummings RC	.10	.05
130T	Ryan Bowen	.10	.05
131T	John Powell RC USA	.10	.05
132T	Checklist 1-132	.10	.05

1994 Topps

	MINT	NRMT
COMPLETE SET (792)	40.00	18.00
COMP.FACT.SET (808)	50.00	22.00
COMP.BAKER SET (818)	60.00	27.00
COMPLETE SERIES 1 (396)	20.00	9.00
COMPLETE SERIES 2 (396)	20.00	9.00

No.	Player	MINT	NRMT
1	Mike Piazza	1.25	.55
2	Bernie Williams	.40	.18
3	Kevin Rogers	.10	.05
4	Paul Carey	.10	.05
5	Ozzie Guillen	.10	.05
6	Derrick May	.10	.05
7	Jose Mesa	.10	.05
8	Todd Hundley	.10	.05
9	Chris Haney	.10	.05
10	John Olerud	.15	.07
11	Andujar Cedeno	.10	.05
12	John Smiley	.10	.05
13	Phil Plantier	.10	.05
14	Willie Banks	.10	.05
15	Jay Bell	.15	.07
16	Doug Henry	.10	.05
17	Lance Blankenship	.10	.05
18	Greg W. Harris	.10	.05
19	Scott Livingstone	.10	.05
20	Bryan Harvey	.10	.05
21	Wil Cordero	.10	.05
22	Roger Pavlik	.10	.05
23	Mark Lemke	.10	.05
24	Jeff Nelson	.10	.05
25	Todd Zeile	.10	.05
26	Billy Hatcher	.10	.05
27	Joe Magrane	.10	.05
28	Tony Longmire	.10	.05
29	Omar Daal	.10	.05
30	Kirt Manwaring	.10	.05
31	Melido Perez	.10	.05
32	Tim Hulett	.10	.05
33	Jeff Schwartz	.10	.05
34	Nolan Ryan	2.00	.90
35	Jose Guzman	.10	.05
36	Felix Fermin	.10	.05
37	Jeff Innis	.10	.05
38	Brett Mayne	.10	.05
39	Huck Flener RC	.10	.05
40	Jeff Bagwell	.50	.23
41	Kevin Wickander	.10	.05
42	Ricky Gutierrez	.10	.05
43	Pat Mahomes	.10	.05
44	Jeff King	.10	.05
45	Cal Eldred	.10	.05
46	Craig Paquette	.10	.05
47	Richie Lewis	.10	.05
48	Tony Phillips	.10	.05
49	Armando Reynoso	.10	.05
50	Moises Alou	.15	.07
51	Manuel Lee	.10	.05
52	Otis Nixon	.10	.05
53	Billy Ashley	.10	.05
54	Mark Whiten	.10	.05
55	Jeff Russell	.10	.05
56	Chad Curtis	.10	.05
57	Kevin Stocker	.10	.05
58	Mike Jackson	.10	.05
59	Matt Nokes	.10	.05
60	Chris Bosio	.10	.05
61	Damon Buford	.10	.05
62	Tim Belcher	.10	.05
63	Glenallen Hill	.10	.05
64	Bill Wertz	.10	.05
65	Eddie Murray	.40	.18
66	Tom Gordon	.10	.05
67	Alex Gonzalez	.10	.05
68	Eddie Taubensee	.10	.05
69	Jacob Brumfield	.10	.05
70	Andy Benes	.10	.05
71	Rich Becker	.10	.05
72	Steve Cooke	.10	.05
73	Billy Spiers	.10	.05
74	Scott Brosius	.15	.07
75	Alan Trammell	.25	.11
76	Luis Aquino	.10	.05
77	Jerald Clark	.10	.05
78	Mel Rojas	.10	.05
79	Outfield Prospects Billy Masse Stanton Cameron Tim Clark Craig McClure RC	.10	.05
80	Jose Canseco	.40	.18
81	Greg McMichael	.10	.05
82	Brian Turang RC	.10	.05
83	Tom Urbani	.10	.05
84	Garret Anderson	.15	.07
85	Tony Pena	.10	.05
86	Ricky Jordan	.10	.05
87	Jim Gott	.10	.05
88	Pat Kelly	.10	.05
89	Bud Black	.10	.05
90	Robin Ventura	.15	.07
91	Rick Sutcliffe	.15	.07
92	Jose Bautista	.10	.05
93	Bob Ojeda	.10	.05
94	Phil Hiatt	.10	.05
95	Tim Pugh	.10	.05
96	Randy Knorr	.10	.05
97	Todd Jones	.10	.05
98	Ryan Thompson	.10	.05
99	Tim Mauser	.10	.05
100	Kirby Puckett	1.00	.45
101	Mark Dewey	.10	.05
102	B.J. Surhoff	.15	.07
103	Sterling Hitchcock	.10	.05
104	Alex Arias	.10	.05
105	David Wells	.15	.07
106	Daryl Boston	.10	.05
107	Mike Stanton	.10	.05
108	Gary Redus	.10	.05
109	Delino DeShields	.10	.05
110	Lee Smith	.15	.07
111	Greg Litton	.10	.05
112	Frankie Rodriguez	.10	.05
113	Russ Springer	.10	.05
114	Mitch Williams	.10	.05
115	Eric Karros	.15	.07
116	Jeff Brantley	.10	.05
117	Jack Voigt	.10	.05
118	Jason Bere	.10	.05
119	Kevin Roberson	.10	.05
120	Jimmy Key	.15	.07
121	Reggie Jefferson	.10	.05
122	Jeromy Burnitz	.15	.07
123	Billy Brewer	.10	.05
124	Willie Canate	.10	.05
125	Greg Swindell	.10	.05
126	Hal Morris	.10	.05
127	Brad Ausmus	.10	.05
128	George Tsamis	.10	.05
129	Denny Neagle	.15	.07
130	Pat Listach	.10	.05
131	Steve Karsay	.10	.05
132	Bret Barberie	.10	.05
133	Mark Leiter	.10	.05
134	Greg Colbrunn	.10	.05
135	David Nied	.10	.05
136	Dean Palmer	.15	.07
137	Steve Avery	.10	.05
138	Bill Haselman	.10	.05
139	Tripp Cromer	.10	.05
140	Frank Viola	.15	.07
141	Rene Gonzales	.10	.05
142	Curt Schilling	.40	.18
143	Tim Wallach	.10	.05
144	Bobby Munoz	.10	.05
145	Brady Anderson	.15	.07
146	Rod Beck	.10	.05
147	Mike LaValliere	.10	.05
148	Greg Hibbard	.10	.05
149	Kenny Lofton	.15	.07
150	Dwight Gooden	.15	.07
151	Greg Gagne	.10	.05
152	Ray McDavid	.10	.05
153	Chris Donnels	.10	.05
154	Dan Wilson	.10	.05
155	Todd Stottlemyre	.10	.05
156	David McCarty	.10	.05
157	Paul Wagner	.10	.05
158	Shortstop Prospects Orlando Miller Brandon Wilson Derek Jeter Mike Neal	2.00	.90
159	Mike Fetters	.10	.05
160	Scott Lydy	.10	.05
161	Darrell Whitmore	.10	.05
162	Bob MacDonald	.10	.05
163	Vinny Castilla	.15	.07
164	Denis Boucher	.10	.05
165	Ivan Rodriguez	.40	.18
166	Ron Gant	.10	.05
167	Tim Davis	.10	.05
168	Steve Dixon	.10	.05
169	Scott Fletcher	.10	.05
170	Terry Mulholland	.10	.05
171	Greg Myers	.10	.05
172	Brett Butler	.15	.07
173	Bob Wickman	.10	.05
174	Dave Martinez	.10	.05
175	Fernando Valenzuela	.15	.07
176	Craig Grebeck	.10	.05
177	Shawn Boskie	.10	.05
178	Albie Lopez	.10	.05
179	Butch Huskey	.10	.05
180	George Brett	.75	.35
181	Juan Guzman	.10	.05
182	Eric Anthony	.10	.05
183	Rob Dibble	.10	.05
184	Craig Shipley	.10	.05
185	Kevin Tapani	.10	.05
186	Marcus Moore	.10	.05
187	Graeme Lloyd	.10	.05
188	Mike Bordick	.10	.05
189	Chris Hammond	.10	.05
190	Cecil Fielder	.15	.07
191	Curt Leskanic	.10	.05
192	Lou Frazier	.10	.05
193	Steve Dreyer RC	.10	.05
194	Javier Lopez	.15	.07
195	Edgar Martinez	.25	.11
196	Allen Watson	.10	.05
197	John Flaherty	.10	.05
198	Kurt Stillwell	.10	.05
199	Danny Jackson	.10	.05
200	Cal Ripken	1.50	.70
201	Mike Bell FDP RC	.10	.05
202	Alan Benes FDP RC	.15	.07
203	Matt Farner FDP RC	.10	.05
204	Jeff Granger	.10	.05
205	B.Kieschnick FDP RC	.10	.05
206	Jeremy Lee FDP RC	.10	.05
207	C.Peterson FDP RC	.10	.05
208	Alan Rice FDP RC	.10	.05
209	Billy Wagner FDP RC	.40	.18
210	Kelly Wunsch FDP RC	.10	.05
211	Tom Candiotti	.10	.05
212	Domingo Jean	.10	.05
213	John Burkett	.10	.05
214	George Bell	.10	.05
215	Dan Plesac	.10	.05
216	Manny Ramirez	.60	.25
217	Mike Maddux	.10	.05
218	Kevin McReynolds	.10	.05
219	Pat Borders	.10	.05
220	Doug Drabek	.10	.05
221	Larry Luebbers RC	.10	.05
222	Trevor Hoffman	.15	.07
223	Pat Meares	.10	.05
224	Danny Miceli	.10	.05
225	Greg Vaughn	.15	.07
226	Scott Hemond	.10	.05
227	Pat Rapp	.10	.05
228	Kirk Gibson	.15	.07
229	Lance Painter	.10	.05

❑ 230 Larry Walker .25 .11
❑ 231 Benji Gil .10 .05
❑ 232 Mark Wohlers .10 .05
❑ 233 Rich Amaral .10 .05
❑ 234 Eric Pappas .10 .05
❑ 235 Scott Cooper .10 .05
❑ 236 Mike Butcher .10 .05
❑ 237 Outfield Prospects .50 .23
Curtis Pride
Shawn Green
Mark Sweeney
Eddie Davis
❑ 238 Kim Batiste .10 .05
❑ 239 Paul Assenmacher .10 .05
❑ 240 Will Clark .40 .18
❑ 241 Jose Offerman .10 .05
❑ 242 Todd Frohwirth .10 .05
❑ 243 Tim Raines .15 .07
❑ 244 Rick Wilkins .10 .05
❑ 245 Bret Saberhagen .15 .07
❑ 246 Thomas Howard .10 .05
❑ 247 Stan Belinda .10 .05
❑ 248 Rickey Henderson .75 .35
❑ 249 Brian Williams .10 .05
❑ 250 Barry Larkin .40 .18
❑ 251 Jose Valentin .10 .05
❑ 252 Lenny Webster .10 .05
❑ 253 Blas Minor .10 .05
❑ 254 Tim Teufel .10 .05
❑ 255 Bobby Witt .10 .05
❑ 256 Walt Weiss .10 .05
❑ 257 Chad Kreuter .10 .05
❑ 258 Roberto Mejia .10 .05
❑ 259 Cliff Floyd .15 .07
❑ 260 Julio Franco .15 .07
❑ 261 Rafael Belliard .10 .05
❑ 262 Marc Newfield .10 .05
❑ 263 Gerald Perry .10 .05
❑ 264 Ken Ryan .10 .05
❑ 265 Chili Davis .15 .07
❑ 266 Dave West .10 .05
❑ 267 Royce Clayton .10 .05
❑ 268 Pedro Martinez .60 .25
❑ 269 Mark Hutton .10 .05
❑ 270 Frank Thomas .50 .23
❑ 271 Brad Pennington .10 .05
❑ 272 Mike Harkey .10 .05
❑ 273 Sandy Alomar Jr. .15 .07
❑ 274 Dave Gallagher .10 .05
❑ 275 Wally Joyner .15 .07
❑ 276 Ricky Trlicek .10 .05
❑ 277 Al Osuna .10 .05
❑ 278 Pokey Reese .10 .05
❑ 279 Kevin Higgins .10 .05
❑ 280 Rick Aguilera .10 .05
❑ 281 Orlando Merced .10 .05
❑ 282 Mike Mohler .10 .05
❑ 283 John Jaha .10 .05
❑ 284 Robb Nen .10 .05
❑ 285 Travis Fryman .15 .07
❑ 286 Mark Thompson .10 .05
❑ 287 Mike Lansing .10 .05
❑ 288 Craig Lefferts .10 .05
❑ 289 Damon Berryhill .10 .05
❑ 290 Randy Johnson .50 .23
❑ 291 Jeff Reed .10 .05
❑ 292 Danny Darwin .10 .05
❑ 293 J.T. Snow .15 .07
❑ 294 Tyler Green .10 .05
❑ 295 Chris Hoiles .10 .05
❑ 296 Roger McDowell .10 .05
❑ 297 Spike Owen .10 .05
❑ 298 Salomon Torres .10 .05
❑ 299 Wilson Alvarez .10 .05
❑ 300 Ryne Sandberg .50 .23
❑ 301 Derek Lilliquist .10 .05
❑ 302 Howard Johnson .10 .05
❑ 303 Greg Cadaret .10 .05
❑ 304 Pat Hentgen .10 .05
❑ 305 Craig Biggio .25 .11
❑ 306 Scott Service .10 .05
❑ 307 Melvin Nieves .10 .05
❑ 308 Mike Trombley .10 .05
❑ 309 Carlos Garcia .10 .05
❑ 310 Robin Yount UER .40 .18
(listed with 111 triples in
1988; should be 11)
❑ 311 Marcos Armas .10 .05
❑ 312 Rich Rodriguez .10 .05
❑ 313 Justin Thompson .10 .05
❑ 314 Danny Sheaffer .10 .05
❑ 315 Ken Hill .10 .05
❑ 316 Pitching Prospects .10 .05
Chad Ogea
Duff Brumley
Terrell Wade RC
Chris Michalak
❑ 317 Cris Carpenter .10 .05
❑ 318 Jeff Blauser .10 .05
❑ 319 Ted Power .10 .05
❑ 320 Ozzie Smith .50 .23
❑ 321 John Dopson .10 .05
❑ 322 Chris Turner .10 .05
❑ 323 Pete Incaviglia .10 .05
❑ 324 Alan Mills .10 .05
❑ 325 Jody Reed .10 .05
❑ 326 Rich Monteleone .10 .05
❑ 327 Mark Carreon .10 .05
❑ 328 Donn Pall .10 .05
❑ 329 Matt Walbeck .10 .05
❑ 330 Charles Nagy .10 .05
❑ 331 Jeff McKnight .10 .05
❑ 332 Jose Lind .10 .05
❑ 333 Mike Timlin .10 .05
❑ 334 Doug Jones .10 .05
❑ 335 Kevin Mitchell .10 .05
❑ 336 Luis Lopez .10 .05
❑ 337 Shane Mack .10 .05
❑ 338 Randy Tomlin .10 .05
❑ 339 Matt Mieske .10 .05
❑ 340 Mark McGwire 1.50 .70
❑ 341 Nigel Wilson .10 .05
❑ 342 Danny Gladden .10 .05
❑ 343 Mo Sanford .10 .05
❑ 344 Sean Berry .10 .05
❑ 345 Kevin Brown .15 .07
❑ 346 Greg Olson .10 .05
❑ 347 Dave Magadan .10 .05
❑ 348 Rene Arocha .10 .05
❑ 349 Carlos Quintana .10 .05
❑ 350 Jim Abbott .15 .07
❑ 351 Gary DiSarcina .10 .05
❑ 352 Ben Rivera .10 .05
❑ 353 Carlos Hernandez .10 .05
❑ 354 Darren Lewis .10 .05
❑ 355 Harold Reynolds .10 .05
❑ 356 Scott Ruffcorn .10 .05
❑ 357 Mark Gubicza .10 .05
❑ 358 Paul Sorrento .10 .05
❑ 359 Anthony Young .10 .05
❑ 360 Mark Grace .40 .18
❑ 361 Rob Butler .10 .05
❑ 362 Kevin Bass .10 .05
❑ 363 Eric Helfand .10 .05
❑ 364 Derek Bell .10 .05
❑ 365 Scott Erickson .10 .05
❑ 366 Al Martin .10 .05
❑ 367 Ricky Bones .10 .05
❑ 368 Jeff Branson .10 .05
❑ 369 Third Base Prospects .75 .35
Luis Ortiz
David Bell RC
Jason Giambi
George Arias
❑ 370 Benito Santiago .10 .05
(See also 379)
❑ 371 John Doherty .10 .05
❑ 372 Joe Girardi .10 .05
❑ 373 Tim Scott .10 .05
❑ 374 Marvin Freeman .10 .05
❑ 375 Deion Sanders .15 .07
❑ 376 Roger Salkeld .10 .05
❑ 377 Bernard Gilkey .10 .05
❑ 378 Tony Fossas .10 .05
❑ 379 Mark McLemore UER .10 .05
(Card number is 370)
❑ 380 Darren Daulton .15 .07
❑ 381 Chuck Finley .15 .07
❑ 382 Mitch Webster .10 .05
❑ 383 Gerald Williams .10 .05
❑ 384 Frank Thomas AS .25 .11
Fred McGriff AS
❑ 385 Roberto Alomar AS .15 .07
Robby Thompson AS
❑ 386 Wade Boggs AS .15 .07
Matt Williams AS
❑ 387 Cal Ripken AS .40 .18
Jeff Blauser AS
❑ 388 Ken Griffey Jr. AS .50 .23
Len Dykstra AS
❑ 389 Juan Gonzalez AS .15 .07
David Justice AS
❑ 390 George Belle AS .50 .23
Bobby Bonds AS
❑ 391 Mike Stanley AS .40 .18
Mike Piazza AS
❑ 392 Jack McDowell AS .25 .11
Greg Maddux AS
❑ 393 Jimmy Key AS .15 .07
Tom Glavine AS
❑ 394 Jeff Montgomery AS .10 .05
Randy Myers AS
❑ 395 Checklist 1-198 .10 .05
❑ 396 Checklist 199-396 .10 .05
❑ 397 Tim Salmon .15 .07
❑ 398 Todd Benzinger .10 .05
❑ 399 Frank Castillo .10 .05
❑ 400 Ken Griffey Jr. 1.25 .55
❑ 401 John Kruk .15 .07
❑ 402 Dave Telgheder .10 .05
❑ 403 Gary Gaetti .15 .07
❑ 404 Jim Edmonds .40 .18
❑ 405 Don Slaught .10 .05
❑ 406 Jose Oquendo .10 .05
❑ 407 Bruce Ruffin .10 .05
❑ 408 Phil Clark .10 .05
❑ 409 Joe Klink .10 .05
❑ 410 Lou Whitaker .15 .07
❑ 411 Kevin Seitzer .10 .05
❑ 412 Darrin Fletcher .10 .05
❑ 413 Kenny Rogers .10 .05
❑ 414 Bill Pecota .10 .05
❑ 415 Dave Fleming .10 .05
❑ 416 Luis Alicea .10 .05
❑ 417 Paul Quantrill .10 .05
❑ 418 Damion Easley .10 .05
❑ 419 Wes Chamberlain .10 .05
❑ 420 Harold Baines .15 .07
❑ 421 Scott Radinsky .10 .05
❑ 422 Rey Sanchez .10 .05
❑ 423 Junior Ortiz .10 .05
❑ 424 Jeff Kent .25 .11
❑ 425 Brian McRae .10 .05
❑ 426 Ed Sprague .10 .05
❑ 427 Tom Edens .10 .05
❑ 428 Willie Greene .10 .05
❑ 429 Bryan Hickerson .10 .05
❑ 430 Dave Winfield .40 .18
❑ 431 Pedro Astacio .10 .05
❑ 432 Mike Gallego .10 .05
❑ 433 Dave Burba .10 .05
❑ 434 Bob Walk .10 .05
❑ 435 Darryl Hamilton .10 .05
❑ 436 Vince Horsman .10 .05
❑ 437 Bob Natal .10 .05
❑ 438 Mike Henneman .10 .05
❑ 439 Willie Blair .10 .05
❑ 440 Dennis Martinez .15 .07
❑ 441 Dan Peltier .10 .05
❑ 442 Tony Tarasco .10 .05
❑ 443 John Cummings .10 .05
❑ 444 Geronimo Pena .10 .05
❑ 445 Aaron Sele .15 .07
❑ 446 Stan Javier .10 .05
❑ 447 Mike Williams .10 .05
❑ 448 First Base Prospects .25 .11
Greg Pirkl
Roberto Petagine
D.J.Boston
Shawn Wooten RC
❑ 449 Jim Poole .10 .05
❑ 450 Carlos Baerga .10 .05
❑ 451 Bob Scanlan .10 .05
❑ 452 Lance Johnson .10 .05
❑ 453 Eric Hillman .10 .05
❑ 454 Keith Miller .10 .05
❑ 455 Dave Stewart .15 .07
❑ 456 Pete Harnisch .10 .05

❑ 457 Roberto Kelly .10 .05
❑ 458 Tim Worrell .10 .05
❑ 459 Pedro Munoz .10 .05
❑ 460 Orel Hershiser .15 .07
❑ 461 Randy Velarde .10 .05
❑ 462 Trevor Wilson .10 .05
❑ 463 Jerry Goff .10 .05
❑ 464 Bill Wegman .10 .05
❑ 465 Dennis Eckersley .15 .07
❑ 466 Jeff Conine .10 .05
❑ 467 Joe Boever .10 .05
❑ 468 Dante Bichette .15 .07
❑ 469 Jeff Shaw .10 .05
❑ 470 Rafael Palmeiro .40 .18
❑ 471 Phil Leftwich RC .10 .05
❑ 472 Jay Buhner .15 .07
❑ 473 Bob Tewksbury .10 .05
❑ 474 Tim Naehring .10 .05
❑ 475 Tom Glavine .40 .18
❑ 476 Dave Hollins .10 .05
❑ 477 Arthur Rhodes .10 .05
❑ 478 Joey Cora .10 .05
❑ 479 Mike Morgan .10 .05
❑ 480 Albert Belle .15 .07
❑ 481 John Franco .15 .07
❑ 482 Hipolito Pichardo .10 .05
❑ 483 Duane Ward .10 .05
❑ 484 Luis Gonzalez .40 .18
❑ 485 Joe Oliver .10 .05
❑ 486 Wally Whitehurst .10 .05
❑ 487 Mike Benjamin .10 .05
❑ 488 Eric Davis .15 .07
❑ 489 Scott Kamieniecki .10 .05
❑ 490 Kent Hrbek .15 .07
❑ 491 John Hope RC .10 .05
❑ 492 Jesse Orosco .10 .05
❑ 493 Troy Neel .10 .05
❑ 494 Ryan Bowen .10 .05
❑ 495 Mickey Tettleton .10 .05
❑ 496 Chris Jones .10 .05
❑ 497 John Wetteland .15 .07
❑ 498 David Hulse .10 .05
❑ 499 Greg Maddux 1.00 .45
❑ 500 Bo Jackson .15 .07
❑ 501 Donovan Osborne .10 .05
❑ 502 Mike Greenwell .10 .05
❑ 503 Steve Frey .10 .05
❑ 504 Jim Eisenreich .10 .05
❑ 505 Robby Thompson .10 .05
❑ 506 Leo Gomez .10 .05
❑ 507 Dave Staton .10 .05
❑ 508 Wayne Kirby .10 .05
❑ 509 Tim Bogar .10 .05
❑ 510 David Cone .15 .07
❑ 511 Devon White .10 .05
❑ 512 Xavier Hernandez .10 .05
❑ 513 Tim Costo .10 .05
❑ 514 Gene Harris .10 .05
❑ 515 Jack McDowell .10 .05
❑ 516 Kevin Gross .10 .05
❑ 517 Scott Leius .10 .05
❑ 518 Lloyd McClendon .10 .05
❑ 519 Alex Diaz RC .10 .05
❑ 520 Wade Boggs .40 .18
❑ 521 Bob Welch .10 .05
❑ 522 Henry Cotto .10 .05
❑ 523 Mike Moore .10 .05
❑ 524 Tim Laker .10 .05
❑ 525 Andres Galarraga .25 .11
❑ 526 Jamie Moyer .10 .05
❑ 527 2B Prospects .15 .07
Norberto Martin
Ruben Santana
Jason Hardtke
Chris Sexton RC
❑ 528 Sid Bream .10 .05
❑ 529 Erik Hanson .10 .05
❑ 530 Ray Lankford .10 .05
❑ 531 Rob Deer .10 .05
❑ 532 Rod Correia .10 .05
❑ 533 Roger Mason .10 .05
❑ 534 Mike Devereaux .10 .05
❑ 535 Jeff Montgomery .10 .05
❑ 536 Dwight Smith .10 .05
❑ 537 Jeremy Hernandez .10 .05
❑ 538 Ellis Burks .15 .07
❑ 539 Bobby Jones .10 .05
❑ 540 Paul Molitor .40 .18
❑ 541 Jeff Juden .10 .05
❑ 542 Chris Sabo .10 .05
❑ 543 Larry Casian .10 .05
❑ 544 Jeff Gardner .10 .05
❑ 545 Ramon Martinez .10 .05
❑ 546 Paul O'Neill .40 .18
❑ 547 Steve Hosey .10 .05
❑ 548 Dave Nilsson .10 .05
❑ 549 Ron Darling .10 .05
❑ 550 Matt Williams .25 .11
❑ 551 Jack Armstrong .10 .05
❑ 552 Bill Krueger .10 .05
❑ 553 Freddie Benavides .10 .05
❑ 554 Jeff Fassero .10 .05
❑ 555 Chuck Knoblauch .15 .07
❑ 556 Guillermo Velasquez .10 .05
❑ 557 Joel Johnston .10 .05
❑ 558 Tom Lampkin .10 .05
❑ 559 Todd Van Poppel .10 .05
❑ 560 Gary Sheffield .15 .07
❑ 561 Skeeter Barnes .10 .05
❑ 562 Darren Holmes .10 .05
❑ 563 John Vander Wal .10 .05
❑ 564 Mike Ignasiak .10 .05
❑ 565 Fred McGriff .25 .11
❑ 566 Luis Polonia .10 .05
❑ 567 Mike Perez .10 .05
❑ 568 John Valentin .10 .05
❑ 569 Mike Felder .10 .05
❑ 570 Tommy Greene .10 .05
❑ 571 David Segui .10 .05
❑ 572 Roberto Hernandez .10 .05
❑ 573 Steve Wilson .10 .05
❑ 574 Willie McGee .15 .07
❑ 575 Randy Myers .10 .05
❑ 576 Darrin Jackson .10 .05
❑ 577 Eric Plunk .10 .05
❑ 578 Mike Macfarlane .10 .05
❑ 579 Doug Brocail .10 .05
❑ 580 Steve Finley .15 .07
❑ 581 John Roper .10 .05
❑ 582 Danny Cox .10 .05
❑ 583 Chip Hale .10 .05
❑ 584 Scott Bullett .10 .05
❑ 585 Kevin Reimer .10 .05
❑ 586 Brent Gates .10 .05
❑ 587 Matt Turner .10 .05
❑ 588 Rich Rowland .10 .05
❑ 589 Kent Bottenfield .10 .05
❑ 590 Marquis Grissom .10 .05
❑ 591 Doug Strange .10 .05
❑ 592 Jay Howell .10 .05
❑ 593 Omar Vizquel .15 .07
❑ 594 Rheal Cormier .10 .05
❑ 595 Andre Dawson .25 .11
❑ 596 Hilly Hathaway .10 .05
❑ 597 Todd Pratt .10 .05
❑ 598 Mike Mussina .40 .18
❑ 599 Alex Fernandez .10 .05
❑ 600 Don Mattingly 1.00 .45
❑ 601 Frank Thomas ST .25 .11
❑ 602 Ryne Sandberg ST .25 .11
❑ 603 Wade Boggs ST .15 .07
❑ 604 Cal Ripken ST .75 .35
❑ 605 Barry Bonds ST .50 .23
❑ 606 Ken Griffey Jr. ST .60 .25
❑ 607 Kirby Puckett ST .50 .23
❑ 608 Darren Daulton ST .10 .05
❑ 609 Paul Molitor ST .15 .07
❑ 610 Terry Steinbach .10 .05
❑ 611 Todd Worrell .10 .05
❑ 612 Jim Thome .40 .18
❑ 613 Chuck McElroy .10 .05
❑ 614 John Habyan .10 .05
❑ 615 Sid Fernandez .10 .05
❑ 616 Outfield Prospects .10 .05
Eddie Zambrano
Glenn Murray
Chad Mottola
Jermaine Allensworth RC
❑ 617 Steve Bedrosian .10 .05
❑ 618 Rob Ducey .10 .05
❑ 619 Tom Browning .10 .05
❑ 620 Tony Gwynn .75 .35
❑ 621 Carl Willis .10 .05
❑ 622 Kevin Young .10 .05
❑ 623 Rafael Novoa .10 .05
❑ 624 Jerry Browne .10 .05
❑ 625 Charlie Hough .15 .07
❑ 626 Chris Gomez .10 .05
❑ 627 Steve Reed .10 .05
❑ 628 Kirk Rueter .10 .05
❑ 629 Matt Whiteside .10 .05
❑ 630 David Justice .15 .07
❑ 631 Brad Holman .10 .05
❑ 632 Brian Jordan .15 .07
❑ 633 Scott Bankhead .10 .05
❑ 634 Torey Lovullo .10 .05
❑ 635 Len Dykstra .15 .07
❑ 636 Ben McDonald .10 .05
❑ 637 Steve Howe .10 .05
❑ 638 Jose Vizcaino .10 .05
❑ 639 Bill Swift .10 .05
❑ 640 Darryl Strawberry .15 .07
❑ 641 Steve Farr .10 .05
❑ 642 Tom Kramer .10 .05
❑ 643 Joe Orsulak .10 .05
❑ 644 Tom Henke .10 .05
❑ 645 Joe Carter .15 .07
❑ 646 Ken Caminiti .15 .07
❑ 647 Reggie Sanders .10 .05
❑ 648 Andy Ashby .10 .05
❑ 649 Derek Parks .10 .05
❑ 650 Andy Van Slyke .15 .07
❑ 651 Juan Bell .10 .05
❑ 652 Roger Smithberg .10 .05
❑ 653 Chuck Carr .10 .05
❑ 654 Bill Gullickson .10 .05
❑ 655 Charlie Hayes .10 .05
❑ 656 Chris Nabholz .10 .05
❑ 657 Karl Rhodes .10 .05
❑ 658 Pete Smith .10 .05
❑ 659 Bret Boone .15 .07
❑ 660 Gregg Jefferies .10 .05
❑ 661 Bob Zupcic .10 .05
❑ 662 Steve Sax .10 .05
❑ 663 Mariano Duncan .10 .05
❑ 664 Jeff Tackett .10 .05
❑ 665 Mark Langston .10 .05
❑ 666 Steve Buechele .10 .05
❑ 667 Candy Maldonado .10 .05
❑ 668 Woody Williams .10 .05
❑ 669 Tim Wakefield .10 .05
❑ 670 Danny Tartabull .10 .05
❑ 671 Charlie O'Brien .10 .05
❑ 672 Felix Jose .10 .05
❑ 673 Bobby Ayala .10 .05
❑ 674 Scott Servais .10 .05
❑ 675 Roberto Alomar .40 .18
❑ 676 Pedro A.Martinez RC .10 .05
❑ 677 Eddie Guardado .10 .05
❑ 678 Mark Lewis .10 .05
❑ 679 Jaime Navarro .10 .05
❑ 680 Ruben Sierrra .10 .05
❑ 681 Rick Renteria .10 .05
❑ 682 Storm Davis .10 .05
❑ 683 Cory Snyder .10 .05
❑ 684 Ron Karkovice .10 .05
❑ 685 Juan Gonzalez .40 .18
❑ 686 Catchers Prospects 1.00 .45
Chris Howard
Carlos Delgado
Jason Kendall
Paul Bako
❑ 687 John Smoltz .15 .07
❑ 688 Brian Dorsett .10 .05
❑ 689 Omar Olivares .10 .05
❑ 690 Mo Vaughn .15 .07
❑ 691 Joe Grahe .10 .05
❑ 692 Mickey Morandini .10 .05
❑ 693 Tino Martinez .15 .07
❑ 694 Brian Barnes .10 .05
❑ 695 Mike Stanley .10 .05
❑ 696 Mark Clark .10 .05
❑ 697 Dave Hansen .10 .05
❑ 698 Willie Wilson .10 .05
❑ 699 Pete Schourek .10 .05
❑ 700 Barry Bonds 1.00 .45
❑ 701 Kevin Appier .15 .07
❑ 702 Tony Fernandez .10 .05

	Player	Mint	Nrmt
❑ 703	Darryl Kile	.15	.07
❑ 704	Archi Cianfrocco	.10	.05
❑ 705	Jose Rijo	.10	.05
❑ 706	Brian Harper	.10	.05
❑ 707	Zane Smith	.10	.05
❑ 708	Dave Henderson	.10	.05
❑ 709	Angel Miranda UER	.10	.05
	(no Topps logo on back)		
❑ 710	Orestes Destrade	.10	.05
❑ 711	Greg Gohr	.10	.05
❑ 712	Eric Young	.10	.05
❑ 713	Relief Pitchers	.10	.05
	Prospects		
	Todd Williams		
	Ron Watson		
	Kirk Bullinger		
	Mike Welch		
❑ 714	Tim Spehr	.10	.05
❑ 715	Hank Aaron 715 HR	.50	.23
❑ 716	Nate Minchey	.10	.05
❑ 717	Mike Blowers	.10	.05
❑ 718	Kent Mercker	.10	.05
❑ 719	Tom Pagnozzi	.10	.05
❑ 720	Roger Clemens	1.00	.45
❑ 721	Eduardo Perez	.10	.05
❑ 722	Milt Thompson	.10	.05
❑ 723	Gregg Olson	.10	.05
❑ 724	Kirk McCaskill	.10	.05
❑ 725	Sammy Sosa	.75	.35
❑ 726	Alvaro Espinoza	.10	.05
❑ 727	Henry Rodriguez	.10	.05
❑ 728	Jim Leyritz	.10	.05
❑ 729	Steve Scarsone	.10	.05
❑ 730	Bobby Bonilla	.15	.07
❑ 731	Chris Gwynn	.10	.05
❑ 732	Al Leiter	.15	.07
❑ 733	Bip Roberts	.10	.05
❑ 734	Mark Portugal	.10	.05
❑ 735	Terry Pendleton	.15	.07
❑ 736	Dave Valle	.10	.05
❑ 737	Paul Kilgus	.10	.05
❑ 738	Greg A. Harris	.10	.05
❑ 739	Jon Ratliff DP RC	.10	.05
❑ 740	Kirk Presley DP RC	.10	.05
❑ 741	Josue Estrada DP RC	.10	.05
❑ 742	Wayne Gomes DP RC	.10	.05
❑ 743	Pat Watkins DP RC	.10	.05
❑ 744	Jamey Wright DP RC	.15	.07
❑ 745	Jay Powell DP RC	.10	.05
❑ 746	Ryan McGuire DP RC	.15	.07
❑ 747	Marc Barcelo DP RC	.10	.05
❑ 748	Sloan Smith DP RC	.10	.05
❑ 749	John Wasdin DP RC	.10	.05
❑ 750	Marc Vlades DP	.10	.05
❑ 751	Dan Ehler DP RC	.10	.05
❑ 752	Andre King DP RC	.10	.05
❑ 753	Greg Keagle DP RC	.10	.05
❑ 754	Jason Myers DP RC	.10	.05
❑ 755	Dax Winslett DP RC	.10	.05
❑ 756	Casey Whitten DP RC	.10	.05
❑ 757	Tony Fuduric DP RC	.10	.05
❑ 758	Greg Norton DP RC	.15	.07
❑ 759	Jeff D'Amico DP RC	.40	.18
❑ 760	Ryan Hancock DP RC	.10	.05
❑ 761	David Cooper DP RC	.10	.05
❑ 762	Kevin Orie DP RC	.10	.05
❑ 763	John O'Donoghue	.10	.05
	Mike Oquist		
❑ 764	Cory Bailey RC	.10	.05
	Scott Hatteberg		
❑ 765	Mark Holzemer	.10	.05
	Paul Swingle		
❑ 766	James Baldwin	.10	.05
	Rod Bolton		
❑ 767	Jerry Di Poto	.15	.07
	Julian Tavarez RC		
❑ 768	Danny Bautista	.10	.05
	Sean Bergman		
❑ 769	Bob Hamelin	.10	.05
	Joe Vitiello		
❑ 770	Mark Kiefer	.25	.11
	Troy O'Leary		
❑ 771	Denny Hocking	.10	.05
	Oscar Munoz RC		
❑ 772	Russ Davis	.10	.05
	Brien Taylor		
❑ 773	Kyle Abbott RC	.15	.07
	Miguel Jimenez		
❑ 774	Kevin King	.10	.05
	Eric Plantenberg RC		
❑ 775	Jon Shave	.10	.05
	Desi Wilson		
❑ 776	Domingo Cedeno	.10	.05
	Paul Spoljaric		
❑ 777	Chipper Jones	.75	.35
	Ryan Klesko		
❑ 778	Steve Trachsel	.10	.05
	Turk Wendell		
❑ 779	Johnny Ruffin	.10	.05
	Jerry Spradlin RC		
❑ 780	Jason Bates	.10	.05
	John Burke		
❑ 781	Carl Everett	.25	.11
	Dave Weathers		
❑ 782	Gary Mota	.10	.05
	James Mouton		
❑ 783	Raul Mondesi	.25	.11
	Ben Van Ryn		
❑ 784	Gabe White	.15	.07
	Rondell White		
❑ 785	Brook Fordyce	.15	.07
	Bill Pulsipher		
❑ 786	Kevin Foste RCr	.10	.05
	Gene Schall		
❑ 787	Rich Aude RC	.10	.05
	Midre Cummings		
❑ 788	Brian Barber	.10	.05
	Rich Batchelor		
❑ 789	Brian Johnson RC	.10	.05
	Scott Sanders		
❑ 790	Ricky Faneyte	.10	.05
	J.R. Phillips		
❑ 791	Checklist 3	.10	.05
❑ 792	Checklist 4	.10	.05

1994 Topps Traded

	MINT	NRMT
COMP.FACT.SET (140)	40.00	18.00

	Player	Mint	Nrmt
❑ 1T	Paul Wilson	.10	.05
❑ 2T	Bill Taylor RC	.15	.07
❑ 3T	Dan Wilson	.10	.05
❑ 4T	Mark Smith	.10	.05
❑ 5T	Toby Borland RC	.10	.05
❑ 6T	Dave Clark	.10	.05
❑ 7T	Dennis Martinez	.15	.07
❑ 8T	Dave Gallagher	.10	.05
❑ 9T	Josias Manzanillo	.10	.05
❑ 10T	Brian Anderson RC	.15	.07
❑ 11T	Damon Berryhill	.10	.05
❑ 12T	Alex Cole	.10	.05
❑ 13T	Jacob Shumate RC	.10	.05
❑ 14T	Oddibe McDowell	.10	.05
❑ 15T	Willie Banks	.10	.05
❑ 16T	Jerry Browne	.10	.05
❑ 17T	Donnie Elliott	.10	.05
❑ 18T	Ellis Burks	.15	.07
❑ 19T	Chuck McElroy	.10	.05
❑ 20T	Luis Polonia	.10	.05
❑ 21T	Brian Harper	.10	.05
❑ 22T	Mark Portugal	.10	.05
❑ 23T	Dave Henderson	.10	.05
❑ 24T	Mark Acre RC	.10	.05
❑ 25T	Julio Franco	.15	.07
❑ 26T	Darren Hall RC	.10	.05
❑ 27T	Eric Anthony	.10	.05
❑ 28T	Sid Fernandez	.10	.05
❑ 29T	Rusty Greer RC	2.00	.90
❑ 30T	Riccardo Ingram RC	.10	.05
❑ 31T	Gabe White	.10	.05
❑ 32T	Tim Belcher	.10	.05
❑ 33T	Terrence Long RC	6.00	2.70
❑ 34T	Mark Dalesandro RC	.10	.05
❑ 35T	Mike Kelly	.10	.05
❑ 36T	Jack Morris	.15	.07
❑ 37T	Jeff Brantley	.10	.05
❑ 38T	Larry Barnes RC	.10	.05
❑ 39T	Brian R. Hunter	.10	.05
❑ 40T	Otis Nixon	.10	.05
❑ 41T	Bret Wagner	.10	.05
❑ 42T	Pedro Martinez TR	1.00	.45
	Delino Deshields		
❑ 43T	Heathcliff Slocumb	.10	.05
❑ 44T	Ben Grieve RC	6.00	2.70
❑ 45T	John Hudek RC	.10	.05
❑ 46T	Shawon Dunston	.10	.05
❑ 47T	Greg Colbrunn	.10	.05
❑ 48T	Joey Hamilton	.10	.05
❑ 49T	Marvin Freeman	.10	.05
❑ 50T	Terry Mulholland	.10	.05
❑ 51T	Keith Mitchell	.10	.05
❑ 52T	Dwight Smith	.10	.05
❑ 53T	Shawn Boskie	.10	.05
❑ 54T	Kevin Witt RC	.15	.07
❑ 55T	Ron Gant	.10	.05
❑ 56T	1994 Prospects	1.00	.45
	Trenidad Hubbard		
	Jason Schmidt RC		
	Larry Sutton		
	Stephen Larkin		
❑ 57T	Jody Reed	.10	.05
❑ 58T	Rick Helling	.10	.05
❑ 59T	John Powell	.10	.05
❑ 60T	Eddie Murray	.40	.18
❑ 61T	Joe Hall RC	.10	.05
❑ 62T	Jorge Fabregas	.10	.05
❑ 63T	Mike Mordecai RC	.10	.05
❑ 64T	Ed Vosberg	.10	.05
❑ 65T	Rickey Henderson	1.00	.45
❑ 66T	Tim Grieve RC	.10	.05
❑ 67T	Jon Lieber	.15	.07
❑ 68T	Chris Howard	.10	.05
❑ 69T	Matt Walbeck	.10	.05
❑ 70T	Chan Ho Park RC	5.00	2.20
❑ 71T	Bryan Eversgerd RC	.10	.05
❑ 72T	John Dettmer	.10	.05
❑ 73T	Erik Hanson	.10	.05
❑ 74T	Mike Thurman RC	.10	.05
❑ 75T	Bobby Ayala	.10	.05
❑ 76T	Rafael Palmeiro	.40	.18
❑ 77T	Bret Boone	.15	.07
❑ 78T	Paul Shuey	.10	.05
❑ 79T	Kevin Foster RC	.10	.05
❑ 80T	Dave Magadan	.10	.05
❑ 81T	Bip Roberts	.10	.05
❑ 82T	Howard Johnson	.10	.05
❑ 83T	Xavier Hernandez	.10	.05
❑ 84T	Ross Powell RC	.10	.05
❑ 85T	Doug Million RC	.10	.05
❑ 86T	Geronimo Berroa	.10	.05
❑ 87T	Mark Farris RC	.10	.05
❑ 88T	Butch Henry	.10	.05
❑ 89T	Junior Felix	.10	.05
❑ 90T	Bo Jackson	.15	.07
❑ 91T	Hector Carrasco	.10	.05
❑ 92T	Charlie O'Brien	.10	.05
❑ 93T	Omar Vizquel	.15	.07
❑ 94T	David Segui	.10	.05
❑ 95T	Dustin Hermanson	.15	.07
❑ 96T	Gar Finnvold RC	.10	.05
❑ 97T	Dave Stevens	.10	.05
❑ 98T	Corey Pointer RC	.10	.05
❑ 99T	Felix Fermin	.10	.05
❑ 100T	Lee Smith	.15	.07
❑ 101T	Reid Ryan RC	.15	.07
❑ 102T	Bobby Munoz	.10	.05
❑ 103T	Deion Sanders TR	.15	.07
	Roberto Kelly		
❑ 104T	Turner Ward	.10	.05

❑ 105T W.VanLandingham RC .10 .05
❑ 106T Vince Coleman .10 .05
❑ 107T Stan Javier .10 .05
❑ 108T Darrin Jackson .10 .05
❑ 109T C.J. Nitkowski RC .10 .05
❑ 110T Anthony Young .10 .05
❑ 111T Kurt Miller .10 .05
❑ 112T Paul Konerko RC 6.00 2.70
❑ 113T Walt Weiss .10 .05
❑ 114T Daryl Boston .10 .05
❑ 115T Will Clark .40 .18
❑ 116T Matt Smith RC .10 .05
❑ 117T Mark Leiter .10 .05
❑ 118T Gregg Olson .10 .05
❑ 119T Tony Pena .10 .05
❑ 120T Jose Vizcaino .10 .05
❑ 121T Rick White RC .10 .05
❑ 122T Rich Rowland .10 .05
❑ 123T Jeff Reboulet .10 .05
❑ 124T Greg Hibbard .10 .05
❑ 125T Chris Sabo .10 .05
❑ 126T Doug Jones .10 .05
❑ 127T Tony Fernandez .10 .05
❑ 128T Carlos Reyes RC .10 .05
❑ 129T Kevin L.Brown RC .10 .05
❑ 130T Ryne Sandberg 1.00 .45
Farewell
❑ 131T Ryne Sandberg 1.00 .45
Farewell
❑ 132T Checklist 1-132 .10 .05

1995 Topps

	MINT	NRMT
COMPLETE SET (660)	60.00	27.00
COMP.HOBBY SET (677)	100.00	45.00
COMP.RETAIL SET (677)	80.00	36.00
COMPLETE SERIES 1 (396)	30.00	13.50
COMPLETE SERIES 2 (264)	30.00	13.50

❑ 1 Frank Thomas .75 .35
❑ 2 Mickey Morandini .15 .07
❑ 3 Babe Ruth 100th B-Day 2.00 .90
❑ 4 Scott Cooper .15 .07
❑ 5 David Cone .25 .11
❑ 6 Jacob Shumate .15 .07
❑ 7 Trevor Hoffman .25 .11
❑ 8 Shane Mack .15 .07
❑ 9 Delino DeShields .15 .07
❑ 10 Matt Williams .40 .18
❑ 11 Sammy Sosa 1.25 .55
❑ 12 Gary DiSarcina .15 .07
❑ 13 Kenny Rogers .15 .07
❑ 14 Jose Vizcaino .15 .07
❑ 15 Lou Whitaker .25 .11
❑ 16 Ron Darling .15 .07
❑ 17 Dave Nilsson .15 .07
❑ 18 Chris Hammond .15 .07
❑ 19 Sid Bream .15 .07
❑ 20 Denny Martinez .25 .11
❑ 21 Orlando Merced .15 .07
❑ 22 John Wetteland .25 .11
❑ 23 Mike Devereaux .15 .07
❑ 24 Rene Arocha .15 .07
❑ 25 Jay Buhner .25 .11
❑ 26 Darren Holmes .15 .07
❑ 27 Hal Morris .15 .07
❑ 28 Brian Buchanan RC .15 .07
❑ 29 Keith Miller .15 .07
❑ 30 Paul Molitor .60 .25
❑ 31 Dave West .15 .07
❑ 32 Tony Tarasco .15 .07
❑ 33 Scott Sanders .15 .07
❑ 34 Eddie Zambrano .15 .07
❑ 35 Ricky Bones .15 .07
❑ 36 John Valentin .15 .07
❑ 37 Kevin Tapani .15 .07
❑ 38 Tim Wallach .15 .07
❑ 39 Darren Lewis .15 .07
❑ 40 Travis Fryman .25 .11
❑ 41 Mark Leiter .15 .07
❑ 42 Jose Bautista .15 .07
❑ 43 Pete Smith .15 .07
❑ 44 Bret Barberie .15 .07
❑ 45 Dennis Eckersley .25 .11
❑ 46 Ken Hill .15 .07
❑ 47 Chad Ogea .15 .07
❑ 48 Pete Harnisch .15 .07
❑ 49 James Baldwin .15 .07
❑ 50 Mike Mussina .60 .25
❑ 51 Al Martin .15 .07
❑ 52 Mark Thompson .15 .07
❑ 53 Matt Smith .15 .07
❑ 54 Joey Hamilton .15 .07
❑ 55 Edgar Martinez .40 .18
❑ 56 John Smiley .15 .07
❑ 57 Rey Sanchez .15 .07
❑ 58 Mike Timlin .15 .07
❑ 59 Ricky Bottalico .15 .07
❑ 60 Jim Abbott .25 .11
❑ 61 Mike Kelly .15 .07
❑ 62 Brian Jordan .25 .11
❑ 63 Ken Ryan .15 .07
❑ 64 Matt Mieske .15 .07
❑ 65 Rick Aguilera .15 .07
❑ 66 Ismael Valdes .15 .07
❑ 67 Royce Clayton .15 .07
❑ 68 Junior Felix .15 .07
❑ 69 Harold Reynolds .15 .07
❑ 70 Juan Gonzalez .60 .25
❑ 71 Kelly Stinnett .15 .07
❑ 72 Carlos Reyes .15 .07
❑ 73 Dave Weathers .15 .07
❑ 74 Mel Rojas .15 .07
❑ 75 Doug Drabek .15 .07
❑ 76 Charles Nagy .15 .07
❑ 77 Tim Raines .25 .11
❑ 78 Midre Cummings .15 .07
❑ 79 First Base Prospects .15 .07
Gene Schall
Scott Talanoa
Harold Williams
Ray Brown RC
❑ 80 Rafael Palmeiro .60 .25
❑ 81 Charlie Hayes .15 .07
❑ 82 Ray Lankford .15 .07
❑ 83 Tim Davis .15 .07
❑ 84 C.J. Nitkowski .15 .07
❑ 85 Andy Ashby .15 .07
❑ 86 Gerald Williams .15 .07
❑ 87 Terry Shumpert .15 .07
❑ 88 Heathcliff Slocumb .15 .07
❑ 89 Domingo Cedeno .15 .07
❑ 90 Mark Grace .60 .25
❑ 91 Brad Woodall RC .15 .07
❑ 92 Gar Finnvold .15 .07
❑ 93 Jaime Navarro .15 .07
❑ 94 Carlos Hernandez .15 .07
❑ 95 Mark Langston .15 .07
❑ 96 Chuck Carr .15 .07
❑ 97 Mike Gardiner .15 .07
❑ 98 Dave McCarty .15 .07
❑ 99 Cris Carpenter .15 .07
❑ 100 Barry Bonds 1.50 .70
❑ 101 David Segui .15 .07
❑ 102 Scott Brosius .25 .11
❑ 103 Mariano Duncan .15 .07
❑ 104 Kenny Lofton .25 .11
❑ 105 Ken Caminiti .25 .11
❑ 106 Darrin Jackson .15 .07
❑ 107 Jim Poole .15 .07
❑ 108 Wil Cordero .15 .07
❑ 109 Danny Miceli .15 .07
❑ 110 Walt Weiss .15 .07
❑ 111 Tom Pagnozzi .15 .07
❑ 112 Terrence Long .60 .25
❑ 113 Bret Boone .25 .11
❑ 114 Daryl Boston .15 .07
❑ 115 Wally Joyner .25 .11
❑ 116 Rob Butler .15 .07
❑ 117 Rafael Belliard .15 .07
❑ 118 Luis Lopez .15 .07
❑ 119 Tony Fossas .15 .07
❑ 120 Len Dykstra .25 .11
❑ 121 Mike Morgan .15 .07
❑ 122 Denny Hocking .15 .07
❑ 123 Kevin Gross .15 .07
❑ 124 Todd Benzinger .15 .07
❑ 125 John Doherty .15 .07
❑ 126 Eduardo Perez .15 .07
❑ 127 Dan Smith .15 .07
❑ 128 Joe Orsulak .15 .07
❑ 129 Brent Gates .15 .07
❑ 130 Jeff Conine .15 .07
❑ 131 Doug Henry .15 .07
❑ 132 Paul Sorrento .15 .07
❑ 133 Mike Hampton .25 .11
❑ 134 Tim Spehr .15 .07
❑ 135 Julio Franco .25 .11
❑ 136 Mike Dyer .15 .07
❑ 137 Chris Sabo .15 .07
❑ 138 Rheal Cormier .15 .07
❑ 139 Paul Konerko .60 .25
❑ 140 Dante Bichette .25 .11
❑ 141 Chuck McElroy .15 .07
❑ 142 Mike Stanley .15 .07
❑ 143 Bob Hamelin .15 .07
❑ 144 Tommy Greene .15 .07
❑ 145 John Smoltz .25 .11
❑ 146 Ed Sprague .15 .07
❑ 147 Ray McDavid .15 .07
❑ 148 Otis Nixon .15 .07
❑ 149 Turk Wendell .15 .07
❑ 150 Chris James .15 .07
❑ 151 Derek Parks .15 .07
❑ 152 Jose Offerman .15 .07
❑ 153 Tony Clark .25 .11
❑ 154 Chad Curtis .15 .07
❑ 155 Mark Portugal .15 .07
❑ 156 Bill Pulsipher .15 .07
❑ 157 Troy Neel .15 .07
❑ 158 Dave Winfield .60 .25
❑ 159 Bill Wegman .15 .07
❑ 160 Benito Santiago .15 .07
❑ 161 Jose Mesa .15 .07
❑ 162 Luis Gonzalez .60 .25
❑ 163 Alex Fernandez .15 .07
❑ 164 Freddie Benavides .15 .07
❑ 165 Ben McDonald .15 .07
❑ 166 Blas Minor .15 .07
❑ 167 Bret Wagner .15 .07
❑ 168 Mac Suzuki .15 .07
❑ 169 Roberto Mejia .15 .07
❑ 170 Wade Boggs .60 .25
❑ 171 Pokey Reese .15 .07
❑ 172 Hipolito Pichardo .15 .07
❑ 173 Kim Batiste .15 .07
❑ 174 Darren Hall .15 .07
❑ 175 Tom Glavine .60 .25
❑ 176 Phil Plantier .15 .07
❑ 177 Chris Howard .15 .07
❑ 178 Karl Rhodes .15 .07
❑ 179 LaTroy Hawkins .15 .07
❑ 180 Raul Mondesi .25 .11
❑ 181 Jeff Reed .15 .07
❑ 182 Milt Cuyler .15 .07
❑ 183 Jim Edmonds .40 .18
❑ 184 Hector Fajardo .15 .07
❑ 185 Jeff Kent .40 .18
❑ 186 Wilson Alvarez .15 .07
❑ 187 Geronimo Berroa .15 .07
❑ 188 Billy Spiers .15 .07
❑ 189 Derek Lilliquist .15 .07
❑ 190 Craig Biggio .40 .18
❑ 191 Roberto Hernandez .15 .07
❑ 192 Bob Natal .15 .07
❑ 193 Bobby Ayala .15 .07
❑ 194 Travis Miller RC .15 .07
❑ 195 Bob Tewksbury .15 .07
❑ 196 Rondell White .25 .11

No.	Card	Price	Price
197	Steve Cooke	.15	.07
198	Jeff Branson	.15	.07
199	Derek Jeter	2.50	1.10
200	Tim Salmon	.25	.11
201	Steve Frey	.15	.07
202	Kent Mercker	.15	.07
203	Randy Johnson	.75	.35
204	Todd Worrell	.15	.07
205	Mo Vaughn	.25	.11
206	Howard Johnson	.15	.07
207	John Wasdin	.15	.07
208	Eddie Williams	.15	.07
209	Tim Belcher	.15	.07
210	Jeff Montgomery	.15	.07
211	Kirt Manwaring	.15	.07
212	Ben Grieve	.60	.25
213	Pat Hentgen	.15	.07
214	Shawon Dunston	.15	.07
215	Mike Greenwell	.15	.07
216	Alex Diaz	.15	.07
217	Pat Mahomes	.15	.07
218	Dave Hansen	.15	.07
219	Kevin Rogers	.15	.07
220	Cecil Fielder	.25	.11
221	Andrew Lorraine	.15	.07
222	Jack Armstrong	.15	.07
223	Todd Hundley	.15	.07
224	Mark Acre	.15	.07
225	Darrell Whitmore	.15	.07
226	Randy Milligan	.15	.07
227	Wayne Kirby	.15	.07
228	Darryl Kile	.25	.11
229	Bob Zupcic	.15	.07
230	Jay Bell	.25	.11
231	Dustin Hermanson	.15	.07
232	Harold Baines	.25	.11
233	Alan Benes	.15	.07
234	Felix Fermin	.15	.07
235	Ellis Burks	.25	.11
236	Jeff Brantley	.15	.07
237	Outfield Prospects	.25	.11
	Brian Hunter		
	Jose Malave		
	Karim Garcia RC		
	Shane Pullen		
238	Matt Nokes	.15	.07
239	Ben Rivera	.15	.07
240	Joe Carter	.25	.11
241	Jeff Granger	.15	.07
242	Terry Pendleton	.25	.11
243	Melvin Nieves	.15	.07
244	Frankie Rodriguez	.15	.07
245	Darryl Hamilton	.15	.07
246	Brooks Kieschnick	.15	.07
247	Todd Hollandsworth	.15	.07
248	Joe Rosselli	.15	.07
249	Bill Gullickson	.15	.07
250	Chuck Knoblauch	.25	.11
251	Kurt Miller	.15	.07
252	Bobby Jones	.15	.07
253	Lance Blankenship	.15	.07
254	Matt Whiteside	.15	.07
255	Darrin Fletcher	.15	.07
256	Eric Plunk	.15	.07
257	Shane Reynolds	.15	.07
258	Norberto Martin	.15	.07
259	Mike Thurman	.15	.07
260	Andy Van Slyke	.25	.11
261	Dwight Smith	.15	.07
262	Allen Watson	.15	.07
263	Dan Wilson	.15	.07
264	Brent Mayne	.15	.07
265	Bip Roberts	.15	.07
266	Sterling Hitchcock	.15	.07
267	Alex Gonzalez	.15	.07
268	Greg Harris	.15	.07
269	Ricky Jordan	.15	.07
270	Johnny Ruffin	.15	.07
271	Mike Stanton	.15	.07
272	Rich Rowland	.15	.07
273	Steve Trachsel	.15	.07
274	Pedro Munoz	.15	.07
275	Ramon Martinez	.15	.07
276	Dave Henderson	.15	.07
277	Chris Gomez	.15	.07
278	Joe Grahe	.15	.07
279	Rusty Greer	.25	.11
280	John Franco	.25	.11
281	Mike Bordick	.15	.07
282	Jeff D'Amico	.15	.07
283	Dave Magadan	.15	.07
284	Tony Pena	.15	.07
285	Greg Swindell	.15	.07
286	Doug Million	.15	.07
287	Gabe White	.15	.07
288	Trey Beamon	.15	.07
289	Arthur Rhodes	.15	.07
290	Juan Guzman	.15	.07
291	Jose Oquendo	.15	.07
292	Willie Blair	.15	.07
293	Eddie Taubensee	.15	.07
294	Steve Howe	.15	.07
295	Greg Maddux	1.50	.70
296	Mike Macfarlane	.15	.07
297	Curt Schilling	.60	.25
298	Phil Clark	.15	.07
299	Woody Williams	.15	.07
300	Jose Canseco	.60	.25
301	Aaron Sele	.25	.11
302	Carl Willis	.15	.07
303	Steve Buechele	.15	.07
304	Dave Burba	.15	.07
305	Orel Hershiser	.25	.11
306	Damion Easley	.15	.07
307	Mike Henneman	.15	.07
308	Josias Manzanillo	.15	.07
309	Kevin Seitzer	.15	.07
310	Ruben Sierra	.15	.07
311	Bryan Harvey	.15	.07
312	Jim Thome	.60	.25
313	Ramon Castro RC	.25	.11
314	Lance Johnson	.15	.07
315	Marquis Grissom	.15	.07
316	Starting Pitcher	.15	.07
	Prospects		
	Terrell Wade		
	Juan Acevedo		
	Matt Arrandale		
	Eddie Priest RC		
317	Paul Wagner	.15	.07
318	Jamie Moyer	.15	.07
319	Todd Zeile	.15	.07
320	Chris Bosio	.15	.07
321	Steve Reed	.15	.07
322	Erik Hanson	.15	.07
323	Luis Polonia	.15	.07
324	Ryan Klesko	.25	.11
325	Kevin Appier	.25	.11
326	Jim Eisenreich	.15	.07
327	Randy Knorr	.15	.07
328	Craig Shipley	.15	.07
329	Tim Naehring	.15	.07
330	Randy Myers	.15	.07
331	Alex Cole	.15	.07
332	Jim Gott	.15	.07
333	Mike Jackson	.15	.07
334	John Flaherty	.15	.07
335	Chili Davis	.25	.11
336	Benji Gil	.15	.07
337	Jason Jacome	.15	.07
338	Stan Javier	.15	.07
339	Mike Fetters	.15	.07
340	Rich Renteria	.15	.07
341	Kevin Witt	.15	.07
342	Scott Servais	.15	.07
343	Craig Grebeck	.15	.07
344	Kirk Rueter	.15	.07
345	Don Slaught	.15	.07
346	Armando Benitez	.25	.11
347	Ozzie Smith	.75	.35
348	Mike Blowers	.15	.07
349	Armando Reynoso	.15	.07
350	Barry Larkin	.60	.25
351	Mike Williams	.15	.07
352	Scott Kamieniecki	.15	.07
353	Gary Gaetti	.25	.11
354	Todd Stottlemyre	.15	.07
355	Fred McGriff	.40	.18
356	Tim Mauser	.15	.07
357	Chris Gwynn	.15	.07
358	Frank Castillo	.15	.07
359	Jeff Reboulet	.15	.07
360	Roger Clemens	1.50	.70
361	Mark Carreon	.15	.07
362	Chad Kreuter	.15	.07
363	Mark Farris	.15	.07
364	Bob Welch	.15	.07
365	Dean Palmer	.25	.11
366	Jeromy Burnitz	.25	.11
367	B.J. Surhoff	.25	.11
368	Mike Butcher	.15	.07
369	Relief Pitcher	.25	.11
	Prospects		
	Brad Clontz		
	Steve Phoenix		
	Scott Gentile		
	Bucky Buckles RC		
370	Eddie Murray	.60	.25
371	Orlando Miller	.15	.07
372	Ron Karkovice	.15	.07
373	Richie Lewis	.15	.07
374	Lenny Webster	.15	.07
375	Jeff Tackett	.15	.07
376	Tom Urbani	.15	.07
377	Tino Martinez	.25	.11
378	Mark Dewey	.15	.07
379	Charles O'Brien	.15	.07
380	Terry Mulholland	.15	.07
381	Thomas Howard	.15	.07
382	Chris Haney	.15	.07
383	Billy Hatcher	.15	.07
384	Jeff Bagwell AS	.40	.18
	Frank Thomas AS		
385	Bret Boone AS	.15	.07
	Carlos Baerga AS		
386	Matt Williams AS	.25	.11
	Wade Boggs AS		
387	Wil Cordero AS	.60	.25
	Cal Ripken AS		
388	Barry Bonds AS	1.00	.45
	Ken Griffey AS		
389	Tony Gwynn AS	.25	.11
	Albert Belle AS		
390	Dante Bichette AS	.60	.25
	Kirby Puckett AS		
391	Mike Piazza AS	.40	.18
	Mike Stanley AS		
392	Greg Maddux AS	.25	.11
	David Cone AS		
393	Danny Jackson AS	.15	.07
	Jimmy Key AS		
394	John Franco AS	.15	.07
	Lee Smith AS		
395	Checklist 1-198	.15	.07
396	Checklist 199-396	.15	.07
397	Ken Griffey Jr.	2.00	.90
398	Rick Heiserman RC	.15	.07
399	Don Mattingly	1.50	.70
400	Henry Rodriguez	.15	.07
401	Lenny Harris	.15	.07
402	Ryan Thompson	.15	.07
403	Darren Oliver	.15	.07
404	Omar Vizquel	.25	.11
405	Jeff Bagwell	.75	.35
406	Doug Webb RC	.15	.07
407	Todd Van Poppel	.15	.07
408	Leo Gomez	.15	.07
409	Mark Whiten	.15	.07
410	Pedro A.Martinez	.15	.07
411	Reggie Sanders	.15	.07
412	Kevin Foster	.15	.07
413	Danny Tartabull	.15	.07
414	Jeff Blauser	.15	.07
415	Mike Magnante	.15	.07
416	Tom Candiotti	.15	.07
417	Rod Beck	.15	.07
418	Jody Reed	.15	.07
419	Vince Coleman	.15	.07
420	Danny Jackson	.15	.07
421	Ryan Nye RC	.15	.07
422	Larry Walker	.40	.18
423	Russ Johnson DP	.15	.07
424	Pat Borders	.15	.07
425	Lee Smith	.25	.11
426	Paul O'Neill	.60	.25
427	Devon White	.25	.11
428	Jim Bullinger	.15	.07
429	Starting Pitchers	.15	.07

Prospects
Greg Hansell
Brian Sackinsky
Carey Paige
Rob Welch RC
❑ 430 Steve Avery .15 .07
❑ 431 Tony Gwynn 1.25 .55
❑ 432 Pat Meares .15 .07
❑ 433 Bill Swift .15 .07
❑ 434 David Wells .25 .11
❑ 435 John Briscoe .15 .07
❑ 436 Roger Pavlik .15 .07
❑ 437 Jayson Peterson RC .15 .07
❑ 438 Roberto Alomar .60 .25
❑ 439 Billy Brewer .15 .07
❑ 440 Gary Sheffield .25 .11
❑ 441 Lou Frazier .15 .07
❑ 442 Terry Steinbach .15 .07
❑ 443 Jay Payton RC .50 .23
❑ 444 Jason Bere .15 .07
❑ 445 Denny Neagle .25 .11
❑ 446 Andres Galarraga .40 .18
❑ 447 Hector Carrasco .15 .07
❑ 448 Bill Risley .15 .07
❑ 449 Andy Benes .15 .07
❑ 450 Jim Leyritz .15 .07
❑ 451 Jose Oliva .15 .07
❑ 452 Greg Vaughn .25 .11
❑ 453 Rich Monteleone .15 .07
❑ 454 Tony Eusebio .15 .07
❑ 455 Chuck Finley .25 .11
❑ 456 Kevin Brown .25 .11
❑ 457 Joe Boever .15 .07
❑ 458 Bobby Munoz .15 .07
❑ 459 Bret Saberhagen .25 .11
❑ 460 Kurt Abbott .15 .07
❑ 461 Bobby Witt .15 .07
❑ 462 Cliff Floyd .25 .11
❑ 463 Mark Clark .15 .07
❑ 464 Andujar Cedeno .15 .07
❑ 465 Marvin Freeman .15 .07
❑ 466 Mike Piazza 1.50 .70
❑ 467 Willie Greene .15 .07
❑ 468 Pat Kelly .15 .07
❑ 469 Carlos Delgado .60 .25
❑ 470 Willie Banks .15 .07
❑ 471 Matt Walbeck .15 .07
❑ 472 Mark McGwire 2.50 1.10
❑ 473 M.Christensen RC .15 .07
❑ 474 Alan Trammell .40 .18
❑ 475 Tom Gordon .15 .07
❑ 476 Greg Colbrunn .15 .07
❑ 477 Darren Daulton .25 .11
❑ 478 Albie Lopez .15 .07
❑ 479 Robin Ventura .25 .11
❑ 480 Catcher Prospects .50 .23
Eddie Perez RC
Jason Kendall
Einar Diaz
Bret Hemphill
❑ 481 Bryan Eversgerd .15 .07
❑ 482 Dave Fleming .15 .07
❑ 483 Scott Livingstone .15 .07
❑ 484 Pete Schourek .15 .07
❑ 485 Bernie Williams .60 .25
❑ 486 Mark Lemke .15 .07
❑ 487 Eric Karros .25 .11
❑ 488 Scott Ruffcorn .15 .07
❑ 489 Billy Ashley .15 .07
❑ 490 Rico Brogna .15 .07
❑ 491 John Burkett .15 .07
❑ 492 Cade Gaspar RC .15 .07
❑ 493 Jorge Fabregas .15 .07
❑ 494 Greg Gagne .15 .07
❑ 495 Doug Jones .15 .07
❑ 496 Troy O'Leary .15 .07
❑ 497 Pat Rapp .15 .07
❑ 498 Butch Henry .15 .07
❑ 499 John Olerud .25 .11
❑ 500 John Hudek .15 .07
❑ 501 Jeff King .15 .07
❑ 502 Bobby Bonilla .25 .11
❑ 503 Albert Belle .25 .11
❑ 504 Rick Wilkins .15 .07
❑ 505 John Jaha .15 .07
❑ 506 Nigel Wilson .15 .07
❑ 507 Sid Fernandez .15 .07
❑ 508 Deion Sanders .25 .11
❑ 509 Gil Heredia .15 .07
❑ 510 Scott Elarton RC .50 .23
❑ 511 Melido Perez .15 .07
❑ 512 Greg McMichael .15 .07
❑ 513 Rusty Meacham .15 .07
❑ 514 Shawn Green .60 .25
❑ 515 Carlos Garcia .15 .07
❑ 516 Dave Stevens .15 .07
❑ 517 Eric Young .15 .07
❑ 518 Omar Daal .15 .07
❑ 519 Kirk Gibson .25 .11
❑ 520 Spike Owen .15 .07
❑ 521 Jacob Cruz RC .25 .11
❑ 522 Sandy Alomar Jr. .25 .11
❑ 523 Steve Bedrosian .15 .07
❑ 524 Ricky Gutierrez .15 .07
❑ 525 Dave Veres .15 .07
❑ 526 Gregg Jefferies .15 .07
❑ 527 Jose Valentin .15 .07
❑ 528 Robb Nen .15 .07
❑ 529 Jose Rijo .15 .07
❑ 530 Sean Berry .15 .07
❑ 531 Mike Gallego .15 .07
❑ 532 Roberto Kelly .15 .07
❑ 533 Kevin Stocker .15 .07
❑ 534 Kirby Puckett 1.50 .70
❑ 535 Chipper Jones 1.25 .55
❑ 536 Russ Davis .15 .07
❑ 537 Jon Lieber .15 .07
❑ 538 Trey Moore RC .15 .07
❑ 539 Joe Girardi .15 .07
❑ 540 2Base Prospects .25 .11
Quilvio Veras
Arquimedez Pozo
Miguel Cairo RC
Jason Camilli
❑ 541 Tony Phillips .15 .07
❑ 542 Brian Anderson .15 .07
❑ 543 Ivan Rodriguez .60 .25
❑ 544 Jeff Cirillo .25 .11
❑ 545 Joey Cora .15 .07
❑ 546 Chris Hoiles .15 .07
❑ 547 Bernard Gilkey .15 .07
❑ 548 Mike Lansing .15 .07
❑ 549 Jimmy Key .25 .11
❑ 550 Mark Wohlers .15 .07
❑ 551 Chris Clemons RC .15 .07
❑ 552 Vinny Castilla .25 .11
❑ 553 Mark Guthrie .15 .07
❑ 554 Mike Lieberthal .25 .11
❑ 555 Tommy Davis RC .15 .07
❑ 556 Robby Thompson .15 .07
❑ 557 Danny Bautista .15 .07
❑ 558 Will Clark .60 .25
❑ 559 Rickey Henderson 1.25 .55
❑ 560 Todd Jones .15 .07
❑ 561 Jack McDowell .15 .07
❑ 562 Carlos Rodriguez .15 .07
❑ 563 Mark Eichhorn .15 .07
❑ 564 Jeff Nelson .15 .07
❑ 565 Eric Anthony .15 .07
❑ 566 Randy Velarde .15 .07
❑ 567 Javier Lopez .25 .11
❑ 568 Kevin Mitchell .15 .07
❑ 569 Steve Karsay .15 .07
❑ 570 Brian Meadows RC .25 .11
❑ 571 Rey Ordonez RC .50 .23
Mike Metcalfe
Kevin Orie
Ray Holbert
❑ 572 John Kruk .25 .11
❑ 573 Scott Leius .15 .07
❑ 574 John Patterson .15 .07
❑ 575 Kevin Brown .25 .11
❑ 576 Mike Moore .15 .07
❑ 577 Manny Ramirez .75 .35
❑ 578 Jose Lind .15 .07
❑ 579 Derrick May .15 .07
❑ 580 Cal Eldred .15 .07
❑ 581 Third Base Prospects .25 .11
David Bell
Joel Chelmis
Lino Diaz
Aaron Boone RC
❑ 582 J.T. Snow .25 .11
❑ 583 Luis Sojo .15 .07
❑ 584 Moises Alou .25 .11
❑ 585 Dave Clark .15 .07
❑ 586 Dave Hollins .15 .07
❑ 587 Nomar Garciaparra 3.00 1.35
❑ 588 Cal Ripken 2.50 1.10
❑ 589 Pedro Astacio .15 .07
❑ 590 J.R. Phillips .15 .07
❑ 591 Jeff Frye .15 .07
❑ 592 Bo Jackson .25 .11
❑ 593 Steve Ontiveros .15 .07
❑ 594 David Nied .15 .07
❑ 595 Brad Ausmus .15 .07
❑ 596 Carlos Baerga .15 .07
❑ 597 James Mouton .15 .07
❑ 598 Ozzie Guillen .15 .07
❑ 599 Outfield Prospects .40 .18
Ozzie Timmons
Curtis Goodwin
Johnny Damon
Jeff Abbott RC
❑ 600 Yorkis Perez .15 .07
❑ 601 Rich Rodriguez .15 .07
❑ 602 Mark McLemore .15 .07
❑ 603 Jeff Fassero .15 .07
❑ 604 John Roper .15 .07
❑ 605 Mark Johnson RC .25 .11
❑ 606 Wes Chamberlain .15 .07
❑ 607 Felix Jose .15 .07
❑ 608 Tony Longmire .15 .07
❑ 609 Duane Ward .15 .07
❑ 610 Brett Butler .25 .11
❑ 611 W.VanLandingham .15 .07
❑ 612 Mickey Tettleton .15 .07
❑ 613 Brady Anderson .25 .11
❑ 614 Reggie Jefferson .15 .07
❑ 615 Mike Kingery .15 .07
❑ 616 Derek Bell .15 .07
❑ 617 Scott Erickson .15 .07
❑ 618 Bob Wickman .15 .07
❑ 619 Phil Leftwich .15 .07
❑ 620 David Justice .25 .11
❑ 621 Paul Wilson .15 .07
❑ 622 Pedro Martinez .75 .35
❑ 623 Terry Mathews .15 .07
❑ 624 Brian McRae .15 .07
❑ 625 Bruce Ruffin .15 .07
❑ 626 Steve Finley .25 .11
❑ 627 Ron Gant .15 .07
❑ 628 Rafael Bournigal .15 .07
❑ 629 Darryl Strawberry .25 .11
❑ 630 Luis Alicea .15 .07
❑ 631 Orioles Prospects .15 .07
Mark Smith
Scott Klingenbeck
❑ 632 Red Sox Prospects .15 .07
Cory Bailey
Scott Hatteberg
❑ 633 Angels Prospects .15 .07
Todd Greene
Troy Percival
❑ 634 White Sox Prospects .15 .07
Rod Bolton
Olmedo Saenz
❑ 635 Indians Prospects .15 .07
Steve Kline
Herb Perry
❑ 636 Tigers Prospects .15 .07
Sean Bergman
Shannon Penn
❑ 637 Royals Prospects .15 .07
Joe Randa
Joe Vitiello
❑ 638 Brewers Prospects .15 .07
Jose Mercedes
Duane Singleton
❑ 639 Twins Prospects .15 .07
Marc Barcelo
Marty Cordova
❑ 640 Yankees Prospects .15 .07
Andy Pettitte
Ruben Rivera
❑ 641 Athletics Prospects .15 .07
Willie Adams
Scott Spiezio

❑ 642 Mariners Prospects .... .15 .07
Eddy Diaz RC
Desi Relaford
❑ 643 Rangers Prospects .... .15 .07
Terrell Lowery
Jon Shave
❑ 644 Blue Jays Prospects ...... .15 .07
Angel Martinez
Paul Spoljaric
❑ 645 Braves Prospects .... .15 .07
Tony Graffanino
Damon Hollins
❑ 646 Cubs Prospects.............. .15 .07
Darron Cox
Doug Glanville
❑ 647 Reds Prospects.............. .15 .07
Tim Belk
Pat Watkins
❑ 648 Rockies Propsects .... .15 .07
Rod Pedraza
Phil Schneider
❑ 649 Marlins Prospects .... .15 .07
Vic Darensbourg
Marc Valdes
❑ 650 Astros Prospects............ .15 .07
Rick Huisman
Roberto Petagine
❑ 651 Dodgers Prospects .... .25 .11
Roger Cedeno
Ron Coomer RC
❑ 652 Expos Prospects .... .25 .11
Shane Andrews
Carlos Perez RC
❑ 653 Mets Prospects .... .25 .11
Jason Isringhausen
Chris Roberts
❑ 654 Phillies Prospects .... .15 .07
Wayne Gomes
Kevin Jordan
❑ 655 Pirates Prospects .... .15 .07
Esteban Loiaza
Steve Pegues
❑ 656 Cardinals Prospects ...... .15 .07
Terry Bradshaw
John Frascatore
❑ 657 Padres Prospects .... .15 .07
Andres Berumen
Bryce Florie
❑ 658 Giants Prospects............ .15 .07
Dan Carlson
Keith Williams
❑ 659 Checklist .... .15 .07
❑ 660 Checklist .... .15 .07

1995 Topps Traded

	MINT	NRMT
COMPLETE SET (165)	40.00	18.00

❑ 1T Frank Thomas ATB.......... .40 .18
❑ 2T Ken Griffey Jr. ATB........ 1.00 .45
❑ 3T Barry Bonds ATB .... .75 .35
❑ 4T Albert Belle ATB .... .25 .11
❑ 5T Cal Ripken ATB .... 1.25 .55
❑ 6T Mike Piazza ATB............ .75 .35
❑ 7T Tony Gwynn ATB .... .60 .25
❑ 8T Jeff Bagwell ATB............ .40 .18
❑ 9T Mo Vaughn ATB .... .15 .07
❑ 10T Matt Williams ATB.......... .25 .11
❑ 11T Ray Durham .... .25 .11
❑ 12T Juan LeBron .... 1.00 .45
Card pictures Carlos Beltran instead of Juan LeBron RC
❑ 13T Shawn Green .... .60 .25
❑ 14T Kevin Gross .... .15 .07
❑ 15T Jon Nunnally.................. .15 .07
❑ 16T Brian Maxcy RC .... .15 .07
❑ 17T Mark Kiefer .... .15 .07
❑ 18T Carlos Beltran UER...... 5.00 2.20
Card pictures Juan LeBron instead of Carlos Beltran RC.
❑ 19T Mike Mimbs RC.............. .15 .07
❑ 20T Larry Walker .... .40 .18
❑ 21T Chad Curtis.................... .15 .07
❑ 22T Jeff Barry........................ .15 .07
❑ 23T Joe Oliver .... .15 .07
❑ 24T Tomas Perez RC .... .15 .07
❑ 25T Michael Barrett RC ...... 1.00 .45
❑ 26T Brian McRae .... .15 .07
❑ 27T Derek Bell .... .15 .07
❑ 28T Ray Durham .... .25 .11
❑ 29T Todd Williams .... .15 .07
❑ 30T Ryan Jaroncyk RC .... .15 .07
❑ 31T Todd Steverson.............. .15 .07
❑ 32T Mike Devereaux .... .15 .07
❑ 33T Rheal Cormier................ .15 .07
❑ 34T Benny Santiago.............. .15 .07
❑ 35T Bobby Higginson RC.... 2.00 .90
❑ 36T Jack McDowell .... .15 .07
❑ 37T Mike Macfarlane .... .15 .07
❑ 38T Tony McKnight RC .... .50 .23
❑ 39T Brian Hunter .... .15 .07
❑ 40T Hideo Nomo RC 3.00 1.35
❑ 41T Brett Butler .... .25 .11
❑ 42T Donovan Osborne.......... .15 .07
❑ 43T Scott Karl .... .15 .07
❑ 44T Tony Phillips .... .15 .07
❑ 45T Marty Cordova .... .15 .07
❑ 46T Dave Mlicki .... .15 .07
❑ 47T Bronson Arroyo RC...... 1.00 .45
❑ 48T John Burkett .... .15 .07
❑ 49T J.D. Smart RC................ .15 .07
❑ 50T Mickey Tettleton .... .15 .07
❑ 51T Todd Stottlemyre............ .15 .07
❑ 52T Mike Perez .... .15 .07
❑ 53T Terry Mulholland .... .15 .07
❑ 54T Edgardo Alfonzo .... .60 .25
❑ 55T Zane Smith .... .15 .07
❑ 56T Jacob Brumfield .... .15 .07
❑ 57T Andujar Cedeno .... .15 .07
❑ 58T Jose Parra...................... .15 .07
❑ 59T Manny Alexander .... .15 .07
❑ 60T Tony Tarasco .... .15 .07
❑ 61T Orel Hershiser................ .25 .11
❑ 62T Tim Scott........................ .15 .07
❑ 63T Felix Rodriguez RC........ .25 .11
❑ 64T Ken Hill .... .15 .07
❑ 65T Marquis Grissom............ .15 .07
❑ 66T Lee Smith .... .25 .11
❑ 67T Jason Bates .... .15 .07
❑ 68T Felipe Lira .... .15 .07
❑ 69T Alex Hernandez RC ...... .60 .25
❑ 70T Tony Fernandez .... .15 .07
❑ 71T Scott Radinsky .... .15 .07
❑ 72T Jose Canseco .... .60 .25
❑ 73T Mark Grudzielanek RC 1.00 .45
❑ 74T Ben Davis RC .... 2.00 .90
❑ 75T Jim Abbott...................... .25 .11
❑ 76T Roger Bailey .... .15 .07
❑ 77T Gregg Jefferies .... .15 .07
❑ 78T Erik Hanson .... .15 .07
❑ 79T Brad Radke RC............ 6.00 2.70
❑ 80T Jaime Navarro................ .15 .07
❑ 81T John Wetteland.............. .25 .11
❑ 82T Chad Fonville RC .... .15 .07
❑ 83T John Mabry.................... .15 .07
❑ 84T Glenallen Hill.................. .15 .07
❑ 85T Ken Caminiti .... .25 .11
❑ 86T Tom Goodwin .... .15 .07
❑ 87T Darren Bragg .... .15 .07
❑ 88T Pitching Prospects ...... 1.50 .70
Pat Ahearne
Gary Rath
Larry Wimberly
Robbie Bell RC
❑ 89T Jeff Russell .... .15 .07
❑ 90T Dave Gallagher.............. .15 .07
❑ 91T Steve Finley .... .25 .11
❑ 92T Vaughn Eshelman.......... .15 .07
❑ 93T Kevin Jarvis.................... .15 .07
❑ 94T Mark Gubicza .... .15 .07
❑ 95T Tim Wakefield .... .15 .07
❑ 96T Bob Tewksbury .... .15 .07
❑ 97T Sid Roberson RC .... .15 .07
❑ 98T Tom Henke .... .15 .07
❑ 99T Michael Tucker .... .15 .07
❑ 100T Jason Bates .... .15 .07
❑ 101T Otis Nixon .... .15 .07
❑ 102T Mark Whiten .... .15 .07
❑ 103T Dilson Torres RC .... .15 .07
❑ 104T Melvin Bunch RC .... .15 .07
❑ 105T Terry Pendleton .... .25 .11
❑ 106T Corey Jenkins RC.......... .15 .07
❑ 107T Glenn Dishman RC ...... .15 .07
Rob Grable
❑ 108T Reggie Taylor RC .... .60 .25
❑ 109T Curtis Goodwin .... .15 .07
❑ 110T David Cone .... .25 .11
❑ 111T Antonio Osuna .... .15 .07
❑ 112T Paul Shuey .... .15 .07
❑ 113T Doug Jones.................. .15 .07
❑ 114T Mark McLemore .... .15 .07
❑ 115T Kevin Ritz .... .15 .07
❑ 116T John Kruk .... .25 .11
❑ 117T Trevor Wilson .... .15 .07
❑ 118T Jerald Clark.................... .15 .07
❑ 119T Julian Tavarez................ .15 .07
❑ 120T Tim Pugh........................ .15 .07
❑ 121T Todd Zeile .... .15 .07
❑ 122T Prospects 5.00 2.20
Mark Sweeney UER
George Arias
Richie Sexson RC
Brian Schneider
❑ 123T Bobby Witt...................... .15 .07
❑ 124T Hideo Nomo .... 1.00 .45
❑ 125T Joey Cora .... .15 .07
❑ 126T Jim Scharrer RC .... .15 .07
❑ 127T Paul Quantrill .... .15 .07
❑ 128T Chipper Jones ROY .. 1.00 .45
❑ 129T Kenny James RC .... .15 .07
❑ 130T Lyle Mouton .... .25 .11
Mariano Rivera
❑ 131T Tyler Green.................... .15 .07
❑ 132T Brad Clontz.................... .15 .07
❑ 133T Jon Nunnally.................. .15 .07
❑ 134T Dave Magadan .... .15 .07
❑ 135T Al Leiter.......................... .25 .11
❑ 136T Bret Barberie.................. .15 .07
❑ 137T Bill Swift .... .15 .07
❑ 138T Scott Cooper.................. .15 .07
❑ 139T Roberto Kelly .... .15 .07
❑ 140T Charlie Hayes .... .15 .07
❑ 141T Pete Harnisch .... .15 .07
❑ 142T Rich Amaral .... .15 .07
❑ 143T Rudy Seanez .... .15 .07
❑ 144T Pat Listach .... .15 .07
❑ 145T Quilvio Veras.................. .15 .07
❑ 146T Jose Olmeda RC............ .15 .07
❑ 147T Roberto Petagine .... .15 .07
❑ 148T Kevin Brown .... .25 .11
❑ 149T Phil Plantier.................... .15 .07
❑ 150T Carlos Perez .... .25 .11
❑ 151T Pat Borders.................... .15 .07
❑ 152T Tyler Green.................... .15 .07
❑ 153T Stan Belinda .... .15 .07
❑ 154T Dave Stewart .... .25 .11
❑ 155T Andre Dawson .... .40 .18
❑ 156T Frank Thomas AS .... .40 .18
Fred McGriff UER
(McGriff's team shown as Blue Jays)
❑ 157T Carlos Baerga AS .... .25 .11
Craig Biggio
❑ 158T Wade Boggs AS .... .25 .11
Matt Williams
❑ 159T Cal Ripken AS.............. .60 .25
Ozzie Smith
❑ 160T Ken Griffey Jr. AS .... .75 .35
Tony Gwynn
❑ 161T Albert Belle AS .... .75 .35

		MINT	NRMT
	Barry Bonds		
❑ 162T	Kirby Puckett	.60	.25
	Len Dykstra		
❑ 163T	Ivan Rodriguez AS	.40	.18
	Mike Piazza		
❑ 164T	Randy Johnson AS	1.00	.45
	Hideo Nomo		
❑ 165T	Checklist	.15	.07

1996 Topps

	MINT	NRMT
COMPLETE SET (440)	50.00	22.00
COMP.HOBBY SET (449)	60.00	27.00
COMP.CEREAL SET (444)	50.00	22.00
COMPLETE SERIES 1 (220)	30.00	13.50
COMPLETE SERIES 2 (220)	20.00	9.00

		MINT	NRMT
❑ 1	Tony Gwynn STP	.40	.18
❑ 2	Mike Piazza STP	.50	.23
❑ 3	Greg Maddux STP	.60	.25
❑ 4	Jeff Bagwell STP	.25	.11
❑ 5	Larry Walker STP	.10	.05
❑ 6	Barry Larkin STP	.15	.07
❑ 7	Mickey Mantle	4.00	1.80
❑ 8	Tom Glavine STP UER	.15	.07
	Won 21 games in June 95		
❑ 9	Craig Biggio STP	.15	.07
❑ 10	Barry Bonds STP	.50	.23
❑ 11	H.Slocumb STP	.10	.05
❑ 12	Matt Williams STP	.15	.07
❑ 13	Todd Helton	2.00	.90
❑ 14	Mark Redman	.15	.07
❑ 15	Michael Barrett	.10	.05
❑ 16	Ben Davis	.15	.07
❑ 17	Juan LeDron	.10	.05
❑ 18	Tony McKnight	.10	.05
❑ 19	Ryan Jaroncyk	.10	.05
❑ 20	Corey Jenkins	.10	.05
❑ 21	Jim Scharrer	.10	.05
❑ 22	Mark Bellhorn RC	.10	.05
❑ 23	Jarrod Washburn RC	1.00	.45
❑ 24	Geoff Jenkins RC	2.50	1.10
❑ 25	Sean Casey RC	5.00	2.20
❑ 26	Brett Tomko RC	.15	.07
❑ 27	Tony Fernandez	.10	.05
❑ 28	Rich Becker	.10	.05
❑ 29	Andujar Cedeno	.10	.05
❑ 30	Paul Molitor	.40	.18
❑ 31	Brent Gates	.10	.05
❑ 32	Glenallen Hill	.10	.05
❑ 33	Mike Macfarlane	.10	.05
❑ 34	Manny Alexander	.10	.05
❑ 35	Todd Zeile	.10	.05
❑ 36	Joe Girardi	.10	.05
❑ 37	Tony Tarasco	.10	.05
❑ 38	Tim Belcher	.10	.05
❑ 39	Tom Goodwin	.10	.05
❑ 40	Orel Hershiser	.15	.07
❑ 41	Tripp Cromer	.10	.05
❑ 42	Sean Bergman	.10	.05
❑ 43	Troy Percival	.10	.05
❑ 44	Kevin Stocker	.10	.05
❑ 45	Albert Belle	.15	.07
❑ 46	Tony Eusebio	.10	.05
❑ 47	Sid Roberson	.10	.05
❑ 48	Todd Hollandsworth	.10	.05
❑ 49	Mark Wohlers	.10	.05
❑ 50	Kirby Puckett	1.00	.45
❑ 51	Darren Holmes	.10	.05
❑ 52	Ron Karkovice	.10	.05
❑ 53	Al Martin	.10	.05
❑ 54	Pat Rapp	.10	.05
❑ 55	Mark Grace	.40	.18
❑ 56	Greg Gagne	.10	.05
❑ 57	Stan Javier	.10	.05
❑ 58	Scott Sanders	.10	.05
❑ 59	J.T. Snow	.15	.07
❑ 60	David Justice	.15	.07
❑ 61	Royce Clayton	.10	.05
❑ 62	Kevin Foster	.10	.05
❑ 63	Tim Naehring	.10	.05
❑ 64	Orlando Miller	.10	.05
❑ 65	Mike Mussina	.40	.18
❑ 66	Jim Eisenreich	.10	.05
❑ 67	Felix Fermin	.10	.05
❑ 68	Bernie Williams	.40	.18
❑ 69	Robb Nen	.10	.05
❑ 70	Ron Gant	.10	.05
❑ 71	Felipe Lira	.10	.05
❑ 72	Jacob Brumfield	.10	.05
❑ 73	John Mabry	.10	.05
❑ 74	Mark Carreon	.10	.05
❑ 75	Carlos Baerga	.10	.05
❑ 76	Jim Dougherty	.10	.05
❑ 77	Ryan Thompson	.10	.05
❑ 78	Scott Leius	.10	.05
❑ 79	Roger Pavlik	.10	.05
❑ 80	Gary Sheffield	.15	.07
❑ 81	Julian Tavarez	.10	.05
❑ 82	Andy Ashby	.10	.05
❑ 83	Mark Lemke	.10	.05
❑ 84	Omar Vizquel	.15	.07
❑ 85	Darren Daulton	.15	.07
❑ 86	Mike Lansing	.10	.05
❑ 87	Rusty Greer	.15	.07
❑ 88	Dave Stevens	.10	.05
❑ 89	Jose Offerman	.10	.05
❑ 90	Tom Henke	.10	.05
❑ 91	Troy O'Leary	.10	.05
❑ 92	Michael Tucker	.10	.05
❑ 93	Marvin Freeman	.10	.05
❑ 94	Alex Diaz	.10	.05
❑ 95	John Wetteland	.15	.07
❑ 96	Cal Ripken 2131	2.00	.90
❑ 97	Mike Mimbs	.10	.05
❑ 98	Bobby Higginson	.15	.07
❑ 99	Edgardo Alfonzo	.15	.07
❑ 100	Frank Thomas	.50	.23
❑ 101	Steve Gibralter	.40	.18
	Bob Abreu		
❑ 102	Brian Givens	.10	.05
	T.J. Mathews		
❑ 103	Chris Pritchett	.10	.05
	Trenidad Hubbard		
❑ 104	Eric Owens	.10	.05
	Butch Huskey		
❑ 105	Doug Drabek	.10	.05
❑ 106	Tomas Perez	.10	.05
❑ 107	Mark Leiter	.10	.05
❑ 108	Joe Oliver	.10	.05
❑ 109	Tony Castillo	.10	.05
❑ 110	Checklist (1-110)	.10	.05
❑ 111	Kevin Seitzer	.10	.05
❑ 112	Pete Schourek	.10	.05
❑ 113	Sean Berry	.10	.05
❑ 114	Todd Stottlemyre	.10	.05
❑ 115	Joe Carter	.15	.07
❑ 116	Jeff King	.10	.05
❑ 117	Dan Wilson	.10	.05
❑ 118	Kurt Abbott	.10	.05
❑ 119	Lyle Mouton	.10	.05
❑ 120	Jose Rijo	.10	.05
❑ 121	Curtis Goodwin	.10	.05
❑ 122	Jose Valentin	.10	.05
❑ 123	Ellis Burks	.15	.07
❑ 124	David Cone	.15	.07
❑ 125	Eddie Murray	.40	.18
❑ 126	Brian Jordan	.15	.07
❑ 127	Darrin Fletcher	.10	.05
❑ 128	Curt Schilling	.40	.18
❑ 129	Ozzie Guillen	.10	.05
❑ 130	Kenny Rogers	.10	.05
❑ 131	Tom Pagnozzi	.10	.05
❑ 132	Garret Anderson	.15	.07
❑ 133	Bobby Jones	.10	.05
❑ 134	Chris Gomez	.10	.05
❑ 135	Mike Stanley	.10	.05
❑ 136	Hideo Nomo	.50	.23
❑ 137	Jon Nunnally	.10	.05
❑ 138	Tim Wakefield	.10	.05
❑ 139	Steve Finley	.15	.07
❑ 140	Ivan Rodriguez	.40	.18
❑ 141	Quilvio Veras	.10	.05
❑ 142	Mike Fetters	.10	.05
❑ 143	Mike Greenwell	.10	.05
❑ 144	Bill Pulsipher	.10	.05
❑ 145	Mark McGwire	1.50	.70
❑ 146	Frank Castillo	.10	.05
❑ 147	Greg Vaughn	.15	.07
❑ 148	Pat Hentgen	.10	.05
❑ 149	Walt Weiss	.10	.05
❑ 150	Randy Johnson	.50	.23
❑ 151	David Segui	.10	.05
❑ 152	Benji Gil	.10	.05
❑ 153	Tom Candiotti	.10	.05
❑ 154	Geronimo Berroa	.10	.05
❑ 155	John Franco	.15	.07
❑ 156	Jay Bell	.15	.07
❑ 157	Mark Gubicza	.10	.05
❑ 158	Hal Morris	.10	.05
❑ 159	Wilson Alvarez	.10	.05
❑ 160	Derek Bell	.10	.05
❑ 161	Ricky Bottalico	.10	.05
❑ 162	Bret Boone	.15	.07
❑ 163	Brad Radke	.15	.07
❑ 164	John Valentin	.10	.05
❑ 165	Steve Avery	.10	.05
❑ 166	Mark McLemore	.10	.05
❑ 167	Danny Jackson	.10	.05
❑ 168	Tino Martinez	.15	.07
❑ 169	Shane Reynolds	.10	.05
❑ 170	Terry Pendleton	.15	.07
❑ 171	Jim Edmonds	.25	.11
❑ 172	Esteban Loaiza	.10	.05
❑ 173	Ray Durham	.15	.07
❑ 174	Carlos Perez	.10	.05
❑ 175	Raul Mondesi	.15	.07
❑ 176	Steve Ontiveros	.10	.05
❑ 177	Chipper Jones	.75	.35
❑ 178	Otis Nixon	.10	.05
❑ 179	John Burkett	.10	.05
❑ 180	Gregg Jefferies	.10	.05
❑ 181	Denny Martinez	.15	.07
❑ 182	Ken Caminiti	.15	.07
❑ 183	Doug Jones	.10	.05
❑ 184	Brian McRae	.10	.05
❑ 185	Don Mattingly	1.00	.45
❑ 186	Mel Rojas	.10	.05
❑ 187	Marty Cordova	.10	.05
❑ 188	Vinny Castilla	.15	.07
❑ 189	John Smoltz	.15	.07
❑ 190	Travis Fryman	.15	.07
❑ 191	Chris Hoiles	.10	.05
❑ 192	Chuck Finley	.15	.07
❑ 193	Ryan Klesko	.15	.07
❑ 194	Alex Fernandez	.10	.05
❑ 195	Dante Bichette	.15	.07
❑ 196	Eric Karros	.15	.07
❑ 197	Roger Clemens	1.00	.45
❑ 198	Randy Myers	.10	.05
❑ 199	Tony Phillips	.10	.05
❑ 200	Cal Ripken	1.50	.70
❑ 201	Rod Beck	.10	.05
❑ 202	Chad Curtis	.10	.05
❑ 203	Jack McDowell	.10	.05
❑ 204	Gary Gaetti	.15	.07
❑ 205	Ken Griffey Jr.	1.25	.55
❑ 206	Ramon Martinez	.10	.05
❑ 207	Jeff Kent	.25	.11
❑ 208	Brad Ausmus	.10	.05
❑ 209	Devon White	.15	.07
❑ 210	Jason Giambi	.40	.18
❑ 211	Nomar Garciaparra	1.00	.45
❑ 212	Billy Wagner	.10	.05
❑ 213	Todd Greene	.10	.05
❑ 214	Paul Wilson	.10	.05
❑ 215	Johnny Damon	.15	.07
❑ 216	Alan Benes	.10	.05
❑ 217	Karim Garcia	.10	.05

❑ 218 Dustin Hermanson .10 .05
❑ 219 Derek Jeter 1.50 .70
❑ 220 Checklist (111-220) .10 .05
❑ 221 Kirby Puckett STP .50 .23
❑ 222 Cal Ripken STP .75 .35
❑ 223 Albert Belle STP .15 .07
❑ 224 Randy Johnson STP .25 .11
❑ 225 Wade Boggs STP .15 .07
❑ 226 Carlos Baerga STP .10 .05
❑ 227 Ivan Rodriguez STP .15 .07
❑ 228 Mike Mussina STP .15 .07
❑ 229 Frank Thomas STP .25 .11
❑ 230 Ken Griffey Jr. STP .75 .35
❑ 231 Jose Mesa STP .10 .05
❑ 232 Matt Morris RC 2.00 .90
❑ 233 Craig Wilson RC .10 .05
❑ 234 Alvie Shepherd .10 .05
❑ 235 Randy Winn RC .10 .05
❑ 236 David Yocum RC .10 .05
❑ 237 Jason Brester RC .10 .05
❑ 238 Shane Monahan RC .10 .05
❑ 239 Brian McNichol RC .15 .07
❑ 240 Reggie Taylor .10 .05
❑ 241 Garrett Long .10 .05
❑ 242 Jonathan Johnson .10 .05
❑ 243 Jeff Liefer RC .10 .05
❑ 244 Brian Powell .10 .05
❑ 245 Brian Buchanan .10 .05
❑ 246 Mike Piazza 1.00 .45
❑ 247 Edgar Martinez .25 .11
❑ 248 Chuck Knoblauch .15 .07
❑ 249 Andres Galarraga .25 .11
❑ 250 Tony Gwynn .75 .35
❑ 251 Lee Smith .15 .07
❑ 252 Sammy Sosa .75 .35
❑ 253 Jim Thome .40 .18
❑ 254 Frank Rodriguez .10 .05
❑ 255 Charlie Hayes .10 .05
❑ 256 Bernard Gilkey .10 .05
❑ 257 John Smiley .10 .05
❑ 258 Brady Anderson .15 .07
❑ 259 Rico Brogna .10 .05
❑ 260 Kirt Manwaring .10 .05
❑ 261 Len Dykstra .15 .07
❑ 262 Tom Glavine .40 .18
❑ 263 Vince Coleman .10 .05
❑ 264 John Olerud .15 .07
❑ 265 Orlando Merced .10 .05
❑ 266 Kent Mercker .10 .05
❑ 267 Terry Steinbach .10 .05
❑ 268 Brian L. Hunter .10 .05
❑ 269 Jeff Fassero .10 .05
❑ 270 Jay Buhner .15 .07
❑ 271 Jeff Brantley .10 .05
❑ 272 Tim Raines .15 .07
❑ 273 Jimmy Key .15 .07
❑ 274 Mo Vaughn .15 .07
❑ 275 Andre Dawson .25 .11
❑ 276 Jose Mesa .10 .05
❑ 277 Brett Butler .15 .07
❑ 278 Luis Gonzalez .40 .18
❑ 279 Steve Sparks .10 .05
❑ 280 Chili Davis .15 .07
❑ 281 Carl Everett .15 .07
❑ 282 Jeff Cirillo .15 .07
❑ 283 Thomas Howard .10 .05
❑ 284 Paul O'Neill .40 .18
❑ 285 Pat Meares .10 .05
❑ 286 Mickey Tettleton .10 .05
❑ 287 Rey Sanchez .10 .05
❑ 288 Bip Roberts .10 .05
❑ 289 Roberto Alomar .40 .18
❑ 290 Ruben Sierra .10 .05
❑ 291 John Flaherty .10 .05
❑ 292 Bret Saberhagen .15 .07
❑ 293 Barry Larkin .40 .18
❑ 294 Sandy Alomar Jr. .15 .07
❑ 295 Ed Sprague .10 .05
❑ 296 Gary DiSarcina .10 .05
❑ 297 Marquis Grissom .10 .05
❑ 298 John Frascatore .10 .05
❑ 299 Will Clark .40 .18
❑ 300 Barry Bonds 1.00 .45
❑ 301 Ozzie Smith UER .50 .23
 Padres is listed as Padre
❑ 302 Dave Nilsson .10 .05
❑ 303 Pedro Martinez .50 .23
❑ 304 Joey Cora .10 .05
❑ 305 Rick Aguilera .10 .05
❑ 306 Craig Biggio .25 .11
❑ 307 Jose Vizcaino .10 .05
❑ 308 Jeff Montgomery .10 .05
❑ 309 Moises Alou .15 .07
❑ 310 Robin Ventura .15 .07
❑ 311 David Wells .15 .07
❑ 312 Delino DeShields .10 .05
❑ 313 Trevor Hoffman .15 .07
❑ 314 Andy Benes .10 .05
❑ 315 Deion Sanders .15 .07
❑ 316 Jim Bullinger .10 .05
❑ 317 John Jaha .10 .05
❑ 318 Greg Maddux 1.00 .45
❑ 319 Tim Salmon .15 .07
❑ 320 Ben McDonald .10 .05
❑ 321 Sandy Martinez .10 .05
❑ 322 Dan Miceli .10 .05
❑ 323 Wade Boggs .40 .18
❑ 324 Ismael Valdes .10 .05
❑ 325 Juan Gonzalez .40 .18
❑ 326 Charles Nagy .10 .05
❑ 327 Ray Lankford .10 .05
❑ 328 Mark Portugal .10 .05
❑ 329 Bobby Bonilla .15 .07
❑ 330 Reggie Sanders .10 .05
❑ 331 Jamie Brewington RC .10 .05
❑ 332 Aaron Sele .15 .07
❑ 333 Pete Harnisch .10 .05
❑ 334 Cliff Floyd .15 .07
❑ 335 Cal Eldred .10 .05
❑ 336 Jason Bates .10 .05
❑ 337 Tony Clark .15 .07
❑ 338 Jose Herrera .10 .05
❑ 339 Alex Ochoa .10 .05
❑ 340 Mark Loretta .10 .05
❑ 341 Donne Wall .10 .05
❑ 342 Jason Kendall .15 .07
❑ 343 Shannon Stewart .15 .07
❑ 344 Brooks Kieschnick .10 .05
❑ 345 Chris Snopek .10 .05
❑ 346 Ruben Rivera .10 .05
❑ 347 Jeff Suppan .10 .05
❑ 348 Phil Nevin .15 .07
❑ 349 John Wasdin .10 .05
❑ 350 Jay Payton .10 .05
❑ 351 Tim Crabtree .10 .05
❑ 352 Rick Krivda .10 .05
❑ 353 Bob Wolcott .10 .05
❑ 354 Jimmy Haynes .10 .05
❑ 355 Herb Perry .10 .05
❑ 356 Ryne Sandberg .50 .23
❑ 357 Harold Baines .15 .07
❑ 358 Chad Ogea .10 .05
❑ 359 Lee Tinsley .10 .05
❑ 360 Matt Williams .25 .11
❑ 361 Randy Velarde .10 .05
❑ 362 Jose Canseco .40 .18
❑ 363 Larry Walker .25 .11
❑ 364 Kevin Appier .15 .07
❑ 365 Darryl Hamilton .10 .05
❑ 366 Jose Lima .10 .05
❑ 367 Javy Lopez .15 .07
❑ 368 Dennis Eckersley .15 .07
❑ 369 Jason Isringhausen .15 .07
❑ 370 Mickey Morandini .10 .05
❑ 371 Scott Cooper .10 .05
❑ 372 Jim Abbott .15 .07
❑ 373 Paul Sorrento .10 .05
❑ 374 Chris Hammond .10 .05
❑ 375 Lance Johnson .10 .05
❑ 376 Kevin Brown .15 .07
❑ 377 Luis Alicea .10 .05
❑ 378 Andy Pettitte .15 .07
❑ 379 Dean Palmer .15 .07
❑ 380 Jeff Bagwell .50 .23
❑ 381 Jaime Navarro .10 .05
❑ 382 Rondell White .15 .07
❑ 383 Erik Hanson .10 .05
❑ 384 Pedro Munoz .10 .05
❑ 385 Heathcliff Slocumb .10 .05
❑ 386 Wally Joyner .15 .07
❑ 387 Bob Tewksbury .10 .05
❑ 388 David Bell .10 .05
❑ 389 Fred McGriff .25 .11
❑ 390 Mike Henneman .10 .05
❑ 391 Robby Thompson .10 .05
❑ 392 Norm Charlton .10 .05
❑ 393 Cecil Fielder .15 .07
❑ 394 Benito Santiago .10 .05
❑ 395 Rafael Palmeiro .40 .18
❑ 396 Ricky Bones .10 .05
❑ 397 Rickey Henderson .75 .35
❑ 398 C.J. Nitkowski .10 .05
❑ 399 Shawon Dunston .10 .05
❑ 400 Manny Ramirez .50 .23
❑ 401 Bill Swift .10 .05
❑ 402 Chad Fonville .10 .05
❑ 403 Joey Hamilton .10 .05
❑ 404 Alex Gonzalez .10 .05
❑ 405 Roberto Hernandez .10 .05
❑ 406 Jeff Blauser .10 .05
❑ 407 LaTroy Hawkins .10 .05
❑ 408 Greg Colbrunn .10 .05
❑ 409 Todd Hundley .10 .05
❑ 410 Glenn Dishman .10 .05
❑ 411 Joe Vitiello .10 .05
❑ 412 Todd Worrell .10 .05
❑ 413 Wil Cordero .10 .05
❑ 414 Ken Hill .10 .05
❑ 415 Carlos Garcia .10 .05
❑ 416 Bryan Rekar .10 .05
❑ 417 Shawn Green .40 .18
❑ 418 Tyler Green .10 .05
❑ 419 Mike Blowers .10 .05
❑ 420 Kenny Lofton .15 .07
❑ 421 Denny Neagle .15 .07
❑ 422 Jeff Conine .10 .05
❑ 423 Mark Langston .10 .05
❑ 424 Steve Cox .15 .07
 Jesse Ibarra
 Derrek Lee
 Ron Wright RC
❑ 425 Jim Bonnici 1.50 .70
 Billy Owens
 Richie Sexson
 Daryle Ward RC
❑ 426 Kevin Jordan .10 .05
 Bobby Morris
 Desi Relaford
 Adam Riggs RC
❑ 427 Tim Harkrider .10 .05
 Rey Ordonez
 Neifi Perez
 Enrique Wilson
❑ 428 Bartolo Colon .15 .07
 Doug Million
 Rafael Orellano
 Ray Ricken
❑ 429 Jeff D'Amico .10 .05
 Marty Janzen RC
 Gary Rath
 Clint Sodowsky
❑ 430 Matt Drews .10 .05
 Rich Hunter RC
 Matt Ruebel
 Bret Wagner
❑ 431 Jaime Bluma .50 .23
 David Coggin
 Steve Montgomery
 Brandon Reed RC
❑ 432 Mike Figga .15 .07
 Raul Ibanez
 Paul Konerko
 Julio Mosquera
❑ 433 Brian Barber .10 .05
 Marc Kroon
 Marc Valdes
 Don Wengert
❑ 434 George Arias .75 .35
 Chris Haas RC
 Scott Rolen
 Scott Spiezio
❑ 435 Brian Banks 2.50 1.10
 Vladimir Guerrero
 Andruw Jones
 Billy McMillon
❑ 436 Roger Cedeno 2.00 .90
 Derrick Gibson
 Ben Grieve

	Card	MINT	NRMT
	Shane Spencer RC		
☐ 437	Anton French	.10	.05
	Demond Smith		
	DaRond Stovall RC		
	Keith Williams		
☐ 438	Michael Coleman RC	.15	.07
	Jacob Cruz		
	Richard Hidalgo		
	Charles Peterson		
☐ 439	Trey Beamon	.15	.07
	Yamil Benitez		
	Jermaine Dye		
	Angel Echevarria		
☐ 440	Checklist	.10	.05
☐ F7	M.Mantle Last Day	15.00	6.75
☐ NNO	Mickey Mantle TRIB	3.00	1.35
	Promotes the Mantle Foundation		
	Black and White Photo		

1997 Topps

	MINT	NRMT
COMPLETE SET (495)	60.00	27.00
COMPLETE SERIES 1 (276)	30.00	13.50
COMPLETE SERIES 2 (220)	30.00	13.50

	Card	MINT	NRMT
☐ 1	Barry Bonds	1.00	.45
☐ 2	Tom Pagnozzi	.10	.05
☐ 3	Terrell Wade	.10	.05
☐ 4	Jose Valentin	.10	.05
☐ 5	Mark Clark	.10	.05
☐ 6	Brady Anderson	.15	.07
☐ 8	Wade Boggs	.40	.18
☐ 9	Scott Stahoviak	.10	.05
☐ 10	Andres Galarraga	.25	.11
☐ 11	Steve Avery	.10	.05
☐ 12	Rusty Greer	.15	.07
☐ 13	Derek Jeter	1.50	.70
☐ 14	Ricky Bottalico	.10	.05
☐ 15	Andy Ashby	.10	.05
☐ 16	Paul Shuey	.10	.05
☐ 17	F.P. Santangelo	.10	.05
☐ 18	Royce Clayton	.10	.05
☐ 19	Mike Mohler	.10	.05
☐ 20	Mike Piazza	1.00	.45
☐ 21	Jaime Navarro	.10	.05
☐ 22	Billy Wagner	.10	.05
☐ 23	Mike Timlin	.10	.05
☐ 24	Garret Anderson	.15	.07
☐ 25	Ben McDonald	.10	.05
☐ 26	Mel Rojas	.10	.05
☐ 27	John Burkett	.10	.05
☐ 28	Jeff King	.10	.05
☐ 29	Reggie Jefferson	.10	.05
☐ 30	Kevin Appier	.15	.07
☐ 31	Felipe Lira	.10	.05
☐ 32	Kevin Tapani	.10	.05
☐ 33	Mark Portugal	.10	.05
☐ 34	Carlos Garcia	.10	.05
☐ 35	Joey Cora	.10	.05
☐ 36	David Segui	.10	.05
☐ 37	Mark Grace	.40	.18
☐ 38	Erik Hanson	.10	.05
☐ 39	Jeff D'Amico	.10	.05
☐ 40	Jay Buhner	.15	.07
☐ 41	B.J. Surhoff	.15	.07
☐ 42	Jackie Robinson TRIB	2.00	.90
☐ 43	Roger Pavlik	.10	.05
☐ 44	Hal Morris	.10	.05
☐ 45	Mariano Duncan	.10	.05
☐ 46	Harold Baines	.15	.07
☐ 47	Jorge Fabregas	.10	.05
☐ 48	Jose Herrera	.10	.05
☐ 49	Jeff Cirillo	.15	.07
☐ 50	Tom Glavine	.40	.18
☐ 51	Pedro Astacio	.10	.05
☐ 52	Mark Gardner	.10	.05
☐ 53	Arthur Rhodes	.10	.05
☐ 54	Troy O'Leary	.10	.05
☐ 55	Bip Roberts	.10	.05
☐ 56	Mike Lieberthal	.15	.07
☐ 57	Shane Andrews	.10	.05
☐ 58	Scott Karl	.10	.05
☐ 59	Gary DiSarcina	.10	.05
☐ 60	Andy Pettitte	.15	.07
☐ 61	Kevin Elster	.10	.05
☐ 62	Mark McGwire	1.50	.70
☐ 63	Dan Wilson	.10	.05
☐ 64	Mickey Morandini	.10	.05
☐ 65	Chuck Knoblauch	.15	.07
☐ 66	Tim Wakefield	.10	.05
☐ 67	Raul Mondesi	.15	.07
☐ 68	Todd Jones	.10	.05
☐ 69	Albert Belle	.15	.07
☐ 70	Trevor Hoffman	.15	.07
☐ 71	Eric Young	.10	.05
☐ 72	Robert Perez	.10	.05
☐ 73	Butch Huskey	.10	.05
☐ 74	Brian McRae	.10	.05
☐ 75	Jim Edmonds	.25	.11
☐ 76	Mike Henneman	.10	.05
☐ 77	Frank Rodriguez	.10	.05
☐ 78	Danny Tartabull	.10	.05
☐ 79	Robb Nen	.10	.05
☐ 80	Reggie Sanders	.10	.05
☐ 81	Ron Karkovice	.10	.05
☐ 82	Benito Santiago	.10	.05
☐ 83	Mike Lansing	.10	.05
☐ 84	Mike Fetters UER	.10	.05
	Card numbered 61		
☐ 85	Craig Biggio	.25	.11
☐ 86	Mike Bordick	.10	.05
☐ 87	Ray Lankford	.10	.05
☐ 88	Charles Nagy	.10	.05
☐ 89	Paul Wilson	.10	.05
☐ 90	John Wetteland	.15	.07
☐ 91	Tom Candiotti	.10	.05
☐ 92	Carlos Delgado	.40	.18
☐ 93	Derek Bell	.10	.05
☐ 94	Mark Lemke	.10	.05
☐ 95	Edgar Martinez	.25	.11
☐ 96	Rickey Henderson	.75	.35
☐ 97	Greg Myers	.10	.05
☐ 98	Jim Leyritz	.10	.05
☐ 99	Mark Johnson	.10	.05
☐ 100	Dwight Gooden HL	.10	.05
☐ 101	Al Leiter HL	.10	.05
☐ 102	John Mabry HL	.10	.05
☐ 103	Alex Ochoa HL	.10	.05
☐ 104	Mike Piazza HL	.50	.23
☐ 105	Jim Thome	.40	.18
☐ 106	Ricky Otero	.10	.05
☐ 107	Jamey Wright	.10	.05
☐ 108	Frank Thomas	.50	.23
☐ 109	Jody Reed	.10	.05
☐ 110	Orel Hershiser	.15	.07
☐ 111	Terry Steinbach	.10	.05
☐ 112	Mark Loretta	.10	.05
☐ 113	Turk Wendell	.10	.05
☐ 114	Marvin Benard	.10	.05
☐ 115	Kevin Brown	.15	.07
☐ 116	Robert Person	.10	.05
☐ 117	Joey Hamilton	.10	.05
☐ 118	Francisco Cordova	.10	.05
☐ 119	John Smiley	.10	.05
☐ 120	Travis Fryman	.15	.07
☐ 121	Jimmy Key	.15	.07
☐ 122	Tom Goodwin	.10	.05
☐ 123	Mike Greenwell	.10	.05
☐ 124	Juan Gonzalez	.40	.18
☐ 125	Pete Harnisch	.10	.05
☐ 126	Roger Cedeno	.10	.05
☐ 127	Ron Gant	.10	.05
☐ 128	Mark Langston	.10	.05
☐ 129	Tim Crabtree	.10	.05
☐ 130	Greg Maddux	1.00	.45
☐ 131	W.VanLandingham	.10	.05
☐ 132	Wally Joyner	.15	.07
☐ 133	Randy Myers	.10	.05
☐ 134	John Valentin	.10	.05
☐ 135	Bret Boone	.15	.07
☐ 136	Bruce Ruffin	.10	.05
☐ 137	Chris Snopek	.10	.05
☐ 138	Paul Molitor	.40	.18
☐ 139	Mark McLemore	.10	.05
☐ 140	Rafael Palmeiro	.40	.18
☐ 141	Herb Perry	.10	.05
☐ 142	Luis Gonzalez	.40	.18
☐ 143	Doug Drabek	.10	.05
☐ 144	Ken Ryan	.10	.05
☐ 145	Todd Hundley	.10	.05
☐ 146	Ellis Burks	.15	.07
☐ 147	Ozzie Guillen	.10	.05
☐ 148	Rich Becker	.10	.05
☐ 149	Sterling Hitchcock	.10	.05
☐ 150	Bernie Williams	.40	.18
☐ 151	Mike Stanley	.10	.05
☐ 152	Roberto Alomar	.40	.18
☐ 153	Jose Mesa	.10	.05
☐ 154	Steve Trachsel	.10	.05
☐ 155	Alex Gonzalez	.10	.05
☐ 156	Troy Percival	.10	.05
☐ 157	John Smoltz	.15	.07
☐ 158	Pedro Martinez	.50	.23
☐ 159	Jeff Conine	.10	.05
☐ 160	Bernard Gilkey	.10	.05
☐ 161	Jim Eisenreich	.10	.05
☐ 162	Mickey Tettleton	.10	.05
☐ 163	Justin Thompson	.10	.05
☐ 164	Jose Offerman	.10	.05
☐ 165	Tony Phillips	.10	.05
☐ 166	Ismael Valdes	.10	.05
☐ 167	Ryne Sandberg UER	.50	.23
	Card has him with 252 homers in 1996		
☐ 168	Matt Mieske	.10	.05
☐ 169	Geronimo Berroa	.10	.05
☐ 170	Otis Nixon	.10	.05
☐ 171	John Mabry	.10	.05
☐ 172	Shawon Dunston	.10	.05
☐ 173	Omar Vizquel	.15	.07
☐ 174	Chris Hoiles	.10	.05
☐ 175	Dwight Gooden	.15	.07
☐ 176	Wilson Alvarez	.10	.05
☐ 177	Todd Hollandsworth	.10	.05
☐ 178	Roger Salkeld	.10	.05
☐ 179	Rey Sanchez	.10	.05
☐ 180	Rey Ordonez	.10	.05
☐ 181	Denny Martinez	.15	.07
☐ 182	Ramon Martinez	.10	.05
☐ 183	Dave Nilsson	.10	.05
☐ 184	Marquis Grissom	.10	.05
☐ 185	Randy Velarde	.10	.05
☐ 186	Ron Coomer	.10	.05
☐ 187	Tino Martinez	.15	.07
☐ 188	Jeff Brantley	.10	.05
☐ 189	Steve Finley	.15	.07
☐ 190	Andy Benes	.10	.05
☐ 191	Terry Adams	.10	.05
☐ 192	Mike Blowers	.10	.05
☐ 193	Russ Davis	.10	.05
☐ 194	Darryl Hamilton	.10	.05
☐ 195	Jason Kendall	.15	.07
☐ 196	Johnny Damon	.15	.07
☐ 197	Dave Martinez	.10	.05
☐ 198	Mike Macfarlane	.10	.05
☐ 199	Norm Charlton	.10	.05
☐ 200	Doug Million RC	.10	.05
	Damian Moss		
	Bobby Rodgers		
☐ 201	Geoff Jenkins	.25	.11
	Raul Ibanez		
	Mike Cameron		
☐ 202	Sean Casey	.50	.23
	Jim Bonnici		
	Dmitri Young		
☐ 203	Jed Hansen	.10	.05
	Homer Bush		
	Felipe Crespo		
☐ 204	Kevin Orie	.10	.05

Gabe Alvarez
Aaron Boone
❑ 205 Ben Davis .15 .07
Kevin Brown
Bobby Estalella
❑ 206 Billy McMillon RC .15 .07
Bubba Trammell
Dante Powell
❑ 207 Jarrod Washburn .10 .05
Marc Wilkins RC
Glendon Rusch
❑ 208 Brian Hunter .10 .05
❑ 209 Jason Giambi .40 .18
❑ 210 Henry Rodriguez .10 .05
❑ 211 Edgar Renteria .10 .05
❑ 212 Edgardo Alfonzo .15 .07
❑ 213 Fernando Vina .10 .05
❑ 214 Shawn Green .40 .18
❑ 215 Ray Durham .15 .07
❑ 216 Joe Randa .10 .05
❑ 217 Armando Reynoso .10 .05
❑ 218 Eric Davis .15 .07
❑ 219 Bob Tewksbury .10 .05
❑ 220 Jacob Cruz .10 .05
❑ 221 Glenallen Hill .10 .05
❑ 222 Gary Gaetti .15 .07
❑ 223 Donne Wall .10 .05
❑ 224 Brad Clontz .10 .05
❑ 225 Marty Janzen .10 .05
❑ 226 Todd Worrell .10 .05
❑ 227 John Franco .15 .07
❑ 228 David Wells .15 .07
❑ 229 Gregg Jefferies .10 .05
❑ 230 Tim Naehring .10 .05
❑ 231 Thomas Howard .10 .05
❑ 232 Roberto Hernandez .10 .05
❑ 233 Kevin Ritz .10 .05
❑ 234 Julian Tavarez .10 .05
❑ 235 Ken Hill .10 .05
❑ 236 Greg Gagne .10 .05
❑ 237 Bobby Chouinard .10 .05
❑ 238 Joe Carter .15 .07
❑ 239 Jermaine Dye .15 .07
❑ 240 Antonio Osuna .10 .05
❑ 241 Julio Franco .15 .07
❑ 242 Mike Grace .10 .05
❑ 243 Aaron Sele .15 .07
❑ 244 David Justice .15 .07
❑ 245 Sandy Alomar Jr. .15 .07
❑ 246 Jose Canseco .40 .18
❑ 247 Paul O'Neill .40 .18
❑ 248 Sean Berry .10 .05
❑ 249 Nick Bierbrodt .40 .18
Kevin Sweeney RC
❑ 250 Larry Rodriguez RC .15 .07
Vladimir Nunez RC
❑ 251 Ron Hartman .15 .07
David Hayman RC
❑ 252 Alex Sanchez .15 .07
Matthew Quatraro RC
❑ 253 Ronni Seberino RC .15 .07
Pablo Ortego RC
❑ 254 Rex Hudler .10 .05
❑ 255 Orlando Miller .10 .05
❑ 256 Mariano Rivera .15 .07
❑ 257 Brad Radke .15 .07
❑ 258 Bobby Higginson .15 .07
❑ 259 Jay Bell .15 .07
❑ 260 Mark Grudzielanek .10 .05
❑ 261 Lance Johnson .10 .05
❑ 262 Ken Caminiti .15 .07
❑ 263 J.T. Snow .15 .07
❑ 264 Gary Sheffield .15 .07
❑ 265 Darrin Fletcher .10 .05
❑ 266 Eric Owens .10 .05
❑ 267 Luis Castillo .10 .05
❑ 268 Scott Rolen .40 .18
❑ 269 Todd Noel .25 .11
John Oliver RC
❑ 270 Robert Stratton RC .40 .18
Corey Lee RC
❑ 271 Gil Meche RC .50 .23
Matt Halloran RC
❑ 272 Eric Milton RC .75 .35
Dermal Brown
❑ 273 Josh Garrett .40 .18
Chris Reitsma RC
❑ 274 A.J.Zapp RC .50 .23
Jason Marquis
❑ 275 Checklist .10 .05
❑ 276 Checklist .10 .05
❑ 277 Chipper Jones UER .75 .35
incorrectly numbered 276
❑ 278 Orlando Merced .10 .05
❑ 279 Ariel Prieto .10 .05
❑ 280 Al Leiter .15 .07
❑ 281 Pat Meares .10 .05
❑ 282 Darryl Strawberry .15 .07
❑ 283 Jamie Moyer .10 .05
❑ 284 Scott Servais .10 .05
❑ 285 Delino DeShields .10 .05
❑ 286 Danny Graves .10 .05
❑ 287 Gerald Williams .10 .05
❑ 288 Todd Greene .10 .05
❑ 289 Rico Brogna .10 .05
❑ 290 Derrick Gibson .10 .05
❑ 291 Joe Girardi .10 .05
❑ 292 Darren Lewis .10 .05
❑ 293 Nomar Garciaparra 1.00 .45
❑ 294 Greg Colbrunn .10 .05
❑ 295 Jeff Bagwell .50 .23
❑ 296 Brent Gates .10 .05
❑ 297 Jose Vizcaino .10 .05
❑ 298 Alex Ochoa .10 .05
❑ 299 Sid Fernandez .10 .05
❑ 300 Ken Griffey Jr. 1.25 .55
❑ 301 Chris Gomez .10 .05
❑ 302 Wendell Magee .10 .05
❑ 303 Darren Oliver .10 .05
❑ 304 Mel Nieves .10 .05
❑ 305 Sammy Sosa .75 .35
❑ 306 George Arias .10 .05
❑ 307 Jack McDowell .10 .05
❑ 308 Stan Javier .10 .05
❑ 309 Kimera Bartee .10 .05
❑ 310 James Baldwin .10 .05
❑ 311 Rocky Coppinger .10 .05
❑ 312 Keith Lockhart .10 .05
❑ 313 C.J. Nitkowski .10 .05
❑ 314 Allen Watson .10 .05
❑ 315 Darryl Kile .15 .07
❑ 316 Amaury Telemaco .10 .05
❑ 317 Jason Isringhausen .10 .05
❑ 318 Manny Ramirez .50 .23
❑ 319 Terry Pendleton .15 .07
❑ 320 Tim Salmon .15 .07
❑ 321 Eric Karros .15 .07
❑ 322 Mark Whiten .10 .05
❑ 323 Rick Krivda .10 .05
❑ 324 Brett Butler .15 .07
❑ 325 Randy Johnson .50 .23
❑ 326 Eddie Taubensee .10 .05
❑ 327 Mark Leiter .10 .05
❑ 328 Kevin Gross .10 .05
❑ 329 Ernie Young .10 .05
❑ 330 Pat Hentgen .10 .05
❑ 331 Rondell White .15 .07
❑ 332 Bobby Witt .10 .05
❑ 333 Eddie Murray .40 .18
❑ 334 Tim Raines .15 .07
❑ 335 Jeff Fassero .10 .05
❑ 336 Chuck Finley .15 .07
❑ 337 Willie Adams .10 .05
❑ 338 Chan Ho Park .15 .07
❑ 339 Jay Powell .10 .05
❑ 340 Ivan Rodriguez .40 .18
❑ 341 Jermaine Allensworth .10 .05
❑ 342 Jay Payton .10 .05
❑ 343 T.J. Mathews .10 .05
❑ 344 Tony Batista .15 .07
❑ 345 Ed Sprague .10 .05
❑ 346 Jeff Kent .25 .11
❑ 347 Scott Erickson .10 .05
❑ 348 Jeff Suppan .10 .05
❑ 349 Pete Schourek .10 .05
❑ 350 Kenny Lofton .15 .07
❑ 351 Alan Benes .10 .05
❑ 352 Fred McGriff .25 .11
❑ 353 Charlie O'Brien .10 .05
❑ 354 Darren Bragg .10 .05
❑ 355 Alex Fernandez .10 .05
❑ 356 Al Martin .10 .05
❑ 357 Bob Wells .10 .05
❑ 358 Chad Mottola .10 .05
❑ 359 Devon White .15 .07
❑ 360 David Cone .15 .07
❑ 361 Bobby Jones .10 .05
❑ 362 Scott Sanders .10 .05
❑ 363 Karim Garcia .10 .05
❑ 364 Kirt Manwaring .10 .05
❑ 365 Chili Davis .15 .07
❑ 366 Mike Hampton .15 .07
❑ 367 Chad Ogea .10 .05
❑ 368 Curt Schilling .40 .18
❑ 369 Phil Nevin .15 .07
❑ 370 Roger Clemens 1.00 .45
❑ 371 Willie Greene .10 .05
❑ 372 Kenny Rogers .10 .05
❑ 373 Jose Rijo .10 .05
❑ 374 Bobby Bonilla .15 .07
❑ 375 Mike Mussina .40 .18
❑ 376 Curtis Pride .10 .05
❑ 377 Todd Walker .10 .05
❑ 378 Jason Bere .10 .05
❑ 379 Heathcliff Slocumb .10 .05
❑ 380 Dante Bichette .15 .07
❑ 381 Carlos Baerga .10 .05
❑ 382 Livan Hernandez .10 .05
❑ 383 Jason Schmidt .10 .05
❑ 384 Kevin Stocker .10 .05
❑ 385 Matt Williams .25 .11
❑ 386 Bartolo Colon .15 .07
❑ 387 Will Clark .40 .18
❑ 388 Dennis Eckersley .15 .07
❑ 389 Brooks Kieschnick .10 .05
❑ 390 Ryan Klesko .15 .07
❑ 391 Mark Carreon .10 .05
❑ 392 Tim Worrell .10 .05
❑ 393 Dean Palmer .15 .07
❑ 394 Wil Cordero .10 .05
❑ 395 Javy Lopez .15 .07
❑ 396 Rich Aurilia .15 .07
❑ 397 Greg Vaughn .15 .07
❑ 398 Vinny Castilla .15 .07
❑ 399 Jeff Montgomery .10 .05
❑ 400 Cal Ripken 1.50 .70
❑ 401 Walt Weiss .10 .05
❑ 402 Brad Ausmus .10 .05
❑ 403 Ruben Rivera .10 .05
❑ 404 Mark Wohlers .10 .05
❑ 405 Rick Aguilera .10 .05
❑ 406 Tony Clark .15 .07
❑ 407 Lyle Mouton .10 .05
❑ 408 Bill Pulsipher .10 .05
❑ 409 Jose Rosado .10 .05
❑ 410 Tony Gwynn .75 .35
❑ 411 Cecil Fielder .15 .07
❑ 412 John Flaherty .10 .05
❑ 413 Lenny Dykstra .15 .07
❑ 414 Ugueth Urbina .10 .05
❑ 415 Brian Jordan .15 .07
❑ 416 Bob Abreu .15 .07
❑ 417 Craig Paquette .10 .05
❑ 418 Sandy Martinez .10 .05
❑ 419 Jeff Blauser .10 .05
❑ 420 Barry Larkin .40 .18
❑ 421 Kevin Seitzer .10 .05
❑ 422 Tim Belcher .10 .05
❑ 423 Paul Sorrento .10 .05
❑ 424 Cal Eldred .10 .05
❑ 425 Robin Ventura .15 .07
❑ 426 John Olerud .15 .07
❑ 427 Bob Wolcott .10 .05
❑ 428 Matt Lawton .15 .07
❑ 429 Rod Beck .10 .05
❑ 430 Shane Reynolds .10 .05
❑ 431 Mike James .10 .05
❑ 432 Steve Wojciechowski .10 .05
❑ 433 Vladimir Guerrero .60 .25
❑ 434 Dustin Hermanson .10 .05
❑ 435 Marty Cordova .10 .05
❑ 436 Marc Newfield .10 .05
❑ 437 Todd Stottlemyre .10 .05
❑ 438 Jeffrey Hammonds .10 .05
❑ 439 Dave Stevens .10 .05
❑ 440 Hideo Nomo .40 .18
❑ 441 Mark Thompson .10 .05
❑ 442 Mark Lewis .10 .05

❑ 443 Quinton McCracken ...... .10 .05
❑ 444 Cliff Floyd .... .15 .07
❑ 445 Denny Neagle .... .15 .07
❑ 446 John Jaha .... .10 .05
❑ 447 Mike Sweeney................ .15 .07
❑ 448 John Wasdin .... .10 .05
❑ 449 Chad Curtis .... .10 .05
❑ 450 Mo Vaughn .... .15 .07
❑ 451 Donovan Osborne .... .10 .05
❑ 452 Ruben Sierra .... .10 .05
❑ 453 Michael Tucker .... .10 .05
❑ 454 Kurt Abbott .... .10 .05
❑ 455 Andruw Jones UER........ .50 .23
Birthdate is incorrectly listed as 1-22-67, should be 1-22-77
❑ 456 Shannon Stewart............ .15 .07
❑ 457 Scott Brosius.................. .15 .07
❑ 458 Juan Guzman .... .10 .05
❑ 459 Ron Villone .... .10 .05
❑ 460 Moises Alou.................... .15 .07
❑ 461 Larry Walker .... .25 .11
❑ 462 Eddie Murray SH............ .15 .07
❑ 463 Paul Molitor SH .... .15 .07
❑ 464 Hideo Nomo SH .... .15 .07
❑ 465 Barry Bonds SH .... .50 .23
❑ 466 Todd Hundley SH .... .10 .05
❑ 467 Rheal Cormier................. .10 .05
❑ 468 Jason Conti RC.............. .15 .07
Jhensy Sandoval
❑ 469 Rod Barajas .... .15 .07
Jackie Rexrode RC
❑ 470 Cedric Bowers RC........ 2.00 .90
Jared Sandberg
❑ 471 Chei Gunner RC .... .10 .05
Paul Wilder
❑ 472 Mike Decelle .... .10 .05
Marcus McCain RC
❑ 473 Todd Zeile .... .10 .05
❑ 474 Neifi Perez...................... .10 .05
❑ 475 Jeromy Burnitz .... .15 .07
❑ 476 Trey Beamon.................. .10 .05
❑ 477 Braden Looper RC .... .40 .18
John Patterson
❑ 478 Danny Peoples .... .15 .07
Jake Westbrook RC
❑ 479 Eric Chavez .... 1.25 .55
Adam Eaton RC
❑ 480 Joe Lawrence RC .... .40 .18
Pete Tucci
❑ 481 Kris Benson.................... .60 .25
Billy Koch RC
❑ 482 John Nicholson .... .15 .07
Andy Prater RC
❑ 483 Mark Johnson RC .... .40 .18
Mark Kotsay
❑ 484 Armando Benitez............ .10 .05
❑ 485 Mike Matheny .... .10 .05
❑ 486 Jeff Reed........................ .10 .05
❑ 487 Mark Bellhorn .... .10 .05
Russ Johnson
Enrique Wilson
❑ 488 Ben Grieve .... .15 .07
Richard Hidalgo
Scott Morgan RC
❑ 489 Paul Konerko.................. .15 .07
Derrek Lee UER
spelled Derek on back
Ron Wright
❑ 490 Wes Helms RC .... .25 .11
Bill Mueller
Brad Seitzer
❑ 491 Jeff Abbott...................... .10 .05
Shane Monahan
Edgard Velazquez
❑ 492 Jimmy Anderson RC ...... .10 .05
Ron Blazier
Gerald Witasick
❑ 493 Darin Blood .... .10 .05
Heath Murray
Carl Pavano
❑ 494 Nelson Figueroa RC ...... .40 .18
Mark Redman
Mike Villano
❑ 495 Checklist .... .10 .05
❑ 496 Checklist .... .10 .05
❑ NNO Derek Jeter AU 150.00 70.00

1998 Topps

	MINT	NRMT
COMPLETE SET (503)	50.00	22.00
COMP.HOBBY SET (511)	80.00	36.00
COMP.RETAIL SET (511)	80.00	36.00
COMPLETE SERIES 1 (282)..	25.00	11.00
COMPLETE SERIES 2 (221)..	25.00	11.00

❑ 1 Tony Gwynn .... .75 .35
❑ 2 Larry Walker .... .25 .11
❑ 3 Billy Wagner .... .10 .05
❑ 4 Denny Neagle .... .10 .05
❑ 5 Vladimir Guerrero .... .50 .23
❑ 6 Kevin Brown .... .25 .11
❑ 8 Mariano Rivera .... .15 .07
❑ 9 Tony Clark.......................... .15 .07
❑ 10 Deion Sanders .... .15 .07
❑ 11 Francisco Cordova .... .10 .05
❑ 12 Matt Williams.................... .25 .11
❑ 13 Carlos Baerga .... .10 .05
❑ 14 Mo Vaughn .... .15 .07
❑ 15 Bobby Witt........................ .10 .05
❑ 16 Matt Stairs......................... .10 .05
❑ 17 Chan Ho Park .... .15 .07
❑ 18 Mike Bordick .... .10 .05
❑ 19 Michael Tucker .... .10 .05
❑ 20 Frank Thomas................... .50 .23
❑ 21 Roberto Clemente.......... 1.00 .45
❑ 22 Dmitri Young .... .15 .07
❑ 23 Steve Trachsel .... .10 .05
❑ 24 Jeff Kent .... .25 .11
❑ 25 Scott Rolen .... .40 .18
❑ 26 John Thomson .... .10 .05
❑ 27 Joe Vitiello......................... .10 .05
❑ 28 Eddie Guardado .... .10 .05
❑ 29 Charlie Hayes .... .10 .05
❑ 30 Juan Gonzalez .... .40 .18
❑ 31 Garret Anderson .... .15 .07
❑ 32 John Jaha .... .15 .07
❑ 33 Omar Vizquel .... .15 .07
❑ 34 Brian Hunter .... .10 .05
❑ 35 Jeff Bagwell....................... .50 .23
❑ 36 Mark Lemke .... .10 .05
❑ 37 Doug Glanville................... .10 .05
❑ 38 Dan Wilson .... .10 .05
❑ 39 Steve Cooke .... .10 .05
❑ 40 Chili Davis .... .15 .07
❑ 41 Mike Cameron................... .15 .07
❑ 42 F.P. Santangelo .... .10 .05
❑ 43 Brad Ausmus..................... .10 .05
❑ 44 Gary DiSarcina .... .10 .05
❑ 45 Pat Hentgen .... .10 .05
❑ 46 Wilton Guerrero.................. .10 .05
❑ 47 Devon White .... .10 .05
❑ 48 Danny Patterson .... .10 .05
❑ 49 Pat Meares .... .10 .05
❑ 50 Rafael Palmeiro................. .40 .18
❑ 51 Mark Gardner .... .10 .05
❑ 52 Jeff Blauser .... .10 .05
❑ 53 Dave Hollins .... .10 .05
❑ 54 Carlos Garcia .... .10 .05
❑ 55 Ben McDonald.................... .10 .05
❑ 56 John Mabry .... .10 .05
❑ 57 Trevor Hoffman .... .15 .07
❑ 58 Tony Fernandez .... .15 .05
❑ 59 Rich Loiselle .... .15 .07
❑ 60 Mark Leiter .... .10 .05

❑ 61 Pat Kelly .... .10 .05
❑ 62 John Flaherty .... .10 .05
❑ 63 Roger Bailey .... .10 .05
❑ 64 Tom Gordon .... .15 .07
❑ 65 Ryan Klesko .... .15 .07
❑ 66 Darryl Hamilton .... .10 .05
❑ 67 Jim Eisenreich..................... .10 .05
❑ 68 Butch Huskey .... .10 .05
❑ 69 Mark Grudzielanek .... .10 .05
❑ 70 Marquis Grissom................. .10 .05
❑ 71 Mark McLemore .... .10 .05
❑ 72 Gary Gaetti .... .15 .07
❑ 73 Greg Gagne .... .10 .05
❑ 74 Lyle Mouton........................ .10 .05
❑ 75 Jim Edmonds .... .25 .11
❑ 76 Shawn Green .... .40 .18
❑ 77 Greg Vaughn....................... .15 .07
❑ 78 Terry Adams .... .10 .05
❑ 79 Kevin Polcovich................... .10 .05
❑ 80 Troy O'Leary .... .10 .05
❑ 81 Jeff Shaw .... .10 .05
❑ 82 Rich Becker......................... .10 .05
❑ 83 David Wells......................... .15 .07
❑ 84 Steve Karsay....................... .10 .05
❑ 85 Charles Nagy .... .10 .05
❑ 86 B.J. Surhoff .... .15 .07
❑ 87 Jamey Wright .... .10 .05
❑ 88 James Baldwin .... .10 .05
❑ 89 Edgardo Alfonzo .... .15 .07
❑ 90 Jay Buhner .... .15 .07
❑ 91 Brady Anderson .... .15 .07
❑ 92 Scott Servais........................ .10 .05
❑ 93 Edgar Renteria .... .10 .05
❑ 94 Mike Lieberthal .... .15 .07
❑ 95 Rick Aguilera........................ .10 .05
❑ 96 Walt Weiss .... .15 .07
❑ 97 Deivi Cruz .... .10 .05
❑ 98 Kurt Abbott .... .10 .05
❑ 99 Henry Rodriguez.................. .10 .05
❑ 100 Mike Piazza.................... 1.00 .45
❑ 101 Bill Taylor .... .10 .05
❑ 102 Todd Zeile .... .15 .07
❑ 103 Rey Ordonez.................... .10 .05
❑ 104 Willie Greene.................... .10 .05
❑ 105 Tony Womack................... .10 .05
❑ 106 Mike Sweeney.................. .15 .07
❑ 107 Jeffrey Hammonds .... .10 .05
❑ 108 Kevin Orie .... .10 .05
❑ 109 Alex Gonzalez................... .10 .05
❑ 110 Jose Canseco .... .40 .18
❑ 111 Paul Sorrento .... .10 .05
❑ 112 Joey Hamilton .... .10 .05
❑ 113 Brad Radke........................ .15 .07
❑ 114 Steve Avery........................ .10 .05
❑ 115 Esteban Loaiza .... .10 .05
❑ 116 Stan Javier .... .10 .05
❑ 117 Chris Gomez...................... .10 .05
❑ 118 Royce Clayton................... .10 .05
❑ 119 Orlando Merced .... .10 .05
❑ 120 Kevin Appier .... .15 .07
❑ 121 Mel Nieves .... .10 .05
❑ 122 Joe Girardi.......................... .10 .05
❑ 123 Rico Brogna .... .10 .05
❑ 124 Kent Mercker...................... .10 .05
❑ 125 Manny Ramirez.................. .50 .23
❑ 126 Jeromy Burnitz .... .15 .07
❑ 127 Kevin Foster .... .10 .05
❑ 128 Matt Morris .... .15 .07
❑ 129 Jason Dickson.................... .10 .05
❑ 130 Tom Glavine .... .40 .18
❑ 131 Wally Joyner .... .15 .07
❑ 132 Rick Reed .... .10 .05
❑ 133 Todd Jones .... .10 .05
❑ 134 Dave Martinez.................... .10 .05
❑ 135 Sandy Alomar Jr................ .15 .07
❑ 136 Mike Lansing....................... .10 .05
❑ 137 Sean Berry .... .10 .05
❑ 138 Doug Jones......................... .10 .05
❑ 139 Todd Stottlemyre................ .10 .05
❑ 140 Jay Bell .... .15 .07
❑ 141 Jaime Navarro.................... .10 .05
❑ 142 Chris Hoiles .... .10 .05
❑ 143 Joey Cora .... .10 .05
❑ 144 Scott Spiezio .... .10 .05
❑ 145 Joe Carter .... .15 .07
❑ 146 Jose Guillen .... .10 .05

❑ 147 Damion Easley .10 .05
❑ 148 Lee Stevens .10 .05
❑ 149 Alex Fernandez .10 .05
❑ 150 Randy Johnson .50 .23
❑ 151 J.T. Snow .15 .07
❑ 152 Chuck Finley .15 .07
❑ 153 Bernard Gilkey .10 .05
❑ 154 David Segui .10 .05
❑ 155 Dante Bichette .15 .07
❑ 156 Kevin Stocker .10 .05
❑ 157 Carl Everett .15 .07
❑ 158 Jose Valentin .10 .05
❑ 159 Pokey Reese .10 .05
❑ 160 Derek Jeter 1.50 .70
❑ 161 Roger Pavlik .10 .05
❑ 162 Mark Wohlers .10 .05
❑ 163 Ricky Bottalico .10 .05
❑ 164 Ozzie Guillen .10 .05
❑ 165 Mike Mussina .40 .18
❑ 166 Gary Sheffield .15 .07
❑ 167 Hideo Nomo .40 .18
❑ 168 Mark Grace .40 .18
❑ 169 Aaron Sele .15 .07
❑ 170 Darryl Kile .15 .07
❑ 171 Shawn Estes .15 .07
❑ 172 Vinny Castilla .15 .07
❑ 173 Ron Coomer .10 .05
❑ 174 Jose Rosado .10 .05
❑ 175 Kenny Lofton .15 .07
❑ 176 Jason Giambi .40 .18
❑ 177 Hal Morris .10 .05
❑ 178 Darren Bragg .10 .05
❑ 179 Orel Hershiser .15 .07
❑ 180 Ray Lankford .10 .05
❑ 181 Hideki Irabu .10 .05
❑ 182 Kevin Young .15 .07
❑ 183 Javy Lopez .15 .07
❑ 184 Jeff Montgomery .10 .05
❑ 185 Mike Holtz .10 .05
❑ 186 George Williams .10 .05
❑ 187 Cal Eldred .10 .05
❑ 188 Tom Candiotti .10 .05
❑ 189 Glenallen Hill .10 .05
❑ 190 Brian Giles .15 .07
❑ 191 Dave Mlicki .10 .05
❑ 192 Garrett Stephenson .10 .05
❑ 193 Jeff Frye .10 .05
❑ 194 Joe Oliver .10 .05
❑ 195 Bob Hamelin .10 .05
❑ 196 Luis Sojo .10 .05
❑ 197 LaTroy Hawkins .10 .05
❑ 198 Kevin Elster .10 .05
❑ 199 Jeff Reed .10 .05
❑ 200 Dennis Eckersley .15 .07
❑ 201 Bill Mueller .10 .05
❑ 202 Russ Davis .10 .05
❑ 203 Armando Benitez .10 .05
❑ 204 Quilvio Veras .10 .05
❑ 205 Tim Naehring .10 .05
❑ 206 Quinton McCracken .10 .05
❑ 207 Raul Casanova .10 .05
❑ 208 Matt Lawton .10 .05
❑ 209 Luis Alicea .10 .05
❑ 210 Luis Gonzalez .40 .18
❑ 211 Allen Watson .10 .05
❑ 212 Gerald Williams .10 .05
❑ 213 David Bell .10 .05
❑ 214 Todd Hollandsworth .10 .05
❑ 215 Wade Boggs .40 .18
❑ 216 Jose Mesa .10 .05
❑ 217 Jamie Moyer .10 .05
❑ 218 Darren Daulton .15 .07
❑ 219 Mickey Morandini .10 .05
❑ 220 Rusty Greer .15 .07
❑ 221 Jim Bullinger .10 .05
❑ 222 Jose Offerman .10 .05
❑ 223 Matt Karchner .10 .05
❑ 224 Woody Williams .10 .05
❑ 225 Mark Loretta .10 .05
❑ 226 Mike Hampton .15 .07
❑ 227 Willie Adams .10 .05
❑ 228 Scott Hatteberg .10 .05
❑ 229 Rich Amaral .10 .05
❑ 230 Terry Steinbach .10 .05
❑ 231 Glendon Rusch .10 .05
❑ 232 Bret Boone .15 .07

❑ 233 Robert Person .10 .05
❑ 234 Jose Hernandez .10 .05
❑ 235 Doug Drabek .10 .05
❑ 236 Jason McDonald .10 .05
❑ 237 Chris Widger .10 .05
❑ 238 Tom Martin .10 .05
❑ 239 Dave Burba .10 .05
❑ 240 Pete Rose Jr. .15 .07
❑ 241 Bobby Ayala .10 .05
❑ 242 Tim Wakefield .10 .05
❑ 243 Dennis Springer .10 .05
❑ 244 Tim Belcher .10 .05
❑ 245 Jon Garland .10 .05
Geoff Goetz
❑ 246 Glenn Davis .40 .18
Lance Berkman
❑ 247 Vernon Wells .25 .11
Aaron Akin
❑ 248 Adam Kennedy .10 .05
Jason Romano
❑ 249 Jason Dellaero .10 .05
Troy Cameron
❑ 250 Alex Sanchez .15 .07
Jared Sandberg
❑ 251 Pablo Ortega .10 .05
James Manias
❑ 252 Jason Conti RC .10 .05
Mike Stoner
❑ 253 John Patterson .10 .05
Larry Rodriguez
❑ 254 Adrian Beltre .15 .07
Ryan Minor RC
Aaron Boone
❑ 255 Ben Grieve .15 .07
Brian Buchanan
Dermal Brown
❑ 256 Kerry Wood .40 .18
Carl Pavano
Gil Meche
❑ 257 David Ortiz .15 .07
Daryle Ward
Richie Sexson
❑ 258 Randy Winn .15 .07
Juan Encarnacion
Andrew Vessel
❑ 259 Kris Benson RC .10 .05
Travis Smith
Courtney Duncan
❑ 260 Chad Hermansen RC .40 .18
Brent Butler
Warren Morris
❑ 261 Ben Davis .15 .07
Eli Marrero
Ramon Hernandez
❑ 262 Eric Chavez .15 .07
Russell Branyan
Russ Johnson
❑ 263 Todd Dunwoody RC .10 .05
John Barnes
Ryan Jackson
❑ 264 Matt Clement RC .10 .05
Roy Halladay
Brian Fuentes
❑ 265 Randy Johnson SH .15 .07
❑ 266 Kevin Brown SH .15 .07
❑ 267 Ricardo Rincon SH .10 .05
Francisco Cordova
❑ 268 N.Garciaparra SH .40 .18
❑ 269 Tino Martinez SH .10 .05
❑ 270 Chuck Knoblauch IL .10 .05
❑ 271 Pedro Martinez IL .25 .11
❑ 272 Denny Neagle IL .10 .05
❑ 273 Juan Gonzalez IL .15 .07
❑ 274 Andres Galarraga IL .10 .05
❑ 275 Checklist .10 .05
❑ 276 Checklist .10 .05
❑ 277 Moises Alou WS .10 .05
❑ 278 Sandy Alomar Jr. WS .10 .05
❑ 279 Gary Sheffield WS .10 .05
❑ 280 Matt Williams WS .15 .07
❑ 281 Livan Hernandez WS .10 .05
❑ 282 Chad Ogea WS .10 .05
❑ 283 Marlins Champs .10 .05
❑ 284 Tino Martinez .15 .07
❑ 285 Roberto Alomar .40 .18
❑ 286 Jeff King .10 .05

❑ 287 Brian Jordan .15 .07
❑ 288 Darin Erstad .40 .18
❑ 289 Ken Caminiti .15 .07
❑ 290 Jim Thome .40 .18
❑ 291 Paul Molitor .40 .18
❑ 292 Ivan Rodriguez .40 .18
❑ 293 Bernie Williams .40 .18
❑ 294 Todd Hundley .10 .05
❑ 295 Andres Galarraga .25 .11
❑ 296 Greg Maddux 1.00 .45
❑ 297 Edgar Martinez .25 .11
❑ 298 Ron Gant .15 .07
❑ 299 Derek Bell .10 .05
❑ 300 Roger Clemens 1.00 .45
❑ 301 Rondell White .15 .07
❑ 302 Barry Larkin .40 .18
❑ 303 Robin Ventura .15 .07
❑ 304 Jason Kendall .15 .07
❑ 305 Chipper Jones .75 .35
❑ 306 John Franco .15 .07
❑ 307 Sammy Sosa .75 .35
❑ 308 Troy Percival .10 .05
❑ 309 Chuck Knoblauch .15 .07
❑ 310 Ellis Burks .15 .07
❑ 311 Al Martin .10 .05
❑ 312 Tim Salmon .15 .07
❑ 313 Moises Alou .15 .07
❑ 314 Lance Johnson .10 .05
❑ 315 Justin Thompson .10 .05
❑ 316 Will Clark .40 .18
❑ 317 Barry Bonds 1.00 .45
❑ 318 Craig Biggio .25 .11
❑ 319 John Smoltz .15 .07
❑ 320 Cal Ripken 1.50 .70
❑ 321 Ken Griffey Jr. 1.25 .55
❑ 322 Paul O'Neill .40 .18
❑ 323 Todd Helton .50 .23
❑ 324 John Olerud .15 .07
❑ 325 Mark McGwire 1.50 .70
❑ 326 Jose Cruz Jr. .15 .07
❑ 327 Jeff Cirillo .15 .07
❑ 328 Dean Palmer .15 .07
❑ 329 John Wetteland .15 .07
❑ 330 Steve Finley .15 .07
❑ 331 Albert Belle .15 .07
❑ 332 Curt Schilling .40 .18
❑ 333 Raul Mondesi .15 .07
❑ 334 Andruw Jones .40 .18
❑ 335 Nomar Garciaparra 1.00 .45
❑ 336 David Justice .15 .07
❑ 337 Andy Pettitte .15 .07
❑ 338 Pedro Martinez .50 .23
❑ 339 Travis Miller .10 .05
❑ 340 Chris Stynes .10 .05
❑ 341 Gregg Jefferies .10 .05
❑ 342 Jeff Fassero .10 .05
❑ 343 Craig Counsell .10 .05
❑ 344 Wilson Alvarez .10 .05
❑ 345 Bip Roberts .10 .05
❑ 346 Kelvim Escobar .10 .05
❑ 347 Mark Bellhorn .10 .05
❑ 348 Cory Lidle RC .50 .23
❑ 349 Fred McGriff .25 .11
❑ 350 Chuck Carr .10 .05
❑ 351 Bob Abreu .15 .07
❑ 352 Juan Guzman .10 .05
❑ 353 Fernando Vina .10 .05
❑ 354 Andy Benes .10 .05
❑ 355 Dave Nilsson .10 .05
❑ 356 Bobby Bonilla .15 .07
❑ 357 Ismael Valdes .10 .05
❑ 358 Carlos Perez .10 .05
❑ 359 Kirk Rueter .10 .05
❑ 360 Bartolo Colon .15 .07
❑ 361 Mel Rojas .10 .05
❑ 362 Johnny Damon .15 .07
❑ 363 Geronimo Berroa .10 .05
❑ 364 Reggie Sanders .10 .05
❑ 365 Jermaine Allensworth .10 .05
❑ 366 Orlando Cabrera .10 .05
❑ 367 Jorge Fabregas .10 .05
❑ 368 Scott Stahoviak .10 .05
❑ 369 Ken Cloude .10 .05
❑ 370 Donovan Osborne .10 .05
❑ 371 Roger Cedeno .10 .05
❑ 372 Neifi Perez .10 .05

❑ 373 Chris Holt .10 .05
❑ 374 Cecil Fielder .15 .07
❑ 375 Marty Cordova .10 .05
❑ 376 Tom Goodwin .10 .05
❑ 377 Jeff Suppan .10 .05
❑ 378 Jeff Brantley .10 .05
❑ 379 Mark Langston .10 .05
❑ 380 Shane Reynolds .10 .05
❑ 381 Mike Fetters .10 .05
❑ 382 Todd Greene .10 .05
❑ 383 Ray Durham .15 .07
❑ 384 Carlos Delgado .40 .18
❑ 385 Jeff D'Amico .10 .05
❑ 386 Brian McRae .10 .05
❑ 387 Alan Benes .10 .05
❑ 388 Heathcliff Slocumb .10 .05
❑ 389 Eric Young .10 .05
❑ 390 Travis Fryman .15 .07
❑ 391 David Cone .15 .07
❑ 392 Otis Nixon .10 .05
❑ 393 Jeremi Gonzalez .10 .05
❑ 394 Jeff Juden .10 .05
❑ 395 Jose Vizcaino .10 .05
❑ 396 Ugueth Urbina .10 .05
❑ 397 Ramon Martinez .10 .05
❑ 398 Robb Nen .10 .05
❑ 399 Harold Baines .15 .07
❑ 400 Delino DeShields .10 .05
❑ 401 John Burkett .10 .05
❑ 402 Sterling Hitchcock .10 .05
❑ 403 Mark Clark .10 .05
❑ 404 Terrell Wade .10 .05
❑ 405 Scott Brosius .15 .07
❑ 406 Chad Curtis .10 .05
❑ 407 Brian Johnson .10 .05
❑ 408 Roberto Kelly .10 .05
❑ 409 Dave Dellucci RC .10 .05
❑ 410 Michael Tucker .10 .05
❑ 411 Mark Kotsay .15 .07
❑ 412 Mark Lewis .10 .05
❑ 413 Ryan McGuire .10 .05
❑ 414 Shawon Dunston .10 .05
❑ 415 Brad Rigby .10 .05
❑ 416 Scott Erickson .10 .05
❑ 417 Bobby Jones .10 .05
❑ 418 Darren Oliver .10 .05
❑ 419 John Smiley .10 .05
❑ 420 T.J. Mathews .10 .05
❑ 421 Dustin Hermanson .10 .05
❑ 422 Mike Timlin .10 .05
❑ 423 Willie Blair .10 .05
❑ 424 Manny Alexander .10 .05
❑ 425 Bob Tewksbury .10 .05
❑ 426 Pete Schourek .10 .05
❑ 427 Reggie Jefferson .10 .05
❑ 428 Ed Sprague .10 .05
❑ 429 Jeff Conine .10 .05
❑ 430 Roberto Hernandez .10 .05
❑ 431 Tom Pagnozzi .10 .05
❑ 432 Jaret Wright .10 .05
❑ 433 Livan Hernandez .10 .05
❑ 434 Andy Ashby .10 .05
❑ 435 Todd Dunn .10 .05
❑ 436 Bobby Higginson .15 .07
❑ 437 Rod Beck .10 .05
❑ 438 Jim Leyritz .10 .05
❑ 439 Matt Williams .25 .11
❑ 440 Brett Tomko .10 .05
❑ 441 Joe Randa .10 .05
❑ 442 Chris Carpenter .10 .05
❑ 443 Dennis Reyes .10 .05
❑ 444 Al Leiter .15 .07
❑ 445 Jason Schmidt .10 .05
❑ 446 Ken Hill .10 .05
❑ 447 Shannon Stewart .15 .07
❑ 448 Enrique Wilson .10 .05
❑ 449 Fernando Tatis .10 .05
❑ 450 Jimmy Key .15 .07
❑ 451 Darrin Fletcher .10 .05
❑ 452 John Valentin .10 .05
❑ 453 Kevin Tapani .10 .05
❑ 454 Eric Karros .15 .07
❑ 455 Jay Bell .15 .07
❑ 456 Walt Weiss .15 .07
❑ 457 Devon White .10 .05
❑ 458 Carl Pavano .10 .05
❑ 459 Mike Lansing .10 .05
❑ 460 John Flaherty .10 .05
❑ 461 Richard Hidalgo .15 .07
❑ 462 Quinton McCracken .10 .05
❑ 463 Karim Garcia .10 .05
❑ 464 Miguel Cairo .10 .05
❑ 465 Edwin Diaz .10 .05
❑ 466 Bobby Smith .10 .05
❑ 467 Yamil Benitez .10 .05
❑ 468 Rich Butler .10 .05
❑ 469 Ben Ford RC .15 .07
❑ 470 Bubba Trammell .10 .05
❑ 471 Brent Brede .10 .05
❑ 472 Brooks Kieschnick .10 .05
❑ 473 Carlos Castillo .10 .05
❑ 474 Brad Radke SH .10 .05
❑ 475 Roger Clemens SH .50 .23
❑ 476 Curt Schilling SH .40 .18
❑ 477 John Olerud SH .10 .05
❑ 478 Mark McGwire SH .75 .35
❑ 479 Mike Piazza .50 .23
Ken Griffey Jr. IL
❑ 480 Jeff Bagwell .25 .11
Frank Thomas IL
❑ 481 Chipper Jones .40 .18
Nomar Garciaparra IL
❑ 482 Larry Walker .25 .11
Juan Gonzalez IL
❑ 483 Gary Sheffield .10 .05
Tino Martinez IL
❑ 484 Derrick Gibson .10 .05
Michael Coleman
Norm Hutchins
❑ 485 Braden Looper .10 .05
Cliff Politte
Brian Rose
❑ 486 Eric Milton .15 .07
Jason Marquis
Corey Lee
❑ 487 A.J.Hinch .75 .35
Mark Osborne RC
Robert Fick
❑ 488 Aramis Ramirez .25 .11
Alex Gonzalez
Sean Casey
❑ 489 Donnie Bridges .15 .07
Tim Drew RC
❑ 490 Ntema Ndungidi RC .15 .07
Darnell McDonald
❑ 491 Ryan Anderson RC 1.00 .45
Mark Mangum
❑ 492 J.J.Davis 2.50 1.10
Troy Glaus RC
❑ 493 Jayson Werth RC .40 .18
Dan Reichert
❑ 494 John Curtice RC .60 .25
Michael Cuddyer
❑ 495 Jack Cust RC .60 .25
Jason Standridge
❑ 496 Brian Anderson .10 .05
❑ 497 Tony Saunders .10 .05
❑ 498 Vladimir Nunez .10 .05
Jhensy Sandoval
❑ 499 Brad Penny .15 .07
Nick Bierbrodt
❑ 500 Dustin Carr .15 .07
Luis Cruz RC
❑ 501 Cedric Bowers .15 .07
Marcus McCain
❑ 502 Checklist .10 .05
❑ 503 Checklist .10 .05
❑ 504 Alex Rodriguez 2.00 .90

1999 Topps

	MINT	NRMT
COMPLETE SET (462)	55.00	25.00
COMP.HOBBY SET (462)	60.00	27.00
COMP.X-MAS SET (463)	60.00	27.00
COMPLETE SERIES 1 (241)	30.00	13.50
COMPLETE SERIES 2 (221)	25.00	11.00
COMP.MCGWIRE HR SET (70)	1000.00	450.00
COMP.SOSA HR SET (66)	400.00	180.00

❑ 1 Roger Clemens 1.00 .45
❑ 2 Andres Galarraga .25 .11

❑ 3 Scott Brosius .15 .07
❑ 4 John Flaherty .10 .05
❑ 5 Jim Leyritz .10 .05
❑ 6 Ray Durham .15 .07
❑ 8 Jose Vizcaino .10 .05
❑ 9 Will Clark .40 .18
❑ 10 David Wells .15 .07
❑ 11 Jose Guillen .10 .05
❑ 12 Scott Hatteberg .10 .05
❑ 13 Edgardo Alfonzo .15 .07
❑ 14 Mike Bordick .10 .05
❑ 15 Manny Ramirez .50 .23
❑ 16 Greg Maddux 1.00 .45
❑ 17 David Segui .10 .05
❑ 18 Darryl Strawberry .15 .07
❑ 19 Brad Radke .15 .07
❑ 20 Kerry Wood .40 .18
❑ 21 Matt Anderson .10 .05
❑ 22 Derrek Lee .15 .07
❑ 23 Mickey Morandini .10 .05
❑ 24 Paul Konerko .15 .07
❑ 25 Travis Lee .10 .05
❑ 26 Ken Hill .10 .05
❑ 27 Kenny Rogers .10 .05
❑ 28 Paul Sorrento .10 .05
❑ 29 Quilvio Veras .10 .05
❑ 30 Todd Walker .10 .05
❑ 31 Ryan Jackson .10 .05
❑ 32 John Olerud .15 .07
❑ 33 Doug Glanville .10 .05
❑ 34 Nolan Ryan 2.50 1.10
❑ 35 Ray Lankford .10 .05
❑ 36 Mark Loretta .10 .05
❑ 37 Jason Dickson .10 .05
❑ 38 Sean Bergman .10 .05
❑ 39 Quinton McCracken .10 .05
❑ 40 Bartolo Colon .15 .07
❑ 41 Brady Anderson .15 .07
❑ 42 Chris Stynes .10 .05
❑ 43 Jorge Posada .15 .07
❑ 44 Justin Thompson .10 .05
❑ 45 Johnny Damon .15 .07
❑ 46 Armando Benitez .10 .05
❑ 47 Brant Brown .10 .05
❑ 48 Charlie Hayes .10 .05
❑ 49 Darren Dreifort .10 .05
❑ 50 Juan Gonzalez .40 .18
❑ 51 Chuck Knoblauch .15 .07
❑ 52 Todd Helton .50 .23
❑ 53 Rick Reed .10 .05
❑ 54 Chris Gomez .10 .05
❑ 55 Gary Sheffield .15 .07
❑ 56 Rod Beck .10 .05
❑ 57 Rey Sanchez .10 .05
❑ 58 Garret Anderson .15 .07
❑ 59 Jimmy Haynes .10 .05
❑ 60 Steve Woodard .10 .05
❑ 61 Rondell White .15 .07
❑ 62 Vladimir Guerrero .50 .23
❑ 63 Eric Karros .15 .07
❑ 64 Russ Davis .10 .05
❑ 65 Mo Vaughn .15 .07
❑ 66 Sammy Sosa .75 .35
❑ 67 Troy Percival .10 .05
❑ 68 Kenny Lofton .15 .07
❑ 69 Bill Taylor .10 .05
❑ 70 Mark McGwire 1.50 .70

❑	71	Roger Cedeno	.10	.05
❑	72	Javy Lopez	.15	.07
❑	73	Damion Easley	.10	.05
❑	74	Andy Pettitte	.15	.07
❑	75	Tony Gwynn	.75	.35
❑	76	Ricardo Rincon	.10	.05
❑	77	F.P. Santangelo	.10	.05
❑	78	Jay Bell	.15	.07
❑	79	Scott Servais	.10	.05
❑	80	Jose Canseco	.40	.18
❑	81	Roberto Hernandez	.10	.05
❑	82	Todd Dunwoody	.10	.05
❑	83	John Wetteland	.15	.07
❑	84	Mike Caruso	.10	.05
❑	85	Derek Jeter	1.50	.70
❑	86	Aaron Sele	.15	.07
❑	87	Jose Lima	.10	.05
❑	88	Ryan Christenson	.10	.05
❑	89	Jeff Cirillo	.15	.07
❑	90	Jose Hernandez	.10	.05
❑	91	Mark Kotsay	.10	.05
❑	92	Darren Bragg	.10	.05
❑	93	Albert Belle	.15	.07
❑	94	Matt Lawton	.15	.07
❑	95	Pedro Martinez	.50	.23
❑	96	Greg Vaughn	.15	.07
❑	97	Neifi Perez	.10	.05
❑	98	Gerald Williams	.10	.05
❑	99	Derek Bell	.10	.05
❑	100	Ken Griffey Jr.	1.25	.55
❑	101	David Cone	.15	.07
❑	102	Brian Johnson	.10	.05
❑	103	Dean Palmer	.15	.07
❑	104	Javier Valentin	.10	.05
❑	105	Trevor Hoffman	.15	.07
❑	106	Butch Huskey	.10	.05
❑	107	Dave Martinez	.10	.05
❑	108	Billy Wagner	.10	.05
❑	109	Shawn Green	.40	.18
❑	110	Ben Grieve	.15	.07
❑	111	Tom Goodwin	.10	.05
❑	112	Jaret Wright	.10	.05
❑	113	Aramis Ramirez	.15	.07
❑	114	Dmitri Young	.15	.07
❑	115	Hideki Irabu	.10	.05
❑	116	Roberto Kelly	.10	.05
❑	117	Jeff Fassero	.10	.05
❑	118	Mark Clark UER	.10	.05
		1997 and Career Victory totals are wrong		
❑	119	Jason McDonald	.10	.05
❑	120	Matt Williams	.25	.11
❑	121	Dave Burba	.10	.05
❑	122	Bret Saberhagen	.15	.07
❑	123	Deivi Cruz	.10	.05
❑	124	Chad Curtis	.10	.05
❑	125	Scott Rolen	.40	.18
❑	126	Lee Stevens	.10	.05
❑	127	J.T. Snow	.15	.07
❑	128	Rusty Greer	.15	.07
❑	129	Brian Meadows	.10	.05
❑	130	Jim Edmonds	.25	.11
❑	131	Ron Gant	.15	.07
❑	132	A.J. Hinch	.10	.05
❑	133	Shannon Stewart	.15	.07
❑	134	Brad Fullmer	.15	.07
❑	135	Cal Eldred	.10	.05
❑	136	Matt Walbeck	.10	.05
❑	137	Carl Everett	.15	.07
❑	138	Walt Weiss	.10	.05
❑	139	Fred McGriff	.25	.11
❑	140	Darin Erstad	.40	.18
❑	141	Dave Nilsson	.10	.05
❑	142	Eric Young	.10	.05
❑	143	Dan Wilson	.10	.05
❑	144	Jeff Reed	.10	.05
❑	145	Brett Tomko	.10	.05
❑	146	Terry Steinbach	.10	.05
❑	147	Seth Greisinger	.10	.05
❑	148	Pat Meares	.10	.05
❑	149	Livan Hernandez	.10	.05
❑	150	Jeff Bagwell	.50	.23
❑	151	Bob Wickman	.10	.05
❑	152	Omar Vizquel	.15	.07
❑	153	Eric Davis	.15	.07
❑	154	Larry Sutton	.10	.05
❑	155	Magglio Ordonez	.25	.11
❑	156	Eric Milton	.15	.07
❑	157	Darren Lewis	.10	.05
❑	158	Rick Aguilera	.10	.05
❑	159	Mike Lieberthal	.15	.07
❑	160	Robb Nen	.10	.05
❑	161	Brian Giles	.15	.07
❑	162	Jeff Brantley	.10	.05
❑	163	Gary DiSarcina	.10	.05
❑	164	John Valentin	.10	.05
❑	165	David Dellucci	.10	.05
❑	166	Chan Ho Park	.15	.07
❑	167	Masato Yoshii	.15	.07
❑	168	Jason Schmidt	.10	.05
❑	169	LaTroy Hawkins	.10	.05
❑	170	Bret Boone	.15	.07
❑	171	Jerry DiPoto	.10	.05
❑	172	Mariano Rivera	.15	.07
❑	173	Mike Cameron	.15	.07
❑	174	Scott Erickson	.10	.05
❑	175	Charles Johnson	.15	.07
❑	176	Bobby Jones	.10	.05
❑	177	Francisco Cordova	.10	.05
❑	178	Todd Jones	.10	.05
❑	179	Jeff Montgomery	.10	.05
❑	180	Mike Mussina	.40	.18
❑	181	Bob Abreu	.15	.07
❑	182	Ismael Valdes	.10	.05
❑	183	Andy Fox	.10	.05
❑	184	Woody Williams	.10	.05
❑	185	Denny Neagle	.10	.05
❑	186	Jose Valentin	.10	.05
❑	187	Darrin Fletcher	.10	.05
❑	188	Gabe Alvarez	.10	.05
❑	189	Eddie Taubensee	.10	.05
❑	190	Edgar Martinez	.25	.11
❑	191	Jason Kendall	.15	.07
❑	192	Darryl Kile	.15	.07
❑	193	Jeff King	.10	.05
❑	194	Rey Ordonez	.10	.05
❑	195	Andruw Jones	.40	.18
❑	196	Tony Fernandez	.10	.05
❑	197	Jamey Wright	.10	.05
❑	198	B.J. Surhoff	.15	.07
❑	199	Vinny Castilla	.15	.07
❑	200	David Wells HL	.10	.05
❑	201	Mark McGwire HL	.75	.35
❑	202	Sammy Sosa HL	.40	.18
❑	203	Roger Clemens HL	.50	.23
❑	204	Kerry Wood HL	.15	.07
❑	205	Lance Berkman	.40	.18
		Mike Frank		
		Gabe Kapler		
❑	206	Alex Escobar RC	.75	.35
		Ricky Ledee		
		Mike Stoner		
❑	207	Peter Bergeron RC	.40	.18
		Jeremy Giambi		
		George Lombard		
❑	208	Michael Barrett	.10	.05
		Ben Davis		
		Robert Fick		
❑	209	Pat Cline	.10	.05
		Ramon Hernandez		
		Jayson Werth		
❑	210	Bruce Chen	.15	.07
		Chris Enochs		
		Ryan Anderson		
❑	211	Mike Lincoln	.10	.05
		Octavio Dotel		
		Brad Penny		
❑	212	Chuck Abbott RC	.10	.05
		Brent Butler		
		Danny Klassen		
❑	213	Chris C.Jones	.40	.18
		Jeff Urban RC		
❑	214	Arturo McDowell RC	.40	.18
		Tony Torcato		
❑	215	Josh McKinley RC	.15	.07
		Jason Tyner		
❑	216	Matt Burch	.40	.18
		Seth Etheron RC		
		UER back Etherton		
❑	217	Mamon Tucker RC	.40	.18
		Rick Elder		
❑	218	J.M.Gold	.40	.18
		Ryan Mills RC		
❑	219	Adam Brown	.40	.18
		Choo Freeman RC		
❑	220A	Mark McGwire HR 1	50.00	22.00
❑	220B	Mark McGwire HR 2	20.00	9.00
❑	220C	Mark McGwire HR 3	20.00	9.00
❑	220D	Mark McGwire HR 4	20.00	9.00
❑	220E	Mark McGwire HR 5	20.00	9.00
❑	220F	Mark McGwire HR 6	20.00	9.00
❑	220G	Mark McGwire HR 7	20.00	9.00
❑	220H	Mark McGwire HR 8	20.00	9.00
❑	220I	Mark McGwire HR 9	20.00	9.00
❑	220J	M.McGwire HR 10	20.00	9.00
❑	220K	M.McGwire HR 11	20.00	9.00
❑	220L	M.McGwire HR 12	20.00	9.00
❑	220M	M.McGwire HR 13	20.00	9.00
❑	220N	M.McGwire HR 14	20.00	9.00
❑	220O	M.McGwire HR 15	20.00	9.00
❑	220P	M.McGwire HR 16	20.00	9.00
❑	220Q	M.McGwire HR 17	20.00	9.00
❑	220R	M.McGwire HR 18	20.00	9.00
❑	220S	M.McGwire HR 19	20.00	9.00
❑	220T	M.McGwire HR 20	20.00	9.00
❑	220U	M.McGwire HR 21	20.00	9.00
❑	220V	M.McGwire HR 22	20.00	9.00
❑	220W	M.McGwire HR 23	20.00	9.00
❑	220X	M.McGwire HR 24	20.00	9.00
❑	220Y	M.McGwire HR 25	20.00	9.00
❑	220Z	M.McGwire HR 26	20.00	9.00
❑	220AA	M.McGwire HR 27	20.00	9.00
❑	220AB	M.McGwire HR 28	20.00	9.00
❑	220AC	M.McGwire HR 29	20.00	9.00
❑	220AD	M.McGwire HR 30	20.00	9.00
❑	220AE	M.McGwire HR 31	20.00	9.00
❑	220AF	M.McGwire HR 32	20.00	9.00
❑	220AG	M.McGwire HR 33	20.00	9.00
❑	220AH	M.McGwire HR 34	20.00	9.00
❑	220AI	M.McGwire HR 35	20.00	9.00
❑	220AJ	M.McGwire HR 36	20.00	9.00
❑	220AK	M.McGwire HR 37	20.00	9.00
❑	220AL	M.McGwire HR 38	20.00	9.00
❑	220AM	M.McGwire HR 39	20.00	9.00
❑	220AN	M.McGwire HR 40	20.00	9.00
❑	220AO	M.McGwire HR 41	20.00	9.00
❑	220AP	M.McGwire HR 42	20.00	9.00
❑	220AQ	M.McGwire HR 43	20.00	9.00
❑	220AR	M.McGwire HR 44	20.00	9.00
❑	220AS	M.McGwire HR 45	20.00	9.00
❑	220AT	M.McGwire HR 46	20.00	9.00
❑	220AU	M.McGwire HR 47	20.00	9.00
❑	220AV	M.McGwire HR 48	20.00	9.00
❑	220AW	M.McGwire HR 49	20.00	9.00
❑	220AX	M.McGwire HR 50	20.00	9.00
❑	220AY	M.McGwire HR 51	20.00	9.00
❑	220AZ	M.McGwire HR 52	20.00	9.00
❑	220BB	M.McGwire HR 53	20.00	9.00
❑	220CC	M.McGwire HR 54	20.00	9.00
❑	220DD	M.McGwire HR 55	20.00	9.00
❑	220EE	M.McGwire HR 56	20.00	9.00
❑	220FF	M.McGwire HR 57	20.00	9.00
❑	220GG	M.McGwire HR 58	20.00	9.00
❑	220HH	M.McGwire HR 59	20.00	9.00
❑	220II	M.McGwire HR 60	20.00	9.00
❑	220JJ	M.McGwire HR 61	40.00	18.00
❑	220KK	M.McGwire HR 62	60.00	27.00
❑	220LL	M.McGwire HR 63	20.00	9.00
❑	220MM	M.McGwire HR 64	20.00	9.00
❑	220NN	M.McGwire HR 65	20.00	9.00
❑	220OO	M.McGwire HR 66	20.00	9.00
❑	220PP	M.McGwire HR 67	20.00	9.00
❑	220QQ	M.McGwire HR 68	20.00	9.00
❑	220RR	M.McGwire HR 69	20.00	9.00
❑	220SS	M.McGwire HR 70	125.00	55.00
❑	221	Larry Walker LL	.25	.11
❑	222	Bernie Williams LL	.15	.07
❑	223	Mark McGwire LL	.75	.35
❑	224	Ken Griffey Jr. LL	.60	.25
❑	225	Sammy Sosa LL	.40	.18
❑	226	Juan Gonzalez LL	.15	.07
❑	227	Dante Bichette LL	.10	.05
❑	228	Alex Rodriguez LL	.50	.23
❑	229	Sammy Sosa LL	.40	.18
❑	230	Derek Jeter LL	.75	.35
❑	231	Greg Maddux LL	.50	.23
❑	232	Roger Clemens LL	.50	.23
❑	233	Ricky Ledee WS	.10	.05

Card	Player	Price	Price
❑ 234	Chuck Knoblauch WS	.15	.07
❑ 235	Bernie Williams WS	.15	.07
❑ 236	Tino Martinez WS	.10	.05
❑ 237	Orl. Hernandez WS	.15	.07
❑ 238	Scott Brosius WS	.10	.05
❑ 239	Andy Pettitte WS	.10	.05
❑ 240	Mariano Rivera WS	.15	.07
❑ 241	Checklist 1	.10	.05
❑ 242	Checklist 2	.10	.05
❑ 243	Tom Glavine	.40	.18
❑ 244	Andy Benes	.10	.05
❑ 245	Sandy Alomar Jr.	.15	.07
❑ 246	Wilton Guerrero	.10	.05
❑ 247	Alex Gonzalez	.10	.05
❑ 248	Roberto Alomar	.40	.18
❑ 249	Ruben Rivera	.10	.05
❑ 250	Eric Chavez	.15	.07
❑ 251	Ellis Burks	.15	.07
❑ 252	Richie Sexson	.15	.07
❑ 253	Steve Finley	.15	.07
❑ 254	Dwight Gooden	.15	.07
❑ 255	Dustin Hermanson	.10	.05
❑ 256	Kirk Rueter	.10	.05
❑ 257	Steve Trachsel	.10	.05
❑ 258	Gregg Jefferies	.10	.05
❑ 259	Matt Stairs	.10	.05
❑ 260	Shane Reynolds	.10	.05
❑ 261	Gregg Olson	.10	.05
❑ 262	Kevin Tapani	.10	.05
❑ 263	Matt Morris	.15	.07
❑ 264	Carl Pavano	.10	.05
❑ 265	Nomar Garciaparra	1.00	.45
❑ 266	Kevin Young	.15	.07
❑ 267	Rick Helling	.10	.05
❑ 268	Matt Franco	.10	.05
❑ 269	Brian McRae	.10	.05
❑ 270	Cal Ripken	1.50	.70
❑ 271	Jeff Abbott	.10	.05
❑ 272	Tony Batista	.15	.07
❑ 273	Bill Simas	.10	.05
❑ 274	Brian Hunter	.10	.05
❑ 275	John Franco	.15	.07
❑ 276	Devon White	.10	.05
❑ 277	Rickey Henderson	.75	.35
❑ 278	Chuck Finley	.15	.07
❑ 279	Mike Blowers	.10	.05
❑ 280	Mark Grace	.40	.18
❑ 281	Randy Winn	.10	.05
❑ 282	Bobby Bonilla	.15	.07
❑ 283	David Justice	.15	.07
❑ 284	Shane Monahan	.10	.05
❑ 285	Kevin Brown	.25	.11
❑ 286	Todd Zeile	.15	.07
❑ 287	Al Martin	.10	.05
❑ 288	Troy O'Leary	.10	.05
❑ 289	Darryl Hamilton	.10	.05
❑ 290	Tino Martinez	.15	.07
❑ 291	David Ortiz	.15	.07
❑ 292	Tony Clark	.15	.07
❑ 293	Ryan Minor	.10	.05
❑ 294	Mark Leiter	.10	.05
❑ 295	Wally Joyner	.15	.07
❑ 296	Cliff Floyd	.15	.07
❑ 297	Shawn Estes	.15	.07
❑ 298	Pat Hentgen	.10	.05
❑ 299	Scott Elarton	.10	.05
❑ 300	Alex Rodriguez	1.00	.45
❑ 301	Ozzie Guillen	.10	.05
❑ 302	Hideo Nomo	.40	.18
❑ 303	Ryan McGuire	.10	.05
❑ 304	Brad Ausmus	.10	.05
❑ 305	Alex Gonzalez	.10	.05
❑ 306	Brian Jordan	.15	.07
❑ 307	John Jaha	.10	.05
❑ 308	Mark Grudzielanek	.10	.05
❑ 309	Juan Guzman	.10	.05
❑ 310	Tony Womack	.10	.05
❑ 311	Dennis Reyes	.10	.05
❑ 312	Marty Cordova	.10	.05
❑ 313	Ramiro Mendoza	.10	.05
❑ 314	Robin Ventura	.15	.07
❑ 315	Rafael Palmeiro	.40	.18
❑ 316	Ramon Martinez	.10	.05
❑ 317	Pedro Astacio	.10	.05
❑ 318	Dave Hollins	.10	.05
❑ 319	Tom Candiotti	.10	.05

Card	Player	Price	Price
❑ 320	Al Leiter	.15	.07
❑ 321	Rico Brogna	.10	.05
❑ 322	Reggie Jefferson	.10	.05
❑ 323	Bernard Gilkey	.10	.05
❑ 324	Jason Giambi	.40	.18
❑ 325	Craig Biggio	.25	.11
❑ 326	Troy Glaus	.40	.18
❑ 327	Delino DeShields	.10	.05
❑ 328	Fernando Vina	.10	.05
❑ 329	John Smoltz	.15	.07
❑ 330	Jeff Kent	.25	.11
❑ 331	Roy Halladay	.10	.05
❑ 332	Andy Ashby	.10	.05
❑ 333	Tim Wakefield	.10	.05
❑ 334	Roger Clemens	1.00	.45
❑ 335	Bernie Williams	.40	.18
❑ 336	Desi Relaford	.10	.05
❑ 337	John Burkett	.10	.05
❑ 338	Mike Hampton	.15	.07
❑ 339	Royce Clayton	.10	.05
❑ 340	Mike Piazza	1.00	.45
❑ 341	Jeremi Gonzalez	.10	.05
❑ 342	Mike Lansing	.10	.05
❑ 343	Jamie Moyer	.10	.05
❑ 344	Ron Coomer	.10	.05
❑ 345	Barry Larkin	.40	.18
❑ 346	Fernando Tatis	.10	.05
❑ 347	Chili Davis	.15	.07
❑ 348	Bobby Higginson	.15	.07
❑ 349	Hal Morris	.10	.05
❑ 350	Larry Walker	.25	.11
❑ 351	Carlos Guillen	.10	.05
❑ 352	Miguel Tejada	.15	.07
❑ 353	Travis Fryman	.15	.07
❑ 354	Jarrod Washburn	.10	.05
❑ 355	Chipper Jones	.75	.35
❑ 356	Todd Stottlemyre	.10	.05
❑ 357	Henry Rodriguez	.10	.05
❑ 358	Eli Marrero	.10	.05
❑ 359	Alan Benes	.10	.05
❑ 360	Tim Salmon	.15	.07
❑ 361	Luis Gonzalez	.40	.18
❑ 362	Scott Spiezio	.10	.05
❑ 363	Chris Carpenter	.10	.05
❑ 364	Bobby Howry	.10	.05
❑ 365	Raul Mondesi	.15	.07
❑ 366	Ugueth Urbina	.10	.05
❑ 367	Tom Evans	.10	.05
❑ 368	Kerry Ligtenberg RC	.15	.07
❑ 369	Adrian Beltre	.15	.07
❑ 370	Ryan Klesko	.15	.07
❑ 371	Wilson Alvarez	.10	.05
❑ 372	John Thomson	.10	.05
❑ 373	Tony Saunders	.10	.05
❑ 374	Dave Mlicki	.10	.05
❑ 375	Ken Caminiti	.15	.07
❑ 376	Jay Buhner	.15	.07
❑ 377	Bill Mueller	.10	.05
❑ 378	Jeff Blauser	.10	.05
❑ 379	Edgar Renteria	.10	.05
❑ 380	Jim Thome	.40	.18
❑ 381	Joey Hamilton	.10	.05
❑ 382	Calvin Pickering	.10	.05
❑ 383	Marquis Grissom	.10	.05
❑ 384	Omar Daal	.10	.05
❑ 385	Curt Schilling	.40	.18
❑ 386	Jose Cruz Jr.	.15	.07
❑ 387	Chris Widger	.10	.05
❑ 388	Pete Harnisch	.10	.05
❑ 389	Charles Nagy	.10	.05
❑ 390	Tom Gordon	.10	.05
❑ 391	Bobby Smith	.10	.05
❑ 392	Derrick Gibson	.10	.05
❑ 393	Jeff Conine	.10	.05
❑ 394	Carlos Perez	.10	.05
❑ 395	Barry Bonds	1.00	.45
❑ 396	Mark McLemore	.10	.05
❑ 397	Juan Encarnacion	.15	.07
❑ 398	Wade Boggs	.40	.18
❑ 399	Ivan Rodriguez	.40	.18
❑ 400	Moises Alou	.15	.07
❑ 401	Jeromy Burnitz	.15	.07
❑ 402	Sean Casey	.25	.11
❑ 403	Jose Offerman	.10	.05
❑ 404	Joe Fontenot	.10	.05
❑ 405	Kevin Millwood	.10	.05

Card	Player	Price	Price
❑ 406	Lance Johnson	.10	.05
❑ 407	Richard Hidalgo	.15	.07
❑ 408	Mike Jackson	.10	.05
❑ 409	Brian Anderson	.10	.05
❑ 410	Jeff Shaw	.10	.05
❑ 411	Preston Wilson	.15	.07
❑ 412	Todd Hundley	.10	.05
❑ 413	Jim Parque	.10	.05
❑ 414	Justin Baughman	.10	.05
❑ 415	Dante Bichette	.15	.07
❑ 416	Paul O'Neill	.40	.18
❑ 417	Miguel Cairo	.10	.05
❑ 418	Randy Johnson	.50	.23
❑ 419	Jesus Sanchez	.10	.05
❑ 420	Carlos Delgado	.40	.18
❑ 421	Ricky Ledee	.10	.05
❑ 422	Orlando Hernandez	.15	.07
❑ 423	Frank Thomas	.50	.23
❑ 424	Pokey Reese	.10	.05
❑ 425	Carlos Lee	.15	.07
	Mike Lowell		
	Kit Pellow RC		
❑ 426	Michael Cuddyer	.15	.07
	Mark DeRosa		
	Jerry Hairston Jr.		
❑ 427	Marlon Anderson	.10	.05
	Ron Belliard		
	Orlando Cabrera		
❑ 428	Micah Bowie	.10	.05
	Phil Norton RC		
	Randy Wolf		
❑ 429	Jack Cressend RC	.15	.07
	Jason Rakers		
	John Rocker		
❑ 430	Ruben Mateo	.15	.07
	Scott Morgan		
	Mike Zywica RC		
❑ 431	Jason LaRue	.10	.05
	Matt LeCroy		
	Mitch Meluskey		
❑ 432	Gabe Kapler	.15	.07
	Armando Rios		
	Fernando Seguignol		
❑ 433	Adam Kennedy	.10	.05
	Mickey Lopez RC		
	Jackie Rexrode		
❑ 434	Jose Fernandez RC	.10	.05
	Jeff Liefer		
	Chris Truby		
❑ 435	Corey Koskie	.75	.35
	Doug Mientkiewicz RC		
	Damon Minor		
❑ 436	Roosevelt Brown RC	.40	.18
	Dernell Stenson		
	Vernon Wells		
❑ 437	A.J. Burnett RC	.50	.23
	Billy Koch		
	John Nicholson		
❑ 438	Matt Belisle	.40	.18
	Matt Roney RC		
❑ 439	Austin Kearns	1.25	.55
	Chris George RC		
❑ 440	Nate Bump RC	.60	.25
	Nate Cornejo		
❑ 441	Brad Lidge	.40	.18
	Mike Nannini RC		
❑ 442	Matt Holliday	.40	.18
	Jeff Winchester RC		
❑ 443	Adam Everett	.40	.18
	Chip Ambres RC		
❑ 444	Pat Burrell	1.00	.45
	Eric Valent RC		
❑ 445	Roger Clemens SK	.50	.23
❑ 446	Kerry Wood SK	.15	.07
❑ 447	Curt Schilling SK	.15	.07
❑ 448	Randy Johnson SK	.15	.07
❑ 449	Pedro Martinez SK	.25	.11
❑ 450	Jeff Bagwell AT	.75	.35
	Andres Galarraga		
	Mark McGwire		
❑ 451	John Olerud AT	.15	.07
	Jim Thome		
	Tino Martinez		
❑ 452	Alex Rodriguez AT	.50	.23
	Nomar Garciaparra		
	Derek Jeter		

❑ 453 Vinny Castilla AT .40 .18
Chipper Jones
Scott Rolen
❑ 454 Sammy Sosa AT .60 .25
Ken Griffey Jr.
Juan Gonzalez
❑ 455 Barry Bonds AT .50 .23
Manny Ramirez
Larry Walker
❑ 456 Frank Thomas AT .15 .07
Tim Salmon
David Justice
❑ 457 Travis Lee AT .40 .18
Todd Helton
Ben Grieve
❑ 458 Vladimir Guerrero AT .40 .18
Greg Vaughn
Bernie Williams
❑ 459 Mike Piazza AT .25 .11
Ivan Rodriguez
Jason Kendall
❑ 460 Roger Clemens AT .50 .23
Kerry Wood
Greg Maddux
❑ 461A Sammy Sosa HR 1 20.00 9.00
❑ 461B Sammy Sosa HR 2 8.00 3.60
❑ 461C Sammy Sosa HR 3 8.00 3.60
❑ 461D Sammy Sosa HR 4 8.00 3.60
❑ 461E Sammy Sosa HR 5 8.00 3.60
❑ 461F Sammy Sosa HR 6 8.00 3.60
❑ 461G Sammy Sosa HR 7 8.00 3.60
❑ 461H Sammy Sosa HR 8 8.00 3.60
❑ 461I Sammy Sosa HR 9 8.00 3.60
❑ 461J Sammy Sosa HR 10 8.00 3.60
❑ 461K Sammy Sosa HR 11 8.00 3.60
❑ 461L Sammy Sosa HR 12 8.00 3.60
❑ 461M Sammy Sosa HR 13 8.00 3.60
❑ 461N Sammy Sosa HR 14 8.00 3.60
❑ 461O Sammy Sosa HR 15 8.00 3.60
❑ 461P Sammy Sosa HR 16 8.00 3.60
❑ 461Q Sammy Sosa HR 17 8.00 3.60
❑ 461R Sammy Sosa HR 18 8.00 3.60
❑ 461S Sammy Sosa HR 19 8.00 3.60
❑ 461T Sammy Sosa HR 20 8.00 3.60
❑ 461U Sammy Sosa HR 21 8.00 3.60
❑ 461V Sammy Sosa HR 22 8.00 3.60
❑ 461W Sammy Sosa HR 23 8.00 3.60
❑ 461X Sammy Sosa HR 24 8.00 3.60
❑ 461Y Sammy Sosa HR 25 8.00 3.60
❑ 461Z Sammy Sosa HR 26 8.00 3.60
❑ 461AA S.Sosa HR 27 8.00 3.60
❑ 461AB S.Sosa HR 28 8.00 3.60
❑ 461AC S.Sosa HR 29 8.00 3.60
❑ 461AD S.Sosa HR 30 8.00 3.60
❑ 461AE S.Sosa HR 31 8.00 3.60
❑ 461AF S.Sosa HR 32 8.00 3.60
❑ 461AG S.Sosa HR 33 8.00 3.60
❑ 461AH S.Sosa HR 34 8.00 3.60
❑ 461AI S.Sosa HR 35 8.00 3.60
❑ 461AJ S.Sosa HR 36 8.00 3.60
❑ 461AK S.Sosa HR 37 8.00 3.60
❑ 461AL S.Sosa HR 38 8.00 3.60
❑ 461AM S.Sosa HR 39 8.00 3.60
❑ 461AN S.Sosa HR 40 8.00 3.60
❑ 461AO S.Sosa HR 41 8.00 3.60
❑ 461AP S.Sosa HR 42 8.00 3.60
❑ 461AR S.Sosa HR 43 8.00 3.60
❑ 461AS S.Sosa HR 44 8.00 3.60
❑ 461AT S.Sosa HR 45 8.00 3.60
❑ 461AU S.Sosa HR 46 8.00 3.60
❑ 461AV S.Sosa HR 47 8.00 3.60
❑ 461AW S.Sosa HR 48 8.00 3.60
❑ 461AX S.Sosa HR 49 8.00 3.60
❑ 461AY S.Sosa HR 50 8.00 3.60
❑ 461AZ S.Sosa HR 51 8.00 3.60
❑ 461BB S.Sosa HR 52 8.00 3.60
❑ 461CC S.Sosa HR 53 8.00 3.60
❑ 461DD S.Sosa HR 54 8.00 3.60
❑ 461EE S.Sosa HR 55 8.00 3.60
❑ 461FF S.Sosa HR 56 8.00 3.60
❑ 461GG S.Sosa HR 57 8.00 3.60
❑ 461HH S.Sosa HR 58 8.00 3.60
❑ 461II S.Sosa HR 59 8.00 3.60
❑ 461JJ S.Sosa HR 60 8.00 3.60
❑ 461KK S.Sosa HR 61 20.00 9.00
❑ 461LL S.Sosa HR 62 25.00 11.00
❑ 461MM S.Sosa HR 63 10.00 4.50
❑ 461NN S.Sosa HR 64 10.00 4.50
❑ 461OO S.Sosa HR 65 10.00 4.50
❑ 461PP S.Sosa HR 66 30.00 13.50
❑ 462 Checklist .10 .05
❑ 463 Checklist .10 .05

1999 Topps Traded

	MINT	NRMT
COMP.FACT.SET (122)	40.00	18.00
COMPLETE SET (121)	20.00	9.00

❑ T1 Seth Etherton .15 .07
❑ T2 Mark Harriger RC .10 .05
❑ T3 Matt Wise RC .10 .05
❑ T4 Carlos E. Hernandez RC .15 .07
❑ T5 Julio Lugo RC .60 .25
❑ T6 Mike Nannini .40 .18
❑ T7 Justin Bowles RC .10 .05
❑ T8 Mark Mulder RC 2.00 .90
❑ T9 Roberto Vaz RC .10 .05
❑ T10 Felipe Lopez RC 1.00 .45
❑ T11 Matt Belisle .50 .23
❑ T12 Micah Bowie .10 .05
❑ T13 Ruben Quevedo RC .60 .25
❑ T14 Jose Garcia RC .25 .11
❑ T15 David Kelton RC .75 .35
❑ T16 Phil Norton .15 .07
❑ T17 Corey Patterson RC 1.50 .70
❑ T18 Ron Walker RC .10 .05
❑ T19 Paul Hoover RC .15 .07
❑ T20 Ryan Rupe RC .40 .18
❑ T21 J.D. Closser RC .60 .25
❑ T22 Rob Ryan RC .10 .05
❑ T23 Steve Colyer RC .25 .11
❑ T24 Bubba Crosby RC .15 .07
❑ T25 Luke Prokopec RC .60 .25
❑ T26 Matt Blank RC .15 .07
❑ T27 Josh McKinley .15 .07
❑ T28 Nate Bump .15 .07
❑ T29 G.Chiaramonte RC .40 .18
❑ T30 Arturo McDowell .40 .18
❑ T31 Tony Torcato .60 .25
❑ T32 Dave Roberts RC .10 .05
❑ T33 C.C. Sabathia RC 2.00 .90
❑ T34 Sean Spencer RC .10 .05
❑ T35 Chip Ambres .40 .18
❑ T36 A.J. Burnett .75 .35
❑ T37 Mo Bruce RC .10 .05
❑ T38 Jason Tyner .15 .07
❑ T39 Mamon Tucker .40 .18
❑ T40 Sean Burroughs RC 2.50 1.10
❑ T41 Kevin Eberwein RC .40 .18
❑ T42 Junior Herndon RC .40 .18
❑ T43 Bryan Wolff RC .10 .05
❑ T44 Pat Burrell 1.25 .55
❑ T45 Eric Valent .60 .25
❑ T46 Carlos Pena RC 1.50 .70
❑ T47 Mike Zywica .15 .07
❑ T48 Adam Everett .40 .18
❑ T49 Juan Pena RC .15 .07
❑ T50 Adam Dunn RC 8.00 3.60
❑ T51 Austin Kearns 2.00 .90
❑ T52 Jacobo Sequea RC .25 .11
❑ T53 Choo Freeman .40 .18
❑ T54 Jeff Winchester .15 .07
❑ T55 Matt Burch .15 .07
❑ T56 Chris George .60 .25
❑ T57 Scott Mullen RC .10 .05
❑ T58 Kit Pellow .40 .18
❑ T59 Mark Quinn RC .75 .35
❑ T60 Nate Cornejo 1.00 .45
❑ T61 Ryan Mills .15 .07
❑ T62 Kevin Beirne RC .10 .05
❑ T63 Kip Wells RC .50 .23
❑ T64 Juan Rivera RC 1.25 .55
❑ T65 Alfonso Soriano RC 2.50 1.10
❑ T66 Josh Hamilton RC 2.50 1.10
❑ T67 Josh Girdley RC .40 .18
❑ T68 Kyle Snyder RC .25 .11
❑ T69 Mike Paradis RC .25 .11
❑ T70 Jason Jennings RC .75 .35
❑ T71 David Walling RC .40 .18
❑ T72 Omar Ortiz RC .15 .07
❑ T73 Jay Gehrke RC .15 .07
❑ T74 Casey Burns RC .15 .07
❑ T75 Carl Crawford RC 1.00 .45
❑ T76 Reggie Sanders .10 .05
❑ T77 Will Clark .40 .18
❑ T78 David Wells .15 .07
❑ T79 Paul Konerko .15 .07
❑ T80 Armando Benitez .10 .05
❑ T81 Brant Brown .10 .05
❑ T82 Mo Vaughn .15 .07
❑ T83 Jose Canseco .40 .18
❑ T84 Albert Belle .15 .07
❑ T85 Dean Palmer .15 .07
❑ T86 Greg Vaughn .15 .07
❑ T87 Mark Clark .10 .05
❑ T88 Pat Meares .10 .05
❑ T89 Eric Davis .15 .07
❑ T90 Brian Giles .15 .07
❑ T91 Jeff Brantley .10 .05
❑ T92 Bret Boone .15 .07
❑ T93 Ron Gant .15 .07
❑ T94 Mike Cameron .15 .07
❑ T95 Charles Johnson .15 .07
❑ T96 Denny Neagle .10 .05
❑ T97 Brian Hunter .10 .05
❑ T98 Jose Hernandez .10 .05
❑ T99 Rick Aguilera .10 .05
❑ T100 Tony Batista .15 .07
❑ T101 Roger Cedeno .10 .05
❑ T102 C.Gubanich RC .10 .05
❑ T103 Tim Belcher .10 .05
❑ T104 Bruce Aven .10 .05
❑ T105 Brian Daubach RC .75 .35
❑ T106 Ed Sprague .10 .05
❑ T107 Michael Tucker .10 .05
❑ T108 Homer Bush .10 .05
❑ T109 Armando Reynoso .10 .05
❑ T110 Brook Fordyce .10 .05
❑ T111 Matt Mantei .10 .05
❑ T112 Dave Mlicki .10 .05
❑ T113 Kenny Rogers .10 .05
❑ T114 Livan Hernandez .10 .05
❑ T115 Butch Huskey .10 .05
❑ T116 David Segui .10 .05
❑ T117 Darryl Hamilton .10 .05
❑ T118 Terry Mulholland .10 .05
❑ T119 Randy Velarde .10 .05
❑ T120 Bill Taylor .10 .05
❑ T121 Kevin Appier .15 .07

2000 Topps

	MINT	NRMT
COMPLETE SET (478)	60.00	27.00
COMP.HOBBY SET (478)	60.00	27.00
COMPLETE SERIES 1 (239)	30.00	13.50
COMPLETE SERIES 2 (240)	30.00	13.50
MCGWIRE MM SET (5)	15.00	6.75
AARON MM SET (5)	10.00	4.50
RIPKEN MM SET (5)	15.00	6.75
BOGGS MM SET (5)	5.00	2.20
GWYNN MM SET (5)	8.00	3.60
GRIFFEY MM SET (5)	12.00	5.50
BONDS MM SET (5)	10.00	4.50
SOSA MM SET (5)	8.00	3.60
JETER MM SET (5)	15.00	6.75
A.ROD MM SET (5)	10.00	4.50
❑ 1 Mark McGwire	1.50	.70
❑ 2 Tony Gwynn	.75	.35
❑ 3 Wade Boggs	.40	.18
❑ 4 Cal Ripken	1.50	.70
❑ 5 Matt Williams	.25	.11
❑ 6 Jay Buhner	.15	.07
❑ 7 Does Not Exist	.10	.05
❑ 8 Jeff Conine	.10	.05
❑ 9 Todd Greene	.10	.05
❑ 10 Mike Lieberthal	.15	.07
❑ 11 Steve Avery	.10	.05
❑ 12 Bret Saberhagen	.15	.07
❑ 13 Maggiio Ordonez	.15	.07
❑ 14 Brad Radke	.15	.07
❑ 15 Derek Jeter	1.50	.70
❑ 16 Javy Lopez	.15	.07
❑ 17 Russ Davis	.10	.05
❑ 18 Armando Benitez	.15	.07
❑ 19 B.J. Surhoff	.15	.07
❑ 20 Darryl Kile	.15	.07
❑ 21 Mark Lewis	.10	.05
❑ 22 Mike Williams	.10	.05
❑ 23 Mark McLemore	.10	.05
❑ 24 Sterling Hitchcock	.10	.05
❑ 25 Darin Erstad	.40	.18
❑ 26 Ricky Gutierrez	.10	.05
❑ 27 John Jaha	.10	.05
❑ 28 Homer Bush	.10	.05
❑ 29 Darrin Fletcher	.10	.05
❑ 30 Mark Grace	.40	.18
❑ 31 Fred McGriff	.25	.11
❑ 32 Omar Daal	.10	.05
❑ 33 Eric Karros	.15	.07
❑ 34 Orlando Cabrera	.10	.05
❑ 35 J.T. Snow	.15	.07
❑ 36 Luis Castillo	.10	.05
❑ 37 Rey Ordonez	.10	.05
❑ 38 Bob Abreu	.15	.07
❑ 39 Warren Morris	.10	.05
❑ 40 Juan Gonzalez	.40	.18
❑ 41 Mike Lansing	.10	.05
❑ 42 Chili Davis	.15	.07
❑ 43 Dean Palmer	.15	.07
❑ 44 Hank Aaron	.75	.35
❑ 45 Jeff Bagwell	.50	.23
❑ 46 Jose Valentin	.10	.05
❑ 47 Shannon Stewart	.15	.07
❑ 48 Kent Bottenfield	.10	.05
❑ 49 Jeff Shaw	.10	.05
❑ 50 Sammy Sosa	.75	.35
❑ 51 Randy Johnson	.50	.23
❑ 52 Benny Agbayani	.10	.05
❑ 53 Dante Bichette	.15	.07
❑ 54 Pete Harnisch	.10	.05
❑ 55 Frank Thomas	.50	.23
❑ 56 Jorge Posada	.15	.07
❑ 57 Todd Walker	.10	.05
❑ 58 Juan Encarnacion	.15	.07
❑ 59 Mike Sweeney	.15	.07
❑ 60 Pedro Martinez	.50	.23
❑ 61 Lee Stevens	.10	.05
❑ 62 Brian Giles	.15	.07
❑ 63 Chad Ogea	.10	.05
❑ 64 Ivan Rodriguez	.40	.18
❑ 65 Roger Cedeno	.10	.05
❑ 66 David Justice	.15	.07
❑ 67 Steve Trachsel	.10	.05
❑ 68 Eli Marrero	.10	.05
❑ 69 Dave Nilsson	.10	.05
❑ 70 Ken Caminiti	.15	.07
❑ 71 Tim Raines	.15	.07
❑ 72 Brian Jordan	.15	.07
❑ 73 Jeff Blauser	.10	.05
❑ 74 Bernard Gilkey	.10	.05
❑ 75 John Flaherty	.10	.05
❑ 76 Brent Mayne	.10	.05
❑ 77 Jose Vidro	.15	.07
❑ 78 David Bell	.10	.05
❑ 79 Bruce Aven	.10	.05
❑ 80 John Olerud	.15	.07
❑ 81 Pokey Reese	.10	.05
❑ 82 Woody Williams	.10	.05
❑ 83 Ed Sprague	.10	.05
❑ 84 Joe Girardi	.10	.05
❑ 85 Barry Larkin	.40	.18
❑ 86 Mike Caruso	.10	.05
❑ 87 Bobby Higginson	.10	.05
❑ 88 Roberto Kelly	.10	.05
❑ 89 Edgar Martinez	.25	.11
❑ 90 Mark Kotsay	.10	.05
❑ 91 Paul Sorrento	.10	.05
❑ 92 Eric Young	.10	.05
❑ 93 Carlos Delgado	.40	.18
❑ 94 Troy Glaus	.40	.18
❑ 95 Ben Grieve	.15	.07
❑ 96 Jose Lima	.10	.05
❑ 97 Garret Anderson	.15	.07
❑ 98 Luis Gonzalez	.40	.18
❑ 99 Carl Pavano	.10	.05
❑ 100 Alex Rodriguez	1.00	.45
❑ 101 Preston Wilson	.15	.07
❑ 102 Ron Gant	.15	.07
❑ 103 Brady Anderson	.15	.07
❑ 104 Rickey Henderson	.75	.35
❑ 105 Gary Sheffield	.15	.07
❑ 106 Mickey Morandini	.10	.05
❑ 107 Jim Edmonds	.25	.11
❑ 108 Kris Benson	.15	.07
❑ 109 Adrian Beltre	.15	.07
❑ 110 Alex Fernandez	.10	.05
❑ 111 Dan Wilson	.10	.05
❑ 112 Mark Clark	.10	.05
❑ 113 Greg Vaughn	.15	.07
❑ 114 Neifi Perez	.10	.05
❑ 115 Paul O'Neill	.40	.18
❑ 116 Jermaine Dye	.15	.07
❑ 117 Todd Jones	.10	.05
❑ 118 Terry Steinbach	.10	.05
❑ 119 Greg Norton	.10	.05
❑ 120 Curt Schilling	.40	.18
❑ 121 Todd Zeile	.15	.07
❑ 122 Edgardo Alfonzo	.15	.07
❑ 123 Ryan McGuire	.10	.05
❑ 124 Rich Aurilia	.15	.07
❑ 125 John Smoltz	.15	.07
❑ 126 Bob Wickman	.10	.05
❑ 127 Richard Hidalgo	.15	.07
❑ 128 Chuck Finley	.15	.07
❑ 129 Billy Wagner	.10	.05
❑ 130 Todd Hundley	.10	.05
❑ 131 Dwight Gooden	.15	.07
❑ 132 Russ Ortiz	.15	.07
❑ 133 Mike Lowell	.10	.05
❑ 134 Reggie Sanders	.10	.05
❑ 135 John Valentin	.10	.05
❑ 136 Brad Ausmus	.10	.05
❑ 137 Chad Kreuter	.10	.05
❑ 138 David Cone	.15	.07
❑ 139 Brook Fordyce	.10	.05
❑ 140 Roberto Alomar	.40	.18
❑ 141 Charles Nagy	.10	.05
❑ 142 Brian Hunter	.10	.05
❑ 143 Mike Mussina	.40	.18
❑ 144 Robin Ventura	.25	.11
❑ 145 Kevin Brown	.25	.11
❑ 146 Pat Hentgen	.10	.05
❑ 147 Ryan Klesko	.15	.07
❑ 148 Derek Bell	.10	.05
❑ 149 Andy Sheets	.10	.05
❑ 150 Larry Walker	.25	.11
❑ 151 Scott Williamson	.10	.05
❑ 152 Jose Offerman	.10	.05
❑ 153 Doug Mientkiewicz	.25	.11
❑ 154 John Snyder RC	.25	.11
❑ 155 Sandy Alomar Jr.	.10	.05
❑ 156 Joe Nathan	.10	.05
❑ 157 Lance Johnson	.10	.05
❑ 158 Odalis Perez	.10	.05
❑ 159 Hideo Nomo	.40	.18
❑ 160 Steve Finley	.15	.07
❑ 161 Dave Martinez	.10	.05
❑ 162 Matt Walbeck	.10	.05
❑ 163 Bill Spiers	.10	.05
❑ 164 Fernando Tatis	.10	.05
❑ 165 Kenny Lofton	.15	.07
❑ 166 Paul Byrd	.10	.05
❑ 167 Aaron Sele	.15	.07
❑ 168 Eddie Taubensee	.10	.05
❑ 169 Reggie Jefferson	.10	.05
❑ 170 Roger Clemens	1.00	.45
❑ 171 Francisco Cordova	.10	.05
❑ 172 Mike Bordick	.10	.05
❑ 173 Wally Joyner	.15	.07
❑ 174 Marvin Benard	.10	.05
❑ 175 Jason Kendall	.15	.07
❑ 176 Mike Stanley	.10	.05
❑ 177 Chad Allen	.10	.05
❑ 178 Carlos Beltran	.15	.07
❑ 179 Deivi Cruz	.10	.05
❑ 180 Chipper Jones	.75	.35
❑ 181 Vladimir Guerrero	.50	.23
❑ 182 Dave Burba	.10	.05
❑ 183 Tom Goodwin	.10	.05
❑ 184 Brian Daubach	.15	.07
❑ 185 Jay Bell	.15	.07
❑ 186 Roy Halladay	.10	.05
❑ 187 Migue; Tejada	.15	.07
❑ 188 Armando Rios	.10	.05
❑ 189 Fernando Vina	.10	.05
❑ 190 Eric Davis	.15	.07
❑ 191 Henry Rodriguez	.10	.05
❑ 192 Joe McEwing	.10	.05
❑ 193 Jeff Kent	.25	.11
❑ 194 Mike Jackson	.10	.05
❑ 195 Mike Morgan	.10	.05
❑ 196 Jeff Montgomery	.10	.05
❑ 197 Jeff Zimmerman	.10	.05
❑ 198 Tony Fernandez	.10	.05
❑ 199 Jason Giambi	.40	.18
❑ 200 Jose Canseco	.40	.18
❑ 201 Alex Gonzalez	.10	.05
❑ 202 Jack Cust	.15	.07
Mike Colangelo		
Dee Brown		
❑ 203 Felipe Lopez	.40	.18
Alfonso Soriano		
Pablo Ozuna		
❑ 204 Erubiel Durazo	.40	.18
Pat Burrell		
Nick Johnson		
❑ 205 John Sneed RC	.25	.11
Kip Wells		
Matt Blank		
❑ 206 Josh Kalinowski	.25	.11
Michael Tejera		
Chris Mears RC		
❑ 207 Roosevelt Brown	.40	.18
Corey Patterson		
Lance Berkman		
❑ 208 Kit Pellow	.10	.05
Kevin Barker		
Russ Branyan		
❑ 209 B.J. Garbe	.75	.35
Larry Bigbie RC		
❑ 210 Eric Munson	.60	.25
Bobby Bradley RC		
❑ 211 Josh Girdley	.15	.07
Kyle Snyder		
❑ 212 Chance Caple RC	.40	.18
Jason Jennings		
❑ 213 Ryan Christianson	.60	.25
Brett Myers RC		
❑ 214 Jason Stumm	.40	.18
Rob Purvis RC		
❑ 215 David Walling	.10	.05
Mike Paradis		
❑ 216 Omar Ortiz	.10	.05
Jay Gehrke		
❑ 217 David Cone HL	.15	.07
❑ 218 Jose Jimenez HL	.10	.05
❑ 219 Chris Singleton HL	.10	.05
❑ 220 Fernando Tatis HL	.10	.05

❑	221	Todd Helton HL	.40	.18
❑	222	Kevin Millwood DIV	.10	.05
❑	223	Todd Pratt DIV	.10	.05
❑	224	Orl.Hernandez DIV	.10	.05
❑	225	Pedro Martinez DIV	.50	.23
❑	226	Tom Glavine LCS	.15	.07
❑	227	Bernie Williams LCS	.15	.07
❑	228	Mariano Rivera WS	.10	.05
❑	229	Tony Gwynn 20CB	.75	.35
❑	230	Wade Boggs 20CB	.40	.18
❑	231	Lance Johnson CB	.10	.05
❑	232	Mark McGwire 20CB	1.50	.70
❑	233	R.Henderson 20CB	.75	.35
❑	234	R.Henderson 20CB	.75	.35
❑	235	Roger Clemens 20CB	1.00	.45
❑	236A	M.McGwire MM 1st HR	4.00	1.80
❑	236B	M.McGwire MM 1987 ROY	4.00	1.80
❑	236C	M.McGwire MM 62nd HR	4.00	1.80
❑	236D	M.McGwire MM 70th HR	4.00	1.80
❑	236E	M.McGwire MM 500th HR	4.00	1.80
❑	237A	H.Aaron MM 1st Career HR	2.00	.90
❑	237B	H.Aaron MM 1957 MVP	2.00	.90
❑	237C	H.Aaron MM 3000th Hit	2.00	.90
❑	237D	H.Aaron MM 715th HR	2.00	.90
❑	237E	H.Aaron MM 755th HR	2.00	.90
❑	238A	C.Ripken MM 1982 ROY	4.00	1.80
❑	238B	C.Ripken MM 1991 MVP	4.00	1.80
❑	238C	C.Ripken MM 2131 Game	4.00	1.80
❑	238D	C.Ripken MM Streak Ends	4.00	1.80
❑	238E	C.Ripken MM 400th HR	4.00	1.80
❑	239A	W.Boggs MM 1983 Batting	1.25	.55
❑	239B	W.Boggs MM 1988 Batting	1.25	.55
❑	239C	W.Boggs MM 2000th Hit	1.25	.55
❑	239D	W.Boggs MM 1996 Champs	1.25	.55
❑	239E	W.Boggs MM 3000th Hit	1.25	.55
❑	240A	T.Gwynn MM 1984 Batting	2.00	.90
❑	240B	T.Gwynn MM 1984 NLCS	2.00	.90
❑	240C	T.Gwynn MM 1995 Batting	2.00	.90
❑	240D	T.Gwynn MM 1998 NLCS	2.00	.90
❑	240E	T.Gwynn MM 3000th Hit	2.00	.90
❑	241	Tom Glavine	.40	.18
❑	242	David Wells	.15	.07
❑	243	Kevin Appier	.10	.05
❑	244	Troy Percival	.10	.05
❑	245	Ray Lankford	.10	.05
❑	246	Marquis Grissom	.10	.05
❑	247	Randy Winn	.10	.05
❑	248	Miguel Batista	.10	.05
❑	249	Darren Dreifort	.10	.05
❑	250	Barry Bonds	1.00	.45
❑	251	Harold Baines	.15	.07
❑	252	Cliff Floyd	.15	.07
❑	253	Freddy Garcia	.25	.11
❑	254	Kenny Rogers	.10	.05
❑	255	Ben Davis		
❑	256	Charles Johnson	.15	.07
❑	257	Bubba Trammell	.10	.05
❑	258	Desi Relaford	.10	.05
❑	259	Al Martin	.10	.05
❑	260	Andy Pettitte	.15	.07
❑	261	Carlos Lee	.15	.07
❑	262	Matt Lawton	.10	.05
❑	263	Andy Fox	.10	.05
❑	264	Chan Ho Park	.15	.07
❑	265	Billy Koch	.10	.05
❑	266	Dave Roberts	.10	.05
❑	267	Carl Everett	.15	.07
❑	268	Orel Hershiser	.15	.07
❑	269	Trot Nixon	.15	.07
❑	270	Rusty Greer	.15	.07
❑	271	Will Clark	.40	.18
❑	272	Quilvio Veras	.10	.05
❑	273	Rico Brogna	.10	.05
❑	274	Devon White	.10	.05
❑	275	Tim Hudson	.40	.18
❑	276	Mike Hampton	.15	.07
❑	277	Miguel Cairo	.10	.05
❑	278	Darren Oliver	.10	.05
❑	279	Jeff Cirillo	.15	.07
❑	280	Al Leiter	.10	.05
❑	281	Shane Andrews	.10	.05
❑	282	Carlos Febles	.10	.05
❑	283	Pedro Astacio	.10	.05
❑	284	Juan Guzman	.10	.05
❑	285	Orlando Hernandez	.15	.07
❑	286	Paul Konerko	.15	.07
❑	287	Tony Clark	.15	.07
❑	288	Aaron Boone	.10	.05
❑	289	Ismael Valdes	.10	.05
❑	290	Moises Alou	.15	.07
❑	291	Kevin Tapani	.10	.05
❑	292	John Franco	.15	.07
❑	293	Todd Zeile	.15	.07
❑	294	Jason Schmidt	.10	.05
❑	295	Johnny Damon	.15	.07
❑	296	Scott Brosius	.15	.07
❑	297	Travis Fryman	.15	.07
❑	298	Jose Vizcaino	.10	.05
❑	299	Eric Chavez	.15	.07
❑	300	Mike Piazza	1.00	.45
❑	301	Matt Clement	.10	.05
❑	302	Cristian Guzman	.15	.07
❑	303	C.J. Nitkowski	.10	.05
❑	304	Michael Tucker	.10	.05
❑	305	Brett Tomko	.10	.05
❑	306	Mike Lansing	.10	.05
❑	307	Eric Owens	.10	.05
❑	308	Livan Hernandez	.10	.05
❑	309	Rondell White	.15	.07
❑	310	Todd Stottlemyre	.10	.05
❑	311	Chris Carpenter	.10	.05
❑	312	Ken Hill	.10	.05
❑	313	Mark Loretta	.10	.05
❑	314	John Rocker	.15	.07
❑	315	Richie Sexson	.15	.07
❑	316	Ruben Mateo	.15	.07
❑	317	Joe Randa	.10	.05
❑	318	Mike Sirotka	.10	.05
❑	319	Jose Rosado	.10	.05
❑	320	Matt Mantei	.10	.05
❑	321	Kevin Millwood	.10	.05
❑	322	Gary DiSarcina	.10	.05
❑	323	Dustin Hermanson	.10	.05
❑	324	Mike Stanton	.10	.05
❑	325	Kirk Rueter	.10	.05
❑	326	Damian Miller	.10	.05
❑	327	Doug Glanville	.10	.05
❑	328	Scott Rolen	.40	.18
❑	329	Ray Durham	.15	.07
❑	330	Butch Huskey	.10	.05
❑	331	Mariano Rivera	.15	.07
❑	332	Darren Lewis	.10	.05
❑	333	Mike Timlin	.10	.05
❑	334	Mark Grudzielanek	.10	.05
❑	335	Mike Cameron	.15	.07
❑	336	Kelvim Escobar	.10	.05
❑	337	Bret Boone	.15	.07
❑	338	Mo Vaughn	.15	.07
❑	339	Craig Biggio	.25	.11
❑	340	Michael Barrett	.10	.05
❑	341	Marlon Anderson	.10	.05
❑	342	Bobby Jones	.10	.05
❑	343	John Halama	.10	.05
❑	344	Todd Ritchie	.10	.05
❑	345	Chuck Knoblauch	.15	.07
❑	346	Rick Reed	.10	.05
❑	347	Kelly Stinnett	.10	.05
❑	348	Tim Salmon	.15	.07
❑	349	A.J. Hinch	.10	.05
❑	350	Jose Cruz Jr.	.15	.07
❑	351	Roberto Hernandez	.10	.05
❑	352	Edgar Renteria	.10	.05
❑	353	Jose Hernandez	.10	.05
❑	354	Brad Fullmer	.15	.07
❑	355	Trevor Hoffman	.15	.07
❑	356	Troy O'Leary	.10	.05
❑	357	Justin Thompson	.10	.05
❑	358	Kevin Young	.10	.05
❑	359	Hideki Irabu	.10	.05
❑	360	Jim Thome	.40	.18
❑	361	Steve Karsay	.10	.05
❑	362	Octavio Dotel	.10	.05
❑	363	Omar Vizquel	.15	.07
❑	364	Raul Mondesi	.15	.07
❑	365	Shane Reynolds	.10	.05
❑	366	Bartolo Colon	.15	.07
❑	367	Chris Widger	.10	.05
❑	368	Gabe Kapler	.15	.07
❑	369	Bill Simas	.10	.05
❑	370	Tino Martinez	.15	.07
❑	371	John Thomson	.10	.05
❑	372	Delino DeShields	.10	.05
❑	373	Carlos Perez	.10	.05
❑	374	Eddie Perez	.10	.05
❑	375	Jeromy Burnitz	.15	.07
❑	376	Jimmy Haynes	.10	.05
❑	377	Travis Lee	.10	.05
❑	378	Darryl Hamilton	.10	.05
❑	379	Jamie Moyer	.10	.05
❑	380	Alex Gonzalez	.10	.05
❑	381	John Wetteland	.15	.07
❑	382	Vinny Castilla	.15	.07
❑	383	Jeff Suppan	.10	.05
❑	384	Jim Leyritz	.10	.05
❑	385	Robb Nen	.10	.05
❑	386	Wilson Alvarez	.10	.05
❑	387	Andres Galarraga	.25	.11
❑	388	Mike Remlinger	.10	.05
❑	389	Geoff Jenkins	.15	.07
❑	390	Matt Stairs	.10	.05
❑	391	Bill Mueller	.10	.05
❑	392	Mike Lowell	.10	.05
❑	393	Andy Ashby	.10	.05
❑	394	Ruben Rivera	.10	.05
❑	395	Todd Helton	.50	.23
❑	396	Bernie Williams	.40	.18
❑	397	Royce Clayton	.10	.05
❑	398	Manny Ramirez	.50	.23
❑	399	Kerry Wood	.40	.18
❑	400	Ken Griffey Jr.	1.25	.55
❑	401	Enrique Wilson	.10	.05
❑	402	Joey Hamilton	.10	.05
❑	403	Shawn Estes	.15	.07
❑	404	Ugueth Urbina	.10	.05
❑	405	Albert Belle	.15	.07
❑	406	Rick Helling	.10	.05
❑	407	Steve Parris	.10	.05
❑	408	Eric Milton	.15	.07
❑	409	Dave Mlicki	.10	.05
❑	410	Shawn Green	.40	.18
❑	411	Jaret Wright	.10	.05
❑	412	Tony Womack	.10	.05
❑	413	Vernon Wells	.15	.07
❑	414	Ron Belliard	.10	.05
❑	415	Ellis Burks	.15	.07
❑	416	Scott Erickson	.10	.05
❑	417	Rafael Palmeiro	.40	.18
❑	418	Damion Easley	.10	.05
❑	419	Jamey Wright	.10	.05
❑	420	Corey Koskie	.15	.07
❑	421	Bobby Howry	.10	.05
❑	422	Ricky Ledee	.10	.05
❑	423	Dmitri Young	.15	.07
❑	424	Sidney Ponson	.10	.05
❑	425	Greg Maddux	1.00	.45
❑	426	Jose Guillen	.10	.05
❑	427	Jon Lieber	.10	.05
❑	428	Andy Benes	.10	.05
❑	429	Randy Velarde	.10	.05
❑	430	Sean Casey	.25	.11
❑	431	Torii Hunter	.15	.07
❑	432	Ryan Rupe	.10	.05
❑	433	David Segui	.10	.05

❑ 434 Todd Pratt .10 .05
❑ 435 Nomar Garciaparra 1.00 .45
❑ 436 Denny Neagle .10 .05
❑ 437 Ron Coomer .10 .05
❑ 438 Chris Singleton .10 .05
❑ 439 Tony Batista .15 .07
❑ 440 Andruw Jones .40 .18
❑ 441 Aubrey Huff .40 .18
Sean Burroughs
Adam Piatt
❑ 442 Rafael Furcal .40 .18
Travis Dawkins
Jason Dellaero
❑ 443 Mike Lamb RC .40 .18
Joe Crede
Wilton Veras
❑ 444 Julio Zuleta RC .40 .18
Jorge Toca
Dernell Stenson
❑ 445 Garry Maddox Jr. RC .25 .11
Gary Matthews Jr.
Tim Raines Jr.
❑ 446 Mark Mulder .40 .18
C.C. Sabathia
Matt Riley
❑ 447 Scott Downs RC .25 .11
Chris George
Matt Belisle
❑ 448 Doug Mirabelli .10 .05
Ben Petrick
Jayson Werth
❑ 449 Josh Hamilton .50 .23
Corey Myers RC
❑ 450 Ben Christensen RC .40 .18
Richard Stahl RC
❑ 451 Ben Sheets RC 2.00 .90
Barry Zito
❑ 452 Kurt Ainsworth 1.00 .45
Ty Howington RC
❑ 453 Vince Faison RC .50 .23
Rick Asadoorian
❑ 454 Keith Reed RC .75 .35
Jeff Heaverlo
❑ 455 Mike MacDougal .60 .25
Brad Baker RC
❑ 456 Mark McGwire SH .75 .35
❑ 457 Cal Ripken SH .75 .35
❑ 458 Wade Boggs SH .15 .07
❑ 459 Tony Gwynn SH .40 .18
❑ 460 Jesse Orosco SH .10 .05
❑ 461 Larry Walker .25 .11
Nomar Garciaparra LL
❑ 462 Ken Griffey Jr. .60 .25
Mark McGwire LL
❑ 463 Manny Ramirez .50 .23
Mark McGwire LL
❑ 464 Pedro Martinez .25 .11
Randy Johnson LL
❑ 465 Pedro Martinez .25 .11
Randy Johnson LL
❑ 466 Derek Jeter .50 .23
Luis Gonzalez LL
❑ 467 Larry Walker .25 .11
Manny Ramirez LL
❑ 468 Tony Gwynn 20CB .75 .35
❑ 469 Mark McGwire 20CB 1.50 .70
❑ 470 Frank Thomas 20CB .50 .23
❑ 471 Harold Baines 20CB .15 .07
❑ 472 Roger Clemens 20CB 1.00 .45
❑ 473 John Franco 20CB .15 .07
❑ 474 John Franco 20CB .15 .07
❑ 475A K.Griffey Jr. MM 3.00 1.35
350th HR
❑ 475B K.Griffey Jr. MM 3.00 1.35
1997 MVP
❑ 475C K.Griffey Jr. MM 3.00 1.35
HR Dad
❑ 475D K.Griffey Jr. MM 3.00 1.35
1992 AS MVP
❑ 475E K.Griffey Jr. MM 3.00 1.35
50 HR 1997
❑ 476A B.Bonds MM 2.50 1.10
400HR/400SB
❑ 476B B.Bonds MM 2.50 1.10
40HR/40SB
❑ 476C B.Bonds MM 2.50 1.10
1993 MVP
❑ 476D B.Bonds MM 2.50 1.10
1990 MVP
❑ 476E B.Bonds MM 2.50 1.10
1992 MVP
❑ 477A S.Sosa MM 2.00 .90
20 HR June
❑ 477B S.Sosa MM 2.00 .90
66 HR 1998
❑ 477C S.Sosa MM 2.00 .90
60 HR 1999
❑ 477D S.Sosa MM 2.00 .90
1998 MVP
❑ 477E S.Sosa MM HR's 2.00 .90
61/62
❑ 478A D.Jeter MM 4.00 1.80
1996 ROY
❑ 478B D.Jeter MM 4.00 1.80
Wins 1999 WS
❑ 478C D.Jeter MM 4.00 1.80
Wins 1998 WS
❑ 478D D.Jeter MM 4.00 1.80
Wins 1996 WS
❑ 478E D.Jeter MM 4.00 1.80
17 GM Hit Streak
❑ 479A A.Rodriguez MM 2.50 1.10
40HR/40SB
❑ 479B A.Rodriguez MM 2.50 1.10
100th HR
❑ 479C A.Rodriguez MM 2.50 1.10
1996 POY
❑ 479D A.Rodriguez MM 2.50 1.10
Wins 1 Million
❑ 479E A.Rodriguez MM 2.50 1.10
1996 Batting Leader
❑ NNO Mark McGwire 85 Reprint 6.00 2.70

2000 Topps Limited

	MINT	NRMT
COMP.FACT.SET (619)	200.00	90.00
COMPLETE SET (478)	150.00	70.00

*STARS: 2.5X TO 6X BASIC CARDS
*ROOKIES: 5X TO 10X BASIC CARDS
*MAGIC MOMENTS: 1.25X TO 3X BASIC MM

2000 Topps Traded

	MINT	NRMT
COMP.FACT.SET (136)	30.00	13.50
COMPLETE SET (135)	20.00	9.00

❑ T1 Mike MacDougal .25 .11
❑ T2 Andy Tracy RC .25 .11
❑ T3 Brandon Phillips RC .60 .25
❑ T4 Brandon Inge RC .60 .25
❑ T5 Robbie Morrison RC .25 .11
❑ T6 Josh Pressley RC .25 .11
❑ T7 Todd Moser RC .25 .11
❑ T8 Rob Purvis .25 .11
❑ T9 Chance Caple .25 .11
❑ T10 Ben Sheets 1.00 .45
❑ T11 Russ Jacobson RC .25 .11
❑ T12 Brian Cole RC .25 .11
❑ T13 Brad Baker .60 .25
❑ T14 Alex Cintron RC .40 .18
❑ T15 Lyle Overbay RC .75 .35
❑ T16 Mike Edwards RC .25 .11
❑ T17 Sean McGowan RC .40 .18
❑ T18 Jose Molina .15 .07
❑ T19 Marcos Castillo RC .25 .11
❑ T20 Josue Espada RC .25 .11
❑ T21 Alex Gordon RC .50 .23
❑ T22 Rob Pugmire RC .25 .11
❑ T23 Jason Stumm .40 .18
❑ T24 Ty Howington .60 .25
❑ T25 Brett Myers .40 .18
❑ T26 Maicer Izturis RC .25 .11
❑ T27 John McDonald .15 .07
❑ T28 W.Rodriguez RC .50 .23
❑ T29 Carlos Zambrano RC .60 .25
❑ T30 Alejandro Diaz RC .25 .11
❑ T31 Geraldo Guzman RC .25 .11
❑ T32 J.R. House RC 2.50 1.10
❑ T33 Elvin Nina RC .25 .11
❑ T34 Juan Pierre RC .75 .35
❑ T35 Ben Johnson RC .60 .25
❑ T36 Jeff Bailey RC .25 .11
❑ T37 Miguel Olivo RC .40 .18
❑ T38 F.Rodriguez RC .40 .18
❑ T39 Tony Pena Jr. RC .40 .18
❑ T40 Miguel Cabrera RC 1.00 .45
❑ T41 Asdrubal Oropeza RC .25 .11
❑ T42 Junior Zamora RC .25 .11
❑ T43 Jovanny Cedeno RC .60 .25
❑ T44 John Sneed .25 .11
❑ T45 Josh Kalinowski .25 .11
❑ T46 Mike Young RC .60 .25
❑ T47 Rico Washington RC .40 .18
❑ T48 Chad Durbin RC .25 .11
❑ T49 Junior Brignac RC .25 .11
❑ T50 Carlos Hernandez RC 1.25 .55
❑ T51 Cesar Izturis RC .50 .23
❑ T52 Oscar Salazar RC .50 .23
❑ T53 Pat Strange RC .60 .25
❑ T54 Rick Asadoorian .50 .23
❑ T55 Keith Reed .60 .25
❑ T56 Leo Estrella RC .25 .11
❑ T57 Wascar Serrano RC .40 .18
❑ T58 Richard Gomez RC .50 .23
❑ T59 Ramon Santiago RC .50 .23
❑ T60 Jovanny Sosa RC .40 .18
❑ T61 Aaron Rowand RC .60 .25
❑ T62 Junior Guerrero RC .25 .11
❑ T63 Luis Terrero RC .40 .18
❑ T64 Brian Sanches RC .25 .11
❑ T65 Scott Sobkowiak RC .40 .18
❑ T66 Gary Majewski RC .40 .18
❑ T67 Barry Zito 1.25 .55
❑ T68 Ryan Christianson .60 .25
❑ T69 Cristian Guerrero RC 2.50 1.10
❑ T70 T.De La Rosa RC .25 .11
❑ T71 Andrew Beinbrink RC .25 .11
❑ T72 Ryan Knox RC .40 .18
❑ T73 Alex Graman RC .50 .23
❑ T74 Juan Guzman RC .25 .11
❑ T75 Ruben Salazar RC .60 .25
❑ T76 Luis Matos RC .25 .11
❑ T77 Tony Mota RC .25 .11
❑ T78 Doug Davis .15 .07
❑ T79 Ben Christensen .25 .11
❑ T80 Mike Lamb .40 .18
❑ T81 Adrian Gonzalez RC 2.50 1.10
❑ T82 Mike Stodolka RC .50 .23
❑ T83 Adam Johnson RC .60 .25
❑ T84 Matt Wheatland RC .50 .23
❑ T85 Corey Smith RC .75 .35
❑ T86 Rocco Baldelli RC .60 .25

❑ T87 Keith Bucktrot RC .40 .18
❑ T88 Adam Wainwright RC .75 .35
❑ T89 Scott Thorman RC .50 .23
❑ T90 Tripper Johnson RC .50 .23
❑ T91 Jim Edmonds .40 .18
❑ T92 Masato Yoshii .15 .07
❑ T93 Adam Kennedy .15 .07
❑ T94 Darryl Kile .25 .11
❑ T95 Mark McLemore .15 .07
❑ T96 Ricky Gutierrez .15 .07
❑ T97 Juan Gonzalez .60 .25
❑ T98 Melvin Mora .15 .07
❑ T99 Dante Bichette .25 .11
❑ T100 Lee Stevens .15 .07
❑ T101 Roger Cedeno .15 .07
❑ T102 John Olerud .25 .11
❑ T103 Eric Young .15 .07
❑ T104 Mickey Morandini .15 .07
❑ T105 Travis Lee .15 .07
❑ T106 Greg Vaughn .25 .11
❑ T107 Todd Zeile .25 .11
❑ T108 Chuck Finley .25 .11
❑ T109 Ismael Valdes .15 .07
❑ T110 Reggie Sanders .15 .07
❑ T111 Pat Hentgen .15 .07
❑ T112 Ryan Klesko .25 .11
❑ T113 Derek Bell .15 .07
❑ T114 Hideo Nomo .60 .25
❑ T115 Aaron Sele .25 .11
❑ T116 Fernando Vina .15 .07
❑ T117 Wally Joyner .25 .11
❑ T118 Brian Hunter .15 .07
❑ T119 Joe Girardi .15 .07
❑ T120 Omar Daal .15 .07
❑ T121 Brook Fordyce .15 .07
❑ T122 Jose Valentin .15 .07
❑ T123 Curt Schilling .60 .25
❑ T124 B.J. Surhoff .25 .11
❑ T125 Henry Rodriguez .15 .07
❑ T126 Mike Bordick .15 .07
❑ T127 David Justice .25 .11
❑ T128 Charles Johnson .25 .11
❑ T129 Will Clark .60 .25
❑ T130 Dwight Gooden .25 .11
❑ T131 David Segui .15 .07
❑ T132 Denny Neagle .25 .11
❑ T133 Jose Canseco .60 .25
❑ T134 Bruce Chen .15 .07
❑ T135 Jason Bere .15 .07

2001 Topps

	MINT	NRMT
COMPLETE SET (790)	80.00	36.00
COMP.FACT SET (795)	80.00	36.00
COMP.HTA SET (795)	80.00	36.00
COMPLETE SERIES 1 (405)	40.00	18.00
COMPLETE SERIES 2 (385)	40.00	18.00
COMMON CARD (1-6/8-791)	.10	.05
COMMON (352-376/727-751)	.25	.11

❑ 1 Cal Ripken 1.50 .70
❑ 2 Chipper Jones .75 .35
❑ 3 Roger Cedeno .10 .05
❑ 4 Garret Anderson .15 .07
❑ 5 Robin Ventura .15 .07
❑ 6 Daryle Ward .10 .05
❑ 7 Does Not Exist
❑ 8 Craig Paquette .10 .05
❑ 9 Phil Nevin .15 .07
❑ 10 Jermaine Dye .15 .07
❑ 11 Chris Singleton .10 .05
❑ 12 Mike Stanton .10 .05
❑ 13 Brian Hunter .10 .05
❑ 14 Mike Redmond .10 .05
❑ 15 Jim Thome .40 .18
❑ 16 Brian Jordan .15 .07
❑ 17 Joe Girardi .10 .05
❑ 18 Steve Woodard .10 .05
❑ 19 Dustin Hermanson .10 .05
❑ 20 Shawn Green .40 .18
❑ 21 Todd Stottlemyre .10 .05
❑ 22 Dan Wilson .10 .05
❑ 23 Todd Pratt .10 .05
❑ 24 Derek Lowe .10 .05
❑ 25 Juan Gonzalez .40 .18
❑ 26 Clay Bellinger .10 .05
❑ 27 Jeff Fassero .10 .05
❑ 28 Pat Meares .10 .05
❑ 29 Eddie Taubensee .10 .05
❑ 30 Paul O'Neill .40 .18
❑ 31 Jeffrey Hammonds .10 .05
❑ 32 Pokey Reese .10 .05
❑ 33 Mike Mussina .40 .18
❑ 34 Rico Brogna .10 .05
❑ 35 Jay Buhner .15 .07
❑ 36 Steve Cox .10 .05
❑ 37 Quilvio Veras .10 .05
❑ 38 Marquis Grissom .10 .05
❑ 39 Shigetoshi Hasegawa .15 .07
❑ 40 Shane Reynolds .10 .05
❑ 41 Adam Piatt .15 .07
❑ 42 Luis Polonia .10 .05
❑ 43 Brook Fordyce .10 .05
❑ 44 Preston Wilson .15 .07
❑ 45 Ellis Burks .15 .07
❑ 46 Armando Rios .10 .05
❑ 47 Chuck Finley .15 .07
❑ 48 Dan Plesac .10 .05
❑ 49 Shannon Stewart .15 .07
❑ 50 Mark McGwire 1.50 .70
❑ 51 Mark Loretta .10 .05
❑ 52 Gerald Williams .10 .05
❑ 53 Eric Young .10 .05
❑ 54 Peter Bergeron .10 .05
❑ 55 Dave Hansen .10 .05
❑ 56 Arthur Rhodes .10 .05
❑ 57 Bobby Jones .10 .05
❑ 58 Matt Clement .10 .05
❑ 59 Mike Benjamin .10 .05
❑ 60 Pedro Martinez .50 .23
❑ 61 Jose Canseco .40 .18
❑ 62 Matt Anderson .10 .05
❑ 63 Torii Hunter .15 .07
❑ 64 Carlos Lee UER .15 .07
1999 Charlotte Games Played are wrong
❑ 65 David Cone .15 .07
❑ 66 Rey Sanchez .10 .05
❑ 67 Eric Chavez .15 .07
❑ 68 Rick Helling .10 .05
❑ 69 Manny Alexander .10 .05
❑ 70 John Franco .15 .07
❑ 71 Mike Bordick .15 .07
❑ 72 Andres Galarraga .25 .11
❑ 73 Jose Cruz Jr. .15 .07
❑ 74 Mike Matheny .10 .05
❑ 75 Randy Johnson .50 .23
❑ 76 Richie Sexson .15 .07
❑ 77 Vladimir Nunez .10 .05
❑ 78 Harold Baines .15 .07
❑ 79 Aaron Boone .10 .05
❑ 80 Darin Erstad .40 .18
❑ 81 Alex Gonzalez .10 .05
❑ 82 Gil Heredia .10 .05
❑ 83 Shane Andrews .10 .05
❑ 84 Todd Hundley .10 .05
❑ 85 Bill Mueller .10 .05
❑ 86 Mark McLemore .10 .05
❑ 87 Scott Spiezio .10 .05
❑ 88 Kevin McGlinchy .10 .05
❑ 89 Bubba Trammell .10 .05
❑ 90 Manny Ramirez .50 .23
❑ 91 Mike Lamb .10 .05
❑ 92 Scott Karl .10 .05
❑ 93 Brian Buchanan .10 .05
❑ 94 Chris Turner .10 .05
❑ 95 Mike Sweeney .15 .07
❑ 96 John Wetteland .15 .07
❑ 97 Rob Bell .10 .05
❑ 98 Pat Rapp .10 .05
❑ 99 John Burkett .10 .05
❑ 100 Derek Jeter 1.50 .70
❑ 101 J.D. Drew .40 .18
❑ 102 Jose Offerman .10 .05
❑ 103 Rick Reed .10 .05
❑ 104 Will Clark .40 .18
❑ 105 Rickey Henderson .75 .35
❑ 106 Dave Berg .10 .05
❑ 107 Kirk Rueter .10 .05
❑ 108 Lee Stevens .10 .05
❑ 109 Jay Bell .15 .07
❑ 110 Fred McGriff .25 .11
❑ 111 Julio Zuleta .10 .05
❑ 112 Brian Anderson .10 .05
❑ 113 Orlando Cabrera .10 .05
❑ 114 Alex Fernandez .10 .05
❑ 115 Derek Bell .10 .05
❑ 116 Eric Owens .10 .05
❑ 117 Brian Bohanon .10 .05
❑ 118 Dennys Reyes .10 .05
❑ 119 Mike Stanley .10 .05
❑ 120 Jorge Posada .15 .07
❑ 121 Rich Becker .10 .05
❑ 122 Paul Konerko .15 .07
❑ 123 Mike Remlinger .10 .05
❑ 124 Travis Lee .10 .05
❑ 125 Ken Caminiti .15 .07
❑ 126 Kevin Barker .10 .05
❑ 127 Paul Quantrill .10 .05
❑ 128 Ozzie Guillen .10 .05
❑ 129 Kevin Tapani .10 .05
❑ 130 Mark Johnson .10 .05
❑ 131 Randy Wolf .10 .05
❑ 132 Michael Tucker .10 .05
❑ 133 Darren Lewis .10 .05
❑ 134 Joe Randa .10 .05
❑ 135 Jeff Cirillo .15 .07
❑ 136 David Ortiz .15 .07
❑ 137 Herb Perry .10 .05
❑ 138 Jeff Nelson .10 .05
❑ 139 Chris Stynes .10 .05
❑ 140 Johnny Damon .15 .07
❑ 141 Jeff Reboulet .10 .05
❑ 142 Jason Schmidt .10 .05
❑ 143 Charles Johnson .10 .05
❑ 144 Pat Burrell .15 .07
❑ 145 Gary Sheffield .15 .07
❑ 146 Tom Glavine .40 .18
❑ 147 Jason Isringhausen .10 .05
❑ 148 Chris Carpenter .10 .05
❑ 149 Jeff Suppan .10 .05
❑ 150 Ivan Rodriguez .40 .18
❑ 151 Luis Sojo .10 .05
❑ 152 Ron Villone .10 .05
❑ 153 Mike Sirotka .10 .05
❑ 154 Chuck Knoblauch .15 .07
❑ 155 Jason Kendall .15 .07
❑ 156 Dennis Cook .10 .05
❑ 157 Bobby Estalella .10 .05
❑ 158 Jose Guillen .10 .05
❑ 159 Thomas Howard .10 .05
❑ 160 Carlos Delgado .40 .18
❑ 161 Benji Gil .10 .05
❑ 162 Tim Bogar .10 .05
❑ 163 Kevin Elster .10 .05
❑ 164 Einar Diaz .10 .05
❑ 165 Andy Benes .10 .05
❑ 166 Adrian Beltre .15 .07
❑ 167 David Bell .10 .05
❑ 168 Turk Wendell .10 .05
❑ 169 Pete Harnisch .10 .05
❑ 170 Roger Clemens 1.00 .45
❑ 171 Scott Williamson .10 .05
❑ 172 Kevin Jordan .10 .05
❑ 173 Brad Penny .15 .07
❑ 174 John Flaherty .10 .05
❑ 175 Troy Glaus .40 .18
❑ 176 Kevin Appier .15 .07
❑ 177 Walt Weiss .10 .05

❑	178	Tyler Houston	.10	.05
❑	179	Michael Barrett	.10	.05
❑	180	Mike Hampton	.15	.07
❑	181	Francisco Cordova	.10	.05
❑	182	Mike Jackson	.10	.05
❑	183	David Segui	.10	.05
❑	184	Carlos Febles	.10	.05
❑	185	Roy Halladay	.10	.05
❑	186	Seth Etherton	.10	.05
❑	187	Charlie Hayes	.10	.05
❑	188	Fernando Tatis	.10	.05
❑	189	Steve Trachsel	.10	.05
❑	190	Livan Hernandez	.10	.05
❑	191	Joe Oliver	.10	.05
❑	192	Stan Javier	.10	.05
❑	193	B.J. Surhoff	.15	.07
❑	194	Rob Ducey	.10	.05
❑	195	Barry Larkin	.40	.18
❑	196	Danny Patterson	.10	.05
❑	197	Bobby Howry	.10	.05
❑	198	Dmitri Young	.15	.07
❑	199	Brian Hunter	.10	.05
❑	200	Alex Rodriguez	1.00	.45
❑	201	Hideo Nomo	.40	.18
❑	202	Luis Alicea	.10	.05
❑	203	Warren Morris	.10	.05
❑	204	Antonio Alfonseca	.10	.05
❑	205	Edgardo Alfonzo	.15	.07
❑	206	Mark Grudzielanek	.10	.05
❑	207	Fernando Vina	.10	.05
❑	208	Willie Greene	.10	.05
❑	209	Homer Bush	.10	.05
❑	210	Jason Giambi	.40	.18
❑	211	Mike Morgan	.10	.05
❑	212	Steve Karsay	.10	.05
❑	213	Matt Lawton	.15	.07
❑	214	Wendell Magee Jr.	.10	.05
❑	215	Rusty Greer	.15	.07
❑	216	Keith Lockhart	.10	.05
❑	217	Billy Koch	.10	.05
❑	218	Todd Hollandsworth	.10	.05
❑	219	Raul Ibanez	.10	.05
❑	220	Tony Gwynn	.75	.35
❑	221	Carl Everett	.15	.07
❑	222	Hector Carrasco	.10	.05
❑	223	Jose Valentin	.10	.05
❑	224	Deivi Cruz	.10	.05
❑	225	Bret Boone	.15	.07
❑	226	Kurt Abbott	.10	.05
❑	227	Melvin Mora	.10	.05
❑	228	Danny Graves	.10	.05
❑	229	Jose Jimenez	.10	.05
❑	230	James Baldwin	.10	.05
❑	231	C.J. Nitkowski	.10	.05
❑	232	Jeff Zimmerman	.10	.05
❑	233	Mike Lowell	.15	.07
❑	234	Hideki Irabu	.10	.05
❑	235	Greg Vaughn	.15	.07
❑	236	Omar Daal	.10	.05
❑	237	Darren Dreifort	.10	.05
❑	238	Gil Meche	.10	.05
❑	239	Damian Jackson	.10	.05
❑	240	Frank Thomas	.50	.23
❑	241	Travis Miller	.10	.05
❑	242	Jeff Frye	.10	.05
❑	243	Dave Magadan	.10	.05
❑	244	Luis Castillo	.10	.05
❑	245	Bartolo Colon	.15	.07
❑	246	Steve Kline	.10	.05
❑	247	Shawon Dunston	.10	.05
❑	248	Rick Aguilera	.10	.05
❑	249	Omar Olivares	.10	.05
❑	250	Craig Biggio	.25	.11
❑	251	Scott Schoeneweis	.10	.05
❑	252	Dave Veres	.10	.05
❑	253	Ramon Martinez	.10	.05
❑	254	Jose Vidro	.15	.07
❑	255	Todd Helton	.50	.23
❑	256	Greg Norton	.10	.05
❑	257	Jacque Jones	.15	.07
❑	258	Jason Grimsley	.10	.05
❑	259	Dan Reichert	.10	.05
❑	260	Robb Nen	.10	.05
❑	261	Mark Clark	.10	.05
❑	262	Scott Hatteberg	.10	.05
❑	263	Doug Brocail	.10	.05
❑	264	Mark Johnson	.10	.05
❑	265	Eric Davis	.15	.07
❑	266	Terry Shumpert	.10	.05
❑	267	Kevin Millar	.10	.05
❑	268	Ismael Valdes	.10	.05
❑	269	Richard Hidalgo	.15	.07
❑	270	Randy Velarde	.10	.05
❑	271	Bengie Molina	.10	.05
❑	272	Tony Womack	.10	.05
❑	273	Enrique Wilson	.10	.05
❑	274	Jeff Brantley	.10	.05
❑	275	Rick Ankiel	.25	.11
❑	276	Terry Mulholland	.10	.05
❑	277	Ron Belliard	.10	.05
❑	278	Terrence Long	.15	.07
❑	279	Alberto Castillo	.10	.05
❑	280	Royce Clayton	.10	.05
❑	281	Joe McEwing	.10	.05
❑	282	Jason McDonald	.10	.05
❑	283	Ricky Bottalico	.10	.05
❑	284	Keith Foulke	.10	.05
❑	285	Brad Radke	.15	.07
❑	286	Gabe Kapler	.15	.07
❑	287	Pedro Astacio	.10	.05
❑	288	Armando Reynoso	.10	.05
❑	289	Darryl Kile	.15	.07
❑	290	Reggie Sanders	.10	.05
❑	291	Esteban Yan	.10	.05
❑	292	Joe Nathan	.10	.05
❑	293	Jay Payton	.10	.05
❑	294	Francisco Cordero	.10	.05
❑	295	Gregg Jefferies	.10	.05
❑	296	LaTroy Hawkins	.10	.05
❑	297	Jeff Tam RC	.25	.11
❑	298	Jacob Cruz	.10	.05
❑	299	Chris Holt	.10	.05
❑	300	Vladimir Guerrero	.50	.23
❑	301	Marvin Benard	.10	.05
❑	302	Alex Ramirez	.10	.05
❑	303	Mike Williams	.10	.05
❑	304	Sean Bergman	.10	.05
❑	305	Juan Encarnacion	.15	.07
❑	306	Russ Davis	.10	.05
❑	307	Hanley Frias	.10	.05
❑	308	Ramon Hernandez	.10	.05
❑	309	Matt Walbeck	.10	.05
❑	310	Bill Spiers	.10	.05
❑	311	Bob Wickman	.10	.05
❑	312	Sandy Alomar Jr.	.15	.07
❑	313	Eddie Guardado	.10	.05
❑	314	Shane Halter	.10	.05
❑	315	Geoff Jenkins	.15	.07
❑	316	Brian Meadows	.10	.05
❑	317	Damian Miller	.10	.05
❑	318	Darrin Fletcher	.10	.05
❑	319	Rafael Furcal	.15	.07
❑	320	Mark Grace	.40	.18
❑	321	Mark Mulder	.25	.11
❑	322	Joe Torre MG	.15	.07
❑	323	Bobby Cox MG	.10	.05
❑	324	Mike Scioscia MG	.10	.05
❑	325	Mike Hargrove MG	.10	.05
❑	326	Jimy Williams MG	.10	.05
❑	327	Jerry Manuel MG	.10	.05
❑	328	Buck Showalter MG	.10	.05
❑	329	Charlie Manuel MG	.10	.05
❑	330	Don Baylor MG	.15	.07
❑	331	Phil Garner MG	.10	.05
❑	332	Jack McKeon MG	.10	.05
❑	333	Tony Muser MG	.10	.05
❑	334	Buddy Bell MG	.15	.07
❑	335	Tom Kelly MG	.10	.05
❑	336	John Boles MG	.10	.05
❑	337	Art Howe MG	.10	.05
❑	338	Larry Dierker MG	.10	.05
❑	339	Lou Piniella MG	.15	.07
❑	340	Davey Johnson MG	.10	.05
❑	341	Larry Rothschild MG	.10	.05
❑	342	Davey Lopes MG	.15	.07
❑	343	Johnny Oates MG	.10	.05
❑	344	Felipe Alou MG	.10	.05
❑	345	Jim Fregosi MG	.10	.05
❑	346	Bobby Valentine MG	.10	.05
❑	347	Terry Francona MG	.10	.05
❑	348	Gene Lamont MG	.10	.05
❑	349	Tony LaRussa MG	.10	.05
❑	350	Bruce Bochy MG	.10	.05
❑	351	Dusty Baker MG	.15	.07
❑	352	Adrian Gonzalez	.50	.23
		Adam Johnson		
❑	353	Matt Wheatland	.40	.18
		Bryan Digby		
❑	354	Tripper Johnson	.25	.11
		Scott Thorman		
❑	355	Phil Dumatrait	.40	.18
		Adam Wainwright		
❑	356	Scott Heard	.60	.25
		David Parrish RC		
❑	357	Rocco Baldelli	.75	.35
		Mark Folsom RC		
❑	358	Dominic Rich RC	.50	.23
		Aaron Herr		
❑	359	Mike Stodolka	.40	.18
		Sean Burnett		
❑	360	Derek Thompson	.40	.18
		Corey Smith		
❑	361	Danny Borrell RC	.50	.23
		Jason Bourgeois RC		
❑	362	Chin-Feng Chen	.75	.35
		Corey Patterson		
		Josh Hamilton		
❑	363	Ryan Anderson	.75	.35
		Barry Zito		
		C.C. Sabathia		
❑	364	Scott Sobkowiak	.25	.11
		David Walling		
		Ben Sheets		
❑	365	Ty Howington	.40	.18
		Josh Kalinowski		
		Josh Girdley		
❑	366	Hee Seop Choi RC	1.50	.70
		Aaron McNeal		
		Jason Hart		
❑	367	Bobby Bradley	.15	.07
		Kurt Ainsworth		
		Chin-Hui Tsao		
❑	368	Mike Glendenning	.40	.18
		Kenny Kelly		
		Juan Silvestri		
❑	369	J.R. House	1.00	.45
		Ramon Castro		
		Ben Davis		
❑	370	Chance Caple	.60	.25
		Rafael Soriano RC		
		Pascual Coco		
❑	371	Travis Hafner RC	.40	.18
		Eric Munson		
		Bucky Jacobsen		
❑	372	Jason Conti	.40	.18
		Chris Wakeland		
		Brian Cole		
❑	373	Scott Seabol	.40	.18
		Aubrey Huff		
		Joe Crede		
❑	374	Adam Everett	.25	.11
		Jose Ortiz		
		Keith Ginter		
❑	375	Carlos Hernandez	.40	.18
		Geraldo Guzman		
		Adam Eaton		
❑	376	Bobby Kielty	.40	.18
		Milton Bradley		
		Juan Rivera		
❑	377	Mark McGwire GM	.75	.35
❑	378	Don Larsen GM	.15	.07
❑	379	Bobby Thomson GM	.15	.07
❑	380	Bill Mazeroski GM	.15	.07
❑	381	Reggie Jackson GM	.40	.18
❑	382	Kirk Gibson GM	.15	.07
❑	383	Roger Maris GM	.40	.18
❑	384	Cal Ripken GM	.75	.35
❑	385	Hank Aaron GM	.50	.23
❑	386	Joe Carter GM	.15	.07
❑	387	Cal Ripken SH	1.50	.70
❑	388	Randy Johnson SH	.50	.23
❑	389	Ken Griffey Jr. SH	1.25	.55
❑	390	Troy Glaus SH	.40	.18
❑	391	Kazuhiro Sasaki SH	.15	.07
❑	392	Sammy Sosa	.40	.18
		Troy Glaus		
❑	393	Todd Helton	.25	.11
		Edgar Martinez		

❑ 394 Todd Helton .60 .25
Nomar Garciaparra
❑ 395 Barry Bonds .50 .23
Jason Giambi
❑ 396 Todd Helton .25 .11
Manny Ramirez
❑ 397 Todd Helton .25 .11
Darin Erstad
❑ 398 Kevin Brown .25 .11
Pedro Martinez
❑ 399 Randy Johnson .25 .11
Pedro Martinez
❑ 400 Will Clark HL .50 .23
❑ 401 New York Mets HL .50 .23
❑ 402 New York Yankees HL .75 .35
❑ 403 Seattle Mariners HL .15 .07
❑ 404 Mike Hampton HL .15 .07
❑ 405 New York Yankees HL 1.00 .45
❑ 406 N.Y. Yankees Champs 2.00 .90
❑ 407 Jeff Bagwell .50 .23
❑ 408 Brant Brown .10 .05
❑ 409 Brad Fullmer .15 .07
❑ 410 Dean Palmer .15 .07
❑ 411 Greg Zaun .10 .05
❑ 412 Jose Vizcaino .10 .05
❑ 413 Jeff Abbott .10 .05
❑ 414 Travis Fryman .15 .07
❑ 415 Mike Cameron .15 .07
❑ 416 Matt Mantei .10 .05
❑ 417 Alan Benes .10 .05
❑ 418 Mickey Morandini .10 .05
❑ 419 Troy Percival .10 .05
❑ 420 Eddie Perez .10 .05
❑ 421 Vernon Wells .10 .05
❑ 422 Ricky Gutierrez .10 .05
❑ 423 Carlos Hernandez .10 .05
❑ 424 Chan Ho Park .15 .07
❑ 425 Armando Benitez .15 .07
❑ 426 Sidney Ponson .10 .05
❑ 427 Adrian Brown .10 .05
❑ 428 Ruben Mateo .15 .07
❑ 429 Alex Ochoa .10 .05
❑ 430 Jose Rosado .10 .05
❑ 431 Masato Yoshii .15 .07
❑ 432 Corey Koskie .15 .07
❑ 433 Andy Pettitte .15 .07
❑ 434 Brian Daubach .15 .07
❑ 435 Sterling Hitchcock .10 .05
❑ 436 Timo Perez .10 .05
❑ 437 Shawn Estes .15 .07
❑ 438 Tony Armas Jr. .10 .05
❑ 439 Danny Bautista .10 .05
❑ 440 Randy Winn .10 .05
❑ 441 Wilson Alvarez .10 .05
❑ 442 Rondell White .15 .07
❑ 443 Jeromy Burnitz .15 .07
❑ 444 Kelvim Escobar .10 .05
❑ 445 Paul Bako .10 .05
❑ 446 Javier Vazquez .15 .07
❑ 447 Eric Gagne .10 .05
❑ 448 Kenny Lofton .15 .07
❑ 449 Mark Kotsay .15 .07
❑ 450 Jamie Moyer .10 .05
❑ 451 Delino DeShields .10 .05
❑ 452 Rey Ordonez .10 .05
❑ 453 Russ Ortiz .15 .07
❑ 454 Dave Burba .10 .05
❑ 455 Eric Karros .15 .07
❑ 456 Felix Martinez .10 .05
❑ 457 Tony Batista .15 .07
❑ 458 Bobby Higginson .15 .07
❑ 459 Jeff D'Amico .10 .05
❑ 460 Shane Spencer .10 .05
❑ 461 Brent Mayne .10 .05
❑ 462 Glendon Rusch .10 .05
❑ 463 Chris Gomez .10 .05
❑ 464 Jeff Shaw .10 .05
❑ 465 Damon Buford .10 .05
❑ 466 Mike DiFelice .10 .05
❑ 467 Jimmy Haynes .10 .05
❑ 468 Billy Wagner .10 .05
❑ 469 A.J. Hinch .10 .05
❑ 470 Gary DiSarcina .10 .05
❑ 471 Tom Lampkin .10 .05
❑ 472 Adam Eaton .15 .07
❑ 473 Brian Giles .15 .07
❑ 474 John Thomson .10 .05
❑ 475 Cal Eldred .10 .05
❑ 476 Ramiro Mendoza .10 .05
❑ 477 Scott Sullivan .10 .05
❑ 478 Scott Rolen .40 .18
❑ 479 Todd Ritchie .10 .05
❑ 480 Pablo Ozuna .10 .05
❑ 481 Carl Pavano .10 .05
❑ 482 Matt Morris .15 .07
❑ 483 Matt Stairs .10 .05
❑ 484 Tim Belcher .10 .05
❑ 485 Lance Berkman .40 .18
❑ 486 Brian Meadows .10 .05
❑ 487 Bob Abreu .15 .07
❑ 488 John VanderWal .10 .05
❑ 489 Donnie Sadler .10 .05
❑ 490 Damion Easley .10 .05
❑ 491 David Justice .15 .07
❑ 492 Ray Durham .15 .07
❑ 493 Todd Zeile .15 .07
❑ 494 Desi Relaford .10 .05
❑ 495 Cliff Floyd .15 .07
❑ 496 Scott Downs .10 .05
❑ 497 Barry Bonds 1.00 .45
❑ 498 Jeff D'Amico .10 .05
❑ 499 Octavio Dotel .10 .05
❑ 500 Kent Mercker .10 .05
❑ 501 Craig Grebeck .10 .05
❑ 502 Roberto Hernandez .10 .05
❑ 503 Matt Williams .25 .11
❑ 504 Bruce Aven .10 .05
❑ 505 Brett Tomko .10 .05
❑ 506 Kris Benson .15 .07
❑ 507 Neifi Perez .10 .05
❑ 508 Alfonso Soriano .40 .18
❑ 509 Keith Osik .10 .05
❑ 510 Matt Franco .10 .05
❑ 511 Steve Finley .15 .07
❑ 512 Olmedo Saenz .10 .05
❑ 513 Esteban Loaiza .10 .05
❑ 514 Adam Kennedy .10 .05
❑ 515 Scott Elarton .10 .05
❑ 516 Moises Alou .15 .07
❑ 517 Bryan Rekar .10 .05
❑ 518 Darryl Hamilton .10 .05
❑ 519 Osvaldo Fernandez .10 .05
❑ 520 Kip Wells .10 .05
❑ 521 Bernie Williams .40 .18
❑ 522 Mike Darr .10 .05
❑ 523 Marlon Anderson .10 .05
❑ 524 Derrek Lee .10 .05
❑ 525 Ugueth Urbina .10 .05
❑ 526 Vinny Castilla .15 .07
❑ 527 David Wells .15 .07
❑ 528 Jason Marquis .15 .07
❑ 529 Orlando Palmeiro .10 .05
❑ 530 Carlos Perez .10 .05
❑ 531 J.T. Snow .15 .07
❑ 532 Al Leiter .15 .07
❑ 533 Jimmy Anderson .10 .05
❑ 534 Brett Laxton .10 .05
❑ 535 Butch Huskey .10 .05
❑ 536 Orlando Hernandez .15 .07
❑ 537 Magglio Ordonez .15 .07
❑ 538 Willie Blair .10 .05
❑ 539 Kevin Sefcik .10 .05
❑ 540 Chad Curtis .10 .05
❑ 541 John Halama .10 .05
❑ 542 Andy Fox .10 .05
❑ 543 Juan Guzman .10 .05
❑ 544 Frank Menechino RC .25 .11
❑ 545 Raul Mondesi .15 .07
❑ 546 Tim Salmon .15 .07
❑ 547 Ryan Rupe .10 .05
❑ 548 Jeff Reed .10 .05
❑ 549 Mike Mordecai .10 .05
❑ 550 Jeff Kent .25 .11
❑ 551 Wiki Gonzalez .10 .05
❑ 552 Kenny Rogers .10 .05
❑ 553 Kevin Young .10 .05
❑ 554 Brian Johnson .10 .05
❑ 555 Tom Goodwin .10 .05
❑ 556 Tony Clark .15 .07
❑ 557 Mac Suzuki .15 .07
❑ 558 Brian Moehler .10 .05
❑ 559 Jim Parque .10 .05
❑ 560 Mariano Rivera .15 .07
❑ 561 Trot Nixon .15 .07
❑ 562 Mike Mussina .40 .18
❑ 563 Nelson Figueroa .10 .05
❑ 564 Alex Gonzalez .10 .05
❑ 565 Benny Agbayani .15 .07
❑ 566 Ed Sprague .10 .05
❑ 567 Scott Erickson .10 .05
❑ 568 Abraham Nunez .15 .07
❑ 569 Jerry DiPoto .10 .05
❑ 570 Sean Casey .25 .11
❑ 571 Wilton Veras .10 .05
❑ 572 Joe Mays .15 .07
❑ 573 Bill Simas .10 .05
❑ 574 Doug Glanville .10 .05
❑ 575 Scott Sauerbeck .10 .05
❑ 576 Ben Davis .15 .07
❑ 577 Jesus Sanchez .10 .05
❑ 578 Ricardo Rincon .10 .05
❑ 579 John Olerud .15 .07
❑ 580 Curt Schilling .40 .18
❑ 581 Alex Cora .10 .05
❑ 582 Pat Hentgen .10 .05
❑ 583 Javy Lopez .15 .07
❑ 584 Ben Grieve .15 .07
❑ 585 Frank Castillo .10 .05
❑ 586 Kevin Stocker .10 .05
❑ 587 Mark Sweeney .10 .05
❑ 588 Ray Lankford .10 .05
❑ 589 Turner Ward .10 .05
❑ 590 Felipe Crespo .10 .05
❑ 591 Omar Vizquel .15 .07
❑ 592 Mike Lieberthal .15 .07
❑ 593 Ken Griffey Jr. 1.25 .55
❑ 594 Troy O'Leary .10 .05
❑ 595 Dave Mlicki .10 .05
❑ 596 Manny Ramirez .50 .23
❑ 597 Mike Lansing .10 .05
❑ 598 Rich Aurilia .15 .07
❑ 599 Russell Branyan .15 .07
❑ 600 Russ Johnson .10 .05
❑ 601 Greg Colbrunn .10 .05
❑ 602 Andruw Jones .40 .18
❑ 603 Henry Blanco .10 .05
❑ 604 Jarrod Washburn .10 .05
❑ 605 Tony Eusebio .10 .05
❑ 606 Aaron Sele .15 .07
❑ 607 Charles Nagy .10 .05
❑ 608 Ryan Klesko .15 .07
❑ 609 Dante Bichette .15 .07
❑ 610 Bill Haselman .10 .05
❑ 611 Jerry Spradlin .10 .05
❑ 612 Alex Rodriguez Rangers 1.00 .45
❑ 613 Jose Silva .10 .05
❑ 614 Darren Oliver .10 .05
❑ 615 Pat Mahomes .10 .05
❑ 616 Roberto Alomar .40 .18
❑ 617 Edgar Renteria .10 .05
❑ 618 Jon Lieber .10 .05
❑ 619 John Rocker .15 .07
❑ 620 Miguel Tejada .15 .07
❑ 621 Mo Vaughn .15 .07
❑ 622 Jose Lima .10 .05
❑ 623 Kerry Wood .40 .18
❑ 624 Mike Timlin .10 .05
❑ 625 Wil Cordero .10 .05
❑ 626 Albert Belle .15 .07
❑ 627 Bobby Jones .10 .05
❑ 628 Doug Mirabelli .10 .05
❑ 629 Jason Tyner .10 .05
❑ 630 Andy Ashby .10 .05
❑ 631 Jose Hernandez .10 .05
❑ 632 Devon White .15 .07
❑ 633 Ruben Rivera .10 .05
❑ 634 Steve Parris .10 .05
❑ 635 David McCarty .10 .05
❑ 636 Jose Canseco .40 .18
❑ 637 Todd Walker .10 .05
❑ 638 Stan Spencer .10 .05
❑ 639 Wayne Gomes .10 .05
❑ 640 Freddy Garcia .15 .07
❑ 641 Jeremy Giambi .10 .05
❑ 642 Luis Lopez .10 .05
❑ 643 John Smoltz .15 .07
❑ 644 Kelly Stinnett .10 .05
❑ 645 Kevin Brown .15 .07

❑ 646 Wilton Guerrero .10 .05
❑ 647 Al Martin .10 .05
❑ 648 Woody Williams .10 .05
❑ 649 Brian Rose .10 .05
❑ 650 Rafael Palmeiro .40 .18
❑ 651 Pete Schourek .10 .05
❑ 652 Kevin Jarvis .10 .05
❑ 653 Mark Redman .10 .05
❑ 654 Ricky Ledee .10 .05
❑ 655 Larry Walker .25 .11
❑ 656 Paul Byrd .10 .05
❑ 657 Jason Bere .10 .05
❑ 658 Rick White .10 .05
❑ 659 Calvin Murray .10 .05
❑ 660 Greg Maddux 1.00 .45
❑ 661 Ron Gant .15 .07
❑ 662 Eli Marrero .10 .05
❑ 663 Graeme Lloyd .10 .05
❑ 664 Trevor Hoffman .15 .07
❑ 665 Nomar Garciaparra 1.00 .45
❑ 666 Glenallen Hill .10 .05
❑ 667 Matt LeCroy .10 .05
❑ 668 Justin Thompson .10 .05
❑ 669 Brady Anderson .15 .07
❑ 670 Miguel Batista .10 .05
❑ 671 Erubiel Durazo .10 .05
❑ 672 Kevin Millwood .10 .05
❑ 673 Mitch Meluskey .10 .05
❑ 674 Luis Gonzalez .40 .18
❑ 675 Edgar Martinez .25 .11
❑ 676 Robert Person .10 .05
❑ 677 Benito Santiago .10 .05
❑ 678 Todd Jones .10 .05
❑ 679 Tino Martinez .15 .07
❑ 680 Carlos Beltran .15 .07
❑ 681 Gabe White .10 .05
❑ 682 Bret Saberhagen .15 .07
❑ 683 Jeff Conine .10 .05
❑ 684 Jaret Wright .10 .05
❑ 685 Bernard Gilkey .10 .05
❑ 686 Garrett Stephenson .10 .05
❑ 687 Jamey Wright .10 .05
❑ 688 Sammy Sosa .75 .35
❑ 689 John Jaha .10 .05
❑ 690 Ramon Martinez .10 .05
❑ 691 Robert Fick .10 .05
❑ 692 Eric Milton .15 .07
❑ 693 Denny Neagle .10 .05
❑ 694 Ron Coomer .10 .05
❑ 695 John Valentin .10 .05
❑ 696 Placido Polanco .10 .05
❑ 697 Tim Hudson .40 .18
❑ 698 Marty Cordova .10 .05
❑ 699 Chad Kreuter .10 .05
❑ 700 Frank Catalanotto .10 .05
❑ 701 Tim Wakefield .10 .05
❑ 702 Jim Edmonds .25 .11
❑ 703 Michael Tucker .10 .05
❑ 704 Cristian Guzman .15 .07
❑ 705 Joey Hamilton .10 .05
❑ 706 Mike Piazza 1.00 .45
❑ 707 Dave Martinez .10 .05
❑ 708 Mike Hampton .15 .07
❑ 709 Bobby Bonilla .15 .07
❑ 710 Juan Pierre .15 .07
❑ 711 John Parrish .10 .05
❑ 712 Kory DeHaan .10 .05
❑ 713 Brian Tollberg .10 .05
❑ 714 Chris Truby .10 .05
❑ 715 Emil Brown .10 .05
❑ 716 Ryan Dempster .15 .07
❑ 717 Rich Garces .10 .05
❑ 718 Mike Myers .10 .05
❑ 719 Luis Ordaz .10 .05
❑ 720 Kazuhiro Sasaki .40 .18
❑ 721 Mark Quinn .15 .07
❑ 722 Ramon Ortiz .15 .07
❑ 723 Kerry Ligtenberg .10 .05
❑ 724 Rolando Arrojo .10 .05
❑ 725 Tsuyoshi Shinjo RC 2.00 .90
❑ 726 Ichiro Suzuki RC 20.00 9.00
❑ 727 Roy Oswalt .40 .18
Pat Strange
Jon Rauch
❑ 728 Phil Wilson RC .75 .35
Jake Peavy RC
Darwin Cubillan RC
❑ 729 Steve Smyth RC .50 .23
Mike Bynum
Nathan Haynes
❑ 730 Michael Cuddyer .40 .18
Joe Lawrence
Choo Freeman
❑ 731 Carlos Pena .40 .18
Larry Barnes
DeWayne Wise
❑ 732 Travis Dawkins .50 .23
Erick Almonte
Felipe Lopez
❑ 733 Alex Escobar .40 .18
Eric Valent
Brad Wilkerson
❑ 734 Toby Hall .40 .18
Rod Barajas
Jeff Goldbach
❑ 735 Jason Romano .25 .11
Marcus Giles
Pablo Ozuna
❑ 736 Dee Brown .40 .18
Jack Cust
Vernon Wells
❑ 737 David Espinosa 1.00 .45
Luis Montanez RC
❑ 738 Anthony Pluta RC .75 .35
Justin Wayne RC
❑ 739 Josh Axelson RC .50 .23
Carmen Cali RC
❑ 740 Shaun Boyd RC .75 .35
Chris Morris RC
❑ 741 Tommy Arko RC .50 .23
Dan Moylan RC
❑ 742 Luis Cotto RC .50 .23
Luis Escobar
❑ 743 Brandon Mims RC .75 .35
Blake Williams RC
❑ 744 Chris Russ RC .50 .23
Bryan Edwards
❑ 745 Joe Torres .40 .18
Ben Diggins
❑ 746 Hugh Quattlebaum RC .50 .23
Edwin Encarnacion RC
❑ 747 Brian Bass RC .50 .23
Odannis Ayala RC
❑ 748 Jason Kaanoi .50 .23
Michael Matthews RC
UER name misspelled Mathews
❑ 749 Stuart McFarland RC .50 .23
Adam Sterrett RC
❑ 750 David Krynzel .40 .18
Grady Sizemore
❑ 751 Keith Bucktrot .40 .18
Dane Sardinha
❑ 752 Anaheim Angels TC .15 .07
❑ 753 Ariz. Diamondbacks TC .15 .07
❑ 754 Atlanta Braves TC .15 .07
❑ 755 Baltimore Orioles TC .15 .07
❑ 756 Boston Red Sox TC .15 .07
❑ 757 Chicago Cubs TC .15 .07
❑ 758 Chicago White Sox TC .15 .07
❑ 759 Cincinnati Reds TC .15 .07
❑ 760 Cleveland Indians TC .15 .07
❑ 761 Colorado Rockies TC .15 .07
❑ 762 Detroit Tigers TC .15 .07
❑ 763 Florida Marlins TC .15 .07
❑ 764 Houston Astros TC .15 .07
❑ 765 Kansas City Royals TC .15 .07
❑ 766 Los Angeles Dodgers TC .15 .07
❑ 767 Milwaukee Brewers TC .15 .07
❑ 768 Minnesota Twins TC .15 .07
❑ 769 Montreal Expos TC .15 .07
❑ 770 New York Mets TC .15 .07
❑ 771 New York Yankees TC 1.00 .45
❑ 772 Oakland Athletics TC .15 .07
❑ 773 Philadelphia Phillies TC .15 .07
❑ 774 Pittsburgh Pirates TC .15 .07
❑ 775 San Diego Padres TC .15 .07
❑ 776 San Francisco Giants TC .15 .07
❑ 777 Seattle Mariners TC .15 .07
❑ 778 St. Louis Cardinals TC .15 .07
❑ 779 Tampa Bay Devil Rays TC .15 .07
❑ 780 Texas Rangers TC .15 .07
▲❑ 781 Toronto Blue Jays TC .15 .07
❑ 782 Bucky Dent GM .10 .05
❑ 783 Jackie Robinson GM .40 .18
❑ 784 Roberto Clemente GM .60 .25
❑ 785 Nolan Ryan GM 1.00 .45
❑ 786 Kerry Wood GM .15 .07
❑ 787 Rickey Henderson GM .40 .18
❑ 788 Lou Brock GM .15 .07
❑ 789 David Wells GM .10 .05
❑ 790 Andruw Jones GM .15 .07
❑ 791 Carlton Fisk GM .15 .07
❑ TK Bo Jackson 150.00 70.00
Deion Sanders Bat
❑ NNO Bobby Thomson 100.00 45.00
Ralph Branca
1991 Bowman Autograph

2001 Topps Limited

	MINT	NRMT
COMP.FACT.SET (790)	200.00	90.00

*SINGLES: 2.5X TO 6X BASIC CARDS
*ROOKIES: 1.5X TO 4X BASIC CARDS

2001 Topps Traded

	MINT	NRMT
COMPLETE SET (265)	75.00	34.00

❑ T1 Sandy Alomar Jr. .40 .18
❑ T2 Kevin Appier .40 .18
❑ T3 Brad Ausmus .25 .11
❑ T4 Derek Bell .25 .11
❑ T5 Bret Boone .40 .18
❑ T6 Rico Brogna .25 .11
❑ T7 Ellis Burks .40 .18
❑ T8 Ken Caminiti .40 .18
❑ T9 Roger Cedeno .25 .11
❑ T10 Royce Clayton .25 .11
❑ T11 Enrique Wilson .25 .11
❑ T12 Rheal Cormier .25 .11
❑ T13 Eric Davis .40 .18
❑ T14 Shawon Dunston .25 .11
❑ T15 Andres Galarraga .60 .25
❑ T16 Tom Gordon .25 .11
❑ T17 Mark Grace 1.00 .45
❑ T18 Jeffrey Hammonds .25 .11
❑ T19 Dustin Hermanson .25 .11
❑ T20 Quinton McCracken .25 .11
❑ T21 Todd Hundley .25 .11
❑ T22 Charles Johnson .40 .18

	Card	Mint	NrMt
❑	T23 Marquis Grissom	.25	.11
❑	T24 Jose Mesa	.25	.11
❑	T25 Brian Boehringer	.25	.11
❑	T26 John Rocker	.40	.18
❑	T27 Jeff Frye	.25	.11
❑	T28 Reggie Sanders	.40	.18
❑	T29 David Segui	.25	.11
❑	T30 Mike Sirotka	.25	.11
❑	T31 Fernando Tatis	.25	.11
❑	T32 Steve Trachsel	.25	.11
❑	T33 Ismael Valdes	.25	.11
❑	T34 Randy Velarde	.25	.11
❑	T35 Ryan Kohlmeier	.25	.11
❑	T36 Mike Bordick	.40	.18
❑	T37 Kent Bottenfield	.25	.11
❑	T38 Pat Rapp	.25	.11
❑	T39 Jeff Nelson	.25	.11
❑	T40 Ricky Bottalico	.25	.11
❑	T41 Luke Prokopec	.25	.11
❑	T42 Hideo Nomo	1.00	.45
❑	T43 Bill Mueller	.25	.11
❑	T44 Roberto Kelly	.25	.11
❑	T45 Chris Holt	.25	.11
❑	T46 Mike Jackson	.25	.11
❑	T47 Devon White	.25	.11
❑	T48 Gerald Williams	.25	.11
❑	T49 Eddie Taubensee	.25	.11
❑	T50 Brian Hunter UER Brian R Hunter pictured Brian L Hunter stats	.25	.11
❑	T51 Nelson Cruz	.25	.11
❑	T52 Jeff Fassero	.25	.11
❑	T53 Bubba Trammell	.25	.11
❑	T54 Bo Porter	.25	.11
❑	T55 Greg Norton	.25	.11
❑	T56 Benito Santiago	.25	.11
❑	T57 Ruben Rivera	.25	.11
❑	T58 Dee Brown	.40	.18
❑	T59 Jose Canseco	1.00	.45
❑	T60 Chris Michalak	.25	.11
❑	T61 Tim Worrell	.25	.11
❑	T62 Matt Clement	.25	.11
❑	T63 Bill Pulsipher	.25	.11
❑	T64 Troy Brohawn RC	.50	.23
❑	T65 Mark Kotsay	.40	.18
❑	T66 Jimmy Rollins	.40	.18
❑	T67 Shea Hillenbrand	.40	.18
❑	T68 Ted Lilly	.25	.11
❑	T69 Jermaine Dye	.40	.18
❑	T70 Jerry Hairston Jr.	.25	.11
❑	T71 John Mabry	.25	.11
❑	T72 Kurt Abbott	.25	.11
❑	T73 Eric Owens	.25	.11
❑	T74 Jeff Brantley	.25	.11
❑	T75 Roy Oswalt	1.00	.45
❑	T76 Doug Mientkiewicz	.40	.18
❑	T77 Rickey Henderson	2.00	.90
❑	T78 Jason Grimsley	.25	.11
❑	T79 Christian Parker RC	.50	.23
❑	T80 Donne Wall	.25	.11
❑	T81 Alex Arias	.25	.11
❑	T82 Willis Roberts	.25	.11
❑	T83 Ryan Minor	.25	.11
❑	T84 Jason LaRue	.25	.11
❑	T85 Ruben Sierra	.25	.11
❑	T86 Johnny Damon	.40	.18
❑	T87 Juan Gonzalez	1.00	.45
❑	T88 C.C. Sabathia	.60	.25
❑	T89 Tony Batista	.40	.18
❑	T90 Jay Witasick	.25	.11
❑	T91 Brent Abernathy	.25	.11
❑	T92 Paul LoDuca	.40	.18
❑	T93 Wes Helms	.25	.11
❑	T94 Mark Wohlers	.25	.11
❑	T95 Rob Bell	.25	.11
❑	T96 Tim Redding	.40	.18
❑	T97 Bud Smith RC	3.00	1.35
❑	T98 Adam Dunn	1.25	.55
❑	T99 Ichiro Suzuki Albert Pujols ROY	10.00	4.50
❑	T100 Carlton Fisk 81	1.50	.70
❑	T101 Tim Raines 81	1.00	.45
❑	T102 Juan Marichal 74	1.00	.45
❑	T103 Dave Winfield 81	1.50	.70
❑	T104 Reggie Jackson 82	2.50	1.10
❑	T105 Cal Ripken 82	6.00	2.70
❑	T106 Ozzie Smith 82	2.00	.90
❑	T107 Tom Seaver 83	2.50	1.10
❑	T108 Lou Piniella 74	1.00	.45
❑	T109 Dwight Gooden 84	1.00	.45
❑	T110 Bret Saberhagen 84	1.00	.45
❑	T111 Gary Carter 85	1.00	.45
❑	T112 Jack Clark 85	1.00	.45
❑	T113 Rickey Henderson 85	3.00	1.35
❑	T114 Barry Bonds 86	4.00	1.80
❑	T115 Bobby Bonilla 86	1.00	.45
❑	T116 Jose Canseco 86	1.50	.70
❑	T117 Will Clark 86	1.50	.70
❑	T118 Andres Galarraga 86	1.00	.45
❑	T119 Bo Jackson 86	1.00	.45
❑	T120 Wally Joyner 86	1.00	.45
❑	T121 Ellis Burks 87	1.00	.45
❑	T122 David Cone 87	1.00	.45
❑	T123 Greg Maddux 87	4.00	1.80
❑	T124 Willie Randolph 76	1.00	.45
❑	T125 Dennis Eckersley 87	1.00	.45
❑	T126 Matt Williams 87	1.00	.45
❑	T127 Joe Morgan 81	1.00	.45
❑	T128 Fred McGriff 87	1.00	.45
❑	T129 Roberto Alomar 88	1.50	.70
❑	T130 Lee Smith 88	1.00	.45
❑	T131 David Wells 88	1.00	.45
❑	T132 Ken Griffey Jr. 89	5.00	2.20
❑	T133 Deion Sanders 89	1.00	.45
❑	T134 Nolan Ryan 89	5.00	2.20
❑	T135 David Justice 90	1.00	.45
❑	T136 Joe Carter 91	1.00	.45
❑	T137 Jack Morris 92	1.00	.45
❑	T138 Mike Piazza 93	4.00	1.80
❑	T139 Barry Bonds 93	4.00	1.80
❑	T140 Terrence Long 94	1.00	.45
❑	T141 Ben Grieve 94	1.00	.45
❑	T142 Richie Sexson 95 George Arias Mark Sweeney Brian Schneider	1.00	.45
❑	T143 Sean Burroughs 99	1.50	.70
❑	T144 Alfonso Soriano 99	1.50	.70
❑	T145 Bob Boone MG	.40	.18
❑	T146 Larry Bowa MG	.40	.18
❑	T147 Bob Brenly MG	.25	.11
❑	T148 Buck Martinez MG	.25	.11
❑	T149 Lloyd McClendon MG	.25	.11
❑	T150 Jim Tracy MG	.25	.11
❑	T151 Jared Abruzzo RC	.75	.35
❑	T152 Kurt Ainsworth	.40	.18
❑	T153 Willie Bloomquist	.40	.18
❑	T154 Ben Broussard	.40	.18
❑	T155 Bobby Bradley	.40	.18
❑	T156 Mike Bynum	.25	.11
❑	T157 A.J. Hinch	.25	.11
❑	T158 Ryan Christianson	.40	.18
❑	T159 Carlos Silva	.25	.11
❑	T160 Joe Crede	.40	.18
❑	T161 Jack Cust	.40	.18
❑	T162 Ben Diggins	.40	.18
❑	T163 Phil Dumatrait	.25	.11
❑	T164 Alex Escobar	.40	.18
❑	T165 Miguel Olivo	.25	.11
❑	T166 Chris George	.40	.18
❑	T167 Marcus Giles	.40	.18
❑	T168 Keith Ginter	.40	.18
❑	T169 Josh Girdley	.25	.11
❑	T170 Tony Alvarez	.25	.11
❑	T171 Scott Seabol	.25	.11
❑	T172 Josh Hamilton	1.00	.45
❑	T173 Jason Hart	.60	.25
❑	T174 Israel Alcantara	.25	.11
❑	T175 Jake Peavy	.75	.35
❑	T176 Stubby Clapp RC	.50	.23
❑	T177 D'Angelo Jimenez	.25	.11
❑	T178 Nick Johnson	.40	.18
❑	T179 Ben Johnson	.40	.18
❑	T180 Larry Bigbie	.25	.11
❑	T181 Allen Levrault	.25	.11
❑	T182 Felipe Lopez	.40	.18
❑	T183 Sean Burnett	.25	.11
❑	T184 Nick Neugebauer	1.00	.45
❑	T185 Austin Kearns	.60	.25
❑	T186 Corey Patterson	.40	.18
❑	T187 Carlos Pena	.40	.18
❑	T188 Ricardo Rodriguez RC	1.00	.45
❑	T189 Juan Rivera	.40	.18
❑	T190 Grant Roberts	.25	.11
❑	T191 Adam Pettyjohn RC	.75	.35
❑	T192 Jared Sandberg	.25	.11
❑	T193 Xavier Nady	.60	.25
❑	T194 Dane Sardinha	.25	.11
❑	T195 Shawn Sonnier	.25	.11
❑	T196 Rafael Soriano	.40	.18
❑	T197 Brian Specht RC	.50	.23
❑	T198 Aaron Myette	.25	.11
❑	T199 Juan Uribe RC	1.50	.70
❑	T200 Jayson Werth	.25	.11
❑	T201 Brad Wilkerson	.25	.11
❑	T202 Horacio Estrada	.25	.11
❑	T203 Joel Pineiro	1.00	.45
❑	T204 Matt LeCroy	.25	.11
❑	T205 Michael Coleman	.25	.11
❑	T206 Ben Sheets	.60	.25
❑	T207 Eric Byrnes	.25	.11
❑	T208 Sean Burroughs	1.00	.45
❑	T209 Ken Harvey	.40	.18
❑	T210 Travis Hafner	.60	.25
❑	T211 Erick Almonte	.40	.18
❑	T212 Jason Belcher RC	1.00	.45
❑	T213 Wilson Betemit RC	2.50	1.10
❑	T214 Hank Blalock RC	4.00	1.80
❑	T215 Danny Borrell	.40	.18
❑	T216 John Buck RC	1.00	.45
❑	T217 Freddie Bynum RC	1.00	.45
❑	T218 Noel Devarez RC	.50	.23
❑	T219 Juan Diaz RC	.50	.23
❑	T220 Felix Diaz RC	.75	.35
❑	T221 Josh Fogg RC	.50	.23
❑	T222 Matt Ford RC	.50	.23
❑	T223 Scott Heard	.40	.18
❑	T224 Ben Hendrickson RC	.50	.23
❑	T225 Cody Ross RC	1.00	.45
❑	T226 Adrian Hernandez RC	.50	.23
❑	T227 Alfredo Amezaga RC	.60	.25
❑	T228 Bob Keppel RC	.75	.35
❑	T229 Ryan Madson RC	.75	.35
❑	T230 Octavio Martinez RC	.50	.23
❑	T231 Hee Seop Choi	1.00	.45
❑	T232 Thomas Mitchell	.25	.11
❑	T233 Luis Montanez	.75	.35
❑	T234 Andy Morales RC	.50	.23
❑	T235 Justin Morneau RC	2.00	.90
❑	T236 Toe Nash RC	2.50	1.10
❑	T237 Valentino Pascucci RC	.60	.25
❑	T238 Roy Smith RC	.50	.23
❑	T239 Antonio Perez RC	1.50	.70
❑	T240 Chad Petty RC	1.00	.45
❑	T241 Steve Smyth	.40	.18
❑	T242 Jose Reyes RC	1.00	.45
❑	T243 Eric Reynolds RC	.60	.25
❑	T244 Dominic Rich	.40	.18
❑	T245 Jason Richardson RC	.50	.23
❑	T246 Ed Rogers RC	.75	.35
❑	T247 Albert Pujols RC	10.00	4.50
❑	T248 Esix Snead RC	.50	.23
❑	T249 Luis Torres RC	.50	.23
❑	T250 Matt White RC	.60	.25
❑	T251 Blake Williams	.40	.18
❑	T252 Chris Russ	.40	.18
❑	T253 Joe Kennedy RC	1.00	.45
❑	T254 Jeff Randazzo RC	.50	.23
❑	T255 Beau Hale RC	1.00	.45
❑	T256 Brad Hennessey RC	.60	.25
❑	T257 Jake Gautreau RC	1.25	.55
❑	T258 Jeff Mathis RC	.75	.35
❑	T259 Aaron Heilman RC	1.00	.45
❑	T260 Bronson Sardinha RC	1.50	.70
❑	T261 Irvin Guzman RC	1.50	.70
❑	T262 Gabe Gross RC	2.00	.90
❑	T263 J.D. Martin RC	1.50	.70
❑	T264 Chris Smith RC	.75	.35
❑	T265 Kenny Baugh RC	.75	.35

2002 Topps

	MINT	NRMT
COMPLETE SERIES 1 (365)	40.00	18.00
COMMON CARD (1-306)	.10	.05
COMMON CARD (307-331)	.50	.23
COMMON CARD (332-364)	.50	.23

❑ 1 Pedro Martinez .50 .23
❑ 2 Mike Stanton .10 .05
❑ 3 Brad Penny .15 .07
❑ 4 Mike Matheny .10 .05
❑ 5 Johnny Damon .15 .07
❑ 6 Bret Boone .15 .07
❑ 7 Does Not Exist
❑ 8 Chris Truby .10 .05
❑ 9 B.J. Surhoff .15 .07
❑ 10 Mike Hampton .15 .07
❑ 11 Juan Pierre .15 .07
❑ 12 Mark Buehrle .15 .07
❑ 13 Bob Abreu .15 .07
❑ 14 David Cone .15 .07
❑ 15 Aaron Sele UER .15 .07
Card lists him as being born in New Mexico
He was born in Minnesota
❑ 16 Fernando Tatis .10 .05
❑ 17 Bobby Jones .10 .05
❑ 18 Rick Helling .10 .05
❑ 19 Dmitri Young .15 .07
❑ 20 Mike Mussina UER .40 .18
Career win total is wrong
❑ 21 Mike Sweeney .15 .07
❑ 22 Cristian Guzman .15 .07
❑ 23 Ryan Kohlmeier .10 .05
❑ 24 Adam Kennedy .10 .05
❑ 25 Larry Walker .25 .11
❑ 26 Eric Davis .15 .07
❑ 27 Jason Tyner .10 .05
❑ 28 Eric Young .10 .05
❑ 29 Jason Marquis .10 .05
❑ 30 Luis Gonzalez .40 .18
❑ 31 Kevin Tapani .10 .05
❑ 32 Orlando Cabrera .10 .05
❑ 33 Marty Cordova .10 .05
❑ 34 Brad Ausmus .10 .05
❑ 35 Livan Hernandez .10 .05
❑ 36 Alex Gonzalez .10 .05
❑ 37 Edgar Renteria .15 .07
❑ 38 Bengie Molina .10 .05
❑ 39 Frank Menechino .10 .05
❑ 40 Rafael Palmeiro .40 .18
❑ 41 Brad Fullmer .15 .07
❑ 42 Julio Zuleta .10 .05
❑ 43 Darren Dreifort .10 .05
❑ 44 Trot Nixon .15 .07
❑ 45 Trevor Hoffman .15 .07
❑ 46 Vladimir Nunez .10 .05
❑ 47 Mark Kotsay .15 .07
❑ 48 Kenny Rogers .10 .05
❑ 49 Ben Petrick .10 .05
❑ 50 Jeff Bagwell .50 .23
❑ 51 Juan Encarnacion .15 .07
❑ 52 Ramiro Mendoza .10 .05
❑ 53 Brian Meadows .10 .05
❑ 54 Chad Curtis .10 .05
❑ 55 Aramis Ramirez .15 .07
❑ 56 Mark McLemore .10 .05
❑ 57 Dante Bichette .15 .07
❑ 58 Scott Schoeneweis .10 .05
❑ 59 Jose Cruz Jr. .15 .07
❑ 60 Roger Clemens 1.00 .45
❑ 61 Jose Guillen .10 .05
❑ 62 Darren Oliver .10 .05
❑ 63 Chris Reitsma .10 .05
❑ 64 Jeff Abbott .10 .05
❑ 65 Robin Ventura .15 .07
❑ 66 Denny Neagle .10 .05
❑ 67 Al Martin .10 .05
❑ 68 Benito Santiago .10 .05
❑ 69 Roy Oswalt .25 .11
❑ 70 Juan Gonzalez .40 .18
❑ 71 Garret Anderson .15 .07
❑ 72 Bobby Bonilla .15 .07
❑ 73 Danny Bautista .10 .05
❑ 74 J.T. Snow .15 .07
❑ 75 Derek Jeter 1.50 .70
❑ 76 John Olerud .15 .07
❑ 77 Kevin Appier .15 .07
❑ 78 Phil Nevin .15 .07
❑ 79 Sean Casey .25 .11
❑ 80 Troy Glaus .40 .18
❑ 81 Joe Randa .10 .05
❑ 82 Jose Valentin .10 .05
❑ 83 Ricky Bottalico .10 .05
❑ 84 Todd Zeile .15 .07
❑ 85 Barry Larkin .40 .18
❑ 86 Bob Wickman .10 .05
❑ 87 Jeff Shaw .10 .05
❑ 88 Greg Vaughn .15 .07
❑ 89 Fernando Vina .10 .05
❑ 90 Mark Mulder .15 .07
❑ 91 Paul Bako .10 .05
❑ 92 Aaron Boone .10 .05
❑ 93 Esteban Loaiza .10 .05
❑ 94 Richie Sexson .15 .07
❑ 95 Alfonso Soriano .40 .18
❑ 96 Tony Womack .10 .05
❑ 97 Paul Shuey .10 .05
❑ 98 Melvin Mora .10 .05
❑ 99 Tony Gwynn .75 .35
❑ 100 Vladimir Guerrero .50 .23
❑ 101 Keith Osik .10 .05
❑ 102 Randy Velarde .10 .05
❑ 103 Scott Williamson .10 .05
❑ 104 Daryle Ward .10 .05
❑ 105 Doug Mientkiewicz .15 .07
❑ 106 Stan Javier .10 .05
❑ 107 Russ Ortiz .15 .07
❑ 108 Wade Miller .15 .07
❑ 109 Luke Prokopec .10 .05
❑ 110 Andruw Jones .40 .18
❑ 111 Ron Coomer .10 .05
❑ 112 Dan Wilson .10 .05
❑ 113 Luis Castillo .10 .05
❑ 114 Derek Bell .10 .05
❑ 115 Gary Sheffield .15 .07
❑ 116 Ruben Rivera .10 .05
❑ 117 Paul O'Neill .40 .18
❑ 118 Craig Paquette .10 .05
❑ 119 Chris Michalak .10 .05
❑ 120 Brad Radke .15 .07
❑ 121 Jorge Fabregas .10 .05
❑ 122 Randy Winn .10 .05
❑ 123 Tom Goodwin .10 .05
❑ 124 Jaret Wright .10 .05
❑ 125 Manny Ramirez .50 .23
❑ 126 Al Leiter .10 .05
❑ 127 Ben Davis .10 .05
❑ 128 Frank Catalanotto .10 .05
❑ 129 Jose Cabrera .10 .05
❑ 130 Magglio Ordonez .15 .07
❑ 131 Jose Macias .10 .05
❑ 132 Ted Lilly .10 .05
❑ 133 Chris Holt .10 .05
❑ 134 Eric Milton .15 .07
❑ 135 Shannon Stewart .15 .07
❑ 136 Omar Olivares .10 .05
❑ 137 David Segui .10 .05
❑ 138 Jeff Nelson .10 .05
❑ 139 Matt Williams .25 .11
❑ 140 Ellis Burks .15 .07
❑ 141 Jason Bere .10 .05
❑ 142 Jimmy Haynes .10 .05
❑ 143 Ramon Hernandez .10 .05
❑ 144 Craig Counsell .10 .05
❑ 145 John Smoltz .15 .07
❑ 146 Homer Bush .10 .05
❑ 147 Quilvio Veras .10 .05
❑ 148 Esteban Yan .10 .05
❑ 149 Ramon Ortiz .15 .07
❑ 150 Carlos Delgado .40 .18
❑ 151 Lee Stevens .10 .05
❑ 152 Wil Cordero .10 .05
❑ 153 Mike Bordick .15 .07
❑ 154 John Flaherty .10 .05
❑ 155 Omar Daal .10 .05
❑ 156 Todd Ritchie .10 .05
❑ 157 Carl Everett .15 .07
❑ 158 Scott Sullivan .10 .05
❑ 159 Deivi Cruz .15 .07
❑ 160 Albert Pujols 1.00 .45
❑ 161 Royce Clayton .10 .05
❑ 162 Jeff Suppan .10 .05
❑ 163 C.C. Sabathia .25 .11
❑ 164 Jimmy Rollins .15 .07
❑ 165 Rickey Henderson .75 .35
❑ 166 Rey Ordonez .10 .05
❑ 167 Shawn Estes .15 .07
❑ 168 Reggie Sanders .15 .07
❑ 169 Jon Lieber .15 .07
❑ 170 Armando Benitez .15 .07
❑ 171 Mike Remlinger .10 .05
❑ 172 Billy Wagner .15 .07
❑ 173 Troy Percival .15 .07
❑ 174 Devon White .10 .05
❑ 175 Ivan Rodriguez .40 .18
❑ 176 Dustin Hermanson .15 .07
❑ 177 Brian Anderson .10 .05
❑ 178 Graeme Lloyd .10 .05
❑ 179 Russel Branyan .15 .07
❑ 180 Bobby Higginson .15 .07
❑ 181 Alex Gonzalez .10 .05
❑ 182 John Franco .15 .07
❑ 183 Sidney Ponson .10 .05
❑ 184 Jose Mesa .10 .05
❑ 185 Todd Hollandsworth .10 .05
❑ 186 Kevin Young .10 .05
❑ 187 Tim Wakefield .10 .05
❑ 188 Craig Biggio .25 .11
❑ 189 Jason Isringhausen .15 .07
❑ 190 Mark Quinn .15 .07
❑ 191 Glendon Rusch .10 .05
❑ 192 Damian Miller .10 .05
❑ 193 Sandy Alomar Jr. .15 .07
❑ 194 Scott Brosius .15 .07
❑ 195 Dave Martinez .10 .05
❑ 196 Danny Graves .10 .05
❑ 197 Shea Hillenbrand .15 .07
❑ 198 Jimmy Anderson .10 .05
❑ 199 Travis Lee .15 .07
❑ 200 Randy Johnson .50 .23
❑ 201 Carlos Beltran .15 .07
❑ 202 Jerry Hairston .10 .05
❑ 203 Jesus Sanchez .10 .05
❑ 204 Eddie Taubensee .10 .05
❑ 205 David Wells .15 .07
❑ 206 Russ Davis .10 .05
❑ 207 Michael Barrett .10 .05
❑ 208 Marquis Grissom .10 .05
❑ 209 Byung-Hyun Kim .15 .07
❑ 210 Hideo Nomo .40 .18
❑ 211 Ryan Rupe .10 .05
❑ 212 Ricky Gutierrez .10 .05
❑ 213 Darryl Kile .15 .07
❑ 214 Rico Brogna .10 .05
❑ 215 Terrence Long .15 .07
❑ 216 Mike Jackson .10 .05
❑ 217 Jamey Wright .10 .05
❑ 218 Adrian Beltre .15 .07
❑ 219 Benny Agbayani .10 .05
❑ 220 Chuck Knoblauch .15 .07
❑ 221 Randy Wolf .10 .05
❑ 222 Andy Ashby .10 .05
❑ 223 Corey Koskie .15 .07
❑ 224 Roger Cedeno .10 .05
❑ 225 Ichiro Suzuki 1.50 .70
❑ 226 Keith Foulke .10 .05
❑ 227 Ryan Minor .10 .05
❑ 228 Shawon Dunston .10 .05
❑ 229 Alex Cora .10 .05
❑ 230 Jeromy Burnitz .15 .07
❑ 231 Mark Grace .40 .18
❑ 232 Aubrey Huff .10 .05
❑ 233 Jeffrey Hammonds .10 .05
❑ 234 Olmedo Saenz .10 .05
❑ 235 Brian Jordan .15 .07

❑ 236 Jeremy Giambi .10 .05
❑ 237 Joe Girardi .10 .05
❑ 238 Eric Gagne .10 .05
❑ 239 Masato Yoshii .15 .07
❑ 240 Greg Maddux 1.00 .45
❑ 241 Bryan Rekar .10 .05
❑ 242 Ray Durham .15 .07
❑ 243 Torii Hunter .15 .07
❑ 244 Derrek Lee .10 .05
❑ 245 Jim Edmonds .25 .11
❑ 246 Einar Diaz .10 .05
❑ 247 Brian Bohanon .10 .05
❑ 248 Ron Belliard .10 .05
❑ 249 Mike Lowell .15 .07
❑ 250 Sammy Sosa .75 .35
❑ 251 Richard Hidalgo .15 .07
❑ 252 Bartolo Colon .15 .07
❑ 253 Jorge Posada .15 .07
❑ 254 LaTroy Hawkins .10 .05
❑ 255 Paul LoDuca .15 .07
❑ 256 Carlos Febles .10 .05
❑ 257 Nelson Cruz .10 .05
❑ 258 Edgardo Alfonzo .15 .07
❑ 259 Joey Hamilton .10 .05
❑ 260 Cliff Floyd .15 .07
❑ 261 Wes Helms .10 .05
❑ 262 Jay Bell .15 .07
❑ 263 Mike Cameron .15 .07
❑ 264 Paul Konerko .15 .07
❑ 265 Jeff Kent .25 .11
❑ 266 Robert Fick .10 .05
❑ 267 Allen Levrault .10 .05
❑ 268 Placido Polanco .10 .05
❑ 269 Marlon Anderson .10 .05
❑ 270 Mariano Rivera .15 .07
❑ 271 Chan Ho Park .15 .07
❑ 272 Jose Vizcaino .10 .05
❑ 273 Jeff D'Amico .10 .05
❑ 274 Mark Gardner .10 .05
❑ 275 Travis Fryman .15 .07
❑ 276 Darren Lewis .10 .05
❑ 277 Bruce Bochy MG .10 .05
❑ 278 Jerry Manuel MG .10 .05
❑ 279 Bob Brenly MG .15 .07
❑ 280 Don Baylor MG .15 .07
❑ 281 Dave Lopes MG .15 .07
❑ 282 Jerry Narron MG .10 .05
❑ 283 Tony Muser MG .10 .05
❑ 284 Hal McRae MG .15 .07
❑ 285 Bobby Cox MG .10 .05
❑ 286 Larry Dierker MG .10 .05
❑ 287 Phil Garner MG .10 .05
❑ 288 Jimy Williams MG .10 .05
❑ 289 Bobby Valentine MG .10 .05
❑ 290 Dusty Baker MG .15 .07
❑ 291 Lloyd McClendon MG .10 .05
❑ 292 Mike Scioscia MG .10 .05
❑ 293 Buck Martinez MG .10 .05
❑ 294 Larry Bowa MG .15 .07
❑ 295 Tony LaRussa MG .15 .07
❑ 296 Jeff Torborg MG .10 .05
❑ 297 Tom Kelly MG .10 .05
❑ 298 Mike Hargrove MG .10 .05
❑ 299 Art Howe MG .10 .05
❑ 300 Lou Piniella MG .15 .07
❑ 301 Charlie Manuel MG .10 .05
❑ 302 Buddy Bell MG .10 .05
❑ 303 Tony Perez MG .15 .07
❑ 304 Bob Boone MG .15 .07
❑ 305 Joe Torre MG .15 .07
❑ 306 Jim Tracy MG .10 .05
❑ 307 Jason Lane PROS .50 .23
❑ 308 Chris George PROS .50 .23
❑ 309 Hank Blalock PROS .75 .35
❑ 310 Joe Borchard PROS .75 .35
❑ 311 Marlon Byrd PROS .50 .23
❑ 312 R.ond Cabrera PROS RC .50 .23
❑ 313 F. Sanchez PROS RC .50 .23
❑ 314 Scott Wiggins PROS RC .50 .23
❑ 315 Jason Maule PROS RC .50 .23
❑ 316 Dionys Cesar PROS RC .50 .23
❑ 317 Boof Bonser PROS .75 .35
❑ 318 Juan Tolentino PROS RC .50 .23
❑ 319 Earl Snyder PROS RC .50 .23
❑ 320 Travis Wade PROS RC .50 .23
❑ 321 N. Calzado PROS RC .50 .23
❑ 322 Eric Glaser PROS RC .50 .23
❑ 323 Craig Kuzmic PROS RC .50 .23
❑ 324 Nic Jackson PROS RC .75 .35
❑ 325 Mike Rivera PROS .50 .23
❑ 326 Jason Bay PROS RC .50 .23
❑ 327 Chris Smith DP .50 .23
❑ 328 Jake Gautreau DP .50 .23
❑ 329 Gabe Gross DP .50 .23
❑ 330 Kenny Baugh DP .50 .23
❑ 331 Mike Conroy DP RC .50 .23
❑ 332 Barry Bonds HL 1.00 .45
500th Homer
❑ 333 Rickey Henderson HL .75 .35
Sets record for career walks
❑ 334 Bud Smith HL .50 .23
❑ 335 R. Henderson HL 3000 .75 .35
❑ 336 Barry Bonds HL 1.00 .45
73 homers in a season
❑ 337 Ichiro Suzuki 1.50 .70
Jason Giambi
Roberto Alomar LL
❑ 338 Alex Rodriguez 1.50 .70
Ichiro Suzuki
Bret Boone LL
❑ 339 Alex Rodriguez .50 .23
Jim Thome
Rafael Palmeiro LL
❑ 340 Bret Boone .50 .23
Juan Gonzalez
Alex Rodriguez LL
❑ 341 Freddy Garcia .50 .23
Mike Mussina
Joe Mays LL
❑ 342 Hideo Nomo .50 .23
Mike Mussina
Roger Clemens LL
❑ 343 Larry Walker .50 .23
Todd Helton
Moises Alou#Lance Berkman LL
❑ 344 Sammy Sosa .50 .23
Todd Helton
Barry Bonds LL
❑ 345 Barry Bonds .50 .23
Sammy Sosa
Luis Gonzalez LL
❑ 346 Sammy Sosa .50 .23
Todd Helton
Luis Gonzalez LL
❑ 347 Randy Johnson .50 .23
Curt Schilling
John Burkett LL
❑ 348 Randy Johnson .50 .23
Curt Schilling
Chan Ho Park LL
❑ 349 Seattle Mariners PB .50 .23
❑ 350 Oakland Athletics PB .50 .23
❑ 351 New York Yankees PB .50 .23
❑ 352 Cleveland Indians PB .50 .23
❑ 353 Ariz. Diamondbacks PB .50 .23
❑ 354 Atlanta Braves PB .50 .23
❑ 355 St. Louis Cardinals PB .50 .23
❑ 356 Houston Astros PB .50 .23
❑ 357 Arizona Diamondbacks .50 .23
Houston Astros UWS
❑ 358 Mike Piazza UWS 1.00 .45
❑ 359 Braves-Phillies UWS .50 .23
❑ 360 Curt Schilling UWS .50 .23
❑ 361 Roger Clemens .50 .23
Lee Mazzilli UWS
❑ 362 Sammy Sosa UWS .75 .35
❑ 363 Tom Lampkin 1.50 .70
Ichiro Suzuki
Bret Boone UWS
❑ 364 Barry Bonds .50 .23
Jeff Bagwell UWS
❑ 365 Barry Bonds HR 1 15.00 6.75
❑ 365 Barry Bonds HR 2 10.00 4.50
❑ 365 Barry Bonds HR 3 10.00 4.50
❑ 365 Barry Bonds HR 4 10.00 4.50
❑ 365 Barry Bonds HR 5 10.00 4.50
❑ 365 Barry Bonds HR 6 10.00 4.50
❑ 365 Barry Bonds HR 7 10.00 4.50
❑ 365 Barry Bonds HR 8 10.00 4.50
❑ 365 Barry Bonds HR 9 10.00 4.50
❑ 365 Barry Bonds HR 10 10.00 4.50
❑ 365 Barry Bonds HR 11 10.00 4.50
❑ 365 Barry Bonds HR 12 10.00 4.50
❑ 365 Barry Bonds HR 13 10.00 4.50
❑ 365 Barry Bonds HR 14 10.00 4.50
❑ 365 Barry Bonds HR 15 10.00 4.50
❑ 365 Barry Bonds HR 16 10.00 4.50
❑ 365 Barry Bonds HR 17 10.00 4.50
❑ 365 Barry Bonds HR 18 10.00 4.50
❑ 365 Barry Bonds HR 19 10.00 4.50
❑ 365 Barry Bonds HR 20 10.00 4.50
❑ 365 Barry Bonds HR 21 10.00 4.50
❑ 365 Barry Bonds HR 22 10.00 4.50
❑ 365 Barry Bonds HR 23 10.00 4.50
❑ 365 Barry Bonds HR 24 10.00 4.50
❑ 365 Barry Bonds HR 25 10.00 4.50
❑ 365 Barry Bonds HR 26 10.00 4.50
❑ 365 Barry Bonds HR 27 10.00 4.50
❑ 365 Barry Bonds HR 28 10.00 4.50
❑ 365 Barry Bonds HR 29 10.00 4.50
❑ 365 Barry Bonds HR 30 10.00 4.50
❑ 365 Barry Bonds HR 31 10.00 4.50
❑ 365 Barry Bonds HR 32 10.00 4.50
❑ 365 Barry Bonds HR 33 10.00 4.50
❑ 365 Barry Bonds HR 34 10.00 4.50
❑ 365 Barry Bonds HR 35 10.00 4.50
❑ 365 Barry Bonds HR 36 10.00 4.50
❑ 365 Barry Bonds HR 37 10.00 4.50
❑ 365 Barry Bonds HR 38 10.00 4.50
❑ 365 Barry Bonds HR 39 10.00 4.50
❑ 365 Barry Bonds HR 40 10.00 4.50
❑ 365 Barry Bonds HR 41 10.00 4.50
❑ 365 Barry Bonds HR 42 10.00 4.50
❑ 365 Barry Bonds HR 43 10.00 4.50
❑ 365 Barry Bonds HR 44 10.00 4.50
❑ 365 Barry Bonds HR 45 10.00 4.50
❑ 365 Barry Bonds HR 46 10.00 4.50
❑ 365 Barry Bonds HR 47 10.00 4.50
❑ 365 Barry Bonds HR 48 10.00 4.50
❑ 365 Barry Bonds HR 49 10.00 4.50
❑ 365 Barry Bonds HR 50 10.00 4.50
❑ 365 Barry Bonds HR 51 10.00 4.50
❑ 365 Barry Bonds HR 52 10.00 4.50
❑ 365 Barry Bonds HR 53 10.00 4.50
❑ 365 Barry Bonds HR 54 10.00 4.50
❑ 365 Barry Bonds HR 55 10.00 4.50
❑ 365 Barry Bonds HR 56 10.00 4.50
❑ 365 Barry Bonds HR 57 10.00 4.50
❑ 365 Barry Bonds HR 58 10.00 4.50
❑ 365 Barry Bonds HR 59 10.00 4.50
❑ 365 Barry Bonds HR 60 10.00 4.50
❑ 365 Barry Bonds HR 61 15.00 6.75
❑ 365 Barry Bonds HR 62 10.00 4.50
❑ 365 Barry Bonds HR 63 10.00 4.50
❑ 365 Barry Bonds HR 64 10.00 4.50
❑ 365 Barry Bonds HR 65 10.00 4.50
❑ 365 Barry Bonds HR 66 10.00 4.50
❑ 365 Barry Bonds HR 67 10.00 4.50
❑ 365 Barry Bonds HR 68 10.00 4.50
❑ 365 Barry Bonds HR 69 10.00 4.50
❑ 365 Barry Bonds HR 70 25.00 11.00
❑ 365 Barry Bonds HR 71 10.00 4.50
❑ 365 Barry Bonds HR 72 10.00 4.50
❑ 365 Barry Bonds HR 73 60.00 27.00

2001 Topps American Pie

	MINT	NRMT
COMPLETE SET (150)	40.00	18.00

❑ 1	Al Kaline	1.25	.55
❑ 2	Al Oliver	.40	.18
❑ 3	Andre Dawson	.60	.25
❑ 4	Bert Blyleven	.40	.18
❑ 5	Bill Buckner	.40	.18
❑ 6	Bill Mazeroski	.60	.25
❑ 7	Bob Gibson	1.00	.45
❑ 8	Bill Freehan	.40	.18
❑ 9	Bobby Grich	.40	.18
❑ 10	Bobby Murcer	.40	.18
❑ 11	Bobby Richardson	.40	.18
❑ 12	Boog Powell	.40	.18
❑ 13	Brooks Robinson	1.00	.45
❑ 14	Carl Yastrzemski	1.50	.70
❑ 15	Carlton Fisk	1.00	.45
❑ 16	Clete Boyer	.25	.11
❑ 17	Curt Flood	.40	.18
❑ 18	Dale Murphy	1.00	.45
❑ 19	Tony Conigliaro	.60	.25
❑ 20	Dave Parker	.40	.18
❑ 21	Dave Winfield	1.00	.45
❑ 22	Dick Allen	.40	.18
❑ 23	Dick Groat	.40	.18
❑ 24	Don Drysdale	1.00	.45
❑ 25	Don Sutton	.40	.18
❑ 26	Dwight Evans	.40	.18
❑ 27	Eddie Mathews	1.00	.45
❑ 28	Elston Howard	.40	.18
❑ 29	Frank Howard	.40	.18
❑ 30	Frank Robinson	1.00	.45
❑ 31	Fred Lynn	.40	.18
❑ 32	Gary Carter	.60	.25
❑ 33	Gaylord Perry	.40	.18
❑ 34	Norm Cash	.40	.18
❑ 35	George Brett	2.00	.90
❑ 36	George Foster	.40	.18
❑ 37	Goose Gossage	.40	.18
❑ 38	Graig Nettles	.40	.18
❑ 39	Greg Luzinski	.40	.18
❑ 40	Hank Aaron	2.50	1.10
❑ 41	Harmon Killebrew	1.00	.45
❑ 42	Jack Clark	.40	.18
❑ 43	Jack Morris	.40	.18
❑ 44	Jim Wynn	.40	.18
❑ 45	Jim Kaat	.40	.18
❑ 46	Jim Palmer	1.00	.45
❑ 47	Joe Pepitone	.25	.11
❑ 48	Joe Rudi	.40	.18
❑ 49	Johnny Bench	1.50	.70
❑ 50	Juan Marichal	.60	.25
❑ 51	Keith Hernandez	.40	.18
❑ 52	Bucky Dent	.40	.18
❑ 53	Lou Brock	1.00	.45
❑ 54	Ron Cey	.40	.18
❑ 55	Luis Aparicio	.60	.25
❑ 56	Luis Tiant	.40	.18
❑ 57	Mark Fidrych	.40	.18
❑ 58	Maury Wills	.40	.18
❑ 59	Mickey Lolich	.40	.18
❑ 60	Mickey Rivers	.25	.11
❑ 61	Mike Schmidt	2.00	.90
❑ 62	Moose Skowron	.40	.18
❑ 63	Nolan Ryan	4.00	1.80
❑ 64	Orlando Cepeda	.60	.25
❑ 65	Ozzie Smith	1.25	.55
❑ 66	Phil Niekro	.60	.25
❑ 67	Reggie Jackson	1.50	.70
❑ 68	Reggie Smith	.40	.18
❑ 69	Rico Carty	.25	.11
❑ 70	Roberto Clemente	3.00	1.35
❑ 71	Robin Yount	1.00	.45
❑ 72	Roger Maris	1.50	.70
❑ 73	Rollie Fingers	.40	.18
❑ 74	Ron Guidry	.40	.18
❑ 75	Ron Santo	.60	.25
❑ 76	Ron Swoboda	.40	.18
❑ 77	Sal Bando	.40	.18
❑ 78	Sam McDowell	.40	.18
❑ 79	Steve Carlton	1.00	.45
❑ 80	Thurman Munson	1.50	.70
❑ 81	Tim McCarver	.40	.18
❑ 82	Tom Seaver	1.50	.70
❑ 83	Mike Cuellar	.25	.11
❑ 84	Tony Kubek	.40	.18
❑ 85	Tommy John	.40	.18
❑ 86	Tony Perez	.60	.25
❑ 87	Tug McGraw	.40	.18
❑ 88	Vida Blue	.25	.11
❑ 89	Warren Spahn	1.00	.45
❑ 90	Whitey Ford	1.00	.45
❑ 91	Willie Mays	2.50	1.10
❑ 92	Willie McCovey	1.00	.45
❑ 93	Willie Stargell	.60	.25
❑ 94	Yogi Berra	1.25	.55
❑ 95	Stan Musial	2.00	.90
❑ 96	Jim Piersall	.40	.18
❑ 97	Duke Snider	1.00	.45
❑ 98	Bruce Sutter	.40	.18
❑ 99	Dave Concepcion	.40	.18
❑ 100	Darrell Evans	.40	.18
❑ 101	Dennis Eckersley	.40	.18
❑ 102	Hoyt Wilhelm	.40	.18
❑ 103	Minnie Minoso	.40	.18
❑ 104	Don Newcombe	.40	.18
❑ 105	Richie Ashburn	1.00	.45
❑ 106	Alan Trammell	.60	.25
❑ 107	Jim Hunter	.60	.25
❑ 108	Lou Whitaker	.40	.18
❑ 109	Johnny Podres	.40	.18
❑ 110	Denny Martinez	.40	.18
❑ 111	Willie Horton	.25	.11
❑ 112	Dean Chance	.25	.11
❑ 113	Fergie Jenkins	.40	.18
❑ 114	Cecil Cooper	.40	.18
❑ 115	Rick Reuschel	.25	.11
❑ 116	Civil Rights Movement	.25	.11
❑ 117	Bay of Pigs	.25	.11
❑ 118	Cuban Missile Crisis	.25	.11
❑ 119	N.Y. World's Fair	.25	.11
❑ 120	Atomic Bomb Test Ban Treaty	.25	.11
❑ 121	Kennedy Assassination	1.00	.45
❑ 122	Lyndon Johnson Signs	.25	.11
❑ 123	The Motown Sound	.25	.11
❑ 124	British Music Invasion	.40	.18
❑ 125	U.S. Troops in Vietnam	.25	.11
❑ 126	Space Race	.25	.11
❑ 127	Robert F. Kennedy	.40	.18
❑ 128	Peace Movement	.25	.11
❑ 129	Man On The Moon	.40	.18
❑ 130	Woodstock	.25	.11
❑ 131	Flower Power	.25	.11
❑ 132	Women's Lib Movement	.25	.11
❑ 133	Vietnam Cease Fire	.25	.11
❑ 134	U.S. Gas Shortage	.25	.11
❑ 135	Watergate	.40	.18
❑ 136	Nixon Resigns	.40	.18
❑ 137	Bicentennial	.25	.11
❑ 138	Disco	.25	.11
❑ 139	Three Mile Island	.25	.11
❑ 140	Iran Hostage Crisis	.25	.11
❑ 141	John F. Kennedy	2.00	.90
❑ 142	Marilyn Monroe	2.00	.90
❑ 143	Elvis Presley	2.00	.90
❑ 144	Jimi Hendrix	1.00	.45
❑ 145	Arthur Ashe	.40	.18
❑ 146	Richard Nixon	.40	.18
❑ 147	James Dean	1.00	.45
❑ 148	Janis Joplin	.40	.18
❑ 149	Frank Sinatra	1.00	.45
❑ 150	Malcolm X	.40	.18

2001 Topps Archives

	MINT	NRMT
COMPLETE SET (450)	200.00	90.00
COMPLETE SERIES 1 (225)	100.00	45.00
COMPLETE SERIES 2 (225)	100.00	45.00

❑ 1	Johnny Antonelli 52	.75	.35
❑ 2	Yogi Berra 52 UER Berra's first card was 51 Topps Red Back	2.50	1.10
❑ 3	Dom DiMaggio 52 UER His first Topps card is 1951 Red Back	.75	.35
❑ 4	Carl Erskine 52	.75	.35
❑ 5	Larry Doby 52	.75	.35
❑ 6	Monte Irvin 52	.75	.35
❑ 7	Vernon Law 52	.75	.35
❑ 8	Eddie Mathews 52	2.00	.90
❑ 9	Willie Mays 52	5.00	2.20
❑ 10	Gil McDougald 52	1.25	.55
❑ 11	Andy Pafko 52	1.25	.55
❑ 12	Phil Rizzuto 52	2.00	.90
❑ 13	Preacher Roe 52 UER His first Topps card is 51 Topps Red Back	.75	.35
❑ 14	Hank Sauer 52 UER His first Topps card is 51 Topps Blue Back	.75	.35
❑ 15	Bobby Shantz 52	.75	.35
❑ 16	Enos Slaughter 52 UER His first Topps card is 51 Topps Blue Back	1.25	.55
❑ 17	Warren Spahn 52 UER His First Topps card was 1951 Topps Red Back	2.00	.90
❑ 18	Mickey Vernon 52 UER His First Topps Card was 1951 Topps Blue Back	.75	.35
❑ 19	Early Wynn 52 UER His first Topps card is a 1951 Topps Red Back	.75	.35
❑ 20	Gaylord Perry 62	1.25	.55
❑ 21	Johnny Podres 53	.75	.35
❑ 22	Ernie Banks 54	2.50	1.10
❑ 23	Moose Skowron 54	.75	.35
❑ 24	Harmon Killebrew 55	2.00	.90
❑ 25	Ted Williams 54	6.00	2.70
❑ 26	Jimmy Piersall 56	.75	.35
❑ 27	Frank Thomas 56	.75	.35
❑ 28	Bill Mazeroski 57	2.00	.90
❑ 29	Bobby Richardson 57	1.25	.55
❑ 30	Frank Robinson 57	2.00	.90
❑ 31	Stan Musial 58	3.00	1.35
❑ 32	Johnny Callison 59	.75	.35
❑ 33	Bob Gibson 59	2.00	.90
❑ 34	Frank Howard 60	.75	.35
❑ 35	Willie McCovey 60	2.00	.90
❑ 36	Carl Yastrzemski 60	3.00	1.35
❑ 37	Jim Maloney 61	.75	.35
❑ 38	Ron Santo 61	1.25	.55
❑ 39	Lou Brock 62	2.00	.90
❑ 40	Tim McCarver 62	.75	.35
❑ 41	Joe Pepitone 62	.75	.35
❑ 42	Boog Powell 62	1.25	.55
❑ 43	Bill Freehan 63	.75	.35
❑ 44	Dick Allen 64	.75	.35
❑ 45	Willie Horton 64	.50	.23
❑ 46	Mickey Lolich 64	.75	.35
❑ 47	Wilbur Wood 64	.50	.23
❑ 48	Bert Campaneris 65	.75	.35
❑ 49	Rod Carew 67	2.50	1.10
❑ 50	Luis Aparicio 56	2.00	.90
❑ 51	Joe Morgan 65	2.00	.90
❑ 52	Luis Tiant 65	.75	.35
❑ 53	Bobby Murcer 66	.75	.35
❑ 54	Don Sutton 66	.75	.35
❑ 55	Ken Holtzman 67	.50	.23
❑ 56	Reggie Smith 67	.75	.35
❑ 57	Hal McRae 68	.75	.35
❑ 58	Roy White 68 UER His Rookie Card is 66 Topps	.75	.35
❑ 59	Reggie Jackson 69	3.00	1.35
❑ 60	Graig Nettles 69	.75	.35
❑ 61	Joe Rudi 69	.75	.35
❑ 62	Vida Blue 70	.75	.35
❑ 63	Darrell Evans 70	.75	.35
❑ 64	David Concepcion 71	.75	.35

❑ 65 Bobby Grich 71 .75 .35
❑ 66 Greg Luzinski 71 .75 .35
❑ 67 Ron Cey 72 .75 .35
❑ 68 George Hendrick 72 .50 .23
❑ 69 Dwight Evans 73 1.25 .55
❑ 70 Gary Matthews 73 .50 .23
❑ 71 Mike Schmidt 73 5.00 2.20
❑ 72 Jim Kaat 60 .75 .35
❑ 73 Dave Winfield 74 2.00 .90
❑ 74 Gary Carter 75 2.00 .90
❑ 75 Dennis Eckersley 76 2.00 .90
❑ 76 Kent Tekulve 76 .75 .35
❑ 77 Andre Dawson 77 2.00 .90
❑ 78 Denny Martinez 77 .75 .35
❑ 79 Bruce Sutter 77 .75 .35
❑ 80 Jack Morris 78 .75 .35
❑ 81 Ozzie Smith 80 2.50 1.10
❑ 82 Lee Smith 82 .75 .35
❑ 83 Don Mattingly 84 6.00 2.70
❑ 84 Joe Carter 85 .75 .35
❑ 85 Kirby Puckett 85 5.00 2.20
❑ 86 Joe Adcock 52 .75 .35
❑ 87 Gus Bell 52 UER .50 .23
His first Topps card is 1951
Topps Red Back
❑ 88 Roy Campanella 52 2.50 1.10
❑ 89 Jackie Jensen 52 .75 .35
❑ 90 Johnny Mize 52 1.25 .55
❑ 91 Allie Reynolds 52 .75 .35
❑ 92 Al Rosen 52 UER .75 .35
His first Topps card is a 1951
Topps Red Back
❑ 93 Hal Newhouser 53 .75 .35
❑ 94 Harvey Kuenn 54 .75 .35
❑ 95 Nellie Fox 56 2.00 .90
❑ 96 Elston Howard 56 1.25 .55
❑ 97 Sal Maglie 57 .75 .35
❑ 98 Roger Maris 58 3.00 1.35
❑ 99 Norm Cash 60 UER .75 .35
His Rookie Card was in 1959
Topps
❑ 100 Thurman Munson 70 3.00 1.35
❑ 101 Roy Campanella 57 UER 2.00 .90
His first Topps card is in 1952
❑ 102 Larry Doby 59 .75 .35
❑ 103 Dom Dimaggio 53 .75 .35
❑ 104 Johnny Mize 53 .75 .35
❑ 105 Allie Reynolds 53 .75 .35
❑ 106 Preacher Roe 54 .75 .35
❑ 107 Hal Newhouser 55 .50 .23
❑ 108 Monte Irvin 56 .75 .35
❑ 109 Carl Erskine 59 .75 .35
❑ 110 Enos Slaughter 59 .75 .35
❑ 111 Gil McDougald 60 .75 .35
❑ 112 Andy Pafko 59 .75 .35
❑ 113 Sal Maglie 59 .50 .23
❑ 114 Johnny Antonelli 61 .50 .23
❑ 115 Phil Rizzuto 61 1.25 .55
❑ 116 Yogi Berra 62 2.00 .90
❑ 117 Jim Wynn 77 .50 .23
❑ 118 Mickey Vernon 63 .50 .23
❑ 119 Gus Bell 64 .50 .23
❑ 120 Ted Williams 58 4.00 1.80
❑ 121 Frank Thomas 65 .50 .23
❑ 122 Bobby Richardson 66 .75 .35
❑ 123 Gaylord Perry 83 .75 .35
❑ 124 Vernon Law 67 .50 .23
❑ 125 Jimmy Piersall 67 .50 .23
❑ 126 Moose Skowron 67 .75 .35
❑ 127 Joe Adcock 63 .50 .23
❑ 128 Johnny Podres 69 .75 .35
❑ 129 Ernie Banks 71 2.00 .90
❑ 130 Jim Maloney 72 .50 .23
❑ 131 Johnny Callison 73 .50 .23
❑ 132 Eddie Mathews 68 1.25 .55
❑ 133 Joe Pepitone 73 .75 .35
❑ 134 Warren Spahn 65 1.25 .55
❑ 135 Bill Mazeroski 72 1.25 .55
❑ 136 Norm Cash 74 .75 .35
❑ 137 Bob Gibson 75 1.25 .55
❑ 138 Harmon Killebrew 75 1.25 .55
❑ 139 Frank Robinson 75 1.25 .55
❑ 140 Ron Santo 73 .75 .35
❑ 141 Hank Sauer 59 .50 .23
❑ 142 Bobby Shantz 64 .50 .23
❑ 143 Nellie Fox 65 1.25 .55
❑ 144 Elston Howard 68 .75 .35
❑ 145 Jackie Jensen 61 .75 .35
❑ 146 Al Rosen 56 .75 .35
❑ 147 Dick Allen 76 .50 .23
❑ 148 Bill Freehan 77 .75 .35
❑ 149 Boog Powell 77 .75 .35
❑ 150 Lou Brock 79 UER 1.25 .55
Header for stats on back is
for a pitcher
Brock was an outfielder
❑ 151 Rod Carew 86 2.00 .90
❑ 152 Wilbur Wood 79 .50 .23
❑ 153 Thurman Munson 79 2.00 .90
❑ 154 Ken Holtzman 80 .50 .23
❑ 155 Willie Horton 80 .50 .23
❑ 156 Mickey Lolich 80 .50 .23
❑ 157 Tim McCarver 80 .50 .23
❑ 158 Willie McCovey 80 1.25 .55
❑ 159 Roy White 80 .50 .23
❑ 160 Bobby Murcer 83 .50 .23
❑ 161 Joe Rudi 83 .50 .23
❑ 162 Reggie Smith 83 .50 .23
❑ 163 Luis Tiant 83 .50 .23
❑ 164 Bert Campaneris 84 .50 .23
❑ 165 Frank Howard 73 .50 .23
❑ 166 Harvey Kuenn 66 .50 .23
❑ 167 Greg Luzinski 85 .50 .23
❑ 168 Luis Aparicio 74 1.25 .55
❑ 169 Willie Mays 73 3.00 1.35
❑ 170 Roger Maris 68 2.00 .90
❑ 171 Vida Blue 87 .50 .23
❑ 172 Bobby Grich 87 .50 .23
❑ 173 Reggie Jackson 87 2.00 .90
❑ 174 Hal McRae 87 .50 .23
❑ 175 Carl Yastrzemski 83 2.00 .90
❑ 176 David Concepcion 88 .50 .23
❑ 177 Ron Cey 87 .50 .23
❑ 178 George Hendrick 88 .50 .23
❑ 179 Gary Matthews 88 .50 .23
❑ 180 Stan Musial 63 2.00 .90
❑ 181 Graig Nettles 88 .50 .23
❑ 182 Don Sutton 88 .75 .35
❑ 183 Kent Tekulve 88 .50 .23
❑ 184 Bruce Sutter 89 .75 .35
❑ 185 Darrell Evans 90 .50 .23
❑ 186 Mike Schmidt 89 3.00 1.35
❑ 187 Jim Kaat 83 .50 .23
❑ 188 Dwight Evans 92 .75 .35
❑ 189 Gary Carter 93 1.25 .55
❑ 190 Jack Morris 94 .50 .23
❑ 191 Joe Morgan 85 1.25 .55
❑ 192 Dave Winfield 95 1.25 .55
❑ 193 Andre Dawson 96 1.25 .55
❑ 194 Lee Smith 96 .50 .23
❑ 195 Ozzie Smith 96 2.00 .90
❑ 196 Denny Martinez 97 .50 .23
❑ 197 Don Mattingly 96 4.00 1.80
❑ 198 Joe Carter 98 .75 .35
❑ 199 Dennis Eckersley 98 .75 .35
❑ 200 Kirby Puckett 96 3.00 1.35
❑ 201 Walter Alston MG 56 .75 .35
❑ 202 Casey Stengel MG 60 .75 .35
❑ 203 Sparky Anderson MG 71 .75 .35
❑ 204 Tommy Lasorda MG 88 .75 .35
❑ 205 Whitey Herzog MG 88 .50 .23
❑ 206 AL HR Leaders 70 .75 .35
Harmon Killebrew
Frank Howard
Reggie Jackson
❑ 207 NL HR Leaders 68 3.00 1.35
Hank Aaron
Jim Wynn
Ron Santo
Willie McCovey
❑ 208 AL HR Leaders 67 2.00 .90
Brooks Robinson
Harmon Killebrew
Boog Powell
❑ 209 AL Batting Leaders 65 .75 .35
Tony Oliva
Brooks Robinson
Elston Howard
❑ 210 NL HR Leaders 64 3.00 1.35
Hank Aaron
Willie McCovey
Willie Mays
Orlando Cepeda
❑ 211 NL HR Leaders 63 3.00 1.35
Hank Aaron
Frank Robinson
Willie Mays
Ernie Banks
Orlando Cepeda
❑ 212 AL HR Leaders 68 2.00 .90
Carl Yastrzemski
Harmon Killebrew
Frank Howard
❑ 213 Ernie Banks 59 Thrill 2.00 .90
❑ 214 Hank Aaron 59 Thrill 3.00 1.35
❑ 215 Willie Mays 59 Thrill 3.00 1.35
❑ 216 Al Kaline 59 Thrill 2.00 .90
❑ 217 Stan Musial 59 Thrill 2.00 .90
❑ 218 Duke Snider 59 Thrill 2.00 .90
❑ 219 The Champs 67 2.00 .90
Frank Robinson
Hank Bauer MG
Brooks Robinson UER
All Cards have a 1965 Leaders Back
❑ 220 Pride of the NL 63 3.00 1.35
Willie Mays
Stan Musial
❑ 221 Whitey Ford WS 63 2.00 .90
❑ 222 Jerry Koosman WS 70 .50 .23
❑ 223 Bob Gibson WS 65 1.25 .55
❑ 224 Gil Hodges WS 60 1.25 .55
❑ 225 Reggie Jackson WS 78 2.00 .90
❑ 226 Hank Bauer 52 .75 .35
❑ 227 Ralph Branca 52 .75 .35
❑ 228 Joe Garagiola 52 .75 .35
❑ 229 Bob Feller 52 2.00 .90
❑ 230 Dick Groat 52 .75 .35
❑ 231 George Kell 52 .75 .35
❑ 232 Bob Boone 73 .75 .35
❑ 233 Minnie Minoso 52 .75 .35
❑ 234 Billy Pierce 52 .75 .35
❑ 235 Robin Roberts 52 1.25 .55
❑ 236 Johnny Sain 52 .75 .35
❑ 237 Red Schoendienst 52 .75 .35
❑ 238 Curt Simmons 52 .75 .35
❑ 239 Duke Snider 52 2.50 1.10
❑ 240 Bobby Thomson 52 1.25 .55
❑ 241 Hoyt Wilhelm 52 1.25 .55
❑ 242 Elroy Face 53 .75 .35
❑ 243 Ralph Kiner 53 .75 .35
❑ 244 Hank Aaron 54 6.00 2.70
❑ 245 Al Kaline 54 2.50 1.10
❑ 246 Don Larsen 56 2.00 .90
❑ 247 Tug McGraw 65 .75 .35
❑ 248 Don Newcombe 56 1.25 .55
❑ 249 Herb Score 56 .75 .35
❑ 250 Clete Boyer 57 .75 .35
❑ 251 Lindy McDaniel 57 .50 .23
❑ 252 Brooks Robinson 57 2.50 1.10
❑ 253 Orlando Cepeda 58 1.25 .55
❑ 254 Larry Bowa 70 .75 .35
❑ 255 Mike Cuellar 59 .75 .35
❑ 256 Jim Perry 59 .75 .35
❑ 257 Dave Parker 74 .75 .35
❑ 258 Maury Wills 60 .75 .35
❑ 259 Willie Davis 61 .50 .23
❑ 260 Juan Marichal 61 1.25 .55
❑ 261 Jim Bouton 62 .75 .35
❑ 262 Dean Chance 62 .75 .35
❑ 263 Sam McDowell 62 .75 .35
❑ 264 Whitey Ford 53 4.00 1.80
❑ 265 Bob Uecker 62 2.00 .90
❑ 266 Willie Stargell 63 2.00 .90
❑ 267 Rico Carty 64 .75 .35
❑ 268 Tommy John 64 .75 .35
❑ 269 Phil Niekro 64 1.25 .55
❑ 270 Paul Blair 65 .75 .35
❑ 271 Steve Carlton 65 4.00 1.80
❑ 272 Jim Lonborg 65 .75 .35
❑ 273 Tony Perez 65 1.25 .55
❑ 274 Ron Swoboda 65 .75 .35
❑ 275 Fergie Jenkins 66 1.25 .55
❑ 276 Jim Palmer 66 2.00 .90
❑ 277 Sal Bando 67 .75 .35
❑ 278 Tom Seaver 67 5.00 2.20
❑ 279 Johnny Bench 68 5.00 2.20
❑ 280 Nolan Ryan 68 8.00 3.60
❑ 281 Rollie Fingers 69 1.25 .55

❑ 282 Sparky Lyle 69 .75 .35
❑ 283 Al Oliver 69 .75 .35
❑ 284 Bob Watson 69 .75 .35
❑ 285 Bill Buckner 70 .75 .35
❑ 286 Bert Blyleven 71 1.25 .55
❑ 287 George Foster 71 .75 .35
❑ 288 Al Hrabosky 71 .50 .23
❑ 289 Cecil Cooper 72 .75 .35
❑ 290 Carlton Fisk 72 2.00 .90
❑ 291 Mickey Rivers 72 .75 .35
❑ 292 Goose Gossage 73 .75 .35
❑ 293 Rick Reuschel 73 .75 .35
❑ 294 Bucky Dent 74 .75 .35
❑ 295 Frank Tanana 74 .75 .35
❑ 296 George Brett 75 5.00 2.20
❑ 297 Keith Hernandez 75 .75 .35
❑ 298 Fred Lynn 75 .75 .35
❑ 299 Robin Yount 75 3.00 1.35
❑ 300 Ron Guidry 76 .75 .35
❑ 301 Jack Clark 77 .75 .35
❑ 302 Mark Fidrych 77 .75 .35
❑ 303 Dale Murphy 77 2.00 .90
❑ 304 Willie Hernandez 78 .50 .23
❑ 305 Lou Whitaker 78 .75 .35
❑ 306 Kirk Gibson 81 1.25 .55
❑ 307 Wade Boggs 83 2.00 .90
❑ 308 Ryne Sandberg 83 5.00 2.20
❑ 309 Orel Hershiser 85 .75 .35
❑ 310 Jimmy Key 85 .75 .35
❑ 311 Richie Ashburn 52 1.25 .55
❑ 312 Smoky Burgess 52 .75 .35
❑ 313 Gil Hodges 52 2.00 .90
❑ 314 Ted Kluszewski 52 1.25 .55
❑ 315 Pee Wee Reese 52 2.00 .90
❑ 316 Jackie Robinson 52 4.00 1.80
❑ 317 Jim Wynn 64 .50 .23
❑ 318 Satchel Paige 53 4.00 1.80
❑ 319 Roberto Clemente 55 5.00 2.20
❑ 320 Carl Furillo 56 .75 .35
❑ 321 Don Drysdale 57 2.00 .90
❑ 322 Curt Flood 58 .75 .35
❑ 323 Bob Allison 59 .75 .35
❑ 324 Tony Conigliaro 64 .75 .35
❑ 325 Dan Quisenberry 80 .75 .35
❑ 326 Ralph Branca 52 .50 .23
❑ 327 Bob Feller 53 1.25 .55
❑ 328 Satchel Paige 53 4.00 1.80
❑ 329 George Kell 58 .50 .23
❑ 330 Pee Wee Reese 58 1.25 .55
❑ 331 Bobby Thomson 60 .75 .35
❑ 332 Carl Furillo 60 .50 .23
❑ 333 Hank Bauer 61 .50 .23
❑ 334 Herb Score 62 .50 .23
❑ 335 Richie Ashburn 63 .75 .35
❑ 336 Billy Pierce 64 .50 .23
❑ 337 Duke Snider 64 2.00 .90
❑ 338 Early Wynn 62 .50 .23
❑ 339 Robin Roberts 66 .75 .35
❑ 340 Dick Groat 67 .50 .23
❑ 341 Curt Simmons 67 .50 .23
❑ 342 Bob Uecker 67 1.25 .55
❑ 343 Smoky Burgess 67 .50 .23
❑ 344 Jim Bouton 68 .50 .23
❑ 345 Elroy Face 69 .50 .23
❑ 346 Don Drysdale 69 1.25 .55
❑ 347 Bob Allison 70 .50 .23
❑ 348 Clete Boyer 71 .50 .23
❑ 349 Dean Chance 71 .50 .23
❑ 350 Tony Conigliaro 71 .50 .23
❑ 351 Curt Flood 71 .50 .23
❑ 352 Hoyt Wilhelm 72 .75 .35
❑ 353 Ron Swoboda 73 .50 .23
❑ 354 Roberto Clemente 73 3.00 1.35
❑ 355 Tug McGraw 85 .50 .23
❑ 356 Orlando Cepeda 74 .75 .35
❑ 357 Joe Garagiola 52 .50 .23
❑ 358 Juan Marichal 74 .75 .35
❑ 359 Sam McDowell 74 .50 .23
❑ 360 Johnny Sain 55 .50 .23
❑ 361 Ted Kluszewski 61 .75 .35
❑ 362 Al Kaline 74 2.00 .90
❑ 363 Lindy McDaniel 75 .50 .23
❑ 364 Don Newcombe 60 .75 .35
❑ 365 Jim Perry 75 .50 .23
❑ 366 Hank Aaron 76 4.00 1.80
❑ 367 Don Larsen 65 .75 .35
❑ 368 Mike Cuellar 77 .50 .23
❑ 369 Willie Davis 77 .50 .23
❑ 370 Ralph Kiner 53 .75 .35
❑ 371 Minnie Minoso 64 .75 .35
❑ 372 Larry Bowa 85 .50 .23
❑ 373 Brooks Robinson 77 1.25 .55
❑ 374 Bob Boone 90 .50 .23
❑ 375 Jim Lonborg 79 .50 .23
❑ 376 Paul Blair 80 .50 .23
❑ 377 Rico Carty 80 .50 .23
❑ 378 Sal Bando 81 .50 .23
❑ 379 Mark Fidrych 81 .50 .23
❑ 380 Al Hrabosky 82 .50 .23
❑ 381 Willie Stargell 82 1.25 .55
❑ 382 Johnny Bench 83 3.00 1.35
❑ 383 Dave Parker 91 .50 .23
❑ 384 Sparky Lyle 83 .50 .23
❑ 385 Fergie Jenkins 84 .75 .35
❑ 386 Jim Palmer 84 1.25 .55
❑ 387 Whitey Ford 67 2.50 1.10
❑ 388 Tony Perez 86 .75 .35
❑ 389 Mickey Rivers 85 .50 .23
❑ 390 Bob Watson 85 .50 .23
❑ 391 Rollie Fingers 86 .75 .35
❑ 392 George Foster 86 .50 .23
❑ 393 Al Oliver 86 .50 .23
❑ 394 Tom Seaver 87 3.00 1.35
❑ 395 Maury Wills 72 .50 .23
❑ 396 Steve Carlton 87T 1.25 .55
❑ 397 Cecil Cooper 88 .50 .23
❑ 398 Bill Buckner 88 .50 .23
❑ 399 Phil Niekro 87 .75 .35
❑ 400 Red Schoendienst 62 .75 .35
❑ 401 Ron Guidry 89 .50 .23
❑ 402 Willie Hernandez 89 .50 .23
❑ 403 Tommy John 89 .50 .23
❑ 404 Gil Hodges 63 1.25 .55
❑ 405 Bucky Dent 84 .50 .23
❑ 406 Keith Hernandez 90 .50 .23
❑ 407 Dan Quisenberry 90 .50 .23
❑ 408 Fred Lynn 91 .50 .23
❑ 409 Rick Reuschel 91 .50 .23
❑ 410 Jackie Robinson 56 2.50 1.10
❑ 411 Goose Gossage 92 .50 .23
❑ 412 Bert Blyleven 93 .75 .35
❑ 413 Jack Clark 93 .50 .23
❑ 414 Carlton Fisk 93 1.25 .55
❑ 415 Dale Murphy 93 .75 .35
❑ 416 Frank Tanana 93 .50 .23
❑ 417 George Brett 94 3.00 1.35
❑ 418 Robin Yount 94 2.50 1.10
❑ 419 Kirk Gibson 95 .75 .35
❑ 420 Lou Whitaker 95 .50 .23
❑ 421 Ryne Sandberg 97 UER 3.00 1.35
Card lists 1996 homers as 252
❑ 422 Jimmy Key 98 .50 .23
❑ 423 Nolan Ryan 94 5.00 2.20
❑ 424 Wade Boggs 00 .75 .35
❑ 425 Orel Hershiser 00 .50 .23
❑ 426 Billy Martin MG 84 .75 .35
❑ 427 Ralph Houk MG 62 .75 .35
❑ 428 Chuck Tanner MG 72 .50 .23
❑ 429 Earl Weaver MG 71 .75 .35
❑ 430 Leo Durocher MG 52 .75 .35
❑ 431 AL HR Leaders 66 .75 .35
Tony Conigliaro
Norm Cash
Willie Horton
❑ 432 NL HR Leaders 60 2.00 .90
Ernie Banks
Hank Aaron
Eddie Mathews
Ken Boyer
❑ 433 AL Batting Leaders 62 .75 .35
Norm Cash
Elston Howard
Al Kaline
Jimmy Piersall
❑ 434 Leading Firemen 79 .50 .23
Goose Gossage
Rollie Fingers
❑ 435 Strikeout Leaders 77 3.00 1.35
Nolan Ryan
Tom Seaver
❑ 436 HR Leaders 74 1.25 .55
Reggie Jackson
Willie Stargell
❑ 437 RBI Leaders 73 1.25 .55
Johnny Bench
Dick Allen
❑ 438 Roger Maris 3.00 1.35
Blasts 61st 62
❑ 439 Carl Yastrzemski 2.00 .90
World Series Game Two 68
❑ 440 Nolan Ryan RB 78 5.00 2.20
❑ 441 Baltimore Orioles 70 .75 .35
❑ 442 Tony Perez RB 86 .75 .35
❑ 443 Steve Carlton RB 84 1.25 .55
❑ 444 Wade Boggs RB 89 .75 .35
❑ 445 Andre Dawson RB 89 1.25 .55
❑ 446 Whitey Ford WS 62 2.00 .90
❑ 447 Hank Aaron WS 59 4.00 1.80
❑ 448 Bob Gibson WS 69 1.25 .55
❑ 449 Roberto Clemente WS 72 4.00 1.80
❑ 450 Orioles Brooks Robinson WS 71 1.25 .55

2001 Topps Archives Reserve

	MINT	NRMT
COMPLETE SET (100)	150.00	70.00

❑ 1 Joe Adcock 52 1.25 .55
❑ 2 Brooks Robinson 57 4.00 1.80
❑ 3 Luis Aparicio 56 3.00 1.35
❑ 4 Richie Ashburn 52 2.00 .90
❑ 5 Hank Bauer 52 1.25 .55
❑ 6 Johnny Bench 68 8.00 3.60
❑ 7 Wade Boggs 83 6.00 2.70
❑ 8 Moose Skowron 54 1.25 .55
❑ 9 George Brett 75 8.00 3.60
❑ 10 Lou Brock 62 3.00 1.35
❑ 11 Roy Campanella 52 4.00 1.80
❑ 12 Willie Hernandez 78 1.25 .55
❑ 13 Steve Carlton 65 6.00 2.70
❑ 14 Gary Carter 75 3.00 1.35
❑ 15 Hoyt Wilhelm 52 2.00 .90
❑ 16 Orlando Cepeda 58 2.00 .90
❑ 17 Roberto Clemente 55 8.00 3.60
❑ 18 Dale Murphy 77 3.00 1.35
❑ 19 Dave Concepcion 71 1.25 .55
❑ 20 Dom DiMaggio 52 1.25 .55
❑ 21 Larry Doby 52 1.25 .55
❑ 22 Don Drysdale 57 3.00 1.35
❑ 23 Dennis Eckersley 76 3.00 1.35
❑ 24 Bob Feller 52 3.00 1.35
❑ 25 Rollie Fingers 69 2.00 .90
❑ 26 Carlton Fisk 72 3.00 1.35
❑ 27 Nellie Fox 56 3.00 1.35
❑ 28 Mickey Rivers 72 1.25 .55
❑ 29 Tommy John 64 1.25 .55
❑ 30 Johnny Sain 52 1.25 .55
❑ 31 Keith Hernandez 75 1.25 .55
❑ 32 Gil Hodges 52 3.00 1.35
❑ 33 Elston Howard 56 2.00 .90
❑ 34 Frank Howard 60 1.25 .55
❑ 35 Bob Gibson 59 3.00 1.35
❑ 36 Fergie Jenkins 66 2.00 .90
❑ 37 Jackie Jensen 52 1.25 .55
❑ 38 Al Kaline 54 4.00 1.80
❑ 39 Harmon Killebrew 55 3.00 1.35
❑ 40 Ralph Kiner 53 1.25 .55
❑ 41 Dick Groat 52 1.25 .55
❑ 42 Don Larsen 56 3.00 1.35

❑ 43 Ralph Branca 52 ... 1.25 .55
❑ 44 Mickey Lolich 64 ... 1.25 .55
❑ 45 Juan Marichal 61 ... 2.00 .90
❑ 46 Roger Maris 58 ... 5.00 2.20
❑ 47 Bobby Thomson 52 ... 2.00 .90
❑ 48 Eddie Mathews 52 ... 3.00 1.35
❑ 49 Don Mattingly 84 ... 10.00 4.50
❑ 50 Willie McCovey 60 ... 3.00 1.35
❑ 51 Gil McDougald 52 ... 2.00 .90
❑ 52 Tug McGraw 65 ... 1.25 .55
❑ 53 Billy Pierce 52 ... 1.25 .55
❑ 54 Minnie Minoso 52 ... 1.25 .55
❑ 55 Johnny Mize 52 ... 2.00 .90
❑ 56 Elroy Face 53 ... 1.25 .55
❑ 57 Joe Morgan 65 ... 3.00 1.35
❑ 58 Thurman Munson 70 ... 5.00 2.20
❑ 59 Stan Musial 58 ... 5.00 2.20
❑ 60 Phil Niekro 64 ... 2.00 .90
❑ 61 Paul Blair 65 ... 1.25 .55
❑ 62 Andy Pafko 52 ... 2.00 .90
❑ 63 Satchel Paige 53 ... 6.00 2.70
❑ 64 Tony Perez 65 ... 2.00 .90
❑ 65 Sal Bando 67 ... 1.25 .55
❑ 66 Jimmy Piersall 56 ... 1.25 .55
❑ 67 Kirby Puckett 85 ... 8.00 3.60
❑ 68 Phil Rizzuto 52 ... 3.00 1.35
❑ 69 Robin Roberts 52 ... 2.00 .90
❑ 70 Jackie Robinson 52 ... 6.00 2.70
❑ 71 Ryne Sandberg 83 ... 8.00 3.60
❑ 72 Mike Schmidt 73 ... 8.00 3.60
❑ 73 Red Schoendienst 52 ... 1.25 .55
❑ 74 Herb Score 56 ... 1.25 .55
❑ 75 Enos Slaughter 52 ... 2.00 .90
❑ 76 Ozzie Smith 80 ... 4.00 1.80
❑ 77 Warren Spahn 52 ... 3.00 1.35
❑ 78 Don Sutton 66 ... 1.25 .55
❑ 79 Luis Tiant 65 ... 1.25 .55
❑ 80 Ted Kluszewski 52 ... 2.00 .90
❑ 81 Whitey Ford 53 ... 6.00 2.70
❑ 82 Maury Wills 60 ... 1.25 .55
❑ 83 Dave Winfield 74 ... 3.00 1.35
❑ 84 Early Wynn 52 ... 1.25 .55
❑ 85 Carl Yastrzemski 60 ... 5.00 2.20
❑ 86 Robin Yount 75 ... 5.00 2.20
❑ 87 Bob Allison 59 ... 1.25 .55
❑ 88 Clete Boyer 57 ... 1.25 .55
❑ 89 Reggie Jackson 69 ... 5.00 2.20
❑ 90 Yogi Berra 52 ... 4.00 1.80
❑ 91 Willie Mays 52 ... 8.00 3.60
❑ 92 Jim Palmer 66 ... 3.00 1.35
❑ 93 Pee Wee Reese 52 ... 3.00 1.35
❑ 94 Frank Robinson 57 ... 3.00 1.35
❑ 95 Boog Powell 62 ... 2.00 .90
❑ 96 Willie Stargell 63 ... 3.00 1.35
❑ 97 Nolan Ryan 68 ... 12.00 5.50
❑ 98 Tom Seaver 67 ... 8.00 3.60
❑ 99 Duke Snider 52 ... 4.00 1.80
❑ 100 Bill Mazeroski 57 ... 3.00 1.35

1996 Topps Chrome

	MINT	NRMT
COMPLETE SET (165)	60.00	27.00

❑ 1 Tony Gwynn STP ... 1.50 .70
❑ 2 Mike Piazza STP ... 2.00 .90
❑ 3 Greg Maddux STP ... 2.00 .90
❑ 4 Jeff Bagwell STP ... 1.00 .45
❑ 5 Larry Walker STP ... .40 .18
❑ 6 Barry Larkin STP ... .60 .25
❑ 7 Mickey Mantle COMM ... 10.00 4.50
❑ 8 Tom Glavine STP ... .60 .25
❑ 9 Craig Biggio STP ... .60 .25
❑ 10 Barry Bonds STP ... 2.00 .90
❑ 11 H.Slocumb STP ... .40 .18
❑ 12 Matt Williams STP ... .60 .25
❑ 13 Todd Helton ... 6.00 2.70
❑ 14 Paul Molitor ... 1.50 .70
❑ 15 Glenallen Hill ... .40 .18
❑ 16 Troy Percival ... .40 .18
❑ 17 Albert Belle ... .60 .25
❑ 18 Mark Wohlers ... .40 .18
❑ 19 Kirby Puckett ... 4.00 1.80
❑ 20 Mark Grace ... 1.50 .70
❑ 21 J.T. Snow ... .60 .25
❑ 22 David Justice ... .60 .25
❑ 23 Mike Mussina ... 1.50 .70
❑ 24 Bernie Williams ... 1.50 .70
❑ 25 Ron Gant ... .40 .18
❑ 26 Carlos Baerga ... .40 .18
❑ 27 Gary Sheffield ... .60 .25
❑ 28 Cal Ripken 2131 ... 6.00 2.70
❑ 29 Frank Thomas ... 2.00 .90
❑ 30 Kevin Seitzer ... .40 .18
❑ 31 Joe Carter ... .60 .25
❑ 32 Jeff King ... .40 .18
❑ 33 David Cone ... .60 .25
❑ 34 Eddie Murray ... 1.50 .70
❑ 35 Brian Jordan ... .60 .25
❑ 36 Garret Anderson ... .60 .25
❑ 37 Hideo Nomo ... 2.00 .90
❑ 38 Steve Finley ... .60 .25
❑ 39 Ivan Rodriguez ... 1.50 .70
❑ 40 Quilvio Veras ... .40 .18
❑ 41 Mark McGwire ... 6.00 2.70
❑ 42 Greg Vaughn ... .60 .25
❑ 43 Randy Johnson ... 2.00 .90
❑ 44 David Segui ... .40 .18
❑ 45 Derek Bell ... .40 .18
❑ 46 John Valentin ... .40 .18
❑ 47 Steve Avery ... .40 .18
❑ 48 Tino Martinez ... .60 .25
❑ 49 Shane Reynolds ... .40 .18
❑ 50 Jim Edmonds ... 1.00 .45
❑ 51 Raul Mondesi ... .60 .25
❑ 52 Chipper Jones ... 3.00 1.35
❑ 53 Gregg Jefferies ... .40 .18
❑ 54 Ken Caminiti ... .60 .25
❑ 55 Brian McRae ... .40 .18
❑ 56 Don Mattingly ... 4.00 1.80
❑ 57 Marty Cordova ... .40 .18
❑ 58 Vinny Castilla ... .60 .25
❑ 59 John Smoltz ... .60 .25
❑ 60 Travis Fryman ... .60 .25
❑ 61 Ryan Klesko ... .60 .25
❑ 62 Alex Fernandez ... .40 .18
❑ 63 Dante Bichette ... .60 .25
❑ 64 Eric Karros ... .60 .25
❑ 65 Roger Clemens ... 4.00 1.80
❑ 66 Randy Myers ... .40 .18
❑ 67 Cal Ripken ... 6.00 2.70
❑ 68 Rod Beck ... .40 .18
❑ 69 Jack McDowell ... .40 .18
❑ 70 Ken Griffey Jr. ... 5.00 2.20
❑ 71 Ramon Martinez ... .40 .18
❑ 72 Jason Giambi ... 1.50 .70
❑ 73 Nomar Garciaparra FS ... 4.00 1.80
❑ 74 Billy Wagner ... .40 .18
❑ 75 Todd Greene ... .40 .18
❑ 76 Paul Wilson ... .40 .18
❑ 77 Johnny Damon ... .60 .25
❑ 78 Alan Benes ... .40 .18
❑ 79 Karim Garcia FS ... .40 .18
❑ 80 Derek Jeter FS ... 6.00 2.70
❑ 81 Kirby Puckett STP ... 2.00 .90
❑ 82 Cal Ripken STP ... 3.00 1.35
❑ 83 Albert Belle STP ... .60 .25
❑ 84 Randy Johnson STP ... 1.00 .45
❑ 85 Wade Boggs STP ... .60 .25
❑ 86 Carlos Baerga STP ... .40 .18
❑ 87 Ivan Rodriguez STP ... .60 .25
❑ 88 Mike Mussina STP ... .60 .25
❑ 89 Frank Thomas STP ... 1.00 .45
❑ 90 Ken Griffey Jr. STP ... 2.50 1.10
❑ 91 Jose Mesa STP ... .40 .18
❑ 92 Matt Morris RC ... 10.00 4.50
❑ 93 Mike Piazza ... 4.00 1.80
❑ 94 Edgar Martinez ... 1.00 .45
❑ 95 Chuck Knoblauch ... .60 .25
❑ 96 Andres Galarraga ... 1.00 .45
❑ 97 Tony Gwynn ... 3.00 1.35
❑ 98 Lee Smith ... .60 .25
❑ 99 Sammy Sosa ... 3.00 1.35
❑ 100 Jim Thome ... 1.50 .70
❑ 101 Bernard Gilkey ... .40 .18
❑ 102 Brady Anderson ... .60 .25
❑ 103 Rico Brogna ... .40 .18
❑ 104 Len Dykstra ... .60 .25
❑ 105 Tom Glavine ... 1.50 .70
❑ 106 John Olerud ... .60 .25
❑ 107 Terry Steinbach ... .40 .18
❑ 108 Brian Hunter ... .40 .18
❑ 109 Jay Buhner ... .60 .25
❑ 110 Mo Vaughn ... .60 .25
❑ 111 Jose Mesa ... .40 .18
❑ 112 Brett Butler ... .60 .25
❑ 113 Chili Davis ... .60 .25
❑ 114 Paul O'Neill ... 1.50 .70
❑ 115 Roberto Alomar ... 1.50 .70
❑ 116 Barry Larkin ... 1.50 .70
❑ 117 Marquis Grissom ... .40 .18
❑ 118 Will Clark ... 1.50 .70
❑ 119 Barry Bonds ... 4.00 1.80
❑ 120 Ozzie Smith ... 2.00 .90
❑ 121 Pedro Martinez ... 2.00 .90
❑ 122 Craig Biggio ... 1.00 .45
❑ 123 Moises Alou ... .60 .25
❑ 124 Robin Ventura ... .60 .25
❑ 125 Greg Maddux ... 4.00 1.80
❑ 126 Tim Salmon ... .60 .25
❑ 127 Wade Boggs ... 1.50 .70
❑ 128 Ismael Valdes ... .40 .18
❑ 129 Juan Gonzalez ... 1.50 .70
❑ 130 Ray Lankford ... .40 .18
❑ 131 Bobby Bonilla ... .60 .25
❑ 132 Reggie Sanders ... .40 .18
❑ 133 Alex Ochoa ... .40 .18
❑ 134 Mark Loretta ... .40 .18
❑ 135 Jason Kendall ... .60 .25
❑ 136 Brooks Kieschnick ... .40 .18
❑ 137 Chris Snopek ... .40 .18
❑ 138 Ruben Rivera NOW ... .40 .18
❑ 139 Jeff Suppan ... .40 .18
❑ 140 John Wasdin ... .40 .18
❑ 141 Jay Payton ... .40 .18
❑ 142 Rick Krivda ... .40 .18
❑ 143 Jimmy Haynes ... .40 .18
❑ 144 Ryne Sandberg ... 2.00 .90
❑ 145 Matt Williams ... 1.00 .45
❑ 146 Jose Canseco ... 1.50 .70
❑ 147 Larry Walker ... 1.00 .45
❑ 148 Kevin Appier ... .60 .25
❑ 149 Javy Lopez ... .60 .25
❑ 150 Dennis Eckersley ... .60 .25
❑ 151 Jason Isringhausen ... .60 .25
❑ 152 Dean Palmer ... .60 .25
❑ 153 Jeff Bagwell ... 2.00 .90
❑ 154 Rondell White ... .60 .25
❑ 155 Wally Joyner ... .60 .25
❑ 156 Fred McGriff ... 1.00 .45
❑ 157 Cecil Fielder ... .60 .25
❑ 158 Rafael Palmeiro ... 1.50 .70
❑ 159 Rickey Henderson ... 3.00 1.35
❑ 160 Shawon Dunston ... .40 .18
❑ 161 Manny Ramirez ... 2.00 .90
❑ 162 Alex Gonzalez ... .40 .18
❑ 163 Shawn Green ... 1.50 .70
❑ 164 Kenny Lofton ... .60 .25
❑ 165 Jeff Conine ... .40 .18

1997 Topps Chrome

	MINT	NRMT
COMPLETE SET (165)	70.00	32.00

❑ 1 Barry Bonds ... 4.00 1.80
❑ 2 Jose Valentin ... .40 .18
❑ 3 Brady Anderson ... .60 .25
❑ 4 Wade Boggs ... 1.50 .70
❑ 5 Andres Galarraga ... 1.00 .45

❑ 6 Rusty Greer .60 .25
❑ 7 Derek Jeter 6.00 2.70
❑ 8 Ricky Bottalico .40 .18
❑ 9 Mike Piazza 4.00 1.80
❑ 10 Garret Anderson .60 .25
❑ 11 Jeff King .40 .18
❑ 12 Kevin Appier .60 .25
❑ 13 Mark Grace 1.50 .70
❑ 14 Jeff D'Amico .40 .18
❑ 15 Jay Buhner .60 .25
❑ 16 Hal Morris .40 .18
❑ 17 Harold Baines .60 .25
❑ 18 Jeff Cirillo .60 .25
❑ 19 Tom Glavine 1.50 .70
❑ 20 Andy Pettitte .60 .25
❑ 21 Mark McGwire 6.00 2.70
❑ 22 Chuck Knoblauch .60 .25
❑ 23 Raul Mondesi .60 .25
❑ 24 Albert Belle .60 .25
❑ 25 Trevor Hoffman .60 .25
❑ 26 Eric Young .40 .18
❑ 27 Brian McRae .40 .18
❑ 28 Jim Edmonds 1.00 .45
❑ 29 Robb Nen .40 .18
❑ 30 Reggie Sanders .40 .18
❑ 31 Mike Lansing .40 .18
❑ 32 Craig Biggio 1.00 .45
❑ 33 Ray Lankford .40 .18
❑ 34 Charles Nagy .40 .18
❑ 35 Paul Wilson .40 .18
❑ 36 John Wetteland .60 .25
❑ 37 Derek Bell .40 .18
❑ 38 Edgar Martinez 1.00 .45
❑ 39 Rickey Henderson 3.00 1.35
❑ 40 Jim Thome 1.50 .70
❑ 41 Frank Thomas 2.00 .90
❑ 42 Jackie Robinson 5.00 2.20
❑ 43 Terry Steinbach .40 .18
❑ 44 Kevin Brown .60 .25
❑ 45 Joey Hamilton .40 .18
❑ 46 Travis Fryman .60 .25
❑ 47 Juan Gonzalez 1.50 .70
❑ 48 Ron Gant .40 .18
❑ 49 Greg Maddux 4.00 1.80
❑ 50 Wally Joyner .60 .25
❑ 51 John Valentin .40 .18
❑ 52 Bret Boone .60 .25
❑ 53 Paul Molitor 1.50 .70
❑ 54 Rafael Palmeiro 1.50 .70
❑ 55 Todd Hundley .40 .18
❑ 56 Ellis Burks .60 .25
❑ 57 Bernie Williams 1.50 .70
❑ 58 Roberto Alomar 1.50 .70
❑ 59 Jose Mesa .40 .18
❑ 60 Troy Percival .40 .18
❑ 61 John Smoltz .60 .25
❑ 62 Jeff Conine .40 .18
❑ 63 Bernard Gilkey .40 .18
❑ 64 Mickey Tettleton .40 .18
❑ 65 Justin Thompson .40 .18
❑ 66 Tony Phillips .40 .18
❑ 67 Ryne Sandberg 2.00 .90
❑ 68 Geronimo Berroa .40 .18
❑ 69 Todd Hollandsworth .40 .18
❑ 70 Rey Ordonez .40 .18
❑ 71 Marquis Grissom .40 .18
❑ 72 Tino Martinez .60 .25
❑ 73 Steve Finley .60 .25
❑ 74 Andy Benes .40 .18
❑ 75 Jason Kendall .60 .25
❑ 76 Johnny Damon .60 .25
❑ 77 Jason Giambi 1.50 .70
❑ 78 Henry Rodriguez .40 .18
❑ 79 Edgar Renteria .40 .18
❑ 80 Ray Durham .60 .25
❑ 81 Gregg Jefferies .40 .18
❑ 82 Roberto Hernandez .40 .18
❑ 83 Joe Carter .60 .25
❑ 84 Jermaine Dye .60 .25
❑ 85 Julio Franco .60 .25
❑ 86 David Justice .60 .25
❑ 87 Jose Canseco 1.50 .70
❑ 88 Paul O'Neill 1.50 .70
❑ 89 Mariano Rivera .60 .25
❑ 90 Bobby Higginson .60 .25
❑ 91 Mark Grudzielanek .40 .18
❑ 92 Lance Johnson .40 .18
❑ 93 Ken Caminiti .60 .25
❑ 94 Gary Sheffield .60 .25
❑ 95 Luis Castillo .40 .18
❑ 96 Scott Rolen 1.50 .70
❑ 97 Chipper Jones 3.00 1.35
❑ 98 Darryl Strawberry .60 .25
❑ 99 Nomar Garciaparra 4.00 1.80
❑ 100 Jeff Bagwell 2.00 .90
❑ 101 Ken Griffey Jr. 5.00 2.20
❑ 102 Sammy Sosa 3.00 1.35
❑ 103 Jack McDowell .40 .18
❑ 104 James Baldwin .40 .18
❑ 105 Rocky Coppinger .40 .18
❑ 106 Manny Ramirez 2.00 .90
❑ 107 Tim Salmon .60 .25
❑ 108 Eric Karros .60 .25
❑ 109 Brett Butler .60 .25
❑ 110 Randy Johnson 2.00 .90
❑ 111 Pat Hentgen .40 .18
❑ 112 Rondell White .60 .25
❑ 113 Eddie Murray 1.50 .70
❑ 114 Ivan Rodriguez 1.50 .70
❑ 115 Jermaine Allensworth .40 .18
❑ 116 Ed Sprague .40 .18
❑ 117 Kenny Lofton .60 .25
❑ 118 Alan Benes .40 .18
❑ 119 Fred McGriff 1.00 .45
❑ 120 Alex Fernandez .40 .18
❑ 121 Al Martin .40 .18
❑ 122 Devon White .60 .25
❑ 123 David Cone .60 .25
❑ 124 Karim Garcia .40 .18
❑ 125 Chili Davis .60 .25
❑ 126 Roger Clemens 4.00 1.80
❑ 127 Bobby Bonilla .60 .25
❑ 128 Mike Mussina 1.50 .70
❑ 129 Todd Walker .40 .18
❑ 130 Dante Bichette .60 .25
❑ 131 Carlos Baerga .40 .18
❑ 132 Matt Williams 1.00 .45
❑ 133 Will Clark 1.50 .70
❑ 134 Dennis Eckersley .60 .25
❑ 135 Ryan Klesko .60 .25
❑ 136 Dean Palmer .60 .25
❑ 137 Javy Lopez .60 .25
❑ 138 Greg Vaughn .60 .25
❑ 139 Vinny Castilla .60 .25
❑ 140 Cal Ripken 6.00 2.70
❑ 141 Ruben Rivera .40 .18
❑ 142 Mark Wohlers .40 .18
❑ 143 Tony Clark .60 .25
❑ 144 Jose Rosado .40 .18
❑ 145 Tony Gwynn 3.00 1.35
❑ 146 Cecil Fielder .60 .25
❑ 147 Brian Jordan .60 .25
❑ 148 Bob Abreu .60 .25
❑ 149 Barry Larkin 1.50 .70
❑ 150 Robin Ventura .60 .25
❑ 151 John Olerud .60 .25
❑ 152 Rod Beck .40 .18
❑ 153 Vladimir Guerrero 2.50 1.10
❑ 154 Marty Cordova .40 .18
❑ 155 Todd Stottlemyre .40 .18
❑ 156 Hideo Nomo 1.50 .70
❑ 157 Denny Neagle .60 .25
❑ 158 John Jaha .40 .18
❑ 159 Mo Vaughn .60 .25
❑ 160 Andruw Jones 2.00 .90
❑ 161 Moises Alou .60 .25
❑ 162 Larry Walker 1.00 .45
❑ 163 Eddie Murray SH .60 .25
❑ 164 Paul Molitor SH .60 .25
❑ 165 Checklist .40 .18

1998 Topps Chrome

	MINT	NRMT
COMPLETE SET (503)	250.00	110.00
COMPLETE SERIES 1 (282)	150.00	70.00
COMPLETE SERIES 2 (221)	100.00	45.00

❑ 1 Tony Gwynn 3.00 1.35
❑ 2 Larry Walker 1.00 .45
❑ 3 Billy Wagner .40 .18
❑ 4 Denny Neagle .40 .18
❑ 5 Vladimir Guerrero 2.00 .90
❑ 6 Kevin Brown 1.00 .45
❑ 8 Mariano Rivera .60 .25
❑ 9 Tony Clark .60 .25
❑ 10 Deion Sanders .60 .25
❑ 11 Francisco Cordova .40 .18
❑ 12 Matt Williams 1.00 .45
❑ 13 Carlos Baerga .40 .18
❑ 14 Mo Vaughn .60 .25
❑ 15 Bobby Witt .40 .18
❑ 16 Matt Stairs .40 .18
❑ 17 Chan Ho Park .60 .25
❑ 18 Mike Bordick .40 .18
❑ 19 Michael Tucker .40 .18
❑ 20 Frank Thomas 2.00 .90
❑ 21 Roberto Clemente 5.00 2.20
❑ 22 Dmitri Young .60 .25
❑ 23 Steve Trachsel .40 .18
❑ 24 Jeff Kent 1.00 .45
❑ 25 Scott Rolen 1.50 .70
❑ 26 John Thomson .40 .18
❑ 27 Joe Vitiello .40 .18
❑ 28 Eddie Guardado .40 .18
❑ 29 Charlie Hayes .40 .18
❑ 30 Juan Gonzalez 1.50 .70
❑ 31 Garret Anderson .60 .25
❑ 32 John Jaha .60 .25
❑ 33 Omar Vizquel .60 .25
❑ 34 Brian Hunter .40 .18
❑ 35 Jeff Bagwell 2.00 .90
❑ 36 Mark Lemke .40 .18
❑ 37 Doug Glanville .40 .18
❑ 38 Dan Wilson .40 .18
❑ 39 Steve Cooke .40 .18
❑ 40 Chili Davis .60 .25
❑ 41 Mike Cameron .60 .25
❑ 42 F.P. Santangelo .40 .18
❑ 43 Brad Ausmus .40 .18
❑ 44 Gary DiSarcina .40 .18
❑ 45 Pat Hentgen .40 .18
❑ 46 Wilton Guerrero .40 .18
❑ 47 Devon White .40 .18
❑ 48 Danny Patterson .40 .18
❑ 49 Pat Meares .40 .18
❑ 50 Rafael Palmeiro 1.50 .70
❑ 51 Mark Gardner .40 .18
❑ 52 Jeff Blauser .40 .18
❑ 53 Dave Hollins .40 .18
❑ 54 Carlos Garcia .40 .18

❑ 55 Ben McDonald .40 .18
❑ 56 John Mabry .40 .18
❑ 57 Trevor Hoffman .60 .25
❑ 58 Tony Fernandez .40 .18
❑ 59 Rich Loiselle RC .60 .25
❑ 60 Mark Leiter .40 .18
❑ 61 Pat Kelly .40 .18
❑ 62 John Flaherty .40 .18
❑ 63 Roger Bailey .40 .18
❑ 64 Tom Gordon .60 .25
❑ 65 Ryan Klesko .60 .25
❑ 66 Darryl Hamilton .40 .18
❑ 67 Jim Eisenreich .40 .18
❑ 68 Butch Huskey .40 .18
❑ 69 Mark Grudzielanek .40 .18
❑ 70 Marquis Grissom .40 .18
❑ 71 Mark McLemore .40 .18
❑ 72 Gary Gaetti .60 .25
❑ 73 Greg Gagne .40 .18
❑ 74 Lyle Mouton .40 .18
❑ 75 Jim Edmonds 1.00 .45
❑ 76 Shawn Green 1.50 .70
❑ 77 Greg Vaughn .60 .25
❑ 78 Terry Adams .40 .18
❑ 79 Kevin Polcovich .40 .18
❑ 80 Troy O'Leary .40 .18
❑ 81 Jeff Shaw .40 .18
❑ 82 Rich Becker .40 .18
❑ 83 David Wells .60 .25
❑ 84 Steve Karsay .40 .18
❑ 85 Charles Nagy .40 .18
❑ 86 B.J. Surhoff .60 .25
❑ 87 Jamey Wright .40 .18
❑ 88 James Baldwin .40 .18
❑ 89 Edgardo Alfonzo .60 .25
❑ 90 Jay Buhner .60 .25
❑ 91 Brady Anderson .60 .25
❑ 92 Scott Servais .40 .18
❑ 93 Edgar Renteria .40 .18
❑ 94 Mike Lieberthal .60 .25
❑ 95 Rick Aguilera .40 .18
❑ 96 Walt Weiss .60 .25
❑ 97 Deivi Cruz .40 .18
❑ 98 Kurt Abbott .40 .18
❑ 99 Henry Rodriguez .40 .18
❑ 100 Mike Piazza 4.00 1.80
❑ 101 Billy Taylor .40 .18
❑ 102 Todd Zeile .60 .25
❑ 103 Rey Ordonez .40 .18
❑ 104 Willie Greene .40 .18
❑ 105 Tony Womack .40 .18
❑ 106 Mike Sweeney .60 .25
❑ 107 Jeffrey Hammonds .40 .18
❑ 108 Kevin Orie .40 .18
❑ 109 Alex Gonzalez .40 .18
❑ 110 Jose Canseco 1.50 .70
❑ 111 Paul Sorrento .40 .18
❑ 112 Joey Hamilton .40 .18
❑ 113 Brad Radke .60 .25
❑ 114 Steve Avery .40 .18
❑ 115 Esteban Loaiza .40 .18
❑ 116 Stan Javier .40 .18
❑ 117 Chris Gomez .40 .18
❑ 118 Royce Clayton .40 .18
❑ 119 Orlando Merced .40 .18
❑ 120 Kevin Appier .60 .25
❑ 121 Mel Nieves .40 .18
❑ 122 Joe Girardi .40 .18
❑ 123 Rico Brogna .40 .18
❑ 124 Kent Mercker .40 .18
❑ 125 Manny Ramirez 2.00 .90
❑ 126 Jeromy Burnitz .60 .25
❑ 127 Kevin Foster .40 .18
❑ 128 Matt Morris .60 .25
❑ 129 Jason Dickson .40 .18
❑ 130 Tom Glavine 1.50 .70
❑ 131 Wally Joyner .60 .25
❑ 132 Rick Reed .40 .18
❑ 133 Todd Jones .40 .18
❑ 134 Dave Martinez .40 .18
❑ 135 Sandy Alomar Jr. .60 .25
❑ 136 Mike Lansing .40 .18
❑ 137 Sean Berry .40 .18
❑ 138 Doug Jones .40 .18
❑ 139 Todd Stottlemyre .40 .18
❑ 140 Jay Bell .60 .25
❑ 141 Jaime Navarro .40 .18
❑ 142 Chris Hoiles .40 .18
❑ 143 Joey Cora .40 .18
❑ 144 Scott Spiezio .40 .18
❑ 145 Joe Carter .60 .25
❑ 146 Jose Guillen .40 .18
❑ 147 Damion Easley .40 .18
❑ 148 Lee Stevens .40 .18
❑ 149 Alex Fernandez .40 .18
❑ 150 Randy Johnson 2.00 .90
❑ 151 J.T. Snow .60 .25
❑ 152 Chuck Finley .60 .25
❑ 153 Bernard Gilkey .40 .18
❑ 154 David Segui .40 .18
❑ 155 Dante Bichette .60 .25
❑ 156 Kevin Stocker .40 .18
❑ 157 Carl Everett .60 .25
❑ 158 Jose Valentin .40 .18
❑ 159 Pokey Reese .40 .18
❑ 160 Derek Jeter 6.00 2.70
❑ 161 Roger Pavlik .40 .18
❑ 162 Mark Wohlers .40 .18
❑ 163 Ricky Bottalico .40 .18
❑ 164 Ozzie Guillen .40 .18
❑ 165 Mike Mussina 1.50 .70
❑ 166 Gary Sheffield .60 .25
❑ 167 Hideo Nomo 1.50 .70
❑ 168 Mark Grace 1.50 .70
❑ 169 Aaron Sele .60 .25
❑ 170 Darryl Kile .60 .25
❑ 171 Shawn Estes .60 .25
❑ 172 Vinny Castilla .60 .25
❑ 173 Ron Coomer .40 .18
❑ 174 Jose Rosado .40 .18
❑ 175 Kenny Lofton .60 .25
❑ 176 Jason Giambi 1.50 .70
❑ 177 Hal Morris .40 .18
❑ 178 Darren Bragg .40 .18
❑ 179 Orel Hershiser .60 .25
❑ 180 Ray Lankford .40 .18
❑ 181 Hideki Irabu .40 .18
❑ 182 Kevin Young .60 .25
❑ 183 Javy Lopez .60 .25
❑ 184 Jeff Montgomery .40 .18
❑ 185 Mike Holtz .40 .18
❑ 186 George Williams .40 .18
❑ 187 Cal Eldred .40 .18
❑ 188 Tom Candiotti .40 .18
❑ 189 Glenallen Hill .40 .18
❑ 190 Brian Giles .60 .25
❑ 191 Dave Mlicki .40 .18
❑ 192 Garrett Stephenson .40 .18
❑ 193 Jeff Frye .40 .18
❑ 194 Joe Oliver .40 .18
❑ 195 Bob Hamelin .40 .18
❑ 196 Luis Sojo .40 .18
❑ 197 LaTroy Hawkins .40 .18
❑ 198 Kevin Elster .40 .18
❑ 199 Jeff Reed .40 .18
❑ 200 Dennis Eckersley .60 .25
❑ 201 Bill Mueller .40 .18
❑ 202 Russ Davis .40 .18
❑ 203 Armando Benitez .40 .18
❑ 204 Quilvio Veras .40 .18
❑ 205 Tim Naehring .40 .18
❑ 206 Quinton McCracken .40 .18
❑ 207 Raul Casanova .40 .18
❑ 208 Matt Lawton .40 .18
❑ 209 Luis Alicea .40 .18
❑ 210 Luis Gonzalez 1.50 .70
❑ 211 Allen Watson .40 .18
❑ 212 Gerald Williams .40 .18
❑ 213 David Bell .40 .18
❑ 214 Todd Hollandsworth .40 .18
❑ 215 Wade Boggs 1.50 .70
❑ 216 Jose Mesa .40 .18
❑ 217 Jamie Moyer .40 .18
❑ 218 Darren Daulton .60 .25
❑ 219 Mickey Morandini .40 .18
❑ 220 Rusty Greer .60 .25
❑ 221 Jim Bullinger .40 .18
❑ 222 Jose Offerman .40 .18
❑ 223 Matt Karchner .40 .18
❑ 224 Woody Williams .40 .18
❑ 225 Mark Loretta .40 .18
❑ 226 Mike Hampton .60 .25
❑ 227 Willie Adams .40 .18
❑ 228 Scott Hatteberg .40 .18
❑ 229 Rich Amaral .40 .18
❑ 230 Terry Steinbach .40 .18
❑ 231 Glendon Rusch .40 .18
❑ 232 Bret Boone .60 .25
❑ 233 Robert Person .40 .18
❑ 234 Jose Hernandez .40 .18
❑ 235 Doug Drabek .40 .18
❑ 236 Jason McDonald .40 .18
❑ 237 Chris Widger .40 .18
❑ 238 Tom Martin .40 .18
❑ 239 Dave Burba .40 .18
❑ 240 Pete Rose Jr. RC .60 .25
❑ 241 Bobby Ayala .40 .18
❑ 242 Tim Wakefield .40 .18
❑ 243 Dennis Springer .40 .18
❑ 244 Tim Belcher .40 .18
❑ 245 Jon Garland 1.00 .45
Geoff Goetz
❑ 246 Glenn Davis 2.00 .90
Lance Berkman
❑ 247 Vernon Wells 2.00 .90
Aaron Akin
❑ 248 Adam Kennedy 1.00 .45
Jason Romano
❑ 249 Jason Dellaero 1.00 .45
Troy Cameron
❑ 250 Alex Sanchez 2.00 .90
Jared Sandberg
❑ 251 Pablo Ortega 1.00 .45
James Manias
❑ 252 Jason Conti RC 1.00 .45
Mike Stoner
❑ 253 John Patterson 1.00 .45
Larry Rodriguez
❑ 254 Adrian Beltre 2.00 .90
Ryan Minor RC
Aaron Boone
❑ 255 Ben Grieve 2.00 .90
Brian Buchanan
Dermal Brown
❑ 256 Kerry Wood 2.00 .90
Carl Pavano
Gil Meche
❑ 257 David Ortiz 2.00 .90
Daryle Ward
Richie Sexson
❑ 258 Randy Winn 2.00 .90
Juan Encarnacion
Andrew Vessel
❑ 259 Kris Benson RC 1.00 .45
Travis Smith
Courtney Duncan
❑ 260 Chad Hermansen RC 2.00 .90
Brent Butler
Warren Morris
❑ 261 Ben Davis 2.00 .90
Eli Marrero
Ramon Hernandez
❑ 262 Eric Chavez 2.00 .90
Russell Branyan
Russ Johnson
❑ 263 Todd Dunwoody RC 1.00 .45
John Barnes
Ryan Jackson
❑ 264 Matt Clement RC .40 .18
Roy Halladay
Brian Fuentes
❑ 265 Randy Johnson SH .60 .25
❑ 266 Kevin Brown SH .60 .25
❑ 267 Ricardo Rincon SH .40 .18
❑ 268 N.Garciaparra SH 2.00 .90
❑ 269 Tino Martinez SH .40 .18
❑ 270 Chuck Knoblauch IL .40 .18
❑ 271 Pedro Martinez IL 1.00 .45
❑ 272 Denny Neagle IL .40 .18
❑ 273 Juan Gonzalez IL .60 .25
❑ 274 Andres Galarraga IL .40 .18
❑ 275 Checklist .40 .18
❑ 276 Checklist .40 .18
❑ 277 Moises Alou WS .40 .18
❑ 278 Sandy Alomar Jr. WS .60 .25
❑ 279 Gary Sheffield WS .40 .18
❑ 280 Matt Williams WS 1.00 .45
❑ 281 Livan Hernandez WS .40 .18

- ❑ 282 Chad Ogea WS .40 .18
- ❑ 283 Marlins Champs .60 .25
- ❑ 284 Tino Martinez .60 .25
- ❑ 285 Roberto Alomar 1.50 .70
- ❑ 286 Jeff King .40 .18
- ❑ 287 Brian Jordan .60 .25
- ❑ 288 Darin Erstad 1.50 .70
- ❑ 289 Ken Caminiti .60 .25
- ❑ 290 Jim Thome 1.50 .70
- ❑ 291 Paul Molitor 1.50 .70
- ❑ 292 Ivan Rodriguez 1.50 .70
- ❑ 293 Bernie Williams 1.50 .70
- ❑ 294 Todd Hundley .40 .18
- ❑ 295 Andres Galarraga 1.00 .45
- ❑ 296 Greg Maddux 4.00 1.80
- ❑ 297 Edgar Martinez 1.00 .45
- ❑ 298 Ron Gant .60 .25
- ❑ 299 Derek Bell .40 .18
- ❑ 300 Roger Clemens 4.00 1.80
- ❑ 301 Rondell White .60 .25
- ❑ 302 Barry Larkin 1.50 .70
- ❑ 303 Robin Ventura .60 .25
- ❑ 304 Jason Kendall .60 .25
- ❑ 305 Chipper Jones 3.00 1.35
- ❑ 306 John Franco .60 .25
- ❑ 307 Sammy Sosa 3.00 1.35
- ❑ 308 Troy Percival .40 .18
- ❑ 309 Chuck Knoblauch .60 .25
- ❑ 310 Ellis Burks .60 .25
- ❑ 311 Al Martin .40 .18
- ❑ 312 Tim Salmon .60 .25
- ❑ 313 Moises Alou .60 .25
- ❑ 314 Lance Johnson .40 .18
- ❑ 315 Justin Thompson .40 .18
- ❑ 316 Will Clark 1.50 .70
- ❑ 317 Barry Bonds 4.00 1.80
- ❑ 318 Craig Biggio 1.00 .45
- ❑ 319 John Smoltz .60 .25
- ❑ 320 Cal Ripken 6.00 2.70
- ❑ 321 Ken Griffey Jr. 5.00 2.20
- ❑ 322 Paul O'Neill 1.50 .70
- ❑ 323 Todd Helton 2.00 .90
- ❑ 324 John Olerud .60 .25
- ❑ 325 Mark McGwire 6.00 2.70
- ❑ 326 Jose Cruz Jr. .60 .25
- ❑ 327 Jeff Cirillo .60 .25
- ❑ 328 Dean Palmer .60 .25
- ❑ 329 John Wetteland .60 .25
- ❑ 330 Steve Finley .60 .25
- ❑ 331 Albert Belle .60 .25
- ❑ 332 Curt Schilling 1.50 .70
- ❑ 333 Raul Mondesi .60 .25
- ❑ 334 Andruw Jones 1.50 .70
- ❑ 335 Nomar Garciaparra 4.00 1.80
- ❑ 336 David Justice .60 .25
- ❑ 337 Andy Pettitte .60 .25
- ❑ 338 Pedro Martinez 2.00 .90
- ❑ 339 Travis Miller .40 .18
- ❑ 340 Chris Stynes .40 .18
- ❑ 341 Gregg Jefferies .40 .18
- ❑ 342 Jeff Fassero .40 .18
- ❑ 343 Craig Counsell .40 .18
- ❑ 344 Wilson Alvarez .40 .18
- ❑ 345 Bip Roberts .40 .18
- ❑ 346 Kelvim Escobar .40 .18
- ❑ 347 Mark Bellhorn .40 .18
- ❑ 348 Cory Lidle RC 2.50 1.10
- ❑ 349 Fred McGriff 1.00 .45
- ❑ 350 Chuck Carr .40 .18
- ❑ 351 Bob Abreu .60 .25
- ❑ 352 Juan Guzman .40 .18
- ❑ 353 Fernando Vina .40 .18
- ❑ 354 Andy Benes .40 .18
- ❑ 355 Dave Nilsson .40 .18
- ❑ 356 Bobby Bonilla .60 .25
- ❑ 357 Ismael Valdes .40 .18
- ❑ 358 Carlos Perez .40 .18
- ❑ 359 Kirk Rueter .40 .18
- ❑ 360 Bartolo Colon .60 .25
- ❑ 361 Mel Rojas .40 .18
- ❑ 362 Johnny Damon .60 .25
- ❑ 363 Geronimo Berroa .40 .18
- ❑ 364 Reggie Sanders .40 .18
- ❑ 365 Jermaine Allensworth .40 .18
- ❑ 366 Orlando Cabrera .40 .18
- ❑ 367 Jorge Fabregas .40 .18
- ❑ 368 Scott Stahoviak .40 .18
- ❑ 369 Ken Cloude .40 .18
- ❑ 370 Donovan Osborne .40 .18
- ❑ 371 Roger Cedeno .40 .18
- ❑ 372 Neifi Perez .40 .18
- ❑ 373 Chris Holt .40 .18
- ❑ 374 Cecil Fielder .60 .25
- ❑ 375 Marty Cordova .40 .18
- ❑ 376 Tom Goodwin .40 .18
- ❑ 377 Jeff Suppan .40 .18
- ❑ 378 Jeff Brantley .40 .18
- ❑ 379 Mark Langston .40 .18
- ❑ 380 Shane Reynolds .40 .18
- ❑ 381 Mike Fetters .40 .18
- ❑ 382 Todd Greene .40 .18
- ❑ 383 Ray Durham .60 .25
- ❑ 384 Carlos Delgado 1.50 .70
- ❑ 385 Jeff D'Amico .40 .18
- ❑ 386 Brian McRae .40 .18
- ❑ 387 Alan Benes .40 .18
- ❑ 388 Heathcliff Slocumb .40 .18
- ❑ 389 Eric Young .40 .18
- ❑ 390 Travis Fryman .60 .25
- ❑ 391 David Cone .60 .25
- ❑ 392 Otis Nixon .40 .18
- ❑ 393 Jeremi Gonzalez .40 .18
- ❑ 394 Jeff Juden .40 .18
- ❑ 395 Jose Vizcaino .40 .18
- ❑ 396 Ugueth Urbina .40 .18
- ❑ 397 Ramon Martinez .40 .18
- ❑ 398 Robb Nen .40 .18
- ❑ 399 Harold Baines .60 .25
- ❑ 400 Delino DeShields .40 .18
- ❑ 401 John Burkett .40 .18
- ❑ 402 Sterling Hitchcock .40 .18
- ❑ 403 Mark Clark .40 .18
- ❑ 404 Terrell Wade .40 .18
- ❑ 405 Scott Brosius .60 .25
- ❑ 406 Chad Curtis .40 .18
- ❑ 407 Brian Johnson .40 .18
- ❑ 408 Roberto Kelly .40 .18
- ❑ 409 Dave Dellucci RC .40 .18
- ❑ 410 Michael Tucker .40 .18
- ❑ 411 Mark Kotsay .60 .25
- ❑ 412 Mark Lewis .40 .18
- ❑ 413 Ryan McGuire .40 .18
- ❑ 414 Shawon Dunston .40 .18
- ❑ 415 Brad Rigby .40 .18
- ❑ 416 Scott Erickson .40 .18
- ❑ 417 Bobby Jones .40 .18
- ❑ 418 Darren Oliver .40 .18
- ❑ 419 John Smiley .40 .18
- ❑ 420 T.J. Mathews .40 .18
- ❑ 421 Dustin Hermanson .40 .18
- ❑ 422 Mike Timlin .40 .18
- ❑ 423 Willie Blair .40 .18
- ❑ 424 Manny Alexander .40 .18
- ❑ 425 Bob Tewksbury .40 .18
- ❑ 426 Pete Schourek .40 .18
- ❑ 427 Reggie Jefferson .40 .18
- ❑ 428 Ed Sprague .40 .18
- ❑ 429 Jeff Conine .40 .18
- ❑ 430 Roberto Hernandez .40 .18
- ❑ 431 Tom Pagnozzi .40 .18
- ❑ 432 Jaret Wright .40 .18
- ❑ 433 Livan Hernandez .40 .18
- ❑ 434 Andy Ashby .40 .18
- ❑ 435 Todd Dunn .40 .18
- ❑ 436 Bobby Higginson .60 .25
- ❑ 437 Rod Beck .40 .18
- ❑ 438 Jim Leyritz .40 .18
- ❑ 439 Matt Williams 1.00 .45
- ❑ 440 Brett Tomko .40 .18
- ❑ 441 Joe Randa .40 .18
- ❑ 442 Chris Carpenter .40 .18
- ❑ 443 Dennis Reyes .40 .18
- ❑ 444 Al Leiter .60 .25
- ❑ 445 Jason Schmidt .40 .18
- ❑ 446 Ken Hill .40 .18
- ❑ 447 Shannon Stewart .60 .25
- ❑ 448 Enrique Wilson .40 .18
- ❑ 449 Fernando Tatis .40 .18
- ❑ 450 Jimmy Key .60 .25
- ❑ 451 Darrin Fletcher .40 .18
- ❑ 452 John Valentin .40 .18
- ❑ 453 Kevin Tapani .40 .18
- ❑ 454 Eric Karros .60 .25
- ❑ 455 Jay Bell .60 .25
- ❑ 456 Walt Weiss .60 .25
- ❑ 457 Devon White .40 .18
- ❑ 458 Carl Pavano .40 .18
- ❑ 459 Mike Lansing .40 .18
- ❑ 460 John Flaherty .40 .18
- ❑ 461 Richard Hidalgo .60 .25
- ❑ 462 Quinton McCracken .40 .18
- ❑ 463 Karim Garcia .40 .18
- ❑ 464 Miguel Cairo .40 .18
- ❑ 465 Edwin Diaz .40 .18
- ❑ 466 Bobby Smith .40 .18
- ❑ 467 Yamil Benitez .40 .18
- ❑ 468 Rich Butler RC .40 .18
- ❑ 469 Ben Ford RC .60 .25
- ❑ 470 Bubba Trammell .40 .18
- ❑ 471 Brent Brede .40 .18
- ❑ 472 Brooks Kieschnick .40 .18
- ❑ 473 Carlos Castillo .40 .18
- ❑ 474 Brad Radke SH .40 .18
- ❑ 475 Roger Clemens SH 2.00 .90
- ❑ 476 Curt Schilling SH 1.50 .70
- ❑ 477 John Olerud SH .40 .18
- ❑ 478 Mark McGwire SH 3.00 1.35
- ❑ 479 Mike Piazza IL 2.00 .90
  Ken Griffey Jr.
- ❑ 480 Jeff Bagwell 1.00 .45
  Frank Thomas
- ❑ 481 Chipper Jones 1.50 .70
  Nomar Garciaparra IL
- ❑ 482 Larry Walker IL 1.00 .45
  Juan Gonzalez IL
- ❑ 483 Gary Sheffield IL .60 .25
  Tino Martinez IL
- ❑ 484 Derrick Gibson 1.00 .45
  Michael Coleman
  Norm Hutchins
- ❑ 485 Braden Looper 1.00 .45
  Cliff Politte
  Brian Rose
- ❑ 486 Eric Milton 2.00 .90
  Jason Marquis
  Corey Lee
- ❑ 487 A.J.Hinch 3.00 1.35
  Mark Osborne RC
  Robert Fick
- ❑ 488 Aramis Ramirez 2.00 .90
  Alex Gonzalez
  Sean Casey
- ❑ 489 Donnie Bridges 2.00 .90
  Tim Drew RC
- ❑ 490 Ntema Ndungidi RC 2.00 .90
  Darnell McDonald
- ❑ 491 Ryan Anderson RC 5.00 2.20
  Mark Mangum
- ❑ 492 J.J.Davis 10.00 4.50
  Troy Glaus RC
- ❑ 493 Jayson Werth RC 2.00 .90
  Dan Reichert
- ❑ 494 John Curtice RC 3.00 1.35
  Michael Cuddyer
- ❑ 495 Jack Cust RC 3.00 1.35
  Jason Standridge
- ❑ 496 Brian Anderson 1.00 .45
- ❑ 497 Tony Saunders 1.00 .45
- ❑ 498 Vladimir Nunez 1.00 .45
  Jhensy Sandoval
- ❑ 499 Brad Penny 2.00 .90
  Nick Bierbrodt
- ❑ 500 Dustin Carr 2.00 .90
  Luis Cruz RC
- ❑ 501 Cedric Bowers 2.00 .90
  Marcus McCain
- ❑ 502 Checklist .40 .18
- ❑ 503 Checklist .40 .18
- ❑ 504 Alex Rodriguez 4.00 1.80

1999 Topps Chrome

	MINT	NRMT
COMPLETE SET (462)	200.00	90.00
COMPLETE SERIES 1 (241)	100.00	45.00
COMPLETE SERIES 2 (221)	100.00	45.00
COMMON CARD (1-6/8-463)	.40	.18
COMMON (205-212/425-437)	1.00	.45

COMP.MCGWIRE SET (70)		3000.00	1350.00
COMP.SOSA HR SET (66)		1100.00	500.00
❑ 1	Roger Clemens	4.00	1.80
❑ 2	Andres Galarraga	1.00	.45
❑ 3	Scott Brosius	.60	.25
❑ 4	John Flaherty	.40	.18
❑ 5	Jim Leyritz	.40	.18
❑ 6	Ray Durham	.60	.25
❑ 8	Jose Vizcaino	.40	.18
❑ 9	Will Clark	1.50	.70
❑ 10	David Wells	.60	.25
❑ 11	Jose Guillen	.40	.18
❑ 12	Scott Hatteberg	.40	.18
❑ 13	Edgardo Alfonzo	.60	.25
❑ 14	Mike Bordick	.40	.18
❑ 15	Manny Ramirez	2.00	.90
❑ 16	Greg Maddux	4.00	1.80
❑ 17	David Segui	.40	.18
❑ 18	Darryl Strawberry	.60	.25
❑ 19	Brad Radke	.60	.25
❑ 20	Kerry Wood	1.50	.70
❑ 21	Matt Anderson	.40	.18
❑ 22	Derrek Lee	.60	.25
❑ 23	Mickey Morandini	.40	.18
❑ 24	Paul Konerko	.60	.25
❑ 25	Travis Lee	.40	.18
❑ 26	Ken Hill	.40	.18
❑ 27	Kenny Rogers	.40	.18
❑ 28	Paul Sorrento	.40	.18
❑ 29	Quilvio Veras	.40	.18
❑ 30	Todd Walker	.40	.18
❑ 31	Ryan Jackson	.40	.18
❑ 32	John Olerud	.60	.25
❑ 33	Doug Glanville	.40	.18
❑ 34	Nolan Ryan	8.00	3.60
❑ 35	Ray Lankford	.40	.18
❑ 36	Mark Loretta	.40	.18
❑ 37	Jason Dickson	.40	.18
❑ 38	Sean Bergman	.40	.18
❑ 39	Quinton McCracken	.40	.18
❑ 40	Bartolo Colon	.60	.25
❑ 41	Brady Anderson	.60	.25
❑ 42	Chris Stynes	.40	.18
❑ 43	Jorge Posada	.60	.25
❑ 44	Justin Thompson	.40	.18
❑ 45	Johnny Damon	.60	.25
❑ 46	Armando Benitez	.40	.18
❑ 47	Brant Brown	.40	.18
❑ 48	Charlie Hayes	.40	.18
❑ 49	Darren Dreifort	.40	.18
❑ 50	Juan Gonzalez	1.50	.70
❑ 51	Chuck Knoblauch	.60	.25
❑ 52	Todd Helton	2.00	.90
❑ 53	Rick Reed	.40	.18
❑ 54	Chris Gomez	.40	.18
❑ 55	Gary Sheffield	.60	.25
❑ 56	Rod Beck	.40	.18
❑ 57	Rey Sanchez	.40	.18
❑ 58	Garret Anderson	.60	.25
❑ 59	Jimmy Haynes	.40	.18
❑ 60	Steve Woodard	.40	.18
❑ 61	Rondell White	.60	.25
❑ 62	Vladimir Guerrero	2.00	.90
❑ 63	Eric Karros	.60	.25
❑ 64	Russ Davis	.40	.18
❑ 65	Mo Vaughn	.60	.25
❑ 66	Sammy Sosa	3.00	1.35
❑ 67	Troy Percival	.40	.18
❑ 68	Kenny Lofton	.60	.25
❑ 69	Bill Taylor	.40	.18
❑ 70	Mark McGwire	6.00	2.70
❑ 71	Roger Cedeno	.40	.18
❑ 72	Javy Lopez	.60	.25
❑ 73	Damion Easley	.40	.18
❑ 74	Andy Pettitte	.60	.25
❑ 75	Tony Gwynn	3.00	1.35
❑ 76	Ricardo Rincon	.40	.18
❑ 77	F.P. Santangelo	.40	.18
❑ 78	Jay Bell	.60	.25
❑ 79	Scott Servais	.40	.18
❑ 80	Jose Canseco	1.50	.70
❑ 81	Roberto Hernandez	.40	.18
❑ 82	Todd Dunwoody	.40	.18
❑ 83	John Wetteland	.60	.25
❑ 84	Mike Caruso	.40	.18
❑ 85	Derek Jeter	6.00	2.70
❑ 86	Aaron Sele	.60	.25
❑ 87	Jose Lima	.40	.18
❑ 88	Ryan Christenson	.40	.18
❑ 89	Jeff Cirillo	.60	.25
❑ 90	Jose Hernandez	.40	.18
❑ 91	Mark Kotsay	.40	.18
❑ 92	Darren Bragg	.40	.18
❑ 93	Albert Belle	.60	.25
❑ 94	Matt Lawton	.60	.25
❑ 95	Pedro Martinez	2.00	.90
❑ 96	Greg Vaughn	.60	.25
❑ 97	Neifi Perez	.40	.18
❑ 98	Gerald Williams	.40	.18
❑ 99	Derek Bell	.40	.18
❑ 100	Ken Griffey Jr.	5.00	2.20
❑ 101	David Cone	.60	.25
❑ 102	Brian Johnson	.40	.18
❑ 103	Dean Palmer	.60	.25
❑ 104	Javier Valentin	.40	.18
❑ 105	Trevor Hoffman	.60	.25
❑ 106	Butch Huskey	.40	.18
❑ 107	Dave Martinez	.40	.18
❑ 108	Billy Wagner	.40	.18
❑ 109	Shawn Green	1.50	.70
❑ 110	Ben Grieve	.60	.25
❑ 111	Tom Goodwin	.40	.18
❑ 112	Jaret Wright	.40	.18
❑ 113	Aramis Ramirez	.60	.25
❑ 114	Dmitri Young	.60	.25
❑ 115	Hideki Irabu	.40	.18
❑ 116	Roberto Kelly	.40	.18
❑ 117	Jeff Fassero	.40	.18
❑ 118	Mark Clark	.40	.18
❑ 119	Jason McDonald	.40	.18
❑ 120	Matt Williams	1.00	.45
❑ 121	Dave Burba	.40	.18
❑ 122	Bret Saberhagen	.60	.25
❑ 123	Deivi Cruz	.40	.18
❑ 124	Chad Curtis	.40	.18
❑ 125	Scott Rolen	1.50	.70
❑ 126	Lee Stevens	.40	.18
❑ 127	J.T. Snow	.60	.25
❑ 128	Rusty Greer	.60	.25
❑ 129	Brian Meadows	.40	.18
❑ 130	Jim Edmonds	1.00	.45
❑ 131	Ron Gant	.60	.25
❑ 132	A.J. Hinch	.40	.18
❑ 133	Shannon Stewart	.60	.25
❑ 134	Brad Fullmer	.60	.25
❑ 135	Cal Eldred	.40	.18
❑ 136	Matt Walbeck	.40	.18
❑ 137	Carl Everett	.60	.25
❑ 138	Walt Weiss	.40	.18
❑ 139	Fred McGriff	1.00	.45
❑ 140	Darin Erstad	1.50	.70
❑ 141	Dave Nilsson	.40	.18
❑ 142	Eric Young	.40	.18
❑ 143	Dan Wilson	.40	.18
❑ 144	Jeff Reed	.40	.18
❑ 145	Brett Tomko	.40	.18
❑ 146	Terry Steinbach	.40	.18
❑ 147	Seth Greisinger	.40	.18
❑ 148	Pat Meares	.40	.18
❑ 149	Livan Hernandez	.40	.18
❑ 150	Jeff Bagwell	2.00	.90
❑ 151	Bob Wickman	.40	.18
❑ 152	Omar Vizquel	.60	.25
❑ 153	Eric Davis	.60	.25
❑ 154	Larry Sutton	.40	.18
❑ 155	Magglio Ordonez	1.00	.45
❑ 156	Eric Milton	.60	.25
❑ 157	Darren Lewis	.40	.18
❑ 158	Rick Aguilera	.40	.18
❑ 159	Mike Lieberthal	.60	.25
❑ 160	Robb Nen	.40	.18
❑ 161	Brian Giles	.60	.25
❑ 162	Jeff Brantley	.40	.18
❑ 163	Gary DiSarcina	.40	.18
❑ 164	John Valentin	.40	.18
❑ 165	Dave Dellucci	.40	.18
❑ 166	Chan Ho Park	.60	.25
❑ 167	Masato Yoshii	.60	.25
❑ 168	Jason Schmidt	.40	.18
❑ 169	LaTroy Hawkins	.40	.18
❑ 170	Bret Boone	.60	.25
❑ 171	Jerry DiPoto	.40	.18
❑ 172	Mariano Rivera	.60	.25
❑ 173	Mike Cameron	.60	.25
❑ 174	Scott Erickson	.40	.18
❑ 175	Charles Johnson	.60	.25
❑ 176	Bobby Jones	.40	.18
❑ 177	Francisco Cordova	.40	.18
❑ 178	Todd Jones	.40	.18
❑ 179	Jeff Montgomery	.40	.18
❑ 180	Mike Mussina	1.50	.70
❑ 181	Bob Abreu	.60	.25
❑ 182	Ismael Valdes	.40	.18
❑ 183	Andy Fox	.40	.18
❑ 184	Woody Williams	.40	.18
❑ 185	Denny Neagle	.40	.18
❑ 186	Jose Valentin	.40	.18
❑ 187	Darrin Fletcher	.40	.18
❑ 188	Gabe Alvarez	.40	.18
❑ 189	Eddie Taubensee	.40	.18
❑ 190	Edgar Martinez	1.00	.45
❑ 191	Jason Kendall	.60	.25
❑ 192	Darryl Kile	.60	.25
❑ 193	Jeff King	.40	.18
❑ 194	Rey Ordonez	.40	.18
❑ 195	Andruw Jones	1.50	.70
❑ 196	Tony Fernandez	.40	.18
❑ 197	Jamey Wright	.40	.18
❑ 198	B.J. Surhoff	.60	.25
❑ 199	Vinny Castilla	.60	.25
❑ 200	David Wells HL	.40	.18
❑ 201	Mark McGwire HL	3.00	1.35
❑ 202	Sammy Sosa HL	1.50	.70
❑ 203	Roger Clemens HL	2.00	.90
❑ 204	Kerry Wood HL	.60	.25
❑ 205	Gabe Kapler	1.50	.70
	Lance Berkman		
	Mike Frank		
❑ 206	Alex Escobar RC	5.00	2.20
	Ricky Ledee		
	Mike Stoner		
❑ 207	Peter Bergeron RC	2.00	.90
	Jeremy Giambi		
	George Lombard		
❑ 208	Michael Barrett	1.00	.45
	Ben Davis		
	Robert Fick		
❑ 209	Jayson Werth	1.00	.45
	Ramon Hernandez		
	Pat Cline		
❑ 210	Ryan Anderson	1.25	.55
	Bruce Chen		
	Chris Enochs		
❑ 211	Brad Penny	1.00	.45
	Octavio Dotel		
	Mike Lincoln		
❑ 212	Chuck Abbott RC	1.00	.45
	Brent Butler		
	Danny Klassen		
❑ 213	Chris C.Jones	2.00	.90
	Jeff Urban RC		
❑ 214	Arturo McDowell RC	2.00	.90
	Tony Torcato		
❑ 215	Josh McKinley RC	1.50	.70
	Jason Tyner		
❑ 216	Matt Burch	2.00	.90
	Seth Etherton RC		
❑ 217	Mamon Tucker RC	2.50	1.10

Rick Elder
❑ 218 J.M.Gold .... 2.00 .90
Ryan Mills RC
❑ 219 Andy Brown .... 2.00 .90
Choo Freeman RC
❑ 220A Mark McGwire HR 1 100.00 45.00
❑ 220B Mark McGwire HR 2 50.00 22.00
❑ 220C Mark McGwire HR 3 50.00 22.00
❑ 220D Mark McGwire HR 4 50.00 22.00
❑ 220E Mark McGwire HR 5 50.00 22.00
❑ 220F Mark McGwire HR 6 50.00 22.00
❑ 220G Mark McGwire HR 7 50.00 22.00
❑ 220H Mark McGwire HR 8 50.00 22.00
❑ 220I Mark McGwire HR 9 .. 50.00 22.00
❑ 220J M.McGwire HR 10 .... 50.00 22.00
❑ 220K M.McGwire HR 11 .. 50.00 22.00
❑ 220L M.McGwire HR 12 .... 50.00 22.00
❑ 220M M.McGwire HR 13 .. 50.00 22.00
❑ 220N M.McGwire HR 14 .. 50.00 22.00
❑ 220O M.McGwire HR 15 .. 50.00 22.00
❑ 220P M.McGwire HR 16 .. 50.00 22.00
❑ 220Q M.McGwire HR 17 .. 50.00 22.00
❑ 220R M.McGwire HR 18 .. 50.00 22.00
❑ 220S M.McGwire HR 19 .. 50.00 22.00
❑ 220T M.McGwire HR 20 .... 50.00 22.00
❑ 220U M.McGwire HR 21 .. 50.00 22.00
❑ 220V M.McGwire HR 22 .. 50.00 22.00
❑ 220W M.McGwire HR 23 .. 50.00 22.00
❑ 220X M.McGwire HR 24 .. 50.00 22.00
❑ 220Y M.McGwire HR 25 .. 50.00 22.00
❑ 220Z M.McGwire HR 26 .... 50.00 22.00
❑ 220AA M.McGwire HR 27 50.00 22.00
❑ 220AB M.McGwire HR 28 50.00 22.00
❑ 220AC M.McGwire HR 29 50.00 22.00
❑ 220AD M.McGwire HR 30 50.00 22.00
❑ 220AE M.McGwire HR 31 50.00 22.00
❑ 220AF M.McGwire HR 32 50.00 22.00
❑ 220AG M.McGwire HR 33 50.00 22.00
❑ 220AH M.McGwire HR 34 50.00 22.00
❑ 220AI M.McGwire HR 35 .. 50.00 22.00
❑ 220AJ M.McGwire HR 36 .. 50.00 22.00
❑ 220AK M.McGwire HR 37 50.00 22.00
❑ 220AL M.McGwire HR 38 50.00 22.00
❑ 220AM M.McGwire HR 39 50.00 22.00
❑ 220AN M.McGwire HR 40 50.00 22.00
❑ 220AO M.McGwire HR 41 50.00 22.00
❑ 220AP M.McGwire HR 42 50.00 22.00
❑ 220AQ M.McGwire HR 43 50.00 22.00
❑ 220AR M.McGwire HR 44 50.00 22.00
❑ 220AS M.McGwire HR 45 50.00 22.00
❑ 220AT M.McGwire HR 46 50.00 22.00
❑ 220AU M.McGwire HR 47 50.00 22.00
❑ 220AV M.McGwire HR 48 50.00 22.00
❑ 220AW M.McGwire HR 49 50.00 22.00
❑ 220AX M.McGwire HR 50 50.00 22.00
❑ 220AY M.McGwire HR 51 50.00 22.00
❑ 220AZ M.McGwire HR 52 50.00 22.00
❑ 220BB M.McGwire HR 53 50.00 22.00
❑ 220CC M.McGwire HR 54 50.00 22.00
❑ 220DD M.McGwire HR 55 50.00 22.00
❑ 220EE M.McGwire HR 56 50.00 22.00
❑ 220FF M.McGwire HR 57 50.00 22.00
❑ 220GG M.McGwire HR 58 50.00 22.00
❑ 220HH M.McGwire HR 59 50.00 22.00
❑ 220II M.McGwire HR 60 .... 50.00 22.00
❑ 220JJ M.McGwire HR 61 .. 80.00 36.00
❑ 220KK M.McGwire HR 62 120.00 55.00
❑ 220LL M.McGwire HR 63 .. 60.00 27.00
❑ 220MM M.McGwire HR 64 60.00 27.00
❑ 220NN M.McGwire HR 65 60.00 27.00
❑ 220OO M.McGwire HR 66 60.00 27.00
❑ 220PP M.McGwire HR 67 60.00 27.00
❑ 220QQ M.McGwire HR 68 60.00 27.00
❑ 220RR M.McGwire HR 69 60.00 27.00
❑ 220SS M.McGwire HR 70 250.00 110.00
❑ 221 Larry Walker LL .... 1.00 .45
❑ 222 Bernie Williams LL .... .60 .25
❑ 223 Mark McGwire LL 3.00 1.35
❑ 224 Ken Griffey Jr. LL 2.50 1.10
❑ 225 Sammy Sosa LL .... 1.50 .70
❑ 226 Juan Gonzalez LL .... 1.00 .45
❑ 227 Dante Bichette LL .... .40 .18
❑ 228 Alex Rodriguez LL .... 2.00 .90
❑ 229 Sammy Sosa LL .... 1.50 .70
❑ 230 Derek Jeter LL 3.00 1.35
❑ 231 Greg Maddux LL .... 2.00 .90
❑ 232 Roger Clemens LL .... 2.00 .90
❑ 233 Ricky Ledee WS .... .40 .18
❑ 234 Chuck Knoblauch WS .... .60 .25
❑ 235 Bernie Williams WS .... .60 .25
❑ 236 Tino Martinez WS .... .40 .18
❑ 237 Orl. Hernandez WS .... .60 .25
❑ 238 Scott Brosius WS .... .40 .18
❑ 239 Andy Pettitte WS .... .40 .18
❑ 240 Mariano Rivera WS .... .60 .25
❑ 241 Checklist .... .40 .18
❑ 242 Checklist .... .40 .18
❑ 243 Tom Glavine .... 1.50 .70
❑ 244 Andy Benes .... .40 .18
❑ 245 Sandy Alomar Jr. .... .60 .25
❑ 246 Wilton Guerrero .... .40 .18
❑ 247 Alex Gonzalez .... .40 .18
❑ 248 Roberto Alomar .... 1.50 .70
❑ 249 Ruben Rivera .... .40 .18
❑ 250 Eric Chavez .... .60 .25
❑ 251 Ellis Burks .... .60 .25
❑ 252 Richie Sexson .... .60 .25
❑ 253 Steve Finley .... .60 .25
❑ 254 Dwight Gooden .... .60 .25
❑ 255 Dustin Hermanson .... .40 .18
❑ 256 Kirk Rueter .... .40 .18
❑ 257 Steve Trachsel .... .40 .18
❑ 258 Gregg Jefferies .... .40 .18
❑ 259 Matt Stairs .... .40 .18
❑ 260 Shane Reynolds .... .40 .18
❑ 261 Gregg Olson .... .40 .18
❑ 262 Kevin Tapani .... .40 .18
❑ 263 Matt Morris .... .60 .25
❑ 264 Carl Pavano .... .40 .18
❑ 265 Nomar Garciaparra 4.00 1.80
❑ 266 Kevin Young .... .60 .25
❑ 267 Rick Helling .... .40 .18
❑ 268 Matt Franco .... .40 .18
❑ 269 Brian McRae .... .40 .18
❑ 270 Cal Ripken 6.00 2.70
❑ 271 Jeff Abbott .... .40 .18
❑ 272 Tony Batista .... .60 .25
❑ 273 Bill Simas .... .40 .18
❑ 274 Brian Hunter .... .40 .18
❑ 275 John Franco .... .60 .25
❑ 276 Devon White .... .40 .18
❑ 277 Rickey Henderson 3.00 1.35
❑ 278 Chuck Finley .... .60 .25
❑ 279 Mike Blowers .... .40 .18
❑ 280 Mark Grace .... 1.50 .70
❑ 281 Randy Winn .... .40 .18
❑ 282 Bobby Bonilla .... .60 .25
❑ 283 David Justice .... .60 .25
❑ 284 Shane Monahan .... .40 .18
❑ 285 Kevin Brown .... 1.00 .45
❑ 286 Todd Zeile .... .60 .25
❑ 287 Al Martin .... .40 .18
❑ 288 Troy O'Leary .... .40 .18
❑ 289 Darryl Hamilton .... .40 .18
❑ 290 Tino Martinez .... .60 .25
❑ 291 David Ortiz .... .60 .25
❑ 292 Tony Clark .... .60 .25
❑ 293 Ryan Minor .... .40 .18
❑ 294 Mark Leiter .... .40 .18
❑ 295 Wally Joyner .... .60 .25
❑ 296 Cliff Floyd .... .60 .25
❑ 297 Shawn Estes .... .60 .25
❑ 298 Pat Hentgen .... .40 .18
❑ 299 Scott Elarton .... .40 .18
❑ 300 Alex Rodriguez 4.00 1.80
❑ 301 Ozzie Guillen .... .40 .18
❑ 302 Hideo Nomo .... 1.50 .70
❑ 303 Ryan McGuire .... .40 .18
❑ 304 Brad Ausmus .... .40 .18
❑ 305 Alex Gonzalez .... .40 .18
❑ 306 Brian Jordan .... .60 .25
❑ 307 John Jaha .... .40 .18
❑ 308 Mark Grudzielanek .... .40 .18
❑ 309 Juan Guzman .... .40 .18
❑ 310 Tony Womack .... .40 .18
❑ 311 Dennis Reyes .... .40 .18
❑ 312 Marty Cordova .... .40 .18
❑ 313 Ramiro Mendoza .... .40 .18
❑ 314 Robin Ventura .... .60 .25
❑ 315 Rafael Palmeiro .... 1.50 .70
❑ 316 Ramon Martinez .... .40 .18
❑ 317 Pedro Astacio .... .40 .18
❑ 318 Dave Hollins .... .40 .18
❑ 319 Tom Candiotti .... .40 .18
❑ 320 Al Leiter .... .60 .25
❑ 321 Rico Brogna .... .40 .18
❑ 322 Reggie Jefferson .... .40 .18
❑ 323 Bernard Gilkey .... .40 .18
❑ 324 Jason Giambi .... 1.50 .70
❑ 325 Craig Biggio .... 1.00 .45
❑ 326 Troy Glaus .... 1.50 .70
❑ 327 Delino DeShields .... .40 .18
❑ 328 Fernando Vina .... .40 .18
❑ 329 John Smoltz .... .60 .25
❑ 330 Jeff Kent .... 1.00 .45
❑ 331 Roy Halladay .... .40 .18
❑ 332 Andy Ashby .... .40 .18
❑ 333 Tim Wakefield .... .40 .18
❑ 334 Roger Clemens 4.00 1.80
❑ 335 Bernie Williams .... 1.50 .70
❑ 336 Desi Relaford .... .40 .18
❑ 337 John Burkett .... .40 .18
❑ 338 Mike Hampton .... .60 .25
❑ 339 Royce Clayton .... .40 .18
❑ 340 Mike Piazza 4.00 1.80
❑ 341 Jeremi Gonzalez .... .40 .18
❑ 342 Mike Lansing .... .40 .18
❑ 343 Jamie Moyer .... .40 .18
❑ 344 Ron Coomer .... .40 .18
❑ 345 Barry Larkin .... 1.50 .70
❑ 346 Fernando Tatis .... .40 .18
❑ 347 Chili Davis .... .60 .25
❑ 348 Bobby Higginson .... .60 .25
❑ 349 Hal Morris .... .40 .18
❑ 350 Larry Walker .... 1.00 .45
❑ 351 Carlos Guillen .... .40 .18
❑ 352 Miguel Tejada .... .60 .25
❑ 353 Travis Fryman .... .60 .25
❑ 354 Jarrod Washburn .... .40 .18
❑ 355 Chipper Jones 3.00 1.35
❑ 356 Todd Stottlemyre .... .40 .18
❑ 357 Henry Rodriguez .... .40 .18
❑ 358 Eli Marrero .... .40 .18
❑ 359 Alan Benes .... .40 .18
❑ 360 Tim Salmon .... .60 .25
❑ 361 Luis Gonzalez .... 1.50 .70
❑ 362 Scott Spiezio .... .40 .18
❑ 363 Chris Carpenter .... .40 .18
❑ 364 Bobby Howry .... .40 .18
❑ 365 Raul Mondesi .... .60 .25
❑ 366 Ugueth Urbina .... .40 .18
❑ 367 Tom Evans .... .40 .18
❑ 368 Kerry Ligtenberg RC ...... .60 .25
❑ 369 Adrian Beltre .... .60 .25
❑ 370 Ryan Klesko .... .60 .25
❑ 371 Wilson Alvarez .... .40 .18
❑ 372 John Thomson .... .40 .18
❑ 373 Tony Saunders .... .40 .18
❑ 374 Dave Mlicki .... .40 .18
❑ 375 Ken Caminiti .... .60 .25
❑ 376 Jay Buhner .... .60 .25
❑ 377 Bill Mueller .... .40 .18
❑ 378 Jeff Blauser .... .40 .18
❑ 379 Edgar Renteria .... .40 .18
❑ 380 Jim Thome .... 1.50 .70
❑ 381 Joey Hamilton .... .40 .18
❑ 382 Calvin Pickering .... .40 .18
❑ 383 Marquis Grissom .... .40 .18
❑ 384 Omar Daal .... .40 .18
❑ 385 Curt Schilling .... 1.50 .70
❑ 386 Jose Cruz Jr. .... .60 .25
❑ 387 Chris Widger .... .40 .18
❑ 388 Pete Harnisch .... .40 .18
❑ 389 Charles Nagy .... .40 .18
❑ 390 Tom Gordon .... .40 .18
❑ 391 Bobby Smith .... .40 .18
❑ 392 Derrick Gibson .... .40 .18
❑ 393 Jeff Conine .... .40 .18
❑ 394 Carlos Perez .... .40 .18
❑ 395 Barry Bonds 4.00 1.80
❑ 396 Mark McLemore .... .40 .18
❑ 397 Juan Encarnacion .... .60 .25
❑ 398 Wade Boggs .... 1.50 .70
❑ 399 Ivan Rodriguez .... 1.50 .70
❑ 400 Moises Alou .... .60 .25
❑ 401 Jeromy Burnitz .... .60 .25
❑ 402 Sean Casey .... 1.00 .45
❑ 403 Jose Offerman .... .40 .18

Card	Player	Mint	NrMt
❑ 404	Joe Fontenot	.40	.18
❑ 405	Kevin Millwood	.40	.18
❑ 406	Lance Johnson	.40	.18
❑ 407	Richard Hidalgo	.60	.25
❑ 408	Mike Jackson	.40	.18
❑ 409	Brian Anderson	.40	.18
❑ 410	Jeff Shaw	.40	.18
❑ 411	Preston Wilson	.60	.25
❑ 412	Todd Hundley	.40	.18
❑ 413	Jim Parque	.40	.18
❑ 414	Justin Baughman	.40	.18
❑ 415	Dante Bichette	.60	.25
❑ 416	Paul O'Neill	1.50	.70
❑ 417	Miguel Cairo	.40	.18
❑ 418	Randy Johnson	2.00	.90
❑ 419	Jesus Sanchez	.40	.18
❑ 420	Carlos Delgado	1.50	.70
❑ 421	Ricky Ledee	.40	.18
❑ 422	Orlando Hernandez	.60	.25
❑ 423	Frank Thomas	2.00	.90
❑ 424	Pokey Reese	.40	.18
❑ 425	Carlos Lee	.60	.25
	Mike Lowell		
	Kit Pellow RC		
❑ 426	Michael Cuddyer	1.25	.55
	Mark DeRosa		
	Jerry Hairston Jr.		
❑ 427	Marlon Anderson	1.00	.45
	Ron Belliard		
	Orlando Cabrera		
❑ 428	Micah Bowie	1.00	.45
	Phil Norton RC		
	Randy Wolf		
❑ 429	Jack Cressend RC	.60	.25
	Jason Rakers		
	John Rocker		
❑ 430	Ruben Mateo	1.25	.55
	Scott Morgan		
	Mike Zywica RC		
❑ 431	Jason LaRue	1.00	.45
	Matt LeCroy		
	Mitch Meluskey		
❑ 432	Gabe Kapler	1.25	.55
	Armando Rios		
	Fernando Seguignol		
❑ 433	Adam Kennedy	1.00	.45
	Mickey Lopez RC		
	Jackie Rexrode		
❑ 434	Jose Fernandez RC	1.00	.45
	Jeff Liefer		
	Chris Truby		
❑ 435	Corey Koskie	5.00	2.20
	Doug Mientkiewicz RC		
	Damon Minor		
❑ 436	Roosevelt Brown RC	2.00	.90
	Dernell Stenson		
	Vernon Wells		
❑ 437	A.J. Burnett RC	3.00	1.35
	Billy Koch		
	John Nicholson		
❑ 438	Matt Belisle	2.00	.90
	Matt Roney RC		
❑ 439	Austin Kearns	8.00	3.60
	Chris George RC		
❑ 440	Nate Bump RC	4.00	1.80
	Nate Cornejo		
❑ 441	Brad Lidge	2.00	.90
	Mike Nannini RC		
❑ 442	Matt Holliday	2.00	.90
	Jeff Winchester RC		
❑ 443	Adam Everett	2.00	.90
	Chip Ambres RC		
❑ 444	Pat Burrell	6.00	2.70
	Eric Valent RC		
❑ 445	Roger Clemens SK	2.00	.90
❑ 446	Kerry Wood SK	.60	.25
❑ 447	Curt Schilling SK	.60	.25
❑ 448	Randy Johnson SK	.60	.25
❑ 449	Pedro Martinez SK	1.00	.45
❑ 450	Jeff Bagwell AT	3.00	1.35
	Andres Galarraga		
	Mark McGwire		
❑ 451	John Olerud AT	.60	.25
	Jim Thome		
	Tino Martinez		
❑ 452	Alex Rodriguez AT	2.00	.90
	Nomar Garciaparra		
	Derek Jeter		
❑ 453	Vinny Castilla AT	1.50	.70
	Chipper Jones		
	Scott Rolen		
❑ 454	Sammy Sosa AT	2.50	1.10
	Ken Griffey Jr.		
	Juan Gonzalez		
❑ 455	Barry Bonds AT	2.00	.90
	Manny Ramirez		
	Larry Walker		
❑ 456	Frank Thomas AT	.60	.25
	Tim Salmon		
	David Justice		
❑ 457	Travis Lee AT	1.50	.70
	Todd Helton		
	Ben Grieve		
❑ 458	Vladimir Guerrero AT	1.50	.70
	Greg Vaughn		
	Bernie Williams		
❑ 459	Mike Piazza AT	1.00	.45
	Ivan Rodriguez		
	Jason Kendall		
❑ 460	Roger Clemens AT	2.00	.90
	Kerry Wood		
	Greg Maddux		
❑ 461A	Sammy Sosa HR 1	30.00	13.50
❑ 461B	Sammy Sosa HR 2	15.00	6.75
❑ 461C	Sammy Sosa HR 3	15.00	6.75
❑ 461D	Sammy Sosa HR 4	15.00	6.75
❑ 461E	Sammy Sosa HR 5	15.00	6.75
❑ 461F	Sammy Sosa HR 6	15.00	6.75
❑ 461G	Sammy Sosa HR 7	15.00	6.75
❑ 461H	Sammy Sosa HR 8	15.00	6.75
❑ 461I	Sammy Sosa HR 9	15.00	6.75
❑ 461J	Sammy Sosa HR 10	15.00	6.75
❑ 461K	Sammy Sosa HR 11	15.00	6.75
❑ 461L	Sammy Sosa HR 12	15.00	6.75
❑ 461M	Sammy Sosa HR 13	15.00	6.75
❑ 461N	Sammy Sosa HR 14	15.00	6.75
❑ 461O	Sammy Sosa HR 15	15.00	6.75
❑ 461P	Sammy Sosa HR 16	15.00	6.75
❑ 461Q	Sammy Sosa HR 17	15.00	6.75
❑ 461R	Sammy Sosa HR 18	15.00	6.75
❑ 461S	Sammy Sosa HR 19	15.00	6.75
❑ 461T	Sammy Sosa HR 20	15.00	6.75
❑ 461U	Sammy Sosa HR 21	15.00	6.75
❑ 461V	Sammy Sosa HR 22	15.00	6.75
❑ 461W	Sammy Sosa HR 23	15.00	6.75
❑ 461X	Sammy Sosa HR 24	15.00	6.75
❑ 461Y	Sammy Sosa HR 25	15.00	6.75
❑ 461Z	Sammy Sosa HR 26	15.00	6.75
❑ 461AA	S.Sosa HR 27	15.00	6.75
❑ 461AB	S.Sosa HR 28	15.00	6.75
❑ 461AC	S.Sosa HR 29	15.00	6.75
❑ 461AD	S.Sosa HR 30	15.00	6.75
❑ 461AE	S.Sosa HR 31	15.00	6.75
❑ 461AF	S.Sosa HR 32	15.00	6.75
❑ 461AG	S.Sosa HR 33	15.00	6.75
❑ 461AH	S.Sosa HR 34	15.00	6.75
❑ 461AI	S.Sosa HR 35	15.00	6.75
❑ 461AJ	S.Sosa HR 36	15.00	6.75
❑ 461AK	S.Sosa HR 37	15.00	6.75
❑ 461AL	S.Sosa HR 38	15.00	6.75
❑ 461AM	S.Sosa HR 39	15.00	6.75
❑ 461AN	S.Sosa HR 40	15.00	6.75
❑ 461AO	S.Sosa HR 41	15.00	6.75
❑ 461AP	S.Sosa HR 42	15.00	6.75
❑ 461AR	S.Sosa HR 43	15.00	6.75
❑ 461AS	S.Sosa HR 44	15.00	6.75
❑ 461AT	S.Sosa HR 45	15.00	6.75
❑ 461AU	S.Sosa HR 46	15.00	6.75
❑ 461AV	S.Sosa HR 47	15.00	6.75
❑ 461AW	S.Sosa HR 48	15.00	6.75
❑ 461AX	S.Sosa HR 49	15.00	6.75
❑ 461AY	S.Sosa HR 50	15.00	6.75
❑ 461AZ	S.Sosa HR 51	15.00	6.75
❑ 461BB	S.Sosa HR 52	15.00	6.75
❑ 461CC	S.Sosa HR 53	15.00	6.75
❑ 461DD	S.Sosa HR 54	15.00	6.75
❑ 461EE	S.Sosa HR 55	15.00	6.75
❑ 461FF	S.Sosa HR 56	15.00	6.75
❑ 461GG	S.Sosa HR 57	15.00	6.75
❑ 461HH	S.Sosa HR 58	15.00	6.75
❑ 461II	S.Sosa HR 59	15.00	6.75
❑ 461JJ	S.Sosa HR 60	15.00	6.75
❑ 461KK	S.Sosa HR 61	30.00	13.50
❑ 461LL	S.Sosa HR 62	50.00	22.00
❑ 461MM	S.Sosa HR 63	20.00	9.00
❑ 461NN	S.Sosa HR 64	20.00	9.00
❑ 461OO	S.Sosa HR 65	20.00	9.00
❑ 461PP	S.Sosa HR 66	80.00	36.00
❑ 462	Checklist	.40	.18
❑ 463	Checklist	.40	.18

1999 Topps Chrome Traded

		MINT	NRMT
COMP.FACT SET (121)		110.00	50.00
❑ T1	Seth Etherton	1.50	.70
❑ T2	Mark Harriger RC	.40	.18
❑ T3	Matt Wise RC	.40	.18
❑ T4	Carlos Eduardo Hernandez RC	.60	.25
❑ T5	Julio Lugo RC	2.50	1.10
❑ T6	Mike Nannini	2.50	1.10
❑ T7	Justin Bowles RC	.40	.18
❑ T8	Mark Mulder RC	10.00	4.50
❑ T9	Roberto Vaz RC	.40	.18
❑ T10	Felipe Lopez RC	5.00	2.20
❑ T11	Matt Belisle	2.50	1.10
❑ T12	Micah Bowie	.40	.18
❑ T13	Ruben Quevedo RC	2.50	1.10
❑ T14	Jose Garcia RC	1.25	.55
❑ T15	David Kelton RC	4.00	1.80
❑ T16	Phil Norton	.40	.18
❑ T17	Corey Patterson RC	8.00	3.60
❑ T18	Ron Walker RC	.40	.18
❑ T19	Paul Hoover RC	.75	.35
❑ T20	Ryan Rupe RC	1.25	.55
❑ T21	J.D. Closser RC	2.50	1.10
❑ T22	Rob Ryan RC	.40	.18
❑ T23	Steve Colyer RC	1.25	.55
❑ T24	Bubba Crosby RC	.60	.25
❑ T25	Luke Prokopec RC	3.00	1.35
❑ T26	Matt Blank RC	.60	.25
❑ T27	Josh McKinley	1.50	.70
❑ T28	Nate Bump	1.00	.45
❑ T29	G.Chiaramonte RC	1.25	.55
❑ T30	Arturo McDowell	1.00	.45
❑ T31	Tony Torcato	2.50	1.10
❑ T32	Dave Roberts RC	.40	.18
❑ T33	C.C. Sabathia RC	10.00	4.50
❑ T34	Sean Spencer RC	.40	.18
❑ T35	Chip Ambres	1.50	.70
❑ T36	A.J. Burnett	3.00	1.35
❑ T37	Mo Bruce RC	.40	.18
❑ T38	Jason Tyner	1.50	.70
❑ T39	Mamon Tucker	1.50	.70
❑ T40	Sean Burroughs RC	12.00	5.50
❑ T41	Kevin Eberwein RC	1.25	.55
❑ T42	Junior Herndon RC	1.50	.70
❑ T43	Bryan Wolff RC	.40	.18
❑ T44	Pat Burrell	6.00	2.70
❑ T45	Eric Valent	2.50	1.10
❑ T46	Carlos Pena RC	8.00	3.60
❑ T47	Mike Zywica	.40	.18
❑ T48	Adam Everett	1.50	.70
❑ T49	Juan Pena RC	.60	.25
❑ T50	Adam Dunn RC	30.00	13.50
❑ T51	Austin Kearns	8.00	3.60
❑ T52	Jacobo Sequea RC	1.50	.70
❑ T53	Choo Freeman	1.50	.70

Card	MINT	NRMT
❑ T54 Jeff Winchester	1.50	.70
❑ T55 Matt Burch	.60	.25
❑ T56 Chris George	2.50	1.10
❑ T57 Scott Mullen RC	.40	.18
❑ T58 Kit Pellow	1.50	.70
❑ T59 Mark Quinn RC	4.00	1.80
❑ T60 Nate Cornejo	4.00	1.80
❑ T61 Ryan Mills	1.00	.45
❑ T62 Kevin Beirne RC	.40	.18
❑ T63 Kip Wells RC	2.50	1.10
❑ T64 Juan Rivera RC	6.00	2.70
❑ T65 Alfonso Soriano RC	12.00	5.50
❑ T66 Josh Hamilton RC	15.00	6.75
❑ T67 Josh Girdley RC	2.00	.90
❑ T68 Kyle Snyder RC	1.25	.55
❑ T69 Mike Paradis RC	1.25	.55
❑ T70 Jason Jennings RC	4.00	1.80
❑ T71 David Walling RC	1.50	.70
❑ T72 Omar Ortiz RC	.75	.35
❑ T73 Jay Gehrke RC	.60	.25
❑ T74 Casey Burns RC	.60	.25
❑ T75 Carl Crawford RC	5.00	2.20
❑ T76 Reggie Sanders	.40	.18
❑ T77 Will Clark	1.50	.70
❑ T78 David Wells	.60	.25
❑ T79 Paul Konerko	.60	.25
❑ T80 Armando Benitez	.40	.18
❑ T81 Brant Brown	.40	.18
❑ T82 Mo Vaughn	.60	.25
❑ T83 Jose Canseco	1.50	.70
❑ T84 Albert Belle	.60	.25
❑ T85 Dean Palmer	.60	.25
❑ T86 Greg Vaughn	.60	.25
❑ T87 Mark Clark	.40	.18
❑ T88 Pat Meares	.40	.18
❑ T89 Eric Davis	.60	.25
❑ T90 Brian Giles	.60	.25
❑ T91 Jeff Brantley	.40	.18
❑ T92 Bret Boone	.60	.25
❑ T93 Ron Gant	.60	.25
❑ T94 Mike Cameron	.60	.25
❑ T95 Charles Johnson	.60	.25
❑ T96 Denny Neagle	.40	.18
❑ T97 Brian Hunter	.40	.18
❑ T98 Jose Hernandez	.40	.18
❑ T99 Rick Aguilera	.40	.18
❑ T100 Tony Batista	.60	.25
❑ T101 Roger Cedeno	.40	.18
❑ T102 C.Gubanich RC	.40	.18
❑ T103 Tim Belcher	.40	.18
❑ T104 Bruce Aven	.40	.18
❑ T105 Brian Daubach RC	3.00	1.35
❑ T106 Ed Sprague	.40	.18
❑ T107 Michael Tucker	.40	.18
❑ T108 Homer Bush	.40	.18
❑ T109 Armando Reynoso	.40	.18
❑ T110 Brook Fordyce	.40	.18
❑ T111 Matt Mantei	.40	.18
❑ T112 Dave Mlicki	.40	.18
❑ T113 Kenny Rogers	.40	.18
❑ T114 Livan Hernandez	.40	.18
❑ T115 Butch Huskey	.40	.18
❑ T116 David Segui	.40	.18
❑ T117 Darryl Hamilton	.40	.18
❑ T118 Terry Mulholland	.40	.18
❑ T119 Randy Velarde	.40	.18
❑ T120 Bill Taylor	.40	.18
❑ T121 Kevin Appier	.60	.25

2000 Topps Chrome

	MINT	NRMT
COMPLETE SET (478)	300.00	135.00
COMPLETE SERIES 1 (239)	150.00	70.00
COMPLETE SERIES 2 (240)	150.00	70.00
MCGWIRE MM SET (5)	60.00	27.00
AARON MM SET (5)	40.00	18.00
RIPKEN MM SET (5)	60.00	27.00
BOGGS MM SET (5)	20.00	9.00
GWYNN MM SET (5)	30.00	13.50
GRIFFEY MM SET (5)	50.00	22.00
BONDS MM SET (5)	40.00	18.00
SOSA MM SET (5)	30.00	13.50
JETER MM SET (5)	60.00	27.00
A.ROD MM SET (5)	40.00	18.00

Card	MINT	NRMT
❑ 1 Mark McGwire	6.00	2.70
❑ 2 Tony Gwynn	3.00	1.35
❑ 3 Wade Boggs	1.50	.70
❑ 4 Cal Ripken	6.00	2.70
❑ 5 Matt Williams	1.00	.45
❑ 6 Jay Buhner	.60	.25
❑ 7 Does Not Exist		
❑ 8 Jeff Conine	.40	.18
❑ 9 Todd Greene	.40	.18
❑ 10 Mike Lieberthal	.60	.25
❑ 11 Steve Avery	.40	.18
❑ 12 Bret Saberhagen	.60	.25
❑ 13 Magglio Ordonez	.60	.25
❑ 14 Brad Radke	.60	.25
❑ 15 Derek Jeter	6.00	2.70
❑ 16 Javy Lopez	.60	.25
❑ 17 Russ Davis	.40	.18
❑ 18 Armando Benitez	.60	.25
❑ 19 B.J. Surhoff	.60	.25
❑ 20 Darryl Kile	.60	.25
❑ 21 Mark Lewis	.40	.18
❑ 22 Mike Williams	.40	.18
❑ 23 Mark McLemore	.40	.18
❑ 24 Sterling Hitchcock	.40	.18
❑ 25 Darin Erstad	1.50	.70
❑ 26 Ricky Gutierrez	.40	.18
❑ 27 John Jaha	.40	.18
❑ 28 Homer Bush	.40	.18
❑ 29 Darrin Fletcher	.40	.18
❑ 30 Mark Grace	1.50	.70
❑ 31 Fred McGriff	1.00	.45
❑ 32 Omar Daal	.40	.18
❑ 33 Eric Karros	.60	.25
❑ 34 Orlando Cabrera	.40	.18
❑ 35 J.T. Snow	.60	.25
❑ 36 Luis Castillo	.40	.18
❑ 37 Rey Ordonez	.40	.18
❑ 38 Bob Abreu	.60	.25
❑ 39 Warren Morris	.40	.18
❑ 40 Juan Gonzalez	1.50	.70
❑ 41 Mike Lansing	.40	.18
❑ 42 Chili Davis	.60	.25
❑ 43 Dean Palmer	.60	.25
❑ 44 Hank Aaron	4.00	1.80
❑ 45 Jeff Bagwell	2.00	.90
❑ 46 Jose Valentin	.40	.18
❑ 47 Shannon Stewart	.60	.25
❑ 48 Kent Bottenfield	.40	.18
❑ 49 Jeff Shaw	.40	.18
❑ 50 Sammy Sosa	3.00	1.35
❑ 51 Randy Johnson	2.00	.90
❑ 52 Benny Agbayani	.40	.18
❑ 53 Dante Bichette	.60	.25
❑ 54 Pete Harnisch	.40	.18
❑ 55 Frank Thomas	2.00	.90
❑ 56 Jorge Posada	.60	.25
❑ 57 Todd Walker	.40	.18
❑ 58 Juan Encarnacion	.60	.25
❑ 59 Mike Sweeney	.60	.25
❑ 60 Pedro Martinez	2.00	.90
❑ 61 Lee Stevens	.40	.18
❑ 62 Brian Giles	.60	.25
❑ 63 Chad Ogea	.40	.18
❑ 64 Ivan Rodriguez	1.50	.70
❑ 65 Roger Cedeno	.40	.18
❑ 66 David Justice	.60	.25
❑ 67 Steve Trachsel	.40	.18

Card	MINT	NRMT
❑ 68 Eli Marrero	.40	.18
❑ 69 Dave Nilsson	.40	.18
❑ 70 Ken Caminiti	.60	.25
❑ 71 Tim Raines	.60	.25
❑ 72 Brian Jordan	.60	.25
❑ 73 Jeff Blauser	.40	.18
❑ 74 Bernard Gilkey	.40	.18
❑ 75 John Flaherty	.40	.18
❑ 76 Brent Mayne	.40	.18
❑ 77 Jose Vidro	.60	.25
❑ 78 David Bell	.40	.18
❑ 79 Bruce Aven	.40	.18
❑ 80 John Olerud	.60	.25
❑ 81 Pokey Reese	.40	.18
❑ 82 Woody Williams	.40	.18
❑ 83 Ed Sprague	.40	.18
❑ 84 Joe Girardi	.40	.18
❑ 85 Barry Larkin	1.50	.70
❑ 86 Mike Caruso	.40	.18
❑ 87 Bobby Higginson	.40	.18
❑ 88 Roberto Kelly	.40	.18
❑ 89 Edgar Martinez	1.00	.45
❑ 90 Mark Kotsay	.40	.18
❑ 91 Paul Sorrento	.40	.18
❑ 92 Eric Young	.40	.18
❑ 93 Carlos Delgado	1.50	.70
❑ 94 Troy Glaus	1.50	.70
❑ 95 Ben Grieve	.60	.25
❑ 96 Jose Lima	.40	.18
❑ 97 Garret Anderson	.60	.25
❑ 98 Luis Gonzalez	1.50	.70
❑ 99 Carl Pavano	.40	.18
❑ 100 Alex Rodriguez	4.00	1.80
❑ 101 Preston Wilson	.60	.25
❑ 102 Ron Gant	.60	.25
❑ 103 Brady Anderson	.60	.25
❑ 104 Rickey Henderson	3.00	1.35
❑ 105 Gary Sheffield	.60	.25
❑ 106 Mickey Morandini	.40	.18
❑ 107 Jim Edmonds	1.00	.45
❑ 108 Kris Benson	.60	.25
❑ 109 Adrian Beltre	.60	.25
❑ 110 Alex Fernandez	.40	.18
❑ 111 Dan Wilson	.40	.18
❑ 112 Mark Clark	.40	.18
❑ 113 Greg Vaughn	.60	.25
❑ 114 Neifi Perez	.40	.18
❑ 115 Paul O'Neill	1.50	.70
❑ 116 Jermaine Dye	.60	.25
❑ 117 Todd Jones	.40	.18
❑ 118 Terry Steinbach	.40	.18
❑ 119 Greg Norton	.40	.18
❑ 120 Curt Schilling	1.50	.70
❑ 121 Todd Zeile	.60	.25
❑ 122 Edgardo Alfonzo	.60	.25
❑ 123 Ryan McGuire	.40	.18
❑ 124 Rich Aurilia	.60	.25
❑ 125 John Smoltz	.60	.25
❑ 126 Bob Wickman	.40	.18
❑ 127 Richard Hidalgo	.60	.25
❑ 128 Chuck Finley	.60	.25
❑ 129 Billy Wagner	.40	.18
❑ 130 Todd Hundley	.40	.18
❑ 131 Dwight Gooden	.60	.25
❑ 132 Russ Ortiz	.60	.25
❑ 133 Mike Lowell	.40	.18
❑ 134 Reggie Sanders	.40	.18
❑ 135 John Valentin	.40	.18
❑ 136 Brad Ausmus	.40	.18
❑ 137 Chad Kreuter	.40	.18
❑ 138 David Cone	.60	.25
❑ 139 Brook Fordyce	.40	.18
❑ 140 Roberto Alomar	1.50	.70
❑ 141 Charles Nagy	.40	.18
❑ 142 Brian Hunter	.40	.18
❑ 143 Mike Mussina	1.50	.70
❑ 144 Robin Ventura	1.00	.45
❑ 145 Kevin Brown	1.00	.45
❑ 146 Pat Hentgen	.40	.18
❑ 147 Ryan Klesko	.60	.25
❑ 148 Derek Bell	.40	.18
❑ 149 Andy Sheets	.40	.18
❑ 150 Larry Walker	1.00	.45
❑ 151 Scott Williamson	.40	.18
❑ 152 Jose Offerman	.40	.18
❑ 153 Doug Mientkiewicz	1.00	.45

No.	Player	Price	Price
❑ 154	John Snyder RC	1.25	.55
❑ 155	Sandy Alomar Jr.	.40	.18
❑ 156	Joe Nathan	.40	.18
❑ 157	Lance Johnson	.40	.18
❑ 158	Odalis Perez	.40	.18
❑ 159	Hideo Nomo	1.50	.70
❑ 160	Steve Finley	.60	.25
❑ 161	Dave Martinez	.40	.18
❑ 162	Matt Walbeck	.40	.18
❑ 163	Bill Spiers	.40	.18
❑ 164	Fernando Tatis	.40	.18
❑ 165	Kenny Lofton	.60	.25
❑ 166	Paul Byrd	.40	.18
❑ 167	Aaron Sele	.60	.25
❑ 168	Eddie Taubensee	.40	.18
❑ 169	Reggie Jefferson	.40	.18
❑ 170	Roger Clemens	4.00	1.80
❑ 171	Francisco Cordova	.40	.18
❑ 172	Mike Bordick	.40	.18
❑ 173	Wally Joyner	.60	.25
❑ 174	Marvin Benard	.40	.18
❑ 175	Jason Kendall	.60	.25
❑ 176	Mike Stanley	.40	.18
❑ 177	Chad Allen	.40	.18
❑ 178	Carlos Beltran	.60	.25
❑ 179	Deivi Cruz	.40	.18
❑ 180	Chipper Jones	3.00	1.35
❑ 181	Vladimir Guerrero	2.00	.90
❑ 182	Dave Burba	.40	.18
❑ 183	Tom Goodwin	.40	.18
❑ 184	Brian Daubach	.60	.25
❑ 185	Jay Bell	.60	.25
❑ 186	Roy Halladay	.40	.18
❑ 187	Miguel Tejada	.60	.25
❑ 188	Armando Rios	.40	.18
❑ 189	Fernando Vina	.40	.18
❑ 190	Eric Davis	.60	.25
❑ 191	Henry Rodriguez	.40	.18
❑ 192	Joe McEwing	.40	.18
❑ 193	Jeff Kent	1.00	.45
❑ 194	Mike Jackson	.40	.18
❑ 195	Mike Morgan	.40	.18
❑ 196	Jeff Montgomery	.40	.18
❑ 197	Jeff Zimmerman	.40	.18
❑ 198	Tony Fernandez	.40	.18
❑ 199	Jason Giambi	1.50	.70
❑ 200	Jose Canseco	1.50	.70
❑ 201	Alex Gonzalez	.40	.18
❑ 202	Jack Cust Mike Colangelo Dee Brown	.60	.25
❑ 203	Felipe Lopez Alfonso Soriano Pablo Ozuna	1.50	.70
❑ 204	Erubiel Durazo Pat Burrell Nick Johnson	1.50	.70
❑ 205	John Sneed RC Kip Wells Matt Blank	1.00	.45
❑ 206	Josh Kalinowski Michael Tejera Chris Mears RC	1.00	.45
❑ 207	Roosevelt Brown Corey Patterson Lance Berkman	1.50	.70
❑ 208	Kit Pellow Kevin Barker Russ Branyan	.40	.18
❑ 209	B.J. Garbe Larry Bigbie RC	2.50	1.10
❑ 210	Eric Munson Bobby Bradley RC	2.00	.90
❑ 211	Josh Girdley Kyle Snyder	.60	.25
❑ 212	Chance Caple RC Jason Jennings	1.50	.70
❑ 213	Ryan Christianson Brett Myers RC	2.00	.90
❑ 214	Jason Stumm Rob Purvis RC	1.50	.70
❑ 215	David Walling Mike Paradis	.60	.25
❑ 216	Omar Ortiz Jay Gehrke	.60	.25
❑ 217	David Cone HL	.60	.25
❑ 218	Jose Jimenez HL	.40	.18
❑ 219	Chris Singleton HL	.40	.18
❑ 220	Fernando Tatis HL	.40	.18
❑ 221	Todd Helton HL	1.50	.70
❑ 222	Kevin Millwood DIV	.40	.18
❑ 223	Todd Pratt DIV	.40	.18
❑ 224	Orl. Hernandez DIV	.40	.18
❑ 225	Pedro Martinez DIV	1.00	.45
❑ 226	Tom Glavine LCS	.60	.25
❑ 227	Bernie Williams LCS	.60	.25
❑ 228	Mariano Rivera WS	.40	.18
❑ 229	Tony Gwynn 20CB	3.00	1.35
❑ 230	Wade Boggs 20CB	1.50	.70
❑ 231	Lance Johnson CB	.40	.18
❑ 232	Mark McGwire 20CB	6.00	2.70
❑ 233	R.Henderson 20CB	3.00	1.35
❑ 234	R.Henderson 20CB	3.00	1.35
❑ 235	Roger Clemens 20CB	4.00	1.80
❑ 236A	Mark McGwire MM 1st HR	15.00	6.75
❑ 236B	Mark McGwire MM 1987 ROY	15.00	6.75
❑ 236C	Mark McGwire MM 62nd HR	15.00	6.75
❑ 236D	Mark McGwire MM 70th HR	15.00	6.75
❑ 236E	Mark McGwire MM 500th HR	15.00	6.75
❑ 237A	Hank Aaron MM 1st Career HR	10.00	4.50
❑ 237B	Hank Aaron MM 1957 MVP	10.00	4.50
❑ 237C	Hank Aaron MM 3000th Hit	10.00	4.50
❑ 237D	Hank Aaron MM 715th HR	10.00	4.50
❑ 237E	Hank Aaron MM 755th HR	10.00	4.50
❑ 238A	Cal Ripken MM 1982 ROY	15.00	6.75
❑ 238B	Cal Ripken MM 1991 MVP	15.00	6.75
❑ 238C	Cal Ripken MM 2131 Game	15.00	6.75
❑ 238D	Cal Ripken MM Streak Ends	15.00	6.75
❑ 238E	Cal Ripken MM 400th HR	15.00	6.75
❑ 239A	Wade Boggs MM 1983 Batting	5.00	2.20
❑ 239B	Wade Boggs MM 1988 Batting	5.00	2.20
❑ 239C	Wade Boggs MM 2000th Hit	5.00	2.20
❑ 239D	Wade Boggs MM 1996 Champs	5.00	2.20
❑ 239E	Wade Boggs MM 3000th Hit	5.00	2.20
❑ 240A	Tony Gwynn MM 1984 Batting	8.00	3.60
❑ 240B	Tony Gwynn MM 1984 NLCS	8.00	3.60
❑ 240C	Tony Gwynn MM 1995 Batting	8.00	3.60
❑ 240D	Tony Gwynn MM 1998 NLCS	8.00	3.60
❑ 240E	Tony Gwynn MM 3000th Hit	8.00	3.60
❑ 241	Tom Glavine	1.50	.70
❑ 242	David Wells	.60	.25
❑ 243	Kevin Appier	.40	.18
❑ 244	Troy Percival	.40	.18
❑ 245	Ray Lankford	.40	.18
❑ 246	Marquis Grissom	.40	.18
❑ 247	Randy Winn	.40	.18
❑ 248	Miguel Batista	.40	.18
❑ 249	Darren Dreifort	.40	.18
❑ 250	Barry Bonds	3.00	1.35
❑ 251	Harold Baines	.60	.25
❑ 252	Cliff Floyd	.60	.25
❑ 253	Freddy Garcia	1.00	.45
❑ 254	Kenny Rogers	.40	.18
❑ 255	Ben Davis		
❑ 256	Charles Johnson	.60	.25
❑ 257	Bubba Trammell	.40	.18
❑ 258	Desi Relaford	.40	.18
❑ 259	Al Martin	.40	.18
❑ 260	Andy Pettitte	.60	.25
❑ 261	Carlos Lee	.60	.25
❑ 262	Matt Lawton	.40	.18
❑ 263	Andy Fox	.40	.18
❑ 264	Chan Ho Park	.60	.25
❑ 265	Billy Koch	.40	.18
❑ 266	Dave Roberts	.40	.18
❑ 267	Carl Everett	.60	.25
❑ 268	Orel Hershiser	.60	.25
❑ 269	Trot Nixon	.60	.25
❑ 270	Rusty Greer	.60	.25
❑ 271	Will Clark	1.50	.70
❑ 272	Quilvio Veras	.40	.18
❑ 273	Rico Brogna	.40	.18
❑ 274	Devon White	.40	.18
❑ 275	Tim Hudson	1.50	.70
❑ 276	Mike Hampton	.60	.25
❑ 277	Miguel Cairo	.40	.18
❑ 278	Darren Oliver	.40	.18
❑ 279	Jeff Cirillo	.60	.25
❑ 280	Al Leiter	.40	.18
❑ 281	Shane Andrews	.40	.18
❑ 282	Carlos Febles	.40	.18
❑ 283	Pedro Astacio	.40	.18
❑ 284	Juan Guzman	.40	.18
❑ 285	Orlando Hernandez	.60	.25
❑ 286	Paul Konerko	.60	.25
❑ 287	Tony Clark	.60	.25
❑ 288	Aaron Boone	.40	.18
❑ 289	Ismael Valdes	.40	.18
❑ 290	Moises Alou	.60	.25
❑ 291	Kevin Tapani	.40	.18
❑ 292	John Franco	.60	.25
❑ 293	Todd Zeile	.60	.25
❑ 294	Jason Schmidt	.40	.18
❑ 295	Johnny Damon	.60	.25
❑ 296	Scott Brosius	.60	.25
❑ 297	Travis Fryman	.60	.25
❑ 298	Jose Vizcaino	.40	.18
❑ 299	Eric Chavez	.60	.25
❑ 300	Mike Piazza	4.00	1.80
❑ 301	Matt Clement	.40	.18
❑ 302	Cristian Guzman	.60	.25
❑ 303	C.J. Nitkowski	.40	.18
❑ 304	Michael Tucker	.40	.18
❑ 305	Brett Tomko	.40	.18
❑ 306	Mike Lansing	.40	.18
❑ 307	Eric Owens	.40	.18
❑ 308	Livan Hernandez	.40	.18
❑ 309	Rondell White	.60	.25
❑ 310	Todd Stottlemyre	.40	.18
❑ 311	Chris Carpenter	.40	.18
❑ 312	Ken Hill	.40	.18
❑ 313	Mark Loretta	.40	.18
❑ 314	John Rocker	.60	.25
❑ 315	Richie Sexson	.60	.25
❑ 316	Ruben Mateo	.60	.25
❑ 317	Joe Randa	.40	.18
❑ 318	Mike Sirotka	.40	.18
❑ 319	Jose Rosado	.40	.18
❑ 320	Matt Mantei	.40	.18
❑ 321	Kevin Millwood	.40	.18
❑ 322	Gary DiSarcina	.40	.18
❑ 323	Dustin Hermanson	.40	.18
❑ 324	Mike Stanton	.40	.18
❑ 325	Kirk Rueter	.40	.18
❑ 326	Damian Miller	.40	.18
❑ 327	Doug Glanville	.40	.18
❑ 328	Scott Rolen	1.50	.70
❑ 329	Ray Durham	.60	.25
❑ 330	Butch Huskey	.40	.18
❑ 331	Mariano Rivera	.60	.25
❑ 332	Darren Lewis	.40	.18
❑ 333	Mike Timlin	.40	.18
❑ 334	Mark Grudzielanek	.40	.18
❑ 335	Mike Cameron	.60	.25
❑ 336	Kelvim Escobar	.40	.18
❑ 337	Bret Boone	.60	.25
❑ 338	Mo Vaughn	.60	.25
❑ 339	Craig Biggio	1.00	.45
❑ 340	Michael Barrett	.40	.18
❑ 341	Marlon Anderson	.40	.18
❑ 342	Bobby Jones	.40	.18
❑ 343	John Halama	.40	.18
❑ 344	Todd Ritchie	.40	.18

❑ 345 Chuck Knoblauch .... .60 .25
❑ 346 Rick Reed .... .40 .18
❑ 347 Kelly Stinnett .... .40 .18
❑ 348 Tim Salmon .... .60 .25
❑ 349 A.J. Hinch .... .40 .18
❑ 350 Jose Cruz Jr. .... .60 .25
❑ 351 Roberto Hernandez .... .40 .18
❑ 352 Edgar Renteria .... .40 .18
❑ 353 Jose Hernandez .... .40 .18
❑ 354 Brad Fullmer .... .60 .25
❑ 355 Trevor Hoffman .... .60 .25
❑ 356 Troy O'Leary .... .40 .18
❑ 357 Justin Thompson .... .40 .18
❑ 358 Kevin Young .... .40 .18
❑ 359 Hideki Irabu .... .40 .18
❑ 360 Jim Thome .... 1.50 .70
❑ 361 Steve Karsay .... .40 .18
❑ 362 Octavio Dotel .... .40 .18
❑ 363 Omar Vizquel .... .60 .25
❑ 364 Raul Mondesi .... .60 .25
❑ 365 Shane Reynolds .... .40 .18
❑ 366 Bartolo Colon .... .60 .25
❑ 367 Chris Widger .... .40 .18
❑ 368 Gabe Kapler .... .60 .25
❑ 369 Bill Simas .... .40 .18
❑ 370 Tino Martinez .... .60 .25
❑ 371 John Thomson .... .40 .18
❑ 372 Delino DeShields .... .40 .18
❑ 373 Carlos Perez .... .40 .18
❑ 374 Eddie Perez .... .40 .18
❑ 375 Jeromy Burnitz .... .60 .25
❑ 376 Jimmy Haynes .... .40 .18
❑ 377 Travis Lee .... .40 .18
❑ 378 Darryl Hamilton .... .40 .18
❑ 379 Jamie Moyer .... .40 .18
❑ 380 Alex Gonzalez .... .40 .18
❑ 381 John Wetteland .... .60 .25
❑ 382 Vinny Castilla .... .60 .25
❑ 383 Jeff Suppan .... .40 .18
❑ 384 Jim Leyritz .... .40 .18
❑ 385 Robb Nen .... .40 .18
❑ 386 Wilson Alvarez .... .40 .18
❑ 387 Andres Galarraga .... 1.00 .45
❑ 388 Mike Remlinger .... .40 .18
❑ 389 Geoff Jenkins .... .60 .25
❑ 390 Matt Stairs .... .40 .18
❑ 391 Bill Mueller .... .40 .18
❑ 392 Mike Lowell .... .40 .18
❑ 393 Andy Ashby .... .40 .18
❑ 394 Ruben Rivera .... .40 .18
❑ 395 Todd Helton .... 2.00 .90
❑ 396 Bernie Williams .... 1.50 .70
❑ 397 Royce Clayton .... .40 .18
❑ 398 Manny Ramirez .... 2.00 .90
❑ 399 Kerry Wood .... 1.50 .70
❑ 400 Ken Griffey Jr. 5.00 2.20
❑ 401 Enrique Wilson .... .40 .18
❑ 402 Joey Hamilton .... .40 .18
❑ 403 Shawn Estes .... .60 .25
❑ 404 Ugueth Urbina .... .40 .18
❑ 405 Albert Belle .... .60 .25
❑ 406 Rick Helling .... .40 .18
❑ 407 Steve Parris .... .40 .18
❑ 408 Eric Milton .... .60 .25
❑ 409 Dave Mlicki .... .40 .18
❑ 410 Shawn Green .... 1.50 .70
❑ 411 Jaret Wright .... .40 .18
❑ 412 Tony Womack .... .40 .18
❑ 413 Vernon Wells .... .60 .25
❑ 414 Ron Belliard .... .40 .18
❑ 415 Ellis Burks .... .60 .25
❑ 416 Scott Erickson .... .40 .18
❑ 417 Rafael Palmeiro .... 1.50 .70
❑ 418 Damion Easley .... .40 .18
❑ 419 Jamey Wright .... .40 .18
❑ 420 Corey Koskie .... .60 .25
❑ 421 Bobby Howry .... .40 .18
❑ 422 Ricky Ledee .... .40 .18
❑ 423 Dmitri Young .... .60 .25
❑ 424 Sidney Ponson .... .40 .18
❑ 425 Greg Maddux 4.00 1.80
❑ 426 Jose Guillen .... .40 .18
❑ 427 Jon Lieber .... .40 .18
❑ 428 Andy Benes .... .40 .18
❑ 429 Randy Velarde .... .40 .18
❑ 430 Sean Casey .... 1.00 .45
❑ 431 Torii Hunter .... .60 .25
❑ 432 Ryan Rupe .... .40 .18
❑ 433 David Segui .... .40 .18
❑ 434 Todd Pratt .... .40 .18
❑ 435 Nomar Garciaparra 4.00 1.80
❑ 436 Denny Neagle .... .40 .18
❑ 437 Ron Coomer .... .40 .18
❑ 438 Chris Singleton .... .40 .18
❑ 439 Tony Batista .... .60 .25
❑ 440 Andruw Jones .... 1.50 .70
❑ 441 Aubrey Huff .... 1.50 .70
Sean Burroughs
Adam Piatt
❑ 442 Rafael Furcal .... 1.50 .70
Travis Dawkins
Jason Dellaero
❑ 443 Mike Lamb RC .... 1.50 .70
Joe Crede
Wilton Veras
❑ 444 Julio Zuleta RC .... 1.50 .70
Jorge Toca
Dernell Stenson
❑ 445 Garry Maddox Jr. RC .. 1.00 .45
Gary Matthews Jr.
Tim Raines Jr.
❑ 446 Mark Mulder .... 1.50 .70
C.C. Sabathia
Matt Riley
❑ 447 Scott Downs RC .... 1.00 .45
Chris George
Matt Belisle
❑ 448 Doug Mirabelli .... .40 .18
Ben Petrick
Jayson Werth
❑ 449 Josh Hamilton .... 2.00 .90
Corey Myers RC
❑ 450 Ben Christensen RC .... 1.25 .55
Richard Stahl
❑ 451 Ben Sheets RC 10.00 4.50
Barry Zito RC
❑ 452 Kurt Ainsworth 3.00 1.35
Ty Howington RC
❑ 453 Vince Faison RC 2.50 1.10
Rick Asadoorian
❑ 454 Keith Reed RC 2.50 1.10
Jeff Heaverlo
❑ 455 Mike MacDougal .... 2.00 .90
Brad Baker RC
❑ 456 Mark McGwire SH 3.00 1.35
❑ 457 Cal Ripken SH 3.00 1.35
❑ 458 Wade Boggs SH .... .60 .25
❑ 459 Tony Gwynn SH .... 1.50 .70
❑ 460 Jesse Orosco SH .... .40 .18
❑ 461 Larry Walker .... 1.00 .45
Nomar Garciaparra LL
❑ 462 Ken Griffey Jr. .... 2.00 .90
Mark McGwire LL
❑ 463 Manny Ramirez .... 1.50 .70
Mark McGwire LL
❑ 464 Pedro Martinez .... 1.00 .45
Randy Johnson LL
❑ 465 Pedro Martinez .... 1.00 .45
Randy Johnson LL
❑ 466 Derek Jeter .... 2.00 .90
Luis Gonzalez LL
❑ 467 Larry Walker .... 1.00 .45
Manny Ramirez LL
❑ 468 Tony Gwynn 20CB 3.00 1.35
❑ 469 Mark McGwire 20CB 6.00 2.70
❑ 470 Frank Thomas 20CB .... 2.00 .90
❑ 471 Harold Baines 20CB .... .60 .25
❑ 472 Roger Clemens 20CB .. 4.00 1.80
❑ 473 John Franco 20CB .... .60 .25
❑ 474 John Franco 20CB .... .60 .25
❑ 475A Ken Griffey Jr. MM .. 12.00 5.50
350th HR
❑ 475B Ken Griffey Jr. MM .. 12.00 5.50
1997 MVP
❑ 475C Ken Griffey Jr. MM .. 12.00 5.50
HR Dad
❑ 475D Ken Griffey Jr. MM .. 12.00 5.50
1992 AS MVP
❑ 475E Ken Griffey Jr. MM .. 12.00 5.50
50 HR 1997
❑ 476A Barry Bonds MM 10.00 4.50
400HR/400SB
❑ 476B Barry Bonds MM 10.00 4.50
40HR/40SB
❑ 476C Barry Bonds MM 10.00 4.50
1993 MVP
❑ 476D Barry Bonds MM 10.00 4.50
1990 MVP
❑ 476E Barry Bonds MM 10.00 4.50
1992 MVP
❑ 477A Sammy Sosa 8.00 3.60
MM 20 HR June
❑ 477B Sammy Sosa MM 8.00 3.60
66 HR 1998
❑ 477C Sammy Sosa MM 8.00 3.60
60 HR 1999
❑ 477D Sammy Sosa MM 8.00 3.60
1998 MVP
❑ 477E Sammy Sosa MM 8.00 3.60
HR's 61/62
❑ 478A Derek Jeter MM 15.00 6.75
1996 ROY
❑ 478B Derek Jeter MM 15.00 6.75
Wins 1999 WS
❑ 478C Derek Jeter MM 15.00 6.75
Wins 1998 WS
❑ 478D Derek Jeter MM 15.00 6.75
Wins 1996 WS
❑ 478E Derek Jeter MM 15.00 6.75
17 GM Hit Streak
❑ 479A Alex Rodriguez MM 10.00 4.50
40HR/40SB
❑ 479B Alex Rodriguez MM 10.00 4.50
100th HR
❑ 479C Alex Rodriguez 10.00 4.50
MM 1996 POY
❑ 479D Alex Rodriguez 10.00 4.50
MM Wins 1 Million
❑ 479E Alex Rodriguez MM 10.00 4.50
1996 Batting Leader
❑ NNO M.McGwire 85 Reprint 8.00 3.60

2000 Topps Chrome Traded

	MINT	NRMT
COMP.FACT.SET (135)	80.00	36.00

❑ T1 Mike MacDougal .... .60 .25
❑ T2 Andy Tracy RC .... 1.00 .45
❑ T3 Brandon Phillips RC 3.00 1.35
❑ T4 Brandon Inge RC 3.00 1.35
❑ T5 Robbie Morrison RC .... 1.00 .45
❑ T6 Josh Pressley RC .... 1.50 .70
❑ T7 Todd Moser RC .... 1.00 .45
❑ T8 Rob Purvis .... .60 .25
❑ T9 Chance Caple .... .60 .25
❑ T10 Ben Sheets 4.00 1.80
❑ T11 Russ Jacobson RC .... 1.50 .70
❑ T12 Brian Cole RC .... 1.50 .70
❑ T13 Brad Baker 3.00 1.35
❑ T14 Alex Cintron RC .... 2.00 .90
❑ T15 Lyle Overbay RC 4.00 1.80
❑ T16 Mike Edwards RC .... 1.00 .45
❑ T17 Sean McGowan RC .... 2.00 .90
❑ T18 Jose Molina .... .40 .18
❑ T19 Marcos Castillo RC .... 1.00 .45
❑ T20 Josue Espada RC .... 1.00 .45
❑ T21 Alex Gordon RC 2.50 1.10
❑ T22 Rob Pugmire RC .... 1.00 .45

Card	Player	MINT	NRMT
❑ T23	Jason Stumm	2.00	.90
❑ T24	Ty Howington	2.50	1.10
❑ T25	Brett Myers	2.00	.90
❑ T26	Maicer Izturis RC	1.00	.45
❑ T27	John McDonald	.40	.18
❑ T28	W.Rodriguez RC	2.50	1.10
❑ T29	Carlos Zambrano RC	3.00	1.35
❑ T30	Alejandro Diaz RC	1.50	.70
❑ T31	Geraldo Guzman RC	1.00	.45
❑ T32	J.R. House RC	10.00	4.50
❑ T33	Elvin Nina RC	1.00	.45
❑ T34	Juan Pierre RC	4.00	1.80
❑ T35	Ben Johnson RC	3.00	1.35
❑ T36	Jeff Bailey RC	1.00	.45
❑ T37	Miguel Olivo RC	1.50	.70
❑ T38	F.Rodriguez RC	2.00	.90
❑ T39	Tony Pena Jr. RC	2.00	.90
❑ T40	Miguel Cabrera RC	5.00	2.20
❑ T41	Asdrubal Oropeza RC	1.50	.70
❑ T42	Junior Zamora RC	1.00	.45
❑ T43	Jovanny Cedeno RC	3.00	1.35
❑ T44	John Sneed	.60	.25
❑ T45	Josh Kalinowski	.60	.25
❑ T46	Mike Young RC	3.00	1.35
❑ T47	Rico Washington RC	1.50	.70
❑ T48	Chad Durbin RC	1.00	.45
❑ T49	Junior Brignac RC	1.50	.70
❑ T50	Carlos Hernandez RC	5.00	2.20
❑ T51	Cesar Izturis RC	2.50	1.10
❑ T52	Oscar Salazar RC	2.50	1.10
❑ T53	Pat Strange RC	3.00	1.35
❑ T54	Rick Asadoorian	1.50	.70
❑ T55	Keith Reed	2.00	.90
❑ T56	Leo Estrella RC	1.00	.45
❑ T57	Wascar Serrano RC	2.00	.90
❑ T58	Richard Gomez RC	2.50	1.10
❑ T59	Ramon Santiago RC	2.50	1.10
❑ T60	Jovanny Sosa RC	2.00	.90
❑ T61	Aaron Rowand RC	3.00	1.35
❑ T62	Junior Guerrero RC	1.00	.45
❑ T63	Luis Terrero RC	1.50	.70
❑ T64	Brian Sanches RC	1.00	.45
❑ T65	Scott Sobkowiak RC	2.00	.90
❑ T66	Gary Majewski RC	2.00	.90
❑ T67	Barry Zito	5.00	2.20
❑ T68	Ryan Christianson	3.00	1.35
❑ T69	Cristian Guerrero RC	10.00	4.50
❑ T70	T.De La Rosa RC	1.00	.45
❑ T71	Andrew Beinbrink RC	1.00	.45
❑ T72	Ryan Knox RC	2.00	.90
❑ T73	Alex Graman RC	2.50	1.10
❑ T74	Juan Guzman RC	1.00	.45
❑ T75	Ruben Salazar RC	3.00	1.35
❑ T76	Luis Matos RC	1.50	.70
❑ T77	Tony Mota RC	1.00	.45
❑ T78	Doug Davis	.40	.18
❑ T79	Ben Christensen	1.00	.45
❑ T80	Mike Lamb	.60	.25
❑ T81	Adrian Gonzalez RC	12.00	5.50
❑ T82	Mike Stodolka RC	2.50	1.10
❑ T83	Adam Johnson RC	3.00	1.35
❑ T84	Matt Wheatland RC	2.50	1.10
❑ T85	Corey Smith RC	4.00	1.80
❑ T86	Rocco Baldelli RC	3.00	1.35
❑ T87	Keith Bucktrot RC	2.00	.90
❑ T88	Adam Wainwright RC	4.00	1.80
❑ T89	Scott Thorman RC	2.50	1.10
❑ T90	Tripper Johnson RC	2.50	1.10
❑ T91	Jim Edmonds	1.00	.45
❑ T92	Masato Yoshii	.40	.18
❑ T93	Adam Kennedy	.40	.18
❑ T94	Darryl Kile	.60	.25
❑ T95	Mark McLemore	.40	.18
❑ T96	Ricky Gutierrez	.40	.18
❑ T97	Juan Gonzalez	1.50	.70
❑ T98	Melvin Mora	.40	.18
❑ T99	Dante Bichette	.60	.25
❑ T100	Lee Stevens	.40	.18
❑ T101	Roger Cedeno	.40	.18
❑ T102	John Olerud	.60	.25
❑ T103	Eric Young	.40	.18
❑ T104	Mickey Morandini	.40	.18
❑ T105	Travis Lee	.40	.18
❑ T106	Greg Vaughn	.60	.25
❑ T107	Todd Zeile	.60	.25
❑ T108	Chuck Finley	.60	.25
❑ T109	Ismael Valdes	.40	.18
❑ T110	Reggie Sanders	.40	.18
❑ T111	Pat Hentgen	.40	.18
❑ T112	Ryan Klesko	.60	.25
❑ T113	Derek Bell	.40	.18
❑ T114	Hideo Nomo	1.50	.70
❑ T115	Aaron Sele	.60	.25
❑ T116	Fernando Vina	.40	.18
❑ T117	Wally Joyner	.60	.25
❑ T118	Brian Hunter	.40	.18
❑ T119	Joe Girardi	.40	.18
❑ T120	Omar Daal	.40	.18
❑ T121	Brook Fordyce	.40	.18
❑ T122	Jose Valentin	.40	.18
❑ T123	Curt Schilling	1.50	.70
❑ T124	B.J. Surhoff	.60	.25
❑ T125	Henry Rodriguez	.40	.18
❑ T126	Mike Bordick	.40	.18
❑ T127	David Justice	.60	.25
❑ T128	Charles Johnson	.60	.25
❑ T129	Will Clark	1.50	.70
❑ T130	Dwight Gooden	.60	.25
❑ T131	David Segui	.40	.18
❑ T132	Denny Neagle	.60	.25
❑ T133	Jose Canseco	1.50	.70
❑ T134	Bruce Chen	.40	.18
❑ T135	Jason Bere	.40	.18

2001 Topps Chrome

	MINT	NRMT
COMPLETE SET (661)	300.00	135.00
COMPLETE SERIES 1 (331)	150.00	70.00
COMPLETE SERIES 2 (330)	150.00	70.00

Card	Player	MINT	NRMT
❑ 1	Cal Ripken	6.00	2.70
❑ 2	Chipper Jones	3.00	1.35
❑ 3	Roger Cedeno	.40	.18
❑ 4	Garret Anderson	.60	.25
❑ 5	Robin Ventura	.60	.25
❑ 6	Daryle Ward	.40	.18
❑ 7	Does Not Exist		
❑ 8	Phil Nevin	.60	.25
❑ 9	Jermaine Dye	.60	.25
❑ 10	Chris Singleton	.40	.18
❑ 11	Mike Redmond	.40	.18
❑ 12	Jim Thome	1.50	.70
❑ 13	Brian Jordan	.60	.25
❑ 14	Dustin Hermanson	.40	.18
❑ 15	Shawn Green	1.50	.70
❑ 16	Todd Stottlemyre	.40	.18
❑ 17	Dan Wilson	.40	.18
❑ 18	Derek Lowe	.40	.18
❑ 19	Juan Gonzalez	1.50	.70
❑ 20	Pat Meares	.40	.18
❑ 21	Paul O'Neill	1.50	.70
❑ 22	Jeffrey Hammonds	.40	.18
❑ 23	Pokey Reese	.40	.18
❑ 24	Mike Mussina	1.50	.70
❑ 25	Rico Brogna	.40	.18
❑ 26	Jay Buhner	.60	.25
❑ 27	Steve Cox	.40	.18
❑ 28	Quilvio Veras	.40	.18
❑ 29	Marquis Grissom	.40	.18
❑ 30	Shigetoshi Hasegawa	.60	.25
❑ 31	Shane Reynolds	.40	.18
❑ 32	Adam Piatt	.60	.25
❑ 33	Preston Wilson	.60	.25
❑ 34	Ellis Burks	.60	.25
❑ 35	Armando Rios	.40	.18
❑ 36	Chuck Finley	.60	.25
❑ 37	Shannon Stewart	.60	.25
❑ 38	Mark McGwire	6.00	2.70
❑ 39	Gerald Williams	.40	.18
❑ 40	Eric Young	.40	.18
❑ 41	Peter Bergeron	.40	.18
❑ 42	Arthur Rhodes	.40	.18
❑ 43	Bobby Jones	.40	.18
❑ 44	Matt Clement	.40	.18
❑ 45	Pedro Martinez	2.00	.90
❑ 46	Jose Canseco	1.50	.70
❑ 47	Matt Anderson	.40	.18
❑ 48	Torii Hunter	.60	.25
❑ 49	Carlos Lee	.60	.25
❑ 50	Eric Chavez	.60	.25
❑ 51	Rick Helling	.40	.18
❑ 52	John Franco	.60	.25
❑ 53	Mike Bordick	.60	.25
❑ 54	Andres Galarraga	1.00	.45
❑ 55	Jose Cruz Jr.	.60	.25
❑ 56	Mike Matheny	.40	.18
❑ 57	Randy Johnson	2.00	.90
❑ 58	Richie Sexson	.60	.25
❑ 59	Vladimir Nunez	.40	.18
❑ 60	Aaron Boone	.40	.18
❑ 61	Darin Erstad	1.50	.70
❑ 62	Alex Gonzalez	.40	.18
❑ 63	Gil Heredia	.40	.18
❑ 64	Shane Andrews	.40	.18
❑ 65	Todd Hundley	.40	.18
❑ 66	Bill Mueller	.40	.18
❑ 67	Mark McLemore	.40	.18
❑ 68	Scott Spiezio	.40	.18
❑ 69	Kevin McGlinchy	.40	.18
❑ 70	Manny Ramirez	2.00	.90
❑ 71	Mike Lamb	.40	.18
❑ 72	Brian Buchanan	.40	.18
❑ 73	Mike Sweeney	.60	.25
❑ 74	John Wetteland	.60	.25
❑ 75	Rob Bell	.40	.18
❑ 76	John Burkett	.40	.18
❑ 77	Derek Jeter	6.00	2.70
❑ 78	J.D. Drew	1.50	.70
❑ 79	Jose Offerman	.40	.18
❑ 80	Rick Reed	.40	.18
❑ 81	Will Clark	1.50	.70
❑ 82	Rickey Henderson	3.00	1.35
❑ 83	Kirk Rueter	.40	.18
❑ 84	Lee Stevens	.40	.18
❑ 85	Jay Bell	.60	.25
❑ 86	Fred McGriff	1.00	.45
❑ 87	Julio Zuleta	.40	.18
❑ 88	Brian Anderson	.40	.18
❑ 89	Orlando Cabrera	.40	.18
❑ 90	Alex Fernandez	.40	.18
❑ 91	Derek Bell	.40	.18
❑ 92	Eric Owens	.40	.18
❑ 93	Dennys Reyes	.40	.18
❑ 94	Mike Stanley	.40	.18
❑ 95	Jorge Posada	.60	.25
❑ 96	Paul Konerko	.60	.25
❑ 97	Mike Remlinger	.40	.18
❑ 98	Travis Lee	.40	.18
❑ 99	Ken Caminiti	.60	.25
❑ 100	Kevin Barker	.40	.18
❑ 101	Ozzie Guillen	.40	.18
❑ 102	Randy Wolf	.40	.18
❑ 103	Michael Tucker	.40	.18
❑ 104	Darren Lewis	.40	.18
❑ 105	Joe Randa	.40	.18
❑ 106	Jeff Cirillo	.60	.25
❑ 107	David Ortiz	.60	.25
❑ 108	Herb Perry	.40	.18
❑ 109	Jeff Nelson	.40	.18
❑ 110	Chris Stynes	.40	.18
❑ 111	Johnny Damon	.60	.25
❑ 112	Jason Schmidt	.40	.18
❑ 113	Charles Johnson	.40	.18
❑ 114	Pat Burrell	.60	.25
❑ 115	Gary Sheffield	.60	.25
❑ 116	Tom Glavine	1.50	.70
❑ 117	Jason Isringhausen	.40	.18
❑ 118	Chris Carpenter	.40	.18

❑ 119 Jeff Suppan .40 .18
❑ 120 Ivan Rodriguez 1.50 .70
❑ 121 Luis Sojo .40 .18
❑ 122 Ron Villone .40 .18
❑ 123 Mike Sirotka .40 .18
❑ 124 Chuck Knoblauch .60 .25
❑ 125 Jason Kendall .60 .25
❑ 126 Bobby Estalella .40 .18
❑ 127 Jose Guillen .40 .18
❑ 128 Carlos Delgado 1.50 .70
❑ 129 Benji Gil .40 .18
❑ 130 Einar Diaz .40 .18
❑ 131 Andy Benes .40 .18
❑ 132 Adrian Beltre .60 .25
❑ 133 Roger Clemens 4.00 1.80
❑ 134 Scott Williamson .40 .18
❑ 135 Brad Penny .60 .25
❑ 136 Troy Glaus 1.50 .70
❑ 137 Kevin Appier .60 .25
❑ 138 Walt Weiss .40 .18
❑ 139 Michael Barrett .40 .18
❑ 140 Mike Hampton .60 .25
❑ 141 Francisco Cordova .40 .18
❑ 142 David Segui .40 .18
❑ 143 Carlos Febles .40 .18
❑ 144 Roy Halladay .40 .18
❑ 145 Seth Etherton .40 .18
❑ 146 Fernando Tatis .40 .18
❑ 147 Livan Hernandez .40 .18
❑ 148 B.J. Surhoff .60 .25
❑ 149 Barry Larkin 1.50 .70
❑ 150 Bobby Howry .40 .18
❑ 151 Dmitri Young .60 .25
❑ 152 Brian Hunter .40 .18
❑ 153 Alex Rodriguez Rangers 4.00 1.80
❑ 154 Hideo Nomo 1.50 .70
❑ 155 Warren Morris .40 .18
❑ 156 Antonio Alfonseca .40 .18
❑ 157 Edgardo Alfonzo .60 .25
❑ 158 Mark Grudzielanek .40 .18
❑ 159 Fernando Vina .40 .18
❑ 160 Homer Bush .40 .18
❑ 161 Jason Giambi 1.50 .70
❑ 162 Steve Karsay .40 .18
❑ 163 Matt Lawton .60 .25
❑ 164 Rusty Greer .60 .25
❑ 165 Billy Koch .40 .18
❑ 166 Todd Hollandsworth .40 .18
❑ 167 Raul Ibanez .40 .18
❑ 168 Tony Gwynn 3.00 1.35
❑ 169 Carl Everett .60 .25
❑ 170 Hector Carrasco .40 .18
❑ 171 Jose Valentin .40 .18
❑ 172 Deivi Cruz .40 .18
❑ 173 Bret Boone .60 .25
❑ 174 Melvin Mora .40 .18
❑ 175 Danny Graves .40 .18
❑ 176 Jose Jimenez .40 .18
❑ 177 James Baldwin .40 .18
❑ 178 C.J. Nitkowski .40 .18
❑ 179 Jeff Zimmerman .40 .18
❑ 180 Mike Lowell .60 .25
❑ 181 Hideki Irabu .40 .18
❑ 182 Greg Vaughn .60 .25
❑ 183 Omar Daal .40 .18
❑ 184 Darren Dreifort .40 .18
❑ 185 Gil Meche .40 .18
❑ 186 Damian Jackson .40 .18
❑ 187 Frank Thomas 2.00 .90
❑ 188 Luis Castillo .40 .18
❑ 189 Bartolo Colon .60 .25
❑ 190 Craig Biggio 1.00 .45
❑ 191 Scott Schoeneweis .40 .18
❑ 192 Dave Veres .40 .18
❑ 193 Ramon Martinez .40 .18
❑ 194 Jose Vidro .60 .25
❑ 195 Todd Helton 2.00 .90
❑ 196 Greg Norton .40 .18
❑ 197 Jacque Jones .60 .25
❑ 198 Jason Grimsley .40 .18
❑ 199 Dan Reichert .40 .18
❑ 200 Robb Nen .40 .18
❑ 201 Scott Hatteberg .40 .18
❑ 202 Terry Shumpert .40 .18
❑ 203 Kevin Millar .40 .18
❑ 204 Ismael Valdes .40 .18
❑ 205 Richard Hidalgo .60 .25
❑ 206 Randy Velarde .40 .18
❑ 207 Bengie Molina .40 .18
❑ 208 Tony Womack .40 .18
❑ 209 Enrique Wilson .40 .18
❑ 210 Jeff Brantley .40 .18
❑ 211 Rick Ankiel 1.00 .45
❑ 212 Terry Mulholland .40 .18
❑ 213 Ron Belliard .40 .18
❑ 214 Terrence Long .60 .25
❑ 215 Alberto Castillo .40 .18
❑ 216 Royce Clayton .40 .18
❑ 217 Joe McEwing .40 .18
❑ 218 Jason McDonald .40 .18
❑ 219 Ricky Bottalico .40 .18
❑ 220 Keith Foulke .40 .18
❑ 221 Brad Radke .60 .25
❑ 222 Gabe Kapler .60 .25
❑ 223 Pedro Astacio .40 .18
❑ 224 Armando Reynoso .40 .18
❑ 225 Darryl Kile .60 .25
❑ 226 Reggie Sanders .40 .18
❑ 227 Esteban Yan .40 .18
❑ 228 Joe Nathan .40 .18
❑ 229 Jay Payton .40 .18
❑ 230 Francisco Cordero .40 .18
❑ 231 Gregg Jefferies .40 .18
❑ 232 LaTroy Hawkins .40 .18
❑ 233 Jacob Cruz .40 .18
❑ 234 Chris Holt .40 .18
❑ 235 Vladimir Guerrero 2.00 .90
❑ 236 Marvin Benard .40 .18
❑ 237 Alex Ramirez .40 .18
❑ 238 Mike Williams .40 .18
❑ 239 Sean Bergman .40 .18
❑ 240 Juan Encarnacion .60 .25
❑ 241 Russ Davis .40 .18
❑ 242 Ramon Hernandez .40 .18
❑ 243 Sandy Alomar Jr. .60 .25
❑ 244 Eddie Guardado .40 .18
❑ 245 Shane Halter .40 .18
❑ 246 Geoff Jenkins .60 .25
❑ 247 Brian Meadows .40 .18
❑ 248 Damian Miller .40 .18
❑ 249 Darrin Fletcher .40 .18
❑ 250 Rafael Furcal .60 .25
❑ 251 Mark Grace 1.50 .70
❑ 252 Mark Mulder 1.00 .45
❑ 253 Joe Torre MG .60 .25
❑ 254 Bobby Cox MG .40 .18
❑ 255 Mike Scioscia MG .40 .18
❑ 256 Mike Hargrove MG .40 .18
❑ 257 Jimy Williams MG .40 .18
❑ 258 Jerry Manuel MG .40 .18
❑ 259 Charlie Manuel MG .40 .18
❑ 260 Don Baylor MG .60 .25
❑ 261 Phil Garner MG .40 .18
❑ 262 Tony Muser MG .40 .18
❑ 263 Buddy Bell MG .60 .25
❑ 264 Tom Kelly MG .40 .18
❑ 265 John Boles MG .40 .18
❑ 266 Art Howe MG .40 .18
❑ 267 Larry Dierker MG .40 .18
❑ 268 Lou Piniella MG .60 .25
❑ 269 Larry Rothschild MG .40 .18
❑ 270 Davey Lopes MG .60 .25
❑ 271 Johnny Oates MG .40 .18
❑ 272 Felipe Alou MG .40 .18
❑ 273 Bobby Valentine MG .40 .18
❑ 274 Tony LaRussa MG .40 .18
❑ 275 Bruce Bochy MG .40 .18
❑ 276 Dusty Baker MG .60 .25
❑ 277 Adrian Gonzalez 2.00 .90
Adam Johnson
❑ 278 Matt Wheatland 1.50 .70
Bryan Digby
❑ 279 Tripper Johnson 1.00 .45
Scott Thorman
❑ 280 Phil Dumatrait 1.50 .70
Adam Wainwright
❑ 281 Scott Heard 2.50 1.10
David Parrish RC
❑ 282 Rocco Baldelli 3.00 1.35
Mark Folsom
❑ 283 Dominic Rich RC 2.00 .90
Aaron Herr
❑ 284 Mike Stodolka 1.50 .70
Sean Burnett
❑ 285 Derek Thompson 1.50 .70
Corey Smith
❑ 286 Danny Borrell 2.00 .90
Jason Bourgeois RC
❑ 287 Chin-Feng Chen 3.00 1.35
Corey Patterson
Josh Hamilton
❑ 288 Ryan Anderson 3.00 1.35
Barry Zito
C.C. Sabathia
❑ 289 Scott Sobkowiak 2.00 .90
David Walling
Ben Sheets
❑ 290 Ty Howington 1.50 .70
Josh Kalinowski
Josh Girdley
❑ 291 Hee Seop Choi 8.00 3.60
Aaron McNeal
Jason Hart
❑ 292 Bobby Bradley 1.50 .70
Kurt Ainsworth
Chin-Hui Tsao
❑ 293 Mike Glendenning 1.50 .70
Kenny Kelly
Juan Silvestre
❑ 294 J.R. House 4.00 1.80
Ramon Castro
Ben Davis
❑ 295 Chance Caple 2.50 1.10
Rafael Soriano
Pascual Coco
❑ 296 Travis Hafner RC 1.25 .55
Eric Munson
Bucky Jacobsen
❑ 297 Jason Conti 1.50 .70
Chris Wakeland
Brian Cole
❑ 298 Scott Seabol 1.50 .70
Aubrey Huff
Joe Crede
❑ 299 Adam Everett 2.00 .90
Jose Ortiz
Keith Ginter
❑ 300 Carlos Hernandez 1.50 .70
Geraldo Guzman
Adam Eaton
❑ 301 Bobby Kielty 1.50 .70
Milton Bradley
Juan Rivera
❑ 302 Mark McGwire GM 3.00 1.35
❑ 303 Don Larsen GM .60 .25
❑ 304 Bobby Thomson GM .60 .25
❑ 305 Bill Mazeroski GM .60 .25
❑ 306 Reggie Jackson GM 1.50 .70
❑ 307 Kirk Gibson GM .60 .25
❑ 308 Roger Maris GM 1.50 .70
❑ 309 Cal Ripken GM 3.00 1.35
❑ 310 Hank Aaron GM 2.00 .90
❑ 311 Joe Carter GM .60 .25
❑ 312 Cal Ripken SH 3.00 1.35
❑ 313 Randy Johnson SH 1.00 .45
❑ 314 Ken Griffey Jr. SH 2.50 1.10
❑ 315 Troy Glaus SH 1.50 .70
❑ 316 Kazuhiro Sasaki SH .60 .25
❑ 317 Sammy Sosa 1.50 .70
Troy Glaus LL
❑ 318 Todd Helton 1.00 .45
Edgar Martinez LL
❑ 319 Todd Helton 2.50 1.10
Nomar Garicaparra LL
❑ 320 Barry Bonds 2.00 .90
Jason Giambi LL
❑ 321 Todd Helton 1.00 .45
Manny Ramirez LL
❑ 322 Todd Helton 1.00 .45
Darin Erstad LL
❑ 323 Kevin Brown 1.00 .45
Pedro Martinez LL
❑ 324 Randy Johnson 1.00 .45
Pedro Martinez LL
❑ 325 Will Clark HL 2.00 .90
❑ 326 New York Mets HL 2.00 .90
❑ 327 New York Yankees HL 3.00 1.35
❑ 328 Seattle Mariners HL .60 .25

No.	Player	Price	Price
329	Mike Hampton HL	.60	.25
330	New York Yankees HL	4.00	1.80
331	New York Yankees Champs	8.00	3.60
332	Jeff Bagwell	2.00	.90
333	Andy Pettitte	.60	.25
334	Tony Armas Jr.	.60	.25
335	Jeromy Burnitz	.60	.25
336	Javier Vazquez	.60	.25
337	Eric Karros	.60	.25
338	Brian Giles	.60	.25
339	Scott Rolen	1.50	.70
340	David Justice	.60	.25
341	Ray Durham	.60	.25
342	Todd Zeile	.60	.25
343	Cliff Floyd	.60	.25
344	Barry Bonds	4.00	1.80
345	Matt Williams	1.00	.45
346	Steve Finley	.60	.25
347	Scott Elarton	.40	.18
348	Bernie Williams	1.50	.70
349	David Wells	.60	.25
350	J.T. Snow	.60	.25
351	Al Leiter	.60	.25
352	Magglio Ordonez	.60	.25
353	Raul Mondesi	.60	.25
354	Tim Salmon	.60	.25
355	Jeff Kent	1.00	.45
356	Mariano Rivera	.60	.25
357	John Olerud	.60	.25
358	Javy Lopez	.60	.25
359	Ben Grieve	.60	.25
360	Ray Lankford	.40	.18
361	Ken Griffey Jr.	5.00	2.20
362	Rich Aurilia	.60	.25
363	Andruw Jones	1.50	.70
364	Ryan Klesko	.60	.25
365	Roberto Alomar	1.50	.70
366	Miguel Tejada	.60	.25
367	Mo Vaughn	.60	.25
368	Albert Belle	.60	.25
369	Jose Canseco	1.50	.70
370	Kevin Brown	.60	.25
371	Rafael Palmeiro	1.50	.70
372	Mark Redman	.40	.18
373	Larry Walker	1.00	.45
374	Greg Maddux	4.00	1.80
375	Nomar Garciaparra	4.00	1.80
376	Kevin Millwood	.40	.18
377	Edgar Martinez	1.00	.45
378	Sammy Sosa	3.00	1.35
379	Tim Hudson	1.50	.70
380	Jim Edmonds	1.00	.45
381	Mike Piazza	4.00	1.80
382	Brant Brown	.40	.18
383	Brad Fullmer	.60	.25
384	Alan Benes	.40	.18
385	Mickey Morandini	.40	.18
386	Troy Percival	.40	.18
387	Eddie Perez	.40	.18
388	Vernon Wells	.60	.25
389	Ricky Gutierrez	.40	.18
390	Rondell White	.60	.25
391	Kelvim Escobar	.40	.18
392	Tony Batista	.60	.25
393	Jimmy Haynes	.40	.18
394	Billy Wagner	.40	.18
395	A.J. Hinch	.40	.18
396	Matt Morris	.60	.25
397	Lance Berkman	1.50	.70
398	Jeff D'Amico	.40	.18
399	Octavio Dotel	.40	.18
400	Olmedo Saenz	.40	.18
401	Esteban Loaiza	.40	.18
402	Adam Kennedy	.40	.18
403	Moises Alou	.60	.25
404	Orlando Palmeiro	.40	.18
405	Kevin Young	.40	.18
406	Tom Goodwin	.40	.18
407	Mac Suzuki	.60	.25
408	Pat Hentgen	.40	.18
409	Kevin Stocker	.40	.18
410	Mark Sweeney	.60	.25
411	Tony Eusebio	.40	.18
412	Edgar Renteria	.40	.18
413	John Rocker	.60	.25
414	Jose Lima	.40	.18
415	Kerry Wood	1.50	.70
416	Mike Timlin	.40	.18
417	Jose Hernandez	.40	.18
418	Jeremy Giambi	.40	.18
419	Luis Lopez	.40	.18
420	Mitch Meluskey	.40	.18
421	Garrett Stephenson	.40	.18
422	Jamey Wright	.40	.18
423	John Jaha	.40	.18
424	Placido Polanco	.40	.18
425	Marty Cordova	.40	.18
426	Joey Hamilton	.40	.18
427	Travis Fryman	.60	.25
428	Mike Cameron	.60	.25
429	Matt Mantei	.40	.18
430	Chan Ho Park	.60	.25
431	Shawn Estes	.60	.25
432	Danny Bautista	.40	.18
433	Wilson Alvarez	.40	.18
434	Kenny Lofton	.60	.25
435	Russ Ortiz	.60	.25
436	Dave Burba	.40	.18
437	Felix Martinez	.40	.18
438	Jeff Shaw	.40	.18
439	Mike DiFelice	.40	.18
440	Roberto Hernandez	.40	.18
441	Bryan Rekar	.40	.18
442	Ugueth Urbina	.40	.18
443	Vinny Castilla	.60	.25
444	Carlos Perez	.40	.18
445	Juan Guzman	.40	.18
446	Ryan Rupe	.40	.18
447	Mike Mordecai	.40	.18
448	Ricardo Rincon	.40	.18
449	Curt Schilling	1.50	.70
450	Alex Cora	.40	.18
451	Turner Ward	.40	.18
452	Omar Vizquel	.60	.25
453	Russ Branyan	.60	.25
454	Russ Johnson	.40	.18
455	Greg Colbrunn	.40	.18
456	Charles Nagy	.40	.18
457	Wil Cordero	.40	.18
458	Jason Tyner	.40	.18
459	Devon White	.40	.18
460	Kelly Stinnett	.40	.18
461	Wilton Guerrero	.40	.18
462	Jason Bere	.40	.18
463	Calvin Murray	.40	.18
464	Miguel Batista	.40	.18
466	Luis Gonzalez	1.50	.70
467	Jaret Wright	.40	.18
468	Chad Kreuter	.40	.18
469	Armando Benitez	.60	.25
470	Erubiel Durazo	.40	.18
470	Sidney Ponson	.40	.18
471	Adrian Brown	.40	.18
472	Sterling Hitchcock	.40	.18
473	Timo Perez	.40	.18
474	Jamie Moyer	.40	.18
475	Delino DeShields	.40	.18
476	Glendon Rusch	.40	.18
477	Chris Gomez	.40	.18
478	Adam Eaton	.60	.25
479	Pablo Ozuna	.40	.18
480	Bob Abreu	.60	.25
481	Kris Benson	.60	.25
482	Keith Osik	.40	.18
483	Darryl Hamilton	.40	.18
484	Marlon Anderson	.40	.18
485	Jimmy Anderson	.40	.18
486	John Halama	.40	.18
487	Nelson Figueroa	.40	.18
488	Alex Gonzalez	.40	.18
489	Benny Agbayani	.60	.25
490	Ed Sprague	.40	.18
491	Scott Erickson	.40	.18
492	Doug Glanville	.40	.18
493	Jesus Sanchez	.40	.18
494	Mike Lieberthal	.60	.25
495	Aaron Sele	.60	.25
496	Pat Mahomes	.40	.18
497	Ruben Rivera	.40	.18
498	Wayne Gomes	.40	.18
499	Freddy Garcia	.60	.25
500	Al Martin	.40	.18
501	Woody Williams	.40	.18
502	Paul Byrd	.40	.18
503	Rick White	.40	.18
504	Trevor Hoffman	.60	.25
505	Brady Anderson	.60	.25
506	Robert Person	.40	.18
507	Jeff Conine	.40	.18
508	Chris Truby	.40	.18
509	Emil Brown	.40	.18
510	Ryan Dempster	.60	.25
511	Ruben Mateo	.60	.25
512	Alex Ochoa	.40	.18
513	Jose Rosado	.40	.18
514	Masato Yoshii	.60	.25
515	Brian Daubach	.40	.18
516	Jeff D'Amico	.40	.18
517	Brent Mayne	.40	.18
518	John Thomson	.40	.18
519	Todd Ritchie	.40	.18
520	John VanderWal	.40	.18
521	Neifi Perez	.40	.18
522	Chad Curtis	.40	.18
523	Kenny Rogers	.40	.18
524	Trot Nixon	.60	.25
525	Sean Casey	1.00	.45
526	Wilton Veras	.40	.18
527	Troy O'Leary	.40	.18
528	Dante Bichette	.60	.25
529	Jose Silva	.40	.18
530	Darren Oliver	.40	.18
531	Steve Parris	.40	.18
532	David McCarty	.40	.18
533	Todd Walker	.40	.18
534	Brian Rose	.40	.18
535	Pete Schourek	.40	.18
536	Ricky Ledee	.40	.18
537	Justin Thompson	.40	.18
538	Benito Santiago	.40	.18
539	Carlos Beltran	.60	.25
540	Gabe White	.40	.18
541	Bret Saberhagen	.60	.25
542	Ramon Martinez	.40	.18
543	John Valentin	.40	.18
544	Frank Catalanotto	.40	.18
545	Tim Wakefield	.40	.18
546	Michael Tucker	.40	.18
547	Juan Pierre	.60	.25
548	Rich Garces	.40	.18
549	Luis Ordaz	.40	.18
550	Jerry Spradlin	.40	.18
551	Corey Koskie	.60	.25
552	Cal Eldred	.40	.18
553	Alfonso Soriano	1.50	.70
554	Kip Wells	.40	.18
555	Orlando Hernandez	.60	.25
556	Bill Simas	.40	.18
557	Jim Parque	.40	.18
558	Joe Mays	.60	.25
559	Tim Belcher	.40	.18
560	Shane Spencer	.40	.18
561	Glenallen Hill	.40	.18
562	Matt LeCroy	.40	.18
563	Tino Martinez	.60	.25
564	Eric Milton	.60	.25
565	Ron Coomer	.40	.18
566	Cristian Guzman	.60	.25
567	Kazuhiro Sasaki	1.50	.70
568	Mark Quinn	.60	.25
569	Eric Gagne	.40	.18
570	Kerry Ligtenberg	.40	.18
571	Rolando Arrojo	.40	.18
572	Jon Lieber	.40	.18
573	Jose Vizcaino	.40	.18
574	Jeff Abbott	.40	.18
575	Carlos Hernandez	.40	.18
576	Scott Sullivan	.40	.18
577	Matt Stairs	.40	.18
578	Tom Lampkin	.40	.18
579	Donnie Sadler	.40	.18
580	Desi Relaford	.40	.18
581	Scott Downs	.40	.18
582	Mike Mussina	1.50	.70
583	Ramon Ortiz	.60	.25
584	Mike Myers	.40	.18
585	Frank Castillo	.40	.18
586	Manny Ramirez	2.00	.90

❑ 587	Alex Rodriguez	4.00	1.80
❑ 588	Andy Ashby	.40	.18
❑ 589	Felipe Crespo	.40	.18
❑ 590	Bobby Bonilla	.60	.25
❑ 591	Denny Neagle	.40	.18
❑ 592	Dave Martinez	.40	.18
❑ 593	Mike Hampton	.60	.25
❑ 594	Gary DiSarcina	.40	.18
❑ 595	Tsuyoshi Shinjo RC	6.00	2.70
❑ 596	Albert Pujols RC	40.00	18.00
❑ 597	Roy Oswalt	3.00	1.35
	Pat Strange		
	Jon Rauch		
❑ 598	Phil Wilson RC	3.00	1.35
	Jake Peavy RC		
	Darwin Cubillan RC		
❑ 599	Nathan Haynes	2.00	.90
	Steve Smyth RC		
	Mike Bynum		
❑ 600	Joe Lawrence	1.50	.70
	Choo Freeman		
	Michael Cuddyer		
❑ 601	Larry Barnes	1.50	.70
	DeWayne Wise		
	Carlos Pena		
❑ 602	Feilpe Lopez	2.00	.90
	Gookie Dawkins		
	Eric Almonte RC		
❑ 603	Brad Wilkerson	1.50	.70
	Alex Escobar		
	Eric Valent		
❑ 604	Jeff Goldbach	1.50	.70
	Toby Hall		
	Rod Barajas		
❑ 605	Marcus Giles	1.00	.45
	Pablo Ozuna		
	Jason Romano		
❑ 606	Vernon Wells	1.50	.70
	Jack Cust		
	Dee Brown		
❑ 607	Luis Montanez RC	4.00	1.80
	David Espinosa		
❑ 608	Anthony Pluta RC	3.00	1.35
	Justin Wayne RC		
❑ 609	Josh Axelson RC	2.00	.90
	Carmen Cali RC		
❑ 610	Shaun Boyd RC	3.00	1.35
	Chris Morris RC		
❑ 611	Dan Moylan RC	2.00	.90
	Tommy Arko RC		
❑ 612	Luis Cotto RC	2.00	.90
	Luis Escobar		
❑ 613	Blake Williams RC	3.00	1.35
	Brandon Mims RC		
❑ 614	Chris Russ RC	2.00	.90
	Bryan Edwards		
❑ 615	Joe Torres	1.50	.70
	Ben Diggins		
❑ 616	Hugh Quattlebaum RC	2.00	.90
	Edwin Encarnacion RC		
❑ 617	Brian Bass RC	2.00	.90
	Odannis Ayala RC		
❑ 618	Jason Kaanoi	2.00	.90
	Michael Matthews RC		
	UER name misspelled Mathews		
❑ 619	Stuart McFarland RC	2.00	.90
	Adam Sterrett RC		
❑ 620	David Krynzel	1.50	.70
	Grady Sizemore		
❑ 621	Keith Bucktrot	1.50	.70
	Dane Sardinha		
❑ 622	Anaheim Angels TC	.60	.25
❑ 623	Ariz. Diamondbacks TC	.60	.25
❑ 624	Atlanta Braves TC	.60	.25
❑ 625	Baltimore Orioles TC	.60	.25
❑ 626	Boston Red Sox TC	.60	.25
❑ 627	Chicago Cubs TC	.60	.25
❑ 628	Chicago White Sox TC	.60	.25
❑ 629	Cincinnati Reds TC	.60	.25
❑ 630	Cleveland Indians TC	.60	.25
❑ 631	Colorado Rockies TC	.60	.25
❑ 632	Detroit Tigers TC	.60	.25
❑ 633	Florida Marlins TC	.60	.25
❑ 634	Houston Astros TC	.60	.25
❑ 635	Kansas City Royals TC	.60	.25
❑ 636	Los Angeles Dodgers TC	.60	.25
❑ 637	Milwaukee Brewers TC	.60	.25
❑ 638	Minnesota Twins TC	.60	.25
❑ 639	Montreal Expos TC	.60	.25
❑ 640	New York Mets TC	.60	.25
❑ 641	New York Yankees TC	4.00	1.80
❑ 642	Oakland Athletics TC	.60	.25
❑ 643	Philadelphia Phillies TC	.60	.25
❑ 644	Pittsburgh Pirates TC	.60	.25
❑ 645	San Diego Padres TC	.60	.25
❑ 646	San Francisco Giants TC	.60	.25
❑ 647	Seattle Mariners TC	.60	.25
❑ 648	St. Louis Cardinals TC	.60	.25
❑ 649	T. Bay Devil Rays TC	.60	.25
❑ 650	Texas Rangers TC	.60	.25
❑ 651	Toronto Blue Jays TC	.60	.25
❑ 652	Bucky Dent GM	.40	.18
❑ 653	Jackie Robinson GM	1.50	.70
❑ 654	Roberto Clemente GM	2.50	1.10
❑ 655	Nolan Ryan GM	4.00	1.80
❑ 656	Kerry Wood GM	.60	.25
❑ 657	Rickey Henderson GM	1.50	.70
❑ 658	Lou Brock GM	.60	.25
❑ 659	David Wells GM	.40	.18
❑ 660	Andruw Jones GM	.60	.25
❑ 661	Carlton Fisk GM	.60	.25

2001 Topps Chrome Traded

		MINT	NRMT
COMPLETE SET (266)		200.00	90.00
COMMON REPRINT (100-144)		1.50	.70
❑ T1	Sandy Alomar Jr.	1.25	.55
❑ T2	Kevin Appier	1.25	.55
❑ T3	Brad Ausmus	.75	.35
❑ T4	Derek Bell	.75	.35
❑ T5	Bret Boone	1.25	.55
❑ T6	Rico Brogna	.75	.35
❑ T7	Ellis Burks	1.25	.55
❑ T8	Ken Caminiti	1.25	.55
❑ T9	Roger Cedeno	.75	.35
❑ T10	Royce Clayton	.75	.35
❑ T11	Enrique Wilson	.75	.35
❑ T12	Rheal Cormier	.75	.35
❑ T13	Eric Davis	1.25	.55
❑ T14	Shawon Dunston	.75	.35
❑ T15	Andres Galarraga	2.00	.90
❑ T16	Tom Gordon	.75	.35
❑ T17	Mark Grace	3.00	1.35
❑ T18	Jeffrey Hammonds	.75	.35
❑ T19	Dustin Hermanson	.75	.35
❑ T20	Quinton McCracken	.75	.35
❑ T21	Todd Hundley	.75	.35
❑ T22	Charles Johnson	1.25	.55
❑ T23	Marquis Grissom	.75	.35
❑ T24	Jose Mesa	.75	.35
❑ T25	Brian Boehringer	.75	.35
❑ T26	John Rocker	1.25	.55
❑ T27	Jeff Frye	.75	.35
❑ T28	Reggie Sanders	1.25	.55
❑ T29	David Segui	.75	.35
❑ T30	Mike Sirotka	.75	.35
❑ T31	Fernando Tatis	.75	.35
❑ T32	Steve Trachsel	.75	.35
❑ T33	Ismael Valdes	.75	.35
❑ T34	Randy Velarde	.75	.35
❑ T35	Ryan Kohlmeier	.75	.35
❑ T36	Mike Bordick	1.25	.55
❑ T37	Kent Bottenfield	.75	.35
❑ T38	Pat Rapp	.75	.35
❑ T39	Jeff Nelson	.75	.35
❑ T40	Ricky Bottalico	.75	.35
❑ T41	Luke Prokopec	.75	.35
❑ T42	Hideo Nomo	3.00	1.35
❑ T43	Bill Mueller	.75	.35
❑ T44	Roberto Kelly	.75	.35
❑ T45	Chris Holt	.75	.35
❑ T46	Mike Jackson	.75	.35
❑ T47	Devon White	.75	.35
❑ T48	Gerald Williams	.75	.35
❑ T49	Eddie Taubensee	.75	.35
❑ T50	Brian Hunter UER	.75	.35
	Brian R Hunter pictured		
	Brian L Hunter stats		
❑ T51	Nelson Cruz	.75	.35
❑ T52	Jeff Fassero	.75	.35
❑ T53	Bubba Trammell	.75	.35
❑ T54	Bo Porter	.75	.35
❑ T55	Greg Norton	.75	.35
❑ T56	Benito Santiago	.75	.35
❑ T57	Ruben Rivera	.75	.35
❑ T58	Dee Brown	1.25	.55
❑ T59	Jose Canseco	3.00	1.35
❑ T60	Chris Michalak	.75	.35
❑ T61	Tim Worrell	.75	.35
❑ T62	Matt Clement	.75	.35
❑ T63	Bill Pulsipher	.75	.35
❑ T64	Troy Brohawn RC	1.50	.70
❑ T65	Mark Kotsay	1.25	.55
❑ T66	Jimmy Rollins	1.25	.55
❑ T67	Shea Hillenbrand	1.25	.55
❑ T68	Ted Lilly	.75	.35
❑ T69	Jermaine Dye	1.25	.55
❑ T70	Jerry Hairston Jr.	.75	.35
❑ T71	John Mabry	.75	.35
❑ T72	Kurt Abbott	.75	.35
❑ T73	Eric Owens	.75	.35
❑ T74	Jeff Brantley	.75	.35
❑ T75	Roy Oswalt	3.00	1.35
❑ T76	Doug Mientkiewicz	1.25	.55
❑ T77	Rickey Henderson	6.00	2.70
❑ T78	Jason Grimsley	.75	.35
❑ T79	Christian Parker RC	1.50	.70
❑ T80	Donne Wall	.75	.35
❑ T81	Alex Arias	.75	.35
❑ T82	Willis Roberts	.75	.35
❑ T83	Ryan Minor	.75	.35
❑ T84	Jason LaRue	.75	.35
❑ T85	Ruben Sierra	.75	.35
❑ T86	Johnny Damon	1.25	.55
❑ T87	Juan Gonzalez	3.00	1.35
❑ T88	C.C. Sabathia	2.00	.90
❑ T89	Tony Batista	1.25	.55
❑ T90	Jay Witasick	.75	.35
❑ T91	Brent Abernathy	.75	.35
❑ T92	Paul LoDuca	1.25	.55
❑ T93	Wes Helms	.75	.35
❑ T94	Mark Wohlers	.75	.35
❑ T95	Rob Bell	.75	.35
❑ T96	Tim Redding	1.25	.55
❑ T97	Bud Smith RC	10.00	4.50
❑ T98	Adam Dunn	4.00	1.80
❑ T99	Ichiro Suzuki	20.00	9.00
	Albert Pujols ROY		
❑ T100	Carlton Fisk 81	2.50	1.10
❑ T101	Tim Raines 81	1.50	.70
❑ T102	Juan Marichal 74	1.50	.70
❑ T103	Dave Winfield 81	2.50	1.10
❑ T104	Reggie Jackson 82	4.00	1.80
❑ T105	Cal Ripken 82	10.00	4.50
❑ T106	Ozzie Smith 82	3.00	1.35
❑ T107	Tom Seaver 83	4.00	1.80
❑ T108	Lou Piniella 74	1.50	.70
❑ T109	Dwight Gooden 84	1.50	.70
❑ T110	Bret Saberhagen 84	1.50	.70
❑ T111	Gary Carter 85	1.50	.70
❑ T112	Jack Clark 85	1.50	.70
❑ T113	Rickey Henderson 85	5.00	2.20
❑ T114	Barry Bonds 86	6.00	2.70
❑ T115	Bobby Bonilla 86	1.50	.70
❑ T116	Jose Canseco 86	2.50	1.10
❑ T117	Will Clark 86	2.50	1.10
❑ T118	Andres Galarraga 86	1.50	.70

❑ T119 Bo Jackson 86 .... 1.50 .70
❑ T120 Wally Joyner 86 .... 1.50 .70
❑ T121 Ellis Burks 87 .... 1.50 .70
❑ T122 David Cone 87 .... 1.50 .70
❑ T123 Greg Maddux 87 .... 6.00 2.70
❑ T124 Willie Randolph 76 ..... 1.50 .70
❑ T125 Dennis Eckersley 87 .. 1.50 .70
❑ T126 Matt Williams 87 .... 1.50 .70
❑ T127 Joe Morgan 81 .... 1.50 .70
❑ T128 Fred McGriff 87 .... 1.50 .70
❑ T129 Roberto Alomar 88 .... 2.50 1.10
❑ T130 Lee Smith 88.............. 1.50 .70
❑ T131 David Wells 88 .... 1.50 .70
❑ T132 Ken Griffey Jr. 89 ...... 8.00 3.60
❑ T133 Deion Sanders 89 ...... 1.50 .70
❑ T134 Nolan Ryan 89 .... 10.00 4.50
❑ T135 David Justice 90 .... 1.50 .70
❑ T136 Joe Carter 91 .... 1.50 .70
❑ T137 Jack Morris 92............ 1.50 .70
❑ T138 Mike Piazza 93 .... 6.00 2.70
❑ T139 Barry Bonds 93 .... 6.00 2.70
❑ T140 Terrence Long 94 ...... 1.50 .70
❑ T141 Ben Grieve 94.............. 1.50 .70
❑ T142 Richie Sexson 95 ...... 1.50 .70
George Arias
Mark Sweeney
Brian Schneider
❑ T143 Sean Burroughs 99.... 2.50 1.10
❑ T144 Alfonso Soriano 99 .... 2.50 1.10
❑ T145 Bob Boone MG .... 1.25 .55
❑ T146 Larry Bowa MG.......... 1.25 .55
❑ T147 Bob Brenly MG .... .75 .35
❑ T148 Buck Martinez MG ...... .75 .35
❑ T149 Lloyd McClendon MG .. .75 .35
❑ T150 Jim Tracy MG .... .75 .35
❑ T151 Jared Abruzzo RC...... 2.50 1.10
❑ T152 Kurt Ainsworth............ 1.25 .55
❑ T153 Willie Bloomquist........ 1.25 .55
❑ T154 Ben Broussard .... 1.25 .55
❑ T155 Bobby Bradley............ 1.25 .55
❑ T156 Mike Bynum .... .75 .35
❑ T157 A.J. Hinch .... .75 .35
❑ T158 Ryan Christianson...... 1.25 .55
❑ T159 Carlos Silva................ .75 .35
❑ T160 Joe Crede .... 1.25 .55
❑ T161 Jack Cust .... 1.25 .55
❑ T162 Ben Diggins................ 1.25 .55
❑ T163 Phil Dumatrait .... .75 .35
❑ T164 Alex Escobar.............. 1.25 .55
❑ T165 Miguel Olivo .... .75 .35
❑ T166 Chris George.............. 1.25 .55
❑ T167 Marcus Giles.............. 1.25 .55
❑ T168 Keith Ginter................ 1.25 .55
❑ T169 Josh Girdley .... .75 .35
❑ T170 Tony Alvarez................ .75 .35
❑ T171 Scott Seabol .... .75 .35
❑ T172 Josh Hamilton 3.00 1.35
❑ T173 Jason Hart.................. 2.00 .90
❑ T174 Israel Alcantara .... .75 .35
❑ T175 Jake Peavy 2.50 1.10
❑ T176 Stubby Clapp RC ...... 1.50 .70
❑ T177 D'Angelo Jimenez .... .75 .35
❑ T178 Nick Johnson .... 1.25 .55
❑ T179 Ben Johnson .... 1.25 .55
❑ T180 Larry Bigbie.................. .75 .35
❑ T181 Allen Levrault .... .75 .35
❑ T182 Felipe Lopez .... 1.25 .55
❑ T183 Sean Burnett................ .75 .35
❑ T184 Nick Neugebauer 3.00 1.35
❑ T185 Austin Kearns .... 2.00 .90
❑ T186 Corey Patterson .... 1.25 .55
❑ T187 Carlos Pena .... 1.25 .55
❑ T188 Ricardo Rodriguez RC 3.00 1.35
❑ T189 Juan Rivera................ 1.25 .55
❑ T190 Grant Roberts .... .75 .35
❑ T191 Adam Pettyjohn RC .. 2.50 1.10
❑ T192 Jared Sandberg .... .75 .35
❑ T193 Xavier Nady .... 2.00 .90
❑ T194 Dane Sardinha .... .75 .35
❑ T195 Shawn Sonnier .... .75 .35
❑ T196 Rafael Soriano .... 1.25 .55
❑ T197 Brian Specht RC .... 1.50 .70
❑ T198 Aaron Myette................ .75 .35
❑ T199 Juan Uribe RC 5.00 2.20
❑ T200 Jayson Werth .... .75 .35
❑ T201 Brad Wilkerson .... .75 .35
❑ T202 Horacio Estrada .... .75 .35
❑ T203 Joel Pineiro 3.00 1.35
❑ T204 Matt LeCroy .... .75 .35
❑ T205 Michael Coleman .... .75 .35
❑ T206 Ben Sheets .... 2.00 .90
❑ T207 Eric Byrnes .... .75 .35
❑ T208 Sean Burroughs 3.00 1.35
❑ T209 Ken Harvey .... 1.25 .55
❑ T210 Travis Hafner .... 2.00 .90
❑ T211 Erick Almonte .... 1.25 .55
❑ T212 Jason Belcher RC 3.00 1.35
❑ T213 Wilson Betemit RC 8.00 3.60
❑ T214 Hank Blalock RC...... 12.00 5.50
❑ T215 Danny Borrell .... 1.25 .55
❑ T216 John Buck RC.......... 3.00 1.35
❑ T217 Freddie Bynum RC 3.00 1.35
❑ T218 Noel Devarez RC ...... 1.50 .70
❑ T219 Juan Diaz RC .... 1.50 .70
❑ T220 Felix Diaz RC 2.50 1.10
❑ T221 Josh Fogg RC.......... 1.50 .70
❑ T222 Matt Ford RC .... 1.50 .70
❑ T223 Scott Heard.............. 1.25 .55
❑ T224 Ben Hendrickson RC 1.50 .70
❑ T225 Cody Ross RC 3.00 1.35
❑ T226 Adrian Hernandez RC 1.50 .70
❑ T227 Alfredo Amezaga RC 2.00 .90
❑ T228 Bob Keppel RC.......... 2.50 1.10
❑ T229 Ryan Madson RC 2.50 1.10
❑ T230 Octavio Martinez RC .. 1.50 .70
❑ T231 Hee Seop Choi 3.00 1.35
❑ T232 Thomas Mitchell .... .75 .35
❑ T233 Luis Montanez............ 2.50 1.10
❑ T234 Andy Morales RC ...... 1.50 .70
❑ T235 Justin Morneau RC 6.00 2.70
❑ T236 Toe Nash RC 8.00 3.60
❑ T237 Valentino Pascucci RC 2.00 .90
❑ T238 Roy Smith RC............ 1.50 .70
❑ T239 Antonio Perez RC 5.00 2.20
❑ T240 Chad Petty RC 3.00 1.35
❑ T241 Steve Smyth .... 1.25 .55
❑ T242 Jose Reyes RC.......... 3.00 1.35
❑ T243 Eric Reynolds RC ...... 2.00 .90
❑ T244 Dominic Rich.............. 1.25 .55
❑ T245 Jason Richardson RC 1.50 .70
❑ T246 Ed Rogers RC............ 2.50 1.10
❑ T247 Albert Pujols 20.00 9.00
❑ T248 Esix Snead RC .... 1.50 .70
❑ T249 Luis Torres RC .... 1.50 .70
❑ T250 Matt White RC............ 2.00 .90
❑ T251 Blake Williams............ 1.25 .55
❑ T252 Chris Russ .... 1.25 .55
❑ T253 Joe Kennedy RC........ 3.00 1.35
❑ T254 Jeff Randazzo RC...... 1.50 .70
❑ T255 Beau Hale RC............ 3.00 1.35
❑ T256 Brad Hennessey RC .. 2.00 .90
❑ T257 Jake Gautreau RC 4.00 1.80
❑ T258 Jeff Mathis RC 2.50 1.10
❑ T259 Aaron Heilman RC 3.00 1.35
❑ T260 Bronson Sardinha RC 5.00 2.20
❑ T261 Irvin Guzman RC 5.00 2.20
❑ T262 Gabe Gross RC 6.00 2.70
❑ T263 J.D. Martin RC 5.00 2.20
❑ T264 Chris Smith RC.......... 2.50 1.10
❑ T265 Kenny Baugh RC 2.50 1.10
❑ T266 Ichiro Suzuki RC 50.00 22.00

2001 Topps Fusion

	MINT	NRMT
COMPLETE SET (250)	200.00	90.00
❑ 1 Albert Belle BB	.60	.25
❑ 2 Albert Belle FIN..................	.60	.25
❑ 3 Albert Belle GAL	.60	.25
❑ 4 Nick Bierbrodt GL	.25	.11
❑ 5 Alex Rodriguez Rangers SC	2.50	1.10
❑ 6 Alex Rodriguez Rangers BB	2.50	1.10
❑ 7 A. Rodriguez Rangers FIN	2.50	1.10
❑ 8 A. Rodriguez Rangers GAL	2.50	1.10
❑ 9 Eric Munson GL	.40	.18
❑ 10 Barry Bonds SC	2.50	1.10
❑ 11 Andruw Jones BB	1.00	.45
❑ 12 Antonio Alfonseca FIN	.40	.18
❑ 13 Andres Galarraga GAL	.60	.25
❑ 14 Joe Crede GL	.40	.18
❑ 15 Barry Larkin SC..............	1.00	.45
❑ 16 Barry Bonds BB..............	2.50	1.10
❑ 17 Barry Bonds FIN	2.50	1.10
❑ 18 Andruw Jones GAL	1.00	.45
❑ 19 C.C. Sabathia GL	.60	.25
❑ 20 Bobby Higginson SC	.40	.18
❑ 21 Barry Larkin BB..............	1.00	.45
❑ 22 Ben Grieve FIN	.40	.18
❑ 23 Barry Bonds GAL	2.50	1.10
❑ 24 Corey Patterson GL	.40	.18
❑ 25 Carlos Delgado SC	1.00	.45
❑ 26 Bernie Williams BB	1.00	.45
❑ 27 Brian Giles FIN	.40	.18
❑ 28 Barry Larkin GAL............	1.00	.45
❑ 29 Travis Dawkins GL	.25	.11
❑ 30 Chipper Jones SC	2.00	.90
❑ 31 Brian Giles BB..................	.40	.18
❑ 32 Carlos Delgado FIN........	1.00	.45
❑ 33 Ben Grieve GAL	.40	.18
❑ 34 Geoff Goetz GL................	.25	.11
❑ 35 Cristian Guzman SC	.40	.18
❑ 36 Cal Ripken BB................	4.00	1.80
❑ 37 Chipper Jones FIN	2.00	.90
❑ 38 Bernie Williams GAL	1.00	.45
❑ 39 Pablo Ozuna GL	.25	.11
❑ 40 Dante Bichette SC............	.40	.18
❑ 41 Carlos Delgado BB	1.00	.45
❑ 42 Craig Biggio FIN	.60	.25
❑ 43 Cal Ripken GAL	4.00	1.80
❑ 44 Tim Redding GL	.40	.18
❑ 45 Darin Erstad SC	1.00	.45
❑ 46 Chipper Jones BB	2.00	.90
❑ 47 Darin Erstad FIN	1.00	.45
❑ 48 Carlos Delgado GAL	1.00	.45
❑ 49 Josh Hamilton GL	1.00	.45
❑ 50 Derek Jeter SC	4.00	1.80
❑ 51 Darin Erstad BB	1.00	.45
❑ 52 Dean Palmer FIN	.40	.18
❑ 53 Chipper Jones GAL........	2.00	.90
❑ 54 Chin-Feng Chen GL	.60	.25
❑ 55 Edgar Martinez SC	.60	.25
❑ 56 Derek Jeter BB	4.00	1.80
❑ 57 Derek Jeter FIN..............	4.00	1.80
❑ 58 Craig Biggio GAL	.60	.25
❑ 59 Keith Ginter GL	.40	.18
❑ 60 Edgardo Alfonzo SC	.40	.18
❑ 61 Edgar Martinez BB	.60	.25
❑ 62 Edgardo Alfonzo FIN........	.40	.18
❑ 63 David Justice GAL............	.40	.18
❑ 64 Roy Oswalt GL	1.00	.45
❑ 65 Eric Karros SC	.40	.18
❑ 66 Edgardo Alfonzo BB	.40	.18
❑ 67 Frank Thomas FIN	1.25	.55
❑ 68 Dean Palmer GAL............	.40	.18
❑ 69 Alfonso Soriano GL	1.00	.45
❑ 70 Fernando Vina SC............	.25	.11
❑ 71 Frank Thomas BB	1.25	.55
❑ 72 Garret Anderson FIN........	.40	.18
❑ 73 Derek Jeter GAL	4.00	1.80
❑ 74 Bobby Bradley GL	.40	.18
❑ 75 Frank Thomas SC	1.25	.55
❑ 76 Gary Sheffield BB	.40	.18
❑ 77 Geoff Jenkins FIN	.40	.18
❑ 78 Edgar Martinez GAL	.60	.25
❑ 79 Nick Johnson GL..............	.40	.18
❑ 80 Fred McGriff SC	.60	.25
❑ 81 Geoff Jenkins BB	.40	.18
❑ 82 Greg Maddux FIN	2.50	1.10
❑ 83 Edgardo Alfonzo GAL	.40	.18

	Card	MINT	NRMT
❑	84 Hee Seop Choi GL RC	6.00	2.70
❑	85 Garret Anderson SC	.40	.18
❑	86 Greg Maddux BB	2.50	1.10
❑	87 Ivan Rodriguez FIN	1.00	.45
❑	88 Eric Karros GAL	.40	.18
❑	89 Scott Seabol GL	.25	.11
❑	90 Ivan Rodriguez SC	1.00	.45
❑	91 Ivan Rodriguez BB	1.00	.45
❑	92 J.D. Drew FIN	1.00	.45
❑	93 Frank Thomas GAL	1.25	.55
❑	94 Ryan Anderson GL	.40	.18
❑	95 Jason Giambi SC	1.00	.45
❑	96 Jason Giambi BB	1.00	.45
❑	97 Jason Kendall FIN	.40	.18
❑	98 Gary Sheffield GAL	.40	.18
❑	99 Milton Bradley GL	.25	.11
❑	100 Jason Kendall SC	.40	.18
❑	101 Jason Kendall BB	.40	.18
❑	102 Jeff Bagwell FIN	1.25	.55
❑	103 Greg Maddux GAL	2.50	1.10
❑	104 Sean Burroughs GL	1.00	.45
❑	105 Jay Bell SC	.40	.18
❑	106 Jeff Bagwell BB	1.25	.55
❑	107 Jeffrey Hammonds FIN	.25	.11
❑	108 Ivan Rodriguez GAL	1.00	.45
❑	109 Ben Petrick GL	.25	.11
❑	110 Jeff Bagwell SC	1.25	.55
❑	111 Jeff Cirillo BB	.40	.18
❑	112 Jermaine Dye FIN	.40	.18
❑	113 J.T. Snow GAL	.40	.18
❑	114 Ben Davis GL	.40	.18
❑	115 Jeff Cirillo SC	.40	.18
❑	116 Jeff Kent BB	.60	.25
❑	117 Jeromy Burnitz FIN	.40	.18
❑	118 Jay Bell GAL	.40	.18
❑	119 Jason Hart GL	.60	.25
❑	120 Jeff Kent SC	.60	.25
❑	121 Jermaine Dye BB	.40	.18
❑	122 John Olerud FIN	.40	.18
❑	123 Jeff Bagwell GAL	1.25	.55
❑	124 Jeff Segar GL RC	2.00	.90
❑	125 Jeromy Burnitz SC	.40	.18
❑	126 Jeromy Burnitz BB	.40	.18
❑	127 Johnny Damon FIN	.40	.18
❑	128 Jim Edmonds GAL	.60	.25
❑	129 Tim Christman GL RC	1.00	.45
❑	130 Jim Thome SC	1.00	.45
❑	131 Jim Edmonds BB	.60	.25
❑	132 Jorge Posada FIN	.40	.18
❑	133 Jim Thome GAL	1.00	.45
❑	134 Danny Borrell GL RC	2.00	.90
❑	135 Johnny Damon SC	.40	.18
❑	136 Jim Thome BB	1.00	.45
❑	137 Jose Vidro FIN	.40	.18
❑	138 Ken Griffey Jr. GAL	3.00	1.35
❑	139 Sean Burnett GL	.40	.18
❑	140 Larry Walker SC	.60	.25
❑	141 Jose Vidro BB	.40	.18
❑	142 Ken Griffey Jr. FIN	3.00	1.35
❑	143 Larry Walker GAL	.60	.25
❑	144 Robert Keppel GL RC	2.00	.90
❑	145 Luis Castillo SC	.25	.11
❑	146 Ken Griffey Jr. BB	3.00	1.35
❑	147 Kevin Brown FIN	.40	.18
❑	148 Manny Ramirez GAL	1.25	.55
❑	149 David Parrish GL RC	1.50	.70
❑	150 Manny Ramirez SC	1.25	.55
❑	151 Kevin Brown BB	.40	.18
❑	152 Luis Castillo FIN	.25	.11
❑	153 Mark Grace GAL	1.00	.45
❑	154 Mike Jacobs GL	1.25	.55
❑	155 Mark Grace SC	1.00	.45
❑	156 Larry Walker BB	.60	.25
❑	157 Magglio Ordonez FIN	.40	.18
❑	158 Mark McGwire GAL	4.00	1.80
❑	159 Adam Johnson GL	.40	.18
❑	160 Mark McGwire SC	4.00	1.80
❑	161 Magglio Ordonez BB	.40	.18
❑	162 Mark McGwire FIN	4.00	1.80
❑	163 Matt Williams GAL	.60	.25
❑	164 Oscar Ramirez GL RC	1.50	.70
❑	165 Mike Piazza SC	2.50	1.10
❑	166 Manny Ramirez BB	1.25	.55
❑	167 Mike Piazza FIN	2.50	1.10
❑	168 Mike Mussina GAL	1.00	.45
❑	169 Odannis Ayala GL RC	1.50	.70
❑	170 Mike Sweeney SC	.40	.18
❑	171 Mark McGwire BB	4.00	1.80
❑	172 Nomar Garciaparra FIN	2.50	1.10
❑	173 Mike Piazza GAL	2.50	1.10
❑	174 J.R. House GL	1.00	.45
❑	175 Neifi Perez SC	.25	.11
❑	176 Mike Piazza BB	2.50	1.10
❑	177 Pedro Martinez FIN	1.25	.55
❑	178 Mo Vaughn GAL	.40	.18
❑	179 Shawn Fagan GL RC	2.50	1.10
❑	180 Nomar Garciaparra SC	2.50	1.10
❑	181 Mo Vaughn BB	.40	.18
❑	182 Rafael Palmeiro FIN	1.00	.45
❑	183 Nomar Garciaparra GAL	2.50	1.10
❑	184 Chris Bass GL RC	2.00	.90
❑	185 Raul Mondesi SC	.40	.18
❑	186 Nomar Garciaparra BB	2.50	1.10
❑	187 Randy Johnson FIN	1.25	.55
❑	188 Omar Vizquel GAL	.40	.18
❑	189 Erick Almonte GL RC	1.50	.70
❑	190 Ray Durham SC	.40	.18
❑	191 Pedro Martinez BB	1.25	.55
❑	192 Robb Nen FIN	.25	.11
❑	193 Pedro Martinez GAL	1.25	.55
❑	194 Luis Montanez GL RC	4.00	1.80
❑	195 Ray Lankford SC	.25	.11
❑	196 Rafael Palmeiro BB	1.00	.45
❑	197 Roberto Alomar FIN	1.00	.45
❑	198 Rafael Palmeiro GAL	1.00	.45
❑	199 Chad Petty GL RC	2.00	.90
❑	200 Richard Hidalgo SC	.40	.18
❑	201 Randy Johnson BB	1.25	.55
❑	202 Robin Ventura FIN	.40	.18
❑	203 Randy Johnson GAL	1.25	.55
❑	204 Derek Thompson GL	.25	.11
❑	205 Sammy Sosa SC	2.00	.90
❑	206 Roberto Alomar BB	1.00	.45
❑	207 Sammy Sosa FIN	2.00	.90
❑	208 Raul Mondesi GAL	.40	.18
❑	209 Scott Heard GL	.40	.18
❑	210 Scott Rolen SC	1.00	.45
❑	211 Sammy Sosa BB	2.00	.90
❑	212 Scott Rolen FIN	1.00	.45
❑	213 Roberto Alomar GAL	1.00	.45
❑	214 Dominic Rich GL RC	2.00	.90
❑	215 Sean Casey SC	.60	.25
❑	216 Scott Rolen BB	1.00	.45
❑	217 Sean Casey FIN	.60	.25
❑	218 Robin Ventura GAL	.40	.18
❑	219 William Smith GL RC	1.50	.70
❑	220 Tim Salmon SC	.40	.18
❑	221 Sean Casey BB	.60	.25
❑	222 Shannon Stewart FIN	.40	.18
❑	223 Sammy Sosa GAL	2.00	.90
❑	224 Joel Pineiro GL	1.00	.45
❑	225 Tino Martinez SC	.40	.18
❑	226 Shawn Green BB	1.00	.45
❑	227 Shawn Green FIN	1.00	.45
❑	228 Scott Rolen GAL	1.00	.45
❑	229 Greg Morrison GL RC	1.00	.45
❑	230 Tony Gwynn SC	2.00	.90
❑	231 Todd Helton BB	1.25	.55
❑	232 Steve Finley FIN	.40	.18
❑	233 Scott Williamson GAL	.25	.11
❑	234 Talmadge Nunnari GL	.25	.11
❑	235 Tony Womack SC	.25	.11
❑	236 Tony Batista BB	.40	.18
❑	237 Tim Salmon FIN	.40	.18
❑	238 Shawn Green GAL	1.00	.45
❑	239 Carlos Villalobos GL RC	1.00	.45
❑	240 Troy Glaus SC	1.00	.45
❑	241 Troy Glaus BB	1.00	.45
❑	242 Todd Helton FIN	1.25	.55
❑	243 Tim Salmon GAL	.40	.18
❑	244 Marcos Scutaro GL RC	1.00	.45
❑	245 Troy O'Leary SC	.25	.11
❑	246 Vladimir Guerrero BB	1.25	.55
❑	247 Vladimir Guerrero FIN	1.25	.55
❑	248 Vladimir Guerrero GAL	1.25	.55
❑	249 Horacio Estrada GL	.25	.11
❑	250 Vladimir Guerrero SC	1.25	.55

1996 Topps Gallery

	MINT	NRMT
COMPLETE SET (180)	40.00	18.00

	Card	MINT	NRMT
❑	1 Tom Glavine	1.00	.45
❑	2 Carlos Baerga	.25	.11
❑	3 Dante Bichette	.40	.18
❑	4 Mark Langston	.25	.11
❑	5 Ray Lankford	.25	.11
❑	6 Moises Alou	.40	.18
❑	7 Marquis Grissom	.25	.11
❑	8 Ramon Martinez	.25	.11
❑	9 Steve Finley	.40	.18
❑	10 Todd Hundley	.25	.11
❑	11 Brady Anderson	.40	.18
❑	12 John Valentin	.25	.11
❑	13 Heathcliff Slocumb	.25	.11
❑	14 Ruben Sierra	.25	.11
❑	15 Jeff Conine	.25	.11
❑	16 Jay Buhner	.40	.18
❑	17 Sammy Sosa	2.00	.90
❑	18 Doug Drabek	.25	.11
❑	19 Jose Mesa	.25	.11
❑	20 Jeff King	.25	.11
❑	21 Mickey Tettleton	.25	.11
❑	22 Jeff Montgomery	.25	.11
❑	23 Alex Fernandez	.25	.11
❑	24 Greg Vaughn	.40	.18
❑	25 Chuck Finley	.40	.18
❑	26 Terry Steinbach	.25	.11
❑	27 Rod Beck	.25	.11
❑	28 Jack McDowell	.25	.11
❑	29 Mark Wohlers	.25	.11
❑	30 Len Dykstra	.40	.18
❑	31 Bernie Williams	1.00	.45
❑	32 Travis Fryman	.40	.18
❑	33 Jose Canseco	1.00	.45
❑	34 Ken Caminiti	.40	.18
❑	35 Devon White	.40	.18
❑	36 Bobby Bonilla	.40	.18
❑	37 Paul Sorrento	.25	.11
❑	38 Ryne Sandberg	1.25	.55
❑	39 Derek Bell	.25	.11
❑	40 Bobby Jones	.25	.11
❑	41 J.T. Snow	.40	.18
❑	42 Denny Neagle	.40	.18
❑	43 Tim Wakefield	.25	.11
❑	44 Andres Galarraga	.60	.25
❑	45 David Segui	.25	.11
❑	46 Lee Smith	.40	.18
❑	47 Mel Rojas	.25	.11
❑	48 John Franco	.40	.18
❑	49 Pete Schourek	.25	.11
❑	50 John Wetteland	.40	.18
❑	51 Paul Molitor	1.00	.45
❑	52 Ivan Rodriguez	1.00	.45
❑	53 Chris Hoiles	.25	.11
❑	54 Mike Greenwell	.25	.11
❑	55 Orel Hershiser	.40	.18
❑	56 Brian McRae	.25	.11
❑	57 Geronimo Berroa	.25	.11
❑	58 Craig Biggio	.60	.25
❑	59 David Justice	.40	.18
❑	60 Lance Johnson	.25	.11
❑	61 Andy Ashby	.25	.11
❑	62 Randy Myers	.25	.11
❑	63 Gregg Jefferies	.25	.11
❑	64 Kevin Appier	.40	.18
❑	65 Rick Aguilera	.25	.11
❑	66 Shane Reynolds	.25	.11
❑	67 John Smoltz	.40	.18

❑ 68 Ron Gant	.25	.11
❑ 69 Eric Karros	.40	.18
❑ 70 Jim Thome	1.00	.45
❑ 71 Terry Pendleton	.40	.18
❑ 72 Kenny Rogers	.25	.11
❑ 73 Robin Ventura	.40	.18
❑ 74 Dave Nilsson	.25	.11
❑ 75 Brian Jordan	.40	.18
❑ 76 Glenallen Hill	.25	.11
❑ 77 Greg Colbrunn	.25	.11
❑ 78 Roberto Alomar	1.00	.45
❑ 79 Rickey Henderson	2.00	.90
❑ 80 Carlos Garcia	.25	.11
❑ 81 Dean Palmer	.40	.18
❑ 82 Mike Stanley	.25	.11
❑ 83 Hal Morris	.25	.11
❑ 84 Wade Boggs	1.00	.45
❑ 85 Chad Curtis	.25	.11
❑ 86 Roberto Hernandez	.25	.11
❑ 87 John Olerud	.40	.18
❑ 88 Frank Castillo	.25	.11
❑ 89 Rafael Palmeiro	1.00	.45
❑ 90 Trevor Hoffman	.40	.18
❑ 91 Marty Cordova	.25	.11
❑ 92 Hideo Nomo	1.25	.55
❑ 93 Johnny Damon	.40	.18
❑ 94 Bill Pulsipher	.25	.11
❑ 95 Garret Anderson	.40	.18
❑ 96 Ray Durham	.40	.18
❑ 97 Ricky Bottalico	.25	.11
❑ 98 Carlos Perez	.25	.11
❑ 99 Troy Percival	.25	.11
❑ 100 Chipper Jones	2.00	.90
❑ 101 Esteban Loaiza	.25	.11
❑ 102 John Mabry	.25	.11
❑ 103 Jon Nunnally	.25	.11
❑ 104 Andy Pettitte	.40	.18
❑ 105 Lyle Mouton	.25	.11
❑ 106 Jason Isringhausen	.40	.18
❑ 107 Brian L.Hunter	.25	.11
❑ 108 Quilvio Veras	.25	.11
❑ 109 Jim Edmonds	.60	.25
❑ 110 Ryan Klesko	.40	.18
❑ 111 Pedro Martinez	1.25	.55
❑ 112 Joey Hamilton	.25	.11
❑ 113 Vinny Castilla	.40	.18
❑ 114 Alex Gonzalez	.25	.11
❑ 115 Raul Mondesi	.40	.18
❑ 116 Rondell White	.40	.18
❑ 117 Dan Miceli	.25	.11
❑ 118 Tom Goodwin	.25	.11
❑ 119 Bret Boone	.40	.18
❑ 120 Shawn Green	1.00	.45
❑ 121 Jeff Cirillo	.40	.18
❑ 122 Rico Brogna	.25	.11
❑ 123 Chris Gomez	.25	.11
❑ 124 Ismael Valdes	.25	.11
❑ 125 Javy Lopez	.40	.18
❑ 126 Manny Ramirez	1.25	.55
❑ 127 Paul Wilson	.25	.11
❑ 128 Billy Wagner	.25	.11
❑ 129 Eric Owens	.25	.11
❑ 130 Todd Greene	.25	.11
❑ 131 Karim Garcia	.25	.11
❑ 132 Jimmy Haynes	.25	.11
❑ 133 Michael Tucker	.25	.11
❑ 134 John Wasdin	.25	.11
❑ 135 Brooks Kieschnick	.25	.11
❑ 136 Alex Ochoa	.25	.11
❑ 137 Ariel Prieto	.25	.11
❑ 138 Tony Clark	.40	.18
❑ 139 Mark Loretta	.25	.11
❑ 140 Rey Ordonez	.25	.11
❑ 141 Chris Snopek	.25	.11
❑ 142 Roger Cedeno	.25	.11
❑ 143 Derek Jeter	4.00	1.80
❑ 144 Jeff Suppan	.25	.11
❑ 145 Greg Maddux	2.50	1.10
❑ 146 Ken Griffey Jr.	3.00	1.35
❑ 147 Tony Gwynn	2.00	.90
❑ 148 Darren Daulton	.40	.18
❑ 149 Will Clark	1.00	.45
❑ 150 Mo Vaughn	.40	.18
❑ 151 Reggie Sanders	.25	.11
❑ 152 Kirby Puckett	2.50	1.10
❑ 153 Paul O'Neill	1.00	.45
❑ 154 Tim Salmon	.40	.18
❑ 155 Mark McGwire	4.00	1.80
❑ 156 Barry Bonds	2.50	1.10
❑ 157 Albert Belle	.40	.18
❑ 158 Edgar Martinez	.60	.25
❑ 159 Mike Mussina	1.00	.45
❑ 160 Cecil Fielder	.40	.18
❑ 161 Kenny Lofton	.40	.18
❑ 162 Randy Johnson	1.25	.55
❑ 163 Juan Gonzalez	1.00	.45
❑ 164 Jeff Bagwell	1.25	.55
❑ 165 Joe Carter	.40	.18
❑ 166 Mike Piazza	2.50	1.10
❑ 167 Eddie Murray	1.00	.45
❑ 168 Cal Ripken	4.00	1.80
❑ 169 Barry Larkin	1.00	.45
❑ 170 Chuck Knoblauch	.40	.18
❑ 171 Chili Davis	.40	.18
❑ 172 Fred McGriff	.60	.25
❑ 173 Matt Williams	.60	.25
❑ 174 Roger Clemens	2.50	1.10
❑ 175 Frank Thomas	1.25	.55
❑ 176 Dennis Eckersley	.40	.18
❑ 177 Gary Sheffield	.40	.18
❑ 178 David Cone	.40	.18
❑ 179 Larry Walker	.60	.25
❑ 180 Mark Grace	1.00	.45
❑ NNO M. Mantle Masterpiece	20.00	9.00

1997 Topps Gallery

	MINT	NRMT
COMPLETE SET (180)	50.00	22.00
❑ 1 Paul Molitor	1.00	.45
❑ 2 Devon White	.40	.18
❑ 3 Andres Galarraga	.60	.25
❑ 4 Cal Ripken	4.00	1.80
❑ 5 Tony Gwynn	2.00	.90
❑ 6 Mike Stanley	.25	.11
❑ 7 Orel Hershiser	.40	.18
❑ 8 Jose Canseco	1.00	.45
❑ 9 Chili Davis	.40	.18
❑ 10 Harold Baines	.40	.18
❑ 11 Rickey Henderson	2.00	.90
❑ 12 Darryl Strawberry	.40	.18
❑ 13 Todd Worrell	.25	.11
❑ 14 Cecil Fielder	.40	.18
❑ 15 Gary Gaetti	.40	.18
❑ 16 Bobby Bonilla	.40	.18
❑ 17 Will Clark	1.00	.45
❑ 18 Kevin Brown	.40	.18
❑ 19 Tom Glavine	1.00	.45
❑ 20 Wade Boggs	1.00	.45
❑ 21 Edgar Martinez	.60	.25
❑ 22 Lance Johnson	.25	.11
❑ 23 Gregg Jefferies	.25	.11
❑ 24 Bip Roberts	.25	.11
❑ 25 Tony Phillips	.25	.11
❑ 26 Greg Maddux	2.50	1.10
❑ 27 Mickey Tettleton	.25	.11
❑ 28 Terry Steinbach	.25	.11
❑ 29 Ryne Sandberg	1.25	.55
❑ 30 Wally Joyner	.40	.18
❑ 31 Joe Carter	.40	.18
❑ 32 Ellis Burks	.40	.18
❑ 33 Fred McGriff	.60	.25
❑ 34 Barry Larkin	1.00	.45
❑ 35 John Franco	.40	.18
❑ 36 Rafael Palmeiro	1.00	.45
❑ 37 Mark McGwire	4.00	1.80
❑ 38 Ken Caminiti	.40	.18
❑ 39 David Cone	.40	.18
❑ 40 Julio Franco	.40	.18
❑ 41 Roger Clemens	2.50	1.10
❑ 42 Barry Bonds	2.50	1.10
❑ 43 Dennis Eckersley	.40	.18
❑ 44 Eddie Murray	1.00	.45
❑ 45 Paul O'Neill	1.00	.45
❑ 46 Craig Biggio	.60	.25
❑ 47 Roberto Alomar	1.00	.45
❑ 48 Mark Grace	1.00	.45
❑ 49 Matt Williams	.60	.25
❑ 50 Jay Buhner	.40	.18
❑ 51 John Smoltz	.40	.18
❑ 52 Randy Johnson	1.25	.55
❑ 53 Ramon Martinez	.25	.11
❑ 54 Curt Schilling	1.00	.45
❑ 55 Gary Sheffield	.40	.18
❑ 56 Jack McDowell	.25	.11
❑ 57 Brady Anderson	.40	.18
❑ 58 Dante Bichette	.40	.18
❑ 59 Ron Gant	.25	.11
❑ 60 Alex Fernandez	.25	.11
❑ 61 Moises Alou	.40	.18
❑ 62 Travis Fryman	.40	.18
❑ 63 Dean Palmer	.40	.18
❑ 64 Todd Hundley	.25	.11
❑ 65 Jeff Brantley	.25	.11
❑ 66 Bernard Gilkey	.25	.11
❑ 67 Geronimo Berroa	.25	.11
❑ 68 John Wetteland	.40	.18
❑ 69 Robin Ventura	.40	.18
❑ 70 Ray Lankford	.25	.11
❑ 71 Kevin Appier	.40	.18
❑ 72 Larry Walker	.60	.25
❑ 73 Juan Gonzalez	1.00	.45
❑ 74 Jeff King	.25	.11
❑ 75 Greg Vaughn	.40	.18
❑ 76 Steve Finley	.40	.18
❑ 77 Brian McRae	.25	.11
❑ 78 Paul Sorrento	.25	.11
❑ 79 Ken Griffey Jr.	3.00	1.35
❑ 80 Omar Vizquel	.40	.18
❑ 81 Jose Mesa	.25	.11
❑ 82 Albert Belle	.40	.18
❑ 83 Glenallen Hill	.25	.11
❑ 84 Sammy Sosa	2.00	.90
❑ 85 Andy Benes	.25	.11
❑ 86 David Justice	.40	.18
❑ 87 Marquis Grissom	.25	.11
❑ 88 John Olerud	.40	.18
❑ 89 Tino Martinez	.40	.18
❑ 90 Frank Thomas	1.25	.55
❑ 91 Raul Mondesi	.40	.18
❑ 92 Steve Trachsel	.25	.11
❑ 93 Jim Edmonds	.60	.25
❑ 94 Rusty Greer	.40	.18
❑ 95 Joey Hamilton	.25	.11
❑ 96 Ismael Valdes	.25	.11
❑ 97 Dave Nilsson	.25	.11
❑ 98 John Jaha	.25	.11
❑ 99 Alex Gonzalez	.25	.11
❑ 100 Javy Lopez	.40	.18
❑ 101 Ryan Klesko	.40	.18
❑ 102 Tim Salmon	.40	.18
❑ 103 Bernie Williams	1.00	.45
❑ 104 Roberto Hernandez	.25	.11
❑ 105 Chuck Knoblauch	.40	.18
❑ 106 Mike Lansing	.25	.11
❑ 107 Vinny Castilla	.40	.18
❑ 108 Reggie Sanders	.25	.11
❑ 109 Mo Vaughn	.40	.18
❑ 110 Rondell White	.40	.18
❑ 111 Ivan Rodriguez	1.00	.45
❑ 112 Mike Mussina	1.00	.45
❑ 113 Carlos Baerga	.25	.11
❑ 114 Jeff Conine	.25	.11
❑ 115 Jim Thome	1.00	.45
❑ 116 Manny Ramirez	1.25	.55
❑ 117 Kenny Lofton	.40	.18
❑ 118 Wilson Alvarez	.25	.11
❑ 119 Eric Karros	.40	.18
❑ 120 Robb Nen	.25	.11

		MINT	NRMT
❑ 121	Mark Wohlers	.25	.11
❑ 122	Ed Sprague	.25	.11
❑ 123	Pat Hentgen	.25	.11
❑ 124	Juan Guzman	.25	.11
❑ 125	Derek Bell	.25	.11
❑ 126	Jeff Bagwell	1.25	.55
❑ 127	Eric Young	.25	.11
❑ 128	John Valentin	.25	.11
❑ 129	Al Martin UER Picture of Javy Lopez	.25	.11
❑ 130	Trevor Hoffman	.40	.18
❑ 131	Henry Rodriguez	.25	.11
❑ 132	Pedro Martinez	1.25	.55
❑ 133	Mike Piazza	2.50	1.10
❑ 134	Brian Jordan	.40	.18
❑ 135	Jose Valentin	.25	.11
❑ 136	Jeff Cirillo	.40	.18
❑ 137	Chipper Jones	2.00	.90
❑ 138	Ricky Bottalico	.25	.11
❑ 139	Hideo Nomo	1.00	.45
❑ 140	Troy Percival	.25	.11
❑ 141	Rey Ordonez	.25	.11
❑ 142	Edgar Renteria	.25	.11
❑ 143	Luis Castillo	.25	.11
❑ 144	Vladimir Guerrero	1.50	.70
❑ 145	Jeff D'Amico	.25	.11
❑ 146	Andruw Jones	1.25	.55
❑ 147	Darin Erstad	1.00	.45
❑ 148	Bob Abreu	.40	.18
❑ 149	Carlos Delgado	1.00	.45
❑ 150	Jamey Wright	.25	.11
❑ 151	Nomar Garciaparra	2.50	1.10
❑ 152	Jason Kendall	.40	.18
❑ 153	Jermaine Allensworth	.25	.11
❑ 154	Scott Rolen	1.00	.45
❑ 155	Rocky Coppinger	.25	.11
❑ 156	Paul Wilson	.25	.11
❑ 157	Garret Anderson	.40	.18
❑ 158	Mariano Rivera	.40	.18
❑ 159	Ruben Rivera	.25	.11
❑ 160	Andy Pettitte	.40	.18
❑ 161	Derek Jeter	4.00	1.80
❑ 162	Neifi Perez	.25	.11
❑ 163	Ray Durham	.40	.18
❑ 164	James Baldwin	.25	.11
❑ 165	Marty Cordova	.25	.11
❑ 166	Tony Clark	.40	.18
❑ 167	Michael Tucker	.25	.11
❑ 168	Mike Sweeney	.40	.18
❑ 169	Johnny Damon	.40	.18
❑ 170	Jermaine Dye	.40	.18
❑ 171	Alex Ochoa	.25	.11
❑ 172	Jason Isringhausen	.25	.11
❑ 173	Mark Grudzielanek	.25	.11
❑ 174	Jose Rosado	.25	.11
❑ 175	Todd Hollandsworth	.25	.11
❑ 176	Alan Benes	.25	.11
❑ 177	Jason Giambi	1.00	.45
❑ 178	Billy Wagner	.25	.11
❑ 179	Justin Thompson	.25	.11
❑ 180	Todd Walker	.25	.11

1998 Topps Gallery

		MINT	NRMT
COMPLETE SET (150)		50.00	22.00
❑ 1	Andruw Jones	1.00	.45
❑ 2	Fred McGriff	.60	.25
❑ 3	Wade Boggs	1.00	.45
❑ 4	Pedro Martinez	1.25	.55
❑ 5	Matt Williams	.60	.25
❑ 6	Wilson Alvarez	.25	.11
❑ 7	Henry Rodriguez	.25	.11
❑ 8	Jay Bell	.40	.18
❑ 9	Marquis Grissom	.25	.11
❑ 10	Darryl Kile	.40	.18
❑ 11	Chuck Knoblauch	.40	.18
❑ 12	Kenny Lofton	.40	.18
❑ 13	Quinton McCracken	.25	.11
❑ 14	Andres Galarraga	.60	.25
❑ 15	Brian Jordan	.40	.18
❑ 16	Mike Lansing	.25	.11
❑ 17	Travis Fryman	.40	.18
❑ 18	Tony Saunders	.25	.11
❑ 19	Moises Alou	.40	.18
❑ 20	Travis Lee	.40	.18
❑ 21	Garret Anderson	.40	.18
❑ 22	Ken Caminiti	.40	.18
❑ 23	Pedro Astacio	.25	.11
❑ 24	Ellis Burks	.40	.18
❑ 25	Albert Belle	.40	.18
❑ 26	Alan Benes	.25	.11
❑ 27	Jay Buhner	.40	.18
❑ 28	Derek Bell	.25	.11
❑ 29	Jeromy Burnitz	.40	.18
❑ 30	Kevin Appier	.40	.18
❑ 31	Jeff Cirillo	.40	.18
❑ 32	Bernard Gilkey	.25	.11
❑ 33	David Cone	.40	.18
❑ 34	Jason Dickson	.25	.11
❑ 35	Jose Cruz Jr.	.40	.18
❑ 36	Marty Cordova	.25	.11
❑ 37	Ray Durham	.40	.18
❑ 38	Jaret Wright	.25	.11
❑ 39	Billy Wagner	.25	.11
❑ 40	Roger Clemens	2.50	1.10
❑ 41	Juan Gonzalez	1.00	.45
❑ 42	Jeremi Gonzalez	.25	.11
❑ 43	Mark Grudzielanek	.25	.11
❑ 44	Tom Glavine	1.00	.45
❑ 45	Barry Larkin	1.00	.45
❑ 46	Lance Johnson	.25	.11
❑ 47	Bobby Higginson	.40	.18
❑ 48	Mike Mussina	1.00	.45
❑ 49	Al Martin	.25	.11
❑ 50	Mark McGwire	4.00	1.80
❑ 51	Todd Hundley	.25	.11
❑ 52	Ray Lankford	.25	.11
❑ 53	Jason Kendall	.40	.18
❑ 54	Javy Lopez	.40	.18
❑ 55	Ben Grieve	.40	.18
❑ 56	Randy Johnson	1.25	.55
❑ 57	Jeff King	.25	.11
❑ 58	Mark Grace	1.00	.45
❑ 59	Rusty Greer	.40	.18
❑ 60	Greg Maddux	2.50	1.10
❑ 61	Jeff Kent	.60	.25
❑ 62	Rey Ordonez	.25	.11
❑ 63	Hideo Nomo	1.00	.45
❑ 64	Charles Nagy	.25	.11
❑ 65	Rondell White	.40	.18
❑ 66	Todd Helton	1.25	.55
❑ 67	Jim Thome	1.00	.45
❑ 68	Denny Neagle	.25	.11
❑ 69	Ivan Rodriguez	1.00	.45
❑ 70	Vladimir Guerrero	1.25	.55
❑ 71	Jorge Posada	.40	.18
❑ 72	J.T. Snow	.40	.18
❑ 73	Reggie Sanders	.25	.11
❑ 74	Scott Rolen	1.00	.45
❑ 75	Robin Ventura	.40	.18
❑ 76	Mariano Rivera	.40	.18
❑ 77	Cal Ripken	4.00	1.80
❑ 78	Justin Thompson	.25	.11
❑ 79	Mike Piazza	2.50	1.10
❑ 80	Kevin Brown	.60	.25
❑ 81	Sandy Alomar Jr.	.40	.18
❑ 82	Craig Biggio	.60	.25
❑ 83	Vinny Castilla	.40	.18
❑ 84	Eric Young	.25	.11
❑ 85	Bernie Williams	1.00	.45
❑ 86	Brady Anderson	.40	.18
❑ 87	Bobby Bonilla	.40	.18
❑ 88	Tony Clark	.40	.18
❑ 89	Dan Wilson	.25	.11
❑ 90	John Wetteland	.40	.18
❑ 91	Barry Bonds	2.50	1.10
❑ 92	Chan Ho Park	.40	.18
❑ 93	Carlos Delgado	1.00	.45
❑ 94	David Justice	.40	.18
❑ 95	Chipper Jones	2.00	.90
❑ 96	Shawn Estes	.40	.18
❑ 97	Jason Giambi	1.00	.45
❑ 98	Ron Gant	.40	.18
❑ 99	John Olerud	.40	.18
❑ 100	Frank Thomas	1.25	.55
❑ 101	Jose Guillen	.25	.11
❑ 102	Brad Radke	.40	.18
❑ 103	Troy Percival	.25	.11
❑ 104	John Smoltz	.40	.18
❑ 105	Edgardo Alfonzo	.40	.18
❑ 106	Dante Bichette	.40	.18
❑ 107	Larry Walker	.60	.25
❑ 108	John Valentin	.25	.11
❑ 109	Roberto Alomar	1.00	.45
❑ 110	Mike Cameron	.40	.18
❑ 111	Eric Davis	.40	.18
❑ 112	Johnny Damon	.40	.18
❑ 113	Darin Erstad	1.00	.45
❑ 114	Omar Vizquel	.40	.18
❑ 115	Derek Jeter	4.00	1.80
❑ 116	Tony Womack	.25	.11
❑ 117	Edgar Renteria	.25	.11
❑ 118	Raul Mondesi	.40	.18
❑ 119	Tony Gwynn	2.00	.90
❑ 120	Ken Griffey Jr.	3.00	1.35
❑ 121	Jim Edmonds	.60	.25
❑ 122	Brian Hunter	.25	.11
❑ 123	Neifi Perez	.25	.11
❑ 124	Dean Palmer	.40	.18
❑ 125	Alex Rodriguez	2.50	1.10
❑ 126	Tim Salmon	.40	.18
❑ 127	Curt Schilling	1.00	.45
❑ 128	Kevin Orie	.25	.11
❑ 129	Andy Pettitte	.40	.18
❑ 130	Gary Sheffield	.40	.18
❑ 131	Jose Rosado	.25	.11
❑ 132	Manny Ramirez	1.25	.55
❑ 133	Rafael Palmeiro	1.00	.45
❑ 134	Sammy Sosa	2.00	.90
❑ 135	Jeff Bagwell	1.25	.55
❑ 136	Delino DeShields	.25	.11
❑ 137	Ryan Klesko	.40	.18
❑ 138	Mo Vaughn	.40	.18
❑ 139	Steve Finley	.40	.18
❑ 140	Nomar Garciaparra	2.50	1.10
❑ 141	Paul Molitor	1.00	.45
❑ 142	Pat Hentgen	.25	.11
❑ 143	Eric Karros	.40	.18
❑ 144	Bobby Jones	.25	.11
❑ 145	Tino Martinez	.40	.18
❑ 146	Matt Morris	.40	.18
❑ 147	Livan Hernandez	.25	.11
❑ 148	Edgar Martinez	.60	.25
❑ 149	Paul O'Neill	1.00	.45
❑ 150	Checklist	.25	.11

1999 Topps Gallery

	MINT	NRMT
COMPLETE SET (150)	80.00	36.00

COMP.SET w/o SP's (100)	25.00	11.00
COMMON CARD (1-100)	.15	.07
COMMON CARD (101-150)	.50	.23
❑ 1 Mark McGwire	2.50	1.10
❑ 2 Jim Thome	.60	.25
❑ 3 Bernie Williams	.60	.25
❑ 4 Larry Walker	.40	.18
❑ 5 Juan Gonzalez	.60	.25
❑ 6 Ken Griffey Jr.	2.00	.90
❑ 7 Raul Mondesi	.25	.11
❑ 8 Sammy Sosa	1.25	.55
❑ 9 Greg Maddux	1.50	.70
❑ 10 Jeff Bagwell	.75	.35
❑ 11 Vladimir Guerrero	.75	.35
❑ 12 Scott Rolen	.60	.25
❑ 13 Nomar Garciaparra	1.50	.70
❑ 14 Mike Piazza	1.50	.70
❑ 15 Travis Lee	.15	.07
❑ 16 Carlos Delgado	.60	.25
❑ 17 Darin Erstad	.60	.25
❑ 18 David Justice	.25	.11
❑ 19 Cal Ripken	2.50	1.10
❑ 20 Derek Jeter	2.50	1.10
❑ 21 Tony Clark	.25	.11
❑ 22 Barry Larkin	.60	.25
❑ 23 Greg Vaughn	.25	.11
❑ 24 Jeff Kent	.40	.18
❑ 25 Wade Boggs	.60	.25
❑ 26 Andres Galarraga	.40	.18
❑ 27 Ken Caminiti	.25	.11
❑ 28 Jason Kendall	.25	.11
❑ 29 Todd Helton	.75	.35
❑ 30 Chuck Knoblauch	.25	.11
❑ 31 Roger Clemens	1.50	.70
❑ 32 Jeromy Burnitz	.25	.11
❑ 33 Javy Lopez	.25	.11
❑ 34 Roberto Alomar	.60	.25
❑ 35 Eric Karros	.25	.11
❑ 36 Ben Grieve	.25	.11
❑ 37 Eric Davis	.25	.11
❑ 38 Rondell White	.25	.11
❑ 39 Dmitri Young	.25	.11
❑ 40 Ivan Rodriguez	.60	.25
❑ 41 Paul O'Neill	.60	.25
❑ 42 Jeff Cirillo	.25	.11
❑ 43 Kerry Wood	.60	.25
❑ 44 Albert Belle	.25	.11
❑ 45 Frank Thomas	.75	.35
❑ 46 Manny Ramirez	.75	.35
❑ 47 Tom Glavine	.60	.25
❑ 48 Mo Vaughn	.25	.11
❑ 49 Jose Cruz Jr.	.25	.11
❑ 50 Sandy Alomar Jr.	.25	.11
❑ 51 Edgar Martinez	.40	.18
❑ 52 John Olerud	.25	.11
❑ 53 Todd Walker	.15	.07
❑ 54 Tim Salmon	.25	.11
❑ 55 Derek Bell	.15	.07
❑ 56 Matt Williams	.40	.18
❑ 57 Alex Rodriguez	1.50	.70
❑ 58 Rusty Greer	.25	.11
❑ 59 Vinny Castilla	.25	.11
❑ 60 Jason Giambi	.60	.25
❑ 61 Mark Grace	.60	.25
❑ 62 Jose Canseco	.60	.25
❑ 63 Gary Sheffield	.25	.11
❑ 64 Brad Fullmer	.25	.11
❑ 65 Trevor Hoffman	.25	.11
❑ 66 Mark Kotsay	.15	.07
❑ 67 Mike Mussina	.60	.25
❑ 68 Johnny Damon	.25	.11
❑ 69 Tino Martinez	.25	.11
❑ 70 Curt Schilling	.60	.25
❑ 71 Jay Buhner	.25	.11
❑ 72 Kenny Lofton	.25	.11
❑ 73 Randy Johnson	.75	.35
❑ 74 Kevin Brown	.40	.18
❑ 75 Brian Jordan	.25	.11
❑ 76 Craig Biggio	.40	.18
❑ 77 Barry Bonds	1.50	.70
❑ 78 Tony Gwynn	1.25	.55
❑ 79 Jim Edmonds	.40	.18
❑ 80 Shawn Green	.60	.25
❑ 81 Todd Hundley	.15	.07
❑ 82 Cliff Floyd	.25	.11
❑ 83 Jose Guillen	.15	.07
❑ 84 Dante Bichette	.25	.11
❑ 85 Moises Alou	.25	.11
❑ 86 Chipper Jones	1.25	.55
❑ 87 Ray Lankford	.15	.07
❑ 88 Fred McGriff	.40	.18
❑ 89 Rod Beck	.15	.07
❑ 90 Dean Palmer	.25	.11
❑ 91 Pedro Martinez	.75	.35
❑ 92 Andruw Jones	.60	.25
❑ 93 Robin Ventura	.25	.11
❑ 94 Ugueth Urbina	.15	.07
❑ 95 Orlando Hernandez	.25	.11
❑ 96 Sean Casey	.40	.18
❑ 97 Denny Neagle	.15	.07
❑ 98 Troy Glaus	.60	.25
❑ 99 John Smoltz	.25	.11
❑ 100 Al Leiter	.25	.11
❑ 101 Ken Griffey Jr. MAS	4.00	1.80
❑ 102 Frank Thomas MAS	1.50	.70
❑ 103 Mark McGwire MAS	5.00	2.20
❑ 104 Sammy Sosa MAS	2.50	1.10
❑ 105 Chipper Jones MAS	2.50	1.10
❑ 106 Alex Rodriguez MAS	3.00	1.35
❑ 107 N.Garciaparra MAS	3.00	1.35
❑ 108 Juan Gonzalez MAS	1.25	.55
❑ 109 Derek Jeter MAS	5.00	2.20
❑ 110 Mike Piazza MAS	3.00	1.35
❑ 111 Barry Bonds MAS	3.00	1.35
❑ 112 Tony Gwynn MAS	2.50	1.10
❑ 113 Cal Ripken MAS	5.00	2.20
❑ 114 Greg Maddux MAS	3.00	1.35
❑ 115 Roger Clemens MAS	3.00	1.35
❑ 116 Brad Fullmer ART	.50	.23
❑ 117 Kerry Wood ART	1.25	.55
❑ 118 Ben Grieve ART	.50	.23
❑ 119 Todd Helton ART	1.50	.70
❑ 120 Kevin Millwood ART	.50	.23
❑ 121 Sean Casey ART	.75	.35
❑ 122 V.Guerrero ART	1.50	.70
❑ 123 Travis Lee ART	.50	.23
❑ 124 Troy Glaus ART	1.25	.55
❑ 125 Bartolo Colon ART	.50	.23
❑ 126 Andruw Jones ART	1.25	.55
❑ 127 Scott Rolen ART	1.25	.55
❑ 128 A.Soriano APP RC	8.00	3.60
❑ 129 Nick Johnson APP RC	5.00	2.20
❑ 130 Matt Belisle APP RC	1.25	.55
❑ 131 Jorge Toca APP RC	.75	.35
❑ 132 Masao Kida APP RC	.50	.23
❑ 133 Carlos Pena APP RC	5.00	2.20
❑ 134 Adrian Beltre APP	.50	.23
❑ 135 Eric Chavez APP	.50	.23
❑ 136 Carlos Beltran APP	.50	.23
❑ 137 Alex Gonzalez APP	.50	.23
❑ 138 Ryan Anderson APP	.50	.23
❑ 139 Ruben Mateo APP	.50	.23
❑ 140 Bruce Chen APP	.50	.23
❑ 141 Pat Burrell APP RC	5.00	2.20
❑ 142 Michael Barrett APP	.50	.23
❑ 143 Carlos Lee APP	.50	.23
❑ 144 Mark Mulder APP RC	6.00	2.70
❑ 145 C.Freeman APP RC	1.25	.55
❑ 146 Gabe Kapler APP	.50	.23
❑ 147 J.Encarnacion APP	.50	.23
❑ 148 Jeremy Giambi APP	.50	.23
❑ 149 Jason Tyner APP RC	1.00	.45
❑ 150 George Lombard APP	.50	.23

2000 Topps Gallery

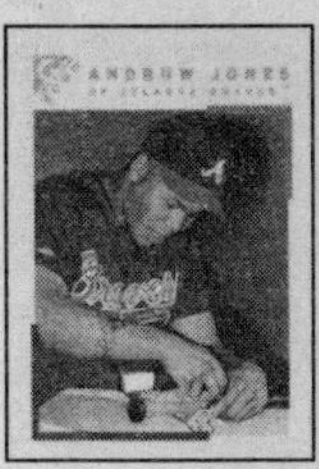

	MINT	NRMT
COMPLETE SET (150)	100.00	45.00
COMP.SET w/o SP's (100)	25.00	11.00
COMMON CARD (1-100)	.15	.07
COMMON CARD (101-150)	1.00	.45
❑ 1 Nomar Garciaparra	1.50	.70
❑ 2 Kevin Millwood	.15	.07
❑ 3 Jay Bell	.25	.11
❑ 4 Rusty Greer	.25	.11
❑ 5 Bernie Williams	.60	.25
❑ 6 Barry Larkin	.60	.25
❑ 7 Carlos Beltran	.25	.11
❑ 8 Damion Easley	.15	.07
❑ 9 Maggio Ordonez	.25	.11
❑ 10 Matt Williams	.40	.18
❑ 11 Shannon Stewart	.25	.11
❑ 12 Ray Lankford	.15	.07
❑ 13 Vinny Castilla	.25	.11
❑ 14 Miguel Tejada	.25	.11
❑ 15 Craig Biggio	.40	.18
❑ 16 Chipper Jones	1.25	.55
❑ 17 Albert Belle	.25	.11
❑ 18 Doug Glanville	.15	.07
❑ 19 Brian Giles	.25	.11
❑ 20 Shawn Green	.60	.25
❑ 21 Bret Boone	.25	.11
❑ 22 Luis Gonzalez	.60	.25
❑ 23 Carlos Delgado	.60	.25
❑ 24 J.D. Drew	.60	.25
❑ 25 Ivan Rodriguez	.60	.25
❑ 26 Tino Martinez	.25	.11
❑ 27 Erubiel Durazo	.25	.11
❑ 28 Scott Rolen	.60	.25
❑ 29 Gary Sheffield	.25	.11
❑ 30 Manny Ramirez	.75	.35
❑ 31 Luis Castillo	.15	.07
❑ 32 Fernando Tatis	.15	.07
❑ 33 Darin Erstad	.60	.25
❑ 34 Tim Hudson	.60	.25
❑ 35 Sammy Sosa	1.25	.55
❑ 36 Jason Kendall	.25	.11
❑ 37 Todd Walker	.15	.07
❑ 38 Orlando Hernandez	.25	.11
❑ 39 Pokey Reese	.15	.07
❑ 40 Mike Piazza	1.50	.70
❑ 41 B.J. Surhoff	.25	.11
❑ 42 Tony Gwynn	1.25	.55
❑ 43 Kevin Brown	.25	.11
❑ 44 Preston Wilson	.25	.11
❑ 45 Kenny Lofton	.25	.11
❑ 46 Rondell White	.25	.11
❑ 47 Frank Thomas	.75	.35
❑ 48 Neifi Perez	.15	.07
❑ 49 Edgardo Alfonzo	.15	.07
❑ 50 Ken Griffey Jr.	2.00	.90
❑ 51 Barry Bonds	1.50	.70
❑ 52 Brian Jordan	.25	.11
❑ 53 Raul Mondesi	.25	.11
❑ 54 Troy Glaus	.60	.25
❑ 55 Curt Schilling	.60	.25
❑ 56 Mike Mussina	.60	.25
❑ 57 Brian Daubach	.25	.11
❑ 58 Roger Clemens	1.50	.70
❑ 59 Carlos Febles	.15	.07
❑ 60 Todd Helton	.75	.35
❑ 61 Mark Grace	.60	.25
❑ 62 Randy Johnson	.75	.35
❑ 63 Jeff Bagwell	.75	.35
❑ 64 Tom Glavine	.60	.25
❑ 65 Adrian Beltre	.25	.11
❑ 66 Rafael Palmeiro	.60	.25
❑ 67 Paul O'Neill	.60	.25
❑ 68 Robin Ventura	.25	.11
❑ 69 Ray Durham	.25	.11
❑ 70 Mark McGwire	2.50	1.10
❑ 71 Greg Vaughn	.25	.11
❑ 72 Javy Lopez	.25	.11
❑ 73 Ryan Klesko	.25	.11
❑ 74 Mike Lieberthal	.25	.11
❑ 75 Cal Ripken	2.50	1.10
❑ 76 Juan Gonzalez	.60	.25

❑ 77	Sean Casey	.40	.18
❑ 78	Jermaine Dye	.25	.11
❑ 79	John Olerud	.25	.11
❑ 80	Jose Canseco	.60	.25
❑ 81	Eric Karros	.25	.11
❑ 82	Roberto Alomar	.60	.25
❑ 83	Ben Grieve	.25	.11
❑ 84	Greg Maddux	1.50	.70
❑ 85	Pedro Martinez	.75	.35
❑ 86	Tony Clark	.25	.11
❑ 87	Richie Sexson	.25	.11
❑ 88	Cliff Floyd	.25	.11
❑ 89	Eric Chavez	.25	.11
❑ 90	Andruw Jones	.60	.25
❑ 91	Vladimir Guerrero	.75	.35
❑ 92	Alex Gonzalez	.15	.07
❑ 93	Jim Thome	.60	.25
❑ 94	Bob Abreu	.25	.11
❑ 95	Derek Jeter	2.50	1.10
❑ 96	Larry Walker	.40	.18
❑ 97	Mike Hampton	.25	.11
❑ 98	Mo Vaughn	.25	.11
❑ 99	Jason Giambi	.60	.25
❑ 100	Alex Rodriguez	1.50	.70
❑ 101	Mark McGwire MAS	5.00	2.20
❑ 102	Sammy Sosa MAS	2.50	1.10
❑ 103	Alex Rodriguez MAS	3.00	1.35
❑ 104	Derek Jeter MAS	5.00	2.20
❑ 105	Greg Maddux MAS	3.00	1.35
❑ 106	Jeff Bagwell MAS	1.50	.70
❑ 107	N.Garciaparra MAS	3.00	1.35
❑ 108	Mike Piazza MAS	3.00	1.35
❑ 109	Pedro Martinez MAS	1.50	.70
❑ 110	Chipper Jones MAS	2.50	1.10
❑ 111	Randy Johnson MAS	1.50	.70
❑ 112	Barry Bonds MAS	3.00	1.35
❑ 113	Ken Griffey Jr. MAS	4.00	1.80
❑ 114	Manny Ramirez MAS	1.50	.70
❑ 115	Ivan Rodriguez MAS	.60	.25
❑ 116	Juan Gonzalez MAS	2.00	.90
❑ 117	V.Guerrero MAS	1.50	.70
❑ 118	Tony Gwynn MAS	2.50	1.10
❑ 119	Larry Walker MAS	1.25	.55
❑ 120	Cal Ripken MAS	5.00	2.20
❑ 121	Josh Hamilton SG	2.50	1.10
❑ 122	Corey Patterson SG	2.00	.90
❑ 123	Pat Burrell SG	2.00	.90
❑ 124	Nick Johnson SG	2.00	.90
❑ 125	Adam Piatt SG	1.25	.55
❑ 126	Rick Ankiel SG	2.00	.90
❑ 127	A.J. Burnett SG	1.00	.45
❑ 128	Ben Petrick SG	1.00	.45
❑ 129	Rafael Furcal SG	2.00	.90
❑ 130	Alfonso Soriano SG	2.00	.90
❑ 131	Dee Brown SG	1.00	.45
❑ 132	Ruben Mateo SG	1.00	.45
❑ 133	Pablo Ozuna SG	1.00	.45
❑ 134	S.Burroughs SG UER Eric Munson's bio on back	2.00	.90
❑ 135	Mark Mulder SG	2.00	.90
❑ 136	Jason Jennings SG	1.00	.45
❑ 137	Eric Munson SG	1.00	.45
❑ 138	Vernon Wells SG	1.00	.45
❑ 139	Brett Myers SG RC	1.50	.70
❑ 140	B.Christensen SG RC	1.00	.45
❑ 141	Bobby Bradley SG RC	2.00	.90
❑ 142	Ruben Salazar SG RC	2.00	.90
❑ 143	R.Christianson SG RC	2.00	.90
❑ 144	Corey Myers SG RC	1.25	.55
❑ 145	Aaron Rowand SG RC	2.00	.90
❑ 146	Julio Zuleta SG RC	1.50	.70
❑ 147	Kurt Ainsworth SG RC	2.00	.90
❑ 148	Scott Downs SG RC	1.00	.45
❑ 149	Larry Bigbie SG RC	1.50	.70
❑ 150	Chance Caple SG RC	1.25	.55

2001 Topps Gallery

	MINT	NRMT
COMPLETE SET (150)	120.00	55.00
COMP.SET w/o SP's (100)	40.00	18.00
COMMON (1-49/51-101)	.40	.18
COMMON CARD (102-150)	3.00	1.35

❑ 1	Darin Erstad	1.00	.45
❑ 2	Chipper Jones	2.00	.90
❑ 3	Nomar Garciaparra	2.50	1.10
❑ 4	Fernando Vina	.40	.18
❑ 5	Bartolo Colon	.40	.18
❑ 6	Bobby Higginson	.40	.18
❑ 7	Antonio Alfonseca	.40	.18
❑ 8	Mike Sweeney	.40	.18
❑ 9	Kevin Brown	.40	.18
❑ 10	Jose Vidro	.40	.18
❑ 11	Derek Jeter	4.00	1.80
❑ 12	Jason Giambi	1.00	.45
❑ 13	Pat Burrell	.40	.18
❑ 14	Jeff Kent	.60	.25
❑ 15	Alex Rodriguez	2.50	1.10
❑ 16	Rafael Palmeiro	1.00	.45
❑ 17	Garret Anderson	.40	.18
❑ 18	Brad Fullmer	.40	.18
❑ 19	Doug Glanville	.40	.18
❑ 20	Mark Quinn	.40	.18
❑ 21	Mo Vaughn	.40	.18
❑ 22	Andruw Jones	1.00	.45
❑ 23	Pedro Martinez	1.25	.55
❑ 24	Ken Griffey Jr.	3.00	1.35
❑ 25	Roberto Alomar	1.00	.45
❑ 26	Dean Palmer	.40	.18
❑ 27	Jeff Bagwell	1.25	.55
❑ 28	Jermaine Dye	.40	.18
❑ 29	Chan Ho Park	.40	.18
❑ 30	Vladimir Guerrero	1.25	.55
❑ 31	Bernie Williams	1.00	.45
❑ 32	Ben Grieve	.40	.18
❑ 33	Jason Kendall	.40	.18
❑ 34	Barry Bonds	2.50	1.10
❑ 35	Jim Edmonds	.60	.25
❑ 36	Ivan Rodriguez	1.00	.45
❑ 37	Javy Lopez	.40	.18
❑ 38	J.T. Snow	.40	.18
❑ 39	Erubiel Durazo	.40	.18
❑ 40	Terrence Long	.40	.18
❑ 41	Tim Salmon	.40	.18
❑ 42	Greg Maddux	2.50	1.10
❑ 43	Sammy Sosa	2.00	.90
❑ 44	Sean Casey	.60	.25
❑ 45	Jeff Cirillo	.40	.18
❑ 46	Juan Gonzalez	1.00	.45
❑ 47	Richard Hidalgo	.40	.18
❑ 48	Shawn Green	1.00	.45
❑ 49	Jeromy Burnitz	.40	.18
❑ 50	Willie Mays HTA	15.00	6.75
❑ 50	Willie Mays RETAIL	40.00	18.00
❑ 51	David Justice	.40	.18
❑ 52	Tim Hudson	1.00	.45
❑ 53	Brian Giles	.40	.18
❑ 54	Robb Nen	.40	.18
❑ 55	Fernando Tatis	.40	.18
❑ 56	Tony Batista	.40	.18
❑ 57	Pokey Reese	.40	.18
❑ 58	Ray Durham	.40	.18
❑ 59	Greg Vaughn	.40	.18
❑ 60	Kazuhiro Sasaki	1.00	.45
❑ 61	Troy Glaus	1.00	.45
❑ 62	Rafael Furcal	.40	.18
❑ 63	Magglio Ordonez	.40	.18
❑ 64	Jim Thome	1.00	.45
❑ 65	Todd Helton	1.25	.55
❑ 66	Preston Wilson	.40	.18
❑ 67	Moises Alou	.40	.18
❑ 68	Gary Sheffield	.40	.18
❑ 69	Geoff Jenkins	.40	.18
❑ 70	Mike Piazza	2.50	1.10
❑ 71	Jorge Posada	.40	.18
❑ 72	Bobby Abreu	.40	.18
❑ 73	Phil Nevin	.40	.18
❑ 74	John Olerud	.40	.18
❑ 75	Mark McGwire	4.00	1.80
❑ 76	Jose Cruz Jr.	.40	.18
❑ 77	David Segui	.40	.18
❑ 78	Neifi Perez	.40	.18
❑ 79	Omar Vizquel	.40	.18
❑ 80	Rick Ankiel	.60	.25
❑ 81	Randy Johnson	1.25	.55
❑ 82	Albert Belle	.40	.18
❑ 83	Frank Thomas	1.25	.55
❑ 84	Manny Ramirez	1.25	.55
❑ 85	Larry Walker	.60	.25
❑ 86	Luis Castillo	.40	.18
❑ 87	Johnny Damon	.40	.18
❑ 88	Adrian Beltre	.40	.18
❑ 89	Cristian Guzman	.40	.18
❑ 90	Jay Payton	.40	.18
❑ 91	Miguel Tejada	.40	.18
❑ 92	Scott Rolen	1.00	.45
❑ 93	Ryan Klesko	.40	.18
❑ 94	Edgar Martinez	.60	.25
❑ 95	Fred McGriff	.60	.25
❑ 96	Carlos Delgado	1.00	.45
❑ 97	Barry Zito	1.00	.45
❑ 98	Mike Lieberthal	.40	.18
❑ 99	Trevor Hoffman	.40	.18
❑ 100	Gabe Kapler	.40	.18
❑ 101	Edgardo Alfonzo	.40	.18
❑ 102	Corey Patterson	3.00	1.35
❑ 103	Alfonso Soriano	4.00	1.80
❑ 104	Keith Ginter	3.00	1.35
❑ 105	Keith Reed	3.00	1.35
❑ 106	Nick Johnson	3.00	1.35
❑ 107	Carlos Pena	3.00	1.35
❑ 108	Vernon Wells	3.00	1.35
❑ 109	Roy Oswalt	4.00	1.80
❑ 110	Alex Escobar	3.00	1.35
❑ 111	Adam Everett	3.00	1.35
❑ 112	Jimmy Rollins	3.00	1.35
❑ 113	Marcus Giles	3.00	1.35
❑ 114	Jack Cust	3.00	1.35
❑ 115	Chin-Feng Chen	3.00	1.35
❑ 116	Pablo Ozuna	3.00	1.35
❑ 117	Ben Sheets	3.00	1.35
❑ 118	Adrian Gonzalez	5.00	2.20
❑ 119	Ben Davis	3.00	1.35
❑ 120	Eric Valent	3.00	1.35
❑ 121	Scott Heard	3.00	1.35
❑ 122	David Parrish RC	3.00	1.35
❑ 123	Sean Burnett	3.00	1.35
❑ 124	Derek Thompson	3.00	1.35
❑ 125	Tim Christman RC	3.00	1.35
❑ 126	Mike Jacobs RC	3.00	1.35
❑ 127	Luis Montanez RC	5.00	2.20
❑ 128	Chris Bass RC	4.00	1.80
❑ 129	William Smith RC	3.00	1.35
❑ 130	Justin Wayne RC	4.00	1.80
❑ 131	Shawn Fagan RC	3.00	1.35
❑ 132	Chad Petty RC	4.00	1.80
❑ 133	J.R. House	4.00	1.80
❑ 134	Joel Pineiro	5.00	2.20
❑ 135	Albert Pujols RC	25.00	11.00
❑ 136	Carmen Cali RC	3.00	1.35
❑ 137	Steve Smyth RC	3.00	1.35
❑ 138	John Lackey	3.00	1.35
❑ 139	Bob Keppel RC	4.00	1.80
❑ 140	Dominic Rich RC	3.00	1.35
❑ 141	Josh Hamilton	4.00	1.80
❑ 142	Nolan Ryan	8.00	3.60
❑ 143	Tom Seaver	5.00	2.20
❑ 144	Reggie Jackson	5.00	2.20
❑ 145	Johnny Bench	5.00	2.20
❑ 146	Warren Spahn	4.00	1.80
❑ 147	Brooks Robinson	4.00	1.80
❑ 148	Carl Yastrzemski	5.00	2.20
❑ 149	Al Kaline	4.00	1.80
❑ 150	Bob Feller	4.00	1.80
❑ 151A	I. Suzuki English RC	40.00	18.00
❑ 151B	Ichiro Suzuki Japan RC	30.00	13.50
❑ NNO	I.Suzuki English EXCH	50.00	22.00
❑ NNO	I.Suzuki Japan EXCH	30.00	13.50

1998 Topps Gold Label Class 1

	MINT	NRMT
COMP.GOLD SET (100)	50.00	22.00
COMMON BLACK (1-100)	2.00	.90
*CLASS 1 BLACK: 3X TO 8X HI COLUMN		
CLASS 1 BLACK STATED ODDS 1:8		
COMMON RED (1-100)	8.00	3.60
*CLASS 1 RED STARS: 12.5X TO 30X HI		
*CLASS 1 RED RC's: 8X TO 20X HI		
CLASS 1 RED STATED ODDS 1:99		
CLASS 1 RED PR.RUN 100 SERIAL #'d SETS		
CLASS 1: FLAT GOLD TEXT ON FRONT		

Card	MINT	NRMT
❑ 1 Kevin Brown	.60	.25
❑ 2 Greg Maddux	2.50	1.10
❑ 3 Albert Belle	.40	.18
❑ 4 Andres Galarraga	.60	.25
❑ 5 Craig Biggio	.60	.25
❑ 6 Matt Williams	.60	.25
❑ 7 Derek Jeter	4.00	1.80
❑ 8 Randy Johnson	1.25	.55
❑ 9 Jay Bell	.40	.18
❑ 10 Jim Thome	1.00	.45
❑ 11 Roberto Alomar	1.00	.45
❑ 12 Tom Glavine	1.00	.45
❑ 13 Reggie Sanders	.25	.11
❑ 14 Tony Gwynn	2.00	.90
❑ 15 Mark McGwire	4.00	1.80
❑ 16 Jeromy Burnitz	.40	.18
❑ 17 Andruw Jones	1.00	.45
❑ 18 Jay Buhner	.40	.18
❑ 19 Robin Ventura	.40	.18
❑ 20 Jeff Bagwell	1.25	.55
❑ 21 Roger Clemens	2.50	1.10
❑ 22 Masato Yoshii RC	1.00	.45
❑ 23 Travis Fryman	.40	.18
❑ 24 Rafael Palmeiro	1.00	.45
❑ 25 Alex Rodriguez	2.50	1.10
❑ 26 Sandy Alomar Jr.	.40	.18
❑ 27 Chipper Jones	2.00	.90
❑ 28 Rusty Greer	.40	.18
❑ 29 Cal Ripken	4.00	1.80
❑ 30 Tony Clark	.40	.18
❑ 31 Derek Bell	.25	.11
❑ 32 Fred McGriff	.60	.25
❑ 33 Paul O'Neill	1.00	.45
❑ 34 Moises Alou	.40	.18
❑ 35 Henry Rodriguez	.25	.11
❑ 36 Steve Finley	.40	.18
❑ 37 Marquis Grissom	.25	.11
❑ 38 Jason Giambi	1.00	.45
❑ 39 Javy Lopez	.40	.18
❑ 40 Damion Easley	.25	.11
❑ 41 Mariano Rivera	.40	.18
❑ 42 Mo Vaughn	.40	.18
❑ 43 Mike Mussina	1.00	.45
❑ 44 Jason Kendall	.40	.18
❑ 45 Pedro Martinez	1.25	.55
❑ 46 Frank Thomas	1.25	.55
❑ 47 Jim Edmonds	.60	.25
❑ 48 Hideki Irabu	.25	.11
❑ 49 Eric Karros	.40	.18
❑ 50 Juan Gonzalez	1.00	.45
❑ 51 Ellis Burks	.40	.18
❑ 52 Dean Palmer	.40	.18
❑ 53 Scott Rolen	1.00	.45
❑ 54 Raul Mondesi	.40	.18
❑ 55 Quinton McCracken	.25	.11
❑ 56 John Olerud	.40	.18
❑ 57 Ken Caminiti	.40	.18
❑ 58 Brian Jordan	.40	.18
❑ 59 Wade Boggs	1.00	.45
❑ 60 Mike Piazza	2.50	1.10
❑ 61 Darin Erstad	1.00	.45
❑ 62 Curt Schilling	1.00	.45
❑ 63 David Justice	.40	.18
❑ 64 Kenny Lofton	.40	.18
❑ 65 Barry Bonds	2.50	1.10
❑ 66 Ray Lankford	.25	.11
❑ 67 Brian Hunter	.25	.11
❑ 68 Chuck Knoblauch	.40	.18
❑ 69 Vinny Castilla	.40	.18
❑ 70 Vladimir Guerrero	1.25	.55
❑ 71 Tim Salmon	.40	.18
❑ 72 Larry Walker	.60	.25
❑ 73 Paul Molitor	1.00	.45
❑ 74 Barry Larkin	1.00	.45
❑ 75 Edgar Martinez	.60	.25
❑ 76 Bernie Williams	1.00	.45
❑ 77 Dante Bichette	.40	.18
❑ 78 Nomar Garciaparra	2.50	1.10
❑ 79 Ben Grieve	.40	.18
❑ 80 Ivan Rodriguez	1.00	.45
❑ 81 Todd Helton	1.25	.55
❑ 82 Ryan Klesko	.40	.18
❑ 83 Sammy Sosa	2.00	.90
❑ 84 Travis Lee	.40	.18
❑ 85 Jose Cruz Jr.	.40	.18
❑ 86 Mark Kotsay	.40	.18
❑ 87 Richard Hidalgo	.40	.18
❑ 88 Rondell White	.40	.18
❑ 89 Greg Vaughn	.40	.18
❑ 90 Gary Sheffield	.40	.18
❑ 91 Paul Konerko	.40	.18
❑ 92 Mark Grace	1.00	.45
❑ 93 Kevin Millwood RC	1.00	.45
❑ 94 Manny Ramirez	1.25	.55
❑ 95 Tino Martinez	.40	.18
❑ 96 Brad Fullmer	.40	.18
❑ 97 Todd Walker	.25	.11
❑ 98 Carlos Delgado	1.00	.45
❑ 99 Kerry Wood	1.00	.45
❑ 100 Ken Griffey Jr.	3.00	1.35

1999 Topps Gold Label Class 1

	MINT	NRMT
COMP.GOLD SET (100)	50.00	22.00
COMMON BLACK (1-100)	1.00	.45
*CLASS 1 BLACK STARS: 1.5X TO 4X HI		
*CLASS 1 BLACK RC'S: 1.25X TO 3X HI		
CLASS 1 BLACK ODDS 1:12 RETAIL, 1:8 HTA		
COMMON RED (1-100)	6.00	2.70
*CLASS 1 RED STARS: 12.5X TO 25X HI		
*CLASS 1 RED RC'S: 5X TO 10X HI		
CLASS 1 RED ODDS 1:148 RETAIL, 1:118 HTA		
CLASS 1 RED PR.RUN 100 SERIAL #'d SETS		
NINE DIFT.ONE TO ONE PARALLELS EXIST		
ONE TO ONE 1:1587 RETAIL, 1:1271 HTA		

Card	MINT	NRMT
❑ 1 Mike Piazza	2.50	1.10
❑ 2 Andres Galarraga	.60	.25
❑ 3 Mark Grace	1.00	.45
❑ 4 Tony Clark	.40	.18
❑ 5 Jim Thome	1.00	.45
❑ 6 Tony Gwynn	2.00	.90
❑ 7 Kelly Dransfeldt RC	.25	.11
❑ 8 Eric Chavez	.40	.18
❑ 9 Brian Jordan	.40	.18
❑ 10 Todd Hundley	.25	.11
❑ 11 Rondell White	.40	.18
❑ 12 Dmitri Young	.40	.18
❑ 13 Jeff Kent	.60	.25
❑ 14 Derek Bell	.25	.11
❑ 15 Todd Helton	1.25	.55
❑ 16 Chipper Jones	2.00	.90
❑ 17 Albert Belle	.40	.18
❑ 18 Barry Larkin	1.00	.45
❑ 19 Dante Bichette	.40	.18
❑ 20 Gary Sheffield	.40	.18
❑ 21 Cliff Floyd	.40	.18
❑ 22 Derek Jeter	4.00	1.80
❑ 23 Jason Giambi	1.00	.45
❑ 24 Ray Lankford	.25	.11
❑ 25 Alex Rodriguez	2.50	1.10
❑ 26 Ruben Mateo	.40	.18
❑ 27 Wade Boggs	1.00	.45
❑ 28 Carlos Delgado	1.00	.45
❑ 29 Tim Salmon	.40	.18
❑ 30 Alfonso Soriano RC	5.00	2.20
❑ 31 Javy Lopez	.40	.18
❑ 32 Jason Kendall	.40	.18
❑ 33 Nick Johnson RC	3.00	1.35
❑ 34 A.J. Burnett RC	1.50	.70
❑ 35 Troy Glaus	1.00	.45
❑ 36 Pat Burrell RC	3.00	1.35
❑ 37 Jeff Cirillo	.40	.18
❑ 38 David Justice	.40	.18
❑ 39 Ivan Rodriguez	1.00	.45
❑ 40 Bernie Williams	1.00	.45
❑ 41 Jay Buhner	.40	.18
❑ 42 Mo Vaughn	.40	.18
❑ 43 Randy Johnson	1.25	.55
❑ 44 Pedro Martinez	1.25	.55
❑ 45 Larry Walker	.60	.25
❑ 46 Todd Walker	.25	.11
❑ 47 Roberto Alomar	1.00	.45
❑ 48 Kevin Brown	.60	.25
❑ 49 Mike Mussina	1.00	.45
❑ 50 Tom Glavine	1.00	.45
❑ 51 Curt Schilling	1.00	.45
❑ 52 Ken Caminiti	.40	.18
❑ 53 Brad Fullmer	.40	.18
❑ 54 Bobby Seay RC	.60	.25
❑ 55 Orlando Hernandez	.40	.18
❑ 56 Sean Casey	.60	.25
❑ 57 Al Leiter	.40	.18
❑ 58 Sandy Alomar Jr.	.40	.18
❑ 59 Mark Kotsay	.25	.11
❑ 60 Matt Williams	.60	.25
❑ 61 Raul Mondesi	.40	.18
❑ 62 Joe Crede RC	10.00	4.50
❑ 63 Jim Edmonds	.60	.25
❑ 64 Jose Cruz Jr.	.40	.18
❑ 65 Juan Gonzalez	1.00	.45
❑ 66 Sammy Sosa	2.00	.90
❑ 67 Cal Ripken	4.00	1.80
❑ 68 Vinny Castilla	.40	.18
❑ 69 Craig Biggio	.60	.25
❑ 70 Mark McGwire	4.00	1.80
❑ 71 Greg Vaughn	.40	.18
❑ 72 Greg Maddux	2.50	1.10
❑ 73 Paul O'Neill	1.00	.45
❑ 74 Scott Rolen	1.00	.45
❑ 75 Ben Grieve	.40	.18
❑ 76 Vladimir Guerrero	1.25	.55
❑ 77 John Olerud	.40	.18
❑ 78 Eric Karros	.40	.18
❑ 79 Jeromy Burnitz	.40	.18
❑ 80 Jeff Bagwell	1.25	.55
❑ 81 Kenny Lofton	.40	.18
❑ 82 Manny Ramirez	1.25	.55
❑ 83 Andruw Jones	1.00	.45
❑ 84 Travis Lee	.25	.11
❑ 85 Darin Erstad	1.00	.45
❑ 86 Nomar Garciaparra	2.50	1.10
❑ 87 Frank Thomas	1.25	.55
❑ 88 Moises Alou	.40	.18
❑ 89 Tino Martinez	.40	.18

Card	MINT	NRMT
❑ 90 Carlos Pena RC	3.00	1.35
❑ 91 Shawn Green	1.00	.45
❑ 92 Rusty Greer	.40	.18
❑ 93 Matt Belisle RC	.75	.35
❑ 94 Adrian Beltre	.40	.18
❑ 95 Roger Clemens	2.50	1.10
❑ 96 John Smoltz	.40	.18
❑ 97 Mark Mulder RC	4.00	1.80
❑ 98 Kerry Wood	1.00	.45
❑ 99 Barry Bonds	2.50	1.10
❑ 100 Ken Griffey Jr.	3.00	1.35

2000 Topps Gold Label Class 1

	MINT	NRMT
COMPLETE SET (100)	100.00	45.00
❑ 1 Sammy Sosa	2.00	.90
❑ 2 Greg Maddux	2.50	1.10
❑ 3 Mark Quinn	.40	.18
❑ 4 Rondell White	.40	.18
❑ 5 Fernando Tatis	.25	.11
❑ 6 Troy Glaus	1.00	.45
❑ 7 Nick Johnson	1.00	.45
❑ 8 Albert Belle	.40	.18
❑ 9 Scott Rolen	1.00	.45
❑ 10 Rafael Palmeiro	1.00	.45
❑ 11 Tony Gwynn	2.00	.90
❑ 12 Kevin Brown	.40	.18
❑ 13 Roberto Alomar	1.00	.45
❑ 14 John Olerud	.40	.18
❑ 15 Rick Ankiel	1.00	.45
❑ 16 Chipper Jones	2.00	.90
❑ 17 Craig Biggio	.60	.25
❑ 18 Mark Mulder	1.00	.45
❑ 19 Carlos Delgado	1.00	.45
❑ 20 Alex Gonzalez	.25	.11
❑ 21 Gabe Kapler	.40	.18
❑ 22 Derek Jeter	4.00	1.80
❑ 23 Carlos Beltran	.40	.18
❑ 24 Todd Helton	1.25	.55
❑ 25 Mark McGwire	4.00	1.80
❑ 26 Ben Grieve	.40	.18
❑ 27 Rafael Furcal	1.00	.45
❑ 28 Vernon Wells	.40	.18
❑ 29 Greg Vaughn	.40	.18
❑ 30 Vladimir Guerrero	1.25	.55
❑ 31 Mike Piazza	2.50	1.10
❑ 32 Roger Clemens	2.50	1.10
❑ 33 Barry Larkin	1.00	.45
❑ 34 Pedro Martinez	1.25	.55
❑ 35 Matt Williams	.60	.25
❑ 36 Mo Vaughn	.40	.18
❑ 37 Tim Hudson	.25	.11
❑ 38 Andruw Jones	1.00	.45
❑ 39 Vinny Castilla	.40	.18
❑ 40 Frank Thomas	1.25	.55
❑ 41 Pokey Reese	.25	.11
❑ 42 Corey Patterson	1.00	.45
❑ 43 Jeromy Burnitz	.40	.18
❑ 44 Preston Wilson	.40	.18
❑ 45 Juan Gonzalez	1.00	.45
❑ 46 Brian Giles	.40	.18
❑ 47 Todd Walker	.25	.11
❑ 48 Magglio Ordonez	.40	.18
❑ 49 Alfonso Soriano	1.00	.45
❑ 50 Ken Griffey Jr.	3.00	1.35
❑ 51 Michael Barrett	.25	.11
❑ 52 Shawn Green	1.00	.45
❑ 53 Erubiel Durazo	.40	.18
❑ 54 Adam Piatt	.60	.25
❑ 55 Pat Burrell	1.00	.45
❑ 56 Mike Mussina	1.00	.45
❑ 57 Bernie Williams	1.00	.45
❑ 58 Sean Casey	.60	.25
❑ 59 Randy Johnson	1.25	.55
❑ 60 Jeff Bagwell	1.25	.55
❑ 61 Eric Chavez	.40	.18
❑ 62 Josh Hamilton	1.25	.55
❑ 63 A.J. Burnett	.40	.18
❑ 64 Jim Thome	1.00	.45
❑ 65 Raul Mondesi	.40	.18
❑ 66 Jason Kendall	.40	.18
❑ 67 Mike Lieberthal	.40	.18
❑ 68 Robin Ventura	.40	.18
❑ 69 Ivan Rodriguez	1.00	.45
❑ 70 Larry Walker	.60	.25
❑ 71 Eric Munson	.40	.18
❑ 72 Brian Jordan	.40	.18
❑ 73 Edgardo Alfonzo	.40	.18
❑ 74 Curt Schilling	1.00	.45
❑ 75 Nomar Garciaparra	2.50	1.10
❑ 76 Mark Grace	1.00	.45
❑ 77 Shannon Stewart	.40	.18
❑ 78 J.D. Drew	1.00	.45
❑ 79 Jack Cust	.40	.18
❑ 80 Cal Ripken	4.00	1.80
❑ 81 Bob Abreu	.40	.18
❑ 82 Ruben Mateo	.40	.18
❑ 83 Orlando Hernandez	.40	.18
❑ 84 Kris Benson	.40	.18
❑ 85 Barry Bonds	2.50	1.10
❑ 86 Manny Ramirez	1.25	.55
❑ 87 Jose Canseco	1.00	.45
❑ 88 Sean Burroughs	1.00	.45
❑ 89 Kevin Millwood	.25	.11
❑ 90 Alex Rodriguez	2.50	1.10
❑ 91 Brett Myers RC	1.00	.45
❑ 92 Rick Asadoorian RC	1.25	.55
❑ 93 Ben Christensen RC	.60	.25
❑ 94 Bobby Bradley RC	1.25	.55
❑ 95 Chris Wakeland RC	.75	.35
❑ 96 Brad Baisley RC	.75	.35
❑ 97 Aaron McNeal RC	.75	.35
❑ 98 Aaron Rowand RC	1.25	.55
❑ 99 Scott Downs RC	.60	.25
❑ 100 Michael Tejera RC	.75	.35
❑ NNO D.Jeter AU Sheet/40 EXCH		

2001 Topps Gold Label Class 1

	MINT	NRMT
COMPLETE SET (115)	200.00	90.00
COMP.SET w/o SP's (100)	50.00	22.00
COMMON CARD (1-115)	.40	.18
COMMON SP	10.00	4.50
❑ 1 Adrian Beltre	.40	.18
❑ 2 Danny Borrell SP RC	10.00	4.50
❑ 3 Albert Belle	.40	.18
❑ 4 Jay Buhner	.40	.18
❑ 5 Alex Rodriguez	2.50	1.10
❑ 6 Andruw Jones	1.00	.45
❑ 7 Antonio Alfonseca	.40	.18
❑ 8 Barry Bonds	2.50	1.10
❑ 9 Barry Larkin	1.00	.45
❑ 10 Ben Grieve	.40	.18
❑ 11 Ben Molina	.40	.18
❑ 12 Bernie Williams	1.00	.45
❑ 13 Bobby Abreu	.40	.18
❑ 14 Bobby Higginson	.40	.18
❑ 15 Brad Fullmer	.40	.18
❑ 16 Brian Giles	.40	.18
❑ 17 Cal Ripken	4.00	1.80
❑ 18 Carlos Delgado	1.00	.45
❑ 19 Chad Petty SP RC	10.00	4.50
❑ 20 Charles Johnson	.40	.18
❑ 21 Chipper Jones	2.00	.90
❑ 22 Cristian Guzman	.40	.18
❑ 23 Darin Erstad	1.00	.45
❑ 24 David Justice	.40	.18
❑ 25 David Segui	.40	.18
❑ 26 Derek Jeter	4.00	1.80
❑ 27 Edgar Martinez	.60	.25
❑ 28 Edgardo Alfonzo	.40	.18
❑ 29 Fernando Tatis	.40	.18
❑ 30 Eric Karros	.40	.18
❑ 31 Eric Munson	.40	.18
❑ 32 Eric Young	.40	.18
❑ 33 Frank Thomas	1.25	.55
❑ 34 Fernando Vina	.40	.18
❑ 35 Garret Anderson	.40	.18
❑ 36 Gary Sheffield	.40	.18
❑ 37 Geoff Jenkins	.40	.18
❑ 38 Greg Maddux	2.50	1.10
❑ 39 Ivan Rodriguez	1.00	.45
❑ 40 J.D. Drew	1.00	.45
❑ 41 J.R. House SP	15.00	6.75
❑ 42 J.T. Snow	.40	.18
❑ 43 Jason Giambi	1.00	.45
❑ 44 Jason Kendall	.40	.18
❑ 45 Jay Payton	.40	.18
❑ 46 Jeff Bagwell	1.25	.55
❑ 47 Jeff Cirillo	.40	.18
❑ 48 Jeff Kent	.60	.25
❑ 49 Chan Ho Park	.40	.18
❑ 50 Jermaine Dye	.40	.18
❑ 51 Jeromy Burnitz	.40	.18
❑ 52 Jim Edmonds	.60	.25
❑ 53 Jim Thome	1.00	.45
❑ 54 John Olerud	.40	.18
❑ 55 Johnny Damon	.40	.18
❑ 56 Jorge Posada	.40	.18
❑ 57 Jose Cruz Jr.	.40	.18
❑ 58 Jose Vidro	.40	.18
❑ 59 Josh Hamilton	1.00	.45
❑ 60 Juan Gonzalez	1.00	.45
❑ 61 Juan Uribe	10.00	4.50
❑ 62 Justin Wayne SP RC	15.00	6.75
❑ 63 Kazuhiro Sasaki	1.00	.45
❑ 64 Ken Griffey Jr.	3.00	1.35
❑ 65 Kevin Brown	.40	.18
❑ 66 Kevin Young	.40	.18
❑ 67 Larry Walker	.60	.25
❑ 68 Luis Castillo	.40	.18
❑ 69 Steve Finley	.40	.18
❑ 70 Magglio Ordonez	.40	.18
❑ 71 Manny Ramirez	1.25	.55
❑ 72 Mark McGwire	4.00	1.80
❑ 73 Mark Quinn	.40	.18
❑ 74 Miguel Tejada	.40	.18
❑ 75 Mike Piazza	2.50	1.10
❑ 76 Mike Sweeney	.40	.18
❑ 77 Mo Vaughn	.40	.18
❑ 78 Moises Alou	.40	.18
❑ 79 Nomar Garciaparra	2.50	1.10
❑ 80 Pat Burrell	.40	.18
❑ 81 Paul Konerko	.40	.18
❑ 82 Pedro Martinez	1.25	.55
❑ 83 Phil Nevin	.40	.18
❑ 84 Preston Wilson	.40	.18
❑ 85 Rafael Furcal	.40	.18
❑ 86 Todd Zeile	.40	.18
❑ 87 Randy Johnson	1.25	.55
❑ 88 Travis Lee	.40	.18
❑ 89 Carl Everett	.40	.18
❑ 90 Quilvio Veras	.40	.18
❑ 91 Rick Ankiel	.60	.25
❑ 92 Rick Brosseau SP RC	10.00	4.50
❑ 93 Robert Keppel SP RC	10.00	4.50

❑ 94	Roberto Alomar	1.00	.45
❑ 95	Ryan Klesko	.40	.18
❑ 96	Sammy Sosa	2.00	.90
❑ 97	Scott Heard SP	10.00	4.50
❑ 98	Scott Rolen	1.00	.45
❑ 99	Sean Casey	.60	.25
❑ 100	Shawn Green	1.00	.45
❑ 101	Terrence Long	.40	.18
❑ 102	Tim Salmon	.40	.18
❑ 103	Todd Helton	1.25	.55
❑ 104	Tom Glavine	1.00	.45
❑ 105	Tony Batista	.40	.18
❑ 106	Travis Baptist SP RC	10.00	4.50
❑ 107	Troy Glaus	1.00	.45
❑ 108	Victor Hall SP RC	10.00	4.50
❑ 109	Vladimir Guerrero	1.25	.55
❑ 110	Tim Hudson	1.00	.45
❑ 111	Brian Roberts SP RC	10.00	4.50
❑ 112	Virgil Chevalier SP RC	10.00	4.50
❑ 113	Fernando Rodney SP RC	10.00	4.50
❑ 114	Paul Phillips SP RC	10.00	4.50
❑ 115	Cesar Bolivar SP RC	10.00	4.50

2000 Topps HD

	MINT	NRMT
COMPLETE SET (100)	80.00	36.00

❑ 1	Derek Jeter	5.00	2.20
❑ 2	Andruw Jones	1.25	.55
❑ 3	Ben Grieve	.50	.23
❑ 4	Carlos Beltran	.50	.23
❑ 5	Randy Johnson	1.50	.70
❑ 6	Javy Lopez	.50	.23
❑ 7	Gary Sheffield	.50	.23
❑ 8	John Olerud	.50	.23
❑ 9	Vinny Castilla	.50	.23
❑ 10	Barry Larkin	1.25	.55
❑ 11	Tony Clark	.50	.23
❑ 12	Roberto Alomar	1.25	.55
❑ 13	Brian Jordan	.50	.23
❑ 14	Wade Boggs	1.25	.55
❑ 15	Carlos Febles	.30	.14
❑ 16	Alfonso Soriano	1.25	.55
❑ 17	A.J. Burnett	.50	.23
❑ 18	Matt Williams	.75	.35
❑ 19	Alex Gonzalez	.30	.14
❑ 20	Larry Walker	.75	.35
❑ 21	Jeff Bagwell	1.50	.70
❑ 22	Al Leiter	.30	.14
❑ 23	Ken Griffey Jr.	4.00	1.80
❑ 24	Ruben Mateo	.50	.23
❑ 25	Mark Grace	1.25	.55
❑ 26	Carlos Delgado	1.25	.55
❑ 27	Vladimir Guerrero	1.50	.70
❑ 28	Kenny Lofton	.50	.23
❑ 29	Rusty Greer	.50	.23
❑ 30	Pedro Martinez	1.50	.70
❑ 31	Todd Helton	1.00	.45
❑ 32	Ray Lankford	.30	.14
❑ 33	Jose Canseco	1.25	.55
❑ 34	Raul Mondesi	.50	.23
❑ 35	Mo Vaughn	.50	.23
❑ 36	Eric Chavez	.50	.23
❑ 37	Manny Ramirez	1.50	.70
❑ 38	Jason Kendall	.50	.23
❑ 39	Mike Mussina	1.25	.55
❑ 40	Dante Bichette	.50	.23
❑ 41	Troy Glaus	1.25	.55
❑ 42	Rickey Henderson	2.50	1.10
❑ 43	Pablo Ozuna	.30	.14
❑ 44	Michael Barrett	.30	.14
❑ 45	Tony Gwynn	2.50	1.10
❑ 46	John Smoltz	.50	.23
❑ 47	Rafael Palmeiro	1.25	.55
❑ 48	Curt Schilling	1.25	.55
❑ 49	Todd Walker	.30	.14
❑ 50	Greg Vaughn	.50	.23
❑ 51	Orlando Hernandez	.50	.23
❑ 52	Jim Thome	1.25	.55
❑ 53	Pat Burrell	1.25	.55
❑ 54	Tim Salmon	.50	.23
❑ 55	Tom Glavine	1.25	.55
❑ 56	Travis Lee	.30	.14
❑ 57	Gabe Kapler	.50	.23
❑ 58	Greg Maddux	3.00	1.35
❑ 59	Scott Rolen	1.25	.55
❑ 60	Cal Ripken	5.00	2.20
❑ 61	Preston Wilson	.50	.23
❑ 62	Ivan Rodriguez	1.25	.55
❑ 63	Johnny Damon	.50	.23
❑ 64	Bernie Williams	1.25	.55
❑ 65	Barry Bonds	3.00	1.35
❑ 66	Sammy Sosa	2.50	1.10
❑ 67	Robin Ventura	.75	.35
❑ 68	Tony Fernandez	.30	.14
❑ 69	Jay Bell	.50	.23
❑ 70	Mark McGwire	5.00	2.20
❑ 71	Jeromy Burnitz	.50	.23
❑ 72	Chipper Jones	2.50	1.10
❑ 73	Josh Hamilton	1.50	.70
❑ 74	Darin Erstad	1.25	.55
❑ 75	Alex Rodriguez	3.00	1.35
❑ 76	Sean Casey	.75	.35
❑ 77	Tino Martinez	.50	.23
❑ 78	Juan Gonzalez	1.25	.55
❑ 79	Cliff Floyd	.50	.23
❑ 80	Craig Biggio	.75	.35
❑ 81	Shawn Green	1.25	.55
❑ 82	Adrian Beltre	.50	.23
❑ 83	Mike Piazza	3.00	1.35
❑ 84	Nomar Garciaparra	3.00	1.35
❑ 85	Kevin Brown	.75	.35
❑ 86	Roger Clemens	3.00	1.35
❑ 87	Frank Thomas	1.50	.70
❑ 88	Albert Belle	.50	.23
❑ 89	Erubiel Durazo	.50	.23
❑ 90	David Walling	.50	.23
❑ 91	John Sneed RC	.75	.35
❑ 92	Larry Bigbie RC	2.00	.90
❑ 93	B.J. Garbe RC	3.00	1.35
❑ 94	Bobby Bradley RC	2.50	1.10
❑ 95	Ryan Christianson RC	2.50	1.10
❑ 96	Jay Gehrke	.30	.14
❑ 97	Jason Stumm RC	2.00	.90
❑ 98	Brett Myers RC	2.00	.90
❑ 99	Chance Caple RC	1.50	.70
❑ 100	Corey Myers RC	1.50	.70

2001 Topps HD

	MINT	NRMT
COMPLETE SET (120)	200.00	90.00
COMP.SET w/o SP's (100)	80.00	36.00
COMMON CARD (1-100)	.30	.14
COMMON CARD (101-120)	3.00	1.35

❑ 1	Derek Jeter	5.00	2.20
❑ 2	Magglio Ordonez	.50	.23
❑ 3	Eric Munson	.50	.23
❑ 4	Jermaine Dye	.50	.23
❑ 5	Larry Walker	.75	.35
❑ 6	Pokey Reese	.30	.14
❑ 7	Pedro Martinez	1.50	.70
❑ 8	Rafael Palmeiro	1.25	.55
❑ 9	Jason Kendall	.50	.23
❑ 10	Mike Lieberthal	.50	.23
❑ 11	Ryan Klesko	.50	.23
❑ 12	Cal Ripken	5.00	2.20
❑ 13	Mike Piazza	3.00	1.35
❑ 14	Adam Sterrett RC	1.00	.45
❑ 15	John Olerud	.50	.23
❑ 16	Manny Ramirez	1.50	.70
❑ 17	Chad Petty RC	1.50	.70
❑ 18	Vladimir Guerrero	1.50	.70
❑ 19	Kevin Brown	.50	.23
❑ 20	Luis Cotto RC	1.00	.45
❑ 21	Josh Hamilton	1.25	.55
❑ 22	Mark Grace	1.25	.55
❑ 23	Mark McGwire	5.00	2.20
❑ 24	Jeromy Burnitz	.50	.23
❑ 25	Andruw Jones	1.25	.55
❑ 26	Raul Mondesi	.50	.23
❑ 27	Stuart McFarland RC	1.00	.45
❑ 28	Craig Biggio	.75	.35
❑ 29	Troy Glaus	1.25	.55
❑ 30	Carlos Delgado	1.25	.55
❑ 31	Rafael Furcal	.50	.23
❑ 32	J.D. Drew	1.25	.55
❑ 33	Corey Patterson	.50	.23
❑ 34	Gary Sheffield	.50	.23
❑ 35	Jeff Kent	.75	.35
❑ 36	Alex Rodriguez	3.00	1.35
❑ 37	Edgardo Alfonzo	.50	.23
❑ 38	Jeff Segar RC	1.50	.70
❑ 39	Bob Abreu	.50	.23
❑ 40	Brian Giles	.50	.23
❑ 41	Jason Smith RC	2.00	.90
❑ 42	Mo Vaughn	.50	.23
❑ 43	Pat Burrell	.50	.23
❑ 44	Barry Larkin	1.25	.55
❑ 45	Carlos Beltran	.50	.23
❑ 46	Eric Mosley RC	1.50	.70
❑ 47	Alfonso Soriano	1.25	.55
❑ 48	Tim Salmon	.50	.23
❑ 49	Jason Giambi	1.25	.55
❑ 50	Greg Maddux	3.00	1.35
❑ 51	Randy Johnson	1.50	.70
❑ 52	Jose Vidro	.50	.23
❑ 53	Edgar Martinez	.75	.35
❑ 54	Albert Belle	.50	.23
❑ 55	Ivan Rodriguez	1.25	.55
❑ 56	Sean Casey	.75	.35
❑ 57	Jorge Posada	.50	.23
❑ 58	Preston Wilson	.50	.23
❑ 59	Paul Konerko	.50	.23
❑ 60	Todd Helton	1.50	.70
❑ 61	Dominick Rich RC	1.00	.45
❑ 62	Tony Gwynn	2.50	1.10
❑ 63	Bernie Williams	1.25	.55
❑ 64	Anthony Brewer RC	2.00	.90
❑ 65	Shawn Green	1.25	.55
❑ 66	Jeff Bagwell	1.50	.70
❑ 67	Jose Cruz Jr.	.50	.23
❑ 68	Darin Erstad	1.25	.55
❑ 69	Jim Edmonds	.75	.35
❑ 70	Frank Thomas	1.50	.70
❑ 71	Ryan Anderson	.50	.23
❑ 72	Scott Rolen	1.25	.55
❑ 73	Jeff Cirillo	.50	.23
❑ 74	Chris Bass RC	1.50	.70
❑ 75	William Smith RC	1.50	.70
❑ 76	Trot Nixon	.50	.23
❑ 77	Bobby Bradley	.50	.23
❑ 78	Odannis Ayala RC	1.00	.45
❑ 79	Jim Thome	1.25	.55
❑ 80	Sammy Sosa	2.50	1.10
❑ 81	Geoff Jenkins	.50	.23
❑ 82	Ben Grieve	.50	.23
❑ 83	Andres Galarraga	.75	.35
❑ 84	Rick Ankiel	.75	.35
❑ 85	Barry Bonds	3.00	1.35

❑ 86 Alex Gonzalez	.30	.14
❑ 87 Sean Burroughs	1.25	.55
❑ 88 Nomar Garciaparra	3.00	1.35
❑ 89 Ken Griffey Jr.	4.00	1.80
❑ 90 Tim Hudson	1.25	.55
❑ 91 Chipper Jones	2.50	1.10
❑ 92 Matt Williams	.75	.35
❑ 93 Roberto Alomar	1.25	.55
❑ 94 Adrian Gonzalez	1.50	.70
❑ 95 Juan Gonzalez	1.25	.55
❑ 96 Brian Bass RC	1.00	.45
❑ 97 Rick Brosseau RC	1.00	.45
❑ 98 Mariano Rivera	.50	.23
❑ 99 James Baldwin	.30	.14
❑ 100 Dean Palmer	.50	.23
❑ 101 Pedro Martinez SS	4.00	1.80
❑ 102 Randy Johnson SS	4.00	1.80
❑ 103 Greg Maddux SS	8.00	3.60
❑ 104 Sammy Sosa SS	6.00	2.70
❑ 105 Mark McGwire SS	12.00	5.50
❑ 106 Ivan Rodriguez SS	3.00	1.35
❑ 107 Mike Piazza SS	8.00	3.60
❑ 108 Chipper Jones SS	6.00	2.70
❑ 109 Vladimir Guerrero SS	4.00	1.80
❑ 110 Alex Rodriguez SS	8.00	3.60
❑ 111 Ken Griffey Jr. SS	10.00	4.50
❑ 112 Cal Ripken SS	12.00	5.50
❑ 113 Derek Jeter SS	12.00	5.50
❑ 114 Barry Bonds SS	8.00	3.60
❑ 115 N.Garciaparra SS	8.00	3.60
❑ 116 Jeff Bagwell SS	4.00	1.80
❑ 117 Todd Helton SS	4.00	1.80
❑ 118 Darin Erstad SS	3.00	1.35
❑ 119 Shawn Green SS	3.00	1.35
❑ 120 Roberto Alomar SS	3.00	1.35

2001 Topps Heritage

	MINT	NRMT
COMP.MASTER SET (487)	600.00	275.00
COMPLETE SET (407)	500.00	220.00
COMP.BASIC SET (230)	80.00	36.00
COMMON CARD (81-310)	.50	.23
COMMON CARD (1-80)	2.50	1.10
COMMON CARD (311-407)	5.00	2.20

Card	MINT	NRMT
❑ 1 Kris Benson	3.00	1.35
❑ 1 Kris Benson Black	3.00	1.35
❑ 2 Brian Jordan	2.50	1.10
❑ 2 Brian Jordan Black	2.50	1.10
❑ 3 Fernando Vina	2.50	1.10
❑ 3 Fernando Vina Black	2.50	1.10
❑ 4 Mike Sweeney	2.50	1.10
❑ 4 Mike Sweeney Black	2.50	1.10
❑ 5 Rafael Palmeiro	3.00	1.35
❑ 5 Rafael Palmeiro Black	3.00	1.35
❑ 6 Paul O'Neill	3.00	1.35
❑ 6 Paul O'Neill Black	3.00	1.35
❑ 7 Todd Helton	4.00	1.80
❑ 7 Todd Helton Black	4.00	1.80
❑ 8 Ramiro Mendoza	2.50	1.10
❑ 8 Ramiro Mendoza Black	2.50	1.10
❑ 9 Kevin Millwood	2.50	1.10
❑ 9 Kevin Millwood Black	2.50	1.10
❑ 10 Chuck Knoblauch	2.50	1.10
❑ 10 Chuck Knoblauch Black	2.50	1.10
❑ 11 Derek Jeter	12.00	5.50
❑ 11 Derek Jeter Black	12.00	5.50
❑ 12 Alex Rodriguez Rangers	8.00	3.60
❑ 12 A.Rod Black Rangers	8.00	3.60
❑ 13 Geoff Jenkins	2.50	1.10
❑ 13 Geoff Jenkins Black	2.50	1.10
❑ 14 David Justice	2.50	1.10
❑ 14 David Justice Black	2.50	1.10
❑ 15 David Cone	2.50	1.10
❑ 15 David Cone Black	2.50	1.10
❑ 16 Andres Galarraga	2.50	1.10
❑ 16 Andres Galarraga Black	2.50	1.10
❑ 17 Garret Anderson	2.50	1.10
❑ 17 Garret Anderson Black	2.50	1.10
❑ 18 Roger Cedeno	2.50	1.10
❑ 18 Roger Cedeno Black	2.50	1.10
❑ 19 Randy Velarde	2.50	1.10
❑ 19 Randy Velarde Black	2.50	1.10
❑ 20 Carlos Delgado	3.00	1.35
❑ 20 Carlos Delgado Black	3.00	1.35
❑ 21 Quilvio Veras	2.50	1.10
❑ 21 Quilvio Veras Black	2.50	1.10
❑ 22 Jose Vidro	2.50	1.10
❑ 22 Jose Vidro Black	2.50	1.10
❑ 23 Corey Patterson	2.50	1.10
❑ 23 Corey Patterson Black	2.50	1.10
❑ 24 Jorge Posada	2.50	1.10
❑ 24 Jorge Posada Black	2.50	1.10
❑ 25 Eddie Perez	2.50	1.10
❑ 25 Eddie Perez Black	2.50	1.10
❑ 26 Jack Cust	2.50	1.10
❑ 26 Jack Cust Black	2.50	1.10
❑ 27 Sean Burroughs	3.00	1.35
❑ 27 Sean Burroughs Black	3.00	1.35
❑ 28 Randy Wolf	2.50	1.10
❑ 28 Randy Wolf Black	2.50	1.10
❑ 29 Mike Lamb	2.50	1.10
❑ 29 Mike Lamb Black	2.50	1.10
❑ 30 Rafael Furcal	2.50	1.10
❑ 30 Rafael Furcal Black	2.50	1.10
❑ 31 Barry Bonds	8.00	3.60
❑ 31 Barry Bonds Black	8.00	3.60
❑ 32 Tim Hudson	3.00	1.35
❑ 32 Tim Hudson Black	1.25	.55
❑ 33 Tom Glavine	3.00	1.35
❑ 33 Tom Glavine Black	3.00	1.35
❑ 34 Javy Lopez	2.50	1.10
❑ 34 Javy Lopez Black	2.50	1.10
❑ 35 Aubrey Huff	2.50	1.10
❑ 35 Aubrey Huff Black	2.50	1.10
❑ 36 Wally Joyner	2.50	1.10
❑ 36 Wally Joyner Black	2.50	1.10
❑ 37 Magglio Ordonez	2.50	1.10
❑ 37 Magglio Ordonez Black	2.50	1.10
❑ 38 Matt Lawton	2.50	1.10
❑ 38 Matt Lawton Black	2.50	1.10
❑ 39 Mariano Rivera	2.50	1.10
❑ 39 Mariano Rivera Black	2.50	1.10
❑ 40 Andy Ashby	2.50	1.10
❑ 40 Andy Ashby Black	2.50	1.10
❑ 41 Mark Buehrle	3.00	1.35
❑ 41 Mark Buehrle Black	3.00	1.35
❑ 42 Esteban Loaiza	2.50	1.10
❑ 42 Esteban Loaiza Black	2.50	1.10
❑ 43 Mark Redman	2.50	1.10
❑ 43 Mark Redman Black	2.50	1.10
❑ 44 Mark Quinn	2.50	1.10
❑ 44 Mark Quinn Black	2.50	1.10
❑ 45 Tino Martinez	2.50	1.10
❑ 45 Tino Martinez Black	2.50	1.10
❑ 46 Joe Mays	2.50	1.10
❑ 46 Joe Mays Black	2.50	1.10
❑ 47 Walt Weiss	2.50	1.10
❑ 47 Walt Weiss Black	2.50	1.10
❑ 48 Roger Clemens	8.00	3.60
❑ 48 Roger Clemens Black	8.00	3.60
❑ 49 Greg Maddux	8.00	3.60
❑ 49 Greg Maddux Black	8.00	3.60
❑ 50 Richard Hidalgo	2.50	1.10
❑ 50 Richard Hidalgo Black	2.50	1.10
❑ 51 Orlando Hernandez	2.50	1.10
❑ 51 Orlando Hernandez Black	2.50	1.10
❑ 52 Chipper Jones	6.00	2.70
❑ 52 Chipper Jones Black	6.00	2.70
❑ 53 Ben Grieve	2.50	1.10
❑ 53 Ben Grieve Black	2.50	1.10
❑ 54 Jimmy Haynes	2.50	1.10
❑ 54 Jimmy Haynes Black	2.50	1.10
❑ 55 Ken Caminiti	2.50	1.10
❑ 55 Ken Caminiti Black	2.50	1.10
❑ 56 Tim Salmon	2.50	1.10
❑ 56 Tim Salmon Black	2.50	1.10
❑ 57 Andy Pettitte	2.50	1.10
❑ 57 Andy Pettitte Black	2.50	1.10
❑ 58 Darin Erstad	3.00	1.35
❑ 58 Darin Erstad Black	3.00	1.35
❑ 59 Marquis Grissom	2.50	1.10
❑ 59 Marquis Grissom Black	2.50	1.10
❑ 60 Raul Mondesi	2.50	1.10
❑ 60 Raul Mondesi Black	2.50	1.10
❑ 61 Bengie Molina	2.50	1.10
❑ 61 Bengie Molina Black	2.50	1.10
❑ 62 Miguel Tejada	2.50	1.10
❑ 62 Miguel Tejada Black	2.50	1.10
❑ 63 Jose Cruz Jr.	2.50	1.10
❑ 63 Jose Cruz Jr. Black	2.50	1.10
❑ 64 Billy Koch	2.50	1.10
❑ 64 Billy Koch Black	2.50	1.10
❑ 65 Troy Glaus	1.25	.55
❑ 65 Troy Glaus Black	1.25	.55
❑ 66 Cliff Floyd	2.50	1.10
❑ 66 Cliff Floyd Black	2.50	1.10
❑ 67 Tony Batista	2.50	1.10
❑ 67 Tony Batista Black	2.50	1.10
❑ 68 Jeff Bagwell	4.00	1.80
❑ 68 Jeff Bagwell Black	4.00	1.80
❑ 69 Billy Wagner	2.50	1.10
❑ 69 Billy Wagner Black	2.50	1.10
❑ 70 Eric Chavez	2.50	1.10
❑ 70 Eric Chavez Black	2.50	1.10
❑ 71 Troy Percival	2.50	1.10
❑ 71 Troy Percival Black	2.50	1.10
❑ 72 Andruw Jones	3.00	1.35
❑ 72 Andruw Jones Black	3.00	1.35
❑ 73 Shane Reynolds	2.50	1.10
❑ 73 Shane Reynolds Black	2.50	1.10
❑ 74 Barry Zito	3.00	1.35
❑ 74 Barry Zito Black	3.00	1.35
❑ 75 Roy Halladay	2.50	1.10
❑ 75 Roy Halladay Black	2.50	1.10
❑ 76 David Wells	2.50	1.10
❑ 76 David Wells Black	2.50	1.10
❑ 77 Jason Giambi	3.00	1.35
❑ 77 Jason Giambi Black	3.00	1.35
❑ 78 Scott Elarton	2.50	1.10
❑ 78 Scott Elarton Black	2.50	1.10
❑ 79 Moises Alou	2.50	1.10
❑ 79 Moises Alou Black	2.50	1.10
❑ 80 Adam Piatt	2.50	1.10
❑ 80 Adam Piatt Black	2.50	1.10
❑ 81 Wilton Veras	.50	.23
❑ 82 Darryl Kile	.50	.23
❑ 83 Johnny Damon	.50	.23
❑ 84 Tony Armas Jr.	.50	.23
❑ 85 Ellis Burks	.50	.23
❑ 86 Jamey Wright	.50	.23
❑ 87 Jose Vizcaino	.50	.23
❑ 88 Bartolo Colon	.50	.23
❑ 89 Carmen Cali RC	.75	.35
❑ 90 Kevin Brown	.50	.23
❑ 91 Josh Hamilton	1.25	.55
❑ 92 Jay Buhner	.50	.23
❑ 93 Scott Pratt RC	1.00	.45
❑ 94 Alex Cora	.50	.23
❑ 95 Luis Montanez RC	2.50	1.10
❑ 96 Dmitri Young	.50	.23
❑ 97 J.T. Snow	.50	.23
❑ 98 Damion Easley	.50	.23
❑ 99 Greg Norton	.50	.23
❑ 100 Matt Wheatland	.50	.23
❑ 101 Chin-Feng Chen	.75	.35
❑ 102 Tony Womack	.50	.23
❑ 103 Adam Kennedy Black	.50	.23
❑ 104 J.D. Drew	1.25	.55
❑ 105 Carlos Febles	.50	.23
❑ 106 Jim Thome	1.25	.55
❑ 107 Danny Graves	.50	.23
❑ 108 Dave Mlicki	.50	.23
❑ 109 Ron Coomer	.50	.23
❑ 110 James Baldwin	.50	.23
❑ 111 Shaun Boyd RC	1.50	.70
❑ 112 Brian Bohanon	.50	.23
❑ 113 Jacque Jones	.50	.23

❑ 114 Alfonso Soriano 1.25 .55
❑ 115 Tony Clark .50 .23
❑ 116 Terrence Long .50 .23
❑ 117 Todd Hundley .50 .23
❑ 118 Kazuhiro Sasaki 1.25 .55
❑ 119 Brian Sellier RC .75 .35
❑ 120 John Olerud .50 .23
❑ 121 Javier Vazquez .50 .23
❑ 122 Sean Burnett .50 .23
❑ 123 Matt LeCroy .50 .23
❑ 124 Erubiel Durazo .50 .23
❑ 125 Juan Encarnacion .50 .23
❑ 126 Pablo Ozuna .50 .23
❑ 127 Russ Ortiz .50 .23
❑ 128 David Segui .50 .23
❑ 129 Mark McGwire 5.00 2.20
❑ 130 Mark Grace 1.25 .55
❑ 131 Fred McGriff .75 .35
❑ 132 Carl Pavano .50 .23
❑ 133 Derek Thompson .50 .23
❑ 134 Shawn Green 1.25 .55
❑ 135 B.J. Surhoff .50 .23
❑ 136 Michael Tucker .50 .23
❑ 137 Jason Isringhausen .50 .23
❑ 138 Eric Milton .50 .23
❑ 139 Mike Stodolka .50 .23
❑ 140 Milton Bradley .50 .23
❑ 141 Curt Schilling 1.25 .55
❑ 142 Sandy Alomar Jr. .50 .23
❑ 143 Brent Mayne .50 .23
❑ 144 Todd Jones .50 .23
❑ 145 Charles Johnson .50 .23
❑ 146 Dean Palmer .50 .23
❑ 147 Masato Yoshii .50 .23
❑ 148 Edgar Renteria .50 .23
❑ 149 Joe Randa .50 .23
❑ 150 Adam Johnson .50 .23
❑ 151 Greg Vaughn .50 .23
❑ 152 Adrian Beltre .50 .23
❑ 153 Glenallen Hill .50 .23
❑ 154 David Parrish RC 1.50 .70
❑ 155 Neifi Perez .50 .23
❑ 156 Pete Harnisch .50 .23
❑ 157 Paul Konerko .50 .23
❑ 158 Dennys Reyes .50 .23
❑ 159 Jose Lima Black .50 .23
❑ 160 Eddie Taubensee .50 .23
❑ 161 Miguel Cairo .50 .23
❑ 162 Jeff Kent .75 .35
❑ 163 Dustin Hermanson .50 .23
❑ 164 Alex Gonzalez .50 .23
❑ 165 Hideo Nomo 1.25 .55
❑ 166 Sammy Sosa 2.50 1.10
❑ 167 C.J. Nitkowski .50 .23
❑ 168 Cal Eldred .50 .23
❑ 169 Jeff Abbott .50 .23
❑ 170 Jim Edmonds .75 .35
❑ 171 Mark Mulder Black .75 .35
❑ 172 Dominic Rich RC 1.00 .45
❑ 173 Ray Lankford .50 .23
❑ 174 Danny Borrell RC 1.50 .70
❑ 175 Rick Aguilera .50 .23
❑ 176 Shannon Stewart Black .50 .23
❑ 177 Steve Finley .50 .23
❑ 178 Jim Parque .50 .23
❑ 179 Kevin Appier Black .50 .23
❑ 180 Adrian Gonzalez 1.50 .70
❑ 181 Tom Goodwin .50 .23
❑ 182 Kevin Tapani .50 .23
❑ 183 Fernando Tatis .50 .23
❑ 184 Mark Grudzielanek .50 .23
❑ 185 Ryan Anderson .50 .23
❑ 186 Jeffrey Hammonds .50 .23
❑ 187 Corey Koskie .50 .23
❑ 188 Brad Fullmer Black .50 .23
❑ 189 Rey Sanchez .50 .23
❑ 190 Michael Barrett .50 .23
❑ 191 Rickey Henderson 2.50 1.10
❑ 192 Jermaine Dye .50 .23
❑ 193 Scott Brosius .50 .23
❑ 194 Matt Anderson .50 .23
❑ 195 Brian Buchanan .50 .23
❑ 196 Derrek Lee .50 .23
❑ 197 Larry Walker .75 .35
❑ 198 Dan Moylan RC .75 .35
❑ 199 Vinny Castilla .50 .23
❑ 200 Ken Griffey Jr. 4.00 1.80
❑ 201 Matt Stairs Black .50 .23
❑ 202 Ty Howington .50 .23
❑ 203 Andy Benes .50 .23
❑ 204 Luis Gonzalez 1.25 .55
❑ 205 Brian Moehler .50 .23
❑ 206 Harold Baines .50 .23
❑ 207 Pedro Astacio .50 .23
❑ 208 Cristian Guzman .50 .23
❑ 209 Kip Wells .50 .23
❑ 210 Frank Thomas 1.50 .70
❑ 211 Jose Rosado .50 .23
❑ 212 Vernon Wells Black .50 .23
❑ 213 Bobby Higginson .50 .23
❑ 214 Juan Gonzalez 1.25 .55
❑ 215 Omar Vizquel .50 .23
❑ 216 Bernie Williams 1.25 .55
❑ 217 Aaron Sele .50 .23
❑ 218 Shawn Estes .50 .23
❑ 219 Roberto Alomar 1.25 .55
❑ 220 Rick Ankiel .75 .35
❑ 221 Josh Kalinowski .50 .23
❑ 222 David Bell .50 .23
❑ 223 Keith Foulke .50 .23
❑ 224 Craig Biggio Black .75 .35
❑ 225 Josh Axelson RC .75 .35
❑ 226 Scott Williamson .50 .23
❑ 227 Ron Belliard .50 .23
❑ 228 Chris Singleton .50 .23
❑ 229 Alex Serrano RC 1.00 .45
❑ 230 Deivi Cruz .50 .23
❑ 231 Eric Munson .50 .23
❑ 232 Luis Castillo .50 .23
❑ 233 Edgar Martinez .75 .35
❑ 234 Jeff Shaw .50 .23
❑ 235 Jeromy Burnitz .50 .23
❑ 236 Richie Sexson .50 .23
❑ 237 Will Clark 1.25 .55
❑ 238 Ron Villone .50 .23
❑ 239 Kerry Wood 1.25 .55
❑ 240 Rich Aurilia .50 .23
❑ 241 Mo Vaughn Black .50 .23
❑ 242 Travis Fryman .50 .23
❑ 243 Manny Ramirez Red Sox 4.00 1.80
❑ 244 Chris Stynes .50 .23
❑ 245 Ray Durham .50 .23
❑ 246 Juan Uribe RC 1.50 .70
❑ 247 Juan Guzman .50 .23
❑ 248 Lee Stevens .50 .23
❑ 249 Devon White .50 .23
❑ 250 Kyle Lohse RC 2.50 1.10
❑ 251 Bryan Wolff .50 .23
❑ 252 Matt Galante RC 1.00 .45
❑ 253 Eric Young .50 .23
❑ 254 Freddy Garcia .50 .23
❑ 255 Jay Bell .50 .23
❑ 256 Steve Cox .50 .23
❑ 257 Torii Hunter .50 .23
❑ 258 Jose Canseco 1.25 .55
❑ 259 Brad Ausmus .50 .23
❑ 260 Jeff Cirillo .50 .23
❑ 261 Brad Penny .50 .23
❑ 262 Antonio Alfonseca .50 .23
❑ 263 Russ Branyan .50 .23
❑ 264 Chris Morris RC 1.50 .70
❑ 265 John Lackey .50 .23
❑ 266 Justin Wayne RC 2.00 .90
❑ 267 Brad Radke .50 .23
❑ 268 Todd Stottlemyre .50 .23
❑ 269 Mark Loretta .50 .23
❑ 270 Matt Williams .75 .35
❑ 271 Kenny Lofton .50 .23
❑ 272 Jeff D'Amico .50 .23
❑ 273 Jamie Moyer .50 .23
❑ 274 Darren Dreifort .50 .23
❑ 275 Denny Neagle .50 .23
❑ 276 Orlando Cabrera .50 .23
❑ 277 Chuck Finley .50 .23
❑ 278 Miguel Batista .50 .23
❑ 279 Carlos Beltran .50 .23
❑ 280 Eric Karros .50 .23
❑ 281 Mark Kotsay .50 .23
❑ 282 Ryan Dempster .50 .23
❑ 283 Barry Larkin 1.25 .55
❑ 284 Jeff Suppan .50 .23
❑ 285 Gary Sheffield .50 .23
❑ 286 Jose Valentin .50 .23
❑ 287 Robb Nen .50 .23
❑ 288 Chan Ho Park .50 .23
❑ 289 John Halama .50 .23
❑ 290 Steve Smyth RC 1.00 .45
❑ 291 Gerald Williams .50 .23
❑ 292 Preston Wilson .50 .23
❑ 293 Victor Hall RC 1.50 .70
❑ 294 Ben Sheets .75 .35
❑ 295 Eric Davis .50 .23
❑ 296 Kirk Rueter .50 .23
❑ 297 Chad Petty RC 1.00 .45
❑ 298 Kevin Millar .50 .23
❑ 299 Marvin Benard .50 .23
❑ 300 Vladimir Guerrero 1.50 .70
❑ 301 Livan Hernandez .50 .23
❑ 302 Travis Baptist RC 1.00 .45
❑ 303 Bill Mueller .50 .23
❑ 304 Mike Cameron .50 .23
❑ 305 Randy Johnson 1.50 .70
❑ 306 Alan Mahaffey RC 1.00 .45
❑ 307 Timo Perez UER .50 .23
No facsimile autograph on card
❑ 308 Pokey Reese .50 .23
❑ 309 Ryan Rupe .50 .23
❑ 310 Carlos Lee .50 .23
❑ 311 Doug Glanville SP 5.00 2.20
❑ 312 Jay Payton SP 5.00 2.20
❑ 313 Troy O'Leary SP 5.00 2.20
❑ 314 Francisco Cordero SP 5.00 2.20
❑ 315 Rusty Greer SP 5.00 2.20
❑ 316 Cal Ripken SP 25.00 11.00
❑ 317 Ricky Ledee SP 5.00 2.20
❑ 318 Brian Daubach SP 5.00 2.20
❑ 319 Robin Ventura SP 5.00 2.20
❑ 320 Todd Zeile SP 5.00 2.20
❑ 321 Francisco Cordova SP 5.00 2.20
❑ 322 Henry Rodriguez SP 5.00 2.20
❑ 323 Pat Meares SP 5.00 2.20
❑ 324 Glendon Rusch SP 5.00 2.20
❑ 325 Keith Osik SP 5.00 2.20
❑ 326 Robert Keppel SP RC 6.00 2.70
❑ 327 Bobby Jones SP 5.00 2.20
❑ 328 Alex Ramirez SP 5.00 2.20
❑ 329 Robert Person SP 5.00 2.20
❑ 330 Ruben Mateo SP 5.00 2.20
❑ 331 Rob Bell SP 5.00 2.20
❑ 332 Carl Everett SP 5.00 2.20
❑ 333 Jason Schmidt SP 5.00 2.20
❑ 334 Scott Rolen SP 5.00 2.20
❑ 335 Jimmy Anderson SP 5.00 2.20
❑ 336 Bret Boone SP 5.00 2.20
❑ 337 Delino DeShields SP 5.00 2.20
❑ 338 Trevor Hoffman SP 5.00 2.20
❑ 339 Bob Abreu SP 5.00 2.20
❑ 340 Mike Williams SP 5.00 2.20
❑ 341 Mike Hampton SP 5.00 2.20
❑ 342 John Wetteland SP 5.00 2.20
❑ 343 Scott Erickson SP 5.00 2.20
❑ 344 Enrique Wilson SP 5.00 2.20
❑ 345 Tim Wakefield SP 5.00 2.20
❑ 346 Mike Lowell SP 5.00 2.20
❑ 347 Todd Pratt SP 5.00 2.20
❑ 348 Brook Fordyce SP 5.00 2.20
❑ 349 Benny Agbayani SP 5.00 2.20
❑ 350 Gabe Kapler SP 5.00 2.20
❑ 351 Sean Casey SP 6.00 2.70
❑ 352 Darren Oliver SP 5.00 2.20
❑ 353 Todd Ritchie SP 5.00 2.20
❑ 354 Kenny Rogers SP 5.00 2.20
❑ 355 Jason Kendall SP 5.00 2.20
❑ 356 John Vander Wal SP 5.00 2.20
❑ 357 Ramon Martinez SP 5.00 2.20
❑ 358 Edgardo Alfonzo SP 5.00 2.20
❑ 359 Phil Nevin SP 5.00 2.20
❑ 360 Albert Belle SP 5.00 2.20
❑ 361 Ruben Rivera SP 5.00 2.20
❑ 362 Pedro Martinez SP 8.00 3.60
❑ 363 Derek Lowe SP 5.00 2.20
❑ 364 Pat Burrell SP 5.00 2.20
❑ 365 Mike Mussina SP 5.00 2.20
❑ 366 Brady Anderson SP 5.00 2.20
❑ 367 Darren Lewis SP 5.00 2.20
❑ 368 Sidney Ponson SP 5.00 2.20
❑ 369 Adam Eaton SP 5.00 2.20
❑ 370 Eric Owens SP 5.00 2.20

Card	MINT	NRMT
371 Aaron Boone SP	5.00	2.20
372 Matt Clement SP	5.00	2.20
373 Derek Bell SP	5.00	2.20
374 Trot Nixon SP	5.00	2.20
375 Travis Lee SP	5.00	2.20
376 Mike Benjamin SP	5.00	2.20
377 Jeff Zimmerman SP	5.00	2.20
378 Mike Lieberthal SP	5.00	2.20
379 Rick Reed SP	5.00	2.20
380 Nomar Garciaparra SP	15.00	6.75
381 Omar Daal SP	5.00	2.20
382 Ryan Klesko SP	5.00	2.20
383 Rey Ordonez SP	5.00	2.20
384 Kevin Young SP	5.00	2.20
385 Rick Helling SP	5.00	2.20
386 Brian Giles SP	5.00	2.20
387 Tony Gwynn SP	12.00	5.50
388 Ed Sprague SP	5.00	2.20
389 J.R. House SP	12.00	5.50
390 Scott Hatteberg SP	5.00	2.20
391 John Valentin SP	5.00	2.20
392 Melvin Mora SP	5.00	2.20
393 Royce Clayton SP	5.00	2.20
394 Jeff Fassero SP	5.00	2.20
395 Manny Alexander SP	5.00	2.20
396 John Franco SP	5.00	2.20
397 Luis Alicea SP	5.00	2.20
398 Ivan Rodriguez SP	5.00	2.20
399 Kevin Jordan SP	5.00	2.20
400 Jose Offerman SP	5.00	2.20
401 Jeff Conine SP	5.00	2.20
402 Seth Etherton SP	5.00	2.20
403 Mike Bordick SP	5.00	2.20
404 Al Leiter SP	5.00	2.20
405 Mike Piazza SP	15.00	6.75
406 Armando Benitez SP	5.00	2.20
407 Warren Morris SP	5.00	2.20
NNO 1952 Card Redemption EXCH		
NNO Replica Hat-Jsy EXCH	100.00	45.00

1998 Topps Opening Day

	MINT	NRMT
COMPLETE SET (165)	50.00	22.00

Card	MINT	NRMT
1 Tony Gwynn	1.50	.70
2 Larry Walker	.50	.23
3 Billy Wagner	.20	.09
4 Denny Neagle	.20	.09
5 Vladimir Guerrero	1.00	.45
6 Kevin Brown	.50	.23
7 Mariano Rivera	.30	.14
8 Tony Clark	.30	.14
9 Deion Sanders	.30	.14
10 Matt Williams	.50	.23
11 Carlos Baerga	.20	.09
12 Mo Vaughn	.30	.14
13 Chan Ho Park	.30	.14
14 Frank Thomas	1.00	.45
15 John Jaha	.30	.14
16 Steve Trachsel	.20	.09
17 Jeff Kent	.50	.23
18 Scott Rolen	.75	.35
19 Juan Gonzalez	.75	.35
20 Garret Anderson	.30	.14
21 Roberto Clemente	2.00	.90
22 Omar Vizquel	.30	.14
23 Brian Hunter	.20	.09
24 Jeff Bagwell	1.00	.45
25 Chili Davis	.30	.14
26 Mike Cameron	.30	.14
27 Pat Hentgen	.20	.09
28 Wilton Guerrero	.20	.09
29 Devon White	.20	.09
30 Rafael Palmeiro	.75	.35
31 Jeff Blauser	.20	.09
32 Dave Hollins	.20	.09
33 Trevor Hoffman	.30	.14
34 Ryan Klesko	.30	.14
35 Butch Huskey	.20	.09
36 Mark Grudzielanek	.20	.09
37 Marquis Grissom	.20	.09
38 Jim Edmonds	.50	.23
39 Greg Vaughn	.30	.14
40 David Wells	.30	.14
41 Charles Nagy	.20	.09
42 B.J. Surhoff	.30	.14
43 Edgardo Alfonzo	.30	.14
44 Jay Buhner	.30	.14
45 Brady Anderson	.30	.14
46 Edgar Renteria	.20	.09
47 Rick Aguilera	.20	.09
48 Henry Rodriguez	.20	.09
49 Mike Piazza	2.00	.90
50 Todd Zeile	.30	.14
51 Rey Ordonez	.20	.09
52 Tony Womack	.20	.09
53 Mike Sweeney	.30	.14
54 Jeffrey Hammonds	.20	.09
55 Kevin Orie	.20	.09
56 Alex Gonzalez	.20	.09
57 Jose Canseco	.75	.35
58 Joey Hamilton	.20	.09
59 Brad Radke	.30	.14
60 Kevin Appier	.30	.14
61 Manny Ramirez	1.00	.45
62 Jeromy Burnitz	.30	.14
63 Matt Morris	.30	.14
64 Jason Dickson	.20	.09
65 Tom Glavine	.75	.35
66 Wally Joyner	.30	.14
67 Todd Jones	.20	.09
68 Sandy Alomar Jr.	.30	.14
69 Mike Lansing	.20	.09
70 Todd Stottlemyre	.20	.09
71 Jay Bell	.30	.14
72 Joey Cora	.20	.09
73 Scott Spiezio	.20	.09
74 Joe Carter	.30	.14
75 Jose Guillen	.20	.09
76 Damion Easley	.20	.09
77 Alex Fernandez	.20	.09
78 Randy Johnson	1.00	.45
79 J.T. Snow	.30	.14
80 Bernard Gilkey	.20	.09
81 David Segui	.20	.09
82 Dante Bichette	.30	.14
83 Derek Jeter	3.00	1.35
84 Mark Wohlers	.20	.09
85 Ricky Bottalico	.20	.09
86 Mike Mussina	.75	.35
87 Gary Sheffield	.30	.14
88 Hideo Nomo	.75	.35
89 Mark Grace	.75	.35
90 Darryl Kile	.30	.14
91 Shawn Estes	.30	.14
92 Vinny Castilla	.30	.14
93 Jose Rosado	.20	.09
94 Kenny Lofton	.30	.14
95 Jason Giambi	.75	.35
96 Ray Lankford	.20	.09
97 Hideki Irabu	.20	.09
98 Javy Lopez	.30	.14
99 Jeff Montgomery	.20	.09
100 Dennis Eckersley	.30	.14
101 Armando Benitez	.20	.09
102 Tim Naehring	.20	.09
103 Luis Gonzalez	.75	.35
104 Todd Hollandsworth	.20	.09
105 Wade Boggs	.75	.35
106 Mickey Morandini	.20	.09
107 Rusty Greer	.30	.14
108 Terry Steinbach	.20	.09
109 Pete Rose Jr.	.30	.14
110 Checklist	.20	.09
111 Tino Martinez	.30	.14
112 Roberto Alomar	.75	.35
113 Jeff King	.20	.09
114 Brian Jordan	.30	.14
115 Darin Erstad	.75	.35
116 Ken Caminiti	.30	.14
117 Jim Thome	.75	.35
118 Paul Molitor	.75	.35
119 Ivan Rodriguez	.75	.35
120 Bernie Williams	.75	.35
121 Todd Hundley	.20	.09
122 Andres Galarraga	.50	.23
123 Greg Maddux	2.00	.90
124 Edgar Martinez	.50	.23
125 Ron Gant	.30	.14
126 Derek Bell	.20	.09
127 Roger Clemens	2.00	.90
128 Rondell White	.30	.14
129 Barry Larkin	.75	.35
130 Robin Ventura	.30	.14
131 Jason Kendall	.30	.14
132 Chipper Jones	1.50	.70
133 John Franco	.30	.14
134 Sammy Sosa	1.25	.55
135 Chuck Knoblauch	.30	.14
136 Ellis Burks	.30	.14
137 Al Martin	.20	.09
138 Tim Salmon	.30	.14
139 Moises Alou	.30	.14
140 Lance Johnson	.20	.09
141 Justin Thompson	.20	.09
142 Will Clark	.75	.35
143 Barry Bonds	2.00	.90
144 Craig Biggio	.50	.23
145 John Smoltz	.30	.14
146 Cal Ripken	3.00	1.35
147 Ken Griffey Jr.	2.50	1.10
148 Paul O'Neill	.75	.35
149 Todd Helton	1.00	.45
150 John Olerud	.30	.14
151 Mark McGwire	3.00	1.35
152 Jose Cruz Jr.	.30	.14
153 Jeff Cirillo	.30	.14
154 Dean Palmer	.30	.14
155 John Wetteland	.30	.14
156 Eric Karros	.30	.14
157 Steve Finley	.30	.14
158 Albert Belle	.30	.14
159 Curt Schilling	.75	.35
160 Raul Mondesi	.30	.14
161 Andruw Jones	.75	.35
162 Nomar Garciaparra	2.00	.90
163 David Justice	.30	.14
164 Andy Pettitte	.30	.14
165 Pedro Martinez	1.00	.45

1999 Topps Opening Day

	MINT	NRMT
COMPLETE SET (165)	40.00	18.00

Card	MINT	NRMT
1 Hank Aaron	2.50	1.10
2 Roger Clemens	2.00	.90
3 Andres Galarraga UER	.50	.23
Card erroneously numbered 2		

❑ 4 Scott Brosius .30 .14
❑ 5 Ray Durham .30 .14
❑ 6 Will Clark .75 .35
❑ 7 David Wells .30 .14
❑ 8 Jose Guillen .20 .09
❑ 9 Edgardo Alfonzo .30 .14
❑ 10 Manny Ramirez 1.00 .45
❑ 11 Greg Maddux 2.00 .90
❑ 12 David Segui .20 .09
❑ 13 Darryl Strawberry .30 .14
❑ 14 Brad Radke .30 .14
❑ 15 Kerry Wood .75 .35
❑ 16 Paul Konerko .30 .14
❑ 17 Travis Lee .20 .09
❑ 18 Kenny Rogers .20 .09
❑ 19 Todd Walker .20 .09
❑ 20 John Olerud .30 .14
❑ 21 Nolan Ryan 5.00 2.20
❑ 22 Ray Lankford .20 .09
❑ 23 Bartolo Colon .30 .14
❑ 24 Brady Anderson .30 .14
❑ 25 Jorge Posada .30 .14
❑ 26 Justin Thompson .20 .09
❑ 27 Juan Gonzalez .75 .35
❑ 28 Chuck Knoblauch .30 .14
❑ 29 Todd Helton 1.00 .45
❑ 30 Gary Sheffield .30 .14
❑ 31 Rod Beck .20 .09
❑ 32 Garret Anderson .30 .14
❑ 33 Rondell White .30 .14
❑ 34 Vladimir Guerrero 1.00 .45
❑ 35 Eric Karros .30 .14
❑ 36 Mo Vaughn .30 .14
❑ 37 Sammy Sosa 1.50 .70
❑ 38 Kenny Lofton .30 .14
❑ 39 Mark McGwire 3.00 1.35
❑ 40 Javy Lopez .30 .14
❑ 41 Damion Easley .20 .09
❑ 42 Andy Pettitte .30 .14
❑ 43 Tony Gwynn 1.50 .70
❑ 44 Jay Bell .30 .14
❑ 45 Jose Canseco .75 .35
❑ 46 John Wetteland .30 .14
❑ 47 Mike Caruso .20 .09
❑ 48 Derek Jeter 3.00 1.35
❑ 49 Aaron Sele .30 .14
❑ 50 Jeff Cirillo .30 .14
❑ 51 Mark Kotsay .20 .09
❑ 52 Albert Belle .30 .14
❑ 53 Matt Lawton .30 .14
❑ 54 Pedro Martinez 1.00 .45
❑ 55 Greg Vaughn .30 .14
❑ 56 Neifi Perez .20 .09
❑ 57 Derek Bell .20 .09
❑ 58 Ken Griffey Jr. 2.50 1.10
❑ 59 David Cone .30 .14
❑ 60 Dean Palmer .30 .14
❑ 61 Trevor Hoffman .30 .14
❑ 62 Billy Wagner .20 .09
❑ 63 Shawn Green .75 .35
❑ 64 Ben Grieve .30 .14
❑ 65 Tom Goodwin .20 .09
❑ 66 Jaret Wright .20 .09
❑ 67 Dmitri Young .30 .14
❑ 68 Hideki Irabu .20 .09
❑ 69 Jeff Fassero .20 .09
❑ 70 Matt Williams .50 .23
❑ 71 Bret Saberhagen .30 .14
❑ 72 Chad Curtis .20 .09
❑ 73 Scott Rolen .75 .35
❑ 74 J.T. Snow .30 .14
❑ 75 Rusty Greer .30 .14
❑ 76 Jim Edmonds .50 .23
❑ 77 Ron Gant .30 .14
❑ 78 A.J. Hinch .20 .09
❑ 79 Shannon Stewart .30 .14
❑ 80 Brad Fullmer .30 .14
❑ 81 Walt Weiss .20 .09
❑ 82 Fred McGriff .50 .23
❑ 83 Darin Erstad .75 .35
❑ 84 Eric Young .20 .09
❑ 85 Livan Hernandez .20 .09
❑ 86 Jeff Bagwell 1.00 .45
❑ 87 Omar Vizquel .30 .14
❑ 88 Eric Davis .30 .14
❑ 89 Maggio Ordonez .50 .23
❑ 90 John Valentin .20 .09
❑ 91 Dave Dellucci .20 .09
❑ 92 Chan Ho Park .30 .14
❑ 93 Masato Yoshii .30 .14
❑ 94 Bret Boone .30 .14
❑ 95 Mariano Rivera .30 .14
❑ 96 Bobby Jones .20 .09
❑ 97 Francisco Cordova .20 .09
❑ 98 Mike Mussina .75 .35
❑ 99 Denny Neagle .20 .09
❑ 100 Edgar Martinez .50 .23
❑ 101 Jason Kendall .30 .14
❑ 102 Jeff King .20 .09
❑ 103 Rey Ordonez .20 .09
❑ 104 Andruw Jones .75 .35
❑ 105 Vinny Castilla .30 .14
❑ 106 Troy Glaus .75 .35
❑ 107 Tom Glavine .75 .35
❑ 108 Moises Alou .30 .14
❑ 109 Carlos Delgado .75 .35
❑ 110 Raul Mondesi .30 .14
❑ 111 Shane Reynolds .20 .09
❑ 112 Jason Giambi .75 .35
❑ 113 Jose Cruz Jr. .30 .14
❑ 114 Craig Biggio .50 .23
❑ 115 Tim Salmon .30 .14
❑ 116 Chipper Jones 1.50 .70
❑ 117 Andy Benes .20 .09
❑ 118 John Smoltz .30 .14
❑ 119 Jeromy Burnitz .30 .14
❑ 120 Randy Johnson 1.00 .45
❑ 121 Mark Grace .75 .35
❑ 122 Henry Rodriguez .20 .09
❑ 123 Ryan Klesko .30 .14
❑ 124 Kevin Milwood .20 .09
❑ 125 Sean Casey .50 .23
❑ 126 Brian Jordan .30 .14
❑ 127 Kevin Brown .50 .23
❑ 128 Orlando Hernandez .30 .14
❑ 129 Barry Bonds 2.00 .90
❑ 130 David Justice .30 .14
❑ 131 Carlos Perez .20 .09
❑ 132 Andy Ashby .20 .09
❑ 133 Paul O'Neill .75 .35
❑ 134 Curt Schilling .75 .35
❑ 135 Alex Rodriguez 2.00 .90
❑ 136 Cliff Floyd .30 .14
❑ 137 Rafael Palmeiro .75 .35
❑ 138 Nomar Garciaparra 2.00 .90
❑ 139 Mike Piazza 2.00 .90
❑ 140 Roberto Alomar .75 .35
❑ 141 Todd Hundley .20 .09
❑ 142 Jeff Kent .50 .23
❑ 143 Barry Larkin .75 .35
❑ 144 Cal Ripken 3.00 1.35
❑ 145 Jay Buhner .30 .14
❑ 146 Kevin Young .30 .14
❑ 147 Ivan Rodriguez .75 .35
❑ 148 Al Leiter .30 .14
❑ 149 Sandy Alomar Jr. .30 .14
❑ 150 Bernie Williams .75 .35
❑ 151 Ellis Burks .30 .14
❑ 152 Wally Joyner .30 .14
❑ 153 Bobby Higginson .30 .14
❑ 154 Tony Clark .30 .14
❑ 155 Larry Walker .50 .23
❑ 156 Frank Thomas 1.00 .45
❑ 157 Tino Martinez .30 .14
❑ 158 Jim Thome .75 .35
❑ 159 Dante Bichette .30 .14
❑ 160 David Wells HL .20 .09
❑ 161 Roger Clemens HL 1.00 .45
❑ 162 Kerry Wood HL .30 .14
❑ 163 Mark McGwire HR 70 8.00 3.60
❑ 164 Sammy Sosa HR 66 4.00 1.80
❑ 165 Checklist UER .20 .09
124 Devon White, 125 Bobby Bonilla
❑ NNO Hank Aaron AU 250.00 110.00

2000 Topps Opening Day

	MINT	NRMT
COMPLETE SET (165)	50.00	22.00

❑ 1 Mark McGwire 3.00 1.35
❑ 2 Tony Gwynn 1.50 .70
❑ 3 Wade Boggs .75 .35
❑ 4 Cal Ripken 3.00 1.35
❑ 5 Matt Williams .50 .23
❑ 6 Jay Buhner .30 .14
❑ 7 Mike Lieberthal .30 .14
❑ 8 Magglio Ordonez .30 .14
❑ 9 Derek Jeter 3.00 1.35
❑ 10 Javy Lopez .30 .14
❑ 11 Armando Benitez .30 .14
❑ 12 Darin Erstad .75 .35
❑ 13 Mark Grace .75 .35
❑ 14 Eric Karros .30 .14
❑ 15 J.T. Snow .30 .14
❑ 16 Luis Castillo .20 .09
❑ 17 Rey Ordonez .20 .09
❑ 18 Bob Abreu .30 .14
❑ 19 Warren Morris .20 .09
❑ 20 Juan Gonzalez .75 .35
❑ 21 Dean Palmer .30 .14
❑ 22 Hank Aaron 2.00 .90
❑ 23 Jeff Bagwell 1.00 .45
❑ 24 Sammy Sosa 1.50 .70
❑ 25 Randy Johnson 1.00 .45
❑ 26 Dante Bichette .30 .14
❑ 27 Frank Thomas 1.00 .45
❑ 28 Pedro Martinez 1.00 .45
❑ 29 Brain Giles .30 .14
❑ 30 Ivan Rodriguez .75 .35
❑ 31 Roger Cedeno .20 .09
❑ 32 David Justice .30 .14
❑ 33 Ken Caminiti .30 .14
❑ 34 Brian Jordan .30 .14
❑ 35 John Olerud .30 .14
❑ 36 Pokey Reese .20 .09
❑ 37 Barry Larkin .75 .35
❑ 38 Edgar Martinez .50 .23
❑ 39 Carlos Delgado .75 .35
❑ 40 Troy Glaus .75 .35
❑ 41 Ben Grieve .30 .14
❑ 42 Jose Lima .20 .09
❑ 43 Luis Gonzalez .75 .35
❑ 44 Alex Rodriguez 2.00 .90
❑ 45 Preston Wilson .30 .14
❑ 46 Rickey Henderson 1.50 .70
❑ 47 Gary Sheffield .30 .14
❑ 48 Jim Edmonds .50 .23
❑ 49 Greg Vaughn .30 .14
❑ 50 Neifi Perez .20 .09
❑ 51 Paul O'Neill .75 .35
❑ 52 Jermaine Dye .30 .14
❑ 53 Curt Schilling .75 .35
❑ 54 Edgardo Alfonzo .30 .14
❑ 55 John Smoltz .30 .14
❑ 56 Chuck Finley .30 .14
❑ 57 Billy Wagner .20 .09
❑ 58 David Cone .30 .14
❑ 59 Roberto Alomar .75 .35
❑ 60 Charles Nagy .20 .09
❑ 61 Mike Mussina .75 .35
❑ 62 Robin Ventura .50 .23
❑ 63 Kevin Brown .50 .23
❑ 64 Pat Hentgen .20 .09
❑ 65 Ryan Klesko .30 .14
❑ 66 Derek Bell .20 .09
❑ 67 Larry Walker .50 .23

Card	Player	MINT	NRMT
❑ 68	Scott Williamson	.20	.09
❑ 69	Jose Offerman	.20	.09
❑ 70	Doug Mientkiewicz	.50	.23
❑ 71	John Snyder RC	.50	.23
❑ 72	Sandy Alomar Jr.	.20	.09
❑ 73	Joe Nathan	.20	.09
❑ 74	Steve Finley	.30	.14
❑ 75	Dave Martinez	.20	.09
❑ 76	Fernando Tatis	.20	.09
❑ 77	Kenny Lofton	.30	.14
❑ 78	Paul Byrd	.20	.09
❑ 79	Aaron Sele	.30	.14
❑ 80	Roger Clemens	2.00	.90
❑ 81	Francisco Cordova	.20	.09
❑ 82	Wally Joyner	.30	.14
❑ 83	Jason Kendall	.30	.14
❑ 84	Carlos Beltran	.30	.14
❑ 85	Chipper Jones	1.50	.70
❑ 86	Vladimir Guerrero	1.00	.45
❑ 87	Tom Goodwin	.20	.09
❑ 88	Brian Daubach	.30	.14
❑ 89	Jay Bell	.30	.14
❑ 90	Roy Halladay	.20	.09
❑ 91	Miguel Tejada	.30	.14
❑ 92	Eric Davis	.30	.14
❑ 93	Henry Rodriguez	.20	.09
❑ 94	Joe McEwing	.20	.09
❑ 95	Jeff Kent	.50	.23
❑ 96	Jeff Zimmerman	.20	.09
❑ 97	Tony Fernandez	.20	.09
❑ 98	Jason Giambi	.75	.35
❑ 99	Jose Canseco	.75	.35
❑ 100	Alex Gonzalez	.20	.09
❑ 101	Erubiel Durazo	.75	.35
	Pat Burrell		
	Nick Johnson		
❑ 102	Lance Berkman	.75	.35
	Corey Patterson		
	Roosevelt Brown		
❑ 103	Bobby Bradley RC	1.00	.45
	Eric Munson		
❑ 104	Josh Hamilton	1.00	.45
	Corey Myers RC		
❑ 105	Mark McGwire MM	3.00	1.35
	70th HR		
❑ 106	Hank Aaron MM	2.00	.90
	715th HR		
❑ 107	Cal Ripken MM	3.00	1.35
	2131st Game		
❑ 108	Wade Boggs MM	.75	.35
	3000th Hit		
❑ 109	Tony Gwynn MM	1.50	.70
	3000th Hit		
❑ 110	Hank Aaron 1954	4.00	1.80
	UER numbered 128		
❑ 111	Tom Glavine	.75	.35
❑ 112	Mo Vaughn	.30	.14
❑ 113	Tino Martinez	.30	.14
❑ 114	Craig Biggio	.50	.23
❑ 115	Tim Hudson	.75	.35
❑ 116	John Wetteland	.30	.14
❑ 117	Ellis Burks	.30	.14
❑ 118	David Wells	.30	.14
❑ 119	Rico Brogna	.20	.09
❑ 120	Greg Maddux	2.00	.90
❑ 121	Jeromy Burnitz	.30	.14
❑ 122	Raul Mondesi	.30	.14
❑ 123	Rondell White	.30	.14
❑ 124	Barry Bonds	2.00	.90
❑ 125	Orlando Hernandez	.30	.14
❑ 126	Bartolo Colon	.30	.14
❑ 127	Tim Salmon	.30	.14
❑ 128	Kevin Young	.20	.09
❑ 129	Troy O'Leary	.20	.09
❑ 130	Jim Thome	.75	.35
❑ 131	Ray Durham	.30	.14
❑ 132	Tony Clark	.30	.14
❑ 133	Mariano Rivera	.30	.14
❑ 134	Omar Vizquel	.30	.14
❑ 135	Ken Griffey Jr.	2.50	1.10
❑ 136	Shawn Green	.75	.35
❑ 137	Cliff Floyd	.30	.14
❑ 138	Al Leiter	.20	.09
❑ 139	Mike Hampton	.30	.14
❑ 140	Mike Piazza	2.00	.90
❑ 141	Andy Pettitte	.30	.14
❑ 142	Albert Belle	.30	.14
❑ 143	Scott Rolen	.75	.35
❑ 144	Rusty Greer	.30	.14
❑ 145	Kevin Millwood	.20	.09
❑ 146	Sean Casey	.50	.23
❑ 147	Nomar Garciaparra	2.00	.90
❑ 148	Denny Neagle	.20	.09
❑ 149	Manny Ramirez	1.00	.45
❑ 150	Vinny Castilla	.30	.14
❑ 151	Andruw Jones	.75	.35
❑ 152	Johnny Damon	.30	.14
❑ 153	Eric Milton	.30	.14
❑ 154	Todd Helton	1.00	.45
❑ 155	Rafael Palmeiro	.75	.35
❑ 156	Damion Easley	.20	.09
❑ 157	Carlos Febles	.20	.09
❑ 158	Paul Konerko	.30	.14
❑ 159	Bernie Williams	.75	.35
❑ 160	Ken Griffey Jr. MM	2.50	1.10
	HR Dad		
❑ 161	Barry Bonds MM	2.00	.90
	400/400		
❑ 162	Sammy Sosa MM	1.50	.70
	20 HR June		
❑ 163	Derek Jeter MM	3.00	1.35
	96 AL ROY		
❑ 164	Alex Rodriguez MM	2.00	.90
	40/40		
❑ 165	Checklist	.20	.09

2001 Topps Opening Day

		MINT	NRMT
COMPLETE SET (165)		50.00	22.00
❑ 1	Cal Ripken	3.00	1.35
❑ 2	Chipper Jones	1.50	.70
❑ 3	Garret Anderson	.30	.14
❑ 4	Robin Ventura	.30	.14
❑ 5	Jermaine Dye	.30	.14
❑ 6	Jim Thome	.75	.35
❑ 7	Brian Jordan	.30	.14
❑ 8	Shawn Green	.75	.35
❑ 9	Juan Gonzalez	.75	.35
❑ 10	Paul O'Neill	.75	.35
❑ 11	Pokey Reese	.20	.09
❑ 12	Mike Mussina	.75	.35
❑ 13	Jay Buhner	.30	.14
❑ 14	Shane Reynolds	.20	.09
❑ 15	Adam Piatt	.30	.14
❑ 16	Preston Wilson	.30	.14
❑ 17	Ellis Burks	.30	.14
❑ 18	Chuck Finley	.30	.14
❑ 19	Shannon Stewart	.30	.14
❑ 20	Mark McGwire	3.00	1.35
❑ 21	Mark Loretta	.20	.09
❑ 22	Bobby Jones	.20	.09
❑ 23	Matt Clement	.20	.09
❑ 24	Pedro Martinez	1.00	.45
❑ 25	Carlos Lee	.30	.14
❑ 26	John Franco	.30	.14
❑ 27	Andres Galarraga	.50	.23
❑ 28	Jose Cruz Jr.	.30	.14
❑ 29	Randy Johnson	1.00	.45
❑ 30	Richie Sexson	.30	.14
❑ 31	Darin Erstad	.75	.35
❑ 32	Manny Ramirez	1.00	.45
❑ 33	Mike Sweeney	.30	.14
❑ 34	John Wetteland	.30	.14
❑ 35	Derek Jeter	3.00	1.35
❑ 36	J.D. Drew	.75	.35
❑ 37	Rick Reed	.20	.09
❑ 38	Jay Bell	.30	.14
❑ 39	Fred McGriff	.50	.23
❑ 40	Orlando Cabrera	.20	.09
❑ 41	Eric Owens	.20	.09
❑ 42	Jorge Posada	.30	.14
❑ 43	Jeff Cirillo	.30	.14
❑ 44	Johnny Damon	.30	.14
❑ 45	Charles Johnson	.20	.09
❑ 46	Pat Burrell	.30	.14
❑ 47	Gary Sheffield	.30	.14
❑ 48	Tom Glavine	.75	.35
❑ 49	Ivan Rodriguez	.75	.35
❑ 50	Chuck Knoblauch	.30	.14
❑ 51	Jason Kendall	.30	.14
❑ 52	Carlos Delgado	.75	.35
❑ 53	Roger Clemens	2.00	.90
❑ 54	Brad Penny	.30	.14
❑ 55	Troy Glaus	.75	.35
❑ 56	Mike Hampton	.30	.14
❑ 57	Carlos Febles	.20	.09
❑ 58	Seth Etherton	.20	.09
❑ 59	Fernando Tatis	.20	.09
❑ 60	Livan Hernandez	.20	.09
❑ 61	Barry Larkin	.75	.35
❑ 62	Alex Rodriguez	2.00	.90
❑ 63	Warren Morris	.20	.09
❑ 64	Antonio Alfonseca	.30	.14
❑ 65	Edgardo Alfonzo	.30	.14
❑ 66	Fernando Vina	.20	.09
❑ 67	Jason Giambi	.75	.35
❑ 68	Matt Lawton	.30	.14
❑ 69	Rusty Greer	.30	.14
❑ 70	Tony Gwynn	1.50	.70
❑ 71	Carl Everett	.30	.14
❑ 72	Bret Boone	.30	.14
❑ 73	James Baldwin	.20	.09
❑ 74	Greg Vaughn	.30	.14
❑ 75	Darren Dreifort	.20	.09
❑ 76	Frank Thomas	1.00	.45
❑ 77	Luis Castillo	.20	.09
❑ 78	Bartolo Colon	.30	.14
❑ 79	Craig Biggio	.50	.23
❑ 80	Jose Vidro	.30	.14
❑ 81	Todd Helton	1.00	.45
❑ 82	Jacque Jones	.30	.14
❑ 83	Robb Nen	.20	.09
❑ 84	Richard Hidalgo	.30	.14
❑ 85	Tony Womack	.20	.09
❑ 86	Rick Ankiel	.50	.23
❑ 87	Terrence Long	.30	.14
❑ 88	Brad Radke	.30	.14
❑ 89	Gabe Kapler	.30	.14
❑ 90	Pedro Astacio	.20	.09
❑ 91	Darryl Kile	.30	.14
❑ 92	Jay Payton	.20	.09
❑ 93	Vladimir Guerrero	1.00	.45
❑ 94	Juan Encarnacion	.30	.14
❑ 95	Ramon Hernandez	.20	.09
❑ 96	Sandy Alomar Jr.	.30	.14
❑ 97	Geoff Jenkins	.30	.14
❑ 98	Rafael Furcal	.30	.14
❑ 99	Mark Grace	.75	.35
❑ 100	Mark Mulder	.50	.23
❑ 101	Jim Edmonds	.50	.23
❑ 102	Tim Salmon	.30	.14
❑ 103	Jeff Bagwell	1.00	.45
❑ 104	Jose Canseco	.75	.35
❑ 105	Ben Grieve	.30	.14
❑ 106	Ryan Klesko	.30	.14
❑ 107	Javy Lopez	.30	.14
❑ 108	Greg Maddux	2.00	.90
❑ 109	Andruw Jones	.75	.35
❑ 110	Jeromy Burnitz	.30	.14
❑ 111	Ray Lankford	.20	.09
❑ 112	Sammy Sosa	1.50	.70
❑ 113	Raul Mondesi	.30	.14
❑ 114	Mike Piazza	2.00	.90
❑ 115	Todd Zeile	.30	.14
❑ 116	Eric Karros	.30	.14
❑ 117	Barry Bonds	2.00	.90
❑ 118	J.T. Snow	.30	.14

❑ 119 Jeff Kent .50 .23
❑ 120 David Justice .50 .23
❑ 121 Matt Williams .50 .23
❑ 122 Brian Giles .30 .14
❑ 123 Edgar Martinez .50 .23
❑ 124 Ken Griffey Jr. 2.50 1.10
❑ 125 Al Leiter .30 .14
❑ 126 Kevin Brown .30 .14
❑ 127 John Olerud .30 .14
❑ 128 Roberto Alomar .75 .35
❑ 129 Rafael Palmeiro .75 .35
❑ 130 Steve Finley .30 .14
❑ 131 Tim Hudson .75 .35
❑ 132 Scott Rolen .75 .35
❑ 133 Nomar Garciaparra 2.00 .90
❑ 134 Mo Vaughn .30 .14
❑ 135 Larry Walker .50 .23
❑ 136 Albert Belle .30 .14
❑ 137 Ray Durham .30 .14
❑ 138 Andy Pettitte .30 .14
❑ 139 Mariano Rivera .30 .14
❑ 140 Bernie Williams .75 .35
❑ 141 David Wells .30 .14
❑ 142 Magglio Ordonez .30 .14
❑ 143 Kevin Millwood .20 .09
❑ 144 Cliff Floyd .30 .14
❑ 145 Rich Aurilia .30 .14
❑ 146 Miguel Tejada .30 .14
❑ 147 Scott Elarton .20 .09
❑ 148 Tony Armas Jr. .30 .14
❑ 149 Mark Redman .20 .09
❑ 150 Javier Vazquez .30 .14
❑ 151 Adrian Gonzalez 1.25 .55
Adam Johnson
❑ 152 Mike Stodolka .30 .14
Sean Burnett
❑ 153 David Walling .50 .23
Ben Sheets
Scott Sobkowiak
❑ 154 Chin-Feng Chen .75 .35
Corey Patterson
Josh Hamilton
❑ 155 Mark McGwire GM 1.50 .70
❑ 156 Bobby Thomson GM .30 .14
❑ 157 Bill Mazeroski GM .30 .14
❑ 158 Cal Ripken GM 1.50 .70
❑ 159 Hank Aaron GM 1.00 .45
❑ 160 Bucky Dent GM .30 .14
❑ 161 Jackie Robinson GM 1.00 .45
❑ 162 Roberto Clemente GM 1.25 .55
❑ 163 Nolan Ryan GM 2.00 .90
❑ 164 Kerry Wood GM .30 .14
❑ 165 Checklist .20 .09

2001 Topps Reserve

	MINT	NRMT
COMP.SET w/o SP's (100)	100.00	45.00
COMMON CARD (1-100)	.75	.35
COMMON (101-151)	10.00	4.50

❑ 1 Darin Erstad 2.00 .90
❑ 2 Moises Alou .75 .35
❑ 3 Tony Batista .75 .35
❑ 4 Andruw Jones 2.00 .90
❑ 5 Edgar Renteria .75 .35
❑ 6 Eric Young .75 .35
❑ 7 Steve Finley .75 .35
❑ 8 Adrian Beltre .75 .35
❑ 9 Vladimir Guerrero 2.50 1.10
❑ 10 Barry Bonds 5.00 2.20
❑ 11 Juan Gonzalez 2.00 .90
❑ 12 Jay Buhner .75 .35
❑ 13 Luis Castillo .75 .35
❑ 14 Cal Ripken 8.00 3.60
❑ 15 Bob Abreu .75 .35
❑ 16 Ivan Rodriguez 2.00 .90
❑ 17 Nomar Garciaparra 5.00 2.20
❑ 18 Todd Helton 2.50 1.10
❑ 19 Bobby Higginson .75 .35
❑ 20 Jorge Posada .75 .35
❑ 21 Tim Salmon .75 .35
❑ 22 Jason Giambi 2.00 .90
❑ 23 Jose Cruz Jr. .75 .35
❑ 24 Chipper Jones 4.00 1.80
❑ 25 Jim Edmonds 1.25 .55
❑ 26 Gerald Williams .75 .35
❑ 27 Randy Johnson 2.50 1.10
❑ 28 Gary Sheffield .75 .35
❑ 29 Jeff Kent 1.25 .55
❑ 30 Jim Thome 2.00 .90
❑ 31 John Olerud .75 .35
❑ 32 Cliff Floyd .75 .35
❑ 33 Mike Lowell .75 .35
❑ 34 Phil Nevin .75 .35
❑ 35 Scott Rolen 2.00 .90
❑ 36 Alex Rodriguez 5.00 2.20
❑ 37 Ken Griffey Jr. 6.00 2.70
❑ 38 Neifi Perez .75 .35
❑ 39 Cristian Guzman .75 .35
❑ 40 Mariano Rivera .75 .35
❑ 41 Troy Glaus 2.00 .90
❑ 42 Johnny Damon .75 .35
❑ 43 Rafael Furcal .75 .35
❑ 44 Jeromy Burnitz .75 .35
❑ 45 Mark McGwire 8.00 3.60
❑ 46 Fred McGriff 1.25 .55
❑ 47 Matt Williams 1.25 .55
❑ 48 Kevin Brown .75 .35
❑ 49 J.T. Snow .75 .35
❑ 50 Kenny Lofton .75 .35
❑ 51 Al Martin .75 .35
❑ 52 Antonio Alfonseca .75 .35
❑ 53 Edgardo Alfonzo .75 .35
❑ 54 Ryan Klesko .75 .35
❑ 55 Pat Burrell .75 .35
❑ 56 Rafael Palmeiro 2.00 .90
❑ 57 Sean Casey 1.25 .55
❑ 58 Jeff Cirillo .75 .35
❑ 59 Ray Durham .75 .35
❑ 60 Derek Jeter 8.00 3.60
❑ 61 Jeff Bagwell 2.50 1.10
❑ 62 Carlos Delgado 2.00 .90
❑ 63 Tom Glavine 2.00 .90
❑ 64 Richie Sexson .75 .35
❑ 65 J.D. Drew 2.00 .90
❑ 66 Ben Grieve .75 .35
❑ 67 Mark Grace 2.00 .90
❑ 68 Shawn Green 2.00 .90
❑ 69 Robb Nen .75 .35
❑ 70 Omar Vizquel .75 .35
❑ 71 Edgar Martinez 1.25 .55
❑ 72 Preston Wilson .75 .35
❑ 73 Mike Piazza 5.00 2.20
❑ 74 Tony Gwynn 4.00 1.80
❑ 75 Jason Kendall .75 .35
❑ 76 Manny Ramirez 2.50 1.10
❑ 77 Pokey Reese .75 .35
❑ 78 Mike Sweeney .75 .35
❑ 79 Magglio Ordonez .75 .35
❑ 80 Bernie Williams 2.00 .90
❑ 81 Richard Hidalgo .75 .35
❑ 82 Brad Fullmer .75 .35
❑ 83 Greg Maddux 5.00 2.20
❑ 84 Geoff Jenkins .75 .35
❑ 85 Sammy Sosa 4.00 1.80
❑ 86 Luis Gonzalez 2.00 .90
❑ 87 Eric Karros .75 .35
❑ 88 Jose Vidro .75 .35
❑ 89 Rich Aurilia .75 .35
❑ 90 Roberto Alomar 2.00 .90
❑ 91 Mike Cameron .75 .35
❑ 92 Mike Mussina 2.00 .90
❑ 93 Barry Zito 2.00 .90
❑ 94 Mike Lieberthal .75 .35
❑ 95 Brian Giles .75 .35
❑ 96 Pedro Martinez 2.50 1.10
❑ 97 Barry Larkin 2.00 .90
❑ 98 Jermaine Dye .75 .35
❑ 99 Frank Thomas 2.50 1.10
❑ 100 David Justice 1.25 .55
❑ 101 Gary Johnson RC 10.00 4.50
❑ 102 Matt Ford RC 10.00 4.50
❑ 103 Albert Pujols RC 60.00 27.00
❑ 104 Brad Cresse 12.00 5.50
❑ 105 Valentino Pascucci RC 10.00 4.50
❑ 106 Bob Keppel RC 12.00 5.50
❑ 107 Luis Torres RC 10.00 4.50
❑ 108 Tony Blanco RC 15.00 6.75
❑ 109 Ronnie Corona RC 10.00 4.50
❑ 110 Phil Wilson RC 10.00 4.50
❑ 111 John Buck RC 12.00 5.50
❑ 112 Jim Journell RC 12.00 5.50
❑ 113 Victor Hall RC 10.00 4.50
❑ 114 Jeff Andra RC 10.00 4.50
❑ 115 Greg Nash RC 20.00 9.00
❑ 116 Travis Hafner RC 12.00 5.50
❑ 117 Casey Fossum RC 15.00 6.75
❑ 118 Miguel Olivo 10.00 4.50
❑ 119 Elpidio Guzman RC 10.00 4.50
❑ 120 Jason Belcher RC 12.00 5.50
❑ 121 Esix Snead RC 10.00 4.50
❑ 122 Joe Thurston RC 10.00 4.50
❑ 123 Rafael Soriano RC 12.00 5.50
❑ 124 Ed Rogers RC 10.00 4.50
❑ 125 Omar Beltre RC 10.00 4.50
❑ 126 Brett Gray RC 10.00 4.50
❑ 127 Deivi Mendez RC 12.00 5.50
❑ 128 Freddie Bynum RC 12.00 5.50
❑ 129 David Krynzel 10.00 4.50
❑ 130 Blake Williams RC 10.00 4.50
❑ 131 Reggie Abercrombie RC 10.00 4.50
❑ 132 Miguel Villilo RC 10.00 4.50
❑ 133 Ryan Madson RC 10.00 4.50
❑ 134 Matt Thompson RC 10.00 4.50
❑ 135 Mark Burnett RC 10.00 4.50
❑ 136 Andy Beal RC 10.00 4.50
❑ 137 Ryan Ludwick RC 15.00 6.75
❑ 138 Roberto Miniel RC 10.00 4.50
❑ 139 Steve Smyth RC 10.00 4.50
❑ 140 Ben Washburn RC 10.00 4.50
❑ 141 Marvin Seale RC 10.00 4.50
❑ 142 Reggie Griggs RC 10.00 4.50
❑ 143 Seung Song RC 15.00 6.75
❑ 144 Chad Petty RC 12.00 5.50
❑ 145 Noel Devarez RC 10.00 4.50
❑ 146 Matt Butler RC 10.00 4.50
❑ 147 Brett Evert RC 12.00 5.50
❑ 148 Cesar Izturis 10.00 4.50
❑ 149 Troy Farnsworth RC 10.00 4.50
❑ 150 Brian Schmitt RC 10.00 4.50
❑ 151 Ichiro Suzuki RC 100.00 45.00

1997 Topps Stars

	MINT	NRMT
COMPLETE SET (125)	50.00	22.00

❑ 1 Larry Walker .40 .18
❑ 2 Tino Martinez .25 .11
❑ 3 Cal Ripken 2.50 1.10
❑ 4 Ken Griffey Jr. 2.00 .90

❑ 5 Chipper Jones .... 1.25 .55
❑ 6 David Justice .... .25 .11
❑ 7 Mike Piazza .... 1.50 .70
❑ 8 Jeff Bagwell .... .75 .35
❑ 9 Ron Gant .... .15 .07
❑ 10 Sammy Sosa .... 1.25 .55
❑ 11 Tony Gwynn .... 1.25 .55
❑ 12 Carlos Baerga .... .15 .07
❑ 13 Frank Thomas .... .75 .35
❑ 14 Moises Alou .... .25 .11
❑ 15 Barry Larkin .... .60 .25
❑ 16 Ivan Rodriguez .... .60 .25
❑ 17 Greg Maddux .... 1.50 .70
❑ 18 Jim Edmonds .... .40 .18
❑ 19 Jose Canseco .... .60 .25
❑ 20 Rafael Palmeiro .... .60 .25
❑ 21 Paul Molitor .... .60 .25
❑ 22 Kevin Appier .... .25 .11
❑ 23 Raul Mondesi .... .25 .11
❑ 24 Lance Johnson .... .15 .07
❑ 25 Edgar Martinez .... .40 .18
❑ 26 Andres Galarraga .... .40 .18
❑ 27 Mo Vaughn .... .25 .11
❑ 28 Ken Caminiti .... .25 .11
❑ 29 Cecil Fielder .... .25 .11
❑ 30 Harold Baines .... .25 .11
❑ 31 Roberto Alomar .... .60 .25
❑ 32 Shawn Estes .... .25 .11
❑ 33 Tom Glavine .... .60 .25
❑ 34 Dennis Eckersley .... .25 .11
❑ 35 Manny Ramirez .... .75 .35
❑ 36 John Olerud .... .25 .11
❑ 37 Juan Gonzalez .... .60 .25
❑ 38 Chuck Knoblauch .... .25 .11
❑ 39 Albert Belle .... .25 .11
❑ 40 Vinny Castilla .... .25 .11
❑ 41 John Smoltz .... .25 .11
❑ 42 Barry Bonds .... 1.50 .70
❑ 43 Randy Johnson .... .75 .35
❑ 44 Brady Anderson .... .25 .11
❑ 45 Jeff Blauser .... .15 .07
❑ 46 Craig Biggio .... .40 .18
❑ 47 Jeff Conine .... .15 .07
❑ 48 Marquis Grissom .... .15 .07
❑ 49 Mark Grace .... .60 .25
❑ 50 Roger Clemens .... 1.50 .70
❑ 51 Mark McGwire 2.50 1.10
❑ 52 Fred McGriff .... .40 .18
❑ 53 Gary Sheffield .... .25 .11
❑ 54 Bobby Jones .... .15 .07
❑ 55 Eric Young .... .15 .07
❑ 56 Robin Ventura .... .25 .11
❑ 57 Wade Boggs .... .60 .25
❑ 58 Joe Carter .... .25 .11
❑ 59 Ryne Sandberg .... .75 .35
❑ 60 Matt Williams .... .40 .18
❑ 61 Todd Hundley .... .15 .07
❑ 62 Dante Bichette .... .25 .11
❑ 63 Chili Davis .... .25 .11
❑ 64 Kenny Lofton .... .25 .11
❑ 65 Jay Buhner .... .25 .11
❑ 66 Will Clark .... .60 .25
❑ 67 Travis Fryman .... .25 .11
❑ 68 Pat Hentgen .... .15 .07
❑ 69 Ellis Burks .... .25 .11
❑ 70 Mike Mussina .... .60 .25
❑ 71 Hideo Nomo .... .60 .25
❑ 72 Sandy Alomar Jr. .... .25 .11
❑ 73 Bobby Bonilla .... .25 .11
❑ 74 Rickey Henderson .... 1.25 .55
❑ 75 David Cone .... .25 .11
❑ 76 Terry Steinbach .... .15 .07
❑ 77 Pedro Martinez .... .75 .35
❑ 78 Jim Thome .... .60 .25
❑ 79 Rod Beck .... .15 .07
❑ 80 Randy Myers .... .15 .07
❑ 81 Charles Nagy .... .15 .07
❑ 82 Mark Wohlers .... .15 .07
❑ 83 Paul O'Neill .... .60 .25
❑ 84 Curt Schilling .... .60 .25
❑ 85 Joey Cora .... .15 .07
❑ 86 John Franco .... .25 .11
❑ 87 Kevin Brown .... .25 .11
❑ 88 Benito Santiago .... .15 .07
❑ 89 Ray Lankford .... .15 .07
❑ 90 Bernie Williams .... .60 .25
❑ 91 Jason Dickson .... .15 .07
❑ 92 Jeff Cirillo .... .25 .11
❑ 93 Nomar Garciaparra .... 1.50 .70
❑ 94 Mariano Rivera .... .25 .11
❑ 95 Javy Lopez .... .25 .11
❑ 96 Tony Womack RC .... 1.25 .55
❑ 97 Jose Rosado .... .15 .07
❑ 98 Denny Neagle .... .25 .11
❑ 99 Darryl Kile .... .25 .11
❑ 100 Justin Thompson .... .15 .07
❑ 101 Juan Encarnacion .... .25 .11
❑ 102 Brad Fullmer .... .25 .11
❑ 103 Kris Benson RC 2.50 1.10
❑ 104 Todd Helton .... 1.00 .45
❑ 105 Paul Konerko .... .25 .11
❑ 106 Travis Lee RC 2.50 1.10
❑ 107 Todd Greene .... .15 .07
❑ 108 Mark Kotsay RC .... 1.50 .70
❑ 109 Carl Pavano .... .15 .07
❑ 110 Kerry Wood RC 8.00 3.60
❑ 111 Jason Romano RC .... 1.00 .45
❑ 112 Geoff Goetz RC .... .60 .25
❑ 113 Scott Hodges RC .... 1.00 .45
❑ 114 Aaron Akin RC .... .25 .11
❑ 115 Vernon Wells RC 4.00 1.80
❑ 116 Chris Stowe RC .... .15 .07
❑ 117 Brett Caradonna RC .... .60 .25
❑ 118 Adam Kennedy RC .... 1.50 .70
❑ 119 Jayson Werth RC .... .60 .25
❑ 120 Glenn Davis RC .... .15 .07
❑ 121 Troy Cameron RC .... .75 .35
❑ 122 J.J. Davis RC .... 1.50 .70
❑ 123 Jason Dellaero RC .... .25 .11
❑ 124 Jason Standridge RC .. 1.00 .45
❑ 125 Lance Berkman RC 20.00 9.00
❑ NNO Checklist .... .15 .07

1998 Topps Stars

	MINT	NRMT
COMP.RED SET (150)	80.00	36.00

❑ 1 Greg Maddux 4.00 1.80
❑ 2 Darryl Kile .... .60 .25
❑ 3 Rod Beck .... .40 .18
❑ 4 Ellis Burks .... .60 .25
❑ 5 Gary Sheffield .... .60 .25
❑ 6 David Ortiz .... .60 .25
❑ 7 Marquis Grissom .... .40 .18
❑ 8 Tony Womack .... .40 .18
❑ 9 Mike Mussina .... 1.50 .70
❑ 10 Bernie Williams .... 1.50 .70
❑ 11 Andy Benes .... .40 .18
❑ 12 Rusty Greer .... .60 .25
❑ 13 Carlos Delgado .... 1.50 .70
❑ 14 Jim Edmonds .... 1.00 .45
❑ 15 Raul Mondesi .... .60 .25
❑ 16 Andres Galarraga .... 1.00 .45
❑ 17 Wade Boggs .... 1.50 .70
❑ 18 Paul O'Neill .... 1.50 .70
❑ 19 Edgar Renteria .... .40 .18
❑ 20 Tony Clark .... .60 .25
❑ 21 Vladimir Guerrero .... 2.00 .90
❑ 22 Moises Alou .... .60 .25
❑ 23 Bernard Gilkey .... .40 .18
❑ 24 Lance Johnson .... .40 .18
❑ 25 Ben Grieve .... .60 .25
❑ 26 Sandy Alomar Jr. .... .60 .25
❑ 27 Ray Durham .... .60 .25
❑ 28 Shawn Estes .... .60 .25
❑ 29 David Segui .... .40 .18
❑ 30 Javy Lopez .... .60 .25
❑ 31 Steve Finley .... .60 .25
❑ 32 Rey Ordonez .... .40 .18
❑ 33 Derek Jeter 6.00 2.70
❑ 34 Henry Rodriguez .... .40 .18
❑ 35 Mo Vaughn .... .60 .25
❑ 36 Richard Hidalgo .... .60 .25
❑ 37 Omar Vizquel .... .60 .25
❑ 38 Johnny Damon .... .60 .25
❑ 39 Brian Hunter .... .40 .18
❑ 40 Matt Williams .... 1.00 .45
❑ 41 Chuck Finley .... .60 .25
❑ 42 Jeromy Burnitz .... .60 .25
❑ 43 Livan Hernandez .... .40 .18
❑ 44 Delino DeShields .... .40 .18
❑ 45 Charles Nagy .... .40 .18
❑ 46 Scott Rolen .... 1.50 .70
❑ 47 Neifi Perez .... .40 .18
❑ 48 John Wetteland .... .60 .25
❑ 49 Eric Milton .... .60 .25
❑ 50 Mike Piazza 4.00 1.80
❑ 51 Cal Ripken 6.00 2.70
❑ 52 Mariano Rivera .... .60 .25
❑ 53 Butch Huskey .... .40 .18
❑ 54 Quinton McCracken .... .40 .18
❑ 55 Jose Cruz Jr. .... .60 .25
❑ 56 Brian Jordan .... .60 .25
❑ 57 Hideo Nomo .... 1.50 .70
❑ 58 Masato Yoshii RC .... 1.25 .55
❑ 59 Cliff Floyd .... .60 .25
❑ 60 Jose Guillen .... .40 .18
❑ 61 Jeff Shaw .... .40 .18
❑ 62 Edgar Martinez .... 1.00 .45
❑ 63 Rondell White .... .60 .25
❑ 64 Hal Morris .... .40 .18
❑ 65 Barry Larkin .... 1.50 .70
❑ 66 Eric Young .... .40 .18
❑ 67 Ray Lankford .... .40 .18
❑ 68 Derek Bell .... .40 .18
❑ 69 Charles Johnson .... .60 .25
❑ 70 Robin Ventura .... .60 .25
❑ 71 Chuck Knoblauch .... .60 .25
❑ 72 Kevin Brown .... 1.00 .45
❑ 73 Jose Valentin .... .40 .18
❑ 74 Jay Buhner .... .60 .25
❑ 75 Tony Gwynn 3.00 1.35
❑ 76 Andy Pettitte .... .60 .25
❑ 77 Edgardo Alfonzo .... .60 .25
❑ 78 Kerry Wood .... 1.50 .70
❑ 79 Darin Erstad .... 1.50 .70
❑ 80 Paul Konerko .... .60 .25
❑ 81 Jason Kendall .... .60 .25
❑ 82 Tino Martinez .... .60 .25
❑ 83 Brad Radke .... .60 .25
❑ 84 Jeff King .... .40 .18
❑ 85 Travis Lee .... .60 .25
❑ 86 Jeff Kent .... 1.00 .45
❑ 87 Trevor Hoffman .... .60 .25
❑ 88 David Cone .... .60 .25
❑ 89 Jose Canseco .... 1.50 .70
❑ 90 Juan Gonzalez .... 1.50 .70
❑ 91 Todd Hundley .... .40 .18
❑ 92 John Valentin .... .40 .18
❑ 93 Sammy Sosa 3.00 1.35
❑ 94 Jason Giambi .... 1.50 .70
❑ 95 Chipper Jones 3.00 1.35
❑ 96 Jeff Blauser .... .40 .18
❑ 97 Brad Fullmer .... .60 .25
❑ 98 Derrek Lee .... .60 .25
❑ 99 Denny Neagle .... .40 .18
❑ 100 Ken Griffey Jr. 5.00 2.20
❑ 101 David Justice .... .60 .25
❑ 102 Tim Salmon .... .60 .25
❑ 103 J.T. Snow .... .60 .25
❑ 104 Fred McGriff .... 1.00 .45
❑ 105 Brady Anderson .... .60 .25
❑ 106 Larry Walker .... 1.00 .45
❑ 107 Jeff Cirillo .... .60 .25
❑ 108 Andruw Jones .... 1.50 .70
❑ 109 Manny Ramirez .... 2.00 .90
❑ 110 Justin Thompson .... .40 .18
❑ 111 Vinny Castilla .... .60 .25
❑ 112 Chan Ho Park .... .60 .25

❑ 113	Mark Grudzielanek	.40	.18
❑ 114	Mark Grace	1.50	.70
❑ 115	Ken Caminiti	.60	.25
❑ 116	Ryan Klesko	.60	.25
❑ 117	Rafael Palmeiro	1.50	.70
❑ 118	Pat Hentgen	.40	.18
❑ 119	Eric Karros	.60	.25
❑ 120	Randy Johnson	2.00	.90
❑ 121	Roberto Alomar	1.50	.70
❑ 122	John Olerud	.60	.25
❑ 123	Paul Molitor	1.50	.70
❑ 124	Dean Palmer	.60	.25
❑ 125	Nomar Garciaparra	4.00	1.80
❑ 126	Curt Schilling	1.50	.70
❑ 127	Jay Bell	.60	.25
❑ 128	Craig Biggio	1.00	.45
❑ 129	Marty Cordova	.40	.18
❑ 130	Ivan Rodriguez	1.50	.70
❑ 131	Todd Helton	2.00	.90
❑ 132	Jim Thome	1.50	.70
❑ 133	Albert Belle	.60	.25
❑ 134	Mike Lansing	.40	.18
❑ 135	Mark McGwire	6.00	2.70
❑ 136	Roger Clemens	4.00	1.80
❑ 137	Tom Glavine	1.50	.70
❑ 138	Ron Gant	.60	.25
❑ 139	Alex Rodriguez	4.00	1.80
❑ 140	Jeff Bagwell	2.00	.90
❑ 141	John Smoltz	.60	.25
❑ 142	Kenny Lofton	.60	.25
❑ 143	Dante Bichette	.60	.25
❑ 144	Pedro Martinez	2.00	.90
❑ 145	Barry Bonds	4.00	1.80
❑ 146	Travis Fryman	.60	.25
❑ 147	Bobby Jones	.40	.18
❑ 148	Bobby Higginson	.60	.25
❑ 149	Reggie Sanders	.40	.18
❑ 150	Frank Thomas	2.00	.90

1999 Topps Stars

		MINT	NRMT
COMPLETE SET (180)		80.00	36.00
❑ 1	Ken Griffey Jr.	4.00	1.80
❑ 2	Chipper Jones	2.50	1.10
❑ 3	Mike Piazza	3.00	1.35
❑ 4	Nomar Garciaparra	3.00	1.35
❑ 5	Derek Jeter	5.00	2.20
❑ 6	Frank Thomas	1.50	.70
❑ 7	Ben Grieve	.50	.23
❑ 8	Mark McGwire	5.00	2.20
❑ 9	Sammy Sosa	2.50	1.10
❑ 10	Alex Rodriguez	3.00	1.35
❑ 11	Troy Glaus	1.25	.55
❑ 12	Eric Chavez	.50	.23
❑ 13	Kerry Wood	1.25	.55
❑ 14	Barry Bonds	3.00	1.35
❑ 15	Vladimir Guerrero	1.50	.70
❑ 16	Albert Belle	.50	.23
❑ 17	Juan Gonzalez	1.25	.55
❑ 18	Roger Clemens	3.00	1.35
❑ 19	Ruben Mateo	.50	.23
❑ 20	Cal Ripken	5.00	2.20
❑ 21	Darin Erstad	1.25	.55
❑ 22	Jeff Bagwell	1.50	.70
❑ 23	Roy Halladay	.30	.14
❑ 24	Todd Helton	1.50	.70
❑ 25	Michael Barrett	.30	.14
❑ 26	Manny Ramirez	1.50	.70
❑ 27	Fernando Seguignol	.30	.14
❑ 28	Pat Burrell RC	2.50	1.10
❑ 29	Andruw Jones	1.25	.55
❑ 30	Randy Johnson	1.50	.70
❑ 31	Jose Canseco	1.25	.55
❑ 32	Brad Fullmer	.50	.23
❑ 33	Alex Escobar RC	2.00	.90
❑ 34	Alfonso Soriano RC	4.00	1.80
❑ 35	Larry Walker	.75	.35
❑ 36	Matt Clement	.30	.14
❑ 37	Mo Vaughn	.50	.23
❑ 38	Bruce Chen	.30	.14
❑ 39	Travis Lee	.30	.14
❑ 40	Adrian Beltre	.50	.23
❑ 41	Alex Gonzalez	.30	.14
❑ 42	Jason Tyner RC	1.25	.55
❑ 43	George Lombard	.30	.14
❑ 44	Scott Rolen	1.25	.55
❑ 45	Mark Mulder RC	3.00	1.35
❑ 46	Gabe Kapler	.50	.23
❑ 47	Choo Freeman RC	.60	.25
❑ 48	Tony Gwynn	2.50	1.10
❑ 49	A.J. Burnett RC	1.25	.55
❑ 50	Matt Belisle RC	.60	.25
❑ 51	Greg Maddux	3.00	1.35
❑ 52	John Smoltz	.50	.23
❑ 53	Mark Grace	1.25	.55
❑ 54	Wade Boggs	1.25	.55
❑ 55	Bernie Williams	1.25	.55
❑ 56	Pedro Martinez	1.50	.70
❑ 57	Barry Larkin	1.25	.55
❑ 58	Orlando Hernandez	.50	.23
❑ 59	Jason Kendall	.50	.23
❑ 60	Mark Kotsay	.30	.14
❑ 61	Jim Thome	1.25	.55
❑ 62	Gary Sheffield	.50	.23
❑ 63	Preston Wilson	.50	.23
❑ 64	Rafael Palmeiro	1.25	.55
❑ 65	David Wells	.50	.23
❑ 66	Shawn Green	1.25	.55
❑ 67	Tom Glavine	1.25	.55
❑ 68	Jeromy Burnitz	.50	.23
❑ 69	Kevin Brown	.75	.35
❑ 70	Rondell White	.50	.23
❑ 71	Roberto Alomar	1.25	.55
❑ 72	Cliff Floyd	.50	.23
❑ 73	Craig Biggio	.75	.35
❑ 74	Greg Vaughn	.50	.23
❑ 75	Ivan Rodriguez	1.25	.55
❑ 76	Vinny Castilla	.50	.23
❑ 77	Todd Walker	.30	.14
❑ 78	Paul Konerko	.50	.23
❑ 79	Andy Brown RC	.60	.25
❑ 80	Todd Hundley	.30	.14
❑ 81	Dmitri Young	.50	.23
❑ 82	Tony Clark	.50	.23
❑ 83	Nick Johnson RC	2.50	1.10
❑ 84	Mike Caruso	.30	.14
❑ 85	David Ortiz	.50	.23
❑ 86	Matt Williams	.75	.35
❑ 87	Raul Mondesi	.50	.23
❑ 88	Kenny Lofton	.50	.23
❑ 89	Miguel Tejada	.50	.23
❑ 90	Dante Bichette	.50	.23
❑ 91	Jorge Posada	.50	.23
❑ 92	Carlos Beltran	.50	.23
❑ 93	Carlos Delgado	1.25	.55
❑ 94	Javy Lopez	.50	.23
❑ 95	Aramis Ramirez	.50	.23
❑ 96	Neifi Perez	.30	.14
❑ 97	Marlon Anderson	.30	.14
❑ 98	David Cone	.50	.23
❑ 99	Moises Alou	.50	.23
❑ 100	John Olerud	.50	.23
❑ 101	Tim Salmon	.50	.23
❑ 102	Jason Giambi	1.25	.55
❑ 103	Sandy Alomar Jr.	.50	.23
❑ 104	Curt Schilling	1.25	.55
❑ 105	Andres Galarraga	.75	.35
❑ 106	Rusty Greer	.50	.23
❑ 107	Bobby Seay RC	.50	.23
❑ 108	Eric Young	.30	.14
❑ 109	Brian Jordan	.50	.23
❑ 110	Eric Davis	.50	.23
❑ 111	Will Clark	1.25	.55
❑ 112	Andy Ashby	.30	.14
❑ 113	Edgardo Alfonzo	.50	.23
❑ 114	Paul O'Neill	1.25	.55
❑ 115	Denny Neagle	.30	.14
❑ 116	Eric Karros	.50	.23
❑ 117	Ken Caminiti	.50	.23
❑ 118	Garret Anderson	.50	.23
❑ 119	Todd Stottlemyre	.30	.14
❑ 120	David Justice	.50	.23
❑ 121	Francisco Cordova	.30	.14
❑ 122	Robin Ventura	.50	.23
❑ 123	Mike Mussina	1.25	.55
❑ 124	Hideki Irabu	.30	.14
❑ 125	Justin Thompson	.30	.14
❑ 126	Mariano Rivera	.50	.23
❑ 127	Delino DeShields	.30	.14
❑ 128	Steve Finley	.50	.23
❑ 129	Jose Cruz Jr.	.50	.23
❑ 130	Ray Lankford	.30	.14
❑ 131	Jim Edmonds	.75	.35
❑ 132	Charles Johnson	.50	.23
❑ 133	Al Leiter	.50	.23
❑ 134	Jose Offerman	.30	.14
❑ 135	Eric Milton	.50	.23
❑ 136	Dean Palmer	.50	.23
❑ 137	Johnny Damon	.50	.23
❑ 138	Andy Pettitte	.50	.23
❑ 139	Ray Durham	.50	.23
❑ 140	Ugueth Urbina	.30	.14
❑ 141	Marquis Grissom	.30	.14
❑ 142	Ryan Klesko	.50	.23
❑ 143	Brady Anderson	.50	.23
❑ 144	Bobby Higginson	.50	.23
❑ 145	Chuck Knoblauch	.50	.23
❑ 146	Rickey Henderson	2.50	1.10
❑ 147	Kevin Millwood	.30	.14
❑ 148	Fred McGriff	.75	.35
❑ 149	Damion Easley	.30	.14
❑ 150	Tino Martinez	.50	.23
❑ 151	Greg Maddux LUM	1.50	.70
❑ 152	Scott Rolen LUM	1.25	.55
❑ 153	Pat Burrell LUM	.75	.35
❑ 154	Roger Clemens LUM	1.50	.70
❑ 155	Albert Belle LUM	.30	.14
❑ 156	Troy Glaus LUM	.50	.23
❑ 157	Cal Ripken LUM	2.50	1.10
❑ 158	Alfonso Soriano LUM	1.25	.55
❑ 159	Manny Ramirez LUM	.75	.35
❑ 160	Eric Chavez LUM	.50	.23
❑ 161	Kerry Wood LUM	.50	.23
❑ 162	Tony Gwynn LUM	1.25	.55
❑ 163	Barry Bonds LUM	1.50	.70
❑ 164	Ruben Mateo LUM	.50	.23
❑ 165	Todd Helton LUM	1.25	.55
❑ 166	Darin Erstad LUM	1.25	.55
❑ 167	Jeff Bagwell LUM	.75	.35
❑ 168	Juan Gonzalez LUM	.50	.23
❑ 169	Mo Vaughn LUM	.50	.23
❑ 170	V.Guerrero LUM	.75	.35
❑ 171	N.Garciaparra SUP	1.50	.70
❑ 172	Derek Jeter SUP	2.50	1.10
❑ 173	Alex Rodriguez SUP	1.50	.70
❑ 174	Ben Grieve SUP	.50	.23
❑ 175	Mike Piazza SUP	1.50	.70
❑ 176	Chipper Jones SUP	1.25	.55
❑ 177	Frank Thomas SUP	.75	.35
❑ 178	Ken Griffey Jr. SUP	2.00	.90
❑ 179	Sammy Sosa SUP	1.25	.55
❑ 180	Mark McGwire SUP	2.50	1.10

2000 Topps Stars

		MINT	NRMT
COMPLETE SET (200)		80.00	36.00
❑ 1	Vladimir Guerrero	1.25	.55
❑ 2	Eric Karros	.40	.18
❑ 3	Omar Vizquel	.40	.18
❑ 4	Ken Griffey Jr.	3.00	1.35
❑ 5	Preston Wilson	.40	.18
❑ 6	Albert Belle	.40	.18
❑ 7	Ryan Klesko	.40	.18
❑ 8	Bob Abreu	.40	.18
❑ 9	Warren Morris	.25	.11
❑ 10	Rafael Palmeiro	1.00	.45

❑ 11 Nomar Garciaparra 2.50 1.10
❑ 12 Dante Bichette .40 .18
❑ 13 Jeff Cirillo .40 .18
❑ 14 Carlos Beltran .40 .18
❑ 15 Tony Clark .40 .18
❑ 16 Ray Durham .40 .18
❑ 17 Mark McGwire 4.00 1.80
❑ 18 Jim Thome 1.00 .45
❑ 19 Todd Walker .25 .11
❑ 20 Richie Sexson .40 .18
❑ 21 Adrian Beltre .40 .18
❑ 22 Jay Bell .40 .18
❑ 23 Craig Biggio .60 .25
❑ 24 Ben Grieve .40 .18
❑ 25 Greg Maddux 2.50 1.10
❑ 26 Fernando Tatis .25 .11
❑ 27 Jeromy Burnitz .40 .18
❑ 28 Vinny Castilla .40 .18
❑ 29 Mark Grace 1.00 .45
❑ 30 Derek Jeter 4.00 1.80
❑ 31 Larry Walker .60 .25
❑ 32 Ivan Rodriguez 1.00 .45
❑ 33 Curt Schilling 1.00 .45
❑ 34 Mike Lamb RC .50 .23
❑ 35 Kevin Brown .40 .18
❑ 36 Andruw Jones 1.00 .45
❑ 37 Chris Mears RC .40 .18
❑ 38 Bartolo Colon .40 .18
❑ 39 Edgardo Alfonzo .40 .18
❑ 40 Brady Anderson .40 .18
❑ 41 Andres Galarraga .60 .25
❑ 42 Scott Rolen 1.00 .45
❑ 43 Manny Ramirez 1.25 .55
❑ 44 Carlos Delgado 1.00 .45
❑ 45 David Cone .40 .18
❑ 46 Carl Everett .40 .18
❑ 47 Chipper Jones 2.00 .90
❑ 48 Barry Bonds 2.50 1.10
❑ 49 Dean Palmer .40 .18
❑ 50 Frank Thomas 1.25 .55
❑ 51 Paul O'Neill 1.00 .45
❑ 52 Mo Vaughn .40 .18
❑ 53 Todd Helton 1.25 .55
❑ 54 Jason Giambi 1.00 .45
❑ 55 Brian Jordan .40 .18
❑ 56 Luis Gonzalez 1.00 .45
❑ 57 Alex Rodriguez 2.50 1.10
❑ 58 J.D. Drew 1.00 .45
❑ 59 Javy Lopez .40 .18
❑ 60 Tony Gwynn 2.00 .90
❑ 61 Jason Kendall .40 .18
❑ 62 Pedro Martinez 1.25 .55
❑ 63 Matt Williams .60 .25
❑ 64 Gary Sheffield .40 .18
❑ 65 Roberto Alomar 1.00 .45
❑ 66 Lyle Overbay RC 1.25 .55
❑ 67 Jeff Bagwell 1.25 .55
❑ 68 Tim Hudson 1.00 .45
❑ 69 Sammy Sosa 2.00 .90
❑ 70 Keith Reed RC .75 .35
❑ 71 Robin Ventura .40 .18
❑ 72 Cal Ripken 4.00 1.80
❑ 73 Alex Gonzalez .25 .11
❑ 74 Aaron McNeal RC .60 .25
❑ 75 Mike Lieberthal .40 .18
❑ 76 Brian Giles .40 .18
❑ 77 Kevin Millwood .25 .11
❑ 78 Troy O'Leary .25 .11
❑ 79 Raul Mondesi .40 .18
❑ 80 John Olerud .40 .18
❑ 81 David Justice .40 .18
❑ 82 Erubiel Durazo .40 .18
❑ 83 Shawn Green 1.00 .45
❑ 84 Tino Martinez .40 .18
❑ 85 Greg Vaughn .40 .18
❑ 86 Tom Glavine 1.00 .45
❑ 87 Jose Canseco 1.00 .45
❑ 88 Kenny Lofton .40 .18
❑ 89 Brian Daubach .40 .18
❑ 90 Mike Piazza 2.50 1.10
❑ 91 Randy Johnson 1.25 .55
❑ 92 Pokey Reese .25 .11
❑ 93 Troy Glaus 1.00 .45
❑ 94 Kerry Wood 1.00 .45
❑ 95 Sean Casey .60 .25
❑ 96 Magglio Ordonez .40 .18
❑ 97 Bernie Williams 1.00 .45
❑ 98 Juan Gonzalez 1.00 .45
❑ 99 Barry Larkin 1.00 .45
❑ 100 Orlando Hernandez .40 .18
❑ 101 Roger Clemens 2.50 1.10
❑ 102 Bob Gibson 1.00 .45
❑ 103 Gary Carter .60 .25
❑ 104 Willie Stargell .60 .25
❑ 105 Joe Morgan 1.00 .45
❑ 106 Brooks Robinson 1.00 .45
❑ 107 Ozzie Smith 1.25 .55
❑ 108 Carl Yastrzemski 1.50 .70
❑ 109 Al Kaline 1.25 .55
❑ 110 Frank Robinson 1.00 .45
❑ 111 Lance Berkman 1.00 .45
❑ 112 Adam Piatt .60 .25
❑ 113 Vernon Wells .40 .18
❑ 114 Rafael Furcal 1.00 .45
❑ 115 Rick Ankiel 1.00 .45
❑ 116 Corey Patterson 1.00 .45
❑ 117 Josh Hamilton 1.25 .55
❑ 118 Jack Cust .40 .18
❑ 119 Josh Girdley .25 .11
❑ 120 Pablo Ozuna .25 .11
❑ 121 Sean Burroughs 1.00 .45
❑ 122 Pat Burrell 1.00 .45
❑ 123 Chad Hermansen .25 .11
❑ 124 Ruben Mateo .40 .18
❑ 125 Ben Petrick .25 .11
❑ 126 Dee Brown .25 .11
❑ 127 Eric Munson .40 .18
❑ 128 Ruben Salazar RC 1.00 .45
❑ 129 Kip Wells .40 .18
❑ 130 Alfonso Soriano 1.00 .45
❑ 131 Mark Mulder 1.00 .45
❑ 132 Roosevelt Brown .25 .11
❑ 133 Nick Johnson 1.00 .45
❑ 134 Kyle Snyder .25 .11
❑ 135 David Walling .25 .11
❑ 136 Geraldo Guzman RC .40 .18
❑ 137 John Sneed RC .40 .18
❑ 138 Ben Christensen RC .50 .23
❑ 139 Corey Myers RC .60 .25
❑ 140 Jose Ortiz RC 5.00 2.20
❑ 141 Ryan Christianson RC 1.00 .45
❑ 142 Brett Myers RC .75 .35
❑ 143 Bobby Bradley RC 1.00 .45
❑ 144 Rick Asadoorian RC 1.00 .45
❑ 145 Julio Zuleta RC .60 .25
❑ 146 Ty Howington RC 1.25 .55
❑ 147 Josh Kalinowski RC .50 .23
❑ 148 B.J. Garbe RC 1.25 .55
❑ 149 Scott Downs RC .50 .23
❑ 150 Dan Wright RC 1.50 .70
❑ 151 Jeff Bagwell SPOT .60 .25
❑ 152 V.Guerrero SPOT .60 .25
❑ 153 Mike Piazza SPOT 1.50 .70
❑ 154 Juan Gonzalez SPOT .40 .18
❑ 155 Ivan Rodriguez SPOT .40 .18
❑ 156 Manny Ramirez SPOT .60 .25
❑ 157 Sammy Sosa SPOT 1.25 .55
❑ 158 Chipper Jones SPOT 1.25 .55
❑ 159 Shawn Green SPOT .40 .18
❑ 160 Ken Griffey Jr. SPOT 2.00 .90
❑ 161 Cal Ripken SPOT 2.50 1.10
❑ 162 N.Garciaparra SPOT 1.50 .70
❑ 163 Derek Jeter SPOT 2.50 1.10
❑ 164 Barry Bonds SPOT 1.25 .55
❑ 165 Greg Maddux SPOT 1.50 .70
❑ 166 Mark McGwire SPOT 2.50 1.10
❑ 167 Roberto Alomar SPOT .40 .18
❑ 168 Alex Rodriguez SPOT 1.50 .70
❑ 169 Randy Johnson SPOT .60 .25
❑ 170 Tony Gwynn SPOT 1.25 .55
❑ 171 Pedro Martinez SPOT .60 .25
❑ 172 Bob Gibson SPOT .60 .25
❑ 173 Gary Carter SPOT .40 .18
❑ 174 Willie Stargell SPOT .40 .18
❑ 175 Joe Morgan SPOT .60 .25
❑ 176 B.Robinson SPOT .60 .25
❑ 177 Ozzie Smith SPOT .60 .25
❑ 178 C.Yastrzemski SPOT .60 .25
❑ 179 Al Kaline SPOT .60 .25
❑ 180 Frank Robinson SPOT .60 .25
❑ 181 Adam Piatt SPOT .40 .18
❑ 182 Alfonso Soriano SPOT .40 .18
❑ 183 Corey Patterson SPOT 1.00 .45
❑ 184 Vernon Wells SPOT .40 .18
❑ 185 Pat Burrell SPOT .40 .18
❑ 186 Mark Mulder SPOT 1.00 .45
❑ 187 Eric Munson SPOT .25 .11
❑ 188 Rafael Furcal SPOT .40 .18
❑ 189 Rick Ankiel SPOT 1.00 .45
❑ 190 Ruben Mateo SPOT .25 .11
❑ 191 S.Burroughs SPOT 1.00 .45
❑ 192 Josh Hamilton SPOT 1.00 .45
❑ 193 Brett Myers SPOT .50 .23
❑ 194 B.Christensen SPOT .40 .18
❑ 195 Ty Howington SPOT .60 .25
❑ 196 R.Asadoorian SPOT 1.00 .45
❑ 197 J.Kalinowski SPOT .40 .18
❑ 198 Corey Myers SPOT .40 .18
❑ 199 R.Christianson SPOT .60 .25
❑ 200 John Sneed SPOT .25 .11

2001 Topps Stars

	MINT	NRMT
COMPLETE SET (200)	80.00	36.00

❑ 1 Darin Erstad 1.00 .45
❑ 2 Luis Gonzalez 1.00 .45
❑ 3 Rafael Furcal .40 .18
❑ 4 Dante Bichette .40 .18
❑ 5 Sammy Sosa 2.00 .90
❑ 6 Ken Griffey Jr. 4.00 1.80
❑ 7 Jim Thome 1.00 .45
❑ 8 Bobby Higginson .40 .18
❑ 9 Cliff Floyd .40 .18
❑ 10 Lance Berkman 1.00 .45
❑ 11 Eric Karros .40 .18
❑ 12 Jeromy Burnitz .40 .18
❑ 13 Jose Vidro .40 .18
❑ 14 Benny Agbayani .40 .18
❑ 15 Jorge Posada .40 .18
❑ 16 Ramon Hernandez .40 .18
❑ 17 Jason Kendall .40 .18
❑ 18 Jeff Kent .60 .25
❑ 19 John Olerud .40 .18
❑ 20 Al Martin .25 .11
❑ 21 Gerald Williams .25 .11
❑ 22 Gabe Kapler .40 .18
❑ 23 Carlos Delgado 1.00 .45
❑ 24 Mariano Rivera .40 .18
❑ 25 Javy Lopez .40 .18

Card	MINT	NRMT
❑ 26 Paul Konerko	.40	.18
❑ 27 Daryle Ward	.25	.11
❑ 28 Mike Lieberthal	.40	.18
❑ 29 Tom Goodwin	.25	.11
❑ 30 Garret Anderson	.40	.18
❑ 31 Steve Finley	.40	.18
❑ 32 Brian Jordan	.40	.18
❑ 33 Nomar Garciaparra	2.50	1.10
❑ 34 Ray Durham	.40	.18
❑ 35 Sean Casey	.60	.25
❑ 36 Kenny Lofton	.40	.18
❑ 37 Dean Palmer	.40	.18
❑ 38 Jeff Bagwell	1.25	.55
❑ 39 Mike Sweeney	.40	.18
❑ 40 Adrian Beltre	.40	.18
❑ 41 Richie Sexson	.40	.18
❑ 42 Vladimir Guerrero	1.25	.55
❑ 43 Derek Jeter	4.00	1.80
❑ 44 Miguel Tejada	.40	.18
❑ 45 Doug Glanville	.25	.11
❑ 46 Brian Giles	.40	.18
❑ 47 Marvin Benard	.25	.11
❑ 48 Edgar Martinez	.60	.25
❑ 49 Edgar Renteria	.25	.11
❑ 50 Fred McGriff	.60	.25
❑ 51 Ivan Rodriguez	1.00	.45
❑ 52 Brad Fullmer	.40	.18
❑ 53 Antonio Alfonseca	.25	.11
❑ 54 Tom Glavine	1.00	.45
❑ 55 Warren Morris	.25	.11
❑ 56 Johnny Damon	.40	.18
❑ 57 Dmitri Young	.40	.18
❑ 58 Mo Vaughn	.40	.18
❑ 59 Randy Johnson	1.25	.55
❑ 60 Greg Maddux	2.50	1.10
❑ 61 Carl Everett	.40	.18
❑ 62 Magglio Ordonez	.40	.18
❑ 63 Pokey Reese	.25	.11
❑ 64 Todd Helton	1.25	.55
❑ 65 Preston Wilson	.40	.18
❑ 66 Richard Hidalgo	.40	.18
❑ 67 Jermaine Dye	.40	.18
❑ 68 Gary Sheffield	.40	.18
❑ 69 Geoff Jenkins	.40	.18
❑ 70 Edgardo Alfonzo	.40	.18
❑ 71 Paul O'Neill	1.00	.45
❑ 72 Terrence Long	.40	.18
❑ 73 Bob Abreu	.40	.18
❑ 74 Kevin Young	.25	.11
❑ 75 J.T. Snow	.40	.18
❑ 76 Alex Rodriguez	2.50	1.10
❑ 77 Jim Edmonds	.60	.25
❑ 78 Mark McGwire	4.00	1.80
❑ 79 Tony Batista	.40	.18
❑ 80 Darrin Fletcher	.25	.11
❑ 81 Robb Nen	.40	.18
❑ 82 Jose Offerman	.25	.11
❑ 83 Travis Fryman	.40	.18
❑ 84 Joe Randa	.25	.11
❑ 85 Omar Vizquel	.40	.18
❑ 86 Tim Salmon	.40	.18
❑ 87 Andruw Jones	1.00	.45
❑ 88 Albert Belle	.40	.18
❑ 89 Manny Ramirez	1.25	.55
❑ 90 Frank Thomas	1.25	.55
❑ 91 Barry Larkin	1.00	.45
❑ 92 Neifi Perez	.25	.11
❑ 93 Luis Castillo	.25	.11
❑ 94 Moises Alou	.40	.18
❑ 95 Mark Quinn	.40	.18
❑ 96 Kevin Brown	.40	.18
❑ 97 Cristian Guzman	.40	.18
❑ 98 Mike Piazza	2.50	1.10
❑ 99 Bernie Williams	1.00	.45
❑ 100 Jason Giambi	1.00	.45
❑ 101 Scott Rolen	1.00	.45
❑ 102 Phil Nevin	.40	.18
❑ 103 Rich Aurilia	.40	.18
❑ 104 Mike Cameron	.40	.18
❑ 105 Fernando Vina	.25	.11
❑ 106 Greg Vaughn	.40	.18
❑ 107 Jose Cruz Jr.	.40	.18
❑ 108 Raul Mondesi	.40	.18
❑ 109 Ben Molina	.25	.11
❑ 110 Pedro Martinez	1.25	.55
❑ 111 Todd Hollandsworth	.25	.11
❑ 112 Jacque Jones	.40	.18
❑ 113 Rickey Henderson	2.00	.90
❑ 114 Troy Glaus	1.00	.45
❑ 115 Chipper Jones	2.00	.90
❑ 116 Delino DeShields	.25	.11
❑ 117 Eric Young	.25	.11
❑ 118 Jose Valentin	.25	.11
❑ 119 Roberto Alomar	1.00	.45
❑ 120 Jeff Cirillo	.40	.18
❑ 121 Mike Lowell	.40	.18
❑ 122 Julio Lugo	.25	.11
❑ 123 Shawn Green	1.00	.45
❑ 124 Marquis Grissom	.25	.11
❑ 125 Matt Lawton	.40	.18
❑ 126 Jay Payton	.25	.11
❑ 127 David Justice	.60	.25
❑ 128 Eric Chavez	.40	.18
❑ 129 Pat Burrell	.40	.18
❑ 130 Ryan Klesko	.40	.18
❑ 131 Barry Bonds	2.50	1.10
❑ 132 Jay Buhner	.40	.18
❑ 133 J.D. Drew	1.00	.45
❑ 134 Rafael Palmeiro	1.00	.45
❑ 135 Shannon Stewart	.40	.18
❑ 136 Juan Gonzalez	1.00	.45
❑ 137 Tony Womack	.25	.11
❑ 138 Carlos Lee	.40	.18
❑ 139 Derrek Lee	.25	.11
❑ 140 Ben Grieve	.40	.18
❑ 141 Ron Belliard	.25	.11
❑ 142 Stan Musial	2.00	.90
❑ 143 Ernie Banks	1.25	.55
❑ 144 Jim Palmer	1.00	.45
❑ 145 Tony Perez	1.00	.45
❑ 146 Duke Snider	1.00	.45
❑ 147 Rod Carew	1.00	.45
❑ 148 Warren Spahn	1.00	.45
❑ 149 Yogi Berra	1.50	.70
❑ 150 Juan Marichal	1.00	.45
❑ 151 Eric Munson	.40	.18
❑ 152 Carlos Pena	.40	.18
❑ 153 Joe Crede	.40	.18
❑ 154 Ryan Anderson	.40	.18
❑ 155 Milton Bradley	.25	.11
❑ 156 Sean Burroughs	1.00	.45
❑ 157 Corey Patterson	.40	.18
❑ 158 C.C. Sabathia	.60	.25
❑ 159 Ben Petrick	.25	.11
❑ 160 Aubrey Huff	.25	.11
❑ 161 Gookie Dawkins	.25	.11
❑ 162 Ben Sheets	.60	.25
❑ 163 Pablo Ozuna	.25	.11
❑ 164 Eric Valent	.25	.11
❑ 165 Rod Barajas	.25	.11
❑ 166 Chin-Feng Chen	.60	.25
❑ 167 Josh Hamilton	1.00	.45
❑ 168 Keith Ginter	.40	.18
❑ 169 Vernon Wells	.40	.18
❑ 170 Dernell Stenson	.25	.11
❑ 171 Alfonso Soriano	1.00	.45
❑ 172 Jason Marquis	.40	.18
❑ 173 Nick Johnson	.40	.18
❑ 174 Adam Everett	.25	.11
❑ 175 Jimmy Rollins	.40	.18
❑ 176 Ben Diggins	.40	.18
❑ 177 John Lackey	.25	.11
❑ 178 Scott Heard	.40	.18
❑ 179 Brian Hitchcox RC	.50	.23
❑ 180 Odannis Ayala RC	.50	.23
❑ 181 Scott Pratt RC	.75	.35
❑ 182 Greg Runser RC	.60	.25
❑ 183 Chris Russ RC	.75	.35
❑ 184 Derek Thompson	.25	.11
❑ 185 Jason Jones RC	.60	.25
❑ 186 Dominic Rich RC	.50	.23
❑ 187 Chad Petty RC	1.00	.45
❑ 188 Steve Smyth RC	.75	.35
❑ 189 Bryan Hebson RC	.50	.23
❑ 190 Danny Borrell RC	1.00	.45
❑ 191 Bob Keppel RC	1.00	.45
❑ 192 Justin Wayne RC	1.25	.55
❑ 193 Reggie Abercrombie RC	.75	.35
❑ 194 Travis Baptist RC	.25	.11
❑ 195 Shawn Fagan RC	.50	.23
❑ 196 Jose Reyes RC	1.00	.45
❑ 197 Chris Bass RC	1.00	.45
❑ 198 Albert Pujols RC	20.00	9.00
❑ 199 Luis Cotto RC	.50	.23
❑ 200 Jake Peavy RC	1.25	.55

2001 UD Reserve

	MINT	NRMT
COMP.SET w/o SP's (180)	40.00	18.00
COMMON CARD (1-180)	.15	.07
COMMON CARD (181-210)	5.00	2.20

Card	MINT	NRMT
❑ 1 Darin Erstad	.60	.25
❑ 2 Tim Salmon	.25	.11
❑ 3 Bengie Molina	.15	.07
❑ 4 Troy Glaus	.60	.25
❑ 5 Glenallen Hill	.15	.07
❑ 6 Garret Anderson	.25	.11
❑ 7 Jason Giambi	.60	.25
❑ 8 Johnny Damon	.25	.11
❑ 9 Eric Chavez	.25	.11
❑ 10 Tim Hudson	.60	.25
❑ 11 Miguel Tejada	.25	.11
❑ 12 Barry Zito	.60	.25
❑ 13 Jose Ortiz	.40	.18
❑ 14 Tony Batista	.25	.11
❑ 15 Carlos Delgado	.60	.25
❑ 16 Shannon Stewart	.25	.11
❑ 17 Raul Mondesi	.25	.11
❑ 18 Ben Grieve	.25	.11
❑ 19 Aubrey Huff	.15	.07
❑ 20 Greg Vaughn	.25	.11
❑ 21 Fred McGriff	.40	.18
❑ 22 Gerald Williams	.15	.07
❑ 23 Bartolo Colon	.25	.11
❑ 24 Roberto Alomar	.60	.25
❑ 25 Jim Thome	.60	.25
❑ 26 Omar Vizquel	.25	.11
❑ 27 Juan Gonzalez	.60	.25
❑ 28 Ellis Burks	.25	.11
❑ 29 Edgar Martinez	.40	.18
❑ 30 Aaron Sele	.25	.11
❑ 31 Jay Buhner	.25	.11
❑ 32 Mike Cameron	.25	.11
❑ 33 Kazuhiro Sasaki	.60	.25
❑ 34 John Olerud	.25	.11
❑ 35 Cal Ripken	2.50	1.10
❑ 36 Brady Anderson	.25	.11
❑ 37 Pat Hentgen	.15	.07
❑ 38 Chris Richard	.15	.07
❑ 39 Jerry Hairston Jr.	.15	.07
❑ 40 Mike Bordick	.25	.11
❑ 41 Ivan Rodriguez	.60	.25
❑ 42 Rick Helling	.25	.11
❑ 43 Rafael Palmeiro	.60	.25
❑ 44 Alex Rodriguez	1.50	.70
❑ 45 Andres Galarraga	.40	.18
❑ 46 Rusty Greer	.25	.11
❑ 47 Ruben Mateo	.25	.11
❑ 48 Ken Caminiti	.25	.11
❑ 49 Nomar Garciaparra	1.50	.70
❑ 50 Pedro Martinez	.75	.35
❑ 51 Manny Ramirez	.75	.35
❑ 52 Carl Everett	.25	.11
❑ 53 Dante Bichette	.25	.11
❑ 54 Hideo Nomo	.60	.25
❑ 55 Mike Sweeney	.25	.11
❑ 56 Carlos Beltran	.25	.11
❑ 57 Jeff Suppan	.15	.07

❑ 58 Jermaine Dye	.25	.11
❑ 59 Mark Quinn	.25	.11
❑ 60 Joe Randa	.15	.07
❑ 61 Bobby Higginson	.25	.11
❑ 62 Tony Clark	.25	.11
❑ 63 Brian Moehler	.15	.07
❑ 64 Dean Palmer	.25	.11
❑ 65 Brandon Inge	.25	.11
❑ 66 Damion Easley	.15	.07
❑ 67 Brad Radke	.25	.11
❑ 68 Corey Koskie	.25	.11
❑ 69 Cristian Guzman	.25	.11
❑ 70 Eric Milton	.25	.11
❑ 71 Jacque Jones	.25	.11
❑ 72 Matt Lawton	.25	.11
❑ 73 Frank Thomas	.75	.35
❑ 74 David Wells	.25	.11
❑ 75 Magglio Ordonez	.25	.11
❑ 76 Paul Konerko	.25	.11
❑ 77 Sandy Alomar Jr.	.25	.11
❑ 78 Ray Durham	.25	.11
❑ 79 Roger Clemens	1.50	.70
❑ 80 Bernie Williams	.60	.25
❑ 81 Derek Jeter	2.50	1.10
❑ 82 David Justice	.40	.18
❑ 83 Paul O'Neill	.60	.25
❑ 84 Mike Mussina	.60	.25
❑ 85 Jorge Posada	.25	.11
❑ 86 Jeff Bagwell	.75	.35
❑ 87 Richard Hidalgo	.25	.11
❑ 88 Craig Biggio	.40	.18
❑ 89 Scott Elarton	.15	.07
❑ 90 Moises Alou	.25	.11
❑ 91 Greg Maddux	1.50	.70
❑ 92 Rafael Furcal	.25	.11
❑ 93 Andruw Jones	.60	.25
❑ 94 Tom Glavine	.60	.25
❑ 95 Chipper Jones	1.25	.55
❑ 96 Javy Lopez	.25	.11
❑ 97 Richie Sexson	.25	.11
❑ 98 Jeromy Burnitz	.25	.11
❑ 99 Jeff D'Amico	.15	.07
❑ 100 Jeffrey Hammonds	.15	.07
❑ 101 Geoff Jenkins	.25	.11
❑ 102 Ben Sheets	.40	.18
❑ 103 Mark McGwire	2.50	1.10
❑ 104 Rick Ankiel	.40	.18
❑ 105 Darryl Kile	.25	.11
❑ 106 Edgar Renteria	.25	.11
❑ 107 Jim Edmonds	.40	.18
❑ 108 J.D. Drew	.60	.25
❑ 109 Sammy Sosa	1.25	.55
❑ 110 Corey Patterson	.25	.11
❑ 111 Kerry Wood	.60	.25
❑ 112 Todd Hundley	.15	.07
❑ 113 Rondell White	.25	.11
❑ 114 Matt Stairs	.15	.07
❑ 115 Randy Johnson	.75	.35
❑ 116 Mark Grace	.60	.25
❑ 117 Steve Finley	.25	.11
❑ 118 Luis Gonzalez	.60	.25
❑ 119 Matt Williams	.40	.18
❑ 120 Curt Schilling	.60	.25
❑ 121 Gary Sheffield	.25	.11
❑ 122 Kevin Brown	.25	.11
❑ 123 Shawn Green	.60	.25
❑ 124 Eric Karros	.25	.11
❑ 125 Chan Ho Park	.25	.11
❑ 126 Adrian Beltre	.25	.11
❑ 127 Vladimir Guerrero	.75	.35
❑ 128 Fernando Tatis	.15	.07
❑ 129 Lee Stevens	.15	.07
❑ 130 Jose Vidro	.25	.11
❑ 131 Peter Bergeron	.15	.07
❑ 132 Michael Barrett	.15	.07
❑ 133 Jeff Kent	.40	.18
❑ 134 Russ Ortiz	.25	.11
❑ 135 Barry Bonds	1.50	.70
❑ 136 J.T. Snow	.25	.11
❑ 137 Livan Hernandez	.25	.11
❑ 138 Rich Aurilia	.25	.11
❑ 139 Preston Wilson	.25	.11
❑ 140 Mike Lowell	.25	.11
❑ 141 Ryan Dempster	.25	.11
❑ 142 Charles Johnson	.25	.11
❑ 143 Matt Clement	.15	.07

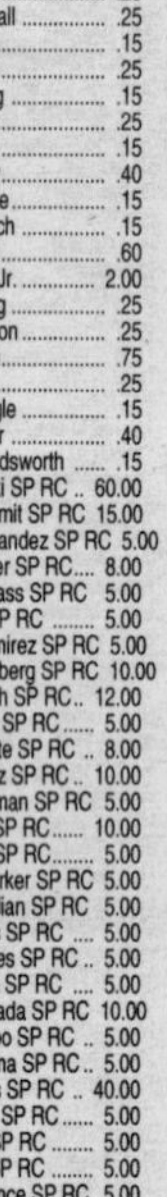

❑ 144 Luis Castillo	.15	.07
❑ 145 Mike Piazza UER	1.50	.70
Card lists him as a Dodger		
❑ 146 Al Leiter	.25	.11
❑ 147 Robin Ventura	.25	.11
❑ 148 Jay Payton	.15	.07
❑ 149 Todd Zeile	.25	.11
❑ 150 Edgardo Alfonzo	.25	.11
❑ 151 Tony Gwynn	1.25	.55
❑ 152 Ryan Klesko	.25	.11
❑ 153 Phil Nevin	.25	.11
❑ 154 Mark Kotsay	.25	.11
❑ 155 Trevor Hoffman	.25	.11
❑ 156 Damian Jackson	.15	.07
❑ 157 Scott Rolen	.60	.25
❑ 158 Mike Lieberthal	.25	.11
❑ 159 Bruce Chen	.15	.07
❑ 160 Bobby Abreu	.25	.11
❑ 161 Pat Burrell	.25	.11
❑ 162 Travis Lee	.25	.11
❑ 163 Jason Kendall	.25	.11
❑ 164 Derek Bell	.15	.07
❑ 165 Kris Benson	.25	.11
❑ 166 Kevin Young	.15	.07
❑ 167 Brian Giles	.25	.11
❑ 168 Pat Meares	.15	.07
❑ 169 Sean Casey	.40	.18
❑ 170 Pokey Reese	.15	.07
❑ 171 Pete Harnisch	.15	.07
❑ 172 Barry Larkin	.60	.25
❑ 173 Ken Griffey Jr.	2.00	.90
❑ 174 Dmitri Young	.25	.11
❑ 175 Mike Hampton	.25	.11
❑ 176 Todd Helton	.75	.35
❑ 177 Jeff Cirillo	.25	.11
❑ 178 Denny Neagle	.15	.07
❑ 179 Larry Walker	.40	.18
❑ 180 Todd Hollandsworth	.15	.07
❑ 181 Ichiro Suzuki SP RC	60.00	27.00
❑ 182 Wilson Betemit SP RC	15.00	6.75
❑ 183 Adrian Hernandez SP RC	5.00	2.20
❑ 184 Travis Hafner SP RC	8.00	3.60
❑ 185 Sean Douglass SP RC	5.00	2.20
❑ 186 Juan Diaz SP RC	5.00	2.20
❑ 187 Horacio Ramirez SP RC	5.00	2.20
❑ 188 Morgan Ensberg SP RC	10.00	4.50
❑ 189 B. Duckworth SP RC	12.00	5.50
❑ 190 Jack Wilson SP RC	5.00	2.20
❑ 191 Erick Almonte SP RC	8.00	3.60
❑ 192 R. Rodriguez SP RC	10.00	4.50
❑ 193 Elpidio Guzman SP RC	5.00	2.20
❑ 194 Juan Uribe SP RC	10.00	4.50
❑ 195 Ryan Freel SP RC	5.00	2.20
❑ 196 Christian Parker SP RC	5.00	2.20
❑ 197 Jackson Melian SP RC	5.00	2.20
❑ 198 Jose Mieses SP RC	5.00	2.20
❑ 199 Andres Torres SP RC	5.00	2.20
❑ 200 Jason Smith SP RC	5.00	2.20
❑ 201 Johnny Estrada SP RC	10.00	4.50
❑ 202 Cesar Crespo SP RC	5.00	2.20
❑ 203 C. Valderrama SP RC	5.00	2.20
❑ 204 Albert Pujols SP RC	40.00	18.00
❑ 205 Wilkin Ruan SP RC	5.00	2.20
❑ 206 Josh Fogg SP RC	5.00	2.20
❑ 207 Bert Snow SP RC	5.00	2.20
❑ 208 Brian Lawrence SP RC	5.00	2.20
❑ 209 Esix Snead SP RC	5.00	2.20
❑ 210 Tsuyoshi Shinjo SP RC	15.00	6.75

1991 Ultra

	MINT	NRMT
COMPLETE SET (400)	20.00	9.00
❑ 1 Steve Avery	.10	.05
❑ 2 Jeff Blauser	.10	.05
❑ 3 Francisco Cabrera	.10	.05
❑ 4 Ron Gant	.10	.05
❑ 5 Tom Glavine	.40	.18
❑ 6 Tommy Gregg	.10	.05
❑ 7 Dave Justice	.40	.18
❑ 8 Oddibe McDowell	.10	.05
❑ 9 Greg Olson	.10	.05
❑ 10 Terry Pendleton	.15	.07
❑ 11 Lonnie Smith	.10	.05
❑ 12 John Smoltz	.15	.07

❑ 13 Jeff Treadway	.10	.05
❑ 14 Glenn Davis	.10	.05
❑ 15 Mike Devereaux	.10	.05
❑ 16 Leo Gomez	.10	.05
❑ 17 Chris Hoiles	.10	.05
❑ 18 Dave Johnson	.10	.05
❑ 19 Ben McDonald	.10	.05
❑ 20 Randy Milligan	.10	.05
❑ 21 Gregg Olson	.10	.05
❑ 22 Joe Orsulak	.10	.05
❑ 23 Bill Ripken	.10	.05
❑ 24 Cal Ripken	1.50	.70
❑ 25 David Segui	.10	.05
❑ 26 Craig Worthington	.10	.05
❑ 27 Wade Boggs	.40	.18
❑ 28 Tom Bolton	.10	.05
❑ 29 Tom Brunansky	.10	.05
❑ 30 Ellis Burks	.15	.07
❑ 31 Roger Clemens	1.00	.45
❑ 32 Mike Greenwell	.10	.05
❑ 33 Greg A. Harris	.10	.05
❑ 34 Daryl Irvine	.10	.05
❑ 35 Mike Marshall UER	.10	.05
(1990 in stats is shown as 990)		
❑ 36 Tim Naehring	.10	.05
❑ 37 Tony Pena	.10	.05
❑ 38 Phil Plantier RC	.10	.05
❑ 39 Carlos Quintana	.10	.05
❑ 40 Jeff Reardon	.15	.07
❑ 41 Jody Reed	.10	.05
❑ 42 Luis Rivera	.10	.05
❑ 43 Jim Abbott	.15	.07
❑ 44 Chuck Finley	.15	.07
❑ 45 Bryan Harvey	.10	.05
❑ 46 Donnie Hill	.10	.05
❑ 47 Jack Howell	.10	.05
❑ 48 Wally Joyner	.15	.07
❑ 49 Mark Langston	.10	.05
❑ 50 Kirk McCaskill	.10	.05
❑ 51 Lance Parrish	.15	.07
❑ 52 Dick Schofield	.10	.05
❑ 53 Lee Stevens	.10	.05
❑ 54 Dave Winfield	.40	.18
❑ 55 George Bell	.10	.05
❑ 56 Damon Berryhill	.10	.05
❑ 57 Mike Bielecki	.10	.05
❑ 58 Andre Dawson	.25	.11
❑ 59 Shawon Dunston	.10	.05
❑ 60 Joe Girardi UER	.10	.05
(Bats right, LH hitter shown is Doug Dascenzo)		
❑ 61 Mark Grace	.40	.18
❑ 62 Mike Harkey	.10	.05
❑ 63 Les Lancaster	.10	.05
❑ 64 Greg Maddux	1.00	.45
❑ 65 Derrick May	.10	.05
❑ 66 Ryne Sandberg	.50	.23
❑ 67 Luis Salazar	.10	.05
❑ 68 Dwight Smith	.10	.05
❑ 69 Hector Villanueva	.10	.05
❑ 70 Jerome Walton	.10	.05
❑ 71 Mitch Williams	.10	.05
❑ 72 Carlton Fisk	.40	.18
❑ 73 Scott Fletcher	.10	.05
❑ 74 Ozzie Guillen	.10	.05
❑ 75 Greg Hibbard	.10	.05

❑ 76 Lance Johnson .10 .05
❑ 77 Steve Lyons .10 .05
❑ 78 Jack McDowell .10 .05
❑ 79 Dan Pasqua .10 .05
❑ 80 Melido Perez .10 .05
❑ 81 Tim Raines .15 .07
❑ 82 Sammy Sosa 1.00 .45
❑ 83 Cory Snyder .10 .05
❑ 84 Bobby Thigpen .10 .05
❑ 85 Frank Thomas .60 .25
(Card says he is
an outfielder)
❑ 86 Robin Ventura .15 .07
❑ 87 Todd Benzinger .10 .05
❑ 88 Glenn Braggs .10 .05
❑ 89 Tom Browning UER .10 .05
(Front photo actually
Norm Charlton)
❑ 90 Norm Charlton .10 .05
❑ 91 Eric Davis .15 .07
❑ 92 Rob Dibble .10 .05
❑ 93 Bill Doran .10 .05
❑ 94 Mariano Duncan UER .10 .05
(Right back photo
is Billy Hatcher)
❑ 95 Billy Hatcher .10 .05
❑ 96 Barry Larkin .40 .18
❑ 97 Randy Myers .10 .05
❑ 98 Hal Morris .10 .05
❑ 99 Joe Oliver .10 .05
❑ 100 Paul O'Neill .40 .18
❑ 101 Jeff Reed .10 .05
(See also 104)
❑ 102 Jose Rijo .10 .05
❑ 103 Chris Sabo .10 .05
(See also 106)
❑ 104 Beau Allred UER .10 .05
(Card number is 101)
❑ 105 Sandy Alomar Jr. .15 .07
❑ 106 Carlos Baerga UER .10 .05
(Card number is 103)
❑ 107 Albert Belle .15 .07
❑ 108 Jerry Browne .10 .05
❑ 109 Tom Candiotti .10 .05
❑ 110 Alex Cole .10 .05
❑ 111 John Farrell .10 .05
(See also 114)
❑ 112 Felix Fermin .10 .05
❑ 113 Brook Jacoby .10 .05
❑ 114 Chris James UER .10 .05
(Card number is 111)
❑ 115 Doug Jones .10 .05
❑ 116 Steve Olin .10 .05
(See also 119)
❑ 117 Greg Swindell .10 .05
❑ 118 Turner Ward RC .15 .07
❑ 119 Mitch Webster UER .10 .05
(Card number is 116)
❑ 120 Dave Bergman .10 .05
❑ 121 Cecil Fielder .15 .07
❑ 122 Travis Fryman .15 .07
❑ 123 Mike Henneman .10 .05
❑ 124 Lloyd Moseby .10 .05
❑ 125 Dan Petry .10 .05
❑ 126 Tony Phillips .10 .05
❑ 127 Mark Salas .10 .05
❑ 128 Frank Tanana .10 .05
❑ 129 Alan Trammell .25 .11
❑ 130 Lou Whitaker .15 .07
❑ 131 Eric Anthony .10 .05
❑ 132 Craig Biggio .25 .11
❑ 133 Ken Caminiti .15 .07
❑ 134 Casey Candaele .10 .05
❑ 135 Andujar Cedeno .10 .05
❑ 136 Mark Davidson .10 .05
❑ 137 Jim Deshaies .10 .05
❑ 138 Mark Portugal .10 .05
❑ 139 Rafael Ramirez .10 .05
❑ 140 Mike Scott .10 .05
❑ 141 Eric Yelding .10 .05
❑ 142 Gerald Young .10 .05
❑ 143 Kevin Appier .15 .07
❑ 144 George Brett .75 .35
❑ 145 Jeff Conine RC .15 .07
❑ 146 Jim Eisenreich .10 .05
❑ 147 Tom Gordon .10 .05
❑ 148 Mark Gubicza .10 .05
❑ 149 Bo Jackson .15 .07
❑ 150 Brent Mayne .10 .05
❑ 151 Mike Macfarlane .10 .05
❑ 152 Brian McRae RC .15 .07
❑ 153 Jeff Montgomery .10 .05
❑ 154 Bret Saberhagen .15 .07
❑ 155 Kevin Seitzer .10 .05
❑ 156 Terry Shumpert .10 .05
❑ 157 Kurt Stillwell .10 .05
❑ 158 Danny Tartabull .10 .05
❑ 159 Tim Belcher .10 .05
❑ 160 Kal Daniels .10 .05
❑ 161 Alfredo Griffin .10 .05
❑ 162 Lenny Harris .10 .05
❑ 163 Jay Howell .10 .05
❑ 164 Ramon Martinez .10 .05
❑ 165 Mike Morgan .10 .05
❑ 166 Eddie Murray .40 .18
❑ 167 Jose Offerman .10 .05
❑ 168 Juan Samuel .10 .05
❑ 169 Mike Scioscia .10 .05
❑ 170 Mike Sharperson .10 .05
❑ 171 Darryl Strawberry .15 .07
❑ 172 Greg Brock .10 .05
❑ 173 Chuck Crim .10 .05
❑ 174 Jim Gantner .10 .05
❑ 175 Ted Higuera .10 .05
❑ 176 Mark Knudson .10 .05
❑ 177 Tim McIntosh .10 .05
❑ 178 Paul Molitor .40 .18
❑ 179 Dan Plesac .10 .05
❑ 180 Gary Sheffield .15 .07
❑ 181 Bill Spiers .10 .05
❑ 182 B.J. Surhoff .15 .07
❑ 183 Greg Vaughn .15 .07
❑ 184 Robin Yount .40 .18
❑ 185 Rick Aguilera .15 .07
❑ 186 Greg Gagne .10 .05
❑ 187 Dan Gladden .10 .05
❑ 188 Brian Harper .10 .05
❑ 189 Kent Hrbek .15 .07
❑ 190 Gene Larkin .10 .05
❑ 191 Shane Mack .10 .05
❑ 192 Pedro Munoz RC .10 .05
❑ 193 Al Newman .10 .05
❑ 194 Junior Ortiz .10 .05
❑ 195 Kirby Puckett 1.00 .45
❑ 196 Kevin Tapani .10 .05
❑ 197 Dennis Boyd .10 .05
❑ 198 Tim Burke .10 .05
❑ 199 Ivan Calderon .10 .05
❑ 200 Delino DeShields .15 .07
❑ 201 Mike Fitzgerald .10 .05
❑ 202 Steve Frey .10 .05
❑ 203 Andres Galarraga .25 .11
❑ 204 Marquis Grissom .10 .05
❑ 205 Dave Martinez .10 .05
❑ 206 Dennis Martinez .15 .07
❑ 207 Junior Noboa .10 .05
❑ 208 Spike Owen .10 .05
❑ 209 Scott Ruskin .10 .05
❑ 210 Tim Wallach .10 .05
❑ 211 Daryl Boston .10 .05
❑ 212 Vince Coleman .10 .05
❑ 213 David Cone .15 .07
❑ 214 Ron Darling .10 .05
❑ 215 Kevin Elster .10 .05
❑ 216 Sid Fernandez .10 .05
❑ 217 John Franco .15 .07
❑ 218 Dwight Gooden .15 .07
❑ 219 Tom Herr .10 .05
❑ 220 Todd Hundley .10 .05
❑ 221 Gregg Jefferies .10 .05
❑ 222 Howard Johnson .10 .05
❑ 223 Dave Magadan .10 .05
❑ 224 Kevin McReynolds .10 .05
❑ 225 Keith Miller .10 .05
❑ 226 Mackey Sasser .10 .05
❑ 227 Frank Viola .15 .07
❑ 228 Jesse Barfield .10 .05
❑ 229 Greg Cadaret .10 .05
❑ 230 Alvaro Espinoza .10 .05
❑ 231 Bob Geren .10 .05
❑ 232 Lee Guetterman .10 .05
❑ 233 Mel Hall .10 .05
❑ 234 Andy Hawkins UER .10 .05
(Back center photo
is not him)
❑ 235 Roberto Kelly .10 .05
❑ 236 Tim Leary .10 .05
❑ 237 Jim Leyritz .10 .05
❑ 238 Kevin Maas .10 .05
❑ 239 Don Mattingly 1.00 .45
❑ 240 Hensley Meulens .10 .05
❑ 241 Eric Plunk .10 .05
❑ 242 Steve Sax .10 .05
❑ 243 Todd Burns .10 .05
❑ 244 Jose Canseco .40 .18
❑ 245 Dennis Eckersley .15 .07
❑ 246 Mike Gallego .10 .05
❑ 247 Dave Henderson .10 .05
❑ 248 Rickey Henderson .75 .35
❑ 249 Rick Honeycutt .10 .05
❑ 250 Carney Lansford .15 .07
❑ 251 Mark McGwire 1.50 .70
❑ 252 Mike Moore .10 .05
❑ 253 Terry Steinbach .10 .05
❑ 254 Dave Stewart .15 .07
❑ 255 Walt Weiss .10 .05
❑ 256 Bob Welch .10 .05
❑ 257 Curt Young .10 .05
❑ 258 Wes Chamberlain RC .10 .05
❑ 259 Pat Combs .10 .05
❑ 260 Darren Daulton .15 .07
❑ 261 Jose DeJesus .10 .05
❑ 262 Len Dykstra .15 .07
❑ 263 Charlie Hayes .10 .05
❑ 264 Von Hayes .10 .05
❑ 265 Ken Howell .10 .05
❑ 266 John Kruk .15 .07
❑ 267 Roger McDowell .10 .05
❑ 268 Mickey Morandini .10 .05
❑ 269 Terry Mulholland .10 .05
❑ 270 Dale Murphy .40 .18
❑ 271 Randy Ready .10 .05
❑ 272 Dickie Thon .10 .05
❑ 273 Stan Belinda .10 .05
❑ 274 Jay Bell .15 .07
❑ 275 Barry Bonds 1.00 .45
❑ 276 Bobby Bonilla .15 .07
❑ 277 Doug Drabek .10 .05
❑ 278 Carlos Garcia RC .10 .05
❑ 279 Neal Heaton .10 .05
❑ 280 Jeff King .10 .05
❑ 281 Bill Landrum .10 .05
❑ 282 Mike LaValliere .10 .05
❑ 283 Jose Lind .10 .05
❑ 284 Orlando Merced RC .10 .05
❑ 285 Gary Redus .10 .05
❑ 286 Don Slaught .10 .05
❑ 287 Andy Van Slyke .15 .07
❑ 288 Jose DeLeon .10 .05
❑ 289 Pedro Guerrero .15 .07
❑ 290 Ray Lankford .15 .07
❑ 291 Joe Magrane .10 .05
❑ 292 Jose Oquendo .10 .05
❑ 293 Tom Pagnozzi .10 .05
❑ 294 Bryn Smith .10 .05
❑ 295 Lee Smith .15 .07
❑ 296 Ozzie Smith UER .50 .23
(Born 12-26, 54,
should have hyphen)
❑ 297 Milt Thompson .10 .05
❑ 298 Craig Wilson .10 .05
❑ 299 Todd Zeile .10 .05
❑ 300 Shawn Abner .10 .05
❑ 301 Andy Benes .10 .05
❑ 302 Paul Faries .10 .05
❑ 303 Tony Gwynn .75 .35
❑ 304 Greg W. Harris .10 .05
❑ 305 Thomas Howard .10 .05
❑ 306 Bruce Hurst .10 .05
❑ 307 Craig Lefferts .10 .05
❑ 308 Fred McGriff .25 .11
❑ 309 Dennis Rasmussen .10 .05
❑ 310 Bip Roberts .10 .05
❑ 311 Benito Santiago .10 .05
❑ 312 Garry Templeton .10 .05
❑ 313 Ed Whitson .10 .05
❑ 314 Dave Anderson .10 .05
❑ 315 Kevin Bass .10 .05

❑ 316 Jeff Brantley .10 .05
❑ 317 John Burkett .10 .05
❑ 318 Will Clark .40 .18
❑ 319 Steve Decker .10 .05
❑ 320 Scott Garrelts .10 .05
❑ 321 Terry Kennedy .10 .05
❑ 322 Mark Leonard .10 .05
❑ 323 Darren Lewis .10 .05
❑ 324 Greg Litton .10 .05
❑ 325 Willie McGee .15 .07
❑ 326 Kevin Mitchell .10 .05
❑ 327 Don Robinson .10 .05
❑ 328 Andres Santana .10 .05
❑ 329 Robby Thompson .10 .05
❑ 330 Jose Uribe .10 .05
❑ 331 Matt Williams .25 .11
❑ 332 Scott Bradley .10 .05
❑ 333 Henry Cotto .10 .05
❑ 334 Alvin Davis .10 .05
❑ 335 Ken Griffey Sr. .15 .07
❑ 336 Ken Griffey Jr. 1.50 .70
❑ 337 Erik Hanson .10 .05
❑ 338 Brian Holman .10 .05
❑ 339 Randy Johnson .60 .25
❑ 340 Edgar Martinez UER .25 .11
(Listed as playing SS)
❑ 341 Tino Martinez .15 .07
❑ 342 Pete O'Brien .10 .05
❑ 343 Harold Reynolds .10 .05
❑ 344 Dave Valle .10 .05
❑ 345 Omar Vizquel .15 .07
❑ 346 Brad Arnsberg .10 .05
❑ 347 Kevin Brown .15 .07
❑ 348 Julio Franco .15 .07
❑ 349 Jeff Huson .10 .05
❑ 350 Rafael Palmeiro .40 .18
❑ 351 Geno Petralli .10 .05
❑ 352 Gary Pettis .10 .05
❑ 353 Kenny Rogers .10 .05
❑ 354 Jeff Russell .10 .05
❑ 355 Nolan Ryan 2.00 .90
❑ 356 Ruben Sierra .10 .05
❑ 357 Bobby Witt .10 .05
❑ 358 Roberto Alomar .40 .18
❑ 359 Pat Borders .10 .05
❑ 360 Joe Carter UER .15 .07
(Reverse negative on back photo)
❑ 361 Kelly Gruber .10 .05
❑ 362 Tom Henke .10 .05
❑ 363 Glenallen Hill .10 .05
❑ 364 Jimmy Key .15 .07
❑ 365 Manny Lee .10 .05
❑ 366 Rance Mulliniks .10 .05
❑ 367 John Olerud UER .25 .11
(Throwing left on card; back has throws right; he does throw lefty)
❑ 368 Dave Stieb .10 .05
❑ 369 Duane Ward .10 .05
❑ 370 David Wells .15 .07
❑ 371 Mark Whiten .10 .05
❑ 372 Mookie Wilson .15 .07
❑ 373 Willie Banks MLP .10 .05
❑ 374 Steve Carter MLP .10 .05
❑ 375 S.Chiamparino MLP .10 .05
❑ 376 Steve Chitren MLP .10 .05
❑ 377 Darrin Fletcher MLP .10 .05
❑ 378 Rich Garces MLP RC .10 .05
❑ 379 Reggie Jefferson MLP .10 .05
❑ 380 Eric Karros MLP RC .75 .35
❑ 381 Pat Kelly MLP RC .10 .05
❑ 382 C.Knoblauch MLP .15 .07
❑ 383 D.Neagle MLP RC .40 .18
❑ 384 Dan Opperman MLP .10 .05
❑ 385 John Ramos MLP .10 .05
❑ 386 H.Rodriguez MLP RC .40 .18
❑ 387 Mo Vaughn MLP .15 .07
❑ 388 G.Williams MLP RC .40 .18
❑ 389 Mike York MLP .10 .05
❑ 390 Eddie Zosky MLP .10 .05
❑ 391 Barry Bonds EP .50 .23
❑ 392 Cecil Fielder EP .10 .05
❑ 393 Rickey Henderson EP .40 .18
❑ 394 Dave Justice EP .15 .07
❑ 395 Nolan Ryan EP 1.00 .45
❑ 396 Bobby Thigpen EP .10 .05
❑ 397 Gregg Jefferies CL .10 .05
❑ 398 Von Hayes CL .10 .05
❑ 399 Terry Kennedy CL .10 .05
❑ 400 Nolan Ryan CL .40 .18

1991 Ultra Update

	MINT	NRMT
COMP.FACT.SET (120)	50.00	22.00

❑ 1 Dwight Evans .50 .23
❑ 2 Chito Martinez .25 .11
❑ 3 Bob Melvin .25 .11
❑ 4 Mike Mussina RC 6.00 2.70
❑ 5 Jack Clark .50 .23
❑ 6 Dana Kiecker .25 .11
❑ 7 Steve Lyons .25 .11
❑ 8 Gary Gaetti .50 .23
❑ 9 Dave Gallagher .25 .11
❑ 10 Dave Parker .50 .23
❑ 11 Luis Polonia .25 .11
❑ 12 Luis Sojo .25 .11
❑ 13 Wilson Alvarez .25 .11
❑ 14 Alex Fernandez .25 .11
❑ 15 Craig Grebeck .25 .11
❑ 16 Ron Karkovice .25 .11
❑ 17 Warren Newson .25 .11
❑ 18 Scott Radinsky .25 .11
❑ 19 Glenallen Hill .25 .11
❑ 20 Charles Nagy .25 .11
❑ 21 Mark Whiten .25 .11
❑ 22 Milt Cuyler .25 .11
❑ 23 Paul Gibson .25 .11
❑ 24 Mickey Tettleton .25 .11
❑ 25 Todd Benzinger .25 .11
❑ 26 Storm Davis .25 .11
❑ 27 Kirk Gibson .50 .23
❑ 28 Bill Pecota .25 .11
❑ 29 Gary Thurman .25 .11
❑ 30 Darryl Hamilton .25 .11
❑ 31 Jaime Navarro .25 .11
❑ 32 Willie Randolph .50 .23
❑ 33 Bill Wegman .25 .11
❑ 34 Randy Bush .25 .11
❑ 35 Chili Davis .50 .23
❑ 36 Scott Erickson .25 .11
❑ 37 Chuck Knoblauch .50 .23
❑ 38 Scott Leius .25 .11
❑ 39 Jack Morris .50 .23
❑ 40 John Habyan .25 .11
❑ 41 Pat Kelly .25 .11
❑ 42 Matt Nokes .25 .11
❑ 43 Scott Sanderson .25 .11
❑ 44 Bernie Williams 5.00 2.20
❑ 45 Harold Baines .50 .23
❑ 46 Brook Jacoby .25 .11
❑ 47 Earnest Riles .25 .11
❑ 48 Willie Wilson .25 .11
❑ 49 Jay Buhner .50 .23
❑ 50 Rich DeLucia .25 .11
❑ 51 Mike Jackson .25 .11
❑ 52 Bill Krueger .25 .11
❑ 53 Bill Swift .25 .11
❑ 54 Brian Downing .25 .11
❑ 55 Juan Gonzalez 10.00 4.50
❑ 56 Dean Palmer 1.00 .45
❑ 57 Kevin Reimer .25 .11
❑ 58 Ivan Rodriguez RC 10.00 4.50
❑ 59 Tom Candiotti .25 .11
❑ 60 Juan Guzman RC .50 .23
❑ 61 Bob MacDonald .25 .11
❑ 62 Greg Myers .25 .11
❑ 63 Ed Sprague .25 .11
❑ 64 Devon White .25 .11
❑ 65 Rafael Belliard .25 .11
❑ 66 Juan Berenguer .25 .11
❑ 67 Brian R. Hunter RC .50 .23
❑ 68 Kent Mercker .25 .11
❑ 69 Otis Nixon .25 .11
❑ 70 Danny Jackson .25 .11
❑ 71 Chuck McElroy .25 .11
❑ 72 Gary Scott .25 .11
❑ 73 Heathcliff Slocumb RC .50 .23
❑ 74 Chico Walker .25 .11
❑ 75 Rick Wilkins RC .25 .11
❑ 76 Chris Hammond .25 .11
❑ 77 Luis Quinones .25 .11
❑ 78 Herm Winningham .25 .11
❑ 79 Jeff Bagwell RC 12.00 5.50
❑ 80 Jim Corsi .25 .11
❑ 81 Steve Finley .50 .23
❑ 82 Luis Gonzalez RC 10.00 4.50
❑ 83 Pete Harnisch .25 .11
❑ 84 Darryl Kile .50 .23
❑ 85 Brett Butler .50 .23
❑ 86 Gary Carter .75 .35
❑ 87 Tim Crews .25 .11
❑ 88 Orel Hershiser .50 .23
❑ 89 Bob Ojeda .25 .11
❑ 90 Bret Barberie RC** .25 .11
❑ 91 Barry Jones .25 .11
❑ 92 Gilberto Reyes .25 .11
❑ 93 Larry Walker .75 .35
❑ 94 Hubie Brooks .25 .11
❑ 95 Tim Burke .25 .11
❑ 96 Rick Cerone .25 .11
❑ 97 Jeff Innis .25 .11
❑ 98 Wally Backman .25 .11
❑ 99 Tommy Greene .25 .11
❑ 100 Ricky Jordan .25 .11
❑ 101 Mitch Williams .25 .11
❑ 102 John Smiley .25 .11
❑ 103 Randy Tomlin RC .25 .11
❑ 104 Gary Varsho .25 .11
❑ 105 Cris Carpenter .25 .11
❑ 106 Ken Hill .25 .11
❑ 107 Felix Jose .25 .11
❑ 108 Omar Olivares RC .50 .23
❑ 109 Gerald Perry .25 .11
❑ 110 Jerald Clark .25 .11
❑ 111 Tony Fernandez .25 .11
❑ 112 Darrin Jackson .25 .11
❑ 113 Mike Maddux .25 .11
❑ 114 Tim Teufel .25 .11
❑ 115 Bud Black .25 .11
❑ 116 Kelly Downs .25 .11
❑ 117 Mike Felder .25 .11
❑ 118 Willie McGee .50 .23
❑ 119 Trevor Wilson .25 .11
❑ 120 Checklist 1-120 .25 .11

1992 Ultra

	MINT	NRMT
COMPLETE SET (600)	30.00	13.50

COMPLETE SERIES 1 (300) .. 20.00 9.00
COMPLETE SERIES 2 (300) .. 10.00 4.50

❑	1	Glenn Davis	.10	.05
❑	2	Mike Devereaux	.10	.05
❑	3	Dwight Evans	.15	.07
❑	4	Leo Gomez	.10	.05
❑	5	Chris Hoiles	.10	.05
❑	6	Sam Horn	.10	.05
❑	7	Chito Martinez	.10	.05
❑	8	Randy Milligan	.10	.05
❑	9	Mike Mussina	.60	.25
❑	10	Billy Ripken	.10	.05
❑	11	Cal Ripken	1.50	.70
❑	12	Tom Brunansky	.10	.05
❑	13	Ellis Burks	.15	.07
❑	14	Jack Clark	.15	.07
❑	15	Roger Clemens	1.00	.45
❑	16	Mike Greenwell	.10	.05
❑	17	Joe Hesketh	.10	.05
❑	18	Tony Pena	.10	.05
❑	19	Carlos Quintana	.10	.05
❑	20	Jeff Reardon	.15	.07
❑	21	Jody Reed	.10	.05
❑	22	Luis Rivera	.10	.05
❑	23	Mo Vaughn	.15	.07
❑	24	Gary DiSarcina	.10	.05
❑	25	Chuck Finley	.15	.07
❑	26	Gary Gaetti	.15	.07
❑	27	Bryan Harvey	.10	.05
❑	28	Lance Parrish	.15	.07
❑	29	Luis Polonia	.10	.05
❑	30	Dick Schofield	.10	.05
❑	31	Luis Sojo	.10	.05
❑	32	Wilson Alvarez	.10	.05
❑	33	Carlton Fisk	.40	.18
❑	34	Craig Grebeck	.10	.05
❑	35	Ozzie Guillen	.10	.05
❑	36	Greg Hibbard	.10	.05
❑	37	Charlie Hough	.15	.07
❑	38	Lance Johnson	.10	.05
❑	39	Ron Karkovice	.10	.05
❑	40	Jack McDowell	.10	.05
❑	41	Donn Pall	.10	.05
❑	42	Melido Perez	.10	.05
❑	43	Tim Raines	.15	.07
❑	44	Frank Thomas	.50	.23
❑	45	Sandy Alomar Jr.	.15	.07
❑	46	Carlos Baerga	.10	.05
❑	47	Albert Belle	.15	.07
❑	48	Jerry Browne UER (Reversed negative on card back)	.10	.05
❑	49	Felix Fermin	.10	.05
❑	50	Reggie Jefferson UER (Born 1968& not 1966)	.10	.05
❑	51	Mark Lewis	.10	.05
❑	52	Carlos Martinez	.10	.05
❑	53	Steve Olin	.10	.05
❑	54	Jim Thome	.40	.18
❑	55	Mark Whiten	.10	.05
❑	56	Dave Bergman	.10	.05
❑	57	Milt Cuyler	.10	.05
❑	58	Rob Deer	.10	.05
❑	59	Cecil Fielder	.15	.07
❑	60	Travis Fryman	.15	.07
❑	61	Scott Livingstone	.10	.05
❑	62	Tony Phillips	.10	.05
❑	63	Mickey Tettleton	.10	.05
❑	64	Alan Trammell	.25	.11
❑	65	Lou Whitaker	.15	.07
❑	66	Kevin Appier	.15	.07
❑	67	Mike Boddicker	.10	.05
❑	68	George Brett	.75	.35
❑	69	Jim Eisenreich	.10	.05
❑	70	Mark Gubicza	.10	.05
❑	71	David Howard	.10	.05
❑	72	Joel Johnson	.10	.05
❑	73	Mike Macfarlane	.10	.05
❑	74	Brent Mayne	.10	.05
❑	75	Brian McRae	.10	.05
❑	76	Jeff Montgomery	.10	.05
❑	77	Danny Tartabull	.10	.05
❑	78	Don August	.10	.05
❑	79	Dante Bichette	.15	.07
❑	80	Ted Higuera	.10	.05
❑	81	Paul Molitor	.40	.18
❑	82	Jaime Navarro	.10	.05
❑	83	Gary Sheffield	.15	.07
❑	84	Bill Spiers	.10	.05
❑	85	B.J. Surhoff	.15	.07
❑	86	Greg Vaughn	.15	.07
❑	87	Robin Yount	.40	.18
❑	88	Rick Aguilera	.15	.07
❑	89	Chili Davis	.15	.07
❑	90	Scott Erickson	.10	.05
❑	91	Brian Harper	.10	.05
❑	92	Kent Hrbek	.15	.07
❑	93	Chuck Knoblauch	.15	.07
❑	94	Scott Leius	.10	.05
❑	95	Shane Mack	.10	.05
❑	96	Mike Pagliarulo	.10	.05
❑	97	Kirby Puckett	1.00	.45
❑	98	Kevin Tapani	.10	.05
❑	99	Jesse Barfield	.10	.05
❑	100	Alvaro Espinoza	.10	.05
❑	101	Mel Hall	.10	.05
❑	102	Pat Kelly	.10	.05
❑	103	Roberto Kelly	.10	.05
❑	104	Kevin Maas	.10	.05
❑	105	Don Mattingly	1.00	.45
❑	106	Hensley Meulens	.10	.05
❑	107	Matt Nokes	.10	.05
❑	108	Steve Sax	.10	.05
❑	109	Harold Baines	.15	.07
❑	110	Jose Canseco	.40	.18
❑	111	Ron Darling	.10	.05
❑	112	Mike Gallego	.10	.05
❑	113	Dave Henderson	.10	.05
❑	114	Rickey Henderson	.75	.35
❑	115	Mark McGwire	1.50	.70
❑	116	Terry Steinbach	.10	.05
❑	117	Dave Stewart	.15	.07
❑	118	Todd Van Poppel	.10	.05
❑	119	Bob Welch	.10	.05
❑	120	Greg Briley	.10	.05
❑	121	Jay Buhner	.15	.07
❑	122	Rick DeLucia	.10	.05
❑	123	Ken Griffey Jr.	1.25	.55
❑	124	Erik Hanson	.10	.05
❑	125	Randy Johnson	.50	.23
❑	126	Edgar Martinez	.25	.11
❑	127	Tino Martinez	.15	.07
❑	128	Pete O'Brien	.10	.05
❑	129	Harold Reynolds	.10	.05
❑	130	Dave Valle	.10	.05
❑	131	Julio Franco	.15	.07
❑	132	Juan Gonzalez	.40	.18
❑	133	Jeff Huson (Shows Jose Canseco sliding into second)	.15	.07
❑	134	Mike Jeffcoat	.10	.05
❑	135	Terry Mathews	.10	.05
❑	136	Rafael Palmeiro	.40	.18
❑	137	Dean Palmer	.15	.07
❑	138	Geno Petralli	.10	.05
❑	139	Ivan Rodriguez	.60	.25
❑	140	Jeff Russell	.10	.05
❑	141	Nolan Ryan	2.00	.90
❑	142	Ruben Sierra	.10	.05
❑	143	Roberto Alomar	.40	.18
❑	144	Pat Borders	.10	.05
❑	145	Joe Carter	.15	.07
❑	146	Kelly Gruber	.10	.05
❑	147	Jimmy Key	.15	.07
❑	148	Manny Lee	.10	.05
❑	149	Rance Mulliniks	.10	.05
❑	150	Greg Myers	.10	.05
❑	151	John Olerud	.15	.07
❑	152	Dave Stieb	.10	.05
❑	153	Todd Stottlemyre	.10	.05
❑	154	Duane Ward	.10	.05
❑	155	Devon White	.10	.05
❑	156	Eddie Zosky	.10	.05
❑	157	Steve Avery	.10	.05
❑	158	Rafael Belliard	.10	.05
❑	159	Jeff Blauser	.10	.05
❑	160	Sid Bream	.10	.05
❑	161	Ron Gant	.10	.05
❑	162	Tom Glavine	.40	.18
❑	163	Brian Hunter	.10	.05
❑	164	Dave Justice	.15	.07
❑	165	Mark Lemke	.10	.05
❑	166	Greg Olson	.10	.05
❑	167	Terry Pendleton	.15	.07
❑	168	Lonnie Smith	.10	.05
❑	169	John Smoltz	.15	.07
❑	170	Mike Stanton	.10	.05
❑	171	Jeff Treadway	.10	.05
❑	172	Paul Assenmacher	.10	.05
❑	173	George Bell	.10	.05
❑	174	Shawon Dunston	.10	.05
❑	175	Mark Grace	.40	.18
❑	176	Danny Jackson	.10	.05
❑	177	Les Lancaster	.10	.05
❑	178	Greg Maddux	1.00	.45
❑	179	Luis Salazar	.10	.05
❑	180	Rey Sanchez RC	.15	.07
❑	181	Ryne Sandberg	.50	.23
❑	182	Jose Vizcaino	.10	.05
❑	183	Chico Walker	.10	.05
❑	184	Jerome Walton	.10	.05
❑	185	Glenn Braggs	.10	.05
❑	186	Tom Browning	.10	.05
❑	187	Rob Dibble	.10	.05
❑	188	Bill Doran	.10	.05
❑	189	Chris Hammond	.10	.05
❑	190	Billy Hatcher	.10	.05
❑	191	Barry Larkin	.40	.18
❑	192	Hal Morris	.10	.05
❑	193	Joe Oliver	.10	.05
❑	194	Paul O'Neill	.40	.18
❑	195	Jeff Reed	.10	.05
❑	196	Jose Rijo	.10	.05
❑	197	Chris Sabo	.10	.05
❑	198	Jeff Bagwell	.75	.35
❑	199	Craig Biggio	.25	.11
❑	200	Ken Caminiti	.15	.07
❑	201	Andujar Cedeno	.10	.05
❑	202	Steve Finley	.15	.07
❑	203	Luis Gonzalez	.40	.18
❑	204	Pete Harnisch	.10	.05
❑	205	Xavier Hernandez	.10	.05
❑	206	Darryl Kile	.15	.07
❑	207	Al Osuna	.10	.05
❑	208	Curt Schilling	.40	.18
❑	209	Brett Butler	.15	.07
❑	210	Kal Daniels	.10	.05
❑	211	Lenny Harris	.10	.05
❑	212	Stan Javier	.10	.05
❑	213	Ramon Martinez	.10	.05
❑	214	Roger McDowell	.10	.05
❑	215	Jose Offerman	.10	.05
❑	216	Juan Samuel	.10	.05
❑	217	Mike Scioscia	.10	.05
❑	218	Mike Sharperson	.10	.05
❑	219	Darryl Strawberry	.15	.07
❑	220	Delino DeShields	.10	.05
❑	221	Tom Foley	.10	.05
❑	222	Steve Frey	.10	.05
❑	223	Dennis Martinez	.15	.07
❑	224	Spike Owen	.10	.05
❑	225	Gilberto Reyes	.10	.05
❑	226	Tim Wallach	.10	.05
❑	227	Daryl Boston	.10	.05
❑	228	Tim Burke	.10	.05
❑	229	Vince Coleman	.10	.05
❑	230	David Cone	.15	.07
❑	231	Kevin Elster	.10	.05
❑	232	Dwight Gooden	.15	.07
❑	233	Todd Hundley	.10	.05
❑	234	Jeff Innis	.10	.05
❑	235	Howard Johnson	.10	.05
❑	236	Dave Magadan	.10	.05
❑	237	Mackey Sasser	.10	.05
❑	238	Anthony Young	.10	.05
❑	239	Wes Chamberlain	.10	.05
❑	240	Darren Daulton	.15	.07
❑	241	Len Dykstra	.15	.07
❑	242	Tommy Greene	.10	.05
❑	243	Charlie Hayes	.10	.05
❑	244	Dave Hollins	.10	.05
❑	245	Ricky Jordan	.10	.05
❑	246	John Kruk	.15	.07
❑	247	Mickey Morandini	.10	.05
❑	248	Terry Mulholland	.10	.05
❑	249	Dale Murphy	.40	.18
❑	250	Jay Bell	.15	.07

❑ 251 Barry Bonds 1.00 .45
❑ 252 Steve Buechele .10 .05
❑ 253 Doug Drabek .10 .05
❑ 254 Mike LaValliere .10 .05
❑ 255 Jose Lind .10 .05
❑ 256 Lloyd McClendon .10 .05
❑ 257 Orlando Merced .10 .05
❑ 258 Don Slaught .10 .05
❑ 259 John Smiley .10 .05
❑ 260 Zane Smith .10 .05
❑ 261 Randy Tomlin .10 .05
❑ 262 Andy Van Slyke .15 .07
❑ 263 Pedro Guerrero .15 .07
❑ 264 Felix Jose .10 .05
❑ 265 Ray Lankford .10 .05
❑ 266 Omar Olivares .10 .05
❑ 267 Jose Oquendo .10 .05
❑ 268 Tom Pagnozzi .10 .05
❑ 269 Bryn Smith .10 .05
❑ 270 Lee Smith UER .15 .07
(1991 record listed as 61-61)
❑ 271 Ozzie Smith UER .50 .23
(Comma before year of birth on card back)
❑ 272 Milt Thompson .10 .05
❑ 273 Todd Zeile .10 .05
❑ 274 Andy Benes .10 .05
❑ 275 Jerald Clark .10 .05
❑ 276 Tony Fernandez .10 .05
❑ 277 Tony Gwynn .75 .35
❑ 278 Greg W. Harris .10 .05
❑ 279 Thomas Howard .10 .05
❑ 280 Bruce Hurst .10 .05
❑ 281 Mike Maddux .10 .05
❑ 282 Fred McGriff .25 .11
❑ 283 Benito Santiago .10 .05
❑ 284 Kevin Bass .10 .05
❑ 285 Jeff Brantley .10 .05
❑ 286 John Burkett .10 .05
❑ 287 Will Clark .40 .18
❑ 288 Royce Clayton .10 .05
❑ 289 Steve Decker .10 .05
❑ 290 Kelly Downs .10 .05
❑ 291 Mike Felder .10 .05
❑ 292 Darren Lewis .10 .05
❑ 293 Kirt Manwaring .10 .05
❑ 294 Willie McGee .15 .07
❑ 295 Robby Thompson .10 .05
❑ 296 Matt Williams .25 .11
❑ 297 Trevor Wilson .10 .05
❑ 298 Checklist 1-100 .10 .05
❑ 299 Checklist 101-200 .10 .05
❑ 300 Checklist 201-300 .10 .05
❑ 301 Brady Anderson .15 .07
❑ 302 Todd Frohwirth .10 .05
❑ 303 Ben McDonald .10 .05
❑ 304 Mark McLemore .10 .05
❑ 305 Jose Mesa .10 .05
❑ 306 Bob Milacki .10 .05
❑ 307 Gregg Olson .10 .05
❑ 308 David Segui .10 .05
❑ 309 Rick Sutcliffe .15 .07
❑ 310 Jeff Tackett .10 .05
❑ 311 Wade Boggs .40 .18
❑ 312 Scott Cooper .10 .05
❑ 313 John Flaherty .10 .05
❑ 314 Wayne Housie .10 .05
❑ 315 Peter Hoy .10 .05
❑ 316 John Marzano .10 .05
❑ 317 Tim Naehring .10 .05
❑ 318 Phil Plantier .10 .05
❑ 319 Frank Viola .15 .07
❑ 320 Matt Young .10 .05
❑ 321 Jim Abbott .15 .07
❑ 322 Hubie Brooks .10 .05
❑ 323 Chad Curtis RC .15 .07
❑ 324 Alvin Davis .10 .05
❑ 325 Junior Felix .10 .05
❑ 326 Von Hayes .10 .05
❑ 327 Mark Langston .10 .05
❑ 328 Scott Lewis .10 .05
❑ 329 Don Robinson .10 .05
❑ 330 Bobby Rose .10 .05
❑ 331 Lee Stevens .10 .05
❑ 332 George Bell .10 .05
❑ 333 Esteban Beltre .10 .05
❑ 334 Joey Cora .10 .05
❑ 335 Alex Fernandez .10 .05
❑ 336 Roberto Hernandez .10 .05
❑ 337 Mike Huff .10 .05
❑ 338 Kirk McCaskill .10 .05
❑ 339 Dan Pasqua .10 .05
❑ 340 Scott Radinsky .10 .05
❑ 341 Steve Sax .10 .05
❑ 342 Bobby Thigpen .10 .05
❑ 343 Robin Ventura .15 .07
❑ 344 Jack Armstrong .10 .05
❑ 345 Alex Cole .10 .05
❑ 346 Dennis Cook .10 .05
❑ 347 Glenallen Hill .10 .05
❑ 348 Thomas Howard .10 .05
❑ 349 Brook Jacoby .10 .05
❑ 350 Kenny Lofton .40 .18
❑ 351 Charles Nagy .10 .05
❑ 352 Rod Nichols .10 .05
❑ 353 Junior Ortiz .10 .05
❑ 354 Dave Otto .10 .05
❑ 355 Tony Perezchica .10 .05
❑ 356 Scott Scudder .10 .05
❑ 357 Paul Sorrento .10 .05
❑ 358 Skeeter Barnes .10 .05
❑ 359 Mark Carreon .10 .05
❑ 360 John Doherty RC .10 .05
❑ 361 Dan Gladden .10 .05
❑ 362 Bill Gullickson .10 .05
❑ 363 Shawn Hare RC .10 .05
❑ 364 Mike Henneman .10 .05
❑ 365 Chad Kreuter .10 .05
❑ 366 Mark Leiter .10 .05
❑ 367 Mike Munoz .10 .05
❑ 368 Kevin Ritz .10 .05
❑ 369 Mark Davis .10 .05
❑ 370 Tom Gordon .10 .05
❑ 371 Chris Gwynn .10 .05
❑ 372 Gregg Jefferies .10 .05
❑ 373 Wally Joyner .15 .07
❑ 374 Kevin McReynolds .10 .05
❑ 375 Keith Miller .10 .05
❑ 376 Rico Rossy .10 .05
❑ 377 Curtis Wilkerson .10 .05
❑ 378 Ricky Bones .10 .05
❑ 379 Chris Bosio .10 .05
❑ 380 Cal Eldred .10 .05
❑ 381 Scott Fletcher .10 .05
❑ 382 Jim Gantner .10 .05
❑ 383 Darryl Hamilton .10 .05
❑ 384 Doug Henry RC .10 .05
❑ 385 Pat Listach RC .15 .07
❑ 386 Tim McIntosh .10 .05
❑ 387 Edwin Nunez .10 .05
❑ 388 Dan Plesac .10 .05
❑ 389 Kevin Seitzer .10 .05
❑ 390 Franklin Stubbs .10 .05
❑ 391 William Suero .10 .05
❑ 392 Bill Wegman .10 .05
❑ 393 Willie Banks .10 .05
❑ 394 Jarvis Brown .10 .05
❑ 395 Greg Gagne .10 .05
❑ 396 Mark Guthrie .10 .05
❑ 397 Bill Krueger .10 .05
❑ 398 Pat Mahomes RC .10 .05
❑ 399 Pedro Munoz .10 .05
❑ 400 John Smiley .10 .05
❑ 401 Gary Wayne .10 .05
❑ 402 Lenny Webster .10 .05
❑ 403 Carl Willis .10 .05
❑ 404 Greg Cadaret .10 .05
❑ 405 Steve Farr .10 .05
❑ 406 Mike Gallego .10 .05
❑ 407 Charlie Hayes .10 .05
❑ 408 Steve Howe .10 .05
❑ 409 Dion James .10 .05
❑ 410 Jeff Johnson .10 .05
❑ 411 Tim Leary .10 .05
❑ 412 Jim Leyritz .10 .05
❑ 413 Melido Perez .10 .05
❑ 414 Scott Sanderson .10 .05
❑ 415 Andy Stankiewicz .10 .05
❑ 416 Mike Stanley .10 .05
❑ 417 Danny Tartabull .10 .05
❑ 418 Lance Blankenship .10 .05
❑ 419 Mike Bordick .10 .05
❑ 420 Scott Brosius RC .50 .23
❑ 421 Dennis Eckersley .15 .07
❑ 422 Scott Hemond .10 .05
❑ 423 Carney Lansford .15 .07
❑ 424 Henry Mercedes .10 .05
❑ 425 Mike Moore .10 .05
❑ 426 Gene Nelson .10 .05
❑ 427 Randy Ready .10 .05
❑ 428 Bruce Walton .10 .05
❑ 429 Willie Wilson .10 .05
❑ 430 Rich Amaral .10 .05
❑ 431 Dave Cochrane .10 .05
❑ 432 Henry Cotto .10 .05
❑ 433 Calvin Jones .10 .05
❑ 434 Kevin Mitchell .10 .05
❑ 435 Clay Parker .10 .05
❑ 436 Omar Vizquel .15 .07
❑ 437 Floyd Bannister .10 .05
❑ 438 Kevin Brown .15 .07
❑ 439 John Cangelosi .10 .05
❑ 440 Brian Downing .10 .05
❑ 441 Monty Fariss .10 .05
❑ 442 Jose Guzman .10 .05
❑ 443 Donald Harris .10 .05
❑ 444 Kevin Reimer .10 .05
❑ 445 Kenny Rogers .10 .05
❑ 446 Wayne Rosenthal .10 .05
❑ 447 Dickie Thon .10 .05
❑ 448 Derek Bell .15 .07
❑ 449 Juan Guzman .10 .05
❑ 450 Tom Henke .10 .05
❑ 451 Candy Maldonado .10 .05
❑ 452 Jack Morris .15 .07
❑ 453 David Wells .15 .07
❑ 454 Dave Winfield .40 .18
❑ 455 Juan Berenguer .10 .05
❑ 456 Damon Berryhill .10 .05
❑ 457 Mike Bielecki .10 .05
❑ 458 Marvin Freeman .10 .05
❑ 459 Charlie Leibrandt .10 .05
❑ 460 Kent Mercker .10 .05
❑ 461 Otis Nixon .10 .05
❑ 462 Alejandro Pena .10 .05
❑ 463 Ben Rivera .10 .05
❑ 464 Deion Sanders .15 .07
❑ 465 Mark Wohlers .10 .05
❑ 466 Shawn Boskie .10 .05
❑ 467 Frank Castillo .10 .05
❑ 468 Andre Dawson .25 .11
❑ 469 Joe Girardi .10 .05
❑ 470 Chuck McElroy .10 .05
❑ 471 Mike Morgan .10 .05
❑ 472 Ken Patterson .10 .05
❑ 473 Bob Scanlan .10 .05
❑ 474 Gary Scott .10 .05
❑ 475 Dave Smith .10 .05
❑ 476 Sammy Sosa .75 .35
❑ 477 Hector Villanueva .10 .05
❑ 478 Scott Bankhead .10 .05
❑ 479 Tim Belcher .10 .05
❑ 480 Freddie Benavides .10 .05
❑ 481 Jacob Brumfield .10 .05
❑ 482 Norm Charlton .10 .05
❑ 483 Dwayne Henry .10 .05
❑ 484 Dave Martinez .10 .05
❑ 485 Bip Roberts .10 .05
❑ 486 Reggie Sanders .10 .05
❑ 487 Greg Swindell .10 .05
❑ 488 Ryan Bowen .10 .05
❑ 489 Casey Candaele .10 .05
❑ 490 Juan Guerrero UER .10 .05
(photo on front is Andujar Cedeno
❑ 491 Pete Incaviglia .10 .05
❑ 492 Jeff Juden .10 .05
❑ 493 Rob Murphy .10 .05
❑ 494 Mark Portugal .10 .05
❑ 495 Rafael Ramirez .10 .05
❑ 496 Scott Servais .10 .05
❑ 497 Ed Taubensee RC .15 .07
❑ 498 Brian Williams RC .10 .05
❑ 499 Todd Benzinger .10 .05
❑ 500 John Candelaria .10 .05
❑ 501 Tom Candiotti .10 .05
❑ 502 Tim Crews .10 .05
❑ 503 Eric Davis .15 .07

No.	Player	Mint	Nrmt
504	Jim Gott	.10	.05
505	Dave Hansen	.10	.05
506	Carlos Hernandez	.10	.05
507	Orel Hershiser	.15	.07
508	Eric Karros	.15	.07
509	Bob Ojeda	.10	.05
510	Steve Wilson	.10	.05
511	Moises Alou	.15	.07
512	Bret Barberie	.10	.05
513	Ivan Calderon	.10	.05
514	Gary Carter	.25	.11
515	Archi Cianfrocco RC	.10	.05
516	Jeff Fassero	.10	.05
517	Darrin Fletcher	.10	.05
518	Marquis Grissom	.10	.05
519	Chris Haney	.10	.05
520	Ken Hill	.10	.05
521	Chris Nabholz	.10	.05
522	Bill Sampen	.10	.05
523	John Vander Wal	.10	.05
524	Dave Wainhouse	.10	.05
525	Larry Walker	.25	.11
526	John Wetteland	.15	.07
527	Bobby Bonilla	.15	.07
528	Sid Fernandez	.10	.05
529	John Franco	.15	.07
530	Dave Gallagher	.10	.05
531	Paul Gibson	.10	.05
532	Eddie Murray	.40	.18
533	Junior Noboa	.10	.05
534	Charlie O'Brien	.10	.05
535	Bill Pecota	.10	.05
536	Willie Randolph	.15	.07
537	Bret Saberhagen	.15	.07
538	Dick Schofield	.10	.05
539	Pete Schourek	.10	.05
540	Ruben Amaro	.10	.05
541	Andy Ashby	.10	.05
542	Kim Batiste	.10	.05
543	Cliff Brantley	.10	.05
544	Mariano Duncan	.10	.05
545	Jeff Grotewold	.10	.05
546	Barry Jones	.10	.05
547	Julio Peguero	.10	.05
548	Curt Schilling	.40	.18
549	Mitch Williams	.10	.05
550	Stan Belinda	.10	.05
551	Scott Bullett RC	.10	.05
552	Cecil Espy	.10	.05
553	Jeff King	.10	.05
554	Roger Mason	.10	.05
555	Paul Miller	.10	.05
556	Denny Neagle	.15	.07
557	Vicente Palacios	.10	.05
558	Bob Patterson	.10	.05
559	Tom Prince	.10	.05
560	Gary Redus	.10	.05
561	Gary Varsho	.10	.05
562	Juan Agosto	.10	.05
563	Cris Carpenter	.10	.05
564	Mark Clark RC	.15	.07
565	Jose DeLeon	.10	.05
566	Rich Gedman	.10	.05
567	Bernard Gilkey	.10	.05
568	Rex Hudler	.10	.05
569	Tim Jones	.10	.05
570	Donovan Osborne	.10	.05
571	Mike Perez	.10	.05
572	Gerald Perry	.10	.05
573	Bob Tewksbury	.10	.05
574	Todd Worrell	.10	.05
575	Dave Eiland	.10	.05
576	Jeremy Hernandez RC	.10	.05
577	Craig Lefferts	.10	.05
578	Jose Melendez	.10	.05
579	Randy Myers	.10	.05
580	Gary Pettis	.10	.05
581	Rich Rodriguez	.10	.05
582	Gary Sheffield	.15	.07
583	Craig Shipley	.10	.05
584	Kurt Stillwell	.10	.05
585	Tim Teufel	.10	.05
586	Rod Beck RC	.40	.18
587	Dave Burba	.10	.05
588	Craig Colbert	.10	.05
589	Bryan Hickerson RC	.10	.05
590	Mike Jackson	.10	.05
591	Mark Leonard	.10	.05
592	Jim McNamara	.10	.05
593	John Patterson	.10	.05
594	Dave Righetti	.15	.07
595	Cory Snyder	.10	.05
596	Bill Swift	.10	.05
597	Ted Wood	.10	.05
598	Checklist 301-400	.10	.05
599	Checklist 401-500	.10	.05
600	Checklist 501-600	.10	.05

1993 Ultra

	MINT	NRMT
COMPLETE SET (650)	30.00	13.50
COMPLETE SERIES 1 (300)	15.00	6.75
COMPLETE SERIES 2 (350)	15.00	6.75

No.	Player	Mint	Nrmt
1	Steve Avery	.15	.07
2	Rafael Belliard	.15	.07
3	Damon Berryhill	.15	.07
4	Sid Bream	.15	.07
5	Ron Gant	.15	.07
6	Tom Glavine	.60	.25
7	Ryan Klesko	.25	.11
8	Mark Lemke	.15	.07
9	Javier Lopez	.25	.11
10	Greg Olson	.15	.07
11	Terry Pendleton	.25	.11
12	Deion Sanders	.25	.11
13	Mike Stanton	.15	.07
14	Paul Assenmacher	.15	.07
15	Steve Buechele	.15	.07
16	Frank Castillo	.15	.07
17	Shawon Dunston	.15	.07
18	Mark Grace	.60	.25
19	Derrick May	.15	.07
20	Chuck McElroy	.15	.07
21	Mike Morgan	.15	.07
22	Bob Scanlan	.15	.07
23	Dwight Smith	.15	.07
24	Sammy Sosa	1.25	.55
25	Rick Wilkins	.15	.07
26	Tim Belcher	.15	.07
27	Jeff Branson	.15	.07
28	Bill Doran	.15	.07
29	Chris Hammond	.15	.07
30	Barry Larkin	.60	.25
31	Hal Morris	.15	.07
32	Joe Oliver	.15	.07
33	Jose Rijo	.15	.07
34	Bip Roberts	.15	.07
35	Chris Sabo	.15	.07
36	Reggie Sanders	.15	.07
37	Craig Biggio	.40	.18
38	Ken Caminiti	.25	.11
39	Steve Finley	.25	.11
40	Luis Gonzalez	.60	.25
41	Juan Guerrero	.15	.07
42	Pete Harnisch	.15	.07
43	Xavier Hernandez	.15	.07
44	Doug Jones	.15	.07
45	Al Osuna	.15	.07
46	Eddie Taubensee	.15	.07
47	Scooter Tucker	.15	.07
48	Brian Williams	.15	.07
49	Pedro Astacio	.15	.07
50	Rafael Bournigal	.15	.07
51	Brett Butler	.25	.11
52	Tom Candiotti	.15	.07
53	Eric Davis	.25	.11
54	Lenny Harris	.15	.07
55	Orel Hershiser	.25	.11
56	Eric Karros	.25	.11
57	Pedro Martinez	1.50	.70
58	Roger McDowell	.15	.07
59	Jose Offerman	.15	.07
60	Mike Piazza	3.00	1.35
61	Moises Alou	.25	.11
62	Kent Bottenfield	.15	.07
63	Archi Cianfrocco	.15	.07
64	Greg Colbrunn	.15	.07
65	Wil Cordero	.15	.07
66	Delino DeShields	.15	.07
67	Darrin Fletcher	.15	.07
68	Ken Hill	.15	.07
69	Chris Nabholz	.15	.07
70	Mel Rojas	.15	.07
71	Larry Walker	.40	.18
72	Sid Fernandez	.15	.07
73	John Franco	.25	.11
74	Dave Gallagher	.15	.07
75	Todd Hundley	.15	.07
76	Howard Johnson	.15	.07
77	Jeff Kent	.60	.25
78	Eddie Murray	.60	.25
79	Bret Saberhagen	.25	.11
80	Chico Walker	.15	.07
81	Anthony Young	.15	.07
82	Kyle Abbott	.15	.07
83	Ruben Amaro	.15	.07
84	Juan Bell	.15	.07
85	Wes Chamberlain	.15	.07
86	Darren Daulton	.25	.11
87	Mariano Duncan	.15	.07
88	Dave Hollins	.15	.07
89	Ricky Jordan	.15	.07
90	John Kruk	.25	.11
91	Mickey Morandini	.15	.07
92	Terry Mulholland	.15	.07
93	Ben Rivera	.15	.07
94	Mike Williams	.15	.07
95	Stan Belinda	.15	.07
96	Jay Bell	.25	.11
97	Jeff King	.15	.07
98	Mike LaValliere	.15	.07
99	Lloyd McClendon	.15	.07
100	Orlando Merced	.15	.07
101	Zane Smith	.15	.07
102	Randy Tomlin	.15	.07
103	Andy Van Slyke	.25	.11
104	Tim Wakefield	.15	.07
105	John Wehner	.15	.07
106	Bernard Gilkey	.15	.07
107	Brian Jordan	.25	.11
108	Ray Lankford	.15	.07
109	Donovan Osborne	.15	.07
110	Tom Pagnozzi	.15	.07
111	Mike Perez	.15	.07
112	Lee Smith	.25	.11
113	Ozzie Smith	.75	.35
114	Bob Tewksbury	.15	.07
115	Todd Zeile	.15	.07
116	Andy Benes	.15	.07
117	Greg W. Harris	.15	.07
118	Darrin Jackson	.15	.07
119	Fred McGriff	.40	.18
120	Rich Rodriguez	.15	.07
121	Frank Seminara	.15	.07
122	Gary Sheffield	.25	.11
123	Craig Shipley	.15	.07
124	Kurt Stillwell	.15	.07
125	Dan Walters	.15	.07
126	Rod Beck	.15	.07
127	Mike Benjamin	.15	.07
128	Jeff Brantley	.15	.07
129	John Burkett	.15	.07
130	Will Clark	.60	.25
131	Royce Clayton	.15	.07
132	Steve Hosey	.15	.07
133	Mike Jackson	.15	.07
134	Darren Lewis	.15	.07
135	Kirt Manwaring	.15	.07
136	Bill Swift	.15	.07

❑ 137 Robby Thompson .15 .07
❑ 138 Brady Anderson .25 .11
❑ 139 Glenn Davis .15 .07
❑ 140 Leo Gomez .15 .07
❑ 141 Chito Martinez .15 .07
❑ 142 Ben McDonald .15 .07
❑ 143 Alan Mills .15 .07
❑ 144 Mike Mussina .60 .25
❑ 145 Gregg Olson .15 .07
❑ 146 David Segui .15 .07
❑ 147 Jeff Tackett .15 .07
❑ 148 Jack Clark .25 .11
❑ 149 Scott Cooper .15 .07
❑ 150 Danny Darwin .15 .07
❑ 151 John Dopson .15 .07
❑ 152 Mike Greenwell .15 .07
❑ 153 Tim Naehring .15 .07
❑ 154 Tony Pena .15 .07
❑ 155 Paul Quantrill .15 .07
❑ 156 Mo Vaughn .25 .11
❑ 157 Frank Viola .25 .11
❑ 158 Bob Zupcic .15 .07
❑ 159 Chad Curtis .15 .07
❑ 160 Gary DiSarcina .15 .07
❑ 161 Damion Easley .15 .07
❑ 162 Chuck Finley .25 .11
❑ 163 Tim Fortugno .15 .07
❑ 164 Rene Gonzales .15 .07
❑ 165 Joe Grahe .15 .07
❑ 166 Mark Langston .15 .07
❑ 167 John Orton .15 .07
❑ 168 Luis Polonia .15 .07
❑ 169 Julio Valera .15 .07
❑ 170 Wilson Alvarez .15 .07
❑ 171 George Bell .15 .07
❑ 172 Joey Cora .15 .07
❑ 173 Alex Fernandez .15 .07
❑ 174 Lance Johnson .15 .07
❑ 175 Ron Karkovice .15 .07
❑ 176 Jack McDowell .15 .07
❑ 177 Scott Radinsky .15 .07
❑ 178 Tim Raines .25 .11
❑ 179 Steve Sax .15 .07
❑ 180 Bobby Thigpen .15 .07
❑ 181 Frank Thomas .75 .35
❑ 182 Sandy Alomar Jr. .25 .11
❑ 183 Carlos Baerga .15 .07
❑ 184 Felix Fermin .15 .07
❑ 185 Thomas Howard .15 .07
❑ 186 Mark Lewis .15 .07
❑ 187 Derek Lilliquist .15 .07
❑ 188 Carlos Martinez .15 .07
❑ 189 Charles Nagy .15 .07
❑ 190 Scott Scudder .15 .07
❑ 191 Paul Sorrento .15 .07
❑ 192 Jim Thome .60 .25
❑ 193 Mark Whiten .15 .07
❑ 194 Milt Cuyler UER .15 .07
(Reversed negative
on card front)
❑ 195 Rob Deer .15 .07
❑ 196 John Doherty .15 .07
❑ 197 Travis Fryman .25 .11
❑ 198 Dan Gladden .15 .07
❑ 199 Mike Henneman .15 .07
❑ 200 John Kiely .15 .07
❑ 201 Chad Kreuter .15 .07
❑ 202 Scott Livingstone .15 .07
❑ 203 Tony Phillips .15 .07
❑ 204 Alan Trammell .40 .18
❑ 205 Mike Boddicker .15 .07
❑ 206 George Brett 1.25 .55
❑ 207 Tom Gordon .15 .07
❑ 208 Mark Gubicza .15 .07
❑ 209 Gregg Jefferies .15 .07
❑ 210 Wally Joyner .25 .11
❑ 211 Kevin Koslofski .15 .07
❑ 212 Brent Mayne .15 .07
❑ 213 Brian McRae .15 .07
❑ 214 Kevin McReynolds .15 .07
❑ 215 Rusty Meacham .15 .07
❑ 216 Steve Shifflett .15 .07
❑ 217 James Austin .15 .07
❑ 218 Cal Eldred .15 .07
❑ 219 Darryl Hamilton .15 .07
❑ 220 Doug Henry .15 .07
❑ 221 John Jaha .15 .07
❑ 222 Dave Nilsson .15 .07
❑ 223 Jesse Orosco .15 .07
❑ 224 B.J. Surhoff .25 .11
❑ 225 Greg Vaughn .25 .11
❑ 226 Bill Wegman .15 .07
❑ 227 Robin Yount UER .60 .25
(Born in Illinois&
not in Virginia)
❑ 228 Rick Aguilera .15 .07
❑ 229 J.T. Bruett .15 .07
❑ 230 Scott Erickson .15 .07
❑ 231 Kent Hrbek .25 .11
❑ 232 Terry Jorgensen .15 .07
❑ 233 Scott Leius .15 .07
❑ 234 Pat Mahomes .15 .07
❑ 235 Pedro Munoz .15 .07
❑ 236 Kirby Puckett 1.50 .70
❑ 237 Kevin Tapani .15 .07
❑ 238 Lenny Webster .15 .07
❑ 239 Carl Willis .15 .07
❑ 240 Mike Gallego .15 .07
❑ 241 John Habyan .15 .07
❑ 242 Pat Kelly .15 .07
❑ 243 Kevin Maas .15 .07
❑ 244 Don Mattingly 1.50 .70
❑ 245 Hensley Meulens .15 .07
❑ 246 Sam Militello .15 .07
❑ 247 Matt Nokes .15 .07
❑ 248 Melido Perez .15 .07
❑ 249 Andy Stankiewicz .15 .07
❑ 250 Randy Velarde .15 .07
❑ 251 Bob Wickman .15 .07
❑ 252 Bernie Williams .60 .25
❑ 253 Lance Blankenship .15 .07
❑ 254 Mike Bordick .15 .07
❑ 255 Jerry Browne .15 .07
❑ 256 Ron Darling .15 .07
❑ 257 Dennis Eckersley .25 .11
❑ 258 Rickey Henderson 1.25 .55
❑ 259 Vince Horsman .15 .07
❑ 260 Troy Neel .15 .07
❑ 261 Jeff Parrett .15 .07
❑ 262 Terry Steinbach .15 .07
❑ 263 Bob Welch .15 .07
❑ 264 Bobby Witt .15 .07
❑ 265 Rich Amaral .15 .07
❑ 266 Bret Boone .25 .11
❑ 267 Jay Buhner .25 .11
❑ 268 Dave Fleming .15 .07
❑ 269 Randy Johnson .75 .35
❑ 270 Edgar Martinez .40 .18
❑ 271 Mike Schooler .15 .07
❑ 272 Russ Swan .15 .07
❑ 273 Dave Valle .15 .07
❑ 274 Omar Vizquel .25 .11
❑ 275 Kerry Woodson .15 .07
❑ 276 Kevin Brown .25 .11
277 Julio Franco .25 .11
❑ 278 Jeff Frye .15 .07
❑ 279 Juan Gonzalez .60 .25
❑ 280 Jeff Huson .15 .07
❑ 281 Rafael Palmeiro .60 .25
❑ 282 Dean Palmer .25 .11
❑ 283 Roger Pavlik .15 .07
❑ 284 Ivan Rodriguez .60 .25
❑ 285 Kenny Rogers .15 .07
❑ 286 Derek Bell .15 .07
❑ 287 Pat Borders .15 .07
❑ 288 Joe Carter .25 .11
❑ 289 Bob MacDonald .15 .07
❑ 290 Jack Morris .25 .11
❑ 291 John Olerud .25 .11
❑ 292 Ed Sprague .15 .07
❑ 293 Todd Stottlemyre .15 .07
❑ 294 Mike Timlin .15 .07
❑ 295 Duane Ward .15 .07
❑ 296 David Wells .25 .11
❑ 297 Devon White .15 .07
❑ 298 Ray Lankford CL .15 .07
❑ 299 Bobby Witt CL .15 .07
❑ 300 Mike Piazza CL .60 .25
❑ 301 Steve Bedrosian .15 .07
❑ 302 Jeff Blauser .15 .07
❑ 303 Francisco Cabrera .15 .07
❑ 304 Marvin Freeman .15 .07
❑ 305 Brian Hunter .15 .07
❑ 306 David Justice .25 .11
❑ 307 Greg Maddux 1.50 .70
❑ 308 Greg McMichael RC .15 .07
❑ 309 Kent Mercker .15 .07
❑ 310 Otis Nixon .15 .07
❑ 311 Pete Smith .15 .07
❑ 312 John Smoltz .25 .11
❑ 313 Jose Guzman .15 .07
❑ 314 Mike Harkey .15 .07
❑ 315 Greg Hibbard .15 .07
❑ 316 Candy Maldonado .15 .07
❑ 317 Randy Myers .15 .07
❑ 318 Dan Plesac .15 .07
❑ 319 Rey Sanchez .15 .07
❑ 320 Ryne Sandberg .75 .35
❑ 321 Tommy Shields .15 .07
❑ 322 Jose Vizcaino .15 .07
❑ 323 Matt Walbeck RC .15 .07
❑ 324 Willie Wilson .15 .07
❑ 325 Tom Browning .15 .07
❑ 326 Tim Costo .15 .07
❑ 327 Rob Dibble .15 .07
❑ 328 Steve Foster .15 .07
❑ 329 Roberto Kelly .15 .07
❑ 330 Randy Milligan .15 .07
❑ 331 Kevin Mitchell .15 .07
❑ 332 Tim Pugh RC .15 .07
❑ 333 Jeff Reardon .25 .11
❑ 334 John Roper .15 .07
❑ 335 Juan Samuel .15 .07
❑ 336 John Smiley .15 .07
❑ 337 Dan Wilson .25 .11
❑ 388 Scott Aldred .15 .07
❑ 339 Andy Ashby .15 .07
❑ 340 Freddie Benavides .15 .07
❑ 341 Dante Bichette .25 .11
❑ 342 Willie Blair .15 .07
❑ 343 Daryl Boston .15 .07
❑ 344 Vinny Castilla .25 .11
❑ 345 Jerald Clark .15 .07
❑ 346 Alex Cole .15 .07
❑ 347 Andres Galarraga .40 .18
❑ 348 Joe Girardi .15 .07
❑ 349 Ryan Hawblitzel .15 .07
❑ 350 Charlie Hayes .15 .07
❑ 351 Butch Henry .15 .07
❑ 352 Darren Holmes .15 .07
❑ 353 Dale Murphy .40 .18
❑ 354 David Nied .15 .07
❑ 355 Jeff Parrett .15 .07
❑ 356 Steve Reed RC .15 .07
❑ 357 Bruce Ruffin .15 .07
❑ 358 Danny Sheaffer RC .15 .07
❑ 359 Bryn Smith .15 .07
❑ 360 Jim Tatum RC .15 .07
❑ 361 Eric Young .15 .07
❑ 362 Gerald Young .15 .07
❑ 363 Luis Aquino .15 .07
❑ 364 Alex Arias .15 .07
❑ 365 Jack Armstrong .15 .07
❑ 366 Bret Barberie .15 .07
❑ 367 Ryan Bowen .15 .07
❑ 368 Greg Briley .15 .07
❑ 369 Cris Carpenter .15 .07
❑ 370 Chuck Carr .15 .07
❑ 371 Jeff Conine .15 .07
❑ 372 Steve Decker .15 .07
❑ 373 Orestes Destrade .15 .07
❑ 374 Monty Fariss .15 .07
❑ 375 Junior Felix .15 .07
❑ 376 Chris Hammond .15 .07
❑ 377 Bryan Harvey .15 .07
❑ 378 Trevor Hoffman .25 .11
❑ 379 Charlie Hough .25 .11
❑ 380 Joe Klink .15 .07
❑ 381 Richie Lewis RC .15 .07
❑ 382 Dave Magadan .15 .07
❑ 383 Bob McClure .15 .07
❑ 384 Scott Pose RC .15 .07
❑ 385 Rich Renteria .15 .07
❑ 386 Benito Santiago .15 .07
❑ 387 Walt Weiss .15 .07
❑ 388 Nigel Wilson .15 .07
❑ 389 Eric Anthony .15 .07
❑ 390 Jeff Bagwell .75 .35

❑ 391 Andujar Cedeno .15 .07
❑ 392 Doug Drabek .15 .07
❑ 393 Darryl Kile .25 .11
❑ 394 Mark Portugal .15 .07
❑ 395 Karl Rhodes .15 .07
❑ 396 Scott Servais .15 .07
❑ 397 Greg Swindell .15 .07
❑ 398 Tom Goodwin .15 .07
❑ 399 Kevin Gross .15 .07
❑ 400 Carlos Hernandez .15 .07
❑ 401 Ramon Martinez .15 .07
❑ 402 Raul Mondesi .25 .11
❑ 403 Jody Reed .15 .07
❑ 404 Mike Sharperson .15 .07
❑ 405 Cory Snyder .15 .07
❑ 406 Darryl Strawberry .25 .11
❑ 407 Rick Trlicek .15 .07
❑ 408 Tim Wallach .15 .07
❑ 409 Todd Worrell .15 .07
❑ 410 Tavo Alvarez .15 .07
❑ 411 Sean Berry .15 .07
❑ 412 Frank Bolick .15 .07
❑ 413 Cliff Floyd .25 .11
❑ 414 Mike Gardiner .15 .07
❑ 415 Marquis Grissom .15 .07
❑ 416 Tim Laker RC .15 .07
❑ 417 Mike Lansing RC .25 .11
❑ 418 Dennis Martinez .25 .11
❑ 419 John Vander Wal .15 .07
❑ 420 John Wetteland .25 .11
❑ 421 Rondell White .25 .11
❑ 422 Bobby Bonilla .25 .11
❑ 423 Jeromy Burnitz .25 .11
❑ 424 Vince Coleman .15 .07
❑ 425 Mike Draper .15 .07
❑ 426 Tony Fernandez .15 .07
❑ 427 Dwight Gooden .25 .11
❑ 428 Jeff Innis .15 .07
❑ 429 Bobby Jones .25 .11
❑ 430 Mike Maddux .15 .07
❑ 431 Charlie O'Brien .15 .07
❑ 432 Joe Orsulak .15 .07
❑ 433 Pete Schourek .15 .07
❑ 434 Frank Tanana .15 .07
❑ 435 Ryan Thompson .15 .07
❑ 436 Kim Batiste .15 .07
❑ 437 Mark Davis .15 .07
❑ 438 Jose DeLeon .15 .07
❑ 439 Len Dykstra .25 .11
❑ 440 Jim Eisenreich .15 .07
❑ 441 Tommy Greene .15 .07
❑ 442 Pete Incaviglia .15 .07
❑ 443 Danny Jackson .15 .07
❑ 444 Todd Pratt RC .25 .11
❑ 445 Curt Schilling .60 .25
❑ 446 Milt Thompson .15 .07
❑ 447 David West .15 .07
❑ 448 Mitch Williams .15 .07
❑ 449 Steve Cooke .15 .07
❑ 450 Carlos Garcia .15 .07
❑ 451 Al Martin .15 .07
❑ 452 Blas Minor .15 .07
❑ 453 Dennis Moeller .15 .07
❑ 454 Denny Neagle .25 .11
❑ 455 Don Slaught .15 .07
❑ 456 Lonnie Smith .15 .07
❑ 457 Paul Wagner .15 .07
❑ 458 Bob Walk .15 .07
❑ 459 Kevin Young .25 .11
❑ 460 Rene Arocha RC .25 .11
❑ 461 Brian Barber .15 .07
❑ 462 Rheal Cormier .15 .07
❑ 463 Gregg Jefferies .15 .07
❑ 464 Joe Magrane .15 .07
❑ 465 Omar Olivares .15 .07
❑ 466 Geronimo Pena .15 .07
❑ 467 Allen Watson .15 .07
❑ 468 Mark Whiten .15 .07
❑ 469 Derek Bell .15 .07
❑ 470 Phil Clark .15 .07
❑ 471 Pat Gomez RC .15 .07
❑ 472 Tony Gwynn 1.25 .55
❑ 473 Jeremy Hernandez .15 .07
❑ 474 Bruce Hurst .15 .07
❑ 475 Phil Plantier .15 .07
❑ 476 Scott Sanders RC .15 .07
❑ 477 Tim Scott .15 .07
❑ 478 Darrell Sherman RC .15 .07
❑ 479 Guillermo Velasquez .15 .07
❑ 480 Tim Worrell RC .15 .07
❑ 481 Todd Benzinger .15 .07
❑ 482 Bud Black .15 .07
❑ 483 Barry Bonds 1.50 .70
❑ 484 Dave Burba .15 .07
❑ 485 Bryan Hickerson .15 .07
❑ 486 Dave Martinez .15 .07
❑ 487 Willie McGee .25 .11
❑ 488 Jeff Reed .15 .07
❑ 489 Kevin Rogers .15 .07
❑ 490 Matt Williams .40 .18
❑ 491 Trevor Wilson .15 .07
❑ 492 Harold Baines .25 .11
❑ 493 Mike Devereaux .15 .07
❑ 494 Todd Frohwirth .15 .07
❑ 495 Chris Hoiles .15 .07
❑ 496 Luis Mercedes .15 .07
❑ 497 Sherman Obando RC .15 .07
❑ 498 Brad Pennington .15 .07
❑ 499 Harold Reynolds .15 .07
❑ 500 Arthur Rhodes .15 .07
❑ 501 Cal Ripken 2.50 1.10
❑ 502 Rick Sutcliffe .25 .11
❑ 503 Fernando Valenzuela .25 .11
❑ 504 Mark Williamson .15 .07
❑ 505 Scott Bankhead .15 .07
❑ 506 Greg Blosser .15 .07
❑ 507 Ivan Calderon .15 .07
❑ 508 Roger Clemens 1.50 .70
❑ 509 Andre Dawson .40 .18
❑ 510 Scott Fletcher .15 .07
❑ 511 Greg A. Harris .15 .07
❑ 512 Billy Hatcher .15 .07
❑ 513 Bob Melvin .15 .07
❑ 514 Carlos Quintana .15 .07
❑ 515 Luis Rivera .15 .07
❑ 516 Jeff Russell .15 .07
❑ 517 Ken Ryan RC .15 .07
❑ 518 Chili Davis .25 .11
❑ 519 Jim Edmonds RC 4.00 1.80
❑ 520 Gary Gaetti .25 .11
❑ 521 Torey Lovullo .15 .07
❑ 522 Troy Percival .25 .11
❑ 523 Tim Salmon .25 .11
❑ 524 Scott Sanderson .15 .07
❑ 525 J.T. Snow RC .75 .35
❑ 526 Jerome Walton .15 .07
❑ 527 Jason Bere .15 .07
❑ 528 Rod Bolton .15 .07
❑ 529 Ellis Burks .25 .11
❑ 530 Carlton Fisk .60 .25
❑ 531 Craig Grebeck .15 .07
❑ 532 Ozzie Guillen .15 .07
❑ 533 Roberto Hernandez .15 .07
❑ 534 Bo Jackson .25 .11
❑ 535 Kirk McCaskill .15 .07
❑ 536 Dave Stieb .15 .07
❑ 537 Robin Ventura .25 .11
❑ 538 Albert Belle .25 .11
❑ 539 Mike Bielecki .15 .07
❑ 540 Glenallen Hill .15 .07
❑ 541 Reggie Jefferson .15 .07
❑ 542 Kenny Lofton .25 .11
❑ 543 Jeff Mutis .15 .07
❑ 544 Junior Ortiz .15 .07
❑ 545 Manny Ramirez 1.50 .70
❑ 546 Jeff Treadway .15 .07
❑ 547 Kevin Wickander .15 .07
❑ 548 Cecil Fielder .25 .11
❑ 549 Kirk Gibson .25 .11
❑ 550 Greg Gohr .15 .07
❑ 551 David Haas .15 .07
❑ 552 Bill Krueger .15 .07
❑ 553 Mike Moore .15 .07
❑ 554 Mickey Tettleton .15 .07
❑ 555 Lou Whitaker .25 .11
❑ 556 Kevin Appier .25 .11
❑ 557 Billy Brewer .15 .07
❑ 558 David Cone .25 .11
❑ 559 Greg Gagne .15 .07
❑ 560 Mark Gardner .15 .07
❑ 561 Phil Hiatt .15 .07
❑ 562 Felix Jose .15 .07
❑ 563 Jose Lind .15 .07
❑ 564 Mike Macfarlane .15 .07
❑ 565 Keith Miller .15 .07
❑ 566 Jeff Montgomery .15 .07
❑ 567 Hipolito Pichardo .15 .07
❑ 568 Ricky Bones .15 .07
❑ 569 Tom Brunansky .15 .07
❑ 570 Joe Kmak .15 .07
❑ 571 Pat Listach .15 .07
❑ 572 Graeme Lloyd RC .25 .11
❑ 573 Carlos Maldonado .15 .07
❑ 574 Josias Manzanillo .15 .07
❑ 575 Matt Mieske .15 .07
❑ 576 Kevin Reimer .15 .07
❑ 577 Bill Spiers .15 .07
❑ 578 Dickie Thon .15 .07
❑ 579 Willie Banks .15 .07
❑ 580 Jim Deshaies .15 .07
❑ 581 Mark Guthrie .15 .07
❑ 582 Brian Harper .15 .07
❑ 583 Chuck Knoblauch .25 .11
❑ 584 Gene Larkin .15 .07
❑ 585 Shane Mack .15 .07
❑ 586 David McCarty .15 .07
❑ 587 Mike Pagliarulo .15 .07
❑ 588 Mike Trombley .15 .07
❑ 589 Dave Winfield .60 .25
❑ 590 Jim Abbott .25 .11
❑ 591 Wade Boggs .60 .25
❑ 592 Russ Davis RC .25 .11
❑ 593 Steve Farr .15 .07
❑ 594 Steve Howe .15 .07
❑ 595 Mike Humphreys .15 .07
❑ 596 Jimmy Key .25 .11
❑ 597 Jim Leyritz .15 .07
❑ 598 Bobby Munoz .15 .07
❑ 599 Paul O'Neill .60 .25
❑ 600 Spike Owen .15 .07
❑ 601 Mike Stanley .15 .07
❑ 602 Danny Tartabull .15 .07
❑ 603 Scott Brosius .25 .11
❑ 604 Storm Davis .15 .07
❑ 605 Eric Fox .15 .07
❑ 606 Rich Gossage .25 .11
❑ 607 Scott Hemond .15 .07
❑ 608 Dave Henderson .15 .07
❑ 609 Mark McGwire 2.50 1.10
❑ 610 Mike Mohler RC .15 .07
❑ 611 Edwin Nunez .15 .07
❑ 612 Kevin Seitzer .15 .07
❑ 613 Ruben Sierra .15 .07
❑ 614 Chris Bosio .15 .07
❑ 615 Norm Charlton .15 .07
❑ 616 Jim Converse RC .15 .07
❑ 617 John Cummings RC .15 .07
❑ 618 Mike Felder .15 .07
❑ 619 Ken Griffey Jr. 2.00 .90
❑ 620 Mike Hampton .60 .25
❑ 621 Erik Hanson .15 .07
❑ 622 Bill Haselman .15 .07
❑ 623 Tino Martinez .25 .11
❑ 624 Lee Tinsley .15 .07
❑ 625 Fernando Vina RC .50 .23
❑ 626 David Wainhouse .15 .07
❑ 627 Jose Canseco .60 .25
❑ 628 Benji Gil .15 .07
❑ 629 Tom Henke .15 .07
❑ 630 David Hulse RC .15 .07
❑ 631 Manuel Lee .15 .07
❑ 632 Craig Lefferts .15 .07
❑ 633 Robb Nen .15 .07
❑ 634 Gary Redus .15 .07
❑ 635 Bill Ripken .15 .07
❑ 636 Nolan Ryan 3.00 1.35
❑ 637 Dan Smith .15 .07
❑ 638 Matt Whiteside RC .15 .07
❑ 639 Roberto Alomar .60 .25
❑ 640 Juan Guzman .15 .07
❑ 641 Pat Hentgen .15 .07
❑ 642 Darrin Jackson .15 .07
❑ 643 Randy Knorr .15 .07
❑ 644 Domingo Martinez RC .15 .07
❑ 645 Paul Molitor .60 .25
❑ 646 Dick Schofield .15 .07
❑ 647 Dave Stewart .25 .11
❑ 648 Rey Sanchez CL .15 .07

	Card	Mint	NrMt
❑	649 Jeremy Hernandez CL	.15	.07
❑	650 Junior Ortiz CL	.15	.07

1994 Ultra

	MINT	NRMT
COMPLETE SET (600)	30.00	13.50
COMPLETE SERIES 1 (300)	15.00	6.75
COMPLETE SERIES 2 (300)	15.00	6.75

	Card	Mint	NrMt
❑	1 Jeffrey Hammonds	.25	.11
❑	2 Chris Hoiles	.15	.07
❑	3 Ben McDonald	.15	.07
❑	4 Mark McLemore	.15	.07
❑	5 Alan Mills	.15	.07
❑	6 Jamie Moyer	.15	.07
❑	7 Brad Pennington	.15	.07
❑	8 Jim Poole	.15	.07
❑	9 Cal Ripken Jr.	2.50	1.10
❑	10 Jack Voigt	.15	.07
❑	11 Roger Clemens	1.50	.70
❑	12 Danny Darwin	.15	.07
❑	13 Andre Dawson	.40	.18
❑	14 Scott Fletcher	.15	.07
❑	15 Greg A. Harris	.15	.07
❑	16 Billy Hatcher	.15	.07
❑	17 Jeff Russell	.15	.07
❑	18 Aaron Sele	.25	.11
❑	19 Mo Vaughn	.25	.11
❑	20 Mike Butcher	.15	.07
❑	21 Rod Correia	.15	.07
❑	22 Steve Frey	.15	.07
❑	23 Phil Leftwich RC	.15	.07
❑	24 Torey Lovullo	.15	.07
❑	25 Ken Patterson	.15	.07
❑	26 Eduardo Perez UER (listed as a Twin instead of Angel)	.15	.07
❑	27 Tim Salmon	.25	.11
❑	28 J.T. Snow	.25	.11
❑	29 Chris Turner	.15	.07
❑	30 Wilson Alvarez	.15	.07
❑	31 Jason Bere	.15	.07
❑	32 Joey Cora	.15	.07
❑	33 Alex Fernandez	.15	.07
❑	34 Roberto Hernandez	.15	.07
❑	35 Lance Johnson	.15	.07
❑	36 Ron Karkovice	.15	.07
❑	37 Kirk McCaskill	.15	.07
❑	38 Jeff Schwarz	.15	.07
❑	39 Frank Thomas	.75	.35
❑	40 Sandy Alomar Jr.	.25	.11
❑	41 Albert Belle	.25	.11
❑	42 Felix Fermin	.15	.07
❑	43 Wayne Kirby	.15	.07
❑	44 Tom Kramer	.15	.07
❑	45 Kenny Lofton	.25	.11
❑	46 Jose Mesa	.15	.07
❑	47 Eric Plunk	.15	.07
❑	48 Paul Sorrento	.15	.07
❑	49 Jim Thome	.60	.25
❑	50 Bill Wertz	.15	.07
❑	51 John Doherty	.15	.07
❑	52 Cecil Fielder	.25	.11
❑	53 Travis Fryman	.25	.11
❑	54 Chris Gomez	.15	.07
❑	55 Mike Henneman	.15	.07
❑	56 Chad Kreuter	.15	.07
❑	57 Bob MacDonald	.15	.07
❑	58 Mike Moore	.15	.07
❑	59 Tony Phillips	.15	.07
❑	60 Lou Whitaker	.25	.11
❑	61 Kevin Appier	.25	.11
❑	62 Greg Gagne	.15	.07
❑	63 Chris Gwynn	.15	.07
❑	64 Bob Hamelin	.15	.07
❑	65 Chris Haney	.15	.07
❑	66 Phil Hiatt	.15	.07
❑	67 Felix Jose	.15	.07
❑	68 Jose Lind	.15	.07
❑	69 Mike Macfarlane	.15	.07
❑	70 Jeff Montgomery	.15	.07
❑	71 Hipolito Pichardo	.15	.07
❑	72 Juan Bell	.15	.07
❑	73 Cal Eldred	.15	.07
❑	74 Darryl Hamilton	.15	.07
❑	75 Doug Henry	.15	.07
❑	76 Mike Ignasiak	.15	.07
❑	77 John Jaha	.15	.07
❑	78 Graeme Lloyd	.15	.07
❑	79 Angel Miranda	.15	.07
❑	80 Dave Nilsson	.15	.07
❑	81 Troy O'Leary	.15	.07
❑	82 Kevin Reimer	.15	.07
❑	83 Willie Banks	.15	.07
❑	84 Larry Casian	.15	.07
❑	85 Scott Erickson	.15	.07
❑	86 Eddie Guardado	.15	.07
❑	87 Kent Hrbek	.25	.11
❑	88 Terry Jorgensen	.15	.07
❑	89 Chuck Knoblauch	.25	.11
❑	90 Pat Meares	.15	.07
❑	91 Mike Trombley	.15	.07
❑	92 Dave Winfield	.60	.25
❑	93 Wade Boggs	.60	.25
❑	94 Scott Kamieniecki	.15	.07
❑	95 Pat Kelly	.15	.07
❑	96 Jimmy Key	.25	.11
❑	97 Jim Leyritz	.15	.07
❑	98 Bobby Munoz	.15	.07
❑	99 Paul O'Neill	.60	.25
❑	100 Melido Perez	.15	.07
❑	101 Mike Stanley	.15	.07
❑	102 Danny Tartabull	.15	.07
❑	103 Bernie Williams	.60	.25
❑	104 Kurt Abbott RC	.25	.11
❑	105 Mike Bordick	.15	.07
❑	106 Ron Darling	.15	.07
❑	107 Brent Gates	.15	.07
❑	108 Miguel Jimenez	.15	.07
❑	109 Steve Karsay	.15	.07
❑	110 Scott Lydy	.15	.07
❑	111 Mark McGwire	2.50	1.10
❑	112 Troy Neel	.15	.07
❑	113 Craig Paquette	.15	.07
❑	114 Bob Welch	.15	.07
❑	115 Bobby Witt	.15	.07
❑	116 Rich Amaral	.15	.07
❑	117 Mike Blowers	.15	.07
❑	118 Jay Buhner	.25	.11
❑	119 Dave Fleming	.15	.07
❑	120 Ken Griffey Jr.	2.00	.90
❑	121 Tino Martinez	.25	.11
❑	122 Marc Newfield	.15	.07
❑	123 Ted Power	.15	.07
❑	124 Mackey Sasser	.15	.07
❑	125 Omar Vizquel	.25	.11
❑	126 Kevin Brown	.25	.11
❑	127 Juan Gonzalez	.60	.25
❑	128 Tom Henke	.15	.07
❑	129 David Hulse	.15	.07
❑	130 Dean Palmer	.25	.11
❑	131 Roger Pavlik	.15	.07
❑	132 Ivan Rodriguez	.60	.25
❑	133 Kenny Rogers	.15	.07
❑	134 Doug Strange	.15	.07
❑	135 Pat Borders	.15	.07
❑	136 Joe Carter	.25	.11
❑	137 Darnell Coles	.15	.07
❑	138 Pat Hentgen	.15	.07
❑	139 Al Leiter	.25	.11
❑	140 Paul Molitor	.60	.25
❑	141 John Olerud	.25	.11
❑	142 Ed Sprague	.15	.07
❑	143 Dave Stewart	.25	.11
❑	144 Mike Timlin	.15	.07
❑	145 Duane Ward	.15	.07
❑	146 Devon White	.15	.07
❑	147 Steve Avery	.15	.07
❑	148 Steve Bedrosian	.15	.07
❑	149 Damon Berryhill	.15	.07
❑	150 Jeff Blauser	.15	.07
❑	151 Tom Glavine	.60	.25
❑	152 Chipper Jones	1.25	.55
❑	153 Mark Lemke	.15	.07
❑	154 Fred McGriff	.40	.18
❑	155 Greg McMichael	.15	.07
❑	156 Deion Sanders	.25	.11
❑	157 John Smoltz	.25	.11
❑	158 Mark Wohlers	.15	.07
❑	159 Jose Bautista	.15	.07
❑	160 Steve Buechele	.15	.07
❑	161 Mike Harkey	.15	.07
❑	162 Greg Hibbard	.15	.07
❑	163 Chuck McElroy	.15	.07
❑	164 Mike Morgan	.15	.07
❑	165 Kevin Roberson	.15	.07
❑	166 Ryne Sandberg	.75	.35
❑	167 Jose Vizcaino	.15	.07
❑	168 Rick Wilkins	.15	.07
❑	169 Willie Wilson	.15	.07
❑	170 Willie Greene	.15	.07
❑	171 Roberto Kelly	.15	.07
❑	172 Larry Luebbers RC	.15	.07
❑	173 Kevin Mitchell	.15	.07
❑	174 Joe Oliver	.15	.07
❑	175 John Roper	.15	.07
❑	176 Johnny Ruffin	.15	.07
❑	177 Reggie Sanders	.15	.07
❑	178 John Smiley	.15	.07
❑	179 Jerry Spradlin RC	.15	.07
❑	180 Freddie Benavides	.15	.07
❑	181 Dante Bichette	.25	.11
❑	182 Willie Blair	.15	.07
❑	183 Kent Bottenfield	.15	.07
❑	184 Jerald Clark	.15	.07
❑	185 Joe Girardi	.15	.07
❑	186 Roberto Mejia	.15	.07
❑	187 Steve Reed	.15	.07
❑	188 Armando Reynoso	.15	.07
❑	189 Bruce Ruffin	.15	.07
❑	190 Eric Young	.15	.07
❑	191 Luis Aquino	.15	.07
❑	192 Bret Barberie	.15	.07
❑	193 Ryan Bowen	.15	.07
❑	194 Chuck Carr	.15	.07
❑	195 Orestes Destrade	.15	.07
❑	196 Richie Lewis	.15	.07
❑	197 Dave Magadan	.15	.07
❑	198 Bob Natal	.15	.07
❑	199 Gary Sheffield	.25	.11
❑	200 Matt Turner	.15	.07
❑	201 Darrell Whitmore	.15	.07
❑	202 Eric Anthony	.15	.07
❑	203 Jeff Bagwell	.75	.35
❑	204 Andujar Cedeno	.15	.07
❑	205 Luis Gonzalez	.60	.25
❑	206 Xavier Hernandez	.15	.07
❑	207 Doug Jones	.15	.07
❑	208 Darryl Kile	.25	.11
❑	209 Scott Servais	.15	.07
❑	210 Greg Swindell	.15	.07
❑	211 Brian Williams	.15	.07
❑	212 Pedro Astacio	.15	.07
❑	213 Brett Butler	.25	.11
❑	214 Omar Daal	.15	.07
❑	215 Jim Gott	.15	.07
❑	216 Raul Mondesi	.25	.11
❑	217 Jose Offerman	.15	.07
❑	218 Mike Piazza	2.00	.90
❑	219 Cory Snyder	.15	.07
❑	220 Tim Wallach	.15	.07
❑	221 Todd Worrell	.15	.07
❑	222 Moises Alou	.25	.11
❑	223 Sean Berry	.15	.07
❑	224 Wil Cordero	.15	.07
❑	225 Jeff Fassero	.15	.07
❑	226 Darrin Fletcher	.15	.07
❑	227 Cliff Floyd	.25	.11
❑	228 Marquis Grissom	.15	.07

❑ 229 Ken Hill .15 .07
❑ 230 Mike Lansing .15 .07
❑ 231 Kirk Rueter .15 .07
❑ 232 John Wetteland .25 .11
❑ 233 Rondell White .25 .11
❑ 234 Tim Bogar .15 .07
❑ 235 Jeromy Burnitz .25 .11
❑ 236 Dwight Gooden .25 .11
❑ 237 Todd Hundley .15 .07
❑ 238 Jeff Kent .40 .18
❑ 239 Josias Manzanillo .15 .07
❑ 240 Joe Orsulak .15 .07
❑ 241 Ryan Thompson .15 .07
❑ 242 Kim Batiste .15 .07
❑ 243 Darren Daulton .25 .11
❑ 244 Tommy Greene .15 .07
❑ 245 Dave Hollins .15 .07
❑ 246 Pete Incaviglia .15 .07
❑ 247 Danny Jackson .15 .07
❑ 248 Ricky Jordan .15 .07
❑ 249 John Kruk .25 .11
❑ 250 Mickey Morandini .15 .07
❑ 251 Terry Mulholland .15 .07
❑ 252 Ben Rivera .15 .07
❑ 253 Kevin Stocker .15 .07
❑ 254 Jay Bell .25 .11
❑ 255 Steve Cooke .15 .07
❑ 256 Jeff King .15 .07
❑ 257 Al Martin .15 .07
❑ 258 Danny Miceli .15 .07
❑ 259 Blas Minor .15 .07
❑ 260 Don Slaught .15 .07
❑ 261 Paul Wagner .15 .07
❑ 262 Tim Wakefield .15 .07
❑ 263 Kevin Young .15 .07
❑ 264 Rene Arocha .15 .07
❑ 265 Richard Batchelor RC .15 .07
❑ 266 Gregg Jefferies .15 .07
❑ 267 Brian Jordan .25 .11
❑ 268 Jose Oquendo .15 .07
❑ 269 Donovan Osborne .15 .07
❑ 270 Erik Pappas .15 .07
❑ 271 Mike Perez .15 .07
❑ 272 Bob Tewksbury .15 .07
❑ 273 Mark Whiten .15 .07
❑ 274 Todd Zeile .15 .07
❑ 275 Andy Ashby .15 .07
❑ 276 Brad Ausmus .15 .07
❑ 277 Phil Clark .15 .07
❑ 278 Jeff Gardner .15 .07
❑ 279 Ricky Gutierrez .15 .07
❑ 280 Tony Gwynn 1.25 .55
❑ 281 Tim Mauser .15 .07
❑ 282 Scott Sanders .15 .07
❑ 283 Frank Seminara .15 .07
❑ 284 Wally Whitehurst .15 .07
❑ 285 Rod Beck .15 .07
❑ 286 Barry Bonds 1.50 .70
❑ 287 Dave Burba .15 .07
❑ 288 Mark Carreon .15 .07
❑ 289 Royce Clayton .15 .07
❑ 290 Mike Jackson .15 .07
❑ 291 Darren Lewis .15 .07
❑ 292 Kirt Manwaring .15 .07
❑ 293 Dave Martinez .15 .07
❑ 294 Billy Swift .15 .07
❑ 295 Salomon Torres .15 .07
❑ 296 Matt Williams .40 .18
❑ 297 Checklist 1-75 .15 .07
❑ 298 Checklist 76-150 .15 .07
❑ 299 Checklist 151-225 .15 .07
❑ 300 Checklist 226-300 .15 .07
❑ 301 Brady Anderson .25 .11
❑ 302 Harold Baines .25 .11
❑ 303 Damon Buford .15 .07
❑ 304 Mike Devereaux .15 .07
❑ 305 Sid Fernandez .15 .07
❑ 306 Rick Krivda RC .15 .07
❑ 307 Mike Mussina .60 .25
❑ 308 Rafael Palmeiro .60 .25
❑ 309 Arthur Rhodes .15 .07
❑ 310 Chris Sabo .15 .07
❑ 311 Lee Smith .25 .11
❑ 312 Gregg Zaun RC .15 .07
❑ 313 Scott Cooper .15 .07
❑ 314 Mike Greenwell .15 .07
❑ 315 Tim Naehring .15 .07
❑ 316 Otis Nixon .15 .07
❑ 317 Paul Quantrill .15 .07
❑ 318 John Valentin .15 .07
❑ 319 Dave Valle .15 .07
❑ 320 Frank Viola .25 .11
❑ 321 Brian Anderson RC .25 .11
❑ 322 Garret Anderson .25 .11
❑ 323 Chad Curtis .15 .07
❑ 324 Chili Davis .25 .11
❑ 325 Gary DiSarcina .15 .07
❑ 326 Damion Easley .15 .07
❑ 327 Jim Edmonds .60 .25
❑ 328 Chuck Finley .25 .11
❑ 329 Joe Grahe .15 .07
❑ 330 Bo Jackson .25 .11
❑ 331 Mark Langston .15 .07
❑ 332 Harold Reynolds .15 .07
❑ 333 James Baldwin .15 .07
❑ 334 Ray Durham RC 1.00 .45
❑ 335 Julio Franco .25 .11
❑ 336 Craig Grebeck .15 .07
❑ 337 Ozzie Guillen .15 .07
❑ 338 Joe Hall RC .15 .07
❑ 339 Darrin Jackson .15 .07
❑ 340 Jack McDowell .15 .07
❑ 341 Tim Raines .25 .11
❑ 342 Robin Ventura .25 .11
❑ 343 Carlos Baerga .15 .07
❑ 344 Derek Lilliquist .15 .07
❑ 345 Dennis Martinez .25 .11
❑ 346 Jack Morris .25 .11
❑ 347 Eddie Murray .60 .25
❑ 348 Chris Nabholz .15 .07
❑ 349 Charles Nagy .15 .07
❑ 350 Chad Ogea .15 .07
❑ 351 Manny Ramirez 1.00 .45
❑ 352 Omar Vizquel .25 .11
❑ 353 Tim Belcher .15 .07
❑ 354 Eric Davis .25 .11
❑ 355 Kirk Gibson .25 .11
❑ 356 Rick Greene .15 .07
❑ 357 Mickey Tettleton .15 .07
❑ 358 Alan Trammell .40 .18
❑ 359 David Wells .25 .11
❑ 360 Stan Belinda .15 .07
❑ 361 Vince Coleman .15 .07
❑ 362 David Cone .25 .11
❑ 363 Gary Gaetti .25 .11
❑ 364 Tom Gordon .15 .07
❑ 365 Dave Henderson .15 .07
❑ 366 Wally Joyner .25 .11
❑ 367 Brent Mayne .15 .07
❑ 368 Brian McRae .15 .07
❑ 369 Michael Tucker .15 .07
❑ 370 Ricky Bones .15 .07
❑ 371 Brian Harper .15 .07
❑ 372 Tyrone Hill .15 .07
❑ 373 Mark Kiefer .15 .07
❑ 374 Pat Listach .15 .07
❑ 375 Mike Matheny RC .15 .07
❑ 376 Jose Mercedes RC .15 .07
❑ 377 Jody Reed .15 .07
❑ 378 Kevin Seitzer .15 .07
❑ 379 B.J. Surhoff .25 .11
❑ 380 Greg Vaughn .25 .11
❑ 381 Turner Ward .15 .07
❑ 382 Wes Weger RC .15 .07
❑ 383 Bill Wegman .15 .07
❑ 384 Rick Aguilera .15 .07
❑ 385 Rich Becker .15 .07
❑ 386 Alex Cole .15 .07
❑ 387 Steve Dunn .15 .07
❑ 388 Keith Garagozzo RC .15 .07
❑ 389 LaTroy Hawkins RC .25 .11
❑ 390 Shane Mack .15 .07
❑ 391 David McCarty .15 .07
❑ 392 Pedro Munoz .15 .07
❑ 393 Derek Parks .15 .07
❑ 394 Kirby Puckett 1.50 .70
❑ 395 Kevin Tapani .15 .07
❑ 396 Matt Walbeck .15 .07
❑ 397 Jim Abbott .25 .11
❑ 398 Mike Gallego .15 .07
❑ 399 Xavier Hernandez .15 .07
❑ 400 Don Mattingly 1.50 .70
❑ 401 Terry Mulholland .15 .07
❑ 402 Matt Nokes .15 .07
❑ 403 Luis Polonia .15 .07
❑ 404 Bob Wickman .15 .07
❑ 405 Mark Acre RC .15 .07
❑ 406 Fausto Cruz RC .15 .07
❑ 407 Dennis Eckersley .25 .11
❑ 408 Rickey Henderson 1.25 .55
❑ 409 Stan Javier .15 .07
❑ 410 Carlos Reyes RC .15 .07
❑ 411 Ruben Sierra .15 .07
❑ 412 Terry Steinbach .15 .07
❑ 413 Bill Taylor RC .25 .11
❑ 414 Todd Van Poppel .15 .07
❑ 415 Eric Anthony .15 .07
❑ 416 Bobby Ayala .15 .07
❑ 417 Chris Bosio .15 .07
❑ 418 Tim Davis .15 .07
❑ 419 Randy Johnson .75 .35
❑ 420 Kevin King RC .15 .07
❑ 421 Anthony Manahan RC .15 .07
❑ 422 Edgar Martinez .40 .18
❑ 423 Keith Mitchell .15 .07
❑ 424 Roger Salkeld .15 .07
❑ 425 Mac Suzuki RC .25 .11
❑ 426 Dan Wilson .15 .07
❑ 427 Duff Brumley RC .15 .07
❑ 428 Jose Canseco .60 .25
❑ 429 Will Clark .60 .25
❑ 430 Steve Dreyer RC .15 .07
❑ 431 Rick Helling .15 .07
❑ 432 Chris James .15 .07
❑ 433 Matt Whiteside .15 .07
❑ 434 Roberto Alomar .60 .25
❑ 435 Scott Brow .15 .07
❑ 436 Domingo Cedeno .15 .07
❑ 437 Carlos Delgado 1.00 .45
❑ 438 Juan Guzman .15 .07
❑ 439 Paul Spoljaric .15 .07
❑ 440 Todd Stottlemyre .15 .07
❑ 441 Woody Williams .15 .07
❑ 442 David Justice .25 .11
❑ 443 Mike Kelly .15 .07
❑ 444 Ryan Klesko .25 .11
❑ 445 Javier Lopez .25 .11
❑ 446 Greg Maddux 1.50 .70
❑ 447 Kent Mercker .15 .07
❑ 448 Charlie O'Brien .15 .07
❑ 449 Terry Pendleton .25 .11
❑ 450 Mike Stanton .15 .07
❑ 451 Tony Tarasco .15 .07
❑ 452 Terrell Wade RC .15 .07
❑ 453 Willie Banks .15 .07
❑ 454 Shawon Dunston .15 .07
❑ 455 Mark Grace .60 .25
❑ 456 Jose Guzman .15 .07
❑ 457 Jose Hernandez .15 .07
❑ 458 Glenallen Hill .15 .07
❑ 459 Blaise Ilsley RC .15 .07
❑ 460 Brooks Kieschnick RC .15 .07
❑ 461 Derrick May .15 .07
❑ 462 Randy Myers .15 .07
❑ 463 Karl Rhodes .15 .07
❑ 464 Sammy Sosa 1.00 .45
❑ 465 Steve Trachsel .15 .07
❑ 466 Anthony Young .15 .07
❑ 467 Eddie Zambrano RC .15 .07
❑ 468 Bret Boone .25 .11
❑ 469 Tom Browning .15 .07
❑ 470 Hector Carrasco .15 .07
❑ 471 Rob Dibble .15 .07
❑ 472 Erik Hanson .15 .07
❑ 473 Thomas Howard .15 .07
❑ 474 Barry Larkin .60 .25
❑ 475 Hal Morris .15 .07
❑ 476 Jose Rijo .15 .07
❑ 477 John Burke .15 .07
❑ 478 Ellis Burks .25 .11
❑ 479 Marvin Freeman .15 .07
❑ 480 Andres Galarraga .40 .18
❑ 481 Greg W. Harris .15 .07
❑ 482 Charlie Hayes .15 .07
❑ 483 Darren Holmes .15 .07
❑ 484 Howard Johnson .15 .07
❑ 485 Marcus Moore .15 .07
❑ 486 David Nied .15 .07

❑ 487 Mark Thompson .15 .07
❑ 488 Walt Weiss .15 .07
❑ 489 Kurt Abbott .25 .11
❑ 490 Matias Carrillo RC .15 .07
❑ 491 Jeff Conine .15 .07
❑ 492 Chris Hammond .15 .07
❑ 493 Bryan Harvey .15 .07
❑ 494 Charlie Hough .25 .11
❑ 495 Yorkis Perez .15 .07
❑ 496 Pat Rapp .15 .07
❑ 497 Benito Santiago .15 .07
❑ 498 David Weathers .15 .07
❑ 499 Craig Biggio .40 .18
❑ 500 Ken Caminiti .25 .11
❑ 501 Doug Drabek .15 .07
❑ 502 Tony Eusebio .15 .07
❑ 503 Steve Finley .25 .11
❑ 504 Pete Harnisch .15 .07
❑ 505 Brian L. Hunter .15 .07
❑ 506 Domingo Jean .15 .07
❑ 507 Todd Jones .15 .07
❑ 508 Orlando Miller .15 .07
❑ 509 James Mouton .15 .07
❑ 510 Roberto Petagine .15 .07
❑ 511 Shane Reynolds .15 .07
❑ 512 Mitch Williams .15 .07
❑ 513 Billy Ashley .15 .07
❑ 514 Tom Candiotti .15 .07
❑ 515 Delino DeShields .15 .07
❑ 516 Kevin Gross .15 .07
❑ 517 Orel Hershiser .25 .11
❑ 518 Eric Karros .25 .11
❑ 519 Ramon Martinez .15 .07
❑ 520 Chan Ho Park RC 1.25 .55
❑ 521 Henry Rodriguez .15 .07
❑ 522 Joey Eischen .15 .07
❑ 523 Rod Henderson .15 .07
❑ 524 Pedro Martinez 1.00 .45
❑ 525 Mel Rojas .15 .07
❑ 526 Larry Walker .40 .18
❑ 527 Gabe White .15 .07
❑ 528 Bobby Bonilla .25 .11
❑ 529 Jonathan Hurst .15 .07
❑ 530 Bobby Jones .15 .07
❑ 531 Kevin McReynolds .15 .07
❑ 532 Bill Pulsipher .25 .11
❑ 533 Bret Saberhagen .25 .11
❑ 534 David Segui .15 .07
❑ 535 Pete Smith .15 .07
❑ 536 Kelly Stinnett RC .25 .11
❑ 537 Dave Telgheder .15 .07
❑ 538 Quilvio Veras .15 .07
❑ 539 Jose Vizcaino .15 .07
❑ 540 Pete Walker RC .15 .07
❑ 541 Ricky Bottalico RC .25 .11
❑ 542 Wes Chamberlain .15 .07
❑ 543 Mariano Duncan .15 .07
❑ 544 Lenny Dykstra .25 .11
❑ 545 Jim Eisenreich .15 .07
❑ 546 Phil Geisler RC .15 .07
❑ 547 Wayne Gomes RC .15 .07
❑ 548 Doug Jones .15 .07
❑ 549 Jeff Juden .15 .07
❑ 550 Mike Lieberthal .25 .11
❑ 551 Tony Longmire .15 .07
❑ 552 Tom Marsh .15 .07
❑ 553 Bobby Munoz .15 .07
❑ 554 Curt Schilling .60 .25
❑ 555 Carlos Garcia .15 .07
❑ 556 Ravelo Manzanillo RC .15 .07
❑ 557 Orlando Merced .15 .07
❑ 558 Will Pennyfeather .15 .07
❑ 559 Zane Smith .15 .07
❑ 560 Andy Van Slyke .25 .11
❑ 561 Rick White .15 .07
❑ 562 Luis Alicea .15 .07
❑ 563 Brian Barber .15 .07
❑ 564 Clint Davis RC .15 .07
❑ 565 Bernard Gilkey .15 .07
❑ 566 Ray Lankford .15 .07
❑ 567 Tom Pagnozzi .15 .07
❑ 568 Ozzie Smith .75 .35
❑ 569 Rick Sutcliffe .25 .11
❑ 570 Allen Watson .15 .07
❑ 571 Dmitri Young .25 .11
❑ 572 Derek Bell .15 .07
❑ 573 Andy Benes .15 .07
❑ 574 Archi Cianfrocco .15 .07
❑ 575 Joey Hamilton .15 .07
❑ 576 Gene Harris .15 .07
❑ 577 Trevor Hoffman .25 .11
❑ 578 Tim Hyers RC .15 .07
❑ 579 Brian Johnson RC .15 .07
❑ 580 Keith Lockhart RC .25 .11
❑ 581 Pedro A. Martinez RC .15 .07
❑ 582 Ray McDavid .15 .07
❑ 583 Phil Plantier .15 .07
❑ 584 Bip Roberts .15 .07
❑ 585 Dave Staton .15 .07
❑ 586 Todd Benzinger .15 .07
❑ 587 John Burkett .15 .07
❑ 588 Bryan Hickerson .15 .07
❑ 589 Willie McGee .25 .11
❑ 590 John Patterson .15 .07
❑ 591 Mark Portugal .15 .07
❑ 592 Kevin Rogers .15 .07
❑ 593 Joe Rosselli .15 .07
❑ 594 Steve Soderstrom RC .15 .07
❑ 595 Robby Thompson .15 .07
❑ 596 125th Anniversary Card .15 .07
❑ 597 Checklist .15 .07
❑ 598 Checklist .15 .07
❑ 599 Checklist .15 .07
❑ 600 Checklist .15 .07
❑ P243 D.Daulton Promo 2.00 .90
❑ P249 John Kruk Promo 2.00 .90

1995 Ultra

	MINT	NRMT
COMPLETE SET (450)	30.00	13.50
COMPLETE SERIES 1 (250)	18.00	8.00
COMPLETE SERIES 2 (200)	12.00	5.50

❑ 1 Brady Anderson .25 .11
❑ 2 Sid Fernandez .15 .07
❑ 3 Jeffrey Hammonds .15 .07
❑ 4 Chris Hoiles .15 .07
❑ 5 Ben McDonald .15 .07
❑ 6 Mike Mussina .60 .25
❑ 7 Rafael Palmeiro .60 .25
❑ 8 Jack Voigt .15 .07
❑ 9 Wes Chamberlain .15 .07
❑ 10 Roger Clemens 1.50 .70
❑ 11 Chris Howard .15 .07
❑ 12 Tim Naehring .15 .07
❑ 13 Otis Nixon .15 .07
❑ 14 Rich Rowland .15 .07
❑ 15 Ken Ryan .15 .07
❑ 16 John Valentin .15 .07
❑ 17 Mo Vaughn .25 .11
❑ 18 Brian Anderson .15 .07
❑ 19 Chili Davis .25 .11
❑ 20 Damion Easley .15 .07
❑ 21 Jim Edmonds .40 .18
❑ 22 Mark Langston .15 .07
❑ 23 Tim Salmon .25 .11
❑ 24 J.T. Snow .25 .11
❑ 25 Chris Turner .15 .07
❑ 26 Wilson Alvarez .15 .07
❑ 27 Joey Cora .15 .07
❑ 28 Alex Fernandez .15 .07
❑ 29 Roberto Hernandez .15 .07
❑ 30 Lance Johnson .15 .07
❑ 31 Ron Karkovice .15 .07
❑ 32 Kirk McCaskill .15 .07
❑ 33 Tim Raines .25 .11
❑ 34 Frank Thomas .75 .35
❑ 35 Sandy Alomar Jr. .25 .11
❑ 36 Albert Belle .25 .11
❑ 37 Mark Clark .15 .07
❑ 38 Kenny Lofton .25 .11
❑ 39 Eddie Murray .60 .25
❑ 40 Eric Plunk .15 .07
❑ 41 Manny Ramirez .75 .35
❑ 42 Jim Thome .60 .25
❑ 43 Omar Vizquel .25 .11
❑ 44 Danny Bautista .15 .07
❑ 45 Junior Felix .15 .07
❑ 46 Cecil Fielder .25 .11
❑ 47 Chris Gomez .15 .07
❑ 48 Chad Kreuter .15 .07
❑ 49 Mike Moore .15 .07
❑ 50 Tony Phillips .15 .07
❑ 51 Alan Trammell .40 .18
❑ 52 David Wells .25 .11
❑ 53 Kevin Appier .25 .11
❑ 54 Billy Brewer .15 .07
❑ 55 David Cone .25 .11
❑ 56 Greg Gagne .15 .07
❑ 57 Bob Hamelin .15 .07
❑ 58 Jose Lind .15 .07
❑ 59 Brent Mayne .15 .07
❑ 60 Brian McRae .15 .07
❑ 61 Terry Shumpert .15 .07
❑ 62 Ricky Bones .15 .07
❑ 63 Mike Fetters .15 .07
❑ 64 Darryl Hamilton .15 .07
❑ 65 John Jaha .15 .07
❑ 66 Graeme Lloyd .15 .07
❑ 67 Matt Mieske .15 .07
❑ 68 Kevin Seitzer .15 .07
❑ 69 Jose Valentin .15 .07
❑ 70 Turner Ward .15 .07
❑ 71 Rick Aguilera .15 .07
❑ 72 Rich Becker .15 .07
❑ 73 Alex Cole .15 .07
❑ 74 Scott Leius .15 .07
❑ 75 Pat Meares .15 .07
❑ 76 Kirby Puckett 1.50 .70
❑ 77 Dave Stevens .15 .07
❑ 78 Kevin Tapani .15 .07
❑ 79 Matt Walbeck .15 .07
❑ 80 Wade Boggs .60 .25
❑ 81 Scott Kamieniecki .15 .07
❑ 82 Pat Kelly .15 .07
❑ 83 Jimmy Key .25 .11
❑ 84 Paul O'Neill .60 .25
❑ 85 Luis Polonia .15 .07
❑ 86 Mike Stanley .15 .07
❑ 87 Danny Tartabull .15 .07
❑ 88 Bob Wickman .15 .07
❑ 89 Mark Acre .15 .07
❑ 90 Geronimo Berroa .15 .07
❑ 91 Mike Bordick .15 .07
❑ 92 Ron Darling .15 .07
❑ 93 Stan Javier .15 .07
❑ 94 Mark McGwire 2.50 1.10
❑ 95 Troy Neel .15 .07
❑ 96 Ruben Sierra .15 .07
❑ 97 Terry Steinbach .15 .07
❑ 98 Eric Anthony .15 .07
❑ 99 Chris Bosio .15 .07
❑ 100 Dave Fleming .15 .07
❑ 101 Ken Griffey Jr. 2.00 .90
❑ 102 Reggie Jefferson .15 .07
❑ 103 Randy Johnson .75 .35
❑ 104 Edgar Martinez .40 .18
❑ 105 Bill Risley .15 .07
❑ 106 Dan Wilson .15 .07
❑ 107 Cris Carpenter .15 .07
❑ 108 Will Clark .60 .25
❑ 109 Juan Gonzalez .60 .25
❑ 110 Rusty Greer .25 .11
❑ 111 David Hulse .15 .07
❑ 112 Roger Pavlik .15 .07
❑ 113 Ivan Rodriguez .60 .25
❑ 114 Doug Strange .15 .07
❑ 115 Matt Whiteside .15 .07

❑	116	Roberto Alomar	.60	.25
❑	117	Brad Cornett	.15	.07
❑	118	Carlos Delgado	.60	.25
❑	119	Alex Gonzalez	.15	.07
❑	120	Darren Hall	.15	.07
❑	121	Pat Hentgen	.15	.07
❑	122	Paul Molitor	.60	.25
❑	123	Ed Sprague	.15	.07
❑	124	Devon White	.25	.11
❑	125	Tom Glavine	.60	.25
❑	126	David Justice	.25	.11
❑	127	Roberto Kelly	.15	.07
❑	128	Mark Lemke	.15	.07
❑	129	Greg Maddux	1.50	.70
❑	130	Greg McMichael	.15	.07
❑	131	Kent Mercker	.15	.07
❑	132	Charlie O'Brien	.15	.07
❑	133	John Smoltz	.25	.11
❑	134	Willie Banks	.15	.07
❑	135	Steve Buechele	.15	.07
❑	136	Kevin Foster	.15	.07
❑	137	Glenallen Hill	.15	.07
❑	138	Rey Sanchez	.15	.07
❑	139	Sammy Sosa	1.25	.55
❑	140	Steve Trachsel	.15	.07
❑	141	Rick Wilkins	.15	.07
❑	142	Jeff Brantley	.15	.07
❑	143	Hector Carrasco	.15	.07
❑	144	Kevin Jarvis	.15	.07
❑	145	Barry Larkin	.60	.25
❑	146	Chuck McElroy	.15	.07
❑	147	Jose Rijo	.15	.07
❑	148	Johnny Ruffin	.15	.07
❑	149	Deion Sanders	.25	.11
❑	150	Eddie Taubensee	.15	.07
❑	151	Dante Bichette	.25	.11
❑	152	Ellis Burks	.25	.11
❑	153	Joe Girardi	.15	.07
❑	154	Charlie Hayes	.15	.07
❑	155	Mike Kingery	.15	.07
❑	156	Steve Reed	.15	.07
❑	157	Kevin Ritz	.15	.07
❑	158	Bruce Ruffin	.15	.07
❑	159	Eric Young	.15	.07
❑	160	Kurt Abbott	.15	.07
❑	161	Chuck Carr	.15	.07
❑	162	Chris Hammond	.15	.07
❑	163	Bryan Harvey	.15	.07
❑	164	Terry Mathews	.15	.07
❑	165	Yorkis Perez	.15	.07
❑	166	Pat Rapp	.15	.07
❑	167	Gary Sheffield	.25	.11
❑	168	Dave Weathers	.15	.07
❑	169	Jeff Bagwell	.75	.35
❑	170	Ken Caminiti	.25	.11
❑	171	Doug Drabek	.15	.07
❑	172	Steve Finley	.25	.11
❑	173	John Hudek	.15	.07
❑	174	Todd Jones	.15	.07
❑	175	James Mouton	.15	.07
❑	176	Shane Reynolds	.15	.07
❑	177	Scott Servais	.15	.07
❑	178	Tom Candiotti	.15	.07
❑	179	Omar Daal	.15	.07
❑	180	Darren Dreifort	.15	.07
❑	181	Eric Karros	.25	.11
❑	182	Ramon J.Martinez	.15	.07
❑	183	Raul Mondesi	.25	.11
❑	184	Henry Rodriguez	.15	.07
❑	185	Todd Worrell	.15	.07
❑	186	Moises Alou	.25	.11
❑	187	Sean Berry	.15	.07
❑	188	Wil Cordero	.15	.07
❑	189	Jeff Fassero	.15	.07
❑	190	Darrin Fletcher	.15	.07
❑	191	Butch Henry	.15	.07
❑	192	Ken Hill	.15	.07
❑	193	Mel Rojas	.15	.07
❑	194	John Wetteland	.25	.11
❑	195	Bobby Bonilla	.25	.11
❑	196	Rico Brogna	.15	.07
❑	197	Bobby Jones	.15	.07
❑	198	Jeff Kent	.40	.18
❑	199	Josias Manzanillo	.15	.07
❑	200	Kelly Stinnett	.15	.07
❑	201	Ryan Thompson	.15	.07
❑	202	Jose Vizcaino	.15	.07
❑	203	Lenny Dykstra	.25	.11
❑	204	Jim Eisenreich	.15	.07
❑	205	Dave Hollins	.15	.07
❑	206	Mike Lieberthal	.25	.11
❑	207	Mickey Morandini	.15	.07
❑	208	Bobby Munoz	.15	.07
❑	209	Curt Schilling	.60	.25
❑	210	Heathcliff Slocumb	.15	.07
❑	211	David West	.15	.07
❑	212	Dave Clark	.15	.07
❑	213	Steve Cooke	.15	.07
❑	214	Midre Cummings	.15	.07
❑	215	Carlos Garcia	.15	.07
❑	216	Jeff King	.15	.07
❑	217	Jon Lieber	.15	.07
❑	218	Orlando Merced	.15	.07
❑	219	Don Slaught	.15	.07
❑	220	Rick White	.15	.07
❑	221	Rene Arocha	.15	.07
❑	222	Bernard Gilkey	.15	.07
❑	223	Brian Jordan	.25	.11
❑	224	Tom Pagnozzi	.15	.07
❑	225	Vicente Palacios	.15	.07
❑	226	Geronimo Pena	.15	.07
❑	227	Ozzie Smith	.75	.35
❑	228	Allen Watson	.15	.07
❑	229	Mark Whiten	.15	.07
❑	230	Brad Ausmus	.15	.07
❑	231	Derek Bell	.15	.07
❑	232	Andy Benes	.15	.07
❑	233	Tony Gwynn	1.25	.55
❑	234	Joey Hamilton	.15	.07
❑	235	Luis Lopez	.15	.07
❑	236	Pedro A.Martinez	.15	.07
❑	237	Scott Sanders	.15	.07
❑	238	Eddie Williams	.15	.07
❑	239	Rod Beck	.15	.07
❑	240	Dave Burba	.15	.07
❑	241	Darren Lewis	.15	.07
❑	242	Kirt Manwaring	.15	.07
❑	243	Mark Portugal	.15	.07
❑	244	Darryl Strawberry	.25	.11
❑	245	Robby Thompson	.15	.07
❑	246	Wm.VanLandingham	.15	.07
❑	247	Matt Williams	.40	.18
❑	248	Checklist	.15	.07
❑	249	Checklist	.15	.07
❑	250	Checklist	.15	.07
❑	251	Harold Baines	.25	.11
❑	252	Bret Barberie	.15	.07
❑	253	Armando Benitez	.25	.11
❑	254	Mike Devereaux	.15	.07
❑	255	Leo Gomez	.15	.07
❑	256	Jamie Moyer	.15	.07
❑	257	Arthur Rhodes	.15	.07
❑	258	Cal Ripken	2.50	1.10
❑	259	Luis Alicea	.15	.07
❑	260	Jose Canseco	.60	.25
❑	261	Scott Cooper	.15	.07
❑	262	Andre Dawson	.40	.18
❑	263	Mike Greenwell	.15	.07
❑	264	Aaron Sele	.25	.11
❑	265	Garret Anderson	.25	.11
❑	266	Chad Curtis	.15	.07
❑	267	Gary DiSarcina	.15	.07
❑	268	Chuck Finley	.25	.11
❑	269	Rex Hudler	.15	.07
❑	270	Andrew Lorraine	.15	.07
❑	271	Spike Owen	.15	.07
❑	272	Lee Smith	.25	.11
❑	273	Jason Bere	.15	.07
❑	274	Ozzie Guillen	.15	.07
❑	275	Norberto Martin	.15	.07
❑	276	Scott Ruffcorn	.15	.07
❑	277	Robin Ventura	.25	.11
❑	278	Carlos Baerga	.15	.07
❑	279	Jason Grimsley	.15	.07
❑	280	Dennis Martinez	.25	.11
❑	281	Charles Nagy	.15	.07
❑	282	Paul Sorrento	.15	.07
❑	283	Dave Winfield	.60	.25
❑	284	John Doherty	.15	.07
❑	285	Travis Fryman	.25	.11
❑	286	Kirk Gibson	.25	.11
❑	287	Lou Whitaker	.25	.11
❑	288	Gary Gaetti	.25	.11
❑	289	Tom Gordon	.15	.07
❑	290	Mark Gubicza	.15	.07
❑	291	Wally Joyner	.25	.11
❑	292	Mike Macfarlane	.15	.07
❑	293	Jeff Montgomery	.15	.07
❑	294	Jeff Cirillo	.25	.11
❑	295	Cal Eldred	.15	.07
❑	296	Pat Listach	.15	.07
❑	297	Jose Mercedes	.15	.07
❑	298	Dave Nilsson	.15	.07
❑	299	Duane Singleton	.15	.07
❑	300	Greg Vaughn	.25	.11
❑	301	Scott Erickson	.15	.07
❑	302	Denny Hocking	.15	.07
❑	303	Chuck Knoblauch	.25	.11
❑	304	Pat Mahomes	.15	.07
❑	305	Pedro Munoz	.15	.07
❑	306	Erik Schullstrom	.15	.07
❑	307	Jim Abbott	.25	.11
❑	308	Tony Fernandez	.15	.07
❑	309	Sterling Hitchcock	.15	.07
❑	310	Jim Leyritz	.15	.07
❑	311	Don Mattingly	1.50	.70
❑	312	Jack McDowell	.15	.07
❑	313	Melido Perez	.15	.07
❑	314	Bernie Williams	.60	.25
❑	315	Scott Brosius	.25	.11
❑	316	Dennis Eckersley	.25	.11
❑	317	Brent Gates	.15	.07
❑	318	Rickey Henderson	1.25	.55
❑	319	Steve Karsay	.15	.07
❑	320	Steve Ontiveros	.15	.07
❑	321	Bill Taylor	.15	.07
❑	322	Todd Van Poppel	.15	.07
❑	323	Bob Welch	.15	.07
❑	324	Bobby Ayala	.15	.07
❑	325	Mike Blowers	.15	.07
❑	326	Jay Buhner	.25	.11
❑	327	Felix Fermin	.15	.07
❑	328	Tino Martinez	.25	.11
❑	329	Marc Newfield	.15	.07
❑	330	Greg Pirkl	.15	.07
❑	331	Alex Rodriguez	2.00	.90
❑	332	Kevin Brown	.25	.11
❑	333	John Burkett	.15	.07
❑	334	Jeff Frye	.15	.07
❑	335	Kevin Gross	.15	.07
❑	336	Dean Palmer	.25	.11
❑	337	Joe Carter	.25	.11
❑	338	Shawn Green	.60	.25
❑	339	Juan Guzman	.15	.07
❑	340	Mike Huff	.15	.07
❑	341	Al Leiter	.25	.11
❑	342	John Olerud	.25	.11
❑	343	Dave Stewart	.25	.11
❑	344	Todd Stottlemyre	.15	.07
❑	345	Steve Avery	.15	.07
❑	346	Jeff Blauser	.15	.07
❑	347	Chipper Jones	1.25	.55
❑	348	Mike Kelly	.15	.07
❑	349	Ryan Klesko	.25	.11
❑	350	Javier Lopez	.25	.11
❑	351	Fred McGriff	.40	.18
❑	352	Jose Oliva	.15	.07
❑	353	Terry Pendleton	.25	.11
❑	354	Mike Stanton	.15	.07
❑	355	Tony Tarasco	.15	.07
❑	356	Mark Wohlers	.15	.07
❑	357	Jim Bullinger	.15	.07
❑	358	Shawon Dunston	.15	.07
❑	359	Mark Grace	.60	.25
❑	360	Derrick May	.15	.07
❑	361	Randy Myers	.15	.07
❑	362	Karl Rhodes	.15	.07
❑	363	Bret Boone	.25	.11
❑	364	Brian Dorsett	.15	.07
❑	365	Ron Gant	.15	.07
❑	366	Brian R.Hunter	.15	.07
❑	367	Hal Morris	.15	.07
❑	368	Jack Morris	.25	.11
❑	369	John Roper	.15	.07
❑	370	Reggie Sanders	.15	.07
❑	371	Pete Schourek	.15	.07
❑	372	John Smiley	.15	.07
❑	373	Marvin Freeman	.15	.07

❑ 374 Andres Galarraga	.40	.18
❑ 375 Mike Munoz	.15	.07
❑ 376 David Nied	.15	.07
❑ 377 Walt Weiss	.15	.07
❑ 378 Greg Colbrunn	.15	.07
❑ 379 Jeff Conine	.15	.07
❑ 380 Charles Johnson	.25	.11
❑ 381 Kurt Miller	.15	.07
❑ 382 Robb Nen	.15	.07
❑ 383 Benito Santiago	.15	.07
❑ 384 Craig Biggio	.40	.18
❑ 385 Tony Eusebio	.15	.07
❑ 386 Luis Gonzalez	.60	.25
❑ 387 Brian L.Hunter	.15	.07
❑ 388 Darryl Kile	.25	.11
❑ 389 Orlando Miller	.15	.07
❑ 390 Phil Plantier	.15	.07
❑ 391 Greg Swindell	.15	.07
❑ 392 Billy Ashley	.15	.07
❑ 393 Pedro Astacio	.15	.07
❑ 394 Brett Butler	.25	.11
❑ 395 Delino DeShields	.15	.07
❑ 396 Orel Hershiser	.25	.11
❑ 397 Garey Ingram	.15	.07
❑ 398 Chan Ho Park	.25	.11
❑ 399 Mike Piazza	1.50	.70
❑ 400 Ismael Valdes	.15	.07
❑ 401 Tim Wallach	.15	.07
❑ 402 Cliff Floyd	.25	.11
❑ 403 Marquis Grissom	.15	.07
❑ 404 Mike Lansing	.15	.07
❑ 405 Pedro Martinez	.75	.35
❑ 406 Kirk Rueter	.15	.07
❑ 407 Tim Scott	.15	.07
❑ 408 Jeff Shaw	.15	.07
❑ 409 Larry Walker	.40	.18
❑ 410 Rondell White	.25	.11
❑ 411 John Franco	.25	.11
❑ 412 Todd Hundley	.15	.07
❑ 413 Jason Jacome	.15	.07
❑ 414 Joe Orsulak	.15	.07
❑ 415 Bret Saberhagen	.25	.11
❑ 416 David Segui	.15	.07
❑ 417 Darren Daulton	.25	.11
❑ 418 Mariano Duncan	.15	.07
❑ 419 Tommy Greene	.15	.07
❑ 420 Gregg Jefferies	.15	.07
❑ 421 John Kruk	.25	.11
❑ 422 Kevin Stocker	.15	.07
❑ 423 Jay Bell	.25	.11
❑ 424 Al Martin	.15	.07
❑ 425 Denny Neagle	.25	.11
❑ 426 Zane Smith	.15	.07
❑ 427 Andy Van Slyke	.25	.11
❑ 428 Paul Wagner	.15	.07
❑ 429 Tom Henke	.15	.07
❑ 430 Danny Jackson	.15	.07
❑ 431 Ray Lankford	.15	.07
❑ 432 John Mabry	.15	.07
❑ 433 Bob Tewksbury	.15	.07
❑ 434 Todd Zeile	.15	.07
❑ 435 Andy Ashby	.15	.07
❑ 436 Andujar Cedeno	.15	.07
❑ 437 Donnie Elliott	.15	.07
❑ 438 Bryce Florie	.15	.07
❑ 439 Trevor Hoffman	.25	.11
❑ 440 Melvin Nieves	.15	.07
❑ 441 Bip Roberts	.15	.07
❑ 442 Barry Bonds	1.50	.70
❑ 443 Royce Clayton	.15	.07
❑ 444 Mike Jackson	.15	.07
❑ 445 John Patterson	.15	.07
❑ 446 J.R. Phillips	.15	.07
❑ 447 Bill Swift	.15	.07
❑ 448 Checklist	.15	.07
❑ 449 Checklist	.15	.07
❑ 450 Checklist	.15	.07

1996 Ultra

	MINT	NRMT
COMPLETE SET (600)	60.00	27.00
COMPLETE SERIES 1 (300)	30.00	13.50
COMPLETE SERIES 2 (300)	30.00	13.50
❑ 1 Manny Alexander	.15	.07

❑ 2 Brady Anderson	.25	.11
❑ 3 Bobby Bonilla	.25	.11
❑ 4 Scott Erickson	.15	.07
❑ 5 Curtis Goodwin	.15	.07
❑ 6 Chris Hoiles	.15	.07
❑ 7 Doug Jones	.15	.07
❑ 8 Jeff Manto	.15	.07
❑ 9 Mike Mussina	.60	.25
❑ 10 Rafael Palmeiro	.60	.25
❑ 11 Cal Ripken	2.50	1.10
❑ 12 Rick Aguilera	.15	.07
❑ 13 Luis Alicea	.15	.07
❑ 14 Stan Belinda	.15	.07
❑ 15 Jose Canseco	.60	.25
❑ 16 Roger Clemens	1.50	.70
❑ 17 Mike Greenwell	.15	.07
❑ 18 Mike Macfarlane	.15	.07
❑ 19 Tim Naehring	.15	.07
❑ 20 Troy O'Leary	.15	.07
❑ 21 John Valentin	.15	.07
❑ 22 Mo Vaughn	.25	.11
❑ 23 Tim Wakefield	.15	.07
❑ 24 Brian Anderson	.15	.07
❑ 25 Garret Anderson	.25	.11
❑ 26 Chili Davis	.25	.11
❑ 27 Gary DiSarcina	.15	.07
❑ 28 Jim Edmonds	.40	.18
❑ 29 Jorge Fabregas	.15	.07
❑ 30 Chuck Finley	.25	.11
❑ 31 Mark Langston	.15	.07
❑ 32 Troy Percival	.15	.07
❑ 33 Tim Salmon	.25	.11
❑ 34 Lee Smith	.25	.11
❑ 35 Wilson Alvarez	.15	.07
❑ 36 Ray Durham	.25	.11
❑ 37 Alex Fernandez	.15	.07
❑ 38 Ozzie Guillen	.15	.07
❑ 39 Roberto Hernandez	.15	.07
❑ 40 Lance Johnson	.15	.07
❑ 41 Ron Karkovice	.15	.07
❑ 42 Lyle Mouton	.15	.07
❑ 43 Tim Raines	.25	.11
❑ 44 Frank Thomas	.75	.35
❑ 45 Carlos Baerga	.15	.07
❑ 46 Albert Belle	.25	.11
❑ 47 Orel Hershiser	.25	.11
❑ 48 Kenny Lofton	.25	.11
❑ 49 Dennis Martinez	.25	.11
❑ 50 Jose Mesa	.15	.07
❑ 51 Eddie Murray	.60	.25
❑ 52 Chad Ogea	.15	.07
❑ 53 Manny Ramirez	.75	.35
❑ 54 Jim Thome	.60	.25
❑ 55 Omar Vizquel	.25	.11
❑ 56 Dave Winfield	.60	.25
❑ 57 Chad Curtis	.15	.07
❑ 58 Cecil Fielder	.25	.11
❑ 59 John Flaherty	.15	.07
❑ 60 Travis Fryman	.25	.11
❑ 61 Chris Gomez	.15	.07
❑ 62 Bob Higginson	.25	.11
❑ 63 Felipe Lira	.15	.07
❑ 64 Brian Maxcy	.15	.07
❑ 65 Alan Trammell	.40	.18
❑ 66 Lou Whitaker	.25	.11
❑ 67 Kevin Appier	.25	.11
❑ 68 Gary Gaetti	.25	.11
❑ 69 Tom Goodwin	.15	.07
❑ 70 Tom Gordon	.15	.07
❑ 71 Jason Jacome	.15	.07
❑ 72 Wally Joyner	.25	.11
❑ 73 Brent Mayne	.15	.07
❑ 74 Jeff Montgomery	.15	.07
❑ 75 Jon Nunnally	.15	.07
❑ 76 Joe Vitiello	.15	.07
❑ 77 Ricky Bones	.15	.07
❑ 78 Jeff Cirillo	.25	.11
❑ 79 Mike Fetters	.15	.07
❑ 80 Darryl Hamilton	.15	.07
❑ 81 David Hulse	.15	.07
❑ 82 Dave Nilsson	.15	.07
❑ 83 Kevin Seitzer	.15	.07
❑ 84 Steve Sparks	.15	.07
❑ 85 B.J. Surhoff	.25	.11
❑ 86 Jose Valentin	.15	.07
❑ 87 Greg Vaughn	.25	.11
❑ 88 Marty Cordova	.15	.07
❑ 89 Chuck Knoblauch	.25	.11
❑ 90 Pat Meares	.15	.07
❑ 91 Pedro Munoz	.15	.07
❑ 92 Kirby Puckett	1.50	.70
❑ 93 Brad Radke	.25	.11
❑ 94 Scott Stahoviak	.15	.07
❑ 95 Dave Stevens	.15	.07
❑ 96 Mike Trombley	.15	.07
❑ 97 Matt Walbeck	.15	.07
❑ 98 Wade Boggs	.60	.25
❑ 99 Russ Davis	.15	.07
❑ 100 Jim Leyritz	.15	.07
❑ 101 Don Mattingly	1.50	.70
❑ 102 Jack McDowell	.15	.07
❑ 103 Paul O'Neill	.60	.25
❑ 104 Andy Pettitte	.25	.11
❑ 105 Mariano Rivera	.25	.11
❑ 106 Ruben Sierra	.15	.07
❑ 107 Darryl Strawberry	.25	.11
❑ 108 John Wetteland	.25	.11
❑ 109 Bernie Williams	.60	.25
❑ 110 Geronimo Berroa	.15	.07
❑ 111 Scott Brosius	.25	.11
❑ 112 Dennis Eckersley	.25	.11
❑ 113 Brent Gates	.15	.07
❑ 114 Rickey Henderson	1.25	.55
❑ 115 Mark McGwire	2.50	1.10
❑ 116 Ariel Prieto	.15	.07
❑ 117 Terry Steinbach	.15	.07
❑ 118 Todd Stottlemyre	.15	.07
❑ 119 Todd Van Poppel	.15	.07
❑ 120 Steve Wojciechowski	.15	.07
❑ 121 Rich Amaral	.15	.07
❑ 122 Bobby Ayala	.15	.07
❑ 123 Mike Blowers	.15	.07
❑ 124 Chris Bosio	.15	.07
❑ 125 Joey Cora	.15	.07
❑ 126 Ken Griffey Jr.	2.00	.90
❑ 127 Randy Johnson	.75	.35
❑ 128 Edgar Martinez	.40	.18
❑ 129 Tino Martinez	.25	.11
❑ 130 Alex Rodriguez	1.50	.70
❑ 131 Dan Wilson	.15	.07
❑ 132 Will Clark	.60	.25
❑ 133 Jeff Frye	.15	.07
❑ 134 Benji Gil	.15	.07
❑ 135 Juan Gonzalez	.60	.25
❑ 136 Rusty Greer	.25	.11
❑ 137 Mark McLemore	.15	.07
❑ 138 Roger Pavlik	.15	.07
❑ 139 Ivan Rodriguez	.60	.25
❑ 140 Kenny Rogers	.15	.07
❑ 141 Mickey Tettleton	.15	.07
❑ 142 Roberto Alomar	.60	.25
❑ 143 Joe Carter	.25	.11
❑ 144 Tony Castillo	.15	.07
❑ 145 Alex Gonzalez	.15	.07
❑ 146 Shawn Green	.60	.25
❑ 147 Pat Hentgen	.15	.07
❑ 148 Sandy Martinez	.15	.07
❑ 149 Paul Molitor	.60	.25
❑ 150 John Olerud	.25	.11
❑ 151 Ed Sprague	.15	.07
❑ 152 Jeff Blauser	.15	.07
❑ 153 Brad Clontz	.15	.07
❑ 154 Tom Glavine	.60	.25

❑	155	Marquis Grissom	.15	.07
❑	156	Chipper Jones	1.25	.55
❑	157	David Justice	.25	.11
❑	158	Ryan Klesko	.25	.11
❑	159	Javier Lopez	.25	.11
❑	160	Greg Maddux	1.50	.70
❑	161	John Smoltz	.25	.11
❑	162	Mark Wohlers	.15	.07
❑	163	Jim Bullinger	.15	.07
❑	164	Frank Castillo	.15	.07
❑	165	Shawon Dunston	.15	.07
❑	166	Kevin Foster	.15	.07
❑	167	Luis Gonzalez	.60	.25
❑	168	Mark Grace	.60	.25
❑	169	Rey Sanchez	.15	.07
❑	170	Scott Servais	.15	.07
❑	171	Sammy Sosa	1.25	.55
❑	172	Ozzie Timmons	.15	.07
❑	173	Steve Trachsel	.15	.07
❑	174	Bret Boone	.25	.11
❑	175	Jeff Branson	.15	.07
❑	176	Jeff Brantley	.15	.07
❑	177	Dave Burba	.15	.07
❑	178	Ron Gant	.15	.07
❑	179	Barry Larkin	.60	.25
❑	180	Darren Lewis	.15	.07
❑	181	Mark Portugal	.15	.07
❑	182	Reggie Sanders	.15	.07
❑	183	Pete Schourek	.15	.07
❑	184	John Smiley	.15	.07
❑	185	Jason Bates	.15	.07
❑	186	Dante Bichette	.25	.11
❑	187	Ellis Burks	.25	.11
❑	188	Vinny Castilla	.25	.11
❑	189	Andres Galarraga	.40	.18
❑	190	Darren Holmes	.15	.07
❑	191	Armando Reynoso	.15	.07
❑	192	Kevin Ritz	.15	.07
❑	193	Bill Swift	.15	.07
❑	194	Larry Walker	.40	.18
❑	195	Kurt Abbott	.15	.07
❑	196	John Burkett	.15	.07
❑	197	Greg Colbrunn	.15	.07
❑	198	Jeff Conine	.15	.07
❑	199	Andre Dawson	.40	.18
❑	200	Chris Hammond	.15	.07
❑	201	Charles Johnson	.25	.11
❑	202	Robb Nen	.15	.07
❑	203	Terry Pendleton	.25	.11
❑	204	Quilvio Veras	.15	.07
❑	205	Jeff Bagwell	.75	.35
❑	206	Derek Bell	.15	.07
❑	207	Doug Drabek	.15	.07
❑	208	Tony Eusebio	.15	.07
❑	209	Mike Hampton	.25	.11
❑	210	Brian L. Hunter	.15	.07
❑	211	Todd Jones	.15	.07
❑	212	Orlando Miller	.15	.07
❑	213	James Mouton	.15	.07
❑	214	Shane Reynolds	.15	.07
❑	215	Dave Veres	.15	.07
❑	216	Billy Ashley	.15	.07
❑	217	Brett Butler	.25	.11
❑	218	Chad Fonville	.15	.07
❑	219	Todd Hollandsworth	.15	.07
❑	220	Eric Karros	.25	.11
❑	221	Ramon Martinez	.15	.07
❑	222	Raul Mondesi	.25	.11
❑	223	Hideo Nomo	.75	.35
❑	224	Mike Piazza	1.50	.70
❑	225	Kevin Tapani	.15	.07
❑	226	Ismael Valdes	.15	.07
❑	227	Todd Worrell	.15	.07
❑	228	Moises Alou	.25	.11
❑	229	Wil Cordero	.15	.07
❑	230	Jeff Fassero	.15	.07
❑	231	Darrin Fletcher	.15	.07
❑	232	Mike Lansing	.15	.07
❑	233	Pedro Martinez	.75	.35
❑	234	Carlos Perez	.15	.07
❑	235	Mel Rojas	.15	.07
❑	236	David Segui	.15	.07
❑	237	Tony Tarasco	.15	.07
❑	238	Rondell White	.25	.11
❑	239	Edgardo Alfonzo	.25	.11
❑	240	Rico Brogna	.15	.07
❑	241	Carl Everett	.25	.11
❑	242	Todd Hundley	.15	.07
❑	243	Butch Huskey	.15	.07
❑	244	Jason Isringhausen	.25	.11
❑	245	Bobby Jones	.15	.07
❑	246	Jeff Kent	.40	.18
❑	247	Bill Pulsipher	.15	.07
❑	248	Jose Vizcaino	.15	.07
❑	249	Ricky Bottalico	.15	.07
❑	250	Darren Daulton	.25	.11
❑	251	Jim Eisenreich	.15	.07
❑	252	Tyler Green	.15	.07
❑	253	Charlie Hayes	.15	.07
❑	254	Gregg Jefferies	.15	.07
❑	255	Tony Longmire	.15	.07
❑	256	Michael Mimbs	.15	.07
❑	257	Mickey Morandini	.15	.07
❑	258	Paul Quantrill	.15	.07
❑	259	Heathcliff Slocumb	.15	.07
❑	260	Jay Bell	.25	.11
❑	261	Jacob Brumfield	.15	.07
❑	262	A.Encarnacion RC	.15	.07
❑	263	John Ericks	.15	.07
❑	264	Mark Johnson	.15	.07
❑	265	Esteban Loaiza	.15	.07
❑	266	Al Martin	.15	.07
❑	267	Orlando Merced	.15	.07
❑	268	Dan Miceli	.15	.07
❑	269	Denny Neagle	.25	.11
❑	270	Brian Barber	.15	.07
❑	271	Scott Cooper	.15	.07
❑	272	Tripp Cromer	.15	.07
❑	273	Bernard Gilkey	.15	.07
❑	274	Tom Henke	.15	.07
❑	275	Brian Jordan	.25	.11
❑	276	John Mabry	.15	.07
❑	277	Tom Pagnozzi	.15	.07
❑	278	Mark Petkovsek	.15	.07
❑	279	Ozzie Smith	.75	.35
❑	280	Andy Ashby	.15	.07
❑	281	Brad Ausmus	.15	.07
❑	282	Ken Caminiti	.25	.11
❑	283	Glenn Dishman	.15	.07
❑	284	Tony Gwynn	1.25	.55
❑	285	Joey Hamilton	.15	.07
❑	286	Trevor Hoffman	.25	.11
❑	287	Phil Plantier	.15	.07
❑	288	Jody Reed	.15	.07
❑	289	Eddie Williams	.15	.07
❑	290	Barry Bonds	1.50	.70
❑	291	Jamie Brewington RC	.15	.07
❑	292	Mark Carreon	.15	.07
❑	293	Royce Clayton	.15	.07
❑	294	Glenallen Hill	.15	.07
❑	295	Mark Leiter	.15	.07
❑	296	Kirt Manwaring	.15	.07
❑	297	J.R. Phillips	.15	.07
❑	298	Deion Sanders	.25	.11
❑	299	Wm. VanLandingham	.15	.07
❑	300	Matt Williams	.40	.18
❑	301	Roberto Alomar	.60	.25
❑	302	Armando Benitez	.15	.07
❑	303	Mike Devereaux	.15	.07
❑	304	Jeffrey Hammonds	.15	.07
❑	305	Jimmy Haynes	.15	.07
❑	306	Scott McClain	.15	.07
❑	307	Kent Mercker	.15	.07
❑	308	Randy Myers	.15	.07
❑	309	B.J. Surhoff	.25	.11
❑	310	Tony Tarasco	.15	.07
❑	311	David Wells	.25	.11
❑	312	Wil Cordero	.15	.07
❑	313	Alex Delgado	.15	.07
❑	314	Tom Gordon	.15	.07
❑	315	Dwayne Hosey	.15	.07
❑	316	Jose Malave	.15	.07
❑	317	Kevin Mitchell	.15	.07
❑	318	Jamie Moyer	.15	.07
❑	319	Aaron Sele	.25	.11
❑	320	Heathcliff Slocumb	.15	.07
❑	321	Mike Stanley	.15	.07
❑	322	Jeff Suppan	.15	.07
❑	323	Jim Abbott	.25	.11
❑	324	George Arias	.15	.07
❑	325	Todd Greene	.15	.07
❑	326	Bryan Harvey	.15	.07
❑	327	J.T. Snow	.25	.11
❑	328	Randy Velarde	.15	.07
❑	329	Tim Wallach	.15	.07
❑	330	Harold Baines	.25	.11
❑	331	Jason Bere	.15	.07
❑	332	Darren Lewis	.15	.07
❑	333	Norberto Martin	.15	.07
❑	334	Tony Phillips	.15	.07
❑	335	Bill Simas	.15	.07
❑	336	Chris Snopek	.15	.07
❑	337	Kevin Tapani	.15	.07
❑	338	Danny Tartabull	.15	.07
❑	339	Robin Ventura	.25	.11
❑	340	Sandy Alomar Jr.	.25	.11
❑	341	Julio Franco	.25	.11
❑	342	Jack McDowell	.15	.07
❑	343	Charles Nagy	.15	.07
❑	344	Julian Tavarez	.15	.07
❑	345	Kimera Bartee	.15	.07
❑	346	Greg Keagle	.15	.07
❑	347	Mark Lewis	.15	.07
❑	348	Jose Lima	.15	.07
❑	349	Melvin Nieves	.15	.07
❑	350	Mark Parent	.15	.07
❑	351	Eddie Williams	.15	.07
❑	352	Johnny Damon	.25	.11
❑	353	Sal Fasano	.15	.07
❑	354	Mark Gubicza	.15	.07
❑	355	Bob Hamelin	.15	.07
❑	356	Chris Haney	.15	.07
❑	357	Keith Lockhart	.15	.07
❑	358	Mike Macfarlane	.15	.07
❑	359	Jose Offerman	.15	.07
❑	360	Bip Roberts	.15	.07
❑	361	Michael Tucker	.15	.07
❑	362	Chuck Carr	.15	.07
❑	363	Bobby Hughes	.15	.07
❑	364	John Jaha	.15	.07
❑	365	Mark Loretta	.15	.07
❑	366	Mike Matheny	.15	.07
❑	367	Ben McDonald	.15	.07
❑	368	Matt Mieske	.15	.07
❑	369	Angel Miranda	.15	.07
❑	370	Fernando Vina	.15	.07
❑	371	Rick Aguilera	.15	.07
❑	372	Rich Becker	.15	.07
❑	373	LaTroy Hawkins	.15	.07
❑	374	Dave Hollins	.15	.07
❑	375	Roberto Kelly	.15	.07
❑	376	Matt Lawton RC	.75	.35
❑	377	Paul Molitor	.60	.25
❑	378	Dan Naulty	.15	.07
❑	379	Rich Robertson	.15	.07
❑	380	Frank Rodriguez	.15	.07
❑	381	David Cone	.25	.11
❑	382	Mariano Duncan	.15	.07
❑	383	Andy Fox	.15	.07
❑	384	Joe Girardi	.15	.07
❑	385	Dwight Gooden	.25	.11
❑	386	Derek Jeter	2.50	1.10
❑	387	Pat Kelly	.15	.07
❑	388	Jimmy Key	.25	.11
❑	389	Matt Luke	.15	.07
❑	390	Tino Martinez	.25	.11
❑	391	Jeff Nelson	.15	.07
❑	392	Melido Perez	.15	.07
❑	393	Tim Raines	.25	.11
❑	394	Ruben Rivera	.15	.07
❑	395	Kenny Rogers	.15	.07
❑	396	Tony Batista RC	2.00	.90
❑	397	Allen Battle	.15	.07
❑	398	Mike Bordick	.15	.07
❑	399	Steve Cox	.15	.07
❑	400	Jason Giambi	.60	.25
❑	401	Doug Johns	.15	.07
❑	402	Pedro Munoz	.15	.07
❑	403	Phil Plantier	.15	.07
❑	404	Scott Spiezio	.15	.07
❑	405	George Williams	.15	.07
❑	406	Ernie Young	.15	.07
❑	407	Darren Bragg	.15	.07
❑	408	Jay Buhner	.25	.11
❑	409	Norm Charlton	.15	.07
❑	410	Russ Davis	.15	.07
❑	411	Sterling Hitchcock	.15	.07
❑	412	Edwin Hurtado	.15	.07

❑ 413 Raul Ibanez RC .15 .07
❑ 414 Mike Jackson .15 .07
❑ 415 Luis Sojo .15 .07
❑ 416 Paul Sorrento .15 .07
❑ 417 Bob Wolcott .15 .07
❑ 418 Damon Buford .15 .07
❑ 419 Kevin Gross .15 .07
❑ 420 Darryl Hamilton UER .15 .07
❑ 421 Mike Henneman .15 .07
❑ 422 Ken Hill .15 .07
❑ 423 Dean Palmer .25 .11
❑ 424 Bobby Witt .15 .07
❑ 425 Tilson Brito RC .15 .07
❑ 426 Giovanni Carrara RC .15 .07
❑ 427 Domingo Cedeno .15 .07
❑ 428 Felipe Crespo .15 .07
❑ 429 Carlos Delgado .60 .25
❑ 430 Juan Guzman .15 .07
❑ 431 Erik Hanson .15 .07
❑ 432 Marty Janzen .15 .07
❑ 433 Otis Nixon .15 .07
❑ 434 Robert Perez .15 .07
❑ 435 Paul Quantrill .15 .07
❑ 436 Bill Risley .15 .07
❑ 437 Steve Avery .15 .07
❑ 438 Jermaine Dye .25 .11
❑ 439 Mark Lemke .15 .07
❑ 440 Marty Malloy RC .15 .07
❑ 441 Fred McGriff .40 .18
❑ 442 Greg McMichael .15 .07
❑ 443 Wonderful Monds RC .15 .07
❑ 444 Eddie Perez .15 .07
❑ 445 Jason Schmidt .15 .07
❑ 446 Terrell Wade .15 .07
❑ 447 Terry Adams .15 .07
❑ 448 Scott Bullett .15 .07
❑ 449 Robin Jennings .15 .07
❑ 450 Doug Jones .15 .07
❑ 451 Brooks Kieschnick .15 .07
❑ 452 Dave Magadan .15 .07
❑ 453 Jason Maxwell RC .15 .07
❑ 454 Brian McRae .15 .07
❑ 455 Rodney Myers RC .15 .07
❑ 456 Jaime Navarro .15 .07
❑ 457 Ryne Sandberg .75 .35
❑ 458 Vince Coleman .15 .07
❑ 459 Eric Davis .25 .11
❑ 460 Steve Gibralter .15 .07
❑ 461 Thomas Howard .15 .07
❑ 462 Mike Kelly .15 .07
❑ 463 Hal Morris .15 .07
❑ 464 Eric Owens .15 .07
❑ 465 Jose Rijo .15 .07
❑ 466 Chris Sabo .15 .07
❑ 467 Eddie Taubensee .15 .07
❑ 468 Trenidad Hubbard .15 .07
❑ 469 Curt Leskanic .15 .07
❑ 470 Quinton McCracken .15 .07
❑ 471 Jayhawk Owens .15 .07
❑ 472 Steve Reed .15 .07
❑ 473 Bryan Rekar .15 .07
❑ 474 Bruce Ruffin .15 .07
❑ 475 Bret Saberhagen .25 .11
❑ 476 Walt Weiss .15 .07
❑ 477 Eric Young .15 .07
❑ 478 Kevin Brown .25 .11
❑ 479 Al Leiter .25 .11
❑ 480 Pat Rapp .15 .07
❑ 481 Gary Sheffield .25 .11
❑ 482 Devon White .25 .11
❑ 483 Bob Abreu .60 .25
❑ 484 Sean Berry .15 .07
❑ 485 Craig Biggio .40 .18
❑ 486 Jim Dougherty .15 .07
❑ 487 Richard Hidalgo .25 .11
❑ 488 Darryl Kile .25 .11
❑ 489 Derrick May .15 .07
❑ 490 Greg Swindell .15 .07
❑ 491 Rick Wilkins .15 .07
❑ 492 Mike Blowers .15 .07
❑ 493 Tom Candiotti .15 .07
❑ 494 Roger Cedeno .15 .07
❑ 495 Delino DeShields .15 .07
❑ 496 Greg Gagne .15 .07
❑ 497 Karim Garcia .15 .07
❑ 498 Wilton Guerrero RC .25 .11
❑ 499 Chan Ho Park .25 .11
❑ 500 Israel Alcantara .15 .07
❑ 501 Shane Andrews .15 .07
❑ 502 Yamil Benitez .15 .07
❑ 503 Cliff Floyd .25 .11
❑ 504 Mark Grudzielanek .15 .07
❑ 505 Ryan McGuire .15 .07
❑ 506 Sherman Obando .15 .07
❑ 507 Jose Paniagua .15 .07
❑ 508 Henry Rodriguez .15 .07
❑ 509 Kirk Rueter .15 .07
❑ 510 Juan Acevedo .15 .07
❑ 511 John Franco .25 .11
❑ 512 Bernard Gilkey .15 .07
❑ 513 Lance Johnson .15 .07
❑ 514 Rey Ordonez .15 .07
❑ 515 Robert Person .15 .07
❑ 516 Paul Wilson .15 .07
❑ 517 Toby Borland .15 .07
❑ 518 David Doster RC .15 .07
❑ 519 Lenny Dykstra .25 .11
❑ 520 Sid Fernandez .15 .07
❑ 521 Mike Grace RC .15 .07
❑ 522 Rich Hunter .15 .07
❑ 523 Benito Santiago .15 .07
❑ 524 Gene Schall .15 .07
❑ 525 Curt Schilling .60 .25
❑ 526 Kevin Sefcik RC .15 .07
❑ 527 Lee Tinsley .15 .07
❑ 528 David West .15 .07
❑ 529 Mark Whiten .15 .07
❑ 530 Todd Zeile .15 .07
❑ 531 Carlos Garcia .15 .07
❑ 532 Charlie Hayes .15 .07
❑ 533 Jason Kendall .25 .11
❑ 534 Jeff King .15 .07
❑ 535 Mike Kingery .15 .07
❑ 536 Nelson Liriano .15 .07
❑ 537 Dan Plesac .15 .07
❑ 538 Paul Wagner .15 .07
❑ 539 Luis Alicea .15 .07
❑ 540 David Bell .15 .07
❑ 541 Alan Benes .15 .07
❑ 542 Andy Benes .15 .07
❑ 543 Mike Busby RC .15 .07
❑ 544 Royce Clayton .15 .07
❑ 545 Dennis Eckersley .25 .11
❑ 546 Gary Gaetti .25 .11
❑ 547 Ron Gant .15 .07
❑ 548 Aaron Holbert .15 .07
❑ 549 Ray Lankford .15 .07
❑ 550 T.J. Mathews .15 .07
❑ 551 Willie McGee .25 .11
❑ 552 Miguel Mejia .15 .07
❑ 553 Todd Stottlemyre .15 .07
❑ 554 Sean Bergman .15 .07
❑ 555 Willie Blair .15 .07
❑ 556 Andujar Cedeno .15 .07
❑ 557 Steve Finley .25 .11
❑ 558 Rickey Henderson 1.25 .55
❑ 559 Wally Joyner .25 .11
❑ 560 Scott Livingstone .15 .07
❑ 561 Marc Newfield .15 .07
❑ 562 Bob Tewksbury .15 .07
❑ 563 Fernando Valenzuela .25 .11
❑ 564 Rod Beck .15 .07
❑ 565 Doug Creek .15 .07
❑ 566 Shawon Dunston .15 .07
❑ 567 O.Fernandez RC .15 .07
❑ 568 Stan Javier .15 .07
❑ 569 Marcus Jensen .15 .07
❑ 570 Steve Scarsone .15 .07
❑ 571 Robby Thompson .15 .07
❑ 572 Allen Watson .15 .07
❑ 573 Roberto Alomar STA .25 .11
❑ 574 Jeff Bagwell STA .40 .18
❑ 575 Albert Belle STA .25 .11
❑ 576 Wade Boggs STA .25 .11
❑ 577 Barry Bonds STA .75 .35
❑ 578 Juan Gonzalez STA .25 .11
❑ 579 Ken Griffey Jr. STA 1.00 .45
❑ 580 Tony Gwynn STA .60 .25
❑ 581 Randy Johnson STA .40 .18
❑ 582 Chipper Jones STA .60 .25
❑ 583 Barry Larkin STA .25 .11
❑ 584 Kenny Lofton STA .15 .07
❑ 585 Greg Maddux STA .75 .35
❑ 586 Raul Mondesi STA .15 .07
❑ 587 Mike Piazza STA .75 .35
❑ 588 Cal Ripken STA 1.25 .55
❑ 589 Tim Salmon STA .15 .07
❑ 590 Frank Thomas STA .40 .18
❑ 591 Mo Vaughn STA .15 .07
❑ 592 Matt Williams STA .25 .11
❑ 593 Marty Cordova RAW .15 .07
❑ 594 Jim Edmonds RAW .25 .11
❑ 595 Cliff Floyd RAW .15 .07
❑ 596 Chipper Jones RAW .60 .25
❑ 597 Ryan Klesko RAW .15 .07
❑ 598 Raul Mondesi RAW .15 .07
❑ 599 Manny Ramirez RAW .40 .18
❑ 600 Ruben Rivera RAW .15 .07
❑ DD1 C. Ripken DD 25.00 11.00
Issued through dealers
Serial numbered to 2131
❑ DD2 Cal Ripken DD 15.00 6.75
Issued through a wrapper redemption

1997 Ultra

	MINT	NRMT
COMPLETE SET (553)	60.00	27.00
COMPLETE SERIES 1 (300)	30.00	13.50
COMPLETE SERIES 2 (253)	30.00	13.50
COMMON CARD (1-450)	.15	.07
COMMON CARD (451-553)	.20	.09

❑ 1 Roberto Alomar .60 .25
❑ 2 Brady Anderson .25 .11
❑ 3 Rocky Coppinger .15 .07
❑ 4 Jeffrey Hammonds .15 .07
❑ 5 Chris Hoiles .15 .07
❑ 6 Eddie Murray .60 .25
❑ 7 Mike Mussina .60 .25
❑ 8 Jimmy Myers .15 .07
❑ 9 Randy Myers .15 .07
❑ 10 Arthur Rhodes .15 .07
❑ 11 Cal Ripken 2.50 1.10
❑ 12 Jose Canseco .60 .25
❑ 13 Roger Clemens 1.50 .70
❑ 14 Tom Gordon .15 .07
❑ 15 Jose Malave .15 .07
❑ 16 Tim Naehring .15 .07
❑ 17 Troy O'Leary .15 .07
❑ 18 Bill Selby .15 .07
❑ 19 Heathcliff Slocumb .15 .07
❑ 20 Mike Stanley .15 .07
❑ 21 Mo Vaughn .25 .11
❑ 22 Garret Anderson .25 .11
❑ 23 George Arias .15 .07
❑ 24 Chili Davis .25 .11
❑ 25 Jim Edmonds .40 .18
❑ 26 Darin Erstad .60 .25
❑ 27 Chuck Finley .25 .11
❑ 28 Todd Greene .15 .07
❑ 29 Troy Percival .15 .07
❑ 30 Tim Salmon .25 .11
❑ 31 Jeff Schmidt .15 .07
❑ 32 Randy Velarde .15 .07
❑ 33 Shad Williams .15 .07
❑ 34 Wilson Alvarez .15 .07
❑ 35 Harold Baines .25 .11
❑ 36 James Baldwin .15 .07
❑ 37 Mike Cameron .25 .11

❑ 38	Ray Durham	.25	.11
❑ 39	Ozzie Guillen	.15	.07
❑ 40	Roberto Hernandez	.15	.07
❑ 41	Darren Lewis	.15	.07
❑ 42	Jose Munoz	.15	.07
❑ 43	Tony Phillips	.15	.07
❑ 44	Frank Thomas	.75	.35
❑ 45	Sandy Alomar Jr.	.25	.11
❑ 46	Albert Belle	.25	.11
❑ 47	Mark Carreon	.15	.07
❑ 48	Julio Franco	.25	.11
❑ 49	Orel Hershiser	.25	.11
❑ 50	Kenny Lofton	.25	.11
❑ 51	Jack McDowell	.15	.07
❑ 52	Jose Mesa	.15	.07
❑ 53	Charles Nagy	.15	.07
❑ 54	Manny Ramirez	.75	.35
❑ 55	Julian Tavarez	.15	.07
❑ 56	Omar Vizquel	.25	.11
❑ 57	Raul Casanova	.15	.07
❑ 58	Tony Clark	.25	.11
❑ 59	Travis Fryman	.25	.11
❑ 60	Bob Higginson	.25	.11
❑ 61	Melvin Nieves	.15	.07
❑ 62	Curtis Pride	.15	.07
❑ 63	Justin Thompson	.15	.07
❑ 64	Alan Trammell	.40	.18
❑ 65	Kevin Appier	.25	.11
❑ 66	Johnny Damon	.25	.11
❑ 67	Keith Lockhart	.15	.07
❑ 68	Jeff Montgomery	.15	.07
❑ 69	Jose Offerman	.15	.07
❑ 70	Bip Roberts	.15	.07
❑ 71	Jose Rosado	.15	.07
❑ 72	Chris Stynes	.15	.07
❑ 73	Mike Sweeney	.25	.11
❑ 74	Jeff Cirillo	.25	.11
❑ 75	Jeff D'Amico	.15	.07
❑ 76	John Jaha	.15	.07
❑ 77	Scott Karl	.15	.07
❑ 78	Mike Matheny	.15	.07
❑ 79	Ben McDonald	.15	.07
❑ 80	Matt Mieske	.15	.07
❑ 81	Marc Newfield	.15	.07
❑ 82	Dave Nilsson	.15	.07
❑ 83	Jose Valentin	.15	.07
❑ 84	Fernando Vina	.15	.07
❑ 85	Rick Aguilera	.15	.07
❑ 86	Marty Cordova	.15	.07
❑ 87	Chuck Knoblauch	.25	.11
❑ 88	Matt Lawton	.25	.11
❑ 89	Pat Meares	.15	.07
❑ 90	Paul Molitor	.60	.25
❑ 91	Greg Myers	.15	.07
❑ 92	Dan Naulty	.15	.07
❑ 93	Kirby Puckett	1.50	.70
❑ 94	Frank Rodriguez	.15	.07
❑ 95	Wade Boggs	.60	.25
❑ 96	Cecil Fielder	.25	.11
❑ 97	Joe Girardi	.15	.07
❑ 98	Dwight Gooden	.25	.11
❑ 99	Derek Jeter	2.50	1.10
❑ 100	Tino Martinez	.25	.11
❑ 101	Ramiro Mendoza RC	.50	.23
❑ 102	Andy Pettitte	.25	.11
❑ 103	Mariano Rivera	.25	.11
❑ 104	Ruben Rivera	.15	.07
❑ 105	Kenny Rogers	.15	.07
❑ 106	Darryl Strawberry	.25	.11
❑ 107	Bernie Williams	.60	.25
❑ 108	Tony Batista	.25	.11
❑ 109	Geronimo Berroa	.15	.07
❑ 110	Bobby Chouinard	.15	.07
❑ 111	Brent Gates	.15	.07
❑ 112	Jason Giambi	.60	.25
❑ 113	Damon Mashore	.15	.07
❑ 114	Mark McGwire	2.50	1.10
❑ 115	Scott Spiezio	.15	.07
❑ 116	John Wasdin	.15	.07
❑ 117	Steve Wojciechowski	.15	.07
❑ 118	Ernie Young	.15	.07
❑ 119	Norm Charlton	.15	.07
❑ 120	Joey Cora	.15	.07
❑ 121	Ken Griffey Jr.	2.00	.90
❑ 122	Sterling Hitchcock	.15	.07
❑ 123	Raul Ibanez	.15	.07
❑ 124	Randy Johnson	.75	.35
❑ 125	Edgar Martinez	.40	.18
❑ 126	Alex Rodriguez	1.50	.70
❑ 127	Matt Wagner	.15	.07
❑ 128	Bob Wells	.15	.07
❑ 129	Dan Wilson	.15	.07
❑ 130	Will Clark	.60	.25
❑ 131	Kevin Elster	.15	.07
❑ 132	Juan Gonzalez	.60	.25
❑ 133	Rusty Greer	.25	.11
❑ 134	Darryl Hamilton	.15	.07
❑ 135	Mike Henneman	.15	.07
❑ 136	Ken Hill	.15	.07
❑ 137	Mark McLemore	.15	.07
❑ 138	Dean Palmer	.25	.11
❑ 139	Roger Pavlik	.15	.07
❑ 140	Ivan Rodriguez	.60	.25
❑ 141	Joe Carter	.25	.11
❑ 142	Carlos Delgado	.60	.25
❑ 143	Alex Gonzalez	.15	.07
❑ 144	Juan Guzman	.15	.07
❑ 145	Pat Hentgen	.15	.07
❑ 146	Marty Janzen	.15	.07
❑ 147	Otis Nixon	.15	.07
❑ 148	Charlie O'Brien	.15	.07
❑ 149	John Olerud	.25	.11
❑ 150	Robert Perez	.15	.07
❑ 151	Jermaine Dye	.25	.11
❑ 152	Tom Glavine	.60	.25
❑ 153	Andruw Jones	.75	.35
❑ 154	Chipper Jones	1.25	.55
❑ 155	Ryan Klesko	.25	.11
❑ 156	Javier Lopez	.25	.11
❑ 157	Greg Maddux	1.50	.70
❑ 158	Fred McGriff	.40	.18
❑ 159	Wonderful Monds	.15	.07
❑ 160	John Smoltz	.25	.11
❑ 161	Terrell Wade	.15	.07
❑ 162	Mark Wohlers	.15	.07
❑ 163	Brant Brown	.15	.07
❑ 164	Mark Grace	.60	.25
❑ 165	Tyler Houston	.15	.07
❑ 166	Robin Jennings	.15	.07
❑ 167	Jason Maxwell	.15	.07
❑ 168	Ryne Sandberg	.75	.35
❑ 169	Sammy Sosa	1.25	.55
❑ 170	Amaury Telemaco	.15	.07
❑ 171	Steve Trachsel	.15	.07
❑ 172	Pedro Valdes RC	.15	.07
❑ 173	Tim Belk	.15	.07
❑ 174	Bret Boone	.25	.11
❑ 175	Jeff Brantley	.15	.07
❑ 176	Eric Davis	.25	.11
❑ 177	Barry Larkin	.60	.25
❑ 178	Chad Mottola	.15	.07
❑ 179	Mark Portugal	.15	.07
❑ 180	Reggie Sanders	.15	.07
❑ 181	John Smiley	.15	.07
❑ 182	Eddie Taubensee	.15	.07
❑ 183	Dante Bichette	.25	.11
❑ 184	Ellis Burks	.25	.11
❑ 185	Andres Galarraga	.40	.18
❑ 186	Curt Leskanic	.15	.07
❑ 187	Quinton McCracken	.15	.07
❑ 188	Jeff Reed	.15	.07
❑ 189	Kevin Ritz	.15	.07
❑ 190	Walt Weiss	.15	.07
❑ 191	Jamey Wright	.15	.07
❑ 192	Eric Young	.15	.07
❑ 193	Kevin Brown	.25	.11
❑ 194	Luis Castillo	.15	.07
❑ 195	Jeff Conine	.15	.07
❑ 196	Andre Dawson	.40	.18
❑ 197	Charles Johnson	.25	.11
❑ 198	Al Leiter	.25	.11
❑ 199	Ralph Milliard	.15	.07
❑ 200	Robb Nen	.15	.07
❑ 201	Edgar Renteria	.15	.07
❑ 202	Gary Sheffield	.25	.11
❑ 203	Bob Abreu	.25	.11
❑ 204	Jeff Bagwell	.75	.35
❑ 205	Derek Bell	.15	.07
❑ 206	Sean Berry	.15	.07
❑ 207	Richard Hidalgo	.25	.11
❑ 208	Todd Jones	.15	.07
❑ 209	Darryl Kile	.25	.11
❑ 210	Orlando Miller	.15	.07
❑ 211	Shane Reynolds	.15	.07
❑ 212	Billy Wagner	.15	.07
❑ 213	Donne Wall	.15	.07
❑ 214	Roger Cedeno	.15	.07
❑ 215	Greg Gagne	.15	.07
❑ 216	Karim Garcia	.15	.07
❑ 217	Wilton Guerrero	.15	.07
❑ 218	Todd Hollandsworth	.15	.07
❑ 219	Ramon Martinez	.15	.07
❑ 220	Raul Mondesi	.25	.11
❑ 221	Hideo Nomo	.60	.25
❑ 222	Chan Ho Park	.25	.11
❑ 223	Mike Piazza	1.50	.70
❑ 224	Ismael Valdes	.15	.07
❑ 225	Moises Alou	.25	.11
❑ 226	Derek Aucoin	.15	.07
❑ 227	Yamil Benitez	.15	.07
❑ 228	Jeff Fassero	.15	.07
❑ 229	Darrin Fletcher	.15	.07
❑ 230	Mark Grudzielanek	.15	.07
❑ 231	Barry Manuel	.15	.07
❑ 232	Pedro Martinez	.75	.35
❑ 233	Henry Rodriguez	.15	.07
❑ 234	Ugueth Urbina	.15	.07
❑ 235	Rondell White	.25	.11
❑ 236	Carlos Baerga	.15	.07
❑ 237	John Franco	.25	.11
❑ 238	Bernard Gilkey	.15	.07
❑ 239	Todd Hundley	.15	.07
❑ 240	Butch Huskey	.15	.07
❑ 241	Jason Isringhausen	.15	.07
❑ 242	Lance Johnson	.15	.07
❑ 243	Bobby Jones	.15	.07
❑ 244	Alex Ochoa	.15	.07
❑ 245	Rey Ordonez	.15	.07
❑ 246	Paul Wilson	.15	.07
❑ 247	Ron Blazier	.15	.07
❑ 248	David Doster	.15	.07
❑ 249	Jim Eisenreich	.15	.07
❑ 250	Mike Grace	.15	.07
❑ 251	Mike Lieberthal	.25	.11
❑ 252	Wendell Magee	.15	.07
❑ 253	Mickey Morandini	.15	.07
❑ 254	Ricky Otero	.15	.07
❑ 255	Scott Rolen	.60	.25
❑ 256	Curt Schilling	.60	.25
❑ 257	Todd Zeile	.15	.07
❑ 258	Jermaine Allensworth	.15	.07
❑ 259	Trey Beamon	.15	.07
❑ 260	Carlos Garcia	.15	.07
❑ 261	Mark Johnson	.15	.07
❑ 262	Jason Kendall	.25	.11
❑ 263	Jeff King	.15	.07
❑ 264	Al Martin	.15	.07
❑ 265	Denny Neagle	.25	.11
❑ 266	Matt Ruebel	.15	.07
❑ 267	Marc Wilkins	.15	.07
❑ 268	Alan Benes	.15	.07
❑ 269	Dennis Eckersley	.25	.11
❑ 270	Ron Gant	.15	.07
❑ 271	Aaron Holbert	.15	.07
❑ 272	Brian Jordan	.25	.11
❑ 273	Ray Lankford	.15	.07
❑ 274	John Mabry	.15	.07
❑ 275	T.J. Mathews	.15	.07
❑ 276	Ozzie Smith	.75	.35
❑ 277	Todd Stottlemyre	.15	.07
❑ 278	Mark Sweeney	.15	.07
❑ 279	Andy Ashby	.15	.07
❑ 280	Steve Finley	.25	.11
❑ 281	John Flaherty	.15	.07
❑ 282	Chris Gomez	.15	.07
❑ 283	Tony Gwynn	1.25	.55
❑ 284	Joey Hamilton	.15	.07
❑ 285	Rickey Henderson	1.25	.55
❑ 286	Trevor Hoffman	.25	.11
❑ 287	Jason Thompson	.15	.07
❑ 288	Fernando Valenzuela	.25	.11
❑ 289	Greg Vaughn	.25	.11
❑ 290	Barry Bonds	1.50	.70
❑ 291	Jay Canizaro	.15	.07
❑ 292	Jacob Cruz	.15	.07
❑ 293	Shawon Dunston	.15	.07
❑ 294	Shawn Estes	.25	.11
❑ 295	Mark Gardner	.15	.07

❑ 296 Marcus Jensen .15 .07
❑ 297 Bill Mueller RC .40 .18
❑ 298 Chris Singleton .15 .07
❑ 299 Allen Watson .15 .07
❑ 300 Matt Williams .40 .18
❑ 301 Rod Beck .15 .07
❑ 302 Jay Bell .25 .11
❑ 303 Shawon Dunston .15 .07
❑ 304 Reggie Jefferson .15 .07
❑ 305 Darren Oliver .15 .07
❑ 306 Benito Santiago .15 .07
❑ 307 Gerald Williams .15 .07
❑ 308 Damon Buford .15 .07
❑ 309 Jeromy Burnitz .25 .11
❑ 310 Sterling Hitchcock .15 .07
❑ 311 Dave Hollins .15 .07
❑ 312 Mel Rojas .15 .07
❑ 313 Robin Ventura .25 .11
❑ 314 David Wells .25 .11
❑ 315 Cal Eldred .15 .07
❑ 316 Gary Gaetti .25 .11
❑ 317 John Hudek .15 .07
❑ 318 Brian Johnson .15 .07
❑ 319 Denny Neagle .25 .11
❑ 320 Larry Walker .40 .18
❑ 321 Russ Davis .15 .07
❑ 322 Delino DeShields .15 .07
❑ 323 Charlie Hayes .15 .07
❑ 324 Jermaine Dye .25 .11
❑ 325 John Ericks .15 .07
❑ 326 Jeff Fassero .15 .07
❑ 327 Nomar Garciaparra 1.50 .70
❑ 328 Willie Greene .15 .07
❑ 329 Greg McMichael .15 .07
❑ 330 Damion Easley .15 .07
❑ 331 Ricky Bones .15 .07
❑ 332 John Burkett .15 .07
❑ 333 Royce Clayton .15 .07
❑ 334 Greg Colbrunn .15 .07
❑ 335 Tony Eusebio .15 .07
❑ 336 Gregg Jefferies .15 .07
❑ 337 Wally Joyner .25 .11
❑ 338 Jim Leyritz .15 .07
❑ 339 Paul O'Neill .60 .25
❑ 340 Bruce Ruffin .15 .07
❑ 341 Michael Tucker .15 .07
❑ 342 Andy Benes .15 .07
❑ 343 Craig Biggio .40 .18
❑ 344 Rex Hudler .15 .07
❑ 345 Brad Radke .25 .11
❑ 346 Deion Sanders .25 .11
❑ 347 Moises Alou .25 .11
❑ 348 Brad Ausmus .15 .07
❑ 349 Armando Benitez .15 .07
❑ 350 Mark Gubicza .15 .07
❑ 351 Terry Steinbach .15 .07
❑ 352 Mark Whiten .15 .07
❑ 353 Ricky Bottalico .15 .07
❑ 354 Brian Giles RC 2.50 1.10
❑ 355 Eric Karros .25 .11
❑ 356 Jimmy Key .25 .11
❑ 357 Carlos Perez .15 .07
❑ 358 Alex Fernandez .15 .07
❑ 359 J.T. Snow .25 .11
❑ 360 Bobby Bonilla .25 .11
❑ 361 Scott Brosius .25 .11
❑ 362 Greg Swindell .15 .07
❑ 363 Jose Vizcaino .15 .07
❑ 364 Matt Williams .40 .18
❑ 365 Darren Daulton .25 .11
❑ 366 Shane Andrews .15 .07
❑ 367 Jim Eisenreich .15 .07
❑ 368 Ariel Prieto .15 .07
❑ 369 Bob Tewksbury .15 .07
❑ 370 Mike Bordick .15 .07
❑ 371 Rheal Cormier .15 .07
❑ 372 Cliff Floyd .25 .11
❑ 373 David Justice .25 .11
❑ 374 John Wetteland .25 .11
❑ 375 Mike Blowers .15 .07
❑ 376 Jose Canseco .60 .25
❑ 377 Roger Clemens 1.50 .70
❑ 378 Kevin Mitchell .15 .07
❑ 379 Todd Zeile .15 .07
❑ 380 Jim Thome .60 .25
❑ 381 Turk Wendell .15 .07
❑ 382 Rico Brogna .15 .07
❑ 383 Eric Davis .25 .11
❑ 384 Mike Lansing .15 .07
❑ 385 Devon White .25 .11
❑ 386 Marquis Grissom .15 .07
❑ 387 Todd Worrell .15 .07
❑ 388 Jeff Kent .40 .18
❑ 389 Mickey Tettleton .15 .07
❑ 390 Steve Avery .15 .07
❑ 391 David Cone .25 .11
❑ 392 Scott Cooper .15 .07
❑ 393 Lee Stevens .15 .07
❑ 394 Kevin Elster .15 .07
❑ 395 Tom Goodwin .15 .07
❑ 396 Shawn Green .60 .25
❑ 397 Pete Harnisch .15 .07
❑ 398 Eddie Murray .60 .25
❑ 399 Joe Randa .15 .07
❑ 400 Scott Sanders .15 .07
❑ 401 John Valentin .15 .07
❑ 402 Todd Jones .15 .07
❑ 403 Terry Adams .15 .07
❑ 404 Brian Hunter .15 .07
❑ 405 Pat Listach .15 .07
❑ 406 Kenny Lofton .25 .11
❑ 407 Hal Morris .15 .07
❑ 408 Ed Sprague .15 .07
❑ 409 Rich Becker .15 .07
❑ 410 Edgardo Alfonzo .25 .11
❑ 411 Albert Belle .30 .14
❑ 412 Jeff King .15 .07
❑ 413 Kirt Manwaring .15 .07
❑ 414 Jason Schmidt .15 .07
❑ 415 Allen Watson .15 .07
❑ 416 Lee Tinsley .15 .07
❑ 417 Brett Butler .25 .11
❑ 418 Carlos Garcia .15 .07
❑ 419 Mark Lemke .15 .07
❑ 420 Jaime Navarro .15 .07
❑ 421 David Segui .15 .07
❑ 422 Ruben Sierra .15 .07
❑ 423 B.J. Surhoff .25 .11
❑ 424 Julian Tavarez .15 .07
❑ 425 Billy Taylor .15 .07
❑ 426 Ken Caminiti .25 .11
❑ 427 Chuck Carr .15 .07
❑ 428 Benji Gil .15 .07
❑ 429 Terry Mulholland .15 .07
❑ 430 Mike Stanton .15 .07
❑ 431 Wil Cordero .15 .07
❑ 432 Chili Davis .25 .11
❑ 433 Mariano Duncan .15 .07
❑ 434 Orlando Merced .15 .07
❑ 435 Kent Mercker .15 .07
❑ 436 John Olerud .25 .11
❑ 437 Quilvio Veras .15 .07
❑ 438 Mike Fetters .15 .07
❑ 439 Glenallen Hill .15 .07
❑ 440 Bill Swift .15 .07
❑ 441 Tim Wakefield .15 .07
❑ 442 Pedro Astacio .15 .07
❑ 443 Vinny Castilla .25 .11
❑ 444 Doug Drabek .15 .07
❑ 445 Alan Embree .15 .07
❑ 446 Lee Smith .25 .11
❑ 447 Darryl Hamilton .15 .07
❑ 448 Brian McRae .15 .07
❑ 449 Mike Timlin .15 .07
❑ 450 Bob Wickman .15 .07
❑ 451 Jason Dickson .20 .09
❑ 452 Chad Curtis .20 .09
❑ 453 Mark Leiter .20 .09
❑ 454 Damon Berryhill .20 .09
❑ 455 Kevin Orie .20 .09
❑ 456 Dave Burba .20 .09
❑ 457 Chris Holt .20 .09
❑ 458 Ricky Ledee RC .60 .25
❑ 459 Mike Devereaux .20 .09
❑ 460 Pokey Reese .20 .09
❑ 461 Tim Raines .30 .14
❑ 462 Ryan Jones .20 .09
❑ 463 Shane Mack .20 .09
❑ 464 Darren Dreifort .15 .07
❑ 465 Mark Parent .20 .09
❑ 466 Mark Portugal .20 .09
❑ 467 Dante Powell .20 .09
❑ 468 Craig Grebeck .20 .09
❑ 469 Ron Villone .20 .09
❑ 470 Dmitri Young .30 .14
❑ 471 Shannon Stewart .30 .14
❑ 472 Rick Helling .20 .09
❑ 473 Bill Haselman .20 .09
❑ 474 Albie Lopez .20 .09
❑ 475 Glendon Rusch .20 .09
❑ 476 Derrick May .20 .09
❑ 477 Chad Ogea .20 .09
❑ 478 Kirk Rueter .20 .09
❑ 479 Chris Hammond .20 .09
❑ 480 Russ Johnson .20 .09
❑ 481 James Mouton .20 .09
❑ 482 Mike Macfarlane .20 .09
❑ 483 Scott Ruffcorn .20 .09
❑ 484 Jeff Frye .20 .09
❑ 485 Richie Sexson .30 .14
❑ 486 Emil Brown RC .20 .09
❑ 487 Desi Wilson .20 .09
❑ 488 Brent Gates .20 .09
❑ 489 Tony Graffanino .20 .09
❑ 490 Dan Miceli .20 .09
❑ 491 Orlando Cabrera RC .50 .23
❑ 492 Tony Womack RC .60 .25
❑ 493 Jerome Walton .20 .09
❑ 494 Mark Thompson .20 .09
❑ 495 Jose Guillen .20 .09
❑ 496 Willie Blair .20 .09
❑ 497 T.J. Staton RC .20 .09
❑ 498 Scott Kamieniecki .20 .09
❑ 499 Vince Coleman .20 .09
❑ 500 Jeff Abbott .20 .09
❑ 501 Chris Widger .20 .09
❑ 502 Kevin Tapani .20 .09
❑ 503 Carlos Castillo RC .20 .09
❑ 504 Luis Gonzalez .60 .25
❑ 505 Tim Belcher .20 .09
❑ 506 Armando Reynoso .20 .09
❑ 507 Jamie Moyer .20 .09
❑ 508 Randall Simon RC .20 .09
❑ 509 Vladimir Guerrero 1.25 .55
❑ 510 Wady Almonte RC .20 .09
❑ 511 Dustin Hermanson .20 .09
❑ 512 Deivi Cruz RC 1.00 .45
❑ 513 Luis Alicea .20 .09
❑ 514 Felix Heredia RC .20 .09
❑ 515 Don Slaught .20 .09
❑ 516 S.Hasegawa RC .50 .23
❑ 517 Matt Walbeck .20 .09
❑ 518 David Arias-Ortiz RC 1.50 .70
❑ 519 Brady Raggio RC .20 .09
❑ 520 Rudy Pemberton .20 .09
❑ 521 Wayne Kirby .20 .09
❑ 522 Calvin Maduro .20 .09
❑ 523 Mark Lewis .20 .09
❑ 524 Mike Jackson .20 .09
❑ 525 Sid Fernandez .20 .09
❑ 526 Mike Bielecki .20 .09
❑ 527 Bubba Trammell RC .30 .14
❑ 528 Brent Brede RC .20 .09
❑ 529 Matt Morris .30 .14
❑ 530 Joe Borowski RC .20 .09
❑ 531 Orlando Miller .20 .09
❑ 532 Jim Bullinger .20 .09
❑ 533 Robert Person .20 .09
❑ 534 Doug Glanville .20 .09
❑ 535 Terry Pendleton .30 .14
❑ 536 Jorge Posada .30 .14
❑ 537 Marc Sagmoen RC .20 .09
❑ 538 Fernando Tatis RC .75 .35
❑ 539 Aaron Sele .30 .14
❑ 540 Brian Banks .20 .09
❑ 541 Derrek Lee .30 .14
❑ 542 John Wasdin .20 .09
❑ 543 Justin Towle RC .20 .09
❑ 544 Pat Cline .20 .09
❑ 545 Dave Magadan .20 .09
❑ 546 Jeff Blauser .20 .09
❑ 547 Phil Nevin .30 .14
❑ 548 Todd Walker .20 .09
❑ 549 Eli Marrero .20 .09
❑ 550 Bartolo Colon .30 .14
❑ 551 Jose Cruz Jr. RC 2.00 .90
❑ 552 Todd Dunwoody .20 .09
❑ 553 Hideki Irabu RC .30 .14

		MINT	NRMT
❑ P11	Cal Ripken Promo Three Card Strip	2.00	.90

1998 Ultra

	MINT	NRMT
COMPLETE SET (501)	160.00	70.00
COMPLETE SERIES 1 (250)	100.00	45.00
COMPLETE SERIES 2 (251)	60.00	27.00
COMP.SER.1 w/o SP's (210)	15.00	6.75
COMP.SER.2 w/o SP's (226)	15.00	6.75
COMMON 1 (1-220/246-250)	.15	.07
COMMON 2 (251-475/501)	.15	.07
COMMON SC (211-220)	2.50	1.10
COMMON PROS (221-245)	3.00	1.35
COMMON PZ (476-500)	.75	.35

	Player	MINT	NRMT
❑ 1	Ken Griffey Jr.	2.00	.90
❑ 2	Matt Morris	.25	.11
❑ 3	Roger Clemens	1.50	.70
❑ 4	Matt Williams	.40	.18
❑ 5	Roberto Hernandez	.15	.07
❑ 6	Rondell White	.25	.11
❑ 7	Tim Salmon	.25	.11
❑ 8	Brad Radke	.25	.11
❑ 9	Brett Butler	.25	.11
❑ 10	Carl Everett	.25	.11
❑ 11	Chili Davis	.25	.11
❑ 12	Chuck Finley	.25	.11
❑ 13	Darryl Kile	.25	.11
❑ 14	Deivi Cruz	.15	.07
❑ 15	Gary Gaetti	.25	.11
❑ 16	Matt Stairs	.15	.07
❑ 17	Pat Meares	.15	.07
❑ 18	Will Cunnane	.15	.07
❑ 19	Steve Woodard	.15	.07
❑ 20	Andy Ashby	.15	.07
❑ 21	Bobby Higginson	.25	.11
❑ 22	Brian Jordan	.25	.11
❑ 23	Craig Biggio	.40	.18
❑ 24	Jim Edmonds	.40	.18
❑ 25	Ryan McGuire	.15	.07
❑ 26	Scott Hatteberg	.15	.07
❑ 27	Willie Greene	.15	.07
❑ 28	Albert Belle	.25	.11
❑ 29	Ellis Burks	.25	.11
❑ 30	Hideo Nomo	.60	.25
❑ 31	Jeff Bagwell	.75	.35
❑ 32	Kevin Brown	.40	.18
❑ 33	Nomar Garciaparra	1.50	.70
❑ 34	Pedro Martinez	.75	.35
❑ 35	Raul Mondesi	.25	.11
❑ 36	Ricky Bottalico	.15	.07
❑ 37	Shawn Estes	.25	.11
❑ 38	Otis Nixon	.15	.07
❑ 39	Terry Steinbach	.15	.07
❑ 40	Tom Glavine	.60	.25
❑ 41	Todd Dunwoody	.15	.07
❑ 42	Deion Sanders	.25	.11
❑ 43	Gary Sheffield	.25	.11
❑ 44	Mike Lansing	.15	.07
❑ 45	Mike Lieberthal	.25	.11
❑ 46	Paul Sorrento	.15	.07
❑ 47	Paul O'Neill	.60	.25
❑ 48	Tom Goodwin	.15	.07
❑ 49	Andruw Jones	.60	.25
❑ 50	Barry Bonds	1.50	.70
❑ 51	Bernie Williams	.60	.25
❑ 52	Jeremi Gonzalez	.15	.07
❑ 53	Mike Piazza	1.50	.70
❑ 54	Russ Davis	.15	.07
❑ 55	Vinny Castilla	.25	.11
❑ 56	Rod Beck	.15	.07
❑ 57	Andres Galarraga	.40	.18
❑ 58	Ben McDonald	.15	.07
❑ 59	Billy Wagner	.15	.07
❑ 60	Charles Johnson	.25	.11
❑ 61	Fred McGriff	.40	.18
❑ 62	Dean Palmer	.25	.11
❑ 63	Frank Thomas	.75	.35
❑ 64	Ismael Valdes	.15	.07
❑ 65	Mark Bellhorn	.15	.07
❑ 66	Jeff King	.15	.07
❑ 67	John Wetteland	.25	.11
❑ 68	Mark Grace	.60	.25
❑ 69	Mark Kotsay	.25	.11
❑ 70	Scott Rolen	.60	.25
❑ 71	Todd Hundley	.15	.07
❑ 72	Todd Worrell	.15	.07
❑ 73	Wilson Alvarez	.15	.07
❑ 74	Bobby Jones	.15	.07
❑ 75	Jose Canseco	.60	.25
❑ 76	Kevin Appier	.25	.11
❑ 77	Neifi Perez	.15	.07
❑ 78	Paul Molitor	.60	.25
❑ 79	Quilvio Veras	.15	.07
❑ 80	Randy Johnson	.75	.35
❑ 81	Glendon Rusch	.15	.07
❑ 82	Curt Schilling	.60	.25
❑ 83	Alex Rodriguez	1.50	.70
❑ 84	Rey Ordonez	.15	.07
❑ 85	Jeff Juden	.15	.07
❑ 86	Mike Cameron	.25	.11
❑ 87	Ryan Klesko	.25	.11
❑ 88	Trevor Hoffman	.25	.11
❑ 89	Chuck Knoblauch	.25	.11
❑ 90	Larry Walker	.40	.18
❑ 91	Mark McLemore	.15	.07
❑ 92	B.J. Surhoff	.25	.11
❑ 93	Darren Daulton	.25	.11
❑ 94	Ray Durham	.25	.11
❑ 95	Sammy Sosa	1.25	.55
❑ 96	Eric Young	.15	.07
❑ 97	Gerald Williams	.15	.07
❑ 98	Javy Lopez	.25	.11
❑ 99	John Smiley	.15	.07
❑ 100	Juan Gonzalez	.60	.25
❑ 101	Shawn Green	.60	.25
❑ 102	Charles Nagy	.15	.07
❑ 103	David Justice	.25	.11
❑ 104	Joey Hamilton	.15	.07
❑ 105	Pat Hentgen	.15	.07
❑ 106	Raul Casanova	.15	.07
❑ 107	Tony Phillips	.15	.07
❑ 108	Tony Gwynn	1.25	.55
❑ 109	Will Clark	.60	.25
❑ 110	Jason Giambi	.60	.25
❑ 111	Jay Bell	.25	.11
❑ 112	Johnny Damon	.25	.11
❑ 113	Alan Benes	.15	.07
❑ 114	Jeff Suppan	.15	.07
❑ 115	Kevin Polcovich	.15	.07
❑ 116	Shigetoshi Hasegawa	.25	.11
❑ 117	Steve Finley	.25	.11
❑ 118	Tony Clark	.25	.11
❑ 119	David Cone	.25	.11
❑ 120	Jose Guillen	.15	.07
❑ 121	Kevin Millwood RC	.60	.25
❑ 122	Greg Maddux	1.50	.70
❑ 123	Dave Nilsson	.15	.07
❑ 124	Hideki Irabu	.15	.07
❑ 125	Jason Kendall	.25	.11
❑ 126	Jim Thome	.60	.25
❑ 127	Delino DeShields	.15	.07
❑ 128	Edgar Renteria	.15	.07
❑ 129	Edgardo Alfonzo	.25	.11
❑ 130	J.T. Snow	.25	.11
❑ 131	Jeff Abbott	.15	.07
❑ 132	Jeffrey Hammonds	.15	.07
❑ 133	Todd Greene	.15	.07
❑ 134	Vladimir Guerrero	.75	.35
❑ 135	Jay Buhner	.25	.11
❑ 136	Jeff Cirillo	.25	.11
❑ 137	Jeromy Burnitz	.25	.11
❑ 138	Mickey Morandini	.15	.07
❑ 139	Tino Martinez	.25	.11
❑ 140	Jeff Shaw	.15	.07
❑ 141	Rafael Palmeiro	.60	.25
❑ 142	Bobby Bonilla	.25	.11
❑ 143	Cal Ripken	2.50	1.10
❑ 144	Chad Fox RC	.15	.07
❑ 145	Dante Bichette	.25	.11
❑ 146	Dennis Eckersley	.25	.11
❑ 147	Mariano Rivera	.25	.11
❑ 148	Mo Vaughn	.25	.11
❑ 149	Reggie Sanders	.15	.07
❑ 150	Derek Jeter	2.50	1.10
❑ 151	Rusty Greer	.25	.11
❑ 152	Brady Anderson	.25	.11
❑ 153	Brett Tomko	.15	.07
❑ 154	Jaime Navarro	.15	.07
❑ 155	Kevin Orie	.15	.07
❑ 156	Roberto Alomar	.60	.25
❑ 157	Edgar Martinez	.40	.18
❑ 158	John Olerud	.25	.11
❑ 159	John Smoltz	.25	.11
❑ 160	Ryne Sandberg	.75	.35
❑ 161	Billy Taylor	.15	.07
❑ 162	Chris Holt	.15	.07
❑ 163	Damion Easley	.15	.07
❑ 164	Darin Erstad	.60	.25
❑ 165	Joe Carter	.25	.11
❑ 166	Kelvim Escobar	.15	.07
❑ 167	Ken Caminiti	.25	.11
❑ 168	Pokey Reese	.15	.07
❑ 169	Ray Lankford	.15	.07
❑ 170	Livan Hernandez	.15	.07
❑ 171	Steve Kline	.15	.07
❑ 172	Tom Gordon	.25	.11
❑ 173	Travis Fryman	.25	.11
❑ 174	Al Martin	.15	.07
❑ 175	Andy Pettitte	.25	.11
❑ 176	Jeff Kent	.40	.18
❑ 177	Jimmy Key	.25	.11
❑ 178	Mark Grudzielanek	.15	.07
❑ 179	Tony Saunders	.15	.07
❑ 180	Barry Larkin	.60	.25
❑ 181	Bubba Trammell	.15	.07
❑ 182	Carlos Delgado	.60	.25
❑ 183	Carlos Baerga	.15	.07
❑ 184	Derek Bell	.15	.07
❑ 185	Henry Rodriguez	.15	.07
❑ 186	Jason Dickson	.15	.07
❑ 187	Ron Gant	.25	.11
❑ 188	Tony Womack	.15	.07
❑ 189	Justin Thompson	.15	.07
❑ 190	Fernando Tatis	.15	.07
❑ 191	Mark Wohlers	.15	.07
❑ 192	Takashi Kashiwada	.25	.11
❑ 193	Garret Anderson	.25	.11
❑ 194	Jose Cruz Jr.	.25	.11
❑ 195	Ricardo Rincon	.15	.07
❑ 196	Tim Naehring	.15	.07
❑ 197	Moises Alou	.25	.11
❑ 198	Eric Karros	.25	.11
❑ 199	John Jaha	.25	.11
❑ 200	Marty Cordova	.15	.07
❑ 201	Ken Hill	.15	.07
❑ 202	Chipper Jones	1.25	.55
❑ 203	Kenny Lofton	.25	.11
❑ 204	Mike Mussina	.60	.25
❑ 205	Manny Ramirez	.75	.35
❑ 206	Todd Hollandsworth	.15	.07
❑ 207	Cecil Fielder	.25	.11
❑ 208	Mark McGwire	2.50	1.10
❑ 209	Jim Leyritz	.15	.07
❑ 210	Ivan Rodriguez	.60	.25
❑ 211	Jeff Bagwell SC	3.00	1.35
❑ 212	Barry Bonds SC	6.00	2.70
❑ 213	Roger Clemens SC	6.00	2.70
❑ 214	N.Garciaparra SC	6.00	2.70
❑ 215	Ken Griffey Jr. SC	8.00	3.60
❑ 216	Tony Gwynn SC	6.00	2.70
❑ 217	Randy Johnson SC	3.00	1.35
❑ 218	Mark McGwire SC	10.00	4.50
❑ 219	Scott Rolen SC	2.50	1.10
❑ 220	Frank Thomas SC	3.00	1.35
❑ 221	Matt Perisho PROS	3.00	1.35
❑ 222	Wes Helms PROS	3.00	1.35
❑ 223	D.Dellucci PROS RC	3.00	1.35

❑ 224 Todd Helton PROS 6.00 2.70
❑ 225 Brian Rose PROS 3.00 1.35
❑ 226 Aaron Boone PROS 3.00 1.35
❑ 227 Keith Foulke PROS 3.00 1.35
❑ 228 Homer Bush PROS 3.00 1.35
❑ 229 S.Stewart PROS 3.00 1.35
❑ 230 R.Hidalgo PROS 3.00 1.35
❑ 231 Russ Johnson PROS 3.00 1.35
❑ 232 H.Blanco PROS RC 3.00 1.35
❑ 233 Paul Konerko PROS 3.00 1.35
❑ 234 A.Williamson PROS 3.00 1.35
❑ 235 S.Bowers PROS RC 3.00 1.35
❑ 236 Jose Vidro PROS 3.00 1.35
❑ 237 Derek Wallace PROS 3.00 1.35
❑ 238 Ricky Ledee PROS SP 4.00 1.80
❑ 239 Ben Grieve PROS 3.00 1.35
❑ 240 Lou Collier PROS 3.00 1.35
❑ 241 Derrek Lee PROS 3.00 1.35
❑ 242 Ruben Rivera PROS 3.00 1.35
❑ 243 J.Velandia PROS SP 5.00 2.20
❑ 244 Andrew Vessel PROS 3.00 1.35
❑ 245 Chris Carpenter PROS 3.00 1.35
❑ 246 Ken Griffey Jr. CL 1.00 .45
❑ 247 Alex Rodriguez CL .75 .35
❑ 248 Diamond Ink CL .15 .07
❑ 249 Frank Thomas CL .40 .18
❑ 250 Cal Ripken CL 1.25 .55
❑ 251 Carlos Perez .15 .07
❑ 252 Larry Sutton .15 .07
❑ 253 Gary Sheffield .25 .11
❑ 254 Wally Joyner .25 .11
❑ 255 Todd Stottlemyre .15 .07
❑ 256 Nerio Rodriguez .15 .07
❑ 257 Charles Johnson .25 .11
❑ 258 Pedro Astacio .15 .07
❑ 259 Cal Eldred .15 .07
❑ 260 Chili Davis .25 .11
❑ 261 Freddy Garcia .15 .07
❑ 262 Bobby Witt .15 .07
❑ 263 Michael Coleman .15 .07
❑ 264 Mike Caruso .15 .07
❑ 265 Mike Lansing .15 .07
❑ 266 Dennis Reyes .15 .07
❑ 267 F.P. Santangelo .15 .07
❑ 268 Darryl Hamilton .15 .07
❑ 269 Mike Fetters .15 .07
❑ 270 Charlie Hayes .15 .07
❑ 271 Royce Clayton .15 .07
❑ 272 Doug Drabek .15 .07
❑ 273 James Baldwin .15 .07
❑ 274 Brian Hunter .15 .07
❑ 275 Chan Ho Park .25 .11
❑ 276 John Franco .25 .11
❑ 277 David Wells .25 .11
❑ 278 Eli Marrero .15 .07
❑ 279 Kerry Wood .60 .25
❑ 280 Donnie Sadler .15 .07
❑ 281 Scott Winchester RC .15 .07
❑ 282 Hal Morris .15 .07
❑ 283 Brad Fullmer .25 .11
❑ 284 Bernard Gilkey .15 .07
❑ 285 Ramiro Mendoza .15 .07
❑ 286 Kevin Brown .40 .18
❑ 287 David Segui .15 .07
❑ 288 Willie McGee .25 .11
❑ 289 Darren Oliver .15 .07
❑ 290 Antonio Alfonseca .15 .07
❑ 291 Eric Davis .25 .11
❑ 292 Mickey Morandini .15 .07
❑ 293 Frank Catalanotto RC .60 .25
❑ 294 Derrek Lee .25 .11
❑ 295 Todd Zeile .25 .11
❑ 296 Chuck Knoblauch .25 .11
❑ 297 Wilson Delgado .15 .07
❑ 298 Bobby Bonilla .25 .11
❑ 299 Orel Hershiser .25 .11
❑ 300 Ozzie Guillen .15 .07
❑ 301 Aaron Sele .25 .11
❑ 302 Joe Carter .25 .11
❑ 303 Darryl Kile .25 .11
❑ 304 Shane Reynolds .15 .07
❑ 305 Todd Dunn .15 .07
❑ 306 Bob Abreu .25 .11
❑ 307 Doug Strange .15 .07
❑ 308 Jose Canseco .60 .25
❑ 309 Lance Johnson .15 .07
❑ 310 Harold Baines .25 .11
❑ 311 Todd Pratt .15 .07
❑ 312 Greg Colbrunn .15 .07
❑ 313 Masato Yoshii RC .50 .23
❑ 314 Felix Heredia .15 .07
❑ 315 Dennis Martinez .25 .11
❑ 316 Geronimo Berroa .15 .07
❑ 317 Darren Lewis .15 .07
❑ 318 Bill Ripken .15 .07
❑ 319 Enrique Wilson .15 .07
❑ 320 Alex Ochoa .15 .07
❑ 321 Doug Glanville .15 .07
❑ 322 Mike Stanley .15 .07
❑ 323 Gerald Williams .15 .07
❑ 324 Pedro Martinez .75 .35
❑ 325 Jaret Wright .15 .07
❑ 326 Terry Pendleton .25 .11
❑ 327 LaTroy Hawkins .15 .07
❑ 328 Emil Brown .15 .07
❑ 329 Walt Weiss .25 .11
❑ 330 Omar Vizquel .25 .11
❑ 331 Carl Everett .25 .11
❑ 332 Fernando Vina .15 .07
❑ 333 Mike Blowers .15 .07
❑ 334 Dwight Gooden .15 .07
❑ 335 Mark Lewis .15 .07
❑ 336 Jim Leyritz .15 .07
❑ 337 Kenny Lofton .25 .11
❑ 338 John Halama RC .50 .23
❑ 339 Jose Valentin .15 .07
❑ 340 Desi Relaford .15 .07
❑ 341 Dante Powell .15 .07
❑ 342 Ed Sprague .15 .07
❑ 343 Reggie Jefferson .15 .07
❑ 344 Mike Hampton .25 .11
❑ 345 Marquis Grissom .15 .07
❑ 346 Heathcliff Slocumb .15 .07
❑ 347 Francisco Cordova .15 .07
❑ 348 Ken Cloude .15 .07
❑ 349 Benito Santiago .15 .07
❑ 350 Denny Neagle .15 .07
❑ 351 Sean Casey .40 .18
❑ 352 Robb Nen .15 .07
❑ 353 Orlando Merced .15 .07
❑ 354 Adrian Brown .15 .07
❑ 355 Gregg Jefferies .15 .07
❑ 356 Otis Nixon .15 .07
❑ 357 Michael Tucker .15 .07
❑ 358 Eric Milton .25 .11
❑ 359 Travis Fryman .25 .11
❑ 360 Gary DiSarcina .15 .07
❑ 361 Mario Valdez .15 .07
❑ 362 Craig Counsell .15 .07
❑ 363 Jose Offerman .15 .07
❑ 364 Tony Fernandez .15 .07
❑ 365 Jason McDonald .15 .07
❑ 366 Sterling Hitchcock .15 .07
❑ 367 Donovan Osborne .15 .07
❑ 368 Troy Percival .15 .07
❑ 369 Henry Rodriguez .15 .07
❑ 370 Dmitri Young .25 .11
❑ 371 Jay Powell .15 .07
❑ 372 Jeff Conine .15 .07
❑ 373 Orlando Cabrera .15 .07
❑ 374 Butch Huskey .15 .07
❑ 375 Mike Lowell RC .75 .35
❑ 376 Kevin Young .25 .11
❑ 377 Jamie Moyer .15 .07
❑ 378 Jeff D'Amico .15 .07
❑ 379 Scott Erickson .15 .07
❑ 380 Magglio Ordonez RC 2.00 .90
❑ 381 Melvin Nieves .15 .07
❑ 382 Ramon Martinez .15 .07
❑ 383 A.J. Hinch .15 .07
❑ 384 Jeff Brantley .15 .07
❑ 385 Kevin Elster .15 .07
❑ 386 Allen Watson .15 .07
❑ 387 Moises Alou .25 .11
❑ 388 Jeff Blauser .15 .07
❑ 389 Pete Harnisch .15 .07
❑ 390 Shane Andrews .15 .07
❑ 391 Rico Brogna .15 .07
❑ 392 Stan Javier .15 .07
❑ 393 David Howard .15 .07
❑ 394 Darryl Strawberry .25 .11
❑ 395 Kent Mercker .15 .07
❑ 396 Juan Encarnacion .25 .11
❑ 397 Sandy Alomar Jr. .25 .11
❑ 398 Al Leiter .25 .11
❑ 399 Tony Graffanino .15 .07
❑ 400 Terry Adams .15 .07
❑ 401 Bruce Aven .15 .07
❑ 402 Derrick Gibson .15 .07
❑ 403 Jose Cabrera RC .15 .07
❑ 404 Rich Becker .15 .07
❑ 405 David Ortiz .25 .11
❑ 406 Brian McRae .15 .07
❑ 407 Bobby Estalella .15 .07
❑ 408 Bill Mueller .15 .07
❑ 409 Dennis Eckersley .25 .11
❑ 410 Sandy Martinez .15 .07
❑ 411 Jose Vizcaino .15 .07
❑ 412 Jermaine Allensworth .15 .07
❑ 413 Miguel Tejada .40 .18
❑ 414 Turner Ward .15 .07
❑ 415 Glenallen Hill .15 .07
❑ 416 Lee Stevens .15 .07
❑ 417 Cecil Fielder .25 .11
❑ 418 Ruben Sierra .15 .07
❑ 419 Jon Nunnally .15 .07
❑ 420 Rod Myers .15 .07
❑ 421 Dustin Hermanson .15 .07
❑ 422 James Mouton .15 .07
❑ 423 Dan Wilson .15 .07
❑ 424 Roberto Kelly .15 .07
❑ 425 Antonio Osuna .15 .07
❑ 426 Jacob Cruz .15 .07
❑ 427 Brent Mayne .15 .07
❑ 428 Matt Karchner .15 .07
❑ 429 Damian Jackson .15 .07
❑ 430 Roger Cedeno .15 .07
❑ 431 Rickey Henderson 1.25 .55
❑ 432 Joe Randa .15 .07
❑ 433 Greg Vaughn .25 .11
❑ 434 Andres Galarraga .40 .18
❑ 435 Rod Beck .15 .07
❑ 436 Curtis Goodwin .15 .07
❑ 437 Brad Ausmus .15 .07
❑ 438 Bob Hamelin .15 .07
❑ 439 Todd Walker .15 .07
❑ 440 Scott Brosius .25 .11
❑ 441 Len Dykstra .25 .11
❑ 442 Abraham Nunez .15 .07
❑ 443 Brian Johnson .15 .07
❑ 444 Randy Myers .25 .11
❑ 445 Bret Boone .25 .11
❑ 446 Oscar Henriquez .15 .07
❑ 447 Mike Sweeney .25 .11
❑ 448 Kenny Rogers .15 .07
❑ 449 Mark Langston .15 .07
❑ 450 Luis Gonzalez .60 .25
❑ 451 John Burkett .15 .07
❑ 452 Bip Roberts .15 .07
❑ 453 Travis Lee .25 .11
❑ 454 Felix Rodriguez .15 .07
❑ 455 Andy Benes .15 .07
❑ 456 Willie Blair .15 .07
❑ 457 Brian Anderson .15 .07
❑ 458 Jay Bell .25 .11
❑ 459 Matt Williams .40 .18
❑ 460 Devon White .15 .07
❑ 461 Karim Garcia .15 .07
❑ 462 Jorge Fabregas .15 .07
❑ 463 Wilson Alvarez .15 .07
❑ 464 Roberto Hernandez .15 .07
❑ 465 Tony Saunders .15 .07
❑ 466 Rolando Arrojo RC .50 .23
❑ 467 Wade Boggs .75 .35
❑ 468 Fred McGriff .40 .18
❑ 469 Paul Sorrento .15 .07
❑ 470 Kevin Stocker .15 .07
❑ 471 Bubba Trammell .15 .07
❑ 472 Quinton McCracken .15 .07
❑ 473 Ken Griffey Jr. CL 1.00 .45
❑ 474 Cal Ripken CL 1.25 .55
❑ 475 Frank Thomas CL .40 .18
❑ 476 Ken Griffey Jr. PZ 6.00 2.70
❑ 477 Cal Ripken PZ 8.00 3.60
❑ 478 Frank Thomas PZ 2.50 1.10
❑ 479 Alex Rodriguez PZ 5.00 2.20
❑ 480 Nomar Garciaparra PZ 5.00 2.20
❑ 481 Derek Jeter PZ 8.00 3.60

	Card	MINT	NRMT
❑	482 Andruw Jones PZ	2.00	.90
❑	483 Chipper Jones PZ	4.00	1.80
❑	484 Greg Maddux PZ	5.00	2.20
❑	485 Mike Piazza PZ	5.00	2.20
❑	486 Juan Gonzalez PZ	.60	.25
❑	487 Jose Cruz Jr. PZ	1.00	.45
❑	488 Jaret Wright PZ	.75	.35
❑	489 Hideo Nomo PZ	2.00	.90
❑	490 Scott Rolen PZ	2.00	.90
❑	491 Tony Gwynn PZ	4.00	1.80
❑	492 Roger Clemens PZ	5.00	2.20
❑	493 Darin Erstad PZ	2.00	.90
❑	494 Mark McGwire PZ	8.00	3.60
❑	495 Jeff Bagwell PZ	2.50	1.10
❑	496 Mo Vaughn PZ	1.00	.45
❑	497 Albert Belle PZ	1.00	.45
❑	498 Kenny Lofton PZ	1.00	.45
❑	499 Ben Grieve PZ	1.00	.45
❑	500 Barry Bonds PZ	5.00	2.20
❑	501 Mike Piazza	1.50	.70
❑	S100 A.Rodriguez AU/750	80.00	36.00

1999 Ultra

	MINT	NRMT
COMPLETE SET (250)	80.00	36.00
COMP.SET w/o SP's (215)	25.00	11.00
COMMON CARD (1-215)	.15	.07
COMMON SC (216-225)	1.00	.45
COMMON PROSPECT (226-250)	2.00	.90

	Card	MINT	NRMT
❑	1 Greg Maddux	1.50	.70
❑	2 Greg Vaughn	.25	.11
❑	3 John Wetteland	.25	.11
❑	4 Tino Martinez	.25	.11
❑	5 Todd Walker	.15	.07
❑	6 Troy O'Leary	.15	.07
❑	7 Barry Larkin	.60	.25
❑	8 Mike Lansing	.15	.07
❑	9 Delino DeShields	.15	.07
❑	10 Brett Tomko	.15	.07
❑	11 Carlos Perez	.15	.07
❑	12 Mark Langston	.15	.07
❑	13 Jamie Moyer	.15	.07
❑	14 Jose Guillen	.15	.07
❑	15 Bartolo Colon	.25	.11
❑	16 Brady Anderson	.25	.11
❑	17 Walt Weiss	.15	.07
❑	18 Shane Reynolds	.15	.07
❑	19 David Segui	.15	.07
❑	20 Vladimir Guerrero	.75	.35
❑	21 Freddy Garcia	.15	.07
❑	22 Carl Everett	.25	.11
❑	23 Jose Cruz Jr.	.25	.11
❑	24 David Ortiz	.25	.11
❑	25 Andruw Jones	.60	.25
❑	26 Darren Lewis	.15	.07
❑	27 Ray Lankford	.15	.07
❑	28 Wally Joyner	.25	.11
❑	29 Charles Johnson	.25	.11
❑	30 Derek Jeter	2.50	1.10
❑	31 Sean Casey	.40	.18
❑	32 Bobby Bonilla	.25	.11
❑	33 Todd Zeile	.25	.11
❑	34 Todd Helton	.75	.35
❑	35 David Wells	.25	.11
❑	36 Darin Erstad	.60	.25
❑	37 Ivan Rodriguez	.60	.25
❑	38 Antonio Osuna	.15	.07
❑	39 Mickey Morandini	.15	.07
❑	40 Rusty Greer	.25	.11
❑	41 Rod Beck	.15	.07
❑	42 Larry Sutton	.15	.07
❑	43 Edgar Renteria	.15	.07
❑	44 Otis Nixon	.15	.07
❑	45 Eli Marrero	.15	.07
❑	46 Reggie Jefferson	.15	.07
❑	47 Trevor Hoffman	.25	.11
❑	48 Andres Galarraga	.40	.18
❑	49 Scott Brosius	.25	.11
❑	50 Vinny Castilla	.25	.11
❑	51 Bret Boone	.25	.11
❑	52 Masato Yoshii	.15	.07
❑	53 Matt Williams	.40	.18
❑	54 Robin Ventura	.25	.11
❑	55 Jay Powell	.15	.07
❑	56 Dean Palmer	.25	.11
❑	57 Eric Milton	.25	.11
❑	58 Willie McGee	.25	.11
❑	59 Tony Gwynn	1.25	.55
❑	60 Tom Gordon	.15	.07
❑	61 Dante Bichette	.25	.11
❑	62 Jaret Wright	.15	.07
❑	63 Devon White	.15	.07
❑	64 Frank Thomas	.75	.35
❑	65 Mike Piazza	1.50	.70
❑	66 Jose Offerman	.15	.07
❑	67 Pat Meares	.15	.07
❑	68 Brian Meadows	.15	.07
❑	69 Nomar Garciaparra	1.50	.70
❑	70 Mark McGwire	2.50	1.10
❑	71 Tony Graffanino	.15	.07
❑	72 Ken Griffey Jr.	2.00	.90
❑	73 Ken Caminiti	.25	.11
❑	74 Todd Jones	.15	.07
❑	75 A.J. Hinch	.15	.07
❑	76 Marquis Grissom	.15	.07
❑	77 Jay Buhner	.25	.11
❑	78 Albert Belle	.25	.11
❑	79 Brian Anderson	.15	.07
❑	80 Quinton McCracken	.15	.07
❑	81 Omar Vizquel	.25	.11
❑	82 Todd Stottlemyre	.15	.07
❑	83 Cal Ripken	2.50	1.10
❑	84 Magglio Ordonez	.40	.18
❑	85 John Olerud	.25	.11
❑	86 Hal Morris	.15	.07
❑	87 Derrek Lee	.25	.11
❑	88 Doug Glanville	.15	.07
❑	89 Marty Cordova	.15	.07
❑	90 Kevin Brown	.25	.11
❑	91 Kevin Young	.25	.11
❑	92 Rico Brogna	.15	.07
❑	93 Wilson Alvarez	.15	.07
❑	94 Bob Wickman	.15	.07
❑	95 Jim Thome	.60	.25
❑	96 Mike Mussina	.60	.25
❑	97 Al Leiter	.25	.11
❑	98 Travis Lee	.15	.07
❑	99 Jeff King	.15	.07
❑	100 Kerry Wood	.60	.25
❑	101 Cliff Floyd	.25	.11
❑	102 Jose Valentin	.15	.07
❑	103 Manny Ramirez	.75	.35
❑	104 Butch Huskey	.15	.07
❑	105 Scott Erickson	.15	.07
❑	106 Ray Durham	.25	.11
❑	107 Johnny Damon	.25	.11
❑	108 Craig Counsell	.15	.07
❑	109 Rolando Arrojo	.15	.07
❑	110 Bob Abreu	.25	.11
❑	111 Tony Womack	.15	.07
❑	112 Mike Stanley	.15	.07
❑	113 Kenny Lofton	.25	.11
❑	114 Eric Davis	.25	.11
❑	115 Jeff Conine	.15	.07
❑	116 Carlos Baerga	.15	.07
❑	117 Rondell White	.25	.11
❑	118 Billy Wagner	.15	.07
❑	119 Ed Sprague	.15	.07
❑	120 Jason Schmidt	.15	.07
❑	121 Edgar Martinez	.40	.18
❑	122 Travis Fryman	.25	.11
❑	123 Armando Benitez	.15	.07
❑	124 Matt Stairs	.15	.07
❑	125 Roberto Hernandez	.15	.07
❑	126 Jay Bell	.25	.11
❑	127 Justin Thompson	.15	.07
❑	128 John Jaha	.15	.07
❑	129 Mike Caruso	.15	.07
❑	130 Miguel Tejada	.25	.11
❑	131 Geoff Jenkins	.25	.11
❑	132 Wade Boggs	.60	.25
❑	133 Andy Benes	.15	.07
❑	134 Aaron Sele	.25	.11
❑	135 Bret Saberhagen	.25	.11
❑	136 Mariano Rivera	.25	.11
❑	137 Neifi Perez	.15	.07
❑	138 Paul Konerko	.25	.11
❑	139 Barry Bonds	1.50	.70
❑	140 Garret Anderson	.25	.11
❑	141 Bernie Williams	.60	.25
❑	142 Gary Sheffield	.25	.11
❑	143 Rafael Palmeiro	.60	.25
❑	144 Orel Hershiser	.25	.11
❑	145 Craig Biggio	.40	.18
❑	146 Dmitri Young	.25	.11
❑	147 Damion Easley	.15	.07
❑	148 Henry Rodriguez	.15	.07
❑	149 Brad Radke	.25	.11
❑	150 Pedro Martinez	.75	.35
❑	151 Mike Lieberthal	.25	.11
❑	152 Jim Leyritz	.15	.07
❑	153 Chuck Knoblauch	.25	.11
❑	154 Darryl Kile	.25	.11
❑	155 Brian Jordan	.25	.11
❑	156 Chipper Jones	1.25	.55
❑	157 Pete Harnisch	.15	.07
❑	158 Moises Alou	.25	.11
❑	159 Ismael Valdes	.15	.07
❑	160 Stan Javier	.15	.07
❑	161 Mark Grace	.60	.25
❑	162 Jason Giambi	.60	.25
❑	163 Chuck Finley	.25	.11
❑	164 Juan Encarnacion	.25	.11
❑	165 Chan Ho Park	.25	.11
❑	166 Randy Johnson	.75	.35
❑	167 J.T. Snow	.25	.11
❑	168 Tim Salmon	.25	.11
❑	169 Brian L.Hunter	.15	.07
❑	170 Rickey Henderson	1.25	.55
❑	171 Cal Eldred	.15	.07
❑	172 Curt Schilling	.60	.25
❑	173 Alex Rodriguez	1.50	.70
❑	174 Dustin Hermanson	.15	.07
❑	175 Mike Hampton	.25	.11
❑	176 Shawn Green	.60	.25
❑	177 Roberto Alomar	.60	.25
❑	178 Sandy Alomar Jr.	.25	.11
❑	179 Larry Walker	.40	.18
❑	180 Mo Vaughn	.25	.11
❑	181 Raul Mondesi	.25	.11
❑	182 Hideki Irabu	.15	.07
❑	183 Jim Edmonds	.40	.18
❑	184 Shawn Estes	.25	.11
❑	185 Tony Clark	.25	.11
❑	186 Dan Wilson	.15	.07
❑	187 Michael Tucker	.15	.07
❑	188 Jeff Shaw	.15	.07
❑	189 Mark Grudzielanek	.15	.07
❑	190 Roger Clemens	1.50	.70
❑	191 Juan Gonzalez	.60	.25
❑	192 Sammy Sosa	1.25	.55
❑	193 Troy Percival	.15	.07
❑	194 Robb Nen	.15	.07
❑	195 Bill Mueller	.15	.07
❑	196 Ben Grieve	.25	.11
❑	197 Luis Gonzalez	.60	.25
❑	198 Will Clark	.60	.25
❑	199 Jeff Cirillo	.25	.11
❑	200 Scott Rolen	.60	.25
❑	201 Reggie Sanders	.15	.07
❑	202 Fred McGriff	.40	.18
❑	203 Denny Neagle	.15	.07
❑	204 Brad Fullmer	.25	.11
❑	205 Royce Clayton	.15	.07
❑	206 Jose Canseco	.60	.25
❑	207 Jeff Bagwell	.75	.35
❑	208 Hideo Nomo	.60	.25
❑	209 Karim Garcia	.15	.07

		MINT	NRMT
❑ 210	Kenny Rogers	.15	.07
❑ 211	Kerry Wood CL	.25	.11
❑ 212	Alex Rodriguez CL	.75	.35
❑ 213	Cal Ripken CL	1.25	.55
❑ 214	Frank Thomas CL	.40	.18
❑ 215	Ken Griffey Jr. CL	1.00	.45
❑ 216	Alex Rodriguez SC	4.00	1.80
❑ 217	Greg Maddux SC	4.00	1.80
❑ 218	Juan Gonzalez SC	1.50	.70
❑ 219	Ken Griffey Jr. SC	5.00	2.20
❑ 220	Kerry Wood SC	1.50	.70
❑ 221	Mark McGwire SC	6.00	2.70
❑ 222	Mike Piazza SC	4.00	1.80
❑ 223	Rickey Henderson SC	3.00	1.35
❑ 224	Sammy Sosa SC	3.00	1.35
❑ 225	Travis Lee SC	1.00	.45
❑ 226	Gabe Alvarez PROS	2.00	.90
❑ 227	Matt Anderson PROS	2.00	.90
❑ 228	Adrian Beltre PROS	2.00	.90
❑ 229	O.Cabrera PROS	2.00	.90
❑ 230	Orl. Hernandez PROS	2.00	.90
❑ 231	A.Ramirez PROS	2.00	.90
❑ 232	Troy Glaus PROS	5.00	2.20
❑ 233	Gabe Kapler PROS	2.00	.90
❑ 234	Jeremy Giambi PROS	2.00	.90
❑ 235	Derrick Gibson PROS	2.00	.90
❑ 236	Carlton Loewer PROS	2.00	.90
❑ 237	Mike Frank PROS	2.00	.90
❑ 238	Carlos Guillen PROS	2.00	.90
❑ 239	Alex Gonzalez PROS	2.00	.90
❑ 240	Enrique Wilson PROS	2.00	.90
❑ 241	J.D. Drew PROS	5.00	2.20
❑ 242	Bruce Chen PROS	2.00	.90
❑ 243	Ryan Minor PROS	2.00	.90
❑ 244	Preston Wilson PROS	2.00	.90
❑ 245	Josh Booty PROS	2.00	.90
❑ 246	Luis Ordaz PROS	2.00	.90
❑ 247	G.Lombard PROS	2.00	.90
❑ 248	Matt Clement PROS	2.00	.90
❑ 249	Eric Chavez PROS	2.00	.90
❑ 250	Corey Koskie PROS	2.00	.90

2000 Ultra

	MINT	NRMT
COMPLETE SET (300)	200.00	90.00
COMP.SET w/o SP's (250)	25.00	11.00
COMMON CARD (1-250)	.15	.07
COMMON PROSPECT (251-300)	4.00	1.80

		MINT	NRMT
❑ 1	Alex Rodriguez	1.50	.70
❑ 2	Shawn Green	.60	.25
❑ 3	Magglio Ordonez	.25	.11
❑ 4	Tony Gwynn	1.25	.55
❑ 5	Joe McEwing	.15	.07
❑ 6	Jose Rosado	.15	.07
❑ 7	Sammy Sosa	1.25	.55
❑ 8	Gary Sheffield	.25	.11
❑ 9	Mickey Morandini	.15	.07
❑ 10	Mo Vaughn	.25	.11
❑ 11	Todd Hollandsworth	.15	.07
❑ 12	Tom Gordon	.15	.07
❑ 13	Charles Johnson	.25	.11
❑ 14	Derek Bell	.15	.07
❑ 15	Kevin Young	.15	.07
❑ 16	Jay Buhner	.25	.11
❑ 17	J.T. Snow	.25	.11
❑ 18	Jay Bell	.25	.11
❑ 19	John Rocker	.25	.11
❑ 20	Ivan Rodriguez	.60	.25
❑ 21	Pokey Reese	.15	.07
❑ 22	Paul O'Neill	.60	.25
❑ 23	Ronnie Belliard	.15	.07
❑ 24	Ryan Rupe	.15	.07
❑ 25	Travis Fryman	.25	.11
❑ 26	Trot Nixon	.25	.11
❑ 27	Wally Joyner	.25	.11
❑ 28	Andy Pettitte	.25	.11
❑ 29	Dan Wilson	.15	.07
❑ 30	Orlando Hernandez	.25	.11
❑ 31	Dmitri Young	.25	.11
❑ 32	Edgar Renteria	.15	.07
❑ 33	Eric Karros	.25	.11
❑ 34	Fernando Seguignol	.15	.07
❑ 35	Jason Kendall	.25	.11
❑ 36	Jeff Shaw	.15	.07
❑ 37	Matt Lawton	.15	.07
❑ 38	Robin Ventura	.40	.18
❑ 39	Scott Williamson	.15	.07
❑ 40	Ben Grieve	.25	.11
❑ 41	Billy Wagner	.15	.07
❑ 42	Javy Lopez	.25	.11
❑ 43	Joe Randa	.15	.07
❑ 44	Neifi Perez	.15	.07
❑ 45	David Justice	.25	.11
❑ 46	Ray Durham	.25	.11
❑ 47	Dustin Hermanson	.15	.07
❑ 48	Andres Galarraga	.40	.18
❑ 49	Brad Fullmer	.25	.11
❑ 50	Nomar Garciaparra	1.50	.70
❑ 51	David Cone	.25	.11
❑ 52	David Nilsson	.15	.07
❑ 53	David Wells	.25	.11
❑ 54	Miguel Tejada	.25	.11
❑ 55	Ismael Valdes	.15	.07
❑ 56	Jose Lima	.15	.07
❑ 57	Juan Encarnacion	.25	.11
❑ 58	Fred McGriff	.40	.18
❑ 59	Kenny Rogers	.15	.07
❑ 60	Vladimir Guerrero	.75	.35
❑ 61	Benito Santiago	.15	.07
❑ 62	Chris Singleton	.15	.07
❑ 63	Carlos Lee	.25	.11
❑ 64	Sean Casey	.40	.18
❑ 65	Tom Goodwin	.15	.07
❑ 66	Todd Hundley	.15	.07
❑ 67	Ellis Burks	.25	.11
❑ 68	Tim Hudson	.60	.25
❑ 69	Matt Stairs	.15	.07
❑ 70	Chipper Jones UER Dodgers logo on the back	1.25	.55
❑ 71	Craig Biggio	.40	.18
❑ 72	Brian Rose	.15	.07
❑ 73	Carlos Delgado	.60	.25
❑ 74	Eddie Taubensee	.15	.07
❑ 75	John Smoltz	.25	.11
❑ 76	Ken Caminiti	.25	.11
❑ 77	Rafael Palmeiro	.60	.25
❑ 78	Sidney Ponson	.15	.07
❑ 79	Todd Helton	.75	.35
❑ 80	Juan Gonzalez	.60	.25
❑ 81	Bruce Aven	.15	.07
❑ 82	Desi Relaford	.15	.07
❑ 83	Johnny Damon	.25	.11
❑ 84	Albert Belle	.25	.11
❑ 85	Mark McGwire	2.50	1.10
❑ 86	Rico Brogna	.15	.07
❑ 87	Tom Glavine	.60	.25
❑ 88	Harold Baines	.25	.11
❑ 89	Chad Allen	.15	.07
❑ 90	Barry Bonds	1.50	.70
❑ 91	Mark Grace	.60	.25
❑ 92	Paul Byrd	.15	.07
❑ 93	Roberto Alomar	.60	.25
❑ 94	Roberto Hernandez	.15	.07
❑ 95	Steve Finley	.25	.11
❑ 96	Bret Boone	.25	.11
❑ 97	Charles Nagy	.15	.07
❑ 98	Eric Chavez	.25	.11
❑ 99	Jamie Moyer	.15	.07
❑ 100	Ken Griffey Jr.	2.00	.90
❑ 101	J.D. Drew	.60	.25
❑ 102	Todd Stottlemyre	.15	.07
❑ 103	Tony Fernandez	.15	.07
❑ 104	Jeromy Burnitz	.25	.11
❑ 105	Jeremy Giambi	.15	.07
❑ 106	Livan Hernandez	.15	.07
❑ 107	Marlon Anderson	.15	.07
❑ 108	Troy Glaus	.60	.25
❑ 109	Troy O'Leary	.15	.07
❑ 110	Scott Rolen	.60	.25
❑ 111	Bernard Gilkey	.15	.07
❑ 112	Brady Anderson	.25	.11
❑ 113	Chuck Knoblauch	.25	.11
❑ 114	Jeff Weaver	.25	.11
❑ 115	B.J. Surhoff	.25	.11
❑ 116	Alex Gonzalez	.15	.07
❑ 117	Vinny Castilla	.25	.11
❑ 118	Tim Salmon	.25	.11
❑ 119	Brian Jordan	.25	.11
❑ 120	Corey Koskie	.25	.11
❑ 121	Dean Palmer	.25	.11
❑ 122	Gabe Kapler	.25	.11
❑ 123	Jim Edmonds	.40	.18
❑ 124	John Jaha	.15	.07
❑ 125	Mark Grudzielanek	.15	.07
❑ 126	Mike Bordick	.15	.07
❑ 127	Mike Lieberthal	.25	.11
❑ 128	Pete Harnisch	.15	.07
❑ 129	Russ Ortiz	.25	.11
❑ 130	Kevin Brown	.40	.18
❑ 131	Troy Percival	.15	.07
❑ 132	Alex Gonzalez	.15	.07
❑ 133	Bartolo Colon	.25	.11
❑ 134	John Valentin	.15	.07
❑ 135	Jose Hernandez	.15	.07
❑ 136	Marquis Grissom	.15	.07
❑ 137	Wade Boggs	.60	.25
❑ 138	Dante Bichette	.25	.11
❑ 139	Bobby Higginson	.15	.07
❑ 140	Frank Thomas	.75	.35
❑ 141	Geoff Jenkins	.25	.11
❑ 142	Jason Giambi	.60	.25
❑ 143	Jeff Cirillo	.25	.11
❑ 144	Sandy Alomar Jr.	.15	.07
❑ 145	Luis Gonzalez	.60	.25
❑ 146	Preston Wilson	.25	.11
❑ 147	Carlos Beltran	.25	.11
❑ 148	Greg Vaughn	.25	.11
❑ 149	Carlos Febles	.15	.07
❑ 150	Jose Canseco	.60	.25
❑ 151	Kris Benson	.25	.11
❑ 152	Chuck Finley	.25	.11
❑ 153	Michael Barrett	.15	.07
❑ 154	Rey Ordonez	.15	.07
❑ 155	Adrian Beltre	.25	.11
❑ 156	Andruw Jones	.60	.25
❑ 157	Barry Larkin	.60	.25
❑ 158	Brian Giles	.25	.11
❑ 159	Carl Everett	.25	.11
❑ 160	Manny Ramirez	.75	.35
❑ 161	Darryl Kile	.25	.11
❑ 162	Edgar Martinez	.40	.18
❑ 163	Jeff Kent	.40	.18
❑ 164	Matt Williams	.40	.18
❑ 165	Mike Piazza	1.50	.70
❑ 166	Pedro Martinez	.75	.35
❑ 167	Ray Lankford	.15	.07
❑ 168	Roger Cedeno	.15	.07
❑ 169	Ron Coomer	.15	.07
❑ 170	Cal Ripken	2.50	1.10
❑ 171	Jose Offerman	.15	.07
❑ 172	Kenny Lofton	.25	.11
❑ 173	Kent Bottenfield	.15	.07
❑ 174	Kevin Millwood	.15	.07
❑ 175	Omar Daal	.15	.07
❑ 176	Orlando Cabrera	.15	.07
❑ 177	Pat Hentgen	.15	.07
❑ 178	Tino Martinez	.25	.11
❑ 179	Tony Clark	.25	.11
❑ 180	Roger Clemens	1.50	.70
❑ 181	Brad Radke	.25	.11
❑ 182	Darin Erstad	.60	.25
❑ 183	Jose Jimenez	.15	.07
❑ 184	Jim Thome	.60	.25
❑ 185	John Wetteland	.25	.11
❑ 186	Justin Thompson	.15	.07
❑ 187	John Halama	.15	.07
❑ 188	Lee Stevens	.15	.07
❑ 189	Miguel Cairo	.15	.07

❑ 190	Mike Mussina	.60	.25
❑ 191	Raul Mondesi	.25	.11
❑ 192	Armando Rios	.15	.07
❑ 193	Trevor Hoffman	.25	.11
❑ 194	Tony Batista	.25	.11
❑ 195	Will Clark	.60	.25
❑ 196	Brad Ausmus	.15	.07
❑ 197	Chili Davis	.25	.11
❑ 198	Cliff Floyd	.25	.11
❑ 199	Curt Schilling	.60	.25
❑ 200	Derek Jeter	2.50	1.10
❑ 201	Henry Rodriguez	.15	.07
❑ 202	Jose Cruz Jr.	.25	.11
❑ 203	Omar Vizquel	.25	.11
❑ 204	Randy Johnson	.75	.35
❑ 205	Reggie Sanders	.15	.07
❑ 206	Al Leiter	.15	.07
❑ 207	Damion Easley	.15	.07
❑ 208	David Bell	.15	.07
❑ 209	Fernando Tatis	.15	.07
❑ 210	Kerry Wood	.60	.25
❑ 211	Kevin Appier	.15	.07
❑ 212	Mariano Rivera	.25	.11
❑ 213	Mike Caruso	.15	.07
❑ 214	Moises Alou	.25	.11
❑ 215	Randy Winn	.15	.07
❑ 216	Roy Halladay	.15	.07
❑ 217	Shannon Stewart	.25	.11
❑ 218	Todd Walker	.15	.07
❑ 219	Jim Parque	.15	.07
❑ 220	Travis Lee	.15	.07
❑ 221	Andy Ashby	.15	.07
❑ 222	Ed Sprague	.15	.07
❑ 223	Larry Walker	.40	.18
❑ 224	Rick Helling	.15	.07
❑ 225	Rusty Greer	.25	.11
❑ 226	Todd Zeile	.25	.11
❑ 227	Freddy Garcia	.40	.18
❑ 228	Hideo Nomo	.60	.25
❑ 229	Marty Cordova	.15	.07
❑ 230	Greg Maddux	1.50	.70
❑ 231	Rondell White	.25	.11
❑ 232	Paul Konerko	.25	.11
❑ 233	Warren Morris	.15	.07
❑ 234	Bernie Williams	.60	.25
❑ 235	Bob Abreu	.25	.11
❑ 236	John Olerud	.25	.11
❑ 237	Doug Glanville	.15	.07
❑ 238	Eric Young	.15	.07
❑ 239	Robb Nen	.15	.07
❑ 240	Jeff Bagwell	.75	.35
❑ 241	Sterling Hitchcock	.15	.07
❑ 242	Todd Greene	.15	.07
❑ 243	Bill Mueller	.15	.07
❑ 244	Rickey Henderson	1.25	.55
❑ 245	Chan Ho Park	.25	.11
❑ 246	Jason Schmidt	.15	.07
❑ 247	Jeff Zimmerman	.15	.07
❑ 248	Jermaine Dye	.25	.11
❑ 249	Randall Simon	.15	.07
❑ 250	Richie Sexson	.25	.11
❑ 251	Micah Bowie PROS	4.00	1.80
❑ 252	Joe Nathan PROS	4.00	1.80
❑ 253	C.Woodward PROS	4.00	1.80
❑ 254	Lance Berkman PROS	6.00	2.70
❑ 255	Ruben Mateo PROS	4.00	1.80
❑ 256	R.Branyan PROS	4.00	1.80
❑ 257	Randy Wolf PROS	4.00	1.80
❑ 258	A.J. Burnett PROS	4.00	1.80
❑ 259	Mark Quinn PROS	4.00	1.80
❑ 260	Buddy Carlyle PROS	4.00	1.80
❑ 261	Ben Davis PROS	4.00	1.80
❑ 262	Yamid Haad PROS	4.00	1.80
❑ 263	Mike Colangelo PROS	4.00	1.80
❑ 264	Rick Ankiel PROS	6.00	2.70
❑ 265	Jacque Jones PROS	4.00	1.80
❑ 266	Kelly Dransfeldt PROS	4.00	1.80
❑ 267	Matt Riley PROS	4.00	1.80
❑ 268	Adam Kennedy PROS	4.00	1.80
❑ 269	Octavio Dotel PROS	4.00	1.80
❑ 270	F.Cordero PROS	4.00	1.80
❑ 271	Wilton Veras PROS	4.00	1.80
❑ 272	C.Pickering PROS	4.00	1.80
❑ 273	Alex Sanchez PROS	4.00	1.80
❑ 274	Tony Armas Jr. PROS	4.00	1.80
❑ 275	Pat Burrell PROS	6.00	2.70
❑ 276	Chad Meyers PROS	4.00	1.80
❑ 277	Ben Petrick PROS	4.00	1.80
❑ 278	R.Hernandez PROS	4.00	1.80
❑ 279	Ed Yarnall PROS	4.00	1.80
❑ 280	Erubiel Durazo PROS	4.00	1.80
❑ 281	Vernon Wells PROS	4.00	1.80
❑ 282	G.Matthews Jr. PROS	4.00	1.80
❑ 283	Kip Wells PROS	4.00	1.80
❑ 284	Peter Bergeron PROS	4.00	1.80
❑ 285	Travis Dawkins PROS	4.00	1.80
❑ 286	Jorge Toca PROS	4.00	1.80
❑ 287	Cole Liniak PROS	4.00	1.80
❑ 288	C.Hermansen PROS	4.00	1.80
❑ 289	Eric Gagne PROS	4.00	1.80
❑ 290	C.Hutchinson PROS	4.00	1.80
❑ 291	Eric Munson PROS	4.00	1.80
❑ 292	Wiki Gonzalez PROS	4.00	1.80
❑ 293	A.Soriano PROS	6.00	2.70
❑ 294	T.Durrington PROS	4.00	1.80
❑ 295	Ben Molina PROS	4.00	1.80
❑ 296	Aaron Myette PROS	4.00	1.80
❑ 297	Wily Pena PROS	6.00	2.70
❑ 298	Kevin Barker PROS	4.00	1.80
❑ 299	Geoff Blum PROS	4.00	1.80
❑ 300	Josh Beckett PROS	8.00	3.60
❑ P1	Alex Rodriguez Promo	1.50	.70
❑ P2	A.Rodriguez Promo 3-D	4.00	1.80

2001 Ultra

	MINT	NRMT
COMPLETE SET (275)	120.00	55.00
COMP.SET w/o SP's (250)	25.00	11.00
COMMON CARD (1-250)	.15	.07
COMMON CARD (251-275)	3.00	1.35

❑ 1	Pedro Martinez	.75	.35
❑ 2	Derek Jeter	2.50	1.10
❑ 3	Cal Ripken	2.50	1.10
❑ 4	Alex Rodriguez	1.50	.70
❑ 5	Vladimir Guerrero	.75	.35
❑ 6	Troy Glaus	.60	.25
❑ 7	Sammy Sosa	1.25	.55
❑ 8	Mike Piazza	1.50	.70
❑ 9	Tony Gwynn	1.25	.55
❑ 10	Tim Hudson	.60	.25
❑ 11	John Flaherty	.15	.07
❑ 12	Jeff Cirillo	.25	.11
❑ 13	Ellis Burks	.25	.11
❑ 14	Carlos Lee	.25	.11
❑ 15	Carlos Beltran	.25	.11
❑ 16	Ruben Rivera	.15	.07
❑ 17	Richard Hidalgo	.25	.11
❑ 18	Omar Vizquel	.25	.11
❑ 19	Michael Barrett	.15	.07
❑ 20	Jose Canseco	.60	.25
❑ 21	Jason Giambi	.60	.25
❑ 22	Greg Maddux	1.50	.70
❑ 23	Charles Johnson	.25	.11
❑ 24	Sandy Alomar Jr.	.25	.11
❑ 25	Rick Ankiel	.40	.18
❑ 26	Richie Sexson	.25	.11
❑ 27	Matt Williams	.40	.18
❑ 28	Joe Girardi	.15	.07
❑ 29	Jason Kendall	.25	.11
❑ 30	Brad Fullmer	.25	.11
❑ 31	Alex Gonzalez	.15	.07
❑ 32	Rick Helling	.15	.07
❑ 33	Mike Mussina	.60	.25
❑ 34	Joe Randa	.15	.07
❑ 35	J.T. Snow	.25	.11
❑ 36	Edgardo Alfonzo	.25	.11
❑ 37	Dante Bichette	.25	.11
❑ 38	Brad Ausmus	.15	.07
❑ 39	Bobby Abreu	.25	.11
❑ 40	Warren Morris	.15	.07
❑ 41	Tony Womack	.15	.07
❑ 42	Russell Branyan	.25	.11
❑ 43	Mike Lowell	.25	.11
❑ 44	Mark Grace	.60	.25
❑ 45	Jeromy Burnitz	.25	.11
❑ 46	J.D. Drew	.60	.25
❑ 47	David Justice	.40	.18
❑ 48	Alex Gonzalez	.15	.07
❑ 49	Tino Martinez	.25	.11
❑ 50	Raul Mondesi	.25	.11
❑ 51	Rafael Furcal	.25	.11
❑ 52	Marquis Grissom	.15	.07
❑ 53	Kevin Young	.15	.07
❑ 54	Jon Lieber	.15	.07
❑ 55	Henry Rodriguez	.15	.07
❑ 56	Dave Burba	.15	.07
❑ 57	Shannon Stewart	.25	.11
❑ 58	Preston Wilson	.25	.11
❑ 59	Paul O'Neill	.60	.25
❑ 60	Jimmy Haynes	.15	.07
❑ 61	Darryl Kile	.25	.11
❑ 62	Bret Boone	.25	.11
❑ 63	Bartolo Colon	.25	.11
❑ 64	Andres Galarraga	.40	.18
❑ 65	Trot Nixon	.25	.11
❑ 66	Steve Finley	.25	.11
❑ 67	Shawn Green	.60	.25
❑ 68	Robert Person	.15	.07
❑ 69	Kenny Rogers	.15	.07
❑ 70	Bobby Higginson	.25	.11
❑ 71	Barry Larkin	.60	.25
❑ 72	Al Martin	.15	.07
❑ 73	Tom Glavine	.60	.25
❑ 74	Rondell White	.25	.11
❑ 75	Ray Lankford	.15	.07
❑ 76	Moises Alou	.25	.11
❑ 77	Matt Clement	.15	.07
❑ 78	Geoff Jenkins	.25	.11
❑ 79	David Wells	.25	.11
❑ 80	Chuck Finley	.25	.11
❑ 81	Andy Pettitte	.25	.11
❑ 82	Travis Fryman	.25	.11
❑ 83	Ron Coomer	.15	.07
❑ 84	Mark McGwire	2.50	1.10
❑ 85	Kerry Wood	.60	.25
❑ 86	Jorge Posada	.25	.11
❑ 87	Jeff Bagwell	.75	.35
❑ 88	Andruw Jones	.60	.25
❑ 89	Ryan Klesko	.25	.11
❑ 90	Mariano Rivera	.25	.11
❑ 91	Lance Berkman	.60	.25
❑ 92	Kenny Lofton	.25	.11
❑ 93	Jacque Jones	.25	.11
❑ 94	Eric Young	.15	.07
❑ 95	Edgar Renteria	.15	.07
❑ 96	Chipper Jones	1.25	.55
❑ 97	Todd Helton	.75	.35
❑ 98	Shawn Estes	.25	.11
❑ 99	Mark Mulder	.40	.18
❑ 100	Lee Stevens	.15	.07
❑ 101	Jermaine Dye	.25	.11
❑ 102	Greg Vaughn	.25	.11
❑ 103	Chris Singleton	.15	.07
❑ 104	Brady Anderson	.25	.11
❑ 105	Terrence Long	.25	.11
❑ 106	Quilvio Veras	.15	.07
❑ 107	Magglio Ordonez	.25	.11
❑ 108	Johnny Damon	.25	.11
❑ 109	Jeffrey Hammonds	.15	.07
❑ 110	Fred McGriff	.40	.18
❑ 111	Carl Pavano	.15	.07
❑ 112	Bobby Estalella	.15	.07
❑ 113	Todd Hundley	.15	.07
❑ 114	Scott Rolen	.60	.25
❑ 115	Robin Ventura	.25	.11
❑ 116	Pokey Reese	.15	.07
❑ 117	Luis Gonzalez	.60	.25
❑ 118	Jose Offerman	.15	.07

	#	Player	MINT	NRMT
❑	119	Edgar Martinez	.40	.18
❑	120	Dean Palmer	.25	.11
❑	121	David Segui	.15	.07
❑	122	Troy O'Leary	.15	.07
❑	123	Tony Batista	.25	.11
❑	124	Todd Zeile	.25	.11
❑	125	Randy Johnson	.75	.35
❑	126	Luis Castillo	.15	.07
❑	127	Kris Benson	.25	.11
❑	128	John Olerud	.25	.11
❑	129	Eric Karros	.25	.11
❑	130	Eddie Taubensee	.15	.07
❑	131	Neifi Perez	.15	.07
❑	132	Matt Stairs	.15	.07
❑	133	Luis Alicea	.15	.07
❑	134	Jeff Kent	.40	.18
❑	135	Javier Vazquez	.25	.11
❑	136	Garret Anderson	.25	.11
❑	137	Frank Thomas	.75	.35
❑	138	Carlos Febles	.15	.07
❑	139	Albert Belle	.25	.11
❑	140	Tony Clark	.25	.11
❑	141	Pat Burrell	.25	.11
❑	142	Mike Sweeney	.25	.11
❑	143	Jay Buhner	.25	.11
❑	144	Gabe Kapler	.25	.11
❑	145	Derek Bell	.15	.07
❑	146	B.J. Surhoff	.25	.11
❑	147	Adam Kennedy	.15	.07
❑	148	Aaron Boone	.15	.07
❑	149	Todd Stottlemyre	.15	.07
❑	150	Roberto Alomar	.60	.25
❑	151	Orlando Hernandez	.25	.11
❑	152	Jason Varitek	.25	.11
❑	153	Gary Sheffield	.25	.11
❑	154	Cliff Floyd	.25	.11
❑	155	Chad Hermansen	.15	.07
❑	156	Carlos Delgado	.60	.25
❑	157	Aaron Sele	.25	.11
❑	158	Sean Casey	.40	.18
❑	159	Ruben Mateo	.25	.11
❑	160	Mike Bordick	.15	.07
❑	161	Mike Cameron	.25	.11
❑	162	Doug Glanville	.15	.07
❑	163	Damion Easley	.15	.07
❑	164	Carl Everett	.25	.11
❑	165	Bengie Molina	.15	.07
❑	166	Adrian Beltre	.25	.11
❑	167	Tom Goodwin	.15	.07
❑	168	Rickey Henderson	1.25	.55
❑	169	Mo Vaughn	.25	.11
❑	170	Mike Lieberthal	.25	.11
❑	171	Ken Griffey Jr.	2.00	.90
❑	172	Juan Gonzalez	.60	.25
❑	173	Ivan Rodriguez	.60	.25
❑	174	Al Leiter	.25	.11
❑	175	Vinny Castilla	.25	.11
❑	176	Peter Bergeron	.15	.07
❑	177	Pedro Astacio	.15	.07
❑	178	Paul Konerko	.25	.11
❑	179	Mitch Meluskey	.15	.07
❑	180	Kevin Millwood	.15	.07
❑	181	Ben Grieve	.25	.11
❑	182	Barry Bonds	1.50	.70
❑	183	Rusty Greer	.25	.11
❑	184	Miguel Tejada	.25	.11
❑	185	Mark Quinn	.25	.11
❑	186	Larry Walker	.40	.18
❑	187	Jose Valentin	.15	.07
❑	188	Jose Vidro	.25	.11
❑	189	Delino DeShields	.15	.07
❑	190	Darin Erstad	.60	.25
❑	191	Bill Mueller	.15	.07
❑	192	Ray Durham	.25	.11
❑	193	Ken Caminiti	.25	.11
❑	194	Jim Thome	.60	.25
❑	195	Javy Lopez	.25	.11
❑	196	Fernando Vina	.15	.07
❑	197	Eric Chavez	.25	.11
❑	198	Eric Owens	.15	.07
❑	199	Brad Radke	.25	.11
❑	200	Travis Lee	.15	.07
❑	201	Tim Salmon	.25	.11
❑	202	Rafael Palmeiro	.60	.25
❑	203	Nomar Garciaparra	1.50	.70
❑	204	Mike Hampton	.25	.11
❑	205	Kevin Brown	.25	.11
❑	206	Juan Encarnacion	.25	.11
❑	207	Danny Graves	.15	.07
❑	208	Carlos Guillen	.15	.07
❑	209	Phil Nevin	.25	.11
❑	210	Matt Lawton	.25	.11
❑	211	Manny Ramirez	.75	.35
❑	212	James Baldwin	.15	.07
❑	213	Fernando Tatis	.15	.07
❑	214	Craig Biggio	.40	.18
❑	215	Brian Jordan	.25	.11
❑	216	Bernie Williams	.60	.25
❑	217	Ryan Dempster	.25	.11
❑	218	Roger Clemens	1.50	.70
❑	219	Jose Cruz Jr.	.25	.11
❑	220	John Valentin	.15	.07
❑	221	Dmitri Young	.25	.11
❑	222	Curt Schilling	.60	.25
❑	223	Jim Edmonds	.40	.18
❑	224	Chan Ho Park	.25	.11
❑	225	Brian Giles	.25	.11
❑	226	Jimmy Anderson Tike Redman	.15	.07
❑	227	Adam Piatt Jose Ortiz	.40	.18
❑	228	Kenny Kelly Aubrey Huff	.15	.07
❑	229	Randy Choate Craig Dingman	.15	.07
❑	230	Eric Cammack Grant Roberts	.15	.07
❑	231	Yovanny Lara Andy Tracy	.15	.07
❑	232	Wayne Franklin Scott Linebrink	.15	.07
❑	233	Cameron Cairncross Chan Perry	.15	.07
❑	234	J.C. Romero Matt LeCroy	.15	.07
❑	235	Geraldo Guzman Jason Conti	.15	.07
❑	236	Morgan Burkhart Paxton Crawford	.15	.07
❑	237	Pasqual Coco Leo Estrella	.15	.07
❑	238	John Parrish Fernando Lunar	.15	.07
❑	239	Keith McDonald Justin Brunette	.15	.07
❑	240	Carlos Casimiro Ivanon Coffie	.15	.07
❑	241	Daniel Garibay Ruben Quevedo	.15	.07
❑	242	Sang-Hoon Lee Tomo Ohka	.25	.11
❑	243	Hector Ortiz Jeff D'Amico	.15	.07
❑	244	Jeff Sparks Travis Harper	.15	.07
❑	245	Jason Boyd David Coggin	.15	.07
❑	246	Mark Buehrle Lorenzo Barcelo	.60	.25
❑	247	Adam Melhuse Ben Petrick	.15	.07
❑	248	Kane Davis Paul Rigdon	.15	.07
❑	249	Mike Darr Kory DeHaan	.15	.07
❑	250	Vicente Padilla Mark Brownson	.15	.07
❑	251	Barry Zito PROS	5.00	2.20
❑	252	Tim Drew PROS	3.00	1.35
❑	253	Luis Matos PROS	3.00	1.35
❑	254	Alex Cabrera PROS	3.00	1.35
❑	255	Jon Garland PROS	3.00	1.35
❑	256	Milton Bradley PROS	3.00	1.35
❑	257	Juan Pierre PROS	4.00	1.80
❑	258	Ismael Villegas PROS	3.00	1.35
❑	259	Eric Munson PROS	4.00	1.80
❑	260	T.De la Rosa PROS	3.00	1.35
❑	261	Chris Richard PROS	4.00	1.80
❑	262	Jason Tyner PROS	3.00	1.35
❑	263	B.J. Waszgis PROS	3.00	1.35
❑	264	Jason Marquis PROS	4.00	1.80
❑	265	Dusty Allen PROS	3.00	1.35
❑	266	C.Patterson PROS	4.00	1.80
❑	267	Eric Byrnes PROS	3.00	1.35
❑	268	Xavier Nady PROS	4.00	1.80
❑	269	G.Lombard PROS	3.00	1.35
❑	270	Timo Perez PROS	3.00	1.35
❑	271	G.Matthews Jr. PROS	3.00	1.35
❑	272	Chad Durbin PROS	3.00	1.35
❑	273	Tony Armas Jr. PROS	4.00	1.80
❑	274	F.Cordero PROS	3.00	1.35
❑	275	A.Soriano PROS	5.00	2.20

2002 Ultra

	MINT	NRMT
COMPLETE SET (285)	180.00	80.00
COMP.SET w/o SP's (200)	25.00	11.00
COMMON CARD (1-200)	.15	.07
COMMON CARD (201-220)	1.00	.45
COMMON CARD (221-250)	1.00	.45
COMMON CARD (251-285)	3.00	1.35

	#	Player	MINT	NRMT
❑	1	Jeff Bagwell	.75	.35
❑	2	Derek Jeter	2.50	1.10
❑	3	Alex Rodriguez	1.50	.70
❑	4	Eric Chavez	.25	.11
❑	5	Tsuyoshi Shinjo	.40	.18
❑	6	Chris Stynes	.15	.07
❑	7	Ivan Rodriguez	.60	.25
❑	8	Cal Ripken	2.50	1.10
❑	9	Freddy Garcia	.25	.11
❑	10	Chipper Jones	1.25	.55
❑	11	Hideo Nomo	.60	.25
❑	12	Rafael Furcal	.25	.11
❑	13	Preston Wilson	.25	.11
❑	14	Jimmy Rollins	.25	.11
❑	15	Cristian Guzman	.25	.11
❑	16	Garret Anderson	.25	.11
❑	17	Todd Helton	.75	.35
❑	18	Moises Alou	.25	.11
❑	19	Tony Gwynn	1.25	.55
❑	20	Jorge Posada	.25	.11
❑	21	Sean Casey	.40	.18
❑	22	Kazuhiro Sasaki	.60	.25
❑	23	Ray Lankford	.25	.11
❑	24	Manny Ramirez	.75	.35
❑	25	Barry Bonds	1.50	.70
❑	26	Fred McGriff	.40	.18
❑	27	Vladimir Guerrero	.75	.35
❑	28	Jermaine Dye	.25	.11
❑	29	Adrian Beltre	.25	.11
❑	30	Ken Griffey Jr.	2.00	.90
❑	31	Ramon Hernandez	.15	.07
❑	32	Kerry Wood	.60	.25
❑	33	Greg Maddux	1.50	.70
❑	34	Rondell White	.25	.11
❑	35	Mike Mussina	.60	.25
❑	36	Jim Edmonds	.40	.18
❑	37	Scott Rolen	.60	.25
❑	38	Mike Lowell	.25	.11
❑	39	Al Leiter	.25	.11
❑	40	Tony Clark	.25	.11
❑	41	Joe Mays	.25	.11
❑	42	Mo Vaughn	.25	.11
❑	43	Geoff Jenkins	.25	.11
❑	44	Curt Schilling	.60	.25
❑	45	Pedro Martinez	.75	.35
❑	46	Andy Pettitte	.25	.11
❑	47	Tim Salmon	.25	.11

❑	48 Carl Everett	.25	.11
❑	49 Lance Berkman	.60	.25
❑	50 Troy Glaus	.60	.25
❑	51 Ichiro Suzuki	2.50	1.10
❑	52 Alfonso Soriano	.60	.25
❑	53 Tomo Ohka	.25	.11
❑	54 Dean Palmer	.25	.11
❑	55 Kevin Brown	.25	.11
❑	56 Albert Pujols	1.50	.70
❑	57 Homer Bush	.15	.07
❑	58 Tim Hudson	.60	.25
❑	59 Frank Thomas	.75	.35
❑	60 Joe Randa	.15	.07
❑	61 Chan Ho Park	.25	.11
❑	62 Bobby Higginson	.25	.11
❑	63 Bartolo Colon	.25	.11
❑	64 Aramis Ramirez	.25	.11
❑	65 Jeff Cirillo	.25	.11
❑	66 Roberto Alomar	.60	.25
❑	67 Mark Kotsay	.25	.11
❑	68 Mike Cameron	.25	.11
❑	69 Mike Hampton	.25	.11
❑	70 Trot Nixon	.25	.11
❑	71 Juan Gonzalez	.60	.25
❑	72 Damian Rolls	.15	.07
❑	73 Brad Fullmer	.25	.11
❑	74 David Ortiz	.15	.07
❑	75 Brandon Inge	.25	.11
❑	76 Orlando Hernandez	.25	.11
❑	77 Matt Stairs	.15	.07
❑	78 Jay Gibbons	.25	.11
❑	79 Greg Vaughn	.25	.11
❑	80 Brady Anderson	.25	.11
❑	81 Jim Thome	.60	.25
❑	82 Ben Sheets	.25	.11
❑	83 Rafael Palmeiro	.60	.25
❑	84 Edgar Renteria	.25	.11
❑	85 Doug Mientkiewicz	.25	.11
❑	86 Raul Mondesi	.25	.11
❑	87 Shane Reynolds	.15	.07
❑	88 Steve Finley	.25	.11
❑	89 Jose Cruz Jr.	.25	.11
❑	90 Edgardo Alfonzo	.25	.11
❑	91 Jose Valentin	.15	.07
❑	92 Mark McGwire	2.50	1.10
❑	93 Mark Grace	.60	.25
❑	94 Mike Lieberthal	.25	.11
❑	95 Barry Larkin	.60	.25
❑	96 Chuck Knoblauch	.25	.11
❑	97 Deivi Cruz	.15	.07
❑	98 Jeromy Burnitz	.25	.11
❑	99 Shannon Stewart	.25	.11
❑	100 David Wells	.25	.11
❑	101 Brook Fordyce	.15	.07
❑	102 Rusty Greer	.25	.11
❑	103 Andruw Jones	.60	.25
❑	104 Jason Kendall	.25	.11
❑	105 Nomar Garciaparra	1.50	.70
❑	106 Shawn Green	.60	.25
❑	107 Craig Biggio	.40	.18
❑	108 Masato Yoshii	.25	.11
❑	109 Ben Petrick	.15	.07
❑	110 Gary Sheffield	.25	.11
❑	111 Travis Lee	.25	.11
❑	112 Matt Williams	.40	.18
❑	113 Billy Wagner	.25	.11
❑	114 Robin Ventura	.25	.11
❑	115 Jerry Hairston	.15	.07
❑	116 Paul LoDuca	.25	.11
❑	117 Darin Erstad	.60	.25
❑	118 Ruben Sierra	.15	.07
❑	119 Ricky Gutierrez	.15	.07
❑	120 Bret Boone	.25	.11
❑	121 John Rocker	.25	.11
❑	122 Roger Clemens	1.50	.70
❑	123 Eric Karros	.25	.11
❑	124 J.D. Drew	.60	.25
❑	125 Carlos Delgado	.60	.25
❑	126 Jeffrey Hammonds	.15	.07
❑	127 Jeff Kent	.40	.18
❑	128 David Justice	.40	.18
❑	129 Cliff Floyd	.25	.11
❑	130 Omar Vizquel	.25	.11
❑	131 Matt Morris	.25	.11
❑	132 Rich Aurilia	.25	.11
❑	133 Larry Walker	.40	.18
❑	134 Miguel Tejada	.25	.11
❑	135 Eric Young	.15	.07
❑	136 Aaron Sele	.25	.11
❑	137 Eric Milton	.25	.11
❑	138 Travis Fryman	.25	.11
❑	139 Maggio Ordonez	.25	.11
❑	140 Sammy Sosa	1.25	.55
❑	141 Pokey Reese	.15	.07
❑	142 Adam Eaton	.25	.11
❑	143 Adam Kennedy	.15	.07
❑	144 Mike Piazza	1.50	.70
❑	145 Larry Barnes	.15	.07
❑	146 Darryl Kile	.25	.11
❑	147 Tom Glavine	.60	.25
❑	148 Ryan Klesko	.25	.11
❑	149 Jose Vidro	.25	.11
❑	150 Joe Kennedy	.15	.07
❑	151 Bernie Williams	.60	.25
❑	152 C.C. Sabathia	.40	.18
❑	153 Alex Ochoa	.15	.07
❑	154 A.J. Pierzynski	.15	.07
❑	155 Johnny Damon	.25	.11
❑	156 Omar Daal	.15	.07
❑	157 A.J. Burnett	.25	.11
❑	158 Eric Munson	.25	.11
❑	159 Fernando Vina	.15	.07
❑	160 Chris Singleton	.15	.07
❑	161 Juan Pierre	.25	.11
❑	162 John Olerud	.25	.11
❑	163 Randy Johnson	.75	.35
❑	164 Paul Konerko	.25	.11
❑	165 Tino Martinez	.25	.11
❑	166 Richard Hidalgo	.25	.11
❑	167 Luis Gonzalez	.60	.25
❑	168 Ben Grieve	.25	.11
❑	169 Matt Lawton	.25	.11
❑	170 Gabe Kapler	.25	.11
❑	171 Mariano Rivera	.25	.11
❑	172 Kenny Lofton	.25	.11
❑	173 Brian Jordan	.25	.11
❑	174 Brian Giles	.25	.11
❑	175 Mark Quinn	.25	.11
❑	176 Neifi Perez	.15	.07
❑	177 Ellis Burks	.25	.11
❑	178 Bobby Abreu	.25	.11
❑	179 Jeff Weaver	.25	.11
❑	180 Andres Galarraga	.40	.18
❑	181 Javy Lopez	.25	.11
❑	182 Todd Walker	.15	.07
❑	183 Fernando Tatis	.15	.07
❑	184 Charles Johnson	.25	.11
❑	185 Pat Burrell	.25	.11
❑	186 Jay Bell	.25	.11
❑	187 Aaron Boone	.15	.07
❑	188 Jason Giambi	.60	.25
❑	189 Jay Payton	.15	.07
❑	190 Carlos Lee	.25	.11
❑	191 Phil Nevin	.25	.11
❑	192 Mike Sweeney	.25	.11
❑	193 J.T. Snow	.25	.11
❑	194 Dmitri Young	.25	.11
❑	195 Richie Sexson	.25	.11
❑	196 Derrek Lee	.15	.07
❑	197 Corey Koskie	.25	.11
❑	198 Edgar Martinez	.40	.18
❑	199 Wade Miller	.25	.11
❑	200 Tony Batista	.25	.11
❑	201 John Olerud AS	1.00	.45
❑	202 Bret Boone AS	1.00	.45
❑	203 Cal Ripken AS	5.00	2.20
❑	204 Alex Rodriguez AS	3.00	1.35
❑	205 Ichiro Suzuki AS	5.00	2.20
❑	206 Manny Ramirez AS	1.50	.70
❑	207 Juan Gonzalez AS	1.25	.55
❑	208 Ivan Rodriguez AS	1.25	.55
❑	209 Roger Clemens AS	3.00	1.35
❑	210 Edgar Martinez AS	1.00	.45
❑	211 Todd Helton AS	1.50	.70
❑	212 Jeff Kent AS	1.00	.45
❑	213 Chipper Jones AS	2.50	1.10
❑	214 Rich Aurilia AS	1.00	.45
❑	215 Barry Bonds AS	3.00	1.35
❑	216 Sammy Sosa AS	2.50	1.10
❑	217 Luis Gonzalez AS	1.25	.55
❑	218 Mike Piazza AS	3.00	1.35
❑	219 Randy Johnson AS	1.50	.70
❑	220 Larry Walker AS	1.00	.45
❑	221 Todd Helton	1.50	.70
	Juan Uribe		
❑	222 Pat Burrell	1.00	.45
	Eric Valent		
❑	223 Edgar Martinez	5.00	2.20
	Ichiro Suzuki		
❑	224 Ben Grieve	1.00	.45
	Jason Tyner		
❑	225 Mark Quinn	1.00	.45
	Dee Brown		
❑	226 Cal Ripken	5.00	2.20
	Brian Roberts		
❑	227 Cliff Floyd	1.00	.45
	Abraham Nunez		
❑	228 Jeff Bagwell	1.50	.70
	Adam Everett		
❑	229 Mark McGwire	5.00	2.20
	Albert Pujols		
❑	230 Doug Mientkewicz	1.00	.45
	Luis Rivas		
❑	231 Juan Gonzalez	1.25	.55
	Danny Peoples		
❑	232 Kevin Brown	1.00	.45
	Luke Prokopec		
❑	233 Richie Sexson	1.00	.45
	Ben Sheets		
❑	234 Jason Giambi	1.25	.55
	Jason Hart		
❑	235 Barry Bonds	3.00	1.35
	Carlos Valderrama		
❑	236 Tony Gwynn	2.50	1.10
	Cesar Crespo		
❑	237 Ken Griffey Jr.	4.00	1.80
	Adam Dunn		
❑	238 Frank Thomas	1.50	.70
	Joe Crede		
❑	239 Derek Jeter	5.00	2.20
	Drew Henson		
❑	240 Chipper Jones	2.50	1.10
	Wilson Betemit		
❑	241 Luis Gonzalez	1.25	.55
	Junior Spivey		
❑	242 Bobby Higginson	1.00	.45
	Andres Torres		
❑	243 Carlos Delgado	1.25	.55
	Vernon Wells		
❑	244 Sammy Sosa	2.50	1.10
	Corey Patterson		
❑	245 Nomar Garciaparra	3.00	1.35
	Shea Hillenbrand		
❑	246 Alex Rodriguez	3.00	1.35
	Jason Romano		
❑	247 Troy Glaus	1.25	.55
	David Eckstein		
❑	248 Mike Piazza	3.00	1.35
	Alex Escobar		
❑	249 Brian Giles	1.00	.45
	Jack Wilson		
❑	250 Vladimir Guerrero	1.50	.70
	Scott Hodges		
❑	251 Bud Smith PROS	6.00	2.70
❑	252 Juan Diaz PROS	3.00	1.35
❑	253 Wilkin Ruan PROS	3.00	1.35
❑	254 Chris Spurling PROS RC	3.00	1.35
❑	255 Toby Hall PROS	3.00	1.35
❑	256 Jason Jennings PROS	3.00	1.35
❑	257 George Perez PROS	3.00	1.35
❑	258 D'Angelo Jimenez PROS	3.00	1.35
❑	259 Jose Acevedo PROS	3.00	1.35
❑	260 Josue Perez PROS	3.00	1.35
❑	261 Brian Rogers PROS	3.00	1.35
❑	262 C. Maldonado PROS RC	3.00	1.35
❑	263 Travis Phelps PROS	3.00	1.35
❑	264 Rob Mackowiak PROS	3.00	1.35
❑	265 Ryan Drese PROS	3.00	1.35
❑	266 Carlos Garcia PROS	3.00	1.35
❑	267 Alexis Gomez PROS	3.00	1.35
❑	268 Jeremy Affeldt PROS	3.00	1.35
❑	269 Scott Podsednik PROS	3.00	1.35
❑	270 Adam Johnson PROS	3.00	1.35
❑	271 Pedro Santana PROS	3.00	1.35
❑	272 Les Walrond PROS	3.00	1.35
❑	273 Jackson Melian PROS	3.00	1.35
❑	274 Carlos Hernandez PROS	3.00	1.35
❑	275 M. Nussbeck PROS RC	3.00	1.35

❑ 276 Cory Aldridge PROS 3.00 1.35
❑ 277 Troy Mattes PROS 3.00 1.35
❑ 278 Brent Abernathy PROS 3.00 1.35
❑ 279 J.J. Davis PROS 3.00 1.35
❑ 280 B. Duckworth PROS 3.00 1.35
❑ 281 Kyle Lohse PROS 3.00 1.35
❑ 282 Justin Kaye PROS 3.00 1.35
❑ 283 Cody Ransom PROS .. 3.00 1.35
❑ 284 Dave Williams PROS .. 3.00 1.35
❑ 285 Luis Lopez PROS 3.00 1.35

1989 Upper Deck

Orel Hershiser

	MINT	NRMT
COMPLETE SET (800)	150.00	70.00
COMP.FACT.SET (800)	200.00	90.00
COMPLETE LO SET (700)	140.00	65.00
COMPLETE HI SET (100)	10.00	4.50
COMP.HI FACT.SET (100)	8.00	3.60

❑ 1 Ken Griffey Jr. RC 80.00 36.00
❑ 2 Luis Medina .... .20 .09
❑ 3 Tony Chance .... .20 .09
❑ 4 Dave Otto .... .20 .09
❑ 5 S.Alomar Jr. RC UER ...... 1.00 .45
Born 6/16/66,
should be 6/18/66
❑ 6 Rolando Roomes .... .20 .09
❑ 7 Dave West RC .... .20 .09
❑ 8 Cris Carpenter RC .... .20 .09
❑ 9 Gregg Jefferies .... .30 .14
❑ 10 Doug Dascenzo .... .20 .09
❑ 11 Ron Jones .... .20 .09
❑ 12 Luis DeLosSantos .... .20 .09
❑ 13 Gary Sheffield COR RC 5.00 2.20
❑ 13A G.Sheffield RC ERR 5.00 2.20
SS upside down
on card front
❑ 14 Mike Harkey RC .... .20 .09
❑ 15 Lance Blankenship RC .... .20 .09
❑ 16 William Brennan .... .20 .09
❑ 17 John Smoltz RC .... 2.00 .90
❑ 18 Ramon Martinez RC .... .75 .35
❑ 19 Mark Lemke RC .... .50 .23
❑ 20 Juan Bell RC .... .20 .09
❑ 21 Rey Palacios .... .20 .09
❑ 22 Felix Jose RC .... .20 .09
❑ 23 Van Snider .... .20 .09
❑ 24 Dante Bichette RC .... 2.00 .90
❑ 25 Randy Johnson RC 15.00 6.75
❑ 26 Carlos Quintana RC .... .20 .09
❑ 27 Star Rookie CL .... .20 .09
❑ 28 Mike Schooler .... .20 .09
❑ 29 Randy St.Claire .... .20 .09
❑ 30 Jerald Clark RC .... .20 .09
❑ 31 Kevin Gross .... .20 .09
❑ 32 Dan Firova .... .20 .09
❑ 33 Jeff Calhoun .... .20 .09
❑ 34 Tommy Hinzo .... .20 .09
❑ 35 Ricky Jordan RC .... .30 .14
❑ 36 Larry Parrish .... .20 .09
❑ 37 Bret Saberhagen UER ..... .30 .14
Hit total 931,&
should be 1031
❑ 38 Mike Smithson .... .20 .09
❑ 39 Dave Dravecky .... .30 .14
❑ 40 Ed Romero .... .20 .09
❑ 41 Jeff Musselman .... .20 .09
❑ 42 Ed Hearn .... .20 .09
❑ 43 Rance Mulliniks .... .20 .09
❑ 44 Jim Eisenreich .... .20 .09
❑ 45 Sil Campusano .... .20 .09
❑ 46 Mike Krukow .... .20 .09
❑ 47 Paul Gibson .... .20 .09
❑ 48 Mike LaCoss .... .20 .09
❑ 49 Larry Herndon .... .20 .09
❑ 50 Scott Garrelts .... .20 .09
❑ 51 Dwayne Henry .... .20 .09
❑ 52 Jim Acker .... .20 .09
❑ 53 Steve Sax .... .20 .09
❑ 54 Pete O'Brien .... .20 .09
❑ 55 Paul Runge .... .20 .09
❑ 56 Rick Rhoden .... .20 .09
❑ 57 John Dopson .... .20 .09
❑ 58 Casey Candaele UER ...... .20 .09
(No stats for Astros
for '88 season)
❑ 59 Dave Righetti .... .20 .09
❑ 60 Joe Hesketh .... .20 .09
❑ 61 Frank DiPino .... .20 .09
❑ 62 Tim Laudner .... .20 .09
❑ 63 Jamie Moyer .... .20 .09
❑ 64 Fred Toliver .... .20 .09
❑ 65 Mitch Webster .... .20 .09
❑ 66 John Tudor .... .20 .09
❑ 67 John Cangelosi .... .20 .09
❑ 68 Mike Devereaux .... .20 .09
❑ 69 Brian Fisher .... .20 .09
❑ 70 Mike Marshall .... .20 .09
❑ 71 Zane Smith .... .20 .09
❑ 72A Brian Holton ERR .... .75 .35
(Photo actually
Shawn Hillegas)
❑ 72B Brian Holton COR .... .30 .14
❑ 73 Jose Guzman .... .20 .09
❑ 74 Rick Mahler .... .20 .09
❑ 75 John Shelby .... .20 .09
❑ 76 Jim Deshaies .... .20 .09
❑ 77 Bobby Meacham .... .20 .09
❑ 78 Bryn Smith .... .20 .09
❑ 79 Joaquin Andujar .... .20 .09
❑ 80 Richard Dotson .... .20 .09
❑ 81 Charlie Lea .... .20 .09
❑ 82 Calvin Schiraldi .... .20 .09
❑ 83 Les Straker .... .20 .09
❑ 84 Les Lancaster .... .20 .09
❑ 85 Allan Anderson .... .20 .09
❑ 86 Junior Ortiz .... .20 .09
❑ 87 Jesse Orosco .... .20 .09
❑ 88 Felix Fermin .... .20 .09
❑ 89 Dave Anderson .... .20 .09
❑ 90 Rafael Belliard UER .... .20 .09
(Born '61, not '51)
❑ 91 Franklin Stubbs .... .20 .09
❑ 92 Cecil Espy .... .20 .09
❑ 93 Albert Hall .... .20 .09
❑ 94 Tim Leary .... .20 .09
❑ 95 Mitch Williams .... .20 .09
❑ 96 Tracy Jones .... .20 .09
❑ 97 Danny Darwin .... .20 .09
❑ 98 Gary Ward .... .20 .09
❑ 99 Neal Heaton .... .20 .09
❑ 100 Jim Pankovits .... .20 .09
❑ 101 Bill Doran .... .20 .09
❑ 102 Tim Wallach .... .20 .09
❑ 103 Joe Magrane .... .20 .09
❑ 104 Ozzie Virgil .... .20 .09
❑ 105 Alvin Davis .... .20 .09
❑ 106 Tom Brookens .... .20 .09
❑ 107 Shawon Dunston .... .20 .09
❑ 108 Tracy Woodson .... .20 .09
❑ 109 Nelson Liriano .... .20 .09
❑ 110 Devon White UER .... .30 .14
(Doubles total 46,
should be 56)
❑ 111 Steve Balboni .... .20 .09
❑ 112 Buddy Bell .... .30 .14
❑ 113 German Jimenez .... .20 .09
❑ 114 Ken Dayley .... .20 .09
❑ 115 Andres Galarraga .... .50 .23
❑ 116 Mike Scioscia .... .20 .09
❑ 117 Gary Pettis .... .20 .09
❑ 118 Ernie Whitt .... .20 .09
❑ 119 Bob Boone .... .30 .14
❑ 120 Ryne Sandberg .... 1.00 .45
❑ 121 Bruce Benedict .... .20 .09
❑ 122 Hubie Brooks .... .20 .09
❑ 123 Mike Moore .... .20 .09
❑ 124 Wallace Johnson .... .20 .09
❑ 125 Bob Horner .... .20 .09
❑ 126 Chili Davis .... .30 .14
❑ 127 Manny Trillo .... .20 .09
❑ 128 Chet Lemon .... .20 .09
❑ 129 John Cerutti .... .20 .09
❑ 130 Orel Hershiser .... .30 .14
❑ 131 Terry Pendleton .... .20 .09
❑ 132 Jeff Blauser .... .30 .14
❑ 133 Mike Fitzgerald .... .20 .09
❑ 134 Henry Cotto .... .20 .09
❑ 135 Gerald Young .... .20 .09
❑ 136 Luis Salazar .... .20 .09
❑ 137 Alejandro Pena .... .20 .09
❑ 138 Jack Howell .... .20 .09
❑ 139 Tony Fernandez .... .20 .09
❑ 140 Mark Grace .... .75 .35
❑ 141 Ken Caminiti .... .30 .14
❑ 142 Mike Jackson .... .20 .09
❑ 143 Larry McWilliams .... .20 .09
❑ 144 Andres Thomas .... .20 .09
❑ 145 Nolan Ryan 3X 4.00 1.80
❑ 146 Mike Davis .... .20 .09
❑ 147 DeWayne Buice .... .20 .09
❑ 148 Jody Davis .... .20 .09
❑ 149 Jesse Barfield .... .20 .09
❑ 150 Matt Nokes .... .20 .09
❑ 151 Jerry Reuss .... .20 .09
❑ 152 Rick Cerone .... .20 .09
❑ 153 Storm Davis .... .20 .09
❑ 154 Marvell Wynne .... .20 .09
❑ 155 Will Clark .... .75 .35
❑ 156 Luis Aguayo .... .20 .09
❑ 157 Willie Upshaw .... .20 .09
❑ 158 Randy Bush .... .20 .09
❑ 159 Ron Darling .... .20 .09
❑ 160 Kal Daniels .... .20 .09
❑ 161 Spike Owen .... .20 .09
❑ 162 Luis Polonia .... .20 .09
❑ 163 Kevin Mitchell UER .... .30 .14
('88/total HR's 18/52,
should be 19/53)
❑ 164 Dave Gallagher .... .20 .09
❑ 165 Benito Santiago .... .20 .09
❑ 166 Greg Gagne .... .20 .09
❑ 167 Ken Phelps .... .20 .09
❑ 168 Sid Fernandez .... .20 .09
❑ 169 Bo Diaz .... .20 .09
❑ 170 Cory Snyder .... .20 .09
❑ 171 Eric Show .... .20 .09
❑ 172 Robby Thompson .... .20 .09
❑ 173 Marty Barrett .... .20 .09
❑ 174 Dave Henderson .... .20 .09
❑ 175 Ozzie Guillen .... .20 .09
❑ 176 Barry Lyons .... .20 .09
❑ 177 Kelvin Torve .... .20 .09
❑ 178 Don Slaught .... .20 .09
❑ 179 Steve Lombardozzi .... .20 .09
❑ 180 Chris Sabo RC .... .20 .09
❑ 181 Jose Uribe .... .20 .09
❑ 182 Shane Mack .... .20 .09
❑ 183 Ron Karkovice .... .20 .09
❑ 184 Todd Benzinger .... .20 .09
❑ 185 Dave Stewart .... .30 .14
❑ 186 Julio Franco .... .20 .09
❑ 187 Ron Robinson .... .20 .09
❑ 188 Wally Backman .... .20 .09
❑ 189 Randy Velarde .... .20 .09
❑ 190 Joe Carter .... .50 .23
❑ 191 Bob Welch .... .20 .09
❑ 192 Kelly Paris .... .20 .09
❑ 193 Chris Brown .... .20 .09
❑ 194 Rick Reuschel .... .20 .09
❑ 195 Roger Clemens .... 2.00 .90
❑ 196 Dave Concepcion .... .30 .14
❑ 197 Al Newman .... .20 .09
❑ 198 Brook Jacoby .... .20 .09
❑ 199 Mookie Wilson .... .30 .14
❑ 200 Don Mattingly .... 2.00 .90
❑ 201 Dick Schofield .... .20 .09
❑ 202 Mark Gubicza .... .20 .09
❑ 203 Gary Gaetti .... .30 .14

❑ 204	Dan Pasqua	.20	.09
❑ 205	Andre Dawson	.50	.23
❑ 206	Chris Speier	.20	.09
❑ 207	Kent Tekulve	.20	.09
❑ 208	Rod Scurry	.20	.09
❑ 209	Scott Bailes	.20	.09
❑ 210	R.Henderson UER Throws Right	1.50	.70
❑ 211	Harold Baines	.30	.14
❑ 212	Tony Armas	.20	.09
❑ 213	Kent Hrbek	.30	.14
❑ 214	Darrin Jackson	.20	.09
❑ 215	George Brett	1.50	.70
❑ 216	Rafael Santana	.20	.09
❑ 217	Andy Allanson	.20	.09
❑ 218	Brett Butler	.30	.14
❑ 219	Steve Jeltz	.20	.09
❑ 220	Jay Buhner	.30	.14
❑ 221	Bo Jackson	.50	.23
❑ 222	Angel Salazar	.20	.09
❑ 223	Kirk McCaskill	.20	.09
❑ 224	Steve Lyons	.20	.09
❑ 225	Bert Blyleven	.30	.14
❑ 226	Scott Bradley	.20	.09
❑ 227	Bob Melvin	.20	.09
❑ 228	Ron Kittle	.20	.09
❑ 229	Phil Bradley	.20	.09
❑ 230	Tommy John	.30	.14
❑ 231	Greg Walker	.20	.09
❑ 232	Juan Berenguer	.20	.09
❑ 233	Pat Tabler	.20	.09
❑ 234	Terry Clark	.20	.09
❑ 235	Rafael Palmeiro	.75	.35
❑ 236	Paul Zuvella	.20	.09
❑ 237	Willie Randolph	.30	.14
❑ 238	Bruce Fields	.20	.09
❑ 239	Mike Aldrete	.20	.09
❑ 240	Lance Parrish	.20	.09
❑ 241	Greg Maddux	3.00	1.35
❑ 242	John Moses	.20	.09
❑ 243	Melido Perez	.20	.09
❑ 244	Willie Wilson	.20	.09
❑ 245	Mark McLemore	.20	.09
❑ 246	Von Hayes	.20	.09
❑ 247	Matt Williams	.50	.23
❑ 248	John Candelaria UER Listed as Yankee for part of '87, should be Mets	.20	.09
❑ 249	Harold Reynolds	.20	.09
❑ 250	Greg Swindell	.20	.09
❑ 251	Juan Agosto	.20	.09
❑ 252	Mike Felder	.20	.09
❑ 253	Vince Coleman	.20	.09
❑ 254	Larry Sheets	.20	.09
❑ 255	George Bell	.20	.09
❑ 256	Terry Steinbach	.30	.14
❑ 257	Jack Armstrong RC	.20	.09
❑ 258	Dickie Thon	.20	.09
❑ 259	Ray Knight	.20	.09
❑ 260	Darryl Strawberry	.30	.14
❑ 261	Doug Sisk	.20	.09
❑ 262	Alex Trevino	.20	.09
❑ 263	Jeffrey Leonard	.20	.09
❑ 264	Tom Henke	.20	.09
❑ 265	Ozzie Smith	1.00	.45
❑ 266	Dave Bergman	.20	.09
❑ 267	Tony Phillips	.20	.09
❑ 268	Mark Davis	.20	.09
❑ 269	Kevin Elster	.20	.09
❑ 270	Barry Larkin	.75	.35
❑ 271	Manny Lee	.20	.09
❑ 272	Tom Brunansky	.20	.09
❑ 273	Craig Biggio RC	3.00	1.35
❑ 274	Jim Gantner	.20	.09
❑ 275	Eddie Murray	.75	.35
❑ 276	Jeff Reed	.20	.09
❑ 277	Tim Teufel	.20	.09
❑ 278	Rick Honeycutt	.20	.09
❑ 279	Guillermo Hernandez	.20	.09
❑ 280	John Kruk	.30	.14
❑ 281	Luis Alicea RC	.20	.09
❑ 282	Jim Clancy	.20	.09
❑ 283	Billy Ripken	.20	.09
❑ 284	Craig Reynolds	.20	.09
❑ 285	Robin Yount	.75	.35
❑ 286	Jimmy Jones	.20	.09
❑ 287	Ron Oester	.20	.09
❑ 288	Terry Leach	.20	.09
❑ 289	Dennis Eckersley	.50	.23
❑ 290	Alan Trammell	.50	.23
❑ 291	Jimmy Key	.30	.14
❑ 292	Chris Bosio	.20	.09
❑ 293	Jose DeLeon	.20	.09
❑ 294	Jim Traber	.20	.09
❑ 295	Mike Scott	.20	.09
❑ 296	Roger McDowell	.20	.09
❑ 297	Garry Templeton	.20	.09
❑ 298	Doyle Alexander	.20	.09
❑ 299	Nick Esasky	.20	.09
❑ 300	Mark McGwire UER (Doubles total 52, should be 51)	5.00	2.20
❑ 301	Darryl Hamilton RC	.20	.09
❑ 302	Dave Smith	.20	.09
❑ 303	Rick Sutcliffe	.30	.14
❑ 304	Dave Stapleton	.20	.09
❑ 305	Alan Ashby	.20	.09
❑ 306	Pedro Guerrero	.20	.09
❑ 307	Ron Guidry	.30	.14
❑ 308	Steve Farr	.20	.09
❑ 309	Curt Ford	.20	.09
❑ 310	Claudell Washington	.20	.09
❑ 311	Tom Prince	.20	.09
❑ 312	Chad Kreuter RC	.20	.09
❑ 313	Ken Oberkfell	.20	.09
❑ 314	Jerry Browne	.20	.09
❑ 315	R.J. Reynolds	.20	.09
❑ 316	Scott Bankhead	.20	.09
❑ 317	Milt Thompson	.20	.09
❑ 318	Mario Diaz	.20	.09
❑ 319	Bruce Ruffin	.20	.09
❑ 320	Dave Valle	.20	.09
❑ 321A	Gary Varsho ERR (Back photo actually Mike Bielecki bunting)	2.00	.90
❑ 321B	Gary Varsho COR (In road uniform)	.20	.09
❑ 322	Paul Mirabella	.20	.09
❑ 323	Chuck Jackson	.20	.09
❑ 324	Drew Hall	.20	.09
❑ 325	Don August	.20	.09
❑ 326	Israel Sanchez	.20	.09
❑ 327	Denny Walling	.20	.09
❑ 328	Joel Skinner	.20	.09
❑ 329	Danny Tartabull	.20	.09
❑ 330	Tony Pena	.20	.09
❑ 331	Jim Sundberg	.20	.09
❑ 332	Jeff D. Robinson	.20	.09
❑ 333	Oddibe McDowell	.20	.09
❑ 334	Jose Lind	.20	.09
❑ 335	Paul Kilgus	.20	.09
❑ 336	Juan Samuel	.20	.09
❑ 337	Mike Campbell	.20	.09
❑ 338	Mike Maddux	.20	.09
❑ 339	Darnell Coles	.20	.09
❑ 340	Bob Dernier	.20	.09
❑ 341	Rafael Ramirez	.20	.09
❑ 342	Scott Sanderson	.20	.09
❑ 343	B.J. Surhoff	.30	.14
❑ 344	Billy Hatcher	.20	.09
❑ 345	Pat Perry	.20	.09
❑ 346	Jack Clark	.20	.09
❑ 347	Gary Thurman	.20	.09
❑ 348	Tim Jones	.20	.09
❑ 349	Dave Winfield	.75	.35
❑ 350	Frank White	.30	.14
❑ 351	Dave Collins	.20	.09
❑ 352	Jack Morris	.30	.14
❑ 353	Eric Plunk	.20	.09
❑ 354	Leon Durham	.20	.09
❑ 355	Ivan DeJesus	.20	.09
❑ 356	Brian Holman RC	.20	.09
❑ 357A	Dale Murphy ERR (Front has reverse negative)	30.00	13.50
❑ 357B	Dale Murphy COR	.30	.14
❑ 358	Mark Portugal	.20	.09
❑ 359	Andy McGaffigan	.20	.09
❑ 360	Tom Glavine	.75	.35
❑ 361	Keith Moreland	.20	.09
❑ 362	Todd Stottlemyre	.50	.23
❑ 363	Dave Leiper	.20	.09
❑ 364	Cecil Fielder	.30	.14
❑ 365	Carmelo Martinez	.20	.09
❑ 366	Dwight Evans	.30	.14
❑ 367	Kevin McReynolds	.20	.09
❑ 368	Rich Gedman	.20	.09
❑ 369	Len Dykstra	.30	.14
❑ 370	Jody Reed	.20	.09
❑ 371	Jose Canseco UER (Strikeout total 391, should be 491)	.75	.35
❑ 372	Rob Murphy	.20	.09
❑ 373	Mike Henneman	.20	.09
❑ 374	Walt Weiss	.20	.09
❑ 375	Rob Dibble RC	.30	.14
❑ 376	Kirby Puckett (Mark McGwire in background)	2.00	.90
❑ 377	Dennis Martinez	.30	.14
❑ 378	Ron Gant	.30	.14
❑ 379	Brian Harper	.20	.09
❑ 380	Nelson Santovenia	.20	.09
❑ 381	Lloyd Moseby	.20	.09
❑ 382	Lance McCullers	.20	.09
❑ 383	Dave Stieb	.20	.09
❑ 384	Tony Gwynn	1.50	.70
❑ 385	Mike Flanagan	.20	.09
❑ 386	Bob Ojeda	.20	.09
❑ 387	Bruce Hurst	.20	.09
❑ 388	Dave Magadan	.20	.09
❑ 389	Wade Boggs	.75	.35
❑ 390	Gary Carter	.50	.23
❑ 391	Frank Tanana	.20	.09
❑ 392	Curt Young	.20	.09
❑ 393	Jeff Treadway	.20	.09
❑ 394	Darrell Evans	.30	.14
❑ 395	Glenn Hubbard	.20	.09
❑ 396	Chuck Cary	.20	.09
❑ 397	Frank Viola	.20	.09
❑ 398	Jeff Parrett	.20	.09
❑ 399	Terry Blocker	.20	.09
❑ 400	Dan Gladden	.20	.09
❑ 401	Louie Meadows	.20	.09
❑ 402	Tim Raines	.30	.14
❑ 403	Joey Meyer	.20	.09
❑ 404	Larry Andersen	.20	.09
❑ 405	Rex Hudler	.20	.09
❑ 406	Mike Schmidt	1.50	.70
❑ 407	John Franco	.30	.14
❑ 408	Brady Anderson RC	2.00	.90
❑ 409	Don Carman	.20	.09
❑ 410	Eric Davis	.30	.14
❑ 411	Bob Stanley	.20	.09
❑ 412	Pete Smith	.20	.09
❑ 413	Jim Rice	.30	.14
❑ 414	Bruce Sutter	.20	.09
❑ 415	Oil Can Boyd	.20	.09
❑ 416	Ruben Sierra	.20	.09
❑ 417	Mike LaValliere	.20	.09
❑ 418	Steve Buechele	.20	.09
❑ 419	Gary Redus	.20	.09
❑ 420	Scott Fletcher	.20	.09
❑ 421	Dale Sveum	.20	.09
❑ 422	Bob Knepper	.20	.09
❑ 423	Luis Rivera	.20	.09
❑ 424	Ted Higuera	.20	.09
❑ 425	Kevin Bass	.20	.09
❑ 426	Ken Gerhart	.20	.09
❑ 427	Shane Rawley	.20	.09
❑ 428	Paul O'Neill	.75	.35
❑ 429	Joe Orsulak	.20	.09
❑ 430	Jackie Gutierrez	.20	.09
❑ 431	Gerald Perry	.20	.09
❑ 432	Mike Greenwell	.20	.09
❑ 433	Jerry Royster	.20	.09
❑ 434	Ellis Burks	.50	.23
❑ 435	Ed Olwine	.20	.09
❑ 436	Dave Rucker	.20	.09
❑ 437	Charlie Hough	.30	.14
❑ 438	Bob Walk	.20	.09
❑ 439	Bob Brower	.20	.09
❑ 440	Barry Bonds	3.00	1.35
❑ 441	Tom Foley	.20	.09
❑ 442	Rob Deer	.20	.09
❑ 443	Glenn Davis	.20	.09
❑ 444	Dave Martinez	.20	.09

❑ 445 Bill Wegman .20 .09
❑ 446 Lloyd McClendon .20 .09
❑ 447 Dave Schmidt .20 .09
❑ 448 Darren Daulton .30 .14
❑ 449 Frank Williams .20 .09
❑ 450 Don Aase .20 .09
❑ 451 Lou Whitaker .30 .14
❑ 452 Rich Gossage .30 .14
❑ 453 Ed Whitson .20 .09
❑ 454 Jim Walewander .20 .09
❑ 455 Damon Berryhill .20 .09
❑ 456 Tim Burke .20 .09
❑ 457 Barry Jones .20 .09
❑ 458 Joel Youngblood .20 .09
❑ 459 Floyd Youmans .20 .09
❑ 460 Mark Salas .20 .09
❑ 461 Jeff Russell .20 .09
❑ 462 Darrell Miller .20 .09
❑ 463 Jeff Kunkel .20 .09
❑ 464 Sherman Corbett .20 .09
❑ 465 Curtis Wilkerson .20 .09
❑ 466 Bud Black .20 .09
❑ 467 Cal Ripken 3.00 1.35
❑ 468 John Farrell .20 .09
❑ 469 Terry Kennedy .20 .09
❑ 470 Tom Candiotti .20 .09
❑ 471 Roberto Alomar 1.25 .55
❑ 472 Jeff M. Robinson .20 .09
❑ 473 Vance Law .20 .09
❑ 474 Randy Ready UER .20 .09
(Strikeout total 136& should be 115)
❑ 475 Walt Terrell .20 .09
❑ 476 Kelly Downs .20 .09
❑ 477 Johnny Paredes .20 .09
❑ 478 Shawn Hillegas .20 .09
❑ 479 Bob Brenly .20 .09
❑ 480 Otis Nixon .20 .09
❑ 481 Johnny Ray .20 .09
❑ 482 Geno Petralli .20 .09
❑ 483 Stu Cliburn .20 .09
❑ 484 Pete Incaviglia .20 .09
❑ 485 Brian Downing .20 .09
❑ 486 Jeff Stone .20 .09
❑ 487 Carmen Castillo .20 .09
❑ 488 Tom Niedenfuer .20 .09
❑ 489 Jay Bell .50 .23
❑ 490 Rick Schu .20 .09
❑ 491 Jeff Pico .20 .09
❑ 492 Mark Parent .20 .09
❑ 493 Eric King .20 .09
❑ 494 Al Nipper .20 .09
❑ 495 Andy Hawkins .20 .09
❑ 496 Daryl Boston .20 .09
❑ 497 Ernie Riles .20 .09
❑ 498 Pascual Perez .20 .09
❑ 499 Bill Long UER .20 .09
(Games started total 70& should be 44)
❑ 500 Kirt Manwaring .20 .09
❑ 501 Chuck Crim .20 .09
❑ 502 Candy Maldonado .20 .09
❑ 503 Dennis Lamp .20 .09
❑ 504 Glenn Braggs .20 .09
❑ 505 Joe Price .20 .09
❑ 506 Ken Williams .20 .09
❑ 507 Bill Pecota .20 .09
❑ 508 Rey Quinones .20 .09
❑ 509 Jeff Bittiger .20 .09
❑ 510 Kevin Seitzer .20 .09
❑ 511 Steve Bedrosian .20 .09
❑ 512 Todd Worrell .30 .14
❑ 513 Chris James .20 .09
❑ 514 Jose Oquendo .20 .09
❑ 515 David Palmer .20 .09
❑ 516 John Smiley .20 .09
❑ 517 Dave Clark .20 .09
❑ 518 Mike Dunne .20 .09
❑ 519 Ron Washington .20 .09
❑ 520 Bob Kipper .20 .09
❑ 521 Lee Smith .30 .14
❑ 522 Juan Castillo .20 .09
❑ 523 Don Robinson .20 .09
❑ 524 Kevin Romine .20 .09
❑ 525 Paul Molitor .75 .35
❑ 526 Mark Langston .20 .09
❑ 527 Donnie Hill .20 .09
❑ 528 Larry Owen .20 .09
❑ 529 Jerry Reed .20 .09
❑ 530 Jack McDowell .30 .14
❑ 531 Greg Mathews .20 .09
❑ 532 John Russell .20 .09
❑ 533 Dan Quisenberry .20 .09
❑ 534 Greg Gross .20 .09
❑ 535 Danny Cox .20 .09
❑ 536 Terry Francona .30 .14
❑ 537 Andy Van Slyke .30 .14
❑ 538 Mel Hall .20 .09
❑ 539 Jim Gott .20 .09
❑ 540 Doug Jones .20 .09
❑ 541 Craig Lefferts .20 .09
❑ 542 Mike Boddicker .20 .09
❑ 543 Greg Brock .20 .09
❑ 544 Atlee Hammaker .20 .09
❑ 545 Tom Bolton .20 .09
❑ 546 Mike Macfarlane RC .20 .09
❑ 547 Rich Renteria .20 .09
❑ 548 John Davis .20 .09
❑ 549 Floyd Bannister .20 .09
❑ 550 Mickey Brantley .20 .09
❑ 551 Duane Ward .20 .09
❑ 552 Dan Petry .20 .09
❑ 553 Mickey Tettleton UER .20 .09
(Walks total 175, should be 136)
❑ 554 Rick Leach .20 .09
❑ 555 Mike Witt .20 .09
❑ 556 Sid Bream .20 .09
❑ 557 Bobby Witt .20 .09
❑ 558 Tommy Herr .20 .09
❑ 559 Randy Milligan .20 .09
❑ 560 Jose Cecena .20 .09
❑ 561 Mackey Sasser .20 .09
❑ 562 Carney Lansford .30 .14
❑ 563 Rick Aguilera .30 .14
❑ 564 Ron Hassey .20 .09
❑ 565 Dwight Gooden .30 .14
❑ 566 Paul Assenmacher .20 .09
❑ 567 Neil Allen .20 .09
❑ 568 Jim Morrison .20 .09
❑ 569 Mike Pagliarulo .20 .09
❑ 570 Ted Simmons .30 .14
❑ 571 Mark Thurmond .20 .09
❑ 572 Fred McGriff .75 .35
❑ 573 Wally Joyner .30 .14
❑ 574 Jose Bautista .20 .09
❑ 575 Kelly Gruber .20 .09
❑ 576 Cecilio Guante .20 .09
❑ 577 Mark Davidson .20 .09
❑ 578 Bobby Bonilla UER .30 .14
(Total steals 2 in '87, should be 3)
❑ 579 Mike Stanley .20 .09
❑ 580 Gene Larkin .20 .09
❑ 581 Stan Javier .20 .09
❑ 582 Howard Johnson .20 .09
❑ 583A Mike Gallego ERR .75 .35
(Front reversed negative)
❑ 583B Mike Gallego COR .75 .35
❑ 584 David Cone .30 .14
❑ 585 Doug Jennings .20 .09
❑ 586 Charles Hudson .20 .09
❑ 587 Dion James .20 .09
❑ 588 Al Leiter .75 .35
❑ 589 Charlie Puleo .20 .09
❑ 590 Roberto Kelly .30 .14
❑ 591 Thad Bosley .20 .09
❑ 592 Pete Stanicek .20 .09
❑ 593 Pat Borders RC .30 .14
❑ 594 Bryan Harvey RC .20 .09
❑ 595 Jeff Ballard .20 .09
❑ 596 Jeff Reardon .30 .14
❑ 597 Doug Drabek .20 .09
❑ 598 Edwin Correa .20 .09
❑ 599 Keith Atherton .20 .09
❑ 600 Dave LaPoint .20 .09
❑ 601 Don Baylor .30 .14
❑ 602 Tom Pagnozzi .20 .09
❑ 603 Tim Flannery .20 .09
❑ 604 Gene Walter .20 .09
❑ 605 Dave Parker .30 .14
❑ 606 Mike Diaz .20 .09
❑ 607 Chris Gwynn .20 .09
❑ 608 Odell Jones .20 .09
❑ 609 Carlton Fisk .75 .35
❑ 610 Jay Howell .20 .09
❑ 611 Tim Crews .20 .09
❑ 612 Keith Hernandez .30 .14
❑ 613 Willie Fraser .20 .09
❑ 614 Jim Eppard .20 .09
❑ 615 Jeff Hamilton .20 .09
❑ 616 Kurt Stillwell .20 .09
❑ 617 Tom Browning .20 .09
❑ 618 Jeff Montgomery .30 .14
❑ 619 Jose Rijo .20 .09
❑ 620 Jamie Quirk .20 .09
❑ 621 Willie McGee .30 .14
❑ 622 Mark Grant UER .20 .09
(Glove on wrong hand)
❑ 623 Bill Swift .20 .09
❑ 624 Orlando Mercado .20 .09
❑ 625 John Costello .20 .09
❑ 626 Jose Gonzalez .20 .09
❑ 627A Bill Schroeder ERR .75 .35
(Back photo actually Ronn Reynolds buckling shin guards)
❑ 627B Bill Schroeder COR .75 .35
❑ 628A Fred Manrique ERR .75 .35
(Back photo actually Ozzie Guillen throwing)
❑ 628B Fred Manrique COR .20 .09
(Swinging bat on back)
❑ 629 Ricky Horton .20 .09
❑ 630 Dan Plesac .20 .09
❑ 631 Alfredo Griffin .20 .09
❑ 632 Chuck Finley .30 .14
❑ 633 Kirk Gibson .30 .14
❑ 634 Randy Myers .30 .14
❑ 635 Greg Minton .20 .09
❑ 636A Herm Winningham .75 .35
ERR (W1nningham on back)
❑ 636B H.Winningham COR .20 .09
❑ 637 Charlie Leibrandt .20 .09
❑ 638 Tim Birtsas .20 .09
❑ 639 Bill Buckner .30 .14
❑ 640 Danny Jackson .20 .09
❑ 641 Greg Booker .20 .09
❑ 642 Jim Presley .20 .09
❑ 643 Gene Nelson .20 .09
❑ 644 Rod Booker .20 .09
❑ 645 Dennis Rasmussen .20 .09
❑ 646 Juan Nieves .20 .09
❑ 647 Bobby Thigpen .20 .09
❑ 648 Tim Belcher .20 .09
❑ 649 Mike Young .20 .09
❑ 650 Ivan Calderon .20 .09
❑ 651 Oswaldo Peraza .20 .09
❑ 652A Pat Sheridan ERR 2.00 .90
(No position on front)
❑ 652B Pat Sheridan COR .20 .09
❑ 653 Mike Morgan .20 .09
❑ 654 Mike Heath .20 .09
❑ 655 Jay Tibbs .20 .09
❑ 656 Fernando Valenzuela .30 .14
❑ 657 Lee Mazzilli .20 .09
❑ 658 Frank Viola AL CY .20 .09
❑ 659A J.Canseco AL MVP .30 .14
Eagle logo in black
❑ 659B J.Canseco AL MVP .30 .14
Eagle logo in blue
❑ 660 Walt Weiss AL ROY .20 .09
❑ 661 Orel Hershiser NL CY .30 .14
❑ 662 Kirk Gibson NL MVP .20 .09
❑ 663 Chris Sabo NL ROY .20 .09
❑ 664 Dennis Eckersley .20 .09
ALCS MVP
❑ 665 Orel Hershiser .30 .14
NLCS MVP
❑ 666 Kirk Gibson WS .75 .35
❑ 667 O.Hershiser WS MVP .30 .14
❑ 668 Wally Joyner TC .20 .09
❑ 669 Nolan Ryan TC 1.25 .55
❑ 670 Jose Canseco TC .30 .14
❑ 671 Fred McGriff TC .30 .14
❑ 672 Dale Murphy TC .30 .14

❑ 673	Paul Molitor TC	.30	.14
❑ 674	Ozzie Smith TC	.50	.23
❑ 675	Ryne Sandberg TC	.50	.23
❑ 676	Kirk Gibson TC	.20	.09
❑ 677	Andres Galarraga TC	.20	.09
❑ 678	Will Clark TC	.30	.14
❑ 679	Cory Snyder TC	.20	.09
❑ 680	Alvin Davis TC	.20	.09
❑ 681	Darryl Strawberry TC	.20	.09
❑ 682	Cal Ripken TC	1.00	.45
❑ 683	Tony Gwynn TC	.75	.35
❑ 684	Mike Schmidt TC	.30	.14
❑ 685	A.Van Slyke TC UER 96 Junior Ortiz	.20	.09
❑ 686	Ruben Sierra TC	.20	.09
❑ 687	Wade Boggs TC	.30	.14
❑ 688	Eric Davis TC	.20	.09
❑ 689	George Brett TC	.75	.35
❑ 690	Alan Trammell TC	.20	.09
❑ 691	Frank Viola TC	.20	.09
❑ 692	Harold Baines TC	.20	.09
❑ 693	Don Mattingly TC	.50	.23
❑ 694	Checklist 1-100	.20	.09
❑ 695	Checklist 101-200	.20	.09
❑ 696	Checklist 201-300	.20	.09
❑ 697	Checklist 301-400	.20	.09
❑ 698	CL 401-500 UER 467 Cal Ripkin Jr.	.20	.09
❑ 699	CL 501-600 UER 543 Greg Booker	.20	.09
❑ 700	Checklist 601-700	.20	.09
❑ 701	Checklist 701-800	.20	.09
❑ 702	Jesse Barfield	.20	.09
❑ 703	Walt Terrell	.20	.09
❑ 704	Dickie Thon	.20	.09
❑ 705	Al Leiter	.75	.35
❑ 706	Dave LaPoint	.20	.09
❑ 707	Charlie Hayes RC	.75	.35
❑ 708	Andy Hawkins	.20	.09
❑ 709	Mickey Hatcher	.20	.09
❑ 710	Lance McCullers	.20	.09
❑ 711	Ron Kittle	.20	.09
❑ 712	Bert Blyleven	.30	.14
❑ 713	Rick Dempsey	.20	.09
❑ 714	Ken Williams	.20	.09
❑ 715	Steve Rosenberg	.20	.09
❑ 716	Joe Skalski	.20	.09
❑ 717	Spike Owen	.20	.09
❑ 718	Todd Burns	.20	.09
❑ 719	Kevin Gross	.20	.09
❑ 720	Tommy Herr	.20	.09
❑ 721	Rob Ducey	.20	.09
❑ 722	Gary Green	.20	.09
❑ 723	Gregg Olson RC	.75	.35
❑ 724	Greg W. Harris RC	.20	.09
❑ 725	Craig Worthington	.20	.09
❑ 726	Tom Howard RC	.20	.09
❑ 727	Dale Mohorcic	.20	.09
❑ 728	Rich Yett	.20	.09
❑ 729	Mel Hall	.20	.09
❑ 730	Floyd Youmans	.20	.09
❑ 731	Lonnie Smith	.20	.09
❑ 732	Wally Backman	.20	.09
❑ 733	Trevor Wilson RC	.20	.09
❑ 734	Jose Alvarez	.20	.09
❑ 735	Bob Milacki	.20	.09
❑ 736	Tom Gordon RC	1.00	.45
❑ 737	Wally Whitehurst RC	.20	.09
❑ 738	Mike Aldrete	.20	.09
❑ 739	Keith Miller	.20	.09
❑ 740	Randy Milligan	.20	.09
❑ 741	Jeff Parrett	.20	.09
❑ 742	Steve Finley RC	2.00	.90
❑ 743	Junior Felix RC	.20	.09
❑ 744	Pete Harnisch RC	.75	.35
❑ 745	Bill Spiers RC	.20	.09
❑ 746	Hensley Meulens RC	.20	.09
❑ 747	Juan Bell	.20	.09
❑ 748	Steve Sax	.20	.09
❑ 749	Phil Bradley	.20	.09
❑ 750	Rey Quinones	.20	.09
❑ 751	Tommy Gregg	.20	.09
❑ 752	Kevin Brown	.75	.35
❑ 753	Derek Lilliquist RC	.20	.09
❑ 754	Todd Zeile RC	1.00	.45
❑ 755	Jim Abbott RC	.75	.35

Triple exposure

❑ 756	Ozzie Canseco	.20	.09
❑ 757	Nick Esasky	.20	.09
❑ 758	Mike Moore	.20	.09
❑ 759	Rob Murphy	.20	.09
❑ 760	Rick Mahler	.20	.09
❑ 761	Fred Lynn	.20	.09
❑ 762	Kevin Blankenship	.20	.09
❑ 763	Eddie Murray	.75	.35
❑ 764	Steve Searcy	.20	.09
❑ 765	Jerome Walton RC	.75	.35
❑ 766	Erik Hanson RC	.30	.14
❑ 767	Bob Boone	.30	.14
❑ 768	Edgar Martinez	.50	.23
❑ 769	Jose DeJesus	.20	.09
❑ 770	Greg Briley	.20	.09
❑ 771	Steve Peters	.20	.09
❑ 772	Rafael Palmeiro	.75	.35
❑ 773	Jack Clark	.20	.09
❑ 774	Nolan Ryan (Throwing football)	4.00	1.80
❑ 775	Lance Parrish	.20	.09
❑ 776	Joe Girardi RC	.75	.35
❑ 777	Willie Randolph	.30	.14
❑ 778	Mitch Williams	.20	.09
❑ 779	Dennis Cook RC	.20	.09
❑ 780	Dwight Smith RC	.30	.14
❑ 781	Lenny Harris RC	.30	.14
❑ 782	Torey Lovullo RC	.20	.09
❑ 783	Norm Charlton RC	.30	.14
❑ 784	Chris Brown	.20	.09
❑ 785	Todd Benzinger	.20	.09
❑ 786	Shane Rawley	.20	.09
❑ 787	Omar Vizquel RC	2.50	1.10
❑ 788	LaVel Freeman	.20	.09
❑ 789	Jeffrey Leonard	.20	.09
❑ 790	Eddie Williams	.20	.09
❑ 791	Jamie Moyer	.20	.09
❑ 792	Bruce Hurst UER (Workd Series)	.20	.09
❑ 793	Julio Franco	.20	.09
❑ 794	Claudell Washington	.20	.09
❑ 795	Jody Davis	.20	.09
❑ 796	Oddibe McDowell	.20	.09
❑ 797	Paul Kilgus	.20	.09
❑ 798	Tracy Jones	.20	.09
❑ 799	Steve Wilson	.20	.09
❑ 800	Pete O'Brien	.20	.09

1990 Upper Deck

	MINT	NRMT
COMPLETE SET (800)	30.00	13.50
COMP.FACT.SET (800)	30.00	13.50
COMPLETE LO SET (700)	25.00	11.00
COMPLETE HI SET (100)	5.00	2.20
COMP.HI FACT.SET (100)	4.00	1.80

❑ 1	Star Rookie Checklist	.10	.05
❑ 2	Randy Nosek	.10	.05
❑ 3	Tom Drees UER (11th line, hulred, should be hurled	.10	.05
❑ 4	Curt Young	.10	.05
❑ 5	Devon White TC	.10	.05
❑ 6	Luis Salazar	.10	.05
❑ 7	Von Hayes TC	.10	.05
❑ 8	Jose Bautista	.10	.05
❑ 9	Marquis Grissom RC	.15	.07
❑ 10	Orel Hershiser TC	.10	.05
❑ 11	Rick Aguilera	.15	.07
❑ 12	Benito Santiago TC	.10	.05
❑ 13	Deion Sanders	.40	.18
❑ 14	Marvell Wynne	.10	.05
❑ 15	Dave West	.10	.05
❑ 16	Bobby Bonilla TC	.10	.05
❑ 17	Sammy Sosa RC	8.00	3.60
❑ 18	Steve Sax TC	.10	.05
❑ 19	Jack Howell	.10	.05
❑ 20	Mike Schmidt Special UER (Suprising, should be surprising)	.75	.35
❑ 21	Robin Ventura UER (Samta Maria)	.40	.18
❑ 22	Brian Meyer	.10	.05
❑ 23	Blaine Beatty	.10	.05
❑ 24	Ken Griffey Jr. TC	.75	.35
❑ 25	Greg Vaughn UER (Association misspelled as assiocation)	.40	.18
❑ 26	Xavier Hernandez RC	.10	.05
❑ 27	Jason Grimsley RC	.10	.05
❑ 28	Eric Anthony RC UER (Ashville, should be Asheville)	.10	.05
❑ 29	Tim Raines TC UER (Wallach listed before Walker)	.10	.05
❑ 30	David Wells	.15	.07
❑ 31	Hal Morris	.10	.05
❑ 32	Bo Jackson TC	.15	.07
❑ 33	Kelly Mann	.10	.05
❑ 34	Nolan Ryan Special	1.00	.45
❑ 35	Scott Service UER (Born Cincinati on 7/27/67, should be Cincinnati 2/27)	.10	.05
❑ 36	Mark McGwire TC	.75	.35
❑ 37	Tino Martinez	.40	.18
❑ 38	Chili Davis	.15	.07
❑ 39	Scott Sanderson	.10	.05
❑ 40	Kevin Mitchell TC	.10	.05
❑ 41	Lou Whitaker TC	.10	.05
❑ 42	Scott Coolbaugh UER (Definately)	.10	.05
❑ 43	Jose Cano UER (Born 9/7/62, should be 3/7/62)	.10	.05
❑ 44	Jose Vizcaino RC	.25	.11
❑ 45	Bob Hamelin RC	.40	.18
❑ 46	Jose Offerman RC UER (Posesses)	.15	.07
❑ 47	Kevin Blankenship	.10	.05
❑ 48	Kirby Puckett TC	.50	.23
❑ 49	Tommy Greene RC UER (Livest, should be liveliest)	.10	.05
❑ 50	Will Clark Special UER (Perenial, should be perennial)	.15	.07
❑ 51	Rob Nelson	.10	.05
❑ 52	C.Hammond RC UER Chatanooga	.10	.05
❑ 53	Joe Carter TC	.10	.05
❑ 54A	B.McDonald RC ERR No Rookie designation on card front	2.00	.90
❑ 54B	B.McDonald COR RC	.25	.11
❑ 55	Andy Benes UER (Whichita)	.10	.05
❑ 56	John Olerud RC	1.00	.45
❑ 57	Roger Clemens TC	.50	.23
❑ 58	Tony Armas	.10	.05
❑ 59	George Canale	.10	.05
❑ 60A	Mickey Tettleton TC ERR (683 Jamie Weston)	2.00	.90
❑ 60B	Mickey Tettleton TC COR (683 Mickey Weston)	.10	.05
❑ 61	Mike Stanton RC	.10	.05
❑ 62	Dwight Gooden TC	.10	.05
❑ 63	Kent Mercker RC UER (Albuguerque)	.10	.05
❑ 64	Francisco Cabrera	.10	.05
❑ 65	Steve Avery UER (Born NJ, should be MI,	.10	.05

Merker should be Mercker
❑ 66 Jose Canseco .40 .18
❑ 67 Matt Merullo .10 .05
❑ 68 Vince Coleman TC UER .10 .05
(Guerrero)
❑ 69 Ron Karkovice .10 .05
❑ 70 Kevin Maas RC .15 .07
❑ 71 Dennis Cook UER .10 .05
(Shown with righty
glove on card back)
❑ 72 Juan Gonzalez RC UER 4.00 1.80
(135 games for Tulsa
in '89, should be 133)
❑ 73 Andre Dawson TC .15 .07
❑ 74 Dean Palmer RC UER .75 .35
(Permanent misspelled
as perminant)
❑ 75 Bo Jackson Special .15 .07
UER (Monsterous,
should be monstrous)
❑ 76 Rob Richie .10 .05
❑ 77 Bobby Rose UER .10 .05
(Pickin, should
be pick in)
❑ 78 Brian DuBois UER .10 .05
(Commiting)
❑ 79 Ozzie Guillen TC .10 .05
❑ 80 Gene Nelson .10 .05
❑ 81 Bob McClure .10 .05
❑ 82 Julio Franco TC .10 .05
❑ 83 Greg Minton .10 .05
❑ 84 John Smoltz TC UER .10 .05
(Oddibe not Odibbe)
❑ 85 Willie Fraser .10 .05
❑ 86 Neal Heaton .10 .05
❑ 87 Kevin Tapani RC UER .40 .18
(24th line has excpet,
should be except)
❑ 88 Mike Scott TC .10 .05
❑ 89A Jim Gott ERR 2.00 .90
(Photo actually
Rick Reed)
❑ 89B Jim Gott COR .10 .05
❑ 90 Lance Johnson .10 .05
❑ 91 Robin Yount TC UER .15 .07
(Checklist on back has
178 Rob Deer and
176 Mike Felder)
❑ 92 Jeff Parrett .10 .05
❑ 93 Julio Machado UER .10 .05
(Valenzuelan, should
be Venezuelan)
❑ 94 Ron Jones .10 .05
❑ 95 George Bell TC .10 .05
❑ 96 Jerry Reuss .10 .05
❑ 97 Brian Fisher .10 .05
❑ 98 Kevin Ritz UER .10 .05
(Amercian)
❑ 99 Barry Larkin TC .15 .07
❑ 100 Checklist 1-100 .10 .05
❑ 101 Gerald Perry .10 .05
❑ 102 Kevin Appier .25 .11
❑ 103 Julio Franco .10 .05
❑ 104 Craig Biggio .25 .11
❑ 105 Bo Jackson UER .15 .07
('89 BA wrong,
should be .256)
❑ 106 Junior Felix .10 .05
❑ 107 Mike Harkey .10 .05
❑ 108 Fred McGriff .40 .18
❑ 109 Rick Sutcliffe .15 .07
❑ 110 Pete O'Brien .10 .05
❑ 111 Kelly Gruber .10 .05
❑ 112 Dwight Evans .15 .07
❑ 113 Pat Borders .10 .05
❑ 114 Dwight Gooden .15 .07
❑ 115 Kevin Batiste .10 .05
❑ 116 Eric Davis .15 .07
❑ 117 Kevin Mitchell UER .10 .05
(Career HR total 99,
should be 100)
❑ 118 Ron Oester .10 .05
❑ 119 Brett Butler .15 .07
❑ 120 Danny Jackson .10 .05
❑ 121 Tommy Gregg .10 .05
❑ 122 Ken Caminiti .15 .07
❑ 123 Kevin Brown .40 .18
❑ 124 George Brett UER .75 .35
(133 runs, should
be 1300)
❑ 125 Mike Scott .10 .05
❑ 126 Cory Snyder .10 .05
❑ 127 George Bell .10 .05
❑ 128 Mark Grace .40 .18
❑ 129 Devon White .10 .05
❑ 130 Tony Fernandez .10 .05
❑ 131 Don Aase .10 .05
❑ 132 Rance Mulliniks .10 .05
❑ 133 Marty Barrett .10 .05
❑ 134 Nelson Liriano .10 .05
❑ 135 Mark Carreon .10 .05
❑ 136 Candy Maldonado .10 .05
❑ 137 Tim Birtsas .10 .05
❑ 138 Tom Brookens .10 .05
❑ 139 John Franco .15 .07
❑ 140 Mike LaCoss .10 .05
❑ 141 Jeff Treadway .10 .05
❑ 142 Pat Tabler .10 .05
❑ 143 Darrell Evans .15 .07
❑ 144 Rafael Ramirez .10 .05
❑ 145 O.McDowell UER .10 .05
Misspelled Odibbe
❑ 146 Brian Downing .10 .05
❑ 147 Curt Wilkerson .10 .05
❑ 148 Ernie Whitt .10 .05
❑ 149 Bill Schroeder .10 .05
❑ 150 Domingo Ramos UER .10 .05
(Says throws right,
but shows him
throwing lefty)
❑ 151 Rick Honeycutt .10 .05
❑ 152 Don Slaught .10 .05
❑ 153 Mitch Webster .10 .05
❑ 154 Tony Phillips .10 .05
❑ 155 Paul Kilgus .10 .05
❑ 156 Ken Griffey Jr. UER 2.50 1.10
(Simultaniously)
❑ 157 Gary Sheffield .15 .07
❑ 158 Wally Backman .10 .05
❑ 159 B.J. Surhoff .15 .07
❑ 160 Louie Meadows .10 .05
❑ 161 Paul O'Neill .40 .18
❑ 162 Jeff McKnight .10 .05
❑ 163 Alvaro Espinoza .10 .05
❑ 164 Scott Scudder .10 .05
❑ 165 Jeff Reed .10 .05
❑ 166 Gregg Jefferies .15 .07
❑ 167 Barry Larkin .40 .18
❑ 168 Gary Carter .25 .11
❑ 169 Robby Thompson .10 .05
❑ 170 Rolando Roomes .10 .05
❑ 171 Mark McGwire UER 1.50 .70
(Total games 427 and
hits 479, should be
467 and 427)
❑ 172 Steve Sax .10 .05
❑ 173 Mark Williamson .10 .05
❑ 174 Mitch Williams .10 .05
❑ 175 Brian Holton .10 .05
❑ 176 Rob Deer .10 .05
❑ 177 Tim Raines .15 .07
❑ 178 Mike Felder .10 .05
❑ 179 Harold Reynolds .10 .05
❑ 180 Terry Francona .15 .07
❑ 181 Chris Sabo .10 .05
❑ 182 Darryl Strawberry .15 .07
❑ 183 Willie Randolph .15 .07
❑ 184 Bill Ripken .10 .05
❑ 185 Mackey Sasser .10 .05
❑ 186 Todd Benzinger .10 .05
❑ 187 Kevin Elster UER .10 .05
(16 homers in 1989,
should be 10)
❑ 188 Jose Uribe .10 .05
❑ 189 Tom Browning .10 .05
❑ 190 Keith Miller .10 .05
❑ 191 Don Mattingly 1.00 .45
❑ 192 Dave Parker .15 .07
❑ 193 Roberto Kelly UER .10 .05
(96 RBI, should be 62)
❑ 194 Phil Bradley .10 .05
❑ 195 Ron Hassey .10 .05
❑ 196 Gerald Young .10 .05
❑ 197 Hubie Brooks .10 .05
❑ 198 Bill Doran .10 .05
❑ 199 Al Newman .10 .05
❑ 200 Checklist 101-200 .10 .05
❑ 201 Terry Puhl .10 .05
❑ 202 Frank DiPino .10 .05
❑ 203 Jim Clancy .10 .05
❑ 204 Bob Ojeda .10 .05
❑ 205 Alex Trevino .10 .05
❑ 206 Dave Henderson .10 .05
❑ 207 Henry Cotto .10 .05
❑ 208 Rafael Belliard UER .10 .05
(Born 1961, not 1951)
❑ 209 Stan Javier .10 .05
❑ 210 Jerry Reed .10 .05
❑ 211 Doug Dascenzo .10 .05
❑ 212 Andres Thomas .10 .05
❑ 213 Greg Maddux 1.00 .45
❑ 214 Mike Schooler .10 .05
❑ 215 Lonnie Smith .10 .05
❑ 216 Jose Rijo .10 .05
❑ 217 Greg Gagne .10 .05
❑ 218 Jim Gantner .10 .05
❑ 219 Allan Anderson .10 .05
❑ 220 Rick Mahler .10 .05
❑ 221 Jim Deshaies .10 .05
❑ 222 Keith Hernandez .15 .07
❑ 223 Vince Coleman .10 .05
❑ 224 David Cone .15 .07
❑ 225 Ozzie Smith .50 .23
❑ 226 Matt Nokes .10 .05
❑ 227 Barry Bonds 1.00 .45
❑ 228 Felix Jose .10 .05
❑ 229 Dennis Powell .10 .05
❑ 230 Mike Gallego .10 .05
❑ 231 Shawon Dunston UER .10 .05
('89 stats are
Andre Dawson's)
❑ 232 Ron Gant .15 .07
❑ 233 Omar Vizquel .40 .18
❑ 234 Derek Lilliquist .10 .05
❑ 235 Erik Hanson .10 .05
❑ 236 Kirby Puckett UER 1.00 .45
(824 games, should
be 924)
❑ 237 Bill Spiers .10 .05
❑ 238 Dan Gladden .10 .05
❑ 239 Bryan Clutterbuck .10 .05
❑ 240 John Moses .10 .05
❑ 241 Ron Darling .10 .05
❑ 242 Joe Magrane .10 .05
❑ 243 Dave Magadan .10 .05
❑ 244 Pedro Guerrero UER .10 .05
(Misspelled Guererro)
❑ 245 Glenn Davis .10 .05
❑ 246 Terry Steinbach .10 .05
❑ 247 Fred Lynn .10 .05
❑ 248 Gary Redus .10 .05
❑ 249 Ken Williams .10 .05
❑ 250 Sid Bream .10 .05
❑ 251 Bob Welch UER .10 .05
(2587 career strike-
outs, should be 1587)
❑ 252 Bill Buckner .10 .05
❑ 253 Carney Lansford .15 .07
❑ 254 Paul Molitor .40 .18
❑ 255 Jose DeJesus .10 .05
❑ 256 Orel Hershiser .15 .07
❑ 257 Tom Brunansky .10 .05
❑ 258 Mike Davis .10 .05
❑ 259 Jeff Ballard .10 .05
❑ 260 Scott Terry .10 .05
❑ 261 Sid Fernandez .10 .05
❑ 262 Mike Marshall .10 .05
❑ 263 Howard Johnson UER .10 .05
(192 SO, should be 592)
❑ 264 Kirk Gibson UER .15 .07
(659 runs, should
be 669)
❑ 265 Kevin McReynolds .10 .05
❑ 266 Cal Ripken 1.50 .70
❑ 267 Ozzie Guillen UER .10 .05
(Career triples 27,
should be 29)
❑ 268 Jim Traber .10 .05

- ❑ 269 Bobby Thigpen UER .10 .05 (31 saves in 1989, should be 34)
- ❑ 270 Joe Orsulak .10 .05
- ❑ 271 Bob Boone .15 .07
- ❑ 272 Dave Stewart UER .15 .07 (Totals wrong due to omission of '86 stats)
- ❑ 273 Tim Wallach .10 .05
- ❑ 274 Luis Aquino UER .10 .05 (Says throws lefty, but shows him throwing righty)
- ❑ 275 Mike Moore .10 .05
- ❑ 276 Tony Pena .10 .05
- ❑ 277 Eddie Murray UER .40 .18 (Several typos in career total stats)
- ❑ 278 Milt Thompson .10 .05
- ❑ 279 Alejandro Pena .10 .05
- ❑ 280 Ken Dayley .10 .05
- ❑ 281 Carmen Castillo .10 .05
- ❑ 282 Tom Henke .10 .05
- ❑ 283 Mickey Hatcher .10 .05
- ❑ 284 Roy Smith .10 .05
- ❑ 285 Manny Lee .10 .05
- ❑ 286 Dan Pasqua .10 .05
- ❑ 287 Larry Sheets .10 .05
- ❑ 288 Garry Templeton .10 .05
- ❑ 289 Eddie Williams .10 .05
- ❑ 290 Brady Anderson UER .40 .18 (Home: Silver Springs, not Siver Springs)
- ❑ 291 Spike Owen .10 .05
- ❑ 292 Storm Davis .10 .05
- ❑ 293 Chris Bosio .10 .05
- ❑ 294 Jim Eisenreich .10 .05
- ❑ 295 Don August .10 .05
- ❑ 296 Jeff Hamilton .10 .05
- ❑ 297 Mickey Tettleton .10 .05
- ❑ 298 Mike Scioscia .10 .05
- ❑ 299 Kevin Hickey .10 .05
- ❑ 300 Checklist 201-300 .10 .05
- ❑ 301 Shawn Abner .10 .05
- ❑ 302 Kevin Bass .10 .05
- ❑ 303 Bip Roberts .10 .05
- ❑ 304 Joe Girardi .25 .11
- ❑ 305 Danny Darwin .10 .05
- ❑ 306 Mike Heath .10 .05
- ❑ 307 Mike Macfarlane .10 .05
- ❑ 308 Ed Whitson .10 .05
- ❑ 309 Tracy Jones .10 .05
- ❑ 310 Scott Fletcher .10 .05
- ❑ 311 Darnell Coles .10 .05
- ❑ 312 Mike Brumley .10 .05
- ❑ 313 Bill Swift .10 .05
- ❑ 314 Charlie Hough .15 .07
- ❑ 315 Jim Presley .10 .05
- ❑ 316 Luis Polonia .10 .05
- ❑ 317 Mike Morgan .10 .05
- ❑ 318 Lee Guetterman .10 .05
- ❑ 319 Jose Oquendo .10 .05
- ❑ 320 Wayne Tolleson .10 .05
- ❑ 321 Jody Reed .10 .05
- ❑ 322 Damon Berryhill .10 .05
- ❑ 323 Roger Clemens 1.00 .45
- ❑ 324 Ryne Sandberg .50 .23
- ❑ 325 Benito Santiago UER .10 .05 (Misspelled Santago on card back)
- ❑ 326 Bret Saberhagen UER .15 .07 (1140 hits, should be 1240; 56 CG, should be 52)
- ❑ 327 Lou Whitaker .15 .07
- ❑ 328 Dave Gallagher .10 .05
- ❑ 329 Mike Pagliarulo .10 .05
- ❑ 330 Doyle Alexander .10 .05
- ❑ 331 Jeffrey Leonard .10 .05
- ❑ 332 Torey Lovullo .10 .05
- ❑ 333 Pete Incaviglia .10 .05
- ❑ 334 Rickey Henderson .75 .35
- ❑ 335 Rafael Palmeiro .40 .18
- ❑ 336 Ken Hill .15 .07
- ❑ 337 Dave Winfield UER .40 .18 (1418 RBI, should be 1438)
- ❑ 338 Alfredo Griffin .10 .05
- ❑ 339 Andy Hawkins .10 .05
- ❑ 340 Ted Power .10 .05
- ❑ 341 Steve Wilson .10 .05
- ❑ 342 Jack Clark UER .15 .07 (916 BB, should be 1006; 1142 SO, should be 1130)
- ❑ 343 Ellis Burks .25 .11
- ❑ 344 Tony Gwynn UER .75 .35 (Doubles stats on card back are wrong)
- ❑ 345 Jerome Walton UER .10 .05 (Total At Bats 476, should be 475)
- ❑ 346 Roberto Alomar UER .40 .18 (61 doubles, should be 51)
- ❑ 347 Carlos Martinez UER .10 .05 (Born 8/11/64, should be 8/11/65)
- ❑ 348 Chet Lemon .10 .05
- ❑ 349 Willie Wilson .10 .05
- ❑ 350 Greg Walker .10 .05
- ❑ 351 Tom Bolton .10 .05
- ❑ 352 German Gonzalez .10 .05
- ❑ 353 Harold Baines .15 .07
- ❑ 354 Mike Greenwell .10 .05
- ❑ 355 Ruben Sierra .10 .05
- ❑ 356 Andres Galarraga .25 .11
- ❑ 357 Andre Dawson .25 .11
- ❑ 358 Jeff Brantley .10 .05
- ❑ 359 Mike Bielecki .10 .05
- ❑ 360 Ken Oberkfell .10 .05
- ❑ 361 Kurt Stillwell .10 .05
- ❑ 362 Brian Holman .10 .05
- ❑ 363 Kevin Seitzer UER .10 .05 (Career triples total does not add up)
- ❑ 364 Alvin Davis .10 .05
- ❑ 365 Tom Gordon .15 .07
- ❑ 366 Bobby Bonilla UER .15 .07 (Two steals in 1987, should be 3)
- ❑ 367 Carlton Fisk .40 .18
- ❑ 368 Steve Carter UER .10 .05 (Charlotesville)
- ❑ 369 Joel Skinner .10 .05
- ❑ 370 John Cangelosi .10 .05
- ❑ 371 Cecil Espy .10 .05
- ❑ 372 Gary Wayne .10 .05
- ❑ 373 Jim Rice .15 .07
- ❑ 374 Mike Dyer .10 .05
- ❑ 375 Joe Carter .15 .07
- ❑ 376 Dwight Smith .10 .05
- ❑ 377 John Wetteland .40 .18
- ❑ 378 Earnie Riles .10 .05
- ❑ 379 Otis Nixon .10 .05
- ❑ 380 Vance Law .10 .05
- ❑ 381 Dave Bergman .10 .05
- ❑ 382 Frank White .15 .07
- ❑ 383 Scott Bradley .10 .05
- ❑ 384 Israel Sanchez UER .10 .05 (Totals don't include '89 stats)
- ❑ 385 Gary Pettis .10 .05
- ❑ 386 Donn Pall .10 .05
- ❑ 387 John Smiley .10 .05
- ❑ 388 Tom Candiotti .10 .05
- ❑ 389 Junior Ortiz .10 .05
- ❑ 390 Steve Lyons .10 .05
- ❑ 391 Brian Harper .10 .05
- ❑ 392 Fred Manrique .10 .05
- ❑ 393 Lee Smith .15 .07
- ❑ 394 Jeff Kunkel .10 .05
- ❑ 395 Claudell Washington .10 .05
- ❑ 396 John Tudor .10 .05
- ❑ 397 Terry Kennedy UER .10 .05 (Career totals all wrong)
- ❑ 398 Lloyd McClendon .10 .05
- ❑ 399 Craig Lefferts .10 .05
- ❑ 400 Checklist 301-400 .10 .05
- ❑ 401 Keith Moreland .10 .05
- ❑ 402 Rich Gedman .10 .05
- ❑ 403 Jeff D. Robinson .10 .05
- ❑ 404 Randy Ready .10 .05
- ❑ 405 Rick Cerone .10 .05
- ❑ 406 Jeff Blauser .10 .05
- ❑ 407 Larry Andersen .10 .05
- ❑ 408 Joe Boever .10 .05
- ❑ 409 Felix Fermin .10 .05
- ❑ 410 Glenn Wilson .10 .05
- ❑ 411 Rex Hudler .10 .05
- ❑ 412 Mark Grant .10 .05
- ❑ 413 Dennis Martinez .15 .07
- ❑ 414 Darrin Jackson .10 .05
- ❑ 415 Mike Aldrete .10 .05
- ❑ 416 Roger McDowell .10 .05
- ❑ 417 Jeff Reardon .15 .07
- ❑ 418 Darren Daulton .15 .07
- ❑ 419 Tim Laudner .10 .05
- ❑ 420 Don Carman .10 .05
- ❑ 421 Lloyd Moseby .10 .05
- ❑ 422 Doug Drabek .10 .05
- ❑ 423 Lenny Harris UER .10 .05 (Walks 2 in '89, should be 20)
- ❑ 424 Jose Lind .10 .05
- ❑ 425 Dave Johnson (P) .10 .05
- ❑ 426 Jerry Browne .10 .05
- ❑ 427 Eric Yelding .10 .05
- ❑ 428 Brad Komminsk .10 .05
- ❑ 429 Jody Davis .10 .05
- ❑ 430 Mariano Duncan .10 .05
- ❑ 431 Mark Davis .10 .05
- ❑ 432 Nelson Santovenia .10 .05
- ❑ 433 Bruce Hurst .10 .05
- ❑ 434 Jeff Huson RC .10 .05
- ❑ 435 Chris James .10 .05
- ❑ 436 Mark Guthrie .10 .05
- ❑ 437 Charlie Hayes .10 .05
- ❑ 438 Shane Rawley .10 .05
- ❑ 439 Dickie Thon .10 .05
- ❑ 440 Juan Berenguer .10 .05
- ❑ 441 Kevin Romine .10 .05
- ❑ 442 Bill Landrum .10 .05
- ❑ 443 Todd Frohwirth .10 .05
- ❑ 444 Craig Worthington .10 .05
- ❑ 445 Fernando Valenzuela .15 .07
- ❑ 446 Joey Belle .40 .18
- ❑ 447 Ed Whited UER .10 .05 (Ashville, should be Asheville)
- ❑ 448 Dave Smith .10 .05
- ❑ 449 Dave Clark .10 .05
- ❑ 450 Juan Agosto .10 .05
- ❑ 451 Dave Valle .10 .05
- ❑ 452 Kent Hrbek .15 .07
- ❑ 453 Von Hayes .10 .05
- ❑ 454 Gary Gaetti .15 .07
- ❑ 455 Greg Briley .10 .05
- ❑ 456 Glenn Braggs .10 .05
- ❑ 457 Kirt Manwaring .10 .05
- ❑ 458 Mel Hall .10 .05
- ❑ 459 Brook Jacoby .10 .05
- ❑ 460 Pat Sheridan .10 .05
- ❑ 461 Rob Murphy .10 .05
- ❑ 462 Jimmy Key .15 .07
- ❑ 463 Nick Esasky .10 .05
- ❑ 464 Rob Ducey .10 .05
- ❑ 465 Carlos Quintana UER .10 .05 (Internatinoal)
- ❑ 466 Larry Walker RC 1.50 .70
- ❑ 467 Todd Worrell .10 .05
- ❑ 468 Kevin Gross .10 .05
- ❑ 469 Terry Pendleton .15 .07
- ❑ 470 Dave Martinez .10 .05
- ❑ 471 Gene Larkin .10 .05
- ❑ 472 Len Dykstra UER .15 .07 ('89 and total runs understated by 10)
- ❑ 473 Barry Lyons .10 .05
- ❑ 474 Terry Mulholland .10 .05
- ❑ 475 Chip Hale .10 .05
- ❑ 476 Jesse Barfield .10 .05
- ❑ 477 Dan Plesac .10 .05
- ❑ 478A Scott Garrelts ERR 2.00 .90 (Photo actually Bill Bathe)
- ❑ 478B Scott Garrelts COR .10 .05

No.	Player	Mint	Nr. Mint
❑ 479	Dave Righetti	.10	.05
❑ 480	Gus Polidor UER (Wearing 14 on front& but 10 on back)	.10	.05
❑ 481	Mookie Wilson	.15	.07
❑ 482	Luis Rivera	.10	.05
❑ 483	Mike Flanagan	.10	.05
❑ 484	Dennis Boyd	.10	.05
❑ 485	John Cerutti	.10	.05
❑ 486	John Costello	.10	.05
❑ 487	Pascual Perez	.10	.05
❑ 488	Tommy Herr	.10	.05
❑ 489	Tom Foley	.10	.05
❑ 490	Curt Ford	.10	.05
❑ 491	Steve Lake	.10	.05
❑ 492	Tim Teufel	.10	.05
❑ 493	Randy Bush	.10	.05
❑ 494	Mike Jackson	.10	.05
❑ 495	Steve Jeltz	.10	.05
❑ 496	Paul Gibson	.10	.05
❑ 497	Steve Balboni	.10	.05
❑ 498	Bud Black	.10	.05
❑ 499	Dale Sveum	.10	.05
❑ 500	Checklist 401-500	.10	.05
❑ 501	Tim Jones	.10	.05
❑ 502	Mark Portugal	.10	.05
❑ 503	Ivan Calderon	.10	.05
❑ 504	Rick Rhoden	.10	.05
❑ 505	Willie McGee	.15	.07
❑ 506	Kirk McCaskill	.10	.05
❑ 507	Dave LaPoint	.10	.05
❑ 508	Jay Howell	.10	.05
❑ 509	Johnny Ray	.10	.05
❑ 510	Dave Anderson	.10	.05
❑ 511	Chuck Crim	.10	.05
❑ 512	Joe Hesketh	.10	.05
❑ 513	Dennis Eckersley	.25	.11
❑ 514	Greg Brock	.10	.05
❑ 515	Tim Burke	.10	.05
❑ 516	Frank Tanana	.10	.05
❑ 517	Jay Bell	.15	.07
❑ 518	Guillermo Hernandez	.10	.05
❑ 519	Randy Kramer UER (Codiroli misspelled as Codoroli)	.10	.05
❑ 520	Charles Hudson	.10	.05
❑ 521	Jim Corsi Word "originally" is misspelled on back	.10	.05
❑ 522	Steve Rosenberg	.10	.05
❑ 523	Cris Carpenter	.10	.05
❑ 524	Matt Winters	.10	.05
❑ 525	Melido Perez	.10	.05
❑ 526	Chris Gwynn UER (Albeguergue)	.10	.05
❑ 527	Bert Blyleven UER (Games career total is wrong, should be 644)	.15	.07
❑ 528	Chuck Cary	.10	.05
❑ 529	Daryl Boston	.10	.05
❑ 530	Dale Mohorcic	.10	.05
❑ 531	Geronimo Berroa	.10	.05
❑ 532	Edgar Martinez	.25	.11
❑ 533	Dale Murphy	.40	.18
❑ 534	Jay Buhner	.15	.07
❑ 535	John Smoltz UER (HEA Stadium)	.15	.07
❑ 536	Andy Van Slyke	.15	.07
❑ 537	Mike Henneman	.10	.05
❑ 538	Miguel Garcia	.10	.05
❑ 539	Frank Williams	.10	.05
❑ 540	R.J. Reynolds	.10	.05
❑ 541	Shawn Hillegas	.10	.05
❑ 542	Walt Weiss	.10	.05
❑ 543	Greg Hibbard RC	.10	.05
❑ 544	Nolan Ryan	2.00	.90
❑ 545	Todd Zeile	.15	.07
❑ 546	Hensley Meulens	.10	.05
❑ 547	Tim Belcher	.10	.05
❑ 548	Mike Witt	.10	.05
❑ 549	Greg Cadaret UER (Aquiring, should be Acquiring)	.10	.05
❑ 550	Franklin Stubbs	.10	.05
❑ 551	Tony Castillo	.10	.05
❑ 552	Jeff M. Robinson	.10	.05
❑ 553	Steve Olin RC	.15	.07
❑ 554	Alan Trammell	.25	.11
❑ 555	Wade Boggs 4X (Bo Jackson in background)	.40	.18
❑ 556	Will Clark	.40	.18
❑ 557	Jeff King	.10	.05
❑ 558	Mike Fitzgerald	.10	.05
❑ 559	Ken Howell	.10	.05
❑ 560	Bob Kipper	.10	.05
❑ 561	Scott Bankhead	.10	.05
❑ 562A	Jeff Innis ERR (Photo actually David West)	2.00	.90
❑ 562B	Jeff Innis COR	.10	.05
❑ 563	Randy Johnson	.75	.35
❑ 564	Wally Whitehurst	.10	.05
❑ 565	Gene Harris	.10	.05
❑ 566	Norm Charlton	.10	.05
❑ 567	Robin Yount UER (7602 career hits, should be 2606)	.15	.07
❑ 568	Joe Oliver UER (Fl.orida)	.10	.05
❑ 569	Mark Parent	.10	.05
❑ 570	John Farrell UER (Loss total added wrong)	.10	.05
❑ 571	Tom Glavine	.40	.18
❑ 572	Rod Nichols	.10	.05
❑ 573	Jack Morris	.15	.07
❑ 574	Greg Swindell	.10	.05
❑ 575	Steve Searcy	.10	.05
❑ 576	Ricky Jordan	.10	.05
❑ 577	Matt Williams	.25	.11
❑ 578	Mike LaValliere	.10	.05
❑ 579	Bryn Smith	.10	.05
❑ 580	Bruce Ruffin	.10	.05
❑ 581	Randy Myers	.15	.07
❑ 582	Rick Wrona	.10	.05
❑ 583	Juan Samuel	.10	.05
❑ 584	Les Lancaster	.10	.05
❑ 585	Jeff Musselman	.10	.05
❑ 586	Rob Dibble	.10	.05
❑ 587	Eric Show	.10	.05
❑ 588	Jesse Orosco	.10	.05
❑ 589	Herm Winningham	.10	.05
❑ 590	Andy Allanson	.10	.05
❑ 591	Dion James	.10	.05
❑ 592	Carmelo Martinez	.10	.05
❑ 593	Luis Quinones	.10	.05
❑ 594	Dennis Rasmussen	.10	.05
❑ 595	Rich Yett	.10	.05
❑ 596	Bob Walk	.10	.05
❑ 597A	A.McGaffigan ERR Photo actually Rich Thompson	.15	.07
❑ 597B	A.McGaffigan COR	.10	.05
❑ 598	Billy Hatcher	.10	.05
❑ 599	Bob Knepper	.10	.05
❑ 600	CL 501-600 UER 599 Bob Kneppers	.10	.05
❑ 601	Joey Cora	.15	.07
❑ 602	Steve Finley	.15	.07
❑ 603	Kal Daniels UER (12 hits in '87, should be 123; 335 runs, should be 235)	.10	.05
❑ 604	Gregg Olson	.15	.07
❑ 605	Dave Stieb	.15	.07
❑ 606	Kenny Rogers (Shown catching football)	.15	.07
❑ 607	Zane Smith	.10	.05
❑ 608	Bob Geren UER (Origionally)	.10	.05
❑ 609	Chad Kreuter	.10	.05
❑ 610	Mike Smithson	.10	.05
❑ 611	Jeff Wetherby	.10	.05
❑ 612	Gary Mielke	.10	.05
❑ 613	Pete Smith	.10	.05
❑ 614	Jack Daugherty UER (Born 7/30/60, should be 7/3/60)	.10	.05
❑ 615	Lance McCullers	.10	.05
❑ 616	Don Robinson	.10	.05
❑ 617	Jose Guzman	.10	.05
❑ 618	Steve Bedrosian	.10	.05
❑ 619	Jamie Moyer	.10	.05
❑ 620	Atlee Hammaker	.10	.05
❑ 621	Rick Luecken UER (Innings pitched wrong)	.10	.05
❑ 622	Greg W. Harris	.10	.05
❑ 623	Pete Harnisch	.10	.05
❑ 624	Jerald Clark	.10	.05
❑ 625	Jack McDowell UER (Career totals for Games and GS don't include 1987 season)	.10	.05
❑ 626	Frank Viola	.10	.05
❑ 627	Teddy Higuera	.10	.05
❑ 628	Marty Pevey	.10	.05
❑ 629	Bill Wegman	.10	.05
❑ 630	Eric Plunk	.10	.05
❑ 631	Drew Hall	.10	.05
❑ 632	Doug Jones	.10	.05
❑ 633	Geno Petralli UER (Sacremento)	.10	.05
❑ 634	Jose Alvarez	.10	.05
❑ 635	Bob Milacki	.10	.05
❑ 636	Bobby Witt	.10	.05
❑ 637	Trevor Wilson	.10	.05
❑ 638	Jeff Russell UER (Shutout stats wrong)	.10	.05
❑ 639	Mike Krukow	.10	.05
❑ 640	Rick Leach	.10	.05
❑ 641	Dave Schmidt	.10	.05
❑ 642	Terry Leach	.10	.05
❑ 643	Calvin Schiraldi	.10	.05
❑ 644	Bob Melvin	.10	.05
❑ 645	Jim Abbott	.25	.11
❑ 646	Jaime Navarro	.10	.05
❑ 647	Mark Langston UER (Several errors in stats totals)	.10	.05
❑ 648	Juan Nieves	.10	.05
❑ 649	Damaso Garcia	.10	.05
❑ 650	Charlie O'Brien	.10	.05
❑ 651	Eric King	.10	.05
❑ 652	Mike Boddicker	.10	.05
❑ 653	Duane Ward	.10	.05
❑ 654	Bob Stanley	.10	.05
❑ 655	Sandy Alomar Jr.	.15	.07
❑ 656	Danny Tartabull UER (395 BB, should be 295)	.10	.05
❑ 657	Randy McCament	.10	.05
❑ 658	Charlie Leibrandt	.10	.05
❑ 659	Dan Quisenberry	.10	.05
❑ 660	Paul Assenmacher	.10	.05
❑ 661	Walt Terrell	.10	.05
❑ 662	Tim Leary	.10	.05
❑ 663	Randy Milligan	.10	.05
❑ 664	Bo Diaz	.10	.05
❑ 665	Mark Lemke UER (Richmond misspelled as Richomond)	.10	.05
❑ 666	Jose Gonzalez	.10	.05
❑ 667	Chuck Finley UER (Born 11/16/62, should be 11/26/62)	.15	.07
❑ 668	John Kruk	.15	.07
❑ 669	Dick Schofield	.10	.05
❑ 670	Tim Crews	.10	.05
❑ 671	John Dopson	.10	.05
❑ 672	John Orton RC	.10	.05
❑ 673	Eric Hetzel	.10	.05
❑ 674	Lance Parrish	.10	.05
❑ 675	Ramon Martinez	.10	.05
❑ 676	Mark Gubicza	.10	.05
❑ 677	Greg Litton	.10	.05
❑ 678	Greg Mathews	.10	.05
❑ 679	Dave Dravecky	.15	.07
❑ 680	Steve Farr	.10	.05
❑ 681	Mike Devereaux	.10	.05
❑ 682	Ken Griffey Sr.	.15	.07
❑ 683A	Mickey Weston ERR (Listed as Jamie on card)	2.00	.90
❑ 683B	Mickey Weston COR (Technically still an error as birthdate is listed as 3/26/81)	.10	.05
❑ 684	Jack Armstrong	.10	.05

❑ 685 Steve Buechele .10 .05
❑ 686 Bryan Harvey .10 .05
❑ 687 Lance Blankenship .10 .05
❑ 688 Dante Bichette .40 .18
❑ 689 Todd Burns .10 .05
❑ 690 Dan Petry .10 .05
❑ 691 Kent Anderson .10 .05
❑ 692 Todd Stottlemyre .15 .07
❑ 693 Wally Joyner UER .15 .07
(Several stats errors)
❑ 694 Mike Rochford .10 .05
❑ 695 Floyd Bannister .10 .05
❑ 696 Rick Reuschel .10 .05
❑ 697 Jose DeLeon .10 .05
❑ 698 Jeff Montgomery .15 .07
❑ 699 Kelly Downs .10 .05
❑ 700A Checklist 601-700 2.00 .90
(683 Jamie Weston)
❑ 700B Checklist 601-700 .10 .05
(683 Mickey Weston)
❑ 701 Jim Gott .10 .05
❑ 702 Rookie Threats .40 .18
Delino DeShields
Marquis Grissom
Larry Walker
❑ 702A Mike Witt 10.00 4.50
Black rectangle covers much of back
❑ 703 Alejandro Pena .10 .05
❑ 704 Willie Randolph .15 .07
❑ 705 Tim Leary .10 .05
❑ 706 Chuck McElroy RC .10 .05
❑ 707 Gerald Perry .10 .05
❑ 708 Tom Brunansky .10 .05
❑ 709 John Franco .15 .07
❑ 710 Mark Davis .10 .05
❑ 711 David Justice RC 1.25 .55
❑ 712 Storm Davis .10 .05
❑ 713 Scott Ruskin .10 .05
❑ 714 Glenn Braggs .10 .05
❑ 715 Kevin Bearse .10 .05
❑ 716 Jose Nunez .10 .05
❑ 717 Tim Layana .10 .05
❑ 718 Greg Myers .10 .05
❑ 719 Pete O'Brien .10 .05
❑ 720 John Candelaria .10 .05
❑ 721 Craig Grebeck RC .10 .05
❑ 722 Shawn Boskie RC .10 .05
❑ 723 Jim Leyritz RC .15 .07
❑ 724 Bill Sampen .10 .05
❑ 725 Scott Radinsky RC .10 .05
❑ 726 Todd Hundley RC .40 .18
❑ 727 Scott Hemond RC .10 .05
❑ 728 Lenny Webster RC .10 .05
❑ 729 Jeff Reardon .15 .07
❑ 730 Mitch Webster .10 .05
❑ 731 Brian Bohanon RC .10 .05
❑ 732 Rick Parker .10 .05
❑ 733 Terry Shumpert .10 .05
❑ 734A Ryan's 6th No-Hitter .. 3.00 1.35
(No stripe on front)
❑ 734B Ryan's 6th No-Hitter .. 1.00 .45
(stripe added on card
front for 300th win)
❑ 735 John Burkett .10 .05
❑ 736 Derrick May RC .15 .07
❑ 737 Carlos Baerga RC .15 .07
❑ 738 Greg Smith .10 .05
❑ 739 Scott Sanderson .10 .05
❑ 740 Joe Kraemer .10 .05
❑ 741 Hector Villanueva RC .10 .05
❑ 742 Mike Fetters RC .10 .05
❑ 743 Mark Gardner RC .10 .05
❑ 744 Matt Nokes .10 .05
❑ 745 Dave Winfield .40 .18
❑ 746 Delino DeShields RC .40 .18
❑ 747 Dann Howitt .10 .05
❑ 748 Tony Pena .10 .05
❑ 749 Oil Can Boyd .10 .05
❑ 750 Mike Benjamin .10 .05
❑ 751 Alex Cole RC .10 .05
❑ 752 Eric Gunderson .10 .05
❑ 753 Howard Farmer .10 .05
❑ 754 Joe Carter .15 .07
❑ 755 Ray Lankford RC .50 .23
❑ 756 Sandy Alomar Jr. .15 .07
❑ 757 Alex Sanchez .10 .05
❑ 758 Nick Esasky .10 .05
❑ 759 Stan Belinda RC .10 .05
❑ 760 Jim Presley .10 .05
❑ 761 Gary DiSarcina RC .25 .11
❑ 762 Wayne Edwards .10 .05
❑ 763 Pat Combs .10 .05
❑ 764 Mickey Pina .10 .05
❑ 765 Wilson Alvarez RC .15 .07
❑ 766 Dave Parker .15 .07
❑ 767 Mike Blowers RC .15 .07
❑ 768 Tony Phillips .10 .05
❑ 769 Pascual Perez .10 .05
❑ 770 Gary Pettis .10 .05
❑ 771 Fred Lynn .10 .05
❑ 772 Mel Rojas RC .15 .07
❑ 773 David Segui RC .50 .23
❑ 774 Gary Carter .25 .11
❑ 775 Rafael Valdez .10 .05
❑ 776 Glenallen Hill .10 .05
❑ 777 Keith Hernandez .15 .07
❑ 778 Billy Hatcher .10 .05
❑ 779 Marty Clary .10 .05
❑ 780 Candy Maldonado .10 .05
❑ 781 Mike Marshall .10 .05
❑ 782 Billy Joe Robidoux .10 .05
❑ 783 Mark Langston .10 .05
❑ 784 Paul Sorrento RC .25 .11
❑ 785 Dave Hollins RC .40 .18
❑ 786 Cecil Fielder .15 .07
❑ 787 Matt Young .10 .05
❑ 788 Jeff Huson .10 .05
❑ 789 Lloyd Moseby .10 .05
❑ 790 Ron Kittle .10 .05
❑ 791 Hubie Brooks .10 .05
❑ 792 Craig Lefferts .10 .05
❑ 793 Kevin Bass .10 .05
❑ 794 Bryn Smith .10 .05
❑ 795 Juan Samuel .10 .05
❑ 796 Sam Horn .10 .05
❑ 797 Randy Myers .15 .07
❑ 798 Chris James .10 .05
❑ 799 Bill Gullickson .10 .05
❑ 800 Checklist 701-800 .10 .05

1991 Upper Deck

	MINT	NRMT
COMPLETE SET (800)	20.00	9.00
COMP.FACT.SET (800)	25.00	11.00
COMPLETE LO SET (700)	16.00	7.25
COMPLETE HI SET (100)	4.00	1.80

❑ 1 Star Rookie Checklist .05 .02
❑ 2 Phil Plantier RC .05 .02
❑ 3 D.J. Dozier .05 .02
❑ 4 Dave Hansen .05 .02
❑ 5 Maurice Vaughn .10 .05
❑ 6 Leo Gomez .05 .02
❑ 7 Scott Aldred .05 .02
❑ 8 Scott Chiamparino .05 .02
❑ 9 Lance Dickson RC .05 .02
❑ 10 Sean Berry RC .10 .05
❑ 11 Bernie Williams .25 .11
❑ 12 Brian Barnes UER .05 .02
(Photo either not him
or in wrong jersey)
❑ 13 Narciso Elvira .05 .02
❑ 14 Mike Gardiner .05 .02
❑ 15 Greg Colbrunn RC .10 .05
❑ 16 Bernard Gilkey .05 .02
❑ 17 Mark Lewis .05 .02
❑ 18 Mickey Morandini .05 .02
❑ 19 Charles Nagy .05 .02
❑ 20 Geronimo Pena .05 .02
❑ 21 Henry Rodriguez RC .20 .09
❑ 22 Scott Cooper .05 .02
❑ 23 Andujar Cedeno UER .05 .02
(Shown batting left,
back says right)
❑ 24 Eric Karros RC .50 .23
❑ 25 Steve Decker UER .05 .02
Lewis-Clark State
College, not Lewis
and Clark
❑ 26 Kevin Belcher .05 .02
❑ 27 Jeff Conine RC .10 .05
❑ 28 Dave Stewart TC .05 .02
❑ 29 Carlton Fisk TC .10 .05
❑ 30 Rafael Palmeiro TC .10 .05
❑ 31 Chuck Finley TC .05 .02
❑ 32 Harold Reynolds TC .05 .02
❑ 33 Bret Saberhagen TC .05 .02
❑ 34 Gary Gaetti TC .05 .02
❑ 35 Scott Leius .05 .02
❑ 36 Neal Heaton .05 .02
❑ 37 Terry Lee .05 .02
❑ 38 Gary Redus .05 .02
❑ 39 Barry Jones .05 .02
❑ 40 Chuck Knoblauch .10 .05
❑ 41 Larry Andersen .05 .02
❑ 42 Darryl Hamilton .05 .02
❑ 43 Mike Greenwell TC .05 .02
❑ 44 Kelly Gruber TC .05 .02
❑ 45 Jack Morris TC .05 .02
❑ 46 Sandy Alomar Jr. TC .05 .02
❑ 47 Gregg Olson TC .05 .02
❑ 48 Dave Parker TC .05 .02
❑ 49 Roberto Kelly TC .05 .02
❑ 50 Top Prospect Checklist .05 .02
❑ 51 Kyle Abbott .05 .02
❑ 52 Jeff Juden .05 .02
❑ 53 T.Van Poppel UER RC .05 .02
Born Arlington and
attended John Martin HS,
should say Hinsdale and
James Martin HS
❑ 54 Steve Karsay RC .10 .05
❑ 55 Chipper Jones RC 2.50 1.10
❑ 56 Chris Johnson RC UER .. .05 .02
(Called Tim on back)
❑ 57 John Ericks .05 .02
❑ 58 Gary Scott .05 .02
❑ 59 Kiki Jones .05 .02
❑ 60 Wil Cordero RC .10 .05
❑ 61 Royce Clayton .05 .02
❑ 62 Tim Costo RC .05 .02
❑ 63 Roger Salkeld .05 .02
❑ 64 Brook Fordyce RC .05 .02
❑ 65 Mike Mussina RC 2.00 .90
❑ 66 Dave Staton RC .05 .02
❑ 67 Mike Lieberthal RC .50 .23
❑ 68 Kurt Miller RC .05 .02
❑ 69 Dan Peltier RC .05 .02
❑ 70 Greg Blosser .05 .02
❑ 71 Reggie Sanders RC .50 .23
❑ 72 Brent Mayne .05 .02
❑ 73 Rico Brogna .05 .02
❑ 74 Willie Banks .05 .02
❑ 75 Len Brutcher .05 .02
❑ 76 Pat Kelly RC .05 .02
❑ 77 Chris Sabo TC .05 .02
❑ 78 Ramon Martinez TC .05 .02
❑ 79 Matt Williams TC .10 .05
❑ 80 Roberto Alomar TC .10 .05
❑ 81 Glenn Davis TC .05 .02
❑ 82 Ron Gant TC .05 .02
❑ 83 Cecil Fielder FEAT .05 .02
❑ 84 Orlando Merced RC .05 .02
❑ 85 Domingo Ramos .05 .02
❑ 86 Tom Bolton .05 .02
❑ 87 Andres Santana .05 .02
❑ 88 John Dopson .05 .02
❑ 89 Kenny Williams .05 .02
❑ 90 Marty Barrett .05 .02

91	Tom Pagnozzi	.05	.02
92	Carmelo Martinez	.05	.02
93	Bobby Thigpen SAVE	.05	.02
94	Barry Bonds TC	.25	.11
95	Gregg Jefferies TC	.05	.02
96	Tim Wallach TC	.05	.02
97	Len Dykstra TC	.05	.02
98	Pedro Guerrero TC	.05	.02
99	Mark Grace TC	.10	.05
100	Checklist 1-100	.05	.02
101	Kevin Elster	.05	.02
102	Tom Brookens	.05	.02
103	Mackey Sasser	.05	.02
104	Felix Fermin	.05	.02
105	Kevin McReynolds	.05	.02
106	Dave Stieb	.05	.02
107	Jeffrey Leonard	.05	.02
108	Dave Henderson	.05	.02
109	Sid Bream	.05	.02
110	Henry Cotto	.05	.02
111	Shawon Dunston	.05	.02
112	Mariano Duncan	.05	.02
113	Joe Girardi	.05	.02
114	Billy Hatcher	.05	.02
115	Greg Maddux	.50	.23
116	Jerry Browne	.05	.02
117	Juan Samuel	.05	.02
118	Steve Olin	.05	.02
119	Alfredo Griffin	.05	.02
120	Mitch Webster	.05	.02
121	Joel Skinner	.05	.02
122	Frank Viola	.10	.05
123	Cory Snyder	.05	.02
124	Howard Johnson	.05	.02
125	Carlos Baerga	.05	.02
126	Tony Fernandez	.05	.02
127	Dave Stewart	.10	.05
128	Jay Buhner	.10	.05
129	Mike LaValliere	.05	.02
130	Scott Bradley	.05	.02
131	Tony Phillips	.05	.02
132	Ryne Sandberg	.25	.11
133	Paul O'Neill	.20	.09
134	Mark Grace	.20	.09
135	Chris Sabo	.05	.02
136	Ramon Martinez	.05	.02
137	Brook Jacoby	.05	.02
138	Candy Maldonado	.05	.02
139	Mike Scioscia	.05	.02
140	Chris James	.05	.02
141	Craig Worthington	.05	.02
142	Manny Lee	.05	.02
143	Tim Raines	.10	.05
144	Sandy Alomar Jr.	.10	.05
145	John Olerud	.15	.07
146	Ozzie Canseco (With Jose)	.10	.05
147	Pat Borders	.05	.02
148	Harold Reynolds	.05	.02
149	Tom Henke	.05	.02
150	R.J. Reynolds	.05	.02
151	Mike Gallego	.05	.02
152	Bobby Bonilla	.10	.05
153	Terry Steinbach	.05	.02
154	Barry Bonds	.50	.23
155	Jose Canseco	.20	.09
156	Gregg Jefferies	.05	.02
157	Matt Williams	.15	.07
158	Craig Biggio	.15	.07
159	Daryl Boston	.05	.02
160	Ricky Jordan	.05	.02
161	Stan Belinda	.05	.02
162	Ozzie Smith	.25	.11
163	Tom Brunansky	.05	.02
164	Todd Zeile	.05	.02
165	Mike Greenwell	.05	.02
166	Kal Daniels	.05	.02
167	Kent Hrbek	.10	.05
168	Franklin Stubbs	.05	.02
169	Dick Schofield	.05	.02
170	Junior Ortiz	.05	.02
171	Hector Villanueva	.05	.02
172	Dennis Eckersley	.10	.05
173	Mitch Williams	.05	.02
174	Mark McGwire	.75	.35
175	F.Valenzuela 3X	.10	.05
176	Gary Carter	.15	.07
177	Dave Magadan	.05	.02
178	Robby Thompson	.05	.02
179	Bob Ojeda	.05	.02
180	Ken Caminiti	.10	.05
181	Don Slaught	.05	.02
182	Luis Rivera	.05	.02
183	Jay Bell	.10	.05
184	Jody Reed	.05	.02
185	Wally Backman	.05	.02
186	Dave Martinez	.05	.02
187	Luis Polonia	.05	.02
188	Shane Mack	.05	.02
189	Spike Owen	.05	.02
190	Scott Bailes	.05	.02
191	John Russell	.05	.02
192	Walt Weiss	.05	.02
193	Jose Oquendo	.05	.02
194	Carney Lansford	.10	.05
195	Jeff Huson	.05	.02
196	Keith Miller	.05	.02
197	Eric Yelding	.05	.02
198	Ron Darling	.05	.02
199	John Kruk	.10	.05
200	Checklist 101-200	.05	.02
201	John Shelby	.05	.02
202	Bob Geren	.05	.02
203	Lance McCullers	.05	.02
204	Alvaro Espinoza	.05	.02
205	Mark Salas	.05	.02
206	Mike Pagliarulo	.05	.02
207	Jose Uribe	.05	.02
208	Jim Deshaies	.05	.02
209	Ron Karkovice	.05	.02
210	Rafael Ramirez	.05	.02
211	Donnie Hill	.05	.02
212	Brian Harper	.05	.02
213	Jack Howell	.05	.02
214	Wes Gardner	.05	.02
215	Tim Burke	.05	.02
216	Doug Jones	.05	.02
217	Hubie Brooks	.05	.02
218	Tom Candiotti	.05	.02
219	Gerald Perry	.05	.02
220	Jose DeLeon	.05	.02
221	Wally Whitehurst	.05	.02
222	Alan Mills	.05	.02
223	Alan Trammell	.15	.07
224	Dwight Gooden	.10	.05
225	Travis Fryman	.10	.05
226	Joe Carter	.10	.05
227	Julio Franco	.10	.05
228	Craig Lefferts	.05	.02
229	Gary Pettis	.05	.02
230	Dennis Rasmussen	.05	.02
231A	Brian Downing ERR (No position on front)	.05	.02
231B	Brian Downing COR (DH on front)	.20	.09
232	Carlos Quintana	.05	.02
233	Gary Gaetti	.10	.05
234	Mark Langston	.05	.02
235	Tim Wallach	.05	.02
236	Greg Swindell	.05	.02
237	Eddie Murray	.20	.09
238	Jeff Manto	.05	.02
239	Lenny Harris	.05	.02
240	Jesse Orosco	.05	.02
241	Scott Lusader	.05	.02
242	Sid Fernandez	.05	.02
243	Jim Leyritz	.05	.02
244	Cecil Fielder	.10	.05
245	Darryl Strawberry	.10	.05
246	Frank Thomas UER (Comiskey Park misspelled Comisky)	.30	.14
247	Kevin Mitchell	.05	.02
248	Lance Johnson	.05	.02
249	Rick Reuschel	.05	.02
250	Mark Portugal	.05	.02
251	Derek Lilliquist	.05	.02
252	Brian Holman	.05	.02
253	Rafael Valdez UER (Born 4/17/68, should be 12/17/67)	.05	.02
254	B.J. Surhoff	.10	.05
255	Tony Gwynn	.40	.18
256	Andy Van Slyke	.10	.05
257	Todd Stottlemyre	.05	.02
258	Jose Lind	.05	.02
259	Greg Myers	.05	.02
260	Jeff Ballard	.05	.02
261	Bobby Thigpen	.05	.02
262	Jimmy Kremers	.05	.02
263	Robin Ventura	.10	.05
264	John Smoltz	.10	.05
265	Sammy Sosa	.50	.23
266	Gary Sheffield	.10	.05
267	Len Dykstra	.10	.05
268	Bill Spiers	.05	.02
269	Charlie Hayes	.05	.02
270	Brett Butler	.10	.05
271	Bip Roberts	.05	.02
272	Rob Deer	.05	.02
273	Fred Lynn	.05	.02
274	Dave Parker	.10	.05
275	Andy Benes	.05	.02
276	Glenallen Hill	.05	.02
277	Steve Howard	.05	.02
278	Doug Drabek	.05	.02
279	Joe Oliver	.05	.02
280	Todd Benzinger	.05	.02
281	Eric King	.05	.02
282	Jim Presley	.05	.02
283	Ken Patterson	.05	.02
284	Jack Daugherty	.05	.02
285	Ivan Calderon	.05	.02
286	Edgar Diaz	.05	.02
287	Kevin Bass	.05	.02
288	Don Carman	.05	.02
289	Greg Brock	.05	.02
290	John Franco	.10	.05
291	Joey Cora	.05	.02
292	Bill Wegman	.05	.02
293	Eric Show	.05	.02
294	Scott Bankhead	.05	.02
295	Garry Templeton	.05	.02
296	Mickey Tettleton	.05	.02
297	Luis Sojo	.05	.02
298	Jose Rijo	.05	.02
299	Dave Johnson	.05	.02
300	Checklist 201-300	.05	.02
301	Mark Grant	.05	.02
302	Pete Harnisch	.05	.02
303	Greg Olson	.05	.02
304	Anthony Telford	.05	.02
305	Lonnie Smith	.05	.02
306	Chris Hoiles	.05	.02
307	Bryn Smith	.05	.02
308	Mike Devereaux	.05	.02
309A	Milt Thompson ERR (Under yr information has print dot)	.20	.09
309B	Milt Thompson COR (Under yr information says 86)	.05	.02
310	Bob Melvin	.05	.02
311	Luis Salazar	.05	.02
312	Ed Whitson	.05	.02
313	Charlie Hough	.10	.05
314	Dave Clark	.05	.02
315	Eric Gunderson	.05	.02
316	Dan Petry	.05	.02
317	Dante Bichette UER (Assists misspelled as assissts)	.10	.05
318	Mike Heath	.05	.02
319	Damon Berryhill	.05	.02
320	Walt Terrell	.05	.02
321	Scott Fletcher	.05	.02
322	Dan Plesac	.05	.02
323	Jack McDowell	.05	.02
324	Paul Molitor	.20	.09
325	Ozzie Guillen	.05	.02
326	Gregg Olson	.05	.02
327	Pedro Guerrero	.10	.05
328	Bob Milacki	.05	.02
329	John Tudor UER ('90 Cardinals, should be '90 Dodgers)	.05	.02
330	Steve Finley UER (Born 3/12/65,	.10	.05

should be 5/12)

- ❑ 331 Jack Clark .10 .05
- ❑ 332 Jerome Walton .05 .02
- ❑ 333 Andy Hawkins .05 .02
- ❑ 334 Derrick May .05 .02
- ❑ 335 Roberto Alomar .20 .09
- ❑ 336 Jack Morris .10 .05
- ❑ 337 Dave Winfield .20 .09
- ❑ 338 Steve Searcy .05 .02
- ❑ 339 Chili Davis .10 .05
- ❑ 340 Larry Sheets .05 .02
- ❑ 341 Ted Higuera .05 .02
- ❑ 342 David Segui .05 .02
- ❑ 343 Greg Cadaret .05 .02
- ❑ 344 Robin Yount .20 .09
- ❑ 345 Nolan Ryan 1.00 .45
- ❑ 346 Ray Lankford .10 .05
- ❑ 347 Cal Ripken .75 .35
- ❑ 348 Lee Smith .10 .05
- ❑ 349 Brady Anderson .10 .05
- ❑ 350 Frank DiPino .05 .02
- ❑ 351 Hal Morris .05 .02
- ❑ 352 Deion Sanders .10 .05
- ❑ 353 Barry Larkin .20 .09
- ❑ 354 Don Mattingly .50 .23
- ❑ 355 Eric Davis .10 .05
- ❑ 356 Jose Offerman .05 .02
- ❑ 357 Mel Rojas .05 .02
- ❑ 358 Rudy Seanez .05 .02
- ❑ 359 Oil Can Boyd .05 .02
- ❑ 360 Nelson Liriano .05 .02
- ❑ 361 Ron Gant .05 .02
- ❑ 362 Howard Farmer .05 .02
- ❑ 363 David Justice .20 .09
- ❑ 364 Delino DeShields .10 .05
- ❑ 365 Steve Avery .05 .02
- ❑ 366 David Cone .10 .05
- ❑ 367 Lou Whitaker .10 .05
- ❑ 368 Von Hayes .05 .02
- ❑ 369 Frank Tanana .05 .02
- ❑ 370 Tim Teufel .05 .02
- ❑ 371 Randy Myers .05 .02
- ❑ 372 Roberto Kelly .05 .02
- ❑ 373 Jack Armstrong .05 .02
- ❑ 374 Kelly Gruber .05 .02
- ❑ 375 Kevin Maas .05 .02
- ❑ 376 Randy Johnson .30 .14
- ❑ 377 David West .05 .02
- ❑ 378 Brent Knackert .05 .02
- ❑ 379 Rick Honeycutt .05 .02
- ❑ 380 Kevin Gross .05 .02
- ❑ 381 Tom Foley .05 .02
- ❑ 382 Jeff Blauser .05 .02
- ❑ 383 Scott Ruskin .05 .02
- ❑ 384 Andres Thomas .05 .02
- ❑ 385 Dennis Martinez .10 .05
- ❑ 386 Mike Henneman .05 .02
- ❑ 387 Felix Jose .05 .02
- ❑ 388 Alejandro Pena .05 .02
- ❑ 389 Chet Lemon .05 .02
- ❑ 390 Craig Wilson .05 .02
- ❑ 391 Chuck Crim .05 .02
- ❑ 392 Mel Hall .05 .02
- ❑ 393 Mark Knudson .05 .02
- ❑ 394 Norm Charlton .05 .02
- ❑ 395 Mike Felder .05 .02
- ❑ 396 Tim Layana .05 .02
- ❑ 397 Steve Frey .05 .02
- ❑ 398 Bill Doran .05 .02
- ❑ 399 Dion James .05 .02
- ❑ 400 Checklist 301-400 .05 .02
- ❑ 401 Ron Hassey .05 .02
- ❑ 402 Don Robinson .05 .02
- ❑ 403 Gene Nelson .05 .02
- ❑ 404 Terry Kennedy .05 .02
- ❑ 405 Todd Burns .05 .02
- ❑ 406 Roger McDowell .05 .02
- ❑ 407 Bob Kipper .05 .02
- ❑ 408 Darren Daulton .10 .05
- ❑ 409 Chuck Cary .05 .02
- ❑ 410 Bruce Ruffin .05 .02
- ❑ 411 Juan Berenguer .05 .02
- ❑ 412 Gary Ward .05 .02
- ❑ 413 Al Newman .05 .02
- ❑ 414 Danny Jackson .05 .02
- ❑ 415 Greg Gagne .05 .02
- ❑ 416 Tom Herr .05 .02
- ❑ 417 Jeff Parrett .05 .02
- ❑ 418 Jeff Reardon .10 .05
- ❑ 419 Mark Lemke .05 .02
- ❑ 420 Charlie O'Brien .05 .02
- ❑ 421 Willie Randolph .10 .05
- ❑ 422 Steve Bedrosian .05 .02
- ❑ 423 Mike Moore .05 .02
- ❑ 424 Jeff Brantley .05 .02
- ❑ 425 Bob Welch .05 .02
- ❑ 426 Terry Mulholland .05 .02
- ❑ 427 Willie Blair .05 .02
- ❑ 428 Darrin Fletcher .05 .02
- ❑ 429 Mike Witt .05 .02
- ❑ 430 Joe Boever .05 .02
- ❑ 431 Tom Gordon .05 .02
- ❑ 432 Pedro Munoz RC .05 .02
- ❑ 433 Kevin Seitzer .05 .02
- ❑ 434 Kevin Tapani .05 .02
- ❑ 435 Bret Saberhagen .10 .05
- ❑ 436 Ellis Burks .10 .05
- ❑ 437 Chuck Finley .10 .05
- ❑ 438 Mike Boddicker .05 .02
- ❑ 439 Francisco Cabrera .05 .02
- ❑ 440 Todd Hundley .05 .02
- ❑ 441 Kelly Downs .05 .02
- ❑ 442 Dann Howitt .05 .02
- ❑ 443 Scott Garrelts .05 .02
- ❑ 444 Rickey Henderson 3X .40 .18
- ❑ 445 Will Clark .20 .09
- ❑ 446 Ben McDonald .05 .02
- ❑ 447 Dale Murphy .20 .09
- ❑ 448 Dave Righetti .10 .05
- ❑ 449 Dickie Thon .05 .02
- ❑ 450 Ted Power .05 .02
- ❑ 451 Scott Coolbaugh .05 .02
- ❑ 452 Dwight Smith .05 .02
- ❑ 453 Pete Incaviglia .05 .02
- ❑ 454 Andre Dawson .15 .07
- ❑ 455 Ruben Sierra .05 .02
- ❑ 456 Andres Galarraga .15 .07
- ❑ 457 Alvin Davis .05 .02
- ❑ 458 Tony Castillo .05 .02
- ❑ 459 Pete O'Brien .05 .02
- ❑ 460 Charlie Leibrandt .05 .02
- ❑ 461 Vince Coleman .05 .02
- ❑ 462 Steve Sax .05 .02
- ❑ 463 Omar Olivares RC .10 .05
- ❑ 464 Oscar Azocar .05 .02
- ❑ 465 Joe Magrane .05 .02
- ❑ 466 Karl Rhodes .05 .02
- ❑ 467 Benito Santiago .05 .02
- ❑ 468 Joe Klink .05 .02
- ❑ 469 Sil Campusano .05 .02
- ❑ 470 Mark Parent .05 .02
- ❑ 471 Shawn Boskie UER .05 .02
  (Depleted misspelled as depleated)
- ❑ 472 Kevin Brown .10 .05
- ❑ 473 Rick Sutcliffe .10 .05
- ❑ 474 Rafael Palmeiro .20 .09
- ❑ 475 Mike Harkey .05 .02
- ❑ 476 Jaime Navarro .05 .02
- ❑ 477 Marquis Grissom UER .05 .02
  (DeShields misspelled as DeSheilds)
- ❑ 478 Marty Clary .05 .02
- ❑ 479 Greg Briley .05 .02
- ❑ 480 Tom Glavine .20 .09
- ❑ 481 Lee Guetterman .05 .02
- ❑ 482 Rex Hudler .05 .02
- ❑ 483 Dave LaPoint .05 .02
- ❑ 484 Terry Pendleton .10 .05
- ❑ 485 Jesse Barfield .05 .02
- ❑ 486 Jose DeJesus .05 .02
- ❑ 487 Paul Abbott RC .10 .05
- ❑ 488 Ken Howell .05 .02
- ❑ 489 Greg W. Harris .05 .02
- ❑ 490 Roy Smith .05 .02
- ❑ 491 Paul Assenmacher .05 .02
- ❑ 492 Geno Petralli .05 .02
- ❑ 493 Steve Wilson .05 .02
- ❑ 494 Kevin Reimer .05 .02
- ❑ 495 Bill Long .05 .02
- ❑ 496 Mike Jackson .05 .02
- ❑ 497 Oddibe McDowell .05 .02
- ❑ 498 Bill Swift .05 .02
- ❑ 499 Jeff Treadway .05 .02
- ❑ 500 Checklist 401-500 .05 .02
- ❑ 501 Gene Larkin .05 .02
- ❑ 502 Bob Boone .10 .05
- ❑ 503 Allan Anderson .05 .02
- ❑ 504 Luis Aquino .05 .02
- ❑ 505 Mark Guthrie .05 .02
- ❑ 506 Joe Orsulak .05 .02
- ❑ 507 Dana Kiecker .05 .02
- ❑ 508 Dave Gallagher .05 .02
- ❑ 509 Greg A. Harris .05 .02
- ❑ 510 Mark Williamson .05 .02
- ❑ 511 Casey Candaele .05 .02
- ❑ 512 Mookie Wilson .10 .05
- ❑ 513 Dave Smith .05 .02
- ❑ 514 Chuck Carr .05 .02
- ❑ 515 Glenn Wilson .05 .02
- ❑ 516 Mike Fitzgerald .05 .02
- ❑ 517 Devon White .05 .02
- ❑ 518 Dave Hollins .05 .02
- ❑ 519 Mark Eichhorn .05 .02
- ❑ 520 Otis Nixon .05 .02
- ❑ 521 Terry Shumpert .05 .02
- ❑ 522 Scott Erickson .05 .02
- ❑ 523 Danny Tartabull .05 .02
- ❑ 524 Orel Hershiser .10 .05
- ❑ 525 George Brett .40 .18
- ❑ 526 Greg Vaughn .10 .05
- ❑ 527 Tim Naehring .05 .02
- ❑ 528 Curt Schilling .20 .09
- ❑ 529 Chris Bosio .05 .02
- ❑ 530 Sam Horn .05 .02
- ❑ 531 Mike Scott .05 .02
- ❑ 532 George Bell .05 .02
- ❑ 533 Eric Anthony .05 .02
- ❑ 534 Julio Valera .05 .02
- ❑ 535 Glenn Davis .05 .02
- ❑ 536 Larry Walker UER .15 .07
  (Should have comma after Expos in text)
- ❑ 537 Pat Combs .05 .02
- ❑ 538 Chris Nabholz .05 .02
- ❑ 539 Kirk McCaskill .05 .02
- ❑ 540 Randy Ready .05 .02
- ❑ 541 Mark Gubicza .05 .02
- ❑ 542 Rick Aguilera .10 .05
- ❑ 543 Brian McRae RC .10 .05
- ❑ 544 Kirby Puckett .50 .23
- ❑ 545 Bo Jackson .10 .05
- ❑ 546 Wade Boggs .20 .09
- ❑ 547 Tim McIntosh .05 .02
- ❑ 548 Randy Milligan .05 .02
- ❑ 549 Dwight Evans .10 .05
- ❑ 550 Billy Ripken .05 .02
- ❑ 551 Erik Hanson .05 .02
- ❑ 552 Lance Parrish .10 .05
- ❑ 553 Tino Martinez .10 .05
- ❑ 554 Jim Abbott .10 .05
- ❑ 555 Ken Griffey Jr. UER .75 .35
  (Second most votes for 1991 All-Star Game)
- ❑ 556 Milt Cuyler .05 .02
- ❑ 557 Mark Leonard .05 .02
- ❑ 558 Jay Howell .05 .02
- ❑ 559 Lloyd Moseby .05 .02
- ❑ 560 Chris Gwynn .05 .02
- ❑ 561 Mark Whiten .05 .02
- ❑ 562 Harold Baines .10 .05
- ❑ 563 Junior Felix .05 .02
- ❑ 564 Darren Lewis .05 .02
- ❑ 565 Fred McGriff .15 .07
- ❑ 566 Kevin Appier .10 .05
- ❑ 567 Luis Gonzalez RC 2.50 1.10
- ❑ 568 Frank White .10 .05
- ❑ 569 Juan Agosto .05 .02
- ❑ 570 Mike Macfarlane .05 .02
- ❑ 571 Bert Blyleven .10 .05
- ❑ 572 Ken Griffey Sr. .40 .18
  Ken Griffey Jr.
- ❑ 573 Lee Stevens .05 .02
- ❑ 574 Edgar Martinez .15 .07
- ❑ 575 Wally Joyner .10 .05
- ❑ 576 Tim Belcher .05 .02
- ❑ 577 John Burkett .05 .02
- ❑ 578 Mike Morgan .05 .02

❑ 579 Paul Gibson .05 .02
❑ 580 Jose Vizcaino .05 .02
❑ 581 Duane Ward .05 .02
❑ 582 Scott Sanderson .05 .02
❑ 583 David Wells .10 .05
❑ 584 Willie McGee .10 .05
❑ 585 John Cerutti .05 .02
❑ 586 Danny Darwin .05 .02
❑ 587 Kurt Stillwell .05 .02
❑ 588 Rich Gedman .05 .02
❑ 589 Mark Davis .05 .02
❑ 590 Bill Gullickson .05 .02
❑ 591 Matt Young .05 .02
❑ 592 Bryan Harvey .05 .02
❑ 593 Omar Vizquel .10 .05
❑ 594 Scott Lewis RC .05 .02
❑ 595 Dave Valle .05 .02
❑ 596 Tim Crews .05 .02
❑ 597 Mike Bielecki .05 .02
❑ 598 Mike Sharperson .05 .02
❑ 599 Dave Bergman .05 .02
❑ 600 Checklist 501-600 .05 .02
❑ 601 Steve Lyons .05 .02
❑ 602 Bruce Hurst .05 .02
❑ 603 Donn Pall .05 .02
❑ 604 Jim Vatcher .05 .02
❑ 605 Dan Pasqua .05 .02
❑ 606 Kenny Rogers .05 .02
❑ 607 Jeff Schulz .05 .02
❑ 608 Brad Arnsberg .05 .02
❑ 609 Willie Wilson .05 .02
❑ 610 Jamie Moyer .05 .02
❑ 611 Ron Oester .05 .02
❑ 612 Dennis Cook .05 .02
❑ 613 Rick Mahler .05 .02
❑ 614 Bill Landrum .05 .02
❑ 615 Scott Scudder .05 .02
❑ 616 Tom Edens .05 .02
❑ 617 1917 Revisited .10 .05
(White Sox vintage uniforms)
❑ 618 Jim Gantner .05 .02
❑ 619 Darrel Akerfelds .05 .02
❑ 620 Ron Robinson .05 .02
❑ 621 Scott Radinsky .05 .02
❑ 622 Pete Smith .05 .02
❑ 623 Melido Perez .05 .02
❑ 624 Jerald Clark .05 .02
❑ 625 Carlos Martinez .05 .02
❑ 626 Wes Chamberlain RC .05 .02
❑ 627 Bobby Witt .05 .02
❑ 628 Ken Dayley .05 .02
❑ 629 John Barfield .05 .02
❑ 630 Bob Tewksbury .05 .02
❑ 631 Glenn Braggs .05 .02
❑ 632 Jim Neidlinger .05 .02
❑ 633 Tom Browning .05 .02
❑ 634 Kirk Gibson .10 .05
❑ 635 Rob Dibble .05 .02
❑ 636 Rickey Henderson SB .20 .09
Lou Brock
May 1, 1991 on front
❑ 636A R.Henderson SB .40 .18
Lou Brock
no date on card
❑ 637 Jeff Montgomery .05 .02
❑ 638 Mike Schooler .05 .02
❑ 639 Storm Davis .05 .02
❑ 640 Rich Rodriguez .05 .02
❑ 641 Phil Bradley .05 .02
❑ 642 Kent Mercker .05 .02
❑ 643 Carlton Fisk .20 .09
❑ 644 Mike Bell .05 .02
❑ 645 Alex Fernandez .05 .02
❑ 646 Juan Gonzalez .25 .11
❑ 647 Ken Hill .05 .02
❑ 648 Jeff Russell .05 .02
❑ 649 Chuck Malone .05 .02
❑ 650 Steve Buechele .05 .02
❑ 651 Mike Benjamin .05 .02
❑ 652 Tony Pena .05 .02
❑ 653 Trevor Wilson .05 .02
❑ 654 Alex Cole .05 .02
❑ 655 Roger Clemens .50 .23
❑ 656 Mark McGwire BASH .40 .18
❑ 657 Joe Grahe RC .05 .02
❑ 658 Jim Eisenreich .05 .02
❑ 659 Dan Gladden .05 .02
❑ 660 Steve Farr .05 .02
❑ 661 Bill Sampen .05 .02
❑ 662 Dave Rohde .05 .02
❑ 663 Mark Gardner .05 .02
❑ 664 Mike Simms .05 .02
❑ 665 Moises Alou .10 .05
❑ 666 Mickey Hatcher .05 .02
❑ 667 Jimmy Key .10 .05
❑ 668 John Wetteland .10 .05
❑ 669 John Smiley .05 .02
❑ 670 Jim Acker .05 .02
❑ 671 Pascual Perez .05 .02
❑ 672 Reggie Harris UER .05 .02
(Opportunity misspelled
as oppurtinty)
❑ 673 Matt Nokes .05 .02
❑ 674 Rafael Novoa .05 .02
❑ 675 Hensley Meulens .05 .02
❑ 676 Jeff M. Robinson .05 .02
❑ 677 Ground Breaking .10 .05
(New Comiskey Park;
Carlton Fisk and
Robin Ventura)
❑ 678 Johnny Ray .05 .02
❑ 679 Greg Hibbard .05 .02
❑ 680 Paul Sorrento .05 .02
❑ 681 Mike Marshall .05 .02
❑ 682 Jim Clancy .05 .02
❑ 683 Rob Murphy .05 .02
❑ 684 Dave Schmidt .05 .02
❑ 685 Jeff Gray .05 .02
❑ 686 Mike Hartley .05 .02
❑ 687 Jeff King .05 .02
❑ 688 Stan Javier .05 .02
❑ 689 Bob Walk .05 .02
❑ 690 Jim Gott .05 .02
❑ 691 Mike LaCoss .05 .02
❑ 692 John Farrell .05 .02
❑ 693 Tim Leary .05 .02
❑ 694 Mike Walker .05 .02
❑ 695 Eric Plunk .05 .02
❑ 696 Mike Fetters .05 .02
❑ 697 Wayne Edwards .05 .02
❑ 698 Tim Drummond .05 .02
❑ 699 Willie Fraser .05 .02
❑ 700 Checklist 601-700 .05 .02
❑ 701 Mike Heath .05 .02
❑ 702 Rookie Threats 1.00 .45
Luis Gonzalez
Karl Rhodes
Jeff Bagwell
❑ 703 Jose Mesa .05 .02
❑ 704 Dave Smith .05 .02
❑ 705 Danny Darwin .05 .02
❑ 706 Rafael Belliard .05 .02
❑ 707 Rob Murphy .05 .02
❑ 708 Terry Pendleton .10 .05
❑ 709 Mike Pagliarulo .05 .02
❑ 710 Sid Bream .05 .02
❑ 711 Junior Felix .05 .02
❑ 712 Dante Bichette .10 .05
❑ 713 Kevin Gross .05 .02
❑ 714 Luis Sojo .05 .02
❑ 715 Bob Ojeda .05 .02
❑ 716 Julio Machado .05 .02
❑ 717 Steve Farr .05 .02
❑ 718 Franklin Stubbs .05 .02
❑ 719 Mike Boddicker .05 .02
❑ 720 Willie Randolph .10 .05
❑ 721 Willie McGee .10 .05
❑ 722 Chili Davis .10 .05
❑ 723 Danny Jackson .05 .02
❑ 724 Cory Snyder .05 .02
❑ 725 MVP Lineup .15 .07
Andre Dawson
George Bell
Ryne Sandberg
❑ 726 Rob Deer .05 .02
❑ 727 Rich DeLucia .05 .02
❑ 728 Mike Perez RC .05 .02
❑ 729 Mickey Tettleton .05 .02
❑ 730 Mike Blowers .05 .02
❑ 731 Gary Gaetti .10 .05
❑ 732 Brett Butler .10 .05
❑ 733 Dave Parker .10 .05
❑ 734 Eddie Zosky .05 .02
❑ 735 Jack Clark .10 .05
❑ 736 Jack Morris .10 .05
❑ 737 Kirk Gibson .10 .05
❑ 738 Steve Bedrosian .05 .02
❑ 739 Candy Maldonado .05 .02
❑ 740 Matt Young .05 .02
❑ 741 Rich Garces RC .05 .02
❑ 742 George Bell .05 .02
❑ 743 Deion Sanders .10 .05
❑ 744 Bo Jackson .10 .05
❑ 745 Luis Mercedes RC .05 .02
❑ 746 Reggie Jefferson UER .05 .02
(Throwing left on card;
back has throws right)
❑ 747 Pete Incaviglia .05 .02
❑ 748 Chris Hammond .05 .02
❑ 749 Mike Stanton .05 .02
❑ 750 Scott Sanderson .05 .02
❑ 751 Paul Faries .05 .02
❑ 752 Al Osuna RC .05 .02
❑ 753 Steve Chitren .05 .02
❑ 754 Tony Fernandez .05 .02
❑ 755 Jeff Bagwell RC UER 2.50 1.10
(Strikeout and walk
totals reversed)
❑ 756 K.Dressendorfer RC .05 .02
❑ 757 Glenn Davis .05 .02
❑ 758 Gary Carter .15 .07
❑ 759 Zane Smith .05 .02
❑ 760 Vance Law .05 .02
❑ 761 Denis Boucher RC .05 .02
❑ 762 Turner Ward RC .10 .05
❑ 763 Roberto Alomar .20 .09
❑ 764 Albert Belle .10 .05
❑ 765 Joe Carter .10 .05
❑ 766 Pete Schourek RC .05 .02
❑ 767 H.Slocumb RC .10 .05
❑ 768 Vince Coleman .05 .02
❑ 769 Mitch Williams .05 .02
❑ 770 Brian Downing .05 .02
❑ 771 Dana Allison .05 .02
❑ 772 Pete Harnisch .05 .02
❑ 773 Tim Raines .10 .05
❑ 774 Darryl Kile .10 .05
❑ 775 Fred McGriff .15 .07
❑ 776 Dwight Evans .10 .05
❑ 777 Joe Slusarski .05 .02
❑ 778 Dave Righetti .10 .05
❑ 779 Jeff Hamilton .05 .02
❑ 780 Ernest Riles .05 .02
❑ 781 Ken Dayley .05 .02
❑ 782 Eric King .05 .02
❑ 783 Devon White .05 .02
❑ 784 Beau Allred .05 .02
❑ 785 Mike Timlin RC .10 .05
❑ 786 Ivan Calderon .05 .02
❑ 787 Hubie Brooks .05 .02
❑ 788 Juan Agosto .05 .02
❑ 789 Barry Jones .05 .02
❑ 790 Wally Backman .05 .02
❑ 791 Jim Presley .05 .02
❑ 792 Charlie Hough .10 .05
❑ 793 Larry Andersen .05 .02
❑ 794 Steve Finley .10 .05
❑ 795 Shawn Abner .05 .02
❑ 796 Jeff M. Robinson .05 .02
❑ 797 Joe Bitker .05 .02
❑ 798 Eric Show .05 .02
❑ 799 Bud Black .05 .02
❑ 800 Checklist 701-800 .05 .02
❑ HH1 H.Aaron Hologram 1.50 .70
❑ SP1 Michael Jordan SP 10.00 4.50
(Shown batting in
White Sox uniform)
❑ SP2 Rickey Henderson 3.00 1.35
Nolan Ryan
May 1, 1991 Records

1991 Upper Deck Final Edition

	MINT	NRMT
COMP.FACT.SET (100)	12.00	5.50

No.	Card	Mint	NrMt
❑ 1F	Ryan Klesko CL Reggie Sanders	.10	.05
❑ 2F	Pedro Martinez RC	8.00	3.60
❑ 3F	Lance Dickson	.05	.02
❑ 4F	Royce Clayton	.05	.02
❑ 5F	Scott Bryant	.05	.02
❑ 6F	Dan Wilson RC	.10	.05
❑ 7F	Dmitri Young RC	.50	.23
❑ 8F	Ryan Klesko RC	.75	.35
❑ 9F	Tom Goodwin	.05	.02
❑ 10F	Rondell White RC	.40	.18
❑ 11F	Reggie Sanders	.50	.23
❑ 12F	Todd Van Poppel	.05	.02
❑ 13F	Arthur Rhodes RC	.10	.05
❑ 14F	Eddie Zosky	.05	.02
❑ 15F	Gerald Williams RC	.20	.09
❑ 16F	Robert Eenhoorn RC	.05	.02
❑ 17F	Jim Thome RC	1.25	.55
❑ 18F	Marc Newfield RC	.05	.02
❑ 19F	Kerwin Moore RC	.05	.02
❑ 20F	Jeff McNeely RC	.05	.02
❑ 21F	Frankie Rodriguez RC	.05	.02
❑ 22F	Andy Mota	.05	.02
❑ 23F	Chris Haney RC	.05	.02
❑ 24F	Kenny Lofton RC	.50	.23
❑ 25F	Dave Nilsson RC	.10	.05
❑ 26F	Derek Bell	.10	.05
❑ 27F	Frank Castillo RC	.10	.05
❑ 28F	Candy Maldonado	.05	.02
❑ 29F	Chuck McElroy	.05	.02
❑ 30F	Chito Martinez	.05	.02
❑ 31F	Steve Howe	.05	.02
❑ 32F	Freddie Benavides	.05	.02
❑ 33F	Scott Kamieniecki RC	.05	.02
❑ 34F	Denny Neagle RC	.20	.09
❑ 35F	Mike Humphreys RC	.05	.02
❑ 36F	Mike Remlinger	.05	.02
❑ 37F	Scott Coolbaugh	.05	.02
❑ 38F	Darren Lewis	.05	.02
❑ 39F	Thomas Howard	.05	.02
❑ 40F	John Candelaria	.05	.02
❑ 41F	Todd Benzinger	.05	.02
❑ 42F	Wilson Alvarez	.05	.02
❑ 43F	Patrick Lennon RC	.05	.02
❑ 44F	Rusty Meacham RC	.05	.02
❑ 45F	Ryan Bowen RC	.05	.02
❑ 46F	Rick Wilkins RC	.05	.02
❑ 47F	Ed Sprague	.05	.02
❑ 48F	Bob Scanlan	.05	.02
❑ 49F	Tom Candiotti	.05	.02
❑ 50F	Dennis Martinez (Perfecto)	.10	.05
❑ 51F	Oil Can Boyd	.05	.02
❑ 52F	Glenallen Hill	.05	.02
❑ 53F	Scott Livingstone RC	.05	.02
❑ 54F	Brian R. Hunter RC	.10	.05
❑ 55F	Ivan Rodriguez RC	1.50	.70
❑ 56F	Keith Mitchell RC	.05	.02
❑ 57F	Roger McDowell	.05	.02
❑ 58F	Otis Nixon	.05	.02
❑ 59F	Juan Bell	.05	.02
❑ 60F	Bill Krueger	.05	.02
❑ 61F	Chris Donnels	.05	.02
❑ 62F	Tommy Greene	.05	.02
❑ 63F	Doug Simons	.05	.02
❑ 64F	Andy Ashby RC	.20	.09
❑ 65F	Anthony Young RC	.05	.02
❑ 66F	Kevin Morton	.05	.02
❑ 67F	Bret Barberie RC**	.05	.02
❑ 68F	Scott Servais RC	.10	.05
❑ 69F	Ron Darling	.05	.02
❑ 70F	Tim Burke	.05	.02
❑ 71F	Vicente Palacios	.05	.02
❑ 72F	Gerald Alexander	.05	.02
❑ 73F	Reggie Jefferson	.05	.02
❑ 74F	Dean Palmer	.10	.05
❑ 75F	Mark Whiten	.05	.02
❑ 76F	Randy Tomlin RC	.05	.02
❑ 77F	Mark Wohlers RC	.10	.05
❑ 78F	Brook Jacoby	.05	.02
❑ 79F	Ken Griffey Jr. CL Ryne Sandberg	.40	.18
❑ 80F	Jack Morris AS	.05	.02
❑ 81F	Sandy Alomar Jr. AS	.05	.02
❑ 82F	Cecil Fielder AS	.05	.02
❑ 83F	Roberto Alomar AS	.10	.05
❑ 84F	Wade Boggs AS	.10	.05
❑ 85F	Cal Ripken AS	.40	.18
❑ 86F	Rickey Henderson AS	.20	.09
❑ 87F	Ken Griffey Jr. AS	.40	.18
❑ 88F	Dave Henderson AS	.05	.02
❑ 89F	Danny Tartabull AS	.05	.02
❑ 90F	Tom Glavine AS	.10	.05
❑ 91F	Benito Santiago AS	.05	.02
❑ 92F	Will Clark AS	.10	.05
❑ 93F	Ryne Sandberg AS	.15	.07
❑ 94F	Chris Sabo AS	.05	.02
❑ 95F	Ozzie Smith AS	.15	.07
❑ 96F	Ivan Calderon AS	.05	.02
❑ 97F	Tony Gwynn AS	.20	.09
❑ 98F	Andre Dawson AS	.10	.05
❑ 99F	Bobby Bonilla AS	.05	.02
❑ 100F	Checklist 1-100	.05	.02

1992 Upper Deck

	MINT	NRMT
COMPLETE SET (800)	15.00	6.75
COMPLETE LO SET (700)	12.00	5.50
COMPLETE HI SET (100)	3.00	1.35

No.	Card	Mint	NrMt
❑ 1	Ryan Klesko CL Jim Thome	.25	.11
❑ 2	Royce Clayton SR	.05	.02
❑ 3	Brian Jordan SR RC	.50	.23
❑ 4	Dave Fleming SR	.05	.02
❑ 5	Jim Thome SR	.20	.09
❑ 6	Jeff Juden SR	.05	.02
❑ 7	Roberto Hernandez SR	.05	.02
❑ 8	Kyle Abbott SR	.05	.02
❑ 9	Chris George SR	.05	.02
❑ 10	Rob Maurer SR	.05	.02
❑ 11	Donald Harris SR	.05	.02
❑ 12	Ted Wood SR	.05	.02
❑ 13	Patrick Lennon SR	.05	.02
❑ 14	Willie Banks SR	.05	.02
❑ 15	Roger Salkeld SR UER (Bill was his grand- father, not his father)	.05	.02
❑ 16	Wil Cordero SR	.05	.02
❑ 17	Arthur Rhodes SR	.05	.02
❑ 18	Pedro Martinez SR	1.50	.70
❑ 19	Andy Ashby SR	.05	.02
❑ 20	Tom Goodwin SR	.05	.02
❑ 21	Braulio Castillo SR	.05	.02
❑ 22	Todd Van Poppel SR	.05	.02
❑ 23	Brian Williams SR RC	.05	.02
❑ 24	Ryan Klesko SR	.10	.05
❑ 25	Kenny Lofton SR	.20	.09
❑ 26	Derek Bell SR	.10	.05
❑ 27	Reggie Sanders SR	.05	.02
❑ 28	Dave Winfield's 400th	.10	.05
❑ 29	David Justice TC	.10	.05
❑ 30	Rob Dibble TC	.05	.02
❑ 31	Craig Biggio TC	.10	.05
❑ 32	Eddie Murray TC	.10	.05
❑ 33	Fred McGriff TC	.10	.05
❑ 34	Willie McGee TC	.05	.02
❑ 35	Shawon Dunston TC	.05	.02
❑ 36	Delino DeShields TC	.05	.02
❑ 37	Howard Johnson TC	.05	.02
❑ 38	John Kruk TC	.05	.02
❑ 39	Doug Drabek TC	.05	.02
❑ 40	Todd Zeile TC	.05	.02
❑ 41	Steve Avery Playoff Perfection	.05	.02
❑ 42	Jeremy Hernandez RC	.05	.02
❑ 43	Doug Henry RC	.05	.02
❑ 44	Chris Donnels	.05	.02
❑ 45	Mo Sanford	.05	.02
❑ 46	Scott Kamieniecki	.05	.02
❑ 47	Mark Lemke	.05	.02
❑ 48	Steve Farr	.05	.02
❑ 49	Francisco Oliveras	.05	.02
❑ 50	Ced Landrum	.05	.02
❑ 51	Rondell White CL Mark Newfield	.10	.05
❑ 52	Eduardo Perez TP RC	.05	.02
❑ 53	Tom Nevers TP	.05	.02
❑ 54	David Zancanaro TP	.05	.02
❑ 55	Shawn Green TP RC	2.00	.90
❑ 56	Mark Wohlers TP	.05	.02
❑ 57	Dave Nilsson TP	.05	.02
❑ 58	Dmitri Young TP	.10	.05
❑ 59	Ryan Hawblitzel TP RC	.05	.02
❑ 60	Raul Mondesi TP	.20	.09
❑ 61	Rondell White TP	.10	.05
❑ 62	Steve Hosey TP	.05	.02
❑ 63	Manny Ramirez TP RC	2.50	1.10
❑ 64	Marc Newfield TP	.05	.02
❑ 65	Jeromy Burnitz TP	.10	.05
❑ 66	Mark Smith TP RC	.05	.02
❑ 67	Joey Hamilton TP RC	.10	.05
❑ 68	Tyler Green TP RC	.05	.02
❑ 69	Jon Farrell TP RC	.05	.02
❑ 70	Kurt Miller TP	.05	.02
❑ 71	Jeff Plympton TP	.05	.02
❑ 72	Dan Wilson TP	.05	.02
❑ 73	Joe Vitiello TP RC	.05	.02
❑ 74	Rico Brogna TP	.05	.02
❑ 75	David McCarty TP RC	.10	.05
❑ 76	Bob Wickman TP	.05	.02
❑ 77	Carlos Rodriguez TP	.05	.02
❑ 78	Jim Abbott Stay In School	.05	.02
❑ 79	Ramon Martinez Pedro Martinez	.20	.09
❑ 80	Kevin Mitchell Keith Mitchell	.05	.02
❑ 81	Sandy Alomar Jr. Roberto Alomar	.10	.05
❑ 82	Cal Ripken Billy Ripken	.50	.23
❑ 83	Tony Gwynn Chris Gwynn	.20	.09
❑ 84	Dwight Gooden Gary Sheffield	.05	.02
❑ 85	Ken Griffey Sr. Ken Griffey Jr. Craig Griffey	.40	.18
❑ 86	Jim Abbott TC	.05	.02
❑ 87	Frank Thomas TC	.15	.07
❑ 88	Danny Tartabull TC	.05	.02
❑ 89	Scott Erickson TC	.05	.02
❑ 90	Rickey Henderson TC	.20	.09
❑ 91	Edgar Martinez TC	.10	.05
❑ 92	Nolan Ryan TC	.50	.23
❑ 93	Ben McDonald TC	.05	.02
❑ 94	Ellis Burks TC	.05	.02
❑ 95	Greg Swindell TC	.05	.02
❑ 96	Cecil Fielder TC	.05	.02

❑ 97 Greg Vaughn TC .05 .02
❑ 98 Kevin Maas TC .05 .02
❑ 99 Dave Stieb TC .05 .02
❑ 100 Checklist 1-100 .05 .02
❑ 101 Joe Oliver .05 .02
❑ 102 Hector Villanueva .05 .02
❑ 103 Ed Whitson .05 .02
❑ 104 Danny Jackson .05 .02
❑ 105 Chris Hammond .05 .02
❑ 106 Ricky Jordan .05 .02
❑ 107 Kevin Bass .05 .02
❑ 108 Darrin Fletcher .05 .02
❑ 109 Junior Ortiz .05 .02
❑ 110 Tom Bolton .05 .02
❑ 111 Jeff King .05 .02
❑ 112 Dave Magadan .05 .02
❑ 113 Mike LaValliere .05 .02
❑ 114 Hubie Brooks .05 .02
❑ 115 Jay Bell .10 .05
❑ 116 David Wells .10 .05
❑ 117 Jim Leyritz .05 .02
❑ 118 Manuel Lee .05 .02
❑ 119 Alvaro Espinoza .05 .02
❑ 120 B.J. Surhoff .10 .05
❑ 121 Hal Morris .05 .02
❑ 122 Shawon Dawson .05 .02
❑ 123 Chris Sabo .05 .02
❑ 124 Andre Dawson .15 .07
❑ 125 Eric Davis .10 .05
❑ 126 Chili Davis .10 .05
❑ 127 Dale Murphy .20 .09
❑ 128 Kirk McCaskill .05 .02
❑ 129 Terry Mulholland .05 .02
❑ 130 Rick Aguilera .10 .05
❑ 131 Vince Coleman .05 .02
❑ 132 Andy Van Slyke .10 .05
❑ 133 Gregg Jefferies .05 .02
❑ 134 Barry Bonds .50 .23
❑ 135 Dwight Gooden .10 .05
❑ 136 Dave Stieb .05 .02
❑ 137 Albert Belle .10 .05
❑ 138 Teddy Higuera .05 .02
❑ 139 Jesse Barfield .05 .02
❑ 140 Pat Borders .05 .02
❑ 141 Bip Roberts .05 .02
❑ 142 Rob Dibble .05 .02
❑ 143 Mark Grace .20 .09
❑ 144 Barry Larkin .20 .09
❑ 145 Ryne Sandberg .25 .11
❑ 146 Scott Erickson .05 .02
❑ 147 Luis Polonia .05 .02
❑ 148 John Burkett .05 .02
❑ 149 Luis Sojo .05 .02
❑ 150 Dickie Thon .05 .02
❑ 151 Walt Weiss .05 .02
❑ 152 Mike Scioscia .05 .02
❑ 153 Mark McGwire .75 .35
❑ 154 Matt Williams .15 .07
❑ 155 Rickey Henderson .40 .18
❑ 156 Sandy Alomar Jr. .10 .05
❑ 157 Brian McRae .05 .02
❑ 158 Harold Baines .10 .05
❑ 159 Kevin Appier .10 .05
❑ 160 Felix Fermin .05 .02
❑ 161 Leo Gomez .05 .02
❑ 162 Craig Biggio .15 .07
❑ 163 Ben McDonald .05 .02
❑ 164 Randy Johnson .25 .11
❑ 165 Cal Ripken .75 .35
❑ 166 Frank Thomas .25 .11
❑ 167 Delino DeShields .05 .02
❑ 168 Greg Gagne .05 .02
❑ 169 Ron Karkovice .05 .02
❑ 170 Charlie Leibrandt .05 .02
❑ 171 Dave Righetti .10 .05
❑ 172 Dave Henderson .05 .02
❑ 173 Steve Decker .05 .02
❑ 174 Darryl Strawberry .10 .05
❑ 175 Will Clark .20 .09
❑ 176 Ruben Sierra .05 .02
❑ 177 Ozzie Smith .25 .11
❑ 178 Charles Nagy .05 .02
❑ 179 Gary Pettis .05 .02
❑ 180 Kirk Gibson .10 .05
❑ 181 Randy Milligan .05 .02
❑ 182 Dave Valle .05 .02
❑ 183 Chris Hoiles .05 .02
❑ 184 Tony Phillips .05 .02
❑ 185 Brady Anderson .10 .05
❑ 186 Scott Fletcher .05 .02
❑ 187 Gene Larkin .05 .02
❑ 188 Lance Johnson .05 .02
❑ 189 Greg Olson .05 .02
❑ 190 Melido Perez .05 .02
❑ 191 Lenny Harris .05 .02
❑ 192 Terry Kennedy .05 .02
❑ 193 Mike Gallego .05 .02
❑ 194 Willie McGee .10 .05
❑ 195 Juan Samuel .05 .02
❑ 196 Jeff Huson .10 .05
(Shows Jose Canseco sliding into second)
❑ 197 Alex Cole .05 .02
❑ 198 Ron Robinson .05 .02
❑ 199 Joel Skinner .05 .02
❑ 200 Checklist 101-200 .05 .02
❑ 201 Kevin Reimer .05 .02
❑ 202 Stan Belinda .05 .02
❑ 203 Pat Tabler .05 .02
❑ 204 Jose Guzman .05 .02
❑ 205 Jose Lind .05 .02
❑ 206 Spike Owen .05 .02
❑ 207 Joe Orsulak .05 .02
❑ 208 Charlie Hayes .05 .02
❑ 209 Mike Devereaux .05 .02
❑ 210 Mike Fitzgerald .05 .02
❑ 211 Willie Randolph .10 .05
❑ 212 Rod Nichols .05 .02
❑ 213 Mike Boddicker .05 .02
❑ 214 Bill Spiers .05 .02
❑ 215 Steve Olin .05 .02
❑ 216 David Howard .05 .02
❑ 217 Gary Varsho .05 .02
❑ 218 Mike Harkey .05 .02
❑ 219 Luis Aquino .05 .02
❑ 220 Chuck McElroy .05 .02
❑ 221 Doug Drabek .05 .02
❑ 222 Dave Winfield .20 .09
❑ 223 Rafael Palmeiro .20 .09
❑ 224 Joe Carter .10 .05
❑ 225 Bobby Bonilla .10 .05
❑ 226 Ivan Calderon .05 .02
❑ 227 Gregg Olson .05 .02
❑ 228 Tim Wallach .05 .02
❑ 229 Terry Pendleton .10 .05
❑ 230 Gilberto Reyes .05 .02
❑ 231 Carlos Baerga .05 .02
❑ 232 Greg Vaughn .10 .05
❑ 233 Bret Saberhagen .10 .05
❑ 234 Gary Sheffield .10 .05
❑ 235 Mark Lewis .05 .02
❑ 236 George Bell .05 .02
❑ 237 Danny Tartabull .05 .02
❑ 238 Willie Wilson .05 .02
❑ 239 Doug Dascenzo .05 .02
❑ 240 Bill Pecota .05 .02
❑ 241 Julio Franco .10 .05
❑ 242 Ed Sprague .05 .02
❑ 243 Juan Gonzalez .20 .09
❑ 244 Chuck Finley .10 .05
❑ 245 Ivan Rodriguez .25 .11
❑ 246 Len Dykstra .10 .05
❑ 247 Deion Sanders .10 .05
❑ 248 Dwight Evans .10 .05
❑ 249 Larry Walker .15 .07
❑ 250 Billy Ripken .05 .02
❑ 251 Mickey Tettleton .05 .02
❑ 252 Tony Pena .05 .02
❑ 253 Benito Santiago .05 .02
❑ 254 Kirby Puckett .50 .23
❑ 255 Cecil Fielder .10 .05
❑ 256 Howard Johnson .05 .02
❑ 257 Andujar Cedeno .05 .02
❑ 258 Jose Rijo .05 .02
❑ 259 Al Osuna .05 .02
❑ 260 Todd Hundley .05 .02
❑ 261 Orel Hershiser .10 .05
❑ 262 Ray Lankford .05 .02
❑ 263 Robin Ventura .10 .05
❑ 264 Felix Jose .05 .02
❑ 265 Eddie Murray .20 .09
❑ 266 Kevin Mitchell .05 .02
❑ 267 Gary Carter .15 .07
❑ 268 Mike Benjamin .05 .02
❑ 269 Dick Schofield .05 .02
❑ 270 Jose Uribe .05 .02
❑ 271 Pete Incaviglia .05 .02
❑ 272 Tony Fernandez .05 .02
❑ 273 Alan Trammell .15 .07
❑ 274 Tony Gwynn .40 .18
❑ 275 Mike Greenwell .05 .02
❑ 276 Jeff Bagwell .40 .18
❑ 277 Frank Viola .10 .05
❑ 278 Randy Myers .05 .02
❑ 279 Ken Caminiti .10 .05
❑ 280 Bill Doran .05 .02
❑ 281 Dan Pasqua .05 .02
❑ 282 Alfredo Griffin .05 .02
❑ 283 Jose Oquendo .05 .02
❑ 284 Kal Daniels .05 .02
❑ 285 Bobby Thigpen .05 .02
❑ 286 Robby Thompson .05 .02
❑ 287 Mark Eichhorn .05 .02
❑ 288 Mike Felder .05 .02
❑ 289 Dave Gallagher .05 .02
❑ 290 Dave Anderson .05 .02
❑ 291 Mel Hall .05 .02
❑ 292 Jerald Clark .05 .02
❑ 293 Al Newman .05 .02
❑ 294 Rob Deer .05 .02
❑ 295 Matt Nokes .05 .02
❑ 296 Jack Armstrong .05 .02
❑ 297 Jim Deshaies .05 .02
❑ 298 Jeff Innis .05 .02
❑ 299 Jeff Reed .05 .02
❑ 300 Checklist 201-300 .05 .02
❑ 301 Lonnie Smith .05 .02
❑ 302 Jimmy Key .10 .05
❑ 303 Junior Felix .05 .02
❑ 304 Mike Heath .05 .02
❑ 305 Mark Langston .05 .02
❑ 306 Greg W. Harris .05 .02
❑ 307 Brett Butler .10 .05
❑ 308 Luis Rivera .05 .02
❑ 309 Bruce Ruffin .05 .02
❑ 310 Paul Faries .05 .02
❑ 311 Terry Leach .05 .02
❑ 312 Scott Brosius RC .50 .23
❑ 313 Scott Leius .05 .02
❑ 314 Harold Reynolds .05 .02
❑ 315 Jack Morris .10 .05
❑ 316 David Segui .05 .02
❑ 317 Bill Gullickson .05 .02
❑ 318 Todd Frohwirth .05 .02
❑ 319 Mark Leiter .05 .02
❑ 320 Jeff M. Robinson .05 .02
❑ 321 Gary Gaetti .10 .05
❑ 322 John Smoltz .10 .05
❑ 323 Andy Benes .05 .02
❑ 324 Kelly Gruber .05 .02
❑ 325 Jim Abbott .10 .05
❑ 326 John Kruk .10 .05
❑ 327 Kevin Seitzer .05 .02
❑ 328 Darrin Jackson .05 .02
❑ 329 Kurt Stillwell .05 .02
❑ 330 Mike Maddux .05 .02
❑ 331 Dennis Eckersley .10 .05
❑ 332 Dan Gladden .05 .02
❑ 333 Jose Canseco .20 .09
❑ 334 Kent Hrbek .10 .05
❑ 335 Ken Griffey Sr. .10 .05
❑ 336 Greg Swindell .05 .02
❑ 337 Trevor Wilson .05 .02
❑ 338 Sam Horn .05 .02
❑ 339 Mike Henneman .05 .02
❑ 340 Jerry Browne .05 .02
❑ 341 Glenn Braggs .05 .02
❑ 342 Tom Glavine .20 .09
❑ 343 Wally Joyner .10 .05
❑ 344 Fred McGriff .15 .07
❑ 345 Ron Gant .05 .02
❑ 346 Ramon Martinez .05 .02
❑ 347 Wes Chamberlain .05 .02
❑ 348 Terry Shumpert .05 .02
❑ 349 Tim Teufel .05 .02
❑ 350 Wally Backman .05 .02
❑ 351 Joe Girardi .05 .02
❑ 352 Devon White .05 .02

❑ 353 Greg Maddux .50 .23
❑ 354 Ryan Bowen .05 .02
❑ 355 Roberto Alomar .20 .09
❑ 356 Don Mattingly .50 .23
❑ 357 Pedro Guerrero .10 .05
❑ 358 Steve Sax .05 .02
❑ 359 Joey Cora .05 .02
❑ 360 Jim Gantner .05 .02
❑ 361 Brian Barnes .05 .02
❑ 362 Kevin McReynolds .05 .02
❑ 363 Bret Barberie .05 .02
❑ 364 David Cone .10 .05
❑ 365 Dennis Martinez .10 .05
❑ 366 Brian Hunter .05 .02
❑ 367 Edgar Martinez .15 .07
❑ 368 Steve Finley .10 .05
❑ 369 Greg Briley .05 .02
❑ 370 Jeff Blauser .05 .02
❑ 371 Todd Stottlemyre .05 .02
❑ 372 Luis Gonzalez .20 .09
❑ 373 Rick Wilkins .05 .02
❑ 374 Darryl Kile .10 .05
❑ 375 John Olerud .10 .05
❑ 376 Lee Smith .10 .05
❑ 377 Kevin Maas .05 .02
❑ 378 Dante Bichette .10 .05
❑ 379 Tom Pagnozzi .05 .02
❑ 380 Mike Flanagan .05 .02
❑ 381 Charlie O'Brien .05 .02
❑ 382 Dave Martinez .05 .02
❑ 383 Keith Miller .05 .02
❑ 384 Scott Ruskin .05 .02
❑ 385 Kevin Elster .05 .02
❑ 386 Alvin Davis .05 .02
❑ 387 Casey Candaele .05 .02
❑ 388 Pete O'Brien .05 .02
❑ 389 Jeff Treadway .05 .02
❑ 390 Scott Bradley .05 .02
❑ 391 Mookie Wilson .10 .05
❑ 392 Jimmy Jones .05 .02
❑ 393 Candy Maldonado .05 .02
❑ 394 Eric Yelding .05 .02
❑ 395 Tom Henke .05 .02
❑ 396 Franklin Stubbs .05 .02
❑ 397 Milt Thompson .05 .02
❑ 398 Mark Carreon .05 .02
❑ 399 Randy Velarde .05 .02
❑ 400 Checklist 301-400 .05 .02
❑ 401 Omar Vizquel .10 .05
❑ 402 Joe Boever .05 .02
❑ 403 Bill Krueger .05 .02
❑ 404 Jody Reed .05 .02
❑ 405 Mike Schooler .05 .02
❑ 406 Jason Grimsley .05 .02
❑ 407 Greg Myers .05 .02
❑ 408 Randy Ready .05 .02
❑ 409 Mike Timlin .05 .02
❑ 410 Mitch Williams .05 .02
❑ 411 Garry Templeton .05 .02
❑ 412 Greg Cadaret .05 .02
❑ 413 Donnie Hill .05 .02
❑ 414 Wally Whitehurst .05 .02
❑ 415 Scott Sanderson .05 .02
❑ 416 Thomas Howard .05 .02
❑ 417 Neal Heaton .05 .02
❑ 418 Charlie Hough .10 .05
❑ 419 Jack Howell .05 .02
❑ 420 Greg Hibbard .05 .02
❑ 421 Carlos Quintana .05 .02
❑ 422 Kim Batiste .05 .02
❑ 423 Paul Molitor .20 .09
❑ 424 Ken Griffey Jr. .60 .25
❑ 425 Phil Plantier .05 .02
❑ 426 Denny Neagle .10 .05
❑ 427 Von Hayes .05 .02
❑ 428 Shane Mack .05 .02
❑ 429 Darren Daulton .10 .05
❑ 430 Dwayne Henry .05 .02
❑ 431 Lance Parrish .10 .05
❑ 432 Mike Humphreys .05 .02
❑ 433 Tim Burke .05 .02
❑ 434 Bryan Harvey .05 .02
❑ 435 Pat Kelly .05 .02
❑ 436 Ozzie Guillen .05 .02
❑ 437 Bruce Hurst .05 .02
❑ 438 Sammy Sosa .40 .18
❑ 439 Dennis Rasmussen .05 .02
❑ 440 Ken Patterson .05 .02
❑ 441 Jay Buhner .10 .05
❑ 442 Pat Combs .05 .02
❑ 443 Wade Boggs .20 .09
❑ 444 George Brett .40 .18
❑ 445 Mo Vaughn .10 .05
❑ 446 Chuck Knoblauch .10 .05
❑ 447 Tom Candiotti .05 .02
❑ 448 Mark Portugal .05 .02
❑ 449 Mickey Morandini .05 .02
❑ 450 Duane Ward .05 .02
❑ 451 Otis Nixon .05 .02
❑ 452 Bob Welch .05 .02
❑ 453 Rusty Meacham .05 .02
❑ 454 Keith Mitchell .05 .02
❑ 455 Marquis Grissom .05 .02
❑ 456 Robin Yount .20 .09
❑ 457 Harvey Pulliam .05 .02
❑ 458 Jose DeLeon .05 .02
❑ 459 Mark Gubicza .05 .02
❑ 460 Darryl Hamilton .05 .02
❑ 461 Tom Browning .05 .02
❑ 462 Monty Fariss .05 .02
❑ 463 Jerome Walton .05 .02
❑ 464 Paul O'Neill .20 .09
❑ 465 Dean Palmer .10 .05
❑ 466 Travis Fryman .10 .05
❑ 467 John Smiley .05 .02
❑ 468 Lloyd Moseby .05 .02
❑ 469 John Wehner .05 .02
❑ 470 Skeeter Barnes .05 .02
❑ 471 Steve Chitren .05 .02
❑ 472 Kent Mercker .05 .02
❑ 473 Terry Steinbach .05 .02
❑ 474 Andres Galarraga .15 .07
❑ 475 Steve Avery .05 .02
❑ 476 Tom Gordon .05 .02
❑ 477 Cal Eldred .05 .02
❑ 478 Omar Olivares .05 .02
❑ 479 Julio Machado .05 .02
❑ 480 Bob Milacki .05 .02
❑ 481 Les Lancaster .05 .02
❑ 482 John Candelaria .05 .02
❑ 483 Brian Downing .05 .02
❑ 484 Roger McDowell .05 .02
❑ 485 Scott Scudder .05 .02
❑ 486 Zane Smith .05 .02
❑ 487 John Cerutti .05 .02
❑ 488 Steve Buechele .05 .02
❑ 489 Paul Gibson .05 .02
❑ 490 Curtis Wilkerson .05 .02
❑ 491 Marvin Freeman .05 .02
❑ 492 Tom Foley .05 .02
❑ 493 Juan Berenguer .05 .02
❑ 494 Ernest Riles .05 .02
❑ 495 Sid Bream .05 .02
❑ 496 Chuck Crim .05 .02
❑ 497 Mike Macfarlane .05 .02
❑ 498 Dale Sveum .05 .02
❑ 499 Storm Davis .05 .02
❑ 500 Checklist 401-500 .05 .02
❑ 501 Jeff Reardon .10 .05
❑ 502 Shawn Abner .05 .02
❑ 503 Tony Fossas .05 .02
❑ 504 Cory Snyder .05 .02
❑ 505 Matt Young .05 .02
❑ 506 Allan Anderson .05 .02
❑ 507 Mark Lee .05 .02
❑ 508 Gene Nelson .05 .02
❑ 509 Mike Pagliarulo .05 .02
❑ 510 Rafael Belliard .05 .02
❑ 511 Jay Howell .05 .02
❑ 512 Bob Tewksbury .05 .02
❑ 513 Mike Morgan .05 .02
❑ 514 John Franco .10 .05
❑ 515 Kevin Gross .05 .02
❑ 516 Lou Whitaker .10 .05
❑ 517 Orlando Merced .05 .02
❑ 518 Todd Benzinger .05 .02
❑ 519 Gary Redus .05 .02
❑ 520 Walt Terrell .05 .02
❑ 521 Jack Clark .10 .05
❑ 522 Dave Parker .10 .05
❑ 523 Tim Naehring .05 .02
❑ 524 Mark Whiten .05 .02
❑ 525 Ellis Burks .10 .05
❑ 526 Frank Castillo .05 .02
❑ 527 Brian Harper .05 .02
❑ 528 Brook Jacoby .05 .02
❑ 529 Rick Sutcliffe .10 .05
❑ 530 Joe Klink .05 .02
❑ 531 Terry Bross .05 .02
❑ 532 Jose Offerman .05 .02
❑ 533 Todd Zeile .05 .02
❑ 534 Eric Karros .10 .05
❑ 535 Anthony Young .05 .02
❑ 536 Milt Cuyler .05 .02
❑ 537 Randy Tomlin .05 .02
❑ 538 Scott Livingstone .05 .02
❑ 539 Jim Eisenreich .05 .02
❑ 540 Don Slaught .05 .02
❑ 541 Scott Cooper .05 .02
❑ 542 Joe Grahe .05 .02
❑ 543 Tom Brunansky .05 .02
❑ 544 Eddie Zosky .05 .02
❑ 545 Roger Clemens .50 .23
❑ 546 David Justice .10 .05
❑ 547 Dave Stewart .10 .05
❑ 548 David West .05 .02
❑ 549 Dave Smith .05 .02
❑ 550 Dan Plesac .05 .02
❑ 551 Alex Fernandez .05 .02
❑ 552 Bernard Gilkey .05 .02
❑ 553 Jack McDowell .05 .02
❑ 554 Tino Martinez .10 .05
❑ 555 Bo Jackson .10 .05
❑ 556 Bernie Williams .20 .09
❑ 557 Mark Gardner .05 .02
❑ 558 Glenallen Hill .05 .02
❑ 559 Oil Can Boyd .05 .02
❑ 560 Chris James .05 .02
❑ 561 Scott Servais .05 .02
❑ 562 Rey Sanchez RC .10 .05
❑ 563 Paul McClellan .05 .02
❑ 564 Andy Mota .05 .02
❑ 565 Darren Lewis .05 .02
❑ 566 Jose Melendez .05 .02
❑ 567 Tommy Greene .05 .02
❑ 568 Rich Rodriguez .05 .02
❑ 569 Heathcliff Slocumb .05 .02
❑ 570 Joe Hesketh .05 .02
❑ 571 Carlton Fisk .20 .09
❑ 572 Erik Hanson .05 .02
❑ 573 Wilson Alvarez .05 .02
❑ 574 Rheal Cormier .05 .02
❑ 575 Tim Raines .10 .05
❑ 576 Bobby Witt .05 .02
❑ 577 Roberto Kelly .05 .02
❑ 578 Kevin Brown .10 .05
❑ 579 Chris Nabholz .05 .02
❑ 580 Jesse Orosco .05 .02
❑ 581 Jeff Brantley .05 .02
❑ 582 Rafael Ramirez .05 .02
❑ 583 Kelly Downs .05 .02
❑ 584 Mike Simms .05 .02
❑ 585 Mike Remlinger .05 .02
❑ 586 Dave Hollins .05 .02
❑ 587 Larry Andersen .05 .02
❑ 588 Mike Gardiner .05 .02
❑ 589 Craig Lefferts .05 .02
❑ 590 Paul Assenmacher .05 .02
❑ 591 Bryn Smith .05 .02
❑ 592 Donn Pall .05 .02
❑ 593 Mike Jackson .05 .02
❑ 594 Scott Radinsky .05 .02
❑ 595 Brian Holman .05 .02
❑ 596 Geronimo Pena .05 .02
❑ 597 Mike Jeffcoat .05 .02
❑ 598 Carlos Martinez .05 .02
❑ 599 Geno Petralli .05 .02
❑ 600 Checklist 501-600 .05 .02
❑ 601 Jerry Don Gleaton .05 .02
❑ 602 Adam Peterson .05 .02
❑ 603 Craig Grebeck .05 .02
❑ 604 Mark Guthrie .05 .02
❑ 605 Frank Tanana .05 .02
❑ 606 Hensley Meulens .05 .02
❑ 607 Mark Davis .05 .02
❑ 608 Eric Plunk .05 .02
❑ 609 Mark Williamson .05 .02
❑ 610 Lee Guetterman .05 .02

❑ 611 Bobby Rose	.05	.02
❑ 612 Bill Wegman	.05	.02
❑ 613 Mike Hartley	.05	.02
❑ 614 Chris Beasley	.05	.02
❑ 615 Chris Bosio	.05	.02
❑ 616 Henry Cotto	.05	.02
❑ 617 Chico Walker	.05	.02
❑ 618 Russ Swan	.05	.02
❑ 619 Bob Walk	.05	.02
❑ 620 Bill Swift	.05	.02
❑ 621 Warren Newson	.05	.02
❑ 622 Steve Bedrosian	.05	.02
❑ 623 Ricky Bones	.05	.02
❑ 624 Kevin Tapani	.05	.02
❑ 625 Juan Guzman	.05	.02
❑ 626 Jeff Johnson	.05	.02
❑ 627 Jeff Montgomery	.05	.02
❑ 628 Ken Hill	.05	.02
❑ 629 Gary Thurman	.05	.02
❑ 630 Steve Howe	.05	.02
❑ 631 Jose DeJesus	.05	.02
❑ 632 Kirk Dressendorfer	.05	.02
❑ 633 Jaime Navarro	.05	.02
❑ 634 Lee Stevens	.05	.02
❑ 635 Pete Harnisch	.05	.02
❑ 636 Bill Landrum	.05	.02
❑ 637 Rich DeLucia	.05	.02
❑ 638 Luis Salazar	.05	.02
❑ 639 Rob Murphy	.05	.02
❑ 640 Jose Canseco CL	.20	.09
Rickey Henderson		
❑ 641 Roger Clemens DS	.25	.11
❑ 642 Jim Abbott DS	.05	.02
❑ 643 Travis Fryman DS	.05	.02
❑ 644 Jesse Barfield DS	.05	.02
❑ 645 Cal Ripken DS	.40	.18
❑ 646 Wade Boggs DS	.10	.05
❑ 647 Cecil Fielder DS	.05	.02
❑ 648 Rickey Henderson DS	.20	.09
❑ 649 Jose Canseco DS	.10	.05
❑ 650 Ken Griffey Jr. DS	.50	.23
❑ 651 Kenny Rogers	.05	.02
❑ 652 Luis Mercedes	.05	.02
❑ 653 Mike Stanton	.05	.02
❑ 654 Glenn Davis	.05	.02
❑ 655 Nolan Ryan	1.00	.45
❑ 656 Reggie Jefferson	.05	.02
❑ 657 Javier Ortiz	.05	.02
❑ 658 Greg A. Harris	.05	.02
❑ 659 Mariano Duncan	.05	.02
❑ 660 Jeff Shaw	.05	.02
❑ 661 Mike Moore	.05	.02
❑ 662 Chris Haney	.05	.02
❑ 663 Joe Slusarski	.05	.02
❑ 664 Wayne Housie	.05	.02
❑ 665 Carlos Garcia	.05	.02
❑ 666 Bob Ojeda	.05	.02
❑ 667 Bryan Hickerson RC	.05	.02
❑ 668 Tim Belcher	.05	.02
❑ 669 Ron Darling	.05	.02
❑ 670 Rex Hudler	.05	.02
❑ 671 Sid Fernandez	.05	.02
❑ 672 Chito Martinez	.05	.02
❑ 673 Pete Schourek	.05	.02
❑ 674 Armando Reynoso RC	.10	.05
❑ 675 Mike Mussina	.30	.14
❑ 676 Kevin Morton	.05	.02
❑ 677 Norm Charlton	.05	.02
❑ 678 Danny Darwin	.05	.02
❑ 679 Eric King	.05	.02
❑ 680 Ted Power	.05	.02
❑ 681 Barry Jones	.05	.02
❑ 682 Carney Lansford	.10	.05
❑ 683 Mel Rojas	.05	.02
❑ 684 Rick Honeycutt	.05	.02
❑ 685 Jeff Fassero	.05	.02
❑ 686 Cris Carpenter	.05	.02
❑ 687 Tim Crews	.05	.02
❑ 688 Scott Terry	.05	.02
❑ 689 Chris Gwynn	.05	.02
❑ 690 Gerald Perry	.05	.02
❑ 691 John Barfield	.05	.02
❑ 692 Bob Melvin	.05	.02
❑ 693 Juan Agosto	.05	.02
❑ 694 Alejandro Pena	.05	.02
❑ 695 Jeff Russell	.05	.02
❑ 696 Carmelo Martinez	.05	.02
❑ 697 Bud Black	.05	.02
❑ 698 Dave Otto	.05	.02
❑ 699 Billy Hatcher	.05	.02
❑ 700 Checklist 601-700	.05	.02
❑ 701 Clemente Nunez RC	.05	.02
❑ 702 Rookie Threats	.05	.02
Mark Clark		
Donovan Osborne		
Brian Jordan		
❑ 703 Mike Morgan	.05	.02
❑ 704 Keith Miller	.05	.02
❑ 705 Kurt Stillwell	.05	.02
❑ 706 Damon Berryhill	.05	.02
❑ 707 Von Hayes	.05	.02
❑ 708 Rick Sutcliffe	.10	.05
❑ 709 Hubie Brooks	.05	.02
❑ 710 Ryan Turner RC	.05	.02
❑ 711 Barry Bonds CL	.25	.11
Andy Van Slyke		
❑ 712 Jose Rijo DS	.05	.02
❑ 713 Tom Glavine DS	.10	.05
❑ 714 Shawon Dunston DS	.05	.02
❑ 715 Andy Van Slyke DS	.05	.02
❑ 716 Ozzie Smith DS	.15	.07
❑ 717 Tony Gwynn DS	.20	.09
❑ 718 Will Clark DS	.10	.05
❑ 719 Marquis Grissom DS	.05	.02
❑ 720 Howard Johnson DS	.05	.02
❑ 721 Barry Bonds DS	.25	.11
❑ 722 Kirk McCaskill	.05	.02
❑ 723 Sammy Sosa	.75	.35
❑ 724 George Bell	.05	.02
❑ 725 Gregg Jefferies	.05	.02
❑ 726 Gary DiSarcina	.05	.02
❑ 727 Mike Bordick	.05	.02
❑ 728 Eddie Murray	.10	.05
400 Home Run Club		
❑ 729 Rene Gonzales	.05	.02
❑ 730 Mike Bielecki	.05	.02
❑ 731 Calvin Jones	.05	.02
❑ 732 Jack Morris	.10	.05
❑ 733 Frank Viola	.10	.05
❑ 734 Dave Winfield	.20	.09
❑ 735 Kevin Mitchell	.05	.02
❑ 736 Bill Swift	.05	.02
❑ 737 Dan Gladden	.05	.02
❑ 738 Mike Jackson	.05	.02
❑ 739 Mark Carreon	.05	.02
❑ 740 Kirt Manwaring	.05	.02
❑ 741 Randy Myers	.05	.02
❑ 742 Kevin McReynolds	.05	.02
❑ 743 Steve Sax	.05	.02
❑ 744 Wally Joyner	.10	.05
❑ 745 Gary Sheffield	.10	.05
❑ 746 Danny Tartabull	.05	.02
❑ 747 Julio Valera	.05	.02
❑ 748 Denny Neagle	.10	.05
❑ 749 Lance Blankenship	.05	.02
❑ 750 Mike Gallego	.05	.02
❑ 751 Bret Saberhagen	.10	.05
❑ 752 Ruben Amaro	.05	.02
❑ 753 Eddie Murray	.20	.09
❑ 754 Kyle Abbott	.05	.02
❑ 755 Bobby Bonilla	.10	.05
❑ 756 Eric Davis	.10	.05
❑ 757 Eddie Taubensee RC	.10	.05
❑ 758 Andres Galarraga	.15	.07
❑ 759 Pete Incaviglia	.05	.02
❑ 760 Tom Candiotti	.05	.02
❑ 761 Tim Belcher	.05	.02
❑ 762 Ricky Bones	.05	.02
❑ 763 Bip Roberts	.05	.02
❑ 764 Pedro Munoz	.05	.02
❑ 765 Greg Swindell	.05	.02
❑ 766 Kenny Lofton	.20	.09
❑ 767 Gary Carter	.15	.07
❑ 768 Charlie Hayes	.05	.02
❑ 769 Dickie Thon	.05	.02
❑ 770 Donovan Osborne DD CL	.05	.02
❑ 771 Bret Boone DD	.75	.35
❑ 772 Archi Cianfrocco DD RC	.05	.02
❑ 773 Mark Clark DD RC	.10	.05
❑ 774 Chad Curtis DD RC	.10	.05
❑ 775 Pat Listach DD RC	.10	.05
❑ 776 Pat Mahomes DD RC	.05	.02
❑ 777 Donovan Osborne DD	.05	.02
❑ 778 John Patterson DD	.05	.02
❑ 779 Andy Stankiewicz DD	.05	.02
❑ 780 Turk Wendell DD RC	.10	.05
❑ 781 Bill Krueger	.05	.02
❑ 782 Rickey Henderson	.20	.09
Grand Theft		
❑ 783 Kevin Seitzer	.05	.02
❑ 784 Dave Martinez	.05	.02
❑ 785 John Smiley	.05	.02
❑ 786 Matt Stairs RC	.10	.05
❑ 787 Scott Scudder	.05	.02
❑ 788 John Wetteland	.10	.05
❑ 789 Jack Armstrong	.05	.02
❑ 790 Ken Hill	.05	.02
❑ 791 Dick Schofield	.05	.02
❑ 792 Mariano Duncan	.05	.02
❑ 793 Bill Pecota	.05	.02
❑ 794 Mike Kelly RC	.05	.02
❑ 795 Willie Randolph	.10	.05
❑ 796 Butch Henry	.05	.02
❑ 797 Carlos Hernandez	.05	.02
❑ 798 Doug Jones	.05	.02
❑ 799 Melido Perez	.05	.02
❑ 800 Checklist 701-800	.05	.02
❑ HH2 T.Williams Hologram	2.00	.90
Top left corner says		
91 Upper Deck 92		
❑ SP3 Deion Sanders FB/BB	.50	.23
❑ SP4 Tom Selleck	1.00	.45
Frank Thomas SP		
(Mr. Baseball)		

1993 Upper Deck

	MINT	NRMT
COMPLETE SET (840)	40.00	18.00
COMP.FACT.SET (840)	50.00	22.00
COMPLETE SERIES 1 (420)	15.00	6.75
COMPLETE SERIES 2 (420)	25.00	11.00

❑ 1 Tim Salmon CL	.10	.05
❑ 2 Mike Piazza SR	2.00	.90
❑ 3 Rene Arocha SR RC	.15	.07
❑ 4 Willie Greene SR	.10	.05
❑ 5 Manny Alexander	.10	.05
❑ 6 Dan Wilson	.15	.07
❑ 7 Dan Smith	.10	.05
❑ 8 Kevin Rogers	.10	.05
❑ 9 Kurt Miller SR	.10	.05
❑ 10 Joe Vitko	.10	.05
❑ 11 Tim Costo	.10	.05
❑ 12 Alan Embree SR	.10	.05
❑ 13 Jim Tatum SR RC	.10	.05
❑ 14 Cris Colon	.10	.05
❑ 15 Steve Hosey	.10	.05
❑ 16 Sterling Hitchcock SR RC	.15	.07
❑ 17 Dave Mlicki	.10	.05
❑ 18 Jessie Hollins	.10	.05
❑ 19 Bobby Jones SR	.15	.07
❑ 20 Kurt Miller	.10	.05
❑ 21 Melvin Nieves SR	.10	.05
❑ 22 Billy Ashley SR	.10	.05
❑ 23 J.T. Snow SR RC	.50	.23
❑ 24 Chipper Jones SR	1.00	.45
❑ 25 Tim Salmon SR	.15	.07
❑ 26 Tim Pugh SR RC	.10	.05
❑ 27 David Nied SR	.10	.05

❑ 28 Mike Trombley .10 .05
❑ 29 Javier Lopez SR .15 .07
❑ 30 Jim Abbott CH CL .10 .05
❑ 31 Jim Abbott CH .10 .05
❑ 32 Dale Murphy CH .15 .07
❑ 33 Tony Pena CH .10 .05
❑ 34 Kirby Puckett CH .50 .23
❑ 35 Harold Reynolds CH .10 .05
❑ 36 Cal Ripken CH .75 .35
❑ 37 Nolan Ryan CH 1.00 .45
❑ 38 Ryne Sandberg CH .25 .11
❑ 39 Dave Stewart CH .10 .05
❑ 40 Dave Winfield CH .15 .07
❑ 41 Joe Carter CL .40 .18
Mark McGwire
❑ 42 Blockbuster Trade .15 .07
Joe Carter
Roberto Alomar
❑ 43 Brew Crew .15 .07
Paul Molitor
Pat Listach
Robin Yount
❑ 44 Iron and Steel .40 .18
Cal Ripken
Brady Anderson
❑ 45 Youthful Tribe .25 .11
Albert Belle
Sandy Alomar Jr.
Jim Thome
Carlos Baerga
Kenny Lofton
❑ 46 Motown Mashers .10 .05
Cecil Fielder
Mickey Tettleton
❑ 47 Yankee Pride .15 .07
Roberto Kelly
Don Mattingly
❑ 48 Boston Cy Sox .25 .11
Frank Viola
Roger Clemens
❑ 49 Bash Brothers .40 .18
Ruben Sierra
Mark McGwire
❑ 50 Twin Titles .25 .11
Kent Hrbek
Kirby Puckett
❑ 51 Southside Sluggers .25 .11
Robin Ventura
Frank Thomas
❑ 52 Latin Stars .15 .07
Juan Gonzalez
Jose Canseco
Ivan Rodriguez
Rafael Palmeiro
❑ 53 Lethal Lefties .10 .05
Mark Langston
Jim Abbott
Chuck Finley
❑ 54 Royal Family .10 .05
Wally Joyner
Gregg Jefferies
George Brett
❑ 55 Pacific Sock Exchange .40 .18
Kevin Mitchell
Ken Griffey Jr.
Jay Buhner
❑ 56 George Brett .75 .35
❑ 57 Scott Cooper .10 .05
❑ 58 Mike Maddux .10 .05
❑ 59 Rusty Meacham .10 .05
❑ 60 Wil Cordero .10 .05
❑ 61 Tim Teufel .10 .05
❑ 62 Jeff Montgomery .10 .05
❑ 63 Scott Livingstone .10 .05
❑ 64 Doug Dascenzo .10 .05
❑ 65 Bret Boone .15 .07
❑ 66 Tim Wakefield .10 .05
❑ 67 Curt Schilling .40 .18
❑ 68 Frank Tanana .10 .05
❑ 69 Len Dykstra .15 .07
❑ 70 Derek Lilliquist .10 .05
❑ 71 Anthony Young .10 .05
❑ 72 Hipolito Pichardo .10 .05
❑ 73 Rod Beck .10 .05
❑ 74 Kent Hrbek .15 .07
❑ 75 Tom Glavine .40 .18
❑ 76 Kevin Brown .15 .07
❑ 77 Chuck Finley .15 .07
❑ 78 Bob Walk .10 .05
❑ 79 Rheal Cormier UER .10 .05
(Born in New Brunswick,
not British Columbia)
❑ 80 Rick Sutcliffe .15 .07
❑ 81 Harold Baines .15 .07
❑ 82 Lee Smith .15 .07
❑ 83 Geno Petralli .10 .05
❑ 84 Jose Oquendo .10 .05
❑ 85 Mark Gubicza .10 .05
❑ 86 Mickey Tettleton .10 .05
❑ 87 Bobby Witt .10 .05
❑ 88 Mark Lewis .10 .05
❑ 89 Kevin Appier .15 .07
❑ 90 Mike Stanton .10 .05
❑ 91 Rafael Belliard .10 .05
❑ 92 Kenny Rogers .10 .05
❑ 93 Randy Velarde .10 .05
❑ 94 Luis Sojo .10 .05
❑ 95 Mark Leiter .10 .05
❑ 96 Jody Reed .10 .05
❑ 97 Pete Harnisch .10 .05
❑ 98 Tom Candiotti .10 .05
❑ 99 Mark Portugal .10 .05
❑ 100 Dave Valle .10 .05
❑ 101 Shawon Dunston .10 .05
❑ 102 B.J. Surhoff .15 .07
❑ 103 Jay Bell .15 .07
❑ 104 Sid Bream .10 .05
❑ 105 Frank Thomas CL .25 .11
❑ 106 Mike Morgan .10 .05
❑ 107 Bill Doran .10 .05
❑ 108 Lance Blankenship .10 .05
❑ 109 Mark Lemke .10 .05
❑ 110 Brian Harper .10 .05
❑ 111 Brady Anderson .15 .07
❑ 112 Bip Roberts .10 .05
❑ 113 Mitch Williams .10 .05
❑ 114 Craig Biggio .25 .11
❑ 115 Eddie Murray .40 .18
❑ 116 Matt Nokes .10 .05
❑ 117 Lance Parrish .15 .07
❑ 118 Bill Swift .10 .05
❑ 119 Jeff Innis .10 .05
❑ 120 Mike LaValliere .10 .05
❑ 121 Hal Morris .10 .05
❑ 122 Walt Weiss .10 .05
❑ 123 Ivan Rodriguez .40 .18
❑ 124 Andy Van Slyke .15 .07
❑ 125 Roberto Alomar .40 .18
❑ 126 Robby Thompson .10 .05
❑ 127 Sammy Sosa .75 .35
❑ 128 Mark Langston .10 .05
❑ 129 Jerry Browne .10 .05
❑ 130 Chuck McElroy .10 .05
❑ 131 Frank Viola .15 .07
❑ 132 Leo Gomez .10 .05
❑ 133 Ramon Martinez .10 .05
❑ 134 Don Mattingly 1.00 .45
❑ 135 Roger Clemens 1.00 .45
❑ 136 Rickey Henderson .75 .35
❑ 137 Darren Daulton .15 .07
❑ 138 Ken Hill .10 .05
❑ 139 Ozzie Guillen .10 .05
❑ 140 Jerald Clark .10 .05
❑ 141 Dave Fleming .10 .05
❑ 142 Delino DeShields .10 .05
❑ 143 Matt Williams .25 .11
❑ 144 Larry Walker .25 .11
❑ 145 Ruben Sierra .10 .05
❑ 146 Ozzie Smith .50 .23
❑ 147 Chris Sabo .10 .05
❑ 148 Carlos Hernandez .10 .05
❑ 149 Pat Borders .10 .05
❑ 150 Orlando Merced .10 .05
❑ 151 Royce Clayton .10 .05
❑ 152 Kurt Stillwell .10 .05
❑ 153 Dave Hollins .10 .05
❑ 154 Mike Greenwell .10 .05
❑ 155 Nolan Ryan 2.00 .90
❑ 156 Felix Jose .10 .05
❑ 157 Junior Felix .10 .05
❑ 158 Derek Bell .10 .05
❑ 159 Steve Buechele .10 .05
❑ 160 John Burkett .10 .05
❑ 161 Pat Howell .10 .05
❑ 162 Milt Cuyler .10 .05
❑ 163 Terry Pendleton .15 .07
❑ 164 Jack Morris .15 .07
❑ 165 Tony Gwynn .75 .35
❑ 166 Deion Sanders .15 .07
❑ 167 Mike Devereaux .10 .05
❑ 168 Ron Darling .10 .05
❑ 169 Orel Hershiser .15 .07
❑ 170 Mike Jackson .10 .05
❑ 171 Doug Jones .10 .05
❑ 172 Dan Walters .10 .05
❑ 173 Darren Lewis .10 .05
❑ 174 Carlos Baerga .10 .05
❑ 175 Ryne Sandberg .50 .23
❑ 176 Gregg Jefferies .10 .05
❑ 177 John Jaha .10 .05
❑ 178 Luis Polonia .10 .05
❑ 179 Kirt Manwaring .10 .05
❑ 180 Mike Magnante .10 .05
❑ 181 Billy Ripken .10 .05
❑ 182 Mike Moore .10 .05
❑ 183 Eric Anthony .10 .05
❑ 184 Lenny Harris .10 .05
❑ 185 Tony Pena .10 .05
❑ 186 Mike Felder .10 .05
❑ 187 Greg Olson .10 .05
❑ 188 Rene Gonzales .10 .05
❑ 189 Mike Bordick .10 .05
❑ 190 Mel Rojas .10 .05
❑ 191 Todd Frohwirth .10 .05
❑ 192 Darryl Hamilton .10 .05
❑ 193 Mike Fetters .10 .05
❑ 194 Omar Olivares .10 .05
❑ 195 Tony Phillips .10 .05
❑ 196 Paul Sorrento .10 .05
❑ 197 Trevor Wilson .10 .05
❑ 198 Kevin Gross .10 .05
❑ 199 Ron Karkovice .10 .05
❑ 200 Brook Jacoby .10 .05
❑ 201 Mariano Duncan .10 .05
❑ 202 Dennis Cook .10 .05
❑ 203 Daryl Boston .10 .05
❑ 204 Mike Perez .10 .05
❑ 205 Manuel Lee .10 .05
❑ 206 Steve Olin .10 .05
❑ 207 Charlie Hough .15 .07
❑ 208 Scott Scudder .10 .05
❑ 209 Charlie O'Brien .10 .05
❑ 210 Barry Bonds CL .50 .23
❑ 211 Jose Vizcaino .10 .05
❑ 212 Scott Leius .10 .05
❑ 213 Kevin Mitchell .10 .05
❑ 214 Brian Barnes .10 .05
❑ 215 Pat Kelly .10 .05
❑ 216 Chris Hammond .10 .05
❑ 217 Rob Deer .10 .05
❑ 218 Cory Snyder .10 .05
❑ 219 Gary Carter .25 .11
❑ 220 Danny Darwin .10 .05
❑ 221 Tom Gordon .10 .05
❑ 222 Gary Sheffield .15 .07
❑ 223 Joe Carter .15 .07
❑ 224 Jay Buhner .15 .07
❑ 225 Jose Offerman .10 .05
❑ 226 Jose Rijo .10 .05
❑ 227 Mark Whiten .10 .05
❑ 228 Randy Milligan .10 .05
❑ 229 Bud Black .10 .05
❑ 230 Gary DiSarcina .10 .05
❑ 231 Steve Finley .15 .07
❑ 232 Dennis Martinez .15 .07
❑ 233 Mike Mussina .40 .18
❑ 234 Joe Oliver .10 .05
❑ 235 Chad Curtis .10 .05
❑ 236 Shane Mack .10 .05
❑ 237 Jaime Navarro .10 .05
❑ 238 Brian McRae .10 .05
❑ 239 Chili Davis .15 .07
❑ 240 Jeff King .10 .05
❑ 241 Dean Palmer .15 .07
❑ 242 Danny Tartabull .10 .05
❑ 243 Charles Nagy .10 .05
❑ 244 Ray Lankford .10 .05
❑ 245 Barry Larkin .40 .18

❑ 246 Steve Avery .10 .05
❑ 247 John Kruk .15 .07
❑ 248 Derrick May .10 .05
❑ 249 Stan Javier .10 .05
❑ 250 Roger McDowell .10 .05
❑ 251 Dan Gladden .10 .05
❑ 252 Wally Joyner .15 .07
❑ 253 Pat Listach .10 .05
❑ 254 Chuck Knoblauch .15 .07
❑ 255 Sandy Alomar Jr. .15 .07
❑ 256 Jeff Bagwell .50 .23
❑ 257 Andy Stankiewicz .10 .05
❑ 258 Darrin Jackson .10 .05
❑ 259 Brett Butler .15 .07
❑ 260 Joe Orsulak .10 .05
❑ 261 Andy Benes .10 .05
❑ 262 Kenny Lofton .15 .07
❑ 263 Robin Ventura .15 .07
❑ 264 Ron Gant .10 .05
❑ 265 Ellis Burks .15 .07
❑ 266 Juan Guzman .10 .05
❑ 267 Wes Chamberlain .10 .05
❑ 268 John Smiley .10 .05
❑ 269 Franklin Stubbs .10 .05
❑ 270 Tom Browning .10 .05
❑ 271 Dennis Eckersley .15 .07
❑ 272 Carlton Fisk .40 .18
❑ 273 Lou Whitaker .15 .07
❑ 274 Phil Plantier .10 .05
❑ 275 Bobby Bonilla .15 .07
❑ 276 Ben McDonald .10 .05
❑ 277 Bob Zupcic .10 .05
❑ 278 Terry Steinbach .10 .05
❑ 279 Terry Mulholland .10 .05
❑ 280 Lance Johnson .10 .05
❑ 281 Willie McGee .15 .07
❑ 282 Bret Saberhagen .15 .07
❑ 283 Randy Myers .10 .05
❑ 284 Randy Tomlin .10 .05
❑ 285 Mickey Morandini .10 .05
❑ 286 Brian Williams .10 .05
❑ 287 Tino Martinez .15 .07
❑ 288 Jose Melendez .10 .05
❑ 289 Jeff Huson .10 .05
❑ 290 Joe Grahe .10 .05
❑ 291 Mel Hall .10 .05
❑ 292 Otis Nixon .10 .05
❑ 293 Todd Hundley .10 .05
❑ 294 Casey Candaele .10 .05
❑ 295 Kevin Seitzer .10 .05
❑ 296 Eddie Taubensee .10 .05
❑ 297 Moises Alou .15 .07
❑ 298 Scott Radinsky .10 .05
❑ 299 Thomas Howard .10 .05
❑ 300 Kyle Abbott .10 .05
❑ 301 Omar Vizquel .15 .07
❑ 302 Keith Miller .10 .05
❑ 303 Rick Aguilera .10 .05
❑ 304 Bruce Hurst .10 .05
❑ 305 Ken Caminiti .15 .07
❑ 306 Mike Pagliarulo .10 .05
❑ 307 Frank Seminara .10 .05
❑ 308 Andre Dawson .25 .11
❑ 309 Jose Lind .10 .05
❑ 310 Joe Boever .10 .05
❑ 311 Jeff Parrett .10 .05
❑ 312 Alan Mills .10 .05
❑ 313 Kevin Tapani .10 .05
❑ 314 Darryl Kile .15 .07
❑ 315 Will Clark CL .15 .07
❑ 316 Mike Sharperson .10 .05
❑ 317 John Orton .10 .05
❑ 318 Bob Tewksbury .10 .05
❑ 319 Xavier Hernandez .10 .05
❑ 320 Paul Assenmacher .10 .05
❑ 321 John Franco .15 .07
❑ 322 Mike Timlin .10 .05
❑ 323 Jose Guzman .10 .05
❑ 324 Pedro Martinez 1.00 .45
❑ 325 Bill Spiers .10 .05
❑ 326 Melido Perez .10 .05
❑ 327 Mike Macfarlane .10 .05
❑ 328 Ricky Bones .10 .05
❑ 329 Scott Bankhead .10 .05
❑ 330 Rich Rodriguez .10 .05
❑ 331 Geronimo Pena .10 .05
❑ 332 Bernie Williams .40 .18
❑ 333 Paul Molitor .40 .18
❑ 334 Carlos Garcia .10 .05
❑ 335 David Cone .15 .07
❑ 336 Randy Johnson .50 .23
❑ 337 Pat Mahomes .10 .05
❑ 338 Erik Hanson .10 .05
❑ 339 Duane Ward .10 .05
❑ 340 Al Martin .10 .05
❑ 341 Pedro Munoz .10 .05
❑ 342 Greg Colbrunn .10 .05
❑ 343 Julio Valera .10 .05
❑ 344 John Olerud .15 .07
❑ 345 George Bell .10 .05
❑ 346 Devon White .10 .05
❑ 347 Donovan Osborne .10 .05
❑ 348 Mark Gardner .10 .05
❑ 349 Zane Smith .10 .05
❑ 350 Wilson Alvarez .10 .05
❑ 351 Kevin Koslofski .10 .05
❑ 352 Roberto Hernandez .10 .05
❑ 353 Glenn Davis .10 .05
❑ 354 Reggie Sanders .10 .05
❑ 355 Ken Griffey Jr. 1.25 .55
❑ 356 Marquis Grissom .10 .05
❑ 357 Jack McDowell .10 .05
❑ 358 Jimmy Key .15 .07
❑ 359 Stan Belinda .10 .05
❑ 360 Gerald Williams .10 .05
❑ 361 Sid Fernandez .10 .05
❑ 362 Alex Fernandez .10 .05
❑ 363 John Smoltz .15 .07
❑ 364 Travis Fryman .15 .07
❑ 365 Jose Canseco .40 .18
❑ 366 David Justice .15 .07
❑ 367 Pedro Astacio .10 .05
❑ 368 Tim Belcher .10 .05
❑ 369 Steve Sax .10 .05
❑ 370 Gary Gaetti .15 .07
❑ 371 Jeff Frye .10 .05
❑ 372 Bob Wickman .10 .05
❑ 373 Ryan Thompson .10 .05
❑ 374 David Hulse RC .10 .05
❑ 375 Cal Eldred .10 .05
❑ 376 Ryan Klesko .15 .07
❑ 377 Damion Easley .10 .05
❑ 378 John Kiely .10 .05
❑ 379 Jim Bullinger .10 .05
❑ 380 Brian Bohanon .10 .05
❑ 381 Rod Brewer .10 .05
❑ 382 Fernando Ramsey RC .10 .05
❑ 383 Sam Militello .10 .05
❑ 384 Arthur Rhodes .10 .05
❑ 385 Eric Karros .15 .07
❑ 386 Rico Brogna .10 .05
❑ 387 John Valentin .10 .05
❑ 388 Kerry Woodson .10 .05
❑ 389 Ben Rivera .10 .05
❑ 390 Matt Whiteside RC .10 .05
❑ 391 Henry Rodriguez .10 .05
❑ 392 John Wetteland .15 .07
❑ 393 Kent Mercker .10 .05
❑ 394 Bernard Gilkey .10 .05
❑ 395 Doug Henry .10 .05
❑ 396 Mo Vaughn .15 .07
❑ 397 Scott Erickson .10 .05
❑ 398 Bill Gullickson .10 .05
❑ 399 Mark Guthrie .10 .05
❑ 400 Dave Martinez .10 .05
❑ 401 Jeff Kent .40 .18
❑ 402 Chris Hoiles .10 .05
❑ 403 Mike Henneman .10 .05
❑ 404 Chris Nabholz .10 .05
❑ 405 Tom Pagnozzi .10 .05
❑ 406 Kelly Gruber .10 .05
❑ 407 Bob Welch .10 .05
❑ 408 Frank Castillo .10 .05
❑ 409 John Dopson .10 .05
❑ 410 Steve Farr .10 .05
❑ 411 Henry Cotto .10 .05
❑ 412 Bob Patterson .10 .05
❑ 413 Todd Stottlemyre .10 .05
❑ 414 Greg A. Harris .10 .05
❑ 415 Denny Neagle .15 .07
❑ 416 Bill Wegman .10 .05
❑ 417 Willie Wilson .10 .05
❑ 418 Terry Leach .10 .05
❑ 419 Willie Randolph .15 .07
❑ 420 Mark McGwire CL .40 .18
❑ 421 Calvin Murray CL .10 .05
❑ 422 Pete Janicki TP RC .10 .05
❑ 423 Todd Jones TP .10 .05
❑ 424 Mike Neill TP .10 .05
❑ 425 Carlos Delgado TP .75 .35
❑ 426 Jose Oliva TP .10 .05
❑ 427 Tyrone Hill TP .10 .05
❑ 428 Dmitri Young TP .15 .07
❑ 429 Derek Wallace TP RC .10 .05
❑ 430 Michael Moore TP RC .10 .05
❑ 431 Cliff Floyd TP .15 .07
❑ 432 Calvin Murray TP .10 .05
❑ 433 Manny Ramirez TP 1.00 .45
❑ 434 Marc Newfield TP .10 .05
❑ 435 Charles Johnson TP .15 .07
❑ 436 Butch Huskey TP .10 .05
❑ 437 Brad Pennington TP .10 .05
❑ 438 Ray McDavid TP RC .10 .05
❑ 439 Chad McConnell TP .10 .05
❑ 440 M.Cummings TP RC .10 .05
❑ 441 Benji Gil TP .10 .05
❑ 442 Frankie Rodriguez TP .10 .05
❑ 443 Chad Mottola TP RC .10 .05
❑ 444 John Burke TP RC .10 .05
❑ 445 Michael Tucker TP .10 .05
❑ 446 Rick Greene TP .10 .05
❑ 447 Rich Becker TP .10 .05
❑ 448 Mike Robertson TP .10 .05
❑ 449 Derek Jeter TP RC 15.00 6.75
❑ 450 Ivan Rodriguez CL .15 .07
David McCarty
❑ 451 Jim Abbott IN .10 .05
❑ 452 Jeff Bagwell IN .25 .11
❑ 453 Jason Bere IN .10 .05
❑ 454 Delino DeShields IN .10 .05
❑ 455 Travis Fryman IN .10 .05
❑ 456 Alex Gonzalez IN .10 .05
❑ 457 Phil Hiatt IN .10 .05
❑ 458 Dave Hollins IN .10 .05
❑ 459 Chipper Jones IN .40 .18
❑ 460 David Justice IN .10 .05
❑ 461 Ray Lankford IN .10 .05
❑ 462 David McCarty IN .10 .05
❑ 463 Mike Mussina IN .15 .07
❑ 464 Jose Offerman IN .10 .05
❑ 465 Dean Palmer IN .10 .05
❑ 466 Geronimo Pena IN .10 .05
❑ 467 Eduardo Perez IN .10 .05
❑ 468 Ivan Rodriguez IN .15 .07
❑ 469 Reggie Sanders IN .10 .05
❑ 470 Bernie Williams IN .15 .07
❑ 471 Barry Bonds CL .40 .18
Matt Williams
Will Clark
❑ 472 Strike Force .40 .18
Greg Maddux
Steve Avery
John Smoltz
Tom Glavine
❑ 473 Red October .10 .05
Jose Rijo
Rob Dibble
Roberto Kelly
Reggie Sanders
Barry Larkin
❑ 474 Four Corners .25 .11
Gary Sheffield
Phil Plantier
Tony Gwynn
Fred McGriff
❑ 475 Shooting Stars .15 .07
Doug Drabek
Craig Biggio
Jeff Bagwell
❑ 476 Giant Sticks .50 .23
Will Clark
Barry Bonds
Matt Williams
❑ 477 Boyhood Friends .15 .07
Eric Davis
Darryl Strawberry
❑ 478 Rock Solid Foundation .25 .11
Dante Bichette

David Nied
Andres Galarraga
❑ 479 Inaugural Catch .10 .05
Dave Magadan
Orestes Destrade
Bret Barberie
Jeff Conine
❑ 480 Steel City Champions .10 .05
Tim Wakefield
Andy Van Slyke
Jay Bell
❑ 481 Les Grandes Etoiles .10 .05
Marquis Grissom
Delino DeShields
Dennis Martinez
Larry Walker
❑ 482 Runnin' Redbirds .40 .18
Geronimo Pena
Ray Lankford
Ozzie Smith
Bernard Gilkey
❑ 483 Ivy Leaguers .15 .07
Randy Myers
Ryne Sandberg
Mark Grace
❑ 484 Eddie Murray .10 .05
Howard Johnson
Bobby Bonilla
Big Apple Power Switch
❑ 485 Hammers and Nails .10 .05
John Kruk
Dave Hollins
Darren Daulton
Len Dykstra
❑ 486 Barry Bonds AW .50 .23
❑ 487 Dennis Eckersley AW .10 .05
❑ 488 Greg Maddux AW .50 .23
❑ 489 Dennis Eckersley AW .10 .05
❑ 490 Eric Karros AW .10 .05
❑ 491 Pat Listach AW .10 .05
❑ 492 Gary Sheffield AW .10 .05
❑ 493 Mark McGwire AW .75 .35
❑ 494 Gary Sheffield AW .10 .05
❑ 495 Edgar Martinez AW .15 .07
❑ 496 Fred McGriff AW .15 .07
❑ 497 Juan Gonzalez AW .15 .07
❑ 498 Darren Daulton AW .10 .05
❑ 499 Cecil Fielder AW .10 .05
❑ 500 Brent Gates CL .10 .05
❑ 501 Tavo Alvarez DD .10 .05
❑ 502 Rod Bolton .10 .05
❑ 503 J.Cummings DD RC .10 .05
❑ 504 Brent Gates DD .10 .05
❑ 505 Tyler Green .10 .05
❑ 506 Jose Martinez DD RC .10 .05
❑ 507 Troy Percival .15 .07
❑ 508 Kevin Stocker DD .10 .05
❑ 509 Matt Walbeck DD RC .10 .05
❑ 510 Rondell White DD .15 .07
❑ 511 Billy Ripken .10 .05
❑ 512 Mike Moore .10 .05
❑ 513 Jose Lind .10 .05
❑ 514 Chito Martinez .10 .05
❑ 515 Jose Guzman .10 .05
❑ 516 Kim Batiste .10 .05
❑ 517 Jeff Tackett .10 .05
❑ 518 Charlie Hough .15 .07
❑ 519 Marvin Freeman .10 .05
❑ 520 Carlos Martinez .10 .05
❑ 521 Eric Young .10 .05
❑ 522 Pete Incaviglia .10 .05
❑ 523 Scott Fletcher .10 .05
❑ 524 Orestes Destrade .10 .05
❑ 525 Ken Griffey Jr. CL .40 .18
❑ 526 Ellis Burks .15 .07
❑ 527 Juan Samuel .10 .05
❑ 528 Dave Magadan .10 .05
❑ 529 Jeff Parrett .10 .05
❑ 530 Bill Krueger .10 .05
❑ 531 Frank Bolick .10 .05
❑ 532 Alan Trammell .25 .11
❑ 533 Walt Weiss .10 .05
❑ 534 David Cone .15 .07
❑ 535 Greg Maddux 1.00 .45
❑ 536 Kevin Young .15 .07
❑ 537 Dave Hansen .10 .05
❑ 538 Alex Cole .10 .05
❑ 539 Greg Hibbard .10 .05
❑ 540 Gene Larkin .10 .05
❑ 541 Jeff Reardon .15 .07
❑ 542 Felix Jose .10 .05
❑ 543 Jimmy Key .15 .07
❑ 544 Reggie Jefferson .10 .05
❑ 545 Gregg Jefferies .10 .05
❑ 546 Dave Stewart .15 .07
❑ 547 Tim Wallach .10 .05
❑ 548 Spike Owen .10 .05
❑ 549 Tommy Greene .10 .05
❑ 550 Fernando Valenzuela .15 .07
❑ 551 Rich Amaral .10 .05
❑ 552 Bret Barberie .10 .05
❑ 553 Edgar Martinez .25 .11
❑ 554 Jim Abbott .15 .07
❑ 555 Frank Thomas .50 .23
❑ 556 Wade Boggs .40 .18
❑ 557 Tom Henke .10 .05
❑ 558 Milt Thompson .10 .05
❑ 559 Lloyd McClendon .10 .05
❑ 560 Vinny Castilla .15 .07
❑ 561 Ricky Jordan .10 .05
❑ 562 Andujar Cedeno .10 .05
❑ 563 Greg Vaughn .15 .07
❑ 564 Cecil Fielder .15 .07
❑ 565 Kirby Puckett 1.00 .45
❑ 566 Mark McGwire 1.50 .70
❑ 567 Barry Bonds 1.00 .45
❑ 568 Jody Reed .10 .05
❑ 569 Todd Zeile .10 .05
❑ 570 Mark Carreon .10 .05
❑ 571 Joe Girardi .10 .05
❑ 572 Luis Gonzalez .40 .18
❑ 573 Mark Grace .40 .18
❑ 574 Rafael Palmeiro .40 .18
❑ 575 Darryl Strawberry .15 .07
❑ 576 Will Clark .40 .18
❑ 577 Fred McGriff .25 .11
❑ 578 Kevin Reimer .10 .05
❑ 579 Dave Righetti .15 .07
❑ 580 Juan Bell .10 .05
❑ 581 Jeff Brantley .10 .05
❑ 582 Brian Hunter .10 .05
❑ 583 Tim Naehring .10 .05
❑ 584 Glenallen Hill .10 .05
❑ 585 Cal Ripken 1.50 .70
❑ 586 Albert Belle .15 .07
❑ 587 Robin Yount .40 .18
❑ 588 Chris Bosio .10 .05
❑ 589 Pete Smith .10 .05
❑ 590 Chuck Carr .10 .05
❑ 591 Jeff Blauser .10 .05
❑ 592 Kevin McReynolds .10 .05
❑ 593 Andres Galarraga .25 .11
❑ 594 Kevin Maas .10 .05
❑ 595 Eric Davis .15 .07
❑ 596 Brian Jordan .15 .07
❑ 597 Tim Raines .15 .07
❑ 598 Rick Wilkins .10 .05
❑ 599 Steve Cooke .10 .05
❑ 600 Mike Gallego .10 .05
❑ 601 Mike Munoz .10 .05
❑ 602 Luis Rivera .10 .05
❑ 603 Junior Ortiz .10 .05
❑ 604 Brent Mayne .10 .05
❑ 605 Luis Alicea .10 .05
❑ 606 Damon Berryhill .10 .05
❑ 607 Dave Henderson .10 .05
❑ 608 Kirk McCaskill .10 .05
❑ 609 Jeff Fassero .10 .05
❑ 610 Mike Harkey .10 .05
❑ 611 Francisco Cabrera .10 .05
❑ 612 Rey Sanchez .10 .05
❑ 613 Scott Servais .10 .05
❑ 614 Darrin Fletcher .10 .05
❑ 615 Felix Fermin .10 .05
❑ 616 Kevin Seitzer .10 .05
❑ 617 Bob Scanlan .10 .05
❑ 618 Billy Hatcher .10 .05
❑ 619 John Vander Wal .10 .05
❑ 620 Joe Hesketh .10 .05
❑ 621 Hector Villanueva .10 .05
❑ 622 Randy Milligan .10 .05
❑ 623 Tony Tarasco RC .10 .05
❑ 624 Russ Swan .10 .05
❑ 625 Willie Wilson .10 .05
❑ 626 Frank Tanana .10 .05
❑ 627 Pete O'Brien .10 .05
❑ 628 Lenny Webster .10 .05
❑ 629 Mark Clark .10 .05
❑ 630 Roger Clemens CL .50 .23
❑ 631 Alex Arias .10 .05
❑ 632 Chris Gwynn .10 .05
❑ 633 Tom Bolton .10 .05
❑ 634 Greg Briley .10 .05
❑ 635 Kent Bottenfield .10 .05
❑ 636 Kelly Downs .10 .05
❑ 637 Manuel Lee .10 .05
❑ 638 Al Leiter .15 .07
❑ 639 Jeff Gardner .10 .05
❑ 640 Mike Gardiner .10 .05
❑ 641 Mark Gardner .10 .05
❑ 642 Jeff Branson .10 .05
❑ 643 Paul Wagner .10 .05
❑ 644 Sean Berry .10 .05
❑ 645 Phil Hiatt .10 .05
❑ 646 Kevin Mitchell .10 .05
❑ 647 Charlie Hayes .10 .05
❑ 648 Jim Deshaies .10 .05
❑ 649 Dan Pasqua .10 .05
❑ 650 Mike Maddux .10 .05
❑ 651 Domingo Martinez RC .10 .05
❑ 652 Greg McMichael RC .10 .05
❑ 653 Eric Wedge RC .10 .05
❑ 654 Mark Whiten .10 .05
❑ 655 Roberto Kelly .10 .05
❑ 656 Julio Franco .15 .07
❑ 657 Gene Harris .10 .05
❑ 658 Pete Schourek .10 .05
❑ 659 Mike Bielecki .10 .05
❑ 660 Ricky Gutierrez .10 .05
❑ 661 Chris Hammond .10 .05
❑ 662 Tim Scott .10 .05
❑ 663 Norm Charlton .10 .05
❑ 664 Doug Drabek .10 .05
❑ 665 Dwight Gooden .15 .07
❑ 666 Jim Gott .10 .05
❑ 667 Randy Myers .10 .05
❑ 668 Darren Holmes .10 .05
❑ 669 Tim Spehr .10 .05
❑ 670 Bruce Ruffin .10 .05
❑ 671 Bobby Thigpen .10 .05
❑ 672 Tony Fernandez .10 .05
❑ 673 Darrin Jackson .10 .05
❑ 674 Gregg Olson .10 .05
❑ 675 Rob Dibble .10 .05
❑ 676 Howard Johnson .10 .05
❑ 677 Mike Lansing RC .15 .07
❑ 678 Charlie Leibrandt .10 .05
❑ 679 Kevin Bass .10 .05
❑ 680 Hubie Brooks .10 .05
❑ 681 Scott Brosius .15 .07
❑ 682 Randy Knorr .10 .05
❑ 683 Dante Bichette .15 .07
❑ 684 Bryan Harvey .10 .05
❑ 685 Greg Gohr .10 .05
❑ 686 Willie Banks .10 .05
❑ 687 Robb Nen .10 .05
❑ 688 Mike Scioscia .10 .05
❑ 689 John Farrell .10 .05
❑ 690 John Candelaria .10 .05
❑ 691 Damon Buford .10 .05
❑ 692 Todd Worrell .10 .05
❑ 693 Pat Hentgen .10 .05
❑ 694 John Smiley .10 .05
❑ 695 Greg Swindell .10 .05
❑ 696 Derek Bell .10 .05
❑ 697 Terry Jorgensen .10 .05
❑ 698 Jimmy Jones .10 .05
❑ 699 David Wells .15 .07
❑ 700 Dave Martinez .10 .05
❑ 701 Steve Bedrosian .10 .05
❑ 702 Jeff Russell .10 .05
❑ 703 Joe Magrane .10 .05
❑ 704 Matt Mieske .10 .05
❑ 705 Paul Molitor .40 .18
❑ 706 Dale Murphy .25 .11
❑ 707 Steve Howe .10 .05
❑ 708 Greg Gagne .10 .05
❑ 709 Dave Eiland .10 .05

❑ 710	David West	.10	.05
❑ 711	Luis Aquino	.10	.05
❑ 712	Joe Orsulak	.10	.05
❑ 713	Eric Plunk	.10	.05
❑ 714	Mike Felder	.10	.05
❑ 715	Joe Klink	.10	.05
❑ 716	Lonnie Smith	.10	.05
❑ 717	Monty Fariss	.10	.05
❑ 718	Craig Lefferts	.10	.05
❑ 719	John Habyan	.10	.05
❑ 720	Willie Blair	.10	.05
❑ 721	Darnell Coles	.10	.05
❑ 722	Mark Williamson	.10	.05
❑ 723	Bryn Smith	.10	.05
❑ 724	Greg W. Harris	.10	.05
❑ 725	Graeme Lloyd RC	.15	.07
❑ 726	Cris Carpenter	.10	.05
❑ 727	Chico Walker	.10	.05
❑ 728	Tracy Woodson	.10	.05
❑ 729	Jose Uribe	.10	.05
❑ 730	Stan Javier	.10	.05
❑ 731	Jay Howell	.10	.05
❑ 732	Freddie Benavides	.10	.05
❑ 733	Jeff Reboulet	.10	.05
❑ 734	Scott Sanderson	.10	.05
❑ 735	Ryne Sandberg CL	.25	.11
❑ 736	Archi Cianfrocco	.10	.05
❑ 737	Daryl Boston	.10	.05
❑ 738	Craig Grebeck	.10	.05
❑ 739	Doug Dascenzo	.10	.05
❑ 740	Gerald Young	.10	.05
❑ 741	Candy Maldonado	.10	.05
❑ 742	Joey Cora	.10	.05
❑ 743	Don Slaught	.10	.05
❑ 744	Steve Decker	.10	.05
❑ 745	Blas Minor	.10	.05
❑ 746	Storm Davis	.10	.05
❑ 747	Carlos Quintana	.10	.05
❑ 748	Vince Coleman	.10	.05
❑ 749	Todd Burns	.10	.05
❑ 750	Steve Frey	.10	.05
❑ 751	Ivan Calderon	.10	.05
❑ 752	Steve Reed RC	.10	.05
❑ 753	Danny Jackson	.10	.05
❑ 754	Jeff Conine	.10	.05
❑ 755	Juan Gonzalez	.40	.18
❑ 756	Mike Kelly	.10	.05
❑ 757	John Doherty	.10	.05
❑ 758	Jack Armstrong	.10	.05
❑ 759	John Wehner	.10	.05
❑ 760	Scott Bankhead	.10	.05
❑ 761	Jim Tatum	.10	.05
❑ 762	Scott Pose RC	.10	.05
❑ 763	Andy Ashby	.10	.05
❑ 764	Ed Sprague	.10	.05
❑ 765	Harold Baines	.15	.07
❑ 766	Kirk Gibson	.15	.07
❑ 767	Troy Neel	.10	.05
❑ 768	Dick Schofield	.10	.05
❑ 769	Dickie Thon	.10	.05
❑ 770	Butch Henry	.10	.05
❑ 771	Junior Felix	.10	.05
❑ 772	Ken Ryan RC	.10	.05
❑ 773	Trevor Hoffman	.15	.07
❑ 774	Phil Plantier	.10	.05
❑ 775	Bo Jackson	.15	.07
❑ 776	Benito Santiago	.10	.05
❑ 777	Andre Dawson	.25	.11
❑ 778	Bryan Hickerson	.10	.05
❑ 779	Dennis Moeller	.10	.05
❑ 780	Ryan Bowen	.10	.05
❑ 781	Eric Fox	.10	.05
❑ 782	Joe Kmak	.10	.05
❑ 783	Mike Hampton	.40	.18
❑ 784	Darrell Sherman RC	.10	.05
❑ 785	J.T. Snow	.40	.18
❑ 786	Dave Winfield	.40	.18
❑ 787	Jim Austin	.10	.05
❑ 788	Craig Shipley	.10	.05
❑ 789	Greg Myers	.10	.05
❑ 790	Todd Benzinger	.10	.05
❑ 791	Cory Snyder	.10	.05
❑ 792	David Segui	.10	.05
❑ 793	Armando Reynoso	.10	.05
❑ 794	Chili Davis	.15	.07
❑ 795	Dave Nilsson	.10	.05
❑ 796	Paul O'Neill	.40	.18
❑ 797	Jerald Clark	.10	.05
❑ 798	Jose Mesa	.10	.05
❑ 799	Brain Holman	.10	.05
❑ 800	Jim Eisenreich	.10	.05
❑ 801	Mark McLemore	.10	.05
❑ 802	Luis Sojo	.10	.05
❑ 803	Harold Reynolds	.10	.05
❑ 804	Dan Plesac	.10	.05
❑ 805	Dave Stieb	.10	.05
❑ 806	Tom Brunansky	.10	.05
❑ 807	Kelly Gruber	.10	.05
❑ 808	Bob Ojeda	.10	.05
❑ 809	Dave Burba	.10	.05
❑ 810	Joe Boever	.10	.05
❑ 811	Jeremy Hernandez	.10	.05
❑ 812	Tim Salmon TC	.10	.05
❑ 813	Jeff Bagwell TC	.25	.11
❑ 814	Dennis Eckersley TC	.10	.05
❑ 815	Roberto Alomar TC	.15	.07
❑ 816	Steve Avery TC	.10	.05
❑ 817	Pat Listach TC	.10	.05
❑ 818	Gregg Jefferies TC	.10	.05
❑ 819	Sammy Sosa TC	.40	.18
❑ 820	Darryl Strawberry TC	.10	.05
❑ 821	Dennis Martinez TC	.10	.05
❑ 822	Robby Thompson TC	.10	.05
❑ 823	Albert Belle TC	.15	.07
❑ 824	Randy Johnson TC	.25	.11
❑ 825	Nigel Wilson TC	.10	.05
❑ 826	Bobby Bonilla TC	.10	.05
❑ 827	Glenn Davis TC	.10	.05
❑ 828	Gary Sheffield TC	.10	.05
❑ 829	Darren Daulton TC	.10	.05
❑ 830	Jay Bell TC	.10	.05
❑ 831	Juan Gonzalez TC	.15	.07
❑ 832	Andre Dawson TC	.15	.07
❑ 833	Hal Morris TC	.10	.05
❑ 834	David Nied TC	.10	.05
❑ 835	Felix Jose TC	.10	.05
❑ 836	Travis Fryman TC	.10	.05
❑ 837	Shane Mack TC	.10	.05
❑ 838	Robin Ventura TC	.10	.05
❑ 839	Danny Tartabull TC	.10	.05
❑ 840	Roberto Alomar CL	.15	.07
❑ SP5	George Brett Robin Yount 3,000th Hit	1.00	.45
❑ SP6	Nolan Ryan	2.50	1.10

1994 Upper Deck

	MINT	NRMT
COMPLETE SET (550)	50.00	22.00
COMPLETE SERIES 1 (280)	30.00	13.50
COMPLETE SERIES 2 (270)	20.00	9.00

No.	Player	MINT	NRMT
❑ 1	Brian Anderson RC	.25	.11
❑ 2	Shane Andrews	.15	.07
❑ 3	James Baldwin	.15	.07
❑ 4	Rich Becker	.15	.07
❑ 5	Greg Blosser	.15	.07
❑ 6	Ricky Bottalico RC	.25	.11
❑ 7	Midre Cummings	.15	.07
❑ 8	Carlos Delgado	.75	.35
❑ 9	Steve Dreyer RC	.15	.07
❑ 10	Joey Eischen	.15	.07
❑ 11	Carl Everett	.25	.11
❑ 12	Cliff Floyd UER (text indicates he throws left; should be right)	.25	.11
❑ 13	Alex Gonzalez	.15	.07
❑ 14	Jeff Granger	.15	.07
❑ 15	Shawn Green	.75	.35
❑ 16	Brian L. Hunter	.15	.07
❑ 17	Butch Huskey	.15	.07
❑ 18	Mark Hutton	.15	.07
❑ 19	Michael Jordan RC	10.00	4.50
❑ 20	Steve Karsay	.15	.07
❑ 21	Jeff McNeely	.15	.07
❑ 22	Marc Newfield	.15	.07
❑ 23	Manny Ramirez	1.00	.45
❑ 24	Alex Rodriguez RC	15.00	6.75
❑ 25	Scott Ruffcorn UER (photo on back is Robert Ellis)	.15	.07
❑ 26	Paul Spoljaric UER (Expos logo on back)	.15	.07
❑ 27	Salomon Torres	.15	.07
❑ 28	Steve Trachsel	.15	.07
❑ 29	Chris Turner	.15	.07
❑ 30	Gabe White	.15	.07
❑ 31	Randy Johnson FT	.40	.18
❑ 32	John Wetteland FT	.15	.07
❑ 33	Mike Piazza FT	1.00	.45
❑ 34	Rafael Palmeiro FT	.25	.11
❑ 35	Roberto Alomar FT	.25	.11
❑ 36	Matt Williams FT	.25	.11
❑ 37	Travis Fryman FT	.15	.07
❑ 38	Barry Bonds FT	.75	.35
❑ 39	Marquis Grissom FT	.15	.07
❑ 40	Albert Belle FT	.25	.11
❑ 41	Steve Avery FUT	.15	.07
❑ 42	Jason Bere FUT	.15	.07
❑ 43	Alex Fernandez FUT	.15	.07
❑ 44	Mike Mussina FUT	.25	.11
❑ 45	Aaron Sele FUT	.15	.07
❑ 46	Rod Beck FUT	.15	.07
❑ 47	Mike Piazza FUT	1.00	.45
❑ 48	John Olerud FUT	.15	.07
❑ 49	Carlos Baerga FUT	.15	.07
❑ 50	Gary Sheffield FUT	.15	.07
❑ 51	Travis Fryman FUT	.15	.07
❑ 52	Juan Gonzalez FUT	.25	.11
❑ 53	Ken Griffey Jr. FUT	1.00	.45
❑ 54	Tim Salmon FUT	.15	.07
❑ 55	Frank Thomas FUT	.40	.18
❑ 56	Tony Phillips	.15	.07
❑ 57	Julio Franco	.25	.11
❑ 58	Kevin Mitchell	.15	.07
❑ 59	Raul Mondesi	.25	.11
❑ 60	Rickey Henderson	1.25	.55
❑ 61	Jay Buhner	.25	.11
❑ 62	Bill Swift	.15	.07
❑ 63	Brady Anderson	.25	.11
❑ 64	Ryan Klesko	.25	.11
❑ 65	Darren Daulton	.25	.11
❑ 66	Damion Easley	.15	.07
❑ 67	Mark McGwire	2.50	1.10
❑ 68	John Roper	.15	.07
❑ 69	Dave Telgheder	.15	.07
❑ 70	David Nied	.15	.07
❑ 71	Mo Vaughn	.25	.11
❑ 72	Tyler Green	.15	.07
❑ 73	Dave Magadan	.15	.07
❑ 74	Chili Davis	.25	.11
❑ 75	Archi Cianfrocco	.15	.07
❑ 76	Joe Girardi	.15	.07
❑ 77	Chris Hoiles	.15	.07
❑ 78	Ryan Bowen	.15	.07
❑ 79	Greg Gagne	.15	.07
❑ 80	Aaron Sele	.25	.11
❑ 81	Dave Winfield	.60	.25
❑ 82	Chad Curtis	.15	.07
❑ 83	Andy Van Slyke	.25	.11
❑ 84	Kevin Stocker	.15	.07
❑ 85	Deion Sanders	.25	.11
❑ 86	Bernie Williams	.60	.25
❑ 87	John Smoltz	.25	.11
❑ 88	Ruben Santana	.15	.07
❑ 89	Dave Stewart	.25	.11
❑ 90	Don Mattingly	1.50	.70
❑ 91	Joe Carter	.25	.11
❑ 92	Ryne Sandberg	.75	.35
❑ 93	Chris Gomez	.15	.07

❑ 94 Tino Martinez .25 .11
❑ 95 Terry Pendleton .25 .11
❑ 96 Andre Dawson .40 .18
❑ 97 Wil Cordero .15 .07
❑ 98 Kent Hrbek .25 .11
❑ 99 John Olerud .25 .11
❑ 100 Kirt Manwaring .15 .07
❑ 101 Tim Bogar .15 .07
❑ 102 Mike Mussina .60 .25
❑ 103 Nigel Wilson .15 .07
❑ 104 Ricky Gutierrez .15 .07
❑ 105 Roberto Mejia .15 .07
❑ 106 Tom Pagnozzi .15 .07
❑ 107 Mike Macfarlane .15 .07
❑ 108 Jose Bautista .15 .07
❑ 109 Luis Ortiz .15 .07
❑ 110 Brent Gates .15 .07
❑ 111 Tim Salmon .25 .11
❑ 112 Wade Boggs .60 .25
❑ 113 Tripp Cromer .15 .07
❑ 114 Denny Hocking .15 .07
❑ 115 Carlos Baerga .15 .07
❑ 116 J.R. Phillips .15 .07
❑ 117 Bo Jackson .25 .11
❑ 118 Lance Johnson .15 .07
❑ 119 Bobby Jones .15 .07
❑ 120 Bobby Witt .15 .07
❑ 121 Ron Karkovice .15 .07
❑ 122 Jose Vizcaino .15 .07
❑ 123 Danny Darwin .15 .07
❑ 124 Eduardo Perez .15 .07
❑ 125 Brian Looney RC .15 .07
❑ 126 Pat Hentgen .15 .07
❑ 127 Frank Viola .25 .11
❑ 128 Darren Holmes .15 .07
❑ 129 Wally Whitehurst .15 .07
❑ 130 Matt Walbeck .15 .07
❑ 131 Albert Belle .25 .11
❑ 132 Steve Cooke .15 .07
❑ 133 Kevin Appier .25 .11
❑ 134 Joe Oliver .15 .07
❑ 135 Benji Gil .15 .07
❑ 136 Steve Buechele .15 .07
❑ 137 Devon White .15 .07
❑ 138 S.Hitchcock UER .15 .07
two losses for career; should be four
❑ 139 Phil Leftwich RC .15 .07
❑ 140 Jose Canseco .60 .25
❑ 141 Rick Aguilera .15 .07
❑ 142 Rod Beck .15 .07
❑ 143 Jose Rijo .15 .07
❑ 144 Tom Glavine .60 .25
❑ 145 Phil Plantier .15 .07
❑ 146 Jason Bere .15 .07
❑ 147 Jamie Moyer .15 .07
❑ 148 Wes Chamberlain .15 .07
❑ 149 Glenallen Hill .15 .07
❑ 150 Mark Whiten .15 .07
❑ 151 Bret Barberie .15 .07
❑ 152 Chuck Knoblauch .25 .11
❑ 153 Trevor Hoffman .25 .11
❑ 154 Rick Wilkins .15 .07
❑ 155 Juan Gonzalez .60 .25
❑ 156 Ozzie Guillen .15 .07
❑ 157 Jim Eisenreich .15 .07
❑ 158 Pedro Astacio .15 .07
❑ 159 Joe Magrane .15 .07
❑ 160 Ryan Thompson .15 .07
❑ 161 Jose Lind .15 .07
❑ 162 Jeff Conine .15 .07
❑ 163 Todd Benzinger .15 .07
❑ 164 Roger Salkeld .15 .07
❑ 165 Gary DiSarcina .15 .07
❑ 166 Kevin Gross .15 .07
❑ 167 Charlie Hayes .15 .07
❑ 168 Tim Costo .15 .07
❑ 169 Wally Joyner .25 .11
❑ 170 Johnny Ruffin .15 .07
❑ 171 Kirk Rueter .15 .07
❑ 172 Lenny Dykstra .25 .11
❑ 173 Ken Hill .15 .07
❑ 174 Mike Bordick .15 .07
❑ 175 Billy Hall .15 .07
❑ 176 Rob Butler .15 .07
❑ 177 Jay Bell .25 .11
❑ 178 Jeff Kent .40 .18
❑ 179 David Wells .25 .11
❑ 180 Dean Palmer .25 .11
❑ 181 Mariano Duncan .15 .07
❑ 182 Orlando Merced .15 .07
❑ 183 Brett Butler .25 .11
❑ 184 Milt Thompson .15 .07
❑ 185 Chipper Jones 1.25 .55
❑ 186 Paul O'Neill .60 .25
❑ 187 Mike Greenwell .15 .07
❑ 188 Harold Baines .25 .11
❑ 189 Todd Stottlemyre .15 .07
❑ 190 Jeromy Burnitz .25 .11
❑ 191 Rene Arocha .15 .07
❑ 192 Jeff Fassero .15 .07
❑ 193 Robby Thompson .15 .07
❑ 194 Greg W. Harris .15 .07
❑ 195 Todd Van Poppel .15 .07
❑ 196 Jose Guzman .15 .07
❑ 197 Shane Mack .15 .07
❑ 198 Carlos Garcia .15 .07
❑ 199 Kevin Roberson .15 .07
❑ 200 David McCarty .15 .07
❑ 201 Alan Trammell .40 .18
❑ 202 Chuck Carr .15 .07
❑ 203 Tommy Greene .15 .07
❑ 204 Wilson Alvarez .15 .07
❑ 205 Dwight Gooden .25 .11
❑ 206 Tony Tarasco .15 .07
❑ 207 Darren Lewis .15 .07
❑ 208 Eric Karros .25 .11
❑ 209 Chris Hammond .15 .07
❑ 210 Jeffrey Hammonds .25 .11
❑ 211 Rich Amaral .15 .07
❑ 212 Danny Tartabull .15 .07
❑ 213 Jeff Russell .15 .07
❑ 214 Dave Staton .15 .07
❑ 215 Kenny Lofton .25 .11
❑ 216 Manuel Lee .15 .07
❑ 217 Brian Koelling .15 .07
❑ 218 Scott Lydy .15 .07
❑ 219 Tony Gwynn 1.25 .55
❑ 220 Cecil Fielder .25 .11
❑ 221 Royce Clayton .15 .07
❑ 222 Reggie Sanders .15 .07
❑ 223 Brian Jordan .25 .11
❑ 224 Ken Griffey Jr. 2.00 .90
❑ 225 Fred McGriff .40 .18
❑ 226 Felix Jose .15 .07
❑ 227 Brad Pennington .15 .07
❑ 228 Chris Bosio .15 .07
❑ 229 Mike Stanley .15 .07
❑ 230 Willie Greene .15 .07
❑ 231 Alex Fernandez .15 .07
❑ 232 Brad Ausmus .15 .07
❑ 233 Darrell Whitmore .15 .07
❑ 234 Marcus Moore .15 .07
❑ 235 Allen Watson .15 .07
❑ 236 Jose Offerman .15 .07
❑ 237 Rondell White .25 .11
❑ 238 Jeff King .15 .07
❑ 239 Luis Alicea .15 .07
❑ 240 Dan Wilson .15 .07
❑ 241 Ed Sprague .15 .07
❑ 242 Todd Hundley .15 .07
❑ 243 Al Martin .15 .07
❑ 244 Mike Lansing .15 .07
❑ 245 Ivan Rodriguez .60 .25
❑ 246 Dave Fleming .15 .07
❑ 247 John Doherty .15 .07
❑ 248 Mark McLemore .15 .07
❑ 249 Bob Hamelin .15 .07
❑ 250 Curtis Pride RC .25 .11
❑ 251 Zane Smith .15 .07
❑ 252 Eric Young .15 .07
❑ 253 Brian McRae .15 .07
❑ 254 Tim Raines .25 .11
❑ 255 Javier Lopez .25 .11
❑ 256 Melvin Nieves .15 .07
❑ 257 Randy Myers .15 .07
❑ 258 Willie McGee .25 .11
❑ 259 Jimmy Key UER .25 .11
(birthdate missing on back)
❑ 260 Tom Candiotti .15 .07
❑ 261 Eric Davis .25 .11
❑ 262 Craig Paquette .15 .07
❑ 263 Robin Ventura .25 .11
❑ 264 Pat Kelly .15 .07
❑ 265 Gregg Jefferies .15 .07
❑ 266 Cory Snyder .15 .07
❑ 267 David Justice HFA .15 .07
❑ 268 Sammy Sosa HFA .60 .25
❑ 269 Barry Larkin HFA .25 .11
❑ 270 Andres Galarraga HFA .25 .11
❑ 271 Gary Sheffield HFA .15 .07
❑ 272 Jeff Bagwell HFA .40 .18
❑ 273 Mike Piazza HFA 1.00 .45
❑ 274 Larry Walker HFA .15 .07
❑ 275 Bobby Bonilla HFA .15 .07
❑ 276 John Kruk HFA .15 .07
❑ 277 Jay Bell HFA .15 .07
❑ 278 Ozzie Smith HFA .40 .18
❑ 279 Tony Gwynn HFA .60 .25
❑ 280 Barry Bonds HFA .75 .35
❑ 281 Cal Ripken Jr. HFA 1.25 .55
❑ 282 Mo Vaughn HFA .15 .07
❑ 283 Tim Salmon HFA .15 .07
❑ 284 Frank Thomas HFA .40 .18
❑ 285 Albert Belle HFA .25 .11
❑ 286 Cecil Fielder HFA .15 .07
❑ 287 Wally Joyner HFA .15 .07
❑ 288 Greg Vaughn HFA .15 .07
❑ 289 Kirby Puckett HFA .75 .35
❑ 290 Don Mattingly HFA .75 .35
❑ 291 Terry Steinbach HFA .15 .07
❑ 292 Ken Griffey Jr. HFA 1.00 .45
❑ 293 Juan Gonzalez HFA .25 .11
❑ 294 Paul Molitor HFA .25 .11
❑ 295 Tavo Alvarez UDC .15 .07
❑ 296 Matt Brunson UDC .15 .07
❑ 297 Shawn Green UDC .25 .11
❑ 298 Alex Rodriguez UDC 2.50 1.10
❑ 299 S.Stewart UDC .60 .25
❑ 300 Frank Thomas .75 .35
❑ 301 Mickey Tettleton .15 .07
❑ 302 Pedro Munoz .15 .07
❑ 303 Jose Valentin .15 .07
❑ 304 Orestes Destrade .15 .07
❑ 305 Pat Listach .15 .07
❑ 306 Scott Brosius .25 .11
❑ 307 Kurt Miller .15 .07
❑ 308 Rob Dibble .15 .07
❑ 309 Mike Blowers .15 .07
❑ 310 Jim Abbott .25 .11
❑ 311 Mike Jackson .15 .07
❑ 312 Craig Biggio .40 .18
❑ 313 Kurt Abbott RC .25 .11
❑ 314 Chuck Finley .25 .11
❑ 315 Andres Galarraga .40 .18
❑ 316 Mike Moore .15 .07
❑ 317 Doug Strange .15 .07
❑ 318 Pedro Martinez 1.00 .45
❑ 319 Kevin McReynolds .15 .07
❑ 320 Greg Maddux 1.50 .70
❑ 321 Mike Henneman .15 .07
❑ 322 Scott Leius .15 .07
❑ 323 John Franco .25 .11
❑ 324 Jeff Blauser .15 .07
❑ 325 Kirby Puckett 1.50 .70
❑ 326 Darryl Hamilton .15 .07
❑ 327 John Smiley .15 .07
❑ 328 Derrick May .15 .07
❑ 329 Jose Vizcaino .15 .07
❑ 330 Randy Johnson .75 .35
❑ 331 Jack Morris .25 .11
❑ 332 Graeme Lloyd .15 .07
❑ 333 Dave Valle .15 .07
❑ 334 Greg Myers .15 .07
❑ 335 John Wetteland .25 .11
❑ 336 Jim Gott .15 .07
❑ 337 Tim Naehring .15 .07
❑ 338 Mike Kelly .15 .07
❑ 339 Jeff Montgomery .15 .07
❑ 340 Rafael Palmeiro .60 .25
❑ 341 Eddie Murray .60 .25
❑ 342 Xavier Hernandez .15 .07
❑ 343 Bobby Munoz .15 .07
❑ 344 Bobby Bonilla .25 .11
❑ 345 Travis Fryman .25 .11
❑ 346 Steve Finley .25 .11
❑ 347 Chris Sabo .15 .07
❑ 348 Armando Reynoso .15 .07

❑ 349 Ramon Martinez .15 .07
❑ 350 Will Clark .60 .25
❑ 351 Moises Alou .25 .11
❑ 352 Jim Thome .60 .25
❑ 353 Bob Tewksbury .15 .07
❑ 354 Andujar Cedeno .15 .07
❑ 355 Orel Hershiser .25 .11
❑ 356 Mike Devereaux .15 .07
❑ 357 Mike Perez .15 .07
❑ 358 Dennis Martinez .25 .11
❑ 359 Dave Nilsson .15 .07
❑ 360 Ozzie Smith .75 .35
❑ 361 Eric Anthony .15 .07
❑ 362 Scott Sanders .15 .07
❑ 363 Paul Sorrento .15 .07
❑ 364 Tim Belcher .15 .07
❑ 365 Dennis Eckersley .25 .11
❑ 366 Mel Rojas .15 .07
❑ 367 Tom Henke .15 .07
❑ 368 Randy Tomlin .15 .07
❑ 369 B.J. Surhoff .25 .11
❑ 370 Larry Walker .40 .18
❑ 371 Joey Cora .15 .07
❑ 372 Mike Harkey .15 .07
❑ 373 John Valentin .15 .07
❑ 374 Doug Jones .15 .07
❑ 375 David Justice .25 .11
❑ 376 Vince Coleman .15 .07
❑ 377 David Hulse .15 .07
❑ 378 Kevin Seitzer .15 .07
❑ 379 Pete Harnisch .15 .07
❑ 380 Ruben Sierra .15 .07
❑ 381 Mark Lewis .15 .07
❑ 382 Bip Roberts .15 .07
❑ 383 Paul Wagner .15 .07
❑ 384 Stan Javier .15 .07
❑ 385 Barry Larkin .60 .25
❑ 386 Mark Portugal .15 .07
❑ 387 Roberto Kelly .15 .07
❑ 388 Andy Benes .15 .07
❑ 389 Felix Fermin .15 .07
❑ 390 Marquis Grissom .15 .07
❑ 391 Troy Neel .15 .07
❑ 392 Chad Kreuter .15 .07
❑ 393 Gregg Olson .15 .07
❑ 394 Charles Nagy .15 .07
❑ 395 Jack McDowell .15 .07
❑ 396 Luis Gonzalez .60 .25
❑ 397 Benito Santiago .15 .07
❑ 398 Chris James .15 .07
❑ 399 Terry Mulholland .15 .07
❑ 400 Barry Bonds 1.50 .70
❑ 401 Joe Grahe .15 .07
❑ 402 Duane Ward .15 .07
❑ 403 John Burkett .15 .07
❑ 404 Scott Servais .15 .07
❑ 405 Bryan Harvey .15 .07
❑ 406 Bernard Gilkey .15 .07
❑ 407 Greg McMichael .15 .07
❑ 408 Tim Wallach .15 .07
❑ 409 Ken Caminiti .25 .11
❑ 410 John Kruk .25 .11
❑ 411 Darrin Jackson .15 .07
❑ 412 Mike Gallego .15 .07
❑ 413 David Cone .25 .11
❑ 414 Lou Whitaker .25 .11
❑ 415 Sandy Alomar Jr. .25 .11
❑ 416 Bill Wegman .15 .07
❑ 417 Pat Borders .15 .07
❑ 418 Roger Pavlik .15 .07
❑ 419 Pete Smith .15 .07
❑ 420 Steve Avery .15 .07
❑ 421 David Segui .15 .07
❑ 422 Rheal Cormier .15 .07
❑ 423 Harold Reynolds .15 .07
❑ 424 Edgar Martinez .40 .18
❑ 425 Cal Ripken Jr. 2.50 1.10
❑ 426 Jaime Navarro .15 .07
❑ 427 Sean Berry .15 .07
❑ 428 Bret Saberhagen .25 .11
❑ 429 Bob Welch .15 .07
❑ 430 Juan Guzman .15 .07
❑ 431 Cal Eldred .15 .07
❑ 432 Dave Hollins .15 .07
❑ 433 Sid Fernandez .15 .07
❑ 434 Willie Banks .15 .07
❑ 435 Darryl Kile .25 .11
❑ 436 Henry Rodriguez .15 .07
❑ 437 Tony Fernandez .15 .07
❑ 438 Walt Weiss .15 .07
❑ 439 Kevin Tapani .15 .07
❑ 440 Mark Grace .60 .25
❑ 441 Brian Harper .15 .07
❑ 442 Kent Mercker .15 .07
❑ 443 Anthony Young .15 .07
❑ 444 Todd Zeile .15 .07
❑ 445 Greg Vaughn .25 .11
❑ 446 Ray Lankford .15 .07
❑ 447 Dave Weathers .15 .07
❑ 448 Bret Boone .25 .11
❑ 449 Charlie Hough .25 .11
❑ 450 Roger Clemens 1.50 .70
❑ 451 Mike Morgan .15 .07
❑ 452 Doug Drabek .15 .07
❑ 453 Danny Jackson .15 .07
❑ 454 Dante Bichette .25 .11
❑ 455 Roberto Alomar .60 .25
❑ 456 Ben McDonald .15 .07
❑ 457 Kenny Rogers .15 .07
❑ 458 Bill Gullickson .15 .07
❑ 459 Darrin Fletcher .15 .07
❑ 460 Curt Schilling .60 .25
❑ 461 Billy Hatcher .15 .07
❑ 462 Howard Johnson .15 .07
❑ 463 Mickey Morandini .15 .07
❑ 464 Frank Castillo .15 .07
❑ 465 Delino DeShields .15 .07
❑ 466 Gary Gaetti .25 .11
❑ 467 Steve Farr .15 .07
❑ 468 Roberto Hernandez .15 .07
❑ 469 Jack Armstrong .15 .07
❑ 470 Paul Molitor .60 .25
❑ 471 Melido Perez .15 .07
❑ 472 Greg Hibbard .15 .07
❑ 473 Jody Reed .15 .07
❑ 474 Tom Gordon .15 .07
❑ 475 Gary Sheffield .25 .11
❑ 476 John Jaha .15 .07
❑ 477 Shawon Dunston .15 .07
❑ 478 Reggie Jefferson .15 .07
❑ 479 Don Slaught .15 .07
❑ 480 Jeff Bagwell .75 .35
❑ 481 Tim Pugh .15 .07
❑ 482 Kevin Young .15 .07
❑ 483 Ellis Burks .25 .11
❑ 484 Greg Swindell .15 .07
❑ 485 Mark Langston .15 .07
❑ 486 Omar Vizquel .25 .11
❑ 487 Kevin Brown .25 .11
❑ 488 Terry Steinbach .15 .07
❑ 489 Mark Lemke .15 .07
❑ 490 Matt Williams .40 .18
❑ 491 Pete Incaviglia .15 .07
❑ 492 Karl Rhodes .15 .07
❑ 493 Shawn Green .75 .35
❑ 494 Hal Morris .15 .07
❑ 495 Derek Bell .15 .07
❑ 496 Luis Polonia .15 .07
❑ 497 Otis Nixon .15 .07
❑ 498 Ron Darling .15 .07
❑ 499 Mitch Williams .15 .07
❑ 500 Mike Piazza 2.00 .90
❑ 501 Pat Meares .15 .07
❑ 502 Scott Cooper .15 .07
❑ 503 Scott Erickson .15 .07
❑ 504 Jeff Juden .15 .07
❑ 505 Lee Smith .25 .11
❑ 506 Bobby Ayala .15 .07
❑ 507 Dave Henderson .15 .07
❑ 508 Erik Hanson .15 .07
❑ 509 Bob Wickman .15 .07
❑ 510 Sammy Sosa 1.25 .55
❑ 511 Hector Carrasco .15 .07
❑ 512 Tim Davis .15 .07
❑ 513 Joey Hamilton .15 .07
❑ 514 Robert Eenhoorn .15 .07
❑ 515 Jorge Fabregas .15 .07
❑ 516 Tim Hyers RC .15 .07
❑ 517 John Hudek RC .15 .07
❑ 518 James Mouton .15 .07
❑ 519 Herbert Perry RC .25 .11
❑ 520 Chan Ho Park RC 1.25 .55
❑ 521 W.Va Landingham RC .15 .07
❑ 522 Paul Shuey .15 .07
❑ 523 Ryan Hancock RC .15 .07
❑ 524 Billy Wagner RC .50 .23
❑ 525 Jason Giambi .75 .35
❑ 526 Jose Silva RC .25 .11
❑ 527 Terrell Wade RC .15 .07
❑ 528 Todd Dunn .15 .07
❑ 529 Alan Benes RC .25 .11
❑ 530 B.Kieschnick RC .15 .07
❑ 531 T.Hollandsworth .15 .07
❑ 532 Brad Fullmer RC 1.00 .45
❑ 533 S.Soderstrom RC .15 .07
❑ 534 Daron Kirkreit .15 .07
❑ 535 Arquimedez Pozo RC .15 .07
❑ 536 Charles Johnson .25 .11
❑ 537 Preston Wilson .60 .25
❑ 538 Alex Ochoa .15 .07
❑ 539 Derrek Lee RC .50 .23
❑ 540 Wayne Gomes RC .15 .07
❑ 541 J.Allensworth RC .15 .07
❑ 542 Mike Bell RC .15 .07
❑ 543 Trot Nixon RC 1.25 .55
❑ 544 Pokey Reese .15 .07
❑ 545 Neifi Perez RC .50 .23
❑ 546 Johnny Damon .60 .25
❑ 547 Matt Brunson RC .15 .07
❑ 548 L.Hawkins RC .25 .11
❑ 549 Eddie Pearson RC .15 .07
❑ 550 Derek Jeter 3.00 1.35
❑ A298 Alex Rodriguez AU 200.00 90.00
❑ P224 K.Griffey Jr. Promo 2.50 1.10
❑ GM1 Ken Griffey Jr. AU 1200.00 550.00
Mickey Mantle AU/1000
❑ KG1 K.Griffey Jr. AU/1000 250.00 110.00
❑ MM1 M.Mantle AU/1000 600.00 275.00

1995 Upper Deck

	MINT	NRMT
COMP.MASTER SET (495)	80.00	36.00
COMPLETE SET (450)	60.00	27.00
COMPLETE SERIES 1 (225)	30.00	13.50
COMPLETE SERIES 2 (225)	30.00	13.50
COMMON CARD (1-450)	.15	.07
COMP.TRADE SET (45)	25.00	11.00
COMMON TRADE (451T-495T)	.50	.23

❑ 1 Ruben Rivera .15 .07
❑ 2 Bill Pulsipher .15 .07
❑ 3 Ben Grieve .60 .25
❑ 4 Curtis Goodwin .15 .07
❑ 5 Damon Hollins .15 .07
❑ 6 Todd Greene .15 .07
❑ 7 Glenn Williams .15 .07
❑ 8 Bret Wagner .15 .07
❑ 9 Karim Garcia RC .25 .11
❑ 10 Nomar Garciaparra 3.00 1.35
❑ 11 Raul Casanova RC .15 .07
❑ 12 Matt Smith .15 .07
❑ 13 Paul Wilson .15 .07
❑ 14 Jason Isringhausen .25 .11
❑ 15 Reid Ryan .25 .11
❑ 16 Lee Smith .25 .11
❑ 17 Chili Davis .25 .11
❑ 18 Brian Anderson .15 .07
❑ 19 Gary DiSarcina .15 .07
❑ 20 Bo Jackson .25 .11

❑ 21 Chuck Finley .25 .11
❑ 22 Darryl Kile .25 .11
❑ 23 Shane Reynolds .15 .07
❑ 24 Tony Eusebio .15 .07
❑ 25 Craig Biggio .40 .18
❑ 26 Doug Drabek .15 .07
❑ 27 Brian L. Hunter .15 .07
❑ 28 James Mouton .15 .07
❑ 29 Geronimo Berroa .15 .07
❑ 30 Rickey Henderson 1.25 .55
❑ 31 Steve Karsay .15 .07
❑ 32 Steve Ontiveros .15 .07
❑ 33 Ernie Young .15 .07
❑ 34 Dennis Eckersley .25 .11
❑ 35 Mark McGwire 2.50 1.10
❑ 36 Dave Stewart .25 .11
❑ 37 Pat Hentgen .15 .07
❑ 38 Carlos Delgado .60 .25
❑ 39 Joe Carter .25 .11
❑ 40 Roberto Alomar .60 .25
❑ 41 John Olerud .25 .11
❑ 42 Devon White .25 .11
❑ 43 Roberto Kelly .15 .07
❑ 44 Jeff Blauser .15 .07
❑ 45 Fred McGriff .40 .18
❑ 46 Tom Glavine .60 .25
❑ 47 Mike Kelly .15 .07
❑ 48 Javier Lopez .25 .11
❑ 49 Greg Maddux 1.50 .70
❑ 50 Matt Mieske .15 .07
❑ 51 Troy O'Leary .15 .07
❑ 52 Jeff Cirillo .25 .11
❑ 53 Cal Eldred .15 .07
❑ 54 Pat Listach .15 .07
❑ 55 Jose Valentin .15 .07
❑ 56 John Mabry .15 .07
❑ 57 Bob Tewksbury .15 .07
❑ 58 Brian Jordan .25 .11
❑ 59 Gregg Jefferies .15 .07
❑ 60 Ozzie Smith .75 .35
❑ 61 Geronimo Pena .15 .07
❑ 62 Mark Whiten .15 .07
❑ 63 Rey Sanchez .15 .07
❑ 64 Willie Banks .15 .07
❑ 65 Mark Grace .60 .25
❑ 66 Randy Myers .15 .07
❑ 67 Steve Trachsel .15 .07
❑ 68 Derrick May .15 .07
❑ 69 Brett Butler .25 .11
❑ 70 Eric Karros .25 .11
❑ 71 Tim Wallach .15 .07
❑ 72 Delino DeShields .15 .07
❑ 73 Darren Dreifort .15 .07
❑ 74 Orel Hershiser .25 .11
❑ 75 Billy Ashley .15 .07
❑ 76 Sean Berry .15 .07
❑ 77 Ken Hill .15 .07
❑ 78 John Wetteland .25 .11
❑ 79 Moises Alou .25 .11
❑ 80 Cliff Floyd .25 .11
❑ 81 Marquis Grissom .15 .07
❑ 82 Larry Walker .40 .18
❑ 83 Rondell White .25 .11
❑ 84 W.VanLandingham .15 .07
❑ 85 Matt Williams .40 .18
❑ 86 Rod Beck .15 .07
❑ 87 Darren Lewis .15 .07
❑ 88 Robby Thompson .15 .07
❑ 89 Darryl Strawberry .25 .11
❑ 90 Kenny Lofton .25 .11
❑ 91 Charles Nagy .15 .07
❑ 92 Sandy Alomar Jr. .25 .11
❑ 93 Mark Clark .15 .07
❑ 94 Dennis Martinez .25 .11
❑ 95 Dave Winfield .60 .25
❑ 96 Jim Thome .60 .25
❑ 97 Manny Ramirez .75 .35
❑ 98 Goose Gossage .25 .11
❑ 99 Tino Martinez .25 .11
❑ 100 Ken Griffey Jr. 2.00 .90
❑ 101 Greg Maddux ANA .75 .35
❑ 102 Randy Johnson ANA .40 .18
❑ 103 Barry Bonds ANA .75 .35
❑ 104 Juan Gonzalez ANA .25 .11
❑ 105 Frank Thomas ANA .40 .18
❑ 106 Matt Williams ANA .25 .11
❑ 107 Paul Molitor ANA .25 .11
❑ 108 Fred McGriff ANA .25 .11
❑ 109 Carlos Baerga ANA .15 .07
❑ 110 Ken Griffey Jr. ANA 1.00 .45
❑ 111 Reggie Jefferson .15 .07
❑ 112 Randy Johnson .75 .35
❑ 113 Marc Newfield .15 .07
❑ 114 Robb Nen .15 .07
❑ 115 Jeff Conine .15 .07
❑ 116 Kurt Abbott .15 .07
❑ 117 Charlie Hough .25 .11
❑ 118 Dave Weathers .15 .07
❑ 119 Juan Castillo .15 .07
❑ 120 Bret Saberhagen .25 .11
❑ 121 Rico Brogna .15 .07
❑ 122 John Franco .25 .11
❑ 123 Todd Hundley .15 .07
❑ 124 Jason Jacome .15 .07
❑ 125 Bobby Jones .15 .07
❑ 126 Bret Barberie .15 .07
❑ 127 Ben McDonald .15 .07
❑ 128 Harold Baines .25 .11
❑ 129 Jeffrey Hammonds .15 .07
❑ 130 Mike Mussina .60 .25
❑ 131 Chris Hoiles .15 .07
❑ 132 Brady Anderson .25 .11
❑ 133 Eddie Williams .15 .07
❑ 134 Andy Benes .15 .07
❑ 135 Tony Gwynn 1.25 .55
❑ 136 Bip Roberts .15 .07
❑ 137 Joey Hamilton .15 .07
❑ 138 Luis Lopez .15 .07
❑ 139 Ray McDavid .15 .07
❑ 140 Lenny Dykstra .25 .11
❑ 141 Mariano Duncan .15 .07
❑ 142 Fernando Valenzuela .25 .11
❑ 143 Bobby Munoz .15 .07
❑ 144 Kevin Stocker .15 .07
❑ 145 John Kruk .25 .11
❑ 146 Jon Lieber .15 .07
❑ 147 Zane Smith .15 .07
❑ 148 Steve Cooke .15 .07
❑ 149 Andy Van Slyke .25 .11
❑ 150 Jay Bell .25 .11
❑ 151 Carlos Garcia .15 .07
❑ 152 John Dettmer .15 .07
❑ 153 Darren Oliver .15 .07
❑ 154 Dean Palmer .25 .11
❑ 155 Otis Nixon .15 .07
❑ 156 Rusty Greer .25 .11
❑ 157 Rick Helling .15 .07
❑ 158 Jose Canseco .60 .25
❑ 159 Roger Clemens 1.50 .70
❑ 160 Andre Dawson .40 .18
❑ 161 Mo Vaughn .25 .11
❑ 162 Aaron Sele .25 .11
❑ 163 John Valentin .15 .07
❑ 164 Brian R. Hunter .15 .07
❑ 165 Bret Boone .25 .11
❑ 166 Hector Carrasco .15 .07
❑ 167 Pete Schourek .15 .07
❑ 168 Willie Greene .15 .07
❑ 169 Kevin Mitchell .15 .07
❑ 170 Deion Sanders .25 .11
❑ 171 John Roper .15 .07
❑ 172 Charlie Hayes .15 .07
❑ 173 David Nied .15 .07
❑ 174 Ellis Burks .25 .11
❑ 175 Dante Bichette .25 .11
❑ 176 Marvin Freeman .15 .07
❑ 177 Eric Young .15 .07
❑ 178 David Cone .25 .11
❑ 179 Greg Gagne .15 .07
❑ 180 Bob Hamelin .15 .07
❑ 181 Wally Joyner .25 .11
❑ 182 Jeff Montgomery .15 .07
❑ 183 Jose Lind .15 .07
❑ 184 Chris Gomez .15 .07
❑ 185 Travis Fryman .25 .11
❑ 186 Kirk Gibson .25 .11
❑ 187 Mike Moore .15 .07
❑ 188 Lou Whitaker .25 .11
❑ 189 Sean Bergman .15 .07
❑ 190 Shane Mack .15 .07
❑ 191 Rick Aguilera .15 .07
❑ 192 Denny Hocking .15 .07
❑ 193 Chuck Knoblauch .25 .11
❑ 194 Kevin Tapani .15 .07
❑ 195 Kent Hrbek .25 .11
❑ 196 Ozzie Guillen .15 .07
❑ 197 Wilson Alvarez .15 .07
❑ 198 Tim Raines .25 .11
❑ 199 Scott Ruffcorn .15 .07
❑ 200 Michael Jordan 2.50 1.10
❑ 201 Robin Ventura .25 .11
❑ 202 Jason Bere .15 .07
❑ 203 Darrin Jackson .15 .07
❑ 204 Russ Davis .15 .07
❑ 205 Jimmy Key .25 .11
❑ 206 Jack McDowell .15 .07
❑ 207 Jim Abbott .25 .11
❑ 208 Paul O'Neill .60 .25
❑ 209 Bernie Williams .60 .25
❑ 210 Don Mattingly 1.50 .70
❑ 211 Orlando Miller .15 .07
❑ 212 Alex Gonzalez .15 .07
❑ 213 Terrell Wade .15 .07
❑ 214 Jose Oliva .15 .07
❑ 215 Alex Rodriguez 2.00 .90
❑ 216 Garret Anderson .25 .11
❑ 217 Alan Benes .15 .07
❑ 218 Armando Benitez .25 .11
❑ 219 Dustin Hermanson .15 .07
❑ 220 Charles Johnson .25 .11
❑ 221 Julian Tavarez .15 .07
❑ 222 Jason Giambi .60 .25
❑ 223 LaTroy Hawkins .15 .07
❑ 224 Todd Hollandsworth .15 .07
❑ 225 Derek Jeter 2.50 1.10
❑ 226 Hideo Nomo RC 2.00 .90
❑ 227 Tony Clark .25 .11
❑ 228 Roger Cedeno .15 .07
❑ 229 Scott Stahoviak .15 .07
❑ 230 Michael Tucker .15 .07
❑ 231 Joe Rosselli .15 .07
❑ 232 Antonio Osuna .15 .07
❑ 233 Bobby Higginson RC 1.25 .55
❑ 234 Mark Grudzielanek RC .25 .11
❑ 235 Ray Durham .25 .11
❑ 236 Frank Rodriguez .15 .07
❑ 237 Quilvio Veras .15 .07
❑ 238 Darren Bragg .15 .07
❑ 239 Ugueth Urbina .15 .07
❑ 240 Jason Bates .15 .07
❑ 241 David Bell .15 .07
❑ 242 Ron Villone .15 .07
❑ 243 Joe Randa .15 .07
❑ 244 Carlos Perez RC .25 .11
❑ 245 Brad Clontz .15 .07
❑ 246 Steve Rodriguez .15 .07
❑ 247 Joe Vitiello .15 .07
❑ 248 Ozzie Timmons .15 .07
❑ 249 Rudy Pemberton .15 .07
❑ 250 Marty Cordova .15 .07
❑ 251 Tony Graffanino .15 .07
❑ 252 Mark Johnson RC .25 .11
❑ 253 Tomas Perez RC .15 .07
❑ 254 Jimmy Hurst .15 .07
❑ 255 Edgardo Alfonzo .60 .25
❑ 256 Jose Malave .15 .07
❑ 257 Brad Radke RC 2.50 1.10
❑ 258 Jon Nunnally .15 .07
❑ 259 Dilson Torres RC .15 .07
❑ 260 Esteban Loaiza .15 .07
❑ 261 Freddy Adrian Garcia RC .15 .07
❑ 262 Don Wengert .15 .07
❑ 263 Robert Person RC .50 .23
❑ 264 Tim Unroe RC .15 .07
❑ 265 Juan Acevedo RC .15 .07
❑ 266 Eduardo Perez .15 .07
❑ 267 Tony Phillips .15 .07
❑ 268 Jim Edmonds .40 .18
❑ 269 Jorge Fabregas .15 .07
❑ 270 Tim Salmon .25 .11
❑ 271 Mark Langston .15 .07
❑ 272 J.T. Snow .25 .11
❑ 273 Phil Plantier .15 .07
❑ 274 Derek Bell .15 .07
❑ 275 Jeff Bagwell .75 .35
❑ 276 Luis Gonzalez .60 .25
❑ 277 John Hudek .15 .07
❑ 278 Todd Stottlemyre .15 .07

	Card	Mint	NrMt
❑ 279	Mark Acre	.15	.07
❑ 280	Ruben Sierra	.15	.07
❑ 281	Mike Bordick	.15	.07
❑ 282	Ron Darling	.15	.07
❑ 283	Brent Gates	.15	.07
❑ 284	Todd Van Poppel	.15	.07
❑ 285	Paul Molitor	.60	.25
❑ 286	Ed Sprague	.15	.07
❑ 287	Juan Guzman	.15	.07
❑ 288	David Cone	.25	.11
❑ 289	Shawn Green	.60	.25
❑ 290	Marquis Grissom	.15	.07
❑ 291	Kent Mercker	.15	.07
❑ 292	Steve Avery	.15	.07
❑ 293	Chipper Jones	1.25	.55
❑ 294	John Smoltz	.25	.11
❑ 295	David Justice	.25	.11
❑ 296	Ryan Klesko	.25	.11
❑ 297	Joe Oliver	.15	.07
❑ 298	Ricky Bones	.15	.07
❑ 299	John Jaha	.15	.07
❑ 300	Greg Vaughn	.25	.11
❑ 301	Dave Nilsson	.15	.07
❑ 302	Kevin Seitzer	.15	.07
❑ 303	Bernard Gilkey	.15	.07
❑ 304	Allen Battle	.15	.07
❑ 305	Ray Lankford	.15	.07
❑ 306	Tom Pagnozzi	.15	.07
❑ 307	Allen Watson	.15	.07
❑ 308	Danny Jackson	.15	.07
❑ 309	Ken Hill	.15	.07
❑ 310	Todd Zeile	.15	.07
❑ 311	Kevin Roberson	.15	.07
❑ 312	Steve Buechele	.15	.07
❑ 313	Rick Wilkins	.15	.07
❑ 314	Kevin Foster	.15	.07
❑ 315	Sammy Sosa	1.25	.55
❑ 316	Howard Johnson	.15	.07
❑ 317	Greg Hansell	.15	.07
❑ 318	Pedro Astacio	.15	.07
❑ 319	Rafael Bournigal	.15	.07
❑ 320	Mike Piazza	1.50	.70
❑ 321	Ramon Martinez	.15	.07
❑ 322	Raul Mondesi	.25	.11
❑ 323	Ismael Valdes	.15	.07
❑ 324	Wil Cordero	.15	.07
❑ 325	Tony Tarasco	.15	.07
❑ 326	Roberto Kelly	.15	.07
❑ 327	Jeff Fassero	.15	.07
❑ 328	Mike Lansing	.15	.07
❑ 329	Pedro Martinez	.75	.35
❑ 330	Kirk Rueter	.15	.07
❑ 331	Glenallen Hill	.15	.07
❑ 332	Kirt Manwaring	.15	.07
❑ 333	Royce Clayton	.15	.07
❑ 334	J.R. Phillips	.15	.07
❑ 335	Barry Bonds	1.50	.70
❑ 336	Mark Portugal	.15	.07
❑ 337	Terry Mulholland	.15	.07
❑ 338	Omar Vizquel	.25	.11
❑ 339	Carlos Baerga	.15	.07
❑ 340	Albert Belle	.25	.11
❑ 341	Eddie Murray	.60	.25
❑ 342	Wayne Kirby	.15	.07
❑ 343	Chad Ogea	.15	.07
❑ 344	Tim Davis	.15	.07
❑ 345	Jay Buhner	.25	.11
❑ 346	Bobby Ayala	.15	.07
❑ 347	Mike Blowers	.15	.07
❑ 348	Dave Fleming	.15	.07
❑ 349	Edgar Martinez	.40	.18
❑ 350	Andre Dawson	.40	.18
❑ 351	Darrell Whitmore	.15	.07
❑ 352	Chuck Carr	.15	.07
❑ 353	John Burkett	.15	.07
❑ 354	Chris Hammond	.15	.07
❑ 355	Gary Sheffield	.25	.11
❑ 356	Pat Rapp	.15	.07
❑ 357	Greg Colbrunn	.15	.07
❑ 358	David Segui	.15	.07
❑ 359	Jeff Kent	.40	.18
❑ 360	Bobby Bonilla	.25	.11
❑ 361	Pete Harnisch	.15	.07
❑ 362	Ryan Thompson	.15	.07
❑ 363	Jose Vizcaino	.15	.07
❑ 364	Brett Butler	.25	.11
❑ 365	Cal Ripken Jr.	2.50	1.10
❑ 366	Rafael Palmeiro	.60	.25
❑ 367	Leo Gomez	.15	.07
❑ 368	Andy Van Slyke	.25	.11
❑ 369	Arthur Rhodes	.15	.07
❑ 370	Ken Caminiti	.25	.11
❑ 371	Steve Finley	.25	.11
❑ 372	Melvin Nieves	.15	.07
❑ 373	Andujar Cedeno	.15	.07
❑ 374	Trevor Hoffman	.25	.11
❑ 375	Fernando Valenzuela	.25	.11
❑ 376	Ricky Bottalico	.15	.07
❑ 377	Dave Hollins	.15	.07
❑ 378	Charlie Hayes	.15	.07
❑ 379	Tommy Greene	.15	.07
❑ 380	Darren Daulton	.25	.11
❑ 381	Curt Schilling	.60	.25
❑ 382	Midre Cummings	.15	.07
❑ 383	Al Martin	.15	.07
❑ 384	Jeff King	.15	.07
❑ 385	Orlando Merced	.15	.07
❑ 386	Denny Neagle	.25	.11
❑ 387	Don Slaught	.15	.07
❑ 388	Dave Clark	.15	.07
❑ 389	Kevin Gross	.15	.07
❑ 390	Will Clark	.60	.25
❑ 391	Ivan Rodriguez	.60	.25
❑ 392	Benji Gil	.15	.07
❑ 393	Jeff Frye	.15	.07
❑ 394	Kenny Rogers	.15	.07
❑ 395	Juan Gonzalez	.60	.25
❑ 396	Mike Macfarlane	.15	.07
❑ 397	Lee Tinsley	.15	.07
❑ 398	Tim Naehring	.15	.07
❑ 399	Tim Vanegmond	.15	.07
❑ 400	Mike Greenwell	.15	.07
❑ 401	Ken Ryan	.15	.07
❑ 402	John Smiley	.15	.07
❑ 403	Tim Pugh	.15	.07
❑ 404	Reggie Sanders	.15	.07
❑ 405	Barry Larkin	.60	.25
❑ 406	Hal Morris	.15	.07
❑ 407	Jose Rijo	.15	.07
❑ 408	Lance Painter	.15	.07
❑ 409	Joe Girardi	.15	.07
❑ 410	Andres Galarraga	.40	.18
❑ 411	Mike Kingery	.15	.07
❑ 412	Roberto Mejia	.15	.07
❑ 413	Walt Weiss	.15	.07
❑ 414	Bill Swift	.15	.07
❑ 415	Larry Walker	.40	.18
❑ 416	Billy Brewer	.15	.07
❑ 417	Pat Borders	.15	.07
❑ 418	Tom Gordon	.15	.07
❑ 419	Kevin Appier	.25	.11
❑ 420	Gary Gaetti	.25	.11
❑ 421	Greg Gohr	.15	.07
❑ 422	Felipe Lira	.15	.07
❑ 423	John Doherty	.15	.07
❑ 424	Chad Curtis	.15	.07
❑ 425	Cecil Fielder	.25	.11
❑ 426	Alan Trammell	.40	.18
❑ 427	David McCarty	.15	.07
❑ 428	Scott Erickson	.15	.07
❑ 429	Pat Mahomes	.15	.07
❑ 430	Kirby Puckett	1.50	.70
❑ 431	Dave Stevens	.15	.07
❑ 432	Pedro Munoz	.15	.07
❑ 433	Chris Sabo	.15	.07
❑ 434	Alex Fernandez	.15	.07
❑ 435	Frank Thomas	.75	.35
❑ 436	Roberto Hernandez	.15	.07
❑ 437	Lance Johnson	.15	.07
❑ 438	Jim Abbott	.25	.11
❑ 439	John Wetteland	.25	.11
❑ 440	Melido Perez	.15	.07
❑ 441	Tony Fernandez	.15	.07
❑ 442	Pat Kelly	.15	.07
❑ 443	Mike Stanley	.15	.07
❑ 444	Danny Tartabull	.15	.07
❑ 445	Wade Boggs	.60	.25
❑ 446	Robin Yount	.60	.25
❑ 447	Ryne Sandberg	.75	.35
❑ 448	Nolan Ryan	3.00	1.35
❑ 449	George Brett	1.25	.55
❑ 450	Mike Schmidt	1.00	.45
❑ 451	Jim Abbott TRADE	.75	.35
❑ 452	D.Tartabull TRADE	.50	.23
❑ 453	Ariel Prieto TRADE	.50	.23
❑ 454	Scott Cooper TRADE	.50	.23
❑ 455	Tom Henke TRADE	.50	.23
❑ 456	Todd Zeile TRADE	.50	.23
❑ 457	Brian McRae TRADE	.50	.23
❑ 458	Luis Gonzalez TRADE	2.00	.90
❑ 459	Jaime Navarro TRADE	.50	.23
❑ 460	Todd Worrell TRADE	.50	.23
❑ 461	Roberto Kelly TRADE	.50	.23
❑ 462	Chad Fonville TRADE	.50	.23
❑ 463	S.Andrews TRADE	.50	.23
❑ 464	David Segui TRADE	.50	.23
❑ 465	Deion Sanders TRADE	.75	.35
❑ 466	Orel Hershiser TRADE	.75	.35
❑ 467	Ken Hill TRADE	.50	.23
❑ 468	Andy Benes TRADE	.50	.23
❑ 469	T.Pendleton TRADE	.75	.35
❑ 470	Bobby Bonilla TRADE	.75	.35
❑ 471	Scott Erickson TRADE	.50	.23
❑ 472	Kevin Brown TRADE	.75	.35
❑ 473	G.Dishman TRADE	.50	.23
❑ 474	Phil Plantier TRADE	.50	.23
❑ 475	G.Jefferies TRADE	.50	.23
❑ 476	Tyler Green TRADE	.50	.23
❑ 477	H. Slocumb TRADE	.50	.23
❑ 478	Mark Whiten TRADE	.50	.23
❑ 479	M.Tettleton TRADE	.50	.23
❑ 480	Tim Wakefield TRADE	.50	.23
❑ 481	V. Eshelman TRADE	.50	.23
❑ 482	Rick Aguilera TRADE	.50	.23
❑ 483	Erik Hanson TRADE	.50	.23
❑ 484	Willie McGee TRADE	.75	.35
❑ 485	Troy O'Leary TRADE	.50	.23
❑ 486	B.Santiago TRADE	.50	.23
❑ 487	Darren Lewis TRADE	.50	.23
❑ 488	Dave Burba TRADE	.50	.23
❑ 489	Ron Gant TRADE	.50	.23
❑ 490	B.Saberhagen TRADE	.75	.35
❑ 491	Vinny Castilla TRADE	.75	.35
❑ 492	F.Rodriguez TRADE	.50	.23
❑ 493	Andy Pettitte TRADE	.75	.35
❑ 494	Ruben Sierra TRADE	.50	.23
❑ 495	David Cone TRADE	.75	.35
❑ J159	R. Clemens Jumbo AU	40.00	18.00
❑ J215	A. Rodriguez Jumbo AU	80.00	36.00
❑ P100	K.Griffey Jr. Promo	2.50	1.10

1996 Upper Deck

	MINT	NRMT
COMPLETE SET (480)	50.00	22.00
COMP.FACT.SET (510)	60.00	27.00
COMPLETE SERIES 1 (240)	25.00	11.00
COMPLETE SERIES 2 (240)	25.00	11.00
COMMON CARD (1-480)	.15	.07
COMP.UPDATE SET (30)	20.00	9.00
COMMON UPDATE (481U-510U)	.50	.23

	Card	Mint	NrMt
❑ 1	Cal Ripken 2131	4.00	1.80
❑ 2	Eddie Murray 3000 Hits	.60	.25
❑ 3	Mark Wohlers	.15	.07
❑ 4	David Justice	.25	.11
❑ 5	Chipper Jones	1.25	.55
❑ 6	Javier Lopez	.25	.11
❑ 7	Mark Lemke	.15	.07
❑ 8	Marquis Grissom	.15	.07

❑ 9 Tom Glavine .60 .25
❑ 10 Greg Maddux 1.50 .70
❑ 11 Manny Alexander .15 .07
❑ 12 Curtis Goodwin .15 .07
❑ 13 Scott Erickson .15 .07
❑ 14 Chris Hoiles .15 .07
❑ 15 Rafael Palmeiro .60 .25
❑ 16 Rick Krivda .15 .07
❑ 17 Jeff Manto .15 .07
❑ 18 Mo Vaughn .25 .11
❑ 19 Tim Wakefield .15 .07
❑ 20 Roger Clemens 1.50 .70
❑ 21 Tim Naehring .15 .07
❑ 22 Troy O'Leary .15 .07
❑ 23 Mike Greenwell .15 .07
❑ 24 Stan Belinda .15 .07
❑ 25 John Valentin .15 .07
❑ 26 J.T. Snow .25 .11
❑ 27 Gary DiSarcina .15 .07
❑ 28 Mark Langston .15 .07
❑ 29 Brian Anderson .15 .07
❑ 30 Jim Edmonds .40 .18
❑ 31 Garret Anderson .25 .11
❑ 32 Orlando Palmeiro .15 .07
❑ 33 Brian McRae .15 .07
❑ 34 Kevin Foster .15 .07
❑ 35 Sammy Sosa 1.25 .55
❑ 36 Todd Zeile .15 .07
❑ 37 Jim Bullinger .15 .07
❑ 38 Luis Gonzalez .60 .25
❑ 39 Lyle Mouton .15 .07
❑ 40 Ray Durham .25 .11
❑ 41 Ozzie Guillen .15 .07
❑ 42 Alex Fernandez .15 .07
❑ 43 Brian Keyser .15 .07
❑ 44 Robin Ventura .25 .11
❑ 45 Reggie Sanders .15 .07
❑ 46 Pete Schourek .15 .07
❑ 47 John Smiley .15 .07
❑ 48 Jeff Brantley .15 .07
❑ 49 Thomas Howard .15 .07
❑ 50 Bret Boone .25 .11
❑ 51 Kevin Jarvis .15 .07
❑ 52 Jeff Branson .15 .07
❑ 53 Carlos Baerga .15 .07
❑ 54 Jim Thome .60 .25
❑ 55 Manny Ramirez .75 .35
❑ 56 Omar Vizquel .25 .11
❑ 57 Jose Mesa .15 .07
❑ 58 Julian Tavarez UER .15 .07
❑ 59 Orel Hershiser .25 .11
❑ 60 Larry Walker .40 .18
❑ 61 Bret Saberhagen .25 .11
❑ 62 Vinny Castilla .25 .11
❑ 63 Eric Young .15 .07
❑ 64 Bryan Rekar .15 .07
❑ 65 Andres Galarraga .40 .18
❑ 66 Steve Reed .15 .07
❑ 67 Chad Curtis .15 .07
❑ 68 Bobby Higginson .25 .11
❑ 69 Phil Nevin .25 .11
❑ 70 Cecil Fielder .25 .11
❑ 71 Felipe Lira .15 .07
❑ 72 Chris Gomez .15 .07
❑ 73 Charles Johnson .25 .11
❑ 74 Quilvio Veras .15 .07
❑ 75 Jeff Conine .15 .07
❑ 76 John Burkett .15 .07
❑ 77 Greg Colbrunn .15 .07
❑ 78 Terry Pendleton .25 .11
❑ 79 Shane Reynolds .15 .07
❑ 80 Jeff Bagwell .75 .35
❑ 81 Orlando Miller .15 .07
❑ 82 Mike Hampton .25 .11
❑ 83 James Mouton .15 .07
❑ 84 Brian L. Hunter .15 .07
❑ 85 Derek Bell .15 .07
❑ 86 Kevin Appier .25 .11
❑ 87 Joe Vitiello .15 .07
❑ 88 Wally Joyner .25 .11
❑ 89 Michael Tucker .15 .07
❑ 90 Johnny Damon .25 .11
❑ 91 Jon Nunnally .15 .07
❑ 92 Jason Jacome .15 .07
❑ 93 Chad Fonville .15 .07
❑ 94 Chan Ho Park .25 .11
❑ 95 Hideo Nomo .75 .35
❑ 96 Ismael Valdes .15 .07
❑ 97 Greg Gagne .15 .07
❑ 98 Arizona Diamondbacks .60 .25
Tampa Bay Devil Rays
❑ 99 Raul Mondesi .25 .11
❑ 100 Dave Winfield YH .25 .11
❑ 101 Dennis Eckersley YH .15 .07
❑ 102 Andre Dawson YH .25 .11
❑ 103 Dennis Martinez YH .15 .07
❑ 104 Lance Parrish YH .15 .07
❑ 105 Eddie Murray YH .25 .11
❑ 106 Alan Trammell YH .25 .11
❑ 107 Lou Whitaker YH .15 .07
❑ 108 Ozzie Smith YH .40 .18
❑ 109 Paul Molitor YH .25 .11
❑ 110 Rickey Henderson YH .60 .25
❑ 111 Tim Raines YH .15 .07
❑ 112 Harold Baines YH .15 .07
❑ 113 Lee Smith YH .15 .07
❑ 114 F.Valenzuela YH .15 .07
❑ 115 Cal Ripken YH 1.25 .55
❑ 116 Tony Gwynn YH .60 .25
❑ 117 Wade Boggs .60 .25
❑ 118 Todd Hollandsworth .15 .07
❑ 119 Dave Nilsson .15 .07
❑ 120 Jose Valentin .15 .07
❑ 121 Steve Sparks .15 .07
❑ 122 Chuck Carr .15 .07
❑ 123 John Jaha .15 .07
❑ 124 Scott Karl .15 .07
❑ 125 Chuck Knoblauch .25 .11
❑ 126 Brad Radke .25 .11
❑ 127 Pat Meares .15 .07
❑ 128 Ron Coomer .15 .07
❑ 129 Pedro Munoz .15 .07
❑ 130 Kirby Puckett 1.50 .70
❑ 131 David Segui .15 .07
❑ 132 Mark Grudzielanek .15 .07
❑ 133 Mike Lansing .15 .07
❑ 134 Sean Berry .15 .07
❑ 135 Rondell White .25 .11
❑ 136 Pedro Martinez .75 .35
❑ 137 Carl Everett .25 .11
❑ 138 Dave Mlicki .15 .07
❑ 139 Bill Pulsipher .15 .07
❑ 140 Jason Isringhausen .25 .11
❑ 141 Rico Brogna .15 .07
❑ 142 Edgardo Alfonzo .25 .11
❑ 143 Jeff Kent .40 .18
❑ 144 Andy Pettitte .25 .11
❑ 145 Mike Piazza BO .75 .35
❑ 146 Cliff Floyd BO .15 .07
❑ 147 J.Isringhausen BO .15 .07
❑ 148 Tim Wakefield BO .15 .07
❑ 149 Chipper Jones BO .60 .25
❑ 150 Hideo Nomo BO .25 .11
❑ 151 Mark McGwire BO 1.25 .55
❑ 152 Ron Gant BO .15 .07
❑ 153 Gary Gaetti BO .15 .07
❑ 154 Don Mattingly 1.50 .70
❑ 155 Paul O'Neill .60 .25
❑ 156 Derek Jeter 2.50 1.10
❑ 157 Joe Girardi .15 .07
❑ 158 Ruben Sierra .15 .07
❑ 159 Jorge Posada .25 .11
❑ 160 Geronimo Berroa .15 .07
❑ 161 Steve Ontiveros .15 .07
❑ 162 George Williams .15 .07
❑ 163 Doug Johns .15 .07
❑ 164 Ariel Prieto .15 .07
❑ 165 Scott Brosius .25 .11
❑ 166 Mike Bordick .15 .07
❑ 167 Tyler Green .15 .07
❑ 168 Mickey Morandini .15 .07
❑ 169 Darren Daulton .25 .11
❑ 170 Gregg Jefferies .15 .07
❑ 171 Jim Eisenreich .15 .07
❑ 172 Heathcliff Slocumb .15 .07
❑ 173 Kevin Stocker .15 .07
❑ 174 Esteban Loaiza .15 .07
❑ 175 Jeff King .15 .07
❑ 176 Mark Johnson .15 .07
❑ 177 Denny Neagle .25 .11
❑ 178 Orlando Merced .15 .07
❑ 179 Carlos Garcia .15 .07
❑ 180 Brian Jordan .25 .11
❑ 181 Mike Morgan .15 .07
❑ 182 Mark Petkovsek .15 .07
❑ 183 Bernard Gilkey .15 .07
❑ 184 John Mabry .15 .07
❑ 185 Tom Henke .15 .07
❑ 186 Glenn Dishman .15 .07
❑ 187 Andy Ashby .15 .07
❑ 188 Bip Roberts .15 .07
❑ 189 Melvin Nieves .15 .07
❑ 190 Ken Caminiti .25 .11
❑ 191 Brad Ausmus .15 .07
❑ 192 Deion Sanders .25 .11
❑ 193 Jamie Brewington RC .15 .07
❑ 194 Glenallen Hill .15 .07
❑ 195 Barry Bonds 1.50 .70
❑ 196 Wm. Van Landingham .15 .07
❑ 197 Mark Carreon .15 .07
❑ 198 Royce Clayton .15 .07
❑ 199 Joey Cora .15 .07
❑ 200 Ken Griffey Jr. 2.00 .90
❑ 201 Jay Buhner .25 .11
❑ 202 Alex Rodriguez 1.50 .70
❑ 203 Norm Charlton .15 .07
❑ 204 Andy Benes .15 .07
❑ 205 Edgar Martinez .40 .18
❑ 206 Juan Gonzalez .60 .25
❑ 207 Will Clark .60 .25
❑ 208 Kevin Gross .15 .07
❑ 209 Roger Pavlik .15 .07
❑ 210 Ivan Rodriguez .60 .25
❑ 211 Rusty Greer .25 .11
❑ 212 Angel Martinez .15 .07
❑ 213 Tomas Perez .15 .07
❑ 214 Alex Gonzalez .15 .07
❑ 215 Joe Carter .25 .11
❑ 216 Shawn Green .60 .25
❑ 217 Edwin Hurtado .15 .07
❑ 218 Edgar Martinez .15 .07
Tony Pena CL
❑ 219 Chipper Jones .60 .25
Barry Larkin CL
❑ 220 Orel Hershiser CL .15 .07
❑ 221 Mike Devereaux CL .15 .07
❑ 222 Tom Glavine CL .25 .11
❑ 223 Karim Garcia .15 .07
❑ 224 Arquimedez Pozo .15 .07
❑ 225 Billy Wagner .15 .07
❑ 226 John Wasdin .15 .07
❑ 227 Jeff Suppan .15 .07
❑ 228 Steve Gibralter .15 .07
❑ 229 Jimmy Haynes .15 .07
❑ 230 Ruben Rivera .15 .07
❑ 231 Chris Snopek .15 .07
❑ 232 Alex Ochoa .15 .07
❑ 233 Shannon Stewart .25 .11
❑ 234 Quinton McCracken .15 .07
❑ 235 Trey Beamon .15 .07
❑ 236 Billy McMillon .15 .07
❑ 237 Steve Cox .15 .07
❑ 238 George Arias .15 .07
❑ 239 Yamil Benitez .15 .07
❑ 240 Todd Greene .15 .07
❑ 241 Jason Kendall .25 .11
❑ 242 Brooks Kieschnick .15 .07
❑ 243 O. Fernandez RC .15 .07
❑ 244 Livan Hernandez RC .75 .35
❑ 245 Rey Ordonez .15 .07
❑ 246 Mike Grace RC .15 .07
❑ 247 Jay Canizaro .15 .07
❑ 248 Bob Wolcott .15 .07
❑ 249 Jermaine Dye .25 .11
❑ 250 Jason Schmidt .15 .07
❑ 251 Mike Sweeney RC 2.50 1.10
❑ 252 Marcus Jensen .15 .07
❑ 253 Mendy Lopez .15 .07
❑ 254 Wilton Guerrero RC .25 .11
❑ 255 Paul Wilson .15 .07
❑ 256 Edgar Renteria .15 .07
❑ 257 Richard Hidalgo .25 .11
❑ 258 Bob Abreu .60 .25
❑ 259 Robert Smith RC .25 .11
❑ 260 Sal Fasano .15 .07
❑ 261 Enrique Wilson .15 .07
❑ 262 Rich Hunter RC .15 .07
❑ 263 Sergio Nunez .15 .07

❑ 264 Dan Serafini .15 .07
❑ 265 David Doster .15 .07
❑ 266 Ryan McGuire .15 .07
❑ 267 Scott Spiezio .15 .07
❑ 268 Rafael Orellano .15 .07
❑ 269 Steve Avery .15 .07
❑ 270 Fred McGriff .40 .18
❑ 271 John Smoltz .25 .11
❑ 272 Ryan Klesko .25 .11
❑ 273 Jeff Blauser .15 .07
❑ 274 Brad Clontz .15 .07
❑ 275 Roberto Alomar .60 .25
❑ 276 B.J. Surhoff .25 .11
❑ 277 Jeffrey Hammonds .15 .07
❑ 278 Brady Anderson .25 .11
❑ 279 Bobby Bonilla .25 .11
❑ 280 Cal Ripken 2.50 1.10
❑ 281 Mike Mussina .60 .25
❑ 282 Wil Cordero .15 .07
❑ 283 Mike Stanley .15 .07
❑ 284 Aaron Sele .25 .11
❑ 285 Jose Canseco .60 .25
❑ 286 Tom Gordon .15 .07
❑ 287 Heathcliff Slocumb .15 .07
❑ 288 Lee Smith .25 .11
❑ 289 Troy Percival .15 .07
❑ 290 Tim Salmon .25 .11
❑ 291 Chuck Finley .25 .11
❑ 292 Jim Abbott .25 .11
❑ 293 Chili Davis .25 .11
❑ 294 Steve Trachsel .15 .07
❑ 295 Mark Grace .60 .25
❑ 296 Rey Sanchez .15 .07
❑ 297 Scott Servais .15 .07
❑ 298 Jaime Navarro .15 .07
❑ 299 Frank Castillo .15 .07
❑ 300 Frank Thomas .75 .35
❑ 301 Jason Bere .15 .07
❑ 302 Danny Tartabull .15 .07
❑ 303 Darren Lewis .15 .07
❑ 304 Roberto Hernandez .15 .07
❑ 305 Tony Phillips .15 .07
❑ 306 Wilson Alvarez .15 .07
❑ 307 Jose Rijo .15 .07
❑ 308 Hal Morris .15 .07
❑ 309 Mark Portugal .15 .07
❑ 310 Barry Larkin .60 .25
❑ 311 Dave Burba .15 .07
❑ 312 Ed Taubensee .15 .07
❑ 313 Sandy Alomar Jr. .25 .11
❑ 314 Dennis Martinez .25 .11
❑ 315 Albert Belle .25 .11
❑ 316 Eddie Murray .60 .25
❑ 317 Charles Nagy .15 .07
❑ 318 Chad Ogea .15 .07
❑ 319 Kenny Lofton .25 .11
❑ 320 Dante Bichette .25 .11
❑ 321 Armando Reynoso .15 .07
❑ 322 Walt Weiss .15 .07
❑ 323 Ellis Burks .25 .11
❑ 324 Kevin Ritz .15 .07
❑ 325 Bill Swift .15 .07
❑ 326 Jason Bates .15 .07
❑ 327 Tony Clark .25 .11
❑ 328 Travis Fryman .25 .11
❑ 329 Mark Parent .15 .07
❑ 330 Alan Trammell .40 .18
❑ 331 C.J. Nitkowski .15 .07
❑ 332 Jose Lima .15 .07
❑ 333 Phil Plantier .15 .07
❑ 334 Kurt Abbott .15 .07
❑ 335 Andre Dawson .40 .18
❑ 336 Chris Hammond .15 .07
❑ 337 Robb Nen .15 .07
❑ 338 Pat Rapp .15 .07
❑ 339 Al Leiter .25 .11
❑ 340 Gary Sheffield UER .25 .11
(HR total says 17
❑ 341 Todd Jones .15 .07
❑ 342 Doug Drabek .15 .07
❑ 343 Greg Swindell .15 .07
❑ 344 Tony Eusebio .15 .07
❑ 345 Craig Biggio .40 .18
❑ 346 Darryl Kile .25 .11
❑ 347 Mike Macfarlane .15 .07
❑ 348 Jeff Montgomery .15 .07
❑ 349 Chris Haney .15 .07
❑ 350 Bip Roberts .15 .07
❑ 351 Tom Goodwin .15 .07
❑ 352 Mark Gubicza .15 .07
❑ 353 Joe Randa .15 .07
❑ 354 Ramon Martinez .15 .07
❑ 355 Eric Karros .25 .11
❑ 356 Delino DeShields .15 .07
❑ 357 Brett Butler .25 .11
❑ 358 Todd Worrell .15 .07
❑ 359 Mike Blowers .15 .07
❑ 360 Mike Piazza 1.50 .70
❑ 361 Ben McDonald .15 .07
❑ 362 Ricky Bones .15 .07
❑ 363 Greg Vaughn .25 .11
❑ 364 Matt Mieske .15 .07
❑ 365 Kevin Seitzer .15 .07
❑ 366 Jeff Cirillo .25 .11
❑ 367 LaTroy Hawkins .15 .07
❑ 368 Frank Rodriguez .15 .07
❑ 369 Rick Aguilera .15 .07
❑ 370 Roberto Alomar BG .25 .11
❑ 371 Albert Belle BG .25 .11
❑ 372 Wade Boggs BG .25 .11
❑ 373 Barry Bonds BG .75 .35
❑ 374 Roger Clemens BG .75 .35
❑ 375 Dennis Eckersley BG .15 .07
❑ 376 Ken Griffey Jr. BG 1.00 .45
❑ 377 Tony Gwynn BG .60 .25
❑ 378 Rickey Henderson BG .60 .25
❑ 379 Greg Maddux BG .75 .35
❑ 380 Fred McGriff BG .25 .11
❑ 381 Paul Molitor BG .25 .11
❑ 382 Eddie Murray BG .25 .11
❑ 383 Mike Piazza BG .75 .35
❑ 384 Kirby Puckett BG .75 .35
❑ 385 Cal Ripken BG 1.25 .55
❑ 386 Ozzie Smith BG .40 .18
❑ 387 Frank Thomas BG .40 .18
❑ 388 Matt Walbeck .15 .07
❑ 389 Dave Stevens .15 .07
❑ 390 Marty Cordova .15 .07
❑ 391 Darrin Fletcher .15 .07
❑ 392 Cliff Floyd .25 .11
❑ 393 Mel Rojas .15 .07
❑ 394 Shane Andrews .15 .07
❑ 395 Moises Alou .25 .11
❑ 396 Carlos Perez .15 .07
❑ 397 Jeff Fassero .15 .07
❑ 398 Bobby Jones .15 .07
❑ 399 Todd Hundley .15 .07
❑ 400 John Franco .25 .11
❑ 401 Jose Vizcaino .15 .07
❑ 402 Bernard Gilkey .15 .07
❑ 403 Pete Harnisch .15 .07
❑ 404 Pat Kelly .15 .07
❑ 405 David Cone .25 .11
❑ 406 Bernie Williams .60 .25
❑ 407 John Wetteland .25 .11
❑ 408 Scott Kamieniecki .15 .07
❑ 409 Tim Raines .25 .11
❑ 410 Wade Boggs .60 .25
❑ 411 Terry Steinbach .15 .07
❑ 412 Jason Giambi .60 .25
❑ 413 Todd Van Poppel .15 .07
❑ 414 Pedro Munoz .15 .07
❑ 415 Eddie Murray SBT .25 .11
❑ 416 Dennis Eckersley SBT .15 .07
❑ 417 Bip Roberts SBT .15 .07
❑ 418 Glenallen Hill SBT .15 .07
❑ 419 John Hudek SBT .15 .07
❑ 420 Derek Bell SBT .15 .07
❑ 421 Larry Walker SBT .15 .07
❑ 422 Greg Maddux SBT .75 .35
❑ 423 Ken Caminiti SBT .15 .07
❑ 424 Brent Gates .15 .07
❑ 425 Mark McGwire 2.50 1.10
❑ 426 Mark Whiten .15 .07
❑ 427 Sid Fernandez .15 .07
❑ 428 Ricky Bottalico .15 .07
❑ 429 Mike Mimbs .15 .07
❑ 430 Lenny Dykstra .25 .11
❑ 431 Todd Zeile .15 .07
❑ 432 Benito Santiago .15 .07
❑ 433 Danny Miceli .15 .07
❑ 434 Al Martin .15 .07
❑ 435 Jay Bell .25 .11
❑ 436 Charlie Hayes .15 .07
❑ 437 Mike Kingery .15 .07
❑ 438 Paul Wagner .15 .07
❑ 439 Tom Pagnozzi .15 .07
❑ 440 Ozzie Smith .75 .35
❑ 441 Ray Lankford .15 .07
❑ 442 Dennis Eckersley .25 .11
❑ 443 Ron Gant .15 .07
❑ 444 Alan Benes .15 .07
❑ 445 Rickey Henderson 1.25 .55
❑ 446 Jody Reed .15 .07
❑ 447 Trevor Hoffman .25 .11
❑ 448 Andujar Cedeno .15 .07
❑ 449 Steve Finley .25 .11
❑ 450 Tony Gwynn 1.25 .55
❑ 451 Joey Hamilton .15 .07
❑ 452 Mark Leiter .15 .07
❑ 453 Rod Beck .15 .07
❑ 454 Kirt Manwaring .15 .07
❑ 455 Matt Williams .40 .18
❑ 456 Robby Thompson .15 .07
❑ 457 Shawon Dunston .15 .07
❑ 458 Russ Davis .15 .07
❑ 459 Paul Sorrento .15 .07
❑ 460 Randy Johnson .75 .35
❑ 461 Chris Bosio .15 .07
❑ 462 Luis Sojo .15 .07
❑ 463 Sterling Hitchcock .15 .07
❑ 464 Benji Gil .15 .07
❑ 465 Mickey Tettleton .15 .07
❑ 466 Mark McLemore .15 .07
❑ 467 Darryl Hamilton .15 .07
❑ 468 Ken Hill .15 .07
❑ 469 Dean Palmer .25 .11
❑ 470 Carlos Delgado .60 .25
❑ 471 Ed Sprague .15 .07
❑ 472 Otis Nixon .15 .07
❑ 473 Pat Hentgen .15 .07
❑ 474 Juan Guzman .15 .07
❑ 475 John Olerud .25 .11
❑ 476 Buck Showalter CL .15 .07
❑ 477 Bobby Cox CL .15 .07
❑ 478 Tommy Lasorda CL .25 .11
❑ 479 Buck Showalter CL .15 .07
❑ 480 Sparky Anderson CL .25 .11
❑ 481U Randy Myers .50 .23
❑ 482U Kent Mercker .50 .23
❑ 483U David Wells .75 .35
❑ 484U Kevin Mitchell .50 .23
❑ 485U Randy Velarde .50 .23
❑ 486U Ryne Sandberg 2.50 1.10
❑ 487U Doug Jones .50 .23
❑ 488U Terry Adams .50 .23
❑ 489U Kevin Tapani .50 .23
❑ 490U Harold Baines .75 .35
❑ 491U Eric Davis .75 .35
❑ 492U Julio Franco .75 .35
❑ 493U Jack McDowell .50 .23
❑ 494U Devon White .75 .35
❑ 495U Kevin Brown .75 .35
❑ 496U Rick Wilkins .50 .23
❑ 497U Sean Berry .50 .23
❑ 498U Keith Lockhart .50 .23
❑ 499U Mark Loretta .50 .23
❑ 500U Paul Molitor 2.00 .90
❑ 501U Roberto Kelly .50 .23
❑ 502U Lance Johnson .50 .23
❑ 503U Tino Martinez .75 .35
❑ 504U Kenny Rogers .50 .23
❑ 505U Todd Stottlemyre .50 .23
❑ 506U Gary Gaetti .75 .35
❑ 507U Royce Clayton .50 .23
❑ 508U Andy Benes .50 .23
❑ 509U Wally Joyner .75 .35
❑ 510U Erik Hanson .50 .23

1997 Upper Deck

	MINT	NRMT
COMP.MASTER SET (550)	220.00	100.00
COMPLETE SET (490)	120.00	55.00
COMPLETE SERIES 1 (240)	40.00	18.00
COMPLETE SERIES 2 (250)	80.00	36.00
COMP.SER.2 w/o GHL (240)	20.00	9.00
COMMON (1-240/271-520)	.15	.07

COMP.UPDATE SET (30)	80.00	36.00
COMMON UPDATE (241-270)	1.00	.45
COMMON GHL (415-424)	1.50	.70
COMP.TRADE SET (30)	20.00	9.00
COMMON TRADE (521-550)	.50	.23

❑ 1 Jackie Robinson The Beginnings	.50	.23
❑ 2 Jackie Robinson Breaking the Barrier	.50	.23
❑ 3 Jackie Robinson The MVP Season, 1949	.50	.23
❑ 4 Jackie Robinson 1951 season	.50	.23
❑ 5 Jackie Robinson 1952 and 1953 seasons	.50	.23
❑ 6 Jackie Robinson 1954 season	.50	.23
❑ 7 Jackie Robinson 1955 season	.50	.23
❑ 8 Jackie Robinson 1956 season	.50	.23
❑ 9 Jackie Robinson Hall of Fame	.50	.23
❑ 10 Chipper Jones	1.25	.55
❑ 11 Marquis Grissom	.15	.07
❑ 12 Jermaine Dye	.25	.11
❑ 13 Mark Lemke	.15	.07
❑ 14 Terrell Wade	.15	.07
❑ 15 Fred McGriff	.40	.18
❑ 16 Tom Glavine	.60	.25
❑ 17 Mark Wohlers	.15	.07
❑ 18 Randy Myers	.15	.07
❑ 19 Roberto Alomar	.60	.25
❑ 20 Cal Ripken	2.50	1.10
❑ 21 Rafael Palmeiro	.60	.25
❑ 22 Mike Mussina	.60	.25
❑ 23 Brady Anderson	.25	.11
❑ 24 Jose Canseco	.60	.25
❑ 25 Mo Vaughn	.25	.11
❑ 26 Roger Clemens	1.50	.70
❑ 27 Tim Naehring	.15	.07
❑ 28 Jeff Suppan	.15	.07
❑ 29 Troy Percival	.15	.07
❑ 30 Sammy Sosa	1.25	.55
❑ 31 Amaury Telemaco	.15	.07
❑ 32 Rey Sanchez	.15	.07
❑ 33 Scott Servais	.15	.07
❑ 34 Steve Trachsel	.15	.07
❑ 35 Mark Grace	.60	.25
❑ 36 Wilson Alvarez	.15	.07
❑ 37 Harold Baines	.25	.11
❑ 38 Tony Phillips	.15	.07
❑ 39 James Baldwin	.15	.07
❑ 40 Frank Thomas UER Bio information is Ken Griffey Jr.'s	.75	.35
❑ 41 Lyle Mouton	.15	.07
❑ 42 Chris Snopek	.15	.07
❑ 43 Hal Morris	.15	.07
❑ 44 Eric Davis	.25	.11
❑ 45 Barry Larkin	.60	.25
❑ 46 Reggie Sanders	.15	.07
❑ 47 Pete Schourek	.15	.07
❑ 48 Lee Smith	.25	.11
❑ 49 Charles Nagy	.15	.07
❑ 50 Albert Belle	.25	.11
❑ 51 Julio Franco	.25	.11
❑ 52 Kenny Lofton	.25	.11
❑ 53 Orel Hershiser	.25	.11
❑ 54 Omar Vizquel	.25	.11
❑ 55 Eric Young	.15	.07
❑ 56 Curtis Leskanic	.15	.07
❑ 57 Quinton McCracken	.15	.07
❑ 58 Kevin Ritz	.15	.07
❑ 59 Walt Weiss	.15	.07
❑ 60 Dante Bichette	.25	.11
❑ 61 Mark Lewis	.15	.07
❑ 62 Tony Clark	.25	.11
❑ 63 Travis Fryman	.25	.11
❑ 64 John Smoltz SF	.15	.07
❑ 65 Greg Maddux SF	.75	.35
❑ 66 Tom Glavine SF	.25	.11
❑ 67 Mike Mussina SF	.25	.11
❑ 68 Andy Pettitte SF	.15	.07
❑ 69 Mariano Rivera SF	.15	.07
❑ 70 Hideo Nomo SF	.25	.11
❑ 71 Kevin Brown SF	.15	.07
❑ 72 Randy Johnson SF	.40	.18
❑ 73 Felipe Lira	.15	.07
❑ 74 Kimera Bartee	.15	.07
❑ 75 Alan Trammell	.40	.18
❑ 76 Kevin Brown	.25	.11
❑ 77 Edgar Renteria	.15	.07
❑ 78 Al Leiter	.25	.11
❑ 79 Charles Johnson	.25	.11
❑ 80 Andre Dawson	.40	.18
❑ 81 Billy Wagner	.15	.07
❑ 82 Donne Wall	.15	.07
❑ 83 Jeff Bagwell	.75	.35
❑ 84 Keith Lockhart	.15	.07
❑ 85 Jeff Montgomery	.15	.07
❑ 86 Tom Goodwin	.15	.07
❑ 87 Tim Belcher	.15	.07
❑ 88 Mike Macfarlane	.15	.07
❑ 89 Joe Randa	.15	.07
❑ 90 Brett Butler	.25	.11
❑ 91 Todd Worrell	.15	.07
❑ 92 Todd Hollandsworth	.15	.07
❑ 93 Ismael Valdes	.15	.07
❑ 94 Hideo Nomo	.60	.25
❑ 95 Mike Piazza	1.50	.70
❑ 96 Jeff Cirillo	.25	.11
❑ 97 Ricky Bones	.15	.07
❑ 98 Fernando Vina	.15	.07
❑ 99 Ben McDonald	.15	.07
❑ 100 John Jaha	.15	.07
❑ 101 Mark Loretta	.15	.07
❑ 102 Paul Molitor	.60	.25
❑ 103 Rick Aguilera	.15	.07
❑ 104 Marty Cordova	.15	.07
❑ 105 Kirby Puckett	1.50	.70
❑ 106 Dan Naulty	.15	.07
❑ 107 Frank Rodriguez	.15	.07
❑ 108 Shane Andrews	.15	.07
❑ 109 Henry Rodriguez	.15	.07
❑ 110 Mark Grudzielanek	.15	.07
❑ 111 Pedro Martinez	.75	.35
❑ 112 Ugueth Urbina	.15	.07
❑ 113 David Segui	.15	.07
❑ 114 Rey Ordonez	.15	.07
❑ 115 Bernard Gilkey	.15	.07
❑ 116 Butch Huskey	.15	.07
❑ 117 Paul Wilson	.15	.07
❑ 118 Alex Ochoa	.15	.07
❑ 119 John Franco	.25	.11
❑ 120 Dwight Gooden	.25	.11
❑ 121 Ruben Rivera	.15	.07
❑ 122 Andy Pettitte	.25	.11
❑ 123 Tino Martinez	.25	.11
❑ 124 Bernie Williams	.60	.25
❑ 125 Wade Boggs	.60	.25
❑ 126 Paul O'Neill	.60	.25
❑ 127 Scott Brosius	.25	.11
❑ 128 Ernie Young	.15	.07
❑ 129 Doug Johns	.15	.07
❑ 130 Geronimo Berroa	.15	.07
❑ 131 Jason Giambi	.60	.25
❑ 132 John Wasdin	.15	.07
❑ 133 Jim Eisenreich	.15	.07
❑ 134 Ricky Otero	.15	.07
❑ 135 Ricky Bottalico	.15	.07
❑ 136 Mark Langston DG	.15	.07
❑ 137 Greg Maddux DG	.75	.35
❑ 138 Ivan Rodriguez DG	.25	.11
❑ 139 Charles Johnson DG	.15	.07
❑ 140 J.T. Snow DG	.15	.07
❑ 141 Mark Grace DG	.25	.11
❑ 142 Roberto Alomar DG	.25	.11
❑ 143 Craig Biggio DG	.25	.11
❑ 144 Ken Caminiti DG	.15	.07
❑ 145 Matt Williams DG	.25	.11
❑ 146 Omar Vizquel DG	.15	.07
❑ 147 Cal Ripken DG	1.25	.55
❑ 148 Ozzie Smith DG	.40	.18
❑ 149 Rey Ordonez DG	.15	.07
❑ 150 Ken Griffey Jr. DG	1.00	.45
❑ 151 Devon White DG	.15	.07
❑ 152 Barry Bonds DG	.75	.35
❑ 153 Kenny Lofton DG	.15	.07
❑ 154 Mickey Morandini	.15	.07
❑ 155 Gregg Jefferies	.15	.07
❑ 156 Curt Schilling	.60	.25
❑ 157 Jason Kendall	.25	.11
❑ 158 Francisco Cordova	.15	.07
❑ 159 Dennis Eckersley	.25	.11
❑ 160 Ron Gant	.15	.07
❑ 161 Ozzie Smith	.75	.35
❑ 162 Brian Jordan	.25	.11
❑ 163 John Mabry	.15	.07
❑ 164 Andy Ashby	.15	.07
❑ 165 Steve Finley	.25	.11
❑ 166 Fernando Valenzuela	.25	.11
❑ 167 Archi Cianfrocco	.15	.07
❑ 168 Wally Joyner	.25	.11
❑ 169 Greg Vaughn	.25	.11
❑ 170 Barry Bonds	1.50	.70
❑ 171 W.VanLandingham	.15	.07
❑ 172 Marvin Benard	.15	.07
❑ 173 Rich Aurilia	.25	.11
❑ 174 Jay Canizaro	.15	.07
❑ 175 Ken Griffey Jr.	2.00	.90
❑ 176 Bob Wells	.15	.07
❑ 177 Jay Buhner	.25	.11
❑ 178 Sterling Hitchcock	.15	.07
❑ 179 Edgar Martinez	.40	.18
❑ 180 Rusty Greer	.25	.11
❑ 181 Dave Nilsson GI	.15	.07
❑ 182 Larry Walker GI	.15	.07
❑ 183 Edgar Renteria GI	.15	.07
❑ 184 Rey Ordonez GI	.15	.07
❑ 185 Rafael Palmeiro GI	.25	.11
❑ 186 Osvaldo Fernandez GI	.15	.07
❑ 187 Raul Mondesi GI	.15	.07
❑ 188 Manny Ramirez GI	.40	.18
❑ 189 Sammy Sosa GI	.60	.25
❑ 190 Robert Eenhoorn GI	.15	.07
❑ 191 Devon White GI	.15	.07
❑ 192 Hideo Nomo GI	.25	.11
❑ 193 Mac Suzuki GI	.15	.07
❑ 194 Chan Ho Park GI	.15	.07
❑ 195 F.Valenzuela GI	.15	.07
❑ 196 Andruw Jones GI	.40	.18
❑ 197 Vinny Castilla GI	.15	.07
❑ 198 Dennis Martinez GI	.15	.07
❑ 199 Ruben Rivera GI	.15	.07
❑ 200 Juan Gonzalez GI	.25	.11
❑ 201 Roberto Alomar GI	.25	.11
❑ 202 Edgar Martinez GI	.25	.11
❑ 203 Ivan Rodriguez GI	.25	.11
❑ 204 Carlos Delgado GI	.25	.11
❑ 205 Andres Galarraga GI	.25	.11
❑ 206 Ozzie Guillen GI	.15	.07
❑ 207 Midre Cummings GI	.15	.07
❑ 208 Roger Pavlik	.15	.07
❑ 209 Darren Oliver	.15	.07
❑ 210 Dean Palmer	.25	.11
❑ 211 Ivan Rodriguez	.60	.25
❑ 212 Otis Nixon	.15	.07
❑ 213 Pat Hentgen	.15	.07
❑ 214 Ozzie Smith Andre Dawson Kirby Puckett HL/CL (1-27)	.25	.11
❑ 215 Barry Bonds Gary Sheffield Brady Anderson HL/CL (28-54)	.25	.11
❑ 216 Ken Caminiti SH CL	.15	.07
❑ 217 John Smoltz SH CL	.15	.07

❑ 218 Eric Young SH CL .... .15 .07
❑ 219 Juan Gonzalez SH CL.... .25 .11
❑ 220 Eddie Murray SH CL ...... .25 .11
❑ 221 Tommy Lasorda SH CL.. .15 .07
❑ 222 Paul Molitor SH CL .... .25 .11
❑ 223 Luis Castillo .... .15 .07
❑ 224 Justin Thompson .... .15 .07
❑ 225 Rocky Coppinger .... .15 .07
❑ 226 Jermaine Allensworth .... .15 .07
❑ 227 Jeff D'Amico .... .15 .07
❑ 228 Jamey Wright .... .15 .07
❑ 229 Scott Rolen .... .60 .25
❑ 230 Darin Erstad .... .60 .25
❑ 231 Marty Janzen .... .15 .07
❑ 232 Jacob Cruz .... .15 .07
❑ 233 Raul Ibanez .... .15 .07
❑ 234 Nomar Garciaparra ...... 1.50 .70
❑ 235 Todd Walker .... .15 .07
❑ 236 Brian Giles RC .... 2.00 .90
❑ 237 Matt Beech .... .15 .07
❑ 238 Mike Cameron .... .25 .11
❑ 239 Jose Paniagua .... .15 .07
❑ 240 Andruw Jones .... .75 .35
❑ 241 Brant Brown UPD .... 1.00 .45
❑ 242 Robin Jennings UPD .... 1.00 .45
❑ 243 Willie Adams UPD .... 1.00 .45
❑ 244 Ken Caminiti UPD .... 1.50 .70
❑ 245 Brian Jordan UPD .... 1.50 .70
❑ 246 Chipper Jones UPD 8.00 3.60
❑ 247 Juan Gonzalez UPD 4.00 1.80
❑ 248 Bernie Williams UPD 4.00 1.80
❑ 249 Roberto Alomar UPD .. 4.00 1.80
❑ 250 Bernie Williams UPD 4.00 1.80
❑ 251 David Wells UPD .... 1.50 .70
❑ 252 Cecil Fielder UPD .... 1.50 .70
❑ 253 D.Strawberry UPD .... 1.50 .70
❑ 254 Andy Pettitte UPD .... 1.50 .70
❑ 255 Javier Lopez UPD .... 1.50 .70
❑ 256 Gary Gaetti UPD .... 1.50 .70
❑ 257 Ron Gant UPD .... 1.00 .45
❑ 258 Brian Jordan UPD .... 1.50 .70
❑ 259 John Smoltz UPD .... 1.50 .70
❑ 260 Greg Maddux UPD 10.00 4.50
❑ 261 Tom Glavine UPD 4.00 1.80
❑ 262 Andruw Jones UPD 5.00 2.20
❑ 263 Greg Maddux UPD 10.00 4.50
❑ 264 David Cone UPD .... 1.50 .70
❑ 265 Jim Leyritz UPD .... 1.00 .45
❑ 266 Andy Pettitte UPD .... 1.50 .70
❑ 267 John Wetteland UPD .... 1.50 .70
❑ 268 Dario Veras UPD .... 1.00 .45
❑ 269 Neifi Perez UPD .... 1.00 .45
❑ 270 Bill Mueller UPD 2.50 1.10
❑ 271 Vladimir Guerrero .... 1.00 .45
❑ 272 Dmitri Young .... .25 .11
❑ 273 Nerio Rodriguez RC ...... .15 .07
❑ 274 Kevin Orie .... .15 .07
❑ 275 Felipe Crespo .... .15 .07
❑ 276 Danny Graves .... .15 .07
❑ 277 Rod Myers .... .15 .07
❑ 278 Felix Heredia RC .... .15 .07
❑ 279 Ralph Milliard .... .15 .07
❑ 280 Greg Norton .... .15 .07
❑ 281 Derek Wallace .... .15 .07
❑ 282 Trot Nixon .... .25 .11
❑ 283 Bobby Chouinard .... .15 .07
❑ 284 Jay Witasick .... .15 .07
❑ 285 Travis Miller .... .15 .07
❑ 286 Brian Bevil RC .... .15 .07
❑ 287 Bobby Estalella .... .15 .07
❑ 288 Steve Soderstrom .... .15 .07
❑ 289 Mark Langston .... .15 .07
❑ 290 Tim Salmon .... .25 .11
❑ 291 Jim Edmonds .... .40 .18
❑ 292 Garret Anderson .... .25 .11
❑ 293 George Arias .... .15 .07
❑ 294 Gary DiSarcina .... .15 .07
❑ 295 Chuck Finley .... .25 .11
❑ 296 Todd Greene .... .15 .07
❑ 297 Randy Velarde .... .15 .07
❑ 298 David Justice .... .25 .11
❑ 299 Ryan Klesko .... .25 .11
❑ 300 John Smoltz .... .25 .11
❑ 301 Javier Lopez .... .25 .11
❑ 302 Greg Maddux .... 1.50 .70
❑ 303 Denny Neagle .... .25 .11
❑ 304 B.J. Surhoff .... .25 .11
❑ 305 Chris Hoiles .... .15 .07
❑ 306 Eric Davis .... .25 .11
❑ 307 Scott Erickson .... .15 .07
❑ 308 Mike Bordick .... .15 .07
❑ 309 John Valentin .... .15 .07
❑ 310 Heathcliff Slocumb .... .15 .07
❑ 311 Tom Gordon .... .15 .07
❑ 312 Mike Stanley .... .15 .07
❑ 313 Reggie Jefferson .... .15 .07
❑ 314 Darren Bragg .... .15 .07
❑ 315 Troy O'Leary .... .15 .07
❑ 316 John Mabry SH CL .... .15 .07
❑ 317 Mark Whiten SH CL .... .15 .07
❑ 318 Edgar Martinez SH CL .. .25 .11
❑ 319 Alex Rodriguez SH CL .. .75 .35
❑ 320 Mark McGwire SH CL .. 1.25 .55
❑ 321 Hideo Nomo SH CL .... .25 .11
❑ 322 Todd Hundley SH CL .... .15 .07
❑ 323 Barry Bonds SH CL .... .75 .35
❑ 324 Andruw Jones SH CL .... .40 .18
❑ 325 Ryne Sandberg .... .75 .35
❑ 326 Brian McRae .... .15 .07
❑ 327 Frank Castillo .... .15 .07
❑ 328 Shawon Dunston .... .15 .07
❑ 329 Ray Durham .... .25 .11
❑ 330 Robin Ventura .... .25 .11
❑ 331 Ozzie Guillen .... .15 .07
❑ 332 Roberto Hernandez .... .15 .07
❑ 333 Albert Belle .... .25 .11
❑ 334 Dave Martinez .... .15 .07
❑ 335 Willie Greene .... .15 .07
❑ 336 Jeff Brantley .... .15 .07
❑ 337 Kevin Jarvis .... .15 .07
❑ 338 John Smiley .... .15 .07
❑ 339 Eddie Taubensee .... .15 .07
❑ 340 Bret Boone .... .25 .11
❑ 341 Kevin Seitzer .... .15 .07
❑ 342 Jack McDowell .... .15 .07
❑ 343 Sandy Alomar Jr. .... .25 .11
❑ 344 Chad Curtis .... .15 .07
❑ 345 Manny Ramirez .... .75 .35
❑ 346 Chad Ogea .... .15 .07
❑ 347 Jim Thome .... .60 .25
❑ 348 Mark Thompson .... .15 .07
❑ 349 Ellis Burks .... .25 .11
❑ 350 Andres Galarraga .... .40 .18
❑ 351 Vinny Castilla .... .25 .11
❑ 352 Kirt Manwaring .... .15 .07
❑ 353 Larry Walker .... .40 .18
❑ 354 Omar Olivares .... .15 .07
❑ 355 Bobby Higginson .... .25 .11
❑ 356 Melvin Nieves .... .15 .07
❑ 357 Brian Johnson .... .15 .07
❑ 358 Devon White .... .25 .11
❑ 359 Jeff Conine .... .15 .07
❑ 360 Gary Sheffield .... .25 .11
❑ 361 Robb Nen .... .15 .07
❑ 362 Mike Hampton .... .25 .11
❑ 363 Bob Abreu .... .25 .11
❑ 364 Luis Gonzalez .... .60 .25
❑ 365 Derek Bell .... .15 .07
❑ 366 Sean Berry .... .15 .07
❑ 367 Craig Biggio .... .40 .18
❑ 368 Darryl Kile .... .25 .11
❑ 369 Shane Reynolds .... .15 .07
❑ 370 Jeff Bagwell CF .... .40 .18
❑ 371 Ron Gant CF .... .15 .07
❑ 372 Andy Benes CF .... .15 .07
❑ 373 Gary Gaetti CF .... .15 .07
❑ 374 Ramon Martinez CF ...... .15 .07
❑ 375 Raul Mondesi CF .... .15 .07
❑ 376 Steve Finley CF .... .15 .07
❑ 377 Ken Caminiti CF .... .15 .07
❑ 378 Tony Gwynn CF .... .60 .25
❑ 379 Dario Veras RC .... .15 .07
❑ 380 Andy Pettitte CF .... .15 .07
❑ 381 Ruben Rivera CF .... .15 .07
❑ 382 David Cone CF .... .15 .07
❑ 383 Roberto Alomar CF .... .25 .11
❑ 384 Edgar Martinez CF .... .25 .11
❑ 385 Ken Griffey Jr. CF .... 1.00 .45
❑ 386 Mark McGwire CF .... 1.25 .55
❑ 387 Rusty Greer CF .... .15 .07
❑ 388 Jose Rosado .... .15 .07
❑ 389 Kevin Appier .... .25 .11
❑ 390 Johnny Damon .... .25 .11
❑ 391 Jose Offerman .... .15 .07
❑ 392 Michael Tucker .... .15 .07
❑ 393 Craig Paquette .... .15 .07
❑ 394 Bip Roberts .... .15 .07
❑ 395 Ramon Martinez .... .15 .07
❑ 396 Greg Gagne .... .15 .07
❑ 397 Chan Ho Park .... .25 .11
❑ 398 Karim Garcia .... .15 .07
❑ 399 Wilton Guerrero .... .15 .07
❑ 400 Eric Karros .... .25 .11
❑ 401 Raul Mondesi .... .25 .11
❑ 402 Matt Mieske .... .15 .07
❑ 403 Mike Fetters .... .15 .07
❑ 404 Dave Nilsson .... .15 .07
❑ 405 Jose Valentin .... .15 .07
❑ 406 Scott Karl .... .15 .07
❑ 407 Marc Newfield .... .15 .07
❑ 408 Cal Eldred .... .15 .07
❑ 409 Rich Becker .... .15 .07
❑ 410 Terry Steinbach .... .15 .07
❑ 411 Chuck Knoblauch .... .25 .11
❑ 412 Pat Meares .... .15 .07
❑ 413 Brad Radke .... .25 .11
❑ 414 Kirby Puckett UER ...... 1.50 .70
Card numbered 415
❑ 415 A.Jones GHL SP 3.00 1.35
❑ 416 C.Jones GHL SP 5.00 2.20
❑ 417 Mo Vaughn GHL SP .... 1.50 .70
❑ 418 F.Thomas GHL SP 3.00 1.35
❑ 419 Albert Belle GHL SP .... 1.50 .70
❑ 420 M.McGwire GHL SP .. 10.00 4.50
❑ 421 Derek Jeter GHL SP .. 10.00 4.50
❑ 422 A.Rodriguez GHL SP .. 6.00 2.70
❑ 423 J.Gonzalez GHL SP 2.50 1.10
❑ 424 K.Griffey Jr. GHL SP 8.00 3.60
❑ 425 Rondell White .... .25 .11
❑ 426 Darrin Fletcher .... .15 .07
❑ 427 Cliff Floyd .... .25 .11
❑ 428 Mike Lansing .... .15 .07
❑ 429 F.P. Santangelo .... .15 .07
❑ 430 Todd Hundley .... .15 .07
❑ 431 Mark Clark .... .15 .07
❑ 432 Pete Harnisch .... .15 .07
❑ 433 Jason Isringhausen .... .15 .07
❑ 434 Bobby Jones .... .15 .07
❑ 435 Lance Johnson .... .15 .07
❑ 436 Carlos Baerga .... .15 .07
❑ 437 Mariano Duncan .... .15 .07
❑ 438 David Cone .... .25 .11
❑ 439 Mariano Rivera .... .25 .11
❑ 440 Derek Jeter 2.50 1.10
❑ 441 Joe Girardi .... .15 .07
❑ 442 Charlie Hayes .... .15 .07
❑ 443 Tim Raines .... .25 .11
❑ 444 Darryl Strawberry .... .25 .11
❑ 445 Cecil Fielder .... .25 .11
❑ 446 Ariel Prieto .... .15 .07
❑ 447 Tony Batista .... .25 .11
❑ 448 Brent Gates .... .15 .07
❑ 449 Scott Spiezio .... .15 .07
❑ 450 Mark McGwire 2.50 1.10
❑ 451 Don Wengert .... .15 .07
❑ 452 Mike Lieberthal .... .25 .11
❑ 453 Lenny Dykstra .... .25 .11
❑ 454 Rex Hudler .... .15 .07
❑ 455 Darren Daulton .... .25 .11
❑ 456 Kevin Stocker .... .15 .07
❑ 457 Trey Beamon .... .15 .07
❑ 458 Midre Cummings .... .15 .07
❑ 459 Mark Johnson .... .15 .07
❑ 460 Al Martin .... .15 .07
❑ 461 Kevin Elster .... .15 .07
❑ 462 Jon Lieber .... .15 .07
❑ 463 Jason Schmidt .... .15 .07
❑ 464 Paul Wagner .... .15 .07
❑ 465 Andy Benes .... .15 .07
❑ 466 Alan Benes .... .15 .07
❑ 467 Royce Clayton .... .15 .07
❑ 468 Gary Gaetti .... .25 .11
❑ 469 Curt Lyons RC .... .15 .07
❑ 470 Eugene Kingsale DD ...... .15 .07
❑ 471 Damian Jackson DD ...... .15 .07
❑ 472 Wendell Magee DD .... .15 .07
❑ 473 Kevin L. Brown DD .... .15 .07
❑ 474 Raul Casanova DD .... .15 .07

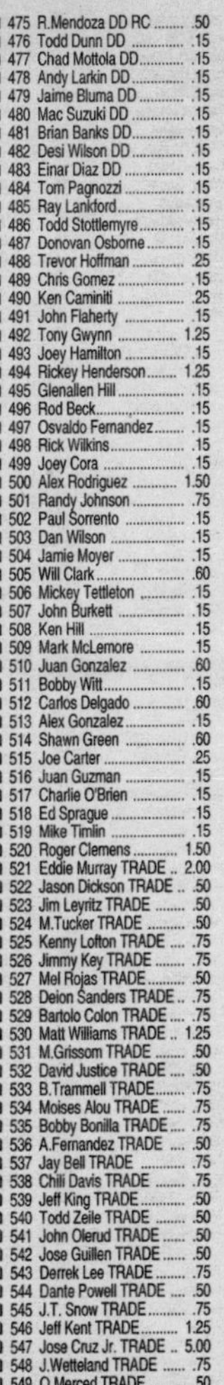

❑ 475 R.Mendoza DD RC .50 .23
❑ 476 Todd Dunn DD .15 .07
❑ 477 Chad Mottola DD .15 .07
❑ 478 Andy Larkin DD .15 .07
❑ 479 Jaime Bluma DD .15 .07
❑ 480 Mac Suzuki DD .15 .07
❑ 481 Brian Banks DD .15 .07
❑ 482 Desi Wilson DD .15 .07
❑ 483 Einar Diaz DD .15 .07
❑ 484 Tom Pagnozzi .15 .07
❑ 485 Ray Lankford .15 .07
❑ 486 Todd Stottlemyre .15 .07
❑ 487 Donovan Osborne .15 .07
❑ 488 Trevor Hoffman .25 .11
❑ 489 Chris Gomez .15 .07
❑ 490 Ken Caminiti .25 .11
❑ 491 John Flaherty .15 .07
❑ 492 Tony Gwynn 1.25 .55
❑ 493 Joey Hamilton .15 .07
❑ 494 Rickey Henderson 1.25 .55
❑ 495 Glenallen Hill .15 .07
❑ 496 Rod Beck .15 .07
❑ 497 Osvaldo Fernandez .15 .07
❑ 498 Rick Wilkins .15 .07
❑ 499 Joey Cora .15 .07
❑ 500 Alex Rodriguez 1.50 .70
❑ 501 Randy Johnson .75 .35
❑ 502 Paul Sorrento .15 .07
❑ 503 Dan Wilson .15 .07
❑ 504 Jamie Moyer .15 .07
❑ 505 Will Clark .60 .25
❑ 506 Mickey Tettleton .15 .07
❑ 507 John Burkett .15 .07
❑ 508 Ken Hill .15 .07
❑ 509 Mark McLemore .15 .07
❑ 510 Juan Gonzalez .60 .25
❑ 511 Bobby Witt .15 .07
❑ 512 Carlos Delgado .60 .25
❑ 513 Alex Gonzalez .15 .07
❑ 514 Shawn Green .60 .25
❑ 515 Joe Carter .25 .11
❑ 516 Juan Guzman .15 .07
❑ 517 Charlie O'Brien .15 .07
❑ 518 Ed Sprague .15 .07
❑ 519 Mike Timlin .15 .07
❑ 520 Roger Clemens 1.50 .70
❑ 521 Eddie Murray TRADE 2.00 .90
❑ 522 Jason Dickson TRADE .50 .23
❑ 523 Jim Leyritz TRADE .50 .23
❑ 524 M.Tucker TRADE .50 .23
❑ 525 Kenny Lofton TRADE .75 .35
❑ 526 Jimmy Key TRADE .75 .35
❑ 527 Mel Rojas TRADE .50 .23
❑ 528 Deion Sanders TRADE .75 .35
❑ 529 Bartolo Colon TRADE .75 .35
❑ 530 Matt Williams TRADE 1.25 .55
❑ 531 M.Grissom TRADE .50 .23
❑ 532 David Justice TRADE .50 .23
❑ 533 B.Trammell TRADE .75 .35
❑ 534 Moises Alou TRADE .75 .35
❑ 535 Bobby Bonilla TRADE .75 .35
❑ 536 A.Fernandez TRADE .50 .23
❑ 537 Jay Bell TRADE .75 .35
❑ 538 Chili Davis TRADE .75 .35
❑ 539 Jeff King TRADE .50 .23
❑ 540 Todd Zeile TRADE .50 .23
❑ 541 John Olerud TRADE .50 .23
❑ 542 Jose Guillen TRADE .50 .23
❑ 543 Derrek Lee TRADE .75 .35
❑ 544 Dante Powell TRADE .50 .23
❑ 545 J.T. Snow TRADE .75 .35
❑ 546 Jeff Kent TRADE 1.25 .55
❑ 547 Jose Cruz Jr. TRADE 5.00 2.20
❑ 548 J.Wetteland TRADE .75 .35
❑ 549 O.Merced TRADE .50 .23
❑ 550 Hideki Irabu TRADE .75 .35

1998 Upper Deck

	MINT	NRMT
COMPLETE SET (751)	225.00	100.00
COMPLETE SERIES 1 (270)	50.00	22.00
COMPLETE SERIES 2 (270)	50.00	22.00
COMPLETE SERIES 3 (211)	125.00	55.00
COMMON (1-600/631-750)	.15	.07
COMMON EP (601-630)	2.00	.90

❑ 1 Tino Martinez HIST .15 .07
❑ 2 Jimmy Key HIST .15 .07
❑ 3 Jay Buhner HIST .15 .07
❑ 4 Mark Gardner HIST .15 .07
❑ 5 Greg Maddux HIST .75 .35
❑ 6 Pedro Martinez HIST .40 .18
❑ 7 Hideo Nomo HIST .25 .11
❑ 8 Sammy Sosa HIST .60 .25
❑ 9 Mark McGwire GHL 1.25 .55
❑ 10 Ken Griffey Jr. GHL 1.00 .45
❑ 11 Larry Walker GHL .40 .18
❑ 12 Tino Martinez GHL .25 .11
❑ 13 Mike Piazza GHL .75 .35
❑ 14 Jose Cruz Jr. GHL .25 .11
❑ 15 Tony Gwynn GHL .60 .25
❑ 16 Greg Maddux GHL .75 .35
❑ 17 Roger Clemens GHL .75 .35
❑ 18 Alex Rodriguez GHL .75 .35
❑ 19 Shigetoshi Hasegawa .25 .11
❑ 20 Eddie Murray .60 .25
❑ 21 Jason Dickson .15 .07
❑ 22 Darin Erstad .60 .25
❑ 23 Chuck Finley .25 .11
❑ 24 Dave Hollins .15 .07
❑ 25 Garret Anderson .25 .11
❑ 26 Michael Tucker .15 .07
❑ 27 Kenny Lofton .25 .11
❑ 28 Javier Lopez .25 .11
❑ 29 Fred McGriff .40 .18
❑ 30 Greg Maddux 1.50 .70
❑ 31 Jeff Blauser .15 .07
❑ 32 John Smoltz .25 .11
❑ 33 Mark Wohlers .15 .07
❑ 34 Scott Erickson .15 .07
❑ 35 Jimmy Key .25 .11
❑ 36 Harold Baines .25 .11
❑ 37 Randy Myers .25 .11
❑ 38 B.J. Surhoff .25 .11
❑ 39 Eric Davis .25 .11
❑ 40 Rafael Palmeiro .60 .25
❑ 41 Jeffrey Hammonds .15 .07
❑ 42 Mo Vaughn .25 .11
❑ 43 Tom Gordon .25 .11
❑ 44 Tim Naehring .15 .07
❑ 45 Darren Bragg .15 .07
❑ 46 Aaron Sele .25 .11
❑ 47 Troy O'Leary .15 .07
❑ 48 John Valentin .15 .07
❑ 49 Doug Glanville .15 .07
❑ 50 Ryne Sandberg .75 .35
❑ 51 Steve Trachsel .15 .07
❑ 52 Mark Grace .60 .25
❑ 53 Kevin Foster .15 .07
❑ 54 Kevin Tapani .15 .07
❑ 55 Kevin Orie .15 .07
❑ 56 Lyle Mouton .15 .07
❑ 57 Ray Durham .25 .11
❑ 58 Jaime Navarro .15 .07
❑ 59 Mike Cameron .25 .11
❑ 60 Albert Belle .25 .11
❑ 61 Doug Drabek .15 .07
❑ 62 Chris Snopek .15 .07
❑ 63 Ed Taubensee .15 .07
❑ 64 Terry Pendleton .25 .11
❑ 65 Barry Larkin .60 .25
❑ 66 Willie Greene .15 .07
❑ 67 Deion Sanders .25 .11
❑ 68 Pokey Reese .15 .07
❑ 69 Jeff Shaw .15 .07
❑ 70 Jim Thome .60 .25
❑ 71 Orel Hershiser .25 .11
❑ 72 Omar Vizquel .25 .11
❑ 73 Brian Giles .25 .11
❑ 74 David Justice .25 .11
❑ 75 Bartolo Colon .25 .11
❑ 76 Sandy Alomar Jr. .25 .11
❑ 77 Neifi Perez .15 .07
❑ 78 Dante Bichette .25 .11
❑ 79 Vinny Castilla .25 .11
❑ 80 Eric Young .15 .07
❑ 81 Quinton McCracken .15 .07
❑ 82 Jamey Wright .15 .07
❑ 83 John Thomson .15 .07
❑ 84 Damion Easley .15 .07
❑ 85 Justin Thompson .15 .07
❑ 86 Willie Blair .15 .07
❑ 87 Raul Casanova .15 .07
❑ 88 Bobby Higginson .25 .11
❑ 89 Bubba Trammell .15 .07
❑ 90 Tony Clark .25 .11
❑ 91 Livan Hernandez .15 .07
❑ 92 Charles Johnson .25 .11
❑ 93 Edgar Renteria .15 .07
❑ 94 Alex Fernandez .15 .07
❑ 95 Gary Sheffield .25 .11
❑ 96 Moises Alou .25 .11
❑ 97 Tony Saunders .15 .07
❑ 98 Robb Nen .15 .07
❑ 99 Darryl Kile .25 .11
❑ 100 Craig Biggio .40 .18
❑ 101 Chris Holt .15 .07
❑ 102 Bob Abreu .25 .11
❑ 103 Luis Gonzalez .60 .25
❑ 104 Billy Wagner .15 .07
❑ 105 Brad Ausmus .15 .07
❑ 106 Chili Davis .25 .11
❑ 107 Tim Belcher .15 .07
❑ 108 Dean Palmer .25 .11
❑ 109 Jeff King .15 .07
❑ 110 Jose Rosado .15 .07
❑ 111 Mike Macfarlane .15 .07
❑ 112 Jay Bell .25 .11
❑ 113 Todd Worrell .15 .07
❑ 114 Chan Ho Park .25 .11
❑ 115 Raul Mondesi .25 .11
❑ 116 Brett Butler .25 .11
❑ 117 Greg Gagne .15 .07
❑ 118 Hideo Nomo .60 .25
❑ 119 Todd Zeile .25 .11
❑ 120 Eric Karros .25 .11
❑ 121 Cal Eldred .15 .07
❑ 122 Jeff D'Amico .15 .07
❑ 123 Antone Williamson .15 .07
❑ 124 Doug Jones .15 .07
❑ 125 Dave Nilsson .15 .07
❑ 126 Gerald Williams .15 .07
❑ 127 Fernando Vina .15 .07
❑ 128 Ron Coomer .15 .07
❑ 129 Matt Lawton .15 .07
❑ 130 Paul Molitor .60 .25
❑ 131 Todd Walker .15 .07
❑ 132 Rick Aguilera .15 .07
❑ 133 Brad Radke .25 .11
❑ 134 Bob Tewksbury .15 .07
❑ 135 Vladimir Guerrero .75 .35
❑ 136 Tony Gwynn DG .60 .25
❑ 137 Roger Clemens DG .75 .35
❑ 138 Dennis Eckersley DG .15 .07
❑ 139 Brady Anderson DG .15 .07
❑ 140 Ken Griffey Jr. DG 1.00 .45
❑ 141 Derek Jeter DG 1.25 .55
❑ 142 Ken Caminiti DG .15 .07
❑ 143 Frank Thomas DG .40 .18
❑ 144 Barry Bonds DG .75 .35
❑ 145 Cal Ripken DG 1.25 .55
❑ 146 Alex Rodriguez DG .75 .35
❑ 147 Greg Maddux DG .75 .35
❑ 148 Kenny Lofton DG .15 .07
❑ 149 Mike Piazza DG .75 .35
❑ 150 Mark McGwire DG 1.25 .55
❑ 151 Andruw Jones DG .25 .11
❑ 152 Rusty Greer DG .15 .07
❑ 153 F.P. Santangelo DG .15 .07

❑ 154 Mike Lansing .15 .07
❑ 155 Lee Smith .25 .11
❑ 156 Carlos Perez .15 .07
❑ 157 Pedro Martinez .75 .35
❑ 158 Ryan McGuire .15 .07
❑ 159 F.P. Santangelo .15 .07
❑ 160 Rondell White .25 .11
❑ 161 T.Kashiwada RC .15 .07
❑ 162 Butch Huskey .15 .07
❑ 163 Edgardo Alfonzo .25 .11
❑ 164 John Franco .25 .11
❑ 165 Todd Hundley .15 .07
❑ 166 Rey Ordonez .15 .07
❑ 167 Armando Reynoso .15 .07
❑ 168 John Olerud .25 .11
❑ 169 Bernie Williams .60 .25
❑ 170 Andy Pettitte .25 .11
❑ 171 Wade Boggs .60 .25
❑ 172 Paul O'Neill .60 .25
❑ 173 Cecil Fielder .25 .11
❑ 174 Charlie Hayes .15 .07
❑ 175 David Cone .25 .11
❑ 176 Hideki Irabu .15 .07
❑ 177 Mark Bellhorn .15 .07
❑ 178 Steve Karsay .15 .07
❑ 179 Damon Mashore .15 .07
❑ 180 Jason McDonald .15 .07
❑ 181 Scott Spiezio .15 .07
❑ 182 Ariel Prieto .15 .07
❑ 183 Jason Giambi .60 .25
❑ 184 Wendell Magee .15 .07
❑ 185 Rico Brogna .15 .07
❑ 186 Garrett Stephenson .15 .07
❑ 187 Wayne Gomes .15 .07
❑ 188 Ricky Bottalico .15 .07
❑ 189 Mickey Morandini .15 .07
❑ 190 Mike Lieberthal .25 .11
❑ 191 Kevin Polcovich .15 .07
❑ 192 Francisco Cordova .15 .07
❑ 193 Kevin Young .25 .11
❑ 194 Jon Lieber .15 .07
❑ 195 Kevin Elster .15 .07
❑ 196 Tony Womack .15 .07
❑ 197 Lou Collier .15 .07
❑ 198 Mike Difelice RC .15 .07
❑ 199 Gary Gaetti .25 .11
❑ 200 Dennis Eckersley .25 .11
❑ 201 Alan Benes .15 .07
❑ 202 Willie McGee .25 .11
❑ 203 Ron Gant .25 .11
❑ 204 Fernando Valenzuela .25 .11
❑ 205 Mark McGwire 2.50 1.10
❑ 206 Archi Cianfrocco .15 .07
❑ 207 Andy Ashby .15 .07
❑ 208 Steve Finley .25 .11
❑ 209 Quilvio Veras .15 .07
❑ 210 Ken Caminiti .25 .11
❑ 211 Rickey Henderson 1.25 .55
❑ 212 Joey Hamilton .15 .07
❑ 213 Derrek Lee .25 .11
❑ 214 Bill Mueller .15 .07
❑ 215 Shawn Estes .25 .11
❑ 216 J.T. Snow .25 .11
❑ 217 Mark Gardner .15 .07
❑ 218 Terry Mulholland .15 .07
❑ 219 Dante Powell .15 .07
❑ 220 Jeff Kent .40 .18
❑ 221 Jamie Moyer .15 .07
❑ 222 Joey Cora .15 .07
❑ 223 Jeff Fassero .15 .07
❑ 224 Dennis Martinez .25 .11
❑ 225 Ken Griffey Jr. 2.00 .90
❑ 226 Edgar Martinez .40 .18
❑ 227 Russ Davis .15 .07
❑ 228 Dan Wilson .15 .07
❑ 229 Will Clark .60 .25
❑ 230 Ivan Rodriguez .60 .25
❑ 231 Benji Gil .15 .07
❑ 232 Lee Stevens .15 .07
❑ 233 Mickey Tettleton .15 .07
❑ 234 Julio Santana .15 .07
❑ 235 Rusty Greer .25 .11
❑ 236 Bobby Witt .15 .07
❑ 237 Ed Sprague .15 .07
❑ 238 Pat Hentgen .15 .07
❑ 239 Kelvim Escobar .15 .07
❑ 240 Joe Carter .25 .11
❑ 241 Carlos Delgado .60 .25
❑ 242 Shannon Stewart .25 .11
❑ 243 Benito Santiago .15 .07
❑ 244 Tino Martinez SH .15 .07
❑ 245 Ken Griffey Jr. SH 1.00 .45
❑ 246 Kevin Brown SH .25 .11
❑ 247 Ryne Sandberg SH .40 .18
❑ 248 Mo Vaughn SH .25 .11
❑ 249 Darryl Hamilton SH .15 .07
❑ 250 Randy Johnson SH .25 .11
❑ 251 Steve Finley SH .15 .07
❑ 252 Bobby Higginson SH .15 .07
❑ 253 Brett Tomko .15 .07
❑ 254 Mark Kotsay .25 .11
❑ 255 Jose Guillen .15 .07
❑ 256 Eli Marrero .15 .07
❑ 257 Dennis Reyes .15 .07
❑ 258 Richie Sexson .25 .11
❑ 259 Pat Cline .15 .07
❑ 260 Todd Helton .75 .35
❑ 261 Juan Melo .15 .07
❑ 262 Matt Morris .25 .11
❑ 263 Jeremi Gonzalez .15 .07
❑ 264 Jeff Abbott .15 .07
❑ 265 Aaron Boone .15 .07
❑ 266 Todd Dunwoody .15 .07
❑ 267 Jaret Wright .15 .07
❑ 268 Derrick Gibson .15 .07
❑ 269 Mario Valdez .15 .07
❑ 270 Fernando Tatis .15 .07
❑ 271 Craig Counsell .15 .07
❑ 272 Brad Rigby .15 .07
❑ 273 Danny Clyburn .15 .07
❑ 274 Brian Rose .15 .07
❑ 275 Miguel Tejada .40 .18
❑ 276 Jason Varitek .25 .11
❑ 277 Dave Dellucci RC .15 .07
❑ 278 Michael Coleman .15 .07
❑ 279 Adam Riggs .15 .07
❑ 280 Ben Grieve .25 .11
❑ 281 Brad Fullmer .25 .11
❑ 282 Ken Cloude .15 .07
❑ 283 Tom Evans .15 .07
❑ 284 Kevin Millwood RC .60 .25
❑ 285 Paul Konerko .25 .11
❑ 286 Juan Encarnacion .25 .11
❑ 287 Chris Carpenter .15 .07
❑ 288 Tom Fordham .15 .07
❑ 289 Gary DiSarcina .15 .07
❑ 290 Tim Salmon .25 .11
❑ 291 Troy Percival .15 .07
❑ 292 Todd Greene .15 .07
❑ 293 Ken Hill .15 .07
❑ 294 Dennis Springer .15 .07
❑ 295 Jim Edmonds .40 .18
❑ 296 Allen Watson .15 .07
❑ 297 Brian Anderson .15 .07
❑ 298 Keith Lockhart .15 .07
❑ 299 Tom Glavine .60 .25
❑ 300 Chipper Jones 1.25 .55
❑ 301 Randall Simon .15 .07
❑ 302 Mark Lemke .15 .07
❑ 303 Ryan Klesko .25 .11
❑ 304 Denny Neagle .15 .07
❑ 305 Andruw Jones .60 .25
❑ 306 Mike Mussina .60 .25
❑ 307 Brady Anderson .25 .11
❑ 308 Chris Hoiles .15 .07
❑ 309 Mike Bordick .15 .07
❑ 310 Cal Ripken 2.50 1.10
❑ 311 Geronimo Berroa .15 .07
❑ 312 Armando Benitez .15 .07
❑ 313 Roberto Alomar .60 .25
❑ 314 Tim Wakefield .15 .07
❑ 315 Reggie Jefferson .15 .07
❑ 316 Jeff Frye .15 .07
❑ 317 Scott Hatteberg .15 .07
❑ 318 Steve Avery .15 .07
❑ 319 Robinson Checo .15 .07
❑ 320 Nomar Garciaparra 1.50 .70
❑ 321 Lance Johnson .15 .07
❑ 322 Tyler Houston .15 .07
❑ 323 Mark Clark .15 .07
❑ 324 Terry Adams .15 .07
❑ 325 Sammy Sosa 1.25 .55
❑ 326 Scott Servais .15 .07
❑ 327 Manny Alexander .15 .07
❑ 328 Norberto Martin .15 .07
❑ 329 Scott Eyre .15 .07
❑ 330 Frank Thomas .75 .35
❑ 331 Robin Ventura .25 .11
❑ 332 Matt Karchner .15 .07
❑ 333 Keith Foulke .15 .07
❑ 334 James Baldwin .15 .07
❑ 335 Chris Stynes .15 .07
❑ 336 Bret Boone .25 .11
❑ 337 Jon Nunnally .15 .07
❑ 338 Dave Burba .15 .07
❑ 339 Eduardo Perez .15 .07
❑ 340 Reggie Sanders .15 .07
❑ 341 Mike Remlinger .15 .07
❑ 342 Pat Watkins .15 .07
❑ 343 Chad Ogea .15 .07
❑ 344 John Smiley .15 .07
❑ 345 Kenny Lofton .25 .11
❑ 346 Jose Mesa .15 .07
❑ 347 Charles Nagy .15 .07
❑ 348 Enrique Wilson .15 .07
❑ 349 Bruce Aven .15 .07
❑ 350 Manny Ramirez .75 .35
❑ 351 Jerry DiPoto .15 .07
❑ 352 Ellis Burks .25 .11
❑ 353 Kirt Manwaring .15 .07
❑ 354 Vinny Castilla .25 .11
❑ 355 Larry Walker .40 .18
❑ 356 Kevin Ritz .15 .07
❑ 357 Pedro Astacio .15 .07
❑ 358 Scott Sanders .15 .07
❑ 359 Deivi Cruz .15 .07
❑ 360 Brian L. Hunter .15 .07
❑ 361 Pedro Martinez HM .40 .18
❑ 362 Tom Glavine HM .25 .11
❑ 363 Willie McGee HM .15 .07
❑ 364 J.T. Snow HM .15 .07
❑ 365 Rusty Greer HM .15 .07
❑ 366 Mike Grace HM .15 .07
❑ 367 Tony Clark HM .25 .11
❑ 368 Ben Grieve HM .25 .11
❑ 369 Gary Sheffield HM .15 .07
❑ 370 Joe Oliver .15 .07
❑ 371 Todd Jones .15 .07
❑ 372 Frank Catalanotto RC .60 .25
❑ 373 Brian Moehler .15 .07
❑ 374 Cliff Floyd .25 .11
❑ 375 Bobby Bonilla .25 .11
❑ 376 Al Leiter .25 .11
❑ 377 Josh Booty .15 .07
❑ 378 Darren Daulton .25 .11
❑ 379 Jay Powell .15 .07
❑ 380 Felix Heredia .15 .07
❑ 381 Jim Eisenreich .15 .07
❑ 382 Richard Hidalgo .25 .11
❑ 383 Mike Hampton .25 .11
❑ 384 Shane Reynolds .15 .07
❑ 385 Jeff Bagwell .75 .35
❑ 386 Derek Bell .15 .07
❑ 387 Ricky Gutierrez .15 .07
❑ 388 Bill Spiers .15 .07
❑ 389 Jose Offerman .15 .07
❑ 390 Johnny Damon .25 .11
❑ 391 Jermaine Dye .25 .11
❑ 392 Jeff Montgomery .15 .07
❑ 393 Glendon Rusch .15 .07
❑ 394 Mike Sweeney .25 .11
❑ 395 Kevin Appier .25 .11
❑ 396 Joe Vitiello .15 .07
❑ 397 Ramon Martinez .15 .07
❑ 398 Darren Dreifort .15 .07
❑ 399 Wilton Guerrero .15 .07
❑ 400 Mike Piazza 1.50 .70
❑ 401 Eddie Murray .60 .25
❑ 402 Ismael Valdes .15 .07
❑ 403 Todd Hollandsworth .15 .07
❑ 404 Mark Loretta .15 .07
❑ 405 Jeromy Burnitz .25 .11
❑ 406 Jeff Cirillo .25 .11
❑ 407 Scott Karl .15 .07
❑ 408 Mike Matheny .15 .07
❑ 409 Jose Valentin .15 .07
❑ 410 John Jaha .25 .11
❑ 411 Terry Steinbach .15 .07

❑ 412 Torii Hunter .25 .11
❑ 413 Pat Meares .15 .07
❑ 414 Marty Cordova .15 .07
❑ 415 Jaret Wright PH .15 .07
❑ 416 Mike Mussina PH .25 .11
❑ 417 John Smoltz PH .15 .07
❑ 418 Devon White PH .15 .07
❑ 419 Denny Neagle PH .15 .07
❑ 420 Livan Hernandez PH .15 .07
❑ 421 Kevin Brown PH .25 .11
❑ 422 Marquis Grissom PH .15 .07
❑ 423 Mike Mussina PH .25 .11
❑ 424 Eric Davis PH .15 .07
❑ 425 Tony Fernandez PH .15 .07
❑ 426 Moises Alou PH .15 .07
❑ 427 Sandy Alomar Jr. PH .15 .07
❑ 428 Gary Sheffield PH .15 .07
❑ 429 Jaret Wright PH .15 .07
❑ 430 Livan Hernandez PH .15 .07
❑ 431 Chad Ogea PH .15 .07
❑ 432 Edgar Renteria PH .15 .07
❑ 433 LaTroy Hawkins .15 .07
❑ 434 Rich Robertson .15 .07
❑ 435 Chuck Knoblauch .25 .11
❑ 436 Jose Vidro .25 .11
❑ 437 Dustin Hermanson .15 .07
❑ 438 Jim Bullinger .15 .07
❑ 439 Orlando Cabrera .15 .07
❑ 440 Vladimir Guerrero .75 .35
❑ 441 Ugueth Urbina .15 .07
❑ 442 Brian McRae .15 .07
❑ 443 Matt Franco .15 .07
❑ 444 Bobby Jones .15 .07
❑ 445 Bernard Gilkey .15 .07
❑ 446 Dave Mlicki .15 .07
❑ 447 Brian Bohanon .15 .07
❑ 448 Mel Rojas .15 .07
❑ 449 Tim Raines .25 .11
❑ 450 Derek Jeter 2.50 1.10
❑ 451 Roger Clemens UE .75 .35
❑ 452 N.Garciaparra UE .75 .35
❑ 453 Mike Piazza UE .75 .35
❑ 454 Mark McGwire UE 1.25 .55
❑ 455 Ken Griffey Jr. UE 1.00 .45
❑ 456 Larry Walker UE .40 .18
❑ 457 Alex Rodriguez UE .75 .35
❑ 458 Tony Gwynn UE .60 .25
❑ 459 Frank Thomas UE .40 .18
❑ 460 Tino Martinez .25 .11
❑ 461 Chad Curtis .15 .07
❑ 462 Ramiro Mendoza .15 .07
❑ 463 Joe Girardi .15 .07
❑ 464 David Wells .25 .11
❑ 465 Mariano Rivera .25 .11
❑ 466 Willie Adams .15 .07
❑ 467 George Williams .15 .07
❑ 468 Dave Telgheder .15 .07
❑ 469 Dave Magadan .15 .07
❑ 470 Matt Stairs .15 .07
❑ 471 Bill Taylor .15 .07
❑ 472 Jimmy Haynes .15 .07
❑ 473 Gregg Jefferies .15 .07
❑ 474 Midre Cummings .15 .07
❑ 475 Curt Schilling .60 .25
❑ 476 Mike Grace .15 .07
❑ 477 Mark Leiter .15 .07
❑ 478 Matt Beech .15 .07
❑ 479 Scott Rolen .60 .25
❑ 480 Jason Kendall .25 .11
❑ 481 Esteban Loaiza .15 .07
❑ 482 Jermaine Allensworth .15 .07
❑ 483 Mark Smith .15 .07
❑ 484 Jason Schmidt .15 .07
❑ 485 Jose Guillen .15 .07
❑ 486 Al Martin .15 .07
❑ 487 Delino DeShields .15 .07
❑ 488 Todd Stottlemyre .15 .07
❑ 489 Brian Jordan .25 .11
❑ 490 Ray Lankford .15 .07
❑ 491 Matt Morris .25 .11
❑ 492 Royce Clayton .15 .07
❑ 493 John Mabry .15 .07
❑ 494 Wally Joyner .25 .11
❑ 495 Trevor Hoffman .25 .11
❑ 496 Chris Gomez .15 .07
❑ 497 Sterling Hitchcock .15 .07
❑ 498 Pete Smith .15 .07
❑ 499 Greg Vaughn .25 .11
❑ 500 Tony Gwynn 1.25 .55
❑ 501 Will Cunnane .15 .07
❑ 502 Darryl Hamilton .15 .07
❑ 503 Brian Johnson .15 .07
❑ 504 Kirk Rueter .15 .07
❑ 505 Barry Bonds 1.50 .70
❑ 506 Osvaldo Fernandez .15 .07
❑ 507 Stan Javier .15 .07
❑ 508 Julian Tavarez .15 .07
❑ 509 Rich Aurilia .25 .11
❑ 510 Alex Rodriguez 1.50 .70
❑ 511 David Segui .15 .07
❑ 512 Rich Amaral .15 .07
❑ 513 Raul Ibanez .15 .07
❑ 514 Jay Buhner .25 .11
❑ 515 Randy Johnson .75 .35
❑ 516 Heathcliff Slocumb .15 .07
❑ 517 Tony Saunders .15 .07
❑ 518 Kevin Elster .15 .07
❑ 519 John Burkett .15 .07
❑ 520 Juan Gonzalez .60 .25
❑ 521 John Wetteland .25 .11
❑ 522 Domingo Cedeno .15 .07
❑ 523 Darren Oliver .15 .07
❑ 524 Roger Pavlik .15 .07
❑ 525 Jose Cruz Jr. .25 .11
❑ 526 Woody Williams .15 .07
❑ 527 Alex Gonzalez .15 .07
❑ 528 Robert Person .15 .07
❑ 529 Juan Guzman .15 .07
❑ 530 Roger Clemens 1.50 .70
❑ 531 Shawn Green .60 .25
❑ 532 Francisco Cordova SH .15 .07
Ricardo Rincon
Mark Smith
❑ 533 N.Garciaparra SH .75 .35
❑ 534 Roger Clemens SH .75 .35
❑ 535 Mark McGwire SH 1.25 .55
❑ 536 Larry Walker SH .40 .18
❑ 537 Mike Piazza SH .75 .35
❑ 538 Curt Schilling SH .60 .25
❑ 539 Tony Gwynn SH .60 .25
❑ 540 Ken Griffey Jr. SH 1.00 .45
❑ 541 Carl Pavano .15 .07
❑ 542 Shane Monahan .15 .07
❑ 543 Gabe Kapler RC 1.00 .45
❑ 544 Eric Milton .25 .11
❑ 545 Gary Matthews Jr. RC .25 .11
❑ 546 Mike Kinkade RC .25 .11
❑ 547 Ryan Christenson RC .25 .11
❑ 548 Corey Koskie RC .75 .35
❑ 549 Norm Hutchins .15 .07
❑ 550 Russell Branyan .25 .11
❑ 551 Masato Yoshii RC .50 .23
❑ 552 Jesus Sanchez RC .25 .11
❑ 553 Anthony Sanders .15 .07
❑ 554 Edwin Diaz .15 .07
❑ 555 Gabe Alvarez .15 .07
❑ 556 Carlos Lee RC 1.00 .45
❑ 557 Mike Darr .15 .07
❑ 558 Kerry Wood .60 .25
❑ 559 Carlos Guillen .15 .07
❑ 560 Sean Casey .40 .18
❑ 561 Manny Aybar RC .25 .11
❑ 562 Octavio Dotel .15 .07
❑ 563 Jarrod Washburn .15 .07
❑ 564 Mark L. Johnson .15 .07
❑ 565 Ramon Hernandez .15 .07
❑ 566 Rich Butler RC .15 .07
❑ 567 Mike Caruso .15 .07
❑ 568 Cliff Politte .15 .07
❑ 569 Scott Elarton .15 .07
❑ 570 Magglio Ordonez RC 2.00 .90
❑ 571 Adam Butler RC .25 .11
❑ 572 Marlon Anderson .15 .07
❑ 573 Julio Ramirez RC .25 .11
❑ 574 Darron Ingram RC .25 .11
❑ 575 Bruce Chen .15 .07
❑ 576 Steve Woodard .15 .07
❑ 577 Hiram Bocachica .15 .07
❑ 578 Kevin Witt .15 .07
❑ 579 Javier Vazquez .25 .11
❑ 580 Alex Gonzalez .15 .07
❑ 581 Brian Powell .15 .07
❑ 582 Wes Helms .15 .07
❑ 583 Ron Wright .15 .07
❑ 584 Rafael Medina .15 .07
❑ 585 Daryle Ward .15 .07
❑ 586 Geoff Jenkins .25 .11
❑ 587 Preston Wilson .25 .11
❑ 588 Jim Chamblee RC .15 .07
❑ 589 Mike Lowell RC .75 .35
❑ 590 A.J. Hinch .15 .07
❑ 591 Francisco Cordero RC .40 .18
❑ 592 Rolando Arrojo RC .50 .23
❑ 593 Braden Looper .15 .07
❑ 594 Sidney Ponson .15 .07
❑ 595 Matt Clement .25 .11
❑ 596 Carlton Loewer .15 .07
❑ 597 Brian Meadows .15 .07
❑ 598 Danny Klassen .15 .07
❑ 599 Larry Sutton .15 .07
❑ 600 Travis Lee .25 .11
❑ 601 Randy Johnson EP 2.50 1.10
❑ 602 Greg Maddux EP 5.00 2.20
❑ 603 Roger Clemens EP 5.00 2.20
❑ 604 Jaret Wright EP 2.00 .90
❑ 605 Mike Piazza EP 5.00 2.20
❑ 606 Tino Martinez EP 2.00 .90
❑ 607 Frank Thomas EP 2.50 1.10
❑ 608 Mo Vaughn EP 2.00 .90
❑ 609 Todd Helton EP 2.50 1.10
❑ 610 Mark McGwire EP 8.00 3.60
❑ 611 Jeff Bagwell EP 2.50 1.10
❑ 612 Travis Lee EP 2.00 .90
❑ 613 Scott Rolen EP 2.00 .90
❑ 614 Cal Ripken EP 8.00 3.60
❑ 615 Chipper Jones EP 4.00 1.80
❑ 616 Nomar Garciaparra EP 5.00 2.20
❑ 617 Alex Rodriguez EP 5.00 2.20
❑ 618 Derek Jeter EP 8.00 3.60
❑ 619 Tony Gwynn EP 4.00 1.80
❑ 620 Ken Griffey Jr. EP 6.00 2.70
❑ 621 Kenny Lofton EP 2.00 .90
❑ 622 Juan Gonzalez EP 2.00 .90
❑ 623 Jose Cruz Jr. EP 2.00 .90
❑ 624 Larry Walker EP 2.00 .90
❑ 625 Barry Bonds EP 5.00 2.20
❑ 626 Ben Grieve EP 2.00 .90
❑ 627 Andruw Jones EP 2.00 .90
❑ 628 Vladimir Guerrero EP 2.50 1.10
❑ 629 Paul Konerko EP 2.00 .90
❑ 630 Paul Molitor EP 2.00 .90
❑ 631 Cecil Fielder .25 .11
❑ 632 Jack McDowell .15 .07
❑ 633 Mike James .15 .07
❑ 634 Brian Anderson .15 .07
❑ 635 Jay Bell .25 .11
❑ 636 Devon White .15 .07
❑ 637 Andy Stankiewicz .15 .07
❑ 638 Tony Batista .25 .11
❑ 639 Omar Daal .15 .07
❑ 640 Matt Williams .40 .18
❑ 641 Brent Brede .15 .07
❑ 642 Jorge Fabregas .15 .07
❑ 643 Karim Garcia .15 .07
❑ 644 Felix Rodriguez .15 .07
❑ 645 Andy Benes .15 .07
❑ 646 Willie Blair .15 .07
❑ 647 Jeff Suppan .15 .07
❑ 648 Yamil Benitez .15 .07
❑ 649 Walt Weiss .25 .11
❑ 650 Andres Galarraga .40 .18
❑ 651 Doug Drabek .15 .07
❑ 652 Ozzie Guillen .15 .07
❑ 653 Joe Carter .25 .11
❑ 654 Dennis Eckersley .25 .11
❑ 655 Pedro Martinez .75 .35
❑ 656 Jim Leyritz .15 .07
❑ 657 Henry Rodriguez .15 .07
❑ 658 Rod Beck .15 .07
❑ 659 Mickey Morandini .15 .07
❑ 660 Jeff Blauser .15 .07
❑ 661 Ruben Sierra .15 .07
❑ 662 Mike Sirotka .15 .07
❑ 663 Pete Harnisch .15 .07
❑ 664 Damian Jackson .15 .07
❑ 665 Dmitri Young .25 .11
❑ 666 Steve Cooke .15 .07
❑ 667 Geronimo Berroa .15 .07

❑	668 Shawon Dunston	.15	.07
❑	669 Mike Jackson	.15	.07
❑	670 Travis Fryman	.25	.11
❑	671 Dwight Gooden	.15	.07
❑	672 Paul Assenmacher	.15	.07
❑	673 Eric Plunk	.15	.07
❑	674 Mike Lansing	.15	.07
❑	675 Darryl Kile	.25	.11
❑	676 Luis Gonzalez	.60	.25
❑	677 Frank Castillo	.15	.07
❑	678 Joe Randa	.15	.07
❑	679 Bip Roberts	.15	.07
❑	680 Derrek Lee	.25	.11
❑	681 Mike Piazza SP New York Mets	4.00	1.80
❑	681A Mike Piazza SP Florida Marlins	4.00	1.80
❑	682 Sean Berry	.15	.07
❑	683 Ramon Garcia	.15	.07
❑	684 Carl Everett	.25	.11
❑	685 Moises Alou	.25	.11
❑	686 Hal Morris	.15	.07
❑	687 Jeff Conine	.15	.07
❑	688 Gary Sheffield	.25	.11
❑	689 Jose Vizcaino	.15	.07
❑	690 Charles Johnson	.25	.11
❑	691 Bobby Bonilla	.25	.11
❑	692 Marquis Grissom	.15	.07
❑	693 Alex Ochoa	.15	.07
❑	694 Mike Morgan	.15	.07
❑	695 Orlando Merced	.15	.07
❑	696 David Ortiz	.25	.11
❑	697 Brent Gates	.15	.07
❑	698 Otis Nixon	.15	.07
❑	699 Trey Moore	.15	.07
❑	700 Derrick May	.15	.07
❑	701 Rich Becker	.15	.07
❑	702 Al Leiter	.25	.11
❑	703 Chili Davis	.25	.11
❑	704 Scott Brosius	.25	.11
❑	705 Chuck Knoblauch	.25	.11
❑	706 Kenny Rogers	.15	.07
❑	707 Mike Blowers	.15	.07
❑	708 Mike Fetters	.15	.07
❑	709 Tom Candiotti	.15	.07
❑	710 Rickey Henderson	1.25	.55
❑	711 Bob Abreu	.25	.11
❑	712 Mark Lewis	.15	.07
❑	713 Doug Glanville	.15	.07
❑	714 Desi Relaford	.15	.07
❑	715 Kent Mercker	.15	.07
❑	716 Kevin Brown	.40	.18
❑	717 James Mouton	.15	.07
❑	718 Mark Langston	.15	.07
❑	719 Greg Myers	.15	.07
❑	720 Orel Hershiser	.25	.11
❑	721 Charlie Hayes	.15	.07
❑	722 Robb Nen	.15	.07
❑	723 Glenallen Hill	.15	.07
❑	724 Tony Saunders	.15	.07
❑	725 Wade Boggs	.60	.25
❑	726 Kevin Stocker	.15	.07
❑	727 Wilson Alvarez	.15	.07
❑	728 Albie Lopez	.15	.07
❑	729 Dave Martinez	.15	.07
❑	730 Fred McGriff	.40	.18
❑	731 Quinton McCracken	.15	.07
❑	732 Bryan Rekar	.15	.07
❑	733 Paul Sorrento	.15	.07
❑	734 Roberto Hernandez	.15	.07
❑	735 Bubba Trammell	.15	.07
❑	736 Miguel Cairo	.15	.07
❑	737 John Flaherty	.15	.07
❑	738 Terrell Wade	.15	.07
❑	739 Roberto Kelly	.15	.07
❑	740 Mark McLemore	.15	.07
❑	741 Danny Patterson	.15	.07
❑	742 Aaron Sele	.25	.11
❑	743 Tony Fernandez	.15	.07
❑	744 Randy Myers	.25	.11
❑	745 Jose Canseco	.60	.25
❑	746 Darrin Fletcher	.15	.07
❑	747 Mike Stanley	.15	.07
❑	748 M.Grissom SH CL	.15	.07
❑	749 Fred McGriff SH CL	.25	.11
❑	750 Travis Lee SH CL	.25	.11

1999 Upper Deck

	MINT	NRMT
COMPLETE SET (525)	100.00	45.00
COMPLETE SERIES 1 (255)	60.00	27.00
COMPLETE SERIES 2 (270)	40.00	18.00
COMMON (19-255/293-535)	.15	.07
COMMON SER.2 SR (266-292)	.30	.14

❑	1 Troy Glaus SR	2.50	1.10
❑	2 Adrian Beltre SR	.60	.25
❑	3 Matt Anderson SR	.40	.18
❑	4 Eric Chavez SR	.60	.25
❑	5 Jin Ho Cho SR	.40	.18
❑	6 Robert Smith SR	.40	.18
❑	7 George Lombard SR	.40	.18
❑	8 Mike Kinkade SR	.40	.18
❑	9 Seth Greisinger SR	.40	.18
❑	10 J.D. Drew SR	2.00	.90
❑	11 Aramis Ramirez SR	.50	.23
❑	12 Carlos Guillen SR	.40	.18
❑	13 Justin Baughman SR	.40	.18
❑	14 Jim Parque SR	.40	.18
❑	15 Ryan Jackson SR	.40	.18
❑	16 Ramon E.Martinez SR RC	.40	.18
❑	17 Orlando Hernandez SR	.60	.25
❑	18 Jeremy Giambi SR	.40	.18
❑	19 Gary DiSarcina	.15	.07
❑	20 Darin Erstad	.60	.25
❑	21 Troy Glaus	.60	.25
❑	22 Chuck Finley	.25	.11
❑	23 Dave Hollins	.15	.07
❑	24 Troy Percival	.15	.07
❑	25 Tim Salmon	.25	.11
❑	26 Brian Anderson	.15	.07
❑	27 Jay Bell	.25	.11
❑	28 Andy Benes	.15	.07
❑	29 Brent Brede	.15	.07
❑	30 David Dellucci	.15	.07
❑	31 Karim Garcia	.15	.07
❑	32 Travis Lee	.15	.07
❑	33 Andres Galarraga	.40	.18
❑	34 Ryan Klesko	.25	.11
❑	35 Keith Lockhart	.15	.07
❑	36 Kevin Millwood	.15	.07
❑	37 Denny Neagle	.15	.07
❑	38 John Smoltz	.25	.11
❑	39 Michael Tucker	.15	.07
❑	40 Walt Weiss	.15	.07
❑	41 Dennis Martinez	.25	.11
❑	42 Javy Lopez	.25	.11
❑	43 Brady Anderson	.25	.11
❑	44 Harold Baines	.25	.11
❑	45 Mike Bordick	.15	.07
❑	46 Roberto Alomar	.60	.25
❑	47 Scott Erickson	.15	.07
❑	48 Mike Mussina	.60	.25
❑	49 Cal Ripken	2.50	1.10
❑	50 Darren Bragg	.15	.07
❑	51 Dennis Eckersley	.25	.11
❑	52 Nomar Garciaparra	1.50	.70
❑	53 Scott Hatteberg	.15	.07
❑	54 Troy O'Leary	.15	.07
❑	55 Bret Saberhagen	.25	.11
❑	56 John Valentin	.15	.07
❑	57 Rod Beck	.15	.07
❑	58 Jeff Blauser	.15	.07
❑	59 Brant Brown	.15	.07

❑	60 Mark Clark	.15	.07
❑	61 Mark Grace	.60	.25
❑	62 Kevin Tapani	.15	.07
❑	63 Henry Rodriguez	.15	.07
❑	64 Mike Cameron	.25	.11
❑	65 Mike Caruso	.15	.07
❑	66 Ray Durham	.25	.11
❑	67 Jaime Navarro	.15	.07
❑	68 Magglio Ordonez	.40	.18
❑	69 Mike Sirotka	.15	.07
❑	70 Sean Casey	.40	.18
❑	71 Barry Larkin	.60	.25
❑	72 Jon Nunnally	.15	.07
❑	73 Paul Konerko	.25	.11
❑	74 Chris Stynes	.15	.07
❑	75 Brett Tomko	.15	.07
❑	76 Dmitri Young	.25	.11
❑	77 Sandy Alomar Jr.	.25	.11
❑	78 Bartolo Colon	.25	.11
❑	79 Travis Fryman	.25	.11
❑	80 Brian Giles	.25	.11
❑	81 David Justice	.25	.11
❑	82 Omar Vizquel	.25	.11
❑	83 Jaret Wright	.15	.07
❑	84 Jim Thome	.60	.25
❑	85 Charles Nagy	.15	.07
❑	86 Pedro Astacio	.15	.07
❑	87 Todd Helton	.75	.35
❑	88 Darryl Kile	.25	.11
❑	89 Mike Lansing	.15	.07
❑	90 Neifi Perez	.15	.07
❑	91 John Thomson	.15	.07
❑	92 Larry Walker	.40	.18
❑	93 Tony Clark	.25	.11
❑	94 Deivi Cruz	.15	.07
❑	95 Damion Easley	.15	.07
❑	96 Brian L.Hunter	.15	.07
❑	97 Todd Jones	.15	.07
❑	98 Brian Moehler	.15	.07
❑	99 Gabe Alvarez	.15	.07
❑	100 Craig Counsell	.15	.07
❑	101 Cliff Floyd	.25	.11
❑	102 Livan Hernandez	.15	.07
❑	103 Andy Larkin	.15	.07
❑	104 Derrek Lee	.25	.11
❑	105 Brian Meadows	.15	.07
❑	106 Moises Alou	.25	.11
❑	107 Sean Berry	.15	.07
❑	108 Craig Biggio	.40	.18
❑	109 Ricky Gutierrez	.15	.07
❑	110 Mike Hampton	.25	.11
❑	111 Jose Lima	.15	.07
❑	112 Billy Wagner	.15	.07
❑	113 Hal Morris	.15	.07
❑	114 Johnny Damon	.25	.11
❑	115 Jeff King	.15	.07
❑	116 Jeff Montgomery	.15	.07
❑	117 Glendon Rusch	.15	.07
❑	118 Larry Sutton	.15	.07
❑	119 Bobby Bonilla	.25	.11
❑	120 Jim Eisenreich	.15	.07
❑	121 Eric Karros	.25	.11
❑	122 Matt Luke	.15	.07
❑	123 Ramon Martinez	.15	.07
❑	124 Gary Sheffield	.25	.11
❑	125 Eric Young	.15	.07
❑	126 Charles Johnson	.25	.11
❑	127 Jeff Cirillo	.25	.11
❑	128 Marquis Grissom	.15	.07
❑	129 Jeromy Burnitz	.25	.11
❑	130 Bob Wickman	.15	.07
❑	131 Scott Karl	.15	.07
❑	132 Mark Loretta	.15	.07
❑	133 Fernando Vina	.15	.07
❑	134 Matt Lawton	.25	.11
❑	135 Pat Meares	.15	.07
❑	136 Eric Milton	.25	.11
❑	137 Paul Molitor	.60	.25
❑	138 David Ortiz	.25	.11
❑	139 Todd Walker	.15	.07
❑	140 Shane Andrews	.15	.07
❑	141 Brad Fullmer	.25	.11
❑	142 Vladimir Guerrero	.75	.35
❑	143 Dustin Hermanson	.15	.07
❑	144 Ryan McGuire	.15	.07
❑	145 Ugueth Urbina	.15	.07

❑ 146 John Franco .25 .11
❑ 147 Butch Huskey .15 .07
❑ 148 Bobby Jones .15 .07
❑ 149 John Olerud .25 .11
❑ 150 Rey Ordonez .15 .07
❑ 151 Mike Piazza 1.50 .70
❑ 152 Hideo Nomo .60 .25
❑ 153 Masato Yoshii .25 .11
❑ 154 Derek Jeter 2.50 1.10
❑ 155 Chuck Knoblauch .25 .11
❑ 156 Paul O'Neill .60 .25
❑ 157 Andy Pettitte .25 .11
❑ 158 Mariano Rivera .25 .11
❑ 159 Darryl Strawberry .25 .11
❑ 160 David Wells .25 .11
❑ 161 Jorge Posada .25 .11
❑ 162 Ramiro Mendoza .15 .07
❑ 163 Miguel Tejada .25 .11
❑ 164 Ryan Christenson .15 .07
❑ 165 Rickey Henderson 1.25 .55
❑ 166 A.J. Hinch .15 .07
❑ 167 Ben Grieve .25 .11
❑ 168 Kenny Rogers .15 .07
❑ 169 Matt Stairs .15 .07
❑ 170 Bob Abreu .25 .11
❑ 171 Rico Brogna .15 .07
❑ 172 Doug Glanville .15 .07
❑ 173 Mike Grace .15 .07
❑ 174 Desi Relaford .15 .07
❑ 175 Scott Rolen .60 .25
❑ 176 Jose Guillen .15 .07
❑ 177 Francisco Cordova .15 .07
❑ 178 Al Martin .15 .07
❑ 179 Jason Schmidt .15 .07
❑ 180 Turner Ward .15 .07
❑ 181 Kevin Young .25 .11
❑ 182 Mark McGwire 2.50 1.10
❑ 183 Delino DeShields .15 .07
❑ 184 Eli Marrero .15 .07
❑ 185 Tom Lampkin .15 .07
❑ 186 Ray Lankford .15 .07
❑ 187 Willie McGee .25 .11
❑ 188 Matt Morris .25 .11
❑ 189 Andy Ashby .15 .07
❑ 190 Kevin Brown .40 .18
❑ 191 Ken Caminiti .25 .11
❑ 192 Trevor Hoffman .25 .11
❑ 193 Wally Joyner .25 .11
❑ 194 Greg Vaughn .25 .11
❑ 195 Danny Darwin .15 .07
❑ 196 Shawn Estes .25 .11
❑ 197 Orel Hershiser .25 .11
❑ 198 Jeff Kent .40 .18
❑ 199 Bill Mueller .15 .07
❑ 200 Robb Nen .15 .07
❑ 201 J.T. Snow .25 .11
❑ 202 Ken Cloude .15 .07
❑ 203 Russ Davis .15 .07
❑ 204 Jeff Fassero .15 .07
❑ 205 Ken Griffey Jr. 2.00 .90
❑ 206 Shane Monahan .15 .07
❑ 207 David Segui .15 .07
❑ 208 Dan Wilson .15 .07
❑ 209 Wilson Alvarez .15 .07
❑ 210 Wade Boggs .60 .25
❑ 211 Miguel Cairo .15 .07
❑ 212 Bubba Trammell .15 .07
❑ 213 Quinton McCracken .15 .07
❑ 214 Paul Sorrento .15 .07
❑ 215 Kevin Stocker .15 .07
❑ 216 Will Clark .60 .25
❑ 217 Rusty Greer .25 .11
❑ 218 Rick Helling .15 .07
❑ 219 Mark McLemore .15 .07
❑ 220 Ivan Rodriguez .60 .25
❑ 221 John Wetteland .25 .11
❑ 222 Jose Canseco .60 .25
❑ 223 Roger Clemens 1.50 .70
❑ 224 Carlos Delgado .60 .25
❑ 225 Darrin Fletcher .15 .07
❑ 226 Alex Gonzalez .15 .07
❑ 227 Jose Cruz Jr. .25 .11
❑ 228 Shannon Stewart .25 .11
❑ 229 Rolando Arrojo FF .15 .07
❑ 230 Livan Hernandez FF .15 .07
❑ 231 Orlando Hernandez FF .25 .11
❑ 232 Raul Mondesi FF .25 .11
❑ 233 Moises Alou FF .25 .11
❑ 234 Pedro Martinez FF .75 .35
❑ 235 Sammy Sosa FF 1.25 .55
❑ 236 Vladimir Guerrero FF .75 .35
❑ 237 Bartolo Colon FF .25 .11
❑ 238 Miguel Tejada FF .25 .11
❑ 239 Ismael Valdes FF .15 .07
❑ 240 Mariano Rivera FF .25 .11
❑ 241 Jose Cruz Jr. FF .25 .11
❑ 242 Juan Gonzalez FF .60 .25
❑ 243 Ivan Rodriguez FF .60 .25
❑ 244 Sandy Alomar Jr. FF .25 .11
❑ 245 Roberto Alomar FF .60 .25
❑ 246 Magglio Ordonez FF .40 .18
❑ 247 Kerry Wood SH CL .25 .11
❑ 248 Mark McGwire SH CL 2.50 1.10
❑ 249 David Wells SH CL .25 .11
❑ 250 Rolando Arrojo SH CL .15 .07
❑ 251 Ken Griffey Jr. SH CL 2.00 .90
❑ 252 T.Hoffman SH CL .25 .11
❑ 253 Travis Lee SH CL .15 .07
❑ 254 R.Alomar SH CL .60 .25
❑ 255 Sammy Sosa SH CL 1.25 .55
❑ 266 Pat Burrell SR RC 2.00 .90
❑ 267 S.Hillenbrand SR RC 1.00 .45
❑ 268 Robert Fick SR .30 .14
❑ 269 Roy Halladay SR .30 .14
❑ 270 Ruben Mateo SR .50 .23
❑ 271 Bruce Chen SR .30 .14
❑ 272 Angel Pena SR .30 .14
❑ 273 Michael Barrett SR .30 .14
❑ 274 Kevin Witt SR .30 .14
❑ 275 Damon Minor SR .30 .14
❑ 276 Ryan Minor SR .30 .14
❑ 277 A.J. Pierzynski SR .30 .14
❑ 278 A.J. Burnett SR RC 1.00 .45
❑ 279 Dermal Brown SR .30 .14
❑ 280 Joe Lawrence SR .50 .23
❑ 281 Derrick Gibson SR .30 .14
❑ 282 Carlos Febles SR .30 .14
❑ 283 Chris Haas SR .30 .14
❑ 284 Cesar King SR .30 .14
❑ 285 Calvin Pickering SR .30 .14
❑ 286 Mitch Meluskey SR .30 .14
❑ 287 Carlos Beltran SR .50 .23
❑ 288 Ron Belliard SR .30 .14
❑ 289 Jerry Hairston Jr. SR .50 .23
❑ 290 F.Seguignol SR .30 .14
❑ 291 Kris Benson SR .50 .23
❑ 292 C.Hutchinson SR RC .50 .23
❑ 293 Jarrod Washburn .15 .07
❑ 294 Jason Dickson .15 .07
❑ 295 Mo Vaughn .25 .11
❑ 296 Garret Anderson .25 .11
❑ 297 Jim Edmonds .40 .18
❑ 298 Ken Hill .15 .07
❑ 299 Shigetoshi Hasegawa .15 .07
❑ 300 Todd Stottlemyre .15 .07
❑ 301 Randy Johnson .75 .35
❑ 302 Omar Daal .15 .07
❑ 303 Steve Finley .25 .11
❑ 304 Matt Williams .40 .18
❑ 305 Danny Klassen .15 .07
❑ 306 Tony Batista .25 .11
❑ 307 Brian Jordan .25 .11
❑ 308 Greg Maddux 1.50 .70
❑ 309 Chipper Jones 1.25 .55
❑ 310 Bret Boone .25 .11
❑ 311 Ozzie Guillen .15 .07
❑ 312 John Rocker .25 .11
❑ 313 Tom Glavine .60 .25
❑ 314 Andruw Jones .60 .25
❑ 315 Albert Belle .25 .11
❑ 316 Charles Johnson .25 .11
❑ 317 Will Clark .60 .25
❑ 318 B.J. Surhoff .25 .11
❑ 319 Delino DeShields .15 .07
❑ 320 Heathcliff Slocumb .15 .07
❑ 321 Sidney Ponson .15 .07
❑ 322 Juan Guzman .15 .07
❑ 323 Reggie Jefferson .15 .07
❑ 324 Mark Portugal .15 .07
❑ 325 Tim Wakefield .15 .07
❑ 326 Jason Varitek .25 .11
❑ 327 Jose Offerman .15 .07
❑ 328 Pedro Martinez .75 .35
❑ 329 Trot Nixon .25 .11
❑ 330 Kerry Wood .60 .25
❑ 331 Sammy Sosa 1.25 .55
❑ 332 Glenallen Hill .15 .07
❑ 333 Gary Gaetti .15 .07
❑ 334 Mickey Morandini .15 .07
❑ 335 Benito Santiago .15 .07
❑ 336 Jeff Blauser .15 .07
❑ 337 Frank Thomas .75 .35
❑ 338 Paul Konerko .25 .11
❑ 339 Jaime Navarro .15 .07
❑ 340 Carlos Lee .25 .11
❑ 341 Brian Simmons .15 .07
❑ 342 Mark Johnson .15 .07
❑ 343 Jeff Abbott .15 .07
❑ 344 Steve Avery .15 .07
❑ 345 Mike Cameron .25 .11
❑ 346 Michael Tucker .15 .07
❑ 347 Greg Vaughn .25 .11
❑ 348 Hal Morris .15 .07
❑ 349 Pete Harnisch .15 .07
❑ 350 Denny Neagle .15 .07
❑ 351 Manny Ramirez .75 .35
❑ 352 Roberto Alomar .60 .25
❑ 353 Dwight Gooden .25 .11
❑ 354 Kenny Lofton .25 .11
❑ 355 Mike Jackson .15 .07
❑ 356 Charles Nagy .15 .07
❑ 357 Enrique Wilson .15 .07
❑ 358 Russ Branyan .25 .11
❑ 359 Richie Sexson .25 .11
❑ 360 Vinny Castilla .25 .11
❑ 361 Dante Bichette .25 .11
❑ 362 Kirt Manwaring .15 .07
❑ 363 Darryl Hamilton .15 .07
❑ 364 Jamey Wright .15 .07
❑ 365 Curtis Leskanic .15 .07
❑ 366 Jeff Reed .15 .07
❑ 367 Bobby Higginson .25 .11
❑ 368 Justin Thompson .15 .07
❑ 369 Brad Ausmus .15 .07
❑ 370 Dean Palmer .25 .11
❑ 371 Gabe Kapler .25 .11
❑ 372 Juan Encarnacion .25 .11
❑ 373 Karim Garcia .15 .07
❑ 374 Alex Gonzalez .15 .07
❑ 375 Braden Looper .15 .07
❑ 376 Preston Wilson .25 .11
❑ 377 Todd Dunwoody .15 .07
❑ 378 Alex Fernandez .15 .07
❑ 379 Mark Kotsay .15 .07
❑ 380 Matt Mantei .15 .07
❑ 381 Ken Caminiti .25 .11
❑ 382 Scott Elarton .15 .07
❑ 383 Jeff Bagwell .75 .35
❑ 384 Derek Bell .15 .07
❑ 385 Ricky Gutierrez .15 .07
❑ 386 Richard Hidalgo .25 .11
❑ 387 Shane Reynolds .15 .07
❑ 388 Carl Everett .25 .11
❑ 389 Scott Service .15 .07
❑ 390 Jeff Suppan .15 .07
❑ 391 Joe Randa .15 .07
❑ 392 Kevin Appier .25 .11
❑ 393 Shane Halter .15 .07
❑ 394 Chad Kreuter .15 .07
❑ 395 Mike Sweeney .25 .11
❑ 396 Kevin Brown .40 .18
❑ 397 Devon White .15 .07
❑ 398 Todd Hollandsworth .15 .07
❑ 399 Todd Hundley .15 .07
❑ 400 Chan Ho Park .25 .11
❑ 401 Mark Grudzielanek .15 .07
❑ 402 Raul Mondesi .25 .11
❑ 403 Ismael Valdes .15 .07
❑ 404 Rafael Roque RC .25 .11
❑ 405 Sean Berry .15 .07
❑ 406 Kevin Barker .15 .07
❑ 407 Dave Nilsson .15 .07
❑ 408 Geoff Jenkins .25 .11
❑ 409 Jim Abbott .25 .11
❑ 410 Bobby Hughes .15 .07
❑ 411 Corey Koskie .25 .11
❑ 412 Rick Aguilera .15 .07
❑ 413 LaTroy Hawkins .15 .07

❑ 414 Ron Coomer .15 .07
❑ 415 Denny Hocking .15 .07
❑ 416 Marty Cordova .15 .07
❑ 417 Terry Steinbach .15 .07
❑ 418 Rondell White .25 .11
❑ 419 Wilton Guerrero .15 .07
❑ 420 Shane Andrews .15 .07
❑ 421 Orlando Cabrera .15 .07
❑ 422 Carl Pavano .15 .07
❑ 423 Javier Vazquez .25 .11
❑ 424 Chris Widger .15 .07
❑ 425 Robin Ventura .25 .11
❑ 426 Rickey Henderson 1.25 .55
❑ 427 Al Leiter .25 .11
❑ 428 Bobby Jones .15 .07
❑ 429 Brian McRae .15 .07
❑ 430 Roger Cedeno .15 .07
❑ 431 Bobby Bonilla .25 .11
❑ 432 Edgardo Alfonzo .25 .11
❑ 433 Bernie Williams .60 .25
❑ 434 Ricky Ledee .15 .07
❑ 435 Chili Davis .25 .11
❑ 436 Tino Martinez .25 .11
❑ 437 Scott Brosius .25 .11
❑ 438 David Cone .25 .11
❑ 439 Joe Girardi .15 .07
❑ 440 Roger Clemens 1.50 .70
❑ 441 Chad Curtis .15 .07
❑ 442 Hideki Irabu .15 .07
❑ 443 Jason Giambi .60 .25
❑ 444 Scott Spiezio .15 .07
❑ 445 Tony Phillips .15 .07
❑ 446 Ramon Hernandez .15 .07
❑ 447 Mike Macfarlane .15 .07
❑ 448 Tom Candiotti .15 .07
❑ 449 Billy Taylor .15 .07
❑ 450 Bobby Estalella .15 .07
❑ 451 Curt Schilling .60 .25
❑ 452 Carlton Loewer .15 .07
❑ 453 Marlon Anderson .15 .07
❑ 454 Kevin Jordan .15 .07
❑ 455 Ron Gant .25 .11
❑ 456 Chad Ogea .15 .07
❑ 457 Abraham Nunez .15 .07
❑ 458 Jason Kendall .25 .11
❑ 459 Pat Meares .15 .07
❑ 460 Brant Brown .15 .07
❑ 461 Brian Giles .25 .11
❑ 462 Chad Hermansen .15 .07
❑ 463 Freddy Adrian Garcia .15 .07
❑ 464 Edgar Renteria .15 .07
❑ 465 Fernando Tatis .15 .07
❑ 466 Eric Davis .25 .11
❑ 467 Darren Bragg .15 .07
❑ 468 Donovan Osborne .15 .07
❑ 469 Manny Aybar .15 .07
❑ 470 Jose Jimenez .15 .07
❑ 471 Kent Mercker .15 .07
❑ 472 Reggie Sanders .15 .07
❑ 473 Ruben Rivera .15 .07
❑ 474 Tony Gwynn 1.25 .55
❑ 475 Jim Leyritz .15 .07
❑ 476 Chris Gomez .15 .07
❑ 477 Matt Clement .15 .07
❑ 478 Carlos Hernandez .15 .07
❑ 479 Sterling Hitchcock .15 .07
❑ 480 Ellis Burks .25 .11
❑ 481 Barry Bonds 1.50 .70
❑ 482 Marvin Benard .15 .07
❑ 483 Kirk Rueter .15 .07
❑ 484 F.P. Santangelo .15 .07
❑ 485 Stan Javier .15 .07
❑ 486 Jeff Kent .40 .18
❑ 487 Alex Rodriguez 1.50 .70
❑ 488 Tom Lampkin .15 .07
❑ 489 Jose Mesa .15 .07
❑ 490 Jay Buhner .25 .11
❑ 491 Edgar Martinez .40 .18
❑ 492 Butch Huskey .15 .07
❑ 493 John Mabry .15 .07
❑ 494 Jamie Moyer .15 .07
❑ 495 Roberto Hernandez .15 .07
❑ 496 Tony Saunders .15 .07
❑ 497 Fred McGriff .40 .18
❑ 498 Dave Martinez .15 .07
❑ 499 Jose Canseco .60 .25
❑ 500 Rolando Arrojo .15 .07
❑ 501 Esteban Yan .15 .07
❑ 502 Juan Gonzalez .60 .25
❑ 503 Rafael Palmeiro .60 .25
❑ 504 Aaron Sele .25 .11
❑ 505 Royce Clayton .15 .07
❑ 506 Todd Zeile .25 .11
❑ 507 Tom Goodwin .15 .07
❑ 508 Lee Stevens .15 .07
❑ 509 Esteban Loaiza .15 .07
❑ 510 Joey Hamilton .15 .07
❑ 511 Homer Bush .15 .07
❑ 512 Willie Greene .15 .07
❑ 513 Shawn Green .60 .25
❑ 514 David Wells .25 .11
❑ 515 Kelvim Escobar .15 .07
❑ 516 Tony Fernandez .15 .07
❑ 517 Pat Hentgen .15 .07
❑ 518 Mark McGwire AR 1.25 .55
❑ 519 Ken Griffey Jr. AR 1.00 .45
❑ 520 Sammy Sosa AR .60 .25
❑ 521 Juan Gonzalez AR .25 .11
❑ 522 J.D. Drew AR .60 .25
❑ 523 Chipper Jones AR .60 .25
❑ 524 Alex Rodriguez AR .75 .35
❑ 525 Mike Piazza AR .75 .35
❑ 526 N.Garciaparra AR .75 .35
❑ 527 Mark McGwire SH CL 1.25 .55
❑ 528 Sammy Sosa SH CL .60 .25
❑ 529 Scott Brosius SH CL .15 .07
❑ 530 Cal Ripken SH CL 1.25 .55
❑ 531 Barry Bonds SH CL .75 .35
❑ 532 Roger Clemens SH CL .75 .35
❑ 533 Ken Griffey Jr. SH CL 1.00 .45
❑ 534 Alex Rodriguez SH CL .75 .35
❑ 535 Curt Schilling SH CL .25 .11
❑ NNO Ken Griffey Jr. 1200.00 550.00
1989 AU/100

2000 Upper Deck

	MINT	NRMT
COMPLETE SET (540)	100.00	45.00
COMPLETE SERIES 1 (270)	50.00	22.00
COMPLETE SERIES 2 (270)	50.00	22.00
COMMON CARD (1-540)	.15	.07
COMMON SR (1-28/271-297)	.25	.11

❑ 1 Rick Ankiel SR 1.00 .45
❑ 2 Vernon Wells SR .40 .18
❑ 3 Ryan Anderson SR .40 .18
❑ 4 Ed Yarnall SR .25 .11
❑ 5 Brian McNichol SR .25 .11
❑ 6 Ben Petrick SR .25 .11
❑ 7 Kip Wells SR .40 .18
❑ 8 Eric Munson SR .40 .18
❑ 9 Matt Riley SR .25 .11
❑ 10 Peter Bergeron SR .25 .11
❑ 11 Eric Gagne SR .25 .11
❑ 12 Ramon Ortiz SR .40 .18
❑ 13 Josh Beckett SR 1.25 .55
❑ 14 Alfonso Soriano SR 1.00 .45
❑ 15 Jorge Toca SR .25 .11
❑ 16 Buddy Carlyle SR .25 .11
❑ 17 Chad Hermansen SR .25 .11
❑ 18 Matt Perisho SR .25 .11
❑ 19 Tomokazu Ohka SR RC .75 .35
❑ 20 Jacque Jones SR .40 .18
❑ 21 Josh Paul SR .25 .11
❑ 22 Dermal Brown SR .25 .11
❑ 23 Adam Kennedy SR .15 .07
❑ 24 Chad Harville SR .25 .11
❑ 25 Calvin Murray SR .25 .11
❑ 26 Chad Meyers SR .25 .11
❑ 27 Brian Cooper SR .25 .11
❑ 28 Troy Glaus .60 .25
❑ 29 Ben Molina .15 .07
❑ 30 Troy Percival .15 .07
❑ 31 Ken Hill .15 .07
❑ 32 Chuck Finley .25 .11
❑ 33 Todd Greene .15 .07
❑ 34 Tim Salmon .25 .11
❑ 35 Gary DiSarcina .15 .07
❑ 36 Luis Gonzalez .60 .25
❑ 37 Tony Womack .15 .07
❑ 38 Omar Daal .15 .07
❑ 39 Randy Johnson .75 .35
❑ 40 Erubiel Durazo .25 .11
❑ 41 Jay Bell .25 .11
❑ 42 Steve Finley .25 .11
❑ 43 Travis Lee .15 .07
❑ 44 Greg Maddux 1.50 .70
❑ 45 Bret Boone .25 .11
❑ 46 Brian Jordan .25 .11
❑ 47 Kevin Millwood .15 .07
❑ 48 Odalis Perez .15 .07
❑ 49 Javy Lopez .25 .11
❑ 50 John Smoltz .25 .11
❑ 51 Bruce Chen .15 .07
❑ 52 Albert Belle .25 .11
❑ 53 Jerry Hairston Jr. .15 .07
❑ 54 Will Clark .60 .25
❑ 55 Sidney Ponson .15 .07
❑ 56 Charles Johnson .25 .11
❑ 57 Cal Ripken 2.50 1.10
❑ 58 Ryan Minor .15 .07
❑ 59 Mike Mussina .60 .25
❑ 60 Tom Gordon .15 .07
❑ 61 Jose Offerman .15 .07
❑ 62 Trot Nixon .25 .11
❑ 63 Pedro Martinez .75 .35
❑ 64 John Valentin .15 .07
❑ 65 Jason Varitek .25 .11
❑ 66 Juan Pena .15 .07
❑ 67 Troy O'Leary .15 .07
❑ 68 Sammy Sosa 1.25 .55
❑ 69 Henry Rodriguez .15 .07
❑ 70 Kyle Farnsworth .15 .07
❑ 71 Glenallen Hill .15 .07
❑ 72 Lance Johnson .15 .07
❑ 73 Mickey Morandini .15 .07
❑ 74 Jon Lieber .15 .07
❑ 75 Kevin Tapani .15 .07
❑ 76 Carlos Lee .25 .11
❑ 77 Ray Durham .25 .11
❑ 78 Jim Parque .15 .07
❑ 79 Bob Howry .15 .07
❑ 80 Magglio Ordonez .25 .11
❑ 81 Paul Konerko .25 .11
❑ 82 Mike Caruso .15 .07
❑ 83 Chris Singleton .15 .07
❑ 84 Sean Casey .40 .18
❑ 85 Barry Larkin .60 .25
❑ 86 Pokey Reese .15 .07
❑ 87 Eddie Taubensee .15 .07
❑ 88 Scott Williamson .15 .07
❑ 89 Jason LaRue .15 .07
❑ 90 Aaron Boone .15 .07
❑ 91 Jeffrey Hammonds .15 .07
❑ 92 Omar Vizquel .25 .11
❑ 93 Manny Ramirez .75 .35
❑ 94 Kenny Lofton .25 .11
❑ 95 Jaret Wright .15 .07
❑ 96 Einar Diaz .15 .07
❑ 97 Charles Nagy .15 .07
❑ 98 David Justice .25 .11
❑ 99 Richie Sexson .25 .11
❑ 100 Steve Karsay .15 .07
❑ 101 Todd Helton .75 .35
❑ 102 Dante Bichette .25 .11
❑ 103 Larry Walker .40 .18
❑ 104 Pedro Astacio .15 .07
❑ 105 Neifi Perez .15 .07
❑ 106 Brian Bohanon .15 .07

❑	107	Edgard Clemente	.15	.07
❑	108	Dave Veres	.15	.07
❑	109	Gabe Kapler	.25	.11
❑	110	Juan Encarnacion	.25	.11
❑	111	Jeff Weaver	.25	.11
❑	112	Damion Easley	.15	.07
❑	113	Justin Thompson	.15	.07
❑	114	Brad Ausmus	.15	.07
❑	115	Frank Catalanotto	.15	.07
❑	116	Todd Jones	.15	.07
❑	117	Preston Wilson	.25	.11
❑	118	Cliff Floyd	.25	.11
❑	119	Mike Lowell	.15	.07
❑	120	Antonio Alfonseca	.15	.07
❑	121	Alex Gonzalez	.15	.07
❑	122	Braden Looper	.15	.07
❑	123	Bruce Aven	.15	.07
❑	124	Richard Hidalgo	.25	.11
❑	125	Mitch Meluskey	.15	.07
❑	126	Jeff Bagwell	.75	.35
❑	127	Jose Lima	.15	.07
❑	128	Derek Bell	.15	.07
❑	129	Billy Wagner	.15	.07
❑	130	Shane Reynolds	.15	.07
❑	131	Moises Alou	.25	.11
❑	132	Carlos Beltran	.25	.11
❑	133	Carlos Febles	.15	.07
❑	134	Jermaine Dye	.25	.11
❑	135	Jeremy Giambi	.15	.07
❑	136	Joe Randa	.15	.07
❑	137	Jose Rosado	.15	.07
❑	138	Chad Kreuter	.15	.07
❑	139	Jose Vizcaino	.15	.07
❑	140	Adrian Beltre	.25	.11
❑	141	Kevin Brown	.40	.18
❑	142	Ismael Valdes	.15	.07
❑	143	Angel Pena	.15	.07
❑	144	Chan Ho Park	.25	.11
❑	145	Mark Grudzielanek	.15	.07
❑	146	Jeff Shaw	.15	.07
❑	147	Geoff Jenkins	.25	.11
❑	148	Jeromy Burnitz	.25	.11
❑	149	Hideo Nomo	.60	.25
❑	150	Ron Belliard	.15	.07
❑	151	Sean Berry	.15	.07
❑	152	Mark Loretta	.15	.07
❑	153	Steve Woodard	.15	.07
❑	154	Joe Mays	.25	.11
❑	155	Eric Milton	.25	.11
❑	156	Corey Koskie	.25	.11
❑	157	Ron Coomer	.15	.07
❑	158	Brad Radke	.25	.11
❑	159	Terry Steinbach	.15	.07
❑	160	Cristian Guzman	.25	.11
❑	161	Vladimir Guerrero	.75	.35
❑	162	Wilton Guerrero	.15	.07
❑	163	Michael Barrett	.15	.07
❑	164	Chris Widger	.15	.07
❑	165	Fernando Seguignol	.15	.07
❑	166	Ugueth Urbina	.15	.07
❑	167	Dustin Hermanson	.15	.07
❑	168	Kenny Rogers	.15	.07
❑	169	Edgardo Alfonzo	.25	.11
❑	170	Orel Hershiser	.25	.11
❑	171	Robin Ventura	.25	.11
❑	172	Octavio Dotel	.15	.07
❑	173	Rickey Henderson	1.25	.55
❑	174	Roger Cedeno	.15	.07
❑	175	John Olerud	.25	.11
❑	176	Derek Jeter	2.50	1.10
❑	177	Tino Martinez	.25	.11
❑	178	Orlando Hernandez	.25	.11
❑	179	Chuck Knoblauch	.25	.11
❑	180	Bernie Williams	.60	.25
❑	181	Chili Davis	.25	.11
❑	182	David Cone	.25	.11
❑	183	Ricky Ledee	.15	.07
❑	184	Paul O'Neill	.60	.25
❑	185	Jason Giambi	.60	.25
❑	186	Eric Chavez	.25	.11
❑	187	Matt Stairs	.15	.07
❑	188	Miguel Tejada	.25	.11
❑	189	Olmedo Saenz	.15	.07
❑	190	Tim Hudson	.60	.25
❑	191	John Jaha	.15	.07
❑	192	Randy Velarde	.15	.07
❑	193	Rico Brogna	.15	.07
❑	194	Mike Lieberthal	.25	.11
❑	195	Marlon Anderson	.15	.07
❑	196	Bob Abreu	.25	.11
❑	197	Ron Gant	.25	.11
❑	198	Randy Wolf	.15	.07
❑	199	Desi Relaford	.15	.07
❑	200	Doug Glanville	.15	.07
❑	201	Warren Morris	.15	.07
❑	202	Kris Benson	.25	.11
❑	203	Kevin Young	.15	.07
❑	204	Brian Giles	.25	.11
❑	205	Jason Schmidt	.15	.07
❑	206	Ed Sprague	.15	.07
❑	207	Francisco Cordova	.15	.07
❑	208	Mark McGwire	2.50	1.10
❑	209	Jose Jimenez	.15	.07
❑	210	Fernando Tatis	.15	.07
❑	211	Kent Bottenfield	.15	.07
❑	212	Eli Marrero	.15	.07
❑	213	Edgar Renteria	.15	.07
❑	214	Joe McEwing	.15	.07
❑	215	J.D. Drew	.60	.25
❑	216	Tony Gwynn	1.25	.55
❑	217	Gary Matthews Jr.	.15	.07
❑	218	Eric Owens	.15	.07
❑	219	Damian Jackson	.15	.07
❑	220	Reggie Sanders	.15	.07
❑	221	Trevor Hoffman	.25	.11
❑	222	Ben Davis	.25	.11
❑	223	Shawn Estes	.25	.11
❑	224	F.P. Santangelo	.15	.07
❑	225	Livan Hernandez	.15	.07
❑	226	Ellis Burks	.25	.11
❑	227	J.T. Snow	.25	.11
❑	228	Jeff Kent	.40	.18
❑	229	Robb Nen	.15	.07
❑	230	Marvin Benard	.15	.07
❑	231	Ken Griffey Jr.	2.00	.90
❑	232	John Halama	.15	.07
❑	233	Gil Meche	.15	.07
❑	234	David Bell	.15	.07
❑	235	Brian Hunter	.15	.07
❑	236	Jay Buhner	.25	.11
❑	237	Edgar Martinez	.40	.18
❑	238	Jose Mesa	.15	.07
❑	239	Wilson Alvarez	.15	.07
❑	240	Wade Boggs	.60	.25
❑	241	Fred McGriff	.40	.18
❑	242	Jose Canseco	.60	.25
❑	243	Kevin Stocker	.15	.07
❑	244	Roberto Hernandez	.15	.07
❑	245	Bubba Trammell	.15	.07
❑	246	John Flaherty	.15	.07
❑	247	Ivan Rodriguez	.60	.25
❑	248	Rusty Greer	.25	.11
❑	249	Rafael Palmeiro	.60	.25
❑	250	Jeff Zimmerman	.15	.07
❑	251	Royce Clayton	.15	.07
❑	252	Todd Zeile	.25	.11
❑	253	John Wetteland	.25	.11
❑	254	Ruben Mateo	.25	.11
❑	255	Kelvim Escobar	.15	.07
❑	256	David Wells	.25	.11
❑	257	Shawn Green	.60	.25
❑	258	Homer Bush	.15	.07
❑	259	Shannon Stewart	.25	.11
❑	260	Carlos Delgado	.60	.25
❑	261	Roy Halladay	.15	.07
❑	262	Fernando Tatis SH CL	.15	.07
❑	263	Jose Jimenez SH CL	.15	.07
❑	264	Tony Gwynn SH CL	.60	.25
❑	265	Wade Boggs SH CL	.25	.11
❑	266	Cal Ripken SH CL	1.25	.55
❑	267	David Cone SH CL	.25	.11
❑	268	Mark McGwire SH CL	1.50	.70
❑	269	Pedro Martinez SH CL	.40	.18
❑	270	N. Garciaparra SH CL	.75	.35
❑	271	Nick Johnson SR	1.00	.45
❑	272	Mark Quinn SR	.40	.18
❑	273	Roosevelt Brown SR	.25	.11
❑	274	Terrence Long SR	.40	.18
❑	275	Jason Marquis SR	.40	.18
❑	276	K.Sasaki SR RC	2.00	.90
❑	277	Aaron Myette SR	.40	.18
❑	278	Danys Baez SR RC	.75	.35
❑	279	Travis Dawkins SR	.40	.18
❑	280	Mark Mulder SR	1.00	.45
❑	281	Chris Haas SR	.25	.11
❑	282	Milton Bradley SR	.25	.11
❑	283	Brad Penny SR	.40	.18
❑	284	Rafael Furcal SR	1.00	.45
❑	285	Luis Matos SR RC	.50	.23
❑	286	Victor Santos SR RC	.40	.18
❑	287	R.Washington SR RC	.50	.23
❑	288	Rob Bell SR	.25	.11
❑	289	Joe Crede SR	.40	.18
❑	290	Pablo Ozuna SR	.25	.11
❑	291	W.Serrano SR RC	.60	.25
❑	292	S-H. Lee SR RC	.40	.18
❑	293	C.Wakeland SR RC	.40	.18
❑	294	Luis Rivera SR	.25	.11
❑	295	Mike Lamb SR RC	.75	.35
❑	296	Wily Mo Pena SR	1.00	.45
❑	297	Mike Meyers SR RC	.50	.23
❑	298	Mo Vaughn	.25	.11
❑	299	Darin Erstad	.60	.25
❑	300	Garret Anderson	.25	.11
❑	301	Tim Belcher	.15	.07
❑	302	Scott Spiezio	.15	.07
❑	303	Kent Bottenfield	.15	.07
❑	304	Orlando Palmeiro	.15	.07
❑	305	Jason Dickson	.15	.07
❑	306	Matt Williams	.40	.18
❑	307	Brian Anderson	.15	.07
❑	308	Hanley Frias	.15	.07
❑	309	Todd Stottlemyre	.15	.07
❑	310	Matt Mantei	.15	.07
❑	311	David Dellucci	.15	.07
❑	312	Armando Reynoso	.15	.07
❑	313	Bernard Gilkey	.15	.07
❑	314	Chipper Jones	1.25	.55
❑	315	Tom Glavine	.60	.25
❑	316	Quilvio Veras	.15	.07
❑	317	Andruw Jones	.60	.25
❑	318	Bobby Bonilla	.25	.11
❑	319	Reggie Sanders	.15	.07
❑	320	Andres Galarraga	.40	.18
❑	321	George Lombard	.15	.07
❑	322	John Rocker	.25	.11
❑	323	Wally Joyner	.25	.11
❑	324	B.J. Surhoff	.25	.11
❑	325	Scott Erickson	.15	.07
❑	326	Delino DeShields	.15	.07
❑	327	Jeff Conine	.15	.07
❑	328	Mike Timlin	.15	.07
❑	329	Brady Anderson	.25	.11
❑	330	Mike Bordick	.15	.07
❑	331	Harold Baines	.25	.11
❑	332	Nomar Garciaparra	1.50	.70
❑	333	Bret Saberhagen	.25	.11
❑	334	Ramon Martinez	.15	.07
❑	335	Donnie Sadler	.15	.07
❑	336	Wilton Veras	.15	.07
❑	337	Mike Stanley	.15	.07
❑	338	Brian Rose	.15	.07
❑	339	Carl Everett	.25	.11
❑	340	Tim Wakefield	.15	.07
❑	341	Mark Grace	.60	.25
❑	342	Kerry Wood	.60	.25
❑	343	Eric Young	.15	.07
❑	344	Jose Nieves	.15	.07
❑	345	Ismael Valdes	.15	.07
❑	346	Joe Girardi	.15	.07
❑	347	Damon Buford	.15	.07
❑	348	Ricky Gutierrez	.15	.07
❑	349	Frank Thomas	.75	.35
❑	350	Brian Simmons	.15	.07
❑	351	James Baldwin	.15	.07
❑	352	Brook Fordyce	.15	.07
❑	353	Jose Valentin	.15	.07
❑	354	Mike Sirotka	.15	.07
❑	355	Greg Norton	.15	.07
❑	356	Dante Bichette	.25	.11
❑	357	Deion Sanders	.25	.11
❑	358	Ken Griffey Jr.	2.00	.90
❑	359	Denny Neagle	.25	.11
❑	360	Dmitri Young	.25	.11
❑	361	Pete Harnisch	.15	.07
❑	362	Michael Tucker	.15	.07
❑	363	Roberto Alomar	.60	.25
❑	364	Dave Roberts	.15	.07

No.	Player	MINT	NRMT
365	Jim Thome	.60	.25
366	Bartolo Colon	.25	.11
367	Travis Fryman	.25	.11
368	Chuck Finley	.25	.11
369	Russell Branyan	.25	.11
370	Alex Ramirez	.15	.07
371	Jeff Cirillo	.25	.11
372	Jeffrey Hammonds	.15	.07
373	Scott Karl	.15	.07
374	Brent Mayne	.15	.07
375	Tom Goodwin	.15	.07
376	Jose Jimenez	.15	.07
377	Rolando Arrojo	.15	.07
378	Terry Shumpert	.15	.07
379	Juan Gonzalez	.60	.25
380	Bobby Higginson	.25	.11
381	Tony Clark	.25	.11
382	Dave Mlicki	.15	.07
383	Deivi Cruz	.15	.07
384	Brian Moehler	.15	.07
385	Dean Palmer	.25	.11
386	Luis Castillo	.15	.07
387	Mike Redmond	.15	.07
388	Alex Fernandez	.15	.07
389	Brant Brown	.15	.07
390	Dave Berg	.15	.07
391	A.J. Burnett	.25	.11
392	Mark Kotsay	.15	.07
393	Craig Biggio	.40	.18
394	Daryle Ward	.15	.07
395	Lance Berkman	.60	.25
396	Roger Cedeno	.15	.07
397	Scott Elarton	.15	.07
398	Octavio Dotel	.15	.07
399	Ken Caminiti	.25	.11
400	Johnny Damon	.25	.11
401	Mike Sweeney	.25	.11
402	Jeff Suppan	.15	.07
403	Rey Sanchez	.15	.07
404	Blake Stein	.15	.07
405	Ricky Bottalico	.15	.07
406	Jay Witasick	.15	.07
407	Shawn Green	.60	.25
408	Orel Hershiser	.25	.11
409	Gary Sheffield	.25	.11
410	Todd Hollandsworth	.15	.07
411	Terry Adams	.15	.07
412	Todd Hundley	.15	.07
413	Eric Karros	.25	.11
414	F.P. Santangelo	.15	.07
415	Alex Cora	.15	.07
416	Marquis Grissom	.15	.07
417	Henry Blanco	.15	.07
418	Jose Hernandez	.15	.07
419	Kyle Peterson	.15	.07
420	John Snyder RC	.40	.18
421	Bob Wickman	.15	.07
422	Jamey Wright	.15	.07
423	Chad Allen	.15	.07
424	Todd Walker	.15	.07
425	J.C. Romero RC	.40	.18
426	Butch Huskey	.15	.07
427	Jacque Jones	.25	.11
428	Matt Lawton	.25	.11
429	Rondell White	.25	.11
430	Jose Vidro	.25	.11
431	Hideki Irabu	.15	.07
432	Javier Vazquez	.25	.11
433	Lee Stevens	.15	.07
434	Mike Thurman	.15	.07
435	Geoff Blum	.15	.07
436	Mike Hampton	.25	.11
437	Mike Piazza	1.50	.70
438	Al Leiter	.25	.11
439	Derek Bell	.15	.07
440	Armando Benitez	.25	.11
441	Rey Ordonez	.15	.07
442	Todd Zeile	.25	.11
443	Roger Clemens	1.50	.70
444	Ramiro Mendoza	.15	.07
445	Andy Pettitte	.25	.11
446	Scott Brosius	.25	.11
447	Mariano Rivera	.25	.11
448	Jim Leyritz	.15	.07
449	Jorge Posada	.25	.11
450	Omar Olivares	.15	.07

No.	Player	MINT	NRMT
451	Ben Grieve	.25	.11
452	A.J. Hinch	.15	.07
453	Gil Heredia	.15	.07
454	Kevin Appier	.25	.11
455	Ryan Christenson	.15	.07
456	Ramon Hernandez	.15	.07
457	Scott Rolen	.60	.25
458	Alex Arias	.15	.07
459	Andy Ashby	.15	.07
460	K.Jordan UER 474	.15	.07
461	Robert Person	.15	.07
462	Paul Byrd	.15	.07
463	Curt Schilling	.60	.25
464	Mike Jackson	.15	.07
465	Jason Kendall	.25	.11
466	Pat Meares	.15	.07
467	Bruce Aven	.15	.07
468	Todd Ritchie	.15	.07
469	Wil Cordero	.15	.07
470	Aramis Ramirez	.25	.11
471	Andy Benes	.15	.07
472	Ray Lankford	.15	.07
473	Fernando Vina	.15	.07
474	Jim Edmonds	.40	.18
475	Craig Paquette	.15	.07
476	Pat Hentgen	.15	.07
477	Darryl Kile	.25	.11
478	Sterling Hitchcock	.15	.07
479	Ruben Rivera	.15	.07
480	Ryan Klesko	.25	.11
481	Phil Nevin	.25	.11
482	Woody Williams	.15	.07
483	Carlos Hernandez	.15	.07
484	Brian Meadows	.15	.07
485	Bret Boone	.25	.11
486	Barry Bonds	1.50	.70
487	Russ Ortiz	.15	.07
488	Bobby Estalella	.15	.07
489	Rich Aurilia	.25	.11
490	Bill Mueller	.15	.07
491	Joe Nathan	.15	.07
492	Russ Davis	.15	.07
493	John Olerud	.25	.11
494	Alex Rodriguez	1.50	.70
495	Freddy Garcia	.40	.18
496	Carlos Guillen	.15	.07
497	Aaron Sele	.25	.11
498	Brett Tomko	.15	.07
499	Jamie Moyer	.15	.07
500	Mike Cameron	.25	.11
501	Vinny Castilla	.25	.11
502	Gerald Williams	.15	.07
503	Mike DiFelice	.15	.07
504	Ryan Rupe	.15	.07
505	Greg Vaughn	.25	.11
506	Miguel Cairo	.15	.07
507	Juan Guzman	.15	.07
508	Jose Guillen	.15	.07
509	Gabe Kapler	.25	.11
510	Rick Helling	.15	.07
511	David Segui	.15	.07
512	Doug Davis	.15	.07
513	Justin Thompson	.15	.07
514	Chad Curtis	.15	.07
515	Tony Batista	.25	.11
516	Billy Koch	.15	.07
517	Raul Mondesi	.25	.11
518	Joey Hamilton	.15	.07
519	Darrin Fletcher	.15	.07
520	Brad Fullmer	.25	.11
521	Jose Cruz Jr.	.25	.11
522	Kevin Witt	.15	.07
523	Mark McGwire AUT	1.25	.55
524	Roberto Alomar AUT	.25	.11
525	Chipper Jones AUT	.60	.25
526	Derek Jeter AUT	1.25	.55
527	Ken Griffey Jr. AUT	1.00	.45
528	Sammy Sosa AUT	.60	.25
529	Manny Ramirez AUT	.40	.18
530	Ivan Rodriguez AUT	.25	.11
531	Pedro Martinez AUT	.40	.18
532	Mariano Rivera CL	.25	.11
533	Sammy Sosa CL	.60	.25
534	Cal Ripken CL	1.25	.55
535	Vladimir Guerrero CL	.40	.18
536	Tony Gwynn CL	.60	.25
537	Mark McGwire CL	1.25	.55
538	Bernie Williams CL	.25	.11
539	Pedro Martinez CL	.40	.18
540	Ken Griffey Jr. CL	1.00	.45

2001 Upper Deck

	MINT	NRMT
COMPLETE SET (450)	90.00	40.00
COMPLETE SERIES 1 (270)	40.00	18.00
COMPLETE SERIES 2 (180)	50.00	22.00
COMMON (46-270/300-450)	.15	.07
COMMON SR (1-45/271-300)	.50	.23
1 Jeff DaVanon SR	.50	.23
2 Aubrey Huff SR	.50	.23
3 Pasqual Coco SR	.50	.23
4 Barry Zito SR	1.00	.45
5 Augie Ojeda SR	.50	.23
6 Chris Richard SR	.50	.23
7 Josh Phelps SR	.50	.23
8 Kevin Nicholson SR	.50	.23
9 Juan Guzman SR	.50	.23
10 Brandon Kolb SR	.50	.23
11 Johan Santana SR	.50	.23
12 Josh Kalinowski SR	.50	.23
13 Tike Redman SR	.50	.23
14 Ivanon Coffie SR	.50	.23
15 Chad Durbin SR	.50	.23
16 Derrick Turnbow SR	.50	.23
17 Scott Downs SR	.50	.23
18 Jason Grilli SR	.50	.23
19 Mark Buehrle SR	1.00	.45
20 Paxton Crawford SR	.50	.23
21 Bronson Arroyo SR	.50	.23
22 Tomas De la Rosa SR	.50	.23
23 Paul Rigdon SR	.50	.23
24 Rob Ramsay SR	.50	.23
25 Damian Rolls SR	.50	.23
26 Jason Conti SR	.50	.23
27 John Parrish SR	.50	.23
28 Geraldo Guzman SR	.50	.23
29 Tony Mota SR	.50	.23
30 Luis Rivas SR	.50	.23
31 Brian Tollberg SR	.50	.23
32 Adam Bernero SR	.50	.23
33 Michael Cuddyer SR	.50	.23
34 Josue Espada SR	.50	.23
35 Joe Lawrence SR	.50	.23
36 Chad Moeller SR	.50	.23
37 Nick Bierbrodt SR	.50	.23
38 DeWayne Wise SR	.50	.23
39 Javier Cardona SR	.50	.23
40 Hiram Bocachica SR	.50	.23
41 G.Chiaramonte SR	.50	.23
42 Alex Cabrera SR	.50	.23
43 Jimmy Rollins SR	.50	.23
44 Pat Flury SR RC	.50	.23
45 Leo Estrella SR	.50	.23
46 Darin Erstad	.60	.25
47 Seth Etherton	.15	.07
48 Troy Glaus	.60	.25
49 Brian Cooper	.15	.07
50 Tim Salmon	.25	.11
51 Adam Kennedy	.15	.07
52 Bengie Molina	.15	.07
53 Jason Giambi	.60	.25
54 Miguel Tejada	.25	.11

No.	Player	Price	Price
❑ 55	Tim Hudson	.60	.25
❑ 56	Eric Chavez	.25	.11
❑ 57	Terrence Long	.25	.11
❑ 58	Jason Isringhausen	.15	.07
❑ 59	Ramon Hernandez	.15	.07
❑ 60	Raul Mondesi	.25	.11
❑ 61	David Wells	.25	.11
❑ 62	Shannon Stewart	.25	.11
❑ 63	Tony Batista	.25	.11
❑ 64	Brad Fullmer	.25	.11
❑ 65	Chris Carpenter	.15	.07
❑ 66	Homer Bush	.15	.07
❑ 67	Gerald Williams	.15	.07
❑ 68	Miguel Cairo	.15	.07
❑ 69	Ryan Rupe	.15	.07
❑ 70	Greg Vaughn	.25	.11
❑ 71	John Flaherty	.15	.07
❑ 72	Dan Wheeler	.15	.07
❑ 73	Fred McGriff	.40	.18
❑ 74	Roberto Alomar	.60	.25
❑ 75	Bartolo Colon	.25	.11
❑ 76	Kenny Lofton	.25	.11
❑ 77	David Segui	.15	.07
❑ 78	Omar Vizquel	.25	.11
❑ 79	Russ Branyan	.25	.11
❑ 80	Chuck Finley	.25	.11
❑ 81	Manny Ramirez UER Back photo is of David Segui	.75	.35
❑ 82	Alex Rodriguez	1.50	.70
❑ 83	John Halama	.15	.07
❑ 84	Mike Cameron	.25	.11
❑ 85	David Bell	.15	.07
❑ 86	Jay Buhner	.25	.11
❑ 87	Aaron Sele	.25	.11
❑ 88	Rickey Henderson	1.25	.55
❑ 89	Brook Fordyce	.15	.07
❑ 90	Cal Ripken	2.50	1.10
❑ 91	Mike Mussina	.60	.25
❑ 92	Delino DeShields	.15	.07
❑ 93	Melvin Mora	.15	.07
❑ 94	Sidney Ponson	.15	.07
❑ 95	Brady Anderson	.25	.11
❑ 96	Ivan Rodriguez	.60	.25
❑ 97	Ricky Ledee	.15	.07
❑ 98	Rick Helling	.15	.07
❑ 99	Ruben Mateo	.25	.11
❑ 100	Luis Alicea	.15	.07
❑ 101	John Wetteland	.25	.11
❑ 102	Mike Lamb	.15	.07
❑ 103	Carl Everett	.25	.11
❑ 104	Troy O'Leary	.15	.07
❑ 105	Wilton Veras	.15	.07
❑ 106	Pedro Martinez	.75	.35
❑ 107	Rolando Arrojo	.15	.07
❑ 108	Scott Hatteberg	.15	.07
❑ 109	Jason Varitek	.25	.11
❑ 110	Jose Offerman	.15	.07
❑ 111	Carlos Beltran	.25	.11
❑ 112	Johnny Damon	.25	.11
❑ 113	Mark Quinn	.25	.11
❑ 114	Rey Sanchez	.15	.07
❑ 115	Mac Suzuki	.15	.07
❑ 116	Jermaine Dye	.25	.11
❑ 117	Chris Fussell	.15	.07
❑ 118	Jeff Weaver	.25	.11
❑ 119	Dean Palmer	.25	.11
❑ 120	Robert Fick	.15	.07
❑ 121	Brian Moehler	.15	.07
❑ 122	Damion Easley	.15	.07
❑ 123	Juan Encarnacion	.25	.11
❑ 124	Tony Clark	.25	.11
❑ 125	Cristian Guzman	.25	.11
❑ 126	Matt LeCroy	.15	.07
❑ 127	Eric Milton	.25	.11
❑ 128	Jay Canizaro	.15	.07
❑ 129	David Ortiz	.25	.11
❑ 130	Brad Radke	.25	.11
❑ 131	Jacque Jones	.25	.11
❑ 132	Magglio Ordonez	.25	.11
❑ 133	Carlos Lee	.25	.11
❑ 134	Mike Sirotka	.15	.07
❑ 135	Ray Durham	.25	.11
❑ 136	Paul Konerko	.25	.11
❑ 137	Charles Johnson	.25	.11
❑ 138	James Baldwin	.15	.07
❑ 139	Jeff Abbott	.15	.07
❑ 140	Roger Clemens	1.50	.70
❑ 141	Derek Jeter	2.50	1.10
❑ 142	David Justice	.40	.18
❑ 143	Ramiro Mendoza	.15	.07
❑ 144	Chuck Knoblauch	.25	.11
❑ 145	Orlando Hernandez	.25	.11
❑ 146	Alfonso Soriano	.60	.25
❑ 147	Jeff Bagwell	.75	.35
❑ 148	Julio Lugo	.15	.07
❑ 149	Mitch Meluskey	.15	.07
❑ 150	Jose Lima	.15	.07
❑ 151	Richard Hidalgo	.25	.11
❑ 152	Moises Alou	.25	.11
❑ 153	Scott Elarton	.15	.07
❑ 154	Andruw Jones	.60	.25
❑ 155	Quilvio Veras	.15	.07
❑ 156	Greg Maddux	1.50	.70
❑ 157	Brian Jordan	.25	.11
❑ 158	Andres Galarraga	.40	.18
❑ 159	Kevin Millwood	.15	.07
❑ 160	Rafael Furcal	.25	.11
❑ 161	Jeromy Burnitz	.25	.11
❑ 162	Jimmy Haynes	.15	.07
❑ 163	Mark Loretta	.15	.07
❑ 164	Ron Belliard	.15	.07
❑ 165	Richie Sexson	.25	.11
❑ 166	Kevin Barker	.15	.07
❑ 167	Jeff D'Amico	.15	.07
❑ 168	Rick Ankiel	.40	.18
❑ 169	Mark McGwire	2.50	1.10
❑ 170	J.D. Drew	.60	.25
❑ 171	Eli Marrero	.15	.07
❑ 172	Darryl Kile	.25	.11
❑ 173	Edgar Renteria	.15	.07
❑ 174	Will Clark	.60	.25
❑ 175	Eric Young	.15	.07
❑ 176	Mark Grace	.60	.25
❑ 177	Jon Lieber	.15	.07
❑ 178	Damon Buford	.15	.07
❑ 179	Kerry Wood	.60	.25
❑ 180	Rondell White	.25	.11
❑ 181	Joe Girardi	.15	.07
❑ 182	Curt Schilling	.60	.25
❑ 183	Randy Johnson	.75	.35
❑ 184	Steve Finley	.25	.11
❑ 185	Kelly Stinnett	.15	.07
❑ 186	Jay Bell	.25	.11
❑ 187	Matt Mantei	.15	.07
❑ 188	Luis Gonzalez	.60	.25
❑ 189	Shawn Green	.60	.25
❑ 190	Todd Hundley	.15	.07
❑ 191	Chan Ho Park	.25	.11
❑ 192	Adrian Beltre	.25	.11
❑ 193	Mark Grudzielanek	.15	.07
❑ 194	Gary Sheffield	.25	.11
❑ 195	Tom Goodwin	.15	.07
❑ 196	Lee Stevens	.15	.07
❑ 197	Javier Vazquez	.25	.11
❑ 198	Milton Bradley	.15	.07
❑ 199	Vladimir Guerrero	.75	.35
❑ 200	Carl Pavano	.15	.07
❑ 201	Orlando Cabrera	.15	.07
❑ 202	Tony Armas Jr.	.25	.11
❑ 203	Jeff Kent	.40	.18
❑ 204	Calvin Murray	.15	.07
❑ 205	Ellis Burks	.25	.11
❑ 206	Barry Bonds	1.50	.70
❑ 207	Russ Ortiz	.25	.11
❑ 208	Marvin Benard	.15	.07
❑ 209	Joe Nathan	.15	.07
❑ 210	Preston Wilson	.25	.11
❑ 211	Cliff Floyd	.25	.11
❑ 212	Mike Lowell	.25	.11
❑ 213	Ryan Dempster	.25	.11
❑ 214	Brad Penny	.25	.11
❑ 215	Mike Redmond	.15	.07
❑ 216	Luis Castillo	.15	.07
❑ 217	Derek Bell	.15	.07
❑ 218	Mike Hampton	.25	.11
❑ 219	Todd Zeile	.25	.11
❑ 220	Robin Ventura	.25	.11
❑ 221	Mike Piazza	1.50	.70
❑ 222	Al Leiter	.25	.11
❑ 223	Edgardo Alfonzo	.25	.11
❑ 224	Mike Bordick	.15	.07
❑ 225	Phil Nevin	.25	.11
❑ 226	Ryan Klesko	.25	.11
❑ 227	Adam Eaton	.25	.11
❑ 228	Eric Owens	.15	.07
❑ 229	Tony Gwynn	1.25	.55
❑ 230	Matt Clement	.15	.07
❑ 231	Wiki Gonzalez	.15	.07
❑ 232	Robert Person	.15	.07
❑ 233	Doug Glanville	.15	.07
❑ 234	Scott Rolen	.60	.25
❑ 235	Mike Lieberthal	.25	.11
❑ 236	Randy Wolf	.15	.07
❑ 237	Bob Abreu	.25	.11
❑ 238	Pat Burrell	.25	.11
❑ 239	Bruce Chen	.15	.07
❑ 240	Kevin Young	.15	.07
❑ 241	Todd Ritchie	.15	.07
❑ 242	Adrian Brown	.15	.07
❑ 243	Chad Hermansen	.15	.07
❑ 244	Warren Morris	.15	.07
❑ 245	Kris Benson	.25	.11
❑ 246	Jason Kendall	.25	.11
❑ 247	Pokey Reese	.15	.07
❑ 248	Rob Bell	.15	.07
❑ 249	Ken Griffey Jr.	2.00	.90
❑ 250	Sean Casey	.40	.18
❑ 251	Aaron Boone	.15	.07
❑ 252	Pete Harnisch	.15	.07
❑ 253	Barry Larkin	.60	.25
❑ 254	Dmitri Young	.25	.11
❑ 255	Todd Hollandsworth	.15	.07
❑ 256	Pedro Astacio	.15	.07
❑ 257	Todd Helton	.75	.35
❑ 258	Terry Shumpert	.15	.07
❑ 259	Neifi Perez	.15	.07
❑ 260	Jeffrey Hammonds	.15	.07
❑ 261	Ben Petrick	.15	.07
❑ 262	Mark McGwire SH	1.25	.55
❑ 263	Derek Jeter SH	1.25	.55
❑ 264	Sammy Sosa SH	.60	.25
❑ 265	Cal Ripken SH	1.25	.55
❑ 266	Pedro Martinez SH	.40	.18
❑ 267	Barry Bonds SH	.75	.35
❑ 268	Fred McGriff SH	.25	.11
❑ 269	Randy Johnson SH	.40	.18
❑ 270	Darin Erstad SH	.25	.11
❑ 271	Ichiro Suzuki SR RC	20.00	9.00
❑ 272	Wilson Betemit SR RC	2.00	.90
❑ 273	Corey Patterson SR	.50	.23
❑ 274	Sean Douglass SR RC	.50	.23
❑ 275	Mike Penney SR RC	.50	.23
❑ 276	Nate Teut SR RC	.50	.23
❑ 277	R. Rodriguez SR RC	.75	.35
❑ 278	B. Duckworth SR RC	2.00	.90
❑ 279	Rafael Soriano SR RC	1.00	.45
❑ 280	Juan Diaz SR RC	.50	.23
❑ 281	Horacio Ramirez SR RC	.75	.35
❑ 282	Tsuyoshi Shinjo SR RC	2.00	.90
❑ 283	Keith Ginter SR	.50	.23
❑ 284	Esix Snead SR RC	.50	.23
❑ 285	Erick Almonte SR RC	.75	.35
❑ 286	Travis Hafner SR RC	1.00	.45
❑ 287	Jason Smith SR RC	.50	.23
❑ 288	Jackson Melian SR RC	.50	.23
❑ 289	Tyler Walker SR RC	.75	.35
❑ 290	Jason Standridge SR	.50	.23
❑ 291	Juan Uribe SR RC	1.00	.45
❑ 292	Adrian Hernandez SR RC	.75	.35
❑ 293	Jason Michaels SR RC	.50	.23
❑ 294	Jason Hart SR	.60	.25
❑ 295	Albert Pujols SR RC	12.00	5.50
❑ 296	Morgan Ensberg SR RC	1.00	.45
❑ 297	Brandon Inge SR	.50	.23
❑ 298	Jesus Colome SR	.50	.23
❑ 299	Kyle Kessel SR RC	.75	.35
❑ 300	Timo Perez SR	.50	.23
❑ 301	Mo Vaughn	.25	.11
❑ 302	Ismael Valdes	.15	.07
❑ 303	Glenallen Hill	.15	.07
❑ 304	Garret Anderson	.25	.11
❑ 305	Johnny Damon	.25	.11
❑ 306	Jose Ortiz	.40	.18
❑ 307	Mark Mulder	.40	.18
❑ 308	Adam Piatt	.25	.11
❑ 309	Gil Heredia	.15	.07
❑ 310	Mike Sirotka	.15	.07
❑ 311	Carlos Delgado	.60	.25

❑ 312 Alex Gonzalez .15 .07
❑ 313 Jose Cruz Jr. .25 .11
❑ 314 Darrin Fletcher .15 .07
❑ 315 Ben Grieve .25 .11
❑ 316 Vinny Castilla .25 .11
❑ 317 Wilson Alvarez .15 .07
❑ 318 Brent Abernathy .15 .07
❑ 319 Ellis Burks .25 .11
❑ 320 Jim Thome .60 .25
❑ 321 Juan Gonzalez .60 .25
❑ 322 Ed Taubensee .15 .07
❑ 323 Travis Fryman .25 .11
❑ 324 John Olerud .25 .11
❑ 325 Edgar Martinez .40 .18
❑ 326 Freddy Garcia .25 .11
❑ 327 Bret Boone .25 .11
❑ 328 Kazuhiro Sasaki .60 .25
❑ 329 Albert Belle .25 .11
❑ 330 Mike Bordick .25 .11
❑ 331 David Segui .15 .07
❑ 332 Pat Hentgen .15 .07
❑ 333 Alex Rodriguez 1.50 .70
❑ 334 Andres Galarraga .40 .18
❑ 335 Gabe Kapler .25 .11
❑ 336 Ken Caminiti .25 .11
❑ 337 Rafael Palmeiro .60 .25
❑ 338 Manny Ramirez .75 .35
❑ 339 David Cone .25 .11
❑ 340 Nomar Garciaparra 1.50 .70
❑ 341 Trot Nixon .25 .11
❑ 342 Derek Lowe .15 .07
❑ 343 Roberto Hernandez .15 .07
❑ 344 Mike Sweeney .25 .11
❑ 345 Carlos Febles .15 .07
❑ 346 Jeff Suppan .15 .07
❑ 347 Roger Cedeno .15 .07
❑ 348 Bobby Higginson .25 .11
❑ 349 Deivi Cruz .15 .07
❑ 350 Mitch Meluskey .15 .07
❑ 351 Matt Lawton .25 .11
❑ 352 Mark Redman .15 .07
❑ 353 Jay Canizaro .15 .07
❑ 354 Corey Koskie .25 .11
❑ 355 Matt Kinney .15 .07
❑ 356 Frank Thomas .75 .35
❑ 357 Sandy Alomar Jr. .25 .11
❑ 358 David Wells .25 .11
❑ 359 Jim Parque .15 .07
❑ 360 Chris Singleton .15 .07
❑ 361 Tino Martinez .25 .11
❑ 362 Paul O'Neill .60 .25
❑ 363 Mike Mussina .60 .25
❑ 364 Bernie Williams .60 .25
❑ 365 Andy Pettitte .25 .11
❑ 366 Mariano Rivera .25 .11
❑ 367 Brad Ausmus .15 .07
❑ 368 Craig Biggio .40 .18
❑ 369 Lance Berkman .60 .25
❑ 370 Shane Reynolds .15 .07
❑ 371 Chipper Jones 1.25 .55
❑ 372 Tom Glavine .60 .25
❑ 373 B.J. Surhoff .25 .11
❑ 374 John Smoltz .25 .11
❑ 375 Rico Brogna .15 .07
❑ 376 Geoff Jenkins .25 .11
❑ 377 Jose Hernandez .15 .07
❑ 378 Tyler Houston .15 .07
❑ 379 Henry Blanco .15 .07
❑ 380 Jeffrey Hammonds .15 .07
❑ 381 Jim Edmonds .40 .18
❑ 382 Fernando Vina .15 .07
❑ 383 Andy Benes .15 .07
❑ 384 Ray Lankford .15 .07
❑ 385 Dustin Hermanson .15 .07
❑ 386 Todd Hundley .15 .07
❑ 387 Sammy Sosa 1.25 .55
❑ 388 Tom Gordon .15 .07
❑ 389 Bill Mueller .15 .07
❑ 390 Ron Coomer .15 .07
❑ 391 Matt Stairs .15 .07
❑ 392 Mark Grace .60 .25
❑ 393 Matt Williams .40 .18
❑ 394 Todd Stottlemyre .15 .07
❑ 395 Tony Womack .15 .07
❑ 396 Erubiel Durazo .15 .07
❑ 397 Reggie Sanders .25 .11
❑ 398 Andy Ashby .15 .07
❑ 399 Eric Karros .25 .11
❑ 400 Kevin Brown .25 .11
❑ 401 Darren Dreifort .15 .07
❑ 402 Fernando Tatis .15 .07
❑ 403 Jose Vidro .25 .11
❑ 404 Peter Bergeron .15 .07
❑ 405 Geoff Blum .15 .07
❑ 406 J.T. Snow .25 .11
❑ 407 Livan Hernandez .25 .11
❑ 408 Robb Nen .25 .11
❑ 409 Bobby Estalella .15 .07
❑ 410 Rich Aurilia .25 .11
❑ 411 Eric Davis .25 .11
❑ 412 Charles Johnson .25 .11
❑ 413 Alex Gonzalez .15 .07
❑ 414 A.J. Burnett .25 .11
❑ 415 Antonio Alfonseca .15 .07
❑ 416 Derek Lee .15 .07
❑ 417 Jay Payton .15 .07
❑ 418 Kevin Appier .25 .11
❑ 419 Steve Trachsel .15 .07
❑ 420 Rey Ordonez .15 .07
❑ 421 Darryl Hamilton .15 .07
❑ 422 Ben Davis .25 .11
❑ 423 Damian Jackson .15 .07
❑ 424 Mark Kotsay .25 .11
❑ 425 Trevor Hoffman .25 .11
❑ 426 Travis Lee .25 .11
❑ 427 Omar Daal .15 .07
❑ 428 Paul Byrd .15 .07
❑ 429 Reggie Taylor .15 .07
❑ 430 Brian Giles .25 .11
❑ 431 Derek Bell .15 .07
❑ 432 Francisco Cordova .15 .07
❑ 433 Pat Meares .15 .07
❑ 434 Scott Williamson .15 .07
❑ 435 Jason LaRue .15 .07
❑ 436 Michael Tucker .15 .07
❑ 437 Wilton Guerrero .15 .07
❑ 438 Mike Hampton .25 .11
❑ 439 Ron Gant .25 .11
❑ 440 Jeff Cirillo .25 .11
❑ 441 Denny Neagle .15 .07
❑ 442 Larry Walker .40 .18
❑ 443 Juan Pierre .25 .11
❑ 444 Todd Walker .15 .07
❑ 445 Jason Giambi SH CL .25 .11
❑ 446 Jeff Kent SH CL .25 .11
❑ 447 Mariano Rivera SH CL .15 .07
❑ 448 Edgar Martinez SH CL .25 .11
❑ 449 Troy Glaus SH CL .25 .11
❑ 450 Alex Rodriguez SH CL .75 .35

2002 Upper Deck

	MINT	NRMT
COMPLETE SET (500)	100.00	45.00

❑ 1 Mark Prior SR 5.00 2.20
❑ 2 Mark Teixeira SR 2.50 1.10
❑ 3 Brian Roberts SR .50 .23
❑ 4 Jason Romano SR .50 .23
❑ 5 Dennis Stark SR .50 .23
❑ 6 Oscar Salazar SR .50 .23
❑ 7 John Patterson SR .50 .23
❑ 8 Shane Loux SR .50 .23
❑ 9 Marcus Giles SR .50 .23
❑ 10 Juan Cruz SR .60 .25
❑ 11 Jorge Julio SR .50 .23
❑ 12 Adam Dunn SR 1.50 .70
❑ 13 Delvin James SR .50 .23
❑ 14 Jeremy Affeldt SR .50 .23
❑ 15 Tim Raines Jr. SR .50 .23
❑ 16 Luke Hudson SR .50 .23
❑ 17 Todd Sears SR .50 .23
❑ 18 George Perez SR .50 .23
❑ 19 Wilmy Caceres SR .50 .23
❑ 20 Abraham Nunez SR .50 .23
❑ 21 Mike Amrhein SR RC .50 .23
❑ 22 Carlos Hernandez SR .50 .23
❑ 23 Scott Hodges SR .50 .23
❑ 24 Brandon Knight SR .50 .23
❑ 25 Geoff Goetz SR .50 .23
❑ 26 Carlos Garcia SR .50 .23
❑ 27 Luis Pineda SR .50 .23
❑ 28 Chris Gissell SR .50 .23
❑ 29 Jae Weong Seo SR .50 .23
❑ 30 Paul Phillips SR .50 .23
❑ 31 Cory Aldridge SR .50 .23
❑ 32 Aaron Cook SR RC .50 .23
❑ 33 Rendy Espina SR RC .50 .23
❑ 34 Jason Phillips SR .50 .23
❑ 35 Carlos Silva SR .50 .23
❑ 36 Ryan Mills SR .50 .23
❑ 37 Pedro Santana SR .50 .23
❑ 38 John Grabow SR .50 .23
❑ 39 Cody Ransom SR .50 .23
❑ 40 Orlando Woodards SR .50 .23
❑ 41 Bud Smith SR 1.00 .45
❑ 42 Junior Guerrero SR .50 .23
❑ 43 David Brous SR .50 .23
❑ 44 Steve Green SR .50 .23
❑ 45 Brian Rogers SR .50 .23
❑ 46 Juan Figueroa SR RC .50 .23
❑ 47 Nick Punto SR .50 .23
❑ 48 Junior Herndon SR .50 .23
❑ 49 Justin Kaye SR .50 .23
❑ 50 Jason Karnuth SR .50 .23
❑ 51 Troy Glaus .60 .25
❑ 52 Bengie Molina .15 .07
❑ 53 Ramon Ortiz .25 .11
❑ 54 Adam Kennedy .15 .07
❑ 55 Jarrod Washburn .15 .07
❑ 56 Troy Percival .25 .11
❑ 57 David Eckstein .15 .07
❑ 58 Ben Weber .15 .07
❑ 59 Larry Barnes .15 .07
❑ 60 Ismael Valdes .15 .07
❑ 61 Benji Gil .15 .07
❑ 62 Scott Schoeneweis .15 .07
❑ 63 Pat Rapp .15 .07
❑ 64 Jason Giambi .60 .25
❑ 65 Mark Mulder .25 .11
❑ 66 Ron Gant .25 .11
❑ 67 Johnny Damon .25 .11
❑ 68 Adam Piatt .15 .07
❑ 69 Jermaine Dye .25 .11
❑ 70 Jason Hart .25 .11
❑ 71 Eric Chavez .25 .11
❑ 72 Jim Mecir .15 .07
❑ 73 Barry Zito .25 .11
❑ 74 Jason Isringhausen .25 .11
❑ 75 Jeremy Giambi .15 .07
❑ 76 Olmedo Saenz .15 .07
❑ 77 Terrence Long .25 .11
❑ 78 Ramon Hernandez .15 .07
❑ 79 Chris Carpenter .15 .07
❑ 80 Raul Mondesi .25 .11
❑ 81 Carlos Delgado .60 .25
❑ 82 Billy Koch .15 .07
❑ 83 Vernon Wells .25 .11
❑ 84 Darrin Fletcher .15 .07
❑ 85 Homer Bush .15 .07
❑ 86 Pasqual Coco .15 .07
❑ 87 Shannon Stewart .25 .11
❑ 88 Chris Woodward .15 .07
❑ 89 Joe Lawrence .15 .07
❑ 90 Esteban Loaiza .15 .07
❑ 91 Cesar Izturis .15 .07
❑ 92 Kelvim Escobar .15 .07
❑ 93 Greg Vaughn .25 .11
❑ 94 Brent Abernathy .15 .07
❑ 95 Tanyon Sturtze .15 .07

- ❑ 96 Steve Cox .15 .07
- ❑ 97 Aubrey Huff .15 .07
- ❑ 98 Jesus Colome .15 .07
- ❑ 99 Ben Grieve .25 .11
- ❑ 100 Esteban Yan .15 .07
- ❑ 101 Joe Kennedy .15 .07
- ❑ 102 Felix Martinez .15 .07
- ❑ 103 Nick Bierbrodt .15 .07
- ❑ 104 Damian Rolls .15 .07
- ❑ 105 Russ Johnson .15 .07
- ❑ 106 Toby Hall .25 .11
- ❑ 107 Roberto Alomar .60 .25
- ❑ 108 Bartolo Colon .25 .11
- ❑ 109 John Rocker .25 .11
- ❑ 110 Juan Gonzalez .60 .25
- ❑ 111 Einar Diaz .15 .07
- ❑ 112 Chuck Finley .25 .11
- ❑ 113 Kenny Lofton .25 .11
- ❑ 114 Danys Baez .15 .07
- ❑ 115 Travis Fryman .25 .11
- ❑ 116 C.C. Sabathia .40 .18
- ❑ 117 Paul Shuey .15 .07
- ❑ 118 Marty Cordova .15 .07
- ❑ 119 Ellis Burks .25 .11
- ❑ 120 Bob Wickman .15 .07
- ❑ 121 Edgar Martinez .40 .18
- ❑ 122 Freddy Garcia .25 .11
- ❑ 123 Ichiro Suzuki 2.50 1.10
- ❑ 124 John Olerud .25 .11
- ❑ 125 Gil Meche .15 .07
- ❑ 126 Dan Wilson .15 .07
- ❑ 127 Aaron Sele .25 .11
- ❑ 128 Kazuhiro Sasaki .60 .25
- ❑ 129 Mark McLemore .15 .07
- ❑ 130 Carlos Guillen .15 .07
- ❑ 131 Al Martin .15 .07
- ❑ 132 David Bell .15 .07
- ❑ 133 Jay Buhner .25 .11
- ❑ 134 Stan Javier .15 .07
- ❑ 135 Tony Batista .25 .11
- ❑ 136 Jason Johnson .15 .07
- ❑ 137 Brook Fordyce .15 .07
- ❑ 138 Mike Kinkade .15 .07
- ❑ 139 Willis Roberts .15 .07
- ❑ 140 David Segui .15 .07
- ❑ 141 Josh Towers .25 .11
- ❑ 142 Jeff Conine .25 .11
- ❑ 143 Chris Richard .15 .07
- ❑ 144 Pat Hentgen .15 .07
- ❑ 145 Melvin Mora .15 .07
- ❑ 146 Jerry Hairston Jr. .15 .07
- ❑ 147 Calvin Maduro .15 .07
- ❑ 148 Brady Anderson .25 .11
- ❑ 149 Alex Rodriguez 1.50 .70
- ❑ 150 Kenny Rogers .15 .07
- ❑ 151 Chad Curtis .15 .07
- ❑ 152 Ricky Ledee .15 .07
- ❑ 153 Rafael Palmeiro .60 .25
- ❑ 154 Rob Bell .15 .07
- ❑ 155 Rick Helling .15 .07
- ❑ 156 Doug Davis .15 .07
- ❑ 157 Mike Lamb .15 .07
- ❑ 158 Gabe Kapler .25 .11
- ❑ 159 Jeff Zimmerman .15 .07
- ❑ 160 Bill Haselman .15 .07
- ❑ 161 Tim Crabtree .15 .07
- ❑ 162 Carlos Pena .25 .11
- ❑ 163 Nomar Garciaparra 1.50 .70
- ❑ 164 Shea Hillenbrand .25 .11
- ❑ 165 Hideo Nomo .60 .25
- ❑ 166 Manny Ramirez .75 .35
- ❑ 167 Jose Offerman .15 .07
- ❑ 168 Scott Hatteberg .15 .07
- ❑ 169 Trot Nixon .25 .11
- ❑ 170 Darren Lewis .15 .07
- ❑ 171 Derek Lowe .15 .07
- ❑ 172 Troy O'Leary .15 .07
- ❑ 173 Tim Wakefield .15 .07
- ❑ 174 Chris Stynes .15 .07
- ❑ 175 John Valentin .15 .07
- ❑ 176 David Cone .25 .11
- ❑ 177 Neifi Perez .15 .07
- ❑ 178 Brent Mayne .15 .07
- ❑ 179 Dan Reichert .15 .07
- ❑ 180 A.J. Hinch .15 .07
- ❑ 181 Chris George .15 .07
- ❑ 182 Mike Sweeney .25 .11
- ❑ 183 Jeff Suppan .15 .07
- ❑ 184 Roberto Hernandez .15 .07
- ❑ 185 Joe Randa .15 .07
- ❑ 186 Paul Byrd .15 .07
- ❑ 187 Luis Ordaz .15 .07
- ❑ 188 Kris Wilson .15 .07
- ❑ 189 Dee Brown .25 .11
- ❑ 190 Tony Clark .25 .11
- ❑ 191 Matt Anderson .15 .07
- ❑ 192 Robert Fick .25 .11
- ❑ 193 Juan Encarnacion .25 .11
- ❑ 194 Dean Palmer .25 .11
- ❑ 195 Victor Santos .15 .07
- ❑ 196 Damion Easley .15 .07
- ❑ 197 Jose Lima .15 .07
- ❑ 198 Deivi Cruz .15 .07
- ❑ 199 Roger Cedeno .15 .07
- ❑ 200 Jose Macias .15 .07
- ❑ 201 Jeff Weaver .25 .11
- ❑ 202 Brandon Inge .25 .11
- ❑ 203 Brian Moehler .15 .07
- ❑ 204 Brad Radke .25 .11
- ❑ 205 Doug Mientkiewicz .25 .11
- ❑ 206 Cristian Guzman .25 .11
- ❑ 207 Corey Koskie .25 .11
- ❑ 208 LaTroy Hawkins .15 .07
- ❑ 209 J.C. Romero .15 .07
- ❑ 210 Chad Allen .15 .07
- ❑ 211 Torii Hunter .25 .11
- ❑ 212 Travis Miller .15 .07
- ❑ 213 Joe Mays .25 .11
- ❑ 214 Todd Jones .15 .07
- ❑ 215 David Ortiz .15 .07
- ❑ 216 Brian Buchanan .15 .07
- ❑ 217 A.J. Pierzynski .15 .07
- ❑ 218 Carlos Lee .25 .11
- ❑ 219 Gary Glover .15 .07
- ❑ 220 Jose Valentin .15 .07
- ❑ 221 Aaron Rowand .25 .11
- ❑ 222 Sandy Alomar Jr. .25 .11
- ❑ 223 Herbert Perry .15 .07
- ❑ 224 Jon Garland .25 .11
- ❑ 225 Mark Buehrle .25 .11
- ❑ 226 Chris Singleton .15 .07
- ❑ 227 Kip Wells .25 .11
- ❑ 228 Ray Durham .25 .11
- ❑ 229 Joe Crede .25 .11
- ❑ 230 Keith Foulke .15 .07
- ❑ 231 Royce Clayton .15 .07
- ❑ 232 Andy Pettitte .25 .11
- ❑ 233 Derek Jeter 2.50 1.10
- ❑ 234 Jorge Posada .25 .11
- ❑ 235 Roger Clemens 1.50 .70
- ❑ 236 Paul O'Neill .60 .25
- ❑ 237 Nick Johnson .25 .11
- ❑ 238 Gerald Williams .15 .07
- ❑ 239 Mariano Rivera .25 .11
- ❑ 240 Alfonso Soriano .60 .25
- ❑ 241 Ramiro Mendoza .15 .07
- ❑ 242 Mike Mussina .60 .25
- ❑ 243 Luis Sojo .15 .07
- ❑ 244 Scott Brosius .25 .11
- ❑ 245 David Justice .40 .18
- ❑ 246 Wade Miller .25 .11
- ❑ 247 Brad Ausmus .15 .07
- ❑ 248 Jeff Bagwell .75 .35
- ❑ 249 Daryle Ward .15 .07
- ❑ 250 Shane Reynolds .15 .07
- ❑ 251 Chris Truby .15 .07
- ❑ 252 Billy Wagner .25 .11
- ❑ 253 Craig Biggio .40 .18
- ❑ 254 Moises Alou .25 .11
- ❑ 255 Vinny Castilla .25 .11
- ❑ 256 Tim Redding .25 .11
- ❑ 257 Roy Oswalt .25 .11
- ❑ 258 Julio Lugo .15 .07
- ❑ 259 Chipper Jones 1.25 .55
- ❑ 260 Greg Maddux 1.50 .70
- ❑ 261 Ken Caminiti .25 .11
- ❑ 262 Kevin Millwood .15 .07
- ❑ 263 Keith Lockhart .15 .07
- ❑ 264 Rey Sanchez .15 .07
- ❑ 265 Jason Marquis .15 .07
- ❑ 266 Brian Jordan .25 .11
- ❑ 267 Steve Karsay .15 .07
- ❑ 268 Wes Helms .15 .07
- ❑ 269 B.J. Surhoff .25 .11
- ❑ 270 Wilson Betemit .40 .18
- ❑ 271 John Smoltz .25 .11
- ❑ 272 Rafael Furcal .25 .11
- ❑ 273 Jeromy Burnitz .25 .11
- ❑ 274 Jimmy Haynes .15 .07
- ❑ 275 Mark Loretta .15 .07
- ❑ 276 Jose Hernandez .15 .07
- ❑ 277 Paul Rigdon .15 .07
- ❑ 278 Alex Sanchez .15 .07
- ❑ 279 Chad Fox .15 .07
- ❑ 280 Devon White .15 .07
- ❑ 281 Tyler Houston .15 .07
- ❑ 282 Ronnie Belliard .15 .07
- ❑ 283 Luis Lopez .15 .07
- ❑ 284 Ben Sheets .25 .11
- ❑ 285 Curtis Leskanic .15 .07
- ❑ 286 Henry Blanco .15 .07
- ❑ 287 Mark McGwire 2.50 1.10
- ❑ 288 Edgar Renteria .25 .11
- ❑ 289 Matt Morris .25 .11
- ❑ 290 Gene Stechschulte .15 .07
- ❑ 291 Dustin Hermanson .15 .07
- ❑ 292 Eli Marrero .15 .07
- ❑ 293 Albert Pujols 1.50 .70
- ❑ 294 Luis Saturria .15 .07
- ❑ 295 Bobby Bonilla .25 .11
- ❑ 296 Garrett Stephenson .15 .07
- ❑ 297 Jim Edmonds .40 .18
- ❑ 298 Rick Ankiel .40 .18
- ❑ 299 Placido Polanco .15 .07
- ❑ 300 Dave Veres .15 .07
- ❑ 301 Sammy Sosa 1.25 .55
- ❑ 302 Eric Young .15 .07
- ❑ 303 Kerry Wood .60 .25
- ❑ 304 Jon Lieber .25 .11
- ❑ 305 Joe Girardi .15 .07
- ❑ 306 Fred McGriff .40 .18
- ❑ 307 Jeff Fassero .15 .07
- ❑ 308 Julio Zuleta .15 .07
- ❑ 309 Kevin Tapani .15 .07
- ❑ 310 Rondell White .25 .11
- ❑ 311 Julian Tavarez .15 .07
- ❑ 312 Tom Gordon .15 .07
- ❑ 313 Corey Patterson .25 .11
- ❑ 314 Bill Mueller .15 .07
- ❑ 315 Randy Johnson .75 .35
- ❑ 316 Chad Moeller .15 .07
- ❑ 317 Tony Womack .15 .07
- ❑ 318 Erubiel Durazo .15 .07
- ❑ 319 Luis Gonzalez .60 .25
- ❑ 320 Brian Anderson .15 .07
- ❑ 321 Reggie Sanders .25 .11
- ❑ 322 Greg Colbrunn .15 .07
- ❑ 323 Robert Ellis .15 .07
- ❑ 324 Jack Cust .25 .11
- ❑ 325 Bret Prinz .15 .07
- ❑ 326 Steve Finley .25 .11
- ❑ 327 Byung-Hyun Kim .25 .11
- ❑ 328 Albie Lopez .15 .07
- ❑ 329 Gary Sheffield .25 .11
- ❑ 330 Mark Grudzielanek .15 .07
- ❑ 331 Paul LoDuca .25 .11
- ❑ 332 Tom Goodwin .15 .07
- ❑ 333 Andy Ashby .15 .07
- ❑ 334 Hiram Bocachica .15 .07
- ❑ 335 Dave Hansen .15 .07
- ❑ 336 Kevin Brown .25 .11
- ❑ 337 Marquis Grissom .15 .07
- ❑ 338 Terry Adams .15 .07
- ❑ 339 Chan Ho Park .25 .11
- ❑ 340 Adrian Beltre .25 .11
- ❑ 341 Luke Prokopec .15 .07
- ❑ 342 Jeff Shaw .15 .07
- ❑ 343 Vladimir Guerrero .75 .35
- ❑ 344 Orlando Cabrera .15 .07
- ❑ 345 Tony Armas Jr. .25 .11
- ❑ 346 Michael Barrett .15 .07
- ❑ 347 Geoff Blum .15 .07
- ❑ 348 Ryan Minor .15 .07
- ❑ 349 Peter Bergeron .15 .07
- ❑ 350 Graeme Lloyd .15 .07
- ❑ 351 Jose Vidro .25 .11
- ❑ 352 Javier Vazquez .25 .11
- ❑ 353 Matt Blank .15 .07

No.	Player	MINT	NRMT
354	Masato Yoshii	.25	.11
355	Carl Pavano	.15	.07
356	Barry Bonds	1.50	.70
357	Shawon Dunston	.15	.07
358	Livan Hernandez	.15	.07
359	Felix Rodriguez	.15	.07
360	Pedro Feliz	.15	.07
361	Calvin Murray	.15	.07
362	Robb Nen	.25	.11
363	Marvin Benard	.15	.07
364	Russ Ortiz	.25	.11
365	Jason Schmidt	.15	.07
366	Rich Aurilia	.25	.11
367	John Vanderwal	.15	.07
368	Benito Santiago	.15	.07
369	Ryan Dempster	.15	.07
370	Charles Johnson	.25	.11
371	Alex Gonzalez	.15	.07
372	Luis Castillo	.15	.07
373	Mike Lowell	.25	.11
374	Antonio Alfonseca	.15	.07
375	A.J. Burnett	.25	.11
376	Brad Penny	.25	.11
377	Jason Grilli	.15	.07
378	Derrek Lee	.15	.07
379	Matt Clement	.15	.07
380	Eric Owens	.15	.07
381	Vladimir Nunez	.15	.07
382	Cliff Floyd	.25	.11
383	Mike Piazza	1.50	.70
384	Lenny Harris	.15	.07
385	Glendon Rusch	.15	.07
386	Todd Zeile	.25	.11
387	Al Leiter	.25	.11
388	Armando Benitez	.25	.11
389	Alex Escobar	.25	.11
390	Kevin Appier	.25	.11
391	Matt Lawton	.25	.11
392	Bruce Chen	.15	.07
393	John Franco	.25	.11
394	Tsuyoshi Shinjo	.40	.18
395	Rey Ordonez	.15	.07
396	Joe McEwing	.15	.07
397	Ryan Klesko	.25	.11
398	Brian Lawrence	.15	.07
399	Kevin Walker	.15	.07
400	Phil Nevin	.25	.11
401	Bubba Trammell	.15	.07
402	Wiki Gonzalez	.15	.07
403	D'Angelo Jimenez	.15	.07
404	Rickey Henderson	1.25	.55
405	Mike Darr	.15	.07
406	Trevor Hoffman	.25	.11
407	Damian Jackson	.15	.07
408	Santiago Perez	.15	.07
409	Cesar Crespo	.15	.07
410	Robert Person	.15	.07
411	Travis Lee	.25	.11
412	Scott Rolen	.60	.25
413	Turk Wendell	.15	.07
414	Randy Wolf	.15	.07
415	Kevin Jordan	.15	.07
416	Jose Mesa	.15	.07
417	Mike Lieberthal	.25	.11
418	Bobby Abreu	.25	.11
419	Tomas Perez	.15	.07
420	Doug Glanville	.15	.07
421	Reggie Taylor	.15	.07
422	Jimmy Rollins	.25	.11
423	Brian Giles	.25	.11
424	Rob Mackowiak	.15	.07
425	Bronson Arroyo	.15	.07
426	Kevin Young	.15	.07
427	Jack Wilson	.15	.07
428	Adrian Brown	.15	.07
429	Chad Hermansen	.15	.07
430	Jimmy Anderson	.15	.07
431	Aramis Ramirez	.25	.11
432	Todd Ritchie	.15	.07
433	Pat Meares	.15	.07
434	Warren Morris	.15	.07
435	Derek Bell	.15	.07
436	Ken Griffey Jr.	2.00	.90
437	Elmer Dessens	.15	.07
438	Ruben Rivera	.15	.07
439	Jason LaRue	.15	.07
440	Sean Casey	.40	.18
441	Pete Harnisch	.15	.07
442	Danny Graves	.15	.07
443	Aaron Boone	.15	.07
444	Dmitri Young	.25	.11
445	Brandon Larson	.15	.07
446	Pokey Reese	.15	.07
447	Todd Walker	.15	.07
448	Juan Castro	.15	.07
449	Todd Helton	.75	.35
450	Ben Petrick	.15	.07
451	Juan Pierre	.25	.11
452	Jeff Cirillo	.25	.11
453	Juan Uribe	.25	.11
454	Brian Bohanon	.15	.07
455	Terry Shumpert	.15	.07
456	Mike Hampton	.25	.11
457	Shawn Chacon	.15	.07
458	Adam Melhuse	.15	.07
459	Greg Norton	.15	.07
460	Gabe White	.15	.07
461	Ichiro Suzuki WS	1.25	.55
462	Carlos Delgado WS	.25	.11
463	Manny Ramirez WS	.40	.18
464	Miguel Tejada WS	.15	.07
465	Tsuyoshi Shinjo WS	.25	.11
466	Bernie Williams WS	.25	.11
467	Juan Gonzalez WS	.25	.11
468	Andruw Jones WS	.25	.11
469	Ivan Rodriguez WS	.25	.11
470	Larry Walker WS	.40	.18
471	Hideo Nomo WS	.25	.11
472	Albert Pujols WS	.75	.35
473	Pedro Martinez WS	.40	.18
474	Vladimir Guerrero WS	.40	.18
475	Tony Batista WS	.15	.07
476	Kazuhiro Sasaki WS	.25	.11
477	Richard Hidalgo WS	.15	.07
478	Carlos Lee WS	.15	.07
479	Roberto Alomar WS	.25	.11
480	Rafael Palmeiro WS	.25	.11
481	Ken Griffey Jr. GG	1.00	.45
482	Ken Griffey Jr. GG	1.00	.45
483	Ken Griffey Jr. GG	1.00	.45
484	Ken Griffey Jr. GG	1.00	.45
485	Ken Griffey Jr. GG	1.00	.45
486	Ken Griffey Jr. GG	1.00	.45
487	Ken Griffey Jr. GG	1.00	.45
488	Ken Griffey Jr. GG	1.00	.45
489	Ken Griffey Jr. GG	1.00	.45
490	Ken Griffey Jr. GG	1.00	.45
491	Barry Bonds CL	.75	.35
492	Hideo Nomo CL	.25	.11
493	Ichiro Suzuki CL	1.25	.55
494	Cal Ripken CL	1.25	.55
495	Tony Gwynn CL	.60	.25
496	Randy Johnson CL	.40	.18
497	A.J. Burnett CL	.15	.07
498	Rickey Henderson CL	.60	.25
499	Albert Pujols CL	.75	.35
500	Luis Gonzalez CL	.25	.11

2001 Upper Deck Decade 1970's

	MINT	NRMT
COMPLETE SET (180)	50.00	22.00

No.	Player	MINT	NRMT
1	Nolan Ryan	5.00	2.20
2	Don Baylor	.50	.23
3	Bobby Grich	.50	.23
4	Reggie Jackson	2.00	.90
5	Catfish Hunter	1.25	.55
6	Gene Tenace	.30	.14
7	Rollie Fingers	.50	.23
8	Sal Bando	.50	.23
9	Bert Campaneris	.30	.14
10	John Mayberry	.30	.14
11	Rico Carty	.30	.14
12	Gaylord Perry	.50	.23
13	Andre Thornton	.30	.14
14	Buddy Bell	.50	.23
15	Dennis Eckersley	.50	.23
16	Ruppert Jones	.30	.14
17	Brooks Robinson	1.25	.55
18	Tommy Davis	.30	.14
19	Eddie Murray	1.25	.55
20	Boog Powell	.50	.23
21	Al Oliver	.50	.23
22	Jeff Burroughs	.30	.14
23	Mike Hargrove	.50	.23
24	Dwight Evans	.50	.23
25	Fred Lynn	.50	.23
26	Rico Petrocelli	.30	.14
27	Carlton Fisk	1.25	.55
28	Luis Aparicio	.75	.35
29	Amos Otis	.30	.14
30	Hal McRae	.50	.23
31	Jason Thompson	.30	.14
32	Al Kaline	1.50	.70
33	Jim Perry	.30	.14
34	Bert Blyleven	.50	.23
35	Harmon Killebrew	1.25	.55
36	Wilbur Wood	.30	.14
37	Jim Kaat	.50	.23
38	Ron Guidry	.50	.23
39	Thurman Munson	2.00	.90
40	Graig Nettles	.50	.23
41	Bobby Murcer	.50	.23
42	Chris Chambliss	.50	.23
43	Roy White	.30	.14
44	J.R. Richard	.50	.23
45	Jose Cruz	.50	.23
46	Hank Aaron	3.00	1.35
47	Phil Niekro	.75	.35
48	Bob Horner	.30	.14
49	Darrell Evans	.50	.23
50	Gorman Thomas	.50	.23
51	Don Money	.30	.14
52	Robin Yount	1.25	.55
53	Joe Torre	.50	.23
54	Tim McCarver	.50	.23
55	Lou Brock	1.25	.55
56	Keith Hernandez	.50	.23
57	Bill Madlock	.50	.23
58	Ron Santo	.75	.35
59	Billy Williams	.75	.35
60	Ferguson Jenkins	.50	.23
61	Steve Garvey	.75	.35
62	Bill Russell UER Trivia question has several wrong answers	.50	.23
63	Maury Wills	.50	.23
64	Ron Cey	.50	.23
65	Manny Mota	.30	.14
66	Ron Fairly	.30	.14
67	Steve Rogers	.30	.14
68	Gary Carter	.75	.35
69	Andre Dawson	.75	.35
70	Bobby Bonds	.50	.23
71	Jack Clark	.50	.23
72	Willie McCovey	1.25	.55
73	Tom Seaver	2.00	.90
74	Bud Harrelson	.50	.23
75	Dave Kingman	.50	.23
76	Jerry Koosman	.50	.23
77	Jon Matlack	.30	.14
78	Randy Jones	.30	.14
79	Ozzie Smith	1.50	.70
80	Garry Maddox	.30	.14
81	Mike Schmidt	2.50	1.10
82	Greg Luzinski	.50	.23
83	Tug McGraw	.50	.23
84	Willie Stargell	.75	.35

❑ 85 Dave Parker .50 .23
❑ 86 Roberto Clemente 4.00 1.80
❑ 87 Johnny Bench 2.00 .90
❑ 88 Joe Morgan 1.25 .55
❑ 89 George Foster .50 .23
❑ 90 Ken Griffey Sr. .50 .23
❑ 91 Carlton Fisk RF 1.25 .55
❑ 92 Andre Dawson RF .75 .35
❑ 93 Fred Lynn RF .50 .23
❑ 94 Eddie Murray RF 1.25 .55
❑ 95 Bob Horner RF .30 .14
❑ 96 Jon Matlack RF .30 .14
❑ 97 Mike Hargrove RF .50 .23
❑ 98 Robin Yount RF 1.25 .55
❑ 99 Mike Schmidt RF 1.25 .55
❑ 100 Gary Carter RF .75 .35
❑ 101 Ozzie Smith RF .75 .35
❑ 102 Paul Molitor RF 1.25 .55
❑ 103 Dennis Eckersley RF .50 .23
❑ 104 Dale Murphy RF .75 .35
❑ 105 Bert Blyleven RF .50 .23
❑ 106 Thurman Munson RF 1.25 .55
❑ 107 Dave Parker RF .50 .23
❑ 108 Jack Clark RF .50 .23
❑ 109 Keith Hernandez RF .50 .23
❑ 110 Ron Cey RF .50 .23
❑ 111 Billy Williams DD .50 .23
❑ 112 Tom Seaver DD 1.25 .55
❑ 113 Reggie Jackson DD 1.25 .55
❑ 114 Bobby Bonds DD .30 .14
❑ 115 Willie Stargell DD .50 .23
❑ 116 Harmon Killebrew DD .50 .23
❑ 117 Roberto Clemente DD 2.00 .90
❑ 118 Wilbur Wood DD .30 .14
❑ 119 Billy Williams DD .50 .23
❑ 120 Nolan Ryan DD 2.50 1.10
❑ 121 Ron Blomberg DD .30 .14
❑ 122 Hank Aaron DD 1.50 .70
❑ 123 Lou Brock DD .50 .23
❑ 124 Al Kaline DD UER .75 .35
Kaline got his 3,000 hit in 1974, not 1964
❑ 125 Brooks Robinson DD .50 .23
❑ 126 Bill Madlock DD .30 .14
❑ 127 Rennie Stennett DD .30 .14
❑ 128 Carlton Fisk DD .50 .23
❑ 129 Chris Chambliss DD .30 .14
❑ 130 Ruppert Jones DD .30 .14
❑ 131 Ron Fairly DD .30 .14
❑ 132 George Foster DD .30 .14
❑ 133 Reggie Jackson DD 1.25 .55
❑ 134 Ron Guidry DD .30 .14
❑ 135 Gaylord Perry DD .30 .14
❑ 136 Bucky Dent DD .30 .14
❑ 137 Dave Kingman DD .30 .14
❑ 138 Lou Brock DD .50 .23
❑ 139 Thurman Munson DD 1.25 .55
❑ 140 Willie Stargell DD .50 .23
❑ 141 Johnny Bench AW 1.25 .55
❑ 142 Boog Powell AW .30 .14
❑ 143 Jim Perry AW .30 .14
❑ 144 Joe Torre AW .30 .14
❑ 145 Chris Chambliss AW .30 .14
❑ 146 Ferguson Jenkins AW .30 .14
❑ 147 Carlton Fisk AW .50 .23
❑ 148 Gaylord Perry AW .30 .14
❑ 149 Johnny Bench AW 1.25 .55
❑ 150 Reggie Jackson AW 1.25 .55
❑ 151 Tom Seaver AW 1.25 .55
❑ 152 Thurman Munson AW 1.25 .55
❑ 153 Steve Garvey AW .50 .23
❑ 154 Catfish Hunter AW .50 .23
❑ 155 Mike Hargrove AW .30 .14
❑ 156 Joe Morgan AW .50 .23
❑ 157 Fred Lynn AW .30 .14
❑ 158 Tom Seaver AW 1.25 .55
❑ 159 Thurman Munson AW 1.25 .55
❑ 160 Randy Jones AW .30 .14
❑ 161 Joe Morgan AW .50 .23
❑ 162 George Foster AW .30 .14
❑ 163 Eddie Murray AW .50 .23
❑ 164 Andre Dawson AW .50 .23
❑ 165 Gaylord Perry AW .30 .14
❑ 166 Ron Guidry AW .30 .14
❑ 167 Dave Parker AW .30 .14
❑ 168 Don Baylor AW .30 .14
❑ 169 Bruce Sutter AW .30 .14
❑ 170 Willie Stargell AW .50 .23
❑ 171 Brooks Robinson WS .50 .23
❑ 172 Roberto Clemente WS 2.00 .90
❑ 173 Gene Tenace WS .30 .14
❑ 174 Reggie Jackson WS 1.25 .55
❑ 175 Rollie Fingers WS .30 .14
❑ 176 Carlton Fisk WS .50 .23
❑ 177 Johnny Bench WS 1.25 .55
❑ 178 Reggie Jackson WS 1.25 .55
❑ 179 Bucky Dent WS .30 .14
❑ 180 Willie Stargell WS .50 .23

2001 Upper Deck Evolution

	MINT	NRMT
COMP.SET w/o SP's (90)	20.00	9.00
COMMON CARD (1-90)	.25	.11
COMMON CARD (91-120)	5.00	2.20

❑ 1 Darin Erstad .60 .25
❑ 2 Troy Glaus .60 .25
❑ 3 Jason Giambi .60 .25
❑ 4 Tim Hudson .60 .25
❑ 5 Jermaine Dye .25 .11
❑ 6 Barry Zito .60 .25
❑ 7 Carlos Delgado .60 .25
❑ 8 Shannon Stewart .25 .11
❑ 9 Jose Cruz Jr. .25 .11
❑ 10 Greg Vaughn .25 .11
❑ 11 Juan Gonzalez .60 .25
❑ 12 Roberto Alomar .60 .25
❑ 13 Omar Vizquel .25 .11
❑ 14 Jim Thome .60 .25
❑ 15 Edgar Martinez .40 .18
❑ 16 John Olerud .25 .11
❑ 17 Kazuhiro Sasaki .60 .25
❑ 18 Cal Ripken 2.50 1.10
❑ 19 Alex Rodriguez 1.50 .70
❑ 20 Ivan Rodriguez .60 .25
❑ 21 Rafael Palmeiro .60 .25
❑ 22 Pedro Martinez .75 .35
❑ 23 Nomar Garciaparra 2.00 .90
❑ 24 Manny Ramirez .75 .35
❑ 25 Carl Everett .25 .11
❑ 26 Mark Quinn .25 .11
❑ 27 Mike Sweeney .25 .11
❑ 28 Neifi Perez .25 .11
❑ 29 Tony Clark .25 .11
❑ 30 Eric Milton .25 .11
❑ 31 Doug Mientkiewicz .25 .11
❑ 32 Corey Koskie .25 .11
❑ 33 Frank Thomas .75 .35
❑ 34 David Wells .25 .11
❑ 35 Magglio Ordonez .25 .11
❑ 36 Derek Jeter 2.50 1.10
❑ 37 Mike Mussina .60 .25
❑ 38 Bernie Williams .60 .25
❑ 39 Roger Clemens 1.50 .70
❑ 40 David Justice .40 .18
❑ 41 Jeff Bagwell .75 .35
❑ 42 Richard Hidalgo .25 .11
❑ 43 Wade Miller .25 .11
❑ 44 Chipper Jones 1.25 .55
❑ 45 Greg Maddux 1.50 .70
❑ 46 Andruw Jones .60 .25
❑ 47 Rafael Furcal .25 .11
❑ 48 Geoff Jenkins .25 .11
❑ 49 Jeromy Burnitz .25 .11
❑ 50 Ben Sheets .40 .18
❑ 51 Richie Sexson .25 .11
❑ 52 Mark McGwire 2.50 1.10
❑ 53 Jim Edmonds .40 .18
❑ 54 Darryl Kile .25 .11
❑ 55 J.D. Drew .60 .25
❑ 56 Sammy Sosa 1.25 .55
❑ 57 Kerry Wood .60 .25
❑ 58 Randy Johnson .75 .35
❑ 59 Luis Gonzalez .60 .25
❑ 60 Matt Williams .40 .18
❑ 61 Kevin Brown .25 .11
❑ 62 Gary Sheffield .25 .11
❑ 63 Shawn Green .60 .25
❑ 64 Chan Ho Park .25 .11
❑ 65 Vladimir Guerrero .75 .35
❑ 66 Jose Vidro .25 .11
❑ 67 Fernando Tatis .25 .11
❑ 68 Barry Bonds 1.50 .70
❑ 69 Jeff Kent .40 .18
❑ 70 Russ Ortiz .25 .11
❑ 71 Preston Wilson .25 .11
❑ 72 Ryan Dempster .25 .11
❑ 73 Charles Johnson .25 .11
❑ 74 Mike Piazza 1.50 .70
❑ 75 Edgardo Alfonzo .25 .11
❑ 76 Robin Ventura .25 .11
❑ 77 Jay Payton .25 .11
❑ 78 Tony Gwynn 1.25 .55
❑ 79 Phil Nevin .25 .11
❑ 80 Pat Burrell .25 .11
❑ 81 Scott Rolen .60 .25
❑ 82 Bob Abreu .25 .11
❑ 83 Brian Giles .25 .11
❑ 84 Jason Kendall .25 .11
❑ 85 Ken Griffey Jr. 2.00 .90
❑ 86 Barry Larkin .60 .25
❑ 87 Sean Casey .40 .18
❑ 88 Todd Helton .75 .35
❑ 89 Larry Walker .40 .18
❑ 90 Mike Hampton .25 .11
❑ 91 Ichiro Suzuki PROS RC 60.00 27.00
❑ 92 Albert Pujols PROS RC 40.00 18.00
❑ 93 Wilson Betemit PROS RC 15.00 6.75
❑ 94 Jay Gibbons PROS RC 8.00 3.60
❑ 95 Juan Uribe PROS RC 10.00 4.50
❑ 96 M. Ensberg PROS RC 10.00 4.50
❑ 97 Christian Parker PROS RC 5.00 2.20
❑ 98 Tsuyoshi Shinjo PROS RC 20.00 9.00
❑ 99 Jack Wilson PROS RC 5.00 2.20
❑ 100 D. Mendez PROS RC 8.00 3.60
❑ 101 Ryan Freel PROS RC 5.00 2.20
❑ 102 Juan Diaz PROS RC 5.00 2.20
❑ 103 H. Ramirez PROS RC 5.00 2.20
❑ 104 R. Rodriguez PROS RC 10.00 4.50
❑ 105 Erick Almonte PROS RC 8.00 3.60
❑ 106 Josh Towers PROS RC 10.00 4.50
❑ 107 Adr.Hernandez PROS RC 5.00 2.20
❑ 108 B..Duckworth PROS RC 12.00 5.50
❑ 109 Travis Hafner PROS RC 8.00 3.60
❑ 110 Martin Vargas PROS RC 5.00 2.20
❑ 111 Kris Keller PROS RC 5.00 2.20
❑ 112 B. Lawrence PROS RC 5.00 2.20
❑ 113 Esix Snead PROS RC 5.00 2.20
❑ 114 Wilkin Ruan PROS RC 5.00 2.20
❑ 115 Jose Mieses PROS RC 5.00 2.20
❑ 116 J. Estrada PROS RC 10.00 4.50
❑ 117 E. Guzman PROS RC 5.00 2.20
❑ 118 S. Douglass PROS RC 5.00 2.20
❑ 119 Billy Sylvester PROS RC 5.00 2.20
❑ 120 Bret Prinz PROS RC 5.00 2.20

2001 Upper Deck Gold Glove

	MINT	NRMT
COMP.SET w/o SP'S (90)	30.00	13.50
COMMON CARD (1-90)	.50	.23
COMMON CARD (91-129)	10.00	4.50
COMMON CARD (130-135)	25.00	11.00

❑ 1 Troy Glaus 1.25 .55
❑ 2 Darin Erstad 1.25 .55
❑ 3 Jason Giambi 1.25 .55
❑ 4 Tim Hudson 1.25 .55
❑ 5 Jermaine Dye .50 .23
❑ 6 Raul Mondesi .50 .23
❑ 7 Carlos Delgado 1.25 .55
❑ 8 Shannon Stewart .50 .23
❑ 9 Greg Vaughn .50 .23
❑ 10 Aubrey Huff .50 .23
❑ 11 Juan Gonzalez 1.25 .55
❑ 12 Roberto Alomar 1.25 .55
❑ 13 Omar Vizquel .50 .23
❑ 14 Jim Thome 1.25 .55
❑ 15 John Olerud .50 .23
❑ 16 Edgar Martinez .75 .35
❑ 17 Kazuhiro Sasaki 1.25 .55
❑ 18 Aaron Sele .50 .23
❑ 19 Cal Ripken 5.00 2.20
❑ 20 Chris Richard .50 .23
❑ 21 Ivan Rodriguez 1.25 .55
❑ 22 Rafael Palmeiro 1.25 .55
❑ 23 Alex Rodriguez 3.00 1.35
❑ 24 Pedro Martinez 1.50 .70
❑ 25 Nomar Garciaparra 3.00 1.35
❑ 26 Manny Ramirez 1.50 .70
❑ 27 Neifi Perez .50 .23
❑ 28 Mike Sweeney .50 .23
❑ 29 Bobby Higginson .50 .23
❑ 30 Dean Palmer .50 .23
❑ 31 Tony Clark .50 .23
❑ 32 Doug Mientkiewicz .50 .23
❑ 33 Brad Radke .50 .23
❑ 34 Joe Mays .50 .23
❑ 35 Frank Thomas 1.50 .70
❑ 36 Magglio Ordonez .50 .23
❑ 37 Carlos Lee .50 .23
❑ 38 Bernie Williams 1.25 .55
❑ 39 Mike Mussina 1.25 .55
❑ 40 Derek Jeter 5.00 2.20
❑ 41 Roger Clemens 3.00 1.35
❑ 42 Craig Biggio .75 .35
❑ 43 Jeff Bagwell 1.50 .70
❑ 44 Lance Berkman 1.25 .55
❑ 45 Andruw Jones 1.25 .55
❑ 46 Greg Maddux 3.00 1.35
❑ 47 Chipper Jones 2.50 1.10
❑ 48 Geoff Jenkins .50 .23
❑ 49 Ben Sheets .75 .35
❑ 50 Jeromy Burnitz .50 .23
❑ 51 Jim Edmonds .75 .35
❑ 52 Mark McGwire 5.00 2.20
❑ 53 Mike Matheny .50 .23
❑ 54 J.D. Drew 1.25 .55
❑ 55 Sammy Sosa 2.50 1.10
❑ 56 Kerry Wood 1.25 .55
❑ 57 Fred McGriff .75 .35
❑ 58 Randy Johnson 1.50 .70
❑ 59 Steve Finley .50 .23
❑ 60 Mark Grace 1.25 .55
❑ 61 Matt Williams .75 .35
❑ 62 Luis Gonzalez 1.25 .55
❑ 63 Shawn Green 1.25 .55
❑ 64 Kevin Brown .50 .23
❑ 65 Gary Sheffield .50 .23
❑ 66 Vladimir Guerrero 1.50 .70
❑ 67 Tony Armas Jr. .50 .23
❑ 68 Barry Bonds 3.00 1.35
❑ 69 J.T. Snow .50 .23
❑ 70 Jeff Kent .75 .35
❑ 71 Charles Johnson .50 .23
❑ 72 Preston Wilson .50 .23
❑ 73 Cliff Floyd .50 .23
❑ 74 Robin Ventura .50 .23
❑ 75 Mike Piazza 3.00 1.35
❑ 76 Edgardo Alfonzo .50 .23
❑ 77 Tony Gwynn 2.50 1.10
❑ 78 Ryan Klesko .50 .23
❑ 79 Scott Rolen 1.25 .55
❑ 80 Mike Lieberthal .50 .23
❑ 81 Pat Burrell .50 .23
❑ 82 Jason Kendall .50 .23
❑ 83 Brian Giles .50 .23
❑ 84 Ken Griffey Jr. 4.00 1.80
❑ 85 Barry Larkin 1.25 .55
❑ 86 Pokey Reese .50 .23
❑ 87 Larry Walker .75 .35
❑ 88 Mike Hampton .50 .23
❑ 89 Juan Pierre .50 .23
❑ 90 Todd Helton 1.50 .70
❑ 91 Mike Penney GD RC 10.00 4.50
❑ 92 Wilkin Ruan GD RC 10.00 4.50
❑ 93 Greg Miller GD RC 10.00 4.50
❑ 94 Johnny Estrada GD RC 12.00 5.50
❑ 95 Tsuyoshi Shinjo GD RC 25.00 11.00
❑ 96 Josh Towers GD RC 12.00 5.50
❑ 97 Horacio Ramirez GD RC 10.00 4.50
❑ 98 Ryan Freel GD RC 10.00 4.50
❑ 99 Morgan Ensberg GD RC 12.00 5.50
❑ 100 Adrian Hernandez GD RC 10.00 4.50
❑ 101 Juan Uribe GD RC 12.00 5.50
❑ 102 Jose Mieses GD RC 10.00 4.50
❑ 103 Jack Wilson GD RC 10.00 4.50
❑ 104 Cesar Crespo GD RC 10.00 4.50
❑ 105 Bud Smith GD RC 25.00 11.00
❑ 106 Erick Almonte GD RC 10.00 4.50
❑ 107 Elpidio Guzman GD RC 10.00 4.50
❑ 108 B. Duckworth GD RC 15.00 6.75
❑ 109 Juan Diaz GD RC 10.00 4.50
❑ 110 Kris Keller GD RC 10.00 4.50
❑ 111 Jason Michaels GD RC 10.00 4.50
❑ 112 Bret Prinz GD RC 10.00 4.50
❑ 113 Henry Mateo GD RC 10.00 4.50
❑ 114 R. Rodriguez GD RC 10.00 4.50
❑ 115 Travis Hafner GD RC 10.00 4.50
❑ 116 Nate Teut GD RC 10.00 4.50
❑ 117 Alexis Gomez GD RC 10.00 4.50
❑ 118 Billy Sylvester GD RC 10.00 4.50
❑ 119 Adam Pettyjohn GD RC 10.00 4.50
❑ 120 Josh Fogg GD RC 10.00 4.50
❑ 121 Juan Cruz GD RC 20.00 9.00
❑ 122 C. Valderrama GD RC 10.00 4.50
❑ 123 Jay Gibbons GD RC 10.00 4.50
❑ 124 Donaldo Mendez GD RC 10.00 4.50
❑ 125 Bill Ortega GD RC 10.00 4.50
❑ 126 Sean Douglass GD RC 10.00 4.50
❑ 127 Christian Parker GD RC 10.00 4.50
❑ 128 Grant Balfour GD RC 10.00 4.50
❑ 129 Joe Kennedy GD RC 10.00 4.50
❑ 130 Albert Pujols GD RC 80.00 36.00
❑ 131 Wilson Betemit GD RC 25.00 11.00
❑ 132 Mark Teixeira GD RC 60.00 27.00
❑ 133 Mark Prior GD RC 40.00 18.00
❑ 134 Dewon Brazelton GD RC 25.00 11.00
❑ 135 Ichiro Suzuki GD RC 180.00 80.00

2001 Upper Deck Hall of Famers

	MINT	NRMT
COMPLETE SET (90)	20.00	9.00
❑ 1 Reggie Jackson	.60	.25
❑ 2 Hank Aaron	1.25	.55
❑ 3 Eddie Mathews	.50	.23
❑ 4 Warren Spahn	.50	.23
❑ 5 Robin Yount	.50	.23
❑ 6 Lou Brock	.50	.23
❑ 7 Dizzy Dean	.50	.23
❑ 8 Bob Gibson	.50	.23
❑ 9 Stan Musial	1.00	.45
❑ 10 Enos Slaughter	.20	.09
❑ 11 Rogers Hornsby	.50	.23
❑ 12 Ernie Banks	.60	.25

❑ 13 Fergie Jenkins .20 .09
❑ 14 Roy Campanella .60 .25
❑ 15 Pee Wee Reese .50 .23
❑ 16 Jackie Robinson 1.00 .45
❑ 17 Juan Marichal .30 .14
❑ 18 Christy Mathewson .50 .23
❑ 19 Willie Mays 1.25 .55
❑ 20 Hoyt Wilhelm .20 .09
❑ 21 Buck Leonard .20 .09
❑ 22 Bob Feller .50 .23
❑ 23 Cy Young .50 .23
❑ 24 Satchel Paige .60 .25
❑ 25 Tom Seaver .75 .35
❑ 26 Brooks Robinson .50 .23
❑ 27 Mike Schmidt 1.00 .45
❑ 28 Roberto Clemente 1.50 .70
❑ 29 Ralph Kiner .20 .09
❑ 30 Willie Stargell .30 .14
❑ 31 Honus Wagner .75 .35
❑ 32 Josh Gibson .50 .23
❑ 33 Nolan Ryan 2.50 1.10
❑ 34 Carlton Fisk .50 .23
❑ 35 Jimmie Foxx .60 .25
❑ 36 Johnny Bench .75 .35
❑ 37 Joe Morgan .50 .23
❑ 38 George Brett 1.00 .45
❑ 39 Walter Johnson .50 .23
❑ 40 Cool Papa Bell .20 .09
❑ 41 Ty Cobb 1.25 .55
❑ 42 Al Kaline .50 .23
❑ 43 Harmon Killebrew .50 .23
❑ 44 Luis Aparicio .30 .14
❑ 45 Yogi Berra .60 .25
❑ 46 Joe DiMaggio 1.50 .70
❑ 47 Whitey Ford .50 .23
❑ 48 Lou Gehrig 1.50 .70
❑ 49 Mickey Mantle 2.50 1.10
❑ 50 Babe Ruth 2.50 1.10
❑ 51 Josh Gibson OG .20 .09
❑ 52 Honus Wagner OG .50 .23
❑ 53 Hoyt Wilhelm OG .20 .09
❑ 54 Cy Young OG .20 .09
❑ 55 Walter Johnson OG .20 .09
❑ 56 Satchel Paige OG .30 .14
❑ 57 Rogers Hornsby OG .20 .09
❑ 58 Christy Mathewson OG .20 .09
❑ 59 Tris Speaker OG .50 .23
❑ 60 Nap Lajoie OG .50 .23
❑ 61 Mickey Mantle NP 1.25 .55
❑ 62 Jackie Robinson NP .50 .23
❑ 63 Nolan Ryan NP 1.25 .55
❑ 64 Josh Gibson NP .20 .09
❑ 65 Yogi Berra NP .30 .14
❑ 66 Brooks Robinson NP .20 .09
❑ 67 Stan Musial NP .50 .23
❑ 68 Mike Schmidt NP .50 .23
❑ 69 Joe DiMaggio NP .75 .35
❑ 70 Ernie Banks NP .30 .14
❑ 71 Willie Stargell NP .20 .09
❑ 72 Johnny Bench NP .50 .23
❑ 73 Willie Mays NP .60 .25
❑ 74 Satchel Paige NP .30 .14
❑ 75 Bob Gibson NP .20 .09
❑ 76 Harmon Killebrew NP .20 .09
❑ 77 Al Kaline NP .30 .14
❑ 78 Carlton Fisk NP .20 .09
❑ 79 Tom Seaver NP .50 .23

#	Player	MINT	NRMT
❑ 80	Reggie Jackson NP	.30	.14
❑ 81	Bob Gibson HR	.20	.09
❑ 82	Nolan Ryan HR	1.25	.55
❑ 83	Walter Johnson HR	.20	.09
❑ 84	Stan Musial HR	.50	.23
❑ 85	Josh Gibson HR	.20	.09
❑ 86	Cy Young HR	.20	.09
❑ 87	Joe DiMaggio HR	.75	.35
❑ 88	Hoyt Wilhelm HR	.20	.09
❑ 89	Lou Brock HR	.20	.09
❑ 90	Mickey Mantle HR	1.25	.55

2000 Upper Deck Legends

	MINT	NRMT
COMPLETE SET (135)	100.00	45.00
COMP.SET w/o SP'S (90)	20.00	9.00
COMMON CARD (1-90)	.25	.11
COMMON CARD (91-105)	2.00	.90
COMMON CARD (106-135)	2.00	.90

#	Player	MINT	NRMT
❑ 1	Darin Erstad	.60	.25
❑ 2	Troy Glaus	.60	.25
❑ 3	Mo Vaughn	.25	.11
❑ 4	Craig Biggio	.40	.18
❑ 5	Jeff Bagwell	.75	.35
❑ 6	Reggie Jackson	.75	.35
❑ 7	Tim Hudson	.60	.25
❑ 8	Jason Giambi	.60	.25
❑ 9	Hank Aaron	1.50	.70
❑ 10	Greg Maddux	1.50	.70
❑ 11	Chipper Jones	1.25	.55
❑ 12	Andres Galarraga	.40	.18
❑ 13	Robin Yount	.60	.25
❑ 14	Jeromy Burnitz	.25	.11
❑ 15	Paul Molitor	.60	.25
❑ 16	David Wells	.25	.11
❑ 17	Carlos Delgado	.60	.25
❑ 18	Ernie Banks	.75	.35
❑ 19	Sammy Sosa	1.25	.55
❑ 20	Kerry Wood	.60	.25
❑ 21	Stan Musial	1.00	.45
❑ 22	Bob Gibson	.60	.25
❑ 23	Mark McGwire	2.50	1.10
❑ 24	Fernando Tatis	.25	.11
❑ 25	Randy Johnson	.75	.35
❑ 26	Matt Williams	.40	.18
❑ 27	Jackie Robinson	1.25	.55
❑ 28	Sandy Koufax	2.00	.90
❑ 29	Shawn Green	.60	.25
❑ 30	Kevin Brown	.40	.18
❑ 31	Gary Sheffield	.25	.11
❑ 32	Greg Vaughn	.25	.11
❑ 33	Jose Canseco	.60	.25
❑ 34	Gary Carter	.40	.18
❑ 35	Vladimir Guerrero	.75	.35
❑ 36	Willie Mays	1.50	.70
❑ 37	Barry Bonds	1.50	.70
❑ 38	Jeff Kent	.40	.18
❑ 39	Bob Feller	.60	.25
❑ 40	Roberto Alomar	.60	.25
❑ 41	Jim Thome	.60	.25
❑ 42	Manny Ramirez	.75	.35
❑ 43	Alex Rodriguez	1.50	.70
❑ 44	Preston Wilson	.25	.11
❑ 45	Tom Seaver	1.00	.45
❑ 46	Robin Ventura	.25	.11
❑ 47	Mike Piazza	1.50	.70
❑ 48	Mike Hampton	.25	.11
❑ 49	Brooks Robinson	.60	.25
❑ 50	Frank Robinson	.60	.25
❑ 51	Cal Ripken	2.50	1.10
❑ 52	Albert Belle	.25	.11
❑ 53	Eddie Murray	.60	.25
❑ 54	Tony Gwynn	1.25	.55
❑ 55	Roberto Clemente	1.50	.70
❑ 56	Willie Stargell	.40	.18
❑ 57	Brian Giles	.25	.11
❑ 58	Jason Kendall	.25	.11
❑ 59	Mike Schmidt	1.25	.55
❑ 60	Bob Abreu	.25	.11
❑ 61	Scott Rolen	.60	.25
❑ 62	Curt Schilling	.60	.25
❑ 63	Johnny Bench	1.00	.45
❑ 64	Sean Casey	.40	.18
❑ 65	Barry Larkin	.60	.25
❑ 66	Ken Griffey Jr.	2.00	.90
❑ 67	George Brett	1.25	.55
❑ 68	Carlos Beltran	.25	.11
❑ 69	Nolan Ryan	3.00	1.35
❑ 70	Ivan Rodriguez	.60	.25
❑ 71	Rafael Palmeiro	.60	.25
❑ 72	Larry Walker	.40	.18
❑ 73	Todd Helton	.75	.35
❑ 74	Jeff Cirillo	.25	.11
❑ 75	Carl Everett	.25	.11
❑ 76	Nomar Garciaparra	1.50	.70
❑ 77	Pedro Martinez	.75	.35
❑ 78	Harmon Killebrew	.60	.25
❑ 79	Corey Koskie	.25	.11
❑ 80	Ty Cobb	1.25	.55
❑ 81	Dean Palmer	.25	.11
❑ 82	Juan Gonzalez	.60	.25
❑ 83	Carlton Fisk	.60	.25
❑ 84	Frank Thomas	.75	.35
❑ 85	Magglio Ordonez	.25	.11
❑ 86	Lou Gehrig	2.00	.90
❑ 87	Babe Ruth	3.00	1.35
❑ 88	Derek Jeter	2.50	1.10
❑ 89	Roger Clemens	1.50	.70
❑ 90	Bernie Williams	.60	.25
❑ 91	Rick Ankiel Y2K	2.50	1.10
❑ 92	Kip Wells Y2K	2.00	.90
❑ 93	Pat Burrell Y2K	.60	.25
❑ 94	Mark Quinn Y2K	2.00	.90
❑ 95	Ruben Mateo Y2K	2.00	.90
❑ 96	Adam Kennedy Y2K	2.00	.90
❑ 97	Brad Penny Y2K	2.00	.90
❑ 98	K.Sasaki Y2K RC	2.50	1.10
❑ 99	Peter Bergeron Y2K	2.00	.90
❑ 100	Rafael Furcal Y2K	2.50	1.10
❑ 101	Eric Munson Y2K	2.00	.90
❑ 102	Nick Johnson Y2K	2.50	1.10
❑ 103	Rob Bell Y2K	2.00	.90
❑ 104	Vernon Wells Y2K	2.00	.90
❑ 105	Ben Petrick Y2K	2.00	.90
❑ 106	Babe Ruth 20C	8.00	3.60
❑ 107	Mark McGwire 20C	6.00	2.70
❑ 108	Nolan Ryan 20C	8.00	3.60
❑ 109	Hank Aaron 20C	4.00	1.80
❑ 110	Barry Bonds 20C	4.00	1.80
❑ 111	N.Garciaparra 20C	4.00	1.80
❑ 112	Roger Clemens 20C	4.00	1.80
❑ 113	Johnny Bench 20C	2.50	1.10
❑ 114	Alex Rodriguez 20C	4.00	1.80
❑ 115	Cal Ripken 20C	6.00	2.70
❑ 116	Willie Mays 20C	4.00	1.80
❑ 117	Mike Piazza 20C	4.00	1.80
❑ 118	Reggie Jackson 20C	2.00	.90
❑ 119	Tony Gwynn 20C	3.00	1.35
❑ 120	Cy Young 20C	2.00	.90
❑ 121	George Brett 20C	3.00	1.35
❑ 122	Greg Maddux 20C	4.00	1.80
❑ 123	Yogi Berra 20C	2.00	.90
❑ 124	Sammy Sosa 20C	3.00	1.35
❑ 125	Randy Johnson 20C	2.00	.90
❑ 126	Bob Gibson 20C	2.00	.90
❑ 127	Lou Gehrig 20C	5.00	2.20
❑ 128	Ken Griffey Jr. 20C	5.00	2.20
❑ 129	Derek Jeter 20C	6.00	2.70
❑ 130	Mike Schmidt 20C	3.00	1.35
❑ 131	Pedro Martinez 20C	2.00	.90
❑ 132	Jackie Robinson 20C	3.00	1.35
❑ 133	Jose Canseco 20C	2.00	.90
❑ 134	Ty Cobb 20C	3.00	1.35
❑ 135	Stan Musial 20C	2.50	1.10

2001 Upper Deck Legends

	MINT	NRMT
COMPLETE SET (90)	20.00	9.00

#	Player	MINT	NRMT
❑ 1	Darin Erstad	.60	.25
❑ 2	Troy Glaus	.60	.25
❑ 3	Nolan Ryan	3.00	1.35
❑ 4	Reggie Jackson	.75	.35
❑ 5	Catfish Hunter	.40	.18
❑ 6	Jason Giambi	.60	.25
❑ 7	Tim Hudson	.60	.25
❑ 8	Miguel Tejada	.25	.11
❑ 9	Carlos Delgado	.60	.25
❑ 10	Shannon Stewart	.25	.11
❑ 11	Greg Vaughn	.25	.11
❑ 12	Larry Doby	.25	.11
❑ 13	Jim Thome	.60	.25
❑ 14	Juan Gonzalez	.60	.25
❑ 15	Roberto Alomar	.60	.25
❑ 16	Edgar Martinez	.40	.18
❑ 17	John Olerud	.25	.11
❑ 18	Eddie Murray	.60	.25
❑ 19	Cal Ripken	2.50	1.10
❑ 20	Alex Rodriguez	1.50	.70
❑ 21	Ivan Rodriguez	.60	.25
❑ 22	Rafael Palmeiro	.60	.25
❑ 23	Jimmie Foxx	.75	.35
❑ 24	Cy Young	.75	.35
❑ 25	Manny Ramirez	.75	.35
❑ 26	Pedro Martinez	.75	.35
❑ 27	Nomar Garciaparra	1.50	.70
❑ 28	George Brett	1.25	.55
❑ 29	Mike Sweeney	.25	.11
❑ 30	Jermaine Dye	.25	.11
❑ 31	Ty Cobb	1.25	.55
❑ 32	Dean Palmer	.25	.11
❑ 33	Harmon Killebrew	.60	.25
❑ 34	Matt Lawton	.25	.11
❑ 35	Luis Aparicio	.40	.18
❑ 36	Frank Thomas	.75	.35
❑ 37	Magglio Ordonez	.25	.11
❑ 38	David Wells	.25	.11
❑ 39	Mickey Mantle	3.00	1.35
❑ 40	Joe DiMaggio	2.50	1.10
❑ 41	Roger Maris	1.00	.45
❑ 42	Babe Ruth	3.00	1.35
❑ 43	Derek Jeter	2.50	1.10
❑ 44	Roger Clemens	1.50	.70
❑ 45	Bernie Williams	.60	.25
❑ 46	Jeff Bagwell	.75	.35
❑ 47	Richard Hidalgo	.25	.11
❑ 48	Warren Spahn	.60	.25
❑ 49	Greg Maddux	1.50	.70
❑ 50	Chipper Jones	1.25	.55
❑ 51	Andruw Jones	.60	.25
❑ 52	Robin Yount	.60	.25
❑ 53	Jeromy Burnitz	.25	.11
❑ 54	Jeffrey Hammonds	.25	.11
❑ 55	Ozzie Smith	.75	.35
❑ 56	Stan Musial	1.00	.45
❑ 57	Mark McGwire	2.50	1.10
❑ 58	Jim Edmonds	.40	.18

❑ 59	Sammy Sosa	1.25	.55
❑ 60	Ernie Banks	.75	.35
❑ 61	Kerry Wood	.60	.25
❑ 62	Randy Johnson	.75	.35
❑ 63	Luis Gonzalez	.60	.25
❑ 64	Don Drysdale	.40	.18
❑ 65	Jackie Robinson	1.25	.55
❑ 66	Gary Sheffield	.25	.11
❑ 67	Kevin Brown	.25	.11
❑ 68	Vladimir Guerrero	.75	.35
❑ 69	Willie Mays	1.50	.70
❑ 70	Mel Ott	.60	.25
❑ 71	Jeff Kent	.40	.18
❑ 72	Barry Bonds	1.50	.70
❑ 73	Preston Wilson	.25	.11
❑ 74	Ryan Dempster	.25	.11
❑ 75	Tom Seaver	1.00	.45
❑ 76	Mike Piazza	1.50	.70
❑ 77	Robin Ventura	.25	.11
❑ 78	Dave Winfield	.60	.25
❑ 79	Tony Gwynn	1.25	.55
❑ 80	Bob Abreu	.25	.11
❑ 81	Scott Rolen	.60	.25
❑ 82	Mike Schmidt	1.25	.55
❑ 83	Roberto Clemente	1.50	.70
❑ 84	Brian Giles	.25	.11
❑ 85	Ken Griffey Jr.	2.00	.90
❑ 86	Frank Robinson	.60	.25
❑ 87	Johnny Bench	1.00	.45
❑ 88	Todd Helton	.75	.35
❑ 89	Larry Walker	.40	.18
❑ 90	Mike Hampton	.25	.11

1999 Upper Deck MVP

		MINT	NRMT
COMPLETE SET (220)		25.00	11.00
❑ 1	Mo Vaughn	.15	.07
❑ 2	Tim Belcher	.10	.05
❑ 3	Jack McDowell	.10	.05
❑ 4	Troy Glaus	.40	.18
❑ 5	Darin Erstad	.40	.18
❑ 6	Tim Salmon	.15	.07
❑ 7	Jim Edmonds	.25	.11
❑ 8	Randy Johnson	.50	.23
❑ 9	Steve Finley	.15	.07
❑ 10	Travis Lee	.10	.05
❑ 11	Matt Williams	.25	.11
❑ 12	Todd Stottlemyre	.10	.05
❑ 13	Jay Bell	.15	.07
❑ 14	David Dellucci	.10	.05
❑ 15	Chipper Jones	.75	.35
❑ 16	Andruw Jones	.40	.18
❑ 17	Greg Maddux	1.00	.45
❑ 18	Tom Glavine	.40	.18
❑ 19	Javy Lopez	.15	.07
❑ 20	Brian Jordan	.15	.07
❑ 21	George Lombard	.10	.05
❑ 22	John Smoltz	.15	.07
❑ 23	Cal Ripken	1.50	.70
❑ 24	Charles Johnson	.15	.07
❑ 25	Albert Belle	.15	.07
❑ 26	Brady Anderson	.15	.07
❑ 27	Mike Mussina	.40	.18
❑ 28	Calvin Pickering	.10	.05
❑ 29	Ryan Minor	.10	.05
❑ 30	Jerry Hairston Jr.	.15	.07
❑ 31	Nomar Garciaparra	1.00	.45
❑ 32	Pedro Martinez	.50	.23
❑ 33	Jason Varitek	.15	.07
❑ 34	Troy O'Leary	.10	.05
❑ 35	Donnie Sadler	.10	.05
❑ 36	Mark Portugal	.10	.05
❑ 37	John Valentin	.10	.05
❑ 38	Kerry Wood	.40	.18
❑ 39	Sammy Sosa	.75	.35
❑ 40	Mark Grace	.40	.18
❑ 41	Henry Rodriguez	.10	.05
❑ 42	Rod Beck	.10	.05
❑ 43	Benito Santiago	.10	.05
❑ 44	Kevin Tapani	.10	.05
❑ 45	Frank Thomas	.50	.23
❑ 46	Mike Caruso	.10	.05
❑ 47	Magglio Ordonez	.25	.11
❑ 48	Paul Konerko	.15	.07
❑ 49	Ray Durham	.15	.07
❑ 50	Jim Parque	.10	.05
❑ 51	Carlos Lee	.15	.07
❑ 52	Denny Neagle	.10	.05
❑ 53	Pete Harnisch	.10	.05
❑ 54	Michael Tucker	.10	.05
❑ 55	Sean Casey	.25	.11
❑ 56	Eddie Taubensee	.10	.05
❑ 57	Barry Larkin	.40	.18
❑ 58	Pokey Reese	.10	.05
❑ 59	Sandy Alomar Jr.	.15	.07
❑ 60	Roberto Alomar	.40	.18
❑ 61	Bartolo Colon	.15	.07
❑ 62	Kenny Lofton	.15	.07
❑ 63	Omar Vizquel	.15	.07
❑ 64	Travis Fryman	.15	.07
❑ 65	Jim Thome	.40	.18
❑ 66	Manny Ramirez	.50	.23
❑ 67	Jaret Wright	.10	.05
❑ 68	Darryl Kile	.15	.07
❑ 69	Kirt Manwaring	.10	.05
❑ 70	Vinny Castilla	.15	.07
❑ 71	Todd Helton	.50	.23
❑ 72	Dante Bichette	.15	.07
❑ 73	Larry Walker	.25	.11
❑ 74	Derrick Gibson	.10	.05
❑ 75	Gabe Kapler	.15	.07
❑ 76	Dean Palmer	.15	.07
❑ 77	Matt Anderson	.10	.05
❑ 78	Bobby Higginson	.15	.07
❑ 79	Damion Easley	.10	.05
❑ 80	Tony Clark	.15	.07
❑ 81	Juan Encarnacion	.15	.07
❑ 82	Livan Hernandez	.10	.05
❑ 83	Alex Gonzalez	.10	.05
❑ 84	Preston Wilson	.15	.07
❑ 85	Derrek Lee	.15	.07
❑ 86	Mark Kotsay	.10	.05
❑ 87	Todd Dunwoody	.10	.05
❑ 88	Cliff Floyd	.15	.07
❑ 89	Ken Caminiti	.15	.07
❑ 90	Jeff Bagwell	.50	.23
❑ 91	Moises Alou	.15	.07
❑ 92	Craig Biggio	.25	.11
❑ 93	Billy Wagner	.10	.05
❑ 94	Richard Hidalgo	.15	.07
❑ 95	Derek Bell	.10	.05
❑ 96	Hipolito Pichardo	.10	.05
❑ 97	Jeff King	.10	.05
❑ 98	Carlos Beltran	.15	.07
❑ 99	Jeremy Giambi	.10	.05
❑ 100	Larry Sutton	.10	.05
❑ 101	Johnny Damon	.15	.07
❑ 102	Dee Brown	.10	.05
❑ 103	Kevin Brown	.25	.11
❑ 104	Chan Ho Park	.15	.07
❑ 105	Raul Mondesi	.15	.07
❑ 106	Eric Karros	.15	.07
❑ 107	Adrian Beltre	.15	.07
❑ 108	Devon White	.10	.05
❑ 109	Gary Sheffield	.15	.07
❑ 110	Sean Berry	.10	.05
❑ 111	Alex Ochoa	.10	.05
❑ 112	Marquis Grissom	.10	.05
❑ 113	Fernando Vina	.10	.05
❑ 114	Jeff Cirillo	.15	.07
❑ 115	Geoff Jenkins	.15	.07
❑ 116	Jeromy Burnitz	.15	.07
❑ 117	Brad Radke	.15	.07
❑ 118	Eric Milton	.15	.07
❑ 119	A.J. Pierzynski	.10	.05
❑ 120	Todd Walker	.10	.05
❑ 121	David Ortiz	.15	.07
❑ 122	Corey Koskie	.15	.07
❑ 123	Vladimir Guerrero	.50	.23
❑ 124	Rondell White	.15	.07
❑ 125	Brad Fullmer	.15	.07
❑ 126	Ugueth Urbina	.10	.05
❑ 127	Dustin Hermanson	.10	.05
❑ 128	Michael Barrett	.10	.05
❑ 129	Fernando Seguignol	.10	.05
❑ 130	Mike Piazza	1.00	.45
❑ 131	Rickey Henderson	.75	.35
❑ 132	Rey Ordonez	.10	.05
❑ 133	John Olerud	.15	.07
❑ 134	Robin Ventura	.15	.07
❑ 135	Hideo Nomo	.40	.18
❑ 136	Mike Kinkade	.10	.05
❑ 137	Al Leiter	.15	.07
❑ 138	Brian McRae	.10	.05
❑ 139	Derek Jeter	1.50	.70
❑ 140	Bernie Williams	.40	.18
❑ 141	Paul O'Neill	.40	.18
❑ 142	Scott Brosius	.15	.07
❑ 143	Tino Martinez	.15	.07
❑ 144	Roger Clemens	1.00	.45
❑ 145	Orlando Hernandez	.15	.07
❑ 146	Mariano Rivera	.15	.07
❑ 147	Ricky Ledee	.10	.05
❑ 148	A.J. Hinch	.10	.05
❑ 149	Ben Grieve	.15	.07
❑ 150	Eric Chavez	.15	.07
❑ 151	Miguel Tejada	.15	.07
❑ 152	Matt Stairs	.10	.05
❑ 153	Ryan Christenson	.10	.05
❑ 154	Jason Giambi	.40	.18
❑ 155	Curt Schilling	.40	.18
❑ 156	Scott Rolen	.40	.18
❑ 157	Pat Burrell RC	1.00	.45
❑ 158	Doug Glanville	.10	.05
❑ 159	Bobby Abreu	.15	.07
❑ 160	Rico Brogna	.10	.05
❑ 161	Ron Gant	.15	.07
❑ 162	Jason Kendall	.15	.07
❑ 163	Aramis Ramirez	.15	.07
❑ 164	Jose Guillen	.10	.05
❑ 165	Emil Brown	.10	.05
❑ 166	Pat Meares	.10	.05
❑ 167	Kevin Young	.15	.07
❑ 168	Brian Giles	.15	.07
❑ 169	Mark McGwire	1.50	.70
❑ 170	J.D. Drew	.40	.18
❑ 171	Edgar Renteria	.10	.05
❑ 172	Fernando Tatis	.10	.05
❑ 173	Matt Morris	.15	.07
❑ 174	Eli Marrero	.10	.05
❑ 175	Ray Lankford	.10	.05
❑ 176	Tony Gwynn	.75	.35
❑ 177	Sterling Hitchcock	.10	.05
❑ 178	Ruben Rivera	.10	.05
❑ 179	Wally Joyner	.15	.07
❑ 180	Trevor Hoffman	.15	.07
❑ 181	Jim Leyritz	.10	.05
❑ 182	Carlos Hernandez	.10	.05
❑ 183	Barry Bonds UER Uniform number 24 on front, 25 on back	1.00	.45
❑ 184	Ellis Burks	.15	.07
❑ 185	F.P. Santangelo	.10	.05
❑ 186	J.T. Snow	.15	.07
❑ 187	Ramon E.Martinez RC	.10	.05
❑ 188	Jeff Kent	.25	.11
❑ 189	Robb Nen	.10	.05
❑ 190	Ken Griffey Jr.	1.25	.55
❑ 191	Alex Rodriguez	1.00	.45
❑ 192	Shane Monahan	.10	.05
❑ 193	Carlos Guillen	.10	.05
❑ 194	Edgar Martinez	.25	.11
❑ 195	David Segui	.10	.05
❑ 196	Jose Mesa	.10	.05
❑ 197	Jose Canseco	.40	.18

❑ 198 Rolando Arrojo .10 .05
❑ 199 Wade Boggs .40 .18
❑ 200 Fred McGriff .25 .11
❑ 201 Quinton McCracken .10 .05
❑ 202 Bobby Smith .10 .05
❑ 203 Bubba Trammell .10 .05
❑ 204 Juan Gonzalez .40 .18
❑ 205 Ivan Rodriguez .40 .18
❑ 206 Rafael Palmeiro .40 .18
❑ 207 Royce Clayton .10 .05
❑ 208 Rick Helling .10 .05
❑ 209 Todd Zeile .15 .07
❑ 210 Rusty Greer .15 .07
❑ 211 David Wells .15 .07
❑ 212 Roy Halladay .10 .05
❑ 213 Carlos Delgado .40 .18
❑ 214 Darrin Fletcher .10 .05
❑ 215 Shawn Green .40 .18
❑ 216 Kevin Witt .10 .05
❑ 217 Jose Cruz Jr. .15 .07
❑ 218 Ken Griffey Jr. CL .60 .25
❑ 219 Sammy Sosa CL .40 .18
❑ 220 Mark McGwire CL .75 .35
❑ S3 Ken Griffey Jr. Sample .75 .35

2000 Upper Deck MVP

	MINT	NRMT
COMPLETE SET (220)	25.00	11.00

❑ 1 Garret Anderson .15 .07
❑ 2 Mo Vaughn .15 .07
❑ 3 Tim Salmon .15 .07
❑ 4 Ramon Ortiz .15 .07
❑ 5 Darin Erstad .40 .18
❑ 6 Troy Glaus .40 .18
❑ 7 Troy Percival .10 .05
❑ 8 Jeff Bagwell .50 .23
❑ 9 Ken Caminiti .15 .07
❑ 10 Daryle Ward .10 .05
❑ 11 Craig Biggio .25 .11
❑ 12 Jose Lima .10 .05
❑ 13 Moises Alou .15 .07
❑ 14 Octavio Dotel .10 .05
❑ 15 Ben Grieve .15 .07
❑ 16 Jason Giambi .40 .18
❑ 17 Tim Hudson .40 .18
❑ 18 Eric Chavez .15 .07
❑ 19 Matt Stairs .10 .05
❑ 20 Miguel Tejada .15 .07
❑ 21 John Jaha .10 .05
❑ 22 Chipper Jones .75 .35
❑ 23 Kevin Millwood .10 .05
❑ 24 Brian Jordan .15 .07
❑ 25 Andruw Jones .40 .18
❑ 26 Andres Galarraga .25 .11
❑ 27 Greg Maddux 1.00 .45
❑ 28 Reggie Sanders .10 .05
❑ 29 Javy Lopez .15 .07
❑ 30 Jeromy Burnitz .15 .07
❑ 31 Kevin Barker .10 .05
❑ 32 Jose Hernandez .10 .05
❑ 33 Ron Belliard .10 .05
❑ 34 Henry Blanco .10 .05
❑ 35 Marquis Grissom .10 .05
❑ 36 Geoff Jenkins .15 .07
❑ 37 Carlos Delgado .40 .18
❑ 38 Raul Mondesi .15 .07
❑ 39 Roy Halladay .10 .05
❑ 40 Tony Batista .15 .07
❑ 41 David Wells .15 .07
❑ 42 Shannon Stewart .15 .07
❑ 43 Vernon Wells .15 .07
❑ 44 Sammy Sosa .75 .35
❑ 45 Ismael Valdes .10 .05
❑ 46 Joe Girardi .10 .05
❑ 47 Mark Grace .40 .18
❑ 48 Henry Rodriguez .10 .05
❑ 49 Kerry Wood .40 .18
❑ 50 Eric Young .10 .05
❑ 51 Mark McGwire 1.50 .70
❑ 52 Darryl Kile .15 .07
❑ 53 Fernando Vina .10 .05
❑ 54 Ray Lankford .10 .05
❑ 55 J.D. Drew .40 .18
❑ 56 Fernando Tatis .10 .05
❑ 57 Rick Ankiel .40 .18
❑ 58 Matt Williams .25 .11
❑ 59 Erubiel Durazo .15 .07
❑ 60 Tony Womack .10 .05
❑ 61 Jay Bell .15 .07
❑ 62 Randy Johnson .50 .23
❑ 63 Steve Finley .15 .07
❑ 64 Matt Mantei .10 .05
❑ 65 Luis Gonzalez .40 .18
❑ 66 Gary Sheffield .15 .07
❑ 67 Eric Gagne .10 .05
❑ 68 Adrian Beltre .15 .07
❑ 69 Mark Grudzielanek .10 .05
❑ 70 Kevin Brown .15 .07
❑ 71 Chan Ho Park .15 .07
❑ 72 Shawn Green .40 .18
❑ 73 Vinny Castilla .15 .07
❑ 74 Fred McGriff .25 .11
❑ 75 Wilson Alvarez .10 .05
❑ 76 Greg Vaughn .15 .07
❑ 77 Gerald Williams .10 .05
❑ 78 Ryan Rupe .10 .05
❑ 79 Jose Canseco .40 .18
❑ 80 Vladimir Guerrero .50 .23
❑ 81 Dustin Hermanson .10 .05
❑ 82 Michael Barrett .10 .05
❑ 83 Rondell White .15 .07
❑ 84 Tony Armas Jr. .15 .07
❑ 85 Wilton Guerrero .10 .05
❑ 86 Jose Vidro .15 .07
❑ 87 Barry Bonds 1.00 .45
❑ 88 Russ Ortiz .10 .05
❑ 89 Ellis Burks .15 .07
❑ 90 Jeff Kent .25 .11
❑ 91 Russ Davis .10 .05
❑ 92 J.T. Snow .15 .07
❑ 93 Roberto Alomar .40 .18
❑ 94 Manny Ramirez .50 .23
❑ 95 Chuck Finley .15 .07
❑ 96 Kenny Lofton .15 .07
❑ 97 Jim Thome .40 .18
❑ 98 Bartolo Colon .15 .07
❑ 99 Omar Vizquel .15 .07
❑ 100 Richie Sexson .15 .07
❑ 101 Mike Cameron .15 .07
❑ 102 Brett Tomko .10 .05
❑ 103 Edgar Martinez .25 .11
❑ 104 Alex Rodriguez 1.00 .45
❑ 105 John Olerud .15 .07
❑ 106 Freddy Garcia .25 .11
❑ 107 Kazuhiro Sasaki RC 1.25 .55
❑ 108 Preston Wilson .15 .07
❑ 109 Luis Castillo .10 .05
❑ 110 A.J. Burnett .15 .07
❑ 111 Mike Lowell .10 .05
❑ 112 Cliff Floyd .15 .07
❑ 113 Brad Penny .15 .07
❑ 114 Alex Gonzalez .10 .05
❑ 115 Mike Piazza 1.00 .45
❑ 116 Derek Bell .10 .05
❑ 117 Edgardo Alfonzo .15 .07
❑ 118 Rickey Henderson .75 .35
❑ 119 Todd Zeile .15 .07
❑ 120 Mike Hampton .15 .07
❑ 121 Al Leiter .15 .07
❑ 122 Robin Ventura .15 .07
❑ 123 Cal Ripken 1.50 .70
❑ 124 Mike Mussina .40 .18
❑ 125 B.J. Surhoff .15 .07
❑ 126 Jerry Hairston Jr. .10 .05
❑ 127 Brady Anderson .15 .07
❑ 128 Albert Belle .15 .07
❑ 129 Sidney Ponson .10 .05
❑ 130 Tony Gwynn .75 .35
❑ 131 Ryan Klesko .15 .07
❑ 132 Sterling Hitchcock .10 .05
❑ 133 Eric Owens .10 .05
❑ 134 Trevor Hoffman .15 .07
❑ 135 Al Martin .10 .05
❑ 136 Bret Boone .15 .07
❑ 137 Brian Giles .15 .07
❑ 138 Chad Hermansen .10 .05
❑ 139 Kevin Young .10 .05
❑ 140 Kris Benson .15 .07
❑ 141 Warren Morris .10 .05
❑ 142 Jason Kendall .15 .07
❑ 143 Wil Cordero .10 .05
❑ 144 Scott Rolen .40 .18
❑ 145 Curt Schilling .40 .18
❑ 146 Doug Glanville .10 .05
❑ 147 Mike Lieberthal .15 .07
❑ 148 Mike Jackson .10 .05
❑ 149 Rico Brogna .10 .05
❑ 150 Andy Ashby .10 .05
❑ 151 Bob Abreu .15 .07
❑ 152 Sean Casey .25 .11
❑ 153 Pete Harnisch .10 .05
❑ 154 Dante Bichette .15 .07
❑ 155 Pokey Reese .10 .05
❑ 156 Aaron Boone .10 .05
❑ 157 Ken Griffey Jr. 1.25 .55
❑ 158 Barry Larkin .40 .18
❑ 159 Scott Williamson .10 .05
❑ 160 Carlos Beltran .15 .07
❑ 161 Jermaine Dye .15 .07
❑ 162 Jose Rosado .10 .05
❑ 163 Joe Randa .10 .05
❑ 164 Johnny Damon .15 .07
❑ 165 Mike Sweeney .15 .07
❑ 166 Mark Quinn .15 .07
❑ 167 Ivan Rodriguez .40 .18
❑ 168 Rusty Greer .15 .07
❑ 169 Ruben Mateo .15 .07
❑ 170 Doug Davis .10 .05
❑ 171 Gabe Kapler .15 .07
❑ 172 Justin Thompson .10 .05
❑ 173 Rafael Palmeiro .40 .18
❑ 174 Larry Walker .25 .11
❑ 175 Neifi Perez .10 .05
❑ 176 Rolando Arrojo .10 .05
❑ 177 Jeffrey Hammonds .10 .05
❑ 178 Todd Helton .50 .23
❑ 179 Pedro Astacio .10 .05
❑ 180 Jeff Cirillo .15 .07
❑ 181 Pedro Martinez .50 .23
❑ 182 Carl Everett .15 .07
❑ 183 Troy O'Leary .10 .05
❑ 184 Nomar Garciaparra 1.00 .45
❑ 185 Jose Offerman .10 .05
❑ 186 Bret Saberhagen .15 .07
❑ 187 Trot Nixon .15 .07
❑ 188 Jason Varitek .15 .07
❑ 189 Todd Walker .10 .05
❑ 190 Eric Milton .15 .07
❑ 191 Chad Allen .10 .05
❑ 192 Jacque Jones .15 .07
❑ 193 Brad Radke .15 .07
❑ 194 Corey Koskie .15 .07
❑ 195 Joe Mays .15 .07
❑ 196 Juan Gonzalez .40 .18
❑ 197 Jeff Weaver .15 .07
❑ 198 Juan Encarnacion .15 .07
❑ 199 Deivi Cruz .10 .05
❑ 200 Damion Easley .10 .05
❑ 201 Tony Clark .15 .07
❑ 202 Dean Palmer .15 .07
❑ 203 Frank Thomas .50 .23
❑ 204 Carlos Lee .15 .07
❑ 205 Mike Sirotka .10 .05
❑ 206 Kip Wells .15 .07
❑ 207 Magglio Ordonez .15 .07
❑ 208 Paul Konerko .15 .07
❑ 209 Chris Singleton .10 .05
❑ 210 Derek Jeter 1.50 .70

❑ 211	Tino Martinez	.15	.07
❑ 212	Mariano Rivera	.15	.07
❑ 213	Roger Clemens	1.00	.45
❑ 214	Nick Johnson	.40	.18
❑ 215	Paul O'Neill	.40	.18
❑ 216	Bernie Williams	.40	.18
❑ 217	David Cone	.15	.07
❑ 218	Ken Griffey Jr. CL	.60	.25
❑ 219	Sammy Sosa CL	.40	.18
❑ 220	Mark McGwire CL	.75	.35

2001 Upper Deck MVP

	MINT	NRMT
COMPLETE SET (330)	40.00	18.00

	Player	MINT	NRMT
❑ 1	Mo Vaughn	.15	.07
❑ 2	Troy Percival	.10	.05
❑ 3	Adam Kennedy	.10	.05
❑ 4	Darin Erstad	.40	.18
❑ 5	Tim Salmon	.15	.07
❑ 6	Bengie Molina	.10	.05
❑ 7	Troy Glaus	.40	.18
❑ 8	Garret Anderson	.15	.07
❑ 9	Ismael Valdes	.10	.05
❑ 10	Glenallen Hill	.10	.05
❑ 11	Tim Hudson	.40	.18
❑ 12	Eric Chavez	.15	.07
❑ 13	Johnny Damon	.15	.07
❑ 14	Barry Zito	.40	.18
❑ 15	Jason Giambi	.40	.18
❑ 16	Terrence Long	.15	.07
❑ 17	Jason Hart	.25	.11
❑ 18	Jose Ortiz	.25	.11
❑ 19	Miguel Tejada	.15	.07
❑ 20	Jason Isringhausen	.10	.05
❑ 21	Adam Piatt	.15	.07
❑ 22	Jeremy Giambi	.10	.05
❑ 23	Tony Batista	.15	.07
❑ 24	Darrin Fletcher	.10	.05
❑ 25	Mike Sirotka	.10	.05
❑ 26	Carlos Delgado	.40	.18
❑ 27	Billy Koch	.10	.05
❑ 28	Shannon Stewart	.15	.07
❑ 29	Raul Mondesi	.15	.07
❑ 30	Brad Fullmer	.15	.07
❑ 31	Jose Cruz Jr.	.15	.07
❑ 32	Kelvim Escobar	.10	.05
❑ 33	Greg Vaughn	.15	.07
❑ 34	Aubrey Huff	.10	.05
❑ 35	Albie Lopez	.10	.05
❑ 36	Gerald Williams	.10	.05
❑ 37	Ben Grieve	.15	.07
❑ 38	John Flaherty	.10	.05
❑ 39	Fred McGriff	.25	.11
❑ 40	Ryan Rupe	.10	.05
❑ 41	Travis Harper	.10	.05
❑ 42	Steve Cox	.10	.05
❑ 43	Roberto Alomar	.40	.18
❑ 44	Jim Thome	.40	.18
❑ 45	Russell Branyan	.15	.07
❑ 46	Bartolo Colon	.15	.07
❑ 47	Omar Vizquel	.15	.07
❑ 48	Travis Fryman	.15	.07
❑ 49	Kenny Lofton	.15	.07
❑ 50	Chuck Finley	.15	.07
❑ 51	Ellis Burks	.15	.07
❑ 52	Eddie Taubensee	.10	.05
❑ 53	Juan Gonzalez	.40	.18
❑ 54	Edgar Martinez	.25	.11
❑ 55	Aaron Sele	.15	.07
❑ 56	John Olerud	.15	.07
❑ 57	Jay Buhner	.15	.07
❑ 58	Mike Cameron	.15	.07
❑ 59	John Halama	.10	.05
❑ 60	Ichiro Suzuki RC	15.00	6.75
❑ 61	David Bell	.10	.05
❑ 62	Freddy Garcia	.15	.07
❑ 63	Carlos Guillen	.10	.05
❑ 64	Bret Boone	.15	.07
❑ 65	Al Martin	.10	.05
❑ 66	Cal Ripken	1.50	.70
❑ 67	Delino DeShields	.10	.05
❑ 68	Chris Richard	.15	.07
❑ 69	Sean Douglass RC	.40	.18
❑ 70	Melvin Mora	.10	.05
❑ 71	Luis Matos	.10	.05
❑ 72	Sidney Ponson	.10	.05
❑ 73	Mike Bordick	.10	.05
❑ 74	Brady Anderson	.15	.07
❑ 75	David Segui	.10	.05
❑ 76	Jeff Conine	.10	.05
❑ 77	Alex Rodriguez	1.00	.45
❑ 78	Gabe Kapler	.15	.07
❑ 79	Ivan Rodriguez	.40	.18
❑ 80	Rick Helling	.10	.05
❑ 81	Kenny Rogers	.10	.05
❑ 82	Andres Galarraga	.25	.11
❑ 83	Rusty Greer	.15	.07
❑ 84	Justin Thompson	.10	.05
❑ 85	Ken Caminiti	.15	.07
❑ 86	Rafael Palmeiro	.40	.18
❑ 87	Ruben Mateo	.15	.07
❑ 88	Travis Hafner RC	.50	.23
❑ 89	Manny Ramirez	.50	.23
❑ 90	Pedro Martinez	.50	.23
❑ 91	Carl Everett	.15	.07
❑ 92	Dante Bichette	.15	.07
❑ 93	Derek Lowe	.10	.05
❑ 94	Jason Varitek	.15	.07
❑ 95	Nomar Garciaparra	1.00	.45
❑ 96	David Cone	.15	.07
❑ 97	Tomokazu Ohka	.15	.07
❑ 98	Troy O'Leary	.10	.05
❑ 99	Trot Nixon	.15	.07
❑ 100	Jermaine Dye	.15	.07
❑ 101	Joe Randa	.10	.05
❑ 102	Jeff Suppan	.10	.05
❑ 103	Roberto Hernandez	.10	.05
❑ 104	Mike Sweeney	.15	.07
❑ 105	Mac Suzuki	.15	.07
❑ 106	Carlos Febles	.10	.05
❑ 107	Jose Rosado	.10	.05
❑ 108	Mark Quinn	.15	.07
❑ 109	Carlos Beltran	.15	.07
❑ 110	Dean Palmer	.15	.07
❑ 111	Mitch Meluskey	.10	.05
❑ 112	Bobby Higginson	.15	.07
❑ 113	Brandon Inge	.15	.07
❑ 114	Tony Clark	.15	.07
❑ 115	Brian Moehler	.10	.05
❑ 116	Juan Encarnacion	.15	.07
❑ 117	Damion Easley	.10	.05
❑ 118	Roger Cedeno	.10	.05
❑ 119	Jeff Weaver	.15	.07
❑ 120	Matt Lawton	.15	.07
❑ 121	Jay Canizaro	.10	.05
❑ 122	Eric Milton	.15	.07
❑ 123	Corey Koskie	.15	.07
❑ 124	Mark Redman	.10	.05
❑ 125	Jacque Jones	.15	.07
❑ 126	Brad Radke	.15	.07
❑ 127	Cristian Guzman	.15	.07
❑ 128	Joe Mays	.15	.07
❑ 129	Denny Hocking	.10	.05
❑ 130	Frank Thomas	.50	.23
❑ 131	David Wells	.15	.07
❑ 132	Ray Durham	.15	.07
❑ 133	Paul Konerko	.15	.07
❑ 134	Joe Crede	.15	.07
❑ 135	Jim Parque	.10	.05
❑ 136	Carlos Lee	.15	.07
❑ 137	Magglio Ordonez	.15	.07
❑ 138	Sandy Alomar Jr.	.15	.07
❑ 139	Chris Singleton	.10	.05
❑ 140	Jose Valentin	.10	.05
❑ 141	Roger Clemens	1.00	.45
❑ 142	Derek Jeter	1.50	.70
❑ 143	Orlando Hernandez	.15	.07
❑ 144	Tino Martinez	.15	.07
❑ 145	Bernie Williams	.40	.18
❑ 146	Jorge Posada	.15	.07
❑ 147	Mariano Rivera	.15	.07
❑ 148	David Justice	.25	.11
❑ 149	Paul O'Neill	.40	.18
❑ 150	Mike Mussina	.40	.18
❑ 151	Christian Parker RC	.40	.18
❑ 152	Andy Pettitte	.15	.07
❑ 153	Alfonso Soriano	.40	.18
❑ 154	Jeff Bagwell	.50	.23
❑ 155	Morgan Ensberg RC	.75	.35
❑ 156	Daryle Ward	.10	.05
❑ 157	Craig Biggio	.25	.11
❑ 158	Richard Hidalgo	.15	.07
❑ 159	Shane Reynolds	.10	.05
❑ 160	Scott Elarton	.10	.05
❑ 161	Julio Lugo	.10	.05
❑ 162	Moises Alou	.15	.07
❑ 163	Lance Berkman	.40	.18
❑ 164	Chipper Jones	.75	.35
❑ 165	Greg Maddux	1.00	.45
❑ 166	Javy Lopez	.15	.07
❑ 167	Andruw Jones	.40	.18
❑ 168	Rafael Furcal	.15	.07
❑ 169	Brian Jordan	.15	.07
❑ 170	Wes Helms	.10	.05
❑ 171	Tom Glavine	.40	.18
❑ 172	B.J. Surhoff	.15	.07
❑ 173	John Smoltz	.15	.07
❑ 174	Quilvio Veras	.10	.05
❑ 175	Rico Brogna	.10	.05
❑ 176	Jeromy Burnitz	.15	.07
❑ 177	Jeff D'Amico	.10	.05
❑ 178	Geoff Jenkins	.15	.07
❑ 179	Henry Blanco	.10	.05
❑ 180	Mark Loretta	.10	.05
❑ 181	Richie Sexson	.15	.07
❑ 182	Jimmy Haynes	.10	.05
❑ 183	Jeffrey Hammonds	.10	.05
❑ 184	Ron Belliard	.10	.05
❑ 185	Tyler Houston	.10	.05
❑ 186	Mark McGwire	1.50	.70
❑ 187	Rick Ankiel	.25	.11
❑ 188	Darryl Kile	.10	.05
❑ 189	Jim Edmonds	.25	.11
❑ 190	Mike Matheny	.10	.05
❑ 191	Edgar Renteria	.10	.05
❑ 192	Ray Lankford	.10	.05
❑ 193	Garrett Stephenson	.10	.05
❑ 194	J.D. Drew	.40	.18
❑ 195	Fernando Vina	.10	.05
❑ 196	Dustin Hermanson	.10	.05
❑ 197	Sammy Sosa	.75	.35
❑ 198	Corey Patterson	.15	.07
❑ 199	Jon Lieber	.10	.05
❑ 200	Kerry Wood	.40	.18
❑ 201	Todd Hundley	.10	.05
❑ 202	Kevin Tapani	.10	.05
❑ 203	Rondell White	.15	.07
❑ 204	Eric Young	.10	.05
❑ 205	Matt Stairs	.10	.05
❑ 206	Bill Mueller	.10	.05
❑ 207	Randy Johnson	.50	.23
❑ 208	Mark Grace	.40	.18
❑ 209	Jay Bell	.15	.07
❑ 210	Curt Schilling	.40	.18
❑ 211	Erubiel Durazo	.10	.05
❑ 212	Luis Gonzalez	.40	.18
❑ 213	Steve Finley	.15	.07
❑ 214	Matt Williams	.25	.11
❑ 215	Reggie Sanders	.10	.05
❑ 216	Tony Womack	.10	.05
❑ 217	Gary Sheffield	.15	.07
❑ 218	Kevin Brown	.15	.07
❑ 219	Adrian Beltre	.15	.07
❑ 220	Shawn Green	.40	.18
❑ 221	Darren Dreifort	.10	.05
❑ 222	Chan Ho Park	.15	.07
❑ 223	Eric Karros	.15	.07
❑ 224	Alex Cora	.10	.05

No.	Player	MINT	NRMT
❑ 225	Mark Grudzielanek	.15	.07
❑ 226	Andy Ashby	.10	.05
❑ 227	Vladimir Guerrero	.50	.23
❑ 228	Tony Armas Jr.	.15	.07
❑ 229	Fernando Tatis	.10	.05
❑ 230	Jose Vidro	.15	.07
❑ 231	Javier Vazquez	.15	.07
❑ 232	Lee Stevens	.10	.05
❑ 233	Milton Bradley	.10	.05
❑ 234	Carl Pavano	.10	.05
❑ 235	Peter Bergeron	.10	.05
❑ 236	Wilton Guerrero	.10	.05
❑ 237	Ugueth Urbina	.10	.05
❑ 238	Barry Bonds	1.00	.45
❑ 239	Livan Hernandez	.15	.07
❑ 240	Jeff Kent	.25	.11
❑ 241	Pedro Feliz	.10	.05
❑ 242	Bobby Estalella	.10	.05
❑ 243	J.T. Snow	.15	.07
❑ 244	Shawn Estes	.15	.07
❑ 245	Robb Nen	.15	.07
❑ 246	Rich Aurilia	.15	.07
❑ 247	Russ Ortiz	.15	.07
❑ 248	Preston Wilson	.15	.07
❑ 249	Brad Penny	.15	.07
❑ 250	Cliff Floyd	.15	.07
❑ 251	A.J. Burnett	.15	.07
❑ 252	Mike Lowell	.15	.07
❑ 253	Luis Castillo	.10	.05
❑ 254	Ryan Dempster	.15	.07
❑ 255	Derrek Lee	.10	.05
❑ 256	Charles Johnson	.15	.07
❑ 257	Pablo Ozuna	.10	.05
❑ 258	Antonio Alfonseca	.10	.05
❑ 259	Mike Piazza	1.00	.45
❑ 260	Robin Ventura	.15	.07
❑ 261	Al Leiter	.15	.07
❑ 262	Timo Perez	.10	.05
❑ 263	Edgardo Alfonzo	.15	.07
❑ 264	Jay Payton	.10	.05
❑ 265	Tsuyoshi Shinjo RC	1.50	.70
❑ 266	Todd Zeile	.15	.07
❑ 267	Armando Benitez	.15	.07
❑ 268	Glendon Rusch	.10	.05
❑ 269	Rey Ordonez	.10	.05
❑ 270	Kevin Appier	.15	.07
❑ 271	Tony Gwynn	.75	.35
❑ 272	Phil Nevin	.15	.07
❑ 273	Mark Kotsay	.15	.07
❑ 274	Ryan Klesko	.15	.07
❑ 275	Adam Eaton	.15	.07
❑ 276	Mike Darr	.10	.05
❑ 277	Damian Jackson	.10	.05
❑ 278	Woody Williams	.10	.05
❑ 279	Chris Gomez	.10	.05
❑ 280	Trevor Hoffman	.15	.07
❑ 281	Xavier Nady	.25	.11
❑ 282	Scott Rolen	.40	.18
❑ 283	Bruce Chen	.10	.05
❑ 284	Pat Burrell	.15	.07
❑ 285	Mike Lieberthal	.15	.07
❑ 286	Brandon Duckworth RC	1.25	.55
❑ 287	Travis Lee	.15	.07
❑ 288	Bobby Abreu	.15	.07
❑ 289	Jimmy Rollins	.15	.07
❑ 290	Robert Person	.10	.05
❑ 291	Randy Wolf	.10	.05
❑ 292	Jason Kendall	.15	.07
❑ 293	Derek Bell	.10	.05
❑ 294	Brian Giles	.15	.07
❑ 295	Kris Benson	.15	.07
❑ 296	John VanderWal	.10	.05
❑ 297	Todd Ritchie	.10	.05
❑ 298	Warren Morris	.10	.05
❑ 299	Kevin Young	.10	.05
❑ 300	Francisco Cordova	.10	.05
❑ 301	Aramis Ramirez	.15	.07
❑ 302	Ken Griffey Jr.	1.25	.55
❑ 303	Pete Harnisch	.10	.05
❑ 304	Aaron Boone	.10	.05
❑ 305	Sean Casey	.25	.11
❑ 306	Jackson Melian RC	.50	.23
❑ 307	Rob Bell	.10	.05
❑ 308	Barry Larkin	.40	.18
❑ 309	Dmitri Young	.15	.07
❑ 310	Danny Graves	.10	.05
❑ 311	Pokey Reese	.10	.05
❑ 312	Leo Estrella	.10	.05
❑ 313	Todd Helton	.50	.23
❑ 314	Mike Hampton	.15	.07
❑ 315	Juan Pierre	.15	.07
❑ 316	Brent Mayne	.10	.05
❑ 317	Larry Walker	.25	.11
❑ 318	Denny Neagle	.10	.05
❑ 319	Jeff Cirillo	.15	.07
❑ 320	Pedro Astacio	.10	.05
❑ 321	Todd Hollandsworth	.10	.05
❑ 322	Neifi Perez	.10	.05
❑ 323	Ron Gant	.10	.05
❑ 324	Todd Walker	.10	.05
❑ 325	Alex Rodriguez CL	.50	.23
❑ 326	Ken Griffey Jr. CL	.60	.25
❑ 327	Mark McGwire CL	.75	.35
❑ 328	Pedro Martinez CL	.25	.11
❑ 329	Derek Jeter CL	.75	.35
❑ 330	Mike Piazza CL	.50	.23

1999 Upper Deck Ovation

	MINT	NRMT
COMPLETE SET (90)	80.00	36.00
COMP.SET w/o SP's (60)	25.00	11.00
COMMON CARD (1-60)	.20	.09
COMMON WP (61-80)	1.50	.70
COMMON SS (81-90)	2.00	.90

No.	Player	MINT	NRMT
❑ 1	Ken Griffey Jr.	2.50	1.10
❑ 2	Rondell White	.30	.14
❑ 3	Tony Clark	.30	.14
❑ 4	Barry Bonds	2.00	.90
❑ 5	Larry Walker	.50	.23
❑ 6	Greg Vaughn	.30	.14
❑ 7	Mark Grace	.75	.35
❑ 8	John Olerud	.30	.14
❑ 9	Matt Williams	.50	.23
❑ 10	Craig Biggio	.50	.23
❑ 11	Quinton McCracken	.20	.09
❑ 12	Kerry Wood	.75	.35
❑ 13	Derek Jeter	3.00	1.35
❑ 14	Frank Thomas	1.00	.45
❑ 15	Tino Martinez	.30	.14
❑ 16	Albert Belle	.30	.14
❑ 17	Ben Grieve	.30	.14
❑ 18	Cal Ripken	3.00	1.35
❑ 19	Johnny Damon	.30	.14
❑ 20	Jose Cruz Jr.	.30	.14
❑ 21	Barry Larkin	.75	.35
❑ 22	Jason Giambi	.75	.35
❑ 23	Sean Casey	.50	.23
❑ 24	Scott Rolen	.75	.35
❑ 25	Jim Thome	.75	.35
❑ 26	Curt Schilling	.75	.35
❑ 27	Moises Alou	.30	.14
❑ 28	Alex Rodriguez	2.00	.90
❑ 29	Mark Kotsay	.20	.09
❑ 30	Darin Erstad	.75	.35
❑ 31	Mike Mussina	.75	.35
❑ 32	Todd Walker	.20	.09
❑ 33	Nomar Garciaparra	2.00	.90
❑ 34	Vladimir Guerrero	1.00	.45
❑ 35	Jeff Bagwell	1.00	.45
❑ 36	Mark McGwire	3.00	1.35
❑ 37	Travis Lee	.20	.09
❑ 38	Dean Palmer	.30	.14
❑ 39	Fred McGriff	.50	.23
❑ 40	Sammy Sosa	1.50	.70
❑ 41	Mike Piazza	2.00	.90
❑ 42	Andres Galarraga	.50	.23
❑ 43	Pedro Martinez	1.00	.45
❑ 44	Juan Gonzalez	.75	.35
❑ 45	Greg Maddux	2.00	.90
❑ 46	Jeromy Burnitz	.30	.14
❑ 47	Roger Clemens	2.00	.90
❑ 48	Vinny Castilla	.30	.14
❑ 49	Kevin Brown	.50	.23
❑ 50	Mo Vaughn	.30	.14
❑ 51	Raul Mondesi	.30	.14
❑ 52	Randy Johnson	1.00	.45
❑ 53	Ray Lankford	.20	.09
❑ 54	Jaret Wright	.20	.09
❑ 55	Tony Gwynn	1.50	.70
❑ 56	Chipper Jones	1.50	.70
❑ 57	Gary Sheffield	.30	.14
❑ 58	Ivan Rodriguez	.75	.35
❑ 59	Kenny Lofton	.30	.14
❑ 60	Jason Kendall	.30	.14
❑ 61	J.D. Drew WP	4.00	1.80
❑ 62	Gabe Kapler WP	1.50	.70
❑ 63	Adrian Beltre WP	1.50	.70
❑ 64	Carlos Beltran WP	1.50	.70
❑ 65	Eric Chavez WP	1.50	.70
❑ 66	Mike Lowell WP	1.50	.70
❑ 67	Troy Glaus WP	3.00	1.35
❑ 68	George Lombard WP	1.50	.70
❑ 69	Alex Gonzalez WP	1.50	.70
❑ 70	Mike Kinkade WP	1.50	.70
❑ 71	Jeremy Giambi WP	1.50	.70
❑ 72	Bruce Chen WP	1.50	.70
❑ 73	Preston Wilson WP	1.50	.70
❑ 74	Kevin Witt WP	1.50	.70
❑ 75	Carlos Guillen WP	1.50	.70
❑ 76	Ryan Minor WP	1.50	.70
❑ 77	Corey Koskie WP	1.50	.70
❑ 78	Robert Fick WP	1.50	.70
❑ 79	Michael Barrett WP	1.50	.70
❑ 80	Calvin Pickering WP	1.50	.70
❑ 81	Ken Griffey Jr. SS	6.00	2.70
❑ 82	Mark McGwire SS	8.00	3.60
❑ 83	Cal Ripken SS	8.00	3.60
❑ 84	Derek Jeter SS	8.00	3.60
❑ 85	Chipper Jones SS	4.00	1.80
❑ 86	Nomar Garciaparra SS	5.00	2.20
❑ 87	Sammy Sosa SS	4.00	1.80
❑ 88	Juan Gonzalez SS	2.00	.90
❑ 89	Mike Piazza SS	5.00	2.20
❑ 90	Alex Rodriguez SS	5.00	2.20
❑ MICL	M.Mantle Legendary Cut/1		

2000 Upper Deck Ovation

	MINT	NRMT
COMPLETE SET (89)	100.00	45.00
COMP.SET w/o SP's (60)	20.00	9.00
COMMON CARD (1-60)	.20	.09
COMMON WP (61-80)	2.00	.90
COMMON SS (81-90)	3.00	1.35

No.	Player	MINT	NRMT
❑ 1	Mo Vaughn	.30	.14
❑ 2	Troy Glaus	.75	.35
❑ 3	Jeff Bagwell	1.00	.45

	MINT	NRMT
❑ 4 Craig Biggio	.50	.23
❑ 5 Mike Hampton	.30	.14
❑ 6 Jason Giambi	.75	.35
❑ 7 Tim Hudson	.75	.35
❑ 8 Chipper Jones	1.50	.70
❑ 9 Greg Maddux	2.00	.90
❑ 10 Kevin Millwood	.20	.09
❑ 11 Brian Jordan	.30	.14
❑ 12 Jeromy Burnitz	.30	.14
❑ 13 David Wells	.30	.14
❑ 14 Carlos Delgado	.75	.35
❑ 15 Sammy Sosa	1.50	.70
❑ 16 Mark McGwire	3.00	1.35
❑ 17 Matt Williams	.50	.23
❑ 18 Randy Johnson	1.00	.45
❑ 19 Erubiel Durazo	.30	.14
❑ 20 Kevin Brown	.50	.23
❑ 21 Shawn Green	.75	.35
❑ 22 Gary Sheffield	.30	.14
❑ 23 Jose Canseco	.75	.35
❑ 24 Vladimir Guerrero	1.00	.45
❑ 25 Barry Bonds	2.00	.90
❑ 26 Manny Ramirez	1.00	.45
❑ 27 Roberto Alomar	.75	.35
❑ 28 Richie Sexson	.30	.14
❑ 29 Jim Thome	.75	.35
❑ 30 Alex Rodriguez	2.00	.90
❑ 31 Ken Griffey Jr.	2.50	1.10
❑ 32 Preston Wilson	.30	.14
❑ 33 Mike Piazza	2.00	.90
❑ 34 Al Leiter	.20	.09
❑ 35 Robin Ventura	.50	.23
❑ 36 Cal Ripken	3.00	1.35
❑ 37 Albert Belle	.30	.14
❑ 38 Tony Gwynn	1.50	.70
❑ 39 Brian Giles	.30	.14
❑ 40 Jason Kendall	.30	.14
❑ 41 Scott Rolen	.75	.35
❑ 42 Bob Abreu	.30	.14
❑ 43 Ken Griffey Jr. Reds	2.50	1.10
❑ 44 Sean Casey	.50	.23
❑ 45 Carlos Beltran	.30	.14
❑ 46 Gabe Kapler	.30	.14
❑ 47 Ivan Rodriguez	.75	.35
❑ 48 Rafael Palmeiro	.75	.35
❑ 49 Larry Walker	.50	.23
❑ 50 Nomar Garciaparra	2.00	.90
❑ 51 Pedro Martinez	1.00	.45
❑ 52 Eric Milton	.30	.14
❑ 53 Juan Gonzalez	.75	.35
❑ 54 Tony Clark	.30	.14
❑ 55 Frank Thomas	1.00	.45
❑ 56 Magglio Ordonez	.30	.14
❑ 57 Roger Clemens	2.00	.90
❑ 58 Derek Jeter	3.00	1.35
❑ 59 Bernie Williams	.75	.35
❑ 60 Orlando Hernandez	.30	.14
❑ 61 Rick Ankiel WP	5.00	2.20
❑ 62 Josh Beckett WP	6.00	2.70
❑ 63 Vernon Wells WP	2.50	1.10
❑ 64 Alfonso Soriano WP	5.00	2.20
❑ 65 Pat Burrell WP	5.00	2.20
❑ 66 Eric Munson WP	2.50	1.10
❑ 67 Chad Hutchinson WP	2.00	.90
❑ 68 Eric Gagne WP	2.00	.90
❑ 69 Peter Bergeron WP	2.00	.90
❑ 70 Ryan Anderson WP SP	200.00	90.00
❑ 71 A.J. Burnett WP	2.50	1.10
❑ 72 Jorge Toca WP	2.00	.90
❑ 73 Matt Riley WP	2.00	.90
❑ 74 Chad Hermansen WP	2.00	.90
❑ 75 Doug Davis WP	2.00	.90
❑ 76 Jim Morris WP	2.00	.90
❑ 77 Ben Petrick WP	2.00	.90
❑ 78 Mark Quinn WP	2.50	1.10
❑ 79 Ed Yarnall WP	2.00	.90
❑ 80 Ramon Ortiz WP	2.50	1.10
❑ 81 Ken Griffey Jr. SS	8.00	3.60
❑ 82 Mark McGwire SS	10.00	4.50
❑ 83 Derek Jeter SS	10.00	4.50
❑ 84 Jeff Bagwell SS	3.00	1.35
❑ 85 Nomar Garciaparra SS	6.00	2.70
❑ 86 Sammy Sosa SS	5.00	2.20
❑ 87 Mike Piazza SS	6.00	2.70
❑ 88 Alex Rodriguez SS	6.00	2.70
❑ 89 Cal Ripken SS	10.00	4.50
❑ 90 Pedro Martinez SS	3.00	1.35

2001 Upper Deck Ovation

	MINT	NRMT
COMP.SET w/o SP'S (60)	25.00	11.00
COMMON CARD (1-60)	.30	.14
COMMON WP (61-90)	8.00	3.60

❑ 1 Troy Glaus	.75	.35
❑ 2 Darin Erstad	.75	.35
❑ 3 Jason Giambi	.75	.35
❑ 4 Tim Hudson	.75	.35
❑ 5 Eric Chavez	.30	.14
❑ 6 Carlos Delgado	.75	.35
❑ 7 David Wells	.30	.14
❑ 8 Greg Vaughn	.30	.14
❑ 9 Omar Vizquel Travis Fryman is pictured on card front UER	.30	.14
❑ 10 Jim Thome	.75	.35
❑ 11 Roberto Alomar	.75	.35
❑ 12 John Olerud	.30	.14
❑ 13 Edgar Martinez	.50	.23
❑ 14 Cal Ripken	3.00	1.35
❑ 15 Alex Rodriguez	2.00	.90
❑ 16 Ivan Rodriguez	.75	.35
❑ 17 Manny Ramirez	1.00	.45
❑ 18 Nomar Garciaparra	2.00	.90
❑ 19 Pedro Martinez	1.00	.45
❑ 20 Jermaine Dye	.30	.14
❑ 21 Juan Gonzalez	.75	.35
❑ 22 Matt Lawton	.30	.14
❑ 23 Frank Thomas	1.00	.45
❑ 24 Magglio Ordonez	.30	.14
❑ 25 Bernie Williams	.75	.35
❑ 26 Derek Jeter	3.00	1.35
❑ 27 Roger Clemens	2.00	.90
❑ 28 Jeff Bagwell	1.00	.45
❑ 29 Richard Hidalgo	.30	.14
❑ 30 Chipper Jones	1.50	.70
❑ 31 Greg Maddux	2.00	.90
❑ 32 Andruw Jones	.75	.35
❑ 33 Jeromy Burnitz	.30	.14
❑ 34 Mark McGwire	3.00	1.35
❑ 35 Jim Edmonds	.50	.23
❑ 36 Sammy Sosa	1.50	.70
❑ 37 Kerry Wood	.75	.35
❑ 38 Randy Johnson	1.00	.45
❑ 39 Steve Finley	.30	.14
❑ 40 Gary Sheffield	.30	.14
❑ 41 Kevin Brown	.30	.14
❑ 42 Shawn Green	.75	.35
❑ 43 Vladimir Guerrero	1.00	.45
❑ 44 Jose Vidro	.30	.14
❑ 45 Barry Bonds	2.00	.90
❑ 46 Jeff Kent	.50	.23
❑ 47 Preston Wilson	.30	.14
❑ 48 Luis Castillo	.30	.14
❑ 49 Mike Piazza	2.00	.90
❑ 50 Edgardo Alfonzo	.30	.14
❑ 51 Tony Gwynn	1.50	.70
❑ 52 Ryan Klesko	.30	.14
❑ 53 Scott Rolen	.75	.35
❑ 54 Bob Abreu	.30	.14
❑ 55 Jason Kendall	.30	.14
❑ 56 Brian Giles	.30	.14
❑ 57 Ken Griffey Jr.	2.50	1.10
❑ 58 Barry Larkin	.75	.35
❑ 59 Todd Helton	1.00	.45
❑ 60 Mike Hampton	.30	.14
❑ 61 Corey Patterson WP	8.00	3.60
❑ 62 Timo Perez WP	8.00	3.60
❑ 63 Toby Hall WP	8.00	3.60
❑ 64 Brandon Inge WP	8.00	3.60
❑ 65 Joe Crede WP	8.00	3.60
❑ 66 Xavier Nady WP	8.00	3.60
❑ 67 Adam Pettyjohn WP RC	8.00	3.60
❑ 68 Keith Ginter WP	8.00	3.60
❑ 69 Brian Cole WP	8.00	3.60
❑ 70 Tyler Walker WP RC	8.00	3.60
❑ 71 Juan Uribe WP RC	15.00	6.75
❑ 72 Alex Hernandez WP	8.00	3.60
❑ 73 Leo Estrella WP	8.00	3.60
❑ 74 Joey Nation WP	8.00	3.60
❑ 75 Aubrey Huff WP	8.00	3.60
❑ 76 Ichiro Suzuki WP RC	120.00	55.00
❑ 77 Jay Spurgeon WP	8.00	3.60
❑ 78 Sun Woo Kim WP	8.00	3.60
❑ 79 Pedro Feliz WP	8.00	3.60
❑ 80 Pablo Ozuna WP	8.00	3.60
❑ 81 Hiram Bocachica WP	8.00	3.60
❑ 82 Brad Wilkerson WP	8.00	3.60
❑ 83 Rocky Biddle WP	8.00	3.60
❑ 84 Aaron McNeal WP	8.00	3.60
❑ 85 Adam Bernero WP	8.00	3.60
❑ 86 Danys Baez WP	8.00	3.60
❑ 87 Dee Brown WP	8.00	3.60
❑ 88 Jimmy Rollins WP	8.00	3.60
❑ 89 Jason Hart WP	8.00	3.60
❑ 90 Ross Gload WP	8.00	3.60

2000 Upper Deck Pros and Prospects

	MINT	NRMT
COMPLETE SET (192)	1150.00	525.00
COMP.BASIC SET (132)	750.00	350.00
COMP.UPDATE SET (60)	400.00	180.00
COMP.BASIC w/o SP's (90)	20.00	9.00
COMP.UPDATE w/o SP'S (30)	10.00	4.50
COMMON CARD (1-90)	.20	.09
COMMON PS (91-120)	8.00	3.60
COMMON PF (121-132)	12.00	5.50
COMMON PS (133-162)	10.00	4.50
COMMON CARD (163-192)	.30	.14

❑ 1 Darin Erstad	.75	.35
❑ 2 Troy Glaus	.75	.35
❑ 3 Mo Vaughn	.30	.14
❑ 4 Jason Giambi	.75	.35
❑ 5 Tim Hudson	.75	.35
❑ 6 Ben Grieve	.30	.14
❑ 7 Eric Chavez	.30	.14
❑ 8 Shannon Stewart	.30	.14
❑ 9 Raul Mondesi	.30	.14
❑ 10 Carlos Delgado	.75	.35
❑ 11 Jose Canseco	.75	.35
❑ 12 Fred McGriff	.50	.23
❑ 13 Greg Vaughn	.30	.14
❑ 14 Manny Ramirez	1.00	.45
❑ 15 Roberto Alomar	.75	.35
❑ 16 Jim Thome	.75	.35

Card	MINT	NRMT
17 Alex Rodriguez	2.00	.90
18 Freddy Garcia	.50	.23
19 John Olerud	.30	.14
20 Cal Ripken	3.00	1.35
21 Albert Belle	.30	.14
22 Mike Mussina	.75	.35
23 Ivan Rodriguez	.75	.35
24 Rafael Palmeiro	.75	.35
25 Ruben Mateo	.30	.14
26 Gabe Kapler	.30	.14
27 Pedro Martinez	1.00	.45
28 Nomar Garciaparra	2.00	.90
29 Carl Everett	.30	.14
30 Carlos Beltran	.30	.14
31 Jermaine Dye	.30	.14
32 Johnny Damon UER	.30	.14
Picture on front is Joe Randa		
33 Juan Gonzalez	.75	.35
34 Juan Encarnacion	.30	.14
35 Dean Palmer	.30	.14
36 Jacque Jones	.30	.14
37 Matt Lawton	.20	.09
38 Frank Thomas	1.00	.45
39 Paul Konerko	.30	.14
40 Magglio Ordonez	.30	.14
41 Derek Jeter	3.00	1.35
42 Bernie Williams	.75	.35
43 Mariano Rivera	.30	.14
44 Roger Clemens	2.00	.90
45 Jeff Bagwell	1.00	.45
46 Craig Biggio	.50	.23
47 Richard Hidalgo	.30	.14
48 Chipper Jones	1.50	.70
49 Andres Galarraga	.50	.23
50 Andruw Jones	.75	.35
51 Greg Maddux	2.00	.90
52 Jeromy Burnitz	.30	.14
53 Geoff Jenkins	.30	.14
54 Mark McGwire	3.00	1.35
55 Jim Edmonds	.50	.23
56 Fernando Tatis	.20	.09
57 J.D. Drew	.75	.35
58 Sammy Sosa	1.50	.70
59 Kerry Wood	.75	.35
60 Randy Johnson	1.00	.45
61 Matt Williams	.30	.14
62 Erubiel Durazo	.30	.14
63 Shawn Green	.75	.35
64 Kevin Brown	.30	.14
65 Gary Sheffield	.30	.14
66 Adrian Beltre	.30	.14
67 Vladimir Guerrero	1.00	.45
68 Jose Vidro	.30	.14
69 Barry Bonds	2.00	.90
70 Jeff Kent	.50	.23
71 Preston Wilson	.30	.14
72 Ryan Dempster	.30	.14
73 Mike Lowell	.30	.14
74 Mike Piazza	2.00	.90
75 Robin Ventura	.30	.14
76 Edgardo Alfonzo	.30	.14
77 Derek Bell	.20	.09
78 Tony Gwynn	1.50	.70
79 Matt Clement	.20	.09
80 Scott Rolen	.50	.23
81 Bobby Abreu	.30	.14
82 Curt Schilling	.75	.35
83 Brian Giles	.30	.14
84 Jason Kendall	.30	.14
85 Kris Benson	.30	.14
86 Ken Griffey Jr.	2.50	1.10
87 Sean Casey	.50	.23
88 Pokey Reese	.20	.09
89 Larry Walker	.50	.23
90 Todd Helton	1.00	.45
91 Rick Ankiel PS	10.00	4.50
92 Milton Bradley PS	8.00	3.60
93 Vernon Wells PS	8.00	3.60
94 Rafael Furcal PS	10.00	4.50
95 Kazuhiro Sasaki PS RC	20.00	9.00
96 Joe Torres PS RC	10.00	4.50
97 Adam Kennedy PS	8.00	3.60
98 Adam Piatt PS	8.00	3.60
99 Matt Wheatland PS RC	10.00	4.50
100 Alex Cabrera PS RC	10.00	4.50
101 Barry Zito PS RC	40.00	18.00
102 Mike Lamb PS RC	10.00	4.50
103 Scott Heard PS RC	10.00	4.50
104 Danys Baez PS RC	10.00	4.50
105 Matt Riley PS	8.00	3.60
106 Mark Mulder PS	10.00	4.50
107 W.Rodriguez PS RC	8.00	3.60
108 Luis Matos PS RC	8.00	3.60
109 Alfonso Soriano PS	10.00	4.50
110 Pat Burrell PS	10.00	4.50
111 Mike Tonis PS RC	10.00	4.50
112 Aaron McNeal PS RC	8.00	3.60
113 Dave Krynzel PS RC	10.00	4.50
114 Josh Beckett PS	15.00	6.75
115 Sean Burnett PS RC	10.00	4.50
116 Eric Munson PS	8.00	3.60
117 Scott Downs PS RC	8.00	3.60
118 Brian Tollberg PS RC	8.00	3.60
119 Nick Johnson PS	10.00	4.50
120 Leo Estrella PS RC	8.00	3.60
121 Ken Griffey Jr. PF	30.00	13.50
122 Frank Thomas PF	12.00	5.50
123 Cal Ripken PF	40.00	18.00
124 Ivan Rodriguez PF	15.00	6.75
125 Derek Jeter PF	40.00	18.00
126 Mark McGwire PF	40.00	18.00
127 Pedro Martinez PF	15.00	6.75
128 Chipper Jones PF	20.00	9.00
129 Sammy Sosa PF	20.00	9.00
130 Alex Rodriguez PF	25.00	11.00
131 Vladimir Guerrero PF	12.00	5.50
132 Jeff Bagwell PF	15.00	6.75
133 Dane Artman PS RC	10.00	4.50
134 Juan Pierre PS RC	12.00	5.50
135 Jace Brewer PS RC	10.00	4.50
136 Sun Woo Kim PS RC	10.00	4.50
137 Jon Rauch PS RC	15.00	6.75
138 Juan Guzman PS RC	10.00	4.50
139 Daylan Holt PS RC	10.00	4.50
140 R.Washington PS RC	10.00	4.50
141 Ben Diggins PS RC	12.00	5.50
142 Mike Meyers PS RC	10.00	4.50
143 C.Wakeland PS RC	10.00	4.50
144 Cory Vance PS RC	10.00	4.50
145 Keith Ginter PS RC	12.00	5.50
146 Koyie Hill PS RC	10.00	4.50
147 Julio Zuleta PS RC	10.00	4.50
148 G.Guzman PS RC	10.00	4.50
149 Jay Spurgeon PS RC	10.00	4.50
150 Ross Gload PS RC	10.00	4.50
151 Ben Sheets PS RC	25.00	11.00
152 J.Kalinowski PS RC	10.00	4.50
153 Kurt Ainsworth PS RC	12.00	5.50
154 P.Crawford PS RC	10.00	4.50
155 Xavier Nady PS RC	25.00	11.00
156 B.Wilkerson PS RC	10.00	4.50
157 Kris Wilson PS RC	10.00	4.50
158 Paul Rigdon PS RC	10.00	4.50
159 R.Kohlmeier PS RC	10.00	4.50
160 Dane Sardinha PS RC	10.00	4.50
161 Javier Cardona PS RC	10.00	4.50
162 Brad Cresse PS RC	20.00	9.00
163 Ron Gant	.30	.14
164 Mark Mulder	1.25	.55
165 David Wells	.50	.23
166 Jason Tyner	.30	.14
167 David Segui	.30	.14
168 Al Martin	.30	.14
169 Melvin Mora	.30	.14
170 Ricky Ledee	.30	.14
171 Rolando Arrojo	.30	.14
172 Mike Sweeney	.50	.23
173 Bobby Higginson	.50	.23
174 Eric Milton	.50	.23
175 Charles Johnson	.50	.23
176 David Justice	.50	.23
177 Moises Alou	.50	.23
178 Andy Ashby	.30	.14
179 Richie Sexson	.50	.23
180 Will Clark	1.25	.55
181 Rondell White	.50	.23
182 Curt Schilling	1.25	.55
183 Tom Goodwin	.30	.14
184 Lee Stevens	.30	.14
185 Ellis Burks	.50	.23
186 Henry Rodriguez	.30	.14
187 Mike Bordick	.30	.14
188 Ryan Klesko	.50	.23
189 Travis Lee	.30	.14
190 Kevin Young	.30	.14
191 Barry Larkin	1.25	.55
192 Jeff Cirillo	.50	.23

2001 Upper Deck Pros and Prospects

	MINT	NRMT
COMP.SET w/o SP's (90)	20.00	9.00
COMMON CARD (1-90)	.30	.14
COMMON CARD (91-135)	8.00	3.60
COMMON CARD (136-141)	30.00	13.50

Card	MINT	NRMT
1 Troy Glaus	.75	.35
2 Darin Erstad	.75	.35
3 Tim Hudson	.75	.35
4 Jason Giambi	.75	.35
5 Jermaine Dye	.30	.14
6 Barry Zito	.75	.35
7 Carlos Delgado	.75	.35
8 Shannon Stewart	.30	.14
9 Raul Mondesi	.30	.14
10 Greg Vaughn	.30	.14
11 Ben Grieve	.30	.14
12 Roberto Alomar	.75	.35
13 Juan Gonzalez	.75	.35
14 Jim Thome	.75	.35
15 C.C. Sabathia	.50	.23
16 Edgar Martinez	.50	.23
17 Kazuhiro Sasaki	.75	.35
18 Aaron Sele	.30	.14
19 John Olerud	.30	.14
20 Cal Ripken	3.00	1.35
21 Rafael Palmeiro	.75	.35
22 Ivan Rodriguez	.75	.35
23 Alex Rodriguez	2.00	.90
24 Manny Ramirez	1.00	.45
25 Pedro Martinez	1.00	.45
26 Carl Everett	.30	.14
27 Nomar Garciaparra	2.00	.90
28 Neifi Perez	.30	.14
29 Mike Sweeney	.30	.14
30 Bobby Higginson	.30	.14
31 Tony Clark	.30	.14
32 Doug Mientkiewicz	.30	.14
33 Cristian Guzman	.30	.14
34 Brad Radke	.30	.14
35 Magglio Ordonez	.30	.14
36 Carlos Lee	.30	.14
37 Frank Thomas	1.00	.45
38 Roger Clemens	2.00	.90
39 Bernie Williams	.75	.35
40 Derek Jeter	3.00	1.35
41 Tino Martinez	.30	.14
42 Wade Miller	.30	.14
43 Jeff Bagwell	1.00	.45
44 Lance Berkman	.30	.14
45 Richard Hidalgo	.30	.14
46 Greg Maddux	2.00	.90
47 Andruw Jones	.75	.35
48 Chipper Jones	1.50	.70
49 Rafael Furcal	.30	.14
50 Jeromy Burnitz	.30	.14
51 Geoff Jenkins	.30	.14
52 Ben Sheets	.30	.14
53 Mark McGwire	3.00	1.35

	MINT	NRMT
❑ 54 Jim Edmonds	.50	.23
❑ 55 J.D. Drew	.75	.35
❑ 56 Fred McGriff	.50	.23
❑ 57 Sammy Sosa	1.50	.70
❑ 58 Kerry Wood	.75	.35
❑ 59 Randy Johnson	1.00	.45
❑ 60 Luis Gonzalez	.75	.35
❑ 61 Curt Schilling	.75	.35
❑ 62 Kevin Brown	.30	.14
❑ 63 Shawn Green	.75	.35
❑ 64 Gary Sheffield	.30	.14
❑ 65 Vladimir Guerrero	1.00	.45
❑ 66 Jose Vidro	.30	.14
❑ 67 Barry Bonds	2.00	.90
❑ 68 Jeff Kent	.50	.23
❑ 69 Rich Aurilia	.30	.14
❑ 70 Preston Wilson	.30	.14
❑ 71 Charles Johnson	.30	.14
❑ 72 Cliff Floyd	.30	.14
❑ 73 Mike Piazza	2.00	.90
❑ 74 Al Leiter	.30	.14
❑ 75 Matt Lawton	.30	.14
❑ 76 Tony Gwynn	1.50	.70
❑ 77 Ryan Klesko	.30	.14
❑ 78 Phil Nevin	.30	.14
❑ 79 Scott Rolen	.75	.35
❑ 80 Pat Burrell	.30	.14
❑ 81 Jimmy Rollins	.30	.14
❑ 82 Jason Kendall	.30	.14
❑ 83 Brian Giles	.30	.14
❑ 84 Aramis Ramirez	.30	.14
❑ 85 Ken Griffey Jr.	2.50	1.10
❑ 86 Barry Larkin	.75	.35
❑ 87 Sean Casey	.50	.23
❑ 88 Larry Walker	.30	.14
❑ 89 Todd Helton	1.00	.45
❑ 90 Mike Hampton	.30	.14
❑ 91 Juan Cruz PS RC	15.00	6.75
❑ 92 Brian Lawrence PS RC	8.00	3.60
❑ 93 Brandon Lyon PS RC	8.00	3.60
❑ 94 Adrian Hernandez PS RC	8.00	3.60
❑ 95 Jose Mieses PS RC	8.00	3.60
❑ 96 Juan Uribe PS RC	10.00	4.50
❑ 97 Morgan Ensberg PS RC	10.00	4.50
❑ 98 Wilson Betemit PS RC	15.00	6.75
❑ 99 Ryan Freel PS RC	8.00	3.60
❑ 100 Jack Wilson PS RC	8.00	3.60
❑ 101 Cesar Crespo PS RC	8.00	3.60
❑ 102 Bret Prinz PS RC	8.00	3.60
❑ 103 Horacio Ramirez PS RC	8.00	3.60
❑ 104 Elpidio Guzman PS RC	8.00	3.60
❑ 105 Josh Towers PS RC	10.00	4.50
❑ 106 B. Duckworth PS RC	12.00	5.50
❑ 107 Esix Snead PS RC	8.00	3.60
❑ 108 Billy Sylvester PS RC	8.00	3.60
❑ 109 Alexis Gomez PS RC	8.00	3.60
❑ 110 Johnny Estrada PS RC	10.00	4.50
❑ 111 Joe Kennedy PS RC	8.00	3.60
❑ 112 Travis Hafner PS RC	8.00	3.60
❑ 113 Martin Vargas PS RC	8.00	3.60
❑ 114 Jay Gibbons PS RC	8.00	3.60
❑ 115 Andres Torres PS RC	8.00	3.60
❑ 116 Sean Douglass PS RC	8.00	3.60
❑ 117 Juan Diaz PS RC	8.00	3.60
❑ 118 Greg Miller PS RC	8.00	3.60
❑ 119 C. Valderrama PS RC	8.00	3.60
❑ 120 Bill Ortega PS RC	8.00	3.60
❑ 121 Josh Fogg PS RC	8.00	3.60
❑ 122 Wilken Ruan PS RC	8.00	3.60
❑ 123 Kris Keller PS RC	8.00	3.60
❑ 124 Erick Almonte PS RC	8.00	3.60
❑ 125 R. Rodriguez PS RC	8.00	3.60
❑ 126 Grant Balfour PS RC	8.00	3.60
❑ 127 Nick Maness PS RC	8.00	3.60
❑ 128 Jeremy Owens PS RC	8.00	3.60
❑ 129 Doug Nickle PS RC	8.00	3.60
❑ 130 Bert Snow PS RC	8.00	3.60
❑ 131 Jason Smith PS RC	8.00	3.60
❑ 132 Henry Mateo PS RC	8.00	3.60
❑ 133 Mike Penney PS RC	8.00	3.60
❑ 134 Bud Smith PS RC	20.00	9.00
❑ 135 Junior Spivey PS RC	8.00	3.60
❑ 136 Ichiro Suzuki JSY RC	200.00	90.00
❑ 137 Albert Pujols JSY RC	100.00	45.00
❑ 138 Mark Teixeira JSY RC	100.00	45.00
❑ 139 Dewon Brazelton JSY RC	30.00	13.50
❑ 140 Mark Prior JSY RC	60.00	27.00
❑ 141 Tsuyoshi Shinjo JSY RC	50.00	22.00

2001 Upper Deck Prospect Premieres

	MINT	NRMT
COMP.SET w/o SP's (90)	40.00	18.00
COMMON CARD (1-90)	.50	.23
COMMON AUTO (91-102)	50.00	22.00

❑ 1 Jeff Mathis XRC	.75	.35
❑ 2 Jake Woods XRC	.50	.23
❑ 3 Dallas McPherson XRC	.75	.35
❑ 4 Steven Shell XRC	.50	.23
❑ 5 Ryan Budde XRC	.50	.23
❑ 6 Kirk Saarloos XRC	.50	.23
❑ 7 Ryan Stegall XRC	.50	.23
❑ 8 Bobby Crosby XRC	.75	.35
❑ 9 J.T. Stotts XRC	.50	.23
❑ 10 Neal Cotts XRC	.50	.23
❑ 11 Jeremy Bonderman XRC	.75	.35
❑ 12 Brandon League XRC	.75	.35
❑ 13 Tyrell Godwin XRC	.75	.35
❑ 14 Gabe Gross XRC	2.00	.90
❑ 15 Chris Neylan XRC	.50	.23
❑ 16 Macay McBride XRC	.75	.35
❑ 17 Josh Burrus XRC	.75	.35
❑ 18 Adam Stern XRC	.50	.23
❑ 19 Richard Lewis XRC	.50	.23
❑ 20 Cole Barthel XRC	.75	.35
❑ 21 Mike Jones XRC	.75	.35
❑ 22 J.J. Hardy XRC	.50	.23
❑ 23 Jon Steitz XRC	.50	.23
❑ 24 Brad Nelson XRC	.60	.25
❑ 25 Justin Pope XRC	.75	.35
❑ 26 Dan Haren XRC	.60	.25
❑ 27 Andy Sisco XRC	.50	.23
❑ 28 Ryan Theriot XRC	.75	.35
❑ 29 Ricky Nolasco XRC	.50	.23
❑ 30 Jon Switzer XRC	.50	.23
❑ 31 Justin Wechsler XRC	.50	.23
❑ 32 Mike Gosling XRC	.50	.23
❑ 33 Scott Hairston XRC	1.00	.45
❑ 34 Brian Pilkington XRC	.50	.23
❑ 35 Kole Strayhorn XRC	.75	.35
❑ 36 David Taylor XRC	.50	.23
❑ 37 Donald Levinski XRC	.50	.23
❑ 38 Mike Hinckley XRC	.50	.23
❑ 39 Nick Long XRC	.50	.23
❑ 40 Brad Hennessey XRC	.60	.25
❑ 41 Noah Lowry XRC	.60	.25
❑ 42 Josh Cram XRC	.50	.23
❑ 43 Jesse Foppert XRC	1.00	.45
❑ 44 Julian Benavidez XRC	1.00	.45
❑ 45 Dan Denham XRC	1.00	.45
❑ 46 Travis Foley XRC	.75	.35
❑ 47 Mike Conroy XRC	.60	.25
❑ 48 Jake Dittler XRC	.60	.25
❑ 49 Rene Rivera XRC	.50	.23
❑ 50 John Cole XRC	.50	.23
❑ 51 Lazaro Abreu XRC	.50	.23
❑ 52 David Wright XRC	.75	.35
❑ 53 Aaron Heilman XRC	1.00	.45
❑ 54 Len DiNardo XRC	.50	.23
❑ 55 Alhaji Turay XRC	.50	.23
❑ 56 Chris Smith XRC	.75	.35
❑ 57 Rommie Lewis XRC	.60	.25
❑ 58 Bryan Bass XRC	1.00	.45
❑ 59 David Crouthers XRC	.50	.23
❑ 60 Josh Barfield XRC	.75	.35
❑ 61 Jake Peavy XRC	.75	.35
❑ 62 Ryan Howard XRC	.50	.23
❑ 63 Gavin Floyd XRC	2.00	.90
❑ 64 Michael Floyd XRC	.50	.23
❑ 65 Stefan Bailie XRC	.50	.23
❑ 66 Jon DeVries XRC	.50	.23
❑ 67 Steve Kelly XRC	.75	.35
❑ 68 Alan Moye XRC	.50	.23
❑ 69 Justin Gillman XRC	.60	.25
❑ 70 Jayson Nix XRC	.60	.25
❑ 71 John Draper XRC	.50	.23
❑ 72 Kenny Baugh XRC	.75	.35
❑ 73 Michael Woods XRC	.50	.23
❑ 74 Preston Larrison XRC	.50	.23
❑ 75 Matt Coenen XRC	.50	.23
❑ 76 Scott Tyler XRC	.50	.23
❑ 77 Jose Morales XRC	.50	.23
❑ 78 Corwin Malone XRC	1.25	.55
❑ 79 Dennis Ulacia XRC	.60	.25
❑ 80 Andy Gonzalez XRC	.60	.25
❑ 81 Kris Honel XRC	.75	.35
❑ 82 Wyatt Allen XRC	.50	.23
❑ 83 Ryan Wing XRC	.50	.23
❑ 84 Sean Henn XRC	.75	.35
❑ 85 John-Ford Griffin XRC	1.50	.70
❑ 86 Bronson Sardinha XRC	1.50	.70
❑ 87 Jon Skaggs XRC	.60	.25
❑ 88 Shelley Duncan XRC	.60	.25
❑ 89 Jason Arnold XRC	1.25	.55
❑ 90 Aaron Rifkin XRC	1.00	.45
❑ 91 Colt Griffin AU XRC	50.00	22.00
❑ 92 J.D. Martin AU XRC	50.00	22.00
❑ 93 Justin Wayne AU XRC	50.00	22.00
❑ 94 J. VanBenschoten AU XRC	50.00	22.00
❑ 95 Chris Burke AU XRC	50.00	22.00
❑ 96 Casey Kotchman AU XRC	100.00	45.00
❑ 97 M. Garciaparra AU XRC	60.00	27.00
❑ 98 Jake Gautreau AU XRC	50.00	22.00
❑ 99 Jerome Williams AU XRC	50.00	22.00
❑ 100 Toe Nash AU XRC	60.00	27.00
❑ 101 Joe Borchard AU XRC	100.00	45.00
❑ 102 Mark Prior AU XRC	120.00	55.00

1999 Upper Deck Retro

	MINT	NRMT
COMPLETE SET (110)	25.00	11.00

❑ 1 Mo Vaughn	.25	.11
❑ 2 Troy Glaus	.60	.25
❑ 3 Tim Salmon	.25	.11
❑ 4 Randy Johnson	.75	.35
❑ 5 Travis Lee	.15	.07
❑ 6 Matt Williams	.40	.18
❑ 7 Greg Maddux	1.50	.70
❑ 8 Chipper Jones	1.25	.55
❑ 9 Andruw Jones	.60	.25
❑ 10 Tom Glavine	.60	.25
❑ 11 Javy Lopez	.25	.11
❑ 12 Albert Belle	.25	.11
❑ 13 Cal Ripken	2.50	1.10
❑ 14 Brady Anderson	.25	.11
❑ 15 Nomar Garciaparra	1.50	.70
❑ 16 Pedro Martinez	.75	.35

Card		
☐ 17 Sammy Sosa	1.25	.55
☐ 18 Mark Grace	.60	.25
☐ 19 Frank Thomas	.75	.35
☐ 20 Ray Durham	.25	.11
☐ 21 Sean Casey	.40	.18
☐ 22 Greg Vaughn	.25	.11
☐ 23 Barry Larkin	.60	.25
☐ 24 Manny Ramirez	.75	.35
☐ 25 Jim Thome	.60	.25
☐ 26 Jaret Wright	.15	.07
☐ 27 Kenny Lofton	.25	.11
☐ 28 Larry Walker	.40	.18
☐ 29 Todd Helton	.75	.35
☐ 30 Vinny Castilla	.25	.11
☐ 31 Tony Clark	.25	.11
☐ 32 Juan Encarnacion	.25	.11
☐ 33 Dean Palmer	.25	.11
☐ 34 Mark Kotsay	.15	.07
☐ 35 Alex Gonzalez	.15	.07
☐ 36 Shane Reynolds	.15	.07
☐ 37 Ken Caminiti	.25	.11
☐ 38 Jeff Bagwell	.75	.35
☐ 39 Craig Biggio	.40	.18
☐ 40 Carlos Febles	.15	.07
☐ 41 Carlos Beltran	.25	.11
☐ 42 Jeremy Giambi	.15	.07
☐ 43 Raul Mondesi	.25	.11
☐ 44 Adrian Beltre	.25	.11
☐ 45 Kevin Brown	.40	.18
☐ 46 Jeromy Burnitz	.25	.11
☐ 47 Jeff Cirillo	.25	.11
☐ 48 Corey Koskie	.25	.11
☐ 49 Todd Walker	.15	.07
☐ 50 Vladimir Guerrero	.75	.35
☐ 51 Michael Barrett	.15	.07
☐ 52 Mike Piazza	1.50	.70
☐ 53 Robin Ventura	.25	.11
☐ 54 Edgardo Alfonzo	.25	.11
☐ 55 Derek Jeter	2.50	1.10
☐ 56 Roger Clemens	1.50	.70
☐ 57 Tino Martinez	.25	.11
☐ 58 Orlando Hernandez	.25	.11
☐ 59 Chuck Knoblauch	.25	.11
☐ 60 Bernie Williams	.60	.25
☐ 61 Eric Chavez	.25	.11
☐ 62 Ben Grieve	.25	.11
☐ 63 Jason Giambi	.60	.25
☐ 64 Scott Rolen	.60	.25
☐ 65 Curt Schilling	.60	.25
☐ 66 Bobby Abreu	.25	.11
☐ 67 Jason Kendall	.25	.11
☐ 68 Kevin Young	.25	.11
☐ 69 Mark McGwire	2.50	1.10
☐ 70 J.D. Drew	.60	.25
☐ 71 Eric Davis	.25	.11
☐ 72 Tony Gwynn	1.25	.55
☐ 73 Trevor Hoffman	.25	.11
☐ 74 Barry Bonds	1.50	.70
☐ 75 Robb Nen	.15	.07
☐ 76 Ken Griffey Jr.	2.00	.90
☐ 77 Alex Rodriguez	1.50	.70
☐ 78 Jay Buhner	.25	.11
☐ 79 Carlos Guillen	.15	.07
☐ 80 Jose Canseco	.60	.25
☐ 81 Bobby Smith	.15	.07
☐ 82 Juan Gonzalez	.60	.25
☐ 83 Ivan Rodriguez	.60	.25
☐ 84 Rafael Palmeiro	.60	.25
☐ 85 Rick Helling	.15	.07
☐ 86 Jose Cruz Jr.	.25	.11
☐ 87 David Wells	.25	.11
☐ 88 Carlos Delgado	.60	.25
☐ 89 Nolan Ryan	4.00	1.80
☐ 90 George Brett	1.25	.55
☐ 91 Robin Yount	.60	.25
☐ 92 Paul Molitor	.60	.25
☐ 93 Dave Winfield	.60	.25
☐ 94 Steve Garvey	.40	.18
☐ 95 Ozzie Smith	.75	.35
☐ 96 Ted Williams	2.50	1.10
☐ 97 Don Mattingly	1.50	.70
☐ 98 Mickey Mantle	3.00	1.35
☐ 99 Harmon Killebrew	.60	.25
☐ 100 Rollie Fingers	.25	.11
☐ 101 Kirk Gibson	.25	.11
☐ 102 Bucky Dent	.25	.11
☐ 103 Willie Mays	1.50	.70
☐ 104 Babe Ruth	3.00	1.35
☐ 105 Gary Carter	.40	.18
☐ 106 Reggie Jackson	.75	.35
☐ 107 Frank Robinson	.60	.25
☐ 108 Ernie Banks	.75	.35
☐ 109 Eddie Murray	.60	.25
☐ 110 Mike Schmidt	1.25	.55

2001 Upper Deck Sweet Spot

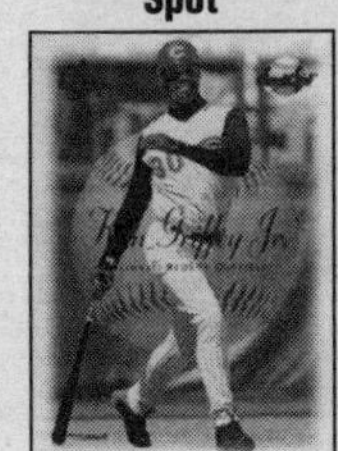

	MINT	NRMT
COMP.BASIC w/o SP's (60)	25.00	11.00
COMMON CARD (1-60)	.40	.18
COMMON CARD (61-90)	10.00	4.50

Card		
☐ 1 Troy Glaus	.75	.35
☐ 2 Darin Erstad	.75	.35
☐ 3 Jason Giambi	.75	.35
☐ 4 Tim Hudson	.75	.35
☐ 5 Ben Grieve	.40	.18
☐ 6 Carlos Delgado	.75	.35
☐ 7 David Wells	.40	.18
☐ 8 Greg Vaughn	.40	.18
☐ 9 Roberto Alomar	.75	.35
☐ 10 Jim Thome	.75	.35
☐ 11 John Olerud	.40	.18
☐ 12 Edgar Martinez	.50	.23
☐ 13 Cal Ripken	3.00	1.35
☐ 14 Albert Belle	.40	.18
☐ 15 Ivan Rodriguez	.75	.35
☐ 16 Alex Rodriguez Rangers	4.00	1.80
☐ 17 Pedro Martinez	1.00	.45
☐ 18 Nomar Garciaparra	2.00	.90
☐ 19 Manny Ramirez	1.00	.45
☐ 20 Jermaine Dye	.40	.18
☐ 21 Juan Gonzalez	.75	.35
☐ 22 Dean Palmer	.40	.18
☐ 23 Matt Lawton	.40	.18
☐ 24 Eric Milton	.40	.18
☐ 25 Frank Thomas	1.00	.45
☐ 26 Magglio Ordonez	.40	.18
☐ 27 Derek Jeter	3.00	1.35
☐ 28 Bernie Williams	.75	.35
☐ 29 Roger Clemens	2.00	.90
☐ 30 Jeff Bagwell	1.00	.45
☐ 31 Richard Hidalgo	.40	.18
☐ 32 Chipper Jones	1.50	.70
☐ 33 Greg Maddux	2.00	.90
☐ 34 Richie Sexson	.40	.18
☐ 35 Jeromy Burnitz	.40	.18
☐ 36 Mark McGwire	3.00	1.35
☐ 37 Jim Edmonds	.50	.23
☐ 38 Sammy Sosa	1.50	.70
☐ 39 Randy Johnson	1.00	.45
☐ 40 Steve Finley	.40	.18
☐ 41 Gary Sheffield	.40	.18
☐ 42 Shawn Green	.75	.35
☐ 43 Vladimir Guerrero	1.00	.45
☐ 44 Jose Vidro	.40	.18
☐ 45 Barry Bonds	2.00	.90
☐ 46 Jeff Kent	.50	.23
☐ 47 Preston Wilson	.40	.18
☐ 48 Luis Castillo	.40	.18
☐ 49 Mike Piazza	2.00	.90
☐ 50 Edgardo Alfonzo	.40	.18
☐ 51 Tony Gwynn	1.50	.70
☐ 52 Ryan Klesko	.40	.18
☐ 53 Scott Rolen	.75	.35
☐ 54 Bob Abreu	.40	.18
☐ 55 Jason Kendall	.40	.18
☐ 56 Brian Giles	.40	.18
☐ 57 Ken Griffey Jr.	2.50	1.10
☐ 58 Barry Larkin	.75	.35
☐ 59 Todd Helton	1.00	.45
☐ 60 Mike Hampton Card back has batting header lines UER	.40	.18
☐ 61 Corey Patterson SB	10.00	4.50
☐ 62 Ichiro Suzuki SB RC	250.00	110.00
☐ 63 Jason Grilli SB	10.00	4.50
☐ 64 Brian Cole SB	10.00	4.50
☐ 65 Juan Pierre SB	10.00	4.50
☐ 66 Matt Ginter SB	10.00	4.50
☐ 67 Jimmy Rollins SB	10.00	4.50
☐ 68 Jason Smith SB RC	10.00	4.50
☐ 69 Israel Alcantara SB	10.00	4.50
☐ 70 Adam Pettyjohn SB RC	10.00	4.50
☐ 71 Luke Prokopec SB	10.00	4.50
☐ 72 Barry Zito SB	12.00	5.50
☐ 73 Keith Ginter SB	10.00	4.50
☐ 74 Sun Woo Kim SB	10.00	4.50
☐ 75 Ross Gload SB	10.00	4.50
☐ 76 Matt Wise SB	10.00	4.50
☐ 77 Aubrey Huff SB	10.00	4.50
☐ 78 Ryan Franklin SB	10.00	4.50
☐ 79 Brandon Inge SB	10.00	4.50
☐ 80 Wes Helms SB	10.00	4.50
☐ 81 Junior Spivey SB RC	10.00	4.50
☐ 82 Ryan Vogelsong SB	10.00	4.50
☐ 83 John Parrish SB	10.00	4.50
☐ 84 Joe Crede SB	10.00	4.50
☐ 85 Damian Rolls SB	10.00	4.50
☐ 86 Esix Snead SB RC	10.00	4.50
☐ 87 Rocky Biddle SB	10.00	4.50
☐ 88 Brady Clark SB	10.00	4.50
☐ 89 Timo Perez SB	10.00	4.50
☐ 90 Jay Spurgeon SB	10.00	4.50

1999 Upper Deck Victory

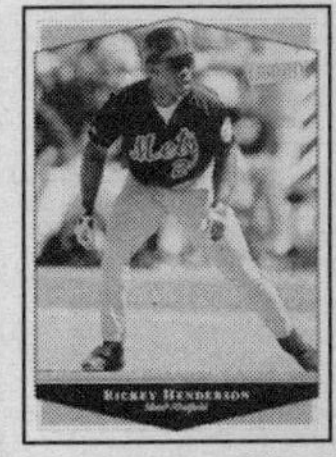

	MINT	NRMT
COMPLETE SET (470)	75.00	34.00
COMMON CARD (1-470)	.10	.05
COMMON MCGWIRE (421-450)	1.00	.45

Card		
☐ 1 Anaheim Angels TC	.10	.05
☐ 2 Mark Harriger RC	.10	.05
☐ 3 Mo Vaughn PT	.15	.07
☐ 4 Darin Erstad BP	.15	.07
☐ 5 Troy Glaus	.40	.18
☐ 6 Tim Salmon	.15	.07
☐ 7 Mo Vaughn	.15	.07
☐ 8 Darin Erstad	.40	.18
☐ 9 Garret Anderson	.15	.07
☐ 10 Todd Greene	.10	.05
☐ 11 Troy Percival	.10	.05
☐ 12 Chuck Finley	.15	.07
☐ 13 Jason Dickson	.10	.05
☐ 14 Jim Edmonds	.25	.11
☐ 15 Ariz. Diamondbacks TC	.10	.05
☐ 16 Randy Johnson	.50	.23
☐ 17 Matt Williams	.25	.11
☐ 18 Travis Lee	.10	.05

❑	19	Jay Bell	.15	.07
❑	20	Tony Womack	.10	.05
❑	21	Steve Finley	.15	.07
❑	22	Bernard Gilkey	.10	.05
❑	23	Tony Batista	.15	.07
❑	24	Todd Stottlemyre	.10	.05
❑	25	Omar Daal	.10	.05
❑	26	Atlanta Braves TC	.10	.05
❑	27	Bruce Chen	.10	.05
❑	28	George Lombard	.10	.05
❑	29	Chipper Jones PT	.40	.18
❑	30	Chipper Jones BP	.40	.18
❑	31	Greg Maddux	1.00	.45
❑	32	Chipper Jones	.75	.35
❑	33	Javy Lopez	.15	.07
❑	34	Tom Glavine	.40	.18
❑	35	John Smoltz	.15	.07
❑	36	Andruw Jones	.40	.18
❑	37	Brian Jordan	.15	.07
❑	38	Walt Weiss	.10	.05
❑	39	Bret Boone	.15	.07
❑	40	Andres Galarraga	.25	.11
❑	41	Baltimore Orioles TC	.10	.05
❑	42	Ryan Minor	.10	.05
❑	43	Jerry Hairston Jr.	.15	.07
❑	44	Calvin Pickering	.10	.05
❑	45	Cal Ripken HM	.75	.35
❑	46	Cal Ripken	1.50	.70
❑	47	Charles Johnson	.15	.07
❑	48	Albert Belle	.15	.07
❑	49	Delino DeShields	.10	.05
❑	50	Mike Mussina	.40	.18
❑	51	Scott Erickson	.10	.05
❑	52	Brady Anderson	.15	.07
❑	53	B.J. Surhoff	.15	.07
❑	54	Harold Baines	.15	.07
❑	55	Will Clark	.40	.18
❑	56	Boston Red Sox TC	.10	.05
❑	57	Shea Hillenbrand RC	.50	.23
❑	58	Trot Nixon	.15	.07
❑	59	Jin Ho Cho	.10	.05
❑	60	Nomar Garciaparra PT	.50	.23
❑	61	Nomar Garciaparra BP	.50	.23
❑	62	Pedro Martinez	.50	.23
❑	63	Nomar Garciaparra	1.00	.45
❑	64	Jose Offerman	.10	.05
❑	65	Jason Varitek	.15	.07
❑	66	Darren Lewis	.10	.05
❑	67	Troy O'Leary	.10	.05
❑	68	Donnie Sadler	.10	.05
❑	69	John Valentin	.10	.05
❑	70	Tim Wakefield	.10	.05
❑	71	Bret Saberhagen	.15	.07
❑	72	Chicago Cubs TC	.10	.05
❑	73	Kyle Farnsworth RC	.40	.18
❑	74	Sammy Sosa PT	.40	.18
❑	75	Sammy Sosa BP	.40	.18
❑	76	Sammy Sosa HM	.40	.18
❑	77	Kerry Wood HM	.15	.07
❑	78	Sammy Sosa	.75	.35
❑	79	Mark Grace	.40	.18
❑	80	Kerry Wood	.40	.18
❑	81	Kevin Tapani	.10	.05
❑	82	Benito Santiago	.10	.05
❑	83	Gary Gaetti	.10	.05
❑	84	Mickey Morandini	.10	.05
❑	85	Glenallen Hill	.10	.05
❑	86	Henry Rodriguez	.10	.05
❑	87	Rod Beck	.10	.05
❑	88	Chicago White Sox TC	.10	.05
❑	89	Carlos Lee	.15	.07
❑	90	Mark Johnson	.10	.05
❑	91	Frank Thomas PT	.25	.11
❑	92	Frank Thomas	.50	.23
❑	93	Jim Parque	.10	.05
❑	94	Mike Sirotka	.10	.05
❑	95	Mike Caruso	.10	.05
❑	96	Ray Durham	.15	.07
❑	97	Maggio Ordonez	.25	.11
❑	98	Paul Konerko	.15	.07
❑	99	Bob Howry	.10	.05
❑	100	Brian Simmons	.10	.05
❑	101	Jaime Navarro	.10	.05
❑	102	Cincinnati Reds TC	.10	.05
❑	103	Denny Neagle	.10	.05
❑	104	Pete Harnisch	.10	.05
❑	105	Greg Vaughn	.15	.07
❑	106	Brett Tomko	.10	.05
❑	107	Mike Cameron	.15	.07
❑	108	Sean Casey	.25	.11
❑	109	Aaron Boone	.10	.05
❑	110	Michael Tucker	.10	.05
❑	111	Dmitri Young	.15	.07
❑	112	Barry Larkin	.40	.18
❑	113	Cleveland Indians TC	.10	.05
❑	114	Russ Branyan	.15	.07
❑	115	Jim Thome PT	.40	.18
❑	116	Manny Ramirez PT	.25	.11
❑	117	Manny Ramirez	.50	.23
❑	118	Jim Thome	.40	.18
❑	119	David Justice	.15	.07
❑	120	Sandy Alomar Jr.	.15	.07
❑	121	Roberto Alomar	.40	.18
❑	122	Jaret Wright	.10	.05
❑	123	Bartolo Colon	.15	.07
❑	124	Travis Fryman	.15	.07
❑	125	Kenny Lofton	.15	.07
❑	126	Omar Vizquel	.15	.07
❑	127	Colorado Rockies TC	.10	.05
❑	128	Derrick Gibson	.10	.05
❑	129	Larry Walker BP	.25	.11
❑	130	Larry Walker	.25	.11
❑	131	Dante Bichette	.15	.07
❑	132	Todd Helton	.50	.23
❑	133	Neifi Perez	.10	.05
❑	134	Vinny Castilla	.15	.07
❑	135	Darryl Kile	.15	.07
❑	136	Pedro Astacio	.10	.05
❑	137	Darryl Hamilton	.10	.05
❑	138	Mike Lansing	.10	.05
❑	139	Kirt Manwaring	.10	.05
❑	140	Detroit Tigers TC	.10	.05
❑	141	Jeff Weaver RC	.50	.23
❑	142	Gabe Kapler	.15	.07
❑	143	Tony Clark PT	.15	.07
❑	144	Tony Clark	.15	.07
❑	145	Juan Encarnacion	.15	.07
❑	146	Dean Palmer	.15	.07
❑	147	Damion Easley	.10	.05
❑	148	Bobby Higginson	.15	.07
❑	149	Karim Garcia	.10	.05
❑	150	Justin Thompson	.10	.05
❑	151	Matt Anderson	.10	.05
❑	152	Willie Blair	.10	.05
❑	153	Brian Hunter	.10	.05
❑	154	Florida Marlins TC	.10	.05
❑	155	Alex Gonzalez	.10	.05
❑	156	Mark Kotsay	.10	.05
❑	157	Livan Hernandez	.10	.05
❑	158	Cliff Floyd	.15	.07
❑	159	Todd Dunwoody	.10	.05
❑	160	Alex Fernandez	.10	.05
❑	161	Matt Mantei	.10	.05
❑	162	Derrek Lee	.15	.07
❑	163	Kevin Orie	.10	.05
❑	164	Craig Counsell	.10	.05
❑	165	Rafael Medina	.10	.05
❑	166	Houston Astros TC	.10	.05
❑	167	Daryle Ward	.10	.05
❑	168	Mitch Meluskey	.10	.05
❑	169	Jeff Bagwell PT	.25	.11
❑	170	Jeff Bagwell	.50	.23
❑	171	Ken Caminiti	.15	.07
❑	172	Craig Biggio	.25	.11
❑	173	Derek Bell	.10	.05
❑	174	Moises Alou	.15	.07
❑	175	Billy Wagner	.10	.05
❑	176	Shane Reynolds	.10	.05
❑	177	Carl Everett	.15	.07
❑	178	Scott Elarton	.10	.05
❑	179	Richard Hidalgo	.15	.07
❑	180	K.C Royals TC	.10	.05
❑	181	Carlos Beltran	.15	.07
❑	182	Carlos Febles	.10	.05
❑	183	Jeremy Giambi	.10	.05
❑	184	Johnny Damon	.15	.07
❑	185	Joe Randa	.10	.05
❑	186	Jeff King	.10	.05
❑	187	Hipolito Pichardo	.10	.05
❑	188	Kevin Appier	.15	.07
❑	189	Chad Kreuter	.10	.05
❑	190	Rey Sanchez	.10	.05
❑	191	Larry Sutton	.10	.05
❑	192	Jeff Montgomery	.10	.05
❑	193	Jermaine Dye	.15	.07
❑	194	L.A. Dodgers TC	.10	.05
❑	195	Adam Riggs	.10	.05
❑	196	Angel Pena	.10	.05
❑	197	Todd Hundley	.10	.05
❑	198	Kevin Brown	.25	.11
❑	199	Ismael Valdes	.10	.05
❑	200	Chan Ho Park	.15	.07
❑	201	Adrian Beltre	.15	.07
❑	202	Mark Grudzielanek	.10	.05
❑	203	Raul Mondesi	.15	.07
❑	204	Gary Sheffield	.15	.07
❑	205	Eric Karros	.15	.07
❑	206	Devon White	.10	.05
❑	207	Milw. Brewers TC	.10	.05
❑	208	Ron Belliard	.10	.05
❑	209	Rafael Roque RC	.15	.07
❑	210	Jeromy Burnitz	.15	.07
❑	211	Fernando Vina	.10	.05
❑	212	Scott Karl	.10	.05
❑	213	Jim Abbott	.15	.07
❑	214	Sean Berry	.10	.05
❑	215	Marquis Grissom	.10	.05
❑	216	Geoff Jenkins	.15	.07
❑	217	Jeff Cirillo	.15	.07
❑	218	Dave Nilsson	.10	.05
❑	219	Jose Valentin	.10	.05
❑	220	Minnesota Twins TC	.10	.05
❑	221	Corey Koskie	.15	.07
❑	222	Cristian Guzman	.15	.07
❑	223	A.J. Pierzynski	.10	.05
❑	224	David Ortiz	.15	.07
❑	225	Brad Radke	.15	.07
❑	226	Todd Walker	.10	.05
❑	227	Matt Lawton	.15	.07
❑	228	Rick Aguilera	.10	.05
❑	229	Eric Milton	.15	.07
❑	230	Marty Cordova	.10	.05
❑	231	Torii Hunter	.15	.07
❑	232	Ron Coomer	.10	.05
❑	233	LaTroy Hawkins	.10	.05
❑	234	Montreal Expos TC	.10	.05
❑	235	Fernando Seguignol	.10	.05
❑	236	Michael Barrett	.10	.05
❑	237	Vladimir Guerrero BP	.25	.11
❑	238	Vladimir Guerrero	.50	.23
❑	239	Brad Fullmer	.15	.07
❑	240	Rondell White	.15	.07
❑	241	Ugueth Urbina	.10	.05
❑	242	Dustin Hermanson	.10	.05
❑	243	Orlando Cabrera	.10	.05
❑	244	Wilton Guerrero	.10	.05
❑	245	Carl Pavano	.10	.05
❑	246	Javier Vazquez	.15	.07
❑	247	Chris Widger	.10	.05
❑	248	New York Mets TC	.10	.05
❑	249	Mike Kinkade	.10	.05
❑	250	Octavio Dotel	.10	.05
❑	251	Mike Piazza PT	.50	.23
❑	252	Mike Piazza	1.00	.45
❑	253	Rickey Henderson	.75	.35
❑	254	Edgardo Alfonzo	.15	.07
❑	255	Robin Ventura	.15	.07
❑	256	Al Leiter	.15	.07
❑	257	Brian McRae	.10	.05
❑	258	Rey Ordonez	.10	.05
❑	259	Bobby Bonilla	.15	.07
❑	260	Orel Hershiser	.15	.07
❑	261	John Olerud	.15	.07
❑	262	New York Yankees TC	.10	.05
❑	263	Ricky Ledee	.10	.05
❑	264	Bernie Williams BP	.15	.07
❑	265	Derek Jeter BP	.75	.35
❑	266	Scott Brosius HM	.10	.05
❑	267	Derek Jeter	1.50	.70
❑	268	Roger Clemens	1.00	.45
❑	269	Orlando Hernandez	.15	.07
❑	270	Scott Brosius	.15	.07
❑	271	Paul O'Neill	.40	.18
❑	272	Bernie Williams	.40	.18
❑	273	Chuck Knoblauch	.15	.07
❑	274	Tino Martinez	.15	.07
❑	275	Mariano Rivera	.15	.07
❑	276	Jorge Posada	.15	.07

❑ 277 Oakland Athletics TC .10 .05
❑ 278 Eric Chavez .15 .07
❑ 279 Ben Grieve HM .15 .07
❑ 280 Jason Giambi .40 .18
❑ 281 John Jaha .10 .05
❑ 282 Miguel Tejada .15 .07
❑ 283 Ben Grieve .15 .07
❑ 284 Matt Stairs .10 .05
❑ 285 Ryan Christenson .10 .05
❑ 286 A.J. Hinch .10 .05
❑ 287 Kenny Rogers .10 .05
❑ 288 Tom Candiotti .10 .05
❑ 289 Scott Spiezio .10 .05
❑ 290 Phi. Phillies TC .10 .05
❑ 291 Pat Burrell RC 1.00 .45
❑ 292 Marlon Anderson .10 .05
❑ 293 Scott Rolen BP .40 .18
❑ 294 Scott Rolen .40 .18
❑ 295 Doug Glanville .10 .05
❑ 296 Rico Brogna .10 .05
❑ 297 Ron Gant .15 .07
❑ 298 Bobby Abreu .15 .07
❑ 299 Desi Relaford .10 .05
❑ 300 Curt Schilling .40 .18
❑ 301 Chad Ogea .10 .05
❑ 302 Kevin Jordan .10 .05
❑ 303 Carlton Loewer .10 .05
❑ 304 Pittsburgh Pirates TC .10 .05
❑ 305 Kris Benson .15 .07
❑ 306 Brian Giles .15 .07
❑ 307 Jason Kendall .15 .07
❑ 308 Jose Guillen .10 .05
❑ 309 Pat Meares .10 .05
❑ 310 Brant Brown .10 .05
❑ 311 Kevin Young .15 .07
❑ 312 Ed Sprague .10 .05
❑ 313 Francisco Cordova .10 .05
❑ 314 Aramis Ramirez .15 .07
❑ 315 Freddy Adrian Garcia .10 .05
❑ 316 St. Louis Cardinals TC .10 .05
❑ 317 J.D. Drew .40 .18
❑ 318 Chad Hutchinson RC .25 .11
❑ 319 Mark McGwire PT .75 .35
❑ 320 J.D. Drew PT .40 .18
❑ 321 Mark McGwire BP .75 .35
❑ 322 Mark McGwire HM .75 .35
❑ 323 Mark McGwire 1.50 .70
❑ 324 Fernando Tatis .10 .05
❑ 325 Edgar Renteria .10 .05
❑ 326 Ray Lankford .10 .05
❑ 327 Willie McGee .15 .07
❑ 328 Ricky Bottalico .10 .05
❑ 329 Eli Marrero .10 .05
❑ 330 Matt Morris .15 .07
❑ 331 Eric Davis .15 .07
❑ 332 Darren Bragg .10 .05
❑ 333 San Diego Padres TC .10 .05
❑ 334 Matt Clement .10 .05
❑ 335 Ben Davis .15 .07
❑ 336 Gary Matthews Jr. .10 .05
❑ 337 Tony Gwynn BP .40 .18
❑ 338 Tony Gwynn HM .40 .18
❑ 339 Tony Gwynn .75 .35
❑ 340 Reggie Sanders .10 .05
❑ 341 Ruben Rivera .10 .05
❑ 342 Wally Joyner .15 .07
❑ 343 Sterling Hitchcock .10 .05
❑ 344 Carlos Hernandez .10 .05
❑ 345 Andy Ashby .10 .05
❑ 346 Trevor Hoffman .15 .07
❑ 347 Chris Gomez .10 .05
❑ 348 Jim Leyritz .10 .05
❑ 349 S.F. Giants TC .10 .05
❑ 350 Armando Rios .10 .05
❑ 351 Barry Bonds PT .50 .23
❑ 352 Barry Bonds BP .50 .23
❑ 353 Barry Bonds HM .50 .23
❑ 354 Robb Nen .10 .05
❑ 355 Bill Mueller .10 .05
❑ 356 Barry Bonds 1.00 .45
❑ 357 Jeff Kent .25 .11
❑ 358 J.T. Snow .15 .07
❑ 359 Ellis Burks .15 .07
❑ 360 F.P. Santangelo .10 .05
❑ 361 Marvin Benard .10 .05
❑ 362 Stan Javier .10 .05
❑ 363 Shawn Estes .15 .07
❑ 364 Seattle Mariners TC .10 .05
❑ 365 Carlos Guillen .10 .05
❑ 366 Ken Griffey Jr. PT .60 .25
❑ 367 Alex Rodriguez PT .50 .23
❑ 368 Ken Griffey Jr. BP .60 .25
❑ 369 Alex Rodriguez BP .50 .23
❑ 370 Ken Griffey Jr. HM .60 .25
❑ 371 Alex Rodriguez HM .50 .23
❑ 372 Ken Griffey Jr. 1.25 .55
❑ 373 Alex Rodriguez 1.00 .45
❑ 374 Jay Buhner .15 .07
❑ 375 Edgar Martinez .25 .11
❑ 376 Jeff Fassero .10 .05
❑ 377 David Bell .10 .05
❑ 378 David Segui .10 .05
❑ 379 Russ Davis .10 .05
❑ 380 Dan Wilson .10 .05
❑ 381 Jamie Moyer .10 .05
❑ 382 T.B. Devil Rays TC .10 .05
❑ 383 Roberto Hernandez .10 .05
❑ 384 Bobby Smith .10 .05
❑ 385 Wade Boggs .40 .18
❑ 386 Fred McGriff .25 .11
❑ 387 Rolando Arrojo .10 .05
❑ 388 Jose Canseco .40 .18
❑ 389 Wilson Alvarez .10 .05
❑ 390 Kevin Stocker .10 .05
❑ 391 Miguel Cairo .10 .05
❑ 392 Quinton McCracken .10 .05
❑ 393 Texas Rangers TC .10 .05
❑ 394 Ruben Mateo .15 .07
❑ 395 Cesar King .10 .05
❑ 396 Juan Gonzalez PT .15 .07
❑ 397 Juan Gonzalez BP .15 .07
❑ 398 Ivan Rodriguez .40 .18
❑ 399 Juan Gonzalez .40 .18
❑ 400 Rafael Palmeiro .40 .18
❑ 401 Rick Helling .10 .05
❑ 402 Aaron Sele .15 .07
❑ 403 John Wetteland .15 .07
❑ 404 Rusty Greer .15 .07
❑ 405 Todd Zeile .15 .07
❑ 406 Royce Clayton .10 .05
❑ 407 Tom Goodwin .10 .05
❑ 408 Toronto Blue Jays TC .10 .05
❑ 409 Kevin Witt .10 .05
❑ 410 Roy Halladay .10 .05
❑ 411 Jose Cruz Jr. .15 .07
❑ 412 Carlos Delgado .40 .18
❑ 413 Willie Greene .10 .05
❑ 414 Shawn Green .40 .18
❑ 415 Homer Bush .10 .05
❑ 416 Shannon Stewart .15 .07
❑ 417 David Wells .15 .07
❑ 418 Kelvim Escobar .10 .05
❑ 419 Joey Hamilton .10 .05
❑ 420 Alex Gonzalez .10 .05
❑ 421 Mark McGwire MM 1.00 .45
❑ 422 Mark McGwire MM 1.00 .45
❑ 423 Mark McGwire MM 1.00 .45
❑ 424 Mark McGwire MM 1.00 .45
❑ 425 Mark McGwire MM 1.00 .45
❑ 426 Mark McGwire MM 1.00 .45
❑ 427 Mark McGwire MM 1.00 .45
❑ 428 Mark McGwire MM 1.00 .45
❑ 429 Mark McGwire MM 1.00 .45
❑ 430 Mark McGwire MM 1.00 .45
❑ 431 Mark McGwire MM 1.00 .45
❑ 432 Mark McGwire MM 1.00 .45
❑ 433 Mark McGwire MM 1.00 .45
❑ 434 Mark McGwire MM 1.00 .45
❑ 435 Mark McGwire MM 1.00 .45
❑ 436 Mark McGwire MM 1.00 .45
❑ 437 Mark McGwire MM 1.00 .45
❑ 438 Mark McGwire MM 1.00 .45
❑ 439 Mark McGwire MM 1.00 .45
❑ 440 Mark McGwire MM 1.00 .45
❑ 441 Mark McGwire MM 1.00 .45
❑ 442 Mark McGwire MM 1.00 .45
❑ 443 Mark McGwire MM 1.00 .45
❑ 444 Mark McGwire MM 1.00 .45
❑ 445 Mark McGwire MM 1.00 .45
❑ 446 Mark McGwire MM 1.00 .45
❑ 447 Mark McGwire MM 1.00 .45
❑ 448 Mark McGwire MM 1.00 .45
❑ 449 Mark McGwire MM 1.00 .45
❑ 450 Mark McGwire MM 1.00 .45
❑ 451 Chipper Jones RF .40 .18
❑ 452 Cal Ripken RF .75 .35
❑ 453 Roger Clemens RF .50 .23
❑ 454 Wade Boggs RF .15 .07
❑ 455 Greg Maddux RF .50 .23
❑ 456 Frank Thomas RF .25 .11
❑ 457 Jeff Bagwell RF .25 .11
❑ 458 Mike Piazza RF .50 .23
❑ 459 Randy Johnson RF .15 .07
❑ 460 Mo Vaughn RF .15 .07
❑ 461 Mark McGwire RF .75 .35
❑ 462 Rickey Henderson RF .40 .18
❑ 463 Barry Bonds RF .50 .23
❑ 464 Tony Gwynn RF .40 .18
❑ 465 Ken Griffey Jr. RF .60 .25
❑ 466 Alex Rodriguez RF .50 .23
❑ 467 Sammy Sosa RF .40 .18
❑ 468 Juan Gonzalez RF .15 .07
❑ 469 Kevin Brown RF .15 .07
❑ 470 Fred McGriff RF .15 .07

2000 Upper Deck Victory

	MINT	NRMT
COMPLETE SET (440)	20.00	9.00
COMP.FACT.SET (466)	20.00	9.00
COMMON CARD (1-390)	.10	.05
COMMON GRIFFEY (391-440)	.50	.23
COMMON USA (441-466)	.50	.23

❑ 1 Mo Vaughn .15 .07
❑ 2 Garret Anderson .15 .07
❑ 3 Tim Salmon .15 .07
❑ 4 Troy Percival .10 .05
❑ 5 Orlando Palmeiro .10 .05
❑ 6 Darin Erstad .40 .18
❑ 7 Ramon Ortiz .15 .07
❑ 8 Ben Molina .10 .05
❑ 9 Troy Glaus .40 .18
❑ 10 Jim Edmonds .25 .11
❑ 11 Mo Vaughn .15 .07
Troy Percival CL
❑ 12 Craig Biggio .25 .11
❑ 13 Roger Cedeno .10 .05
❑ 14 Shane Reynolds .10 .05
❑ 15 Jeff Bagwell .50 .23
❑ 16 Octavio Dotel .10 .05
❑ 17 Moises Alou .15 .07
❑ 18 Jose Lima .10 .05
❑ 19 Ken Caminiti .15 .07
❑ 20 Richard Hidalgo .15 .07
❑ 21 Billy Wagner .10 .05
❑ 22 Lance Berkman .40 .18
❑ 23 Jeff Bagwell .10 .05
Jose Lima CL
❑ 24 Jason Giambi .40 .18
❑ 25 Randy Velarde .10 .05
❑ 26 Miguel Tejada .15 .07
❑ 27 Matt Stairs .10 .05
❑ 28 A.J. Hinch .10 .05
❑ 29 Olmedo Saenz .10 .05
❑ 30 Ben Grieve .15 .07
❑ 31 Ryan Christenson .10 .05
❑ 32 Eric Chavez .15 .07
❑ 33 Tim Hudson .40 .18

❑ 34	John Jaha	.10	.05
❑ 35	Jason Giambi	.40	.18
	Matt Stairs CL		
❑ 36	Raul Mondesi	.15	.07
❑ 37	Tony Batista	.15	.07
❑ 38	David Wells	.15	.07
❑ 39	Homer Bush	.10	.05
❑ 40	Carlos Delgado	.40	.18
❑ 41	Billy Koch	.10	.05
❑ 42	Darrin Fletcher	.10	.05
❑ 43	Tony Fernandez	.10	.05
❑ 44	Shannon Stewart	.15	.07
❑ 45	Roy Halladay	.10	.05
❑ 46	Chris Carpenter	.10	.05
❑ 47	Carlos Delgado	.15	.07
	David Wells CL		
❑ 48	Chipper Jones	.75	.35
❑ 49	Greg Maddux	1.00	.45
❑ 50	Andruw Jones	.40	.18
❑ 51	Andres Galarraga	.25	.11
❑ 52	Tom Glavine	.40	.18
❑ 53	Brian Jordan	.15	.07
❑ 54	John Smoltz	.15	.07
❑ 55	John Rocker	.15	.07
❑ 56	Javy Lopez	.15	.07
❑ 57	Eddie Perez	.10	.05
❑ 58	Kevin Millwood	.10	.05
❑ 59	Chipper Jones	.40	.18
	Greg Maddux CL		
❑ 60	Jeromy Burnitz	.15	.07
❑ 61	Steve Woodard	.10	.05
❑ 62	Ron Belliard	.10	.05
❑ 63	Geoff Jenkins	.15	.07
❑ 64	Bob Wickman	.10	.05
❑ 65	Marquis Grissom	.10	.05
❑ 66	Henry Blanco	.10	.05
❑ 67	Mark Loretta	.10	.05
❑ 68	Alex Ochoa	.10	.05
❑ 69	Marquis Grissom	.15	.07
	Jeromy Burnitz CL		
❑ 70	Mark McGwire	1.50	.70
❑ 71	Edgar Renteria	.10	.05
❑ 72	Dave Veres	.10	.05
❑ 73	Eli Marrero	.10	.05
❑ 74	Fernando Tatis	.10	.05
❑ 75	J.D. Drew	.40	.18
❑ 76	Ray Lankford	.10	.05
❑ 77	Darryl Kile	.15	.07
❑ 78	Kent Bottenfield	.10	.05
❑ 79	Joe McEwing	.10	.05
❑ 80	Mark McGwire	.75	.35
	Ray Lankford CL		
❑ 81	Sammy Sosa	.75	.35
❑ 82	Jose Nieves	.10	.05
❑ 83	Jon Lieber	.10	.05
❑ 84	Henry Rodriguez	.10	.05
❑ 85	Mark Grace	.40	.18
❑ 86	Eric Young	.10	.05
❑ 87	Kerry Wood	.40	.18
❑ 88	Ismael Valdes	.10	.05
❑ 89	Glenallen Hill	.10	.05
❑ 90	Sammy Sosa	.40	.18
	Mark Grace CL		
❑ 91	Greg Vaughn	.15	.07
❑ 92	Fred McGriff	.25	.11
❑ 93	Ryan Rupe	.10	.05
❑ 94	Bubba Trammell	.10	.05
❑ 95	Miguel Cairo	.10	.05
❑ 96	Roberto Hernandez	.10	.05
❑ 97	Jose Canseco	.40	.18
❑ 98	Wilson Alvarez	.10	.05
❑ 99	John Flaherty	.10	.05
❑ 100	Vinny Castilla	.15	.07
❑ 101	Jose Canseco	.15	.07
	Ramon Hernandez CL		
❑ 102	Randy Johnson	.50	.23
❑ 103	Matt Williams	.25	.11
❑ 104	Matt Mantei	.10	.05
❑ 105	Steve Finley	.15	.07
❑ 106	Luis Gonzalez	.40	.18
❑ 107	Travis Lee	.10	.05
❑ 108	Omar Daal	.10	.05
❑ 109	Jay Bell	.15	.07
❑ 110	Erubiel Durazo	.15	.07
❑ 111	Tony Womack	.10	.05
❑ 112	Todd Stottlemyre	.10	.05
❑ 113	Randy Johnson	.15	.07
	Matt Williams CL		
❑ 114	Gary Sheffield	.15	.07
❑ 115	Adrian Beltre	.15	.07
❑ 116	Kevin Brown	.25	.11
❑ 117	Todd Hundley	.10	.05
❑ 118	Eric Karros	.15	.07
❑ 119	Shawn Green	.40	.18
❑ 120	Chan Ho Park	.15	.07
❑ 121	Mark Grudzielanek	.10	.05
❑ 122	Todd Hollandsworth	.10	.05
❑ 123	Jeff Shaw	.10	.05
❑ 124	Darren Dreifort	.10	.05
❑ 125	Gary Sheffield	.15	.07
	Kevin Brown CL		
❑ 126	Vladimir Guerrero	.50	.23
❑ 127	Michael Barrett	.10	.05
❑ 128	Dustin Hermanson	.10	.05
❑ 129	Jose Vidro	.15	.07
❑ 130	Chris Widger	.10	.05
❑ 131	Mike Thurman	.10	.05
❑ 132	Wilton Guerrero	.10	.05
❑ 133	Brad Fullmer	.15	.07
❑ 134	Rondell White	.15	.07
❑ 135	Ugueth Urbina	.10	.05
❑ 136	Vladimir Guerrero	.15	.07
	Rondell White CL		
❑ 137	Barry Bonds	1.00	.45
❑ 138	Russ Ortiz	.15	.07
❑ 139	J.T. Snow	.15	.07
❑ 140	Joe Nathan	.10	.05
❑ 141	Rich Aurilia	.15	.07
❑ 142	Jeff Kent	.25	.11
❑ 143	Armando Rios	.10	.05
❑ 144	Ellis Burks	.15	.07
❑ 145	Robb Nen	.10	.05
❑ 146	Marvin Benard	.10	.05
❑ 147	Barry Bonds	.50	.23
	Russ Ortiz CL		
❑ 148	Manny Ramirez	.50	.23
❑ 149	Bartolo Colon	.15	.07
❑ 150	Kenny Lofton	.15	.07
❑ 151	Sandy Alomar Jr.	.10	.05
❑ 152	Travis Fryman	.15	.07
❑ 153	Omar Vizquel	.15	.07
❑ 154	Roberto Alomar	.40	.18
❑ 155	Richie Sexson	.15	.07
❑ 156	David Justice	.15	.07
❑ 157	Jim Thome	.40	.18
❑ 158	Manny Ramirez	.15	.07
	Roberto Alomar CL		
❑ 159	Ken Griffey Jr.	1.25	.55
❑ 160	Edgar Martinez	.25	.11
❑ 161	Freddy Garcia	.25	.11
❑ 162	Alex Rodriguez	1.00	.45
❑ 163	John Halama	.10	.05
❑ 164	Russ Davis	.10	.05
❑ 165	David Bell	.10	.05
❑ 166	Gil Meche	.10	.05
❑ 167	Jamie Moyer	.10	.05
❑ 168	John Olerud	.15	.07
❑ 169	Ken Griffey Jr.	.60	.25
	Freddy Garcia CL		
❑ 170	Preston Wilson	.15	.07
❑ 171	Antonio Alfonseca	.10	.05
❑ 172	A.J. Burnett	.15	.07
❑ 173	Luis Castillo	.10	.05
❑ 174	Mike Lowell	.10	.05
❑ 175	Alex Fernandez	.10	.05
❑ 176	Mike Redmond	.10	.05
❑ 177	Alex Gonzalez	.10	.05
❑ 178	Vladimir Nunez	.10	.05
❑ 179	Mark Kotsay	.10	.05
❑ 180	Preston Wilson	.10	.05
	Luis Castillo CL		
❑ 181	Mike Piazza	1.00	.45
❑ 182	Darryl Hamilton	.10	.05
❑ 183	Al Leiter	.10	.05
❑ 184	Robin Ventura	.25	.11
❑ 185	Rickey Henderson	.75	.35
❑ 186	Rey Ordonez	.10	.05
❑ 187	Edgardo Alfonzo	.15	.07
❑ 188	Derek Bell	.10	.05
❑ 189	Mike Hampton	.15	.07
❑ 190	Armando Benitez	.15	.07
❑ 191	Mike Piazza	.60	.25
	Rickey Henderson CL		
❑ 192	Cal Ripken	1.50	.70
❑ 193	B.J. Surhoff	.15	.07
❑ 194	Mike Mussina	.40	.18
❑ 195	Albert Belle	.15	.07
❑ 196	Jerry Hairston Jr.	.10	.05
❑ 197	Will Clark	.40	.18
❑ 198	Sidney Ponson	.10	.05
❑ 199	Brady Anderson	.15	.07
❑ 200	Scott Erickson	.10	.05
❑ 201	Ryan Minor	.10	.05
❑ 202	Cal Ripken	.75	.35
	Albert Belle CL		
❑ 203	Tony Gwynn	.75	.35
❑ 204	Bret Boone	.15	.07
❑ 205	Ryan Klesko	.15	.07
❑ 206	Ben Davis	.15	.07
❑ 207	Matt Clement	.10	.05
❑ 208	Eric Owens	.10	.05
❑ 209	Trevor Hoffman	.15	.07
❑ 210	Sterling Hitchcock	.10	.05
❑ 211	Phil Nevin	.15	.07
❑ 212	Tony Gwynn	.40	.18
	Trevor Hoffman CL		
❑ 213	Scott Rolen	.40	.18
❑ 214	Bob Abreu	.15	.07
❑ 215	Curt Schilling	.40	.18
❑ 216	Rico Brogna	.10	.05
❑ 217	Robert Person	.10	.05
❑ 218	Doug Glanville	.10	.05
❑ 219	Mike Lieberthal	.15	.07
❑ 220	Andy Ashby	.10	.05
❑ 221	Randy Wolf	.10	.05
❑ 222	Bob Abreu	.15	.07
	Curt Schilling CL		
❑ 223	Brian Giles	.15	.07
❑ 224	Jason Kendall	.15	.07
❑ 225	Kris Benson	.15	.07
❑ 226	Warren Morris	.10	.05
❑ 227	Kevin Young	.10	.05
❑ 228	Al Martin	.10	.05
❑ 229	Wil Cordero	.10	.05
❑ 230	Bruce Aven	.10	.05
❑ 231	Todd Ritchie	.10	.05
❑ 232	Jason Kendall	.10	.05
	Brian Giles CL		
❑ 233	Ivan Rodriguez	.40	.18
❑ 234	Rusty Greer	.15	.07
❑ 235	Ruben Mateo	.15	.07
❑ 236	Justin Thompson	.10	.05
❑ 237	Rafael Palmeiro	.40	.18
❑ 238	Chad Curtis	.10	.05
❑ 239	Royce Clayton UER	.10	.05
	Mark McLemore pictured on back		
❑ 240	Gabe Kapler	.15	.07
❑ 241	Jeff Zimmerman	.10	.05
❑ 242	John Wetteland	.15	.07
❑ 243	Ivan Rodriguez	.15	.07
	Rafael Palmeiro CL		
❑ 244	Nomar Garciaparra	1.00	.45
❑ 245	Pedro Martinez	.50	.23
❑ 246	Jose Offerman	.10	.05
❑ 247	Jason Varitek	.15	.07
❑ 248	Troy O'Leary	.10	.05
❑ 249	John Valentin	.10	.05
❑ 250	Trot Nixon	.15	.07
❑ 251	Carl Everett	.15	.07
❑ 252	Wilton Veras	.10	.05
❑ 253	Bret Saberhagen	.15	.07
❑ 254	Nomar Garciaparra	.50	.23
	Pedro Martinez CL		
❑ 255	Sean Casey	.25	.11
❑ 256	Barry Larkin	.40	.18
❑ 257	Pokey Reese	.10	.05
❑ 258	Pete Harnisch	.10	.05
❑ 259	Aaron Boone	.10	.05
❑ 260	Dante Bichette	.15	.07
❑ 261	Scott Williamson	.10	.05
❑ 262	Steve Parris	.10	.05
❑ 263	Dmitri Young	.15	.07
❑ 264	Mike Cameron	.15	.07
❑ 265	Sean Casey	.10	.05
	Scott Williamson CL		
❑ 266	Larry Walker	.25	.11
❑ 267	Rolando Arrojo	.10	.05
❑ 268	Pedro Astacio	.10	.05

❑ 269	Todd Helton	.50	.23
❑ 270	Jeff Cirillo	.15	.07
❑ 271	Neifi Perez	.10	.05
❑ 272	Brian Bohanon	.10	.05
❑ 273	Jeffrey Hammonds	.10	.05
❑ 274	Tom Goodwin	.10	.05
❑ 275	Larry Walker	.15	.07
	Todd Helton CL		
❑ 276	Carlos Beltran	.15	.07
❑ 277	Jermaine Dye	.15	.07
❑ 278	Mike Sweeney	.15	.07
❑ 279	Joe Randa	.10	.05
❑ 280	Jose Rosado	.10	.05
❑ 281	Carlos Febles	.10	.05
❑ 282	Jeff Suppan	.10	.05
❑ 283	Johnny Damon	.15	.07
❑ 284	Jeremy Giambi	.10	.05
❑ 285	Mike Sweeney	.15	.07
	Carlos Beltran CL		
❑ 286	Tony Clark	.15	.07
❑ 287	Damion Easley	.10	.05
❑ 288	Jeff Weaver	.15	.07
❑ 289	Dean Palmer	.15	.07
❑ 290	Juan Gonzalez	.40	.18
❑ 291	Juan Encarnacion	.15	.07
❑ 292	Todd Jones	.10	.05
❑ 293	Karim Garcia	.10	.05
❑ 294	Deivi Cruz	.10	.05
❑ 295	Dean Palmer	.10	.05
	Juan Encarnacion CL		
❑ 296	Corey Koskie	.15	.07
❑ 297	Brad Radke	.15	.07
❑ 298	Doug Mientkiewicz	.25	.11
❑ 299	Ron Coomer	.10	.05
❑ 300	Joe Mays	.15	.07
❑ 301	Eric Milton	.15	.07
❑ 302	Jacque Jones	.15	.07
❑ 303	Chad Allen	.10	.05
❑ 304	Cristian Guzman	.15	.07
❑ 305	Jason Ryan	.10	.05
❑ 306	Todd Walker	.10	.05
❑ 307	Corey Koskie	.15	.07
	Eric Milton CL		
❑ 308	Frank Thomas	.50	.23
❑ 309	Paul Konerko	.15	.07
❑ 310	Mike Sirotka	.10	.05
❑ 311	Jim Parque	.10	.05
❑ 312	Magglio Ordonez	.15	.07
❑ 313	Bob Howry	.10	.05
❑ 314	Carlos Lee	.15	.07
❑ 315	Ray Durham	.15	.07
❑ 316	Chris Singleton	.10	.05
❑ 317	Brook Fordyce	.10	.05
❑ 318	Frank Thomas	.25	.11
	Magglio Ordonez CL		
❑ 319	Derek Jeter	1.50	.70
❑ 320	Roger Clemens	1.00	.45
❑ 321	Paul O'Neill	.40	.18
❑ 322	Bernie Williams	.40	.18
❑ 323	Mariano Rivera	.15	.07
❑ 324	Tino Martinez	.15	.07
❑ 325	David Cone	.15	.07
❑ 326	Chuck Knoblauch	.15	.07
❑ 327	Darryl Strawberry	.15	.07
❑ 328	Orlando Hernandez	.15	.07
❑ 329	Ricky Ledee	.10	.05
❑ 330	Derek Jeter	.75	.35
	Bernie Williams CL		
❑ 331	Pat Burrell	.40	.18
❑ 332	Alfonso Soriano	.40	.18
❑ 333	Josh Beckett	.50	.23
❑ 334	Matt Riley	.10	.05
❑ 335	Brian Cooper	.10	.05
❑ 336	Eric Munson	.15	.07
❑ 337	Vernon Wells	.15	.07
❑ 338	Juan Pena	.10	.05
❑ 339	Mark DeRosa	.10	.05
❑ 340	Kip Wells	.15	.07
❑ 341	Roosevelt Brown	.10	.05
❑ 342	Jason LaRue	.10	.05
❑ 343	Ben Petrick	.10	.05
❑ 344	Mark Quinn	.15	.07
❑ 345	Julio Ramirez	.10	.05
❑ 346	Rod Barajas	.10	.05
❑ 347	Robert Fick	.10	.05
❑ 348	David Newhan	.10	.05
❑ 349	Eric Gagne	.10	.05
❑ 350	Jorge Toca	.10	.05
❑ 351	Mitch Meluskey	.10	.05
❑ 352	Ed Yarnall	.10	.05
❑ 353	Chad Hermansen	.10	.05
❑ 354	Peter Bergeron	.10	.05
❑ 355	Dernal Brown	.10	.05
❑ 356	Adam Kennedy	.10	.05
❑ 357	Kevin Barker	.10	.05
❑ 358	Francisco Cordero	.10	.05
❑ 359	Travis Dawkins	.15	.07
❑ 360	Jeff Williams RC	.25	.11
❑ 361	Chad Hutchinson	.10	.05
❑ 362	D'Angelo Jimenez	.15	.07
❑ 363	Derrick Gibson	.10	.05
❑ 364	Calvin Murray	.10	.05
❑ 365	Doug Davis	.10	.05
❑ 366	Rob Ramsay	.10	.05
❑ 367	Mark Redman	.10	.05
❑ 368	Rick Ankiel	.40	.18
❑ 369	Domingo Guzman RC	.25	.11
❑ 370	Eugene Kingsale	.10	.05
❑ 371	N.Garciaparra BPM	.50	.23
❑ 372	Ken Griffey Jr. BPM	.60	.25
❑ 373	Randy Johnson BPM	.25	.11
❑ 374	Jeff Bagwell BPM	.25	.11
❑ 375	Ivan Rodriguez BPM	.15	.07
❑ 376	Derek Jeter BPM	.75	.35
❑ 377	Carlos Beltran BPM	.15	.07
❑ 378	V.Guerrero BPM	.25	.11
❑ 379	Sammy Sosa BPM	.40	.18
❑ 380	Barry Bonds BPM	.50	.23
❑ 381	Pedro Martinez BPM	.25	.11
❑ 382	Chipper Jones BPM	.40	.18
❑ 383	Mo Vaughn BPM	.15	.07
❑ 384	Mike Piazza BPM	.50	.23
❑ 385	Alex Rodriguez BPM	.50	.23
❑ 386	Manny Ramirez BPM	.25	.11
❑ 387	Mark McGwire BPM	.75	.35
❑ 388	Tony Gwynn BPM	.40	.18
❑ 389	Sean Casey BPM	.25	.11
❑ 390	Cal Ripken BPM	.75	.35
❑ 391	Ken Griffey Jr. JC	.50	.23
❑ 392	Ken Griffey Jr. JC	.50	.23
❑ 393	Ken Griffey Jr. JC	.50	.23
❑ 394	Ken Griffey Jr. JC	.50	.23
❑ 395	Ken Griffey Jr. JC	.50	.23
❑ 396	Ken Griffey Jr. JC	.50	.23
❑ 397	Ken Griffey Jr. JC	.50	.23
❑ 398	Ken Griffey Jr. JC	.50	.23
❑ 399	Ken Griffey Jr. JC	.50	.23
❑ 400	Ken Griffey Jr. JC	.50	.23
❑ 401	Ken Griffey Jr. JC	.50	.23
❑ 402	Ken Griffey Jr. JC	.50	.23
❑ 403	Ken Griffey Jr. JC	.50	.23
❑ 404	Ken Griffey Jr. JC	.50	.23
❑ 405	Ken Griffey Jr. JC	.50	.23
❑ 406	Ken Griffey Jr. JC	.50	.23
❑ 407	Ken Griffey Jr. JC	.50	.23
❑ 408	Ken Griffey Jr. JC	.50	.23
❑ 409	Ken Griffey Jr. JC	.50	.23
❑ 410	Ken Griffey Jr. JC	.50	.23
❑ 411	Ken Griffey Jr. JC	.50	.23
❑ 412	Ken Griffey Jr. JC	.50	.23
❑ 413	Ken Griffey Jr. JC	.50	.23
❑ 414	Ken Griffey Jr. JC	.50	.23
❑ 415	Ken Griffey Jr. JC	.50	.23
❑ 416	Ken Griffey Jr. JC	.50	.23
❑ 417	Ken Griffey Jr. JC	.50	.23
❑ 418	Ken Griffey Jr. JC	.50	.23
❑ 419	Ken Griffey Jr. JC	.50	.23
❑ 420	Ken Griffey Jr. JC	.50	.23
❑ 421	Ken Griffey Jr. JC	.50	.23
❑ 422	Ken Griffey Jr. JC	.50	.23
❑ 423	Ken Griffey Jr. JC	.50	.23
❑ 424	Ken Griffey Jr. JC	.50	.23
❑ 425	Ken Griffey Jr. JC	.50	.23
❑ 426	Ken Griffey Jr. JC	.50	.23
❑ 427	Ken Griffey Jr. JC	.50	.23
❑ 428	Ken Griffey Jr. JC	.50	.23
❑ 429	Ken Griffey Jr. JC	.50	.23
❑ 430	Ken Griffey Jr. JC	.50	.23
❑ 431	Ken Griffey Jr. JC	.50	.23
❑ 432	Ken Griffey Jr. JC	.50	.23
❑ 433	Ken Griffey Jr. JC	.50	.23
❑ 434	Ken Griffey Jr. JC	.50	.23
❑ 435	Ken Griffey Jr. JC	.50	.23
❑ 436	Ken Griffey Jr. JC	.50	.23
❑ 437	Ken Griffey Jr. JC	.50	.23
❑ 438	Ken Griffey Jr. JC	.50	.23
❑ 439	Ken Griffey Jr. JC	.50	.23
❑ 440	Ken Griffey Jr. JC	.50	.23
❑ 441	T.Lasorda USA MG	1.00	.45
❑ 442	Sean Burroughs USA	1.50	.70
❑ 443	Rick Krivda USA	.50	.23
❑ 444	Ben Sheets USA RC	4.00	1.80
❑ 445	Pat Borders USA	.50	.23
❑ 446	B.Abernathy USA RC	1.50	.70
❑ 447	Tim Young USA	.50	.23
❑ 448	Adam Everett USA	.50	.23
❑ 449	Anthony Sanders USA	.50	.23
❑ 450	Ernie Young USA	.50	.23
❑ 451	B.Wilkerson USA RC	1.25	.55
❑ 452	K.Ainsworth USA RC	2.00	.90
❑ 453	Ryan Franklin USA RC	1.00	.45
❑ 454	Todd Williams USA	.50	.23
❑ 455	Jon Rauch USA RC	2.50	1.10
❑ 456	Roy Oswalt USA RC	6.00	2.70
❑ 457	S.Heams USA RC	1.00	.45
❑ 458	Chris George USA	.50	.23
❑ 459	Bobby Seay USA	.50	.23
❑ 460	Mike Kinkade USA	.50	.23
❑ 461	Marcus Jensen USA	.50	.23
❑ 462	Travis Dawkins USA	.50	.23
❑ 463	D.Mientkiewicz USA	1.00	.45
❑ 464	John Cotton USA RC	1.00	.45
❑ 465	Mike Neill USA	.50	.23
❑ 466	Team Photo USA	2.00	.90
❑ NNO	Japanese Checklist	.25	.11
❑ NNO	Jap. Product Info.	.25	.11

2001 Upper Deck Victory

		MINT	NRMT
COMPLETE SET (660)		50.00	22.00
❑ 1	Troy Glaus	.40	.18
❑ 2	Scott Spiezio	.10	.05
❑ 3	Gary DiSarcina	.10	.05
❑ 4	Darin Erstad	.40	.18
❑ 5	Tim Salmon	.15	.07
❑ 6	Troy Percival	.10	.05
❑ 7	Ramon Ortiz	.15	.07
❑ 8	Orlando Palmeiro	.10	.05
❑ 9	Tim Belcher	.10	.05
❑ 10	Mo Vaughn	.15	.07
❑ 11	Bengie Molina	.10	.05
❑ 12	Benji Gil	.10	.05
❑ 13	Scott Schoeneweis	.10	.05
❑ 14	Garret Anderson	.15	.07
❑ 15	Matt Wise	.10	.05
❑ 16	Adam Kennedy	.10	.05
❑ 17	Jarrod Washburn	.10	.05
❑ 18	Darin Erstad	.15	.07
	Troy Percival CL		
❑ 19	Jason Giambi	.40	.18
❑ 20	Tim Hudson	.40	.18
❑ 21	Ramon Hernandez	.10	.05
❑ 22	Eric Chavez	.15	.07
❑ 23	Gil Heredia	.10	.05
❑ 24	Jason Isringhausen	.10	.05
❑ 25	Jeremy Giambi	.10	.05
❑ 26	Miguel Tejada	.15	.07

❑ 27 Barry Zito .40 .18
❑ 28 Terrence Long .15 .07
❑ 29 Ryan Christenson .10 .05
❑ 30 Mark Mulder .25 .11
❑ 31 Olmedo Saenz .10 .05
❑ 32 Adam Piatt .15 .07
❑ 33 Ben Grieve .15 .07
❑ 34 Omar Olivares .10 .05
❑ 35 John Jaha .10 .05
❑ 36 Jason Giambi .15 .07
Tim Hudson CL
❑ 37 Carlos Delgado .40 .18
❑ 38 Esteban Loaiza .10 .05
❑ 39 Brad Fullmer .15 .07
❑ 40 David Wells .15 .07
❑ 41 Chris Woodward .10 .05
❑ 42 Billy Koch .10 .05
❑ 43 Shannon Stewart .15 .07
❑ 44 Chris Carpenter .10 .05
❑ 45 Steve Parris .10 .05
❑ 46 Darrin Fletcher .10 .05
❑ 47 Joey Hamilton .10 .05
❑ 48 Jose Cruz Jr. .15 .07
❑ 49 Vernon Wells .15 .07
❑ 50 Raul Mondesi .15 .07
❑ 51 Kelvim Escobar .10 .05
❑ 52 Tony Batista .15 .07
❑ 53 Alex Gonzalez .10 .05
❑ 54 Carlos Delgado .15 .07
David Wells CL
❑ 55 Greg Vaughn .15 .07
❑ 56 Albie Lopez .10 .05
❑ 57 Randy Winn .10 .05
❑ 58 Ryan Rupe .10 .05
❑ 59 Steve Cox .10 .05
❑ 60 Vinny Castilla .15 .07
❑ 61 Jose Guillen .10 .05
❑ 62 Wilson Alvarez .10 .05
❑ 63 Bryan Rekar .10 .05
❑ 64 Gerald Williams .10 .05
❑ 65 Esteban Yan .10 .05
❑ 66 Felix Martinez .10 .05
❑ 67 Fred McGriff .25 .11
❑ 68 John Flaherty .10 .05
❑ 69 Jason Tyner .10 .05
❑ 70 Russ Johnson .10 .05
❑ 71 Roberto Hernandez .10 .05
❑ 72 Greg Vaughn .10 .05
Albie Lopez CL
❑ 73 Eddie Taubensee .10 .05
❑ 74 Bob Wickman .10 .05
❑ 75 Ellis Burks .15 .07
❑ 76 Kenny Lofton .15 .07
❑ 77 Einar Diaz .10 .05
❑ 78 Travis Fryman .15 .07
❑ 79 Omar Vizquel .15 .07
❑ 80 Jason Bere .10 .05
❑ 81 Bartolo Colon .15 .07
❑ 82 Jim Thome .40 .18
❑ 83 Roberto Alomar .40 .18
❑ 84 Chuck Finley .15 .07
❑ 85 Steve Woodard .10 .05
❑ 86 Russ Branyan .15 .07
❑ 87 Dave Burba .10 .05
❑ 88 Jaret Wright .10 .05
❑ 89 Jacob Cruz .10 .05
❑ 90 Steve Karsay .10 .05
❑ 91 Manny Ramirez .15 .07
Bartolo Colon CL
❑ 92 Raul Ibanez .10 .05
❑ 93 Freddy Garcia .15 .07
❑ 94 Edgar Martinez .25 .11
❑ 95 Jay Buhner .15 .07
❑ 96 Jamie Moyer .10 .05
❑ 97 John Olerud .15 .07
❑ 98 Aaron Sele .15 .07
❑ 99 Kazuhiro Sasaki .50 .23
❑ 100 Mike Cameron .15 .07
❑ 101 John Halama .10 .05
❑ 102 David Bell .10 .05
❑ 103 Gil Meche .10 .05
❑ 104 Carlos Guillen .10 .05
❑ 105 Mark McLemore .10 .05
❑ 106 Stan Javier .10 .05
❑ 107 Al Martin .10 .05
❑ 108 Dan Wilson .10 .05
❑ 109 Alex Rodriguez .50 .23
Kazuhiro Sasaki CL
❑ 110 Cal Ripken 1.50 .70
❑ 111 Delino DeShields .10 .05
❑ 112 Sidney Ponson .10 .05
❑ 113 Albert Belle .15 .07
❑ 114 Jose Mercedes .10 .05
❑ 115 Scott Erickson .10 .05
❑ 116 Jerry Hairston Jr. .15 .07
❑ 117 Brook Fordyce .10 .05
❑ 118 Luis Matos .10 .05
❑ 119 Eugene Kingsale .10 .05
❑ 120 Jeff Conine .10 .05
❑ 121 Chris Richard .15 .07
❑ 122 Fernando Lunar .10 .05
❑ 123 John Parrish .10 .05
❑ 124 Brady Anderson .15 .07
❑ 125 Ryan Kohlmeier .10 .05
❑ 126 Melvin Mora .10 .05
❑ 127 Albert Belle .15 .07
Jose Mercedes CL
❑ 128 Ivan Rodriguez .40 .18
❑ 129 Justin Thompson .10 .05
❑ 130 Kenny Rogers .10 .05
❑ 131 Rafael Palmeiro .40 .18
❑ 132 Rusty Greer .15 .07
❑ 133 Gabe Kapler .15 .07
❑ 134 John Wetteland .15 .07
❑ 135 Mike Lamb .10 .05
❑ 136 Doug Davis .10 .05
❑ 137 Ruben Mateo .15 .07
❑ 138 Alex Rodriguez Rangers 2.00 .90
❑ 139 Chad Curtis .10 .05
❑ 140 Rick Helling .10 .05
❑ 141 Ryan Glynn .10 .05
❑ 142 Andres Galarraga .25 .11
❑ 143 Ricky Ledee .10 .05
❑ 144 Frank Catalanotto .10 .05
❑ 145 Rafael Palmeiro .10 .05
Rick Helling CL
❑ 146 Pedro Martinez .50 .23
❑ 147 Wilton Veras .10 .05
❑ 148 Manny Ramirez Red Sox 1.00 .45
❑ 149 Rolando Arrojo .10 .05
❑ 150 Nomar Garciaparra 1.00 .45
❑ 151 Darren Lewis .10 .05
❑ 152 Troy O'Leary .10 .05
❑ 153 Tomokazu Ohka .15 .07
❑ 154 Carl Everett .15 .07
❑ 155 Jason Varitek .15 .07
❑ 156 Frank Castillo .10 .05
❑ 157 Pete Schourek .10 .05
❑ 158 Jose Offerman .10 .05
❑ 159 Derek Lowe .10 .05
❑ 160 John Valentin .10 .05
❑ 161 Dante Bichette .15 .07
❑ 162 Trot Nixon .15 .07
❑ 163 Nomar Garciaparra .50 .23
Pedro Martinez CL
❑ 164 Jermaine Dye .15 .07
❑ 165 Dave McCarty .10 .05
❑ 166 Jose Rosado .10 .05
❑ 167 Mike Sweeney .15 .07
❑ 168 Rey Sanchez .10 .05
❑ 169 Jeff Suppan .10 .05
❑ 170 Chad Durbin .10 .05
❑ 171 Carlos Beltran .15 .07
❑ 172 Brian Meadows .10 .05
❑ 173 Todd Dunwoody .10 .05
❑ 174 Johnny Damon .15 .07
❑ 175 Blake Stein .10 .05
❑ 176 Carlos Febles .10 .05
❑ 177 Joe Randa .10 .05
❑ 178 Mac Suzuki .15 .07
❑ 179 Mark Quinn .15 .07
❑ 180 Gregg Zaun .10 .05
❑ 181 Mike Sweeney .10 .05
Jeff Suppan
❑ 182 Juan Gonzalez .40 .18
❑ 183 Dean Palmer .15 .07
❑ 184 Wendell Magee .10 .05
❑ 185 Todd Jones .10 .05
❑ 186 Bobby Higginson .15 .07
❑ 187 Brian Moehler .10 .05
❑ 188 Juan Encarnacion .15 .07
❑ 189 Tony Clark .15 .07
❑ 190 Rich Becker .10 .05
❑ 191 Roger Cedeno .10 .05
❑ 192 Mitch Meluskey .10 .05
❑ 193 Shane Halter .10 .05
❑ 194 Jeff Weaver .15 .07
❑ 195 Deivi Cruz .15 .07
❑ 196 Damion Easley .10 .05
❑ 197 Robert Fick .10 .05
❑ 198 Matt Anderson .10 .05
❑ 199 Bobby Higginson .10 .05
Brian Moehler
❑ 200 Brad Radke .15 .07
❑ 201 Mark Redman .10 .05
❑ 202 Corey Koskie .15 .07
❑ 203 Matt Lawton .15 .07
❑ 204 Eric Milton .15 .07
❑ 205 Chad Moeller .10 .05
❑ 206 Jacque Jones .15 .07
❑ 207 Matt Kinney .10 .05
❑ 208 Jay Canizaro .10 .05
❑ 209 Torii Hunter .15 .07
❑ 210 Ron Coomer .10 .05
❑ 211 Chad Allen .10 .05
❑ 212 Denny Hocking .10 .05
❑ 213 Cristian Guzman .15 .07
❑ 214 LaTroy Hawkins .10 .05
❑ 215 Joe Mays .15 .07
❑ 216 David Ortiz .15 .07
❑ 217 Matt Lawton .10 .05
Eric Milton CL
❑ 218 Frank Thomas .50 .23
❑ 219 Jose Valentin .10 .05
❑ 220 Mike Sirotka .10 .05
❑ 221 Kip Wells .10 .05
❑ 222 Magglio Ordonez .15 .07
❑ 223 Herbert Perry .10 .05
❑ 224 James Baldwin .10 .05
❑ 225 Jon Garland .10 .05
❑ 226 Sandy Alomar Jr. .15 .07
❑ 227 Chris Singleton .10 .05
❑ 228 Keith Foulke .10 .05
❑ 229 Paul Konerko .15 .07
❑ 230 Jim Parque .10 .05
❑ 231 Greg Norton .10 .05
❑ 232 Carlos Lee .15 .07
❑ 233 Cal Eldred .10 .05
❑ 234 Ray Durham .15 .07
❑ 235 Jeff Abbott .10 .05
❑ 236 Frank Thomas .25 .11
Mike Sirotka CL
❑ 237 Derek Jeter 1.50 .70
❑ 238 Glenallen Hill .10 .05
❑ 239 Roger Clemens 1.00 .45
❑ 240 Bernie Williams .40 .18
❑ 241 David Justice .25 .11
❑ 242 Luis Sojo .10 .05
❑ 243 Orlando Hernandez .15 .07
❑ 244 Mike Mussina .40 .18
❑ 245 Jorge Posada .15 .07
❑ 246 Andy Pettitte .15 .07
❑ 247 Paul O'Neill .40 .18
❑ 248 Scott Brosius .15 .07
❑ 249 Alfonso Soriano .40 .18
❑ 250 Mariano Rivera .15 .07
❑ 251 Chuck Knoblauch .15 .07
❑ 252 Ramiro Mendoza .10 .05
❑ 253 Tino Martinez .15 .07
❑ 254 David Cone .15 .07
❑ 255 Derek Jeter .75 .35
Andy Pettite CL
❑ 256 Jeff Bagwell .50 .23
❑ 257 Lance Berkman .40 .18
❑ 258 Craig Biggio .25 .11
❑ 259 Scott Elarton .10 .05
❑ 260 Bill Spiers .10 .05
❑ 261 Moises Alou .15 .07
❑ 262 Billy Wagner .10 .05
❑ 263 Shane Reynolds .10 .05
❑ 264 Tony Eusebio .10 .05
❑ 265 Julio Lugo .10 .05
❑ 266 Jose Lima .10 .05
❑ 267 Octavio Dotel .10 .05
❑ 268 Brad Ausmus .10 .05
❑ 269 Daryle Ward .10 .05
❑ 270 Glen Barker .10 .05
❑ 271 Wade Miller .15 .07

272	Richard Hidalgo	.15	.07
273	Chris Truby	.10	.05
274	Jeff Bagwell Scott Elarton CL	.15	.07
275	Greg Maddux	1.00	.45
276	Chipper Jones	.75	.35
277	Tom Glavine	.40	.18
278	Brian Jordan	.15	.07
279	Andruw Jones	.40	.18
280	Kevin Millwood	.10	.05
281	Rico Brogna	.10	.05
282	George Lombard	.10	.05
283	Reggie Sanders	.10	.05
284	John Rocker	.15	.07
285	Rafael Furcal	.15	.07
286	John Smoltz	.15	.07
287	Javy Lopez	.15	.07
288	Walt Weiss	.10	.05
289	Quilvio Veras	.10	.05
290	Eddie Perez	.10	.05
291	B.J. Surhoff	.15	.07
292	Chipper Jones Tom Glavine CL	.25	.11
293	Jeromy Burnitz	.15	.07
294	Charlie Hayes	.10	.05
295	Jeff D'Amico	.10	.05
296	Jose Hernandez	.10	.05
297	Richie Sexson	.15	.07
298	Tyler Houston	.10	.05
299	Paul Rigdon	.10	.05
300	Jamey Wright	.10	.05
301	Mark Loretta	.10	.05
302	Geoff Jenkins	.15	.07
303	Luis Lopez	.10	.05
304	John Snyder	.10	.05
305	Henry Blanco	.10	.05
306	Curtis Leskanic	.10	.05
307	Ron Belliard	.10	.05
308	Jimmy Haynes	.10	.05
309	Marquis Grissom	.10	.05
310	Geoff Jenkins Jeff D'Amico CL	.10	.05
311	Mark McGwire	1.50	.70
312	Rick Ankiel	.25	.11
313	Dave Veres	.10	.05
314	Carlos Hernandez	.10	.05
315	Jim Edmonds	.25	.11
316	Andy Benes	.10	.05
317	Garrett Stephenson	.10	.05
318	Ray Lankford	.10	.05
319	Dustin Hermanson	.10	.05
320	Steve Kline	.10	.05
321	Mike Matheny	.10	.05
322	Edgar Renteria	.10	.05
323	J.D. Drew	.40	.18
324	Craig Paquette	.10	.05
325	Darryl Kile	.15	.07
326	Fernando Vina	.10	.05
327	Eric Davis	.15	.07
328	Placido Polanco	.10	.05
329	Jim Edmonds Darryl Kile CL	.15	.07
330	Sammy Sosa	.75	.35
331	Rick Aguilera	.10	.05
332	Willie Greene	.10	.05
333	Kerry Wood	.40	.18
334	Todd Hundley	.10	.05
335	Rondell White	.15	.07
336	Julio Zuleta	.10	.05
337	Jon Lieber	.10	.05
338	Joe Girardi	.10	.05
339	Damon Buford	.10	.05
340	Kevin Tapani	.10	.05
341	Ricky Gutierrez	.10	.05
342	Bill Mueller	.10	.05
343	Ruben Quevedo	.10	.05
344	Eric Young	.10	.05
345	Gary Matthews Jr.	.10	.05
346	Daniel Garibay	.10	.05
347	Sammy Sosa Jon Lieber CL	.25	.11
348	Randy Johnson	.50	.23
349	Matt Williams	.25	.11
350	Kelly Stinnett	.10	.05
351	Brian Anderson	.10	.05
352	Steve Finley	.15	.07
353	Curt Schilling	.40	.18
354	Erubiel Durazo	.10	.05
355	Todd Stottlemyre	.10	.05
356	Mark Grace	.40	.18
357	Luis Gonzalez	.40	.18
358	Danny Bautista	.10	.05
359	Matt Mantei	.10	.05
360	Tony Womack	.10	.05
361	Armando Reynoso	.10	.05
362	Greg Colbrunn	.10	.05
363	Jay Bell	.15	.07
364	Byung-Hyun Kim	.15	.07
365	Luis Gonzalez Randy Johnson CL	.40	.18
366	Gary Sheffield	.15	.07
367	Eric Karros	.15	.07
368	Jeff Shaw	.10	.05
369	Jim Leyritz	.10	.05
370	Kevin Brown	.15	.07
371	Alex Cora	.10	.05
372	Andy Ashby	.10	.05
373	Eric Gagne	.10	.05
374	Chan Ho Park	.15	.07
375	Shawn Green	.40	.18
376	Kevin Elster	.10	.05
377	Mark Grudzielanek	.10	.05
378	Darren Dreifort	.10	.05
379	Dave Hansen	.10	.05
380	Bruce Aven	.10	.05
381	Adrian Beltre	.15	.07
382	Tom Goodwin	.10	.05
383	Gary Sheffield Chan Ho Park CL	.10	.05
384	Vladimir Guerrero	.50	.23
385	Ugueth Urbina	.10	.05
386	Michael Barrett	.10	.05
387	Geoff Blum	.10	.05
388	Fernando Tatis	.10	.05
389	Carl Pavano	.10	.05
390	Jose Vidro	.15	.07
391	Orlando Cabrera	.10	.05
392	Terry Jones	.10	.05
393	Mike Thurman	.10	.05
394	Lee Stevens	.10	.05
395	Tony Armas Jr.	.15	.07
396	Wilton Guerrero	.10	.05
397	Peter Bergeron	.10	.05
398	Milton Bradley	.10	.05
399	Javier Vazquez	.15	.07
400	Fernando Seguignol	.10	.05
401	Vladimir Guerrero Dustin Hermanson CL	.25	.11
402	Barry Bonds	1.00	.45
403	Russ Ortiz	.15	.07
404	Calvin Murray	.10	.05
405	Armando Rios	.10	.05
406	Livan Hernandez	.10	.05
407	Jeff Kent	.25	.11
408	Bobby Estalella	.10	.05
409	Felipe Crespo	.10	.05
410	Shawn Estes	.15	.07
411	J.T. Snow	.15	.07
412	Marvin Benard	.10	.05
413	Joe Nathan	.10	.05
414	Robb Nen	.10	.05
415	Shawon Dunston	.10	.05
416	Mark Gardner	.10	.05
417	Kirk Rueter	.10	.05
418	Rich Aurilia	.15	.07
419	Doug Mirabelli	.10	.05
420	Russ Davis	.10	.05
421	Barry Bonds Livan Hernandez CL	.50	.23
422	Cliff Floyd	.15	.07
423	Luis Castillo	.10	.05
424	Antonio Alfonseca	.15	.07
425	Preston Wilson	.15	.07
426	Ryan Dempster	.15	.07
427	Jesus Sanchez	.10	.05
428	Derrek Lee	.15	.07
429	Brad Penny	.15	.07
430	Mark Kotsay	.15	.07
431	Alex Fernandez	.10	.05
432	Mike Lowell	.15	.07
433	Chuck Smith	.10	.05
434	Alex Gonzalez	.10	.05
435	Dave Berg	.10	.05
436	A.J. Burnett	.15	.07
437	Charles Johnson	.10	.05
438	Reid Cornelius	.10	.05
439	Mike Redmond	.10	.05
440	Preston Wilson Ryan Dempster CL	.10	.05
441	Mike Piazza	1.00	.45
442	Kevin Appier	.15	.07
443	Jay Payton	.10	.05
444	Steve Trachsel	.10	.05
445	Al Leiter	.15	.07
446	Joe McEwing	.10	.05
447	Armando Benitez	.15	.07
448	Edgardo Alfonzo	.15	.07
449	Glendon Rusch	.10	.05
450	Mike Bordick	.15	.07
451	Lenny Harris	.10	.05
452	Matt Franco	.10	.05
453	Darryl Hamilton	.10	.05
454	Bobby Jones	.10	.05
455	Robin Ventura	.15	.07
456	Todd Zeile	.15	.07
457	John Franco	.15	.07
458	Mike Piazza Al Leiter CL	.50	.23
459	Tony Gwynn	.75	.35
460	John Mabry	.10	.05
461	Trevor Hoffman	.15	.07
462	Phil Nevin	.15	.07
463	Ryan Klesko	.15	.07
464	Wiki Gonzalez	.10	.05
465	Matt Clement	.10	.05
466	Alex Arias	.10	.05
467	Woody Williams	.10	.05
468	Ruben Rivera	.10	.05
469	Sterling Hitchcock	.10	.05
470	Ben Davis	.15	.07
471	Bubba Trammell	.10	.05
472	Jay Witasick	.10	.05
473	Eric Owens	.10	.05
474	Damian Jackson	.10	.05
475	Adam Eaton	.15	.07
476	Mike Darr	.10	.05
477	Phil Nevin Trevor Hoffman CL	.10	.05
478	Scott Rolen	.40	.18
479	Robert Person	.10	.05
480	Mike Lieberthal	.15	.07
481	Reggie Taylor	.10	.05
482	Paul Byrd	.10	.05
483	Bruce Chen	.10	.05
484	Pat Burrell	.15	.07
485	Kevin Jordan	.10	.05
486	Bobby Abreu	.15	.07
487	Randy Wolf	.10	.05
488	Kevin Sefcik	.10	.05
489	Brian Hunter	.10	.05
490	Doug Glanville	.10	.05
491	Kent Bottenfield	.10	.05
492	Travis Lee	.15	.07
493	Jeff Brantley	.10	.05
494	Omar Daal	.10	.05
495	Bobby Abreu Randy Wolf CL	.10	.05
496	Jason Kendall	.15	.07
497	Adrian Brown	.10	.05
498	Warren Morris	.10	.05
499	Brian Giles	.15	.07
500	Jimmy Anderson	.10	.05
501	John VanderWal	.10	.05
502	Mike Williams	.10	.05
503	Aramis Ramirez	.15	.07
504	Pat Meares	.10	.05
505	Jason Schmidt	.10	.05
506	Todd Ritchie	.10	.05
507	Abraham Nunez	.10	.05
508	Jose Silva	.10	.05
509	Francisco Cordova	.10	.05
510	Kevin Young	.10	.05
511	Derek Bell	.10	.05
512	Kris Benson	.15	.07
513	Brian Giles Jose Silva CL	.10	.05
514	Ken Griffey Jr.	1.25	.55
515	Scott Williamson	.10	.05

❑ 516 Dmitri Young .15 .07
❑ 517 Sean Casey .25 .11
❑ 518 Barry Larkin .40 .18
❑ 519 Juan Castro .10 .05
❑ 520 Danny Graves .10 .05
❑ 521 Aaron Boone .10 .05
❑ 522 Pokey Reese .10 .05
❑ 523 Elmer Dessens .10 .05
❑ 524 Michael Tucker .10 .05
❑ 525 Benito Santiago .10 .05
❑ 526 Pete Harnisch .10 .05
❑ 527 Alex Ochoa .10 .05
❑ 528 Gookie Dawkins .10 .05
❑ 529 Seth Etherton .10 .05
❑ 530 Rob Bell .10 .05
❑ 531 Ken Griffey Jr. .60 .25
Steve Parris CL
❑ 532 Todd Helton .50 .23
❑ 533 Jose Jimenez .10 .05
❑ 534 Todd Walker .10 .05
❑ 535 Ron Gant .15 .07
❑ 536 Neifi Perez .10 .05
❑ 537 Butch Huskey .10 .05
❑ 538 Pedro Astacio .10 .05
❑ 539 Juan Pierre .15 .07
❑ 540 Jeff Cirillo .15 .07
❑ 541 Ben Petrick .10 .05
❑ 542 Brian Bohanon .10 .05
❑ 543 Larry Walker .25 .11
❑ 544 Masato Yoshii .15 .07
❑ 545 Denny Neagle .10 .05
❑ 546 Brent Mayne .10 .05
❑ 547 Mike Hampton .15 .07
❑ 548 Todd Hollandsworth .10 .05
❑ 549 Brian Rose .10 .05
❑ 550 Todd Helton .15 .07
Pedro Astacio CL
❑ 551 Jason Hart .25 .11
❑ 552 Joe Crede .15 .07
❑ 553 Timo Perez .10 .05
❑ 554 Brady Clark .10 .05
❑ 555 Adam Pettyjohn RC .75 .35
❑ 556 Jason Grilli .10 .05
❑ 557 Paxton Crawford .10 .05
❑ 558 Jay Spurgeon .10 .05
❑ 559 Hector Ortiz .10 .05
❑ 560 Vernon Wells .15 .07
❑ 561 Aubrey Huff .10 .05
❑ 562 Xavier Nady .25 .11
❑ 563 Billy McMillon .10 .05
❑ 564 Ichiro Suzuki RC 20.00 9.00
❑ 565 Tomas De la Rosa .10 .05
❑ 566 Matt Ginter .15 .07
❑ 567 Sun Woo Kim .15 .07
❑ 568 Nick Johnson .15 .07
❑ 569 Pablo Ozuna .10 .05
❑ 570 Tike Redman .10 .05
❑ 571 Brian Cole .15 .07
❑ 572 Ross Gload .10 .05
❑ 573 Dee Brown .10 .05
❑ 574 Tony McKnight .10 .05
❑ 575 Allen Levrault .10 .05
❑ 576 Lesli Brea .10 .05
❑ 577 Adam Bernero .10 .05
❑ 578 Tom Davey .10 .05
❑ 579 Morgan Burkhart .10 .05
❑ 580 Britt Reames .10 .05
❑ 581 Dave Coggin .10 .05
❑ 582 Trey Moore .10 .05
❑ 583 Matt Kinney .10 .05
❑ 584 Pedro Feliz .10 .05
❑ 585 Brandon Inge .15 .07
❑ 586 Alex Hernandez .10 .05
❑ 587 Toby Hall .15 .07
❑ 588 Grant Roberts .10 .05
❑ 589 Brian Sikorski .10 .05
❑ 590 Aaron Myette .10 .05
❑ 591 Derek Jeter PM 1.50 .70
❑ 592 Ivan Rodriguez PM .15 .07
❑ 593 Alex Rodriguez PM 1.00 .45
❑ 594 Carlos Delgado PM .15 .07
❑ 595 Mark McGwire PM 1.50 .70
❑ 596 Troy Glaus PM .40 .18
❑ 597 Sammy Sosa PM .75 .35
❑ 598 Vladimir Guerrero PM .50 .23
❑ 599 Manny Ramirez PM .25 .11
❑ 600 Pedro Martinez PM .25 .11
❑ 601 Chipper Jones PM .75 .35
❑ 602 Jason Giambi PM .15 .07
❑ 603 Frank Thomas PM .50 .23
❑ 604 Ken Griffey Jr. PM 1.25 .55
❑ 605 Nomar Garciaparra PM 1.00 .45
❑ 606 Randy Johnson PM .25 .11
❑ 607 Mike Piazza PM 1.00 .45
❑ 608 Barry Bonds PM 1.00 .45
❑ 609 Todd Helton PM .25 .11
❑ 610 Jeff Bagwell PM .25 .11
❑ 611 Ken Griffey Jr. VB 1.25 .55
❑ 612 Carlos Delgado VB .15 .07
❑ 613 Jeff Bagwell VB .25 .11
❑ 614 Jason Giambi VB .15 .07
❑ 615 Cal Ripken VB 1.50 .70
❑ 616 Brian Giles VB .10 .05
❑ 617 Bernie Williams VB .15 .07
❑ 618 Greg Maddux VB 1.00 .45
❑ 619 Troy Glaus VB .40 .18
❑ 620 Greg Vaughn VB .10 .05
❑ 621 Sammy Sosa VB .75 .35
❑ 622 Pat Burrell VB .10 .05
❑ 623 Ivan Rodriguez VB .15 .07
❑ 624 Chipper Jones VB .75 .35
❑ 625 Barry Bonds VB 1.00 .45
❑ 626 Roger Clemens VB 1.00 .45
❑ 627 Jim Edmonds VB .15 .07
❑ 628 Nomar Garciaparra VB 1.00 .45
❑ 629 Frank Thomas VB .50 .23
❑ 630 Mike Piazza VB 1.00 .45
❑ 631 Randy Johnson VB .25 .11
❑ 632 Andruw Jones VB .15 .07
❑ 633 David Wells VB .10 .05
❑ 634 Manny Ramirez VB .25 .11
❑ 635 Preston Wilson VB .10 .05
❑ 636 Todd Helton VB .25 .11
❑ 637 Kerry Wood VB .15 .07
❑ 638 Albert Belle VB .15 .07
❑ 639 Juan Gonzalez VB .15 .07
❑ 640 Vladimir Guerrero VB .50 .23
❑ 641 Gary Sheffield VB .15 .07
❑ 642 Larry Walker VB .25 .11
❑ 643 Magglio Ordonez VB .10 .05
❑ 644 Jermaine Dye VB .10 .05
❑ 645 Scott Rolen VB .15 .07
❑ 646 Tony Gwynn VB .75 .35
❑ 647 Shawn Green VB .15 .07
❑ 648 Roberto Alomar VB .15 .07
❑ 649 Eric Milton VB .10 .05
❑ 650 Mark McGwire VB 1.50 .70
❑ 651 Tim Hudson VB .15 .07
❑ 652 Jose Canseco VB .15 .07
❑ 653 Tom Glavine VB .15 .07
❑ 654 Derek Jeter VB 1.50 .70
❑ 655 Alex Rodriguez VB 1.00 .45
❑ 656 Darin Erstad VB .15 .07
❑ 657 Jason Kendall VB .10 .05
❑ 658 Pedro Martinez VB .25 .11
❑ 659 Richie Sexson VB .10 .05
❑ 660 Rafael Palmeiro VB .15 .07

2001 Upper Deck Vintage

	MINT	NRMT
COMPLETE SET (400)	50.00	22.00
COMMON (1-340/371-400)	.15	.07
COMMON CARD (341-370)	.50	.23

❑ 1 Darin Erstad .60 .25
❑ 2 Seth Etherton .15 .07
❑ 3 Troy Glaus .60 .25
❑ 4 Bengie Molina .15 .07
❑ 5 Mo Vaughn .25 .11
❑ 6 Tim Salmon .25 .11
❑ 7 Ramon Ortiz .25 .11
❑ 8 Adam Kennedy .15 .07
❑ 9 Garret Anderson .25 .11
❑ 10 Troy Percival .15 .07
❑ 11 California Angels .15 .07
Tim Salmon
Bengie Molina
MoVaughn
Adam Kennedy
Troy Glaus
Kevin Stocker
Darin Erstad
Garret Anderson
Ron Gant CL
❑ 12 Jason Giambi .60 .25
❑ 13 Tim Hudson .60 .25
❑ 14 Adam Piatt .25 .11
❑ 15 Miguel Tejada .25 .11
❑ 16 Mark Mulder .40 .18
❑ 17 Eric Chavez .25 .11
❑ 18 Ramon Hernandez .25 .11
❑ 19 Terrence Long .25 .11
❑ 20 Jason Isringhausen .25 .11
❑ 21 Barry Zito .60 .25
❑ 22 Ben Grieve .25 .11
❑ 23 Oakland Athletics .25 .11
Olmedo Saenz
Ramon Hernandez
Jason Giambi
Randy Velarde
Eric Chavez
Miguel Tejada
Ben Grieve
Terrence Long
Adam Piatt CL
❑ 24 David Wells .25 .11
❑ 25 Raul Mondesi .25 .11
❑ 26 Darrin Fletcher .15 .07
❑ 27 Shannon Stewart .25 .11
❑ 28 Kelvim Escobar .15 .07
❑ 29 Tony Batista .25 .11
❑ 30 Carlos Delgado .60 .25
❑ 31 Brad Fullmer .25 .11
❑ 32 Billy Koch .15 .07
❑ 33 Jose Cruz Jr. .25 .11
❑ 34 Toronto Blue Jays .25 .11
Brad Fullmer
Darrin Fletcher
Carlos Delgado
Homer Bush
Tony Batista
Alex Gonzalez
Shannon Stewart
Jose Cruz Jr.
Raul Mondesi CL
❑ 35 Greg Vaughn .25 .11
❑ 36 Roberto Hernandez .15 .07
❑ 37 Vinny Castilla .25 .11
❑ 38 Gerald Williams .15 .07
❑ 39 Aubrey Huff .15 .07
❑ 40 Bryan Rekar .15 .07
❑ 41 Albie Lopez .15 .07
❑ 42 Fred McGriff .40 .18
❑ 43 Miguel Cairo .15 .07
❑ 44 Ryan Rupe .15 .07
❑ 45 Tampa Bay Devil Rays .25 .11
Greg Vaughn
John Flaherty
Fred McGriff
Miguel Cairo
Vinny Castilla
Felix Martinez
Gerald Williams
Jose Guillen
Steve Cox CL
❑ 46 Jim Thome .60 .25
❑ 47 Roberto Alomar .60 .25
❑ 48 Bartolo Colon .25 .11

❑ 49 Omar Vizquel .25 .11
❑ 50 Travis Fryman .25 .11
❑ 51 Manny Ramirez .75 .35
Picture is off David Segui UER
❑ 52 Dave Burba .15 .07
❑ 53 Chuck Finley .25 .11
❑ 54 Russ Branyan .25 .11
❑ 55 Kenny Lofton .25 .11
❑ 56 Cleveland Indians .25 .11
Russell Branyan
Sandy Alomar Jr.
Jim Thome
Roberto Alomar
Travis Fryman
Omar Vizquel
Wil Cordero
Kenny Lofton
Manny Ramirez
Picture is off David Segui CL UER
❑ 57 Alex Rodriguez 1.50 .70
❑ 58 Jay Buhner .25 .11
❑ 59 Aaron Sele .25 .11
❑ 60 Kazuhiro Sasaki .60 .25
❑ 61 Edgar Martinez .40 .18
❑ 62 John Halama .15 .07
❑ 63 Mike Cameron .25 .11
❑ 64 Freddy Garcia .25 .11
❑ 65 John Olerud .25 .11
❑ 66 Jamie Moyer .15 .07
❑ 67 Gil Meche .15 .07
❑ 68 Seattle Mariners .25 .11
Edgar Martinez
Joe Oliver
John Olerud
David Bell
Carlos Guillen
Alex Rodriguez
Jay Buhner
Mike Cameron
Al Martin CL
❑ 69 Cal Ripken 2.50 1.10
❑ 70 Sidney Ponson .15 .07
❑ 71 Chris Richard .25 .11
❑ 72 Jose Mercedes .15 .07
❑ 73 Albert Belle .25 .11
❑ 74 Mike Mussina .60 .25
❑ 75 Brady Anderson .25 .11
❑ 76 Delino DeShields .15 .07
❑ 77 Melvin Mora .15 .07
❑ 78 Luis Matos .15 .07
❑ 79 Brook Fordyce .15 .07
❑ 80 Baltimore Orioles .25 .11
Jeff Conine
Brook Fordyce
Chris Richard
Delino DeShields
Cal Ripken
Melvin Mora
Luis Matos
Brady Anderson
Albert Belle CL
❑ 81 Rafael Palmeiro .60 .25
❑ 82 Rick Helling .15 .07
❑ 83 Ruben Mateo .25 .11
❑ 84 Rusty Greer .25 .11
❑ 85 Ivan Rodriguez .60 .25
❑ 86 Doug Davis .15 .07
❑ 87 Gabe Kapler .25 .11
❑ 88 Mike Lamb .15 .07
❑ 89 Alex Rodriguez Rangers 4.00 1.80
❑ 90 Kenny Rogers .15 .07
❑ 91 Texas Rangers .15 .07
David Segui
Ivan Rodriguez
Rafael Palmeiro
Frank Catalanotto
Mike Lamb
Royce Clayton
Ruben Mateo
Gabe Kapler
Rusty Greer CL
❑ 92 Nomar Garciaparra 1.50 .70
❑ 93 Trot Nixon .25 .11
❑ 94 Tomokazu Ohka .25 .11
❑ 95 Pedro Martinez .75 .35
❑ 96 Dante Bichette .25 .11
❑ 97 Jason Varitek .25 .11
❑ 98 Rolando Arrojo .15 .07
❑ 99 Carl Everett .25 .11
❑ 100 Derek Lowe .15 .07
❑ 101 Troy O'Leary .15 .07
❑ 102 Tim Wakefield .15 .07
❑ 103 Boston Red Sox .25 .11
Troy O'Leary
Jason Varitek
Jose Offerman
Mike Lansing
Wilton Veras
Nomar Garciaparra
Carl Everett
Trot Nixon
Dante Bichette CL
❑ 104 Mike Sweeney .25 .11
❑ 105 Carlos Febles .15 .07
❑ 106 Joe Randa .15 .07
❑ 107 Jeff Suppan .15 .07
❑ 108 Mac Suzuki .15 .07
❑ 109 Jermaine Dye .25 .11
❑ 110 Carlos Beltran .25 .11
❑ 111 Mark Quinn .25 .11
❑ 112 Johnny Damon .25 .11
❑ 113 Kansas City Royals .25 .11
Mark Quinn
Gregg Zaun
Mike Sweeney
Carlos Febles
Joe Randa
Rey Sanchez
Carlos Beltran
Johnny Damon
Jermaine Dye CL
❑ 114 Tony Clark .25 .11
❑ 115 Dean Palmer .25 .11
❑ 116 Brian Moehler .15 .07
❑ 117 Brad Ausmus .15 .07
❑ 118 Juan Gonzalez .60 .25
❑ 119 Juan Encarnacion .25 .11
❑ 120 Jeff Weaver .25 .11
❑ 121 Bobby Higginson .25 .11
❑ 122 Todd Jones .15 .07
❑ 123 Deivi Cruz .15 .07
❑ 124 Detroit Tigers .25 .11
Juan Gonzalez
Brad Ausmus
Tony Clark
Damion Easley
Dean Palmer
Deivi Cruz
Bobby Higginson
Juan Encarnacion
Rich Becker CL
❑ 125 Corey Koskie .25 .11
❑ 126 Matt Lawton .25 .11
❑ 127 Mark Redman .15 .07
❑ 128 David Ortiz .25 .11
❑ 129 Jay Canizaro .15 .07
❑ 130 Eric Milton .25 .11
❑ 131 Jacque Jones .25 .11
❑ 132 J.C. Romero .15 .07
❑ 133 Ron Coomer .15 .07
❑ 134 Brad Radke .25 .11
❑ 135 Minnesota Twins .25 .11
David Ortiz
Matt LeCroy
Ron Coomer
Jay Canizaro
Corey Koskie
Cristian Guzman
Jacque Jones
Matt Lawton
Torii Hunter CL
❑ 136 Carlos Lee .25 .11
❑ 137 Frank Thomas .75 .35
❑ 138 Mike Sirotka .15 .07
❑ 139 Charles Johnson .25 .11
❑ 140 James Baldwin .15 .07
❑ 141 Magglio Ordonez .25 .11
❑ 142 Jon Garland .15 .07
❑ 143 Paul Konerko .25 .11
❑ 144 Ray Durham .25 .11
❑ 145 Keith Foulke .15 .07
❑ 146 Chris Singleton .15 .07
❑ 147 Chicago White Sox .15 .07
Frank Thomas
Charles Johnson
Paul Konerko
Ray Durham
Herbert Perry
Jose Valentin
Carlos Lee
Magglio Ordonez
Chris Singleton CL
❑ 148 Bernie Williams .60 .25
❑ 149 Orlando Hernandez .25 .11
❑ 150 David Justice .40 .18
❑ 151 Andy Pettitte .25 .11
❑ 152 Mariano Rivera .25 .11
❑ 153 Derek Jeter 2.50 1.10
❑ 154 Jorge Posada .25 .11
❑ 155 Jose Canseco .60 .25
❑ 156 Glenallen Hill .15 .07
❑ 157 Paul O'Neill .60 .25
❑ 158 Denny Neagle .15 .07
❑ 159 Chuck Knoblauch .25 .11
❑ 160 Roger Clemens 1.50 .70
❑ 161 New York Yankees .75 .35
Glenallen Hill
Jorge Posada
Tino Martinez
Chuck Knoblauch
Scott Brosius
Derek Jeter
Paul O'Neill
Bernie Williams
David Justice CL
❑ 162 Jeff Bagwell .75 .35
❑ 163 Moises Alou .25 .11
❑ 164 Lance Berkman .60 .25
❑ 165 Shane Reynolds .15 .07
❑ 166 Ken Caminiti .25 .11
❑ 167 Craig Biggio .40 .18
❑ 168 Jose Lima .15 .07
❑ 169 Octavio Dotel .15 .07
❑ 170 Richard Hidalgo .25 .11
❑ 171 Scott Elarton .15 .07
❑ 172 Houston Astros .40 .18
Scott Elarton
Mitch Meluskey
Jeff Bagwell
Craig Biggio
Bill Spiers
Julio Lugo
Moises Alou
Richard Hidalgo
Lance Berkman CL
❑ 173 Rafael Furcal .25 .11
❑ 174 Greg Maddux 1.50 .70
❑ 175 Quilvio Veras .15 .07
❑ 176 Chipper Jones 1.25 .55
❑ 177 Andres Galarraga .40 .18
❑ 178 Brian Jordan .25 .11
❑ 179 Tom Glavine .60 .25
❑ 180 Kevin Millwood .15 .07
❑ 181 Javier Lopez .25 .11
❑ 182 B.J. Surhoff .25 .11
❑ 183 Andruw Jones .60 .25
❑ 184 Andy Ashby .15 .07
❑ 185 Atlanta Braves .25 .11
Tom Glavine
Javy Lopez
Andres Galarraga
Quilvio Veras
Chipper Jones
Rafael Furcal
Reggie Sanders
Brian Jordan
Andruw Jones CL
❑ 186 Richie Sexson .25 .11
❑ 187 Jeff D'Amico .15 .07
❑ 188 Ron Belliard .15 .07
❑ 189 Jeromy Burnitz .25 .11
❑ 190 Jimmy Haynes .15 .07
❑ 191 Marquis Grissom .15 .07
❑ 192 Jose Hernandez .15 .07
❑ 193 Geoff Jenkins .25 .11
❑ 194 Jamey Wright .15 .07
❑ 195 Mark Loretta .15 .07
❑ 196 Milwaukee Brewers .25 .11

Jeff D'Amico
Henry Blanco
Richie Sexson
Ron Belliard
Tyler Houston
Mark Loretta
Jeromy Burnitz
Marquis Grissom
Geoff Jenkins CL
❑ 197 Rick Ankiel .40 .18
❑ 198 Mark McGwire 2.50 1.10
❑ 199 Fernando Vina .15 .07
❑ 200 Edgar Renteria .15 .07
❑ 201 Darryl Kile .25 .11
❑ 202 Jim Edmonds .40 .18
❑ 203 Ray Lankford .15 .07
❑ 204 Garrett Stephenson .15 .07
❑ 205 Fernando Tatis .15 .07
❑ 206 Will Clark .60 .25
❑ 207 J.D. Drew .60 .25
❑ 208 St. Louis Cardinals .60 .25
Darryl Kile
Mike Matheny
Mark McGwire
Fernando Vina
Fernando Tatis
Edgar Renteria
Ray Lankford
Jim Edmonds
J.D. Drew CL
❑ 209 Mark Grace .60 .25
❑ 210 Eric Young .15 .07
❑ 211 Sammy Sosa 1.25 .55
❑ 212 Jon Lieber .15 .07
❑ 213 Joe Girardi .15 .07
❑ 214 Kevin Tapani .15 .07
❑ 215 Ricky Gutierrez .15 .07
❑ 216 Kerry Wood .60 .25
❑ 217 Rondell White .25 .11
❑ 218 Damon Buford .15 .07
❑ 219 Chicago Cubs .25 .11
Jon Lieber
Joe Girardi
Mark Grace
Eric Young
Willie Greene
Ricky Gutierrez
Sammy Sosa
Damon Bufford
Rondell White CL
❑ 220 Luis Gonzalez .60 .25
❑ 221 Randy Johnson .75 .35
❑ 222 Jay Bell .25 .11
❑ 223 Erubiel Durazo .15 .07
❑ 224 Matt Williams .40 .18
❑ 225 Steve Finley .25 .11
❑ 226 Curt Schilling .60 .25
❑ 227 Todd Stottlemyre .15 .07
❑ 228 Tony Womack .15 .07
❑ 229 Brian Anderson .15 .07
❑ 230 Arizona Diamondbacks .25 .11
Randy Johnson
Kelly Stinnett
Greg Colbrunn
Jay Bell
Matt Williams
Tony Womack
Luis Gonzalez
Steve Finley
Danny Bautista CL
❑ 231 Gary Sheffield .25 .11
❑ 232 Adrian Beltre .25 .11
❑ 233 Todd Hundley .15 .07
❑ 234 Chan Ho Park .25 .11
❑ 235 Shawn Green .60 .25
❑ 236 Kevin Brown .25 .11
❑ 237 Tom Goodwin .15 .07
❑ 238 Mark Grudzielanek .15 .07
❑ 239 Ismael Valdes .15 .07
❑ 240 Eric Karros .25 .11
❑ 241 Los Angeles Dodgers .15 .07
Kevin Brown
Todd Hundley
Eric Karros
Mark Grudzielanek
Adrian Beltre
Alex Cora
Gary Sheffield
Shawn Green
Tom Goodwin CL
❑ 242 Jose Vidro .25 .11
❑ 243 Javier Vazquez .25 .11
❑ 244 Orlando Cabrera .15 .07
❑ 245 Peter Bergeron .15 .07
❑ 246 Vladimir Guerrero .75 .35
❑ 247 Dustin Hermanson .15 .07
❑ 248 Tony Armas Jr. .25 .11
❑ 249 Lee Stevens .15 .07
❑ 250 Milton Bradley .15 .07
❑ 251 Carl Pavano .15 .07
❑ 252 Montreal Expos .25 .11
Dustin Hermanson
Michael Barrett
Lee Stevens
Jose Vidro
Geoff Jenkins
Orlando Cabrera
Vladimir Guerrero
Peter Bergeron
Milton Bradley CL
❑ 253 Ellis Burks .25 .11
❑ 254 Robb Nen .25 .11
❑ 255 J.T. Snow .25 .11
❑ 256 Barry Bonds 1.50 .70
❑ 257 Shawn Estes .25 .11
❑ 258 Jeff Kent .40 .18
❑ 259 Kirk Rueter .15 .07
❑ 260 Bill Mueller .15 .07
❑ 261 Livan Hernandez .25 .11
❑ 262 Rich Aurilia .25 .11
❑ 263 San Francisco Giants .15 .07
Livan Hernadez
Bobby Estalella
J.T. Snow
Jeff Kent
Bill Mueller
Rich Aurilia
Barry Bonds
Marvin Benard
Ellis Burks CL
❑ 264 Ryan Dempster .25 .11
❑ 265 Cliff Floyd .25 .11
❑ 266 Mike Lowell .25 .11
❑ 267 A.J. Burnett .25 .11
❑ 268 Preston Wilson .25 .11
❑ 269 Luis Castillo .15 .07
❑ 270 Henry Rodriguez .15 .07
❑ 271 Antonio Alfonseca .15 .07
❑ 272 Derrek Lee .15 .07
❑ 273 Mark Kotsay .25 .11
❑ 274 Brad Penny .25 .11
❑ 275 Florida Marlins .25 .11
Ryan Dempster
Mike Redmond
Derrek Lee
Luis Castillo
Mike Lowell
Alex Gonzalez
Cliff Floyd
Mark Kotsay
Preston Wilson CL
❑ 276 Mike Piazza 1.50 .70
❑ 277 Jay Payton .15 .07
❑ 278 Al Leiter .25 .11
❑ 279 Mike Bordick .25 .11
❑ 280 Armando Benitez .25 .11
❑ 281 Todd Zeile .25 .11
❑ 282 Mike Hampton .25 .11
❑ 283 Edgardo Alfonzo .25 .11
❑ 284 Derek Bell .15 .07
❑ 285 Robin Ventura .25 .11
❑ 286 New York Mets .15 .07
Mike Hampton
Mike Piazza
Todd Zeile
Edgardo Alfonzo
Robin Ventura
Mike Bordick
Derek Bell
Jay Payton
Timo Perez CL
❑ 287 Tony Gwynn 1.25 .55
❑ 288 Trevor Hoffman .25 .11
❑ 289 Ryan Klesko .25 .11
❑ 290 Phil Nevin .25 .11
❑ 291 Matt Clement .15 .07
❑ 292 Ben Davis .25 .11
❑ 293 Ruben Rivera .15 .07
❑ 294 Bret Boone .25 .11
❑ 295 Adam Eaton .25 .11
❑ 296 Eric Owens .15 .07
❑ 297 San Diego Padres .25 .11
Matt Clemente
Ben Davis
Ryan Klesko
Bret Boone
Phil Nevin
Damian Jackson
Ruben Rivera
Eric Owens
Tony Gwynn CL
❑ 298 Bob Abreu .25 .11
❑ 299 Mike Lieberthal .25 .11
❑ 300 Robert Person .15 .07
❑ 301 Scott Rolen .60 .25
❑ 302 Randy Wolf .15 .07
❑ 303 Bruce Chen .15 .07
❑ 304 Travis Lee .15 .07
❑ 305 Kent Bottenfield .15 .07
❑ 306 Pat Burrell .25 .11
❑ 307 Doug Glanville .15 .07
❑ 308 Philadelphia Phillies .15 .07
Robert Person
Mike Lieberthal
Pat Burrell
Kevin Jordan
Scott Rolen
Alex Arias
Bob Abreu
Doug Glanville
Travis Lee CL
❑ 309 Brian Giles .25 .11
❑ 310 Todd Ritchie .15 .07
❑ 311 Warren Morris .15 .07
❑ 312 John VanderWal .15 .07
❑ 313 Kris Benson .25 .11
❑ 314 Jason Kendall .25 .11
❑ 315 Kevin Young .15 .07
❑ 316 Francisco Cordova .15 .07
❑ 317 Jimmy Anderson .15 .07
❑ 318 Pittsburgh Pirates .25 .11
Kris Benson
Jason Kendall
Kevin Young
Warren Morris
Mike Benjamin
Pat Meares
John VanderWal
Brian Giles
Adrian Brown CL
❑ 319 Ken Griffey Jr. 2.00 .90
❑ 320 Pokey Reese .15 .07
❑ 321 Chris Stynes .15 .07
❑ 322 Barry Larkin .60 .25
❑ 323 Steve Parris .15 .07
❑ 324 Michael Tucker .15 .07
❑ 325 Dmitri Young .25 .11
❑ 326 Pete Harnisch .15 .07
❑ 327 Danny Graves .15 .07
❑ 328 Aaron Boone .15 .07
❑ 329 Sean Casey .40 .18
❑ 330 Cincinnati Reds .15 .07
Steve Parris
Ed Taubensee
Sean Casey
Pokey Reese
Aaron Boone
Barry Larkin
Ken Griffey Jr.
Dmitri Young
Michael Tucker CL
❑ 331 Todd Helton .75 .35
❑ 332 Pedro Astacio .15 .07
❑ 333 Larry Walker .40 .18
❑ 334 Ben Petrick .15 .07
❑ 335 Brian Bohanon .15 .07
❑ 336 Juan Pierre .25 .11
❑ 337 Jeffrey Hammonds .15 .07

	No.	Card	Nm	Ex
❑	338	Jeff Cirillo	.25	.11
❑	339	Todd Hollandsworth	.15	.07
❑	340	Colorado Rockies	.40	.18
		Pedro Astacio		
		Brent Mayne		
		Todd Helton		
		Todd Walker		
		Jeff Cirillo		
		Neifi Perez		
		Larry Walker		
		Jeffrey Hammonds		
		Juan Pierre CL		
❑	341	Matt Wise	.50	.23
		Keith Luuola		
		Derrick Turnbow		
❑	342	Jason Hart	.60	.25
		Jose Ortiz		
		Mario Encarnacion		
❑	343	Vernon Wells	.50	.23
		Pasqual Coco		
		Josh Phelps		
❑	344	Travis Harper	.50	.23
		Kenny Kelley		
		Toby Hall		
❑	345	Danys Baez	.60	.25
		Tim Drew		
		Martin Vargas		
❑	346	Ichiro Suzuki	15.00	6.75
		Ryan Franklin		
		Ryan Christianson		
❑	347	Jay Spurgeon	.50	.23
		Lesli Brea		
		Carlos Casimiro		
❑	348	B.J. Waszgis	.50	.23
		Brian Sikorski		
		Joaquin Benoit		
❑	349	Sun-Woo Kim	.50	.23
		Paxton Crawford		
		Steve Lomasney		
❑	350	Kris Wilson	.50	.23
		Orber Moreno		
		Dee Brown		
❑	351	Mark Johnson	.50	.23
		Brandon Inge		
		Adam Bernero		
❑	352	Danny Ardoin	.50	.23
		Matt Kinney		
		Jason Ryan		
❑	353	Rocky Biddle	.50	.23
		Joe Crede		
		Josh Paul		
❑	354	Nick Johnson	.50	.23
		D'Angelo Jimenez		
		Wily Mo Pena		
❑	355	Tony McKnight	.50	.23
		Aaron McNeal		
		Keith Ginter		
❑	356	Mark DeRosa	.50	.23
		Jason Marquis		
		Wes Helms		
❑	357	Allen Levrault	.50	.23
		Horacio Estrada		
		Santiago Perez		
❑	358	Luis Saturria	.50	.23
		Gene Stechschulte		
		Britt Reames		
❑	359	Joey Nation	.50	.23
		Corey Patterson		
		Cole Liniak		
❑	360	Alex Cabrera	.50	.23
		Geraldo Guzman		
		Nelson Figuero		
❑	361	Hiram Bocachica	.50	.23
		Mike Judd		
		Luke Prokopec		
❑	362	Tomas de la Rosa	.50	.23
		Yohanny Valera		
		Talmadge Nunnari		
❑	363	Ryan Vogelsong	.50	.23
		Juan Melo		
		Chad Zerbe		
❑	364	Jason Grilli	.50	.23
		Pablo Ozuna		
		Ramon Castro		
❑	365	Timo Perez	.50	.23
		Grant Roberts		
		Brian Cole		
❑	366	Tom Davey	.75	.35
		Xavier Nady		
		Dave Maurer		
❑	367	Jimmy Rollins	.50	.23
		Mark Brownson		
		Reggie Taylor		
❑	368	Alex Hernandez	.50	.23
		Adam Hyzdu		
		Tike Redman		
❑	369	Brady Clark	.50	.23
		John Riedling		
		Mike Bell		
❑	370	Giovanni Carrara	.50	.23
		Josh Kalinowski		
		Craig House		
❑	371	Jim Edmonds SH	.25	.11
❑	372	Edgar Martinez SH	.25	.11
❑	373	Rickey Henderson SH	.60	.25
❑	374	Barry Zito SH	.60	.25
❑	375	Tino Martinez SH	.15	.07
❑	376	J.T. Snow SH	.15	.07
❑	377	Bobby Jones SH	.15	.07
❑	378	Alex Rodriguez SH	.75	.35
❑	379	Mike Hampton SH	.15	.07
❑	380	Roger Clemens SH	.75	.35
❑	381	Jay Payton SH	.15	.07
❑	382	John Olerud SH	.15	.07
❑	383	David Justice SH	.25	.11
❑	384	Mike Hampton SH	.15	.07
❑	385	New York Yankees SH	.75	.35
❑	386	Jose Vizcaino SH	.15	.07
❑	387	Roger Clemens SH	.75	.35
❑	388	Todd Zeile SH	.15	.07
❑	389	Derek Jeter SH	1.25	.55
❑	390	New York Yankees SH	.75	.35
❑	391	Nomar Garciaparra	.75	.35
		Darin Erstad		
		Manny Ramirez		
		Derek Jeter		
		Carlos Delgado LL		
❑	392	Todd Helton	.40	.18
		Luis Castillo		
		Jeffrey Hammonds		
		Vladimir Guerrero		
		Moises Alou LL		
❑	393	Troy Glaus	.25	.11
		Frank Thomas		
		Alex Rodriguez		
		Jason Giambi		
		David Justice LL		
❑	394	Sammy Sosa	.75	.35
		Jeff Bagwell		
		Barry Bonds		
		Vladimir Guerrero		
		Richard Hidalgo LL		
❑	395	Edgar Martinez	.25	.11
		Mike Sweeney		
		Frank Thomas		
		Carlos Delgado		
		Jason Giambi LL		
❑	396	Todd Helton	.40	.18
		Jeff Kent		
		Brian Giles		
		Sammy Sosa		
		Jeff Bagwell LL		
❑	397	Pedro Martinez	.60	.25
		Roger Clemens		
		Mike Mussina		
		Bartolo Colon		
		Mike Sirotka LL		
❑	398	Kevin Brown	.15	.07
		Randy Johnson		
		Jeff D'Amico		
		Greg Maddux		
		Mike Hampton LL		
❑	399	Tim Hudson	.25	.11
		David Wells		
		Aaron Sele		
		Andy Pettitte		
		Pedro Martinez LL		
❑	400	Tom Glavine	.25	.11
		Darryl Kile		
		Randy Johnson		
		Chan Ho Park		
		Greg Maddux LL		
❑	S30	Ken Griffey Jr. Sample	1.50	.70

Acknowledgments

Each year we refine the process of developing the most accurate and up-to-date information for this book. I believe this year's Price Guide is our best yet. Thanks again to all the contributors nationwide (listed below) as well as our staff here in Dallas.

Those who have worked closely with us on this and many other books have again proven themselves invaluable: Ed Allan, Frank and Vivian Barning, Levi Bleam and Jim Fleck (707 Sportscards), T. Scott Brandon, Peter Brennan, Ray Bright, Card Collectors Co., Dwight Chapin, Theo Chen, Barry Colla, Bill and Diane Dodge, Brett Domue, Dan Even, David Festberg, Fleer/SkyBox (Josh Perlman), Steve Freedman, Gervise Ford, Larry and Jeff Fritsch, Tony Galovich, Georgia Music and Sports (Dick DeCourcey), Dick Gilkeson, Steve Gold (AU Sports), Bill Goodwin (St. Louis Baseball Cards), Mike and Howard Gordon, George Grauer, Steve Green (STB Sports), John Greenwald, Greg's Cards, Bill Henderson, Jerry and Etta Hersh, Mike Hersh, Neil Hoppenworth, Hunt Auction,Mike Jaspersen, Jay and Mary Kasper (Jay's Emporium), Jerry Katz, Pete Kennedy, David Kohler (SportsCards Plus), Terry Knouse (Tik and Tik), Tom Leon, Paul Lewicki, Robert Lifsen (Robert Edward Auction), Lew Lipset (Four Base Hits), Mike Livingston (U-Trading Cards), Mark Macrae, Bill Madden, Bill Mastro, Dr.William McAvoy, Michael McDonald, Mid-Atlantic Sports Cards (Bill Bossert), Gary Mills, Ernie Montella, Brian Morris, Mike Mosier (Columbia City Collectibles Co.), B.A. Murry, Ralph Nozaki, Mike O'Brien, Oldies and Goodies (Nigel Spill), Oregon Trail Auctions, Pacific Trading Cards (Mike Cramer and Mike Monson), Playoff Trading Cards (Ben Ecklar), Jack Pollard, Jeff Prillaman, Pat Quinn, Jerald Reichstein (Fabulous Cardboard), Steve Judd, Tom Reid, Gavin Riley, Clifton Rouse, John Rumierz, Pat Blandford, Lonn Passon and Kevin Savage (Sports Gallery), Gary Sawatski and Jim Justus (The Wizards of Odd), Mike Schechter, Bill and Darlene Shafer, Barry Sloate, John E. Spalding, Phil Spector, Murvin Sterling, Ted Taylor, Lee Temanson, Topps (Marty Appel), Treat (Harold Anderson), Ed Twombly, Upper Deck (Justin Kanoya), Wayne Varner, Bill Vizas, Bill Wesslund (Portland Sports Card Co.), Kit Young, Rick Young, Ted Zanidakis, Robert Zanze (Z-Cards and Sports), Bill Zimpleman and Dean Zindler. Finally we give a special acknowledgment to the late Dennis W. Eckes, "Mr. Sport Americana." The success of the Beckett Price Guides has always been the result of a team effort.

It is very difficult to be "accurate" - one can only do one's best. But this job is especially difficult since we're shooting at a moving target: Prices are fluctuating all the time. Having several full-time pricing experts has definitely proven to be better than just one, and I thank all of them for working together to provide you, our readers, with the most accurate prices possible.

Many people have provided price input, illustrative material, checklist verifications, errata, and/or background information. We should like to individually thank AbD Cards (Dale Wesolewski), Action Card Sales, Jerry Adamic, Johnny and Sandy Adams, Mehdi Ahlei, Alex's MVP Cards & Comics, Doug Allen, Will Allison, Dennis Anderson, Ed Anderson, Shane Anderson, Ellis Anmuth, Alan Applegate, Ric Apter, Clyde Archer, Randy Archer, Burl Armstrong, Neil Armstrong, B and J Sportscards, Jeremy Bachman, Dave Bailey, Ball Four Cards (Frank and Steve Pemper), Bob Bartosz, Bubba Bennett, Carl Berg, Beulah Sports (Jeff Blatt), B..J. Sportscollectables, David Boedicker (The Wild Pitch Inc.), Louis Bollman, Tim Bond Andrew Bosarge, Terry Boyd, Dan Brandenberry, Jeff Breitenfield, John Brigandi, Scott Brockleman, John Broggi, Virgil Burns, Greg Bussineau, David Byer, California Card Co., Capital Cards, Danny Cariseo, Carl Carlson (C.T.S.), Jim Carr, Ira Cetron, Sandy Chan, Ric Chandgie, Ray Cherry, Bigg Wayne Christian, Josh Chidester, Michael and Abe Citron, Dr. Jeffrey Clair, Michael Cohen, Tom Cohoon (Cardboard Dreams), Gary Collett, Rick Cosmen (RC Card Co.), Lou Costanzo (Champion Sports), Mike Coyne, Tony Craig (T.C. Card Co.), Solomon Cramer, Kevin Crane, Taylor Crane, Chad Cripe, Scott Crump, Allen Custer, Dave Dame, Scott Dantio, Dee's Baseball Cards (Dee Robinson), Joe Delgrippo, Mike DeLuca, Ken Dinerman (California Cruizers), Rob DiSalvatore, Cliff Dolgins, Discount Dorothy, Richard Dolloff (Dolloff Coin Center), Joe Donato, Jerry Dong, Pat Dorsey, Double Play Baseball Cards, Joe Drelich, Richard Duglin (Baseball Cards-N-More), The Dugout, Ken Edick (Home Plate of Utah), Brad Englehardt, Doak Ewing, Terry Falkner, Mike and Chris Fanning, Linda Ferrigno and Mark Mezzardi, Jay Finglass, Bob Flitter, Fremont Fong, Paul Franzetti, Ron Frasier, Tom Freeman, Bob Frye, Bill Fusaro, Chris Gala, Richard Galasso, David Garza, David Gaumer, Georgetown Card Exchange, David Giove, Dick Goddard, Jeff Goldstein, Ron Gomez, Rich Gove, Jay and Jan Grinsby, Bob Grissett, Gerry Guenther, Neil Gubitz (What-A-Card), Hall's Nostalgia, Hershell Hanks, Gregg Hara, Todd Harrell, Robert Harrison, Steve Hart, Floyd Haynes (H and H Baseball Cards), Kevin Heffner, Joel Hellman, Hit and Run Cards (Jon, David, and Kirk Peterson), Vinny Ho, Johnny Hustle Card Co., John Inouye, Vern Isenberg, Dale Jackson, Marshall Jackson, Mike Jardina, Paul Jastrzembski, Jeff's Sports Cards, Donn Jennings Cards, George Johnson, Craig Jones, Chuck Juliana, Nick Kardoulias, Scott Kashner, Frank and Rose Katen, Kevin's Kards, Kingdom Collectibles, Inc., John Klassnik, Steve Kluback, Don Knutsen, Gregg Kohn, Mike Kohlhas, Bob & Bryan Kornfield, Carl and Maryanne Laron, Howard Lau, Richard S. Lawrence, William Lawrence, Brent Lee, Morley Leeking, Irv Lerner, Larry and Sally Levine, Larry Loeschen (A and J Sportscards), Neil Lopez, Kendall

Loyd (Orlando Sportscards South), Steve Lowe, Jim Macie, Peter Maltin, Paul Marchant, Brian Marcy, Scott Martinez, James S. Maxwell Jr., McDag Productions Inc., Bob McDonald, Steve McHenry, Tony McLaughlin, Mendal Mearkle, Carlos Medina, Ken Melanson, William Mendel, Blake Meyer (Lone Star Sportscards), Tim Meyer, Joe Michalowicz, Lee Milazzo, Cary S. Miller, George Miller, Wayne Miller, Dick Millerd, Frank Mineo, Mitchell's Baseball Cards, John Morales, William Munn, Mark Murphy, Robert Nappe, National Sportscard Exchange, Roger Neufeldt, Steve Novella, Bud Obermeyer, John O'Hara, Glenn Olson, Scott Olson, Ron Oser, Luther Owen, Earle Parrish, Clay Pasternack, Michael Perrotta, Tom Pfirrmann, Don Phlong, Loran Pulver, Bob Ragonese, Bryan Rappaport, Don and Tom Ras, Robert M. Ray, Phil Regli, Rob Resnick, Dave Reynolds, Carson Ritchey, Bill Rodman, Craig Roehrig, Mike Sablow, Terry Sack, Thomas Salem, Barry Sanders, Jon Sands, Tony Scarpa, John Schad, Dave Schau (Baseball Cards), Masa Shinohara, Eddie Silard, Mike Slepcevic, Sam Sliheet, Art Smith, Lynn and Todd Solt, Jerry Sorice, Don Spagnolo, Sports Card Fan-Attic, The Sport Hobbyist, Norm Stapleton, Bill Steinberg, Lisa Stellato (Never Enough Cards), Rob Stenzel, Jason Stern, Andy Stoltz, Rob Stenzel, Bill Stone, Ted Straka, Tim Strandberg (East Texas Sports Cards), Edward Strauss, Strike Three, Richard Strobino, Kevin Struss, Superior Sport Card, Dr. Richard Swales, George Tahinos, Brent Thorton, Ian Taylor, The The Thirdhand Shoppe, Brent Thornton, Paul Thornton, Jim and Sally Thurtell, Bud Tompkins (Minnesota Connection), Philip J. Tremont, Ralph Triplette, Umpire's Choice Inc., Eric Unglaub, Hoyt Vanderpool, Steven Wagman, T. Wall, Gary A. Walter, Joe and John Weisenburger (The Wise Guys), Brian and Mike Wentz (BMW Sportscards), Richard West, Mike Wheat, Richard Wiercinski, Don Williams (Robin's Nest of Dolls), Jeff Williams, John Williams, Kent Williams, Craig Williamson, Rich Wojtasick, John Wolf Jr., Jay Wolt (Cavalcade of Sports), Joe Yanello, Peter Yee, Tom Zocco, Mark Zubrensky and Tim Zwick.

Every year we make active solicitations for expert input. We are particularly appreciative of help (however extensive or cursory) provided for this volume. We receive many inquiries, comments and questions regarding material within this book. In fact, each and every one is read and digested. Time constraints, however, prevent us from personally replying. But keep sharing your knowledge. Your letters and input are part of the "big picture" of hobby information we can pass along to readers in our books and magazines. Even though we cannot respond to each letter, you are making significant contributions to the hobby through your interest and comments.

The effort to continually refine and improve this book also involves a growing number of people and types of expertise on our home team. Our company boasts a substantial Sports Data Publishing team, which strengthens our ability to provide comprehensive analysis of the marketplace. SDP capably handled numerous technical details and provided able assistance in the preparation of this edition.

Our baseball analysts played a major part in compiling this year's book, traveling thousands of miles during the past year to attend sports card shows and visit card shops around the United States and Canada. The Beckett baseball specialists are, Wayne Grove, Rich Klein, Dave Porter, Grant Sandground (Senior Price Guide Editor), and Tim Trout. Their pricing analysis and careful proofreading were key contributions to the accuracy of this annual.

Grant Sandground's coordination and reconciling of prices as Beckett Baseball Card Monthly Price Guide Editor helped immeasurably. Rich Klein, as research analyst, contributed detailed pricing analysis and hours of proofing.

The effort was led by the Senior Manager of Sports Data Publishing Dan Hitt. They were ably assisted by the rest of the Price Guide analysts: Clint Hall, Keith Hower, Tony Joseph, Denny Parsons, Bill Sutherland and Joe White.

The price gathering and analytical talents of this fine group of hobbyists have helped make our Beckett team stronger, while making this guide and its companion monthly Price Guide more widely recognized as the hobby's most reliable and relied upon sources of pricing information.

The Beckett Interactive Division played a critical role in technology. They spent countless hours programming, testing, and implementing it to simplify the handling of thousands of prices that must be checked and updated for each edition.

In the years since this guide debuted, Beckett Publications has grown beyond any rational expectation. A great many talented and hard working individuals have been instrumental in this growth and success. Our whole team is to be congratulated for what we together have accomplished.

The whole Beckett Publications team has my thanks for jobs well done. Thank you, everyone.

HOUSE OF COLLECTIBLES SERIES

THE OFFICIAL PRICE GUIDES TO

tle	ISBN	Price	Author
ction Figures, 2nd ed.	0676601790	$21.95	Stuart Wells & Main Toys
ntique Clocks, 3rd ed.	0876375131	$12.00	Roy Erhardt
ntiques & Collectibles, 18th ed.	0676601855	$16.00	Rinker Enterprises
eatles Records & Memorabilia, 2nd ed.	0676601812	$18.95	Perry Cox
ottles, 13th ed.	0676601847	$17.95	Jim Megura
ivil War Collectibles, 2nd ed.	067660160X	$17.95	Richard Friz
ollectible Card Games	0676601456	$17.95	Tony Lee & Timothy Brown
ollecting Books, 4th ed.	0609807692	$18.00	Marie Tedford & Pat Goudey
ollector Knives, 13th ed.	0676601898	$17.95	C. Houston Price
ollector Plates, 7th ed.	0676601545	$19.95	Rinker Enterprises
innerware of the 20th Century	0676600859	$29.95	Harry L. Rinker
lvis Presley Records & Memorabilia, 2nd ed.	0676601413	$17.00	Jerry Osborne
lassware, 3rd ed.	067660188X	$17.00	Mark Pickvet
lilitary Collectibles, 6th ed.	0676600522	$20.00	Richard Austin
verstreet Comic Books, 31st ed.	0609808206	$22.00	Robert M. Overstreet
verstreet Indian Arrowheads, 7th ed.	0609808699	$24.00	Robert M. Overstreet
ottery & Porcelain, 8th ed.	0876378939	$18.00	Harvey Duke
ecords 2001	0676601871	$25.95	Jerry Osborne
inker Collectibles, 4th ed.	0676601596	$19.95	Harry L. Rinker
R. L. Wilson Gun Collecting, 3rd ed.	0676601537	$24.95	R. L. Wilson
Silverware of the 20th Century	0676600867	$24.95	Harry L. Rinker
Star Wars Collectibles, 4th ed.	0876379951	$19.95	Sue Cornwell & Mike Kott
Stemware of the 20th Century	0676600840	$24.95	Harry L. Rinker
Vintage Fashion & Fabrics	0609808133	$17.00	Pamela Smith

THE OFFICIAL GUIDES TO

Title	ISBN	Price	Author
America s State Quarters	0609807706	$5.99	David L. Ganz
Coin Grading & Counterfeit Detection	0676600409	$29.95	Prof. Coin Grading Service
Flea Market Prices	0609807722	$14.95	Harry L. Rinker
How to Buy Jewelry Wholesale	067660126X	$10.95	Frank J. Adler
How to Make Money in Coins Right Now, 2nd ed.	0609807463	$14.95	Scott Travers
Official Directory to U.S. Flea Markets, 7th ed.	0676601901	$10.00	Kitty Werner
One-Minute Coin Expert, 4th ed.	0609807471	$7.99	Scott Travers

THE OFFICIAL BECKETT SPORTS CARDS PRICE GUIDES TO

Title	ISBN	Price	Author
Baseball Cards 2002, 21st ed.	0609807641	$7.99	Dr. James Beckett
Basketball Cards 2002, 11th ed.	0609808427	$6.99	Dr. James Beckett
Football Cards 2002, 21st ed.	0609808435	$7.99	Dr. James Beckett

THE OFFICIAL BLACKBOOK PRICE GUIDES TO

Title	ISBN	Price	Author
U.S. Coins 2002, 40th ed.	0676601731	$6.99	Marc & Tom Hudgeons
U.S. Paper Money 2002, 34th ed.	0676601677	$6.99	Marc & Tom Hudgeons
U.S. Postage Stamps 2002, 24th ed.	0676601707	$7.99	Marc & Tom Hudgeons
World Coins 2002, 5th ed.	0676601766	$7.99	Marc & Tom Hudgeons

Available in bookstores everywhere